The Sport

NATIONAL
HUNT

RESULTS IN FULL 1993–94

Published 1994 by The Sporting Life
One Canada Square, Canary Wharf, London E14 5AP

ISBN 0 901091 72 3

Editorial and Production by Martin Pickering Bloodstock Services
Cover designed by Reprosharp Ltd, London EC1
Cover printed by Robert Pearce & Co Ltd, Orpington, Kent
Preliminaries typeset by LBJ Enterprises Ltd, of Chilcompton and
     Aldermaston
Text printed by Bath Press Ltd, Bath and London

Cover picture
Action from the 1994 Mandarin Chase at Newbury. Eventual winner Bishops Island (No 3), ridden by Adrian Maguire, is headed over the water-jump by Brendan Powell on Rathvinden House
(Photo: Trevor Jones)

Contents

National Hunt Average Times 1993–94

(Revised up to and including 1992–93 season)

SPORTING LIFE Adjusted Average Times represent the theoretical time a top class horse can be expected to clock under ideal conditions carrying 12 stone.

They embrace previous fast times over each individual course and distance, are adjusted to compensate for the state of the ground, weight carried, calibre of horse and revised to 12 stone. They provide an accurate and reliable benchmark for each individual trip and track with which we can compare the actual times recorded at a meeting.

ASCOT
Chases

About 2m	3m 47.5s
2m about 3f 110yds	4m 41.5s
3m about 110yds	6m 3.5s
3m about 5f	7m 19s

Hurdles

2m about 110 yds	3m 46s
2m about 4f	4m 41s
About 3m	5m 33s
3m about 1f 110yds	5m 59s

AYR
Chases

About 2m	3m 48s
2m about 4f	4m 47s
2m about 5f 110yds	5m 5s
3m about 1f	6m
3m about 3f 110yds	6m 43s
4m about 1f	8m 4s

Hurdles

About 2m	3m 37s
2m about 4f	4m 39s
2m about 6f	5m 10s
3m about 110yds	5m 46s
3m about 2f 110yds	6m 13s

BANGOR
Chases

2m about 1f 110yds	4m 6s
2m about 4f 110yds	4m 51s
3m about 110yds	5m 50s
3m about 6f	7m 15s

Hurdles

2m about 1f	3m 50s
2m about 4f	4m 36s
2m about 7f 110yds	5m 32s

CARLISLE
Chases

About 2m	3m 59s
2m about 4f 110yds	5m 3s
About 3m	5m 59s
3m about 2f	6m 30s

Hurdles

2m about 1f	4m 7s
2m about 4f 110yds	4m 53s
3m about 110yds	5m 53s

CARTMEL
Chases

2m about 1f 110yds	4m 13s
2m about 5f 110yds	5m 12s
3m about 2f	6m 17s

Hurdles

2m about 1f 110yds	4m
2m 6f	5m 5s
3m about 2f	5m 58s

CATTERICK
Chases

About 2m	3m 49s
3m about 1f 110yds	6m 15s
3m about 4f 110yds	7m 2s

Hurdles

About 2m	3m 41s
3m about 1f 110yds	6m 1s

CHELTENHAM (New Course)
Chases

2m about 110yds	3m 56s
2m about 5f	5m 4s
3m about 1f 110yds	6m 16s
3m about 2f 110yds	6m 33s
3m about 4f 110yds	7m 2s
4m about 1f	8m 17s

Hurdles

2m about 1f	3m 54.5s
2m about 5f 110yds	5m 1.5s
3m about 110yds	5m 40s

CHELTENHAM (Old Course)
Chases

About 2m	3m 53s
2m about 4f 110yds	5m
3m about 1f	6m 6s
3m about 2f	6m 23s
3m about 3f 110yds	6m 47s
About 4m	8m 5s

Hurdles

2m about 110yds	3m 51s
2m about 5f	4m 59s
3m about 2f	6m 19s

CHELTENHAM (Park Course)
Chases

2m about 110 yds	4m 6s
2m 5f	5m 10s
3m 1f 110yds	6m 17s

Hurdles

2m 110yds	3m 59s
2m 5f 110yds	5m 11s
2m 7f 110yds	5m 38s

CHEPSTOW
Chases

2m about 110yds	3m 59s
2m about 3f 110yds	4m 47s
About 3m	5m 50s
3m about 2f 110yds	6m 35s
3m 5f about 110yds	7m 26s

Hurdles

2m about 110yds	3m 46s
2m about 4f 110yds	4m 41s
About 3m	5m 38s

DONCASTER
Chases

2m about 110yds	3m 55s
2m about 3f 110yds	4m 46s
About 3m	5m 54s
3m about 2f	6m 19s
About 4m	7m 59s

Hurdles

2m about 110yds	3m 50.5s
2m 4f	4m 38s
3m about 110yds	5m 40s

EDINBURGH
Chases

About 2m	3m 50s
2m about 4f	4m 50s
About 3m	5m 50s

Hurdles

About 2m	3m 38s
2m about 4f	4m 38s
About 3m	5m 40s

EXETER (Summer Course)
Chases

2m about 1f 110yds	4m 6s
2m about 3f	4m 29s
2m about 6f 110yds	5m 21s
3m about 1f	5m 58s

Hurdles

2m about 1f 110yds	3m 57s
2m about 3f	4m 19s
2m about 6f	5m

(Winter Course)
Chases

2m about 2f	4m 11s
2m about 3f 110yds	4m 34s
2m about 7f 110yds	5m 35s
3m about 1f 110yds	6m 4s

Hurdles

2m about 2f	4m
2m about 3f 110yds	4m 22s

FAKENHAM
Chases

2m about 110yds	3m 57s
2m 5f about 110yds	5m 12s
About 3m	5m 52s

Hurdles

2m about 110 yds	3m 50s
2m about 5f	4m 53s
3m about 110yds	5m 42s

FOLKESTONE
Chases

About 2m	3m 55s
2m about 5f	5m 10s
3m about 2f	6m 12s
3m about 7f	7m 30s

Hurdles

2m about 1f 110yds	3m 57s
2m about 6f 110yds	5m 14s
3m about 4f	6m 33s

FONTWELL
Chases

2m about 2f	4m 20s
2m about 3f	4m 35s
3m about 2f 110yds	6m 30s

Hurdles

2m about 2f	4m 10s
2m about 6f	5m 9s
3m about 2f 110yds	6m 17s

HAYDOCK
Chases

About 2m	3m 59s
2m about 4f	4m 58s
About 3m	6m 6s
3m about 4f 110yds	7m 16s
4m about 110yds	8m 20s

Hurdles

About 2m	3m 40s
2m about 4f	4m 38.5s
2m about 6f	5m 8s
2m about 7f 110yds	5m 31s

HEREFORD
Chases

About 2m	3m 49s
2m about 3f	4m 30s
3m about 1f 110yds	6m 12s

Hurdles

2m about 1f	3m 46s
2m about 3f 110yds	4m 21s
3m about 2f	6m

HEXHAM
Chases

2m about 110yds	3m 58s
2m about 4f 110yds	5m 1s
3m about 1f	6m 5s
4m	7m 59s

Hurdles

About 2m	3m 50s
2m about 4f 110yds	4m 53s
About 3m	5m 47s

HUNTINGDON
Chases

2m about 110 yds	3m 58s
2m about 4f 110yds	4m 55s
About 3m	5m 48s

Hurdles

2m about 110yds	3m 47s
2m about 5f 110yds	4m 55s
3m about 2f	6m 1s

AVERAGE TIMES FOR COURSES

KELSO
Chases

2m about 1f 4m 6s
2m about 6f 110yds 5m 27s
3m about 1f 6m 2s
3m about 4f 6m 50s

Hurdles

2m about 110yds 3m 43s
2m about 2f 4m 7s
2m about 4f 110yds 4m 42s
2m about 6f 110yds 5m 11s
3m about 3f 6m 14s

KEMPTON
Chases

About 2m 3m 47s
2m about 4f 110yds 4m 53s
About 3m 5m 49s

Hurdles

About 2m 3m 40s
2m about 5f 4m 53s
3m about 110yds 5m 47s

LEICESTER
Chases

2m about 1f 4m 9s
2m about 4f 110yds 5m 3s
About 3m 5m 52s

Hurdles

About 2m 3m 43s
2m about 4f 110yds 4m 48s
About 3m 5m 47s

LEOPARDSTOWN
Chases

2m 1f 4m 15s
2m 3f 4m 43s
2m 5f 5m 14s
2m 6f 5m 30s
2m 7f 5m 45s
3m 6m 12s

Hurdles

2m 3m 48s
2m 2f 4m 16s
2m 4f 4m 45s
2m 6f 5m 12s
3m 5m 42s

LINGFIELD (A.W.)
Hurdles

2m 3m 33s
2m 2f 4m 1s
2m 4f 4m 31s
2m 6f 4m 59s
3m 5m 27s

LINGFIELD (Turf)
Chases

About 2m 3m 54s
2m about 4f 110yds 5m 1s
About 3m 5m 53s

Hurdles

2m about 110yds 3m 51s
2m about 3f 110yds 4m 34s

LIVERPOOL
Chases
National Course

2m about 6f 5m 28s
3m 3f 6m 44s
4m about 4f 8m 58s

Mildmay Course

About 2m 3m 49s
2m about 4f 4m 50s
3m about 1f 6m 5s

Hurdles

2m about 110yds 3m 48s
2m about 4f 4m 38s
3m about 110yds 5m 47.5s

LUDLOW
Chases

About 2m 3m 52s
2m about 4f 4m 51s
About 3m 5m 49s

Hurdles

About 2m 3m 37s
2m about 5f 110yds 4m 57s
3m about 1f 110yds 5m 56s

MARKET RASEN
Chases

2m about 1f 110yds 4m 14s
2m about 4f 4m 52s
2m 6f 110yds 5m 28s
3m about 1f 6m 1s
3m about 4f 110yds 7m
4m about 1f 8m 6s
4m about 3f 110yds 8m 46s

Hurdles

2m about 1f 110yds 4m 2s
2m about 3f 110yds 4m 33s
2m about 5f 110yds 5m 4s
About 3m 5m 42s

NEWBURY
Chases

2m about 1f 4m 1s
2m about 4f 4m 50s
About 3m 5m 48s
3m 2f about 110yds 6m 28s

Hurdles

2m about 110yds 3m 49s
2m about 5f 4m 53s
3m about 110yds 5m 49s

NEWCASTLE
Chases

2m about 110yds 4m 1s
2m about 4f 4m 51s
About 3m 5m 50s
3m about 6f 7m 25s
4m about 1f 8m 11s

Hurdles

2m about 110yds 3m 53s
2m about 4f 4m 43s
About 3m 5m 42s

NEWTON ABBOT
Chases

2m about 110yds 3m 57s
2m about 5f 5m
3m about 2f 110yds 6m 20s

AVERAGE TIMES FOR COURSES

Hurdles

2m about 1f	3m 50s
2m about 6f	4m 59s
3m about 3f	6m 14s

NOTTINGHAM
Chases

About 2m	3m 51s
2m about 5f 110yds	5m 13s
3m about 110yds	5m 55s
3m about 3f 110yds	6m 48s

Hurdles

About 2m	3m 44s
2m about 5f 110yds	5m 2s
3m about 110yds	5m 48s
3m about 4f	6m 40s

PERTH
Chases

About 2m	3m 51s
2m about 4f 110yds	4m 58s
About 3m	5m 57s

Hurdles

2m about 110yds	3m 44s
2m about 4f 110yds	4m 45s
3m about 110yds	5m 45s

PLUMPTON
Chases

About 2m	3m 50s
2m 2f	4m 19s
2m about 5f	5m 5s
3m about 1f 110yds	6m 12s

Hurdles

2m about 1f	3m 52s
2m about 4f	4m 37s

SANDOWN
Chases

About 2m	3m 48.5s
2m about 4f 110yds	4m 59.5s
3m about 110yds	5m 59s
3m 5f about 110yds	7m 13s

Hurdles

2m about 110yds	3m 47s
2m about 6f	5m 6s

SEDGEFIELD
Chases

2m about 1f	4m 5s
2m about 5f	5m 4s
3m about 3f	6m 39s
3m about 4f	6m 56s

Hurdles

2m about 1f 110yds	3m 55s
2m about 5f 110yds	4m 51s
3m 3f 110yds	6m 26s

SOUTHWELL (A.W.)
Hurdles

2m	3m 46s
2m 2f	4m 12s
2m 4f	4m 41s
2m 6f	5m 9s
3m	5m 37s

SOUTHWELL (Turf)
Chases

About 2m	3m 59s
2m about 4f 110yds	5m 3s
2m about 6f	5m 22s
3m about 110yds	5m 58s

Hurdles

About 2m	3m 52s
2m 2f	4m 21s
2m about 4f 110yds	4m 53.5s
2m about 6f	5m 15s
3m about 110yds	5m 50s

STRATFORD
Chases

2m about 1f 110yds	4m 4s
2m about 4f	4m 42s
2m about 5f 110yds	5m 3s
About 3m	5m 47s
3m about 4f	6m 45s

Hurdles

2m about 110yds	3m 49s
2m about 6f 110yds	5m 12s
3m about 3f	6m 19s

TAUNTON
Chases

2m about 110yds	3m 58s
2m about 3f	4m 34s
About 3m	5m 47s
3m about 3f	6m 35s
3m about 6f	7m 17s
4m about 2f 110yds	8m 25s

Hurdles

2m about 1f	3m 47s
2m about 3f 110yds	4m 21s
3m about 110yds	5m 34.5s

TOWCESTER
Chases

2m about 110 yds	4m 2s
2m about 6f	5m 26s
3m about 1f	6m 15s

Hurdles

About 2m	3m 43s
2m about 5f	4m 59s
About 3m	5m 46s

UTTOXETER
Chases

2m	3m 49s
2m about 5f	5m
2m about 7f	5m 30s
3m about 2f	6m 16s
4m about 2f	8m 28s

Hurdles

About 2m	3m 39s
2m about 4f 110yds	4m 43s
2m about 6f 110yds	5m 11s
3m about 110yds	5m 39s

WARWICK
Chases

About 2m	3m 52s
2m about 4f 110yds	4m 55s
3m about 2f	6m 14s
3m about 5f	7m 9s
4m about 1f 110yds	8m 19s

AVERAGE TIMES FOR COURSES

Hurdles

About 2m 3m 40s
2m about 4f 110yds 4m 47.5s

WETHERBY
Chases

About 2m 3m 52s
2m about 5f 5m 4s
3m about 110yds 6m 6s
3m about 5f 7m 17s

Hurdles

About 2m 3m 41s
2m about 4f 110yds 4m 47s
3m about 1f 5m 55s

WINCANTON
Chases

About 2m 3m 51s
2m about 5f 5m 6s
3m about 1f 110yds 6m 16s

Hurdles

About 2m 3m 37s
2m about 6f 5m 6s

WINDSOR
Chases

About 2m 3m 56s
2m about 5f 5m 11s
About 3m 5m 55s
3m about 4f 110yds 7m 2s

Hurdles

About 2m 3m 45s
2m about 6f 110yds 5m 19s

WORCESTER
Chases

About 2m 3m 49s
2m about 4f 110yds 5m 3s
2m about 7f 5m 44s
3m about 4f 110yds 6m 59s

Hurdles

About 2m 3m 41s
2m about 2f 4m 8s
2m about 5f 110yds 4m 54s
About 3m 5m 36s

National Hunt Jockeys' Weights

* Jockeys shown with an asterisk hold a "conditional" licence or a claiming licence. They are entitled to claim 7lb. until they have won 15 races, thereafter 5lb. until they have won 30 races and thereafter 3lb. until they have won 55 races.

† Restricted to Conditional Jockeys Races and National Hunt Flat Races only.

	st	lb
Ahern, M J	10	0
Akehurst, J C	10	2
*Appleby, M	9	10
Armytage, Gee	9	7
†Arnold, L G	9	7
*Arnold, S P	9	7
*Aspell, L	8	10
*Bastiman, H J	8	10
*Bates, A	9	9
*Bazin, G N	9	11
†Becton, T B	9	7
Beggan, R J	10	2
Bellamy, R J	10	0
*Bentley, D B	9	9
*Bentley, N A	9	11
*Berry, M	10	2
*Billany, Miss A L	8	6
†Blythe, W S	9	7
*Bohan, D J	9	7
*Bond, J M	9	0
Bosley, M R	10	3
Bradley, G J	10	2
*Brand, Miss L E	8	12
Brennan, M J	10	0
Bridgwater, D G	9	9
*Brown, J J	9	7
*Brown, K	9	7
†Brown, M	8	5
Burchell, D J	10	0
*Burke, J H	10	2
*Burnett-Wells, C P	9	10
Burrough, S C	10	1
*Burrows, D J	9	7
Byrne, D C	10	0
Byrne, E M	10	0
Caldwell, P A	10	2
Caldwell, Peter H	10	2
Callaghan, J G	10	0
Campbell, R	10	1
†Carey, D M	9	7
*Carey, P D	9	7
*Carr, P A	9	7
Carroll, A W	10	0
†Carroll, G J	9	7
Charlton, A	10	0
*Clarke, M J	9	7
Clay, Miss D L	10	0

	st	lb
Clifford, B M	9	7
†Clinton, M A	9	3
*Colles, R A	9	7
*Collum, N C	9	7
Conlon, P S	9	7
Coogan, A B	10	7
†Cook, Miss K A	8	10
Corkell, J D	10	1
†Creech, D P	9	7
*Crone, G S	9	0
Crosse, M J	10	1
*Curran, J M	9	7
†Currie, W A	9	7
*Cuthbert, Miss Carol	9	0
*Dace, L A	9	7
Da Costa, J W	10	0
Dalton, B P	10	0
*Darke, E R	10	0
*Dascombe, T G	9	7
†Davies, C A W	9	0
Davies, H J	10	3
*Davies, Miss J A	9	7
*Davies, K	9	7
*Davis, Miss K J	9	7
*Davis, R J	9	10
Dawe, N J	10	0
Dennis, C P	10	0
*Dicken, A R	9	12
Dobbin, A G	9	11
Doughty, D N	10	6
*Dowling, A G	9	7
*Doyle, M A	9	7
*Drake, S T	9	0
*Driscoll, J P	9	10
Duggan, J	10	4
Dunwoody, T R	10	1
Dwan, W J	10	0
Dwyer, M P	10	3
Earle, S A	10	0
*Edwards, R	9	0
Elderfield, W G	10	0
*Eley, T J	9	9
†Elliott, C J	9	2
*Farrant, R A	9	9
FitzGerald, M A	10	0
*FitzGerald, M P	9	7

	st	lb
†Fogarty, J M	9	7
*Fordham, J R	9	7
*Fortt, D L	10	0
Foster, M R	10	0
*Fox, S	9	11
Frost, J D	10	4
*Fry, W S	9	7
Gallagher, D T	10	0
Garrity, R J	10	1
*Godsafe, M S B	9	7
Grant, C	10	0
Grantham, T O'D	10	0
*Grattan, B D	8	12
Greene, R J	10	0
†Griffiths, M J	9	0
Guest, R C	10	1
*Harding, B P	9	7
Harker, G A	10	0
Harley, P M	10	0
Harris, J A	10	0
†Harris, J E	9	0
*Harris, M P	9	0
Harvey, L J	10	0
Hawke, N	10	0
Hawkins, C	10	0
*Haworth, S M	9	7
*Herrington, M	9	7
*Hide, P E	9	11
Hoad, M R	10	1
Hobbs, P D	10	0
Hodge, R J	9	10
Hodgson, S P	10	0
†Hogg, S R	9	10
Holley, P S	9	10
Hourigan, M P	9	10
*Huggan, C H	9	10
Humphreys, W G	10	0
*Husband, E L	9	3
Irvine, W S	9	7
*Issac, N D	8	7
*James, J L	9	2
*Jardine, I J	9	7
Jarvis, T O	10	0
Jenkins, H L	10	0
*Jenks, T P	9	9

NATIONAL HUNT JOCKEYS

	st	lb
†John, R B	9	10
Johnson, K	10	0
Jones, A E	10	0
Jones, K	10	2
*Juckes, N R	9	7
Kavanagh, J R	9	7
*Keighley, M H	9	7
Keightley, S L	9	7
†Kennedy, P E	9	7
Kent, T J	10	0
Kersey, Miss Susan	9	10
*Knott, S T	8	2
Knox, W D R	10	10
†Lane, M A P	9	7
†Large, A W	9	7
*Larnach, A A	9	11
Lawrence, I R	9	7
*Leahy, D	9	9
*Leahy, F T	9	7
*Lee, G M	9	7
Leech, J P	10	0
Leech, P J	10	0
*Lees, D W	9	4
Leonard, E A	8	5
*Lewis, G M	9	7
*Linton, A	9	7
Llewellyn, C	10	0
*Lonergan, J G	9	7
Long, Miss Leesa	9	7
Lower, J A	10	0
†Lucas, A K	9	5
*Lycett, S	9	7
Lyons, Gary	10	0
*Lyons, S C	9	10
Mackey, S C	10	0
*Maddock, P J	9	7
Maguire, A	10	0
*Maher, P J	9	7
Mann, N J W	10	0
Marley, R J	10	0
Marston, W J	9	7
*Mason, S T	9	7
*Massey, R I	9	7
*Matthews, D D	9	12
Maude, C G	10	0
McCabe, A J	9	7
*McCarthy, J A	9	9
McCourt, G M	10	5
McDermott, P S	10	0
*McDougall, S J	9	7
*McEntee, P L P	10	7
McFarland, W J	10	0
*McGrath, R	9	7
McKeown, D W E	9	12

	st	lb
McKinley, E M	9	9
McLaughlin, J F S	8	7
*McLoughlin, P J	9	7
McNeill, S R O	10	0
Meade, D N	9	7
*Melia, P C	9	7
*Melrose, S	9	10
*Meredith, D	9	0
Merrigan, A T A	10	0
*Midgley, P T	10	5
*Moffatt, D J	9	10
*Molloy, M J	9	4
Moloney, M J	10	0
*Moore, P A	9	7
*Moore, R W	9	9
*Moran, M P	9	5
Morgan, G P	9	7
Morris, Derrick	10	0
Mulholland, A B	10	0
†Mullen, G B	9	2
*Munday, M D	9	7
*Murphy, B J	10	0
Murphy, D J	10	0
Murphy, E R	10	0
*Murphy, P T J	9	7
*Murphy, T C	9	7
Naughton, P J	10	0
*Neaves, J P	9	7
†Newton, M J	9	7
Niven, P D	10	2
*O'Dowd, B	9	7
O'Hagan, A T	10	0
O'Hara, L S	10	0
*O'Hare, L N P	9	7
Oliver, Miss Jacqueline		
....	10	0
Orkney, R A	10	0
Osborne, J A	10	0
O'Sullivan, D K	10	4
†Pearce, Miss H C	8	0
Pears, O J	8	12
*Perratt, W F	9	7
Perrett, M E	9	0
Pitman, M A	10	5
†Porritt, S	9	7
Powell, B G	9	7
*Procter, A R	8	9
Quinlan, C A	9	10
Railton, J A	10	2
Ranger, M	10	0
Reed, W T	10	3

	st	lb
*Rees, D C	9	10
*Reynolds, L R	9	7
*Rice, J A	10	0
Richards, M R	9	12
*Richmond, D S	9	7
*Roberts, M A	9	7
*Robertson, G N	9	7
Robinson, M I	10	0
*Roche, A J	9	0
*Rourke, R R	9	7
Rowe, G T	10	0
Rowell, R	10	3
*Ryan, D A	8	2
Ryan, J B	10	0
*Ryan, S	9	7
*Salter, D G	9	7
*Sellars, Miss K	9	7
*Shakespeare, A L	9	0
Sharratt, M R	10	0
Shoemark, I W	10	0
Skyrme, D V	10	0
Slattery, J V	8	7
Smith, A S	10	0
Smith, C N	10	0
Smith, V	8	9
Smith-Eccles, S	10	4
*Spence, S D	9	7
Stevens, M	10	1
*Stocks, N A	10	0
Stokell, Miss Ann	9	7
Storey, B	10	0
*Supple, J A	9	7
Supple, R J	10	0
*Taylor, S D	9	7
Telfer, D M	10	2
*Thompson, P A	9	7
*Thompson, T P	9	7
*Thornton, A R	10	0
*Tierney, E	9	7
*Tolhurst, E J	9	7
*Tormey, G E	9	7
Tory, A S	10	0
*Towler, D L	9	7
Turner, S	10	0
Turner, Miss T J	9	7
†Turton, W	9	7
Upton, G	10	1
Vincent, Miss Lorna	8	10
*Waggott, P	9	9
*Walker, R W	9	7

NATIONAL HUNT JOCKEYS

	st	lb
Wall, T R	8	11
*Walsh, W J	9	0
*Ward, P D	9	7
†Waters, D M	10	7
†Watt, A R	8	7
Webb, A	10	0
*Webb, C L	9	7
*Webb, D C	9	7

	st	lb
Wilkinson, D	9	7
*Wilkinson, R D J	9	7
*Williams, P D	10	0
Williams, S D	8	3
Williamson, N	10	0
*Williamson, R E	9	7
*Willmington, N S	9	7

	st	lb
*Winter, D	9	7
*Woodall, C	9	9
Worthington, W M	10	0
Wright, B J	10	10
†Wright, C D	9	7
Wyer, L A	10	0
*Wynne, S	9	0

Index to Meetings

Abandoned Meetings

Wed.	Oct.	13	Uttoxeter	Waterlogged
Sat.	Nov.	20	Ascot	Frost
			Catterick	Frost
			Towcester	Frost
Mon.	Nov.	22	Catterick	Snow
			Folkestone	Frost
Tues.	Nov.	23	Stratford	Fog
Wed.	Nov.	24	Hereford	Frost
			Hexham	Snow
Thurs.	Nov.	25	Carlisle	Frost
Fri.	Nov.	26	Newbury	Fog
Sat.	Nov.	27	Newcastle	Snow and Frost
Mon.	Nov.	29	Kelso	Frost
Wed.	Dec.	8	Clonmel	Abandoned after 5th race due to gale force winds
Fri.	Dec.	10	Hexham	Waterlogged
Wed.	Dec.	15	Bangor-on-Dee	Waterlogged
Thurs.	Dec.	16	Clonmel	Waterlogged
Mon.	Dec.	20	Lingfield	Waterlogged
Wed.	Dec.	22	Hexham	Frost
Mon.	Dec.	27	Ayr	Frost
			Hereford	Frost
			Sedgefield	Snow
			Wincanton	Frost
Tues.	Dec.	28	Wetherby	Snow
Wed.	Dec.	29	Plumpton	Waterlogged
Thurs.	Dec.	30	Fontwell	Abandoned after 4th race due to waterlogging
			Taunton	Last two Chases abandoned due to waterlogging
Fri.	Dec.	31	Folkestone	Waterlogged
Sat.	Jan.	1	Catterick	Frost
Tues.	Jan.	4	Newton Abbot	Waterlogged
Wed.	Jan.	5	Lingfield	Waterlogged
			Sedgefield	Frost
Thurs.	Jan.	6	Lingfield	Last two races abandoned
			Market Rasen	Waterlogged
			Thurles	Frost
			Worcester	Flooded
Fri.	Jan.	7	Towcester	Waterlogged
Sat.	Jan.	8	Haydock	Frost
			Sandown	Waterlogged
Mon.	Jan.	10	Lingfield	Waterlogged
Tues.	Jan.	11	Chepstow	Waterlogged
			Leicester	Waterlogged
Wed.	Jan.	12	Plumpton	Waterlogged
Fri.	Jan.	14	Ascot	Waterlogged
Sat.	Jan.	15	Ascot	Waterlogged
			Newcastle	Waterlogged
Mon.	Jan.	17	Carlisle	Frost

ABANDONED MEETINGS

Wed.	Jan.	19	Windsor	Flooded
Thurs.	Jan.	20	Taunton	Waterlogged
Thurs.	Jan.	27	Newton Abbot	Waterlogged
Fri.	Jan.	28	Uttoxeter	Waterlogged
Thurs.	Feb.	3	Lingfield	2.40 race abandoned
			Towcester	Waterlogged
Fri.	Feb.	11	Bangor-on-Dee	Waterlogged
Mon.	Feb.	14	Hereford	Frost
			Plumpton	Frost
Tues.	Feb.	15	Newton Abbot	Snow
			Towcester	Frost
Wed.	Feb.	16	Sedgefield	Frost
			Worcester	Frost and Snow
Fri.	Feb.	18	Edinburgh	Frost
Sat.	Feb.	19	Chepstow	Waterlogged
			Newcastle	Frost and Snow
Mon.	Feb.	21	Fontwell	Frost
Tues.	Feb.	22	Huntingdon	Frost
			Sedgefield	Frost
Wed.	Feb.	23	Doncaster	Frost
			Southwell	Poor visibility and Snow
			Tipperary	Waterlogged
			Warwick	Snow
Thurs.	Feb.	24	Catterick	Snow and Frost
Fri.	Feb.	25	Haydock	Frost and Snow
Sat.	Feb.	26	Haydock	Frost and Snow
			Market Rasen	Waterlogged
Sun.	Feb.	27	Fairyhouse	Waterlogged
Mon.	Feb.	28	Leicester	Waterlogged
Tues.	Mar.	1	Hexham	Waterlogging and Frost
Wed.	Mar.	2	Southwell	Cancelled by Jockey Club
			Worcester	Flooded
Thurs.	Mar.	3	Clonmel	Waterlogged
			Lingfield	Cancelled by Jockey Club
Mon.	Mar.	28	Hexham	Waterlogged
Mon.	Apr.	4	Carlisle	Waterlogged
			Chepstow	Waterlogged
			Huntingdon	Snow
			Mallow	Waterlogged
			Plumpton	Waterlogged
			Towcester	Waterlogged
			Uttoxeter	Waterlogged
Tues.	Apr.	5	Chepstow	Waterlogged
Thurs.	Apr.	7	Tipperary	Waterlogged
Mon.	Apr.	25	Sligo	Engineering Work

QUEST CANCER RESEARCH

We wish to thank the York Racecourse Executive
for allowing the Charity to hold a collection at
entrances and exits to the course on Thursday 12 May.

**Also, we thank Sheikh Mohammed for his generosity that day
in donating the prize-money from his 1st, 2nd and 3rd
in the Michael Seely Memorial Glasgow Condition Stakes.**

Quest funds medical research to develop routine testing for early
signs of cancer in both adults and children.

Most cancers are diagnosed only when there are symptoms and
tests currently available often fail to detect cancer
early enough for effective treatment.

We are already helping to save lives
but each form of cancer requires separate research
and it is a constant struggle to raise the money needed.

PLEASE HELP TO PREVENT MORE TRAGEDY
by contributing generously

QUEST CANCER RESEARCH
Woodbury
Harlow Road
Roydon
Harlow
Essex CM19 5HF

No animals are used in the research

Registered Charity No. 284526

The Sporting Life
BOOKS

National Hunt Results 1993-94

DUNDALK (IRE) (soft)
Friday June 11th

1 Carrickarnon Handicap Hurdle (0-102 4-y-o and up) £2,245 2½m 153yds..........(5:30)

SENSITIVE KING (Ire) [-] 5-10-5 (3*) J Collins, ... (33 to 1)	1
SONG OF CAEDMON (Ire) [-] 5-10-8 C F Swan, ... (8 to 1)	2
SALLOW GLEN [-] 7-10-8 T Horgan, ... (6 to 1)	3
GOLDEN RAPPER [-] (bl) 8-11-0 J F Titley, ... (5 to 1)	4
HOSTETLER [-] 4-10-10 (3*,5ex) P Carberry, ... (4 to 1)	5
FAUGHAN LODGE [-] 6-10-0 (7*) K P Gaule, ... (16 to 1)	6
JOEY KELLY [-] 8-10-9 C O'Dwyer, ... (2 to 1 fav)	7
LUCKY ENOUGH [-] 8-10-7 F Woods, ... (10 to 1)	8
SUNSHINE SEAL [-] 6-11-2 P L Malone, ... (8 to 1)	9
MRS COOPS [-] 6-10-7 K F O'Brien, ... (12 to 1)	10
KAFKAN (Ire) [-] 5-10-8 B Sheridan, ... (12 to 1)	11
MABES TOWN (Ire) [-] 5-10-11 N Byrne, ... (12 to 1)	12
PERSIAN GLEN [-] 6-11-2 H Rogers, ... (25 to 1)	13
MISS SPLENDOUR (Ire) [-] 5-10-2 (5*) T J Mitchell, (10 to 1)	14
WINDOVER LODGE [-] 6-11-4 L P Cusack, ... (20 to 1)	15
CHEERFUL CALLER [-] 6-10-1 (7*) C O'Brien, ... (20 to 1)	16
NANCYS LAD [-] 6-10-3 (7*) G Lee, ... (14 to 1)	su
ICANSEEFORMILES (Ire) [-] 5-10-9 C N Bowens, . . (25 to 1)	pu

Dist: 2½l, nk, 5½l, hd. 5m 13.60s. (18 Ran).

(J C Harley), J C Harley

2 Fane Hurdle (4-y-o and up) £2,245 2m 135yds..............................(6:00)

FABRICATOR 7-11-8 K F O'Brien, ... (8 to 1)	1
LIFE SAVER (Ire) 4-11-3 (3*) P Carberry, ... (4 to 1)	2
DIPIE (Ire) 5-11-0 (7*) H Taylor, ... (8 to 1)	3
HIS WAY (Ire) 4-11-6 C F Swan, ... (11 to 10 fav)	4
RATTLE AND HUM 6-11-8 P L Malone, ... (8 to 1)	5
KAZKAR (Ire) 5-11-7 B Sheridan, ... (12 to 1)	6
FINGAL BOY (Ire) 5-11-2 (5*) Mr P J Casey, ... (50 to 1)	7
KHAZARI (USA) 5-11-13 C O'Dwyer, ... (10 to 1)	8
GONE BY (Ire) 5-11-0 (7*) Mr J Connolly, ... (14 to 1)	9
ARDNAMONA 6-11-4 (5*) D P Geoghegan, ... (33 to 1)	10
TADILA (Ire) 4-10-9 J Shortt, ... (12 to 1)	11
KORACLE BAY (bl) 6-11-2 (7*) P Mulligan, ... (16 to 1)	12
PYR FOUR 6-11-8 K Morgan, ... (8 to 1)	13
LARGE PROFILE 5-11-7 T Horgan, ... (16 to 1)	14
BELLAGHY BRIDGE 6-11-3 A Powell, ... (50 to 1)	15

Dist: 1½l, 15l, 2½l, sht-hd. 4m 17.40s. (15 Ran).

(Mrs C Marks), J T R Dreaper

3 Faughart Flat Race (4-y-o and up) £2,245 2m 135yds............................(8:30)

D'S FANCY (Ire) 5-11-6 (7*) Mr M Brennan, ... (33 to 1)	1
MASTER CRUSADER 7-11-7 (7*) Mr J A Nash, (7 to 4 fav)	2
JOKERS THREE (Ire) 4-10-13 (7*) Mr A F Doherty, . . (6 to 1)	3
KEY WEST (Ire) 4-10-13 (7*) Mr M O'Connor, ... (12 to 1)	4
DOGS DILEMMA (Ire) 4-11-6 Mr P F Graffin, ... (12 to 1)	5
PILS INVADER (Ire) 5-11-8 Mr M McNulty, ... (12 to 1)	6
CASTLE LORD (Ire) 4-10-13 (7*) Mr G J Harford, ... (8 to 1)	7
CARLINGFORD GEM 7-11-6 (3*) Mr R Neylon, ... (20 to 1)	8
RED BARONS LADY (Ire) 4-10-12 (3*) Mrs S McCarthy,	
. . . . (5 to 2)	9
WILLCHRIS 6-11-7 (7*) Mr C A McBratney, ... (20 to 1)	10
INACTUALFACT (Ire) 4-11-1 (5*) Mr L Lennon, . . . (16 to 1)	11
DECEMBER BRIDE (Ire) 5-11-1 (7*) Mr E Magee, . (50 to 1)	12
BOGGLE HOLE (Ire) (bl) 5-11-10 (3*) Mr D Marnane,	
. . . . (33 to 1)	13
THE PARSONS ROSE (Ire) 5-11-5 (3*) Mr P McMahon,	
. . . . (25 to 1)	14
BRAVE STAR 7-11-7 (7*) Mr D J Kavanagh, ... (33 to 1)	15
WISHING'N'HOPING (Ire) 4-10-13³ (7*) Mr B Potts, (16 to 1)	16
SALVATION 6-12-0 Mr J P Dempsey, ... (8 to 1)	17
CARDINALS LADY (Ire) 4-10-8 (7*) Mr J Bright, . . . (33 to 1)	18

Dist: 8l, 1½l, 1½l, 4l. 4m 20.90s. (18 Ran).

(R J Walshe), J H Scott

CLONMEL (IRE) (yielding to soft (races 1,2,3), soft (4))
Tuesday June 15th

4 Cahir Maiden Hurdle (4-y-o and up) £2,245 2m...................................(5:30)

SOLBA (USA) 4-11-6 G M O'Neill, ... (5 to 1 fav)	1
STEEL MIRROR 4-11-1 J Shortt, ... (16 to 1)	2
HURRICANE EDEN 6-10-10 (5*) C P Dunne, ... (8 to 1)	3
BACK TO BLACK (Ire) 4-10-5 (5*) M G Cleary, ... (10 to 1)	4
PUNTERS BAR 6-12-0 C O'Dwyer, ... (5 to 1)	5
IDEAL RISK (Ire) 4-11-1 C F Swan, ... (14 to 1)	6
FULL MOON FEVER (Ire) 4-11-1 K F O'Brien, ... (20 to 1)	7
FAHA GIG (Ire) 4-10-10 S H O'Donovan, ... (20 to 1)	8
IRELANDS GEM 5-11-5 F J Flood, ... (10 to 1)	9
BRAVE STAR 7-11-1 (5*) T J Mitchell, ... (25 to 1)	10
JOHNOTHELODGE (Ire) 5-11-5 A J Slattery, ... (14 to 1)	11
VICTORY TOAST (Ire) 4-11-1 H Rogers, ... (4 to 1)	12
DRIPSEY QUAY (Ire) (bl) 5-10-7 (7*) Mr D Marke, . (20 to 1)	13
PEGUS PRINCE (Ire) 4-10-8 (7*) C O'Brien, ... (25 to 1)	14
ARAQUEEPA (Ire) 5-11-5 F Woods, ... (33 to 1)	15

Dist: 2½l, nk, 1l, hd. 4m 17.60s. (15 Ran).

(Three Counties Syndicate), Augustine Leahy

5 Sportsmans Handicap Hurdle (0-116 4-y-o and up) £2,245 2m....................(6:00)

WATERLOO LADY [-] 6-10-0 (3*) P Carberry, ... (14 to 1)	1
BUCKINGHAM BOY [-] 7-10-3 (7*) Mrs C Harrison, (16 to 1)	2
AQUINAS [-] 7-10-8 (7*) R A Hennessy, ... (5 to 1)	3
THE MAN FROM COOKS [-] 4-11-1 T Horgan, ... (8 to 1)	4
SERJITAK [-] 6-10-6 C F Swan, ... (6 to 4 fav)	5
SNOWDRIFTER [-] 6-10-6 (7*) J R Barry, ... (7 to 2)	6
NO TAKERS [-] 4-10-3 L P Cusack, ... (14 to 1)	7
COOLBAWN CASTLE [-] 10-10-0 (7*) C O'Brien, . . (16 to 1)	8
FUR N MONEY [-] 7-10-1 (7*) J P Broderick, ... (33 to 1)	9
BALLYTIGUE LORD [-] 7-11-5 G M O'Neill, ... (6 to 1)	10

Dist: 3½l, 4l, 10l, 10l. 4m 8.00s. (10 Ran).

(John Philip Kelly), James Joseph Mangan

6 Dungarvan Novice Chase (5-y-o and up) £2,245 2¼m.......................(7:00)

TUSKER LADY 8-11-9 C O'Dwyer, ... (4 to 1 fav)	1
AHEEMA COTTAGE 7-12-0 F J Flood, ... (5 to 1)	2
HISTORY GRADUATE 7-11-7 (7*) Mr G Hogan, . . . (11 to 2)	3
TIGH AN CHEOIL 9-12-0 A J O'Brien, ... (12 to 1)	4
BALLYHEIGUE 7-11-7 (7*) Mr J T McNamara, ... (10 to 1)	5
TWO BOB 9-12-0 S H O'Donovan, ... (14 to 1)	6
DOCTER MAC 6-11-7 (7*) T Horgan, ... (20 to 1)	7
ASHBOURNE CLASSIC (bl) 6-11-4 (5*) D Leahy, . . (20 to 1)	8
BALLYBRIT BOY 7-12-0 L P Cusack, ... (7 to 1)	9
EDWARD'S DOLLY 8-11-4 (5*) M G Cleary, ... (14 to 1)	10
BOHOLA EXPRESS 6-11-7 (7*) Mr C A Leavy, ... (20 to 1)	11
SMOOTH COUP 7-11-2 (7*) Mr D K Budds, ... (20 to 1)	12
LISNAGREE BOY (Ire) 5-11-7 K F O'Brien, ... (25 to 1)	13
TOLL BRIDGE 6-11-9 H Rogers, ... (16 to 1)	14
LUCYS LAW (bl) 7-11-9 F Woods, ... (16 to 1)	15

Dist: 3½l, 4l, 3½l, 7l. 4m 54.50s. (15 Ran).

(Patrick Day), Patrick Day

7 Park INH Flat Race (4-y-o and up) £2,245 2m...................................(8:30)

CHANCERY QUEEN (Ire) 4-11-1 Mr A P O'Brien,	
. . . . (11 to 8 fav)	1
THE WICKED CHICKEN (Ire) 4-10-12 (3*) Mrs S McCarthy,	
. . . . (9 to 2)	2
MISS POLLERTON (Ire) 5-11-1 (7*) Mr K O'Sullivan, (14 to 1)	3
SUMMER FOX 6-11-11 (3*) Mrs M Olivefalk, ... (8 to 1)	4
LE SEPT 6-11-2 (7*) Mr R Foley, ... (16 to 1)	5
IRISH PERRY 6-11-2 (7*) Mr M Comber, ... (25 to 1)	6
TWO IN TUNE (Ire) 5-11-6 (7*) Mr D Keane, ... (20 to 1)	7
PAT'S VALENTINE (Ire) 5-11-1 (7*) Mr G Hogan, . . (25 to 1)	8
I'D SAY HARDLY 6-12-0 Mr T Mullins, ... (7 to 1)	9
MILFORD MATCH (Ire) 5-11-3 (5*) Mrs J M Mullins, (10 to 1)	10
FIFTYBETWEENYE (Ire) 5-11-6 (7*) Mr D Duggan, (33 to 1)	11
MISTER DRUM (Ire) 4-11-6 Mr E Bolger, ... (8 to 1)	12
BALLYDAY SNOW (Ire) 4-10-11³ (7*) Mr J P Walsh, (16 to 1)	13
BELLE LAKE 5-11-1 (7*) Mr P A Roche, ... (33 to 1)	14
D'S AND DO'S (Ire) 4-10-10 (5*) Mr J P Berry, ... (14 to 1)	15
SMART DECISION 5-11-1 (7*) Mr R J Curran, ... (8 to 1)	pu

Dist: 5½l, 4l, 2l, 2½l. 4m 6.30s. (16 Ran).

(Richard O'Gorman), A P O'Brien

NAAS (IRE) (soft)
Thursday June 17th

8 Grange Con Handicap Hurdle (0-123 4-y-o and up) £3,107 2m....................(6:35)

SHEAMY'S DREAM (Ire) [-] (bl) 5-12-0 J Shortt, . .(5 to 2 jt-
fav)
EMARRCEEVEESS [-] 6-11-7 (3ª) P Carberry, ... (7 to 1) 2
1 WINDOVER LODGE [-] 6-10-5 L P Cusack, ... (20 to 1) 3
27 FINGAL BOY (Ire) [-] 5- (5ª) T J Mitchell, ... (16 to 1) 4
DEGO DANCER [-] 6-9-13 F Woods, ... (4 to 1) 5
PENNINE PASS [-] (bl) 4-10-1 B Sheridan, ... (7 to 1) 6
DARCARI ROSE (Ire) [-] 4-9-11 P McWilliams, ...(20 to 1) 7
FINE PRINT (Ire) [-] 5-10-7 H Rogers, ... (9 to 1) 8
TOUCHDOWN [-] 6-10-0 C F Swan, ...(5 to 2 jt-fav) f
Dist: 1½l, 1½l, 1½l. 4m 5.40s. (9 Ran).

(Mrs A Hughes), J G Coogan

9 Ballytore Flat Race (4-y-o and up) £3,107 2m
. . . .(8:30)

SCALLYROUGE (Ire) 4-10-13 (7ª) Mr G A Kingston, (10 to 1) 1
THE DICTATOR (Ire) 4-11-1 (5ª) Mr A E Lacy, ...(9 to 2) 2
BLAST FREEZE (Ire) 4-10-8 (7ª) Mr J A Nash, . . (5 to 4 fav) 3
PEARL'S CHOICE (Ire) 5-11-1 (7ª) Mr G Harford, . . (7 to 1) 4
EMPTY VANITY (Ire) 4-11-3 (3ª) Mr A R Coonan, . .(20 to 1) 5
LADY FONTAINE (Ire) 4-11-1 Mr S R Murphy, ...(16 to 1) 6
TODDY MARK (Ire) (bl) 4-10-13 (7ª) Mr J P Kilfeather,
. . . .(10 to 1) 7
SIMPLISTIC (Ire) 4-11-1 Mr J P Dempsey, ...(7 to 2) 8
NAMESTAKEN 7-11-7 (7ª) Mr B M Cash, ...(25 to 1) 9
BALLYDAVIN 6-12-0 Mr P Fenton, ...(20 to 1) 10
SIMPLY GOOD (Ire) 5-11-5⁴ (7ª) Mr B Deegan, . . (20 to 1) 11
Dist: 3½l, 2l, ¾l, 4½l. 4m 13.90s. (11 Ran).

(G A Kingston), Mrs John Harrington

GOWRAN PARK (IRE) (yielding to soft)
Friday June 18th

10 Rhone-Poulenc Maiden Hurdle (5-y-o and up) £3,452 2m. . . . .(5:30)

PAGET 6-11-7 (7ª) Mr A K Wyse, ...(5 to 4 fav) 1
DANCING COURSE (Ire) 5-11-8 K Morgan, ...(5 to 1) 2
KENMAC 6-11-6 M P Hourigan, ...(16 to 1) 3
OH SO GRUMPY 5-11-5 C F Swan, ...(5 to 1) 4
BRAVEFOOT 5-11-8 (5ª) T J Mitchell, ...(7 to 1) 5
FULL SCHEDULAL 6-11-6 J F Titley, ...(20 to 1) 6
COMBINE CALL 6-12-0 C O'Dwyer, ...(10 to 1) 7
UNCLE BART (Ire) 5-10-12 (7ª) R A Hennessy, ... (14 to 1) 8
MANDAVINCI (Ire) 5-10-7 (7ª) C O'Brien, ...(33 to 1) 9
UPPINGHAM 7-11-8¹ (7ª) Mr M F Mennin, ...(14 to 1) 10
CLARA BRIDGE 6-11-1 C N Bowens, ...(20 to 1) 11
BAMANYAR (Ire) 5-10-12 (7ª) Mr E Sheehy, ...(12 to 1) 12
4 JOHNOTHELODGE (Ire) 5-11-0 (5ª) A J Slattery, . . .(50 to 1) 13
COOL COOPER 6-11-1 W T Slattery Jnr, ...(50 to 1) 14
CASTLEROE LAD 6-11-6 P Kavanagh, ...(50 to 1) 15
BOLEREE (Ire) 5-11-0 S H O'Donovan, ...(14 to 1) 16
KINGS RIVER LAD 9-11-9 (5ª) M A Davey, ...(14 to 1) 17
EASY TERMS (bl) 7-10-8 (7ª) T P Treacy, ...(50 to 1) 18
BOLD BREW (Ire) 5-11-5 Mr D M O'Brien, ...(12 to 1) pu
Dist: ¾l, 2l, ½l, 1l. 3m 59.30s. (19 Ran).

(A P Wyse), A Redmond

11 Prix Du Loin D'Angers Handicap Hurdle (0-130 4-y-o and up) £4,142 3m. . . . . . . (6:00)

TERZIA [-] 6-10-3 T Horgan, ...(6 to 1) 1
CUILIN BUI (Ire) [-] 5-10-2 (7ª) C O'Brien, ...(8 to 1) 2
MUST DO [-] 7-10-3 (5ª) T J Mitchell, ...(10 to 1) 3
CARES OF TOMORROW [-] 6-10-13 N Byrne, ...(10 to 1) 4
DUNBOY CASTLE (Ire) [-] 5-10-13 (6ex) R Supple,
. . . .(4 to 1 fav) 5
GOODNIGHT IRENE (Ire) [-] 4-9-5¹ (5ª) M J Holbrook,
. . . .(50 to 1) 6
FOXBROOK [-] 7-11-6 C F Swan, ...(14 to 1) 7
AISEIRI [-] 6-10-8 A Powell, ...(8 to 1) 8
MOUNTAIN BLOOM (Ire) [-] 5-10-10 J F Titley, ...(8 to 1) 9
MARYS COURSE [-] 7-11-9 M P Hourigan, ...(10 to 1) 10
ERMESHKA [-] 7-9-10 (7ª) K P Gaule, ...(33 to 1) 11
VINEYARD SPECIAL [-] 7-11-2 K Morgan, ...(6 to 1) 12
PERSIAN HAZE (Ire) [-] 4-9-12 (7ª) J Butler, ...(14 to 1) 13
SOMERSET DANCER (USA) [-] 6-10-11 (6ex) S H O'Don-
ovan, ...(10 to 1) 14
ONE FOR LUCK (Ire) [-] 5-9-12 F J Flood, ... (16 to 1) pu
Dist: ½l, 6l, 9l, 2l. 6m 1.70s. (15 Ran).

(P Hughes), P Hughes

12 Kilkenny Vintners INH Flat Race (4-y-o and up) £3,107 2m. . . . .(8:30)

CLASHWILLIAM GIRL (Ire) 5-11-3 (5ª) Mr T Lombard,
. . . .(5 to 1) 1
MOOREFIELD GIRL (Ire) 4-10-8 (7ª) Miss F M Crowley,
. . . .(7 to 1) 2
7² THE WICKED CHICKEN (Ire) 4-10-12 (3ª) Mrs S McCarthy,
. . . .(2 to 1 fav) 3
TOUREEN GIRL (Ire) 4-10-14 (5ª) Mrs J M Mullins, . . .(10 to 1) 4
THE DASHER DOYLE (Ire) 5-11-13 Mr P J Healy, . . (7 to 1) 5
RHOMAN FUN (Ire) 4-10-13 (7ª) Mr M G Hartrey, . .(12 to 1) 6
GIVEN BEST (Ire) 4-11-6 Mr J P Durkan, ...(14 to 1) 7

AR AIS ARIS (Ire) 4-10-8 (7ª) Mr P A Roche, ...(14 to 1) 8
HANG A RIGHT 6-12-0 Mr T Mullins, ...(20 to 1) 9
COMINOLE (Ire) 4-10-12 (3ª) Mr R O'Neill, ...(20 to 1) 10
CARRAIG LIATH (Ire) 4-10-12 (3ª) Mrs M Mullins, . . .(9 to 4) pu
Dist: 10l, 6l, 12l, ¾l. 3m 49.20s. (11 Ran).

(P Walsh), Thomas G Walsh

GOWRAN PARK (IRE) (good to yielding)
Saturday June 19th

13 Jack Duggan Memorial Handicap Hurdle (3,4,5-y-o) £4,830 2m. . . . .(2:00)

NORDIC SUN (Ire) [-] 5-10-10 (2ex) J F Titley, ...(4 to 1) 1
SHAREEF ALLIANCE (Ire) [-] 4-9-13 (7ª) J P Broderick,
. . . .(5 to 1) 2
CHOISYA (Ire) [-] 5-10-5 (12ex) C F Swan, . . (2 to 1 fav) 3
SMOULDER (USA) [-] 5-9-6 (7ª,3ex) R A Hennessy, (6 to 1) 4
CASTLE KNIGHT [-] 7-9-11 W T Slattery Jnr, ...(7 to 1) 5
KEPPOLS PRINCE [-] 6-10-11 P L Malone, ...(12 to 1) 6
HERE IT IS [-] 6-10-2 B Sheridan, ...(14 to 1) 7
CLOGS [-] (bl) 9-9-7 F Woods, ...(33 to 1) 8
Dist: 3l, sht-hd, 7l, 6l. 3m 51.30s. (8 Ran).

(D Bernie), J S Bolger

14 Aubergine Handicap Chase (4-y-o and up) £3,450 2m 5f. . . . .(4:00)

CITIZEN LEVEE [-] 7-9-12 N Williamson, ...(9 to 4 fav) 1
KINGSTON WAY [-] 7-10-9 A J O'Brien, ...(7 to 1) 2
QUIVERING MELODY [-] 6-9-13 J R Kavanagh, ...(8 to 1) 3
HARRISTOWN LADY [-] 6-10-1 A Powell, ...(9 to 2) 4
NOBODYS SON [-] 7-9-1 (7ª,5eex) C O'Brien, ...(6 to 1) 5
PROVERB PRINCE [-] 9-9-11 C F Swan, ...(4 to 1) 6
COURSING GUY [-] 11-9-10 F Woods, ...(33 to 1) 7
Dist: 4l, 10l, 8l, 1l. 5m 42.10s. (7 Ran).

(E J O'Sullivan), Eugene M O'Sullivan

15 Thomastown Traders Summer Flat Race (5-y-o and up) £3,450 2½m. . . . .(5:00)

WOLF WINTER 8-11-7 (7ª) Mr P A Roche, ...(7 to 1) 1
OX EYE DAISY (Ire) 5-11-5 (3ª) Mrs M Mullins, ...(6 to 1) 2
THE LITTLE LADY 6-11-4 (5ª) Mr D P Murphy, ...(10 to 1) 3
MERRY PEOPLE (Ire) 5-11-13 Mr J Queally, ...(5 to 1 fav) 4
CLYDE PRINCE 8-12-0 Mr J P Dempsey, ...(25 to 1) 5
GOOLDS GOLD 7-12-0 Mr P F Graffin, ...(11 to 2) 6
ASHTON'S VENTURE (Ire) 5-11-3 (5ª) Mrs J M Mullins,
. . . .(8 to 1) 7
MILLER'S CROSSING 6-11-9 Mr T Doyle, ...(11 to 2) 8
BALLINGOWAN STAR 6-11-2 (7ª) Mr S O'Donnell, (12 to 1) 9
DEISE MARSHALL (Ire) 5-11-6 (7ª) Mr P A Dunphy, (40 to 1) 10
DOCTRINAIRE 7-11-9 (5ª) Mr D Valentine, ...(16 to 1) 11
KILMOUNTAIN DAWN (Ire) 5-11-1 (7ª) Mr R J Foley, (20 to 1) 12
FANCY DISH 7-11-9 Mr J A Berry, ...(14 to 1) 13
STRONG CHERRY 7-11-2 (7ª) Mr K Taylor, ...(14 to 1) 14
IDEAL 8-11-7 (7ª) Miss E Kennedy, ...(14 to 1) 15
BALLYDAY DAWN 6-11-2 (7ª) Mr J P Walsh, ...(14 to 1) 16
FRAGRANCE MOUNTAIN 7-11-2 (7ª) Miss A Sloane,
. . . .(40 to 1) pu
HIGH IDEALS 7-11-7 (7ª) Mr M McGrath, ...(40 to 1) pu
Dist: 6l, 2l, 4½l, 2½l. 4m 55.80s. (18 Ran).

(Mrs R Baly), H de Bromhead

AUTEUIL (FR) (soft)
Sunday June 20th

16 Grand Steeple-Chase de Paris (5-y-o and up) £119,474 3m 5f. . . . .(3:25)

UCELLO II (Fr) 8-10-1 C Aubert, ... 1
AL CAPONE II (Fr) 5-9-11 J-Y Beaurain, ... 2
VORETIN (Fr) 9-10-1 D Mescam, ... 3
SIRTA (Fr) 9-, ... 4
THE FELLOW (Fr) 8-, ... 5
UTELLO II (Fr) 7-, ... 6
UTIN DU MOULIN (Fr) 7-, ... 7
SUPER MAX (Fr) 8-, ... 8
TZAMBUKO (Fr) 9-, ... 9
Dist: 6l, 1l, 8l, 1l, 1½l, 1l. 7m 16.00s. (9 Ran).

(Marquesa de Moratalla), F Doumen

KILBEGGAN (IRE) (good to yielding)
Monday June 21st

17 Tyrellspass Maiden Hurdle (4-y-o and up) £2,245 2m 3f. . . . .(5:30)

LET IT RIDE 4-11-6 T Horgan, ...(6 to 4 on) 1
7⁴ SUMMER FOX 6-11-6 C F Swan, ...(5 to 2) 2
BELLS HILL LAD 6-11-6 B Sheridan, ...(16 to 1) 3
THE VERY MAN 7-11-7 (7ª) T P Treacy, ...(9 to 1) 4
PARSONS EYRE (Ire) 5-10-9 (5ª) T J Mitchell, ...(14 to 1) 5
BUMBLY BROOK 6-11-6 N Byrne, ...(25 to 1) 6

AERODYNAMIC 7-11-6 M Flynn, ...(25 to 1) 7
RATHNAGEERA GIRL (Ire) 5-11-1 (7") M P Halbrook,

. . . .(10 to 1) 8
HODGESTOWN 6-10-8 (7") A P Sweeney, ...(20 to 1) 9
BRAE (Ire) 5-11-0 C O'Dwyer, ...(14 to 1) 10
THE COBH GALE 6-11-1 H Rogers, ... (20 to 1) 11
SWEET KILDARE 6-11-1 A Powell, ... (33 to 1) 12
KAMTARA 7-10-13 (7") G Lee, ... (33 to 1) 13
CANDY IS DANDY (Ire) 4-10-7 (3") J Collins, ... (50 to 1) 14
REMAINDER LASS (Ire) 4-10-10 S H O'Donovan, (14 to 1) 15
DECENT DUAL (Ire) (bl) 5-11-0 J Shortt, ...(25 to 1) 16
RECORD BILLY 6-10-13 (7") Mr P Bohan, ...(100 to 1) 17
BELLAGHY BRIDGE 6-11-1 Satoshi Oehara, ...(100 to 1) 19
2 BELLAGHY BRIDGE 6-11-1 Satoshi Oehara, ...(100 to 1) 19
Dist: 5l, sht-hd, 3l, 4½l. 4m 45.40s. (18 Ran).

(J S Gutkin), E J O'Grady

18 C.T.V. Maiden Hurdle (Div 1) (5-y-o and up) £2,762 3m. . . . . (6:00)

BITACRACK 6-11-6 P McWilliams, ... (5 to 1) 1
REFINED HEIR 5-11-10 (3") P Carberry, ... (2 to 1 on) 2
KIL KIL CASTLE 6-11-1 (5") P O'Sullivan, ... (14 to 1) 3
ANYTHING FOR YOU 9-10-13 (7") T P Treacy, ...(66 to 1) 4
PARALIGHT 7-10-10 (5") C P Dunne, ... (14 to 1) 5
COURIER DESPATCH (Ire) 5-10-12 (7") C O'Brien, . .(7 to 1) 6
DADS HOBBY 7-10-8 (7") E G Callaghan, ... (66 to 1) 7
EASE THE BURDEN (Ire) 5-11-0 G M O'Neill, ...(20 to 1) 8
PAR-BAR (Ire) 5-11-0 A Maguire, ...(10 to 1) 9
MR MIAVI (Ire) 5-11-0 (5") D Leahy, ...(33 to 1) 10
COLLON MISSION 6-10-10 (5") M G Cleary, ... (33 to 1) 11
Dist: 1l, 10l, 14l, 15l. 6m 15.20s. (11 Ran).

(Bita Syndicate), I R Ferguson

19 C.T.V. Maiden Hurdle (Div 2) (5-y-o and up) £2,762 3m. . . . . (6:30)

1 MISS SPLENDOUR (Ire) 5-10-9 (5") T J Mitchell, . . (12 to 1) 1
BUCKSHOT ROBERTS 7-11-6 J Shortt, ...(8 to 1) 2
BEST MY TRY 6-11-6 M Flynn, ...(7 to 1) 3
TRINIVER 6-11-6 K Morgan, ... (14 to 1) 4
SILVER LIGHT (Ire) 5-11-5 J F Titley, ... (20 to 1) 5
CROGHAN DEW 6-11-1 F Woods, ... (14 to 1) 6
RED SHOON 7-11-1 H Rogers, ... (100 to 1) 7
MUTUAL BENEFIT 6-10-13 (7") Mr D E Finn, ...(14 to 1) 8
BALLAGH COUNTESS 6-11-9 A Maguire, ... (9 to 4) f
MOUNTHENRY STAR (Ire) 5-11-5 G M O'Neill,   (5 to 4 fav) f
Dist: Sht-hd, 11l, 9l, 15l. 6m 26.00s. (10 Ran).

(John W Byrne), John W Byrne

20 William Glynn Memorial Handicap Hurdle (0-116 4-y-o and up) £2,245 2m 3f. . . . . .(7:00)

AMID BIRDS OF PREY [-] 6-10-8 C O'Dwyer, ... (20 to 1) 1
FARMER'S CROSS [-] 9-11-12 M Flynn, ... (25 to 1) 2
MERRY JOHN [-] 7-11-5 N Byrne, ...(14 to 1) 3
RUNAWAY GOLD [-] 6-10-9 (5") T J Mitchell, ...(8 to 1) 4
LAY ONE ON YA (Ire) [-] 5-11-8 C F Swan, ... (4 to 1) 5
GARYS GIRL [-] 6-10-3 (7") Mr G Finlay, ... (20 to 1) 6
PRINCE TAUFAN (Ire) [-] 4-10-6 A Maguire, ... (5 to 1) 7
PEARLTWIST [-] 7-11-6 P L Malone, ...(6 to 1) 8
FLYING SOUTH (Ire) [-] 5-11-5 (3") P Carberry, . .(3 to 1 fav) 9
RUBY LODGE [-] 10-10-12 F Woods, ...(14 to 1) 10
HAVE TO THINK [-] 5-11-2 T J Taaffe, ... (9 to 1) 11
ARDEE FLO JO (Ire) [-] 5-10-2 (7") C O'Neill, ... (7 to 1) 12
LODATO [-] 9-10-6 (7") M Kelly, ... (20 to 1) 13
GALES JEWEL [-] 7-10-4 T Horgan, ...(50 to 1) 14
BE HOME SHARP [-] 6-9-12 (7") D A McLoughlin, (33 to 1) ur
Dist: 2l, 1½l, 8l, 9l. 4m 45.70s. (15 Ran).

(Mrs Mairead Higgins), Francis Berry

21 Bloomfield House Hotel Handicap Hurdle (0-102 4-y-o and up) £2,762 2m 5f. . . . . .(7:30)

DANCINGCINDERELLA [-] 9-9-9 J R Kavanagh, ...(5 to 1) 1
HIGHBABS [-] 7-10-4 T Horgan, ... (6 to 1) 2
CLOSE AT HAND [-] 8-9-8 (3") K B Walsh, ... (10 to 1) 3
CAPINCUR BOY [-] (bl) 11-11-4 J F Titley, ...(10 to 1) 4
REHEY LADY [-] 7-9-7 (5") T J O'Sullivan, ... (20 to 1) 5
GLITTER GREY [-] 7-11-6 (5") T J Mitchell, ...(9 to 1) 6
DOWN TOWN TO-NIGHT [-] 8-10-1 (7") Mr A Daly, (50 to 1) 7
ANNETTE'S DELIGHT [-] 14-9-7 (7") Miss Z Davison, (8 to 1) 8
QUEEN OF THE SWANS [-] 9-11-7 R Dunne, ...(16 to 1) 9
FERGAL'S DELIGHT [-] (bl) 10-10-9 H Rogers, . . .(9 to 4 fav) 10
LUCAS COURT [-] (bl) 7-11-9 C F Swan, ... (12 to 1) 11
BALLYBRIKEN CASTLE [-] 6-9-7 (7") C O'Brien, . . .(8 to 1) pu
Dist: 5l, 6l, 2½l, 4l. 5m 29.60s. (12 Ran).

(M F Murray), Michael Hourigan

22 Old Distillery Novice Chase (5-y-o and up) £2,590 2m 5f. . . . . (8:00)

LIGHT THE WICK 7-11-9 C F Swan, ...(2 to 1 fav) 1
INCH MAID 7-11-9 T Horgan, ...(4 to 1) 2
FESTIVAL DREAMS 8-12-0 J Shortt, ... (8 to 1) 3
INCA CHIEF 9-12-0 T J Taaffe, ... (10 to 1) 4
GLYNN RIVER (Ire) 5-10-6 (7") Mr J Bright, ...(20 to 1) 5
HAPPY ELIZA 10-10-11 (7") Mr J P Codd, ... (50 to 1) 6
BILLMAR 6-11-4 H Rogers, ... (33 to 1) 7

FURRY STAR 7-12-0 C O'Dwyer, ... (6 to 1) 8
PALMROCK DONNA 6-11-4 K Morgan, ...(20 to 1) 9
BALLY O ROURKE 7-11-9 F Woods, ...(25 to 1) 10
GRANGE PRIZE 7-11-2 (7") J Butler, ... (33 to 1) 11
RESTLESS ONE 6-11-9 P M Verling, ...(50 to 1) 12
FIX IT 6-11-2 (7") Mr G J Harford, ... (14 to 1) f
TRASSEY BRIDGE 6-11-9 A Powell, ...(20 to 1) f
KINGOFSPANCILHILL 6-11-9 J F Titley, ...(20 to 1) pu
ASTOUNDED 6-11-4 (5") T J Mitchell, ... (33 to 1) pu
Dist: 5l, 2l, 3l, 9l. 5m 23.90s. (16 Ran).

(Mrs J Downey), D T Hughes

23 Coola Mills INH Flat Race (4-y-o and up) £2,245 2m 3f. . . . . (8:30)

ANMACA (Ire) 5-11-1 (7") Mr E Norris, ... (5 to 2 fav) 1
12 SONG OF CAEDMON (Ire) 5-11-13 Mr S R Murphy, (11 to 4) 2
GAYLOIRE (Ire) 4-10-13 (7") Mr T J Murphy, ... (14 to 1) 3
DONT GAMBLE 7-12-0 Mr T Mullins, ...(7 to 1) 4
BEL SHAN 7-11-2 (7") Mr K Whelan, ... (14 to 1) 5
ANNFIELD LADY (Ire) 5-11-5 (3") Mr A R Coonan, . .(14 to 1) 6
ALANSFORD 6-11-7 (7") Mr J Bright, ... (16 to 1) 7
PRAGMATAR 6-12-0 Mr M McNulty, ... (6 to 1) 8
MEXICAN WAVE 6-11-2 (7") Mr A Daly, ... (10 to 1) 9
HAZEL PARK 6-11-1 (7") Mr P Henley, ... (16 to 1) 10
GOLDEN ARRANGEMENT 8-11-7 (7") Mr G Hogan,

. . . .(14 to 1) 11
STONELEIGH TURBO (Ire) 4-11-1 (5") Mr P M Kelly, (6 to 1) 12
MANAMOUR 6-11-7 (7") Mr P A Roche, ... (16 to 1) 13
ARDFALLON (Ire) 4-10-10 (5") Mr J P Berry, ... (20 to 1) 14
ODELL ROSE 6-11-4 (5") Mr D P Murphy, ... (50 to 1) 15
THE BOOTER 8-11-7 (7") Mr L Mannerings, ... (66 to 1) 16
GLASHA BRIDGE (Ire) 5-11-6 (7") Mr D M Christie, (66 to 1) 17
CRAZY LADY 7-11-6 (3") Miss M Olivefalk, ... (50 to 1) 18
Dist: 5l, 3½l, 13l, 6l. 4m 38.50s. (18 Ran).

(Mrs M D Murphy), Patrick Joseph Flynn

SLIGO (IRE) (yielding to soft)
Tuesday June 22nd

24 Garavogue Maiden Hurdle (4-y-o and up) £2,245 2m. . . . . (5:30)

10 BRAVEFOOT 5-11-8 (5") T J Mitchell, ... (4 to 1) 1
FION CORN 6-11-6 T J Taaffe, ... (11 to 10 fav) 2
OYSTER LANE 7-10-12 (3") G Kilfeather, ... (14 to 1) 3
8 DARCARI ROSE (Ire) 4-10-10 F Woods, ...(14 to 1) 4
CREGGYCONNELL 7-10-13 (7") Mr R Pugh, ... (20 to 1) 5
CAT FIGHT 6-10-8 (7") Mr A Daly, ... (16 to 1) 6
PALLASKENRY (Ire) 5-11-5 Mr E Bolger, ...(20 to 1) 7
OZONE RIVER (Ire) 5-11-0 L P Cusack, ... (14 to 1) 8
KEASHILL (Ire) 4-10-10 P L Malone, ...(33 to 1) 9
HINTERLAND 6-11-3 (3") P Carberry, ...(3 to 1) pu
Dist: 6l, 7l, ½l, 12l. 4m 5.90s. (10 Ran).

(S Macklin), J H Scott

25 Ballysodare Handicap Hurdle (0-102 4-y-o and up) £2,245 2m. . . . . (6:00)

11 TERZIA [-] 6-11-8 (6ex) T Horgan, ...(3 to 1 fav) 1
2 RATTLE AND HUM [-] 6-11-3 P L Malone, ... (8 to 1) 2
15 HOSTETLER [-] 4-10-11 (3") P Carberry, ... (4 to 1) 3
DAVY CROCKETT [-] 6-10-12† (7",6ex) Mr R Pugh, (7 to 1) 4
KINDERSLEIGH [-] 6-10-7 (5") Mr A E Lacy, ... (7 to 1) 5
MARY OG [-] 6-9-11 (7") T Martin, ... (33 to 1) 6
1 MABES TOWN [-] 5-10-12 N Byrne, ... (16 to 1) 7
1 MRS COOPS [-] 6-10-3 (5") T J Mitchell, ... (16 to 1) 8
BANKONIT (Ire) [-] (bl) 5-11-1 (3") J Magee, ... (9 to 2) 9
CRAGHAN CRAFTY (Ire) [-] 5-10-1 (3") G Kilfeather, (20 to 1) pu
Dist: 4½l, nk, sht-hd, 3l. 4m 6.60s. (10 Ran).

(P Hughes), P Hughes

26 Martin Reilly Fiat Connaught National Chase (0-114 4-y-o and up) £2,762 2½m. . . . . . (8:00)

RUSTY COIN [-] 8-11-13 T Horgan, ...(Evens fav) 1
LOUGHLINSTOWN BOY [-] 8-11-5 T J Taaffe, ...(10 to 1) 2
PORTLAND LAD [-] 8-9-12 F Woods, ... (25 to 1) 3
CHARDEN [-] 7-9-7 (7") C O'Brien, ...(7 to 1) 4
MIDNIGHT MISS (NZ) [-] 9-10-5 L P Cusack, ... (10 to 1) 5
THURSDAY SWEEP [-] 7-11-3 (7") J P Broderick, . .(16 to 1) 6
TREAT ME GOOD [-] 10-10-12 (5") T J Mitchell, ...(7 to 1) pu
MAYE FANE [-] 9-11-10 (3") G Kilfeather, ...(5m 30.30s) pu
Dist: 5l, 10l, sht-hd, 4½l. 5m 30.30s. (8 Ran).

(P Hughes), P Hughes

27 Grange INH Flat Race (4-y-o and up) £2,245 2m. . . . . (8:30)

BOLD CRYSTAL (Ire) 4-11-3 (7") Mr J A Nash, (10 to 9 on) 1
CASH CHASE (Ire) 5-11-2 (7") Mr S O'Donnell, ...(3 to 1) 2
BEAU GRANDE (Ire) 5-11-5 (5") Mr D Valentine, . . .(6 to 1) 3
CARRIGANS LAD (Ire) 5-11-3 (7") Mr A Daly, ... (20 to 1) 4
BARR NA CRANEY (Ire) 5-11-3 (7") Mrs D McDonogh,

. . . .(14 to 1) 5
CLON CAW (Ire) 5-11-3 (7") Mr G Hogan, ...(10 to 1) 6

CHUCK'S TREASURE (Ire) 4-10-10 (7*) Mr J P Fahey,
....(20 to 1) 7
THYNE OWN GIRL (Ire) 4-10-10[5] (7*) Mr R Pugh, ..(14 to 1) 8
9[7] TODDY MARK (Ire) (bl) 4-10-10 (7*) Mr J P Kilfeather,
....(12 to 1) 9
CLANMANY (Ire) 4-11-3 Mr E Bolger, ...(10 to 1) 10
Dist: 10l, ¾l, 6l, 15l. 4m 8.80s. (10 Ran).

(High Seas Leisure Limited), Patrick Prendergast

WEXFORD (IRE) (good to yielding)
Wednesday June 23rd

28
Stanley Cooker Maiden Hurdle (4-y-o and up) £2,762 2m...........................(6:00)

NIMBLE WIND (bl) 7-11-9 A J O'Brien, ...(8 to 1) 1
MARIYDA (Ire) 4-11-1 P McWilliams, ...(6 to 1) 2
SEARCHLIGHT (Ire) 5-11-13 C F Swan, ... (5 to 4 fav) 3
7 SMART DECISION (Ire) 5-10-7 (7*) K P Gaule, ...(8 to 1) 4
DAWN APPEAL 6-11-9 T J Taaffe, ...(10 to 1) 5
ZORIA (Ire) 5-10-11 (3*) P Carberry, ...(12 to 1) 6
2[3] DIPIE (Ire) 5-10-12 (7*) H Taylor, ...(9 to 2) 7
10 CASTLEROE LAD 6-11-6 P Kavanagh, ...(66 to 1) 8
FROMTHEGETGO (Ire) (bl) 4-11-6 P L Malone, ...(20 to 1) 9
LAVINS THATCH 7-11-1 J F Titley, ...(25 to 1) 10
WINCHLING 8-11-6 N Byrne, ...(20 to 1) 11
ALL YOURS (Ire) 4-11-6 L P Cusack, ...(12 to 1) 12
SEZ HE SEZ I 9-11-7 (7*) Miss C E Hyde, ...(33 to 1) 13
FARAGHAN (Ire) 4-11-6 T Horgan, ...(20 to 1) 14
CASEY'S SHADOW (Ire) 4-10-5 (5*) Mr P J Casey, (20 to 1) 15
Dist: ½l, 2½l, 2l, 4l. 3m 52.70s. (15 Ran).

(Mrs D J Tarrant), Francis M O'Brien

29
Hilary Murphy Travel Handicap Hurdle (4-y-o and up) £2,762 2¼m.............(6:30)

DIRECT LADY (Ire) [-] 4-10-11 J F Titley, ...(6 to 4 fav) 1
MILLENIUM LASS (Ire) [-] 5-9-8 N Williamson, ...(20 to 1) 2
HI MILLIE [-] 7-10-8 P L Malone, ...(7 to 1) 3
ANOTHER CONTACT [-] 7-9-12 (5*) T J Mitchell, ..(7 to 1) 4
CREWS CASTLE [-] 6-9-1 (7*) Mr J Connolly, ...(8 to 1) 5
5* WATERLOO LADY [-] 6-9-10 (3*,6ex) P Carberry, ..(9 to 2) 6
NICE AND SIMPLE [-] 6-10-0 A J O'Brien, ...(14 to 1) 7
11 ERMESHKA [-] 7-9-6 (7*) K P Gaule, ...(25 to 1) 8
MOTILITY [-] 6-10-2 (5*) M J Holbrook, ...(8 to 1) 9
PRINCE JUAN [-] 6-10-2 (7*) J Butler, ...(10 to 1) 10
7[5] LE SEPT [-] 6-9-7 T Horgan, ...(20 to 1) 11
MANDEVILLE LANE [-] 7-9-7 (5*) A J Roche, ...(20 to 1) pu
Dist: ¾l, 12l, 10l, 10l. 4m 8.60s. (12 Ran).

(Mrs D Mahony), J S Bolger

30
Waterford Stanley Cooker Maiden Hurdle (4-y-o and up) £2,762 2½m.............(7:00)

HOUSE OF ROSES (Ire) 5-11-13 J F Titley, ...(3 to 1 fav) 1
THE JEWELLER 6-11-9 (5*) Mr T P Hyde, ...(8 to 1) 2
CARRABAWN 7-11-2 (7*) Mr P O'Keeffe, ...(9 to 2) 3
1 KAFKAN (Ire) 5-11-13 H Rogers, ...(6 to 1) 4
AWBEG ROVER (Ire) 5-11-13 T Horgan, ...(16 to 1) 5
4[8] FAHA GIG (Ire) 4-11-0 S H O'Donovan, ...(8 to 1) 6
HEY LAD (Ire) 5-11-13 P M Verling, ...(20 to 1) 7
BARTS CASTLE 7-11-9 (5*) A J Roche, ...(12 to 1) 8
WALKERS LADY (Ire) 5-11-3 (5*) D T Evans, ...(12 to 1) 9
THE PLEDGER 6-11-9 C F Swan, ...(8 to 1) 10
6 BOHOLA EXPRESS 6-11-7 (7*) Mr C A Leavy, ...(25 to 1) 11
DECENTRUN (Ire) 5-11-1 (7*) Mr K F O'Donnell, ..(10 to 1) 12
BELGRADE (Ire) 5-11-13 P Kavanagh, ...(20 to 1) 13
TIMELY NUN (Ire) 5-11-8 A J O'Brien, ...(20 to 1) pu
LOT OF STYLE (Ire) 5-11-13 J Shortt, ...(12 to 1) pu
Dist: Hd, 7l, 10l, 3l. 4m 49.90s. (15 Ran).

(Cornelius Rice), E Bolger

31
Talbot Hotel INH Flat Race (4 & 5-y-o) £2,762 2m..................................(8:30)

9[3] BLAST FREEZE (Ire) 4-10-8 (7*) Mr J A Nash, (11 to 10 fav) 1
MR GREY FELLOW (Ire) 5-11-13 Mr A P O'Brien, ..(10 to 1) 2
HERE NOW (Ire) 4-10-13 (7*) Mr P Henley, ...(16 to 1) 3
ANOTHER COURSE (Ire) 5-11-6 (7*) Mr P M Cloke, (3 to 1) 4
LITTLE BUCK (Ire) 5-11-6 (7*) Mr M McGrath, ...(40 to 1) 5
QUEEN KAM (Ire) 4-10-10 (5*) Mr J P Berry, ...(14 to 1) 6
PRYS PAUPER (Ire) 5-11-6 (7*) Miss Julia Murphy, (14 to 1) 7
GREENFIELD LODGE (Ire) 4-11-6 Mr J P Durkan, (16 to 1) 8
CROGHAN BRIDGE (Ire) 4-10-13 (7*) Mr W P Doyle,
....(50 to 1) 9
DONT RISE ME (Ire) 4-10-13 (7*) Mr D K Budds, ..(8 to 1) 10
ARKS PRINCESS (Ire) 4-10-8 (7*) Mr G P FitzGerald,
....(16 to 1) 11
RING WING (Ire) 4-11-1 Mr S R Murphy, ...(20 to 1) 12
LADY SALLY (Ire) 4-10-8 (7*) Mr G R Ryan, ...(14 to 1) 13
SONIC EXPERIENCE (Ire) 5-11-5 (3*) Mr R Neylon, (50 to 1) 14
JUDY RUN HOME (Ire) (bl) 5-11-1 (7*) Mr P English, (25 to 1) 15
Dist: 2l, 5½l, 3l, sht-hd. 3m 48.30s. (15 Ran).

(Mrs E Queally), J G Coogan

THURLES (IRE) (good)
Thursday June 24th

32
Tipperary Novice Hurdle (4-y-o and up) £2,245 2m........................(5:30)

CAN'T THINK WHAT 6-10-6 (7*) T P Treacy, ...(8 to 1) 1
10 UPPINGHAM 7-11-4 C O'Dwyer, ...(12 to 1) 2
JOHNSTON'S JET 9-11-4 J F Titley, ...(3 to 1) 3
OXFORD QUILL 6-11-4 T J Taaffe, ...(5 to 2 fav) 4
PERSIAN TACTICS 4-10-10 B Sheridan, ...(8 to 1) 5
TAKE IT EASY KID (Ire) 5-10-12 C F Swan, ...(5 to 1) 6
FAIRYHILL RUN (Ire) 5-10-5 (7*) Mr D A Harney, ..(12 to 1) 7
10[9] MANDAVINCI (Ire) 5-10-5 (7*) C O'Brien, ...(25 to 1) 8
SUMMER JANE (Ire) 5-10-9 (3*) J Collins, ...(16 to 1) 9
4 DRIPSEY QUAY (Ire) 5-10-5 (7*) Mr D Keane, ...(33 to 1) 10
PRINCE CHANTER 9-11-4 Mr T Doyle, ...(33 to 1) 11
KINCOR (Ire) 4-10-0 (5*) T P Rudd, ...(33 to 1) 12
MILLIES GIRL (Ire) 5-10-5 (7*) Mr J T McNamara, ..(16 to 1) f
THE FUN OF IT 8-11-4 T Horgan, ...(16 to 1) pu
Dist: 3l, ½l, 2½l, 14l. 3m 48.90s. (14 Ran).

(Mrs P Mullins), P Mullins

33
Moycarkey Novice Chase (5-y-o and up) £2,245 2¾m........................(6:00)

MUZAHIM (USA) 9-12-0 T J Taaffe, ...(5 to 4 fav) 1
QUAYSIDE BUOY 10-12-0 M Dwyer, ...(7 to 1) 2
MUSIC SCORE 7-12-0 G M O'Neill, ...(7 to 1) 3
18[6] COURIER DESPATCH (Ire) 5-10-6 (7*) C O'Brien, ..(12 to 1) 4
BALADINE 6-11-4 W T Slattery Jnr, ...(33 to 1) 5
HURRYUP 6-11-4 (5*) T J Mitchell, ...(14 to 1) 6
6 EDWARD'S DOLLY 8-10-13 (5*) M G Cleary, ...(20 to 1) 7
6[4] TIGH AN CHEOIL 9-12-0 A J O'Brien, ...(8 to 1) 8
22 BALLY O ROURKE 7-11-9 F Woods, ...(20 to 1) 9
BUCKTAN 7-10-13 (5*) M A Davey, ...(20 to 1) 10
6[6] TWO BOB 9-12-0 S H O'Donovan, ...(12 to 1) 11
MANOR RHYME 6-11-2 (7*) Mr D Keane, ...(50 to 1) 12
TINKERS CORNER 8-11-9 N Williamson, ...(20 to 1) f
MISS CORINTHIAN (bl) 6-11-4 T Horgan, ...(20 to 1) f
22 RESTLESS ONE 6-11-9 P M Verling, ...(33 to 1) ur
BIT OF A TOUCH 7-11-9 (5*) T J O'Sullivan, ...(9 to 1) pu
Dist: 3l, 1½l, 10l, 6l. 5m 26.20s. (16 Ran).

(J F Ryan), A L T Moore

34
Shannon Handicap Hurdle (0-116 4-y-o and up) £2,245 2m....................(6:30)

THE LADY'S KNIGHT [-] 7-11-6 (7*) C O'Brien, ...(7 to 1) 1
13[5] CASTLE KNIGHT [-] 7-11-2 W T Slattery Jnr, ...(8 to 1) 2
BANAAYKA (Ire) [-] 4-11-11 C O'Dwyer, ...(5 to 4 fav) 3
8[8] FINE PRINT (Ire) [-] 5-11-1 H Rogers, ...(10 to 1) 4
RUSTIC GENT (Ire) [-] 5-10-8 A J O'Brien, ...(8 to 1) 5
DANGEROUS REEF (Ire) [-] 5-10-9 (5*) T P Rudd, ..(7 to 1) 6
JUST FOUR (Ire) [-] 4-10-2 B Sheridan, ...(25 to 1) 7
1[9] SUNSHINE SEAL [-] 6-10-11 P L Malone, ...(12 to 1) 8
LEVERACH [-] 6-9-9 (5*) T J Mitchell, ...(20 to 1) 9
5[9] FUR N MONEY [-] 7-9-12 (7*) J P Broderick, ...(40 to 1) 10
SUNDAY WORLD (USA) [-] 7-10-12 C F Swan, ...(14 to 1) 11
5[2] BUCKINGHAM BOY [-] 7-10-0 (7*) Mrs C Harrison, (8 to 1) f
Dist: 15l, 2l, 2l, 1l. 3m 42.90s. (12 Ran).

(F X Doyle), F X Doyle

35
Golden Vale Handicap Chase (4-y-o and up) £2,245 2m........................(7:30)

THATS THE LIFE [-] 8-11-6 T J Taaffe, ...(10 to 1) 1
LA MODE LADY [-] 8-9-7 W T Slattery Jnr, ...(14 to 1) 2
ARDUBH [-] 6-9-7 N Williamson, ...(10 to 1) 3
BEST VINTAGE [-] 9-11-7 A O'Donovan, ...(10 to 1) 4
TURNBERRY LAKE [-] 7-9-11 A J O'Brien, ...(14 to 1) 5
CROSS CANNON [-] 7-11-7 Mr P F Graffin, ...(7 to 2) 6
BLENHEIM PALACE (USA) [-] 6-9-7 F Woods, ...(8 to 1) 7
FLUSTERED (USA) [-] 7-11-7 M Dwyer, ...(3 to 1 fav) 8
GRANVILLE GRILL [-] 8-9-4 (5*) T J Mitchell, ...(12 to 1) 9
MOLDAVIA [-] (bl) 7-9-6 (7*) C O'Brien, ...(10 to 1) f
ORIENT MELODY [-] 11-9-10 P McWilliams, ...(14 to 1) pu
Dist: 1½l, sht-hd, 2½l, 6l. 3m 58.60s. (11 Ran).

(C Nolan), A L T Moore

36
Devils Bit Flat Race (4-y-o and up) £2,245 2m..(8:30)

PROFIT MOTIVE 4-11-6 Mr S R Murphy, ...(5 to 1) 1
TAYLORS QUAY (Ire) 5-11-6 (7*) Mr K Whelan, (11 to 8 fav) 2
THE LODGER (Ire) 4-10-13 (7*) Mr D A Harney, ...(8 to 1) 3
KINGS DECREE (Ire) 4-11-3 (7*) Mr J T McNamara,
....(12 to 1) 4
BALLYGIBLIN LADY 9-11-9 Mr P Fenton, ...(10 to 1) 5
7[3] MISS POLLERTON (Ire) 5-11-1 (7*) Mr M J Bowe, (10 to 1) 6
CILL CHUILLINN (Ire) 5-11-6 (7*) Mr M A Cahill, ..(20 to 1) 7
WOLVER LAD (Ire) 5-11-13 Mr T Doyle, ...(6 to 1) 8
DONT BE SHORT (Ire) 4-10-8 (7*) Mr D Keane, ..(10 to 1) 9
TOURIG LE MOSS 6-11-2 (7*) Mr R Foley, ...(33 to 1) 10
ABDUL EMIR 6-11-9 (5*) Mr C T G Kinane, ...(33 to 1) 11

4

SLEMISH MINSTREL 7-11-7 (7") Mr I Johnston, . . .(50 to 1) 12
ORGAN MELODY 6-11-2 (7") Miss A Rohan, ...(40 to 1) 13
ORANGE FLAME 7-11-7 (7") Mr S Mulcaire, ... (40 to 1) 14
WISE STATEMENT (Ire) 4-11-1 (5") Mr J T Berry, . . .(8 to 1) 15
FIRST SET (USA) 4-10-12 (3") Miss M Olivefalk, . . .(6 to 1) 16
CAPTAIN GREG 6-12-0 Mr E Bolger, ...(25 to 1) 17
23 GOLDEN ARRANGEMENT 8-11-7 (7") Mr M McGrath,

. . . .(20 to 1) 18
GROGAN CREST (Ire) 5-11-3 (5") Mr D P Murphy, (33 to 1) 19
THE BLACK MEADOW (Ire) 5-11-5 (3") Mr D Marnane,

. . . .(20 to 1) 20
LADY BUDD (Ire) 5-11-5 (3") Mr A R Coonan, ... (16 to 1) 21
Dist: Nk, 3½l, 5½l, 1½l. 3m 38.60s. (21 Ran).

(Patrick O'Leary), Patrick O'Leary

DUNDALK (IRE) (good to soft)
Friday June 25th

37 Annagassan Maiden Hurdle (4-y-o and up) £2,245 2m 135yds. . . . . (5:30)

VICOSA (Ire) 4-11-1 (5") T F Lacy Jnr, ... (8 to 1) 1
4² STEEL MIRROR 4-11-1 J Shortt, ... (3 to 1) 2
CUBAN QUESTION 6-11-6 C F Swan, ... (20 to 1) 3
CLASSIC MATCH (Ire) 5-11-10 (3") P Carberry, (9 to 4 fav) 4
BULLANGUERO (Ire) (bl) 4-10-8 (7") D M McCullagh,

. . . .(14 to 1) 5
8⁶ PENNINE PASS (Ire) 4-11-6 B Sheridan, ...(10 to 1) 6
MOSARAT (Ire) 4-10-3 (7") D M Bean, ...(33 to 1) 7
8³ WINDOVER LODGE 6-11-6 L P Cusack, ... (7 to 2) 8
PRINCE ROCKAWAY (Ire) 5-11-5 K Morgan, ...(20 to 1) 9
FIGHTING TALK (USA) 4-11-1 T J Taaffe, ...(14 to 1) 10
SLIM-N-LITE 7-11-1 H Rogers, ...(66 to 1) 11
ARI'S FASHION 8-11-1 F Woods, ... (20 to 1) 12
MERSEY RACING 6-11-1 (5") T J O'Sullivan, ...(66 to 1) 13
LORD LOVING (Ire) 4-11-1 T Horgan, ...(20 to 1) 14
MOORCLOUGH VIEW (Ire) 5-10-7 (7") G McGivern, .(50 to 1) 15
ARDLEA HOUSE (Ire) 4-10-13 (7") R A Hennessy, . .(16 to 1) 16
FOXHILL 7-11-1 (5") D T Evans, ...(66 to 1) 17
PEARLY CASTLE (Ire) 5-11-0 P McWilliams, ...(25 to 1) su
3 SALVATION 6-11-6 A Powell, ...(14 to 1) pu
Dist: ½l, 4l, 2l, 2½l. 4m 6.20s. (19 Ran).

(T F Lacy), T F Lacy

38 Dunleer Handicap Hurdle (0-109 4-y-o and up) £2,245 2½m 153yds. . . . . (6:00)

BALLINDERRY GLEN [-] 7-11-1 L P Cusack, ...(16 to 1) 1
1* SENSITIVE KING [-] 5-11-2 (3",6ex) J Collins, . . (7 to 1) 2
COQ HARDI SMOKEY (Ire) [-] 5-11-5 (3") P Carberry, (5 to 1) 3
16 FAUGHAN LODGE [-] 6-10-2 (7") K P Gaule, ... (14 to 1) 4
20⁴ RUNAWAY GOLD [-] 6-10-13 (7") R A Hennessy, . . .(8 to 1) 5
25⁶ MARY OG [-] 6-10-1 (7") T Martin, ...(25 to 1) 6
2 TADILA (Ire) [-] 4-11-2 B Sheridan, ...(10 to 1) 7
IDENTITY CRISIS [-] (bl) 8-10-10 (7") H Taylor, ...(25 to 1) 8
19* MISS SPLENDOUR (Ire) [-] 5-11-2 (6ex) C F Swan, (10 to 1) 9
LET THE RIVER RUN [-] 7-11-2 C O'Dwyer, ...(12 to 1) 10
1³ SALLOW GLEN [-] 7-10-13 T Horgan, ... (7 to 2 jt-fav) 11
3 WILLCHRIS [-] 6-10-12 F Woods, ...(50 to 1) 12
1 PERSIAN GALLERY [-] 6-11-7 H Rogers, ...(33 to 1) 13
ANNAGH QUEEN [-] 7-11-5 (7") C O'Brien, ...(50 to 1) 14
COQUALLA [-] (bl) 8-10-9 (7") D M Bean, ...(25 to 1) 15
11³ MUST DO [-] 7-11-6 (5") T J Mitchell, ...(7 to 2 jt-fav) f
Dist: 1l, 1l, 3½l, 2l. 5m 4.20s. (16 Ran).

(K Killian), T F Lacy

39 Louth INH Flat Race (4-y-o and up) £2,245 2m 135yds. . . . . (8:30)

HAUNTING ANGLE (Ire) 4-10-12 (3") Mr A R Coonan,

. . . .(3 to 1 fav) 1
PEACEFULL RIVER (Ire) 4-10-8 (7") Mr T J Beattie, (14 to 1) 2
KICKALONG 7-11-4 (5") Mr P J Casey, ...(10 to 1) 3
3⁴ KEY WEST (Ire) 4-11-1 (5") Mr D McGoona, ...(10 to 1) 4
3⁵ DOCS DILEMMA 4-11-6 Mr P F Graffin, ... (7 to 1) 5
TRAP ONE (Ire) 5-11-6 (7") Mr D J Kavanagh, ...(5 to 1) 6
QUEENS HALL (Ire) 5-11-8 Mr M McNulty, ... (12 to 1) 7
3³ JOKERS THREE (Ire) 4-10-13 (7") Mr A F Doherty, . .(9 to 2) 8
MAUREEN MAC (Ire) 4-10-8 (7") Mr M Brennan, ...(10 to 1) 9
PROUD KITTEN (Ire) 4-10-8 (7") Mr J A Nash, ...(5 to 1) 10
CURRAGH GALE (Ire) 5-11-1 (7") Mr P J Kelly, ...(20 to 1) 11
SPOUTING INSPECTOR (Ire) 5-11-6 (7") Mr M Budds,

. . . .(8 to 1) 12
MADAM NODDY 6-11-9 Mr S R Murphy, ...(25 to 1) 13
3 INACTUALFACT (Ire) 4-11-1 (5") Mr L Lennon, ...(16 to 1) 14
BELLE DE SEUL 6-11-2 (7") Mr P J McCrickard, . . .(66 to 1) 15
TOUCHER (Ire) 5-11-6 (7") Mr J Bright, ...(66 to 1) 16
OLDTOWN GIRL (Ire) 4-10-8 (7") Mr J Mulvaney, . .(25 to 1) 17
3 THE PARSONS ROSE (Ire) 5-11-5 (3") Mr P McMahon,

. . . .(33 to 1) su
Dist: 3l, 2l, 6l, ¾l. 4m 10.00s. (18 Ran).

(Glassdrummon Racing Syndicate), Patrick Martin

LIMERICK (IRE) (good)
Monday June 28th

40 Punch's Pub & Restaurant Handicap Hurdle (0-123 4-y-o and up) £3,452 2m. . . . . . . (6:30)

24⁷ BRAVEFOOT [-] 5-10-6 (5",6ex) T J Mitchell, ... (6 to 1) 1
13² SHAREEF ALLIANCE [-] 4-10-11 (7") J P Broderick,

. . . .(9 to 4) 2
5⁵ SERJITAK [-] 6-9-3 (7") T P Treacy, ...(4 to 1) 3
THATCH AND GOLD (Ire) [-] 5-11-2 (5") J R Barry,

. . . .(7 to 4 fav) 4
BELIEVE THE BEST (Ger) [-] 8-9-7 F Woods, ...(25 to 1) 5
29⁷ NICE AND SIMPLE [-] 6-10-2 A J O'Brien, ...(12 to 1) 6
Dist: 1½l, 2l, 4½l, hd. 3m 48.00s. (6 Ran).

(S Macklin), J H Scott

41 Armitage Shanks Maiden Hurdle (4-y-o and up) £3,452 2¼m. . . . . (7:00)

4⁶ IDEAL RISK (Ire) 4-11-1 F J Flood, ...(11 to 2) 1
20⁷ PRINCE TAUFAN (Ire) 4-11-1 A Maguire, ...(7 to 2 jt-fav) 2
THUNDERSTRUCK 7-11-6 J F Titley, ...(5 to 1) 3
4⁷ FULL MOON FEVER (Ire) 4-11-1 K F O'Brien, ...(10 to 1) 4
RATHBRAN (Ire) 4-10-8 (7") C O'Brien, ... (20 to 1) 5
HAVEN LIGHT 6-11-6 N Williamson, ... (20 to 1) 6
ALLOW GOLD 6-11-3 (3") P Carberry, ... (20 to 1) 7
32 MILLIES GIRL (Ire) 5-11-1 (7") Mr J T McNamara, . .(8 to 1) 8
MASTER BATT (Ire) 4-10-12 (3") J Magee, ... (10 to 1) 9
REGULAR PAL 10-10-10 (5") A J Roche, ...(20 to 1) 10
32⁹ SUMMER JANE (Ire) 5-10-11 (3") J Collins, ...(20 to 1) 11
KILLEEN COUNTESS (Ire) 5-11-0 L P Cusack, ...(25 to 1) 12
MAGNIFICENT OAK (NZ) 5-11-0 (5") C P Dunne, . .(20 to 1) 13
BARRINGTONS CASTLE (Ire) 5-11-13 B Sheridan, (8 to 1) 14
RAISE THE BANNER (Ire) 4-10-10 J R Kavanagh, (12 to 1) 15
RUSSIAN GALE (Ire) 5-10-9 (5") M G Cleary, ... (25 to 1) 16
CASTLE CELEBRITY (Ire) 4-10-10 M P Hourigan, (12 to 1) f
KINGS CHERRY (Ire) 5-11-3 S H O'Donovan, ...(6 to 1) ro
10⁶ FULL SCHEDUAL 6-11-6 A Powell, ... (7 to 2 jt-fav) pu
DERRING DREAM 6-10-13 (7") Mr J A Nash, ...(20 to 1) pu
Dist: 2l, nk, 2l, 4l. 4m 7.80s. (20 Ran).

(Mrs E Queally), Mrs John Harrington

42 B.D.O. Binder/G.N.P. Handicap Hurdle (4-y-o and up) £3,452 2m 5f. . . . . (7:30)

11² CUILIN BUI (Ire) [-] 5-9-11 (7") C O'Brien, ...(11 to 2) 1
20⁸ PEARLTWIST [-] 7-10-5 P L Malone, ...(10 to 1) 2
LANTERN LUCK (Ire) [-] (bl) 5-9-2 (7") J P Broderick,

. . . .(10 to 1) 3
MARILYN [-] 4-9-11 (5") T J Mitchell, ...(7 to 4 fav) 4
14² KINGSTON WAY [-] 7-10-5 A J O'Brien, ...(10 to 1) 5
14³ QUIVERING MELODY [-] 6-10-3 M P Hourigan, . . . (12 to 1) 6
M MACG (Ire) [-] 4-9-5¹ (3") J Magee, ...(25 to 1) 7
MOBILE MAN [-] 6-10-3 B Sheridan, ...(14 to 1) 8
29³ HI MILLIE [-] 7-10-6 A Powell, ...(12 to 1) 9
JOHNJOES PRIDE [-] 9-10-1 (7") K P Gaule, ...(25 to 1) 10
GRANADOS (USA) [-] 5-10-0 F Woods, ...(10 to 1) 11
6⁹ BALLYHEIGUE [-] 7-9-13 (7") Mr J T McNamara, . .(12 to 1) 12
WAR DEVIL [-] 7-9-8¹ (3") J Jones, ...(16 to 1) 13
29⁸ ERMESHKA [-] 7-9-8 (3") P Carberry, ...(14 to 1) 14
WILL YOU STOP VI [-] 10-10-9 (5") M A Davey, . . .(33 to 1) f
FIXED ASSETS [-] 6-10-6 N Williamson, ...(7 to 1) bd
TELL A TALE [-] 6-10-1 A Maguire, ...(9 to 1) bd
Dist: 1l, 3½l, 3l, ½l. 4m 52.20s. (17 Ran).

(Miss E Kiely), David J McGrath

43 J.P. McManus Bookmaker INH Flat Race (5 & 6-y-o) £3,452 2m. (8:30)

CARLINGFORD RUN 6-11-2 (7") Mr D Murphy, ...(12 to 1) 1
PAPRS GALE (Ire) 5-11-8 Mr P Fenton, ...(Evens fav) 2
DADDY LONG LEGGS 6-12-0 Mr A P O'Brien, ... (4 to 1) 3
KING OF THE WORLD (Ire) 5-11-6 (7") Mr D E Finn, (10 to 1) 4
THE TENANT 6-12-0 Mr S R Murphy, ...(14 to 1) 5
MAKE A LINE 5-11-6 (7") Mr A H Lillingston, ...(8 to 1) 6
23⁹ MEXICAN WAVE 6-11-2 (7") Mr A Daly, ...(14 to 1) 7
23 HAZEL PARK 5-11-1 (7") Mr P Henly, ...(20 to 1) 8
36⁷ CILL CHUILLINN (Ire) 5-11-6 (7") Mr M A Cahill, . . (12 to 1) 9
15⁷ ASHTON'S VENTURE (Ire) 5-11-3 (5") Mrs J M Mullins,

. . . .(10 to 1) 10
7 FIFTYBETWEENYE (Ire) 5-11-1 (7") Mr D Duggan, (33 to 1) 11
MINERS DREAM 6-11-2 (7") Mr D Keane, ...(14 to 1) 12
TAR AND CEMENT (Ire) 5-11-13 Mr D M O'Brien, (14 to 1) 13
10³ KENMAC 6-12-0 Mr E Bolger, ... (8 to 1) 14
HAZEL BROOK LAD (Ire) 5-11-6 (7") Mr N C Kelleher,

. . . .(14 to 1) 15
36 THE BLACK MEADOW (Ire) 5-11-5 (3") Mr D Marnane,

. . . .(25 to 1) su
Dist: 1l, ¾l, 6l, nk. 3m 29.30s. (16 Ran).

(Timothy Carver), Thomas Carver

GOWRAN PARK (IRE) (firm (race 1), good (2,3))
Wednesday June 30th

44 Standard Life Handicap Chase (0-116 5-y-o and up) £3,452 2¾m. . . . .(7:15)

14^6	PROVERB PRINCE [-] 9-10-12 J F Titley,	(10 to 1)	1
	OCTOBER FLAME [-] 10-10-9 K Morgan,	(9 to 4 fav)	2
	JAMES PIGG [-] 6-10-10 A J O'Brien,	(10 to 1)	3
21^2	HIGHBABS [-] 7-9-7 T Horgan,	(6 to 1)	4
	ANN'S PRINCE [-] 10-9-11^3 H Rogers,	(16 to 1)	5
	DESELBY'S CHOICE [-] 8-10-4 M Flynn,	(5 to 1)	6
11^7	FOXBROOK [-] (bl) 7-10-12 N Williamson,	(8 to 1)	7
33	BUCKTAN [-] 7-9-0 (7*) C O'Brien,	(20 to 1)	8
21^8	ANNETTE'S DELIGHT [-] 14-9-0 (7*) Miss Z Davison,	(12 to 1)	9
	GOLDEN SEE [-] 9-10-5 N Byrne,	(12 to 1)	10
	LIFE OF A LORD [-] 7-11-7 S H O'Donovan,	(14 to 1)	f
	KILSHEELAN LAD [-] 10-10-10 (5*) T J Mitchell,	(8 to 1)	pu
	TEMPLE MARY [-] 6-9-11 M P Hourigan,	(12 to 1)	pu
	ST ELMO'S FIRE (NZ) [-] 8-11-4 L P Cusack,	(14 to 1)	pu

Dist: ½l, 8l, 8l, 6l. 5m 22.00s. (14 Ran).

(M H Burke), Michael Cunningham

45 Kilkenny Block Maiden Hurdle (5-y-o and up) £3,107 2½m. . . . . (7:40)

17^4	THE VERY MAN 7-11-7 (7*) T P Treacy,	(6 to 4 fav)	1
	UGOLIN DE LA WERA (Fr) 7-12-0 N Williamson,	(10 to 1)	2
20^2	FARMER'S CROSS 9-12-0 M Flynn,	(3 to 1)	3
10^8	UNCLE BART (Ire) 5-10-12 (7*) R A Hennessy,	(14 to 1)	4
	SILVERWEIR 10-10-13 (7*) K P Gaule,	(8 to 1)	5
4^5	PUNTERS BAR 6-11-7 (7*) C O'Brien,	(10 to 1)	6
10	BAMANYAR (Ire) 5-10-12 (7*) Mr E Sheehy,	(14 to 1)	7
	MICHAEL'S STAR (Ire) 5-11-5 A Powell,	(14 to 1)	8
	LODGE PARTY (Ire) 5-11-0 D P Fagen,	(12 to 1)	9
15^4	MERRY PEOPLE (Ire) 5-11-5 T Horgan,	(12 to 1)	10
	CRACKLE N POP (Ire) 5-11-5 C N Bowens,	(33 to 1)	11
17^7	AERODYNAMIC 7-11-6 K F O'Brien,	(25 to 1)	12
28^8	CASTLEROE LAD 6-11-6 P Kavanagh,	(33 to 1)	13
17^8	RATHNAGEERA GIRL (Ire) 5-11-3 (5*) M J Holbrook,	(10 to 1)	14
10	BOLEREE (Ire) 5-11-0 S H O'Donovan,	(14 to 1)	15
10	JOHNOTHELODGE (Ire) 5-11-5 Mr P Fenton,	(25 to 1)	16
10	EASY TERMS 7-11-1 F Woods,	(5 to 1)	17
	SILVER BATCHELOR 11-12-0 C O'Dwyer,	(12 to 1)	18
	CROCKALAWN (Ire) 5-10-12 (7*) Mr D Keane,	(33 to 1)	19
20	BE HOME SHARP 6-11-6 K Morgan,	(16 to 1)	pu

Dist: 5l, 1½l, 1½l, 2l. 4m 49.90s. (20 Ran).

(F P Taaffe), P Mullins

46 John M.Foley Novice Handicap Hurdle (4-y-o and up) £3,176 2m. . . . .(8:05)

13*	NORDIC SUN (Ire) [-] 5-11-10 (6ex) J F Titley,	(11 to 4 fav)	1
13^4	SMOULDER (USA) [-] 5-9-13 (7*) R A Hennessy,	(8 to 1)	2
	ULTRA MAGIC [-] 6-9-4^2 (5*) A J Roche,	(16 to 1)	3
	PALACE GEM [-] 6-10-12 K F O'Brien,	(8 to 1)	4
2^4	HIS WAY (Ire) [-] 4-10-6 M Flynn,	(9 to 1)	5
25^7	MABES TOWN (Ire) [-] 5-9-8 N Byrne,	(16 to 1)	6
	PARTNERS IN CRIME [-] 5-10-4 (7*) B Bowens,	(5 to 1)	7
2*	FABRICATOR [-] 7-11-0 K Morgan,	(9 to 2)	8
22^8	FURRY STAR [-] 7-12-0 C O'Dwyer,	(9 to 1)	9
	MELTEMI [-] 7-10-11 D P Fagen,	(16 to 1)	10
	LE HACHETTE [-] 6-9-9 F Woods,	(20 to 1)	11
	MINI FASHION (Ire) [-] 5-9-0 (7*) T P Treacy,	(33 to 1)	12

Dist: 2½l, ½l, 12l, 1½l. 3m 44.60s. (12 Ran).

(D Bernie), J S Bolger

TIPPERARY (IRE) (good) Thursday July 1st

47 Royal Hotel/Carlsberg Handicap Hurdle (4-y-o and up) £3,452 2m. . . . . (8:30)

5	BALLYTIGUE LORD [-] 7-10-4 G M O'Neill,	(9 to 4 fav)	1
11	VINEYARD SPECIAL [-] 7-10-11 K Morgan,	(7 to 2)	2
13^8	CLOGS [-] (bl) 9-9-12 T Horgan,	(16 to 1)	3
	J-TEC BOY [-] 7-9-7 N Byrne,	(12 to 1)	4
35^8	FLUSTERED (USA) [-] 7-11-7 (7*) C O'Brien,	(3 to 1)	5
34	FUR N MONEY [-] 7-9-0 (7*) J P Broderick,	(16 to 1)	6
37^8	WINDOVER LODGE [-] 6-10-1 L P Cusack,	(6 to 1)	7
	SON OF SARAH [-] 9-10-11 A J O'Brien,	(14 to 1)	8

Dist: 3½l, 2l, 1½l, nk. 3m 57.20s. (8 Ran).

(Mrs Mary O'Connor), Augustine Leahy

48 Pierse Motors Flat Race (4-y-o and up) £3,452 2m. . . . . (9:00)

	WILD FANTASY (Ire) 5-11-12 Mr A P O'Brien,	(8 to 1)	1
	HIGHLANDER (Ire) 4-11-4 Mr J P Durkan,	(7 to 4 on)	2
	A FEW GOOD MEN (Ire) 4-11-4 Mr E Bolger,	(14 to 1)	3
34	BUCKINGHAM BOY 7-11-11 (7*) Miss C Harrison,	(10 to 1)	4
	PRACTICE RUN (Ire) 5-11-10 (7*) Mr D J Donegan,	(14 to 1)	5
36	TOURIG LE MOSS 6-10-13 (7*) Mr R J Foley,	(25 to 1)	6
	DUN OENGUS (Ire) 4-10-6 (7*) Mr K Whelan,	(14 to 1)	7
	US AND SAM (Ire) 4-10-11 (7*) Mr P A Roche,	(14 to 1)	8
15^2	OX EYE DAISY (Ire) 5-11-2 (3*) Mrs M Mullins,	(8 to 1)	9
12^3	THE WICKED CHICKEN (Ire) 4-10-10 (3*) Mrs S McCarthy,	(13 to 2)	10
31	RING VIEW (Ire) 4-10-13 Mr S R Murphy,	(20 to 1)	11
	ABBEY TRINITY (Ire) 4-10-10 (3*) Mr A R Coonan,	(20 to 1)	12
31	ARKS PRINCESS (Ire) 4-10-6 (7*) Mr G P FitzGerald,	(25 to 1)	13

Dist: 1½l, 10l, ½l, 6l. 3m 42.70s. (13 Ran).

(L F Curtin), A P O'Brien

WEXFORD (IRE) (good to firm) Friday July 2nd

49 Nick O'Donnell Memorial Maiden Hurdle (4-y-o and up) £3,452 2m. . . . . (5:30)

10^7	COMBINE CALL 6-11-7 (7*) T P Treacy,	(15 to 2)	1
32^3	JOHNSTON'S JET 9-12-0 J F Titley,	(9 to 4 fav)	2
	HUGH DANIELS 5-10-12 (7*) M P Moran,	(14 to 1)	3
	PAKOL (Ire) 4-10-5 (5*) D T Evans,	(20 to 1)	4
	TOP GENERATION 4-10-10 N Williamson,	(8 to 1)	5
37^4	CLASSIC MATCH (Ire) 5-11-10 (3*) P Carberry,	(5 to 2)	6
28	ALL YOURS (Ire) 4-11-6 L P Cusack,	(10 to 1)	7
	SHYNAWILL 9-12-0 C O'Dwyer,	(8 to 1)	8
28	FARAGHAN (Ire) 4-11-6 T Horgan,	(16 to 1)	9
	NORDIC RACE 6-11-6 H Rogers,	(16 to 1)	10
4^9	IRELANDS GALE (Ire) 5-11-5 F J Flood,	(12 to 1)	11
12^8	AR AIS ARIS (Ire) 4-10-7 (3*) J Magee,	(20 to 1)	12
	DUNSFORD 7-12-0 F Woods,	(20 to 1)	13
34^7	JUST FOUR (Ire) 4-10-10 B Sheridan,	(14 to 1)	f

Dist: 1l, 2l, 3½l, hd. 3m 58.00s. (14 Ran).

(Rory F Larkin), P Mullins

50 Waterford Co-Op (Mares) Maiden Hurdle (5-y-o and up) £3,452 2¼m. . . . . (6:00)

	TERINGETTE (Hun) 5-11-13 L P Cusack,	(5 to 1)	1
5^7	NO TAKERS 6-11-6 K F O'Brien,	(16 to 1)	2
	WINNING HEART 6-12-0 B Sheridan,	(5 to 4 fav)	3
9^4	PEARL'S CHOICE (Ire) 5-11-5 A Maguire,	(8 to 1)	4
	JOHNS ROSE (Ire) 5-11-2 (3*) J Collins,	(33 to 1)	5
32^6	TAKE IT EASY KID (Ire) 5-11-13 N Williamson,	(6 to 1)	6
33	MISS CORINTHIAN (bl) 6-11-6 T Horgan,	(25 to 1)	7
7	MILFORD MATCH (Ire) 5-11-5 P M Verling,	(14 to 1)	8
10	CLARA BRIDGE 6-11-6 C N Bowens,	(20 to 1)	9
	BAR LASS 6-10-13 (7*) M J Molloy,	(14 to 1)	10
17^5	PARSONS EYRE (Ire) 5-11-5 J P Byrne,	(8 to 1)	11
37	ARI'S FASHION 8-11-6 F Woods,	(25 to 1)	f
	SHEHEREZADE (Ire) 5-11-5 A J O'Brien,	(20 to 1)	f
	MYSTIC MEG (Ire) 5-10-12 (7*) Mr L B Murphy,	(25 to 1)	bd
	WAY LADY 7-11-6 S H O'Donovan,	(33 to 1)	pu

Dist: 3½l, 2l, 2½l, 4l. 4m 17.60s. (15 Ran).

(D W Samuel), Michael Robinson

51 Campile Oil Products Opportunity Handicap Hurdle (0-102 4-y-o and up) £3,452 2m (6:30)

25^5	KINDERSLEIGH [-] 6-11-2 (2*) T F Lacy Jnr,	(10 to 1)	1
29^2	MILLENIUM LASS (Ire) [-] 5-10-11 (4*) F Byrne,	(6 to 1)	2
	RATHBRIDES JOY [-] 6-11-10 (4*) D J Bunyan,	(9 to 2)	3
	CELTIC GOLD [-] 9-11-6 (2*) T P Rudd,	(20 to 1)	4
5^3	AQUINAS [-] 7-11-6 (4*) R A Hennessy,	(5 to 2 fav)	5
20^6	GARYS GIRL [-] 6-11-2 (2*) T J Mitchell,	(14 to 1)	6
	ST DONAVINT [-] 6-11-7 (4*) B Bowens,	(12 to 1)	7
29^6	WATERLOO LADY [-] 6-11-4 (6ex) P Carberry,	(9 to 1)	8
23^6	ANNFIELD LADY (Ire) [-] 5-10-10 (4*) T Martin,	(16 to 1)	9
	MURPHY'S TROUBLE (Ire) [-] 5-10-12 (4*) P O Casey,	(20 to 1)	10
	DELIFFIN [-] 7-11-8 (4*) J K McCarthy,	(20 to 1)	f
	MAGIC GLOW (Ire) [-] 4-10-10 (4*) G Lee,	(16 to 1)	f
33^8	TIGH AN CHEOIL [-] 9-11-12 J Magee,	(12 to 1)	pu
	GREEK MAGIC [-] 6-11-7 J Collins,	(10 to 1)	pu

Dist: 2½l, 7l, 2l, 4½l. 3m 46.80s. (14 Ran).

(Mrs T F Lacy), T F Lacy

52 William Neville & Sons Ltd. Handicap Chase (4-y-o and up) £4,142 2½m. . . . .(7:00)

	NEVER BE GREAT [-] 11-11-7 F J Flood,	(12 to 1)	1
14^5	NOBODYS SON [-] 7-10-3 (7*) C O'Brien,	(7 to 1)	2
6*	TUSKER LADY [-] 8-10-5 (6ex) C O'Dwyer,	(6 to 1)	3
	MAC'S GLEN [-] 9-11-10 J F Titley,	(10 to 1)	4
35^2	LA MODE LADY [-] 8-9-12 T Horgan,	(9 to 1)	5
21	FERGAL'S DELIGHT [-] (bl) 10-9-10 W T Slattery Jnr,	(12 to 1)	6
35^5	TURNBERRY LAKE [-] 7-10-0 A J O'Brien,	(12 to 1)	7
35^4	BEST VINTAGE [-] 9-11-12 S H O'Donovan,	(7 to 1)	8
21^6	GLITTER GREY [-] 7-10-7 (5*) T J Mitchell,	(12 to 1)	9
42	WILL YOU STOP VI [-] 10-11-13 A Powell,	(33 to 1)	10
26^6	THURSDAY SWEEP [-] 7-11-1 (7*) J P Broderick,	(20 to 1)	11
	LITTLE TOM [-] 8-9-13 M P Hourigan,	(9 to 4 fav)	ur
	CASTLE WINDOWS [-] (bl) 10-10-12 (5*) C P Dunne,	(33 to 1)	pu
40^5	BELIEVE THE BEST (Ger) [-] 8-9-7 F Woods,	(20 to 1)	pu

Dist: Sht-hd, 4½l, 5½l, 9l. 4m 44.50s. (14 Ran).

(Patrick McAteer), F Flood

53 Chadwicks INH Flat Race (6-y-o and up) £2,762 2m. . . . . (8:00)

12[4] TOUREEN GIRL 6-11-4 (5*) Mrs J M Mullins, ...(5 to 1) 1
45[5] SILVERWEIR 10-12-0 Mr A P O'Brien, ...(8 to 1) 2
37[3] CUBAN QUESTION 6-12-0 Mr S R Murphy, ...(5 to 1) 3
LOUGH ATALIA 6-11-7 (7*) Mr P A Roche, ...(25 to 1) 4
AR AGHAIDH LEATH 7-11-11 (3*) Mr A R Coonan, (20 to 1) 5
23[4] DONT GAMBLE 7-12-0 Mr T Mullins, ...(2 to 1 fav) 6
36 SLEMISH MINSTREL 7-11-7 (7*) Mr I Johnston, . . .(25 to 1) 7
FLOWER OF GRANGE 6-11-2 (7*) Mr P English, . . (20 to 1) 8
32 THE FUN OF IT 8-12-0 Mr P Fenton, ...(16 to 1) 9
23[5] BEL SHAN 7-11-2 (7*) Mr K Whelan, ...(10 to 1) 10
MOON-FROG 6-11-7 (7*) Miss Julia Murphy, ... (25 to 1) 11
WHISTLERS PRIDE 10-11-7 (7*) T J Beattie, ...(20 to 1) 12
7[9] I'D SAY HARDLY 6-11-7 (7*) Mr B Lennon, ...(10 to 1) 13
36 ABDUL EMIR 6-11-7 (7*) Mr A H Lillingston, ... (25 to 1) 14
RAMDON ROCKS 6-11-9 (5*) Mr D P Murphy, ... (6 to 1) 15

Dist: 3½l, ¾l, nk, 20l. 3m 41.10s. (15 Ran).

(Colm Murray), W P Mullins

AUTEUIL (FR) (soft)
Saturday July 3rd

54 Grand Course de Haies d'Auteuil (Hurdle) (5-y-o and up) £71,685 3m 1f 110yds. . . (4:25)

UBU III (Fr) 7-10-5 A Kondrat, ... 1
TRUE BRAVE (USA) 5-10-1 C Aubert, ... 2
GABARRET (Fr) 6-10-5 D Mescam, ... 3
SWEET GLOW (Fr) 6-10-5 J Osborne, *al beh*. 0
RULING (USA) 7-10-5 P Niven, *pld up one m out*. . . . . pu
LORD RELIC (NZ) 7-10-5 R Dunwoody, *trkd ldr till fdd 3 fs out*. 8

Dist: 2½l, 2½l, 4l, 2½l, 1l, 2½l, 8l, 1½l, 4l. 6m 26.00s. (14 Ran).

(Marquesa de Moratalla), F Doumen

NAAS (IRE) (good)
Saturday July 3rd

55 Kildare INH Flat Race (4-y-o and up) £3,105 2m. . . . .(5:00)

FLEMCUR (Ire) 5-11-6 (7*) Mr J A Nash, ...(8 to 1) 1
9[8] SIMPLISTIC (Ire) 4-11-2 Mr J P Dempsey, ... (8 to 1) 2
43[6] MAKE A LINE 5-11-6 (7*) Mr A H Lillingston, ...(9 to 1) 3
PORT RISING (Ire) 4-11-4 (3*) Mr D Marnane, . . (3 to 1 fav) 4
CLASS OF NINETYTWO (Ire) 4-11-7 Mr M McNulty, (8 to 1) 5
31[7] PRYS PAUPER (Ire) 5-11-6 (7*) Miss Julia Murphy, (20 to 1) 6
GETA LEGUP 4-11-7 Mr P F Graffin, ...(16 to 1) 7
PRIORITY GALE (Ire) 4-11-2 Mr P Fenton, ...(7 to 2) 8
ASKASILLA (Ire) 5-11-3 (5*) Mr D P Murphy, ... (33 to 1) 9
SHUIL SHELL (Ire) 4-10-11 (5*) Mrs J M Mullins, ...(8 to 1) 10
BERT HOUSE 7-12-0 Mr E Bolger, ...(6 to 1) 11
39[9] MAUREEN MAC (Ire) 4-10-9 (7*) Mr M Brennan, . . .(12 to 1) 12
31 SONIC EXPERIENCE (Ire) 5-11-5 (3*) Mr R Neylon, (50 to 1) 13
WEDDING DREAM (Ire) 4-11-2 (5*) Mr D Valentine, (33 to 1) pu

Dist: 5l, 1½l, 1½l, 1l. 3m 44.30s. (14 Ran).

(Patrick Fleming), D K Weld

ROSCOMMON (IRE) (good)
Monday July 5th

56 Harrison Maiden Hurdle (4-y-o and up) £2,762 2m. . . . . (5:30)

10[4] OH SO GRUMPY 5-11-5 M Dwyer, ...(9 to 2 fav) 1
NANARCH (USA) 9-12-0 E A Leonard, ... (10 to 1) 2
24[2] FION CORN 6-11-6 T J Taaffe, ...(11 to 2) 3
SUNSHINES TAXI 6-11-6 S H O'Donovan, ...(20 to 1) 4
MARTIN'S MARTINA (Ire) 4-10-11 N Byrne, ...(20 to 1) 5
37[2] STEEL MIRROR 4-11-2 J Shortt, ...(5 to 1) 6
SIR SOOJE (Ire) 4-11-2 G M O'Neill, ...(7 to 1) 7
SILVER GIPSEY 7-11-9 P L Malone, ... (14 to 1) 8
41 KINGS CHERRY (Ire) 5-11-5 C O'Dwyer, ... (10 to 1) 9
10[2] DANCING COURSE (Ire) 5-11-8 K Morgan, ... (11 to 2) 10
OLD MAN RIVER 8-12-0 B Sheridan, ... (12 to 1) 11
ROSSMANAGHER (Ire) 4-10-9 (7*) C O'Brien, ...(20 to 1) 12
17 REMAINDER LASS (Ire) 4-10-6 (5*) M J Holbrook, (20 to 1) 13
DAMHSA (Den) 4-10-4 (7*) C McCormack, ... (16 to 1) 14
ERNEST MORSE (Ire) 5-11-0 (5*) T P Rudd, ... (33 to 1) 15
4[4] BACK TO BLACK (Ire) 4-10-6 (5*) M G Cleary, ...(12 to 1) 16
SIRAJAO (Ire) 4-10-4 (7*) S N Donohoe, ...(33 to 1) 17
SQUARE GALE (Ire) 5-10-9 (5*) Susan A Finn, ...(25 to 1) 18
OLD BOLEY (Ire) (bl) 5-11-5 L P Cusack, ... (33 to 1) 19
27[5] BARR NA CRANEY (Ire) 5-11-5 H Rogers, ...(33 to 1) pu

Dist: 1l, 2½l, ½l, 4l. 3m 50.30s. (20 Ran).

(Mrs E Queally), Mrs John Harrington

57 Runabracken Handicap Hurdle (0-123 4-y-o and up) £2,762 2m. . . . .(6:00)

32* CAN'T THINK WHAT [-] 6-10-7 (7*,6ex) T P Treacy, (6 to 1) 1
29* DIRECT LADY (Ire) [-] (bl) 4-11-5 (6ex) J F Titley, ...(5 to 1) 2
28[3] SEARCHLIGHT (Ire) [-] 5-10-5 N Williamson, ...(9 to 2) 3
NATALIES FANCY [-] 7-12-0 C O'Dwyer, ...(10 to 1) 4
46[3] ULTRA MAGIC [-] 6-9-10 S H O'Donovan, ...(14 to 1) 5
8[5] DEGO DANCER [-] 6-9-6 (7*) J P Broderick, ... (10 to 1) 6
2 ARDNAMONA [-] 6-9-9[2] (5*) T J Mitchell, ...(33 to 1) 7
PRETTY NICE (Ire) [-] 5-11-6 P L Malone, ...(8 to 1) 8
LINCOLNS INN (USA) [-] 8-10-4 (5*) D P Geoghegan, ...(20 to 1) 9
SWEET CHARMER [-] 10-11-8 (5*) A J Roche, ... (8 to 1) 10
20 LODATO [-] 9-9-8 (7*) M Kelly, ...(50 to 1) 11
8[2] EMARRCEEVEESS [-] 6-11-11 J Shortt, ... (4 to 1 fav) pu

Dist: 1½l, 4l, 2l, 3½l. 3m 41.10s. (12 Ran).

(Mrs P Mullins), P Mullins

58 Castle Pro-Am INH Flat Race (4-y-o and up) £2,762 2m. . . . . (8:30)

COMMON POLICY (Ire) 4-11-0 (7*) Mr J A Nash, (2 to 1 fav) 1
WHAT IT IS (Ire) 4-10-9 (7*) Mr M Brennan, ... (10 to 1) 2
VON CARTY (Ire) 4-10-9 (7*) Mr J T McNamara, ... (8 to 1) 3
THE REGAL ROYAL (Ire) 5-11-8 (5*) Mrs J M Mullins, (6 to 1) 4
53[9] THE FUN OF IT (bl) 8-11-7 (7*) K P Gaule, ... (20 to 1) 5
23 STONELEIGH TURBO (Ire) 4-11-2 (5*) Mr P M Kelly, (10 to 1) 6
24[8] OZONE RIVER (Ire) 5-11-1 (7*) Mr S O'Donnell, . . . (20 to 1) 7
MOUNT SACKVILLE 6-11-2 (7*) Mr D Groome, ...(50 to 1) 8
HIGHLAND SUPREME (Ire) 4-11-0 (7*) C O'Brien, . . (3 to 1) 9
39[6] TRAP ONE (Ire) 5-11-6 (7*) Mr D J Kavanagh, ... (7 to 1) 10
15[5] CLYDE PRINCE 8-11-7 (7*) Mr G J Harford, ...(5 to 1) 11
ORIENT ROVER 9-11-7 (7*) Mr A Daly, ...(33 to 1) 12
HASSLE FREE 6-11-7 (7*) Mr D M Christie, ...(66 to 1) 13
MR MOSS TROOPER (Ire) 5-11-6 (7*) Mr A F Doherty, ...(12 to 1) 14
48 ABBEY TRINITY (Ire) 4-10-9 (7*) Mr E Norris, ...(20 to 1) 15
23 THE BOOTER 8-11-7 (7*) Mr L Mannerings, ... (66 to 1) 16
27 CLANMANY (Ire) 4-11-0 (7*) J P Broderick, ... (50 to 1) 17
GLADUATE (Ire) 4-10-9 (7*) M Kelly, ...(20 to 1) su

Dist: ¾l, 1½l, 3l, 4l. 3m 45.50s. (18 Ran).

(Patrick O'Leary), Patrick O'Leary

BELLEWSTOWN (IRE) (good to firm)
Tuesday July 6th

59 Hilltown Hurdle (4-y-o and up) £2,245 2½m . . . .(6:00)

CABRA TOWERS 6-10-6 (5*) M M Mackin, ... (25 to 1) 1
BASSETJA (Ire) 4-10-7 A Maguire, ...(9 to 4) 2
11 SOMERSET DANCER (USA) 6-11-6 S H O'Donovan, (7 to 1) 3
39[2] PEACEFULL RIVER (Ire) 4-9-5 (7*) H Taylor, ...(7 to 1) 4
BOLD FLYER 10-11-2 K Morgan, ...(11 to 1) 5
STAR ROSE 11-10-8 (7*) J Butler, ...(7 to 4 fav) 6
BARRYMORE BOY 6-10-11 C F Swan, ... (14 to 1) 7
37 SLIM-N-LITE 7-10-6 H Rogers, ... (33 to 1) f
3[8] CARLINGFORD GEM 7-10-6 P L Malone, ... (33 to 1) pu
CLEAN SHEETS VI (Ire) 5-10-10 N Byrne, ... (33 to 1) pu

Dist: 2l, 3½l, 5½l, nk. 5m 0.70s. (10 Ran).

(J G Cosgrave), J G Cosgrave

60 Bolies Handicap Hurdle (4-y-o and up) £2,245 3m. . . . . (7:30)

42[2] PEARLTWIST [-] 7-10-2 P L Malone, ...(9 to 2) 1
BANOUR (USA) [-] (bl) 5-11-7 A Maguire, ...(8 to 1) 2
DANCE OF WORDS (Ire) [-] 4-10-9 P McWilliams, . . (9 to 2) 3
THE BULL MCCABE [-] 8-11-7 C F Swan, ... (4 to 1 fav) 4
HAWKFIELD (Ire) [-] (bl) 4-10-4 B Sheridan, ...(12 to 1) 5
38[5] RUNAWAY GOLD [-] 6-9-3 (7*) R A Hennessy, ...(10 to 1) 6
ALTAR BOY [-] 9-10-11 S H O'Donovan, ...(10 to 1) 7
51 MURPHY'S TROUBLE (Ire) [-] 5-9-0 (7*) P O Casey, (20 to 1) 8
38[6] MARY OG [-] 6-9-0 (7*) T Martin, ... (33 to 1) 9
38[9] MISS SPLENDOUR (Ire) [-] 5-9-11 (4ex) F Woods, (12 to 1) 10
COBBLERS ROCK [-] 7-9-1[1] (7*) T P Treacy, ...(33 to 1) 11
11 ONE FOR LUCK (Ire) [-] 5-9-0 (7*) Mr D J Kavanagh, (20 to 1) 12
17[3] BELLS HILL LAD [-] 6-9-10 T Horgan, ...(8 to 1) 13
33[7] EDWARD'S DOLLY [-] (bl) 8-9-4 (3*) M G Cleary, . . .(20 to 1) 14

Dist: ½l, 2½l, 2l, 7l. 5m 54.80s. (14 Ran).

(Jeremiah John O'Neill), Jeremiah John O'Neill

61 McLoughlin Oil INH Flat Race (5-y-o and up) £2,762 2m 1f. . . . . (8:30)

FIRST SESSION (Ire) 5-11-3 (5*) Mrs J M Mullins, . . .(8 to 1) 1
BAVARD DIEU (Ire) 5-11-13 Mr A J Martin, ... (7 to 2 fav) 2
39[3] KICKALONG 7-11-4 (5*) Mr P J Casey, ...(11 to 2) 3
50[4] PEARL'S CHOICE (Ire) 5-11-1 (7*) Mr G J Harford, . . (5 to 1) 4
LORD GREYSTONES 6-11-7 (7*) Mr A D Evans, . . .(25 to 1) 5
23[8] PRAGMATAR 6-11-7 (7*) Mr M O'Connor, ... (14 to 1) 6
53[7] SLEMISH MINSTREL 7-11-7 (7*) Mr I Johnston, . . .(33 to 1) 7
RALPH SQUARE 5-11-6 (7*) Mr T J Beattie, ... (20 to 1) 8
RIYASHA (Ire) 5-11-1 (7*) Mr J A Nash, ... (14 to 1) 9
17 SWEET KILDARE 6-11-2 (7*) Mr J P Harvey, ... (25 to 1) 10
SARACEN'S BOY (Ire) 5-11-13 Mr P Fenton, ...(14 to 1) 11
EXPRESS TRAVEL (Ire) 5-11-13 Mr J P Dempsey, (25 to 1) 12
CROGHAN MIST (Ire) 5-11-5 (3*) Mr A R Coonan, (14 to 1) 13
WESTCARNE LAD (Ire) 5-11-13 Mr M McNulty, . . . (10 to 1) 14

DOWNS DELIGHT (Ire) 5-11-8 (5*) Mr H F Cleary, . . .(5 to 1)   15
MOUNTAINFOOT GIRL 6-11-2 (7*) Mr R Pugh, . . .(25 to 1)   16
Dist: Hd, 9l, 4½l, 1½l. 3m 48.80s. (16 Ran).

(John A Mernagh), W P Mullins

BELLEWSTOWN (IRE) (good to firm)
Wednesday July 7th

62 Michael Moore Car Sales Hurdle (4-y-o)
£2,762 2m 1f. . . . . (5:00)

46⁵ HIS WAY (Ire) 11-7 M Flynn, ...(4 to 1)   1
38⁷ TADILA (Ire) 10-9 B Sheridan, ...(10 to 1)   2
17* LET IT RIDE (Ire) 11-7 T Horgan, ... (6 to 4 on)   3
4 VICTORY TOAST (Ire) 10-9 H Rogers, ...(9 to 1)   4
41* IDEAL RISK (Ire) 11-7 F J Flood, ...(6 to 1)   5
3⁷ CASTLE LORD (Ire) 11-0 C F Swan, ...(14 to 1)   6
COUNTESS PAHLEN (Ire) 10-9 A Powell, ...(50 to 1)   7
37 LORD LOVING (Ire) 10-7 (7*) C O'Brien, ...(33 to 1)   8
Dist: 3l, 9l, 1l, 15l. 4m 1.50s. (8 Ran).

(Robert Scott), Kevin Prendergast

63 Tayto Growers Handicap Hurdle (4-y-o and
up) £3,452 2m 1f. . . . . (7:30)

51⁵ AQUINAS [-] 7-9-10 (7*) R A Hennessy, ...(5 to 1)   1
46⁶ MABES TOWN (Ire) [-] 5-9-11 N Byrne, ...(10 to 1)   2
BALLYCANN [-] 6-10-12 (7*) P Mulligan, ...(4 to 1 fav)   3
SANTA PONSA BAY [-] 6-10-3 P McWilliams, ... (5 to 1)   4
28 SEZ HE SEZ I [-] 9-9-6 (7*) Miss C E Hyde, ...(16 to 1)   5
2⁸ KHAZARI (USA) [-] 5-10-10 C O'Dwyer, ...(9 to 2)   6
RAYSULID [-] (bl) 8-11-11 M Flynn, ...(7 to 1)   7
25⁸ MRS COOPS [-] 6-9-0 (7*) T Martin, ...(16 to 1)   8
34⁸ SUNSHINE SEAL [-] (bl) 6-10-3 P L Malone, ...(14 to 1)   9
PYLON SPARKS [-] (bl) 8-10-13 A Maguire, ...(9 to 2)   ur
Dist: 7l, 3½l, 1l, 1½l. 3m 57.30s. (10 Ran).

(W Hennessy), Anthony Mullins

BELLEWSTOWN (IRE) (firm)
Thursday July 8th

64 Bookmakers Maiden Hurdle (4-y-o and up)
£2,762 2m 1f. . . . . (6:00)

OPEN MARKET (USA) 4-11-7 B Sheridan, ...(9 to 2)   1
32⁴ OXFORD QUILL 6-12-0 T J Taaffe, ...(4 to 1)   2+
45⁴ UNCLE BART (Ire) 5-10-12 (7*) R A Hennessy, . . . (11 to 2)   2+
OLD TALKA RIVER 6-12-0 C F Swan, ... (11 to 4 fav)   4
HE'S A FLYER 9-12-0 A Maguire, ...(20 to 1)   5
30⁴ KAFKAN (Ire) 5-11-5 K F O'Brien, ...(14 to 1)   6
END GAME (Ire) 4-10-13 (3*) P Carberry, ... (8 to 1)   7
JUST BLUSH 6-11-9 H Rogers, ...(20 to 1)   8
1⁸ LUCKY ENOUGH 8-11-1 F Woods, ...(14 to 1)   9
ASK THE FAIRIES (Ire) 5-10-11 (3*) K B Walsh, ...(66 to 1)   10
37 SALVATION 6-11-6 A Powell, ...(14 to 1)   11
RUFO'S COUP 6-11-6 G M O'Neill, ...(16 to 1)   12
ANOTHER BONNY 7-11-1 (5*) C P Dunne, ...(20 to 1)   13
I HAVE HIM 6-11-6 C O'Dwyer, ...(33 to 1)   14
37 FOXHILL 7-11-1 (5*) D T Evans, ...(50 to 1)   15
Dist: 2½l, dd-ht, 12l, 1l. 4m 3.70s. (15 Ran).

(S Creaven), D K Weld

65 Tipperary Water Novice Hurdle (4-y-o and
up) £2,762 2½m. (7:00)

MORNING DREAM 6-11-6 G M O'Neill, ... (7 to 4)   1
IFALLELSEFAILS 5-11-5 Mr A J Martin, ...(11 to 8 fav)   2
LE GERARD 8-11-6 C O'Dwyer, ...(7 to 1)   3
HURRICANE TOMMY (bl) 6-11-6 J F Titley, ...(6 to 1)   4
HILL RANGER 6-10-8 (7*) Mr J P Brennan, ...(14 to 1)   5
FINAL OPTION (Ire) 5-11-0² (7*) Mr T J Nagle Jnr, . .(25 to 1)   6
18⁷ DADS HOBBY 7-11-1 F Woods, ...(25 to 1)   7
Dist: ½l, 4l, 7l, dist. 5m 14.10s. (7 Ran).

(Donal Hassett), Donal Hassett

66 Seamus Mulvaney Crockafotha Handicap
Hurdle (0-102 4-y-o and up) £2,762 2½m
. . . .(7:30)

23² SONG OF CAEDMON (Ire) [-] 5-10-9 C F Swan,
. . . .(100 to 30 fav)   1
38² SENSITIVE KING [-] 5-10-8 (3*) J Collins, ...(7 to 1)   2
1⁷ JOEY KELLY [-] 8-10-9 C O'Dwyer, ...(7 to 1)   3
29⁵ CREWS CASTLE [-] 6-10-3 (5*) D P Geoghegan, . .(12 to 1)   4
34⁴ FINE PRINT (Ire) [-] 5-11-6 H Rogers, ...(10 to 1)   5
42⁷ M MACG (Ire) [-] 4-10-6 (3*) J Magee, ...(16 to 1)   6
CHARLIES DELIGHT (Ire) [-] 5-11-5 K F O'Brien, . . .(6 to 1)   7
25³ HOSTETLER [-] 4-10-10 (3*) P Carberry, ...(4 to 1)   8
38 PERSIAN GLEN [-] (bl) 6-11-0 N Byrne, ...(25 to 1)   9
37 MERSEY RACING [-] 6-9-12 (5*) T J O'Sullivan, . . .(50 to 1)   10
GEROLAS (Ire) [-] 5-11-3 A Maguire, ...(16 to 1)   11
38 SALLOW GLEN [-] 7-10-8 J Shortt, ...(8 to 1)   12
38 COQUALLA [-] (bl) 8-10-4 (7*) D M Bean, ...(25 to 1)   13
57 LODATO [-] 9-10-7 (7*) P Mulligan, ...(50 to 1)   14
CONNELLICO (Ire) [-] 5-9-11 (5*) T J Mitchell, ...(33 to 1)   15

38* BALLINDERRY GLEN [-] 7-11-1 (6ex) L P Cusack, . . .(7 to 1)   pu
Dist: 2½l, 4l, 4l, sht-hd. 5m 7.60s. (16 Ran).

(Mrs T M Moriarty), D T Hughes

67 V.Keating (Oil Distributor) Flat Race (4-y-o
and up) £3,602 2m 1f. . . . . (8:30)

CLOGHANS BAY (Ire) 4-11-4 (7*) Mr J A Nash, (6 to 4 fav)   1
31* BLAST FREEZE (Ire) 4-10-13 (7*) Mr G J Harford, . . .(5 to 1)   2
39* HAUNTING ANGLE 4-11-1 (5*) Mr A E Lacy, . . . (7 to 1)   3
48⁵ PRACTICE RUN (Ire) 5-11-10 (7*) Mr D J Donegan, (16 to 1)   4
SWANING AROUND 4-11-1 (3*) Mr D Marnane,
. . . .(40 to 1)   5
48⁸ OX EYE DAISY (Ire) 5-11-2 (3*) Mrs M Mullins, . . (10 to 1)   6
KARABAKH (Ire) 4-10-13 (5*) Mrs J M Mullins, . . . (4 to 1)   7
55⁴ PORT RISING (Ire) 4-11-4 Mr S R Murphy, ...(8 to 1)   8
3* D'S FANCY (Ire) 5-11-10 (7*) Mr M Brennan, ...(10 to 1)   9
SUIL AWAIN (Ire) 4-10-6 (7*) Mr S Mahon, ...(33 to 1)   10
BALLYGRANT 6-11-11 (7*) Mr B Foster, ...(20 to 1)   11
DELLA WEE (Ire) 5-11-12 Mr A J Martin, ...(20 to 1)   12
HAUGHTON LAD (Ire) 4-10-11 (7*) Mr G Behan, . . .(20 to 1)   su
SHANES GREY (Ire) 4-10-8 (5*) Mr P J Casey, . . . (33 to 1)   su
Dist: Sht-hd, 7l, 1½l, 2l. 3m 53.10s. (14 Ran).

(Mrs Patrick Prendergast), Patrick Prendergast

DUNDALK (IRE) (firm)
Monday July 12th

68 Carrickdale Hotel Hurdle (4-y-o and up)
£2,762 2m 135yds. . . . . (5:00)

49² JOHNSTON'S JET 9-11-0 J F Titley, ...(2 to 1)   1
56² NANARCH (USA) 9-11-0 E A Leonard, ...(5 to 4 fav)   2
MEJEVE 5-10-13 C F Swan, ...(3 to 1)   3
64 ASK THE FAIRIES (Ire) 5-10-5 (3*) K B Walsh, ...(50 to 1)   4
37⁹ PRINCE ROCKAWAY (Ire) 5-10-13 K Morgan, ...(8 to 1)   5
NOBLE PEACE (Ire) 5-10-10 (3*) D Bromley, ...(16 to 1)   6
51 DELIFFIN 7-10-7 (7*) J K McCarthy, ...(25 to 1)   ur
Dist: ¾l, 10l, 15l, dist. 4m 1.40s. (7 Ran).

(Frank McKevitt), M J P O'Brien

69 Dundalk Supporters Club Handicap Hurdle
(0-116 4-y-o and up) £2,762 2½m 153yds
. . . .(5:30)

38³ COQ HARDI SMOKEY (Ire) [-] 5-10-11 (3*) P Carberry,
. . . .(5 to 2 fav)   1
66⁴ CREWS CASTLE [-] 6-10-0 (5*) D P Geoghegan, . . (8 to 1)   2
TULLY BOY [-] 6-10-2 (7*) Mr D McCartan, ...(14 to 1)   3
1⁴ GOLDEN RAPPER [-] (bl) 8-10-11 J F Titley, ...(6 to 1)   4
1 NANCYS LAD [-] 6-9-13 (7*) H Taylor, ...(10 to 1)   5
63⁴ SANTA PONSA BAY [-] 6-10-13 P McWilliams, ...(6 to 1)   6
38⁴ FAUGHAN LODGE [-] 6-9-13 J P Byrne, ...(10 to 3)   7
KILIAN MY BOY [-] 5-10-13 C O'Dwyer, ...(14 to 1)   8
51⁶ GARYS GIRL [-] 6-10-8 F Woods, ...(14 to 1)   9
KLICKITAT [-] 6-12-0 C N Bowens, ...(14 to 1)   10
BETH'S PRINCE [-] (bl) 8-11-6 C F Swan, ...(8 to 1)   11
DIAMOND SPRITE (USA) [-] 6-10-1 (5*) T J O'Sullivan,
. . . .(16 to 1)   su
Dist: 5½l, 10l, 9l, 4l. 4m 44.60s. (12 Ran).

(Mrs Catherine Howard), Noel Meade

70 Mullacrew INH Flat Race (5-y-o and up)
£2,245 2½m 153yds. . . . .(8:00)

53³ CUBAN QUESTION 6-12-0 Mr S R Murphy, ...(6 to 4 fav)   1
SHEER MIRTH 8-11-7 (7*) Miss Sarah Taaffe, ...(14 to 1)   2
HAWAIIAN GODDESS (USA) 6-11-4 (5*) Mr D McGoona,
. . . .(14 to 1)   3
30² THE JEWELLER 6-11-9 (5*) Mr T P Hyde, ...(10 to 1)   4
53⁶ DONT GAMBLE 7-12-0 Mr T Mullins, ...(9 to 2)   5
DUNDOCK WOOD 5-11-5 (3*) Mr A R Coonan, ...(7 to 1)   6
61⁸ RALPH SQUARE 5-11-6 (7*) Mr T J Beattie, ...(20 to 1)   7
39 CURRAGH GALE (Ire) 5-11-1 (7*) Mr P J Kelly, ...(10 to 1)   8
NEWBRISTY (bl) 6-11-2 (7*) Mr D Kiernan, ...(50 to 1)   9
SKIN GRAFT (bl) 7-11-2 (7*) Mr P J Mackin, ...(50 to 1)   10
PAVLOVA RUN (Ire) 5-11-6 (7*) Mr C M Healy, ...(33 to 1)   11
WE WONT FALL OUT (Ire) 5-11-6 (7*) Mr J P Hayden,
. . . .(33 to 1)   12
IM OK (Ire) 5-11-1 (7*) Miss F Loughran, ...(20 to 1)   13
SPURIOUS 7-11-7 (7*) Mr J Bright, ...(10 to 1)   pu
Dist: Hd, 15l, 2l, 1½l. 4m 41.20s. (14 Ran).

(Laurence Byrne), D T Hughes

KILLARNEY (IRE) (good to yielding)
Monday July 12th

71 Bourne Vincent Memorial Park Maiden Hurdle (4-y-o and up) £3,452 2m 1f. . . . .(5:30)

WALK RITE BACK (Ire) 4-11-2 K F O'Brien, ...(4 to 1)   1
19 MOUNTHENRY STAR (Ire) 5-11-5 G M O'Neill, (5 to 2 fav)   2
WALNEY ISLAND 4-11-2 A Maguire, ...(16 to 1)   3
NORDIC BEAT (Ire) 4-11-7 M P Hourigan, ...(10 to 1)   4
AUTHENTICITY 5-11-0 T Horgan, ...(33 to 1)   5

```
   IRISH ROVER (Ire) 5-11-0 (5") D T Evans, .........(14 to 1)    6
   TRIPLE ACE (Ire) 4-10-9 (7") Mr N D Fehily, .......(33 to 1)   7
   BOLTON SARAH 6-10-8 (7") T P Treacy, .........(20 to 1)        8
   PEJAWI 6-11-1 A J O'Brien, ...................(12 to 1)        9
   NOBODYS FLAME (Ire) 5-11-5 T Grantham, ........(6 to 1)        10
41 BARRINGTONS CASTLE (Ire) 5-11-13 B Sheridan,  (5 to 1)         11
41 KILLEEN COUNTESS (Ire) 5-11-0 L P Cusack, ....(50 to 1)        12
   COOLGREEN (Ire) 5-11-5 Mr W T Slattery Jnr, ....(33 to 1)      13
   FAHA STAR (Ire) 4-11-2 S H O'Donovan, ........(16 to 1)        14
17 CANDY IS DANDY (Ire) 4-10-11 N Williamson, ....(50 to 1)       15
   MARIENS TREASURE (Ire) 4-10-11 A Powell, ......(25 to 1)       16
64 ANOTHER BONNY 7-11-1 (5") C P Dunne, .........(14 to 1)        17
   TERRY'S PRIDE 7-11-1 G Bradley, ..............(14 to 1)        18
   TYARA 7-11-1 J R Kavanagh, ...................(14 to 1)        19
56 SQUARE GALE (Ire) 5-10-9 (5") Susan A Finn, ....(50 to 1)      pu
Dist: 2l, 6l, 11l, 1l. 4m 21.00s. (20 Ran).
```
(D H W Dobson), J S Bolger

72 Diners Club Mares Novice Chase (5-y-o and up) £3,452 2¾m. . . . . (8:00)

```
22²  INCH MAID 7-12-0 T Horgan, ..............(5 to 2 jt-fav)     1
21³  CLOSE AT HAND 8-11-9 A Maguire, ...............(8 to 1)      2
42³  LANTERN LUCK (Ire) 5-11-7 K F O'Brien, ....(5 to 2 jt-fav)   3
44⁴  HIGHBABS 7-12-0 N Williamson, ...............(9 to 2)        4
33⁵  BALADINE 6-11-9 W T Slattery Jnr, ...........(14 to 1)       5
22⁶  HAPPY ELIZA 10-11-9 D H O'Connor, ...........(14 to 1)       6
     HELENIUM GALE 6-11-2 (7") Mr W M O'Sullivan, ..(16 to 1)     7
22⁷  BILLMAR 6-11-9 H Rogers, ....................(20 to 1)       8
6⁸   ASHBOURNE CLASSIC (bl) 6-11-2 (7") D Leahy, ..(50 to 1)      9
50⁷  MISS CORINTHIAN (bl) 6-11-9 S H O'Donovan, ...(33 to 1)      10
6    LUCYS LAW (bl) 7-11-9 A J O'Brien, ..........(33 to 1)       ur
     ANOTHER DUO 9-11-4 (5") M A Davey, ..........(14 to 1)       pu
     EYESEE 7-11-9 G Bradley, ....................(14 to 1)       pu
22⁹  PALMROCK DONNA 6-11-9 A Powell, ............(20 to 1)        pu
     MERRY RIVER 6-11-9 C O'Brien, ...............(20 to 1)       pu
Dist: 2½l, 8l, 1l, 15l. 5m 47.10s. (15 Ran).
```
(William P O'Neill), W J Burke

73 Michael Lynch Plant Hire INH Flat Race (4-y-o and up) £3,452 2m 1f. . . . . (8:30)

```
     MORE DASH (Ire) 5-11-1 (7") Mr J Nash, .........(12 to 1)    1
     KELLSEIGHTHUNDRED (Ire) 4-11-7 Mr A P O'Brien,
     .........................................(5 to 4 fav)        2
     OLD ARCHIVES (Ire) 4-11-7 Mr J P Durkin, .......(8 to 1)     3
7⁶   IRISH PERRY 6-11-2 (7") Mr M J Comber, .......(12 to 1)      4
32   DRIPSEY QUAY (Ire) 5-11-1 (7") Mr D Keane, .....(25 to 1)    5
     BULGADEN CASTLE 5-11-6 (7") Mr B Moran, .....(33 to 1)       6
     FULL SCORE 4-11-2 (5") Mr T Lombard, .........(33 to 1)      7
     RIGHT AND REASON (Ire) 4-10-9 (7") Miss C E Hyde,
     .......................................(20 to 1)             8
     IF SO 7-11-7 (7") Miss A M McMahon, ..........(12 to 1)      9
43²  PAPRS GALE (Ire) 5-11-8 Mr P Fenton, ..........(5 to 2)      10
     LAFFAN'S BRIDGE (Ire) 4-10-9 (7") Mr P A Roche, (10 to 1)    11
43   HAZEL BROOK LAD (Ire) 5-11-6 (7") Mr N C Kelleher,
     .......................................(33 to 1)             12
     GOLDEN SLEIGH (Ire) 5-11-1 (7") Mr A J Kennedy, (25 to 1)    13
     LARRYS PENNY (Ire) 4-11-2 Mr J M Roche, ......(16 to 1)      14
     DOVEGROVE HOUSE (Ire) 5-11-6 (7") Mr J T McNamara,
     .......................................(14 to 1)             15
55²  SIMPLISTIC (Ire) 4-11-2 Mr J P Dempsey, .......(7 to 1)      16
     PARK BOREEN (Ire) 4-11-7 Mr T S Costello, .....(10 to 1)     17
43⁷  MEXICAN WAVE 6-11-2 (7") Mr A Daly, ..........(14 to 1)      18
41   SUMMER JANE 5-11-1 (7") Mr G Hogan, .........(33 to 1)       19
Dist: 3½l, 2l, 8l, 3l. 4m 11.40s. (19 Ran).
```
(Mrs Louisa Mangan), James Joseph Mangan

DOWN ROYAL (IRE) (good to firm)
Tuesday July 13th

74 First National Building Society Hurdle (4-y-o and up) £1,380 2m. . . . . (1:50)

```
5⁴   THE MAN FROM COOKS (Ire) 4-10-11 (3") P Carberry,
     .......................................(2 to 1 fav)          1
51⁷  ST DONAVINT 6-11-7 C N Bowens, ..............(3 to 1)        2
     CAOIMSEACH (Ire) 5-11-1 (5") Mr J A Nash, .....(8 to 1)      3
8⁴   FINGAL BOY (Ire) 5-11-1 (5") T J Mitchell, .....(11 to 2)    4
64   SALVATION 6-11-7 A Powell, ...................(12 to 1)      5
     GREEK CHIME (Ire) 4-10-9 P McWilliams, ........(6 to 1)      6
17   KAMTARA 7-11-7 Mr K Ross, ...................(25 to 1)       7
     RAGS RAGOUILLE 7-11-0 (7") Mr J Bryson, ......(33 to 1)      8
66   MERSEY RACING 6-11-4 (3") K B Walsh, .........(33 to 1)      9
     ROVANIEMI (Ire) 5-11-6 C F Swan, .............(8 to 1)       10
64   FOXHILL 7-11-2 (5") D T Evans, ................(33 to 1)     11
Dist: Hd, 1l, nk, hd. (Time not taken) (11 Ran).
```
(P Senezio), E J O'Grady

75 Northern Ireland Tourist Board Handicap Chase (4-y-o and up) £6,900 2½m. . . . . (2:45)

```
     EASTER SIXTEEN [-] 7-11-4 J Shortt, ...........(4 to 1)      1
59⁵  BOLD FLYER [-] 10-11-9 K Morgan, .............(12 to 1)      2
22*  LIGHT THE WICK [-] 7-10-4 C F Swan, .........(2 to 1 fav)    3
52⁴  MAC'S GLEN [-] 9-10-13 P McWilliams, .........(10 to 1)      4
```

```
66³  JOEY KELLY [-] 8-9-12⁵ C O'Dwyer, .............(8 to 1)      5
33³  MUSIC SCORE [-] 7-9-9 (3") J Collins, ..........(10 to 1)    6
     FOUR TRIX [-] 12-11-7 B Powell, ................(6 to 1)     7
26   TREAT ME GOOD [-] (bl) 10-9-13 (5") T J Mitchell,  (12 to 1) 8
     SAM WELLER [-] 8-10-0 C N Bowens, ...........(25 to 1)       9
     MAPLE DANCER [-] (bl) 7-11-3 F Woods, ........(4 to 1)       f
Dist: 1½l, 6l, 1l, 7l. (Time not taken) (10 Ran).
```
(Michael B Moore), Patrick Prendergast

KILLARNEY (IRE) (yielding to soft)
Tuesday July 13th

76 Torc Great Southern Handicap Chase (4-y-o and up) £3,452 2¾m. . . . . (5:30)

```
21*  DANCINGCINDERELLA [-] 9-9-0 (7") J P Broderick,  (9 to 2)    1
14⁴  HARRISTOWN LADY [-] (bl) 6-9-7 N Williamson, ...(5 to 1)     2
     DESERT LORD [-] 7-9-5 (7") C O'Brien, .........(4 to 1)      3
44   LIFE OF A LORD [-] 7-9-13 S H O'Donovan, ......(10 to 1)     4
     BISHOPS HALL [-] 7-11-9 G Bradley, ............(7 to 2 fav)  5
     WATERLOO ANDY [-] 7-9-3¹ (5") T J O'Sullivan, ..(33 to 1)    6
44³  JAMES PIGG [-] 6-9-7 N Byrne, .................(9 to 1)      7
52   THURSDAY SWEEP [-] 7-9-12 W T Slattery Jnr, ....(20 to 1)    8
     GOOD FOR A LAUGH [-] 9-11-1 T J Taaffe, ........(9 to 2)     pu
Dist: Sht-hd, 3l, 15l, 1l. 5m 55.60s. (9 Ran).
```
(M F Murray), Michael Hourigan

77 Parknasilla Great Southern Novices' Chase (4-y-o and up) £3,452 2½m. . . . . (6:00)

```
44⁷  FOXBROOK (bl) 7-11-8 N Williamson, ...........(8 to 1)       1
     TAKE THE TOWN 8-11-8 J F Titley, ..........(15 to 8 fav)     2
41³  THUNDERSTRUCK 7-11-8 G Bradley, ............(5 to 1)         3
     RACHELS ROCKER 6-10-10 (7") K F O'Brien, .....(10 to 1)      4
33⁶  HURRYUP 6-11-8 L P Cusack, .................(10 to 1)        5
47⁸  SON OF SARAH 9-11-8 W T Slattery Jnr, ........(12 to 1)      6
     TANAISTE (USA) 4-10-0 (5") T J O'Sullivan, .....(14 to 1)    7
33⁴  COURIER DESPATCH (Ire) 5-10-8 (7") C O'Brien, ..(10 to 1)    8
6²   AHEEMA COTTAGE 7-11-8 F J Flood, ............(4 to 1)        f
34⁵  RUSTIC GENT (Ire) 5-11-1 A J O'Brien, .........(12 to 1)     f
33   BIT OF A TOUCH (bl) 7-11-8 G M O'Neill, .......(12 to 1)     pu
72   EYESEE 7-11-3 A Maguire, ....................(14 to 1)       pu
6    TOLL BRIDGE 6-11-3 H Rogers, ................(33 to 1)       pu
     CIARA'S STAR 6-11-8 T Horgan, ................(33 to 1)      pu
     NOTTODAY (Ire) 5-11-1 T Grantham, ...........(33 to 1)       pu
Dist: 12l, 6l, 1l, 25l. 5m 35.70s. (15 Ran).
```
(Mrs P F N Fanning), M F Morris

78 Killarney Gt.S'thern Long Dist Handicap Hdle (4-y-o and up) £4,142 2¾m. . . . . . (6:30)

```
42*  CUILIN BUI (Ire) [-] 5-9-10 (7",2ex) C O'Brien, .. (7 to 4 fav)  1
     MARBLE CITY GIRL [-] 8-9-0 (7") J P Broderick, ..(16 to 1)   2
     RISING WATERS (Ire) [-] 5-11-4 (5") C P Dunne, ..(9 to 2)    3
26²  LOUGHLINSTOWN BOY [-] 8-12-0 T J Taaffe, ......(7 to 1)      4
42⁶  QUIVERING MELODY [-] (bl) 6-9-11 M P Hourigan,  (7 to 1)     5
11⁴  CARES OF TOMORROW [-] 6-10-3 N Byrne, .......(6 to 1)        6
42   FIXED ASSETS [-] 6-10-0 A J O'Brien, ..........(14 to 1)     7
34   SANDY WORLD (USA) [-] (bl) 7-9-7 N Williamson, (20 to 1)     8
     ACTION DANCER [-] 7-10-9 L P Cusack, ........(14 to 1)       pu
Dist: 1l, 9l, 1l, 1l. 5m 46.50s. (9 Ran).
```
(Miss E Kiely), David J McGrath

79 Rosslare Gt.S'thern Ladies Q.R.Flat Race (6-y-o and up) £3,452 2m 1f. . . . . (8:30)

```
     QUEENIES CHILD 6-11-6 (3") Miss C Hutchinson,
     ........................................(10 to 9 on)         1
43⁵  THE TENANT 6-11-11 (3") Miss M Olivefalk, ......(7 to 1)     2
43   KENMAC 6-11-7 (7") Mrs S Hobbs, .............(10 to 1)       3
     ROOKS ROCK 6-11-7 (7") Miss L Townsley, ......(11 to 2)      4
15⁸  MILLER'S CROSSING 6-11-2 (7") Mrs C Doyle, ...(11 to 2)      5
     KIZZY ROSE 6-11-2 (7") Miss C Hourigan, .......(8 to 1)      6
     THE FENIAN SON 7-11-7 (7") Miss A Sloane, .....(33 to 1)     7
     TORLOUGH 8-11-7 (7") Miss V Hugton, ..........(20 to 1)      8
22   KINGOFSPANCILHILL 6-11-7 (7") Mrs K Walsh, ...(20 to 1)      9
     WINDMILL CROSS 6-11-7 (7") Miss C O'Donovan, (20 to 1)       10
     BLACK MALACHA VI 10-11-2 (7") Mrs H O'Keeffe-Daly,
     ........................................(20 to 1)            11
     BEAT THE RAP 7-11-7 (7") Miss C E Hyde, ......(33 to 1)      12
41   FULL SCHEDUAL 6-11-7 (7") Miss A M McMahon, (8 to 1)         13
41   DERRING DREAM 6-11-7 (7") Miss L E A Doyle, ..(50 to 1)      14
     MILLWOOD STREAM 8-11-2 (7") Miss L Gough, ...(16 to 1)       15
     PARSONS TOI 8-11-2 (7") Miss J Riordan, .......(33 to 1)     16
     GENISTA 8-11-7 (7") Miss A L Moore, ..........(10 to 1)      17
Dist: Hd, 2l, 12l, sht-hd. 4m 30.80s. (17 Ran).
```
(Mrs E Donoghue), C P Donoghue

DOWN ROYAL (IRE) (good to yielding)
Wednesday July 14th

80 Archers (Mares) Maiden Hurdle (4-y-o and up) £1,380 2m. . . . . (6:00)

```
56⁸  SILVER GIPSEY 7-12-0 P L Malone, .............(7 to 1)       1
```

9

50	PARSONS EYRE (Ire) 5-11-0 (5") T J Mitchell, ... (10 to 1)	2+
62²	TADILA (Ire) 4-11-7 B Sheridan, ...(2 to 1 fav)	2+
	POLLY PLUM (Ire) 5-11-2 (3") Mr A R Coonan, ... (4 to 1)	4
61⁴	PEARL'S CHOICE (Ire) 5-11-0 (5") Mr A J Nash, ... (5 to 1)	5
49	JUST FOUR (Ire) 4-10-11 (5") D P Geoghegan, ... (16 to 1)	6
	BELLECARA 6-11-11 (3") D Bromley, ... (12 to 1)	7
50	ARI'S FASHION 8-11-3 (3") P Carberry, ... (20 to 1)	8
61	SWEET KILDARE 6-11-8 A Powell, ... (20 to 1)	9
50⁹	CLARA BRIDGE 6-11-6 C N Bowens, ...(14 to 1)	10
37	PEARLY CASTLE (Ire) 5-11-5 P McWilliams, ...(20 to 1)	11
56⁵	MARTIN'S MARTINA (Ire) 4-11-2 K F O'Brien, ...(12 to 1)	12

Dist: 3l, dd-ht, 3½l, 3l. (Time not taken) (12 Ran).

(Noel Brannigan), M J Grassick

81 Sullivans INH Flat Race (4-y-o and up) £1,380
2m. . . . . (8:30)

	MRS RUMPOLE (Ire) 4-10-11 (5") Mr A Nash, (5 to 4 fav)	1
	PENNYBRIDGE (Ire) 4-11-7 Mr P F Graffin, ...(5 to 2)	2
	SCRABO VIEW (Ire) 5-11-10 (3") Mr B R Hamilton, (20 to 1)	3
17	BRAE (Ire) 5-11-1 (7") Mr D McCann, ...(14 to 1)	4
63⁸	MRS COOPS 6-11-2 (7") Mr D M Christie, ... (16 to 1)	5
	NEW DIRECTIONS 6-11-6 (3") Mr A R Coonan, ...(10 to 1)	6
	STRAWTALDI (Ire) 5-11-6 (7") Mr J D O'Connell, . . .(33 to 1)	7
39⁵	DOCS DILEMMA 5-11-6 (7") Mr J J Lambe, ...(8 to 1)	8
27⁷	CHUCK'S TREASURE (Ire) 4-11-0 (7") Mr J P Fahey, (8 to 1)	9
3	DECEMBER BRIDE (Ire) 5-11-1 (7") Mr E Magee, . . (33 to 1)	10
	KILMACREW 6-11-8¹ (7") Mr J Johnston, ...(50 to 1)	11
	TALENT SPOTTER 6-11-7 (7") Mr C A McBratney, (10 to 1)	12
3	WISHING'N'HOPING (Ire) 3-10-9 (7") Mr K Ross, . .(33 to 1)	13
	DRUMCOLLIHER 6-11-7 (7") Mr I A Gault, ...(33 to 1)	14
	OZONE LASS 5-11-8 Mr A J Martin, ...(10 to 1)	15
	STANDAROUND (Ire) 4-10-9 (7") Mr A K Wyse, ...(14 to 1)	bd
39	BELLE DE SEUL 6-11-2 (7") Mr J McCrickard, ... (33 to 1)	su
	DARA KNIGHT (Ire) 4-11-0 (7") Mr C Andrews, ... (20 to 1)	pu

Dist: 1l, 15l, 3l, 1l. (Time not taken) (18 Ran).

(Mrs M T Quinn), Victor Bowens

KILLARNEY (IRE) (soft)
Wednesday July 14th

82 Famous Grouse Handicap Chase (0-116 4-y-
o and up) £3,450 2m 1f. . . . .(2:30)

	GRATTAN PARK [-] 8-9-12 A Maguire, ...(5 to 1)	1
72⁴	HIGHBABS [-] 7-9-7 T Horgan, ...(6 to 1)	2
35³	ARDUBH [-] 6-9-12 N Williamson, ... (8 to 1)	3
	FROZEN FRIEND [-] 10-10-8 (5") T J O'Sullivan, . . .(20 to 1)	4
52²	NOBODYS SON [-] 7-10-3 (7") C O'Brien, ... (5 to 1)	5
51	TIGH AN CHEOIL [-] 9-10-0 K F O'Brien, ...(12 to 1)	6
52⁵	LA MODE LADY [-] 8-9-12 A J O'Brien, ... (8 to 1)	7
26	MAYE FANE [-] 9-11-7 (3") G Kilfeather, ...(20 to 1)	pu
21	LUCAS COURT [-] 7-10-6 (3") Miss M Olivefalk, . . . (10 to 1)	pu
	CHILIPOUR [-] 6-10-10 C F Swan, ...(7 to 4 fav)	pu

Dist: 8l, sht-hd, 1l, nk. 4m 28.80s. (10 Ran).

(O B P Carroll), John Brassil

83 Doyle Brothers Chase (5-y-o and up) £3,450
2½m. . . . . (3:00)

	MAJIRIYOUN (Ire) 5-11-1 M Flynn, ...(7 to 2)	1
42⁵	KINGSTON WAY 7-11-8 A J O'Brien, ...(5 to 2)	2
26"	RUSTY COIN 8-11-11 T Horgan, ...(11 to 8 on)	3
44	TEMPLE MARY 6-11-8 M P Hourigan, ...(10 to 1)	4
	BETWEEN THE LINES 11-11-4 G Bradley, ...(16 to 1)	pu

Dist: 3l, dist, 4l. 5m 26.30s. (5 Ran).

(G Moore), Declan Gillespie

84 Murphy's Irish Stout Handicap Hurdle (4-y-o
and up) £9,750 2m 1f. . . . . (3:30)

63"	AQUINAS [-] 7-9-7 (6ex) N Williamson, ...(10 to 1)	1
8"	SHEAMY'S DREAM (Ire) [-] (bl) 5-11-2 J Shortt, ... (4 to 1)	2
46"	NORDIC SUN (Ire) [-] 5-11-4 (8ex) J F Titley, ... (7 to 1)	3
40²	SHAREEF ALLIANCE (Ire) [-] 4-10-3 K F O'Brien, . . . (5 to 1)	4
	NATIVE PORTRAIT [-] 6-11-2 A Maguire, ...(9 to 4 fav)	5
13³	CHOISYA (Ire) [-] (bl) 5-10-1 C F Swan, ...(5 to 1)	6
46⁹	FURRY STAR [-] 7-11-1 T J Taaffe, ...(12 to 1)	7
	TRY A BRANDY [-] 11-10-11 C O'Dwyer, ...(10 to 1)	8

Dist: 2½l, hd, 2l, 2½l. 4m 29.90s. (8 Ran).

(W Hennessy), Anthony Mullins

KILLARNEY (IRE) (heavy)
Thursday July 15th

85 Travel Choice Ireland Hurdle (4-y-o and up)
£3,450 2m 1f. . . . . (2:00)

	LOVE AND PORTER (Ire) 5-10-10 D H O'Connor, (2 to 1 fav)	1
56"	OH SO GROUPY 5-11-8 C F Swan, ...(9 to 4)	2
41	CASTLE CELEBRITY (Ire) 4-10-4 K F O'Brien, ...(25 to 1)	3
71⁴	NORDIC BEAT (Ire) 4-10-9 M P Hourigan, ... (8 to 1)	4
41⁹	MASTER BATT (Ire) 4-10-6 (3") J Magee, ...(16 to 1)	5
79	FULL SCHEDUAL 6-11-2 J F Titley, ...(8 to 1)	6
28"	NIMBLE WIND (bl) 7-11-4 A J O'Brien, ...(9 to 2)	7

41	RAISE THE BANNER (Ire) 4-10-4 J R Kavanagh, . . . (33 to 1)	8
	OFF N'BACKAGAIN (Ire) 4-10-2 (7") C O'Brien, . .(33 to 1)	f
	TENDERENE (Ire) 5-10-4¹ (7") Mr P O'Keeffe, ...(25 to 1)	pu

Dist: 8l, 2l, 13l, 2l. 4m 34.70s. (10 Ran).

(The Schooner Syndicate), James Joseph O'Connor

86 Bowler/Londis Handicap Hurdle (0-116 4-y-o
and up) £3,450 2m 1f. . . . .(2:30)

	THE HEARTY CARD (Ire) [-] 5-10-10 D H O'Connor, (6 to 1)	1
	BROOK COTTAGE (Ire) [-] 5-10-13 K F O'Brien, (4 to 1 fav)	2
51⁸	WATERLOO LADY [-] 6-10-4 (3") P Carberry, ...(10 to 1)	3
57⁶	DEGO DANCER [-] 6-10-0 (7") J P Broderick, ... (8 to 1)	4
73⁹	IF SO [-] 7-10-6 C F Swan, ...(12 to 1)	5
49"	COMBINE CALL [-] 6-10-10 (7",6ex) T P Treacy, ... (6 to 1)	6
40⁶	NICE AND SIMPLE [-] 6-10-8 A J O'Brien, ...(12 to 1)	7
	CLONEENVERB [-] 9-9-6 (7") C O'Brien, ...(33 to 1)	8
48⁶	TOURIG LE MOSS [-] 6-10-11 J R Kavanagh, ... (20 to 1)	9
49⁷	ALL YOURS [-] 4-10-7 L P Cusack, ...(16 to 1)	10
41²	PRINCE TAUFAN (Ire) [-] 4-10-1 A Maguire, ... (5 to 1)	11
	CLASSY MACHINE (Ire) [-] 5-10-9 P M Verling, ...(10 to 1)	12
29	PRINCE JUAN [-] (bl) 6-10-11 (7") J Butler, ...(12 to 1)	13
	TRANSCRIBER (USA) [-] 6-12-0 G Bradley, ...(14 to 1)	pu

Dist: 1½l, 5l, ¾l, 2l. 4m 29.50s. (14 Ran).

(E O'Dwyer), James Joseph O'Connor

87 Menvier-Swain Handicap Hurdle (0-123 4-y-
o and up) £3,450 2¾m. . . . . (3:00)

25"	TERZIA [-] 6-11-0 T Horgan, ...(5 to 2 fav)	1
66"	SONG OF CAEDMON (Ire) [-] 5-10-1 (4ex) C F Swan, (3 to 1)	2
19⁵	SILVER LIGHT [-] 5-9-0 (7") J P Broderick, ...(33 to 1)	3
42	TELL A TALE [-] 6-10-5 K F O'Brien, ... (7 to 1)	4
72³	LANTERN LUCK (Ire) [-] (bl) 5-9-13 M P Hourigan, . .(7 to 2)	5
34²	CASTLE KNIGHT [-] 7-10-6 W T Slattery Jnr, ... (8 to 1)	6
	MINERAL DUST [-] 10-10-2⁹ (7") Mr P Cashman, . .(25 to 1)	7
47⁶	FUR N MONEY [-] 7-9-4³ (7") C O'Brien, ... (20 to 1)	8
	KINDLY KING [-] 9-10-8 (3") J Magee, ...(16 to 1)	9
29	MANDEVILLE LANE [-] 7-10-0 N Williamson, ...(33 to 1)	pu

Dist: 13l, 13l, 2½l, 3l. 5m 53.70s. (10 Ran).

(P Hughes), P Hughes

88 Woodfab Flat Race (Qualifer) (4-y-o and up)
£4,140 2m 1f. . . . . (3:30)

7"	CHANCERY QUEEN (Ire) 4-11-6 Mr A P O'Brien, (9 to 4 fav)	1
43⁴	KING OF THE WORLD (Ire) 5-11-5² (7") Mr D E Finn,	
	. . . . (20 to 1)	2
79"	QUEENIES CHILD 6-11-6 (7") Mr G J Harford, ... (12 to 1)	3
12"	CLASHWILLIAM GIRL (Ire) 5-11-9 (3") Mr T Lombard,	
	. . . . (10 to 3)	4
56	DANCING COURSE (Ire) 5-11-5 (7") Mr P A Roche, (10 to 1)	5
67²	BLAST FREEZE (Ire) 4-11-1 (5") Mr J A Nash, ... (7 to 2)	6
36⁴	KINGS DECREE (Ire) 4-10-11 (7") Mr J T McNamara,	
	. . . . (12 to 1)	7
73"	MOON DASH (Ire) 5-11-12 Mr S R Murphy, ... (8 to 1)	8
	IF YOU SAY YES (Ire) 5-11-7 (5") Mrs J M Mullins, (10 to 1)	9
7⁸	PAT'S VALENTINE (Ire) 5-10-12 (7") Mr G Hogan, . .(33 to 1)	10

Dist: 5l, 2½l, ½l, 9l. 4m 26.10s. (10 Ran).

(Richard O'Gorman), A P O'Brien

KILBEGGAN (IRE) (yielding)
Friday July 16th

89 Tyrrellspass Maiden Hurdle (6-y-o and up)
£2,245 2m 3f. . . . .(6:00)

32²	UPPINGHAM 7-11-7 (7") C O'Dwyer, ...(3 to 1)	1
	MASAI WARRIOR 6-11-11 (3") J Collins, ... (100 to 30)	2
53"	TOUREEN GIRL 6-11-9 C F Swan, ...(5 to 2 fav)	3
18³	KIL KIL CASTLE 6-11-1 (5") T J O'Sullivan, ...(12 to 1)	4
60	BELLS HILL LAD 6-11-6 B Sheridan, ...(10 to 1)	5
79⁸	TORLOUGH 8-10-13 (7") Mr A J Kennedy, ...(33 to 1)	6
45	AERODYNAMIC (bl) 7-11-6 M Flynn, ...(25 to 1)	7
	TOM HENRY 6-11-1 (5") C P Dunne, ...(33 to 1)	8
64⁸	JUST BLUSH 6-11-9 H Rogers, ...(9 to 1)	9
18⁴	ANYTHING FOR YOU 9-10-13 (7") T P Treacy, ...(14 to 1)	10

Dist: ¾l, 3l, 15l, 1½l. 4m 44.00s. (10 Ran).

(W Fennin), W Fennin

90 Loughnagore Maiden Hurdle (4 & 5-y-o)
£2,245 2m 3f. . . . .(6:30)

61"	FIRST SESSION (Ire) 5-11-8 C F Swan, ...(6 to 4 fav)	1
45⁸	MICHAEL'S STAR (Ire) 5-11-5 C O'Dwyer, ... (8 to 1)	2
12⁵	THE DASHER DOYLE (Ire) 5-11-5 Mr P J Healy, ... (4 to 1)	3
30⁹	WALKERS LADY (Ire) 5-10-9 (5") D T Evans, ...(10 to 1)	4
30⁷	HEY LAD (Ire) 5-11-5 P M Verling, ...(20 to 1)	5
	GRAND SCENERY (Ire) 5-10-12 (7") M Kelly, ... (10 to 1)	6
65⁶	FINAL OPTION (Ire) 5-10-12 (7") Mr J Nagle Jnr, . .(33 to 1)	7
41⁴	FULL MOON FEVER (Ire) 4-11-2 K F O'Brien, ...(7 to 2)	8
50⁸	MILFORD MATCH (Ire) 5-10-7 (7") P Morris, ...(14 to 1)	bd
	LADY DIGA (Ire) 5-10-7 (7") Mr S O'Callaghan, ...(25 to 1)	bd
	LUCKY MINSTREL (Ire) 5-11-0 N Williamson, ...(14 to 1)	su

Dist: 2½l, 8l, 2l, 2l. 4m 46.70s. (11 Ran).

(John A Mernagh), W P Mullins

91 Leinster Petroleum Handicap Hurdle (0-116 4-y-o and up) £2,762 2m 3f.................(7:00)

50*	TERINGETTE (Hun) [-] 5-10-12 (6ex) L P Cusack, ...(7 to 1)	1
47²	VINEYARD SPECIAL [-] 7-11-6 K Morgan, ...(5 to 1)	2
66⁵	FINE PRINT (Ire) [-] 5-10-12 H Rogers, ...(7 to 1)	3
69³	TULLY BOY [-] 6-9-12 (7*) Mr D McCartan, ...(12 to 1)	4
20*	AMID BIRDS OF PREY [-] 6-10-7 C O'Dwyer, ...(9 to 2 fav)	5
	JOE WHITE [-] 7-10-12 (3*) P Carberry, ...(8 to 1)	6
66	COQUALLA [-] (bl) 8-9-9 (7*) D M Bean, ...(25 to 1)	7
66⁸	M MAGIC (Ire) [-] 4-9-13 (3*) J Magee, ...(12 to 1)	8
	CLASS ACT [-] 7-10-0 (7*) J M Donnelly, ...(33 to 1)	9
17⁹	HODGESTOWN [-] 6-9-6 (7*) A P Sweeney, ...(25 to 1)	10
	THE BOURDA [-] 7-10-5 F Woods, ...(14 to 1)	11
22	FIX IT [-] 6-10-7 J F Titley, ...(12 to 1)	12
	OLDE CRESCENT [-] 7-10-10 C F Swan, ...(7 to 1)	13

Dist: Hd, ½l, 3l, 11l. 4m 40.60s. (13 Ran).

(D W Samuel), Michael Robinson

92 Ryans Hardware Novice Chase (5-y-o and up) £2,590 2m 5f...................(7:30)

33²	QUAYSIDE BUOY 10-12-0 A Maguire, ...(5 to 4 fav)	1
22⁴	INCA CHIEF 9-12-0 T J Taaffe, ...(3 to 1)	2
	BIRDIE'S PRINCE 8-11-9 C O'Dwyer, ...(50 to 1)	3
	LADY DIAMOND 7-10-13 (5*) D Leahy, ...(25 to 1)	4
	CLASSIC CHEER (Ire) 5-10-13 N Williamson, ...(12 to 1)	5
6	LINAGREE BOY (Ire) 5-10-13 F J Flood, ...(7 to 1)	6
60	COBBLERS ROCK 7-11-9 L P Cusack, ...(25 to 1)	7
	HARRY'S BOREEN 6-11-9 K Morgan, ...(8 to 1)	8
33	TINKERS CORNER 8-11-2 (7*) S N Donohoe, ...(25 to 1)	9
9⁹	NAMESTAKEN 7-11-9 F Woods, ...(33 to 1)	10
24³	OYSTER LANE 7-11-1 (3*) G Kilfeather, ...(10 to 1)	f
45	SILVER BATCHELOR 11-11-9 D H O'Connor, ...(12 to 1)	pu
	MAJESTIC PARK 8-11-9 J Shortt, ...(33 to 1)	pu
	GERRYMANDER 7-11-9 G M O'Neill, ...(25 to 1)	pu

Dist: 9l, 8l, 10l, 10l. 5m 34.50s. (14 Ran).

(J L Needham), Declan Queally

93 Locks Whiskey Handicap Chase (0-102 4-y-o and up) £2,245 3m 1f................(8:00)

72²	CLOSE AT HAND [-] 8-9-9 A Maguire, ...(11 to 8 fav)	1
52⁶	FERGAL'S DELIGHT [-] (bl) 10-10-8 J F Titley, ...(11 to 2)	2
	ROSSBEIGH CREEK [-] 6-10-11 F J Flood, ...(13 to 2)	3
26⁴	CHARDEN [-] 7-10-3 (7*) C O'Brien, ...(11 to 2)	4
	BENS DILEMMA [-] 8-9-9 (7*) J P Broderick, ...(14 to 1)	5
	MARY GINA [-] 8-9-10 (5*) T J O'Sullivan, ...(14 to 1)	6
	BARRACILLA [-] 8-10-2 (3*) J Magee, ...(10 to 1)	7
	ABBEY JACK [-] 6-10-6 H Rogers, ...(20 to 1)	8
	BOG LEAF VI [-] 10-10-0 C F Swan, ...(33 to 1)	pu

Dist: 10l, 3l, 15l, 15l. 6m 41.60s. (9 Ran).

(M W McPhilemy), James O'Haire

94 Coola Mills INH Flat Race (4-y-o and up) £2,245 2m 3f...................(8:30)

23³	GAYLOIRE (Ire) 4-11-0 (7*) Mr T J Murphy, ...(5 to 2 fav)	1
31⁶	QUEEN KAM (Ire) 4-10-11 (5*) Mr J P Berry, ...(7 to 1)	2
36⁶	MISS POLLERTON (Ire) 5-11-1 (7*) Mr M J Bowe, ..(7 to 1)	3
65⁴	HURRICANE TOMMY (bl) 6-11-7 (7*) Mr G J Harford,	
	....(12 to 1)	4
	MILLROAD 7-11-4 (5*) Mr D P Murphy, ...(20 to 1)	5
53	BEL SHAN 7-11-2 (7*) Mr P A Roche, ...(8 to 1)	6
55	SHUIL SHELL (Ire) 4-11-0 (5*) Mrs J M Mullins, ...(5 to 1)	7
	SLANEY VISON (Ire) 5-11-3 (5*) Mr H F Cleary, ...(10 to 1)	8
	GLAD GIRL (Ire) 4-10-9 (7*) Mr E Keena, ...(33 to 1)	9
32	KINCOR (Ire) 4-10-9 (7*) Mr P English, ...(33 to 1)	10
58	THE BOOTER 8-11-7 (7*) Mr L Mannerings, ...(50 to 1)	11
	ARISTOLIGHT (Ire) 4-10-9 (7*) Mr V P O'Brien, ...(50 to 1)	12
	SUNRISE SARAH 7-11-9 Mr M McNulty, ...(7 to 1)	pu

Dist: 5½l, 4l, 6l, 5l. 4m 43.10s. (13 Ran).

(George Halford), M Halford

LEOPARDSTOWN (IRE) (good to firm)
Saturday July 17th

95 Silverpark INH Flat Race (4-y-o and up) £3,105 2m.......................(5:00)

	FERRAGOSTO (Ire) 4-11-7 Mr A P O'Brien, ...(2 to 1)	1
48²	HIGHLANDER (Ire) 4-11-7 Mr J P Durkan, ...(11 to 10 fav)	2
31³	HERE NOW (Ire) 4-11-0 (7*) Mr P Healy, ...(10 to 1)	3
36⁸	WOLVER LAD (Ire) 5-11-13 Mr T Doyle, ...(12 to 1)	4
28	WINCHLING 8-11-7 (7*) Miss C Rogers, ...(20 to 1)	5
31⁹	CROGHAN BRIDGE (Ire) 4-11-2 (5*) Mr D P Murphy,	
	....(50 to 1)	6
9⁵	EMPTY VANITY (Ire) 4-11-4 (3*) Mr A R Coonan, ..(33 to 1)	7
55⁵	CLASS OF NINETYTWO (Ire) 4-11-9 Mr M McNulty, (12 to 1)	8
55⁸	PRIORITY GALE (Ire) 4-11-2 Mr P Fenton, ...(8 to 1)	9
	KINGQUILLO (Ire) 4-11-7 Mr J P Dempsey, ...(14 to 1)	10
	CUCHULLAINS GOLD (Ire) 5-11-6 (7*) Mr D C Cullen,	
	....(20 to 1)	11
53	MOON-FROG 6-11-7 (7*) Mrs J Crosby, ...(50 to 1)	12

	GENE OF THE GLEN (Ire) 4-10-9 (7*) Mr J P Kilfeather,	
	....(33 to 1)	13
58⁵	THE FUN OF IT (bl) 8-12-0 Mr S R Murphy, ...(14 to 1)	14

Dist: 2l, 4½l, 2½l, ½l. 3m 60.70s. (14 Ran).

(D H W Dobson), J S Bolger

BALLINROBE (IRE) (good (race 1), good to soft (2,3))
Monday July 19th

96 Derks Maiden Hurdle (5-y-o and up) £2,245 2m.......................(5:30)

68²	NANARCH (USA) 9-12-0 C F Swan, ...(5 to 4 on)	1
27²	CASH CHASE (Ire) 5-11-0 L P Cusack, ...(3 to 1)	2
64⁶	KAFKAN (Ire) 5-10-12 (7*) C O'Brien, ...(8 to 1)	3
50⁵	JOHNS ROSE (Ire) 5-10-7 (7*) Mr W M O'Sullivan, ..(8 to 1)	4
71	ANOTHER BONNY 7-11-1 (5*) C P Dunne, ...(33 to 1)	5
41⁶	HAVEN LIGHT 6-11-6 N Williamson, ...(16 to 1)	6
	BOBBIE MAGEE (Ire) 5-11-0 F Woods, ...(33 to 1)	7
80⁸	ARI'S FASHION 8-10-10 (5*) T J Mitchell, ...(14 to 1)	8
	KALONA 6-11-6 J F Titley, ...(9 to 1)	f

Dist: 2l, 15l, 15l, ¾l. 4m 8.80s. (9 Ran).

(Mrs Kevin Prendergast), Kevin Prendergast

97 Cong Novice Chase (5-y-o and up) £2,245 2m 1f.......................(7:00)

35⁷	BLENHEIM PALACE (USA) 6-12-0 H Rogers, ...(6 to 1)	1
72	PALMROCK DONNA 6-11-9 K Morgan, ...(16 to 1)	2
	GONZALO 10-12-0 A Powell, ...(7 to 2)	3
79³	KENMAC 6-12-0 K F O'Brien, ...(2 to 1 fav)	4
	MIRROMARK (Ire) 5-11-7 P M Verling, ...(14 to 1)	5
	SCORPIO GIRL 8-11-9 A J O'Brien, ...(16 to 1)	6
	THE WEST'S ASLEEP 8-11-7 (7*) C O'Brien, ...(7 to 1)	7
58	ORIENT ROVER 9-11-7 (7*) Mr A Daly, ...(12 to 1)	8
27⁴	CARRIGANS LAD (Ire) 5-11-4 (3*) G Kilfeather, ...(16 to 1)	9
	BALLINAVEEN BRIDGE 6-12-0 S H O'Donovan, ...(16 to 1)	10
6⁷	DOCTER MAC 6-12-0 N Williamson, ...(14 to 1)	11
	SECRET GALE 6-11-9 T Horgan, ...(12 to 1)	12
	COOLMOREEN (Ire) 5-11-7 J F Titley, ...(20 to 1)	13
92⁷	COBBLERS ROCK 7-12-0 L P Cusack, ...(20 to 1)	su

Dist: 1l, 2½l, 11l, 5l. 4m 37.30s. (14 Ran).

(Damien Shine), J P Byrne

98 Loughcarra I.N.H. Flat Race (4-y-o and up) £2,245 2m.......................(8:30)

7	MISTER DRUM (Ire) 4-11-0 (7*) Mr J T McNamara, (11 to 2)	1
41	MAGNIFICENT OAK (NZ) 5-11-8 (5*) Mr C T G Kinane,	
	....(14 to 1)	2
56	REMAINDER LASS (Ire) 4-10-9 (7*) Mr M P Dunne, (16 to 1)	3
	DROP THE HAMMER (Ire) 4-11-0 (7*) Mr R Pugh, (12 to 1)	4
	NOELEENS DELIGHT (Ire) 4-10-9 (7*) Mr G J Harford,	
	....(10 to 1)	5
58⁷	OZONE RIVER (Ire) 5-11-1 (7*) Mr S O'Donnell, ...(14 to 1)	6
73²	KELLSEIGHTHUNDRED (Ire) 4-11-7 Mr A P O'Brien,	
	....(11 to 8 on)	7
58	ABBEY TRINITY (Ire) 4-10-9 (7*) Mr E Norris, ...(33 to 1)	8
	QUAINT HONOUR 4-10-9 (7*) Miss S Kiernan, ...(20 to 1)	9
58	CLANMANY (Ire) (bl) 4-11-0 (7*) Mr B O Lennon, ..(20 to 1)	10
	BRIGADIER SUPREME (Ire) 4-11-7 Mr T S Costello,	
	....(11 to 1)	11
	CLADDAGH CRYSTAL 6-11-7 (7*) Mr R Monroe, ..(33 to 1)	12
27⁸	THYNE OWN GIRL (Ire) 4-11-2 Mr E Bolger, ...(16 to 1)	13
61	MOUNTAINFOOT GIRL 6-11-2 (7*) Mr A Daly, ...(33 to 1)	14
	REASKA SURPRISE (Ire) 4-10-13 (3*) Mr D Marnane,	
	....(20 to 1)	bd
	MARCHING SEASON (Ire) 5-11-1 (7*) Mr D A Harney,	
	....(20 to 1)	su
	RATHCARRICK LASS (Ire) (bl) 4-10-11 (5*) Mr J A Nash,	
	....(20 to 1)	pu

Dist: 9l, 2l, 4½l. 4m 2.20s. (17 Ran).

(A J McNamara), A J McNamara

BALLINROBE (IRE) (good)
Tuesday July 20th

99 Bowers Maiden Hurdle (4-y-o and up) £2,245 2m.......................(5:30)

28⁹	FROMTHEGETGO (Ire) 4-11-7 P L Malone, ...(10 to 1)	1
17⁶	BUMBLY BROOK 6-10-13 (7*) J M McCormack, ...(4 to 1)	2
	CLONALEENAN 4-11-2 N Williamson, ...(10 to 1)	3
81⁴	BRAE (Ire) 5-10-7 (7*) Mr D McCann, ...(8 to 1)	4
24⁶	CAT FIGHT 6-10-8 (7*) Mr A Daly, ...(14 to 1)	5
	DEB'S TURN (Ire) 4-11-2 A Powell, ...(33 to 1)	6
	MAJESTIC MAIGUE (Ire) 4-10-11 T Grantham, ...(14 to 1)	7
	TOMBARA (Ire) 5-11-13 J Shortt, ...(Evens fav)	8

Dist: 2l, 13l, 3l, 13l. 4m 8.50s. (8 Ran).

(J Crowley), M J Grassick

100 Summer Handicap Hurdle (0-102 4-y-o and up) £2,245 2½m..................(6:00)

76* DANCINGCINDERELLA [-] 9-10-8 M P Hourigan,
.... (2 to 1 fav) 1
66[2] SENSITIVE KING [-] 5-10-12 (3*) J Collins, ... (7 to 2) 2
38 MUST DO [-] 7-11-1 (5*) T J Mitchell, ... (11 to 2) 3
63[5] SEZ HE SEZ I [-] 9-10-5 (7*) Miss C E Hyde, ... (12 to 1) 4
78[2] MARBLE CITY GIRL [-] 8-10-4 (7*) J P Broderick, (11 to 2) 5
69 GARYS GIRL [-] 6-10-2 (7*) Mr G Finlay, ... (20 to 1) 6
66 BALLINDERRY GLEN [-] 7-10-12 L P Cusack, ... (13 to 2) 7
ANA CRUSIS (Ire) [-] 5-10-5 A Powell, ... (20 to 1) 8
24[7] PALLASKENRY (Ire) [-] 5-10-8 F Woods, ... (20 to 1) 9
Dist: 2l, 2l, 1l, 2l. 5m 12.60s. (9 Ran).

(M F Murray), Michael Hourigan

101 Cloon Gowla Handicap Chase (0-109 4-y-o and up) £2,245 2m 1f. .... (6:30)

82* GRATTAN PARK [-] 8-10-12 (6ex) A Maguire, ... (7 to 4 fav) 1
21[4] CAPINCUR BOY [-] 11-10-11 J F Titley, ... (10 to 1) 2
MACK A DAY [-] 6-11-1 A J O'Brien, ... (12 to 1) 3
GERTIES PRIDE [-] 9-11-6 F Woods, ... (12 to 1) 4
93[5] BENS DILEMMA [-] 8-9-4 (7*) J P Broderick, ... (25 to 1) 5
WHO'S FOOLING WHO [-] (bl) 7-10-11 N Williamson,
.... (8 to 1) 6
56[4] SUNSHINES TAXI [-] 6-11-12 S H O'Donovan, ... (10 to 1) 7
52[9] GLITTER GREY [-] 7-11-5 J Shortt, ... (12 to 1) 8
79 BLACK MALACHA VI [-] 10-9-6[2] (3*) J Collins, ... (25 to 1) 9
26[3] PORTLAND LAD [-] 8-10-3 A Powell, ... (12 to 1) 10
14* CITIZEN LEVEE [-] 7-11-5 (7*) Mr W M O'Sullivan, .. (4 to 1) ur
76[8] THURSDAY SWEEP [-] 7-11-9 (5*) T J Mitchell, ... (33 to 1) pu
78[5] QUIVERING MELODY [-] 6-11-8 K F O'Brien, ... (10 to 1) pu
Dist: 6l, 7l, 4½l, 3l. 4m 25.70s. (13 Ran).

(O B P Carroll), John Brassil

WEXFORD (IRE) (good)
Tuesday July 20th

102 Carne & Kilmore Maiden Hurdle (4-y-o and up) £2,245 2m. .... (5:30)

ANSEO [-] 4-11-7 T Horgan, ... (4 to 1) 1
GILT DIMENSION 6-12-0 C F Swan, ... (4 to 1) 2
37[7] MOSARAT (Ire) 4-10-4 (7*) D M Bean, ... (14 to 1) 3
64[5] HE'S A FLYER 9-11-11 (3*) J Magee, ... (9 to 1) 4
50[3] WINNING HEART 6-11-9 B Sheridan, ... (7 to 4 fav) 5
LAKE HOTEL 4-11-2 M Flynn, ... (14 to 1) 6
CARBON FIVE (Ire) 4-10-8 (3*) P Carberry, ... (8 to 1) 7
COCKNEY LAD (Ire) 4-10-9 (7*) F Byrne, ... (16 to 1) 8
31[8] GREENFIELD LODGE (Ire) 4-11-2 D H O'Connor, ... (20 to 1) 9
73 LAFFAN'S BRIDGE (Ire) 4-10-11 C O'Dwyer, ... (16 to 1) 10
TURALITY 4-11-2[2] P Kavanagh, ... (16 to 1) 11
56 SIRAJAO (Ire) 4-10-4 (7*) S N Donohoe, ... (16 to 1) 12
IMOKILLY PEOPLE (Ire) 5-11-0 N Byrne, ... (20 to 1) 13
12[7] GIVEN BEST (Ire) 4-10-11 (5*) M A Davey, ... (20 to 1) ur
THE APPRENTICE 7-11-6 J P Banahan, ... (10 to 1) ur
Dist: ¾l, 2l, 3½l, 8l. 3m 56.30s. (15 Ran).

(L Thompson), E J O'Grady

103 Horse And Hound Mares Maiden Hurdle (5-y-o and up) £2,762 2¼m. .... (6:00)

SUSTENANCE 6-11-6 D H O'Connor, ... (10 to 1) 1
80[5] PEARL'S CHOICE (Ire) 5-11-2 (3*) P Carberry, ... (9 to 2) 2
71[9] PEJAWI 6-11-6 C O'Dwyer, ... (10 to 1) 3
LILY ROSE VI 9-11-1 (5*) T J O'Sullivan, ... (14 to 1) 4
QUITE A FIGHTER 6-11-1 (5*) D T Evans, ... (20 to 1) 5
17 THE COBH GALE 6-11-6 H Rogers, ... (12 to 1) 6
41 REGULAR PAL 10-11-1 (5*) A J Roche, ... (16 to 1) 7
20 GALES JEWEL 7-11-6 A Powell, ... (16 to 1) 8
RHINESTALL 6-11-1 (5*) T F Lacy Jnr, ... (3 to 1 jt-fav) 9
70[9] NEWBRISTY 6-10-13 (7*) J Pearse, ... (20 to 1) 10
80[7] BELLECARA 6-11-11 (3*) D Bromley, ... (5 to 1) 11
65[5] HILL RANGER 6-10-13 (7*) Mr J P Brennan, ... (20 to 1) 12
BOUNTIFUL HOLLOW (Ire) 5-11-5 C F Swan, (3 to 1 jt-fav) f
Dist: 4½l, 12l, 8l, ½l. 4m 15.70s. (13 Ran).

(J P Rossiter), J P Rossiter

104 Ryans O Rosslare Handicap Hurdle (0-109 4-y-o and up) £2,762 2m. .... (6:30)

51[4] CELTIC GOLD [-] 9-11-0 C F Swan, ... (100 to 30) 1
86 PRINCE JUAN [-] (bl) 6-11-0 (7*) J Butler, ... (8 to 1) 2
91 THE BLACKED [-] 7-10-11 K Morgan, ... (9 to 1) 3
91[4] TULLY BOY [-] 6-10-4 (7*) Mr D McCartan, ... (13 to 2) 4
GARRYDOOLIS [-] 7-10-7 C O'Dwyer, ... (10 to 1) 5
74[4] FINGAL BOY (Ire) [-] 5-10-6 J P Banahan, ... (6 to 1) 6
1 ICANSEEFORMILES (Ire) [-] 5-10-4 O N Bowens, ... (12 to 1) 7
84* AQUINAS [-] 7-10-4 (7*,12ex) R A Hennessy, ... (9 to 4 fav) 8
KIARA DEE [-] 7-10-1[9] (7*) J P Deegan, ... (20 to 1) 9
45 CASTLEROE LAD [-] 6-10-5 P Kavanagh, ... (16 to 1) 10
Dist: Nk, ¾l, ½l, 10l. 3m 51.70s. (10 Ran).

(Patrick Joseph Hogan), Michael J Carroll

105 Whitford House Hotel INH Flat Race (4-y-o and up) £2,770 2m. .... (8:30)

64[2] UNCLE BART (Ire) 5-11-6 (7*) R A Hennessy, ... (Evens fav) 1
94 SIMPLY SARAH 7-11-2 (7*) D A McLoughlin, ... (10 to 1) 2
15 FRAGRANCE MOUNTAIN 7-11-2 (7*) C O'Brien, .. (16 to 1) 3
81[9] CHUCK'S TREASURE (Ire) 4-11-0 (7*) Mr J P Fahey,
.... (12 to 1) 4
61[5] LORD GREYSTONES 5-11-13[6] (7*) Mr A D Evans, (12 to 1) 5
81[7] STRAWTALDI (Ire) 5-11-6 (7*) Mr J D O'Connell, ... (12 to 1) 6
90[6] GRAND SCENERY (Ire) 5-11-8 (5*) Mrs J M Mullins, (6 to 1) 7
LADY BLUE ROSE (bl) 6-11-2 (7*) J Pearse, ... (16 to 1) 8
61[7] SLEMISH MINSTREL 7-11-7 (7*) Mr I Johnston, .. (16 to 1) 9
BALMY GALE 7-11-9 (5*) Mr D P Murphy, ... (7 to 2) 10
23 ODELL ROSE 6-11-4 (5*) Mr H F Cleary, ... (14 to 1) 11
PENNY SHUFFLE (Ire) 5-11-1 (7*) Mr J D O'Neill, .. (12 to 1) 12
GAYLE HOUSE (Ire) 5-11-3 (5*) Mr J P Berry, ... (10 to 1) 13
61 CROGHAN MIST (Ire) 5-11-1 (7*) Mrs J Crosby, ... (14 to 1) 14
SAN REMO 6-11-7 (7*) Mr P M Cloke, ... (12 to 1) 15
Dist: 8l, 9l, 2½l, hd. 3m 44.80s. (15 Ran).

(W Hennessy), Anthony Mullins

NAAS (IRE) (good to yielding)
Wednesday July 21st

106 Halfway House Handicap Hurdle (0-123 4-y-o and up) £3,107 2m. .... (6:30)

57[2] DIRECT LADY (Ire) [-] (bl) 4-11-1 J F Titley, ... (11 to 2) 1
68* JOHNSTON'S JET [-] 9-10-3 (7*,6ex) C O'Brien, ... (7 to 1) 2
40* BRAVEFOOT [-] 5-10-7 (5*) T J Mitchell, ... (7 to 1) 3
PERKNAPP [-] 6-10-12 (3*) P Carberry, ... (6 to 1) 4
46[4] PALACE GEM [-] (bl) 6-11-0 B Sheridan, ... (8 to 1) 5
67[4] PRACTICE RUN (Ire) [-] 5-10-1 M Flynn, ... (7 to 1) 6
86[2] BROOK COTTAGE (Ire) [-] 5-10-3 K F O'Brien, ... (9 to 1) 7
75[7] FOUR TRIX [-] 12-10-8 (7*) B D Grattan, ... (25 to 1) 8
47[4] J-TEC BOY [-] 7-9-8 N Byrne, ... (16 to 1) 9
46 MELTEMI [-] 7-10-11 D P Fagan, ... (20 to 1) 10
29[4] ANOTHER CONTACT [-] 7-9-11 (5*) M J Holbrook, (12 to 1) 11
80[6] JUST FOUR (Ire) [-] 4-9-2[2] (7*) T P Treacy, ... (33 to 1) 12
8 TOUCHDOWN [-] 6-10-2 C F Swan, ... (5 to 1 fav) f
SONG OF THE WOODS [-] 4-9-8 F Woods, ... (25 to 1) pu
Dist: Hd, hd, 1l, 1½l. 3m 51.10s. (14 Ran).

(Mrs D Mahony), J S Bolger

107 Kill INH Flat Race (4-y-o and up) £3,107 2m
.... (8:30)

HERBERT LODGE (Ire) 4-11-2 (5*) Mr P M Kelly, ... (10 to 1) 1
67[7] KARABAKH (Ire) 4-11-2 (5*) Mrs J M Mullins, ... (5 to 1) 2
32[7] FAIRYHILL RUN (Ire) 5-11-1 (7*) Mr D A Harney, ... (12 to 1) 3
48 THE WICKED CHICKEN (Ire) 4-10-13 (3*) Mrs S McCarthy,
.... (8 to 1) 4
45 MERRY PEOPLE (Ire) 5-11-13 Mr J Queally, ... (12 to 1) 5
CAILIN RUA (Ire) 5-11-3 (5*) Mr A E Lacy, ... (12 to 1) 6
64 RUFO'S COUP 6-12-0 Mr S R Murphy, ... (12 to 1) 7
55[7] GETA LEGUP 4-11-7 Mr P F Graffin, ... (9 to 1) 8
58[8] MOUNT SACKVILLE 6-11-2 (7*) Mr D Groome, ... (12 to 1) 9
FERRYCARRIGCRYSTAL (Ire) 5-11-13 Mr A P O'Brien,
.... (3 to 1 fav) 10
55 SONIC EXPERIENCE (Ire) 5-11-5 (3*) Mr R Neylon, (33 to 1) 11
47[7] WINDOVER LODGE 6-11-7 (7*) M Brennan, ... (10 to 1) 12
CORYMANDEL (Ire) 4-11-0 (7*) Mr R Roche, ... (9 to 2) 13
QUARTER MARKER (Ire) 5-11-6 (7*) Mr P English, (33 to 1) 14
CAIRDE MHAITH 6-11-7 (7*) Mr A Henley, ... (14 to 1) 15
YES YOUR HONOUR 6-11-2 (7*) Mr A J Kennedy, (33 to 1) 16
TIME UP (Ire) 5-11-0 (3*) Mr A R Coonan, ... (25 to 1) 17
32 PRINCE CHANTER 9-12-0 Mr T Doyle, ... (33 to 1) 18
BENTLEY'S FLYER (Ire) 4-10-9 (7*) Mr G Ryan, ... (10 to 1) 19
70 PAVLOVA RUN (Ire) 5-11-6 (7*) Mr C M Healy, ... (33 to 1) 20
LADY OF THE RIVER (Ire) 4-10-11 (5*) Mr D Valentine,
.... (33 to 1) 21
MUNINNABANE QUIZ 9-11-2 (7*) Mr B M Cash, .. (33 to 1) 22
Dist: Sht-hd, ¾l, 12l, hd. 3m 43.90s. (22 Ran).

(Stephen Hayden), J C Hayden

TIPPERARY (IRE) (good)
Thursday July 22nd

108 Sturakeen Maiden Hurdle (4-y-o and up) £2,762 2m. .... (8:00)

KILSHANNON SPRINGS 7-11-6 T J Taaffe, ... (5 to 4 fav) 1
4[3] HURRICANE EDEN 6-11-1 K F O'Brien, ... (7 to 1) 2
55 BERT HOUSE 7-11-6 T Kinane Jnr, ... (12 to 1) 3
71 BARRINGTONS CASTLE (Ire) 5-11-13 C F Swan, (10 to 1) 4
WHITE OFF 7-12-0 C O'Dwyer, ... (14 to 1) 5
71[8] BOLTON SARAH 6-10-8 (7*) T P Treacy, ... (16 to 1) 6
90 FULL MOON FEVER (Ire) 4-11-2 A Maguire, ... (8 to 1) 7
71[7] TRIPLE ACE (Ire) 4-10-9 (7*) Mr N D Fehily, ... (25 to 1) 8
56 DAMHSA (Den) 4-10-4 (7*) C McCormack, ... (16 to 1) 9
71[3] WALNEY ISLAND 4-11-2 T Horgan, ... (3 to 1) 10
TESALIA (Spa) 4-11-2 A Powell, ... (16 to 1) 11
43 MINERS DREAM 6-11-0[6] (7*) Mr D E Finn, ... (33 to 1) 12
71 TERRY'S PRIDE 7-11-1 H Rogers, ... (33 to 1) 13
DALGORIAN (Ire) 4-10-11 A J O'Brien, ... (33 to 1) 14
79 DERRING DREAM 6-11-1 (5*) Mr J A Nash, ... (33 to 1) 15
56[9] KINGS CHERRY (Ire) 5-11-5 F Woods, ... (10 to 1) 16
PAULMATIC 6-11-6 Mr J A Flynn, ... (40 to 1) 17

Dist: 2l, 4½l, 2½l, 1½l. 3m 58.80s. (17 Ran).

(P Fitzpatrick), A L T Moore

109 Donohill Flat Race (4-y-o and up) £2,762 2m .... (8:30)

	TEMPLERAINEY (Ire) 5-11-13 Mr A P O'Brien, . . (6 to 4 on)		1
	THE BRIDGE TAVERN (Ire) 4-11-0 (7") Miss C Duggan,		
	....(25 to 1)		2
58⁴	THE REGAL ROYAL (Ire) 5-11-8 (5") Mrs J M Mullins, (4 to 1)		3
	ARISE (Ire) 4-11-4 (3") Mr T Lombard, ...(25 to 1)		4
95⁴	WOLVER LAD (Ire) 5-11-13 Mr T Doyle, ...(12 to 1)		5
58³	VON CARTY (Ire) 4-10-9 (7") Mr J T McNamara, ..(14 to 1)		6
48³	A FEW GOOD MEN (Ire) 4-11-7 Mr E Bolger, ...(13 to 2)		7
	SUNSET RUN 7-12-0 Mr J A Berry, ...(20 to 1)		8
67	HAUGHTON LAD (Ire) 4-11-0 (7") Mr D Groome, ..(20 to 1)		9
43	FIFTYBETWEENYE (Ire) 5-11-1 (7") Mr D Duggan, (33 to 1)		10
36	ORANGE FLAME 7-11-9 (5") Mr J A Nash, ...(25 to 1)		11
73	GOLDEN SLEIGH (Ire) 5-11-1 (7") Mr A J Kennedy, (33 to 1)		12
73⁴	IRISH PERRY 6-11-9 Mr T S Costello, ...(16 to 1)		13
12	COMINOLE (Ire) 4-10-13 (3") Mr R O'Neill, ...(33 to 1)		14
	TROPICAL GABRIEL (Ire) 5-11-13 Mr P J Healy, ..(25 to 1)		15
36³	THE LODGER (Ire) 4-11-0 (7") Mr D A Harney, ...(12 to 1)		16
	MODEL BEHAVIOUR 4-11-7 Mr S R Murphy, ...(12 to 1)		17
	DINNYS DELIGHT (Ire) 4-11-0 (7") Mr D E Finn, ...(25 to 1)		18

Dist: Sht-hd, 4l, ¾l, 5½l. 3m 45.40s. (18 Ran).

(T Conroy), A P O'Brien

TIPPERARY (IRE) (good to yielding) Friday July 23rd

110 Power Solicitors Handicap Hurdle (4-y-o and up) £3,452 2m .... (8:00)

57*	CAN'T THINK WHAT [-] 6-10-0 (7",10ex) T P Treacy,		
	....(6 to 4 fav)		1
86³	WATERLOO LADY [-] 6-9-7 C F Swan, ...(7 to 1)		2
84³	NORDIC SUN (Ire) [-] 5-11-9 J F Titley, ...(5 to 2)		3
78	ACTION DANCER [-] 7-10-1 (7") C O'Brien, ...(14 to 1)		4
	RANDOM PRINCE [-] 9-11-11 (3") P Carberry, ...(7 to 1)		5
	PREMIER LEAP (Ire) [-] 4-9-9 (7") D M Duggan, ...(6 to 1)		6
34⁶	DANGEROUS REEF (Ire) [-] 5-9-7⁴ (5") T P Rudd, ..(10 to 1)		7
68	DELIFFIN [-] 7-9-8 C N Bones, ...(25 to 1)		8

Dist: 2½l, 7l, 1l, ¾l. 3m 51.10s. (8 Ran).

(Mrs P Mullins), P Mullins

111 Grange Stud Maiden Hurdle (4-y-o and up) £3,452 2½m .... (8:30)

	STRONG PLATINUM (Ire) 5-10-12 (7") Mr J Connolly,		
	....(5 to 4 fav)		1D
53²	SILVERWEIR 10-11-6 K F O'Brien, ...(3 to 1)		1
94⁵	MILLROAD 7-10-8 (7") C O'Brien, ...(16 to 1)		2
90²	MICHAEL'S STAR (Ire) 5-11-5 C O'Dwyer, ...(7 to 2)		3
30⁵	AWBEG ROVER (Ire) 5-11-5 A A Powell, ...(14 to 1)		4
	FERRIC FORTRESS 7-11-1 A J O'Brien, ...(25 to 1)		5
	JO-SU-KI 6-11-6 C F Swan, ...(14 to 1)		6
41⁸	MILLIES GIRL 5-11-1 (7") Mr J T McNamara, ...(10 to 1)		7
	PERCY BRENNAN 6-11-6 D H O'Connor, ...(20 to 1)		8
61	SARACEN'S BOY (Ire) 5-11-0 (5") T J O'Sullivan, ..(20 to 1)		9
44⁸	BUCKTAN 7-10-10 (5") M A Davey, ...(14 to 1)		10
	ANOTHER GROUSE 6-11-1 L P Cusack, ...(10 to 1)		11
85⁸	RAISE THE BANNER (Ire) 4-10-4 (7") J P Broderick, (16 to 1)		12
56	ERNEST MORSE (Ire) 5-11-0 (5") T P Rudd, ...(20 to 1)		13
	LOSLANN (Ire) 5-11-5 Mr P J Healy, ...(20 to 1)		14
	CHESTNUT SHOON 7-11-1 F Woods, ...(20 to 1)		15

Dist: 1l, dist, 11l, 5l. 4m 49.40s. (16 Ran).

(W J Purcell), A P O'Brien

GALWAY (IRE) (good to yielding (race 1), soft (2,3)) Monday July 26th

112 GPT Sligo Maiden Hurdle (6-y-o and up) £4,142 2½m .... (5:00)

87⁴	TELL A TALE 6-11-1 K F O'Brien, ...(15 to 2)		1
	THE EXAMINER 7-11-3 (3") J Magee, ...(33 to 1)		2
96	KALONA 6-10-13 (7") Mr G J Harford, ...(20 to 1)		3
74²	ST DONAVINT 6-12-0 C N Bowens, ...(9 to 2)		4
86⁵	IF SO 7-11-6 N Williamson, ...(16 to 1)		5
70⁵	DONT GAMBLE 7-10-13 (7") T P Treacy, ...(10 to 1)		6
	WHATASUCCESS 6-11-6 (3") P Carberry, ...(7 to 1)		7
	REDONDO BEACH 8-11-1 M Duffy, ...(25 to 1)		8
92	OYSTER LANE 7-10-12 (3") G Kilfeather, ...(20 to 1)		9
	ALLOON BAWN 7-11-1 T Horgan, ...(25 to 1)		10
41⁷	ALLOW GOLD 6-11-6 J F Titley, ...(20 to 1)		11
70²	SHEER MIRTH 8-10-13 (7") Mr D W Cullen, ...(8 to 1)		12
19	BALLAGH COUNTESS 6-11-9 A Maguire, ...(8 to 1)		13
45²	UGOLIN DE LA WERA (Fr) 7-12-0 C F Swan, ...(9 to 4 fav)		14
	JOHNNY SCATTERCASH 11-11-6 H Rogers, ...(20 to 1)		15
	I SUPPOSE (bl) 8-11-6 Mr A J Martin, ...(25 to 1)		16
52	BELIEVE THE BEST (Ger) 8-10-13 (7") Mr M Costello,		
	....(33 to 1)		17

65³ LE GERARD 8-11-6 C O'Dwyer, ...(14 to 1) — 18
ANOTHER BRIDGE 7-10-13 (7") B Bowens, ...(33 to 1) — 19
79 WINDMILL CROSS 6-11-6 J R Kavanagh, ...(50 to 1) — 20
92 GERRYMANDER 7-11-6 T Grantham, ...(33 to 1) — 21
19³ BEST MY TRY 6-11-6 B Sheridan, ...(10 to 1) — f
30³ CARRABAWN 7-10-8 (7") Mr P O'Keeffe, ...(16 to 1) — pu

Dist: 11l, 4l, 2½l, 6l. 5m 17.50s. (23 Ran).

(Mrs H C Taylor), Michael Hourigan

113 G.P.T. Dublin Handicap Hurdle (0-123 4-y-o and up) £4,142 2m .... (5:35)

57⁵	ULTRA MAGIC [-] 6-9-9 (5") A J Roche, ...(14 to 1)		1
	DUHARRA (Ire) [-] 5-12-0 A Maguire, ...(4 to 1 fav)		2
20⁹	FLYING SOUTH (Ire) [-] 5-10-9 J Shortt, ...(10 to 1)		3
	MARIAN YEAR [-] 7-10-9 (3") J Collins, ...(14 to 1)		4
50²	NO TAKERS [-] 6-9-7 N Williamson, ...(14 to 1)		5
89³	TOUREEN GIRL [-] 6-10-5 T Horgan, ...(12 to 1)		6
37⁵	BULLANGUERO (Ire) [-] (bl) 4-9-2 (7") D M McCullagh,		
	....(14 to 1)		7
71*	WALK RITE BACK (Ire) [-] 4-11-0 (6ex) K F O'Brien, (7 to 1)		8
86⁶	COMBINE CALL [-] 6-9-13 (7") T P Treacy, ...(12 to 1)		9
86⁷	NICE AND SIMPLE [-] 6-9-11 A J O'Brien, ...(20 to 1)		10
63²	MABES TOWN (Ire) [-] 5-9-10 N Byrne, ...(12 to 1)		11
69*	COQ HARDI SMOKEY (Ire) [-] 5-10-6 (3",6ex) P Carberry,		
	....(6 to 1)		12
85⁴	NORDIC BEAT (Ire) [-] 4-9-9 (7") J P Broderick, ...(25 to 1)		13
85²	OH SO GRUMPY [-] 5-10-4 C F Swan, ...(16 to 1)		14
69⁶	SANTA PONSA BAY [-] (bl) 6-10-2 P McWilliams, ..(10 to 1)		15
86	PRINCE TAUFAN (Ire) [-] 4-9-4 (7") C O'Brien, ...(10 to 1)		16
	SPECIAL CORNER (Ire) [-] 5-10-10 M Dwyer, ...(14 to 1)		17
106³	BRAVEFOOT [-] 5-10-7 (5") T J Mitchell, ...(15 to 2)		18

Dist: 1½l, 3½l, 4l, 1l. 4m 0.70s. (18 Ran).

(T A Kent), T A Kent

114 GPT Contractors Plant INH Flat Race (4-y-o and up) £3,797 2m .... (8:35)

	BANNTOWN BILL (Ire) 4-11-7 Mr A P O'Brien, ...(7 to 1)		1
98³	REMAINDER LASS (Ire) 4-10-9 (7") Mr M P Dunne, (33 to 1)		2
	SAME DIFFERENCE (Ire) 5-11-13 Mr S R Murphy, (16 to 1)		3
	DROMOD POINT (Ire) 4-11-0 (7") Mr E Norris, ...(10 to 1)		4
58²	WHAT IT IS (Ire) 4-10-11 (5") Mr J A Nash, ...(5 to 2 fav)		5
58⁹	HIGHLAND SUPREME (Ire) 4-11-7 Mr T S Costello, (10 to 1)		6
	HAYMAKERS JIG (Ire) 5-11-8 Mr E Bolger, ...(8 to 1)		7
	BEGLAWELLA 6-11-4 (5") Mr J P O'Brien, ...(50 to 1)		8
95⁷	EMPTY VANITY 4-11-4 (3") Mr A R Coonan, ...(14 to 1)		9
53⁴	LOUGH ATALIA 6-11-7 (7") Mr P A Roche, ...(16 to 1)		10
95	CUCHULLAINS GOLD (Ire) 5-11-6 (7") Mr D W Cullen,		
	....(50 to 1)		11
	JENNYELLEN (Ire) 4-11-2 Mr A J Martin, ...(14 to 1)		12
81²	PENNYBRIDGE (Ire) 4-11-0 (7") Mr P F Graffin, ...(7 to 1)		13
	TIM'S RUN 6-12-0 Mr P Fenton, ...(14 to 1)		14
58⁶	STONELEIGH TURBO (Ire) 4-11-2 (5") Mr P M Kelly, (20 to 1)		15
48⁷	DUN OENGUS (Ire) 4-10-9 (7") Mr K Whelan, ...(12 to 1)		16
	WE PAY MORE (Ire) 4-10-9 (7") Mr F McGirr, ...(20 to 1)		17
	LONG'S EXPRESS (Ire) 5-11-5 (3") Mrs M Mullins, (50 to 1)		18
94⁹	GLAD GIRL (Ire) 4-10-9 (7") Mr E Keena, ...(66 to 1)		19
88	PAT'S VALENTINE (Ire) 5-11-1 (7") Mr G Hogan, ..(33 to 1)		20
	CABLE BEACH (Ire) 4-11-0 (7") Mr G J Harford, ...(11 to 2)		21
73⁷	FULL SCORE (Ire) 4-11-2 (5") A J Slattery, ...(25 to 1)		22
58	GLADUATE (Ire) 4-10-9 (7") Mr D Naughton, ...(50 to 1)		23
	SHANAHOE STAR 7-11-2 (7") Mr T J Murphy, ...(50 to 1)		24
73	SIMPLISTIC (Ire) (bl) 4-11-2 Mr J P Dempsey, ...(14 to 1)		25
	CEOL NA RI (Ire) 4-11-0 (7") Mr B Hassett, ...(50 to 1)		26
98	THYNE OWN GIRL (Ire) 4-10-12³ (7") Mr R Pugh, ..(66 to 1)		27

Dist: Hd, 12l, ½l, nk. 4m 6.00s. (27 Ran).

(T Conroy), A P O'Brien

GALWAY (IRE) (soft) Tuesday July 27th

115 Albatros N-Rich Maiden Hurdle (4-y-o and up) £4,142 2m .... (5:00)

32⁵	PERSIAN TACTICS 4-11-7 B Sheridan, ...(5 to 2 fav)		1
	DERRYMOYLE (Ire) 4-11-7 W T Slattery Jnr, ...(12 to 1)		2
81*	MRS RUMPOLE (Ire) 4-11-2 C N Bowens, ...(4 to 1)		3
56	ROSSMANAGHER (Ire) 4-10-9 (7") C O'Brien, ...(20 to 1)		4
107	WINDOVER LODGE 6-11-1 (5") T J Mitchell, ...(14 to 1)		5
101⁷	SUNSHINES TAXI 6-11-6 S H O'Donovan, ...(10 to 1)		6
	NEXT TYCOON (Ire) 5-11-13 K F O'Brien, ...(8 to 1)		7
71	NOBODYS FLAME (Ire) 5-11-5 T Grantham, ...(12 to 1)		8
	SIR HENRY KNYVET (Ire) 4-11-2 N Williamson, ...(12 to 1)		9
	PURPLE EMPEROR (Fr) 4-11-2 (5") C P Dunne, ...(10 to 1)		10
103⁵	QUITE A FIGHTER 6-10-10 (5") D T Evans, ...(25 to 1)		11
18⁸	EASE THE BURDEN (Ire) 5-10-9 (5") T J O'Sullivan, (14 to 1)		12
	FANE PARK (Ire) 5-11-2 (3") P Carberry, ...(16 to 1)		13
111⁸	PERCY BRENNAN 6-11-1 (5") T P Rudd, ...(33 to 1)		14
96⁷	BOBBIE MAGEE (Ire) 5-11-0 F Woods, ...(33 to 1)		15
74	ROVANIEMI (Ire) 5-11-5 P McWilliams, ...(25 to 1)		16
	CORRAVOGGY (Ire) 4-11-2 J F Titley, ...(25 to 1)		17
70*	CUBAN QUESTION 6-12-0 C F Swan, ...(15 to 2)		18
89	MILFORD MATCH (Ire) 5-11-0 M Dwyer, ...(12 to 1)		19
	SHINDWA (Ire) 4-10-8 (3") J Jones, ...(50 to 1)		20
	POSEHILL 6-10-13 (7") K P Gaule, ...(10 to 1)		21

KODAK LADY (Ire) 4-10-4 (7*) J P Broderick, ... (25 to 1) 22
85 OFF N'BACKAGAIN (Ire) 4-10-11 (5*) D P Geoghegan,
. . . . (25 to 1) pu
Dist: Sht-hd, 4½l, 4l, 2l. 4m 14.20s. (23 Ran).
(Michael W J Smurfit), D K Weld

116 Albatros Chase (4-y-o and up) £5,177 2¾m
. . . . (6:10)

100* DANCINGCINDERELLA 9-11-9 K F O'Brien, ... (4 to 1) 1
92* QUAYSIDE BUOY 10-11-11 M Dwyer, ... (5 to 2 fav) 2
97⁷ THE WEST'S ASLEEP 8-11-1 (7*) C O'Brien, ... (16 to 1) 3
CHESTNUT JEWEL (Ire) 5-11-1 P McWilliams, . . . (33 to 1) 4
52⁷ TURNBERRY LAKE 7-12-0 A J O'Brien, ... (25 to 1) 5
SCREEN PRINTER (Ire) 4-10-0 J R Kavanagh, ... (50 to 1) 6
93⁴ CHARDEN 7-11-3 (5*) T J Mitchell, ... (16 to 1) f
72* INCH MAID 7-11-6 T Horgan, ... (6 to 1) f
77² TAKE THE TOWN 8-11-8 J F Titley, ... (6 to 1) f
72⁶ HAPPY ELIZA (bl) 10-11-3 D H O'Connor, ... (25 to 1) ur
77* FOXBROOK (bl) 7-11-11 N Williamson, ...(4 to 1) pu
97 BALLINAVEEN BRIDGE 6-11-8 S H O'Donovan, . . (33 to 1) pu
Dist: 1½l, 14l, dist, 1½l. 5m 53.60s. (12 Ran).
(M F Murray), Michael Hourigan

GALWAY (IRE) (yielding)
Wednesday July 28th

117 Digital Decsite Hurdle (4-y-o and up) £4,140 2m . . . . (1:50)

2² LIFE SAVER (Ire) 4-11-1 (3*) P Carberry, ... (6 to 1) 1
85* LOVE AND PORTER (Ire) 5-11-5 D H O'Connor, . . . (4 to 1) 2
PRINCIPLE MUSIC (USA) 5-11-3 B Sheridan, . . (2 to 1 fav) 3
HEAD OF CHAMBERS (Ire) 5-11-13 J P Banahan, . . (8 to 1) 4
84⁷ FURRY STAR 7-12-0 C F Swan, ...(9 to 2) 5
87⁶ CASTLE KNIGHT 7-11-11 W T Slattery Jnr, ... (20 to 1) 6
FLASHY BUCK 9-11-7 (7*) Mr H P Murphy, ... (9 to 1) 7
110⁸ DELIFFIN 7-11-4 C N Bowens, ... (33 to 1) pu
Dist: 1l, 2l, 6l, 1l. 3m 58.90s. (8 Ran).
(Mrs H A Hegarty), Noel Meade

118 Digital VAX Handicap Hurdle (4-y-o and up) £4,140 2¼m. . . . . (2:25)

62² HIS WAY (Ire) [-] 4-10-3 M Flynn, ... (11 to 4) 1
100⁷ BALLINDERRY GLEN [-] 7-9-2 (5*) M G Cleary, ...(9 to 1) 2
63³ BALLYCANN [-] 6-10-2 (7*) P Mulligan, ...(4 to 1) 3
66⁷ CHARLIES DELIGHT (Ire) [-] 5-9-3 (7*) K P Gaule, . .(6 to 1) 4
22³ FESTIVAL DREAMS [-] 8-10-2 J Shortt, ... (4 to 1 fav) 5
112 ANOTHER BRIDGE [-] 7-9-0 (7*) B Bowens, ... (50 to 1) 6
Dist: ¾l, 2½l, 2l, dist. 4m 35.00s. (6 Ran).
(Robert Scott), Kevin Prendergast

119 Digital Galway Plate (Handicap Chase) (Listed Race-Grade II) (4-y-o and up) £22,100 2¾m. . . . . (3:50)

GENERAL IDEA [-] 8-12-0 A Maguire, wl plcd, prog into
second 3 out, led aftr last, ran on strly. . . . . . (9 to 2 fav) 1
76² HARRISTOWN LADY [-] (bl) 6-9-7 J R Kavanagh, mid-div till
prog into 4th bef 3 out, 3rd o'r last, wknd r-in. (33 to 1) 2
GALEVILLA EXPRESS [-] 6-10-6 C N Bowens, led 7th till
hdd nxt, led ag'n 9th till headed shrtly aftr last, wknd
r-in. . . . . (7 to 1) 3
106⁸ FOUR TRIX [-] 12-10-2 J P Banahan, rear till styd on wl
frm 4 out. . . . . (25 to 1) 4
83² KINGSTON WAY [-] 7-9-8 A J O'Brien, mid-div till prog
into 8th betw last 2, wknd r-in. . . . . (25 to 1) 5
52* NEVER BE GREAT [-] 11-9-9 F J Flood, prog frm rear 5 out,
4th whn lost ch with blund 2 out, sn btn. . . . . (16 to 1) 6
CASTLE KING [-] 6-9-10 B Powell, trkd ldrs, ev ch in 4th 3
out, wknd nxt. . . . . (10 to 1) 7
76⁴ LIFE OF A LORD [-] 7-9-7 S H O'Donovan, rear, styd on frm
4 out without rching ldrs. . . . . (20 to 1) 8
76³ DESERT LORD [-] 7-9-7 C F Swan, mstks, mid-div whn
rdn and wknd bef 3 out. . . . . (10 to 1) 9
83³ RUSTY COIN [-] 8-10-2 T Horgan, mid-div, nvr rchd ldrs.
. . . . (20 to 1) 10
44² OCTOBER FLAME [-] 10-9-7 C O'Brien, trkd ldrs, prog into
second 9th, wknd 3 out. . . . . (25 to 1) 11
FINAL TUB [-] 10-10-6 C O'Dwyer, led till mstk and hdd
6th, led ag'n 8th, hdd nxt, grad wknd. (20 to 1) 12
101⁴ GERTIES PRIDE [-] (bl) 9-9-7 N Byrne, al rear. . . . (66 to 1) 13
91⁶ JOE WHITE [-] (bl) 7-10-4 P Carberry, trkd ldrs till lost pl
7th, no dngr aftr. . . . . (13 to 2) 14
75 MAPLE DANCER [-] (bl) 7-9-12 F Woods, mstk 1st, al rear.
. . . . (25 to 1) 15
83² EASTER SIXTEEN [-] 7-10-3 (4ex) J Shortt, al rear. (14 to 1) 16
87⁹ KINDLY KING [-] (bl) 9-9-12 J Magee, rear, lost tch hfwy.
. . . . (33 to 1) 17
101 CITIZEN LEVEE [-] 7-9-7 J Collins, mid-div and btn whn f 2
out. . . . . (10 to 1) f
75⁴ MAC'S GLEN [-] 9-9-8 P McWilliams, uns rdr 3rd. (25 to 1) ur
33* MUZAHIM (USA) [-] (bl) 9-9-7 N Williamson, trkd ldrs till pld
up 5 out. . . . . (10 to 1) pu

THE GOOSER [-] 10-10-11 R Dunwoody, mstks, rdn hfwy,
pld up bef 3 out. . . . . (14 to 1) pu
Dist: 6l, nk, sht-hd, 3½l, 7l, 14l. 5m 37.90s. (21 Ran).
(Michael W J Smurfit), D K Weld

GALWAY (IRE) (yielding)
Thursday July 29th

120 Harp Lager Novice Hurdle (4-y-o and up) £4,140 2½m. . . . . (1:50)

105* UNCLE BART (Ire) 5-11-6 (7*) R A Hennessy, . . .(7 to 4 fav) 1
101⁶ WHO'S FOOLING WHO 7-12-0 C F Swan, ... (12 to 1) 2
90³ THE DASHER DOYLE (Ire) 5-11-5 Mr P J Healy, . . (14 to 1) 3
71² MOUNTHENRY STAR (Ire) 5-11-6 G M O'Neill, . . . (9 to 2) 4
107⁵ MERRY PEOPLE (Ire) 5-11-5 T Horgan, ... (10 to 1) 5
97⁴ KENMAC 6-10-13 (7*) J P Broderick, ... (10 to 1) 6
STEEL CHIMES (Ire) (bl) 4-11-6 B Sheridan, . . . (11 to 2) 7
99² BUMBLY BROOK 6-11-6 C Swan, ...(7 to 1) 8
96⁴ JOHNS ROSE (Ire) 5-10-11 (3*) J Collins, ... (25 to 1) 9
83⁴ TEMPLE MARY 6-12-0 K F O'Brien, ... (16 to 1) 10
MISS FLINTSTONE VI (Ire) 5-11-0 J F Titley, . . . (66 to 1) 11
Dist: 3l, 2½l, 7l, 7l. 5m 16.30s. (11 Ran).
(W Hennessy), Anthony Mullins

121 Guinness Chase (4-y-o and up) £4,140 2m 1f. . . . . (2:25)

101³ MACK A DAY 6-11-11 A J O'Brien, ... (8 to 1) 1
35* THATS THE LIFE 8-12-0 T J Taaffe, ... (7 to 4) 2
97³ GONZALO 10-11-7 A Powell, ... (10 to 1) 3
THIRD QUARTER 8-12-0 C O'Dwyer, ... (Evens fav) 4
49 ORIENT ROVER 9-11-0 (7*) M A Daly, ... (20 to 1) 5
82 MAYE FANE 9-11-8 (3*) G Kilfeather, ... (12 to 1) 6
Dist: 5½l, 11l, 4l, 10l. 4m 45.00s. (6 Ran).
(C John McCarthy), Michael Condon

122 St. James's Gate Handicap Hurdle (0-123 4-y-o and up) £4,140 3m. . . . . (3:00)

87* TERZIA [-] 6-11-2 (4ex) T Horgan, ... (15 to 2) 1
87⁷ MINERAL DUST [-] 10-9-13 N Williamson, ... (20 to 1) 2
91² VINEYARD SPECIAL [-] 7-10-13 K Morgan, ... (10 to 1) 3
87² SONG OF CAEDMON (Ire) [-] 5-10-0 C F Swan, (4 to 1 fav) 4
87³ SILVER LIGHT (Ire) [-] 5-9-0 (7*) J P Broderick, . . (20 to 1) 5
42⁸ MOBILE MAN [-] 6-10-5 A Maguire, ... (13 to 2) 6
100² SENSITIVE KING (Ire) [-] 5-9-12 (3*) J Collins, . . . (10 to 1) 7
87⁵ LANTERN LUCK (Ire) [-] 6-9-1 J R Kavanagh, . . . (12 to 1) 8
100³ MUST DO [-] 7-10-1 (5*) T J Mitchell, ... (10 to 1) 9
86* THE HEARTY CARD (Ire) [-] 5-10-4 (4ex) D H O'Connor,
. . . . (10 to 1) 10
112* TELL A TALE [-] 6-10-7 (4ex) K F O'Brien, ...(6 to 1) 11
60 EDWARD'S DOLLY [-] 8-9-2 (5*) M G Cleary, ... (33 to 1) 12
69⁴ GOLDEN RAPPER [-] 8-9-7 (7*) N T Egan, ... (20 to 1) 13
SWEET DOWNS [-] 12-10-1 C O'Dwyer, ... (33 to 1) 14
17 BIT OF A TOUCH [-] 7-10-11 G M O'Neill, ... (20 to 1) 15
74⁹ MERSEY RACING [-] 6-9-6² (3*) K B Walsh, ... (50 to 1) 16
PROVERBS GIRL [-] 8-9-4 (3*) P Carberry, ... (20 to 1) 17
111⁵ FERRIC FORTRESS [-] 7-9-7 W T Slattery Jnr, . . . (25 to 1) 18
42 JOHNJOES PRIDE [-] (bl) 9-10-10 J F Titley, ... (20 to 1) 19
100⁹ PALLASKENRY (Ire) [-] (bl) 5-9-8 F Woods, ... (33 to 1) 20
91 HODGESTOWN [-] (bl) 6-9-4 (3*) J Magee, ... (66 to 1) 21
66 LODATO [-] 9-9-0 (7*) Mr S Durack, ... (100 to 1) 22
CAHERWALTER [-] 9-9-2² (7*) M J Molloy, ... (50 to 1) bd
WINSTON MURPHY [-] 7-7-12 H Rogers, ... (50 to 1) su
112 BELIEVE THE BEST (Ger) [-] 8-9-4 (3*) D Bromley, (50 to 1) su
46 MINION FASHION (Ire) [-] 5-9-1¹ (7*) T P Treacy, . . (50 to 1) pu
Dist: Hd, 4½l, hd, ½l. 6m 4.80s. (26 Ran).
(P Hughes), P Hughes

123 Guinness Galway Hurdle Handicap (Listed Race - Grade II) (4-y-o and up) £21,700 2m . . . . (3:50)

CAMDEN BUZZ (Ire) [-] 5-10-12 C F Swan, hld up, prog to
track ldrs aftr 3 out, slight advantage appr last, quick-
ened r-in. . . . . (4 to 1) 1
MUBADIR (USA) [-] 5-11-13 P Carberry, wl plcd, led aftr 2
out till appr last, ran on well. . . . . (12 to 1) 2
84⁵ NATIVE PORTRAIT [-] 6-11-10 Mr P Fenton, mid-div till gd
prog into 4th betw last 2, no extr r-in. . . . . (20 to 1) 3
84² SHAREEF ALLIANCE (Ire) [-] 4-10-9 K F O'Brien, wl plcd,
rdn to go second 2 out, styd on und pres. . . . . (16 to 1) 4
NAMELOC [-] 9-11-2 Mr J A Flynn, mid-div till some late
prog strt. . . . . (25 to 1) 5
57⁴ NATALIES FANCY [-] 7-11-3 J F Titley, hld up, styd on frm 2
out without rching ldrs. . . . . (14 to 1) 6
110* CAN'T THINK WHAT [-] 6-11-1 (7ex) T P Treacy, mid-div,
rdn and no imprsn frm 2 out. . . . . (14 to 1) 7
106⁴ PERKNAPP [-] 6-10-6 R Dunwoody, mid-div, nvr rch ldrs.
. . . . (25 to 1) 8
13⁶ KEPPOLS PRINCE [-] 6-10-11 K Morgan, led 1st till appr
4th, rdn and wknd 3 out. . . . . (12 to 1) 9
113 BRAVEFOOT [-] 5-10-3 T J Mitchell, mid-div till prog to
track ldrs bef 3 out, 5th into strt, wknd last. . . (25 to 1) 10

84² SHEAMY'S DREAM (Ire) [-] (bl) 5-11-8 J Shortt, *trkd ldrs, 4th 2 out, wknd nxt*.............................(14 to 1) 11

69⁸ KILIAN MY BOY [-] 10-10-6 S H O'Donovan, *rear, nvr rch ldrs*...(40 to 1) 12

NASSAU [-] 6-11-1 B Sheridan, *mid-div, shrtlvd effrt 4 out, btn nxt*..(16 to 1) 13

118³ BALLYCANN [-] 6-10-9 P Mulligan, *al rear*..........(33 to 1) 14

34⁴ THE LADY'S KNIGHT [-] 7-11-1 Mr T Doyle, *wl plcd to hfwy, rdn and no imprsn frm 3 out*.............(33 to 1) 15

BIG MATT [-] 5-11-5 C O'Dwyer, *led 4th till aftr 2 out, wknd quickly*...(6 to 1) 16

47⁵ BALLYTIGUE LORD [-] 7-10-2 T Horgan, *al rear*..(25 to 1) 17

BACK DOOR JOHNNY [-] (bl) 7-11-7 D H O'Connor, *trkd ldrs till prog into 4th four out, rdn and wknd nxt*.
....(40 to 1) 18

110⁵ RANDOM PRINCE [-] 9-12-0 M Dwyer, *mid-div whn hmpd 3rd, no imprsn aftr*................................(33 to 1) 19

113 PRINCE TAUFAN (Ire) [-] (bl) 4-9-7 N Byrne, *mid-div till wknd 3 out*...(50 to 1) 20

CRAZY GAIL [-] 6-9-11 N Williamson, *mid-div whn f 3rd*.
....(16 to 1) f

JUDICIAL FIELD (Ire) [-] (bl) 4-11-4 A Maguire, *mid-div whn brght dwn 3rd*..(7 to 2 fav) bd

Dist: 2½l, 6l, 1l, 4½l, 1½l, ½l. 3m 56.50s. (22 Ran).
(Miss Carmel Byrne), P Mullins

124 Arthur Guinness INH Flat Race (5-y-o and up) £4,140 2¼m........................(5:00)

36² TAYLORS QUAY (Ire) 5-11-6 (7") Mr K Whelan, *..(5 to 7 op 2 to 1)* 1

67⁶ OX EYE DAISY (Ire) 5-11-3 (5") Mrs M Mullins, ...(10 to 1) 2

61² BAVARD DIEU (Ire) 5-11-6 (7") Mr G J Harford, ...(5 to 1) 3

LE BRAVE 7-11-7 (7") Mr M Brennan, ...(14 to 1) 4

MAKES YOU WONDER (Ire) 5-11-13 Mr P F Graffin,
....(16 to 1) 5

94³ MISS POLLERTON (Ire) 5-11-1 (7") Mr M J Bowe, (14 to 1) 6

88² KING OF THE WORLD (Ire) 5-11-6 (7") Mr D E Finn, (10 to 1) 7

ICED HONEY 6-12-0 Mr A J Martin, ...(7 to 1) 8

FIFI'S MAN 7-11-7 (7") Mr P A Roche, ...(25 to 1) 9

79⁴ ROOKS ROCK 6-11-11 (3") Mr D Marnane, ...(14 to 1) 10

94⁸ SLANEY VISON (Ire) 5-11-3 (5") Mr H F Cleary, ...(25 to 1) 11

109 IRISH PERRY 6-11-2 (7") Mr J Kelleher, ...(20 to 1) 12

105⁷ GRAND SCENERY (Ire) 5-11-8 (5") Mrs J M Mullins, (20 to 1) 13

115⁵ WINDOVER LODGE 6-11-9 (5") Mr J A Nash, ...(14 to 1) 14

79⁷ THE TENANT 6-11-3 (7") Miss M Olivefalk, ...(8 to 1) 15

DESPERADO 5-11-9 (5") Mr D McGoona, ...(25 to 1) 16

114 TIM'S RUN 6-11-7 (7") Mr W Ewing, ...(20 to 1) 17

70⁶ DUNDOCK WOOD (Ire) 5-11-7 (7") Miss A Reilly, ..(20 to 1) 18

BELGRAVIA BOY (Ire) 5-11-13 Mr P Fenton, ...(8 to 1) 19

107 TIME UP (Ire) 5-11-8 (7") Mr A R Coonan, ...(33 to 1) 20

POLLANEDIN 9-11-7 (7") Mr B Deegan, ...(33 to 1) 21

73 PAPRS GALE (Ire) 5-11-1 (7") Mr E Norris, ...(8 to 1) 22

OAK COURT (Ire) 5-11-1 (7") Mr R M Murphy, ...(33 to 1) 23

TOECURLER (Ire) 5-11-1 (7") Mr G Hogan, ...(25 to 1) pu

Dist: 2l, 5½l, 2l, ¾l. 4m 29.10s. (24 Ran).
(P J Murphy), David J McGrath

BANGOR (good to firm)
Friday July 30th
Going Correction: NIL

125 Fred Archer Conditional Jockeys' Handicap Hurdle (0-115 4-y-o and up) £2,668 2½m........................(3:35)

LITTLE BIG [82] 6-11-1 (3") A Flannigan, *al handily plcd, chsd ldr 6th, led appr 3 out, sn clr, eased r-in*.
...................................(11 to 2 op 9 to 2 tchd 6 to 1) 1

NOUVELLE CUISINE [88] 5-11-10 N Bentley, *hld up in rear, improved 6th, chsd wnr frm 3 out, no imprsn*.
.....................................(7 to 4 fav op 11 to 8) 2

PANATHINAIKOS (USA) [77] 8-10-13 R Davis, *hld up, no real prog frm 3 out*............................(25 to 1 op 20 to 1) 3

STORM WARRIOR [67] (bl) 8-9-11 (6") N Juckes, *wl beh 7th, styd on frm 3 out, not rch ldrs*.

COMING ALIVE [86] 6-11-5 (3") J Supple, *wl plcd to 8th*.
....(7 to 2 op 6 to 1) 5

FOREST LORD [66] 9-10-2 D Walsh, *led, clr 3rd, hdd appr 3 out, sn lost pl*...............................(33 to 1 op 20 to 1) 6

CRAZY HORSE DANCER (USA) [80] 5-10-10 (6") M Doyle, *no ch frm 7th*......................................(14 to 1 op 20 to 1) 7

SAN PIER NICETO [85] 6-11-7 S Lyons, *wl plcd till hrd drvn and wknd 8th, tld off*...............(5 to 1 op 4 to 1) 8

Dist: 15l, 4l, ½l, ½l, 5l, 4l, 15l. 4m 44.20s. a 8.20s (8 Ran).
SR: 8/-/-/-/-/ (Christopher P J Brown), C D Broad

126 B.B.C. Radio Merseyside Selling Hurdle (3-y-o and up) £1,812 2m 1f........(4:05)

MOYMET 4-11-9 G McCourt, *led till aftr 1st, remained prmnt, led 3 out, sn forged clr, ran on wl*.....(7 to 2 jt-fav op 9 to 4) 1

ALICANTE 6-11-4 (3") D Walsh, *al wl plcd, chsd wnr frm 3 out, no imprsn whn mstk last*.
..................................(14 to 1 op 10 to 1 tchd 16 to 1) 2

KINLET VISION (Ire) 5-10-13 (5") T Jenks, *wtd wth in rear, prog appr 3 out, kpt on same pace frm nxt*.
..................................(16 to 1 op 12 to 1) 3

ABSOLUTELY RIGHT 5-11-2 (7") K Comerford, *took str hold, hdwy to join ldrs 6th, ev ch 3 out, sn btn*.
....(4 to 1 op 5 to 1) 4

GIN AND ORANGE 7-11-9 J Osborne, *hld up, improved 3 out, nvr able to chal*..................(7 to 2 jt-fav tchd 3 to 1) 5

FAIRFORD 4-11-7 Gary Lyons, *cl up, led 6th to 3 out, wknd quickly*......................................(6 to 1) 6

ALAMIR (USA) (bl) 5-11-9 J Railton, *pressed ldrs to 5th*.
....(33 to 1 op 25 to 1) 7

MONTAGNE 4-10-13 (3") R Greene, *pld hrd, led aftr 1st, hdd 6th, sn lost pl*.............................(33 to 1 op 25 to 1) 8

SLY PROSPECT (USA) 5-11-9 T Wall, *mstks 1st and 3rd, al in rear*..(9 to 1) 9

MANULIFE 4-11-7 D Bridgwater, *mstk 6th, al beh, tld off whn pld up bef 2 out*.........(11 to 4 op 9 to 8 tchd 12 to 1) pu

SHARDRA 4-11-2 S McNeill, *cl up till wknd quickly 4th, pld up bef nxt, collapsed, dead....* (14 to 1 op 12 to 1) pu

Dist: 8l, 3½l, 4l, ½l, 10l, 3l, 5l, 6l. 4m 6.20s. a 16.20s (11 Ran).
(E J Mangan), K R Burke

127 Daily Post Handicap Chase (0-130 5-y-o and up) £3,355 3m 110yds.........(4:35)

OK CORRAL (USA) [112] (bl) 6-10-13 A Maguire, *hld up, chsd clr ldr frm 13th, led 2 out, drvn clear r-in*.
.....................(6 to 5 on op 5 to 4 on tchd 11 to 10 on) 1

EMRYS [103] 10-10-4 D J Burchell, *led, sn wl clr, slight mstk tenth, hdd 2 out, hrd rdn r-in, no extr*.
.....................................(5 to 1 tchd 11 to 2) 2

KIRSTY'S BOY [127] 10-12-0 L O'Hara, *wl beh, poor 3rd whn mstk 2 out*..........................(4 to 1 op 7 to 2) 3

SANDSTONE ARCH [103] 10-10-4² Pat Caldwell, *chsd ldr to 13th, wknd 15th, pld up and lft remote 4th last, continued*....................(11 to 2 op 5 to 1 tchd 16 to 1) 4

SPIRITED HOLME (Fr) [99] 8-9-7 (7") Miss S Higgins, *beh, toiling frm 12th, remote 5th whn f last*.
....(50 to 1 op 33 to 1) f

CLARES HORSE [99] 6-10-13 R Supple, *struggling frm 13th, remote 4th whn f last*.........(12 to 1 op 10 to 1) f

DUNRAVEN ROYAL [99] 10-10-0 D Morris, *al beh, tld off whn pld up bef 13th*.................(25 to 1 tchd 33 to 1) pu

Dist: 6l, 25l, dist. 6m 3.20s. a 13.20s (7 Ran).
(Mrs C M Dartford), J White

128 Marcher Sound Novices' Claiming Hurdle (3-y-o) £2,242 2m 1f.............(5:05)

MR GENEAOLOGY (USA) (bl) 11-7 A Maguire, *hld up, slightly hmpd 3 out, led and crrd rght 2 out, kpt on wl*.
.....................................(6 to 4 on tchd 7 to 4 on) 1

KESANTA 10-4 R Dunwoody, *al cl up, slight ld 3 out, wnt lft and hdd nxt, no extr*. (7 to 1 op 6 to 1 tchd 8 to 1) 2

ASTRAC TRIO (USA) 11-3 P Niven, *led to 3rd, ev ch 3 out, one pace*............................(7 to 1 op 5 to 1 tchd 8 to 1) 3

BECKY'S GIRL 10-9 D Bridgwater, *hld up and beh, jmpd rght second, hmpd 3 out, nvr a factor*........(50 to 1) 4

MAGIC FAN (Ire) (v) 10-13 J Railton, *wl plcd, beh, sn drvn alng, wknd appr 3 out*.....(33 to 1 op 20 to 1) 5

BOHEMIAN QUEEN 10-3 (3") V Slattery, *pressed ldr, led 3rd, narrowly hdd and f 3 out*......(10 to 1 op 7 to 1) 6

CASHABLE 11-3 S Smith Eccles, *hld up, slight mstk and uns rdr 4th*.........................(15 to 2 op 6 to 1 tchd 8 to 1) ur

Dist: 3½l, 10l, 8l, 15l. 4m 0.90s. a 20.90s (7 Ran).
(Mrs P A White), J White

129 Chronicle Newspapers Novices' Chase (5-y-o and up) £2,710 2m 1f 110yds....(5:35)

CASTLE DIAMOND 6-11-0 J A Harris, *chsd ldr, hit 7th, rdn to ld 3 out, mstk last, ran on wl und pres*.
.....................(3 to 1 op 11 to 4 tchd 100 to 30) 1

SALMAN (USA) 7-11-0 C Llewellyn, *led, sn clr, hit 3 out, still jmp wl and ev ch betw last 2, rdn and no extr r-in*.
.....................................(11 to 4 tchd 3 to 1 and 5 to 2) 2

AT PEACE 7-11-0 A Maguire, *al handily plcd, rdn to chal appr 2 out, wknd frm last*.
.....................................(9 to 4 fav op 5 to 2 tchd 3 to 1) 3

WEEKDAY CROSS (Ire) 14-11-0 S Smith Eccles, *took str hold, struggling frm 9th, tld off*.....................(7 to 2) 4

HAZEL HILL 7-10-4 (5") T Eley, *mstk 3rd, al in rear, tld off frm 8th*..............................(50 to 1 op 33 to 1) 5

CRAFTY CHAPLAIN 7-10-9 (5") Mr D McCain, *improved to chase clr ldr 4th, cl fourth whn heavy fall 3 out*.
.....................................(12 to 1 tchd 16 to 1) f

GOOD EGG 7-10-9 Gary Lyons, *not jump wl, took keen hold, tld off whn pld up bef 2 out.* (50 to 1 op 33 to 1) pu

Dist: 2½l, 6l, 20l, 20l. 4m 15.10s. a 9.10s (7 Ran).
(Mrs S Kavanagh), H M Kavanagh

130 Buy Wise Novices' Hurdle (4-y-o and up) £2,179 2½m......................(6:05)

JALORE 4-10-8 (3") R Greene, *gd prog to join ldrs 6th, styd on to ld r-in, rdn out*..........(3 to 1 op 5 to 2) 1

15

QUIET RIOT 11-11-0 A Maguire, *improved 4th, led 3 out, hrd drvn betw last 2, hdd and no extr r-in.*
..................(5 to 2 fav op 9 to 4 tchd 11 to 4) 2
RUN MILADY 5-10-9 D Wilkinson, *hdwy 7th, kpt on same pace frm 3 out.* ....(9 to 2 op 4 to 1) 3
PLEASANT COMPANY 6-10-2 (7*) S Lycett, *pressed ldr, led appr 4th, wknd and pres approaching 2 out.*
.... (40 to 1 op 33 to 1 tchd 50 to 1) 4
LEANDER LAD 8-10-9 (5*) D Walsh, *led till appr 4th, wknd approaching 3 out, tld off.*........(25 to 1 op 12 to 1) 5
KING OF THE WOOD 8-11-0 R Dunwoody, *chsd ldrs to hfwy, sn struggling, tld off.*........(20 to 1 op 16 to 1) 6
WASSLS MILLION 7-10-7 (7*) A Harrington, *handily plcd to hfwy, tld off whn pld up bef 3 out.* (8 to 1 op 13 to 1) pu
RAPID ROULETTE (Ire) 5-10-9 R Supple, *prmnt till pld up aftr 3rd, broke leg, dead.* (9 to 2 op 5 to 1 tchd 6 to 1) pu
BUCKNALL GIRL 5-10-9 D Bridgwater, *al in rear, tld off whn pld up bef 2 out.*...............(20 to 1 op 16 to 1) pu
Dist: 3l, 8l, 15l, 30l, 8l. 4m 48.20s. a 12.20s (9 Ran).

(Mrs J Coathup), S Coathup

GALWAY (IRE) (good to yielding)
Friday July 30th

131 Budweiser Q.R. Handicap Hurdle (0-116 4-y-o and up) £4,142 2¼m......... (5:15)

112⁴ ST DONAVINT [-] 6-10-8 (7*) Mr J P Durkan, ... (6 to 1) 1
64* OPEN MARKET (USA) [-] 4-10-11 (5*) Mr J A Nash,
.... (4 to 1 jt-fav) 2
100⁸ ANA CRUSIS (Ire) [-] 5-9-12 (7*) Mr A Daly, ... (33 to 1) 3
51* KINDERSLEIGH [-] 6-10-10 (5*) Mr A E Lacy, ... (10 to 1) 4
113⁴ MARIAN YEAR [-] 7-11-5 (7*) Mr B Moran, ...(10 to 1) 5
113³ FLYING SOUTH (Ire) [-] 5-11-2 (7*) Mr G J Harford, (8 to 1) 6
45⁷ BAMANYAR (Ire) [-] 5-10-0 (7*) Mr John J Murphy, (25 to 1) 7
113⁵ NO TAKERS [-] 6-10-3³ (3*) Mr D Marnane, ...(12 to 1) 8
91⁹ CLASS ACT [-] 7-10-11 (3*) Miss M Olivefalk, ...(33 to 1) 9
10* PAGET [-] 6-11-3 (7*) Mr A A Wyse, ...(4 to 1 jt-fav) 10
4* SOLBA (USA) [-] 4-11-3 (7*) Mr G P FitzGerald, ...(7 to 1) 11
122 GOLDEN RAPPER [-] 8-11-0 Mr A J Martin, ...(14 to 1) 12
MAKE ME AN ISLAND [-] 8-11-0 Mr J P Dempsey, (25 to 1) 13
PRIDE OF ERIN [-] (bl) 9-12-0 (3*) Mr A R Coonan, (20 to 1) 14
93⁶ MARY GINA [-] (bl) 8-9-12 (7*) Mr G Hogan, ...(33 to 1) 15
114 LOUGH ATALIA [-] 6-9-13 (7*) Mr A Roche, ...(16 to 1) 16
BEAU JOHN (Ire) [-] 5-10-7 (7*) Mr D Murphy, ...(20 to 1) pu
66⁸ HOSTETLER [-] (bl) 4-10-13 Mr S R Murphy, ...(8 to 1) pu
Dist: Hd, ½l, 4½l, 1l. 4m 27.30s. (18 Ran).

(P A McMahon), Victor Bowens

132 Tony O'Malley Memorial Handicap Chase (4-y-o and up) £5,822 2m 1f........ (6:25)

101* GRATTAN PARK [-] 8-9-11 (12ex) C F Swan, ... (7 to 4 fav) 1
FRANTESA [-] 7-10-3 T Horgan, ...(13 to 2) 2
119 MAC'S GLEN [-] 9-10-11 J F Titley, ...(7 to 1) 3
77³ THUNDERSTRUCK [-] 7-9-12 (7*) C O'Brien, ...(16 to 1) 4
104⁵ GARRYDOOLIS [-] 7-10-0 C O'Dwyer, ...(16 to 1) 5
76 GOOD FOR A LAUGH [-] 9-11-11 T J Taaffe, ...(14 to 1) 6
THE RIDGE BOREEN [-] 9-12-0 N Byrne, ...(10 to 1) 7
101 PORTLAND LAD [-] 8-9-7 F Woods, ...(33 to 1) 8
82 CHILIPOUR [-] 6-9-10⁴ (5*) A J Roche, ...(12 to 1) 9
75² BOLD FLYER [-] 10-11-7 K Morgan, ...(11 to 2) 10
OH JACKO [-] (bl) 6-9-7 P McWilliams, ...(25 to 1) 11
PARGALE [-] 7-10-5 K F O'Brien, ...(8 to 1) pu
Dist: 6l, 6l, 4½l, 1½l. 4m 35.00s. (12 Ran).

(O B P Carroll), John Brassil

GALWAY (IRE) (good to yielding)
Saturday July 31st

133 Jockeys Association Novice Chase (4-y-o and up) £4,485 2m 1f.............. (1:30)

NORTHERN HIDE 7-12-0 T J Taaffe, ...(3 to 1) 1
108³ BERT HOUSE 7-11-9 T Kinane Jnr, ...(8 to 1) 2
92⁴ LADY DIAMOND 7-10-10 (7*) C N Bowens, ...(25 to 1) 3
DINNY'S SISTER 7-11-4 A J O'Brien, ...(25 to 1) 4
STRAIGHT TALK 6-11-9 B Sheridan, ...(8 to 1) 5
77⁹ AHEEMA COTTAGE 7-12-0 F J Flood, ...(9 to 2) 6
79⁹ KINGOFSPANCILHILL 6-11-2 (7*) Mr G P FitzGerald,
.... (20 to 1) 7
91 FIX IT 6-11-9 A Powell, ...(10 to 1) 8
106⁹ J-TEC BOY 7-11-7 (7*) C O'Brien, ...(16 to 1) 9
41 RUSSIAN GALE (Ire) (bl) 5-10-4 (7*) Mr G Mulcaire, (50 to 1) 10
77 TOLL BRIDGE 6-11-4 H Rogers, ...(14 to 1) 11
106² JOHNSTON'S JET 9-12-0 J F Titley, ...(5 to 2 fav) f
77⁷ TANAISTE (USA) 4-10-4 Mr C P Dunne, ...(25 to 1) f
23 MANAMOUR 6-11-9 G Bradley, ...(20 to 1) f
116⁴ CHESTNUT JEWEL (Ire) 5-11-2 P McWilliams, ...(25 to 1) f
86 TRANSCRIBER (USA) 6-12-0 C F Swan, ...(33 to 1) bd
92⁵ CLASSIC CHEER (Ire) 5-10-13 (3*) J Jones, ...(14 to 1) pu
97⁹ CARRIGANS LAD 5-10-13 (3*) G Kilfeather, ...(33 to 1) pu
Dist: 20l, 10l, 4l, 2l. 4m 36.90s. (18 Ran).

(T Ryan), A L T Moore

134 Oranmore Dairies Freshmilk Handicap Chase (0-116 4-y-o and up) £4,140 2¾m
....(2:00)

75⁵ JOEY KELLY [-] 8-10-6 C O'Dwyer, ...(8 to 1) 1
SKY RANGE [-] 8-11-4 T Horgan, ...(10 to 1) 2
76⁶ WATERLOO ANDY [-] 7-10-6 F J Flood, ...(33 to 1) 3
116* DANCINGCINDERELLA [-] 9-10-1 (8ex) K F O'Brien,
.... (5 to 4 fav) 4
MALACHYS BAR [-] 9-9-13 (3*) D Bromley, ...(33 to 1) 5
101⁵ BENS DILEMMA [-] 8-9-0 (7*) J P Broderick, ...(25 to 1) 6
119 GERTIES PRIDE [-] (bl) 9-10-7 (7*) C O'Brien, ...(16 to 1) 7
VAVASIR [-] 7-10-13 T J Taaffe, ...(10 to 1) 8
97* BLENHEIM PALACE (USA) [-] 6-10-1 (4ex) H Rogers,
.... (12 to 1) 9
116 HAPPY ELIZA [-] (bl) 10-9-7 W T Slattery Jun, ...(20 to 1) 10
76⁷ JAMES PIGG [-] 6-10-13 A J O'Brien, ...(16 to 1) 11
122 LODATO [-] (bl) 9-9-0 (7*) Mr S Durack, ...(50 to 1) 12
82² HIGHBABS [-] 7-9-7 S H O'Donovan, ...(12 to 1) 13
93* CLOSE AT HAND [-] 8-9-6 (5*,4ex) T J Mitchell, ...(10 to 1) 14
75⁹ SAM WELLER [-] 8-10-13 B Sheridan, ...(25 to 1) 15
21⁵ REHEY LADY [-] 7-9-0 (7*) T J O'Sullivan, ...(20 to 1) 0
116 FOXBROOK [-] (bl) 7-11-5 (4ex) J F Titley, ...(6 to 1) f
75³ LIGHT THE WICK [-] 7-11-3 C F Swan, ...(6 to 1) f
FRABER GLEN [-] 9-10-3 F Woods, ...(14 to 1) f
Dist: 6l, 1l, ½l, 4l. 5m 40.60s. (19 Ran).

(Stephen A O'Hara), W Rock

135 Oranmore Dairies Handicap Hurdle (4-y-o and up) £8,925 2m 5f 190yds........ (2:30)

106⁶ PRACTICE RUN [-] 5-9-12 P McWilliams, ...(14 to 1) 1
78* CUILIN BUI (Ire) [-] 5-10-13 (6ex) C O'Brien, ...(7 to 1) 2
106* DIRECT LADY (Ire) [-] (bl) 4-11-5 (1ex) J F Titley, ...(8 to 1) 3
84⁶ CHOISYA (Ire) [-] (bl) 5-11-0 C F Swan, ...(12 to 1) 4
123⁶ NATALIES FANCY [-] 7-11-9 G Bradley, ...(10 to 1) 5
123 SHEAMY'S DREAM (Ire) [-] 5-12-0 J Shortt, ...(12 to 1) 6
78³ RISING WATERS (Ire) [-] 5-12-0 G Lee, ...(20 to 1) 7
60³ DANCE OF WORDS (Ire) [-] 4-10-11 T J Mitchell, ..(10 to 1) 8
110⁴ ACTION DANCER [-] 7-11-0 J Collins, ...(40 to 1) 9
113² DUHARRA (Ire) [-] (bl) 5-11-11 B Sheridan, ...(13 to 2) 10
18² REFINED HEIR [-] 5-11-0 A P Carberry, ...(14 to 1) 11
HIGH-SPEC [-] 7-11-3 J Magee, ...(40 to 1) 12
78⁶ CARES OF TOMORROW [-] 6-10-8 N Byrne, ...(16 to 1) 13
69 KLUCKITAT [-] (bl) 6-11-0 C N Bowens, ...(33 to 1) 14
78⁸ SUNDAY WORLD (USA) [-] 7-9-12 A J O'Brien, ..(50 to 1) 15
66 SALLOW GLEN [-] 7-9-7 T J O'Sullivan, ...(33 to 1) 16
65* MORNING DREAM [-] 6-9-12 S H O'Donovan, ...(13 to 2) 17
PRINCE YAZA [-] 6-11-7 M Dwyer, ...(8 to 1) 18
122 SWEET DOWNS [-] 12-9-12 F J Flood, ...(50 to 1) 19
45* THE VERY MAN [-] 7-10-12 T P Treacy, ...(6 to 1 fav) 20
118⁴ CHARLIES DELIGHT (Ire) [-] (bl) 5-10-2 T Horgan, (20 to 1) 21
123 KILIAN MY BOY [-] 10-10-12 C O'Dwyer, ...(33 to 1) 22
113 COQ HARDI SMOKEY (Ire) [-] 5-10-5 (5ex) F Woods,
.... (14 to 1) 23
91³ FINE PRINT (Ire) [-] 5-10-1 H Rogers, ...(14 to 1) pu
Dist: 8l, 1½l, 4l, 1l. 5m 15.40s. (24 Ran).

(D Donegan), Patrick Phelan

136 Oranmore Dairies Low Fat Milk INH Flat Race (4-y-o and up) £4,140 2m...... (4:30)

15* WOLF WINTER 8-11-11 (7*) Mr P A Roche, ...(12 to 1) 1
STRONG CASE (Ire) 5-12-3 (3*) Mr D Marnane, (7 to 4 fav) 2
48* WILD FANTASY (Ire) 5-12-1 Mr A P O'Brien, ...(5 to 2) 3
58* COMMON POLICY (Ire) 4-11-4 (7*) Mr D J Kavanagh,
.... (10 to 1) 4
107⁴ THE WICKED CHICKEN (Ire) 4-10-10 (3*) Mrs S McCarthy,
.... 5
48⁴ BUCKINGHAM BOY 7-11-11 (7*) Miss C A Harrison,
.... (33 to 1) 6
ARCTIC LIFE (Ire) 4-10-11 (7*) Mr J Connolly, ...(10 to 1) 7
109⁹ HAUGHTON LAD (Ire) 4-10-11 (7*) Mr D Groome, (50 to 1) 8
55* FLEMCUR (Ire) 5-11-12 (5*) Mr J A Nash, ...(4 to 1) 9
124 DESPERADO 5-11-11 Mr A J Martin, ...(66 to 1) 10
Dist: 2l, 11l, 4½l, 15l. 3m 43.50s. (10 Ran).

(Mrs R Baly), H de Bromhead

MARKET RASEN (good to firm)
Saturday July 31st
Going Correction: MINUS 0.30 sec. per fur.

137 'Sport For The Disabled' Junior Selling Hurdle (3 & 4-y-o) £1,674 2m 1f 110yds
....(6:15)

BATTUTA 4-10-11 (5*) P Midgley, *nvr far away, led 3rd, shaken up and draw crl betw last 2, kpt on wl r-in.*
.................................(9 to 1 op 8 to 1) 1
CYRILL HENRY (Ire) 4-11-7 A Merrigan, *patiently rdn, improved on bit bef 3 out, slpd aftr three out sn reco'red, effrt 2 out, soon outpcd, kpt on stnly r-in.*
.................................(6 to 1 tchd 7 to 1) 2
SUNTAN (Fr) 4-11-7 L Wyer, *made most to 3rd, styd hndy, chlgd 2 out, outpcd bef nxt.*......(3 to 1 fav op 7 to 2) 3

16

ABSOLUTLEY FOXED 4-11-2 T Wall, *pressed ldg grp, out-pcd aftr 3 out, no imprsn frm nxt.* (20 to 1 op 16 to 1) 4
CHAJOTHELYTBRIGADE (Ire) 3-10-5⁹ R Garritty, *hld up in tch, took clr order aftr 3rd, outpcd bef 3 out, eased and tld off before nxt.*......................... (25 to 1) 5
PALACEGATE SUNSET 3-10-5 M Moloney, *handily plcd, drvn alng bef 3 out, sn btn, tld off frm nxt.*
.... (7 to 2 op 3 to 1) 6
REACH FOR GLORY 4-11-7 C Grant, *jmpd slwly, mid-div, lost pl aftr 3rd, tld off.*............. (5 to 1 tchd 6 to 1) 7
MANULEADER 4-11-0 (7⁷) W Fry, *beh, lost tch aftr 3rd, tld off.*.......................... (14 to 1) 8
RESTLESS MINSTREL (USA) 4-11-7 S Keightley, *in tch, jnd issue aftr 3rd, outpcd bef 3 out, hld whn blun and uns rdr last.*......................... (11 to 1 op 8 to 1) ur
RUANO 3-10-5 A Carroll, *al beh, detached bef second, tld off whn pld up before 5th.*...........(11 to 1 op 9 to 1) pu
Dist: 2l, 3¹⁄₄l, 12l, 20l, 8l, dist, 5l. 4m 5.20s. a 3.20s (10 Ran).

SR: 4/7/3/-/-/-/ (Miss K Watson), G R Oldroyd

138 Louth Rural Activities Centre Maiden Hurdle (3-y-o and up) £2,136 2m 1f 110yds
....(6:45)

SAFARI PARK 4-11-4 L Wyer, *al chasing ldr, rdn to ld bef last, hit last, pushed out.*
.... (11 to 1 op 10 to 1 tchd 12 to 1) 1
WELL APPOINTED (Ire) 4-11-9 A S Smith, *in tch, improved on bit 3 out, styd on frm last.*......... (9 to 2 op 4 to 1) 2
YAAKUM 4-11-9 S Keightley, *set gd pace, led, rdn whn blun 2 out, hdd bef last, not quicken.*
.... (6 to 4 fav op 11 to 8 on) 3
TROOPER THORN 9-11-9 (3⁷) A Thornton, *prmnt in chasing grp, drvn alng bef 3 out, sn outpcd.*
.... (16 to 1 op 20 to 1) 4
ON GOLDEN POND (Ire) 3-9-11 (3⁷) N Bentley, *beh, hit 3rd, struggling frm hfwy, tld off.*....... (5 to 1 op 8 to 1) 5
SCOTTISH PARK 4-11-4 C Grant, *not fluent, beh, drvn alng 5th, tld off.*................... (4 to 1 op 7 to 2) 6
VAL DE RAMA (Ire) 4-11-4 (5⁷) P Waggott, *beh, struggling frm 4th, tld off.*......(10 to 1 op 20 to 1 tchd 25 to 1) 7
GOLDSMITH 5-11-5 (7⁷) D Towler, *al beh, lost tch 3rd, blun nxt, tld off whn pld up bef 5th.*....(50 to 1 op 33 to 1) pu
Dist: 3l, 2l, 15l, 12l, 20l, 2l. 4m 4.90s. a 2.90s (8 Ran).

SR: 9/11/9/-/-/ (R A Bethell), B S Rothwell

139 Louth Rural Activities Centre Novices' Chase (5-y-o and up) £2,654 2½m... (7:15)

COUNTERPOINT (v) 6-11-4 N Williamson, *wth ldr, stumbled on landing 3 out, led nxt, rdn clr.*
.... (7 to 4 fav op 6 to 4 tchd 2 to 1) 1
SOLICITOR'S CHOICE 10-11-4 J Railton, *led 1st, slight ld, hdd 2 out, rdn and sn one pace.*
.... (7 to 1 op 8 to 1 tchd 10 to 1) 2
NISHKINA 5-11-0 L Wyer, *led to 1st, blun badly nxt, styd hndy, lost pl quickly 9th, sn struggling, tld off fnl 4.*
.... (9 to 2 op 3 to 1) 3
CAREFREE TIMES (v) 6-11-4 A Mulholland, *beh, mstk 6th, struggling frm hfwy, tld off.*............ 4
KILDOWNEY HILL 7-11-4 P Niven, *nvr far away, outpcd aftr tenth, tld off frm nxt.*........ (9 to 2 op 5 to 1) 5
EBORNEAZER'S DREAM 10-11-4 D Telfer, *beh, reminders and lost tch aftr 8th, tld off.*... (50 to 1 op 25 to 1) 6
WEE WILLIE DICKINS 6-11-4 J A Harris, *beh whn f 1st.*
.... (33 to 1 op 5 to 1) f
SIGNOR SASSIE (USA) 5-11-0 G McCourt, *in tch, early reminders, outpcd hfwy, sn struggling, tld off whn pld up lme aftr last.*............ (7 to 2 tchd 4 to 1) pu
Dist: 12l, 2l, sht-hd, ¾l, 5l. 4m 58.60s. a 6.60s (8 Ran).

(Howard Parker), J A C Edwards

140 Rotary Club Of Market Rasen Handicap Hurdle (0-115 4-y-o and up) £2,407 2m 1f 110yds............................... (7:45)

WHO'S TEF (Ire) [105] 5-11-10 L Wyer, *nvr far away, improved on bit to ld betw last 2, pushed out r-in.*
.... (11 to 10 op 11 to 8 on tchd Evens) 1
KRONPRINZ (Ire) [82] 5-10-1 W Worthington, *hld up, took clr order hfwy, rdn and outpcd jst aftr 2 out, styd on frm last.*..................... (9 to 2 op 4 to 1) 2
ULLSWATER [81] 7-10-0 N Williamson, *led til hdd betw last 2, rdn and one pace frm last.*......(12 to 1 op 10 to 1) 3
SAINT BENE'T (Ire) [84] 5-10-3 J Ryan, *in tch, cld aftr 3rd, ev ch appr 2 out, rdn and not quicken frm last.*
.... (4 to 1 op 6 to 1) 4
COLORADO INSIGHT [81] 5-9-12⁵ (7⁷) C Woodall, *trkd ldrs, effrt and rdn bef 2 out, wknd betw last 2.*
.... 5
PHALAROPE (Ire) [81] 5-10-0 Mr A Walton, *sddl slpd early, took keen hold, chsd ldrs on outer, wknd frm 5th, tld off entering strt.*.................(12 to 1 op 14 to 1) 6
Dist: 1½l, 3l, 1l, 15l, 12l. 4m 2.60s. a 0.60s (6 Ran).

SR: 38/13/9/11/-/-/ (T E F Freight (Scarborough) Ltd), M H Easterby

141 Louth Rural Activities Centre Handicap Chase (0-115 4-y-o and up) £3,470 2m 1f 110yds......................... (8:15)

35⁶ CROSS CANNON [114] 7-11-10 (3⁷) A Larnach, *patiently rdn, improved bef 3 out, effrt and ridden betw last 2, led r-in, kpt on wl.*.................. (8 to 1 op 6 to 1) 1
MR-PAW [93] 10-10-6¹³ (7⁷) B Murphy, *nvr far away, improved to chal bef 3 out, led 2 out, sn rdn, hdd r-in, one pace.*....................... (9 to 2 op 4 to 1) 2
DRUMSTICK [115] 7-12-0 N Williamson, *led, mstk 4 out, jnd 3 out, hdd 2 out, rallied, one, pace last 75 yards.*
....................(6 to 4 fav op 11 to 8 tchd 7 to 4) 3
MIAMI BEAR [99] 7-10-12 Gary Lyons, *trkd ldr, rdn alng 3 out, not quicken frm nxt.*.......... (10 to 1 op 8 to 1) 4
RUPPLES [89] 6-10-2 W Worthington, *beh, outpcd aftr 8th, styd on fnl 2, nrst finish.*.........(7 to 1 tchd 8 to 1) 5
NEWMARKET SAUSAGE [87] 12-10-0 J Callaghan, *mid-div, outpcd and struggling fnl 5, tld off entering strt.*
.... (50 to 1) 6
ENSHARP (USA) [98] 7-10-11 M Brennan, *hld up, hit 8th, sn struggling, tld off entering strt.*............(12 to 1) 7
MARKET LEADER [87] 13-9-12¹ (3⁷) R Greene, *prmnt whn f 3rd.*....................... (4 to 1 op 5 to 1) f
STORMGUARD [87] 10-9-11² (5⁷) T Eley, *handily plcd, drvn alng bef 3 out, sn wknd, pld up before last.*
.... (33 to 1) pu
Dist: 1½l, ½l, ½l, 8l, 20l, ¾l. 4m 23.80s. a 9.80s (9 Ran).

(J A Hellens), J A Hellens

142 'Riding For The Disabled' Novices' Hurdle (4-y-o and up) £2,010 2m 5f 110yds.. (8:45)

PURITAN (Can) 4-10-11 G McCourt, *patiently rdn, cld bef 6th, led 3 out, clr before nxt, very easily.*
.................(4 to 1 op 5 to 1 on tchd 7 to 2 on) 1
WAYWARD EDWARD (bl) 7-11-0 D Telfer, *led, jnd aftr 5th, hdd 3 out, rdn and outpcd.*
.................(4 to 1 op 9 to 2 tchd 5 to 1) 2
MERCERS MAGIC (Ire) 5-11-0 J Ryan, *jmpd badly, chsd ldr, jnd issue aftr 5th, lost pl nxt, struggling 3 out, eased entering strt, tld off.*........ (9 to 1 tchd 9 to 1) 3
Dist: 15l, 20l. 5m 14.50s. a 10.50s (3 Ran).

(J Parks), N Tinkler

NEWTON ABBOT (good to firm)
Saturday July 31st
Going Correction: MINUS 0.50 sec. per fur.

143 Dimplex Canterbury Handicap Chase (0-115 5-y-o and up) £3,117 2m 5f....(2:25)

SKIPPING TIM [120] 14-11-10 R Dunwoody, *jmpd wl, made all, styd on strly whn chlgd 3 out, rdn out.*
.................(7 to 4 fav op 6 to 4 tchd 9 to 4) 1
KARAKTER REFERENCE [117] 11-11-4 (3⁷) D O'Sullivan, *trkd ldg pair, rdn 4 out, styd on to take second pl aftr 2 out, not quicken appr last.*
.................(11 to 4 op 6 to 1 tchd 7 to 2) 2
TOUCHING STAR [97] (bl) 8-9-12 (3⁷) M Hourigan, *hld up, hdwy aftr tenth, cl up and ev ch 3 out, sn rdn and one pace.*....................... (4 to 1 op 3 to 1) 3
BLUECHIPENTERPRISE [96] (bl) 7-10-0 J R Kavanagh, *chsd ldrs, wnt second tenth, ev ch 3 out, wknd nxt.*
.................(40 to 1 op 25 to 1 tchd 50 to 1) 4
OWEN [96] 9-10-0 B Powell, *jmpd slwly 1st 2, hdwy to chase ldrs aftr 9th, sn rdn and wknd 4 out, tld off.*
.................(4 to 1 op 3 to 1 tchd 9 to 2) 5
SAILOR'S DELIGHT [97] 9-10-1 C Llewellyn, *pressed ldr til lost pl aftr 9th, sn beh, tld off 5 out.*
.... (20 to 1 tchd 16 to 1) 6
ABBREVIATION [104] 10-10-8 D Morris, *hld up, pushed alng aftr 8th, beh whn mstk tenth, tld off when pld up bef 3 out.*............(17 to 2 op 4 to 1 tchd 12 to 1) pu
Dist: 3l, 7l, nk, 20l, 30l. 5m 3.30s. a 3.30s (7 Ran).

(Miss H A Bisgrove), M C Pipe

144 Dimplex Comfort Control TM Selling Handicap Hurdle (4-y-o and up) £1,889 2m 1f
....(2:55)

BONDAID [78] 9-11-0 A Maguire, *hld up, hit rng rail aftr 4th, hdwy to track ldrs after nxt, rdn to ld appr 2 out, drvn out.*................(13 to 8 fav op 5 to 4 tchd 2 to 1) 1
DISTANT MEMORY [64] 4-9-7 (7⁷) N Parker, *hld up, hdwy aftr 5th, second whn mstk 2 out, staying on when mistake last, not trble wnr.*
.... (12 to 1 op 10 to 1 tchd 14 to 1) 2
SEE NOW [66] 8-10-2 S McNeill, *mid-div, cl up and ev ch frm 3 out, rdn and styd on from nxt, no imprsn.*
.... (10 to 1 op 7 to 1) 3
LOCH DUICH [75] 7-10-11 R Dunwoody, *chsd clr ldr til led 5th, hdd appr 2 out, sn btn.*
.................(9 to 2 op 4 to 1 tchd 7 to 2) 4

NATIONAL HUNT RESULTS 1993-94

DOTS DEE [64] 4-9-9 (5*) R Farrant, *hld up, mstk second, hdwy to track ldg grp aftr 5th, no imprsn frm 2 out.*
.... (25 to 1 op 16 to 1 tchd 33 to 1) 5
AMBASSADOR ROYALE (Ire) [68] (bl) 5-11-10 N Mann, *hld up, hdwy to chase ldrs aftr 5th, second whn pckd 3 out, rdn and rallied appr nxt, second but held when hit last.*..................(100 to 10 op 5 to 2 tchd 4 to 1) 6
KATHY FAIR (Ire) [64] 4-10-0 L Harvey, *took str hold, led and clr to 3rd, hdd 5th, wknd aftr nxt.*
.... (25 to 1 op 14 to 1 tchd 33 to 1) 7
BLUE AEROPLANE [64] (bl) 5-11-0 C Maude, *hld up, mstk 4th, sn beh, rdn and rallied aftr 3 out, soon btn.*
.... (7 to 1 op 5 to 1 tchd 8 to 1) 8
STAPLEFORD LADY [65] 5-10-1 B Powell, *chsd ldrs, hmpd aftr 4th, lost pl and reminders, sn beh.*
.... (20 to 1 op 16 to 1 tchd 25 to 1) 9
DANNY'S LUCK (NZ) [65] 11-10-0⁶ (7*) Mr Richard White, *prmnt till lost pl aftr 4th, sn beh, tld off whn pld up after 3 out.*.................. (50 to 1 op 25 to 1) pu
Dist: 6l, 2½l, ½l, 1l, 4l, 15l, 1½l, 25l. 3m 54.70s. a 4.70s (10 Ran).

(A J Allright), J White

145 Dimplex Optiflame TM Novices' Chase (5-y-o and up) £2,684 2m 110yds...... (3:30)

NORSTOCK 6-10-12 A Maguire, *chsd lng pair, wnt second aftr 6th, led after 4 out, drw clr after 2 out, styd on wl.*
.... (5 to 4 fav tchd 6 to 4) 1
CARELESS LAD 7-11-3 D Skyrme, *led til hdd aftr 4 out, rdn and styd on one pace, no imprsn.*
.... (9 to 2 op 5 to 2 tchd 5 to 1) 2
GILSTON LASS 6-10-12 J R Kavanagh, *chsd ldr to 6th, 3rd whn slight mstk nxt, no imprsn frm 4 out.*
.... (9 to 4 op 2 to 1 tchd 5 to 2) 3
PAPPA DONT PREACH (Ire) 5-11-0 R Supple, *hld up, lost tch aftr 5th, tld off 6 out.*.......... (9 to 1 op 6 to 1) 4
ASSEMBLY DANCER 6-10-12 (5*) R Davis, *lost tch aftr 5th, mstks, tld off whn pld up bef 4 out.*
.... (16 to 1 op 10 to 1 tchd 20 to 1) pu
IRISH GOSSIP 7-11-3 B Powell, *hld up, lost tch aftr 5th, tld off whn mstk 5 out, pld up bef 2 out.*
.... (16 to 1 op 12 to 1 tchd 20 to 1) pu
Dist: 10l, 10l, dist. 3m 55.40s. b 1.60s (6 Ran).

SR: 18/13/-/

(Nick Quesnel), J White

146 Dimplex Twin Sensor TM Claiming Hurdle (4 - 7-y-o) £2,093 2m 1f........... (4:05)

SAFETY (USA) (bl) 6-11-6 D Skyrme, *trkd lng grp, led appr 2 out, rdn clr betw last two, styd on strly.*
.... (5 to 2 op 2 to 1 tchd 3 to 1) 1
LITMORE DANCER 5-10-1 (5*) R Farrant, *mid-div, rdn and styd on aftr 3 out, took second pl appr last, no imprsn.*
.... (25 to 1 op 12 to 1) 2
STAR MOVER 4-10-9 G Upton, *led 1st, sn hdd, trkd ldr in second pl til led briefly aftr 3 out, soon headed and one pace.*.............. (10 to 1 op 12 to 1 tchd 8 to 1) 3
MISS EQUILIA (USA) 7-11-1 R Dunwoody, *hld up, mstk 3rd, steady hdwy appr 5th, rdn and kpt on one pace aftr 3 out.*...... (11 to 10 on Evens tchd 5 to 4 on) 4
PLAY THE BLUES 6-11-1 J Frost, *hld up, styd on one pace frm 4 out, not trble ldrs.*............ (14 to 1 op 8 to 1) 5
MASTER REACH (bl) 4-11-4 (5*) J McCarthy, *led aftr 1st, hdd after 3 out, rdn and wknd quickly appr nxt.*
.... (7 to 1 op 5 to 1 tchd 9 to 1) 6
ZAMANAYN (Ire) 5-11-12 R Supple, *slwly away, beh til styd on one pace aftr 3 out.*
.... (12 to 1 op 8 to 1 tchd 14 to 1) 7
WRETS (bl) 4-10-7 (7*) Mr S Joynes, *chsd ldg pair til wknd rpdly aftr 4 out, tld off whn mstk last.*
.... (50 to 1 op 33 to 1 tchd 100 to 1) 8
YOUNG JAMES 5-11-0 L Harvey, *hld up, pushed along aftr 4th, lost tch after nxt, tld off whn pld bef 2 out.*
.... (33 to 1 op 20 to 1) pu
Dist: 12l, 1½l, 3½l, 10l, nk, nk, dist. 3m 53.60s. a 3.60s (9 Ran).

(Keith Sturgis), J White

147 Dimplex Whisperheat TM Juvenile Novices' Hurdle (3-y-o) £1,830 2m 1f.... (4:35)

THE EXECUTOR 10-12 R Dunwoody, *al hndy, slight ld 3 out, drw clr betw last 2, cmftbly.*.......... (7 to 2 on p 3 to 1 on tchd 9 to 4 on and 4 to 1 on) 1
NOMADIC FIRE 10-7 (5*) R Davis, *hld up, hdwy to track ldr aftr 5th, cl up and ev ch appr 2 out, not quicken.*
.... (9 to 2 op 4 to 1 tchd 11 to 2) 2
CALIBRATE 10-12 B Powell, *pld hrd early, al prmnt, led 5th to nxt, 3rd whn untidy 2 out, one pace.*
.... (9 to 1 op 8 to 1 tchd 10 to 1) 3
APACHEE FLOWER 10-0 (7*) Mr G Lewis, *lost pl appr 5th, rdn and rallied aftr 3 out, kpt on one pace.*
.... (40 to 1 op 33 to 1 tchd 50 to 1) 4
STAR MARKET 10-12 W McFarland, *hld up, hmpd aftr 4th, hdwy to chase ldrs after 5th, wknd appr 2 out.*
.... (66 to 1 op 20 to 1) 5

IRISH DOMINION 10-12 N Hawke, *hld up, hdwy to chase ldg grp aftr 5th, sn wknd.*
.... (12 to 1 op 16 to 1 tchd 20 to 1) 6
DOOGAREY 10-5 (7*) P McLoughlin, *led til hdd 5th, rdn and wknd quickly.*.. (12 to 1 op 10 to 1 tchd 14 to 1) 7
ANNIE ROSE (bl) 10-7 J Frost, *hld up in last pl, niggled alng aftr 4th, sn beh.*............. (20 to 1 op 33 to 1) 8
Dist: 8l, 5l, 15l, 10l, 8l, ¾l, 20l. 3m 57.30s. a 7.30s (8 Ran).

(Jack Joseph), M C Pipe

148 Dimplex H.E.A.T. Handicap Hurdle (0-125 4-y-o and up) £2,528 2¾m......... (5:05)

NUNS JEWEL [87] 7-9-9 (5*) R Farrant, *led 3rd, made rst, styd on gmely whn chlgd appr last, hld on nr finish.*
.... (5 to 2 op 6 to 1 tchd 8 to 1) 1
CARPET CAPERS (USA) [87] 9-10-0 A Maguire, *trkd ldr frm 4th, rdn and ev ch 2 out, chlgd last, hrd ridden and not quicken nr finish.*
.... (13 to 2 op 10 to 1 tchd 14 to 1 and 6 to 1) 2
MIDFIELDER [115] 7-12-0 Peter Hobbs, *hld up, wnt 3rd 6th, rdn aftr 3 out, third whn pckd nxt, no imprsn.*
.... (3 to 1 op 5 to 2 tchd 7 to 2) 3
SCOTONI [107] 7-11-3 (3*) D O'Sullivan, *led to 3rd, trkd ldg pair til drvn alng aftr 4 out, rallied after nxt, sn wknd.*
.... (6 to 4 fav tchd 11 to 10) 4
WINDSOR PARK (USA) [96] 7-10-6 (3*) V Slattery, *hld up, drvn alng aftr 4 out, wknd quickly after nxt.*
.... (3 to 1 op 5 to 2 tchd 7 to 2) 5
Dist: ¾l, 7l, 10l, 20l. 5m 10.5s. a 11.10s (5 Ran).

(R H Williams), J M Bradley

LINGFIELD (A.W) (std)
Sunday August 1st
Going Correction: MINUS 0.30 sec. per fur.

149 Holiday Club Pontins Claiming Hurdle (4-y-o and up) £2,802 2½m........... (2:15)

BEN ZABEEDY 8-11-3 G McCourt, *trkd ldrs, drw 8th and lost pl, sn reco'red, hdwy to ld appr last, ran on wl....* 1
SAKIL (Ire) 5-10-12 (5*) A Dicken, *nvr far away, led aftr 4 out, rdn and hdd appr last, kpt on one pace...........* 2
CARFAX 8-11-9 M Hoad, *sn tracking ldr, wknd aftr 1st, in cl tch till wknd 3 out........................* 3
MILLIE BELLE (v) 7-10-6 A Maguire, *led till aftr 1st, in cl tch till wknd 5 out.*...................... 4
SAILOR BOY (bl) 7-10-11 N Williamson, *al beh............* 5
WINGCOMMANDER EATS 8-10-11 Peter Hobbs, *led aftr 1st til after 4 out, drpd out quickly.................* 6
YIMKIN BOOKRA 5-11-6 M Richards, *hld up rear, lost tch sn aftr hfwy.................................* 7
LYN'S RETURN (Ire) 4-11-9 D Gallagher, *chsd ldrs, lost pl 5th, rallied briefly 7th, sn beh, tld off whn pld up bef 3 out....................................* pu
Dist: 2l, 15l, 2½l, 10l, hd, 1½l. 4m 48.00s. a 16.00s (8 Ran).

(Richard Armstrong), R Akehurst

LEOPARDSTOWN (IRE) (good)
Monday August 2nd

150 Scalp INH Flat Race (4-y-o and up) £3,105 2½m............................. (5:30)

112 BEST MY TRY 6-11-9 (5*) Mr J A Nash, ... (6 to 1) 1
115⁹ SIR HENRY KNYVET (Ire) 4-11-7 Mr S R Murphy, ...(3 to 1) 2
55³ MAKE A LINE 5-11-7 (7*) Mr A H Lillingston, ...(8 to 1) 3
GENERAL TONIC 6-12-0 Mr J A Berry,...........(12 to 1) 4
105² SIMPLY SARAH 7-11-9 Mr M McNulty, ...(25 to 1) 5
70³ HAWAIIAN GODDESS (USA) 6-11-2 (7*) Mr G J Harford, ...(12 to 1) 6
102 PEARL'S CHOICE (Ire) 5-11-4 (5*) Mr H F Cleary, ...(8 to 1) 7
STEVE BUGU 6-11-7 (7*) Mr K D Cotter, ...(9 to 1) 8
109³ THE REGAL ROYAL (Ire) 5-11-9 (5*) Mr J M Mullins, ...(2 to 1 fav) 9
105³ FRAGRANCE MOUNTAIN 7-11-2 (7*) Mr P A Roche, ...(20 to 1) 10
95 MOON-FROG 6-11-7 (7*) Mrs J Crosbie, ...(33 to 1) 11
45 CRACKLE N POP (Ire) 5-11-7 (7*) Mr P English, ...(20 to 1) 12
WHARFINGER (Ire) 5-11-7 (7*) Mr T Barry, ...(16 to 1) 13
58 MR MOSS TROOPER (Ire) 5-11-11 (3*) Mr A R Coonan, ...(16 to 1) 14
95⁶ CROGHAN BRIDGE (Ire) 4-11-2 (5*) Mr D P Murphy, ...(14 to 1) 15
SPRINGFIELDS JILL (Ire) 5-11-2 (7*) Mr D McDonnell, ...(25 to 1) 16
Dist: Nk, 7l, 2l, 1½l. 4m 41.10s. (16 Ran).

(John C O'Malley), D K Weld

NEWTON ABBOT (good to firm)
Monday August 2nd
Going Correction: MINUS 0.40 sec. per fur.

18

151 South Zeal Novices' Hurdle (4-y-o and up) £1,880 2m 1f. . . . . (2:45)

MERLINS WISH (USA) 4-10-11 R Dunwoody, *trkd ldrs, led aftr 3 out, clr frm 2 out, cmftbly.*
. . . . (10 to 3 on op 3 to 1 on tchd 5 to 2 on and 7 to 2 on) 1
SUPER SARENA (Ire) 4-10-6 J Frost, *led to 3 out, styd on, no ch wth unr*. . . . . (5 to 1 op 4 to 1 tchd 6 to 1) 2
KELLY'S DARLING 7-11-0 D Bridgwater, *steadied in rear, hdwy appr 5th, wknd approaching 2 out.*
. . . . (25 to 1 op 20 to 1) 3
PRIVATE JET (Ire) 4-10-11 A Maguire, *hdwy 5th, wknd aftr 3 out*. . . . .(14 to 1 op 10 to 1 tchd 16 to 1) 4
LA REINE ROUGE (Ire) 5-10-9 S McNeill, *chsd ldrs, led 3 out, sn hdd and wknd*. . . . .(16 to 1 op 8 to 1) 5
LONG FURLONG 5-11-0 N Hawke, *al beh.*
. . . . (20 to 1 op 10 to 1) 6
THARIF 5-11-0 M A FitzGerald, *mstk 1st and rdr lost iron, chsd ldr to 4th, wknd rpdly nxt, tld off.*
. . . . (50 to 1 op 20 to 1 tchd 66 to 1) 7
DAZZLING FIRE (Ire) 4-10-6 M Richards, *in tch whn f 4th.*
. . . . (16 to 1 op 8 to 1) f
NOW BOARDING 6-10-2 (7*) Mr N Bradley, *beh whn brght dwn 4th*. . . . .(66 to 1 op 20 to 1) bd
Dist: 6l, 15l, 7l, 15l, ¾l. dist. 3m 55.10s. a 5.10s (9 Ran).
(Malcolm B Jones), M C Pipe

152 Border Fox Challenge Trophy Chase (5-y-o and up) £3,189 2m 110yds
. . . .(3:15)

RIVER HOUSE [114] 11-12-0 A Maguire, *rcd in 3rd till trkd ldr 7th, led 9th, clr 3 out, eased to a walk cl hme.*
. . . . (Evens fav op 5 to 4 tchd 11 to 8) 1
FLYING ZIAD (Can) [96] 10-10-10 D Morris, *led, hdd briefly 4th, clr aftr 6th, headed 9th, sn outpcd.*
. . . . (3 to 1 op 5 to 2 tchd 100 to 30) 2
POLDER [96] 7-10-0¹ (5*) R Davis, *chsd ldr till led briefly 4th, wknd 9th*. . . . .(4 to 1 op 5 to 2 tchd 9 to 2) 3
IRISH VELVET [96] 7-10-10 J Frost, *rcd up freely till pld up bef 6th, dismouted*. . . . .(6 to 1 op 9 to 1) pu
Dist: 5l, 10l. 3m 58.00s. a 1.00s (4 Ran).
SR: 24/1/-/-/ (Ms M Horan), J White

153 Les Fletcher Memorial Challenge Trophy Handicap Hurdle (0-125 4-y-o and up) £2,540 2m 1f. . . . . (3:45)

WELSHMAN [129] 7-11-13 D Gallagher, *chsd ldrs, drvn alng aftr 5th, led 2 out, driven out.*
. . . .(5 to 4 fav op 6 to 4 tchd 11 to 10) 1
MOHANA [130] 4-12-0 R Dunwoody, *led till hdd aftr 3 out, rdn and styd on one pace frm 2 out.*
. . . . (11 to 8 op 5 to 4 on) 2
AMBASSADOR ROYALE (Ire) [96] (bl) 5-10-0 N Mann, *chlgd 3rd to 4th, led aftr 3 out, hdd 2 out, sn outpcd, fnshd lme*. . . . .(6 to 1 tchd 10 to 1) 3
WINDSOR PARK (USA) [102] 7-9-11 (3*) V Slattery, *pld hrd, chsd ldrs, rdn aftr 3 out, sn one pace.*
. . . . (16 to 1 op 7 to 1) 4
CLWYD LODGE [102] (bl) 6-10-0 T Wall, *beh frm 4th, lost tch nxt, tld off*. . . . .(100 to 1 op 20 to 1) 5
Dist: 2½l, 3l, 4l, dist. 3m 49.10s. b 0.90s (5 Ran).
SR: 40/38/7/3/-/ (Brian Oxton), M Blanshard

154 Torbryan Selling Handicap Chase (5-y-o and up) £2,392 2m 110yds. . . . . (4:15)

JACK THE HIKER [89] 10-10-10 M Richards, *beh, steady hdwy 9th, chlgd 2 out, sn led, drvn out.*
. . . . (20 to 1 op 10 to 1) 1
GABISH [89] 8-10-10 J R Kavanagh, *hdwy 8th, chalg whn lft in ld 3 out, hdd aftr 2 two out, styd on same pace.*
. . . . (14 to 1 op 8 to 1 tchd 16 to 1) 2
SOHAIL (USA) [101] 10-11-8 A Maguire, *hdwy 7th, led 9th till blun 3 out (water), rallied ag'n r-in.*
. . . . (100 to 30 op 5 to 1 tchd 9 to 4) 3
BARTONDALE [85] 8-10-1 (5*) R Farrant, *beh 6th, rdn nxt, one pace*. . . . .(11 to 2 op 7 to 1 tchd 6 to 1) 4
TAKEMETHERE [107] 9-12-0 R Dunwoody, *chsd ldrs, hit tenth, rdn aftr 4 out, sn wknd.*
. . . .(11 to 8 on op 5 to 4 tchd 6 to 4 on) 5
TAFFY JONES [85] 14-10-6 C Maude, *beh 6th, rdn and wknd 8th*. . . . .(16 to 1 op 10 to 1) 6
RONOCCO [85] 11-10-6 N Hawke, *sn prmnt, chlgd 4th to 8th, sn wknd*. . . . .(10 to 1 op 10 to 1) 7
DANNY'S LUCK (NZ) [85] 11-10-6 S Mackey, *al wl beh.*
. . . . (66 to 1 op 16 to 1) 8
DREAMCOAT (USA) [86] 12-10-7 L Harvey, *led to 9th, sn wknd*. . . . .(33 to 1 op 14 to 1) 9
Dist: 2l, 1½l, 12l, 1½l, 8l, 10l, 6l, 4l. 3m 59.30s. a 2.30s (9 Ran).
SR: -/-/1/-/-/-/ (John Bowen), T B Hallett

155 Holsworthy Conditional Jockeys' Novices' Hurdle (4-y-o and up) £1,813 2¾m. . .(4:45)

SILVERCROSS LAD 10-10-7 (7*) N Juckes, *not fluent, led second, hit 6th, clr appr 2 out, hit last, cmftbly.*
. . . . (16 to 1 op 10 to 1) 1
APACHE PRINCE (bl) 6-11-0 M Hourigan, *chlgd 4th to 6th, styd chasing wnr, rdn and no imprsn frm 3 out.*
. . . . (3 to 1 tchd 4 to 1 and 11 to 4) 2
SUNDAY JIM 9-10-11 (3*) D Meade, *hdwy 7th, no prog frm 3 out*. . . . .(9 to 1 op 6 to 1) 3
WHERE ARE WE 7-11-0 R Davis, *rdn aftr 5th, wknd 3 out.*
. . . . (14 to 1 op 7 to 1) 4
DOUBLE THE BLACK 8-10-6 (3*) R Darke, *led to second, chlgd 4th to 5th, weakened nxt*. . . . .(16 to 1 op 8 to 1) 5
QUIET RIOT (bl) 11-10-11 (3*) K Comerford, *in tch whn sddl slpd and uns rdr 4th*. . . . .(7 to 4 on op 2 to 1 on) ur
Dist: 12l, 8l, 25l, 1½l. 5m 9.00s. a 10.00s (6 Ran).
(Mrs Angela Turner), R T Juckes

156 Ogwell Handicap Hurdle (0-115 4-y-o and up) £2,540 3m 3f. . . . . (5:15)

AAHSAYLAD [122] (bl) 7-12-0 A Maguire, *chsd ldr 3 out, chlgd 2 out, easily*. . . . .(4 to 1 on op 8 to 1 on) 1
CARPET CAPERS (USA) [94] 9-10-0 J R Kavanagh, *led 5th till aftr 6th, led 7th till after 8th, led 9th, hdd sn after 2 out, not quicken*. . . . . . . (7 to 2 op 4 to 1 tchd 5 to 1) 2
TRUST DEED (USA) [94] 5-10-0 S McNeill, *set poor pace till hdd 5th, led ag'n aftr 6th, headed nxt, led again after 8th, headed 9th, sn wknd.*
. . . .(10 to 1 op 12 to 1 tchd 14 to 1) 3
Dist: 2½l, 15l. 6m 58.60s. a 44.60s (3 Ran).
(Ms M Horan), J White

TIPPERARY (IRE) (good to yielding (races 1,2), good (3))
Monday August 2nd

157 Muskry Maiden Hurdle (4 & 5-y-o) £2,760 2m. . . . . (4:30)

CASH CHASE (Ire) 5-11-1 L P Cusack, ...(5 to 2) 1
NOBODYS FLAME (Ire) 5-11-6 C F Swan, ... (2 to 1 fav) 2
HUGH DANIELS 5-10-13 (7*) D R Thompson, ...(7 to 1) 3
WALNEY ISLAND 4-11-4 T Horgan, ...(8 to 1) 4
PURPLE EMPEROR (Fr) 4-11-4 (5*) C P Dunne, . . (8 to 1) 5
SLANEY FAYRE (Ire) 5-11-6 C O'Dwyer, ...(14 to 1) 6
PENNINE PASS (Ire) 4-11-9 B Sheridan, ...(10 to 1) 7
TURALITY (Ire) 4-11-4 S H O'Donovan, ...(20 to 1) 8
IMOKILLY PEOPLE (Ire) 5-11-1 H Rogers, ...(20 to 1) 9
DALGORIAN (Ire) (bl) 4-10-13 A J O'Brien, ...(20 to 1) 10
ONTHEROADAGAIN (Ire) 5-11-1 (3*) J Collins, ...(6 to 1) 11
MANALESCO (Ire) 4-10-11 (7*) Mr D Keane, ...(20 to 1) 12
BRIGHT IDEA (Ire) 4-11-4 M Flynn, ...(20 to 1) 13
CIARRAI (Ire) 4-11-4 G M O'Neill, ...(12 to 1) 14
Dist: Hd, 6l, 7l, 4½l. 4m 6.80s. (14 Ran).
(A J Keane), A J Keane

158 Ferndale Hurdle (4-y-o and up) £2,760 2½m. . . . . (5:00)

REDONDO BEACH 8-10-13 M Duffy, ...(20 to 1) 1
MASAI WARRIOR 6-11-1 (3*) J Collins, ...(9 to 2) 2
SUSTENANCE 6-11-6 D H O'Connor, ...(10 to 1) 3
KILSHANNON SPRINGS 7-11-11 T J Taaffe, . . . (9 to 4 fav) 4
MOUNTHENRY STAR (Ire) 5-11-4 G M O'Neill, ...(7 to 1) 5
THE COBH GALE 6-10-13 H Rogers, ...(14 to 1) 6
HURRICANE MILLIE (Ire) 5-10-13 A J O'Brien, . . .(10 to 1) 7
UGOLIN DE LA WERA (Fr) 7-11-4 C F Swan, ...(5 to 1) 8
REGULAR PAL 10-10-8 (5*) A J Roche, ...(20 to 1) 9
DAILY BREAD (Ire) 4-10-4 (7*) Mr J T McNamara, . . .(20 to 1) 10
ANSEO (Ire) 4-11-4 T Horgan, ...(7 to 2) 11
HURRICANE GIRL (Ire) 4-9-13 (7*) C F O'Brien, ...(20 to 1) 12
LADY BUDD (Ire) 5-10-13 C N Bowens, ...(20 to 1) 13
Dist: 1½l, ½l, 7l, 1½l. 5m 4.60s. (13 Ran).
(Michael C Gunn), Michael C Gunn

159 Knockmealdown INH Flat Race (5-y-o and up) £2,760 2m. . . . .(5:30)

BEAU GRANDE (Ire) 5-11-9 (5*) Mr D Valentine, (5 to 4 fav) 1
SLEMISH MINSTREL 7-11-7 (7*) Mr I Johnston, . . .(16 to 1) 2
CAILIN RUA (Ire) 5-11-4 (5*) Mr A E Lacy, ...(7 to 2) 3
GIFTED FELLOW (Ire) 6-11-11 (3*) Mr D Marnane, (16 to 1) 4
OZONE RIVER (Ire) 8-11-2 (7*) Mr S O'Donnell, (10 to 1) 5
LISCAHILL HIGHWAY 6-11-7 (7*) Mr R McGrath, . .(16 to 1) 6
MOUNT SACKVILLE 6-11-2 (7*) Mr D Groome, ...(14 to 1) 7
SONIC EXPERIENCE (Ire) 5-11-6 (3*) Mr R Neylon, (20 to 1) 8
CONQUIRO (Ire) 5-12-0 Mr A P O'Brien, ...(3 to 1) 9
COSTLY BUST 6-11-7 (7*) Mr K Whelan, ...(10 to 1) 10
Dist: 4l, 2½l, 3½l, 9l. 4m 3.40s. (10 Ran).
(M McAuliffe), P D Osborne

ROSCOMMON (IRE) (yielding)
Tuesday August 3rd

160 Elphin Maiden Hurdle (4-y-o and up) £2,762 2m. (5:30)

67*	CLOGHANS BAY (Ire) 4-11-9 J Shortt, ...(7 to 4 fav)	1
	SWALLOWS NEST 6-12-0 D H O'Connor, ...(6 to 1)	2
112²	WHATASUCCESS 6-11-9 P Carberry, ...(6 to 1)	3
104³	THE BOURDA 7-12-0 K Morgan, ...(10 to 1)	4
	FREEWAY HALO (Ire) 4-10-8 (5") T J Mitchell, ...(50 to 1)	5
64²	CROFTON QUILL 6-12-0 T J Taaffe, ...(3 to 1)	6
49⁵	TOP GENERATION 4-10-13 C F Swan, ...(10 to 1)	7
108⁹	DAMHSA (Den) 4-10-6 (7") C McCormack, ...(16 to 1)	8
58	CLYDE PRINCE 8-11-6 Mr J P Dempsey, ...(20 to 1)	9
115	PERCY BRENNAN 6-11-1 (5") T P Rudd, ...(33 to 1)	10
99⁴	BRAE (Ire) 5-10-8 (7") Mr D McCann, ...(16 to 1)	11
115	SHINDWA (Ire) 4-10-10 (3") J Jones, ...(33 to 1)	12
	PETRASHAR 6-11-6 P McWilliams, ...(50 to 1)	13

Dist: 1½l, 4½l, 1l, 2l. 3m 59.20s. (13 Ran).

(Mrs Patrick Prendergast), Patrick Prendergast

161 Castle Handicap Hurdle (0-123 4-y-o and up) £2,762 2m. (6:00)

95⁵	WINCHLING [-] 8-9-10 N Byrne, ...(20 to 1)	1
113	NICE AND SIMPLE [-] 6-9-4 (7") C O'Brien, ...(14 to 1)	2
46⁸	FABRICATOR [-] 7-11-3 K Morgan, ...(7 to 1)	3
123⁸	PERKNAPP [-] 6-11-2 T Horgan, ...(9 to 2)	4
74³	CAOIMSEACH (Ire) [-] 5-9-12 F Woods, ...(8 to 1)	5
	JUST ONE CANALETTO [-] 5-10-5 K F O'Brien, ...(8 to 1)	6
102²	GILT DIMENSION [-] 6-10-12 C F Swan, ...(7 to 2 fav)	7
104²	TULLY BOY [-] 6-9-4 (7") Mr D McCartan, ...(8 to 1)	8
100⁴	SEZ HE SEZ I [-] 9-9-2 (7") Miss C E Hyde, ...(12 to 1)	9
110²	WATERLOO LADY [-] 6-9-12 P Carberry, ...(5 to 1)	10
	PICK'N HILL (Ire) [-] 5-9-2 (5") M G Cleary, ...(33 to 1)	11
70	WE WONT FALL OUT (Ire) [-] 5-9-8 P McWilliams, ...(50 to 1)	12
113	MABES TOWN [-] 5-9-13 H Rogers, ...(10 to 1)	13

Dist: Nk, ¾l, 1½l, sht-hd. 3m 52.50s. (13 Ran).

(David Price), A J Maxwell

162 Midland Oil Company Flat Race (4-y-o and up) £3,452 2m. (8:00)

115²	DERRYMOYLE (Ire) 4-11-2 (7") Mr G J Harford, (5 to 4 fav)	1
	BAY MISCHIEF (Ire) 4-11-2 (7") Mr J Connolly, ...(9 to 2)	2
81⁶	NEW DIRECTIONS 6-11-2 (7") Mr B M Cash, ...(20 to 1)	3
73³	OLD ARCHIVES (Ire) 4-11-9 Mr J P Durkan, ...(5 to 1)	4
	FURTHER APPRAISAL (Ire) 4-11-0¹ (5") Mr P J Dreeling,	
	....(14 to 1)	5
114⁸	BEGLAWELLA 6-11-4 (5") Mr J O'Brien, ...(14 to 1)	6
61	WESTCARNE LAD (Ire) 5-12-0 Mr M McNulty, ...(20 to 1)	7
65²	IFALLELSEFAILS 5-12-0 Mr A J Martin, ...(7 to 2)	8
	RING DONG LASS (Ire) 4-11-2 Mr D M O'Brien, ...(50 to 1)	9
	WHIZ ON BOBBY (Ire) 5-12-0 Mr D M O'Brien, ...(14 to 1)	10
	JODONLEE (Ire) 4-10-11 (7") Mr A K Wyse, ...(50 to 1)	11
98⁸	ABBEY TRINITY (Ire) 4-10-11 (7") Mr E Norris, ...(50 to 1)	12
98	MOUNTAINFOOT GIRL 6-11-2 (7") Mr R Pugh, ...(66 to 1)	13

Dist: 4½l, 5½l, 2l, 2½l. 3m 57.70s. (13 Ran).

(Herb M Stanley), Michael Cunningham

EXETER (firm)
Wednesday August 4th
Going Correction: MINUS 0.40 sec. per fur.

163 Bonusprint Novices' Hurdle (4-y-o and up) £1,875 2m 3f. (2:10)

	PERFORATE (bl) 4-10-11 L Harvey, al prmnt, led ater 2 out,	
	drvn out..................(12 to 1 tchd 20 to 1)	1
	TRUMPET 4-10-11 M A FitzGerald, trkd ldr, led 2 out, sn	
	hdd, rallied and ev ch last, not quicken nr finish.	
	..........................(5 to 1 op 3 to 1 tchd 11 to 2)	2
146³	STAR MOVER 4-10-6 G Upton, led til hdd 2 out, sn rdn	
	and one paced..........(9 to 2 op 5 to 1 tchd 6 to 1)	3
	MISTY VIEW 4-10-6 A Maguire, hld up, pld hrd, sddl slpd,	
	jmpd slwly 5th, chsd ldrs frm nxt, one paced 2 out.	
	..........................(5 to 4 fav op 5 to 4 on)	4
	IL BAMBINO 5-10-7 (7") Mr Richard White, hld up, outpcd 3	
	out, rdn and effrt nxt, sn btn........(3 to 1 tchd 4 to 1)	5
126	MANULIFE 4-10-11 D Bridgwater, hld up, pushed alng frm	
	4th, wknd quickly aftr four out, tld off whn pld up bef	
	2 out................(50 to 1 op 33 to 1)	pu

Dist: Nk, 12l, 4l, 12l. 4m 30.80s. a 11.80s (6 Ran).

(Mrs Merrilyn Rowe), R J Baker

164 Tripleprint Claiming Hurdle (4-y-o and up) £1,908 2m 1f 110yds. (2:40)

	EMMA VICTORIA 5-10-13 D Bridgwater, trkd ldr frm 3rd,	
	jnd lder aftr 3 out, led betw last 2, mstk last, drvn clr.	
	..........................(6 to 1 op 5 to 1 tchd 13 to 2)	1
	CELCIUS (Ire) 4-11-8 R Dunwoody, set slow pace to 3rd,	
	quickened nxt, hdd betw last 2, sn rdn, btn whn mstk	
	last...................(6 to 1 on tchd 5 to 4 on)	2
	MEADOW GAME (Ire) 4-10-12 G Upton, chsd ldr to 3rd,	
	trkd ldg pair, rdn and rallied appr 2 out, sn wknd, tld	
	off...................(10 to 1 op 6 to 1 tchd 12 to 1)	3

Dist: 8l, 25l. 4m 12.60s. a 15.60s (3 Ran).

(Mrs P Catlin), R Brotherton

165 Bonusprint Novices' Chase (5-y-o and up) £2,736 2m 3f. (3:10)

145*	NORSTOCK 6-11-2 (5ex) A Maguire, wtd wth, wnt second	
	8th, led nxt, styd on wl, lft clr 3 out, unchlgd.	
	..........................(5 to 2 op 6 to 4 on tchd 15 to 8 on)	1
	WOODLAND FIREFLY 12-10-11 Miss A Turner, hld up, beh	
	til rdn alng aftr 8th, mstk tenth, lft moderate 3rd 3 out,	
	fnshd lme............(16 to 1 op 10 to 1 tchd 20 to 1)	2
	VICTORIOUS KING 7-11-2 R Dunwoody, led 4th to 9th, rdn	
	alng aftr 5 out, lft moderate second and jmpd badly left	
	3 out, sn wknd..............(3 to 1 op 9 to 4)	3
	NEEDS MUST 6-11-2 J Frost, trkd ldr frm 5th, ev ch 7 out,	
	dsptd second but hld whn f 3 out. (20 to 1 op 10 to 1)	f
	WEST LODGE LADY 8-10-4 (7") J Neaves, hld up and beh,	
	hrd rdn aftr 5 out, moderate 5th whn blun and uns rdr	
	3 out.....................(20 to 1 op 10 to 1)	ur
	THE BARREN ARCTIC 7-11-2 B Powell, led to 4th, trkd	
	ldrs, wnt second 7 out, disputing second whn hmpd	
	and uns rdr 3 out.....(11 to 1 op 10 to 1 tchd 12 to 1)	ur
	COMIC LINE 8-11-3⁶ (5") Mr A Farrant, beh, jmpd very	
	slwly 6th and nxt, sn tld off, pld up 8th.	
	..........................(25 to 1 op 14 to 1)	pu

Dist: 15l, 20l. 4m 45.50s. a 16.50s (7 Ran).

(Nick Quesnel), J White

166 Tripleprint Selling Handicap Hurdle (4-y-o and up) £1,610 2m 3f. (3:40)

156³	TRUST DEED (USA) [74] (bl) 5-10-13 M A FitzGerald, trkd	
	ldr, hrd rdn aftr 3 out, jnd lder 2 out, ridden to lead run	
	in, all out.	
	..........................(7 to 2 op 4 to 1 tchd 5 to 1 and 100 to 30)	1
	WELL DONE RORY [89] 4-11-7 (7") P McLoughlin, led, hit	
	second, rdn appr 2 out, hdd aftr last, not quicken.	
	..........................(9 to 4 op 6 to 1)	2
	PEARLY WHITE [63] 4-9-9 (7") Mr Richard White, lost tch	
	aftr 5th, beh til hdwy aftr 3 out, sn wknd, tld off, sddl	
	slpd..................(14 to 1 op 12 to 1 tchd 25 to 1)	3
	MILLROUS [79] (bl) 5-11-4 R Dunwoody, hld up, mstk 4th,	
	pld up and dismounted.	
	..........................(5 to 4 on op 11 to 10 tchd 5 to 4)	pu

Dist: 1½l, 30l. 4m 29.00s. a 10.00s (4 Ran).

(Fred Camis), Mrs A Knight

167 Bonusprint Handicap Chase (5-y-o and up) £2,723 2¾m 110yds. (4:10)

	MISTER FEATHERS [91] 12-10-3 (5") D Leahy, hld up, wnt	
	second tenth, led aftr 5 out, sn drw clr, hit last, eased	
	nr finish..............(5 to 1 op 4 to 1 tchd 11 to 2)	1
	ROYAL CRAFTSMAN [91] 12-10-8 Peter Hobbs, hld up,	
	hdwy 7th, 3rd whn mstk tenth, rdn and styd on aftr 5	
	out, no ch whn wnr....(9 to 2 op 4 to 1 tchd 11 to 2)	2
	THEY ALL FORGOT ME [89] 6-10-6 D Bridgwater, not flu-	
	ent, wnt 3rd aftr tenth, rdn and styd on frm 3 out, no	
	ch whn wnr........(7 to 2 op 3 to 1 tchd 4 to 1)	3
	CLEANING UP [86] 11-10-3 B Powell, chsd ldrs til wknd	
	aftr 7 out, btn whn mstk 4 out.....(20 to 1 op 12 to 1)	4
	MY CUP OF TEA [107] 10-11-10 R Dunwoody, led til hdd	
	aftr 5 out, wknd quickly aftr nxt, sn beh.	
	..........................(5 to 1 op 7 to 1 tchd 8 to 1 and 9 to 2)	5
	VALASSY [86] 10-10-3 A Maguire, prmnt whn f 5th.	
	..........................(9 to 4 fav op 11 to 4 tchd 11 to 4)	f
	SAMSUN [97] 11-11-0 M A FitzGerald, prmnt to 5th,	
	reminders aftr 8th, sn tld off, pld up bef 4 out.	
	..........................(8 to 1 op 6 to 1 tchd 11 to 1)	pu

Dist: 2½l, 1½l, 20l, 15l. 5m 39.70s. a 18.70s (7 Ran).

(Mrs M Forde), J S King

168 Tripleprint Handicap Hurdle (0-115 4-y-o and up) £2,520 2m 1f 110yds. (4:40)

	ATHAR (Ire) [83] 4-10-11 L Harvey, hld up, rapid hdwy aftr	
	4th, led appr 2 out, rdn clr.	
	..........................(11 to 10 on op Evens tchd 11 to 8)	1
153⁴	WINDSOR PARK (USA) [96] 7-11-7 (3") V Slattery, hld up,	
	rdn aftr 5th, ev ch 2 out, sn one paced.	
	..........................(5 to 1 tchd 11 to 2)	2
	KILLULA CHIEF [100] (bl) 6-12-0 M A FitzGerald, led aftr 1st,	
	hdd appr 2 out, sn wknd..........(4 to 1 op 11 to 2)	3
	FASHION PRINCESS [73] 7-9-8 (7") D Matthews, lost pl aftr	
	4th, styd on one pace after 3 out.	
	..........................(14 to 1 op 10 to 1 tchd 20 to 1)	4
	IMPERIAL FLIGHT [97] 8-11-8 (3") M Hourigan, mstk 4th, sn	
	lost tch, tld off..................(10 to 1 op 8 to 1)	5
	SNOOKER TABLE [79] 10-10-7 D Gallagher, led til aftr 1st,	
	chsd ldr til outpcd frm 5th, rdn and styd on ag'n after 2	
	out, disputing 3rd whn f after last.	
	..........................(8 to 1 tchd 10 to 1 and 6 to 1)	f

Dist: 5l, 20l, 15l, dist. 3m 57.20s. a 0.20s (6 Ran).
SR: 11/19/3/

(J W Buxton), R J Baker

MALLOW (IRE) (good to firm)

Thursday August 5th

169 Mitchelstown Maiden Hurdle (4-y-o and up) £2,245 2m 5f.................. (5:30)

111^4 AWBEG ROVER (Ire) 5-11-3 (3*) Mr T Lombard,... (10 to 1) 1
86^9 TOURIG LE MOSS 6-10-8 (7*) Mr R Foley,........(12 to 1) 2
36^5 BALLYGIBLIN LADY 9-10-12 (3*) J Collins,.....(4 to 1 fav) 3
97^5 MIRROMARK (Ire) 5-11-6 C F Swan,..............(9 to 2) 4
91^8 M MACG (Ire) 4-10-13 (3*) J Magee,..............(7 to 1) 5
90^4 WALKERS LADY (Ire) 5-10-10 (5*) D T Evans,.....(10 to 1) 6
103^8 GALES JEWEL 7-11-1 P Carberry,...............(10 to 1) 7
122 EDWARD'S DOLLY 8-11-1 J F Titley,..............(8 to 1) 8
103^3 PEJAWI 6-11-1 A J O'Brien,.....................(6 to 1) 9
OLDCOURT LADY 7-10-8 (7*) Mr A O'Shea,......(16 to 1) 10
108^6 BOLTON SARAH 6-11-1 K F O'Brien,.............(7 to 1) 11
90^7 FINAL OPTION (Ire) (bl) 5-10-13 (7*) Mr T J Nagle Jnr, ...(20 to 1) 12
109 TROPICAL GABRIEL (Ire) 5-11-6 Mr P J Healy,....(20 to 1) 13
INCH GALE 6-11-1 T Horgan,...................(10 to 1) 14
CITSIROMA 9-10-8 (7*) Mr P O'Keeffe,...........(20 to 1) 15
BRAVE SHARON 9-11-2 (7*) Mr J M Collier,...... (20 to 1) 16
GROVE WALK (bl) 7-10-8 (7*) J A Nagle,......... (20 to 1) 17
112 ALLOW GOLD 6-11-6 F Woods,.................(20 to 1) 18
124 TOECURLER (Ire) 5-10-8 (7*) C O'Brien,..........(20 to 1) 19
109 GOLDEN SLEIGH (Ire) 5-11-1 S H O'Donovan,....(20 to 1) f
108 TERRY'S PRIDE 7-11-1 H Rogers,...............(10 to 1) pu
Dist: 2l, sht-hd, 1½l, hd. 5m 18.80s. (21 Ran).
(Cornelius O'Keeffe), Cornelius O'Keeffe

170 Rathluirc Handicap Chase (0-109 4-y-o and up) £2,245 2½m.................... (6:30)

93^3 ROSSBEIGH CREEK [-] 6-10-4 F J Flood,.........(6 to 1) 1
52^3 TUSKER LADY [-] 8-10-8 (3*) J Magee,............(6 to 1) 2
101^8 GLITTER GREY [-] 7-11-4 K F O'Brien,...........(10 to 1) 3
77^5 HURRYUP [-] 6-10-4 (5*) T J Mitchell,............(12 to 1) 4
KNOCKELLY CASTLE [-] 13-11-1 (7*) Miss C E Hyde, ...(12 to 1) 5
93^7 BARRACILLA [-] 8-9-7 (3*) J Collins,.............(14 to 1) 6
134^7 GERTIES PRIDE [-] 9-11-5 F Woods,..............(10 to 1) 7
131 MARY GINA [-] 8-9-3 (5*) T J O'Sullivan,..........(12 to 1) 8
21^9 QUEEN OF THE SWANS [-] 9-10-11 (5*) Susan A Finn, ...(14 to 1) 9
119 OCTOBER FLAME [-] 10-11-8 K Morgan,......(9 to 4 fav) f
132^5 GARRYDOOLIS [-] 7-11-6 C O'Dwyer,............ (5 to 1) f
44^9 ANNETTE'S DELIGHT [-] 14-9-3^2 (7*) Miss Z Davison, ...(10 to 1) ur
72^7 HELENIUM GALE [-] 6-9-8 C F Swan,............(14 to 1) ur
77^8 COURIER DESPATCH (Ire) [-] (bl) 5-9-5 (7*) C O'Brien, ...(10 to 1) pu
JACKI'S DREAM [-] 8-9-8 T Horgan,.............(20 to 1) pu
Dist: 3½l, 5l, 1l, dist. 4m 58.90s. (15 Ran).
(H Ferguson), F Flood

171 Sean Graham Bookmakers QR Ladies Flat Race (4-y-o and up) £2,935 2m...... (8:00)

107^2 KARABAKH (Ire) 4-11-0 (5*) Mrs J M Mullins, (6 to 4 jt-fav) 1
136^5 THE WICKED CHICKEN (Ire) 4-10-11 (3*) Mrs S McCarthy, ...(8 to 1) 2
114 DUN OENGUS (Ire) 4-10-11 (3*) Miss C Hutchinson, ...(16 to 1) 3
109^2 THE BRIDGE TAVERN (Ire) 4-10-12 (7*) Miss C Duggan, ...(6 to 4 jt-fav) 4
124 THE TENANT 6-11-7 (3*) Miss M Olivefalk,........ (7 to 1) 5
WOODFIELD ROSE 4-10-7 (7*) Miss S J Leahy,... (20 to 1) 6
112^5 IF SO 7-11-3 (7*) Miss A M McMahon,............ (14 to 1) 7
CASTLE CLUB (Ire) 4-10-7 (7*) Miss C O'Neill,.... (20 to 1) 8
103 BOUNTIFUL HOLLOW (Ire) 5-10-12 (7*) Miss F M Crowley, ...(10 to 1) 9
97 COOLMOREEN (Ire) (bl) 5-11-3 (7*) Mrs M Tyner,.. (50 to 1) 10
Dist: 3l, 1½l, sht-hd, 2l. 3m 31.20s. (10 Ran).
(J P M O'Connor), W P Mullins

172 Cork INH Flat Race (4-y-o and up) £2,245 2m................................(8:30)

95^2 HIGHLANDER (Ire) 4-10-12 (7*) Mr G J Harford, (11 to 8 fav) 1
BAWNROCK (Ire) 4-11-12 Mr A P O'Brien,.........(7 to 4) 2
43* CARLINGFORD RUN 6-11-5 (7*) Mr D Murphy,....(12 to 1) 3
36* PROFIT MOTIVE (Ire) 4-11-12 Mr S R Murphy,.... (10 to 3) 4
OAT BRAN 7-11-6^3 (7*) Mr R J Curran,...........(25 to 1) 5
67^9 D'S FANCY (Ire) 5-11-10 (7*) Mr M Brennan,...... (14 to 1) 6
Dist: 3l, 7l, 5l, ½l. 3m 28.20s. (6 Ran).
(Yoshiki Akazawa), P Aspell

KILBEGGAN (IRE) (good)
Friday August 6th

173 Moate Maiden Hurdle (4-y-o and up) £2,245 2m 3f...................... (5:30)

111^3 MICHAEL'S STAR (Ire) 5-11-1 (5*) T J Mitchell,..... (6 to 1) 1
113 NORDIC BEAT (Ire) 4-11-2 (7*) J P Broderick,..... (12 to 1) 2
102^3 MOSARAT (Ire) 4-10-6 (7*) D M Bean,............. (7 to 1) 3
108^5 WRITE IT OFF 7-12-0 C O'Dwyer,.............(6 to 4 fav) 4
115 FANE PARK (Ire) 5-11-6 P Carberry,...............(8 to 1) 5
120^6 KENMAC 6-11-6 K F O'Brien,....................(4 to 1) 6
79 GENISTA 8-11-6 T J Taaffe,......................(10 to 1) 7
111 ERNEST MORSE (Ire) 5-11-1 (5*) T P Rudd,...... (40 to 1) 8
115 QUITE A FIGHTER 6-10-10 (5*) D T Evans,....... (25 to 1) ur
74^7 KAMTARA 7-10-13 (7*) Mr K Ross,.............. (20 to 1) su
Dist: ¾l, 3l, 4l, 4l. 4m 36.50s. (10 Ran).
(F Malone), Francis Berry

174 Sean Graham Mares Maiden Hurdle (4-y-o and up) £2,762 2m 3f............... (6:00)

88^5 DANCING COURSE (Ire) 5-11-9 (5*) Mr G J Harford, ...(3 to 1 fav) 1
80^4 POLLY PLUM (Ire) 5-11-3 (3*) Mr A R Coonan,..... (8 to 1) 2
89^9 JUST BLUSH 6-12-0 H Rogers,....................(25 to 1) 3
131^3 ANA CRUSIS (Ire) 5-10-13 (7*) Mr A Daly,..........(6 to 1) 4
KAITLIN (Ire) 4-11-9 P L Malone,................ (12 to 1) 5
80^2 PARSONS EYRE (Ire) 5-11-1 (5*) T J Mitchell,....... (6 to 1) 6
106 JUST FOUR (Ire) 4-11-4 B Sheridan,.............(16 to 1) 7
111^2 MILLROAD 7-10-13 (7*) C O'Brien,...............(10 to 1) 8
160^7 TOP GENERATION 4-11-4 C F Swan,.............(8 to 1) 9
103^4 LILY ROSE VI 9-11-3 (3*) J Collins,............... (14 to 1) 10
43^8 HAZEL PARK 5-10-13 (7*) Mr P Henley,.......... (16 to 1) 11
85^3 CASTLE CELEBRITY (Ire) 4-11-4 K F O'Brien,.....(11 to 2) 12
162^3 NEW DIRECTIONS 6-11-6 F Woods,..............(8 to 1) 13
CALAMITY CANE (Ire) 5-11-6 M Moran,..........(14 to 1) 14
CLANROSIE (Ire) 4-10-11 (7*) D M Bean,.........(20 to 1) 15
LADY GENERAL 9-11-9 (5*) C P Dunne,..........(14 to 1) 16
HOLME LATER (Ire) 4-10-11 (7*) Mr T J Barry,.....(25 to 1) pu
90 LADY DIGA (Ire) 5-10-13 (7*) Mr S O'Callaghan,... (25 to 1) pu
Dist: 2l, 1l, 3l, 4l. 4m 35.00s. (18 Ran).
(Martin Higgins), Martin Higgins

175 Sean Graham Handicap Hurdle (0-102 4-y-o and up) £2,762 2m 3f..............(6:30)

135* PRACTICE RUN (Ire) [-] 5-11-7 (6ex) P McWilliams, ...(7 to 4 fav) 1
80* SILVER GIPSEY [-] 7-11-5 P L Malone,...........(13 to 2) 2
91* TERINGETTE (Hun) [-] 5-11-6 L P Cusack,.........(7 to 1) 3
85^7 NIMBLE WIND [-] (bl) 7-11-3 A J O'Brien,.........(10 to 1) 4
40^3 SERJITAK [-] 6-10-0 (7*) T P Treacy,...............(5 to 1) 5
161^8 TULLY BOY [-] 6-10-3 (7*) Mr D McCartan,........ (16 to 1) 6
122^6 MOBILE MAN [-] 6-11-5 C F Swan,..............(13 to 2) 7
79^5 MILLER'S CROSSING [-] 6-10-3 (7*) C O'Brien,... (14 to 1) 8
89^8 TOM HENRY [-] 6-9-13 (5*) C P Dunne,.......... (33 to 1) 9
91^5 AMID BIRDS OF PREY [-] 6-11-0 C O'Dwyer,..... (12 to 1) 10
86 CLASSY MACHINE (Ire) [-] 5-10-12 P M Verling,...(16 to 1) 11
Dist: ½l, 6l, 2½l, sht-hd. 4m 34.00s. (11 Ran).
(D Donegan), Patrick Phelan

176 Flat Novice Chase (Div 1) (4-y-o and up) £2,762 2m 5f....................... (7:00)

117^5 FURRY STAR 7-12-0 C F Swan,..................(9 to 4) 1
122^3 VINEYARD SPECIAL 7-12-0 T Horgan,............(7 to 2) 2
92^2 INCA CHIEF 9-12-0 T J Taaffe,............... (13 to 8 fav) 3
33 MANOR RHYME 6-11-7 (7*) C O'Brien,.......... (50 to 1) 4
33^9 BALLY O ROURKE 7-11-9 (5*) D P Georghegan,.. (20 to 1) 5
64^9 LUCKY ENOUGH 8-11-9 F Woods,..............(10 to 1) 6
92^8 HARRY'S BOREEN 6-12-0 K Morgan,............ (10 to 1) 7
THE VIBES 10-11-7 (7*) Mr G W Barry,...........(25 to 1) f
97 SECRET GALE 6-11-9 H Rogers,.................(25 to 1) f
97 COBBLERS ROCK 7-12-0 G M O'Neill,.......... (25 to 1) f
133 RUSSIAN GALE (Ire) (bl) 5-11-0 (3*) J Jones,......(33 to 1) ur
Dist: ½l, dist, 6l, 15l. 5m 19.40s. (11 Ran).
(Thomas J Farrell), P Mullins

177 Flat Novice Chase (Div 2) (4-y-o and up) £2,762 2m 5f...................... (7:30)

118^5 FESTIVAL DREAMS 8-12-0 J Shortt,......... (10 to 9 on) 1
94^4 HURRICANE TOMMY 6-12-0 T J Taaffe,.......... (7 to 1) 2
133^3 LADY DIAMOND 7-11-9 C F Swan,...............(5 to 1) 3
89^6 TORLOUGH 8-11-7 (7*) Mr A J Kennedy,.........(25 to 1) 4
89^4 KIL KIL CASTLE 6-11-9 (5*) T J O'Sullivan,....... (12 to 1) 5
97^2 PALMROCK DONNA 6-11-9 K Morgan,........... (4 to 1) 6
79 BEAT THE RAP 7-12-0 C O'Dwyer,.............. (25 to 1) 7
90^5 HEY LAD (Ire) 5-11-8 P M Verling,................(20 to 1) f
GIVE IT A MISS 7-11-9 (5*) Mr D P Murphy,.......(25 to 1) ur
92 NAMESTAKEN 7-11-9 (5*) T J Mitchell,...........(25 to 1) pu
Dist: 5l, sht-hd, ¾l, 1½l. 5m 24.10s. (10 Ran).
(Mrs Nerys Dutfield), Patrick Prendergast

178 Joe Cooney Memorial Handicap Chase (0-102 4-y-o and up) £2,245 2m 5f....(8:00)

170* ROSSBEIGH CREEK [-] 6-11-3 F J Flood,..... (9 to 4 fav) 1
35^9 GRANVILLE GRILL [-] 8-11-0 C O'Dwyer,.........(10 to 1) 2
BALLYVERANE [-] 7-10-8 (5*) D P Geoghegan,....(12 to 1) 3
77^4 RACHELS ROCKER [-] 6-10-10 (7*) Mr B Moran,..(10 to 1) 4
44 GOLDEN SEE [-] 9-11-5 N Byrne,................ (16 to 1) 5
134 LODATO [-] (bl) 9-9-10 (7*) Mr S Durack,..........(25 to 1) 6
134^9 BLENHEIM PALACE (USA) [-] 6-11-1 (4ex) H Rogers, ...(10 to 1) 7
93^8 ABBEY JACK [-] 6-10-5 T Horgan,...............(33 to 1) 8

134⁶ BENS DILEMMA [-] 8-9-12 (7") J P Broderick, ...(10 to 1) 9
44⁵ ANN'S PRINCE [-] 10-10-8 K F O'Brien, ...(10 to 1) 10
66⁹ PERSIAN GLEN [-] (bl) 6-10-10 (5") T J Mitchell, ...(20 to 1) 11
MELISSAS PRIDE [-] 8-10-13 A J O'Brien, ...(16 to 1) 12
147 COURSING GUY [-] 11-11-8 F Woods, ...(25 to 1) 13
101² CAPINCUR BOY [-] 11-11-5 J F Titley, ...(5 to 2) ur
134⁵ MALACHYS BAR [-] 9-10-13 (3") D Bromley, ...(12 to 1) ur
ENNIS SEVEN FIFTY [-] 6-11-0 G M O'Neill, ...(16 to 1) pu
Dist: 8l, 6l, 2l, 5l. 5m 21.10s. (16 Ran).

(H Ferguson), F Flood

179 Tom Birmingham Menswear INH Flat (4-y-o and up) £2,762 2m 3f...........(8:30)

124³ BAVARD DIEU (Ire) 5-11-9 (5") Mr G J Harford, (11 to 8 fav) 1
150⁵ SIMPLY SARAH 7-11-9 Mr M McNulty, ...(5 to 1) 2
KARA'S DREAM (Ire) 5-11-2 (7") Mr J B Slevin, ...(12 to 1) 3
94² QUEEN KAM (Ire) 4-10-13 (5") Mr J P Berry, ...(4 to 1) 4
70⁷ RALPH SQUARE 5-11-7 (7") Mr T J Beattie, ...(25 to 1) 5
124⁶ MISS POLLERTON (Ire) 5-11-2 (7") Mr M J Bowe, .. (8 to 1) 6
39⁷ QUEENS HALL (Ire) 5-11-2 (7") Mr C J Stafford, ...(12 to 1) 7
58 TRAP ONE (Ire) 5-11-7 (7") Mr D J Kavanagh, ...(12 to 1) 8
109⁸ SUNSET RUN 7-12-0 Mr J A Berry, ...(8 to 1) 9
107 LADY OF THE RIVER (Ire) 4-10-13 (5") Mr D Valentine,
....(25 to 1) 10
DAYLIGHT LADY 6-11-2 (7") Mr K Kirwan, ...(33 to 1) su
MAURADONNA (Ire) 4-10-11 (7") Mr D Groome, ...(25 to 1) pu
Dist: 11l, 2l, 6l, sht-hd. 4m 27.30s. (12 Ran).

(Seamus Maccrosain), Michael Cunningham

PLUMPTON (firm)
Friday August 6th
Going Correction: MINUS 0.40 sec. per fur.

180 Jevington Juvenile Novices' Hurdle (3-y-o) £1,763 2m 1f.....................(2:10)

128* MR GENEAOLOGY (USA) (bl) 11-3 A Maguire, not fluent,
trkd ldrs, wnt second 6th, led appr 2 out, sn clr.
....(13 to 8 on op 6 to 4 on tchd 11 to 8 on and 15 to 8 on) 1
LADY OF SHADOWS 10-2 (5") A Dicken, hld up, hdwy frm
7th, wnt second appr last, no ch wth unr. 2
....(16 to 1 op 7 to 1)
WILL HYDE 10-12 Peter Hobbs, trkd ldr, lft in ld 5th,
already hdd whn mstk 2 out, btn 3rd when blun last.
..................................(50 to 1 op 33 to 1 tchd 66 to 1) 3
DICKINS 10-12 M A FitzGerald, chsd ldrs, rdn and lost pl
hfwy, kpt on past btn horses frm 3 out.
...................................(33 to 1 tchd 50 to 1) 4
SWIFT REVENGE 10-7 Lorna Vincent, mstk second, al beh,
tld off...............(33 to 1 op 20 to 1 tchd 50 to 1) 5
GENERAL BROOKS (Ire) 10-12 T Wall, sn beh, mstk 6th, tld
off........................(50 to 1 op 20 to 1) 6
MUNNASIB (Fr) 10-12 G McCourt, chsd ldrs till wknd appr
3 out, eased whn btn, tld off.........(7 to 2 op 5 to 1) 7
147³ CALIBRATE 10-12 B Powell, hld up, mstk 3rd, hdwy appr
nxt, wknd aftr 6th, beh whn blun 3 out, tld off.
...................................(9 to 2 tchd 7 to 1) 8
147⁷ DOOGAREY 10-5 (7") P McLoughlin, led till ran out 5th.
.................................(66 to 1 op 33 to 1) ro
JIM CANTLE 10-12 M Hoad, al beh, tld off whn pld up bef
7th...............(66 to 1 op 50 to 1) pu
Dist: 8l, 10l, 8l, 20l, 2½l, 8l, 12l. 4m 6.70s. a 14.70s (10 Ran).

(Mrs P A White), J White

181 Streat Selling Handicap Hurdle (4-y-o and up) £1,733 2m 1f.................(2:40)

MANHATTAN BOY [95] 11-11-10 A Maguire, hld up in tch,
outpcd appr 7th, sn rdn, rallied gmely approaching 2
out, ran on to ld r-in......................(7 to 2 op 9 to 4) 1
SALAR'S SPIRIT [75] 7-10-4⁴ G Upton, hld up in tch,
steady hdwy frm 5th, led 3 out, sn clr, wknd appr last,
edgd rght and hdd r-in.
...................................(7 to 1 op 10 to 1 tchd 12 to 1) 2
KEY BEAR (Fr) [77] 6-10-6 T Wall, al prmnt, wnt second 3
out, ran on one pace frm nxt.
...................................(6 to 1 op 7 to 1 tchd 8 to 1 and 10 to 1) 3
WILTOSKI [86] 5-11-1 R Campbell, chsd ldr, ev ch 3 out,
one pace.................(13 to 2 op 5 to 1 tchd 7 to 1) 4
NORTHERN CONQUEROR (Ire) [80] 5-10-9 D Morris, hld up
in tch, hdwy 7th, ev ch 3 out, sn btn.
...................................(7 to 4 fav op 9 to 4 tchd 5 to 2) 5
SALMONID [90] 7-11-5 B Powell, jmpd rght, mstk 3rd, led
till hdd 3 out, btn whn mistake nxt.
...................................(6 to 1 op 3 to 1 tchd 13 to 2) 6
TAPESTRY DANCER [71] 5-10-0 D Skyrme, pld hrd, wl beh
frm 6th.................(25 to 1 op 14 to 1) 7
Dist: 1½l, 2l, 10l, 6l, 3l, 6l. 4m 0.50s. a 8.50s (7 Ran).

(Mrs D R Hunnisett), J Ffitch-Heyes

182 Superform National Hunt Annual Handicap Chase (0-115 4-y-o and up) £2,364 2m
....(3:10)

COURT RAPIER [86] 11-11-0 A Maguire, hld up in tch,
outpcd 4 out, hrd rdn frm nxt, ran on to ld nr finish.
...................................(3 to 1 op 4 to 1 tchd 11 to 4) 1
154² GABISH [89] 8-11-3 J R Kavanagh, towards rear early, sn
in tch, wnt second 7th, rdn to ld appr last, one pace
and ct nr finish...........(7 to 1 op 5 to 1 tchd 8 to 1) 2
COTAPAXI [96] 8-11-10 R Dunwoody, led till hdd appr last,
sn btn.......(6 to 1 op 5 to 1 tchd 13 to 2 and 7 to 1) 3
146* SAFETY (USA) [90] (bl) 6-11-4 D Skyrme, wtd wth in tch, ev
ch whn mstk 3 out, sn btn.
...................................(5 to 4 fav tchd 6 to 4 and 13 to 8) 4
BLUE ENSIGN [90] 8-11-4 C Llewellyn, blun second, al
beh, tld off...........(9 to 1 op 10 to 1 tchd 16 to 1) 5
BEN TIRRAN [93] 9-11-7 D Telfer, prmnt early, mstks and
sn beh, tld off frm 4 out.
...................................(20 to 1 op 10 to 1 tchd 25 to 1) 6
SLIPPERY MAX [90] 9-11-4 J Osborne, chsd ldr to 7th,
wknd appr 4 out, tld off.(5 to 1 op 7 to 1 tchd 8 to 1) 7
Dist: 1½l, 10l, ½l, 15l, ¾l, 1½l. 3m 50.80s. a 0.80s (7 Ran).
SR: 14/15/12/5/

(H V Perry), R H Alner

183 Alfred McAlpine Construction Handicap Hurdle (0-135 4-y-o and up) £1,635 2m 1f
....(3:40)

NORDIC FLASH [98] 6-12-0 A Maguire, hld up in rear, took
clr order frm 4th, wnt second appr 3 out, rdn to ld
approaching last, drvn out. (11 to 10 on op 11 to 10) 1
STRIDING EDGE [90] 8-11-6 R Dunwoody, led, quickened
pace 4 out, rdn and hdd appr last, one pace r-in.
...................................(7 to 4 op 6 to 4 tchd 2 to 1) 2
MABTHUL (USA) [78] 5-10-8 N Williamson, chsd ldr till
wknd quickly appr 3 out, sn eased, tld off.
...................................(4 to 1 op 5 to 2) 3
Dist: 2½l, dist. 4m 1.10s. a 9.10s (3 Ran).

(D Borrows), T J Naughton

184 Berwick Novices' Chase (4-y-o and up) £1,987 2m.....................(4:10)

PEARLS BEAU 6-11-7 S Smith Eccles, made all, drw clr
frm 3 out, unchlgd......(9 to 2 op 4 to 1 tchd 6 to 1) 1
ILEWIN 6-11-7 M A Ahern, hld up, making hdwy whn mstk
8th, headway to chase wnr frm nxt, no imprsn from 2
out...(Evens op 5 to 4 on tchd 5 to 4 and 11 to 8) 2
JESSOP 8-11-7 S Earle, in tch till outpcd frm 7th.
...................................(11 to 1 op 7 to 1 tchd 10 to 1) 3
145⁴ PAPPA DONT PREACH (Ire) 5-11-5 R Supple, mstks, chsd
wnr till wknd 9th, lft poor 3rd 2 out, fnshd tired.
...................................(12 to 1 op 7 to 1 tchd 8 to 1) 4
DECIDING BID 7-11-7 R Rowell, chsd ldrs till wknd
quickly appr 4 out... (14 to 1 op 12 to 1 tchd 20 to 1) 5
MIRAGE DANCER 10-11-7 I Lawrence, al in rear, wl beh
frm 7th.................(20 to 1 op 12 to 1 tchd 25 to 1) 6
151⁴ PRIVATE JET (Ire) 4-10-5 J R Kavanagh, beh till hdwy frm
8th, hld in 3rd whn f 2 out.
...................................(13 to 2 op 4 to 1 tchd 8 to 1) f
Dist: 6l, 30l, 2l, 27/4l, 12l. 3m 51.00s. a 1.00s (7 Ran).
SR: 19/13/-/-/-/

(Mrs T McCoubrey), J R Jenkins

185 Hove Novices' Hurdle (4-y-o and up) £1,660 2½m.....................(4:40)

DEBACLE (USA) 4-10-11 D Murphy, trkd ldrs, wnt second
8th, led appr last, rdn clr.......(6 to 4 fav op 2 to 1) 1
149² SAKIL (Ire) 5-10-9 (5") A Dicken, hld up in rear, hdwy 4
out, drvn alng appr 2 out, wnt second r-in.
...................................(15 to 8 op 2 to 1) 2
NIDOMI (v) 6-11-0 A Maguire, chsd ldr, led appr 8th, hrd
rdn and hdd approaching last, one pace r-in.
...................................(5 to 1 op 4 to 1 tchd 6 to 1) 3
WEDNESDAYS AUCTION (Ire) 5-10-9 (5") C Burnett-Wells,
towards rear till effrt 4 out, wknd aftr nxt, tld off.
...................................(8 to 1 op 7 to 1 tchd 12 to 1) 4
142² WAYWARD EDWARD (bl) 7-11-0 D Telfer, led till hdd appr
8th, sn wknd, tld off...........(20 to 1 op 10 to 1) 5
CANBRACK (Ire) (bl) 4-10-11 Leesa Long, jmpd poorly in
rear, tld off frm hfwy...........(10 to 1 op 50 to 1) 6
135⁵ CLWYD LODGE 6-10-7 (7") N Juckes, al beh, tld off.
...................................(100 to 1 tchd 200 to 1) 7
155² APACHE PRINCE 6-11-0 J R Kavanagh, prmnt early, blun
4th, pld up lme bef nxt.............(14 to 1 op 7 to 1) pu
Dist: 6l, ¾l, 30l, 7l, 15l, 12l. 4m 41.70s. a 4.70s (8 Ran).

(Mrs Lisa Olley), B J McMath

WORCESTER (good to firm)
Saturday August 7th
Going Correction: MINUS 0.20 sec. per fur.

186 Polly Garter Selling Handicap Hurdle (4-y-o and up) £1,557 2m.............(5:40)

126* MOYMET [85] 7-11-10 G McCourt, trkd ldrs, ev ch 3 out, cl
second whn lft in ld last, hld on nr finish, all out.
...................................(4 to 1 jt-fav op 7 to 2 tchd 9 to 2) 1

146[7] ZAMANAYN (Ire) [80] 5-11-5 R Supple, *net muzzle, pld hrd, hld up, mstk 4th, hdwy aftr 3 out, ran on after last, jst fld*..............................(10 to 1 op 5 to 1) 2
144[2] DISTANT MEMORY [64] 4-9-10 (7*) N Parker, *hld up and beh, hdwy whn hmpd 3 out, styd on betw last 2, fnshd strly*..............(4 to 1 jt-fav op 3 to 1 tchd 9 to 2) 3
COLWAY PRINCE (Ire) [80] 5-11-5 G Upton, *hld up, beh 4th, some hdwy aftr four out, not trble ldrs.* ....(10 to 1 op 8 to 1) 4
SHREWD JOHN [74] 7-10-13 R Garritty, *trkd ldrs, cl up and ev ch 3 out, sn rdn and unbl to quicken aftr nxt, one pace*..............(5 to 1 op 6 to 1 tchd 7 to 1) 5
CONE LANE [84] 7-11-2 (7*) P McLoughlin, *led second, mstk 5th, hdd aftr 3 out, one pace.* ....(16 to 1 op 12 to 1 tchd 20 to 1) 6
PERSIAN VALLEY [83] 8-11-1 (7*) M Doyle, *hld up, beh 3rd, lost tch aftr 5th, sn behind*.......(20 to 1 op 14 to 1) 7
STYLISH GENT [68] 6-10-7 A Jones, *chsd ldrs til wknd quickly aftr 5th, sn beh.* ....(12 to 1 tchd 20 to 1 and 10 to 1) 8
EVERSO IRISH [84] 4-11-9 A Maguire, *led to second, pressed ldr til led aftr 4 out, hng rght and hrd rdn whn f last*..............................(6 to 1 tchd 8 to 1) f
137[3] SUNTAN (Fr) [70] (bl) 4-10-9 M Dwyer, *trkd ldrs, wnt second aftr 4 out, 5th and wkng whn f nxt.* ....(8 to 1 op 5 to 1) f

Dist: Nk, 1½l, 3l, 3½l, 10l, 2½l, 10l. 3m 46.20s. a 5.20s (10 Ran).
SR: 12/6/-/1/-/-/ (E J Mangan), K R Burke

187 Dylan Thomas Handicap Chase (0-125 5-y-o and up) £2,409 2m.................(6:10)

141[3] DRUMSTICK [115] 7-12-0 N Williamson, *made all, drw clr aftr 2 out, eased r-in, cmftbly.* (6 to 4 on op 7 to 4 on) 1
TINAS LAD [105] 10-11-4 J Osborne, *trkd ldr, lft second 4 out, sn rdn and no imprsn*...........(5 to 2 op 2 to 1) 2
WILL'S BOUNTY [87] 10-9-11 (3*) V Slattery, *jmpd badly, pressed ldr til mstk 5th, rallied to go second and blun 4 out, sn tld off*.......... (7 to 1 op 5 to 1 tchd 8 to 1) 3
SHARP ORDER [95] 8-10-8 Pat Caldwell, *3rd whn f 4th.* ....(14 to 1 op 10 to 1 tchd 20 to 1) f

Dist: 3l, 30l. 3m 59.60s. a 10.60s (4 Ran).
(Sarah Lady Allendale), K C Bailey

188 Nogood Boyo Juvenile Novices' Hurdle (3-y-o) £1,480 2m.....................(6:40)

BEAT THE BAGMAN (Ire) 10-12 L Harvey, *trkd ldr, wnt 3rd appr 3 out, jnd lder nxt, swtchd, wndrd and bumped approaching last, hng rght and drvn clr* ....(14 to 1 op 8 to 1) 1
BUGLET 10-7 R Dunwoody, *led, jmpd slwly 3rd, rdn 3 out, bumped appr last, not quicken.* ....(6 to 4 on tchd 11 to 8 on) 2
FREE DANCER 10-7 D Bridgwater, *hld up, hdwy aftr 3 out, styd on one pace, not trble 1st 2* ....(66 to 1 op 25 to 1) 3
MRS DAWSON 10-7 A S Smith, *prmnt, jmpd slwly and lost pl 3rd, mstk 5th, hdwy aftr 3 out, styd on one pace.* ....(9 to 2 op 5 to 1 tchd 7 to 1 and 4 to 1) 4
MY BALLYBOY 10-12 N Mann, *hld up, hdwy whn hmpd 3 out, wknd nxt*..................(20 to 1 op 12 to 1) 5
RUSHALONG 10-12 R Garritty, *pressed ldr til wknd appr 3 out*..............................(50 to 1 op 20 to 1) 6
NO SHOW (Ire) 10-12 W Humphreys, *prmnt to 5th, sn beh.* ....(100 to 1 op 33 to 1) 7
QUEENS CONTRACTOR 10-12 S Keightley, *mstk 1st, sn beh, no ch frm 4 out*...............(12 to 1 op 8 to 1) 8
LADY GAIL 10-7 A Webb, *pushed alng aftr second, hdwy 5th, wnt 4th appr 3 out wknd quickly.* ....(14 to 1 op 10 to 1 tchd 20 to 1) 9
MAD MYTTON 10-12 S Smith Eccles, *trkd ldr, wnt second 4th, mstk nxt, wknd quickly aftr 3 out, virtually pld up r-in*..............................(14 to 1 op 8 to 1) 10

Dist: 6l, 12l, 4l, 8l, 3l, 1l, ¾l, 2½l, nk. 3m 48.40s. a 7.40s (10 Ran).
(David Sweet), J Akehurst

189 Captain Cat Novices' Chase (5-y-o and up) £1,811 2½m 110yds................. (7:10)

STRONG MEDICINE 6-11-2 N Williamson, *trkd ldr in second pl, led and pckd 4 out, drw clr aftr nxt, styd on wl.* ....(5 to 4 on tchd 11 to 10 on) 1
145[3] GILSTON LASS (bl) 6-10-11 A Maguire, *led til hdd 4 out, sn rdn and one pace*........ (7 to 2 op 3 to 1 tchd 4 to 1) 2
HELMAR (NZ) 7-11-2 R Supple, *hld up, mstks, styd on aftr 5 out, not trble 1st 2*...... (8 to 1 op 7 to 1 tchd 9 to 1) 3
TEKLA (Fr) 8-11-2 B Powell, *mstks, chsd ldrs to 8th, no ch frm nxt, fnshd lme*..................(33 to 1 op 20 to 1) 4
125[4] STORM WARRIOR (bl) 8-11-2 T Wall, *jmpd badly, hit 8th, sn beh*..............................(25 to 1 op 12 to 1) 5
139[2] SOLICITOR'S CHOICE 10-11-2 J Railton, *mstks, chsd ldg pair til wknd 8th, sn beh*........... (7 to 1 op 4 to 1) 6
WAR BEAT 5-10-12 M A FitzGerald, *mstks and jmpd rght, al beh, tld off*..............................(20 to 1 op 14 to 1) 7

Dist: 10l, 5l, 2½l, 8l, 1½l, dist. 5m 7.80s. a 4.80s (7 Ran).
(Dr D B A Silk), K C Bailey

190 Llareggyb Handicap Hurdle (0-115 4-y-o and up) £1,841 2¼m.................(7:40)

MAN FROM MARS [87] 7-10-11 B Clifford, *trkd ldr, ev ch 3 out, rdn to ld last, drvn out r-in, jst hld on.* ....(16 to 1 op 10 to 1) 1
129* CASTLE DIAMOND [97] 6-11-7 J A Harris, *prmnt, wnt second 4 out, led appr nxt til hdd last, rdn and rallied r-in, not quicken nr finish*................(5 to 1 op 7 to 2) 2
COURT CIRCULAR [100] (bl) 4-11-10 Diane Clay, *hld up in tch, hdwy aftr 4 out, chlgd after nxt, rdn and unbl to quicken*..............................(13 to 2 op 5 to 1) 3
VIAGGIO [95] 5-11-5 J Osborne, *led til hdd appr 3 out, sn one pace*..............................(9 to 1 op 7 to 1) 4
AEDEAN [91] 4-11-1 D Murphy, *trkd ldrs, in tch 4 out, one pace frm nxt*........... (7 to 1 op 6 to 1 tchd 8 to 1) 5
KASHAN (Ire) [87] 5-10-11 L Harvey, *chsd ldrs til lost pl aftr 4 out, tld off*...................... (16 to 1 op 12 to 1) 6
THUNDER BUG (USA) [80] 5-10-4 R Bellamy, *hld up, rdn alng and no response aftr 5th, tld off 3 out.* ....(11 to 2 op 5 to 1 tchd 13 to 2) 7
CORINTHIAN GOD (Ire) [80] 4-10-4 A Maguire, *pressed ldr in second pl til wknd quickly 3 out, tld off* ....(4 to 1 fav op 3 to 1 tchd 5 to 1) 8
SECRET LIASON [93] 7-11-3 D Bridgwater, *hld up, rdn alng and no response aftr 5th, tld off 3 out.* ....(7 to 1 op 10 to 1 tchd 14 to 1 and 6 to 1) 9
MASTER BOSTON (Ire) [80] 5-10-2[5] (7*) J Driscoll, *trkd ldrs til rdn and lost pl aftr 5th, sn tld off.* ....(16 to 1 op 10 to 1) 10

Dist: ½l, 4l, 4l, 5l, 25l, 3½l, 2l, 20l, 4l. 4m 10.90s. a 2.90s (10 Ran).
SR: 18/27/26/17/8/-/ (P J Hobbs), P J Hobbs

191 Milk Wood Novices' Hurdle (4-y-o and up) £1,480 2m......................... (8:10)

BILLY BORU 5-11-0 D Gallagher, *hld up in tch, wnt 4th appr 3 out, led 2 out, drvn clr and quicken r-in, styd on strly*................(5 to 2 fav op 2 to 1 tchd 3 to 1) 1
CLASS ATTRACTION (USA) 4-10-6 R Dunwoody, *hld up, hdwy to track ldrs aftr 5th, ev ch 3 out, not quicken appr last*..............................(4 to 1 op 5 to 2) 2
CLASSICAL STAR 4-10-11 N Williamson, *trkd ldrs, wnt second appr 3 out, ev ch til wknd approaching last.* ....(10 to 1 op 6 to 1) 3
CHRIS'S GLEN 4-10-6 (5*) R Farrant, *mid-div, hdwy to chase ldrs aftr 5th, one pace after 3 out.* ....(50 to 1 op 33 to 1) 4
STERLING BUCK (USA) 6-10-9 (5*) D Leahy, *mid-div, hdwy whn hmpd 3 out, sn one pace.* ....(12 to 1 op 8 to 1 tchd 14 to 1) 5
SHAYNA MAIDEL 4-10-6 A Jones, *pressed ldr til led 3rd to 5th, wknd 3 out*..................(20 to 1 op 12 to 1) 6
KIMS SELECTION (Ire) 4-10-11 R Garritty, *mid-div, mstk 5th, beh frm 4 out*.................(16 to 1 op 25 to 1) 7
HATAAL (Ire) 4-10-6 T Wall, *beh frm 4th, nvr trbld ldrs.* ....(66 to 1 op 33 to 1) 8
MALINDI BAY 5-11-0 D Murphy, *wl beh frm 3rd.* ....(20 to 1 op 16 to 1) 9
MY HARRY BOY 6-11-0 G Upton, *trkd ldrs, wnt 3rd aftr 4 out, hmpd after nxt, wknd quickly.* ....(66 to 1 op 33 to 1) 10
WELL SHOD 5-10-6 (3*) W Marston, *hdwy 3rd, chsd ldrs til wknd 5th, sn beh.* ....(9 to 1 op 8 to 1 tchd 10 to 1 and 7 to 1) 11
ALTO PRINCESS 4-10-6 H Davies, *slwly away, beh frm 3rd, tld off 3 out*..................(33 to 1 op 20 to 1) 12
PADDY'S GOLD (Ire) 5-11-0 G Rowe, *chsd ldrs til wknd quickly aftr 4th, tld off*...........(66 to 1 op 25 to 1) 13
FAIR BABE 7-11-0 M A FitzGerald, *beh frm second, tld off 4 out*..............................(25 to 1 op 14 to 1) 14
138[2] WELL APPOINTED (Ire) 4-10-11 A S Smith, *led to 3rd, led ag'n 5th til f 3 out*..................(4 to 1 op 3 to 1) f
FAMILY ROSE 4-10-11 G McCourt, *beh second, al rear, tld off whn pld up bef 3 out.* ....(16 to 1 op 12 to 1 tchd 20 to 1) pu

Dist: 8l, 10l, 3l, 1l, 8l, 20l, sht-hd, 2½l, nk, 12l. 3m 46.00s. a 5.00s (16 Ran).
SR: 4/-/-/-/-/-/ (Ron Butler), R Simpson

CLAIREFONTAINE (FR) (soft)
Monday August 9th

192 Prix Jacques Peillon (Hurdle) (4-y-o and up) £7,168 2m 1f.................. (1:01)

BOKARO (Fr) 7-10-2[1] G Bradley, *made all, pushed out, very easily*..................................... 1
PAMPILLO (Fr) 5-10-5 D Leblond,...................... 2
LENNOX AVENUE (USA) 5-10-10 R Chotard,............. 3

Dist: 15l, 6l, 7l, dist, nk, dist, dist, dist. 3m 58.60s. (10 Ran).
(Lady Joseph), C P E Brooks

WORCESTER (good to firm)
Monday August 9th

Going Correction: PLUS 0.05 sec. per fur.

193 Nimrod Novices' Selling Hurdle (3-y-o) £1,480 2m........................ (2:15)

128 CASHABLE 10-12 S Smith Eccles, *made virtually all, drvn appr 2 out, rdn out.* .... (13 to 2 op 5 to 1 tchd 7 to 1) 1
GLEAM OF GOLD 10-4 (3*) D Meredith, *chsd ldrs, ev ch 3 out, rdn and styd on one pace aftr 2 out.* .... (20 to 1 op 16 to 1) 2
SIAN WYN 10-7 R Supple, *veered badly second, mstk 4th, styd on frm 3 out, not quicken r-in*............ (8 to 1) 3
MINTEEN 10-7 A Maguire, *mid-div, pushed alng and hdwy 3 out, sn one pace*......... (5 to 1 fav op 9 to 2) 4
SOLAR KNIGHT 10-7 D Bridgwater, *beh frm 3rd, moderate prog from 3 out*.................. (25 to 1 op 20 to 1) 5
KENNINGTON PROTON (bl) 10-7 T Wall, *beh, moderate prog frm 2 out*.....................(33 to 1 op 25 to 1) 6
DOCTOR-J (Ire) 10-12 S Keightley, *chsd ldrs till wknd appr 2 out*...........................(8 to 1 op 7 to 1) 7
KUTAN (Ire) 10-12 D Gallagher, *mstk 4th, hrd drvn appr 3 out, sn wknd*.......................(11 to 2 op 4 to 1) 8
DUKE OF BUDWORTH 10-12 D Murphy, *prmnt till wknd appr 3 out*...........................(11 to 2 op 4 to 1) 9
FLYING AMY 10-7 R Dunwoody, *prmnt till wknd quickly 3 out*............................... (10 to 1 op 8 to 1) 10
WOODLANDS ELECTRIC 10-7 (5*) R Davis, *beh most of way*.................................. (12 to 1 op 16 to 1) 11
147[8] ANNIE ROSE (bl) 10-7 J Frost, *prmnt to 5th, tld off whn pld up bef 2 out*...............................(33 to 1) pu
CLAR DUBH (Ire) 10-9[2] R Campbell, *al beh, tld off whn pld up bef 3 out*......................... (8 to 1 op 7 to 1) pu

Dist: 5l, ½l, 10l, 2½l, nk, 15l, 3l, 12l, 12l, 15l. 3m 57.80s. a 16.80s (13 Ran).
(R P Turf Accountants), J R Jenkins

194 Pomp And Circumstance Novices' Chase (4-y-o and up) £2,490 2m........... (2:45)

FASTBIT 6-11-9 N Williamson, *trkd ldrs, led aftr 5th, mstk 8th and hdd, led ag'n 4 out, sn clr, easily.* ....(5 to 1 tchd 9 to 2) 1
129[3] AT PEACE 7-11-9 A Maguire, *chsd ldrs, led aftr 8th, hdd 4 out, sn rdn, styd on, no ch wth wnr.* ....(13 to 8 fav tchd 2 to 1 and 6 to 4) 2
129[4] WEEKDAY CROSS (Ire) 5-11-7 S Smith Eccles, *mid-div, hdwy 7th, effrt 3 out, no ch whn rdn and wnt rght last.* .... (9 to 1 op 7 to 1 tchd 10 to 1) 3
DARK DEEP DAWN 6-10-11 (7*) Mr T Byrne, *mstk second, beh, tld off 8th, shaken up and ran on wl frm 3 out.* .... (10 to 1 op 7 to 1 tchd 12 to 1) 4
129 CRAFTY CHAPLAIN 7-11-4 (5*) Mr D McCain, *in tch, hit 7th, wkng whn mstk 3 out.* .... (7 to 1 op 5 to 1 tchd 15 to 2) 5
125[7] CRAZY HORSE DANCER (USA) 5-11-7 R Supple, *chsd ldrs till wknd and mstk 4 out*.......... (20 to 1 op 14 to 1) 6
BRYNHILL ALERT 7-11-9 M Brennan, *in tch till wknd 4 out, tld off*........................(14 to 1 op 20 to 1) 7
FURRY LOCH 7-11-9 J A Harris, *led, mstk 1st, f 3rd.* .... (33 to 1 op 25 to 1) f
DARING CLASS 7-11-4 I Shoemark, *lft in ld 3rd, hit 5th, sn hdd, blun 6th, wknd aftr 8th, fifth and tld off whn blunded and uns rdr last*........ (14 to 1 tchd 16 to 1) ur
181[4] WILTOSKI (bl) 5-11-7 R Campbell, *beh whn blun and uns rdr 5th*..............................(10 to 1 op 7 to 1) ur

Dist: 20l, 1½l, ¾l, 1½l, 20l, dist. 4m 2.00s. a 13.00s (10 Ran).
(K C Bailey), K C Bailey

195 Enigma Conditional Jockeys' Handicap Hurdle (0-115 4-y-o and up) £1,579 2m ....(3:15)

ROWHEDGE [80] 7-10-8 (3*) S Curran, *wth ldr till led aftr 3rd, styd pressing ldrs, rdn after 3 out, chlgd 2 out, led last, all out*..................... (16 to 1 tchd 14 to 1) 1
LUSTREMAN [96] 6-11-13 W Marston, *led 4th, hdd appr 3 out, rdn 2 out, rallied r-in, kpt on*... (9 to 2 op 4 to 1) 2
144* BONDAID [85] 9-10-11 (5*) K Comerford, *hld up in tch, led appr 3 out, sn clr, rdn 2 out, hdd last, soon btn.* .... (2 to 1 on tchd 15 to 8 on) 3
168[5] IMPERIAL FLIGHT [97] 8-12-0 D Leahy, *made most till hdd aftr 3rd, rdn and wknd 4th, sn tld off.* ....(9 to 2 op 3 to 1) 4

Dist: 1½l, 2½l, dist. 3m 51.30s. a 10.30s (4 Ran).
SR: -/2/-/-/ (Miss Jacqueline S Doyle), Miss Jacqueline S Doyle

196 Edward Elgar Handicap Chase (0-115 5-y-o and up) £2,950 2m 7f..............(3:45)

COPPER MINE [122] 7-12-0 J Osborne, *made all, blun 3 out, sn clr, rdn r-in, jst hld on.* ....(3 to 1 op 5 to 2 tchd 7 to 2) 1
TRI FOLENE (Fr) [118] (v) 7-11-10 R Dunwoody, *prmnt, chsd wnr aftr 9th, hit 4 out, outpcd nxt, rallied and ev ch last, kpt on, not quicken cl hme.* (6 to 4 fav op 2 to 1) 2
GALA'S IMAGE [106] 13-10-12 S McNeill, *al in tch, outpcd frm 4 out*..............(15 to 2 op 5 to 1 tchd 8 to 1) 3
127 CLARES HORSE [94] 6-10-0 R Supple, *hit tenth, beh, no ch whn blun 13th*................. (20 to 1 op 16 to 1) 4
SIRISAT [94] 9-10-0 Mr K Hollowell, *mstk 1st, al beh, tld off*...................................(50 to 1 op 33 to 1) 5
143 ABBREVIATION [104] 10-10-10 D Morris, *beh, losing tch whn refused tenth*................ (50 to 1 op 25 to 1) ref
127* OK CORRAL (USA) [117] (bl) 6-11-9 A Maguire, *chsd wnr, 3rd whn pld up aftr 9th, dismounted.* (5 to 2 op 2 to 1) pu

Dist: Nk, 25l, 5l, ¾l. 5m 51.10s. a 7.10s (7 Ran).
SR: 41/36/-/-/ (J Dougall), O Sherwood

197 Chanson Novices' Hurdle (4-y-o and up) £1,480 2m 5f 110yds................(4:15)

CLASSIC CONTACT 7-10-7 (7*) J Supple, *hld up in tch, chlgd 3 out, led 2 out.* ....(9 to 4 fav op 2 to 1 tchd 5 to 2) 1
69[2] CREWS CASTLE 6-11-0 S Smith Eccles, *in tch, led 3 out, hdd but ev ch nxt, outpcd frm last.* ....(11 to 4 op 5 to 2 tchd 100 to 30) 2
130* JALORE 4-10-13 (3*) R Greene, *hdwy 4th, chlgd 3 out till not quicken appr last*............(5 to 2 tchd 11 to 4) 3
155* SILVERCROSS LAD 10-10-7 (7*) N Juckes, *led 3rd till hdd 3 out, wknd rpdly*.................. (13 to 2 op 5 to 1) 4
CLASSICAL BLUE (bl) 7-11-0 J Frost, *lost tch frm 5th, tld off*.. (16 to 1) 5
MY SPARKLING RING 7-11-0 R Dunwoody, *led till aftr 1st, wknd 6th, tld off*................ (20 to 1 tchd 16 to 1) 6
PREMIER MAJOR (Ire) 4-10-11 I Shoemark, *mstk and beh 5th, tld off whn pld up aftr 7th, dismounted.* .... (20 to 1 op 16 to 1) pu
MASH THE TEA (Ire) 4-10-11 V Smith, *led aftr 1st till hdd 3rd, wknd 6th, tld off whn pld up bef 3 out.* .... (100 to 1 op 50 to 1) pu

Dist: 2½l, 3l, 20l, dist, 2l. 5m 6.20s. a 11.20s (8 Ran).
(N B Mason), N B Mason

198 Gerontius Handicap Chase (0-125 5-y-o and up) £2,768 2½m 110yds.........(4:45)

52 LITTLE TOM [93] 8-10-7 J R Kavanagh, *made all, clr whn hit 3 out, rdn frm 2 out, all out, fnshd tired.* ....(9 to 4 op 2 to 1) 1
KITTINGER [104] 12-11-4 Peter Hobbs, *chsd ldrs, mstk 9th, chased wnr frm 3 out, ev ch appr last, rdn r-in, no extr, fnshd tired*.................(9 to 2 op 4 to 1) 2
CORRARDER [105] 9-11-5 Mr J Smyth-Osbourne, *mstk 3rd, prmnt, chsd wnr frm 9th till aftr 4 out, sn one paced.* .... (9 to 1 op 7 to 1 tchd 10 to 1) 3
143[4] BLUECHIPENTERPRISE [86] (bl) 7-9-11 (3*) M Hourigan, *chsd ldrs 3rd, chlgd 6th, jmpd slwly and wknd 8th.* .... (10 to 1 op 16 to 1) 4
152* RIVER HOUSE [119] 11-12-5 (5ex) A Maguire, *in tch whn blun badly 5th, drpd rear, sn lost touch, tld off when pld up appr 4 out*...(11 to 8 fav op 5 to 4 tchd 6 to 4) pu

Dist: 4l, 7l, 30l. 5m 12.10s. a 9.10s (5 Ran).
SR: -/5/ (Mark O'Connor), J S King

SLIGO (IRE) (soft)
Tuesday August 10th

199 Yeats Country Hotel Handicap Hurdle (0-109 4-y-o and up) £2,762 2½m.... (5:30)

131* ST DONAVINT [-] 6-11-9 (6ex) C N Bowens, ...(5 to 2 fav) 1
57[3] SEARCHLIGHT (Ire) [-] 5-11-8 C F Swan, ... (3 to 1) 2
122[9] MUST DO [-] 7-11-8 J F Titley, ... (6 to 1) 3
118[2] BALLINDERRY GLEN [-] 7-10-9 (5*) T P Rudd, ... (3 to 1) 4
122[8] LANTERN LUCK (Ire) [-] (bl) 5-10-13 K F O'Brien, ...(7 to 1) 5
122 PALLASKENRY (Ire) [-] (bl) 5-10-7 H Rogers, ... (33 to 1) 6
113 SPECIAL CORNER (Ire) [-] 5-11-5 (7*) J J McKeon, (20 to 1) 7
91[7] COQUALLA [-] (bl) 8-10-1 (7*) D M Bean, ...(20 to 1) 8

Dist: 7l, 5l, hd, 1l. 5m 3.10s. (8 Ran).
(P A McMahon), Victor Bowens

200 Golden Pages 25th Anniversary Novice Chase (5-y-o and up) £2,762 2½m... (7:00)

135 PRINCE YAZA 6-11-11 (3*) J Magee, ... (100 to 30) 1
121[3] GONZALO 10-12-0 C F Swan, ... (2 to 1 fav) 2
51 GREEK MAGIC 6-12-0 T Horgan, ... (12 to 1) 3
131 MAKE ME AN ISLAND 8-11-9 J F Titley, ...(20 to 1) 4
176[7] HARRY'S BOREEN 6-12-0 K Morgan, ... (14 to 1) 5
176[3] INCA CHIEF 9-12-0 T J Taaffe, ... (5 to 2) 6
112[3] KALONA 6-11-9 (5*) Mr G J Harford, ... (6 to 1) 7
92[3] BIRDIE'S PRINCE 8-12-0 C O'Dwyer, ...(20 to 1) ur
133 CLASSIC CHEER (Ire) 5-11-5 (3*) J Jones, ...(20 to 1) pu
133 CHESTNUT JEWEL (Ire) 5-11-8 P McWilliams, ... (14 to 1) pu
PEBBLE BROOK 6-12-0 K F O'Brien, ... (20 to 1) pu

Dist: ¾l, 20l, 6l, 6l. 5m 39.30s. (11 Ran).
(Aidan Comerford), A Redmond

201 Summer INH Flat Race (4-y-o and up) £2,245 2½m..................... (8:30)

124[4] LE BRAVE 7-11-7 (7*) Mr M Brennan, ... (Evens fav) 1

109⁷ A FEW GOOD MEN (Ire) (bl) 4-11-7 Mr E Bolger, ...(7 to 2) 2
133 CARRIGANS LAD (Ire) 5-11-7 (7") Mr R Pugh, ...(25 to 1) 3
114 JENNYELLEN (Ire) 4-11-12 Mr A J Martin, ...(10 to 1) 4
79⁶ KIZZY ROSE 6-11-12 (7") Miss C Hourigan, ...(6 to 1) 5
98² MAGNIFICENT OAK (NZ) 5-11-9 (5") Mr C T G Kinane,
....(7 to 1) 6
150⁶ HAWAIIAN GODDESS (USA) 6-11-4 (5") Mr G J Harford,
....(12 to 1) 7
53⁵ AR AGHAIDH LEATH 7-11-11 (3") Mr A R Coonan, (20 to 1) 8
112⁹ OYSTER LANE 7-11-4 (5") Mr J A Nash, ...(14 to 1) 9
ALWAYS YOU (Ire) 5-11-2 (7") Mr P J Walsh, ...(10 to 1) 10
98 CLANMANY (Ire) (bl) 4-11-0 (7") Mr B Lennon, ... (50 to 1) 11
Dist: ¾l, 4l, 6l, 11l. 5m 12.50s. (11 Ran).

(D Cox), J H Scott

FONTWELL (firm)
Wednesday August 11th
Going Correction: MINUS 0.45 sec. per fur.

202 County Ground Novices' Claiming Hurdle
(4-y-o and up) £1,704 2¾m.........(2:00)

155 QUIET RIOT 11-10-12 A Maguire, hld up, 3rd 4 out, led 2
out, rdn out.................... (2 to 1 on op 6 to 4 on) 1
197⁴ SILVERCROSS LAD (bl) 10-11-3 (7") N Juckes, led aftr 1st
till aftr 3 out, btn whn mstk last.
.... (14 to 1 op 8 to 1 tchd 16 to 1) 2
LONDON EXPRESS 9-10-7 Peter Hobbs, trkd ldr, led aftr
3 out, pckd and hdd nxt, one pace... (6 to 1 op 7 to 1) 3
185 APACHE PRINCE (bl) 6-11-1 M A FitzGerald, led and jmpd
slwly 1st, sn hdd, lost pl aftr 7th, no ch 4 out, tld off.
....(10 to 1 tchd 8 to 1) 4
SUKEY TAWDRY 7-10-81 W Elderfield, hld up, hday to
chase ldr 7th, sn rdn and wknd quickly 4 out, tld off.
..............................(100 to 1 op 50 to 1) 5
165³ VICTORIOUS KING (bl) 7-11-1 R Dunwoody, hld up, hdway
7th, chsd ldr till rdn and wknd aftr 3 out, pld up and
dismounted r-in, lme.... (6 to 1 op 9 to 1 tchd 7 to 1) pu
165 COMIC LINE 8-10-8 (7") Miss S Mitchell, jmpd big, lost tch
aftr 4th, sn tld off, sddl slpd and pld up aftr 3 out.
..............................(100 to 1 op 50 to 1) pu
Dist: 6l, 3l, 20l, 25l. 5m 18.90s. a 9.90s (7 Ran).

(Ms M Horan), J White

203 Lord Walberton Novices' Selling Handicap
Hurdle (4-y-o and up) £1,748 2¼m... (2:30)

BILLY LOMOND (Ire) [70] 5-10-9 Peter Hobbs, trkd ldrs, led
5th, made rst, rdn and styd on whn chlgd aftr 2 out, all
out..............(9 to 4 jt-fav op 11 to 4 tchd 2 to 1) 1
186⁴ MOYMET [91] (bl) 7-11-2 (6ex) G McCourt, jnd ldr 3 out, ev
ch whn mstk last, rdn and rallied r-in, not quicken nr
finish.......... (9 to 4 jt-fav op 7 to 4 tchd 11 to 4) 2
BROUGHTON BLUES (Ire) [65] 5-10-4 D Murphy, mstks,
trkd ldr till dsptd 4 out, jmpd slwly nxt, sn rdn and
wknd.......................... (6 to 1 op 5 to 1) 3
SUNLEY SPARKLE [61] 5-10-0 A Smith, hld up, effrt and
chsd ldrs aftr 5th, one pace 4 out.
.............................(7 to 2 op 4 to 1 tchd 9 to 2) 4
ELEGANT TOUCH [69] (bl) 4-10-8 R Dunwoody, led till 5th,
sn rdn and reluctant to race, tld off. (7 to 1 op 4 to 1) 5
151 NOW BOARDING [61] 6-9-81 (7") Mr N Bradley, hld up,
mstks 1st and 3rd, lost tch aftr 4th, tld off whn pld up
bef 6th.............(25 to 1 op 33 to 1 tchd 20 to 1) pu
Dist: 1l, 20l, 15l, dist. 4m 12.00s. a 2.00s (6 Ran).

(P J Hobbs), P J Hobbs

204 Foreign And Colonial Novices' Chase (4-
y-o and up) £2,163 2¼m........... (3:00)

184⁴ PEARLS BEAU 6-12-0 S Smith Eccles, jmpd boldly, made
all, clr aftr 8th, eased r-in, unchlgd.
.....................................(5 to 1 on op 4 to 1 on) 1
184⁵ DECIDING BID 7-11-7 A Maguire, chsd ldr till 8th, no ch
aftr nxt, one pace 5 out. (9 to 2 op 7 to 1 tchd 4 to 1) 2
APRIL'S BABY 9-11-2 I Lawrence, al last, jmpd slwly 4th,
beh 8th, one pace four out.
..............................(12 to 1 op 8 to 1 tchd 14 to 1) 3
Dist: 3½l, 8l. 4m 37.00s. a 17.00s (3 Ran).

(Mrs T McCoubrey), J R Jenkins

205 Greenwood Googly Handicap Hurdle
(0-125 4-y-o and up) £1,780 2¼m.... (3:30)

RULING DYNASTY [105] (bl) 9-11-10 H Davies, hld up in
last, steady hdwy to cl on ldrs 3 out, led last, pushed clr
r-in, styd on wl.
..........(10 to 1 op 5 to 1 tchd 11 to 1 and 12 to 1) 1
183² STRIDING EDGE [90] 8-10-9 R Dunwoody, trkd ldg pair, cl
up and ev ch 3 out, took second appr nxt, sn hrd rdn,
not quicken..........(9 to 2 tchd 5 to 1 and 4 to 1) 2
149⁴ BEN ZABEEDY [103] 8-11-8 (6ex) G McCourt, hld up,
pushed alng to track ldrs 5th, led aftr 3 out, wknd from
hdd last, unbl to quicken...... (2 to 1 fav tchd 9 to 4) 3

156² CARPET CAPERS (USA) [86] 9-10-5 A Maguire, led till aftr
1st, pressed ldr, led 3 out, sn hdd and wknd.
.... (11 to 4 op 4 to 1) 4
ALICE'S MIRROR [92] 4-10-11 W McFarland, led aftr 1st,
hit 4 out, hdd nxt, sn rdn and btn. (11 to 4 op 5 to 2) 5
Dist: 7l, nk, 10l, 3l. 4m 10.00s. (5 Ran).
SR: 15/-/5/-/-/   (Carl West-Meads), M D I Usher

206 G.P.S. Print Ltd Handicap Chase (0-125
5-y-o and up) £2,269 2¼m....... (4:00)

ST ATHANS LAD [125] (bl) 8-12-0 D Morris, made all, hrd
rdn aftr 3 out, styd on wl..................(11 to 8 jt-
fav op Evens tchd 6 to 4) 1
GLASS MOUNTAIN [97] (bl) 10-10-0 A Maguire, pressed ldr
till 8th, rallied and took second aftr tenth, ev ch 3 out,
rdn and no imprsn r-in.
.... (8 to 1 op 10 to 1 tchd 14 to 1) 2
143³ TOUCHING WOOD (bl) 8-9-11 (3") M Hourigan, hld up,
took 3rd aftr 8th, rdn and no imprsn after 4 out.
................................(11 to 8 jt-fav op 7 to 4) 3
DEVIL'S VALLEY [118] (bl) 10-11-7 H Davies, trkd ldg pair,
mstk 3rd, took second nxt, mistake nxt, wknd quickly.
tld off 4 out..................(14 to 1 op 7 to 1 tchd 16 to 1) 4
HEIGHT OF FUN [101] 9-10-44 M A FitzGerald, tld off aftr
second..............................(10 to 1 op 8 to 1) 5
Dist: 2l, 12l, dist, 4l. 4m 23.20s. a 3.20s (5 Ran).

(Geyer Estates Limited (St Athans Hotel)), R Curtis

207 Sussex Young Cricketers Novices' Hurdle
(3-y-o and up) £1,689 2¼m......... (4:30)

SINGING DETECTIVE (v) 6-11-3 (7") G Crone, led, sn clr,
rdn 2 out, styd on wl, unchlgd.
.......................(7 to 1 op 5 to 1 tchd 8 to 1) 1
191 WELL APPOINTED (Ire) 4-11-7 A S Smith, chsd ldr, rdn aftr
3 out, mstk nxt, sn no imprsn. soon no impression, one
pace.....................(7 to 4 fav op 6 to 4 tchd 2 to 1) 2
EASY TOOMEY 5-11-10 S Smith Eccles, hld up, hdwy aftr
6th, no imprsn appr 2 out, tld off.
...........................(20 to 1 op 12 to 1 tchd 25 to 1) 3
FRANK'S THE NAME 4-11-7 T Grantham, chsd ldr to 6th,
sn wknd, tld off 3 out................ (11 to 2 op 4 to 1) 4
ROCKY ROMANCE 6-11-10 D Morris, chsd ldrs, wnt 3rd
6th, sn wknd, tld off...............(25 to 1 op 14 to 1) 5
COVEN MOON 3-10-0 M Richards, hld up, mstk second,
sn lost tch, tld off 5th. (10 to 1 op 6 to 1 tchd 12 to 1) 6
WEST END GIRL 3-10-0 C Llewellyn, sn beh, tld off 5th,
blun last.............................(25 to 1 tchd 16 to 1) 7
ROSEMARY'S MEMORY (Ire) 3-9-92 (7") P Moore, jmpd rght
1st, ran wide bend aftr 4th, beh whn f nxt.
.... (33 to 1 op 20 to 1) f
GREAT HAND 7-11-5 (5") C Burnett-Wells, hld up, lost tch
5th, sn tld off, pld up bef 2 out.
.............................(9 to 4 op 5 to 2 tchd 2 to 1) pu
MASTAMIST (bl) 4-11-4 (3") D O'Sullivan, jmpd poorly, lost
tch aftr 3rd, sn tld off, pld up bef 3 out.
.............................(50 to 1 op 16 to 1) pu
Dist: 20l, dist, 20l, 2l, 20l. 4m 9.70s. b 0.30s (10 Ran).
SR: 18/-/-/-/-/-/   (Elaine Mills & K Powell), P M McEntee

SLIGO (IRE) (heavy)
Wednesday August 11th

208 Strandhill Maiden Hurdle (4-y-o and up)
£2,243 2m........................... (2:30)

GREEN GLEN (USA) 4-11-9 C F Swan, ... (9 to 4 on) 1
124 WINDOVER LODGE 6-11-6 J F Titley, ...(4 to 1) 2
160⁹ CLYDE PRINCE 8-11-6 J Shortt, ...(10 to 1) 3
99⁵ CAT FIGHT 6-10-8 (7") M A Ryan, ...(20 to 1) 4
102 SIRAJAO (Ire) 4-10-8 (5") T P Rudd, ...(33 to 1) 5
WEE RIVER (Ire) 4-11-4 Mr T S Costello, ...(7 to 1) 6
160 SHINDWA (Ire) 4-10-10 (3") J Jones, ...(33 to 1) pu
94 ARISTOLIGHT (Ire) 4-10-6 (7") J P Broderick, ...(33 to 1) pu
115 ROVANIEMI (Ire) 5-11-6 P McWilliams, ...(20 to 1) pu
Dist: 4l, 6l, dist, 7l. 4m 27.40s. (9 Ran).

(Neil S McGrath), Neil S McGrath

209 Heineken Novice Hurdle (4-y-o and up)
£2,760 2m........................... (3:00)

ROSE APPEAL 7-11-8 C F Swan, ...(5 to 1) 1
37⁴ VICOSA (Ire) 4-11-4 (5") T F Lacy Jnr, ...(10 to 1) 2
161³ FABRICATOR 7-12-0 K Morgan, ...(7 to 4 jt-fav) 3
62³ LET IT RIDE (Ire) 4-11-9 P Carberry, ...(7 to 4 jt-fav) 4
MAY WE DANCE (Ire) 4-10-12 J P Banahan, ...(20 to 1) 5
Dist: 8l, 3½l, 15l, dist. 2m 24.20s. (5 Ran).

(Mrs P Mullins), P Mullins

210 Heineken Sligo Handicap Chase (0-116
4-y-o and up) £3,278 2½m.......... (4:00)

BUNNINADDEN [-] 10-9-7 W T Slattery Jnr, ...(12 to 1) 1
119⁸ LIFE OF A LORD [-] 7-11-10 C O'Dwyer, ...(2 to 1) 2
121²¹ MAYE FANE [-] 9-11-6 (3") G Kilfeather, ...(5 to 1) 3

25

120² WHO'S FOOLING WHO [-] 7-10-5 C F Swan, ... (Evens fav)   4
178 COURSING GUY [-] (bl) 11-10-9 M Flynn, ... (14 to 1)   5
Dist: 2l, hd, 4½l, dist. 5m 58.70s. (5 Ran).

(L Gormley), John J Walsh

211   Mullaghmore INH Flat Race (4-y-o and up) £2,243 2m . . . . (5:30)

NORA ANN (Ire) 4-10-13 (5") Mr G J Harford, ... (3 to 1)   1
98⁴ DROP THE HAMMER (Ire) 4-11-2 (7") Mr R Pugh, . . . (7 to 1)   2
159⁵ OZONE RIVER (Ire) 5-11-2 (7") Mr S O'Donnell, ... (8 to 1)   3
162⁵ FURTHER APPRAISAL (Ire) 4-10-11 (7") Mr P J Dreeling,
. . . . (5 to 1)   4
114⁵ WHAT IT IS (Ire) 4-10-13 (5") Mr J A Nash, ... (6 to 1 fav)   5
MISS CIRCLE (Ire) 4-10-11 (7") Mr J Bright, ... (20 to 1)   6
98 BRIGADIER SUPREME (Ire) 4-11-9 Mr T S Costello,
. . . . (20 to 1)   7
162⁹ RING DONG LASS (Ire) 4-10-11 (7") Mr A Daly, ... (16 to 1)   8
162 ABBEY TRINITY (Ire) 4-10-11 (7") Mr D J Kavanagh, (33 to 1)   9
98 MARCHING SEASON (Ire) 5-11-2 (7") Mr D A Harney,
. . . . (16 to 1)   10
70 IM OK (Ire) 5-11-9 Mr A J Martin, ... (20 to 1)   11
TORMORE LADY (Ire) 5-11-2 (7") Mr P J Tynan, . . (14 to 1)   pu
Dist: 2l, 8l, dist. 4m 30.30s. (12 Ran).

(Mrs Ann Ennis), Francis Ennis

TRAMORE (IRE) (good (races 1,2,4), good to firm (3))
Wednesday August 11th

212   Strand QR Maiden Hurdle (4-y-o and up) £2,245 2½m . . . . (5:30)

120⁵ MERRY PEOPLE (Ire) 5-11-6 Mr E Bolger, ... (5 to 1)   1
124⁷ TAYLORS QUAY (Ire) 5-11-7 (7") Mr K Whelan, . . (5 to 4 on)   2
94* GAYLOIRE (Ire) 4-11-0 (7") Mr T J Murphy, ... (13 to 2)   3
MOUNTAIN SKY 7-11-4 (5") Mr J P Berry, ... (9 to 1)   4
FOR KEVIN 6-10-13 (7") Mr K Taylor, ... (14 to 1)   5
108⁸ TRIPLE ACE (Ire) 4-10-9 (7") Mr N D Fehily, ... (20 to 1)   6
SILENTBROOK 8-11-1 Mr P J Healy, ... (20 to 1)   7
111 BUCKTAN (bl) 7-10-8 (7") Mr T N Cloke, ... (14 to 1)   8
96⁵ ANOTHER BONNY 7-11-1 (5") Mr C T G Kinane, . . (16 to 1)   9
79 PARSONS TOI 8-10-8 (7") Mr M Leahy, ... (33 to 1)   10
73⁶ BULGADEN CASTLE 5-10-13 (7") Mr B Moran, . . . (14 to 1)   11
GOING DOWN 8-10-8 (7") Mr K O'Sullivan, ... (25 to 1)   12
169 CITSIROMA (bl) 9-10-8 (7") Mr P O'Keeffe, ... (25 to 1)   su
BE CREATIVE (Ire) 5-10-13 (7") Mr A K Wyse, ... (16 to 1)   pu
169 FINAL OPTION (Ire) (bl) 5-11-0¹ (7") Mr T J Nagle Jnr,
. . . . (33 to 1)   pu
Dist: 1l, 2½l, 1l, 6l. 4m 44.10s. (15 Ran).

(Karl Casey), John Queally

213   Lismore Handicap Hurdle (95-123 4-y-o and up) £2,245 2½m . . . . (6:00)

135 THE VERY MAN [-] 7-11-4 (7") T P Treacy, ... (5 to 2 jt-fav)   1
90* FIRST SESSION [-] 5-11-5 K F O'Brien, ... (3 to 1)   2
175² SILVER GIPSEY [-] 7-11-1 P L Malone, ... (5 to 2 jt-fav)   3
135 CHARLIES DELIGHT [-] 5-11-1 T Horgan, ... (7 to 1)   4
100⁵ MARBLE CITY GIRL [-] 8-10-10 A J O'Brien, ... (8 to 1)   5
135⁹ ACTION DANCER [-] 7-11-4 (7") C O'Brien, ... (12 to 1)   6
MISS EUROLINK [-] 6-11-1 Mr S R Murphy, ... (14 to 1)   7
Dist: 2½l, 6l, 11l, 4l. 4m 36.60s. (7 Ran).

(F P Taaffe), P Mullins

214   Park Hotel Festival Handicap Chase (4-y-o and up) £2,590 2½m . . . . (6:30)

178 ANN'S PRINCE [-] 10-9-13 H Rogers, ... (12 to 1)   1
121* MACK A DAY [-] 6-11-7 (7ex) A J O'Brien, ... (100 to 30)   2
134³ WATERLOO ANDY [-] 7-10-11 F J Flood, ... (4 to 1)   3
134 JAMES PIGG [-] 6-11-4 T Horgan, ... (8 to 1)   4
178³ BALLYVERANE [-] 7-9-13 (5") D P Geoghegan, ... (7 to 1)   5
116² QUAYSIDE BUOY [-] 10-11-11 K F O'Brien, ... (6 to 4 fav)   6
Dist: Sht-hd, 4l, 2l, 3l. 4m 54.00s. (6 Ran).

(Bernard Stack), Gerard Stack

215   Dungarvan INH Flat Race (4-y-o and up) £2,245 2m . . . . (8:00)

AFGHANI (Ire) 4-11-4 (5") Mrs J M Mullins, ... (2 to 1)   1
124² OX EYE DAISY (Ire) 5-11-6 (3") Mrs M Mullins, . . (6 to 4 fav)   2
31⁴ ANOTHER COURSE (Ire) 5-11-7 (7") Mr P M Cloke, (6 to 1)   3
107 QUARTER MARKER (Ire) 5-11-7 (7") Mr P English, (14 to 1)   4
159² SLEMISH MINSTREL 7-11-7 (7") Mr I Johnston, . . . (9 to 1)   5
55 WEDDING DREAM (Ire) 4-11-2 (7") Mr D Valentine, (33 to 1)   6
CALL THE KING (Ire) 4-11-2 (7") Mr J McNamara, (7 to 1)   7
DRUID'S DAWN 8-11-4 (5") Mr J Wyse, ... (14 to 1)   8
174 CASTLE CELEBRITY (Ire) 4-10-11 (7") Mr R Burns, (10 to 1)   9
53 ABDUL EMIR 6-11-7 (7") Mr A H Lillingston, ... (14 to 1)   10
179 DAYLIGHT LADY (bl) 6-11-9 Mr D M O'Brien, ... (33 to 1)   11
Dist: 12l, 9l, 5½l, 9l. 3m 48.40s. (11 Ran).

(Mrs J M Mullins), W P Mullins

NEWTON ABBOT (good to firm)

Thursday August 12th
Going Correction: NIL

216   Wallabrook Novices' Hurdle (4-y-o and up) £1,948 2m 1f . . . . (2:00)

168* ATHAR (Ire) 4-10-12 L Harvey, hld up, hdwy 5th, wnt second aftr 3 out, slight ld 2 out, drvn out r-in.
. . . . (9 to 4 op 7 to 4 tchd 5 to 2)   1
151* MERLINS WISH (USA) 4-11-3 R Dunwoody, trkd ldrs, led aftr 3 out, hdd nxt, rdn and not quicken.
. . . . (5 to 2 on op 2 to 1 on tchd 11 to 4 on)   2
JR'S PET 6-10-4 (5") R Davis, hld up, hdwy to chase ldrs aftr 5th, wnt 3rd appr 2 out, no imprsn on 1st two.
. . . . (50 to 1 op 16 to 1)   3
191 MY HARRY BOY 6-11-0 G Upton, hld up, hdwy 4th, led appr nxt til hdd aftr 3 out, sn rdn and wknd quickly.
. . . . (20 to 1 tchd 40 to 1)   4
JACKSON SQUARE (Ire) 5-11-0 S Burrough, pressed ldrs til wknd quickly aftr 5th, sn tld off. (100 to 1 op 20 to 1)   5
SEASIDE MINSTREL 5-10-9 (5") D Leahy, set slow pace til hdd aftr second, pressed ldr until wknd quickly after 5th, sn tld off, fifth and no ch whn f last.
. . . . (100 to 1 op 20 to 1)   f
INTUITIVE JOE 6-11-0 B Powell, led aftr second til appr 5th, wknd rpdly, tld off whn pld up bef 2 out.
. . . . (100 to 1 op 20 to 1)   pu
BRACE OF PHEASANTS 4-10-6 D Skyrme, jmpd slwly 1st, lost tch aftr 4th, sn tld off, pld up bef 2 out.
. . . . (66 to 1 op 16 to 1)   pu
Dist: 5l, 25l, 10l, dist. 4m 9.80s. a 19.80s (8 Ran).

(J W Buxton), R J Baker

217   Avon Selling Handicap Hurdle (4-y-o and up) £1,838 2¾m . . . . (2:30)

STANE STREET (Ire) [78] 5-10-4 J Railton, led second til aftr 6th, led ag'n nxt, all out.
. . . . (13 to 2 op 5 to 1 tchd 8 to 1)   1
195* ROWHEDGE [80] 7-9-13 (7") S Curran, trkd ldr, led aftr 6th til nxt, cl up and ev ch 3 out, rdn and not quicken nr finish. . . . . (5 to 2 fav op 3 to 1)   2
166* TRUST DEED (USA) [81] (bl) 5-10-7 (7ex) M A FitzGerald, trkd ldg pair, cl up and ev ch 4 out, rdn appr 2 out, styd on aftr last, not quicken nr finish.
. . . . (13 to 2 op 4 to 1 tchd 15 to 2)   3
164* EMMA VICTORIA [75] 5-10-11 (7ex) D Gallagher, hld up in tch, chsd ldrs frm 4 out, rdn and one pace betw last 2.
. . . . (8 to 1 op 5 to 1)   4
164² CELCIUS [102] (bl) 9-12-0 R Dunwoody, hld up, hdwy to chase ldrs aftr 4 out, rdn and no imprsn appr 2 out, wknd approaching last. (7 to 2 op 3 to 1 tchd 4 to 1)   5
144⁹ STAPLEFORD LADY [74] 5-9-9 (5") D Leahy, hld up in last pl, lost tch aftr 6th, tld off. . . . . . (50 to 1 op 20 to 1)   6
125³ PANATHINAIKOS (USA) [75] 8-10-1 B Powell, hld up, pld up lme aftr 6th. . . . . (7 to 1 tchd 8 to 1)   pu
168 SNOOKER TABLE [79] 10-10-5 D Gallagher, led to second, sn lost pl, wl beh 6th, tld off whn pld up bef 4 out.
. . . . (8 to 1 tchd 10 to 1)   pu
168⁴ FASHION PRINCESS [74] 7-9-7 (7") D Matthews, chsd ldrs, wnt 4th at 6th, wknd aftr four out, beh whn pld up bef 2 out. . . . . (14 to 1 op 8 to 1)   pu
Dist: Nk, nk, 2½l, 20l. 5m 15.00s. a 16.00s (9 Ran).

(Jim Reade), R T Phillips

218   South West Racing Club Novices' Chase (5-y-o and up) £2,762 2m 5f . . . . (3:00)

BELAFONTE 6-11-4 G Bradley, hld up, hdwy 8th, wnt second appr nxt, chsd ldr til led 2 out, drvn clr r-in.
. . . . (11 to 8 op 11 to 10 tchd 6 to 4)   1
OLD BRIG (bl) 7-11-4 R Dunwoody, led jmpd slwly tenth, hdd 2 out, not quicken.
. . . . (6 to 5 fav op Evens tchd 11 to 8)   2
165 NEEDS MUST 6-11-4 J Frost, chsd ldrs, wnt moderate 3rd 4 out, no imprsn on 1st 2.
. . . . (11 to 1 op 8 to 1 tchd 12 to 1)   3
154⁸ DANNY'S LUCK (NZ) 11-11-4 S Mackey, mstk 7th, reminders aftr nxt, sn lost tch, tld off 5 out.
. . . . (50 to 1 op 33 to 1)   4
CORNISH COSSACK (NZ) 6-10-13 (5") R Davis, pressed ldr til wknd aftr 8th, tld off 5 out.
. . . . (8 to 1 op 6 to 1 tchd 10 to 1)   5
WIN ELECTRIC 7-10-13 Mr W Henderson, tld off aftr second, pld up aftr 8th. . . . . (33 to 1 op 16 to 1)   pu
ROUCHEAL 8-11-4 N Hawke, pressed ldrs til wknd quickly aftr 7th, sn tld off, pld up aftr 9th.
. . . . (33 to 1 op 16 to 1)   pu
Dist: 7l, 25l, 8l, 15l. 5m 7.20s. a 7.20s (7 Ran).
SR: 18/11/-/-/

(A P Boden), C P E Brooks

219   Aller Park Handicap Hurdle (4-y-o and up) £2,563 2m 1f . . . . (3:30)

MISTER LAWSON [93] 7-10-0 I Shoemark, hld up, hdwy 5th, 3rd whn untidy 3 out, led appr 2 out, rdn clr r-in.
. . . . (2 to 1 fav op 5 to 2)   1

PHARLY STORY [115] (bl) 5-11-8 R Dunwoody, *hld up, wnt second appr 5th, pressed ldr and ev ch aftr 3 out, rdn and no imprsn frm 2 out*.............(5 to 2 op 6 to 4)   2
SHALCHLO BOY [100] 9-10-7 N Williamson, *prmnt to 4th, lost pl, styd on ag'n aftr 3 out, nvr nrr.*
.................................(20 to 1 op 12 to 1)   3
TIGER CLAW (USA) [117] 7-11-10 M A FitzGerald, *chsd ldrs to 5th, wknd quickly, sn beh.*
.................................(100 to 30 op 5 to 2 tchd 7 to 2)   4
INNOCENT PRINCESS (NZ) [93] 6-10-0⁵ (5*) R Davis, *led, sn clr, wknd rpdly aftr 3 out*...........(9 to 2 op 7 to 1)   5
KADAN (Ger) [117] 9-11-10 Tracy Turner, *hld up, wnt second 4th, mstk nxt, sn beh*...........(12 to 1 op 8 to 1)   6
Dist: 6l, 20l, 5l, 1l, 10l. 4m 3.50s. a 13.50s (6 Ran).

(W McKibbin), B Forsey

220 Pine Lodge Challenge Trophy Handicap Chase (0-125 5-y-o and up) £3,074 3¼m 110yds..........................(4:00)

MR TITTLE TATTLE [97] (bl) 7-10-0 N Williamson, *trkd ldr, wnt second 6th, ev ch frm six out, hrd rdn to ld betw last 2, drvn out r-in, styd on wl.*
.................(11 to 8 op 6 to 4 tchd 15 to 8)   1
143* SKIPPING TIM [125] 14-12-0 R Dunwoody, *led, rallied whn chlgd 3 out, hdd betw last 2, not quicken.*
.................(6 to 5 fav op Evens tchd 5 to 4)   2
154* JACK THE HIKER [97] 10-10-0 (7ex) M Richards, *wnt 3rd 11th, chsd 1st 2 til wknd quickly 6 out, tld off.*
.................................(8 to 1 op 5 to 1)   3
167 SAMSUN [102] 11-10-5⁵ M A FitzGerald, *reminders aftr 6th, drpd rear 8th, tld off 14th.*
.................(12 to 1 op 10 to 1 tchd 14 to 1)   4
167⁴ CLEANING UP [97] 11-10-0 B Powell, *3rd whn blun tenth, sn reco'red, chsd ldrs til wknd 14th, tld off.*
.................................(20 to 1 op 10 to 1)   5
127 DUNRAVEN ROYAL [97] (bl) 10-10-0 D Morris, *jmpd slwly 3rd, rear and reminders 13th, tld off whn pld up bef 6 out.*...................(25 to 1 op 14 to 1)   pu
Dist: 4l, dist, 3½l, 15l. 6m 31.50s. a 11.50s (6 Ran).

(Mrs J K Newton), K C Bailey

221 Knowles Hill Juvenile Novices' Hurdle (3-y-o) £1,822 2m 1f..................(4:30)

147* THE EXECUTOR 11-4 R Dunwoody, *trkd ldr, led appr 2 out, clr last, drvn out r-in.*
.................(7 to 1 on op 5 to 1 on tchd 8 to 1 on)   1
188³ FREE DANCER 10-7 D Bridgwater, *beh, pushed alng appr 5th, wnt 3rd nxt, hrd rdn approaching 2 out, btn whn mstk last*...............(13 to 2 op 6 to 1 tchd 7 to 1)   2
147⁴ APACHEE FLOWER 10-0 (7*) Mr G Lewis, *wnt 3rd 4th, chsd ldr, rdn and styd on one pace aftr 3 out.*
.................................(20 to 1 op 16 to 1 tchd 40 to 1)   3
VENTURE PRINTS 10-12 R Bellamy, *hld up, beh whn blun 3 out, styd on appr nxt, nvr nrr...* (66 to 1 op 25 to 1)   4
188⁸ QUEENS CONTRACTOR (bl) 10-12 S Keightley, *led, sn clr, hdd aftr 3 out, wknd quickly.*
.................(16 to 1 op 14 to 1 tchd 20 to 1)   5
GREAT PLOVER 10-12 S Burrough, *tld off 3rd, mstk 5th, pld up bef 2 out*.............(66 to 1 op 20 to 1)   pu
Dist: 8l, ½l, 10l, 12l. 4m 8.50s. a 18.50s (6 Ran).

(Jack Joseph), M C Pipe

UTTOXETER (good to firm)
Thursday August 12th
Going Correction: MINUS 0.40 sec. per fur.

222 Famous Grouse Conditional Jockeys' Handicap Hurdle (0-115 5-y-o and up) £1,532 3m 110yds.................(5:45)

BRIDGE PLAYER [85] 6-11-3 D J Moffatt, *in tch, lost pos 8th, gd hdwy nxt, led 3 out, pushed out.*
.................................(4 to 1 op 5 to 1)   1
SMILES AHEAD [88] 5-11-6 N Bentley, *made most to 6th, styd pressing ldr till led 8th, hdd 3 out, stayed on.*
.................(11 to 2 op 5 to 1 tchd 6 to 1)   2
190⁶ KASHAN (Ire) [87] 5-11-5 R Farrant, *al frnt rnk, chlgd 3 out, styd on same pace frm nxt.* (20 to 1 tchd 16 to 1)   3
125* LITTLE BIG [90] 6-11-3 (5*) A Flannagan, *with ldrs, lost pl aftr 8th, ran on appr 3 out, sn rdn, no imprsn.*
.................(7 to 2 fav op 9 to 4)   4
STROKED AGAIN [78] 8-10-10 A Thornton, *chsd ldrs 4th, rdn and no prog frm 9th*...............(33 to 1)   5
THARSIS [95] 8-11-13 S Taylor, *prmnt, wth ldr 3rd till led 6th, hdd 8th, wknd aftr 8th*.....(7 to 1 op 4 to 1)   6
KHOJOHN [96] 5-11-9 (5*) C Woodall, *hdwy to chase ldrs 7th, wknd aftr 8th......* (6 to 1 op 4 to 1 tchd 13 to 2)   7
GRACE MOORE [90] 9-11-8 R Greene, *beh frm 7th.*
.................................(10 to 1)   8
125⁵ COMING ALIVE [84] 6-11-2 J Supple, *mstk 1st, beh, hdwy 8th, 4th and wl hld whn f 2 out*...............(10 to 1)   f

167³ THEY ALL FORGOT ME [85] 6-11-3 J McCarthy, *chsd ldrs till wknd quickly 7th, tld off whn pld up bef 2 out.*
.................................(7 to 1 op 6 to 1)   pu
Dist: 5l, 2l, 7l, 15l, 4l, 2l, 4l. 5m 50.00s. a 18.00s (10 Ran).

(D A & M Lambert And Partners), D Moffatt

223 Bunnahabhain Novices' Chase (5-y-o and up) £1,707 2m 5f..................(6:15)

168³ KILLULA CHIEF 6-11-10 M Dwyer, *chsd ldr 6th, led 7th, hdd 8th, led ag'n 3 out, mstk last, ran on wl.*
.................................(2 to 1 op 5 to 2)   1
165* NORSTOCK 6-11-7 A Maguire, *hld up, hdwy to chal 7th, led 8th, hdd 3 out, sn drvn, btn appr last.*
.................(13 to 8 on op 11 to 4 on)   2
MOURNE WARRIOR 10-11-0 A O'Hagan, *chsd ldr to 6th, sn rdn, wknd 8th, tld off*.....(20 to 1 op 12 to 1)   3
189⁶ SOLICITOR'S CHOICE (bl) 10-11-0 J Railton, *led and sn clr, hdd 7th, soon btn, tld off.*
.................(9 to 1 op 8 to 1 tchd 10 to 1)   4
139⁴ CAREFREE TIMES (v) 6-11-0 A Mulholland, *al beh, mstk second, hit 5th, tld off 6th*.......(33 to 1 op 20 to 1)   5
Dist: 4l, dist, ¾l, 20l. 5m 2.20s. a 2.20s (5 Ran).

(T G K Construction Ltd), J G M O'Shea

224 Highland Park Selling Hurdle (4,5,6-y-o) £1,119 2½m 110yds.................(6:45)

ON THE SAUCE (bl) 6-11-10 R Dunwoody, *made most till hdd 6th, sn led ag'n, clr 2 out, eased r-in.*
.................(5 to 2 on op 9 to 4 on tchd 7 to 4 on)   1
SHOW THE FLAG 5-11-0 (7*) N Juckes, *took str hold, chsd ldrs, chased wnr frm 3 out, no imprsn.*
.................(6 to 1 op 4 to 1 tchd 13 to 2)   2
GREEN'S SEAGO (USA) 5-11-1 J A Harris, *beh, drvn alng frm 6th, styd on and pres frm 3 out.*
.................................(20 to 1 op 14 to 1)   3
BAYBEEJAY 6-11-2 G McCourt, *beh, drvn alng appr 6th, no imprsn*.................(9 to 1 op 14 to 1)   4
RAAWI 5-11-1 A Maguire, *pressed wnr, second till led briefly 6th, sn hdd, wknd appr 3 out.*
.................(11 to 2 op 4 to 1 tchd 6 to 1)   5
126⁷ ALAMIR (USA) 5-11-1 J Railton, *in tch, rdn appr 6th, 4th and one pace whn f 7th.*
.................(40 to 1 op 33 to 1 tchd 50 to 1)   f
Dist: 4l, nk, 1l, 3l, 6l. 4m 55.60s. a 12.60s (6 Ran).

(Goldsmith, Langham & Thompson Partners), M C Pipe

225 Famous Grouse Handicap Chase (0-125 5-y-o and up) £2,158 2m.................(7:15)

MEGA BLUE [112] 8-11-12 P Niven, *drpd out in rear, smooth hdwy aftr 6th, led 4 out, readily.*
.................................(5 to 2 op 9 to 4)   1
152³ POLDER [90] 7-9-13 (5*) R Davis, *chsd ldrs, styd on to chase wnr and mstk 2 out, one pace.*
.................(6 to 1 op 7 to 1 tchd 9 to 1)   2
187² TINAS LAD [105] 10-11-5 N Williamson, *pressed ldr till led 5th, blun 6th, hdd 4 out, sn outpcd aftr 3 out.*
.................(6 to 4 fav op 5 to 4 tchd 7 to 4)   3
141 STORMGUARD [86] 10-9-13⁴ (5*) T Eley, *beh, effrt aftr 6th, sn wknd*.................(33 to 1)   4
182³ COTAPAXI [96] 8-10-10 R Dunwoody, *made most till hdd whn pace whn f 7th.*.....(3 to 1 op 5 to 2)   5
Dist: 7l, 4l, 12l, ¾l. 3m 49.10s. a 0.10s (5 Ran).
SR: 33/4/15/-/-/

(Tony Yates), Mrs V A Aconley

226 Tamdhu Trophy Claiming Hurdle (4-y-o and up) £1,553 2m.................(7:45)

166 MILLROUS (bl) 5-10-7 R Dunwoody, *hld up, hdwy frm 6th, styd on chal last, sn led, pushed out.*
.................(4 to 1 fav op 5 to 2 tchd 9 to 2)   1
JAMESTOWN BOY (bl) 5-11-10 T Wall, *beh, losing pl and drvn 6th, hdwy appr 3 out, wnt nxt, hdd sn aftr last, not quicken*.........................(9 to 2 op 7 to 2)   2
NEARCTIC BAY (USA) 7-10-9 (3*) M Hourigan, *chsd ldrs, rdn frm 5th, led 3 out, hdd and ev ch nxt, sn one pace.*
.................(6 to 1 op 7 to 1)   3
NORTHERN NATION 5-12-0 Diane Clay, *beh and mstk 5th, hdwy appr 3 out, ev ch 2 out, wknd approaching last.*
....   4
181³ KEY DEAR (Fr) 6-11-3 (7*) N Juckes, *chsd ldrs till led 5th, hdd 3 out, wknd 2 out*.....(6 to 1 tchd 13 to 2)   5
IMMORTAL IRISH 8-11-0 M A FitzGerald, *led to 5th, rdn appr 3 out, wknd approaching 2 out.*
.................(8 to 1 op 5 to 1 tchd 33 to 1)   6
BRECKENBROUGH LAD 6-10-11 (7*) A Flannigan, *chsd ldrs rdn frm 3 out, wknd 2 out*...........(11 to 2 tchd 6 to 1)   7
CHEEKA 4-11-3 M Ranger, *in tch, rdn 6th, wknd 3 out, tld off whn pld up bef last*.....(16 to 1 op 14 to 1)   pu
Dist: 1l, 10l, hd, 8l, 3½l, 8l. 3m 48.80s. a 9.80s (8 Ran).

(Martin Pipe Racing Club), M C Pipe

227 Highland Park Novices' Hurdle (4-y-o and up) £1,626 2m.................(8:15)

ICE STRIKE (USA) 4-10-11 J Railton, *trkd ldrs, led aftr 6th,*
clr appr 2 out, easily. . . . . (11 to 2 op 5 to 2) 1
MUST BE MAGICAL (USA) 5-11-0 A Maguire, *hdwy to*
chase ldrs 6th, styd on und pres frm 3 out, no ch wth
wnr. . . . . (4 to 1 op 6 to 1) 2
151 DAZZLING FIRE (Ire) 4-10-6 M Richards, *hdwy 6th, styd on*
und pres frm 2 out, not trble wnr. (14 to 1 op 12 to 1) 3
MAPLE BAY (Ire) 4-10-11 A O'Hagan, *hdwy 6th, staying*
on one pace whn mstk 2 out. . . . . . (25 to 1 op 20 to 1) 4
191³ CLASSICAL STAR 4-10-11 N Williamson, *led to 3rd, styd on*
prmnt, chlgd 6th, rdn 3 out, sn btn 2 out.
. . . . (7 to 5 fav tchd 9 to 4) 5
JOTO 4-11-0 S Smith Eccles, *beh 4th, styd on frm 3 out,*
not a dngr. . . . . (16 to 1 op 20 to 1) 6
191⁸ HATAAL (Ire) 4-10-6 T Wall, *in tch, drvn alng frm 5th,*
wknd 3 out. . . . . (50 to 1) 7
ARCTIC LINE (v) 5-11-0 L Harvey, *chsd ldrs, rdn 5th, wknd*
aftr nxt. . . . . (33 to 1) 8
LITTLE THYNE 8-11-0 Dr P Pritchard, *beh frm 4th.* (50 to 1) 9
MAJOR RISK 4-10-8 (3*) N Bentley, *chsd ldrs, rdn aftr 5th,*
wknd 6th. . . . . (8 to 1 op 7 to 1) 10
DOCTOR DUNKLIN (USA) 4-10-11 C Llewellyn, *beh frm 4th.*
. . . . (14 to 1 op 12 to 1) 11
FRIENDLY HOUSE (Ire) 4-10-11 H Davies, *beh frm 4th.*
. . . . (14 to 1 op 7 to 1) 12
139 WEE WILLIE DICKINS 6-11-0 J A Harris, *chsd ldrs to 5th.*
. . . . (50 to 1 op 33 to 1) 13
LORD VIVIENNE (Ire) 4-10-11 C Hawkins, *pld hrd, led 3rd,*
hdd aftr 6th, wknd rpdly. . . . . (14 to 1 op 10 to 1) 14
Dist: 12l, 2l, 2l, 3l, 10l, ¾l, ½l, 6l, 2½l, ¾l. 3m 49.20s. a 10.20s (14 Ran).

(C R Nelson), J W Hills

TRAMORE (IRE) (good)
Thursday August 12th

228 Richard Power Maiden Hurdle (3-y-o)
£2,590 2m. . . . . (6:00)

THE BERUKI (Ire) 9-7 (7*) T P Treacy, ... (2 to 1 fav) 1
BENGALI (Ire) 9-12 (7*) J M Sullivan, ... (10 to 1) 2
TROPICAL LANE (Ire) 9-7 (7*) J P Broderick, ... (6 to 1) 3
NORDIC MINE (Ire) 10-5 K F O'Brien, ... (7 to 1) 4
GIFT OF PEACE (Ire) 10-0 C F Swan, ... (9 to 2) 5
ROOTSMAN (Ire) 10-5 P L Malone, ... (12 to 1) 6
PERCY LANE (Ire) 10-5 C N Bowens, ... (20 to 1) 7
ANY MINUTE NOW (Ire) 9-12 (7*) P J Ryan, ... (10 to 1) 8
SWEET PEACH (Ire) 9-10³ (7*) Mr J A Shehan, ... (33 to 1) 9
CARHUE STAR (Ire) 9-9 (5*) T J O'Sullivan, ... (14 to 1) 10
PHILIP PATRICK (Ire) 5 C O'Dwyer, ... (16 to 1) 11
GIG TIME (Ire) 9-7 (7*) C O'Brien, ... (33 to 1) 12
BRASS BUTTON (Ire) 9-7 (7*) Mr R D McGrath, . . (33 to 1) 13
Dist: 1l, hd, 2l, 2l. 3m 59.50s. (13 Ran).

(Mrs Geraldine Treacy), S J Treacy

229 Cross Q.R. Handicap Hurdle (0-102 4-y-o
and up) £2,590 2½m. . . . .(6:30)

120* UNCLE BART (Ire) [-] 5-11-10 (7*,6ex) Mr B Lennon,
. . . . (6 to 4 fav) 1
86⁸ CLONEENVEEN (Ire) [-] 5-10-7 Mr D P Murphy, ...(14 to 1) 2
116 CHARDEN [-] 7-10-10 (7*) Mr P Roche, ... (10 to 1) 3
62⁵ IDEAL RISK (Ire) [-] 4-11-2 (5*) Mr J A Nash, ... (5 to 1) 4
174 LILY ROSE VI [-] 9-10-8 (7*) Mr G P FitzGerald, . .(20 to 1) 5
175⁸ MILLER'S CROSSING [-] 6-11-4 Mr T Doyle, ...(5 to 1) 6
169² TOURIG LE MOSS [-] 6-10-3 (7*) Mr R J Foley, ...(5 to 1) 7
170⁸ MARY GINA [-] (bl) 8-10-6 (7*) Mr G Hogan, ...(16 to 1) 8
169 BRAVE SHARON [-] 9-10-12 Mr S R Murphy, ...(25 to 1) 9
122 CAHERWALTER [-] 9-10-8 (3*) Mr A R Coonan, . .(16 to 1) 10
Dist: 6l, 6l, 2l, sht-hd. 4m 43.60s. (10 Ran).

(W Hennessy), Anthony Mullins

230 Richard Power Handicap Hurdle (4-y-o
and up) £4,142 2m. . . . .(7:00)

113⁶ TOUREEN GIRL [-] 6-10-4 C F Swan, ... (9 to 4 fav) 1
161² NICE AND SIMPLE [-] 6-9-2 (7*) C O'Brien, ... (8 to 1) 2
SHAYISTA [-] 8-10-4 (7*) Mr P A Roche, ... (8 to 1) 3
123 BRAVEFOOT [-] 5-10-12 K F O'Brien, ... (7 to 1) 4
113* ULTRA MAGIC [-] 6-10-2 (5,8ex) A J Roche, ... (5 to 1) 5
161 WATERLOO LADY [-] 6-10-1 F J Flood, ... (10 to 1) 6
110⁶ PREMIER LEAP [-] 4-10-8 D M O'Neill, ... (5 to 1) 7
106⁵ PALACE GEM [-] (bl) 6-10-7 (5*) Mr P J Casey, . . . (10 to 1) 8
Dist: 2l, 2l, 2½l, 8l. 3m 53.00s. (8 Ran).

(Colm Murray), W P Mullins

DUNDALK (IRE) (good)
Friday August 13th

231 Cullaville Maiden Hurdle (4-y-o and up)
£2,245 2½m 153yds. . . . . (5:15)

112² THE EXAMINER 7-11-3 (3*) J Magee, ... (6 to 4 fav) 1
174³ JUST BLUSH 6-11-9 H Rogers, ... (10 to 1) 2
96³ KAFKAN (Ire) 5-10-13 (7*) C O'Brien, ... (10 to 1) 3
115 CUBAN QUESTION 6-12-0 C F Swan, ... (3 to 1) 4

112 LE GERARD 8-11-6 C O'Dwyer, ... (12 to 1) 5
161⁹ SEZ HE SEZ I 9-11-7 (7*) Miss C E Hyde, ...(10 to 1) 6
67⁸ PORT RISING (Ire) 4-11-2 K F O'Brien, ...(11 to 2) 7
THEKINDWORD VI (bl) 8-11-6 J P Banahan, ...(33 to 1) 8
81 STANDAROUND (Ire) 4-11-2 J P Byrne, ...(33 to 1) 9
150 CRACKLE N POP (Ire) 5-11-6 C N Bowens, ...(16 to 1) 10
THE BOLD FOAL (Ire) 5-11-3 (3*) D Bromley, ...(16 to 1) 11
Dist: 5½l, 3l, 5½l, 8l. 4m 53.80s. (11 Ran).

(J Queally), John Queally

232 Warrenpoint Handicap Hurdle (0-116 4-y-o
and up) £2,245 2m 135yds. . . . . (5:45)

230⁴ BRAVEFOOT [-] 5-11-11 K F O'Brien, ... (4 to 1) 1
175⁶ TULLY BOY [-] 6-11-0 (7*) Mr D McCartan, ...(8 to 1) 2
51² MILLENIUM LASS (Ire) [-] 5-10-10 C F Swan, ... (11 to 4) 3
131⁴ KINDERSLEIGH [-] 6-10-8 (5*) Mr A E Lacy, . . . (5 to 2 fav) 4
161 MABES TOWN (Ire) [-] 5-10-10 N Byrne, ...(10 to 1) 5
174⁶ PARSONS EYRE (Ire) [-] 5-10-4 J P Byrne, ...(15 to 2) 6
106 MELTEMI [-] 7-11-7 D P Fagan, ... (8 to 1) 7
24⁴ DARCARI ROSE (Ire) [-] 4-10-4 H Rogers, ...(16 to 1) 8
161⁵ CAOIMSEACH (Ire) [-] 5-10-4 (5*) Mr J A Nash, ... (7 to 1) 9
Dist: ¾l, sht-hd, 6l, 5½l. 4m 0.60s. (9 Ran).

(S Macklin), J H Scott

233 Carnlough Flat Race (4-y-o and up) £2,245
2m 135yds. . . . . (7:45)

114 STONELEIGH TURBO (Ire) 4-11-4 (5*) Mr P M Kelly, (4 to 1) 1
BALLYWILLIAM (Ire) 4-11-6 (3*) Mr A R Coonan, . . .(5 to 1) 2
81⁸ DOCS DILEMMA (Ire) 4-11-9 Mr P F Graffin, . . (3 to 1 fav) 3
BOLD TED (Ire) 4-11-2 (7*) Mr G A Kingston, ...(9 to 2) 4
162⁷ WESTCARNE LAD (Ire) 5-12-0 Mr M McNulty, ...(4 to 1) 5
159⁸ SONIC EXPERIENCE (Ire) 5-11-6 (3*) Mr R Neylon, (20 to 1) 6
98 RATHCARNICK LASS (Ire) 4-10-13 (5*) Mr J A Nash,
. . . . (14 to 1) 7
81 DECEMBER BRIDE (Ire) 5-11-2 (7*) Mr E Magee, . .(25 to 1) 8
HIGHCLIFF HOTEL (Ire) 5-11-9 Mr S R Murphy, . . .(7 to 1) 9
MONGIE (Ire) 4-11-2 (7*) Mr D J McAteer, ... (16 to 1) 10
HIGHLAND BREEZE 4-11-2 (7*) Mr J Bright, ...(20 to 1) 11
81 DARA KNIGHT (Ire) 4-11-64 (7*) Mr S McFerran, . .(50 to 1) 12
SHESAHUNNY (Ire) 4-11-4 Mr J P Dempsey, ...(20 to 1) pu
Dist: 3½l, ½l, ½l, 2l. 3m 57.20s. (13 Ran).

(John A Doyle), P A Fahy

TRAMORE (IRE) (good to firm)
Friday August 13th

234 Riverstown Maiden Hurdle (4-y-o and up)
£2,245 2m. . . . . (5:30)

215³ ANOTHER COURSE (Ire) 5-11-6 P McWilliams, (2 to 1 fav) 1
174⁵ KAITLIN (Ire) 4-11-4 P L Malone, ... (9 to 2) 2
115 EASE THE BURDEN (Ire) 5-10-10 (5*) T J O'Sullivan,
. . . . (20 to 1) 3
104⁹ KIARA DEE 7-10-8 (7*) J P Deegan, ... (20 to 1) 4
68⁴ ASK THE FAIRIES (Ire) 5-10-12 (3*) K B Walsh, . . .(16 to 1) 5
DANE ST LADY (Ire) 5-11-1 G M O'Neill, ... (16 to 1) 6
102⁷ CARBON FIVE (Ire) 4-10-13 A J O'Brien, ... (7 to 1) 7
160 PERCY BRENNAN 6-11-1 (5*) T P Rudd, ... (16 to 1) 8
174⁷ JUST FOUR (Ire) 4-10-13 B Sheridan, ... (10 to 1) 9
RED FOUNTAIN (Ire) 4-11-4 D H O'Connor, ... (9 to 2) 10
109 FIFTYBETWEENYE (Ire) 5-10-10 (5*) J R Barry, . . . (20 to 1) 11
PRINCE GOAL 6-10-13 (7*) J Pearse, ...(20 to 1) 12
NEVER WRONG 6-12-0 J Shortt, ... (10 to 1) 13
GO DEAS 6-11-9 M Moran, ...(8 to 1) f
VALS CHOICE (Ire) 4-10-13 D Duggan, ...(8 to 1) ur
Dist: 3½l, 7l, hd, 2½l. 3m 55.90s. (15 Ran).

(Patrick Heffernan), Patrick Heffernan

235 Cheekpoint Handicap Chase (0-116 4-y-o
and up) £2,245 2m. . . . .(7:00)

119⁶ NEVER BE GREAT [-] 11-12-0 F J Flood, ...(Evens fav) 1
82⁷ LA MODE LADY [-] 8-10-0 A J O'Brien, ...(7 to 2) 2
92⁶ LISNAGREE BOY (Ire) [-] 5-9-11 (7*) T P Treacy, . . . (6 to 1) 3
GRANVILLE HOTEL [-] 9-10-9 W Slattery Jnr, . . . (10 to 1) 4
70 SKIN GRAFT [-] (bl) 7-9-5¹ (3*) J Collins, ...(20 to 1) f
82⁶ TIGH AN CHEOIL [-] (bl) 9-10-0 P McWilliams, ...(9 to 2) pu
Dist: 6l, 3½l, dist. 3m 56.70s. (6 Ran).

(Patrick McAteer), F Flood

236 Holiday Mares Flat Race (4-y-o and up)
£2,245 2m. . . . . (8:00)

115 MILFORD MATCH (Ire) 5-11-9 (5*) Mrs J M Mullins, (7 to 1) 1
109⁶ VON CARTY (Ire) 4-11-2 (7*) Mr J T McNamara, . . (4 to 1) 2
171² THE WICKED CHICKEN (Ire) 4-11-6 (3*) Mrs S McCarthy,
. . . . (Evens fav) 3
174 HAZEL PARK 5-11-7 (7*) Mr P Henley, ...(12 to 1) 4
109 COMINOLE (Ire) 4-11-6 (3*) Mr R O'Neill, ...(20 to 1) 5
114 LONG'S EXPRESS (Ire) 5-11-7 (7*) Mr B Lennon, . .(7 to 1) 6
174 LADY DIGA (Ire) 5-11-7 (7*) Mr S O'Callaghan, . . .(20 to 1) 7
GOOD OLD SQUIDGY (Ire) 4-11-4 (5*) D T Evans, (20 to 1) 8
105⁸ LADY BLUE ROSE (bl) 6-11-7 (7*) J Pearse, ... (20 to 1) 9
179³ KARA'S DREAM (Ire) 5-11-7 (7*) Mr J B Slevin, ...(8 to 1) 10

215⁸ DRUID'S DAWN (bl) 8-11-9 (5*) Mr J P Berry, ... (12 to 1) 11
KATES CASTLE 6-11-7 (7*) Mr K O'Sullivan, ... (20 to 1) 12
7 D'S AND DO'S (Ire) 4-11-2 (7*) Mr D A Harney, ... (16 to 1) 13
102 LAFFAN'S BRIDGE (Ire) (bl) 4-11-2 (7*) Mr P A Roche,
. . . .(12 to 1) 14
94 KINCOR (Ire) 4-11-2 (7*) Mr P English, ... (20 to 1) 15
Dist: 2l, nk, 3½l, ½l. 3m 47.80s. (15 Ran).

(V J Fitzpatrick), W P Mullins

BANGOR (good to firm)
Saturday August 14th
Going Correction: NIL

237 Conwy Novices' Hurdle (4-y-o and up)
£2,092 2½m. . . . . (2:25)

LABURNUM 5-11-0 R Dunwoody, hld up in tch, cl up and
ev ch 3 out, pressed ldr til slight ld last, drvn out.
. . . .(9 to 2 op 3 to 1) 1
142* PURITAN (Can) 4-11-4 G McCourt, hld up, hdwy and mstk
5 out, ch frm nxt, rdn to ld 2 out, hdd last, rallied
and not quicken nr finish.
. . . .(11 to 4 on on tchd 3 to 1 on and 2 to 1 on) 2
MAGSOOD (bl) 8-11-0 S Earle, led, clr 3rd, hdd appr 2 out,
sn rdn and one pace. . . . .(10 to 1 op 7 to 1) 3
130³ RUN MILADY 5-10-9 D Wilkinson, hld up, wnt moderate
4th, sn rdn and one pace. . . . .(20 to 1 op 12 to 1) 4
MITTON SPRINGS 4-10-11 Gary Lyons, chsd ldr, wknd
quickly aftr 4 out, tld off. . . . .(40 to 1 op 20 to 1) 5
BROWN MYSTIQUE 7-10-2 (7*) A Flannigan, mstk 1st, chsd
ldr til pckd 5th, wknd quickly nxt, tld off whn pld up
bef 2 out. . . . . (100 to 1 op 66 to 1) pu
GLEN MOSELLE 7-11-0 Mr J Cambidge, hld up, wnt sec-
ond 5th, pressed ldr til wknd quickly aftr 4 out, sn tld
off. . . . . (150 to 1 op 66 to 1) pu
Dist: 1l, 15l, 8l, dist. 4m 49.60s. a 13.60s (7 Ran).

(The Icy Fire Partnership), C J Mann

238 Denbigh Conditional Jockeys' Selling Hurdle (4-y-o and up) £1,780 2m 1f. . . . . (2:55)

SAYMORE 7-11-7 S Wynne, trkd ldr frm 3rd, wnt second
6th, led appr 2 out, clr last, cmftbly.
. . . . (13 to 8 on op 6 to 4 on tchd 7 to 4 on and 5 to 4 on) 1
181² SALAR'S SPIRIT 7-10-11 (3*) R Darke, hld up, hdwy 5th,
trkd ldr, wnt second appr 2 out, sn rdn, no imprsn.
. . . .(11 to 4 op 2 to 1 tchd 3 to 1) 2
HELLO SAM 10-11-0 R Greene, led til hdd appr 2 out, sn
rdn and wknd. . . . . (10 to 1 op 6 to 1 tchd 11 to 1) 3
THEM TIMES 4-10-3 (3*) M Doyle, hld up, hdwy 6th,
chsd ldr, rdn and wknd quickly aftr 3 out.
. . . .(14 to 1 op 7 to 1) 4
164³ MEADOW GAME (Ire) 4-9-13 (7*) T Murphy, prmnt til mstk
5th, wknd quickly aftr nxt, sn beh. (33 to 1 op 16 to 1) 5
138 GOLDSMITH 5-10-11 (3*) R Wilkinson, not fluent, rcd
wide, lost tch aftr 3rd, tld off frm nxt.
. . . .(66 to 1 op 25 to 1) 6
Dist: 10l, 8l, 10l, 15l, dist. 4m 1.20s. a 11.20s (6 Ran).

(D Manning), R Hollinshead

239 Construction Services Novices' Chase (5-
y-o and up) £2,789 2m 1f 110yds. . . . .(3:25)

DULZURA 5-10-6 T Jarvis, led and mstk 3rd, jmpd rght
nxt, lft in ld 7th, mistake 3 out, clr whn hit last, all out,
disqualified. . . . . (5 to 1 tchd 9 to 1) 1D
HEAD LAD 10-10-7 (7*) Judy Davies, chsd 1st 2, lft second
7th, rdn and one pace aftr 3 out, finish tired, finished
second, awarded race. . . . .(11 to 1 op 7 to 1) 1
129² SALMAN (USA) 7-11-0 C Llewellyn, led to 3rd, led ag'n 5th
til f 7th. . . . .(11 to 4 on op 5 to 2 on tchd 3 to 1 on) f
MENAGHI 6-10-9 G Bradley, sn last, hdwy aftr 6th, in tch
whn lft 3rd 7th, f nxt. (14 to 1 op 12 to 1 tchd 16 to 1) f
Dist: 15l. 4m 26.80s. a 20.80s (4 Ran).

(F Lloyd), F Lloyd

240 Royal Welch Fusiliers Trophy Handicap
Hurdle (0-125 4-y-o and up) £2,684 2m 1f
. . . .(3:55)

195² LUSTREMAN [101] 6-10-0 T Wall, hld up, wnt 3rd 3 out,
led nxt, mstk last, drvn out. . . . .(16 to 1 op 14 to 1) 1
153* WELSHMAN [129] 7-12-0 D Gallagher, chsd ldr, wnt second 6th, ev ch 2 out, rdn and not quicken appr last.
. . . .(2 to 1 fav op 6 to 4 tchd 9 to 4) 2
CLEEVELAND LADY [103] 6-10-2² R Dunwoody, chsd 1st 2,
cl up and ev ch 3 out, rdn and not quicken betw last
two. . . . . (14 to 1 op 12 to 1) 3
RINGLAND (USA) [101] 5-9-12¹ (3*) D J Moffatt, chsd clr ldr,
lft in ld 4 out, hdd 2 out, not quicken.
. . . .(3 to 1 tchd 4 to 1) 4
190³ COURT CIRCULAR [101] (bl) 4-10-0 Diane Clay, hld up,
outpcd aftr 3 out, rdn and styd on ag'n betw last 2.
. . . .(9 to 4 op 5 to 2 tchd 11 to 4) 5

ELEGANT KING (Ire) [110] 4-10-9 T Jarvis, led, jmpd badly
rght, sn clr, sddl slpd aftr 4th, ran wide aftr nxt, soon
pld, beh whn blun and uns rdr 3 out (8 to 1 op 5 to 1) ur
Dist: 2l, 3½l, ½l, 1½l. 3m 56.70s. a 6.70s (6 Ran).
SR: 5/31/1/ (R A B Brassey), J H Peacock

241 Dee Handicap Chase (0-130 4-y-o and up)
£3,015 2½m 110yds. . . . . (4:25)

CLEVER FOLLY [107] 13-10-11 R Dunwoody, made all, lft
clr 2 out, eased run in, unchlgd.
. . . . . .(6 to 5 on op Evens tchd 11 to 10 and 5 to 4 on) 1
JOYFUL NOISE [134] 10-11-7 (7*) P Naughton, chsd ldr, cl
up whn jmpd slwly tenth, wknd nxt, styd on one pace
frm 3 out, lft moderate second next. (7 to 2 op 3 to 1) 2
141⁴ MIAMI BEAR [107] 7-10-11 Gary Lyons, chsd ldr, wnt second 6 out, rdn 4 out, second but hld whn f 2 out.
. . . .(5 to 2 op 9 to 4) f
COINAGE [111] (bl) 10-10-5⁵ Mr G Johnson Houghton, last
whn blun and uns rdr 3rd. . . . .(14 to 1 op 10 to 1) ur
Dist: 5l. 5m 4.20s. a 13.20s (4 Ran).

(N B Mason (Farms) Ltd), G Richards

242 Showtime Novices' Handicap Hurdle (4-
y-o and up) £2,211 2m 1f. . . . .(5:00)

FRANKUS [74] 4-10-9 S Earle, made all, jmpd wl, found
extr whn chlgd 2 out, drvn out run in.
. . . .(7 to 1 op 6 to 1) 1
SAINT CIEL (USA) [75] 5-10-10 R Supple, chsd clr ldr, wnt
second 4 out, chlgd 2 out, sn rdn and unbl to quicken
appr last.
. . . .(15 to 8 fav op 2 to 1 tchd 7 to 4 and 9 to 4) 2
RISING TEMPO (Ire) [77] 5-10-12 M A FitzGerald, hld up
and beh, hdwy aftr 3 out, styd on betw last 2, unbl to
quicken. . . . .(9 to 2 op 4 to 1 tchd 5 to 1) 3
JON'S CHOICE [75] (bl) 5-10-10 T Wall, chsd clr ldr til rdn
and one pace aftr 3 out. (7 to 1 op 12 to 1 tchd 14 to 1) 4
ANOTHER VINTAGE [76] 4-10-11 R Dunwoody, hld up,
hdwy aftr 5th, chsd ldr til wknd appr 2 out.
. . . .(10 to 1 op 8 to 1) 5
151³ KELLY'S DARLING [84] 7-11-5 D Bridgwater, hld up in tch,
hdwy aftr 5th, chsd ldr til wknd quickly after 3 out.
. . . .(4 to 1 op 8 to 1 tchd 7 to 2) 6
OUR MAN IN HAVANA [93] 4-12-0 J Railton, hld up, wnt
3rd aftr 4th, chsd ldr til wknd quickly 3 out, sn beh.
. . . .(10 to 1 op 8 to 1) 7
Dist: 2l, 7l, 1l, 10l, nk, 10l. 4m 5.40s. a 15.40s (7 Ran).

(H C S Group), S Mellor

MARKET RASEN (good)
Saturday August 14th
Going Correction: MINUS 0.35 sec. per fur.

243 Ladies Night Conditional Jockeys' Novices' Hurdle (4-y-o and up) £2,066 2m 1f
110yds. . . . . (5:50)

YOUNG GEORGE 6-11-0 M Hourigan, wth ldr, led 5th till
hdd 2 out, rgned ld last, sn headed and swtchd lft,
rallied to edge ahead post. . . . .(6 to 1 op 7 to 2) 1
138* SAFARI PARK 4-10-7 (5*) G Cahill, jmpd wl, led to 5th, led 2
out to last, gd jump to rgn advantage, edgd rght, wknd
and ct post. . . . .(85 to 40 op 9 to 4 tchd 5 to 2) 2
BARTON PRIDE (Ire) 4-10-11 D Bentley, pld hrd, handily
plcd, rdn alng aftr 3 out, one pace. (12 to 1 op 8 to 1) 3
163² TRUMPET (bl) 4-10-11 A Thornton, hld up in tch, effrt 3
out, sn rdn, not keen and no hdwy.
. . . . (11 to 8 fav tchd 13 to 8) 4
191⁴ CHRIS'S GLEN 4-10-11 R Farrant, tucked in hndy till
niggled alng aftr 3 out, sn wknd.
. . . .(13 to 2 op 5 to 1 tchd 7 to 1) 5
NOT GORDONS (bl) 4-10-6 (5*) N Juckes, hld up in last pl,
rdn appr 2 out, sn no imprsn. . . . . . .(25 to 1 op 20 to 1) 6
Dist: Sht-hd, 8l, sht-hd, 15l, nk. 4m 15.10s. a 13.10s (6 Ran).

(J A Wynn-Williams), M Dods

244 Champagne And Roses Selling Hurdle (4-
y-o and up) £1,628 2m 1f 110yds. . . . .(6:20)

137² CYRILL HENRY (Ire) 10-12 A Merrigan, patiently rdn,
hdwy 5th, chlgd appr 2 out, ridden to ld r-in, pushed
out. . . . .(6 to 1 op 5 to 1) 1
137* BATTUTA 10-9² (5*) P Midgley, dsptd ld, definite advantage appr 2 out, hdd and no extr r-in. (4 to 1 op 5 to 1) 2
RED INK 10-12 S Smith Eccles, hld up, hdwy 5th, rdn
appr 2 out, unbl to quicken. . . . .(9 to 2 op 4 to 1) 3
FULL SHILLING (USA) 10-12 G McCourt, hld up in tch,
effrt 3 out, rdn appr nxt, sn btn. . . . . .(7 to 1 op 8 to 1) 4
AUNTIE LORNA 10-7 C Grant, prmnt to 3rd, sn lost pl,
some late hdwy. . . . .(9 to 4 fav op 11 to 10) 5
166² WELL DONE RORY (bl) 11-7 A Maguire, dsptd ld till rdn
and wknd appr 2 out. . . . .(7 to 4 fav op 11 to 10) 6
KICK ON MAJESTIC (Ire) (bl) 10-12 P Niven, in tch till wknd
appr 3 out. . . . .(20 to 1 op 16 to 1) 7
Dist: 1½l, 6l, 7l, 6l, 8l, 2l. 4m 3.50s. a 1.50s (7 Ran).

NATIONAL HUNT RESULTS 1993-94

SR: 8/6/-/-/   (Mrs C E Dods), M Dods

245 Singleton Birch Handicap Chase (0-115 4-y-o and up) £3,080 2m 1f 110yds...(6:50)

141⁵ RUPPLES [87] 6-11-1 W Worthington, *hld up and beh, ran on appr 3 out, second and clsg whn lft clr last, drvn out*.................................(6 to 1 op 9 to 2) 1
141² MR-PAW [93] 10-11-0 (7*) B Murphy, *hld up in tch, rdn aftr 4 out, lft second and hmpd nxt unbl to quicken.*
.................................(11 to 10 fav op Evens tchd 5 to 4) 2
141 MARKET LEADER [87] 13-10-12 (3*) R Greene, *trkd ldrs, rdn aftr 4 out, lft 3rd last, no extr*....(4 to 1 op 3 to 1) 3
BILL AND COUP [88] 8-11-2 A S Smith, *trkd ldr till wknd aftr 4 out*.....................(13 to 2 op 5 to 1) 4
LAPIAFFE [95] 9-11-9 C Grant, *led till hdd and f 3 out.*
....................................(9 to 1 op 10 to 1 tchd 12 to 1) f
141⁷ ENSHARP (USA) [96] 7-11-10 A Maguire, *chsd ldr, led and lft clr 3 out, 4 ls up but tiring whn f last.*
....................................(11 to 1 op 12 to 1 tchd 16 to 1) f
Dist: 5l, 3½l, 12l. 4m 25.30s. a 11.30s (6 Ran).

(C Hague), M C Chapman

246 Racing Post Novices' Chase (5-y-o and up) £2,713 2½m.....................(7:20)

139* COUNTERBID (v) 6-11-6 N Williamson, *made all, clr 4 out, unchlgd*.............(11 to 4 on tchd 5 to 2 on) 1
CAMAN 6-11-0 G McCourt, *hld up, hdwy tenth, sn chasing wnr, no imprsn frm 3 out.*
....................................(10 to 1 op 7 to 1 tchd 11 to 1) 2
139⁶ EBORNEEZER'S DREAM (v) 10-11-0 D Telfer, *in tch till lost pl frm 11th, ran on same pace*..... (25 to 1 op 20 to 1) 3
140⁶ PHALAROPE (Ire) 5-10-11 Mr A Walton, *not fluent, al beh, tld off*..................(11 to 2 op 6 to 1 tchd 7 to 1) 4
194⁷ BRYNHILL ALERT 7-11-0 C Grant, *nvr gng wl, tld off whn pld up bef 6th*....................(20 to 1 op 10 to 1) pu
BROTHER MINSTREL 6-11-0 Mr A Pickering, *chsd ldr till wknd frm tenth, beh whn pld up bef 2 out.*
....................................(66 to 1 op 25 to 1) pu
Dist: 5l, 5l, dist. 5m 3.60s. a 11.60s (6 Ran).

(Howard Parker), J A C Edwards

247 Tote-Racing Post 'Ten To Follow' Juvenile Novices' Hurdle (3-y-o) £2,174 2m 1f 110yds.........................(7:50)

ITS UNBELIEVABLE 10-12 N Williamson, *made all, clr appr 2 out, unchlgd*........(11 to 4 op 3 to 1 tchd 7 to 2) 1
SIMPLY SUPERB 10-5 (7*) J Driscoll, *hld up and beh, hdwy aftr 3 out, staying on whn hit last, nvr nrr.*
....................................(14 to 1 op 10 to 1) 2
ROSCOMMON JOE (Ire) 10-12 M Dwyer, *hld up and beh till gd hdwy appr 2 out, fnshd wl, nvr plcd to chal.*
....................................(7 to 1 op 10 to 1 tchd 6 to 1) 3
GRANDERISE (Ire) 10-12 G McCourt, *pld hrd, chsd ldrs, rdn appr 2 out, not quicken*.....(10 to 1 tchd 14 to 1) 4
IMAGERY 10-7 D Murphy, *chsd ldr, rdn aftr 3 out, sn btn.*
....................................(14 to 1 op 12 to 1) 5
SUMMERS DREAM 10-7 D Byrne, *rear till effrt appr 3 out, no further hdwy*................(14 to 1 op 12 to 1) 6
KISS IN THE DARK 10-7 P Niven, *not fluent, hld up and beh, some hdwy appr 2 out, nvr nr to chal.*
....................................(7 to 1 fav op 5 to 2 tchd 3 to 1) 7
PAAJIB (Ire) 10-12 A Mulholland, *in tch to hfwy, sn lost pl.*
....................................(33 to 1 op 25 to 1) 8
137⁵ CHAJOTHELYTBRIGADE (Ire) 10-7 R Garritty, *hdwy second and sn prmnt till wknd 3 out*.....(25 to 1 op 16 to 1) 9
WALSHAM WITCH 10-7 M Ranger, *midfield till some hdwy 5th, wknd aftr nxt*...(12 to 1 op 10 to 1 tchd 14 to 1) 10
PETERED OUT 10-5 (7*) W Fry, *in tch to hfwy, sn wknd.*
....................................(33 to 1 op 25 to 1) 11
CONTRAC COUNTESS (Ire) 10-7 R Dunwoody, *midfield til rdn and wknd 5th*.................(14 to 1 op 12 to 1) 12
BIG GEM 10-12 W Worthington, *wl beh frm hfwy, tld off whn pld up bef 2 out*.....(33 to 1 op 20 to 1) pu
Dist: 10l, 5l, nk, 6l, nk, 8l, 8l, 6l, 2½l, 1½l. 4m 7.60s. a 5.60s (13 Ran).

(Gerald Hopkins), J White

248 Pretty Woman Handicap Hurdle (0-125 4-y-o and up) £2,574 2m 5f 110yds......(8:20)

BAHRAIN QUEEN (Ire) [93] 5-10-0 M Ranger, *in tch, hdwy aftr 3 out, led last, hng rght r-in, all out*......(12 to 1) 1
MILIYEL [95] 4-10-2 R Dunwoody, *al hndy, moved up appr 2 out, sn ev ch, rallied r-in*......(7 to 4 fav op 5 to 2) 2
SEA BREAKER (Ire) [96] 5-10-3³ D Murphy, *patiently rdn, beh till smooth hdwy 7th, chlgd last, no extr.*
....................................(7 to 2 op 4 to 1 tchd 6 to 1 and 7 to 1) 3
148* NUNS JEWEL [93] 7-9-9 (5*) R Farrant, *nvr far away, led aftr 3 out, hdd last and no extr*...............(4 to 1) 4
140² KRONPRINZ (Ire) [93] 5-10-0 W Worthington, *beh, rdn appr 2 out, kpt on aftr last, no dngr*.......(8 to 1 op 7 to 1) 5
ROSGILL [117] 7-11-10 M Dwyer, *hld up, some hdwy aftr 3 out, nvr able to chal*.............(5 to 2 op 2 to 1) 6
138⁴ TROOPER THORN [93] 9-9-7 (7*) Mr D Parker, *wth ldr, led 7th till aftr nxt, sn btn*..................(33 to 1) 7

182⁶ BEN TIRRAN [93] 9-10-0 D Telfer, *prmnt till lost pl 6th, sn beh*....................................(20 to 1) 8
MISS TIMBER TOPPER [93] 9-9-11⁴ (7*) C Woodall, *made most till hdd 7th, wknd quickly frm nxt.*
....................................(50 to 1 op 33 to 1) 9
Dist: 1l, 2½l, 3½l, 1½l, 4l, 7l, 4l, 20l. 5m 13.10s. a 9.10s (9 Ran).

(David J Thompson), C Smith

TRAMORE (IRE) (good to firm)
Saturday August 14th

249 Tramore Handicap Hurdle (0-109 4-y-o and up) £2,243 2m.....................(2:00)

175⁴ NIMBLE WIND [-] (bl) 7-11-3 A J O'Brien, ...(11 to 2) 1
113⁹ COMBINE CALL [-] 6-11-6 C F Swan, ...(11 to 4 fav) 2
115⁶ SUNSHINES TAXI [-] 6-10-12 B Sheridan, ...(9 to 1) 3
89* UPPINGHAM [-] 7-11-10 C O'Dwyer, ...(10 to 3) 4
175 CLASSY MACHINE (Ire) [-] 5-10-12 P M Verling, ...(14 to 1) 5
106⁷ BROOK COTTAGE (Ire) [-] 5-11-6 K F O'Brien, ...(9 to 2) 6
117 DELIFFIN [-] 7-10-7 (7*) J K McCarthy, ...(20 to 1) 7
TWO MAGPIES [-] 6-10-8 P L Malone, ...(14 to 1) su
160⁴ THE BOURDA [-] 7-10-11 N Byrne, ...(5 to 1) su
Dist: 4½l, hd, 12l, 1l. 4m 1.50s. (9 Ran).

(Mrs D J Tarrant), Francis M O'Brien

250 O'Shaughnessy & Co Ltd Handicap Chase (0-109 4-y-o and up) £2,588 2¾m....(3:00)

170⁴ HURRYUP [-] 6-10-6 (7*) C O'Brien, ...(8 to 1) 1
214* ANN'S PRINCE [-] 10-10-7 (4ex) H Rogers, ...(6 to 1) 2
214⁵ BALLYVERANE [-] 7-10-3 (5*) D P Geoghegan, ...(5 to 1) 3
134 HIGHBABS [-] 7-10-1 T Horgan, ...(9 to 2) 4
132⁹ CHILIPOUR [-] 6-11-7 C F Swan, ...(4 to 1 jt-fav) 5
178² GRANVILLE GRILL [-] 8-10-9 C O'Dwyer, ...(4 to 1 jt-fav) 6
101⁹ BLACK MALACHA VI [-] 10-9-4 (3*) J Collins, ...(12 to 1) f
93 BOG LEAF VI [-] 10-9-5 (5*) T J O'Sullivan, ...(20 to 1) pu
WOODEN MINSTREL [-] 7-9-13 (5*) D T Evans, ...(14 to 1) pu
Dist: 5½l, 4½l, 2l, 10l. 5m 25.80s. (9 Ran).

(C Mitchell), Edward P Mitchell

251 Gain Novice Chase (4-y-o and up) £2,760 2m....................................(3:30)

77 RUSTIC GENT [-] 7-10-7 (7*) C O'Brien, ...(8 to 1) 1
42 BALLYHEIGUE 7-11-0 (7*) Mr J T McNamara, ...(6 to 1) 2
169⁵ M MACG (Ire) 4-10-6 J Magee, ...(10 to 1) 3
138⁸ FIX IT 6-11-7 C O'Dwyer, ...(10 to 1) 4
200 CLASSIC CHEER (Ire) (bl) 5-10-12 (3*) J Jones, ...(16 to 1) 5
213⁷ MISS EUROLINK (bl) 6-11-2 Mr S R Murphy, ...(7 to 1) 6
235³ LISNAGREE BOY (Ire) 5-11-1 F J Flood, ...(5 to 1) 7
LAW COURSE (Ire) 5-10-10 J P Banahan, ...(25 to 1) 8
133 TANAISTE (USA) 4-10-1 (5*) C P Dunne, ...(14 to 1) 9
176 RUSSIAN GALE (Ire) 5-10-10 T Horgan, ...(20 to 1) 10
133⁴ DINNY'S SISTER 7-11-2 A J O'Brien, ...(12 to 1) f
87 MANDEVILLE LANE 7-11-2 J F Titley, ...(12 to 1) ref
169 INCH GALE 6-11-2 W T Slattery Jnr, ...(16 to 1) su
MIDNIGHT COURT (USA) 10-11-7 K F O'Brien, ...(7 to 1) pu
CEDAR COURT (Ire) 5-11-1 C F Swan, ...(14 to 1) pu
Dist: 1l, 9l, 1l, 15l. 4m 3.80s. (15 Ran).

(John Sheehan), David J McGrath

252 TSB (Waterford) INH Flat Race (4-y-o and up) £2,588 2m.....................(4:30)

88⁹ IF YOU SAY YES (Ire) 5-11-7 (5*) Mrs J M Mullins, ..(6 to 1) 1
136⁴ COMMON POLICY (Ire) 4-11-5 (7*) Mr G O'Leary, ..(7 to 1) 2
88⁶ BLAST FREEZE (Ire) 4-11-2 (5*) Mr J A Nash, ...(5 to 2) 3
88⁴ CLASHWILLIAM GIRL (Ire) 5-11-9 (3*) Mr T Lombard,
....................................(6 to 4 fav) 4
98* MISTER DRUM (Ire) 4-11-5 (7*) Mr J T McNamara, ..(7 to 1) 5
211* NORA ANN (Ire) 4-11-2 (5*) Mr G J Harford, ...(10 to 1) 6
MARYJO (Ire) 4-10-7 (7*) P P Curran, ...(20 to 1) 7
136⁶ BUCKINGHAM BOY 7-11-10 (7*) Miss C Harrison, ..(14 to 1) 8
124 POLLANEDIN 9-11-3 (7*) J P Deegan, ...(25 to 1) 9
162 WHIZ ON BOBBY (Ire) 5-11-10 Mr D M O'Brien, ...(20 to 1) 10
Dist: Nk, 2½l, 15l, 3½l. 3m 53.90s. (10 Ran).

(F N Doyle), W P Mullins

ROSCOMMON (IRE) (good)
Monday August 16th

253 Sallymount 3-Y-O Maiden Hurdle (3-y-o) £2,762 2m.......................(5:15)

MICKS DELIGHT (Ire) 10-10 P Carberry, ...(Evens fav) 1
CALL MY GUEST (Ire) 10-10 E A Leonard, ...(6 to 1) 2
ASSERT STAR 10-10 C F Swan, ...(3 to 1) 3
228⁶ ROOTSMAN (Ire) 10-10 P L Malone, ...(10 to 1) 4
PULMICORT 10-10 J Shortt, ...(14 to 1) 5
228⁸ ANY MINUTE NOW (Ire) 10-3 (7*) A P Sweeney, ..(16 to 1) 6
MONTEJUSTICE (Ire) 10-5 N Byrne, ...(33 to 1) 7
CHRISTY MOORE (Ire) 10-3 (7*) R Dolan, ...(25 to 1) 8
TRILLICK (Ire) 9-12 (7*) Mr F McGirr, ...(12 to 1) 9
RUEPPELLII (Ire) 10-3 (7*) Mr D J Barry, ...(25 to 1) 10

30

TANDRAGEE LADY (Ire) 10-5 P McWilliams, ... (66 to 1) 11
228 CARHUE STAR (Ire) 10-5 T J O'Sullivan, ...(25 to 1) ur
Dist: 1l, sht-hd, 20l, ½l. 3m 57.10s. (12 Ran).

(M J McCarthy), Noel Meade

254 Lough Key Handicap Hurdle (4-y-o and up)
£2,762 3m. . . . . (5:45)

157⁷ MOBILE MAN [-] 6-10-4 C F Swan, ... (7 to 4 fav) 1
135 KILIAN MY BOY [-] 10-10-12 J F Titley, ...(12 to 1) 2
122 TELL A TALE [-] 6-10-6 K F O'Brien, ... (8 to 1) 3
135² CUILIN BUI (Ire) [-] 5-10-10 (7*) C O'Brien, ...(9 to 4) 4
150⁷ PEARL'S CHOICE (Ire) [-] 5-9-7 T Horgan, ...(20 to 1) 5
171⁷ IF SO [-] 7-9-9 P McWilliams, ...(16 to 1) 6
119 RUSTY COIN [-] 8-11-9 (7*) Mr T R Hughes, ... (14 to 1) 7
213⁶ ACTION DANCER [-] 7-10-11 (3*) J Collins, ...(14 to 1) 8
MERLYNS CHOICE [-] 9-10-3 (7*) K P Gaule, ...(25 to 1) 9
158* REDONDO BEACH [-] 8-9-11 (4ex) M Duffy, ...(10 to 1) 10
135 COQ HARDI SMOKEY (Ire) [-] 5-10-7 P Carberry, . .(12 to 1) 11
119 FINAL TUB [-] 10-10-12 C O'Dwyer, ...(12 to 1) 12
178⁶ LODATO [-] (bl) 9-9-0 (7*) Mr S Durack, ...(66 to 1) 13
DRUMALDA [-] 11-10-9 (7*) T P Treacy, ...(25 to 1) 14
GRILLADIN (Fr) [-] 9-10-10 (7*) Mr P Henley, ... (20 to 1) pu
161 WE WONT FALL OUT (Ire) [-] 5-9-9² P P Kinane, . .(66 to 1) pu
Dist: 1l, 8l, nk, 3½l. 5m 59.40s. (16 Ran).

(Donal Smith), A P O'Brien

255 Mayo Roscommon Hospice Foundation INH Flat Race (4-y-o and up) £3,452 2m
. . . .(8:15)

KING WAH GLORY (Ire) 4-11-2 (7*) Mr J Connolly,
. . . .(5 to 4 on) 1
114² REMAINDER LASS (Ire) 4-10-11 (7*) Mr M P Dunne, (4 to 1) 2
114 CUCHULLAINS GOLD (Ire) 5-11-7 (7*) Mr D W Cullen,
. . . .(16 to 1) 3
179² SIMPLY SARAH 7-11-9 Mr M McNulty, ...(6 to 1) 4
LOVE FOR LYDIA (Ire) 4-10-11 (7*) Mr B Heffernan, (14 to 1) 5
159³ CAILIN RUA (Ire) 5-11-4 (5*) Mr A E Lacy, ...(13 to 2) 6
176⁵ BALLY O ROURKE 7-11-9 (5*) Mr P M Kelly, ...(40 to 1) 7
114 WE PAY MORE (Ire) 4-11-4 Mr P Fenton, ...(10 to 1) 8
DRESSED IN BLACK (Ire) 5-11-7 (7*) Mr B M Cash, (33 to 1) 9
150 FRAGRANCE MOUNTAIN 7-11-2 (7*) Mr P A Roche,
. . . .(16 to 1) 10
FLIP THE LID (Ire) 4-10-11 (7*) Miss H McCourt, . . .(20 to 1) 11
ROYAL OPINION 6-11-9 (5*) Mr G J Harford, ...(10 to 1) 12
95 GENE OF THE GLEN (Ire) 4-10-11 (7*) Mr J P Kilfeather,
. . . .(33 to 1) 13
94⁶ BEL SHAN (bl) 7-11-2 (7*) Mr K Whelan, ...(16 to 1) 14
Dist: 7l, ½l, 4l, hd. 3m 58.30s. (14 Ran).

(Dr Steven Tam), P Burke

LAYTOWN (IRE) (hard)
Tuesday August 17th

256 Woodchester Credit Lyonnais INH Flat Race (4-y-o and up) £3,762 2m. . . . . . (6:00)

114 SIMPLISTIC (Ire) (bl) 4-11-1 Mr J P Dempsey, ...(10 to 1) 1
MULLAGHMEEN 7-11-1 (5*) Mr J Barry, ...(14 to 1) 2
200³ GREEK MAGIC 6-11-11 (7*) Mr B M Cash, ...(14 to 1) 3
SWEET THUNDER 7-11-6 (7*) Mr R Brabazon, ...(12 to 1) 4
74⁵ SALVATION 6-11-11 Mr A J Martin, ...(4 to 1) 5
234⁵ ASK THE FAIRIES (Ire) 5-10-13 (7*) Miss F Loughran,
. . . .(33 to 1) 6
176⁶ LUCKY ENOUGH 8-11-1 (5*) Mr H F Cleary, ...(20 to 1) 7
53 WHISTLERS PRIDE 10-11-8 (3*) Mr A R Coonan, . .(25 to 1) 8
211⁵ WHAT IT IS (Ire) 4-10-10 (5*) Mr J A Nash, ...(11 to 4) 9
109 MODEL BEHAVIOUR 4-11-3 (3*) Mr D Marnane, . .(14 to 1) 10
235 SKIN GRAFT (bl) 7-11-03 (7*) Mr M Callaghan, ...(33 to 1) 11
114⁷ HAYMAKERS JIG (Ire) 5-11-6 Mr E Bolger, ...(11 to 8 fav) 12
105 BALNEY GALE 7-11-6 (5*) Mr D P Murphy, ...(16 to 1) 13
BASSIANESE (Ire) 4-10-10 (5*) Mr G J Harford, . . .(12 to 1) 14
GALE FORCE NINE 7-11-6 Mr S R Murphy, ...(25 to 1) 15
Dist: 6l, 2l, 4l, 2l. (Time not taken) (15 Ran).

(B C C B Syndicate), M Halford

GOWRAN PARK (IRE) (good)
Wednesday August 18th

257 Old Leighlin Maiden Hurdle (4-y-o and up) £2,762 2m. . . . . (5:15)

PADASHPAN (USA) 4-11-2 (7*) P Morris, ...(7 to 4 fav) 1
102⁸ COCKNEY LAD (Ire) 4-10-11 (7*) F Byrne, ...(10 to 1) 2
MIA GEORGINA (Ire) 4-11-4 J F Titley, ...(6 to 1) 3
55⁶ PRYS PAUPER (Ire) 5-11-9 (5*) Mr D P Murphy, . . .(20 to 1) 4
WHEATSTONE BRIDGE 7-12-0 K Morgan, ...(7 to 1) 5
115⁴ ROSSMANAGHER (Ire) 4-10-11 (7*) C O'Brien, ...(8 to 1) 6
JUNGLE STAR (Ire) 5-11-6 M Flynn, ...(33 to 1) 7
TOP RUN (Ire) 5-11-6 H Rogers, ...(16 to 1) 8
NORDIC SIGN (Ire) 4-11-9 K F O'Brien, ...(12 to 1) 9
SHEBA'S PAL 6-10-8 (7*) T P Treacy, ...(33 to 1) 10
Dist: ½l, 4½l, 3l, 2l. 3m 48.30s. (10 Ran).

(William Brennan), W P Mullins

258 Fenniscourt Flat Race (4-y-o and up) £2,762 2½m. . . . . (8:15)

114* BANNTOWN BILL (Ire) 4-11-11 Mr A P O'Brien, (9 to 4 fav) 1
171⁵ THE TENANT 6-11-8 (3*) Miss M Olivefalk, ...(14 to 1) 2
201* LE BRAVE 7-11-11 (7*) Mr M Brennan, ...(10 to 1) 3
136⁸ HAUGHTON LAD (Ire) 7-11-4 M P D Groome, (20 to 1) 4
88⁸ MORE DASH (Ire) 5-11-8 (5*) Mr J A Nash, ...(10 to 1) 5
124 ROOKS ROCK 6-11-4 (7*) Mr K Whelan, ...(14 to 1) 6
172⁴ PROFIT MOTIVE (Ire) 4-11-4 (7*) Mr G O'Leary, . . .(6 to 1) 7
215² OX EYE DAISY (Ire) 5-11-3 (3*) Mrs M Mullins, . . .(11 to 4) 8
107⁷ RUFO'S COUP 6-11-11 Mr S R Murphy, ...(4 to 1) 9
201⁸ AR AGHAIDH LEATH 7-11-8 (3*) Mr A R Coonan, . .(20 to 1) 10
150 MOON-FROG 6-11-4 (7*) Miss L E A Doyle, ...(33 to 1) 11
30 DECENTRUN (Ire) 5-10-13 (7*) Mr K F O'Donnell, . .(20 to 1) 12
159⁶ LISCAHILL HIGHWAY 6-11-11 Mr W P Mullins, . . .(14 to 1) pu
Dist: 2l, 1l, 20l, 4½l. 4m 39.10s. (13 Ran).

(T Conroy), A P O'Brien

HEREFORD (firm)
Wednesday August 18th
Going Correction: MINUS 0.30 sec. per fur.

259 Much Marcle Novices' Hurdle (4-y-o and up) £1,630 2m 3f 110yds. . . . . (5:25)

185³ NIDOMI (v) 6-11-0 R Dunwoody, hld up, hdwy aftr 4 out, wnt second nxt, led appr last, drvn out.
. . . .(7 to 1 op 6 to 1) 1
RIVER CONSORT (USA) 5-11-0 C Maude, hld up, hdwy aftr 4 out, chsd ldr after nxt, ev ch last, wknd r-in, fnshd lme. . . . . . .(6 to 4 fav op 9 to 4 tchd 11 to 4) 2
226 CHEEKA (bl) 4-10-11 M Ranger, chsd ldr, wnt 3rd 4th, led four out, ran wide bend aftr 2 out, kpt on one pace.
. . . .(20 to 1 op 12 to 1 tchd 25 to 1) 3
202 COMIC LINE 8-10-7 (7*) Miss S Mitchell, chsd ldr til wknd appr 7th, rdn and rallied 3 out, weakened aftr nxt, tld off. . . . .(100 to 1 op 50 to 1) 4
197³ JALORE 4-11-1 (3*) R Greene, lost pl aftr second, last and reminders 6th, sn tld off. . . . .(4 to 1 op 5 to 2) 5
ON THE JAR (Ire) 5-11-0 S Earle, led, jmpd slwly 3rd, hdd 4 out, wknd quickly, tld off. . . . .(50 to 1 op 33 to 1) 6
CROSULA 5-11-0 G Upton, wnt second 4th, chsd ldr til wknd four out, 6th and btn whn 4 out.
. . . .(66 to 1 op 50 to 1) f
DEXTER CHIEF 4-10-11 A Maguire, hld up, some hdwy aftr 7th, sn lost pl, rallied after 3 out, 4th and btn whn pld up and dismounted after 2 out, lme.
. . . .(7 to 4 op 5 to 4 tchd 15 to 8) pu
Dist: 4l, 2½l, 25l, 15l, 1½l. 4m 44.20s. a 19.20s (8 Ran).

(D Leon), G P Enright

260 Border Selling Hurdle (3-y-o and up) £1,742 2m 1f. . . . . (5:55)

238² SALAR'S SPIRIT 7-11-3 (7*) R Darke, al prmnt, led 4th, drw clr aftr nxt, unchlgd. . . . .(10 to 1 op 8 to 1) 1
OTHET 9-10-12 N Hawke, hld up, hdwy aftr 4 out, styd on frm nxt, wnt second appr last, no imprsn.
. . . .(5 to 1 op 5 to 1 tchd 5 to 1) 2
226⁸ IMMORTAL IRISH 8-11-10 M A FitzGerald, hld up, rapid hdwy aftr 5th, chsd ldr, one pace frm 2 out.
. . . .(4 to 1 op 2 to 1) 3
146⁴ MISS EQUILIA (USA) 7-11-13 R Dunwoody, hld up, rdn and effrt aftr 4 out, no imprsn frm 2 out.
. . . .(4 to 1 op 2 to 1) 4
186⁷ PERSIAN VALLEY 8-11-3 (7*) M Doyle, beh, hdwy aftr 4 out, styd on one pace frm nxt.
. . . .(14 to 1 op 12 to 1 tchd 16 to 1) 5
OYSTON'S LIFE 4-11-8 J Railton, pld hrd, pressed ldr til wknd aftr 4 out, one pace. . . . . . .(33 to 1 op 20 to 1) 6
217⁴ EMMA VICTORIA 5-11-9 D Bridgwater, pressed ldr, rdn and wknd quickly 4 out.
. . . .(15 to 2 op 14 to 1 tchd 7 to 1) 7
151⁷ THARIF 5-11-3 (7*) N Downs, wl beh 3rd, styd on one pace aftr 3 out. . . . . . .(40 to 1 op 33 to 1 tchd 50 to 1) 8
194² AT PEACE 7-11-10 A Maguire, mid-div, rdn and effrt aftr 4 out, sn btn. . . . . .(85 to 40 fav op 7 to 2 tchd 4 to 1) 9
FLYING CONNECTION 5-11-10 Diane Clay, nvr rchd ldrs, rdn 4 out, no imprsn. . . . .(16 to 1 op 20 to 1) 10
203 NOW BOARDING 6-10-12 (7*) Mr N Bradley, beh frm 3rd, tld off 3 out. . . . .(50 to 1 op 33 to 1) 11
194 FURRY LOCH 7-11-10 J A Harris, led til aftr 1st, pressed ldr until wknd quickly after 5th, sn beh.
. . . .(66 to 1 op 50 to 1) 12
188⁹ LADY GAIL (bl) 3-10-0 A Webb, took str hold, led second to 6th, sn rdn and wknd quickly. . . . .(33 to 1) 13
WESSEX WARRIOR (v) 7-12-0 G McCourt, lost tch frm 4th, tld off aftr four out. . . .(5 to 1 op 4 to 1 tchd 11 to 2) 14
SABEEL 3-10-0 N Williamson, mstks., al beh.
. . . .(20 to 1 op 14 to 1) 15
216 INTUITIVE JOE 6-11-10 B Powell, lost tch frm 5th, tld off 3 out. . . . .(50 to 1 op 33 to 1) 16
SWIFT ASCENT (USA) 11-11-10 S Burrough, beh frm 3rd, tld off 3 out. . . . .(50 to 1) 17

NATIONAL HUNT RESULTS 1993-94

ANGEL'S WING 4-11-3 S McNeill, *beh frm 3rd, tld off 3
out*..(33 to 1) 18
Dist: 15l, 3½l, 1½l, 3½l, 4l, 7l, hd, 12l, 1l, 3l. 3m 49.20s. a 3.20s (18 Ran).
SR: 13/2/-/-/-/-/   (P F Coombes), W G M Turner

261 Malvern Link Handicap Chase (0-125 4-y-o and up) £2,696 2m 3f............... (6:25)

182* COURT RAPIER [89] 11-10-9 A Maguire, *jmpd wl, made all,
styd on well frm 2 out.*
...........................(13 to 8 on op 6 to 4 on tchd 7 to 4 on) 1
     YORKSHIREMAN (USA) [104] 8-11-10 M Ahern, *chsd ldr,
jmpd lft and reminders aftr 6th, pressed lder frm 8th, ev
ch 3 out, rdn and not quicken appr last.*
....(7 to 4 op 11 to 8) 2
154⁹ DREAMCOAT (USA) [85] 12-9-12 (7*) Leanne Eldredge, *wnt
second 4th, pressed ldr and ev ch till wknd 2 out.*
....(33 to 1 op 20 to 1) 3
     ANOTHER BARNEY [85] 9-10-5 W Irvine, *cl up whn blun
and uns rdr 3rd.*.....................(10 to 1 tchd 14 to 1) ur
Dist: 2½l, 15l. 4m 34.20s. a 4.20s (4 Ran).
    (H V Perry), R H Alner

262 Wheatsheaf Inn Amateur Riders' Handicap Hurdle (0-115 4-y-o and up) £2,221 3¼m .... (6:55)

224* ON THE SAUCE [108] (bl) 6-12-2 (5*,7ex) Mr A Farrant, *made
all, drw clr appr last, styd on strly.*............(9 to 4 jt-
fav op 6 to 4 tchd 5 to 2) 1
     MR MURDOCK [100] 8-11-6 (7*) Mr P Henley, *jmpd slwly
6th, wnt 3rd 9th, chsd wnr 3 out, mstk nxt, one pace.*
...............(9 to 4 jt-fav op 5 to 2 tchd 3 to 1) 2
222³ KASHAN (Ire) [82] 5-10-4 (5*) Mr G Johnson Houghton,
*pressed ldr till rdn and one pace aftr 4 out, styd on ag'n
appr last, not quicken.*
..................(3 to 1 op 5 to 2 tchd 100 to 30) 3
167 VALASSY [78] 10-9-12 (7*) Mr N Miles, *beh 4th, rear till
styd on one pace frm 3 out, tld off.*
......................(10 to 1 op 6 to 1 tchd 11 to 1) 4
185⁷ CLWYD LODGE [73] 6-9-7 (7*) Miss S Higgins, *tld off frm
7th.*..............................(100 to 1 op 33 to 1) 5
     AVONMOUTHSECRETARY [95] 7-11-1 (7*) Mr G Lewis,
*pressed ldr, jmpd slwly 6th and nxt, lost tch aftr 5 out,
eased whn btn appr 3 out.*
.........................(7 to 1 op 6 to 1 tchd 8 to 1) 6
     SANDMOOR PRINCE [73] 10-9-11+4 (7*) Dr P Pritchard, *hld
up, hdwy aftr 8th, chsd ldr, wknd quickly 4 out, tld off.*
................................(25 to 1 op 10 to 1) 7
143⁶ SAILOR'S DELIGHT [75] 9-9-9 (7*) Mr S Joynes, *pressed ldr
till wknd quickly and rdn aftr 7th, tld off whn pld up
bef 3 out.*.........................(33 to 1 op 14 to 1) pu
Dist: 4l, 2½l, 25l, 5l, 10l, 7l. 6m 12.60s. a 12.60s (8 Ran).
    (Goldsmith, Langham & Thompson Partners), M C Pipe

263 Aconbury Novices' Chase (5-y-o and up) £2,203 3m 1f 110yds............... (7:25)

     PANICSUN 8-11-3 D Bridgwater, *trkd ldr in second pl till
led aftr 11th, drw clr aftr 3 out, unchlgd.*
.............(11 to 8 fav op 6 to 4 tchd 7 to 4) 1
     TANBER LASS 12-10-12 J Frost, *led, jmpd lft second,
jumped slwly 6th, jumped left and hdd aftr 11th, rallied and ev ch 4 out, kpt on one pace.*
.............................(2 to 1 op 7 to 4 tchd 9 to 4) 2
165 WEST LODGE LADY 8-10-5 (7*) J Neaves, *lost tch and
outpcd aftr 13th, styd on to take moderate 3rd after 2
out.*.............................(25 to 1 op 14 to 1) 3
184³ JESSOP 8-11-3 S Earle, *trkd ldg pair, ev ch 5 out, sn rdn
and wknd 3 out.*...................(9 to 4 op 5 to 4) 4
Dist: 12l, 5l, 2l. 6m 23.00s. a 11.00s (4 Ran).
    (R Hicks), K S Bridgwater

264 Cherry Novices' Handicap Hurdle (0-100 4-y-o and up) £1,480 2m 1f....... (7:55)

     CLYRO [65] 5-10-11 N Mann, *very slwly away, sn
reco'red, hdwy 4th, trkd ldrs, cl up and ev ch four out,
led aftr nxt, clr appr last.*
..........................(8 to 1 op 10 to 1 tchd 12 to 1) 1
     KNIGHTLY ARGUS [73] 6-11-5 G Upton, *trkd ldrs, cl up
and ev ch 3 out, rdn and unbl to quicken aftr 2 out.*
..................(11 to 10 fav op 6 to 4 tchd 7 to 4) 2
     BOXING MATCH [56] 6-10-2 L Harvey, *led till hdd aftr 3
out, rdn and styd on one pace after 2 out.*
.............................(33 to 1 op 20 to 1) 3
     TIBBS INN [78] 4-11-10 M Ranger, *hld up, hdwy aftr 5th,
cl up and ev ch 3 out, rdn and wknd after nxt.*
..........................(11 to 2 op 6 to 1 tchd 5 to 1) 4
     ALICE SMITH [73] 6-10-12 (7*) D Meade, *hld up, mstk 3rd,
beh aftr nxt, styd on after 2 out, nvr nrr.*
.............................(7 to 1 op 4 to 1) 5
197 MASH THE TEA (Ire) [63] 4-10-9 V Smith, *lost tch aftr 4th,
no ch frm four out.*...............(50 to 1 op 20 to 1) 6
     MING BLUE [63] 4-10-4 (5*) R Farrant, *hld up, rdn and lost
tch aftr 4th, no ch frm four out.*.....(13 to 2 op 4 to 1) 7

243⁶ NOT GORDONS [68] (bl) 4-10-7 (7*) N Juckes, *pressed ldr in
second pl till rdn and wknd rpdly aftr 5th, tld off 3 out.*
.............................(14 to 1 op 16 to 1) 8
     VICTORY WIND [65] 8-10-4 (7*) A Flannigan, *blun and uns
rdr 1st.*................(25 to 1 op 10 to 1 tchd 33 to 1) ur
Dist: 5l, 10l, 2½l, 15l, 15l, 2½l, 25l. 3m 50.10s. a 4.10s (9 Ran).
    (Conway Lloyd), P G Murphy

TIPPERARY (IRE) (good)
Thursday August 19th

265 Cahir Hurdle (4-y-o and up) £2,762 2m .... (7:45)

51³ RATHBRIDES JOY 6-11-4 B Sheridan,.............(4 to 1) 1
158² MASAI WARRIOR 6-11-1 (3*) J Collins,.......(9 to 4 fav) 2
111* SILVERWEIR 10-11-8 K F O'Brien,..............(7 to 2) 3
249⁴ UPPINGHAM 7-11-8 C O'Dwyer,.............(100 to 30) 4
172³ CARLINGFORD RUN 6-10-6 (7*) Mr D Murphy,.....(7 to 1) 5
234⁴ KIARA DEE 7-10-6 (7*) J P Deegan,.............(16 to 1) 6
     UP FOR RANSOME (Ire) 4-10-6 (7*) C O'Brien,.....(20 to 1) 7
115 OFF N'BACKAGAIN (Ire) (bl) 4-10-6 (7*) M G Quigley,
.............................(33 to 1) 8
Dist: 2½l, 7l, dist, 10l. 3m 58.00s. (8 Ran).
    (Mrs Chris Harrington), A P O'Brien

266 Kilmurry Flat Race (4-y-o and up) £2,762 2m.................................. (8:15)

12² MOOREFIELD GIRL (Ire) 4-10-11 (7*) Miss F Crowley,
.............................(7 to 4 fav) 1
109⁵ WOLVER LAD (Ire) 5-12-0 Mr T Doyle,...........(7 to 2) 2
114³ SAME DIFFERENCE (Ire) 5-11-9 (5*) Mr J A Nash,
.............................(100 to 30) 3
124 TIM'S RUN 6-11-7 (7*) Mr W Ewing,...........(10 to 1) 4
     HAZY SPELL (Ire) 4-11-4 Mr P Fenton,.........(9 to 1) 5
215⁵ SLEMISH MINSTREL 7-11-7 (7*) Mr I Johnston,...(12 to 1) 6
48⁸ US AND SAM (Ire) 4-11-2 (7*) Mr P A Roche,......(9 to 1) 7
158 DAILY BREAD (Ire) 4-11-2 (7*) Mr J McNamara,..(25 to 1) 8
     DUNHILL IDOL 6-12-0 Mr P J Healy,.............(20 to 1) 9
     CARRIGANN HOTEL (Ire) 5-11-2 (7*) Mr G Hogan, (16 to 1) 10
     TELEMANN 7-11-7 Mr A Ryan,.................(25 to 1) 11
     MILL BELLE (Ire) 4-11-4 Mr M McNulty,.........(14 to 1) 12
Dist: 8l, 7l, sht-hd, ¾l. 4m 2.60s. (12 Ran).
    (Joseph Crowley), A P O'Brien

CLAIREFONTAINE (FR) (good)
Friday August 20th

267 Prix des Troenes (Hurdles) (4-y-o and up) £6,571 2m 1f..................... (5:00)

192* BOKARO (Fr) 7-10-6 G Bradley, *made all, wnt clr frm thee
fs out, cmftbly.*......................... 1
     IKITHAI (Fr) 4-9-13 G Gombeau,................... 2
     TURTURILLA (Fr) 6-10-6 G Landau,................. 3
     SOUVAROV 5-9-13 F Fiquet,...................... 4
     GABURN (Fr) 5-10-1 Beatrice Marie,.............. 5
     LAC AUX FEES (Fr) 5-9-13 L Gerard,............... 6
     LE CLOS MARVILLE (Fr) 9-10-5 A Pommier,........ 7
     NASR LOVE (USA) 4-9-13 L de La Rosa,............ 8
     DEEPSY (Fr) 4-10-3 A Bohan,.................... 9
     JULIJUMP (Fr) 4-9-8 C Martin,.................. 10
Dist: 12l, 2l, 13l, 10l, 8l, nk. 3m 55.80s. (10 Ran).
    (Lady Joseph), C P E Brooks

PERTH (good to firm)
Friday August 20th
Going Correction: MINUS 0.15 sec. per fur.

268 Abtrust Atlas Gold Novices' Hurdle (4-y-o and up) £2,165 2m 110yds....... (2:20)

     MARTINI EXECUTIVE (bl) 5-11-0 A Maguire, *trkd ldr, led
appr 2 out, styd on wl frm last.......*(8 to 1 op 5 to 1) 1
     LADY DONOGHUE (USA) 4-10-8² P Niven, *hld up, smooth
hdwy to track ldrs 5th, chlgd 2 out, ev ch last, no extr.*
...............(4 to 1 jt-fav op 3 to 1 tchd 9 to 2) 2
     TRUBEN (USA) 4-10-6 L O'Hara, *chsd ldrs, pushed alng
hfwy, kpt on frm 2 out.*......................(4 to 1 to 2) 3
                              fav op 5 to 1 tchd 7 to 1)
     LINDA'S FEELINGS 5-10-9 P Harley, *in tch, rdn on same
pace frm 3 out.*......................(25 to 1 op 20 to 1) 4
     DAPHNIS (USA) 4-10-11 R Dunwoody, *trkd ldrs, rdn aftr 2
out, sn btn.* (11 to 2 op 4 to 1 tchd 6 to 1 and 7 to 1) 5
     MONBODDO 4-10-11 M Dwyer, *in tch, effrt aftr 3 out, sn
rdn and btn.*.......................(20 to 1 op 12 to 1) 6
     MIDDLEHAM CASTLE 4-10-4 (7*) F Perratt, *nvr dngrs.*
.............................(16 to 1 op 12 to 1 tchd 20 to 1) 7
     COMMON COUNCIL (v) 4-10-11 C Grant, *led till hdd appr
2 out, sn wknd.*....................(11 to 2 op 4 to 1) 8
     SARANNPOUR (Ire) 4-10-11 G McCourt, *mstk 4th, al beh.*
.............................(7 to 1 op 8 to 1 tchd 6 to 1) 9

32

CALL KENTONS 7-11-0 B Storey, *chsd ldrs till wknd appr 2 out*............................(33 to 1 op 20 to 1) 10
BALZINO (USA) 4-10-11 Mr S Swiers, *beh whn f second.*
.................................(5 to 1 op 6 to 1 tchd 8 to 1) f
PUBLIC APPEAL (bl) 4-10-11 C Hawkins, *mstks, beh whn pld up bef 5th*...................(100 to 1 op 33 to 1) pu
Dist: 3½l, 7l, 3l, 1½l, 2½l, ½l, 4l, 7l, 2½l. 3m 51.20s. a 7.20s (12 Ran).
(Miss A M Smith), B E Wilkinson

269 Abtrust Unit Trust Managers Novices' Chase (5-y-o and up) £2,320 2m.....(2:50)

194* FASTBIT 6-11-7 N Williamson, *made all, clr 3 out, rdn appr last, styd on wl*........(3 to 1 on tchd 5 to 2 on) 1
186⁵ SHREWD JOHN 7-11-0 R Garritty, *in tch, rdn to go second appr 2 out, kpt on frm last.*
................................(10 to 1 op 8 to 1) 2
THE RAMBLING MAN 6-11-0 R Dunwoody, *mstk 1st, cl up till fdd frm 3 out, btn whn blun last and rdr lost reins.*
................................(10 to 1 op 8 to 1) 3
194⁴ DARK DEEP DAWN 6-10-9 R Supple, *mstks, in tch till blun 9th, sn lost touch, tld off*.......(4 to 1 op 7 to 2) 4
SECOND ATTEMPT 9-11-0 B Storey, *sn lost tch, wl tld off whn pld up bef 3 out*..............(50 to 1 op 25 to 1) pu
Dist: 3l, 10l, dist. 3m 56.10s. a 5.10s (5 Ran).
SR: 18/8/ (K C Bailey), K C Bailey

270 Abtrust Personal Equity Plan Handicap Hurdle (4-y-o and up) £2,179 2½m 110yds ....(3:20)

248⁴ NUNS JEWEL [92] 7-9-9 (5*) P Farrant, *trkd ldrs, led 2 out, styd on wl*...............(7 to 1 tchd 8 to 1 and 6 to 1) 1
222⁶ THARSIS [95] 8-9-11¹ (7*) S Taylor, *led till hdd 2 out, rdn and kpt on*..............(11 to 2 op 5 to 1 tchd 6 to 1) 2
BAY TERN (USA) [120] 7-12-0 P Harley, *cl up, rdn appr 2 out, sn btn*.......(5 to 4 on op 11 to 10 on tchd Evens) 3
TRONCHETTO (Ire) [99] (bl) 4-10-7³ G McCourt, *hld up, reminder appr 4 out, wknd aftr nxt, tld off.*
................................(5 to 2 tchd 11 to 4 and 9 to 4) 4
Dist: ¾l, 15l, 25l. 4m 49.90s. a 4.90s (4 Ran).
SR: -/-/4/-/ (R H Williams), J M Bradley

271 Aberdeen Trust Plc Handicap Chase (0-120 5-y-o and up) £3,030 2½m 110yds ....(3:50)

CHARMING GALE [103] 6-10-4² (5*) P Williams, *wth ldr frm 3rd, rdn appr last, slight ld r-in, all out.*
...................................(4 to 1 op 7 to 2) 1
241* CLEVER FOLLY [104] 13-10-5 (4ex) R Dunwoody, *slight ld, rdn appr last, hdd r-in, no extr und pres.*
...................(6 to 4 fav op Evens tchd 13 to 8) 2
154⁴ BARTONDALE [99] 8-9-9 (5*) R Farrant, *in tch, effrt whn hit 4 out, btn nxt*.....(16 to 1 op 12 to 1 tchd 20 to 1) 3
127³ KIRSTY'S BOY [127] 10-12-0 L O'Hara, *mstks, beh, blun 6th, some hdwy appr 3 out, sn btn.*
....................(7 to 2 tchd 4 to 1 and 3 to 1) 4
DEEP DARK DAWN [116] 8-11-3 R Supple, *in tch, effrt whn hit 4 out, btn nxt, lost touch, tld off.*
................................(3 to 1 op 4 to 1) 5
Dist: ½l, 15l, ¾l, dist. 5m 0.10s. a 21.10s (5 Ran).
SR: 24/24/4/31/-/ (Mrs John Etherton), Mrs S C Bradburne

272 Aberdeen Portfolio Services Novices' Claiming Hurdle (3-y-o) £1,850 2m 110yds ....(4:20)

MOONSHINE DANCER 11-4 P Niven, *in tch, hdwy to track ldrs hfwy, rdn to ld 2 out, kpt on und pres.*
...................(7 to 2 op 4 to 1 tchd 9 to 2) 1
247⁴ GRANDERISE (Ire) 10-10 G McCourt, *hld up, effrt aftr 3 out, chsd wnr after nxt, kpt on, no imprsn.*
................................(5 to 4 fav op 6 to 4) 2
ARE YOU HAPPY (Ire) 10-5 R Supple, *prmnt, chlgd 2 out, sn rdn and one paced.*
....................(12 to 1 op 10 to 1 tchd 14 to 1) 3
DUSKY DUCHESS (Ire) 10-3 L O'Hara, *led till blun and hdd 2 out, sn btn*..............................(33 to 1) 4
BRAXTON BRAGG (Ire) 10-8 P Harley, *chsd ldrs till pushed alng and lost pl aftr 4th, no dngr after.*
..................(13 to 2 op 5 to 1 tchd 7 to 1) 5
RACHAEL'S OWEN 11-4 P Harley, *in tch till wknd appr 2 out*...............(14 to 1 op 12 to 1 tchd 16 to 1) 6
GRUMPY'S GRAIN (Ire) 10-12 R Dunwoody, *cl up till wknd aftr 3 out.*..............(6 to 1 op 5 to 1) 7
188⁶ RUSHALONG 10-10 R Garritty, *al beh, lost tch frm 3 out, tld off.*.........(10 to 1 op 14 to 1 tchd 16 to 1) 8
Dist: 2l, 8l, 2½l, 2½l, 10l, 2l, 20l. 3m 59.50s. a 15.50s (8 Ran).
(Peter Colquhoun), Mrs M Reveley

273 Abtrust Fund Managers Novices' Hurdle (4-y-o and up) £2,060 2½m 110yds...(4:50)

TOPFORMER 6-11-0 C Grant, *in tch, hdwy to chase ldr appr 7th, led 2 out, drvn out.*
....................(6 to 1 op 4 to 1 tchd 13 to 2) 1

LUKS AKURA 5-11-0 R Dunwoody, *led till hdd 2 out, kpt on same pace...* (11 to 8 fav op 11 to 10 tchd 13 to 8) 2
190 MASTER BOSTON (Ire) 5-11-0 P Niven, *beh frm 4th, tld off.*
................................(8 to 1 op 5 to 1) 3
GREAT HEIGHTS (bl) 6-11-0 M Dwyer, *dugs toes in and refused to race sn aftr strt.*
..............................(2 to 1 op 7 to 4 tchd 9 to 4) ref
KILLYMADDY (Ire) 4-10-6 (5*) P Williams, *dsptd ld aftr 3rd till wknd appr 7th, wl beh whn pld up bef 2 out.*
....................(11 to 2 op 6 to 1 tchd 5 to 1) pu
Dist: 10l, 30l. 4m 59.10s. a 14.10s (5 Ran).
(M D Hetherington (Packaging) Ltd), F Watson

WEXFORD (IRE) (good)
Friday August 20th

274 Culleton Insurances Maiden Hurdle (4-y-o and up) £2,762 2m.................(5:15)

SHIRWAN (Ire) 4-11-9 C O'Dwyer, ...(9 to 2) 1
173³ MOSARAT (Ire) 4-10-6 (7*) D M Bean, ...(14 to 1) 2
LAUREL VALLEY 6-11-2 (7*) K P Gaule, ...(4 to 1) 3
FURTHER NOTICE (Ire) (bl) 4-11-4 J F Titley, ...(20 to 1) 4
102⁶ LAKE HOTEL (Ire) 4-11-4 B Sheridan, ...(10 to 1) 5
YOUR UNCLE STANLEY (Ire) 4-11-4 K F O'Brien, (16 to 1) 6
212 BE CREATIVE (Ire) 5-10-13 (7*) Mr A K Wyse, ...(25 to 1) f
157 MANALESCO (Ire) 4-10-11 (7*) C O'Brien, ...(50 to 1) bd
249 THE BOURDA 7-12-0 K Morgan, ...(10 to 1) bd
160² SWALLOWS NEST 6-12-0 D H O'Connor, ...(5 to 4 on) su
212 BULGADEN CASTLE 5-11-6 P Carberry, ...(25 to 1) su
236⁷ LADY DIGA (Ire) 5-10-10 (5*) D T Evans, ...(50 to 1) su
234 FIFTYBETWEENYE (Ire) 5-10-8 (7*) Mr D Duggan, (50 to 1) pu
Dist: 2½l, 6l, 6l, 1l. 3m 56.50s. (13 Ran).
(Anthony Kennedy), Francis Ennis

275 Eagle Star Life Opportunity Handicap Hurdle (0-102 4-y-o and up) £2,762 2¼m (5:45)

249² COMBINE CALL [-] 6-11-6 (4*) T P Treacy, ...(9 to 4 fav) 1
249⁶ BROOK COTTAGE (Ire) [-] 5-11-6 (4*) J P Broderick,
..................................(10 to 1) 2
192³ SEARCHLIGHT (Ire) [-] 5-11-6 (4*) J J McKeon, ...(5 to 1) 3
199* ST DONAVINT [-] 6-11-11 (4*,6ex) B Bowens, ...(100 to 30) 4
199⁴ BALLINDERRY GLEN [-] 7-11-4 (2*) T F Lacy Jnr, ..(9 to 1) 5
110⁷ DANGEROUS REEF (Ire) [-] 5-11-4 (2*) T P Rudd, (20 to 1) 6
KOI CARP [-] 9-10-11 (4*) J P Deegan, ...(25 to 1) 7
131 HOSTETLER [-] 4-11-2 J Collins, ...(12 to 1) 8
BEAUFORT LASS [-] 7-11-7 (2*) D T Evans, ...(16 to 1) 9
69 BETH'S PRINCE [-] (bl) 8-11-5 (4*) R Dolan, ...(16 to 1) 10
230² NICE AND SIMPLE [-] 6-10-10 (4*) C O'Brien, ...(6 to 1) su
Dist: 1l, nk, 1l, 15l. 4m 24.00s. (11 Ran).
(Rory F Larkin), P Mullins

276 Misys Financial Systems Maiden Hurdle (4-y-o and up) £2,762 2¼m.........(6:15)

157³ HUGH DANIELS 5-11-7 (7*) Mr P Moran, ...(5 to 1) 1
BOB'S GIRL (Ire) 4-11-7 T Horgan, ...(5 to 1) 2
131⁷ BAMANYAR (Ire) 5-11-7 (7*) Mr John J Murphy, ...(7 to 1) 3
173⁵ FANE PARK (Ire) 5-12-0 P Carberry, ...(8 to 1) 4
ROYAL OUTING 4-11-4 (5*) T P Rudd, ...(7 to 1) 5
229² CLONEENVERB 9-11-4 (5*) Mr D P Murphy, ...(7 to 1) 6
179⁹ TOM HENRY 6-11-9 (5*) C P Dunne, ...(20 to 1) 7
LINWOOD LADY (Ire) 4-10-11 (7*) H Taylor, .. (4 to 1 fav) 8
131⁸ NO TAKERS 6-11-9 K F O'Brien, ...(7 to 1) 9
231³ KAFKAN (Ire) 5-12-0 J Titley, ...(7 to 1) 10
208 SHINDWA (Ire) 4-11-1 (3*) J Jones, ...(33 to 1) 11
PAVLARIOS 4-11-4 (3*) J Jones, ...(20 to 1) 12
SYLVIA'S SAFFRON 6-11-6 (3*) J Collins, ... (10 to 1) ur
215⁴ QUARTER MARKER (Ire) 5-11-9 (5*) M J Holbrook, (14 to 1) su
Dist: 6l, 4l, 1l, 4½l. 4m 19.10s. (14 Ran).
(Mrs A L T Moore), A L T Moore

277 Lombard & Ulster Bank INH Flat (4-y-o and up) £2,762 2m....................(8:15)

GLAD'S NIGHT (Ire) 4-10-13 (5*) Mrs J M Mullins, (11 to 4) 1
150⁴ GENERAL TONIC 6-12-0 Mr J A Berry, ...(2 to 1 fav) 2
BLOW IT (Ire) 5-12-0 Mr M McNulty, ...(3 to 1) 3
179⁹ SUNSET RUN 7-11-9 (5*) Mr J P Berry, ...(10 to 1) 4
THAT'S A SECRET 5-11-7 (7*) Mr P English, ...(10 to 1) 5
236⁵ COMINOLE (Ire) 4-11-1 (3*) Mr R O'Neill, ...(7 to 1) 6
PEPPERONI EXPRESS (Ire) 4-11-2 (7*) Mr H Dunlop, (8 to 1) 7
215⁶ WEDDING DREAM (Ire) 4-11-4 (5*) Mr D Valentine, (16 to 1) 8
233⁵ WESTCARNE LAD (Ire) 5-11-7 (7*) Mr C J Stafford, (10 to 1) 9
105 CROGHAN MIST (Ire) 5-11-2 (7*) Miss L E A Doyle, (33 to 1) 10
108 DERRING DREAM (bl) 6-11-7 (7*) Mr P P O'Brien, (50 to 1) 11
Dist: 1l, 1½l, 1½l, ½l. 3m 53.30s. (11 Ran).
(D A Pim), W P Mullins

PERTH (good to firm)
Saturday August 21st
Going Correction: MINUS 0.35 sec. per fur.

278 **Glenisla Juvenile Novices' Hurdle (3-y-o) £2,165 2m 110yds.................(2:20)**

CONTRACT ELITE (Ire) 10-12 D Wilkinson, *led aftr 1st, clr 3rd, unchlgd....*(5 to 4 on op 11 to 10 on tchd Evens) 1
BRANCEPETH BELLE (Ire) 10-0 (7*) J Supple, *beh till styd on frm 3 out, nrst finish*...........(25 to 1 op 20 to 1) 2
BONUS POINT 10-12 P Niven, *in tch, hdwy to join chasing grp 5th, chsd wnr frm 2 out, no imprsn, eased cl hme*..................................(2 to 1 op 3 to 1) 3
PEEDIE PEAT 10-12 M Dwyer, *sn chasing wnr, one pace frm 2 out*...........................(16 to 1 op 12 to 1) 4
GLINT OF AYR 10-7 K Johnson, *mstk second, in tch, wkng whn blun 2 out*..................(50 to 1 tchd 100 to 1) 5
TOM THE TANK 10-12 G McCourt, *led till aftr 1st, wth chasing grp till wknd after 3 out.*
........................(14 to 1 op 3 to 1 tchd 16 to 1) 6
FLORA LADY 10-7 K Jones, *sn beh, tld off.*
.........................(66 to 1 op 50 to 1 tchd 100 to 1) 7
PHILNIC 10-12 C Grant, *in tch, sn pushed alng, wknd 5th, tld off*............(10 to 1 op 8 to 1 tchd 12 to 1) 8
TAYBRIDGE TOSH 10-12 P Harley, *in tch whn f 4th.*
.............................(33 to 1 op 16 to 1 tchd 40 to 1) f
Dist: 10l, hd, 2½l, 25l, hd, dist, 5l. 3m 56.80s. a 12.80s (9 Ran).
(Brian Whitelaw), C W Thornton

279 **James Halstead Claiming Chase (5-y-o and up) £2,723 2m.................(2:50)**

269* FASTBIT 6-11-13 N Williamson, *nvr far away, led 4 out, clr aftr 2 out, styd on wl.*
........................(5 to 2 op 2 to 1 tchd 11 to 4) 1
SONSIE MO 8-10-12 (5*) P Williams, *cl up, led 5th, hdd 4 out, outpcd appr 2 out, kpt on r-in.*
.............................(2 to 1 op 7 to 4 tchd 9 to 4) 2
206² GLASS MOUNTAIN (bl) 11-10-11 A Maguire, *prmnt, kpt on same pace frm 4 out.*............(6 to 4 fav op 5 to 4) 3
269⁴ DARK DEEP DAWN 6-10-8 R Supple, *mstks, al beh, tld off.*
....(16 to 1 op 10 to 1) 4
PRESSURE GAME 10-10-11 B Storey, *led to 5th, sn lost pl and beh, tld off*..................(33 to 1 op 20 to 1) 5
CLONADRUM 9-10-2 (7*) A Linton, *al beh, blun and uns rdr 2 out.*..........................(66 to 1 op 33 to 1) ur
Dist: 4l, 6l, dist, dist. 3m 52.60s. a 1.60s (6 Ran).
SR: 27/13/1/ (K C Bailey), K C Bailey

280 **Scottish Racing Club Handicap Hurdle (0-125 4-y-o and up) £2,190 2m 110yds ....(3:20)**

SRIVIJAYA [113] 6-11-10 P Niven, *made all, ran on wl frm last*....................(2 to 1 op 9 to 4 tchd 5 to 2) 1
KING WILLIAM [106] 8-11-3 A Maguire, *hld up, effrt appr 2 out, ran on wl, no imprsn on wnr frm last.*
.........................(7 to 4 fav op 13 to 8 tchd 2 to 1) 2
HEIR OF EXCITEMENT [92] (v) 8-10-3 R Dunwoody, *chsd ldrs, effrt appr 2 out, sn hrd rdn and btn.*
..........................(5 to 1 op 4 to 1 tchd 11 to 2) 3
KALKO [105] 4-11-2 C Grant, *chsd ldr till wknd aftr 2 out.*
...........................(11 to 4 op 5 to 2) 4
DOCTOR'S REMEDY [89] 7-10-0 D Morris, *in tch, rdn aftr 3 out, sn btn*....................(66 to 1 op 50 to 1) 5
Dist: 1½l, 8l, 7l, 2l. 4m 0.20s. a 16.20s (5 Ran).
(K Holder), Mrs M Reveley

281 **Polyflor Novices' Chase (5-y-o and up) £2,671 2½m 110yds.............. (3:50)**

VALIANT WARRIOR 5-10-10 C Grant, *trkd ldr, led betw last 2, drvn out*.........(15 to 8 op 7 to 4 tchd 2 to 1) 1
204* PEARLS BEAU 6-12-0 S Smith Eccles, *led till hdd betw last 2, ecnr und pres*.........(6 to 4 on op 5 to 4 on) 2
246² CAMAN 6-11-0 G McCourt, *in tch, hit 7th, wknd aftr 4 out*...................(11 to 2 op 4 to 1 tchd 6 to 1) 3
269 SECOND ATTEMPT 9-11-0 B Storey, *in tch till wknd quickly aftr 4 out....*(33 to 1 op 50 to 1 tchd 66 to 1) 4
Dist: 12l, 15l, 15l. 5m 4.30s. a 6.30s (4 Ran).
(P Sellars), M D Hammond

282 **Craigvinean Claiming Hurdle (4-y-o and up) £1,892 2m 110yds.............. (4:20)**

EXPLOSIVE SPEED (USA) 5-11-4 (5*) D Bentley, *made all, quickened aftr 3 out, wl clr last, eased r-in.*
.........................(6 to 4 op Evens tchd 13 to 8) 1
186⁸ STYLISH GENT 6-11-0 G McCourt, *chsd ldrs, rdn and outpcd 3 out, styd on ag'n frm nxt, no ch wth wnr.*
..............................(16 to 1 op 12 to 1) 2
FLING IN SPRING 7-11-4 (5*) P Williams, *chsd ldrs, outpcd 3 out, no dngr aftr*.............(8 to 1 tchd 9 to 1) 3
BLACKDOWN 11-3 P Harley, *chsd wnr, mstk 3 out, wknd appr nxt*.................(11 to 10 fav op 5 to 4) 4
MARIAN EVANS 6-11-0 (7*) F Perratt, *hld up, effrt whn mstk and uns rdr 4th*.................(20 to 1 op 16 to 1) ur
TREASURE BEACH 4-9-13¹ (7*) A Linton, *in tch till wknd quickly hfwy, tld off whn pld up bef 3 out.*
.........................(66 to 1 op 33 to 1) pu

Dist: 7l, 6l, 7l. 3m 48.20s. a 4.20s (6 Ran).
(Wetherby Racing Bureau Plc), M D Hammond

283 **Errochty Amateur Riders' Handicap Hurdle (0-115 4-y-o and up) £2,179 3m 110yds ....(4:50)**

AS D'EBOLI (Fr) [85] 6-9-13 (7*) Mr C Bonner, *beh, pushed alng aftr 8th, hdwy to chal 2 out, led appr last, all out.*
.............................(3 to 1 op 2 to 1) 1
OFF THE BRU [103] 8-11-5 (5*) Mr J Bradburne, *made most till hdd 8th, reminders to stay in tch, rallied aftr 2 out, kpt on wl und pres frm last.*
.........................(11 to 2 op 9 to 2 tchd 7 to 1) 2
270* NUNS JEWEL [87] 7-10-1 (7*) Mr G Lewis, *trkd ldrs, led 8th, hdd appr last, no extr.*
.........................(14 to 1 op 6 to 4 on tchd 13 to 8 on and 11 to 10 on) 3
270⁴ TRONCHETTO (Ire) [96] (bl) 4-11-3 Mr S Swiers, *prmnt till wknd quickly 8th, tld off whn pld up bef 3 out.*
.........................(6 to 1 op 5 to 1 tchd 8 to 1) pu
Dist: 1½l, 4l. 5m 48.60s. a 3.60s (4 Ran).
(Ecudawn), M D Hammond

HEXHAM (firm)
Monday August 23rd
Going Correction: MINUS 0.10 sec. per fur.

284 **Methven House Novices' Hurdle (4-y-o and up) £1,731 3m.................(2:00)**

243⁴ TRUMPET 4-10-11 M A FitzGerald, *al hndy, led and quickened clr betw last 2, styd on strly.*
.............................(6 to 1 op 5 to 1) 1
OVER THE STREAM 7-11-0 C Grant, *co'red up on rins, outpcd and lost grnd quickly 5 out, rallied betw last 2, kpt on*.............(5 to 2 op 3 to 1 tchd 7 to 2) 2
248⁷ TROOPER THORN 9-11-0 R Dunwoody, *nvr far away, ev ch and bustled alng frm 2 out, outpcd from last.*
.........................(14 to 1 op 12 to 1 tchd 16 to 1) 3
TRUE DILEMMA 6-11-0 R Marley, *patiently rdn, improved to nose ahead appr 2 out, hdd betw last two, fdd.*
.............................(25 to 1) 4
STINGRAY CITY (USA) 4-10-4 (7*) F Perratt, *jmpd novicey, ran in snatches, ev ch and rdn appr 2 out, btn frm last.*
.........................(15 to 8 fav op 6 to 4 tchd 9 to 4) 5
202² SILVERCROSS LAD 10-10-7 (7*) N Juckes, *led, blun and almost uns rdr 4 out, hdd frm 2 out, sn btn.*
.........................(11 to 2 op 5 to 1 tchd 6 to 1) 6
DAUNTLESS KNIGHT (USA) (bl) 5-11-0 Peter Hobbs, *trkd ldrs, ev ch and drvn alng aftr 4 out, sn lost tch, tld off.*
.........................(7 to 1 op 8 to 1) 7
185⁵ WAYWARD EDWARD (bl) 7-11-0 D Telfer, *wth ldrs to hfwy, wknd quickly aftr 4 out, tld off....*(25 to 1 op 20 to 1) 8
Dist: 6l, 7l, 1l, 6l, 3l, 12l, nk. 5m 57.50s. a 10.50s (8 Ran).
(Mrs M Roper), J G M O'Shea

285 **English Estates Juvenile Novices' Hurdle (3-y-o) £1,828 2m.................(2:30)**

WANZA 10-12 C Grant, *jmpd wl, made all, quickened up frm 2 out, readily.............*(3 to 1 co-fav tchd 7 to 1) 1
138⁵ ON GOLDEN POND (Ire) 10-4 (3*) N Bentley, *wth wnr, bustled alng whn pace quickened betw last 2, rallied r-in*...............................(12 to 1) 2
PRINCIPAL PLAYER (USA) 10-9 (3*) A Dobbin, *patiently rdn, took clr order 3 out, hit last, no extr r-in.*
.............................(14 to 1) 3
147² NOMADIC FIRE 10-12 R Dunwoody, *wtd wth, improved hfwy, effrt and rdn 2 out, no imprsn*.......(3 to 1 co-fav op 5 to 2) 4
SUMMER FLOWER 10-2 (5*) T Eley, *in tch, pushed alng to improve appr 3 out, styd on, not pace to chal.* (33 to 1) 5
DUKE OF DREAMS 10-12 P Niven, *settled midfield, effrt and pushed alng appr 3 out, nvr able to chal.*
.............................(7 to 1 op 5 to 1 tchd 8 to 1) 6
247³ ROSCOMMON JOE (Ire) 10-12 M Dwyer, *settled in midfield, steady hdwy hfwy, lost grnd frm 3 out, sn btn.*
.............................(3 to 1 co-fav) 7
128⁵ MAGIC FAN (Ire) (bl) 10-12 J Railton, *pressed ldg pair, drvn alng and lost grnd appr 2 out, sn btn, tld off.* (33 to 1) 8
247 CONTRAC COUNTESS (Ire) 10-7 R Supple, *struggling to go pace hfwy, nvr a serious threat........*(33 to 1) 9
247 WALSHAM WITCH 10-7 M Ranger, *in tch, struggling to keep up hfwy, tld off......*(25 to 1 op 20 to 1) 10
247⁶ SUMMERS DREAM 10-7 D Byrne, *chasing ldg trio whn swrvd badly rght and uns rdr 3rd.*
.........................(25 to 1 op 20 to 1 tchd 33 to 1) ur
Dist: 3½l, 3l, 2l, 6l, 2l, 12l, 15l, 20l, 12l. 4m 0.50s. a 10.50s (11 Ran).
(J D Gordon), M D Hammond

286 **St George's Novices' Chase (4-y-o and up) £2,115 2m 110yds.................(3:00)**

NATIONAL HUNT RESULTS 1993-94

223* KILLULA CHIEF 6-12-0 M Dwyer, *settled gng wl, steady
  hdwy aftr 3 out, hrd drvn and looked btn betw last 2,
  styd on to ld r-in.*
  .... (5 to 4 on op 11 to 8 on tchd 6 to 4 on and 6 to 5 on) 1
  KEEP SHARP 7-11-7 L Wyer, *jmpd wl, wth ldr till led aftr
  5th, 6 ls clr betw last 2, wknd and ct r-in.*
  ....(7 to 2 op 5 to 1) 2
  VIRGINIA'S BAY 7-11-7 A Orkney, *struggling to go pace
  aftr 4th, plodded round a fence beh.*
  .... (25 to 1 op 20 to 1) 3
246³ EBORNEEZER'S DREAM (v) 10-11-7 D Telfer, *struggling to
  go pace frm 3rd, tld off from hfwy.*
  .... (14 to 1 op 12 to 1 tchd 16 to 1) 4
  DIZZY DEALER 6-11-2 D Morris, *slight ld till hdd aftr 5th,
  styd hndy till wknd quickly frm 4 out, tld off.*
  .... (12 to 1 op 8 to 1) 5
  WEST WITH THE WIND 6-11-7 T Reed, *blun and uns rdr*
  .... (4 to 1 op 5 to 2 tchd 9 to 2) ur
Dist: 3l, dist, 6l, 8l. 4m 4.50s. a 6.50s (6 Ran).
SR: 20/10/-/ (T G K Construction Ltd), J G M O'Shea

287 Team Valley Selling Handicap Hurdle (4-y-o and up) £1,675 2½m 110yds..... (3:30)

237⁴ RUN MILADY [65] 5-10-8 D Wilkinson, *drpd out strt, hit
  second, steady hdwy to join issue 3 out, led aftr last,
  styd on.*
  .... (6 to 1 tchd 7 to 1 and 11 to 2) 1
217* STANE STREET (Ire) [81] 5-11-10 J Railton, *wth ldr, ev ch
  and drvn alng frm 2 out, kpt on same pace.*
  ....(6 to 1 op 4 to 1) 2
  JUBILATA (USA) [74] 5-11-3 C Dennis, *patiently rdn, gd
  hdwy fnl circuit, ev ch till not quicken r-in...* (10 to 1) 3
  ALAMIR (USA) [59] (bl) 5-10-2¹ H Dunwoody, *tried to make
  all, hdd and ran appr last, no extr.* (20 to 1 op 16 to 1) 4
224³ GREEN'S SEAGO (USA) [65] 5-10-8¹ J A Harris, *settled
  midfield, bustled alng to improve frm 3 out, nvr nr to
  chal.*........................ (11 to 2 op 6 to 1 tchd 13 to 2) 5
  WHATCOMESNATURALLY (USA) [75] 4-11-4 C Grant, *trkd
  ldg pair, feeling pace and lost grnd aftr one circuit, no
  dngr after*...................... (5 to 1 fav op 4 to 1) 6
225⁵ STROKED AGAIN [74] 8-11-3 A Maguire, *struggling to keep
  in tch aftr one circuit, tld off.*
  .... (9 to 1 op 10 to 1 tchd 12 to 1) 7
  SPANISH WHISPER [82] 6-11-8 (3*) W Marston, *settled midfield, effrt and drvn alng aftr one circuit, tld off frm 3
  out.*..(6 to 1) 8
  SWANK GILBERT [57] 7-9-7 (7*) Carol Cuthbert, *in tch for
  one circuit, sn tld off.*......................... (20 to 1) 9
202³ LONDON EXPRESS [60] 9-10-3 Peter Hobbs, *chsd ldg
  bunch for a circuit, tld off.*...........(6 to 1 op 5 to 1) 10
191⁶ SHAYNA MAIDEL [73] 4-11-2 G McCourt, *struggling frm
  hfwy, tld off.*................... (8 to 1 op 14 to 1) 11
Dist: 1½l, 1½l, 1½l, 20l, 8l, 1½l, 2l, 8l, 8l, 10l. 4m 59.00s. a 6.00s (11 Ran).
SR: -/14/5/-/-/-/ (Scotnorth Racing Ltd), Mrs S M Austin

288 English Estates Handicap Chase (0-115 5-y-o and up) £2,733 2½m 110yds... (4:00)

206³ TOUCHING STAR [91] 8-10-5 (3*) M Hourigan, *nvr far
  away, drvn to nose ahead betw last 2, styd on grimly
  r-in.*................................ (3 to 1 tchd 7 to 2) 1
  ABSAILOR [91] 9-10-3 (5*) P Williams, *al hndy, rdn to join
  wnr betw last 2, kpt on same pace r-in.*
  .... (11 to 2 op 6 to 4 on tchd Evens) 2
  PALMRUSH [107] 9-11-10 C Grant, *jmpd wl, tried to make
  all, hdd and rdn betw last 2, one pace.*
  .... (11 to 10 on op 5 to 4 on tchd Evens) 3
241 MAIAN BEAR [97] 7-11-0 Gary Lyons, *mstks, nvr far away,
  ev ch till hit 2 out, no extr...........* (5 to 1 op 7 to 2) 4
  MR PANACHE [85] 11-9-11 (5*) D Bentley, *sn struggling, tld
  off.*.................................. (50 to 1 op 33 to 1) 5
Dist: 1½l, 3½l, 8l, dist. 5m 7.00s. a 6.00s (5 Ran).
SR: -/-/10/-/-/ (Anthony Palmer), P J Hobbs

289 Chartered Surveyors Handicap Hurdle (0-120 4-y-o and up) £2,108 2m...... (4:30)

  WEE WIZARD (Ire) [87] 4-9-13 (3*) A Dobbin, *patiently rdn,
  drvn up to join ldrs 3 out, led betw last 2, ran on wl.*
  .... (5 to 1 op 4 to 1 tchd 3 to 1) 1
  AZUREUS (Ire) [111] 5-11-12 P Niven, *jmpd badly, bustled
  alng hfwy, styd on grimly frm 2 out, not pace to chal.*
  .... (Evens fav op 6 to 4 tchd 2 to 1) 2
  CASUAL PASS [105] 10-11-6 T Reed, *settled off the pace,
  shaken up and steady hdwy frm 2 out, fnshd wl.*
  ....(6 to 1 op 5 to 1) 3
  BALLYANTO [85] 8-9-7 (7*) Mr D Parker, *patiently rdn, jnd
  issue hfwy, led aftr 3 till betw last 2, one pace.*
  .... (12 to 1 op 10 to 1) 4
  ARCTIC OATS [110] 8-11-6 (5*) S Lyons, *led to 3rd, rgned ld
  briefly 3 out, outpcd appr last...* (20 to 1 op 16 to 1) 5
  RED JAM JAR [85] 8-9-12⁵ (7*) Mr S Bell, *wth ldr, led 3rd to
  3 out, fdd last 2........................* (10 to 1 op 7 to 1) 6
  CHIEF RAIDER (Ire) [88] 5-10-11 A Maguire, *trkd ldrs, rdn 3
  out, btn bef nxt....................* (7 to 1 op 6 to 1) 7
  TALATON FLYER [92] 7-10-7 Peter Hobbs, *pressed ldrs to
  hfwy, tld off whn pld up bef 2 out.* (14 to 1 op 12 to 1) pu

  35

LOCHNDOM [85] 8-10-0 R Hodge, *struggling to keep up
  hfwy, tld off whn pld up bef 2 out.* (50 to 1 op 33 to 1) pu
Dist: 3l, 4l, 2l, 3l, 1½l, 12l. 3m 55.30s. a 5.30s (9 Ran).
SR: 5/26/16/-/16/-/ (Armstrong/Greenwell), M A Barnes

TRALEE (IRE) (good (race 1), firm (2,3))
Monday August 23rd

290 Kellihers Electrical Maiden Hurdle (3-y-o) £3,797 2m......................... (5:00)

253⁸ ASSERT STAR 10-10 C F Swan, ...(9 to 1) 1
253² CALL MY GUEST (Ire) 10-10 J Shortt, ...(7 to 2) 2
  LUSTRINO (USA) (bl) 10-10 B Sheridan, ... (6 to 4 fav) 3
  CARRICK PIKE (USA) 10-5 K F O'Brien, ...(6 to 1) 4
  DUNANY ROSE (Ire) 9-9 (5*) A J Roche, ...(12 to 1) 5
228⁹ SWEET PEACH (Ire) 9-10³ (7*) Mr J A Sheehan, ... (33 to 1) 6
253⁸ CHRISTY MOORE (Ire) 9-12 (7*) R Dolan, ...(33 to 1) 7
  INNOCENT MAN (Ire) 10-5 C O'Dwyer, ...(20 to 1) 8
  SLAINTA (Ire) 10-5 T Horgan, ...(50 to 1) 9
  DRESS DANCE (Ire) 9-12 (7*) H Taylor, ...(33 to 1) f
  JAZZY REFRAIN (Ire) 9-7 (7*) C O'Brien, ...(14 to 1) pu
  RUN MY ROSIE (Ire) 10-0 P McWilliams, ...(33 to 1) pu
Dist: 5l, 25l, 15l, 6l. 3m 49.50s. (12 Ran).
(Ms M Hogan), A P O'Brien

291 Barrett Bookmakers Q.R. Handicap Hurdle (4-y-o and up) £3,797 2¾m......... (5:30)

135 CARES OF TOMORROW [-] 6-10-8 Mr D J Kavanagh,
  .... (12 to 1) 1
265³ SILVERWREN [-] 10-10-3 (5*) Mr P M Kelly, ...(12 to 1) 2
158⁵ MOUNTHENRY STAR (Ire) [-] 5-9-8 (7*) Mr G F FitzGerald,
  .... (14 to 1) 3
254* MOBILE MAN [-] 6-10-2 (5*,4ex) Mr J A Nash,. . (5 to 1 fav) 4
134 FOXBROOK [-] (bl) 7-11-2 Mr S R Murphy, ...(12 to 1) 5
230³ SHAYISTA [-] 8-10-8 (3*) Mr R O'Neill, ...(10 to 1) 6
101 QUIVERING MELODY [-] 6-9-9 (7*) Mr P A Roche, (14 to 1) 7
119⁴ FOUR TRIX [-] 12-10-8 (3*) Mr D Marnane, ...(7 to 1) 8
135 HIGH-SPEC [-] 7-10-12 (7*) Mr J M Fleming, ...(14 to 1) 9
122 BIT OF A TOUCH [-] 7-10-0 (7*) Mr J T McNamara, (25 to 1) 10
201⁷ HAWAIIAN GODDESS (USA) [-] 6-9-9 (5*) Mr D McGoona,
  .... (25 to 1) 11
175* PRACTICE RUN (Ire) [-] 5-10-12 Mr P Fenton, ...(11 to 2) 12
122* TERZIA [-] 6-11-1 (7*) Mr T R Hughes, ...(7 to 1) 13
  GUESSWORK [-] 7-10-13 Mr P J Healy, ...(20 to 1) 14
42 WAR DEVIL [-] 7-9-10³ (7*) Mr D C O'Connor, ...(33 to 1) 15
229³ CHARDON [-] 7-9-9² (7*) Mr J A Sheehan, ...(20 to 1) f
213* THE VERY MAN [-] 7-11-4 (4ex) Mr T Mullins, ...(11 to 2) f
135 SWEET DOWNS [-] 12-9-7 (7*) Mr K Walsh, ...(33 to 1) pu
111 ANOTHER GROUSE [-] 6-9-7 (7*) Mrs K Walsh, ...(25 to 1) pu
Dist: 1½l, 6l, 2l, 2l. 5m 15.60s. (19 Ran).
(Mrs J S Bolger), J S Bolger

292 Festival Mares Flat Race (4-y-o and up) £3,457 2m......................... (8:00)

  KILADANTE (Ire) 4-11-9 Mr A P O'Brien, ... (5 to 4 on) 1
236² VON CARTY (Ire) 4-11-2 (7*) Mr J T McNamara, .. (10 to 1) 2
107³ FAIRYHILL RUN (Ire) 5-11-7 (7*) Mr D A Harney, ...(8 to 1) 3
  SPOUT HOUSE (Ire) 4-11-2 (7*) Mr J P Hunter, ...(7 to 1) 4
255² REMAINDER LASS (Ire) 4-11-4 (5*) Mr P M Kelly, ... (8 to 1) 5
201⁴ JENNYELLEN (Ire) 4-11-9 Mr A J Martin, ...(14 to 1) 6
95⁹ PRIORITY GALE (Ire) 4-11-9 Mr P Fenton, ...(14 to 1) 7
98⁵ NOELEENS DELIGHT (Ire) 4-11-6 (3*) Mr D Marnane,
  .... (14 to 1) 8
50 MYSTIC MEG (Ire) 5-11-7 (7*) Mr L B Murphy, ...(50 to 1) 9
179⁶ MISS POLLERTON (Ire) 5-11-7 (7*) Mr M J Bowe, (12 to 1) 10
158⁹ REGULAR PAL 10-11-11 (3*) Miss M Olivefalk, ...(50 to 1) 11
201⁵ KIZZY ROSE 6-11-7 (7*) Miss C Hourigan, ...(14 to 1) 12
61⁹ RIYASHA (Ire) 5-11-9 (5*) Mr J A Nash, ...(33 to 1) 13
211 MARCHING SEASON (Ire) 5-11-7 (7*) Mr S O'Donnell,
  .... (25 to 1) 14
236 KATES CASTLE 6-11-7 (7*) Mr K O'Sullivan, ...(100 to 1) 15
255 FRAGRANCE MOUNTAIN 7-11-7 (7*) Mr P A Roche,
  .... (25 to 1) 16
179⁴ QUEEN KAM (Ire) 4-11-4 (5*) Mr J P Berry, ...(14 to 1) 17
211⁴ FURTHER APPRAISAL (Ire) 4-11-4 (5*) Mr P J Dreeling,
  .... (10 to 1) 18
236 D'S AND DO'S (Ire) 4-11-6 (3*) Mr T M Bergin, ...(33 to 1) 19
236³ THE WICKED CHICKEN (Ire) 4-11-6 (3*) Mrs S McCarthy,
  .... (7 to 1) su
Dist: 3l, nk, sht-hd, sht-hd. 3m 38.40s. (20 Ran).
(William Feighery), A P O'Brien

TRALEE (IRE) (good)
Tuesday August 24th

293 Lee Strand Arthur Blennerhassett Memorial Novice Chase (4-y-o and up) £3,797 2½m.......................... (5:30)

178 MALACHYS BAR 9-12-0 F Woods, ...(16 to 1) 1
123 BACK DOOR JOHNNY 7-12-0 D H O'Connor, ...(8 to 1) 2
135⁶ SHEAMY'S DREAM (Ire) 5-11-8 J Shortt, ... (2 to 1 fav) 3

122² MINERAL DUST 10-11-7 (7ʰ) Mr P Cashman, ... (8 to 1) 4
97 DOCTER MAC 6-11-7 (7ʰ) C O'Brien, ... (16 to 1) 5
INK BY THE DRUM (USA) 5-11-8 C F Swan, ... (4 to 1) 6
123 RANDOM PRINCE 9-12-0 C O'Dwyer, ... (6 to 1) 7
DOONEGA (Ire) 5-11-8 T Horgan, ... (7 to 1) 8
77 CIARA'S STAR (bl) 6-12-0 A J O'Brien, ... (50 to 1) 9
200 CHESTNUT JEWEL (Ire) 5-11-8 P McWilliams, ... (25 to 1) 10
79 MILLWOOD STREAM 8-11-2 (7ʰ) Miss L Gough, .. (25 to 1) 11
GLOBE HABIT 7-11-9 (5ʰ) T J O'Sullivan, ... (33 to 1) 12
176⁴ MANOR RHYME 6-11-7 (7ʰ) Mr D Keane, ... (33 to 1) 13
135 KLICKITAT 6-11-9 C N Bowens, ... (16 to 1) 14
122 JOHNJOES PRIDE 9-12-0 K F O'Brien, ... (12 to 1) f
200⁴ MAKE ME AN ISLAND 8-11-9 J F Titley, ... (14 to 1) f
Dist: 1l, nk, 12l, 1½l. 5m 10.40s. (16 Ran).
(Patrick J F Hassett), Patrick J F Hassett

294 WinElectric Handicap Hurdle (Listed - Grade 3) (4-y-o and up) £6,900 2m 1f (6:00)

135 DUHARRA [-] (bl) 5-11-9 A Maguire, *wl plcd, prog to ld appr 2 out, ran on well und pres frm last.*.......(8 to 1) 1
249* NIMBLE WIND [-] (bl) 7-9-12 (4ex) A J O'Brien, *rear to hfwy, prog 4 out, chlgd appr last, styd on strly r-in, jst fld.*
....(16 to 1) 2
LOSHIAN (Ire) [-] 4-11-5 R Dunwoody, *wl plcd, mstk two out, styd on und pres r-in.*.......................... (7 to 4 fav) 3
135⁴ CHOISYA (Ire) [-] 5-10-2 (7ʰ) K P Gaule, *mid-div, prog into 5th pl appr 2 out, styd on.*................... (8 to 1) 4
230* TOUREEN GIRL [-] 6-10-3 (6ex) C F Swan, *mid-div, prog into 3rd pl 3 out, rdn and wknd betw last 2......*(7 to 1) 5
CAN'T THINK WHAT [-] 6-10-8 (7ʰ) T P Treacy, *trkd ldrs, 4th and wknd 3 out, fdd r-in....*.................. (10 to 1) 6
230⁶ WATERLOO LADY [-] 6-9-7 T Horgan, *led till appr 3rd, rdn and wknd approaching 2 out.*.................. (33 to 1) 7
117² LOVE AND PORTER [-] [-] 5-10-1 D H O'Connor, *led 3rd till aftr 5th, wknd 3 out.*............................ (10 to 1) 8
135⁷ RISING WATERS (Ire) [-] 5-11-2 (7ʰ) G Lee, *rear, styd on frm 4 out, not rch ldrs.*.............................. (14 to 1) 9
135⁵ NATALIES FANCY [-] 7-11-3 J F Titley, *mid-div, prog 4 out, no imprsn strt.*............................... (14 to 1) 10
131⁵ MARIAN YEAR [-] 7-10-0 (3ʰ) J Collins, *mid-div till rdn and wknd 3 out.*.......................... (20 to 1) 11
57⁸ PRETTY NICE [-] 5-10-10 P L Malone, *al rear.* (16 to 1) 12
157² NOBODYS FLAME (Ire) [-] 5-9-8 J Magee, *mid-div till lost tch 4 out.*...................................... (20 to 1) 13
BEAU BEAUCHAMP [-] 6-11-7 P Carberry, *al rear.* (14 to 1) 14
135 MORNING DREAM [-] 6-9-7 M Duffy, *al rear......* (16 to 1) 15
123⁴ SHAREEF ALLIANCE (Ire) [-] 4-10-10 K F O'Brien, *wl plcd whn pld up lme aftr 5th.*......................(10 to 1) pu
Dist: Nk, 4l, ¾l, 1½l. 3m 54.00s. (16 Ran).
(Mrs M Togher), D K Weld

295 Noel Browne Mares Maiden Hurdle (5-y-o and up) £3,797 2m 1f. (6:30)

256 HAYMAKERS JIG (Ire) 5-11-6 K F O'Brien, ...(8 to 1) 1
108² HURRICANE EDEN 6-11-6 T Horgan, ... (5 to 2 fav) 2
232⁶ PARSONS EYRE (Ire) 5-11-1 (5ʰ) T J Mitchell, ... (10 to 1) 3
265⁵ CARLINGFORD RUN 6-11-7 (7ʰ) Mr D Murphy, ...(7 to 1) 4
FORTUNE'S GIRL 5-12-0 J Shortt, ... (11 to 2) 5
174² FOLLY PRIEST (Ire) 5-11-3 (3ʰ) Mr A R Coonan, ... (7 to 1) 6
120 MISS FLINTSTONE VI (Ire) 5-11-6 J F Titley, ... (33 to 1) 7
236* MILFORD MATCH (Ire) 5-12-0 C F Swan, ...(7 to 2) 8
169 BOLTON SARAH 6-10-13 (7ʰ) T P Treacy, ...(25 to 1) 9
112 ALLOON LAWN 7-11-6 R Byrne, ... (25 to 1) 10
234⁶ DANE ST LADY (Ire) 5-11-6 G M O'Neill, ... (16 to 1) 11
50⁶ TAKE IT EASY KID (Ire) 5-12-0 R Dunwoody, ...(8 to 1) 12
71 SQUARE GALE (Ire) 5-11-1 (5ʰ) Susan A Finn, ...(25 to 1) pu
Dist: 5l, 1l, 2l, ¾l. 4m 1.40s. (13 Ran).
(Edward M Travers), Michael Hourigan

EXETER (firm)
Wednesday August 25th
Going Correction: MINUS 0.35 sec. per fur.

296 Marsh Barton Juvenile Novices' Hurdle (3-y-o) £1,992 2m 1f 110yds. . . . . (2:00)

EUPHONIC 10-12 J Frost, *trkd ldrs, wnt 3rd 4th, cl up and ev ch 2 out, shaken up to ld last 50 yards, styd on wl.*..............(11 to 10 on op 5 to 4 on tchd Evens) 1
188* BEAT THE BAGMAN (Ire) 11-3 L Harvey, *al hndy, wnt second 3 out, led nxt, sn rdn, hdd and not quicken last 50 yards....*(13 to 2 op 5 to 1 tchd 7 to 1 and 8 to 1) 2
STAR MINSTREL (Ire) 10-12 R Dunwoody, *trkd ldrs, jmpd slwly 4th, wnt fourth 3 out, cl up and ev ch frm nxt, sn rdn and one pace......*..........(20 to 1 op 12 to 1) 3
247* ITS UNBELIEVABLE 11-3 N Williamson, *led aftr second till hdd 2 out, sn btn.*...................................... 4
MASTER BEVELED 10-12 G Upton, *hld up, beh 3rd, hdwy aftr 4 out, styd on frm nxt, one pace.*
.... (33 to 1 op 20 to 1) 5
221² FREE DANCER 10-7 D Bridgwater, *hld up, beh 3rd, hdwy aftr 5th, chsd ldrs and ev ch frm nxt, wknd 2 out.*
.... (20 to 1 op 12 to 1) 6

ROWLANDSONS GOLD (Ire) 10-7 Lorna Vincent, *beh 3rd, no ch frm 4 out.*....................(25 to 1 op 14 to 1) 7
GROGFRYN 10-7 M A FitzGerald, *hld up, beh 3rd, lost tch aftr 5th, sn behind.*......................(50 to 1 op 33 to 1) 8
207 ROSEMARY'S MEMORY (Ire) 10-7 W McFarland, *led till aftr second, pressed ldr till wknd after 5th, no ch frm 3 out.*.......................... (50 to 1 op 33 to 1) 9
MONDAY AT THREE 10-12 N Hawke, *pld hrd, beh whn blun 5th, sn tld off.*.................(50 to 1 op 25 to 1) 10
MY SET PEACE (v) 10-7 G Bradley, *mstk 1st, beh frm 3rd, sn tld off, pld up bef 2 out.*....... (33 to 1 op 16 to 1) pu
Dist: 1l, 15l, 2l, ¾l, 1½l, 15l, 1l, 20l. 3m 57.40s. a 0.40s (11 Ran).
SR: 19/23/3/6/-/-/ (Paul Stamp), I A Balding

297 Countess Wear Selling Handicap Hurdle (4-y-o and up) £1,644 2m 1f 110yds. . (2:30)

ITS ALL OVER NOW [68] 9-10-5 S McNeill, *al prmnt, wnt second 5th, led 2 out, drvn out, styd on wl.*
...............................(9 to 2 op 5 to 1 tchd 6 to 1) 1
226* MILLROUS [87] (bl) 5-11-10 R Dunwoody, *hld up, hdwy appr 2 out, ev ch frm nxt, rdn to chal last, not qicken r-in.....* (3 to 1 op 2 to 1 tchd 100 to 30 and 7 to 2) 2
260* SALAR'S SPIRIT [79] 7-10-9 (7ʰ,5ex) R Darke, *hld up, wnt 4th 3 out, rdn frm nxt, styd on betw last 2, no imprsn.*
...............................(9 to 4 fav op 7 to 4) 3
218⁵ CORNISH COSSACK (NZ) [73] 6-10-10 J Frost, *al prmnt, cl up and ev ch appr 2 out, sn rdn, one pace betw last two.*
.................................(12 to 1 tchd 16 to 1) 4
144⁴ LOCH DUICH [72] 7-10-9 G McCourt, *hld up in last pl, hdwy 3 out, cl up and ev ch nxt, sn hrd rdn and wknd.*
...............................(5 to 1 op 4 to 1 tchd 11 to 2) 5
217 FASHION PRINCESS [70] 7-10-0 (7ʰ) D Matthews, *led till aftr second, led ag'n 4th til 2 out, sn wknd.*
...............................(20 to 1 op 14 to 1 tchd 25 to 1) 6
198⁴ BLUECHIPENTERPRISE [82] (bl) 7-11-5 J R Kavanagh, *led second, hdd 4th, pressed ldr till rdn and wknd 2 out.*..................................(25 to 1 op 14 to 1) 7
GREEN'S STUBBS [63] 6-10-0 A Maguire, *chsd ldrs frm 3rd till wknd rpdly aftr 5th, sn tld off.* (20 to 1 op 14 to 1) 8
Dist: 1l, 12l, 3l, 3l, 1½l, 10l, 20l. 3m 59.10s. a 2.10s (8 Ran).
SR: -/13/-/-/-/ (Moor Farm Racing), Mrs A L M King

298 Westcountry Live Novices' Chase (5-y-o and up) £2,736 2m 1f 110yds. . . . . (3:00)

195³ BONDAID 9-11-3 A Maguire, *badly hmpd 1st, several slow jumps, wnt 3rd 5th, chsd ldr, rdn to ld last, all out.*
...............................(5 to 2 tchd 3 to 1) 1
218³ NEEDS MUST 6-11-3 J Frost, *jmpd lft, pressed ldr in second pl, ev ch frm 4 out, rdn and not quicken r-in.*
.................................(17 to 2 op 6 to 1 tchd 10 to 1) 2
TITUS ANDRONICUS 6-11-3 R Supple, *wnt 3rd 4th, mstk nxt, chsd ldr, ev ch 4 out, rdn and one pace appr last.*
...............................(100 to 30 op 2 to 1) 3
TUDOR WEDDING 8-11-3 S Earle, *led til blun and hdd last, not reco'r.*......................... (25 to 1 op 14 to 1) 4
168² WINDSOR PARK (USA) 7-11-0 (3ʰ) V Slattery, *hld up in tch, ev ch whn stumbled and uns rdr aftr 6 out.*
...............................(9 to 4 fav tchd 5 to 2) ur
194 DARING CLASS 7-11-0 L Shoemark, *blun badly 1st, jmpd slwly nxt, cld up to ld 5 out, 5th and ev ch whn blunded and uns rdr next..................*.....(12 to 1 op 8 to 1) ur
JET (bl) 7-11-3 M A FitzGerald, *lost pl and wknd rpdly aftr 4th, tld off frm nxt, pld up bef four out.*
.................................(33 to 1 op 20 to 1) pu
Dist: 1½l, 5l, 7l. 4m 16.60s. a 10.60s (7 Ran).
(A J Allright), J White

299 Westcountry Television Claiming Chase (5-y-o and up) £2,710 2¾m 110yds. . . (3:30)

PIGEON ISLAND 11-10-6 (7ʰ) D Meade, *slwly away, last til hdwy aftr 9th, wnt moderate 3rd 7 out, headway after 3 out, rdn to ld nr finish....*........... (16 to 1 op 10 to 1) 1
220² GROPPING TIM 14-11-12 R Dunwoody, *led 3rd till mstk and hdd 9th, led ag'n 11th to nxt, led 5 out, hit 2 out, wknd and headed nr finish.*
...................(3 to 1 op 11 to 4 on tchd 7 to 2 on) 2
263² DANDY LASS 12-10-7 J Frost, *led second to nxt, led 9th to 11th, led nxt to 5 out, ev ch till rdn and not quicken appr last.*..............(9 to 1 op 10 to 1 tchd 12 to 1) 3
220⁴ SAMSUN (bl) 11-11-2 M A FitzGerald, *reminder aftr 6th, lost tch after 11th, tld off.*
...............................(7 to 1 op 8 to 1 tchd 14 to 1) 4
220⁵ CLEANING UP 11-11-2 B Powell, *mstks, wnt 3rd 9th, jmpd slwly nxt, sn wknd, tld off frm 6 out.*
.................................(33 to 1 op 16 to 1) 5
196⁵ SIRISAT 9-11-0 Mr K Hollowell, *mstk 8th, sn lost pl, wnt moderate 4th aftr four out, soon wknd, tld off.*
....6
MARLBOROUGH LADY 7-10-9 S Burrough, *hld up, hdwy appr tenth, wnt moderate 4th 7 out, wknd aftr 6 out, beh whn pld up bef 3 out.*.......... (33 to 1 op 20 to 1) pu
Dist: 1l, 2½l, dist, 10l, 2½l. 5m 34.00s. a 13.00s (7 Ran).
(J W Browne), G F H Charles-Jones

300 John & Ruth Baker Memorial Handicap Hurdle (0-120 4-y-o and up) £2,599 2m 1f 110yds. . . . . (4:00)

217^{3} TRUST DEED (USA) [89] (bl) 5-10-3^{3} M A FitzGerald, *wnt 3rd appr 4th, pressed ldr, pushed alng 3 out, hrd rdn to ld aftr last, all out*. . . . . (12 to 1 op 10 to 1 tchd 14 to 1) 1
FROSTY RECEPTION [98] (bl) 8-10-12 L Harvey, *led aftr 3rd, hrd rdn 2 out, hdd and unbl to quicken after last.* . . . . (7 to 4 fav op 9 to 4) 2
MADRAJ (Ire) [87] 5-10-1 W McFarland, *al chasing ldrs, rdn frm 3 out, kpt on one pace*. . . . . (10 to 1 op 6 to 1) 3
219^{2} PHARLY STORY [114] (v) 5-12-0 R Dunwoody, *hld up, hdwy 5th, rdn 2 out, unbl to quicken.* . . . . (100 to 30 op 5 to 2 tchd 7 to 2) 4
219^{3} SHALCHLO BOY [95] 9-10-9 N Williamson, *led till aftr 3rd, wknd after 4 out, styd on ag'n, one pace after 2 out.* . . . . (14 to 1 op 7 to 1) 5
NOVA SPIRIT [94] 5-10-8 S Mackey, *hld up, hdwy 5th, wnt 3rd 3 out, sn rdn and wknd aftr nxt.* . . . . (11 to 2 op 9 to 2 tchd 6 to 1) 6
AMPHIGORY [88] (v) 5-9-9 (7*) T Thompson, *hld up, not fluent, rdn and lost tch aftr 4th, sn beh, styd on one pace frm 2 out*. . . . . (8 to 1 op 6 to 1) 7

Dist: 1½l, 2l, 8l, 3l, 1½l, 2l. 3m 58.60s. a 1.60s (7 Ran).
SR: -/5/-/11/ (Fred Camis), Mrs A Knight

301 Crediton Novices' Hurdle (4-y-o and up) £1,992 2m 1f 110yds. . . . . (4:30)

MUSTAHIL (Ire) 4-10-11 R Dunwoody, *mstk 4th, reminders, styd on frm 2 out, led last, drvn clr r-in.* . . . . (11 to 2 op 5 to 1) 1
216* ATHAR (Ire) 4-11-2 L Harvey, *hld up, wnt 3rd 4th, ev ch frm 3 out, sn rdn, every chance whn pckd last, not quicken r-in*. . . . . (5 to 4 fav tchd 6 to 4 on) 2
SUDANOR (Ire) 4-10-11 N Hawke, *led, clr aftr 3rd, mstk 5th, rdn and hdd last, wknd r-in.* . . . . (25 to 1 op 16 to 1 tchd 33 to 1) 3
SOUL TRADER 4-10-6 S Burrough, *al chasing ldrs, in tch 3 out, no imprsn frm nxt*. . . . . (33 to 1 op 14 to 1) 4
FIELDRIDGE (bl) 4-10-11 G Bradley, *trkd ldr, cl up and ev ch 5th, wknd appr 2 out*. . . . . (2 to 1 op 5 to 4) 5
CHICKABIDDY 5-10-2 (7*) Mr N Moore, *sn wl beh, hdwy aftr 3 out, nvr nrr*. . . . . (66 to 1 op 33 to 1) 6
BROWNHALL 5-10-7 (7*) Mr B Pollock, *mid-div till lost pl aftr 4th, sn beh*. . . . . (66 to 1 op 33 to 1) 7
NEW STATESMAN 5-11-0 N Mann, *chsd ldr to 4th, wknd quickly, tld off*. . . . . (33 to 1 op 20 to 1) 8
BARE HIGHLANDER 7-11-0 W Irvine, *pushed alng aftr 3rd, sn beh, tld off*. . . . . (66 to 1 op 33 to 1) 9
216^{4} MY HARRY BOY 6-11-0 G Upton, *beh frm 4th, sn tld off, blun last*. . . . . (66 to 1 op 33 to 1) 10
216^{3} JR'S PET 6-10-4 (5*) R Davis, *hld up, hdwy aftr 4th, chsd ldr till wknd quickly appr 3 out, tld off.* . . . . (25 to 1 op 20 to 1 tchd 33 to 1) 11

Dist: 7l, 3l, 3½l, 15l, 8l, 1½l, dist, 2½l, nk, 5l. 3m 58.30s. a 1.30s (11 Ran).
SR: 9/7/-/-/-/-/ (Unity Farm Holiday Centre Ltd), R J Hodges

TRALEE (IRE) (good)
Wednesday August 25th

302 Paddy Macs And Jacks Pubs Maiden Hurdle (5-y-o and up) £3,795 2½m. . . . . . (2:30)

117^{3} PRINCIPLE MUSIC (USA) (bl) 5-11-11 B Sheridan, ... (6 to 4 on) 1
135 REFINED HEIR 5-11-11 P Carberry, ... (4 to 1) 2
173^{6} KENMAC 6-11-3 K F O'Brien, ... (12 to 1) 3
131^{9} CLASS ACT 7-11-11 C F Swan, ... (5 to 1) 4
169^{6} WALKERS LADY (Ire) 5-10-7 (5*) D T Evans, ... (20 to 1) 5
234^{3} EASE THE BURDEN (Ire) 5-10-7 (5*) T J O'Sullivan, (25 to 1) 6
LADY GALE BRIDGE 6-10-12 G M O'Neill, ... (25 to 1) 7
FAIR GO 7-10-10 (7*) C O'Brien, ... (16 to 1) 8
295^{7} MISS FLINTSTONE VI (Ire) 5-10-5 (7*) J P Broderick, ... (50 to 1) 9
MERRY FRIENDS 7-10-12 C O'Dwyer, ... (14 to 1) 10
96^{6} HAVEN LIGHT 6-10-10 (7*) K P Gaule, ... (33 to 1) 11
150^{3} MAKE A LINE 5-10-10 (7*) Mr A H Lillingston, ... (12 to 1) pu

Dist: 13l, hd, 5l, 11l. 4m 49.60s. (12 Ran).
(Michael W J Smurfit), D K Weld

303 Boyle Brothers Grand Hotel Handicap Chase (4-y-o and up) £3,795 2¼m. . . (3:00)

200^{2} GONZALO [-] 10-10-3 C F Swan, ... (11 to 2) 1+
119 EASTER SIXTEEN [-] 7-11-11 J Shortt, ... (7 to 4 fav) 1+
132^{3} MAC'S GLEN [-] 9-10-9 (5*) Mr G J Harford, ... (5 to 1) 3
132^{2} FRANTESA [-] 7-10-9 T Horgan, ... (3 to 1) 4
170 GARRYDOOLIS [-] 7-10-4 C O'Dwyer, ... (14 to 1) 5
235 TIGH AN CHEOIL [-] 9-9-7 P McWilliams, ... (20 to 1) 6
235^{2} LA MODE LADY [-] 8-9-0 (7*) C O'Brien, ... (10 to 1) 7
235^{4} GRANVILLE HOTEL [-] 9-9-12 W T Slattery, ... (14 to 1) 8
178 CAPINCUR BOY [-] 11-9-12 J Magee, ... (10 to 1) f

Dist: Dd-ht, 2l, 1½l, 13l. 4m 33.60s. (9 Ran).
(F Lacy & Michael B Moore), F J Lacy & Patrick Prendergast

304 Earl Of Desmond INH Flat Race (5-y-o and up) £3,795 2m 1f. . . . . (5:30)

SKEOUGH (Ire) 5-12-0 Mr A P O'Brien, ... (8 to 1) 1
266^{3} SAME DIFFERENCE (Ire) 5-11-9 (5*) Mr J A Nash, . . (6 to 1) 2
BRAVE HENRY 5-11-7 (7*) Mr J T McNamara, ... (6 to 1) 3
59 CLEAN SHEETS VI (Ire) 5-12-0 Mr S R Murphy, ... (25 to 1) 4
124^{9} FIFI'S MAN 7-11-7 (7*) Mr P A Roche, ... (100 to 30) 5
159^{4} GIFTED FELLOW (Ire) 6-11-11 (3*) Mr D Marnane, (12 to 1) 6
107 CAIRDE MHAITH 6-11-7 (7*) Mr P Henley, ... (14 to 1) 7
MUILEAR OIRGE 6-12-0 Mr E Bolger, ... (6 to 4 fav) 8
136 DESPERADO 5-11-9 (5*) Mr G J Harford, ... (25 to 1) 9
266 TELEMANN 7-11-7 (7*) Mr A Ryan, ... (33 to 1) 10

Dist: ½l, 1l, 8l, 2½l. 3m 53.00s. (10 Ran).
(Joseph Crowley), A P O'Brien

TRALEE (IRE) (good)
Thursday August 26th

305 John J. O'Donnell Memorial Maiden Hurdle (5-y-o and up) £3,795 2m 1f. . . . . (2:30)

AIYBAK (Ire) 5-12-0 B Sheridan, ... (5 to 4 on) 1
274 SWALLOWS NEST 6-12-0 M Flynn, ... (4 to 1) 2
258^{2} THE TENANT 6-11-6 C F Swan, ... (12 to 1) 3
CITIZEN BAND (Ire) 5-11-6 M Dwyer, ... (13 to 2) 4
111^{6} JO-SU-KI 6-11-1 (5*) M A Davey, ... (20 to 1) 5
BLAKES FOLLY (Ire) 5-11-6 J Magee, ... (14 to 1) 6
85^{6} FULL SCHEDUAL 6-11-6 C O'Dwyer, ... (25 to 1) 7
DEEP IN TIME (Ire) 5-11-6 K F O'Brien, ... (25 to 1) 8
111 LOSLANN (Ire) 5-11-6 Mr P J Healy, ... (33 to 1) 9
PERSIAN HALO (Ire) 5-12-0 D H O'Connor, ... (11 to 2) f

Dist: ½l, 6l, 11l, 9l. 4m 0.20s. (10 Ran).
(Michael W J Smurfit), D K Weld

306 Denny Gold Medal Handicap Chase (Listed - Grade 3) (4-y-o and up) £8,280 2½m . . . . (3:30)

132* GRATTAN PARK [-] 8-10-6 C F Swan, *mid-div till prog into 6th bef 12th, travelling wl in 4th 2 out, led last, quickened r-in*. . . . . (9 to 2 fav) 1
214^{2} MACK A DAY [-] 6-10-2 A J O'Brien, *rear till steady prog 11th to take 3rd 3 out, led nxt, hdd appr last, not pace of wnr r-in*. . . . . (12 to 1) 2
119^{2} HARRISTOWN LADY [-] (bl) 6-10-12 P McWilliams, *trkd ldrs, ev ch in 3rd 2 out, rdn and wknd appr last.* (5 to 1) 3
119^{5} KINGSTON WAY [-] 7-10-10 C O'Dwyer, *wl plcd, prog into second 3 out, rdn and wknd betw last 2*. . . . . . . (11 to 1) 4
291 GUESSWORK [-] 7-11-8 Mr P J Healy, ... (14 to 1) 5
82^{4} FROZEN FRIEND [-] 10-9-7 (5*) T J O'Sullivan, *rear till styd on 3 out wthout rching ldrs*. . . . . (33 to 1) 6
134^{2} SKY RANGE [-] 8-10-7 T Horgan, *mid-div till prog to track ldrs 12th, wknd nxt*. . . . . (6 to 1) 7
119 THE GOOSER [-] 10-12-0 F Woods, *led 4th, mstk tenth, hdd bef four out, sn wknd*. (14 to 1) 8
134^{4} DANCINGCINDERELLA [-] 9-9-12 (7*) J P Broderick, *mid-div, some prog 12th, nvr rch ldrs*. . . . . (11 to 2) 9
303^{5} GARRYDOOLIS [-] 7-9-7 (7*) C O'Brien, *mid-div, rdn and fdd 11th*. . . . . (20 to 1) 10
FOR WILLIAM [-] 7-11-12 K F O'Brien, *mid-div, mstk 11th, sn wknd*. . . . . (10 to 1) 11
170^{9} QUEEN OF THE SWANS [-] (bl) 9-9-8 P Carberry, *wl plcd till mstk tenth, sn btn*. . . . . (66 to 1) 12
214^{6} QUAYSIDE BUOY [-] 10-10-6 M Dwyer, *tld 8th, pld up bef tenth*. . . . . (14 to 1) pu
235* NEVER BE GREAT [-] 11-11-2 (3ex) F J Flood, *al rear, pld up bef 3 out*. . . . . (7 to 1) pu

Dist: 1l, 3½l, 9l, sht-hd. 4m 59.50s. (14 Ran).
(O B P Carroll), John Brassil

WORCESTER (good to firm)
Thursday August 26th
Going Correction: MINUS 0.20 sec. per fur.

307 Hartlebury Selling Handicap Hurdle (4-y-o and up) £1,748 2¼m. . . . . (2:00)

186^{4} COLWAY PRINCE (Ire) [80] 5-11-2 G Upton, *hld up, steady hdwy aftr 4th, kicked clr after four out, styd on strly.* . . . . (5 to 1 co-fav op 4 to 1 tchd 11 to 2) 1
126^{3} KINLET VISION (Ire) [70] 5-10-1 (5*) T Jenks, *hld up in mid-div, hdwy to chase ldr aftr 4 out, rdn and not quicken appr last*. . . . . (5 to 1 co-fav op 6 to 1 tchd 9 to 2) 2
217^{2} ROWHEDGE [82] 7-10-11 (7*) S Curran, *al prmnt, led 5th, hdd and sn pushed alng aftr 4 out, styd on after 2 out, one pace*. . . . . (5 to 1 co-fav op 9 to 2 tchd 11 to 2) 3
CHAMOIS BOY [90] 9-11-9 (3*) D O'Sullivan, *pushed alng aftr 3rd, lost pl after nxt, styd on frm 3 out, nrst finish.* . . . . (5 to 1 co-fav op 8 to 1 tchd 7 to 2) 4

NATIONAL HUNT RESULTS 1993-94

260⁵ PERSIAN VALLEY [79] 8-10-8 (7") M Doyle, *pressed ldr to 5th, sn outpcd, styd on frm 3 out, one pace.*
...............................(14 to 1 tchd 16 to 1) 5
140³ ULLSWATER [79] 7-11-1 A Maguire, *led, hit 3rd, hdd 5th, no ch frm 3 out*...................(11 to 2 op 4 to 1) 6
THE HIDDEN CITY [83] 7-11-5 S Earle, *pressed ldg pair til wknd aftr 5th, sn beh.*
...............................(14 to 1 op 12 to 1 tchd 16 to 1) 7
226⁵ KEY DEAR (Fr) [77] (bl) 6-10-13 T Wall, *hld up tch aftr 5th, sn beh*...........(10 to 1 op 8 to 1 tchd 12 to 1) 8
HOMILE [74] (bl) 5-10-10 G McCourt, *hld up, lost tch frm 5th, sn beh*.............(13 to 2 op 5 to 1 tchd 7 to 1) 9
CISTOLENA [65] 7-10-1 Diane Clay, *al rear, jmpd badly, tld off 4 out*..........(40 to 1 op 33 to 1 tchd 50 to 1) 10
Dist: 3½l, 4l, ½l, 10l, 1l, 1½l, ¾l, 12l, 10l. 4m 11.20s. a 3.20s (10 Ran).
SR: 19/5/13/20/-/-/1/-/-/   (A A King), A P Jones

308 Redditch Conditional Jockeys' Handicap Chase (0-115 5-y-o and up) £2,709 2½m 110yds.............................(2:30)

143² KARAKTER REFERENCE [118] 11-12-0 D O'Sullivan, *trkd ldr, led 11th, rdn r-in, all out.*
...............................(2 to 1 op 7 to 4 tchd 9 to 4) 1
167" MISTER FEATHERS [93] 12-10-3 D Leahy, *mstk 3rd, making hdwy whn hit 4 out, kpt on one pace.*
...............................(5 to 4 on tchd 11 to 10 on) 2
222 THEY ALL FORGOT ME [90] 6-10-0 J McCarthy, *al abt same pl, mstk tenth, no ch aftr*............(6 to 1 op 5 to 1) 3
184⁶ MIRAGE DANCER [90] 10-10-0 S Wynne, *mstks, lost tch frm 7th*......................(66 to 1 op 33 to 1) 4
BELL DIP [90] 12-10-0 M Hourigan, *led till blun badly 11th, not reco'r, tld off whn pld up bef 3 out.*
...............................(9 to 1 op 14 to 1) pu
Dist: 1½l, 7l, 6l. 5m 6.50s. a 3.50s (5 Ran).
SR: 24/-/   (Mrs R J Doorgachurn), R J O'Sullivan

309 Droitwich Handicap Chase (0-120 5-y-o and up) £2,846 2m.................(3:00)

225" MEGA BLUE [115] 8-11-11 P Niven, *hld up in tch, wnt second appr 8th, led 4 out, went clr frm nxt, easily.*
(6 to 5 on 11 to 10 on tchd 5 to 4 and 5 to 4 on) 1
FEATHER YOUR NEST [96] 8-10-6 N Williamson, *mstks 1st and 3rd, led till mistake and hdd 4 out, sn btn, eased r-in, fnshd tired*.........(11 to 8 op Evens tchd 7 to 4) 2
154⁷ RONOCCO [91] 11-10-1¹ S McNeill, *trkd ldr till wknd appr 8th, sn btn*.....(20 to 1 op 16 to 1 tchd 25 to 1) 3
194³ WEEKDAY CROSS (Ire) [90] 5-10-0 A Maguire, *hld up in last pl, f 7th*...........................(9 to 1 op 9 to 2) 4
Dist: 12l, 1½l. 3m 53.40s. a 4.40s (4 Ran).
SR: 21/   (Tony Yates), Mrs V A Aconley

310 Wychavon Novices' Hurdle (4-y-o and up) £1,480 2m 5f 110yds...............(3:30)

163² PERFORATE (bl) 4-11-3 L Harvey, *pld hrd, nvr far off pace, rdn in 3rd pl appr last, str run to ld r-in.*
...............................(7 to 4 op 2 to 1 tchd 5 to 2) 1
157⁷ PENNINE PASS (Ire) 4-10-6 (5") R Davis, *led 4th to 6th, styd in cl tch, hng rght appr last, led briefly sn aftr, not pace of wnr*.......................(8 to 1 op 10 to 1) 2
RICH AND RED 7-10-9 N Williamson, *al prmnt, led 6th, hng rght frm 2 out, hdd sn aftr last, no extr.*
...............................(9 to 1 op 5 to 1 tchd 10 to 1) 3
155³ SUNDAY JIM 9-11-0 M Bosley, *set steady pace to 4th, one pace frm 3 out*.......(25 to 1 op 20 to 1 tchd 33 to 1) 4
227 DOCTOR DUNKLIN (USA) 4-10-11 D Gallagher, *hld up, hdwy 7th, wknd nxt*...............(16 to 1 op 12 to 1) 5
SKY VENTURE 9-11-0 S Earle, *al towards rear, wkng whn mstk 6th, sn lost tch, tld off.*
...............(20 to 1 op 25 to 1 tchd 33 to 1 and 14 to 1) 6
LAST CONQUEST (Ire) 4-10-11 C Llewellyn, *hld up in rear, steady hdwy frm 5th, wknd quickly and pld up bef 3 out, lme*..........(13 to 8 fav op Evens tchd 7 to 4) pu
Dist: 4l, 2½l, 12l, 7l, 20l. 5m 1.50s. a 6.50s (7 Ran).
(Mrs Merrilyn Rowe), R J Baker

311 Alcester Novices' Chase (5-y-o and up) £2,672 2m 7f.......................(4:00)

ISLAND FOREST (USA) 7-11-0 G Bradley, *hld up early, hdwy to ld aftr 8th, hdd 13th, led nxt, styd on wl.*
...............................(7 to 1 op 5 to 1) 1
204³ APRIL'S BABY 9-10-9 J Lawrence, *al frnt rnk, led 13th, hdd nxt, one pace frm 3 out*.......(50 to 1 op 33 to 1) 2
BADBURY LAD 7-11-0 B Powell, *led, clr 5th, distracted by loose horse and jmpd badly rght 8th, sn hdd, rdn 5 out, wknd*.................(8 to 1 op 7 to 1 tchd 11 to 1) 3
248⁹ MISS TIMBER PIPPER 9-10-9 J Callaghan, *al beh, tld off frm hfwy*......................(50 to 1 op 33 to 1) 4
189" STRONG MEDICINE 6-11-6 N Williamson, *mstk 1st, blun and uns rdr nxt*...........(6 to 4 on tchd 11 to 8 on) ur
HUGLI 6-11-0 J Osborne, *jmpd badly in rear, tld off whn refused 3 out*..........(4 to 1 op 3 to 1 tchd 11 to 4) ref
STRONG SUSPECT 8-11-0 S Earle, *al beh, tld off whn pld up bef 4 out*...............(33 to 1 tchd 25 to 1) pu

Dist: 7l, 20l, dist. 5m 51.60s. a 7.60s (7 Ran).
(Commander Peter Longhurst), P F Nicholls

312 Malvern Handicap Hurdle (0-115 4-y-o and up) £2,343 3m.....................(4:30)

143⁵ OWEN [92] 9-10-0 B Powell, *hld up, gd hdwy to go second 4 out, led appr nxt, rdn out.*
...............................(8 to 1 op 10 to 1 tchd 12 to 1) 1
STORM DRUM [103] 4-10-11 N Williamson, *hld up in rear, mstk 8th, hdwy frm nxt, chlgd 2 out, rdn and slight mistake last, edgd rght, ran on cl hme.*
...............................(7 to 1 op 4 to 1) 2
CHUCKLESTONE [110] 10-11-4 J R Kavanagh, *trkd ldr, rdn and lost pl 4 out, styd on one pace frm 2 out.*
...............................(6 to 4 fav tchd 15 to 8) 3
SMARTIE LEE [99] 6-10-7 A Maguire, *hld up in tch, one pace frm 3 out*.........(8 to 1 tchd 10 to 1) 4
ELITE REG [120] (bl) 4-12-0 R Dunwoody, *led, rdn and hdd whn mstk 3 out, sn btn.* (5 to 2 op 2 to 1 tchd 11 to 4) 5
MOUNTSHANNON [92] 7-10-0 S Earle, *al prmnt, wknd 3 out*.......................(20 to 1 op 16 to 1) 6
222⁸ GRACE MOORE [92] 9-10-0³ (3") R Greene, *prmnt early, in rear frm 4th*..........(20 to 1 op 16 to 1 tchd 25 to 1) 7
189⁷ WAR BEAT [96] 5-10-4⁴ M A FitzGerald, *beh till hdwy 5th, rdn and wknd quickly 8th, tld off.*
...............................(40 to 1 op 33 to 1 tchd 100 to 1) 8
149⁵ SAILOR BOY [92] (bl) 7-9-11 (3") M Hourigan, *al beh, tld off frm hfwy*.........(25 to 1 op 20 to 1 tchd 33 to 1) 9
Dist: 1½l, 15l, 4l, 15l, 10l, 5l, dist, 6l. 5m 38.80s. a 0.80s (9 Ran).
SR: 16/25/17/2/8/-/   (Burt & Travica Contractors Ltd), B Smart

TRALEE (IRE) (good)
Friday August 27th

313 Bank Of Ireland Handicap Hurdle (0-123 4-y-o and up) £3,797 2m...........(7:30)

123 NASSAU [-] 6-11-13 A Maguire, ...(5 to 4 fav) 1
230⁵ ULTRA MAGIC [-] 6-10-4 (5") A J Roche, ...(10 to 1) 2
275" COMBINE CALL [-] 6-10-12 (5",6ex) T P Treacy, ...(4 to 1) 3
275 NICE AND SIMPLE [-] 6-10-2 K F O'Brien, ...(7 to 1) 4
161" WINCHLING [-] 8-10-2 N Byrne, ...(7 to 1) 5
232" BRAVEFOOT [-] 5-11-5 (5",6ex) T J Mitchell, ...(7 to 1) 6
275² BROOK COTTAGE (Ire) [-] 5-10-4 (7") J P Broderick, (8 to 1) 7
252⁸ BUCKINGHAM BOY [-] 7-9-11 (7") C O'Brien, ...(20 to 1) 8
PARTY SIGN [-] 6-11-2 C F Swan, ...(10 to 1) 9
Dist: 4l, 6l, 1½l, 5l. 3m 40.00s. (9 Ran).
(Michael W J Smurfit), D K Weld

314 White Sands Hotel Maiden Hurdle (4-y-o) £3,797 2m 1f.....................(8:00)

95" FERRAGOSTO (Ire) 11-9 K F O'Brien, ...(7 to 1) 1
PRIVATE GUY (Ire) 11-9 A Maguire, ...(11 to 8 on) 2
DOMINO'S RING (Ire) 11-9 D O'Connor, ...(9 to 1) 3
252⁵ MISTER DRUM (Ire) 11-2 (7") Mr J T McNamara, .. (16 to 1) 4
212⁶ TRIPLE ACE (Ire) 10-11 (7") Mr N D Fehily, ...(33 to 1) 5
NOT MY LINE (Ire) 10-11 C O'Brien, ...(33 to 1) 6
208⁶ WEE RIVER (Ire) 11-4 Mr T S Costello, ...(20 to 1) 7
265⁷ UP FOR RANSOME (Ire) 11-4 B Sheridan, ...(50 to 1) 8
108⁷ FULL MOON FEVER (Ire) 11-4 J Shortt, ...(20 to 1) f
Dist: 11l, 7l, 1½l, ½l. 3m 55.60s. (9 Ran).
(D H W Dobson), J S Bolger

CARTMEL (firm)
Saturday August 28th
Going Correction: MINUS 0.30 sec. per fur.

315 EBF 'National Hunt' Novices' Hurdle Qualifier (4,5,6-y-o) £1,847 2m 1f 110yds (2:20)

DARK FOUNTAIN 6-11-0 L O'Hara, *slight ld to 3rd, remained cl up, slight lead last, kpt on wnd pres.*
...............................(7 to 1 op 5 to 1) 1
MELLOW GOLD 6-10-9 R Dunwoody, *dsptd ld, slight advantage aftr 3rd till hdd last, ev ch r-in, no extr.*
...............................(6 to 4 on op 5 to 4 on tchd Evens) 2
FAUSTINA 5-10-9 D Telfer, *chsd ldrs, styd on frm 2 out, not able to chal*..................(33 to 1 op 25 to 1) 3
JOYFUL SMITH 4-10-1² (7") Mr R Hale, *chsd ldrs till lost tch frm 5th*........................(40 to 1 op 20 to 1) 4
ABSOLUTE DANCER 4-10-6 A Maguire, *not fluent, al beh.*
...............................(8 to 1 op 7 to 1 tchd 9 to 1) 5
MAJESTIC GOLD 5-11-0 R Supple, *pld hrd, hld up till led 3rd, jmpd rght and ran out.*
...............................(11 to 4 op 5 to 2 tchd 3 to 1) ro
Dist: 5l, 5l, dist, 1l. 4m 18.90s. a 18.90s (6 Ran).
(Mrs E M Dixon), J E Dixon

316 Chas Kendall Selling Handicap Hurdle (4-y-o and up) £1,748 2m 1f 110yds...(2:55)

BATTLE STANDARD (Can) [80] 6-11-3 (7") J Burke, *al prmnt, slight ld 3 out, rdn out.* (9 to 2 op 5 to 1 tchd 4 to 1) 1

38

GOLDEN MADJAMBO [62] 7-10-6 R Supple, *al prmnt, dsptd ld 2 out, ev ch r-in, styd on.*
..................................(12 to 1 tchd 14 to 1) 2
244* CYRILL HENRY (Ire) [73] 4-11-3 A Merrigan, *al prmnt, chsd ldrs frm 3 out, effrt r-in, not get on terms.*
......................(5 to 4 fav op 6 to 4 tchd 7 to 4) 3
287^{9} SWANK GILBERT [56] 7-9-7 (7*) Carol Cuthbert, *prmnt till wknd 3 out*.....................................(33 to 1) 4
NEVENTER (Fr) [56] 4-10-0 W Worthington, *prmnt, led 3rd to 3 out, sn wknd*..............................(25 to 1) 5
280^{5} DOCTOR'S REMEDY [75] 7-11-5 D Morris, *led 1st to 3rd, lost tch nxt*......................(13 to 2 op 6 to 1) 6
HEAVENLY HOOFER [63] 10-10-7 C Dennis, *prmnt till wknd aftr 4th*........(14 to 1 op 16 to 1 tchd 20 to 1) 7
BALLY FLAME [59] 7-10-3 Mrs M Kendall, *mstk 3rd, cl up till wknd 3 out*....................(25 to 1 op 20 to 1) 8
186 SUNTAN (Fr) [70] (bl) 4-11-0 L Wyer, *led, propped 1st and second, lost pl, beh 3rd, tld off*......(11 to 2 op 5 to 1) 9
DEVIL'S SOUL [72] 5-10-9 (7*) A Linton, *reluctant to race, refused 1st*.........................(16 to 1 op 14 to 1) ref
MARANDISA [60] 6-10-4 J Callaghan, *al beh, tld off hfwy, pld up 3 out*..........................(16 to 1 op 14 to 1) pu
Dist: Hd, 3½l, 20l, 7l, 3l, 12l, 8l, dist. 4m 7.30s. a 7.30s (11 Ran).
(M Stanners), Mrs S A Bramall

317 Bet With The Tote Handicap Chase (0-115 5-y-o and up) £2,730 3¼m.......... (3:30)

LOCAL CUSTOMER [95] 8-10-2 W Humphreys, *trkd ldr, dsptd ld 3 out to 2 out, lft clr aftr last.*
............................(6 to 4 tchd 7 to 4 and 5 to 4) 1
248^{8} BEN TIRRAN [95] (v) 9-10-2^{2} D Telfer, *trkd ldr, mstk 3rd, ev ch 3 out, wknd nxt*.................(13 to 2 op 5 to 1) 2
288^{5} MR PANACHE [93] 11-9-9 (5*) D Bentley, *hld up beh, mstk 6th, blun tenth and nxt, lost tch 4 out.*
.....................(16 to 1 op 20 to 1 tchd 33 to 1) 3
198 RIVER HOUSE [121] 11-12-0 A Maguire, *led, 3 ls clr whn broke dwn aftr last, pld up.*
...................(5 to 4 on op 6 to 4 on tchd Evens) pu
Dist: 10l, dist. 6m 30.20s. a 13.20s (4 Ran).
(Paul Bradley), P Bradley

318 Tote Credit Handicap Hurdle (0-130 4-y-o and up) £2,364 2m 1f 110yds........ (4:05)

BEAUCADEAU [112] 7-9-11 (3*) A Dobbin, *trkd ldr gng wl, dsptd ld 2 out, sn led, clr last, easily.*
.........................(3 to 1 op 4 to 1 tchd 5 to 1) 1
280* SRIVIJAYA [116] 6-10-4 P Niven, *led till hdd and wknd aftr 2 out*.....................(7 to 4 fav tchd 6 to 4) 2
240 ELEGANT KING (Ire) [112] 4-10-0 T Jarvis, *in tch, effrt 3 out, wknd nxt*.......................(9 to 2 op 3 to 1) 3
BALAAT (USA) [112] 5-10-0 W Worthington, *beh, styd on one pace frm 2 out*..............(20 to 1 tchd 25 to 1) 4
QUALITAIR SOUND (Ire) [124] 5-10-12 D Byrne, *trkd ldr, ev ch 3 out, wknd nxt*......(9 to 2 op 7 to 2 tchd 5 to 1) 5
ABLE PLAYER (USA) [120] 6-10-1 (7*) Mr D Parker, *trkd ldrs, cld 3 out, effrt nxt, sn rdn and btn.*
...........(11 to 2 op 6 to 1 tchd 7 to 1 and 5 to 1) 6
Dist: 12l, 3l, 3½l, 2l, 3½l. 4m 0.40s. a 0.40s (6 Ran).
SR: 16/8/1/-/7/-/ (T A Barnes), M A Barnes

319 Lakeland Pennine Linen And Workware Rental Novices' Chase (5-y-o and up) £2,548 2m 5f 110yds................ (4:35)

246* COUNTERBID (v) 6-11-12 A Maguire, *made all, hit 2 out, rdn out*....................(11 to 10 on op 5 to 4 on) 1
189^{3} HELMAR (NZ) 7-11-2 R Supple, *hld up beh, chsd ldr frm 5 out, styd on from last.* (11 to 4 op 5 to 2 tchd 3 to 1) 2
281^{4} SECOND ATTEMPT 9-11-2 B Storey, *trkd ldr till appr 4 out*..(20 to 1) 3
269^{3} THE RAMBLING MAN 6-11-2 M Dwyer, *trkd ldr, mstk 8th, wknd 5 out, mistake nxt, tld off whn f last.*
.......................(11 to 4 op 5 to 2 tchd 3 to 1) f
Dist: 1½l, 10l. 5m 13.10s. a 1.10s (4 Ran).
SR: 23/11/1/-/ (Howard Parker), J A C Edwards

320 Cumbria Tourist Board Juvenile Novices' Hurdle for the Army Benevolent Challenge Cup (3-y-o) £2,005 2m 1f 110yds.....(5:10)

BURNT IMP (USA) 11-0 J Callaghan, *led second, clr 2 out, readily*................(11 to 2 op 5 to 1 tchd 6 to 1) 1
WHO'S THE BEST (Ire) 11-0 T Jarvis, *in tch, prog to chase ldr aftr 3 out, kpt on one pace.*
.......................(5 to 1 op 4 to 1 tchd 11 to 2) 2
180* MR GENEAOLOGY (USA) (bl) 11-9 A Maguire, *in tch, cl up 5th, blun 3 out, rdn and wknd nxt.*
....................(Evens fav op 11 to 10 tchd 5 to 4) 3
247^{7} KISS IN THE DARK 10-9 P Niven, *jmpd slwly 1st, trkd ldr 3rd till wknd 3 out*................(6 to 1 tchd 5 to 1) 4
COMMANCHE CREEK 10-11 (3*) A Larnach, *in tch till mstk 5th, sn rdn and btn*......(7 to 2 op 5 to 1 tchd 7 to 1) 5
247 BIG GEM 11-0 W Worthington, *led to second, cl up till wknd aftr 4th*..................(33 to 1 tchd 50 to 1) 6
TINA'S DOMAIN 10-2 (7*) Mr D Parker, *al rear*.....(33 to 1) 7
MYNYOSS 11-0 M Moloney, *al rear*. (25 to 1 op 20 to 1) 8
Dist: 8l, 12l, 3l, 8l, 8l, 12l, 3l. 4m 1.80s. a 1.80s (8 Ran).
SR: 16/8/5/-/-/ (N B Mason (Farms) Ltd), G M Moore

HEREFORD (good to firm)
Saturday August 28th
Going Correction: MINUS 0.15 sec. per fur.

321 Eardisland Selling Hurdle (3,4,5-y-o) £1,521 2m 1f....................... (5:25)

244^{6} WELL DONE RORY 4-11-5 (7*) P McLoughlin, *led till aftr 4 out, led nxt, hrd rdn and wndrd appr last, drvn out, all out*.................(5 to 4 fav op 6 to 4 tchd 6 to 5) 1
193^{7} DOCTOR-J (Ire) 3-10-5 S Keightley, *pld hrd, trkd ldr, cl up and ev ch 3 out, chlgd last, not quicken.*
.....................(16 to 1 op 12 to 1 tchd 20 to 1) 2
COOCHIE (bl) 4-11-2 L Harvey, *hld up, chsd ldr frm 3 out, chlgd appr last, sn one pace*.........(7 to 2 op 7 to 4) 3
LILY SUGARS (bl) 5-11-2 (7*) N Juckes, *hld up, lost tch and hrd rdn aftr 4th, tld off whn tried to refuse and f nxt, broke leg, dead*...... (14 to 1 op 10 to 1 tchd 16 to 1) f
ALL'A BLAZE 4-11-2 D Gallagher, *pressed ldr frm 3rd, led aftr 4 out, sn hdd, ev ch 2 out, fourth and btn whn f last*...............................(12 to 1 op 8 to 1) f
FEELING FOOLISH (Ire) 4-11-7 I Shoemark, *in tch whn f second*...........................(4 to 1 tchd 6 to 1) f
DAWN POPPY 5-11-4 M A FitzGerald, *hld up, beh whn mstk 5th, sn tld off, jmpd slwly 3 out, pld up bef nxt.*
.....................(12 to 1 op 10 to 1 tchd 14 to 1) pu
Dist: 1l, 2½l. 3m 59.10s. a 13.10s (7 Ran).
(Chiltern Hills Racing Club), J White

322 Whitecross Handicap Chase (0-130 5-y-o and up) £2,528 2m 3f............... (5:55)

245^{3} MARKET LEADER [85] 13-10-12 L Harvey, *hld up in last pl, wnt 3rd 9th, rdn whn hit 2 out, led last, all out.*
..................................(11 to 4 tchd 7 to 2) 1
SOCKS DOWNE [90] 14-11-3 B Powell, *led, rdn alng frm 3 out, hdd last, rallied r-in, not quicken nr finish.*
....(4 to 1 op 3 to 1) 2
261* COURT RAPIER [92] 11-11-5 J R Kavanagh, *trkd ldr, mstk 5th, rdn alng frm 5 out, ev ch 3 out, not quicken appr last*......... (13 to 8 on op 2 to 1 on tchd 6 to 4 on) 3
262 SAILOR'S DELIGHT [97] 9-11-3 (7*) Mr S Joynes, *pressed ldr, 5th to 9th, wknd frm nxt, tld off appr 3 out.*
..................................(20 to 1 op 10 to 1) 4
Dist: ¾l, 1l, dist. 4m 38.60s. a 8.60s (4 Ran).
(Ernie Fiello), R Lee

323 Yarsop Conditional Jockeys' Novices' Hurdle (4-y-o and up) £1,480 2m 1f.. (6:25)

227* ICE STRIKE (USA) 4-11-5 A Thornton, *hld up in tch, wnt second aftr 4 out, led after 3 out, clr last, easily.*
..............................(6 to 4 on op 2 to 1 on) 1
WINGED WHISPER (USA) 4-10-12 T Eley, *led 3rd, clr aftr nxt, hdd after 3 out, sn one pace.* (33 to 1 op 25 to 1) 2
FORTINA'S SONG 6-11-0 M Hourigan, *wl beh 3rd, gd hdwy appr 2 out, styd on well approaching last, prmsg.*
..................................(50 to 1 op 20 to 1) 3
187^{3} WILL'S BOUNTY 10-11-0 V Slattery, *led to 3rd, pressed ldr til pushed alng and outpcd aftr 5th, styd on ag'n one pace after 3 out*..................(16 to 1 op 12 to 1) 4
EARLY DRINKER 5-11-0 J McCarthy, *beh 3rd, not fluent, chsd ldr aftr 5th, rdn and one pace 3 out.*
.....................(100 to 30 op 3 to 1 tchd 5 to 1) 5
242^{4} JON'S CHOICE (bl) 5-11-0 T Jenks, *hld up in mid-div, hdwy and in tch aftr 5th, rdn and one pace 3 out.*
....(8 to 1 op 6 to 1) 6
227^{8} ARCTIC LINE (v) 5-11-0 R Farrant, *mstk second, prmnt whn mistake 5th, chsd ldr til one pace 3 out.*
.....................(33 to 1 op 20 to 1 tchd 50 to 1) 7
260^{8} THARIF 5-10-7 (7*) N Downs, *chsd ldr, hmpd 5th, beh aftr nxt*.....(25 to 1 op 20 to 1 tchd 33 to 1 and 14 to 1) 8
GRUBBY 4-10-7 S Wynne, *wl beh frm 3rd, tld off 5th.*
..................................(25 to 1 op 12 to 1) 9
191 WELL SHOD 5-10-9 W Marston, *beh frm 3rd, lost tch aftr nxt, tld off 4 out*...................(20 to 1 op 10 to 1) 10
PRECISION RACER 5-10-6 (3*) D Walsh, *nvr rchd ldrs, beh frm 3rd, tld off aftr 5th*...........(50 to 1 op 25 to 1) 11
Dist: 15l, 6l, 10l, 6l, 4l, 4l, ½l, 25l, dist. 3m 51.50s. a 5.50s (11 Ran).
SR: 11/-/-/-/-/-/ (C R Nelson), J W Hills

324 Abergavenny Claiming Hurdle (4-y-o and up) £1,651 2m 3f 110yds............ (6:55)

JOHNSTED 7-11-1 Diane Clay, *hld up, wnt 3rd 5th, led 4 out, rdn and styd on wl 2 out, hit last, drvn out, fnshd lme*....................... (11 to 2 op 8 to 1 tchd 5 to 1) 1
THE BLACK MONK (Ire) (v) 5-11-9 R Dunwoody, *hld up, hdwy aftr 5th, jnd ldr after 3 out, rdn 2 out, not quicken appr last.*
..............(15 to 8 on op 5 to 2 on tchd 7 to 4 on) 2

190^{4} VIAGGIO 5-11-5 J Osborne, *led to 4 out, sn rdn and btn, one pace aftr four out*.. (9 to 2 op 7 to 2 tchd 5 to 1) 3

245 LAPIAFFE 9-11-2 (7*) S Taylor, *pressed ldr, pushed alng aftr 5 out, styd on one pace frm 4 out.* .... (9 to 1 op 7 to 1 tchd 10 to 1) 4

227^{7} HATAAL (Ire) (bl) 4-10-2 T Wall, *hld up, jmpd slwly second, sn rdn alng, reminder aftr 4th, lost tch after 6th, soon tld off*........ (40 to 1 op 33 to 1 tchd 50 to 1) 5

TRENTSIDE VALOUR (v) 8-10-7 M Ranger, *prmnt til pushed alng and lost pl aftr 5th, sn tld off, pld up bef 3 out*........ (50 to 1 op 20 to 1) pu

Dist: 1l, 12l, 1½l, dist. 4m 25.20s. a 4.20s (6 Ran).
SR: 16/23/7/9/-/-/ (P Riley), W Clay

325 Hole In The Wall Novices' Chase (5-y-o and up) £2,333 2m........(7:25)

298 WINDSOR PARK (USA) 7-11-3 R Dunwoody, *hld up in tch, trkd ldrs frm 6 out, led 2 out, drvn out.* .... (7 to 4 op 2 to 1 tchd 6 to 4) 1

194^{5} CRAFTY CHAPLAIN 7-10-12 (5*) Mr D McCain, *hld up, hdwy 6th, led 5 out, mstk and hdd 2 out, ev ch whn mistake last, styd on nr finish.* .... (11 to 2 op 6 to 1 tchd 7 to 1) 2

239 MENAGHI 6-10-12 G Bradley, *hld up, hdwy aftr 6 out, ev ch frm 3 out, one pace appr last.* .... (20 to 1 op 16 to 1 tchd 25 to 1) 3

PECCAVI 9-11-3 R Bellamy, *chsd ldr til lft in ld 6th, hdd 5 out, ev ch whn mstk 2 out, not quicken appr last.* .... (50 to 1 op 25 to 1) 4

BARDESAN 7-11-3 J Osborne, *jmpd badly lft, led, jumped slwly 5th, mstk and hdd nxt, rdn and effrt 5 out, one pace aftr 4 out, eased whn btn.* .... (Evens fav op 7 to 4 on tchd 11 to 10) 5

227^{9} LITTLE THYNE 8-11-3 Dr P Pritchard, *hld up, reminders and lost pl 7th, sn beh, f last*...... (50 to 1 op 20 to 1) f

COUNTY CONTRACTOR 6-11-3 S McNeill, *pressed ldr and ev ch til wknd aftr 4 out, beh whn brght dwn last.* .... (50 to 1 op 33 to 1) bd

Dist: 1½l, 4l, hd, dist. 4m 1.90s. a 12.90s (7 Ran).
(Mrs S J Brookhouse), K S Bridgwater

326 Tarrington Handicap Hurdle (0-115 4-y-o and up) £2,274 2m 1f........ (7:55)

240* LUSTREMAN [101] 6-11-5 T Wall, *hld up, hdwy aftr 4th, led 3 out, quickened whn chlgd last, drvn out.* .... (4 to 1 op 3 to 1 tchd 5 to 1) 1

186^{2} ZAMANAYN (Ire) [84] 5-9-9 (7*) J James, *very slwly away, beh til hdwy aftr 5th, ev ch after 3 out, chlgd last, not quicken r-in*........ (7 to 1 op 5 to 1) 2

240^{5} COURT CIRCULAR [99] (v) 4-11-3 Diane Clay, *wnt second 4th, hmpd nxt, led 6th, hdd 3 out, rdn and styd on one pace appr last*........ (13 to 2 op 5 to 1 tchd 7 to 1) 3

FINAL SOUND [82] (bl) 8-10-0 L Harvey, *slwly away, hld up, hdwy aftr 4th, wnt fourth 3 out, rdn and no extr.* .... (10 to 1 op 12 to 1 tchd 14 to 1) 4

SINGING REPLY (USA) [82] 5-10-0 J Osborne, *lft in ld 3rd, hmpd by loose horse 5th, hdd nxt, rdn and rallied 3 out, wknd*........ (3 to 1 fav tchd 7 to 2 and 5 to 2) 5

KING'S RARITY [90] 7-10-8 D Bridgwater, *chsd ldr, lft 3rd at third, pushed alng aftr 6th, hrd rdn after 3 out, no imprsn*........ (20 to 1 op 10 to 1) 6

219* MISTER LAWSON [98] 7-11-2 I Shoemark, *pld hrd, hld up, wnt 3rd 4th, ev ch four out, rdn and wknd aftr nxt.* .... (9 to 2 op 3 to 1 tchd 5 to 1) 7

FAST CRUISE [90] 8-10-8 R Bellamy, *chsd ldrs til hrd rdn aftr 5th, wknd 3 out*........ (20 to 1 op 12 to 1) 8

MINT-MASTER [84] 8-9-9 (7*) P Maddock, *hld up in mid-div, lost tch frm 5th, tld off*........ (33 to 1 op 12 to 1) 9

239 SALMAN (USA) [106] 7-11-5 (5*) R Davis, *led, clr whn ran out 3rd*........ (7 to 1 op 4 to 1) ro

Dist: 1½l, 1½l, 3½l, 5l, 4l, 1l, 10l, dist. 3m 51.80s. a 5.80s (10 Ran).
SR: 8/-/2/-/-/-/ (R A B Brassey), J H Peacock

TRALEE (IRE) (good)
Saturday August 28th

327 Ballybeggan Racegoers Club Belvedere Mares Novice Chase (5-y-o and up) £3,450 2m........(1:30)

294 NATALIES FANCY 7-11-11 J F Titley,........ (5 to 4 fav) 1
250^{4} HIGHBABS 7-11-11 T Horgan,........ (4 to 1) 2
251 INCH GALE 6-11-11 W T Slattery Jnr,........ (16 to 1) 3
276^{6} CLONEENVERB 9-11-6 (5*) D P Murphy,........ (12 to 1) 4
71 KILLEEN COUNTESS (Ire) 5-11-0 (5*) T J Mitchell, (25 to 1) 5
254^{4} CUILIN BUI (Ire) 5-10-12 (7*) C O'Brien,........ (4 to 1) 6
251^{6} MISS EUROLINK (bl) 6-11-11 G M O'Neill,........ (10 to 1) 7
250 WOODEN MINSTREL 7-11-6 (5*) D T Evans,........ (14 to 1) 8
SQUIRRELLSDAUGHTER 6-11-4 (7*) Mr N D Fehily,........ (25 to 1) 9
251 MANDEVILLE LANE 7-11-11 C O'Dwyer,........ (14 to 1) 10
251^{8} LAW COURSE (Ire) 5-11-5 J P Banahan,........ (20 to 1) 11
276^{9} NO TAKERS (bl) 6-11-11 K F O'Brien,........ (8 to 1) pu
Dist: 15l, 11l, 3l, 15l. 3m 52.30s. (12 Ran).
(Mrs Eileen Crowe), Patrick G Kelly

328 Barrys Bakery Novice Hurdle (4-y-o and up) £4,140 2m........(2:00)

115* PERSIAN TACTICS 4-11-13 B Sheridan,........ (6 to 4) 1
RISZARD (USA) 4-11-9 K F O'Brien,........ (11 to 8 fav) 2
131 PAGET 6-11-11 (7*) Mr A K Wyse,........ (7 to 1) 3
274* SHIRWAN (Ire) 4-11-13 C O'Dwyer,........ (4 to 1) 4
Dist: Sht-hd, 2½l, 4½l. 3m 46.70s. (4 Ran).
(Michael W J Smurfit), D K Weld

329 Mount Brandon Hotel Handicap Hurdle (4-y-o) £4,485 2m........ (2:30)

117* LIFE SAVER (Ire) [-] 11-0 P Carberry,........ (6 to 4) 1
AEGEAN FANFARE (Ire) [-] (bl) 10-9 (5*) T J Mitchell, (16 to 1) 2+
123 JUDICIAL FIELD (Ire) [-] (bl) 12-0 B Sheridan, (11 to 10 fav) 2+
209^{2} VICOSA (Ire) [-] 10-9 C O'Dwyer,........ (20 to 1) 4
208* GREEN GLEN (USA) [-] 11-8 C F Swan,........ (13 to 2) 5
157^{5} PURPLE EMPEROR (Fr) [-] 10-1 (5*) C P Dunne,.. (20 to 1) 6
113^{8} WALK RITE BACK (Ire) [-] 10-9 K F O'Brien,........ (12 to 1) pu
Dist: 2½l, dd-ht, 9l, 3l. 3m 38.50s. (7 Ran).
(Mrs H A Hegarty), Noel Meade

330 Paddy Kearns Memorial Handicap Hurdle (0-102 4-y-o and up) £3,550 2½m.... (3:00)

293^{4} MINERAL DUST [-] 10-11-2 T Horgan,........(9 to 4 fav) 1
199^{5} LANTERN LUCK (Ire) [-] (bl) 5-10-1 (7*) J P Broderick,........ (8 to 1) 2
169* AWBEG ROVER (Ire) [-] 5-10-0 (7*) C O'Brien,........(10 to 1) 3
251^{2} BALLYHEIGUE [-] 7-10-11 (7*) Mr J T McNamara,.. (8 to 1) 4
291 ANOTHER GROUSE [-] 6-10-2 (5*) T J Mitchell,.... (14 to 1) 5
291 WAR DEVIL [-] 7-10-6 (3*) J Jones,........ (16 to 1) 6
232^{2} TULLY BOY [-] 6-10-1 (7*) Mr D McCartan,........ (8 to 1) 7
302^{4} CLASS ACT [-] (bl) 7-10-10 C F Swan,........ (10 to 1) 8
122 FERRIC FORTRESS [-] 7-10-1 A J O'Brien,........ (20 to 1) 9
254^{3} TELL A TALE [-] 6-11-4 K F O'Brien,........ (11 to 2) 10
229^{5} LILY ROSE VI [-] (bl) 9-9-12 (3*) J Collins,........ (12 to 1) 11
122 THE HEARTY CARD (Ire) [-] 5-11-3 D H O'Connor,..(7 to 1) 12
BROWN TOP [-] 6-10-4 G M O'Neill,........(12 to 1) 13
275 BETH'S PRINCE [-] (bl) 8-11-3 C O'Dwyer,........ (14 to 1) 14
Dist: 3l, 3l, 2l, 1l. 4m 43.90s. (14 Ran).
(Liam Cashman), Liam Cashman

331 Ballybeggan Racegoers Club Tralee I.N.H. Flat Race (4 & 5-y-o) £3,450 2m 1f... (3:30)

98^{7} KELLSEIGHTHUNDRED (Ire) 4-11-9 Mr A P O'Brien, (7 to 2) 1
95^{3} HERE NOW (Ire) 4-11-2 (7*) Mr P Henley,.... (11 to 10 fav) 2
292^{3} FAIRYHILL RUN (Ire) 5-11-2 (7*) Mr D A Harney,.... (7 to 1) 3
BLACK AVENUE (Ire) 5-11-4 (5*) Mr H F Cleary,.... (6 to 1) 4
HILL OF TULLOW (Ire) 4-11-6 (3*) Mr M F Barrett, (14 to 1) 5
201^{2} A FEW GOOD MEN (Ire) (bl) 4-11-9 Mr E Bolger,.. (13 to 2) 6
266^{2} WOLVER LAD (Ire) 5-12-0 Mr T Doyle,........ (10 to 1) 7
215^{7} CALL THE KING (Ire) 4-11-2 (7*) Mr J T McNamara, (14 to 1) 8
124 OAK COURT (Ire) 5-11-2 (7*) Mr R M Murphy,.....(25 to 1) 9
COOMACHEO (Ire) 4-11-9 Mr S R Murphy,........ (10 to 1) 10
Dist: ¾l, 5l, 1½l, 7l. 3m 51.20s. (10 Ran).
(Kells Sports & Social Club), A P O'Brien

332 Ballybeggan Racegoers Club Paget Cup Handicap Chase (0-109 4-y-o and up) £3,450 2¾m........ (4:00)

250^{2} ANN'S PRINCE [-] 10-10-0 (4ex) H Rogers,........(10 to 1) 1
TURBULENT WIND [-] 6-10-10 T J Taaffe,........(14 to 1) 2
250* HURRYUP [-] 6-10-3 (7*,4ex) C O'Brien,........(8 to 1) 3
214^{4} JAMES PIGG [-] 6-11-2 P McWilliams,........(12 to 1) 4
178* ROSSBEIGH CREEK [-] 6-11-0 F J Flood,....... (Evens fav) 5
210^{4} WHO'S FOOLING WHO [-] (bl) 7-10-8 C F Swan,..(13 to 2) 6
132^{4} THUNDERSTRUCK [-] 7-11-8 J F Titley,........(10 to 1) 7
254^{9} MERLYNS CHOICE [-] 9-10-0 T Horgan,........ (12 to 1) 8
255^{7} BALLY O ROURKE [-] 7-9-8 F Woods,........ (16 to 1) 9
303 CAPINCUR BOY [-] 11-10-12 D H O'Connor,..... (12 to 1) 10
21 BALLYBRIKEN CASTLE [-] 6-9-8 W T Slattery Jnr, (16 to 1) 11
178 MELISSAS PRIDE [-] (bl) 8-10-3 A J O'Brien,......(16 to 1) 12
250^{5} CHILIPOUR [-] 6-11-2 C O'Dwyer,........(12 to 1) 13
CHARLIE CHEVAL [-] 14-10-12 Mr J A Flynn,..... (14 to 1) 14
170 HELENIUM GALE [-] 6-9-11 (7*) J P Broderick,.... (20 to 1) 15
214^{3} WATERLOO ANDY [-] 7-10-11 G M O'Neill,........(10 to 1) pu
Dist: ½l, 8l, 4l, 3½l. 5m 30.40s. (16 Ran).
(Bernard Stack), Gerard Stack

333 Woodfab INH Flat Race (4-y-o and up) £4,735 2m 1f........ (4:30)

172^{2} BAWNROCK (Ire) 4-11-13 Mr A P O'Brien,..... (5 to 1 on) 1
258^{5} MORE DASH (Ire) 5-11-8 (5*) Mr J A Nash,........(4 to 1) 2
304^{5} FIFI'S MAN 7-11-4 (7*) Mr P A Roche,........(8 to 1) 3
BEAU CINQ (Ire) 4-11-6 Mr S R Murphy,........ (14 to 1) 4
Dist: 10l, 4½l, dist. 3m 49.00s. (4 Ran).
(New Road Syndicate), A P O'Brien

CARTMEL (firm)

Monday August 30th
Going Correction: MINUS 0.40 sec. per fur.

334 Crowther Homes Selling Hurdle (4,5,6-y-o) £1,733 2m 1f 110yds . . . . (2:15)

	SAOIRSE (Ire) 5-10-13 (3") D J Moffatt, *trkd ldr, cld up 3 out, led nxt, clr last, eased bef finish.* (4 to 1 op 3 to 1)	1
287	SHAYNA MAIDEL 4-10-6 L O'Hara, *trkd ldr, cld up 3 out, ev ch nxt, kpt on one pace.* . . . . (9 to 1 op 7 to 1)	2
	VERBAL WARNING 5-11-0 K Johnson, *in tch, cld up 3 out, effrt nxt, sn rdn and btn.* . . . . (33 to 1 op 25 to 1)	3
	WAWEEWAWOO (Ire) 5-10-9 A Orkney, *nvr gng wl, blun second, jmpd slwly 3rd, sn beh.* . . . . . (8 to 1 op 12 to 1)	4
244[5]	AUNTIE LORNA 4-10-6 C Grant, *whipped round and badly lft strt, al wl beh.* . . . . (3 to 1 op 4 to 1)	5
	BENGAL TIGER (Ire) (v) 5-11-0 B Clifford, *led till 2 out, btn second whn f last, dead.*	
	. . . . (11 to 10 fav op Evens tchd 5 to 4)	f
	KABELIA 5-10-7[1] (3") R Greene, *whipped round and badly lft strt, al tld off, pld up bef last.*	
	. . . . (50 to 1 op 33 to 1)	pu

Dist: 8l, 25l, 20l, ½l. 4m 8.80s. a 8.80s (7 Ran).

(T A Charlesworth), D Moffatt

335 BBC Radio Cumbria Conditional Jockeys' Handicap Hurdle (0-115 4-y-o and up) £1,952 2m 1f 110yds . . . . (2:50)

318*	BEAUCADEAU [111] 7-12-1 (7ex) A Dobbin, *trkd ldr gng wl, slight ld 2 out, pushed out aftr last.*	
	. . . . (11 to 10 fav tchd 5 to 4)	1
318[3]	ELEGANT KING (Ire) [110] 4-11-7 (7") P Naughton, *al prmnt, pushed into ld appr 5th, hdd 2 out, ev ch aftr last, no extr.* . . . . (8 to 1 op 6 to 1)	2
240[4]	RINGLAND (USA) [97] 5-11-1 D J Moffatt, *in tch in rear, cld up 5th, kpt on one pace frm 3 out.* (2 to 1 tchd 7 to 4)	3
	JUST PULHAM [82] 8-9-11 (3") J Supple, *in tch in rear till wknd 5th.* . . . . (25 to 1 op 20 to 1)	4
	MASTER'S CROWN (USA) [99] 5-11-3 A Larnach, *led till appr 5th, sn pushed alng, rdn and wknd 3 out.*	
	. . . . (4 to 1 op 3 to 1)	5

Dist: 2l, 12l, 3l, nk. 4m 0.70s. a 0.70s (5 Ran).
SR: 24/21/

(T A Barnes), M A Barnes

336 John Calvert Insurance Handicap Chase (0-130 5-y-o and up) £2,820 2m 1f 110yds . . . . (3:25)

271[2]	CLEVER FOLLY [104] 13-10-0 B Storey, *made all, styd on wl frm last, cmftbly.* . . . . (6 to 4 on op 7 to 4 on)	1
241[2]	JOYFUL NOISE [126] 10-11-1 (7") P Naughton, *trkd ldr, effrt 3 out, rdn aftr last, no imprsn.* (5 to 1 op 7 to 2)	2
132[6]	GOOD FOR A LAUGH [132] 9-11-7 (7") J Burke, *trkd ldr, effrt 3 out, rdn nxt, no imprsn r-in...* (7 to 1 op 5 to 1)	3
245*	RUPPLES [104] 6-10-0 W Worthington, *in tch, mstk 8th, kpt on one pace aftr last.* . . . . (3 to 1 op 7 to 2)	4

Dist: 3½l, sht-hd, 1½l. 4m 13.90s. a 0.90s (4 Ran).
SR: -/11/17/-/

(N B Mason (Farms) Ltd), G Richards

337 Libra Gravure International Spinal Research Trust Handicap Hurdle (0-115 4-y-o and up) £2,385 3¼m . . . . (4:00)

248[5]	KRONPRINZ (Ire) [82] 5-10-2 W Worthington, *hld up beh, cld up gng wl 3 out, eased into ld close hme, readily.*	
	. . . . (4 to 1 op 3 to 1)	1
283*	AS D'EBOLI (Fr) [88] 6-10-8 C Grant, *trkd ldr, led and quickened aftr 2 out, rdn r-in, hdd and no extr cl hme.*	
	. . . . (6 to 4 fav tchd 7 to 4)	2
60	ONE FOR LUCK (Ire) [95] 5-11-1 L Wyer, *hld up, trkd ldrs, cld up 3 out, ev ch 2 out, kpt on one pace.*	
	. . . . (12 to 1 op 6 to 1)	3
	DESERT MIST [108] (bl) 4-11-9 (5") P Waggott, *set slow pace, quickened and hit 3 out, hdd aftr nxt, sn wknd.*	
	. . . . (3 to 1 op 5 to 2)	4
	JOHN SHAW (USA) [95] 5-11-1 M Dwyer, *hld up, trkd ldrs, cld up 3 out, ev ch whn pld up lme aftr 2 out.*	
	. . . . (7 to 2 tchd 3 to 1)	pu

Dist: Nk, 6l, 8l. 6m 16.30s. a 18.30s (5 Ran).

(Market Rasen Racing Club), M C Chapman

338 Viktor Emlyn Hughes Novices' Chase (5-y-o and up) £2,422 2m 1f 110yds . . . . . (4:35)

	STRONG VIEWS 6-11-0 N Williamson, *chsd ldr, led 8th, mstk nxt (water), drw clr 3 out, easily.*	
	. . . . (6 to 4 on op 6 to 4 on tchd Evens)	1
286[2]	KEEP SHARP 7-11-0 L Wyer, *chsd ldr, mstk 5th, no ch whn mistake last, styd on to take second r-in.*	
	. . . . (7 to 4 op 6 to 4 tchd 15 to 8)	2
239	DULZURA 5-11-4 T Jarvis, *led and sn wl clr, mstk and hdd 8th, wknd 3 out.* . . . . (9 to 1 op 5 to 1 tchd 6 to 1)	3
	SAY NO MORE 7-11-0 A Orkney, *al beh, mstks and tld off hfwy.* . . . . (14 to 1 op 16 to 1 tchd 12 to 1)	4

Dist: 8l, 4l, dist. 4m 11.90s. b 1.10s (4 Ran).

---

339 British Nuclear Fuels Novices' Hurdle (4-y-o and up) £1,987 2¾m . . . . (5:10)

284[5]	STINGRAY CITY (USA) 4-10-4 (7") F Perratt, *chsd ldrs, led 5th, drw clr 3 out, pushed out.* . . . . (4 to 1 tchd 3 to 1)	1
	SUGEMAR 7-11-0 W Worthington, *hld up beh, prog 4 out, chsd ldr 2 out, no imprsn r-in.*	
	. . . . (3 to 1 tchd 11 to 4 and 7 to 2)	2
	HIGH CASTE (v) 6-11-0 Lorna Vincent, *chsd ldrs frm hfwy, rdn and no imprsn 2 out.* . . . . (33 to 1 op 25 to 1)	3
243[3]	BARTON PRIDE (Ire) 4-10-11 C Grant, *al abt same pl, nvr dngrs.* . . . . (3 to 1 op 5 to 1)	4
	INVISIBLE ARMOUR 4-10-11 J Callaghan, *pressed ldr, led 4th to nxt, chsd lder aftr till wknd quickly 2 out.*	
	. . . . (5 to 2 fav op 2 to 1)	5
273	GREAT HEIGHTS (bl) 6-11-0 M Dwyer, *refused to race.*	
	. . . . (5 to 1 op 9 to 2 tchd 11 to 2)	ref
	PERSIAN EMPEROR 8-10-11 (3") R Greene, *led to 4th, wknd quickly nxt, tld off whn pld up 8th.*	
	. . . . (25 to 1 op 20 to 1)	pu

Dist: 8l, 10l, 3½l, 10l. 5m 18.00s. a 13.00s (7 Ran).

(Mrs B Lungo), L Lungo

DOWNPATRICK (IRE) (good to firm)
Monday August 30th

340 Rea's Bar & Restaurant Handicap Hurdle (0-116 4-y-o and up) £1,380 2¾m . . . . (2:30)

127[7]	SENSITIVE KING (Ire) [-] 5-11-2 (3") J Collins, . . (5 to 4 on)	1
125[5]	SILVER LIGHT (Ire) [-] 5-10-2 (7") J P Broderick, ... (5 to 2)	2
295	SHREWD MOVE [-] (bl) 4-10-10 (3") J Jones, ... (5 to 1)	3
577	ALLOON BAWN [-] 7-10-9 R Byrne, ... (16 to 1)	4
69	ARDNAMONA [-] 6-10-6 (5") D P Geoghegan, ... (16 to 1)	5
	DIAMOND SPRITE (USA) [-] 6-10-7 (5") T J O'Sullivan,	
	. . . . (25 to 1)	pu

Dist: 9l, 6l, 20l, dist. (Time not taken) (6 Ran).

(J C Harley), J C Harley

341 Newcastle Maiden Hurdle (4-y-o and up) £1,380 2m 1f 172yds . . . . (3:00)

265[2]	MASAI WARRIOR 6-12-0 J Collins, ... (Evens fav)	1
104[6]	FINGAL BOY (Ire) 5-12-0 J P Banahan, ... (7 to 2)	2
160[5]	FREEWAY HALO (Ire) 4-10-13 F Woods, ... (7 to 1)	3
274[2]	MOSARAT (Ire) 4-10-7 (7") D M Bean, ... (11 to 4)	4
232[8]	DARCARI ROSE (Ire) 4-10-8 (5") T J Mitchell, ... (9 to 1)	5
208	ROVANIEMI (Ire) 5-11-1 (5") D T Evans, ... (25 to 1)	6
115	BOBBIE MAGEE (Ire) 5-10-8 (7") G Lee, ... (16 to 1)	7
	GONE LIKE THE WIND 6-11-1 (5") D P Geoghegan, (40 to 1)	8
	MAWTVICA 6-10-12 (3") Mr P McMahon, ... (33 to 1)	9
	VISIONARY (Ire) 5-10-13 (7") E G Callaghan, ... (20 to 1)	10
	BO MULLEN (Ire) 5-10-8 (7") G McGivern, ... (33 to 1)	11
162	JODONLEE (Ire) 4-10-13 R Byrne, ... (16 to 1)	f

Dist: 8l, 3l, ¾l, 10l. (Time not taken) (12 Ran).

(J C Harley), J C Harley

342 Moyola Mattress Company Novice Chase (5-y-o and up) £1,380 2½m . . . . (3:30)

256[3]	GREEK MAGIC 6-12-0 F Woods, ... (9 to 4)	1
177[3]	LADY DIAMOND 7-11-9 J P Banahan, ... (2 to 1 fav)	2
177[7]	BEAT THE RAP 7-11-11 (3") J Jones, ... (25 to 1)	3
63[9]	SUNSHINE SEAL 6-11-4 (5") T J Mitchell, ... (7 to 1)	4
256[7]	LUCKY ENOUGH 8-11-9 F Flood, ... (8 to 1)	5
66	GEROLAS (Ire) (bl) 5-11-8 J Magee, ... (8 to 1)	6
74[8]	RAGS RAGOUILLE 7-11-9 (5") D T Evans, ... (25 to 1)	7
258	AR AGHAIDH LEATH 7-11-7 (7") M B Cash, . . . (20 to 1)	ur

Dist: 5l, 3l, hd, 9l. (Time not taken) (8 Ran).

(Mrs Vera O'Brien), Peter McCreery

343 Heart Of Down Mares INH Flat Race (4-y-o and up) £1,380 2m 1f 172yds . . . . (5:00)

61[3]	KICKALONG 7-11-9 (5") Mr P J Casey, ... (11 to 4)	1
100[6]	GARYS GIRL 6-11-7 (7") Mr G Finlay, ... (10 to 1)	2
256[2]	MULLAGHMEEN 7-11-5 Mr J P Berry, ... (9 to 4 fav)	3
233[8]	DECEMBER BRIDE (Ire) 5-11-9 (5") Mr B R Hamilton,	
	. . . . (33 to 1)	4
236[4]	HAZEL PARK 5-11-7 (7") Mr P Henley, ... (5 to 1)	5
255	ONE OF THE GLEN (Ire) 4-11-4 (5") Mr A Nash, (33 to 1)	6
	LITTLE BALLYWOODEN (Ire) 5-11-7 (7") Mr E Magee,	
	. . . . (33 to 1)	7
212	PARSONS TOI 8-11-7 (7") Mr M Leahy, ... (16 to 1)	8
	BRACKENAIR 6-11-7 (7") Mr J Bryson, ... (33 to 1)	9
236[8]	GOOD OLD SQUIDGY (Ire) 4-11-4 (5") Mr D Ballentine,	
	. . . . (12 to 1)	10
231[9]	STANDAROUND (Ire) 4-11-2 (7") Mr A K Wyse, (12 to 1)	11
	SALINA BAY 7-11-9 (5") Mr D McGoona, ... (6 to 1)	12
	LITTLE MOON 4-11-9 Mr P F Graffin, ... (12 to 1)	13
81	WISHING'N'HOPING (Ire) 3-11-9 Mr S R Murphy, (33 to 1)	pu

Dist: Sht-hd, ¾l, nk, 3½l. (Time not taken) (14 Ran).

(Liam McAteer), Liam McAteer

HUNTINGDON (good to firm)
Monday August 30th
Going Correction: MINUS 0.20 sec. per fur.

344 Alconbury Conditional Jockeys' Selling Handicap Hurdle (4-y-o and up) £1,494 2m 110yds............................(2:15)

297* ITS ALL OVER NOW [75] 9-11-1 (7ex) W Marston, *al prmnt gng wl, led last, drvn out*....... (9 to 4 fav op 2 to 1)   1
183³ MABTHUL (USA) [75] 5-11-1 M Hourigan, *dwlt, sn in tch, led 2 out, hdd last, ev ch r-in, no extr nr finish*.
................................(11 to 2 op 5 to 1 tchd 8 to 1)   2
264³ BOXING MATCH [60] 6-10-0 R Farrant, *led 3rd till hdd 2 out, sn one pace*............. (14 to 1 op 10 to 1)   3
307³ ROWHEDGE [82] 7-11-8 S Curran, *led to 3rd, cl up, hrd rdn and wknd o'r 2 out*..........(11 to 2 op 3 to 1)   4
242⁶ KELLY'S DARLING [78] 7-11-4 T Jenks, *took keen hold, trkd ldrs, pushed alng appr 3 out, wknd nxt*.
................................(11 to 2 op 8 to 1 tchd 12 to 1)   5
THE GANNOCHY (USA) [60] (bl) 7-10-0 R Davis, *al beh*.
................................(40 to 1 op 33 to 1)   6
224² SHOW THE FLAG [84] 5-11-10 P Midgley, *in tch till reminders and drpd rear 5th, tld off*.
................................(100 to 30 op 12 to 1)   7
Dist: 1l, 10l, 4l, 3l, 15l, 15l. 3m 52.00s. a 5.00s (7 Ran).
SR: 4/3/-/-/   (Moor Farm Racing), Mrs A L M King

345 Hemingford Handicap Chase (0-115 5-y-o and up) £2,611 2½m 110yds........(2:45)

245² MR-PAW [93] 10-10-6 (7*) B Murphy, *wth ldr, led aftr 9th, made rst, clr after 2 out, fnshd tired*.
................................(2 to 1 fav op 9 to 4 tchd 3 to 1)   1
261² YORKSHIREMAN (USA) [104] 8-11-10 M Ahern, *led till hdd aftr 9th, wth wnr, mstk 12th and sn rdn alng, one pace frm 2 out*....................(3 to 1 op 7 to 4)   2
271³ BARTONDALE [85] 8-10-0 (5*) R Farrant, *chsd ldg pair, mstks 9th and 12th, wknd aftr 3 out, hit last, ran on to take 3rd r-in*..........(6 to 1 op 10 to 1 tchd 11 to 1)   3
AMONG FRIENDS [103] 8-11-4 (5*) R Davis, *chsd ldg pair, no imprsn aftr 3 out*....(11 to 4 op 5 to 2 tchd 3 to 1)   4
CURAHEEN BOY [92] 13-10-12 Miss J Butler, *al beh, sn tld off*......................(9 to 1 op 6 to 1)   5
THE FRUIT [85] 14-10-5 Mrs N Ledger, *mstk second, al beh, sn tld off, pld up r-in*.............(33 to 1 op 20 to 1)   pu
Dist: 3l, 3½l, 25l, dist. 4m 56.50s. a 1.50s (6 Ran).
SR: 29/34/12/26/-/-/   (G A Hubbard), F Murphy

346 Diddington Novices' Hurdle (4-y-o and up) £1,480 2m 110yds................(3:15)

244² BATTUTA 4-10-10³ (5*) P Midgley, *led 1st, led ag'n aftr 4th, made rst, ran on gmely frm 2 out*.
................................(5 to 1 op 8 to 1 tchd 10 to 1)   1
EDIREPUS 5-11-0 P Niven, *al prmnt, hrd rdn and ev ch last, one pace*...........(9 to 4 op 6 to 4 tchd 5 to 2)   2
326² ZAMANAYN (Ire) 5-11-0 R Supple, *hld up, steady hdwy frm 4th, rdn and one pace from 2 out*.
................................(15 to 8 fav op 7 to 4 tchd 2 to 1)   3
JUVENARA 7-10-9 (5*) T Eley, *trkd ldrs, hit 2 out, one pace*.............................(16 to 1 op 12 to 1)   4
264⁴ TIBBS INN 4-10-11 M Ranger, *trkd ldrs till wknd 3 out*.
................................(10 to 1 op 8 to 1)   5
ALPHONSO 4-10-11 D Murphy, *strted slwly, nvr on terms*.
................................(16 to 1 op 8 to 1 tchd 20 to 1)   6
SALLY SOHAM (Ire) 5-10-2 (7*) P Murphy, *al beh, tld off*.
................................(14 to 1 op 8 to 1)   7
227⁴ MAPLE BAY (Ire) 4-10-11 A O'Hagan, *mid-div whn f 3rd*.
................................(9 to 1 op 6 to 1 tchd 10 to 1)   f
HIGH STREET BLUES 6-11-0 A Coogan, *sn tld off, pld up bef 2 out*..................(50 to 1 op 20 to 1)   pu
RELATIVELY RISKY 4-10-6 M Ahern, *rcd very freely, led aftr 1st, sn clr, wknd and hdd after 4th, pld up bef 3 out*........................(33 to 1 op 25 to 1)   pu
SHAURNI GIRL 5-10-9 S Keightley, *chsd ldrs till 4th, beh whn pld up bef 2 out*............(50 to 1 op 25 to 1)   pu
THAT'S SPECIAL 4-10-11 R Campbell, *sn tld off, pld up bef 5th*...................(20 to 1 op 12 to 1)   pu
Dist: 2l, ½l, 6l, 20l, 3½l, 12l. 3m 52.40s. a 5.40s (12 Ran).
(Miss K Watson), G R Oldroyd

347 Three Horseshoes, Gt Stukeley Novices' Chase (5-y-o and up) £2,154 2½m 110yds
................................(3:50)

307⁶ ULLSWATER 7-11-3 J Ryan, *led 3rd to 5th, cl up, led ag'n 2 out, rdn and ran on wl*..........(6 to 1 op 9 to 2)   1
MR GEE (bl) 8-11-3 P Niven, *led second to 3rd, led ag'n 5th, pushed alng 3 out, hdd 2 out, hrd rdn and no extr r-in*....................(7 to 2 tchd 4 to 1)   2
184⁴ PAPPA DONT PREACH (Ire) 5-11-3 R Supple, *chsd ldrs, cld o'r 3 out, one pace whn mstk 2 out*.
................................(100 to 30 op 7 to 2 tchd 3 to 1)   3

190⁹ SECRET LIASON 7-11-3 W Humphreys, *nvr on terms*.
................................(5 to 2 fav tchd 11 to 4 and 3 to 1)   4
DANRIBO 10-10-10 (7*) Mr M Gingell, *led to second, beh 8th, jmpd slwly tenth, tld off*......(20 to 1 op 16 to 1)   5
194 WILTOSKI 5-11-0 R Campbell, *jmpd slwly 1st, beh whn refused 4th*............................(7 to 2 op 5 to 2)   ref
Dist: Nk, 10l, 15l, dist. 5m 0.70s. a 5.70s (6 Ran).
(Mrs F M Reid), A S Reid

348 Huntingdon 'Antiques Drive-in' Handicap Hurdle (0-115 4-y-o and up) £1,795 2m 5f 110yds............................(4:20)

FAIRWAYS ON TARGET [120] 7-12-0 P Niven, *wth ldr, led 4 out, hit last, ran on wl*..............(2 to 1 op Evens)   1
248* BAHRAIN QUEEN (Ire) [92] 5-10-0 M Ranger, *hld up, hdwy 4 out, kpt on wl frm last*.
................................(3 to 1 tchd 100 to 30 and 7 to 2)   2
248³ SEA BREAKER (Ire) [93] 5-10-1 D Murphy, *hld up, hdwy to track wnr 3 out, hit nxt, ev ch last, swshd tail and no extr und pres*.......(7 to 4 fav op 9 to 4 tchd 5 to 2)   3
283³ NUNS JEWEL [92] 7-9-9 (5*) R Farrant, *led till hdd 4 out, wknd nxt*......................(11 to 2 op 7 to 1)   4
312⁹ SAILOR BOY [92] (v) 7-10-0 J Ryan, *not fluent, drpd rear 6th, tld off whn pld up bef 2 out*... (25 to 1 op 20 to 1)   pu
Dist: 6l, ½l, 15l. 4m 57.10s. a 2.10s (5 Ran).
SR: 36/2/2/-/-/   (G Fawcett), Mrs M Reveley

349 Godmanchester Juvenile Novices' Hurdle (3-y-o) £1,480 2m 110yds.........(4:55)

285⁵ SUMMER FLOWER 10-2 (5*) T Eley, *trkd ldrs, led appr 2 out, rdn out*...........................(11 to 2 op 3 to 1)   1
147⁵ STAR MARKET 10-9 (3*) W Marston, *al cl up, ev ch last, one pace*............(16 to 1 op 12 to 1 tchd 20 to 1)   2
285 SUMMERS DREAM 10-7 D Byrne, *cl up till mstk 4th and lost pl, closed o'r 2 out, ev ch appr last, one pace*.
................................(10 to 1 op 12 to 1 tchd 8 to 1)   3
272³ ARE YOU HAPPY (Ire) 10-7 R Supple, *led til hdd appr 2 out, one pace approaching last*.
................................(2 to 1 fav op 7 to 4 tchd 5 to 2)   4
MARAT (USA) 10-12 D Murphy, *hld up in tch, pushed alng 3 out, sn one pace*...(11 to 4 op 2 to 1 tchd 3 to 1)   5
187 NO SHOW (Ire) 10-12 W Humphreys, *hld up, nvr on terms wth ldrs*......................(25 to 1 op 16 to 1)   6
BAYFAN (Ire) 10-12 A Charlton, *hld up in tch, wknd quickly 3 out, tld off*..........(16 to 1 op 12 to 1)   7
DOONE BRAES (Ire) 10-7 (5*) R Farrant, *in tch, pushed alng 4 out, sn wknd, pld up bef 2 out*.
................................(7 to 2 op 5 to 2 tchd 4 to 1)   pu
Dist: 3l, 6l, nk, 3½l, 2l, dist. 4m 3.20s. a 16.20s (8 Ran).
(Target Racing), A L Forbes

NEWTON ABBOT (good to firm)
Monday August 30th
Going Correction: MINUS 0.15 sec. per fur.

350 Passage House Hotel Novices' Chase (5-y-o and up) £2,434 2m 110yds......(2:25)

PARBOLD HILL 5-11-0 M A FitzGerald, *jmpd wl, made all, rdn appr last, ran on strly r-in*.
................................(7 to 2 op 4 to 1 tchd 9 to 4)   1
BUMPTIOUS BOY 9-11-2 D Bridgwater, *3rd aftr 4th, mstk 9th, chlgd 2 out, not quicken r-in*.
................................(2 to 1 fav op Evens tchd 9 to 4)   2
259⁴ COMIC LINE (bl) 8-11-2 S Burrough, *chsd ldr, drvn alng 7th, slight mstk 3 out, one pace*.
................................(7 to 1 op 10 to 1 tchd 16 to 1)   3
286³ VIRGINIA'S BAY 7-11-2 Mr N Miles, *trkd ldrs, struggling 9th*...........................(6 to 1 op 7 to 1 tchd 8 to 1)   4
218⁴ DANNY'S LUCK (NZ) 11-11-2 S Mackey, *mstk 7th, no ch aftr*.....................(6 to 1 op 4 to 1)   5
ARCTICFLOW (USA) (bl) 8-10-9 (7*) J Neaves, *jmpd slwly 3rd, al tld off*....(20 to 1 op 10 to 1 tchd 25 to 1)   6
WOODLANDS CROWN 10-11-2 N Mann, *al rear, tld off 9th*........................(33 to 1 op 25 to 1)   7
Dist: 6l, 2l, 11½l, dist, 10l. 4m 0.70s. a 3.70s (7 Ran).
SR: 24/16/4/-/   (Glenn Martin), K R Burke

351 H. A. Fox Rolls Royce Handicap Hurdle (0-115 4-y-o and up) £2,284 2¾m....(2:55)

284* TRUMPET [90] 4-10-7 (6ex) M A FitzGerald, *chsd ldr second, led appr 2 out, pushed out r-in*.
................................(6 to 4 fav op 7 to 4 tchd 2 to 1)   1
219⁵ INNOCENT PRINCESS (NZ) [91] 8-11-8 J Frost, *hld up, took 3rd 5th, short of room appr 2 out, ev ch whn hit last, ran on*......(2 to 1 op 7 to 4 tchd 5 to 2)   2
RICH PICKINGS [83] 4-10-0 N Hawke, *led, sddl slpd aftr 1st, wnt clr after 6th till appr 2 out, wknd*.
................................(5 to 1 op 6 to 1 tchd 4 to 1)   3
KNIGHTON COOMBE (NZ) [107] 7-11-4 C Llewellyn, *drpd rear 5th, rallied appr 7th, wknd nxt, tld off*.
................................(4 to 1 op 2 to 1)   4
Dist: 1½l, 7l, 13l. 5m 13.80s. a 14.80s (4 Ran).

(Mrs M Roper), J G M O'Shea

352 Flynn's Bistro Juvenile Novices' Hurdle (3-y-o) £1,830 2m 1f.....................(3:25)

GLOWING PATH 10-12 G McCourt, *hld up, hdwy aftr 3rd, chlgd 3 out till slight advantage nxt, mstk 2 out, drvn out r-in*...........................(2 to 1 op 6 to 4) 1

221³ APACHEE FLOWER 10-0 (7") Mr G Lewis, *led till second, remained prmnt, led 6th to 2 out, ran on*.
................(12 to 1 op 8 to 1 tchd 14 to 1) 2

ALLEGATION 10-12 J Lower, *dsptd ld second to 3rd, led 5th to 6th, sn hdd and one pace*.
................(6 to 5 on op 5 to 4 on tchd 11 to 10) 3

221⁴ VENTURE PRINTS 10-10 R Bellamy, *beh 4th, tld off*.
................(14 to 1 op 20 to 1 tchd 12 to 1) 4

WORKING TITLE (Ire) 10-12 J Osborne, *mid-div, rdn and ev ch 3 out, wknd appr nxt, virtually pld up r-in, lme*.
................(7 to 1 op 5 to 1) 5

147⁶ IRISH DOMINION 10-12 N Hawke, *led second till appr 5th, wknd quickly nxt, tld off whn pld up bef 2 out*.
................(33 to 1 op 20 to 1) pu

Dist: 1l, 12l, 25l, 5l. 3m 57.40s. a 7.40s (6 Ran).

(P Slade), R J Hodges

353 Passage House Hotel Claiming Hurdle (4 - 7-y-o) £1,794 2m 1f.................(3:55)

203² MOYMET 7-11-6 G McCourt, *chsd ldrs till wnt second appr 2 out, drvn to ld two out, drw clr und pres r-in*.
................(3 to 1 tchd 7 to 1) 1

182⁴ SAFETY (USA) (bl) 6-11-8 D Skyrme, *trkd ldr till led sn aftr 3 out, hdd nxt, one pace r-in*........(7 to 2 op 7 to 4) 2

CHARLY PHARLY (Fr) 6-11-0 J Frost, *led till sn aftr 3 out, one pace nxt*......................(7 to 2 tchd 9 to 2) 3

EMERALD MOON 6-11-0 S Burrough, *prmnt, rdn and ev ch sn aftr 3 out, btn appr last*.
................(14 to 1 op 8 to 1 tchd 16 to 1) 4

297² MILLROUS (bl) 5-10-7 J Lower, *hld up, some hdwy aftr 4th, mstks 5th and 6th, sn btn, pld up and dismounted r-in, lme*............(7 to 4 fav op 5 to 4 on tchd 9 to 4) pu

Dist: 4l, 2½l, 5l. 4m 1.80s. a 11.80s (5 Ran).

(E J Mangan), K R Burke

354 Passage House Hotel Handicap Chase (5-y-o and up) £2,920 2m 5f...........(4:25)

MAJOR MATCH (NZ) [115] 11-11-4 H Davies, *trkd ldr till led 11th, styd on strly 3 out*.........(7 to 4 on op 6 to 4 on) 1

196⁴ COPPER MINE [125] 7-12-0 J Osborne, *led, blun 5th, hdd 11th, no ch frm 2 out*.
...........(5 to 4 on op 6 to 4 on tchd 11 to 10 on) 2

PLAYPEN [102] 9-10-5 J Frost, *bumped 1st, al rear*.
................(9 to 2 op 5 to 1 tchd 11 to 2) 3

Dist: 8l, 4l. 5m 7.90s. a 7.90s (3 Ran).

(Mrs M Wiggin), Capt T A Forster

355 Westomatic Novices' Handicap Hurdle (0-100 4-y-o and up) £1,880 2m 1f....(4:55)

LITTLE NOD [82] 4-11-3 (7") P McLoughlin, *wtd wth, hdwy to ld appr 2 out, sn drw clr*.
................(5 to 2 op 3 to 1 tchd 7 to 2) 1

244⁴ FULL SHILLING (USA) [69] 4-10-11 G McCourt, *hdwy and ev ch 3 out, took second appr nxt, not pace of wnr*.
................(5 to 1 op 3 to 1) 2

264* CLYRO [73] 5-11-1 N Mann, *led 4th to jst aftr 3 out, wknd, styd on ag'n r-in*......(5 to 2 op 7 to 4 tchd 11 to 4) 3

242* FRANKUS [77] 4-11-5 S Earle, *led, sn clr, hdd 4th, led briefly aftr 3 out, wknd*.
................(15 to 8 fav op 2 to 1 tchd 5 to 2) 4

260 NOW BOARDING [58] 6-9-8¹ (7") Mr N Bradley, *rdn and wknd appr 5th, tld off whn pld up bef 2 out*.
................(33 to 1 op 20 to 1) pu

Dist: 12l, 15l, 1½l. 3m 59.20s. a 9.20s (5 Ran).

(Mrs H J Hollamby), J White

PLUMPTON (firm)
Monday August 30th
Going Correction: MINUS 0.10 sec. per fur.

356 Shaef Juvenile Novices' Hurdle (3-y-o) £1,405 2m 1f......................(2:30)

PYRRHIC DANCE 10-12 J Railton, *trkd ldrs, prog 3 out, led last, jst hld on*.......(5 to 1 op 3 to 1 tchd 6 to 1) 1

CONVOY (bl) 10-12 D Gallagher, *mstk 7th, prmnt, led 2 out till last, rallied flt*................(7 to 1 tchd 5 to 2) 2

193* CASHABLE 11-4 S Smith Eccles, *led, mstk 3 out, hdd and wknd nxt*.......(11 to 8 fav op Evens tchd 6 to 4) 3

180⁴ DICKINS 10-5 (7") G Crone, *chsd ldrs till wknd 7th, kpt on frm 2 out*.......(10 to 1 op 7 to 1 tchd 14 to 1) 4

193 FLYING AMY 10-7 G Upton, *prog 7th, wknd aftr 3 out*.
................(50 to 1 op 20 to 1) 5

193⁴ MINTEEN 10-7 A Maguire, *prmnt till wknd o'r 3 out*.
................(6 to 1 op 7 to 2 tchd 13 to 2) 6

Dist: Sht-hd, 12l, 5l, 5l, 10l. 4m 7.20s. a 15.20s (6 Ran).

(The Pyrrhic Dance Partnership), J W Hills

357 'Poethlyn' Novices' Chase (5-y-o and up) £1,672 2m 5f.....................(3:00)

STAR OF OUGHTERARD (bl) 8-11-2 W McFarland, *jmpd rght, chsd ldr, led last, drvn clr*.
................(7 to 1 op 6 to 1 tchd 8 to 1) 1

223² NORSTOCK 6-11-9 A Maguire, *blun 12th, led till last, not quicken*.......(9 to 4 on op 5 to 2 on tchd 2 to 1 on) 2

149⁴ MILLIE BELLE (v) 7-10-11 M Richards, *al last, tld off frm 3 out*.......(9 to 4 op 7 to 4 tchd 5 to 2) 3

Dist: 6l, 25l. 5m 10.00s. a 5.00s (3 Ran).
SR: 17/18/-/

(Quicksteel Ltd), T P McGovern

358 Evening Argus Challenge Cup Handicap Hurdle (0-115 4-y-o and up) £1,576 2m 1f ....(3:30)

300³ MADRAJ (Ire) [87] 5-10-5 W McFarland, *prog 7th, lft in ld nxt, clr 2 out, jst hld on*.(4 to 1 tchd 7 to 2 tchd 9 to 2) 1

205² STRIDING EDGE [89] 8-10-4 (3") D O'Sullivan, *prmnt, lft second 2 out, outpcd nxt, rallied last, no eztr nr finish*.
................(11 to 4 op 3 to 1 tchd 7 to 2) 2

190⁵ AEDEAN [89] 4-10-7 A Maguire, *hld up, 3rd and no imprsn frm 3 out*......(5 to 1 op 3 to 1 tchd 11 to 1) 3

TELE THON [99] (v) 6-10-12 (5") D Leahy, *led, half l up whn f 3 out*............(6 to 4 fav op 2 to 1 tchd 9 to 4) f

204⁴ DEVIL'S VALLEY [106] (bl) 10-11-3 (7") L Dace, *prmnt til wknd rpdly 4th, tld off and pld up bef 2 out*.
................(10 to 1 tchd 14 to 1 and 9 to 1) pu

Dist: Hd, 20l. 3m 58.90s. a 6.90s (5 Ran).

(P Slade), R J Hodges

359 Peacehaven Selling Handicap Hurdle (3-y-o and up) £1,171 2½m............(4:00)

181* MANHATTAN BOY [100] 11-11-10 A Maguire, *second till led 9th, clr 2 out, unchlgd*.
......(13 to 8 on op 6 to 4 on tchd 11 to 8 on and 7 to 4 on) 1

DESERT PALM [86] (bl) 8-11-3 (7") T Thompson, *led till 9th, mstk nxt, no imprsn aftr*.
................(5 to 1 tchd 4 to 1 tchd 6 to 1) 2

190⁸ BIRTHNIGHT GOD (Ire) [78] 4-10-2 L Harvey, *cl up, mstk 9th, beh aftr*......(5 to 2 op 7 to 4 tchd 3 to 1) 3

181⁷ TAPESTRY DANCER [77] 5-10-1¹ W McFarland, *in tch till outpcd aftr 9th*......(10 to 1 op 14 to 1 tchd 9 to 1) 4

Dist: 5l, 4l, 5l. 4m 51.40s. a 14.40s (4 Ran).

(Mrs D R Hunnisett), J Ffitch-Heyes

360 'Plum Jam' Handicap Chase (0-115 4-y-o and up) £2,115 2m.................(4:30)

281² PEARLS BEAU [97] 6-11-10 S Smith Eccles, *jmpd wl, made all, easily*...(2 to 1 on op 6 to 4 on tchd 11 to 8 on) 1

225⁵ COTAPAXI [96] 8-11-9 W Irvine, *cl up till mstk 9th, wknd 3 out*.........(6 to 4 op 11 to 10 tchd 13 to 8) 2

Won by 8l. 3m 56.50s. a 6.50s (2 Ran).
SR: 15/6/

(Mrs T McCoubrey), J R Jenkins

361 Buxted Novices' Hurdle (4-y-o and up) £1,443 2½m.........................(4:55)

207* SINGING DETECTIVE (v) 6-10-13 (7") G Crone, *clr ldr til hdd appr last, led ag'n r-in, all out*. (9 to 4 op Evens) 1

ACROBATE (USA) 4-10-12 P Holley, *chsd ldr, rdn to ld appr last, hdd and not quicken r-in*.
................(6 to 4 on op Evens) 2

ALLE-ROY 5-11-0 D Gallagher, *lost tch 9th, sn tld off*.
................(25 to 1 op 16 to 1 tchd 50 to 1) 3

AUNT ADA 4-10-7 G Rowe, *al beh, tld off*.
................(9 to 1 op 7 to 1 tchd 10 to 1) 4

Dist: 1l, 30l, 15l. 4m 46.40s. a 9.40s (4 Ran).

(Elaine Mills & K Powell), P M McEntee

ROSCOMMON (IRE) (good to firm)
Monday August 30th

362 Shannon Handicap Hurdle (4-y-o and up) £3,107 2m.......................(4:45)

PUESTO DEL SOL (Ire) [-] 5-11-9 C F Swan, ...(13 to 2) 1
118* HIS WAY (Ire) [-] 4-11-1 K F O'Brien, ...(4 to 1) 2
294² NIMBLE WIND [-] 7-10-6 A J O'Brien, ...(7 to 4 fav) 3
SORRY ABOUT THAT [-] 7-10-11 P Carberry, ...(6 to 1) 4
NORTHERN BREGA [-] 6-9-7 P L Malone, ...(20 to 1) 5
160⁸ DAMHSA (Den) [-] 4-10-0 (7") C McCormack, ...(20 to 1) 6
20³ MERRY JOHN [-] 7-10-7 N Byrne, ...(7 to 1) 7
99 TOMBARA (Ire) [-] (bl) 5-10-4 J Short, ...(12 to 1) 8
KNOCNAGORE (Ire) [-] 4-9-11 T Horgan, ...(20 to 1) 9
249⁷ DELIFFIN [-] 7-9-4 (7") J K McCarthy, ...(20 to 1) 10
37 ARDLEA HOUSE (Ire) [-] 4-9-4 (7") R A Hennessy, (14 to 1) 11

Dist: 1l, sht-hd, ½l, 11l. 3m 46.00s. (11 Ran).

(Mrs J R Mullion), D T Hughes

363 Lenabane Hurdle (4-y-o and up) £3,452 2½m. (5:15)

123	THE LADY'S KNIGHT 7-11-7 (7°) C O'Brien, ... (11 to 2)	1
305²	SWALLOWS NEST 6-11-2 M Flynn, ... (10 to 9 on)	2
254	FINAL TUB 10-11-2 C O'Dwyer, ...(12 to 1)	3
177°	FESTIVAL DREAMS 8-11-8 J Shortt, ...(7 to 2)	4
213⁵	MARBLE CITY GIRL (bl) 8-10-12 (5°) T P Treacy, . . (16 to 1)	5
	SUPER TACTICS (Ire) 5-10-11 (5°) C P Dunne, ... (9 to 1)	6
	STRONG ROSE (bl) 6-10-11 N Byrne, ...(25 to 1)	7
178	ENNIS SEVEN FIFTY 6-11-2 T Horgan, ...(16 to 1)	8
	ITS YOUR CHOICE (Ire) 4-9-11 (7°) J Kelly, ... (10 to 1)	9
112	GERRYMANDER 7-11-2 K F O'Brien, ...(50 to 1)	10
	BALLYBROWN FLASH (Ire) 5-11-2 C F Swan, ...(25 to 1)	11
257⁸	TOP RUN (Ire) 5-11-2 H Rogers, ...(25 to 1)	12

Dist: ½sl, 3l, 1½l, 4½l. 4m 32.10s. (12 Ran).

(F X Doyle), F X Doyle

364 Percy French Handicap Chase (4-y-o and up) £3,452 3m. (6:15)

210²	LIFE OF A LORD [-] (bl) 7-11-0 G M O'Neill, ...(10 to 1)	1
293°	MALACHYS BAR [-] 9-9-13 (6ex) T Horgan, ...(10 to 1)	2
132	BOLD FLYER [-] 10-12-0 K F O'Brien, ...(10 to 1)	3
306⁴	KINGSTON WAY [-] 7-11-2 A J O'Brien, ...(6 to 1)	4
250³	BALLYVERANE [-] 7-9-7 P L Malone, ... (14 to 1)	5
178⁵	GOLDEN SEE [-] 9-9-9 N Byrne, ... (14 to 1)	6
134	CLOSE AT HAND [-] 8-9-7 P McWilliams, ...(14 to 1)	7
	HO FRETTA [-] 7-9-0 (7°) C O'Brien, ...(33 to 1)	8
303°	EASTER SIXTEEN [-] 7-12-1 (2ex) J Shortt, ... (5 to 1)	9
134°	JOEY KELLY [-] 8-10-5 C O'Dwyer, ... (100 to 30 fav)	pu
134	LIGHT THE WICK [-] 7-10-8 C F Swan, ...(9 to 2)	pu

Dist: 2l, 8l, 10l, 15l. 5m 52.70s. (11 Ran).

(M J Clancy), T Costello

365 Lough Derg INH Flat Race (4-y-o and up) £3,107 2m. (7:15)

162²	BAY MISCHIEF (Ire) 4-10-13 (7°) Mr J Connolly, (7 to 4 fav)	1
266°	MOOREFIELD GIRL (Ire) 4-11-1 (7°) Miss F M Crowley,	
	. . . . (2 to 1)	2
162°	DERRYMOYLE (Ire) 4-11-8 (5°) Mr G J Harford, . . (15 to 8)	3
	GOOD DEER (Ire) 5-11-11 Mr J P Dempsey, ... (25 to 1)	4
	RUSHEEN BAY (Ire) 4-10-13 (7°) Mr A Daly, ... (25 to 1)	5
266	CARRIGANN HOTEL (Ire) 5-10-13 (7°) Mr P Doyle, (25 to 1)	6

Dist: 4½l, 1½l, 13l, 13l. 3m 36.10s. (6 Ran).

(T Harty), P Burke

SOUTHWELL (good to firm)
Monday August 30th
Going Correction: NIL

366 British Coal Claiming Chase (5-y-o and up) £1,865 2m. (3:30)

288²	ABSAILOR 9-11-1 (5°) P Williams, al prmnt, hit 5th, led 5 out, styd on wl frm 2 out.	
	. . . . (7 to 4 fav op 2 to 1 tchd 9 to 4)	1
	MAGIC SOLDIER 8-11-10 R Marley, in tch, hdwy 5th, effrt and ev ch 3 out, rdn and one pace appr nxt.	
	. . . . (7 to 1 op 5 to 1)	2
309³	RONOCCO 11-10-10 S McNeill, chsd ldrs, rdn alng whn hmpd 5 out, kpt on same pace. . . . . (4 to 1 op 3 to 1)	3
261	ANOTHER BARNEY 9-10-12 I Lawrence, prmnt, hit 4th, rdn appr 5 out, sn wknd.	
	. . . . (11 to 2 op 6 to 1 tchd 7 to 1)	4
223⁴	SOLICITOR'S CHOICE (v) 10-10-10 Mr R Armson, led and f 1st. . . . .(4 to 1 op 5 to 1 tchd 7 to 2)	f
286⁵	DIZZY DEALER 6-10-11 D Morris, led, rdn 6 out, hdd and f nxt. . . . .(12 to 1 op 10 to 1)	f
	RUFUS BOY 7-10-10 M Brennan, chsd ldrs, blun 4th, sn beh, pld up bef 6th. . . . .(20 to 1)	pu
246	BROTHER MINSTREL 6-11-4 Mr A Pickering, sn beh, tld off 3rd, pld up bef 7th. . . . .(33 to 1)	pu

Dist: 12l, 5l, 15l. 4m 10.10s. a 11.10s (8 Ran).

(Lady Harris), Mrs S C Bradburne

367 Newark Handicap Chase (0-115 5-y-o and up) £1,917 3m 110yds. (4:00)

283²	OFF THE BRU [106] 8-12-0 Mr J Bradburne, al prmnt, led 4th, clr four out, unchlgd. . . . (9 to 4 on op 7 to 4 on)	1
196⁴	CLARES HORSE [94] 6-10-9 (7°) Mr T Byrne, hld up, hit 6th, hdwy hfwy, hit 11th, rdn to chase wnr 4 out, kpt on one pace. . . . .(7 to 2 op 3 to 1)	2
	KNOX'S CORNER [96] 8-11-4 D Morris, led to 4th, cl up till rdn to 5 out and grad wknd, poor 3rd whn refused last, retrd steps and fnshd third. . . . .(20 to 1 tchd 33 to 1)	3
	FIESTA DANCE [88] 10-10-9 M Robinson, chsd ldrs, hit tenth, wknd and beh 12th, pld up bef 6 out.	
	. . . . (16 to 1 op 14 to 1)	pu
	ANOTHER CORNER [87] 10-10-9 M R Armson, in tch, hit 4th and sn lost pl, tld off 8th, pld up bef 12th.	
	. . . .(10 to 1 tchd 8 to 1)	pu

Dist: Dist, dist. 6m 38.90s. a 40.90s (5 Ran).

(G Lochtie), Mrs S C Bradburne

SOUTHWELL (A.W) (std)
Monday August 30th
Going Correction: PLUS 0.40 sec. per fur.

368 Hopeful Novices' Handicap Hurdle (4-y-o and up) £1,492 2½m. (2:30)

	EMERALD VENTURE [78] 6-12-0 Peter Caldwell, in tch, hdwy and hit 4th, led 6th, rdn 2 out, styd on wl.	
	. . . . (9 to 1 op 8 to 1)	1
243²	SAFARI PARK [75] 4-11-4 (7°) G Cahill, al cl up, effrt and ev ch 3 out, rdn and hit nxt, wknd last.	
	. . . . (11 to 4 op 5 to 2)	2
	REEL OF TULLOCH (Ire) [72] 4-11-3 (5°) D Bentley, hld up in tch, hdwy hfwy, ev ch 4 out, rdn appr nxt, kpt on one pace. . . . . (2 to 1 fav op 9 to 4 tchd 11 to 4)	3
	ALIZARI (USA) [60] (bl) 4-10-10 M Robinson, cl up, rdn 5 out, wknd aftr nxt. . . . . (16 to 1 tchd 20 to 1)	4
287⁵	JUBILATA (USA) [74] 5-11-10 C Dennis, cl up, hit 5th, sn rdn and lost pl, beh frm 5 out.	
	. . . . (9 to 4 op 11 to 4 tchd 3 to 1)	5
262⁷	SANDMOOR PRINCE [68] 10-11-4 Dr P Pritchard, led to 6th, sn rdn, wknd and beh frm 5 out. . . (9 to 1 op 8 to 1)	6
289	LOCHNDON [60] 8-10-10 R Hodge, in tch, rdn alng 6th and sn lost pl, pld up aftr 7th. . . . .(50 to 1)	pu

Dist: 4l, nk, dist, 15l, 25l. 5m 9.40s. a 28.40s (7 Ran).

(Jack Simmons), T H Caldwell

369 Staythorpe Novices' Selling Hurdle (4-y-o and up) £1,380 2m. (3:00)

226⁷	BRECKENBROUGH LAD 6-11-4 J A Harris, al prmnt, hit 5 out, effrt and hdwy to ld 3 out, sn rdn and ran on.	
	. . . . (11 to 4 op 2 to 1)	1
307	CISTOLENA (v) 7-10-13 Diane Clay, al prmnt, led 4 out, sn rdn and hdd 3 out, kpt on und pres. (8 to 1 op 14 to 1)	2
227	MAJOR RISK 4-10-12 (3°) N Bentley, led, hit 4th, rdn and hdd four out, sn wknd. . . . . . .(7 to 4 jt-fav op 2 to 1)	3
	BLUEJACKET (Ire) 5-11-4 G Bradley, beh till reminders and hdwy 4th, rdn appr four out, sn btn. . . .(7 to 4 jt-fav op 5 to 2)	4
	HIGH WATER 6-11-4 R Hodge, in tch, till lost pl and beh frm hfwy, tld off whn pld up bef 3 out. . . . . . . (33 to 1)	pu

Dist: 2l, 30l, 10l. 4m 11.30s. a 25.30s (5 Ran).

(Mrs A W Turner), D T Turner

370 Rose County Handicap Hurdle (0-115 4-y-o and up) £1,506 2m. (4:30)

226⁴	NORTHERN NATION [95] 5-10-5 Diane Clay, trkd ldrs, hdwy hfwy, led appr 3 out, rdn nxt and ran on wl.	
	. . . . (5 to 4 fav op 3 to 1)	1
	KING'S SHILLING (USA) [118] 6-12-0 Jacqui Oliver, in tch, hdwy 6th, effrt to chal 3 out, sn rdn and kpt on one pace. . . . .(4 to 1 tchd 9 to 2)	2
	HAVE A NIGHTCAP [95] 4-10-5³ J A Harris, chsd ldr, led 6th, rdn and hdd appr 3 out, sn one pace.	
	. . . . (5 to 1 op 5 to 2)	3
226²	JAMESTOWN BOY [90] (bl) 5-10-0 T Wall, al beh, nvr a factor. . . . .(7 to 2 op 3 to 1)	4
	BLUE DISC [92] 8-10-2 Gary Lyons, led, hdd and hit 6th, wknd nxt, sn beh. . . . . (12 to 1 op 11 to 1)	5
	ELDER PRINCE [100] 7-10-10 G Harker, in tch, rdn and lost pl bef 3 out, sn tld off and pld up bef 3 out.	
	. . . . (12 to 1 op 14 to 1 tchd 20 to 1)	pu

Dist: 3½l, 2l, 15l, 12l. 3m 58.00s. a 12.00s (6 Ran).
SR: 21/40/15/ (Ed Weetman (Haulage & Storage) Ltd), W Clay

371 Averham Amateur Riders' Hurdle (4-y-o and up) £1,478 2½m. (5:00)

	HIRAM B BIRDBATH (bl) 7-11-0 (5°) Mrs P Nash, al prmnt, chsd ldr frm 7th, smooth hdwy 3 out, led appr last, sn clr.	1
	SULUK (USA) 8-11-9 (5°) Mr M Buckley, led to 3rd, led aftr 6th, rdn and jmpd rght 3 out, hdd and wknd appr last, fnshd lme. . . . . (6 to 4 on tchd 5 to 4 on)	2
	LA FONTAINBLEAU (Ire) 5-11-0² (7°) Mr A Rebori, prmnt, hit 5th and sn lost pl, tld off frm 7th. . .(6 to 1 tchd 7 to 1)	3
189⁵	STORM WARRIOR (bl) 8-10-12 (7°) Miss L Boswell, prmnt, hit second, led 3rd till aftr 6th, rdn whn hit 7th and uns rdr. . . . . (12 to 1 op 14 to 1 tchd 10 to 1)	ur

Dist: 8l, dist. 5m 7.90s. a 26.90s (4 Ran).

(Steven Astaire), J A Glover

WAREGEM (BEL) (good to firm)
Tuesday August 31st

372 Prix Andre du Monceau de Bergendal (Chase) (5-y-o and up) £11,928 2m 3f (2:25)

	GEOELITA (Fr) 7-9-11 G Goffart, ...	1
	ACROPOLIS (Fr) 5-9-11 A Chayrigues, ...	2

```
    AZURE V (Fr) 5-9-11 P Esnault, . . . . . . . . . . . . . . . . . . . . . .  3
127 SPIRITED HOLME (Fr) 8-9-10 R Davis, jmpd wl, hdwy into
    4th hfwy, wknd 3 fs out, bhn. . . . . . . . . . . . . . . . . . . . . .  0
182² GABISH 8-9-10 A Maguire, almost refused and f 1st. . . . . .  f
    ALLENROID 14-9-10 L Flynn, beh whn f 6th. . . . . . . . . . . .  f
    BOREEN BRIDGE 8-9-10 D Bromley, rear whn refused
    7th. . . . . . . . . . . . . . . . . . . . . . . . . . . . . . . . . . . . . . . . . ref
Dist: 15l, 3l, 15l, 2l. (Time not taken) (21 Ran).
```
(A de Mieulle), A de Mieulle

373 Prix Jacques du Roy de Blicquy (Handicap Chase) (5-y-o and up) £15,905 2m 7f (3:20)

```
    CARAIBE (Fr) 6-10-5 D Beck, . . . . . . . . . . . . . . . . . . . . . . . .  1
    STEWBALL DE FROSSE (Fr) 9-10-5 J Manceau, . . . . . . . . . .  2
    BENTHOS (Fr) 7-10-5 C Chapdelaine, . . . . . . . . . . . . . . . . .  3
262⁵ CLWYD LODGE 6-9-6 V Slattery, mid-div whn f 6th, broke
    destroyed. . . . . . . . . . . . . . . . . . . . . . . . . . . . . . . . . . . . . .  f
284⁶ SILVERCROSS LAD 10-10-1 T Wall, rear whn brght dwn
    6th. . . . . . . . . . . . . . . . . . . . . . . . . . . . . . . . . . . . . . . . . . . . bd
Dist: 4l, 5l, 5l, 1l, 1l. (Time not taken) (16 Ran).
```
(M Pichaud), A Chayrigues

374 Prix Felix de Ruyck (Handicap Hurdle) (4-y-o and up) £5,964 2m 1f. (4:00)

```
    MISTER ALTO (Fr) 6-11-2 H Blois, . . . . . . . . . . . . . . . . . . . .  1
    LUCEA (Fr) 5-10-6 G Legland, . . . . . . . . . . . . . . . . . . . . . . .  2
    BON VIVANT (Fr) 4-10-10 N Van Hecka, . . . . . . . . . . . . . .  3
    CAPDOO LADY (Ire) 5-9-6 L Flynn, hdwy hfwy, 4th whn f 2
    out. . . . . . . . . . . . . . . . . . . . . . . . . . . . . . . . . . . . . . . . . . . .  4
225² POLDER 7-9-6 R Davis, led second till f 3 out. . . . . . . . . . .  f
264⁸ NOT GORDONS 4-9-6 T Wall, sddl slpd and uns rdr 1st.   ur
310² PENNINE PASS (Ire) 4-9-6 G Brown, beh whn pld up 4 out.  pu
107 MUNINNABANE QUIZ 9-9-6 D Bromley, tld off whn pld up
    3 out. . . . . . . . . . . . . . . . . . . . . . . . . . . . . . . . . . . . . . . . . . pu
Dist: 4l, 8l, 1l, 12l, 5l. (Time not taken) (19 Ran).
```
(Ecurie Cheval Atlantique), Y Fertillet

BALLINROBE (IRE) (good to firm)
Wednesday September 1st

375 Ballinrobe Maiden Hurdle (3-y-o) £2,245 2m. (4:30)

```
    MILLERS MILL (Ire) 10-11 (3*) J Jones, . . . . . . . . . . . (12 to 1)  1
228² BENGALI (Ire) 11-0 C F Swan, . . . . . . . . . . . . . . . . . . (11 to 8)  2
290³ LUSTRINO (USA) (bl) 11-0 B Sheridan, . . . . . . . . . (5 to 4 fav)  3
290 DRESS DANCE (Ire) 11-0 J P Banahan, . . . . . . . . . . . . (6 to 1)  4
228⁷ PERCY LANE (Ire) 10-7 (7*) B Bowens, . . . . . . . . . . . . (12 to 1)  5
Dist: Sht-hd, 1½l, 3½l, ¾l. 4m 24.20s. (5 Ran).
```
(L M K Racing Club), E McNamara

376 Claremorris Handicap Hurdle (0-116 4-y-o and up) £2,245 2m. (5:00)

```
313⁶ BRAVEFOOT [-] 5-11-10 K F O'Brien, . . . . . . . . . . . . . (6 to 1)  1
313⁴ NICE AND SIMPLE [-] 6-10-8 A J O'Brien, . . . (4 to 1 jt-fav)  2
249³ SUNSHINES TAXI [-] 6-10-7 B Sheridan, . . . . . . . . . . (5 to 1)  3
294 NOBODYS FLAME (Ire) [-] 5-10-12 J Magee, . . . . . . . (7 to 1)  4
254² KILIAN MY BOY [-] 10-11-8 J F Titley, . . . . . . (4 to 1 jt-fav)  5
    WIND ZING [-] 9-10-5 W T Slattery Jnr, . . . . . . . . . . (20 to 1)  6
274⁴ FURTHER NOTICE (Ire) [-] (bl) 4-10-2 C O'Dwyer, . (16 to 1)  7
249 TWO MAGPIES [-] 6-10-4 P L Malone, . . . . . . . . . . . (10 to 1)  8
    TOAST AND HONEY (Ire) [-] 4-10-8 (7*) T Martin, . . (12 to 1)  9
174⁴ ANA CRUSIS (Ire) [-] 5-10-2 F Woods, . . . . . . . . . . . . (7 to 1) 10
212⁹ ANOTHER BONNY [-] 7-9-6 (7*) C O'Brien, . . . . . . . (25 to 1) 11
    TRUE BILL [-] (bl) 6-9-7 (7*) J P Broderick, . . . . . . . (10 to 1) pu
Dist: Hd, ¾l, 13l, 13l. 4m 1.70s. (12 Ran).
```
(S Macklin), J H Scott

377 Healys Of Pontoon Novice Chase (5-y-o and up) £2,762 2m 1f. (7:00)

```
293⁶ INK BY THE DRUM (USA) 5-11-9 C F Swan, . . . (5 to 4 fav)  1
293⁷ RANDOM PRINCE 9-12-0 C O'Dwyer, . . . . . . . . . . . . (6 to 1)  2
    NO WORD 6-12-0 J F Titley, . . . . . . . . . . . . . . . . . . . (20 to 1)  3
330⁴ BALLYHEIGUE 7-11-7 (7*) Mr J T McNamara, . . . . . . (7 to 1)  4
    TORENAGA HILL 9-11-2 (7*) Mr A Daly, . . . . . . . . . (25 to 1)  5
    CHARMING EXCUSE 9-11-9 (5*) C P Dunne, . . . . . . (7 to 2)  6
    FAIRY PARK 8-12-0 T J Taaffe, . . . . . . . . . . . . . . . . . . (7 to 1)  f
251 CEDAR COURT (Ire) 5-11-9 K F O'Brien, . . . . . . . . . . (8 to 1) ref
332⁹ BALLY O ROURKE (bl) 7-12-0 F Woods, . . . . . . . . . . (20 to 1) pu
Dist: 1½l, 14l, 11l, dist. 4m 26.00s. (9 Ran).
```
(William Dixon), E J O'Grady

378 Mayo/Roscommon Hospice Foundation INH Flat Race (5-y-o and up) £2,935 2½m (7:30)

```
291³ MOUNTHENRY STAR (Ire) 5-11-7 (7*) Mr G P FitzGerald,
    . . . . . . . . . . . . . . . . . . . . . . . . . . . . . . . . . . . . . . . . . . (5 to 2)  1
276³ BAMANYAR (Ire) 5-11-7 (7*) Mr John J Murphy, (100 to 30)  2
124⁵ MAKES YOU WONDER (Ire) 5-12-0 Mr P F Graffin,
    . . . . . . . . . . . . . . . . . . . . . . . . . . . . . . . . . . . . . (5 to 4 fav)  3
121⁵ ORIENT ROVER 9-11-7 (7*) Mr A Daly, . . . . . . . . . (12 to 1)  4
```

```
124 TIME UP (Ire) 5-11-7 (7*) Mr R Monroe, . . . . . . . . . . (25 to 1)  5
201³ CARRIGANS LAD (Ire) 5-11-7 (7*) Mr R Pugh, . . . . . (8 to 1)  6
    CARTRON HOUSE 6-11-7 (7*) Mr M Jennings, . . . . . (16 to 1)  7
201 ALWAYS YOU (Ire) 5-11-2 (7*) Mr J K Connolly, . . . (10 to 1) su
    ALMONTO 6-11-5³ (7*) Mr S Stagg, . . . . . . . . . . . . . . (25 to 1) pu
Dist: 25l, 4l, 9l, 6l. 4m 53.20s. (9 Ran).
```
(Mrs M Reidy), Augustine Leahy

FONTWELL (firm)
Wednesday September 1st
Going Correction: MINUS 0.65 sec. per fur.

379 Fishbourne Novices' Claiming Hurdle (3-y-o) £1,675 2¼m. (2:20)

```
260 LADY GAIL 10-2 A Webb, hld up, gd hdwy 2 out, led appr
    last, sn clr. . . . . . . . . . . (25 to 1 op 16 to 1 tchd 33 to 1)  1
193³ SIAN WYN 10-8 R Supple, led to 3rd, styd in tch, rdn 2
    out, outpcd r-in. . . . . . . . . . (7 to 2 op 9 to 2 tchd 5 to 1)  2
180⁵ SWIFT REVENGE 9-11 (5*) J McCarthy, rcd in tch, lft in ld
    5th, hdd sn aftr 3 out, rdn and one pace frm nxt,
    . . . . . . . . . . . . . . . . . . . . . . . . . (33 to 1 op 16 to 1)  3
    PATONG BEACH 10-12 A Maguire, hld up in rear, hdwy 4
    out, led sn aftr nxt, rdn and hdd appr last, wknd
    quickly. . . . . . . . . . . . . . . . . . . . . (5 to 4 on op 7 to 4 on)  4
349⁷ BAYFAN (Ire) 10-9 A Charlton, hld up in rear, lost tch 3
    out, virtually pld up r-in, tld off. (33 to 1 op 12 to 1)  5
    JAFETICA 10-9¹ G McCourt, pld hrd, trkd ldrs, led 3rd till
    f 5th. . . . . . . . . . . . . . . . . . . . . . . . (8 to 1 op 5 to 1)  f
298⁶ GROGFRYN 9-13 (7*) N Downs, in tch till f 5th.
    . . . . . . . . . . . . . . . . . . . . (8 to 1 op 12 to 1 tchd 14 to 1)  f
Dist: 12l, nk, 5l, dist. 4m 19.30s. a 9.30s (7 Ran).
```
(Mrs Marilyn Olden), J L Spearing

380 Bow Hill Novices' Hurdle (4-y-o and up) £1,601 2¾m. (2:50)

```
237² PURITAN (Can) 4-11-3 G McCourt, trkd ldr, cld 4 out, mstk
    2 out, led last, rdn out. . . . . . . . . . . (5 to 4 op 7 to 4 on)  1
361* SINGING DETECTIVE (v) 6-11-5 (7*,6ex) G Crone, led sn
    clr, rdn and hdd last, one pace r-in. (11 to 4 op 7 to 4)  2
    UP ALL NIGHT 4-10-6 D Morris, jmpd poorly in rear, tld
    off frm 6th. . . . . . . . . . . . . . . . . . (25 to 1 op 20 to 1)  3
207⁴ FRANK'S THE NAME 4-10-11 T Grantham, rcd in 3rd til
    lost pl appr 4 out, tld off. . . . . . . . . (33 to 1 op 20 to 1)  4
    POLLY MINOR 6-10-9 A Maguire, al beh, tld off frm 4th,
    pld up bef 6th.
    . . . . . . . . (12 to 1 op 10 to 1 tchd 8 to 1 and 14 to 1) pu
Dist: 2½l, dist, 25l. 5m 8.00s. b 1.00s (5 Ran).
```
(J Parks), N Tinkler

381 Fons Selling Hurdle (Div I) (3-y-o and up) £1,572 2¼m. (3:20)

```
238³ HELLO SAM 10-11-9 C Llewellyn, made all, drw clr appr
    last, cmftbly. . . . . . . . . . . (2 to 1 op 9 to 4 tchd 5 to 2)  1
    BETALONGABILL 4-11-7 A Maguire, hld up, hdwy to track
    wnr appr 4 out, rdn and outpcd approaching last.
    . . . . . . . . . . . (2 to 1 op 9 to 4 tchd 5 to 2 and 11 to 4)  2
203* BILLY LOMOND (Ire) 5-11-11 (3*) W Marston, trkd wnr til
    appr 4 out, rdn and wknd aftr nxt.
    . . . . . . . . . . . . . . . . . . . . . (11 to 8 fav op Evens tchd 6 to 4)  3
269⁶ ROSEMARY'S MEMORY (Ire) 3-10-3³ W McFarland, jmpd
    rght, al last, lost tch frm 4 out.
    . . . . . . . . . . . . . . . . . . (20 to 1 op 12 to 1 tchd 25 to 1)  4
Dist: 5l, 12l, 4l. 4m 19.80s. a 9.80s (4 Ran).
```
(P W Bennett), J A Bennett

382 Slindon Handicap Chase (0-125 5-y-o and up) £2,247 2¼m. (3:50)

```
308³ THEY ALL FORGOT ME [97] 6-10-0 A Maguire, trkd ldrs till
    second, wnt second ag'n 6th, hrd rdn appr last, led sn
    aftr, drvn out. . . . . . . . . (15 to 8 op 7 to 4 tchd 9 to 4)  1
360* PEARLS BEAU [103] 6-10-6 (6ex) S Smith Eccles, led, mstk
    4th, rdn appr last, hdd sn aftr, one pace.
    . . . . . . . . . . . . (2 to 1 on op 5 to 4 on and 13 to 8 on)  2
261³ DREAMCOAT (USA) [97] 12-9-7 (7*) Leanne Eldredge, chsd
    ldrs frm second, hit nxt, lost frm 6th, lost tch tenth, tld
    off. . . . . . . . . . . . . . . . (16 to 1 op 10 to 1 tchd 20 to 1)  3
Dist: 4l, 25l. 4m 29.60s. a 9.60s (3 Ran).
```
(Jim McCarthy), T Casey

383 Fons Selling Hurdle (Div II) (3-y-o and up) £1,593 2¼m. (4:20)

```
202* QUIET RIOT 11-12-0 A Maguire, hld up, lft second 3 out,
    hrd rdn to ld last, all out.
    . . . . . . . . . . . . . . (15 to 8 op 6 to 4 tchd 9 to 4)  1
185⁴ WEDNESDAYS AUCTION (Ire) (bl) 5-11-4 (5*) C Burnett-
    Wells, al in tch, lft in ld 3 out, mstk nxt, rdn and hdd
    last, no imprsn r-in. . . . . . . (7 to 1 op 4 to 1 tchd 8 to 1)  2
    MAMALAMA 5-11-1 (3*) D O'Sullivan, made most till f 3
    out. . . . . . . . . . . . . . . . . . (5 to 4 fav op Evens tchd 6 to 4)  f
```

EMERALD EARS 4-10-9 (7") G Crone, *led aftr 1st, nrly refused and hdd nxt, jmpd wildly rght but led betw flights to 4th, last whn f four out.*
..............................(12 to 1 op 10 to 1 tchd 20 to 1) f
Dist: ½l. 4m 6.60s. b 3.40s (4 Ran).
SR: 17/11/-/-/
(Ms M Horan), J White

384 **Chichester Handicap Hurdle (0-125 4-y-o and up) £1,715 2¼m................(4:50)**

ABSENT RELATIVE [119] 5-12-0 A Maguire, *hld up, hdwy 3 out, led 2 out, hng lft r-in, all out.*
..............................(13 to 8 op 5 to 4 tchd 7 to 4) 1
205* RULING DYNASTY [112] (bl) 9-11-7 H Davies, *hld up, some hdwy 4th, outpcd appr 2 out, rallied to go second r-in.*
..............................(5 to 4 fav tchd 11 to 10 and 11 to 8) 2
LUSTY LAD [110] 8-11-5 G McCourt, *led appr second, hdd 2 out, ev ch last, one pace r-in.*
..............................(6 to 1 op 5 to 1 tchd 8 to 1) 3
NEWTON POINT [101] 4-10-10 Peter Hobbs, *led till hdd appr second, mstk 3 out, ev ch till wknd r-in, eased.*
..............................(5 to 1 op 6 to 1 tchd 10 to 1) 4
Dist: 2l, 20l, 12l. 4m 10.80s. a 0.80s (4 Ran).
(Mrs J L Froome), Miss B Sanders

NEWTON ABBOT (good to firm)
Wednesday September 1st
Going Correction: MINUS 0.05 sec. per fur.

385 **Forches Cross Claiming Chase (5-y-o and up) £2,336 2m 110yds............ (2:10)**

225³ TINAS LAD 10-11-8 N Williamson, *chsd ldr, chlgd 7th, led 9th, drvn clr frm 3 out. Subsequently disqualified.*
..............................(13 to 8 fav op Evens tchd 7 to 4) 1D
167⁵ MY CUP OF TEA 10-10-8 R Dunwoody, *led, mstk 6th, hdd 9th, chalg whn blun tenth, rdn and no extr frm 3 out, fnshd second, awarded race.*
..............................(4 to 1 op 3 to 1 tchd 5 to 2) 1
298 DARING CLASS 7-10-9 I Shoemark, *sn rear, mstk 3rd, hit 7th, jmpd slwly and lost tch 8th, no ch whn blun 2 out, fnshd third, plcd second............(11 to 1 op 7 to 1) 2
SWINGTIME BELLE 6-10-3 S McNeill, *in tch, jmpd slwly 3rd and 4th, wknd 6th, tld off whn jumped slowly 8th, fnshd fourth, plcd third.*
..............................(14 to 1 op 12 to 1 tchd 16 to 1) 3
220³ JACK THE HIKER 10-10-10 M Richards, *chsd ldr briefly 6th, sn wknd, pld up aftr 3 out.....(3 to 1 op 9 to 4) pu
Dist: 8l, 20l, 10l. 4m 2.70s. a 5.70s (5 Ran).
SR: 29/7/
(Mrs E King), M C Pipe

386 **Cooper Callas Bathroom Distributors Handicap Chase (0-115 5-y-o and up) £2,684 3¼m 110yds............ (2:40)**

300⁵ SHALCHLO BOY [88] 9-11-1 R Dunwoody, *chsd ldr, led 11th, hdd nxt, led 13th, headed 2 out, rallied to ld ag'n last, styd on wl............................(2 to 1 fav) 1
FATHER DOWLING [101] 6-11-9 (5") R Davis, *in tch, chlgd 14th, led 2 out, hdd last, sn one pace. (3 to 1 op 6 to 1) 2
206⁵ HEIGHT OF FUN [93] (bl) 9-11-6 M A FitzGerald, *chsd ldrs till lost tch frm 4 out.....(9 to 2 op 4 to 1 tchd 5 to 1) 3
170⁶ BARRACILLA [85] 8-10-12 S Hodgson, *hdwy 7th, lost tch 14th.........................(8 to 1 tchd 10 to 1) 4
299⁶ SIRISAT [86] 9-10-6 (7") Mr T Byrne, *beh, jmpd slwly 4th, mstk 8th, lost tch 14th.*
..............................(25 to 1 op 20 to 1 tchd 33 to 1) 5
262⁴ VALASSY [86] 10-10-6 (7") P McLoughlin, *led, mstk 8th, hdd 11th, led 12th, headed 13th, hit 16th, wkng whn jmpd slwly 4 out......(15 to 2 op 5 to 1 tchd 8 to 1) 6
299⁴ SAMSUN [96] (bl) 11-11-9 S McNeill, *rdn frm 6th, lost tch 11th, tld off whn pld up bef 3 out.*
..............................(20 to 1 op 16 to 1 tchd 25 to 1) pu
Dist: 3l, 25l, 1l, 20l, 20l. 6m 32.50s. a 12.50s (7 Ran).
(S N Burfield), W G M Turner

387 **Cooper Callas Bathroom Distributors Conditional Jockeys' Selling Handicap Hurdle (4-y-o and up) £1,768 2m 1f........ (3:10)**

217⁵ CELCIUS [97] (bl) 9-11-9 (5") T Dascombe, *hld up, hdwy 3 out, str run flt to ld last strds.....(11 to 2 op 4 to 1) 1
163³ STAR MOVER [75] 4-10-6 D Leahy, *set poor pace, shaken up 3 out, rdn r-in, ct last strds.*
..............................(11 to 4 tchd 3 to 1 and 5 to 2) 2
186³ DISTANT MEMORY [69] 4-9-7 (7") N Parker, *hld up, hdwy 3 out, rdn 2 out, sn one pace.*
..............................(6 to 4 fav tchd 13 to 8 and 7 to 4) 3
146⁵ PLAY THE BLUES [85] 6-10-13 (3") R Darke, *chsd ldrs till outpcd aftr 3 out, no imprsn after.*
..............................(5 to 1 tchd 4 to 1 and 4 to 1) 4
301 MY HARRY BOY [69] 6-9-7 (7") T Murphy, *hdwy to chase ldrs 3rd, chlgd 5th, rdn 3 out, sn outpcd.*
..............................(16 to 1 op 10 to 1) 5
260 SWIFT ASCENT (USA) [69] 11-9-11 (3") T Thompson, *al beh, lost tch 3 out.........(25 to 1 op 12 to 1 tchd 33 to 1) 6

Dist: Sht-hd, 5l, 5l, 1½l, dist. 4m 35.20s. a 45.20s (6 Ran).
(Martin Pipe Racing Club), M C Pipe

388 **Armitage Shanks Bathrooms Handicap Hurdle (0-115 4-y-o and up) £2,179 2m 1f**
..............................(3:40)

VA UTU [89] 5-10-12 Lorna Vincent, *made all, rdn and styd on wl frm 2 out.*
..............................(15 to 8 fav op 2 to 1 tchd 9 to 4 and 5 to 1) 1
326⁴ FINAL SOUND [79] (bl) 8-10-2 L Harvey, *took str hold, steadied in rear, hdwy appr 2 out, strong chal last, hrd drvn and not quicken............(11 to 4 op 9 to 4) 2
JUST ROSIE [100] 4-11-9 S McNeill, *chsd ldrs, ev ch 2 out, sn outpcd...........(100 to 30 op 5 to 2 tchd 7 to 2) 3
307* COLWAY PRINCE (Ire) [86] 5-10-9 (6ex) G Upton, *hld up, hdwy to chase wnr appr 5th, chlgd 3 out, wknd approaching 2 out, lme.*
..............................(5 to 1 op 4 to 1 tchd 11 to 2) 4
ABU MUSLAB [105] 9-12-0 R Dunwoody, *trkd ldrs till wknd frm 5th.......(12 to 1 op 8 to 1 tchd 14 to 1) 5
RED SOMBRERO [77] 4-10-0 D Bridgwater, *pld hrd, prmnt till wknd 5th......................(50 to 1 op 20 to 1) 6
Dist: 1½l, 10l, 6l, 6l, 15l. 4m 0.70s. a 10.70s (6 Ran).
(M Quinn), M R Channon

389 **H.E.A.T. Novices' Chase (5-y-o and up) £2,346 3¼m 110yds............... (4:10)**

OCEAN LINK 9-11-2 S Earle, *made all, hrd drvn frm 2 out, hld on gmely r-in..................(7 to 2 tchd 9 to 2) 1
218² OLD BRIG (bl) 7-11-2 R Dunwoody, *chsd wnr frm 7th, hrd drvn from 3 out, not much room 2 out, rallied r-in, no extr...(6 to 5 fav op 5 to 4 tchd 6 to 4 and 11 to 10) 2
262³ KASHAN (Ire) 5-10-7 (5") R Farrant, *chsd wnr to 7th, lost pos 16th, styd on ag'n frm 3 out.*
..............................(8 to 1 op 6 to 1 tchd 9 to 1) 3
263³ WEST LODGE LADY 8-10-4 (7") J Neaves, *al beh, lost tch 15th......................(66 to 1 op 33 to 1) 4
311 STRONG MEDICINE 6-11-7 N Williamson, *jmpd slwly 1st and second, tld off whn refused 3rd.*
..............................(2 to 1 op 5 to 4 tchd 9 to 4) ref
Dist: 1l, 4l, 25l. 6m 45.50s. a 25.50s (5 Ran).
(N H S New), R H Alner

390 **Exe Novices' Hurdle (4-y-o and up) £1,768 2¾m..........................(4:40)**

264² KNIGHTLY ARGUS 6-11-0 J Osborne, *led, sn clr, steadied 7th, quickened ag'n appr 2 out, easily.*
..............................(3 to 1 op 9 to 4) 1
CALGARY REDEYE 6-11-0 J R Kavanagh, *hdwy 6th, chsd wnr 7th, rdn appr 2 out, wknd approaching last, lme.*
..............................(2 to 1 fav op 11 to 8 tchd 7 to 4 and 5 to 2) 2
301⁴ SOUL TRADER 4-10-7 S Burrough, *hdwy 4th, chsd wnr 5th to 7th, sn rdn, no imprsn.*
..............................(100 to 30 op 3 to 1 tchd 11 to 4) 3
227⁵ CLASSICAL STAR 4-10-12 N Williamson, *hld up, effrt 7th, sn wknd.................(5 to 2 tchd 3 to 1) 4
298 JET (bl) 7-11-0 S McNeill, *chsd wnr to 5th, wknd quickly, pld up bef 7th.............(50 to 1 op 33 to 1) pu
AN BUCHAILL LIATH (Ire) 4-10-9 (3") R Greene, *prmnt, hit 3rd, wknd 4th, tld off whn pld up bef 7th.*
..............................(50 to 1 op 25 to 1) pu
Dist: 12l, ½l, 12l. 5m 11.90s. a 12.90s (6 Ran).
(South Wales Argus Limited), S E Sherwood

GOWRAN PARK (IRE) (good)
Thursday September 2nd

391 **Mount Juliet Beginners 3-Y-O Hurdle (3-y-o) £3,105 2m....................(3:00)**

290* ASSERT STAR 11-1 C F Swan, ...(6 to 4) 1
253* MICKS DELIGHT (Ire) 11-1 P Carberry, ...(11 to 10 fav) 2
NORDIC THORN (Ire) 10-11 J F Titley, ...(10 to 1) 3
253⁶ ANY MINUTE NOW (Ire) 10-11 C O'Dwyer, ...(25 to 1) 4
290 JAZZY REFRAIN (Ire) 9-13 (7") C O'Brien, ...(50 to 1) 5
290⁴ CARRICK PIKE (USA) 10-11 K F O'Brien, ...(10 to 1) 6
253 RUEPPELLII (Ire) 10-4 (7") Mr T J Barry, ...(33 to 1) 7
253⁹ TRILLICK (Ire) 9-13 (7") Mr F McGirr, ...(16 to 1) 8
NURSE MAID (Ire) 10-6 J Jones, ...(8 to 1) 9
Dist: 2½l, 15l, 13l, 20l. 3m 55.50s. (9 Ran).
(Ms M Hogan), A P O'Brien

392 **Mount Juliet Handicap Hurdle (4-y-o and up) £3,105 2m....................(3:30)**

113 OH SO GRUMPY [-] 5-10-7 (5") T J Mitchell, ...(10 to 1) 1
232³ MILLENIUM LASS (Ire) [-] 5-9-8 (7") F Byrne, ...(12 to 1) 2
275³ GAYOR BRIGHT (Ire) [-] 5-9-0 C F Swan, ...(5 to 1) 3
WILL PHONE [-] 7-11-7 J F Titley, ...(9 to 2 jt-fav) 4
234* ANOTHER COURSE (Ire) [-] 5-10-2 P McWilliams, ..(10 to 1) 5
294⁵ TOUREEN GIRL [-] 6-10-7 (7") M P Kelly, ...(9 to 2 jt-fav) 6
161⁴ PERKNAPP [-] 6-11-2 T Horgan, ...(10 to 1) 7
341⁵ DARCARI ROSE (Ire) [-] 4-9-0 (7") T Martin, ...(50 to 1) 8

46

363* THE LADY'S KNIGHT [-] 7-11-6 (7") C O'Brien, ... (7 to 1) 9
232⁶ MABES TOWN (Ire) [-] 5-9-13 N Byrne, ... (25 to 1) 10
362² HIS WAY (Ire) [-] 4-11-4 M Flynn, ... (5 to 1) 11
265⁴ UPPINGHAM [-] 7-10-13 C O'Dwyer, ... (14 to 1) 12
362 DELIFFIN [-] 7-9-7 (7") J K McCarthy, ... (50 to 1) 13
Dist: 3l, 2l, 1½l, 5l. 3m 51.60s. (13 Ran).

(Mrs E Queally), Mrs John Harrington

393 Kilkenny INH Flat Race (4-y-o and up) £2,760 2m......................... (6:30)

277⁷ PEPPERONI EXPRESS (Ire) 4-11-2 (7") Mr G A Kingston,
.... (14 to 1) 1
277⁴ SUNSET RUN 7-11-9 (5") Mr J P Berry, ... (5 to 1) 2
BALLYBRAZIL BOY (Ire) 4-11-2 (7") Mr M Brennan, (10 to 1) 3
266⁶ SLEMISH MINSTREL 7-11-7 (7") Mr I Johnston, ... (10 to 1) 4
172⁵ OAT BRAN 7-11-7 (7") Mr K Whelan, ... (8 to 1) 5
277⁸ WEDDING DREAM (Ire) 4-11-4 (5") Mr D Valentine, (25 to 1) 6
SLANEY GENT (Ire) 4-11-2 (7") Miss L E A Doyle, .. (14 to 1) 7
PADDY'S RAMBO (Ire) 4-11-2 (7") Mr J M O'Brien, (33 to 1) 8
277 DERRING DREAM (bl) 6-11-7 (7") Mr B Moran, ... (33 to 1) 9
266⁵ HAZY SPELL (Ire) 4-11-4 Mr P Fenton, ... (7 to 1) 10
MALTESE CROSS (Ire) 4-11-2 (7") Mr T J Nagle Jnr, (25 to 1) 11
THANKS ALCOT (Ire) 4-11-9 Mr A P O'Brien, ... (6 to 4 fav) su
POLLYKENDU (Ire) 5-11-7 (7") Mr P M Cloke, ... (14 to 1) su
266⁴ TIM'S RUN 6-11-7 (7") Mr W Ewing, ... (33 to 1) pu
TAITS CLOCK (Ire) 4-11-4 (5") Mr G J Harford, ... (10 to 1) pu
Dist: 13l, 3½l, nk, 2l. 3m 56.10s. (15 Ran).

(Mrs E Queally), Mrs John Harrington

SEDGEFIELD (firm)
Friday September 3rd
Going Correction: NIL

394 Britvic Soft Drinks Conditional Jockeys' Selling Hurdle (3-y-o and up) £1,749 2m 1f 110yds........................... (2:30)

STAGS FELL 8-11-3 (3") N Stocks, led second, clr betw last
2, styd on wl...................... (9 to 2 op 5 to 1) 1
SHARP SENSATION 3-10-5 S Lyons, in tch, chasing ldrs
whn slpd aftr 3 out, no imprsn aftr......... (2 to 1 jt-
fav op 5 to 4) 2
226³ NEARCTIC BAY (USA) 7-11-6 M Hourigan, led till aftr 1st,
chsd ldrs, one pace 3 out..................... (2 to 1 jt-
fav op 5 to 2 tchd 11 to 4) 3
BELFORT PRINCE 6-11-6 P Williams, in tch till wknd aftr
5th, tld off........................ (14 to 1 op 12 to 1) 4
316⁸ BALLY FLAME 7-11-6 A Thornton, mstks, led aftr 1st till
second, chsd wnr till wknd quickly, blun and uns rdr 3
out..................... (50 to 1 op 20 to 1) ur
334² SHAYNA MAIDEL 4-11-0 D J Moffatt, slpd up bend appr
second............... (11 to 2 op 5 to 1 tchd 6 to 1) su
IMPERIAL FLAME 7-11-1 R Davis, blun 1st, sn beh, tld off
whn pld up aftr 4th........ (50 to 1 op 33 to 1) pu
Dist: 10l, 4l, dist. 4m 3.60s. a 8.60s (7 Ran).
SR: 6/-/-/-/ (Richard Johnson), G M Moore

395 Bulmers Cider Novices' Hurdle (4-y-o and up) £1,764 2m 5f 110yds........... (3:00)

FREE TRANSFER (Ire) 4-10-12 J Callaghan, cl up, jnd ldr
aftr 3 out, led betw last 2, styd on und pres.
.... (13 to 8 op 5 to 4 tchd 7 to 4) 1
284³ TROOPER THORN 9-11-0 A Maguire, led 3rd, hdd betw
last 2, kpt on wl und pres........ (3 to 1 tchd 11 to 4) 2
273² LUKS AKURA (bl) 5-11-0 R Dunwoody, not fluent, made
most till 3rd, outpcd and rdn aftr 2 out, kpt on towards
finish.................. (5 to 4 fav op 11 to 10 tchd 6 to 4) 3
Dist: 1½l, 1½l. 5m 1.10s. a 10.10s (3 Ran).

(A Graham), G M Moore

396 Guinness Novices' Chase (5-y-o and up) £2,238 2m 5f........................ (3:35)

DROMINA STAR 12-10-9 (5") P Williams, slwly into strd,
led second till aftr 11th, rdn betw last 2, hdd betw
towards finish..................... (12 to 1 op 7 to 1) 1
139³ NISHKINA 5-10-11 L Wyer, slight ld to second, trkd wnr,
reminder aftr 11th, sn tld, rdn betw last 2, hdd and no
extr towards finish.
.... (6 to 4 on op 13 to 8 on tchd 11 to 8 on) 2
319² SECOND ATTEMPT 9-11-0 B Storey, dsptd ld to second,
lost tch and reminder aftr 7th, tld off 11th.
.... (6 to 4 op 7 to 4) 3
Dist: ½l, 30l. 5m 16.70s. a 12.70s (3 Ran).

(Mrs S C Bradburne), Mrs S C Bradburne

397 Castle Eden Ale Chilton Club Handicap Chase (0-125 5-y-o and up) £2,928 2m 5f
.... (4:05)

RED UNDER THE BED [97] 6-10-12 (7") J Burke, made all,
clr 3 out, cmftbly.................... (3 to 1 op 7 to 2) 1

345³ BARTONDALE [85] 8-10-2 (5") R Farrant, in tch, reminder
hfwy, chsd wnr frm 11th, rdn betw last 2, styd on, no
imprsn........................ (100 to 30 op 9 to 4) 2
271* CHARMING GALE [104] 6-11-7 (5") P Williams, cl up, slpd
bends appr 7th and tenth, blun 11th, sn lost tch, no
dngr aftr.................... (6 to 4 on op 7 to 4 on) 3
Dist: 4l, 12l. 5m 14.80s. a 10.80s (3 Ran).

(M Stanners), Mrs S A Bramall

398 Whitbread Best Scotch Handicap Hurdle (0-125 4-y-o and up) £2,538 2m 5f 110yds
.... (4:35)

MR REINER (Ire) [99] 5-11-3 (7") D Ryan, made all, slpd
bends aftr 3 out and appr nxt, rdn betw last 2, styd on
wl........................ (11 to 8 op Evens tchd 6 to 4) 1
NOTABLE EXCEPTION [90] 4-11-7 R Niven, trkd wnr, mstk
and stumbled 3 out, sn pushed alng, rdn betw last 2, ch
last, no extr...................... (13 to 8 on op 11 to 8 on) 2
Won by 1½l. 5m 8.50s. a 17.50s (2 Ran).
SR: -/-/ (John Wade), J Wade

399 Whitbread Trophy Special Novices' Hurdle (4-y-o and up) £1,844 2m 1f 110yds.. (5:10)

FATHER DAN (Ire) 4-10-12 A Maguire, prmnt, led appr 2
out, styd on und pres frm last.
.... (9 to 2 op 5 to 2 tchd 3 to 1) 1
268² LADY DONOGHUE (USA) 4-10-7 P Niven, sn chasing ldr,
led 3 out, slight hmp and hdd appr nxt, ev ch approaching last, no extr und pres......... (11 to 8 fav op 2 to 1) 2
PERSIAN LION 4-10-12 K Johnson, hld up in tch, styd on
2 out, nvr nr to chal................. (25 to 1 op 16 to 1) 3
268⁸ COMMON COUNCIL (v) 4-10-12 C Grant, led till wknd 3
out...................... (10 to 1 op 8 to 1 tchd 11 to 1) 4
CRESELLY 6-10-9 B Storey, hld up in tch, jnd ldrs aftr
5th, lost pl after nxt, no dngr after...(7 to 1 op 7 to 2) 5
POCKETPICKER (Ire) 5-11-0 A Merrigan, sn lost tch, wl tld
off hfwy.................... (100 to 1 op 50 to 1) 6
268³ TRUBEN (USA) 4-10-7 G McCourt, chsd ldrs, blun 1st,
tried to refuse and uns rdr appr 4th. (7 to 2 op 3 to 1) ur
JOVIAL KATE (USA) 6-10-9 A Orkney, jmpd slwly, sn tld
off, pld up bef 4th....(12 to 1 op 20 to 1 tchd 33 to 1) pu
Dist: 1½l, 6l, 7l, 7l, dist. 4m 3.60s. a 8.60s (8 Ran).

(Roldvale Limited), Miss Gay Kelleway

FAIRYHOUSE (IRE) (good to firm)
Saturday September 4th

400 Rathbeggan INH Flat Race (4-y-o and up) £3,105 2¼m........................ (5:00)

256⁴ SWEET THUNDER 7-11-6 (7") Mr R Brabazon, ... (14 to 1) 1
179³ BAVARD DIEU (Ire) 5-11-13 (5") Mr G J Harford, ... (7 to 1) 2
109⁷ TEMPLERAINEY (Ire) 5-11-13 (5"), ... (10 to 9 on) 3
114 PENNYBRIDGE (Ire) 4-11-6 Mr P F Graffin, ... (7 to 1) 4
343⁴ DECEMBER BRIDE (Ire) 5-11-3 (7") Mr E Meage, (33 to 1) 5
LANDENSTOWN (Ire) 5-11-4 (7") Mr A Weld, ... (16 to 1) 6
233⁶ SONIC EXPERIENCE (Ire) 5-11-3 (5") Mr R Neylon, (25 to 1) 7
FURRY TIPP 7-11-4 (7") Mr J K Connolly, ... (12 to 1) 8
233⁹ HIGHCLIFF HOTEL (Ire) 5-10-13 (7") Mr M O'Connor,
.... (16 to 1) 9
Dist: ¾l, nk, 4l, 15l. 4m 19.00s. (9 Ran).

(R Brabazon), W M Roper

STRATFORD (good to firm)
Saturday September 4th
Going Correction: MINUS 0.20 sec. per fur.

401 Black Prince Conditional Jockeys' Selling Handicap Hurdle (4-y-o and up) £1,772 2 ¾m 110yds........................ (2:20)

SPARKLER GEBE [91] (bl) 7-11-4 D O'Sullivan, made all,
drw clr frm 2 out............ (2 to 1 jt-fav tchd 13 to 8) 1
BRIGTINA [73] 5-10-0 R Farrant, settled in rear, hdwy 3
out, hrd rdn to go second r-in.
.... (11 to 2 op 9 to 2 tchd 6 to 1) 2
287⁷ STROKED AGAIN [73] 8-10-0 A Thornton, prmnt, one pace
frm 3 out.......................... (16 to 1 op 8 to 1) 3
ROCHE [73] 7-10-0 R Davis, hld up in rear, gd hdwy 3
out, lft second nxt, hrd rdn and one pace r-in.
.... (50 to 1 op 33 to 1) 4
307⁵ PERSIAN VALLEY [75] (bl) 8-9-9 (7") M Doyle, in tch, chsd
wnr 5th till wknd 4 out, hdd nxt, tld off.
.... (9 to 1 op 6 to 1 tchd 11 to 1) 5
FILM LIGHTING GIRL [73] 7-9-7 (7") J James, chsd ldrs,
mstk and lost pl 4th, rallied 3 out, staying on one pace
whn sddl slpd and uns rdr appr last. (25 to 1 op 14 to 1) ur
205³ BEN ZABEEDY [101] 8-11-7 (7") S Ryan, hld up in tch,
hdwy to go second 3 out, blun and uns rdr nxt.
.... (2 to 1 jt-fav tchd 3 to 1) ur

MANDALAY PRINCE [82] 9-10-9 W Marston, *trkd wnr to 5th, sn beh, blun 7th, pld up bef nxt.*
....(14 to 1 op 10 to 1) pu
Dist: 15l, ½l, hd, dist. 5m 24.00s. a 12.00s (8 Ran).
(Sparkler Filters (Great Britain) Ltd), R J O'Sullivan

402 BBC CWR Novices' Hurdle (4-y-o and up) £1,996 2m 110yds................. (2:50)

TOP SPIN 4-11-0 S Smith Eccles, *trkd ldrs, al gng wl, led 3 out, drvn clr, eased r-in*........(11 to 8 on op 5 to 4) 1
NORTHERN TRIAL (USA) 5-11-2 R Supple, *hld up in rear, hdwy 3 out, styd on to go second appr last.*
....(10 to 1 op 8 to 1) 2
ASTERIX 5-11-2 L Harvey, *hld up in rear, hdwy frm 4th, styd on, no ch wth 1st 2*.........(20 to 1 op 10 to 1) 3
323² WINGED WHISPER (USA) 4-10-9 (5*) T Eley, *led, mstk 3rd, hdd 3 out, wkng whn mistake last.* (10 to 1 op 8 to 1) 4
SIR PAGEANT 4-11-0 D Bridgwater, *chsd ldrs, outpcd 3 out, sn btn*........................(20 to 1 op 10 to 1) 5
VALIANT WORDS (bl) 6-11-2 G McCourt, *hld up in tch, hdwy 4th, rdn appr 3 out, sn btn...* (12 to 1 op 6 to 1) 6
207⁵ ROCKY ROMANCE 6-11-2 D Morris, *hld up, hdwy 4th, wknd quickly 3 out*.............(100 to 1 op 50 to 1) 7
PALM SWIFT 7-10-11 B Powell, *slwly away, al in rear.*
....(33 to 1 op 20 to 1 tchd 50 to 1) 8
SEA PRODIGY 4-11-0 D Gallagher, *mstk 1st, al beh, tld off frm 3 out*...................(100 to 1 op 33 to 1) 9
MISS CRESTA 4-10-2 (7*) P McLoughlin, *slwly away, tld off frm 5th, pld up bef last.....* (100 to 1 op 50 to 1) pu
TADORA (Ire) 4-11-0 A Maguire, *hld up, effrt 5th, wknd quickly appr 2 out, pld up bef last.*
....(10 to 1 op 7 to 1 tchd 12 to 1) pu
259⁶ ON THE JAR (Ire) 5-11-2 S Earle, *not jump wl, prmnt till ran wide appr 3 out, sn tld off, pld up bef last.*
....(100 to 1 op 33 to 1) pu
259 CROSULA 5-11-2 G Upton, *al beh, tld off whn pld up bef last.*........................(100 to 1 op 50 to 1) pu
MUSICAL TREND (Ire) 5-11-2 J Osborne, *prmnt till wknd 3 out, eased, pld up bef last.*
....(9 to 2 op 7 to 2 tchd 7 to 1) pu
LIAM OG (Ire) 5-11-2 W McFarland, *al beh, tld off whn pld up bef last.*.................(100 to 1 op 33 to 1) pu
Dist: 5l, 8l, 4l, 3l, 10l, 3l, nk, 20l. 3m 51.70s. a 2.70s (15 Ran).
SR: 26/23/15/9/6/-/   *(J M Long), J R Jenkins*

403 Earl Leofric Handicap Chase (0-125 5-y-o and up) £2,967 2m 1f 110yds....... (3:20)

STAY AWAKE [97] 7-10-7 P Niven, *hld up, slight mstk 5th, wnt second nxt, led 4 out, drw clr, very easily.*
....(11 to 10 fav op Evens tchd 6 to 5) 1
358² STRIDING EDGE [92] 8-10-2 R Dunwoody, *trkd ldr to 6th, outpcd 8th, cld 3 out, sn outpaced ag'n, no ch whn mstk nxt*...............(7 to 1 op 8 to 1 tchd 9 to 1) 2
187* DRUMSTICK [118] 7-12-0 N Williamson, *led, rdn and hdd 4 out, wknd quickly nxt, tld off...* (6 to 5 op 4 to 4 tchd 5 to 4) 3
Dist: 5l, dist. 4m 12.60s. a 8.60s (3 Ran).
(Austin Donnellon), Mrs M Reveley

404 Dick Francis 'Decider' Novices' Chase (5-y-o and up) £2,802 2m 5f 110yds... (3:50)

WHATAGALE 6-10-9 J Osborne, *lft second 3rd, hit 7th, rdn and led appr 2 out, styd on wl r-in.*
....(4 to 1 op 3 to 1 tchd 9 to 2) 1
311* ISLAND FOREST (USA) 7-11-6 G Bradley, *hld up, mstk 9th, led 5 out, hrd rdn and hdd appr 2 out, no extr r-in.*
....(7 to 4 fav tchd 2 to 1 and 9 to 4) 2
325* WINDSOR PARK 5-11-6 R Dunwoody, *hld up, out-pcd frm 5 out.............*(4 to 1 op 7 to 2 tchd 9 to 2) 3
SHUTAFUT 7-11-0 C Llewellyn, *led aftr 1st, hit tenth, hdd 5 out, wkng whn mstk nxt...........*(25 to 1 op 16 to 1) 4
CAIRNEYMOUNT 7-11-0 Peter Hobbs, *blun second, al beh, tld off frm tenth...............*(25 to 1 op 16 to 1) 5
389 STRONG MEDICINE 6-11-6 N Williamson, *led till aftr 1st, second whn refused 3rd.........*(8 to 1 op 6 to 1) ref
Dist: 6l, 20l, 15l, 30l. 5m 16.60s. a 13.60s (6 Ran).
(C Coxen), O Sherwood

405 City Of Coventry Trophy Handicap Chase (0-125 5-y-o and up) £2,932 3m..... (4:20)

288* TOUCHING STAR [93] 8-10-3 (3*) M Hourigan, *led to 6th, led sn aftr 3 out, drvn clr r-in.*
....(3 to 1 fav tchd 6 to 4 and 7 to 4) 1
148⁴ SCOTONI [109] 7-11-5 (3*) D O'Sullivan, *hld up, cld on ldrs tenth, hdwy appr 5 out, hdd nxt, not pace of wnr approaching last..............*(2 to 1 tchd 9 to 4) 2
DOONLOUGHAN [113] 8-11-12 J Frost, *trkd ldr, led 6th till appr 3 out, led nxt, hdd sn aftr 3 out, one pace after.*
....(2 to 1 op 13 to 8) 3
Dist: 5l, 6l. 6m 0.20s. a 13.20s (3 Ran).
(P J Hobbs), P J Hobbs

406 Don Thorne Birthday Juvenile Novices' Hurdle (3-y-o) £2,010 2m 110yds.... (4:50)

MOST EQUAL 10-12 R Dunwoody, *al prmnt, led sn aftr last, drvn out.......................*(14 to 1 op 10 to 1) 1
RECORD LOVER (Ire) (bl) 10-12 J Osborne, *trkd ldr, disputing ld whn nrly refused 6th, drvn to lead appr 2 out, hdd sn aftr last, no extr.* (9 to 2 op 4 to 1 tchd 5 to 1) 2
278³ BONUS POINT 10-12 P Niven, *hld up, hdwy 4th, mstk 3 out, styd on frm nxt.*
....(7 to 2 op 5 to 1 tchd 4 to 1 and 3 to 1) 3
PRESS GALLERY 10-12 T Kent, *prmnt, not fluent 3rd and 4th, hmpd nxt, rallied appr 2 out, wknd aftr.*
....(9 to 4 fav op 7 to 4 tchd 5 to 2) 4
379* LADY GAIL 10-13 (6ex) A Webb, *chsd ldrs, one pace frm 3 out........................*(14 to 1 op 12 to 1) 5
349⁶ NO SHOW (Ire) 10-12 W Humphreys, *mid-div, no hdwy frm 3 out..................*(33 to 1 op 25 to 1) 6
PYRAMIS PRINCE (Ire) 10-12 M A FitzGerald, *mstk second, in tch till wknd appr 3 out......*(6 to 1 op 7 to 1) 7
GUNNER BE GOOD 10-7 N Williamson, *slwly away, nvr on terms...................*(66 to 1 op 50 to 1) 8
188 MAD MYTTON 10-12 S Smith Eccles, *led till hdd appr 2 out, wknd quickly................*(33 to 1 op 20 to 1) 9
BONITA BEE 10-7 A Maguire, *chsd ldrs, wkng quickly whn mstk 2 out....................*(25 to 1 op 14 to 1) 10
GOLDEN TARGET (USA) 10-7 D Bridgwater, *al in rear.*
....(66 to 1 op 50 to 1) 11
379 JAFETICA 10-12 G McCourt, *al beh.* (33 to 1 op 25 to 1) 12
TIME OF GRACE (Ire) 10-12 R Bellamy, *al beh.*
....(50 to 1 op 33 to 1) 13
NIKITRIA 10-7 S McNeill, *early mstks, beh frm 4th, tld off.*
....(33 to 1 op 14 to 1) 14
LADY MAGADI 10-7 D Byrne, *al beh, tld off frm 4th.*
....(66 to 1) 15
Dist: 4l, 10l, 1½l, 10l, 1l, sht-hd, 3l, 1½l, ¾l, hd. 3m 56.20s. a 7.20s (15 Ran).
(Heeru Kirpalani), M C Pipe

407 Garrick Jubilee Challenge Cup Handicap Hurdle (0-125 4-y-o and up) £1,870 2m 110yds......................... (5:20)

240³ CLEVELAND LADY [91] 6-10-11 R Dunwoody, *hld up in tch, trkd ldr frm 5th, rdn to ld last, drvn clr.*
....(7 to 4 fav op 5 to 2) 1
NIKITAS [117] 8-11-13 S McNeill, *chsd ldrs, outpcd 3 out, rallied r-in to go second on line.*
....(100 to 30 op 9 to 4 tchd 7 to 2) 2
326 MADRAS (USA) [106] 7-10-11 (5*) R Davis, *led 1st, clr 3 out, hdd last, wknd r-in.....*(8 to 1 op 6 to 1 tchd 9 to 1) 3
370² KING'S SHILLING (USA) [118] 6-12-0 Jacqui Oliver, *hld up, mstk 3rd, hdwy to go third 3 out, rallied nxt, kpt on one pace r-in..................*(12 to 1 op 10 to 1) 4
MIDDAY SHOW (USA) [90] 6-10-0 A Maguire, *al beh, lost tch 3 out, tld off.............*(12 to 1 op 10 to 1) 5
279⁴ DARK DEEP DAWN [90] 6-9-7 (7*) J James, *al beh, effrt 3 out, wknd quickly aftr nxt, tld off.* (33 to 1 op 20 to 1) 6
MOMSER [110] 7-11-6 J Ryan, *led to 1st, wknd appr 5th, pld up bef nxt............*(13 to 2 op 6 to 1 tchd 7 to 1) pu
Dist: 8l, nk, hd, 30l, 3l. 3m 52.10s. a 3.10s (7 Ran).
SR: 9/27/15/27/   *(Mrs Philomena Reich), W G M Turner*

DIEPPE (FR) (good to firm)
Monday September 6th

408 Prix Alain du Breil (Hurdle) (4-y-o) £11,947 2m 1f.............................. (3:15)

323* ICE STRIKE (USA) 9-10 J Osborne, *al prmnt, led appr strt, cmftbly.......................* 1
MARIE POMME (Fr) 9-13 R Chotard, ... 2
267² IKITHAI (Fr) 9-11² C Gombeau, ... 3
Dist: ½l, 8l, 4l, nk, 1½l, 1l. (Time not taken) (15 Ran).
(C R Nelson), J W Hills

GALWAY (IRE) (good to firm)
Monday September 6th

409 Kenny Development Group Maiden Hurdle (4-y-o and up) £3,452 2m........... (4:00)

304* SKEOUGH (Ire) 5-11-7 (7*) K P Gaule, ...(4 to 1) 1
NEMURO (USA) 5-12-0 J Shortt, ...(3 to 1) 2
302² REFINED HEIR 5-12-0 P Carberry, ...(7 to 4 fav) 3
28⁶ ZORIA (Ire) 5-11-1 C F Swan, ...(5 to 1) 4
257⁷ JUNGLE STAR (Ire) 5-11-6 N Byrne, ...(50 to 1) 5
LEATH LA EILE (Ire) 4-10-6 (7*) J P Broderick, ...(50 to 1) 6
SLANEY SAUCE (Ire) 5-10-13 (7*) Miss L E A Doyle, (14 to 1) 7
COSHLA EXPRESSO (Ire) 5-11-6 W T Slattery Jnr, (20 to 1) 8
234⁷ CARBON FIVE (Ire) 4-10-13 B Sheridan, ...(8 to 1) 9
302⁹ MISS FLINTSTONE VI (Ire) 5-11-1 J F Titley, ...(25 to 1) 10
365⁵ RUSHEEN BAY (Ire) 4-11-4 T Horgan, ...(25 to 1) 11
Dist: ¾l, 2½l, 25l, 3l. 3m 55.40s. (11 Ran).
(Joseph Crowley), A P O'Brien

410 Connacht Security Group Handicap Hurdle (4-y-o and up) £3,452 3m........... (4:30)

327[6] CUILIN BUI (Ire) [-] 5-10-6 (7*) C O'Brien, ... (8 to 1) 1
376[5] KILIAN MY BOY [-] 10-10-12 J F Titley, ... (7 to 1) 2
291[2] SILVERWEIR [-] 10-10-5 K F O'Brien, ... (5 to 1) 3
329[2] AEGEAN FANFARE (Ire) [-] (bl) 4-10-6 (3*) T J Mitchell,
.... (10 to 1) 4
212* MERRY PEOPLE (Ire) [-] 5-9-10 T Horgan, ... (10 to 1) 5
254 COQ HARDI SMOKEY (Ire) [-] 5-10-3 P Carberry, .. (12 to 1) 6
FISSURE SEAL [-] 7-12-0 C F Swan, ... (13 to 2) 7
229[8] MARY GINA [-] (bl) 8-9-2 (5*) T J O'Sullivan, ... (50 to 1) 8
291* CARES OF TOMORROW [-] 6-10-2 (7*,4ex) Mr D J Kavanagh,
.... (7 to 2 fav) 9
176[2] VINEYARD SPECIAL [-] 7-10-9 B Sheridan, ... (13 to 2) 10
169[9] PEJAWI [-] 6-9-7 F Woods, ... (40 to 1) 11
291 CHARDEN [-] 7-9-0 (7*) J P Broderick, ... (20 to 1) 12
291[9] HIGH-SPEC [-] 7-11-2 J Magee, ... (10 to 1) f
Dist: 1l, 2l, 3l, 13l. 5m 57.10s. (13 Ran).

(Miss E Kiely), David J McGrath

411 Connacht Tribune Novice Chase (4-y-o and up) £3,797 2¾m. .... (5:00)

293[2] BACK DOOR JOHNNY 7-12-0 D H O'Connor, .. (7 to 4 fav) 1
332[7] THUNDERSTRUCK 7-11-7 (7*) C O'Brien, ... (11 to 2) 2
200[7] KALONA 6-12-0 A Powell, ... (14 to 1) 3
293 CHESTNUT JEWEL 5-11-1 (7*) J P Broderick, ... (25 to 1) 4
293 JOHNJOES PRIDE 9-12-0 T Horgan, ... (12 to 1) 5
116 BALLINAVEEN BRIDGE 6-12-0 W T Slattery Jnr, .. (33 to 1) 6
293 MANOR RHYME 6-11-7 (7*) Mr N C Kelleher, ... (33 to 1) 7
177[2] HURRICANE TOMMY 4-11-2 T J Taaffe, ... (7 to 1) 8
291[4] MOBILE MAN 6-12-0 C F Swan, ... (5 to 2) f
377[3] NO WORD 6-12-0 J F Titley, ... (10 to 1) f
200 BIRDIE'S PRINCE 8-12-0 K F O'Brien, ... (14 to 1) pu
45 CROCKALAWN (Ire) 5-11-8 A J O'Brien, ... (50 to 1) pu
Dist: 3½l, 15l, hd, 20l. 5m 32.60s. (12 Ran).

(Mrs S Guerin), M Halford

GALWAY (IRE) (good to firm (races 1,3), good (2))
Tuesday September 7th

412 Great Southern Hotels Galway Chase (4-y-o and up) £3,452 2m 1f. .... (4:00)

327* NATALIES FANCY 7-11-7 J F Titley, ... (6 to 4 fav) 1
133* NORTHERN HIDE 7-11-12 T J Taaffe, ... (7 to 4) 2
377[2] RANDOM PRINCE 9-11-5 C O'Dwyer, ... (5 to 1) 3
251* RUSTIC GENT (Ire) 5-11-2 (5*) C O'Brien, ... (14 to 1) 4
176* FURRY STAR 7-11-12 C F Swan, ... (5 to 1) f
Dist: 12l, dist, 15l. 4m 26.00s. (5 Ran).

(Mrs Eileen Crowe), Patrick G Kelly

413 C.T. Electric E.B.F. Handicap Hurdle (Listed) (4-y-o and up) £4,832 2m. ...... (4:30)

123[2] MUBADIR (USA) [-] 5-11-12 P Carberry, trkd ldr, prog to
dispute ld at 4th, advantage 3 out, quickened 6 ls clr
aftr nxt, eased r-in........................ (Evens fav) 1
362[3] NIMBLE WIND [-] (bl) 7-9-8 A J O'Brien, hld up, prog 5th,
rdn appr 2 out, kpt on one pace, no threat to wnr.
.... (7 to 1) 2
SHANKORAN [-] 6-11-11 (3*) T J Mitchell, mid-div, rdn and
lost pl 3 out, styd on ag'n in strt, no threat to wnr.
.... (8 to 1) 3
313* NASSAU [-] 6-11-2 (7ex) A Maguire, wl plcd, rdn appr 2
out, kpt on one pace.......................... (7 to 2) 4
174* DANCING COURSE (Ire) [-] 5-9-7 F Woods, mid-div, prog to
track ldrs 5th, rdn and no extr appr 2 out, kpt on.
.... (20 to 1) 5
294[6] CAN'T THINK WHAT [-] 6-10-5 (5*) T P Treacy, hld up, prog
appr 5th, rdn 3 out, wknd aftr nxt........... (7 to 1) 6
CARA DEILISH [-] 7-9-5 (5*) C O'Brien, mid-div, prog to
dispute ld 5th, rdn and hdd 3 out, sn wknd... (20 to 1) 7
294[4] CHOISYA (Ire) [-] 5-10-4 C F Swan, led, jnd 5th, rdn and
wknd quickly appr 3 out...................... (7 to 1) 8
Dist: 3½l, hd, ½l, 2½l. 3m 55.90s. (8 Ran).

(Liam Keating), Noel Meade

414 Paddy Murphy Flat Race (5-y-o and up) £3,452 2m. .... (7:00)

DIRECT RUN 6-12-0 Mr E Bolger, ... (6 to 4) 1
255[3] CUCHULLAINS GOLD (Ire) 5-11-7 (7*) Mr D W Cullen,
.... (5 to 4 fav) 2
255[9] DRESSED IN BLACK (Ire) 5-11-7 (7*) Mr B M Cash, (14 to 1) 3
292 KIZZY ROSE 6-11-4 (5*) Mr B F Murphy, ... (4 to 1) 4
TENESA 6-11-2 (7*) Mr A Daly, ... (14 to 1) 5
Dist: 6l, 4l, 15l, dist. 4m 3.80s. (5 Ran).

(Mrs Sara Bolger), E Bolger

EXETER (firm)
Wednesday September 8th
Going Correction: NIL

415 Stella Artois Conditional Jockeys' Novices' Hurdle (4-y-o and up) £1,788 2m 3f
.... (2:10)

EID (USA) 4-11-0 W Marston, made all, set poor pace till
quickened aftr 3rd, came clr frm 2 out, winning easily
whn lft clear last.
.... (5 to 4 op 6 to 4 tchd 7 to 4 and Evens) 1
DUNKERY BEACON 7-11-2 R Davis, chsd ldrs, effrt 5th,
poor 3rd whn lft second at last.
.... (10 to 1 op 8 to 1 tchd 9 to 1 and 6 to 1) 2
301[9] BARE HIGHLANDER 7-10-13 (3*) T Thompson, blun second, beh frm 5th, no ch aftr........ (66 to 1 op 25 to 1) 3
203[5] ELEGANT TOUCH (bl) 4-10-2 (7*) O Burrows, beh and nvr
dngrs frm 4th.................... (14 to 1 tchd 25 to 1) 4
390 AN BUCHAILL LIATH (Ire) 4-11-0 R Greene, sn wl beh, tld
off frm 4th...................... (100 to 1 op 33 to 1) 5
191[2] CLASS ATTRACTION (USA) 4-10-9 D Richmond, with wnr
4th, till wknd quickly frm 2 out, remote second whn
mstk and uns rdr last.
.... (Evens fav op 6 to 4 on tchd 6 to 5) ur
Dist: 25l, 3½l, 12l, dist. 4m 46.20s. a 27.20s (6 Ran).

(Ladyswood Racing Club), Martyn Meade

416 Boddingtons Bitter Novices' Claiming Hurdle (4-y-o and up) £1,822 2m 1f 110yds
.... (2:40)

387[3] DISTANT MEMORY 4-10-8 (7*) N Parker, sn in tch, jmpd
slwly 3rd, chsd ldr 5th, led 2 out, edgd lft appr last,
pushed out....................... (5 to 2 op 6 to 1) 1
163[4] MISTY VIEW 4-10-12 (7*) P McLoughlin, chsd ldrs, drvn
alng aftr 3 out, hrd driven and found no extr appr last.
.... (Evens fav op 5 to 4 op 2 to 1 on) 2
GILBERT (Ire) 5-10-4 (7*) A Flannigan, led clr 4th, hdd 2 out,
rdn and styd on same pace....... (33 to 1 op 20 to 1) 3
260 INTUITIVE JOE 6-10-8 B Powell, chsd ldr to 5th, sn wknd.
.... (8 to 1 op 5 to 1) 4
COPPER BEACH LADY 7-10-6 P Holley, sn beh, hit second,
tld off whn pld up bef 3 out.
.... (13 to 2 op 4 to 1 tchd 7 to 1) pu
Dist: 3l, nk, 20l. 4m 7.90s. a 10.90s (5 Ran).

(Mrs Ann Weston), P J Hobbs

417 Murphys Irish Stout Novices' Chase (5-y-o and up) £2,872 2¾m 110yds. .... (3:15)

189[2] GILSTON LASS 6-10-13 J R Kavanagh, made all, clr tenth,
unchlgd........................... (9 to 4 op 7 to 4) 1
298[3] TITUS ANDRONICUS 6-11-4 C Llewellyn, chsd wnr, jmpd
hesitantly and lft, no imprsn frm 4 out.
.... (15 to 8 tchd 2 to 1) 2
BARGAIN AND SALE 8-11-4 C Maude, chsd ldrs till lost
tch frm 11th...... (11 to 4 op 5 to 2 tchd 100 to 30) 3
299 MARLBOROUGH LADY 7-10-13 S Burrough, al beh, tld off.
.... (16 to 1 op 12 to 1 tchd 20 to 1) 4
310[4] SUNDAY JIM 9-11-4 M Bosley, not fluent, beh whn f 12th.
.... (12 to 1 op 7 to 1 tchd 14 to 1) f
Dist: 30l, 25l, dist. 5m 48.20s. a 27.20s (5 Ran).

(Marlborough Racing Partnership), J S King

418 Trophy Bitter Selling Handicap Hurdle (4-y-o and up) £1,593 2m 1f 110yds. .... (3:45)

353[4] EMERALD MOON [70] 6-11-0 S Burrough, beh, hdwy 5th,
disputing poor second whn clr ldr f last, drvn to ld cl
hme......................... (4 to 1 op 5 to 1 tchd 7 to 2) 1
344* ITS ALL OVER NOW [73] 9-11-3 S McNeill, chsd ldrs till rdn
and lost pl 3 out, rallied to dispute poor second whn clr
ldr f last, one pace.
.... (6 to 5 on op 6 to 4 on tchd 5 to 4) 2
385[2] DARING CLASS [78] 7-11-8 I Shoemark, hdwy 4th, chsd
ldr appr 2 out, poor second whn lft in ld last, sn rdn, ct
cl hme......................... (6 to 1 op 5 to 1 tchd 7 to 1) 3
297[6] FASHION PRINCESS [67] (bl) 7-10-4 (7*) D Matthews, led till
hdd 3 out, sn wknd. (12 to 1 op 10 to 1 tchd 14 to 1) 4
297[4] CORNISH COSSACK (NZ) [78] 6-11-3 J Frost, chsd ldr till
led 3 out, clr frm 2 out till f last, unlucky.
.... (13 to 2 op 4 to 1) f
IMBIBER [60] 7-10-4 Ann Stokell, beh frm 4th, blun 3 out
and pld up........... (40 to 1 op 20 to 1 tchd 50 to 1) pu
HENBURY HALL (Ire) [80] (v) 5-11-10 M A FitzGerald, drpd
rear 4th, sn lost tch, tld off whn pld up bef last.
.... (10 to 1 op 6 to 1) pu
Dist: ½l, nk, 12l. 4m 14.00s. a 17.00s (7 Ran).

(P C N Heywood), W G Turner

419 Heineken Handicap Chase (0-130 5-y-o and up) £3,220 2m 3f. .... (4:15)

308[2] MISTER FEATHERS [92] 12-10-0 J R Kavanagh, made all,
came clr frm 3 out...... (11 to 10 op Evens tchd 6 to 5) 1
GREEN ISLAND (USA) [120] 7-12-0 Peter Hobbs, not fluent
5th or 6th, hdwy to chase wnr 9th, no imprsn frm 3 out.
.... (Evens fav op 5 to 4 on) 2

NATIONAL HUNT RESULTS 1993-94

154⁶ TAFFY JONES [92] 14-10-0 C Maude, *chsd wnr to 9th and mstk, wknd appr 4 out.*
....(14 to 1 op 10 to 1 tchd 16 to 1) 3
Dist: 12l, 25l. 4m 47.70s. a 18.70s (3 Ran).

(Mrs M Forde), J S King

420 Whitbread Best Bitter Handicap Hurdle (0-120 4-y-o and up) £2,505 2m 3f. . . .(4:45)

300* TRUST DEED (USA) [89] (bl) 5-11-10 M A FitzGerald, *pressed ldr, chlgd 3rd, led appr 5th, drvn and ran on wl frm 2 out.*..........................(5 to 4 fav tchd 11 to 10) 1
300⁷ AMPHIGORY [87] 5-11-1 (7*) T Thompson, *rcd in 3rd till hdwy to chase wnr appr 5th, rdn frm 2 out, no imprsn r-in.*..............................(7 to 2 op 3 to 1) 2
358* MADRAJ (Ire) [92] 5-11-13 (5ex) W McFarland, *moved into 3rd 5th, gng wl 3 out, rdn 2 out, sn btn.*
....(2 to 1 op 3 to 1 tchd 9 to 4) 3
ONENINEFIVE [70] 7-10-5 B Powell, *led till hdd and wknd rpdly appr 5th, sn tld off, pld up bef 2 out.*
....(11 to 1 op 10 to 1 tchd 16 to 1) pu
Dist: 1½l, 4l. 4m 34.90s. a 15.90s (4 Ran).

(Fred Camis), Mrs A Knight

GALWAY (IRE) (good to firm)
Wednesday September 8th

421 Northern Telecom North Star Maiden Hurdle (5-y-o and up) £3,450 2m. . . . . . .(2:30)

258⁹ RUFO'S COUP 6-11-6 P Carberry, ...(6 to 1) 1
ESPRIT D'ETOILE (USA) 8-11-11 (3*) J C Barker, ...(3 to 1) 2
120³ THE DASHER DOYLE (Ire) 5-11-6 Mr P J Healy, ...(4 to 1) 3
376³ SUNSHINES TAXI 6-11-6 B Sheridan, ...(2 to 1 fav) 4
330⁶ CLASS ACT (bl) 7-12-0 C F Swan, ...(4 to 1) 5
208⁴ CAT FIGHT 6-10-8 (7*) Mr A Daly, ...(50 to 1) 6
THE ROCKING CHAIR (Ire) 5-11-6 F Woods, ...(25 to 1) 7
Dist: 1½l, 3l, 5l, 1l. 3m 51.80s. (7 Ran).

(M Tunney), Noel Meade

422 N. Telecom Meridian Mail EBF H'cap Chase (Listed - Grade 3) (4-y-o and up) £5,820 2¾m. . . . .(3:30)

364* LIFE OF A LORD [-] (bl) 7-10-8 (5ex) G M O'Neill, *trkd ldr, prog tenth, travelling wl beh lder 2 out, sn led aftr last, eased cl hme.*............................(8 to 1) 1
306³ HARRISTOWN LADY [-] (bl) 6-10-7 A Powell, *hld up, prog appr 2 out, rdn and no extr aftr last, kpt on. (7 to 2 jt-fav) 2
76⁵ BISHOPS HALL [-] 7-12-0 C F Swan, *mid-div, mstk second, prog appr 2 out, kpt on one pace frm last, not trble wnr.*
....(7 to 2 jt-fav) 3
306 FOR WILLIAM [-] 7-11-7 K F O'Brien, *trkd ldr, slight mstk 4 out, rdn aftr nxt, no extr and wknd aftr last.* (10 to 1) 4
364³ BOLD FLYER [-] 10-11-3 F Woods, *led, 8 ls clr 5th, rdn appr 2 out, wknd and hdd aftr last, wknd.*........(7 to 2) 5
303⁷ LA MODE LADY [-] 8-9-9² A J O'Brien, *mid-div, rdn appr 2 out, wknd frm last.*.......................(20 to 1) 6
306⁵ GUESSWORK [-] 7-11-3 P M Verling, *mid-div, prog 6th, rdn 3 out, no extr and wknd aftr last.*.......(10 to 1) 7
306⁷ SKY RANGE [-] 8-10-2 T Horgan, *al rear, lost tch aftr 5 out.*.............................(8 to 1) 8
303³ MAC'S GLEN [-] 9-10-5 W T Slattery Jnr, *mid-div whn bad mstk and 9th.*..........................(8 to 1) f
363³ FINAL TUB [-] 10-11-2 C O'Dwyer, *mid-div whn brght dwn 9th.*.................................(8 to 1) bd
306⁶ FROZEN FRIEND [-] 10-9-2 (5*) T J O'Sullivan, *mid-div, lost pl 9th, sn rdn, tld off and pld up bef 2 out.*....(20 to 1) pu
Dist: 3½l, hd, 6l, 3l. 5m 25.30s. (11 Ran).

(M J Clancy), T Costello

423 Anglo Printers INH Flat Race (4-y-o and up) £3,795 2m. . . . .(5:30)

252² COMMON POLICY (Ire) 4-11-6 (7*) Mr J Connolly, ..(9 to 4) 1
WATERLOO BALL (Ire) 4-10-8 (7*) Mr G R Ryan, (6 to 4 fav) 2
277* GLAD'S NIGHT (Ire) 4-11-3 (5*) Mrs J M Mullins, ..(9 to 2) 3
292⁶ JENNYELLEN (Ire) 4-11-1 Mr A J Martin, ...(8 to 1) 4
233* STONELEIGH TURBO (Ire) 4-11-8 (5*) Mr P M Kelly, (12 to 1) 5
FRUIT TOWN (Ire) 4-11-1 (5*) Mr G J Harford, ...(25 to 1) 6
256* SIMPLISTIC (Ire) (bl) 4-11-8 Mr J P Dempsey, ...(7 to 1) 7
Dist: Nk, 15l, nk, 5l. 3m 41.40s. (7 Ran).

(Patrick O'Leary), Patrick O'Leary

UTTOXETER (good to firm (races 1,2,3), good (4,5,6))
Wednesday September 8th
Going Correction: PLUS 0.15 sec. per fur.

424 Roe Byfield Advertising Handicap Hurdle (0-115 4-y-o and up) £2,778 3m 110yds
....(2:20)

312² STORM DRUM [104] (bl) 4-11-7 N Williamson, *hld up beh, smooth hdwy 4 out, led nxt, rdn appr last, ran on strly.*
....(5 to 2 fav op 2 to 1) 1
222* BRIDGE PLAYER [89] 6-10-3 (3*) D J Moffatt, *hld up, hdwy o'r 4 fs out, ev ch over 2 out, sn rdn and one pace.*
....(11 to 4 op 5 to 2) 2
273³ MASTER BOSTON (Ire) [84] 5-10-11 R Dunwoody, *prmnt, reminders aftr 7th, led briefly 9th, rdn and ev ch 3 out, sn outpcd.*...........................(16 to 1) 3
222² SMILES AHEAD [88] 5-10-2 (3*) N Bentley, *cl up till rdn and one pace appr 3 out.*...............(5 to 1 op 4 to 1) 4
289⁵ ARCTIC OATS [107] 8-11-5 (5*) S Lyons, *led till hdd 8th, wknd appr 3 out, ran on frm last.*
....(15 to 2 op 5 to 1 tchd 8 to 1) 5
PEAK DISTRICT [83] 7-10-0 A Maguire, *prmnt till wknd o'r 3 out.*........................(10 to 1 op 12 to 1 tchd 8 to 1) 6
SUEZ CANAL (Ire) [98] 4-11-1 R Supple, *prmnt, hit 6th, rdn and wknd aftr nxt, sn tld off.*...(12 to 1 op 10 to 1) 7
THE HILL [84] 11-10-1¹ A Carroll, *cl up till drpd rear aftr 7th, pld up bef 4 out.*..............(33 to 1 op 25 to 1) pu
IAMA ZULU [97] 8-11-0 B Clifford, *prmnt till wknd quickly o'r 4 out, pld up bef 2 out.*.......(13 to 2 op 12 to 1) pu
Dist: 5l, 8l, 5l, sht-hd, 25l, dist. 5m 49.00s. a 10.00s (9 Ran).
SR: 30/10/-/-/15/-/

(Mrs Shelley Fergusson), K C Bailey

425 BBC In Midlands Selling Handicap Hurdle (4-y-o and up) £1,801 2½m 110yds. . .(2:50)

217 SNOOKER TABLE [82] 10-10-0 D Gallagher, *al prmnt, rdn to ld whn wnt lft appr last, ran on, fnshd lme.*
....(12 to 1 op 10 to 1) 1
BURN BRIDGE (USA) [88] (v) 7-10-6² Peter Caldwell, *trkd ldrs, led 6th till hdd appr last, one pace.*
....(4 to 1 tchd 7 to 2 and 9 to 2) 2
MASTER DANCER [110] 6-12-0 Miss S A Billot, *in tch till outpcd frm 6th.*.....................(3 to 1 op 9 to 4) 3
312⁸ WAR BEAT [82] (v) 5-10-0 A Maguire, *cl up, ev ch 4 out, sn outpcd.*...........................(8 to 1 op 5 to 1) 4
307² KINLET VISION (Ire) [82] 5-9-12³ (5*) T Jenks, *wtd wth beh ldrs, outpcd frm o'r 4 out.*
....(11 to 4 fav op 3 to 1) 5
369² CISTOLENA [82] (v) 7-10-0 Diane Clay, *sn wl beh, rapid hdwy aftr 4 out, staying on modest 3rd whn f last.*
....(10 to 1 op 8 to 1) f
287⁴ ALAMIR (USA) [84] (bl) 5-10-2² J Railton, *led to 6th, rdn and wknd o'r 4 out, tld off whn pld up bef last.*
....(12 to 1 op 16 to 1 tchd 10 to 1) pu
346 HIGH STREET BLUES [94] 6-10-12¹² A Coogan, *sn beh, mstk 4th, tld off whn pld up bef 6th.*
....(50 to 1 op 33 to 1) pu
Dist: 2l, dist, nk, 8l. 4m 57.30s. a 14.30s (8 Ran).

(Miss Alyson Yeo), A M Forte

426 Greenhill Chemicals Handicap Chase (5-y-o and up) £3,436 2m 5f. . . . .(3:20)

371* HIRAM B BIRDBATH [100] (bl) 7-9-9 (5*) Mrs P Nash, *hld up in last pl, sstnd hdwy frm 4 out, reminders appr last, quickened to ld r-in, cmftbly.*.....(8 to 1 tchd 10 to 1) 1
KUSHBALOO [119] 8-11-5 B Storey, *took keen hold, cl up, led 8th till hdd and no extr r-in.*
....(100 to 30 op 3 to 1 tchd 7 to 2) 2
PERSIAN HOUSE [115] 6-11-1 M Dwyer, *cld on ldrs aftr 8th, pushed alng o'r 4 out, kpt on one pace and pres frm last.*........................(3 to 1 jt-fav op 11 to 4) 3
336* CLEVER FOLLY [109] 13-10-9 (5ex) R Dunwoody, *led to 8th, cl up, pushed alng and ev ch 4 out, styd on one pace.*
....(3 to 1 jt-fav op 5 to 2 tchd 100 to 30) 4
284⁴ MIAMI BEAR [102] 7-10-2² Gary Lyons, *chsd ldrs, pushed alng o'r 5 out, styd on one pace frm 3 out.*
....(14 to 1 op 10 to 1) 5
WIGTOWN BAY [100] 10-10-0 N Williamson, *hld up in tch till wknd 4 out.*................(7 to 1 op 6 to 1) 6
ICARUS (USA) [124] (bl) 7-11-10 Mr A Rebori, *cl up, outpcd frm 4 out, eased whn btn.*
....(15 to 2 op 6 to 1 tchd 8 to 1) 7
Dist: 3l, 2½l, 1l, sht-hd, 15l, ¾l. 5m 8.60s. a 8.60s (7 Ran).
SR: 18/34/27/20/13/-/19/

(Steven Astaire), J A Glover

427 Borough Of East Staffordshire Novices' Chase (5-y-o and up) £2,710 2m 5f. . .(3:50)

319* COUNTERBID (v) 6-11-9 N Williamson, *made all, quickened pace 11th, mstk 3 out, unchlgd, eased r-in.*
....(11 to 10 fav op 6 to 4 on tchd 5 to 4) 1
281³ CAMAN 6-11-3 B Storey, *chsd wnr, rdn aftr 4 out, one pace frm nxt.*...............(4 to 1 op 6 to 1 tchd 10 to 1) 2
TROPNEVAD 11-10-11 M Dwyer, *hld up in last pl, rdn o'r 3 out, one pace.*....................(14 to 1 op 10 to 1) 3
319² HELMAR (NZ) 7-11-0 R Supple, *rcd in 3rd pl, mstk tenth, pushed alng 12th, reminders and one pace aftr 4 out.*
....(7 to 4 tchd 9 to 4) 4
Dist: 15l, nk, 4l. 5m 20.60s. a 20.60s (4 Ran).

(Howard Parker), J A C Edwards

428 Robins Central Conditional Jockeys' Handicap Hurdle (0-125 4-y-o and up)

£1,829 2m . . . . **(4:20)**

316* BATTLE STANDARD (Can) [84] 6-11-6 J Burke, *in cl tch, led 3 out, drvn out.* . . . . (5 to 2) 1
227² MUST BE MAGICAL (USA) [85] 5-11-7 T Eley, *al second, took keen hold, hld up in cl tch, rdn o'r 2 out, kpt on und pres.* . . . . (2 to 1 fav op 9 to 4) 2
280³ HEIR OF INVENTION [88] 8-11-10 A Larnach, *in tch, out-pcd 4 out, kpt on one pace und pres frm last.* . . . . (9 to 2 op 4 to 1) 3
AFRICAN SAFARI [70] 9-9-13 (7*) D Towler, *set steady pace, hdd 3 out, one pace.* . . . . (20 to 1 op 16 to 1) 4
J R JONES [82] 6-11-4 S Wynne, *cl up till wknd o'r 2 out.* . . . . (10 to 1 op 8 to 1) 5
MY LINDIANNE [74] 6-10-10 M Hourigan, *hld up, cld 4 out, disputing second and ev ch whn stumbled and uns rdr aftr second last.* . . . . (5 to 1 op 4 to 1) ur
Dist: 1l, 2½l, 2l, ½l. 3m 58.50s. a 19.50s (6 Ran).

(M Stanners), Mrs S A Bramall

429 Provident Life Novices' Hurdle (4-y-o and up) £1,976 2m . . . . (4:50)

DANCING DOVE (Ire) 5-10-0 (7*) B Harding, *chsd ldrs, smooth hdwy frm o'r 4 out, led appr 2 out, ran on wl.* . . . . (8 to 1) 1
DOCTOR FOSTER (Ire) 5-10-12 Gary Lyons, *chsd ldrs, cld aftr 4 out, ev ch 2 out, one pace appr last.* . . . . (25 to 1 op 20 to 1) 2
402² NORTHERN TRIAL (USA) 5-10-12 R Supple, *hdwy to chase ldrs o'r 4 out, ch 2 out, one pace.* . . . . (9 to 4 fav op 2 to 1 tchd 3 to 1) 3
CIRCUIT COURT (Ire) 5-10-12 S Smith Eccles, *nvr far away, took keen hold, led aftr 4 out till hdd appr 2 out, one pace.* . . . . (8 to 1 op 5 to 1) 4
227⁶ JOTO 6-10-12 G Bradley, *beh, hdwy 4 out, no imprsn frm nxt.* . . . . (10 to 1 op 25 to 1) 5
69⁷ FAUGHAN LODGE 6-10-12 Diane Clay, *beh till styd on frm 2 out, nrst finish.* . . . . (20 to 1 op 16 to 1) 6
DON'T FORSAKE ME 4-10-5 J Osborne, *led till hdd aftr 4 out, sn wknd.* . . . . (4 to 1 op 9 to 2) 7
SHAKE TOWN (USA) 5-10-12 N Williamson, *chsd ldrs, effrt o'r 4 out, sn btn.* . . . . (10 to 1 op 8 to 1) 8
MURASIL (USA) 4-10-10 A Orkney, *chsd ldrs till wknd o'r 4 out.* . . . . (25 to 1 op 20 to 1) 9
346 MAPLE BAY (Ire) 4-10-10 G McCourt, *beh, shrtlvd effrt o'r 4 out.* . . . . (10 to 1 op 12 to 1 tchd 9 to 1) 10
GRAND RAPIDS (USA) 6-10-12 H Davies, *wth ldr till wknd o'r 4 out.* . . . . (20 to 1 op 14 to 1) 11
268⁷ MIDDLEHAM CASTLE 4-10-10 R Dunwoody, *chsd ldrs till wknd o'r 2 out.* . . . . (6 to 1 op 7 to 1 tchd 5 to 1) 12
346⁴ JUVENARA 7-10-7 (5*) T Eley, *al beh, tld off whn pld up bef 2 out.* . . . . (10 to 1 op 6 to 1) pu
388⁶ RED SOMBRERO 4-10-10 D Bridgwater, *al beh, tld off whn pld up bef 3 out.* . . . . (25 to 1 op 20 to 1) pu
191⁷ KIMS SELECTION (Ire) 4-10-10 R Garritty, *chsd ldrs to 5th, sn beh, tld off whn pld up bef 3 out.* . . . . (40 to 1 op 33 to 1) pu
Dist: 3½l, ½l, 5l, 10l, 1½l, 15l, 3½l, 8l, 4l, 3½l. 3m 51.70s. a 12.70s (15 Ran).

(Dr Kenneth S Fraser), G Richards

CLONMEL (IRE) (good)
Thursday September 9th

430 Giants Grave Novice Chase (4-y-o and up) £2,243 2½m . . . . (5:30)

410 VINEYARD SPECIAL 7-12-0 N Williamson, ... (4 to 1) 1
392⁷ PERKNAPP 6-12-0 C F Swan, ... (5 to 1) 2
411⁵ JOHNJOES PRIDE (bl) 9-12-0 T Horgan, ... (12 to 1) 3
116⁶ SCREEN PRINTER (Ire) (bl) 4-10-1 K F O'Brien, . . . (16 to 1) 4
377 FAIRY PARK 8-11-9 F Woods, ... (6 to 1) 5
293⁶ DOONEGA (Ire) 5-11-8 M Dwyer, ... (3 to 1 fav) 6
COUMEENOOLE LADY 6-11-2 (7*) J M Donnelly, (10 to 1) 7
330⁹ FERRIC FORTRESS 7-11-4 A J O'Brien, ... (20 to 1) 8
MISCHIEF MOON 8-11-9 D H O'Connor, ... (25 to 1) 9
BROTHER HUGH 8-12-3 (7*) P A Roche, ... (33 to 1) 10
293 GLOBE HABIT 7-11-4 (5*) T J O'Sullivan, ... (33 to 1) 11
77⁶ SON OF SARAH (bl) 9-12-0 Mr D M O'Brien, ... (16 to 1) 12
377⁴ BALLYHEIGUE 7-11-7 (7*) Mr J T McNamara, ... (7 to 1) f
251⁵ CLASSIC CHEER (Ire) (bl) 5-10-11 (3*) J Jones, . . . (14 to 1) pu
327⁹ SQUIRRELLSDAUGHTER 6-10-11 (7*) Mr N D Fehily, ... (33 to 1) pu
Dist: 3½l, 15l, 15l, nk. 5m 7.80s. (15 Ran).

(D N Carey), W J Burke

431 Bank Of Ireland Clonmel Maiden Hurdle (4-y-o) £2,243 2m . . . . (6:00)

NISHIKI (USA) 10-11 N Williamson, ... (12 to 1) 1
292⁹ VON CARTY (Ire) 11-2 K F O'Brien, ... (7 to 4 fav) 2
231⁷ PORT RISING (Ire) 11-2 T J Taaffe, ... (10 to 3) 3
234 VALS CHOICE (Ire) 10-6 (5*) A J Roche, ... (7 to 1) 4
314⁵ TRIPLE ACE (Ire) 11-2 C F Swan, ... (8 to 1) 5
NINE O THREE (Ire) 11-2 Mr W P Mullins, ... (8 to 1) 6
314⁶ NOT MY LINE (Ire) 11-2 G Bradley, ... (14 to 1) 7

SHUILNAMON (Ire) 10-11 B Sheridan, ... (12 to 1) 8
FINISK DANCER (Ire) 11-2 M Dwyer, ... (12 to 1) 9
BROWNFARTH KING (Ire) 11-2 M Flynn, ... (10 to 1) 10
OUT THE DOOR (Ire) 11-2 P Malone, ... (14 to 1) 11
BONE IDOL (Ire) 10-11 (5*) D P Murphy, ... (14 to 1) 12
102 GIVEN BEST (Ire) 11-2 S Smith Eccles, ... (10 to 1) pu
Dist: 2½l, sht-hd, 3½l, 3½l. 4m 0.60s. (13 Ran).

(Winners Circle Racing Club), Augustine Leahy

432 Bank Of Ireland Rathronan November Handicap Hurdle (4-y-o and up) £2,243 2m . . . . (6:30)

313³ COMBINE CALL [-] 6-11-0 G Bradley, ... (6 to 4 fav) 1
295² HURRICANE EDEN [-] 6-10-4 K F O'Brien, ... (6 to 1) 2
313⁷ BROOK COTTAGE (Ire) [-] 5-10-2 S Smith Eccles, (11 to 2) 3
POOR TIMES (Ire) [-] 5-10-2 B Sheridan, ... (25 to 1) 4
392 HIS WAY (Ire) [-] 4-11-6 M Dwyer, ... (5 to 1) 5
327 NO TAKERS [-] (bl) 6-9-10 C F Swan, ... (14 to 1) 6
392⁸ ANOTHER COURSE (Ire) [-] 5-10-9 P McWilliams, . . (5 to 1) 7
Dist: 4l, 3½l, hd, 10l. 3m 55.00s. (7 Ran).

(Rory F Larkin), P Mullins

433 Mylerstown Flat Race (5-y-o and up) £2,243 2m . . . . (7:00)

162⁶ BEGLAWELLA 6-11-2 (7*) Mr P English, ... (10 to 1) 1
305³ THE TENANT 6-11-11 (3*) Miss M Olivefalk, . . . (11 to 8 fav) 2
302⁶ EASE THE BURDEN (Ire) 5-11-2 (7*) Mr G P FitzGerald, ... (12 to 1) 3
304³ BRAVE HENRY 5-11-7 (7*) Mr J T McNamara, ... (10 to 1) 4
393 POLLYKENDU (Ire) 5-11-11 (3*) Mr D Marnane, . . . (20 to 1) 5
258 MOON-FROG 6-11-7 (7*) Miss L E A Gunne, ... (50 to 1) 6
257⁴ PRYS PAUPER (Ire) 5-11-9 (5*) Mr H F Cleary, ... (10 to 1) 7
393² SUNSET RUN 7-11-9 (5*) Mr J P Berry, ... (11 to 2) 8
MISS KAREN 6-11-2 (7*) Mr D Kavanagh, ... (16 to 1) 9
393⁴ SLEMISH MINSTREL 7-11-7 (7*) Mr I Johnston, . . (10 to 1) 10
274 BE CREATIVE (Ire) 6-11-7 (7*) Mr A K Wyse, . . . (20 to 1) 11
RATHNURE LADY (Ire) 5-11-9 Mr S R Murphy, . . . (14 to 1) 12
159 COSTLY BUST 6-12-0 Mr P Fenton, ... (25 to 1) 13
393⁹ DERRING DREAM 6-11-7 (7*) Mr B Moran, ... (50 to 1) 14
Dist: 8l, 5l, sht-hd, 1½l. 3m 49.20s. (14 Ran).

(Thomas Keane), Thomas Foley

NEWTON ABBOT (good to soft)
Thursday September 9th
Going Correction: PLUS 0.50 sec. per fur.

434 Stowells Of Chelsea Novices' Hurdle (4-y-o and up) £1,838 2m 1f . . . . (2:20)

301² ATHAR (Ire) 4-11-7 L Harvey, *took str hold, improved to track ldrs 4th, chlgd 2 out, sn led, ran on wl.* . . . . (7 to 2 op 5 to 2) 1
355* LITTLE NOD 4-10-12 (7*) P McLoughlin, *gd hdwy 5th, led aftr 3 out, hdd aftr 2 out, sn one pace.* . . . . (15 to 8 fav op 5 to 2 tchd 7 to 4) 2
SINGERS IMAGE 4-10-12 J Railton, *beh 4th, hdwy frm 5th, styd on same pace frm 2 out.* . . . . (11 to 2 op 3 to 1 tchd 5 to 2) 3
NOEL (Ire) 4-10-12 M A FitzGerald, *chsd ldr, led 3rd, hdd nxt, led ag'n 3 out, headed appr 2 out, sn outpcd.* . . . . (11 to 2 op 4 to 1 tchd 8 to 1) 4
DEVONIAN (USA) 4-10-5 (7*) S Curran, *jmpd slwly 1st, chsd ldrs till wknd appr 3 out.* . . . . (50 to 1 op 16 to 1) 5
STAND AT EASE 8-11-0 B Powell, *led to 4th, led ag'n 5th, hdd and wknd quickly 3 out.* . . . . (11 to 1 op 16 to 1 tchd 25 to 1) 6
TRECOMETTI 5-10-4 (5*) R Davis, *beh, smooth hdwy 3 out, hdd whn mstk 2 out.* . . . . (33 to 1 op 20 to 1) 7
BEAM ME UP SCOTTY (Ire) 4-10-12 N Hawke, *beh frm 5th, tld off whn pld up bef 2 out.* . . . (14 to 1 op 17 to 8 on) pu
ALFREE 5-11-0 S McNeill, *al beh, tld off whn pld up bef 2 out.* . . . . (50 to 1 op 20 to 1) pu
Dist: 6l, 10l, 1½l, 8l, 5l, 12l. 4m 11.60s. a 21.60s (9 Ran).

(J W Buxton), R J Baker

435 Diet Pepsi Selling Hurdle (4-y-o and up) £1,838 2m 1f . . . . (2:50)

384² RULING DYNASTY (bl) 9-11-9 H Davies, *in tch, lost pos aftr 4th, gd hdwy 3 out, chlgd for ld appr 2 out till forged ahead r-in.* . . . . (5 to 4 on op Evens) 1
HEAD TURNER 5-11-4 P Holley, *pld hrd in rear, hdwy 3 out, ran on to dispute ld appr 2 out till outpcd r-in.* . . . . (15 to 2 op 5 to 1 tchd 15 to 2) 2
BROWN SAUCE (NZ) 7-10-13 (3*) W Marston, *chsd ldrs, led 5th, clr 3 out, hdd and wknd appr 2 out.* . . . . (7 to 2 op 4 to 1 tchd 5 to 1) 3
260² OTHET 9-11-9 N Hawke, *led to 5th, sn wknd.* . . . . (5 to 1 op 4 to 1) 4
FANATICAL (USA) (bl) 7-11-2 L Harvey, *hld up, some prog 3 out, nvr dngrs.* . . . . (20 to 1 op 16 to 1) 5
112 I SUPPOSE 8-11-2 Tracy Turner, *mstk 1st, chsd ldrs, disputing ld whn mistake 5th, sn wknd.* . . . . (40 to 1 op 20 to 1) 6

51

350[5] DANNY'S LUCK (NZ) 11-11-2 S Mackey, *prmnt, steadied 3rd, hdwy 5th, sn wknd*.......... (66 to 1 op 20 to 1) 7
191 FAIR BABE 7-11-2 M A FitzGerald, *chsd ldrs to 5th*. .... (20 to 1 op 12 to 1) 8
Dist: 1l, 20l, 15l, 1½l, 8l, 1½l, 7l. 4m 14.70s. a 24.70s (8 Ran).
(Midweek Racing), M D I Usher

436 Champagne Lanson Handicap Chase (5-y-o and up) £2,960 3¼m 110yds..... (3:25)

286* KILLULA CHIEF [97] 6-10-7 M A FitzGerald, *rcd in 3rd till hdwy to go second 15th, led 16th, kpt on readily frm 2 out*...................... (2 to 1 jt-fav tchd 100 to 30) 1
196[2] TRI FOLENE (Fr) [118] (v) 7-12-0 R Dunwoody, *chsd ldr till led 15th, hdd nxt, styd on one pace frm 3 out*. (2 to 1 jt-fav op 6 to 4 tchd 9 to 4) 2
BUDDY HOLLY (NZ) [101] 8-10-11 T Grantham, *led till mstk and hdd 15th, sn wknd*.............. (5 to 1 op 3 to 1) 3
405[3] DOONLOUGHAN [113] 8-11-9 J Frost, *4th thrght, lost tch frm 15th*............ (100 to 30 op 5 to 2 tchd 7 to 2) 4
Dist: 1½l, 30l, 7l. 6m 46.70s. a 26.70s (4 Ran).
(T G K Construction Ltd), J G M O'Shea

437 Teachers Highland Cream Whisky Handicap Hurdle (4-y-o and up) £2,528 3m 3f .... (3:55)

337* KRONPRINZ (Ire) [88] 5-10-0 (6ex) W Worthington, *hld up al gng wl in 4th, chlgd 3 out, led appr 2 out, sn clr, canter*. .... (2 to 1 op 6 to 4) 1
351* TRUMPET [93] 4-10-5 (6ex) M A FitzGerald, *trkd ldrs, chlgd 3 out, rdn appr 2 out, sn btn*......... (9 to 4 op 6 to 4) 2
307[4] CHAMOIS BOY [88] 9-10-0 C Llewellyn, *led, not fluent 5th, hdd appr 2 out, sn btn*. .... (7 to 4 fav op 2 to 1 tchd 13 to 8) 3
312[7] GRACE MOORE [88] 9-10-0[3] (3*) R Greene, *pressed ldr and jmpd rght, rdn appr 9th, wknd quickly 3 out, tld off whn refused last*....... (9 to 1 op 8 to 1 tchd 14 to 1) ref
Dist: 20l, 12l. 6m 51.70s. a 37.70s (4 Ran).
(Market Rasen Racing Club), M C Chapman

438 Pure Genius Novices' Chase (5-y-o and up) £2,684 2m 110yds.............. (4:25)

350[3] COMIC LINE (bl) 8-11-2 S Burrough, *chsd ldr till led 4th, hdd 6th, chlgd frm 3 out till led last, styd on wl*. .... (20 to 1 op 16 to 1) 1
184[2] ILEWIN 6-11-2 M Ahern, *prmnt, hit 3rd, led 7th, hdd last, found nothing*................................. (5 to 1 op 5 to 2) 2
350* PARBOLD HILL 5-11-6 M A FitzGerald, *led to 4th, led ag'n 6th to 7th, styd on same pace frm 2 out*. .... (5 to 2 fav op 3 to 1) 3
298[2] NEEDS MUST 6-11-2 J Frost, *chsd ldrs till wknd 9th*. .... (9 to 2 op 6 to 1) 4
NOBLE INSIGHT (bl) 6-11-2 R Dunwoody, *al beh*. .... (7 to 2 op 7 to 4) 5
388[5] ABU MUSLAB 9-11-2 C Maude, *beh frm 7th*. .... (5 to 1 op 3 to 1) 6
OBLATION (USA) 8-11-2 Miss S Barraclough, *lost tch 6th, tld off whn pld up bef 4 out*....... (33 to 1 op 20 to 1) pu
Dist: 2½l, 3l, 8l, 4l, 25l. 4m 12.40s. (7 Ran).
SR: 6/3/4/-/ (M R Churches), M R Churches

439 Gaymers Olde English Novices' Handicap Hurdle (0-100 4-y-o and up) £1,838 2¾m .... (4:55)

390* KNIGHTLY ARGUS [79] 6-11-0 (6ex) J Osborne, *led till hdd aftr 3 out, rallied to chal last, hrd drvn but in command whn lft clr last*............. (13 to 8 on op 9 to 4 on) 1
326[9] MINT-MASTER [78] 8-10-6 (7*) P Maddock, *chsd wnr till wknd appr 7th*........................ (12 to 1 op 6 to 1) 2
122 PROVERBS GIRL [93] 8-11-9 (5*) R Davis, *rcd in 3rd till chsd wnr appr 7th, led aftr 3 out till hdd and hld whn blun and uns rdr last, rmntd*..... (3 to 1 tchd 11 to 4) 3
HIDDEN FLOWER [73] 4-10-5 (3*) M Hourigan, *al in 4th, tld off 5th, pld up bef 7th*. (10 to 1 op 8 to 1 tchd 12 to 1) pu
Dist: Dist, dist. 5m 34.70s. a 35.70s (4 Ran).
(South Wales Argus Limited), S E Sherwood

AUTEUIL (FR) (soft)
Friday September 10th

440 Prix Jean Doumen (Hurdle) (5-y-o and up) £13,142 2m 3f 110yds............... (4:40)

267* BOKARO (Fr) 7-10-5 G Bradley, *made all, clr aftr 5 fs, rdn whn lft clear last*....................................... 1
ALLUTED (Fr) 5-10-1 D Mescam,........................ 2
LEBODEW (Fr) 6-10-3 P Prouet,........................ 3
Dist: 8l, 1l, 5l, 4l, sht-nk, 6l, 4l, 1l, 10l. 4m 44.00s. (15 Ran).
(Lady Joseph), C P E Brooks

WORCESTER (good to firm)
Friday September 10th

Going Correction: PLUS 0.10 sec. per fur.

441 Oddingley Novices' Hurdle (4-y-o and up) £1,480 2m 5f 110yds................ (2:25)

185* DEBACLE (USA) 4-11-4 D Murphy, *hld up and al gng wl, cruised into ld appr 2 out, clr whn slight mstk last, very easily*. (11 to 8 fav op 6 to 4 tchd 13 to 8 and 7 to 4) 1
GRAIN MERCHANT (v) 7-11-0 D Gallagher, *prmnt, led 3rd to 4th, outpcd 7th, styd on aftr 2 out to go second r-in*. .... (11 to 1 op 5 to 1 tchd 12 to 1) 2
302 MAKE A LINE 5-10-7 (7*) Mr Andrew Lillingston, *pld hrd, prmnt frm 4th, ev ch 2 out, one paced aftr*. .... (7 to 2 op 6 to 1) 3
264[5] ALICE SMITH 6-10-4 (5*) R Farrant, *hld up, hdwy 4 out, sn rdn, outpcd frm nxt*... (11 to 1 op 5 to 1 tchd 12 to 1) 4
323[4] WILL'S BOUNTY 10-10-7 (7*) Mr A Phillips, *al prmnt, led 6th, wkng whn hdd appr 2 out, blun last*. .... (16 to 1 op 10 to 1) 5
310[5] DOCTOR DUNKLIN (USA) 4-10-7 (5*) R Davis, *hld up in mid-div, no hdwy frm 3 out*.................. (25 to 1) 6
STORM FLIGHT 7-11-0 B Powell, *led to 3rd, led 4th to 6th, wknd quickly aftr nxt, tld off*. ....(16 to 1 op 12 to 1 tchd 25 to 1 and 33 to 1) 7
RAGTIME BOY 5-11-0 N Mann, *al in rear, tld off*. .... (7 to 1 op 7 to 2) 8
191 PADDY'S GOLD (Ire) 5-11-0 G Rowe, *prmnt till lost pl aftr 4th, wl beh frm 6th, tld off*........ (50 to 1 op 33 to 1) 9
207[3] EASY TOOMEY 5-11-0 S Smith Eccles, *prmnt till mstk 4th, reminders aftr, beh frm nxt, tld off whn pld up bef 3 out*......................... (20 to 1 op 14 to 1) pu
237 GLEN MOSELLE 7-11-0 Mr J Cambidge, *al beh, tld off frm 5th, pld up bef 3 out*.................. (50 to 1 op 33 to 1) pu
NORDIC FLIGHT 5-11-0 A Maguire, *al beh, tld off frm 5th, pld sn aftr nxt*.................. (33 to 1 op 25 to 1) pu
BROTHER HAROLD 4-10-9 (3*) W Marston, *al beh, tld off whn pld up bef 3 out*............. (33 to 1 op 20 to 1) pu
Dist: 10l, 1½l, 5l, 10l, 6l, dist, 1½l, sht-hd. 5m 6.80s. a 12.80s (13 Ran).
(Mrs Lisa Olley), B J McMath

442 Hindlip Novices' Chase (4-y-o and up) £2,318 2m......................... (2:55)

325[5] BARDESAN 7-11-7 J Osborne, *trkd ldr, led sn aftr 8th, hdd briefly 2 out, faltered r-in, hrd rdn, all out*. ....(11 to 4 jt-fav op 2 to 1 tchd 3 to 1) 1
MISTY (NZ) 6-11-7 C Llewellyn, *al in tch, rdn 3 out, rallied to press wnr r-in*............. (11 to 4 jt-fav op 7 to 4) 2
309 WEEKDAY CROSS (Ire) 5-11-5 S Smith Eccles, *hld up, cld on ldrs aftr 5th, lost pl after 8th, rallied 2 out, wknd r-in*............................... (7 to 1 tchd 11 to 2) 3
325[3] MENAGHI 6-11-2 G McCourt, *hld up in tch, rdn to ld briefly 2 out, sn wknd*... (7 to 2 op 9 to 2 tchd 3 to 1) 4
325[4] PECCAVI 9-11-7 R Bellamy, *hld up in rear, blun and uns rdr 5th*............................ (7 to 1 tchd 8 to 1) ur
PANDORA'S PRIZE 7-11-2 T Wall, *led till hdd and wknd sn aftr 8th, pld up lme bef 2 out*. .... (12 to 1 op 10 to 1 tchd 16 to 1) pu
Dist: Nk, 8l, 2l. 4m 3.50s. a 14.50s (6 Ran).
(A Boyd-Rochfort), O Sherwood

443 North Piddle Handicap Hurdle (0-125 4-y-o and up) £1,970 3m................. (3:25)

312* OWEN [94] 9-10-6 B Powell, *hld in in rear al gng wl, steady hdwy frm 7th, led appr 2 out, rdn and ran on well r-in*. .... (13 to 8 fav op 7 to 4 tchd 2 to 1 and 9 to 4) 1
KANO WARRIOR [90] 6-10-2 C Llewellyn, *hld up in tch, wnt second 2 out, pressed wnr r-in till no extr cl hme*. .... (7 to 2 op 3 to 1) 2
BANKROLL [112] 6-11-3 (7*) Mr G Lewis, *pld hrd and not fluent, trkd ldr, made most frm 5th till hdd appr 2 out, sn btn*.................................. (7 to 1 op 6 to 1) 3
312[6] MOUNTSHANNON [88] 7-10-0 S Earle, *hld up, hdwy 4 out, wknd nxt*...................... (25 to 1 tchd 33 to 1) 4
CLASSIC STATEMENT [105] 7-11-3 A Maguire, *hld up, hdwy to go second briefly 4 out, rdn and wknd nxt*. .... (9 to 1 op 5 to 1) 5
311 HUGLI [104] (bl) 6-11-2 J Osborne, *led to 5th, wth ldr till wknd quickly 3 out, tld off*. .... (12 to 1 op 8 to 1 tchd 14 to 1) 6
300[2] FROSTY RECEPTION [98] (bl) 8-10-10 R Dunwoody, *hit 1st, in tch till wknd 8th, sn tld off*. ....(9 to 2 op 4 to 1 tchd 5 to 1 and 11 to 2) 7
Dist: ¾l, 20l, 10l, ½l, 15l, 12l. 5m 46.40s. a 10.40s (7 Ran).
(Burt & Travica Contractors Ltd), B Smart

444 Stonehall Handicap Chase (0-115 5-y-o and up) £2,695 2m.................. (3:55)

403[3] DRUMSTICK [118] 7-11-10 N Williamson, *chsd ldrs, wnt second 4 out, led nxt, edgd rght r-in, drvn out*. .... (9 to 1 op 6 to 1 tchd 10 to 1) 1
403* STAY AWAKE [103] 7-10-9 (6ex) P Niven, *hld up, outpcd and jmpd slwly frm 4th, gd hdwy aftr 3 out, chlgd r-in, no imprsn cl hme*........ (11 to 10 on op 11 to 10 on) 2

309² FEATHER YOUR NEST [96] 8-10-2 J Railton, *led to 5th, led ag'n appr 4 out, hdd nxt, one pace frm 2 out, fnshd lme.*
.................................(8 to 1 op 6 to 1)   3
336⁴ RUPPLES [94] 6-10-0 W Worthington, *beh, styd on one pace frm 4 out*..............(14 to 1 op 8 to 1)   4
KNIGHT'S SPUR (USA) [101] 6-10-7 G McCourt, *mid-divs hdwy to chase ldr 8th, wkng whn mstk 3 out.*
...........................(11 to 2 op 5 to 1 tchd 8 to 1)   5
TIGERS PET [107] 9-10-13 S Smith Eccles, *trkd ldrs till lost tch 6th.*..................(12 to 1 op 10 to 1)   6
187 SHARP ORDER [96] 8-10-2¹ Pat Caldwell, *al beh, tld off 8th, pld up bef 2 out.* (33 to 1 op 25 to 1)   pu
TRY ME NOW [94] 7-9-7 (7*) J Supple, *pld hrd, mstks, trkd ldrs, ld 5th, hdd appr 4 out, wknd quickly, pulled up bef last.*........................(66 to 1 op 50 to 1)   pu
271⁵ DEEP DARK DAWN [116] 8-11-8 R Supple, *al towards rear, pld up bef 2 out.*..............(14 to 1 op 16 to 1)   pu
Dist: ½l, 6l, 5l, 6l, 12l. 3m 56.10s. a 7.10s (9 Ran).
SR: 41/25/12/5/6/-/   (Sarah Lady Allendale), K C Bailey

445 Pirton Novices' Hurdle (4-y-o and up) £1,480 3m........................ (4:25)

OUTFIELD 7-10-9 G McCourt, *hld up in rear, hdwy to go second 4 out, led aftr lnxt, sn clr, rdn out.*
.................................(14 to 1 op 10 to 1)   1
262² MR MURDOCK 8-11-0 S Earle, *al prmnt, jmpd slwly 7th, rallied appr last, no imprsn r-in.*
..............................(11 to 8 fav op 6 to 4 tchd 7 to 4)   2
301⁷ BROWNHALL 5-10-7 (7*) Mr B Pollock, *led 3rd, mstk 8th, hdd sn aftr 3 out, one pace.*......(50 to 1 op 33 to 1)   3
301⁸ NEW STATESMAN 5-11-0 N Mann, *al in rear, lost tch 4 out.*............................(50 to 1 op 25 to 1)   4
284⁷ DAUNTLESS KNIGHT (USA) 5-11-0 Peter Hobbs, *led to 3rd, styd in tch, wkng whn hmpd 3 out.* (20 to 1 op 16 to 1)   5
310* PERFORATE (bl) 4-11-10 L Harvey, *hld up in tch, mstk 6th, nvr gng wl aftr.*........(11 to 2 op 4 to 1 tchd 6 to 1)   6
310³ RICH AND RED 7-10-9 N Williamson, *in tch till wknd appr 3 out, wl beh whn eased r-in.*......(11 to 2 op 4 to 1)   7
EXARCH (USA) 4-10-12 C Llewellyn, *prmnt, dsptd ld 7th to 4 out, wknd whn f nxt...* (5 to 2 op 3 to 1 tchd 9 to 4)   f
Dist: 2½l, 6l, 10l, 3l, 20l, 15l. 5m 52.50s. a 16.50s (8 Ran).
                                            (Mrs Mary Grant), J Webber

446 Wyre Piddle Handicap Hurdle (0-115 4-y-o and up) £2,022 2m.................(4:55)

407* CLEEVELAND LADY [95] 6-11-5 (7ex) R Dunwoody, *trkd ldrs, led 2 out, rdn clr.*
..................................(13 to 8 on op 5 to 4 tchd 7 to 4)   1
POWER HAPPY [77] 8-10-1 D Gallagher, *led 3rd, jmpd rght 3 out and ag'n whn hdd nxt, one pace aftr.*
.................................(6 to 1 tchd 9 to 1)   2
DONOSTI [109] 9-11-0 A Maguire, *hld up, hdwy frm 5th, rdn and one pace frm 2 out.*........(9 to 2 op 5 to 1)   3
SUNSET REINS FREE [89] 8-10-13 K Jones, *hld up, outpcd 5th, kpt on frm 2 out.* (14 to 1 op 10 to 1 tchd 20 to 1)   4
289 TALATON FLYER [89] 7-10-13 Peter Hobbs, *led to 3rd, in cl tch till wknd quickly appr 2 out...* (10 to 1 op 6 to 1)   5
Dist: 2½l, 6l, nk, nk. 3m 50.10s. a 9.10s (5 Ran).
SR: 16/-/11/-/-/   (Mrs Philomena Reich), W G M Turner

BANGOR (good)
Saturday September 11th
Going Correction: PLUS 0.40 sec. per fur. (races 1,2,-4,6,7), PLUS 0.25 (3,5)

447 Dead Cert Conditional Jockeys' Selling Hurdle (4-y-o and up) £1,906 2½m...(2:10)

387* CELCIUS (bl) 9-11-4 (5*) T Dascombe, *hld up, hdwy aftr 7th, lft second and hmpd 3 out, styd on to chal frm nxt, led after last, kpt on wl.*
.................................(6 to 4 fav op 2 to 1 tchd 11 to 8)   1
370⁴ JAMESTOWN BOY (bl) 5-11-6 T Jenks, *led second to 6th, pressed ldr, lft in ld 3 out, rdn nxt, hdd aftr last, not quicken nr finish...*......(9 to 2 op 4 to 1 tchd 11 to 2)   2
339⁴ BARTON PRIDE (Ire) 4-10-12 P Williams, *chsd ldg pair til wknd aftr 7th, no ch whn hmpd 3 out, tld off.*
.................................(10 to 1 op 5 to 1)   3
307⁷ THE HIDDEN CITY 7-11-0 T Eley, *led to second, not fluent aftr, mstk 5th, led 6th til f 3 out.*
.................................(9 to 1 op 8 to 1 tchd 10 to 1)   f
425² BURN BRIDGE (USA) (v) 7-11-1 (5*) D Walsh, *hld up, hdwy 7th, chsd ldrs frm nxt, cl 3rd and ev ch whn brght dwn 3 out...*.......................(11 to 2 op 7 to 1 tchd 11 to 2)   bd
COLONIAL OFFICE (USA) (bl) 7-11-0 V Slattery, *pushed alng aftr 4th, not much room appr nxt, sn hrd rdn and tld off, pld after four out........* (20 to 1 tchd 25 to 1)   pu
Dist: ½l, 30l. 4m 51.20s. a 15.20s (6 Ran).
SR: 23/19/-/-/   (Martin Pipe Racing Club), M C Pipe

448 Dick Francis Three Year Old Novices' Hurdle (Div I) £2,442 2m 1f............ (2:40)

LEGAL ARTIST (Ire) 10-12 D Murphy, *hld up, trkd ldrs frm 4 out, led 2 out, sn drw clr, cmftbly.*
.................................(6 to 4 fav tchd 2 to 1)   1
285⁴ NOMADIC FIRE 10-7 (5*) T Jenks, *sn prmnt, led aftr 3rd, hdd 3 out, led ag'n briefly appr 2 out, soon headed and one pace...*.............(5 to 1 op 5 to 2 tchd 7 to 2)   2
349* SUMMER FLOWER 10-8 (5*) T Eley, *trkd ldrs, cl up and ev ch 6th, jmpd slwly 3 out, led appr 2 out, hdd and hit two out, sn one pace...*...........(5 to 1 op 7 to 2)   3
THE SECRET SEVEN 10-7 B Clifford, *hld up, cl up and ev ch appr 3 out, rdn frm nxt, one pace.*
.................................(50 to 1 op 25 to 1)   4
247⁸ PAAJIB (Ire) 10-5 (7*) W Fry, *hld up, hdwy aftr 5th, chsd ldrs 3 out, wknd frm nxt..........*(33 to 1 op 25 to 1)   5
406⁹ MAD MYTTON 10-12 N Mann, *led til aftr 3rd, pressed ldr, led ag'n 3 out, sn hdd and wknd...*(8 to 1 op 20 to 1)   6
AWESTRUCK 10-12 T Wall, *not fluent, rear 4th and reminders, sn beh........*(33 to 1 op 20 to 1)   7
AMGANTY 10-7 K Jones, *jmpd badly, lost tch aftr 4th, sn tld off...........................*(33 to 1 op 25 to 1)   8
SICILY OAK 10-12 (5*) C Llewellyn, *f 1st.*
.................................(33 to 1 op 25 to 1)   f
278⁶ TOM THE TANK 10-12 G McCourt, *hld up, hdwy 4 out, chsd ldrs, btn whn mstk 2 out, pld up bef last.*
.................................(12 to 1 tchd 14 to 1)   pu
Dist: 8l, sht-hd, 1½l, 4l, 20l, 10l. dist. 4m 6.60s. a 16.60s (10 Ran).
                                            (Tony Briam), N A Graham

449 Greenalls Handicap Chase (0-130 5-y-o and up) £3,306 3m 110yds......... (3:10)

WONT BE GONE LONG [134] 11-12-0 R Dunwoody, *led to 3rd, trkd ldrs til rdn and outpcd aftr 5 out, rallied after 3 out, not much room appr last, led r-in.*
.................................(11 to 1 op 5 to 2)   1
KILHALLON CASTLE [106] 10-9-11 (3*) N Bentley, *hld up, wnt 3rd 11th, led 2 out, hdd aftr last, not quicken.*
.................................(5 to 1 op 6 to 1 tchd 7 to 1)   2
397³ CHARMING GALE [107] 6-10-10 (5*) P Williams, *pressed ldr til led 8th, hdd 11th, led ag'n 13th to 2 out, ev ch last, not quicken r-in...........*(4 to 1 op 3 to 1)   3
367* OFF THE BRU [112] 8-10-8¹ Mr A Bradburne, *led 3rd to 8th, led ag'n 11th to 13th, rdn and wknd 4 out.*
.................................(15 to 8 fav op 2 to 1 tchd 7 to 4)   4
271⁴ KIRSTY'S BOY [123] 10-11-3 G McCourt, *hld up, reminder and pushed alng aftr 12th, cld up 5 out, disputing ld whn blun 3 out, not reco'r.*
.................................(7 to 2 op 2 to 1 tchd 5 to 1)   5
Dist: 1½l, hd, 10l, 12l. 6m 7.50s. a 17.50s (5 Ran).
                                            (Robert Waley-Cohen), N J Henderson

450 Gordon Mytton Homes Handicap Hurdle (0-135 4-y-o and up) £2,645 2m 1f....(3:40)

326* LUSTREMAN [108] 6-10-0 T Wall, *hld up, swtchd aftr 3 out, rdn to ld last, drvn out.*
.................................(11 to 8 fav op 5 to 4 tchd 6 to 4)   1
MONTPELIER LAD [136] 6-12-0 R Dunwoody, *led, jmpd big and rght, hdd aftr 3 out, rallied betw last 2, not quicken...........*(13 to 8 op 7 to 4 tchd 6 to 4)   2
238² SAYMORE [108] 7-9-11 (3*) S Wynne, *hld up in last pl, rapid hdwy to ld appr 2 out, hdd last, sn one pace.*
.................................(5 to 1 op 4 to 1 tchd 6 to 1)   3
280⁴ KALKO [108] 4-9-9 (5*) D Bentley, *hld up, wnt second 3 out, rdn and wknd appr nxt.*
.................................(11 to 2 op 4 to 1 tchd 6 to 1)   4
Dist: 3l, 3l, 3l. 4m 1.00s. a 11.00s (4 Ran).
SR: 30/55/24/21/   (R A B Brassey), J H Peacock

451 Harrison Hedge Hoppers Novices' Chase (4-y-o and up) £2,762 2½m 110yds...(4:10)

281* VALIANT WARRIOR 5-11-12 C Grant, *trkd ldrs, wnt 3rd 6th, led 2 out, styd on wl.*
.................................(13 to 8 fav op Evens tchd 7 to 4)   1
325² CRAFTY CHAPLAIN 7-11-3 (5*) Mr D McCain, *hld up, hdwy aftr tenth, chsd ldr frm nxt, not quicken appr last.*
.................................(8 to 1 op 7 to 1)   2
396² NISHKINA 5-11-6 L Wyer, *pressed ldr in second pl, ev ch 4 out, not quicken aftr 2 out........*(11 to 2 op 4 to 1)   3
396* DROMINA STAR 12-11-9 (5*) P Williams, *led til hdd 2 out, not quicken.................*(10 to 1 op 6 to 1)   4
404⁴ SHUTAFUT 7-11-8 C Llewellyn, *hld up, hdwy tenth, cl up whn mstk 3 out, rallied nxt, sn wknd.*
.................................(3 to 1 op 6 to 1)   5
SMALLMEAD LAD 6-11-8 P Holley, *hld up, cld on ldg grp 5 out, ev ch aftr 3 out, second but rdn whn f last.*
.................................(16 to 1 op 12 to 1 tchd 20 to 1)   f
REVILLER'S GLORY 9-11-8 Mrs A Farrell, *blun and uns rdr 3rd.........................*(10 to 1 tchd 9 to 1)   ur
BEN RHYDDING 6-11-8 K Jones, *jmpd slwly, wl beh frm 5th, tld off whn pld up bef 5 out...* (66 to 1 op 50 to 1)   pu
Dist: 6l, 2½l, 6l, 8l, 15l. 5m 3.00s. a 12.00s (8 Ran).
SR: 29/19/14/16/2/   (P Sellars), M D Hammond

452 Decider Novices' Handicap Hurdle (4-y-o and up) £2,071 2½m................(4:40)

POWLEYVALE [108] 6-11-12 R Dunwoody, *trkd ldg pair frm 3rd, wnt second 6th, led appr 2 out, sn clr, rdn out.*
................................(3 to 1 op 5 to 1) 1

242³ RISING TEMPO (Ire) [82] 5-10-0 N Mann, *hld up, outpcd aftr 5 out, rdn and styd on after 2 out, lft moderate second at last.*...............(4 to 1 tchd 9 to 2) 2

CROIX VAL MER [82] 6-10-0 C Llewellyn, *pressed ldr till wknd quickly aftr 4 out, styd on one pace frm 2 out, lft moderate 3rd at last.*.............(6 to 1 op 5 to 1) 3

390⁴ CLASSICAL STAR [82] (bl) 4-10-0 N Williamson, *hld up, wknd quickly aftr 4 out, sn beh, tld off.*
.....................................(5 to 2 op 2 to 1) 4

323³ FORTINA'S SONG [82] 6-9-11² (5*) T Jenks, *led, not fluent, hdd appr 2 out, second but no ch whn f last.*
......................(9 to 4 fav op 5 to 2 tchd 3 to 1) f

Dist: 12l, 1½l, dist. 4m 57.00s. a 21.00s (5 Ran).

(M G St Quinton), B S Rothwell

453 Dick Francis Three Year Old Novices' Hurdle (Div II) £2,431 2m 1f. . . . . (5:10)

TOMSK 10-12 C Llewellyn, *chsd clr ldr frm second, led appr 2 out, clear from nxt, styd on wl.*
...............................(2 to 1 op 7 to 4 tchd 9 to 4) 1

PREROGATIVE (v) 10-12 R Dunwoody, *led, wndrd appr second, clr aftr 4th, hdd approaching 2 out, sn btn.*
..............................(6 to 4 fav op 5 to 4 tchd 7 to 4) 2

CREAGMHOR 10-5 (7*) Mr J L Llewellyn, *chsd ldg pair till outpcd aftr 5th, no ch frm 3 out.*
.........................(25 to 1 op 20 to 1 tchd 33 to 1) 3

MOUSE BIRD (Ire) 10-12 P Holley, *hld up, hdwy aftr 5th, wknd after nxt.*...............(13 to 2 op 4 to 1) 4

TRY N' FLY (Ire) 10-12 P Niven, *beh frm 3rd, tld off aftr 5th.*.............................(6 to 1 op 4 to 1) 5

193² GLEAM OF GOLD 10-7 G McCourt, *chsd ldr to 4th, wknd quickly, sn tld off.*................(14 to 1 op 20 to 1) 6

ARABIAN CASTLE 10-12 N Mann, *al beh, tld off aftr 3rd.*
.....................................(25 to 1 op 20 to 1) 7

KINCADE 10-12 Mr J Cambidge, *slwly away, beh whn f second.*........................(50 to 1) f

278⁷ FLORA LINO 10-7 C Grant, *mstk 1st, beh whn hmpd aftr nxt, pld up bef 3rd.*....................(50 to 1) pu

Dist: 8l, 25l, 8l, 25l, 12l, dist. 4m 6.70s. a 16.70s (9 Ran).

(Jack Joseph), N A Twiston-Davies

WORCESTER (good (race 1), good to firm (2,3,4,5,6))
Saturday September 11th
Going Correction: MINUS 0.15 sec. per fur. (races 1,3,6), MINUS 0.10 (2,4,5)

454 Blackpole Selling Handicap Hurdle (4,5,6-y-o) £1,431 2m. . . . . (2:25)

244³ RED INK [73] 4-10-11 S Smith Eccles, *hmpd 1st, hdwy to chase ldrs 5th, chlgd 3 out till hdd last, all out.*
.................(100 to 30 jt-fav op 3 to 1 tchd 7 to 2) 1

NAJEB (USA) [73] 4-10-11 M A FitzGerald, *hmpd and lft in ld 1st, hdd 3rd, led 5th, rdn aftr 2 out, headed and not fluent last, outpcd.*..............(12 to 1 op 7 to 1) 2

242⁵ ANOTHER VINTAGE [70] 4-10-8 J Osborne, *hld up, hdwy 2 out, kpt on same pace appr last.*
.......................(7 to 2 op 9 to 2 tchd 5 to 1) 3

191 ALTO PRINCESS [70] 4-10-8 H Davies, *beh till hdwy 3 out, one pace frm 2 out.*.....................(20 to 1) 4

TRENDY AUCTIONEER (Ire) [72] 5-10-10 A Maguire, *chsd ldrs, effrt frm 3 out till wknd appr last.*
....................................(9 to 2 op 3 to 1) 5

PRIME MOVER [78] (v) 5-11-2 R Campbell, *prmnt till jmpd slwly 3rd, hdwy to chase ldrs 5th, wknd 3 out.*
................(100 to 30 jt-fav op 3 to 1 tchd 7 to 2) 6

166³ PEARLY WHITE [67] 4-10-5⁴ M Bosley, *wth ldr till led 3rd, hdd and jmpd slwly 5th, sn wknd.* (20 to 1 op 11 to 1) 7

ELWAZIR (USA) [62] 4-9-10¹ (5*) J McCarthy, *led, jmpd badly rght, hdd and tried to refuse 1st, refused nxt and uns rdr.*............................(33 to 1 op 20 to 1) ref

Dist: ¾l, 3l, 2l, ½l, 20l, 20l. 3m 56.40s. a 15.40s (8 Ran).

(James Hughes), J R Jenkins

455 Henwick Novices' Chase (5-y-o and up) £1,892 2m 7f. . . . . (2:55)

404* WHATAGALE 6-11-1 J Osborne, *jmpd wl, made virtually all, quickened frm 4 out, eased nr finish.*
.............................(Evens fav op 5 to 4) 1

139⁵ KILDOWNEY HILL 7-11-0 A Maguire, *chsd wnr most of way, not fluent 12th, effrt 4 out, outpcd frm 2 out.*
..............................(10 to 1 op 8 to 1 tchd 12 to 1) 2

347³ PAPPA DONT PREACH (Ire) 5-10-10 R Supple, *not fluent early, beh tenth, rallied 14th, mstk 3 out, sn one pace.*
.................................(20 to 1 op 14 to 1) 3

389³ KASHAN (Ire) 5-10-5 (5*) R Farrant, *in tch, chsd ldrs 7th, still wl th whn blun 13th, not reco'r.* (15 to 2 op 9 to 1) 4

MIRAMAC 12-11-0 J Frost, *al beh and nvr a factor, hit 9th, mstk 2 out.*.......(20 to 1 op 16 to 1 tchd 25 to 1) 5

WELLANE BOY (Ire) 5-10-7 (3*) W Marston, *al beh, mstk tenth, tld off whn blun last.*......(25 to 1 op 16 to 1) 6

TOP IT ALL 5-10-10 D Bridgwater, *dsptd ld and f 1st.*
....................................(4 to 1 tchd 3 to 1) f

351⁴ KNIGHTON COOMBE (NZ) 7-11-0 H Davies, *badly hmpd 1st, wl beh whn jmpd slwly second, tld off when pld up bef 6th.*.....................(2 to 1 op 6 to 1 tchd 9 to 1) pu

Dist: 2½l, 15l, 8l, 10l, dist. 5m 55.20s. a 11.20s (8 Ran).

(C Coxen), O Sherwood

456 Hallow Novices' Hurdle (4-y-o and up) £1,480 2m. . . . . (3:25)

NATIVE CHIEFTAIN 4-10-12 H Davies, *beh till gd headewy frm 5th, trkd ldrs aftr 2 out, chlgd last, sn led, ran on wl.*...............................(12 to 1 op 10 to 1) 1

191* BILLY BORU 5-11-6 D Gallagher, *took str hold in tch, led aftr 2 out, till hdd sn after last, one pace.*
..................(Evens fav op 6 to 5 on tchd 11 to 10) 2

MULL HOUSE 6-11-0 E Murphy, *sn tracking ldrs, chlgd 3 out, soon led, mstk 2 out, soon hdd, one pace.*
...............................(11 to 4 op 7 to 2 tchd 4 to 1) 3

CONCINNITY (USA) 4-10-12 A Maguire, *led till hdd sn aftr 3 out, styd on same pace.*........(16 to 1 op 14 to 1) 4

DANCE PARTOUT (Ire) 5-11-0 Peter Hobbs, *hdwy 5th, nvr dngrs.*...............................(12 to 1 op 6 to 1) 5

402⁵ SIR PAGEANT 4-10-12 W Humphreys, *prmnt till wknd appr 3 out.*.....................(20 to 1 op 25 to 1) 6

191⁵ STERLING BUCK (USA) 6-10-9 (5*) D Leahy, *chsd ldr, rdn 5th, wknd 3 out.*......(18 to 1 op 12 to 1 tchd 20 to 1) 7

HULLO MARY DOLL. 4-10-7 S Earle, *slwly into strd, al beh.*....................................(50 to 1) 8

126⁶ PICKWICK 4-10-12 Gary Lyons, *al beh.*.......(50 to 1) 9

323⁷ ARCTIC LINE (bl) 5-10-9 (5*) R Farrant, *in tch to 5th.*
....................................(66 to 1) 10

81 TALENT SPOTTER 6-11-0 D Bridgwater, *chsd ldrs, mstk 5th, sn weakened.*.........(16 to 1 tchd 20 to 1) 11

MARTINOSKY 7-10-11 (3*) M Hourigan, *beh frm 4th.*
....................................(25 to 1) 12

BID FOR SIX (USA) 4-10-12 M A FitzGerald, *sn beh, whn soon no ch whn f last.*..........(50 to 1 op 40 to 1) f

MASRUR (USA) 4-10-12 S McNeill, *blun 3rd and beh, tld off whn pld up bef 3 out.*....................(33 to 1) pu

STRAWBERRY FOOL 4-10-7 A Webb, *beh frm 5th, tld off whn pld up bef 3 out.*...............(66 to 1) pu

SQUIRREL CITY 9-10-6 (3*) W Marston, *mstk 1st, al bebind, tld off whn pulles up bef 3 out.*...(33 to 1) pu

Dist: 3½l, 7l, 3½l, 6l, 12l, 3½l, 10l, 6l, 6l, 10l. 3m 44.80s. a 3.80s (16 Ran).

SR: 22/26/13/7/3/-/ (Mrs S R Crowe), S Dow

457 Medallion Homes Handicap Chase (0-120 5-y-o and up) £1,970 2½m 110yds. . . (3:55)

COMEDY ROAD [99] 9-10-0 L Harvey, *chsd ldrs, led 2 out, drvn out.*......................(11 to 1 op 7 to 1) 1

198* LITTLE TOM [99] 8-10-0 J R Kavanagh, *led to 5th, chsd ldr till lft in ld tenth, hdd 2 out, not quicken.*
....................................(100 to 30 tchd 7 to 1) 2

345⁴ AMONG FRIENDS [103] 8-9-13 (5*) R Davis, *beh 6th, hit 7th, styd on appr 4 out, no imprsn frm 3 out.*
....................(7 to 1 tchd 8 to 1 and 9 to 1) 3

354* MAJOR MATCH (NZ) [120] 11-11-7 H Davies, *beh, rdn alng frm 8th, no imprsn from 4 out.*
....................(6 to 4 fav tchd 13 to 8 and 11 to 8) 4

182⁷ SLIPPERY MAX [99] 9-10-0 A Maguire, *al beh, tld off.*
....................................(25 to 1 op 20 to 1) 5

PALM READER [127] 9-12-0 M A FitzGerald, *led 5th and rcd freely aftr, sn clr till f tenth.*
....................................(25 to 1 op 5 to 1 tchd 6 to 1) f

IN THE ZONE [101] 8-10-2² Peter Hobbs, *prmnt, hit 9th and lost tch, hit 11th, tld off whn pld up bef 2 out.*
....................................(25 to 1 op 16 to 1) pu

Dist: 6l, 2l, 8l, dist. 5m 6.50s. a 3.50s (7 Ran).

SR: 16/10/12/21/ (Winsbury Livestock), R Lee

458 Bromsgrove Handicap Chase (5-y-o and up) £2,406 2m 7f. . . . . (4:25)

354² COPPER MINE [125] 7-12-0 J Osborne, *jmpd wl, led 4th, came clr frm 2 out, pushed out r-in.*
............................(15 to 8 fav op 11 to 8 tchd 2 to 1) 1

317* LOCAL CUSTOMER [97] 8-10-0 W Humphreys, *chsd wnr frm 6th, chlgd 8th, rdn from 3 out, no ch with winner.*
....................................(4 to 1 tchd 9 to 2) 2

405* TOUCHING STAR [97] 8-9-11 (3*) M Hourigan, *hdwy 9th, not pace 12th, headway appr 4 out, one pace frm nxt.*
....................................(9 to 4 op 2 to 1) 3

386⁴ BARRACILLA [99] 8-10-2² S Hodgson, *chsd ldrs, rdn tenth, lost pl 11th, hit 14th, no imprsn frm 4 out.*
....................................(16 to 1 op 12 to 1 tchd 20 to 1) 4

382* THEY ALL FORGOT ME [97] 6-10-0 A Maguire, *led to 4th, pressed wnr to 6th, drvn and one pace frm four out.*
....................(5 to 1 tchd 6 to 1 and 13 to 2) 5

385³ SWINGTIME BELLE [98] 6-10-1¹ S McNeill, *beh frm 9th, tld off whn pld up bef 14th, dismounted.*
....................................(50 to 1 op 33 to 1) pu

Dist: 2½l, 6l, 1½l, 2l. 5m 47.90s. a 3.90s (6 Ran).

SR: 38/7/1/1/-/-/   (J Dougall), O Sherwood

459 Stourbridge Handicap Hurdle (0-125 4-y-o and up) £1,733 2m 5f 110yds....... (4:55)

384[4] NEWTON POINT [98] 4-10-6 A Maguire, *mstk 1st in tch, chsd ldr appr 3 out, sn led, drvn out r-in.*
.................................(5 to 1 tchd 6 to 1)   1
148[3] MIDFIELDER [112] 7-11-6 Peter Hobbs, *led to 3 out, rdn to chal last, found little.*................(3 to 1 op 7 to 2)   2
NAHAR [120] 8-11-9 (5') A Dicken, *hld up, hdwy appr 3 out, kpt on.*.........(16 to 1 op 12 to 1 tchd 10 to 1)   3
LASTING MEMORY [102] 7-10-10 J Frost, *beh, tld off 6th, ran on frm 3 out, not a dngr.*
.................................(13 to 2 op 8 to 1 tchd 6 to 1)   4
407[2] NIKITAS [115] 8-11-9 S McNeill, *chsd ldr, mstk 3rd, rdn appr 3 out, sn wknd.* (2 to 1 fav op 7 to 4 tchd 9 to 4)   5
348[4] NUNS JEWEL [92] 7-9-9 (5') R Farrant, *chsd ldrs till riden and wknd 7th, tld off.* (13 to 2 op 5 to 1 tchd 8 to 1)   6
401 MANDALAY PRINCE [92] 9-9-11 (3') W Marston, *in tch till wknd rpdly, refused and uns rdr 5th.*
.................................(66 to 1 op 25 to 1)   ref
Dist: 4l, 1½l, 10l, dist. 5m 0.70s. a 6.70s (7 Ran).
           (Pps Racing Partnership), T R George

PLUMPTON (good to firm)
Monday September 13th
Going Correction: PLUS 0.20 sec. per fur.

460 Patcham Selling Handicap Hurdle (4-y-o and up) £1,182 2m 1f.............. (2:10)

STRIKING IMAGE (Ire) [71] 4-10-1[1] W McFarland, *made virtually all, blun 2 out, drvn out.*
.................................(9 to 2 op 4 to 1 tchd 5 to 1)   1
359* MANHATTAN BOY [105] 11-12-0 (7') J Clarke, *chsd ldrs till lost pl 4 out, rallied appr 2 out, wnt second last.*
.................................(9 to 2 op 4 to 1 tchd 11 to 2)   2
387[2] STAR MOVER [75] 4-10-5 R Dunwoody, *trkd wnr to 5th, one pace frm 3 out.*................(11 to 4 op 5 to 2)   3
316[3] CYRILL HENRY (Ire) [73] 4-10-3 A Maguire, *hld up, mstk 6th, hrd rdn to go second appr 2 out, ridden and wknd bef last.*................(6 to 4 fav op 2 to 1 tchd 9 to 4)   4
SUMMERHILL SCOOP [70] 5-9-7 (7') K Goble, *prmnt frm 4th, dsptd ld 4th till mstk and lost pl nxt, rdr lost irons.*
.................................(10 to 1 tchd 12 to 1)   5
L'ENCHERE [77] 8-10-7[4] (7') Paul McEntee, *beh frm strt, nvr on terms, tld off.* (25 to 1 op 16 to 1 tchd 33 to 1)   6
BEACHOLME BOY (Ire) [74] 5-10-4[7] (3') D O'Sullivan, *al beh, rdn aftr hit 5th, tld off whn pld up bef 2 out.*
.................................(66 to 1 op 20 to 1)   pu
Dist: 1½l, 3½l, hd, 20l, dist. 4m 9.60s. a 17.60s (7 Ran).
           (Flahive Brickwork Ltd), J S Moore

461 George Poole Novices' Chase (5-y-o and up) £1,746 3m 1f 110yds........... (2:40)

357* STAR OF OUGHTERARD (bl) 8-11-7 W McFarland, *al prmnt, hit 6 out, hrd drvn to ld appr 3 out, rdn clr.*
.................................(15 to 8 op 9 to 4 tchd 5 to 2)   1
389* OCEAN LINK 9-11-7 S Earle, *al prmnt, led 9th till hdd appr 3 out, one pace aftr.*
.................................(11 to 10 on op 5 to 4 on tchd Evens)   2
357[3] MILLIE BELLE (v) 7-10-11 A Maguire, *led to 9th, rallied 5 out, outpcd appr 3 out.* (8 to 1 op 7 to 1 tchd 10 to 1)   3
KELLY OWENS 8-11-2 W Irvine, *jmpd slwly 4th, hld up in tch, outpcd frm four out.*
.................................(11 to 1 op 8 to 1 tchd 12 to 1)   4
347[5] DANRIBO 10-10-9 (7') Mr M Gingell, *al beh, lost tch frm 14th.*.................................(100 to 1 op 33 to 1)   5
BE PATIENT MY SON 12-11-2 I Lawrence, *beh frm 8th, tld off whn pld up bef 6 out.*........(100 to 1 op 33 to 1)   pu
373 SILVERCROSS LAD 10-11-2 T Wall, *not jump wl, al in rear, tld off whn pld up bef 3 out.*
.................................(20 to 1 op 12 to 1 tchd 25 to 1)   pu
Dist: 7l, 8l, 6l, 30l. 6m 31.80s. a 19.80s (7 Ran).
           (Quicksteel Ltd), T P McGovern

462 A. R. Dennis Bookmakers Juvenile Novices' Hurdle (3-y-o) £1,764 2m 1f.... (3:10)

320[3] MR GENEALOGY (USA) (bl) 11-8 A Maguire, *hld up, hdwy to ld appr 3 out, wnt clr bef nxt....* (4 to 1 tchd 9 to 2)   1
HILLSDOWN BOY (Ire) 10-12 H Davies, *wtd wth in rear, steady hdwy frm 3 out to go second appr last.*
.................................(7 to 1 op 5 to 1 tchd 8 to 1)   2
356* PYRRHIC DANCE 11-3 R Dunwoody, *al prmnt, cld 4 out, outpcd aftr nxt.*......(11 to 2 op 3 to 1 tchd 6 to 1)   3
WONDERFUL YEARS (USA) 10-12 J P Kavanagh, *mid-div, mstk 5th, outpcd frm 4 out.*........(20 to 1 op 8 to 1)   4
TAAHHUB (Ire) 10-12 D Skyrme, *wl in rear, some hdwy frm 4 out, nvr dngrs.*................(14 to 1 op 6 to 1)   5
CHIPPENDALE LADD (Can) (bl) 10-12 J Osborne, *rcd keenly, led till hdd aftr 6th, sn btn.*
.................................(5 to 2 fav op 7 to 4 tchd 4 to 1)   6

HUESCA 10-7 M Richards, *trkd ldr, swshd tail thrght, led aftr 6th, hdd appr 3 out, wknd quickly.*
.................................(33 to 1 op 20 to 1 tchd 50 to 1)   7
ERLKING (Ire) 10-12 S Earle, *hld up in tch, wknd appr 4 out.*.................................(3 to 1 op 5 to 2 tchd 7 to 2)   8
180[6] GENERAL BROOKS (Ire) 10-12 T Wall, *in tch to 5th, tld off whn pld up bef nxt.*......(100 to 1 op 33 to 1)   pu
Dist: 3l, 10l, 30l, 4l, 2½l, 2½l, 1½l. 4m 12.30s. a 20.30s (9 Ran).
           (Mrs P A White), J White

463 Master Brew Bitter Handicap Hurdle (0-125 4-y-o and up) £1,702 2½m.... (3:40)

404 STRONG MEDICINE [106] 6-11-10 N Williamson, *al gng wl, led appr 3 out, drw clr frm nxt, cmftbly.*
.................................(5 to 1 op 5 to 1 tchd 6 to 1)   1
GALLANT EFFORT (Ire) [106] 5-11-10 H Davies, *hld up, hdwy 7th, rdn to chal 2 out, sn btn.*........(3 to 1 jt-fav op 4 to 1 tchd 11 to 4)   2
358 TEL E THON [99] (v) 6-10-12 (5') D Leahy, *led till hdd appr 3 out, wknd bef nxt.*.................................(3 to 1 jt-fav op 9 to 4 tchd 100 to 30)   3
205[4] CARPET CAPERS (USA) [83] 9-10-1 A Maguire, *prmnt till wknd appr 4 out, sn beh.*
.................................(5 to 1 op 4 to 1 tchd 11 to 2)   4
ROGER'S PAL [83] 6-9-10[2] (7') J Clarke, *mstks in rear, lost tch appr 4 out.*........(12 to 1 op 7 to 1 tchd 14 to 1)   5
205[5] ALICE'S MIRROR [90] 4-10-8 W McFarland, *al beh, lost tch appr 4 out.*.................................(4 to 1 op 5 to 1)   6
Dist: 5l, 10l, 15l, 20l, ¾l. 4m 50.00s. a 13.00s (6 Ran).
SR: 6/1/-/   (Dr D B A Silk), K C Bailey

464 Lindfield Novices' Chase (5-y-o and up) £1,522 2m 5f.................... (4:10)

CHARLIE JOHNSON (bl) 9-11-3 A Maguire, *led to 4th, led 9th, hrd rdn appr 2 out, drvn out....* (10 to 1 op 8 to 1)   1
404[2] ISLAND FOREST (USA) 7-11-8 G Bradley, *trkd ldrs, chsd wnr frm 5 out, hrd rdn and no imprsn from 2 out.*
.................................(9 to 4 on op 2 to 1 on tchd 5 to 2 on)   2
404[5] CAIRNEYMOUNT 7-11-3 Peter Hobbs, *al prmnt, ev ch 6 out till wknd aftr 4 out.* (9 to 1 op 7 to 1 tchd 10 to 1)   3
19[8] MUTUAL BENEFIT 6-11-3 R Dunwoody, *al beh, tld off frm tenth.*........(11 to 2 op 4 to 1 tchd 6 to 1)   4
TRUE FINESSE 11-10-12 S Earle, *blun badly 1st, led 4th to 9th, lost tch nxt, tld off whn pld up bef 5 out.*
.................................(25 to 1 op 20 to 1)   pu
Dist: 4l, 30l, dist. 5m 19.20s. a 14.20s (5 Ran).
           (Christopher Harris), J White

465 Pease Pottage Novices' Handicap Hurdle (0-100 4-y-o and up) £1,368 2½m.... (4:40)

185[2] SAKIL (Ire) [75] 5-11-1 H Davies, *wtd wth, gd hdwy to chal 3 out, sn led, hit nxt, ran on wl.*
.................................(11 to 8 fav op 6 to 4 tchd 5 to 4)   1
383[2] WEDNESDAYS AUCTION (Ire) [66] 5-10-1 (5') C Burnett-Wells, *trkd ldr, made most frm 8th till hdd sn aftr 3 out, rdn and one pace....* (100 to 30 op 4 to 1 tchd 3 to 1)   2
JARZON DANCER [62] 5-10-2 D Murphy, *chsd ldrs, wkng whn mstk 2 out.*.........(9 to 2 op 5 to 1 tchd 4 to 1)   3
380[2] SINGING DETECTIVE [84] (v) 6-11-7 (7') G Crone, *led, blun badly 7th, hdd nxt, rallied 4 out, rdn and sn wknd.*
.................................(100 to 30 op 2 to 1 tchd 7 to 2)   4
EASTERN EVENING [82] 8-11-8 Mr J Poulton, *al beh, tld off whn pld up bef 2 out.* (40 to 1 op 25 to 1 tchd 50 to 1)   pu
BRUCE BUCKLEY [70] 5-10-10 S Smith Eccles, *al off, tld off whn pld up bef 2 out.*
.................................(16 to 1 op 8 to 1 tchd 20 to 1)   pu
Dist: 8l, 8l, 6l. 4m 58.10s. a 21.10s (6 Ran).
           (Mrs M Devine), S Dow

ROSCOMMON (IRE) (good to firm)
Monday September 13th

466 Lough Ree Maiden Hurdle (6-y-o and up) £2,760 2m...................... (2:30)

362[4] SORRY ABOUT THAT 7-12-0 P Carberry, ... (5 to 4 fav)   1
421[4] SUNSHINES TAXI 6-11-6 B Sheridan, ...(9 to 2)   2
112 JOHNNY SCATTERCASH 11-11-1 (5') C O'Brien, (14 to 1)   3
RATHCORE 6-12-0 C O'Dwyer, ...(5 to 1)   4
161[7] GILT DIMENSION 6-12-0 Mr W P Mullins, ...(4 to 1)   5
363[8] ENNIS SEVEN FIFTY 8-11-11 (3') D Bromley, ... (14 to 1)   6
362[5] NORTHERN BREGA 6-11-6 P L Malone, ...(12 to 1)   7
HIGHLAND MINSTREL 6-11-1 L P Cusack, ...(16 to 1)   8
276 SYLVIA'S SAFFRON 6-11-1 J Collins, ...(14 to 1)   9
255 ROYAL OPTION 6-11-6 T J Taaffe, ...(20 to 1)   10
302 MERRY FRIENDS 7-11-1 A J O'Brien, ...(20 to 1)   pu
Dist: ¾l, 1l, 14l, 5l. 3m 47.20s. (11 Ran).
           (D Mulvihill), Thomas Carberry

467 Ballymurray Handicap Hurdle (0-123 4-y-o and up) £2,760 2m................(3:00)

413[2] NIMBLE WIND [-] (bl) 7-10-11 A J O'Brien, ...(11 to 10 fav)   1

FOR JUSTIN [-] 6-10-12 T Horgan, ... (5 to 1) 2
WESBEST (Ire) [-] 4-9-3 (8") D M McCullagh, ... (5 to 1) 3
313⁵ WINCHLING [-] 8-9-13 N Byrne, ... (3 to 1) 4
330⁷ TULLY BOY [-] 6-9-4 (7") Mr D McCartan, ... (7 to 1) 5
362⁶ DAMHSA (Den) [-] (bl) 4-10-1 (7") C McCormack, . . (12 to 1) 6
Dist: 2l, 1½sl, sht-hd, nk. 3m 55.03s. (6 Ran).

(Mrs D J Tarrant), Francis M O'Brien

468 Pat Fallon Memorial Handicap Chase (0-109 4-y-o and up) £2,760 2½m. . . . (4:30)

332" ANN'S PRINCE [-] 10-10-10 H Rogers, ... (11 to 2) 1
332³ HURRYUP [-] 6-10-9 (5") C O'Brien, ... (8 to 1) 2
332⁵ ROSSBEIGH CREEK [-] 6-11-2 F J Flood, ... (9 to 4 fav) 3
210" BUNNINADDEN [-] 10-10-2 W T Slattery Jnr, ... (7 to 1) 4
364² MALACHYS BAR [-] 9-11-0 F Woods, ... (3 to 1) 5
PINEWOOD LAD [-] 6-11-0 C O'Dwyer, ... (12 to 1) 6
332 BALLYBRIKEN CASTLE [-] 9-9-3 (7") J P Broderick, (14 to 1) 7
250 BOG LEAF VI [-] (bl) 10-9-7 T Horgan, ... (33 to 1) 8
332 MELISSAS PRIDE [-] (bl) 8-10-2 A J O'Brien, ... (25 to 1) 9
132⁸ PORTLAND LAD [-] 8-9-13 (3") T J Mitchell, ... (12 to 1) 10
LADY BYE-BYE [-] 7-11-6 C F Swan, ... (10 to 1) pu
72⁸ BILLMAR [-] 6-9-7 (3") D Bromley, ... (20 to 1) pu
Dist: 4½l, 12l, 8l, 1l 4m 40.50s. (12 Ran).

(Bornard Stack), Gerard Stack

469 Silver Bawn INH Flat Race (4-y-o and up) £2,760 2m. . . . . (6:00)

HOWABOUTTHATNOW 6-12-0 Mr J A Berry, . . (7 to 2 fav) 1
UNRULY YOUTH 8-11-7 (7") Mr J Connolly, ... (12 to 1) 2
DOONAGLERAGH (Ire) 4-10-11 (7") Mr A Daly, ... (20 to 1) 3
JOHNSON 7-11-7 (7") Mr C A Leavy, ... (6 to 1) 4
PLASSY BOY (Ire) 4-11-9 Mr A J Martin, ... (9 to 2) 5
KILLINISKY (Ire) 5-11-7 (7") Mr F Cowman, ... (5 to 1) 6
RAHEEN FLOWER (Ire) 5-11-9 Mr D M O'Brien, . . (12 to 1) 7
PLEASE CALL (Ire) 4-11-2 (7") Mr D J Kavanagh, . (10 to 1) 8
292 MARCHING SEASON (Ire) 5-11-2 (7") Mr S O'Donnell,
. . . . (20 to 1) 9
114⁹ EMPTY VANITY (Ire) 4-11-9 Mr P Fenton, ... (8 to 1) 10
12⁶ RHOMAN FUN (Ire) 4-11-2 (7") Mr M T Harney, . . . (10 to 1) 11
233⁷ RATHCARRICK LASS (Ire) 4-11-4 Mr M McNulty, . (14 to 1) 12
343⁶ GENE OF THE GLEN (Ire) 4-10-11 (7") Mr J P Kilfeather,
. . . . (12 to 1) 13
331⁹ OAK COURT (Ire) 5-11-2 (7") Mr R M Murphy, ... (50 to 1) 14
233 MONGIE (Ire) 4-11-2 (7") Mr D J McAteer, ... (20 to 1) 15
LOCAL SILK (Ire) 4-10-13 (5") Mr J A Nash, ... (9 to 2) 16
AMOROUS HUG (Ire) 4-10-13 (5") Mr J G Kinane, (12 to 1) 17
211⁷ BRIGADIER SUPREME (Ire) 4-11-4 (5") Mr A E Lacy,
. . . . (14 to 1) 18
SAMSMEDAD 7-11-6 (3") Mrs M Mullins, ... (20 to 1) pu
Dist: 1½l, hd, 7l, 3l. 3m 37.80s. (19 Ran).

(Leo Schwyter), P M Berry

ROSCOMMON (IRE) (firm)
Tuesday September 14th

470 Kilsallagh Three Year Old Maiden Hurdle £2,760 2m. . . . . (4:00)

BIZANA (Ire) 11-0 P Carberry, ... (11 to 8 on) 1
375² BENGALI (Ire) 10-7 (7") J M Sullivan, ... (11 to 8) 2
290⁷ CHRISTY MOORE (Ire) 11-0 A Powell, ... (20 to 1) 3
RED MICKS WIFE (Ire) 10-2 (7") F Byrne, ... (14 to 1) 4
290 RUN MY ROSIE (Ire) 10-9 F Woods, ... (25 to 1) 5
TOP DIVER (Ire) 11-0 A J O'Brien, ... (16 to 1) 6
Dist: 2½l, 15l, 15l, 4l. 3m 53.20s. (6 Ran).

(Breffni Syndicate), Noel Meade

471 Emmoo Hurdle (4-y-o and up) £2,760 2m . . . . (4:30)

341" MASAI WARRIOR 6-11-8 J Collins, ... (7 to 2) 1
376" BRAVEFOOT 5-11-3 (3") T J Mitchell, ... (11 to 4 jt-fav) 2
409⁴ ZORIA (Ire) 5-10-13 P Carberry, ... (10 to 1) 3
328³ PAGET 6-11-7 (7") Mr A K Wyse, ... (11 to 4 jt-fav) 4
295" HAYMAKERS JIG (Ire) 5-11-3 K F O'Brien, ... (6 to 1) f
432⁵ HIS WAY (Ire) 4-11-2 (7") J M Sullivan, ... (9 to 2) bd
Dist: 1½l, ¾l, 8l. 4m 11.50s. (6 Ran).

(J C Harley), J C Harley

472 Glinsk Maiden Hurdle (4 & 5-y-o) £2,760 2m. . . . . (5:00)

363 BALLYBROWN FLASH (Ire) 5-11-1 (5") C O'Brien, (12 to 1) 1
409⁷ SLANEY SAUCE (Ire) (bl) 5-11-6 C O'Dwyer, (5 to 1 co-fav) 2
421⁷ THE ROCKING CHAIR (Ire) 5-10-13 (7") P A Roche, (7 to 1) 3
409⁶ COSHLA EXPRESSO (Ire) 5-11-6 W T Slattery Jnr,
. . . . (5 to 1 co-fav) 4
274 BULGADEN CASTLE 5-11-6 P Carberry, . . (5 to 1 co-fav) 5
REASON TO BELIEVE (Ire) 4-10-10 (3") T J Mitchell, (8 to 1) 6
90 LUCKY MINSTREL (Ire) 5-11-1 B Sheridan, ... (7 to 1) 7
FOR SHONA (Ire) 5-11-1 K F O'Brien, ... (7 to 1) 8
DELIGHTFUL CHOICE 5-11-1 A Powell, ... (8 to 1) 9
409⁶ LEATH LA EILE (Ire) 4-10-6 (7") J P Broderick, . (5 to 1 co-
fav) pu

Dist: 8l, 10l, 4l, 5½sl. 3m 51.00s. (10 Ran).

(Mrs A Long), Edward P Mitchell

473 Villiger Handicap Hurdle (0-116 4-y-o and up) £3,278 2½m. . . . . (5:30)

42⁴ MARILYN (Ire) [-] 4-10-11 J P Banahan, ... (5 to 1) 1
275⁶ DANGEROUS REEF (Ire) [-] 5-10-2 (5") T P Rudd, (10 to 1) 2
392⁴ WILL PHONE [-] 7-11-6 (5") Mr D Valentine, . . (5 to 4 fav) 3
275⁵ WHEATSTONE BRIDGE [-] 7-10-12 F Woods, ... (8 to 1) 4
409 MISS FLINTSTONE VI (Ire) [-] 5-9-4 (7") J P Broderick,
. . . . (33 to 1) 5
340" SENSITIVE KING (Ire) [-] 5-11-1 (6ex) J Collins, . . . (2 to 1) f
Dist: ½sl, hd, 15l, dist. 4m 29.40s. (6 Ran).

(Kildare Racing Club), M A O'Toole

474 Kilbegnet Handicap Chase (0-116 4-y-o and up) £2,760 2m. . . . . (6:00)

422⁶ LA MODE LADY [-] 8-9-9 A J O'Brien, ... (10 to 1) 1
303⁴ FRANTESA [-] 7-11-2 T Horgan, ... (9 to 4) 2
377⁶ CHARMING EXCUSE [-] 9-10-8 (5") C P Dunne, . . (8 to 1) 3
303" GONZALO [-] 10-10-12 C F Swan, ... (5 to 4 fav) 4
PROPUNT [-] 8-12-0 C O'Dwyer, ... (10 to 1) 5
177⁶ PALMROCK DONNA [-] 6-9-4 (7") P A Roche, ... (6 to 1) pu
Dist: 6l, ½l, 5½sl, hd. 3m 56.90s. (6 Ran).

(D J Power), Francis M O'Brien

475 County Novice Chase (5 & 6-y-o) £2,760 2m . . . . (6:30)

392" OH SO GRUMPY 5-11-9 C F Swan, ... (5 to 4 on) 1
430² REENKNAPP 6-12-0 T Horgan, ... (2 to 1) 2
MISTRESS GALE 5-10-13 (5") C O'Brien, ... (33 to 1) 3
411⁶ BALLINAVEEN BRIDGE 6-12-0 W T Slattery Jnr, . (20 to 1) 4
WAR OFFICE 6-11-6 (3") J Jones, ... (14 to 1) 5
327⁵ KILLEEN COUNTESS (Ire) 5-11-1 (3") T J Mitchell, (16 to 1) 6
BUGLERS BEST 6-11-2 (7") Mr K Taylor, ... (25 to 1) 7
467⁵ TULLY BOY 6-11-7 (7") Mr D McCartan, ... (7 to 1) pu
Dist: 9l, 13l, 4½sl, ¾l. 3m 59.40s. (8 Ran).

(Mrs E Queally), Mrs John Harrington

476 Roscommon INH Flat Race (4-y-o and up) £2,760 2m. . . . . (7:00)

292" KILADANTE (Ire) 4-11-8 Mr A P O'Brien, ... (7 to 4 on) 1
RHABDOMANCY (Ire) 5-11-6 (7") Mr A Daly, ... (6 to 1) 2
343" KICKALONG 7-11-6 (7") Mr N L Glennon, ... (7 to 1) 3
231⁴ CUBAN QUESTION 6-11-11 (7") Miss J Lewis, ... (8 to 1) 4
SLANEY FOOD 6-11-11 (7") Miss L E A Doyle, ... (8 to 1) 5
Dist: 1½sl, 1l. 4m 3.70s. (5 Ran).

(William Feighery), A P O'Brien

SEDGEFIELD (good)
Tuesday September 14th
Going Correction: PLUS 0.45 sec. per fur.

477 John Wade Hino Truck Selling Handicap Hurdle (4-y-o and up) £1,213 2m 5f 110yds . . . . (2:10)

HUNMANBY GAP [76] 8-10-6 C Hawkins, in tch, hdwy
hfwy, led aftr 7th, hld on wl frm 2 out.
. . . . (9 to 1 op 8 to 1 tchd 10 to 1) 1
289⁶ RED JAM JAR [85] 8-11-1 R Dunwoody, hld up, smooth
hdwy to track wnr 3 out, rdn aftr nxt, no imprsn.
. . . . (5 to 1 op 4 to 1) 2
401² BRIGTINA [70] 5-9-10† (5") R Farrant, ev ch 3 out, kpt on
same pace. . . . . (16 to 1 op 14 to 1) 3
394" STAGS FELL [84] 8-10-7 (7") N Stocks, cl up, led 5th, hdd
nxt, prmnt till wknd appr 2 out.
. . . . (3 to 1 fav op 5 to 2 tchd 100 to 30) 4
316⁶ DOCTOR'S REMEDY [70] 7-10-0 D Morris, in tch, pushed
alng aftr 7th, nvr dngrs. . . . . (16 to 1) 5
STATION EXPRESS (Ire) [75] 5-10-5 A Orkney, beh, some
hdwy aftr 7th, nvr dngrs. . . . . (11 to 2 op 6 to 1) 6
MY TATA [71] (v) 7-10-1† J Corkell, prmnt till wknd appr 3
out. . . . . (50 to 1) 7
264⁶ MASH THE TEA (Ire) [70] (v) 4-10-0 V Smith, cl up, led 6th
till hdd aftr nxt, wknd appr 3 out. . . . . (66 to 1) 8
SPEEDY SIOUX [70] (bl) 4-9-11 (3") A Dobbin, tld off frm
7th. . . . . (9 to 1) 9
311⁴ MISS TIMBER TOPPER [70] 9-10-0 A Maguire, led till hdd
5th, sn wknd, tld off frm 7th. . . . . (16 to 1 op 12 to 1) 10
287² STANE STREET (Ire) [83] 5-10-13 J Railton, prmnt, wkng
whn f 3 out. . . . . f
324⁴ LAPIAFFE [98] 9-11-7 (7") S Taylor, prmnt whn hmpd and
ran out second. . . . . ro
394 BALLY FLAME [70] 7-10-0 B Storey, prmnt early, tld off
whn pld up aftr 7th. . . . . pu
Dist: 4l, 8l, ¾l, 10l, ½l, 6l, 3½sl, dist, 6l. 5m 11.70s. a 20.70s (13 Ran).

(John Wiles), P Beaumont

478 Burmah Petroleum Fuels Handicap Hurdle (0-130 4-y-o and up) £1,847 3m 3f 110yds

· ·**(2:40)**

SCOTTISH GOLD [93] 9-10-5 A Maguire, *made all, hrd rdn
aftr last, all out*. . . . . (9 to 4 op 7 to 4 tchd 5 to 1) 1
GATHERING TIME [112] 7-11-10 B Storey, *trkd ldr, outpcd
aftr 3 out, rallied appr last, styd on wl towards finish*.
· (5 to 4 on op 11 to 8 on) 2
IT'S A PRY [88] 12-10-0 K Johnson, *trkd ldr, slightly
outpcd aftr tenth, rallied to chal after 3 out, wknd
after nxt*. (16 to 1 op 8 to 1) 3
JUSTICE LEA [88] 13-9-7 (7*) Carol Cuthbert, *lost tch appr
7th, tld off*. . . . . (9 to 2 op 7 to 2) 4
Dist: ½l, 4l, dist. 7m 8.00s. (4 Ran).

(Miss L A Perratt), Miss L A Perratt

479 Raisby Quarries Handicap Chase (0-125 4-y-o and up) £2,217 2m 5f. . . . . (3:10)

141* CROSS CANNON [117] 7-11-0 (3*) A Larnach, *trkd ldrs, led
appr 2 out, hdd r-in, styd on unl pres to ld nr finish*.
· · · · · · · · · · · · · · · · (11 to 8 fav op Evens tchd 6 to 4) 1
MILITARY SECRET [100] 7-10-0 K Johnson, *trkd ldrs, effrt
aftr 3 out, jnd wnr betw last 2, slight ld r-in, no extr
und pres towards finish*. . . . . (6 to 1 op 4 to 1) 2
336³ GOOD FOR A LAUGH [128] 9-11-7 (7*) J Burke, *dsptd ld till
led 12th, hdd appr 2 out, sn rdn and btn*.
· (3 to 1 tchd 2 to 1) 3
141⁶ NEWMARKET SAUSAGE [100] 12-10-0 J Callaghan, *made
most till mstk 12th, wknd quickly*. (50 to 1 op 25 to 1) 4
BARKISLAND [101] 9-10-11 R Dunwoody, *al beh, mstk 6th,
lost tch frm 9th*. . . . .(3 to 1 op 5 to 2) 5
Dist: Hd, 12l, 20l, 6l. 5m 31.40s. a 27.40s (5 Ran).

(J A Hellens), J A Hellens

480 Johnny Ridley Memorial Novices' Chase (5-y-o and up) £1,713 2m 1f. . . . . (3:40)

286 WEST WITH THE WIND 6-11-0 T Reed, *trkd ldrs, mstk 8th,
shaken up aftr last, led towards finish*.
· · · · · · · · · · · · · · · · · · ·(9 to 2 op 3 to 1 tchd 5 to 1) 1
282* EXPLOSIVE SPEED (USA) 5-10-12 C Grant, *led till hdd aftr
3 out, led ag'n betw last 2, rdn after last, headed and
no extr towards finish*. . . . . (11 to 8 fav op Evens) 2
318⁶ ABLE PLAYER (USA) 6-10-8¹ (7*) J Burke, *cl up frm 5th,
slight ld aftr 3 out, hdd betw last 2, sn btn*.
· (6 to 4 op 11 to 8) 3
UPWELL 9-11-0 K Johnson, *beh, pushed alng aftr 5th,
lost tch after 8th, tld off*. . . . . (20 to 1 op 16 to 1) 4
366 DIZZY DEALER 6-10-9 D Morris, *in tch till wknd aftr 8th,
tld off*. . . . . (16 to 1 op 14 to 1) 5
Dist: 1l, 7l, dist. 15l. 4m 19.60s. a 14.60s (5 Ran).
SR: 17/14/9/-/-/

(A G Watson), M Dods

481 Federation Brewery L.C.L. Pils Lager Juvenile Novices' Hurdle (3-y-o) £1,150 2m 1f 110yds. . . . . (4:10)

285² ON GOLDEN POND (Ire) 10-4 (3*) N Bentley, *made all,
reminder aftr 3 out, styd on wl frm nxt*.
· (5 to 4 fav op 6 to 4) 1
394² SHARP SENSATION 10-12 C Grant, *trkd ldrs, effrt aftr 3
out, sn chasing wnr, no imprsn*.
· · · · · · · · · · · · · · · · · · · ·(3 to 1 op 9 to 4 tchd 7 to 2) 2
CHALLENGER ROW (Ire) 10-12 D Wilkinson, *with wnr,
pushed alng appr 5th, wknd approaching 2 out*.
· (2 to 1 tchd 9 to 4) 3
272⁵ BRAXTON BRAGG (Ire) 10-7 (5*) D Bentley, *trkd ldrs,
pushed alng appr 3 out, sn wknd, tld off*.
· (10 to 1 op 5 to 1) 4
Dist: 10l, 7l, dist. 4m 18.40s. a 23.40s (4 Ran).

(N B Mason (Farms) Ltd), G M Moore

482 Battle Of Britain Wings Appeal Novices' Hurdle (4-y-o and up) £1,213 2m 5f 110yds . . . .(4:40)

339* STINGRAY CITY (USA) 4-10-12 (7*) F Perratt, *cl up, led appr
7th, styd on wl frm 2 out*.
· · · · · · · · · · · · · · · · · · ·(13 to 8 fav op 7 to 4 tchd 2 to 1) 1
287* RUN MILADY 5-11-2 D Wilkinson, *in tch, effrt appr 3 out,
styd on frm nxt, not rch wnr*. . . . . . (10 to 1 op 8 to 1) 2
45³ FARMER'S CROSS 9-11-0 Mrs A Farrell, *trkd ldrs, jnd wnr
3 out, ev ch till no extr appr last*. . . . . (9 to 4 op 6 to 4) 3
TWIN STATES 4-10-5 (7*) W Fry, *hld up in tch, gd hdway to
join ldrs 3 out, wknd appr last*. . . . .(33 to 1) 4
424³ MASTER BOSTON (Ire) 5-11-0 R Dunwoody, *al prmnt,
pushed alng appr 2 out, rdn whn slpd badly last, not
reco'r*. . . . . (9 to 2 op 4 to 1 tchd 5 to 1) 5
HIGH PENHOWE 5-10-2 (7*) C Woodall, *hld up, effrt appr
3 out, no hdwy*. . . . . (16 to 1 op 14 to 1) 6
138⁷ VAL DE RAMA (Ire) 4-10-7 (5*) P Waggott, *chsd ldrs till
wknd 3 out*. . . . .(25 to 1 op 20 to 1) 7
334⁵ AUNTIE LORNA 4-10-7 C Grant, *al beh*.
· (25 to 1 op 14 to 1) 8
SANDEDGE 6-10-6 (3*) A Thornton, *in tch till wknd 3 out,
tld off*. . . . . (33 to 1 op 20 to 1) 9

CHERYL'S GIRL 7-10-6 (3*) A Larnach, *al beh, tld off*.
· ·(20 to 1) 10
LAFANTA (Ire) 4-10-12 K Jones, *trkd ldrs, pushed alng
appr 3 out, wknd quickly, wl tld off*. . . . . (33 to 1) 11
399 JOVIAL KATE (USA) 6-10-9 A Orkney, *led till hdd appr 7th,
sn wknd, tld off whn pld up bef 2 out*.
· · · · · · · · · · · · · · · · · · · (25 to 1 op 14 to 1 tchd 33 to 1) pu
DERWENT MIST 7-10-9 B Storey, *prmnt till wknd quickly
hfwy, tld off bef 6th*. . . . . (33 to 1) pu
Dist: 2½l, nk, 3l, 12l, 7l, 5l, 1½l, 30l, ½l. 5m 19.60s. a 28.60s (13 Ran).

(Mrs B Lungo), L Lungo

EXETER (good)
Wednesday September 15th
Going Correction: PLUS 0.10 sec. per fur.

483 All Wool Axminster Novices' Hurdle (4-y-o and up) £1,516 2m 3f. . . . . (2:15)

KING UBAD (USA) 4-10-12 A Maguire, *made all, quickened
frm 2 out, eased r-in*. . . (12 to 1 op 8 to 1 tchd 14 to 1) 1
URBAN COWBOY 6-11-0 S McNeill, *hld up in mid-div,
hdwy to go second appr 2 out, rdn, no ch wth wnr*.
· · · · · · · · · · · · · · · · · · (6 to 1 tchd 9 to 2 and 13 to 2) 2
301⁶ CHICKABIDDY 5-10-9 M A FitzGerald, *hld up in mid-div,
hdwy to stay on frm 2 out, nvr nrr*. (66 to 1 op 33 to 1) 3
390³ SOUL TRADER (bl) 4-10-7 S Burrough, *chsd ldrs, rdn appr
2 out, one pace*. . . . . (11 to 1 op 8 to 1 tchd 12 to 1) 4
DRUMCEVA (Ire) 7-11-0 J Railton, *blun second, chsd wnr till
wknd aftr 3 out*. . . . . (7 to 1 op 6 to 1 tchd 15 to 2) 5
PECTORUS (Ire) 5-11-0 R Dunwoody, *chsd ldrs, hdwy to
go second aftr 3 out, rdn and wknd bef nxt*.
· · · · · · · · · · · · · · (7 to 4 on op 6 to 4 on tchd 5 to 4 on) 6
FROZEN DROP 6-11-0 J Frost, *hld up, effrt appr 5th,
wknd approaching last, tld off*.
· · · · · · · · · · · · · · · · · · · (10 to 1 op 6 to 1 tchd 14 to 1) 7
TINKLING STAR 9-11-0 B Powell, *in tch to 4th, sn beh, tld
off*. . . . .(66 to 1 op 33 to 1) 8
DARKTOWN STRUTTER (bl) 7-11-0 Tracy Turner, *prmnt
early, tld off whn pld up bef 3 out*.
· (100 to 1 op 50 to 1) pu
RAHEEN HILL 8-11-0 D Gallagher, *al beh, tld off whn pld up
up bef 6th*. . . . . (50 to 1 op 25 to 1) pu
374 NOT GORDONS 4-10-12 T Wall, *al beh, tld off whn pld up
bef 2 out*. . . . . (66 to 1 op 33 to 1) pu
TAKE CHANCES 5-11-0 P Holley, *al towards rear, beh
whn pld up bef last*. . . . .(25 to 1 tchd 33 to 1) pu
Dist: 14/9/-/-/-/-/ (A J Richards), K O Cunningham-Brown

484 Royal Seaton Claiming Hurdle (4-y-o and up) £1,544 2m 1f 110yds. . . . . (2:45)

ARRAN VIEW 7-10-11 (7*) Mr J L Llewellyn, *trkd ldr, led
aftr 3rd, drw clr appr 2 out, easily*.
· · · · · · · · · · · · · · · · · · (13 to 2 op 9 to 2 tchd 7 to 1) 1
PREENKA GIRL (Fr) 4-11-5 R Dunwoody, *led till hdd aftr
3rd, chsd wnr after, no imprsn frm 2 out*.
· · · · · · · · · · · · · · · · · ·(11 to 8 fav op 2 to 1 tchd 5 to 2) 2
418³ DARING CLASS 7-11-1 I Shoemark, *hld up, hdwy to go
3rd 3 out, one pace frm nxt*. . . . . (7 to 1 op 4 to 1) 3
316² GOLDEN MADJAMBO 7-11-2 R Supple, *hld up, hdwy 5th,
rdn 2 out, kpt on one pace*.
· (5 to 1 op 4 to 1 tchd 11 to 2) 4
418⁴ FASHION PRINCESS 7-10-11 S Burrough, *chsd ldrs till
wknd 4th, sn tld off*. (20 to 1 op 12 to 1 tchd 25 to 1) 5
435⁶ I SUPPOSE 8-10-13 Tracy Turner, *mstks in rear, tld off frm
3rd*. (33 to 1 op 20 to 1) 6
321* WELL DONE RORY 4-11-1 (7*) P McLoughlin, *al rear, tld
off aftr hmpd 5th*. . . . . (5 to 1 op 3 to 1) 7
387⁴ PLAY THE BLUES 6-11-5 J Frost, *prmnt to 3rd, wkng whn
f 5th, broke neck, died*. . .(7 to 1 op 6 to 1 tchd 8 to 1) f
Dist: 10l, 3l, hd, dist, 3l, 30l. 4m 8.60s. a 11.60s (8 Ran).

(B J Llewellyn), B J Llewellyn

485 Tote Novices' Chase (5-y-o and up) £2,390 2m 3f. . . . .(3:15)

417² TITUS ANDRONICUS (bl) 6-11-3 R Supple, *wtd wth, gd
hdwy frm 7th, led tenth, clr 4 out*. (3 to 1 tchd 11 to 4) 1
438* COMIC LINE (bl) 8-11-9 S Burrough, *dsptd ld, wnt ahead
5th, hdd tenth, mstk nxt, on ch frm 4 out*.
· · · · · · · · · · · · · · · · · · · (2 to 1 fav op 7 to 4 tchd 5 to 2) 2
SHARPRIDGE 9-11-3 M Pitman, *in tch, wnt second 7th to
nxt, one pace frm 11th*.
· (12 to 1 op 10 to 1) 3
350⁴ VIRGINIA'S BAY 7-11-3 Mr N Miles, *beh, some hdwy frm 4
out, mstk last*. . . . . (14 to 1 op 10 to 1) 4
438⁴ NEEDS MUST 6-11-3 J Frost, *jmpd badly lft, made most
to 5th, lost tch 9th*. . . . . (7 to 1 op 4 to 1 tchd 8 to 1) 5
307⁸ KEY DEAR (Fr) 6-11-3 T Wall, *jmpd badly in rear, tld off*.
· · · · · · · · · · · · · · · · · · · (10 to 1 op 12 to 1 tchd 14 to 1) 6
Dist: 25l, 10l, 8l, sht-hd, 12l. 4m 45.70s. a 16.70s (6 Ran).

(Julian Belfrage), N A Gaselee

486 Axminster Tamar Novices' Selling Hurdle (3 - 6-y-o) £1,292 2m 1f 110yds...... (3:45)

	OCTOBER BREW (USA) 3-10-5 R Dunwoody, *nvr far away, wndrd lft und pres appr 2 out, led sn aftr, rdn out*...................................(9 to 1 op 6 to 1)	1
418	CORNISH COSSACK (NZ) 6-11-2 (7") Mr G Shenkin, *al prmnt, led appr 4th, rdn and hdd sn aftr 2 out, one pace*...................... (9 to 2 op 7 to 2 tchd 6 to 1)	2
	MATHAL (USA) 4-11-7 A Maguire, *hld up in tch, hdwy 5th, one pace frm 2 out*............... (5 to 2 fav op 4 to 1)	3
227³	DAZZLING FIRE (Ire) 4-11-2 M Richards, *trkd ldr to 3rd, styd in tch, rdn appr 2 out, one pace*........................ (100 to 30 op 4 to 1 tchd 3 to 1)	4
321	FEELING FOOLISH (Ire) 4-11-7 I Shoemark, *hld up in tch, ev ch till wknd appr 2 out*............ (9 to 1 op 8 to 1 tchd 6 to 1 and 10 to 1)	5
406⁵	LADY GAIL 3-10-5 A Webb, *chsd ldrs, no hdwy frm 3 out*............ (9 to 1 op 7 to 1 tchd 10 to 1)	6
352	IRISH DOMINION 3-10-5 N Hawke, *al beh*............ (40 to 1 op 25 to 1 tchd 50 to 1)	7
	VIS-A-VIS 4-11-7 J Osborne, *al beh*... (14 to 1 op 8 to 1)	8
324⁵	HATAAL (Ire) (bl) 4-11-2 T Wall, *pld hrd, led, jmpd slwly 3rd, hdd bef nxt, sn btn*........................ (40 to 1 op 20 to 1 tchd 50 to 1)	9
	LAID BACK BEN 3-10-2 (3") R Greene, *al beh, tld off*.........................(25 to 1 op 20 to 1)	10
	MINT FRESH 6-11-9 S McNeill, *blun 1st, beh whn pld up bef 4th*........(33 to 1 op 25 to 1 tchd 50 to 1)	pu
	SHAMROCK DANCER (Ire) 3-10-0 L Harvey, *beh frm 3rd, tld off whn pld up bef 2 out*....... (20 to 1 op 14 to 1)	pu

Dist: 4l, 2l, 10l, 10l, 4l, 10l, 5l, 5l, 15l. 4m 10.10s. a 13.10s (12 Ran).

(M C Pipe), M C Pipe

487 Axminster From Axminster Handicap Chase (0-125 5-y-o and up) £2,602 2m 1f 110yds..................................... (4:15)

444*	DRUMSTICK [122] 7-11-10 (5ex) N Williamson, *hld up, mstk 7th, hdwy to go second 4 out, led nxt, pushed out, cmftbly*....................(9 to 4 op 11 to 8 tchd 5 to 2)	1
323³	COURT RAPIER [98] 11-10-0 A Maguire, *mstk 1st, made most till hdd 3 out, one pace aftr*..................... (4 to 1 op 6 to 1 tchd 7 to 1)	2
	ARDCRONEY CHIEF [101] 7-10-3 P Holley, *hld up, hdwy 8th, ev ch 4 out, one pace aftr*...................... (5 to 1 op 6 to 1 tchd 8 to 1 and 4 to 1)	3
322²	SOCKS DOWNE [98] 14-10-0 B Powell, *pressed ldr, rdn appr 4 out, wknd nxt*. (17 to 2 op 8 to 1 tchd 14 to 1)	4
	ACRE HILL [126] 9-12-0 M A FitzGerald, *hld up, hdwy 5th, rdn and rallied 4 out, btn whn blun 2 out*..................... (2 to 1 fav op 7 to 4 tchd 5 to 2)	5

Dist: 6l, 5l, 25l, 20l. 4m 13.60s. a 7.60s (5 Ran).

SR: 38/8/6/-/-/ (Sarah Lady Allendale), K C Bailey

488 Torbay Amateur Riders' Handicap Hurdle South-West Racecourses Series - Round 1 (0-125 4-y-o and up) £1,880 2m 1f 110yds .... (4:45)

153²	MOHANA [128] 4-11-7 (7") Mr N Moore, *led till aftr 3rd, led ag'n after nxt, pushed clr frm 2 out, cmftbly*....................(6 to 4 fav op 6 to 4 on)	1
420²	AMPHIGORY [100] (bl) 5-9-7 (7") Miss S Cobden, *hld up, hdwy 5th, kpt on one pace frm 2 out*............ (9 to 1 op 10 to 1 tchd 14 to 1 and 8 to 1)	2
388²	FINAL SOUND [100] (bl) 8-9-13⁶ (7") Mr Richard White, *hld up, hdwy to go second 3 out, rdn nxt, no extr*..................... (5 to 1 op 10 to 1)	3
	REDGRAVE GIRL [104] 11-9-12¹ (7") Mr B Pollock, *hld up in tch, ev ch appr 2 out, wknd, fnshd lme*.......................... (5 to 1 op 6 to 1)	4
30*	HOUSE OF ROSES (Ire) [104] 5-10-1⁴ (7") Miss J Brackenbury, *pld hrd, in tch till one pace frm 2 out*.......................(8 to 1 op 5 to 1)	5
435⁴	OTHET [100] 9-9-7 (7") Mr G Lewis, *in tch till wknd aftr 5th*.............. (14 to 1 op 10 to 1 tchd 16 to 1)	6
439³	PROVERBS GIRL [103] 8-10-3¹⁰ (7") Mr J Thatcher, *al beh, tld off frm 3rd*...............(7 to 4 op 4 to 1)	7
	NO DAW [105] 9-10-5¹² (7") Mr D Sheridan, *prmnt, led aftr 3rd, hdd after nxt, sn wknd, pld up bef last*.......................(33 to 1 op 25 to 1 tchd 50 to 1)	pu

Dist: 7l, 5l, 8l, nk, 10l, 30l. 4m 3.70s. a 6.70s (8 Ran).

SR: 51/16/11/7/6/ (Martin Pipe Racing Club), M C Pipe

DOWNPATRICK (IRE) (good)
Wednesday September 15th

489 S.P. Graham Maiden Hurdle (5-y-o and up) £1,380 2m 1f 172yds............... (4:00)

	ENQELAAB (USA) 8-12-0 J P Banahan,....... (5 to 4 fav)	1
295³	PARSONS EYRE (Ire) 5-10-12 (3") T J Mitchell,..... (5 to 1)	2
208²	WINDOVER LODGE 6-11-6 C F Swan,............. (4 to 1)	3
	LOAVES AND FISHES 5-11-7 (7") K P Gaule,...... (7 to 1)	4

208³	CLYDE PRINCE 8-11-6 J Shortt,................. (12 to 1)	5
256⁵	SALVATION 6-11-6 A Powell,................... (7 to 1)	6
400⁵	DECEMBER BRIDE (Ire) 5-10-12 (3") K B Walsh,.. (16 to 1)	7
341⁶	ROVANIEMI (Ire) 5-11-1 (5") D T Evans,........ (25 to 1)	8
343	SALINA BAY 7-10-8 (7") A Wall,............... (14 to 1)	9
59	SLIM-N-LITE 7-10-12 (3") Mr P McMahon,....... (50 to 1)	10

Dist: 2½l, 2½l, 10l, 8l. (Time not taken) (10 Ran).

(Kildare Racing Club), M A O'Toole

490 S.P. Graham Handicap Hurdle (0-102 4-y-o and up) £1,380 2m 1f 172yds........ (4:30)

74⁶	GREEK CHIME (Ire) [-] 4-11-1 P McWilliams, ... (6 to 4 fav)	1
392⁸	DARCARI ROSE (Ire) [-] 4-10-4 (7") Mr T Martin, ...(10 to 1)	2
340⁴	ALLOON BAWN [-] 7-10-10 C F Swan,...........(10 to 1)	3
341³	FREEWAY HALO (Ire) [-] 4-10-12 F Woods,........ (5 to 2)	4
	FILL MY GLASS [-] 9-11-9 A Powell,.............(8 to 1)	5
	SLAVOMER [-] 8-10-11 (7") Mr F C O'Keeffe,......(6 to 1)	6

Dist: ¾l, 15l, nk, 10l. (Time not taken) (6 Ran).

(Mrs M A O'Toole), M A O'Toole

491 S.P. Graham INH Flat Race (4-y-o and up) £1,380 2m 1f 172yds............... (6:00)

343²	GARYS GIRL 6-11-2 (7") Mr G Finlay,.......... (9 to 2)	1
400⁴	PENNYBRIDGE (Ire) 4-11-9 Mr P F Graffin, ...(7 to 4 on)	2
	AMME ENACK (Ire) 4-10-11 (7") Mr G Kane,......(3 to 1)	3
179⁵	RALPH SQUARE (bl) 5-11-7 (7") Mr T J Beattie,...(13 to 2)	4
343⁷	LITTLE BALLYWOODEN (Ire) 5-11-2 (7") Mr E Magee,...............................(25 to 1)	5
343⁹	BRACKENAIR 6-11-2 (7") Mr J T Bryson,........(33 to 1)	6
81	BELLE DE SEUL 6-11-2 (7") Mr P J McCrickard, .. (20 to 1)	7
	KEEP THEM KEEN (Ire) 5-11-7 (7") Mr L Madine, .. (25 to 1)	8
	HILLHEAD PRINCE (Ire) 5-11-7 (7") Miss V K Ferris, (25 to 1)	pu

Dist: 8l, ¾l, 1½l, dist. (Time not taken) (9 Ran).

(G Finlay), Noel T Chance

492 S.P. Graham Novice Chase (5-y-o and up) £1,380 2¼m........................ (6:30)

291	HAWAIIAN GODDESS (USA) 6-11-9 C O'Dwyer, ...(3 to 1)	1
	MAGIC MILLION 7-12-0 J P Banahan,.......... (2 to 1 on)	2
342	AR AGHAIDH LEATH 7-12-0 F Woods,...........(16 to 1)	3
342⁷	RAGS RAGOUILLE 7-11-9 (5") D T Evans,........(33 to 1)	f
430	CLASSIC CHEER (Ire) (bl) 5-11-9 J Jones,........(8 to 1)	f

Dist: 1½l, dist. (Time not taken) (5 Ran).

(Matthew McGoona), Francis Ennis

DUNDALK (IRE) (good to firm (race 1), good (2,3,4))
Thursday September 16th

493 Cooley Handicap Hurdle (0-116 4-y-o and up) £2,243 2m 135yds............. (2:30)

392	MABES TOWN (Ire) [-] (bl) 5-10-7 N Byrne,....... (12 to 1)	1
295⁵	FORTUNE'S GIRL [-] 5-10-12 J Shortt,............(5 to 2)	2
103	BELLECARA [-] 6-9-13 (3") D Bromley,...........(12 to 1)	3
63⁶	KHAZARI (USA) [-] (bl) 5-11-5 C O'Dwyer,........(8 to 1)	4
231²	JUST BLUSH [-] 6-10-12 H Rogers,...............(6 to 1)	5
490⁶	SLAVOMER [-] 8-10-1 (7") P Stafford,............(20 to 1)	6
275⁵	BALLINDERRY GLEN [-] 7-10-6 (5") M G Cleary,... (11 to 2)	7
131⁶	FLYING SOUTH (Ire) [-] 5-11-5 P Carberry,......(7 to 4 fav)	pu

Dist: 2l, 12l, 9l, hd. 3m 54.30s. (8 Ran).

(Mrs L Skelly), Laurence Skelly

494 Heinz Custom Foods Maiden Hurdle (3-y-o) £2,768 2m 135yds............. (3:00)

470²	BENGALI (Ire) 10-10 C F Swan,................. (Evens fav)	1
	TOUCHING MOMENT (Ire) 10-5 (5") T P Rudd,....(7 to 2)	2
375⁴	DRESS DANCE (Ire) 10-10 J P Banahan,......... (15 to 2)	3
	ARAN EXILE (bl) 10-5 P Carberry,...............(7 to 2)	4
	RUNNING SLIPPER (Ire) 10-5 (5") M G Cleary, ... (20 to 1)	5
	SISTER CARMEL (Ire) 10-5 C O'Dwyer,...........(8 to 1)	6

Dist: Sht-hd, 8l, 15l. 3m 56.70s. (6 Ran).

(Peter Hill), Kevin Prendergast

495 Rostrevor Pro-Am Flat Race (4-y-o and up) £2,243 2m 135yds................... (5:00)

	GOLDEN CLAW 6-11-9 (5") Mr H F Cleary, ...(9 to 2)	1
277³	BLOW IT (Ire) 5-11-9 (5") Mr J A Nash,.........(5 to 4 on)	2
258⁴	HAUGHTON LAD (Ire) 4-11-2 (7") Mr D Groome, ... (10 to 1)	3
39⁸	JOKERS THREE (Ire) 4-11-2 (7") Mr A F Doherty, ... (7 to 2)	4
	CURRAGH ROSE 6-11-2 (7") J Butler,............(16 to 1)	5
105⁵	LORD GREYSTONES 6-11-9 (5") Mr D Valentine, ... (12 to 1)	6
400⁷	SONIC EXPERIENCE (Ire) 5-11-2 (7") Mr R Lawler,... (25 to 1)	7
	LADY HOSTESS (Ire) 4-10-11 (7") Mr P J Kelly, ... (12 to 1)	8
	QUEENSEAL (Ire) 4-10-11 (7") Mr E Gibney,......(20 to 1)	9
	GARWELL (Ire) 7-11-2 (7") Mr D J Geraghty,......(16 to 1)	pu

Dist: 3l, 7l, 6l, 6l. 3m 53.10s. (10 Ran).

(Castle Syndicate), F Flood

496 Newry Novice Chase (5-y-o and up) £2,243 2m 1f........................... (5:30)

VISIBLE DIFFERENCE 7-12-0 C F Swan, ... (5 to 2)	1
412³ RANDOM PRINCE 9-12-0 C O'Dwyer, ... (11 to 10 fav)	2
200⁶ INCA CHIEF 9-12-0 T J Taaffe, ... (3 to 1)	3
377⁵ TORENAGA HILL 9-11-2 (7⁰) Mr A Daly, ... (16 to 1)	4
254 GRILLADIN (Fr) 9-12-0 J Shortt, ... (16 to 1)	5

Dist: 1l, 3½l, 1l, dist. 4m 28.70s. (5 Ran).

(Patrick Heffernan), Patrick Heffernan

HUNTINGDON (good to firm (races 1,3,6), good (2,4,5))
Friday September 17th
Going Correction: MINUS 0.10 sec. per fur.

497 Upwood Novices' Selling Hurdle (3-y-o) £1,480 2m 110yds. . . . . (2:20)

SOUTHAMPTON 10-12 J Railton, *beh, sstnd hdwy frm o'r 3 out, led r-in, ran on wl.* . . . . (14 to 1 op 8 to 1 tchd 16 to 1)	1
MY SISTER LUCY 10-7 T Jarvis, *al prmnt, ev ch last, ran on.* . . . . (25 to 1 op 20 to 1 tchd 33 to 1)	2
320⁴ KISS IN THE DARK 10-7 P Niven, *not fluent, trkd ldrs, led and jmpd lft 2 out, hit last and rdr lost irons, sn hdd, ran on, fnshd 3rd, plcd 4th.* . . . . (13 to 2 op 5 to 1 tchd 7 to 1)	3D
180² LADY OF SHADOWS 10-2 (5⁰) A Dicken, *chsd ldrs, ev ch whn hmpd appr last, one pace, fnshd 4th, plcd 3rd.* . . . . (13 to 2 op 9 to 2 tchd 10 to 1)	3
321² DOCTOR-J (Ire) 10-12 S Keightley, *al prmnt, led 5th to 6th, one pace.* . . . . (20 to 1 op 16 to 1)	5
193⁵ SOLAR KNIGHT 10-7 W Humphreys, *beh, hdwy 5th, one pace frm 2 out.* . . . . (33 to 1 op 20 to 1)	6
448² NOMADIC FIRE (bl) 10-12 A Maguire, *strted slwly, hdwy 4th, led 3 out, sn hdd, mstk 2 out and wknd.* . . . . (5 to 2 fav op 3 to 1)	7
272² GRANDERISE (Ire) 10-12 G McCourt, *beh, hrd rdn 3 out, kpt on und pres r-in.* . . . . (9 to 2 op 4 to 1 tchd 5 to 1)	8
453⁶ GLEAM OF GOLD 10-4 (3⁰) D Meredith, *trkd ldrs till wknd appr 2 out.* . . . . (20 to 1)	9
486⁶ LADY GAIL 11-0 A Webb, *mid-div, effrt and struggling whn mstk 3 out, no imprsn.* . . . . (20 to 1 op 14 to 1 tchd 25 to 1)	10
MISTER BLAKE 10-12 R Campbell, *al beh.* . . . . (8 to 1 op 14 to 1)	11
356³ CASHABLE 11-5 S Smith Eccles, *led to 5th, cl up, ev ch o'r 2 out, wknd quickly.* . . . . (16 to 1 op 12 to 1)	12
406 GOLDEN TARGET (USA) 10-7 D Bridgwater, *beh, hdwy o'r 3 out, wknd und pres over 2 out.* . . . . (14 to 1 op 25 to 1 tchd 33 to 1)	13
OLICANA (Ire) 10-12 C Grant, *pld hrd in mid-div, jmpd slwly 4th and lost pl, no dngr aftr.* . . . . (8 to 1 op 6 to 1 tchd 10 to 1)	14
349⁴ ARE YOU HAPPY (Ire) 10-7 R Supple, *al beh, tld off.* . . . . (14 to 1 op 10 to 1)	15

Dist: 2l, ½l, ¾l, 1½l, hd, 1l, sht-hd, ½l, 20l, 2½l. 4m 1.40s. a 14.40s (15 Ran).

(G B Balding), G B Balding

498 Tote/Racing Post Ten To Follow Novices' Chase (5-y-o and up) £2,196 2m 110yds . . . . (2:50)

480³ ABLE PLAYER 6-10-7 (7⁰) J Burke, *in cl tch, pckd 4th, led r-in, rdn out.* . . . . (5 to 4 on op 6 to 4 on tchd Evens)	1
BUSTINELLO (Ire) 5-10-12 A Maguire, *in cl tch, mstks 5th and 7th (water), led and hit last, sn hdd, ran on.* . . . . (5 to 4 op 6 to 4 tchd Evens)	2
407⁵ MIDDAY SHOW (USA) 6-11-0 S Smith Eccles, *led, pckd 4th, hdd and wknd appr last, eased.* . . . . . . (9 to 1 op 6 to 1)	3

Dist: Hd, 20l. 4m 9.90s. a 11.90s (3 Ran).

(Miss K S Bramall), Mrs S A Bramall

499 Goodliff Handicap Hurdle (0-115 4-y-o and up) £2,127 2m 110yds. . . . . (3:20)

280² KING WILLIAM [107] 8-11-1 A Maguire, *hld up towards rear, cld 5th, ran on und pres to ld post.* . . . . (4 to 1 op 7 to 2)	1
318² SRIVIJAYA [116] 6-11-10 P Niven, *prmnt, took keen hold, led 3 out, rdn alng r-in, ct post.* . . . . (5 to 1 op 4 to 1 tchd 6 to 1)	2
DENNINGTON (Ire) [92] 5-9-7 (7⁰) P Murphy, *chsd clr ldr to o'r 4 out, cl up, ev ch 2 out, one pace appr last.* . . . . (14 to 1 op 10 to 1)	3
HATS HIGH [94] (bl) 6-10-2² M Crosse, *hld up, rdn and hdwy 3 out, mstk nxt, one pace und pres.* . . . . (33 to 1 op 20 to 1)	4
388³ JUST ROSIE [98] 4-10-6 S McNeill, *trkd ldrs, wnt second appr 4 out, ev ch 2 out, wknd approaching last.* . . . . (4 to 1 op 7 to 2 tchd 9 to 2)	5
384³ LUSTY LAD [110] 8-11-4 R Marley, *chsd ldrs, hdwy and ev ch 3 out, wknd appr nxt.* . . . . . (9 to 4 fav op 2 to 1)	6
WINDWARD ARIOM [102] 7-10-10 R Marley, *mid-div, rdn alng and no hdwy frm 3 out.* . . . . . . (14 to 1 op 20 to 1)	7

HALLO MAM (Ire) [92] 4-10-0 M Brennan, *hld up beh, cld to track ldrs 5th, outpcd frm o'r 2 out.* (12 to 1 op 7 to 1)	8
FAILAND [92] 6-10-0 D Bridgwater, *hld up, effrt o'r 3 out, no imprsn.* . . . . (10 to 1 op 25 to 1)	9
CASTLERICHARDKING [92] 8-10-0 W Humphreys, *rcd freely, led, clr 4th, hdd and wknd aftr nxt.* . . . (33 to 1)	10
SILENT CHANT [94] 9-10-2¹ R Dunwoody, *chsd ldrs, wkng whn mstk 4th, sn tld off.* . . . . (20 to 1 tchd 25 to 1)	11

Dist: Sht-hd, 4l, 2½l, ½l, 10l, ½l, 1½l, 15l, 2½l, dist. 3m 56.20s. a 9.20s (11 Ran).

(Group 1 Racing (1991) Ltd), J L Spearing

500 Old Fletton Claiming Chase (5-y-o and up) £2,427 2m 110yds. . . . . (3:55)

279⁰ FASTBIT 6-11-8 N Williamson, *hld up in rear, hdwy 3 out, led last, rdn clr, easily.* . . . . (5 to 2 op 7 to 4)	1
VULRORY'S CLOWN 15-10-10 M Brennan, *led second to 5th, ev ch appr last, kpt on r-in.* . . . (14 to 1 op 10 to 1)	2
366² MAGIC SOLDIER 8-11-10 R Marley, *cl up, led 5th till hdd appr last, edgd rght und pres, one pace.* . . . . (16 to 1 op 10 to 1)	3
AL HASHIMI 9-11-8 R Dunwoody, *trkd ldrs, hrd rdn aftr 2 out, one paced.* . . . . (6 to 4 fav op 2 to 1)	4
385 TINAS LAD 10-11-8 A Maguire, *cl up, ev ch 3 out, mstk nxt, wknd.* . . . . (5 to 1 op 9 to 4 tchd 11 to 2)	5
374 POLDER 7-10-13 (5⁰) R Davis, *trkd ldrs till outpcd frm 3 out.* . . . . (16 to 1 op 10 to 1)	6
338³ DULZURA 5-10-7 T Jarvis, *not fluent, hld up, outpcd frm o'r 4 out, tld off.* . . . . (16 to 1 op 14 to 1 tchd 20 to 1)	7
245⁴ BILL AND COUP 8-10-6 A S Smith, *al beh, tld off.* . . . . (12 to 1 op 10 to 1)	8
444 SHARP ORDER 8-11-0 Pat Caldwell, *al beh, mstk 5th, tld off.* . . . . (25 to 1 op 20 to 1 tchd 33 to 1)	9
428⁴ AFRICAN SAFARI 9-11-0 J Callaghan, *nvr gng wl, pushed alng and lost tch aftr 4th, tld off.* . . . . (25 to 1 op 16 to 1 tchd 33 to 1)	10

Dist: 8l, ¾l, 1½l, 8l, nk, 20l, 15l, 8l, dist. 4m 2.60s. a 4.60s (10 Ran).

SR: 32/12/25/21/13/8/ (Leeds Plywood And Doors Ltd), K C Bailey

501 Holbeach Handicap Chase (0-115 5-y-o and up) £2,635 3m. . . . . (4:25)

458² LOCAL CUSTOMER [95] 8-10-2 W Humphreys, *in cl tch, al gng wl, led 4 out, ran on well.* . . . . (5 to 2 op 3 to 1 tchd 7 to 2)	1
419⁰ MISTER FEATHERS [99] 12-10-6 (8ex) J R Kavanagh, *hld up in cl tch, mstks tenth and 12th, led 14th till hdd 4 out, ev ch 2 out, one pace.* . . . . (3 to 1 tchd 7 to 2)	2
GLEBE PRINCE [93] 13-9-7 (7⁰) L Dace, *cl up, led aftr 12th till hdd 14th, lost tch nxt, tld off.* (25 to 1 op 20 to 1)	3
SOUTHERLY BUSTER [115] 10-11-8 J Osborne, *jmpd wl in main, made most till hdd aftr 12th, second whn f nxt.* . . . . (7 to 4 fav tchd 2 to 1 and 9 to 4)	f
ASSAGLAWI [121] 11-12-0 R Dunwoody, *cl up whn pld up aftr 4th.* . . . . (7 to 2 op 2 to 1)	pu

Dist: 7l, dist. 5m 58.20s. a 10.20s (5 Ran).

(Paul Bradley), P Bradley

502 Spalding Novices' Hurdle (4-y-o and up) £1,480 2m 5f 110yds. . . . . (5:00)

415⁰ EID (USA) 4-10-9 (3⁰) W Marston, *pld hrd, led to 4th, led ag'n 3 out, clr appr nxt, eased r-in.* . . . . (4 to 4 fav tchd 7 to 4 op 11 to 8)	1
WHISTLING BUCK (Ire) 5-11-0 H Davies, *beh, hdwy o'r 4 out, wnt second over 2 out, no imprsn on wnr.* . . . . (7 to 2 op 5 to 1)	2
PERSIAN SOLDIER 6-11-0 P Niven, *cl up, led 4th till hdd 3 out, sn outpcd.* . . . . (9 to 2 op 2 to 1)	3
THE MAN FROM CLARE (Ire) 5-11-0 T Jarvis, *hld up beh ldrs, outpcd frm 4 out.* . . . . (5 to 1 op 16 to 1)	4
268⁰ SARANNPOUR (Ire) 4-10-12 G McCourt, *hld up in rear, reminders 4th, al beh.* . . . . (7 to 2 op 5 to 1)	5
145 ASSEMBLY DANCER 6-10-9 (5⁰) R Davis, *hld up towards rear, nvr plcd to chal.* . . . . (50 to 1 op 20 to 1)	6
402⁷ ROCKY ROMANCE 6-11-0 D Morris, *trkd ldrs till wknd aftr 5th, tld off.* . . . . (50 to 1 op 20 to 1)	7
346⁷ SALLY SOHAM (Ire) 5-10-2 (7⁰) P Murphy, *trkd ldrs till drpd rear 6th, tld off.* . . . (25 to 1 op 16 to 1 tchd 33 to 1)	8
415³ BARE HIGHLANDER 7-11-0 R Dunwoody, *trkd ldrs till drpd rear 6th, tld off.* . . . (16 to 1 op 6 to 1 tchd 20 to 1)	9
BOULEY BAY 5-11-0 L Harvey, *sn rdn alng in rear, tld off whn refused 2 out.* . . . . (50 to 1 op 20 to 1)	ref
310⁶ SKY VENTURE (bl) 9-11-0 S Earle, *al beh, reminders 5th, tld off whn pld up bef 2 out.* . . . . (33 to 1)	pu
429⁵ JOTO 6-11-0 S Smith Eccles, *chsd ldrs to o'r 4 out, wknd quickly, pld up lme bef nxt.* . . . . (9 to 2 op 4 to 1 tchd 5 to 1)	pu

Dist: 6l, 5l, 15l, 3l, 6l, dist, 12l, 20l, 6l. 5m 6.00s. a 15.00s (12 Ran).

(Ladyswood Racing Club), Martyn Meade

KILBEGGAN (IRE) (good to firm)
Friday September 17th

59

NATIONAL HUNT RESULTS 1993-94

503 Tullamore Claiming Maiden Hurdle (4-y-o and up) £2,243 2m 3f.............. (4:00)

234² KAITLIN (Ire) 4-10-2 P L Malone, ... (11 to 10 fav)	1
99³ CLONALEENAN 4-10-5 B Sheridan, ... (6 to 1)	2
174⁹ TOP GENERATION 4-10-6 J P Banahan, ... (5 to 1)	3
340³ SHREWD MOVE (bl) 4-10-5 J Jones, ...(5 to 1)	4
274 LADY DIGA (Ire) 5-10-2⁴ (7") Mr S O'Callaghan, .. (16 to 1)	5
212⁷ SILENTBROOK 8-10-5 Mr P J Healy, ... (10 to 1)	6
343⁸ PARSONS TOI 8-10-5 D H O'Connor, ...(12 to 1)	7
393⁶ WEDDING DREAM (Ire) 4-10-0 (5") D T Evans, ... (20 to 1)	8
265⁶ KIARA DEE 7-10-4 (7") J P Deegan, ...(16 to 1)	9
CONNIE FOLEY 7-11-0 J F Titley, ... (16 to 1)	10
157 BRIGHT IDEA (Ire) 4-10-5 M Flynn, ... (25 to 1)	11

Dist: Sht-hd, 2l, 12l, sht-hd. 4m 32.00s. (11 Ran).

(J Crowley), M J Grassick

504 Stan Moran Memorial Maiden Hurdle (4-y-o) £2,760 2m 3f.............. (4:30)

365³ DERRYMOYLE (Ire) 11-9 C F Swan, ... (2 to 1 on)	1
314⁴ MISTER DRUM (Ire) 11-2 (7") Mr J T McNamara, .. (7 to 2)	2
431⁷ NOT MY LINE (Ire) 10-13 (5") C O'Brien, ...(14 to 1)	3
362⁹ KNOCNAGORE (Ire) 11-4 M Flynn, ...(14 to 1)	4
431 OUT THE DOOR (Ire) 10-11 (7") Mr K Whelan, ...(25 to 1)	5
MOOHONO (Ire) 10-13 B Sheridan, ...(8 to 1)	6
ORTHORHOMBUS 11-2 (7") P A Roche, ...(10 to 1)	7
292⁸ NOELEENS DELIGHT (Ire) 10-13 J P Banahan, ... (16 to 1)	8

Dist: ¾l, 9l, 2l, 13l. 4m 31.90s. (8 Ran).

(Herb M Stanley), Michael Cunningham

505 Tara Meats Maiden Hurdle (5-y-o and up) £2,760 2m 3f....................(5:00)

400² BARRAD DIEU (Ire) 5-12-0 C F Swan, ...(6 to 4 jt-fav)	1
378⁷ MOUNTHENRY STAR (Ire) 5-12-0 G M O'Neill, (6 to 4 jt-fav)	2
160⁶ OXFORD QUILL 6-12-0 T J Taaffe, ...(3 to 1)	3
363⁷ STRONG ROSE (bl) 6-10-10 (5") C O'Brien, ...(25 to 1)	4
433⁶ MOON-FROG 6-11-1 (5") D P Murphy, ...(25 to 1)	5
275⁷ KOI CORP 9-10-8 (7") J P Deegan, ...(25 to 1)	6

Dist: 1½l, 1½l, 5l, 14l. 4m 31.70s. (6 Ran).

(Seamus Maccrosain), Michael Cunningham

506 Pat Doyle Memorial Handicap Hurdle (0-116 4-y-o and up) £2,243 2m 3f.... (5:30)

410⁵ MERRY PEOPLE (Ire) [-] 5-11-2 T Horgan, ...(5 to 2)	1
213⁵ SILVER GIPSEY [-] 7-11-9 P L Malone, ... (9 to 4 fav)	2
430⁴ SCREEN PRINTER (Ire) [-] (bl) 4-9-13 (7") J P Broderick, ...(12 to 1)	3
230⁸ PALACE GEM [-] (bl) 6-11-9 (5") Mr P J Casey, .. (10 to 1)	4
430 BALLYHEIGUE [-] 7-11-0 (7") Mr J T McNamara, .. (8 to 1)	5
410⁶ COQ HARDI SMOKEY (Ire) [-] 5-11-9 P Carberry, .. (9 to 2)	6
392 UPPINGHAM [-] 7-11-10 C F Swan, ... (6 to 1)	pu

Dist: 2½l, 4½l, ½l, 2l. 4m 26.20s. (8 Ran).

(Karl Casey), John Queally

507 Bank Of Ireland Novice Chase (5-y-o and up) £2,760 2m 5f.................(6:00)

411⁸ HURRICANE TOMMY (bl) 6-11-9 T J Taaffe, ... (10 to 1)	1
KNOW HOW 7-11-9 P M Verling, ...(20 to 1)	2
430⁶ FAIRY PARK (bl) 8-11-9 F Woods, ...(6 to 1)	3
293⁵ DOCTER MAC 6-11-4 (5") C O'Brien, ...(10 to 1)	4
430³ JOHNJOES PRIDE 9-12-0 C F Swan, ...(9 to 2)	5
430⁷ COUMEENOOLE LADY 6-11-2 (7") J M Donnelly, .. (10 to 1)	6
432³ BROOK COTTAGE (Ire) 5-11-8 K F O'Brien, ...(4 to 1)	7
YVONNES PRINCESS 6-11-4 T Horgan, ...(3 to 1 fav)	8
430 BROTHER HUGH 8-11-2 (7") P A Roche, ...(33 to 1)	9
177⁵ KIL KIL CASTLE 6-11-4 (5") T J O'Sullivan, ...(12 to 1)	10
92⁹ TINKERS CORNER 8-11-9 H Rogers, ...(33 to 1)	11
327⁸ WOODEN MINSTREL 7-10-13 (5") D T Evans, ...(33 to 1)	f
411³ KALONA 6-11-9 A Powell, ...(7 to 1)	f

Dist: 8l, ¾l, 4½l, 4½l. 5m 17.90s. (13 Ran).

(Seamus Maccrosain), Michael Cunningham

508 Innkeepers INH Flat Race (4-y-o and up) £2,760 2m 3f.....................(6:30)

276 QUARTER MARKER (Ire) 5-11-7 (7") Mr P English, (10 to 1)	1
COURT MASTER (Ire) 5-11-7 (7") Mr B Moran, ...(7 to 1)	2
295⁶ POLLY PLUM (Ire) 5-11-6 (3") Mr A R Coonan, ...(4 to 1)	3
BIT OF A FUSS 6-11-9 (5") Mrs J M Mullins, ...(8 to 1)	4
469⁸ PLEASE CALL (Ire) 4-11-2 (7") Mr D J Kavanagh, .. (10 to 1)	5
GOODLUCKTOYA (Ire) 4-10-11 (7") Mr J M O'Brien, ...(10 to 1)	6
FORTFIELD GUY 8-11-7 (7") Mr P J Kennedy, ...(16 to 1)	7
MINUS TWO (Ire) 5-11-6 (3") Miss M Olivefalk, ...(12 to 1)	8
ROSEMARY MAC (Ire) 4-10-11 (7") Mr F McGirr, .. (Evens fav)	bd
277 CROGHAN MIST (Ire) 5-11-2 (7") Miss L E A Doyle, (33 to 1)	su
393 TAITS CLOCK (Ire) 4-11-4 (5") Mr G J Harford, ... (8 to 1)	su

Dist: 9l, 1l, 14l, 4½l. 4m 25.60s. (11 Ran).

(Mrs M Balding), Thomas Foley

509 Bridge House Handicap Chase (4-y-o and up) £2,760 2m 5f.................(7:00)

468⁴ ANN'S PRINCE [-] 10-10-10 H Rogers, ...(6 to 4 fav)	1
422⁸ SKY RANGE [-] 8-11-13 T Horgan, ...(9 to 2)	2
116 INCH MAID [-] 7-11-1 C F Swan, ...(3 to 1)	3
332⁴ JAMES PIGG [-] 6-11-3 P McWilliams, ...(7 to 2)	4
CAPTAIN LYNDSEY [-] 12-9-13 N Byrne, ...(25 to 1)	5

Dist: 4½l, 15l, 20l, ½l. 5m 14.90s. (5 Ran).

(Bernard Stack), Gerard Stack

DOWN ROYAL (IRE) (good to firm (race 1), good (2,3,4)) Saturday September 18th

510 James Nicholson Oxford Landing Wine Maiden Hurdle (5-y-o and up) £1,380 2½m ....(2:30)

409⁵ JUNGLE STAR (Ire) 5-11-6 M Flynn, ...(7 to 2)	1
59⁷ BARRYMORE BOY (bl) 6-11-6 C F Swan, ...(5 to 2)	2
489 SLIM-N-LITE 7-10-12 (3") Mr P McMahon, ...(20 to 1)	3
231⁸ THEKINDWORD VI (bl) 8-11-6 J P Banahan, ...(20 to 1)	4
231⁵ LE GERARD 8-11-6 C O'Dwyer, ...(7 to 4 fav)	5
173 KAMTARA 7-10-13 (7") Mr K Ross, ...(12 to 1)	6
341 BO MULLEN (Ire) 5-10-12 (3") D Bromley, ...(20 to 1)	7

Dist: 7l, 4½l, 2l, 7l. (Time not taken) (7 Ran).

(John Weafer), M V Manning

511 Brown Thomas E.B.F. Mares Novice Chase (5-y-o and up) £2,415 2½m... (3:30)

11⁹ MOUNTAIN BLOOM (Ire) (bl) 5-11-8 J F Titley, ...(11 to 2)	1
TITIAN BLONDE (Ire) 5-11-8 C F Swan, ...(6 to 4 on)	2
175 AMID BIRDS OF PREY 6-12-0 C O'Dwyer, ...(6 to 1)	3
342⁴ SUNSHINE SEAL 6-11-7 (7") A Wall, ...(8 to 1)	4
256 SKIN GRAFT (bl) 7-12-0 H Rogers, ...(20 to 1)	5
NORDIC BLUE (Ire) 5-11-5 (3") T J Mitchell, ...(14 to 1)	6

Dist: Dist, dist, 15l, ½l. (Time not taken) (6 Ran).

(Miss G Maher), M J P O'Brien

512 James Nicholson Macallen The Malt Opportunity Handicap Chase (0-102 5-y-o and up) £1,380 2½m....................(4:30)

342¹ GREEK MAGIC [-] 6-11-3 (6ex) T J Mitchell, ...(2 to 1 on)	1
178⁹ BENS DILEMMA [-] 8-9-12 (4") J P Broderick, ...(8 to 1)	2
250⁶ GRANVILLE GRILL [-] 8-10-11 (2") C O'Brien, ...(11 to 4)	3
364⁸ HO FRETTA [-] 7-10-3 (2") T P Rudd, ...(20 to 1)	4
MID-DAY GAMBLE [-] 9-11-10 (2") L Flynn, ...(7 to 1)	5
332⁶ WHO'S FOOLING WHO [-] (bl) 7-11-0 (2") M G Cleary, ...(7 to 2)	6
CARTOON TIME (Fr) [-] 9-9-12¹ (3") D P Geoghegan, ...(20 to 1)	pu

Dist: Hd, 3½l, 5l, 5l. (Time not taken) (7 Ran).

(Mrs Vera O'Brien), Peter McCreery

513 James Nicholson Piper Heidsieck Champagne INH Flat Race (4 & 5-y-o) £1,380 2m ....(5:00)

400⁶ LANDENSTOWN (Ire) 5-11-7 (7") Mr A Merrigan, (10 to 1)	1
495³ HAUGHTON LAD (Ire) 4-11-2 (7") Mr D Groome, ...(4 to 1)	2
160 BRAE (Ire) 5-11-9 Mr A J Martin, ...(5 to 1)	3
FOULKSCOURT DUKE (Ire) 5-12-0 Mr P Fenton, .. (3 to 1)	4
378³ MAKES YOU WONDER (Ire) 5-12-0 Mr P F Graffin, ...(6 to 4 fav)	5
489⁷ DECEMBER BRIDE (Ire) 5-11-4 (5") Mr B R Hamilton, ...(12 to 1)	6
HIDDEN PLAY (Ire) 5-11-4 Mr J Patton, ...(10 to 1)	7
233 HIGHLAND BREEZE 4-11-2 (7") Mr J Bright, ...(20 to 1)	8

Dist: Hd, 1½l, 3½l, 4l. (Time not taken) (8 Ran).

(J Weld), J Weld

MARKET RASEN (good) Saturday September 18th
Going Correction: PLUS 0.45 sec. per fur.

514 EIC Selling Handicap Hurdle (3 & 4-y-o) £1,618 2m 1f 110yds...............(2:15)

460⁴ CYRILL HENRY (Ire) [73] 4-11-6 A Merrigan, hld up, smooth hdwy 3 out, led nxt, rdn r-in, all out. ....(3 to 1 fav op 5 to 2)	1
456⁶ SIR PAGEANT [81] 4-11-9 (5") D Leahy, set steady pace, quickened 3 out, hdd nxt, rdn last, rallied wl flt. ....(9 to 2 op 4 to 1)	2
368⁴ ALIZARI (USA) [55] (bl) 4-10-2 M Robinson, cl up, mstk 3rd, hit 5th and lost pl, sn rdn, styd on appr last. ....(16 to 1 op 20 to 1)	3
448³ SUMMER FLOWER [68] 3-10-10 (5") T Eley, hld up, effrt and hdwy 3 out, rdn nxt, one pace last. ....(7 to 2 op 3 to 1 tchd 4 to 1)	4
349³ SUMMERS DREAM [60] 3-10-7 D Byrne, trkd ldrs, rdn alng aftr 3 out, one pace nxt......(5 to 1 tchd 11 to 2)	5
447³ BARTON PRIDE (Ire) [62] (bl) 4-10-9 C Grant, chsd ldr, rdn 3 out, sn wknd. ....(4 to 1)	6

60

Dist: Nk, 3½l, ¾l, 4l, 12l. 4m 21.10s. a 19.10s (6 Ran).

(Mrs Jill Winkworth), P Winkworth

515 Associated British Ports Handicap Chase (0-120 4-y-o and up) £3,586 2m 1f 110yds ....(2:45)

309* MEGA BLUE [115] 8-11-7 P Niven, *led second to 3rd, hit 8th, led and hit 3 out, rdn clr.*
................(9 to 4 on op 5 to 2 on tchd 2 to 1 on) 1
EMSEE-H [127] 8-11-7 (7*) B Murphy, *led to second, led 3rd till hdd and hit 3 out, sn wknd....*(7 to 4 tchd 15 to 8) 2
Won by 12l. 4m 36.40s. a 22.40s (2 Ran).

SR: -/-/

(Tony Yates), Mrs V A Aconley

516 Exxtor Group Juvenile Novices' Hurdle (3-y-o) £2,372 2m 1f 110yds ....(3:15)

448* LEGAL ARTIST (Ire) 11-4 D Murphy, *trkd ldrs, smooth hdwy 3 out, led appr nxt, clr whn hit last, ran on.*
....(4 to 1 op 7 to 2) 1
MISTROY 10-7 C Grant, *al in tch, hdwy 3 out, rdn to chase wnr 2 out, hit last, kpt on flt.* (7 to 1 op 9 to 2) 2
CARELESS FARMER 10-7 C Llewellyn, *jmpd badly lft 1st and beh, hdwy 4 out, rdn and styd on frm 2 out.*
....................(100 to 30 tac op 5 to 1 tchd 3 to 1) 3
448 TOM THE TANK 10-5 (7*) E Husband, *al chasing ldrs, rdn 2 out, kpt on one pace.*.............(33 to 1 op 25 to 1) 4
MR VINCENT 10-12 A S Smith, *chsd ldrs, effrt and rdn appr 2 out, ssn one pace.* (4 to 1 op 3 to 1 tchd 9 to 2) 5
BILJAN (USA) 10-12 P Niven, *chsd ldr, effrt to chal and ev ch 3 out, sn rdn, hit 2 out and wknd quickly appr last.*
....(8 to 1 tchd 10 to 1) 6
448⁵ PAAJIB (Ire) 10-5 (7*) W Fry, *chsd ldrs, rdn 3 out, wknd appr nxt.*...........................(25 to 1 op 20 to 1) 7
406² RECORD LOVER (Ire) (bl) 10-12 J Osborne, *led, rdn and hdd appr 2 out, wknd quickly.*........(4 to 1 op 3 to 1) 8
320⁶ BIG GEM 10-12 W Worthington, *beh, rdn alng 4th, sn tld off.*.................................(50 to 1 op 33 to 1) 9
MONASTIC FLIGHT (Ire) 10-12 B Storey, *sn beh, tld off frm 4th.*.................................(20 to 1 op 16 to 1) 10
WESTRAY (Fr) 10-5 (7*) J Driscoll, *hld up, mstk 4th, sn wl beh.*................(16 to 1 op 14 to 1 tchd 20 to 1) 11
GETYERKITON (Ire) 10-9 (3*) A Dobbin, *beh, effrt and some hdwy 5th, rdn and wknd nxt, behind whn f last.*
......................................(20 to 1 op 16 to 1) f
SALLY OF THE ALLEY 10-0 (7*) D Towler, *al rear, tried to refuse and uns rdr bef 3 out.*.......(50 to 1 op 33 to 1) ref
Dist: 2l, 2½l, 1l, 3½l, dist, 1l, 3l, 5l, 2l, 12l. 4m 19.60s. a 17.60s (13 Ran).

(Tony Briam), N A Graham

517 Swallow Stevedores Novices' Chase (5-y-o and up) £2,860 2½m. ....(3:45)

DEEP DECISION 7-11-2 K Johnson, *prmnt, outpcd and pushed alng 4 out, hdwy to chal and lft clr 2 out, ran on wl.*.........................(7 to 2 op 3 to 1) 1
451² CRAFTY CHAPLAIN 7-10-11 (5*) Mr D McCain, *hld up, jmpd slwly second, gd hdwy to chase ldr 5 out, clsg and ev ch whn blun 3 out, kpt on...* (3 to 1 tchd 100 to 30) 2
451 SMALLMEAD LAD 6-11-2 P Holley, *hld up, hdwy and hit 9th, rdn nxt, styd on one pace frm 3 out.*
................(13 to 8 fav op 6 to 4 tchd 7 to 4) 3
246⁴ PHALAROPE (Ire) 5-10-13 M Brennan, *chsd ldr, rdn 5 out, hit 3 out and wknd.*................(5 to 1 op 6 to 1) 4
WHISKEY BLUES 8-11-2 D Byrne, *prmnt till lost pl and beh frm 8th.*...........(4 to 1 tchd 5 to 1) 5
CANTGETOUT 7-10-11 Gary Lyons, *led, sn clr, rdn 3 out, jnd and f nxt.*................(16 to 1 op 12 to 1) f
HADLEIGHS CHOICE 6-11-2 M Robinson, *prmnt whn blun and uns rdr 5th.*...................(33 to 1 op 25 to 1) ur
Dist: 5l, hd, dist, 8l. 5m 11.40s. a 19.40s (7 Ran).

(Alan Cairns), P Cheesbrough

518 DFDS 'Flyer' Handicap Chase (0-120 5-y-o and up) £3,817 3m 1f. ....(4:20)

477 LAPIAFFE [100] 9-10-0 B Storey, *prmnt, led 5th, clr aftr 4 out, styd on wl frm 2 out.*
......................(10 to 1 op 7 to 1 tchd 11 to 1) 1
426⁷ ICARUS (USA) [124] 7-11-10 Mr A Rebori, *trkd ldrs, blun 9th, hdwy 4 out, chsd wnr nxt sn rdn and kpt on one pace.*......................(4 to 1 op 3 to 1) 2
KNIGHT OIL [128] (bl) 10-12-0 J Osborne, *hit 1st and second, hdwy 6th, jnd ldr 13th, mstk 5 out, sn rdn, wknd 3 out.*.................(7 to 4 fav op 2 to 1) 3
426⁵ MIAMI BEAR [101] 7-10-11 Gary Lyons, *led to 3rd, prmnt, hdwy to chase wnr whn blun badly 4 out, not reco'r.*.............................(7 to 1 tchd 9 to 1) 4
SMOOTH ESCORT [115] (v) 9-11-11 D Murphy, *prmnt, led 3rd to 5th, rdn and wknd bef 4 out.* (7 to 2 op 11 to 4) 5
NOTARY-NOWELL [100] 7-9-7 (7*) P Murphy, *in tch till rdn alng and lost pl appr 5 out, beh whn f last.*
......................(9 to 1 op 7 to 1) f
Dist: 10l, 8l, 2½l, 12l. 6m 26.40s. a 25.40s (6 Ran).

(Mrs B Ramsden), A Harrison

519 UECC Handicap Hurdle (0-125 4-y-o and up) £2,947 2m 3f 110yds ....(4:50)

289* WEE WIZARD (Ire) [93] 4-10-3 (3*) A Dobbin, *al prmnt, hdwy on inner whn hmpd aftr 3 out, led appr 2 out, hrd rdn and pckd last, ran on wl flt.*
...............(100 to 30 fav op 3 to 1 tchd 4 to 1) 1
318⁴ BALAAT (USA) [90] 5-10-3 A Orkney, *hld up, steady hdwy 3 out, rdn and ev ch last, no extr flt.*
...........................(9 to 2 op 7 to 2 tchd 5 to 1) 2
STORMHEAD [115] 5-12-0 J Osborne, *led, mstk 3rd, rdn aftr 3 out, hdd appr nxt, wnt lft und pres approaching last, no extr flt.*........(4 to 1 op 11 to 4 tchd 9 to 2) 3
MASTER OF THE ROCK [87] 4-10-0 C Hawkins, *hld up, hdwy and hit 6th, effrt and ev ch 2 out, sn rdn, kpt on one pace.*......................(16 to 1 tchd 20 to 1) 4
60⁵ HAWKFIELD (Ire) [107] 4-11-6 C Llewellyn, *hld up, steady hdwy aftr 3 out, ch whn hmpd appr last, 3rd when eased nr finish, lme.*..............(14 to 1 op 10 to 1) 5
JOLI'S GREAT [89] 5-10-2 J Ryan, *hld up, hdwy appr 3 out, rdn nxt, one pace approaching last.*
...............................(7 to 1 op 6 to 1 tchd 15 to 2) 6
140⁵ COLORADO INSIGHT [87] 5-10-0 J Callaghan, *chsd ldrs, rdn and outpcd 3 out, styd on and ev ch nxt, wknd appr last.*...........................(25 to 1 tchd 20 to 1) 7
HAMANAKA (USA) [94] (v) 4-10-7 C Grant, *trkd ldr, rdn 3 out, wknd appr nxt.*............(7 to 1 op 6 to 1) 8
FORWARD GLEN [110] 6-11-9 K Johnson, *in tch, sn rdn and wknd bef 3 out.*...............(14 to 1 op 12 to 1) 9
437² KRONPRINZ (Ire) [94] 5-10-7 W Worthington, *prmnt whn pld up appr 5th.*.................(11 to 2 op 9 to 2) pu
Dist: 3l, 1l, 1½l, 1½l, 1½l, 1l, nk, dist. 4m 47.90s. a 14.90s (10 Ran).

SR: 17/11/35/6/25/5/2/8/-/

(Armstrong/Greenwell), M A Barnes

STRATFORD (good to firm)
Saturday September 18th
Going Correction: MINUS 0.05 sec. per fur.

520 Michaelmas Selling Hurdle (4 & 5-y-o) £1,308 2m 110yds. ....(2:25)

SMART DEBUTANTE (Ire) 4-10-7 G McCourt, *trkd ldrs, wnt second 5th, rdn to ld appr last, drvn out, all out.*
...........................(7 to 2 op 5 to 1 tchd 3 to 1) 1
307⁹ HOMILE 5-10-7 (7*) S Lycett, *led, hit 3rd, clr aftr nxt, hdd appr last, rallied r-in, not quicken.*
..................................(33 to 1 op 20 to 1) 2
454² NAJEB (USA) 4-10-12 M A FitzGerald, *al prmnt, rdn alng aftr 5th, one pace after 3 out.*....(7 to 1 op 4 to 1) 3
434⁵ DEVONIAN (USA) 4-10-5 (7*) S Curran, *hld up and beh, hdwy and rdn aftr 3 out, styd on betw last 2, nvr nrr.*.........................(14 to 1 op 8 to 1 tchd 16 to 1) 4
429⁸ SHAKE TOWN (USA) 5-11-0 N Williamson, *chsd ldrs, out-pcd aftr 5th, styd on ag'n frm 2 out.*(12 to 1 op 8 to 1) 5
415 CLASS ATTRACTION (USA) 4-10-7 R Dunwoody, *hld up, wnt 3rd 5th, chsd ldg pair and no imprsn til wknd aftr 3 out.*....................(15 to 8 fav op 6 to 4 tchd 9 to 4) 6
454⁶ PRIME MOVER (v) 5-11-6 R Campbell, *hld up, chsd ldrs frm 4th, sn rdn and wknd aftr nxt.* (14 to 1 op 5 to 1) 7
QUIETLY IMPRESSIVE (Ire) 5-10-9 A Carroll, *hld up, lost tch aftr 5th, sn beh.*...............(20 to 1 op 12 to 1) 8
SIMON ELLIS (Ire) 4-10-12 G Upton, *beh, mstks, lost tch aftr 4th, sn behind.*...............(7 to 1 op 20 to 1) 9
460 BEACHOLME BOY (Ire) (bl) 5-10-11 (3*) D O'Sullivan, *prmnt til lost pl and rdn aftr 3rd, blun nxt, sn beh.*
...............................(50 to 1 op 33 to 1 tchd 66 to 1) 10
227 FRIENDLY HOUSE (Ire) 4-10-12 H Davies, *nvr rchd ldrs, tld off aftr 5th.*................(9 to 1 op 12 to 1 tchd 10 to 1) 11
429⁹ SEA PRODIGY (bl) 4-10-12 S McNeill, *prmnt til aftr 3rd, wknd quickly 5th, sn beh.*....(50 to 1 op 33 to 1) 12
BALLYMONEYBOY 4-10-12 M Ahern, *slwly away, rapid hdwy to chase ldrs aftr 3rd, lost pl nxt, wl beh whn blun 5th, sn tld off.*........(20 to 1 op 14 to 1 tchd 25 to 1) 13
TAX THE DEVIL 5-10-9 (5*) A Dicken, *mid-div, beh whn f 3rd.*.............................(14 to 1 op 10 to 1) f
321 DAWN POPPY 5-10-2 (7*) T Thompson, *beh whn blun 4th, pld up bef nxt.*......................(66 to 1 op 33 to 1) pu
Dist: 1½l, 15l, 1½l, 1½l, 1½l, 1½l, 8l, 8l. 3m 55.10s. a 6.10s (15 Ran).

SR: 10/15/-/-/-/-/

(Gilberts Animal Feed Products), Miss S J Wilton

521 Anthony Robinson Memorial Trophy Novices' Chase (5-y-o and up) £2,477 2m 1f 110yds. ....(2:55)

338* STRONG VIEWS 6-11-6 A Maguire, *hld up, hdwy 6th, wnt 3rd 4 out, went second nxt, jnd ldr and lft clr 2 out, styd on wl.*..................(Evens fav tchd 6 to 5) 1
DEXTRA DOVE 6-11-0 S Earle, *hld up, wnt second aftr 8th, hit 3 out, no imprsn whn lft second 2 out.*
...............................(4 to 1 tchd 9 to 2) 2
CANDLE KING (Ire) 5-10-12 M Bosley, *hld up and beh, mstk 6th, hdwy aftr 5 out, staying on whn lft moderate 3rd 2 out.*...........................(50 to 1 tchd 33 to 1) 3

195^{4} IMPERIAL FLIGHT 8-11-0 J R Kavanagh, *hld up, effrt aftr 8th, sn no imprsn, lft moderate 4th 2 out.* .... (25 to 1 op 33 to 1) 4

MR HAPPY FEET 6-11-0 R Bellamy, *al beh, lost tch frm 8th*............................ (100 to 1 op 33 to 1) 5

KILKILMARTIN 11-10-7 (7*) Mr Richard White, *rear whn mstk 7th, sn beh*................. (50 to 1 op 33 to 1) 6

GLENSHANE LAD 7-11-0 N Williamson, *trkd ldr til led aftr 8th, rdn after 3 out, jnd and f 2 out.* .... (3 to 1 op 7 to 2 tchd 11 to 4) f

350^{2} BUMPTIOUS BOY 9-11-0 D Bridgwater, *al chasing ldrs, ev ch 4 out, sn rdn and one pace, fourth and btn whn badly hmpd and rdr knocked out of sddl.* .... (14 to 1 op 12 to 1 tchd 16 to 1) bd

AS GOOD AS GOLD 7-11-0 J Railton, *pressed ldr til wknd 6th, pld up aftr nxt*.............. (50 to 1 op 33 to 1) pu

382^{2} PEARLS BEAU 6-11-10 S Smith Eccles, *led til hdd aftr 8th, wknd quickly after 5 out, beh whn pld up bef 2 out.* .... (9 to 1 op 7 to 1 tchd 10 to 1) pu

Dist: 6l, 15l, 3½l, 20l, 4l. 4m 12.70s. a 8.70s (10 Ran).

(Ms M Horan), J White

522 B. M. Limited Lady Riders' Handicap Hurdle (0-115 4-y-o and up) £1,828 2m 110yds .... (3:25)

ROMOLA NIJINSKY [71] 5-10-5 Gee Armytage, *set steady pace and clr, quickened 3 out, clear appr last, unchlgd.* .... (9 to 4 fav op 2 to 1) 1

298* BONDAID [85] 9-11-5 Lorna Vincent, *hld up, rdn and hdwy aftr 5th, wnt second after last, no imprsn.* .... (9 to 2 op 4 to 1 tchd 5 to 1) 2

428 MY LINDIANNE [74] 6-10-8 Mrs A Farrell, *hld up, hdwy aftr 5th, wnt second appr 2 out, rdn and no imprsn.* .... (5 to 1 tchd 13 to 2) 3

454^{5} TRENDY AUCTIONEER (Ire) [72] (v) 5-10-1 (5*) Mrs P Nash, *chsd clr ldr frm 3rd till wknd aftr 2 out.* .... (8 to 1 op 7 to 1) 4

420^{3} MADRAJ (Ire) [89] 5-11-2 (7*) Miss S Mitchell, *hld up, rdn alng aftr 5th, no imprsn frm 2 out.* .... (10 to 1 op 8 to 1 tchd 11 to 1) 5

BAND OF HOPE (USA) [87] (v) 6-11-7 Diane Clay, *wnt second aftr 5th, sn rdn and wknd after 3 out.* .... (7 to 1 op 6 to 1) 6

ALWAYS READY [90] 7-11-3 (7*) Leanne Eldredge, *drpd rear aftr 4th, sn beh, no ch frm nxt*...... (11 to 1 op 8 to 1) 7

WAAZA (USA) [75] 4-10-9 Mrs S Bosley, *drpd rear and rdn alng aftr 5th, sn beh*.............. (16 to 1 op 20 to 1) 8

Dist: 6l, 1l, 7l, 1½l, 5l, 2l, 15l. 4m 1.80s. a 12.80s (8 Ran).

(Mrs E A Dawson), P D Evans

523 Colette's Restaurant Handicap Chase (0-130 5-y-o and up) £2,818 2½m.... (3:55)

336^{2} JOYFUL NOISE [122] 10-11-9 A Maguire, *hld up, mstk second, trkd ldrs frm 8th, ev ch 4 out, lft second 2 out, hrd rdn to ld nr finish*............. (13 to 2 op 6 to 1) 1

457 PALM READER [127] 9-12-0 M A FitzGerald, *hld up in tch, wnt second 4 out, lft in ld 2 out, hdd and not quicken nr finish*.......................... (5 to 2 fav tchd 2 to 1) 2

308* KARAKTER REFERENCE [119] 11-11-3 (3*) D O'Sullivan, *lft in ld 3rd, hdd 5 out, one pace 3 out, left third nxt.* .... (5 to 1 op 9 to 2 tchd 11 to 2) 3

426* HIRAM B BIRDBATH [103] (bl) 7-9-13 (5*) Mrs P Nash, *prmnt til lost pl 8th, no ch frm 6 out, tld off.* .... (9 to 2 op 7 to 2 tchd 5 to 1) 4

UNEX-PLAINED [100] 10-10-1[1] Lorna Vincent, *hld up, lost tch 9th, sn beh, tld off*............ (16 to 1 op 10 to 1) 5

444 TRY ME NOW [99] 7-10-0 R Supple, *hld up, beh whn mstk tenth, sn tld off*.................. (50 to 1 op 33 to 1) 6

119^{7} CASTLE KING [122] 6-11-9 B Powell, *wnt second 5th, trkd ldr til led 5 out, 2 ls clr whn f two out.* .... (11 to 4 op 9 to 4 tchd 7 to 2) f

MIGHTY PRINCE [99] (bl) 8-10-0 N Williamson, *led, clr aftr second, pld up lme bef nxt*........ (33 to 1 op 20 to 1) pu

Dist: 1½l, 10l, 5l, 25l, 6l. 4m 56.40s. a 14.40s (8 Ran).

(A Godrich), A P Jarvis

524 Damsels Mares' Novices' Hurdle (4-y-o and up) £1,730 2m 110yds.......... (4:30)

SWIFT CONVEYANCE (Ire) 4-10-10 K Jones, *al prmnt, led 5th, rdn and styd on wl frm 2 out, all out.* .... (33 to 1 tchd 40 to 1) 1

383 MAMALAMA 5-10-9 (3*) D O'Sullivan, *chsd ldr frm 5th, rdn alng appr 3 out, wnt second approaching last, kpt on r-in, not quicken*................. (14 to 1 op 12 to 1) 2

429^{7} DON'T FORSAKE ME 4-10-10 J Railton, *hld up, beh 3rd, hdwy aftr 3 out, styd on one pace.* (12 to 1 op 6 to 1) 3

KADARI 4-10-10 Diane Clay, *chsd ldg grp aftr 4th, rdn and styd on one pace after 2 out, no imprsn.* .... (9 to 2 tchd 7 to 2) 4

500^{7} DULZURA 5-10-12 T Jarvis, *led to second, led aftr 4th to nxt, chsd ldr in second pl till wknd after 2 out.* .... (20 to 1 op 16 to 1 tchd 28 to 1) 5

429* DANCING DOVE (Ire) 5-10-12 (7*) B Harding, *led second to nxt, chsd ldrs till rdn and no imprsn aftr 3 out.* .... (7 to 4 fav tchd 2 to 1) 6

BLUE LYZANDER 4-10-10 D Bridgwater, *hld up, hdwy aftr 5th, sn rdn and no imprsn after 3 out.* .... (100 to 1 op 50 to 1) 7

PRUDENT PEGGY 6-10-12 J Frost, *hld up, beh 3rd, steady hdwy aftr 2 out, nvr nrr*...................... (25 to 1) 8

KICKING BIRD 6-10-12 N Williamson, *hld up, beh 3rd, rear whn badly hmpd 2 out, styd on one pace.* .... (25 to 1 op 20 to 1 tchd 33 to 1) 9

COOL COQUELIN (Ire) 5-10-12 S Smith Eccles, *beh frm 3rd, nvr rchd ldrs*..................... (33 to 1 op 16 to 1) 10

IZITALLWORTHIT 4-10-10 R Dunwoody, *hld up, hdwy aftr 4th, chsd ldg grp till wknd quickly after 3 out.* .... (9 to 1 op 7 to 1 tchd 10 to 1) 11

FAIRGROUNDPRINCESS 5-10-12 Lorna Vincent, *prmnt, led 3rd till aftr 4th, wknd nxt, sn tld off.* .... (20 to 1 op 16 to 1) 12

DAL MISS 6-10-12 M Bosley, *hld up, wl beh 3rd, mstk 5th, sn tld off*...................... (100 to 1 op 50 to 1) 13

MISS CRUSTY 5-10-9 (3*) V Slattery, *hld up, hdwy to chase ldg grp aftr 5th, mid-div and wkng whn f 2 out.* .... (16 to 1 op 12 to 1) f

BOCELLIE 5-10-12 D J Burchell, *lost tch aftr 4th, wl beh whn f 2 out*..................... (16 to 1 op 14 to 1) f

FIABA 5-10-12 E Murphy, *wl beh 3rd, sn tld off, pld up bef last*.............................. (25 to 1 op 33 to 1) pu

WOODSIDE LADY (Ire) 5-10-12 A Maguire, *wl beh frm 3rd, tld off whn pld up bef 3 out.* .... (11 to 1 op 7 to 1 tchd 12 to 1) pu

Dist: 2l, 12l, 2l, 3l, 3l, 3½l, 7l, 8l, 1l, ½l. 3m 54.90s. a 5.90s (17 Ran).

SR: 15/15/1/-/-/2/ (J B Mitchell), W T Kemp

525 Shottery Claiming Chase (5-y-o and up) £2,705 3m......................... (5:00)

299^{2} SKIPPING TIM 14-10-12 R Dunwoody, *led, styd on wl frm 3 out, mstk nxt, sn drw clr, cmftbly.* .... (13 to 8 on op 7 to 4 on tchd 11 to 8 on) 1

308 BELL DIP 12-10-12 N Williamson, *wnt second 5th, mstk 9th, chsd ldr, rdn 3 out, styd on to take second aftr last, no imprsn*......................... (16 to 1 op 14 to 1) 2

CHANCERY BUCK 10-11-0 J Frost, *wnt 3rd 13th, chsd ldr, went second appr 2 out, sn rdn and one pace.* .... (13 to 2 op 6 to 1 tchd 7 to 1) 3

397^{2} BARTONDALE 8-10-0 (5*) R Farrant, *chsd ldr, rdn alng aftr 11th, no hdwy frm 5 out*........ (8 to 1 op 6 to 1) 4

386 SAMSUN (bl) 11-10-12 M A FitzGerald, *chsd ldg pair to tenth, rdn alng and reminders aftr nxt, sn beh.* .... (50 to 1 op 33 to 1) 5

194^{6} CRAZY HORSE DANCER (USA) 5-10-12 R Supple, *not fluent early, hdwy aftr tenth, sn wknd, wl beh after 13th.* .... (33 to 1 op 20 to 1) 6

218 ROUCHEAL 8-11-8 N Hawke, *hld up, some hdwy aftr 7th, f 9th*............................ (100 to 1 op 66 to 1) f

299* PIGEON ISLAND 11-10-3 (7*) D Meade, *refused to race.* .... (6 to 1 op 5 to 1) ref

MILK QUOTA 10-10-11 W McFarland, *lost tch aftr 5th, tld off tenth, pld up bef 2 out*........ (33 to 1 op 20 to 1) pu

325 LITTLE THYNE 8-10-13 Dr P Pritchard, *jmpd badly, sn last and tld off aftr 7th, pld up bef 2 out*.......... (50 to 1) pu

Dist: 10l, 2l, 8l, 4l, ½l. 5m 59.40s. a 12.40s (10 Ran).

(Bisgrove Partnership), M C Pipe

526 Clifford Chambers Handicap Hurdle (0-115 4-y-o and up) £1,926 2¾m 110yds... (5:30)

NORTHERN VILLAGE [107] 6-11-8 (5*) A Dicken, *hld up, trkd ldrs frm 6th, reminders 4 out, dsptd ld nxt, led aftr 2 out, quickened clr, cmftbly.* .... (11 to 2 op 7 to 2 tchd 6 to 1) 1

BARLEY MOW [80] 7-10-0 N Mann, *chsd ldrs til outpcd aftr 4 out, rdn and rallied appr last, styd on r-in, not rch wnr*.......................... (40 to 1 op 33 to 1) 2

STAR QUEST [105] 6-11-11 S Smith Eccles, *al cl up, rdn aftr 7th, disputing ld whn jmpd slwly and lost pl after 3 out, sn hrd ridden and kpt on.* (2 to 1 fav tchd 5 to 2) 3

424^{6} PEAK DISTRICT [80] 7-10-0 A Maguire, *trkd ldrs, cl up and ev ch 3 out, rdn frm nxt, not quicken.* .... (8 to 1 tchd 11 to 1) 4

FUSSY LADY [87] 6-10-7 L Harvey, *chsd clr ldr, cl up and ev ch 4 out, one pace aftr 3 out*.... (16 to 1 op 25 to 1) 5

SIR CRUSTY [108] 11-11-7 (7*) P Maddock, *hld up and beh, hdwy to chase ldg grp aftr 7th, wknd after 3 out.* .... (20 to 1 op 12 to 1 tchd 25 to 1) 6

VOLCANIC DANCER (USA) [103] 7-11-9 N Williamson, *hld up, pushed alng and outpcd aftr 7th, no ch frm 3 out.* .... (20 to 1 op 14 to 1 tchd 25 to 1) 7

401^{4} ROCHE [80] 7-10-0 A Webb, *hld up and beh, drpd rear and rdn alng 7th, nvr dngrs aftr*............. (50 to 1) 8

353^{3} CHARLY PHARLY (Fr) [92] 6-10-12 J Frost, *led, clr second, hdd 3 out, wknd quickly*............ (9 to 2 op 5 to 1) 9

437^{3} CHAMOIS BOY [86] 9-10-6 D Skyrme, *hld up in last pl, tld off frm 3rd*......................... (12 to 1 op 8 to 1) 10

JIMBALOU [106] 10-11-12 W Humphreys, *hld up, hdwy to cl on ldrs aftr 7th, ev ch frm nxt, in tch but wkng whn f 2 out*....... (9 to 1 op 8 to 1 tchd 7 to 1 and 10 to 1) f
Dist: 8l, 2½l, 2½l, 6l, 10l, 10l, 6l, 15l, dist. 5m 25.70s. a 13.70s (11 Ran).

(Visual Identity Ltd-Design Studio), S Dow

LISTOWEL (IRE) (good to yielding)
Monday September 20th

527 Louis O'Connell Memorial Novice Chase (5-y-o and up) £4,340 2m.......... (3:55)

DORAN'S TOWN LAD 6-11-5 G Bradley,...... (5 to 2 fav)	1
330 THE HEARTY CARD (Ire) 5-11-0 D H O'Connor,... (10 to 1)	2
492* HAWAIIAN GODDESS (USA) 6-11-4 C O'Dwyer,.. (10 to 1)	3
254⁷ RUSTY COIN 8-11-13 T Horgan,................ (3 to 1)	4
ST COLEMAN'S WELL 10-11-5 A Maguire,....... (10 to 1)	5
LONGSHOREMAN 6-11-5 A Powell,.............. (33 to 1)	6
302³ KENMAC 6-11-5 K F O'Brien,.................... (10 to 1)	7
254⁶ IF SO 7-11-5 N Williamson,................... (14 to 1)	f
430 SON OF SARAH (bl) 9-11-5 A J O'Brien,....... (14 to 1)	ur
110³ NORDIC SUN 5-11-0 J F Titley,................ (3 to 1)	ur

Dist: 2l, 15l, 6l, 20l. 4m 6.10s. (10 Ran).

(T J Doran), Anthony Mullins

528 Bank Of Ireland Handicap Hurdle (5-y-o and up) £4,830 2m.................(4:30)

313² ULTRA MAGIC [-] 6-9-9 (5*) A J Roche,......... (11 to 2)	1
157* CASH CHASE [-] 5-9-2 (5*) C O'Brien,........(12 to 1)	2
466² SUNSHINES TAXI [-] 6-9-7 T Horgan,......... (12 to 1)	3
392⁶ TOUREEN GIRL [-] 6-10-3 C F Swan,......... (3 to 1 fav)	4
432⁷ ANOTHER COURSE (Ire) [-] 5-9-11 P McWilliams, (12 to 1)	5
330⁶ WAR DEVIL [-] 7-9-7 J Jones,................. (33 to 1)	6
471 HAYMAKERS JIG (Ire) [-] 5-9-7 (7*) J P Broderick, (10 to 1)	7
229* UNCLE BART (Ire) [-] 5-10-2 (5*) R A Hennessy,..... (5 to 1)	8
413⁶ CAN'T THINK WHAT [-] 6-10-11 (5*) T P Treacy,.... (7 to 1)	9
ASSURING (Ire) [-] (bl) 5-11-9 K F O'Brien,.........(7 to 1)	10
SPEAKING TOUR (USA) [-] 5-10-6 D H O'Connor, (14 to 1)	11
13⁷ HERE IT IS [-] 6-10-4 N Williamson,............. (14 to 1)	f

Dist: 5½l, 1l, 8l, 5½l. 4m 6.60s. (12 Ran).

(T A Kent), T A Kent

529 Devon Inn Maiden Hurdle (3-y-o) £3,795 2m.................................(5:00)

228³ TROPICAL LAKE (Ire) 11-0 K F O'Brien,....... (7 to 4 fav)	1
391³ NORDIC THORN (Ire) 11-0 J F Titley,..............(5 to 1)	2
375³ LUSTRINO (USA) (bl) 11-0 A Maguire,..........(5 to 2)	3
GARDENVALE VIC (Ire) 11-0 J Shortt,............. (14 to 1)	4
391⁵ JAZZY REFRAIN (Ire) 10-9 H Rogers,............ (33 to 1)	5
TEMPLEMARY BOY (Ire) 11-0 T Horgan,............ (20 to 1)	6
WARREN STREET (Ire) 11-0 C O'Dwyer,............(16 to 1)	7
290⁸ INNOCENT MAN (Ire) 11-0 N Williamson,........ (33 to 1)	8
MISS MURPHY (Ire) 10-2 (7*) J P Broderick,..... (33 to 1)	9
RYE HILL QUEEN (Ire) 10-9 B Sheridan,..........(25 to 1)	10
228 GIG TIME (Ire) 10-4 (5*) C P Dunne,.............(33 to 1)	11
LAUNCH INTO SONG (Ire) 11-0 M Dwyer,........(20 to 1)	12
RATES RELIEF (Ire) 10-9 (5*) C O'Brien,..........(20 to 1)	13
ALIBAR'S PET (Ire) 10-2 (7*) K P Gaule,............(7 to 1)	f
FESTIVAL GIRL (Ire) 10-9 H Hughes,............(12 to 1)	pu

Dist: 7l, 10l, 8l, 5½l. 4m 11.80s. (15 Ran).

(G Redford), Michael Hourigan

530 John F. McGuire INH Flat Race (Div I) (4-y-o) £3,795 2m.....................(5:30)

THE SUBBIE (Ire) 11-0 (7*) Mr D J Kavanagh,...... (4 to 1)	1
JUPITER JIMMY 11-7 Mr J A Flynn,...............(8 to 1)	2
431⁶ NINE O THREE (Ire) 11-0 (7*) Mr B Moran,......(16 to 1)	3
107 CORYMANDEL (Ire) 11-0 (7*) Mr D Casey,...... (16 to 1)	4
AN MAINEACH (Ire) 11-4 (3*) Miss M Olivefalk,.... (8 to 1)	5
331⁵ HILL OF TULLOW (Ire) 11-4 (3*) Mr M F Barrett,... (20 to 1)	6
MAJOR GALE (Ire) 11-0 (7*) Mr A J Foley,......... (14 to 1)	7
LEISURE CENTRE (Ire) 10-10¹ (7*) Mr R P Cody,.. (25 to 1)	8
KING'S DECREE (Ire) 11-7 Mr E Bolger,...........(6 to 1)	9
GALE TOI (Ire) 11-4 (3*) Mrs S McCarthy,..........(6 to 1)	10
469⁵ PLASSY BOY (Ire) 11-7 Mr A J Martin,.............(8 to 1)	11
MR SNAGGLE (Ire) 11-0 (7*) Miss M Quigley,...... (16 to 1)	12
DESERT WALTZ (Ire) 11-7 Mr J P Dempsey,...... (14 to 1)	13
171⁸ CASTLE CLUB (Ire) 10-13 (3*) Mr R O'Neill,......(33 to 1)	14
JACK'S BAR (Ire) 11-0 (7*) Mr W M O'Sullivan,....(33 to 1)	15
FATHER RECTOR (Ire) 11-4 (3*) Mrs M Mullins, (20 to 1)	16
KING OF SHERWOOD (Ire) 11-0 (7*) Mr B Hassett, (14 to 1)	17
393 MALTESE CROSS (Ire) 11-7 Mr J Nagle Jnr, (50 to 1)	18
508 ROSEMARY MAC (Ire) 11-2 Mr A P O'Brien,...... (8 to 1)	su

Dist: 8l, sht-hd, 6l, sht-hd. 4m 3.80s. (19 Ran).

(T Miley), Francis Ennis

531 John F. McGuire INH Flat Race (Div II) (4-y-o) £3,795 2m.....................(6:00)

431² VON CARTY (Ire) 11-2 Mr E Bolger,.............(11 to 2)	1
423² WATERLOO BALL (Ire) 11-2 Mr A P O'Brien,... (5 to 4 fav)	2
TREASURE AGAIN (Ire) 11-4 (3*) Mrs M Mullins,... (12 to 1)	3
171³ DUN OENGUS (Ire) 10-13 (3*) Miss C Hutchinson,... (8 to 1)	4

393⁷ SLANEY GENT (Ire) 11-2 (5*) Mr H F Cleary,...... (10 to 1)	5
3⁹ RED BARONS LADY (Ire) 10-13 (3*) Mrs S McCarthy,	
....(16 to 1)	6
PRECEPTOR (Ire) 11-0 (7*) Mr D A Harney,...... (10 to 1)	7
KARTLOS (Ire) 11-0 (7*) Mr J H Hayes,............ (8 to 1)	8
OZEYCAZEY (Ire) 11-0 (7*) Mr A Nash,.......... (10 to 1)	9
431⁵ TRIPLE ACE (Ire) 11-0 (7*) Mr N C Kelliher,........(16 to 1)	10
PALLASOWN GALE (Ire) 10-11 (5*) Mrs J M Mullins,	
....(14 to 1)	11
SCANLONS TOWN (Ire) 11-0 Mr R Burns,.......(14 to 1)	12
233⁴ BOLD TED (Ire) 11-0 (7*) Mr G A Kingston,........(10 to 1)	13
BRONTE BEAT (Ire) 11-2 (7*) Mr T J Nagle Jnr,.. (33 to 1)	14
MOSSY'S SLAVE (Ire) 11-0 (7*) Mr T J O'Mara,...(25 to 1)	15
LORD MONTE (Ire) 11-4 (3*) Mr D Marnane,...... (20 to 1)	16
A WINDY CITIZEN (Ire) 10-9 (7*) Mr W M O'Sullivan, (33 to 1)	17
266⁷ US AND SAM (Ire) 11-4 (3*) Mr J Nash,...........(7 to 1)	su
BRISTOL SPIRIT (Ire) 11-2 Mr J Boland,...........(20 to 1)	pu

Dist: 1l, ¾l, nk, 10l. 4m 9.30s. (19 Ran).

(C Meehan), A J McNamara

LISTOWEL (IRE) (soft)
Tuesday September 21st

532 McElligott Oils Maxol Handicap Chase (4-y-o and up) £3,795 2½m............. (3:45)

119⁹ DESERT LORD [-] 7-10-9 C F Swan,.......... (2 to 1 fav)	1
468³ ROSSBEIGH CREEK [-] 6-9-9 F J Flood,......... (8 to 1)	2
306⁹ DANCINGCINDERELLA [-] 9-10-4 K F O'Brien,.....(9 to 2)	3
132 PARGALE [-] 7-10-5 N Williamson,............. (10 to 1)	4
411⁴ CHESTNUT JEWEL [-] 5-9-0 (7*) J P Broderick, (50 to 1)	5
306 GARRYDOOLIS [-] (bl) 7-9-4 (5*) C O'Brien,......(16 to 1)	6
121⁴ THIRD QUARTER [-] 8-11-5 C O'Dwyer,...........(7 to 1)	7
332 CAPINCUR BOY [-] 11-9-7 J Magee,.......... (14 to 1)	f
474⁴ GONZALO [-] 10-10-0 A Powell,...............(10 to 1)	f
306 QUEEN OF THE SWANS [-] (bl) 9-9-4² (5*) T J O'Sullivan,	
....(50 to 1)	f
468 PORTLAND LAD [-] 8-9-7 W T Slattery Jnr,.... (33 to 1)	pu
509² SKY RANGE [-] 8-10-6 T Horgan,...............(7 to 1)	pu

Dist: Sht-hd, 1½l, 1l, 11l. 5m 29.90s. (12 Ran).

(P A Keogh), A J McNamara

533 Listowel Races Supporters Club Lartigue Hurdled Handicap (Listed) (4-y-o) £11,500 2m.................................... (4:20)

329* LIFE SAVER (Ire) [-] 11-6 P Carberry, *hld up in rear, steady prog frm 4 out to chal appr last, rdn to ld nr line.*	
....	1
294³ LOSHIAN (Ire) [-] 11-13 R Dunwoody, *led second, rdn and slight advantage last, hdd cl home*...............(7 to 2)	2
329⁵ GREEN GLEN (USA) [-] 11-6 C F Swan, *rear til prog to chase ldrs 4 out, styd on wthout rching chalg pos.*	
....(16 to 1)	3
329² JUDICIAL FIELD (Ire) [-] (bl) 12-0 A Maguire, *wl plcd, prog to go second 3 out, rdn and wknd nxt*...............(7 to 2)	4
329⁴ VICOSA (Ire) [-] 10-6 A Powell, *mid-div, rdn and styd on wthout troubling ldrs*.........................(25 to 1)	5
TITLED DANCER (Ire) [-] 11-11 J Shortt, *mid-div till rdn and wknd 3 out*...............................(7 to 2)	6
328⁴ SHIRWAN (Ire) [-] 10-4 C O'Dwyer, *led till hdd second, mstks, rdn and wknd 3 out*.....................(16 to 1)	7
IMPERIAL CALL (Ire) [-] 11-2 G M O'Neill, *al in rear*	
....(16 to 1)	8

Dist: Nk, 5l, 5l, 7l. 4m 17.40s. (8 Ran).

(Mrs H A Hegarty), Noel Meade

534 T.J. Cross Maiden Hurdle (Div 1) (4 & 5-y-o) £3,845 2m.......................(4:55)

PADRE MIO (Ire) 5-12-0 G Bradley,.............. (13 to 2)	1
328² RISZARD (USA) 4-11-9 K F O'Brien,.......... (5 to 4 on)	2
305 PERSIAN HALO (Ire) 5-12-0 D H O'Connor,...... (10 to 1)	3
GRAND TOUR (NZ) 5-12-0 L P Cusack,.......... (20 to 1)	4
WHAT A QUESTION (Ire) 5-11-9 R Dunwoody,...... (7 to 1)	5
376⁴ NOBODY'S FLAME (Ire) 5-11-6 J Magee,........(16 to 1)	6
EAGLE ROCK (USA) 5-11-9 (5*) C O'Brien,........ (10 to 1)	7
ANOTHER SHUIL (Ire) 5-11-1 Mr J A Flynn,...... (33 to 1)	8
471³ ZORIA (Ire) 5-11-1 P Carberry,................. (14 to 1)	9
211³ OZONE RIVER (Ire) 5-10-8 (7*) C McCormack,.. (16 to 1)	10
FINE TUNING (Ire) 5-11-6 T J Taaffe,.............. (14 to 1)	11
157⁶ SLANEY FAYRE (Ire) 5-11-6 C O'Dwyer,.........(16 to 1)	12
333² MORE DASH (Ire) 5-11-2 (7*) P A Roche,........ (20 to 1)	13
159* BEAU GRANDE (Ire) 5-12-0 P L Malone,........ (20 to 1)	14
THE SILVER ROLLS 5-11-6 T Horgan,............. (25 to 1)	15
KEEPHERGOING (Ire) 4-10-6 (7*) J P Broderick,.. (33 to 1)	16
RAINBOW ALLIANCE (Ire) 5-10-10 (5*) C P Dunne, (33 to 1)	17
295 DANE ST LADY (Ire) 5-10-8 (7*) B D Duggan,.... (33 to 1)	ur
409 RUSHEEN BAY (Ire) 4-11-1 (3*) T J Mitchell,...... (100 to 1)	pu

Dist: 9l, nk, 8l, nk. 4m 20.60s. (19 Ran).

(Paddy Fennelly), Anthony Mullins

535 T.J. Cross Maiden Hurdle (Div 2) (4 & 5-y-o) £3,845 2m.......................(5:30)

DORANS PRIDE 4-11-9 K F O'Brien,...... (7 to 4 fav)	1

ERSILLAS (Fr) 5-11-6 Mr S R Murphy, ... (16 to 1) 2
COOL CHARACTER (Ire) 5-12-0 J F Titley, ...(6 to 1) 3
REGALING (Ire) 5-11-6 T J Taaffe, ... (14 to 1) 4
314^{7} WEE RIVER (Ire) 4-11-4 G M O'Neill, ... (16 to 1) 5
BRIDEPARK ROSE (Ire) 5-10-8 (7*) P A Roche, ... (33 to 1) 6
SHOW YOUR HAND (Ire) 5-11-6 T Horgan, ... (33 to 1) 7
PANDA (Ire) 5-11-9 C F Swan, ...(3 to 1) 8
472^{7} LUCKY MINSTREL (Ire) 5-11-1 B Sheridan, ... (50 to 1) 9
BALLYHYLAND (Ire) 4-11-4 G Bradley, ... (7 to 1) 10
PLUNDERING STAR (Ire) 5-11-6 R Dunwoody, ... (12 to 1) 11
365^{6} CARRIGANN HOTEL (Ire) 5-10-10 (5*) C O'Brien, ..(50 to 1) 12
SYLVIES MISSILES (Ire) 4-10-8 (5*) C P Dunne, ... (33 to 1) 13
OLYMPIC D'OR (Ire) 5-11-1 (5*) M A Davey, ... (20 to 1) 14
ROSCEEN BUI (Ire) 4-10-6 (7*) J P Broderick, ... (33 to 1) 15
472^{2} SLANEY SAUCE (Ire) 5-11-6 C O'Dwyer, ... (25 to 1) 16
SARAKIN (Ire) 5-10-10 (5*) D T Evans, ... (33 to 1) 17
TYLERS CABIN (Ire) 5-10-13 (7*) T M O'Donovan, (40 to 1) 18
BUCKS IMAGE (Ire) 5-10-10 (5*) A J Slattery, ... (50 to 1) 19
Dist: ¾l, 1½l, 10l, 1l. 4m 30.30s. (19 Ran).
(T J Doran), Michael Hourigan

536 Aer Rianta Shannon Duty Free INH Flat Race (5-y-o and up) £4,830 2½m.... (6:00)

370^{2} BAMANYAR (Ire) 5-11-7 (7*) Mr John J Murphy, ... (10 to 1) 1
124^{7} KING OF THE WORLD (Ire) 5-12-0 Mr P Fenton, ... (8 to 1) 2
333^{3} FIFI'S MAN 7-12-0 Mr E Bolger, ... (12 to 1) 3
414^{2} CUCHULLAINS GOLD (Ire) 5-12-0 Mr A J Martin, (10 to 1) 4
433^{2} THE TENANT 6-11-11 (3*) Miss M Olivefalk, ... (4 to 1) 5
15^{9} BALLINGOWAN STAR 6-11-2 (7*) Mr S O'Donnell, (33 to 1) 6
174 CALAMITY CANE (Ire) 5-11-2 (7*) Mr R P Cody, ... (33 to 1) 7
433^{5} POLLYKENDU (Ire) 5-11-11 (3*) Mr D Marnane, ... (10 to 1) 8
466^{3} JOHNNY SCATTERCASH 11-11-7 (7*) Mr P O'Keeffe, ...(10 to 1) 9
15^{6} GOOLDS GOLD 7-11-7 (7*) Mr K Whelan, ... (12 to 1) 10
472^{3} THE ROCKING CHAIR (Ire) 5-11-9 (5*) Mr G J Harford, ...(14 to 1) 11
343^{3} MULLAGHMEEN 7-11-4 (5*) Mr J P Berry, ... (16 to 1) 12
103^{9} RHINESTALL 6-11-4 (5*) Mr A E Lacy, ... (16 to 1) 13
469^{6} KILLINISKY (Ire) 5-12-0 Mr A P O'Brien, ... (7 to 2 fav) 14
236^{6} LONG'S EXPRESS (Ire) 5-11-6 (3*) Mrs M Mullins, (12 to 1) 15
THIRD SCHEDULE (Ire) 5-11-7 (7*) Mr P Henley, .. (33 to 1) 16
304^{2} SAME DIFFERENCE (Ire) 5-11-9 (5*) Mr J A Nash, .. (8 to 1) 17
304^{4} CLEAN SHEETS VI (Ire) 5-12-0 Mr S R Murphy, ... (20 to 1) 18
CASTLEPOOK 6-11-7 (7*) Mr B Walsh, ... (33 to 1) 19
258 LISCAHILL HIGHWAY 6-11-9 (5*) Mr H F Cleary, .. (33 to 1) pu
Dist: ½l, 9l, sht-hd, 7l. 5m 57.00s. (20 Ran).
(John J Murphy), W P Mullins

LISTOWEL (IRE) (soft)
Wednesday September 22nd

537 Foran Equine Products Hurdle (4-y-o and up) £4,635 2m..................... (2:00)

SECOND SCHEDUAL 8-12-0 C F Swan, ... (5 to 4 on) 1
305* AIYBAK (Ire) 5-12-0 B Sheridan, ... (9 to 2) 2
466* SORRY ABOUT THAT 7-12-0 P Carberry, ... (5 to 1) 3
SUPER MIDGE 6-12-0 J Magee, ... (8 to 1) 4
TUG OF PEACE 6-12-0 F Woods, ... (12 to 1) 5
174 NEW DIRECTIONS 6-11-2 H Rogers, ... (33 to 1) 6
131 SOLBA (USA) 4-11-9 G M O'Neill, ... (10 to 1) 7
CALL ME HENRY 4-10-11 (5*) C O'Brien, ... (50 to 1) 8
256^{6} ASK THE FAIRIES (Ire) 5-10-13 (3*) K B Walsh, ... (33 to 1) 9
CELTIC BUCK 7-11-7 (7*) Mr P O'Keeffe, ... (20 to 1) 10
Dist: ¾l, 12l, 20l, 1½l. 4m 7.90s. (10 Ran).
(Hugh McMahon), Hugh McMahon

538 Cliff House Hotel Maiden Hurdle (6-y-o and up) £3,795 2¾m.................... (2:35)

MINELLA LAD 7-12-0 T Horgan, ... (8 to 1) 1
304^{8} MUILEAR OIRGE 6-11-6 T J Taaffe, ... (10 to 1) 2
GRANDONHILL 6-12-0 K F O'Brien, ... (20 to 1) 3
536 GOOLDS GOLD 7-10-13 (7*) P A Roche, ... (14 to 1) 4
414* DIRECT RUN 6-12-0 J F Titley, ... (4 to 1 fav) 5
414^{4} KIZZY ROSE 6-11-1 P Niven, ... (33 to 1) 6
330^{5} ANOTHER GROUSE 6-10-10 (5*) C O'Brien, ... (20 to 1) 7
476^{4} CUBAN QUESTION 6-12-0 C F Swan, ... (10 to 1) 8
295^{4} CARLINGFORD RUN 6-11-2 (7*) Mr D Murphy, ... (14 to 1) 9
410 CHARDEN 7-11-11 (3*) T J Mitchell, ... (33 to 1) 10
CLOSUTTON EXPRESS 7-12-0 N Williamson, ... (12 to 1) 11
466^{4} RATHCORE 6-12-0 C O'Dwyer, ... (8 to 1) 12
495* GOLDEN CLAW 6-12-0 F J Flood, ... (9 to 2) 13
508^{4} BIT OF A FUSS 6-11-6 A J O'Brien, ... (25 to 1) 14
WATERLAND LADY 6-11-9 Mr P Fenton, ... (9 to 2) 15
HEROIC MYTH 8-12-0 A Powell, ... (10 to 1) 16
DEL MONTE BOY (bl) 8-11-6 G M O'Neill, ... (14 to 1) f
DRINK UP DAN 6-11-6 P Carberry, ... (33 to 1) f
67 BALLYGRANT 6-12-0 P L Malone, ... (20 to 1) pu
SISTER EMU 6-11-1 G Bradley, ... (33 to 1) pu
Dist: 3l, 13l, 7l, 6l. 5m 54.60s. (20 Ran).
(John J Nallen), A P O'Brien

539 Guinness Kerry National Handicap Chase (Listed) (4-y-o and up) £14,375 3m...(3:15)

DEEP BRAMBLE [-] 6-11-6 P Niven, *trkd ldrs, prog into second aftr 3 out, led nxt, styd on strly*........ (7 to 1) 1
422^{4} FOR WILLIAM [-] 7-11-6 K F O'Brien, *led bef 7th till aftr 11th, led 13th till mstk and hdd 4 out, ran on.* (10 to 1) 2
422* LIFE OF A LORD [-] (bl) 7-11-0 (7ex) G M O'Neill, *led 1st till aftr 6th, led 12th till appr nxt, lft in ld after 4 out, hdd after next, ran on*.................................(8 to 1) 3
422^{3} BISHOPS HALL [-] 7-12-0 N Williamson, *mid-div, styd on wl frm 5 out, not rch ldrs*.................... (14 to 1) 4
ALLEZMOSS [-] 7-11-2 J F Titley, *wl plcd, mstk 12th, rdn 4 out, styd on*.................................. (14 to 1) 5
412 FURRY STAR [-] 7-10-3 J Jones, *wl plcd till rdn and wknd bef 3 out*.......................................(25 to 1) 6
119 JOE WHITE [-] 7-11-1 P Carberry, *trkd ldrs till rdn and wknd 4 out*.................................. (14 to 1) 7
474^{5} PROPUNT [-] 8-10-11 C O'Dwyer, *mid-div, prog to track ldrs 9th, rdn and wknd 4 out*................. (16 to 1) 8
ASK THE BOYS [-] 7-10-1 F Woods, *rear, rdn 5 out, some late prog strt*................................ (20 to 1) 9
422^{2} HARRISTOWN LADY [-] (bl) 6-10-6 A Powell, *al rear.* .... (10 to 1) 10
306^{2} MACK A DAY [-] 6-10-1 A J O'Brien, *al rear*...... (14 to 1) 11
306* GRATTAN PARK [-] 8-10-7 C F Swan, *mid-div till rdn and wknd 4 out*............................... (9 to 2 fav) 12
INCH LADY [-] 8-10-9 T Horgan, *al rear*.......... (33 to 1) 13
LAURA'S BEAU [-] 9-11-10 B Sheridan, *al rear*.... (33 to 1) 14
291^{8} FOUR TRIX [-] 12-11-0 J P Banahan, *mid-div to hfwy, sn rdn, tld off 12th*............................ (16 to 1) 15
410^{7} FISSURE SEAL [-] 7-11-9 G Bradley, *mid-div whn f tenth.* .... (6 to 1) f
306 NEVER BE GREAT [-] 11-10-10 F J Flood, *mstk 3rd, drpd rear, tld off whn pld up bef 2 out*............. (25 to 1) pu
60^{4} THE BULL MCCABE [-] (bl) 8-10-4 Mr S R Murphy, *rear whn pld up 6th*.................................... (16 to 1) pu
Dist: 4l, 4½l, 1l, 2½l. 6m 31.80s. (18 Ran).
(J F Mernagh), Michael Hourigan

540 Listowel Golf And Country Club Flat Race (5-y-o and up) £3,795 2m........... (6:00)

BADEN (Ire) 5-11-9 Mr T Mullins, ... (2 to 1 fav) 1
277^{2} GENERAL TONIC 6-12-0 Mr J A Berry, ... (5 to 1) 2
469^{2} UNRULY YOUTH 8-11-7 (7*) Mr J Connolly, ... (8 to 1) 3
HI-WAY'S GALE 6-11-2 (7*) Mr J R Ryan, ... (14 to 1) 4
HIGHLY SUSPICIOUS 6-11-7 (7*) Mr K Whelan, ... (16 to 1) 5
469^{9} MARCHING SEASON (Ire) 5-11-2 (7*) Mr S O'Donnell, ...(16 to 1) 6
CAPWELL LADY 6-11-3[1] (7*) Mr D G Murphy, ... (33 to 1) 7
FINNEGANS WAKE 6-12-0 Mr A P O'Brien, ... (5 to 1) 8
MAN O'WORDS 7-11-7 (7*) Mr E Norris, ... (20 to 1) 9
433^{4} BRAVE HENRY 5-11-7 (7*) Mr J T McNamara, ... (10 to 1) 10
DESMOND GOLD (Ire) 5-12-0 Mr T S Costello, ... (20 to 1) 11
331^{3} FAIRYHILL RUN (Ire) 5-11-2 (7*) Mr D A Harney, ... (6 to 1) 12
COMERAGH MOUNTAIN 6-12-0 Mr P Fenton, ... (14 to 1) 13
508^{7} FORTFIELD GUY 8-11-7 (7*) Mr P J Kennedy, ... (25 to 1) 14
TYPHOON JOE (Ire) 5-12-0 Mrs J M Mullins, ... (10 to 1) 15
SAMANTHABROWNTHORN 6-11-2 (7*) Mr B Moran, ...(16 to 1) 16
414^{3} DRESSED IN BLACK (Ire) 5-11-7 (7*) Mr B M Cash, (33 to 1) 17
DALUA RIVER (Ire) 5-11-6 (3*) Mrs M Mullins, ... (10 to 1) 18
159^{9} CONQUIRO (Ire) (bl) 5-11-7 (7*) Mr D J Kavanagh, (50 to 1) 19
FIALADY 8-11-2 (7*) Mr A J Normile, ... (33 to 1) 20
Dist: 2½l, 2l, ½l, 13l, 1l. 3m 58.40s. (20 Ran).
(Max Hauri), P Mullins

PERTH (good to firm)
Wednesday September 22nd
Going Correction: PLUS 0.15 sec. per fur.

541 EBF 'National Hunt' Novices' Hurdle Qualifier for the John McKie Challenge Cup (4,5,6-y-o) £2,223 2m 110yds........ (2:20)

TWIST 'N' SCU 5-11-0 D Bridgwater, *made all, hrd pressed frm 2 out, kpt on wl.* ....(13 to 2 op 7 to 1 tchd 8 to 1 and 9 to 1) 1
MAJOR TROOP 4-10-5 (7*) J Supple, *chsd ldrs, rdn aftr 2 out, kpt on wl towards finish*.............. (33 to 1) 2
THE PATTERS MAGIC 6-11-0 C Grant, *trkd ldr, rdn appr 2 out, ev ch whn hng lft approaching last, no extr r-in.* ....(2 to 1 op 5 to 4) 3
ROYAL SURPRISE 6-11-0 K Johnson, *in tch, outpcd and lost pl hfwy, rallied 3 out, rdn aftr nxt, kpt on same pace*........................... (16 to 1 op 20 to 1) 4
SHANNON KING (Ire) 5-11-0 R Dunwoody, *trkd ldrs gng wl, rdn appr 2 out, sn btn.* ....(11 to 10 on op 6 to 4 tchd 5 to 4 on) 5
STANWICK FORT 4-10-2 (5*) S Lyons, *mstks, sn beh, tld off whn pld up bef 2 out*........................ (50 to 1) pu
Dist: ¾l, sht-hd, 1l, 8l. 4m 3.80s. a 19.80s (6 Ran).
(F J Mills), N A Twiston-Davies

542 Gaymers Olde English Cyder Novices' Chase Glengoyne Highland Malt Tamerosia Series Qualifier (5-y-o and up)

£2,814 2½m 110yds............... (2:50)

CAPITAL PUNISHMENT 7-11-0 C Grant, *trkd ldrs, led aftr 2 out, styd on*.................... (3 to 1 op 4 to 1) 1
BOOK OF RUNES 8-11-0 D Bridgwater, *cl up, mstk 4th, led 6th, hdd aftr 2 out, no extr*.....(11 to 10 on op 5 to 4) 2
TARTAN TRADEWINDS 6-11-0 N Doughty, *al prmnt, ev ch 3 out, kpt on same pace*............ (7 to 2 op 9 to 4) 3
EDEN SUNSET 7-11-0 Mr Chris Wilson, *trkd ldrs, effrt appr 3 out, wknd betw last 2*.............(33 to 1) 4
COUNT SURVEYOR 6-11-0 K Johnson, *in tch till outpcd aftr 11th, no dngr after*..........(25 to 1 op 33 to 1) 5
451⁴ DROMINA STAR 12-11-1 (5⁺) P Williams, *led till blun 6th, lost pl, wl beh whn pld up bef tenth.*
.... (16 to 1 op 14 to 1) pu
THE WALTZING MOUSE (bl) 10-11-0 T Reed, *al beh, tld off whn pld up bef last.*.............. (20 to 1 op 25 to 1) pu
ZARBANO 7-11-0 A Merrigan, *in tch till wknd aftr tenth, tld off whn pld up bef last.*........(25 to 1 op 16 to 1) pu
BENNAN MARCH 6-11-0 A Orkney, *sn wl beh, tld off whn pld up bef last.*................... (50 to 1 op 33 to 1) pu
Dist: 1½l, ½l, 8l, ¾l. 5m 10.40s. a 12.40s (9 Ran).

(J N Hinchliffe), M D Hammond

543 Tennents Handicap Hurdle (0-115 4-y-o and up) £2,892 2m 110yds........... (3:20)

335⁵ BEAUCADEAU [116] 7-11-4 (3⁺) A Dobbin, *trkd ldrs, led appr 2 out, ran on strly frm last*................(3 to 1) 1
PERSUASIVE [123] 6-11-9 (5⁺) Mr M Buckley, *hld up, hdwy appr 2 out, ev ch whn mstk last, sn btn, eased cl hme.*
................................(7 to 4 fav op 6 to 4) 2
FLOWING RIVER (USA) [104] 7-10-9 B Storey, *hld up, hdwy aftr 3 out, styd on frm nxt, nrst finish.*
....................................(9 to 1 op 8 to 1) 3
SKOLERN [100] (v) 9-10-5 J Callaghan, *prmnt, ev ch 2 out, kpt on same pace*..............(8 to 1 op 10 to 1) 4
GOLDEN ISLE [115] 9-11-6 K Johnson, *trkd ldrs, effrt appr 2 out, grad wknd*.................(12 to 1 op 10 to 1) 5
428³ HEIR OF EXCITEMENT [97] 8-10-2⁵ (3⁺) A Larnach, *prmnt, effrt appr 2 out, sn rdn and btn*...............(33 to 1) 6
EASBY MANDRINA [97] 6-10-2² R Garritty, *hld up, effrt appr 2 out, no hdwy*......................(16 to 1) 7
THE GREEN FOOL [109] 6-11-0 A Merrigan, *led till hdd and wknd appr 2 out*...................(16 to 1 op 14 to 1) 8
268⁷ MARTINI EXECUTIVE [95] (bl) 5-10-0 R Dunwoody, *prmnt till wknd quickly appr 3 out, tld off.*
....................................(9 to 2 op 5 to 1 tchd 4 to 1) 9
KING OF NORMANDY (Ire) [95] 4-9-7 (7⁺) F Perratt, *sn wl beh, tld off whn pld up bef 3 out.*............(100 to 1) pu
Dist: 7l, hd, 4l, 6l, 1½l, 6l, 7l, 25l. 3m 51.30s. a 7.30s (10 Ran).
SR: 45/45/26/18/27/7/1/6/-/   (T A Barnes), M A Barnes

544 Avebe Handicap Chase (0-120 5-y-o and up) £3,550 3m.................... (3:50)

OVER THE DEEL [110] 7-11-0 B Storey, *trkd ldrs, led 14th, hrd pressed frm nxt, wknd towards finish, jst hld on.*
....................................(12 to 1 op 8 to 1) 1
RU VALENTINO [110] 9-11-0 D Bridgwater, *prmnt, hmpd 5th, chlgd 15th, slightly outpcd aftr 3 out, kpt on und pres towards finish, jst fld.*... (6 to 4 fav tchd 11 to 8) 2
449⁴ OFF THE BRU [109] (v) 8-10-13 Mr J Bradburne, *led till hdd 14th, outpcd and lost pl till rallied strly frm last.*
....................................(6 to 1) 3
449⁵ KIRSTY'S BOY [123] 10-11-13 G McCourt, *mstks, hld up in tch, wknd 15th*......................(5 to 1) 4
SPEECH [108] 10-10-12⁴ T Reed, *cl up whn f 5th.*
....................................(66 to 1 op 50 to 1) f
PORTAVOGIE [96] (bl) 9-9-7 (7⁺) Mr D Parker, *trkd ldrs, pushed alng whn mstk and uns rdr 14th.*
....................................(33 to 1 op 20 to 1) ur
BISHOPDALE [124] 12-12-0 C Grant, *al beh, slightly hmpd 5th, tld off whn pld up bef 13th.* (33 to 1 tchd 25 to 1) pu
450² MONTPELIER LAD [115] 6-11-5 N Doughty, *in tch till lost pl quickly and pld up bef 13th, lme.* (5 to 2 op 7 to 4) pu
Dist: Nk, ¾l, 30l. 6m 10.20s. a 13.20s (8 Ran).

(George Tobitt), J H Johnson

545 Tony Charlton Memorial Novices' Claiming Hurdle (4-y-o and up) £2,169 3m 110yds ....(4:20)

445 EXARCH (USA) (bl) 4-11-6 D Bridgwater, *dsptd ld to second, cl up, pushed alng to lead aftr 3 out, drw clr frm nxt.*....................(5 to 2 op 2 to 1) 1
482⁶ STINGRAY CITY (USA) 4-11-2 F Perratt, *sn cl up, led appr 8th, mstk 3 out, soon hdd, rdn approaching nxt, no imprsn*....................(5 to 2 on tchd 3 to 1 on) 2
TIPPERARY ROSE (Ire) 5-10-9 M Dwyer, *led till hdd appr 8th, sn outpcd and lost tch, wl tld off frm 3 out.* (8 to 1) 3
Dist: 15l, dist. 6m 4.30s. a 19.30s (3 Ran).

(J T Morris), N A Twiston-Davies

546 Gig Handicap Chase for the Fair Maids Challenge Trophy (0-115 4-y-o and up)

£3,081 2m........................ (4:50)

ALGARI [101] 6-10-12 M Moloney, *trkd ldrs, wnt second 8th, led 2 out, drvn out.*.................... (3 to 1) 1
POSITIVE ACTION [95] 7-10-3 (3⁺) A Dobbin, *chsd ldrs till blun and lost pl 4th, hdwy 9th, styd on wl frm 2 out, nrst finish.*................................(6 to 1) 2
STRONG FANCY [91] 10-10-2² R Garritty, *cl up, led appr 5th, hdd 2 out, kpt on und pres*....(14 to 1 op 10 to 1) 3
479⁴ CROSS CANNON [120] 7-12-0 (3⁺,3ex) A Larnach, *trkd ldrs, effrt aftr 3 out, kpt on same pace*.... (4 to 1 op 3 to 1) 4
279² SONSIE MO [105] 8-10-11 (5⁺) P Williams, *prmnt, effrt aftr 9th, no imprsn*.......(9 to 4 fav op 2 to 1 tchd 5 to 2) 5
ANTINOUS [111] 9-11-8 B Storey, *hld up, hdwy aftr 8th, mstk and lost pl nxt, not reco'r*....(6 to 1 tchd 7 to 1) 6
EBRO [92] 7-10-3³ A Merrigan, *al beh, lost tch frm 6th, tld off*....................(100 to 1 op 50 to 1) 7
279⁵ PRESSURE GAME [90] 10-10-1¹ C Grant, *mstks, led till hdd appr 5th, lost tch frm 7th, tld off.*
....................................(50 to 1 op 33 to 1) 8
Dist: 1½l, sht-hd, 4l, 4l, 30l. 3m 59.90s. a 8.90s (8 Ran).
SR: 19/11/7/32/13/   (C J Allan), G Richards

547 Grunwick Stakes National Hunt Flat Race (4,5,6-y-o) £1,516 1m 5f 110yds..... (5:20)

THREE STRONG (Ire) 4-10-11 (3⁺) D J Moffatt, *al prmnt, led o'r 2 out, styd on wl*.............. (6 to 1 tchd 7 to 1) 1
TOPPING TOM (Ire) 4-10-11 (3⁺) V Slattery, *trkd ldrs, stumbled 5 out, chsd wnr frm o'r 2 out, no imprsn.*
................................(6 to 5 fav op 5 to 4 on tchd 5 to 4) 2
ORD GALLERY (Ire) 4-10-7 (7⁺) A Linton, *al prmnt, ev ch 3 out, sn hrd rdn, hng rght 2 out, one pace.*
................................(6 to 1 op 8 to 1) 3
TOTAL UP (Ire) 4-10-9 (5⁺) Mr D McCain, *in tch, hdwy to track ldrs hfwy, outpcd o'r 2 out*...............(7 to 1) 4
SILVER FANCY (Ire) 4-10-7 (7⁺) F Perratt, *in tch till outpcd o'r 2 out*..............(5 to 2 op 7 to 2 tchd 9 to 4) 5
WEY I MAN (Ire) 4-10-11 (3⁺) A Larnach, *in tch till outpcd 3 out*....................(50 to 1 op 33 to 1) 6
FUNNY WORRY 4-10-11 (3⁺) A Dobbin, *led till hdd o'r 2 out, wknd quickly*................(14 to 1 tchd 12 to 1) 7
RED RHAPSODY 4-10-2 (7⁺) Mark Roberts, *al beh.*
....................................(14 to 1 op 8 to 1) 8
LONDON HILL 5-10-11 (5⁺) P Williams, *trkd ldrs till wknd 3 out.*....................................(100 to 1) 9
WEE WARRIOR 5-10-11 (5⁺) D Bentley, *beh frm hfwy.*
....................................(50 to 1 op 33 to 1) 10
CUMINESTOWN 4-10-4 (5⁺) W Dwan, *al beh, tld off.*
....................................(25 to 1 op 20 to 1) 11
Dist: 4l, 2½l, 25l, ¾l, sht-hd, 3l, 1½l, 3l, 10l, dist. 3m 14.10s. (11 Ran).
(The Braw Partnership), J H Johnson

SOUTHWELL (good)
Wednesday September 22nd
Going Correction: PLUS 0.40 sec. per fur.

548 Hepworth Minerals And Chemicals Ltd Handicap Chase (0-115 5-y-o and up) £2,432 3m 110yds................... (3:10)

386³ HEIGHT OF FUN [91] (bl) 9-10-12 M A FitzGerald, *made all, mstk 5th, hit 6th, lft clr nxt, styd on wl frm 3 out.*
....................................(7 to 2 op 3 to 1 tchd 4 to 1) 1
ARD T'MATCH [95] (v) 8-11-2 Gary Lyons, *hld up, lft second 7th, cld up 9th, hit 14th and sn rdn alng, one pace frm 4 out*.............(5 to 1 op 9 to 2 tchd 7 to 1) 2
SCOTTISH REFORM [96] 6-11-3 L Wyer, *f 1st.*
....................................(9 to 2 op 3 to 1) f
427⁷ COUNTERBID [103] (v) 6-11-10 A Maguire, *trkd wnr, hit 6th, f nxt*......(11 to 10 on op 11 to 8 on tchd Evens) f
Dist: 15l. 6m 47.20s. a 49.20s (4 Ran).

(A Staple), C L Popham

549 Coca Cola & Schweppes Novices' Chase (5-y-o and up) £2,173 2m........... (3:40)

338² KEEP SHARP 7-11-0 L Wyer, *made all, blun 8th, rdn appr last and ran on wl.* (11 to 8 fav op 6 to 4 tchd 7 to 4) 1
442⁶ BARDESAN 7-11-7 J Osborne, *jmpd slwly 1st 2, trkd ldrs, chsd wnr frm 3 out, effrt and rdn last, not run on.*
....................................(9 to 4 op 6 to 4) 2
442³ WEEKDAY CROSS (Ire) 5-10-12 A Maguire, *hld up, hdwy hfwy, 3rd whn blun 3 out, no ch aftr.* (4 to 1 op 3 to 1) 3
485⁶ KEY DEAR (Fr) 6-11-0 T Wall, *chsd wnr, hit 7th, second and rdn whn f 4 out*..................(20 to 1 op 12 to 1) f
202² DECIDING BID 7-11-0 M A FitzGerald, *in tch till wknd and hit 6th, sn beh, tld off whn pld up bef 8th.*
....................................(11 to 1 op 8 to 1 tchd 14 to 1) pu
488 NO DAW 9-11-0 B Powell, *jmpd badly 1st 2, pld up bef 3rd*....................(20 to 1 op 16 to 1) pu
ROCKY TYRONE 6-11-0 J Railton, *al rear, tld off whn pld up bef 8th*..................(14 to 1 op 10 to 1) pu
Dist: 2½l, 30l. 4m 21.20s. a 22.20s (7 Ran).
(Hart & Co Insurance Brokers Ltd), Mrs S J Smith

550 Iggesund Timber Conditional Jockeys' Handicap Chase (0-115 5-y-o and up) £2,163 2½m 110yds............... (4:10)

444⁶ TIGERS PET [103] 9-11-12 M Hourigan, *chsd ldrs, hdwy 8th, led 2 out, rdn clr last, ran on wl.*
....(11 to 2 op 6 to 1) 1
SECRET SUMMIT (USA) [94] (v) 7-11-3 T Eley, *blun 1st, chsd ldrs, hdwy to ld 3 out, hdd and blunded nxt, hrd rdn and blundered last.*
....(9 to 2 op 5 to 1 tchd 11 to 2) 2
426⁴ CLEVER FOLLY [105] 13-11-9 (5*) B Harding, *led to second, chsd ldr till blun and lft in ld tenth, rdn and hdd 3 out, blunded nxt, sn btn.*................(4 to 1 op 3 to 1) 3
OLD ROAD (USA) [94] 7-11-3 R Davis, *beh frm 6th.*
....(12 to 1 op 7 to 1) 4
517 CANTGETOUT [85] 7-10-8 A Thornton, *prmnt, hit second, f 3rd.*..................................(10 to 1 op 7 to 1) f
397* RED UNDER THE BED [98] 6-11-4 (3*) J Burke, *cl up, led second till f tenth...*(9 to 4 fav op 13 to 8 tchd 5 to 2) f
ORCHIPEDZO [89] 8-10-9 (3*) Judy Davies, *al rear, hit 5th and sn beh, pld up 7th.*..........(16 to 1 tchd 14 to 1) pu
Dist: 4l, 25l, 15l. 5m 35.40s. a 32.40s (7 Ran).
(Mrs C Bissill), W H Bissill

SOUTHWELL (A.W) (std)
Wednesday September 22nd
Going Correction: PLUS 0.60 sec. per fur.

551 Provident Mutual Novices' Hurdle (4-y-o and up) £1,689 2m................(2:10)

BLAZON OF TROY 4-10-12 S Smith Eccles, *al prmnt, hdwy to chal 4 out, led appr 2 out, rdn and ran on last.*
....(3 to 1 op 7 to 4 tchd 100 to 30 and 7 to 1) 1
207² WELL APPOINTED (Ire) 4-10-12 A Maguire, *led, jnd 4 out, rdn nxt, sn hdd, hit 2 out and last, no extr flt.*
....(11 to 4 fav op 5 to 2 tchd 9 to 4) 2
323⁵ EARLY DRINKER 5-11-0 J Osborne, *in tch, effrt and hdwy 4 out, rdn appr nxt, sn one pace.*
....(9 to 2 op 6 to 1 tchd 4 to 1) 3
355⁴ FRANKUS 4-11-5 M Perrett, *hit second, hdwy 6th, rdn and one pace appr 3 out.*..........(8 to 1 tchd 9 to 1) 4
429⁹ MURASIL (USA) 4-10-12 R Supple, *chsd ldrs, rdn hfwy, lost tch 4 out.*.........................(33 to 1 op 25 to 1) 5
DAUPHIN BLEU (Fr) 7-11-0 Dr P Pritchard, *hit 1st, cl up, hit 6th and 7th, sn wknd.*...........(50 to 1 op 33 to 1) 6
HIGHLAND FLAME 4-10-12 V Smith, *cl up till rdn 5 and sn lost pl.*....................................(33 to 1 op 25 to 1) 7
RUTLAND WATER (USA) 6-11-0 J A Harris, *chsd ldrs, rdn alng and hit 6th, sn wknd, tld off whn pld up bef 3 out.*
....(5 to 1 tchd 11 to 2 and 6 to 1) pu
MY GIRL FRIDAY 4-10-7 L Wyer, *al rear, tld off hfwy, pld up bef 3 out.*.................................(33 to 1) pu
TELMAR SYSTEMS 4-10-12 S McNeill, *mstks and al beh, tld off hfwy, pld up 3 out.*.....................(16 to 1) pu
Dist: 5l, 12l, ½l, 20l, 8l, 15l. 4m 1.70s. a 15.70s (10 Ran).
SR: 23/18/8/12/-/-/ (David F Wilson), T Thomson Jones

552 British Coal Midlands Selling Handicap Hurdle (4-y-o and up) £1,660 2¼m.. (2:40)

370³ HAVE A NIGHTCAP [90] 4-12-0 J A Harris, *al prmnt, chsd ldr whn hit 7th and sn rdn alng, hdwy to ld 3 out, hrd drvn last, ran on wl flt.*
....(100 to 30 fav op 5 to 2 tchd 4 to 1) 1
447 BURN BRIDGE (USA) [86] (v) 7-11-10 Peter Caldwell, *hld up, steady hdwy hfwy, hit 4 out, effrt appr last and sn ev ch, rdn and kpt on flt.*............(9 to 2 op 7 to 2) 2
287⁵ GREEN'S SEAGO (USA) [62] 5-9-9 (5*) T Eley, *hld up, gd hdwy hfwy, chlgd and ev ch 3 out, rdn nxt, one pace last...* (15 to 2 op 8 to 1 tchd 9 to 1 and 7 to 1) 3
344² MABTHUL (USA) [75] 5-10-10 (3*) M Hourigan, *al prmnt and gng wl, hit 4th, smooth hdwy to ld four out, hdd nxt, rdn 2 out, sn wknd.*..........(5 to 1 op 7 to 2) 4
425 CISTOLENA [62] (v) 7-10-0 Diane Clay, *beh, rdn and some hdwy 5 out, nvr a factor.*........(6 to 1 op 10 to 1) 5
514³ ALIZARI (USA) [62] (bl) 4-10-0 M Robinson, *prmnt, rdn 5th and sn lost pl, hrd drvn, wl beh frm 7th.*
....(16 to 1 op 14 to 1) 6
401³ STROKED AGAIN [68] 8-10-3 (3*) A Thornton, *prmnt till rdn and lost pl 5 out, sn beh.*.............(10 to 1 op 8 to 1) 7
477⁸ MASH THE TEA (Ire) [62] (v) 4-10-0 V Smith, *led, rdn and hdd 4 out, sn wknd.*............(16 to 1 op 33 to 1) 8
459 MANDALAY PRINCE [70] 9-10-8 M A FitzGerald, *jmpd slwly 1st and second, beh whn refused 3rd.*........(10 to 1) ref
ARTHURS STONE [90] 7-11-8 A Maguire, *mstks, al beh, tld off hfwy, pld up bef 3 out.*......(10 to 1 op 5 to 1) pu
Dist: ¾l, 5l, 25l, 15l, 1l, 15l. 4m 31.20s. a 19.20s (10 Ran).
SR: 16/11/-/-/-/-/ (R A M Racecourses Ltd), J L Harris

553 Garbo's Nightclub Handicap Hurdle (0-125 4-y-o and up) £1,731 2½m......... (4:40)

ELLTEE-ESS [85] 8-10-13 A Maguire, *chsd ldrs, outpcd and pushed alng 8th, rdn and hdwy to chase ldr 3 out, led nxt, ran on wl and pres flt......*(12 to 1 op 6 to 1) 1
RED CARDINAL [90] 7-11-4 S Smith Eccles, *led, rdn 3 out, hdd nxt, no extr und pres flt......*(8 to 1 op 14 to 1) 2
465* SAKIL (Ire) [81] 5-10-9 (6ex) H Davies, *al prmnt, chsd ldr 4 out, rdn bef nxt, sn wknd.*
....(15 to 8 fav op 11 to 8 tchd 2 to 1) 3
326³ COURT CIRCULAR [99] (bl) 4-11-13 Diane Clay, *hit second, reminders 5th and sn wl beh, some late hdwy.*
....(2 to 1 op 9 to 4 tchd 5 to 2) 4
519⁶ JOLI'S GREAT [89] 5-11-3 J Ryan, *chsd ldrs, lost pl 7th, tld off whn pld up bef 3 out.*............(7 to 2 op 3 to 1) pu
Dist: 3½l, 20l, 3l. 5m 7.40s. a 26.40s (5 Ran).
(D A Johnson), R J Weaver

LISTOWEL (IRE) (good to yielding)
Thursday September 23rd

554 Ansers Boutique and Libra Designs Mares Novices' Chase (4-y-o and up) £3,795 2¾m
....(2:35)

SULLANE RIVER (Ire) 5-11-8 D H O'Connor, ...(5 to 2) 1
327⁴ HIGHBASS 7-12-0 T Horgan, ...(6 to 1) 2
293 MAKE ME AN ISLAND 8-12-0 C O'Dwyer, ...(14 to 1) 3
507⁶ COUMEENOOLE LADY 6-12-0 C F Swan, ...(6 to 1) 4
RAINY MISS (Ire) 5-11-0 W J Slattery Jnr, ...(20 to 1) 5
MCMAHON'S RIVER 6-11-9 H Rogers, ...(14 to 1) 6
430 SQUIRRELLSDAUGHTER (bl) 6-11-9 J Jones, ...(50 to 1) 7
327 MANDEVILLE LANE 7-11-7 (7*) P A Roche, ...(33 to 1) f
430⁸ FERRIC FORTRESS 7-11-9 A J O'Brien, ...(33 to 1) f
473³ WILL PHONE 7-12-0 J F Titley, ...(2 to 1 fav) f
503⁵ LADY DIGA (Ire) 5-10-9 (5*) D T Evans, ...(25 to 1) f
GLENGARRA PRINCESS 6-11-2 (7*) Mr D K Budds,
....(20 to 1) ur
342² LADY DIAMOND 7-11-9 J P Banahan, ...(10 to 1) bd
MONKS AIR 6-11-9 L P Cusack, ...(20 to 1) ref
BOTHA BOCHT 6-11-2 (7*) K M O'Callaghan, ...(33 to 1) pu
Dist: 25l, 15l, 20l, 5½l. 6m 13.90s. (15 Ran).
(S Lucey), David J McGrath

555 Coleman Tunnelling Maiden Hurdle (4-y-o) £4,140 2m.................... (3:10)

257² COCKNEY LAD (Ire) 11-5 C F Swan, ...(10 to 1) 1
504² MISTER DRUM (Ire) 10-12 (7*) Mr J T McNamara, (12 to 1) 2
56⁶ STEEL MIRROR 11-5 J Shortt, ...(12 to 1) 3
333* BAWNROCK (Ire) 11-5 T Horgan, ...(7 to 4 fav) 4
314³ DOMINO'S RING (Ire) 11-5 D H O'Connor, ...(8 to 1) 5
SIDCUP HILL (Ire) 11-0 T J Taaffe, ...(33 to 1) 6
314² PRIVATE GUY (Ire) 11-5 B Sheridan, ...(5 to 2) 7
252⁶ NORA ANN (Ire) 11-0 C O'Dwyer, ...(10 to 1) 8
TALE A TALE (Ire) 10-12 (7*) J P Broderick, ...(33 to 1) 9
MR GERAN (Ire) 11-5 F Woods, ...(25 to 1) 10
THE ODD TIME (Ire) 11-5 J Magee, ...(33 to 1) 11
257⁹ NORDIC SIGN (Ire) (bl) 11-5 K F O'Brien, ...(16 to 1) 12
409⁹ CARBON FIVE (Ire) 11-0 G Bradley, ...(33 to 1) 13
JIMMY THE WEED (Ire) 10-12 (7*) J Butler, ...(33 to 1) 14
531 TRIPLE ACE (Ire) 11-5 J Jones, ...(33 to 1) 15
HAVE A BRANDY (Ire) 11-5 A J O'Brien, ...(14 to 1) 16
274⁶ YOUR UNCLE STANLEY (Ire) 11-5 Mr D M O'Brien, (33 to 1) 17
504⁷ ORTHORHOMBUS 10-12 (7*) P A Roche, ...(33 to 1) 18
JOHNSTONS BUCK (Ire) 11-0 (5*) Mr D Valentine, (16 to 1) 19
234⁹ JUST FOUR (Ire) 10-12 (7*) Mr C M Healy, ...(20 to 1) 20
Dist: 3½l, 5½l, ¾l, 5l, 9l. 4m 9.90s. (20 Ran).
(D Daly), W M Roper

556 Smithwicks Beer Handicap Hurdle (5-y-o and up) £8,880 2m................(3:45)

123* CAMDEN BUZZ (Ire) [-] 5-10-13 C F Swan, ...(5 to 4 on) 1
123 BIG MATT (Ire) [-] 5-10-5 (5*) C O'Brien, ...(5 to 1) 2
528⁴ TOUREEN GIRL [-] 6-9-7 P Carberry, ...(10 to 1) 3
528* ULTRA MAGIC [-] 6-9-3¹ (5*,3ex) A J Roche, ...(7 to 1) 4
527* DORAN'S TOWN LAD [-] 6-10-11 G Bradley, ...(9 to 2) 5
527 NORDIC SUN (Ire) [-] (bl) 5-11-3 J F Titley, ...(10 to 1) 6
475* FLUSTERED (USA) [-] (bl) 7-10-12 A Powell, ...(20 to 1) 7
Dist: 2l, 9l, ½l, dist. 4m 5.90s. (7 Ran).
(Miss Carmel Byrne), P Mullins

557 Spectra Photo Labs Handicap Hurdle (4-y-o and up) £4,485 2¾m........... (4:20)

294⁸ LOVE AND PORTER (Ire) [-] 5-10-6 D H O'Connor, ..(7 to 1) 1
506* MERRY PEOPLE [-] 6-9-13 (4ex) C F Swan, ...(6 to 1) 2
330* MINERAL DUST [-] 10-10-4 T Horgan, ...(7 to 1) 3
275⁴ ST DONAVINT [-] 6-10-6 C N Bowens, ...(6 to 1) 4
410² KILIAN MY BOY [-] 10-10-10 J F Titley, ...(4 to 1 fav) 5
THE CRAZY BISHOP (Ire) [-] 5-11-2 G Bradley, ...(7 to 1) 6
505* MOUNTHENRY STAR (Ire) [-] 5-9-3 (7*) Mr G P FitzGerald,
....(10 to 1) 7
410 HIGH-SPEC [-] 7-11-3 J Magee, ...(14 to 1) 8
363⁵ MARBLE CITY GIRL [-] (bl) 8-9-2 (5*) T P Treacy, (20 to 1) 9
2⁶ KAZKAR (Ire) [-] 5-9-12 F Woods, ...(20 to 1) 10
430⁶ DOONEGA (Ire) [-] 5-10-8 (5*) C O'Brien, ...(12 to 1) 11

330³ AWBEG ROVER (Ire) [-] 5-9-3³ (7*) P A Roche, ... (25 to 1) 12
169⁷ GALES JEWEL [-] 7-9-7 P Carberry, ... (50 to 1) 13
410⁸ MARY GINA [-] 8-9-4² (5*) T J O'Sullivan, ... (66 to 1) 14
      QUIET CITY [-] 6-9-11 (7*) Mr J T McNamara, ... (33 to 1) 15
376² WIND ZING [-] 9-9-7 W T Slattery Jnr, ... (33 to 1) 16
 69⁵ NANCYS LAD [-] 6-9-0 (7*) G Lee, ... (33 to 1) 17
      PORT TIME [-] 6-11-9 T J Taaffe, ... (16 to 1) pu
Dist: 2l, 1½l, sht-hd, 8l. 5m 48.80s. (18 Ran).

(The Schooner Syndicate), James Joseph O'Connor

558 Woodfab Flat Race Final (4-y-o and up) £8,780 2m........................ (5:30)

215* AFGHANI (Ire) 4-11-5 (5*) Mrs J M Mullins, ...(Evens fav) 1
423* COMMON POLICY (Ire) 4-11-6 (7*) Mr J Connolly, (14 to 1) 2
534 MORE DASH (Ire) 5-11-3 (7*) Mr D J Kavanagh, ... (50 to 1) 3
 88* CHANCERY QUEEN (Ire) 4-11-8 Mr A P O'Brien, ... (7 to 2) 4
136* WOLF WINTER 8-12-4 Mr S R Murphy, ... (6 to 1) 5
      EALING COURT 4-11-5 (5*) Mr G J Harford, ... (7 to 2) 6
158⁷ HURRICANE MILLIE (Ire) 5-11-5 (5*) Mr J A Nash, (50 to 1) 7
Dist: 9l, 6l, 2l, 2½l. 4m 5.40s. (7 Ran).

(Mrs Violet O'Leary), W P Mullins

PERTH (good to firm)
Thursday September 3rd
Going Correction: PLUS 0.30 sec. per fur.

559 Highland Spring Novices' Hurdle (4-y-o and up) £2,739 2½m.......... (2:15)

MERRY NUTKIN 7-11-0 P Niven, trkd ldrs gng wl, led 3 out, drw clr frm nxt, easily.
............(5 to 4 on tchd 6 to 5 on and 11 to 8 on) 1
282³ FLING IN SPRING (v) 7-10-9 (5*) P Williams, hld up, smooth hdwy to chase wnr appr 2 out, sn rdn and no imprsn.
..................(10 to 1 op 14 to 1) 2
JOHNS THE BOY 7-10-7 (7*) J Supple, pld hrd, trkd ldrs till outpcd appr 3 out, styd on frm nxt.
.............................(50 to 1 tchd 66 to 1) 3
RED TEMPEST (Ire) 5-10-7² F Perratt, beh, hdwy aftr 3 out, styd on and not rch ldrs..... (66 to 1 op 50 to 1) 4
BLUEBELL TRACK (bl) 7-10-9 A Merrigan, trkd ldrs, effrt appr 2 out, sn btn................ (50 to 1 op 33 to 1) 5
SHUT UP 4-10-7 A Orkney, in tch, pushed alng aftr 6th, wknd aftr 3 out, tld off.......... (50 to 1 op 33 to 1) 6
SEE WHAT I MEAN 6-10-11 (3*) A Thornton, in tch till wknd quickly aftr 3 out, tld off................. (50 to 1) 7
LIME STREET 5-11-0 D Bridgwater, cl up, chsng 3 out, sn wknd, eased whn btn aftr nxt, tld off.
................(4 op 4 to 4 tchd 2 to 1) 8
DONEGAL STYLE (Ire) 5-11-0 B Storey, led till hdd 3 out, wknd quickly, tld off..............(12 to 1 op 10 to 1) 9
Dist: 8l, 1½l, 10l, 12l, dist, 1l, 4l, 2½l. 5m 4.00s. a 19.00s (9 Ran).

(Robert F S Newall), Mrs M Reveley

560 Perthshire Challenge Cup Handicap Chase (0-115 5-y-o and up) £3,078 2½m 110yds........................ (2:45)

GRANGE BRAKE [117] 7-12-0 D Bridgwater, made all, rdn aftr 3 out, mstk nxt, styd on wl.
.................(13 to 8 fav op 5 to 4 tchd 7 to 4) 1
BOARDING SCHOOL [103] 6-11-0 B Storey, chsd wnr, blun 6th, rdn aftr 3 out, no imprsn...(2 to 1 op 3 to 1) 2
366⁶ ABSAILOR [91] 9-10-2⁵ (5*) P Williams, whipped round strt, started slwly, beh, effrt aftr 4 out, sn rdn, no hdwy..................(7 to 2 op 3 to 1 tchd 4 to 1) 3
NIGHT GUEST [106] 11-11-0 (3*) A Dobbin, in tch, pushed alng aftr tenth, wknd appr 3 out.... (7 to 1 op 6 to 1) 4
Dist: 7l, 6l, 4l. 5m 10.00s. a 12.00s (4 Ran).
SR: 41/20/2/13/

(Mrs J Mould), N A Twiston-Davies

561 Harcros Scottish Juvenile Championship Qualifier Three Years Old Novices' Hurdle £2,221 2m 110yds.............. (3:15)

406³ BONUS POINT 10-12 P Niven, trkd ldrs, wnt second aftr 5th, led appr last, styd on wl.
...................(5 to 1 op 4 to 1 tchd 11 to 2) 1
285* WANZA 11-4 C Grant, hld up, hld appr last, kpt on.
...................(5 to 4 fav op 11 to 8 tchd 6 to 4) 2
DEMILUNE (USA) 10-8 D Bridgwater, not jump wl, mstks second and 3rd, effrt aftr 3 out, sn rdn and btn.
.........................(7 to 4 op 9 to 1) 3
481* ON GOLDEN POND (Ire) 10-10 (3*) N Bentley, cl up till outpcd aftr 3 out, no dngr after.
...................(5 to 2 op 9 to 4 tchd 4 to 1) 4
278 TAYBRIDGE TOSH (bl) 10-5 (7*) A Linton, reminders and lost tch aftr 4th, tld off whn pld up bef 2 out.
.......................(50 to 1 tchd 100 to 1) pu
Dist: 1l, 12l, sht-hd. 3m 58.60s. a 14.60s (5 Ran).

(D B O'Connor), Mrs M Reveley

562 Highland Spring Scottish Celebration Handicap Hurdle (0-125 4-y-o and up)

£3,355 2½m 110yds............... (3:45)

519⁴ MASTER OF THE ROCK [99] (v) 4-10-0 C Hawkins, prmnt, wnt second 6th, chlgd 3 out, led nxt, drvn out.
..............................(6 to 1 op 7 to 1) 1
543² PERSUASIVE [123] 6-11-5 (5*) Mr M Buckley, hld up in tch gng wl, chlgd 2 out, sn pushed alng and swtchd, no extr.......(5 to 4 on tchd 11 to 10 on tchd 13 to 8 on) 2
DAWADAR (USA) [113] 6-10-7 (7*) F Perratt, slwly into strd, sn cl up, outpcd appr 3 out, styd on ag'n approaching last.......................(6 to 1 op 3 to 1) 3
HAZEL LEAF [99] 7-10-0 R Hodge, made most till hdd 2 out, sn wknd........ (100 to 30 op 9 to 2 tchd 3 to 1) 4
Dist: 3l, 3l, 2l. 5m 4.80s. a 19.80s (4 Ran).

(L C Maultby), Mrs P A Barker

563 Faulds Advertising Novices' Chase (5-y-o and up) £2,723 3m................(4:15)

478* SCOTTISH GOLD 9-11-4 G McCourt, in tch, pushed alng aftr 12th, gd hdwy appr 4 out, let nxt, clr betw last 2, styd on wl.........................(6 to 1 op 3 to 1) 1
396³ SECOND ATTEMPT 9-11-4 A Merrigan, cl up, led 13th, hdd 3 out, sn btn.............(33 to 1 op 25 to 1) 2
EARTH SUMMIT 5-11-0 D Bridgwater, jmpd deliberately, led till ran wide bend aftr 11th, blun nxt and lost pl, no dngr after. (6 to 4 on 11 to 10 on tchd 13 to 8 on) 3
CLARE LAD 10-11-4 B Storey, prmnt, led aftr 11th, hdd 13th, wknd quickly appr 4 out, tld off..........(6 to 1) 4
279 CLONADRUM 9-10-11 (7*) A Linton, f 1st.
.........................(50 to 1 tchd 50 to 1) f
CELTIC WATERS 8-10-13 C Dennis, mstks, al beh, tld off frm 14th, pld up bef 2 out...........(14 to 1 op 12 to 1) pu
DROMIN (Ire) 5-11-0 C Grant, in tch, mstk tenth, wknd quickly aftr 12th, tld off whn pld up bef nxt.
.......................(12 to 1 op 8 to 1) pu
Dist: 30l, 2½l, 30l. 6m 21.50s. a 24.50s (7 Ran).

(Miss L A Perratt), Miss L A Perratt

564 Travail Employment Group Conditional Jockeys' Handicap Hurdle (0-115 4-y-o and up) £2,221 3m 110yds............. (4:45)

443² KANO WARRIOR [96] 6-10-12 V Slattery, made all, rdn aftr 2 out, styd on wl............(13 to 8 on op 11 to 8 on) 1
CHARLOTTE'S EMMA [100] 6-11-2 P Waggott, prmnt, jmpd rght thrght, mstk 6th, chsd wnr appr 2 out, kpt on, no imprsn.........(4 to 1 tchd 7 to 2 and 9 to 2) 2
478² GATHERING TIME [112] 7-12-0 D J Moffatt, with ldr, pushed alng aftr 9th, hrd rdn and lost pl aftr 3 out, styd on ag'n appr last................(4 to 1 op 7 to 2) 3
SILVER HELLO [99] 7-11-1 P Williams, hld up and beh, gd hdwy to join ldrs 9th, rdn appr 2 out, sn btn.
.......................(12 to 1 op 10 to 1 tchd 14 to 1) 4
478³ IT'S A PRY [84] 12-10-0 E Husband, in tch till outpcd appr 9th, no dngr aftr....................(33 to 1 op 25 to 1) 5
Dist: 2½l, 3l, ¾l, 8l. 6m 8.20s. a 23.20s (5 Ran).

(D Jones), N A Twiston-Davies

TAUNTON (firm)
Thursday September 23rd
Going Correction: MINUS 0.65 sec. per fur.

565 Broadway Novices' Hurdle (4-y-o and up) £1,689 2m 3f 110yds............... (2:20)

RIVER RED 7-11-0 A Maguire, al frnt rnk, led 7th, hrd rdn frm 2 out, all out............(2 to 1 jt-fav tchd 5 to 2) 1
486² CORNISH COSSACK (NZ) 6-10-7 (7*) Mr G Shenkin, hld up, hdwy 5th, pressed wnr frm 3 out, swtchd rght r-in, ran on.........................(6 to 1 tchd 7 to 1) 2
445⁴ NEW STATESMAN 5-11-0 B Clifford, hld up in rear, styd on appr 2 out, nvr nrr..............(25 to 1 op 14 to 1) 3
445⁵ DAUNTLESS KNIGHT (USA) 5-11-0 Peter Hobbs, hld up in rear, hdwy frm 3 out, styd on one pace.
.......................(25 to 1 op 16 to 1) 4
441⁵ WILL'S BOUNTY 10-10-7 (7*) Mr A Phillips, led chasing grp, making hdwy whn hmpd 6th, sn in tch ag'n, wknd appr 2 out...................(20 to 1 tchd 25 to 1) 5
416³ GILBERT (Ire) 5-10-7 (7*) A Flannigan, prmnt, led aftr 5th, hdd 7th, mstk nxt, wknd.....................(25 to 1) 6
ANNABEL'S BABY (Ire) 4-10-2 (5*) R Davis, jmpd slwly second, in rear till hdwy appr 6th, wknd approaching 2 out.........................(14 to 1 op 7 to 1) 7
MAC THE BAT (Ire) 5-10-7 (7*) D Meade, al in rear.
.......................(9 to 1 op 6 to 1 tchd 10 to 1) 8
483⁶ TINKLING STAR 9-11-0 B Powell, al beh.......... (9 to 1) 9
301³ SUDANOR (Ire) 4-10-12 N Hawke, led till aftr 5th, cl second whn f nxt....(2 to 1 jt-fav op 11 to 4 tchd 9 to 4) f
JELLY MORTON 8-11-0 N Mann, wl in rear till hdwy 3 out, btn whn hit nxt, pld up lme r-in.
.......................(25 to 1 op 12 to 1) pu
Dist: ½l, 7l, 4l, 2½l, 3l, 6l, 12l, hd. 4m 28.50s. a 7.50s (11 Ran).

(J Huckle), J White

67

566 William Stansell Trophy Handicap Chase (0-120 5-y-o and up) £2,866 3m...... (2:50)

436* KILLULA CHIEF [102] 6-10-9 M A FitzGerald, *hld up, hdwy frm 13th, wnt second 4 out, led nxt, sn clr.*
......................(6 to 5 fav op 6 to 4 tchd 13 to 8) 1
POWDER BOY [94] 8-10-1¹ R Dunwoody, *led second to 5th, led ag'n nxt, mstk 11th, rdn and hdd 3 out, hld whn hit next*.................. (9 to 2 tchd 5 to 1 and 4 to 1) 2
457³ AMONG FRIENDS [99] 8-10-1 (5") R Davis, *prmnt, led 5th to 6th, wknd appr 4 out.* (7 to 2 op 3 to 1 tchd 4 to 1) 3
458³ TOUCHING STAR [95] (v) 8-9-13 (3") M Hourigan, *led to second, mstk 6th and lost pl, hdwy 11th, wknd 14th.*
......................(7 to 1 op 5 to 1 tchd 8 to 1) 4
457⁴ MAJOR MATCH (NZ) [117] 11-11-10 H Davies, *blun and uns rdr 1st*.................. (7 to 1 op 4 to 1) ur
Dist: 10l, 20l, 15l. 5m 46.10s. b 0.90s (5 Ran).

(T G K Construction Ltd), J G M O'Shea

567 Taunton Castle Novices' Selling Hurdle (4-y-o and up) £1,763 2m 1f............... (3:20)

321³ COOCHIE (bl) 4-10-7 L Harvey, *al in tch, led appr 3 out, rdn nxt, ran on*...... (17 to 2 op 8 to 1 tchd 10 to 1) 1
TAUNTING (Ire) 5-11-0 D Gallagher, *hld up, hdwy frm 6th, ev ch 2 out, one pace aftr.*
......................(4 to 1 op 9 to 2 tchd 6 to 1) 2
SHALOU 4-10-12 R Dunwoody, *hld up in rear, hdwy appr 6th, wnt second nxt, no extr approaching 2 out.*
......................(6 to 1 op 4 to 1) 3
429 JUVENARA 7-10-9 (5") T Eley, *hld up in rear, hdwy 6th, wknd appr 2 out.*...... (7 to 1 op 6 to 1 tchd 10 to 1) 4
416² MISTY VIEW 4-10-0 (7") P McLoughlin, *trkd ldr, led appr 3rd, clr 5th, rdn and hdd approaching 3 out, btn frm nxt*...... (11 to 4 fav op 5 to 2 tchd 9 to 4 and 3 to 1) 5
WILL BONNY (NZ) 6-10-7 (7") T Murphy, *hld up in rear, hdwy appr 2 out, nvr dngrs*..................(33 to 1) 6
454⁴ ALTO PRINCESS 4-10-7 H Davies, *hld up in tch, hdwy 6th, rdn appr 2 out, eased whn btn.*
......................(6 to 1 op 5 to 1 tchd 8 to 1) 7
287 LONDON EXPRESS 9-10-9 Peter Hobbs, *led till hdd appr 3rd, styd prmnt till wknd quickly 3 out.*
......................(14 to 1 op 12 to 1) 8
HONEY'S FORTUNE 6-11-0 N Hawke, *mid-div, wknd 3 out*..................(40 to 1 op 33 to 1 tchd 50 to 1) 9
456 MASRUR (USA) 4-10-7 (5") J McCarthy, *chsd ldrs till wknd quickly 6th, tld off*...(25 to 1 op 16 to 1 tchd 33 to 1) 10
483 DARKTOWN STRUTTER (bl) 7-11-0 S McNeill, *prmnt till lost pl 3rd, ran wide on bend bef 5th, sn tld off.*
......................(100 to 1 op 66 to 1) 11
216 SEASIDE MINSTREL (bl) 5-10-7 (7") A Flannigan, *pld hrd, prmnt till lost pl 5th, tld off whn pulled up bef 2 out.*
......................(33 to 1 op 20 to 1) pu
323⁸ THARIF 5-11-0 M A FitzGerald, *al beh, tld off whn pld up bef 2 out*............(33 to 1 op 20 to 1) pu
Dist: 4l, 2l, 10l, hd, 3½l, 2l, 1½l, 8l, 30l, 30l. 3m 49.90s. a 2.90s (13 Ran).

(S M McCausland), R J Baker

568 Grunwick Novices' Chase (5-y-o and up) £2,450 2m 110yds................. (3:50)

MARCHMAN 8-11-2 J R Kavanagh, *trkd ldrs, chalg whn bumped and lft in ld 4 out, sn clr, one pace r-in, shaken up cl hme.*..................(7 to 2 op 11 to 4) 1
MUSIC BOX 7-11-2 I Lawrence, *hld up in tch, making hdwy whn lft second 4 out, hrd rdn and ran on r-in, no extr cl hme.*..................(25 to 1 op 20 to 1) 2
404³ WINDSOR PARK (USA) 7-11-7 R Dunwoody, *wtd wth, hdwy whn 7th, not pace to chal frm 4 out.*
......................(5 to 2 op 3 to 1) 3
446⁵ TALATON FLYER 7-11-2 Peter Hobbs, *chsd ldrs, hit 8th, outpcd frm 4 out*...... (10 to 1 op 8 to 1 tchd 12 to 1) 4
451⁵ SHUTAFUT (bl) 7-11-2 A Maguire, *led till aftr second, blun badly 6th, hit nxt, sn beh, tld off.*
......................(2 to 1 fav op 5 to 2 tchd 11 to 4) 5
FREE EXPRESSION 8-10-11 N Hawke, *al beh, tld off frm 7th*..................(50 to 1 op 33 to 1) 6
NUCLEAR EXPRESS 6-11-2 W Knox, *prmnt, led aftr second, mstk and hdd 7th, hit nxt, sn btn, tld off.*
......................(25 to 1 op 20 to 1 tchd 33 to 1) 7
325 COUNTY CONTRACTOR 6-11-2 S McNeill, *al beh, tld off frm 6th*..................(50 to 1 op 33 to 1 tchd 66 to 1) 8
CELTIC CATCH 7-11-2 M Bosley, *f second.*
......................(12 to 1 op 14 to 1 tchd 16 to 1) f
TARMON (Ire) (bl) 5-11-0 W Irvine, *hld up, hdwy to ld 7th, blun nxt, jmpd lft, bumped wnr and uns rdr 4 out.*
......................(33 to 1 op 20 to 1) ur
Dist: 1l, 8l, 2½l, dist, 2½l, ½l, 6l. 4m 0.80s. a 2.80s (10 Ran).

(Mrs P M King), J S King

569 Summerfield Handicap Hurdle (0-115 4-y-o and up) £2,696 2m 1f............... (4:20)

388* VA UTU [95] 5-10-0 Lorna Vincent, *al prmnt, trkd ldr frm 5th, hrd rdn to ld one hundred yards out, all out.*
......................(5 to 1 tchd 13 to 2) 1

NOCATCHIM [123] (bl) 4-12-0 J Osborne, *made most till hrd rdn and hdd one hundred yards out, rallied cl hme.*............(17 to 2 op 6 to 1 tchd 9 to 1) 2
SPRING TO GLORY [95] 6-9-9 (5") A Procter, *hld up in rear, hdwy 6th, rdn and styd on one pace frm 2 out.*
......................(33 to 1 op 20 to 1) 3
463³ TEL E THON [99] (bl) 6-9-13 (5") D Leahy, *prmnt, dsptd ld 3rd to 5th, rdn appr 2 out, one pace.*
......................(9 to 1 op 7 to 1 tchd 10 to 1) 4
WOLVER GOLD [95] 6-10-0 C Maude, *hld up in rear, steady hdwy frm 6th, 3rd whn rdn and wknd appr 2 out.*......................(9 to 1 op 16 to 1) 5
MIDNIGHT STRIKE (USA) [102] (bl) 9-10-7 W McFarland, *hld up in rear, effrt 6th, one pace frm 3 out.*
......................(16 to 1 op 10 to 1) 6
HIDDEN OATS [100] 6-10-5 B Powell, *al in rear, no hdwy frm 3 out*..................(14 to 1 op 10 to 1) 7
446³ CLEEVELAND LADY [99] 6-10-4 R Dunwoody, *chsd ldrs, rdn 7th, eased whn btn appr 2 out, tld off*...(3 to 1 jt-fav tchd 7 to 2 and 4 to 1) 8
434⁴ ATHAR (Ire) [98] 4-10-3 L Harvey, *hld up, slpd up on bend aftr 4th*..................(3 to 1 jt-fav op 5 to 2) su
Dist: Nk, 10l, 3l, 1l, 5l, ½l, 20l. 3m 41.20s. b 5.80s (9 Ran).
SR: 19/46/8/9/4/6/3/-/-/   (M Quinn), M R Channon

570 Wiveliscombe Juvenile Novices' Hurdle (3-y-o) £1,815 2m 1f............... (4:50)

C D SHAREPLAN (USA) 10-12 Lorna Vincent, *trkd ldr, led 3 out, rdn nxt, ran on wl*..................(25 to 1 op 14 to 1) 1
296² BEAT THE BAGMAN (Ire) 11-3 L Harvey, *al prmnt, wnt second appr 5th, hrd rdn frm 2 out, no imprsn r-in.*
......................(2 to 1 fav op 6 to 4 tchd 9 to 4) 2
GREEN CHILI 10-7 J Osborne, *hld up, hdwy 5th, styd on one pace frm 3 out.*......(10 to 1 op 14 to 1) 3
HOMEMAKER 10-7 E Byrne, *hld up in rear, steady hdwy frm 3 out, nvr nrr.* (8 to 1 op 6 to 1 tchd 10 to 1) 4
296⁴ ITS UNBELIEVABLE 11-3 A Maguire, *led till hdd 3 out, sn btn*..................(5 to 2 op 5 to 1) 5
296³ STAR MINSTREL (Ire) 10-12 M Perrett, *in tch till one pace frm 3 out*..................(9 to 1 op 7 to 1 tchd 10 to 1) 6
IS SHE QUICK 10-7 N Dawe, *chsd ldrs, rdn and cl 4th whn blun 3 out, no ch aftr*...... (50 to 1 op 20 to 1) 7
SHARED GOLD 10-7 M Bosley, *slwly away, al beh, tld off*..................(50 to 1 op 33 to 1) 8
SABO'S EXPRESS 10-9 (3") W Marston, *beh frm 5th, tld off*..................(50 to 1 op 33 to 1) 9
STANFORD AVENUE 10-7 M Richards, *slwly away, al in rear, tld off*..................(50 to 1 op 33 to 1) 10
MUSICAL PHONE 10-12 M A FitzGerald, *pld hrd, chsd ldrs till wknd 6th, tld off*...... (50 to 1 op 33 to 1) 11
WESSHAUN 10-2² (7") R Darke, *chsd ldrs till wknd quickly appr 6th, tld off*......(20 to 1 op 25 to 1) 12
LOVE IN THE MIST (USA) 10-7 R Dunwoody, *prmnt till wknd 6th, beh whn virtually pld up r-in, tld off.*
......................(6 to 1 op 4 to 1) 13
MERCH FACH (Ire) 10-7 C Maude, *al beh, rdn 5th, tld off whn pld up bef 2 out*..................(50 to 1) pu
Dist: 4l, 10l, ¾l, 3l, 3l, 2½l, 20l, 25l, 6l, 6l. 3m 45.20s. b 1.80s (14 Ran).
(Circular Distributors Ltd), M R Channon

LISTOWEL (IRE) (good to yielding) Friday September 24th

571 John J. Galvin Maiden Hurdle (Div 1) (5-y-o and up) £3,795 2½m............... (2:00)

363² SWALLOWS NEST 6-12-0 M Flynn, ...(6 to 4) 1
421³ THE DASHER DOYLE (Ire) 5-11-6 Mr P J Healy, ...(12 to 1) 2
120⁸ BUMBLY BROOK 6-10-13 (7") J M McCormack, .. (14 to 1) 3
432⁴ POOR TIMES (Ire) 5-10-10 (5") C P Dunne, ...(12 to 1) 4
RICH TRADITION (Ire) 5-12-0 G Bradley, ...(11 to 8 fav) 5
DONERAILE PARK 6-12-0 T Horgan, ...(20 to 1) 6
COOLREE (Ire) 5-12-0 K F O'Brien, ...(20 to 1) 7
158⁶ THE COBH GALE 6-11-1 H Rogers, ...(20 to 1) 8
295 TAKE IT EASY KID (Ire) 5-11-2 (7") Mr D A Harney, (12 to 1) 9
302⁷ LADY GALE BRIDGE 6-11-1 G M O'Neill, ...(20 to 1) 10
KINGS LORD 6-11-6 C O'Dwyer, ...(33 to 1) 11
472⁹ DELIGHTFUL CHOICE 5-11-1 A Powell, ...(50 to 1) 12
ASTON BLAKE 6-11-6 L P Cusack, ...(33 to 1) pu
BROWN GILLETTE 6-10-10 (5") D T Evans, ...(50 to 1) pu
Dist: 2l, 8l, 5½l, 3½l. 5m 27.40s. (14 Ran).
(T W Nicholson), John W Nicholson

572 John J. Galvin Maiden Hurdle (Div 2) (5-y-o and up) £3,795 2½m............... (2:35)

538³ GRANDONHILL 6-12-0 K F O'Brien, ...(5 to 1) 1
363⁶ SUPER TACTICS (Ire) 5-11-1 (5") C P Dunne, .. (7 to 2) 2
505³ OXFORD QUILL 6-12-0 T J Taaffe, ...(7 to 1) 3
535⁷ SHOW YOUR HAND (Ire) 5-11-6 T Horgan, .. (2 to 1 fav) 4
254⁵ PEARL'S CHOICE (Ire) 5-11-1 B Sheridan, ...(8 to 1) 5
169⁴ MIRROMARK (Ire) 5-10-13 (7") Mr W M O'Sullivan, (16 to 1) 6
302⁵ WALKERS LADY (Ire) 5-10-10 (5") D T Evans, ...(33 to 1) 7
252¹ IF YOU SAY YES (Ire) 5-11-9 C F Swan, ...(7 to 2) 8
BRILLIANT VENTURE (Ire) 5-11-1 G Bradley, ... (10 to 1) 9

GOLDEN NUGGET 6-11-1 (5*) C O'Brien, ... (10 to 1) 10
274 FIFTYBETWEENYE (Ire) 5-10-10 (5*) J R Barry, ... (66 to 1) 11
SEPRIMO (Ire) 5-11-1 D H O'Connor, ... (33 to 1) 12
EXILE RUN (Ire) 5-11-6 A Maguire, ... (10 to 1) 13
CLASHREAGH (Ire) 5-10-8 (7*) Mr K O'Sullivan, ... (33 to 1) 14
Dist: Nk, 1l, 12l, ¾l. 5m 36.40s. (14 Ran).
(M P O'Grady), Michael Hourigan

573 Southampton Goodwill Handicap Chase (0-116 4-y-o and up) £4,140 2½m.... (3:10)

PATS MINSTREL [-] (bl) 8-11-0 A Maguire, ... (3 to 1) 1
WINNING CHARLIE [-] 7-10-11 K F O'Brien, ... (12 to 1) 2
332[2] TURBULENT WIND [-] 6-10-12 T J Taaffe, ... (2 to 1 fav) 3
WAIT NO LONGER [-] 7-9-11 T Horgan, ... (10 to 1) 4
468[4] BUNNINADDEN [-] 10-9-9 W T Slattery Jnr, ... (7 to 1) 5
ANTRIM COUNTY [-] 8-11-10 G Bradley, ... (7 to 1) 6
MARKET SURVEY [-] 12-9-5[3] (5*) T J O'Sullivan, .. (16 to 1) 7
ENCHANTED QUEEN [-] 7-9-3 (7*) J P Broderick, (50 to 1) f
506[5] BALLYHEIGUE [-] 7-9-12 (5*) C O'Brien, ... (12 to 1) f
210[3] MAYE FANE [-] 9-11-2 (3*) G Kilfeather, ... (12 to 1) pu
492 CLASSIC CHEER (Ire) [-] (bl) 5-9-13 J Jones, ... (16 to 1) pu
Dist: Sht-hd, 9l, 15l, 5l. 5m 33.20s. (11 Ran).
(K J Hunt), R Champion

574 Listowel Autos (Opportunity) Handicap Hurdle (0-109 4-y-o and up) £4,140 2m .... (3:45)

294 MORNING DREAM [-] 6-10-10 T J Mitchell, ... (6 to 1) 1
413[5] DANCING COURSE (Ire) [-] 5-11-0 (4*) P A Roche, ... (11 to 2 jt-fav) 2
294[7] WATERLOO LADY [-] 6-10-12 (2*) D P Murphy, ... (12 to 1) 3
432[2] HURRICANE EDEN [-] 6-10-10 (2*) C P Dunne, (11 to 2 jt-fav) 4
20 HAVE TO THINK [-] 5-10-13 (2*) T P Rudd, ... (12 to 1) 5
503[4] SHREWD MOVE [-] (bl) 4-10-4 (2*) D T Evans, ... (12 to 1) 6
249[5] CLASSY MACHINE (Ire) [-] 5-10-6 (2*) A J Roche, (20 to 1) 7
431* NISHIKI (USA) [-] 4-10-10 (2*,6ex) C O'Brien, ... (6 to 1) 8
493[7] BALLINDERRY GLEN [-] 7-10-11 (2*) M G Cleary, (10 to 1) 9
ASHBORO (Ire) [-] 4-10-12 (2*) T J O'Sullivan, ... (20 to 1) 10
DUNSTER DAME (Ire) [-] 5-10-11 (4*) J M Donnelly, (8 to 1) 11
KHULM [-] (bl) 6-10-9 (2*) D P Geoghegan, ... (33 to 1) 12
295[8] MILFORD MATCH (Ire) [-] 5-10-2 (4*) P Morris, ... (10 to 1) 13
232[4] KINDERSLEIGH [-] 6-10-12 (2*) T P Lacy Jnr, ... (8 to 1) 14
SOLAR FLASH (Ire) [-] 4-10-7 (4*) B Bowens, ... (16 to 1) 15
507[7] BROOK COTTAGE (Ire) [-] 5-11-2 (4*) J P Broderick, ... (10 to 1) f
131 LOUGH ATALIA [-] 6-9-12 (4*) K P Gaule, ... (25 to 1) ur
Dist: 3½l, 4½l, 4½l, sht-hd. 4m 3.30s. (17 Ran).
(Leo Harvey), Donal Hassett

575 E.S.B. Win Electric Novice S'ch Series (4-y-o and up) £6,900 2¼m 110yds..... (4:55)

CHIRKPAR 6-12-0 K F O'Brien, ... (4 to 1) 1
FRIENDS OF GERALD 7-12-0 C F Swan, ... (6 to 4 fav) 2
293[3] SHEAMY'S DREAM (Ire) 5-11-9 J Shortt, ... (7 to 1) 3
411[2] THUNDERSTRUCK 7-12-0 A Maguire, ... (10 to 1) 4
468[6] PINEWOOD LAD 6-12-0 J P Banahan, ... (20 to 1) 5
CHIC AND ELITE 6-11-9 P P Kinane, ... (50 to 1) 6
BORN DEEP 7-12-0 T Horgan, ... (12 to 1) f
WINDS OF WAR 8-12-0 G Bradley, ... (10 to 1) f
496[2] RANDOM PRINCE 9-12-0 C O'Dwyer, ... (12 to 1) ur
507[9] BROTHER HUGH 8-11-7 (7*) Mr K Whelan, ... (50 to 1) ur
116[3] THE WEST'S ASLEEP 8-11-9 (5*) C O'Brien, ... (25 to 1) bd
327[3] INCH GALE 6-11-9 W T Slattery Jnr, ... (20 to 1) su
133 TRANSCRIBER (USA) 6-11-7 (7*) P A Roche, ... (12 to 1) pu
OUT OF COURT 8-12-0 T J Taaffe, ... (8 to 1) pu
Dist: 1l, 2l, dist, 1½l. 4m 41.70s. (14 Ran).
(Michael W J Smurfit), J S Bolger

576 Lee Strand Flat Race (4-y-o and up) £4,140 2m................................ (6:00)

433* BEGLAWELLA 6-11-6 (7*) Mr P English, ... (7 to 1) 1
88[3] QUEENIES CHILD 6-11-8 (5*) Mr H F Cleary, ... (10 to 1) 2
COURT MELODY (Ire) 5-12-4 Mr E Bolger, ... (11 to 8) 3
423[3] GLAD'S NIGHT (Ire) 4-11-3 (5*) Mrs J M Mullins, ... (8 to 1) 4
IDIOTS VENTURE 6-12-4 Mr A P O'Brien, ... (11 to 10 fav) 5
REGAL DAUGHTER (Ire) 4-10-8 (7*) Mr R P Cody, (20 to 1) 6
SINEADS FANCY (Ire) 4-10-8 (7*) Mr N Moran, ... (25 to 1) 7
Dist: ½l, sht-hd, hd, 3½l. 4m 3.10s. (7 Ran).
(Thomas Keane), Thomas Foley

CARLISLE (good to firm)
Saturday September 25th
Going Correction: MINUS 0.20 sec. per fur.

577 Brotherswater Novices' Hurdle (4-y-o and up) £1,841 2½m 110yds............ (2:10)

ROYAL VACATION 4-10-12 J Callaghan, *hld up, hit 5th, hdwy 4 out, chlgd 2 out, sn led, ran on wl frm last.* .... (9 to 4 fav op 3 to 1 tchd 7 to 2) 1
GREEN TRIX (Ire) 5-11-0 B Storey, *prmnt, led 7th, rdn 2 out, sn hdd, hng lft appr last, one pace.* ...... (8 to 1) 2
SATIN LAKE (USA) 6-10-9 R Garritty, *led to second, cl up, led 6th to nxt, outpcd 3 out, styd on und pres appr last.* .... (25 to 1 op 16 to 1) 3
DENIM BLUE 4-10-13[1] T Reed, *hld up, hdwy 3 out, rdn nxt, kpt on one pace.* .... (11 to 2 op 5 to 1) 4
445[3] BROWNHALL 5-10-7 (7*) Mr B Pollock, *cl up, led second to 6th, ev ch and rdn 2 out, sn wknd.* (11 to 2 op 5 to 1) 5
DOUCE ECLAIR 7-10-9 C Grant, *in tch, hdwy 3 out, sn rdn and btn.* .... (14 to 1 op 12 to 1) 6
482[4] TWIN STATES 4-10-5 (7*) W Fry, *hld up, hdwy and blun 7th, rdn 3 out, sn btn.* .... (9 to 2 op 4 to 1) 7
RUSHING BURN 7-10-9 K Johnson, *blun 1st, some hdwy hfwy, sn rdn and wknd.* .... (33 to 1) 8
WHEELIES NEWMEMBER 10-11-0 Miss J Thurlow, *prmnt, lost pl aftr 5th, tld off bef 4 out.* ... (16 to 1 op 14 to 1) 9
JOYFUL IMP 6-10-2 (7*) Mr R Hale, *chsd ldrs, rdn 4 out, sn wknd.* .... (25 to 1) 10
Dist: 6l, 1l, ¾l, ¾l, 5l, 15l, 2½l, 20l, dist. 4m 56.20s. a 3.20s (10 Ran).
SR: 11/7/1/4/4/-/ (G P Edwards), G M Moore

578 Bassenthwaite Lake Claiming Hurdle (3-y-o) £1,604 2m 1f.................. (2:40)

497 KISS IN THE DARK 11-2 P Niven, *hld up, hdwy to go prmnt 4th, led appr last, drvn out.* .... (5 to 4 fav op 2 to 1 tchd 9 to 4) 1
497[8] GRANDERISE (Ire) 10-11 C Grant, *led, quickened 4th, rdn and hdd appr last, kpt on.* .... (3 to 1 op 2 to 1) 2
TINSTONE 10-6 R Garritty, *pld hrd, in tch, hdwy aftr 3 out, ev ch appr last, sn rdn and one pace.* .... (9 to 1 op 7 to 1) 3
128[3] ASTRAC TRIO (USA) 11-6 (3*) A Dobbin, *in tch, effrt appr 3 out, rdn and one pace nxt.* .... (6 to 1 op 5 to 1 tchd 7 to 1) 4
BELFORTON 11-1 (3*) N Bentley, *beh hfwy, hdwy 4 out, rdn and wknd aftr nxt.* .... (6 to 1 op 4 to 1) 5
COBBS CROSS 11-5 Peter Caldwell, *al rear.* .... (20 to 1 op 16 to 1) 6
BALLACASCADE 10-7 J Callaghan, *chsd ldr, hit 4th, rdn aftr 3 out, sn wknd.* .... (12 to 1 tchd 10 to 1) 7
HIGHLAND SUNBEAM 10-8 (3*) D J Moffatt, *sn prmnt, pld hrd, rdn aftr 4 out, soon wknd.* .... (16 to 1 op 14 to 1 tchd 20 to 1) 8
Dist: 2½l, 5l, 1½l, 3½l, 12l, 3l, 7l. 4m 23.20s. a 16.20s (8 Ran).
(R Meredith), Mrs M Reveley

579 'Red Rum' Handicap Chase (0-125 5-y-o and up) £2,898 3m.................. (3:10)

426[2] KUSHBALOO [119] 8-11-10 B Storey, *hld up in tch, hdwy to join ldrs 11th, led last, ran on wl.* .... (15 to 8 fav op 7 to 4 tchd 2 to 1) 1
449[3] CHARMING GALE [104] 6-10-4 (5*) P Williams, *cl up, led 9th, rdn 3 out, hdd last, kpt on.* .... (9 to 2 tchd 4 to 1) 2
449[2] KILHALLON CASTLE [105] 10-10-7 (3*) N Bentley, *in tch, hdwy 5 out, effrt and ev ch 2 out, rdn and btn whn hit last.* .... (4 to 1 op 7 to 2) 3
MOUNTEBOR [100] 9-10-5 J Callaghan, *hld up beh, rdn 4 out, styd on 2 out, nvr dngrs.* ..... (16 to 1 op 12 to 1) 4
518* LAPIAFFE [100] 9-10-5 A Orkney, *led to 9th, cl up till rdn and wknd appr 4 out, kpt on frm last.* .... (5 to 1 tchd 6 to 1) 5
284[2] OVER THE STREAM [96] 7-10-1 C Grant, *in tch, rdn alng and hit 5 out, sn one pace.* .... (9 to 2) 6
TRUELY ROYAL [95] 9-10-0 K Johnson, *chsd ldrrs, hit 11th, weakend nxt, sn beh.* .... (8 to 1 tchd 9 to 1) 7
Dist: 7l, 5l, 2l, hd, 7l, 25l. 6m 5.50s. a 6.50s (7 Ran).
(Raymond Anderson Green), C Parker

580 Rydal Water Handicap Hurdle (0-115 4-y-o and up) £2,200 2½m 110yds......... (3:40)

MYSTIC MEMORY [93] 4-11-10 P Niven, *trkd ldrs, hdwy 5th, led 2 out, pushed clr r-in.* .... (11 to 10 fav op 5 to 4 tchd 6 to 4) 1
446[4] SUNSET REINS FREE [86] 8-11-3 K Jones, *al cl up, led 3 out to nxt, hrd rdn and not quicken r-in.* .... (14 to 1 op 12 to 1) 2
477* HUNMANBY GAP [81] 8-10-12 C Hawkins, *hld up in tch, hit second, mstk 6th, pushed alng 4 out, rdn and styd on wl 2 out.* .... (5 to 1) 3
477[9] SPEEDY SIOUX [69] (bl) 4-9-7 (7*) F Perratt, *prmnt, hit 4th and nxt, sn lost pl, wl beh four out.* .... (33 to 1) 4
SHERMAGO [70] 11-10-1 A Orkney, *led to 7th, wknd 4 out.* .... (25 to 1 op 16 to 1) 5
289[4] BALLYANTO [80] 8-10-11 B Storey, *hld up, hmpd second, hdwy 6th, led nxt to 3 out, sn wknd.* (9 to 2 op 4 to 1) 6
337[2] AS D'EBOLI (Fr) [89] 6-10-13 (7*) S Hogg, *blun and uns rdr 1st.* .... (9 to 2 op 3 to 1) ur
Dist: 2½l, ½l, 25l, hd, 2l. 4m 55.50s. a 2.50s (7 Ran).
SR: 30/20/14/-/ (Carnoustie Racing Club Ltd), Mrs M Reveley

581 Thirlmere Novices' Chase (5-y-o and up) £2,193 2m....................... (4:10)

WILD ATLANTIC 10-11-0 K Jones, *trkd ldr, led 5th, clr 2*
out, styd on wl frm last..................(3 to 1) 1
NORTHERN SQUIRE 5-10-7 (5*) P Williams, *in tch, chsd*
wnr 5 out, rdn 2 out, kpt on frm last. (7 to 2 op 3 to 1) 2
338⁴ SAY NO MORE 7-11-0 A Orkney, *led to 5th, hit 6th and*
nxt, sn beh...........................(6 to 1 op 12 to 1) 3
THE COUNTRY TRADER 7-11-0 N Doughty, *mstk and uns*
rdr second.....(Evens fav op 11 to 8 on tchd 11 to 10) ur
Dist: 1½l, dist. 4m 4.80s. a 5.80s (4 Ran).

(Albert Cardy), S G Payne

582 Ullswater Novices' Hurdle (4-y-o and up) £1,918 2m 1f. ....(4:40)

INFERRING 5-10-9 (5*) P Midgley, *hld up, hdwy 3 out, led*
appr last, sn rdn, ran on wl.
..........................(14 to 1 op 12 to 1 tchd 16 to 1) 1
GREAT MAX (Ire) 4-10-12 B Storey, *prmnt, led 4th to 6th,*
led nxt, rdn and hdd appr last, one pace.
..............................(7 to 4 on op 6 to 4 on) 2
MARKED CARD 5-11-0 Mrs M Kendall, *led to 4th, cl up till*
rdn and kpt on one pace 2 out.
.............................(10 to 1 op 8 to 1 tchd 12 to 1) 3
BROUGHPARK AZALEA 4-10-12 P Niven, *wl beh hfwy,*
styd on frm 2 out, nrst finish...... (12 to 1 op 14 to 1) 4
SMOKE 7-10-13⁴ T Reed, *chsd ldrs, rdn alng and outpcd*
5th, hdwy and ch 2 out, sn drvn, wknd appr last.
..............................(25 to 1 op 20 to 1) 5
242⁷ OUR MAN IN HAVANA 4-10-12 C Grant, *chsd ldrs, hdwy 3*
out, ev ch nxt, rdn last, 3rd whn broke dwn r-in, fnshd
lme..........................(15 to 2 op 8 to 1 tchd 7 to 1) 6
TIGHTER BUDGET (USA) 6-11-0 K Johnson, *in tch, rdn 4*
out, sn wknd............................(33 to 1) 7
NORTH OF WATFORD 8-11-0 C Dennis, *beh hfwy.*
..............................(25 to 1 op 20 to 1) 8
TIME PIECE (Ire) 5-10-7 (7*) J Supple, *al beh, tld off hfwy.*
..............................(16 to 1 op 14 to 1) 9
452² RISING TEMPO (Ire) (v) 5-11-0 T Wall, *cl up, led 4 out till*
hdd and hit nxt, sn rdn and wknd.
.............................(5 to 1 tchd 11 to 2) 10
315⁴ JOYFUL SMITH 4-10-7 L O'Hara, *prmnt to hfwy, sn lost*
pl, tld off whn pld up bef 3 out..............(33 to 1) pu
Dist: 5l, 5l, 5l, 1½l, nk, 25l, 1½l, 8l, 3l. 4m 10.70s. a 3.70s (11 Ran).
SR: 15/8/5/-/-/-/ (G A Chagoury), J S Wainwright

LISTOWEL (IRE) (yielding to soft) Saturday September 25th

583 Kerry Petroleum Chase (4-y-o and up) £4,140 2½m. ....(2:30)

AMERICAN EYRE 8-11-7 C O'Dwyer, ...(16 to 1) 1
509³ INCH MAID 7-11-6 C F Swan, ...(6 to 1) 2
507³ FAIRY PARK (bl) 8-11-7 F Woods, ...(10 to 1) 3
475⁴ BALLINAVEEN BRIDGE 6-11-7 W T Slattery Jnr, .. (25 to 1) 4
SHUIL LE CHEILE 6-10-11 (5*) C O'Brien, ...(25 to 1) 5
200* PRINGE YAZA 6-11-11 J Magee, ...(5 to 1) 6
527 IF SO 7-11-7 K F O'Brien, ...(20 to 1) 7
CARDAN 7-11-7 J Short, ...(50 to 1) 8
DANNIGALE 7-11-4 (3*) Mr M Phillips, ...(14 to 1) 9
557³ MINERAL DUST 10-11-0 (7*) Mr P Cashman, ...(6 to 1) ur
DEE ELL 7-11-7 T J Taaffe, ...(11 to 8 fav) ur
430 GLOBE HABIT 7-11-7 Mr P J Healy, ...(66 to 1) pu
QUIET MONEY 6-11-2 (5*) D P Geoghegan, ...(16 to 1) pu
Dist: 4½l, 14l, 15l, 2l. 5m 34.00s. (13 Ran).
(Mrs S Neville), Seamus Neville

584 Golden Vale Milk Handicap Hurdle (5-y-o and up) £7,200 3m. ....(3:30)

537* SECOND SCHEDUAL [-] 8-10-11 C F Swan, ... (7 to 4 fav) 1
291 PRACTICE RUN [-] 5-9-7 P McWilliams, ...(10 to 1) 2
528⁸ UNCLE BART (Ire) [-] 5-9-2 (5*) T P Treacy, ...(9 to 1) 3
294⁹ RISING WATERS (Ire) [-] 5-9-13 (7*) G Lee, ...(7 to 1) 4
410* CUILIN BUI (Ire) [-] 5-9-6 (5*, 5ex) C O'Brien, ...(4 to 1) 5
TRAPPER JOHN [-] 9-12-0 G Bradley, ...(8 to 1) 6
527⁴ RUSTY COIN [-] 8-10-3 T Horgan, ...(10 to 1) 7
511² TITIAN BLONDE (Ire) [-] 8-9-7 F Woods, ...(6 to 1) 8
HAVE A BARNEY [-] 12-9-11 (5*) D P Geoghegan, ..(25 to 1) 9
528⁶ WAR DEVIL [-] 7-9-7 J Jones, ...(25 to 1) 10
Dist: Sht-hd, 4l, ¾l, 2l. 6m 29.10s. (10 Ran).
(Hugh McMahon), Hugh McMahon

585 Edmond Whelan Memorial Maiden Hurdle (4-y-o and up) £5,520 2m. ....(4:00)

409² NEMURO (USA) 5-12-0 J Shortt, ...(7 to 1) 1D
HORNER WATER (Ire) 5-11-1 K F O'Brien, ...(3 to 1) 1
535⁸ PANDA (Ire) 5-11-9 C F Swan, ...(7 to 2) 3
534³ PERSIAN HALO (Ire) 5-12-0 D H O'Connor, ... (2 to 1 fav) 4
493² FORTUNE'S GIRL 5-11-4 (5*) C O'Brien, ...(7 to 1) 5
MAY GALE (Ire) 5-11-1 F Woods, ...(10 to 1) 6
472⁸ FOR SHONA (Ire) 5-11-1 A J O'Brien, ...(50 to 1) 7
LEGATISSIMO (Ire) 5-11-1 T J Taaffe, ...(14 to 1) f
534 DANE ST LADY (Ire) 5-10-8 (7*), ...(25 to 1) f
DON'T ASK JOHNNY (Ire) 4-10-13 Mr J A Flynn, .. (14 to 1) pu

Dist: Sht-hd, ½l, 5l, 2l. 4m 10.20s. (10 Ran).
(P M Prior-Wandesforde), Michael Hourigan

MARKET RASEN (good) Saturday September 25th
Going Correction: PLUS 0.40 sec. per fur.

586 Jolly Fisherman Novices' Chase (5-y-o and up) £3,093 2½m. ....(2:20)

498² BUSTINELLO (Ire) 5-10-4 (7*) B Murphy, *trkd ldr, cl up and*
ev ch 6 out, led 4 out, lft clr 2 out, cmftbly.
..............................(5 to 4 fav op 11 to 10 tchd 11 to 8) 1
477³ BRIGTINA 5-10-6 (5*) R Farrant, *al prmnt, ev ch 6 out, rdn*
and wknd 4 out, lft moderate second 2 out, no chance
with wnr...........................(12 to 1 tchd 14 to 1) 2
517⁴ PHALAROPE (Ire) (v) 5-10-11 Mr A Walton, *prmnt, lft in ld*
7th, hdd 4 out, sn one pace, wknd before 3rd 2 out.
..............................(14 to 1 op 12 to 1) 3
MISS SHAW 7-10-9 R Bellamy, *led till 7th.*
..............................(7 to 1 op 10 to 1 tchd 12 to 1) f
498* ABLE PLAYER (USA) 6-10-13 (7*) Mr D Parker, *hld up, mstk*
1st, not fluent aftr, hdwy 6 out, chlgd 3 out, cl second
whn blun and uns rdr nxt...........(7 to 4 op 6 to 4) ur
517⁵ WHISKEY BLUES 8-11-0 D Byrne, *lost tch aftr 7th, beh*
whn pld up after nxt................(16 to 1 op 33 to 1) pu
517 HADLEIGHS CHOICE 6-11-0 M Robinson, *not fluent, chsd*
ldrs til wknd tenth, tld off whn pld up bef 3 out.
..............................(66 to 1 op 50 to 1 tchd 100 to 1) pu
Dist: 15l, 7l. 5m 9.50s. a 17.50s (7 Ran).
(G A Hubbard), F Murphy

587 Audrey Buttery Retirement Novices' Handicap Hurdle (0-100 4-y-o and up) £2,528 2m 3f 110yds. ....(2:55)

STRONG JOHN (Ire) [86] 5-11-3 (7*) P Murphy, *led, rdn 2*
out, hdd and drifted lft r-in, ridden and rallied to ld nr
finish, all out...........................(8 to 1 tchd 9 to 1) 1
368² SAFARI PARK [75] 4-10-13 L Wyer, *chsd ldr, rdn 2 out, led*
r-in, ct nr finish....................(9 to 2 tchd 5 to 1) 2
NORTHERN RAINBOW [66] 5-10-4 R Campbell, *hld up,*
trkd ldrs frm 4th, ev ch appr 2 out, sn rdn and no
imprsn............................(8 to 1 op 11 to 2) 3
MAUREEN'S FANCY [70] 8-10-8 N Smith, *chsd ldrs, rdn 3*
out, styd on one pace appr nxt.... (20 to 1 op 16 to 1) 4
SUPPOSIN [65] 5-9-10 (7*) R Wilkinson, *hld up in mid-div,*
rdn alng aftr 5th, no hdwy frm 3 out.
..............................(33 to 1 op 20 to 1) 5
ON CUE [62] 6-10-0 W Worthington, *hld up, pushed alng*
aftr 4th, sn wknd, tld off after four out.
..............................(25 to 1 op 20 to 1 tchd 33 to 1) 6
ELITE DESIGN [82] 6-11-6 M Brennan, *beh and reminder*
aftr 3rd, sn lost tch, tld off out... (14 to 1 op 10 to 1) 7
COURT OF KINGS [73] 4-10-6 (5*) R Farrant, *chsd ldrs to*
4th, sn wknd, tld off 3 out...........(14 to 1 op 12 to 1) 8
520⁵ SHAKE TOWN (USA) [75] (h) 5-10-8 (5*) T Eley, *cl up whn f*
3rd...........................(12 to 1 op 8 to 1) f
380* PURITAN (Can) [86] 4-11-10 C McCourt, *hld up, in tch whn*
bght dwn 3rd...(11 to 10 fav op 5 to 4 tchd 11 to 8) bd
Dist: Nk, 4l, 8l, 1l, 30l, 25l, 5l. 4m 48.50s. a 15.50s (10 Ran).
SR: 19/7/-/-/-/-/ (G A Hubbard), F Murphy

588 BBC Radio Lincolnshire Juvenile Novices' Hurdle (3-y-o) £2,530 2m 1f 110yds. .. (3:30)

CHIAPPUCCI (Ire) (bl) 10-12 A Maguire, *hld up, trkd ldrs*
5th, smooth hdwy to ld appr 2 out, sn clr, cmftbly.
..............................(13 to 8 jt-fav op 2 to 1 tchd 6 to 4) 1
497 MISTER BLAKE 10-12 R Campbell, *led till appr 2 out, 3rd*
and btn whn lft second at last....(25 to 1 op 16 to 1) 2
SIDE BAR 10-12 J Ryan, *chsd ldr, ev ch 4 out, sn rdn,*
fourth and btn whn lft 3rd at last... (9 to 1 op 8 to 1) 3
CANNY LAD 10-12 M Dwyer, *hld up, hdwy to chase ldrs*
aftr 4th, rdn 3 out, 5th and btn whn lft fourth at last.
..............................(8 to 1 tchd 6 to 1) 4
516⁹ BIG GEM 10-12 W Worthington, *pressed ldr til rdn and*
wknd aftr 4 out, 6th and btn whn lft 5th at last.
..............................(50 to 1 op 33 to 1) 5
AVIATOR'S DREAM 10-12 D Byrne, *chsd ldr, rdn and*
wknd 4 out, 7th and btn whn lft 6th at last.
..............................(16 to 1 op 14 to 1 tchd 20 to 1) 6
516 MONASTIC FLIGHT (Ire) 10-12 M Brennan, *beh 5th, no ch*
frm 4 out..........................(50 to 1 op 33 to 1) 7
BLAKES BEAU 10-12 L Wyer, *hld up, lost tch aftr 4th, sn*
beh.............................(16 to 1 op 14 to 1) 8
285 WALSHAM WITCH (bl) 10-7 M Ranger, *chsd ldr, mstk 3rd,*
sn beh, lost tch aftr 5th.
..............................(40 to 1 op 20 to 1 tchd 50 to 1) 9
406* MOST EQUAL 11-4 R Dunwoody, *trkd ldrs, ev ch 4 out,*
chlgd appr 2 out, sn outpcd, btn second whn blun and
uns rdr last..........................(13 to 8 jt-fav tchd 7 to 4) su
LARKSPUR LEGEND 10-7 (5*) T Eley, *lost tch aftr 4th, tld*
off whn pld up bef 2 out.
..............................(40 to 1 op 33 to 1 tchd 50 to 1) pu
Dist: 4l, 12l, 3½l, 10l, 12l, 4l, 3l, 12l. 4m 17.00s. a 15.00s (11 Ran).

SR: 4/-/-/-/-/-/   (Ms M Horan), J White

589 Evening Telegraph Claiming Chase (5-y-o and up) £2,747 2¾m 110yds........(4:05)

525° SKIPPING TIM 14-11-4 R Dunwoody, *trkd ldr, led 8th, drw clr aftr 4 out, cmftbly*....... (9 to 4 on tchd 2 to 1 on)   1
457⁵ SLIPPERY MAX 9-11-7 A Maguire, *wnt second 8th, chsd ldr, rdn appr 3 out, sn no imprsn, one pace.*
.... (8 to 1 op 7 to 1 tchd 9 to 1)   2
461⁵ DANRIBO 10-10-9 (7°) Mr M Gingell, *lost to aftr 7th, tld off, styd on to take 3rd pl nr finish.*
.... (33 to 1 op 25 to 1 tchd 50 to 1)   3
500² VULRORY'S CLOWN 9-11-0 M Brennan, *drpd rear aftr 9th, wnt second briefly after 4 out, sn wknd, jmpd slwly nxt, eased and lost 3rd pl nr finish.*
.... (5 to 2 tchd 11 to 4)   4
Dist: 12l, 20l, 1l. 5m 48.80s. a 20.80s (4 Ran).

(Bisgrove Partnership), M C Pipe

590 Market Rasen Chamber Of Trade And Commerce Handicap Chase (0-120 4-y-o and up) £3,584 2m 1f 110yds....... (4:40)

CLARES OWN [99] 9-10-0 A Maguire, *jmpd wl, made all, drw clr aftr 3 out, eased nr finish, cmftbly.*
.... (7 to 4 op 2 to 1)   1
515² EMSEE-H [127] 8-11-7 (7°) B Murphy, *trkd ldr, ev ch 4 out, sn rdn and no imprsn, ran on aftr last, not rch wnr.*
.... (11 to 10 fav op Evens)   2
479³ GOOD FOR A LAUGH [125] 9-11-12 Mr S Brisby, *cl up whn f 5th.*.................... (7 to 2 op 3 to 1 tchd 4 to 1)   f
Dist: 2½l. 4m 32.50s. a 18.50s (3 Ran).

(John Wade), J Wade

591 Lincolnshire Echo Handicap Hurdle (0-120 4-y-o and up) £3,020 2m 1f 110yds... (5:10)

TAYLORS PRINCE [89] (v) 6-10-9 V Smith, *al prmnt, ev ch 3 out, rdn to ld aftr last, jst hld on.*
.... (9 to 2 op 4 to 1 tchd 5 to 1)   1
519² BALAAT (USA) [90] 5-10-10 W Worthington, *trkd ldrs, rdn 2 out, ev ch last, ridden and styd on nr finish, jst fld.*
.... (5 to 2 fav op 3 to 1 tchd 7 to 2)   2
450³ SAYMORE [95] 7-10-12 (3°) S Wynne, *hld up in mid-div, chsd ldrs 4 out, rdn appr 2 out, styd on nr finish.*
.... (5 to 1 op 7 to 2 tchd 11 to 2)   3
ASTURIAS [90] 10-10-7 A Larnach, *hld up beh, rdn and hdwy aftr 3 out, no imprsn betw last 2.*
....   4
522³ MY LINDIANNE [80] 6-10-0 A Maguire, *chsd ldrs, ev ch 3 out, led appr nxt, blun last, hdd and not quicken r-in.*
.... (12 to 1 op 10 to 1 tchd 14 to 1)   5
407³ SALMAN (USA) [105] 7-11-6 (5°) J McCarthy, *led, sn clr, hdd appr 2 out, soon wknd.*
.... (12 to 1 op 7 to 1 tchd 14 to 1)   6
450⁴ KALKO [100] 4-10-13 (7°) Mr C Bonner, *hld up, pushed alng aftr 5th, sn no imprsn.*....... (12 to 1 op 10 to 1)   7
KEV'S LASS (Ire) [93] 5-10-6 (7°) P Murphy, *lost pl aftr 4th, sn beh, no chn 3 out.*.................... (16 to 1 op 10 to 1)   8
KIND'A SMART [98] 8-11-4 A S Smith, *hld up, lost to aftr 4th, sn beh.*.................... (20 to 1 op 12 to 1)   9
346⁵ TIBBS INN [80] 4-10-0 M Ranger, *lost tch aftr 4th, sn beh.*.................... (33 to 1 op 20 to 1)   10
499⁸ HALLO MAM (Ire) [85] 4-10-5 M Brennan, *hld up in mid-div, rdn alng aftr 4th, sn lost tch....* (9 to 2 op 6 to 1)   11
DEMOKOS (Fr) [85] 8-10-5 N Smith, *lost tch aftr 5th, btn whn f 2 out.*.................... (25 to 1 op 12 to 1)   f
Dist: Hd, nk, 8l, 5l, 1½l, 8l, 3½l, 7l, 2l, 3½l. 4m 14.70s. a 12.70s (12 Ran).
SR: 24/25/29/16/12/14/24/11/-/-/   (H J Collingridge), H J Collingridge

WORCESTER (good)
Saturday September 25th
Going Correction: PLUS 0.20 sec. per fur. (races 1,3,6), PLUS 0.15 (2,4,5)

592 Excelnir Novices' Selling Hurdle (4-y-o and up) £1,480 2¼m............... (2:30)

429 GRAND RAPIDS (USA) 6-11-0 H Davies, *hld up, hdwy appr 3 out, lft clr nxt, edgd rght and tired r-in.*
.... (10 to 1 tchd 12 to 1)   1
MALLYAN 6-10-4 (5°) R Davis, *hld up, hdwy frm 3 out, rdn and ran on from nxt.*.......... (50 to 1 op 33 to 1)   2
454⁷ PEARLY WHITE 4-10-1¹ (7°) Mr Richard White, *mid-div, styd on one pace frm 3 out, nvr dngrs.*
.... (50 to 1 op 33 to 1)   3
465² WEDNESDAYS AUCTION (Ire) 5-11-0 J Osborne, *in rear till styd on frm 3 out, nvr nrr.*.......... (8 to 1 op 5 to 1)   4
LAW FACULTY (Ire) 4-10-12 S Mackey, *chsd ldrs till no hdwy appr 3 out.*.................... (33 to 1)   5
434⁸ STAND AT EASE 8-11-0 B Powell, *led to second, in frnt rnk till wknd appr 3 out....* (16 to 1 op 14 to 1)   6
435⁸ FAIR BABE (bl) 7-10-7 (7°) Mr N Bradley, *beh whn blun second, hdwy 4th, wknd aftr 6th.*.......... (50 to 1)   7
526⁸ ROCHE 7-11-0 A Webb, *al beh.*...... (16 to 1 op 33 to 1)   8

344³ BOXING MATCH 6-11-0 L Harvey, *in tch to 4th, sn beh, tld off.*.................... (18 to 1 op 16 to 1 tchd 20 to 1)   9
PEWTER PETA 9-10-2 (7°) P Maddock, *in rear whn blun and uns rdr 3rd.*.................... (50 to 1 op 40 to 1)   ur
520² HOMILE 5-10-7 (7°) S Lycett, *prmnt, led appr 4th, clr whn jmpd rght 2 out, jockey unbalanced, uns rdr.*
.... (9 to 2 op 7 to 2 tchd 5 to 1 and 11 to 2)   ur
DRAW LOTS 9-11-0 I Shoemark, *tld off frm 4th, pld up bef 3 out.*.................... (50 to 1 op 33 to 1)   pu
PANDY (bl) 7-11-0 D Bridgwater, *prmnt till wknd quickly 6th, pld up bef 3 out.*
.... (9 to 4 fav op 5 to 2 tchd 3 to 1 and 7 to 2)   pu
520 BEACHOLME BOY (Ire) (bl) 5-10-11 (3°) D O'Sullivan, *chsd ldrs till wknd 5th, tld off whn pld up bef last.*
.... (100 to 1 op 66 to 1)   pu
126⁹ SLY PROSPECT (USA) (bl) 5-11-0 A O'Hagan, *led second, hdd appr 4th, mstk nxt, sn btn, tld off whn pld up bef 3 out.*.................... (16 to 1 op 20 to 1 tchd 25 to 1)   pu
520 SEA PRODIGY 4-10-12 D Gallagher, *al beh, tld off whn pld up bef 3 out.*.................... (33 to 1)   pu
186 EVERSO IRISH 4-10-12 M A FitzGerald, *hld up in tch, hdwy 4th, wknd quickly appr 3 out, pld up bef nxt.*
.... (9 to 2 op 3 to 1 tchd 5 to 1)   pu
ALLIED'S TEAM 6-10-9 D Skyrme, *slwly away, al beh, tld off whn pld up bef 3 out....* (100 to 1 op 66 to 1)   pu
Dist: 4l, 7l, nk, 2½l, 5l, 2l, 1½l, 25l. 4m 23.20s. a 15.20s (18 Ran).
(Gilberts Animal Feed Products), Miss S J Wilton

593 Worcester Rowing Club Novices' Chase (5-y-o and up) £2,006 2m 7f......... (3:05)

GREAT MILL 6-11-0 N Williamson, *hdwy to chase ldrs frm 7th, mstk 13th, pressed 1der from 2 out, led last, hrd rdn, ran on....* (7 to 4 fav op 5 to 2 tchd 3 to 1)   1
HOWARYAFXD 6-11-0 J Osborne, *led to 9th, led ag'n nxt, hrd rdn 2 out, hdd last, rallied gmely, no extr nr finish.*
.... (9 to 2 op 3 to 1 tchd 33 to 1)   2
CONGREGATION 7-11-0 H Davies, *al prmnt, led 9th to nxt, ev ch 3 out till wknd aftr next.*
.... (25 to 1 op 20 to 1 tchd 33 to 1)   3
217⁶ STAPLEFORD LADY 5-9-12 (7°) A Flannigan, *hld up, hdwy hfwy, rdn and wknd appr 3 out....* (66 to 1 op 33 to 1)   4
438⁵ NOBLE INSIGHT (bl) 6-11-0 M Foster, *beh whn blun tenth, hdwy aftr 5 out, wl btn when blunded 3 out.*
.... (10 to 1 op 8 to 1 tchd 12 to 1)   5
417³ BARGAIN AND SALE 8-11-0 C Maude, *al beh, tld off.*
.... (25 to 1 op 20 to 1)   6
KEMMY DARLING 6-10-9 I Lawrence, *f 1st.*
.... (66 to 1 op 33 to 1)   f
LIZZIES LASS 8-10-9 M Crosse, *jmpd badly in rear, tld off whn blun and uns rdr 13th....* (66 to 1 op 33 to 1)   ur
461° STAR OF OUGHTERARD (bl) 8-10-9 M McFarland, *hdwy 5th, mstk tenth, beh whn his 13th, tld off when pld up bef 4 out.*.................... (8 to 1 op 5 to 1)   pu
HASTY SALVO 9-10-9 S Earle, *al beh, tld off whn pld up bef 4 out.*.................... (50 to 1 op 33 to 1)   pu
STAR OF BLADON 8-10-4 (5°) Mrs P Nash, *prmnt till wknd 12th, tld off whn pld up bef 4 out.* (25 to 1 op 16 to 1)   pu
454⁴ KASHAN (Ire) 5-10-10 L Harvey, *al beh, tld off whn pld up bef 8th....* (9 to 1 op 5 to 1 tchd 10 to 1)   pu
BUTTON BOX (bl) 7-10-9 W Irvine, *jmpd badly rght, al beh, tld off whn pld up bef tenth.* (66 to 1 op 33 to 1)   pu
QUEENS CURATE 6-10-9 B Powell, *in tch to hfwy, tld off whn pld up bef 3 out.*.................... (50 to 1 op 33 to 1)   pu
442² MISTY (NZ) 6-11-0 J Railton, *hmpd 1st, al beh, tld off whn pld up bef 11th.*.................... (7 to 2 op 11 to 4)   pu
GAME SET 7-11-0 A Webb, *in tch to hfwy, sn beh, pld up bef 4 out.*.................... (50 to 1 op 33 to 1)   pu
Dist: 1l, 30l, 12l, 12l, 20l. 5m 55.10s. a 11.10s (16 Ran).
SR: 10/9/-/-/-/-/   (Mrs Harry J Duffey), K C Bailey

594 John Whitt Memorial Handicap Hurdle (0-115 4-y-o and up) £2,553 2m 5f 110yds
.... (3:40)

STAUNCH RIVAL (USA) [112] 6-11-10 D Bridgwater, *hld up in tch, hdwy 4 out, rdn to ld sn aftr last, drvn out.*
.... (10 to 1 op 8 to 1 tchd 12 to 1)   1
MYHAMET [98] 6-10-10 Peter Hobbs, *hld up, hdwy frm 4th, led appr last, mstk and sn hdd, one pace.*
.... (9 to 2 op 7 to 2)   2
459° NEWTON POINT [101] 4-10-13 D Gallagher, *al prmnt, hmpd 5th, reco'red aftr nxt, styd on frm 2 out.*
.... (11 to 4 fav op 5 to 2 tchd 3 to 1)   3
NEW ARRANGEMENT [108] 7-11-6 S Smith Eccles, *hld up, pressed ldrs frm 4th, led appr 2 out, hdd sn aftr, one pace.*.................... (5 to 1 op 14 to 1)   4
ANNA VALLEY [94] 7-10-1 (5°) R Davis, *hld up in rear, hdwy appr 3 out, hrd rdn and ran on r-in.*
.... (6 to 1 tchd 13 to 2)   5
TEMPORALE [88] 7-10-9 R Supple, *hld up in tch, no hdwy frm 3 out....* (8 to 1 tchd 25 to 1)   6
BRIGGS LAD (Ire) [103] (bl) 4-11-1 N Williamson, *hld up in rear, effrt appr 3 out, wknd quickly appr 2 out.*.................... (7 to 1 op 5 to 1 tchd 9 to 1)   7
424⁵ ARCTIC OATS [104] 8-10-11 (5°) S Lyons, *chsd ldrs, led 4th till hdd and wknd quickly appr 2 out.*
....   8

MARIE BABY [88] 9-10-0 J R Kavanagh, *set steady pace till hdd 4th, jmpd slwly nxt, wknd 3 out, tld off.*
.... (50 to 1 op 33 to 1) 9
488[3] FINAL SOUND [88] (bl) 8-10-0 L Harvey, *in rear, hdwy 6th, wknd quickly appr 3 out, tld off*.... (10 to 1 op 7 to 1) 10
Dist: 2½l, 1l, 2l, sht-hd, 7l, 5l, 2l, dist, 4l. 5m 16.80s. a 22.80s (10 Ran).
(C Humphry), G Thorner

595 Sabrina Handicap Chase (0-115 5-y-o and up) £2,364 2½m 110yds............(4:15)

LAKE MISSION [110] 8-11-9 J Osborne, *track ldr, led 9th to 5 out, steadied, led 3 out, drw clr appr last, ran on.*
.... (11 to 4 tchd 5 to 2 and 3 to 1) 1
521 GLENSHANE LAD [100] 7-10-13 N Williamson, *hit 1st, hld up, making hdwy whn hit tenth, rallied appr 4 out, ev ch 2 out, rdn and one pace.*
.... (11 to 4 tchd 5 to 2 and 3 to 1) 2
487[2] COURT RAPIER [92] 11-10-5 T Grantham, *led to 9th, led 5 out to 3 out, wknd appr last.*
.... (6 to 1 op 5 to 1 tchd 7 to 1) 3
457[*] COMEDY ROAD [102] 9-11-1 L Harvey, *wtd wth, gd hdwy to go second 5 out, ev ch till wknd aftr 2 out.* (9 to 4 jt-fav op 2 to 1 tchd 5 to 2) 4
LOVE ANEW (USA) [104] 8-11-3 E Murphy, *hld up, lost tch frm 7th, tld off*....... (14 to 1 op 12 to 1 tchd 16 to 1) 5
ENVOPAK TOKEN [115] 12-12-0 Peter Hobbs, *in tch till wknd 4 out, jmpd rght and uns rdr nxt.*
.... (33 to 1 op 20 to 1) ur
Dist: 3½l, 8l, 12l, dist. 5m 12.00s. a 9.00s (6 Ran).
SR: 36/22/6/4/-/-/ (W T Montgomery), S E Sherwood

596 Stour Conditional Jockeys' Handicap Chase (0-115 5-y-o and up) £1,952 2m
.... (4:50)

BALLAD RULER [87] 7-10-0 R Davis, *hld up in rear, steady hdwy to go second aftr 8th, led appr last, kpt on und str pres r-in*.... (40 to 1 op 33 to 1) 1
523[6] TRY ME NOW [87] 7-9-10[1] (5[*]) P Ward, *hld up in rear, hdwy 6th, led aftr 5 out, rdn and hdd appr last, ran on und pres r-in*................. (25 to 1 tchd 33 to 1) 2
500[*] FASTBIT [115] 6-12-0 A Thornton, *hld up in tch, hdwy appr 4 out, cl 3rd whn hit last, no imprsn r-in.*
.... (6 to 4 fav tchd 7 to 4) 3
ACHILLIBUIE [87] 9-10-0 R Greene, *trkd ldr to 5 out, lost pl, kpt on one pace frm 3 out.*
.... (6 to 1 op 5 to 1 tchd 7 to 1) 4
FATHER PADDY [87] 11-10-0 W Marston, *led till hdd sn aftr 5 out, wknd 3 out.*
.... (33 to 1 op 16 to 1 tchd 40 to 1) 5
PINEMARTIN [113] 10-11-9 (3[*]) N Leach, *not jump wl, in tch till wknd appr 4 out.*
.... (5 to 1 op 4 to 1 tchd 11 to 2) 6
385[*] MY CUP OF TEA [89] 10-9-11 (5[*]) L Reynolds, *hit 1st, al beh, lost tch 7........* (7 to 1 op 8 to 1 tchd 9 to 1) 7
BILL QUILL [94] 9-10-2 (5[*]) R Darke, *in tch till wknd appr 4 out*.............. (14 to 1 op 12 to 1 tchd 16 to 1) 8
550 ORCHIPEDZO [89] 8-9-13 (3[*]) Judy Davies, *trkd ldrs till wknd quickly appr 4 out.*........... (33 to 1 op 25 to 1) 9
550[*] TIGERS PET [110] 9-11-9 (7ex) M Hourigan, *in rear whn f 4th*.............................. (3 to 1 op 4 to 1) f
Dist: ¾l, 2l, 5l, 4l, 12l, 12l, 6l, 10l. 4m 0.40s. a 11.40s (10 Ran).
SR: -/-/7/-/-/-/ (Woodlands (Worcestershire) Ltd), P A Pritchard

597 Boathouse Novices' Hurdle (4-y-o and up) £1,480 2m...................... (5:25)

MUSKORA (Ire) 4-10-12 Peter Hobbs, *hld up, gd hdwy on outsd appr 3 out, led approaching last, quickened wl, cmftbly*............. (7 to 1 op 8 to 1 tchd 12 to 1) 1
JOVIAL MAN (Ire) 4-10-12 M Perrett, *nvr far away, hdwy 3 out, styd on frm nxt*..............(20 to 1 op 16 to 1) 2
IRON BARON (Ire) 4-10-5 (7[*]) C Woodall, *hld up towards rear, hdwy 4th, outpcd appr 3 out, rallied and styd on frm nxt*.............. (16 to 1 op 14 to 1 tchd 20 to 1) 3
STYLE AND CLASS 4-10-12 T Grantham, *chsd ldrs, ev ch 2 out, kpt on one pace.*...... (14 to 1 op 12 to 1) 4
402[*] TOP SPIN 4-11-4 S Smith Eccles, *chsd ldrs, rdn to ld appr 2 out, hdd bef last, wknd.*
.... (13 to 8 on op 5 to 4 tchd 11 to 10 on) 5
ROCKY BAY 4-10-0 (7[*]) Mr J L Llewellyn, *pld hrd, led appr 3 out, rdn and hdd bef nxt, sn btn.* (25 to 1 op 33 to 1) 6
MARINERS COVE 5-11-0 W Humphreys, *hld up, styd on frm 5th, nvr nr to chal*.....................(33 to 1) 7
GRANGE CHIEF (Ire) 5-11-0 J Osborne, *hld up, hdwy 5th, wknd aftr 2 out*.......... (9 to 1 op 10 to 1 tchd 11 to 1) 8
429[3] NORTHERN TRIAL (USA) 5-11-0 R Supple, *beh till hdwy appr 3 out, wknd aftr nxt.*
.... (9 to 1 op 7 to 1 tchd 10 to 1) 9
THE GREYSMITH 6-11-0 L Harvey, *nvr on terms.* (33 to 1) 10
434[7] TRECOMETTI 5-10-4 (5[*]) R Davis, *al beh.*
.... (25 to 1 op 20 to 1 tchd 33 to 1) 11
429[6] FAUGHAN LODGE 6-11-0 Diane Clay, *beh frm hfwy, tld off*............................... (20 to 1) 12
DARINGLY 4-10-12 S McNeill, *led to second, prmnt till wknd aftr 5th, tld off*.......... (50 to 1 op 33 to 1) 13

THE OVERTRUMPER 6-11-0 N Williamson, *al beh, tld off.*
.... (66 to 1 op 50 to 1) 14
MR POPPLETON 4-10-12 D Bridgwater, *led second, sn clr, hdd appr 3 out, wknd quickly, tld off.*
.... (50 to 1 op 33 to 1) 15
136[7] ARCTIC LIFE (Ire) 4-10-12 D Skyrme, *not jump wl in rear, sn tld off*....................(33 to 1 tchd 50 to 1) 16
OLIVIPET 4-10-7 M Crosse, *al beh, tld off.*
.... (66 to 1 op 50 to 1) 17
MINSTRALS BOYO 6-11-0 G Upton, *al beh, tld off whn pld up bef last.*............. (66 to 1 op 50 to 1) pu
RHAZYA 5-10-6 (3[*]) D O'Sullivan, *chsd ldrs till wknd quickly 4th, tld off whn pld up bef 3 out.*
.... (66 to 1 op 50 to 1) pu
Dist: 2½l, 2½l, nk, 7l, 2l, 4l, 1½l, 2½l, 2l, 2½l. 3m 50.30s. a 9.30s (19 Ran).
SR: 23/20/17/16/15/2/5/3/-/ (N C Savery), P J Hobbs

OVREVOLL (NOR) (soft)
Sunday September 26th

598 Mercedes Benz Champion Hurdle (4-y-o and up) £9,551 2m 1f 165yds........ (2:10)

270[3] BAY TERN (USA) 7-10-6 P Harley, *led bef hfwy, ran on wl fnl 2 fs, cmftbly*........................... 1
STEPPIN STONE (Swe) 5-10-6 J Twomey,................. 2
DARDO (Pol) 6-10-8 D Byrne,........................ 3
Dist: 5½l, 5½l, 3½l, 16l, 1l, 25l, 25l. 4m 18.80s. (10 Ran).
(Thomas Dyer), T Dyer

FONTWELL (good to firm)
Monday September 27th
Going Correction: PLUS 0.30 sec. per fur.

599 Highland Park Selling Hurdle (4-y-o) £1,719 2¼m...................... (2:20)

KALAMOSS 10-7 (7[*]) Miss S Mitchell, *al frnt rnk, rdn to chal last, sn led, ran on wl.*
.... (7 to 1 op 6 to 1 tchd 8 to 1) 1
359[3] CORINTHIAN GOD (Ire) 11-5 R Dunwoody, *hld up, hdwy 5th, led sn aftr 3 out, rdn and btn sn aftr last, one pace*.............. (7 to 1 op 5 to 1 tchd 8 to 1) 2
514[*] CYRILL HENRY (Ire) 11-10 A Merrigan, *hld up in tch, hdwy appr 6th, ev ch 2 out, wknd r-in.* (8 to 1 tchd 10 to 1) 3
PIE HATCH (Ire) 10-9 D Murphy, *hld up in rear, not fluent, hdwy 6th, mstk and lost pl 3 out, btn whn jmpd badly rght last.*...................(5 to 4 fav op 6 to 4) 4
381[2] BETALONGABILL 11-0 A Maguire, *hld up in tch, rdn appr 3 out, one pace aftr....* (6 to 1 op 5 to 1 tchd 13 to 2) 5
185[6] CANBRACK (Ire) 11-0 Leesa Long, *hld up, rdn and wknd appr 3 out.*.......... (100 to 1 op 50 to 1) 6
DANCING DANCER 10-9 J Frost, *al in rear.*
.... (16 to 1 op 14 to 1 tchd 20 to 1) 7
FORTUNE STAR (Ire) 10-11 (3[*]) D O'Sullivan, *prmnt, led aftr 5th, hdd sn aftr 3 out, wknd quickly.*
.... (66 to 1 op 50 to 1 tchd 100 to 1) 8
402 TADORA (Ire) 11-0 D Morris, *made most till aftr 5th, rdn and wknd 3 out*......(16 to 1 op 10 to 1 tchd 20 to 1) 9
LER CRU (Ire) 11-0 M A FitzGerald, *hld up in rear, lost tch 3 out, virtually pld up r-in, tld off.*
.... (9 to 1 op 6 to 1 tchd 10 to 1) 10
Dist: 5l, 5l, 2l, 7l, ½l, hd, 8l, 1½l, dist. 4m 24.70s. a 14.70s (10 Ran).
(N R Mitchell), N R Mitchell

600 Highland Park Handicap Chase (0-115 5-y-o and up) £2,684 3¼m 110yds....... (2:50)

501[3] GLEBE PRINCE [87] 13-10-0[1] (5[*]) C Burnett-Wells, *jump wl, led second, made rst, quickened clr frm 16th, eased r-in, cmftbly*.............(12 to 1 op 8 to 1 tchd 14 to 1) 1
YIRAGAN [111] 11-11-9 (5[*]) R Davis, *hld up, styd on to chase wnr frm 4 out, rdn and ran on r-in, nvr nrr.*
.... (4 to 1 op 7 to 2 tchd 9 to 2) 2
436[4] DOONLOUGHAN [109] 8-11-12 J Frost, *wtd wth, styd on one pace frm 4 out....* (11 to 4 op 3 to 1 tchd 9 to 2) 3
SAM SHORROCK [99] 11-11-2 D Bridgwater, *led to second, outpcd frm 16th..............* (10 to 1 op 5 to 1) 4
461[3] MILLIE BELLE [85] (v) 7-10-2 A Maguire, *ran in snatches, al in rear, wl beh frm 16th.* (8 to 1 op 6 to 1 tchd 9 to 1) 5
464[3] CAIRNEYMOUNT [87] 7-10-4[2] Peter Hobbs, *in rear frm 8th, lost tch 16th, tld off.*
.... (7 to 1 op 16 to 1 tchd 33 to 1) 6
BETTY HAYES [100] 9-11-3 S Earle, *prmnt, chsd wnr frm 9th to 4 out, sn wknd, pld up bef last.*
.... (9 to 1 op 7 to 1 tchd 10 to 1) pu
Dist: 1l, 12l, 12l, ¾l, 30l. 6m 53.30s. a 23.30s (7 Ran).
(T Hale), R Rowe

601 Famous Grouse Handicap Hurdle for the Rank Challenge Cup (0-115 4-y-o and up) £2,145 2¼m...................... (3:20)

PONTOON BRIDGE [95] 6-10-3 M Perrett, *made all, drw clr 3 out, easily*...................(11 to 10 fav op 2 to 1) 1
FOTOEXPRESS [116] 5-11-3 (7*) L Dace, *chsd wnr frm 4th, styd on one pace 2 out*.............(10 to 1 op 6 to 1) 2
499[6] LUSTY LAD [108] 8-11-2 G McCourt, *hld up, hdwy 4th, rdn and chsd 1st 2 frm 3 out.*
.........................(7 to 1 op 5 to 1 tchd 8 to 1) 3
435* RULING DYNASTY [112] (bl) 9-11-6 H Davies, *wtd wth, styd on frm 3 out, nvr nr to chal*.....(9 to 2 op 3 to 1) 4
463[4] CARPET CAPERS (USA) [92] 9-10-0 J R Kavanagh, *rear, some hdwy 3 out, nvr dngrs*.......(33 to 1 op 16 to 1) 5
SING THE BLUES [92] 9-10-0 D Morris, *frnt rnk till rdn and wknd 3 out*......(33 to 1 op 16 to 1 tchd 40 to 1) 6
HALLOW FAIR [94] 8-10-2[2] M A FitzGerald, *mid-div, out-pcd 6th*...............(15 to 2 op 6 to 1 tchd 8 to 1) 7
MY SENOR [109] 4-11-3 A Maguire, *chsd wnr to 4th, wknd appr 3 out*...........(11 to 1 op 7 to 1 tchd 12 to 1) 8
COLORTAG [95] 7-10-3[3] J Akehurst, *tld off 5th, pld up bef 2 out*..............................(100 to 1 op 50 to 1) pu
PADIORD [96] 6-10-2 (5*) R Davis, *in tch till pld up aftr 5th, broke leg, destroyed.*
.........................(16 to 1 op 10 to 1 tchd 25 to 1) pu
Dist: 8l, 3½l, 6l, 8l, 12l, 5l, 25l. 4m 20.30s. a 10.30s (10 Ran).
SR: 26/39/27/25/-/-/ (Peter Wiegand), G Harwood

602 Famous Grouse Handicap Chase (0-125 5-y-o and up) £2,562 2¼m.........(3:50)

206* ST ATHANS LAD [125] (bl) 8-12-0 D Morris, *led aftr 1st, rdn appr 2 out, ran on gmely r-in.* (Evens fav op 7 to 4 on) 1
458[5] THEY ALL FORGOT ME [98] 6-10-1[1] R Dunwoody, *outpcd 4 out, sn rdn, ran on und pres to go second ct hme.*
.........................(13 to 2 op 6 to 1 tchd 7 to 1) 2
279[3] GLASS MOUNTAIN [97] (bl) 11-10-0 A Maguire, *led till aftr 1st, chsd wnr till wknd and lost second ct hme.*
.........................(9 to 2 op 4 to 1 tchd 11 to 2) 3
372 GABISH [99] 8-10-2[2] M A FitzGerald, *rear, effrt 9th, wknd appr 3 out*...........(14 to 1 op 16 to 1 tchd 20 to 1) 4
KISU KALI [99] 8-10-2 J R Kavanagh, *al beh, lost tch 4 out, tld off*............................(3 to 1 op 4 to 1) 5
Dist: 2½l, nk, 20l, 30l. 4m 35.40s. a 15.40s (5 Ran).
(Geyer Estates Limited (St Athans Hotel)), R Curtis

603 Bunnahabhain Novices' Chase (5-y-o and up) £1,974 2¼m..................(4:20)

LUNABELLE 5-10-7 J Frost, *hld up in rear, steady hdwy frm 9th, led 3 out, sn clr, cmftbly.*
...............(Evens fav op 6 to 4 on tchd 11 to 10) 1
SQUEEZE PLAY (bl) 8-11-0 Peter Hobbs, *hld up, hdwy appr 4 out, chsd wnr aftr nxt*......(4 to 1 tchd 9 to 2) 2
465 EASTERN EVENING 8-11-0 R Rowell, *led to second, led 4th to 3 out, outpcd aftr.* (50 to 1 op 33 to 1 tchd 66 to 1) 3
438[3] PARBOLD HILL 5-11-4 M A FitzGerald, *in tch, wnt second 9th, ev ch till wknd appr 3 out.*
.........................(3 to 1 op 4 to 1 tchd 8 to 1) 4
498[3] MIDDAY SHOW (USA) 6-11-0 S Smith Eccles, *trkd ldr, led second to 4th, wknd tenth, sn wl beh.*
.........................(13 to 2 op 7 to 1 tchd 8 to 1) 5
Dist: 10l, 10l, 12l. 4m 39.50s. a 19.50s (5 Ran).
(Queen Elizabeth), I A Balding

604 Tamdhu Juvenile Novices' Hurdle (3-y-o) £1,763 2¼m....................(4:50)

SATIN DANCER 10-12 M Perrett, *al gng wl, led 3 out, sn clr, cmftbly*..................(5 to 4 fav op 5 to 4 on) 1
462[4] WONDERFUL YEARS (USA) 10-12 A Maguire, *led to 3 out, rdn and edgd rght aftr nxt, one pace.*
.........................(20 to 1 op 16 to 1 tchd 25 to 1) 2
356[2] CONVOY (bl) 10-12 R Dunwoody, *chsd ldr, rdn aftr 3 out, wkng whn hmpd and switchd lft after nxt, edgd left r-in.*............(100 to 30 op 5 to 1 tchd 11 to 2) 3
DARSING 10-12 S Smith Eccles, *hmpd strt, rear till styd on one pace frm 3 out*......(20 to 1 op 14 to 1) 4
247[5] IMAGERY 10-7 L Harvey, *trkd ldrs till wknd 3 out.*
.........................(20 to 1 op 25 to 1 tchd 33 to 1) 5
296 MY SET PEACE 10-7 M A FitzGerald, *al beh.*
.........................(33 to 1 tchd 50 to 1) 6
IVORY HUTCH 10-9 (3*) D O'Sullivan, *al rear, lost tch appr 3 out, tld off*......................(33 to 1 op 20 to 1) 7
462[6] CHIPPENDALE LADD (Can) (bl) 10-12 J Osborne, *hdwy 5th, pressed ldrs till wknd rpdly aftr 3 out, tld off.*
.........................(7 to 1 op 8 to 1 tchd 10 to 1) 8
379[3] SWIFT REVENGE 10-7 Lorna Vincent, *chsd ldrs till wknd 5th, tld off*...............(33 to 1 tchd 50 to 1) 9
462[5] TAAHHUB (Ire) 10-12 D Skyrme, *al beh, tld off 5th.*
.........................(12 to 1 op 16 to 1 tchd 20 to 1) 10
JUST JAMIE 10-12 M Richards, *al beh, tld off whn pld up bef last*..........(15 to 2 op 6 to 1 tchd 8 to 1) pu
Dist: 12l, 2½l, 20l, 15l, 5l, 20l. 4m 26.60s. a 16.60s (11 Ran).
(G Harwood), G Harwood

EXETER (good)
Tuesday September 28th
Going Correction: PLUS 0.15 sec. per fur. (races 1,2,-

4,6), PLUS 0.35 (3,5)

605 Dominion Oils Ltd Novices' Hurdle (4-y-o and up) £1,544 2¾m...............(2:20)

KING'S TREASURE (USA) 4-10-12 J Frost, *hld up in mid-div, hdwy appr 6th, wnt 3rd 3 out, led last, all out.*
.........................(13 to 8 fav op 7 to 4 tchd 2 to 1) 1
502* EID (USA) 4-11-0 (3*) W Marston, *al prmnt, wnt second 6th, led appr 2 out, hdd last, rdn and rallied r-in.*
.........................(7 to 4 op 2 to 1 tchd 13 to 8) 2
439* KNIGHTLY ARGUS 6-11-10 J Osborne, *led 3rd till hdd appr 2 out, one pace aftr.*
.........................(8 to 1 op 6 to 1 tchd 9 to 1) 3
483[3] CHICKABIDDY 5-10-9 M A FitzGerald, *beh till hdwy frm 6th, ev ch appr 2 out, rdn and one pace aftr.*
.........................(12 to 1 op 16 to 1 tchd 10 to 1) 4
TAURUS 7-11-0 B Powell, *mid-div, hdwy frm 6th, rdn 3 out, wknd aftr nxt*................(25 to 1 op 14 to 1) 5
483[4] SOUL TRADER 4-10-7 S Burrough, *wl in rear till styd on frm 3 out, nvr nrr*.....(10 to 1 op 14 to 1 tchd 25 to 1) 6
DICIEMBRE 4-10-12 W McFarland, *in rear, some hdwy 3 out, wknd nxt*.......(40 to 1 op 33 to 1 tchd 50 to 1) 7
441[8] RAGTIME BOY 5-11-0 A Maguire, *chsd ldrs till wknd 7th, tld off*.............(14 to 1 tchd 16 to 1 and 20 to 1) 8
439 HIDDEN FLOWER 4-10-0 (7*) P McLoughlin, *prmnt till wknd 6th, tld off*.................(66 to 1 op 50 to 1) 9
GUITING GIRL 4-10-7 C Llewellyn, *chsd ldrs till wknd 6th, tld off*................(11 to 1 op 6 to 1 tchd 12 to 1) 10
GAMBLERS REFRAIN 8-11-0 S McNeill, *chsd ldrs till wknd appr 6th, tld off whn pld up bef 2 out.*
.........................(100 to 1 op 50 to 1) pu
ROATH PARK 8-10-9 (5*) R Farrant, *mstks in rear, tld off whn pld up bef 3 out*...........(100 to 1 op 50 to 1) pu
445[6] PERFORATE (bl) 4-11-8 L Harvey, *led to 3rd, sn beh, tld off whn pld up bef 3 out*...........(20 to 1 op 12 to 1) pu
Dist: 1l, 7l, 1½l, 6l, 8l, 1l, 20l, 10l, 1½l. 5m 18.30s. a 18.30s (13 Ran).
(Paul Mellon), I A Balding

606 Dominion Oils Ltd Juvenile Novices' Hurdle (3-y-o) £1,509 2m 1f 110yds.....(2:50)

GENERAL CHASE 10-7 D J Burchell, *trkd ldrs, al gng wl, led 3 out, drw clr frm nxt, very easily.*
.........................(12 to 1 op 6 to 1) 1
352[3] ALLEGATION (bl) 10-12 R Dunwoody, *nvr far away, cld on ldrs 3 out, wnt second nxt, no ch wth wnr whn jmpd lft last.*.................(9 to 2 op 7 to 2 tchd 7 to 1) 2
POLLY LEACH 10-7 B Powell, *made most till hdd 3 out, outpcd frm nxt*........(25 to 1 op 14 to 1 tchd 33 to 1) 3
ROMALITO 10-12 D Gallagher, *towards rear till styd on aftr 3 out*........(6 to 1 op 7 to 2 tchd 13 to 2) 4
352[2] APACHEE FLOWER 10-0 (7*) Mr G Lewis, *in frnt rnk till wknd appr 2 out*......(11 to 1 op 8 to 1 tchd 14 to 1) 5
ALDERNEY PRINCE (USA) 10-12 H Davies, *in tch till out-pcd frm 3 out*...........(3 to 1 op 5 to 2 tchd 5 to 1) 6
LITTLE PORKY 10-7 (5*) D Leahy, *al in rear.*
.........................(50 to 1 op 25 to 1) 7
516[3] CARELESS FARMER 10-7 C Llewellyn, *mstk second, jnd ldr nxt, wknd appr 3 out, tld off.*
.........................(7 to 4 fav op 6 to 4 tchd 11 to 10) 8
WATERLOO (Ire) 10-12 S Keightley, *mstks 1st 2, uns rdr nxt*....................(16 to 1 op 10 to 1 tchd 20 to 1) ur
APOLLO DE ORIENTE 10-12 L Harvey, *al beh, lost tch aftr 4th, tld off whn pld up bef 2 out*...(50 to 1 op 20 to 1) pu
Dist: 6l, 8l, 15l, nk, 5l, 12l, 20l. 4m 13.40s. a 16.40s (10 Ran).
(Eamonn O'Malley), D Burchell

607 Dominion Oils Ltd Novices' Chase (5-y-o and up) £2,289 2¾m 110yds.........(3:20)

417* GILSTON LASS 6-11-2 J R Kavanagh, *made virtually all, styd on wl r-in*.......(100 to 30 op 5 to 2 tchd 7 to 2) 1
461[2] OCEAN LINK 9-11-7 S Earle, *sn trkd wnr, upsides 4 out till one pace r-in*.........(11 to 2 op 4 to 1) 2
485* TITUS ANDRONICUS (bl) 6-11-7 R Supple, *nvr far away, chsd on one pace frm 4 out.*
.........................(3 to 1 fav tchd 11 to 4 and 7 to 2) 3
488[5] HOUSE OF ROSES (Ire) 5-11-0 G Bradley, *hld up, hdwy 7th, ev ch 4 out, one pace frm 2 out, prmsg.*
.........................(6 to 1 op 5 to 1) 4
483[5] DRUMCEVA 7-11-2 J Railton, *hld up, hdwy appr tenth, wknd approaching 3 out*........(8 to 1 op 5 to 1) 5
LAVALIGHT 6-11-2 R Dunwoody, *chsd ldrs till wknd appr 4 out*.......................(14 to 1 op 10 to 1) 6
586[2] BRIGTINA 5-10-9 (5*) R Farrant, *mid-div, wkng whn f 4 out*.................(11 to 1 op 7 to 1 tchd 16 to 1) f
JHAL FREZI 5-11-0 W Irvine, *beh whn blun and uns rdr 9th.*...........................(50 to 1 op 25 to 1) ur
485[3] SHARPRIDGE 9-11-2 W McFarland, *chsd ldrs till wknd 11th, beh whn barely jmpd 5 out, pld up bef nxt.*
.........................(11 to 1 op 8 to 1 tchd 12 to 1) pu
526[2] BARLEY MOW 7-11-2 N Mann, *al beh, lost tch 12th, pld up bef 4 out*....(14 to 1 op 12 to 1 tchd 20 to 1) pu
PABREY 7-11-2 B Powell, *prmnt to 4th, beh frm 8th, tld off whn pld up bef 5 out*..........(25 to 1 op 20 to 1) pu

ARUBA (Fr) 5-11-0 P Holley, *al beh, blun 11th, tld off whn pld up bef 4 out*..................(50 to 1 op 25 to 1) pu
Dist: 1l, 2½l, ½l, 10l, 6l. 5m 43.20s. a 22.20s (12 Ran).
(Marlborough Racing Partnership), J S King

608 Dominion Oils Ltd Conditional Jockeys' Novices' Selling Hurdle (3 - 6-y-o) £1,236 2m 1f 110yds..................... (3:50)

416* DISTANT MEMORY (bl) 4-11-8 (5*) N Parker, *led, sn clr, wkng whn stumbled and mstk last, jst hld on.*
..................(100 to 30 op 5 to 2 tchd 7 to 2) 1
486* OCTOBER BREW (USA) (bl) 3-10-7 (5*) T Dascombe, *hld up, hdwy appr 4th, wnt second 3 out, rdn approaching nxt, kpt on one pace, jst fld...* (6 to 4 on op 5 to 4 on) 2
379 GROGFRYN 3-10-2 R Farrant, *prmnt, chsd wnr 5th till wknd aftr nxt..........*(8 to 1 op 7 to 1 tchd 9 to 1) 3
415* ELEGANT TOUCH (bl) 4-10-10 (7*) O Burrows, *chsd wnr till wknd quickly appr 5th, tld off.*
..................(12 to 1 op 10 to 1 tchd 14 to 1) 4
HAZY DAZY 3-9-9 (7*) T Becton, *blun 4th, al beh, tld off.*
..................(25 to 1 op 14 to 1) 5
567 THARIF (bl) 5-11-2 (7*) N Downs, *al beh, lost tch appr 4th, blun 3 out, tld off..........*(33 to 1 op 25 to 1) 6
MY BOOKS ARE BEST (Ire) 4-11-3 D O'Sullivan, *prmnt till wknd quickly appr 4th, tld off whn pld up bef 2 out.*
..................(12 to 1 op 8 to 1) pu
Dist: Nk, 25l, 20l, 6l, 15l. 4m 12.30s. a 15.30s (7 Ran).
(Mrs Ann Weston), P J Hobbs

609 Dominion Oils Ltd Handicap Chase (0-120 5-y-o and up) £2,645 2m 3f......... (4:20)

487³ ARDCRONEY CHIEF [101] 7-10-4 P Holley, *trkd ldr, led tenth, rdn appr last, edgd lft r-in, ran on.*
..................(9 to 2 op 4 to 1 tchd 5 to 1) 1
419² GREEN ISLAND (USA) [119] 7-11-8 Peter Hobbs, *al in tch, dsptd ld 2 out, sn rdn, rallied r-in.* ....(7 to 5 co-fav op 5 to 2 tchd 4 to 1) 2
SARTORIUS [112] 7-11-1 H Davies, *hld up, gd hdwy 9th, dsptd ld appr 4 out, ev ch till wknd r-in.....*(7 to 2 co-fav op 2 to 1) 3
566³ AMONG FRIENDS [99] 8-10-2 A Maguire, *hld up in rear, making gd hdwy whn blun 4 out, mstk nxt, rallied, wknd appr last....................*(5 to 1 op 4 to 1) 4
501² MISTER FEATHERS [97] 12-10-0 J R Kavanagh, *led to fav on 4 out, wknd and sn btn.....*(7 to 2 co-fav 4 to 1 tchd 5 to 1) 5
500⁴ AL HASHIMI [125] 9-12-0 R Dunwoody, *not fluent, in tch till rdn and wknd 3 out.*
..................(10 to 1 op 8 to 1 tchd 11 to 1) 6
Dist: 2l, 3l, 4l, 8l, 1l. 4m 41.30s. a 12.30s (6 Ran).
(W H Dore), D R Gandolfo

610 Dominion Oils Ltd Handicap Hurdle (0-125 4-y-o and up) £1,830 2m 1f 110yds... (4:50)

ROC COLOR (Fr) [95] 4-11-11 G Bradley, *hld up, mstk 5th, rdn and hdwy appr 2 out, chlgd last, sn led, ran on.*
..................(7 to 2 op 4 to 1 tchd 9 to 2) 1
418* EMERALD MOON [72] 6-10-2² S Burrough, *hld up, gd hdwy to go second sn aftr 3 out, led nxt, rdn and hdd soon after last, no extr.*
..................(11 to 2 op 5 to 1 tchd 13 to 2) 2
569* VA UTU [98] 5-12-0 (6ex) Lorna Vincent, *trkd ldr, led sn aftr 3 out, hdd nxt, ev ch till rdn and wknd appr last.*
..................(3 to 1 fav op 5 to 2 tchd 100 to 30) 3
GREENWINE (USA) [85] 7-11-1 M Richards, *nvr far away, cld on ldrs 5th, ev ch till rdn and wknd appr last.*
..................(8 to 1 op 7 to 1 tchd 10 to 1) 4
420* TRUST DEED (USA) [91] (bl) 5-11-7 M A FitzGerald, *chsd ldrs till wknd appr 2 out.................*(6 to 1 op 5 to 1) 5
PRIZE MATCH [95] 4-11-11 C Llewellyn, *al beh, nvr on terms...................*(8 to 1 op 5 to 1 tchd 9 to 1) 6
ATHASSEL ABBEY [70] 7-10-0 N Williamson, *al beh, jmpd slwly 3rd, tld off frm 3 out...*(66 to 1 op 33 to 1) 7
484⁵ FASHION PRINCESS [70] (bl) 7-9-10³ (7*) D Matthews, *led till hdd sn aftr 3 out, wknd quickly, tld off.*
..................(50 to 1 op 33 to 1) 8
Dist: 2l, 5l, 2½l, 10l, 10l, 12l, 12l. 4m 5.70s. a 8.70s (8 Ran).
SR: 36/11/32/16/12/6/-/-/ (Mrs Susan McCarthy), C P E Brooks

CHELTENHAM (good to firm)
Wednesday September 29th
Going Correction: MINUS 0.60 sec. per fur.

611 Neville Russell Three Yrs Old Novices' Hurdle £2,018 2m 110yds.......... (2:10)

462* MR GENEAOLOGY (USA) (bl) 11-6 A Maguire, *prmnt, lft second 6th, led and mstk 2 out, drvn clr appr last.*
..................(100 to 30 op 5 to 2 tchd 4 to 1) 1
516* LEGAL ARTIST (Ire) 11-6 D Murphy, *trkd ldrs, cld up aftr 6th, rdn and not quicken appr last.*
..................(5 to 2 op 9 to 4 tchd 11 to 4) 2

278* CONTRACT ELITE (Ire) 11-3 D Wilkinson, *pld hrd, wth ldr till led 5th, hdd 2 out, no extr appr last.*
..................(9 to 4 fav op 2 to 1 tchd 5 to 2) 3
462⁸ ERLKING (Ire) 10-12 M Perrett, *keen hold and hld up, effrt aftr 6th, nvr nr to chal..............*(25 to 1 op 16 to 1) 4
HOT OFF THE PRESS 10-12 R J Beggan, *chsd ldrs till outpcd aftr 6th, no prog after....* (20 to 1 op 14 to 1) 5
MOSHAAJIR (USA) 10-12 M Ranger, *not jump wl, in tch to 6th, no ch aftr.......* (12 to 1 op 7 to 1 tchd 14 to 1) 6
349² STAR MARKET 10-9 (3*) W Marston, *hmpd strt, beh till styd on frm 2 out, nvr dngrs......*(25 to 1 op 16 to 1) 7
128⁴ BECKY'S GIRL 10-7 D Bridgwater, *al beh, tld off frm 3 out.*
..................(50 to 1 op 25 to 1) 8
TOUCH SILVER 10-12 M Bosley, *whipped round strt, al beh, tld off frm 5th..................*(50 to 1 op 25 to 1) 9
462³ PYRRHIC DANCE 11-3 J Osborne, *al beh, tld off frm 3 out.*
..................(16 to 1 op 12 to 1 tchd 20 to 1) 10
570⁶ STAR MINSTREL (Ire) 10-12 R Dunwoody, *led to 5th, cl second whn crashed through wing nxt.*
..................(14 to 1 op 7 to 1) ro
OUR NIKKI 10-7 I Shoemark, *in tch till pld up aftr 3rd, sddl slpd..................*(50 to 1 op 33 to 1) pu
356⁴ DICKINS 10-12 M A FitzGerald, *chsd ldrs, rdn 5th, 4th whn pld up suddenly aftr nxt....*(33 to 1 op 20 to 1) pu
Dist: 6l, 1½l, 10l, 2l, 10l, 6l, 20l, 2½l, 15l. 4m 0.10s. a 1.10s (13 Ran).
(Mrs P A White), J White

612 Notgrove Novices' Chase (5-y-o and up) £3,436 2m 110yds.................. (2:45)

MINE'S AN ACE (NZ) 6-11-1 J Frost, *wtd wth, steady prog frm tenth, clsg whn mstk last, ran on wl to ld nr finish.*
..................(7 to 1 op 6 to 1 tchd 8 to 1) 1
521* STRONG VIEWS 6-11-5 A Maguire, *hld up, prog 6th, led gng wl 2 out, hrd rdn and put head in air aftr last, hdd finish...............*(6 to 5 fav op Evens tchd 5 to 4) 2
596³ FASTBIT 6-11-5 N Williamson, *led to 2 out, hrd rdn and ev ch last, wknd nr finish.* (9 to 4 op 7 to 4 tchd 5 to 2) 3
521³ CANDLE KING (Ire) 5-11-0 M Bosley, *hld up and beh, mstk 3rd, steady prog tenth, nvr rchd ldrs.*
..................(20 to 1 op 33 to 1) 4
442 PECCAVI 9-11-1 R Bellamy, *chsd ldr frm 4th till mstk tenth, wknd rpdly...............*(50 to 1 op 33 to 1) 5
485⁴ VIRGINIA'S BAY 7-11-1 Mr N Miles, *mstk 1st, chsd ldr to 4th, sn beh, tld off frm 5th........*(66 to 1 op 50 to 1) 6
549² BARDESAN 7-11-5 J Osborne, *chsd ldrs, jmpd slwly 6th, sn lost pl, mstks aftr. tld off frm 9th.*
..................(10 to 1 op 12 to 1 tchd 14 to 1) 7
435³ BROWN SAUCE (NZ) 7-10-12 (3*) W Marston, *hld up rear, in tch whn f 5th...................*(14 to 1 tchd 20 to 1) f
Dist: 2½l, 2l, 20l, 20l, 8l, 25l. 4m 2.00s. b 4.00s (8 Ran).
SR: 28/29/27/2/-/ (D H Barons), D H Barons

613 Allied Dunbar Assurance Handicap Hurdle (0-125 4-y-o and up) £2,883 2m 7f 110yds
..................................(3:15)

443³ BANKROLL [110] 6-10-4 (7*) Mr G Lewis, *trkd ldr, led 7th, mstk 2 out and sn hdd, rallied to ld aftr last, hld on wl.*
..................(12 to 1) 1
594³ NEWTON POINT [101] 4-10-2 Peter Hobbs, *trkd ldrs, effrt 3 out, led appr last, hdd r-in, not quicken cl hme.*
..................(11 to 2 op 5 to 1 tchd 6 to 1) 2
335² ELEGANT KING (Ire) [108] 4-10-9 T Jarvis, *hld up in tch, jnd ldrs 8th, rdn and wknd aftr 3 out, lft poor 3rd, blun last.........................*(10 to 1 op 7 to 1) 3
526⁶ SIR CRUSTY [104] 11-10-2 (3*) V Slattery, *beh, rdn and effrt 9th, sn no ch, ran on to take poor 4th aftr last.*
..................(16 to 1 op 14 to 1 tchd 20 to 1) 4
60² BANOUR (USA) [127] (bl) 5-12-0 C Llewellyn, *chsd ldrs till lost tch aftr 9th, tld off frm nxt...* (6 to 1 tchd 11 to 2) 5
MICKEEN [105] 6-10-6 J Osborne, *led to 7th, wknd frm 9th, tld off 3 out......................*(12 to 1) 6
BRORA ROSE (Ire) [99] 5-10-0¹ Shoemark, *in tch till hmpd and lost pl bend aftr 7th, tld off after 9th.*
..................(100 to 1 op 33 to 1) 7
443³ OWEN [101] 9-10-2 B Powell, *hld up last, effrt 8th, rdn and no prog nxt, tld off 3 out.* (4 to 1 jt-fav op 3 to 1) 8
ARR EFF BEE [99] (bl) 6-9-9 (5*) D Leahy, *in tch till hmpd and lost pl bend aftr 7th, tld off after 9th.*
..................(25 to 1 op 12 to 1) 9
463² GALLANT EFFORT (Ire) [106] (v) 5-10-7 H Davies, *hld up, prog to chase ldrs 8th, rdn and wknd aftr nxt, sn tld off...................................*(10 to 1) 10
463* STRONG MEDICINE [111] 6-10-12 N Williamson, *hld up in tch, jnd ldrs 8th, led briefly aftr 2 out, cl 3rd but btn whn f last...................*(4 to 1 jt-fav tchd 7 to 2) f
Dist: Hd, dist, 12l, 1½l, 4½l, ¾l, 1l, 12l, 12l. 5m 29.90s. b 8.10s (11 Ran).
SR: 23/14/-/-/-/-/ (Ian S Steers), P J Hobbs

614 Nailsworth Intermediate Handicap Chase (0-130 5-y-o and up) £3,967 3m 1f 110yds
..................................(3:45)

MERE CLASS [115] 7-11-2 G Bradley, *trkd ldrs, wnt second 12th, led 3 out, pushed out r-in cmftbly.*
..................(7 to 4 fav tchd 15 to 8) 1

74

458* COPPER MINE [127] 7-12-0 J Osborne, *led to 3 out, kpt on*
one pace aftr.........(9 to 4 op 2 to 1 tchd 15 to 8) 2
CAMELOT KNIGHT [114] 7-11-1 C Llewellyn, *chsd ldr to*
12th, blun 14th, btn frm 3 out........(9 to 4 op 7 to 4) 3
THEO'S FELLA [99] 9-10-0 S Hodgson, *al last, lost tch 4th,*
tld off frm 9th......................(10 to 1 op 7 to 1) 4
Dist: 8l, 12l, dist. 6m 16.40s. b 0.60s (4 Ran).

(Miss M Talbot), C P E Brooks

615 Cirencester Handicap Chase (0-125 5-y-o and up) £4,104 2m 5f.............. (4:15)

436² TRI FOLENE (Fr) [118] (bl) 7-11-2 R Dunwoody, *led to 9th, sn*
pushed alng, rallied 3 out, led aftr last, styd on wl.
....................(9 to 4 fav op 5 to 2 tchd 3 to 1) 1
457² LITTLE TOM [102] 8-10-0 J R Kavanagh, *trkd ldr till led*
9th, rdn aftr 2 out, hdd and wknd after last.
.... (11 to 1 op 7 to 1 tchd 12 to 1) 2
518² ICARUS (USA) [124] 7-11-8 Mr A Rebori, *trkd ldrs, rdn and*
one pace frm 3 out.... (10 to 1 op 6 to 1 tchd 12 to 1) 3
KENTISH PIPER [120] 8-11-4 C Llewellyn, *wtd wth, mstks*
9th and 12th and lost tch, styd on frm 3 out, no dngr.
..............................(4 to 1 op 3 to 1 tchd 9 to 2) 4
523* JOYFUL NOISE [124] 10-11-8 A Maguire, *cl up, chsd ldr*
13th, sn rdn and wknd..................(7 to 2 tchd 4 to 1) 5
523² PALM READER [127] 9-11-11 M A FitzGerald, *hld up, prog*
to join ldrs, rdn and wknd 13th.
.... (7 to 2 tchd 3 to 1 and 4 to 1) 6
POPESWOOD [103] 10-10-1 Peter Hobbs, *in tch to 12th,*
sn beh.................................(50 to 1 op 25 to 1) 7
Dist: 6l, 12l, 5l, 1½l, 8l, 7l. 5m 5.90s. b 4.10s (7 Ran).
SR: -/-/-/-/   (David L'Estrange), M C Pipe

616 Eagle Pest Control Novices' Hurdle (4-y-o and up) £2,081 2m 110yds...... (4:50)

160¹ CLOGHANS BAY (Ire) 4-11-9 R Dunwoody, *cl up, jnd ldrs 3*
out, hrd rdn appr last, ran to ld last strd.
..............................(15 to 8 fav op 11 to 10) 1
WILD STRAWBERRY 4-10-9 M Richards, *cl up, led aftr*
6th, rdn appr last, ran on r-in, hdd last strd.
...............................(5 to 1 tchd 11 to 2) 2
SOUND CARRIER (USA) 5-11-1 J Osborne, *prmnt till out-*
pcd aftr 6th, ran on ag'n frm 2 out, prmsg.
.................................(16 to 1 op 6 to 1) 3
GLENFINN PRINCESS 5-10-10 D Bridgwater, *strted slwly,*
hld up, effrt 6th, kpt on one pace frm 2 out, nvr rchd
ldrs.............(7 to 1 op 12 to 1 tchd 20 to 1) 4
399* FATHER DAN (Ire) 4-11-5 A Maguire, *prmnt, ev ch 3 out, sn*
wknd...............................(10 to 1 op 5 to 1) 5
TREASSOWE MARINER 5-11-1 H Davies, *rear, lost tch*
6th, no prog aftr.... (50 to 1 op 20 to 1 tchd 66 to 1) 6
BERTONE (Ire) 4-11-0 G Bradley, *wtd wth, prog to join*
ldrs aftr 6th, wknd 3 out, no ch when blun nxt.
..................(5 to 1 op 2 op 1 tchd 3 to 1) 7
551⁶ DAUPHIN BLEU (Fr) 7-11-1 Dr P Pritchard, *mstk second, al*
rear, lost tch 5th, sn tld off......(100 to 1 op 33 to 1) 8
452 FORTINA'S SONG 6-11-1 M A FitzGerald, *al rear, lost tch*
frm 6th, sn tld off...............(33 to 1 op 14 to 1) 9
KAYRUZ 5-11-1 Mr N Miles, *not fluent, led till aftr 6th,*
wknd rpdly, sn tld off............(66 to 1 op 20 to 1) 10
SNOWSHILL SHAKER 4-11-0 C Llewellyn, *al rear, tld off*
frm 6th...........................(14 to 1 op 5 to 1) 11
441 BROTHER HAROLD 4-10-11 (3*) R Bellamy, *beh frm 4th, tld*
off frm 6th.........................(66 to 1 op 16 to 1) 12
429⁴ CIRCUIT COURT (Ire) 5-11-1 S Smith Eccles, *rear till pld*
up bef 4th....................(14 to 1 op 8 to 1) pu
DUNNICKS WELL 4-11-0 C Maude, *strted slwly, al beh,*
tld off 5th, pld up bef 2 out....(100 to 1 op 33 to 1) pu
Dist: Sht-hd, 25l, 2½l, hd, 12l, hd, 7l, 3½l, 30l, 8l. 3m 54.40s. b 4.50s (14 Ran).
SR: 41/27/8/-/9/-/   (Sid Williams), M C Pipe

FAIRYHOUSE (IRE) (good to yielding)
Wednesday September 29th

617 Birch Hurdle (3-y-o) £3,105 2m...... (3:00)

470* BIZANA (Ire) 11-2 P Carberry, ...(11 to 8 on) 1
375¹ MILLERS MILL (Ire) 11-2 J Jones, ... (9 to 2) 2
BOB THE YANK 10-10 P P Kinane, ... (20 to 1) 3
529² NORDIC THORN (Ire) 10-10 J F Titley, ...(2 to 1) 4
TORC MOUNTAIN (Ire) 10-10 B Sheridan, ...(10 to 1) 5
494⁶ SISTER CARMEL (Ire) 10-5 C O'Dwyer, ... (12 to 1) 6
Dist: 1½l, 1½l, 1½l, 20l. 4m 14.80s. (6 Ran).

(Breffni Syndicate), Noel Meade

618 Rossmore Maiden Hurdle (5-y-o and up) £3,105 2¾m..................... (3:30)

KILBRICKEN STAR 6-10-4 D H O'Connor, ...(16 to 1) 1
258³ LE BRAVE 7-11-3 C F Swan, ...(11 to 10 fav) 2
469⁴ JOHNSON 7-10-2 (7*) Mr C A Leavy, ...(4 to 1) 3
STRONG DILEMMA (Ire) 5-10-4 (5*) T P Rudd, ...(10 to 1) 4
15 FANCY DISH 7-9-13 (5*) D P Murphy, ...(14 to 1) 5
DARING STAR 7-10-9 C N Bowens, ... (6 to 1) 6

341⁹ MAWTVICA 6-10-1 (3*) Mr P McMahon, ...(33 to 1) 7
495⁵ CURRAGH ROSE 6-9-11 (7*) J Butler, ... (12 to 1) 8
SPEAK OF THE DEVIL 6-11-3 H Rogers, ... (6 to 1) 9
466 ROYAL OPTION 6-10-9 K F O'Brien, ...(25 to 1) 10
508 CROGHAN MIST (Ire) 5-10-4 F Woods, ... (25 to 1) 11
BELLACORICK (Ire) 5-10-9 D P Fagan, ...(10 to 1) f
Dist: 5l, 1½l, 3l, 12l. (Time not taken) (12 Ran).

(Derek O'Keeffe), Derek O'Keeffe

619 Chestnut E.B.F. Novice Chase (5-y-o and up) £4,140 2½m................... (5:00)

412² NORTHERN HIDE 7-11-11 T J Taaffe, ... (9 to 4 jt-fav) 1
496* VISIBLE DIFFERENCE 7-11-11 C F Swan, .. (9 to 4 jt-fav) 2
475² PERKNAPP 6-11-7 K F O'Brien, ...(7 to 1) 3
199³ MUST DO 7-11-4 (3*) T J Mitchell, ...(16 to 1) 4
539⁶ FURRY STAR 7-11-11 J Jones, ... (5 to 2) 5
506⁶ COQ HARDI SMOKEY (Ire) 5-11-1 G M O'Neill, .. (12 to 1) 6
FARNEY GLEN 7-11-2 J Magee, ... (10 to 1) f
Dist: ½l, 14l, 20l, 9l. 5m 4.10s. (7 Ran).

(T Ryan), A L T Moore

620 Sycamore INH Flat Race (4-y-o and up) £3,105 2m..................... (5:30)

GORYTSS SALA (Ity) 4-11-4 (5*) Mr A E Lacy, ...(12 to 1) 1
508 TAITS CLOCK (Ire) 4-11-4 (5*) Mr J G Harford, ... (7 to 1) 2
JIMMY O'GOBLIN 6-12-0 Mr A J Martin, ... (100 to 30 fav) 3
BUCKLESFORDBERRY 4-11-6 (3*) Miss C Hutchinson,
......................................(8 to 1) 4
3² MASTER CRUSADER 7-11-7 (7*) Mr M Brennan, ...(8 to 1) 5
CONQUINN (Ire) 4-11-9 Mr P F Graffin, ...(7 to 1) 6
SWINGER (Ire) 4-11-2 (7*) Mr D A Harney, ...(6 to 1) 7
NO DOZING (Ire) 4-11-4 (5*) Mr B R Hamilton, ... (10 to 1) 8
540⁸ FINNEGANS WAKE 6-12-0 Mr A O'Brien, ...(10 to 1) 9
495² BLOW IT (Ire) 5-12-0 Mr M McNulty, ...(5 to 1) 10
531⁶ RED BARONS LADY (Ire) 4-11-3 (3*) Mrs M Mullins, (8 to 1) 11
RAHAN BRIDGE (Ire) 4-11-1 (3*) Mr A R Coonan, ... (5 to 1) 12
536 THE ROCKING CHAIR (Ire) 5-11-7 (7*) Mr V P O'Brien,
......................................(20 to 1) 13
TONDUFF PRINCE 7-12-0 Mr P Fenton, ...(20 to 1) 14
495 GARWELL (Ire) 5-11-2 (7*) Mr D J Geraghty, ...(33 to 1) 15
THE GUNNER 6-12-0 Mr J P Dempsey, ...(8 to 1) 16
495⁶ LORD GREYSTONES 6-11-9 (5*) Mr D Valentine, ..(25 to 1) 17
540⁶ MARCHING SEASON (Ire) 5-11-2 (7*) Mr S O'Donnell,
......................................(16 to 1) 18
SCEAL SIOG (Ire) 4-10-13 (5*) Mr J A Nash, ...(6 to 1) 19
DRAPERY SHOP (Ire) 5-11-7 (7*) Mr R M Murphy, ..(25 to 1) 20
531 LORD MONTE (Ire) 4-11-6 (3*) Mr D Marnane, ...(20 to 1) 21
Dist: ¾l, 2l, 5½l, 1½l. 3m 58.80s. (21 Ran).

(Pierce Boyce), Robert Norris

LYON (FR) (heavy)
Wednesday September 29th

621 Prix du Mont-Ventoux Hurdle (4-y-o) £11,947 2m 1f.................... (1:00)

ALLEZ WIJINS (USA) 11-7 D Mescam, ... 1
QUARTZ (Fr) 11-3 C Aubert, ... 2
MADRIKO (Fr) 9-13 M Linores, ... 3
408* ICE STRIKE (USA) 10-8 J Railton, *al beh*................ 0
Dist: 3½l, 2l, 2l, 5l, hd, 1l. (Time not taken) (16 Ran).

(D Tsui), H-A Pantall

SEDGEFIELD (good to firm)
Wednesday September 29th
Going Correction: MINUS 0.05 sec. per fur.

622 Stonegrave Aggregates Novices' Selling Hurdle (3-y-o and up) £1,339 2m 1f 110yds
.... (2:20)

339⁵ INVISIBLE ARMOUR 4-11-8 J Callaghan, *al chasing ldrs,*
pushed alng frm hfwy, styd on wl und press to ld r-in.
.................................(9 to 2 op 4 to 1) 1
GOLDMIRE 3-10-14 (3*) A Thornton, *sn tracking ldrs gng*
wl, smooth hdwy to ld betw last 2, hit last, hdd
and no extr r-in.......................(33 to 1) 2
516⁴ TOM THE TANK 3-10-5 G McCourt, *hld up in tch, hdwy to*
track ldrs appr 3 out, slight ld aftr nxt, sn hdd, kpt on
same pace..........(11 to 4 fav op 5 to 2 tchd 3 to 1) 3
477⁷ MY TATA (v) 7-11-9 J Corkell, *wth ldr, slight ld appr 2 out,*
sn hdd, kpt on same pace...................(33 to 1) 4
JUMPING CACTUS 4-11-3 (5*) P Waggott, *chsd ldrs,*
pushed alng aftr 3 out, no extr frm nxt.
.................................(14 to 1 op 12 to 1) 5
402⁴ WINGED WHISPER (USA) 4-11-3 (5*) T Eley, *slight ld till*
hdd appr 2 out, btn whn stumbled aftr last
.................................(9 to 2 op 4 to 1) 6
GREY COMMANDER (v) 5-11-9 P Niven, *chsd ldrs, rdn*
appr 3 out, grad wknd...........(9 to 2 op 7 to 2) 7
PREMIER ENVELOPE (Ire) 4-11-8 C Hawkins, *nvr nr to*
chal...............................(33 to 1) 8

482 LAFANTA (Ire) 4-11-8 K Jones, *chsd ldrs till wknd appr 2
out*..(33 to 1) 9
GREY REALM 5-11-4 N Smith, *in tch till wknd appr 2 out.*
....(25 to 1) 10
344³ VERBAL WARNING 5-11-9 K Johnson, *al beh*......(25 to 1) 11
482 JOVIAL KATE (USA) 6-11-4 A Orkney, *prmnt till wknd appr
2 out*...(20 to 1 tchd 25 to 1) 12
315⁵ ABSOLUTE DANCER 4-10-10 (7*) S Taylor, *sn beh*. (50 to 1) 13
547⁸ RED RHAPSODY 4-10-10 (7*) Mark Roberts, *sn beh.*
....(20 to 1 op 10 to 1) 14
PRINCE ALI (bl) 4-11-8 T Reed, *sn beh, tld off whn pld up
bef last*...(50 to 1) pu
Dist: 1l, 4l, 4l, 2l, 3l, 5l, hd, 1½l, 6l, 5l. 4m 1.70s. a 6.70s (15 Ran).
SR: 18/-/-/10/7/4/ (Dunnington, Shaw & Smart), P C Haslam

623 Red Onion Handicap Hurdle (0-115 4-y-o and up) £2,040 2m 5f 110yds....... (2:50)

398* MR REINER (Ire) [100] 5-10-2 (7*) D Ryan, *made virtually
all, styd on wl und pres frm 2 out*....(3 to 1 op 5 to 2) 1
PINISI [91] 8-10-0³ (3*) A Larnach, *hld up in tch, effrt whn
hmpd 3 out, styd on frm nxt, not rch wnr.*
....(25 to 1 op 20 to 1) 2
398² NOTABLE EXCEPTION [91] 4-9-10¹ (5*) Mr M Buckley, *sn
tracking ldrs, effrt 3 out, styd on same pace frm nxt.*
......................................(2 to 1 fav op 9 to 4 tchd 5 to 2) 3
CHEEKY POT [91] (v) 5-9-12³ (5*) P Waggott, *hld up in tch,
hdwy hfwy, chsd wnr frm 3 out till wknd appr last.*
....(8 to 1 op 10 to 1 tchd 12 to 1) 4
SEXY MOVER [100] 6-10-9 K Johnson, *prmnt, reminders
hfwy, pushed alng aftr, wknd frm 3 out.*
....(6 to 1 op 5 to 1 tchd 13 to 2) 5
564³ GATHERING TIME [111] 7-11-3 (3*) D J Moffatt, *in tch till
rdn and outpcd 7th, no dngr aftr....* (9 to 1 op 7 to 1) 6
MILL DE LEASE [91] 8-9-11 (3*) M Hourigan, *dsptd ld, wkng
and losing tch whn hamperd 3 out.*
....(50 to 1 op 33 to 1) 7
TOP VILLAIN [95] 7-10-4 B Storey, *hld up in tch, hdwy
7th, ev ch whn f 3 out.*.......................(16 to 1) f
NO SID NO STARS (USA) [103] 5-10-12 J Callaghan, *hld up,
some hdwy hfwy, wknd 7th, wl beh whn pld up bef
last*...(7 to 1 op 5 to 1) pu
Dist: 2½l, 1½l, 2l, 8l, 8l, 15l. 4m 57.20s. a 6.20s (9 Ran).
SR: 8/-/-/-/-/-/ (John Wade), J Wade

624 Desert Orchid Handicap Chase (0-115 5-y-o and up) £1,917 3m 3f........ (3:20)

RADICAL LADY [103] 9-11-0 (7*) J Supple, *made all, drw clr
betw last 2, easily*...............................(9 to 1) 1
FOSBURY [106] 8-11-10 C Grant, *in tch, chsd wnr frm
15th, ev ch 2 out, sn btn*..........(4 to 1 tchd 7 to 2) 2
579⁴ MOUNTEBOR [100] 9-11-4 J Callaghan, *in tch, ev ch 3 out,
sn wknd.*...(7 to 4 fav op 6 to 4) 3
286⁴ EBORNEEZER'S DREAM [87] (v) 10-10-5² D Telfer, *in tch till
wknd appr 3 out*..............................(25 to 1 op 20 to 1) 4
461⁴ KELLY OWENS [85] 8-10-0 (3*) M Hourigan, *prmnt till
mstks and lost grnd 15th and 16th, rdn appr 4 out, btn
nxt*...(8 to 1 op 7 to 1) 5
544 SPEECH [104] 10-11-8 T Reed, *blun 1st, hld up and beh,
lost tch frm 16th, tld off.*..........(14 to 1 tchd 16 to 1) 6
Dist: 6l, 6l, 5l, 3l, 15l. 6m 57.10s. a 18.10s (6 Ran).
(N B Mason), N B Mason

625 Oakley Mitsubishi Shogun Novices' Chase (5-y-o and up) £1,843 2m 5f....... (3:50)

DOWN THE ROAD 6-11-0 B Storey, *chsd ldrs, led tenth,
clr betw last 2, styd on wl.*
......................................(Evens fav op 11 to 8 on tchd 11 to 10) 1
KEEP BIDDING 7-11-11 T Reed, *sn beh, blun 12th, ran on
strly frm 2 out, not rch wnr*.........(10 to 1 op 16 to 1) 2
STAIGUE FORT (Ire) 5-11-2 (5*) P Waggott, *in tch, hmpd
11th, chsd wnr aftr till wknd frm 2 out.*
....(10 to 1 tchd 12 to 1) 3
LA MOLINILLA 10-10-2 (7*) Miss S Lamb, *chsd ldr till grad
lost pl frm 12th and tenth, tld off*...............(20 to 1) 4
RISEUPWILLIEREILLY 7-11-0 N Smith, *led, hit 8th, held
tenth, cl second whn f nxt*............(25 to 1 op 16 to 1) f
MAJOR FOUNTAIN 7-11-0 G Harker, *mstk 1st, sn beh, cld
up hfwy, in tch whn f 11th, dead.* (25 to 1 op 16 to 1) f
347⁷ ULLSWATER 7-11-7 J Ryan, *lost tch, pld up and dismounted appr 8th*..........................(7 to 4 tchd 6 to 4) pu
Dist: 2½l, 12l, 25l. 5m 16.70s. a 12.70s (7 Ran).
(R J Crake), J H Johnson

626 George Bolam Conditional Jockeys' Novices' Handicap Hurdle (0-100 4-y-o and up) £1,618 2m 1f 110yds............... (4:20)

546³ STRONG FANCY [72] 10-10-9 (5*) Mark Roberts, *cl up,
slight ld 2 out, styd on wl frm last.*
....(5 to 2 fav op 9 to 4) 1
482⁶ HIGH PENHOWE [73] 5-10-12 (3*) C Woodall, *in tch, effrt
and ch 2 out, sn rdn, styd on towards finish.*
....(11 to 2 op 9 to 2) 2

ROAD TO THE WEIR [58] 6-10-0 A Dobbin, *led, hdd 2 out,
ev ch till veered l/t aftr last.......*(33 to 1 tchd 50 to 1) 3
FELL WARDEN [68] (bl) 5-10-10 A Larnach, *trkd ldrs,
pushed alng appr 2 out, one pace....* (9 to 2 op 7 to 1) 4
316⁹ SUNTAN (Fr) [68] 4-10-3 (7*) K Davies, *prmnt, rdn and
outpcd aftr 3 out, kpt on frm nxt...........*(10 to 1) 5
BELIEVE IT [81] 4-11-9 P Waggott, *chsd ldrs till wknd 2
out...*(9 to 2 op 7 to 1) 6
316⁴ SWANK GILBERT [58] 7-9-9 (5*) Carol Cuthbert, *in tch till
wknd 3 out...............................*(16 to 1 op 20 to 1) 7
259⁵ JALORE [86] 4-11-7 (7*) S Lycett, *strted slwly, al beh.*
....(5 to 1 op 4 to 1) 8
LUGER (Ire) [70] 5-10-12 M Hourigan, *in tch wknd 3
out...*(5 to 1 op 4 to 1) 9
Dist: 1½l, nk, 3½l, 3½l, 15l, 2½l, ½l. 4m 2.10s. a 7.10s (9 Ran).
SR: 6/5/-/-/-/-/ (Northumbria Leisure Ltd), S E Kettlewell

627 Easington Novices' Hurdle (4-y-o and up) £1,140 2m 5f 110yds............... (4:50)

197* CLASSIC CONTACT 7-11-0 (7*) J Supple, *made all, jnd 2
out, styd on wl appr last.*
.....................................(6 to 4 on op 2 to 1 on tchd 11 to 8 on) 1
FOUR DEEP (Ire) 5-11-0 B Storey, *hld up in tch, hdwy to
track ldrs 6th, chlgd 2 out, rdn and no extr appr last.*
..............................(9 to 4 op 5 to 2 tchd 2 to 1 and 11 to 4) 2
NOBLE BRONZE 5-10-9 P Niven, *in tch, ev ch appr 2 out,
one pace*...(10 to 1) 3
482⁹ SANDEDGE 6-10-6 (3*) A Thornton, *prmnt till wknd 3 out.*
....(25 to 1 op 12 to 1) 4
DUNREIDY BAY (Ire) 5-11-0 K Jones, *in tch till wknd appr
3 out...*(10 to 1 op 8 to 1) 5
WEDDICAR LADY 7-10-9 T Reed, *wl beh frm 5th.*
....(14 to 1 op 20 to 1) 6
Dist: 5l, 6l, 12l, 12l, 15l. 5m 2.60s. a 11.60s (6 Ran).
(N B Mason), N B Mason

CHELTENHAM (good (races 1,2,3,4,5), good to soft (6,7))
Thursday September 30th
Going Correction: MINUS 0.25 sec. per fur.

628 Willow Trust Novices' Hurdle (4-y-o and up) £1,882 2m 5f 110yds........... (2:10)

FUZZY LOGIC (Ire) 5-11-1 C Llewellyn, *trkd ldr, led appr
4th, hdd 7th, led ag'n sn aftr nxt, styd on frm 2 out.*
....(3 to 1 op 9 to 4) 1
441⁶ DEBACLE (USA) 4-11-5 D Murphy, *hld up in rear, gd hdwy
4 out, cld on wnr appr 2 out, sn rdn, no imprsn.*
....(11 to 8 on op 6 to 4 on tchd 5 to 4 on) 2
OATS N BARLEY 4-11-0 I Shoemark, *mstk second, hld up,
hdwy 6th, wknd appr 3 out, tld off.*
....(16 to 1 op 14 to 1) 3
THE MINE CAPTAIN 6-11-1 E Murphy, *pld hrd, hdwy 4th,
led 7th, hdd sn aftr nxt, wknd quickly appr 2 out, tld
off.....................................*(7 to 2 op 4 to 1 tchd 6 to 1) 4
368⁶ SANDMOOR PRINCE 10-11-1 Dr P Pritchard, *led till hdd
appr 4th, wl beh frm 6th, tld off...* (50 to 1 op 33 to 1) 5
JACK'S BARN (bl) 9-11-1 M Bosley, *chsd ldrs till wknd
5th, sn beh, tld off................*(33 to 1 op 20 to 1) 6
Dist: 7l, dist, 5l, 5l, 10l. 5m 22.70s. a 11.70s (6 Ran).
(Cheltenham Racing Ltd), N A Twiston-Davies

629 Tewkesbury Handicap Hurdle (0-135 4-y-o and up) £2,753 2m 110yds......... (2:40)

LEOTARD [123] 6-10-13 J Osborne, *al gng wl, trkd ldr frm
3rd, led 6th, quickened clr from 2 out, cmftbly.*
.........................(100 to 30 fav op 5 to 2 tchd 7 to 2) 1
459³ NAHAR [119] 8-10-9 H Davies, *trkd ldrs, lost pl 6th, rallied appr 2 out, ran on wl to go second r-in.*
....(4 to 1 op 3 to 1 tchd 9 to 2) 2
384* ABSENT RELATIVE [121] 5-10-11 A Maguire, *hld up in tch,
hdwy 6th, pressed wnr 3 out, wkng whn slight mstk
last...*(7 to 2 op 3 to 1) 3
407⁴ KING'S SHILLING (USA) [117] 6-10-7 Jacqui Oliver, *nvr far
away, rdn appr 2 out, one pace.*
....(11 to 2 op 5 to 1 tchd 6 to 1) 4
601⁴ RULING DYNASTY [112] (bl) 9-10-2 N Williamson, *hld up in
rear, hdwy appr 3 out, one pace aftr.*
....(10 to 1 op 8 to 1 tchd 12 to 1) 5
ROYAL SQUARE (Can) [128] 7-11-4 I Shoemark, *led second
to 6th, rdn appr 2 out, wknd quickly.*
....(10 to 1 op 8 to 1 tchd 12 to 1) 6
189⁴ TEKLA (Fr) [110] 8-10-0 B Powell, *led to second, wkng whn
mstk 5th, tld off...................................*(100 to 1) 7
450* LUSTREMAN [110] 6-10-0 T Wall, *pld hrd, mstks in rear,
no ch whn f 2 out.................................*(7 to 1 op 5 to 1) f
Dist: 6l, 2½l, 2l, 8l, 12l, 25l. 4m 1.90s. a 2.90s (8 Ran).
SR: 15/5/4/-/-/ (Christopher Heath), O Sherwood

630 Cotswold BMW Chase Handicap (5-y-o and up) £4,162 3m 1f 110yds........ (3:15)

ROCKTOR (NZ) [124] 8-10-13 J Frost, *hld up, cld on ldrs tenth, led 5 out, styd on wl*...............(4 to 1 op 5 to 1) 1
FAR SENIOR [135] 7-11-10 N Williamson, *wtd wth, hdwy to ld briefly 3 out, rdn appr last, one pace r-in.*
.................(100 to 30 jt-fav op 3 to 1 tchd 7 to 2) 2
544² RU VALENTINO [111] 9-10-0 C Llewellyn, *hld up in tch, hdwy to press ldrs 4 out, blun nxt, sn btn.* (100 to 30 jt-fav op 9 to 4 tchd 7 to 2) 3
CARRICKROVADDY [111] (bl) 7-10-0 B Powell, *made most till hdd 5 out, one pace aftr.*
..................(16 to 1 op 12 to 1 tchd 20 to 1) 4
WELKNOWN CHARACTER [119] 11-10-8 G Bradley, *hld up, gd hdwy 9th, outpcd and lost pl 14th, rallied 4 out, wknd appr 2 out.*........(9 to 2 op 4 to 1 tchd 5 to 1) 5
449² WONT BE GONE LONG [134] 11-11-9 R Dunwoody, *dsptd ld till mstk 9th, last whn blun badly 11th, not reco'r, pld up.*.............................(4 to 1 op 7 to 2) pu
Dist: 3½l, 8l, 5l, 5l. 6m 25.20s. a 8.20s (6 Ran).

(Mrs G Watkinson-Yull), D H Barons

631 Studd Challenge Cup Chase Handicap (5-y-o and up) £4,143 2m 110yds....... (3:45)

487* DRUMSTICK [125] 7-10-4 N Williamson, *hld up, hdwy appr 4 out, rdn approaching last, led r-in, all out.*
.......(15 to 8 fav op 9 to 4 tchd 5 to 2 and 7 to 4) 1
SPACE FAIR [149] 10-12-0 L Harvey, *nvr far away, led 2 out, rdn and hdd r-in, rallied gmely, no extr cl hme.*
...................(9 to 5 op 5 to 1 tchd 8 to 1) 2
SETTER COUNTRY [127] 9-10-6 R Dunwoody, *hld up, gd hdwy 7th, trkd ldr frm 9th, led briefly 2 out, ev ch till wknd r-in.*...............(7 to 1 op 6 to 1 tchd 8 to 1) 3
BOUTZDAROFF [140] 11-11-5 M Dwyer, *hld up in tch, hdwy 7th, wknd 3 out.*.............(7 to 1 op 9 to 2) 4
HOWE STREET [133] 10-10-12 B Storey, *led, mstk 7th, hdd and wknd appr 2 out.*...........(7 to 1 op 12 to 1) 5
121² THATS THE LIFE [121] 8-10-0 A Maguire, *pld hrd, prmnt 3rd till aftr 5th, sn beh.*............(7 to 1 tchd 8 to 1) 6
487* ACRE HILL [126] 9-10-5 M A FitzGerald, *trkd ldr to 7th, wknd quickly appr 4 out, tld off whn pld up bef last.*
.................................(8 to 1 op 5 to 1) pu
Dist: ½l, 10l, 5l, 3l, 4l. 4m 5.00s. b 1.00s (7 Ran).
SR: 45/68/36/44/32/16/-/ (Sarah Lady Allendale), K C Bailey

632 Frenchie Nicholson Conditional Jockeys' Handicap Hurdle (0-115 4-y-o and up) £1,976 2m 5f 110yds............... (4:15)

289⁷ CHIEF RAIDER (Ire) [93] 5-10-3 (3") D Bentley, *made all, drw clr frm 2 out, unchlgd...*(7 to 4 fav op 6 to 4 tchd 8 to 1) 1
THE MRS [87] 7-10-0 R Davis, *hld up in rear, steady hdwy frm 6th, chsd wnr aftr 4 out, hit nxt, btn whn mstk last.*............................(9 to 2 op 4 to 1) 2
594² STAUNCH RIVAL (USA) [118] 6-12-3 (6ex) R Farrant, *in tch, hdwy 7th, wknd appr 2 out, fnshd tired.....*(5 to 2 jt-fav op 2 to 1) 3
428⁵ J R JONES [87] 6-10-0 S Wynne, *al beh, tld off frm 7th.*
...................(12 to 1 op 16 to 1 tchd 10 to 1) 4
CAROMANDOO (Ire) [92] (v) 5-9-13 (6") T Thompson, *al beh, tld off aftr mstk 5th.....*(9 to 1 tchd 10 to 1) 5
443⁷ FROSTY RECEPTION [98] (bl) 8-10-11 V Slattery, *trkd wnr frm second till rdn and wknd 4 out.* (9 to 1 op 6 to 1) 6
526⁷ NORTHERN VILLAGE [115] 6-11-11 (3") A Dicken, *trkd wnr to second, 3rd whn f 6th...*(5 to 2 jt-fav op 2 to 1) f
439² MINT-MASTER [87] 8-9-8 (6") P Maddock, *al beh, tld off frm 6th, pld up bef 2 out...*(50 to 1 op 25 to 1) pu
Dist: 12l, 25l, dist, 8l, dist. 5m 22.00s. a 11.00s (8 Ran).

(John Wade), J Wade

633 Cheltenham Sponsorship Club Novices' Chase (5-y-o and up) £3,517 2m 5f...(4:45)

GAELSTROM 6-10-11 C Llewellyn, *made all, clr 3rd, steadied 5 out, clear ag'n 3 out, eased r-in.*
...............(11 to 8 on op 7 to 4 on tchd 5 to 4 on) 1
451* VALIANT WARRIOR 5-11-4 C Grant, *trkd wnr 3rd to 8th, wnt second ag'n tenth, ev ch whn hit 4 out, mstk nxt, sn btn.*..........(9 to 4 op 2 to 1 tchd 5 to 2) 2
PICKETSTONE 6-11-2 G McCourt, *al prmnt, trkd wnr 8th to tenth, ev ch till wknd aftr 4 out, tld off.*
...............................(14 to 1 op 16 to 1) 3
485² COMIC LINE (bl) 8-11-6 S Burrough, *chsd wnr to 3rd, wknd 7th, tld off.*...............(14 to 1 op 10 to 1) 4
593 KASHAN (Ire) 5-10-9 (5") R Farrant, *jmpd badly in rear, tld off whn pld up bef 8th.*
...................(16 to 1 op 14 to 1 tchd 20 to 1) pu
607 JHAL FREZI 5-10-11 (3") A Thornton, *al beh, tld off 9th, blun 3 out, sn pld up...*(50 to 1 op 20 to 1) pu
Dist: 1½l, dist, hd. 5m 24.90s. a 14.90s (6 Ran).

(Mrs J K Powell), N A Twiston-Davies

634 Grunwick Stakes National Hunt Flat Race (4,5,6-y-o) £1,842 2m 110yds........ (5:15)

GOOD INSIGHT (Ire) 5-10-13 (7") M Berry, *hld up in rear, rapid hdwy 5 fs out, rdn and styd on to ld ins last.*
....................(15 to 2 op 9 to 2 tchd 8 to 1) 1

BELL ONE (USA) 4-11-2 (3") M Hourigan, *al prmnt, wnt second 5 fs out, led 2 out, hdd ins last.*
...............(6 to 1 op 4 to 1 tchd 8 to 1) 2
FLAMEWOOD 4-10-7 (7") Mr G Haine, *led, sn clr, rdn 3 fs out, hdd 2 out, one pace.....*(14 to 1 op 7 to 1) 3
SOLAR KESTREL (Ire) 5-10-13 (7") Mr C Vigors, *in chasing grp till wknd wl o'r 2 fs out.*
...............(2 to 1 fav op 5 to 2 tchd 7 to 2) 4
SOLO GENT 4-11-5 Mr S Bush, *prmnt till lost pl hfwy, styd on ins 3 fs.*.....................(33 to 1) 5
ROCKCLIFFE LAD 4-10-12 (7") Mr M Rimell, *prmnt till wknd 4 fs out, tld off...*(7 to 2 op 5 to 1 tchd 9 to 1) 6
SUNGIA (Ire) 4-11-2 (3") W Marston, *prmnt till wknd 4 fs out, tld off.....*(14 to 1 op 20 to 1 tchd 25 to 1) 7
BALLYMGYR 4-11-0 (5") A Procter, *chsd ldr till wknd 5 fs out, tld off.*...........(10 to 1 op 8 to 1) 8
WHAT A RATTLE 4-10-12 (7") Mr Richard White, *al beh, tld off...*.............(33 to 1 op 20 to 1) 9
SILVER SUMAL 4-11-5 V Slattery, *prmnt till wknd hfwy, tld off...*................(10 to 1 op 8 to 1) 10
HEZEKIAH 5-10-13 (7") K Comerford, *prmnt till wknd sn aftr hfwy, tld off...*(16 to 1 op 10 to 1 tchd 20 to 1) 11
MARINERS MEMORY 5-11-3 (3") D Meredith, *al beh, tld off.....*......................(50 to 1 op 33 to 1) 12
REG'S HOLLOA (Ire) 5-10-13 (7") Mr T Byrne, *in rear whn stumbled and uns rdr aftr 4 fs...* (12 to 1 tchd 10 to 1) ur
Dist: 2l, 12l, 8l, 7l, 20l, 3l, nk, ½l, 20l, 8l. 4m 3.30s. (13 Ran).

(Insight Cartons Ltd), C P E Brooks

GOWRAN PARK (IRE) (heavy) Thursday September 30th

635 Careys Cottage Novice Chase (5-y-o and up) £2,960 3m 1f................ (4:00)

575 BORN DEEP 7-11-4 T Horgan, ...(7 to 1) 1
575 WINDS OF WAR 8-11-4 C F Swan, ...(6 to 1) 2
539² ASK THE BOYS 7-11-4 K F O'Brien, ...(5 to 1) 3
583³ FAIRY PARK (bl) 8-11-4 F Woods, ...(10 to 1) 4
411* BACK DOOR JOHNNY 7-11-8 D H O'Connor, ..(5 to 2 fav) 5
538 DEL MONTE BOY 8-11-4 G M O'Neill, ...(14 to 1) 6
546 MCMAHON'S RIVER 6-10-13 H Rogers, ...(16 to 1) 7
583⁶ PRINCE YAZA 8-11-8 F J Flood, ...(8 to 1) 8
543³ MAKE ME AN ISLAND 8-10-13 J F Titley, ...(12 to 1) 9
575 THE WEST'S ASLEEP 8-10-13 (5") C O'Brien, ...(16 to 1) 10
554 LADY DIAMOND 7-10-13 J P Banahan, ...(14 to 1) 11
507⁵ JOHNJOES PRIDE 9-10-11 (7") K P Gaule, ...(14 to 1) 12
583⁸ CARDAN 7-10-11 (7") P A Roche, ...(50 to 1) 13
557⁸ HIGH-SPEC 7-11-4 J Magee, ...(14 to 1) f
507* SUITS ME FINE 10-11-1 (3") T J Mitchell, ...(16 to 1) pu
411 BIRDIE'S PRINCE 8-10-13 (5") D P Murphy, ...(33 to 1) pu
SIRANA 7-10-13 P L Malone, ...(33 to 1) pu
Dist: 2l, 8l, 7l, 2½l. 6m 51.70s. (18 Ran).

(Mrs C McGuirk), A P O'Brien

636 Bagenalstown Maiden Hurdle (5-y-o) £2,760 2m........................ (4:30)

534⁷ EAGLE ROCK (USA) 11-9 (5") C O'Brien, ...(8 to 1) 1
136³ WILD FANTASY (Ire) 11-2 (7") K P Gaule, ...(3 to 1) 2
534⁵ WHAT A QUESTION (Ire) 11-9 C F Swan, ...(15 to 8 fav) 3
45 BOLEREE (Ire) 11-1 C O'Dwyer, ...(20 to 1) 4
BOLERO DANCER (Ire) 11-7 (7") C O'Neill, ...(20 to 1) 5
534⁴ GRAND TOUR (NZ) 12-0 L P Cusack, ...(5 to 1) 6
ROSEPERRINE (Ire) 10-10 (5") D T Evans, ...(20 to 1) 7
363 TOP RUN (Ire) 11-6 H Rogers, ...(66 to 1) 8
IDIOTS DANCE 11-6 J Magee, ...(20 to 1) 9
JOHNNY THE FOX (Ire) 11-6 T Horgan, ...(66 to 1) 10
508* QUARTER MARKER (Ire) 11-9 (5") T P Treacy, ...(10 to 1) 11
534 OZONE RIVER (Ire) 10-8 (7") C McCormack, ...(20 to 1) 12
535 PLUNDERING STAR (Ire) (bl) 11-6 P Carberry, ...(20 to 1) 13
GREAT ADVENTURE (Ire) 11-6 P McWilliams, ...(20 to 1) 14
341 VISIONARY (Ire) 10-13 (7") E G Callaghan, ...(33 to 1) 15
535 BUCKS IMAGE (Ire) 10-10 (5") A J Slattery, ...(14 to 1) 16
BALLYRANEBOW (Ire) 10-10 (5") D P Murphy, ...(33 to 1) 17
572 CLASHREAGH (Ire) 10-8 (7") Mr K O'Sullivan, ...(66 to 1) pu
Dist: 5l, ¾l, 8l, 1½l. 4m 17.60s. (18 Ran).

(P J Kinsella), L Young

637 Milford Handicap Hurdle (4-y-o and up) £2,760 2½m........................ (5:00)

528² CASH CHASE (Ire) [-] 5-9-2 (5") C O'Brien, ...(5 to 1) 1
557* LOVE AND PORTER (Ire) [-] 5-10-12 (6ex) D H O'Connor,
..........................(5 to 4 fav) 2
CARRON HILL [-] 6-9-7 P Carberry, ...(16 to 1) 3
557 NANCYS LAD [-] 6-9-7 F Woods, ...(14 to 1) 4
SO PINK [-] 5-10-8 C F Swan, ...(4 to 1) 5
471² BRAVEFOOT [-] 5-10-12 K F O'Brien, ...(10 to 1) 6
BELEEK CASTLE [-] 7-10-7 P McWilliams, ...(14 to 1) 7
42⁹ HI MILLIE [-] 7-10-3 P L Malone, ...(10 to 1) 8
ENNEREILLY RIVER [-] 10-11-1 C O'Dwyer, ...(12 to 1) 9

292 REGULAR PAL [-] 10-9-4 (3") Miss M Olivefalk, ...(25 to 1) 10
GLEN OG LANE [-] 10-9-7 J Magee, ...(10 to 1) 11
ENERGANCE (Ire) [-] 5-10-10 F J Flood, ...(10 to 1) pu
Dist: 3l, 1l, 2½l, hd. 5m 30.20s. (12 Ran).

(A J Keane), A J Keane

638 Dungarvan I.N.H. Flat Race (4-y-o and up) £2,760 2m. . . . . (5:30)

531² WATERLOO BALL (Ire) 4-11-4 Mr A P O'Brien, (6 to 4 fav) 1
WILD VENTURE (Ire) 5-11-2 (7") Ms W Fox, ...(7 to 2) 2
KESS (Ire) 4-10-13 (5") Mr H F Cleary, ...(8 to 1) 3
530 CASTLE CLUB (Ire) 4-11-1 (3") Mr R O'Neill, ...(16 to 1) 4
SAMMIES DOZER (Ire) 5-11-2 (7") Mr P English, . . .(12 to 1) 5
114 FULL SCORE (Ire) 4-11-4 (5") Mr J P Berry, ...(33 to 1) 6
530⁸ LEISURE CENTRE (Ire) 4-10-11 (7") Mr R P Cody, (10 to 1) 7
536⁶ BALLINGOWAN STAR 6-11-2 (7") Mr S O'Donnell, (10 to 1) 8
124 BELGRAVIA BOY (Ire) 5-12-0 Mr P Fenton, ...(8 to 1) 9
VEG LANE (Ire) 5-11-2 (7") Mr T J O'Mara, ...(8 to 1) 10
BOB MONEY (Ire) 5-11-7 (7") Mr P J Lambert, ...(10 to 1) 11
393³ BALLYBRAZIL BOY (Ire) 4-11-2 (7") Mr M Brennan, (8 to 1) 12
433 RATHNURE LADY (Ire) 5-11-9 Mr S R Murphy, ...(20 to 1) 13
469 LOCAL SILK (Ire) 4-10-13 (5") Mr J A Nash, ...(12 to 1) 14
RATH CULBIN 6-11-2 (7") Mr T R Hughes, ...(12 to 1) pu
MAN O' WORDS 7-11-7 (7") Mr E Norris, ...(12 to 1) pu
SWEET DEMOND 8-11-7 (7") Mr H Murphy, ...(25 to 1) pu
508⁶ MINUS TWO (Ire) 5-11-6 (3") Miss M Olivefalk, . . .(12 to 1) pu
Dist: 1l, 6l, 15l, 4l. 4m 15.50s. (18 Ran).

(J Smyth), A P O'Brien

HEXHAM (good)
Friday October 1st
Going Correction: PLUS 0.25 sec. per fur.

639 Hydrochem Water Treatment Novices' Handicap Hurdle (0-100 4-y-o and up) £1,892 2½m 110yds. . . . . (2:00)

LARAPINTA (Ire) [71] 5-10-11 A Maguire, made most frm
second, jnd 3 out, quickened clr betw last 2, easily. . . . .(14 to 1 tchd 16 to 1) 1
KILMINFOYLE [73] 6-10-13 P Niven, veered badly lft 1st,
reco'red and al hndy, rdn and outpcd frm betw last 2. . . . .(8 to 1 op 6 to 1) 2
587⁵ SUPPOSIN [68] 5-10-8³ Richard Guest, patiently rdn,
improved to join issue aftr 3 out, ridden and not
quicken betw last 2. . . . .(8 to 1 op 5 to 1) 3
482⁵ MASTER BOSTON (Ire) [75] 5-11-1 R Dunwoody, wth wnr,
ev ch 3 out, rdn and no extr frm betw last 2. . . . .(6 to 1 op 5 to 1) 4
482² RUN MILADY [75] 5-11-1 D Wilkinson, outpcd and
scrubbed alng frm 5th, styd on grimly from 3 out, nvr
nrr. . . . .(5 to 1 op 4 to 1) 5
JIM-JOE [74] 8-10-7 (7") J Supple, patiently rdn, improved
to join ldrs 3 out, wknd quickly betw last 2. . . . .(13 to 2 op 7 to 1 tchd 8 to 1) 6
ROLLING THE BONES (USA) [72] (v) 4-10-12 A Orkney, chsd
ldg bunch, effrt hfwy, rdn and outpcd aftr 3 out, no
imprsn. . . . .(9 to 2 fav op 7 to 1 tchd 8 to 1) 7
OVER THE ODDS (Ire) [70] 4-10-10 K Jones, led to second,
styd hndy, feeling pace and drvn alng aftr 3 out, tld
off. . . . .(8 to 1 op 4 to 1) 8
502⁶ ASSEMBLY DANCER [60] (v) 6-9-13⁴ (5") R Davis, trkd ldg
quartet, feeling pace and lost grnd aftr 3 out, pld up bef
last. . . . .(14 to 1 op 12 to 1) pu
563 CLANDRUM [61] 9-10-1⁸ (7") A Linton, in tch, struggling
to keep up aftr 5th, tld off whn pld up bef last. (33 to 1) pu
SWEET NOBLE (Ire) [84] 4-11-10 M Dwyer, settled gng wl,
smooth hdwy to join issue hfwy, lost grnd aftr 3 out,
pld up bef last. . . . .(6 to 1 op 4 to 1) pu
Dist: 8l, 3l, 1l, 1½l, 4l, 5l, dist. 5m 7.60s. a 14.60s (11 Ran).

(Thomas Harty), J H Johnson

640 Tentec Bolting Technology Novices' Hurdle (4-y-o and up) £1,989 2m. . . . . . . (2:35)

AMERICAN HERO 5-11-0 B Storey, jmpd wl, made all, well
clr frm hfwy, eased considerably r-in. . . . .(3 to 1 tchd 7 to 2) 1
RELUCTANT SUITOR 4-10-13 C Grant, patiently rdn,
steady hdwy to chase wnr aftr 3 out, flttened last, styd
on, nvr nrr. . . . .(7 to 4 fav op 5 to 4) 2
JIM'S WISH (Ire) (bl) 5-10-7 (7") Carol Cuthbert, chsd alng to
go pace hfwy, kpt on grimly frm 2 out, nrst finish. . . . .(20 to 1 op 14 to 1) 3
524⁴ KADARI 4-10-8 Diane Clay, settled wth chasing bunch,
effrt and drvn alng hfwy, fdd und pres betw last 2. . . . .(7 to 2 op 3 to 1) 4
434⁸ NOEL (Ire) 4-10-13 M A FitzGerald, chsd alng in midfield,
effrt hfwy, struggling appr 2 out, sn btn. . . . .(9 to 1 op 8 to 1) 5
TASMIN GAYLE (Ire) 5-10-12³ T Reed, chsd alng to keep in
tch, struggling frm 3 out, nvr dngrs. . . . .(16 to 1 op 14 to 1) 6
EMPEROR ALEXANDER (Ire) 5-11-0 R Dunwoody, chsd clr
ldg pair to hfwy, struggling aftr 3 out, sn btn. . . . .(16 to 1 op 14 to 1) 7

577 JOYFUL IMP 6-10-2 (7") Mr R Hale, struggling to go pace
hfwy, tld off frm 3 out. . . . .(50 to 1 op 25 to 1) 8
541⁵ SHANNON KING (Ire) 5-11-0 D Byrne, chsd wnr most of
way, feeling pace aftr 3 out, sn lost tch. . . . .(12 to 1 tchd 14 to 1) 9
HIGHCLIFFE JESTER 4-10-13 C Hawkins, chsd ldg pair
hfwy, blun 4 out, sn lost tch, tld off. . . . .(50 to 1 op 33 to 1) 10
PRICELESS HOLLY 5-11-0 Mr S Brisby, al beh, tld off whn
pld up bef 2 out. . . . .(33 to 1 op 1) pu
Dist: 6l, 12l, 15l, 6l, 5l, nk, nk, 1l. 3m 59.70s. a 9.70s (11 Ran).
SR: 29/22/11/-/-/-/- (David S Leggate), R Allan

641 Conway Robinson Quality Assurance Novices' Chase (4-y-o and up) £2,173 2m 110yds. . . . . (3:05)

480² EXPLOSIVE SPEED (USA) 5-11-5 C Grant, led till hdd 3rd
(water) hit nxt, led ag'n 6th, drvn clr betw last 2,
easily. . . . .(5 to 4 fav op Evens) 1
BEST EFFORT 7-11-6 A Orkney, nvr far away, ev ch frm 3
out, rdn and no extr betw last 2. . . . .(14 to 1 op 16 to 1 tchd 20 to 1) 2
CAPTAIN CUTE 8-11-6 D Byrne, patiently rdn, improved
frm midfield aftr 4 out, staying on at one pace whn lft
3rd last. . . . .(14 to 1 op 8 to 1) 3
JUNIORS CHOICE 10-11-6 Miss J Thurlow, nvr far away,
effrt whn hit 4 out, rallied, no extr last 2. . . . .(16 to 1 op 12 to 1) 4
546⁷ EBRO 7-11-6 A Merrigan, in tch, chsd alng whn pace
lifted 4 out, nvr able to chal. . . . .(50 to 1) 5
542 DROMINA STAR 12-11-8 (5") P Williams, chsd ldg bunch,
effrt hfwy, struggling frm 4 out. . . .(16 to 1 op 12 to 1) 6
SEMINOFF (Fr) 7-11-3 (3") A Dobbin, wth ldr, led 3rd
(water), hdd 6th, rallied third and tired whn f last. . . . .(25 to 1 op 20 to 1 tchd 33 to 1) f
SPACE CAPTAIN 6-11-3 (3") N Bentley, patiently rdn,
imprvg on bit whn o'rmpd and f 5 out. . . . .(13 to 9 op 4 to 1 tchd 6 to 4) f
Dist: 12l, 5l, 12l, 10l, hd. 4m 13.00s. a 15.00s (8 Ran).
(Wetherby Racing Bureau Plc), M D Hammond

642 Kielder Marketing Group Selling Hurdle (3-y-o and up) £1,876 2m. . . . . (3:35)

SKITTLE ALLEY 7-12-0 Diane Clay, al travelling wl, led bef
2 out, drvn clr betw last two, styd on. (4 to 1 op 6 to 1) 1
128 BOHEMIAN QUEEN 3-10-2 A Maguire, wtd wth, improved
frm midfield aftr 3 out, ev ch nxt, one pace appr last. . . . .(7 to 2 co-fav op 3 to 1) 2
BOLD MELODY 4-11-8 J Callaghan, nvr far away, jnd ldg
pair aftr 3 out, rdn and not quicken betw last 2. . . . .(7 to 2 co-fav op 3 to 1 tchd 4 to 1) 3
399⁴ COMMON COUNCIL 4-11-9 C Grant, settled off the pace,
gd hdwy to chal aftr 3 out, rdn frm nxt, no extr. . . . .(7 to 2 co-fav op 6 to 4 tchd 4 to 1) 4
CARDENDEN (Ire) 5-11-10 R Dunwoody, chsd ldr, feeling
pace aftr 3 out, sn btn. . . . .(8 to 1 op 4 to 1) 5
626⁷ SWANK GILBERT 7-11-3 (7") Carol Cuthbert, chsd ldrs,
effrt and drvn alng appr 3 out, sn outpcd. . . .(33 to 1) 6
THOMPSON FLYER 6-11-10 Mrs F Needham, hit 1st, drvn
alng in midfield hfwy, lost tch frm 4 out. . . . .(33 to 1 op 20 to 1) 7
SRADARA (Ire) 5-10-12 (7") A Linton, sn clr ldr, wknd and
hdd appr 2 out, tld off. . . . .(33 to 1) 8
BONNY PRINCESS 3-10-2 K Johnson, al struggling, tld
off frm hfwy. . . . .(20 to 1) 9
CINDERS GIRL 3-9-13 (3") A Dobbin, struggling frm 3rd,
tld off. . . . .(33 to 1) 10
RICH HEIRESS (Ire) 4-11-4 A Merrigan, struggling and
reminders 3rd, tld off. . . . .(33 to 1) 11
Dist: 7l, 5l, 6l, 12l, 3l, 10l, 8l, 3½l. 4m 8.00s. a 18.00s (11 Ran).
(P Riley), W Clay

643 Kielder Marketing Group Handicap Chase (0-115 5-y-o and up) £2,905 2m 110yds . . . .(4:05)

546² POSITIVE ACTION [95] 7-10-12 (3") A Dobbin, patiently
rdn, improved gng wl hfwy, quickened ahead betw last
2, ran on well. . . . .(11 to 4 op 7 to 2 tchd 5 to 2) 1
546⁵ SONSIE MO [105] 8-11-6 (5") P Williams, al hndy, led
briefly 3rd, drvn alng 3 out, styd on. (9 to 1 op 6 to 1) 2
444² STAY AWAKE [104] 7-11-10 P Niven, wtd wth, improved to
go hndy aftr 4 out, drvn alng last 2, one pace. . . . .(5 to 4 fav op 11 to 8 tchd 13 to 8) 3
546⁸ PRESSURE GAME [87] 10-10-7¹ A Merrigan, al wl plcd, led
4th, sn clr, wknd and hdd betw last 2, no extr. . . . .(40 to 1 op 33 to 1) 4
MOSS BEE [92] 6-10-12³ T Reed, settled to track ldrs, lost
grnd aftr 3 out, rng on ag'n finish. . . . .(14 to 1 op 12 to 1 tchd 16 to 1) 5
SIR PETER LELY [104] 6-11-10 C Grant, pressed ldrs, rdn
whn pace quickened aftr 4 out, no extr. . . . .(8 to 1 op 5 to 1) 6
500 AFRICAN SAFARI [86] 9-10-6 Gary Lyons, led to 3rd, drvn
alng frm 4 out, sn outpcd. . . . . . .(33 to 1 tchd 40 to 1) 7

78

500⁶ POLDER [90] 7-10-5 (5*) R Davis, *not fluent, ran in snatches, effrt appr 3 out, fdd* .....(10 to 1 op 12 to 1) 8
579⁹ WHEELIES NEWMEMBER [95] 10-11-1 R Dunwoody, *chasing ldrs whn drvn alng and f 5 out*.(16 to 1 op 14 to 1) f
317³ MR PANACHE [85] 11-10-0 (5*) D Bentley, *struggling bef hfwy, tld off whn pld up before 5 out.*
.................................(66 to 1 op 33 to 1) pu
Dist: 3l, 12l, 4l, 2l, 5l, 10l, 4l. 4m 9.30s. a 11.30s (10 Ran).
SR: 15/22/9/-/-/-/ (G Campbell), M A Barnes

644 Lords Of Harrogate Handicap Hurdle (0-125 4-y-o and up) £2,186 3m ..... (4:35)

MARRA'S ROSCOE [105] 7-11-10 P Niven, *al hndy, led gng wl betw last 2, wnt clr, idled r-in, jst lasted.*
.................(7 to 4 fav op 5 to 4 tchd 2 to 1) 1
SHELTON ABBEY [105] 7-11-7 (3*) A Larnach, *with ldrs till badly outpcd and lost grnd 8th, made up 15 ls frm betw last 2, fnshd wl.*.........(9 to 4 op 3 to 1 tchd 2 to 1) 2
CELTIC BREEZE [104] (v) 10-11-6 (3*) A Dobbin, *tried to make all, reminders 5 out, rallied, hdd betw last 2, one pace.*.................(13 to 2 op 4 to 1 tchd 7 to 1) 3
543⁸ THE GREEN FOOL [109] 6-12-0 A Merrigan, *settled gng wl, looked dngrs aftr 3 out, wknd quickly frm nxt.*
.................................(7 to 1 op 5 to 1 tchd 8 to 1) 4
519⁸ HAMANAKA (USA) [94] (v) 4-10-13 C Grant, *with ldrs, rdn fnl circuit, fdd frm 2 out.*
.................................(6 to 1 op 4 to 1 tchd 13 to 2) 5
Dist: Nk, 3½l, 15l, 8l. 6m 12.00s. a 25.00s (5 Ran).
(Mrs Dorothy Horner), Mrs M Reveley

645 Grunwick Stakes National Hunt Flat Race (4,5,6-y-o) £1,420 2m .... (5:05)

FIVE FLAGS (Ire) 5-10-13 (7*) R Wilkinson, *led for 5 fs, lost grnd whn pace quickened 4 out, rallied to ld last 100 yards, kpt on.*................(25 to 1 op 16 to 1) 1
THE WEATHERMAN 5-11-3 (3*) N Bentley, *led aftr 5 fs, hrd drvn and hdd last 100 yards, one pace.*
.................................(8 to 1 op 4 to 1) 2
STAGGERING (Ire) 4-10-11 (3*) A Dobbin, *patiently rdn, drvn up to draw level last 2 fs, not quicken cl hme.*
.................(13 to 2 op 6 to 1 tchd 8 to 1) 3
MISCHICOUS GIRL 5-11-1 Mrs F Needham, *nvr far away, rdn last 2 fs, one pace.*....(16 to 1 op 14 to 1) 4
MANILA RUN (Ire) 4-11-0 (5*) W Dwan, *slightly hmpd strt, al hndy, ev ch and rdn o'r 2 fs out, no extr.*
.................................(11 to 2 op 3 to 1) 5
AMBER HOLLY 4-10-7 (7*) Mr R Hale, *badly hmpd strt, reco'red to show up wl till lost tch last 4 fs.*
.................................(50 to 1 op 20 to 1) 6
FARM TRACK 4-10-7 (7*) Mr A Parker, *pressed ldrs, rdn o'r 2 fs out, sn btn.*..................(50 to 1 op 16 to 1) 7
Dist: ½l, 4l, hd, 2l, dist, 2l. 4m 18.50s. (7 Ran).
(Mrs S Smith), Mrs S J Smith

CHEPSTOW (good)
Saturday October 2nd
Going Correction: PLUS 0.60 sec. per fur. (races 1,3,-5,6), PLUS 0.55 (2,4)

646 Swansea Hurdle Handicap (4-y-o and up) £3,522 3m .... (2:00)

DESPERATE [115] 5-11-5 C Llewellyn, *led to 5th, led ag'n sn aftr 8th, rdn and edgd rght appr last, all out.*
.................................(2 to 1 op 9 to 4) 1
526 JIMBALOU [106] 10-10-10 W Humphreys, *hld up, gd hdwy to chase wnr frm 8th, rdn and swtchd lft appr last, ran on r-in.*.........................(9 to 1 op 14 to 1) 2
424* STORM DRUM [112] (bl) 4-11-2 R Dunwoody, *hld up in rear, hdwy 8th, rdn appr nxt, styd on frm 2 out.*
.........(6 to 4 fav op 7 to 4 tchd 2 to 1 and 9 to 4) 3
312³ CHUCKLESTONE [107] 10-10-11 J R Kavanagh, *trkd ldrs, rdn 6th, in tch till wknd 3 out.*
.................(10 to 1 op 8 to 1 tchd 11 to 1) 4
HURRICANE BLAKE [120] 5-11-10 J Railton, *wtd with, in tch till wknd 4 out.*................(10 to 1 op 8 to 1) 5
593⁵ NOBLE INSIGHT [103] (bl) 6-10-7 M Foster, *prmnt, led 5th till rdn and sn hdd aftr 8th, soon beh, tld off.*
.................................(14 to 1 op 12 to 1) 6
443⁵ CLASSIC STATEMENT [101] (v) 7-10-5 L Harvey, *prmnt till wknd quickly aftr 8th, tld off whn pld up bef 3 out.*
.................................(12 to 1 op 10 to 1) pu
455 KNIGHTON COOMBE (NZ) [105] (bl) 7-10-4 (5*) R Farrant, *al beh, wknd 7th, tld off whn pld up bef 3 out.*
.................................(9 to 1 op 14 to 1) pu
Dist: ¾l, 2½l, 12l, 2½l, 15l. 6m 1.50s. a 23.50s (8 Ran).
(The Desperate Partnership), N A Twiston-Davies

647 Mercedes Benz Chase Handicap (5-y-o and up) £5,735 3m .... (2:35)

ESPY [146] 10-11-5 G Bradley, *hld up in rear, hdwy o-go 3rd appr 5 out, lft second 2 out, quickened to ld r-in, jst held on.*...............(3 to 1 op 5 to 2 tchd 7 to 2) 1

DAKYNS BOY [144] 8-11-3 C Llewellyn, *trkd ldr, led aftr 7th, mstk and lft clr 2 out, hdd r-in, rallied nr finish.*
.................(Evens 5o to 4 tchd 11 to 10 on) 2
TOPSHAM BAY [155] 10-12-0 J Frost, *led, jmpd rght sth and 5th, hdd aftr 7th, rdn 13th, wkng whn hit 5 out.*
.................................(7 to 2 op 5 to 2) 3
PIPER O'DRUMMOND [127] 6-10-0 B Powell, *hld up in rear, lost tch appr 5 out, tld off*....(33 to 1 op 25 to 1) 4
THATCHER ROCK (NZ) [127] 8-10-0 R Dunwoody, *trkd ldrs, wnt second aftr 13th, chalg and gng wl whn f 2 out.*
.................................(7 to 1 op 5 to 1) f
Dist: Sht-hd, 30l, dist. 6m 17.80s. a 27.80s (5 Ran).
(R E A Bott (Wigmore St) Ltd), C P E Brooks

648 Free Handicap Hurdle (4-y-o) £7,253 2m 110yds .... (3:10)

CULTURED [122] 10-8 D Murphy, *hld up in tch, gd hdwy to ld appr 2 out, sn clr, cmftbly.*(9 to 4 jt-fav op 2 to 1) 1
BO KNOWS BEST (Ire) [130] 11-2 M Perrett, *chsd ldr, rdn appr 2 out, one pace aftr.*
.................................(11 to 4 op 5 to 2 tchd 3 to 1) 2
488* MOHANA [134] 11-6 (4ex) R Dunwoody, *led till rdn and hdd appr 2 out, one pace aftr.*.........(9 to 4 jt-fav op 5 to 2 tchd 11 to 4) 3
601⁸ MY SENOR [114] 10-0 J R Kavanagh, *chsd ldrs till wknd appr 4 out, tld off.*.....................(33 to 1) 4
MAJOR BUGLER (Ire) [138] 11-10 J Railton, *hld up in rear, rdn appr 4 out, sn tld off.*...........(7 to 1 op 7 to 2) 5
ALCOY (Ire) [114] 9-9 (5*) A Bates, *jmpd slwly second, al in rear, rdn aftr 4th, sn tld off.*
.................................(11 to 1 op 10 to 1 tchd 12 to 1) 6
Dist: 5l, 3½l, 30l, 10l, 12l. 3m 59.50s. a 13.50s (6 Ran).
SR: 44/47/47/-/11/-/ (B Whitehorn), J White

649 Autumn Novices' Chase (5-y-o and up) £2,557 2m 3f 110yds .... (3:45)

LUSTY LIGHT 7-11-0 B Powell, *trkd ldr frm 5th, ran on strly from 2 out, drvn out to ld r-in.*
.................(6 to 4 fav op 5 to 4 tchd 13 to 8) 1
WILLIE MCGARR (USA) 8-11-0 R Dunwoody, *led, mstk 8th, clr frm nxt, rdn and edgd rght appr last, wknd and hdd r-in.*.................(5 to 1 op 11 to 2 tchd 9 to 2) 2
BABIL 8-11-0 C Llewellyn, *not fluent, chsd ldr till mstk 5th, wknd appr 5 out.*...........(4 to 1 tchd 9 to 2) 3
GOLDEN FARE 8-11-0 L Harvey, *chsd ldrs, mstk 4th, wknd 5 out.*...........(11 to 2 op 5 to 1 tchd 6 to 1) 4
464 TRUE FINESSE 11-10-9 S Earle, *in rear whn f 8th.*
.................................(50 to 1 op 33 to 1) f
568⁴ TALATON FLYER 7-11-0 P Hobbs, *in tch to 6th, tld off whn blun and uns rdr 2 out.*
.................(12 to 1 op 14 to 1 tchd 16 to 1) ur
GENEROUS SCOT 9-11-0 R Bellamy, *mstk 1st, in rear whn blun 5th, sn pld up.*..........(20 to 1 op 16 to 1) pu
568 TARMON (Ire) (bl) 5-11-0 W McFarland, *al beh, tld off whn pld up bef 3 out.*..........(16 to 1 op 12 to 1) pu
BLUE BURTON LADY 8-10-9 S Mackey, *tld off frm 5th, pld up aftr 11th.*.................(66 to 1 op 50 to 1) pu
Dist: 1½l, 30l, 30l. 5m 3.30s. a 16.30s (9 Ran).
SR: 30/28/-/-/-/-/ (B R H Burrough), Mrs J Pitman

650 Armfield Novices' Hurdle (4-y-o and up) £1,863 2½m 110yds .... (4:20)

456⁵ DANCE PARTOUT (Ire) 5-11-0 P Hobbs, *al prmnt, jmpd into ld 4 out, rdn appr last. drvn out.*
.................................(3 to 1 fav op 6 to 4) 1
DOROBO (NZ) 5-11-0 C Llewellyn, *hld up, hdwy frm 7th, ev ch last, hrd rdn, one pace nr finish.*
.................................(14 to 1 op 10 to 1) 2
GRAHAM GOOCH 7-11-0 J Railton, *nvr far away, kpt on one pace frm 3 out.*...........(6 to 1 op 4 to 1) 3
597⁷ MARINERS COVE 5-11-0 W Humphreys, *hld up, hdwy appr 4 out. one pace frm nxt.*
.................(8 to 1 op 10 to 1 tchd 16 to 1) 4
MOBILE MESSENGER (NZ) 5-11-0 J Frost, *in rear, hdwy appr 4 out, rdn nxt, wknd 2 out.*
.................(8 to 1 op 10 to 1 tchd 16 to 1) 5
TRYING AGAIN 5-11-0 P Holley, *prmnt, led 6th to 4 out, sn btn, tld off.*
.................(100 to 30 op 5 to 1 tchd 6 to 1 and 3 to 1) 6
DOWRY SQUARE (Ire) 5-11-0 E Byrne, *al beh, tld off frm 4 out.*.................(25 to 1 op 20 to 1) 7
MAJOR KINSMAN 8-11-0 L Harvey, *f second.*
.................................(5 to 1 op 7 to 2) f
GENERALLY JUST 8-11-0 Mr S Stickland, *pld hrd, led 5th, jmpd rght and hdd nxt, sn wknd, tld off whn pulled up bef 4 out.*.................................(50 to 1) pu
PHAROAH'S SON 7-10-7 (7*) D Meade, *led till jmpd rght and hdd 5th, jumped right nxt 2, sn beh, pld up bef 4 out.*.................(33 to 1 tchd 50 to 1) pu
441⁷ STORM FLIGHT 11-0 B Powell, *prmnt till wknd 5th, tld off whn pld up bef 4 out.*....(20 to 1 op 25 to 1) pu
441 NORDIC FLIGHT 5-10-9 (5*) R Farrant, *prmnt to 5th, jmpd rght aftr, pld up after 3 out.*....(50 to 1) pu

79

OUR WIZZER (Ire) 4-10-12 S Earle, *al beh, mstk 7th, tld off whn pld up bef 4 out*............ (20 to 1 tchd 33 to 1) pu
Dist: 2l, 4l, 10l, hd, 20l, 30l. 4m 59.70s. a 18.70s (13 Ran).

SR: 22/20/16/6/6/-/ (J Tudor), P J Hobbs

651 **South-West Racecourses Amateur Riders' Series - Round 2 Handicap Hurdle (0-120 4-y-o and up) £1,737 2m 110yds..... (4:50)**

484* ARRAN VIEW [88] 7-10-2 (7*) Mr J L Llewellyn, *made all, shaken up appr last, ran on wl.*
.... (15 to 8 op 7 to 4 tchd 9 to 4) 1
488² AMPHIGORY [87] 5-10-1 (7*) Miss S Cobden, *hld up in rear, hdwy 4 out, ran on frm 2 out, wnt second on line.*
.....................(7 to 1 op 5 to 1 tchd 8 to 1) 2
JAMES THE FIRST [103] 5-11-3 (7*) Mr G Lewis, *not fluent, hld up in tch, wnt second appr 4 out, edging lft whn hit last, lost second pl on line.*..... (11 to 8 fav tchd Evens) 3
488⁷ PROVERBS GIRL [93] 8-10-7 (7*) Mr J Thatcher, *al beh, sn tld off aftr mstk 4th.*............... (14 to 1 op 8 to 1) 4
592³ PEARLY WHITE [86] 4-10-0 (7*) Mr Richard White, *chsd wnr to second, wknd aftr nxt, tld off.*
.... (25 to 1 op 33 to 1 tchd 20 to 1) 5
526² PEAK DISTRICT [86] 7-10-2 (5*) Mrs P Nash, *chsd wnr frm second till wknd appr 4 out, tld off whn pld up bef last.*
.... (6 to 1 tchd 7 to 1) pu
SR: -/-/6/ (B J Llewellyn), B J Llewellyn

KELSO (good)
Saturday October 2nd
Going Correction: MINUS 0.05 sec. per fur.

652 **Tamdhu Single Malt Juvenile Novices' Hurdle (3-y-o) £1,590 2m 110yds.... (2:20)**

285³ PRINCIPAL PLAYER (USA) 10-9 (3*) A Dobbin, *patiently rdn, improved to join issue aftr 3 out, led betw last 2, hit last, sn clr.*.......... (11 to 2 op 4 to 1 tchd 6 to 1) 1
DEVILRY 10-12 J Callaghan, *nvr far away, led gng wl 2 out, sn hdd, hit last, one pace.*
......................(7 to 2 op 3 to 1 tchd 9 to 4) 2
HYDE'S HAPPY HOUR 10-12 G McCourt, *wtd wth, drvn up to chal 3 out, rdn and not quicken betw last 2.*
......................(7 to 2 op 5 to 1) 3
COEUR BATTANT (Fr) 10-12 R Garritty, *settled to track ldrs, improved aftr 3 out, styd on, nvr nrr.*
.... (50 to 1 op 25 to 1) 4
PINKERTON'S SILVER 10-12 L Wyer, *settled off the pace, improved to go hndy aftr 3 out, wknd betw last 2.*
.... (33 to 1 op 16 to 1) 5
CORNFLAKE 10-2 (5*) P Waggott, *wth ldrs, led 1st till hdd 2 out, fdd.*............(11 to 1 op 12 to 1 tchd 10 to 1) 6
PERSIAN CHARMER (Ire) 10-12 P Niven, *led or dsptd ld to 4th, struggling to hold pl aftr 3 out, fdd.*
.... (7 to 1 tchd 8 to 1) 7
FESTIN (bl) 10-7 (5*) D Bentley, *led or dsptd ld to 4th, fdd und pres frm 3 out.*... (25 to 1 op 16 to 1 tchd 33 to 1) 8
516² MISTROY 10-7 C Grant, *trkd ldg quartet, hrd at work appr 3 out, sn lost tch.*
.... (9 to 4 op 5 to 2 tchd 3 to 1) 9
453 FLORA LADY 10-9 K Jones, *jmpd badly, tld off frm 3rd, pld up aftr 3 out.*............ (200 to 1 op 33 to 1) pu
Dist: 7l, ½l, 4l, 2½l, 5l, 3l, dist, 3l. 3m 50.00s. a 7.00s (10 Ran).

SR: 6/-/-/-/-/-/ (Mrs Jean Neilson), P Monteith

653 **Highland Park 12 Y.O. Single Malt Novices' Chase (5-y-o and up) £1,697 3m 1f .... (2:55)**

563⁴ CLARE LAD 10-11-0 B Storey, *settled gng wl, led 4 out, clr last, shaken up, cleverly.*
.... (9 to 2 op 5 to 1 tchd 11 to 2) 1
VELEDA II (Fr) 6-11-0 C Grant, *jmpd wl, ran in snatches, hmpd by faller 12th, outpcd aftr 3 out, rallied, jst fld.*
.... (9 to 4 tchd 15 to 8) 2
542 THE WALTZING MOUSE (bl) 10-11-0 T Reed, *led or dsptd ld, reminders 4 out, rallied und str pres, one pace r-in.*
.... (16 to 1 op 12 to 1) 3
563² SECOND ATTEMPT 9-11-0 A Merrigan, *led or dsptd ld to 4 out, rallied gmely till wknd r-in.*..... (5 to 1 op 4 to 1) 4
542⁴ EDEN SUNSET 7-11-0 Mr Chris Wilson, *pressing ldrs whn f 12th.*...............(9 to 4 tchd 2 to 1 and 5 to 2) f
Dist: Sht-hd, 2½l, 12l. 6m 32.00s. a 30.00s (5 Ran).

(C Rogers), R Allan

654 **Coopers & Lybrand Handicap Hurdle (0-115 4-y-o and up) £2,005 2¾m 110yds .... (3:25)**

562⁴ HAZEL LEAF [89] 7-10-0 R Hodge, *led till hdd 3 out, rallied und pres, led ag'n r-in, styd on wl.*
.... (14 to 1 op 8 to 1 tchd 16 to 1) 1

TAROUDANT [117] 6-12-0 P Niven, *settled gng wl, jmpd ahead 3 out, jnd nxt, hdd and rdn r-in, no extr.*
.... (9 to 4 fav op 7 to 4 tchd 5 to 2) 2
580 AS D'EBOLI (Fr) [89] 6-9-7 (7*) Kate Sellars, *patiently rdn, last hfwy, styd on wl frm 2 out, nrst finish.*
.... (16 to 1 op 10 to 1) 3
564² CHARLOTTE'S EMMA [100] 6-10-11 B Storey, *nvr far away, nrly f 3rd, rallied frm nxt, styd on same pace from 2 out.*...........(3 to 1 op 7 to 2 tchd 4 to 1) 4
334* SAOIRSE (Ire) [89] 5-9-12¹ (3*) D J Moffatt, *wth ldr, hrd at work appr 3 out, one pace frm nxt.* (16 to 1 op 12 to 1) 5
519* WEE WIZARD (Ire) [98] 4-10-6 (3*) A Dobbin, *patiently rdn, drvn up to take clr order hfwy, ridden and btn 2 out.*
.... (5 to 2 op 3 to 1 tchd 9 to 4) 6
SPANISH FAIR (Ire) [93] 5-10-4 C Grant, *took str hold in midfield, effrt and rdn 3 out, fdd...*(8 to 1 tchd 9 to 1) 7
ON THE HOOCH [110] 8-11-2 (5*) P Williams, *pressed ldg pair, ev ch 4 out, rdn and outpcd frm nxt.*
.... (25 to 1 op 16 to 1) 8
GLEMOT (Ire) [89] 5-9-8¹ (7*) F Perratt, *trkd ldrs, feeling pace and rdn aftr 3 out, 3rd and staying on whn f nxt.*
.... (25 to 1 op 16 to 1) f
Dist: 1½l, 2l, ¾l, 3½l, 7l, 5l, 5l. 5m 27.80s. a 16.80s (9 Ran).

(R McDonald), R McDonald

655 **Famous Grouse Handicap Chase (0-125 5-y-o and up) £2,617 3m 1f......... (3:55)**

543³ OFF THE BRU [109] (v) 8-11-3 Mr J Bradburne, *dsptd ld, led second to 8th, led ag'n 6 out, clr last 3, hld on gmely r-in.*...................... (7 to 2 op 4 to 1 tchd 9 to 2) 1
EASTERN OASIS [103] 10-10-6 (5*) P Williams, *wth ldrs, led 8th to 6 out, rallied gmely last 3, kpt on r-in.*
.... (11 to 1 op 8 to 1 tchd 12 to 1) 2
544* OVER THE DEEL [112] 7-11-6 T Reed, *patiently rdn, steady hdwy fnl circuit, ev ch and ridden 3 out, rallied last, one pace r-in.* (7 to 4 fav op 6 to 4 tchd 15 to 8) 3
PINK GIN [104] 6-10-12 C Grant, *trkd ldg trio, blun 13th and mstk nxt, struggling frm 4 out, no imprsn.*
.... (8 to 1 op 7 to 1) 4
WHAAT FETTLE [120] 8-12-0 M Moloney, *led to second, settled gng wl, blun and lost grnd 11th, wknd quickly frm 4 out.* (11 to 4 op 5 to 2 tchd 11 to 4 and 3 to 1) 5
544⁴ KIRSTY'S BOY [119] 10-11-13 G McCourt, *last and hld up, jmpd stickily 6th and 7th, effrt whn slpd badly 4 out, tld off.*.....................(16 to 1 op 20 to 1) 6
Dist: 1½l, 3l, 10l, 5l, 25l. 6m 16.60s. a 14.60s (6 Ran).

(G Lochtie), Mrs S C Bradburne

656 **Christie's Scotland Novices' Hurdle (4-y-o and up) £1,702 2¼m............... (4:25)**

WESTHOLME (USA) 5-11-0 L Wyer, *settled gng wl, quickened to ld hfwy, drw clr last 2, unchlgd......*(3 to 1 jt-fav op 5 to 2 tchd 7 to 2) 1
559² FLING IN SPRING (v) 7-10-9 (5*) P Williams, *trkd ldrs, improved hfwy, feeling pace aftr 3 out, styd on no ch wth wnr.*......................(16 to 1 op 14 to 1) 2
ELLIOTTS CHARM (Ire) 5-11-0 G McCourt, *settled last travelling wl, steady hdwy on bit aftr 3 out, one to note.*...................... (8 to 1 op 7 to 1 tchd 9 to 1) 3
PIRATE HOOK 5-11-0 B Storey, *nvr far away, rdn whn pace lifted aftr 3 out, one pace r-in.* (8 to 1 op 5 to 1) 4
502³ PERSIAN SOLDIER 6-11-0 P Niven, *patiently rdn, quickened up to join issue hfwy, ridden to chase wnr last 2, fdd r-in.*...................... (9 to 1 jt-fav tchd 7 to 2) 5
STRONG MEASURE (Ire) 5-11-0 K Johnson, *settled midfield, improved to go hndy hfwy, rdn and outpcd frm 3 out.*...................... (20 to 1 op 16 to 1) 6
GROUSE-N-HEATHER 4-10-5 (3*) A Dobbin, *chsd ldg bunch, bustled up to take clr order aftr 3 out, no imprsn.*......................(40 to 1 op 25 to 1) 7
ARIADLER (Ire) 5-11-0 C Grant, *jmpd novicely, outpcd and struggling hfwy, styd on stdly towards finish.*
.... (33 to 1 op 25 to 1) 8
CARROLLS MARC (Ire) 5-11-0 J Callaghan, *settled off the pace, pushed alng appr 4 out, nvr a threat.*
.... (10 to 1 op 8 to 1) 9
MACMURPHY 8-11-0 R Hodge, *pressed ldrs, struggling to hold pl hfwy, lost tch frm 4 out.* (40 to 1 op 50 to 1) 10
582⁵ SMOKE 7-10-12¹³ T Reed, *tucked away on ins, effrt appr 4 out, fdd aftr nxt.*...............(25 to 1 op 20 to 1) 11
HERBALIST 4-10-12¹ A Larnach, *led, clr 3rd, hld hfwy, remained hndy till wknd aftr 3 out.*
.... (7 to 2 op 5 to 1 tchd 6 to 1) 12
268 CALL KENTONS (bl) 7-10-11 (3*) D J Moffatt, *wth ldrs, struggling to keep up 4 out, sn lost tch.*
.... (40 to 1 op 50 to 1) 13
Dist: 10l, ¾l, 5l, 3l, 5l, 6l, 3l, sht-hd, nk, 1½l. 4m 25.60s. a 18.60s (13 Ran).

(T H Bennett), M H Easterby

657 **Bunnahabhain 12 Year Old Malt Handicap Hurdle (0-125 4-y-o and up) £1,952 2m 110yds........................... (5:00)**

543* BEAUCADEAU [123] 7-11-11 (3*) A Dobbin, *jmpd wl, led aftr 4th, sn clr, easily.*............. (3 to 1 op 11 to 4) 1

591⁴ ASTURIAS [95] 10-10-0³ (3") A Larnach, *patiently rdn, improved aftr 3 out, sayed on r-in, no ch wth wnr.*
.................................(16 to 1 op 12 to 1 tchd 20 to 1) 2
543³ FLOWING RIVER (USA) [104] 7-10-9 B Storey, *settled gng wl, improved to chase wnr aftr 4th, rdn and found nothing betw last 2.* (2 to 1 fav op 9 to 4 tchd 5 to 2) 3
499² SRIVIJAYA [118] 6-11-9 P Niven, *chsd ldg bunch, effrt and drvn alng aftr 3 out, not pace to chal.*
.................................(8 to 2 tchd 5 to 1) 4
MASTER OFTHE HOUSE [98] 7-10-3 C Grant, *wtd wth, effrt and pushed alng appr 3 out, nvr able to chal.*
.................................(8 to 1 op 7 to 1) 5
COMSTOCK [95] 6-10-0 L Wyer, *chsd ldrs, struggling whn pace quickened aftr 3 out, sn btn...*(7 to 1 tchd 8 to 1) 6
RAPID MOVER [95] (bl) 6-10-0 R Hodge, *chsd ldg pair to hfwy, wknd quickly frm 3 out.....*(25 to 1 op 20 to 1) 7
OLD MORTALITY [95] 7-10-0 J Callaghan, *led and clr till hdd aftr 4th, lost tch frm four out.* (33 to 1 op 20 to 1) 8
COOL DUDE [96] 7-9-13¹ (3") D J Moffatt, *chsd alng in midfield, no imprsn whn f last................*(10 to 1) f
Dist: 7l, 7l, 3l, 3½l, 3l, hd, 20l. 3m 46.90s. a 3.90s (9 Ran).
SR: 53/18/20/31/7/1/1/-/-/ (T A Barnes), M A Barnes

Going Correction: PLUS 0.75 sec. per fur. (races 1,2,- 5,7), PLUS 0.60 (3,4,6)

658 Evening Sentinel Novices' Hurdle (4-y-o and up) £2,897 2m...............................(2:05)

MOZEMO 6-10-12 J Osborne, *wl beh till steady hdwy appr 3 out, shaken up approaching last, led r-in, pushed out...................*(12 to 1 op 7 to 1) 1
MILZIG (USA) (bl) 4-10-8 (3") D O'Sullivan, *in tch, led aftr 3 out, not fluent last, rdn, found nothing and hdd r-in.*
.................(3 to 1 fav op 11 to 4 tchd 100 to 30) 2
323⁶ JON'S CHOICE (bl) 5-10-12 T Wall, *beh, hdwy 6th, ran on und pres frm 3 out..........................*(25 to 1) 3
346³ ZAMANAYN (Ire) 5-10-12 R Supple, *beh, hdwy and rdn appr 3 out, sn one pace.............*(9 to 1 op 8 to 1) 4
DESERT PEACE (Ire) 4-10-11 R Campbell, *chsd ldrs till outpcd frm 3 out,...................*(10 to 1 op 6 to 1) 5
173² NORDIC BEAT (Ire) 4-10-11 Diane Clay, *mid-div, rdn 6th, nvr dngrs..............................*(11 to 1 op 7 to 1) 6
COL BUCKMORE (Ire) 5-10-12 N Doughty, *led, hit second, hdd 3 out, btn whn blun 2 out.*
.................(10 to 1 op 6 to 1 tchd 12 to 1) 7
591 TIBBS 10-10-11 M Ranger, *beh, effrt appr 3 out, sn wknd........................*(25 to 1 op 20 to 1) 8
520* SMART DEBUTANTE (Ire) 4-10-13 H Davies, *prmnt to 6th.*
.................(7 to 1 op 11 to 1) 9
WORDY'S WONDER 5-10-7 A Maguire, *chsd ldrs to 6th, sn wknd.....................*(20 to 1 op 14 to 1) 10
NONCOMMITAL 6-10-12 N Williamson, *al beh.*
.................(16 to 1 op 10 to 1) 11
BUSMAN (Ire) 4-10-11 M Richards, *hdwy to track ldrs, led 3 out, sn hdd, wknd rpdly and no ch whn f last.*
.........(100 to 30 op 3 to 1 tchd 5 to 2 and 7 to 2) f
SEPTEMBER DAWN 8-10-5 (7") Mr N Bradley, *blun and uns rdr second.....................*(50 to 1 op 25 to 1) ur
STORMING RUN (Ire) 5-10-9 (3") A Thornton, *prmnt, wkng whn blun 7th, no ch when veered rght blunded and uns rdr 3 out............*(25 to 1 op 20 to 1) ur
TOMASHENKO 4-10-6 (5") T Eley, *sn beh, tld off whn pld up bef 3 out..................................*(20 to 1) pu
Dist: 1l, 5l, 6l, 1½l, 4l, 2l, nk, 4l, 20l. 3m 57.00s. a 18.00s (15 Ran).
SR: 24/22/18/12/9/5/4/2/-/ (Codan Trust Company Limited), O Sherwood

659 North Staffordshire Advertiser Selling Handicap Hurdle sponsored by Evening Sentinel (4-y-o and up) £1,843 3m 110yds ....(2:35)

OK RECORDS [72] 6-10-6 N Mann, *steady hdwy 4 out led 2 out, edgd rght and drvn out r-in.*
.................(7 to 1 op 8 to 1 tchd 6 to 1) 1
447 THE HIDDEN CITY [82] 7-11-2 A Maguire, *in tch, hdwy 9th, ev ch 3 out, rdn and styd on one pace r-in.*
.................(8 to 1 op 7 to 1) 2
401 FILM LIGHTING GIRL [66] 7-9-8¹ (7") P Ward, *prmnt, chlgd tenth, ev ch frm 3 out till not quicken r-in.*
.................(50 to 1 op 25 to 1) 3
SUASANAN SIOSANA [66] 8-10-0 R Supple, *beh, hdwy tenth, styd on one pace und pres frm 2 out.*
.................(12 to 1 op 12 to 1) 4
394³ NEARCTIC BAY (USA) [75] 7-10-6 (3") M Hourigan, *hdwy 9th, styd on frm 2 out..................*(8 to 1 op 6 to 1) 5
344⁷ SHOW THE FLAG [95] 5-11-2 T Wall, *beh, rdn 3 out, styd on und pres frm 2 out.............*(9 to 1 op 8 to 1) 6
SAFARI KEEPER [68] (v) 7-9-9 (7") W Fry, *chsd ldrs, chlgd tenth, wknd frm 3 out.....................*(14 to 1) 7
224⁴ BAYBEEJAY [76] 6-10-10 D Bridgwater, *prmnt till wknd aftr 3 out.............*(9 to 1 op 14 to 1 tchd 8 to 1) 8

527⁷ STROKED AGAIN [66] 8-10-0 D Byrne, *led to 2 out, wknd quickly............................*(20 to 1 op 14 to 1) 9
477⁶ STATION EXPRESS (Ire) [75] 5-10-9 A Orkney, *beh till gd hdwy tenth, wknd 3 out.....................*(7 to 1) 10
597 FAUGHAN LODGE [88] 6-11-8 Diane Clay, *prmnt, steadied aftr 8th, nvr plcd to chal after..........*(12 to 1) 11
552² BURN BRIDGE (USA) [89] (v) 7-11-9 Peter Caldwell, *in tch till mstk and wknd 4 out........*(13 to 2 fav op 5 to 1) 12
ENCHANTED FLYER [66] 6-9-9 (5") T Eley, *mid-div, effrt tenth, wknd 3 out..........................*(25 to 1) 13
INVITE D'HONNEUR (NZ) [66] 11-11-6 Jacqui Oliver, *drpd rear 8th, nvr dngrs aftr..................*(7 to 1 op 5 to 1) 14
APPLIED GRAPHICS (Ire) [68] 5-10-2 N Williamson, *chsd ldrs, chlgd 4 out, wknd quickly 3 out.*
.................(14 to 1 op 12 to 1 tchd 16 to 1) 15
ANOTHER CRUISE [90] 8-11-7 (3") R Greene, *al beh.*
.................(25 to 1 op 16 to 1 tchd 33 to 1) 16
DEEP DAWN RUN [66] 7-9-11 (3") W Marston, *effrt tenth, wknd appr 3 out............*(25 to 1 tchd 33 to 1) 17
592⁷ FAIR BABE [66] 7-9-8¹ (7") Mr N Bradley, *drpd rear tenth, tld off whn pld up bef 3 out....*(25 to 1 tchd 33 to 1) pu
Dist: 3½l, ½l, nk, 2½l, 1½l, ¾l, sht-hd, 2l, ¾l, sht-hd. 6m 23.30s. a 44.30s (18 Ran).
(S W Bristow), M Williams

660 Staffordshire Yeomanry Challenge Cup Novices' Chase sponsored by Evening Sentinel (5-y-o and up) £3,306 2m 7f (3:05)

FARDROSS 7-11-0 N Williamson, *blun second, hdwy 5th, mstks 7th and 8th, led 3 out, easily.* (11 to 2 op 7 to 2) 1
452² KILDOWNEY HILL 7-11-0 A Maguire, *chsd ldrs till led 4 out, hdd 3 out, kpt on not pace of wnr.*
.................(7 to 1 op 6 to 1) 2
455* WHATAGALE 6-11-7 J Osborne, *led to 4 out, wknd aftr 3 out.............................*(9 to 4 fav op 7 to 4) 3
455³ PAPPA DONT PREACH (Ire) 5-10-12 R Supple, *sn beh, tld off........................*(16 to 1 op 14 to 1) 4
586 WHISKEY BLUES 8-11-0 D Byrne, *sn beh, tld off.*
.................(50 to 1 op 33 to 1) 5
455 TOP IT ALL 5-10-12 D Bridgwater, *prmnt, rdn, 9th, sn wknd, tld off...................*(11 to 2 op 5 to 1) 6
526⁷ VOLCANIC DANCER (USA) 7-11-0 M A FitzGerald, *in tch till wknd tenth, no ch whn f 12th.....*(14 to 1 op 16 to 1) f
543³ TARTAN TRADEWINDS 6-11-0 N Doughty, *chsd ldrs till f 9th...............*(5 to 2 op 3 to 1 tchd 7 to 2) f
SOLDIER EVE 7-10-9 M Bosley, *beh 8th, tld off whn pld up bef 11th....................*(50 to 1 op 33 to 1) pu
KATIE PARSON 6-10-9 A Webb, *sn beh, tld off whn pld up bef 12th..................*(50 to 1 op 33 to 1) pu
Dist: 1½l, 4l, dist, 2l, 10l. 5m 50.10s. a 20.10s (10 Ran).
SR: 23/21/24/-/-/-/ (I M S Racing), K C Bailey

661 Technic Group Plc Handicap Chase For Duke Of Edinburgh's Award Challenge Trophy (5-y-o and up) £5,239 3¼m.. (3:35)

SPRINGALEAK [133] 8-11-3 J Osborne, *chsd ldr, led 2 out styd, on wl...............................*(7 to 2 op 11 to 4) 1
WIND FORCE [140] 8-11-10 N Doughty, *led, blun 13th, hdd and slpd 2 out, one pace....* (2 to 1 fav tchd 7 to 4) 2
KILLBANON [122] 11-10-6 S McNeill, *chsd ldrs till drpd rear 14th...................*(14 to 1 op 16 to 1) 3
BONSAI BUD [123] 10-10-7 D Gallagher, *hdwy 14th, dsptd ld 4 out, 3rd and rdn and blun and uns rdr 2 out.*
.................(5 to 1 tchd 6 to 1) ur
566* KILLULA CHIEF [117] 6-10-11 M A FitzGerald, *drpd rear 5th, hdwy and chasing ldrs whn blun and uns rdr 15th.*
.................(5 to 2 op 2 to 1 tchd 9 to 4) ur
Dist: 4l, dist. 6m 43.30s. a 27.30s (5 Ran).
(Rashleigh Arms Charlestown St Austell), O Sherwood

662 Staffordshire Regiment Challenge Cup Handicap Hurdle sponsored by Evening Sentinel (0-125 4-y-o and up) £2,827 2m ....(4:05)

RED INDIAN [107] 7-10-12 D Byrne, *gd hdwy frm 3 out, str run to ld last, drvn out............*(7 to 1 op 6 to 1) 1
LE METAYER (Fr) [116] 5-11-7 N Williamson, *trkd ldrs gng wl, led 2 out, hdd last, ev ch r-in, no extr.*
.................(3 to 1 fav op 5 to 2 tchd 11 to 4) 2
447² JAMESTOWN BOY [95] 5-10-0 T Wall, *beh, sn rdn alng, rapid hdwy appr last, fnshd wl.* (13 to 1 tchd 14 to 1) 3
569³ SPRING TO GLORY [95] 6-9-9 (5") A Procter, *prmnt, chlgd frm 3 out till wknd r-in...........*(10 to 1 op 8 to 1) 4
STAR OF THE GLEN [122] 7-11-13 A Maguire, *beh, hdwy 3 way out, one pace frm 2 out.........*(6 to 1 op 5 to 1) 5
428² MUST BE MAGICAL (USA) [96] 5-10-1¹ M A FitzGerald, *led to second, styd chasing ldrs till wknd aftr 3 out.*
.................(8 to 1 tchd 9 to 1) 6
499⁷ WINDWARD ARIOM [98] 7-10-3 R Marley, *prmnt till wknd aftr 3 out...................*(20 to 1 op 16 to 1) 7
MIDDLE MARKER (Ire) [119] 4-11-10 Diane Clay, *beh till took str hold and hdwy 5th, led 4 out, hdd 2 out, sn wknd.......................*(6 to 1 op 8 to 1) 8

SWEET CITY [105] 8-10-10 N Doughty, *in tch till weakneed appr 3 out*............................(10 to 1 op 8 to 1) 9
MAJOR'S LAW (Ire) [100] 4-10-5 R Campbell, *led second till hdd 4 out, sn wknd, off whn pld up bef 2 out.*
............................(9 to 1 op 12 to 1) pu
Dist: 1l, 2½l, sht-hd, 5l, ½l, 8l, 1½l, dist. 4m 0.50s. a 21.50s (10 Ran).

(Dave Marshall), W W Haigh

663 Queen's Royal Lancers Challenge Cup Handicap Chase sponsored by Evening Sentinel (0-125 5-y-o and up) £3,582 2m 5f
...................................(4:35)

BALLYROE LADY [109] 7-11-3 S McNeill, *wnt prmnt 5th, led 2 out, pushed out.*
..................(25 to 1 op 12 to 1 tchd 33 to 1) 1
TOUREEN PRINCE [120] 10-12-10 Mr J M Pritchard, *trkd ldrs till lost pl 11th, rallied and ev ch frm 4 out, till not quicken r-in.*........................(7 to 1 op 5 to 1) 2
PARDON ME MUM [109] (bl) 8-11-3 J Osborne, *hld up, hdwy 11th, led appr 4 out, hdd 2 out, one pace.*
...................(11 to 2 op 7 to 1 tchd 9 to 2) 3
426[6] WIGTOWN BAY [99] 10-10-7 M A FitzGerald, *mid-div, hdwy 12th, hit 3 out, kpt on same pace.*
..................(12 to 1 op 8 to 1 tchd 14 to 1) 4
515* MEGA BLUE [117] 8-11-11 D Byrne, *mstks 1st and second, reminders aftr 3rd, effrt and mistake 9th, hit 4 out, wknd 3 out.*...........(9 to 2 op 3 to 1 tchd 5 to 1) 5
SIRRAH JAY [116] 13-11-10 A Maguire, *led till hdd appr 4 out, sn wknd.*.....................(8 to 1 op 7 to 1) 6
426[3] PERSIAN HOUSE [115] 6-11-9 M Dwyer, *chsd ldrs, rdn 11th, wknd appr 4 out.*
...................(9 to 4 fav op 5 to 2 tchd 3 to 1) 7
FALSE ECONOMY [108] 8-11-10 N Williamson, *in tch, hit 12th, wknd appr 4 out.*...........(10 to 1 op 6 to 1) 8
JIMMY O'DEA [100] (bl) 6-10-3 (5*) T Eley, *hit 6th, rdn aftr 8th, tld off whn pld up bef tenth.*
...................(12 to 1 op 10 to 1 tchd 16 to 1) pu
Dist: 1½l, 6l, 7l, hd, 20l, 7l, 5l. 5m 19.30s. a 19.30s (9 Ran).
SR: 22/31/14/-/15/-/   (T J Whitley), D R Gandolfo

664 Green'un Sports Final Novices' Hurdle sponsored by Evening Sentinel (4-y-o and up) £2,739 2¾m 110yds............(5:05)

NEEDWOOD POPPY 5-10-7 B Clifford, *hld up in mid-div, chsd ldrs aftr 4 out, led 2 out, sn drw clr, cmftbly.*
..................(12 to 1 tchd 10 to 1) 1
CLASSIC HUNTER (NZ) 5-10-7 (5*) R Davis, *hld up, mstk second, beh 6th, hdwy 4 out, chsd ldrs appr nxt, styd on to take second pl, no ch wth wnr.*
.....................(7 to 1 op 6 to 1 tchd 8 to 1) 2
502[5] SARANNPOUR (Ire) 4-10-3 (7*) E Husband, *hld up, hdwy to chase ldg grp aftr 4 out, styd on appr last, not quicken.*
.......................(20 to 1) 3
MISS NOSEY OATS 5-10-7 M A FitzGerald, *trkd ldrs, cl up and ev ch 4 out, led nxt, sn hdd, one pace.*
..................(25 to 1 op 20 to 1) 4
DUNDEE PRINCE (NZ) 5-10-12 N Williamson, *hld up, steady hdwy aftr 8th, in tch appr 3 out, ev ch whn pckd last, sn drvn and btn when pecked last.*
.......................(9 to 1 op 5 to 1) 5
445* OUTFIELD 7-10-11 (3*) W Marston, *trkd ldrs, wnt 3rd aftr 5 out, lost pl after nxt, effrt and styd on 2 out, sn btn.*
.......................(6 to 1 op 9 to 2) 6
POP ABROAD 8-10-4 (3*) N Bentley, *pressed ldr, ev ch 4 out, wknd aftr 3 out.*...........(16 to 1 op 12 to 1) 7
LONG REACH 5-10-12 D Bridgwater, *led, mstks 5th and nxt, hdd 3 out, stdly wknd.*.........(6 to 1 op 5 to 1) 8
237* LABURNUM 5-11-5 A Maguire, *hld up, beh 6th, hdwy to chase ldrs appr 3 out, rdn and wknd quickly betw last 2.*..............(2 to 1 fav op 5 to 2 tchd 11 to 4) 9
WANDERLINE 6-10-12 S McNeill, *beh 6th, wknd quickly and sn tld off aftr 8th.*........................(33 to 1) 10
LEARNER DRIVER 6-10-12 R Marley, *pressed ldr to 5th, wknd quickly aftr 7th, tld off 3 out.*
..................(16 to 1 op 14 to 1) 11
TRICYCLE (Ire) 4-10-10 Gary Lyons, *prmnt to 5th, wkng whn jmpd slwly and pld up aftr 7th.*...........(33 to 1) pu
MILL BURN 4-10-10 R Campbell, *hdwy 5th, wnt second nxt, pressed ldr til wknd quickly aftr 8th, beh whn pld up bef 3 out.*....................(25 to 1 op 20 to 1) pu
Dist: 15l, ½l, 1½l, nk, 4l, 3½l, 2l, 8l, 15l. 5m 41.10s. a 30.10s (13 Ran).

(Tim Leadbeater), B C Morgan

PLUMPTON (good)
Monday October 4th
Going Correction: PLUS 0.60 sec. per fur.

665 Firle Handicap Chase (0-115 4-y-o and up) £1,917 2m...........................(2:15)

ALKINOR REX [125] 8-12-0 M Perrett, *made all, shaken up and mstk 2 out, rdn clr frm last.*
..............(5 to 4 on op 11 to 8 on tchd 11 to 10) 1

LUCKY AGAIN [98] 6-10-1 S McNeill, *trkd wnr frm 7th, ev ch from 2 out, not quicken last*......(4 to 1 op 5 to 2) 2
MR FELIX [99] 7-10-2 B Powell, *chsd wnr to 7th, outpcd nxt, poor 3rd whn blun 4 out.*
..................(3 to 1 op 7 to 2 tchd 4 to 1) 3
602[4] GABISH [99] 8-10-2[2] M A FitzGerald, *al outpcd, tld off frm 7th.*..................(20 to 1 op 14 to 1) 4
523[5] UNEX-PLAINED [97] 10-10-0 Lorna Vincent, *blun 1st, al outpcd, sn tld off....* (12 to 1 op 10 to 1 tchd 14 to 1) 5
WOLFHANGAR [97] 11-10-0 D Morris, *blun and uns rdr 1st, dead.*.........(50 to 1 op 25 to 1 tchd 66 to 1) ur
Dist: 10l, 30l, 30l, 30l. 4m 4.30s. a 14.30s (6 Ran).
SR: 53/16/-/   (M C Peraticos), G Harwood

666 October Selling Hurdle (4,5,6-y-o) £1,364 2m 1f..........................(2:45)

MISS MARIGOLD 4-10-13 R Dunwoody, *wl in tch, led aftr 3 out, sn well clr, eased r-in.*
.....................(5 to 1 op 7 to 2 tchd 11 to 2) 1
SALISONG 4-10-13 R Campbell, *chsd ldrs, led 3 out, sn hdd and outpcd, mstk last....* (5 to 2 jt-fav op 6 to 1) 2
463[5] ROGER'S PAL 6-10-12 (7*) K Goble, *hld up towards rear, prog 7th, no imprsn on wnr frm 2 out.*
.....................(6 to 1 op 4 to 1 tchd 7 to 1) 3
KAURI 6-11-10 Peter Hobbs, *mid-div, hdwy 7th, one pace frm 3 out.*...........(5 to 2 jt-fav tchd 11 to 4) 4
OH SO HANDY 5-11-0 D Morris, *hld up towards rear, effrt appr 3 out, no ch wth wnr........*(33 to 1 op 20 to 1) 5
599[5] BETALONGABILL (v) 4-10-13 J R Kavanagh, *chsd ldrs til wknd frm 8th.*...........(20 to 1 op 7 to 1) 6
184 PRIVATE JET (Ire) 4-10-13 M A FitzGerald, *prmnt till lost pl quickly 3rd, nvr dngrs aftrwards.* (20 to 1 op 12 to 1) 7
499[9] FAILAND 6-11-0 J Osborne, *hdwy 3rd, wknd frm 7th.*
..................(10 to 1 op 6 to 1 tchd 14 to 1) 8
567[6] WILL BONNY (NZ) 6-10-7 (7*) R Darke, *led briefly 1st, pckd 4th, cl up till wknd appr 3 out.*
..................(20 to 1 op 12 to 1 tchd 25 to 1) 9
458[8] HULLO MARY DOLL 4-10-8 M Perrett, *al rear grp.*
..................(20 to 1 op 12 to 1 tchd 25 to 1) 10
441 EASY TOOMEY (bl) 5-11-0 H Davies, *led aftr 1st, hdd 3 out, moderate 4th whn f nxt.......*(33 to 1 op 16 to 1) f
PRINCESS JESSICA 6-10-6 (3*) M Hourigan, *lost tch frm 4th, tld off whn pld up bef 7th....*(20 to 1 op 14 to 1) pu
ALTON BELLE 4-10-5 (3*) D O'Sullivan, *beh most of way, tld off whn pld up bef 2 out.*...(20 to 1 op 20 to 1) pu
LAD OF LANGTON 4-10-13 Leesa Long, *prmnt till wknd aftr 4th, pld up aftr 2 out.*........(33 to 1 op 20 to 1) pu
Dist: 25l, 2½l, 5l, ¾l, hd, 5l, 4l, 8l, 10l. 4m 24.00s. a 32.00s (14 Ran).

(Mrs Angela Fayers), R J Hodges

667 Newick Novices' Chase (5-y-o and up) £1,540 2m..........................(3:15)

KALANSKI 7-11-0 J Osborne, *hld up, led 8th, jmpd slwly tenth, clr nxt, eased r-in.*
.....................(5 to 4 on op 6 to 4 on tchd Evens) 1
525[5] MADRAJ (Ire) 5-10-12 R Dunwoody, *hdwy 9th, wnt second 2 out, no imprsn on wnr.*
..............(4 to 1 op 7 to 2 tchd 9 to 2) 2
568 CELTIC CATCH 7-11-0 M Bosley, *led second, jmpd rght 5th, hdd 8th, outpcd frm 3 out.*
.................(5 to 1 op 4 to 1 tchd 7 to 1 and 9 to 2) 3
SMART DRESSER 8-11-0 J R Kavanagh, *not jump wl, al in rear, tld off frm 7th.* (20 to 1 op 14 to 1 tchd 25 to 1) 4
521 PEARLS BEAU 6-12-4 H Davies, *wl plcd till wknd frm 7th, pld up bef 9th..........*(13 to 2 op 3 to 1 tchd 7 to 1) pu
593 GAME SET (bl) 7-11-0 A Webb, *led second, trkd ldrs till wknd 7th, pld up bef 4 out........*(50 to 1 op 25 to 1) pu
Dist: 20l, 12l, 20l. 4m 9.30s. a 19.30s (6 Ran).

(I Kerman), C R Egerton

668 Hove Three Yrs Old Novices' Hurdle £1,413 2m 1f..........................(3:45)

SIR THOMAS BEECHAM 10-12 H Davies, *wl plcd, led appr 2 out, clr last, cmftbly....*(9 to 2 op 7 to 2 tchd 5 to 1) 1
570* C D SHAREPLAN (USA) 11-5 Lorna Vincent, *led till appr 2 out, one pace approaching last....* (3 to 1 tchd 7 to 2) 2
588* CHIAPPUCCI (Ire) (bl) 11-5 J Osborne, *pressed ldr, ev ch and not much room appr 2 out, no extr approaching last.*
.........(11 to 10 on op 11 to 10 tchd 5 to 4 and 5 to 4 on) 3
406[4] PRESS GALLERY 10-12 T Kent, *hld up rear, prog 5th, wknd aftr 3 out, sn lost tch.*
.....................(8 to 1 op 5 to 1 tchd 9 to 1) 4
GEORGE ROPER 10-12 H Jenkins, *mid-div, wknd 3 out, fnshd 5th, collapsed and died.*
..................(25 to 1 op 12 to 1 tchd 33 to 1) 5
DO BE WARE 10-9 (3*) A Thornton, *chsd ldrs till lost tch frm 7th.......*(50 to 1 op 20 to 1 tchd 66 to 1) 6
BARTON ROYAL (Ire) 10-12 A Charlton, *beh 5th, tld off.*
..................(50 to 1 op 25 to 1 tchd 66 to 1) 7
462[7] HUESCA 10-7 M Richards, *swshd tail thrght, al beh, pld up bef last.*........(33 to 1 op 20 to 1 tchd 50 to 1) pu
Dist: 6l, 4l, 30l, 4l, 1½l, 30l. 4m 24.20s. a 32.20s (8 Ran).

(Mrs Heather Chakko), S Dow

669 Uckfield Handicap Chase (0-115 5-y-o and up) £1,795 3m 1f 110yds........... (4:15)

KINGFISHER BAY [92] 8-11-11 M A FitzGerald, *led to second, chsd ldr, mstks 13th and 17th, rdn to ld last, drvn out*..................(5 to 4 fav op 11 to 10 tchd 7 to 4) 1
FIGHTING DAYS (USA) [95] 7-11-7 (7*) J Clarke, *hld up, mstk 8th, led 14th till rdn and hdd last, no extr r-in.*
........................(5 to 1 op 7 to 2 tchd 11 to 2) 2
525⁵ SAMSUN [87] (bl) 11-11-6 R Dunwoody, *led second, hdd 14th, styd on one pace frm 3 out.*
........................(9 to 1 op 10 to 1 tchd 14 to 1) 3
458⁴ BARRACILLA [85] 8-11-4 S Hodgson, *pressed ldrs, blun 7th, drpd rear tenth, shaken up 13th, one pace frm 4 out.*..................(7 to 4 tchd 11 to 8) 4
Dist: 3½l, sht-hd, 1½l. 6m 53.10s. a 41.10s (4 Ran).
(D W Chilcott), J White

670 Hadlow Down Handicap Hurdle (0-115 4-y-o and up) £1,537 2½m............. (4:45)

CANOSCAN [94] 8-11-3 E Murphy, *hld up in rear, hdwy aftr 9th, led appr last, sn clr.*
........................(11 to 2 op 7 to 2 tchd 5 to 1) 1
460² MANHATTAN BOY [105] 11-12-0 J R Kavanagh, *hld up, chsd ldr frm 9th, led 2 out, hdd and not quicken appr last.*..................(11 to 1 op 5 to 1 tchd 12 to 1) 2
599* KALAMOSS [86] 4-10-2 (7*,6ex) Miss S Mitchell, *in tch till lost pl 5th, ran on appr 3 out, one pace approaching last.*..................(10 to 1 op 5 to 1 tchd 11 to 1) 3
NICK THE DREAMER [103] 8-11-12 R Dunwoody, *chsd ldr, led 9th, hdd 2 out, sn btn.*
........................(8 to 1 op 7 to 1 tchd 10 to 1) 4
401* SPARKLER GEBE [95] (bl) 7-11-1 (3*) D O'Sullivan, *chsd ldrs frm 4th, wknd appr 3 out.*......(5 to 1 op 4 to 1) 5
THUHOOL [101] 5-11-3 (7*) L Dace, *mstk second, hdwy 4th, wknd 8th.*...........(7 to 1 op 5 to 1 tchd 8 to 1) 6
JOKER JACK [85] 8-10-3 (5*) A Procter, *drpd rear 5th, lost tch 7th.*...........(11 to 2 op 8 to 1 tchd 5 to 1) 7
TOUCHING TIMES [79] 5-10-2 G Rowe, *led till hdd and f 9th.*.............(3 to 1 fav op 7 to 2 tchd 4 to 1) f
Dist: 7l, 2½l, 7l, 15l, 5l, 3l. 5m 13.40s. a 36.40s (8 Ran).
(Nigel Clutton), Lady Herries

ROSCOMMON (IRE) (yielding)
Monday October 4th

671 Montelado Maiden Hurdle (4-y-o) £3,105 2m........................... (2:30)

FABULIST (Ire) 11-3 T Horgan, ... (10 to 1) 1
120⁷ STEEL CHIMES (Ire) (bl) 11-8 C F Swan, ...(9 to 2) 2
56 BACK TO BLACK (Ire) 10-7 (5*) C O'Brien, ...(5 to 1) 3
SHAWAR (Ire) 11-8 J Evans, ...(8 to 1) 4
274⁵ LAKE HOTEL (Ire) 11-3 B Sheridan, ...(12 to 1) 5
555⁸ NORA ANN (Ire) 10-12 (5*) M A Davey, ...(7 to 1) 6
MOSCOW DUKE (Ire) 11-3 J Jones, ...(14 to 1) 7
393* PEPPERONI EXPRESS (Ire) 11-8 J F Titley, ... (4 to 1 fav) 8
255⁵ LOVE FOR LYDIA (Ire) 10-5 (7*) F Byrne, ...(14 to 1) 9
535 BALLYHYLAND (Ire) 11-3 P Worthington, ...(10 to 1) 10
627 COUNTESS PAHLEN (Ire) 10-12 A Powell, ...(20 to 1) 11
376⁷ FURTHER NOTICE (Ire) (bl) 11-3 S Jenkins, ...(16 to 1) 12
NORA'S ERROR (Ire) 10-12 (5*) Mr J Harford, ..(14 to 1) 13
558⁴ CHANCERY QUEEN (Ire) 11-3 M Patton, ...(6 to 1) 14
365² MOOREFIELD GIRL (Ire) 11-3 M Moran, ...(8 to 1) 15
SON OF TEMPO (Ire) 11-3 J Magee, ...(10 to 1) 16
331⁸ CALL THE KING (Ire) 11-8 K F O'Brien, ...(12 to 1) 17
MIDDLE SUSIE (Ire) 10-7 (5*) T P Treacy, ...(20 to 1) 18
472⁶ REASON TO BELIEVE (Ire) 10-12 F Woods, ...(33 to 1) 19
TOO YOUNG (Ire) 11-3 P McWilliams, ...(33 to 1) 20
Dist: Sht-hd, 6l, 3½l, 2l. 4m 1.80s. (20 Ran).
(Mrs C A Moore), P Mullins

672 Irish National Hunt Novice Hurdle (4-y-o and up) £4,140 2m................. (3:00)

534* PADRE MIO 5-11-6 G Bradley, ...(6 to 4 fav) 1
257* PADASHPAN (USA) 4-11-1 C F Swan, ...(9 to 4) 2
538* MINELLA LAD 7-11-6 T Horgan, ...(7 to 2) 3
THE BURSER 7-11-2 K F O'Brien, ...(20 to 1) 4
471* MASAI WARRIOR 6-11-9 J Collins, ...(9 to 1) 5
538 RATHCORE 6-11-2 C O'Dwyer, ...(20 to 1) 6
FAMBO LAD 5-11-2 Mr J A Berry, ...(25 to 1) 7
SHY GREEN (Ire) 5-10-11 G M O'Neill, ...(50 to 1) 8
Dist: 2l, 12l, 5½l, 4l. 3m 58.00s. (8 Ran).
(Paddy Fennelly), Anthony Mullins

673 Ballinlough Handicap Hurdle (0-130 4-y-o and up) £2,760 2m................. (3:30)

637⁶ BRAVEFOOT [-] 5-11-0 P Worthington, ...(15 to 2) 1
574² DANCING COURSE (Ire) 5-10-1 J Evans, ...(4 to 1) 2
585⁵ FORTUNE'S GIRL [-] 5-10-0 C F Swan, ...(8 to 1) 3
392³ SEARCHLIGHT (Ire) [-] 5-10-3 S Jenkins, ...(5 to 1) 4
117⁴ HEAD OF CHAMBERS (Ire) [-] 5-11-9 J F Titley, ...(8 to 1) 5

534⁶ NOBODYS FLAME (Ire) [-] 5-9-11 M Patton, ... (8 to 1) 6
533⁷ SHIRWAN (Ire) [-] 4-10-2 T Horgan, ...(9 to 4 fav) 7
466⁶ ENNIS SEVEN FIFTY [-] 5-9-9 F Woods, ...(33 to 1) 8
LILLIPUT QUEEN [-] 5-10-7 K F O'Brien, ... (9 to 1) 9
Dist: Hd, 1l, 6l, 3l. 4m 3.40s. (9 Ran).
(S Macklin), J H Scott

674 WinElectric Novice Chase (5-y-o and up) £6,900 2m................... (5:00)

209³ FABRICATOR 7-11-2 K F O'Brien, ...(10 to 1) 1
619⁶ FURRY STAR 7-11-6 J Jones, ...(10 to 1) 2
LADY OLEIN (Ire) 5-10-7 C F Swan, ...(5 to 4 fav) 3
556⁵ DORAN'S TOWN LAD 6-11-8 G Bradley, ...(3 to 1) 4
BEE-FRIEND 9-11-2 T Horgan, ...(16 to 1) 5
575⁵ PINEWOOD LAD 6-11-2 C O'Dwyer, ...(12 to 1) 6
TAWNEY FLAME 7-11-2 M Dwyer, ...(6 to 1) 7
474 PALMROCK DONNA 6-11-4 (7*) P A Roche, ...(20 to 1) 8
467⁴ WINCHLING 8-11-2 F Woods, ...(16 to 1) f
635 SUITS ME FINE 10-11-2 J Shortt, ...(20 to 1) pu
Dist: 5l, ¾l, 4½l, 8l. 4m 7.60s. (10 Ran).
(Mrs C Marks), J T R Dreaper

675 Irish National Bookmakers INH Flat Race (5-y-o) £3,450 2m.................(5:30)

BETTYS THE BOSS (Ire) 11-4 (5*) Mr H F Cleary, ..(10 to 1) 1
513⁴ FOULKSCOURT DUKE (Ire) 11-9 (5*) Mr J A Nash, (12 to 1) 2
BLAZING TRAIL (Ire) 11-7 (7*) Mr M P Dunne, ...(4 to 1) 3
536⁴ CUCHULLAINS GOLD (Ire) 12-0 Mr A J Martin, ...(7 to 1) 4
292 MISS POLLERTON (Ire) 11-2 (7*) Mr M J Bowe, ...(12 to 1) 5
536² KING OF THE WORLD (Ire) 12-0 Mr P Fenton, ...(5 to 4 fav) 6
SHEELIN LAD (Ire) 11-7 (7*) Mr D A Harney, ...(12 to 1) 7
536 LONG'S EXPRESS (Ire) 11-2 (7*) Mr B Lennon, ...(16 to 1) 8
TULLOVIN CASTLE (Ire) 11-2 (7*) Mr P O'Connell, (33 to 1) 9
536⁷ CALAMITY CANE (Ire) 11-9 Mr A P O'Brien, ...(12 to 1) 10
VALMAR (Ire) 11-7 (7*) Mr A K Wyse, ...(20 to 1) 11
BREFFNI MELODY (Ire) 11-9 (5*) Mr G J Harford, ..(14 to 1) 12
534 THE SILVER ROLLS 11-7 (7*) Mr R M Murphy, ...(16 to 1) 13
255⁶ CAILIN RUA (Ire) 11-4 (5*) Mr A E Lacy, ...(14 to 1) 14
540 DESMOND GOLD (Ire) 12-0 Mr J A Berry, ...(14 to 1) 15
SAFRANE 11-11 (3*) Mr A R Coonan, ...(12 to 1) 16
FRIENDLY BID (Ire) 11-2 (7*) Mr N Moran, ...(33 to 1) 17
540 TYPHOON JOE (Ire) 11-9 (5*) Mrs J M Mullins, ...(6 to 1) 18
LADY JOANNE (Ire) 11-2 (7*) Mr A Daly, ...(33 to 1) 19
491 HILLHEAD PRINCE (Ire) 11-7 (7*) Miss V K Ferris, (50 to 1) 20
Dist: ½l, sht-hd, 5l, 3l. 3m 55.50s. (20 Ran).
(South Teffia Racing Club), F Flood

SOUTHWELL (good to soft)
Monday October 4th
Going Correction: PLUS 1.20 sec. per fur.

676 Friends Provident Handicap Chase (0-115 5-y-o and up) £1,987 2m........... (3:50)

BELSTONE FOX [115] 8-12-0 A Maguire, *trkd ldr, led 4 out, sn clr, eased r-in.* (5 to 2 fav op 13 to 8 tchd 11 to 4) 1
521 BUMPTIOUS BOY [90] 9-10-3 D Bridgwater, *hld up, hdwy 5 out, styd on frm 3 out, no ch wth wnr.*
........................(12 to 1 tchd 16 to 1) 2
500³ MAGIC SOLDIER [95] 8-10-8 R Marley, *led, rdn and hdd 4 out, one pace and btn whn hit nxt.*
........................(5 to 1 op 6 to 1 tchd 9 to 2) 3
ISLAND JETSETTER [105] 7-10-13 (5*) T Eley, *chsd ldrs, rdn and hit 6 out, sn wknd.* (6 to 1 op 5 to 1) 4
596 TIGERS PET [107] 9-11-6 S Smith Eccles, *not fluent, al beh.*.................(11 to 2 op 4 to 1) 5
445⁸ KNIGHT'S SPUR (USA) [101] 6-11-0 G McCourt, *chsd ldrs till f 6th.*........(100 to 30 op 7 to 2 tchd 4 to 1) f
SINGING SAM [90] 8-10-3 A Merrigan, *in tch, hit second, blun and uns rdr 4th.*..........(20 to 1 op 14 to 1) ur
Dist: 6l, 5l, 2l, 8l. 4m 23.80s. a 24.80s (7 Ran).
SR: 44/13/13/21/15/-/-/ (Mrs M P Sutton), D Nicholson

677 Holsten Pils & L.V. Schools Handicap Chase (0-115 5-y-o and up) £1,935 2½m 110yds........................... (4:20)

595² GLENSHANE LAD [100] 7-11-5 N Williamson, *hld up, hit second and beh, hdwy 8th, led 2 out, ran on wl.*
........................(3 to 1 op 5 to 2 tchd 7 to 2) 1
BALTIC BROWN [105] 8-11-10 Gary Lyons, *led second to tenth, rdn and outpcd 4 out, kpt on wl frm 2 out.*
........................(7 to 1 op 8 to 1) 2
SANDYBRAES [109] 8-12-0 A Maguire, *prmnt, led tenth, rdn and hdd 2 out, wknd appr last.* (7 to 2 op 9 to 4) 3
544 PORTAVOGIE [92] (bl) 9-10-4 (7*) Mr D Parker, *in tch till outpcd and beh hfwy, styd on frm 4 out.*......(14 to 1) 4
550² SECRET SUMMIT (USA) [94] (v) 7-10-8 (5*) T Eley, *chsd ldrs, pushed alng 7th, hit 9th and tenth, sn lost pl, beh whn blun last.*..................(11 to 2 op 4 to 1) 5
317² BEN TIRRAN [91] (v) 9-10-10 D Telfer, *al beh, tld off hfwy.*
........................(16 to 1 op 14 to 1) 6
DRAGONS DEN [107] 7-11-12 G Upton, *led till hdd and f second.*...........(9 to 4 fav op 3 to 1 tchd 7 to 2) f

Dist.: 4l, 2½l, 4l, 20l, 2l. 5m 35.80s. a 32.80s (7 Ran).
SR: 9/10/11/-/   (Mrs Harry J Duffey), K C Bailey

SOUTHWELL (A.W) (std)
Monday October 4th
Going Correction: PLUS 0.85 sec. per fur.

678 **Carmen Novices' Hurdle (4-y-o and up) £1,087 3m.................(2:20)**

BALLYLEMON (Ire) 5-10-12 S Smith Eccles, *cl up, led 6th, rdn alng 5 out, drvn clr appr 3 out, fnshd lme.*
...............(2 to 1 on op 3 to 1 on tchd 4 to 1 on)   1
VALATCH 5-10-12 B Dalton, *led to 6th, cl up till rdn appr 3 out, styd on one pace, fnshd tired.* (16 to 1 op 14 to 1)   2
552³ GREEN'S SEAGO (USA) 5-10-12 G McCourt, *in tch, rdn alng tenth, sn one pace.* (3 to 1 op 4 to 1 tchd 5 to 1)   3
SIANISKI 4-10-5 D Murphy, *cl up, hit 8th, sn lost pl, beh whn pld up bef tenth....*(5 to 1 op 6 to 1 tchd 7 to 1)   pu
Dist: 5l, 15l. 6m 28.30s. a 51.30s (4 Ran).

(David F Wilson), T Thomson Jones

679 **Tosca Handicap Hurdle (0-115 4-y-o and up) £1,464 2½m.................(2:50)**

553* ELLTEE-ESS [92] (bl) 8-11-6 A Maguire, *made all, sn clr, hit 3 out, styd on wl, unchlgd.*.................(6 to 4 jt-fav op 5 to 4 tchd 13 to 8)   1
523³ HIRAM B BIRDBATH [100] (bl) 7-11-9 (5*) Mrs P Nash, *hld up, hit 6th, mstk 8th, sn rdn alng, no imprsn.* (6 to 4 jt-fav tchd 13 to 8)   2
347⁴ SECRET LIASON [91] 7-11-5 D Bridgwater, *prmnt, chsd wnr frm 3rd, hit 7th, rdn 9th, styd on one pace.*
................(3 to 1 tchd 7 to 2)   3
370 ELDER PRINCE [86] 7-11-0 R Garritty, *in tch, reminders and lost pl 6th, tld off nxt.*......(20 to 1 op 10 to 1)   4
Dist: 20l, 4l, 15l. 5m 10.40s. a 29.40s (4 Ran).

(D A Johnson), R J Weaver

680 **East Midlands Electricity Plc Claiming Hurdle (4-y-o and up) £1,129 2¼m...(3:20)**

552* HAVE A NIGHTCAP 4-11-0 G McCourt, *al prmnt, pushed alng 7th, led 4 out, sn rdn clr, unchlgd.*
................(13 to 8 fav op 6 to 4 tchd 2 to 1)   1
353² SAFETY (USA) (bl) 6-11-5 D Skyrme, *chsd ldr, led 6th to 4 out, sn rdn, no ch wth wnr.*......(11 to 4 op 2 to 1)   2
KARAMOJA 4-11-8 D Murphy, *prmnt, hit 7th and 8th, sn wknd, tld off 4 out.*................(5 to 2 op 4 to 1)   3
323⁹ GRUBBY 4-10-4 (3*) S Wynne, *led to 6th, wknd quickly and tld off 4 out.*................(33 to 1 op 20 to 1)   4
580⁶ BALLYANTO 8-10-2 (7*) Mr D Parker, *mstks, al beh, tld off bef 7th, pld up before 4 out.*.......(6 to 1 tchd 7 to 1)   pu
Dist: 25l, 8l, 1½l. 4m 33.30s. a 21.30s (5 Ran).
SR: 26/6/1/-/-/   (R A M Racecourses Ltd), J L Harris

681 **Madame Butterfly Handicap Hurdle (0-120 4-y-o and up) £1,660 2m...........(4:50)**

522² BONDAID [85] 9-11-1 A Maguire, *led to 6th, cl up, led 3 out, rdn and quickened appr last, ran on wl.*
................(5 to 4 op Evens)   1
370* NORTHERN NATION [97] 5-11-13 Diane Clay, *cl up pulling hrd, led 6th to 3 out, rdn and hit nxt, not quicken r-in.*
................(6 to 4 on op 11 to 8 on tchd 5 to 4 on)   2
Won by 5l. 4m 12.60s. a 26.60s (2 Ran).
SR: -/-/   (A J Allright), J White

NEWTON ABBOT (soft)
Tuesday October 5th
Going Correction: PLUS 0.95 sec. per fur.

682 **Knowles Hill Conditional Jockeys' Selling Handicap Chase (5-y-o and up) £1,453 2m 110yds.................(2:20)**

BARONESS ORKZY [85] 7-11-5 R Greene, *chsd ldr, hit 9th, led 3 out, not fluent last, styd on.*
.........(10 to 1 op 12 to 1 tchd 14 to 1 and 7 to 1)   1
596⁷ MY CUP OF TEA [87] (bl) 10-11-4 (3*) L Reynolds, *led, hit 8th and 9th, hdd 3 out, sn btn.....* (7 to 1 op 4 to 1)   2
598⁸ BILL QUILL [94] 9-11-11 (3*) R Darke, *beh, hdwy frm 3 out, no imprsn on ldrs.......* (9 to 4 op 5 to 2 tchd 3 to 1)   3
PALACE GARDENS [85] 9-11-5 R Farrant, *rcd in 3rd, rdn 7th, wknd 3 out.*................(10 to 1 op 6 to 1)   4
602³ GLASS MOUNTAIN [91] (bl) 11-11-8 (3*) P McLoughlin, *nvr gng wl, al beh, rdn and no response frm 6th.*
................(7 to 4 fav op 5 to 4)   5
568⁶ FREE EXPRESSION [85] 8-11-5 M Hourigan, *al beh.*
................(16 to 1 op 12 to 1)   6
KILLELAN LAD [85] 11-11-5 W Marston, *not fluent, al beh, rdn and no response frm 6th....*(12 to 1 op 20 to 1)   7
Dist: 7l, 10l, 12l, 2½l, 25l, 5l. 4m 20.20s. a 23.20s (7 Ran).
SR: 16/11/8/-/   (C I A Paterson), P F Nicholls

683 **Higher Humber Novices' Hurdle (4-y-o and up) £1,516 2¾m.................(2:50)**

TEXAN BABY (Bel) 4-10-13 C Llewellyn, *chsd ldr, led aftr 6th, jmpd slwly 7th and 3 out, drvn clr appr 2 out, pushed out.*................(5 to 4 fav op 6 to 4)   1
524⁸ PRUDENT PEGGY 6-10-9 J Frost, *led, hdd aftr 6th, chlgd 7th to nxt, styd on one pace.......*(5 to 1 tchd 7 to 1)   2
483⁷ FROZEN DROP 6-11-0 Richard Guest, *hdwy to chase ldrs 7th, styd on same pace frm 3 out....*(10 to 1 op 5 to 1)   3
415² DUNKERY BEACON 7-10-9 (5*) R Davis, *hld up, effrt and wnt 3rd 3 out, wknd 2 out.*
................(16 to 1 op 12 to 1 tchd 20 to 1)   4
587⁸ COURT OF KINGS 4-10-8 (5*) R Farrant, *chsd ldrs to 7th.*
................(14 to 1 op 12 to 1 tchd 20 to 1)   5
SHOREHAM LADY 8-10-9 H Davies, *al beh, tld off whn pld up bef 2 out.*................(33 to 1 op 20 to 1)   pu
565⁴ DAUNTLESS KNIGHT (USA) 5-11-0 Peter Hobbs, *in tch, niggled alng aftr 4th, wknd 7th, tld off whn pld up bef 2 out.*................(10 to 1 op 5 to 1)   pu
PAPER STAR 6-10-9 G Bradley, *al beh, tld off whn pld up bef 3 out.*................(10 to 1 op 5 to 1)   pu
REALLY A RASCAL 6-11-0 P Holley, *hld up, hdwy 6th, shaken up 3 out, sn wknd, tld off whn pld up bef nxt.*
................(6 to 1 op 3 to 1)   pu
Dist: 12l, 10l, 8l, 2½l. 5m 44.40s. a 45.40s (9 Ran).

(John McKenna), N A Twiston-Davies

684 **Les Seward Memorial Challenge Trophy Handicap Chase (5-y-o and up) £2,788 2m 5f.................(3:20)**

DIS TRAIN [123] 9-11-8 J Osborne, *jmpd wl, made all, unchlgd.*
.....(11 to 10 on op Evens tchd 5 to 4 and 5 to 4 on)   1
WIDE BOY [125] 11-11-3 (7*) Mr G Lewis, *chsd wnr frm 5th, nvr on terms.*.........(11 to 4 op 5 to 2 tchd 3 to 1)   2
566 MAJOR MATCH (NZ) [117] 11-11-2 H Davies, *chsd wnr 3rd to 5th, effrt and hit 9th, sn btn.....* (5 to 1 op 3 to 1)   3
CAMDEN BELLE [101] 11-10-0 M A FitzGerald, *drpd rear 3rd, tld off frm 9th.*..........(6 to 1 tchd 8 to 1)   4
Dist: 8l, 12l, dist. 5m 24.20s. a 24.20s (4 Ran).
SR: 52/46/26/-/   (M L Oberstein), S E Sherwood

685 **Wynnards Mead Claiming Hurdle (4,5,6-y-o) £1,488 2m 1f.................(3:50)**

AUVILLAR (USA) (v) 5-10-12 D J Burchell, *dsptd second till led 5th, drvn clr frm 2 out.*.........(5 to 1 tchd 4 to 1)   1
552⁴ MABTHUL (USA) 5-10-13 M A FitzGerald, *dsptd second till chsd wnr aftr 5th, no imprsn frm 2 out.*
................(8 to 1 op 7 to 1 tchd 10 to 1)   2
312⁵ ELITE REG (bl) 4-11-5 H Dunwoody, *led to 5th, sn rdn, found nothing.*............(7 to 4 on op 5 to 4)   3
567⁹ HONEY'S FORTUNE 6-10-11 N Hawke, *sn toiling in 4th pl, rdn aftr fourth, tld off whn pld up bef 3 out.*
................(25 to 1 op 20 to 1 tchd 14 to 1)   pu
484² PREENKA GIRL (Fr) 4-11-4 J Lower, *al wl beh, tld off whn pld up aftr 3 out.*........(4 to 1 op 3 to 1 tchd 5 to 2)   pu
Dist: 10l, 15l. 4m 23.20s. a 33.20s (5 Ran).

(Mrs J M Snape), D Burchell

686 **Bowring Marsh McLennan Novices' Chase (5-y-o and up) £1,722 3¼m 110yds.................(4:20)**

DON'T LIGHT UP 7-11-3 G Bradley, *hit 3rd, steadied rear, hdwy 13th, led 3 out, drvn out.......*(7 to 4 op 6 to 4)   1
563³ EARTH SUMMIT 5-11-0 C Llewellyn, *not fluent 3rd, in tch, pressing ldrs whn hit 4 out, outpcd 2 out, rallied and ev ch last, no extr.....* (13 to 8 fav op 5 to 4 tchd 7 to 2)   2
593 HASTY SALVO 9-10-12 S Earle, *led to 7th, led ag'n 16th, hdd 3 out, sn btn.......*(8 to 1 op 6 to 1 tchd 10 to 1)   3
593 MISTY (NZ) (bl) 6-11-3 B Powell, *dsptd ld 4th, led 7th, hdd and hit 16th, sn btn.............*(3 to 1 tchd 7 to 2)   4
525 ROUCHEAL 8-11-3 N Hawke, *sn beh, lost tch 13th, tld off whn pld up bef nxt...............*(33 to 1 op 20 to 1)   pu
Dist: Hd, 30l, 8l. 7m 1.90s. a 41.90s (5 Ran).

(Geoffrey Solman), P F Nicholls

687 **Mothecombe Handicap Hurdle (0-120 4-y-o and up) £1,855 2¾m.................(4:50)**

MEDITATOR [100] (bl) 9-11-3 (7*) S Curran, *dsptd ld, led 6th, came clr frm 3 out, easily....*(10 to 1 op 7 to 1)   1
SPECIAL ACCOUNT [99] 7-11-9 N Mann, *sn in tch, styd on frm 3 out, no ch wth wnr........*(5 to 2 fav op 7 to 4)   2
IVYCHURCH (USA) [83] 7-10-7³ J Frost, *beh, moderate prog appr 2 out, ran on, not a dngr.*
................(16 to 1 op 10 to 1 tchd 20 to 1)   3
SILVER AGE (USA) [93] 7-10-12 (5*) R Farrant, *hdwy to chase ldrs 3rd, rdn 2 out, wknd r-in.*
................(9 to 2 op 7 to 2 tchd 5 to 1)   4
629⁷ TEKLA (Fr) [83] 8-10-7 B Powell, *in tch, pressed ldrs 7th, sn wknd.*..............(12 to 1 op 16 to 1 tchd 25 to 1)   5

KNIGHT IN SIDE [88] 7-10-12 C Maude, *made most, hdd 6th, hmpd bend appr 7th, sn rdn, btn 3 out, tld off.*
.......................(3 to 1 op 2 to 1 tchd 7 to 2) 6
569[6] MIDNIGHT STRIKE (USA) [99] (bl) 9-11-9 W McFarland, *hld up, jmpd slwly 3rd, in tch whn mstk and pld up 3 out.*
.......................(5 to 1 op 7 to 2) pu
Dist: 12l, 6l, hd, 25l, dist. 5m 38.70s. a 39.70s (7 Ran).
(Miss Jacqueline S Doyle), Miss Jacqueline S Doyle

MALLOW (IRE) (good to yielding)
Wednesday October 6th

688   County Cork 3-Y-O Claiming Hurdle £2,243 2m.................................(2:30)

529[6] TEMPLEVARY BOY (Ire) 10-9 T Horgan, ...	(7 to 1)	1
DANCING VISION (Ire) 11-1 G M O'Neill, ...	(7 to 2)	2
GLOWING LINES 9-11 (5*) C P Dunne, ...	(8 to 1)	3
529[4] GARDENVALE VIC (Ire) 10-4 (5*) M G Cleary, ...	(7 to 2)	4
617[5] TORC MOUNTAIN (Ire) (bl) 10-11 B Sheridan, ...	(10 to 1)	5
529 ALIBAR'S PET (Ire) 10-7 (7*) K P Gaule, ...	(10 to 3 fav)	6
470[3] CHRISTY MOORE (Ire) 10-9 A Powell, ...	(14 to 1)	7
REGAL PRETENDER (Ire) 10-9 H Rogers, ...	(8 to 1)	8
RED ROOSTER (Ire) 10-6 (5*) M A Davey, ...	(20 to 1)	9
290[6] SWEET PEACH (Ire) 9-9 (7*) J P Broderick, ...	(25 to 1)	10
VLADIVOSTOK 10-5 J Magee, ...	(10 to 1)	11
SYGNE OF RICHES (Ire) 10-7 (7*) P A Roche, ...	(25 to 1)	f
GROUND CONTROL (Ire) 10-4 (5*) D P Murphy, ...	(14 to 1)	f
Dist: 3½l, 3½l, nk, 2½l. 3m 52.80s. (13 Ran).
(C Munnelly), A J Martin

689   Kerry Handicap Hurdle (0-116 4-y-o and up) £2,243 2m 5f.................(3:00)

557[5] KILIAN MY BOY [-] 10-12-0 J Evans, ...	(8 to 1)	1
637[3] CARRON HILL [-] 6-10-6 C F Swan, ...	(4 to 1)	2
574 BROOK COTTAGE (Ire) [-] 5-11-1 P Worthington, ..	(10 to 1)	3
557[9] MARBLE CITY GIRL [-] 8-10-0 (5*) C O'Brien, ...	(20 to 1)	4
557 AWBEG ROVER (Ire) [-] 5-9-10 (7*) P A Roche, ..	(16 to 1)	5
557 MARY GINA [-] (bl) 8-9-4 (5*) T J O'Sullivan, ...	(25 to 1)	6
571[4] POOR TIMES (Ire) [-] 5-9-12 (5*) C P Dunne, ...	(20 to 1)	7
574[6] SHREWD MOVE [-] (bl) 4-9-13 J Jones, ...	(14 to 1)	8
571[8] THE COBH GALE [-] 6-9-11 H Rogers, ...	(20 to 1)	9
574[8] NISHIKI (USA) [-] 4-10-7 S Jenkins, ...	(12 to 1)	10
557 GALES JEWEL [-] 7-9-3 (5*) M G Cleary, ...	(20 to 1)	11
637[4] NANCYS LAD [-] 6-10-0 F Woods, ...	(10 to 1)	12
532[3] DANCINGCINDERELLA [-] (bl) 9-10-9 M Patton,	(7 to 2 fav)	13
466[9] SYLVIA'S SAFFRON [-] 6-10-3 J Collins, ...	(20 to 1)	14
THE MAD MONK [-] 8-11-6 T Horgan, ...	(20 to 1)	15
ABBEY EMERALD [-] 7-9-10 (5*) T P Treacy, ...	(33 to 1)	16
571 KINGS LORD [-] 6-10-2 C O'Dwyer, ...	(20 to 1)	17
302[8] FAIR GO [-] 7-9-12 (7*) Miss C A Harrison, ...	(20 to 1)	18
538 CLOSUTTON EXPRESS [-] 7-9-11 (7*) M Kelly, ...	(10 to 1)	19
229[9] BRAVE SHARON [-] 9-9-1 (7*) J P Broderick, ..	(33 to 1)	20
135 SUNDAY WORLD (USA) [-] 7-10-5 A J O'Brien, ...	(20 to 1)	21
574 ASHBORO (Ire) [-] 4-10-11 J F Titley, ...	(20 to 1)	22
MYELLA PRINCE (Ire) [-] 4-10-8 K F O'Brien, ...	(16 to 1)	su
584 WAR DEVIL [-] 7-10-4 N Byrne, ...	(20 to 1)	pu
Dist: ¾l, 6l, 7l, ½l. 5m 23.90s. (24 Ran).
(Mrs Eileen Crowe), Patrick G Kelly

690   Buttevant E.B.F. Novice Chase (5-y-o and up) £2,760 2½m.................(3:30)

575[2] FRIENDS OF GERALD 7-12-0 C F Swan, ...	(2 to 1 on)	1
572* GRANDONHILL 6-11-7 (7*) J P Broderick, ...	(8 to 1)	2
NEW CO (Ire) 4-11-10 T Horgan, ...	(4 to 1)	3
251 RUSSIAN GALE (Ire) 5-11-5 J Collins, ...	(33 to 1)	4
327[4] CLONEENVERB 9-11-4 (5*) D P Murphy, ...	(14 to 1)	5
FEATHERED GALE 6-12-0 T J Taaffe, ...	(10 to 1)	6
635[9] MAKE ME AN ISLAND 8-11-9 G M O'Neill, ...	(14 to 1)	7
475[5] WAR OFFICE 6-11-9 J Jones, ...	(33 to 1)	8
507[2] KNOW HOW 7-12-0 P M Verling, ...	(20 to 1)	9
574* MORNING DREAM 6-12-0 J F Titley, ...	(8 to 1)	10
583 QUIET MONEY 6-11-9 (5*) D P Geoghegan, ...	(20 to 1)	11
507 KIL KIL CASTLE 6-11-9 (5*) T J O'Sullivan, ...	(25 to 1)	12
BLACKPOOL BRIDGE 8-12-0 C O'Brien, ...	(25 to 1)	13
507 WOODEN MINSTREL 7-11-4 (5*) D T Evans, ...	(25 to 1)	14
15 STRONG CHERRY 7-11-2 (7*) Mr K Taylor, ...	(12 to 1)	ur
Dist: 2½l, 10l, 3½l, ½l. 5m 16.10s. (15 Ran).
(R Sheehan), J E Kiely

691   Lee Racecall Australian/Irish Challenge Handicap Chase (0-102 4-y-o and up) £2,243 2½m.................(4:00)

512[2] BENS DILEMMA [-] 8-9-10 (7*) J P Broderick, ...	(7 to 1)	1
583[2] INCH MAID [-] 7-11-5 J Evans, ...	(2 to 1 fav)	2
532[6] GARRYDOOLIS [-] 7-11-9 J F Titley, ...	(12 to 1)	3
468[8] BOG LEAF VI [-] (bl) 10-9-4 (5*) C O'Brien, ...	(10 to 1)	4
573[5] BUNNINADDEN [-] 10-10-9 P Worthington, ...	(7 to 1)	5
CROW RUN [-] 11-10-0 C O'Dwyer, ...	(20 to 1)	6
178[8] ABBEY JACK [-] (bl) 6-10-2 F Woods, ...	(20 to 1)	7
ALTNABROCKY [-] 9-11-3 T Horgan, ...	(12 to 1)	8
303[6] TIGH AN CHEOIL [-] (bl) 9-10-6 A J O'Brien, ...	(12 to 1)	9
635[6] DEL MONTE BOY [-] 8-11-2 S Jenkins, ...	(8 to 1)	10

---

170 ANNETTE'S DELIGHT [-] 14-9-11 (5*) M A Davey,	(20 to 1)	bd
474* LA MODE LADY [-] 8-10-7 (7*) P A Roche, ...	(8 to 1)	bd
JO-JA [-] 7-10-7 M Patton, ...	(20 to 1)	su
LA CERISE [-] (bl) 10-10-0 F J Flood, ...	(12 to 1)	pu
COOLADERRA LADY [-] 7-10-9 C F Swan, ...	(14 to 1)	pu
Dist: 7l, 3l, 12l, 3l. 5m 15.30s. (15 Ran).
(Liam McAteer), Liam McAteer

692   Mallow INH Flat Race (4-y-o) £2,243 2m ....(5:30)

CALLISOE BAY (Ire) 11-9 Mr P Fenton, ...	(9 to 2 fav)	1
530[6] HILL OF TULLOW (Ire) 11-6 (3*) Mr M F Barrett, ...	(10 to 1)	2
BUTCHES BOY (Ire) 11-9 Mr M Dunne, ...	(8 to 1)	3
531[4] DUN OENGUS (Ire) 11-1 (3*) Miss C Hutchinson, ..	(5 to 1)	4
504[3] NOT MY LINE (Ire) 11-9 Mr J P Dempsey, ...	(10 to 1)	5
UNSINKABLE BOXER (Ire) 11-2 (7*) Mr K Whelan,	(20 to 1)	6
TWO HILLS FOLLY (Ire) 10-13 (5*) Mr J A Nash, ...	(16 to 1)	7
BRIDGE PEARL (Ire) 11-9 Mr A J Martin, ...	(10 to 1)	8
LITTLE AND OFTEN (Ire) 10-11 (7*) Mr D J Kavanagh,		
....	(12 to 1)	9
555 THE ODD TIME (Ire) 11-9 Mr J E Kiely, ...	(6 to 1)	10
JO JO BOY (Ire) 11-4 (5*) Mr H F Cleary, ...	(5 to 1)	11
SIOBHAILIN DUBH (Ire) 11-4 Mr A P O'Brien, ...	(7 to 1)	12
530 JACK'S BAR (Ire) 11-2 (7*) Mr W M O'Sullivan, ...	(25 to 1)	13
620 RED BARONS LADY (Ire) 10-11 (7*) Mr J Connolly,	(10 to 1)	14
638 BALLYBRAZIL BOY (Ire) 11-2 (7*) Mr M Brennan, ..	(14 to 1)	15
508[6] GOODLUCKTOYA (Ire) 10-13 (7*) Mr J M O'Brien,	(12 to 1)	16
THE CRIOSRA (Ire) 11-9 Mr S R Murphy, ...	(12 to 1)	17
COOLBAWN ROSE (Ire) 11-4 Mr M Phillips, ...	(20 to 1)	18
531 BRONTE BEAT (Ire) 10-13[2] (7*) Mr T J Nagle, ...	(33 to 1)	19
BOLD CAT (Ire) 11-2 (7*) Mr J Lombard, ...	(20 to 1)	20
535[5] WEE RIVER (Ire) 11-9 Mr T S Costello, ...	(13 to 2)	21
COOLBAWN BRAMBLE (Ire) 11-4 Mr P J Healy, ...(20 to 1)		22
Dist: Hd, 13l, nk, 12l. 3m 41.30s. (22 Ran).
(Donal Kenneally), Michael O'Connor

TOWCESTER (soft)
Wednesday October 6th
Going Correction: PLUS 0.50 sec. per fur. (races 1,3,6), PLUS 0.60 (2,4,5)

693   Park Selling Hurdle (4-y-o and up) £1,822 2m.................................(2:20)

642* SKITTLE ALLEY 7-11-13 Diane Clay, *chsd ldg pair frm 4th, led appr 2 out, rdn out.* (11 to 4 op 2 to 1 tchd 3 to 1)		1
526[5] FUSSY LADY 6-11-1 L Harvey, *chsd ldg pair frm 4th, styd on from 2 out.*...........(11 to 4 op 5 to 2 tchd 4 to 1)		2
324[3] VIAGGIO 5-11-6 J Osborne, *led second till tired and hdd appr 2 out, no extr...*(7 to 4 fav op 5 to 4 tchd 2 to 1)		3
SHAFAYIF 4-11-0 M Bosley, *chsd ldrs till outpcd frm 4th, styd on from 2 out...*...........(14 to 1 op 7 to 1)		4
SINGING GOLD 7-11-6 G Rowe, *took keen hold early, settled in rear, beh 4th, hdwy o'r 2 out, nvr nrr.* .... (25 to 1 op 20 to 1 tchd 33 to 1)		5
HELLO VANOS 5-10-10 (3*) W Marston, *in cl tch till outpcd frm 4th.*...........(25 to 1 op 16 to 1 tchd 33 to 1)		6
207 GREAT HAND 7-10-13 T Grantham, *led 1st, wth ldr, ev ch 3 out, sn wknd.*...........(16 to 1 op 12 to 1)		7
460[6] L'ENCHERE 8-11-1 (7*) Paul McEntee, *al beh, tld off frm 4th.*...........(33 to 1 op 20 to 1)		8
BE THE BEST 5-10-6 (7*) Mr M Gingell, *al beh, tld off frm 4th.*...........(25 to 1 op 14 to 1)		9
Dist: 6l, sht-hd, 10l, 4l, ½l, 3½l, dist, 12l. 4m 3.60s. a 20.60s (9 Ran).
(P Riley), W Clay

694   BBC Radio Northampton Novices' Chase (5-y-o and up) £2,604 2m 110yds.... (2:50)

SOCIAL CLIMBER 9-11-0 S McNeill, *made virtually all, rdn out.*...........(7 to 1 op 6 to 1 tchd 15 to 2)		1
521[12] DEXTRA DOVE 6-11-0 S Earle, *nvr far away, cld o'r 3 out, ev ch last, no extr.*......(2 to 1 fav op 5 to 4 tchd 3 to 10)		2
677* GLENSHANE LAD 7-11-7 (7ex) N Williamson, *in cl tch till lost pl 5th, hdwy 5 out, styd on.* .... (13 to 8 fav op 6 to 4 tchd 7 to 4)		3
586 ABLE PLAYER (USA) 6-11-7 C Grant, *in cl tch til wknd o'r 4 out...*...........(5 to 1 op 4 to 1)		4
464[4] MUTUAL BENEFIT 6-11-0 R Dunwoody, *wth wnr, led briefly 7th, ev ch 4 out, wknd nxt.* (20 to 1 op 10 to 1)		5
MONAUGHTY MAN 7-10-7 (7*) P McLoughlin, *beh frm 7th.* .... (50 to 1 op 33 to 1)		6
HAIRY MAC 7-11-0 B Clifford, *cld up, blun badly 5th, reco'ring whn hmpd and uns rdr.* .... (11 to 1 op 20 to 1 tchd 33 to 1 and 10 to 1)		ur
Dist: 4l, 12l, 5l, 15l, 5l. 4m 19.10s. a 17.10s (7 Ran).
SR: 14/10/5/-/ (L G Kimber), Andrew Turnell

695   Wellingborough Novices' Hurdle (4-y-o and up) £1,480 2m.................(3:20)

LINPAC WEST 7-10-13 A Maguire, *hld up in mid-div, smooth hdwy to ld o'r 2 out, hrd held.*
.... (5 to 2 on tchd 9 to 4 on and 2 to 1 on) 1

SIMPLY (Ire) 4-10-12 G McCourt, *chsd ldrs, cld 3 out, ev ch last, sn rdn and no imprsn on wnr*...(8 to 1 op 6 to 1) 2
ROAD TO FAME 6-10-13 P Holley, *led second till hdd o'r 2 out, one pace*.................. (20 to 1 op 12 to 1) 3
483² URBAN COWBOY 6-10-13 S McNeill, *hld up in tch, styd on frm 2 out*............(8 to 1 op 7 to 1 tchd 9 to 1) 4
597 ARCTIC LIFE (Ire) 4-11-1³ Mr P Graffin, *led 1st, cl up till wknd 3 out*.......... (16 to 1 op 33 to 1 tchd 66 to 1) 5
456⁴ CONCINNITY (USA) 4-10-12 R Dunwoody, *trkd ldrs till wkng o'r 3 out*.................... (10 to 1 op 7 to 1) 6
MILLIES OWN 6-10-13 M Perrett, *trkd ldrs, rdn alng and mstk 3 out, sn btn*.................(33 to 1 op 20 to 1) 7
BARELY BLACK 5-10-13 W Humphreys, *beh, hdwy o'r 3 out, wknd nxt*................... (50 to 1 op 33 to 1) 8
ALWAYS ALLIED (Ire) 5-10-13 D Skyrme, *trkd ldrs till wknd quickly o'r 3 out*.............(66 to 1 op 33 to 1) 9
233² BALLYWILLIAM (Ire) 4-10-12 S Smith Eccles, *al beh, tld off whn pld up bef 2 out.* (14 to 1 op 12 to 1 tchd 16 to 1) pu
RBF ARIANNE 5-10-1 (7") N Collum, *al beh, tld off 4th, pld up bef last*...................(33 to 1 op 20 to 1) pu
Dist: 1l, 10l, nk, 1l, 3½l, 6l, 6l, 6l. 3m 58.70s. a 15.70s (11 Ran).
SR: 8/6/-/-/-/-/ (Group 1 Racing (1991) Ltd), C W C Elsey

696 Carling Black Label Handicap Chase (0-125 5-y-o and up) £3,080 3m 1f....(3:50)

TORT [109] 9-10-0 (3") W Marston, *made all, jmpd rght and hit last, ran on wl*................... (12 to 1 op 7 to 1) 1
518³ KNIGHT OIL [125] (bl) 10-11-5 J Osborne, *hld up in tch, hdwy o'r 5 out, no extr und pres.*
.... (5 to 1 op 4 to 1 tchd 11 to 2) 2
OVERHEREOVERTHERE [107] 10-10-1 R Supple, *beh, hdwy appr 3 out, styd on.*
.....................(8 to 1 op 7 to 1 tchd 9 to 1 and 10 to 1) 3
624¹ RADICAL LADY [110] 9-9-11 (7",7ex) J Supple, *trkd ldrs till wknd o'r 2 out.*.....(9 to 4 fav op 4 to 1 tchd 5 to 2) 4
RIO HAINA [110] 8-10-4 C Llewellyn, *cl up till wknd 4 out.*
.... (10 to 1 op 4 to 1) 5
LAUDERDALE LAD [106] 11-10-0 J R Kavanagh, *jmpd slwly second, in tch till blun badly and lost pl 6th, tld off frm 13th*................... (25 to 1 op 20 to 1) 6
DERRING VALLEY [107] (bl) 8-10-1¹ Peter Hobbs, *cl up, second and ev ch whn f 4 out*... (10 to 1 tchd 12 to 1) f
600² YIRAGAN [111] 11-10-0 (5") R Davis, *cl up whn blun and uns rdr 3rd*...(5 to 2 tchd 9 to 4 and 11 to 4) ur
Dist: 1½l, 15l, 4l, 10l, 6l. 6m 35.80s. a 20.80s (8 Ran).
SR: 17/31/-/-/-/ (R A H Perkins), P T Dalton

697 Permit Trainers' Association Amateur Riders' Handicap Chase (0-115 5-y-o and up) £2,733 2¾m................. (4:20)

SUNBEAM TALBOT [112] 12-11-7 (7") Mr S Bush, *trkd ldrs, ran on to ld nr finish*............ (7 to 4 fav op 2 to 1) 1
A LAD INSANE [102] 12-11-4 Mr M Armytage, *cl up, led aftr tenth till hdd nr finish.*
.....................(11 to 1 op 5 to 1 tchd 12 to 1) 2
FRISCO CITY [94] 7-10-3 (7") Mr M Rimell, *cl up till drpd rear 9th, sn rallied, ev ch 3 out, btn appr last.*
.....................(2 to 1 op 7 to 4 tchd 9 to 4) 3
602² THEY ALL FORGOT ME [89] 6-9-12 (7") Mr G Lewis, *in cl tch till wknd o'r 3 out.*
................(3 to 1 op 2 to 1 tchd 100 to 30 and 7 to 2) 4
596⁵ FATHER PADDY [85] 11-9-8 (7") Miss K Ellis, *led til hdd aftr tenth, cl up till wknd o'r 3 out.*
.....................(5 to 1 op 4 to 1 tchd 16 to 1) 5
345⁵ CURAHEEN BOY [92] 13-10-1 (7") Miss J Butler, *trkd ldrs till mstk and lost pl 12th (water), tld off.*
....................(14 to 1 op 8 to 1 tchd 16 to 1) 6
Dist: ½l, 5l, 15l, 3½l, 30l. 5m 52.60s. a 26.60s (6 Ran).
(Mrs R Legouix), A P Jones

698 Tote Credit Handicap Hurdle (0-115 4-y-o and up) £2,232 2m.................(4:50)

610* ROC COLOR (Fr) [102] 4-10-10 (7ex) G Bradley, *trkd ldrs, led appr 2 out, ran on wl.*............ (7 to 2 op 2 to 1) 1
591* TAYLORS PRINCE [92] (v) 6-10-0 V Smith, *hld up, hdwy o'r 2 out, kpt on und pres r-in.*
.... (2 to 1 fav op 3 to 1 tchd 100 to 30) 2
401 BEN ZABEEDY [101] 8-10-9 G McCourt, *in tch, cld o'r 3 out, ev ch 2 out, sn hrd rdn and no extr.*
.....................(2 to 1 op 7 to 4 tchd 9 to 2) 3
499⁵ JUST ROSIE [96] 4-10-4 S McNeill, *chsd ldrs, one pace frm o'r 2 out.*................ (15 to 2 op 6 to 1 tchd 8 to 1) 4
569⁵ WOLVER GOLD [94] 6-10-2 C Maude, *beh, hdwy o'r 2 out, styd on.*..................... (10 to 1 op 7 to 1) 5
CHILD OF THE MIST [116] 7-11-10 R Dunwoody, *cl up, led 4th till hdd appr 2 out, wknd.*......... (6 to 1 op 8 to 1) 6
569⁷ HIDDEN OATS [99] 6-10-7 B Powell, *hld up in tch, one pace frm o'r 2 out.*.................(14 to 1 op 10 to 1) 7
443¹ MOUNTSHANNON [92] 7-10-0 A Maguire, *trkd ldrs till wknd 3 out.*......................(16 to 1 op 12 to 1) 8
I'M CONFIDENT [100] 9-10-8 S Earle, *led to 4th, sn wknd.*
.....................(33 to 1 op 25 to 1) 9
FRONT PAGE [104] 6-10-12 L Harvey, *prmnt till wknd 4 out.*..................(17 to 2 op 6 to 1 tchd 9 to 1) 10

DRIVING FORCE [108] 7-11-2 D Gallagher, *in tch till drpd rear 5th.*............................(14 to 1 op 12 to 1) 11
499 SILENT CHANT [93] 9-10-1¹ (7") Mr R Griffiths, *al beh, tld off frm 4th*......................(50 to 1 op 25 to 1) 12
MASTER BUSTER [92] 8-10-0 D Skyrme, *al beh, tld off.*
.....................(50 to 1 op 33 to 1) 13
Dist: 2l, 2l, 2l, 2l, nk, nk, ½l, 3½l, 5l, 10l. 3m 55.60s. a 12.60s (13 Ran).
SR: 36/24/31/24/20/41/23/4/8/ (Mrs Susan McCarthy), C P E Brooks

LUDLOW (good)
Thursday October 7th
Going Correction: PLUS 0.05 sec. per fur. (races 1,3,-4,6,7), PLUS 0.30 (2,5)

699 Bridgnorth Novices' Selling Hurdle (4,5,6-y-o) £1,480 2m 5f 110yds...........(2:20)

592⁹ BOXING MATCH 6-10-9 (7") Mr G Lewis, *trkd ldrs, wnt second aftr 4 out, led after 2 out, hit last, drvn out.*
.... (33 to 1 op 14 to 1) 1
565³ NEW STATESMAN 5-11-2 Richard Guest, *trkd ldr aftr 5th, pckd 4 out, hdd aftr 2 out, mstk last, rallied r-in, unbl to quicken.*......................... (3 to 1 op 5 to 2) 2
592⁵ LAW FACULTY (Ire) 4-11-0 S Mackey, *hld up in tch, wnt 3rd 3 out, hrd rdn appr nxt, btn whn mstk last.*
.................(14 to 1 op 8 to 1 tchd 16 to 1) 3
ALDINGTON CHAPPLE 5-11-2 T Wall, *hld up and pld hrd, beh till hdwy und pres aftr 4 out, btn whn mstk last.*
.................(25 to 1 op 20 to 1 tchd 33 to 1) 4
592² MALLYAN 6-10-6 (5") R Davis, *trkd ldrs, wkng whn mstk 3 out, sn beh.*......................(7 to 2 op 5 to 2) 5
YATOO (Ire) 4-11-0 W Knox, *pld hrd, chsd ldrs, hit 4th, wknd aftr 6th, sn beh, tld off whn pulled up after 3 out.*
...........................(33 to 1 op 16 to 1) pu
565² CORNISH COSSACK (NZ) 6-10-9 (7") Mr G Shenkin, *hld up and beh, tld off aftr 4 out, pld up bef 3 out.*
..........(11 to 8 fav op Evens tchd 6 to 4 and 7 to 4) pu
WASTEOFTIME 6-10-11 R Supple, *led, jmpd slwly, hdd 5th, jumped slowly nxt, wknd quickly, beh whn pld up and dismounted bef 2 out.*........ (33 to 1 op 16 to 1) pu
Dist: 2½l, 10l, 4l, 15l. 5m 22.50s. a 25.50s (8 Ran).
(S J Merrick), J M Bradley

700 Invershin Handicap Chase (0-115 4-y-o and up) £2,976 2½m................(2:50)

595* LAKE MISSION [113] 8-11-10 M Richards, *led to 3rd, led ag'n aftr 4th, made rst, styd on wl frm 2 out.*
.... (13 to 8 fav op 6 to 4 tchd 7 to 4 and 2 to 1) 1
BLUSTERY FELLOW [107] 8-11-4 W Humphreys, *slwly away, hld up, wnt 3rd tenth, pressed ldr frm nxt, ev ch appr 3 out, rdn and not quicken betw last 2.*
...................(9 to 2 op 4 to 1 tchd 5 to 1) 2
609¹ ARDCRONEY CHIEF [108] 7-11-5 (7ex) P Holley, *in tch, wnt second 8th, rdn alng frm 6 out, mstk 3 out, one pace.*
...................(7 to 2 op 5 to 2 tchd 4 to 1) 3
198² KITTINGER [104] 12-11-1 Peter Hobbs, *lost pl aftr 9th, rdn and rallied after 5 out, not quicken frm 3 out.*
...................(6 to 1 op 5 to 1 tchd 7 to 1) 4
525³ CHANCERY BUCK [94] 10-10-3 J Frost, *hld up, hdwy aftr 5 out, ev ch appr 3 out, wknd nxt.*...(7 to 1 op 5 to 1) 5
487⁴ SOCKS DOWNE [89] 14-10-0 A Webb, *led 3rd till aftr nxt, chsd ldr till wknd appr 3 out.*....(20 to 1 op 12 to 1) 6
382³ DREAMCOAT (USA) [89] 12-9-10³ (7") Leanne Eldredge, *chsd ldrs, mstk tenth, sn wknd, tld off aftr 5 out.*
.....................(50 to 1 op 20 to 1) 7
Dist: 4l, 2l, 3½l, 8l, 10l, dist. 5m 2.60s. a 11.60s (7 Ran).
SR: 40/30/29/21/3/-/-/ (W T Montgomery), S E Sherwood

701 Radio Shropshire Stayers' Handicap Hurdle (0-125 4-y-o and up) £2,232 3m 1f 110yds.............................. (3:20)

443⁶ HUGLI [99] (bl) 6-10-11 M Richards, *led, drw clr aftr 2 out, drvn out.*..................(14 to 1 op 8 to 1 tchd 16 to 1) 1
601⁵ CARPET CAPERS (USA) [88] 9-10-0 N Williamson, *chsd ldg pair, wnt second 7th, ev ch 4 out, rdn and one pace 2 out.*......(20 to 1 op 16 to 1 tchd 25 to 1 and 33 to 1) 2
437² TRUMPET [91] (bl) 4-9-12 (5") R Davis, *chsd ldg trio, wnt second 8th, ev ch 3 out, one pace frm nxt.*
.................(2 to 1 op 5 to 2 tchd 6 to 1) 3
CAIRNCASTLE [116] 8-12-0 N Mann, *hld up and beh, pushed alng aftr 8th, styd on aftr 3 out, nvr nrr.*
.................(15 to 2 op 5 to 1 tchd 8 to 1) 4
HAWWAR (USA) [88] 6-9-11 (3") W Marston, *chsd ldg quartett till wknd aftr 7th, sn rdn and lost tch.*
.....................(33 to 1 op 16 to 1) 5
459⁴ LASTING MEMORY [99] 7-10-11 J Frost, *hld up and beh, niggled along aftr 6th, some hdwy after nxt, chsd ldr till wknd 4 out, eased whn btn after 2 out.*
...................(9 to 4 fav op 11 to 4) 6
592⁸ ROCHE [88] 7-10-0 A Webb, *hld up and beh, rdn alng aftr 5th, lost tch after 5 out.*.................. (50 to 1) 7

633 KASHAN (Ire) [88] 5-9-7 (7*) Mr G Lewis, *jmpd slwly, chsd ldr in second pl till wknd quickly aftr 7th, sn beh*.
.... (16 to 1 op 12 to 1)   8
REAL PROGRESS (Ire) [104] (bl) 5-11-2 Peter Hobbs, *pld hrd, hld up till hdwy aftr 6th, 4th and rdn whn slpd up bend after 3 out*.................... (3 to 1 op 6 to 4)   su
Dist: 20l, 15l, 6l, 15l, 3½l, 6l, 10l. 6m 11.00s. a 15.00s (9 Ran).
(Viscountess Boyne), S E Sherwood

702 BBC Hereford And Worcester Claiming Hurdle (3-y-o) £1,605 2m............(3:50)

570⁴ HOMEMAKER 10-7 (7*) D Matthews, *chsd ldg pair frm 3rd, slight ld 2 out, drw clr aftr last, cmftbly*.
.... (2 to 1 fav op 6 to 4 tchd 9 to 4)   1
SWISS MOUNTAIN (v) 9-11 (5*) T Eley, *hld up, rapid hdwy to chase ldrs aftr 4th, wnt second appr 2 out, rdn and one pace betw last two*............ (10 to 1 op 8 to 1)   2
497⁵ DOCTOR-J (Ire) 11-5 S Keightley, *pressed ldr, second pl till led aftr 3 out, sn hdd and wknd*..... (8 to 1 op 7 to 1)   3
MAASTRICHT 11-1 D J Burchell, *hld up, hdwy to chase ldrs aftr 5th, cl up and ev ch appr 2 out, sn rdn and wknd*................................ (7 to 2 op 5 to 2)   4
606⁷ LITTLE PORKY 10-10 (5*) D Leahy, *chsd ldg pair, mstk 3rd, pushed alng and outpcd aftr 5th, no ch appr 2 out*.
.... (33 to 1)   5
497 GOLDEN TARGET (USA) 10-8 V Slattery, *mstks, lost tch aftr 5th, tld off 3 out*............ (20 to 1 op 16 to 1)   6
570⁵ ITS UNBELIEVABLE 11-5 N Williamson, *led till hdd aftr 3 out, wknd rpdly*....... (11 to 4 op 3 to 1 tchd 7 to 2)   7
YOSHAARIK (Ire) 10-10 Gary Lyons, *jmpd rght second, sn beh, tld off 3 out, refused and uns rdr nxt*...... (33 to 1)   ref
CLARE'S BOY 10-9 L Harvey, *chsd ldrs till rdn and wknd quickly aftr 4th, sn tld off, pld up bef 2 out*.
.... (20 to 1 op 16 to 1)   pu
ANIL AMIT 10-8 J Railton, *beh whn bumped second, lost tch aftr 4th, tld off 3 out, pld up bef nxt*.
.... (40 to 1 op 25 to 1)   pu
Dist: 10l, 25l, 10l, 4l, 10l, 5l. 3m 45.10s. a 8.10s (10 Ran).
SR: 13/-/-/-/-/-/   (Racecourse Farm Racing), P G Murphy

703 Radnor Novices' Chase (4-y-o and up) £2,424 2m....................... (4:20)

442⁴ MENAGHI 6-11-2 G McCourt, *hld up in tch, trkd ldrs frm 7th, led 3 out, drvn out*.
.... (12 to 1 op 10 to 1 tchd 14 to 1)   1
SANDAIG (bl) 7-11-7 N Williamson, *led till hdd 8th, led ag'n 4 out, headed nxt, rdn and styd on one pace*.
.... (4 to 1 fav op 5 to 2 tchd 9 to 2)   2
WEST BAY 7-11-7 S Smith Eccles, *trkd ldr, led 8th till aftr 4 out, ev ch frm nxt, rdn and unbl to quicken betw last 2*.................... (6 to 1 op 4 to 1)   3
596* BALLAD RULER 7-11-2 (5*) R Davis, *hld up, hdwy aftr 5 out, cl up and ev ch appr 3 out, no imprsn*.
.... (7 to 1 op 7 to 2 tchd 8 to 1)   4
568³ WINDSOR PARK (USA) 7-11-13 V Slattery, *hld up in mid-div, pushed alng aftr 7th, ev ch appr 3 out, sn wknd*.
.... (8 to 1 op 6 to 1)   5
WALLISTRANO 6-11-7 R Supple, *mstk 1st, sn beh, lost tch aftr 6th, tld off*.................... (16 to 1 op 14 to 1)   6
612⁵ PECCAVI 9-11-7 R Bellamy, *mstk 1st, chsd ldg pair, jmpd slwly 6th, wknd quickly 4 out, tld off*.
.... (25 to 1 op 20 to 1)   7
612⁴ CANDLE KING (Ire) 5-11-5 M Bosley, *hld up, mstk second, hdwy 6th, cl up and ev ch aftr 4 out, close fourth whn f 2 out*.................... (8 to 1 op 6 to 1)   f
FLUIDITY (USA) 5-11-2 (3*) W Marston, *hld up, effrt whn jmpd slwly 6th and 7th, hmpd and f aftr 5 out*.
.... (9 to 2 op 4 to 1)   f
SALESMAN 6-11-7 L Harvey, *jmpd badly, sn beh, tld off whn pld up bef 4 out*.............. (66 to 1 op 50 to 1)   pu
Dist: 2½l, 3l, 8l, 1l, dist. 4m 5.80s. a 13.80s (10 Ran).
(Mrs Mary Webb), D McCain

704 Ludford Novices' Hurdle (Div I) (4-y-o and up) £1,480 2m....................... (4:50)

616⁷ BERTONE (Ire) 4-10-12 N Williamson, *trkd ldrs, led 2 out, pushed clr betw last two, rily last, cmftbly*.
.... (11 to 8 on op 6 to 4 on tchd 5 to 4 on)   1
597 TRECOMETTI 5-10-4 (5*) R Davis, *hld up, steady hdwy to track ldg grp appr 3 out, rdn and styd on to take second pl aftr last, no ch wth wnr*........ (10 to 1 op 7 to 1)   2
344⁵ KELLY'S DARLING 7-11-0 W McFarland, *hld up, wnt 3rd aftr 3 out, ev ch appr nxt, unbl to quicken*.
.... (7 to 1 op 6 to 1 tchd 8 to 1)   3
429 MAPLE BAY (Ire) 4-10-12 G McCourt, *hld up, hdwy to chase ldg grp aftr 6th, ev ch appr nxt, sn one pace*.
.... (11 to 2 op 9 to 2)   4
GOTT'S DESIRE 7-10-7 (7*) A Flannigan, *hdwy 4th, trkd ldr till led 3 out, sn hdd, fourth and btn whn mstk last*.
.... (11 to 2 op 9 to 2)   5
616 KAYRUZ 5-10-7 (7*) Mr G Lewis, *pld hrd, trkd ldrs, ev ch appr 2 out, sn wknd*.................... (33 to 1 op 16 to 1)   6
524⁷ BLUE LYZANDER 4-10-7 V Slattery, *lft in ld 3rd, hdd 3 out, sn wknd*.................... (20 to 1 op 16 to 1)   7

GIVE ALL 7-10-7 (7*) M Appleby, *slwly away, beh till hdwy to chase ldg grp aftr 5th, ev ch appr 2 out, sn rdn and btn*............ (100 to 1 op 33 to 1)   8
BIG CHANCE 4-10-12 Richard Guest, *lost pl aftr 4th, sn beh, tld off 3 out*................ (25 to 1 op 12 to 1)   9
IN A WHIRL (USA) 5-10-9 Mr P Hamer, *jmpd badly, led till jumped lft and hdd 3rd, sn beh, tld off whn pld up bef 2 out*.................... (33 to 1 op 16 to 1)   pu
Dist: 10l, 1½l, 8l, ½l, 2½l, 6l, 25l, 2½l. 3m 48.80s. a 11.80s (10 Ran).
(Mrs Harry J Duffey), K C Bailey

705 Ludford Novices' Hurdle (Div II) (4-y-o and up) £1,480 2m....................... (5:20)

KHALIDI (Ire) 4-10-12 P Holley, *trkd ldr in second pl till led 5th, styd on wl frm 2 out, cmftbly*.... (4 to 1 op 5 to 2)   1
551* BLAZON OF TROY 4-11-5 S Smith Eccles, *trkd ldg pair, hit second, mstk 3rd, ev ch frm 3 out, btn second whn mistake last*.
.... (11 to 10 on op 6 to 4 on tchd Evens and 11 to 10)   2
551³ EARLY DRINKER 5-10-9 (5*) J McCarthy, *hld up and beh, hdwy aftr 3 out, styd on frm nxt, not rch ldrs*.
.... (4 to 1 tchd 5 to 1 and 11 to 2)   3
SOLE CONTROL 5-10-9 J Railton, *hld up, hdwy 4th, chsd ldr frm nxt, ev ch appr 2 out, 3rd and btn whn mstk last*.................... (40 to 1 op 20 to 1)   4
ICE MAGIC 6-11-0 N Williamson, *trkd ldg grp frm 4th, wnt 3rd appr 2 out, wknd betw last two*.
.... (12 to 1 op 16 to 1)   5
434 BEAM ME UP SCOTTY (Ire) 4-10-12 N Hawke, *beh, hdwy und pres appr 2 out, kpt on one pace*.
.... (33 to 1 op 16 to 1)   6
402⁸ PALM SWIFT 7-10-9 A Webb, *mid-div till rdn and effrt 3 out, sn wknd*.................... (25 to 1 op 16 to 1)   7
BUSTLING AROUND 6-10-9 M Bosley, *chsd ldrs frm 4th, wnt 3rd nxt, styd in tch till wknd quickly appr 2 out*.
.... (33 to 1 op 16 to 1)   8
MAGGOTS GREEN 6-10-9 L Harvey, *trkd ldg trio, in tch till wknd quickly aftr 3 out*.
.... (12 to 1 op 10 to 1 tchd 20 to 1)   9
HOW HUMBLE (Ire) 4-10-7 T Wall, *al last, lost tch aftr 3rd, tld off 3 out*................ (100 to 1 op 50 to 1)   10
Dist: 8l, 6l, 3½l, 8l, ½l, 10l, 1½l, 3l. 3m 43.30s. a 6.30s (10 Ran).
SR: 29/28/17/8/5/2/   (T J Whitley), D R Gandolfo

PUNCHESTOWN (IRE) (heavy)
Thursday October 7th

706 Ballyshannon Racecall Australian/Irish Challenge Maiden (3-y-o) £3,105 2m (4:00)

529³ LUSTRINO (USA) 10-11 M Patton, ...(10 to 3)   1
DOYROY (Ire) 10-1 (5*) C O'Brien, ... (8 to 1)   2
529⁵ JAZZY REFRAIN (Ire) 10-6 T Horgan, ... (14 to 1)   3
CREHELP EXPRESS (Ire) 10-6 J Evans, ... (12 to 1)   4
529⁹ MISS MURPHY (Ire) 9-13 (7*) J P Broderick, ... (16 to 1)   5
GLAS AGUS OH (Ire) (bl) 10-6 P Worthington, ... (6 to 1)   6
BRIGENSER (Ire) 10-1 C F Swan, ... (11 to 4 jt-fav)   7
POUNDWORLD (Ire) 10-1 (5*) T P Rudd, ... (25 to 1)   8
470⁵ RUN MY ROSIE (Ire) 10-6 F Woods, ... (33 to 1)   9
PRINTOUT (Ire) 10-6 H Rogers, ... (8 to 1)   10
529 RATES RELIEF (Ire) 10-1 C F Swan, ... (11 to 4 jt-fav)   11
SHANGANOIR (Ire) 10-6 P Carberry, ... (11 to 4 jt-fav)   f
290⁹ SLAINTA (Ire) 10-11 S Jenkins, ... (20 to 1)   f
Dist: 12l, 15l, 3l, sht-hd. 4m 3.90s. (13 Ran).
(Mrs Michael Watt), D K Weld

707 Ingoldsby Chase (5-y-o and up) £3,795 2m .... (4:30)

554 WILL PHONE 7-10-8 (5*) Mr D Valentine, ... (3 to 1)   1
475* OH SO GRUMPY 5-11-6 Mr S R Murphy, ...(6 to 1)   2
COMMERCIAL ARTIST 7-11-10 Mr P F Graffin, (6 to 4 fav)   3
MERAPI 7-11-2 (3*) Mr A R Coonan, ... (4 to 1)   4
FRIENDLY ARGUMENT 8-11-5 (5*) Mr H F Cleary, (14 to 1)   5
619 FARNEY GLEN 6-10-11 (7*) Mr D A Harney, ... (12 to 1)   6
DOORSLAMMER 8-10-13 Mr J A Berry, ... (16 to 1)   7
468 LADY BYE-BYE 7-11-2 (3*) Miss M Olivefalk, ... (12 to 1)   8
511⁴ SUNSHINE SEAL 6-10-9¹ (5*) Mr A J Martin, ... (16 to 1)   9
Dist: 6l, 3l, 11l, 4l. 4m 17.00s. (9 Ran).
(Miss G Maher), M J P O'Brien

708 Knockadoo Hurdle (5-y-o and up) £3,105 2 ½m....................... (5:00)

537⁵ TUG OF PEACE 6-11-4 (5*) C O'Brien, ... (6 to 1)   1
557 KAZKAR 5-11-5 M Flynn, ... (16 to 1)   2
571⁵ RICH TRADITION (Ire) 5-11-5 C O'Dwyer, ...(6 to 1)   3
TEMPLEROAN PRINCE 6-11-12 C F Swan, ... (12 to 1)   4
538⁵ DIRECT RUN 6-11-5 Mr E Bolger, ... (12 to 1)   5
576⁵ IDIOTS VENTURE 6-11-5 B Sheridan, ...(7 to 4 fav)   6
538 DRINK UP DAN 6-11-5 P Carberry, ... (50 to 1)   7
ROWAN REX 8-11-9 J F Titley, ... (50 to 1)   8
618⁹ SPEAK OF THE DEVIL 6-11-5 H Rogers, ... (16 to 1)   9
DOWN THE BACK 6-10-7 (7*) P J Ryan, ... (16 to 1)   10
422⁵ BOLD FLYER 10-11-5 S Jenkins, ...(16 to 1)   11

252⁹ POLLANEDIN 9-10-12 (7") J P Deegan, ... (50 to 1) 12
618 BELLACORICK (Ire) 5-11-5 T Horgan, ...(50 to 1) 13
RUFUS SYNTHIA 6-11-5 J P Banahan, ... (25 to 1) 14
BUMBO HALL VI (Ire) 5-11-5 F J Flood, ... (20 to 1) 15
378⁵ TIME UP (Ire) 5-11-5 A J O'Brien, ...(50 to 1) 16
70⁸ CURRAGH GALE (Ire) 5-11-0 A Powell, ... (50 to 1) 17
585 NEMURO (USA) 5-11-3 J Shortt, ... (7 to 1) f
537⁴ SUPER MIDGE 6-11-9 P Worthington, ... (8 to 1) pu
585* HORNER WATER (Ire) 5-11-7 M Patton, ... (7 to 1) pu
Dist: 15l, 2½l, 1l, 5½l. 5m 23.50s. (20 Ran).

(W J Austin), W J Austin

709 Killashee Flat Race (4-y-o) £3,105 2m
. . . .(5:30)

530 GALE TOI (Ire) 9-11-9 Mr W P Mullins, ...(7 to 4 fav) 1
GREAT SVENGALI (Ire) 11-2 (7") Mr E Norris, ...(3 to 1) 2
WHATTABOB (Ire) 11-2 (7") Mr J Kelly, ...(20 to 1) 3
530⁴ CORYMANDEL (Ire) 10-12 (7") Mr D Carey, ...(8 to 1) 4
VARYKINOV (Ire) 11-9 Mr S R Murphy, ... (16 to 1) 5
STRONG SERENADE (Ire) 10-13 (5") Mr P M Kelly, (14 to 1) 6
530 PLASSY BOY (Ire) 11-9 Mr A J Martin, ... (20 to 1) 7
431 BROWNRATH KING (Ire) 11-2 (7") Mr D K Budds, (20 to 1) 8
FOUR MOONS (Ire) 10-11 (7") Mr D Bolger, ... (20 to 1) 9
620⁷ SWINGER (Ire) 11-2 (7") Mr D A Harney, ...(10 to 1) 10
530² JUPITER JIMMY 11-9 Mr J A Flynn, ...(5 to 1) 11
530⁵ AN MAINEACH (Ire) 11-6 (3") Miss M Olivefalk, ...(8 to 1) 12
531⁷ PRECEPTOR (Ire) 11-4 (5") Mr J A Nash, ...(14 to 1) 13
530⁷ MAJOR GALE (Ire) 11-2 (7") Mr R J Foley, ...(14 to 1) 14
469 GENE OF THE GLEN (Ire) 10-11 (7") Mr J P Kilfeather,
. . . .(40 to 1) 15
73 LARRYS PENNY (Ire) 10-13 (5") Mr H F Cleary, ...(40 to 1) 16
292⁷ PRIORITY GALE (Ire) 11-4 Mr F Fenton, ...(14 to 1) 17
SWIFT GLIDER (Ire) 11-4⁷ (7") Mr R P O'Keeffe, . . .(20 to 1) 18
98⁹ QUAINT HONOUR 10-11 (7") Miss S Kiernan, ...(25 to 1) 19
MUMMY'S PRAYER (Ire) 10-11 (7") Mr J Treacy, . . .(25 to 1) 20
BALLYHOOK (Ire) 10-11 (7") Mr D J Kavanagh, ...(14 to 1) 21
PUSH GENTLY (Ire) 10-11 (7") Mr B M Cash, ...(14 to 1) 22
WITHOUT TRACE (Ire) 11-4 (5") Mr G J Harford, . . .(12 to 1) pu
Dist: 1l, 4l, 6l, hd. 4m 3.30s. (23 Ran).

(Mrs M O'Leary), P Mullins

WINCANTON (good)
Thursday October 7th
Going Correction: PLUS 0.10 sec. per fur. (races 1,3,5), MINUS 0.05 (2,4,6,7)

710 Hatherleigh Novices' Chase (5-y-o and up) £3,054 2m 5f. . . . . (2:15)

PRINCE'S COURT 10-11-7 (7") D Fortt, al hndy, mstk 7th,
effrt 13th, chlgd appr 3 out, second and btn whn lft clr
last. . . . .(10 to 1 op 8 to 1 tchd 11 to 1) 1
TURNING TRIX 6-11-0 J Osborne, wth ldr thrght, led
12th, lft clr 4 out, jnd nxt, 3 ls clear whn sprawled on
landing last, not reco'r. (9 to 4 op 6 to 4 tchd 5 to 2) 2
CASTLE BLUE 6-11-0 M A FitzGerald, hld up in tch, effrt
13th, niggled alng frm nxt, styd on same pace.
. . . . (20 to 1 op 16 to 1 tchd 25 to 1) 3
326⁶ KING'S RARITY 7-11-0 D Bridgwater, outpcd 11th, sn
struggling, tld off. . . . .(25 to 1 op 20 to 1) 4
633⁴ COMIC LINE (bl) 8-11-7 S Burrough, lft in ld 1st, hdd 12th,
sn rdn and wknd, tld off. . . . .
GABRIELLA MIA 8-10-9 T Jarvis, hld up in tch, hdwy to go
second frm 12th, ev ch whn f 4 out.
. . . .(12 to 1 op 8 to 1 tchd 14 to 1) f
DEEPENDABLE 6-11-0 R Dunwoody, hmpd and f 1st.
. . . .(8 to 1 op 5 to 1 tchd 9 to 1) f
BARGE BOY 9-11-0 T Grantham, blun and uns rdr 1st.
. . . . (6 to 4 fav op 2 to 1 tchd 9 to 4 and 11 to 8) ur
607 PABREY (bl) 7-11-0 B Powell, not jump wl, led to 1st, sn
lost pl, tld off whn pld up bef 11th. . . . . (50 to 1) pu
Dist: 5l, 2l, dist, 15l. 5m 18.00s. a 12.00s (9 Ran).

(Court Jesters Partnership), Andrew Turnell

711 Shaftesbury Claiming Hurdle (3-y-o) £2,005 2m. . . . . (2:45)

MISS MICHELLE 10-10 S Earle, hld up and beh till gd
hdwy 2 out, led sn aftr last, quickened clr.
. . . .(16 to 1 op 10 to 1 tchd 20 to 1) 1
453³ CREAGMHOR 10-8 (7") Mr J L Llewellyn, wth ldr till led
aftr 3 out, hdd sn after last and not pace of wnr.
. . . .(12 to 1 op 8 to 1) 2
349⁵ MARAT (USA) (v) 11-1 A Maguire, mid-field till gd hdwy
appr 6th, sn ev ch, one pace last. . . . .(8 to 1 op 6 to 1) 3
570 MUSICAL PHONE 10-6 (5") R Farrant, chsd ldg bunch, gd
hdwy aftr 3 out, ev ch whn jmpd lft nxt, unbl to
quicken. . . . .(50 to 1 op 20 to 1) 4
497² MY SISTER LUCY 10-8 T Jarvis, chsd ldrs, mstk 5th, sn
btn. . . . . (6 to 1 tchd 5 to 1 and 13 to 2) 5
406 TIME OF GRACE (Ire) 11-1 S McNeill, trkd ldrs, ev ch appr
3 out, wknd bef nxt. . . . .(50 to 1 op 20 to 1) 6

570³ GREEN CHILI 11-4 J Osborne, hld up in tch, smooth
hdwy to track ldrs aftr 3 out, sn rdn and wknd.
. . . .(7 to 1 op 4 to 1 tchd 3 to 1) 7
611 OUR NIKKI 10-10 I Shoemark, struggling frm 4th.
. . . . (10 to 1 op 33 to 1) 8
RISK PROOF 11-1 M A FitzGerald, al beh, tld off.
. . . . (14 to 1 op 8 to 1) 9
FITZROY LAD 10-11 Lorna Vincent, not fluent, led till hdd
aftr 3 out, sn wknd and pld up bef nxt.
. . . .(12 to 1 op 7 to 1) pu
AMY COME HOME 11-0 E Murphy, pld hrd, in tch till
wknd quickly appr 3 out, pulled up bef nxt.
. . . .(10 to 1 op 12 to 1 tchd 20 to 1) pu
Dist: 5l, 2l, hd, 8l, 1½l, 1½l, 12l, 20l. 3m 53.10s. a 16.10s (11 Ran).

(T M Bowser), S Mellor

712 Oak Conditional Jockeys' Handicap Chase (0-115 5-y-o and up) £3,782 2m 5f. . . .(3:15)

424 IAMA ZULU [97] 8-10-0 M Hourigan, trkd ldr, led 8th, clr
13th, unchlgd. . . . .(25 to 1 op 20 to 1) 1
609⁴ AMONG FRIENDS [97] 8-10-0 A Dobbin, chsd ldg bunch,
wnt second appr 4 out, sn rdn and no imprsn fnl 3.
. . . . (10 to 1 op 8 to 1) 2
595³ COURT RAPIER [97] 11-9-10 (4") P Carey, mstk 1st, led 3rd
to 8th, rdn 13th, styd on same pace.
. . . .(10 to 1 op 7 to 1 tchd 12 to 1) 3
566² POWDER BOY [97] 8-10-0 A Thornton, in tch, hdwy to
chase wnr 12th, rdn aftr nxt and wknd.
. . . . (6 to 1 op 4 to 1) 4
464² ISLAND FOREST (USA) [97] 7-10-0 R Greene, trkd ldg
bunch, rdn 13th, btn whn mstks 3 out and nxt.
. . . . (9 to 2 tchd 5 to 1 and 4 to 1) 5
CHAMPAGNE LAD [122] 7-11-11 P Hide, led to 3rd, styd in
tch till niggled alng appr 11th, sn no hdwy.
. . . . (2 to 1 fav op 5 to 2) 6
609⁶ AL HASHIMI [125] 9-11-10 (4") T Thompson, al beh.
. . . . (25 to 1 op 16 to 1) 7
523³ KARAKTER REFERENCE [118] 11-11-7 D O'Sullivan, beh
whn mstk 7th, no hdwy. . . . .(10 to 1 op 5 to 1) 8
615⁵ JOYFUL NOISE [124] 10-11-6 (7") P Naughton, jmpd slwly
5th, rdn alng appr 9th, sn wknd, pld up bef 13th.
. . . . (7 to 1 op 6 to 1) pu
Dist: 12l, 4l, 12l, sht-hd, 8l, 4l, 2l. 5m 14.00s. a 8.00s (9 Ran).
SR: 13/1/-/-/-/2/1/-/-/

(Mrs Anona Taylor), P J Hobbs

713 Orchard FM Handicap Hurdle (0-120 4-y-o and up) £2,406 2m. . . . . (3:45)

NIGHT WIND [95] 6-9-9 (5") R Farrant, tucked away, hdwy
appr 6th, quickened to ld 2 out, drvn clr r-in. (7 to 2 jt-
fav tchd 3 to 1) 1
662⁵ STAR OF THE GLEN [122] 7-11-13 A Maguire, hdwy 4th, led
nxt, hdd 2 out, not pace of wnr. (7 to 2 jt-fav op 5 to 2) 2
PHILIP'S WOODY [98] 5-10-3 J R Kavanagh, hld up and
beh, hdwy appr 6th, ev ch bef nxt, kpt on same pace.
. . . . (13 to 2 op 6 to 1 tchd 7 to 1) 3
610³ VA UTU [97] 5-10-2 Lorna Vincent, led to second, styd
hndy and ev ch appr 2 out, not quicken.
. . . .(4 to 1 op 7 to 2 tchd 9 to 2) 4
446² POWER HAPPY [95] 8-10-0 D Gallagher, trkd ldrs till mstk
3 out, sn lost pl, kpt on ag'n r-in. (25 to 1 op 20 to 1) 5
NORTHERN SADDLER [98] 6-10-3 R Dunwoody, hld up,
jmpd slwly 3rd, effrt nxt, rdn aftr 3 out and sn btn.
. . . .(4 to 1 op 3 to 1 tchd 5 to 1) 6
FLY BY NORTH (USA) [104] 5-10-2 (7") M Keighley, in tch to
5th, sn wknd. . . . .(16 to 1 op 12 to 1 tchd 20 to 1) 7
PALACE WOLF (NZ) [123] 9-12-0 J Osborne, led second to
5th, lost pl nxt. . . . .(16 to 1 op 10 to 1) 8
Dist: 7l, 3l, 7l, 3l, 2½l, 1½l, 7l. 3m 40.30s. a 3.30s (8 Ran).
SR: 31/51/24/16/9/9/13/25/

(Pell-Mell Partners), Andrew Turnell

714 Portman Handicap Chase (0-120 5-y-o and up) £4,029 3m 1f 110yds. . . . . (4:15)

566⁴ TOUCHING STAR [93] 8-9-11 (3") M Hourigan, hld up till gd
hdwy 13th, sn chasing ldr, ev ch whn slight mstk last,
hrd rdn to ld last 100 yards.
. . . . (10 to 1 tchd 8 to 1 and 11 to 1) 1
TIPP MARINER [97] 8-10-0 A G Upton, chsd ldr, mstk 16th,
reco'red to ld appr 3 out, hdd last 100 yards.
. . . .(7 to 1 op 8 to 1) 2
DELGANY RUN [101] 9-10-8 J Osborne, jmpd fluently, led
till hdd appr 3 out, awkward nxt and no extr, better for
race. . . . . (4 to 1 op 3 to 1) 3
LIGHT VENEER [117] 8-11-10 D Gallagher, hld up, hdwy
16th, hit nxt and sn rdn alng, wknd appr 3 out.
. . . .(7 to 4 op 5 to 2 tchd 9 to 2) 4
600³ DOONLOUGHAN [109] 8-11-2 A Maguire, chsd ldrs, mstks
4th and 12th, wknd appr four out.
. . . .(25 to 12 tchd 5 to 1) 5
262⁶ AVONMOUTHSECRETARY [93] 7-9-13² (3") R Greene, trkd
ldg pair till lost pl 11th, no further hdwy.
. . . . (10 to 1 op 7 to 1 tchd 33 to 1) 6
445² MR MURDOCK [111] 8-11-4 S Earle, not fluent, beh most
of way. . . . .(3 to 1 fav tchd 7 to 2 and 5 to 2) 7

88

TRUSTY FRIEND [109] 11-11-2 M A FitzGerald, *in tch till f 8th*................... (25 to 1 op 16 to 1 tchd 33 to 1) f
Dist: 1½l, 12l, 10l, 15l, 2l, 6l. 6m 28.50s. a 12.50s (8 Ran).
(P J Hobbs), P J Hobbs

715 Wincanton Novices' Hurdle (Div I) (4-y-o and up) £2,127 2m..................(4:45)

FATACK 4-10-6 (7") S Curran, *trkd ldr till hmpd and lft in ld bend aftr 3rd, clr 6th, hit last, unchlgd*.
.... (9 to 1 op 10 to 1 tchd 14 to 1 and 8 to 1) 1
EURIDICE (Ire) 4-10-8 R Dunwoody, *lft second bend aftr 3rd, no imprsn on wnr appr 2 out*.
.... (10 to 1 op 6 to 1 tchd 11 to 1) 2
CRACKLING ANGELS 6-10-5 B Powell, *trkd ldrs, lft 3rd bend aftr third, no imprsn 3 out...* (8 to 1 tchd 10 to 1) 3
WONDERFULL POLLY (Ire) 5-10-5 G Bradley, *mid-field, hdwy aftr 5th, 3rd and btn whn mstk 2 out*.
.... (14 to 1 op 8 to 1 tchd 20 to 1) 4
524⁹ KICKING BIRD 6-10-5 S McNeill, *nvr able to chal*.
.... (33 to 1 op 25 to 1) 5
INDIAN MAESTRO 7-10-11 (3") M Hourigan, *mstk 1st, beh whn crrd wide bend aftr 3rd, no further imprsn*.
.... (50 to 1 op 33 to 1) 6
LUCKNAM DREAMER 5-11-0 G Morgan, *hld up, crrd very wide bend aftr 3rd, tld off*.......... (33 to 1 op 25 to 1) 7
FATHER FORTUNE 5-10-10 J Osborne, *in tch whn crrd wide bend aftr 3rd, not reco'r, tld off*.
.... (10 to 1 op 7 to 1 tchd 12 to 1) 8
456 BID FOR SIX (USA) 4-10-6 (7") N Downs, *chsd ldrs till brght dwn bend aftr 3rd*.......... (66 to 1 op 20 to 1) bd
MISSY-S (Ire) 4-10-1 (7") Mr J L Llewellyn, *in tch till brght dwn bend aftr 3rd*......(6 to 1 op 4 to 1 tchd 13 to 1) bd
VIOLET'S BOY 6-10-10 C Maude, *in tch till brght dwn bend aftr 3rd*.................... (33 to 1 op 16 to 1) bd
483* KING UBAD (USA) 4-11-6 A Maguire, *led till slpd up bend aftr 3rd*.......... (5 to 4 on op 6 to 4 on tchd Evens) su
ANDARE 4-10-13 S Earle, *hld up, crrd very wide bend aftr 3rd, tld off whn pld up bef 2 out*.
.... (33 to 1 op 20 to 1 tchd 50 to 1) pu
Dist: 10l, 1½l, 3½l, 4l, 1½l, 25l, 15l. 3m 43.20s. a 6.20s (13 Ran).
SR: 15/-/-/-/-/-/ (Jeremy W S Barnett), Miss Jacqueline S Doyle

716 Wincanton Novices' Hurdle (Div II) (4-y-o and up) £2,110 2m..................(5:15)

OLD BRIDGE (Ire) 5-10-10 S McNeill, *al hndy, led 2 out, rdn out*.................... (9 to 2 op 3 to 1) 1
456* NATIVE CHIEFTAN 4-11-6 H Davies, *patiently rdn, gd hdwy appr 2 out, chlgd last, not quicken r-in*.
.... (5 to 2 op 9 to 4 tchd 3 to 1) 2
MASNUN (USA) 8-10-11 (3") D O'Sullivan, *took keen hold, handily plcd till slightly outpcd aftr 3 out, styd on r-in*.
.... (11 to 1 op 16 to 1 tchd 8 to 1) 3
FITNESS FANATIC 5-11-0 D Murphy, *pld hrd, trkd ldrs till rdn and outpcd appr 2 out, kpt on r-in*.
.... (16 to 1 op 33 to 1 tchd 14 to 1) 4
301* MUSTAHIL (Ire) 4-11-6 R Dunwoody, *trkd ldrs, ev ch appr 2 out, sn rdn and wknd*................ (7 to 1 op 9 to 2) 5
GROG (Ire) 4-10-13 J Osborne, *reluctant to line up, trkd ldr till led 4th, hdd 2 out, fourth and btn whn mstk last*.
.... (7 to 4 fav op 2 to 1 tchd 9 to 4) 6
597 DARINGLY 4-10-13 D Gallagher, *chsd ldrs till slpd bend aftr 3rd, sn lost pl*................ (100 to 1 op 33 to 1) 7
EARLY STAR 4-10-10 (3") R Greene, *nvr a threat*.
.... (66 to 1 op 50 to 1 tchd 100 to 1) 8
JUNIPER LODGE 5-10-10 S Earle, *al beh*.
.... (25 to 1 op 14 to 1) 9
434 ALFREE 5-10-7 (3") M Hourigan, *led till hdd 4th, sn wknd*.
.... (100 to 1 op 33 to 1) 10
ROUTING 5-11-0 B Clifford, *mid-field, hdwy whn hmpd aftr 5th, ran out nxt*. (33 to 1 op 20 to 1 tchd 50 to 1) ro
JAY JAYS DREAM 7-10-5 B Powell, *tld off frm 4th, pld up bef 2 out*.................... (100 to 1 op 50 to 1) pu
Dist: 1½l, 1l, 10l, sht-hd, ½l, 10l, 8l, ¾l. 3m 46.70s. a 9.70s (12 Ran).
(K C B Mackenzie), Andrew Turnell

CARLISLE (good)
Friday October 8th
Going Correction: MINUS 0.05 sec. per fur.

717 Shap Novices' Hurdle (4-y-o and up) £1,849 2m 1f....................(1:50)

658⁷ COL BUCKMORE (Ire) 5-11-0 N Doughty, *patiently rdn, steady hdwy thrght, led r-in, ran on wl*.
.... (11 to 10 op 9 to 1 tchd 12 to 1) 1
FALCONS DAWN 6-11-0 B Storey, *nvr far away, drw level 3 out, sn led, hdd and rdn r-in, one pace*.
.... (6 to 1 op 4 to 1) 2
395* FREE TRANSFER (Ire) 4-11-6 J Callaghan, *utd wth, imprvg whn hit 4th, chlgd 3 out, one pace aftr last*.
.... (6 to 1 tchd 4 to 1) 3
LINNGATE 4-10-10² T Reed, *patiently rdn, steady hdwy on ins 3 out, shaken up betw last 2, ran on*.
.... (9 to 4 fav op 2 to 1 tchd 5 to 2) 4

626² HIGH PENHOWE 5-10-2 (7") C Woodall, *settled midfield, effrt and drvn alng 3 out, styd on same pace frm nxt*.
.... (11 to 2 op 4 to 1) 5
MR ROYAL 7-11-0 C Grant, *trkd ldg bunch, checked bend aftr 4 out, effrt and rdn after nxt, one pace*.
.... (16 to 1 op 12 to 1) 6
582²³ MARKED CARD 5-11-0 Mrs M Kendall, *settled gng wl, led 4 out till aftr nxt, fdd betw last 2*. (14 to 1 tchd 16 to 1) 7
394 SHAYNA MAIDEL 4-10-8 L O'Hara, *al wl plcd, ev ch aftr 3 out, fdd appr last*.................... (33 to 1) 8
BRIAR'S DELIGHT 5-11-0 A Orkney, *chsd clr ldr to hfwy, feeling pace aftr 3 out, fdd*.... (16 to 1 op 14 to 1) 9
WELLSY LAD (USA) 6-11-10 N Smith, *in tch, chsd alng appr 3 out, nvr able to chal*.......... (33 to 1 op 25 to 1) 10
RED BEACON 6-11-0 C Dennis, *trkd ldg bunch, ev ch 4 out, fdd aftr nxt*.................... (66 to 1 op 33 to 1) 11
582⁷ TIGHTER BUDGET (USA) 6-11-0 Mrs Diane Sayer, *rcd wide, clr ld till hdd 4 out, wknd quickly*.
.... (200 to 1 op 100 to 1) 12
399² POCKETPICKER (Ire) 5-11-0 A Merrigan, *chsd ldrs till fdd appr 3 out*................ (200 to 1 op 100 to 1) 13
237⁵ MITTON SPRINGS 4-10-6 (7") D Towler, *settled wth chasing grp, drvn alng aftr 3 out, fdd*. (100 to 1 op 66 to 1) 14
RICH FUTURE 4-10-13 K Jones, *jmpd deliberately, al beh, tld off*....................(66 to 1 op 50 to 1) 15
Dist: ¾l, 3l, 1l, 1l, 3l, 4l, 1½l, 4l, 10l, 5l. 4m 16.40s. a 9.40s (15 Ran).
(Brian Buckley), G Richards

718 Tebay Novices' Chase (5-y-o and up) £2,672 2½m 110yds...............(2:25)

660 TARTAN TRADEWINDS 6-11-0 N Doughty, *settled gng wl, drw level 6 out, jmpd clr 3 out, rdn out frm last*.
.... (11 to 10 fav tchd 6 to 5) 1
BUCKWHEAT LAD (Ire) 5-10-11 C Grant, *some mstks, nvr far away, feeling pace 4 out, rallied and jmpd rght last, kpt on same pace*.............. (11 to 1 op 10 to 1) 2
TRUE FAIR 10-11-0 B Storey, *set modest pace, quickened hfwy, hdd and rdn 3 out, outpcd frm betw last 2*.
.... (9 to 1 op 7 to 1) 3
480* WEST WITH THE WIND 6-11-7 T Reed, *trkd ldg pair, ev ch whn hit 4 out, not quicken last 2*.
.... (6 to 4 tchd 7 to 4) 4
542 ZARBANO 7-11-0 A Merrigan, *pressed ldrs, effrt and bustled alng aftr 6 out, lost tch and jmpd slwly last, virtually pld up*.................... (33 to 1) 5
VULPIN DE LAUGERE (Fr) 6-11-0 Mr S Brisby, *patiently rdn, improved to join issue fnl circuit, fdd frm 4 out, pld up bef 2 out*.................... (9 to 1 op 7 to 1) pu
Dist: 2½l, 3l, 2½l, dist. 5m 19.40s. a 16.40s (6 Ran).
(The Edinburgh Woollen Mill Ltd), G Richards

719 Brough Handicap Hurdle (0-115 3-y-o and up) £2,110 2m 1f...................(3:00)

ALL WELCOME [96] 6-11-7 P Niven, *made all, quickened up hfwy, clr appr last, hld on wl*.
.... (9 to 4 fav op 2 to 1 tchd 5 to 2) 1
KINOKO [99] 5-11-7 (3") S Wynne, *nvr far away, drvn alng frm 3 out, str run from last, not go past cl hme*.
.... (9 to 2 op 7 to 2 tchd 5 to 1) 2
REGAL ROMPER (Ire) [90] 5-11-1 Richard Guest, *pressed wnr, drvn betw last 2, fdd*........(7 to 1 tchd 6 to 1) 3
519⁷ COLORADO INSIGHT [76] 5-10-1 J Callaghan, *al tracking ldrs, feeling pace and drvn alng 3 out, fdd betw last 2*.
.... (7 to 2 op 4 to 1) 4
562* MASTER OF THE ROCK [99] (v) 4-11-10 C Hawkins, *nvr far away, drvn appr 3 out, sn outpcd*....(5 to 1 op 4 to 1) 5
STARLIGHT WONDER [75] 7-10-0 N Smith, *jmpd carefully, al beh, tld off frm bef last*. (40 to 1 op 33 to 1) pu
Dist: Hd, 15l, 2l, 1½l. 4m 13.30s. a 6.30s (6 Ran).
SR: 22/25/1/-/6/-/ (Lionville Builders Ltd), Mrs M Reveley

720 Kirkby Stephen Handicap Chase (0-125 5-y-o and up) £2,820 3m...........(3:30)

436³ BUDDY HOLLY (NZ) [106] 8-10-1¹ J Osborne, *made all, nrly uns rdr 5th, clr 5 out, styd on wl r-in*.
.... (11 to 8 fav op 5 to 4 tchd 6 to 4) 1
655⁶ KIRSTY'S BOY [119] 10-11-0 C Grant, *jmpd hesitantly, nvr far away, rdn frm 3 out, rallied r-in*.
.... (9 to 4 op 5 to 2) 2
ON THE OTHER HAND [132] 10-11-13 N Doughty, *trkd wnr, sprawled and lost grnd 6 out, rallied, wknd and jmpd slwly 2 out, needed race*.......... (11 to 4 op 3 to 1) 3
VIVA BELLA (Fr) [105] 6-9-7 (7") Mr D Parker, *pressed ldrs, struggled fnl circuit, losing tch whn blun 7 out*.
.... (9 to 1 op 8 to 1) 4
Dist: 2½l, 15l, 12l. 6m 23.80s. a 24.80s (4 Ran).
(B A J Lake), J A B Old

721 Orton Novices' Hurdle (4-y-o and up) £1,807 2½m 110yds...............(4:05)

577* ROYAL VACATION 4-11-6 J Callaghan, *patiently rdn, drvn up aftr 4 out, hmpd bend bef nxt, sn led, styd on strly r-in*...............(5 to 2 tchd 9 to 4 and 11 to 4) 1

KENILWORTH LAD 5-11-0 P Niven, *wtd wth, improved gng wl aftr 4 out, rdn betw last 2, rallied r-in*.
..(6 to 5 on op 11 to 10 on tchd Evens and 5 to 4 on) 2
MY TURN NEXT 5-10-6 (3") S Wynne, *nvr far away, led briefly bef 4 out, squeezed for room and slpd bend appr 3 out, one pace last 2* .... (16 to 1 tchd 20 to 1) 3
DASHMAR 6-11-0 C Dennis, *nvr far away, bumped 4th, hrd at work frm four out, no imprsn*.
.... (200 to 1 op 100 to 1) 4
BECK COTTAGE 5-11-0 B Storey, *al hndy, led 4 out, edgd rght bend appr nxt, sn hdd, wknd quickly last 2*.
.... (7 to 1 op 10 to 1 tchd 5 to 1) 5
ROAD BY THE RIVER 5-11-0 C Grant, *pressed ldrs, feeling pace and drvn alng aftr 4 out, sn outpcd*.
.... (20 to 1 op 12 to 1) 6
6427 THOMPSON FLYER 6-11-0 Mrs F Needham, *chsd clr ldr, drvn appr 4 out, sn btn* .... (100 to 1) 7
CLASSIC MINSTREL 9-10-7 (7") A Watt, *led and sn clr, hdd appr 4 out, soon lost tch* .... (25 to 1 op 20 to 1) 8
HYDROPIC 6-11-0 N Smith, *chsd ldrs, screwed 4th, lost tch appr four out, pld up bef 3 out* .... (50 to 1) pu
SLIPPITT 6-11-0 A Merrigan, *very backward, reminders 3rd, sn tld off, pld up bef 5 out*. (200 to 1 op 100 to 1) pu
Dist: 1½l, 10l, 8l, 10l, 8l, 8l, 10l. 4m 58.00s. a 5.00s (10 Ran).
SR: 32/24/9/6/-/-/ (G P Edwards), G M Moore

722 Appleby-In-Westmorland Handicap Chase (0-125 5-y-o and up) £2,820 2m...... (4:40)

5603 ABSAILOR [91] 9-10-6 (5") P Williams, *jmpd wl, wth ldr, led aftr 5th, clr last 4, readily* .... (7 to 2 tchd 4 to 1) 1
DOLIKOS [104] 6-11-10 P Niven, *led till hdd aftr 5th, lost grnd whn pace quickened 5 out, rallied to go second r-in*......................... (7 to 2 op 5 to 2) 2
PIMS GUNNER (Ire) [103] 5-11-9 C Grant, *wl plcd till rdn alng and outpcd hfwy, styd on grimly frm 2 out, nxt finish*....................... (8 to 1 op 5 to 1) 3
546" ALGARI [103] 6-11-9 M Moloney, *jmpd stickily, improved to track wnr aftr 4 out, sn rdn alng, wknd r-in*.
.... (6 to 5 on op Evens) 4
Dist: 12l, 2½l, 1½l. 4m 4.20s. a 5.20s (4 Ran).
SR: 23/24/20/18/ (Lady Harris), Mrs S C Bradburne

723 Grunwick Stakes National Hunt Flat Race (4,5,6-y-o) £1,266 2m 1f............. (5:10)

JUNGLE RITES (Ire) 5-10-13 (7") G Tormey, *settled gng wl, improved on bit to ld well o'r 2 fs out, rdn over one out, styd on*.............. (100 to 30 op 3 to 1 tchd 7 to 2) 1
RHOSSILI BAY 5-11-1 (5") Mr M Buckley, *set steady pace, quickened up entering strt, hdd wl o'r 2 out, one pace*.............. (11 to 10 fav op 5 to 4 tchd Evens) 2
5473 ORD GALLERY (Ire) 4-10-12 (7") A Linton, *nvr far away, feeling pace and rdn entering strt, kpt on same pace last 2 fs*.......................... (10 to 1 op 8 to 1) 3
6454 MISCHIEVOUS GIRL 5-11-1 Mrs F Needham, *tucked away on ins, effrt and hng badly lft entering strt, one pace last 2 fs*....................... (16 to 1 op 14 to 1) 4
6452 THE WEATHERMAN 5-10-13 (7") N Stocks, *al in tch, effrt and drvn alng appr strt, no imprsn last 3 fs*.
.... (12 to 1 op 8 to 1) 5
RAYLEO (Ire) 4-11-0 (5") Mr D McCain, *chsd ldr, drvn alng entering strt, sn outpcd*.......... (16 to 1 op 14 to 1) 6
RELENTED 4-10-11 (3") A Larnach, *patiently rdn, shaken up whn pace quickened entering strt, staying on finish*...................... (8 to 1 op 5 to 1) 7
6455 MANILA RUN (Ire) 4-11-0 (5") W Dwan, *trkd ldg pair, pushed alng entering strt, fdd*.....(16 to 1 op 12 to 1) 8
KIRKTON GLEN 4-10-12 (7") Mr A Parker, *chsd ldg 5, drvn entering strt, sn btn*.... (20 to 1 op 25 to 1 tchd 16 to 1) 9
YOUNG ANGUS 4-11-5 Mr T Morrison, *chsd ldrs till wknd quickly appr strt, tld off*.......... (40 to 1 op 33 to 1) 10
Dist: 3½l, 8l, ¾l, 8l, 3l, 1l, 8l, 2l, dist. 4m 16.70s. (10 Ran).
(Mrs B V Eve), J G FitzGerald

MARKET RASEN (good)
Friday October 8th
Going Correction: PLUS 0.55 sec. per fur. (races 1,2,-5,7), PLUS 1.05 (3,4,6)

724 Carling Black Label Selling Hurdle (3,4,5-y-o) £1,795 2m 1f 110yds.......... (2:10)

5144 SUMMER FLOWER 3-9-13 (5") T Eley, *chsd ldrs, mstk 4th, effrt appr 2 out, led and pckd last, rdn and ran on*.
.... (9 to 2 op 7 to 2 tchd 5 to 1) 1
5203 NAJEB (USA) 4-11-8 M A FitzGerald, *wth ldr, rdn alng and outpcd appr 2 out, styd on und pres frm last*.
.... (7 to 1 tchd 8 to 1) 2
5783 TINSTONE 3-10-2² R Garritty, *hld up, hdwy 3 out, rdn appr last, styd on one pace*........ (8 to 1 op 10 to 1) 3
5885 BIG GEM 3-10-5 W Worthington, *made most till appr 2 out, hit two out, kpt on one pace und pres*.
.... (16 to 1 tchd 20 to 1) 4
5893 WALSHAM WITCH (bl) 3-10-0 M Ranger, *prmnt, led appr 2 out, rdn, hdd and hit last, wknd.* (25 to 1 tchd 33 to 1) 5

6586 NORDIC BEAT (Ire) 4-11-8 Diane Clay, *chsd ldrs, rdn and wkng whn hit 2 out*................. (6 to 1 op 5 to 1) 6
5526 ALIZARI (USA) (bl) 4-11-8 M Robinson, *beh, rdn alng hfwy, nvr a factor*........................(33 to 1 op 25 to 1) 7
6223 TOM THE TANK (bl) 3-10-5 G McCourt, *mid-div, some hdwy hfwy, sn rdn, btn bef 3 out*.
.... (7 to 2 fav tchd 3 to 1) 8
CRIMSON CONSORT (Ire) 4-11-8 D Wilkinson, *al beh, tld off 3 out*.................. (33 to 1 op 25 to 1) 9
SOUNDS RISKY 3-10-0 R Dunwoody, *prmnt, rdn and wknd quickly 3 out, tld off*..... (12 to 1 tchd 14 to 1) 10
SEA-AYR (Ire) 3-9-7 (7") F Husband, *prmnt, chlgd and hit 3 out, sn rdn, wknd appr nxt, tld off*.
.... (33 to 1 op 25 to 1) 11
SWYNFORD FLYER 4-11-3 D Byrne, *mstk 1st, al beh, tld off 3 out*....................... (25 to 1) 12
4976 SOLAR KNIGHT 3-10-0 D Bridgwater, *not fluent, al rear, tld off 3 out*......... (8 to 1 op 6 to 1 tchd 9 to 1) 13
LIGHT THE BAY 3-10-0 L Wyer, *al beh, tld off 3 out*.
.... (33 to 1 op 25 to 1) 14
EVENING STABLES 4-11-3 B Dalton, *mstk second, sn chasing ldrs, rdn and wknd hfwy, tld off whn pld up bef 2 out*...........................(33 to 1) pu
Dist: 6l, 2½l, 1½l, 1½l, 1l, 12l, 3l, 1l, 6l, ½l. 4m 21.50s. a 19.50s (15 Ran).
(Target Racing), A L Forbes

725 Furness Builders Merchants Novices' Hurdle (4-y-o and up) £2,464 3m.... (2:45)

5775 BROWNHALL 5-10-5 (7") Mr B Pollock, *prmnt, led second, clr 3 out, styd on wl*........... (7 to 1 op 8 to 1) 1
SQUIRES TALE (Ire) 5-10-12 L Wyer, *al prmnt, hit 8th, rdn to chase wnr 3 out, kpt on one pace*.
.... (3 to 1 op 2 to 1 tchd 100 to 30) 2
4823 FARMER'S CROSS 9-10-12 Mrs A Farrell, *hld up, hdwy hfwy, cl 4th whn hmpd four out, sn rdn, kpt on one pace*...(15 to 8 fav op 6 to 4 tchd 11 to 8 and 2 to 1) 3
5028 SALLY SOHAM (Ire) 5-10-0 (7") P Murphy, *led to second, prmnt till rdn and wknd aftr 3 out*.(20 to 1 op 25 to 1) 4
237 BROWN MYSTIQUE 7-10-0 (7") A Flannigan, *pld hrd, mstks in rear, beh hfwy, tld off whn pulled up bef 2 out*.
.... (50 to 1 op 33 to 1) pu
1295 HAZEL HILL 7-10-7 B Clifford, *mstks, in tch to hfwy, tld off whn pld up bef 2 out*.................(50 to 1) pu
BENGAZEE (Ire) 5-10-12 C Llewellyn, *not fluent, chsd ldrs, hit 6th and 7th, sn drvn alng, mstk 8th, pld up lme*.
.... (9 to 2 op 5 to 1 tchd 7 to 1) pu
Dist: 6l, 3l, 30l. 6m 7.20s. a 25.20s (8 Ran).
(R C Wade), M J Charles

726 William Stones Handicap Chase (0-120 5-y-o and up) £3,980 3m 1f........ (3:15)

TOMPET [100] 7-10-8 C Llewellyn, *al prmnt, led 6 out, rdn 3 out, styd on strly*................ (5 to 1 op 9 to 2) 1
5795 LAPIAFFE [100] 9-10-8 R Dunwoody, *made most to 6 out, cl up and ev ch 3 out, sn rdn and wknd, hit 2 out*.
.... (4 to 1 fav tchd 9 to 2) 2
5185 SMOOTH ESCORT [115] (v) 9-11-9 D Murphy, *chsd ldrs, mstk 5th, rdn alng 5 out, sn one pace*.
.... (11 to 1 op 10 to 1) 3
5482 ARD T'MATCH [93] (v) 8-9-10 (5") T Eley, *beh, mstks, drvn alng and hdwy 6 out, sn all out, no imprsn*.
.... (15 to 2 op 7 to 1 tchd 10 to 1) 4
5184 MIAMI BEAR [93] 7-10-1¹ Gary Lyons, *cl up, rdn appr 5 out, sn wknd*.
.... (11 to 1 op 12 to 1 tchd 14 to 1 and 10 to 1) 5
548 SCOTTISH REFORM [96] 6-10-4 N Williamson, *blun 1st 2, beh and mstks, drvn alng 6 out, hdwy and disputing 3rd whn f 3 out*.................(11 to 1 op 10 to 1) f
6004 SAM SHORROCK [99] (bl) 11-10-7 Mr G Johnson Houghton, *f 3rd*.............................. (11 to 1 op 10 to 1) f
JIMSTER [97] 11-10-5 J R Kavanagh, *mstk second, hit 3rd, hmpd and uns rdr*........................... (8 to 1) ur
6242 FOSBURY [106] 8-11-0 S Smith Eccles, *trkd ldrs, hdwy tenth, ev ch whn blun and uns rdr 6 out*.
.... (6 to 1 op 5 to 1) ur
PEANUTS PET [120] 8-12-0 M Dwyer, *not fluent, al rear, beh whn pld up bef 9th*.
.... (11 to 1 op 10 to 1 tchd 12 to 1) pu
Dist: 2½l, 1½l, 12l, 20l. 6m 33.20s. a 25.20s (10 Ran).
SR: 20/17/17/-/-/-/ (Tom Pettifer Ltd), N A Twiston-Davies

727 Stones Bitter Novices' Chase (5-y-o and up) £3,379 3m 1f................. (3:50)

593" GREAT MILL (bl) 6-11-7 N Williamson, *trkd ldrs, mstk 5th, hdwy 12th, chlgd 3 out, led and lft clr nxt, hit last*.
............(2 to 1 on op 5 to 2 on tchd 9 to 4 on) 1
CROWN EYEGLASS 7-11-3 R Garritty, *led to 3rd, prmnt till rdn and wknd 4 out, lft poor second 2 out*.
.... (20 to 1 tchd 33 to 1) 2
6605 WHISKEY BLUES 8-11-3 D Byrne, *mstks in rear, tld off 12th, lft remote 3rd 2 out*....................... (33 to 1) 3

587^{6} ON CUE 6-11-3 W Worthington, *hld up, hdwy 12th, in tch till rdn and wknd 4 out, poor fourth whn f 3 out.* .... (33 to 1 op 25 to 1) f
SQUIRES PRIVILEGE (Ire) 5-11-0 M Dwyer, *cl up, led 4th, jnd and rdn 3 out, hdd and f nxt.* .... (15 to 2 op 7 to 1 tchd 8 to 1) f
451 REVILLER'S GLORY 9-11-3 Mrs A Farrell, *in tch whn blun and uns rdr 5th.*.................... (8 to 1 op 7 to 1) ur
KILCLOONEY FORREST 11-11-3 Gary Lyons, *prmnt, led 3rd to 4th, cl up till rdn and wknd four out, poor third whn pld up bef nxt.*....(9 to 1 op 8 to 1 tchd 10 to 1) pu
DUKE'S DELIGHT 6-11-3 L Wyer, *mstks in rear, tld off whn pld up aftr 13th.* (40 to 1 op 25 to 1 tchd 50 to 1) pu
Dist: 20l, dist. 6m 46.10s. a 45.10s (8 Ran).
(Mrs Harry J Duffey), K C Bailey

728 Robert Peak Bookmakers Novices' Hurdle (4-y-o and up) £2,407 2m 3f 110yds.. (4:25)

656* WESTHOLME (USA) 5-11-7 L Wyer, *al cl up, led appr 6th, quickened clr aftr 3 out, hit nxt, unchlgd.* .... (11 to 10 on tchd 5 to 4) 1
MAJORITY MAJOR (Ire) 4-10-13 K Johnson, *in tch, hdwy appr 3 out, rdn and one pace nxt, wndrd und pres approaching last, fnshd second, plcd 3rd.* .... (33 to 1 op 25 to 1) 2D
664^{3} SARANNPOUR (Ire) 4-10-13 G McCourt, *hld up beh, hdwy appr 2 out, staying on whn hmpd approaching last, ran on, fnshd 3rd, plcd second....* (14 to 1 op 10 to 1) 2
587^{2} SAFARI PARK 4-11-1 R Dunwoody, *prmnt, chsd wnr 3 out, sn rdn, wknd appr last.*........... (8 to 1 tchd 9 to 1) 4
HENRY VILL (Ire) 5-11-0 C Llewellyn, *rear, blun second, rdn alng and some hdwy 3 out, nvr a factor.* .... (9 to 1 op 6 to 1 tchd 10 to 1) 5
587* STRONG JOHN (Ire) 5-11-2 (5*) B Murphy, *led second till appr 6th, blun nxt, sn rdn and wknd.* ....(7 to 2 tchd 4 to 1) 6
COWLEY 8-11-0 M Brennan, *pld hrd, led to second, beh hfwy, sn tld off.*.................(20 to 1 tchd 25 to 1) 7
LITTLE CONKER 5-11-0 N Williamson, *in tch, hdwy 3 out, sn rdn, wknd nxt, poor 5th whn f last.* ....(20 to 1 tchd 33 to 1) f
DANZARIN (Ire) 5-11-0 R Campbell, *al beh, tld off whn pld up bef 4 out.*..................... (16 to 1 op 14 to 1) pu
Dist: 15l, hd, 5l, 10l, 5l, 30l. 4m 48.60s. a 15.60s (9 Ran).
SR: 44/21/21/18/7/9/ (T H Bennett), M H Easterby

729 Worthington Best Bitter Novices' Chase (4-y-o and up) £3,275 2m 1f 110yds.. (4:55)

517* DEEP DECISION 7-11-9 K Johnson, *led to 4th, prmnt, lft second 3 out, led and left clr nxt, fnshd tired.* ....(6 to 1 op 5 to 1) 1
REVE DE VALSE (USA) 6-11-0 (5*) P Waggott, *chsd ldrs, effrt 5 out, rdn nxt, lft 3rd 3 out, hmpd and left second 2 out, kpt on.*.. (10 to 1) 2
641 SPACE CAPTAIN 6-11-2 (3*) N Bentley, *hld up beh, hdwy whn blun 5 out, hit nxt, wl behind, lft 3rd 2 out.* ....(3 to 1 op 7 to 2 tchd 4 to 1) 3
586^{3} PHALAROPE (Ire) (v) 5-11-4 Mr A Walton, *cl up till lost pl and rdn alng 7th, sn tld off.*......(33 to 1 op 25 to 1) 4
DELPIOMBO 7-11-5 M Dwyer, *hld up beh, hdwy 5 out, staying on in 6th whn f 3 out....* (10 to 1 tchd 11 to 1) f
SAN LORENZO (USA) 5-11-4 N Williamson, *prmnt, led 4th, clr whn f 3 out.*..................(2 to 1 fav op 5 to 2) f
269^{2} SHREWD JOHN 7-11-5 R Garritty, *in tch, hdwy 4 out, rdn and staying on in 5th whn f nxt....* (10 to 1 op 8 to 1) f
586* BUSTINELLO (Ire) 5-11-3 (5*) B Murphy, *trkd ldrs, hdwy 6th, chsd lder 5 out, second and rdn whn hmpd and lft in lead 3 out, jnd and f nxt.*......... (5 to 1 op 4 to 1) f
PASSAGE TO FREEDOM (v) 11-11-0 D Telfer, *prmnt, wknd 5 out, beh whn pld up bef 3 out....* (40 to 1 op 33 to 1) pu
586 HADLEIGHS CHOICE 6-11-5 M Robinson, *in tch, blun 7th, sn beh, tld off whn pld up bef 3 out.* .... (66 to 1 op 50 to 1) pu
Dist: 3l, 8l, 15l. 4m 42.20s. a 28.20s (10 Ran).
(Alan Cairns), P Cheesbrough

730 Diamond Seal Windows Lady Riders Handicap Hurdle (4-y-o and up) £2,259 2m 3f 110yds.......................... (5:25)

587 PURITAN (Can) [86] 4-10-5 (5*) Mrs P Nash, *trkd ldrs gng wl, hdwy to chal 2 out, sn led, clr last.* ....(5 to 1 op 9 to 2) 1
222^{4} LITTLE BIG [87] 6-10-11 Jacqui Oliver, *hld up beh, rdn alng 3 out, hdwy appr 2 out, styd on strly und pres approaching last.*..............(7 to 1 tchd 15 to 2) 2
499^{3} DENNINGTON (Ire) [87] 5-10-11 Gee Armytage, *led, rdn 2 out, sn hdd and one pace.*......... (4 to 1 tchd 7 to 2) 3
591^{2} BALAAT (USA) [92] 5-11-2 Lorna Vincent, *hld up beh, hdwy 4 out, rdn and chsd ldrs 2 out, kpt on one pace.* ....(7 to 2 fav tchd 4 to 1) 4
599^{3} CYRILL HENRY (Ire) [76] 4-9-11 (3*) Miss A Harwood, *hld up, hdwy 4 out, rdn nxt, sn btn.* (12 to 1 tchd 14 to 1) 5
SIMPLE PLEASURE [100] 8-11-10 Mrs A Farrell, *rear, pushed alng hfwy, some hdwy 2 out, nvr dngrs.* ....(11 to 1 op 10 to 1 tchd 12 to 1) 6
QUEENS TOUR [76] 8-10-0 Susan Kersey, *beh 4 out.* .... (25 to 1 op 50 to 1) 7
ASTRABEE [96] 8-10-13 (7*) Judy Davies, *prmnt, rdn and lost pl 6th, sn beh.*.............. (14 to 1 op 25 to 1) 8
224^{5} RAAWI [76] 5-10-0 Ann Stokell, *prmnt, rdn 3 out, sn wknd.* .... (16 to 1 op 14 to 1 tchd 20 to 1) 9
ELISSA [76] 7-9-7 (7*) Miss R Judge, *al rear, tld off hfwy.* .... (100 to 1 op 66 to 1) 10
522* ROMOLA NIJINSKY [79] 5-10-3 Diane Clay, *cl up, chlgd and ev ch whn f 2 out.*.............(4 to 1 tchd 7 to 2) f
Dist: 4l, 1½l, 3½l, 25l, sht-hd, 10l, 2l, 4l, 15l. 4m 52.60s. a 19.60s (11 Ran).
(J Parks), N Tinkler

AYR (good)
Saturday October 9th
Going Correction: MINUS 0.15 sec. per fur.

731 Minishant Novices' Hurdle (4-y-o and up) £2,008 2m......................... (2:10)

TARDA 6-10-7 P Niven, *patiently rdn, improved to ld 3 out, hit last, hld on wl.*..............(7 to 2 op 5 to 2) 1
582^{2} GREAT MAX (Ire) 4-10-11 B Storey, *al hndy, drvn up to chal last 2, ran on und pres, jst fld...*(3 to 1 op 9 to 4) 2
THISTLE PRINCESS 4-9-13 (7*) B Harding, *al hndy, ev ch and bustled alng 3 out, kpt on, prmsg.* .... (6 to 1 op 8 to 1 tchd 10 to 1) 3
IMPERIAL BID (Fr) 5-10-7 (5*) P Waggott, *nvr far away, ev ch 3 out, rdn and not quicken frm nxt.* ....(5 to 2 fav op 2 to 1 tchd 3 to 1) 4
559^{4} RED TEMPEST (Ire) 5-10-5 (7*) F Perratt, *wth ldrs, led briefly hfwy, feeling pace appr 3 out, kpt on same pace.* ....(25 to 1 tchd 33 to 1) 5
541^{3} THE PATTERS MAGIC 6-10-12 C Grant, *made most, hdd briefly aftr 3rd, headed bef 4 out, outpcd frm nxt.* .... (12 to 1 op 10 to 1 tchd 14 to 1) 6
MARCO-PIERRE (Ire) 4-10-11 G McCourt, *trkd ldrs, led appr 4 out to nxt, fdd betw last 2.* (100 to 1 op 50 to 1) 7
CORSTON RACER 5-10-12 Mr J Bradburne, *wtd wth, shaken up appr 3 out, nvr able to chal.* .... (33 to 1 op 25 to 1 tchd 50 to 1) 8
BE AMBITIOUS (Ire) 5-10-12 K Jones, *took keen hold, pressed ldrs till wknd appr 3 out.* ....(50 to 1 tchd 100 to 1) 9
STATE FLYER 5-10-7 (5*) P Midgley, *hld up and beh, nvr nr to chal.*...........................(20 to 1 op 14 to 1) 10
THISONESFORALICE 5-10-12 J Callaghan, *patiently rdn, improved to join issue 3 out, btn aftr nxt.* .... (16 to 1 op 10 to 1 tchd 20 to 1) 11
582^{9} TIME PIECE (Ire) 5-10-5 (7*) J Supple, *rcd freely, led briefly aftr 3rd, feeling pace 4 out, sn lost tch.* .... (100 to 1 op 50 to 1) 12
LOCH SCAVAIG (Ire) 4-10-3 (3*) D J Moffatt, *f 1st.* .... (14 to 1 op 10 to 1 tchd 16 to 1) f
Dist: Nk, 3½l, 2l, 10l, ¾l, 1l, 1½l, ¾l, 2l, hd. 3m 40.80s. a 3.80s (13 Ran).
SR: 17/20/11/15/5/4/2/1/-/ (Mrs Dorothy Horner), Mrs M Reveley

732 Monkton Juvenile Selling Hurdle (3-y-o) £1,892 2m........................ (2:40)

578^{4} ASTRAC TRIO (USA) 10-9 (3*) A Dobbin, *made most till hdd 3 out, rallied to ld ag'n betw last 2, kpt on wl.* ....(4 to 1 op 3 to 1) 1
481^{2} SHARP SENSATION 10-12 C Grant, *took keen hold, nvr far away, led and pckd 3 out, hit nxt, hdd betw last 2, hit last, one pace.*...................(9 to 2 op 7 to 2) 2
BLUE RADIANCE 10-7 J Callaghan, *nvr far away, led briefly appr 3 out, rdn and not quicken betw last 2.* .... (14 to 1 op 12 to 1 tchd 16 to 1) 3
578* KISS IN THE DARK 11-0 P Niven, *mstks, trkd ldrs, ev ch whn hit 5th, fdd appr 3 out.* (11 to 10 fav tchd 6 to 5) 4
REBEL KING 10-7 (5*) P Waggott, *in tch, rdn appr 4 out, sn lost touch.*........(40 to 1 op 20 to 1 tchd 50 to 1) 5
272^{4} DUSKY DUCHESS (Ire) 10-7 G McCourt, *chsd ldrs, rdn whn pace quicken appr 4 out, sn lost tch.* .... (16 to 1 op 14 to 1) 6
481^{3} CHALLENGER ROW (Ire) 10-12 D Wilkinson, *chsd ldg quartet, struggling frm hfwy, tld off whn pld up bef 3 out.* ....(8 to 1 op 5 to 1) pu
Dist: 1½l, 10l, 8l, 12l, 1½l. 3m 42.30s. a 5.30s (7 Ran).
SR: 7/5/-/-/ (Lt-Col W L Monteith), P Monteith

733 Symington Novices' Chase (5-y-o and up) £2,444 3m 1f...................... (3:10)

BRACKENFIELD 7-11-0 P Niven, *jmpd carefully, led 3rd to 6th, settled till led ag'n 11th, clr last 5.* .... (4 to 1 on tchd 7 to 2 on) 1
641^{6} DROMINA STAR 12-11-2 (5*) P Williams, *patiently rdn, improved fnl circuit, lft second 5 out, styd on, not rch wnr.*...(50 to 1 op 20 to 1) 2
563* SCOTTISH GOLD 9-11-7 G McCourt, *wth wnr, led 6th till appr 11th, almost f 5 out, not reco'r.* (4 to 1 op 3 to 1) 3

FLASS VALE 5-10-11 J Callaghan, *led to 3rd, ran in snatches frm hfwy, tld off whn f 3 out.*
.................................(33 to 1 op 25 to 1 tchd 40 to 1) f
563 CELTIC WATERS 8-10-9 C Dennis, *chasing ldg trio whn f 11th.*...............................(20 to 1 op 25 to 1) f
542 BENNAN MARCH 6-10-11 (3") A Dobbin, *pressed ldrs, 3rd and bustled alng whn blun and uns rdr 7 out.*
.................................(100 to 1 op 50 to 1) ur
Dist: 8l, 3½l. 6m 21.80s. a 21.80s (6 Ran).

(Guy Faber), Mrs M Reveley

734 Annbank Maiden Hurdle (4-y-o and up) £1,987 2½m...................... (3:40)

559³ JOHNS THE BOY 7-10-5 (7") J Supple, *wth ldr, led 6th, hdd briefly 3 out, rallied gmely, ran on r-in.*
.................................(12 to 1 op 10 to 1) 1
ALI'S ALIBI 6-10-12 P Niven, *settled gng wl, nosed ahead briefly 3 out, sn pushed alng, one pace frm last.*
.................................(7 to 4 fav tchd 2 to 1) 2
POLITICAL TOWER 6-10-9 (3") A Dobbin, *nvr far away, effrt and drvn alng 3 out, styd on und pres.*
.................................(33 to 1 op 20 to 1 tchd 50 to 1) 3
656² FLING IN SPRING (v) 7-10-7 (5") P Williams, *patiently rdn, improved gng wl aftr 4 out, not quicken after nxt.*
.................................(11 to 2 op 7 to 2) 4
577³ SATIN LAKE (USA) 6-10-8⁶ (5") P Midgley, *slight ld till hdd 6th, rallied, not quicken frm betw last 2.*
.................................(6 to 1 op 5 to 1 tchd 7 to 1) 5
89⁵ BELLS HILL LAD 6-10-12 G McCourt, *settled midfield, pushed alng whn pace quickened 3 out, one pace.*
.................................(12 to 1 op 8 to 1) 6
COQUI LANE 6-10-12 B Storey, *trkd ldrs, hrd at work appr 3 out, sn outpcd.*............(16 to 1 op 12 to 1) 7
547⁹ LONDON HILL 5-10-12 Mr D Mactaggart, *chsd ldg quartet til aftr 4 out, lost tch frm nxt.*....(200 to 1 op 100 to 1) 8
HOTDIGGITY 5-10-12 M Moloney, *pushed alng to keep in tch hfwy, nvr plcd to chal.*.......(50 to 1 op 20 to 1) 9
MAN OF FASHION 7-10-9 (3") N Bentley, *chsd ldg bunch till aftr 4 out, sn btn.*..........(14 to 1 op 12 to 1) 10
HURRICANE HORACE 6-10-12 C Grant, *patiently rdn, steady hdwy aftr 4 out, ridden and fdd frm nxt.*
.................................(7 to 2 op 4 to 1 tchd 9 to 2) 11
Dist: 1½l, 4l, 2½l, 1½l, 1½l, 2½l, 20l, ½l, 1l, 12l. 4m 42.00s. a 3.00s (11 Ran).
SR: 24/22/18/15/9/11/8/-/-/ (N B Mason), N B Mason

735 Tarbolton Handicap Chase (0-135 5-y-o and up) £3,104 2½m............... (4:15)

596⁶ PINEMARTIN [113] 10-11-3 (7") N Leach, *al gng wl, jmpd ahead 7 out, given a breather appr last, cleverly.*
.................................(5 to 1 op 4 to 1 tchd 6 to 1) 1
DEEP DAWN [108] 10-11-5 C Grant, *made most till hdd 7 out, rallied und pres betw last 2, ran on wl.*
.................................(12 to 1 op 6 to 1) 2
560² BOARDING SCHOOL [103] 6-11-0 B Storey, *patiently rdn, disputing second pl whn f 8th.*
.................................(11 to 8 on op 5 to 4 on tchd 11 to 10 on) f
560⁴ NIGHT GUEST [102] 11-10-10 (3") A Dobbin, *dsptd ld, feeling pace and lost grnd fnl circuit, jmpd stickily and pld up bef 7 out.*........................(11 to 4 op 5 to 2) pu
Dist: ½l. 5m 11.60s. a 24.60s (4 Ran).

(Mrs A G Martin), G Richards

736 Crosshill Handicap Hurdle (0-135 4-y-o and up) £2,253 2¾m............... (4:50)

562³ DAWADAR (USA) [112] 6-9-12 (7") F Perratt, *trkd ldrs, improved to ld appr 3 out, styd on wl frm last.*
.................................(5 to 1 op 4 to 1) 1
LEADING PROSPECT [107] 6-10-0 B Storey, *chsd alng to keep in tch, hdwy hfwy, ev ch appr 3 out, kpt on one pace r-in.*
.........(15 to 2 op 12 to 1 tchd 14 to 1 and 16 to 1) 2
DEB'S BALL [140] 7-12-2 (3") D J Moffatt, *last and outpcd, relentless prog fnl circuit, effrt 3 out, no imprsn.*
.................................(4 to 1 op 3 to 1 tchd 5 to 2) 3
654⁸ ON THE HOOCH [108] 8-10-1⁵ (5") P Williams, *chsd alng to go pace, effrt hfwy, reminders aftr 4 out, sn btn.*
.................................(12 to 1 op 10 to 1) 4
598ⁿ BAY TERN (USA) [118] 7-10-11 P Harley, *chsd ldr, l/t in ld 7th, hdd bef 3 out, wknd quickly.....(7 to 1 op 4 to 1) 5
632ⁿ CHIEF RAIDER (Ire) [107] 5-9-9 C Bentley, *set str pace, given a breather hfwy, f 7th.*
.........(15 to 8 fav op 9 to 4 tchd 5 to 2 and 7 to 4) f
Dist: 5l, 8l, 12l, 10l. 5m 13.30s. a 3.30s (6 Ran).
SR: 11/1/26/ (J S Goldie), J S Goldie

BANGOR (soft)
Saturday October 9th
Going Correction: PLUS 1.25 sec. per fur. (races 1,3,-6,7), PLUS 1.10 (2,4,5)

737 Fenns Bank Novices' Handicap Hurdle (4-y-o and up) £2,274 2½m........... (2:20)

514² SIR PAGEANT [83] 4-10-12 (5") D Leahy, *hld up, jmpd slwly 3rd, steady hdwy 7th, wnt second nxt, led 3 out, drvn out r-in.*......................(11 to 2 op 4 to 1) 1
587⁴ MAUREEN'S FANCY [68] 8-10-2 N Smith, *hld up, lost pl and rdn alng frm 6th, hdwy und pres 4 out, wnt second appr 2 out, not rch wnr.*........(5 to 1 op 4 to 1) 2
RIDDLEMEROO [66] 8-9-9 (5") T Eley, *hld up, hdwy to chase ldrs aftr 7th, rdn 3 out, 3rd whn mstk nxt, sn btn.*
.................................(25 to 1 op 33 to 1) 3
626⁸ JALORE [79] 4-10-13 R Greene, *led, hit 5th, hdd 3 out, wknd appr nxt.*...............(11 to 2 op 9 to 2) 4
628⁶ JACK'S BARN [71] (bl) 9-10-5⁵ M Bosley, *chsd ldr, ev ch 6th, wknd aftr 4 out.*............(25 to 1 op 20 to 1) 5
683⁵ COURT OF KINGS [74] 4-9-13 (5") R Farrant, *prmnt frm 4th, rdn and wknd aftr four out.*
.................................(7 to 1 op 6 to 1 tchd 15 to 2) 6
650 MAJOR KINSMAN [90] 8-11-10 L Harvey, *trkd ldr, pushed alng aftr 7th, rdn and wknd 3 out.*
.................................(11 to 8 fav op 6 to 4 tchd 7 to 4) 7
Dist: 1½l, 10l, 10l, 5l, 6l, 3l. 5m 8.00s. a 32.00s (7 Ran).
SR: 19/2/-/-/ (The Dirty Dozen), K S Bridgwater

738 Stadco Handicap Chase (0-135 4-y-o and up) £3,562 2m 1f 110yds........... (2:50)

CLAY COUNTY [137] 8-12-2 R Dunwoody, *led, jmpd boldly, clr aftr 5 out, eased r-in, unchlgd.*
.................................(6 to 5 on op Evens) 1
ATLAAL [125] 8-11-4 J Osborne, *chsd ldr, effrt aftr 6th, wknd after 5 out, tld off.*....(11 to 10 op 5 to 4 on) 2
596⁹ ORCHIPEDZO [107] 8-9-12⁵ (7") Judy Davies, *al last, lost tch aftr 6th, tld off.*..............(20 to 1 tchd 33 to 1) 3
Dist: 30l. 4m 29.00s. a 23.00s (3 Ran).
SR: 65/-/-/ (M C Boyd), R Allan

739 Numark Handicap Hurdle (0-135 4-y-o and up) £3,030 2m 1f................. (3:20)

591³ SAYMORE [97] 7-9-13 (3") S Wynne, *hld up, cld on ldrs 5th, led appr 2 out, rdn to go clr betw last two, styd on wl.*...............(7 to 4 fav op 9 to 4 tchd 5 to 2) 1
657³ FLOWING RIVER (USA) [104] 7-10-9 R Dunwoody, *hld up, pld hrd early, cl up and ev ch 4 out, rdn to chal appr 2 out, no response.....(3 to 1 op 2 to 1 tchd 100 to 30) 2
EASTERN MAGIC [99] 5-9-13 (5") A Procter, *trkd ldrs, cl up and ev ch appr 2 out, sn rdn and unbl to quicken.*
.................................(11 to 2 op 5 to 1 tchd 6 to 1) 3
591⁵ MY LINDIANNE [95] 6-9-11 (3") M Hourigan, *pressed ldr, cl up and ev ch appr 2 out, one pace.*
.................................(12 to 1 tchd 16 to 1) 4
ANDERMATT [121] 6-11-12 J Osborne, *hld up, rdn aftr 4 out, wknd after nxt.....(11 to 2 op 4 to 1 tchd 6 to 1) 5
543⁷ EASBY MANDRINA [97] 6-10-2² R Garritty, *led til hdd appr 2 out, wknd quickly....(9 to 1 op 12 to 1 tchd 8 to 1) 6
Dist: 7l, ¾l, 2½l, 15l, 3½l. 4m 21.10s. a 31.10s (6 Ran).
(D Manning), R Hollinshead

740 Willis Corroon Handicap Chase (0-140 5-y-o and up) £4,417 3m 110yds........ (3:50)

MOSSY FERN [129] 7-11-8 J Osborne, *jmpd wl, made all, styd on strly whn chlgd frm 4 out....(9 to 4 op 2 to 1) 1
614³ CAMELOT KNIGHT [114] 7-10-7 C Llewellyn, *al chasing ldr, wnt second tenth, jmpd slwly 3 out, hrd rdn and unbl to quicken betw last 2, rallied nr finish.*
.................................(Evens fav op 11 to 8 tchd 6 to 4) 2
WHATS THE CRACK [135] 10-11-11 (3") W Marston, *drpd rear 6th, pushed alng to go 3rd tenth, lost tch aftr 12th, sn tld off.*............(9 to 2 op 4 to 1 tchd 11 to 2) 3
SOONER STILL [112] 9-9-12 (7") Judy Davies, *chsd ldrs til wknd and rdn alng aftr 9th, lost tch after 12th, tld off.*
.................................(10 to 1 op 7 to 1) 4
544 BISHOPDALE [124] 12-11-3 K Johnson, *hld up, cld up 6th, rdn and wknd quickly aftr 11th, sn tld off, pld up bef last.*.............(20 to 1 op 16 to 1 tchd 25 to 1) pu
Dist: 1½l, dist, 3l. 6m 21.50s. a 31.50s (5 Ran).
SR: 49/32/ (R Waters), O Sherwood

741 Thelwall Memorial Trophy Novices' Chase (5-y-o and up) £3,241 2½m 110yds...(4:20)

BEACHY HEAD 5-11-0 M Dwyer, *led, blun 4 out, sn reco'red, drw wl clr aftr nxt, unchlgd.*
.................................(Evens fav op 11 to 8 tchd 6 to 4) 1
586 MISS SHAW 7-10-8 (3") A Thornton, *al pressing ldr, cl up and ev ch 5 out, rdn and wknd quickly aftr 3 out, tld off.*..................(14 to 1 op 12 to 1) 2
BOLL WEEVIL 7-11-2 J Osborne, *hld up in last pl, wnt moderate 3rd aftr 9th, no hdwy frm nxt, btn whn jmpd slwly 3 out, tld off.*.............(9 to 4 op 2 to 1) 3
ON THE TEAR 7-11-2 R Dunwoody, *chsd ldg pair til wknd 9th, tld off.*...................(25 to 1 op 16 to 1) 4
517² CRAFTY CHAPLAIN 7-10-11 (5") Mr D McCain, *4th whn f 7th.*.........................(9 to 1 op 6 to 1) f
JUDGES FANCY 9-11-2 C Llewellyn, *chsd ldr, jmpd slwly, drpd rear 6th, poor 4th whn jumped badly rght, blun and uns rdr 9th.*.........(7 to 2 op 3 to 1 tchd 4 to 1) ur
Dist: 30l, 25l, dist. 5m 21.30s. a 30.30s (6 Ran).

SR: 9/-/-/   (M Tabor), J J O'Neill

742   Cock Bank Juvenile Novices' Hurdle (3-y-o) £2,389 2m 1f. . . . .(4:55)

WORDSMITH (Ire) 11-0 D J Burchell, *sn prmnt, wnt 3rd 4th, wndrd appr 6th, led aftr 3 out, clr nxt, drvn out r-in*. . . . . (11 to 1 op 11 to 10 tchd 6 to 4)		1
611 PYRRHIC DANCE 11-4 R Dunwoody, *al in tch, pressed ldr frm 4th, outpcd aftr 3 out, rdn and styd on appr last, not rch wnr*. . . . . (11 to 1 op 6 to 1 tchd 12 to 1)		2
561³ DEMILUNE (USA) 11-0 C Llewellyn, *hld up, hdwy 3rd, wnt second appr 2 out, rdn and kpt on betw last two, not quicken*. (5 to 1 tchd 6 to 1)		3
188⁵ MY BALLYBOY 10-9 (5*) A Procter, *prmnt to 3rd, lost pl nxt, rdn and rallied aftr 3 out, styd on betw last 2, not quicken*. . . . .(20 to 1 op 16 to 1)		4
611⁷ STAR MARKET 10-7 (7*) Mr S Joynes, *led till hdd appr 2 out, one pace betw last 2*. . . . (20 to 1 op 14 to 1)		5
278⁴ PEEDIE PEAT 11-0 M Dwyer, *hld up, chsd ldg grp and in tch frm 5th, no hdwy appr 2 out*. . . . .(6 to 1 op 7 to 1 tchd 8 to 1)		6
TURFMANS VISION 10-11 (3*) S Wynne, *hld up and beh, effrt aftr 5th, wknd 3 out*. . . . .(12 to 1 op 10 to 1 tchd 14 to 1)		7
GUNNER SUE 10-9 S McNeill, *hld up and beh, hdwy to go 4th aftr 5th, wknd quickly after four out*. . . . .(25 to 1 op 20 to 1 tchd 33 to 1)		8
406 BONITA BEE 10-6 (3*) W Marston, *beh frm 3rd, tld off aftr 5th*. . . . . (33 to 1 op 20 to 1 tchd 50 to 1)		9
TARGET LINE (v) 10-9 (5*) M McCain, *pressed ldr to 4th, wknd quickly aftr nxt, tld off four out, pld up bef 2 out*. . . . . (66 to 1 op 33 to 1)		10
ALMONTY (Ire) 10-9 (5*) T Eley, *beh frm 3rd, sn lost tch, tld off aftr 5th, pld up bef 2 out*. . . . . .(25 to 1 op 20 to 1)		pu

Dist: 3l, ½l, hd, 3l, 3l, nk, sht-hd, 10l, dist. 4m 25.10s. a 35.10s (12 Ran).   (P A Leonard), D Burchell

743   EBF Stakes National Hunt Flat Race (4,5,6-y-o) £1,805 2m 1f. . . . .(5:25)

LE GINNO (Fr) 6-11-11 Mr Raymond White, *hld up, hdwy to press ldr aftr 7 fs, led o'r 2 out, sn drw clr, very easily*. . . . .(2 to 1 op 6 to 4)		1
GALES CAVALIER (Ire) 5-10-11 (7*) Mr P Cashman, *hld up in last pl, rapid hdwy aftr one m, 3rd strt, sn rdn and styd on one pace, not trble wnr*. . . . . (9 to 1 op 10 to 1)		2
547² TOPPING TOM (Ire) 4-11-4 V Slattery, *led aftr one furlong, hdd 2 out, rdn and styd on one pace*. . . . . (15 to 8 fav op 7 to 4 tchd 2 to 1)		3
STEEL FABRICATOR 6-11-1 (3*) A Larnach, *hld up and beh, hdwy to chase ldg grp 6 fs out, 5th strt, kpt on one pace*. . . . . (8 to 1 op 6 to 1)		4
KING RUST 5-10-11 (7*) Mr J L Llewellyn, *prmnt aftr 4 fs, trkd ldr, fourth strt, wknd quickly fnl 2 furlongs*. . . . .(25 to 1 op 20 to 1 tchd 33 to 1)		5
LACURVA (Ire) 5-10-11 (7*) P Ward, *prmnt early, mid-div till hdwy 6 fs out, 6th strt, wnr nrr*. (33 to 1 op 20 to 1)		6
BUCKNALL BOY 4-10-11 (7*) A Shakespeare, *prmnt aftr 6 fs, wknd o'r 5 furlongs out*. . . . . . (33 to 1 op 20 to 1)		7
MAYINA 4-10-6 (7*) Mr M Rimell, *hld up and beh, lost tch aftr hfwy, tld off fnl 4 fs*. . . . . . . (11 to 1 op 8 to 1)		8
WESTCOURT FLYER 4-10-11 (7*) J Driscoll, *chsd ldg grp aftr one m, rdn o'r 5 fs out, wknd quickly, tld off fnl 3 furlongs*. . . . .(12 to 1 op 10 to 1 tchd 20 to 1)		9
COMEINTOTHELIGHT (Ire) 5-10-13 (7*) P Hide, *led for 2 fs, chsd ldr til rdn and wknd quickly o'r 6 out, tld off 3 out*. (33 to 1 op 16 to 1)		10
GAYTON RUN (Ire) 4-10-13 (5*) A Procter, *beh aftr 6 fs, tld off hfwy*. . . . .(14 to 1 op 12 to 1)		11
MISTY GREY 4-10-11 (7*) S Lycett, *lost tch aftr 7 fs, tld off*. . . . .(50 to 1 op 25 to 1)		12
TOUGH DEAL (Ire) 5-11-4 Mr B Leavy, *al prmnt, chsd ldrs, 7th strt, wknd rpdly, tld off fnl 2 fs*. . . . . (40 to 1 op 25 to 1 tchd 50 to 1)		13
TAFFY POWELL 6-10-13 (5*) R Farrant, *prmnt 4 fs, tld off aftr one m, pld up 6 furlongs out*. (33 to 1 op 20 to 1)		pu
LIVE A LITTLE 4-10-6 (7*) A Flannigan, *beh, lost tch aftr one m, tld off whn pld up 6 fs out*. . . . . .(50 to 1 op 25 to 1)		pu

Dist: 15l, ½l, 30l, 12l, 5l, 10l, 15l. 4m 10.80s. (15 Ran).   (C P E Brooks), C P E Brooks

DOWN ROYAL (IRE) (good to yielding) Saturday October 9th

744   Major Lloyd Hall-Thompson Memorial Novice Chase (4-y-o and up) £1,207 2m . . . .(2:15)

619⁴ MUST DO 7-11-11 (3*) T J Mitchell, ... (6 to 4 on)		1
489⁹ SALINA BAY 7-11-2 (7*) A Wall, ... (5 to 1)		2
EDENAKILL LAD 6-11-11 (3*) D Bromley, ...(14 to 1)		3
MASTER MILLER 7-12-0 F Woods, ... (9 to 2)		4

GABRIELLE'S BOY 8-12-0 J Shortt, ... (12 to 1)		5

Dist: 8l, 13l, 15l, dist. (Time not taken) (5 Ran).   (Sean Macklin), J H Scott

745   Vat 19 Handicap Hurdle (0-116 5-y-o and up) £1,380 2m. . . . .(2:45)

513³ BRAE [-] 5-9-12 C O'Dwyer, ...(5 to 1)		1
493⁶ SLAVOMER [-] 8-9-13 (7*) P Stafford, ...(10 to 1)		2
489³ WINDOVER LODGE [-] 6-10-8 C F Swan, ...(2 to 1 fav)		3
GLENSHANE PASS [-] 6-10-9 P McWilliams, ...(10 to 1)		4
FAMOUS DANCER [-] 5-10-12 C N Bowens, ...(5 to 1)		5
491* GARYS GIRL [-] 6-9-10 (7*) J McCormack, ...(7 to 2)		6
256 GALE FORCE NINE [-] 7-9-8 (3*) T J Mitchell, ...(20 to 1)		7
GREGORY PECK [-] (bl) 8-10-10 (7*) C O'Neill, ...(20 to 1)		8
CHANUSKA [-] (bl) 10-11-3 F Woods, ...(20 to 1)		9

Dist: Hd, 2½l, 1½l, ½l. (Time not taken) (9 Ran).   (Cecil Ross), Cecil Ross

746   Commerical Refridgeration Maiden Hurdle (4-y-o and up) £1,380 2½m. . . . . .(3:15)

489⁴ LOAVES AND FISHES 5-11-7 (7*) H Taylor, ... (7 to 1)		1
SECRET SCEPTRE 6-12-0 P McWilliams, ... (6 to 1)		2
618² LE BRAVE 7-12-0 C F Swan, ... (5 to 4 on)		3
BELLE O' THE BAY (Ire) 4-10-10 (3*) D Bromley, . .(33 to 1)		4
636⁹ IDIOTS DANCE 5-11-6 J Magee, ... (6 to 1)		5
122 MERSEY REGION 6-11-3 (3*) K B Walsh, ...(20 to 1)		6
EUROTHATCH (Ire) 5-10-13 (7*) Mr I Buchanan, . . .(14 to 1)		7
618⁷ MAWTVICA 6-10-12 (3*) Mr P McMahon, ...(20 to 1)		8
REDELVA 6-10-8 F Woods, ...(14 to 1)		9
DUKES SON 6-11-6 F Woods, ...(14 to 1)		10
341⁸ GONE LIKE THE WIND 6-11-1 (5*) L Flynn, ...(20 to 1)		11
TORSTAR 8-11-6 Mr A J Martin, ...(20 to 1)		12
GAZUMPED 6-10-8 (7*) J P Broderick, ...(20 to 1)		f
504² THEKINDWORD VI (bl) 8-11-6 J P Banahan, ...(14 to 1)		f
LADY RASHEE 6-10-13³ (5*) S McKeever, ...(20 to 1)		pu

Dist: 4½l, 22l, 9l, 10l. (Time not taken) (15 Ran).   (Mrs C Cassidy), Norman Cassidy

747   Banbridge Coachworks INH Flat Race (4 & 5-y-o) £1,380 2m. . . . .(4:45)

256⁹ WHAT IT IS (Ire) 4-10-11 (7*) Mr M Brennan, ... (7 to 1)		1
675⁸ LONG'S EXPRESS (Ire) 5-11-6 (3*) Mrs M Mullins, . .(3 to 1)		2
EXCUSE ME (Ire) 4-11-4 (5*) Mr J A Nash, ...(8 to 1)		3
COTTON CALL (Ire) 4-10-11 (7*) Mr S Laird, ...(16 to 1)		4
491³ AMME ENAEK (Ire) 4-10-11 (7*) Mr G Keane, ...(10 to 1)		5
620⁸ NO DOZING (Ire) 4-11-2 (7*) Mr B R Hamilton, . . .(7 to 4 fav)		6
491⁸ KEEP THEM KEEN (Ire) 5-11-7 (7*) Mr L Madine, . .(20 to 1)		7
495⁴ JOKERS THREE (Ire) 4-11-6 (3*) Mr A R Coonan, . . .(7 to 1)		8
STAR FLYER (Ire) 5-11-6 (3*) Mr P McMahon, ...(16 to 1)		9
THE BREAK (Ire) 4-10-11 (7*) Mr K Ross, ...(12 to 1)		10
513⁷ HIDDEN PLAY (Ire) 5-11-2 (7*) Mr J Bright, ...(12 to 1)		11
513⁶ DECEMBER BRIDE (Ire) 5-11-2 (7*) Mr E Magee, . . .(10 to 1)		12
KISMET DANCER (Ire) 4-10-11 (7*) Mr P English, . . .(8 to 1)		13
THE PARSON'S GIRL (Ire) 4-11-4 Mr M McNulty, . .(12 to 1)		14
PRINCESS DILLY (Ire) 4-10-11 (7*) Mrs A Doran, . .(20 to 1)		15
256 BASSIANESE (Ire) (bl) 4-10-13 (5*) Mr G J Harford, .(10 to 1)		16
MISSING MY POINT (Ire) 5-11-7 (7*) Mr G Martin, . .(14 to 1)		17
DISTANT FRIEND (Ire) 5-12-0 Mr A J Martin, ...(10 to 1)		18
THE GAG O'BRIEN (Ire) 5-11-7 (7*) Mr M Callaghan, ...(20 to 1)		19

Dist: 15l, ½l, 4l, sht-hd. (Time not taken) (19 Ran).   (Mrs M Holleran), J H Scott

WORCESTER (soft) Saturday October 9th

Going Correction: PLUS 0.65 sec. per fur. (races 1,3,6), PLUS 0.85 (2,4,5)

748   Bass Mitchells And Butlers Selling Handicap Hurdle (4-y-o and up) £1,926 2m (2:25)

592 HOMILE [92] 5-11-3 (7*) S Lycett, *made all, sn clr, unchlgd*. . . . . (11 to 1 op 8 to 1 tchd 12 to 1)		1
355² FULL SHILLING (USA) [69] 4-10-1 R Supple, *gd hdwy 5th, chsd wnr frm 2 out, no imprsn*. . . . . (10 to 1)		2
260⁹ AT PEACE [90] 7-11-8 A Maguire, *sn prmnt, effrt frm 3 out, styd on one pace*. . . . . (7 to 1 op 12 to 1 tchd 8 to 1)		3
RUTHS PRIDE [74] 8-9-13 (7*) Mr G Lewis, *al in tch, styd on same pace frm 3 out*. . . . . (10 to 1 op 14 to 1 tchd 16 to 1)		4
ALL PRESENT (Ire) [85] 5-11-3 P Holley, *beh, hdwy 3 out, nrst finish*. . . . . (7 to 1 op 10 to 1)		5
599² CORINTHIAN GOD (Ire) [76] 4-10-8 D Murphy, *prmnt till lost pl 4th, kpt on ag'n frm 2 out, mstk last, kept on*. . . . . (9 to 1 op 7 to 1 tchd 10 to 1)		6
612 BROWN SAUCE (NZ) [85] 7-10-12 (5*) R Davis, *beh, hdwy appr 3 out, no prog frm nxt*. . . . . (8 to 1 op 5 to 1 tchd 10 to 1)		7
520⁶ CLASS ATTRACTION (USA) [83] 4-11-1 M Foster, *chsd ldrs, rdn 3 out, wknd 2 out*. . . . . . . (12 to 1 op 8 to 1)		8
499⁴ HATS HIGH [87] (bl) 8-11-5 M Crosse, *chsd ldrs till wknd appr 3 out*. . . . . (6 to 1 op 9 to 2)		9
693⁸ L'ENCHERE [75] 8-10-7¹² (7*) Paul McEntee, *prmnt to 5th, sn wknd*. . . . . (50 to 1)		10

435⁵ FANATICAL (USA) [75] (bl) 7-10-7 V Slattery, *wnt prmnt 3rd,*
wknd aftr 5th.....................(16 to 1 op 14 to 1) 11
488⁶ OTHET [86] 9-11-4 N Hawke, *prmnt till wknd 5th.*
.............................(14 to 1 op 10 to 1) 12
WAVE MASTER [68] 6-9-7 (7⁷) T Thompson, *effrt 4th, sn*
wknd....................(20 to 1 op 16 to 1 tchd 25 to 1) 13
DOTTEREL (Ire) [68] 5-10-0 W Humphreys, *al beh.* (50 to 1) 14
186⁶ CONE LANE [82] 7-11-0 Richard Guest, *prmnt to 4th, sn*
wknd...........................(14 to 1) 15
MOST INTERESTING [86] 8-11-4 B Clifford, *al beh.*
.............................(16 to 1 op 12 to 1) 16
592 PEWTER PETA [70] 9-10-2² P McDermott, *al beh, tld off*
whn pld up aftr 5th, dismounted..............(66 to 1) pu
SULTAN'S SON [84] 7-11-10 D Bridgwater, *sn beh, tld off*
whn pld up bef 3 out.......................(12 to 1) pu
Dist: 10l, 8l, 4l, 1½l, 3l, 2l, 1½l, 2l, 1½l, 2l. 3m 58.50s. a 17.50s (18 Ran).
SR: 25/-/5/-/-/-/ (G Fierro), G Fierro

749 Bass Special Handicap Chase (0-130 5-y-o and up) £2,807 2½m 110yds........(2:55)

PANTO PRINCE [121] 12-11-5 B Powell, *jmpd wl, made*
virtually all, ran on gmely frm 3 out, fnshd tired.
.............................(3 to 1 tchd 7 to 2) 1
MUSTHAVEASWIG [123] 7-11-7 A Maguire, *prmnt, hit 8th,*
chsd wnr 9th, hit 11th, rdn and no imprsn frm 4 out,
fnshd tired........................(2 to 1 fav tchd 7 to 4) 2
589² SLIPPERY MAX [104] 9-10-2² M A FitzGerald, *chsd wnr to*
9th, wknd appr 4 out.................(20 to 1 op 12 to 1) 3
BRANDESTON [130] 8-11-9 (5⁵) B Murphy, *chsd ldrs, hit*
5th, mstk and drpd rear 7th, lost tch 11th.
.............................(100 to 30 op 2 to 1 tchd 7 to 2) 4
VIRIDIAN [110] 8-10-8 H Davies, *sn wl beh, drvn and effrt*
9th, blun and wknd tenth, tld off whn pld up bef 4 out.
.............................(4 to 1 op 9 to 2 tchd 5 to 1) pu
Dist: 15l, dist, 1l. 5m 24.00s. a 21.00s (5 Ran).
SR: 55/42/ (Mrs L M Warren), C L Popham

750 Bass Mitchells And Butlers Handicap Hurdle (4-y-o and up) £3,785 2m 5f 110yds ....(3:25)

459² MIDFIELDER [113] 7-11-3 Peter Hobbs, *chsd ldrs, led 3*
out, styd on wl frm 2 out.
.............................(10 to 1 op 6 to 1 tchd 11 to 1) 1
RIDWAN [98] 6-10-2 A S Smith, *drpd rear 4th, drvn and*
styd on frm 3 out, rdn r-in, no imprsn on wnr.
.............................(16 to 1 up to 14 to 1) 2
651³ JAMES THE FIRST [103] (bl) 5-10-7 G Bradley, *hld up,*
hdwy 7th, trkd ldrs 3 out, rdn and no imprsn frm 2 out.
.............................(7 to 1 op 5 to 1) 3
526³ STAR QUEST [105] 6-10-9 A Maguire, *beh 4th, hdwy 7th,*
ev ch 3 out, rdn and hng lft aftr 2 out.
.............................(9 to 1 op 7 to 1 tchd 10 to 1) 4
687* MEDITATOR [105] (bl) 9-10-2 (7⁷,5ex) S Curran, *led till aftr*
1st, led appr 3 out, sn hdd, wknd 2 out.
.............................(7 to 2 op 5 to 2) 5
DONT TELL THE WIFE [103] 7-10-7 D Murphy, *chsd ldrs till*
wknd aftr 3 out......................(12 to 1 op 10 to 1) 6
591⁸ KEV'S LASS (Ire) [96] 5-9-7 (7⁷) P Murphy, *led aftr 1st till*
hdd and wknd quickly appr 3 out. (25 to 1 op 20 to 1) 7
LEGAL BEAGLE [115] 6-11-5 M Perrett, *prmnt, rdn 5th,*
hmpd and blun 6th, sn lost tch, tld off whn pld up bef 3
out..........................(8 to 1 op 10 to 1) pu
646* DESPERATE [120] 5-11-10 D Bridgwater, *chsd ldrs, rdn*
5th, sn wknd, tld off whn pld up bef 3 out.
.............................(11 to 4 fav op 2 to 1 tchd 100 to 30 and 7 to 2) pu
Dist: 4l, 7l, 1½l, 8l, 20l, 15l. 5m 14.60s. a 20.60s (9 Ran).
SR: 23/4/2/2/-/-/ (Bournstream '6'), P J Hobbs

751 Carling Black Label Novices' Chase (5-y-o and up) £2,290 2m 7f..............(3:55)

593² HOWARYAFXD 6-11-0 M A FitzGerald, *made all, hit 3 out,*
styd on wl...........(5 to 4 fav op Evens tchd 11 to 8) 1
605⁵ TAURUS 7-11-0 B Powell, *propped and chsd wnr frm*
13th, jmpd lft fnl 2 fences, no imprsn, collapsed and
died aftr race......................(8 to 1 op 10 to 1) 2
649 GENEROUS SCOT 9-11-0 R Bellamy, *prmnt, hit 4th, 5th*
and 9th, lost tch frm 14th, tld off. (25 to 1 op 20 to 1) 3
518 NOTARY-NOWELL (bl) 7-10-9 (5⁵) B Murphy, *mstk 3rd, lft*
second 8th, hit 11th, wknd appr 4 out, tld off.
.............................(10 to 1 op 6 to 1) 4
593 LIZZIES LASS 8-10-9 M Crosse, *f second.*
.............................(100 to 1 op 50 to 1) f
603⁵ MIDDAY SHOW (USA) 6-11-0 S Smith Eccles, *f second.*
.............................(14 to 1 op 16 to 1) f
TARAMOSS 6-11-0 N Williamson, *chsd ldr till f 8th.*
.............................(11 to 4 op 2 to 1) f
660⁴ PAPPA DONT PREACH (Ire) 5-10-11 R Supple, *hit 4th and*
5th, sn rear, beh whn blun and uns rdr tenth.
.............................(12 to 1 op 10 to 1) ur
568⁸ COUNTY CONTRACTOR 6-11-0 P Holley, *sn beh, blun*
tenth, jmpd slwly and pld up aftr nxt.
.............................(66 to 1 op 50 to 1) pu
593 QUEENS CURATE 6-10-9 C Maude, *in tch till wknd 8th,*
tld off whn pld up bef 14th.........(66 to 1 op 50 to 1) pu

Dist: 7l, dist, 3l. 6m 13.60s. a 29.60s (10 Ran).
(V J Adams), Miss H C Knight

752 Worthington Best Bitter Handicap Chase (0-135 5-y-o and up) £2,684 2m......(4:30)

TRIMLOUGH [128] 8-12-0 N Mann, *led second, blun 4th,*
rdn whn lft clr 2 out.
.............................(Evens fav op 11 to 10 on tchd 11 to 10) 1
550⁴ OLD ROAD (USA) [100] 7-10-0 N Williamson, *led to second,*
chsd wnr to 6th, lost tch frm 8th.
.............................(5 to 1 op 7 to 1 tchd 8 to 1) 2
CAMPSEA-ASH [128] 9-11-9 (5⁵) B Murphy, *rcd in 3rd till*
chsd wnr 6th to 8th, sn lost tch....(6 to 1 op 3 to 1) 3
712² AMONG FRIENDS [100] 8-10-0 A Maguire, *rcd in 4th till*
hdwy to chase wnr 8th, str chal frm 3 out, till uns rdr
nxt...........................(9 to 4 op 5 to 2 tchd 11 to 4) ur
Dist: 1½l. 4m 9.60s. a 20.60s (4 Ran).
SR: 30/ (R A H Perkins), P T Dalton

753 Tennents Pilsner Novices' Hurdle (4-y-o and up) £1,480 2¼m...............(5:00)

650* DANCE PARTOUT (Ire) 5-11-4 Peter Hobbs, *prmnt, chlgd*
6th, led 2 out, hdd last, rallied r-in and led nr finish.
.............................(7 to 2 op 3 to 1) 1
695² SIMPLY (Ire) 4-10-11 H Davies, *in tch, pushed along 6th,*
chlgd frm 3 out till led last, hdd and outpcd nr finish.
.............................(9 to 4 fav tchd 3 to 1) 2
THE BUD CLUB (Ire) 5-10-12 N Williamson, *badly hmpd*
1st, sn tld off, gd hdwy frm 6th to track ldrs, edgd and
one pace from 2 out...........(16 to 1 op 8 to 1) 3
SOUND AND FURY 9-10-12 G Bradley, *hdwy 5th, led 6th*
till hdd 2 out, kpt on same pace. (20 to 1 op 16 to 1) 4
616⁴ GLENFINN PRINCESS 5-10-7 W Humphreys, *mstk and*
hmpd 1st, sn tld off. (12 to 1 op 10 to 1 tchd 14 to 1) 5
565⁵ WILL'S BOUNTY 10-10-5 (7⁷) Mr A Phillips, *rdn 6th, sn*
wknd, tld off......................(33 to 1 op 25 to 1) 6
TOTHEWOODS 5-10-12 D Bridgwater, *beh, sn clr, hdd 6th,*
wknd rpdly, tld off........(5 to 1 op 6 to 1 tchd 9 to 2) 7
ARCTIC COURSE (Ire) 5-10-12 A Maguire, *slpd and f 1st.*
.............................(3 to 1 op 5 to 2 tchd 4 to 1) f
597 THE GREYSMITH 6-10-12 L Harvey, *hmpd and uns rdr 1st.*
.............................(25 to 1 op 16 to 1) ur
SENIOR STEWARD 5-10-12 Richard Guest, *slpd badly,*
blun and pld up aftr second......(16 to 1 tchd 20 to 1) pu
Dist: 1l, 6l, 1½l, dist, 12l, 12l. 4m 38.40s. a 30.40s (10 Ran).
(J Tudor), P J Hobbs

CARLISLE (good)
Monday October 11th
Going Correction: MINUS 0.25 sec. per fur. (races 1,2,4,6), NIL (3,5)

754 Blencathra Juvenile Novices' Hurdle (3-y-o) £1,718 2m 1f...................(2:20)

606* GENERAL CHASE 11-1 D J Burchell, *pld hrd, cl up, led*
5th, clr 2 out, eased r-in.
.............................(6 to 4 op 11 to 8 on tchd Evens) 1
611⁵ HOT OFF THE PRESS 11-0 R J Beggan, *with ldr, chsd wnr*
frm 5th, kpt on, no imprsn.........(7 to 2 op 9 to 2) 2
CRIMINAL RECORD (USA) 11-0 Diane Clay, *mid-div, styd*
on same pace 3 out.............(12 to 1 op 7 to 1) 3
DANCE FEVER (Ire) 11-0 M Dwyer, *in tch, no hdwy frm 3*
out...........................(12 to 1 op 10 to 1) 4
278⁵ GLINT OF AYR 11-0 K Johnson, *mid-div, effrt appr 3 out,*
wkng whn hit last... (50 to 1 op 20 to 1 tchd 66 to 1) 5
516 SALLY OF THE ALLEY 10-9 Gary Lyons, *in tch to 5th, fdd nxt.*
.............................(100 to 1 op 50 to 1) 6
TTYFRAN 11-0 T Wall, *al beh*........(8 to 1 op 9 to 1) 7
MISS PIMPERNEL 10-9 L O'Hara, *al beh*....(200 to 1) 8
CAROUSEL MAGIC 11-0 C Grant, *trkd ldrs, pushed alng*
hfwy, beh 3 out.............(12 to 1 op 16 to 1) 9
RED RONNIE 10-9 B Storey, *pld hrd early, al beh, tld off*
whn pulled up bef last........(50 to 1 tchd 100 to 1) pu
Dist: 8l, 8l, 6l, 3l, 2½l, 1½l, 3½l, 12l. 4m 20.90s. a 13.90s (10 Ran).
(Eamonn O'Malley), D Burchell

755 Langdale Pike Claiming Hurdle (4-y-o and up) £1,719 2½m 110yds...........(2:50)

135⁸ DANCE OF WORDS (Ire) 4-10-10 A Maguire, *hld up png wl,*
hdwy 6th, led appr 2 out, sn quickened clr, eased r-in.
.............................(9 to 4 op 7 to 4 tchd 5 to 2) 1
FIRM PRICE 12-11-10 P Niven, *hld up, hdwy 6th, chlgd*
appr 2 out, kpt on, no ch with wnr.
.............................(11 to 10 fav op 11 to 8 tchd 6 to 4) 2
659 FAUGHAN LODGE 6-11-3 Diane Clay, *prmnt, led 8th till*
appr 2 out, one pace..............(9 to 1 op 10 to 1) 3
659 BURN BRIDGE (USA) (v) 7-10-10 Peter Caldwell, *beh, hdwy*
to join ldrs 6th, rdn appr 3 out, wkng whn mstk last.
.............................(20 to 1 op 16 to 1) 4
ELMSTEAD 7-11-0 M Ahern, *prmnt, rdn aftr 3 out, sn*
wknd...........................(16 to 1 op 14 to 1) 5

AFFAIR OF HONOUR (Ire) 5-11-6 M Dwyer, *nvr trble ldrs.*
....(8 to 1 op 6 to 1) 6
580⁴ SPEEDY SIOUX (bl) 4-9-11 (7") F Perratt, *chsd ldr, led appr
6th to 8th, wknd quickly aftr 3 out.*..........(100 to 1) 7
643⁷ AFRICAN SAFARI 9-10-7 (7") D Towler, *led till appr 6th,
wknd nxt*........................(66 to 1 op 50 to 1) 8
622 GREY REALM 5-10-9 N Smith, *mid-div, wknd 7th.*
....(100 to 1) 9
WARWICK SUITE (v) 11-10-12 A Mulholland, *mid-div,
wknd 7th*........................(50 to 1 op 33 to 1) 10
FOX TOWER 7-10-12 A Orkney, *sn beh, tld off whn
refused 6th*.....................(100 to 1 op 50 to 1) ref
319 THE RAMBLING MAN 6-11-6 N Doughty, *chsd ldrs,
reminder aftr 3rd, wknd 6th, beh whn pld up bef 2 out.*
....(25 to 1 op 16 to 1) pu
Dist: 3l, 4l, 10l, 10l, 12l, 2l, 6l, 10l, 3l. 4m 55.10s. a 2.10s (12 Ran).
SR: 10/21/10/-/-/-/ (J Howard Johnson), J H Johnson

756 Old Man Of Coniston Novices' Chase (5-y-o and up) £2,872 3m. . . . . (3:20)

653² VELEDA II (Fr) 6-10-7 (7") J Burke, *cl up, jnd ldr 12th, mstk
and led 3 out, sn rdn, styd on*.....(11 to 4 tchd 5 to 2) 1
625* DOWN THE ROAD 6-11-7 A Maguire, *rcd wide, mstk tenth,
made most to 3 out, rdn betw last 2, no extr.*
....(6 to 5 op on 11 to 10) 2
653³ THE WALTZING MOUSE (bl) 10-10-7 (7") F Perratt, *sn wth
ldr, fdd appr 4 out.*...............(25 to 1 op 20 to 1) 3
IRISH GENT 7-11-0 C Grant, *al beh....* (7 to 1 op 9 to 2) 4
653⁴ SECOND ATTEMPT 9-11-0 A Merrigan, *al beh, lost tch
hfwy, tld off.*......................(9 to 1 op 7 to 1) 5
625³ STAIGUE FORT (Ire) 5-10-6 (5") P Waggott, *in tch till wknd
aftr 13th, beh whn pld up bef 2 out.*
....(8 to 1 tchd 10 to 1) pu
Dist: 8l, 12l, 6l. dist. 6m 17.20s. a 18.20s (6 Ran).
(L H Froomes), Mrs S A Bramall

757 Helvellyn Handicap Hurdle (0-125 4-y-o and up) £2,049 2m 1f. . . . . (3:50)

654² TAROUDANT [120] 6-12-0 P Niven, *hld up gng wl, hdwy
on bit to ld 2 out, shaken up and quickened clr, eased
r-in.*...............(11 to 10 on op Evens tchd 6 to 5) 1
A GENTLEMAN TWO [92] 7-10-0 A Maguire, *made most to 2
out, kpt on, no ch wth wnr, fnshd lme.*
....(14 to 1 tchd 16 to 1) 2
MAKE ME PROUD (Ire) [97] (v) 4-9-12 (7") S Taylor, *chsd ldrs,
outpcd appr 3 out, styd on approaching last.*
....(9 to 1 op 7 to 1) 3
JEFFERBY [93] 6-10-1 M Ahern, *cl up till wknd appr 2 out.*
....(20 to 1 op 14 to 1) 4
CHANTRY BARTLE [108] 7-11-2 D Wilkinson, *prmnt till
wknd appr 2 out......* (13 to 8 op 6 to 4 tchd 11 to 8) 5
Dist: 6l, 7l, 2l, 8l. 4m 8.40s. a 1.40s (5 Ran).
SR: 44/10/8/2/9/ (G A Farndon), Mrs M Reveley

758 Scafell Handicap Chase (0-135 5-y-o and up) £3,143 2½m 110yds. . . . . (4:20)

643⁶ SIR PETER LELY [105] 6-10-7 C Grant, *sn cl up, led 8th to
9th, led nxt, drw clr appr 2 out, easily.*
....(5 to 2 op 2 to 1) 1
CORNET [133] (v) 7-11-9 (5") P Waggott, *in tch, chsd wnr
appr 4 out, sn rdn, wknd approaching 2 out.*
....(9 to 4 op 2 to 1) 2
579² CHARMING GALE [107] 6-10-27 (5") P Williams, *prmnt till
wknd 4 out.*........(11 to 8 fav op 5 to 4 tchd 6 to 4) 3
643 WHEELIES NEWMEMBER [105] 10-10-0 K Johnson, *made
most to tenth, wknd 4 out.*..........(16 to 1 op 12 to 1) 4
Dist: 20l, 1l, 10l. 5m 8.00s. a 5.00s (4 Ran).
SR: 22/30/3/-/ (John Doyle Construction Limited), M D Hammond

759 Skiddaw Handicap Hurdle (0-125 5-y-o and up) £2,124 3m 110yds. . . . . (4:50)

COUNTOROUS [92] 7-10-12 A Maguire, *hld up gng wl,
hdwy appr 3 out, led aftr nxt, styd on well.*
....(9 to 4 op 5 to 2 tchd 3 to 1) 1
644* MARRA'S ROSCOE [108] 7-12-0 P Niven, *in tch, hdwy to
track ldrs 7th, led 2 out, sn hdd, btn whn mstk last.*
....(2 to 1 fav tchd 9 to 4) 2
JOCK'S BURN [88] 7-10-1 (7") N Leach, *hld up, effrt appr 2
out, styd on.*..........(11 to 2 op 6 to 1 tchd 13 to 2) 3
644² SHELTON ABBEY [106] 7-11-9 (3") A Larnach, *wth ldr, led 4
out to 2 out, one pace.*..............(4 to 1 op 3 to 1) 4
INVERINATE [86] 8-10-6¹ Mr C Ewart, *chsd ldrs, one pace 3
out.*...............................(20 to 1 op 16 to 1) 5
580³ HUNMANBY GAP [81] 8-10-1 C Hawkins, *in tch, rdn aftr 3
out, no hdwy.*.........................(6 to 1 op 5 to 1) 6
564⁵ IT'S A PRY [80] 12-10-0 K Johnson, *made most to 4 out,
fdd....*................................(66 to 1 op 33 to 1) 7
337³ ONE FOR LUCK (Ire) [93] 5-10-13 M Dwyer, *trkd ldrs, effrt
aftr 3 out, sn btn.*...................(9 to 1 op 7 to 1) 8
Dist: 4l, ¾l, 3l, 3l, 6l, 1l. 5m 59.10s. a 6.10s (8 Ran).
(D Gill), J H Johnson

FONTWELL (good to soft)

Monday October 11th
**Going Correction: PLUS 1.00 sec. per fur. (races
1,3,5), PLUS 1.25 (2,4,6)**

760 Singleton Juvenile Selling Hurdle (3-y-o) £1,534 2¼m. . . . . (2:10)

608² OCTOBER BREW (USA) (bl) 11-4 R Dunwoody, *trkd ldr, led
o'r 2 out, styd on.*............(2 to 1 fav tchd 5 to 2) 1
588² MISTER BLAKE (v) 10-12 R Campbell, *took keen hold, trkd
ldrs, rdn appr last, kpt on r-in.*
....(3 to 1 op 5 to 2 tchd 9 to 4) 2
OMIDJOY (Ire) 10-7 S Smith Eccles, *mstk 1st, in cl tch till
reminders and outpcd 4 out, styd on wl und pres frm
last...............*.............(13 to 2 op 6 to 1 tchd 8 to 1) 3
668⁶ DO BE WARE 10-9 (3") A Thornton, *trkd ldrs, pushed alng
appr 4 out, one pace frm 2 out.*
....(25 to 1 op 12 to 1 tchd 33 to 1) 4
379² SIAN WYN 10-7 R Supple, *led till hdd o'r 2 out, no extr.*
....(9 to 1 op 10 to 1 tchd 12 to 1 and 8 to 1) 5
611⁹ TOUCH SILVER 10-12 M Bosley, *in tch, hdwy aftr 3 out,
sn no extr.*.........................(50 to 1 op 33 to 1) 6
497³ LADY OF SHADOWS 10-2 (5") A Dicken, *beh, cld 4 out,
wknd aftr nxt.*....(100 to 30 op 11 to 4 tchd 7 to 2) 7
PFAFF'S CELLAR 10-7 A Charlton, *jmpd slwly and drpd
rear 3rd, pld up bef 5th............*..(50 to 1 op 20 to 1) pu
WATER DIVINER 10-12 J Ryan, *hld up in tch, wknd aftr 4
out, tld off whn pld up bef 2 out.*..(50 to 1 op 25 to 1) pu
604⁹ SWIFT REVENGE 10-7 Lorna Vincent, *whipped round strt,
al beh, tld off whn pld up bef 4 out.*(33 to 1 op 16 to 1) pu
Dist: ½l, 1½l, ½l, 4l, 3½l, 12l. 4m 40.90s. a 30.90s (10 Ran).
(M C Pipe), M C Pipe

761 Frank Cundell Challenge Trophy Handicap Chase (0-135 4-y-o and up) £2,846 2m 3f
. . . . (2:40)

HOLTERMANN (USA) [103] 9-10-10 M Richards, *pld early,
settled in tch, cld tenth, led aftr 4 out, brushed through
last 2, all out*............(9 to 4 op 3 to 1 tchd 7 to 2) 1
602⁵ KISU KALI [99] 6-10-6 J R Kavanagh, *hld up in cl tch, wnt
second at 9th, ev ch 4 out, sn one pace, rallied r-in.*
....(4 to 1 op 7 to 2 tchd 9 to 2) 2
AMARI KING [117] 9-11-10 C Llewellyn, *cl up till lost tch
11th, tld off.......*.(2 to 1 fav tchd 5 to 2) 3
GOLD SHAFT [93] 10-10-0 Mrs N Ledger, *led to second, cl
up till lost tch tenth, tld off.*
....(33 to 1 op 20 to 1 tchd 16 to 1) 4
VODKA FIZZ [98] 8-10-5¹ D Murphy, *led second till hdd
aftr 4 out, wknd quickly and pld up bef nxt.*
....(7 to 2 op 3 to 1 tchd 4 to 1) pu
Dist: 3l, 30l, 10l. 5m 9.30s. a 34.30s (5 Ran).
(V & T Ass), Mrs L Richards

762 'Salmon Spray' Challenge Trophy Handicap Hurdle (0-135 4-y-o and up) £3,574 2 ¼m. . . . . (3:10)

CHANGE THE ACT [117] 8-10-11 J Osborne, *wth ldr, given
breather 4 out, led o'r 2 out, hdd r-in, rallied to ld ag'n
nr finish..............*.........(11 to 2 op 7 to 2) 1
629² NAHAR [116] 8-10-10 H Davies, *hld up in cl tch, hdwy o'r
2 out, led briefly r-in, ran on. ....*(2 to 1 jt-
fav op 9 to 4 tchd 5 to 2) 2
PIPERS COPSE [114] 9-10-12 M Perrett, *led till hdd o'r 2
out, sn outpcd......*.(20 to 1 op 14 to 1 tchd 16 to 1) 3
MENEBUCK [127] 7-11-7 E Murphy, *in cl tch, ev ch 4 out,
rdn nxt and sn btn.......*.(4 to 1 op 3 to 1 tchd 5 to 1) 4
601² FOTOEXPRESS [116] 5-10-3 (7") L Dace, *trkd ldrs, mstk 3
out, sn btn.......*.(2 to 1 jt-fav tchd 9 to 4) 5
MAJOR INQUIRY (USA) [125] 7-11-5 D Murphy, *hld up in
tch, wknd aftr 3 out...*.(10 to 1 op 5 to 1 tchd 12 to 1) 6
Dist: 1l, 15l, 1l, 5l, 7l. 4m 32.00s. a 22.00s (6 Ran).
SR: 43/41/44/36/20/22/ (Christopher Heath), O Sherwood

763 Hurlimann Swiss Lager Challenge Trophy Novices' Chase (5-y-o and up) £2,154 2m 3f
. . . . (3:40)

YELLOW SPRING 8-11-2 Peter Hobbs, *cl up, mstk 3rd, led
and hit last, ran on wl.*
....(11 to 8 fav op 5 to 4 tchd 6 to 4) 1
GANDOUGE GLEN 6-11-2 D Murphy, *led 5th till hdd last,
ran on.......*.(5 to 2 op 2 to 1 tchd 11 to 4) 2
THE GOLFING CURATE 8-10-13 H Davies, *beh, mstks 4th
and 8th, hdwy 11th, one pace frm 3 out.*
....(7 to 1 op 8 to 1 tchd 9 to 2) 3
613 GALLANT EFFORT (Ire) 5-11-0 W McFarland, *trkd ldrs,
mstk 11th, one pace frm 4 out.*
....(9 to 2 op 5 to 1 tchd 11 to 2) 4
667⁴ SMART DRESSER 8-10-13 J R Kavanagh, *mstk 5th, hdwy
8th, 4th and wkng whn blun 12th, tld off.*
....(33 to 1 op 25 to 1 tchd 20 to 1) 5
PATRUSIKA 7-10-8 J Akehurst, *led second to 5th, beh frm
9th, tld off.*......................(33 to 1 tchd 50 to 1) 6

521 AS GOOD AS GOLD 7-11-2 J Railton, *mstk second, hld up in rear, beh frm 9th, tld off.*
.... (50 to 1 op 20 to 1 tchd 66 to 1) 7
600⁶ CAIRNEYMOUNT 7-10-13 A Webb, *led to second, in rear whn slpd up on turn aftr 9th.*
.... (50 to 1 op 20 to 1 tchd 66 to 1) su
Dist: 1½l, 15l, 8l, 30l, 30l, 5l. 5m 4.30s. a 29.30s (8 Ran).
SR: 32/30/12/5/-/ (Mrs R Howell), D M Grissell

764 EBF Teddington Cricket Club 'National Hunt' Novices' Hurdle Qualifier (4,5,6-y-o) £1,987 2¼m...................... (4:10)

RIVER LOSSIE 4-11-0 J Osborne, *made all, quickened appr last, ran on wl, not extended.*
.... (9 to 4 op 2 to 1 tchd 11 to 4) 1
PRINCESS HOTPOT (Ire) 5-10-4 (5*) R Farrant, *al prmnt, ev ch o'r 2 out, one pace appr last...* (33 to 1 op 14 to 1) 2
456² BILLY BORU 5-11-5 D Gallagher, *hld up in rear, hdwy whn jmpd slwly 4 out and nxt, one pace frm 2 out.*
.... (13 to 8 fav op 6 to 4 tchd 2 to 1) 3
RELATIVE OCTAVE 4-11-0 Peter Hobbs, *beh, cld aftr 5th, pushed alng 4 out, kpt on one pace.*
.... (3 to 1 tchd 5 to 2 and 4 to 1) 4
GLENCARRIG GALE (Ire) 5-11-0 .I Railton, *cl up, jmpd slwly second, wknd o'r 3 out.*
.... (33 to 1 op 25 to 1 tchd 40 to 1) 5
PILGRIMS WAY (NZ) 6-11-0 D Murphy, *wtd wth, hdwy 4 out, ev ch nxt, wknd appr 2 out.*
.... (8 to 1 op 5 to 1 tchd 9 to 1) 6
634 REG'S HOLLOA (Ire) 5-11-0 R Supple, *al beh.*
.... (20 to 1 op 14 to 1) 7
380 POLLY MINOR 6-10-9 M Perrett, *al beh.*
.... (33 to 1 op 20 to 1 tchd 40 to 1) 8
THE MINISTER (Ire) 4-11-0 M A FitzGerald, *al beh.*
.... (25 to 1 op 14 to 1 tchd 33 to 1) 9
616⁶ TREASSOWE MARINER 5-11-0 H Davies, *trkd ldrs till wknd 4 out..........* (14 to 1 op 16 to 1 tchd 20 to 1) 10
Dist: 6l, 8l, 1½l, 10l, 12l, 2½l, 10l, 8l, 5l. 4m 41.50s. a 31.50s (10 Ran).
(Chris Brasher), C R Egerton

765 Norfolk Challenge Cup Amateur Riders' Handicap Chase (0-125 4-y-o and up) £2,183 3¼m 110yds................ (4:40)

TAMMY'S FRIEND [98] 6-10-10 Mr M Armytage, *cl up, led 15th, clr o'r 4 out, hit 2 out, ran on wl........* (3 to 1 jt-fav op 7 to 4 tchd 9 to 4) 1
CYTHERE [116] 9-11-7 (7*) Mr T McCarthy, *pressed ldrs, chsd wnr aftr 3 out, no imprsn.*
.... (7 to 1 op 5 to 1 tchd 8 to 1) 2
GOLD CAP (Fr) [115] 8-11-6 (7*) Mr G Lewis, *mstks thrght, chsd wnr frm 15th, outpcd o'r 4 out, lost second aftr nxt, rgned second r-in till eased nr finish....* (2 to 1 jt-fav tchd 11 to 4) 3
NO GRANDAD [109] 9-11-0 (7*) Mr T Byrne, *in tch, 4th and wkng whn f four out (water).*
.... (4 to 1 op 9 to 2 tchd 5 to 1) f
600* GLEBE PRINCE [95] 13-10-7\10 (3*) Mr J Durkan, *led till hdd 14th, wknd appr 16th, tld off whn pld up bef 3 out.*
.... (5 to 1 op 3 to 1 tchd 11 to 2) pu
Dist: 20l, nk. 7m 22.60s. a 52.60s (5 Ran).
(Mrs Elizabeth Hitchins), Mrs J Pitman

SEDGEFIELD (soft)
Tuesday October 12th
Going Correction: PLUS 0.80 sec. per fur. (races 1,2,-5,6), PLUS 0.30 (3,4)

766 John Wade Haulage Conditional Jockeys' Selling Hurdle (3-y-o and up) £1,266 2m 1f 110yds...................... (2:20)

626⁴ FELL WARDEN 5-11-9 A Larnach, *al hndy, shaken up whn pace quickened 2 out, styd on to ld cl hme.*
.... (7 to 2 op 5 to 2) 1
626⁵ SUNTAN (Fr) 4-11-2 (7*) K Davies, *trkd ldrs, drvn alng whn pace quickened 2 out, rallied r-in, fnshd wl.*
.... (7 to 1 tchd 6 to 1) 2
514⁵ SUMMERS DREAM 3-10-2 A Thornton, *settled gng wl, led on bit 2 out, sn clr, rdn last, wknd and ct cl hme.*
.... (8 to 1 op 6 to 1) 3
717 WELLSY LAD (USA) 6-11-9 A Dobbin, *patiently rdn, improved gng wl to ld 3 out, hdd nxt, fdd last.*
.... (9 to 1 op 8 to 1) 4
588⁷ MONASTIC FLIGHT (Ire) 3-10-2 (5*) G Cahill, *nvr far away, led and jmpd rght 4th, hdd 3 out, hndy till wknd betw last 2.....................* (20 to 1 op 16 to 1) 5
334⁴ WAWEEWAWOO (Ire) 5-11-4 D J Moffatt, *chsd ldrs, drvn alng to keep up aftr 3 out, no imprsn.*
.... (20 to 1 op 12 to 1) 6
622⁵ JUMPING CACTUS 4-11-9 P Waggott, *wtd wth, jnd ldrs hfwy, bustled alng aftr 3 out, sn btn.*
.... (5 to 2 fav op 3 to 1 tchd 100 to 30) 7

MILO 7-11-6 (3*) C Woodall, *keen hold, dsptd ld to hfwy, wknd quickly 3 out.* (12 to 1 op 33 to 1 tchd 50 to 1) 8
NOBBY 7-11-9 J Supple, *trkd ldrs, struggling to hold pl hfwy, lost tch bef 3 out.....................* (20 to 1) 9
GLASTONDALE 7-11-6 (3*) B Harding, *struggling aftr 3rd, pld up bef 5th.....................* pu
625 RISEUPWILLIEREILLY 7-11-4 (5*) F Leahy, *led to 4th, wknd rpdly four out, pld up aftr nxt......* (9 to 1 op 6 to 1) pu
642 RICH HEIRESS (Ire) (bl) 4-11-4 F Perratt, *chsd ldrs to hfwy, lost tch and pld up aftr 3 out......* (50 to 1 op 33 to 1) pu
Dist: ½l, sht-hd, 6l, 4l, 10l, 20l, 8l, hd. 4m 20.40s. a 25.40s (12 Ran).
(Brian Todd), J A Hellens

767 Plumb Center Handicap Hurdle (0-125 4-y-o and up) £1,935 2m 5f 110yds...... (2:50)

INTEGRITY BOY [89] 6-10-11 L Wyer, *patiently rdn, improved gng wl aftr 3 out, kpt on und pres to ld nr finish................*(40 to 1 op 33 to 1 tchd 50 to 1) 1
283 TRONCHETTO (Ire) [94] (bl) 4-11-2 M Dwyer, *made most, pushed clr appr 2 out, rdn aftr last, ct nr finish.*
.... (16 to 1 op 12 to 1) 2
719² KINOKO [99] 5-11-4 (3*) S Wynne, *settled gng wl, chlgd appr 2 out, rdn and one pace betw last two.*
.... (3 to 1 tchd 7 to 2) 3
MYTHICAL STORM [92] 6-11-0 P Niven, *wtd wth, pushed up to join ldrs appr 4 out, wknd and eased betw last 2.*
.... (6 to 4 fav op 7 to 4 tchd 5 to 4) 4
644⁴ THE GREEN FOOL [105] 6-11-6 (7*) F Perratt, *wtd wth, improved on ins to chal aftr 3 out, fdd betw last 2.*
.... (9 to 1 op 8 to 1 tchd 10 to 1) 5
623* MR REINER (Ire) [106] 5-11-7 (7*) D Ryan, *trkd ldg pair, drvn to draw level 7th, blun nxt, rdn and btn 2 out.*
.... (11 to 2 op 9 to 3 tchd 6 to 1) 6
623⁷ MILL DE LEASE [78] 8-10-0 A Maguire, *pressed ldrs, ev ch appr 3 out, reminders bef nxt, sn btn.*
.... (33 to 1 op 25 to 1) 7
SKIRCOAT GREEN [100] 8-11-1 (7*) G Tormey, *dsptd ld to 4th, struggling to hold pl 3 out, sn btn.*
.... (7 to 1 op 6 to 1) 8
623 NO SID NO STARS (USA) [100] 5-11-8 J Callaghan, *chsd ldrs, hrd drvn appr 4 out, sn lost tch.*
.... (16 to 1 op 12 to 1) 9
Dist: 1l, ¾l, 12l, 4l, 3l, 6l, 5l, dist. 5m 14.70s. a 23.70s (9 Ran).
SR: 18/22/26/7/16/14/ (Nigel Lowrey), R O'Leary

768 Sam Berry Novices' Chase (4-y-o and up) £1,665 2m 5f...................... (3:20)

625² KEEP BIDDING 7-11-7 P Niven, *led till aftr 5th, led 8th to nxt, led after 5 out, drw clr last 2, styd on wl.*
.... (5 to 2 fav op 6 to 4) 1
653* CLARE LAD 10-11-11 B Storey, *patiently rdn, improved to join wnr aftr 4 out, ridden alng aftr nxt, no imprsn whn hit last.....................* (7 to 2 tchd 4 to 1) 2
SHEILAS HILLCREST 7-11-0 (7*) J Supple, *al hndy, led aftr 5th to 8th, led 9th till aftr 5 out, wknd quickly last 3.....................* (10 to 1 op 8 to 1) 3
641⁵ EBRO (bl) 7-11-7 A Merrigan, *chsd ldrs, 4th and bustled alng whn slpd and almost f 5 out, not reco'r, tld off.*
.... (33 to 1) 4
721³ MY TURN NEXT 5-10-12 (3*) N Bentley, *in tch, chasing ldg 4 and rdn whn f 5 out..........* (10 to 1 op 8 to 1) f
653 EDEN SUNSET 7-11-7 Mr Chris Wilson, *settled gng wl, clsg whn f 9th..........* (9 to 2 op 5 to 1 tchd 6 to 1) f
427³ TROPNEVAD (bl) 5-11-6 M Dwyer, *jmpd slwly and lost pl 3rd, struggling to keep up whn blun and uns rdr 9th.*
.... (8 to 1 op 7 to 1) ur
732² DROMINA STAR 12-11-6 (5*) P Williams, *wth ldr till pld up appr 5th.....................* (10 to 1 op 8 to 1 tchd 12 to 1) pu
Dist: 8l, 12l, dist. 5m 34.20s. a 30.20s (8 Ran).
(Ray Craggs), M Dods

769 Archibalds Handicap Chase (0-135 5-y-o and up) £2,586 2m 1f................ (3:50)

LOGAMIMO [125] 7-11-1 (3*) A Larnach, *patiently rdn, hdwy 4 out, led last, ran on strly....* (8 to 1 op 6 to 1) 1
643² SONSIE MO [107] 8-10-0⁵ (5*) P Williams, *nvr far away, chsd wnr 4 out, rdn betw last 2, hdd last, no extr.*
.... (9 to 2 op 7 to 2) 2
MAUDLINS CROSS [120] 8-10-13 P Niven, *wtd wth, shaken up and hdwy appr 4 out, no imprsn nxt.*
.... (7 to 2 op 9 to 4) 3
590* CLARES OWN [107] 9-10-0 B Storey, *chsd ldr frm 3rd, drvn alng to keep up aftr 5 out, lost tch nxt.*
.... (11 to 2 op 4 to 1) 4
BORO SMACKEROO [135] 8-12-0 A Maguire, *wnt freely to post, set str pace, hit 7th, hdd 4 out, btn whn blun nxt.*
.... (13 to 8 fav op 5 to 4 tchd 9 to 4) 5
Dist: 3l, 30l, 12l, 6l. 4m 14.50s. a 9.50s (5 Ran).
SR: 46/25/8/-/5/ (J A Hellens), J A Hellens

770 Ramside Catering Novices' Handicap Hurdle (0-100 4-y-o and up) £1,576 3m 3f 110yds...................... (4:20)

639* LARAPINTA (Ire) [81] 5-11-10 A Maguire, *patiently rdn, led aftr 3 out, ridden frm last, ran on wl.*
....(5 to 4 fav op 6 to 4) 1
639² KILMINFOYLE [75] 6-11-4 P Niven, *rcd keenly, al hndy, ev ch 3 out, kpt on r-in*................(4 to 1 op 3 to 1) 2
659⁴ SUASANAN SIOSANA [66] 8-10-9 R Supple, *wtd wth, hdwy to join ldrs 3 out, outpcd betw last 2.*
....(7 to 1 op 5 to 1) 3
LOOSE WHEELS [72] (v) 7-11-1 A Carroll, *made most, quickened 4 out, hdd aftr nxt, fdd last 2......*(20 to 1) 4
659⁷ SAFARI KEEPER [67] (v) 7-10-3 (7*) W Fry, *with ldr, ev ch and drvn alng aftr 3 out, fdd nxt*.............(16 to 1) 5
737² MAUREEN'S FANCY [68] 8-10-11 N Smith, *settled midfield, effrt and drvn alng appr 3 out, sn struggling.*
....(6 to 1 op 5 to 1 tchd 7 to 1) 6
559⁵ BLUEBELL TRACK [62] (bl) 7-10-5 A Merrigan, *chsd ldrs, struggling to hold pl fnl circuit, tld off.*
....(33 to 1 op 25 to 1) 7
577⁶ DOUCE ECLAIR [73] 7-11-2 C Grant, *chsd ldrs till blun and uns rdr 5 out*................(14 to 1 op 12 to 1) ur
656 MACMURPHY [60] 8-10-3 B Storey, *tubed, settled off the pace, hdwy and ev ch 4 out, wknd quickly and pld up betw last 2*......................(12 to 1 tchd 20 to 1) pu
Dist: ½l, 10l, 12l, 8l, 3l, 6l. 7m 7.00s. a 41.00s (9 Ran).

(Thomas Harty), J H Johnson

771 Quarrinton Novices' Hurdle (4-y-o and up) £1,035 2m 1f 110yds.............(4:50)

JOMOVE 4-10-11 P Niven, *wtd wth, hdwy frm 3 out, rdn last, kpt on wl to ld last 50 yards...* (10 to 1 op 4 to 1) 1
597³ IRON BARON (Ire) 4-10-11 G McCourt, *patiently rdn, led 3 out, drvn alng r-in, ct last 50 yards.*
.......(5 to 4 fav op 11 to 8 tchd 6 to 4 and 11 to 10) 2
616⁵ FATHER DAN (Ire) 4-11-4 A Maguire, *settled gng wl, chlgd on bit appr 2 out, rdn aftr last, one pace.*
....(9 to 2 op 1 tchd 5 to 1) 3
SILVERDALE FOX 6-10-9 (3*) S Wynne, *wtd wth, chlgd appr 2 out, bumped last, not quicken.*
....(33 to 1 op 25 to 1) 4
482⁷ VAL DE RAMA (Ire) 4-10-6 (5*) P Waggott, *settled midfield, wnt hndy hfwy, rdn and one pace 2 out......*(33 to 1) 5
MARCHWOOD 6-10-12 K Johnson, *settled off the pace, improved aftr 3 out, styd on betw last 2......* (25 to 1) 6
BAHER (USA) 4-10-11 C Grant, *nvr far away, led aftr 4 out to nxt, outpcd betw last 2......*(20 to 1 op 14 to 1) 7
MARSDEN ROCK 6-10-0 (7*) J Supple, *hit second, sn reco'red, rdn frm 3 out, kpt on same pace.*
....(6 to 1 op 5 to 1 tchd 7 to 1) 8
PRECIOUS HENRY 4-10-11 J Railton, *trkd ldrs, feeling pace aftr 3 out, fdd..................*(33 to 1 op 16 to 1) 9
559⁹ DONEGAL STYLE (Ire) 5-10-12 G Upton, *settled off the pace, pushed alng appr 3 out, nvr dngrs.*
....(16 to 1 op 14 to 1) 10
656 SMOKE (bl) 7-10-0 (7*) F Perratt, *clr ldr till hdd aftr 4 out, wknd quickly....................*(20 to 1 op 16 to 1) 11
656 HERBALIST 4-10-8 (3*) A Larnach, *settled midfield, effrt whn 4 out..........*(15 to 2 op 6 to 1 tchd 8 to 1) f
SONNY-P 5-10-12 L Wyer, *pld hrd, slpd bend appr second, settled midfield hfwy, wknd quickly and pulled up bef 2 out........................*(33 to 1) pu
482 CHERYL'S GIRL 7-10-7 A Orkney, *pld hrd, pressed ldr till wknd quickly 4 out, pulled up bef 2 out.........*(33 to 1) pu
Dist: 1½l, 1l, hd, 7l, 2½l, 1l, nk, 1½l, 8l, dist. 4m 15.90s. a 20.90s (14 Ran).
SR: 14/12/18/12/4/2/

(Raby Racing), Mrs M Reveley

EXETER (soft (races 1,2,4,5,7), good to soft (3,6))

Wednesday October 13th
Going Correction: PLUS 0.85 sec. per fur. (races 1,2,-4,5,7), PLUS 1.05 (3,6)

772 Dean & Dyball Novices' Hurdle (4-y-o and up) £1,998 2m 3f.................(2:20)

605* MAYS TREASURE (USA) 4-11-4 J Frost, *rcd keenly, trkd ldr frm second, led appr 2 out, clr last, cmftbly.*
....(7 to 4 fav op Evens) 1
715 KING UBAD (USA) 4-11-4 A Maguire, *led till hdd appr 2 out, rdn and outpcd approaching last.*
....(4 to 1 op 11 to 4) 2
COTTAGE WALK (NZ) 6-10-7 (5*) R Davis, *hld up, gd hdwy appr 3rd, ev ch 2 out, rdn and one pace.*
....(11 to 1 op 6 to 1 tchd 10 to 1) 3
628³ OATS IN BARLEY 4-10-11 I Shoemark, *chsd ldrs till wknd appr 2 out......................*(9 to 1 op 16 to 1) 4
SNICKERSNEE 5-10-12 S Hodgson, *al beh, ran on past btn horses r-in......................*(9 to 1 op 14 to 1) 5
DUNNICKS VIEW 4-10-11 C Maude, *chsd ldrs till wknd 3 out................................*(66 to 1) 6
716 JAY JAYS DREAM 7-10-7 A Webb, *al beh, tld off frm 4th.* ....(100 to 1) 7
704 IN A WHIRL (USA) 5-10-7 Mr P Hamer, *al beh, tld off frm 4th*.............(50 to 1 tchd 66 to 1 and 33 to 1) 8

BENJAMIN 5-10-12 C Llewellyn, *in tch till rdn and wknd 4th, pld up aftr nxt......*(2 to 1 op 9 to 4 tchd 5 to 2) pu
ROYAL GIOTTO 7-10-12 M Hourigan, *al beh, tld off whn pld up aftr 3 out...............*(66 to 1 op 25 to 1) pu
Dist: 10l, 5l, 15l, 15l, 3l, ½l, 5l. 4m 47.00s. a 28.00s (10 Ran).

(Paul Mellon), I A Balding

773 Dean & Dyball Novices' Handicap Hurdle (0-100 4-y-o and up) £1,851 2m 1f 110yds ....(2:50)

EDIMBOURG [73] 7-10-3 J Osborne, *made virtually all, drw clr appr 3 out, mstk last, unchlgd.*
....(7 to 2 fav tchd 9 to 2) 1
597⁴ STYLE AND CLASS [95] 4-11-6 (5*) C Burnett-Wells, *hld up in rear, gd hdwy to go second appr 2 out, no ch with wnr......................*(9 to 2 op 4 to 1) 2
710 PABREY [70] 7-9-7 (7*) Miss S Mitchell, *hld up, hdwy frm second, kpt on one pace from 2 out.*
....(10 to 1 op 33 to 1) 3
SPUR BAY [70] 6-10-0 B Powell, *prmnt till wknd appr 2 out....................*(10 to 1 op 9 to 1 tchd 11 to 1) 4
LUCAYAN GOLD [71] 9-10-11 R Greene, *prmnt, chsd wnr frm second to 3 out, sn btn..........*(33 to 1 op 25 to 1) 5
565⁶ GILBERT (Ire) [70] 5-10-0 Lorna Vincent, *pld hrd, prmnt till wknd appr 3 out................*(33 to 1 op 20 to 1) 6
FLY GUARD (NZ) [98] 6-12-0 J Frost, *beh, some hdwy 3 out, nvr dngrs..........*(16 to 1 op 10 to 1 tchd 20 to 1) 7
TEARFUL PRINCE [70] 9-10-0 D Bridgwater, *al in rear.*
....(33 to 1 op 25 to 1 tchd 50 to 1) 8
ROSS GRAHAM [85] 5-11-1 G Morgan, *beh, hdwy appr second, wknd quickly 3 out........*(10 to 1 op 14 to 1) 9
715⁶ INDIAN MAESTRO [71] 7-10-11 M A FitzGerald, *al beh, tld off.......................*(14 to 1 op 12 to 1 tchd 16 to 1) 10
650 NORDIC FLIGHT [70] 5-9-9 (5*) R Farrant, *chsd ldrs to 4th, sn beh, tld off......*(25 to 1 op 50 to 1 tchd 100 to 1) 11
KINDLY LADY [76] 5-10-6 J R Kavanagh, *chsd ldrs till rdn and wknd appr 3 out, tld off.........*(8 to 1 op 7 to 1) 12
NEARLY HONEST [70] 5-10-0 R Dunwoody, *al beh, tld off.*
....(20 to 1 op 10 to 1) 13
MISS SOUTER [86] 4-10-11 (5*) R Davis, *al beh, tld off.*
....(16 to 1 op 10 to 1 tchd 14 to 1) 14
DAVES DELIGHT [74] 7-9-11 (7*) Mr G Shenkin, *beh whn sddl slpd and uns rdr bef second.* (25 to 1 op 12 to 1) ur
HERLIN [84] 5-11-0 C Llewellyn, *hld up, hdwy second, wnt second briefly aftr 3 out, mstk nxt, pld up bef last.*
....(10 to 1 op 8 to 1) pu
Dist: 12l, 20l, 3½l, 8l, 4l, ½l, 5l, 7l. 4m 17.20s. a 20.20s (16 Ran).
SR: 22/32/-/-/-/-/

(Mrs Iva Winton), Miss H C Knight

774 Dean & Dyball Novices' Chase (5-y-o and up) £3,571 2m 3f...................(3:20)

593³ CONGREGATION 7-11-0 H Davies, *jmpd wl, made virtually all, rdn out r-in..........*(6 to 4 op 9 to 4) 1
649* LUSTY LIGHT 7-11-5 B Powell, *al frnt rnk, led briefly 6th to 7th, rdn appr last, no imprsn r-in.*
....(2 to 1 op 11 to 10 tchd 5 to 4 and Evens) 2
649² WILLIE MCGARR (USA) 8-11-0 Mr P Hamer, *tld off in rear till hdwy 7th, 4th whn blun four out, one pace aftr.*
....(6 to 1 op 4 to 1) 3
PLAYING TRUANT 5-10-12 P Holley, *hld up, hdwy to chase ldrs frm 8th, held up in 3rd pl whn hit 3 out, wknd..................................*(10 to 1 op 7 to 1) 4
SUKAAB 8-11-0 R Greene, *al in rear...*(8 to 1 op 6 to 1) 5
593 KEMMY DARLING 6-10-2 (7*) D Matthews, *al beh.*
....(50 to 1 op 33 to 1) 6
MATAWAI (NZ) 6-11-0 J Frost, *hld up, hdwy frm 7th, wknd tenth......................*(20 to 1 op 16 to 1) 7
TRAIN ROBBER 8-11-0 W Irvine, *chsd ldrs till wknd 11th.*
....(14 to 1 op 10 to 1) 8
DEVIOSITY (USA) 6-10-7 (7*) Mr G Lewis, *chsd ldrs till wknd 9th, tld off whn pld up bef 4 out.*
....(50 to 1 op 33 to 1) pu
607⁶ LAVALIGHT 6-11-0 R Dunwoody, *chsd ldrs till wknd 9th, tld off whn pld up bef 4 out....*(14 to 1 op 8 to 1) pu
Dist: 1½l, 15l, 10l, 5l, 12l, sht-hd, hd. 4m 54.70s. a 25.70s (10 Ran).
SR: 29/32/12/-/-/-/

(Mrs B Sheils), R Rowe

775 Dean & Dyball Novices' Selling Hurdle (4,5,6-y-o) £1,704 2m 1f 110yds.....(3:50)

650⁵ MOBILE MESSENGER (NZ) 5-10-12 J Frost, *hld up in tch, gd hdwy 3 out, led appr last, pushed out, cmftbly.* ....(6 to 1 op 5 to 1 tchd 5 to 4) 1
705⁶ BEAM ME UP SCOTTY (Ire) 4-10-11 N Hawke, *hld up in rear, gd hdwy appr 2 out, rdn and ev ch til one pace r-in.....................*(9 to 1 op 1 tchd 10 to 1) 2
592 SEA PRODIGY 4-10-11 D Gallagher, *led to second, led ag'n 3 out till rdn and wknd appr last, no extr.*
....(16 to 1 op 10 to 1) 3
705 MOLLETROIS 5-10-7 Peter Hobbs, *pld hrd, gd hdwy 4th, rdn and wknd 2 out................*(8 to 1 op 6 to 1) 4
THANKSFORTHEOFFER 5-10-5 (7*) G Lewis, *in tch till wknd appr 2 out....................*(7 to 1 op 9 to 2) 5
FORGED PUNT 6-10-12 S Hodgson, *led second to 4th, wknd quickly appr 2 out, tld off....*(12 to 1 op 10 to 1) 6

97

748 WAVE MASTER (bl) 6-10-12 R Dunwoody, *chsd ldrs, wknd 3 out, tld off*............(8 to 1 op 9 to 2 tchd 9 to 1) 7
ROLSTER PRINCESS 4-10-6 I Shoemark, *jmpd wildly lft thrght, tld off frm 4th*............ (33 to 1 op 20 to 1) 8
UNCLE BOBBY 6-10-12 Mr D Verco, *chsd ldrs, led 4th to 3 out, wknd quickly, pld up bef last*. (25 to 1 op 12 to 1) pu
Dist: 5l, 2½l, 10l, sht-hd, 20l, 1½l, dist. 4m 30.00s. a 33.00s (9 Ran).

(J B Wilcox), D H Barons

776 Dean & Dyball Handicap Hurdle (0-130 4-y-o and up) £2,320 2m 1f 110yds...... (4:20)

HYMNE D'AMOUR (USA) [104] 5-10-2 J Osborne, *trkd ldr, led appr 2 out, hdd bef last, rallied gmely and led sn aftr, ran on*.............................(4 to 1 op 7 to 2) 1
698* ROC COLOR (Fr) [105] 4-10-3 (5ex) G Bradley, *trkd ldrs, hld second, wnt second 2 out, led appr last, rdn and hdd sn aftr, one pace*.................(6 to 5 on op 11 to 10) 2
LESBET [102] 8-9-10³ (7*) D Matthews, *hld up in rear, hdwy appr 2 out, styd on wl, nvr nrr.*
.... (33 to 1 op 25 to 1) 3
JEASSU [130] 10-12-0 M A FitzGerald, *hld up in rear, making gd hdwy whn mstk last, no extr r-in.*
.... (16 to 1 op 14 to 1) 4
648³ MOHANA [128] 4-11 12 R Dunwoody, *led till hdd appr 2 out, rdn and sn btn, eased.*
.............................(4 to 1 op 3 to 1 tchd 9 to 2) 5
DOC'S COAT [119] 8-11-3³ B Wright, *chsd ldrs, hit 3rd, wknd aftr nxt, tld off.* (11 to 1 op 7 to 1 tchd 12 to 1) 6
610² EMERALD MOON [105] 6-10-3³ S Burrough, *mid-div, effrt appr 3 out, wknd sn aftr, tld off*.. (33 to 1 op 20 to 1) 7
GLENCOMMON [102] 12-10-0 W McFarland, *beh whn pld up lme bef second*............... (100 to 1 op 20 to 1) pu
Dist: 3½l, 2l, 7l, 10l, 25l, 30l. 4m 17.90s. a 25.90s (8 Ran).
SR: 14/11/6/27/15/

(Lord Chelsea), Miss H C Knight

777 Dean & Dyball Challenge Trophy Handicap Chase (0-145 5-y-o and up) £3,744 2m 1f 110yds........................ (4:50)

712* IAMA ZULU [99] 8-10-0 M Hourigan, *trkd ldr frm 4th, led nxt, rdn clr from 3 out, easily.*
............................(100 to 30 op 9 to 4 tchd 4 to 1) 1
609³ SARTORIUS [112] 7-10-13 C Llewellyn, *wtd wth, hdwy to go second 4 out, one pace frm nxt.*
...................(6 to 4 fav op 5 to 4 tchd 13 to 8) 2
631³ SETTER COUNTRY [127] 9-12-0 W Irvine, *hld up in rear, hdwy frm 7th, one pace from 4 out.*
.................(9 to 2 op 4 to 1 tchd 5 to 1) 3
L'UOMO PIU [100] 9-10-1¹ M A FitzGerald, *led to 5th, in cl tch till rdn appr 4 out, btn whn hit 2 out.*
.... (16 to 1 op 14 to 1) 4
ROSCOE HARVEY [112] 11-10-13 G Bradley, *trkd ldr to 4th, wkng whn mstk 6th, tld off when pld up bef four out*...................(4 to 1 op 7 to 2 tchd 9 to 2) pu
Dist: 6l, 8l, 10l. 4m 29.80s. a 23.80s (5 Ran).
SR: 18/25/32/-/-/

(Mrs Anona Taylor), P J Hobbs

778 Heath Cross Levy Board Stakes National Hunt Flat Race (4,5,6-y-o) £1,925 2m 1f 110yds........................ (5:20)

HENRYS NO PUSHOVER 4-10-7 (7*) D Salter, *hld up, gd hdwy hfwy, led one and a half fs out, drvn clr.*
.... (14 to 1 op 20 to 1 tchd 12 to 1) 1
SEE ENOUGH 5-10-7 (7*) N Parker, *wl in rear, ran on strly ins fnl 3 fs, wnt second inside last.* (33 to 1 op 20 to 1) 2
RAMALLAH 4-10-7 (7*) K Comerford, *al prmnt, led 6 fs out, hrd rdn and hdd one and a half out, sn btn.*
.... (11 to 10 fav op 11 to 10) 3
FERNY BALL (Ire) 5-11-0 M Hourigan, *al prmnt, one pace fnl 3 fs.*........................(12 to 1 op 10 to 1) 4
KRAKATOA 4-10-2 (7*) Tanya Braybrook, *hld up, gd hdwy on outsd hfwy, ev ch 4 fs out, one pace aftr.*
.... (33 to 1 op 20 to 1) 5
BIBBY BEAR 4-10-4 (5*) R Farrant, *mid-div, kpt on one pace fnl 3 fs.*........................(20 to 1 op 10 to 1) 6
634⁵ SOLO GENT 4-11-0 Mr S Bush, *in frnt rnk, wknd wl o'r 2 fs out.*.............(8 to 1 op 6 to 1 tchd 10 to 1) 7
QUAGO 5-10-2 (7*) Mr G Lewis, *mid-div, nvr nr to chal.*
.... (33 to 1 op 20 to 1) 8
PENNYMOOR PRINCE 4-10-7 (7*) R Darke, *prmnt, dsptd ld 7 fs out to 6 out, wknd 3 out.*...(16 to 1 op 14 to 1) 9
BUSH POWDER (NZ) 5-10-7 (7*) Mr Richard White, *in tch till rdn and wknd 3 fs out.*...(14 to 1 op 10 to 1) 10
EMBLEY BUOY 5-10-9 (5*) R Davis, *al towards rear.*
.... (20 to 1 op 10 to 1) 11
COUNTRY LORD 4-10-7 (7*) D Hobbs, *led hfwy to 6 fs out, wknd quickly o'r 3 out*........(5 to 1 op 10 to 1) 12
KINGFISHER BLUES (Ire) 5-10-7 (7*) P McLoughlin, *mid-div, hdwy hfwy, wknd 3 fs out.*
.... (14 to 1 op 11 to 1 tchd 16 to 1) 13
PARSON'S WAY 6-10-7 (7*) Mr C Vigors, *in tch to hfwy, wknd o'r 4 fs out, tld off*.............(12 to 1) 14
FIRE AND REIGN (Ire) 5-11-0 R Greene, *led to hfwy, stdly wknd, tld off*.................(12 to 1 op 6 to 1) 15

ADAJOKE 4-10-7 (7*) D Matthews, *beh till hdwy aftr 6 fs, wknd o'r 4 out, tld off whn pld up and dismounted ins last*..................(25 to 1 op 14 to 1 tchd 33 to 1) pu
HOPEFULL DRUMMER 4-11-0 Mr N Harris, *trkd ldr, wknd sn aftr hfwy, pld up and dismounted ins fnl furlong.*
.... (25 to 1 op 12 to 1) pu
Dist: 10l, 5l, 1½l, 8l, hd, sht-hd, 8l, sht-hd, 5l, 10l. 4m 22.60s. (17 Ran).

(F G Hollis), L G Cottrell

WETHERBY (soft)
Wednesday October 13th
Going Correction: PLUS 0.60 sec. per fur. (races 1,3,6), PLUS 0.30 (2,4,5)

779 Hallfield Novices' Hurdle (4-y-o and up) £2,145 2½m 110yds............... (2:10)

559³ MERRY NUTKIN 7-11-5 P Niven, *in tch gng wl, led appr 3 out, jmpd rght nxt, styd on well.*
...(11 to 10 op 11 to 10 tchd 5 to 4 and 5 to 4 on) 1
452* POWLEYVALE 6-11-0 B Storey, *in tch, effrt aftr 2 out, styd on*...........(100 to 30 op 7 to 2 tchd 5 to 2) 2
AUBURN BOY 6-10-12 L Wyer, *hld up in tch, hdwy to track ldrs 7th, ev ch 3 out, kpt on same pace.*
........................(12 to 1 tchd 20 to 1) 3
SHOOFE (USA) 5-10-12 A S Smith, *trkd ldrs, chlgd 3 out, sn rdn, one pace.*..................(13 to 2 op 4 to 1) 4
SPARROW HALL 6-10-12 M Dwyer, *trkd ldrs, effrt aftr 7th, styd on same pace.*..........(14 to 1 op 10 to 1) 5
639³ SUPPOSIN 5-10-12 Richard Guest, *set slow pace, quickened appr 5th, hdd approaching 3 out, fdd.*
.... (25 to 1 op 20 to 1) 6
AMADEUS (Fr) 5-10-12 C Grant, *in tch till outpcd aftr 6th.*
.... (33 to 1 op 20 to 1) 7
JUKE BOX BILLY (Ire) 5-10-9 (3*) A Larnach, *nvr nr to chal.*
.................................(33 to 1) 8
HAUT-BRION (Ire) 4-10-4 (7*) J Supple, *al beh.*
.... (66 to 1 op 50 to 1) 9
TICO GOLD 5-10-12 K Johnson, *beh most of way.*
.... (50 to 1 op 20 to 1) 10
ROYAL QUARRY 4-10-12 C Dennis, *cl up till wknd aftr 6th.*...........................(66 to 1 op 50 to 1) 11
BUSHTUCKER 5-10-12 P Harley, *pld hrd early, trkd ldrs till wknd quickly hfwy, tld off whn pulled up bef 3 out.*
.... (66 to 1 op 50 to 1) pu
Dist: 3½l, 2l, 1½l, 6l, 4l, 8l, 15l, 3l, 6l, nk. 5m 7.00s. a 20.00s (12 Ran).
SR: 14/5/1/-/-/-/

(Robert F S Newall), Mrs M Reveley

780 Gordon Foster Handicap Chase (0-145 5-y-o and up) £3,496 2½m 110yds...... (2:40)

SWORD BEACH [127] 9-10-12 P Niven, *in tch, drpd rear aftr 6th, hdwy to track ldrs 9th, quickened to ld appr 3 out, sn clr, easily*.........(8 to 2 op 3 to 1 tchd 5 to 1) 1
ARMAGRET [143] 8-12-0 D Byrne, *hld up in tch, jnd ldr 11th, kpt on frm 3 out, no ch wth nnr.*
.... (5 to 1 tchd 11 to 2) 2
631⁵ HOWE STREET [133] 10-11-4 D Murphy, *led till appr 3 out, sn btn*...................(11 to 4 op 2 to 1 tchd 3 to 1) 3
LAST 'O' THE BUNCH [143] 9-12-0 N Doughty, *cl up, mstk 7th, lost tch 11th..* (6 to 4 fav op 7 to 4 tchd 11 to 8) 4
CHOICE CHALLENGE [116] 10-10-1⁶ (5*) S Lyons, *in tch till outpcd aftr tenth, poor 4th whn f last.*
...........................(16 to 1 tchd 20 to 1) f
Dist: 5l, 12l, 6l. 5m 5.90s. a 9.40s (5 Ran).
SR: 52/63/41/45/-/

(Mrs S J Mason), Mrs M Reveley

781 Yorkshire Television Handicap Hurdle (0-135 4-y-o and up) £2,758 2m..... (3:10)

BATABANOO [124] 4-11-10 P Niven, *hld up beh, hdwy 3 out, ran on strly to ld r-in*......... (3 to 1 tchd 7 to 2) 1
662* RED INDIAN [110] 7-10-10 D Byrne, *in tch, led 2 out, pckd last, hdd r-in, shaken up and no extr.*
.......................(3 to 1 tchd 100 to 30) 2
SEAGULL HOLLOW (Ire) [100] 4-10-12 L Wyer, *led, quickened aftr 6th, hdd 2 out, kpt on same pace.*
.........(5 to 2 fav op 11 to 4 tchd 3 to 1 and 9 to 4) 3
IN TRUTH [106] 5-10-6 C Grant, *prmnt, jnd ldr aftr 6th, one pace 2 out.*.....................(9 to 1 op 7 to 2) 4
WAKE UP [107] 6-10-7 M Dwyer, *cl up till pushed alng and lost pl aftr 6th.*.................(7 to 1 tchd 9 to 1) 5
CLURICAN (Ire) [128] 4-12-0 G McCourt, *hld up, effrt 3 out, sn btn.*.......(8 to 1 op 6 to 1 tchd 10 to 1) 6
Dist: 2l, 2½l, 1½l, 3½l, 6l. 4m 0.50s. a 19.50s (6 Ran).

(P D Savill), Mrs M Reveley

782 Bobby Renton Memorial Novices' Chase (5-y-o and up) £2,846 2m........... (3:40)

COULTON 6-11-0 L Wyer, *made all, mstk 4 out, styd on wl*...........(7 to 4 op 2 to 1 on tchd 13 to 8 on) 1
BELLTON 5-10-13 M Dwyer, *al tracking ldr, effrt aftr 2 out, kpt on, no imprsn*...............(13 to 8 op 7 to 4) 2
694⁶ MONAUGHTY MAN 7-10-9 (5*) P Williams, *sn beh, tld off.*
.... (40 to 1 op 33 to 1 tchd 66 to 1) 3

NATIONAL HUNT RESULTS 1993-94

GOLDEN BANKER (Ire) 5-10-13 K Jones, *sn beh, blun 5th, tld off*.............. (40 to 1 op 33 to 1 tchd 50 to 1) 4
Dist: 8l, dist, 15l. 4m 0.90s. a 8.90s (4 Ran).
SR: 45/36/-/-/ (G E Shouler), M W Easterby

783 Askham Richard Handicap Chase (0-135 5-y-o and up) £3,470 3m 110yds..... (4:10)

MR BOSTON [123] 8-11-4 P Niven, *trkd ldrs, wnt second 12th, dsptd ld 4 out, led aftr 2 out, hit last, styd on wl.*
.................(11 to 10 on op 11 to 10 tchd 6 to 5) 1
726 FOSBURY [111] 8-10-6⁵ S McNeill, *led, jnd 4 out, rdn appr 2 out, sn hdd, styd on*........ (7 to 1 tchd 9 to 1) 2
ALL JEFF [129] 9-11-10 S McNeill, *in tch, effrt aftr 4 out, kpt on frm last*......(9 to 4 op 6 to 4 tchd 9 to 4) 3
FEILE NA HINSE [107] 10-10-2 D Murphy, *cl up, ev ch 4 out, blun nxt, sn btn*........(13 to 2 op 7 to 1 tchd 8 to 1) 4
Dist: 2½l, ¾l, 10l. 6m 37.10s. a 31.10s (4 Ran).
(M K Oldham), Mrs M Reveley

784 Goldsborough Juvenile Novices' Hurdle (3-y-o) £2,110 2m...................(4:40)

320⁴ BURNT IMP (USA) 11-5 J Callaghan, *prmnt, jnd ldrs 5th, led appr 3 out, hit nxt, styd on wl.*
.......................(13 to 8 fav op 9 to 4) 1
BLUE LAWS (Ire) 10-12 M Dwyer, *trkd ldrs, pushed alng to chase wnr appr 3 out, rdn approaching nxt, kpt on, no imprsn*........................(3 to 1 op 2 to 1) 2
HASTA LA VISTA 10-12 R Garritty, *jmpd rght, led till aftr 3rd, led 5th till appr 3 out, kpt on same pace.*
........................(9 to 1 op 7 to 1) 3
MALAWI 10-12 B Storey, *beh, styd on wl frm 3 out, nvr nr to chal*........................(33 to 1 op 25 to 1) 5
GENSERIC (Fr) 10-12 D Murphy, *in tch, hdwy appr 3 out, fdd approaching nxt*............(16 to 1 op 14 to 1) 6
516⁵ MR VINCENT 10-12 A S Smith, *in tch till wknd appr 3 out, blun last*........................(9 to 2 op 5 to 1) 7
652⁵ PINKERTON'S SILVER 10-12 C Grant, *trkd ldrs, rdn aftr 6th, sn wknd*........................(14 to 1 op 10 to 1) 8
RAGGERTY (Ire) 10-9 (3⁵) N Bentley, *al beh.*
........................(16 to 1 op 10 to 1) 9
588⁸ BLAKES BEAU 10-12 L Wyer, *beh hfwy, tld off.*
........................(20 to 1 tchd 25 to 1) 10
VANARIO 10-12 D Byrne, *al beh, tld off.*
........................(33 to 1 op 25 to 1) 11
Dist: 3½l, 15l, ¾l, 4l, hd, 5l, 8l, 2½l, 20l, 10l. 3m 56.90s. a 15.90s (11 Ran).
SR: 28/17/2/1/-/-/ (N B Mason (Farms) Ltd), G M Moore

HEXHAM (soft)
Thursday October 14th
Going Correction: PLUS 1.35 sec. per fur. (races 1,3,6), PLUS 1.25 (2,4,5)

785 EBF 'National Hunt' Novices' Hurdle Qualifier (4,5,6-y-o) £1,856 2m.......... (2:00)

SEVEN TOWERS 4-10-13 P Niven, *hld up, not fluent, hit 5th, hdwy nxt, chsd ldr 2 out, rdn to ld appr last, sn clr*.....(2 to 1 on op 9 to 4 on tchd 6 to 4 on) 1
BACK BEFORE DAWN 6-10-11 (3⁵) A Dobbin, *trkd ldrs, effrt and hdwy to ld appr 2 out, rdn hdd and wknd approaching last*......(7 to 2 op 4 to 1 tchd 11 to 4) 2
541⁴ ROYAL SURPRISE 6-11-0 K Johnson, *prmnt, pckd 1st, rdn and wknd aftr 3 out*................(8 to 1 op 6 to 1) 3
THORVALORE 5-11-0 R Hodge, *led and sn clr, wknd and hdd appr 2 out, blun two out and beh whn hit last.*
........................(33 to 1 op 20 to 1) 4
DE JORDAAN 6-11-0 A Merrigan, *hld up, rdn alng 5th and sn lost tch*........................(33 to 1 op 25 to 1) 5
53 I'D SAY HARDLY 6-11-0 B Storey, *chsd ldr till rdn and wknd 3 out*........................(33 to 1 op 20 to 1) 6
VANBRUGH'S ROOM 5-11-0 R Garritty, *prmnt till wknd hfwy, tld off whn pld up bef 2 out.* (50 to 1 op 33 to 1) pu
Dist: 10l, 4l, 30l, ¾l, 20l. 4m 24.40s. a 34.40s (7 Ran).
(James Murray (Ballymena)), Mrs M Reveley

786 Carpets By Huglin Novices' Chase (5-y-o and up) £1,738 3m 1f.............. (2:30)

733 BENNAN MARCH 6-10-11 (3⁵) A Dobbin, *trkd ldrs, hdwy to join ldr tenth, led 13th, clr nxt, rdn appr last, ran on strly*....................(2 to 1 op 4 to 1 tchd 5 to 1) 1
627⁴ SANDEDGE 6-10-9 B Storey, *hld up and beh, steady hdwy 14th, chsd wnr frm nxt, ch 2 out, rdn and one pace appr last*.....................(4 to 1 op 7 to 2) 2
624⁴ EBORNEEZER'S DREAM (v) 10-11-0 D Telfer, *led to 6th, rdn alng and lost pl 12th, plugged on frm 2 out.*
........................(9 to 2 op 5 to 2) 3
756³ THE WALTZING MOUSE (bl) 10-11-0 T Reed, *hld up, hdwy and prmnt 6th, lost pl 13th, sn rdn alng, nvr dngrs.*
........................(5 to 4 fav op 11 to 10 tchd 6 to 4) 4

ALIAS GRAY 6-11-0 K Johnson, *chsd ldr, led 6th till hdd 13th, blun badly nxt, hit 15th, sn lost pl, tld off frm 4 out*........................(25 to 1 op 16 to 1) 5
Dist: 10l, sht-hd, 15l, dist. 6m 59.20s. a 54.20s (5 Ran).
(Brian O'Kane), P Monteith

787 Oakwood Conditional Jockeys' Selling Handicap Hurdle (4-y-o and up) £1,140 2m ....(3:00)

623⁴ CHEEKY POT [85] 5-11-3 P Waggott, *in tch, hdwy 5th, effrt and rdn to ld appr last, sn clr.*
.................(6 to 5 fav op 5 to 4 on tchd 5 to 4) 1
HYPNOTIST [92] 6-11-10 N Bentley, *prmnt, led 5th, rdn 2 out, hdd and wknd appr last*........(8 to 1 op 5 to 1) 2
477⁴ STAGS FELL [82] 8-10-10 (4⁵) N Stocks, *cl up, led second, hdd 5th, close up till rdn and wknd aftr 2 out.*
........................(3 to 1 op 5 to 2 tchd 100 to 30) 3
622 VERBAL WARNING [68] 5-10-0 J Supple, *hit second, in tch till lost pl aftr 5th, tld off appr 2 out.*
........................(25 to 1 op 14 to 1) 4
642⁶ SWANK GILBERT [68] 7-9-10 (4⁵) Carol Cuthbert, *pld hrd, led to second, prmnt till rdn and wknd 5th, sn tld off.*
........................(20 to 1 op 16 to 1) 5
543 KING OF NORMANDY (Ire) [68] 4-10-0 F Perratt, *prmnt till lost pl and beh hfwy, tld off*............... (20 to 1) 6
626⁹ LUGER (Ire) [68] 5-10-0 A Thornton, *hld up, hdwy 5th, hit 3 out and sn wknd, tld off.*
........................(9 to 2 op 4 to 1 tchd 5 to 1) 7
730 ELISSA [68] 7-9-10 (4⁵) P Johnson, *rear whn trying to run and refused 3rd*............... (40 to 1 op 33 to 1) ref
Dist: 6l, 4l, 25l, 20l, 12l, dist. 4m 18.80s. a 28.80s (8 Ran).
SR: 17/18/4/-/-/ (Miss L H Davies), Denys Smith

788 John Eustace Smith Trophy Handicap Chase (0-115 5-y-o and up) £2,012 2m 110yds...........................(3:30)

643⁴ POSITIVE ACTION [97] 7-10-11 (3⁵) A Dobbin, *al prmnt, led 6th, rdn appr last, hdd briefly r-in, rallied wl und pres to ld nr finish.* (5 to 4 on tchd 11 to 10 on and Evens) 1
ONE FOR THE POT [108] 8-11-11 A Orkney, *al prmnt, dsptd ld frm 7th, rdn appr last, led briefly r-in, no extr nr finish*.......(3 to 1 op 5 to 2 tchd 100 to 30) 2
581⁴ WILD ATLANTIC [89] 10-10-6 K Jones, *cl up, hit 5th and 6th, sn outpcd, kpt on und pres frm last.*
........................(9 to 2 op 5 to 1) 3
721⁸ CLASSIC MINSTREL [93] 9-10-5 (5⁵) P Williams, *led to 6th, rdn nxt and outpcd till styd on frm last.*
........................(12 to 1 op 8 to 1) 4
643⁵ MOSS BEE [95] 6-10-12⁶ T Reed, *sn outpcd and wl beh, styd on strly appr last*..............(12 to 1 op 8 to 1) 5
Dist: 1l, 3½l, 1½l, 1l. 4m 23.80s. a 25.80s (5 Ran).
SR: 34/44/21/23/24/ (G Campbell), M A Barnes

789 Anick Handicap Chase (0-120 5-y-o and up) £1,976 3m 1f...................(4:00)

677⁴ PORTAVOGIE [92] (bl) 9-10-10 (7⁵) Mr D Parker, *in tch, hdwy to chase ldr 14th, led 2 out and sn clr, pushed alng r-in, kpt on.....*(100 to 30 op 5 to 1 tchd 3 to 1) 1
ABERCROMBY CHIEF [92] (v) 8-11-3 A Orkney, *led and clr, rdn and blun 3 out, hdd, rallied wl und pres r-in*......................(4 to 1 op 8 to 1 tchd 10 to 1) 2
CHOCTAW [92] 9-11-8 Mrs A Farrell, *rdn alng and outpcd hfwy, hdwy appr 3 out, sn ridden and one paced.*
........................(7 to 2 op 5 to 2 tchd 4 to 1) 3
736⁴ ON THE HOOCH [90] 8-11-10 Mr J Bradburne, *prmnt till rdn and one pace frm 5 out*.......(4 to 1 tchd 9 to 2) 4
SANTELLA BOBKES (USA) [88] 8-10-10 (3⁵) A Dobbin, *prmnt till rdn and wkng whn blun and uns rdr 14th.*
........................(14 to 1 tchd 16 to 1) ur
RUSTINO [97] 7-11-8 P Niven, *in tch, not fluent, rdn 13th and sn beh, tld off whn pld up bef 2 out.*
........................(11 to 4 fav op 6 to 4 tchd 3 to 1) pu
Dist: 2l, 15l, 20l. 6m 58.70s. a 53.70s (6 Ran).
(Raymond Anderson Green), C Parker

790 Carpets By Huglin Juvenile Novices' Hurdle (3-y-o) £1,733 2m.............. (4:30)

RED MARAUDER 10-5 (7⁵) J Supple, *hld up, steady hdwy 3 out, pckd 2 out, effrt and hit last, styd on strly r-in to ld nr finish*..................(9 to 2 op 20 to 1) 1
THE PREMIER EXPRES 10-9 (3⁵) N Bentley, *al prmnt, led 5th, rdn clr appr last, not quicken r-in, nr finish.*
........................(3 to 1 op 7 to 2 tchd 4 to 1) 2
REGAL AURA (Ire) 10-12 J Callaghan, *al prmnt, effrt and hdwy to chal 2 out, rdn and one pace appr last.*
........................(4 to 1 op 3 to 1) 3
MADAM GYMCRAK 10-7 L Wyer, *prmnt, ev ch 2 out, sn rdn and wknd*........(7 to 1 op 4 to 1 tchd 8 to 1) 4
BAYRAK (USA) 10-12 J Railton, *trkd ldrs, hit 3 out, effrt and ev ch nxt, sn rdn and wknd bef last.*
......(6 to 4 fav op 5 to 4 tchd 11 to 10 and 13 to 8) 5
NATIVE WORTH 10-7 (5⁵) P Williams, *mid-div, rdn and wknd uftr 3 out*..................(25 to 1 op 20 to 1) 6

99

578[8] HIGHLAND SUNBEAM 10-9 (3*) D J Moffatt, *led till hdd and hit 5th, rdn and wknd nxt....* (33 to 1 op 20 to 1) 7
JASPER ONE 10-12 R Garritty, *mid-div, effrt and rdn 3 out, sn wknd.......................*(25 to 1 op 12 to 1) 8
RYTHMIC RYMER 10-7 M Dwyer, *al rear, tld off whn pld up bef last.........................* (14 to 1 op 8 to 1) pu
Dist: ¾l, 3l, 6l, ¾l, 20l, 3l, 8l. 4m 22.50s. a 32.50s (9 Ran).

(N B Mason), N B Mason

TAUNTON (good)
Thursday October 14th
Going Correction: PLUS 0.35 sec. per fur. (races 1,3,-5,6), PLUS 0.10 (2,4)

791 Donyatt Conditional Jockeys' Novices' Hurdle (4-y-o and up) £1,710 2m 1f. . (2:15)

715* FATACK 4-11-3 S Curran, *made all, clr 6th, hit 3 out, unchlgd...........*(11 to 4 fav op 5 to 2 tchd 9 to 4) 1
SHIRLEY'S TRAIN (USA) 4-10-10 M Hourigan, *hdwy 6th, hit 2 out, chsd wnr and no imprsn r-in.
....................................*(7 to 1 op 4 to 1) 2
MARTRAJAN 6-10-8 (3*) L O'Hare, *took str hold, chsd wnr, no cls frm 3 out, wknd r-in.
....................................*(9 to 2 op 16 to 1 tchd 8 to 1) 3
BAYSHAM (USA) 7-10-11 D Salter, *prmnt, rdn appr 2 out, sn one pace................* (12 to 1 op 16 to 1 tchd 8 to 1) 4
608[4] ELEGANT TOUCH (bl) 4-9-12 (7*) O Burrows, *in tch, hdwy 6th, no imprsn frm 3 out............*(33 to 1 op 40 to 1) 5
628[4] THE MINE CAPTAIN 6-10-11 R Farrant, *prmnt, rdn 3 out, wknd appr 2 out............*(10 to 1 tchd 12 to 1) 6
666 HULLO MARY DOLL 4-9-12 (7*) Christopher Webb, *beh, nvr rchd ldrs....................*(66 to 1 op 33 to 1) 7
WELSH LUSTRE (Ire) 4-10-5 W Marston, *nvr rchd ldrs.
....................................* (10 to 1 op 7 to 1 tchd 14 to 1) 8
CLEAR COMEDY (Ire) 5-10-3 (3*) R Darke, *al beh.
....................................* (33 to 1 op 50 to 1) 9
567* COOCHIE (bl) 4-10-12 V Slattery, *drvn and effrt 6th, sn wknd.........................* (10 to 1 op 8 to 1 tchd 9 to 1) 10
SAAHI (USA) 4-10-10 D O'Sullivan, *beh, no ch whn blun 6th, wl btn when sprawled badly last.
....................................*(20 to 1 op 16 to 1) 11
524[3] DON'T FORSAKE ME 4-10-5 A Procter, *f second.
....................................*(7 to 1 op 6 to 1 tchd 8 to 1) f
ALL THE GIRLS (Ire) 4-10-5 D Meredith, *al beh, tld off whn pld up bef 2 out................* (50 to 1 op 25 to 1) pu
716 ALFREE 5-10-8 (3*) J Neaves, *chsd ldrs, rdn and wknd ....*(100 to 1 op 66 to 1) pu
Dist: 6l, 10l, 1½l, 1½l, 3l, 7l, 1l, 10l, 15l, 20l. 3m 58.30s. a 11.30s (14 Ran).
SR: 35/22/13/11/3/6/ (Jeremy W S Barnett), Miss Jacqueline S Doyle

792 Lansdowne Chemical Handicap Chase (0-135 5-y-o and up) £2,801 3m...... (2:45)

RATHVINDEN HOUSE (USA) [112] 6-10-5[4] G McCourt, *chsd ldrs till led 11th, clr whn not fluent 15th or 4 out, easily.
....................................* (5 to 4 fav tchd 6 to 4) 1
630 WONT BE GONE LONG [134] (bl) 11-11-13 R Dunwoody, *led 3rd to 11th, styd whn wnr to 14th, stayed on same pace frm 4 out....................*(5 to 1 op 9 to 2) 2
696[2] KNIGHT OIL [125] (bl) 10-11-4 J Osborne, *hdwy 8th, pressed ldrs 13th till jmpd slwly 14th, jumped lft and lost pos totally 15th, ran on appr last, fnshd wl.
....................................*(3 to 1 tchd 100 to 30) 3
714 TRUSTY FRIEND [109] 11-10-2 M A FitzGerald, *beh 6th, styd on frm 3 out, one pace appr last.
....................................*(16 to 1 op 14 to 1 tchd 20 to 1) 4
425[3] MASTER DANCER [107] 6-10-0 D Gallagher, *beh and mstk second, moderate prog appr last...*(20 to 1 op 14 to 1) 5
COLONEL O'KELLY (NZ) [107] 9-10-0 N Hawke, *in tch, chsd ldrs 14th, wknd 4 out...........*(14 to 1 op 25 to 1) 6
669[2] FIGHTING DAYS (USA) [107] 7-9-12[5] (7*) J Clarke, *hit 7th, al beh, tld off.........................*(10 to 1 op 20 to 1) 7
595 ENVOPAK TOKEN [112] (bl) 12-10-5 Peter Hobbs, *prmnt till wknd 5th, pld up bef nxt, lme............*(33 to 1) pu
PEOPLE'S CHOICE [107] 8-10-0 B Powell, *led to 3rd, styd pressing ldrs till mstk 12th (water), wknd 14th, tld off whn pld up bef last, lme..........*(25 to 1 op 40 to 1) pu
Dist: 12l, 1½l, ½l, 6l, nk, dist. 6m 4.00s. a 17.00s (9 Ran).
(Brian Lovrey), T Thomson Jones

793 Watchet Juvenile Novices' Selling Hurdle (3-y-o) £1,679 2m 1f............ (3:15)

711[5] MY SISTER LUCY 10-7 T Jarvis, *trkd ldrs, led 3 out, hdd aftr 2 out, shaken up r-in and led last strds.
....................................*(3 to 1 op 7 to 2 tchd 4 to 1) 1
MISSED THE BOAT (Ire) 10-12 H Davies, *hdwy 5th, led aftr 2 out, rdn r-in, ct last strds...........*(7 to 2 op 5 to 2) 2
711[4] MUSICAL PHONE 10-12 B Powell, *led aftr 5th, mstk 6th, hdd 3 out, ev ch 2 out, one pace.* (5 to 2 fav tchd 3 to 1) 3
604[7] IVORY HUTCH (bl) 10-12 A Charlton, *sn beh, moderate prog frm 2 out..................*(12 to 1 op 8 to 1) 4
711[8] OUR NIKKI 10-7 I Shoemark, *led and mstk 1st, hdd 4th, led ag'n 5th, sn headed and btn...* (33 to 1 op 20 to 1) 5

NANQUIDNO 10-7 J R Kavanagh, *al beh, no ch whn mstk last....................................*(14 to 1 op 8 to 1) 6
486[7] IRISH DOMINION 10-12 N Hawke, *beh most of way.
....................................* (12 to 1 op 8 to 1) 7
SUNBEAM CHARLIE 10-5 (7*) J Clarke, *chsd ldrs, led 4th till hdd 5th, fourth and wknd whn f last.
....................................* (16 to 1 op 14 to 1) f
207[7] WEST END GIRL 10-7 L Harvey, *prmnt, chlgd 4th, wknd 5th, tld off whn pld up bef 3 out...* (25 to 1 op 20 to 1) pu
JIMMY HIMSELF 10-12 R Marley, *prmnt to 4th, tld off whn pld up bef last..................* (12 to 1 op 8 to 1) pu
Dist: Hd, 1½l, 20l, 12l, 1½l, 25l. 4m 5.60s. a 18.60s (10 Ran).
(Mrs Ann Jarvis), A P Jarvis

794 Iseflo Iodine Challenge Cup Novices' Chase (5-y-o and up) £2,476 2m 110yds
....(3:45)

438[6] ABU MUSLAB (bl) 9-11-2 M A FitzGerald, *led second, sn clr, rdn alng frm 2 out, hng lft and hld on wl r-in.
....................................*(20 to 1 op 16 to 1) 1
667* KALANSKI 7-11-9 J Osborne, *blun 3rd, hdwy to track ldrs 7th, chsd wnr 4 out, kpt on r-in, no extr nr finish.
....................................*(13 to 8 jt-fav op 6 to 4 tchd 2 to 1) 2
695[7] MILLIES OWN 6-11-2 M Perrett, *beh, mstk 9th, styd on encouragingly frm 3 out, not a dngr.
....................................*(50 to 1 op 33 to 1) 3
ON ALERT (NZ) 6-11-2 J Frost, *in tch 6th, pushed alng and styd on frm 3 out............* (20 to 1 op 14 to 1) 4
676[2] BUMPTIOUS BOY 9-11-2 D Bridgwater, *chsd ldrs, hit 9th, rdn and hld whn slightly hmpd 2 out.
....................................*(16 to 1 op 12 to 1 tchd 20 to 1) 5
703 CANDLE KING (Ire) 5-11-0 M Bosley, *mstk 1st, wl beind 5th, some prog frm 3 out........*(20 to 1 op 14 to 1) 6
CORRIN HILL 6-11-2 R Dunwoody, *led till hdd and mstk second, chsd wnr till blun 4 out, not reco'r.* (13 to 8 jt-fav op 6 to 4 tchd 7 to 4) 7
VERSATILE 9-11-2 S McNeill, *beh frm 5th.
....................................*(50 to 1 op 25 to 1) 8
RECIDIVIST 7-10-11 A Tory, *al beh...* (50 to 1 op 33 to 1) 9
592* GRAND RAPIDS (USA) 4-11-2 H Davies, *beh frm 5th.
....................................*(20 to 1 op 14 to 1) 10
748 FANATICAL (USA) (bl) 7-11-2 L Harvey, *in tch, pd hdwy frm 9th, 3rd and staying on wl whn f 2 out...........*(33 to 1) f
BLAKE'S TREASURE 6-11-2 S Smith Eccles, *prmnt till blun 3rd, no ch whn blunded and uns rdr 8th.
....................................*(6 to 1 op 25 to 1 tchd 33 to 1) ur
Dist: ½l, 10l, 1l, nk, 10l, 15l, 3l, 8l, 3l. 4m 6.00s. a 8.00s (12 Ran).
SR: 25/31/14/13/12/-/ (G F Edwards), G F Edwards

795 Tiverton Novices' Hurdle (4-y-o and up) £1,752 2m 3f 110yds...........(4:15)

715 VIOLET'S BOY 6-10-12 C Maude, *chsd ldrs, chlgd 5th till led 3 out, drvn out r-in...........*(33 to 1 tchd 50 to 1) 1
TOUR LEADER (NZ) 4-10-10 B Powell, *hdwy 6th, styd on to chase wnr and hit 2 out, not quicken r-in.
....................................*(33 to 1 op 16 to 1) 2
604[5] CHICKABIDDY 5-10-7 M A FitzGerald, *in tch, rdn and styd on frm 3 out, not pace of ldrs.
....................................*(33 to 1 op 16 to 1) 3
628[2] DEBACLE (USA) 4-11-8 D Murphy, *in tch, chsd ldrs and rdn appr 2 out, sn wknd.
....................................*(6 to 4 fav op 5 to 2 tchd 7 to 2) 4
MR WILBUR 7-10-12 J Frost, *hld up in rear, ran on frm 2 out, not a dngr............*(33 to 1 op 25 to 1) 5
605[6] SOUL TRADER 4-10-5 S Burrough, *beh till moderate prog frm 2 out..................*(25 to 1 op 16 to 1) 6
597[2] JOVIAL MAN (Ire) 4-10-10 M Perrett, *led 3rd till mstk and hdd 3 out, 6th and wkng whn hmpd 2 out.
....................................*(9 to 4 op 6 to 4 tchd 5 to 2) 7
NORTHERN CREST 7-10-12 S McNeill, *al beh.
....................................*(25 to 1 op 16 to 1) 8
565 SUDANOR (Ire) 4-10-10 N Hawke, *in tch till mstk 6th, sn wknd..................*(11 to 1 op 7 to 1) 9
695 RBF ARIANNE 5-10-7 N Collum, *beh frm 5th.
....................................*(40 to 1 op 33 to 1) 10
695[9] ALWAYS ALLIED (Ire) 5-10-7 D Skyrme, *led to 3rd, styd pressing ldrs till wknd 6th, tld off.* (66 to 1 op 33 to 1) 11
715[2] EURIDICE (Ire) 4-10-5 R Dunwoody, *chsd ldrs to 3 out, 5th and hld whn f 2 out.........*(5 to 1 op 4 to 1) f
NEVER EVER 8-10-5 (7*) Mr G Lewis, *prmnt early, drpd rear 3rd, tld off whn pld up bef 4 out.
....................................*(66 to 1 op 50 to 1) pu
COUNTRY MISTRESS 6-10-7 Peter Hobbs, *prmnt to 6th, wknd quickly, tld off whn pld up bef 4 out.
....................................*(25 to 1 op 20 to 1) pu
Dist: 1½l, 10l, 6l, 12l, 4l, 1½l, 2½l, 20l, 8l, dist. 4m 35.60s. a 14.60s (14 Ran).
SR: 6/2/-/-/ (R M E Wright), P J Hobbs

796 Resorcinol Handicap Hurdle (0-115 4-y-o and up) £2,400 2m 3f 110yds....... (4:45)

662[4] SPRING TO GLORY [90] 6-10-8 A Maguire, *al tracking ldrs, led aftr 2 out, all out............*(5 to 1 fav op 7 to 1) 1

670⁴ NICK THE DREAMER [103] 8-11-7 R Dunwoody, *prmnt till led 5th, hdd aftr 2 out, rallied und pres and str chal r-in, no extr cl hme*.....(7 to 1 op 8 to 1 tchd 10 to 1) 2
SAILOR BLUE [102] (bl) 6-11-6 L Harvey, *prmnt, drvn alng appr 2 out, styd on*...(12 to 1 op 10 to 1 tchd 14 to 1) 3
190* MAN FROM MARS [91] 7-10-2 (7*) N Parker, *wnt prmnt 5th, chsd ldrs frm nxt, kpt on appr last*............(8 to 1) 4
651² AMPHIGORY [87] 5-10-5 M A FitzGerald, *beh till hdwy 6th, drvn and kpt on same pace appr last*.
..............................(8 to 1 op 10 to 1) 5
610⁴ GREENWINE (USA) [84] 7-10-2 M Richards, *beh till hdwy 7th, styd on frm 2 out*...........(14 to 1 tchd 16 to 1) 6
651⁴ PROVERBS GIRL [89] 8-10-2 (5*) R Davis, *beh, plenty to do 3 out, styd on frm 2 out, nrst finish*.
...............................(14 to 1 tchd 20 to 1) 7
613³ ELEGANT KING (Ire) [106] 4-11-10 T Jarvis, *sn in tch, drvn alng aftr 5th, wknd frm 3 out*.
...............................(9 to 1 op 12 to 1 tchd 8 to 1) 8
687⁴ SILVER AGE (USA) [93] 7-10-6 (5*) R Farrant, *prmnt, rdn 3 out, sn wknd*......................(6 to 1 tchd 7 to 1) 9
MORGANS MAN [92] 4-10-10 N Hawke, *mstk second, al beh*......................................(33 to 1 op 25 to 1) 10
447* CELCIUS [98] (bl) 9-10-9 (7*) T Dascombe, *hld up in tch, wknd 3 out*........................(12 to 1 op 8 to 1) 11
713⁷ FLY BY NORTH (USA) [104] 5-11-1 (7*) R Massey, *al beh*.
...............................(16 to 1 op 14 to 1 tchd 20 to 1) 12
488⁴ REDGRAVE GIRL [100] 11-11-4 R Greene, *al beh*. (12 to 1) 13
COOMBESBURY LANE [85] 7-9-12 (5*) D Leahy, *al beh*.
...............................(25 to 1 op 20 to 1) 14
MOUNTAIN RETREAT [105] 7-11-9 N Mann, *led to 5th, sn wknd and tld off, pld up bef nxt*............(50 to 1 op 33 to 1) pu
COLOUR SCHEME [90] 6-10-8 C Maude, *mstk 1st, sn beh, tld off whn pld up bef 2 out*.......(50 to 1 op 33 to 1) pu
Dist: ½l, 2½l, 1l, 1½l, hd, 1l, 15l, 12l, 5l, hd. 4m 34.30s. a 13.30s (16 Ran).
SR: 15/27/23/11/5/2/6/8/-/ (A J Byrne), P Hayward

THURLES (IRE) (good)
Thursday October 14th

797 Eligorty Handicap Hurdle (0-109 4-y-o and up) £2,243 2m.....................(2:30)

574³ WATERLOO LADY [-] 6-10-8 (5*) D P Murphy, ...(11 to 2) 1
528³ SUNSHINES TAXI [-] 6-10-5 (7*) Mr R M Murphy, ...(7 to 1) 2
574⁴ HURRICANE EDEN [-] 6-10-13 K F O'Brien, ...(6 to 1) 3
493³ BELLECARA [-] 6-10-0 (3*) D Bromley, ...(8 to 1) 4
471⁴ PAGET [-] 6-11-3 (7*) Mr A K Wyse, ...(5 to 1 fav) 5
EYREFIELD ROSE [-] 7-9-12 (7*) P P Curran, ...(20 to 1) 6
574⁷ CLASSY MACHINE (Ire) [-] 5-10-9 P M Verling, ...(16 to 1) 7
506³ SCREEN PRINTER (Ire) [-] (bl) 4-9-10 (7*) J P Broderick,
....(8 to 1) 8
538 CHARDEN [-] 7-10-2 (5*) T J O'Sullivan, ...(20 to 1) 9
157⁴ WALNEY ISLAND [-] 4-11-0 C F Swan, ...(8 to 1) 10
555 JIMMY THE WEED (Ire) [-] 4-9-10 (7*) P A Roche, .(33 to 1) 11
689 SUNDAY WORLD (USA) [-] (bl) 7-10-11 A J O'Brien, (20 to 1) 12
557 WIND ZING [-] 9-10-5 W T Slattery Jnr, ...(16 to 1) 13
689 BRAVE SHARON [-] (bl) 9-9-9 (5*) T P Treacy, ...(33 to 1) 14
557 QUIET CITY [-] 6-11-3 (5*) C O'Brien, ...(12 to 1) pu
Dist: 9l, 2½l, ½l, nk. 3m 51.10s. (15 Ran).
(John Philip Kelly), James Joseph Mangan

798 Tipperary Novice Hurdle (4-y-o and up) £2,243 2¼m..................... (3:00)

MISS LIME 6-10-6 (7*) P A Roche, ...(14 to 1) 1
535* DORANS PRIDE 4-11-3 K F O'Brien, ...(6 to 4 fav) 2
584³ UNCLE BART (Ire) 5-11-4 (7*) R A Hennessy, ...(3 to 1) 3
689⁷ POOR TIMES (Ire) 5-10-8 (5*) M A Davey, ...(16 to 1) 4
535 OLYMPIC D'OR (Ire) 5-11-4 C F Swan, ...(14 to 1) 5
PRECARIUM (Ire) 5-11-4 G Bradley, ...(8 to 1) 6
671 BALLYHYLAND (Ire) 4-10-3 (5*) T P Treacy, ...(14 to 1) 7
636⁷ ROSEPERRIE (Ire) 5-10-8 (5*) D T Evans, ...(10 to 1) 8
692⁹ LITTLE AND OFTEN (Ire) 4-10-8 D H O'Connor, ...(25 to 1) 9
503⁶ SILENTBROOK 8-10-13 Mr P J Healy, ...(25 to 1) 10
572 EXILE RUN (Ire) (bl) 5-11-4 J F Titley, ...(14 to 1) 11
534 BEAU GRANDE (Ire) 5-11-4 L P Cusack, ...(10 to 1) 12
555 HAVE A BRANDY 4-10-13 A J O'Brien, ...(14 to 1) 13
BALLY RIOT (Ire) 5-11-4 J Magee, ...(20 to 1) 14
THATS MY BOY 5-11-4 C N Bowens, ...(14 to 1) 15
THE REAL GAEL (Ire) 5-11-4 C O'Brien, ...(33 to 1) 16
571 ASTON BLAKE 6-10-13 (5*) C P Dunne, ...(14 to 1) 17
692 THE CRIOSRA (Ire) 4-10-13 S H O'Donovan, ...(14 to 1) 18
510* JUNGLE STAR (Ire) 5-11-8 M Flynn, ...(12 to 1) 19
537⁷ SOLBA (USA) 4-11-3 G M O'Neill, ...(8 to 1) 20
Dist: 15l, 2l, 9l, 9l. 4m 25.00s. (20 Ran).
(James Bowe), James Bowe

799 Upperchurch Chase (4-y-o and up) £2,243 2¾m.........................(3:30)

BELVEDERIAN 6-11-5 G Bradley, ...(5 to 2) 1
532⁴ PARGALE 7-11-9 C F Swan, ...(8 to 1) 2
707³ COMMERCIAL ARTIST 7-11-9 C N Bowens, ...(9 to 4 fav) 3
635⁷ MCMAHON'S RIVER 6-11-0 D H O'Connor, ...(20 to 1) 4
NUAFFE 8-11-5 S H O'Donovan, ...(16 to 1) 5
POST MASTER 7-11-0 (5*) M M Treacy, ...(14 to 1) 6

468⁵ MALACHYS BAR 9-11-9 F Woods, ...(12 to 1) 7
ANOTHYS EXCUSE (Ire) 5-10-8 (7*) Mr W M O'Sullivan,
....(12 to 1) 8
583* AMERICAN EYRE 8-11-9 C O'Dwyer, ...(9 to 2) 9
292 KATES CASTLE 6-10-7 (7*) Mr K O'Sullivan, ...(50 to 1) 10
CASTLE BRANDON 7-11-9 F J Flood, ...(16 to 1) 11
635 JOHNJOES PRIDE 9-10-12 (7*) K P Gaule, ...(20 to 1) f
635⁸ PRINCE YAZA 6-11-9 K F O'Brien, ...(12 to 1) pu
473⁴ WHEATSTONE BRIDGE 7-11-0 (5*) C O'Brien, ...(14 to 1) pu
575⁶ CHIC AND ELITE 6-11-0 P P Kinane, ...(33 to 1) pu
635 CARDAN 7-10-12 (7*) P A Roche, ...(20 to 1) pu
Dist: 3l, 1½l, 20l, ½l. 5m 31.10s. (16 Ran).
(A J O'Reilly), M F Morris

800 Thurles Handicap Chase (4-y-o and up) £2,243 2¾m.....................(4:30)

635⁴ FAIRY PARK [-] (bl) 8-9-12 F Woods, ...(14 to 1) 1
532² ROSSBEIGH CREEK [-] 6-10-2 F J Flood, ...(9 to 2) 2
LADY BAR [-] 6-11-0 P M Verling, ...(10 to 1) 3
573³ TURBULENT WIND [-] 6-10-6 C F Swan, ...(7 to 1) 4
573⁶ ANTRIM COUNTY [-] 8-10-13 (3*) T J Mitchell, ...(10 to 1) 5
539 MACK A DAY [-] 6-10-13 A J O'Brien, ...(7 to 1) 6
468² HURRYUP [-] 6-9-9 (5*) C O'Brien, ...(8 to 1) 7
DAGWOOD [-] 8-10-11 (5*) D T Evans, ...(12 to 1) 8
573² WINNING CHARLIE [-] 7-10-9 K F O'Brien, ...(4 to 1 fav) 9
332 WATERLOO ANDY [-] 7-9-12 P L Malone, ...(14 to 1) 10
YERVILLE LASS [-] 6-9-7 W T Slattery Jnr, ...(25 to 1) 11
691³ GARRYDOOLIS [-] 7-9-11 C O'Dwyer, ...(14 to 1) 12
CAPTAIN BRANDY [-] 8-12-2 A Powell, ...(14 to 1) pu
ASK FRANK [-] 7-11-2 G Bradley, ...(7 to 1) pu
691 COOLADERRA LADY [-] 7-9-4 (3*) D Bromley, ...(20 to 1) pu
Dist: 1l, 7l, ¾l, ¾l. 5m 31.60s. (15 Ran).
(Mrs B Ryan), Jeremiah Ryan

801 Liscahill I.N.H. Flat Race (5 & 6-y-o) £2,243 2¼m.......................(5:30)

554 GLENGARRA PRINCESS 6-11-2 (7*) Mr M Budds, (20 to 1) 1
572 GOLDEN NUGGET 6-11-7 (7*) Mr D J Kavanagh, .(10 to 1) 2
277⁵ THATS A SECRET 5-11-7 (7*) Mr P English, ..(3 to 1 jt-fav) 3
124 PAPRS GALE (Ire) 5-11-2 (7*) Mr E Norris, ...(8 to 1) 4
538² MUILEAR OIRGE 6-12-0 Mr R Hurley, ...(3 to 1 jt-fav) 5
ISN'T THAT NICE (Ire) 5-11-7 (7*) Mr M Brennan, ..(14 to 1) 6
675⁵ MISS POLLERTON (Ire) 5-11-2 (7*) Mr J Bowe, ...(12 to 1) 7
540⁴ HI-WAY'S GALE 6-11-9 Mr A P O'Brien, ...(9 to 2) 8
COUNTERBALANCE 6-11-9 Mr P Fenton, ...(14 to 1) 9
540 SAMANTHABROWNTHORN 6-11-2 (7*) Mr B Moran,
....(14 to 1) 10
43 ASHTON'S VENTURE (Ire) 5-11-4 (5*) Mrs J M Mullins,
....(14 to 1) 11
708⁷ DRINK UP DAN 6-12-0 Mr A J Martin, ...(8 to 1) 12
DENNY'S GUEST (Ire) 5-12-0 Mr T S Costello, ...(12 to 1) 13
378⁷ CARTRON HOUSE 6-11-7 (7*) Mr M D Jennings, .(25 to 1) 14
CARRIG DANCER (Ire) 5-11-2 (7*) Mr D K Budds, (20 to 1) 15
675⁹ TULLOVIN CASTLE (Ire) 5-11-2 (7*) Mr P O'Connell,
....(12 to 1) 16
ALL A STRUGGLE (Ire) 5-11-2 (7*) Mr W M O'Sullivan,
....(20 to 1) 17
COLIN'S MAN 6-11-9 (5*) Mr J A Nash, ...(20 to 1) 18
NILE LODGE (Ire) 5-11-6 (3*) Mr M Phillips, ...(14 to 1) 19
536 CASTLEPOOK 6-12-0 Mr P J Healy, ...(25 to 1) 20
MULLENAGLOCH 6-11-7 (7*) Mr M A Cahill, ...(20 to 1) ro
Dist: 7l, ½l, 1l, 10l. 4m 19.10s. (21 Ran).
(P Budds), P Budds

DUNDALK (IRE) (good)
Friday October 15th

802 Kilkerly Maiden Hurdle (3-y-o) £2,243 2m 135yds..........................(2:30)

706³ JAZZY REFRAIN (Ire) 10-9 P Carberry, ...(8 to 1) 1
253 CARHUE STAR (Ire) 10-4 (5*) T J O'Sullivan, ...(16 to 1) 2
228⁴ NORDIC MINE (Ire) 11-0 K F O'Brien, ...(9 to 1) 3
706⁵ MISS MURPHY (Ire) 10-9 (7*) J P Broderick, ...(14 to 1) 4
688⁶ ALIBAR'S PET (Ire) 10-2 (7*) K P Gaule, ...(10 to 1) 5
494² TOUCHING MOMENT (Ire) 10-9 (5*) T P Rudd, .(5 to 2 fav) 6
706 PRINTOUT (Ire) 10-9 D H O'Connor, ...(16 to 1) 7
688⁵ TORC MOUNTAIN (Ire) 11-0 B Sheridan, ...(8 to 1) 8
494⁵ RUNNING SLIPPER (Ire) 11-0 L P Cusack, ...(25 to 1) 9
688 GROUND CONTROL (Ire) 10 9 (5*) D P Murphy, ...(16 to 1) 10
706² DOYROY (Ire) 10-4 (5*) C O'Brien, ...(9 to 1) 11
688⁸ REGAL PRETENDER (Ire) 11-0 H Rogers, ...(14 to 1) 12
706⁷ BRIGENSER (Ire) 11-0 A Powell, ...(14 to 1) 13
706⁸ POUNDWORLD (Ire) 10-9 P L Malone, ...(25 to 1) 14
LETS TWIST AGAIN (Ire) 11-0 P McWilliams, ...(14 to 1) 15
ANNADOT (Ire) 10-9 F J Flood, ...(14 to 1) 16
SANDCHORUS (Ire) 11-0 J P Banahan, ...(20 to 1) 17
BOBROSS (Ire) 11-0 F Woods, ...(7 to 1) 18
DIAMOND CLUSTER 11-0 C O'Dwyer, ...(7 to 1) 19
706⁴ CREHELP EXPRESS (Ire) 10-9 C N Bowens, ...(12 to 1) f
Dist: 2l, 1½l, 3l, 3½l. 4m 4.40s. (20 Ran).
(Mrs Mary M Hayes), Noel Meade

101

803 Annagassan Maiden Hurdle (4-y-o) £2,243 2m 135yds.......................(3:00)

555^{3} STEEL MIRROR 11-9 J Shortt, ... (7 to 2) 1
558^{6} EALING COURT 11-9 A Powell, ... (5 to 2 fav) 2
671^{4} SHAWAR (Ire) 11-9 K F O'Brien, ... (5 to 1) 3
504^{4} KNOCNAGORE (Ire) 11-4 M Flynn, ... (20 to 1) 4
215^{9} CASTLE CELEBRITY (Ire) 10-13 G Bradley, ... (14 to 1) 5
671 COUNTESS PAHLEN (Ire) 10-13 J F Titley, ... (20 to 1) 6
620 SCEAL SIOG (Ire) 10-13 H Rogers, ... (25 to 1) 7
555^{5} DOMINO'S RING (Ire) 11-9 D H O'Connor, ... (8 to 1) 8
490^{4} FREEWAY HALO (Ire) 10-10 (3*) T J Mitchell, ... (16 to 1) 9
671^{2} STEEL CHIMES (Ire) (bl) 11-9 B Sheridan, ... (4 to 1) 10
746^{4} BELLE O' THE BAY (Ire) 10-10 (3*) D Bromley, ... (20 to 1) 11
671 NORA'S ERROR (Ire) 11-4 J P Banahan, ... (25 to 1) 12
671^{9} LOVE FOR LYDIA (Ire) 10-6 (7*) F Byrne, ... (16 to 1) 13
508^{5} PLEASE CALL (Ire) 11-4 C O'Dwyer, ... (25 to 1) 14
671 FURTHER NOTICE (Ire) (bl) 10-13 (5*) C O'Brien, .. (20 to 1) 15
LONG GUE (Fr) 10-13 (5*) D P Geoghegan, ... (25 to 1) 16
555^{9} TALE A TALE (Ire) 10-11 (7*) J P Broderick, ... (10 to 1) 17
LOOK NONCHALANT (Ire) 10-13 M Duffy, ... (16 to 1) 18
208^{5} SIRAJAO (Ire) 10-8 (5*) T P Rudd, ... (25 to 1) 19
671 TOO YOUNG (Ire) 11-4 F Woods, ... (25 to 1) 20

Dist: 3l-hd, 15l, 12l, 2l. 4m 3.80s. (20 Ran).

(Quarrywell Syndicate), M Halford

804 Fane Hurdle (5-y-o and up) £2,243 2m 135yds.............................(3:30)

636* EAGLE ROCK (USA) 5-11-3 (5*) C O'Brien, ... (5 to 4 fav) 1
112 SHEER MIRTH 8-11-4 C O'Dwyer, ... (14 to 1) 2
585^{4} PERSIAN HALO (Ire) 5-11-4 D H O'Connor, ... (9 to 4) 3
HACKETTS CROSS (Ire) 5-11-4 A Powell, ... (5 to 1) 4
JATINGA (Ire) 5-11-4 B Sheridan, ... (12 to 1) 5
AMBER RULER 7-11-4 K F O'Brien, ... (7 to 1) 6
SAGASTINI (USA) 6-11-4 P L Malone, ... (16 to 1) 7
746 GONE LIKE THE WIND 6-10-13 (5*) L Flynn, ... (25 to 1) 8
636^{8} TOP RUN (Ire) 5-11-4 H Rogers, ... (14 to 1) 9
SPITFIRE GIRL 5-10-6 (7*) Mr A K Wyse, ... (33 to 1) 10
618^{8} CURRAGH ROSE 6-10-6 (7*) J Butler, ... (20 to 1) 11

Dist: Hd, 3l, 11l, 13l. 4m 10.40s. (11 Ran).

(P J Kinsella), L Young

805 Castletown Handicap Hurdle (0-102 4-y-o and up) £2,243 2m 135yds..........(4:00)

490^{2} DARCARI ROSE (Ire) [-] 4-10-4 (7*) T Martin, ... (14 to 1) 1
797^{4} BELLECARA [-] 6-10-7 (3*) D Bromley, ... (8 to 1) 2
533^{5} VICOSA (Ire) [-] 4-11-7 (5*) Mr A E Lacy, ... (7 to 1) 3
745^{5} FAMOUS DANCER [-] 5-11-1 (7*) B Bowens, ... (8 to 1) 4
574^{9} BALLINDERRY GLEN [-] 7-11-1 (5*) M G Cleary, ... (12 to 1) 5
493^{4} KHAZARI (USA) [-] (bl) 5-11-12 C O'Dwyer, ... (14 to 1) 6
574 LOUGH ATALIA [-] 6-10-10 A Powell, ... (16 to 1) 7
276* HUGH DANIELS [-] 5-11-0 (7*) D R Thompson, ... (6 to 1) 8
SHY GAL (Ire) [-] 5-10-13 P L Malone, ... (50 to 1) 9
493* MABES TOWN (Ire) [-] (bl) 5-11-7 H Rogers, ... (4 to 1) 10
746 GAZUMPED [-] 6-10-5 (7*) J P Broderick, ... (25 to 1) 11
745^{3} WINDOVER LODGE [-] 6-11-4 K F O'Brien, ... (8 to 1) 12
421* RUFO'S COUP [-] 6-12-0 P Carberry, ... (3 to 1 fav) 13
SHABRA CONNECTION [-] 6-10-11 D H O'Connor, (50 to 1) 14
274 THE BOURDA [-] 7-10-11 (7*) D A McLoughlin, ... (10 to 1) f

Dist: 1l, 7l, 10l, 6l. 4m 5.30s. (15 Ran).

(Mrs G Pennicott), F W Pennicott

806 Newry Handicap Chase (0-109 4-y-o and up) £2,243 2m 3f.................. (4:30)

512^{4} HO FRETTA [-] 7-9-7 (5*) C O'Brien, ... (8 to 1) 1
492^{2} MAGIC MILLION [-] 7-11-8 J P Banahan, ... (5 to 2 fav) 2
509* ANN'S PRINCE [-] 10-11-10 H Rogers, ... (4 to 1) 3
OPRYLAND [-] 8-11-10 F Woods, ... (14 to 1) 4
496^{3} INCA CHIEF [-] 9-11-2 (5*) D P Geoghegan, ... (7 to 1) 5
MR HOY [-] 10-11-12 (7*) Mr J Bright, ... (33 to 1) 6
691* BENS DILEMMA [-] 8-9-13 (7*,6ex) J P Broderick, .. (5 to 1) 7
170^{3} GLITTER GREY [-] 7-11-7 K F O'Brien, ... (10 to 1) 8
200^{5} HARRY'S BOREEN [-] 6-10-3 (7*) P Stafford, ... (10 to 1) 9
573 MAYE FANE [-] 9-11-13 (3*) G Kilfeather, ... (14 to 1) 10
BOB DEVANI [-] 7-11-2 G M O'Neill, ... (8 to 1) 11
WHEELER DEALER [-] (bl) 12-10-7 D H O'Connor, (33 to 1) 12
691 ANNETTE'S DELIGHT [-] 14-9-8 (5*) M A Davey, .. (14 to 1) f
BIG JAMES [-] 11-10-10 (3*) T J Mitchell, ... (14 to 1) f
573^{7} MARKET SURVEY [-] 12-10-3 C O'Dwyer, ... (25 to 1) f
ALL A QUIVER [-] 6-11-0 (7*) B Bowens, ... (10 to 1) f
512 CARTOON TIME (Fr) [-] 9-9-7 L Flynn, ... (50 to 1) pu

Dist: 6l, 6l, 12l, 11l. 4m 52.40s. (17 Ran).

(Derek Bell), Cecil Mahon

807 Rossbracken Novice Chase (4-y-o and up) £2,243 2m 3f...................... (5:00)

OPERA HAT (Ire) 5-11-5 A Powell, ... (4 to 1) 1
574^{5} HAVE TO THINK 5-11-5 (5*) T P Rudd, ... (14 to 1) 2
575^{3} SHEAMY'S DREAM (Ire) (bl) 5-11-10 J Shortt, .. (5 to 4 on) 3
575 RANDOM PRINCE 9-12-0 K F O'Brien, ... (6 to 1) 4
NILOUSHA 6-11-9 C O'Dwyer, ... (10 to 1) 5
744^{3} EDENAKILL LAD 6-11-6 (3*) D Bromley, ... (20 to 1) 6
KINGS HILL 11-11-2 (7*) J Butler, ... (10 to 1) 7
619^{6} COQ HARDI SMOKEY (Ire) (bl) 5-11-10 G M O'Neill, ... (16 to 1) 8
707^{9} SUNSHINE SEAL 6-11-6 (3*) T J Mitchell, ... (16 to 1) 9
DEEP ISLE 7-12-0 F Woods, ... (14 to 1) 10
158^{4} KILSHANNON SPRINGS 7-12-0 L P Cusack, ... (7 to 1) f
BACK BAR (Ire) 5-10-11 (5*) D P Geoghegan, ... (33 to 1) f
FIND OUT MORE (Ire) 5-11-2 P McWilliams, ... (33 to 1) bd
WARASH 7-11-9 D P Fagan, ... (20 to 1) bd

Dist: Hd, 5l, 6l, dist. 4m 56.30s. (14 Ran).

(Mrs T K Cooper), J R H Fowler

808 Lisnawilly INH Flat Race (5-y-o and up) £2,243 2m 135yds.................. (5:30)

620^{5} MASTER CRUSADER 7-11-7 (7*) Mr M Brennan, ... (5 to 2 fav) 1
620^{9} FINNEGANS WAKE 6-11-7 (7*) Mr G F Ryan, ... (10 to 1) 2
675^{3} BLAZING TRAIL (Ire) 5-11-9 (5*) Mr P M Kelly, ... (3 to 1) 3
675 CAILIN RUA (Ire) 5-11-4 (5*) Mr A E Lacy, ... (12 to 1) 4
NED BUTLER VI (Ire) 5-11-7 (7*) Mr E Norris, ... (5 to 1) 5
745^{4} GLENSHANE PASS 6-11-9 (5*) Mr J A Nash, ... (10 to 1) 6
675^{7} SHEELIN LAD (Ire) 5-11-7 (7*) Mr D A Harney, ... (4 to 1) 7
I IS 6-12-0 Mr S R Murphy, ... (8 to 1) 8
231 THE BOLD FOAL (Ire) 5-11-7 (7*) Mr J Quinn, ... (20 to 1) 9
MONKS DEAR VI 6-11-6 (3*) Mr A R Coonan, ... (14 to 1) 10
675 LADY JOANNE (Ire) 5-11-2 (7*) Mr A Daly, ... (33 to 1) 11
620 GARWELL (Ire) 5-11-6 (3*) Miss C Hutchinson, ... (25 to 1) 12
491^{7} BELLE DE SEUL 6-11-2 (7*) Mr E Magee, ... (50 to 1) 13
GORE PORT BAY 6-11-7 (7*) Mr D W Cullen, ... (14 to 1) 14
675 HILLHEAD PRINCE (Ire) 5-11-7 (7*) Miss V K Ferris, (50 to 1) 15
SHABRA SOCKS 7-11-7 (7*) Mr D J Kavanagh, ... (50 to 1) 16
CASHEL PALACE 8-11-2 (7*) Mr J Bright, ... (25 to 1) pu

Dist: 7l, 2l, 5l, 13l. 4m 4.20s. (17 Ran).

(Kilkea Castle Racing Syndicate), J H Scott

LUDLOW (good)
Friday October 15th

Going Correction: MINUS 0.10 sec. per fur. (races 1,4,6,7), PLUS 0.25 (2,3,5)

809 Halford Novices' Hurdle (4-y-o and up) £1,480 2m........................ (1:50)

399^{2} LADY DONOGHUE (USA) 4-10-7 P Niven, *took str hold, hdwy 5th, led appr 2 out, sprawled on landing, sn reco'red, run on wl*..... (6 to 1 op 7 to 2 tchd 13 to 2) 1
BALLYHAMAGE (Ire) 5-10-13 A Maguire, *hdwy 5th, pressed wnr frm 2 out till outpcd r-in*...... (25 to 1 op 16 to 1) 2
SUPER COIN 5-10-13 L Harvey, *al in tch, rdn and kpt on same pace frm 2 out.* (20 to 1 op 33 to 1 tchd 16 to 1) 3
CHAPEL OF BARRAS (Ire) 4-10-12 Peter Hobbs, *in tch, pld hrd, shaken up and no imprsn frm 2 out.* .... (7 to 1 op 6 to 1 tchd 8 to 1 and 9 to 1) 4
658^{4} ZAMANAYN (Ire) 5-10-13 R Supple, *hdwy to chase ldrs 4th, rdn and one pace 2 out.* .... (16 to 1 op 14 to 1 tchd 20 to 1) 5
658^{3} JON'S CHOICE (bl) 5-10-13 T Wall, *sn beh, rdn and hdwy 5th, wknd aftr 3 out*.. (10 to 1 op 8 to 1 tchd 12 to 1) 6
260^{6} OYSTON'S LIFE 4-10-12 J Railton, *led to 4th, lft in ld nxt, hdd and wknd quickly appr 2 out.* .... (100 to 1 op 50 to 1) 7
ORUJO (Ire) 5-10-13 J Osborne, *beh till styd on frm 2 out.* .... (6 to 1 op 3 to 1 tchd 7 to 1) 8
704^{4} MAPLE BAY (Ire) 4-10-12 G McCourt, *nvr dngrs.* .... (25 to 1 op 20 to 1) 9
BROTHERLYAFFECTION 4-10-9 (3*) S Wynne, *took str hold, wknd 3 out*................ (100 to 1 op 66 to 1) 10
PRINCETHORPE 6-10-13 Gary Lyons, *in tch whn mstk 3rd, sn wknd*.................... (100 to 1 op 66 to 1) 11
REEDFINCH 4-10-12 M Richards, *not fluent, al beh.* .... (25 to 1 op 12 to 1) 12
704^{8} GIVE ALL 7-10-6 (7*) M Appleby, *chsd ldrs till wknd 3 out.* .... (100 to 1 op 66 to 1) 13
NONANNO 4-10-12 B Powell, *al beh.* .... (100 to 1 op 66 to 1) 14
705* KHALIDI (Ire) 4-11-4 P Holley, *trkd ldrs, led 4th till slpd badly and uns rdr nxt.* .... (5 to 4 fav tchd 11 to 8 and 6 to 4) ur
MISTRESS BEE (USA) 4-10-7 R Greene, *wth ldr till sddl slpd and pld up bef 3rd*........... (25 to 1 op 20 to 1) pu

Dist: 5l, 2l, 4l, 1l, 12l, 4l, 2l, 2½l, 6l, 3l. 3m 45.80s. a 8.80s (16 Ran).

(C C Buckley), Mrs M Reveley

810 Castle Selling Handicap Chase (5-y-o and up) £2,242 2m...................... (2:25)

712^{7} AL HASHIMI [115] 9-12-7 R Dunwoody, *made all, clr appr 3 out, hit 2 out, easily*.... (17 to 2 op 8 to 1 tchd 9 to 1) 1
525^{4} BARTONDALE [82] 8-9-11 (5*) R Farrant, *al frnt rnk, chsd wnr frm 4 out, no ch from 3 out*..... (10 to 1 op 6 to 1) 2
596^{4} ACHILTIBUIE [87] 9-10-7 D Gallagher, *hdwy 7th, no ch frm 3 out*................. (15 to 2 op 11 to 2 tchd 8 to 1) 3
659 ANOTHER CRUISE [90] 8-10-10 R Greene, *mstk 9th, hrd drvn 4 out, no imprsn*.......... (25 to 1 op 20 to 1) 4
749^{3} SLIPPERY MAX [90] 9-10-10 M A FitzGerald, *beh, effrt 7th, wknd 4 out*.............. (7 to 1 op 6 to 1 tchd 8 to 1) 5

643[8] POLDER [83] 7-9-12 (5") R Davis, *hit 3rd, sn beh.*
....(8 to 1 op 6 to 1) 6

612[6] VIRGINIA'S BAY [80] 7-9-7 (7") Mr G Lewis, *hit 4th, al beh.*
....(33 to 1 op 25 to 1) 7

676[3] MAGIC SOLDIER [95] 8-11-1 R Marley, *chsd ldrs till rdn and wknd 3 out*......(4 to 1 fav op 3 to 1 tchd 9 to 2) 8

632 MINT-MASTER [80] 8-9-9 (5") D Leahy, *nvr gng wl, beh frm 5th*......................(33 to 1 op 25 to 1) 9

521[4] IMPERIAL FLIGHT [80] 8-10-0 J R Kavanagh, *slpd bend appr 1st, trkd ldr 6th, 3rd, staying on but no ch wth wnr whn f 3 out*........(13 to 2 op 8 to 1 tchd 6 to 1) f

360[2] COTAPAXI [92] 8-10-12 A Tory, *beh 6th, no ch whn hit 8th, tld off when pld up bef 3 out*..........(8 to 1 op 7 to 1) pu

Dist: 2l, 8l, ½l, 8l, 10l, nk, 10l, 15l. 4m 4.30s. a 12.30s (11 Ran).
SR: 24/-/-/-/-/ (Major A W C Pearn), R J Hodges

811 Court Of Hill Amateur Riders' Handicap Chase (0-125 5-y-o and up) £2,612 2½m
....(2:55)

198[3] CORRARDER [105] 9-11-3 (7") Mr J Smyth-Osbourne, *in tch early, lost pos 7th, plenty to do 3 out, str run appr last, led nr finish.*.................................(8 to 1) 1

677[3] SANDYBRAES [109] 8-11-7 (7") Mr G Hogan, *prmnt, chlgd 9th, led tenth, hdd 4 out, chald nxt, led 2 out, headed and found no extr r-in.*............(4 to 1 tchd 9 to 2) 2

595[4] COMEDY ROAD [101] 9-11-6 Mr M Armytage, *dsptd ld 7th, led 4 out, hdd 2 out, chlgd last, led ag'n r-in, ct nr finish.*.................................(9 to 1 op 11 to 1) 3

GEMBRIDGE JUPITER [96] 15-11-06 (7") Mr C Trietline, *not fluent, al beh.*.....................(20 to 1 op 4 to 1) 4

697[3] FRISCO CITY (Chi) [94] (bl) 7-10-6 (7") Mr M Rimell, *hit ldr to 6th, lost pl 9th, not fluent and nvr dngrs aftr, tld off.*
....(4 to 1 op 3 to 1) 5

548 COUNTERBID [103] (v) 6-11-3 (5") Mr A Farrant, *nvr gng wl, hit 3rd, lost tch 8th, tld off 12th.....*(11 to 2 op 6 to 1) 6

CENTENARY STAR [105] 8-11-5 (5") Mr M Buckley, *hld up, hdway and hit 4 out, fourth and no prog whn f 3 out.*
....(11 to 4 fav op 2 to 1) f

WALK IN RHYTHM [81] 12-9-7 (7") Miss C Thomas, *made most to tenth, sn wknd, tld off whn pld up bef 3 out.*
....(33 to 1) pu

Dist: 2l, 3½l, dist, ½l, dist. 5m 3.30s. a 12.30s (8 Ran).
SR: 23/25/13/-/-/ (Mrs E T Smyth-Osbourne), J A B Old

812 Ashford Handicap Hurdle (0-125 4-y-o and up) £2,134 2m
....(3:25)

KABAYLI [96] 4-10-1[1] J Railton, *in tch, led aftr 3 out, pushed out and ran on wl r-in*......(6 to 1 op 7 to 2) 1

TARKOVSKY [104] 8-10-9 R Dunwoody, *hdway 5th, str run and hit 2 out, no imprsn on wnr r-in.*

....(10 to 1 op 7 to 1) 2

MOVING OUT [95] 5-10-0 J Osborne, *trkd ldrs, led aftr 3 out, sn hdd, hit 2 out, rdn and no extr r-in.*
....(2 to 1 fav op 9 to 4) 3

522[7] ALWAYS READY [91] 7-10-0 A Maguire, *in tch, rdn and styd on same pace appr 2 out.*......(16 to 1 op 14 to 1) 4

569[2] NOCATCHIM [123] (bl) 4-11-9 (5") J McCarthy, *led to 4th, hdd sn aftr 3 out, btn appr 2 out.*
.........(11 to 4 op 5 to 2 tchd 3 to 1 and 100 to 30) 5

KALZARI (USA) [100] 8-10-5 S Earle, *in tch till wknd aftr 3 out.*.................................(25 to 1 op 20 to 1) 6

FIRST CRACK [103] 8-10-8 R Supple, *al beh.*
....(25 to 1 op 14 to 1) 7

SENSEI [95] 6-10-0 T Wall, *al beh*......(66 to 1 op 33 to 1) 8

713[8] PALACE WOLF (NZ) [123] 9-12-0 R Marley, *chsd ldr to 4th, sn wknd.*..............(33 to 1 op 20 to 1) 9

543[4] SKOLERN [99] (v) 9-10-4 J Callaghan, *sn beh, tld off whn pld up bef 2 out.*..........(8 to 1 op 7 to 1) pu

Dist: 3½l, 5l, 8l, 10l, 7l, 12l, 12l, 20l. 3m 40.20s. a 3.20s (10 Ran).
SR: 25/29/15/7/25/-/ (Elite Racing Club), C R Egerton

813 Arthur Elliott Memorial Novices' Chase (5-y-o and up) £2,879 2½m
....(4:00)

661 KILLULA CHIEF 6-11-12 M A FitzGerald, *led till aftr 4th, led ag'n 3 out, hit last, shaken up and styd on wl.*
....(2 to 1 op 9 to 4) 1

649[4] GOLDEN FARE 8-11-2 A Maguire, *led aftr 4th, hdd 3 out, rdn and ev ch last, not quicken.*
..........(7 to 1 op 10 to 1 tchd 12 to 1 and 13 to 2) 2

SPIRIT OF KIBRIS 8-11-2 W McFarland, *al in tch, pressed ldrs gng wl appr 3 out, sn rdn and btn.*
....(7 to 1 op 9 to 2) 3

WILD BRAMBLE (Ire) 5-10-9 P Niven, *chsd ldrs 9th, lost pl and beh tenth, hdway 11th, hit twelfth and 4 out, rdn and wknd quickly 3 out.*
..........(13 to 8 fav op Evens tchd 7 to 4 and 2 to 1) 4

CWM ARCTIC 6-10-11 Mr M Jackson, *mstk 1st, lost tch 9th, nvr dngrs aftr.*..............(66 to 1 op 50 to 1) 5

607 BRIGTINA 5-10-9 (5") R Farrant, *in tch whn hit tenth, wknd twelfth.*..........................(33 to 1 op 25 to 1) 6

FLYING WILD 7-11-2 N Williamson, *hdway 9th, fdd frm 4 out, tld off.*......................(50 to 1 op 33 to 1) 7

ZACTOO 7-11-2 T Wall, *mstk and uns rdr second.*
....(100 to 1 op 50 to 1) ur

703[3] WEST BAY 7-10-13 (3") A Thornton, *chsd ldrs till mstk and uns rdr 4th*.....................(10 to 1 tchd 12 to 1) ur
SR: 20/7/-/-/-/-/ (T G K Construction Ltd), J G M O'Shea

814 Brimfield Novices' Handicap Hurdle (4-y-o and up) £1,480 2m 5f 110yds.
....(4:35)

OSMOSIS [79] 7-10-9 D Gallagher, *hld up, steady hdwy frm 3 out, chlgd last, drvn to ld r-in, ran on.*
....(7 to 1 op 9 to 2) 1

594[5] ANNA VALLEY [94] 7-11-5 (5") R Davis, *beh till steady hdwy 6th, led r-in, rdn and found no extr.*
....(5 to 2 fav tchd 11 to 4 and 3 to 1) 2

484[4] GOLDEN MADJAMBO [70] 7-9-7 (7") M Doyle, *beh, hdwy 6th, ev ch frm 3 out till hit 2 out, styd on one pace.*
....(6 to 1 op 9 to 2) 3

PRINCE of SALERNO [71] 6-10-1 R Supple, *beh, lost tch 7th, styd on ag'n frm 2 out.*
....(14 to 1 op 12 to 1 tchd 16 to 1) 4

659 ENCHANTED FLYER [70] 6-9-9 (5") T Eley, *chsd ldrs, chlgd 3 out, rdn and wknd appr 2 out.*..(20 to 1 op 16 to 1) 5

699 CORNISH COSSACK (NZ) [80] 6-10-3 (7") Mr G Shenkin, *improved to chase ldrs 3rd, styd prmnt till wknd quickly aftr 3 out.*..................(6 to 1 op 4 to 1) 6

441[6] DOCTOR DUNKLIN (USA) [70] 4-10-0 N Williamson, *in tch 5th, lost touch frm 3 out, tld off.*... (25 to 1 op 20 to 1) 7

565[9] TINKLING STAR [70] 9-10-0 B Powell, *led second, beh frm 6th, tld off.*....................(33 to 1 tchd 20 to 1) 8

WEST MONKTON [70] 7-9-11 (3") W Marston, *chsd ldrs 6th, sn rdn and wknd.*................(12 to 1 op 7 to 1) 9

NORDROSS [70] 5-10-0 T Wall, *led second sn clr, hdd 3 out, wknd rpdly, tld off.*.....................(33 to 1) 10

701[3] TRUMPET [88] (bl) 4-11-4 M A FitzGerald, *drpd rear 4th, lost tch 6th, tld off whn pld up bef 2 out.*
....(9 to 2 op 4 to 1 tchd 5 to 1) pu

Dist: 1½l, 10l, nk, 15l, sht-hd, 2½l, dist, 6l. 5m 15.00s. a 18.00s (11 Ran).
(Michael Mellersh), D J G Murray Smith

815 EBF Ludlow National Hunt Flat Race (4,5,6-y-o) £1,350 2m
....(5:05)

CAPTAIN KHEDIVE 5-11-0 M Hourigan, *race keenly in tch, smooth hdwy to ld ins fnl 2 fs, easily.* 1

TOO SHARP 5-10-9 Mr J M Pritchard, *wnt lft strt, led, hdd ins fnl 2 fs, styd on, no ch wth wnr*..........(10 to 1) 2

SPRING GRASS 5-10-2 (7") D Meade, *wnt lft and lost many ls strt, hdway 4 fs out, ran on wl and pres fnl furlong.*.....................(25 to 1 op 20 to 1) 3

ROSEBERRY TOPPING 4-10-7 (7") M Herrington, *beh, hdwy 6 fs out, hit rail 4 furlongs out, styd on fnl 2 furlongs.*...................(5 to 2 fav op 9 to 4) 4

SHERWOOD BOY 4-11-0 Mrs T Bailey, *hdwy frm 4 fs out, kpt on fnl 2 furlongs.*...............(10 to 1 op 7 to 1) 5

KINGS CHARIOT 6-11-0 Mr J Durkan, *gd hdwy hfwy, pressed ldr 3 fs out, wknd 2 furlongs out.*
....(7 to 1 op 8 to 1) 6

CRUNCH TIME (Ire) 4-10-7 (7") A Flannigan, *mid-div, rdn alng o'r 3 fs out, no imprsn fnl 2 furlongs.*
....(14 to 1 op 20 to 1 tchd 33 to 1) 7

634 SILVER SUMAL 4-10-7 (7") Mr M Rimell, *prmnt 12 fs.*
....(33 to 1 op 20 to 1) 8

BATTY'S ISLAND 4-10-9 (5") P Hide, *prmnt 9 fs.*
....(33 to 1 op 20 to 1) 9

SKYE DUCK 4-10-9 V Slattery, *chsd ldrs till wknd 4 fs out.*.................................(16 to 1 op 12 to 1) 10

HECTOR MARIO 5-10-9 (5") R Davis, *smooth hdwy to chase ldrs 5 fs out, wknd o'r 3 furlongs out.*
....(6 to 1 op 4 to 1) 11

HOT 'N ROSIE 4-10-6 (3") D J Moffatt, *wnt lft and lost many ls strt, al beh.*...............(16 to 1 op 10 to 1) 12

RUKIA 4-10-4 (5") J McCarthy, *al in rear.*
....(9 to 1 op 5 to 1 tchd 10 to 1) 13

ROC SPIRIT 6-10-9 Mr N Miles, *nvr better than mid-div.*
....(33 to 1 op 25 to 1) 14

RELAXED LAD 4-10-7 (7") J Bond, *in tch till wknd quickly hfwy.*.........................(33 to 1 op 25 to 1) 15

VEGETARIANPHEASANT 4-10-4 (5") D Leahy, *chsd ldrs 9 fs.* 16

COME ON LUCY 4-10-6 (3") A Thornton, *wnt lft and lost many ls strt, sn reco'red, prmnt till wknd 6 fs out.* 17

CAPTIVA BAY 4-10-6 (3") S Wynne, *wnt lft and lost many ls strt, al beh.*..............(33 to 1 op 20 to 1) 18

Dist: 12l, nk, 2½l, 4l, 3l, 4l, 4l, 1½l, 2l, ½l. 3m 39.90s. (18 Ran).
(Khedive Partnership), P J Hobbs

AUTEUIL (FR) (heavy)
Saturday October 16th

816 Prix Heros XII (Chase) (5-y-o and up) £35,842 2¾m
....(3:00)

16[5] THE FELLOW (Fr) 8-10-3 A Kondrat, ... 1D

16* UCELLO II (Fr) 8-11-2 C Aubert, ... 1

ROYAL CHANCE (Fr) 6-9-13 B Jollivet, ... 2
Dist: 1½l, hd, 2½l, 10l, 1l, 4l, 6l. 5m 53.00s. (8 Ran).
(Marquesa de Moratalla), F Doumen

BELMONT PARK (USA) (firm)
Saturday October 16th

817 Breeders' Cup Chase (Hurdle) (3-y-o and up) £82,781 2m 5f. . . . . (5:00)

LONESOME GLORY (USA) 5-11-2 Blythe Miller, (held to 10) 1
HIGHLAND BUD 8-11-2 R Dunwoody, ... (10 to 7 on) 2
MISTICO (Chi) 7-11-2 C Thornton, ... (10 to 7 on) 3
Dist: 8½l, 5l, 4l, 14l, ¾l, 23l. 4m 53.49s. (9 Ran).
(Mrs Walter M Jeffords), F Bruce Miller

KELSO (good)
Saturday October 16th
Going Correction: PLUS 0.20 sec. per fur. (races 1,2,- 4,6,7), PLUS 0.45 (3,5)

818 Weatherbys 'Newcomers' Series Claiming Hurdle (4-y-o and up) £2,127 2¼m. . . (2:10)

591⁷ KALKO 4-10-8 (5*) D Bentley, *hld up in tch, chlgd appr last, kpt on wl und pres to ld cl hme.*
. . . . (5 to 1 tchd 4 to 1) 1
657⁴ SRIVIJAYA 6-11-10 P Niven, *hld up, steady hdwy frm hfwy, led appr last, hrd rdn r-in, ct cl hme.*
. . . . (11 to 10 fav op 6 to 4 tchd 7 to 4 and Evens) 2
545² STINGRAY CITY (USA) 4-10-12 (7*) F Perratt, *trkd ldrs, led appr 2 out, hdd approaching last, kpt on same pace,.*
. . . . (9 to 1 op 8 to 1 tchd 10 to 1) 3
654⁵ SAOIRSE (Ire) 5-10-8 (3*) D J Moffatt, *in tch, jnd ldrs 3 out, kpt on same pace frm nxt.*
. . . . (8 to 1 op 7 to 1 tchd 10 to 1) 4
594⁶ TEMPORALE 7-10-11 (7*) J Supple, *beh, kpt on frm 3 out, not rch ldrs.* . . . . (20 to 1 op 16 to 1) 5
TAYLORMADE BOY 10-10-5 (5*) P Waggott, *chsd ldrs, kpt on same pace frm 2 out.* . . . . (12 to 1 op 6 to 1) 6
657 COOL DUDE 7-11-0 A Orkney, *prmnt, led 7th, hdd appr 2 out, sn btn.* . . . . (14 to 1 op 10 to 1) 7
766⁴ FELL WARDEN (bl) 5-10-9 (3*) A Larnach, *prmnt, effrt aftr 3 out, fdd.* . . . . (25 to 1 op 20 to 1) 8
477⁵ DOCTOR'S REMEDY 7-10-12 D Morris, *nvr chngrs.*
. . . . (33 to 1 op 25 to 1) 9
657⁸ OLD MORTALITY 7-11-2 B Storey, *nvr better than mid-div.* . . . . (25 to 1 op 16 to 1) 10
755 WARWICK SUITE 11-10-12 A Mulholland, *led to 7th, wkng whn mstk 3 out.* . . . . (66 to 1 op 16 to 1) 11
640⁷ EMPEROR ALEXANDER (Ire) 5-10-9 S Turner, *prmnt, dsptd ld 7th, wknd aftr 3 out.* . . . . (50 to 1 op 33 to 1) 12
INSPIRED GUESS (USA) 6-11-0 M Dwyer, *nvr nr to chal.*
. . . . (6 to 1 op 4 to 1 tchd 12 to 1) 13
642⁵ CARDENDEN (Ire) 5-10-9 R Hodge, *sn beh, tld off.*
. . . . (50 to 1 op 33 to 1) 14
734⁹ HOTDIGGITTY 5-10-13 (3*) A Dobbin, *beh frm hfwy, tld off.*
. . . . (50 to 1 op 25 to 1) 15
BLUSHING GOLD 4-10-1 (7*) S Taylor, *sn lost tch, wl tld off.* . . . . (66 to 1 op 33 to 1) 16
Dist: Nk, 8l, 8l, hd, 3l, ¾l, 1½l, 5l, 2l, 8l. 4m 23.70s. a 16.70s (16 Ran).
(M J Willan), M D Hammond

819 BBC Radio Newcastle Sport FM Amateur Riders' Handicap Hurdle (0-115 4-y-o and up) £2,075 2¾m 110yds. . . . . (2:40)

730* PURITAN (Can) [92] 4-10-8 (5*) Mrs P Nash, *hld up, steady hdwy to track ldrs hfwy, led appr last, quickened clr r-in.* . . . . (2 to 1 fav op 3 to 1 tchd 7 to 2) 1
662⁹ SWEET CITY [100] 8-11-0 (7*) Mr R Hale, *hld up, hdwy hfwy, chlgd last, kpt on, no ch wth wnr.*
. . . . (16 to 1 tchd 25 to 1) 2
730⁶ SIMPLE PLEASURE [96] 8-11-3 Mr S Swiers, *cl up, dsptd ld 3 out, one pace appr last.* . . . . . . (12 to 1 tchd 14 to 1) 3
COXANN [81] 7-9-9 (7*) Mr E Tolhurst, *hld up, hdwy hfwy, kpt on und pres frm last.* . . . . (33 to 1 op 25 to 1) 4
767² TRONCHETTO (Ire) [94] (bl) 4-10-10 (5*) Mr M Buckley, *cl up, led aftr 4th, hdd appr last, sn btn.* (7 to 1 tchd 8 to 1) 5
736² LEADING PROSPECT [107] 6-11-7 (7*) Mr A Parker, *chsd ldrs, wkng whn mstk last.*
. . . . (11 to 2 op 5 to 1 tchd 6 to 1) 6
654 GLEMOT (Ire) [81] 5-9-9 (7*) Mr D Parker, *hld up, hdwy 8th, wknd appr last.* . . . . (7 to 2 op 3 to 1 tchd 4 to 1) 7
759⁵ INVERINATE [85] 8-10-2³ (7*) Mr C Ewart, *chsd ldrs, rdn aftr 3 out, fdd.* . . . . (12 to 1 op 10 to 1) 8
654³ AS D'EBOLI (Fr) [89] 6-10-3 (7*) Mr C Bonner, *al beh.*
. . . . (10 to 1) 9
HARDIHERO [92] 7-10-6 (7*) Mr G White, *in tch till wknd appr 3 out.* . . . . (33 to 1 op 20 to 1) 10
HERE COMES TIBBY [79] 6-9-11 (3*) Mrs A Farrell, *chsd ldrs till wknd 7th.* . . . . (33 to 1 op 20 to 1) 11
DAWN COYOTE (USA) [80] 10-9-8 (7*) Miss J Thurlow, *beh frm hfwy.* . . . . (33 to 1 op 25 to 1 tchd 50 to 1) 12

625⁴ LA MOLINILLA [79] 10-9-7 (7*) Miss S Lamb, *led till aftr 4th, wknd 7th.* . . . . (100 to 1 op 66 to 1) 13
FIRST EVER (Ire) [106] 4-11-6 (7*) Mr A Manners, *beh frm hfwy.* . . . . (200 to 1 op 100 to 1) 14
Dist: 6l, 5l, 3½l, 1l, 2l, 5l, 6l, 10l, 15l, 6l. 5m 26.60s. a 15.60s (14 Ran).
(J Parks), N Tinkler

820 Royal Caledonian Hunt Novices' Chase (4-y-o and up) £2,428 2m 1f. . . . . (3:15)

CELTIC SONG 6-11-0 T Reed, *in tch, lft in ld 2 out, styd on wl.* . . . . (20 to 1 op 12 to 1) 1
718⁵ ZARBANO 7-11-5 A Merrigan, *chsd clr ldr, slpd bend appr 3 out, chased wnr frm nxt, kpt on, no imprsn.*
. . . . (33 to 1 op 25 to 1) 2
729² REVE DE VALSE (USA) 6-11-0 (5*) P Waggott, *sn beh, styd on appr last, not trble ldrs.* . . . . . (5 to 2 op 2 to 1) 3
NORTHERN VISION 6-11-5 B Storey, *nvr nr to chal.*
. . . . (33 to 1 op 20 to 1) 4
EQUATOR 10-11-5 A Orkney, *sn beh.* (33 to 1 op 20 to 1) 5
MASTER MISCHIEF 6-11-5 K Johnson, *sn beh.*
. . . . (33 to 1 op 20 to 1) 6
HURDY 6-11-0 (5*) J Burke, *reared up and uns rdr strt, deemed not to have started.* . . . . . (5 to 2 tchd 100 to 30) 0
641⁴ EXPLOSIVE SPEED (USA) 5-11-10 C Grant, *led and sn clr, mstk 3 out, blun badly and uns rdr nxt.*
. . . . (2 to 1 fav tchd 5 to 2) ur
581 THE COUNTRY TRADER 7-11-5 N Doughty, *disputing 3rd whn blun and uns rdr 8th.* . . . . . (14 to 1 op 10 to 1) ur
HIGHYRMEN 9-11-0 Miss J Thurlow, *hmpd and strted very slwly, tld off whn refused 3rd.* . . . (50 to 1 op 33 to 1) ref
641 SEMINOFF (Fr) 7-11-2 (3*) A Dobbin, *strted slwly, tld off whn pld up bef 4th, sddl slpd.* . . . (20 to 1 op 16 to 1) pu
Dist: 12l, 4l, 5l, 15l, ½l. 4m 20.70s. a 14.70s (11 Ran).
SR: 16/9/5/-/-/-/ (Miss Rosemary Jeffreys), W G Reed

821 Scottish Racing Club Novices' Hurdle (4-y-o and up) £2,267 2m 110yds. . . . . . (3:45)

BRODESSA 7-11-0 P Niven, *in tch, hdwy to track ldr 4th, led aftr 3 out, ran on wl.*
. . . . (15 to 8 fav op 5 to 2 tchd 6 to 4) 1
640² RELUCTANT SUITOR 4-10-13 C Grant, *chsd ldrs, styd on wl frm 2 out, not rch wnr.* . . . . . (4 to 1 tchd 9 to 2) 2
640* AMERICAN HERO 5-11-6 B Storey, *led till hdd aftr 3 out, kpt on same pace.* . . . . (2 to 1 op 5 to 2) 3
731 LOCH SCAVAIG (Ire) 4-10-5 (3*) D J Moffatt, *beh till styd on frm 3 out, nrst finish.* . . . . . . (16 to 1 op 12 to 1) 4
656⁷ GROUSE-N-HEATHER 4-10-8 T Reed, *beh till styd on frm 3 out, nrst finish.* . . . . (66 to 1) 5
626⁶ BELIEVE IT 4-10-6 (7*) J Supple, *chsd ldrs, outpcd appr 3 out, kpt on frm nxt.* . . . . (50 to 1) 6
TAKE BY STORM (Ire) 4-10-13 M Dwyer, *prmnt, chsd 1st 2 frm 3 out till wknd aftr nxt.* . . . . . (7 to 1 op 5 to 1) 7
731⁵ RED TEMPEST (Ire) 5-10-7 (7*) F Perratt, *nvr nr ldrs.*
. . . . (50 to 1) 8
HICKSONS CHOICE (Ire) 5-11-0 K Jones, *in tch some hdwy appr 3 out, wknd nxt.* . . . . (66 to 1 op 33 to 1) 9
543⁹ MARTINI EXECUTIVE (bl) 5-11-6 D Byrne, *chsd ldrs till grad weakneed frm 3 out.*
. . . . (20 to 1 op 16 to 1 tchd 25 to 1) 10
AYIA NAPA 6-11-0 Mr J Bradburne, *in tch till wknd appr 3 out.* . . . . (66 to 1) 11
FLASH OF REALM (Fr) 7-11-0 A Orkney, *al beh...* (33 to 1) 12
577⁸ RUSHING BURN 7-10-9 K Johnson, *chsd ldrs till wknd appr 3 out.* . . . . (200 to 1) 13
CLEAR FOUNTAIN 6-10-11 (3*) A Dobbin, *chsd ldrs till wknd appr 3 out.* . . . . (50 to 1) 14
CHALKIEFORT 4-10-13 R Hodge, *blun 3rd, sn beh.*
. . . . (33 to 1 op 66 to 1) 15
LAZY RHYTHM (USA) 7-11-0 A Mulholland, *chsd ldrs, till wknd appr 3 out.* . . . . (66 to 1 op 50 to 1) 16
SUPER SANDY 6-10-4 (5*) P Williams, *chsd ldrs till blun 4th, sn beh, tld off.* . . . . (50 to 1) 17
KIRCHWYN LAD 5-11-0 A Merrigan, *sn beh, tld off whn pld up bef last.* . . . . (50 to 1) pu
Dist: 3½l, 3l, 10l, hd, 1½l, ¾l, 7l, 4l, 1l, 1½l. 3m 51.40s. a 8.40s (18 Ran).
SR: 35/30/34/12/12/15/14/8/4/ (R W S Jevon), Mrs M Reveley

822 Greenmantle Ale Anthony Marshall Trophy Handicap Chase (0-125 5-y-o and up) £2,786 3m 1f. . . . . (4:20)

PADAVENTURE [121] 8-11-10 P Niven, *hld up and beh, effrt aftr 2 out, chlgd after last, styd on und pres to ld towards finish.* . . . . (5 to 1 tchd 11 to 2) 1
ZAM BEE [107] 7-10-10⁶ T Reed, *trkd ldrs, lft in ld 4 out, hdd and no extr towards finish...* (16 to 1 op 12 to 1) 2
655⁴ PINK GIN [104] 6-10-7 C Grant, *al prmnt, jnd ldrs 4 out, kpt on same pace frm 2 out.*
. . . . (11 to 1 op 10 to 1 tchd 12 to 1) 3
BLUFF KNOLL [125] 10-12-0 K Johnson, *in tch, mstk 12th, sn rdn alng and lost pl, rallied aftr 2 out, kpt on same pace frm last.* . . . . (12 to 1 op 8 to 1) 4
579* KUSHBALOO [122] 8-11-11 B Storey, *mstks, beh, hdwy 13th, hmpd 4 out, wknd appr last.* (Evens fav op 5 to 4) 5

INTERIM LIB [112] 10-11-1 Mr J Bradburne, *led till hdd 4th,
cl up till wknd betw last 2*.........(20 to 1 op 12 to 1) 6
655² EASTERN OASIS [104] 10-10-2 (5*) P Williams, *cl up, led 4th
till f four out*......................(4 to 1 op 5 to 1) f
LAURIE-O [106] 9-10-9 A Merrigan, *f 6th.*
......................................(33 to 1 op 25 to 1) f
720² KIRSTY'S BOY [114] 10-11-3 L O'Hara, *hld up, brght dwn
6th*...............................(10 to 1 op 8 to 1) bd
Dist: ½l, 3l, ½l, 6l, 12l. 6m 19.30s. a 17.30s (9 Ran).
SR: 35/20/14/34/25/3/   (Mrs J G Fulton), Mrs M Reveley

823 Salvesen Food Services Novices' Hurdle (4-y-o and up) £2,180 2¾m 110yds...(4:50)

627² FOUR DEEP (Ire) 5-10-11 (3*) D J Moffatt, *led second, made
rst, hld on wl towards finish.*
....(15 to 2 op 6 to 1 tchd 10 to 1) 1
BERVIE HOUSE (Ire) 5-11-0 P Niven, *sn tracking ldrs, chsd
wnr frm 3 out, ev ch last, kpt on, no imprsn.*
....(6 to 1 op 5 to 1 tchd 13 to 2) 2
728² SARANNPOUR (Ire) (bl) 4-10-7 (5*) Mrs P Nash, *al prmnt,
rdn aftr 3 out, kpt on same pace.*.....(6 to 1 op 5 to 1) 3
656⁴ PIRATE HOOK 5-10-11 (3*) A Dobbin, *al prmnt, rdn aftr 3
out, ev ch last, kpt on same pace.* (5 to 2 fav op 9 to 2) 4
734⁷ COQUI LANE 6-11-0 Mr J M Dun, *prmnt till outpaced
appr 2 out, kpt on frm last*...........(10 to 1 op 8 to 1) 5
JENDEE (Ire) 5-10-11 (3*) A Larnach, *beh, styd on frm 3
out, wnt right aftr last, nvr trble ldrs.*
....(10 to 1 op 8 to 1) 6
KING MELODY 7-11-0 N Doughty, *beh, styd on frm 3 out,
nvr trble ldrs*.......(25 to 1 op 16 to 1 tchd 33 to 1) 7
CELTIC FOUNTAIN (Ire) 5-10-9 (5*) P Waggott, *nvr dngrs.*
....(33 to 1 op 25 to 1) 8
BUCKLE IT UP 8-11-0 Mr D Mactaggart, *beh frm 7th.*
....(33 to 1 op 16 to 1) 9
CASTLE CROSS 6-11-0 K Johnson, *sn pushed alng, beh
frm 7th.*.............................(33 to 1) 10
622⁹ LAFANTA (Ire) 4-10-12 K Jones, *led to second, in tch till
wknd appr 3 out*....................(40 to 1 op 25 to 1) 11
DOUGAL'S BIRTHDAY 7-11-0 A Merrigan, *beh frm 7th, tld
off*................................(100 to 1 op 66 to 1) 12
731⁸ THE PATTERS MAGIC 6-11-0 C Grant, *tld off whn pld up
bef 7th*.............................(10 to 1 op 8 to 1 tchd 11 to 1) pu
BITOFANITTER 5-11-0 Mr S Love, *sn beh, tld off whn pld
up bef 2 out*........................(50 to 1) pu
577² GREEN TRIX (Ire) 5-11-0 B Storey, *in tch till lost pl and
lost place pld up aftr 8th.*
....(7 to 2 op 3 to 1 tchd 4 to 1) pu
717⁹ BRIAR'S DELIGHT 5-11-0 A Orkney, *beh frm 7th, tld off
whn pld up bef 2 out*................(14 to 1 op 10 to 1) pu
Dist: 1½l, 2½l, sht-hd, 3½l, 8l, 8l, 8l, 1½l, 3l, 15l. 5m 32.70s. a 21.70s (16 Ran).
                                        (The Braw Partnership), J H Johnson

824 Potterton-Myson Handicap Hurdle (0-115 4-y-o and up) £2,022 2m 110yds.....(5:25)

MASTER OF TROY [87] 5-9-13² (7*) Mr A Parker, *hld up and
beh, smooth hdwy appr 2 out, rdn to ld towards finish.*
....(33 to 1 op 20 to 1) 1
623³ NOTABLE EXCEPTION [90] 4-10-2 (5*) Mr M Buckley, *in tch,
hdwy to track ldrs 3 out, led aftr last, hdd and no extr
towards finish*.......(8 to 1 op 7 to 1 tchd 10 to 1) 2
719* ALL WELCOME [102] 6-11-5 P Niven, *cl up, led 5th, hdd
last, kpt on same pace*.............(7 to 4 fav op 6 to 4) 3
657² ASTURIAS [88] 10-10-2 (3*) A Larnach, *hld up, gd hdwy
aftr 3 out, led and pckd last, sn hdd, one pace.*
....(7 to 2 op 4 to 1) 4
657⁷ RAPID MOVER [84] (bl) 6-10-1¹ C Grant, *chsd ldrs, outpcd
appr 2 out, kpt on frm last*.........(20 to 1 op 14 to 1) 5
SEON [111] 7-11-11 (3*) N Bentley, *in tch, effrt appr 2 out,
no hdwy*............................(14 to 1 op 12 to 1) 6
CAPTAIN TANCRED (Ire) [86] 5-10-3¹ A Merrigan, *trkd ldrs,
ev ch 2 out, sn rdn and wknd*.......(33 to 1 op 20 to 1) 7
335⁴ JUST PULHAM [83] 8-9-7 (7*) J Supple, *led till hdd 5th,
weakened appr 2 out*.................(50 to 1 op 33 to 1) 8
INVERTIEL [90] 9-10-7 B Storey, *hld up, effrt appr 2 out,
sn btn*.............................(20 to 1 op 12 to 1) 9
ARAGON AYR [92] 5-10-6 (3*) A Dobbin, *chsd ldrs, wnt
second appr 3 out, wknd quickly approaching nxt.*
....(10 to 1 op 8 to 1) 10
335³ RINGLAND (USA) [94] 5-10-8 (3*) D J Moffatt, *f 3rd.*
....(16 to 1 op 8 to 1) f
Dist: ½l, 6l, nk, ½l, 3l, 6l, ½l, 8l, 10l. 3m 56.40s. a 13.40s (11 Ran).
                                        (Chilton Fawcett), C Parker

KEMPTON (good)
Saturday October 16th
Going Correction: PLUS 0.35 sec. per fur.

825 Ferry Boat Handicap Chase (0-145 5-y-o and up) £4,207 2m.................(2:15)

BILLY BATHGATE [127] 7-11-13 M A FitzGerald, *hld up,
steady hdwy frm 8th, led 2 out, sn clr.*
....(7 to 2 tchd 9 to 2) 1

GENERAL JAMES [106] 10-10-6 D Murphy, *al chasing ldrs,
kpt on same pace frm 3 out*........(16 to 1 op 14 to 1) 2
590² EMSEE-H [127] 8-11-8 (5*) B Murphy, *chsd ldr till led 9th,
hdd 2 out, sn outpcd...* (9 to 1 op 8 to 1 tchd 10 to 1) 3
752³ CAMPSEA-ASH [128] 9-11-7 (7*) P Murphy, *hit 3rd and
beh, lost tch frm 4 out*.............(20 to 1 op 12 to 1) 4
777³ SETTER COUNTRY [127] 9-11-13 W Irvine, *hdwy 9th, rdn 3
out, one pace and hld in 4th whn uns rdr last.*
....(11 to 2 op 5 to 1 tchd 6 to 1) ur
631* DRUMSTICK [126] 7-11-12 G Bradley, *beh till mstk and
uns rdr 4th (water)*................(7 to 2 op 9 to 4) ur
TILDARG [119] 9-11-5 J Osborne, *hld up, jmpd lft, hdd 9th,
rallied 4 out, wknd aftr 3 out, no ch whn pld up bef
last*...........(11 to 4 fav op 7 to 2 tchd 4 to 1 and 5 to 2) pu
Dist: 8l, 5l, 30l. 3m 57.00s. a 10.00s (7 Ran).
SR: 55/26/42/13/   (Michael Buckley), N J Henderson

826 Hippodrome D'Evry Novices' Chase (5-y-o and up) £3,557 2m..................(2:50)

LACKENDARA 6-11-0 J Osborne, *made all, hrd drvn and
hld on gmely r-in*.......(15 to 2 op 5 to 1 tchd 8 to 1) 1
THE GLOW (Ire) 5-10-13 P Holley, *in tch, chsd wnr 9th, str
chal frm 4 out, hrd drvn r-in, jst fld.*
....(9 to 2 op 4 to 1 tchd 6 to 1) 2
EASY BUCK 6-11-0 C Maude, *hld up, hit 3rd, blun 6th,
chlgd 4 out, rdn 3 out, sn wknd.*
....(12 to 1 fav op 9 to 4 tchd 15 to 8) 3
632³ STAUNCH RIVAL (USA) 6-11-0 D Bridgwater, *chsd ldrs till
lost tch frm 8th*......(12 to 1 op 10 to 1 tchd 14 to 1) 4
PRESENT TIMES 7-10-7 (7*) Mr T McCarthy, *hit 6th, sn lost
tch*..............(66 to 1 op 33 to 1 tchd 100 to 1) 5
667² MADRAJ (Ire) 5-10-13 W McFarland, *lost tch 5th, mstk 6th,
tld off*...........................(33 to 1 op 20 to 1) 6
SECRET TURN (USA) 7-11-0 L Harvey, *hit 1st, sn in tch, hit
4 out, wknd and no ch whn f 3 out.*
....(12 to 1 op 8 to 1 tchd 14 to 1) f
612* MINE'S AN ACE (NZ) 6-11-6 J Frost, *chsd wnr to 9th, ev ch
4 out, wknd appr 2 out, 3rd and wl hld whn f last.*
....(5 to 2 op 7 to 4) f
Dist: Hd, 20l, 15l, dist, 20l. 3m 58.10s. a 11.10s (8 Ran).
SR: 31/30/11/-/-/   (Opening Bid Partnership), Miss H C Knight

827 Captain Quist Hurdle (4-y-o and up) £6,961 2m.................................(3:20)

LAND AFAR 6-10-11 W Marston, *chsd ldr till led appr last,
ran on wl.*.........................(9 to 2 op 4 to 1) 1
ROYAL DERBI 8-11-7 D Murphy, *led till hdd appoaching
last, shaken up and kpt on same pace.*
....(2 to 1 fav op 9 to 4) 2
SATIN LOVER 5-11-2 G McCourt, *wnt 3rd aftr 4th, rdn 2
out, not quicken appr last.*........(3 to 1 op 9 to 4) 3
648* CULTURED 4-11-1 J Osborne, *hit second, beh, hdwy 3
out, nvr nrr.*.......................(5 to 2 op 7 to 4 tchd 3 to 1) 4
CABOCHON 6-10-11 J Frost, *in tch, drpd rear 4th, lost
touch frm nxt*........(12 to 1 op 8 to 1 tchd 14 to 1) 5
Dist: 2½l, 1l, ½l, 12l. 3m 47.90s. a 7.90s (5 Ran).
SR: 60/67/61/59/43/   (T J Ford), J Webber

828 Charisma Gold Cup Handicap Chase (5-y-o and up) £10,725 3m...............(3:55)

BLACK HUMOUR [147] 9-11-0 G Bradley, *trkd ldr till led
14th, gng easily whn lft wl clr appr last.*
....(21 to 20 fav op 11 to 8) 1
SIBTON ABBEY [161] 8-11-9 (5*) B Murphy, *rcd in 3rd frm
4th, nvr in contention, lft poor second appr last.*
....(16 to 1 op 10 to 1 tchd 20 to 1) 2
ROMANY KING [153] 9-11-6 Richard Guest, *rcd in 4th,
hmpd 5th, hit 9th, wnt 3rd briefly 13th, wkng whn blun
four out*..........(14 to 1 op 16 to 1 tchd 12 to 1) 3
630* ROCKTOR (NZ) [133] 8-10-0 B Powell, *chsd ldr in 3rd till
blun and uns rdr 4th*...............(7 to 2 op 5 to 2) ur
740* RAVEN FERN [134] 7-10-1¹ J Osborne, *led, sn clr, hdd
14th, outpcd but clear second whn pld up aftr 2 out,
lme*...............(3 to 1 op 5 to 2 tchd 7 to 2) pu
Dist: Dist, 25l. 6m 2.30s. a 13.30s (5 Ran).
SR: 37/-/   (R E A Bott (Wigmore St) Ltd), C P E Brooks

829 Park Handicap Hurdle (0-145 4-y-o and up) £3,652 2m 5f.........................(4:25)

CASTLE COURAGEOUS [134] 6-11-6 E Murphy, *rcd keenly
in tch till mstk and lost pl 6th, sn reco'red, led appr 2
out, cmftbly*.......(15 to 8 fav op 5 to 2 tchd 3 to 1) 1
HEBRIDEAN [142] 6-11-11 (3*) W Marston, *in tch, effrt
and not fluent 2 out, ran on strly but not rch wnr r-in.*
....(13 to 2 op 9 to 2 tchd 7 to 1) 2
750* MIDFIELDER [119] 7-10-5 G McCourt, *in tch till lost pos
aftr 6th, gd hdwy 3 out, rdn and one pace
r-in*...............................(5 to 2 op 5 to 2 tchd 3 to 1) 3
MR MATT (Ire) [115] 5-10-1 Peter Hobbs, *chsd ldrs till led
6th, hdd appr 2 out, sn one pace.*
....(7 to 1 tchd 8 to 1 and 13 to 2) 4

105

646³ STORM DRUM [114] (bl) 4-10-0 J Osborne, *hdwy to track ldrs 6th, shaken up and no headway frm 3 out.*
...................................(10 to 1 op 7 to 1) 5

629⁶ ROYAL SQUARE (Can) [123] 7-10-9 M Perrett, *led till mstk and hdd 6th, styd on one pace frm 2 out.*

POORS WOOD [115] 6-10-11 D Murphy, *hld up in rear, nvr rch ldrs.*..............(9 to 1 op 8 to 1 tchd 12 to 1) 6

SUNSET AND VINE [119] 6-10-5 H Davies, *hit 3rd, al beh.*
...................................(12 to 1 tchd 14 to 1) 7

INDIAN RUN (Ire) [127] 4-10-13 W McFarland, *pressed ldr to 6th, wknd 7th, tld off whn pld up bef last.*
...............(12 to 1 op 8 to 1 tchd 14 to 1) pu
Dist: 3l, 2¹⁄₂l, 3l, 2l, 3l, 2¹⁄₂l, 30l. 5m 4.90s. a 11.90s (9 Ran).
SR: 46/51/25/18/15/21/10/-/-/ (Lady Mary Mumford), Lady Herries

830 Riverdale Juvenile Novices' Hurdle (3-y-o) £2,616 2m.........................(4:55)

WINGS COVE 10-10 E Murphy, *trkd ldrs, gng wl whn lft in ld appr 2 out and not fluent, cmftbly.*
...................................(7 to 2 op 3 to 1 tchd 4 to 1) 1

604* SATIN DANCER 11-1 M Perrett, *led, hit 4th, sn hdd, rdn and styd on one pace frm 2 out.*
...................................(100 to 30 op 3 to 1 tchd 7 to 2) 2

668* SIR THOMAS BEECHAM 11-1 H Davies, *mid-div, rdn and hdwy frm 2 out, not pace to rch ldrs.*
...................................(4 to 1 op 9 to 2 tchd 11 to 2) 3

ONE MORE POUND 10-10 D Murphy, *in tch, rdn appr 2 out, styd on.*.................(50 to 1 op 25 to 1) 4

RICH LIFE (Ire) 10-10 Peter Hobbs, *beh, rdn 5th, styd on frm 3 out.*........(33 to 1 op 20 to 1 tchd 50 to 1) 5

QUICK SILVER BOY 10-10 D J Burchell, *chsd ldrs till rdn and wknd frm 3 out.*............(20 to 1 op 12 to 1) 6

604² WONDERFUL YEARS (USA) 10-10 Richard Guest, *in tch early, lost touch frm 5th.*..........(50 to 1 op 25 to 1) 7

652⁴ COEUR BATTANT (Fr) 10-10 G McCourt, *beh, rdn 5th, no response.*............(12 to 1 op 14 to 1 tchd 25 to 1) 8

AMAZING AIR (USA) 10-10 P Holley, *al beh.*
...................................(25 to 1 op 16 to 1 tchd 33 to 1) 9

STORM FALCON (USA) 10-10 S Earle, *strted slwly, al beh.*
...................................(33 to 1 op 25 to 1 tchd 50 to 1) 10

RAGAZZO (Ire) 10-10 M A FitzGerald, *mid-div, rdn 5th, sn wknd.*..................(50 to 1 op 33 to 1) 11

711 AMY COME HOME 9-12 (7*) D Matthews, *al beh.*
...................................(50 to 1 tchd 66 to 1) 12

604⁴ DARSING 10-10 B Powell, *mstk 1st, al beh.*
...................................(50 to 1 op 25 to 1) 13

453* TOMSK 11-1 D Bridgwater, *prmnt till led aftr 4th, gng wl whn broke leg and pld up appr 2 out, dead.*
...................................(3 to 1 fav tchd 11 to 4) pu
Dist: 7l, 6l, 2l, 3l, 2l, 20l, 6l, 10l, 3l, 2¹⁄₂l, 2¹⁄₂l. 3m a 12.40s (14 Ran).
SR: 14/12/6/-/-/-/ (Edwin N Cohen), Lady Herries

NAAS (IRE) (good to yielding)
Saturday October 16th

831 Coughlan Handicap Hurdle (4-y-o and up) £4,140 2m.........................(3:00)

537² AIYBAK (Ire) [-] 5-11-1 B Sheridan, ...(5 to 2 fav) 1
294 PRETTY NICE (Ire) [-] 5-10-4 P L Malone, ...(14 to 1) 2
673* BRAVEFOOT [-] 5-10-7 (3ex) K F O'Brien, ...(9 to 2) 3
637⁷ BELEEK CASTLE [-] 7-9-13 P McWilliams, ...(8 to 1) 4
DEEP INAGH [-] 7-11-2 D P Fagan, ...(8 to 1) 5
PLUMBOB (Ire) [-] 4-9-11 (5*) T P Rudd, ...(14 to 1) 6
STORM FRONT (Ire) [-] 5-11-4 F Woods, ...(10 to 1) 7
673⁵ HEAD OF CHAMBERS (Ire) [-] 5-10-13 J P Banahan,
...................................(10 to 1) 8
KILLINEY GRADUATE [-] 7-10-8 (7*) M J Molloy, ...(14 to 1) 9
467* NIMBLE WIND [-] (bl) 7-10-0 A J O'Brien, ...(9 to 2) 10
532⁷ THIRD QUARTER [-] 8-10-10 C O'Dwyer, ...(14 to 1) 11
DON LEONE [-] 8-10-9 G M O'Neill, ...(25 to 1) 12
506⁴ PALACE GEM [-] 6-9-9 (3*) T J Mitchell, ...(14 to 1) 13
Dist: 7l, ¾l, 1¹⁄₂l, 2l. 3m 51.50s. (13 Ran).
(Michael W J Smurfit), D K Weld

832 Tend-R-Leen Horse Feed I.N.H. Flat Race (4-y-o and up) £3,795 2m..........(5:00)

530* THE SUBBIE (Ire) 4-11-6 (7*) Mr D J Kavanagh, ...(7 to 2) 1
HEIST 4-11-6 (7*) Mr D A Harney, ...(7 to 1 jt-fav) 2
540* BADEN (Ire) 5-11-13 Mr T Mullins, ...(2 to 1 jt-fav) 3
171* KARABAKH (Ire) 4-11-8 (5*) Mrs J M Mullins, ...(10 to 1) 4
LINDEN'S LOTTO (Ire) 4-11-3 (3*) Mr A R Coonan, (14 to 1) 5
469* HOWABOUTTHATNOW 6-11-13 (5*) Mr J P Berry, (12 to 1) 6
CLOWATER LADY (Ire) 4-10-8 (7*) Mr P English, ...(12 to 1) 7
469³ DOONAGLERAGH (Ire) 4-10-8 (7*) Mr A Daly, ...(14 to 1) 8
158⁶ UGOLIN DE LA WERA (Fr) 7-11-11 (7*) Miss J Lewis,
...................................(16 to 1) 9
JIMMY GORDON (Ire) 4-11-7 (7*) Mr M Brennan, ...(20 to 1) 10
TREANAREE 4-11-6 Mr A P O'Brien, ...(20 to 1) 11
MASTER EYRE (Ire) 5-11-7 (7*) Mr M J Bowe, ...(20 to 1) 12
ABAVARD (Ire) 4-10-13 (7*) Mr M P Dunne, ...(20 to 1) 13
709 PRECEPTOR (Ire) 4-11-6 Mr P Fenton, ...(20 to 1) 14
LADY IMELDA (Ire) 4-10-8 (7*) Mr C N Healy, ...(14 to 1) 15

ELLENOR LAD (Ire) 4-11-3 (3*) Miss M Olivefalk, .. (50 to 1) 16
620 THE GUNNER 6-11-11 Mr J P Dempsey, ...(20 to 1) pu
Dist: ¹⁄₂l, 5l, 9l, 6l. 3m 50.10s. (17 Ran).
(T Miley), Francis Ennis

SOUTHWELL (soft)
Saturday October 16th
Going Correction: PLUS 1.25 sec. per fur.

833 M D Troop Groundwork Contractors Novices' Chase (6-y-o and up) £1,515 2¹⁄₂m 110yds.........................(3:30)

741 CRAFTY CHAPLAIN 7-10-9 (5*) Mr D McCain, *hld up, hdwy 7th, led nxt, lft clr 3 out, hit last.*
...................................(6 to 4 fav op 2 to 1 tchd 9 to 4) 1

698 SILENT CHANT (bl) 8-11-3 (*) Mr R Griffiths, *chsd ldr till lft in ld 7th, hdd nxt, hit 9th and tenth, sn lost pl, left second 3 out.*........(7 to 1 op 5 to 1 tchd 8 to 1) 2

660 VOLCANIC DANCER (USA) 7-11-0 R Garritty, *in tch, rdn 9th an wknd, lft 3rd 3 out.*
...................................(11 to 2 op 4 to 1 tchd 6 to 1) 3

730⁶ WALLISTRANO 6-10-7 (7*) Mr T Byrne, *hld up, mstk second, hdwy 8th, chsd wnr 5 out and 2 ls second whn f 3 out.*........................(8 to 1 op 6 to 1) f

445⁷ RICH AND RED 7-10-6 (3*) A Thornton, *prmnt, hdwy to dispute ld 9th till f 5 out.*...........(5 to 2 op 6 to 1) f

RIDAKA 6-10-9 (5*) T Eley, *not fluent, led and sn clr, f 7th.*
...................................(25 to 1 op 16 to 1 tchd 33 to 1) f
Dist: 15l, 4l. 5m 38.30s. a 35.30s (6 Ran).
(D McCain), D McCain

834 Frances Lilian Riley Memorial Handicap Chase (0-120 5-y-o and up) £1,718 2m ....(4:00)

THE GREEN STUFF [110] 8-11-3 (7*) Mr T Byrne, *in tch, chsd ldr frm 5th, steady hdwy to ld 2 out, rdn and ran on flt.*........(Evens fav op 11 to 10 on tchd 11 to 10) 1

BOSSBURG [90] (bl) 6-10-4 D Gallagher, *led and sn clr, rdn and hdd 2 out, kpt on und pres last.* (3 to 1 op 4 to 1) 2

444⁴ RUPPLES [92] 6-10-6 W Worthington, *beh frm hfwy, tld off 5 out.*......................(11 to 4 op 7 to 4) 3

ROMAN DART [93] 9-10-7 R Bellamy, *chsd ldr to 5th, sn lost pl, tld off 5 out, pld up bef last.* (8 to 1 op 5 to 1) pu
Dist: 3l, 25l. 4m 24.50s. a 25.50s (4 Ran).
SR: 41/18/-/-/ (John R Upson), John R Upson

835 Racecourse Medical Officers Handicap Chase (0-115 5-y-o and up) £1,841 3m 110yds.........................(4:30)

TRIBAL RULER [95] 8-11-7 D Gallagher, *in tch, hdwy to dispute ld 14th, led nxt, pushed clr aftr 3 out, ran on.*
...................................(7 to 2 op 3 to 1) 1

RED AMBER [91] 7-11-3 Mr J Durkan, *cl up, led 11th, jnd 14th, hdd nxt and sn rdn alng, jmpd slwly 4 out, soon one pace.*....................(6 to 5 fav op Evens) 2

NAUGHTY NICKY [89] 9-11-1 A Tory, *led till blun and hdd 11th, hit nxt and sn drvn alng, blundered and wknd 3 out.*........(5 to 1 tchd 11 to 2 and 6 to 1) 3

663 JIMMY O'DEA [98] (v) 6-11-5 (5*) T Eley, *prmnt till blun and uns rdr 4th.*..................(3 to 1 op 9 to 4) ur
Dist: 12l, 15l. 7m 1.90s. a 63.90s (4 Ran).
(John Singleton), D McCain

SOUTHWELL (A.W) (std)
Saturday October 16th
Going Correction: PLUS 0.75 sec. per fur.

836 EBF 'National Hunt' Novices' Hurdle Qualifier (4,5,6-y-o) £1,656 2¹⁄₄m....(2:25)

524* SWIFT CONVEYANCE 14-10-5 (7*) S McDougall, *trkd ldr, led appr 7th, clr 3 out.*
...................................(13 to 8 fav op 7 to 4 tchd 2 to 1) 1

658 WORDY'S WONDER 5-10-4 (5*) R Farrant, *in tch, hdwy to chase wnr 4 out, rdn and hit nxt, sn one pace.*
...................................(9 to 1 op 10 to 1 tchd 11 to 1) 2

699⁴ ALDINGTON CHAPPLE 5-11-0 T Wall, *led till appr 7th, wknd and blun 4 out, sn tld off.*...(3 to 1 op 20 to 1) 3

CZAR NICHOLAS 4-10-7 (5*) S Lyons, *hld up, f 6th.*
...................................(9 to 4 tchd 5 to 2) f

PRINCE OF PREY 5-10-11 (3*) A Thornton, *not jump wl, beh whn f 8th.*......(9 to 4 op 11 to 4 tchd 3 to 1) f

DEMOFONTE 5-11-0 A Coogan, *al rear, tld off whn pld up bef 7th.*..................(33 to 1 op 20 to 1) pu
Dist: 15l, 30l. 4m 31.50s. a 19.50s (6 Ran).
SR: 24/6/-/ (J B Mitchell), W T Kemp

837 Gaswarm Homes Conditional Jockeys' Selling Handicap Hurdle (3-y-o and up) £1,272 2m.........................(2:55)

678³ GREEN'S SEAGO (USA) [62] 5-10-11 A Thornton, *in tch, hdwy to chase ldr 5 out, rdn 3 out, staying on und pres whn lft in ld last*..................(9 to 2 op 7 to 2) 1
622⁶ WINGED WHISPER (USA) [63] 4-10-12 T Eley, *prmnt, hdwy and hit 5th, rdn nxt, one pace frm 4 out, lft poor second last*...............(100 to 30 op 6 to 4 tchd 7 to 2) 2
730⁹ RAAWI [70] 5-11-2 (3*) W Fry, *chsd ldr, led 5th to nxt, sn rdn and wknd 4 out, tld off*......(10 to 1 tchd 12 to 1) 3
659⁵ NEARCTIC BAY (USA) [74] 7-11-9 R Farrant, *led to 5th, sn wknd, tld off frm 4 out*..............(9 to 2 op 4 to 1) 4
425 HIGH STREET BLUES [55] (bl) 6-10-7 (3*) J Neaves, *beh, reminders 3rd, tld off frm 6th*......(33 to 1 op 20 to 1) 5
685² MABTHUL (USA) [75] 5-11-5 (5*) N Juckes, *prmnt, led 6th, clr appr 3 out, rdn and hit nxt, 4 ls clear whn f last*.
.........................(2 to 1 fav op 3 to 1 tchd 7 to 2) f
658 SEPTEMBER DAWN [53] 8-9-13 (3*) D Meade, *mstks in rear, tld off 6th, pld up bef 3 out*.
.....................(8 to 1 op 10 to 1 tchd 7 to 1) pu
Dist: 25l, 30l, 6l, 20l. 4m 8.00s. a 22.00s (7 Ran).

(R Atkinson), J L Harris

838 Acenor UK Ltd Handicap Hurdle (0-115 4-y-o and up) £1,363 2½m............. (5:00)

680* HAVE A NIGHTCAP [95] 4-11-0 D Gallagher, *in tch, hdwy to chase ldr 6th, lft in ld 5 out, rdn clr appr 2 out.*
......................................(5 to 2 op 2 to 1) 1
ALREEF [105] 7-11-10 A Tory, *al prmnt, chsd wnr 4 out, rdn and hit nxt, sn one pace*........(7 to 2 op 9 to 4) 2
679⁴ ELDER PRINCE [89] 7-10-8⁸ R Garritty, *hld up, hdwy 5th, rdn 7th, sn lost tch*................(33 to 1 op 14 to 1) 3
ROPE [100] 7-11-0 (5*) T Eley, *prmnt, rdn 5 out, wknd aftr nxt, fnshd lme*..................(5 to 1 op 4 to 1) 4
679* ELLTEE-ESS [100] (bl) 8-11-2 (3*) A Thornton, *led, pushed alng and ran out through wing 5 out.*
.........................(13 to 8 fav op 7 to 4 tchd 2 to 1) ro
678² VALATCH [81] 5-10-0 B Dalton, *prmnt, hit 3rd, lost pl 5th, tld off 7th, pld up bef last.*
......................(14 to 1 op 10 to 1 tchd 16 to 1) pu
Dist: 8l, 30l, 15l. 5m 3.30s. a 22.30s (6 Ran).
SR: 13/15/-/

(R A M Racecourses Ltd), J L Harris

STRATFORD (good)
Saturday October 16th
Going Correction: PLUS 0.50 sec. per fur. (races 1,3,-6,7), PLUS 0.70 (2,4,5)

839 Ratley Conditional Jockeys' Claiming Hurdle (4,5,6-y-o) £1,842 2m 110yds.... (2:20)

486³ MATHAL (USA) 4-11-5 D Matthews, *trkd ldr, led 5th, clr appr last, rdn out*................(16 to 1 op 20 to 1) 1
662³ JAMESTOWN BOY 5-11-0 R Davis, *hld up, hdwy 5th, rdn appr 2 out, styd on to go second r-in.* (7 to 1 op 6 to 1) 2
658¹⁰ SMART DEBUTANTE (Ire) 4-10-4 D Meredith, *al prmnt, chsd wnr 3 out till weakend r-in*.....(6 to 1 op 5 to 1) 3
693³ VIAGGIO (v) 5-10-10 M Hourigan, *hld up early, hdwy appr 4th, wknd 3 out*......(7 to 2 fav op 9 to 2 tchd 5 to 1) 4
KAGRAM QUEEN 5-10-9 S Mason, *hld up in tch, no hdwy frm 3 out*.....................(4 to 1 op 7 to 2) 5
693⁴ SHAFAYIF 4-10-4 D Leahy, *nvr got into race.*
...............................(14 to 1 tchd 16 to 1) 6
632⁴ J R JONES 6-11-0 S Wynne, *chsd ldrs till wknd 5th.*
....(20 to 1) 7
URSHI-JADE 5-10-5 P McLoughlin, *chsd ldrs till wknd 5th*.......................(33 to 1 op 25 to 1) 8
666⁴ RAFIKI 6-10-10 C Burnett-Wells, *led to 5th, wknd quickly, tld off*............(6 to 1 op 5 to 1 tchd 7 to 1) 9
ALOSAILI 6-11-0 M Stevens, *al towards rear, tld off.*
..................................(16 to 1 op 14 to 1) 10
666⁸ FAILAND 6-10-9 V Slattery, *beh whn hrd rdn 5th, sn tld off*.......................(50 to 1 op 25 to 1) 11
567 MASRUR (USA) 4-10-9 J McCarthy, *al beh, tld off frm 4th.*
.............................(66 to 1 op 50 to 1) 12
456 STRAWBERRY FOOL 4-10-0 (4*) Pat Thompson, *in tch to 4th, wkng whn blun and uns rdr 3 out.*
....................................(66 to 1 op 50 to 1) ur
PLEASE PLEASE ME (Ire) 5-10-5 D O'Sullivan, *prmnt till wknd aftr 4th, tld off whn pld up bef last.*
.........................(14 to 1 op 12 to 1) pu
ARAGONA 4-10-6 R Greene, *al beh, tld off whn pld up bef last*..................(33 to 1 op 20 to 1) pu
Dist: 3½l, 2½l, 25l, ¾l, ½l, 23l, 12l, 8l, nk. 4m 4.00s. a 15.00s (15 Ran).
SR: 24/15/2/-/-/-/

(B Babbage), N M Babbage

840 Arlescote Intermediate Handicap Chase (0-125 5-y-o and up) £2,635 2m 1f 110yds
.... (2:55)

631⁶ THATS THE LIFE [120] 8-11-10 A Maguire, *sn trkd ldr, led appr 2 out, jmpd lft and mstk last, hrd rdn, all out.*
.................................(9 to 1 op 6 to 1) 1
777⁴ L'UOMO PIU [96] 9-10-0 N Williamson, *led to 3rd, sn steadied in beh ldrs, cld 3 out, chlgd last, hrd rdn, jst fld.*
.......................(14 to 1 op 12 to 1 tchd 16 to 1) 2

665² LUCKY AGAIN [98] 6-10-2 J Railton, *led 1st, not fluent, hdd appr 2 out, one pace.*
.................(3 to 1 op 5 to 2 tchd 100 to 30) 3
VAIN PRINCE [117] (bl) 6-11-7 L Wyer, *jmpd slwly in rear, last whn f 4 out*..................(11 to 4 op 2 to 1) f
AROUND THE HORN [109] 6-10-13 S McNeill, *hld up, 4th whn f fourth*.......(5 to 4 fav op 6 to 4 tchd 15 to 8) f
Dist: Hd, 12l. 4m 22.50s. a 18.50s (5 Ran).
SR: 33/9/8/-/-/

(A E Dean), T R George

841 John H. Kenny Memorial Cup Handicap Hurdle (0-130 4-y-o and up) £2,372 2m 110yds........................... (3:25)

739* SAYMORE [98] 7-10-1 (3*) S Wynne, *hld up, hdwy to track ldr frm 4th, led sn aftr 2 out, wnt clr, tired r-in.*
.......................(7 to 2 op 5 to 2 tchd 4 to 1) 1
ALBEMINE (USA) [115] 4-11-7 T Kent, *set steady pace, quickened frm 4th, jmpd lft 2 out, sn hdd, rdn and kpt on one pace*.......(13 to 8 fav op 2 to 1 tchd 6 to 4) 2
WHEELER'S WONDER (Ire) [108] 4-10-7 (7*) Mr J L Llewellyn, *hld up, wl beh 3 out, hdwy appr last to go 3rd r-in.*
..............................(10 to 1 op 8 to 1) 3
PRINCE TINO [100] 5-10-6 R Supple, *hld up, hdwy appr 3 out, nvr nr, rallied and rdn frm 2 out, no extr r-in.*
.......................(10 to 1 op 12 to 1 tchd 8 to 1) 4
643³ STAY AWAKE [118] 7-11-11 L Wyer, *trkd ldr till wknd appr 3 out, tld off*........(6 to 1 op 5 to 1 tchd 13 to 2) 5
SAFFAAH (USA) [110] 6-11-2 M Richards, *trkd ldr till aftr 3 out, wknd quickly appr last, eased, tld off.*
......................(100 to 30 op 3 to 1 tchd 7 to 2) 6
Dist: 4l, 1¼l, 3l, 20l, 25l. 4m 5.10s. a 16.10s (6 Ran).
SR: -/10/1/

(D Manning), R Hollinshead

842 Upton Handicap Chase (0-135 5-y-o and up) £2,843 2m 5f 110yds........... (4:00)

677 DRAGONS DEN [107] 7-10-3 G Upton, *al prmnt, led 6th to 9th, led 5 out, clr 2, jmpd badly right last, hdd r-in, rallied to ld nr finish.*.............(7 to 1 op 5 to 1) 1
GAELIC FROLIC [104] 10-10-0 A Maguire, *hld up in rear, hdwy 5 out, short of room appr 2 out, hrd rdn to ld r-in, faltered and hdd cl hme.*...............(7 to 2 jt-fav op 6 to 1 tchd 3 to 1) 2
CARBISDALE [130] 7-11-12 L Wyer, *trkd ldrs, rdn and one pace frm 2 out*................(13 to 2 op 7 to 1) 3
749 VIRIDIAN [108] (bl) 8-10-4 N Williamson, *led to 6th, led 9th, hit nxt, hdd 5 out, wknd appr 2 out.*
.........................(25 to 1 op 16 to 1) 4
615⁴ KENTISH PIPER [120] 8-11-2 R Supple, *hld up in rear, hdwy 5 out, wknd aftr 3 out.*............(7 to 2 jt-fav op 3 to 1 tchd 4 to 1) 5
SHANNON GLEN [106] 7-10-2 I Lawrence, *mstks, in tch till wknd 5 out, tld off*.......(7 to 1 op 6 to 1) 6
LUMBERJACK (USA) [132] (bl) 9-12-0 J Railton, *hld up, hdwy tenth, cl 3rd whn f 4 out.*.......(12 to 1 op 8 to 1) f
MISS FERN [104] 8-9-11 (3*) D Meredith, *prmnt, mstk 5th, wknd tenth, beh whn bright dwn 4 out.*
.........................(20 to 1 op 14 to 1) bd
CHIP AND RUN [113] 7-10-9 S Burrough, *in tch till blun 7th, sn beh, tld off 5 out, pld up bef 2 out.*
.......................(12 to 1 op 10 to 1) pu
Dist: Nk, 8l, 2l, 8l, dist. 5m 22.20s. a 19.20s (9 Ran).
SR: 34/30/48/24/28/-/

(Christopher Heath), S E Sherwood

843 Clairefontaine Trophy Novices' Chase (5-y-o and up) £2,672 3m............. (4:35)

389² OLD BRIG (bl) 7-10-13 J Lower, *made virtually all, hdd briefly 7th and 4 out, clr whn jmpd slwly last, hrd rdn, jst hld on*.......(5 to 1 op 4 to 1 tchd 11 to 2) 1
683³ FROZEN DROP 6-10-13 A Maguire, *hld up in rear, hdwy frm 13th, wnt second 2 out, hrd rdn and fnshd strly, jst fld*....................(9 to 1 op 8 to 1 tchd 10 to 1) 2
WELL BRIEFED 6-10-13 S McNeill, *al prmnt, led briefly 4 out, wkng whn mstk 2 out, eased, tld off.*
.......................(25 to 1 op 16 to 1 tchd 33 to 1) 3
RINANNA BAY 6-10-8 G Upton, *trkd wnr, led briefly 7th, wknd quickly 3 out, tld off*......(14 to 1 op 20 to 1) 4
607 BARLEY MOW 7-10-13 N Mann, *mstks 3rd and 13th, al beh, tld off*.....................(50 to 1 op 40 to 1) 5
CAPALL AOSTA 10-10-6 (7*) R Darke, *mstks, al beh, tld off*.......................(33 to 1 op 20 to 1) 6
710 GABRIELLA MIA 8-10-8 T Jarvis, *in tch whn f tenth.*
.............................(7 to 1 op 6 to 1) f
660* FARDROSS 7-11-5 N Williamson, *hld up in tch, travelling wl and 4th whn f 14th.*
......................(6 to 4 on op 5 to 4 on tchd 6 to 5 on) f
660 KATIE PARSON 6-10-8 A Webb, *prmnt early, mstks 3rd and 4th, tld off 8th, pld up aftr 13th.*
..........................(66 to 1 op 33 to 1) pu
COAL NOT DOLE (Ire) 5-10-10 R Supple, *mstks in rear, tld off whn pld up bef 2 out*.......(50 to 1 op 50 to 1) pu
Dist: Sht-hd, dist, 6l, dist, 15l. 6m 14.00s. a 27.00s (10 Ran).

(David Jenks), M C Pipe

844 Edgehill 'National Hunt' Novices' Hurdle (4-y-o and up) £1,898 2m 110yds.... (5:05)

BELL STAFFBOY (Ire) 4-10-11 N Williamson, *hld up,
smooth hdwy frm 5th, led 2 out, wnt clr, easily.*
................................(11 to 8 fav op 5 to 2 tchd 11 to 10) 1
EMPEROR BUCK (Ire) 5-10-12 A Maguire, *hld up, mstks
3rd and 4th, rdn 3 out, rallied appr last, styd on to go
second r-in............*(2 to 1 op 6 to 4 tchd 11 to 4) 2
616⁸ DAUPHIN BLEU (Fr) 7-10-12 Dr P Pritchard, *chsd ldr, led 3
out, hdd nxt, tired and lost second r-in......* (50 to 1) 3
715⁶ FATHER FORTUNE (bl) 5-10-7 (5*) J McCarthy, *led, mstk
3rd, sn clr, rdn and hdd 3 out, btn third whn mistake
last.................*(9 to 1 op 7 to 1) 4
GAVASKAR (Ire) 4-10-11 L Wyer, *nvr on terms.*
................................(12 to 1 op 7 to 1) 5
MAC'S LEAP 5-10-12 L Harvey, *chsd ldrs, hdwy 3rd, cl up
whn hit 5th, sn wknd............* (33 to 1 op 20 to 1) 6
DISTINCTIVE (Ire) 4-10-4 (7*) P Ward, *in rear whn f 3rd.*
................................(12 to 1 op 10 to 1) f
CAMPDEN AGAIN 6-10-4 (3*) D Meredith, *in rear whn
brght dwn 3rd..............* (50 to 1 op 33 to 1) bd
RED NEST 5-10-0 (7*) Mr S Joynes, *chsd ldrs to 3rd, sn
beh, pld up bef 2 out...............*(33 to 1) pu
EASY AMANDA 5-10-7 S McNeill, *mstk second, sn beh, tld
off whn pld up appr 2 out.................*(33 to 1) pu
IN DEEP FRIENDSHIP (Ire) 5-10-12 M Richards, *beh, mstk
4th, tld off whn pld up bef 2 out.*
...............................(8 to 1 op 5 to 1 tchd 9 to 1) pu
Dist: 15l, 2½l, 2½l, 2½l, 12l. 4m 8.40s. a 19.40s (11 Ran).
(K W Bell & Son Ltd), C D Broad

845 Autumn Intermediate Handicap Hurdle (0-120 4-y-o and up) £2,024 2¾m 110yds ....(5:35)

613 STRONG MEDICINE [111] 6-11-13 N Williamson, *made all,
rdn frm 2 out, drvn out.* (11 to 4 op 2 to 1 tchd 9 to 4) 1
ASK THE GOVERNOR [107] 7-11-9 A Maguire, *hld up in
rear, gd hdwy to press wnr 3 out, outpcd appr last,
rallied to go second ag'n r-in.*
................................(7 to 1 op 6 to 1) 2
610⁶ PRIZE MATCH [90] 4-10-6 R Supple, *hld up, gd hdwy to go
second appr 2 out, ev ch approaching last, rdn and one
pace n-in.................*(7 to 1 op 6 to 1) 3
796⁸ ELEGANT KING (Ire) [106] 4-11-8 T Jarvis, *sn prmnt, rdn
appr 7th, hit nxt, wknd aftr mstk 2 out.*
................................(8 to 1 op 7 to 1) 4
BADASTAN (Ire) [96] 4-10-12 L Wyer, *chsd wnr to 3 out,
wknd..................*(9 to 2 op 7 to 1) 5
BLASKET HERO [90] (bl) 5-10-6 S McNeill, *hld up, hdwy
5th, rdn and wknd appr 2 out.*
................................(8 to 1 op 6 to 1) 6
LASTOFTHEVIKINGS [84] 8-10-0⁵ (5*) R Davis, *al beh, tld
off..............*(66 to 1 op 50 to 1) 7
613⁷ BRORA ROSE (Ire) [84] 5-10-0 I Shoemark, *sn beh, tld off
frm 7th.............*(20 to 1 op 25 to 1 tchd 33 to 1) 8
MAYFIELD PARK [84] 8-10-0 N Mann, *chsd ldrs till wknd
7th, tld off whn pld up bef 2 out..........* (33 to 1) pu
BENTLEY MANOR [84] 4-10-0 W Humphreys, *prmnt till
mstk 7th, wknd quickly, pld up bef 3 out.*
................................(14 to 1 op 10 to 1) pu
Dist: ½l, 2l, 15l, 1½l, 8l, 25l, 25l. 5m 41.90s. a 29.90s (10 Ran).
(Dr D B A Silk), K C Bailey

FAKENHAM (good)
Monday October 18th
Going Correction: PLUS 0.25 sec. per fur.

846 Walsingham Selling Handicap Hurdle (4-y-o and up) £2,284 2m 110yds......(2:10)

RUTH'S GAMBLE [71] 5-10-0 J R Kavanagh, *chsd ldrs, led 2
out, hrd rdn and hld on wl.*
................................(14 to 1 op 10 to 1 tchd 20 to 1) 1
287⁸ SPANISH WHISPER [81] 6-10-10 N Williamson, *chsd ldrs,
ev ch last, sn rdn, no extr cl hme.*
................................(8 to 1 op 7 to 1 tchd 9 to 1) 2
748⁴ RUTHS PRIDE [74] 8-9-10 (7*) Mr G Lewis, *hdwy appr 3
out, ev ch 2 out, unbl to quicken..........* (6 to 1) 3
553 JOLI'S GREAT [86] 5-11-1 J Ryan, *al prmnt, rdn and ran
on one pace frm 3 out.*(11 to 2 op 4 to 1) 4
WE'RE IN THE MONEY [71] (bl) 9-10-0 B Dalton, *al abt mid-
div...............*(20 to 1 op 14 to 1) 5
587⁷ ELITE DESIGN [79] 6-10-8 M Brennan, *beh till some hdwy
frm 3 out, not trble ldrs.*
................................(12 to 1 op 10 to 1 tchd 14 to 1) 6
685* AUVILLAR (USA) [92] (v) 5-11-7 D J Burchell, *led 3rd, hdd
and wknd appr 2 out..........*(5 to 1 op 4 to 1) 7
282² STYLISH GENT [73] 6-10-2² M A FitzGerald, *led to 3rd, sn
lost pl, no ch frm 6th.* (6 to 1 op 10 to 1 tchd 12 to 1) 8
549³ WEEKDAY CROSS (Ire) [89] 5-11-4 A Maguire, *al rear div.*
................................(4 to 1 op 5 to 1 tchd 9 to 1) 9
693⁹ BE THE BEST [99] 5-11-9 (5*) R Davis, *al beh, tld off.*
................................(25 to 1 op 14 to 1) 10

ELEGANT FRIEND [98] 5-11-6 (7*) P Smith Eccles, *chsd ldrs
till pld up bef 4th, sddld slpd.......* (11 to 2 op 4 to 1) pu
Dist: Sht-hd, 1½l, 2l, 2l, 4l, 1½l, 4l, 4l, 30l. 4m 4.60s. a 14.60s (11 Ran).
(Mrs A Emanuel), Mrs L C Jewell

847 Pudding Norton Conditional Jockeys' Handicap Chase (0-115 6-y-o and up) £2,528 3m.........................(2:40)

703² SANDAIG [89] 7-11-0 A Thornton, *hld up, hmpd 13th,
hdwy frm 15th, styd on und pres to ld cl hme.* (2 to 1 jt-
fav op 7 to 4 tchd 9 to 4) 1
DUO DROM [99] 8-11-10 W Marston, *led second, jmpd
slwly 3rd, hdd 4th, led ag'n 8th, made rst till headed
and no extr cl hme.........*(5 to 2 tchd 11 to 4) 2
751⁴ NOTARY-NOWELL [95] (bl) 7-11-3 (3*) B Murphy, *chsd ldrs,
hmpd 13th, wknd 15th.* (8 to 1 op 5 to 1 tchd 10 to 1) 3
SMOOTH MASTER [76] 8-10-1 D Leahy, *led to second, led 4th
to 8th, bad mstk 13th, sn no ch.*
................................(6 to 1 op 10 to 1 tchd 5 to 1) 4
READY OR NOT [96] 7-11-2 (5*) D Fortt, *4th whn f 12th.*
................................(2 to 1 jt-fav tchd 11 to 4) f
Dist: 1½l, 30l, 15l. 6m 16.60s. a 24.60s (5 Ran).
(Miss Sarah Wills), K C Bailey

848 Wimpey Homes Novices' Chase (5-y-o and up) £2,367 2m 110yds.............(3:10)

PEACEMAN 7-11-2 D Murphy, *hit 1st, chsd ldr till led 8th,
made rst, ran on wl.*
................................(11 to 10 on op 5 to 4 tchd 6 to 4) 1
438² ILEWIN 6-11-2 M Ahern, *chsd ldrs, lft in second pl at 9th,
unbl to quicken appr last.*
..............(3 to 1 op 4 to 1 tchd 9 to 2 and 5 to 1) 2
HIGHLAND POACHER 6-11-2 G McCourt, *prmnt to 8th, sn
no ch....................*(10 to 1) 3
CHAPEL HILL (Ire) 5-10-8 S McNeill, *mstks, nvr trbld ldrs.*
................................(7 to 1 op 4 to 1) 4
DALLISTON (NZ) 7-11-2 A Carroll, *mstks, beh most of way.*
................................(8 to 1 op 5 to 1) 5
569⁴ TEL E THON (v) 6-10-11 (5*) D Leahy, *led to 8th, second
whn f nxt..............*(8 to 1 tchd 10 to 1) f
Dist: 6l, 10l, 4l, 6l. 4m 7.50s. a 10.50s (6 Ran).
SR: 24/18/8/
(Sir Peter Gibbings), Mrs D Haine

849 Michael Scotney Turf Accountant Handicap Hurdle (0-125 4-y-o and up) £2,654 2m 110yds.........................(3:40)

591 HALLO MAM (Ire) [92] 4-10-0 M Brennan, *hdwy frm 5th, led
2 out, ran on wl......*(16 to 1 op 8 to 1 tchd 20 to 1) 1
698⁶ CHILD OF THE MIST [116] 7-11-3 (7*) Mr M Gingell, *hld up,
hdwy frm 5th, chsd wnr from 2 out, unbl to quicken.*
................................(6 to 1 op 9 to 2) 2
597⁹ NORTHERN TRIAL (USA) [95] 5-10-3 R Supple, *hld up, ran
on frm 3 out, not trble ldrs.........*(12 to 1 op 8 to 1) 3
698² TAYLORS PRINCE [92] 6-10-0 V Smith, *hld up, hdwy frm 3
out, ran on one pace.*
................................(9 to 4 fav op 5 to 2 tchd 11 to 4) 4
591⁶ SALMAN (USA) [102] 7-10-5 (5*) R Davis, *led and sn clr,
hdd 2 out, wknd quickly.*
................................(11 to 2 op 6 to 1 tchd 5 to 1) 5
836² WORDY'S WONDER [92] 5-9-9 (5*) R Farrant, *chsd ldrs to
hfwy, gd lost pl.............*(20 to 1 tchd 25 to 1) 6
113 SANTA PONSA BAY [100] 6-10-8 A Maguire, *al abt middle
div..................*(8 to 1 op 7 to 1 tchd 10 to 1) 7
750⁷ KEV'S LASS (Ire) [92] 5-9-7 (7*) P Murphy, *chsd ldr to 5th,
wknd quickly............*(6 to 1 op 8 to 1 tchd 12 to 1) 8
594⁴ NEW ARRANGEMENT [108] 7-11-2 S Smith Eccles, *prmnt
to hfwy, sn lost pl, fnshd lme........*(6 to 1 op 9 to 2) 9
662 MAJOR'S LAW (Ire) [88] 4-10-6 R Campbell, *sn beh, tld off
whn pld up bef 6th....*(11 to 1 op 6 to 1 tchd 10 to 1) pu
Dist: 4l, 7l, 3½l, 4l, 3l, 2½l, 8l, 2½l. 3m 58.80s. a 8.80s (10 Ran).
SR: 25/45/17/10/16/3/7/-/4/
(O Brennan), O Brennan

850 West Norfolk Fuels Handicap Chase (0-120 5-y-o and up) £2,996 2m 5f 110yds...(4:10)

GOLD HAVEN [105] 9-10-13 S McNeill, *chsd ldrs, led 14th,
made rst, ran on wl flt.*
..............(15 to 8 fav op 2 to 1 tchd 7 to 4 and 3 to 1) 1
595⁵ LOVE ANEW (USA) [103] 8-10-11 N Williamson, *mstks, hld
up, hdwy frm 12th, ev ch from 2 out, no extr flt.*
................................(9 to 2 op 3 to 1) 2
663⁶ SIRRAH JAY [114] 13-11-8 A Maguire, *led till hdd aftr
13th, unbl to quicken frm 2 out.*
................................(9 to 4 op 2 to 1 tchd 5 to 2) 3
SPREE CROSS [120] 7-11-2 D Gallagher, *pld hrd, trkd ldr,
led aftr 13th, mstk and hdd nxt, wknd appr 2 out.*
................................(5 to 1 op 9 to 2) 4
679² HIRAM B BIRDBATH [101] (bl) 7-10-9 J Osborne, *sn beh, tld
off whn pld up aftr 12th.........*(4 to 1 tchd 9 to 2) pu
Dist: 3l, 6l, 20l. 5m 28.20s. a 16.20s (5 Ran).
(Pell-Mell Partners), Andrew Turnell

851 Little Snoring Juvenile Novices' Hurdle (3-y-o) £2,284 2m 110yds.............(4:40)

ABJAR 10-2 (5*) A Bates, *al prmnt, led appr 2 out, sn drw clr, cmftbly*.......................... (12 to 1 op 7 to 1) 1
LA VILLA ROSE (Fr) 10-2 A Maguire, *hdwy frm 6th, no ch wth wnr*........................... (14 to 1 tchd 16 to 1) 2
O SO NEET 10-10 D Murphy, *hld up, ran on frm 3 out, not rch ldrs*............................. (9 to 1 op 8 to 1) 3
604³ CONVOY (Ire) 10-10 R Dunwoody, *wth lrs till wknd 2 out*.
....(5 to 1 op 6 to 1) 4
TEEN JAY (bl) 10-10 J Osborne, *chsd ldrs till led 6th, hdd and wknd appr 2 out*............ (5 to 2 tchd 3 to 1) 5
611³ CONTRACT ELITE (Ire) 11-3 D Wilkinson, *led to 6th, no hdwy frm 2 out*.............. (2 to 1 fav op 5 to 2) 6
BOLD ACRE 10-10 D J Burchell, *al prmnt, wknd 2 out*.
.......................(7 to 1 op 6 to 1 tchd 8 to 1) 7
588³ SIDE BAR 10-10 J Ryan, *al mid-div*.
..................................(11 to 1 op 12 to 1 tchd 10 to 1) 8
MULLED ALE (Ire) 10-5 R Campbell, *mid-div whn mstk 6th, nvr dngrs*............. (20 to 1 op 33 to 1) 9
MAJOR TRIUMPH (Ire) 10-2 R J Beggan, *beh frm 6th*.
.................................(14 to 1 tchd 16 to 1) 10
516 WESTRAY (Fr) 10-10 A Carroll, *al beh, tld off*.
.... (40 to 1 op 25 to 1) 11
760 WATER DIVINER 10-5 (5*) R Farrant, *al rear div, tld off*.
.... (40 to 1 op 20 to 1) 12
BITRAN 10-7 A Smith, *in tch whn mstks, 3rd and 4th, sn drpd out, tld off*.................(25 to 1 op 20 to 1) 13
711³ MARAT (USA) (v) 10-7 S Smith Eccles, *prmt to 6th, beh whn pld up bef last*............(16 to 1 op 10 to 1) pu
Dist: 12l, ¾l, 5l, 2l, 5l, 10l, 4l, 4l, 5l, 12l. 4m 0.50s. a 10.50s (14 Ran).
SR: 15/-/5/-/-/-/ (P A Kelleway), P A Kelleway

LIMERICK (IRE) (good to yielding)
Monday October 18th

852 Lancer Boss (Ireland) Ltd Hurdle (5-y-o and up) £3,450 2½m............... (2:30)

672³ MINELLA LAD 7-11-8 T Horgan, ... (10 to 9 on) 1
557² MERRY PEOPLE (Ire) 5-11-11 C F Swan, ...(4 to 1) 2D
535³ COOL CHARACTER (Ire) 5-11-4 J F Titley, ...(9 to 4) 2
690² GRANDONHILL 6-11-1 (7*) J P Broderick, ...(7 to 1) 3
Dist: 1l, sht-hd, hd. 5m 27.90s. (4 Ran).
(John J Nallen), A P O'Brien

853 B.R.C. McMahon Reinforcements Maiden Hurdle (5-y-o and up) £3,450 2½m...(3:00)

801⁵ MUILEAR OIRGE 6-11-6 J F Titley, ... (6 to 1) 1
GIMME FIVE 6-12-0 C F Swan, ... (2 to 1 jt-fav) 2
585³ PANDA (Ire) 5-11-4 (5*) T P Treacy, ...(5 to 1) 3
LEGAL ADVISER 6-11-7 (7*) C Eyre, ... (14 to 1) 4
675 THE SILVER ROLLS 5-11-6 T Horgan, ... (20 to 1) 5
TROPICAL TIMES 7-11-9 Mr P J Healy, ... (12 to 1) 6
572² SUPER TACTICS 5-11-6 G Bradley, ... (2 to 1 jt-fav) 7
571⁷ COOLREE (Ire) 5-12-0 K F O'Brien, ... (12 to 1) 8
571⁶ DONERAILE PARK 6-12-0 H Rogers, ... (12 to 1) 9
MRS HEGARTY 7-11-1 A Powell, ... (12 to 1) 10
GALA VOTE 7-10-10 (5*) D P Geoghegan, ...(33 to 1) 11
801 TULLOVIN CASTLE (Ire) 5-10-8 (7*) K M O'Callaghan,
....(50 to 1) 12
675 DESMOND GOLD (Ire) 5-11-6 J Jones, ...(66 to 1) 13
798 ASTON BLAKE 6-11-1 (5*) C P Dunne, ...(66 to 1) 14
672⁸ SHY GREEN (Ire) 5-11-1 G M O'Neill, ...(66 to 1) 15
638 SWEET DEMOND 8-10-13 (7*) J M Donnelly, ...(66 to 1) 16
690 WOODEN MINSTREL 7-10-8 (7*) Mr A O'Shea, ... (66 to 1) su
536 THIRD SCHEDULE (Ire) 5-11-6 F Woods, ...(20 to 1) pu
535 CARRIGANN HOTEL (Ire) 5-10-10 (5*) T J O'Sullivan,
....(33 to 1) pu
HOLLOW VISION (Ire) 5-10-13 (7*) J P Broderick, (25 to 1) pu
Dist: 1l, 3l, 6l, 12l. 5m 15.40s. (20 Ran).
(Greyhound Syndicate), P P Hogan

854 Pat Chesser Handicap Hurdle (4-y-o and up) £3,450 2m 1f................. (3:30)

689* KILIAN MY BOY [-] 10-11-7 (6ex) J F Titley, ...(9 to 1) 1
637⁵ SO PINK [-] 5-10-10 C F Swan, ...(5 to 2 fav) 2
404* THATCH AND GOLD (Ire) [-] 5-10-10 (5*) J R Barry, (7 to 1) 3
797 QUIET CITY [-] 6-9-13¹ (7*) Mr J T McNamara, ...(12 to 1) 4
673² DANCING COURSE (Ire) [-] 5-9-11 (7*) P A Roche, ..(9 to 2) 5
637* CASH CHASE (Ire) [-] 5-9-13 L P Cusack, ...(12 to 1) 6
797² SUNSHINES TAXI [-] 6-9-9 T Horgan, ... (8 to 1) 7
557 DOONEGA (Ire) [-] 5-10-9 (5*) C O'Brien, ... (10 to 1) 8
421⁵ CLASS ACT [-] 7-9-6 (3*) Miss M Olivefalk, ...(10 to 1) 9
689 NISHIKI (USA) [-] 4-9-10 P Carberry, ... (12 to 1) 10
230⁷ PREMIER LEAP (Ire) [-] 4-10-2 C O'Dwyer, ...(10 to 1) 11
531* VON CARTY (Ire) [-] 4-9-8 F Woods, ... (8 to 1) 12
637 ENERGANCE (Ire) [-] 5-10-12 F J Flood, ...(16 to 1) 13
Dist: 9l, 2½l, ¾l, 2l. 4m 18.10s. (13 Ran).
(Mrs Eileen Crowe), Patrick G Kelly

855 Diners Club Munster National Handicap Chase (5-y-o and up) £5,520 3m..... (4:00)

KING OF THE GALES [-] 6-10-11 (5*) C O'Brien, ...(5 to 1) 1
635³ ASK THE BOYS [-] 7-10-1 F Woods, ... (7 to 1) 2

539 LAURA'S BEAU [-] 9-11-10 C O'Dwyer, ... (20 to 1) 3
539² FOR WILLIAM [-] 7-11-9 K F O'Brien, ... (5 to 4 fav) 4
575⁴ THUNDERSTRUCK [-] 7-9-0 (7*) M G Quigley, ... (14 to 1) 5
539⁸ PROPUNT [-] 8-10-10 T Horgan, ... (8 to 1) f
532* DESERT LORD [-] 7-10-9 C F Swan, ... (3 to 1) f
Dist: 2½l, 1l, 5l, 6l. 6m 8.80s. (7 Ran).
(E P King), J E Kiely

856 Deadly Nightshade E.B.F. Novice Chase (5-y-o and up) £3,450 2¾m..........(4:30)

554* SULLANE RIVER (Ire) 5-11-3 D H O'Connor, ... (Evens fav) 1
635* BORN DEEP 7-11-13 T Horgan, ... (4 to 1) 2
430* VINEYARD SPECIAL 7-11-13 K F O'Brien, ...(7 to 1) 3
690 STRONG CHERRY 7-10-9 (7*) Mr K Taylor, ... (50 to 1) 4
690³ NEW CO (Ire) 4-11-2 G Bradley, ... (25 to 1) 5
AQUAFLAME 6-11-7 J Shortt, ... (25 to 1) 6
554⁴ COUMEENOOLE LADY 6-10-9 (7*) J M Donnelly, (12 to 1) 7
SHEILA NA GIG 7-11-2 G M O'Neill, ... (9 to 1) 8
NEW PUNT 6-11-7 C O'Dwyer, ... (50 to 1) 9
690 MORNING DREAM 6-11-7 J F Titley, ... (12 to 1) 10
589³ DANNIGALE 7-11-4 (3*) Mr M Phillips, ... (16 to 1) pu
Dist: 2l, 3l, 12l, 1½l. 5m 30.00s. (11 Ran).
(S Lucey), David J McGrath

857 A.I.B. Bank Mares INH Flat Race (5-y-o and up) £3,450 2½m................(5:00)

TRIMMER WONDER (Ire) 5-11-6 (5*) Mrs J M Mullins,
....(10 to 1) 1
638² WILD VENTURE (Ire) 5-11-4 (7*) Ms W Fox, ... (2 to 1 fav) 2
638⁸ BALLINGOWAN STAR 6-11-4 (7*) Mr S O'Donnell, (16 to 1) 3
535⁶ BRIDEPARK ROSE (Ire) 5-11-11 Mr P Fenton, ...(6 to 1) 4
690⁴ RUSSIAN GALE 5-11-4 (7*) Mr D P Daly, ... (16 to 1) 5
571 LADY GALE BRIDGE 6-11-4 (7*) Mr G P FitzGerald, (20 to 1) 6
28⁴ SMART DECISION (Ire) 5-11-6² (7*) Mr R J Curran, (7 to 1) 7
PERSPEX GALE (Ire) 5-11-6 (5*) Mr J A Nash, ... (14 to 1) 8
538⁷ ANOTHER GROUSE 6-11-4 (7*) Mrs K Walsh, ... (16 to 1) 9
554 FERRIC FORTRESS 7-11-4 (7*) Mr J Lombard, ... (25 to 1) 10
SEANS SHOON 6-11-4 (7*) Mr K Whelan, ... (25 to 1) 11
675 CALAMITY CANE (Ire) 5-11-11 Mr A P O'Brien, ... (14 to 1) 12
535 SARAKIN (Ire) 5-11-4 (7*) Mr W M O'Sullivan, ...(25 to 1) 13
SHOURNAGH DANCER 7-11-7³ (7*) Mr A Barry, (25 to 1) 14
636 CLASHREAGH (Ire) (bl) 5-11-4 (7*) Mr K O'Sullivan, (50 to 1) 15
540 FIALADY 8-11-4 (7*) Miss A Dawson, ... (25 to 1) 16
LADY PATH 8-11-11 Mr J P Dempsey, ... (10 to 1) pu
489² PARSONS EYRE (Ire) 5-11-4 (7*) Mr J T McNamara, (8 to 1) pu
801⁴ PAPRS GALE 5-11-4 (7*) Mr E Norris, ... (25 to 1) pu
Dist: 5½l, 7l, 8l, ½l. 5m 9.00s. (19 Ran).
(Mrs J M Mullins), W P Mullins

858 Newenham Mulligan INH Flat Race (5-y-o and up) £3,450 2m 1f.............(5:30)

576³ COURT MELODY (Ire) 5-12-4 Mr E Bolger, ...(11 to 10 fav) 1
CALL ME AL 7-11-11 Mr J A Flynn, ... (3 to 1) 2
252⁴ CLASHWILLIAM GIRL (Ire) 5-11-6 (7*) Mr J Lombard,
....(13 to 2) 3
675⁶ KING OF THE WORLD (Ire) 5-11-11 Mr P Fenton, ... (9 to 1) 4
576² QUEENIES CHILD 6-11-8 (5*) Mr H F Cleary, ...(9 to 2) 5
GOSHCA DU (Ire) 5-11-4 (7*) Mr A F Brady, ...(50 to 1) 6
Dist: 2l, 7l, 1l, 2½l. 4m 29.05s. (6 Ran).
(P P Johnson), Michael Hourigan

PLUMPTON (good)
Tuesday October 19th
Going Correction: PLUS 0.90 sec. per fur. (races 1,3,-5,6), PLUS 0.30 (2,4)

859 Dyke Selling Handicap Hurdle (3 - 6-y-o) £1,576 2m 1f..................... (2:10)

666* MISS MARIGOLD [89] 4-12-0 R Dunwoody, *hld up, hdwy 6th, led 3 out, rdn clr nxt, hit last, styd on*.
.... (13 to 8 fav op 7 to 4 tchd 6 to 4) 1
MECADO [78] (v) 6-11-3 D Gallagher, *hdwy frm rear 7th, chsd wnr aftr 2 out, no impression frm last*.
.......................(7 to 1 op 6 to 1) 2
666⁶ BETALONGABILL [65] (v) 4-10-4 A Maguire, *led til hdd 7th, sn rdn alng, styd on ag'n frm 2 out*.
.......................(8 to 1 op 6 to 1 tchd 10 to 1) 3
359⁴ TAPESTRY DANCER [67] 5-10-6 D Skyrme, *hdwy to ld 7th, hdd 3 out, wknd nxt*.... (12 to 1 op 8 to 1 tchd 14 to 1) 4
666⁵ OH SO HANDY [64] 5-10-3 D Morris, *nvr able to chal frm 7th*................ (13 to 2 op 10 to 1 tchd 6 to 1) 5
SLICK CHERRY [75] 6-11-0 M A FitzGerald, *beh, moderate effrt aftr 6th, btn frm 3 out*.
........................(10 to 1 op 6 to 1 tchd 12 to 1) 6
MILDRED SOPHIA [61] 6-9-7 (7*) Miss S Mitchell, *pressed ldrs to 6th, mid-div whn mstk 3 out*.
..................(16 to 1 op 33 to 1 tchd 50 to 1) 7
IT'S NOT MY FAULT (Ire) [80] 5-10-12 (7*) A Flannigan, *in tch to 6th, sn wknd*......(12 to 1 op 6 to 1 tchd 14 to 1) 8
760⁵ SIAN WYN [72] 3-10-11 R Supple, *wl plcd til wknd aftr 6th*..................(16 to 1 op 12 to 1 tchd 20 to 1) 9

460⁵ SUMMERHILL SCOOP [66] 5-9-12 (7") K Goble, *wl plcd whn jmpd slwly 3rd, wkng when hit nth, tld off.*
.....................(20 to 1 op 16 to 1 tchd 33 to 1) 10
Dist: 5l, 1l, 12l, 6l, 7l, ½l, 1½l, hd, 30l. 4m 21.00s. a 29.00s (10 Ran).
(Mrs Angela Fayers), R J Hodges

860 Cowfold Handicap Chase (0-115 5-y-o and up) £2,364 2m 5f.................(2:40)

615² LITTLE TOM [96] 8-11-1 J R Kavanagh, *led to 3rd, led ag'n 6th, lft clr 11th, shaken up 2 up, styd on easily.*
.....................(5 to 2 fav tchd 3 to 1) 1
TROJAN CALL [90] 6-10-9 H Davies, *hld up, prog 8th, effrt appr 3 out, wnt second last, not rch wnr.*
.....................(10 to 1 op 7 to 1 tchd 11 to 1) 2
PURBECK DOVE [87] 8-10-6 G Upton, *in tch, chsd wnr frm 11th to last, one pace.*
............(8 to 1 op 7 to 1 tchd 6 to 1 and 10 to 1) 3
697⁴ THEY ALL FORGOT ME [87] 6-10-6 A Maguire, *not fluent, al beh, tld off frm tenth.* (7 to 1 op 6 to 1 tchd 8 to 1) 4
MASTER GLEASON [99] 10-11-4 R Dunwoody, *ldg grp, in second pl whn f 11th...* (11 to 4 op 7 to 2 tchd 5 to 2) f
726⁵ MIAMI BEAR [87] 7-10-6 Gary Lyons, *handily plcd til f 11th...................*(11 to 1 op 8 to 1 tchd 12 to 1) f
405² SCOTONI [109] 7-11-11 (3") D O'Sullivan, *chsd ldrs til brght dwn 11th...............*(5 to 1 op 4 to 1 tchd 11 to 2) bd
GLENGRIFFIN [86] 8-10-5 D Murphy, *mid-div til brght dwn 11th....................*(25 to 1 op 16 to 1 tchd 33 to 1) bd
SILVER CANNON (USA) [92] 11-10-11 M A FitzGerald, *led 3rd to 6th, wknd quickly 8th, pld up bef tenth.*
.....................(25 to 1 op 20 to 1 tchd 66 to 1) pu
761⁴ GOLD SHAFT [87] 10-10-6 Mrs N Ledger, *cl up til wknd aftr 5th, tld off frm 11th, pld up bef 2 out.*
.....................(50 to 1 tchd 66 to 1) pu
Dist: 3½l, ½l, dist. 5m 17.70s. a 12.70s (10 Ran).
SR: 23/13/9/-/-/-/ (Mark O'Connor), J S King

861 Framfield Handicap Hurdle (0-125 4-y-o and up) £1,764 2½m...............(3:10)

670⁴ CANOSCAN [101] 8-11-5 E Murphy, *hld up in mid-div, hdwy 9th, led appr 2 out, clr last, easily.*
....................(11 to 8 fav op 7 to 4 tchd 5 to 4) 1
670⁷ JOKER JACK [82] 8-9-9 (5") A Procter, *led til mstk and hdd 7th, outpcd 9th, ran on ag'n frm 2 out.*
.....................(20 to 1 tchd 25 to 1) 2
670² MANHATTAN BOY [105] 11-11-9 A Maguire, *in tch til outpcd aftr 8th, hdwy appr 2 out, one pace frm last.*
.....................(8 to 1 tchd 9 to 1) 3
ACCESS SUN [98] 6-11-2 J R Kavanagh, *ldg grp, chsd ldr 9th til 3 out, one paced frm nxt.* (20 to 1 tchd 25 to 1) 4
719³ REGAL ROMPER (Ire) [88] 5-10-6 Richard Guest, *led 7th til appr 2 out, sn wknd.........*(11 to 1 op 5 to 1) 5
DARK HONEY [100] 8-11-4 H Davies, *in tch til outpcd frm 8th.....................* (12 to 1 op 10 to 1) 6
670⁶ THUHOOL [99] 5-10-10 (7") L Dace, *nvr able to chal frm 8th...................*(16 to 1 op 14 to 1 tchd 20 to 1) 7
463⁶ ALICE'S MIRROR [85] 4-10-3 W McFarland, *nvr on terms frm 8th.........*(16 to 1 op 20 to 1) 8
DIRECTORS' CHOICE [97] 8-10-10 (5") A Dicken, *al beh, lost tch frm 8th.......*(25 to 1 op 20 to 1 tchd 33 to 1) 9
347 WILTOSKI [84] 5-10-2 Mrs N Ledger, *mstk 4th, al beh, tld off frm 8th...........*(25 to 1 op 20 to 1 tchd 33 to 1) 10
648⁴ MY SENOR [106] 4-11-10 R Dunwoody, *prmnt til wknd quickly 7th, tld off................*(33 to 1 op 20 to 1) 11
776³ LESBET [95] 8-10-6 (7") D Matthews, *al in rear, lost tch frm 8th, pld up bef last......* (9 to 2 op 4 to 1 tchd 5 to 1) pu
HANDSOME NED [93] 7-10-11 J Railton, *mid-div till lost pl and pld up bef 9th...* (12 to 1 op 10 to 1 tchd 14 to 1) pu
Dist: 5l, 1l, 4l, sht-hd, 15l, ¾l, 6l, 4l, 20l, dist. 5m 0.90s. a 23.90s (13 Ran).
SR: 32/8/30/19/9/6/4/-/-/ (Nigel Clutton), Lady Herries

862 Sheekey's Restaurant Novices' Chase (5-y-o and up) £1,631 3m 1f 110yds.....(3:40)

IMPERIAL BRUSH 9-11-2 A Maguire, *hld up, prog 12th, pckd 15th, led 3 out, shaken up and styd on easily frm last....................* (7 to 2 op 5 to 2 tchd 4 to 1) 1
660³ WHATAGALE 6-11-7 J Osborne, *led till hdd 1st, led ag'n 6th, fdd 3 out, ev ch whn hit last, no extr nr finish.*
.....................(6 to 4 fav tchd 7 to 4) 2
607⁴ HOUSE OF ROSES (Ire) 5-10-13 G Bradley, *ldg grp, not fluent 16th, lost tch frm 3 out.*
..............(3 to 1 op 5 to 2 tchd 100 to 30) 3
PALMO DAYS 7-11-2 J Akehurst, *in tch in mid-div whn blun and uns rdr tenth............*(50 to 1 op 20 to 1) ur
347² MR GEE 8-11-2 M A FitzGerald, *al in tch, rdn alng 15th, prmnt 3rd whn ran out 4 out.*
.........(10 to 1 op 12 to 1 tchd 14 to 1 and 9 to 1) ro
686³ HASTY SALVO 9-10-11 S Earle, *trkd frnt rnk till lost tch 11th, tld off in 4th pl whn pld up bef 3 out.*
.....................(8 to 1 op 9 to 1 tchd 10 to 1) pu
751 LIZZIES LASS 8-10-11 M Crosse, *not jump wl, al beh, tld off whn pld up bef 16th.........*(16 to 1 tchd 66 to 1) pu
763⁶ PATRUSIKA 7-10-4 (7") Mr T McCarthy, *mstk 3rd, al in rear, tld off whn pld up bef 15th.*
.....................(66 to 1 op 50 to 1 tchd 100 to 1) pu

694⁵ MUTUAL BENEFIT 6-11-2 R Dunwoody, *chsd frnt rnk till lost tch 11th, pld up bef 4 out.*
.....................(20 to 1 op 16 to 1 tchd 25 to 1) pu
BISHOPS TRUTH 7-11-2 D Morris, *led 1st to 6th, wknd 11th, pld up bef 15th.* (16 to 1 op 9 to 1 tchd 33 to 1) pu
Dist: 3½l, dist. 6m 36.00s. a 24.00s (10 Ran).
(D Baxter), J White

863 EBF 'National Hunt' Novices' Hurdle Qualifier (4,5,6-y-o) £1,687 2m 1f........(4:10)

716⁴ OLD BRIDGE (Ire) 5-11-3 (7") D Fortt, *hld up gng wl, ran on frm 7th, led 2 out, pushed out.*
..............(11 to 8 fav op 11 to 10 tchd Evens and 6 to 4) 1
695⁵ ARCTIC LIFE (Ire) 4-11-0¹ Mr P Graffin, *led til hdd 5th, ev ch 2 out, not quicken appr last.*
.....................(5 to 1 op 8 to 1 tchd 10 to 1) 2
764⁸ POLLY MINOR 6-10-9 M Perrett, *effrt frm rear 7th, outpcd 3 out, styd on into 3rd pl nr line.*
.....................(20 to 1 op 33 to 1 tchd 50 to 1) 3
FRANK RICH 6-11-0 J Osborne, *led 5th til hdd 2 out, wknd quickly.......................*(2 to 1 op 5 to 2) 4
645* FIVE FLAGS (Ire) 5-11-0 Richard Guest, *not jump fluently, lost tch frm 6th, tld off.* (7 to 1 op 5 to 1 tchd 9 to 1) 5
597 OLIVIPET 4-10-8 M Crosse, *al struggling towards rear, tld off frm 6th.................*(100 to 1 op 50 to 1) 6
YELLOW CORN 4-10-8 Peter Hobbs, *hld up in tch, mstk 6th, clsg on ldrs in 4th pl whn f 2 out.*
..............(14 to 1 op 12 to 1 tchd 20 to 1) f
402 LIAM OG (Ire) 5-11-0 W McFarland, *al beh, tld off whn pld up bef 2 out..............*(100 to 1 op 50 to 1) pu
Dist: 2l, dist, ½l, 15l, dist. 4m 22.60s. a 30.60s (8 Ran).
(K C B Mackenzie), Andrew Turnell

864 Newick Novices' Hurdle (4-y-o and up) £1,618 2½m.....................(4:40)

GAMEFULL GOLD 4-10-8 H Davies, *hld up in rear, str run appr 3 out, led and jmpd lft last, rdn clr.*
.....................(20 to 1 op 12 to 1) 1
NAZZARO 4-10-13 R Dunwoody, *hld up, ran on frm 8th, led 2 out, hdd last, not quicken run in.*
.....................(10 to 1 tchd 14 to 1) 2
THE WHIP 6-11-0 Peter Hobbs, *mstk second, cl up till led 7th, hdd 2 out, rdn and edgd lft appr last, and run in, kpt on same pace......*(8 to 1 op 7 to 1 tchd 10 to 1) 3
MOUNTAIN MASTER 7-11-0 Mr J M Pritchard, *prog frm rear 6th, squeezed for room on ins appr last, and on run in, not reco'r.............*(13 to 2 op 4 to 1 tchd 7 to 1) 4
773³ PABREY 7-10-7 (7") Miss S Mitchell, *chsd ldrs til hit 5th, lost pl, kpt on ag'n frm 3 out.*
.....................(20 to 1 op 12 to 1 tchd 25 to 1) 5
CARRIGLAWN 8-11-0 D Murphy, *ldg grp til outpcd frm 9th.....................*(16 to 1 op 33 to 1) 6
WALTON THORNS 5-11-0 J Osborne, *rcd in mid-div til lost tch frm 7th.* (11 to 10 on op 5 to 4 tchd 5 to 4 on) 7
664⁴ MISS NOSEY OATS 5-10-9 M A FitzGerald, *led til hdd 7th, weakened quickly frm 9th.*
.....................(6 to 1 op 7 to 1 tchd 10 to 1) 8
BALLYGRIFFIN LAD (Ire) 4-10-13 W McFarland, *strted slwly, blun badly 9th, al struggling in rear.*
.....................(50 to 1 tchd 66 to 1) 9
597 THE OVERTRUMPER 6-11-0 P McDermott, *mid-div til lost tch appr 7th..........*(66 to 1 tchd 100 to 1) 10
392 DELIFFIN 7-11-0 A Maguire, *pressed ldrs til wknd appr 8th, tld off whn pld up bef 2 out...*(33 to 1 op 25 to 1) pu
704⁹ BIG CHANCE 4-10-13 Richard Guest, *al rear grp, tld off whn pld up bef 3 out...........*(66 to 1 op 33 to 1) pu
LISSADELL LADY 4-10-8 J R Kavanagh, *slwly into strd, al beh, tld off whn pld up bef 3 out...*(66 to 1 op 50 to 1) pu
Dist: 4l, 2½l, ¾l, 15l, 8l, 12l, 10l, 15l, dist. 5m 6.70s. a 29.70s (13 Ran).
(Graham Brown), S Dow

CHELTENHAM (good)
Wednesday October 20th
Going Correction: MINUS 0.20 sec. per fur.

865 Postlip Amateur Riders' Handicap Chase (0-135 5-y-o and up) £2,801 3m 1f 110yds
.....................(1:50)

MAYORAN (NZ) [106] 9-10-1 (7") Mr G Lewis, *trkd ldrs, hit 5th, rdn frm 12th, led 5 out, hdd nxt, rallied und pres frm next to ld cl hme...........*(7 to 1 op 6 to 1) 1
615* TRI FOLENE (Fr) [122] (bl) 7-11-10 Mr Anthony Martin, *trkd ldr to 7th, settled in beh lders, hdwy 5 out, led sn aftr last, rdn and hdd cl hme.*
.....................(4 to 1 op 11 to 4 tchd 9 to 2) 2
765* TAMMY'S FRIEND [104] 6-10-6 (6ex) Mr M Armytage, *hld up, early mstks, hdwy 8th, wnt second 5 out, blun last, sn hdd, no extr......*(2 to 1 fav op 7 to 4 tchd 9 to 4) 3
696⁶ LAUDERDALE LAD [113] 11-10-0 (5") Mrs P Nash, *led to 5 out, ev ch till wknd 2 out...........*(20 to 1 tchd 25 to 1) 4
GUILDWAY [98] 10-9-13⁶ (7") Mr M Rimell, *chsd ldrs, hit 12th, rdn 3 out, sn wknd............*(9 to 1 op 5 to 1) 5

765 NO GRANDAD [109] 9-10-4 (7") Mr T Byrne, *beh, hdwy 12th, rdn and wknd 3 out.*
.... (12 to 1 op 8 to 1 tchd 14 to 1) 6
697² A LAD INSANE [102] 12-9-11 (7") Mr G Hogan, *not fluent, beh aftr mstk 13th.....*(10 to 1 op 8 to 1 tchd 11 to 1) 7
697' SUNBEAM TALBOT [113] 10-11-11 (5") Mr S Bush, *hit 3rd, al in rear.*............ (6 to 1 op 5 to 1 tchd 13 to 2) 8
IMPECCABLE TIMING [98] 10-9-9² (7") Mr A Mitchell, *al beh, tld off.*........................(50 to 1 op 25 to 1) 9
697⁵ FATHER PADDY [98] 11-9-7 (7") Miss K Ellis, *al beh, tld off.*
.... (66 to 1 op 33 to 1) 10
696 YIRAGAN [111] 11-10-10 (3") Mr J Durkan, *mstk 6th, tld off frm 11th, pld up bef 2 out.*...........(8 to 1 op 6 to 1) pu
Dist: ½l, 1½l, 10l, 1l, 1l, 12l, 5l, 15l, 7l. 6m 23.30s. a 6.30s (11 Ran).
(Rod Hamilton), P J Hobbs

866 Cheltenham Racecourse Of The Year Handicap Chase (5-y-o and up) £4,143 2m 5f............................ (2:20)

BRADBURY STAR [150] 8-11-7 D Murphy, *trkd ldr frm 4th to tenth, wnt second ag'n 5 out, led last, rdn out.*
.... (5 to 4 fav op 6 to 4 tchd 13 to 8) 1
GARRISON SAVANNAH [150] (bl) 10-11-7 B Powell, *jmpd wl, trkd ldr to 4th, led 11th till hdd last, rallied r-in, one pace.*............ (13 to 2 op 4 to 1 tchd 7 to 1) 2
TIPPING TIM [157] 8-12-0 D Bridgwater, *led to 11th, rdn appr 4 out, sn btn, eased.*.......... (11 to 4 op 2 to 1) 3
FOREST SUN [139] 8-10-10 Richard Guest, *mstk second, al last, tld off frm 7th, broke dwn badly.*
.... (3 to 1 op 4 to 1) 4
Dist: 1½l, 30l, dist. 5m 7.70s. b 2.30s (4 Ran).
SR: 74/72/49/-/ (James Campbell), J T Gifford

867 Cheltenham And Three Counties Club Handicap Hurdle (0-140 4-y-o and up) £2,786 2m 7f 110yds............... (2:50)

687² SPECIAL ACCOUNT [99] 7-10-0 N Mann, *trkd ldr frm second, led aftr 4 out, rdn 2 out, drw clr r-in.*
.... (10 to 1 op 7 to 1) 1
613² NEWTON POINT [105] 4-10-6 A Maguire, *hld up in tch, wnt 3rd 8th, chlgd 2 out, ev ch till wknd sn aftr mstk last.*.................. (9 to 4 fav op 5 to 2) 2
759² MARRA'S ROSCOE [108] 7-10-9 R Dunwoody, *hld up, hdwy hfwy, rdn and wknd appr 2 out, eased r-in.*
.... (100 to 30 op 3 to 1 tchd 7 to 2) 3
727' GREAT MILL [121] (bl) 6-11-3 (5") J McCarthy, *trkd ldr till jmpd slwly second, lost pl aftr mstk 7th, passed btn horses frm 2 out.*............ (13 to 2 op 11 to 2) 4
BONANZA [118] 6-11-5 R Hodge, *hld up, rdn 6th, lost tch appr 3 out.*............ (16 to 1 op 12 to 1) 5
NICKLE JOE [107] 7-10-5 (3") W Marston, *sn trkd ldrs, rdn 8th, soon beh.*.......... (20 to 1 op 16 to 1) 6
594² BRIGGS LAD (Ire) [103] (bl) 4-10-4 N Williamson, *mstks second and 5th, tld off frm 4 out.*......(9 to 1 op 7 to 1) 7
613⁵ BANOUR (USA) [127] (bl) 5-12-0 D Bridgwater, *led, sn pushed alng, rdn and hdd aftr 4 out, wknd quickly, tld off.*....................... (10 to 1 op 6 to 1) 8
613⁶ MICKEEN [103] 6-10-4 J Osborne, *hmpd second, lost tch 7th, tld off whn pld up bef 2 out....*(10 to 1 op 7 to 1) pu
Dist: 3l, 15l, 6l, 5l, ¾l, 12l, 30l. 5m 37.10s. b 0.90s (9 Ran).
SR: 34/37/25/32/24/12/ (Tony Fiorillo), C R Barwell

868 Chubb Extinguishers Novices' Chase (5-y-o and up) £3,403 3m 1f 110yds..... (3:25)

633' GAELSTROM 6-11-5 D Bridgwater, *made all, drw clr frm 5 out, very easily.*
............(11 to 4 on op 3 to 1 on tchd 5 to 2 on) 1
607' GILSTON LASS 6-11-2 J R Kavanagh, *trkd wnr to 6th and ag'n frm tenth, no ch from 5 out.* (11 to 2 tchd 6 to 1) 2
607² OCEAN LINK 9-11-7 S Earle, *chsd ldrs, lost tch frm 5 out.*
.... (10 to 1 tchd 11 to 1) 3
614⁴ THEO'S FELLA 9-11-3 S Hodgson, *al in rear, nvr plcd to chal.*.................... (20 to 1 op 14 to 1) 4
ANSTEY GADABOUT 7-11-3 Miss A Turner, *blun 4th, rdr lost irons, sn tld off, came hme in own time.*
.... (50 to 1 op 25 to 1) 5
TOI MARINE 8-11-3 Mr A Hambly, *pld hrd, chsd wnr 6th till hit tenth, wknd nxt, tld off whn pulled up bef 4 out.*
.... (66 to 1) pu
607⁵ DRUMCEVA 7-11-3 J Railton, *mstk second, sn tld off, pld up bef 4 out.*...................(20 to 1 op 12 to 1) pu
Dist: 20l, 12l, 6l, dist. 6m 21.10s. a 4.10s (7 Ran).
(Mrs J K Powell), N A Twiston-Davies

869 Tantara Hats 'National Hunt' Novices' Hurdle (4-y-o and up) £2,050 2m 5f 110yds................................... (3:55)

628' FUZZY LOGIC (Ire) 5-11-5 D Bridgwater, *made all, jmpd rght, hrd rdn and mstk last, kpt on gmely.*
.... 1
721² KENILWORTH LAD 5-11-1 N Williamson, *hld up, hdwy 7th, wnt second appr 2 out, ev ch last, kpt on r-in.*
.... (5 to 1 op 4 to 1 tchd 11 to 2) 2

616' CLOGHANS BAY (Ire) 4-11-8 R Dunwoody, *hld up, hdwy 7th, rdn and outpcd 2 out, rallied and styd on wl r-in.*
.... (13 to 8 fav op 6 to 4 tchd 7 to 4) 3
753 ARCTIC COURSE (Ire) 5-11-1 A Maguire, *hld up in tch, hdwy 7th, ev ch 3 out, wknd nxt.*
.... (9 to 2 op 5 to 1 tchd 11 to 2 and 4 to 1) 4
WELSH COTTAGE 6-11-1 D Murphy, *prmnt, chsd wnr 6th to 8th, wknd appr 3 out.*......... (10 to 1 op 8 to 1) 5
664⁶ OUTFIELD 7-10-11 (3") W Marston, *chsd wnr to 6th and ag'n 8th till wknd appr 3 out.*......(33 to 1 op 20 to 1) 6
650' DOWRY SQUARE (Ire) 5-11-1 E Murphy, *mid-div, mstk 5th, lost tch frm 7th, tld off.*........(50 to 1 op 20 to 1) 7
773⁷ FLY GUARD (NZ) 6-11-1 J Frost, *al beh, tld off frm 6th.*
.... (16 to 1 op 10 to 1 tchd 20 to 1) 8
773⁸ TEARFUL PRINCE 9-11-1 S McNeill, *chsd ldrs till outpcd frm 6th, tld off and mstk 2 out.*........(20 to 1) 9
650 PHAROAH'S SON 7-11-1 S Earle, *al beh, tld off frm 7th.*
.... (100 to 1) 10
POLYNOGAN 7-11-1 B Powell, *f second.......* (100 to 1) f
STAN CARTER 5-11-1 M Ranger, *al towards rear, tld off whn pld up bef 2 out.*................. (100 to 1) pu
634⁴ SOLAR KESTREL (Ire) 5-11-1 M A FitzGerald, *hmpd second, mstk 4th, lost tch 6th, tld off whn pld up bef 2 out.*
.... (14 to 1 op 7 to 1) pu
Dist: 1l, 1½l, 20l, 6l, 2l, 20l, 2½l, 12l, 25l. 5m 11.10s. a 0.10s (13 Ran).
SR: 47/42/48/21/15/12/ (Cheltenham Racing Ltd), N A Twiston-Davies

870 Chubb Fire Juvenile Novices' Hurdle (3-y-o) £1,945 2m 110yds............. (4:25)

611' MR GENEAOLOGY (USA) (bl) 11-5 A Maguire, *al prmnt, trkd ldr frm 4th, chlgd from 3 out, led last, drvn out.*
.... (15 to 8 fav op 5 to 2) 1
SQUIRE YORK 10-12 M A FitzGerald, *hld up in rear, rapid hdwy appr 3 out, rdn and ev ch last, kpt on r-in.*
.... (33 to 1 op 25 to 1) 2
BOLTROSE 10-12 A O'Hagan, *pld hrd, hld up in rear, gd hdwy appr 3 out, rdn and styd on wl r-in.*
.... (33 to 1 op 20 to 1) 3
296' EUPHONIC 11-2 J Frost, *sn led, mstk 3rd, jmpd rght 5th, not fluent and hdd last, fdd r-in....*(5 to 2 op 7 to 4) 4
SEASIDE DREAMER 10-12 Mr A Hambly, *beh, gd hdwy appr 3 out, edgd lft aftr nxt, hld whn mstk last.*
.... (50 to 1 op 25 to 1) 5
MOHAYA (USA) 10-12 S McNeill, *hld up, styd on frm 3 out, nvr nrr.*.................... (50 to 1 op 20 to 1) 6
611 STAR MINSTREL (Ire) 10-12 R Dunwoody, *prmnt till wknd aftr 3 out.*.................... (14 to 1 op 12 to 1) 7
296⁶ FREE DANCER 10-7 D Bridgwater, *mid-div, rdn 6th, nvr dngrs aftr....* (5 to 1 op 16 to 1 tchd 33 to 1) 8
760⁶ TOUCH SILVER 10-5 (7") Mr Richard White, *al towards rear....................* (100 to 1 op 25 to 1) 9
611⁴ ERLKING (Ire) 10-12 S Earle, *beh, hdwywhn jmpd rght 5th, sn wknd, tld off.*........ (11 to 1 op 7 to 1) 10
SHALHOLME 10-7 E Murphy, *pld hrd, al beh, tld off.*
.... (20 to 1 op 14 to 1 tchd 33 to 1) 11
MR COPYFORCE 10-12 M Richards, *hld up in tch, rdn and wknd appr 3 out, tld off.*
.... (20 to 1 op 10 to 1 tchd 33 to 1) 12
GENTLEMAN SID 10-9 (3") D Meredith, *prmnt till wknd aftr 3th, tld off....*(40 to 1 op 25 to 1 tchd 50 to 1) 13
DIDACTE (Fr) 10-12 S Smith Eccles, *made most till mstk second, wknd 5th, pld up bef 2 out.*(20 to 1 op 10 to 1) pu
Dist: 1l, nk, 3l, 2l, 1½l, 8l, 3½l, nk, 6l, 12l. 4m 5.60s. a 6.60s (14 Ran).
(Mrs P A White), J White

NEWCASTLE (good)
Wednesday October 20th
Going Correction: PLUS 0.25 sec. per fur. (races 1,4,6), MINUS 0.10 (2,3,5)

871 Durham Handicap Chase (0-145 4-y-o and up) £5,433 2½m......................... (2:10)

780³ HOWE STREET [133] 10-11-4 G McCourt, *chsd ldr, led 7th, clr betw last 2, wkng towards finish, all out.*
.... (10 to 1 op 8 to 1) 1
780² ARMAGRET [143] 8-12-0 D Byrne, *in tch, outpcd tenth, styd on wl ag'n appr last.*
...................(9 to 2 op 4 to 1 tchd 5 to 1) 2
780' SWORD BEACH [132] 9-11-3 (5ex) P Niven, *led, hit 5th, hdd 7th, wth wnr till blun 3 out, no imprsn aftr.*
.... (11 to 10 on op 11 to 10 tchd 6 to 5) 3
758² CORNET [133] (v) 7-10-13 (5") P Waggott, *mstks, lost tch 12th.*.................... (14 to 1 op 10 to 1) 4
CAPTAIN MOR [120] 11-10-5 A Mulholland, *mstks, lost tch frm 12th.*.................... (33 to 1 op 25 to 1) 5
546⁶ ANTINOUS [115] 9-10-0 Mrs A Farrell, *mstks, beh whn f 7th.*.................... (33 to 1 op 20 to 1) f
769' LOGAMIMO [130] 7-10-12 (3",5ex) A Larnach, *in tch till f 9th....*(9 to 2 op 7 to 2 tchd 5 to 1) f
Dist: 2½l, ¾l, 20l, 6l. 5m 0.60s. a 9.60s (7 Ran).
SR: 44/51/39/20/1/-/-/ (W M G Black), J H Johnson

872 Northumbria Juvenile Novices' Hurdle (3-y-o) £2,280 2m 110yds.............(2:40)

ERZADJAN (Ire) 10-10 G McCourt, *cl up, made most frm second, ran on wl from last*......(13 to 8 on op Evens) 1
790² THE PREMIER EXPRES 10-7 (3*) N Bentley, *hld up, gd hdwy to chase wnr betw last 2, hng lft aftr last, no imprsn*..................(7 to 1 op 6 to 1 tchd 8 to 1) 2
561* BONUS POINT 11-1 P Niven, *in tch, jnd ldr 3rd, mstk 2 out, kpt on same pace*...............(4 to 1 op 3 to 1) 3
754⁶ OUT OF THE ALLEY 10-5 Gary Lyons, *prmnt, rdn aftr 2 out, sn btn*...................(66 to 1 op 50 to 1) 4
JUMBO STAR 10-3 (7*) Mr R Hale, *trkd ldrs frm 3rd, wknd aftr 2 out*....................(100 to 1) 5
GRINNELL 10-10 K Johnson, *in tch till rdn and wknd aftr 2 out*..................(33 to 1 op 25 to 1) 6
BUZZ-B-BABE 10-10 A Orkney, *mstks, led till hdd second, sn beh, tld off frm 6th, f 2 out*......(33 to 1 op 25 to 1) f
652² DEVILRY 10-10 J Callaghan, *sn rdr second*.
...................................(5 to 1 tchd 9 to 2) ur
Dist: 2½sl, 3½sl, 7l, 7l, 10l. 4m 9.70s. a 16.70s (8 Ran).

(D S Hall), N Tinkler

873 'Barbour' Billy Bow Handicap Hurdle (0-135 4-y-o and up) £7,180 2m 110yds ....(3:10)

781* BATABANOO [129] 4-11-10 (5ex) P Niven, *hld up, steady hdwy to ld 2 out, pushed out aftr last, cmftbly*.
...................(7 to 4 fav op 2 to 1 tchd 9 to 4) 1
657⁷ BEAUCADEAU [132] 7-11-10 (3*) A Dobbin, *trkd ldrs, slightly outpcd betw last 2, styd on wl und pres frm last*....................(4 to 1 op 7 to 2 tchd 9 to 2) 2
WILLIE SPARKLE [117] 7-10-7 (5*) P Williams, *trkd ldrs, hit 4th, ev ch 2 out, kpt on same pace*..(20 to 1 op 16 to 1) 3
739² FLOWING RIVER (USA) [105] 7-9-11 (3*) S Wynne, *hld up in rear, effrt aftr 2 out, kpt on, not trble ldrs*.
...................................(10 to 1 op 12 to 1) 4
DAGOBERTIN (Fr) [114] 7-10-9 L Wyer, *hld up, smooth hdwy to chal 2 out, one pace appr last*.
...................................(14 to 1 op 10 to 1) 5
736 CHIEF RAIDER (Ire) [105] 5-9-9 (5*) D Bentley, *cl up till rdn and wknd aftr 2 out*...........(7 to 1 op 6 to 1) 6
NODFORM WONDER [118] 6-10-13 G McCourt, *led till hdd 2 out, grad wknd*......(6 to 1 op 8 to 1 tchd 11 to 2) 7
731² GREAT MAX (Ire) [106] (bl) 4-10-1¹ C Grant, *trkd ldrs, dsptd ld appr 2 out, sn rdn and wknd*.
...................................(13 to 2 op 6 to 1 tchd 7 to 1) 8
Dist: 3½sl, 2½sl, 2l, nk, 3½sl, hd, 8l. 3m 55.40s. a 2.40s (8 Ran).
SR: 56/55/37/23/31/18/31/11/

(P D Savill), Mrs M Reveley

874 Bedale Novices' Chase (5-y-o and up) £2,604 3m........................(3:40)

SANDY ANDY 7-11-3 T Reed, *sn cl up, lft in ld tenth, hdd 2 out, styd on wl to lead towards finish*.
.....................................(25 to 1 tchd 33 to 1) 1
MOYODE REGENT 9-11-3 A Merrigan, *in tch, trkd ldrs frm 4 out, led 2 out, mstk last, hrd rdn r-in, hdd and no extr towards finish*.............................(200 to 1) 2
779⁶ SUPPOSIN 5-11-0 Gary Lyons, *wl beh till styd on strly frm 3 out, nrst finish*...........(33 to 1 op 50 to 1) 3
718³ TRUE FAIR 10-11-3 A Orkney, *prmnt, blun 8th, grad wknd aftr 4 out*.............................(14 to 1) 4
782³ MONAUGHTY MAN 7-10-10 (7*) P McLoughlin, *in tch till wknd 4 out*.................(200 to 1 op 100 to 1) 5
768⁴ EBRO (bl) 7-11-3 K Jones, *sn beh, tld off*......(100 to 1) 6
733* BRACKENFIELD 7-11-10 P Niven, *led till f tenth*.
.........................(5 to 2 op 7 to 2 on tchd 9 to 4 on) f
727 DUKE'S DELIGHT 6-10-10 (7*) G Cahill, *mstks, prmnt till wknd aftr 4 out, poor 3rd whn f 2 out*.
.........................(250 to 1 op 200 to 1) f
733 CELTIC WATERS 8-10-12 C Dennis, *beh whn blun and uns rdr 6th*...........................(33 to 1) ur
ARTHUR'S MINSTREL 6-11-3 K Johnson, *prmnt, chsd wnr frm tenth, chalg for ld whn hmpd by loose horse and crrd out 2 out*....................(9 to 2 op 7 to 2) co
756⁶ SECOND ATTEMPT 9-11-3 L Wyer, *in tch till wknd 13th, wl beh whn pld up bef 4 out*.....(66 to 1 op 100 to 1) pu
770 MACMURPHY 8-11-3 C Grant, *wl beh whn pld up bef tenth*.........................(50 to 1 op 33 to 1) pu
KING CASH 7-10-12 (5*) J Burke, *beh frm 13th, wl behind whn pld up bef 4 out*.............(33 to 1 op 50 to 1) pu
718 VULPIN DE LAUGERE (Fr) 6-11-3 Mr S Brisby, *sn beh, tld off whn pld up bef 3 out*........(100 to 1 op 100 to 1) pu
Dist: 2l, 12l, 1l, 15l, dist. 6m 4.50s. a 14.50s (14 Ran).
SR: 4/2/-/-/-/-/

(T J Summerfield), J K M Oliver

875 Burghley Novices' Hurdle (4-y-o and up) £2,267 2½m.......................(4:15)

SHAWWELL 6-11-2 K Johnson, *trkd ldrs gng wl, led appr 2 out, shaken up betw last two, lft clr last*.
.....................(15 to 2 op 8 to 1 tchd 7 to 1) 1

KAUSAR (USA) 6-11-2 J Callaghan, *in tch, trkd ldrs frm 6th, wknd aftr 3 out, lft poor second last*.
...................................(4 to 1 op 3 to 1) 2
721⁴ DASHMAR 6-11-2 C Dennis, *al chasing ldrs, kpt on same pace frm 3 out*.................(14 to 1 op 20 to 1) 3
640⁸ JOYFUL IMP 6-10-4 (7*) Mr R Hale, *chsd ldrs till wknd 3 out, tld off*.....................(50 to 1 op 33 to 1) 4
ADVENT LADY 6-10-11 A Mulholland, *beh frm 7th, tld off*.................................(66 to 1) 5
BOLD'N 6-10-9 (7*) J Supple, *al beh, tld off*.
...................................(33 to 1 op 20 to 1) 6
717 MITTON SPRINGS 4-10-7 (7*) D Towler, *mstks, led, clr second, hdd appr 6th, sn beh, tld off*......(66 to 1) 7
734³ POLITICAL TOWER 6-10-13 (3*) A Dobbin, *prmnt, led appr 6th, hdd approaching 2 out, rallying und pres whn f last*...................(7 to 2 op 5 to 1) f
SON OF IRIS 5-11-2 P Niven, *beh, pushed alng hfwy, no hdwy, ran out appr 2 out*.
.........................(5 to 2 fav op 9 to 4 tchd 3 to 1) ro
PATROL 4-11-0 G McCourt, *in tch till wknd 6th, wl beh whn pld up bef 2 out*...............(5 to 1 op 7 to 2) pu
SONIC BELLE 4-10-4 (5*) P Waggott, *in tch, effrt appr 7th, sn wknd, wl beh whn pld up bef 2 out*.
...................................(33 to 1 op 25 to 1) pu
755 FOX TOWER 7-11-2 T Reed, *in tch till wknd 7th, tld off whn pld up bef seventh*................(200 to 1) pu
Dist: 6l, 3l, dist, ½l, 5l, 15l. 5m 0.00s. a 17.00s (12 Ran).

(Mrs J J Straker), J I A Charlton

876 W. K. Backhouse Handicap Chase (0-135 5-y-o and up) £2,768 3m...........(4:45)

677² BALTIC BROWN [105] 8-10-4 Gary Lyons, *made virtually all, drw clr frm 3 out, easily*.
...................................(4 to 1 op 3 to 1) 1
720³ ON THE OTHER HAND [129] 10-12-0 N Doughty, *beh, effrt 4 out, styd on wl frm 2 out*.
...................................(3 to 1 op 5 to 2 tchd 7 to 2) 2
822 KIRSTY'S BOY [114] 10-10-13 G McCourt, *hld up and beh, styd on frm 2 out, not trble ldrs*...........(7 to 1) 3
822⁶ INTERIM LIB [112] 10-10-11 Mr J Bradburne, *prmnt, chsd wnr frm 11th, dsptd ld 15th till grad wknd frm 3 out*.
...................................(11 to 2 op 6 to 1 tchd 13 to 2) 4
758⁴ WHEELIES NEWMEMBER [101] 10-10-0 K Johnson, *in tch, outpcd 14th, wknd 3 out, tld off*..(33 to 1 op 25 to 1) 5
655³ OVER THE DEEL [112] 7-10-11 A Orkney, *chsd ldr till f 11th*.............(4 to 1 fav tchd 2 to 1 and 9 to 4) f
720⁴ VIVA BELLA (Fr) [101] 6-9-7 (7*) Mr D Parker, *in tch whn f tenth*.................(33 to 1 op 16 to 1) f
Dist: 15l, 1l, 2l, 30l. 6m 1.40s. a 11.40s (7 Ran).
SR: 22/31/15/11/

(Mrs S Smith), Mrs S J Smith

PUNCHESTOWN (IRE) (yielding) Thursday October 21st

877 Gowran Grange Maiden Hurdle (5-y-o and up) £3,105 2½m.................(3:30)

535⁴ REGALING 5-11-1 (5*) T P Rudd.........(7 to 4 fav) 1
571³ BUMBLY BROOK 6-10-13 (7*) J M McCormack,...(7 to 1) 2
798⁵ OLYMPIC D'OR (Ire) 5-11-6 G Bradley,.........(5 to 1) 3
DEEP THYNE 5-11-3¹ (7*) Mr K F O'Donnell,..(7 to 1) 4
536 LISCAHILL HIGHWAY 6-11-3 T J Mitchell,...(33 to 1) 5
12⁹ HANG A RIGHT 6-11-9 (5*) T P Treacy,........(4 to 1) 6
493⁵ JUST BLUSH 6-11-9 H Rogers,................(10 to 1) 7
798 THATS MY BOY (Ire) 5-10-13 (7*) B Bowens,...(14 to 1) 8
708 BELLACORICK (Ire) (bl) 5-11-6 G M O'Neill,...(33 to 1) 9
CALDARO 6-11-6 L P Cusack,.................(8 to 1) 10
RUBDAN (USA) 6-11-1 (5*) C O'Brien,........(14 to 1) 11
675 BREFFNI MELODY (Ire) 5-11-6 J P Banahan,...(33 to 1) 12
TOT EM UP 6-11-9 T Horgan,.................(8 to 1) 13
TREMEIRCHION 7-11-6 M Duffy,.............(16 to 1) 14
BETTER WAY (Ire) 5-11-6 B Sheridan,........(20 to 1) 15
WITH DIAMONDS 10-10-10 (5*) D P Murphy,...(20 to 1) 16
BUCKFIELD 6-10-8 (7*) Mr A F Doherty,......(20 to 1) 17
Dist: 4½l, 9l, 3l, 1½l. 5m 0.00s. (17 Ran).

(Mrs Rita Hale), A L T Moore

878 Thornton Handicap Chase (5-y-o and up) £3,105 2m.......................(4:00)

806² MAGIC MILLION [-] 7-10-3 J P Banahan,....(5 to 2 fav) 1
474² FRANTESA [-] 7-10-10 T Horgan,............(6 to 1) 2
LASATA [-] 8-12-0 G Bradley,.................(8 to 1) 3
807⁴ RANDOM PRINCE [-] 9-10-8 K F O'Brien,......(7 to 1) 4
474³ CHARMING EXCUSE [-] 9-10-2 (5*) C P Dunne,..(10 to 1) 5
CAPE SPY [-] 7-11-2 G M O'Neill,.............(8 to 1) 6
LADY EILY [-] 8-9-8 F Woods,.................(14 to 1) 7
178⁷ BLENHEIM PALACE (USA) [-] 6-9-7 J K Kinane,..(14 to 1) 8
539 NEVER BE GREAT [-] 11-11-5 F J Flood,........(10 to 1) 9
691 LA MODE LADY [-] 8-9-7 A J O'Brien,..........(8 to 1) 10
707⁵ FRIENDLY ARGUMENT [-] 8-10-0 (5*) C O'Brien,...(10 to 1) ur
Dist: 9l, 1l, 8l, 2l. 4m 7.40s. (11 Ran).

(P J Donohoe), M A O'Toole

879 **Royal Bond Chase (5-y-o and up) £3,105 2 ¼m. . . . . (4:30)**

619² VISIBLE DIFFERENCE 7-11-8 C F Swan, ... (9 to 4 fav) 1
707² OH SO GRUMPY 5-11-1 (3*) T J Mitchell, ... (5 to 2) 2
674² FURRY STAR 7-11-8 J Jones, ... (6 to 1) 3
527² THE HEARTY CARD (Ire) 5-11-0 D H O'Connor, ... (7 to 1) 4
496⁴ TORENAGA HILL 9-10-6 (7*) Mr A Daly, ... (25 to 1) 5
619* NORTHERN HIDE 7-11-11 T Horgan, ... (5 to 2) f
Dist: 5l, 4l, 20l, 20l. 4m 35.90s. (6 Ran).
(Patrick Heffernan), Patrick Heffernan

880 **Dollandstown Wood Handicap Hurdle (4-y-o and up) £3,105 2m. . . . . (5:00)**

FINAL FAVOUR (Ire) [-] 4-11-2 (7*) H Taylor, ... (10 to 1) 1
489* ENQELAAB (USA) [-] 5-10-7 J P Banahan, ... (7 to 4 fav) 2
SIMPLY SWIFT [-] 6-11-9 (5*) T P Treacy, ... (10 to 1) 3
JIMMY THE JACKDAW [-] 6-9-8 P Carberry, ... (13 to 2) 4
805 MABES TOWN (Ire) [-] 5-9-12 N Byrne, ... (12 to 1) 5
805³ VICOSA (Ire) [-] 4-10-3 A Powell, ... (10 to 1) 6
831³ BRAVEFOOT [-] 5-11-4 (3ex) K F O'Brien, ... (11 to 2) 7
467² FOR JUSTIN [-] 6-10-11 T Horgan, ... (5 to 1) 8
NUALA'S PET [-] 8-10-5 (5*) M G Cleary, ... (14 to 1) 9
MR FIVE WOOD (Ire) [-] 5-10-3 C F Swan, ... (10 to 1) 10
HEADBANGER [-] 6-11-1 C O'Dwyer, ... (20 to 1) pu
Dist: 2l, 2½l, 2l, ¾l. 4m 9.30s. (11 Ran).
(Mrs Mary Francis McCall), Daniel J Murphy

881 **Rathmore Hurdle (4-y-o and up) £3,105 2 ¼m. . . . . (5:30)**

636³ WHAT A QUESTION (Ire) 5-11-3 G Bradley, ... (9 to 4 fav) 1
533³ GREEN GLEN (USA) (bl) 4-11-9 C F Swan, ... (3 to 1) 2
302* PRINCIPLE MUSIC (USA) (bl) 5-12-0 B Sheridan, . . . (5 to 2) 3
537³ SORRY ABOUT THAT 7-12-0 P Carberry, ... (9 to 2) 4
808⁸ I IS 6-11-3 (5*) M G Cleary, ... (33 to 1) 5
805 RUFO'S COUP 6-12-0 G M O'Neill, ... (10 to 1) 6
SUTR-MAKE (Ire) 4-11-3 J P Byrne, ... (66 to 1) 7
536 SAME DIFFERENCE (Ire) 5-11-8 P P Kinane, ... (25 to 1) 8
39 SPOUTING INSPECTOR (Ire) 5-11-3 (5*) D P Geoghegan, ... (50 to 1) 9
Dist: 1l, 2½l, 9l, ½l. 4m 23.00s. (9 Ran).
(Mrs Miles Valentine), M F Morris

WINCANTON (good to firm)
Thursday October 21st
Going Correction: PLUS 0.10 sec. per fur. (races 1,3,5), MINUS 0.30 (2,4,6,7)

882 **Nether Wallop Novices' Chase (5-y-o and up) £3,210 2m 5f. . . . . (2:15)**

363⁴ FESTIVAL DREAMS 8-11-6 P Holley, *trkd ldr, led 4 out, not fluent last, styd on wl*. . . (7 to 1 op 6 to 1 tchd 8 to 1) 1
710* PRINCE'S COURT 10-10-13 (7*) D Fortt, *al prmnt, ev ch 5 out, hit nxt, second whn pckd 3 out, styd on and mstk last, not quicken*. . . . (100 to 30 op 5 to 2 tchd 7 to 2) 2
774⁵ SUKAAB 8-11-0 R Greene, *pushed alng aftr 8th, styd on one pace frm 4 out*. . . . . (7 to 1 op 9 to 2) 3
SENDAI 7-10-9 D Murphy, *hld up, mstk 6th, styd on aftr 5 out, not quicken*. . . . . (11 to 4 jt-fav op 9 to 4) 4
WANDERWEG (Fr) 5-10-12 H Davies, *led, jmpd slwly 4th, hdd four out, wknd frm nxt*. . . . . (11 to 4 jt-fav op 4 to 1 tchd 9 to 2) 5
649 TARMON (Ire) 5-10-12 W Irvine, *beh, pushed alng aftr tenth, no ch whn mstk 3 out*. . . . . . (33 to 1 op 14 to 1) 6
774 DEVIOSITY (USA) 6-10-7 (7*) Mr G Lewis, *chsd ldr till wknd aftr 5 out, no ch whn blun and uns rdr 3 out*. . . . . (50 to 1 op 25 to 1) ur
694 HAIRY MAC 7-11-0 B Clifford, *drpd rear aftr 8th, jmpd slwly tenth and nxt, sn beh, tld off whn pld up and dismounted after 5 out*. . . . . (12 to 1 op 8 to 1 tchd 14 to 1) pu
Dist: 2l, 8l, 12l, 6l, 4l. 5m 23.50s. a 17.50s (8 Ran).
(Mrs Nerys Dutfield), Mrs P N Dutfield

883 **K. J. Pike & Sons Mares Only Novices' Hurdle (4-y-o and up) £2,127 2¾m. . . (2:50)**

814² ANNA VALLEY 7-10-12 Richard Guest, *hld up, steady hdwy aftr 6th, trkd ldrs, led after 3 out, hdd nxt, hrd rdn to ld ag'n nr finish, all out*. (15 to 8 fav op 5 to 2) 1
CANAL STREET 4-10-10 Peter Hobbs, *al prmnt, chsd ldr frm 4 out, led 2 out, rdn and hdd nr finish*. . . . . (7 to 1 op 4 to 1) 2
715⁵ KICKING BIRD 6-10-12 N Williamson, *hld up and beh, steady hdwy aftr 6th, styd on to take 3rd pl after 3 out, one pace*. (14 to 1 tchd 16 to 1) 3
659³ FILM LIGHTING GIRL 7-10-5 (7*) P Ward, *jmpd slwly 1st, beh till hdwy aftr 5 out, styd on one pace*. . . . . (25 to 1 op 14 to 1) 4
MUTUAL AGREEMENT 6-10-5 (7*) R Darke, *mid-div, chsd ldrs frm 6th, no hdwy appr 2 out*. (20 to 1 op 14 to 1) 5
VERY LITTLE (Ire) 5-10-12 S Earle, *beh 5th, hdwy to chase ldg grp aftr 7th, wknd after 4 out*. . . (10 to 1 op 6 to 1) 6
NEW PROBLEM 6-10-5 (7*) A Flannigan, *chsd ldr, wknd aftr 4 out, btn whn mstk last*. . . . . (66 to 1 op 33 to 1) 7
795 RBF ARIANNE 5-10-5 (7*) N Collum, *prmnt, chsd ldrs till wknd quickly aftr 7th, tld off*. . . . . (66 to 1 op 33 to 1) 8
MAKING TIME 6-10-12 A Tory, *beh frm 6th, tld off 4 out*. . . . . (33 to 1 op 25 to 1) 9
KIRBY OPPORTUNITY 5-10-12 C Maude, *chsd ldrs till tried to run out 6th, sn lost pl, tld off 4 out*. . . . . (14 to 1 op 10 to 1 tchd 16 to 1) 10
POLLYTICKLE 5-10-5 (7*) Mr K Whiting, *hld up, hmpd and mstk 6th, sn beh, tld off 4 out*. . . . . (66 to 1 op 33 to 1) 11
STATE LADY (Ire) 4-10-10 W Irvine, *pressed ldrs till wknd aftr 7th, tld off*. (33 to 1 op 20 to 1) 12
715³ CRACKLING ANGELS 6-10-12 B Powell, *al prmnt, 3rd and rdn alng 4 out, third and btn whn f 2 out*. . . . . (7 to 2 op 5 to 1 tchd 11 to 2) f
HYMN BOOK (Ire) (bl) 4-10-10 M A FitzGerald, *beh, hrd rdn aftr 5th, sn lost tch, tld off whn pld up bef 2 out*. . . . . (25 to 1 op 16 to 1 tchd 33 to 1) pu
LITTLE BUCKSKIN 6-10-12 D Bridgwater, *mstks, led till hdd aftr 4 out, tld off whn pld up bef 2 out*. . . . . (20 to 1 tchd 25 to 1) pu
524 WOODSIDE LADY (Ire) 5-10-9 (3*) W Marston, *beh 5th, tld off whn pld up bef 2 out*. . . . . (33 to 1 op 20 to 1) pu
Dist: Nk, 15l, ¾l, 12l, 1½l, dist, 8l, 4l. 5m 15.20s. a 9.20s (16 Ran).
(Miss B Swire), G B Balding

884 **Desert Orchid South Western Pattern Chase Grade 2 (5-y-o and up) £15,550 2m 5f. . . . . (3:20)**

749* PANTO PRINCE 12-11-8 S McNeill, *trkd ldrs, pushed alng 5 out, outpcd appr 3 out, rallied to ld aftr last, drvn out*. . . . . (5 to 1 tchd 11 to 2) 1
YOUNG HUSTLER 6-11-8 D Bridgwater, *led aftr 4th, hit 3 out, jmpd slwly and hdd last, one pace*. . . . . (13 to 8 op 5 to 4 tchd 7 to 4) 2
KINGS FOUNTAIN 10-11-8 N Williamson, *not fluent, hld up, wnt 3rd tenth, chsd ldr frm nxt, ev ch 3 out, mstk next, sn one pace*. . . . . (5 to 4 fav op 11 to 10 tchd 11 to 8) 3
SMARTIE EXPRESS 11-11-4 R Dunwoody, *trkd ldg pair till wknd 6 out, some hdwy aftr 4 out, btn whn mstk 2 out*. . . . . (12 to 1 tchd 14 to 1) 4
850³ SIRRAH JAY 13-11-0 A Maguire, *led till aftr 4th, wknd 8th, tld off*. . . . . (33 to 1 op 20 to 1) 5
794* ABU MUSLAB (bl) 9-11-0 M A FitzGerald, *pressed ldrs to 6th, wknd 8th, tld off whn pld up bef last*. . . . . (66 to 1 op 33 to 1) pu
Dist: 5l, 6l, 15l, dist. 5m 11.50s. a 5.50s (6 Ran).
SR: 60/55/49/30/-/-/ (Mrs L M Warren), C L Popham

885 **Travis Perkins Novices' Hurdle (Div I) (4-y-o and up) £2,127 2m. . . . . (3:50)**

AUBURN CASTLE 4-10-12 J Osborne, *sn prmnt, led 3rd to 5th, trkd ldr till led ag'n appr 2 out, shaken up, styd on wl*. . . . . (11 to 4 fav op 7 to 2 tchd 4 to 1) 1
716³ MASNUN (USA) 8-10-9 (3*) D O'Sullivan, *chsd ldrs, ev ch appr 2 out, not fluent last, rdn and not quicken*. . . . . (4 to 1 op 3 to 1 tchd 9 to 2) 2
434³ SINGERS IMAGE (v) 4-10-12 Richard Guest, *hld up in mid-div, drvn alng appr 2 out, styd on betw last two, not quicken*. . . . . (9 to 1 op 6 to 1) 3
VITAL WONDER 5-10-12 P Holley, *hld up, hdwy aftr 5th, cl up and ev ch appr 2 out, sn rdn and btn*. . . . . (4 to 1 op 7 to 2 tchd 9 to 2 and 5 to 1) 4
GLORY BEE 9-10-12 M Richards, *drpd rear aftr second, wl beh till styd on after 3 out, nvr nrr*. . . . . (50 to 1 op 25 to 1) 5
HOLIDAY ISLAND 4-10-12 G McCourt, *chsd ldrs, drvn alng aftr 3 out, wknd after nxt*. . . . . (7 to 1 op 5 to 1 tchd 9 to 1) 6
705⁴ SOLE CONTROL 5-10-7 J Railton, *led till 3rd, trkd ldr in second pl till wknd aftr 3 out*. . . . . (14 to 1 op 16 to 1 tchd 20 to 1) 7
715 ANDARE 4-10-12 S Earle, *beh, hdwy to chase ldg grp aftr 4th, wknd 3 out*. . . . . (50 to 1 op 33 to 1) 8
716⁷ DARINGLY 4-10-12 S McNeill, *al beh*. (50 to 1 op 25 to 1) 9
716 ROUTING 5-10-5 (7*) Mr G Lewis, *pld hrd, hld up, rapid hdwy to ld 5th, hdd appr 2 out, wknd quickly*. . . . . (12 to 1 tchd 16 to 1) 10
SALBYNG 5-10-12 A Maguire, *hld up, lost tch frm 3rd, sn beh*. . . . . (5 to 1 op 9 to 2 tchd 11 to 2) 11
PALACE MAN (USA) 5-10-12 E Murphy, *beh second, lost tch aftr nxt, tld off*. . . . . (50 to 1 op 25 to 1) 12
Dist: 5l, 3½l, 7l, 5l, 8l, 2½l, 1l, 8l, 2l. 3m 39.40s. a 2.40s (12 Ran).
SR: 12/7/3/-/-/-/ (Rashleigh Arms Charlestown St Austell), O Sherwood

886 **Blackdown Handicap Chase (0-135 5-y-o and up) £3,720 3m 1f 110yds. . . . . . . (4:20)**

661 BONSAI BUD [118] 10-10-11 D Gallagher, *hld up, beh tenth, hdwy 14th, trkd ldr till led 3 out, styd on wl*. . . . . (12 to 1 op 8 to 1) 1

NATIONAL HUNT RESULTS 1993-94

792* RATHVINDEN HOUSE (USA) [112] 6-10-5 (4ex) G McCourt,
*al hndy, mstk 11th, wnt second 13th, led 15th, hdd 3
out, no imprsn.*
.......(Evens fav op 11 to 10 tchd 11 to 8 and 6 to 4) 2
DANDY MINSTREL [112] 9-10-5 D Bridgwater, *hld up,
reminders and pushed alng aftr 12th, hdwy 14th, chsd
ldr, mstk 4 out, kpt on one pace....* (12 to 1 op 8 to 1) 3
630² FAR SENIOR [135] 7-12-0 N Williamson, *wnt 3rd 8th, chsd
ldg pair till reminders aftr 5 out, one pace after nxt.*
.............(9 to 4 op 11 to 4 tchd 3 to 1) 4
TOM TROUBADOUR [118] 10-10-11 D Murphy, *hld up,
hdwy 13th, mstk nxt, sn wknd.*
..........(11 to 2 op 6 to 1 tchd 13 to 2 and 7 to 1) 5
WELLINGTON BROWN [115] 9-10-8 P Holley, *led to 3rd,
wknd quickly 13th, beh whn pld up aftr nxt.*
...............(25 to 1 op 20 to 1 tchd 33 to 1) pu
LITTLE GENERAL [109] 10-10-2² H Davies, *led 3rd, clr 6th,
hdd and hit 15th, wknd quickly, tld off whn pld up bef
3 out.................*(33 to 1 op 20 to 1 tchd 40 to 1) pu
Dist: 3l, 15l, 4l, 20l. 6m 26.00s. a 10.00s (7 Ran).
SR: 9/-/-/4/ (P M de Wilde), D J G Murray Smith

887 Blandford Handicap Hurdle (0-125 4-y-o and up) £2,856 2m................(4:50)

EL VOLADOR [95] 6-11-0 A Maguire, *trkd ldrs, wnt 3rd
aftr 3 out, led 2 out, drvn clr r-in, styd on strly.*
......(9 to 4 jt-fav op 5 to 2 tchd 11 to 4 and 3 to 1) 1
MONDAY CLUB [108] 9-11-13 M Richards, *hld up and beh,
hdwy aftr 5th, cl up and ev ch 2 out, not quicken.*
...............(20 to 1 op 12 to 1) 2
713⁴ VA UTU [95] 5-11-0 Lorna Vincent, *hld 1st, beh, rdn and
hdwy appr 2 out, kpt on betw last two.*
.................(14 to 1 op 10 to 1) 3
632⁵ CAROMANDOO (Ire) [88] (v) 5-10-7 M A FitzGerald, *beh 3rd,
rdn and hdwy appr 2 out, styd on betw last two, not
quicken.................*(33 to 1 op 25 to 1 tchd 50 to 1) 4
EASTHORPE [92] 5-10-11 J Osborne, *prmnt, led 3 out, sn
hdd, styd on one pace betw last 2...*(12 to 1 op 7 to 1) 5
713* NIGHT WIND [98] 6-11-3 S McNeill, *hld up, hdwy to track
ldrs aftr 4th, cl up and ev ch appr 2 out, sn rdn and not
quicken.................................*(9 to 4 jt-
fav op 3 to 1 tchd 7 to 2 and 2 to 1) 6
SMILING CHIEF (Ire) [92] 5-10-11 W Irvine, *hld up, rdn and
styd on one pace frm 3 out.........*(20 to 1 op 14 to 1) 7
670³ KALAMOSS [85] 4-9-11 (7*) Miss S Mitchell, *chsd ldrs, rdn
alng 3 out, sn wknd.................* (40 to 1 op 25 to 1) 8
687⁶ KNIGHT IN SIDE [82] 7-10-1 C Maude, *led till hdd 3 out,
led ag'n appr nxt, headed 2 out, wknd quickly.*
........(12 to 1 op 10 to 1 tchd 16 to 1 and 20 to 1) 9
698³ BEN ZABEEDY [101] 8-11-6 G McCourt, *beh frm 3rd, nvr
nr to chal..................*(25 to 1 op 14 to 1) 10
ALWAYS REMEMBER [97] 6-11-2 Peter Hobbs, *hld up,
hdwy 4th, cl up and ev ch appr 2 out, sn rdn, eased
whn btn betw last two..............*(4 to 1 op 6 to 1) 11
646⁶ NOBLE INSIGHT [100] 6-11-5 R Dunwoody, *beh, reminders
aftr second, at rear................*(25 to 1 op 20 to 1) 12
SANDRO [81] (bl) 4-10-0 L Harvey, *sn prmnt, chsd ldrs till
rdn and wknd quickly 3 out.......*(66 to 1 op 33 to 1) 13
Dist: 1½l, 4l, 3l, ½l, 2½l, 1½l, 3l, nk, nk, 10l. 3m 37.10s. a 0.10s (13 Ran).
SR: 37/42/29/21/21/24/16/6/2/ (I A Baker), R J O'Sullivan

888 Travis Perkins Novices' Hurdle (Div II) (4-y-o and up) £2,127 2m...............(5:20)

HAROLDON (Ire) 4-10-12 J Osborne, *hld up, trkd ldrs frm
4th, cl up and ev ch appr 2 out, hrd rdn to ld and
bumped nr finish...................*(8 to 1 op 6 to 1) 1
704* BERTONE (Ire) 4-11-5 N Williamson, *trkd ldrs frm 4th, led
and hit 2 out, edgd lft r-in, hdd and bumped nr finish.*
...............(7 to 4 fav tchd 13 to 8) 2
MULCIBER 5-10-12 M Perrett, *hld up, hdwy 4th, cl up
and ev ch 2 out, wknd appr last.*
...............(13 to 2 op 4 to 1 tchd 7 to 1) 3
BOLD STREET BLUES 6-10-12 L Harvey, *beh, hdwy aftr 3
out, kpt on one pace.* (25 to 1 op 20 to 1 tchd 33 to 1) 4
BEY D'AO (Fr) 5-10-12 S Hodgson, *chsd ldrs frm 4th, led 3
out till hdd nxt, sn wknd.........*(50 to 1 op 33 to 1) 5
RIOCHET (Ire) 5-10-12 A Maguire, *pressed ldr, led 3rd to 3
out, ev ch appr nxt, wknd betw last 2.*
...................................*(7 to 1 op 8 to 1) 6
TELEPHUS 4-10-12 D Murphy, *beh, hdwy to chase ldg grp
appr 2 out, sn wknd...*(12 to 1 op 7 to 1 tchd 14 to 1) 7
COUNT BARACHOIS (USA) 5-10-12 N Mann, *led to 3rd,
pressed ldr till wknd quickly appr 2 out.*
...............(50 to 1 op 33 to 1) 8
UNVEILED 5-10-7 W Irvine, *blun 1st, sn beh, nvr rch ldrs,
tld off 3 out.................*(33 to 1 op 20 to 1) 9
753⁷ TOTHEWOODS 4-10-12 D Bridgwater, *beh, hdwy aftr 5th,
chsd ldrs, sn weakened, btn whn blun last, tld off.*
...............(14 to 1 op 10 to 1 tchd 16 to 1) 10
THE POWER OF ONE 4-10-7 R Dunwoody, *beh, hdwy 3
out, wknd quickly appr nxt.*
...................(5 to 1 op 9 to 2 tchd 6 to 1) 11
MOUGINS (Ire) 4-10-12 P Holley, *refused to race.*
...............(8 to 1 op 7 to 1) f
Dist: Nk, 12l, 2l, 1½l, 20l, ½l, hd, dist. 3m 39.60s. a 2.60s (12 Ran).

SR: 10/16/-/-/-/-/ (Lamb Brook Associates), B Palling

EXETER (good to firm)
Friday October 22nd
Going Correction: PLUS 0.25 sec. per fur.

889 Booker Steed Conditional Jockeys' Novices' Handicap Hurdle (4-y-o and up) £1,961 2¼m....................(2:20)

773* EDIMBOURG [80] 7-10-2 (7ex) J McCarthy, *chsd ldr til led
3rd, made rst, rdn frm 2 out, drvn out.*
...............(2 to 1 on op 7 to 4 on tchd 13 to 8 on) 1
HANDY LASS [78] 4-10-0 D Matthews, *hld up, hdwy 5th,
chsd ldr, ev ch 2 out, not quicken appr last.*
...............(12 to 1 tchd 16 to 1) 2
608* DISTANT MEMORY [78] 4-9-10 (4*) N Parker, *trkd ldrs, ev
ch whn hit 2 out, rdn and not quicken appr last.*
...............(8 to 1 tchd 12 to 1) 3
TALLAND STREAM [79] 6-10-1 R Farrant, *trkd ldrs, ev ch 3
out, rdn appr last, one pace.......*(20 to 1 op 10 to 1) 4
737* SIR PAGEANT [87] 4-10-9 D Leahy, *hld up, hdwy aftr 4th,
chsd ldg grp frm four out, no imprsn from 2 out.*
...............(16 to 1 op 10 to 1 tchd 20 to 1) 5
699* BOXING MATCH [74] 4-10-0 R Greene, *hld up, hdwy 5th,
sn rdn alng, kpt on one pace frm 2 out.*
...............(33 to 1 op 16 to 1) 6
737⁶ COURT OF KINGS [78] 4-10-0 C Burnett-Wells, *hld up in
last pl, wl beh til styd on one pace aftr 3 out.*
...............(50 to 1 op 25 to 1) 7
814⁹ WEST MONKTON [78] 7-10-0 W Marston, *chsd ldrs, outpcd and pushed alng frm 4 out, no imprsn.*
...............(50 to 1 op 25 to 1) 8
775* MOBILE MESSENGER (NZ) [89] 5-10-11 (7ex) R Davis, *mstk
1st, chsd ldr till wknd aftr 5th, sn beh.*
...............(11 to 1 op 10 to 1 tchd 16 to 1) 9
BARE FISTED [78] 5-10-0 A Procter, *beh frm 3rd, al rear.*
...............(66 to 1 op 33 to 1) 10
772² KING UBAD (USA) [106] 4-12-0 A Thornton, *led till hdd 3rd,
wknd quickly aftr nxt, sn beh.......* (12 to 1 op 6 to 1) 11
683⁴ DUNKERY BEACON [78] 7-10-0 M Hourigan, *wl beh frm
3rd, sn lost tch...............*(50 to 1 op 25 to 1) 12
DERRYMOSS [78] (bl) 7-9-10 (4*) L Reynolds, *chsd ldrs frm
second till jmpd slwly nxt, sn beh.*
...............(25 to 1 op 20 to 1 tchd 14 to 1) 13
Dist: 6l, 1½l, 8l, 1l, 10l, 12l, sht-hd, 12l, 5l, 4l. 4m 9.20s. a 9.20s (13 Ran).
SR: 27/19/17/10/17/-/ (Mrs Iva Winton), Miss H C Knight

890 Kraft General Foods Foodservice Juvenile Novices' Hurdle (3-y-o) £1,751 2¼m (2:50)

570² BEAT THE BAGMAN (Ire) 11-1 L Harvey, *hmpd 1st, chsd
ldrs till rdn to ld appr 2 out, styd on wl.*
...............(3 to 1 op 9 to 4) 1
606⁶ ALLEGATION (bl) 10-10 R Dunwoody, *led aftr 1st til ran
very wide and lost pl nxt, sn wl beh, rapid hdwy to
chase ldrs aftr 5th, rdn and no imprsn.*
...............(2 to 1 fav op 7 to 4 tchd 9 to 4 and 5 to 2) 2
606⁵ APACHEE FLOWER 10-6¹ J Frost, *beh, rdn and hdwy aftr
5th, styd on frm 2 out, not rch 1st two.*
...............(20 to 1 op 12 to 1) 3
VELVET HEART (Ire) 10-5 S Burrough, *chsd ldrs frm 3rd, ev
ch aftr 3 out, sn rdn and one pace.*
...............(20 to 1 op 12 to 1 tchd 25 to 1) 4
608³ GROGFRYN 10-0 (5*) R Farrant, *hld up, hdwy 5th, cl up
and ev ch 3 out, sn rdn and wknd.*
...............(33 to 1 op 20 to 1) 5
516⁸ RECORD LOVER (Ire) (bl) 10-10 M Richards, *hld up, trkd
ldg grp and cl up aftr 4th, ev ch 3 out, sn rdn and btn.*
...............(3 to 1 op 4 to 1) 6
THORNHILL 10-5 N Hawke, *chsd ldg grp frm 4th till wknd
quickly aftr four out..............*(50 to 1 op 25 to 1) 7
606³ POLLY LEACH 10-5 S Mackey, *pld hrd, jmpd rght 1st, lft
in ld aftr second, mstk 4th, hdd appr 2 out, btn whn
mistake last.............*(7 to 1 op 5 to 2 tchd 8 to 1) 8
406⁶ NO SHOW (Ire) 10-10 W Humphreys, *nvr rch ldrs, wl beh
frm 5th.................*(50 to 1 op 33 to 1) 9
604⁶ MY SET PEACE 10-5 I Lawrence, *beh frm 4th, nvr rch ldrs.*
...............(33 to 1 op 25 to 1) 10
ABU DANCER (Ire) 10-7 (3*) A Thornton, *trkd ldrs frm 3rd,
in tch till rdn and wknd quickly aftr 3 out.*
...............(33 to 1 op 16 to 1) 11
717⁷ GREEN CHILI 10-5 N Williamson, *led into strt, chsd ldrs,
ev ch 3 out, 3rd and wkng whn f nxt. Dead.*
...............(12 to 1 op 7 to 1 tchd 14 to 1) f
604⁵ IMAGERY 10-5 W McFarland, *beh 3rd, blun and uns rdr
5th.................*(33 to 1 op 16 to 1) ur
760 PFAFF'S CELLAR (bl) 10-5 M Hourigan, *drpd rear aftr
second, wl in last pl, pld up bef 3 out.*
...............(50 to 1 op 33 to 1) pu
Dist: 2½l, 2½l, 3½l, 8l, 3l, 7l, 1l, 12l, 2l, 6l. 4m 14.50s. a 14.50s (14 Ran).
(David Sweet), J Akehurst

891 Kitsons Novices' Selling Hurdle (4 & 5-y-o) £1,639 2m 3f 110yds...............(3:20)

114

773[6] GILBERT (Ire) 5-10-12 Lorna Vincent, *made all, rdn appr 2 out, not fluent last, all out*.......... (9 to 2 op 3 to 1) **1**

699[3] LAW FACULTY (Ire) 4-10-11 S Mackey, *trkd ldr, wnt 3rd 4th, hrd rdn aftr four out, ev ch appr 2 out, one pace.*
....(6 to 1 op 7 to 2) **2**

599[7] DANCING DANCER 4-10-6 J Frost, *hld up, rdn and hdwy aftr 4 out, ev ch 2 out, not quicken appr last.*
....(7 to 1 op 5 to 1 tchd 8 to 1) **3**

724[2] NAJEB (USA) 4-10-11 B Clifford, *al chasing ldr, ev ch 2 out, sn rdn and one pace.*
....(11 to 8 fav op 6 to 4 tchd 9 to 4) **4**

699[2] NEW STATESMAN 5-10-12 Richard Guest, *trkd ldrs, jmpd slwly 4th, sn rdn alng, styd on appr 2 out, not quicken, eased whn btn r-in*.....(11 to 4 op 9 to 4 tchd 3 to 1) **5**

PENNY HOLME 5-10-7 L Harvey, *pushed alng aftr 3rd, sn lost tch, tld off 3 out*............ (25 to 1 op 10 to 1) **6**

MERLS PEARL 4-10-6 Leesa Long, *hld up, mstk 3rd, sn pushed alng and lost pl, tld off 3 out.*
.... (25 to 1 op 12 to 1 tchd 33 to 1) **7**

Dist: 1½l, sht-hd, 1½l, 3½l, dist, 3l. 4m 40.30s. a 18.30s (7 Ran).

(Mrs A Carey), D N Carey

892 Booker Steed Customer Care Duchy Of Cornwall Cup Novices' Chase (5-y-o and up) £3,746 2m 3f 110yds............ (3:50)

IN THE NAVY 7-11-0 R Dunwoody, *lft in ld second, made rst, edgd left appr 2 out, sn hrd rdn, jst hld on, all out.*
.... (11 to 4 op 3 to 1 tchd 5 to 2) **1**

CRYSTAL SPIRIT 6-11-0 J Frost, *prmnt, mstks 3rd and 4th, jmpd slwly 8th, pressed ldr, cl up and ev ch four out, rdn and not quicken last strd.*
....(7 to 4 on op 2 to 1 on tchd 9 to 4 on) **2**

MR SUNBEAM 5-10-12 T Jarvis, *hld up, hdwy aftr 7th, 3rd whn blun 9th, styd on one pace frm 4 out, fnshd lme*....................(16 to 1 op 10 to 1 tchd 20 to 1) **3**

774[7] MATAWAI (NZ) 6-10-9 (5*) R Davis, *hld up and beh, hdwy 8th, mstk nxt, wnt 3rd appr 4 out, sn one pace, third whn mistake last*...................(20 to 1 op 14 to 1) **4**

774[8] TRAIN ROBBER 8-11-0 W Irvine, *mid-div, rdn alng frm 6 out, no hdwy from 4 out*..........(14 to 1 op 10 to 1) **5**

683 PAPER STAR 6-10-9 Richard Guest, *hdwy aftr 7th, mstk nxt, sn rdn alng, wnt 4th 6 out, wknd four out.*
.... (50 to 1 op 33 to 1) **6**

594 FINAL SOUND (bl) 8-11-0 L Harvey, *chsd ldrs til lost pl aftr 9th, sn beh*..................(33 to 1 op 16 to 1) **7**

633 JHAL FREZI 5-10-9 (3*) A Thornton, *hld up, drvn alng aftr 6 out, sn beh*......................(66 to 1 op 33 to 1) **8**

CANTORIS FRATER 6-11-0 N Hawke, *led till blun and uns aftr second*....................(14 to 1 op 20 to 1) **ur**

593[e] BARGAIN AND SALE 8-10-7 (7*) Mr Richard White, *jmpd very slwly, sn last, tld off aftr 7th, pld up after 5 out.*
.... (33 to 1 op 20 to 1) **pu**

650 STORM FLIGHT 7-10-7 (7*) Mr C Bonner, *trkd ldrs till mstk and wknd 5 out, tld off whn pld up bef 2 out.*
.... (33 to 1 op 14 to 1) **pu**

Dist: Sht-hd, 15l, 3l, 4l, 2l, 15l, 5l. 4m 43.30s. a 9.30s (11 Ran).

SR: 42/42/25/24/20/13/3/-/-/ (Vice Admiral Sir Fitzroy Talbot), M C Pipe

893 If You Need It Booker Steed It Handicap Chase (0-145 5-y-o and up) £3,680 2¼m ....(4:20)

777[*] IAMA ZULU [106] 8-10-4 (5ex) M Hourigan, *led, jmpd lft 3 out and nxt, hdd appr last, rdn to ld ag'n r-in, styd on wl*.................... (11 to 10 on op 5 to 4 tchd Evens) **1**

825 DRUMSTICK [126] 7-11-10 N Williamson, *hld up, not fluent early, wnt second aftr 5 out, led appr last, hdd r-in, not quicken*.........................(6 to 4 op Evens) **2**

631 ACRE HILL [124] 9-11-8 R Dunwoody, *trkd ldr, ev ch appr 4 out, wknd aftr 3 out*...........(5 to 1 op 4 to 1) **3**

Dist: ¾l, 15l. 4m 22.20s. a 11.20s (3 Ran).

SR: 9/28/11/ (Mrs Anona Taylor), P J Hobbs

894 Kitsons Handicap Hurdle (0-140 4-y-o and up) £2,726 2¼m...(4:50)

HIGH BARON [136] 6-12-0 M Hourigan, *hld up in last pl, plenty to do aftr 3 out, rapid hdwy to go second appr nxt, quickened to ld r-in, styd on strly.*
.... (4 to 1 op 3 to 1) **1**

601[*] PONTOON BRIDGE [108] 6-10-0 N Williamson, *led, clr aftr 4th, not fluent 3 out, hdd r-in, one pace.*
.... (13 to 8 on op Evens) **2**

MUNKA [108] 7-9-7 (7*) N Parker, *trkd ldg pair, rdn aftr 3 out, chsd ldr, one pace betw last 2.* (3 to 1 tchd 7 to 2) **3**

716[5] MUSTAHIL (Ire) [108] 4-10-0 R Dunwoody, *chsd ldr, rdn alng aftr 3 out, kpt on one pace.*
.... (9 to 2 op 6 to 1 tchd 8 to 1) **4**

610[5] TRUST DEED (USA) [108] (bl) 5-10-0 L Harvey, *trkd ldg trio, wknd aftr 5th, no imprsn appr 2 out.*
.... (14 to 1 op 10 to 1) **5**

Dist: 3l, 3l, ½l, 4l. 4m 8.70s. a 8.70s (5 Ran).

SR: 58/27/24/23/19/ (Miss C A James), R H Alner

NEWBURY (good)

Friday October 22nd

Going Correction: PLUS 0.10 sec. per fur. (races 1,2,-4,6,7), MINUS 0.05 (3,5)

895 October Handicap Hurdle (5-y-o and up) £4,347 3m 110yds...(2:10)

156[*] AAHSAYLAD [122] (bl) 7-11-9 A Maguire, *hld up, hdwy frm 7th, rdn 3 out, mstk and led last, drvn clr.*
...... (11 to 8 op 6 to 4 on tchd 7 to 4 on and 5 to 4 on) **1**

EMERALD SUNSET [108] 8-10-9 D Gallagher, *hld up, hdwy 7th, lft in ld 4 out, rdn and hdd last, no extr.*
.... (16 to 1 op 12 to 1 tchd 20 to 1) **2**

646[6] HURRICANE BLAKE [120] (bl) 5-11-7 J Railton, *trkd ldrs, wnt second 9th, rdn and wknd appr 2 out.*
.... (11 to 2 op 6 to 1 tchd 13 to 2) **3**

PHAROAH'S LAEN [103] 12-10-4 S Earle, *trkd ldr till wknd 8th, sn tld off*..............(33 to 1 tchd 50 to 1) **4**

TOP JAVALIN (NZ) [123] 6-11-3 (7*) R Darke, *in tch, 3rd whn f 7th*..................(9 to 1 op 6 to 1 tchd 10 to 1) **f**

750 LEGAL BEAGLE [111] (bl) 6-10-12 M Perrett, *jmpd poorly in ld till blun and uns ndr 4 out.*
.... (16 to 1 op 12 to 1 tchd 20 to 1) **ur**

CHIEF CELT [106] 7-10-7 G McCourt, *in rear, effrt 4 out, wknd nxt, poor fourth whn pld up and dismounted r-in, lme*.............. (9 to 1 op 6 to 1 tchd 10 to 1) **pu**

Dist: 5l, 10l, dist. 6m 1.10s. a 12.10s (7 Ran).

(Ms M Horan), J White

896 Falcon Catering Equipment Novices' Hurdle (3-y-o) £3,353 2m 110yds...(2:40)

830[2] SATIN DANCER 11-5 G McCourt, *made all, clr whn hit 2 out, untidy last, idle r-in, jst hld on.*
.... (2 to 1 on tchd 7 to 4 on) **1**

GRAND APPLAUSE (Ire) 11-0 D Gallagher, *al in tch, trkd wnr frm 5th, mstk last, rallied and ran on wl r-in, jst fld*.........(5 to 1 op 9 to 2 tchd 4 to 1 and 11 to 2) **2**

754[3] CRIMINAL RECORD (USA) 11-0 Diane Clay, *trkd wnr to 5th, wknd appr 2 out*..(6 to 1 op 5 to 1 tchd 13 to 2) **3**

LA POSADA 10-2 (7*) P Moore, *hld up, jmpd slwly second, wl beh frm 4th*.................. (50 to 1 op 20 to 1) **4**

ACROSS THE BOW (USA) 11-0 Peter Hobbs, *beh whn hit 4th, tld off frm nxt*....................(50 to 1 op 16 to 1) **5**

THE SNOUT 10-9 A Maguire, *al beh, tld off frm 5th.*
.... (10 to 1 op 7 to 1 tchd 12 to 1) **6**

PARIS ROBBER 11-0 A Charlton, *in rear, hit 3rd, sn tld off, pld up bef 5th*.................(33 to 1 op 16 to 1) **pu**

Dist: Nk, 30l, sht-hd, dist, dist. 4m 0.00s. a 11.00s (7 Ran).

(G Harwood), G Harwood

897 Glynwed International Handicap Chase (0-145 5-y-o and up) £7,203 2½m.... (3:10)

GUIBURN'S NEPHEW [130] 11-11-1 C Maude, *made all, not fluent 6th, rdn and drw clr frm 2 out.*
.... (13 to 2 op 5 to 1 tchd 7 to 1) **1**

609[2] GREEN ISLAND (USA) [119] 7-10-4 Peter Hobbs, *hld up, hdwy frm 4 out, styd on to go second r-in.*
.... (15 to 2 op 6 to 1 tchd 8 to 1) **2**

684[*] DIS TRAIN [130] 9-11-1 G Bradley, *trkd wnr till wknd r-in.*
.... (9 to 4 fav op 5 to 2 tchd 11 to 4) **3**

CALAPAEZ [137] 9-11-8 A Maguire, *mid-div, hit 5th, one pace frm 3 out*.............(9 to 1 op 8 to 1 tchd 10 to 1) **4**

MR ENTERTAINER [133] 10-11-4 D Murphy, *in tch, hit wknd appr 4 out, btn whn hmpd by faller nxt, tld off.*
.... (12 to 1 op 10 to 1) **5**

523 CASTLE KING [122] 6-10-7 G McCourt, *slwly away, jmpd rght, wl in rear till hdwy 11th, prog appr 4 out, tld off.*
.... (13 to 2 op 5 to 1 tchd 7 to 1) **6**

FREELINE FINISHING [139] 9-11-10 M A FitzGerald, *hld up in tch, wknd appr 4 out, f nxt.*
.... (9 to 1 op 7 to 1 tchd 10 to 1) **f**

663[*] BALLYROE LADY [115] 7-10-0 P Holley, *hld up, steady hdwy frm ch, 3rd whn f 3 out, broke leg, dead.*
.... (10 to 1 op 8 to 1 tchd 12 to 1) **f**

749[4] BRANDESTON [130] 8-11-0 (5*) B Murphy, *chsd ldrs till wknd 11th, tld off whn pld up bef 3 out.*
.... (13 to 2 op 5 to 1 tchd 7 to 1) **pu**

BE SURPRISED [115] 7-9-10[3] (7*) J Clarke, *beh whn hit 11th, sn tld off, behind when pld up bef 3 out.*
.... (100 to 1 op 50 to 1) **pu**

Dist: 12l, 1l, dist, 5l. 4m 58.30s. a 8.30s (10 Ran).

(Mrs R O Steed), P J Hobbs

898 Flavel-Leisure Four Year Old Hurdle (4-y-o) £3,678 2m 110yds...(3:40)

662[8] MIDDLE MARKER (Ire) 11-0 Diane Clay, *hld up in rear, mstk 3 out, hdwy nxt, rdn and styd on to ld 50 yards out*................. (25 to 1 op 20 to 1 tchd 50 to 1) **1**

716[2] NATIVE CHIEFTAN 11-0 H Davies, *hld up in tch, hdwy 5th, led appr last, rdn and hdd 50 yards out.*
.... (9 to 1 op 8 to 1 tchd 10 to 1) **2**

EDEN'S CLOSE 11-3 D Murphy, *hld up in tch, cld 3 out, ev ch appr last, one pace r-in.* (3 to 1 fav tchd 100 to 30) **3**

ZAMIRAH (Ire) 10-12 D Bridgwater, *hit 1st, led, rdn 2 out, hdd appr last, sn btn*..............(6 to 1 op 4 to 1) 4
KADI (Ger) 11-3 A Maguire, *hld up in tch, hdwy 5th, hrd rdn 2 out, sn wknd*...............(7 to 2 op 3 to 1) 5
DOMINANT SERENADE 11-7 C Grant, *trkd ldrs till 3 out and wknd 3 out*.................. (7 to 2 op 3 to 1) 6
MONA MINE (Ire) 10-9 (5*) B Murphy, *al beh, tld off frm 3 out*....................(14 to 1 tchd 16 to 1) 7
648⁵ MAJOR BUGLER (Ire) (v) 11-3 J Railton, *trkd ldr to 5th, btn whn hit 3 out, tld off...* (13 to 2 op 4 to 1) 8
597⁶ ROCKY BAY 10-2 (7*) Mr J L Llewellyn, *pld hrd, in tch till wknd 3 out, tld off*............(50 to 1 op 33 to 1) 9
DUTY SERGEANT (Ire) 11-0 G Bradley, *al beh, tld off 4th, pld up bef nxt*.........(50 to 1 op 25 to 1 tchd 66 to 1) pu
Dist: 1l, 2½l, 6l, 1½l, nk, 25l, 1½l, 7l. 3m 55.10s. a 6.10s (10 Ran).
SR: 42/41/41/30/33/36/4/5/-/ (Miss M O'Donnell), W Clay

899 Leisure Thinking Sink Novices' Chase (5-y-o and up) £3,626 2m 1f...........(4:10)

AMTRAK EXPRESS 6-11-1 M A FitzGerald, *made virtually all, drw clr frm 2 out*............(7 to 2 fav op 3 to 1) 1
WHAT'S IN ORBIT 8-11-1 G Bradley, *al prmnt, dsptd ld 5 out to nxt, outpcd frm 2 out.*
.........................(4 to 1 op 7 to 2 tchd 9 to 2) 2
PARDON ME SIR 9-11-1 S Hodgson, *mid-div, styd on one pace frm 3 out*.......(25 to 1 op 12 to 1 tchd 33 to 1) 3
DURRINGTON 7-11-1 C Maude, *beh, nvr on terms.*
.........................(25 to 1 op 14 to 1 tchd 33 to 1) 4
694* SOCIAL CLIMBER 9-11-5 S McNeill, *prmnt till wknd appr 4 out*....................(9 to 2 op 6 to 1) 5
633³ PICKETSTONE 6-11-1 G McCourt, *al beh.*
.........................(20 to 1 op 14 to 1) 6
TITUS GOLD 8-11-1 C Grant, *al beh, tld off frm 5 out.*
.........................(20 to 1 op 12 to 1 tchd 25 to 1) 7
710 BARGE BOY 9-11-1 Peter Hobbs, *prmnt, blun badly 4th, sn reco'red, wkng whn hit 3 out, collapsed bef last, dead*..................(9 to 2 op 7 to 2) pu
CAPSIZE 7-11-1 D Murphy, *al beh, tld off whn pld up bef 4 out*................(20 to 1 op 16 to 1 tchd 25 to 1) pu
DREAMERS DELIGHT 7-11-1 A Maguire, *in tch whn became distressed and pld up bef 8th, dead.*
.........................(4 to 1 op 7 to 2 tchd 9 to 2) pu
464* CHARLIE JOHNSON (bl) 9-10-8 (7*) P McLoughlin, *in tch to 7th, tld off whn pld up bef last.*
.........................(11 to 1 op 10 to 1 tchd 12 to 1) pu
Dist: 10l, 10l, 3l, 8l, 30l. 4m 4.50s. a 3.50s (11 Ran).
SR: 44/34/24/-/-/-/ (Amtrak Express Parcels Limited), N J Henderson

900 Seven Barrows Handicap Hurdle (0-145 5-y-o and up) £4,467 2m 110yds.....(4:40)

762² NAHAR [116] 8-10-6 H Davies, *wtd wth, cld on ldr 3rd, mstk nxt, sn led, drvn out r-in.*
.........................(5 to 2 fav tchd 100 to 30) 1
849² CHILD OF THE MIST [116] 7-10-6 J R Kavanagh, *hld up, hdwy 3rd, wnt second appr 5th, ev ch frm nxt till rdn and no imprsn r-in....*(9 to 2 op 4 to 1 tchd 5 to 1) 2
GIVENTIME [138] 5-11-7 (7*) D Fortt, *prmnt, outpcd 3 out, rallied and kpt on r-in.* (13 to 2 op 3 to 1 tchd 7 to 1) 3
MARTHA'S SON [130] 6-11-6 S McNeill, *hld up in rear, gd hdwy appr 3 out, one pace aftr nxt.*
.........................(5 to 1 op 4 to 1 tchd 11 to 2) 4
BIBENDUM [115] 7-10-5 Peter Hobbs, *chsd ldrs, outpcd 5th, styd on one pace frm 2 out.*
.........................(10 to 1 op 12 to 1 tchd 14 to 1) 5
BALLY CLOVER [128] 6-11-4 M A FitzGerald, *led till hdd appr 5th, wknd quickly approaching 2 out.*
.........................(8 to 1 op 6 to 1) 6
WINTER SQUALL [138] 5-12-0 A Maguire, *hld up, effrt appr 3 out, sn btn, eased, tld off.*
.........................(4 to 1 op 5 to 1 tchd 9 to 2) 7
Dist: 1½l, 2½l, 1½l, nk, 8l, dist. 3m 54.60s. a 5.60s (7 Ran).
SR: 39/37/56/46/30/35/-/ (Ralph Cross), S Dow

901 EBF Stakes National Hunt Flat Race (4,5,6-y-o) £2,374 2m 110yds.....(5:10)

MISTER NOVA 4-10-7 (7*) Mr C Vigors, *hld up in mid-div, hdwy 5 fs out, led o'r 2 out, quickened clr, easily.*
.........................(12 to 1 op 5 to 1 tchd 20 to 1) 1
CONEY ROAD 4-10-7 (7*) J Hunter, *hld up in rear, hdwy 6 fs out, ev ch o'r 2 out, outpcd by wnr.*
.........................(9 to 2 op 4 to 1 tchd 7 to 1) 2
634* GOOD INSIGHT (Ire) 5-11-2 (5*) J McCarthy, *hld up, hdwy hfwy, ev ch till outpcd ins fnl 2 fs....*(9 to 2 op 3 to 1) 3
723* JUNGLE RITES (Ire) 5-11-0 (7*) G Tormey, *nvr far away, rdn and ev ch o'r 2 fs out, one pace.*
.........................(7 to 4 fav op 2 to 1) 4+
DEAR DO 6-10-7 (7*) Pat Thompson, *rcd in tch, kpt on one pace fnl 2 fs.*........(20 to 1 op 8 to 1) 4+
GOSPEL (Ire) 4-10-2 (7*) Mr S Joynes, *chsd ldrs, rdn 3 fs out, sn outpcd.*..........(20 to 1 op 12 to 1 tchd 25 to 1) 6
CONNAUGHT CRUSADER 5-11-0 (7*) Mr G Lewis, *prmnt, led o'r 4 fs out, rdn and hdd over 2 out, sn wknd.*
.........................(7 to 1 op 5 to 1 tchd 8 to 1) 7

CRADLERS 5-10-9 (5*) C Burnett-Wells, *mid-div, nvr nr to chal*...........................(33 to 1 op 16 to 1) 8
HURRICANE HANKS 4-11-0 V Slattery, *chsd ldrs, no hdwy fnl 3 fs*...........................(20 to 1 op 9 to 1) 9
FERAL BAY (Ire) 4-11-0 Mr Raymond White, *hld up in rear, styd on fnl 3 fs, nvr dngrs.*.........(20 to 1 op 10 to 1) 10
DREAMLINE 4-10-6* (7*) R Williamson, *al mid-div.*
.........................(33 to 1 tchd 40 to 1) 11
LONZA VALLEY 4-10-11 (3*) W Marston, *nvr nr to chal.*
.........................(25 to 1 op 10 to 1) 12
LOYAL GAIT (NZ) 5-10-7 (7*) K Brown, *al mid-div.*
.........................(25 to 1 op 10 to 1) 13
TREENS FOLLY 4-10-7 (7*) L Dace, *chsd ldrs till wknd 6 fs out.*...........................(40 to 1 op 16 to 1) 14
POLICEMANS PRIDE (Fr) 4-10-7 (7*) J Clarke, *al beh.*
.........................(40 to 1 op 33 to 1) 15
ROYAL GAIT (NZ) 5-10-7 (7*) R Darke, *al beh.*
.........................(16 to 1 op 7 to 1 tchd 20 to 1) 16
743⁵ KING RUST 5-10-7 (7*) Mr J L Llewellyn, *al beh.*
.........................(33 to 1 tchd 25 to 1) 17
31² MR GREY FELLOW (Ire) 5-11-0 Mr J Durkan, *al beh.*
.........................(40 to 1 op 12 to 1 tchd 20 to 1) 18
ASLAR (Ire) 4-10-7 (7*) P Moore, *al in rear.*
.........................(40 to 1 op 16 to 1) 19
COTTAGE RAIDER (Ire) 4-10-11 (3*) D O'Sullivan, *in tch early, beh frm hfwy.*...........(33 to 1 op 20 to 1) 20
WATERBEACH VILLAGE (Ire) 5-10-7 (7*) Mr M Gingell, *led, sn clr, wknd and hdd hfwy, soon in rear.*
.........................(40 to 1 op 20 to 1) 21
AFTICA 6-10-11 (3*) D Meredith, *chsd ldr, led hfwy, hdd o'r 4 fs out, drpd out quickly*......(40 to 1 op 16 to 1) 22
ITS GRAND 4-10-7 (7*) A Flannigan, *beh frm hfwy.*
.........................(40 to 1 op 33 to 1) 23
JIMMY-JADE 4-10-9 (5*) D Leahy, *in tch early, beh frm hfwy.*...........................(40 to 1 op 33 to 1) 24
Dist: 12l, 3l, 1½l, dd-ht, 4l, ½l, 5l, 7l, 2½l, 2l. 3m 48.60s. (24 Ran).
(Lord Matthews), N J Henderson

WEXFORD (IRE) (good)
Friday October 22nd

902 New Ross Maiden Hurdle (4-y-o) £2,243 2¼m 100yds........................(2:30)

798⁷ BALLYHYLAND (Ire) 11-4 S H O'Donovan, ...(5 to 1) 1
257³ MIA GEORGINA (Ire) 11-4 J F Titley, ...(4 to 1 fav) 2
803⁵ CASTLE CELEBRITY (Ire) 10-13 K F O'Brien, ...(7 to 1) 3
692 THE ODD TIME (Ire) 10-13 (5*) C O'Brien, ...(16 to 1) 4
797 JIMMY THE WEED (Ire) 10-11 (7*) P A Roache, ...(33 to 1) 5
671⁸ PEPPERONI EXPRESS (Ire) 11-9 C F Swan, ...(5 to 1) 6
692 JO JO BOY (Ire) 11-4 F J Flood, ...(13 to 2) 7
798³ LITTLE AND OFTEN (Ire) 10-13 D H O'Connor, ...(12 to 1) 8
798 HAVE A BRANDY (Ire) 11-4 A J O'Brien, ...(12 to 1) 9
276⁵ ROYAL OUTING (Ire) 10-13 (5*) T P Rudd, ...(12 to 1) 10
692 WEE RIVER (Ire) 11-4 Mr T S Costello, ...(5 to 1) 11
535 SYLVIES MISSILES (Ire) 10-8 (5*) C P Dunne, ...(33 to 1) 12
803⁴ KNOCNAGORE (Ire) 10-13 Mr D K Budge, ...(10 to 1) f
671 MIDDLE SUSIE (Ire) 10-8 (5*) T P Treacy, ...(33 to 1) ro
Dist: 3½l, 2l, 2½l, 3l. 4m 27.00s. (14 Ran).
(Thomas Lennon), Anthony Mullins

903 Garryrichard Stud Novice Hurdle (Qualifier) (5-y-o and up) £2,933 3m......(3:00)

708³ RICH TRADITION (Ire) 5-12-0 C O'Dwyer, ...(6 to 4 fav) 1
689 CLOSUTTON EXPRESS 7-12-0 Mr W P Mullins, ...(8 to 1) 2
LUMINOUS LIGHT 6-10-12 (3*) Mr M Phillips, ...(20 to 1) 3
538⁴ GOOLDS GOLD 7-10-13 (7*) P A Roche, ...(13 to 2) 4
DUBLIN SAGA 8-10-8 (7*) Mr P English, ...(20 to 1) 5
672⁷ FAMBO LAD (Ire) 5-11-6 Mr J A Berry, ...(10 to 1) 6
KILDERIHEEN 6-11-1 (5*) C O'Brien, ...(20 to 1) 7
572⁴ SHOW YOUR HAND (Ire) 5-11-6 T Horgan, ...(6 to 1) 8
746³ LE BRAVE 7-12-0 C F Swan, ...(4 to 1) 9
53 RAMDON ROCKS 6-11-1 (5*) T P Rudd, ...(16 to 1) 10
572 FIFTYBETWEENYE (Ire) 5-10-10 (5*) J R Barry, ..(33 to 1) 11
DECADAS 7-11-6 S H O'Donovan, ...(20 to 1) 12
638⁹ BELGRAVIA BOY 5-11-6 M Duffy, ...(14 to 1) pu
807 WARASH 7-11-8 D P Fagan, ...(14 to 1) pu
Dist: 7l, ½l, 2½l, ¾l. 6m 14.10s. (14 Ran).
(D R Killian), Anthony Mullins

904 Traynors Hardware Handicap Hurdle (4-y-o and up) £2,760 2¼m 100yds.....(3:30)

689³ BROOK COTTAGE (Ire) [-] 4-10-10 K F O'Brien, ..(13 to 2) 1
708⁴ TEMPLEROAN PRINCE [-] 6-11-5 C F Swan, ...(7 to 2) 2
831⁴ BELEEK CASTLE [-] 7-11-1 P McWilliams, ...(3 to 1 fav) 3
CELTIC SAILS (Ire) [-] 5-10-8 (7*) P O Casey, .(10 to 1) 4
831 PALACE GEM [-] 6-10-9 (5*) Mr P J Casey, ...(7 to 1) 5
ONABUNDA [-] 7-9-1 (7*) F Byrne, ...(25 to 1) 6
805⁸ HUGH DANIELS [-] 5-9-10 (7*) Mr M Warren, ...(10 to 1) 7
MYSTIC GALE (Ire) [-] 5-9-12 (7*) Mr P M Cloke, .(10 to 1) 8
637⁸ HI MILLIE [-] 7-10-11 P L Malone, ...(10 to 1) 9
377 CEDAR COURT (Ire) [-] 5-11-7 (7*) G V Butler, .(12 to 1) 10
528 SPEAKING TOUR (USA) [-] 5-11-2 D H O'Connor, .(25 to 1) 11
797⁶ EYREFIELD ROSE [-] 7-9-8 T Horgan, ...(16 to 1) 12

689 SYLVIA'S SAFFRON [-] (bl) 6-9-5 (7*) M P Moran, . . (25 to 1) 13
689 THE MAD MONK [-] 8-10-8 (7*) Mr D K Budge, ... (20 to 1) 14
Dist: 1½l, 1½l, 4l, ½l. 4m 25.00s. (14 Ran).
(T A O'Doherty), Michael Hourigan

905 Slaney Meats Novice Chase (5-y-o and up) £5,520 2½m. . . . . (4:00)

635^{2} WINDS OF WAR 8-12-0 C F Swan, ... (5 to 4 fav) 1
556^{6} NORDIC SUN (Ire) 5-11-10 J F Titley, ... (9 to 2) 2
575 OUT OF COURT 8-12-0 T Horgan, ... (8 to 1) 3
506^{2} SILVER GIPSEY 7-11-9 P L Malone, ... (10 to 1) 4
799^{4} MCMAHON'S RIVER 6-11-9 D H O'Connor, ... (9 to 1) 5
583^{5} SHUIL LE CHEILE 6-11-4 (5*) C O'Brien, ... (20 to 1) 6
799^{6} POST MASTER 7-11-9 (5*) M M Treacy, ... (10 to 1) 7
CAPINCUR EILE 7-11-7 (7*) Mr N C Kelleher, ... (14 to 1) 8
618^{3} JOHNSON 7-12-0 J Shortt, ... (14 to 1) 9
571^{9} TAKE IT EASY KID (Ire) 5-11-5 F Woods, ... (20 to 1) 10
799 WHEATSTONE BRIDGE 7-12-0 K F O'Brien, ... (14 to 1) 11
690^{5} CLONEENVERB 9-11-4 (5*) D P Murphy, ... (14 to 1) 12
575 TRANSCRIBER (USA) 6-11-7 (7*) P A Roche, ... (12 to 1) pu
799 CARDAN 7-12-0 C O'Dwyer, ... (50 to 1) pu
Dist: 4½l, 3½l, 1l, 12l. 5m 22.80s. (14 Ran).
(Mrs Miles Valentine), M F Morris

906 Somers Mercedes Commercials Handicap Chase (4-y-o and up) £2,760 3m. . . . . (4:30)

800^{2} ROSSBEIGH CREEK [-] 6-10-5 F J Flood, ... (7 to 2 jt-fav) 1
800^{5} ANTRIM COUNTY [-] 8-11-2 (3*) T J Mitchell, ... (10 to 1) 2
512^{5} MID-DAY GAMBLE [-] 9-10-5 L P Cusack, ... (12 to 1) 3
800* FAIRY PARK [-] (bl) 8-10-5 (4ex) F Woods, ... (5 to 1) 4
691^{8} ALTNABROCKY [-] 9-9-12 H Rogers, ... (14 to 1) 5
691^{2} INCH MAID [-] 7-9-8[1] (7*) P A Roche, ... (7 to 2 jt-fav) 6
MARKET MOVER [-] 7-11-12 C F Swan, ... (10 to 1) pu
799 JOHNJOES PRIDE [-] (bl) 9-9-7 T Horgan, ... (8 to 1) pu
800 ASK FRANK [-] 7-11-5 K F O'Brien, ... (12 to 1) pu
430^{9} MISCHIEF MOON [-] 8-9-2 (5*) C O'Brien, ... (33 to 1) pu
635 SIRANA [-] 7-9-2 (5*) M G Cleary, ... (20 to 1) pu
635 LADY DIAMOND [-] 7-9-7 P McWilliams, ... (16 to 1) pu
Dist: 6l, 3½l, 2l, dist. 6m 21.20s. (12 Ran).
(H Ferguson), F Flood

907 Talbot Hotel Mares Flat Race (4-y-o and up) £2,760 2¼m 100yds. . . . . (5:00)

709^{6} STRONG SERENADE (Ire) 4-10-13 (7*) Mr P English, ... (3 to 1 fav) 1
255^{4} SIMPLY SARAH 7-11-6 (5*) Mr H F Cleary, ... (6 to 1) 2
252^{7} MARYJO (Ire) 4-11-1 (5*) Mr J A Nash, ... (14 to 1) 3
229^{7} TOURIG LE MOSS 6-11-4 (7*) Mr R Foley, ... (10 to 1) 4
SHUIL (Ire) 4-10-13 (7*) Mr E J O'Rourke, ... (14 to 1) 5
536 MULLAGHMEEN 7-11-6 (5*) Mr J P Berry, ... (6 to 1) 6
BLAZING COMET 7-11-8 (3*) Mr A R Coonan, ... (7 to 1) 7
638^{4} CASTLE CLUB (Ire) 4-10-13 (7*) Miss C O'Neill, . . . (12 to 1) 8
DRUMCILL LASS (Ire) 5-11-11 Mr S R Murphy, ... (4 to 1) 9
692 SIOBHAILIN DUBH (Ire) 4-11-6 Mr A P O'Brien, ... (6 to 1) 10
801 ASHTON'S VENTURE (Ire) 5-11-8 (3*) Mrs J M Mullins, ... (10 to 1) 11
BETTY BALFOUR 7-11-11 Mr J A Flynn, ... (16 to 1) 12
ANOTHER STAR (Ire) 4-11-6 Mr K D Budds, ... (14 to 1) 13
GALE GRIFFIN (Ire) 4-10-13 (7*) Mr P J Kelly, ... (12 to 1) 14
531 A WINDY CITIZEN (Ire) 4-10-13 (7*) Mr W M O'Sullivan, ... (25 to 1) 15
Dist: 1½l, 5½l, 1l, 1½l. 4m 22.70s. (15 Ran).
(J R Kidd), Thomas Foley

908 Killinick Flat Race (4-y-o and up) £2,243 2¼m 100yds. . . . . (5:30)

801^{3} THATS A SECRET 5-11-4 (7*) Mr P English, ... (5 to 2) 1
801^{6} ISN'T THAT NICE (Ire) 5-11-4 (7*) Mr M Brennan, . . . (5 to 1) 2
576^{4} GLAD'S NIGHT (Ire) 4-11-5 (3*) Mrs J M Mullins, ... (11 to 10 fav) 3
636 GREAT ADVENTURE (Ire) 5-11-8 (3*) Mr D Marnane, ... (12 to 1) 4
709 LARRYS PENNY (Ire) 4-10-10 (5*) Mr H F Cleary, . . (16 to 1) 5
638^{5} SAMMIES DOZER (Ire) 5-10-13 (7*) Mr D J Kavanagh, ... (8 to 1) 6
692 RED BARONS LADY (Ire) 4-10-12 (3*) Mrs S McCarthy, ... (8 to 1) 7
801 MULLENAGLOCH 6-11-4 (7*) Mr M A Cahill, ... (16 to 1) 8
Dist: 2l, 5½l, 11l, ½l. 4m 23.50s. (8 Ran).
(James J Foley), Thomas Foley

CATTERICK (good)
Saturday October 23rd
Going Correction: PLUS 0.05 sec. per fur.

909 St Pauls Novices' Chase (5-y-o and up) £1,618 2m. . . . . (2:20)

BANK VIEW 8-11-0 M Dwyer, *hmpd by faller second, improved to join ldrs appr 4 out, pushed alng approaching last, str run to ld cl hme.* . . . . (Evens fav tchd 11 to 10 on) 1
729 SHREWD JOHN 7-11-0 R Garritty, *settled gng wl, led 2 out, quickened clr appr last, rdn and jst ct.* . . . . (8 to 1 op 6 to 1) 2
VAYRUA (Fr) 8-10-11 (3*) A Larnach, *nvr far away, drvn alng whn pace quickened frm 2 out, kpt on same pace r-in.* . . . . (5 to 1) 3
REEF LARK 8-11-0 K Johnson, *trkd ldrs, effrt aftr 4 out, reminder nxt, kpt on same pace.* . . (33 to 1 op 20 to 1) 4
543^{6} HEIR OF EXCITEMENT 8-11-0 J Callaghan, *al hndy, led 5th to 2 out, rdn and no extr betw last two.* . . . . (20 to 1 op 16 to 1) 5
820 THE COUNTRY TRADER 7-11-0 N Doughty, *jmpd carefully, improved on bit hfwy, eased whn btn aftr 4 out.* . . . . (25 to 1 op 16 to 1) 6
729^{4} PHALAROPE (Ire) (v) 5-10-13 Mr A Walton, *chsd ldrs, feeling pace appr 4 out, fdd.* . . . . (40 to 1 op 25 to 1) 7
819^{8} INVERINATE 8-11-0 T Reed, *chsd alng to keep up hfwy, lost tch frm 5 out, tld off.* . . . . (33 to 1 op 20 to 1) 8
782^{4} GOLDEN BANKER (Ire) 5-10-13 K Jones, *sn tld off, plodded round.* . . . . (66 to 1 op 33 to 1) 9
729 PASSAGE TO FREEDOM (v) 11-10-9 D Telfer, *chsd alng beh ldrs whn f 6th.* . . . . (66 to 1 op 50 to 1) f
SHAMIRANI 7-11-0 A Merrigan, *settled in rear till f second.* . . . . (20 to 1 op 14 to 1) f
RAINHAM 6-11-0 C Grant, *f 1st.* . . . . . (16 to 1 op 14 to 1) f
641^{2} BEST EFFORT 7-11-0 A Orkney, *charged tapes bef strt, led till f second, dead.* . . . . (8 to 1 op 16 to 1) f
820^{4} NORTHERN VISION 6-11-0 B Storey, *chsd ldrs, hrd at work frm hfwy, no imprsn whn f 2 out.* . . . . (33 to 1 op 20 to 1) f
ANOTHER RED 5-10-13 S Turner, *wth ldrs, lft in ld second, hdd 5th, tiring in 6th pl whn f 3 out.* . . . . (33 to 1 op 25 to 1) f
766 RISEUPWILLIEREILLY 7-11-0 N Smith, *midfield whn blun and uns rdr 4th.* . . . . (100 to 1 op 50 to 1) ur
Dist: Nk, 5l, 1l, hd, 12l, 4l, 12l, dist. 3m 59.10s. a 10.10s (16 Ran).
(Date (Bloodstock) Ltd), N Tinkler

910 Picton Novices' Hurdle (Div I) (4-y-o and up) £1,165 2m. . . . . (2:50)

SILVER SAMURAI 4-10-11 D Byrne, *settled gng wl, quickened ahead aftr 3 out, jmpd lft and blun nxt, blunded last, styd on r-in.* (11 to 4 jt-fav op 5 to 2 tchd 3 to 1) 1
771^{5} VAL DE RAMA (Ire) 4-10-6 (5*) P Waggott, *al hndy, led aftr 3 out till hdd nxt, kpt on same pace r-in.* . . . . (20 to 1 op 25 to 1) 2
CALL ME EARLY 8-10-5 (7*) R Moore, *settled midfield, jnd issue appr 3 out, styd on same pace frm betw last 2.* . . . . (33 to 1) 3
HIGH MIND (Fr) 4-10-11 N Doughty, *trkd ldrs, blun 4th, lost grnd aftr 3 out, ran on stdly frm betw last 2, prmsg.* . . . . (16 to 1 op 14 to 1) 4
TREVVEETHAN (Ire) 4-10-11 D Wilkinson, *tucked away beh ldrs, effrt und pres 3 out, kpt on, no imprsn.* . . . . (12 to 1 op 10 to 1) 5
ASTRALEON (Ire) 5-10-12 B Storey, *nvr far away, ev ch appr 3 out, no extr betw last 2.* . . . . . (9 to 2 tchd 5 to 1) 6
721^{5} BECK COTTAGE 5-10-12 J Callaghan, *made most till hdd aftr 3 out, fdd.* . . . . (12 to 1 op 14 to 1 tchd 10 to 1) 7
771* JOMOVE 4-11-4 R Hodge, *settled off the pace, pushed alng hfwy, styd on, nvr able to chal.* . . . . (11 to 4 jt-fav op 3 to 1 tchd 100 to 30) 8
717 RED BEACON 6-10-12 C Dennis, *tucked away in midfield, effrt aftr 4 out, no extr appr 2 out.* . . . . (50 to 1 op 33 to 1) 9
551^{5} MURASIL (USA) 4-10-11 A Orkney, *tucked away in midfield, drvn alng whn pace quickened 3 out, fdd.* . . . . (50 to 1 op 33 to 1) 10
771 DONEGAL STYLE (Ire) (bl) 5-10-9 (3*) D J Moffatt, *wth ldrs, struggling to hold pl aftr 3 out, sn btn.* . . . . (8 to 1 op 12 to 1) 11
821^{5} GROUSE-N-HEATHER 4-9-13 (7*) F Perratt, *not fluent, chsd ldg bunch, struggling appr 4 out, sn lost tch.* . . . . (8 to 1 tchd 9 to 1) 12
771^{8} MARSDEN ROCK (bl) 6-10-0 (7*) J Supple, *trkd ldrs, ev ch aftr 4 out, fdd frm nxt.* . . . . (10 to 1 tchd 12 to 1) 13
SPIDERS DELIGHT 5-10-12 T Reed, *struggling to keep up hfwy, tld off.* . . . . (20 to 1 op 16 to 1) 14
Dist: 4l, 2l, ¾l, 8l, 2½l, hd, 4l, 2½l, 2l, 5l. 3m 48.40s. a 7.40s (14 Ran).
SR: 17/13/12/10/2/-/-/2/-/ (J D Cable), Mrs V A Aconley

911 Darlington And Stockton Times Handicap Chase (0-115 5-y-o and up) £2,022 3m 1f 110yds. . . . . (3:20)

542* CAPITAL PUNISHMENT [95] 7-10-8 R Garritty, *hit 1st, reco'red to track ldrs, led 2 out, styd on strly r-in.* . . . . (3 to 1 fav) 1
579^{7} TRUELY ROYAL [93] 9-10-6 B Storey, *nvr far away, drvn alng aftr 4 out, rallied frm betw last 2, kpt on.* . . . . (10 to 1 op 12 to 1) 2
696^{4} RADICAL LADY [107] 9-10-13 (7*) J Supple, *al hndy, led 11th, jnd 6 out, hdd and rdn 2 out, no extr.* . . . . (9 to 2 op 4 to 1 tchd 5 to 1) 3

726^{2} LAPIAFFE [100] 9-10-13 A Orkney, *wth ldrs, led 3rd to 11th, struggling aftr 4 out, sn outpcd.* ....(4 to 1 op 3 to 1 tchd 9 to 2) 4
789^{3} CHOCTAW [97] 9-10-10 Mrs A Farrell, *settled midfield, outpcd and struggling aftr one circuit, styd on ag'n frm 4 out, no imprsn*.....(9 to 2 op 4 to 1 tchd 5 to 1) 5
ITYFUL [97] (bl) 7-10-5 (5*) D Bentley, *patiently rdn, jnd ldr 6 out, ridden appr 3 out, sn btn*....(20 to 1 op 14 to 1) 6
822 LAURIE-O [106] 9-11-5 A Merrigan, *patiently rdn, took clr order aftr one circuit, feeling pace whn blun 7 out, not reco'r*....(25 to 1 op 33 to 1) 7
539 FOUR TRIX [115] 12-11-7 (7*) B Harding, *pushed alng towards rear whn blun and uns rdr 7th.* ....(10 to 1 op 6 to 1) ur
740^{4} SOONER STILL [108] (v) 9-11-0 (7*) Judy Davies, *trkd ldrs, blun tenth, lost tch and pld up bef 5 out.* ....(20 to 1 op 12 to 1) pu
677^{6} BEN TIRRAN [91] (v) 9-10-4 D Telfer, *slight ld to 3rd, blun badly 8th, not reco'r, pld up bef nxt.* ....(16 to 1 op 25 to 1 tchd 14 to 1) pu
624^{6} SPEECH [98] 10-10-11 T Reed, *al struggling and beh, tld off whn pld up bef 5 out*....(50 to 1 op 33 to 1) pu
786^{4} THE WALTZING MOUSE [87] (bl) 10-9-7 (7*) F Perratt, *sn drvn alng, tld off whn pld up bef 5 out.* ....(50 to 1 op 33 to 1) pu

Dist: ¾l, 12l, 12l, 10l, 10l, 2½l. 6m 30.00s. a 15.00s (12 Ran).
(J N Hinchliffe), M D Hammond

912 Sellfield Selling Hurdle (4-y-o and up) £1,423 2m.......... (3:50)

787^{2} HYPNOTIST 6-11-2 (3*) N Bentley, *wtd wth beh ldrs, gd hdwy 4 out, led appr 2 out, styd on wl r-in.* ....(3 to 1 fav op 5 to 2 tchd 9 to 4 and 7 to 2) 1
BAND SARGEANT (Ire) 4-10-11 N Doughty, *trkd ldrs, rdn 2 chal two out, kpt on same pace r-in.* (5 to 1 op 3 to 1) 2
818^{7} COOL DUDE 7-11-9 (3*) D J Moffatt, *patiently rdn, gd hdwy 3 out, effrt and hng lft und pres aftr last, styd on*....(12 to 1 tchd 10 to 1) 3
J P MORGAN (v) 5-11-5 A Orkney, *al hndy, slight ld 3rd, hdd bef 2 out, one pace*....(6 to 1 op 4 to 1) 4
JOHN NAMAN (Ire) 4-10-13 (5*) P Waggott, *wth ldrs, rdn alng whn pace quickened betw last 2, one pace.* ....(12 to 1 op 25 to 1) 5
659^{2} THE HIDDEN CITY 7-11-5 (7*) J Supple, *nvr far away, hit 4th, rdn frm 3 out, no imprsn*.... (16 to 1 tchd 20 to 1) 6
RICHMOND (Ire) 5-11-5 D Wilkinson, *patiently rdn, improved frm 3 out, eased whn btn aftr nxt*... (25 to 1) 7
766^{4} WELLSY LAD (USA) 6-10-12 R Garritty, *took str hold, improved hfwy, no imprsn on ldrs frm 3 out*... (14 to 1) 8
766^{7} JUMPING CACTUS 4-10-11 A S Smith, *settled off the pace, improved 4 out, fdd last 2.* (25 to 1 tchd 33 to 1) 9
766^{6} WAWEEWAWOO (Ire) 5-10-2 (5*) D Bentley, *in tch, struggling to go pace hfwy, nvr rch ldrs*....(50 to 1) 10
839^{5} KAGRAM QUEEN 5-11-0 R Hodge, *patiently rdn, imprvg whn blun 4 out, hit nxt, not reco'r*... (8 to 1 op 6 to 1) 11
787^{5} SWANK GILBERT 7-10-5 (7*) Carol Cuthbert, *al pressing ldrs, feeling pace whn hit 3 out, sn btn*....(200 to 1) 12
640 HIGHCLIFFE JESTER 4-10-11 C Hawkins, *settled midfield, effrt whn hit 3 out, sn lost tch*....(100 to 1) 13
818 OLD MORTALITY 7-11-5 B Storey, *settled midfield, effrt and feeling pace 4 out, nvr able to chal.* ....(25 to 1 op 33 to 1) 14
622 ABSOLUTE DANCER 4-9-13 (7*) S Taylor, *ran in snatches, lost grnd hfwy, no dngr aftr*....(200 to 1) 15
640^{9} SHANNON KING (Ire) (bl) 5-10-12 D Byrne, *not fluent, trkd ldrs till rdn and btn 3 out*.... (20 to 1 op 25 to 1) 16
ACE REPORTER 4-10-6^{5} (5*) P Midgley, *almost f 1st, beh aftrwards*....(50 to 1) 17
582^{8} NORTH OF WATFORD 8-10-12 C Dennis, *hld up beh ldrs, drvn alng hfwy, nvr a factor*.... (66 to 1) 18
779 BUSHTUCKER 5-10-12 L Wyer, *took keen hold, al beh.* ....(50 to 1) 19
766^{9} NOBBY (bl) 7-10-12 A Mulholland, *wth ldrs, dsptd ld hfwy to 3 out, wknd quickly*....(100 to 1) 20
LADY KHADIJA 7-10-3^{3} (7*) J Driscoll, *led to 3rd, sn struggling, tld off whn pld up bef 2 out*....(200 to 1) pu
818 BLUSHING GOLD (bl) 4-10-6 D Morris, *slwly away, al in rear, tld off whn pld up bef 3 out*.... (200 to 1) pu
WITHOUT LEAVE 4-10-11 A Merrigan, *struggling hfwy, tld off whn pld up bef 2 out*.... (200 to 1) pu

Dist: 2l, hd, 4l, ½l, 3½l, 3½l, 2½l, ½l, 8l, 6l. 3m 48.90s. a 7.90s (23 Ran).
SR: 20/10/25/14/12/16/5/-/-/ (P Goodall), W Bentley

913 St Peters Handicap Chase (0-130 5-y-o and up) £1,970 2m.......... (4:25)

BOSTON ROVER [115] 8-11-4 M Brennan, *nvr far away, led aftr 4 out, clr betw last 2, kpt on strly.* ....(9 to 2 tchd 5 to 1) 1
722^{3} PIMS GUNNER (Ire) [103] 5-10-1 (5*) D Bentley, *trkd ldg trio, drvn alng last 3, styd on und pres.* ....(4 to 1 op 3 to 1 tchd 9 to 2) 2
479^{5} BARKISLAND [98] 9-10-1 L Wyer, *made most to 7th, styd hndy and rdn 3 out, kpt on r-in.* .... (13 to 2 op 8 to 1 tchd 9 to 1) 3
590 GOOD FOR A LAUGH [125] 9-11-7 (7*) Mr D Parker, *al wl plcd, feeling pace 4 out, fdd bef nxt*.... (12 to 1) 4
676 SINGING SAM [102] 8-10-5^{5} K Jones, *jmpd badly rght second, sn struggling, tld off*.... (50 to 1 op 33 to 1) 5
788^{2} ONE FOR THE POT [111] 8-11-0 A Orkney, *patiently rdn, improved to join issue hfwy, ev ch and niggled alng whn f 4 out*....(6 to 4 fav op 5 to 4) f
CIRCULATION [103] 7-10-6 B Storey, *al hndy, led 7th till aftr 4 out, fourth and tired whn f 2 out.* ....(9 to 1 op 8 to 1) f
643^{4} PRESSURE GAME [97] 10-10-0 A Merrigan, *hit second, pressed ldrs to hfwy, losing grnd whn hmpd by faller and uns rdr 4 out*....(20 to 1 tchd 33 to 1) ur

Dist: 10l, 5l, 15l, 25l. 3m 54.80s. a 5.80s (8 Ran).
SR: 40/18/8/20/-/ (P Stoner), O Brennan

914 Ampleforth Handicap Hurdle (0-125 4-y-o and up) £1,772 3m 1f 110yds.......... (5:00)

TROODOS [100] 7-10-5 D Wilkinson, *settled gng wl, slight ld 2 out, hrd pressed r-in, kpt on grimly.* ....(5 to 1 tchd 11 to 2) 1
654* HAZEL LEAF [95] 7-10-0 R Hodge, *nvr far away, led bef 8th, hdd 2 out, rallied aftr last, kpt on.* ....(2 to 1 fav tchd 9 to 4) 2
SERAPHIM (Fr) [96] 4-9-8 (7*) S Taylor, *wtd wth, improved to join issue hfwy, slpd and almost f 8th, rallied, rdn and one pace frm betw last 2*....(6 to 1 tchd 7 to 1) 3
613^{9} ARR EFF BEE [95] (bl) 6-9-9 (5*) D Leahy, *tucked away beh ldrs, hmpd and squeezed out appr 6th, rallied, rdn alng betw last 2, kpt on*.... (20 to 1 op 16 to 1) 4
HUDSON BAY TRADER (USA) [123] 6-11-7 (7*) G Tormey, *patiently rdn, took clr order fnl circuit, outpcd 3 out, styd on ag'n frm betw last 2.* ....(8 to 1 op 7 to 1 tchd 9 to 1) 5
IF YOU SAY SO [95] 7-10-0 A Mulholland, *pld hrd for a circuit, ev ch 3 out, not quicken frm nxt.* ....(33 to 1 op 25 to 1) 6
623^{5} SEXY MOVER [98] 6-10-3 K Johnson, *co'red up in midfield, effrt appr 3 out, rdn and not quicken frm nxt.* ....(12 to 1 op 10 to 1) 7
644^{3} CELTIC BREEZE [103] (v) 10-10-1 (7*) Mr D Parker, *set modest pace, quickened hfwy, hdd bef 8th, wknd quickly frm 3 out*....(7 to 1 tchd 8 to 1) 8
623 TOP VILLAIN [95] 7-10-0 B Storey, *last and gng wl, improved to chal appr 3 out, fdd frm nxt.* ....(12 to 1 tchd 14 to 1 and 10 to 1) 9
478^{4} JUSTICE LEA [95] 13-9-7 (7*) Carol Cuthbert, *pressed ldrs, feeling pace appr 3 out, fdd*.... (100 to 1 op 50 to 1) 10
SHEAN ALAINN (Ire) [95] 5-9-7 (7*) D Ryan, *not fluent, effrt and drvn alng aftr one circuit, nvr dngrs, fnshd lme.* ....(25 to 1 op 16 to 1) 11
779 ROYAL QUARRY [95] 7-10-0 C Dennis, *shwd up wl for a circuit, sn lost tch*.... (200 to 1 op 100 to 1) 12

Dist: 1½l, ¾l, ½l, 5l, 2½l, 5l, 1½l, 6l, 10l, 1l. 6m 30.30s. a 29.30s (12 Ran).
(Scotnorth Racing Ltd), Mrs S M Austin

915 Picton Novices' Hurdle (Div II) (4-y-o and up) £1,165 2m.......... (5:30)

771^{2} IRON BARON (Ire) 4-10-11 J Callaghan, *tucked away in midfield, effrt whn hmpd in melee 4 out, rallied aftr nxt, styd on und pres to ld r-in*.... (4 to 1 op 5 to 2) 1
GORTEERA 7-10-12 M Brennan, *led till aftr 1st, improved on bit to ld after 3 out, rdn and hdd r-in, rallied.* ....(20 to 1 op 14 to 1) 2
JALMUSIQUE 7-10-12 L Wyer, *jmpd wl, patiently rdn, smooth hdwy to chal aftr 3 out, ridden and no extr betw last 2*.... (15 to 8 fav op 6 to 4 tchd 2 to 1) 3
717^{2} FALCONS DAWN 6-10-12 B Storey, *nvr far away, hit 4th, led nxt, hdd aftr 3 out, one pace*... (4 to 1 tchd 9 to 2) 4
836 CZAR NICHOLAS 4-10-11^{5} (5*) S Lyons, *patiently rdn, impeded by fallers 4 out, ran on stdly last 2, prmsg.* ....(20 to 1 op 16 to 1) 5
MAJAL (Ire) 4-10-7^{1} (5*) P Midgley, *trkd ldg bunch, effrt aftr 3 out, outpcd frm nxt*.... (14 to 1 op 8 to 1) 6
723^{8} MANILA RUN (Ire) 4-10-11 D Byrne, *co'red up beh ldrs, effrt hfwy, struggling frm 3 out*....(25 to 1 op 14 to 1) 7
KINDA GROOVY 4-10-11 N Smith, *in tch, bustled alng to keep up hfwy, sn btn*....(16 to 1 op 12 to 1) 8
UNCLES-LAD 5-10-9 (3*) N Bentley, *chsd ldg bunch, feeling pace and rdn 4 out, sn lost tch.* ....(100 to 1 op 66 to 1) 9
547^{5} SILVER FANCY (Ire) 4-10-11 T Reed, *wtd wth, improved frm off the pace 3 out, grad wknd from nxt.* ....(20 to 1 op 14 to 1) 10
WILLUBELONG 4-10-11 S Turner, *struggling to go pace hfwy, tld off*....(100 to 1 op 66 to 1) 11
809 MISTRESS BEE (USA) 4-10-6 A S Smith, *led aftr 1st till hdd and f 4 out*.... (25 to 1 op 14 to 1) f
658^{8} TIBBS INN 4-10-11 M Ranger, *trkd ldg pair till brght dwn 4 out*....(14 to 1 tchd 20 to 1) bd
717* COL BUCKMORE (Ire) 5-11-5 N Doughty, *patiently rdn, imprvg whn brght dwn in melee 4 out.* ....(6 to 1 op 5 to 1) bd

Dist: Hd, 5l, 5l, ½l, 4l, 15l, 5l, 1½l, dist, 6l. 3m 50.00s. a 9.00s (14 Ran).
SR: 1/2/-/-/-/-/ (Raymond Gomersall), Mrs V A Aconley

NATIONAL HUNT RESULTS 1993-94

HUNTINGDON (good to firm)
Saturday October 23rd
Going Correction: PLUS 0.20 sec. per fur. (races 1,3,-5,7), PLUS 0.05 (2,4,6)

916 Henkel Novices' Hurdle (Div I) (4-y-o and up) £1,866 2m 110yds. . . . . (1:55)

705² BLAZON OF TROY 4-11-4 S Smith Eccles, *chsd ldrs, led appr 3 out, clr whn mstk last, styd on wl.*
. . . . (15 to 2 op 5 to 1 tchd 8 to 1)   1
731* TARDA 6-11-0 P Niven, *prog aftr 4th, rdn and one pace frm 2 out* . . . . (4 to 1 op 5 to 2)   2
CARPET SLIPPERS 7-10-7 D Bridgwater, *hdwy 4th, not quicken und pres frm 2 out.*
. . . . (20 to 1 op 10 to 1 tchd 25 to 1)   3
705⁸ BUSTLING AROUND 6-10-7 M Bosley, *prog 5th, styd on one pace appr 2 out.* (40 to 1 op 25 to 1 tchd 50 to 1)   4
SCALP 'EM (Ire) 5-10-12 M A FitzGerald, *pressed ldrs till appr 5th, lost tch frm nxt, mstk 2 out.*
. . . . (16 to 1 op 8 to 1 tchd 20 to 1)   5
CAPTAIN MARMALADE 4-10-11 D Murphy, *wl plcd til hmpd frm 3 out.* . . . . . (16 to 1 op 10 to 1 tchd 20 to 1)   6
SPANISH STORM (Ire) 4-10-11 A Carroll, *hld up towards rear, lost tch frm 5th..* (13 to 2 op 5 to 1 tchd 7 to 1)   7
AMADEUS AES 4-10-11 N Mann, *hld up towards rear, nvr rchd ldrs, tld off....* (16 to 1 op 10 to 1 tchd 20 to 1)   8
SWING LUCKY 8-10-12 B Clifford, *rcd in mid-div to 5th, sn wknd, tld off...................* (50 to 1 op 33 to 1)   9
BALTIC EXCHANGE (Can) 4-10-11 M Richards, *cl up, lft in ld 4th, hdd and wknd 3 out, tld off.*
. . . . (5 to 2 fav op 7 to 4 tchd 4 to 1) 10
LEXUS (Ire) 5-10-12 S McNeill, *wl plcd, second and ev ch whn f 2 out....* (16 to 1 op 6 to 1 tchd 20 to 1)   f
748* HOMILE 5-10-12 (7*) S Lycett, *led til pld up lme 4th.*
. . . . (5 to 1 op 7 to 1) pu
GOLDEN SICKLE (USA) 4-10-13² A Coogan, *settled in rear, mstk 3rd, tld off whn pld up bef 3 out.*
. . . . (100 to 1 op 50 to 1) pu
Dist: 3l, 8l, 8l, 15l, nk, 3½l, 2l, 2l. 3m 57.20s. a 10.20s (13 Ran).
SR: 21/13/5/-/-/-/   (David F Wilson), T Thomson Jones

917 Jaguar Novices' Chase (5-y-o and up) £2,831 3m. . . . . (2:25)

663³ PARDON ME MUM (bl) 8-11-0 S McNeill, *hld up in tch, hit 2 out, quickened to ld last, pushed clr.*
. . . . (11 to 8 fav op 7 to 4 tchd 5 to 4)   1
SQUIRE JIM 9-11-0 D Bridgwater, *hld up in mid-div, prog 16th, rdn and not quicken frm 2 out.* (9 to 2 op 6 to 1)   2
813³ SPIRIT OF KIBRIS 8-11-0 W McFarland, *hld up in tch, rdn and kpt on one pace frm 2 out.*
. . . . (11 to 2 op 5 to 1 tchd 7 to 1)   3
710 DEEPENDABLE 6-11-0 M A FitzGerald, *ldg grp, pckd badly second, led 3 out, hdd and hit last, sn btn.*
. . . . (8 to 1 op 6 to 1)   4
770⁴ LOOSE WHEELS (v) 7-11-0 A Carroll, *led 4th til hdd 3 out, sn btn...................* (14 to 1 op 10 to 1)   5
348³ SEA BREAKER (Ire) 5-10-11 D Murphy, *cld on ldrs 11th, wknd aftr 3 out...............* (12 to 1 op 14 to 1)   6
751 PAPPA DONT PREACH (Ire) 5-10-11 R Supple, *al towards rear, jmpd slwly 16th, tld off.*
. . . . (25 to 1 op 20 to 1 tchd 33 to 1)   7
625 ULLSWATER 7-11-7 J Ryan, *al beh, tld off 13th.*
. . . . (16 to 1 op 14 to 1)   8
728⁶ STRONG JOHN (Ire) 5-10-6 (5*) B Murphy, *beh, f 1st.*
. . . . (7 to 1 op 5 to 1)   f
PHILIPINTOWN LAD 10-10-9 (5*) T Eley, *led aftr 1st to 4th, wknd 16th, tld off whn pld up bef 2 out.*
. . . . (33 to 1 op 20 to 1) pu
792⁵ MASTER DANCER 6-11-0 M Richards, *al beh, tld off whn pld up bef 15th...............* (14 to 1 op 10 to 1) pu
Dist: 3l, nk, 4l, 4l, 4l, dist, 16l. 6m 5.00s. a 17.00s (11 Ran).
(A M Grazebrook), K C Bailey

918 Teroson Handicap Hurdle (0-125 4-y-o and up) £2,831 2m 110yds. . . . . (3:05)

MRS MAYHEW [83] 5-9-12 (7*) P Murphy, *pressed ldrs, led 2 out, rdn out..... (12 to 1 op 8 to 1)   1
771³ FATHER DAN (Ire) [90] 4-10-7 (5*) A Bates, *hld up in mid-div, cld on ldrs 3 out, ev ch whn hit last 2, not quicken r-in........................* (9 to 1 op 8 to 1)   2
824³ ALL WELCOME [102] 6-11-10 P Niven, *led till hdd 2 out, hng lft and no extr aftr last...........* (7 to 2 op 9 to 1)   3
CYPRUS (Fr) [96] (bl) 5-10-13 (5*) S Curran, *hld up gng wl, rdn and found nothing appr 2 out*
. . . . (100 to 30 fav op 3 to 1 tchd 4 to 1)   4
739⁶ EASBY MANDRINA [84] 6-9-13 (7*) Mark Roberts, *strted slwly, beh till moderate prog and hit 2 out, nvr rchd ldrs.*
. . . . (10 to 1 op 6 to 1)   5
RARFY'S DREAM [102] 5-11-10 S Keightley, *beh most of way...................* (16 to 1 op 8 to 1 tchd 20 to 1)   6
ENFANT DU PARADIS (Ire) [83] 5-10-5 B Clifford, *wl plcd till wknd 3 out........................* (10 to 1 op 6 to 1)   7

REVE EN ROSE [90] 7-10-12 M A FitzGerald, *in tch till lost pl frm 3 out.........* (12 to 1 op 10 to 1 tchd 14 to 1)   8
846 ELEGANT FRIEND [98] 5-11-6 D Murphy, *ldg grp till wknd appr 3 out......................* (4 to 1 op 8 to 1)   9
Dist: 3l, 8l, 1½l, shd-hd, 10l, 1l, sht-hd, 20l. 3m 55.70s. a 8.70s (9 Ran).
SR: 23/27/31/23/11/19/-/6/-/   (G A Hubbard), F Murphy

919 Rover Handicap Chase (0-135 4-y-o and up) £3,071 2m 110yds. . . . . (3:35)

738² ATLAAL [125] 8-11-4 S Smith Eccles, *handily plcd, mstk 5th, led aftr last, quickened and styd on wl.*
. . . . (11 to 2 op 5 to 1 tchd 6 to 1)   1
700² BLUSTERY FELLOW [107] 8-10-0 W Humphreys, *hld up, hdwy 8th, led 2 out, hit last, sn hdd and edgd rght r-in.*
. . . . (5 to 1 op 7 to 2)   2
834* THE GREEN STUFF [113] 8-10-6 R Supple, *cld on ldrs frm 3rd, not quicken appr 2 out, styd on wl frm last.*
. . . . (5 to 1 op 9 to 2 tchd 11 to 2)   3
ARDBRIN [128] 10-11-7 D Murphy, *led til hdd 2 out, wknd r-in........................* (8 to 1 op 5 to 1)   4
ANTONIN (Fr) [135] 5-11-9 J Burke, *chsd ldr till rdn alng and lost pl 9th, eased whn btn 2 out.*
. . . . . . (100 to 30 fav op 3 to 1 tchd 11 to 4 and 7 to 2)   5
825³ EMSEE-H [125] 8-10-11 (7*) P Murphy, *wl plcd, jmpd slwly 4th, mstk nxt, lost tch frm 8th..................* (10 to 1)   6
TERRIBLE GEL (Fr) [107] 8-10-0 M A FitzGerald, *hld up in rear, blun and uns rdr 9th.........* (13 to 2 op 5 to 1) ur
Dist: 1½l, ½l, 3l, 12l, 20l. 4m 2.90s. a 4.90s (7 Ran).
SR: 49/29/34/46/41/11/-/   (Oliver Donnelly), J R Jenkins

920 Ford Novices' Hurdle (4-y-o and up) £1,895 3¼m. . . . . (4:10)

OCEAN LEADER 6-10-12 D Murphy, *hld up in rear, prog 8th, led 2 out, pushed out, cleverly..* (5 to 1 op 3 to 1)   1
695⁴ URBAN COWBOY 6-10-12 S McNeill, *hdwy frm rear 8th, dsptd ld aftr 2 out, not quicken nr line.*
. . . . (4 to 1 op 3 to 1)   2
525 LITTLE THYNE 8-10-12 Dr P Pritchard, *trkd ldrs, ev ch whn hit 2 out, one pace frm last........* (50 to 1 op 33 to 1)   3
725* BROWNHALL 5-10-11 (7*) Mr B Pollock, *led to 5th, led 7th, clr nxt, hdd 2 out, no extr.*
. . . . (11 to 2 op 4 to 1 tchd 6 to 1)   4
650² DOROBO (NZ) 5-10-12 M A FitzGerald, *ldg grp till rdn and btn aftr mstk 3 out.* (5 to 4 fav tchd 5 to 2 and 3 to 1)   5
PATROCLUS 8-10-12 A Tory, *wl plcd, moderate prog 9th, no ch wth ldrs....* (16 to 1 op 10 to 1 tchd 20 to 1)   6
765 GLEBE PRINCE 13-10-7 (5*) C Burnett-Wells, *ldg grp, wknd frm 8th.....................* (14 to 1 op 8 to 1)   7
721⁷ THOMPSON FLYER 6-10-12 Mrs F Needham, *nvr nr ldrs.*
. . . . (50 to 1 op 33 to 1)   8
FRAMSDEN 7-10-7 (5*) S Curran, *chsd ldrs till mstk 7th, beh nxt.......................* (50 to 1 op 33 to 1)   9
HICKELTON HOUSE 9-10-12 M Richards, *cl up, led 5th to 7th, wknd aftr nxt, pld up bef 3 out.*
. . . . (50 to 1 op 33 to 1) pu
846 BE THE BEST 5-10-12 B Clifford, *in tch till wknd frm 8th, pld up bef 2 out........* (33 to 1 tchd 25 to 1) pu
MANJACK 5-10-12 E Murphy, *effrt frm rear 7th, wknd aftr nxt, pld up bef 2 out........* (20 to 1 tchd 14 to 1) pu
FINKLE STREET (Ire) 5-10-5 (7*) P Murphy, *in tch in mid-div till lost touch 9th, pld up bef last.* (50 to 1 op 25 to 1) pu
Dist: ½l, 7l, 3l, 4l, 20l, 1l, 15l, 10l. 6m 20.60s. a 19.60s (13 Ran).
(Sir Peter Gibbings), Mrs D Haine

921 Peugeot Handicap Chase (0-130 5-y-o and up) £2,941 3m. . . . . (4:40)

842³ CARBISDALE [128] 7-12-0 P Niven, *hld up, prog aftr 13th, led appr 2 out, clr whn jmpd lft last, unchlgd.*
. . . . (4 to 1 co-fav op 3 to 1 tchd 9 to 2)   1
SCOLE [113] 8-10-6 (7*) P Murphy, *ldg grp, pressed ldr frm 12th, outpcd appr 2 out............* (7 to 1 op 5 to 1)   2
777 ROSCOE HARVEY [109] 11-10-9 M A FitzGerald, *led to 5th, hit nxt, one pace appr 2 out........* (16 to 1 op 10 to 1)   3
STAY ON TRACKS [124] 11-11-3 (7*) Mr N King, *chsd frnt rnk, outpcd frm 15th, kpt on alng r-in 2 out.*
. . . . (10 to 1 op 6 to 1)   4
MR JAMBOREE [118] 7-11-4 D Murphy, *lft in ld 11th till hdd appr 2 out, sn btn........* (4 to 1 co-fav op 7 to 2)   5
726 SAM SHORROCK [100] (bl) 11-10-0 Mr G Johnson Houghton, *hit second, al beh, lost tch frm 13th.*
. . . . (25 to 1 op 16 to 1 tchd 33 to 1)   6
HIGH PADRE [108] 7-10-8 M Dwyer, *al towards rear, lost tch frm 15th........* (16 to 1 op 14 to 1 tchd 20 to 1)   7
630³ RU VALENTINO [110] (bl) 9-10-10 D Bridgwater, *led 5th till o'rjmpd and uns rdr 11th.................* (4 to 1 co-
fav tchd 7 to 2 and 9 to 2) ur
GOOD TONIC [125] 10-11-11 G McCourt, *hld up, cld on ldrs 14th, ev ch 3 out, btn in 6th pl whn pld up appr last, lme..................* (8 to 1 op 6 to 1) pu
Dist: 10l, ½l, nk, 5l, 10l, 1½l. 6m 2.80s. a 14.80s (9 Ran).
(Mrs M Williams), Mrs M Reveley

922 Henkel Novices' Hurdle (Div II) (4-y-o and up) £1,851 2m 110yds. . . . . (5:10)

NATIONAL HUNT RESULTS 1993-94

SOUTHOLT (Ire) 5-10-5 (7*) P Murphy, *3rd, led appr 3 out,*
clr last, easily.....................(20 to 1 op 14 to 1) 1
TROOPING (Ire) 4-10-11 G McCourt, *hdwy 5th, styd on*
one pace frm 2 out.......(9 to 2 op 3 to 1 tchd 5 to 1) 2
753 THE GREYSMITH 6-10-12 L Harvey, *ran on frm rear appr 3*
out, rdn and mstk last, no imprsn on wnr.
....(33 to 1 tchd 40 to 1) 3
658⁵ DESERT PEACE (Ire) 4-10-11 R Campbell, *wl plcd, rdn and*
one pace appr 2 out, btn whn hit last.
....(16 to 1 op 12 to 1) 4
380³ UP ALL NIGHT 4-9-13 (7*) G Crone, *beh and pushed alng*
4th, ran on 3 out, hit last 2, no imprsn.
....(50 to 1 op 33 to 1) 5
TIGER SHOOT 6-10-12 R Supple, *pressed ldr, led 4th till*
appr 3 out, wknd bef last.
....(11 to 1 op 8 to 1 tchd 12 to 1) 6
764⁶ PILGRIMS WAY (NZ) 6-10-12 D Murphy, *prmsg effrt 5th, no*
extr appr 2 out.
....(5 to 1 op 6 to 1 tchd 7 to 1) 7
JUDGE AND JURY 4-10-11 M Richards, *beh to hfwy, mod-*
erate late prog.......(16 to 1 op 10 to 1 tchd 33 to 1) 8
WORTHY MEMORIES 4-10-6 J McLaughlin, *led to 4th,*
wknd frm nxt.....................(50 to 1 op 33 to 1) 9
NATIVE FIELD (Ire) 4-10-11 M Dwyer, *hld up towards rear,*
nvr gng wl.
.........(6 to 5 on op 5 to 4 on tchd Evens and 5 to 4) 10
693⁷ GREAT HAND 7-10-7 (5*) C Burnett-Wells, *chsd ldrs to 4th,*
sn lost pl, tld off.......(50 to 1 op 25 to 1) 11
695 BALLYWILLIAM (Ire) 4-10-11 Mr G Johnson Houghton, *in*
tch to hfwy, tld off whn pld up bef 3 out.
....(25 to 1 tchd 33 to 1) pu
Dist: 5l, 3l, 2½l, 6l, nk, 3½l, 2l, 15l, 2l, dist. 3m 57.10s. a 10.10s (12 Ran).
SR: 16/10/8/4/-/-/   (G A Hubbard), F Murphy

LEOPARDSTOWN (IRE) (good to yielding)
Saturday October 23rd

923 Dundrum INH Flat Race (4-y-o) £3,105 2m
....................................(5:00)

709² GALE TOI (Ire) 11-13 Mr W P Mullins, ...(5 to 4 on) 1
673 HAUNTING ANGLE (Ire) 11-5 (3*) Mr A R Coonan, ..(7 to 1) 2
531⁸ KARTLOS (Ire) 10-13 (7*) Mr J A Hayes, ...(10 to 1) 3
620² TAITS CLOCK (Ire) 11-1 (5*) Mr G J Harford, ...(100 to 30) 4
797 WALNEY ISLAND 11-6 Mr P Fenton, ...(12 to 1) 5
620⁴ BUCKLESFORDBERRY 11-3 (3*) Miss C Hutchinson,
....(5 to 1) 6
Dist: 2l, 1½l, 1l, 5l. 3m 45.30s. (6 Ran).
                                          (Mrs M O'Leary), P Mullins

TRALEE (IRE) (good)
Saturday October 23rd

924 Ballybeggan Racegoers Club Killorglin
Novice Hurdle (4-y-o and up) £3,105 2m 1f
....................................(1:50)

555⁴ COCKNEY LAD (Ire) 4-11-3 C F Swan, ...(11 to 8 fav) 1
797* WATERLOO LADY 6-11-1 (5*) D P Murphy, ...(11 to 2) 2
708 NEMURO (USA) 5-11-4 J Shortt, ...(4 to 1) 3
804* EAGLE ROCK (USA) 5-11-6 (5*) C O'Brien, ...(15 to 8) 4
Dist: 1l, 2l, sht-hd. 4m 16.70s. (4 Ran).
                                           (D Daly), W M Roper

925 Castleisland Maiden Hurdle (4-y-o) £2,760
2m..................................(2:20)

555² MISTER DRUM (Ire) 11-7 (7*) Mr J T McNamara, (7 to 4 fav) 1
SENSE OF VALUE 11-2 B Sheridan, ...(8 to 1) 2
EAST HOUSTON 11-2 W T Slattery, ...(25 to 1) 3
709 JUPITER JIMMY 11-2 C F Swan, ...(7 to 2) 4
171⁶ WOODFIELD ROSE 11-2 G M O'Neill, ...(5 to 1) 5
692⁵ NOT MY LINE (Ire) 10-11 (5*) C O'Brien, ...(12 to 1) 6
534 KEEPHERGOING (Ire) 10-4 (7*) J P Broderick, ...(25 to 1) 7
531⁹ OZEYCAZEY (Ire) 11-2 J Collins, ...(12 to 1) 8
671 CHANCERY QUEEN (Ire) 10-9 (7*) Mr G F Ryan, ...(6 to 1) 9
803 TALE A TALE (Ire) 11-2 K F O'Brien, ...(10 to 1) 10
671² MOSCOW DUKE (Ire) 11-2 J Jones, ...(12 to 1) 11
530 MR SNAGGLE (Ire) 10-11 (5*) T J O'Sullivan, ...(25 to 1) 12
AYDOANALLY (Ire) 11-2 J F Titley, ...(25 to 1) 13
531 MOSSY'S SLAVE (Ire) 10-11 (5*) C P Dunne, ...(25 to 1) 14
LEADING TIME (Fr) 11-2 (5*) M G Cleary, ...(10 to 1) 15
671 SON OF TEMPO (Ire) 11-2 A Powell, ...(12 to 1) 16
RED VERONA 10-11 F Woods, ...(20 to 1) 17
4 PEGUS PRINCE (Ire) 10-11 (5*) T P Rudd, ...(25 to 1) ur
Dist: 4l, 6l, 2l, 4l. 4m 5.10s. (18 Ran).
                                      (A J McNamara), A J McNamara

926 Kingdom Maiden Hurdle (5-y-o and up)
£2,760 2½m...........................(2:50)

903⁴ GOOLDS GOLD 7-10-13 (7*) P A Roche, ...(5 to 1) 1
BEAT THE SECOND (Ire) 5-11-6 G M O'Neill, ...(10 to 1) 2
853⁷ SUPER TACTICS (Ire) 5-11-1 (5*) Mr C T G Kinane,
....(9 to 4 fav) 3

534 FINE TUNING (Ire) 5-11-6 T J Taaffe, ...(6 to 1) 4
689 FAIR GO 7-10-13 (7*) Miss C A Harrison, ...(20 to 1) 5
554 LADY DIGA (Ire) 5-10-8 (7*) Mr S O'Callaghan, ..(20 to 1) 6
808* MASTER CRUSADER 7-12-0 C F Swan, ...(100 to 30) 7
508² COURT MASTER (Ire) 5-11-6 K F O'Brien, ...(7 to 2) 8
618⁵ FANCY DISH 7-10-10 (5*) D P Murphy, ...(10 to 1) 9
853 WOODEN MINSTREL 7-11-1 S H O'Donovan, ...(20 to 1) 10
266⁹ DUNHILL IDOL 6-11-6 Mr P J Healy, ...(20 to 1) 11
BASICALLY (Ire) 5-11-1 Mr M Phillips, ...(25 to 1) pu
CHERISHED PRINCESS (Ire) 5-10-10 (5*) C O'Brien,
....(14 to 1) pu
Dist: 1l, 5½l, 6l, 25l. 5m 13.50s. (13 Ran).
                                       (Mrs L Mangan), James Joseph Mangan

927 Ballybeggan Racegoers Club QR Handicap Hurdle (0-123 4-y-o and up) £3,450 2
¼m...................................(3:20)

852 MERRY PEOPLE [-] 5-10-12 Mr E Bolger, ...(7 to 4 fav) 1
AMARI QUEEN [-] 6-9-7 (7*) Ms J Lewis, ...(10 to 1) 2
123 BALLYTIGUE LORD [-] 7-10-9 (7*) Mr G P FitzGerald,
....(12 to 1) 3
854⁶ CASH CHASE [-] 5-10-0 (7*) Mr S O'Donnell, ...(6 to 1) 4
854* KILIAN MY BOY [-] 10-12-0 (7*,6ex) Mr J Lombard, (5 to 2) 5
EARLY PACE [-] 8-9-9¹ (7*) Mr D K Budds, ...(20 to 1) 6
689⁸ SHREWD MOVE [-] 4-9-4 (7*) Mrs K Walsh, ...(16 to 1) 7
797⁵ PAGET [-] 6-10-8 (7*) Mr A K Wyse, ...(5 to 1) 8
102 THE APPRENTICE [-] 7-9-7 (7*) Mr D J Kavanagh, (12 to 1) pu
Dist: 6l, 5l, 2l, hd. 4m 42.30s. (9 Ran).
                                            (Karl Casey), John Queally

928 Kirby Steakhouse Handicap Chase (4-y-o
and up) £3,450 2½m................(3:50)

690⁷ MAKE ME ON 8-9-0 (7*) J P Broderick, ..(9 to 1) 1
691 DEL MONTE BOY [-] 8-9-7 P L Malone, ...(7 to 1) 2
539 INCH LADY [-] 8-10-9 (5*) C O'Brien, ...(8 to 1) 3
854⁴ QUIET CITY [-] 6-10-3 F Woods, ...(8 to 1) 4
800³ LADY BAR [-] 6-10-8 P M Verling, ...(9 to 4 fav) 5
856³ VINEYARD SPECIAL [-] 7-9-12 T Horgan, ...(5 to 1) 6
NOBLE CLANSMAN (USA) [-] 12-9-4 (5*) T J O'Sullivan,
....(20 to 1) 7
539 HARRISTOWN LADY [-] (bl) 6-10-12 A Powell, ...(5 to 2) 8
WAKE UP LUV [-] 8-10-7 S H O'Donovan, ...(12 to 1) 9
Dist: 1l, 10l, 6l, 15l. 5m 20.60s. (9 Ran).
                                     (John A Mitchell), Patrick G Kelly

929 Ballybeggan Racegoers Club Lee Novice
Chase (4-y-o and up) £3,105 2½m... (4:20)

COMMANCHE NELL (Ire) 5-11-5 G M O'Neill, ...(10 to 1) 1
SCRIBBLER 7-12-0 L P Cusack, ...(8 to 1) 2
571* SWALLOWS NEST 6-12-0 F J Flood, ...(5 to 2) 3
507⁴ DOCTER MAC 6-12-0 J Jones, ...(12 to 1) 4
554⁷ SQUIRRELLSDAUGHTER (bl) 6-11-2 (7*) Mr N D Fehily,
....(33 to 1) 5
807² HAVE TO THINK 5-11-5 (5*) T P Rudd, ...(11 to 2) 6
CARRIGEEN KERRIA (Ire) 5-11-5 Mr P J Healy, ...(10 to 1) 7
707⁷ DOORSLAMMER 8-11-4 (5*) C O'Brien, ...(14 to 1) 8
856⁴ STRONG CHERRY 7-11-2 (7*) Mr K Taylor, ...(10 to 1) 9
SANTAMORE 6-11-4 (5*) P A Roche, ...(16 to 1) 10
NORTHERN ACE (bl) 7-12-0 C O'Dwyer, ...(14 to 1) 11
690 BLACKPOOL BRIDGE 8-12-0 S H O'Donovan, ...(25 to 1) 12
707⁶ FARNEY GLEN 6-12-0 C F Swan, ...(9 to 1) pu
SLOE HILL 7-11-9 T Horgan, ...(14 to 1) pu
852³ GRANDONHILL 6-12-0 K F O'Brien, ...(9 to 4 fav) pu
GODFREYS CROSS (Ire) 5-11-5 P M Verling, ...(20 to 1) pu
Dist: 3½l, 2l, 15l, 2l. 5m 25.70s. (16 Ran).
                                (Lisselan Farms Ltd), Fergus Sutherland

930 Desmond INH Flat Race (4-y-o and up)
£2,760 2m 1f........................(4:50)

540⁵ HIGHLY SUSPICIOUS 6-11-7 (7*) Mr K Whelan, ...(5 to 1) 1
808² FINNEGANS WAKE 6-12-0 Mr A P O'Brien, ...(2 to 1) 2
WASHINGTON HEIGHTS (USA) 4-11-2 (7*) Mr M Brennan,
....(8 to 1) 3
540 FAIRYHILL RUN (Ire) 5-11-2 (7*) Mr D A Harney, ...(8 to 1) 4
MY SUNNY WAY (Ire) 4-11-2 (7*) Mr D K Budds, ..(8 to 1) 5
43 TAR AND CEMENT (Ire) 5-12-0 Mr D M O'Brien, ..(14 to 1) 6
CARRIGEEN (Ire) 5-11-2 (7*) Mr D G Murphy, ...(14 to 1) 7
620³ JIMMY O'GOBLIN 6-12-0 Mr A J Martin, ...(5 to 4 on) 8
CAPTAIN CHARLES (Ire) 5-11-7 (7*) Mr G Mulcaire, (20 to 1) 9
252 WHIZ ON BOBBY (Ire) 5-11-7 (7*) Mr R Johnson, (16 to 1) 10
JEWEL OF ERIN 6-11-2 (7*) Mr N C Kelleher, ...(20 to 1) 11
COPPERALLEY (Ire) 4-10-11 (7*) Mr M Budds, ...(10 to 1) pu
GLEN GALE 6-11-7 (7*) Mr N D Fehily, ...(16 to 1) pu
Dist: 15l, 3l, ½l, 4l. 4m 15.40s. (13 Ran).
                                       (Donal Hassett), Donal Hassett

WORCESTER (good to firm)
Saturday October 23rd
Going Correction: PLUS 0.15 sec. per fur.

931 Three Counties Conditional Jockeys'
Handicap Chase (0-115 5-y-o and up)

120

£2,595 2m. . . . . (2:05)

810* AL HASHIMI [120] 9-12-5 M Hourigan, *not fluent, made all, ran on gmely frm 3 out, mstk last.* . . . . (9 to 2 jt-
 fav op 7 to 1) 1
 DR ROCKET [108] 8-11-7 D Meredith, *hld up in tch, mstk 5th, wnt second nxt, pressed wnr 3 out to line.*
 . . . . (6 to 1 op 5 to 1 tchd 7 to 1) 2
840² L'UOMO PIU [95] 9-10-8 A Thornton, *in rear, rdn hfwy, styd on frm 3 out to go 3rd r-in.* . . . . (9 to 2 jt-
 fav op 4 to 1 tchd 5 to 1) 3
403² STRIDING EDGE [90] 8-10-3¹ D O'Sullivan, *prmnt, lft second briefly 5th, wknd appr 4 out.*
 . . . . (12 to 1 op 10 to 1 tchd 14 to 1) 4
738³ ORCHIPEDZO [87] 8-9-11 (3*) P McLoughlin, *chsd ldrs, hit 4th, rdn and wknd appr four out.* (50 to 1 op 33 to 1) 5
703⁴ BALLAD RULER [88] 7-10-1 R Davis, *hmpd 5th, al beh.*
 . . . . (10 to 1 op 8 to 1) 6
799⁹ RECIDIVIST [87] (bl) 7-9-11 (3*) T Thompson, *not jump wl, beh till rdn and hdwy appr 4 out, wkng whn mstk nxt.*
 . . . . (40 to 1 op 33 to 1) 7
810⁴ ANOTHER CRUISE [87] 8-10-0 R Greene, *in rear whn f 3rd.*
 . . . . (14 to 1 op 12 to 1 tchd 16 to 1) f
 PERSIAN SWORD [87] 7-10-0 W Marston, *in rear whn f 5th.* . . . . (11 to 2 op 5 to 1 tchd 6 to 1) f
 SAILORS LUCK [97] 8-10-7 (3*) D Matthews, *chsd wnr till blun and uns rdr 5th.* . . . . (6 to 1 op 9 to 2) ur
 RAHEEN ROVER [87] 9-9-11 (3*) A Flannigan, *al beh, blun 3 out, pld up bef nxt.* . . . . (50 to 1 op 16 to 1) pu
Dist: Nk, 10l, 1½l, 8l, 6l, 5l. 4m 2.30s. a 13.30s (11 Ran).

(Major A W C Pearn), R J Hodges

932 Rushwick Selling Hurdle (4 & 5-y-o) £1,751
 2m. . . . . (2:35)

 DOUBLE THE STAKES (USA) 4-10-12 D J Burchell, *hld up, hdwy to ld 3 out, rdn clr r-in.* . . . . (7 to 2) 1
651⁵ PEARLY WHITE 4-10-7 R Dunwoody, *hld up in rear, hdwy appr 3 out, rdn and ran on to go second r-in.*
 . . . . (16 to 1 op 12 to 1) 2
 LEGAL WIN (USA) 5-10-13 (7*) Mr G Shenkin, *beh, hrd rdn 5th, hdwy 3 out, one pace frm nxt.* (20 to 1 op 12 to 1) 3
839⁴ VIAGGIO 5-11-6 G Bradley, *chsd ldrs second till aftr 5th, no hdwy frm 3 out.* . . . . (9 to 2 op 5 to 1) 4
 PORT IN A STORM 4-10-12 G McCourt, *hld up in tch, hdwy appr 3 out, ev ch nxt, rdn and wknd r-in.*
 . . . . (100 to 30 tav op 9 to 4 tchd 7 to 2) 5
791 DON'T FORSAKE ME 4-10-7 J Railton, *hld up in rear, hdwy aftr 5th, ev ch 2 out, wknd quickly.*
 . . . . (7 to 2 op 2 to 1 tchd 5 to 1) 6
814 NORDROSS 5-10-8 T Wall, *hld up, hdwy to ld aftr 5th, hdd nxt, wknd quickly.* . . . . (7 to 2 op 4 to 1) 7
659⁶ SHOW THE FLAG 5-11-1 (5*) R Davis, *chsd ldrs till wknd quickly appr 3 out, tld off.* . . . . . . (8 to 1 op 6 to 1) 8
809⁷ OYSTON'S LIFE 4-10-12 A Maguire, *led till beh aftr 5th, wknd quickly, pld up bef 2 out.* . . (14 to 1 op 10 to 1) pu
775³ SEA PRODIGY 4-10-12 D Gallagher, *chsd ldr to second, wknd quickly 4th, tld off whn pld up bef 3 out.*
 . . . . (25 to 1 op 14 to 1) pu
 ALIF 4-10-12 Diane Clay, *beh, wknd 4th, tld off whn pld up bef 2 out.* . . . . . (14 to 1 op 10 to 1 tchd 16 to 1) pu
Dist: 8l, 1l, 2l, 4l, 4l, 10l, dist. 3m 56.00s. a 15.00s (11 Ran).

(T G Brooks), D Burchell

933 Fred Rimell Memorial Novices' Chase (5-
 y-o and up) £4,077 2½m 110yds. . . . . (3:05)

 SEE MORE INDIANS 6-10-12 G Bradley, *mstks 4th and 6th, wnt second nxt, led sn aftr 5 out, rdn appr last, ran on.*
 . . . . (13 to 8 fav op 7 to 4 tchd 6 to 4) 1
 CHICHELL'S HURST 7-10-7 R Marley, *hld up in rear, gd hdwy tenth, chlgd 4 out, no imprsn frm 2 out.*
 . . . . (33 to 1 op 14 to 1) 2
729 SAN LORENZO (USA) 5-10-11 N Williamson, *blun second, hld up, hdwy 9th, ev ch 4 out, btn whn jmpd lft and mstk last.* . . . . (2 to 1 tchd 9 to 4) 3
 GALAXY HIGH 6-10-12 R Dunwoody, *mstk 1st, trkd ldrs, ev ch till wknd aftr 3 out.* . . . . (5 to 1 op 7 to 2) 4
 SHARP ANSWER 6-10-12 I Lawrence, *hld up in rear, rdn 7th, kpt on one pace frm 4 out.* . . . . (66 to 1 op 33 to 1) 5
774³ WILLIE MCGARR (USA) 8-10-12 Richard Guest, *led, blun 5 out, sn hdd, wknd quickly, tld off.*
 6
713⁵ POWER HAPPY 8-10-7 D Gallagher, *beh whn hit 3rd, blun and uns rdr nxt.* . . . . (40 to 1 op 25 to 1) ur
 BLACK CHURCH 12-10-12 H Davies, *pld hrd, mstks, chsd ldrs till blun 7th, sn wknd, pulled up bef tenth.*
 . . . . (14 to 1 op 12 to 1 tchd 16 to 1) pu
741² MISS SHAW 7-10-4 (3*) A Thornton, *chsd ldr to 7th, wknd tenth, tld off whn pld up 4 out.* (33 to 1 op 20 to 1) pu
Dist: 4l, 8l, 8l, 7l, dist. 5m 11.00s. a 8.00s (9 Ran).

SR: 34/25/20/13/6/-/ (Paul K Barber), P F Nicholls

934 Inkberrow Novices' Hurdle (4-y-o and up)
 £1,480 2m 5f 110yds. . . . . (3:40)

CORNER BOY 6-10-11 A Maguire, *hld up, steady hdwy frm 6th, chalg whn hit 2 out, led sn aftr last, all out.*
 . . . . (8 to 1 op 5 to 1) 1
ULURU (Ire) 5-10-11 J R Kavanagh, *al prmnt, wnt second 4 out, led nxt, hrd rdn and hdd sn aftr last.*
 . . . . (14 to 1 op 8 to 1) 2
 SHEARMAC STEEL 6-10-11 R Dunwoody, *jmpd rght, led till hdd 3 out, rdn and sn btn.*
 . . . . (11 to 4 fav op 5 to 2 tchd 3 to 1) 3
456 TALENT SPOTTER 6-10-4 (7*) A Shakespeare, *hdwy to track ldrs frm 4th, rdn appr 3 out, one pace.*
 . . . . (33 to 1 op 20 to 1) 4
695³ ROAD TO FAME 6-10-11 P Holley, *al prmnt, chsd ldr 4th to four out, wknd appr nxt.* . . . . (9 to 1 op 6 to 1) 5
683* TEXAN BABY (Bel) 4-11-3 V Slattery, *chsd ldr to 4th, prmnt till mstk four out, rdn and sn wknd.* (7 to 2 op 3 to 1) 6
 KYTTON CASTLE 6-10-3 (3*) D Meredith, *al towards rear, effrt appr 3 out, nvr dngrs.* . . . . (20 to 1 op 9 to 1) 7
716⁶ GROG (Ire) 4-10-10 G Upton, *slwly away, hit second, hld up in rear, some hdwy aftr 4 out, no imprsn after.*
 . . . . (8 to 1 op 5 to 1) 8
813 ZACTOO 7-10-11 T Wall, *wl in rear, hdwy whn mstk 4 out, sn btn, tld off.* . . . . (100 to 1 op 50 to 1) 9
441³ MAKE A LINE 5-10-4 (7*) Mr Andrew Lillingston, *in tch till blun 5th, sn beh, tld off.* . . . . (20 to 1 op 12 to 1) 10
640⁴ KADARI 4-10-5 Diane Clay, *al beh, tld off.*
 . . . . (9 to 1 op 10 to 1 tchd 11 to 1) 11
705⁵ ICE MAGIC 6-10-11 D Gallagher, *hld up, gd hdwy 4 out, wknd and pld up bef nxt.* . . . . . (33 to 1 op 25 to 1) pu
 HICKELTON LAD 9-10-6 (5*) R Davis, *mid-div till wknd quickly 4 out, tld off whn pld up bef nxt.*
 . . . . (33 to 1 op 25 to 1) pu
 SPRING SPIRIT (Ire) 4-10-10 N Williamson, *in tch till wknd 6th, tld off whn pld up bef 3 out.* . (25 to 1 op 16 to 1) pu
755⁵ ELMSTEAD 7-10-11 M Ahern, *pld hrd, chsd ldrs till mstk 6th, pulled up nxt.* . . . . (25 to 1 op 16 to 1) pu
 BIRCHALL BOY 5-10-11 R Bellamy, *al beh, tld off frm 5th, pld up bef 3 out.* . . . . (66 to 1 op 50 to 1) pu
 SPACE MOLLY 4-10-2 (3*) W Marston, *tld off frm 5th, pld up bef 3 out.* . . . . (50 to 1) pu
Dist: 1½l, 20l, 4l, ¾l, 6l, 6l, nk, 8l, 12l, 8l. 5m 11.00s. a 17.00s (17 Ran).

(Mrs E W Wilson), D Nicholson

935 Aston Villa Handicap Chase (0-130 5-y-o
 and up) £3,158 2½m 110yds. . . . . (4:20)

 STUNNING STUFF [118] 8-11-5 N Williamson, *hld up, hdwy on bit appr 4 out, hit nxt, led sn aftr 2 out, quickened clr.* . . . . (9 to 2 op 3 to 1) 1
 NEVADA GOLD [122] 7-11-9 G Bradley, *hld up, gd hdwy 9th, ev ch 2 out, kept on one pace.* . . (5 to 1 op 4 to 1) 2
749² MUSTHAVEASWIG [123] 7-11-10 A Maguire, *trkd ldrs, led sn aftr 5 out, hdd aftr 2 out, no extr.*
 . . . . (7 to 4 fav op 5 to 2 tchd 5 to 2) 3
700³ ARDCRONEY CHIEF [104] (bl) 7-10-5 P Holley, *hld up, making hdwy whn mstk 7th, one pace frm 4 out.*
 . . . . (9 to 2 op 5 to 1 tchd 6 to 1) 4
 AUCTION LAW (NZ) [120] 9-11-7 J Frost, *hld up in rear, effrt 5 out, wknd aftr nxt, tld off.*
 . . . . (12 to 1 op 8 to 1 tchd 14 to 1) 5
842 CHIP AND RUN [113] 7-11-0 J R Kavanagh, *hld up, mstk 5th, hdwy to go 3rd 8th, dsptd ld tenth and 11th, wknd appr 3 out, tld off.* . . . . (25 to 1 op 20 to 1) 6
 WARNER'S END [99] (bl) 12-10-0 R Bellamy, *trkd ldr till wknd quickly aftr 5 out, blun nxt, tld off.*
 . . . . (40 to 1 op 20 to 1) 7
 WINABUCK [116] (bl) 10-11-3 R Dunwoody, *made most till hdd sn aftr 5 out, wknd quickly, wl beh whn f 2 out.*
 . . . . (12 to 1 op 10 to 1 tchd 14 to 1) f
 BUCKSHEE BOY [107] 11-10-8 Richard Guest, *beh frm 7th, tld off tenth, pld up bef 4 out.*
 . . . . (25 to 1 op 20 to 1 tchd 33 to 1) pu
Dist: 7l, sht-hd, ½l, dist, ¾l, dist. 5m 11.40s. a 8.40s (9 Ran).

SR: 38/35/36/16/-/-/ (Giles Gleadell), K C Bailey

936 City Handicap Hurdle (0-115 4-y-o and up)
 £2,910 2m. . . . . (4:55)

99* FROMTHEGETGO (Ire) [101] 4-10-7 (7*) G Cahill, *hld up in tch, rdn 2 out, switchd lft r-in, str brst to ld last 50 yards, sn clr.* . . . . . (16 to 1 op 14 to 1 tchd 20 to 1) 1
698 DRIVING FORCE [101] 7-11-0 J Railton, *al prmnt, led appr 2 out, clr last, rdn and hdd last 50 yards.*
 . . . . (25 to 1 op 16 to 1) 2
 FRONT STREET [89] 6-10-2² G Upton, *hld up, hdwy 4th, jmpd slwly nxt, led appr 3 out, hdd bef next, rdn and kpt on r-in.* . . . . (7 to 2 op 7 to 2) 3
 FOR HEAVEN'S SAKE (Fr) [89] 8-10-2 T Wall, *hld up in tch, styd on frm 3 out, rdn and ran on r-in.*
 . . . . (50 to 1 op 33 to 1) 4
 FLEURCONE [95] 11-10-8 I Lawrence, *al prmnt, rdn and hdwy appr 3 out, wknd aftr nxt.* . . . . (33 to 1) 5
 IMA DELIGHT [97] 6-10-10 R Marley, *prmnt, rdn appr 3 out, one pace aftr.* . . . . . . (14 to 1 op 12 to 1) 6
698⁸ MOUNTSHANNON [87] 7-10-0 A Maguire, *trkd ldr to 4th, prmnt till wknd appr 2 out.* . . . . (20 to 1 op 25 to 1) 7

COUTURE STOCKINGS [97] 9-10-10 N Williamson, *hld up,*
styd on frm 3 out, nvr nrr . . . . (25 to 1 op 20 to 1) 8
698⁴ JUST ROSIE [95] 4-10-1 (7") D Fortt, *chsd ldrs, wnt second*
4th, led briefly aftr nxt, wknd appr 2 out.
. . . . (11 to 2 op 5 to 1 tchd 7 to 1) 9
698 FRONT PAGE [104] 6-11-3 Richard Guest, *al mid-div.*
. . . . (14 to 1 op 8 to 1) 10
ADMIRALTY WAY [108] 7-11-7 Diane Clay, *hld up in rear,*
nvr on terms . . . . (12 to 1 op to 1 tchd 16 to 1) 11
713⁶ NORTHERN SADDLER [98] 6-10-11 H Davies, *mid-div, rdn*
5th, wknd appr nxt. . . . . (7 to 1) 12
275⁸ HOSTETLER [96] 4-10-6 (3") W Marston, *mid-div, rdn and*
lost tch appr 3 out . . . .(20 to 1 op 16 to 1) 13
TAYLORS CASTLE [87] 6-10-0 Lorna Vincent, *hld up in*
rear, al beh . . . . (33 to 1) 14
WILTSHIRE YEOMAN [87] 13-10-0 Gee Armytage, *chsd ldrs*
till lost pl 4th. . . . . (50 to 1) 15
651 PEAK DISTRICT [87] 7-10-0 R Greene, *al beh, tld off.*
. . . . (33 to 1) 16
MACEDONAS [112] 5-11-11 G Bradley, *hld up in rear, gd*
hdwy 5th, cl fifth whn f 3 out. (4 to 1 fav tchd 5 to 1) f
685³ ELITE REG [115] (bl) 4-12-0 R Dunwoody, *led till hdd aftr*
5th, rdn and wknd quickly, f 2 out.
. . . .(10 to 1 tchd 11 to 1) f
Dist: 3½l, sht-hd, 1l, 6l, 1½l, sht-hd, 6l, hd, 3l, sht-hd. 3m 54.70s. a 13.70s
(18 Ran).

(Riston Stars & Stripes Partnership), B S Rothwell

GALWAY (IRE) (Good to yielding)
Monday October 25th

937 Bank Of Ireland Lifetime Novice Hurdle (4-y-o and up) £4,140 2m . . . . (1:25)

672* PADRE MIO (Ire) 5-11-10 G Bradley, ...(6 to 4 on) 1
858* COURT MELODY (Ire) 5-10-9 (7") J P Broderick, . . .(6 to 1) 2
671* FABULIST (Ire) 4-10-5 (5") T P Treacy, ...(7 to 1) 3
854⁵ DANCING COURSE (Ire) 5-10-10 (5") P A Roche, . .(12 to 1) 4
881² GREEN LEADER (USA) (bl) 4-11-1 C F Swan, ...(7 to 2) 5
Dist: 8l, 3l, 3l, 20l. 3m 55.40s. (5 Ran).

(Paddy Fennelly), Anthony Mullins

938 Investment Bank Of Ireland Handicap Hurdle (4-y-o and up) £7,200 2m 5f 190yds . . . .(2:00)

504* DERRYMOYLE (Ire) [-] 4-9-7 C F Swan, ...(7 to 4 fav) 1
505* BAVARD DIEU (Ire) [-] 5-9-9 P L Malone, ...(8 to 1) 2
584⁴ RISING WATERS (Ire) [-] 5-11-5 K F O'Brien, ...(7 to 1) 3
798³ UNCLE BART (Ire) [-] 5-9-13 (7") R A Hennessy, . .(11 to 4) 4
KERFONTAINE [-] 8-10-7³ G Bradley, ...(10 to 1) 5
584⁸ TITIAN BLONDE (Ire) [-] 5-10-6 M Dwyer, ...(8 to 1) 6
HAKI SAKI [-] 7-10-5 G M O'Neill, ...(8 to 1) 7
IL TROVATORE (USA) [-] 7-10-2 H Rogers, ...(14 to 1) 8
673⁹ LILLIPUT QUEEN (Ire) [-] 5-9-12 F J Flood, ...(8 to 1) 9
Dist: 2l, sht-hd, 2½l, 4l. 5m 28.00s. (9 Ran).

(Herb M Stanley), Michael Cunningham

939 Bank Of Ireland Finance Maiden Hurdle (4-y-o and up) £3,750 2m . . . .(2:25)

852² COOL CHARACTER (Ire) 5-12-0 J F Titley, ...(5 to 4 fav) 1
853³ PANDA (Ire) 5-11-4 (5") T P Treacy, ...(3 to 1) 2
ALOHA (Ire) 4-10-13 M Duffy, ...(10 to 1) 3
572³ OXFORD QUILL 6-12-0 T J Taaffe, ...(7 to 1) 4
SAMANTHA'S FLUTTER 7-12-0 T Horgan, ...(7 to 1) 5
709 AN MAINEACH (Ire) 4-11-4 C F Swan, ...(7 to 1) 6
114 CABLE BEACH (Ire) 4-11-4 P L Malone, ...(12 to 1) 7
BALLYMOE BOY (Ire) 5-10-13 (7") K P Gaule, ...(20 to 1) 8
801 DRINK UP DAN 6-11-6 S H O'Donovan, ...(14 to 1) 9
537⁸ CAL ME HENRY 4-11-4 G M O'Neill, ...(16 to 1) 10
MR GLYNN (Ire) 4-10-11 (7") J P Broderick, ...(16 to 1) 11
534 RUSHEEN BAY (Ire) 4-11-4 A J O'Brien, ...(20 to 1) 12
808⁷ SHEELIN LAD (Ire) 5-11-6 H Rogers, ...(14 to 1) 13
907 A WINDY CITIZEN (Ire) 4-10-6 (7") Mr W M O'Sullivan,
. . . .(20 to 1) 14
798 EXILE RUN (Ire) (bl) 5-11-6 G Bradley, ...(14 to 1) 15
ANNAGH FLUTTER 4-11-4 K F O'Brien, ...(14 to 1) 16
VISTAGE (Ire) 5-12-0 J P Banahan, ...(9 to 1) f
Dist: 1l, 1l, 6l, nk. 3m 55.50s. (17 Ran).

(A J Hogan), E Bolger

940 Bank Of Ire. ICS Build Soc Handicap Chase (4-y-o and up) £7,200 2m 1f. . .(3:40)

422 FINAL TUB [-] 10-10-5 G M O'Neill, ...(7 to 2) 1
KINGS ENGLISH [-] 7-10-2 T Horgan, ... (6 to 4 fav) 2
831⁹ KILLINEY GRADUATE [-] 7-10-4 K F O'Brien, ...(6 to 1) 3
GOOD TEAM [-] 8-10-1 (5") T P Rudd, ...(8 to 1) 4
878 LA MODE LADY [-] 8-9-8¹ A J O'Brien, ...(12 to 1) 5
BLITZKREIG [-] 10-12-0 C F Swan, ...(3 to 1) 6
707⁸ LADY BYE-BYE [-] 7-9-2² (7") J M Donnelly, ...(14 to 1) 7
Dist: 1½l, 2½l, 4l, 7l. 4m 33.70s. (7 Ran).

(Sean O'Brien), V T O'Brien

941 Bank Of Ire Credit Card Serv Novices' Chase (5-y-o and up) £3,750 2¾m. . . (4:10)

MERCIFUL HOUR 6-12-0 T J Taaffe, ...(6 to 1) 1
674⁷ TAWNEY FLAME 7-12-0 M Dwyer, ...(7 to 4 fav) 2
799⁸ ANOTHER EXCUSE (Ire) 5-11-3 (7") Mr W M O'Sullivan,
. . . .(12 to 1) 3
856 DANNIGALE 7-11-6 (3") Mr M Phillips, ...(14 to 1) 4
WALLS COURT 6-11-9 P L Malone, ...(14 to 1) 5
SPUR OF THE MOMENT 6-11-9 J P Banahan, ...(8 to 1) 6
674⁸ PACKROCK DONNA 6-10-13 (5") P A Roche, ...(12 to 1) 7
635 THE WEST'S ASLEEP 8-11-9 J F Titley, ...(14 to 1) 8
WYLDE HIDE 6-11-4 (5") T P Rudd, ...(14 to 1) 9
MINSTREL SAM 7-11-9 A J O'Brien, ...(16 to 1) 10
THREE BROWNIES 6-12-0 G Bradley, ...(8 to 1) 11
690 QUIET MONEY 6-11-9 (5") D P Geoghegan, ...(12 to 1) 12
690⁹ KNOW HOW 7-11-4 P M Verling, ...(12 to 1) f
856⁸ SHEILA NA GIG 7-11-9 G M O'Neill, ...(6 to 1) f
799⁵ NUAFFE 8-12-0 S H O'Donovan, ...(3 to 1) f
583⁴ BALLINAVEEN BRIDGE 6-11-9 W T Slattery Jnr, . .(14 to 1) ur
807 DEEP ISLE 7-12-0 K F O'Brien, ...(20 to 1) pu
856⁷ COUMEENOOLE LADY 6-11-6 (3") Miss M Olivefalk,
. . . .(14 to 1) pu
Dist: 8l, 4½l, 6l, 3½l. 5m 40.10s. (18 Ran).

(Mrs A M Daly), A L T Moore

942 Breast Cancer Research Flat Race (5-y-o and up) £2,760 2m . . . .(4:40)

636² WILD FANTASY (Ire) 5-12-2 Mr A J Martin, ...(5 to 2) 1
576* BEGLAWELLA 6-11-9 (7") Mr P English, ...(3 to 1) 2
572⁸ IF YOU SAY YES (Ire) 5-11-13 (3") Mrs J M Mullins,
. . . . (5 to 4 fav) 3
476² RHABDOMANCY (Ire) 5-11-6 (7") Mr A Daly, ...(11 to 2) 4
LOUGH CULTRA DRIVE (Ire) 5-11-6 (5") Mr J A Nash,
. . . .(14 to 1) 5
801 DENNY'S GUESS (Ire) 5-11-11 Mr T S Costello, ...(14 to 1) 6
SWEET PETEL 6-11-6² (7") Mr N Henley, ...(20 to 1) 7
Dist: 1l, 7l, 9l, 7l. 3m 52.90s. (7 Ran).

(L F Curtin), A P O'Brien

LEOPARDSTOWN (IRE) (good to yielding)
Monday October 25th

943 Leopardstown Golf Course Handicap Chase (5-y-o and up) £4,140 2m 5f. . .(3:00)

539⁴ BISHOPS HALL [-] 7-11-5 C O'Dwyer, ...(7 to 4 fav) 1
CAHERVILLAHOW [-] 9-12-0 N Williamson, ...(5 to 1) 2
SON OF WAR [-] 6-10-13 F Woods, ...(5 to 1) 3
539⁷ JOE WHITE [-] 7-10-4 P Carberry, ...(11 to 2) 4
422⁷ GUESSWORK [-] 7-10-5 A Powell, ...(12 to 1) 5
637 GLEN OG LANE [-] 10-9-2 (5") M G Cleary, ...(25 to 1) 6
799² PARGALE [-] 7-9-2 (5") C O'Brien, ...(7 to 2) f
Dist: ½l, 10l, 5l, nk. 5m 23.90s. a 9.90s (7 Ran).

(Joseph Carroll), H de Bromhead

944 Leopardstown Driving Range Cadogan Handicap Hdle (Listed) (4-y-o and up) £5,865 2m. . . . . (3:30)

556² BIG MATT (Ire) [-] 5-10-8 (5") C O'Brien, *hld up in rear, prog*
into 4th 3 out, led betw last 2, hdd aftr mstk last, rdn to
ld ag'n last strds. . . . .(5 to 1) 1
413* MUBADIR (USA) [-] 5-12-0 P Carberry, *trkd ldr till led aftr 3*
out, rdn and hdd betw last 2, rallied to ld ag'n r-in,
headed cl home. . . . .(Evens fav) 2
SYLVIA FOX [-] 6-9-7 R Hughes, *trkd ldrs, rdn to go second*
appr 2 out, wknd last. . . . .(4 to 1) 3
FAMILY WAY [-] 6-9-10 F Woods, *mid-div, rdn 3 out, no*
imprsn strt. . . . .(14 to 1) 4
SHARP INVITE [-] 6-10-10 (7") M P Kelly, *hld up in rear, rdn*
3 out, not rch ldrs. . . . .(12 to 1) 5
HAPPY ROVER [-] 8-11-3 B Sheridan, *set slow pace in ld*
till hdd aftr 3 out, sn wknd . . . .(16 to 1) 6
MAGNUM STAR (Ire) [-] 4-9-2 (5") M G Cleary, *al in rear.*
. . . .(33 to 1) 7
Dist: Hd, 4l, 6l, 4½l. 3m 45.00s. b 3.00s (7 Ran).
SR: 43/58/19/16/32/–/–/

(Mrs Louise Henry), P Burke

945 Carrickmines Flat Race (5-y-o and up) £3,105 2m. . . . . (4:30)

832³ BADEN (Ire) 5-11-13 Mr T Mullins, ...(7 to 4 jt-fav) 1
ATOURS (USA) 5-11-11 (7") Mr H Murphy, . . .(7 to 4 jt-fav) 2
400³ TEMPLERAINEY (Ire) 5-12-4 Mr A P O'Brien, ...(3 to 1) 3
331⁷ WOLVER LAD (Ire) 5-11-11 Mr T Doyle, ...(14 to 1) 4
708⁹ SPEAK OF THE DEVIL 6-11-11 (7") Mr D McDonnell,
. . . .(16 to 1) 5
832 JIMMY GORDON 5-11-11 (7") Mr M Brennan, ...(20 to 1) 6
708 DOWN THE BACK 5-11-1 (5") C O'Brien, ...(33 to 1) 7
CLOGRECON BOY (Ire) 5-11-11 Mr M McNulty, . . .(16 to 1) 8
FISHING LADY (Ire) 5-11-6 Mr D T Evans, ...(33 to 1) 9
Dist: ½l, 1l, ¾l, hd. 3m 52.90s. (9 Ran).

(Max Hauri), P Mullins

SOUTHWELL (good to soft)
Monday October 25th
Going Correction: PLUS 0.40 sec. per fur.

946 **Caunton Claiming Chase (5-y-o and up) £1,640 2m........................ (2:30)**

WICKFIELD LAD 10-10-9 S Earle, *chsd ldrs, hdwy 4 out, chlgd 2 out, sn led, rdn clr appr last.*
...................................(33 to 1 op 20 to 1) 1
589[4] VULRORY'S CLOWN 15-10-11 M Brennan, *al prmnt, chsd ldr and hit 5 out, rdn and ev ch 2 out, wknd appr last.*
...................................(6 to 1 op 5 to 1) 2
WINGSPAN (USA) 9-11-7 N Mann, *prmnt, led 4th, rdn 3 out, hdd sn aftr nxt, wknd appr last.* (3 to 1 op 5 to 4) 3
676[4] ISLAND JETSETTER 7-11-2 A Maguire, *in tch, blun 6th, hit nxt and sn wknd.*
...................................(11 to 10 fav op 6 to 4 tchd 13 to 8) 4
RATHER SHARP 7-11-4 R Dunwoody, *led to 4th, blun 5th and rdr lost reins, rider reco'red reins bef 7th, wknd nxt, sn beh.*............(17 to 2 op 7 to 1 tchd 9 to 1) 5
682[3] BILL QUILL 9-10-3 (7") R Darke, *f 1st.*
...................................(9 to 1 op 6 to 1 tchd 10 to 1) f
322[4] SAILOR'S DELIGHT 9-10-9 (7") Mr S Joynes, *hmpd and uns rdr 1st.*...................................(25 to 1 op 16 to 1) ur
549 NO DAW 9-11-2 M Sharratt, *al rear, tld off whn pld up bef 5 out.*......................................(33 to 1) pu
Dist: 7l, nk, dist, nk. 4m 12.30s. a 13.30s (8 Ran).
SR: 12/7/16/-/-/-   (R P Craddock), N M Babbage

947 **Farnsfield Handicap Chase (0-115 5-y-o and up) £2,059 3m 110yds......... (3:00)**

811[2] SANDYBRAES [109] 8-12-0 A Maguire, *in tch, hit 8th and tenth, hdwy 13th, jnd ldr nxt, led 4 out, hit 3 out, wnt lft 2 out, clr last....* (15 to 8 fav op 7 to 4 tchd 2 to 1) 1
835* TRIBAL RULER [100] 8-11-5 G McCourt, *hld up, smooth hdwy appr 13th, led nxt, hdd 4 out, rdn 3 out, second and held whn blun last*...........(7 to 2 tchd 9 to 2) 2
842 MISS FERN [97] 8-10-13 (3") D Meredith, *al prmnt, rdn 5 out, kpt on und pres frm 3 out......* (7 to 1 op 12 to 1) 3
696[3] OVERHEREOVERTHERE [107] 10-11-12 R Supple, *hld up in tch, hdwy to join ldrs 7th, mstk 11th, rdn and hit 13th, sn wknd.*....................(11 to 2 op 3 to 1) 4
669[3] SAMSUN [86] (bl) 11-10-5 R Dunwoody, *led to 3rd, cl up, hit 7th, reminders 12th, lost pl nxt, plugged on one pace.*.........................(10 to 1 op 12 to 1) 5
876 VIVA BELLA (Fr) [97] 6-10-11 (5") J Burke, *prmnt, mstks 11th and 12th, led 13th, hdd and hit nxt, sn drvn alng, wknd bef 4 out......*(25 to 1 op 14 to 1 tchd 9 to 2) 6
GENTLEMAN ANGLER [97] (bl) 10-11-2 G Upton, *cl up, led 3rd to 13th, sn wknd, beh whn pld up bef 4 out.*
...................................(7 to 1 op 5 to 1) pu
NATIVE SCOT [86] 7-10-5 M A FitzGerald, *blun badly second, al rear, tld off whn pld up bef 4 out.......*(20 to 1) pu
Dist: 7l, 8l, 4l, 4l, 1l. 6m 41.20s. a 43.20s (8 Ran).
                                        (Mrs Stewart Catherwood), D Nicholson

948 **Upton Novices' Chase (5-y-o and up) £1,765 2½m 110yds.............. (3:30)**

VILLAGE REINDEER (NZ) 6-11-0 T Reed, *mstk 1st, hld up and beh, steady hdwy 7th, hit tenth, mistake 4 out, effrt to chal 2 out, sn led, clr f16....* (4 to 1 tchd 5 to 1) 1
768[3] SHEILAS HILLCREST 7-10-7 (7") J Supple, *led, rdn and hit 3 out, hdd aftr nxt, wknd last....* (20 to 1 op 16 to 1) 2
694[2] DEXTRA DOVE 6-11-0 S Earle, *al prmnt, effrt 3 out, sn rdn and kpt on one pace........*(5 to 2 fav op 6 to 4) 3
POLLERTON'S PRIDE 6-11-0 A Maguire, *mid-div, hdwy 7th, pushed alng and mstk 4 out, rdn nxt, sn one pace.*
...................................(10 to 1 op 8 to 1) 4
683[2] PRUDENT PEGGY 6-10-9 J Frost, *beh, rdn and staying on frm 4 out, nvr dngrs..............*(20 to 1 op 16 to 1) 5
GRAZEMBER 6-11-0 L Wyer, *prmnt, chsd ldr 4th, rdn and hit four out, wknd appr nxt.......*(20 to 1 op 16 to 1) 6
FEARSOME 7-11-0 M A FitzGerald, *chsd ldrs, rdn 5 out, one pace appr 3 out.* (10 to 1 op 7 to 1) 7
833[3] VOLCANIC DANCER (USA) 7-11-0 P Niven, *al rear, tld off 4 out....* (1 to 1 op 14 to 1 tchd 16 to 1) 8
FOX CHAPEL 6-11-0 D Byrne, *hmpd second, mstks 3rd and 4th, hit 6th and sn beh, tld off four out.*
...................................(7 to 1 op 14 to 1) 9
833[2] SILENT CHANT (bl) 9-10-7 (7") Mr R Griffiths, *prmnt whn f second.*......................................(20 to 1) f
757[4] JEFFERBY (bl) 6-11-0 M Ahern, *prmnt, mstk second, hit nxt, blun 5th, grad lost pl, tld off 9th, pld up bef 4 out.*
...................................(8 to 1 tchd 10 to 1) pu
833* CRAFTY CHAPLAIN 7-11-1 (5") Mr D McCain, *hld up, blun 7th and sn pushed alng, al beh and tld off whn pld up bef 3 out.*......................(9 to 1 op 6 to 1) pu
Dist: 6l, ½l, 3l, 4l, 8l, 15l, 1½l, 1½l. 5m 24.40s. a 21.40s (12 Ran).
                                        (J R Chester), P Calver

SOUTHWELL (A.W) (std)

Monday October 25th
Going Correction: PLUS 0.70 sec. per fur.

949 **Laxton Handicap Hurdle (0-120 4-y-o and up) £1,405 2¼m................. (1:30)**

MUNIR (USA) [92] 4-11-7 J A Harris, *al prmnt, hit 8th, rdn and not much room on inner 2 out, swtchd and chlgd last, ridden to ld flt, ran on.*
...................................(7 to 2 op 3 to 1 tchd 5 to 1) 1
846[2] SPANISH WHISPER [81] 6-10-10 A Maguire, *led, quickened 3 out, rdn aftr nxt, hdd and no extr flt.*
...................................(6 to 4 op 1 to 1 tchd 13 to 2) 2
681[2] NORTHERN NATION [95] 5-11-10 Diane Clay, *hld up in tch, effrt and hdwy appr 3 out, sn rdn, styd on one pace approaching last....*(9 to 4 fav op 2 to 1 tchd 11 to 4) 3
LOCAL FLYER [91] 4-11-6 R Dunwoody, *hld up in tch, hit 7th, hdwy to chase ldr 4 out, rdn and ev ch 2 out, wknd appr last.*.......................(9 to 2 op 5 to 2, wknd) 4
818[5] TEMPORALE [77] 7-10-6 R Supple, *hld up in tch, hdwy 5th, rdn 4 out, sn one pace.*
...................................(4 to 1 op 9 to 2 tchd 5 to 1) 5
VAZON EXPRESS [71] 7-10-0 N Mann, *prmnt, jmpd slwly 3rd, lost pl 8th, sn beh.*
...................................(12 to 1 op 16 to 1 tchd 25 to 1 and 10 to 1) 6
Dist: 2l, 6l, 1l, 1½l, 30l. 4m 31.50s. a 19.50s (6 Ran).
SR: 24/11/19/14/-/-/   (J S Gowling), J L Harris

950 **Autumn Novices' Claiming Hurdle (4-y-o and up) £1,363 2m.................(2:00)**

849[6] WORDY'S WONDER 5-11-2 (5") R Farrant, *mid-div, hdwy 6th, effrt and led 3 out, sn rdn and ran on wl.*
...................................(4 to 1 op 7 to 2) 1
771[7] BAHER (USA) 4-11-3 A Maguire, *trkd ldrs, hdwy 6th, led aftr nxt, sn rdn, hit 3 out and hdd, soon one pace.*
...................................(2 to 1 fav op 9 to 4) 2
666[9] WILL BONNY (NZ) 6-10-6 (7") R Darke, *mid-div, pushed alng hfwy, styd on frm 4 out, nrst finish.*
...................................(20 to 1 tchd 25 to 1) 3
680[4] GRUBBY 4-10-4 (3") S Wynne, *led till aftr 1st, prmnt, hit 6th, rdn and one pace frm nxt.....*(16 to 1 op 20 to 1) 4
SHARP DANCE 4-11-0 R Dunwoody, *pld hrd, led aftr 1st, hdd and wknd after 4 out.*
...................................(11 to 1 op 8 to 1 tchd 12 to 1) 5
837[7] GREEN'S SEAGO (USA) 5-10-10 M FitzGerald, *beh, effrt 7th, no hdwy...................*(4 to 1 op 9 to 4) 6
664 LEARNER DRIVER 6-11-7 R Supple, *beh frm hfwy.*
...................................(10 to 1 op 6 to 1 tchd 11 to 1) 7
729 HADLEIGHS CHOICE 6-10-6 M Robinson, *beh frm hfwy.*
...................................(50 to 1) 8
622 JOVIAL KATE (USA) 6-10-8 T Reed, *chsd ldrs, hit 1st, wknd 6th, sn beh....* (20 to 1 op 25 to 1 tchd 33 to 1) 9
755[8] AFRICAN SAFARI 9-11-2 Richard Guest, *prmnt till wknd 5th, tld off whn pld up bef 3 out.* (14 to 1 tchd 16 to 1) pu
CHAGHATAI (USA) (bl) 7-10-13 Diane Clay, *sn beh, blun 3rd, tld off nxt, pld up bef 3 out.....* (16 to 1 op 20 to 1) pu
839 STRAWBERRY FOOL 4-10-2 T Wall, *al rear, tld off hfwy, pld up 3 out.*...................................(50 to 1) pu
Dist: 5l, 15l, 5l, 10l, 10l, 6l, 2l. 4m 5.60s. a 19.60s (12 Ran).
SR: 9/-/-/-/-/-/   (L Wordingham), L Wordingham

951 **Maplebeck Handicap Hurdle (0-115 4-y-o and up) £1,380 3m.................(4:00)**

FETTLE UP [72] 5-10-6 A Maguire, *cl up, led 4th, rdn aftr four out, jmpd rght last 3, kpt on und pres.*
...................................(7 to 2 op 2 to 1) 1
838 VALATCH [68] 5-10-2 B Dalton, *prmnt, chsd wnr frm 6th, rdn bef 3 out, kpt on................*(10 to 1 op 7 to 1) 2
755[4] BURN BRIDGE (USA) [86] (v) 7-11-6 Peter Caldwell, *in tch till outpcd hfwy, styd on und pres frm 5 out, nvr dngrs.*
...................................(4 to 1 op 5 to 2 tchd 9 to 2) 3
701[5] HAWWAR (USA) [78] 6-10-12 R Dunwoody, *prmnt, rdn alng tenth, wknd appr 4 out.....* (7 to 2 op 9 to 4) 4
552[5] CISTOLENA [66] (v) 7-10-0 Diane Clay, *al rear, tld off frm 9th...........................*(12 to 1 op 10 to 1) 5
BRIGHT SAPPHIRE [78] 7-10-5 (7") A Flannigan, *chsd ldrs, rdn alng 9th, sn lost pl, tld off whn pld up bef 3 out.*
...................................(11 to 2 op 4 to 1 tchd 10 to 1) pu
499 CASTLERICHARDKING [75] 8-10-9 W Humphreys, *led to 4th, lost pl 6th, tld off whn pld up bef 9th.*
...................................(20 to 1 op 14 to 1) pu
MAY DAY BABY [92] 7-11-12 R Supple, *al rear, tld off 9th, pld up bef 3 out..............*(11 to 1 op 12 to 1) pu
Dist: 5l, 15l, dist, 15l. 6m 10.80s. a 33.80s (8 Ran).
                                        (Mrs A E Hirst), J Wharton

NEWTON ABBOT (good)
Tuesday October 26th
Going Correction: PLUS 0.35 sec. per fur. (races 1,2,-4,7), PLUS 0.20 (3,5,6)

952 **Holne Novices' Hurdle (4-y-o and up) £1,362 2m 1f........................(1:40)**

BUTLER'S TWITCH 6-11-0 J Osborne, *led till aftr second,*
led 5th, gng wl whn lft clr 2 out. (6 to 4 fav op 11 to 4) 1
524² MAMALAMA 5-10-6 (3") D O'Sullivan, *al in tch, lft second 2*
out, styd on, no imprsn on wnr.... (20 to 1 op 10 to 1) 2
ILDERTON ROAD 6-10-9 P Holley, *hdwy 5th, rdn and hld*
whn hmpd 2 out, sn one pace...... (25 to 1 op 12 to 1) 3
423⁴ JENNYELLEN (Ire) 4-10-8 R Dunwoody, *chsd ldrs, led 4th*
to nxt, mstk 3 out, sn rdn, btn 2 out.
.................................(12 to 1 op 6 to 1 tchd 16 to 1) 4
634² BELL ONE (USA) 4-10-13 C Maude, *beh and mstk 1st, rdn*
5th, nvr dngrs......... (15 to 2 op 4 to 1 tchd 8 to 1) 5
715 MISSY-S (Ire) 4-10-1 (7") Mr J L Llewellyn, *pld 4th, hdwy*
and not fluent 5th, chsd ldrs appr 2 out, sn btn.
....(10 to 1 op 6 to 1 tchd 12 to 1) 6
815 SKYE DUCK 4-10-8 L Harvey, *al rear.* (50 to 1 op 20 to 1) 7
ABSENT MINDS 7-10-8⁶ (7") Miss S Young, *prmnt to 5th.*
....(100 to 1 op 20 to 1) 8
795 EURIDICE (Ire) 4-10-1 (7") R Darke, *al beh.*
....(16 to 1 op 10 to 1) 9
773 NEARLY HONEST 5-10-9 A Tory, *chsd ldrs to 5th.*
....(50 to 1 op 20 to 1) 10
772³ COTTAGE WALK (NZ) 4-10-9 (5") R Davis, *in tch 4th, rdn*
aftr 3 out, 5th and wkng whn f 2 out.
....(15 to 2 op 4 to 1 tchd 8 to 1) f
597* MUSKORA (Ire) 4-11-5 Peter Hobbs, *mid-div, hdwy 5th,*
chasing wnr but hld whn veered rght and f 2 out.
....(2 to 1 tchd 5 to 2) f
MENDIP MIST 5-10-9 N Mann, *pld hrd, led aftr second to*
4th, ran wide and wknd bend after, sn tld off, pulled
up bef 2 out........................ (50 to 1 op 33 to 1) pu
BARONESS BELLE 7-10-9 W Irvine, *al beh, tld off 5th, pld*
up bef 2 out........................ (50 to 1 op 20 to 1) pu
ANA BLAKE 4-10-2 (7") D Matthews, *tld off whn pld up*
aftr 4th........................ (100 to 1 op 25 to 1) pu
Dist: 6l, 20l, hd, 6l, 8l, 8l, 3½l, 3½l, 3½l. 4m 2.00s. a 12.00s (15 Ran).
SR: 25/14/-/-/-/-/ (Christopher Heath), O Sherwood

953 Ilsington Novices' Selling Hurdle (4-y-o and up) £1,369 2m 1f.............. (2:10)

794 FANATICAL (USA) 6-11-0 L Harvey, *hdwy and mstk 5th,*
hrd drvn appr 2 out, str chal last, sn led, all out.
....(5 to 1 op 5 to 1 tchd 13 to 2) 1
814⁶ CORNISH COSSACK (NZ) 6-10-7 (7") Mr G Shenkin, *hdwy*
5th, led aftr 3 out, rdn 2 out, hdd after last, kpt on.
....(7 to 1 op 5 to 1) 2
704³ KELLY'S DARLING 7-11-0 D Gallagher, *hdwy 5th, ev ch 2*
out till outpcd r-in........ (8 to 1 op 7 to 1) 3
REALLY NEAT 7-10-2 (7") D Matthews, *led to second,*
prmnt till wknd aftr 3 out........ (10 to 1 tchd 16 to 1) 4
634⁹ WHAT A RATTLE 4-10-13 Peter Hobbs, *rdn 5th, hdwy 3*
out, sn wknd........................ (16 to 1 op 6 to 1) 5
447 COLONIAL OFFICE (USA) (bl) 7-11-0 T Wall, *rdn aftr 4th, sn*
btn........................ (25 to 1 op 14 to 1) 6
GREAT IMPOSTOR (bl) 5-11-0 R Dunwoody, *beh 4th.*
....(9 to 1 op 6 to 1 tchd 10 to 1) 7
650 GENERALLY JUST 8-10-11 (3") D Meredith, *beh most of*
way........................ (50 to 1 op 25 to 1) 8
699⁵ MALLYAN 6-10-4 (5") R Davis, *prmnt to 4th.*
....(10 to 1 op 8 to 1) 9
791⁵ ELEGANT TOUCH (bl) 4-10-8 M Foster, *in tch, led aftr 4th*
till hdd and wknd after 3 out.... (12 to 1 op 10 to 1) 10
891⁷ MERLS PEARL (bl) 4-10-8 I Lawrence, *f 1st.*
....(50 to 1 op 20 to 1) f
885⁵ GLORY BEE 9-11-0 M Richards, *brght dwn 1st.*
....(100 to 50 fav op 3 to 1 tchd 7 to 2) bd
775² BEAM ME UP SCOTTY (Ire) 4-10-13 N Hawke, *brght dwn*
1st........................ (9 to 1 op 5 to 1 tchd 13 to 2) bd
WESSEX MILORD 8-10-7 (7") A Lucas, *beh 4th, tld off whn*
pld up bef 2 out........................ (50 to 1 op 20 to 1) pu
ENTERPRISE PRINCE 7-10-7 (7") T Thompson, *whipped*
round strt, virtually refused to race, al tld off, pld up
bef 2 out........................ (50 to 1 op 20 to 1) pu
598⁸ FORTUNE STAR (Ire) 4-10-10 (3") D O'Sullivan, *led second*
till aftr 4th, sn wknd, tld off whn pld up bef 2 out.
....(25 to 1 op 12 to 1) pu
Dist: Nk, 2½l, 15l, 10l, 1l, 20l, 3½l, 15l, 4l. 4m 5.70s. a 15.70s (16 Ran).
(Duckhaven Stud), R J Baker

954 Brimley Novices' Chase (Div I) (5-y-o and up) £1,519 2m 5f............. (2:40)

ALEGBYE 7-11-0 R Dunwoody, *made all, jmpd hesitantly*
to 6th, clr tenth, drvn out frm 2 out. (10 to 1 op 5 to 1) 1
HAND OUT 9-10-6 (3") W Marston, *hdwy 9th, chsd wnr*
frm 2 out, styd on one pace........ (16 to 1 op 8 to 1) 2
833 MULTISTRANO 6-11-0 R Supple, *chsd ldrs, jmpd slwly*
5th, rdn 4 out, one pace.
....(12 to 1 op 7 to 1 tchd 14 to 1) 3
694³ GLENSHANE LAD 7-11-7 N Williamson, *beh, shaken up*
aftr 8th, in tch whn hmpd tenth, hit 4 out, ran on frm 2
out........................ (9 to 4 op 2 to 1) 4
794⁴ ON ALERT (NZ) 6-11-0 J Frost, *in tch till lost pl 9th, no*
dngr aftr........................ (15 to 2 op 6 to 1 tchd 8 to 1) 5
CRYSTAL BEAR (NZ) 8-11-0 C Llewellyn, *blun 1st, beh,*
mstk 3rd, hdwy 9th, rdn and wknd nxt.
....(2 to 1 fav op 5 to 4 tchd 9 to 4) 6

810 IMPERIAL FLIGHT 8-11-0 J R Kavanagh, *chsd wnr, chlgd*
4th to nxt, second whn f tenth................ (20 to 1) f
ONLY IN IRELAND 7-11-0 G Bradley, *hld up, hdwy tenth,*
chsd ldrs 4 out, wknd 3 out, pld up bef nxt, lme.
....(14 to 1 op 12 to 1 tchd 8 to 1) pu
751 QUEENS CURATE 6-10-9 M Hourigan, *hit 3rd, tld off 8th,*
pld up bef tenth........................ (50 to 1 op 25 to 1) pu
Dist: 2l, 6l, sht-hd, 6l, 25l. 5m 10.90s. a 10.90s (9 Ran).
SR: 20/13/12/19/6/-/ (Mrs Margaret McGlone), M C Pipe

955 Bulpin Challenge Cup Handicap Hurdle For Amateur Riders (0-120 4-y-o and up) £2,113 2¾m.................. (3:10)

845 MAYFIELD PARK [80] 8-10-0⁷ (7") Mr G Hogan, *prmnt,*
chasing ldr whn lft in ld 7th, shaken up and kpt on wl
frm 2 out........................ (50 to 1 op 33 to 1) 1
796 CELCIUS [87] (bl) 9-10-0 (7") Mr N Moore, *hld up, hdwy*
7th, chsd wnr frm 3 out, no imprsn appr last.
....(7 to 1 op 5 to 1) 2
845⁶ BLASKET HERO [87] (bl) 5-10-0 (7") Mr L Jefford, *beh, styd*
on frm 3 out, not rch ldrs.
....(9 to 1 op 8 to 1 tchd 10 to 1) 3
796⁵ AMPHIGORY [87] 5-10-0 (7") Miss S Cobden, *chsd ldrs till*
lost pl 6th, styd on appr 2 out........ (8 to 1 op 7 to 1) 4
819⁴ COXANN [81] (bl) 7-9-8 (7") Mr E Tolhurst, *beh, bumped*
bend aftr 6th, hdwy 3 out, sn one pace.
....(7 to 1 op 5 to 1) 5
796⁷ PROVERBS GIRL [88] 8-10-5⁴ (7") Mr J Thatcher, *beh, tld off*
6th, styd on frm 3 out. (10 to 1 op 8 to 1 tchd 14 to 1) 6
796² NICK THE DREAMER [105] 8-11-6 (5") Mr A Farrant, *chsd*
ldrs till wknd 3 out. (9 to 4 fav op 11 to 4 tchd 3 to 1) 7
864⁴ MOUNTAIN MASTER [89] 7-10-9¹⁴ (7") Mr J M Pritchard, *al*
beh........................ (6 to 1 op 3 to 1) 8
811⁵ FRISCO CITY (Chi) [85] 7-9-12 (7") Mr M Rimell, *wth ldr, led*
aftr second, hdd appr 3rd and mstk, hit 4th, sn beh.
....(10 to 1 op 8 to 1) 9
359² DESERT PALM [86] 8-9-13 (7") Mr N Miles, *in tch, led aftr*
6th, mstk and uns nxt.
....(10 to 1 op 8 to 1 tchd 12 to 1) ur
FREEMANTLE [92] 8-10-5 (7") Mr G Baines, *led appr 3rd til*
aftr 6th, sn wknd, tld off whn pld up bef 2 out.
....(6 to 1 op 5 to 1) pu
STORMSEAL BOY [80] 7-9-9² (7") Miss M Hill, *led till aftr*
second, beh 5th, tld off 6th, pld up bef nxt.
....(50 to 1 op 33 to 1) pu
Dist: 3½l, 6l, 2½l, 2l, 3l, 12l, 8l, 25l. 5m 14.60s. a 15.60s (12 Ran).
(Robin Barwell), C R Barwell

956 S.W. Shower Supplies Ltd Handicap Chase (0-115 5-y-o and up) £2,754 3¼m 110yds.................. (3:40)

CHANNELS GATE [110] 9-11-10 N Williamson, *al tracking*
ldrs, led 4 out, sn clr, cmftbly........ (5 to 1 op 4 to 1) 1
726 JIMSTER [97] 11-10-11 A Maguire, *chsd ldr, chlgd 14th,*
led 16th to 4 out, styd on same pace. (11 to 2 op 8 to 1) 2
835³ NAUGHTY NICKY [89] 9-10-3 R Greene, *beh, hdwy 11th,*
rdn 13th, headway and hit 15th, no und pres frm 3
out........................ (16 to 1 op 10 to 1) 3
792⁴ TRUSTY FRIEND [105] 11-11-5 M A FitzGerald, *prmnt, rdn*
alng frm 13th, styd on one pace from 4 out.
....(11 to 1 op 8 to 1 tchd 12 to 1) 4
835² RED AMBER [91] (bl) 7-10-5 D Gallagher, *al beh.*
....(6 to 1 op 5 to 1) 5
865 YIRAGAN [111] 11-11-6 (5") R Davis, *chsd ldrs to 6th, drpd*
rear 8th, no dngr aftr, tld off...... (14 to 1 op 12 to 1) 6
860 MASTER GLEASON [99] 10-10-13 R Dunwoody, *chsd ldrs*
to 15th, no ch whn refused 3 out.... (5 to 1 op 4 to 1) ref
865⁶ NO GRANDAD [109] 9-11-9 R Supple, *beh, reminders 6th,*
nvr dngrs, tld off whn pld up bef 3 out.
....(8 to 1 op 6 to 1) pu
810⁹ MINT-MASTER [86] 8-9-9 (5") C Leahy, *drpd rear 6th, tld*
off whn pld up bef 15th........ (33 to 1 op 20 to 1) pu
RUFUS [109] 7-11-9 C Llewellyn, *hit second, tld off 6th,*
pld up bef 4 out........................ (9 to 1 op 6 to 1) pu
INDIAN TONIC [114] 7-12-0 C Maude, *led to 16th, sn wknd,*
tld off whn pld up bef 2 out.
....(4 to 1 fav op 3 to 1 tchd 9 to 2) pu
Dist: 6l, 5l, 3½l, 20l, dist. 6m 35.20s. a 15.20s (11 Ran).
(Cabalva Racing Partnership), J A C Edwards

957 Brimley Novices' Chase (Div II) (5-y-o and up) £1,519 2m 5f............. (4:10)

CROFT MILL 7-11-0 M A FitzGerald, *in tch, led 7th, clr*
appr 3 out, edgd lft last, ran on wl.
....(11 to 8 fav op 6 to 4 tchd 11 to 10) 1
741 JUDGES FANCY 9-11-0 C Llewellyn, *blun 1st, beh, hdwy*
8th, blunded 4 out, str chal whn not much room and
mstk last, not reco'r..... (7 to 1 op 8 to 1 tchd 9 to 1) 2
687³ IVYCHURCH (USA) 7-11-0 J Frost, *chsd ldrs till outpcd 4*
out........................ (7 to 1 op 8 to 1 tchd 13 to 2) 3
751³ GENEROUS SCOT 9-11-0 R Bellamy, *hit 1st, jmpd slwly*
second to 5th, hdwy 9th, no prog frm 11th.
....(20 to 1 op 16 to 1) 4

710⁵ COMIC LINE (bl) 8-11-7 S Burrough, *led till aftr 1st, chsd ldrs till wknd 11th*..................(9 to 1 op 6 to 1) 5
JUDYS LINE 9-10-9 C Maude, *in tch till drpd rear 8th, no dngr aftr*........... (33 to 1 op 16 to 1 tchd 50 to 1) 6
PURPLE POINT (NZ) 8-10-9 (5*) R Davis, *beh, lost tch 8th, tld off whn pld up bef 11th*......... (5 to 1 op 7 to 2) pu
795 NEVER EVER 8-10-7 (7*) Mr G Lewis, *led aftr 1st to 7th, rdn appr 9th, sn wknd, tld off whn pld up bef 2 out.* .... (50 to 1 op 25 to 1) pu
MAJOR ELSTON 8-11-0 Richard Guest, *chsd ldrs, drpd rear 8th, tld off whn pld up bef tenth.* .... (50 to 1 op 25 to 1) pu
Dist: 2l, 25l, 1l, 6l, nk. 5m 24.00s. a 24.00s (9 Ran).
(Lord Chelsea), Miss H C Knight

958 Edgemoor Handicap Hurdle (0-125 4-y-o and up) £1,968 2m 1f............... (4:40)

776⁷ EMERALD MOON [82] 6-10-3³ S Burrough, *hdwy 3 out, led sn aftr last, drvn out*.. (9 to 1 op 5 to 1 tchd 10 to 1) 1
698⁵ WOLVER GOLD [93] 6-11-0 C Maude, *in tch, led appr 2 out till sn aftr last, kpt on same pace*...........(2 to 1 jt-fav op 9 to 4 tchd 7 to 4) 2
812⁶ KALZARI (USA) [98] 8-11-5 A Maguire, *hld up, hdwy appr 2 out, one pace approaching last.* .... (5 to 1 op 4 to 1 tchd 11 to 2) 3
BY FAR (USA) [85] 7-10-6 V Slattery, *led till hdd and wknd aftr 3 out*................(6 to 1 op 5 to 1 tchd 7 to 1) 4
750³ JAMES THE FIRST [102] (bl) 5-11-9 G Bradley, *chsd ldr, led aftr 3 out till appr nxt, sn btn.* (2 to 1 jt-fav op 6 to 4) 5
796 COLOUR SCHEME [85] 6-10-6 Peter Hobbs, *in tch till wknd 3 out, beh whn pld up bef nxt.* .... (16 to 1 op 8 to 1 tchd 20 to 1) pu
Dist: 1l, 5l, 2l, 10l. 4m 4.80s. a 14.80s (6 Ran).
(Paul C N Heywood), W G Turner

FONTWELL (good to firm)
Wednesday October 27th

Going Correction: PLUS 0.20 sec. per fur. (races 1,3,6), PLUS 0.30 (2,4,5)

959 Willis Corroon Selling Handicap Hurdle (3,4,5-y-o) £1,778 2¼m............. (1:30)

716⁴ FITNESS FANATIC [92] 5-11-5 (7*) J J Brown, *led aftr 3rd, jmpd slwly 6th, shaken up and ran on wl frm 2 out.* .... (11 to 2 op 5 to 1 tchd 6 to 1) 1
846* RUTH'S GAMBLE [66] 5-10-0 (5ex) A Maguire, *chsd ldrs, reminder aftr 6th, chlgd 2 out, btn appr last.* ....(11 to 10 fav tchd 11 to 8) 2
846⁴ JOLI'S GREAT [86] 5-11-6 J Ryan, *led till aftr 1st, led ag'n 3rd, sn hdd, drpd rear 6th, rdn and styd on one pace frm 3 out*..............(7 to 1 op 8 to 1 tchd 10 to 1) 3
859⁴ TAPESTRY DANCER [67] 5-10-1 D Skyrme, *beh, hit 5th, hdwy 6th, chsd wnr 3 out, wknd appr 2 out.* .... (10 to 1 op 8 to 1 tchd 12 to 1) 4
837 MABTHUL (USA) [78] 5-10-12 M A FitzGerald, *beh 6th, sn rdn, no response*.... (15 to 2 op 6 to 1 tchd 8 to 1) 5
748⁶ CORINTHIAN GOD (Ire) [75] 4-10-9 D Murphy, *led aftr 1st, hdd 3rd, wknd 6th*... (100 to 30 op 4 to 1 tchd 3 to 1) 6
KARIB [77] (bl) 3-10-11 Leesa Long, *reluctant to race and tld off, pld up bef 2 out.* .... (33 to 1 op 20 to 1 tchd 40 to 1) pu
Dist: 7l, 3l, 8l, 10l, 2½l. 4m 24.70s. a 14.70s (7 Ran).
(A D Weller), J T Gifford

960 Derek Wigan Memorial Novices' Handicap Chase (5-y-o and up) £3,492 2¼m... (2:00)

796⁴ MAN FROM MARS [84] 7-11-2 Peter Hobbs, *in tch, chsd ldr 7th, slight ld whn lft clr 3 out, pushed out.* .... (100 to 30 op 5 to 2 tchd 7 to 2) 1
EMERALD STORM [83] 6-11-1 R Dunwoody, *in tch 8th, gd hdwy and ev ch whn blun badly 3 out, not reco'r.* ....(11 to 8 fav op 6 to 4) 2
794⁶ CANDLE KING (Ire) [75] 5-10-7 A Tory, *hdwy to chase ldrs 8th, rdn and styd on one pace frm 3 out.* .... (14 to 1 op 12 to 1 tchd 16 to 1) 3
899 CHARLIE JOHNSON [92] (bl) 9-11-10 A Maguire, *led to second, lost tch frm 4 out.* .... (11 to 2 op 7 to 2 tchd 6 to 1) 4
MIDNIGHT STORY [89] 8-11-7 D Gallagher, *led second, rdn, narrowly hdd and ev ch whn blun and uns rdr 3 out.* .... (12 to 1 op 8 to 1 tchd 14 to 1) ur
521⁶ KILKILMARTIN [85] 11-11-3 M Bosley, *tld off 5th, pld up bef 9th, dismounted*..............(50 to 1 op 33 to 1) pu
794³ MILLIES OWN [85] 6-11-3 M Perrett, *hit 4th, sn beh, tld off whn pld up bef tenth*....(9 to 2 op 7 to 1 tchd 8 to 1) pu
Dist: 5l, 3½l, 15l. 4m 31.70s. a 11.70s (7 Ran).
SR: 25/19/7/9/ (P J Hobbs), P J Hobbs

961 Vintage Veuve Clicquot Handicap Hurdle (0-140 4-y-o and up) £2,820 2¼m.... (2:30)

629³ ABSENT RELATIVE [119] 5-11-10 A Maguire, *hld up, gd hdwy 6th, led appr 2 out, easily.* ....(5 to 4 on op 11 to 10 tchd 5 to 4) 1
MASROUG [95] 6-9-7 (7*) K Goble, *chsd ldr 5th, led aftr 3 out, hdd appr 2 out, sn outpcd.* ....(14 to 1 op 12 to 1 tchd 16 to 1) 2
601³ LUSTY LAD [106] 8-10-11 H Davies, *chsd ldr 5th, lost pos 6th, drvn and ran on ag'n appr last.* .... (11 to 2 op 9 to 2 tchd 6 to 1) 3
867⁷ BRIGGS LAD (Ire) [103] (bl) 4-10-8 J Osborne, *led, clr aftr 3rd, hdd and wkng quickly after 3 out.* ....(8 to 1 op 5 to 1) 4
861⁹ DIRECTORS' CHOICE [97] 8-9-12¹ (5*) A Dicken, *hit 1st, tld off frm second*....................(16 to 1 op 12 to 1) 5
TIP TOP LAD [99] 6-10-4 Peter Hobbs, *chsd ldrs, 3rd and wkng whn f 2 out*...... (9 to 2 op 4 to 1 tchd 5 to 1) f
FIVE CASTLES [95] 5-10-0 M Perrett, *tld off frm second, pld up bef 2 out*.....(66 to 1 op 50 to 1 tchd 100 to 1) pu
Dist: 4l, ½l, 15l, dist. 4m 17.80s. a 7.80s (7 Ran).
SR: 54/26/36/18/ (Mrs J L Froome), Miss B Sanders

962 Action Research For Crippled Child Novices' Chase (5-y-o and up) £1,856 3¼m 110yds............................ (3:00)

712⁵ ISLAND FOREST (USA) 7-11-6 G Bradley, *hld up, hdwy 13th, hit 18th, pressed ldrs frm 3 out, chlgd last, sn led, all out*.................. (7 to 2 op 5 to 2 tchd 4 to 1) 1
710³ CASTLE BLUE 6-11-0 M A FitzGerald, *led second to 3rd, styd wth ldrs, hit 14th, led aftr 15th, rdn 2 out, hit last and hdd, not quicken*.......... (6 to 4 fav tchd 7 to 4) 2
LUCKY LANE (bl) 9-11-0 C Maude, *in tch, hit 4th and 11th, chsd ldr appr 16th, rdn 3 out, one pace* .... (11 to 4 op 3 to 1 tchd 7 to 2) 3
624⁵ KELLY OWENS 8-11-0 W Irvine, *led to second, beh frm 5th, hit tenth, 11th and 15th, nvr dngrs.* .... (20 to 1 op 16 to 1 tchd 25 to 1) 4
HALF A MO 8-10-9 R Dunwoody, *chsd ldrs, mstk 9th, wknd 15th*........... (10 to 1 op 12 to 1 tchd 14 to 1) 5
MAJOR CUT 7-10-11 (3*) W Marston, *led 3rd till aftr 15th, sn wknd*.............. (25 to 1 op 16 to 1 tchd 33 to 1) 6
SPARTAN FLAPJACK 7-10-7 (7*) Mr B Pollock, *mstks, tld off 5th, pld up bef 16th.* .... (12 to 1 op 8 to 1 tchd 14 to 1) pu
LOWICK LAD 6-11-0 D Bridgwater, *tld off 5th, pld up bef 16th*.............................. (50 to 1 op 33 to 1) pu
Dist: 1½l, 1½l, 30l, 12l, dist. 6m 52.90s. a 22.90s (8 Ran).
(Commander Peter Longhurst), P F Nicholls

963 Willis Corroon Conditional Jockeys' Handicap Chase (0-115 5-y-o and up) £2,196 2 ¼m............................... (3:35)

712³ COURT RAPIER [91] 11-11-2 (4*) P Carey, *led till appr second, styd in tch, smooth prog frm 3 out, chlgd last, sn led, cmftbly*............. (11 to 10 on tchd 11 to 10) 1
792⁷ FIGHTING DAYS (USA) [95] (bl) 7-11-6 (4*) J Clarke, *led appr second, clr approaching 6th, hdd 4 out, rallied und pres approaching last, styd on, no ch wth wnr.* ....(4 to 1 op 3 to 1) 2
810³ ACHILTIBUIE [83] 9-10-12 R Greene, *tld off 5th, hdwy 8th, chsd ldr tenth till led 4 out, hdd r-in, wknd cl hme.* ....(5 to 2 tchd 11 to 4) 3
752² OLD ROAD (USA) [93] 7-11-8 R Davis, *hit 3rd, chsd ldrs 7th, rdn and btn 3 out.* (10 to 1 op 5 to 1 tchd 12 to 1) 4
Dist: 7l, 1½l, 10l. 4m 34.60s. a 14.60s (4 Ran).
(H V Perry), R H Alner

964 'Docker' Hughes Memorial Challenge Trophy Novices' Hurdle (4-y-o and up) £1,475 2¼m.............................. (4:05)

WINNOWING (Ire) 5-10-7 J Osborne, *in tch, outpcd 6th, plenty to do frm 2 out, str run appr last, quickened wl to ld nr finish*........(100 to 30 op 4 to 1 tchd 9 to 4) 1
616² WILD STRAWBERRY 4-10-6 M Richards, *hdwy 5th, rdn 2 out, led r-in, ct nr finish*........ (2 to 1 fav op 6 to 4) 2
809 KHALIDI (Ire) 4-11-3 P Holley, *hdwy 6th, led appr last, hdd r-in, styd on one pace.* (11 to 4 op 2 to 1 tchd 3 to 1) 3
602* ST ATHANS LAD (bl) 8-10-12 D Morris, *dwlt, sn reco'red to ld aftr 1st, soon clr, hdd after 2 out, styd on same pace.* ....(9 to 2 op 5 to 1 tchd 8 to 1) 4
664⁹ LABURNUM 5-11-4 R Dunwoody, *hit second, lost tch frm 3 out*...........................(8 to 1 tchd 10 to 1) 5
864⁵ PABREY 7-10-5 (7*) Miss S Mitchell, *led till hdd aftr 1st, wknd 6th*........................ (50 to 1 op 25 to 1) 6
773 MISS SOUTER 4-10-7¹ J Frost, *beh frm 5th.* .... (33 to 1 op 20 to 1 tchd 50 to 1) 7
FREDWILL 6-10-5 (7*) J Clarke, *tld off 4th, pld up bef 2 out*.............................. (50 to 1 op 20 to 1) pu
Dist: 1½l, ½l, 3½l, 15l, 2½l, 3l. 4m 20.20s. a 10.20s (8 Ran).
SR: 13/10/20/11/2/ (Mrs Basil Samuel), O Sherwood

NAVAN (IRE) (good)
Wednesday October 27th

965 Virginia Chase (5-y-o and up) £3,105 2m ....(2:00)

575* CHIRKPAR 6-11-8 K F O'Brien, ... (11 to 10 fav) 1
929[3] SWALLOWS NEST 6-11-4 M Flynn, ... (8 to 1) 2
674[3] LADY OLEIN (Ire) 5-10-9 C F Swan, ... (3 to 1) 3+
879 NORTHERN HIDE 7-11-11 T J Taaffe, ... (100 to 30) 3+
Dist: 1l, 2½l, dd-ht. 4m 18.50s. (4 Ran).

(Michael W J Smurfit), J S Bolger

966 Wilkinstown Handicap Chase (4-y-o and up) £3,105 2½m.................... (3:00)

800[4] TURBULENT WIND [-] 6-10-11 C F Swan, ... (7 to 2) 1
799[7] MALACHYS BAR [-] 9-10-7 J F Titley, ... (9 to 1) 2
806 BOB DEVANI [-] 7-10-2 P Carberry, ... (5 to 1) 3
878[6] CAPE SPY [-] 7-11-7 G M O'Neill, ... (11 to 2) 4
KNOCKNACARRA LAD [-] 8-10-10 (3*) T J Mitchell, (12 to 1) 5
806* HO FRETTA [-] 7-9-2 (5*,9ex) C O'Brien, ... (11 to 4 fav) 6
635 HURRICANE TOMMY [-] (bl) 6-10-5 P L Malone, .. (14 to 1) 7
JOHNEEN [-] 7-10-5 C O'Dwyer, ... (14 to 1) 8
745[2] SLAVOMER [-] 8-9-12 (7*) P Stafford, ... (14 to 1) 9
Dist: ¾l, 8l, 3l, ¾l. 5m 10.40s. (9 Ran).

(Lady Virginia Petersham), A L T Moore

967 Kingscourt Opportunity Handicap Hurdle (0-130 5-y-o and up) £3,450 2m...... (3:30)

538[8] CUBAN QUESTION [-] 6-9-10 (2*) M G Cleary, ... (10 to 1) 1
904[4] CELTIC SAILS (Ire) [-] 5-10-3 (4*) P O Casey, ... (11 to 2) 2
805[2] BELLECARA [-] 6-9-7 D Bromley, ... (5 to 1) 3
2 PYR FOUR [-] 6-9-8 (4*) D A McLoughlin, ... (12 to 1) 4
636[5] BOLERO DANCER (Ire) [-] 5-9-8 (4*) C O'Neill, ... (9 to 1) 5
798[8] ROSEPERRIE (Ire) [-] 5-9-7[2] (2*) D T Evans, ... (10 to 1) 6
880[4] JIMMY THE JACKDAW [-] 6-9-7 T J Mitchell, .. (9 to 4 fav) 7
805[4] FAMOUS DANCER [-] 5-9-4 (4*) B Bowens, ... (7 to 1) 8
904[7] HUGH DANIELS [-] 5-9-5 (4*) M P Moran, ... (10 to 1) 9
23 CRAZY LADY [-] 7-9-4[1] (4*) J M Donnelly, ... (33 to 1) 10
CENTRE FORWARD [-] 9-9-5 (2*) C O'Brien, ... (16 to 1) 11
IVY GLEN [-] 7-9-7[2] (2*) D P Geoghegan, ... (33 to 1) 12
Dist: 1½l, 1½l, 5l, 1l. 3m 52.30s. (12 Ran).

(Laurence Byrne), D T Hughes

968 Juvenile Hurdle (3-y-o) £3,105 2m... (4:00)

688* TEMPLEMARY BOY (Ire) 11-4 T Horgan, ... (10 to 1) 1
529* TROPICAL LAKE (Ire) 10-13 K F O'Brien, ... (11 to 10 fav) 2
GLOWING VALUE (Ire) 11-0 B Sheridan, ... (10 to 1) 3
617* BIZANA (Ire) 11-7 P Carberry, ... (11 to 4) 4
802[7] PRINTOUT (Ire) 10-9 D H O'Connor, ... (20 to 1) 5
MUSCOVY DUCK (Ire) 10-2 (7*) J P Broderick, ... (20 to 1) 6
802 REGAL PRETENDER (Ire) 11-0 H Rogers, ... (33 to 1) 7
802[2] CARHUE STAR (Ire) 10-4 (5*) T J O'Sullivan, ... (16 to 1) 8
LEOS LITTLE BIT (Ire) (bl) 10-9 G M O'Neill, ... (25 to 1) 9
SPORTSTYLE (Ire) 11-0 J P Banahan, ... (20 to 1) 10
706[6] GLAS AGUS OR (Ire) (bl) 10-9 J F Titley, ... (20 to 1) 11
FURIETTO (Ire) 11-0 C F Swan, ... (10 to 1) 12
688[3] GLOWING LINES (Ire) 10-4 (5*) C P Dunne, ... (20 to 1) 13
AULD STOCK (Ire) 10-9 M Duffy, ... (14 to 1) 14
802 GROUND CONTROL (Ire) 10-9 (5*) D P Murphy, ... (33 to 1) 15
Dist: 2l, 1½l, 2l, 1½l. 4m 0.60s. (15 Ran).

(C Munnelly), A J Martin

969 Oristown Flat Race (6-y-o and up) £3,105 2m................................ (4:30)

804[2] SHEER MIRTH 8-12-0 Mr A J Martin, ... (7 to 2) 1
858[2] CALL ME AL 7-12-0 Mr J A Flynn, ... (5 to 4 fav) 2
BIT OF A CHARACTER 6-11-7 (7*) Mr P M Cloke, (20 to 1) 3
930[2] FINNEGANS WAKE 6-12-0 Mr A P O'Brien, ... (7 to 1) 4
BOLD BARNEY (NZ) 7-11-9 (5*) Mrs C Robinson, (20 to 1) 5
TRUE SON 8-11-9 (5*) Mr J A Nash, ... (20 to 1) 6
NOBLE MINISTER 6-12-0 Mr D M O'Brien, ... (16 to 1) 7
CARRIG BELLE 7-11-4[2] (7*) Mr L Hanbidge, ... (33 to 1) 8
FOUR ZEROS 6-11-11 (3*) Mr A R Coonan, ... (12 to 1) 9
433 SLEMISH MINSTREL 7-11-9 (5*) Mr H F Cleary, ... (14 to 1) 10
807[6] EDENAKILL LAD 6-11-9 (5*) Mr A E Lacy, ... (20 to 1) 11
801 SAMANTHABROWNTHORN 6-11-2 (7*) Mr B Moran, ... (16 to 1) 12
MR BARNEY 6-11-11 (3*) Mr D Marnane, ... (33 to 1) 13
YOUR SHOUT 7-12-0 Mr S R Murphy, ... (14 to 1) 14
FISTFUL OF DOLLARS 6-11-7 (7*) Mr R I Arthur, .. (14 to 1) 15
746 TORSTAR 8-11-7 (7*) Mr F McGirr, ... (20 to 1) 16
WOLF 9-11-11 (3*) Mr J R Banahan, ... (14 to 1) 17
801 CARTRON HOUSE 6-11-7 (7*) Mr M D Jennings, .. (33 to 1) 18
808 SHABRA SOCKS 7-11-7 (7*) Mr D J Kavanagh, ... (33 to 1) 19
808 GORE PORT BAY 6-11-7 (7*) Mr D W Cullen, ... (33 to 1) 20
Dist: 4½l, ½l, 1l, ½l. 3m 44.10s. (20 Ran).

(Peter Sherry), A J Martin

SEDGEFIELD (good to firm)
Wednesday October 27th
Going Correction: PLUS 0.30 sec. per fur.

970 Stonegrave Aggregates Selling Handicap Hurdle (3-y-o and up) £1,880 2m 5f 110yds ....(1:10)

759[6] HUNMANBY GAP [78] 8-10-6 C Hawkins, *trkd ldrs, led 7th, hdd appr 2 out, styd on wl und pres to ld aftr last, all out*.................... (13 to 2 op 6 to 1 tchd 7 to 1) 1
DAWAAM [84] 7-10-12 A Merrigan, *prmnt, led and mstk 2 out, hdd aftr last, no extr*......... (33 to 1 op 25 to 1) 2
717[3] FREE TRANSFER (Ire) [88] 4-11-2 J Callaghan, *in tch, trkd ldrs frm hfwy, led aftr 3 out, hdd nxt, kpt on same pace.* .... (5 to 1 fav op 6 to 1) 3
766[2] SUNTAN (Fr) [72] 4-9-8[1] (7*) K Davies, *in tch, rdn alng appr 3 out, kpt on same pace*.......... (12 to 1 op 10 to 1) 4
659 INVITE D'HONNEUR (NZ) [82] 11-10-10 Jacqui Oliver, *trkd ldrs, pushed alng aftr 3 out, styd on appr last.* .... (12 to 1 op 14 to 1 tchd 10 to 1) 5
368[5] JUBILATA (USA) [75] 5-10-3 C Dennis, *prmnt, effrt aftr 3 out, one pace*................................ (16 to 1) 6
659[9] STROKED AGAIN [72] 8-10-0 D Byrne, *nvr dngrs.* (20 to 1) 7
838[3] ELDER PRINCE [75] 7-10-3[1] R Garritty, *nvr dngrs.* .... (33 to 1 op 25 to 1) 8
839[7] J R JONES [80] 6-10-8 R Bellamy, *led till hdd 7th, hrd rdn appr 2 out, sn btn*.......................... (20 to 1) 9
734[5] SATIN LAKE (USA) [73] 6-10-1[1] C Grant, *sn tracking ldrs, effrt aftr 3 out, soon btn*............ (7 to 1 op 6 to 1) 10
659 STATION EXPRESS (Ire) [73] 5-10-1[1] A Orkney, *hld up in tch, effrt aftr 3 out, no hdwy und pres betw last 2.* .... (15 to 2 op 6 to 1 tchd 8 to 1) 11
717[8] SHAYNA MAIDEL [72] 4-10-0[3] (3*) D J Moffatt, *beh, gd hdwy aftr 3 out, wknd after nxt*............. (33 to 1) 12
818[6] TAYLORMADE BOY [91] 10-11-0 (5*) P Waggott, *in tch till wknd aftr 3 out*................. (8 to 1 tchd 9 to 1) 13
770[5] SAFARI KEEPER [72] 7-9-8[1] (7*) W Fry, *cl up till wknd appr 3 out*............................ (20 to 1 op 16 to 1) 14
846[6] ELITE DESIGN [79] 6-10-7 M Brennan, *beh most of way.* .... (20 to 1 tchd 16 to 1) 15
622[7] GREY COMMANDER [77] (v) 5-10-5 P Niven, *in tch till wknd appr 3 out*................... (10 to 1 op 8 to 1) 16
728 LITTLE CONKER [72] 5-10-0 S Turner, *in tch till wknd appr 3 out*............................ (20 to 1) 17
871 ANTINOUS [105] 9-11-12 (7*) F Perratt, *trkd ldrs, effrt whn blun and lost pl 3 out, no ch aftr.* (16 to 1 op 12 to 1) 18
837[4] NEARCTIC BAY (USA) [72] 7-10-0 M Hourigan, *cl up till wknd hfwy, wl beh whn pld up bef 2 out*...... (12 to 1) pu
Dist: 1l, 3l, sht-hd, 2½l, 5l, 3l, ¾l, 2½l, nk, sht-hd. 5m 13.30s. a 22.30s (19 Ran).

(John Wiles), P Beaumont

971 Sedgefield District Council Juvenile Novices' Hurdle (3-y-o) £1,795 2m 1f 110yds ....(1:40)

790[3] REGAL AURA (Ire) 10-12 J Callaghan, *trkd ldrs, led appr 3 out, grad drw clr.* (5 to 2 fav tchd 11 to 4 and 9 to 4) 1
732* ASTRAC TRIO (USA) (v) 11-2 (3*) A Dobbin, *cl up, led 3rd till hdd and outpcd appr 3 out, kpt on approaching nxt, no ch wth wnr*...... (11 to 1 op 10 to 1 tchd 12 to 1) 2
742[7] PEEDIE PEAT 10-12 M Dwyer, *led to 3rd, cl up till one paced appr 2 out*.................. (10 to 1 op 8 to 1) 3
784[3] HASTA LA VISTA 10-12 L Wyer, *prmnt till outpcd appr 3 out, no dngr aftr*...... (11 to 2 op 4 to 1 tchd 6 to 1) 4
790[6] NATIVE WORTH 10-7 (5*) P Williams, *in tch, kpt on same pace frm 3 out*...... (20 to 1 op 25 to 1 tchd 33 to 1) 5
GOLDEN SAVANNAH 10-5 (7*) J Driscoll, *hld up, steady hdwy appr 3 out, no extr betw last 2.* .... (33 to 1 op 25 to 1) 6
NEGD (USA) 10-12 R Garritty, *in tch, no hdwy frm 3 out.* .... (33 to 1 op 25 to 1) 7
561[2] WANZA 11-5 C Grant, *prmnt till wknd appr 3 out.* .... (7 to 2 tchd 4 to 1) 8
516[7] PAAJIB (Ire) 10-5 (7*) W Fry, *nvr dngrs*.......... (33 to 1) 9
754[8] MISS PIMPERNEL 10-7 A Merrigan, *al wl beh.* .... (50 to 1 op 33 to 1) 10
ROSSCOYNE 10-7 P Niven, *al wl beh.* (7 to 1 op 5 to 1) 11
790 RYTHMIC RYMER 10-4 (3*) D J Moffatt, *al wl beh.* .... (50 to 1 op 33 to 1) 12
SKY WISH 10-12 T Reed, *al wl beh*............ (14 to 1) 13
WEAVER GEORGE (Ire) 10-5 (7*) J Supple, *f 1st.* .... (50 to 1 op 33 to 1) f
NEWGATESKY 10-0 (7*) F Leahy, *brght dwn 1st.* (33 to 1) bd
KEEP BATTLING 10-12 A Orkney, *brght dwn 1st.* .... (33 to 1 op 25 to 1) bd
Dist: 10l, 3½l, 1l, 8l, ½l, 2½l, 8l, 1l, 15l, 1l. 4m 6.20s. a 11.20s (16 Ran).
SR: 25/22/11/10/2/1/ (D J Bushell), G M Moore

972 Rowena Coleman Handicap Hurdle (0-125 3-y-o and up) £2,532 2m 1f 110yds... (2:10)

824[2] NOTABLE EXCEPTION [92] 4-10-7 P Niven, *hld up, gd hdwy hfwy, chlgd 3 out, led last, styd on wl.* .... (3 to 1 fav op 7 to 2) 1
849* HALLO MAM (Ire) [89] 4-10-4 (6ex) M Brennan, *hld up, gd hdwy hfwy, led 3 out, hdd last, no extr.* .... (7 to 2 op 3 to 1 tchd 4 to 1) 2

TIP IT IN [85] 4-10-0 S Turner, *cl up, led aftr 4th till hdd 3 out, rallied betw last 2, no extr run in* . . . .(33 to 1) 3

719[5] MASTER OF THE ROCK [95] 4-10-10 C Hawkins, *cl up, led 4th, sn hdd, outpcd aftr 3 out, kpt on frm nxt.*
. . . .(16 to 1 op 12 to 1) 4

ONLY A ROSE [97] 4-10-12 D Wilkinson, *cl up, chlgd 3 out, sn rdn and outpcd, kpt on frm nxt.* (12 to 1 op 10 to 1) 5

787* CHEEKY POT [94] (bl) 5-10-4 (5*) P Waggott, *chsd ldrs till wknd betw last 2* . . . .(7 to 1 op 6 to 1) 6

787[3] STAGS FELL [85] 8-9-12[1] (3*) N Bentley, *prmnt, chlgd 3 out, grad wknd* . . . .(16 to 1 op 14 to 1) 7

MAGIC BLOOM [91] 7-10-3 (3*) A Larnach, *hld up, styd on frm 3 out, nvr nr to chal.*
. . . .(12 to 1 op 14 to 1 tchd 10 to 1) 8

CURTAIN FACTORY [88] 4-10-3 L Wyer, *in tch till wknd aftr 3 out* . . . .(10 to 1 tchd 9 to 1) 9

824[7] CAPTAIN TANCRED (Ire) [85] 5-10-0 A Merrigan, *hld up in tch, effrt appr 3 out, fdd* . . . .(33 to 1 op 20 to 1) 10

781[5] WAKE UP [104] 6-11-5 M Dwyer, *in tch till wknd 3 out.*
. . . .(7 to 1) 11

824[6] SEON [100] 7-11-5 (5*) D Bentley, *prmnt till outpcd aftr 5th, no dngr after* . . . .(12 to 1 tchd 10 to 1) 12

DUTCH BLUES [85] 6-9-7 (7*) E Husband, *beh frm hfwy.*
. . . .(25 to 1 op 33 to 1) 13

PANDESSA [105] 6-11-1 (5*) Mr M Buckley, *led till hdd 4th, wknd quickly aftr nxt.* . . . .(14 to 1) 14

Dist: 1l, ¾l, 7l, hd, ½l, nk, nk, 3l, 5l, 3l, sht-hd. 4m 6.30s. a 11.30s (14 Ran).
SR: 18/14/9/12/14/10/-/5/-/ (Andrews & Wilson), Mrs M Reveley

973 Vaux Breweries Handicap Chase (0-120 4-y-o and up) £2,464 2m 5f. . . . . (2:40)

735 NIGHT GUEST [99] 11-10-5 (3*) A Dobbin, *trkd ldrs, led 12th, jnd appr 2 out, styd on wl und pres frm last.*
. . . .(12 to 1) 1

546[4] CROSS CANNON [119] 7-11-11 (3*) A Larnach, *trkd ldrs, jnd wnr gng wl 2 out, rdn aftr last, not quicken.*
. . . .(5 to 1 tchd 11 to 2 and 6 to 1) 2

811 CENTENARY STAR [105] 8-11-0 P Niven, *prmnt till grad wknd frm 4 out* . . . .(11 to 4 fav op 5 to 2) 3

647[4] PIPER O'DRUMMOND [105] 6-10-6 (5*) J Burke, *hld up, hdwy tenth, wknd appr 3 out* . . . .(10 to 1 op 8 to 1) 4

788[4] CLASSIC MINSTREL [93] 9-10-2[6] (5*) P Williams, *made most till mstk and hdd 12th, grad wknd* . .(4 to 1 op 7 to 2) 5

788[5] MOSS BEE [99] 6-10-8[8] T Reed, *prmnt till wknd frm 4 out.*
. . . .(11 to 2 op 9 to 2) 6

WHO'S IN CHARGE [91] 9-10-0 A Merrigan, *tld off frm hfwy* . . . .(50 to 1 op 33 to 1) 7

SOUTH CROSS (USA) [93] 8-10-2 M Brennan, *in tch, effrt appr 4 out, blun nxt, 3rd and btn whn pld up lme aftr 2 out.* . . . .(14 to 1 op 12 to 1) pu

MOULTON BULL [93] 7-10-2[2] C Hawkins, *lost tch frm 9th, tld off whn pld up bef 4 out.* . . . . . .(12 to 1 tchd 14 to 1) pu

Dist: 1½l, 15l, 10l, 3l, 7l, dist. 5m 16.60s. a 12.60s (9 Ran).
SR: 17/35/6/-/-/-/ (J A G Fiddes), P Monteith

974 Jayne Thompson Memorial Novices' Chase (5-y-o and up) £2,270 2m 5f. . .(3:10)

627* CLASSIC CONTACT 7-11-0 J Callaghan, *jmpd wl, made all, drw clr betw last 2...*(9 to 2 op 4 to 1 tchd 5 to 1) 1

581[2] NORTHERN SQUIRE 5-10-12 M Dwyer, *in tch, outpcd appr 4 out, kpt on frm 2 out, took second pl cl hme.*
. . . .(10 to 1) 2

909[3] VAYRUA (Fr) 8-11-0 B Storey, *chsd wnr most of way, ev ch appr 2 out, one paced, wknd towards finish.*
. . . .(11 to 4 op 5 to 2) 3

909[8] INVERINATE 8-11-0 T Reed, *in tch, no hdwy frm 4 out.*
. . . .(33 to 1 op 25 to 1) 4

756[2] DOWN THE ROAD 6-11-5 G McCourt, *prmnt till grad wknd appr 4 out.* . . . .(5 to 2 fav op 9 to 4) 5

641[3] CAPTAIN CUTE 8-11-0 D Byrne, *sn wl beh, styd on frm 11th, nvr nr ldrs.* . . . .(14 to 1 op 12 to 1 tchd 16 to 1) 6

694[4] ABLE PLAYER (USA) 6-11-0 (5*) J Burke, *nvr better than mid-div* . . . .(12 to 1 op 10 to 1) 7

733 FLASS VALE 5-10-12 R Garritty, *lost tch frm hfwy, sn wl beh.* . . . .(50 to 1 op 33 to 1) 8

721[6] ROAD BY THE RIVER (Ire) 5-10-12 C Grant, *lost tch 11th, sn wl beh.* . . . .(33 to 1) 9

LORD BERTRAM (Ire) 5-10-9 (3*) A Larnach, *sn wl beh, tld off* . . . .(33 to 1 op 25 to 1) 10

909[9] GOLDEN BANKER (Ire) 5-10-12 K Jones, *sn wl beh, tld off* . . . .(66 to 1 op 50 to 1) 11

CONCERT PAPER 9-11-0 L Wyer, *in tch, reminders hfwy, wknd quickly, wl beh whn pld bef 4 out.*
. . . .(10 to 1 op 12 to 1) pu

787[4] VERBAL WARNING 5-10-12 K Johnson, *sn wl beh, pld up bef 4 out.* . . . .(33 to 1) pu

Dist: 12l, nk, 12l, 5l, 10l, 2½l, 15l, 6l. 5m 15.00s. a 11.00s (13 Ran).
SR: 39/25/26/14/14/-/-1/-/ (N B Mason), N B Mason

975 Night Nurse Trophy Handicap Chase (0-120 5-y-o and up) £2,782 3m 3f. . . .(3:45)

HABTON WHIN [102] 7-10-13 L Wyer, *in tch, chsd ldr frm 3 out, led aftr nxt, clr whn dived lft last, hld on und pres.*
. . . .(10 to 1 op 10 to 1) 1

783[2] FOSBURY [106] 8-10-12 (5*) J Burke, *led, rdn whn blun badly 2 out, sn hdd, kpt on same pace.*
. . . .(13 to 8 fav op 5 to 2 tchd 6 to 4) 2

623[6] GATHERING TIME [99] 7-10-10 G McCourt, *chsd ldr, pushed alng frm 7th, hrd rdn aftr 4 out, one pace.*
. . . .(8 to 1 op 7 to 1) 3

789* PORTAVOGIE [94] (bl) 9-9-12 (7*) Mr D Parker, *hld up and beh, pushed alng aftr 12th, hdwy appr 3 out, no extr betw last 2* . . . .(9 to 2 op 4 to 1 tchd 5 to 1) 4

758[3] CHARMING GALE [102] 6-10-8 (5*) P Williams, *trkd ldrs till grad wknd frm appr 4 out* . . . .(6 to 1 tchd 7 to 1) 5

579[6] OVER THE STREAM [93] 7-10-4 C Grant, *in tch till wknd aftr 15th* . . . .(10 to 1 tchd 12 to 1) 6

789 RUSTINO [97] 7-10-8 P Niven, *in tch, blun 11th, reminder aftr 13th, wknd after 15th.* . . . .(12 to 1 op 8 to 1) 7

BOREEN OWEN [117] 9-12-0 T Reed, *in tch whn f 9th.*
. . . .(12 to 1 op 10 to 1) f

Dist: 6l, 3l, 3l, 4l, 15l, 4l. 7m 2.40s. a 23.40s (8 Ran).
(C H Stevens), M H Easterby

976 Grunwick Stakes National Hunt Flat Race (4,5,6-y-o) £1,792 2m 1f 110yds. . . . . .(4:15)

MAYBE O'GRADY (Ire) 4-10-12 (7*) S Mason, *in tch, led 5 fs out, hdd 2 out, kpt on wl to ld cl hme.*
. . . .(5 to 2 fav op 7 to 2 tchd 9 to 4) 1

DOWN THE FELL 4-10-12 (7*) F Perratt, *prmnt, slightly ld 2 fs out, hdd and no extr cl hme.* . . . . .(14 to 1 op 12 to 1) 2

PHILDAN (Ire) 4-11-2 (3*) D J Moffatt, *hld up and beh, gd hdwy to join ldrs 4 fs out, chlgd o'r 2 out, wknd entering fnl furlong.* . . . .(10 to 1 op 8 to 1) 3

OAKLEY 4-11-0 (5*) P Waggott, *in tch, chsd ldrs frm 4 fs out, no extr und pres fnl 2 furlongs.*
. . . .(14 to 1 op 12 to 1) 4

INDIAN ORCHID 6-10-10 (5*) Mr M Buckley, *hld up, gd hdwy to chase ldrs 3 fs out, no extr fnl 2 furlongs.*
. . . .(5 to 1 op 4 to 1) 5

CLERIC ON BROADWAY (Ire) 5-10-8 (7*) Mark Roberts, *al chasing ldrs, one pace fnl 3 fs.....*(16 to 1 op 14 to 1) 6

IVY HOUSE (Ire) 5-10-13 P B Harding, *prmnt till wknd o'r 2 fs out, eased whn btn.*(8 to 1 op 6 to 1 tchd 10 to 1) 7

WANG HOW 5-10-13 (7*) S Taylor, *in tch, gd hdwy to chase ldrs 6 fs out, wknd o'r 3 out.* . . . .(9 to 1 op 7 to 1) 8

723[6] RAYLEO (Ire) 4-11-0 (5*) Mr D McCain, *prmnt, led hfwy, hdd 5 fs out, sn wknd.* . . . .(7 to 1) 9

ROKER LAD (Ire) 4-10-12 (7*) W Fry, *nvr on terms.*
. . . .(16 to 1 op 14 to 1 tchd 20 to 1) 10

SCOTTISH GAMBLER 4-11-0 (5*) D Bentley, *in tch till wknd o'r 4 fs out.* . . . .(4 to 1 tchd 7 to 2) 11

GINGE 4-10-12 (7*) J Driscoll, *chsd ldrs till wknd 4 fs out.*
. . . .(16 to 1 tchd 20 to 1) 12

UNCLE BENJI (Ire) 4-10-12 (7*) F Leahy, *wl beh frm 5 fs out.* . . . .(33 to 1 op 20 to 1) 13

THYMON THE HORTH 4-10-12 (7*) S Haworth, *lost tch frm 7 fs out, tld off.* . . . .(33 to 1 op 20 to 1) 14

LUCKY WEDSONG 4-10-12 (7*) N Stocks, *lost tch frm hfwy, wl tld off.* . . . .(33 to 1 op 20 to 1) 15

SKIDDAW CALYPSO 4-10-11 (3*) A Dobbin, *sddld slpd, led till hdd hfwy, sn lost pl, wl tld off.* . . . .(33 to 1) 16

Dist: 1½l, 3½l, sht-hd, 2½l, 3½l, 5l, 3l, 4l, 2l, hd. 4m 7.90s. (16 Ran).
(David Bell), Mrs M Reveley

KEMPTON (good to firm)
Thursday October 28th
Going Correction: MINUS 0.05 sec. per fur.

977 Drive-in Car Mart Conditional Jockeys' Handicap Hurdle (0-130 5-y-o and up) £2,690 2m. . . . .(1:40)

CABIN HILL [90] 7-10-9 D Leahy, *chsd ldr, led aftr 3 out, clr nxt, cmftbly.* . . . . . .(10 to 4 op 3 to 1 tchd 4 to 1) 1

SOLEIL DANCER (Ire) [103] 5-11-8 D Fortt, *cl up, ev ch 3 out, one pace appr nxt, no chance whn hit last.*
. . . .(3 to 1 op 2 to 1 tchd 2 to 1) 2

TOP WAVE [109] 5-11-9 (5*) Pat Thompson, *hld up in cl tch, closed and ev ch 3 out, rdn and wknd appr nxt.*
. . . .(5 to 1) 3

PERFAY (USA) [105] 5-11-10 D O'Sullivan, *led, ran wide on bend aftr second, hdd aftr 3 out, sn btn, tld off, broke blood vessel.*. . . . . . .(13 to 8 fav op 7 to 4 tchd 2 to 1) 4

Dist: 12l, 8l, dist. 3m 48.80s. a 8.80s (4 Ran).
(The Kinnersley Crew), S Christian

978 Kempton Antique Fair Novices' Chase (5-y-o and up) £3,817 2½m 110yds. . . . .(2:10)

SOME DAY SOON 8-11-0 G Bradley, *made all, quickened 4 out, shaken up and ran on wl aftr last.*
. . . .(7 to 1 op 1 to 1 tchd 12 to 1) 1

FACTOR TEN [113] 8-11-0 J Osborne, *lft second at 7th, chsd wnr, ev ch r-in, sn one pace.*
. . . .(15 to 8 fav op 6 to 4) 2

843[3] WELL BRIEFED 6-11-0 S McNeill, *chsd tdg trio, lft 3rd at 7th, outpcd aftr 4 out, btn whn mstk 2 out, tld off.*
. . . .(20 to 1 op 12 to 1) 3

882* FESTIVAL DREAMS 8-11-9 P Holley, *beh, cld 11th, rdn and
outpcd frm 13th, tld off*. (9 to 2 op 7 to 2 tchd 5 to 1)   4
847³ NOTARY-NOWELL (bl) 7-10-7 (7*) P Murphy, *al beh, tld off*.
.... (20 to 1 op 14 to 1)   5
774* CONGREGATION 7-11-9 H Davies, *rcd freely, second whn
f 7th*......................(2 to 1 op 5 to 2 tchd 11 to 4)   f
MISSILE RUN 9-11-0 B Clifford, *sn tld off, pld up bef 9th*.
....................................(100 to 1 op 50 to 1)   pu
Dist: 2l, 30l, 20l. dist. 5m 2.40s. a 9.40s (7 Ran).
(D A MacKechnie), M Bradstock

979 Tricia Leigh Craft Fairs Handicap Hurdle (0-135 4-y-o and up) £3,622 3m 110yds
......................................(2:40)

564* KANO WARRIOR [103] 6-10-0 C Llewellyn, *in tch, cld on
ldg pair 4 out, led o'r 2 out, clr appr last, eased r-in*.
......................(3 to 1 jt-fav op 9 to 4 tchd 100 to 30)   1
JAWANI (Ire) [104] 5-10-1 A Carroll, *beh, hdwy 4 out, chsd
wnr appr 2 out, one pace approaching last*.. (3 to 1 jt-
fav tchd 11 to 4 and 7 to 2)   2
701⁴ CAIRNCASTLE [115] 8-10-12 N Mann, *hld up, hdwy 8th,
blun badly nxt, styd on appr last*... (9 to 2 op 4 to 1)   3
827⁵ CABOCHON [131] 6-12-0 J Frost, *led til hdd o'r 2 out, one
pace*............................(7 to 1 op 6 to 1 tchd 15 to 2)   4
829⁵ STORM DRUM [112] (bl) 4-10-9 J Osborne, *hld up in rear,
rdn and hdwy o'r 3 out, sn btn*.....(4 to 1 tchd 9 to 2)   5
848 TEL E THON [103] (v) 6-9-9 (5*) D Leahy, *wth ldr, hrd rdn
and ev ch 3 out, sn lost pl*........ (14 to 1 op 16 to 1)   6
861² JOKER JACK [103] 8-9-9 (5*) A Procter, *cl up, rdn alng and
lost pl aftr 6th, tld off*.
......................(20 to 1 op 16 to 1 tchd 25 to 1)   7
TROJAN ENVOY [103] 5-10-0 Mr W Henderson, *al beh, tld
off whn pld up bef 4 out*.......(50 to 1 tchd 100 to 1)   pu
Dist: 4l, 2½l, 8l, 12l, 10l, 8l. 5m 50.00s. a 3.00s (8 Ran).
SR: 30/27/35/43/12/   (D Jones), N A Twiston-Davies

980 Lushous Mobile Catering Handicap Chase (5-y-o and up) £3,705 3m............. (3:10)

614* MERE CLASS [120] 7-11-9 G Bradley, *pckd 1st, led to
second, trkd ldr, led ag'n 14th, clr appr last, easily*.
...............(9 to 4 on op 2 to 1 on tchd 15 to 8 on)   1
BOLD CHOICE [97] 7-10-0 D Skyrme, *trkd ldg pair, second
and one pace whn blun badly 2 out*.
......................(16 to 1 op 12 to 1 tchd 20 to 1)   2
726² TOMPET [105] 7-10-3 (5*) T Jenks, *jmpd lft, led second till
hdd 14th, rallied 3 out, outpcd nxt*..(5 to 2 op 9 to 4)   3
EASTSHAW [125] 11-12-0 C Llewellyn, *hld up, cld 14th,
blun badly and uns rdr nxt*.
......................(16 to 1 op 10 to 1 tchd 20 to 1)   ur
(Miss M Talbot), C P E Brooks

981 Gibbs Toasty Kitchen Novices' Chase (5-y-o and up) £3,607 2m............. (3:40)

826* LACKENDARA 6-11-10 J Osborne, *pckd 1st, led 3rd, clr 4
out, slight mstk 2 out, easily*.
...............(9 to 2 on op 5 to 1 on tchd 4 to 1 on)   1
POPPETS PET 6-11-0 S Earle, *led to 3rd, lost pl 7th, lft
modest second 9th, cld 3 out, sn outpcd*.
......................(11 to 1 op 10 to 1 tchd 12 to 1)   2
826⁵ PRESENT TIMES 7-10-7 (7*) J Clarke, *beh, blun 8th, lft
modest 3rd nxt, tld off*............(20 to 1 tchd 25 to 1)   3
849⁸ KEV'S LASS (Ire) 5-10-2 (7*) P Murphy, *in tch, awkward
6th, chasing wnr whn f 9th*.
......................(6 to 1 op 5 to 1 tchd 7 to 1)   f
Dist: 10l, dist. 3m 55.90s. a 8.90s (4 Ran).
(Opening Bid Partnership), Miss H C Knight

982 Shen Promotions Psychic Fairs Novices' Hurdle (4-y-o and up) £2,490 2m 5f.. (4:10)

JULIOS GENIUS 6-10-10 D Murphy, *al prmnt, jmpd into ld
4 out, clr appr last, easily*.
.......(11 to 10 op 5 to 4 tchd 8 to 1 and 12 to 1)   1
795² TOUR LEADER (NZ) 4-10-10 S Earle, *hld up, cld 6th, hrd
rdn and chsd wnr appr 2 out, one pace*.
......................(7 to 2 op 3 to 1 tchd 4 to 1)   2
773² STYLE AND CLASS 4-10-5 (5*) C Burnett-Wells, *mstk second, trkd ldrs, pushed alng aftr 3 out, one pace*.
.......(13 to 8 fav op 6 to 4 tchd 11 to 8 and 7 to 4)   3
ATROPOS (Fr) (bl) 5-10-10 G Bradley, *trkd ldr till wknd
appr 2 out*....................(5 to 1 tchd 6 to 1 and 4 to 1)   4
883 CRACKLING ANGELS 6-10-5 J Osborne, *led til hdd 4 out,
wknd aftr nxt*.............(16 to 1 op 10 to 1 tchd 20 to 1)   5
634⁶ ROCKCLIFFE LAD 4-10-10 C Llewellyn, *chsd ldrs till lost
pl 6th*......................(13 to 2 op 10 to 1 tchd 15 to 2)   6
BOOTH'S BOUQUET 5-10-10 M Richards, *hld up in rear,
hdwy o'r 3 out, sn btn*.
......................(25 to 1 op 16 to 1 tchd 33 to 1)   7
NEW YORK BOY 5-10-10 J Frost, *al beh, tld off*.
......................(16 to 1 op 12 to 1 tchd 20 to 1)   8
592 ALLIED'S TEAM 6-10-5 D Skyrme, *al beh, tld off*.
....................................(100 to 1)   9
Dist: 12l, 4l, 10l, 6l, 5l, 7l, 30l, 10l. 4m 59.10s. a 6.10s (9 Ran).

SR: 11/-/-/-/-/-/   (Mrs P Jubert), B J Meehan

STRATFORD (good to firm)
Thursday October 28th
**Going Correction: PLUS 0.10 sec. per fur. (races
1,3,6), PLUS 0.40 (2,4,5)**

983 Pathlow Novices' Hurdle (4-y-o and up) £2,303 2m 110yds................. (2:00)

844* BELL STAFFBOY (Ire) 4-11-2 (3*) W Marston, *trkd ldrs, led 2
out, hit last, drvn out*.
......................(5 to 4 fav op 6 to 4 tchd Evens)   1
597⁵ TOP SPIN 4-11-5 L Wyer, *led till mstk and hdd 3 out,
outpcd frm 2 out and plenty do appr last, rallied und
pres, no extr cl hme*................(10 to 1 op 6 to 1)   2
NED THE HALL (Ire) 5-10-12 N Williamson, *al chasing ldrs,
rdn and styd on appr last, not quicken r-in, edgd lft
run-in, fnshd 3rd, plcd 4th*.......(15 to 2 op 9 to 2)   3D
821* BRODESSA 7-11-5 P Niven, *chsd ldrs, led 3 out, mstk and
hdd 2 out, sn outpcd, hdwy appr last, not much room r-in,
fnshd 4th, plcd 3rd*.....(11 to 4 op 9 to 4 tchd 3 to 1)   3
GESNERA 5-10-7 G McCourt, *beh 3rd, hdwy frm 5th, not
rch ldrs*...............................(50 to 1 op 33 to 1)   5
791² SHIRLEY'S TRAIN (USA) 4-10-12 Peter Hobbs, *in tch, chsd
ldrs 3 out, sn wknd*......(9 to 1 op 14 to 1 tchd 8 to 1)   6
346 THAT'S SPECIAL 4-10-12 A Maguire, *nvr rch ldrs*.
....................................(50 to 1 op 33 to 1)   7
597 MR POPPLETON 4-10-12 D Bridgwater, *in tch till wknd 3
out*....................(150 to 1 op 100 to 1)   8
ANDRATH (Ire) 5-10-12 W Humphreys, *al beh*.
.......(66 to 1 op 100 to 1 tchd 50 to 1)   9
BRIMPTON BERTIE 4-10-12 J Railton, *chsd ldrs to 5th*.
.......(25 to 1 op 16 to 1)   10
CURRAGH PETER 6-10-5 (7*) Leanne Eldredge, *al beh*.
....................................(100 to 1)   11
ROSEN THE BEAU (Ire) 5-10-12 R Supple, *beh frm 3rd, tld
off*....................(66 to 1 op 50 to 1)   12
CLAYDON 5-10-12 R Bellamy, *mstk 1st and second, sn wl
beh, tld off*.......................(66 to 1 op 50 to 1)   13
JACK DIAMOND 5-10-7 (5*) R Davis, *tld off 3rd, pld up bef
3 out*....................(150 to 1 op 100 to 1)   pu
CHETWOOD LASS 5-10-0 (7*) P McLoughlin, *mstk 1st, beh
4th, tld off bef 3 out, pld up bef 3 out*.......(100 to 1)   pu
Dist: 2½l, 2l, ¾l, 10l, 12l, 8l, ¾l, 1½l, 2½l, 6l. 3m 56.00s. a 7.00s (15 Ran).
SR: 38/35/26/32/10/3/   (K W Bell & Son Ltd), C D Broad

984 Bearley Novices' Chase (4-y-o and up) £3,046 2m 5f 110yds............... (2:30)

884 ABU MUSLAB (bl) 9-11-4 M A FitzGerald, *made all, hit 2
out, styd on wl*......................(7 to 1 op 5 to 1)   1
701 REAL PROGRESS (Ire) 5-10-10 Peter Hobbs, *chsd ldr, mstk
9th, hdwy tenth, chsd wnr appr last, no extr*. (7 to 2 jt-
fav op 5 to 2)   2
STAGE PLAYER 7-10-7 (5*) T Eley, *sn prmnt, chsd ldr 12th,
one pace appr last*.......(8 to 1 op 9 to 2 tchd 9 to 1)   3
RYTON GUARD 8-10-12 G Upton, *beh, moderate prog frm
3 out*..............................(4 to 1 op 10 to 1)   4
899⁶ PICKETSTONE 6-10-12 G McCourt, *mstk 1st, rdn tenth, al
beh*... (12 to 1 op 14 to 1 tchd 16 to 1 and 10 to 1)   5
892 CANTORIS FRATER 6-10-12 A Tory, *in tch till drpd rear
8th, no ch whn hit 4 out*.......(25 to 1 op 14 to 1)   6
DEBT OF HONOR 5-10-10 R Greene, *beh, drvn and hdwy
4 out, fourth and al hld whn f out*.
......................(20 to 1 op 10 to 1)   f
VAZON BAY (bl) 9-10-12 R Dunwoody, *prmnt, chsd wnr
11th, sn wknd, tld off whn pld up bef 3 out*. (7 to 2 jt-
fav op 5 to 2)   pu
660⁶ TOP IT ALL (bl) 5-10-10 D Bridgwater, *chsd ldrs, hrd drvn
appr tenth, sn wknd, tld off whn pld up bef 4 out*.
......................(12 to 1 op 8 to 1)   pu
Dist: 1½l, 4l, 15l, 6l, 2½l. 5m 19.20s. a 16.20s (9 Ran).
SR: 14/4/2/-/-/-/   (G F Edwards), G F Edwards

985 Archie Scott Benevolent Fund Gold Cup Handicap Hurdle (0-140 4-y-o and up) £3,542 2¾m 110yds............... (3:00)

580* MYSTIC MEMORY [99] 4-10-2¹ P Niven, *trkd ldrs, drvn
alng frm 2 out, styd on gmely to ld nr finish*.
.......(13 to 8 fav op 6 to 4 tchd 15 to 8 and 7 to 4)   1
845* STRONG MEDICINE [116] 6-11-5 N Williamson, *hld up
tracking ldrs, led out 3 out, drvn appr last, hdd nr
finish, rallied, jst fld*................(9 to 2 op 7 to 2)   2
762⁴ MENEBUCK [125] 7-12-0 E Murphy, *pressed ldr, hit 4th,
chlgd tth till ld appr 3 out, hdd sn aftr three out, ev ch
last, hng rght, one pace*. (9 to 2 op 7 to 2 tchd 5 to 1)   3
845² ASK THE GOVERNOR [110] 7-10-13 A Maguire, *hld up in
rear till f 3rd*....................(2 to 1 tchd 9 to 4)   f
796 MORGANS MAN [98] 4-10-1¹ M A FitzGerald, *made most
till hdd appr 3 out, sn wknd and pld up*.
......................(50 to 1 op 33 to 1)   pu
Dist: Nk, 4l. 5m 27.70s. a 15.70s (5 Ran).
(Carnoustie Racing Club Ltd), Mrs M Reveley

986 Binton Handicap Chase (0-125 5-y-o and up) £3,096 3½m. . . . . (3:30)

720* BUDDY HOLLY (NZ) [103] 8-10-9 Peter Hobbs, *led to 8th, styd prmnt, rdn frm 3 out, chlgd last, sn led, jst hld on.*
. . . . (9 to 4 fav op 5 to 2 tchd 2 to 1) 1
726³ SMOOTH ESCORT [112] (v) 9-11-4 N Williamson, *chsd ldrs, led 12th to 14th, led ag'n 16th to 17th, led 4 out, hdd +in, rallied, jst fld.* 2
726⁴ ARD T'MATCH [96] (v) 8-10-2⁵ Gary Lyons, *beh 6th, hdwy to chase ldrs 14th, rdn and styd on one pace frm 3 out.*
. . . . (12 to 1 tchd 14 to 1) 3
714⁵ DOONLOUGHAN [106] 8-10-12 A Maguire, *chsd ldrs, hit 4th, led 8th to 12th, reminder 13th, led 14th to 16th, led 17th to four out, wknd aftr 3 out.*
. . . . (9 to 1 op 10 to 1 tchd 8 to 1) 4
835 JIMMY O'DEA [98] (v) 6-9-13 (5*) T Eley, *jmpd slowy 1st, hit second, hdwy 9th, wknd frm 16th.* (14 to 1 op 10 to 1) 5
WOODLANDS GENHIRE [96] 8-10-0³ (5*) R Davis, *hdwy to chase ldr 7th, wknd 16th.* . . . . (20 to 1 op 14 to 1) 6
DISTILLATION [95] 8-10-1¹ M A FitzGerald, *beh most of way.* . . . . (11 to 1 op 16 to 1 tchd 10 to 1) 7
765³ GOLD CAP (Fr) [115] 8-11-7 M Hourigan, *pressed ldrs, rdn frm 17th, cl 3rd whn f 2 out.* . . . . . (4 to 1 tchd 9 to 2) f
ROMFUL PRINCE [94] 10-10-0 D Bridgwater, *beh 5th, wknd and pld up bef 14th.* . . . . (14 to 1) pu
Dist: Hd, 1½l, 15l, 12l, 15l, ½l. 7m 10.0s. a 25.10s (9 Ran).

(B A J Lake), J A B Old

987 Oslo Trophy Handicap Chase (0-135 5-y-o and up) £2,882 2m 1f 110yds. . . . . (4:00)

EGYPT MILL PRINCE [133] (bl) 7-12-0 R Dunwoody, *chsd ldr till 1ft in ld 3rd, made rest, came clr frm 3 out, easily.*
. . . . (100 to 30 op 3 to 1 tchd 5 to 2 and 7 to 2) 1
893² DROMASTICK [126] 7-11-7 N Williamson, *chsd wnr frm 3rd, effrt 4 out, outpcd from nxt.*
. . . . (5 to 2 op 2 to 1 tchd 11 to 4) 2
713² STAR OF THE GLEN [113] 7-10-8 A Maguire, *chsd ldrs, rdn and one pace frm 4 out.* . . . . . . (2 to 1 fav tchd 9 to 4) 3
CHAIN SHOT [109] 8-10-4 T Wall, *mstk 1st, beh and hit 7th, no ch whn mistake 9th.* . . . . . . (16 to 1 op 10 to 1) 4
BLUE BUCCANEER [105] 10-10-0 L Harvey, *tld off frm 5th.*
. . . . (16 to 1 op 10 to 1) 5
919 TERRIBLE GEL (Fr) [105] 8-10-0 L Wyer, *led till mstk and uns rdr 3rd.* . . . . (6 to 1 op 4 to 1) ur
Dist: 3½l, nk, 25l, 12l. 4m 15.30s. a 11.30s (6 Ran).
SR: 57/46/32/3/-/-/

(S R Webb), Mrs J Pitman

988 Temple Grafton Novices' Handicap Hurdle (0-100 4-y-o and up) £2,072 2m 110yds . . . . (4:30)

809³ SUPER COIN [85] 5-11-10 A Maguire, *hdwy 5th, drvn to chal 2 out, sn led, pushed out.*
. . . . (11 to 2 op 8 to 1 tchd 5 to 1) 1
753⁶ WILLY'S BOUNTY [70] 10-10-9 N Williamson, *sn tracking ldrs, chsd wnr appr last, no imprsn.*
. . . . (20 to 1 tchd 25 to 1) 2
242² SAINT CIEL (USA) [75] 5-11-0 R Supple, *in tch, drvn to press ldrs 3 out, one pace aftr 2 out.*
. . . . (5 to 1 op 7 to 1 tchd 9 to 1) 3
TURF RUN [65] 6-10-4 S McNeill, *beh, styd on wl appr last, nrst finish.* . . . . (9 to 1 op 10 to 1 tchd 9 to 1) 4
551⁴ FRANKUS [75] 4-11-0 R Dunwoody, *prmnt, pressed ldrs 2 out, sn rdn and wknd.* . . . . (10 to 1 op 7 to 1) 5
773 HERLIN [81] 5-11-11 (5*) R Farrant, *chsd ldrs till wknd 2 out.* 6
MASTER MURPHY [65] 4-10-4 E Murphy, *led till hdd sn aftr 2 out, wknd.* . . . . (8 to 1 op 4 to 1) 7
NOTHINGBUTTROUBLE [65] 9-10-4 L Harvey, *beh till modest prog frm 2 out.* . . . . (50 to 1 op 33 to 1) 8
809⁹ MAPLE BAY (Ire) [75] 4-11-0 G McCourt, *hit 1st, sn beh.*
. . . . (20 to 1 op 16 to 1) 9
748 DOTTEREL (Ire) [61] 5-10-0 W Humphreys, *al beh.*
. . . . (6 to 1 op 50 to 1) 10
AVISHAYES (USA) [75] 6-11-0 P Niven, *hdwy to chase ldrs frm 5th, wknd quickly 2 out.* . . . . . (9 to 2 fav op 11 to 4) 11
839³ SMART DEBUTANTE (Ire) [78] 4-10-10 (7*) Mr S Joynes, *pressed ldrs, chlgd 3 out, wknd 2 out.* (8 to 1 op 7 to 1) 12
705⁹ MAGGOTS GREEN [70] 6-10-2 (7*) Mr G Lewis, *chsd ldrs to 5th.* 13
773 INDIAN MAESTRO [62] 7-10-1¹ M A FitzGerald, *chsd ldrs to 5th.* 14
Dist: 4l, 5l, 2½l, 2l, sht-hd, 2l, 4l, 1½l, 3l, 1l. 4m 5.60s. a 16.60s (14 Ran).

(George Brookes), R Lee

TIPPERARY (IRE) (good to yielding)
Thursday October 28th

989 Barronstown Novice Chase (5-y-o and up) £2,760 2m. . . . . (2:30)

392⁹ THE LADY'S KNIGHT 7-11-9 (5*) C O'Brien, ... (9 to 2) 1D
905² NORDIC SUN (Ire) 5-11-10 J F Titley, ... (Evens fav) 1

990 Limerick Junction Maiden Hurdle (4 & 5-y-o) £2,760 2m. . . . . (3:00)

925³ EAST HOUSTON 4-11-4 W T Slattery Jnr, ... (5 to 1) 1
DOONANDORAS (Ire) 5-11-6 C F Swan, ... (5 to 4 fav) 2
ROYAL OAK LADY (Ire) 5-10-10 (5*) Susan A Finn, . (8 to 1) 3
925⁶ NOT MY LINE (Ire) 4-10-13 (5*) C O'Brien, ... (7 to 1) 4
925 MR SNAGGLE (Ire) 4-10-13 (5*) T J O'Sullivan, . . . (16 to 1) 5
BOHEMIAN CASTLE (Ire) 4-11-4 F Woods, ... (8 to 1) 6
939 MR GLYNN (Ire) 4-10-11 (7*) J P Broderick, ... (12 to 1) 7
MINSTREL FIRE (Ire) 5-11-6 M Dwyer, ... (7 to 1) 8
SYLVANER (Ire) 4-10-8 (5*) P A Roche, ... (6 to 1) 9
798 THE REAL GAEL (Ire) 5-10-10 (5*) C P Dunne, . . . (12 to 1) 10
MOLLIE WOOTTON (Ire) 5-11-1 H Rogers, ... (12 to 1) 11
925 PEGUS PRINCE 4-11-4 K F O'Brien, ... (16 to 1) 12
ENNEL VIEW (Ire) 5-11-1 P J Flood, ... (8 to 1) 13
OLD ABBEY (Ire) 5-11-3 (3*) T Townend, ... (12 to 1) 14
BON VIVEUR 4-11-4 T J Taaffe, ... (6 to 1) 15
801 ALL A STRUGGLE (Ire) 5-10-10 (5*) M A Davey, . . (20 to 1) 16
Dist: Sht-hd, 10l, 7l, 20l. 4m 13.20s. (16 Ran).

(C Duggan), C Duggan

991 Ballykisteen Handicap Hurdle (4-y-o and up) £2,760 2m. . . . . (3:30)

BROCKLEY COURT [-] 6-11-7 J P Banahan, ... (6 to 1) 1
927⁴ CASH CHASE [-] 5-10-1 L P Cusack, ... (8 to 1) 2
854² SO PINK (Ire) [-] 5-10-12 C F Swan, ... (5 to 4 fav) 3
907⁷ BLAZING COMET [-] 7-9-7 F Woods, ... (7 to 1) 4
473² DANGEROUS REEF (Ire) [-] 5-9-8 (5*) T P Rudd, . . (10 to 1) 5
CHELSEA NATIVE [-] 6-10-13 (5*) Susan A Finn, . . (10 to 1) 6
927³ BALLYTIGUE LORD [-] 7-10-10 G M O'Neill, ... (5 to 1) 7
854 PREMIER LEAP (Ire) [-] 4-9-11 P B M Duggan, . . (12 to 1) 8
798⁴ POOR TIMES (Ire) [-] 5-9-2 (5*) C O'Brien, ... (14 to 1) 9
ANOTHER RUSTLE [-] 10-9-10 W T Slattery Jnr, . . (20 to 1) 10
FLEMINGS FOOTMAN [-] 6-10-1 (7*) R Dolan, . . . (14 to 1) 11
Dist: Hd, 4l, 3½l, ¾l. 4m 8.50s. (11 Ran).

(C Cronin), Mrs John Harrington

992 Tipperary Gowla National Handicap Chase (4-y-o and up) £6,900 2¾m. . . (4:00)

539* DEEP BRAMBLE [-] 6-11-10 M Dwyer, ... (6 to 4 fav) 1
GALE AGAIN [-] 6-11-9 (5*) C P Dunne, ... (6 to 1) 2
855 DESERT LORD [-] 7-10-6 C F Swan, ... (3 to 1) 3
806⁴ OPRYLAND [-] 8-9-7 F Woods, ... (16 to 1) 4
855³ LAURA'S BEAU [-] 9-11-7 C O'Dwyer, ... (6 to 1) 5
878³ LASATA [-] 8-10-9 (5*) C O'Brien, ... (7 to 1) 6
NEW MILL HOUSE [-] 10-11-2 T J Taaffe, ... (14 to 1) 7
797⁹ CHARDEN [-] 7-9-2 (5*) T J O'Sullivan, ... (40 to 1) 8
Dist: 1½l, 1l, 20l, 3l. 5m 38.70s. (8 Ran).

(J F Mernagh), Michael Hourigan

993 Cullen Flat Race (5-y-o and up) £2,760 2m . . . . (4:30)

675² FOULKSCOURT DUKE (Ire) 5-11-9 (5*) Mr J A Nash, (7 to 1) 1
NO TAG (Ire) 5-12-0 Mr A J Martin, ... (4 to 1) 2
930⁴ FAIRYHILL RUN (Ire) 6-11-9 Mr D Harney, ... (12 to 1) 3
TULLOVIN (Ire) 5-12-0 Mr J A Berry, ... (12 to 1) 4
536⁸ POLLYKENDU (Ire) 5-11-11 (3*) Mr D Marnane, . . (20 to 1) 5
SEA GALE (Ire) 5-11-9 Mr P Fenton, ... (9 to 4 on) 6
MIGHTY HAGGIS 6-11-7 (7*) Mr N C Kelleher, . . . (25 to 1) 7
801 CARRIG DANCER (Ire) 5-11-2 (7*) Mr K Whelan, . . (20 to 1) 8
857⁴ BRIDEPARK ROSE (Ire) 5-11-9 Mr S R Murphy, . . (10 to 1) 9
908² ISN'T THAT NICE (Ire) 5-11-7 (7*) Mr M Brennan, . (12 to 1) 10
LISNABOY PRINCE 6-11-7 (7*) Mr J Lombard, . . . (25 to 1) 11
832 MASTER EYRE (Ire) 5-11-7 (7*) Mr M J Bowe, . . . (20 to 1) 12
853 TULLOVIN CASTLE (Ire) 5-11-2 (7*) Mr P O'Connell,
. . . . (20 to 1) 13
114 PAT'S VALENTINE (Ire) 5-11-6 (3*) Mr M Phillips, . (25 to 1) 14
927 THE APPRENTICE (bl) 7-11-11 (3*) Mr A R Coonan, (20 to 1) 15
Dist: 3l, 6l, 3½l, hd. 4m 11.90s. (15 Ran).

(J Wilson), Thomas Bergin

BANGOR (good)
Friday October 29th
Going Correction: PLUS 0.55 sec. per fur.

994 Oxton Turf Conditional Jockeys' Selling Hurdle (4-y-o and up) £2,043 2m 1f. . (1:20)

629⁵ RULING DYNASTY (bl) 9-11-5 M Hourigan, *hld up, hdwy 3 out, effrt nxt, rdn last, edgd lft flt, styd on to ld nr line.*
...................................(11 to 8 fav tchd 6 to 4) 1
912² BAND SARGEANT (Ire) 4-10-12 N Leach, *hld up gng wl, smooth hdwy 5th, led aftr 3 out, rdn last, ct on line.*
...................................(7 to 2 op 3 to 1) 2
812⁴ ALWAYS READY (bl) 7-11-5 R Greene, *led till appr second, cl up, effrt to chal 2 out, ev ch flt, not quicken nr finish.*
...................................(6 to 1 op 5 to 1 tchd 13 to 2) 3
846³ RUTHS PRIDE 8-10-11 R Farrant, *hld up, effrt and hdwy 3 out, sn rdn and one pace.*
...................................(11 to 1 op 10 to 1 tchd 12 to 1) 4
567² TAUNTING (Ire) 5-10-7 (5*) S Lycett, *led appr second till approaching nxt, lft in ld aftr 3rd, rdn and hdd 4 out, wknd next..........* (12 to 1 op 10 to 1 tchd 14 to 1) 5
839⁸ URSHI-JADE 5-10-4 (3*) P McLoughlin, *prmnt, blun 5th and sn rdn alng, hit 3 out and wknd.*
...................................(25 to 1 op 16 to 1) 6
GROTIUS 9-11-2 R Davis, *prmnt, hdwy to ld 4 out, hdd aftr nxt, wknd quickly.* (8 to 1 op 6 to 1 tchd 9 to 1) 7
809 BROTHERLYAFFECTION 4-10-12 S Wynne, *pld hrd, led aftr second till ran out after nxt..............* (33 to 1) ro
Dist: Hd, ¾l, 8l, nk, 3½l, 2½l. 4m 16.30s. a 26.30s (8 Ran).
(Midweek Racing), M D I Usher

995 Corbett Bookmakers Handicap Chase (0-140 4-y-o and up) £4,546 2½m 110yds
...................................(1:50)

BETTER TIMES AHEAD [125] 7-11-8 R Dunwoody, *al prmnt, blun 3rd, hit nxt and 9th, effrt to chal 2 out, sn led, quickened clr..................* (9 to 2 op 3 to 1) 1
WASHINGTONCROSSING [127] 7-11-10 S McNeill, *al prmnt, led tenth, rdn 2 out, sn hdd and not quicken, hit last..................* (3 to 1 op 2 to 1) 2
811³ COMEDY ROAD [103] 9-10-0 L Harvey, *trkd ldrs, hit 6th, pushed alng 5 out, rdn and ch appr 2 out, sn one pace.*
..........(9 to 1 op 10 to 1 tchd 12 to 1 and 8 to 1) 3
HEY COTTAGE [115] 8-10-12 G McCourt, *hld up in tch, gd hdwy 5 out, dsptd ld 3 out, sn rdn, wknd appr nxt.*
...................................(11 to 1 op 7 to 1 tchd 12 to 1) 4
842² GAELIC FROLIC [103] 10-10-0 N Williamson, *hld up, smooth hdwy 5 out, ev ch whn f 3 out.*
...................................(7 to 4 fav op 9 to 4 tchd 5 to 2) f
BALDA BOY [124] 9-11-7 H Davies, *led, hdd tenth, rdn and wknd 4 out, uns rdr nxt........* (8 to 1 op 6 to 1) ur
Dist: 8l, 7l, 20l. 5m 7.60s. a 16.60s (6 Ran).
SR: 41/35/4/
(E Briggs), G Richards

996 Tarporley Hunt Club Novices' Handicap Chase (5-y-o and up) £3,550 3m 110yds
...................................(2:20)

847² SANDAIG [89] (bl) 7-11-3 N Williamson, *hld up, hit tenth, blun 13th, hdwy nxt, led aftr 3 out, hdd after next, second and held whn lft clr last.*
...................................(11 to 4 op 9 to 4 tchd 3 to 1) 1
813⁵ CWM ARCTIC [79] 6-10-7¹ Mr M Jackson, *chsd ldr, led 5 out, rdn and hdd aftr 3 out, kpt on one pace.*
...................................(33 to 1 op 20 to 1) 2
727² CROWN EYEGLASS [80] 7-10-8 R Garritty, *chsd ldrs, rdn 4 out, one pace frm nxt..........* (14 to 1 tchd 16 to 1) 3
THE LIGHTER SIDE [89] 7-10-10 (7*) Judy Davies, *chsd ldrs, not fluent and wknd appr 3 out.*
...................................(14 to 1 op 10 to 1 tchd 16 to 1) 4
862² WHATAGALE [97] 6-11-11 J Osborne, *led, hdd 5 out, sn rdn and wknd appr 3 out, esaed.*
...................................(5 to 2 fav tchd 3 to 1) 5
525⁶ CRAZY HORSE DANCER (USA) [72] 5-9-7 (7*) M Doyle, *al rear, not jump wl, blun 12th and sn beh.*
...................................(20 to 1 op 14 to 1) 6
845⁷ LASTOFTHEVIKINGS [75] 8-10-0² (5*) R Davis, *mid-div, pushed alng 9 out, wknd whn f 3 out.*
...................................(20 to 1 op 33 to 1 tchd 16 to 1) f
FIVELEIGH FIRST (Ire) [83] 5-10-11 R Supple, *in tch, gd hdwy 4 out, chlgd 2 out, sn led, two ls clr whn blun badly and uns rdr last.* (15 to 2 op 5 to 1 tchd 8 to 1) ur
517³ SMALLMEAD LAD [85] 6-10-13 P Holley, *in tch, effrt and pushed alng 5 out, wkng whn hmpd 3 out, pld up aftr.*
...................................(9 to 2 op 3 to 1) pu
Dist: 4l, 1½l, 2l, 15l, 1½l. 6m 18.70s. a 28.70s (9 Ran).
(Miss Sarah Wills), K C Bailey

997 Llanmynech Racecourse Juvenile Novices' Hurdle (3-y-o) £2,347 2m 1f.... (2:55)

742² PYRRHIC DANCE 11-4 R Dunwoody, *led, hdd aftr 3 out and sn rdn, led and hit last, jst hld on.*
...................................(7 to 4 op 5 to 4 tchd 12 to 1) 1
702² SWISS MOUNTAIN (v) 10-2 (5*) T Eley, *in tch, pushed alng and hdwy 4 out, outpcd appr 2 out, styd on strly frm last, jst fld..................* (20 to 1 op 16 to 1) 2

870² SQUIRE YORK 10-12 M A FitzGerald, *hld up in tch, mstks second and 5th, hdwy 3 out, rdn nxt and ev ch last, not run on flt..................* (3 to 1 op 7 to 4 tchd 7 to 2) 3
742⁹ GUNNER SUE 10-7 S McNeill, *chsd ldr, rdn alng and outpcd 2 out, rallied and styd on flt.*
...................................(50 to 1 tchd 66 to 1) 4
742² WORDSMITH (Ire) 11-4 D J Burchell, *trkd ldrs, hdwy to ld aftr 3 out, rdn nxt, hdd appr last, no extr flt.*
...................................(11 to 10 on op 5 to 4 tchd 5 to 4 on) 5
870³ BOLTROSE 10-7 A O'Hagan, *in tch, rdn alng 4 out, wknd nxt..................* (9 to 2 op 4 to 1 tchd 5 to 1) 6
742 ALMONTY (Ire) 10-5 (7*) S Lycett, *strted slwly, al rear, tld off frm 4 out..................* (100 to 1 op 50 to 1) 7
MANDALIA MELODY 10-7 (5*) D Walsh, *al rear, tld off 4 out, pld up bef 2 out..........* (100 to 1 op 66 to 1) pu
Dist: Nk, ½l, sht-hd, hd, 6l, dist. 4m 16.80s. a 26.80s (8 Ran).
(T W King), C J Mann

998 Jones Peckover Novices' Chase (5-y-o and up) £3,680 2m 1f 110yds............ (3:25)

909² SHREWD JOHN 7-11-0 R Garritty, *in tch, hdwy 4 out, rdn appr last, led flt, ran on strly.*
...................................(7 to 1 op 6 to 1 tchd 10 to 1) 1
THUMBS UP 7-11-0 R Dunwoody, *chsd ldr, led 5 out, rdn appr last, hdd flt, kpt on.*
...................................(6 to 5 on op Evens tchd 11 to 10) 2
GOOD FOR A LOAN 6-11-0 L Harvey, *al chasing ldrs, rdn aftr 3 out, one pace, lft 3rd last...* (8 to 1 op 4 to 1) 3
703² MENAGHI 6-10-13 G McCourt, *mid-div, steady hdwy 6th, ev ch 4 out, rdn nxt, sn one pace....* (10 to 1 op 7 to 1) 4
HOWGILL 7-10-11 (3*) S Wynne, *not fluent, mid-div and rdn alng 5 out, no hdwy..........* (50 to 1 op 20 to 1) 5
LINGER HILL 6-11-0 R Bellamy, *mid-div till lost pl and beh frm 7th..................* (66 to 1 op 33 to 1) 6
759³ JOCK'S BURN 7-11-0 M Moloney, *mstk second, beh frm 6th..................* (9 to 1 op 5 to 1 tchd 16 to 1) 7
THE WOODEN HUT 10-11-0 Mr M Jackson, *led, hit 3rd, hdd 5 out, cl up till rdn and wknd aftr 3 out.*
...................................(100 to 1 op 33 to 1) 8
744⁴ PLAYING TRUANT 5-11-0 P Holley, *mid-div, hdwy 4 out, rdn 2 out, fourth and staying on whn f last.*
...................................(12 to 1 op 10 to 1 tchd 14 to 1) f
629⁴ KING'S SHILLING (USA) 6-11-0 Jacqui Oliver, *mid-div, gd hdwy 7th, effrt 2 out, rdn and disputing ld whn blun and uns rdr last..................* (8 to 1 tchd 9 to 1) ur
521⁵ MR HAPPY FEET 6-11-0 T Wall, *beh and reminders 3rd, blun badly and uns rdr 6th.*
...................................(66 to 1 op 50 to 1 tchd 100 to 1) ur
BATHWICK BOBBIE 6-11-0 S McNeill, *in tch, mstk 3rd, blun badly and uns rdr 6th.....* (16 to 1 op 10 to 1) ur
813⁷ FLYING WILD 7-11-0 N Williamson, *chsd ldrs till lost pl hfwy, tld off whn pld up bef last.* (66 to 1 op 50 to 1) pu
Dist: 15l, 2½l, ½l, 10l, 4l, 4l. 4m 21.70s. a 15.70s (13 Ran).
SR: 25/23/16/10/3/-/
(R D E Woodhouse), R D E Woodhouse

999 Oswestry Racecourse Intermediate Handicap Hurdle (0-135 4-y-o and up) £2,710 2m 1f................................. (3:55)

728* WESTHOLME (USA) [105] 5-10-2² R Garritty, *trkd ldr gng wl, hdwy to ld aftr 3 out, pushed clr nxt, easily.*
...................................(6 to 5 on op 5 to 4 on tchd Evens) 1
936 ADMIRALTY WAY [108] 7-10-5 Diane Clay, *chsd ldg pair, reminders 5th, hrd rdn appr 2 out, styd on last, no ch wth wnr..................* (7 to 2 op 3 to 1) 2
776⁵ MOHANA [127] 4-11-10 R Dunwoody, *led, hit 5th, rdn alng 3 out and sn hdd, wknd nxt.*
...................................(5 to 2 op 3 to 1 tchd 7 to 2) 3
EDWARD SEYMOUR (USA) [103] 6-9-11² (5*) T Jenks, *al rear, lost tch aftr 4 out..........* (20 to 1 op 14 to 1) 4
Dist: 10l, 5l, 25l. 4m 8.60s. a 18.60s (4 Ran).
(T H Bennett), M H Easterby

WETHERBY (good)
Friday October 29th
Going Correction: PLUS 0.25 sec. per fur. (races 1,4,6), PLUS 0.05 (2,3,5)

1000 Hornshaw Novices' Hurdle (4-y-o and up) £2,127 2½m 110yds........(1:30)

SHAFFIC (Fr) 6-10-12 P Niven, *in tch, trkd ldrs frm 5th, led 2 out, drw clr, cmftbly..........* (5 to 2 fav op 2 to 1) 1
ADMIRAL VENLEUVE 5-10-12 J Railton, *made most till hdd 2 out, kpt on, no ch wth wnr.* (5 to 1 tchd 9 to 2) 2
728⁷ COWLEY 8-10-12 M Brennan, *in tch, styd on und pres frm 3 out..................* (25 to 1) 3
734² JOHNS THE BOY 7-10-12 (7*) B Harding, *cl up, dsptd ld frm 5th till one pace from 2 out, mstk last.*
...................................(100 to 30 op 9 to 2 tchd 5 to 1) 4
TITIAN GIRL (bl) 4-10-6 J Callaghan, *in tch, pushed alng appr 7th, kpt on frm 2 out..........* (11 to 2 op 5 to 1) 5
CLEAR IDEA (Ire) 5-10-12 N Doughty, *pld hrd, trkd ldrs frm 4th, outpcd appr 3 out, kpt on from nxt.*
...................................(10 to 1 op 6 to 1) 6

662[6] MUST BE MAGICAL (USA) 5-10-12 A Maguire, *chsd ldrs till wknd aftr 7th*.......................(5 to 1 op 9 to 2) 7
NAWRIK (Ire) 4-10-11 T Reed, *wl beh frm 5th, tld off*.
.................................(25 to 1 op 10 to 1) 8
EASY RHYTHM 6-10-7 (5") D Bentley, *wl beh frm 5th, tld off*...............................(33 to 1) 9
ARRAGUANIE 7-10-12 A S Smith, *wl beh frm 5th, tld off*.
...................................(33 to 1) 10
TOLLS CHOICE (Ire) 4-10-4 (7") J Driscoll, *bolted bef strt, pld hrd, prmnt to 4th, wknd quickly, pulled up before nxt*............................(20 to 1) pu
Dist: 15l, nk, nk, ¾l, 2½l, 15l, 25l, sht-hd, 6l. 4m 56.80s. a 9.80s (11 Ran).
SR: 37/22/21/27/13/16/1/-/-/ (P Davidson-Brown), Mrs M Reveley

# 1001 Harry Wharton Memorial Handicap Chase (0-145 5-y-o and up) £3,392 2m
.........................(2:00)

KING OF THE LOT [145] 10-12-0 A Maguire, *jmpd wl, made all, ran on well*.....(11 to 8 op 6 to 4 tchd 6 to 4) 1
GENERAL PERSHING [143] 7-11-12 N Doughty, *al tracking wnr, ev ch 3 out, no extr frm nxt*.....(5 to 1 op 4 to 1) 2
769[3] MAUDLINS CROSS [121] 8-10-4[3] P Niven, *beh, some hdwy appr 4 out, no imprsn aftr*...........(4 to 1 op 3 to 1) 3
871 LOGAMIMO [125] 7-10-5 (3") A Larnach, *in tch, outpcd aftr 5th, no dngr after*........(9 to 4 op 5 to 2 tchd 3 to 1) 4
Dist: 8l, 4l, 8l. 3m 55.20s. a 3.20s (4 Ran).
SR: 76/66/40/36/ (Mrs G M Brisbane), D Nicholson

# 1002 Weatherbys 'Newcomers' Series Novices' Chase (5-y-o and up) £3,752 2m
.........................(2:30)

549* KEEP SHARP 7-11-7 Richard Guest, *cl up, led 5th, hdd 8th, mstk 4 out, lft in ld last, jst hld on*.
.....................(9 to 1 op 8 to 1 tchd 10 to 1) 1
820 EXPLOSIVE SPEED (USA) 5-11-7 C Grant, *led till hdd 5th, cl up whn blun 8th, so lost tch, effrt whn mstk last, ran on wl und pres, jst fld*..........(5 to 2 op 9 to 2) 2
782* COULTON 6-11-7 L Wyer, *trkd ldrs, led 8th, jmpd clr 4 out, tunty ls in frnt whn blun and uns rdr last*.
.............(10 to 3 on op 7 to 2 on tchd 3 to 1 on) ur
779[7] AMADEUS (Fr) 5-10-9 (5") S Lyons, *blun and uns rdr 3rd*.
.....................................(33 to 1) ur
Dist: Hd. 4m 4.40s. a 12.40s (4 Ran).
(Hart & Co Insurance Brokers Ltd), Mrs S J Smith

1003 EBF 'National Hunt' Novices' Hurdle Qualifier (4,5,6-y-o) £2,469 2m. . (3:05)

779[3] AUBURN BOY 6-11-0 L Wyer, *trkd ldrs, led gng wl 2 out, ran on und pres appr last*.
....................(2 to 1 fav tchd 9 to 4 and 7 to 4) 1
785* SEVEN TOWERS (Ire) 4-11-5 P Niven, *beh, pushed alng and hdwy aftr 7th, kpt on wl frm 2 out*.
...............................(7 to 2 op 3 to 1) 2
844[2] EMPEROR BUCK (Ire) 5-11-0 A Maguire, *mid-div, steady hdwy to ld 3 out, hdd 2 out, kpt on same pace*.
..................(5 to 2 op 3 to 1 tchd 7 to 2) 3
821[9] HICKSONS CHOICE (Ire) 5-11-0 K Jones, *al chasing ldrs, ev ch 3 out, one paced*....................(50 to 1) 4
656[6] STRONG MEASURE (Ire) 5-11-0 A Johnson, *prmnt, effrt appr 3 out, grad wknd*......................(20 to 1) 5
BASILICUS (Fr) 4-11-0 Gary Lyons, *led to second, lft in ld 5th, hdd 7th, cl up till fdd frm 3 out*..........(33 to 1) 6
BALISTEROS (Fr) 4-10-7 (7") W Fry, *mid-div till outpcd appr 7th, no dngr aftr*....................(50 to 1) 7
OTTOMAN EMPIRE 6-11-0 M Brennan, *prmnt, slight ld 7th, hdd 3 out, sn wknd*..........(20 to 1 op 16 to 1) 8
844 DISTINCTIVE (Ire) 4-10-7 (7") P Ward, *mid-div till wknd appr 3 out*.......................(16 to 1 op 20 to 1) 9
645[3] STAGGERING (Ire) 4-10-6 (3") A Dobbin, *al beh*...(33 to 1) 10
771 HERBALIST 4-10-11 (3") A Larnach, *beh most of way*.
....................(8 to 1 op 9 to 1 tchd 10 to 1) 11
734 HURRICANE HORACE 6-11-0 C Grant, *mid-div, effrt 7th, no imprsn whn f 3 out*..........(14 to 1 op 16 to 1) f
THE ADJUTANT (Ire) 5-10-7 (7") B Harding, *loose bef strt, slwly into strd, led second till ran out*.
...............................(33 to 1 op 25 to 1) ro
315[2] MELLOW GOLD 6-10-11[2] N Doughty, *beh frm hdwy, tld off whn pld up bef 3 out*..........(14 to 1 op 12 to 1) pu
645[7] FARM TRACK 4-10-9 B Storey, *al beh, tld off whn pld up bef 3 out*........................(50 to 1) pu
Dist: 2l, 8l, 6l, 3l, nk, 6l, nk, 2½l, 2½l, 10l. 3m 54.40s. a 13.40s (15 Ran).
(G E Shouler), M W Easterby

1004 'Go Racing In Yorkshire' Handicap Chase (0-135 5-y-o and up) £3,626 3m 110yds.........................(3:35)

783* MR BOSTON [125] 8-11-4 P Niven, *trkd ldrs, led appr 4 out, clr 2 out, styd on wl*.
....................(7 to 4 fav op 2 to 1 tchd 9 to 4) 1
MERRY MASTER [135] 9-12-0 Gee Armytage, *jmpd rght, led 3rd, hdd, mstk tenth, hdd appr 4 out, mistake nxt, kpt on frm next*...........(4 to 1 op 5 to 1 tchd 11 to 2) 2

876[2] ON THE OTHER HAND [129] 10-11-8 N Doughty, *trkd ldrs, chlgd appr 4 out, grad wknd frm nxt*.
.....................(8 to 1 op 7 to 1 tchd 9 to 1) 3
876* BALTIC BROWN [110] 8-10-3 (5ex) Gary Lyons, *mstks, led to 3rd, prmnt till lost pl aftr 11th, rallied appr 4 out, wknd approaching nxt*........(5 to 2 op 2 to 1) 4
822[2] ZAM BEE [117] 7-10-10[10] T Reed, *lost tch frm 11th, tld off*.....................(14 to 1 op 10 to 1) 5
696 DERRING VALLEY [107] (bl) 8-10-0 A Maguire, *mstks, wl beh till cld up hfwy, wknd aftr twelfth, well tld off*.
....(8 to 1) 6
Dist: 6l, 4l, 6l, dist, dist. 6m 21.70s. a 15.70s (6 Ran).
(M K Oldham), Mrs M Reveley

1005 Green Hammerton Handicap Hurdle (0-145 4-y-o and up) £2,905 2½m 110yds.........................(4:05)

757[3] TAROUDANT [127] 6-11-2 P Niven, *pld hrd, in tch, hdwy to track ldrs aftr 5th, led appr 2 out, jmpd lft last, sn hard rdn, jst hld on*......(6 to 4 on op 5 to 4 on) 1
BOLLIN WILLIAM [139] 5-12-0 L Wyer, *led, quickened aftr 7th, mstk 3 out, hdd, sn switchd and rallied und pres after last, jst hld*.......(15 to 2 op 6 to 1 tchd 8 to 1) 2
NORTHUMBRIAN KING [111] 7-10-0 J Callaghan, *in tch, hdwy to chase 1st 2 3 out, kpt on, no imprsn*. (50 to 1) 3
ABBOT OF FURNESS [136] 9-11-11 N Doughty, *cl up till grad wknd appr 3 out*...........(20 to 1 op 12 to 1) 4
757[5] CHANTRY BARTLE [111] 7-10-0 D Wilkinson, *in tch, effrt aftr 7th, no imprsn whn mstk 2 out, fdd*.
.........................(12 to 1 op 10 to 1) 5
NESSFIELD [118] 7-10-7 A S Smith, *prmnt till lost pl aftr 7th, sn wknd*.........(25 to 1 op 20 to 1) 6
739[5] ANDERMATT [119] 6-10-8 A Maguire, *hld up and beh, some hdwy aftr 5th, wknd appr 3 out*.
....................................(9 to 2 op 4 to 1) 7
781[6] CLURICAN (Ire) [126] 4-11-1 M Dwyer, *al beh*.
.........................(10 to 1 op 8 to 1) 8
Dist: Sht-hd, 6l, 15l, 6l, 15l, 1½l, hd. 4m 56.90s. a 9.90s (8 Ran).
SR: 40/52/18/28/-/ (G A Farndon), Mrs M Reveley

ASCOT (good)
Saturday October 30th
Going Correction: PLUS 0.15 sec. per fur. (races 1,2,-5,7), PLUS 0.05 (3,4,6)

1006 Valley Gardens Conditional Jockeys' Handicap Hurdle (4-y-o and up) £3,501 2½m.........................(12:55)

BAS DE LAINE (Fr) [125] 7-10-12 J McCarthy, *set steady pace, hdd appr last, rallied to ld ag'n cl hme*. (5 to 2 jt-fav tchd 11 to 4 and 9 to 4) 1
900* NAHAR [120] 8-10-7 A Dicken, *cl up, led appr last, hdd and no extr close hme*.....(5 to 2 jt-fav op 7 to 4) 2
HIGH ALLTITUDE (Ire) [141] 5-11-7 (7") N Stocks, *in cl tch, rdn alng aftr 6th, sn lost touch, tld off*.
.....................(3 to 1 op 7 to 4 tchd 9 to 4) 3
900[2] CHILD OF THE MIST [117] 7-10-4 R Davis, *cl up, ev ch 3 out, wknd quickly, tld off*.
.....................(100 to 30 op 7 to 2 tchd 4 to 1 and 3 to 1) 4
DUKE DE VENDOME [113] 10-9-12[5] (7") C Huggan, *in cl tch till drpd rear and tld off frm 6th, pld up bef 2 out*.
.................................(50 to 1 op 20 to 1) pu
DERISBAY (Ire) [117] 5-10-4[4] D O'Sullivan, *al beh, tld off frm 4th, pld up bef 2 out*.........(100 to 1 op 66 to 1) pu
Dist: Nk, dist, 20l. 4m 48.80s. a 7.80s (6 Ran).
SR: 36/30/-/ (R K Bids Ltd), O Sherwood

1007 Binfield Juvenile Novices' Hurdle (3-y-o) £2,827 2m 110yds.........................(1:30)

611[6] MOSHAAJIR (USA) 11-0 M Ranger, *pld hrd early, in cl tch, led 4 out, ran on wl*. (14 to 1 op 12 to 1 tchd 16 to 1) 1
MARCO MAGNIFICO (USA) 11-0 M A FitzGerald, *hld up in mid-div, cld 3 out, hrd rdn appr nxt, one pace*.
....................(11 to 8 on op 7 to 4 on tchd 5 to 4 on) 2
870[6] MOHAYA (USA) 11-0 S McNeill, *trkd ldrs, chsd wnr frm 4 out, disputing second whn pckd 2 out, wknd r-in*.
.....................(13 to 2 op 8 to 1 tchd 10 to 1) 3
830 STORM FALCON (USA) 11-0 S Earle, *pld hrd, led second, sn cl, hdd 4 out, wknd nxt*......(33 to 1 op 16 to 1) 4
754[2] HOT OFF THE PRESS 11-0 G Bradley, *led to second, in cl tch till wknd 4 out, tld off*.
.....................(15 to 2 op 6 to 1 tchd 8 to 1) 5
FRANK KNOWS 11-0 Peter Hobbs, *in tch till reminders and drpd rear 4th, tld off*......(50 to 1 op 33 to 1) 6
896[4] LA POSADA 10-9 A Charlton, *al beh, lost tch 4th, tld off*.
.........................(25 to 1 op 20 to 1) 7
890[8] POLLY LEACH 10-9 S Mackey, *drpd rear 4th, blun and uns rdr four out*.............(25 to 1 tchd 33 to 1) ur

JOLIS ABSENT 10-9 S Smith Eccles, *trkd ldrs, hrd rdn whn blun badly 4 out, no ch when pld up bef 2 out.* ....(6 to 1 tchd 7 to 1) pu
Dist: 15l, 4l, 20l, 3l, 20l, hd. 3m 55.50s. a 9.50s (9 Ran).
SR: 16/1/-/-/-/-/ (Steve Macdonald), C Smith

1008 Steel Plate And Sections Young Chasers Qualifier Novices' Chase (4 - 7-y-o) £2,827 2m 3f 110yds......(2:05)

GHIA GNEUIAGH 7-11-5 D Bridgwater, *jmpd soundly, made virtually all, clr 3 out, easily.* (10 to 1 op 6 to 1) 1
763^2 GANDOUGE GLEN 6-11-5 D Murphy, *pressed wnr thrght till mstk 4 out, jmpd lft nxt and one pace.* ....(11 to 4 op 3 to 1 tchd 100 to 30 and 5 to 2) 2
826^2 THE GLOW (Ire) 5-11-4 P Holley, *in tch, outpcd 8th, wnt modest 3rd 5 out, styd on frm o'r 3 out, nvr dngrs.* ....(2 to 1 fav op 9 to 4 tchd 5 to 2) 3
826 MINE'S AN ACE (NZ) 6-11-9 J Frost, *al beh, styd on frm o'r 2 out, nvr nr to chal*....(9 to 1 op 8 to 1 tchd 12 to 1) 4
774 LAVALIGHT 6-11-5 W Irvine, *in tch, outpcd frm 7th, wknd 5 out, tld off*.........(50 to 1 op 33 to 1 tchd 66 to 1) 5
RUN UP THE FLAG 6-11-0 (5*) P Hide, *in cl tch, 3rd whn f 7th*....................(15 to 2 op 7 to 1 tchd 9 to 1) f
GINGER TRISTAN 7-11-5 Peter Hobbs, *in tch whn f 7th.* ....(12 to 1 op 10 to 1) f
826^4 STAUNCH RIVAL (USA) 6-11-5 J Railton, *blun and uns rdr 3rd*..............................(20 to 1 tchd 25 to 1) ur
GIVEITAGO 7-11-5 S McNeill, *in tch whn blun badly 7th, blunded 9th, pld up bef nxt*..........(10 to 1 op 7 to 1) pu
Dist: 10l, 4l, 2½l, 20l. 4m 53.80s. a 12.30s (9 Ran).
(Mrs S A Scott), N A Twiston-Davies

1009 United House Construction Chase Handicap (5-y-o and up) £15,313 2m ....(2:35)

STORM ALERT [148] 7-11-1 S McNeill, *trkd ldr, led appr last, rdn out*..................(9 to 4 jt-fav op 7 to 4) 1
YOUNG SNUGFIT [157] 9-11-10 J Osborne, *led till hdd appr last, kpt on*.......(13 to 2 op 6 to 1 tchd 7 to 1) 2
825 SETTER COUNTRY [140] 9-10-7 W Irvine, *in cl tch, rdn 3 out, outpcd aftr nxt*.............(16 to 1 tchd 25 to 1) 3
919* ATLAAL [140] 8-10-7 S Smith Eccles, *in cl tch, hit 4th, rdn alng appr 2 out, sn wknd*..........(8 to 1 op 10 to 1) 4
825* BILLY BATHGATE [140] 7-10-7 M A FitzGerald, *hld up in cl tch gng wl, rdn and found little frm 2 out*....(9 to 4 jt-fav tchd 2 to 1 and 5 to 2) 5
631^4 BOUTZDAROFF [140] 11-10-7 D Byrne, *hld up in tch, blun and uns rdr 5th*.....................(4 to 1 op 5 to 1) ur
Dist: 1½l, 15l, 6l, 7l. 3m 52.00s. a 4.50s (6 Ran).
SR: 50/57/25/19/12/-/ (Lt Col W Whetherly), Andrew Turnell

1010 Hairy Mary Novices' Hurdle (4-y-o and up) £2,944 2m 110yds.......... (3:05)

TEXAN TYCOON 5-11-0 D Bridgwater, *trkd ldrs, hrd rdn to ld appr 2 out, ridden out.* ....(5 to 2 fav op 7 to 2 tchd 4 to 1) 1
LARGE ACTION (Ire) 5-11-0 J Osborne, *al prmnt, dsptd ld 4 out till hdd appr 2 out, ev ch whn awkward last, no extr*.....................(7 to 2 op 5 to 2 tchd 4 to 1) 2
910^4 HIGH MIND (Fr) 4-10-13 M A FitzGerald, *led till hdd 4 out, wknd und pres aftr nxt*..........(14 to 1 tchd 25 to 1) 3
MOVE A MINUTE (USA) 4-10-8 (5*) P Hide, *chsd ldg grp, one pace and no hdwy whn hmpd by faller 2 out.* ....(25 to 1 op 14 to 1 tchd 33 to 1) 4
773^9 ROSS GRAHAM 5-11-0 G Morgan, *beh, styd on frm 2 out, nrst finish*.....................(50 to 1 tchd 66 to 1) 5
SQUIRE SILK 4-10-13 L Harvey, *took keen hold, hld up in mid-div, no prog frm 3 out*.........(16 to 1 op 8 to 1) 6
952^2 MAMALAMA 5-10-6 (3*) D O'Sullivan, *al prmnt, ev ch 3 out, sn rdn and wknd*..................(33 to 1 op 20 to 1) 7
IVOR'S FLUTTER 4-10-13 P Holley, *nvr nr to chal.* .... (5 to 1 op 3 to 1 tchd 11 to 2) 8
MR JERVIS (Ire) 4-10-13 D Murphy, *in tch till outpcd frm 3 out*..................................(25 to 1 op 10 to 1) 9
888^4 BOLD STREET BLUES 6-11-0 R Greene, *beh, shrtlvd effrt 3 out*..............................(50 to 1 op 33 to 1) 10
ARMATEUR (Fr) 5-11-0 G Bradley, *trkd ldrs to 4th, sn beh, tld off*.............. (33 to 1 op 20 to 1 tchd 40 to 1) 11
MEDINAS SWAN SONG 5-11-0 J Frost, *al beh, tld off.* ....(66 to 1 op 50 to 1) 12
901 WATERBEACH VILLAGE (Ire) 5-10-8[1] (7*) Mr M Gingell, *al beh, tld off*......... (66 to 1 op 50 to 1 tchd 100 to 1) 13
NADJATI (USA) 4-10-13 S McNeill, *trkd ldrs, dsptd ld 4 out till hdd appr 2 out, 3rd and one pace whn f two out.* ....(4 to 1 op 2 to 1 tchd 9 to 2) f
DIAMOND TOPPING 4-10-8 S Earle, *beh whn mstk 3rd, sn tld off, pld up bef last*............(50 to 1 op 20 to 1) pu
Dist: 2l, 20l, 2l, 3l, 3l, 5l, 2l, 1½l, 3l, 10l. 3m 52.60s. a 6.60s (15 Ran).
SR: 45/43/22/20/18/14/5/7/5/ (Les Randall), R Akehurst

1011 Bagshot Handicap Chase (5-y-o and up) £8,208 3m 110yds.......... (3:35)

LATENT TALENT [139] 9-10-4 M Richards, *trkd ldrs, led 5 out, ran on strly*...... (9 to 2 op 5 to 1 tchd 11 to 2) 1
661* SPRINGALEAK [137] 8-10-2 J Osborne, *cl up, led 7th till hdd 12th, sn lost pl, ran on frm 2 out, fnshd wl to take second close hme*............... (9 to 4 fav op 2 to 1) 2
647^3 TOPSHAM BAY [155] 10-11-6 J Frost, *al cl up, wth wnr and ev ch 4 out, one pace frm nxt, hit 2 out, lost second close hme*........................ (16 to 1 op 14 to 1) 3
647^2 DAKYNS BOY [144] 8-10-9 D Bridgwater, *niggled alng thrght, mstk 8th, hdwy to ld 14th, hdd 5 out, wknd appr 2 out*.......... (3 to 1 op 5 to 2 tchd 100 to 30) 4
ROYAL ATHLETE [163] 10-12-0 D Gallagher, *hld up in rear, cld 5 out, btn 3 out*............... (12 to 1 op 10 to 1) 5
647* ESPY [147] 10-10-12 G Bradley, *mstk 3rd, al beh.* ....(5 to 1 tchd 11 to 2) 6
792^2 WONT BE GONE LONG [136] (bl) 11-10-1[1] M A FitzGerald, *led to 7th, mstk nxt, led ag'n 12th to 14th, sn rdn and btn*........................(12 to 1 op 10 to 1 tchd 14 to 1) 7
Dist: 3l, ½l, 15l, 15l, 8l, 5l. 6m 6.00s. a 2.50s (7 Ran).
SR: 63/58/75/49/53/29/13/ (Christopher Heath), S E Sherwood

1012 Copper Horse Handicap Hurdle (4-y-o and up) £4,123 2m 110yds...... (4:10)

829^8 SUNSET AND VINE [114] 6-10-11 H Davies, *hld up in rear, hdwy to ld 2 out, ran on wl*.........(7 to 2 op 4 to 1) 1
762* CHANGE THE ACT [123] 8-11-6 J Osborne, *trkd ldr, ev ch appr last, ran on one pace.* ....(11 to 8 fav op 5 to 4 tchd 6 to 4) 2
BIG BEAT (USA) [127] 5-11-10 P Holley, *led till hdd 2 out, one pace appr last*..................(9 to 4 op 6 to 4) 3
829 INDIAN RUN (Ire) [122] 4-11-5 M A FitzGerald, *in cl tch till rdn and outpcd appr 2 out, tld off.* ....(8 to 1 op 5 to 1 tchd 9 to 1) 4
Dist: 1l, 3½l, 25l. 3m 52.80s. a 6.80s (4 Ran).
SR: 40/48/48/18/ (Sunset & Vine Plc), S Dow

DOWN ROYAL (IRE) (good)
Saturday October 30th

1013 John Turner Memorial E.B.F. Chase (5-y-o and up) £1,380 2½m......(1:45)

746 DUKES SON 6-11-1 (7*) Mr J Bright,.............(14 to 1) 1
WICKET KEEPER 8-11-8 J Shortt,................(3 to 1) 2
969 EDENAKILL LAD 6-11-5 (3*) D Bromley,...........(8 to 1) 3
KARISE BRAVE 7-11-8 H Rogers,................(20 to 1) 4
744* MUST DO 7-11-11 (3*) T J Mitchell,........... (6 to 4 on) f
744^4 MASTER MILLER 7-11-8 C O'Dwyer,.............(12 to 1) f
Dist: ¾l, 2½l, dist. (Time not taken) (6 Ran).
(T J Topping), William Patton

1014 Malone Handicap Hurdle (0-109 4-y-o and up) £1,207 2½m............(2:15)

557^4 ST DONAVINT [-] 6-11-10 C N Bowens,...........(7 to 2) 1
505^4 STRONG ROSE [-] (bl) 6-10-4 L P Cusack,.......(16 to 1) 2
905^4 SILVER GIPSEY [-] 7-11-8 P L Malone,............(7 to 2) 3
364 JOEY KELLY [-] 8-10-8 C O'Dwyer,...............(7 to 1) 4
59^2 BASSETJA (Ire) [-] 4-10-11 (5*) Mr B R Hamilton,..(12 to 1) 5
LA-GREINE [-] 6-10-3 (3*) Mr P McMahon,........(10 to 1) 6
877^7 JUST BLUSH [-] 6-10-11 H Rogers,.............(16 to 1) 7
527^3 HAWAIIAN GODDESS (USA) [-] 6-10-0 (5*) Mr D McGoona, ...(12 to 1) 8
473 SENSITIVE KING (Ire) [-] 5-11-4 J Collins,...(100 to 30 fav) 9
AVOWIN [-] 11-10-6 F J Flood,...................(33 to 1) 10
Dist: ¾l, 7l, 2l, 2l. (Time not taken) (10 Ran).
(P A McMahon), Victor Bowens

1015 Ali And Mohamad Soudavar Memorial Trial Hurdle (4-y-o and up) £1,725 2m ....(2:45)

199^8 COQUALLA (bl) 8-10-9 (7*) Mr J P R Geoghegan, (11 to 2) 1
341 JODONLEE (Ire) 4-10-0 (3*) T J Mitchell,...........(5 to 2) 2
881^7 SUTR-MAKE (Ire) 4-10-8 J P Byrne,.............(10 to 1) 3
63 PYLON SPARKS 8-10-9 (7*) E G O'Callaghan, ..(2 to 1 fav) 4
537^9 ASK THE FAIRIES (Ire) 5-10-8 C O'Dwyer,..........(5 to 1) 5
747 DECEMBER BRIDE (Ire) 5-10-5 (3*) K B Walsh,.....(8 to 1) f
Dist: 4l, 4½l, ½l, 15l. (Time not taken) (6 Ran).
(J Geoghegan), J Geoghegan

1016 Archie Watson Memorial Corinthian Flat Race (4-y-o and up) £1,380 2m ....(3:15)

747* WHAT IT IS (Ire) 4-11-1 (7*) Mr M Brennan,..... (2 to 1 fav) 1
233^3 DOCS DILEMMA (Ire) 4-11-1 (5*) Mr A E Lacy,..... (8 to 1) 2
747^4 COTTON CALL (Ire) 4-10-8 (7*) Mr S Laird,........ (12 to 1) 3
804^5 JATINGA (Ire) 5-11-13 (5*) Mr B R Hamilton,........ (9 to 2) 4
ARCTIC TREASURE (Ire) 4-10-10 (5*) Mr C T G Kinane, ...(20 to 1) 5
COLLIERS HILL (Ire) 5-11-4 (7*) Mr J P Harvey,.... (14 to 1) 6
620^6 CONQUINN (Ire) 4-10-13 (7*) Mr C Rae,............(7 to 1) 7
513^5 MAKES YOU WONDER (Ire) 5-11-11 Mr P F Graffin, (7 to 1) 8
513* LANDENSTOWN (Ire) 5-11-11 (7*) Mr A Weld,......(7 to 1) 9

KEANO (Ire) 4-11-6 Mr A J Martin, ...(10 to 1) 10
747 PRINCESS DILLY (Ire) 4-10-8 (7*) Mrs A Doran, . . . (33 to 1) 11
CELIA'S PET (Ire) 5-10-13 (7*) Mr L Madine, ... (33 to 1) 12
MILLBROOK LAD 5-11-4 (7*) Mr R J Patton, ...(20 to 1) 13
DALWAYS BAWN 6-10-13 (7*) Mr J Bright, ...(25 to 1) 14
747 DISTANT FRIEND (Ire) 5-11-8 (3*) Mr P McMahon, (20 to 1) 15
Dist: 3l, 5l, hd, 1½l. (Time not taken) (15 Ran).

(Mrs M Holleran), J H Scott

NAAS (IRE) (good)
Saturday October 30th

1017 Grange Con Handicap Hurdle (4-y-o and up) £4,485 3m. . . . .(2:25)

746² SECRET SCEPTRE [-] 6-9-7 F Woods, ...(8 to 1) 1
637² LOVE AND PORTER (Ire) [-] 5-10-7 D H O'Connor,
. . . .(5 to 2 fav) 2
938³ RISING WATERS (Ire) [-] 5-11-6 K F O'Brien, ...(7 to 2) 3
473* MARILYN (Ire) [-] 4-9-8 P McWilliams, ...(11 to 4) 4
689⁴ MARBLE CITY GIRL [-] 8-9-2 (5*) C O'Brien, ...(14 to 1) 5
GOLA LADY [-] 6-9-0 (7*) B Bowens, ...(14 to 1) 6
VINCERO [-] 8-9-9 (5*) M G Cleary, ...(14 to 1) 7
DESERT OASIS [-] 6-10-0 C F Swan, ...(7 to 1) pu
Dist: ½l, 2l, 9l, 15l. 6m 2.70s. (8 Ran).

(Mrs J K Ferguson), I R Ferguson

1018 Rossmore Novice Hurdle (4-y-o and up) £3,105 2½m. . . . .(2:55)

852* MINELLA LAD 7-11-10 T Horgan, ...(5 to 4 on) 1
927* MERRY PEOPLE (Ire) 5-11-8 (5*) C O'Brien, ...(9 to 4) 2
877 TOT EM UP 6-10-12 Mr M Phillips, ...(12 to 1) 3
801⁹ COUNTERBALANCE 6-10-12 B Sheridan, ...(16 to 1) 4
CALLERBANK 6-10-12 K F O'Brien, ...(20 to 1) 5
877⁸ THATS MY BOY 5-10-10 (7*) B Bowens, ...(16 to 1) 6
939⁴ OXFORD QUILL 6-11-3 T J Taaffe, ...(10 to 1) 7
798 BALLY RIOT 5-11-3 C F Swan, ...(16 to 1) 8
MISGIVINGS (Ire) 5-10-5 (7*) J M Donnelly, ...(25 to 1) 9
FRIGID COUNTESS 6-10-5 (7*) Mr L A Hurley, ...(12 to 1) 10
945⁵ SPEAK OF THE DEVIL 6-11-3 D H O'Connor, ...(10 to 1) 11
638 RATHNURE LADY (Ire) 5-10-7 P A Roche, ...(20 to 1) 12
Dist: 5l, 10l, 2l, hd. 5m 4.40s. (12 Ran).

(John J Nallen), A P O'Brien

1019 Gouldings Fertilizers Novice Handicap Chase (5-y-o and up) £3,795 2m
. . . .(3:55)

879³ FURRY STAR [-] 7-10-9 J Jones, ...(6 to 1) 1
806⁵ INCA CHIEF [-] 9-9-9 (5*) D P Geoghegan, ...(12 to 1) 2
943 PARGALE [-] 7-10-8 C F Swan, ...(9 to 4 jt-fav) 3
674* FABRICATOR [-] 7-10-12 K F O'Brien, ...(3 to 1) 4
879⁵ TORENAGA HILL [-] 9-9-0 (7*) J P Broderick, ...(25 to 1) 5
878* MAGIC MILLION [-] 7-10-7 (6ex) J P Banahan, (9 to 4 jt-fav) ur
Dist: 1l, ¾l, 5l, 13l. 4m 4.60s. (6 Ran).

(Thomas J Farrell), P Mullins

1020 Philip A.McCartan Memorial INH Flat Race (4-y-o) £3,105 2m. . . . .(4:25)

692³ BUTCHES BOY (Ire) 11-2 (7*) Mr M P Dunne, ...(13 to 2) 1
832² CLOWATER LADY (Ire) 10-11 (7*) Mr P English, (5 to 2 fav) 2
709⁷ PLASSY BOY (Ire) 11-9 Mr J A Berry, ...(6 to 1) 3
930⁵ MY SUNNY WAY (Ire) 11-2 (7*) Mr D K Budds, . . .(8 to 1) 4
555⁶ SIDCUP HILL (Ire) 11-4 Mr J A Flynn, ...(100 to 30) 5
832 ABAVARD (Ire) 11-4 (5*) Mr P M Kelly, ...(10 to 1) 6
GLENDUN (Ire) 11-4 (5*) Mr J A Nash, ...(9 to 2) 7
803 NORA'S ERROR (Ire) 11-4 (5*) Mr G J Harford, ...(16 to 1) 8
COOL ROSE (Ire) 11-4 Mr S R Murphy, ...(6 to 1) 9
WEST BROGUE (Ire) 11-9 Mr J P Dempsey, ...(14 to 1) 10
709 SWIFT GLIDER (Ire) 10-13 (5*) Mr J P Berry, ...(14 to 1) 11
832 LADY IMELDA (Ire) 11-3 (3*) Mr D Marnane, ...(20 to 1) 12
832 ELLENOR LAD (Ire) 11-9 Mr M Phillips, ...(25 to 1) 13
LAURA GALE (Ire) 10-13 (5*) Mr H F Cleary, ...(16 to 1) ur
Dist: 6l, nk, 3l, 3½l. 3m 52.30s. (14 Ran).

(Mrs Bridget Kennedy), P A Fahy

WARWICK (good to firm)
Saturday October 30th
Going Correction: MINUS 0.30 sec. per fur.

1021 St Mary's Juvenile Novices' Hurdle (3-y-o) £1,484 2m. . . . . (1:15)

188² BUGLET 10-7 R Dunwoody, led aftr 4th, made rst, styd on
wl whn chlgd frm 2 out, drvn out.
. . . .(3 to 1 fav tchd 11 to 4 and 100 to 30) 1
DESTINY CALLS 10-12 R Supple, al prmnt, ev ch appr 2
out, hng lft and hit last, rallied r-in, not quicken nr
finish. . . . .(12 to 1 op 10 to 1 tchd 14 to 1) 2
784⁴ SOLOMAN SPRINGS (USA) 10-12 N Williamson, hld up,
hdwy aftr 3rd, chsd ldr and ev ch till no imprsn appr 2
out. . . . .(10 to 1 op 12 to 1) 3

742⁸ TURFMANS VISION 10-9 (3*) S Wynne, hld up, beh 3rd,
hdwy nxt, cl up and ev ch 3 out, no imprsn appr next.
. . . .(14 to 1 tchd 16 to 1) 4
ALYVAIR 10-7 J Ryan, hld up, beh 3rd, hdwy aftr 3 out,
styd on frm nxt, nvr nrr. . . . .(33 to 1 op 16 to 1) 5
TACTICAL TOMMY 10-7 (5*) T Jenks, hld up, hdwy aftr
3rd, chsd ldrs, 5th and wkng whn mstk 2 out.
. . . .(8 to 1 op 6 to 1 tchd 10 to 1) 6
668⁷ BARTON ROYAL (Ire) 10-12 Richard Guest, hld up, rapid
hdwy aftr 4 out, wknd appr 2 out. . . . .(50 to 1) 7
POCONO KNIGHT 10-12 G Upton, mid-div, no hdwy frm 3
out. . . . .(50 to 1) 8
870 SHALHOLME 10-0 (7*) D Matthews, led to second, chsd ldr
till hrd rdn and wknd appr 2 out. (20 to 1 op 16 to 1) 9
830⁴ ONE MORE POUND 10-12 M Perrett, trkd ldrs, wknd
quickly 3 out. . . . .(4 to 1 tchd 5 to 1) 10
742⁶ STAR MARKET 10-5 (7*) Mr S Joynes, hdwy aftr 3rd, chsd
ldr till rdn and wknd quickly aftr 3 out.
. . . .(25 to 1 op 20 to 1) 11
DANGER BABY 10-9 (3*) D Meredith, led second, sn hdd,
chsd ldr till wknd quickly aftr 4 out.
. . . .(14 to 1 op 12 to 1 tchd 16 to 1) 12
SHADES OF CROFT 10-12 E Murphy, led to second, styd
prmnt till wknd quickly 3 out.
. . . .(16 to 1 op 8 to 1 tchd 20 to 1) 13
754⁷ TTYFRAN 10-12 T Wall, beh frm 3rd, al rear.
. . . .(10 to 1 op 25 to 1) 14
870⁸ FREE DANCER 10-7 D J Burchell, trkd ldrs frm 3rd, cl up
and ev ch whn mstk 3 out, not reco'r.
. . . .(33 to 1 op 25 to 1) 15
851 WESTRAY (Fr) 10-12 A Carroll, beh frm 3rd, al rear.
. . . .(50 to 1) 16
702 YOSHAARIK (Ire) 10-7 (5*) T Eley, drpd rear aftr 3rd, nvr
dngrs. . . . .(66 to 1 op 50 to 1) 17
EXCESS BAGGAGE (Ire) 10-12 M Hourigan, led aftr second, hdd 4th, chsd ldr till wknd quickly aftr 3 out.
. . . .(33 to 1) 18
CORNELIUS O'DEA (Ire) 10-12 H Davies, al beh, tld off aftr
3 out. . . . .(33 to 1 op 20 to 1) 19
LEGAL RISK 10-7 N Mann, chsd ldr to 4th, wknd aftr nxt,
tld off after 3 out. . . . .(33 to 1 op 20 to 1) 20
352* GLOWING PATH 11-4 W McFarland, f second.
. . . .(11 to 1 op 8 to 1 tchd 12 to 1) f
Dist: ½l, 12l, 2½l, 2l, nk, 15l, 1l, 1l, nk, sht-hd. 3m 41.20s. a 1.20s (21 Ran).
SR: 20/24/12/9/2/6/ (Miss Helen L Pengelly), M C Pipe

1022 Spillers Racing Mix Handicap Chase (0-120 5-y-o and up) £3,730 2m. . (1:50)

THE SLATER [103] 8-11-4 R Dunwoody, trkd ldr gng wl,
wnt second 4 out, led 2 out, styd on well.
. . . .(2 to 1 fav op 9 to 4) 1
HEARTS ARE WILD [92] 6-10-7 M Perrett, hld up and beh,
hdwy aftr 7th, styd on wl frm 2 out to take second pl
r-in, not rch nnr. . . . .(11 to 1 op 10 to 1 tchd 12 to 1) 2
931³ L'UOMO PIU [92] 9-10-7 N Williamson, trkd ldr, cl up and
ev ch 4 out, rdn and styd on frm 2 out, not quicken.
. . . .(7 to 1 op 6 to 1 tchd 8 to 1) 3
931 SAILORS LUCK [97] 8-10-12 E Murphy, trkd ldr, led aftr 3
out, hdd nxt, rdn and rallied betw last 2, not quicken.
. . . .(3 to 1 op 6 to 1 tchd 11 to 4) 4
788* POSITIVE ACTION [101] 7-10-13 (3*) A Dobbin, trkd ldr, ev
ch 4 out, no hdwy appr 2 out.
. . . .(9 to 2 op 7 to 2 tchd 5 to 1) 5
794⁵ BUMPTIOUS BOY [85] 9-10-0 B Clifford, mid-div, trkd ldrs
frm 7th till rdn and wknd appr 3 out.
. . . .(11 to 1 op 16 to 1 tchd 10 to 1) 6
840³ LUCKY AGAIN [94] 6-10-9 C Maude, mstks, chsd ldr frm
6th till wknd aftr 4 out.
. . . .(25 to 1 op 20 to 1) 7
MURPHY [109] 9-11-10 G Upton, led till hdd aftr 3 out,
styd in tch till wknd quickly after last.
. . . .(33 to 1 op 20 to 1) 8
865 FATHER PADDY [85] (h) 11-9-11 (3*) W Marston, pushed
alng aftr 5th, sn tld off.
. . . .(50 to 1 op 33 to 1 tchd 66 to 1) 9
676 KNIGHT'S SPUR (USA) [101] 6-11-2 R J Beggan, pressed
ldr till wknd quickly aftr 7th, tld off.
. . . .(11 to 1 op 8 to 1 tchd 12 to 1) 10
834 ROMAN DART [93] 10-8 R Bellamy, not jump wl, mstk
5th, tld off aftr nxt. . . . .(33 to 1) 11
RUMBLE (USA) [85] 5-9-9² (7*) D Fortt, hld up, hdwy 6th, cl
sixth whn f 4 out. . . . .(14 to 1 op 8 to 1) f
Dist: 2½l, 2l, ¾l, 2l, 2l, 11l, 25l, 8l, dist. 3m 51.60s. b 0.40s (12 Ran).
SR: 46/32/30/34/36/18/25/39/-/ (Kavanagh Roofing Southern Limited), W G
M Turner

1023 West Oxfordshire Novices' Hurdle (4-y-o and up) £1,473 2½m 110yds (2:20)

ACT OF PARLIAMENT (Ire) 5-10-12 N Williamson, hld up,
wnt second, 4 out, led 2 out, drvn out r-in.
. . . .(7 to 4 op 5 to 4 tchd 15 to 8) 1
RIVER MANDATE 6-10-12 H Davies, hld up gng wl, styd
on frm 4 out, rdn to chal appr last, not quicken r-in.
. . . .(11 to 8 fav op 2 to 1) 2

133

MONKSANDER 7-10-12 Richard Guest, *hld up, hdwy aftr 5th, led 7th till hdd and hit 2 out, not quicken appr last*.............................. (50 to 1) 3

728 DANZARIN (Ire) 5-10-12 R Campbell, *chsd ldrs frm 5th till wknd appr 2 out*..... (16 to 1 op 10 to 1 tchd 20 to 1) 4

809 PRINCETHORPE 6-10-9 (3*) D Meredith, *trkd ldrs, hrd rdn aftr 4 out, sn wknd*.................(33 to 1 op 20 to 1) 5

ROYAL REFRAIN 8-10-7 (5*) R Farrant, *led aftr 6th to nxt, trkd ldrs till wknd aftr 4 out*.
.... (7 to 1 op 5 to 1 tchd 15 to 2) 6

664 WANDERLINE 6-10-12 Peter Caldwell, *lost pl aftr 5th, mstk nxt, rallied to chsd ldrs frm 5 out, wknd after 3 out*.....................(40 to 1 op 20 to 1) 7

ALAPA 6-10-12 A Coogan, *trkd ldrs aftr 6th till rdn and wknd quickly 4 out*..............(100 to 1 op 33 to 1) 8

BLACK ARROW 6-10-12 Mr Raymond White, *prmnt till wknd quickly aftr 7th, sn beh, tld off 3 out*.
..............................(100 to 1 op 33 to 1) 9

SEMINOLE PRINCESS 5-10-0 (7*) Katherine Davies, *sn last, tld off aftr 6th, blun and uns rdr 4 out*.
....(33 to 1 op 16 to 1) ur

844 RED NEST 5-10-0 (7*) Mr S Joynes, *some hdwy aftr 6th, wknd 4 out, beh whn ran out through wing 2 out*.
....(33 to 1 op 20 to 1) ro

698 MASTER BUSTER 8-10-12 D Skyrme, *led 3rd till 4th, mstk 6th, beh whn pld up bef nxt*......(100 to 1 op 50 to 1) pu

773 NORDIC FLIGHT 5-10-12 R Dunwoody, *prmnt till wknd quickly aftr 5 out, beh whn pld up bef 3 out*.
....(33 to 1 op 16 to 1) pu

934 SPACE MOLLY 4-10-4 (3*) W Marston, *led to 3rd, led ag'n 4th till aftr 6th, tld off whn pld up bef four out*.
..............................(40 to 1 op 20 to 1) pu

Dist: ½l, 7l, 12l, 12l, ¾l, 4l, 20l, 30l. 4m 54.20s. a 6.70s (14 Ran).

(J Perris), K C Bailey

1024 Bonusprint Novices' Chase (5-y-o and up) £3,952 2½m 110yds........(2:50)

892² CRYSTAL SPIRIT 6-11-0 R Dunwoody, *led 3rd, drw clr aftr 3 out, unchlgd*.............(9 to 4 on op 5 to 2 on) 1

833 RICH AND RED 7-10-9 N Williamson, *led to 3rd, pressed ldr till hit 4 out, sn wknd, tld off*.......(8 to 1 op 6 to 1) 2

DI MODA 6-11-0 M Bosley, *mstks, beh 5th, tld off whn blun 11th*..........................(33 to 1 op 16 to 1) 3

791³ MARTRAJAN 6-11-0 W McFarland, *3rd whn f 5th*.
....(3 to 1 tchd 7 to 2) f

Dist: 30l, 30l. 5m 1.30s. a 6.30s (4 Ran).

(Paul Mellon), I A Balding

# 1025 Tensator Ltd Handicap Hurdle (0-130 4-y-o and up) £3,938 2½m 110yds
...................................(3:25)

SMITH TOO (Ire) [101] 5-10-0 I Lawrence, *trkd ldrs, led and eddd lft 2 out, drvn out*............(12 to 1 op 8 to 1) 1

829³ MIDFIELDER [119] 7-11-4 R Dunwoody, *dsptd ld till led 5th, hdd and swtchd rght aftr 2 out, rallied r-in, not quicken*...............(5 to 2 tchd 11 to 4 and 3 to 1) 2

776⁴ JEASSU [109] 10-12-0 B Clifford, *hld up and beh, hdwy aftr 3 out, styd on behind last 2, not quicken*.
..............................(9 to 2 op 5 to 1 tchd 4 to 1) 3

677⁵ SECRET SUMMIT (USA) [101] 7-9-9 (5*) T Eley, *trkd ldrs, cl up and ev ch 3 out, rdn and no imprsn betw last 2*.
...............................(25 to 1 op 20 to 1) 4

918⁸ REVE EN ROSE [101] 7-10-0 N Williamson, *hld up, hdwy 5th, chsd ldrs 3 out, styd on one pace*.
..............................(33 to 1 op 25 to 1) 5

936⁴ FOR HEAVEN'S SAKE (Fr) [101] 8-10-0 T Wall, *in tch, pushed alng aftr 6th, one pace appr 2 out*.
..............(14 to 1 op 12 to 1 tchd 16 to 1 and 20 to 1) 6

861* CANOSCAN [110] 8-10-9 E Murphy, *hld up, hdwy to track ldrs aftr 6th, rdn alng aftr 3 out, not quicken betw last 2*..................... (2 to 1 fav op 7 to 4) 7

326⁸ FAST CRUISE [101] 8-10-0 R Bellamy, *beh 5th, styd on one pace frm 3 out*.................(50 to 1) 8

477 STANE STREET (Ire) [101] 5-9-9 (5*) R Farrant, *prmnt till wknd aftr 7th*.......(33 to 1 op 25 to 1 tchd 40 to 1) 9

812⁷ FIRST CRACK [101] 8-10-0 R Supple, *hld up and beh, gd hdwy to track ldrs aftr 4 out, wknd quickly appr 2 out*.
..............................(20 to 1) 10

936⁷ MOUNTSHANNON [104] 7-10-3³ Peter Caldwell, *dsptd ld to 5th, mstk 7th, wknd 3 out, beh whn pld up aftr*.............(33 to 1 op 25 to 1) 11

Dist: 3l, 2½l, 1½l, sht-hd, nk, 2½l, 2½l, 3l, nk, 5l. 4m 49.30s. a 1.80s (11 Ran).

SR: -/8/15/-/-/-/

(Smith Mansfield Meat Co Ltd), Mrs J Pitman

1026 Crosbee And Atkins Handicap Chase (0-140 5-y-o and up) £4,302 3¼m (4:00)

PARSONS GREEN [135] (bl) 9-11-10 R Dunwoody, *chsd ldr, rdn alng and no imprsn 4 out, rallied to chal aftr 2 out, ridden to ld r-in, pushed out*... (9 to 4 fav op 11 to 8) 1

842⁴ VIRIDIAN [111] (bl) 8-10-0 N Williamson, *al chsd whn hit 3 out, wknd and hdd r-in*. (5 to 1 op 6 to 1 tchd 7 to 1) 2

792³ KNIGHT OIL [122] (bl) 10-10-11 Mr J Durkan, *lost tch 9th, hdwy 14th, wknd aftr 15th, jmpd slwly 4 out, no ch frm nxt*.....................(5 to 2 op 2 to 1 tchd 3 to 1) 3

669* KINGFISHER BAY [111] 8-9-7 (7*) P McLoughlin, *hld up and beh, reminder aftr 11th, blun 13th, tld off frm nxt*.
..............................(6 to 1 tchd 11 to 2 and 13 to 2) 4

696⁵ RIO HAINA [111] 8-10-0 M Perrett, *mstk second, 4th whn f 7th*......................(7 to 1 op 4 to 1) f

Dist: 3l, 12l, 20l. 6m 20.70s. a 6.70s (5 Ran).

(Raymond Tooth), N J Henderson

1027 Grunwick Stakes National Hunt Flat Race (4,5,6-y-o) £2,024 2m......(4:30)

NIRVANA PRINCE 4-11-2 (5*) T Jenks, *pld hrd, sn tracking ldrs, 4th strt, led 2 fs out, drvn out*. (8 to 1 tchd 9 to 1) 1

BLACK OPAL (Ire) 4-10-7 (7*) L O'Hare, *hld up, trkd ldg grp aftr one m, 3rd strt, chlgd 2 fs out, not quicken ins fnl furlong*...........................(4 to 1 fav op 3 to 1) 2

BASS ROCK 5-10-9 (7*) R Darke, *pld hrd, hld up in mid-div, trkd ldrs 5 fs out, 6th strt, styd on wl fnl 2 furlongs, not quicken*...........(9 to 2 op 6 to 4 tchd 5 to 1) 3

TWISTED BAR 5-11-2 M Hourigan, *led for one furlong, trkd ldrs, led briefly 3 fs out, sn hdd, second strt, kpt on ins fnl 2 furlongs*.......(13 to 2 op 5 to 1 tchd 7 to 1) 4

815 HOT 'N ROSIE 4-10-6 (3*) W Marston, *hld up and beh, hdwy o'r 4 fs out, 8th strt, styd on wl ins fnl 2 furlongs*.
..............................(20 to 1) 5

FLAPPING FREDA (Ire) 5-10-4 (7*) D Fortt, *hld up in mid-div, hdwy to chase ldg grp aftr one m, pushed alng 3 fs out, 7th strt, styd on*. (14 to 1 op 16 to 1 tchd 20 to 1) 6

SOLO GIRL (Ire) 5-10-4 (7*) Mr C Vigors, *hld up, hdwy hfwy, tenth strt, styd on fnl 2 fs*...........(33 to 1) 7

PHIL'S DREAM 5-10-9 (7*) D Bohan, *hld up and beh, hdwy 4 fs out, styd on wl ins fnl 2 furlongs*.
..............................(8 to 1 op 6 to 1 tchd 9 to 1) 8

HURRICANE SUE 4-10-2 (7*) G McGrath, *hld up, beh, styd on fnl 3 fs, nvr nrr*.....................(16 to 1) 9

GOOD FEELING 4-10-7 (7*) P Naughton, *hld up, trkd ldrs aftr 4 fs, 5th strt, wknd ins fnl 2 furlongs*...(20 to 1) 10

PRINCE RUBEN 6-10-11 (5*) R Farrant, *led aftr one furlong till hdd briefly 3 fs out, wknd quickly o'r 2 furlongs out*........(11 to 1 op 10 to 1 tchd 12 to 1) 11

OUR ARNOLD 6-10-9 (7*) P Maddock, *pld hrd, hld up, hdwy to chase ldg grp aftr one m, 9th strt, sn wknd*.
..............................(25 to 1 op 20 to 1) 12

FOXY LASS 4-10-9 Mr J Cambidge, *beh till styd on one pace fnl 4 fs*..........................(50 to 1) 13

634⁷ SUNGIA (Ire) 4-10-9 (5*) D Leahy, *al beh*.
..............................(25 to 1 op 20 to 1) 14

LEWESDON PRINCESS 5-10-4 (7*) P McLoughlin, *al beh, tld off fnl 5 fs*.......(20 to 1 op 10 to 1 tchd 16 to 1) 15

SUPERFORCE 6-10-9 (7*) J Neaves, *hdwy aftr 5 fs, trkd ldg grp till wknd 3 furlongs out*.............(33 to 1) 16

CREDIT CALL (Ire) 5-10-13 (3*) D Meredith, *hld up and beh, hdwy hfwy, chsd ldg grp till wknd quickly 4 fs out*.
..............................(50 to 1) 17

MAJOR MAC 6-10-11 (5*) R Davis, *al beh*.
..............................(11 to 1 op 10 to 1) 18

CUMREWS NEPHEW 5-11-2 V Slattery, *pld hrd, chsd ldg grp aftr 6 fs, wknd quickly o'r 4 furlongs out*.
..............................(33 to 1 op 25 to 1) 19

ALTESSE ROXANNE 4-10-2 (7*) Pat Thompson, *al beh, tld off fnl 5 fs*.........................(33 to 1) 20

778 HOPEFULL DRUMMER 4-11-0 Mr N Harris, *pld hrd, prmnt till wknd o'r 6 fs out*.................(50 to 1) 21

THE STING 6-11-2 Mr Raymond White, *beh aftr 3 fs, tld off fnl 6 furlongs*.....................(33 to 1) 22

901 DREAMLINE 4-10-2 (7*) R Williamson, *stumbled and uns rdr aftr one furlong*.....................(50 to 1) ur

Dist: 2½l, 5l, 2l, 1½l, 1½l, hd, nk, 5l, nk, hd. 3m 38.10s. (23 Ran).

(D Portman), B Preece

WETHERBY (good)
Saturday October 30th
Going Correction: PLUS 0.20 sec. per fur. (races 1,3,-5,7), PLUS 0.15 (2,4,6)

1028 Mercer Marriage Novices' Hurdle (4-y-o and up) £2,215 3m 1f......(12:50)

DURHAM SUNSET 6-10-7 A Maguire, *cl up, led 8th, lft clr 2 out, styd on wl*.............(33 to 1 op 25 to 1) 1

ANOTHER NICK 7-10-7 (5*) P Williams, *trkd ldrs gng wl, chalg whn blun badly 2 out, sn rdn, kpt on, not reco'r*.
..............................(14 to 1 tchd 16 to 1) 2

779⁴ SHOOFE (USA) 5-10-12 A S Smith, *hld up, hdwy aftr 7th, kpt on same pace frm 3 out*.... (5 to 2 op 9 to 4) 3

721* ROYAL VACATION 4-11-9 J Callaghan, *hld up, pushed alng and hdwy appr 3 out, one pace frm nxt*.
..............................(9 to 4 fav) 4

898⁷ MAN O MINE (Ire) 4-10-4 (7*) P Murphy, *pld hrd, cl up to till wknd aftr 3 out*.............(1 to 1 op 6 to 1) 5

743³ TOPPING TOM (Ire) 4-10-11 C Llewellyn, *trkd ldrs, mstk and lost pl 6th, hdwy appr 9th, wknd approaching 3 out*...........................(7 to 1 op 6 to 1) 6

PORTONIA 9-10-7 P Niven, *led till hdd 8th, wknd quickly aftr nxt*.......................(9 to 2 tchd 5 to 1) 7

639[4] MASTER BOSTON (Ire) 5-10-12 R Garritty, *mstk second,
chsd ldrs till wknd quickly aftr 9th*........... (16 to 1) 8
875[5] ADVENT LADY 6-10-7 A Mulholland, *mstks, blun 8th, sn
lost tch, tld off whn pld up bef 3 out.*
.............................(100 to 1 op 50 to 1) pu
Dist: 5l, 3l, 5l, 2½l, 12l, 15l, 10l. 6m 11.30s. a 16.30s (9 Ran).
(W M G Black), J H Johnson

1029 Wighill Handicap Chase (0-140 5-y-o and up) £3,835 2½m 110yds.....(1:25)

USHERS ISLAND [122] 7-11-1 A Maguire, *cl up, led 5th,
blun 11th, styd on wl and pres frm last.*
.............................(12 to 1 op 10 to 1) 1
DAWSON CITY [135] 6-12-0 L Wyer, *in tch, chsd wnr frm 4
out, rdn betw last 2, kpt on, no imprsn.*
.............................(7 to 2 op 3 to 1) 2
SOUTHERN MINSTREL [117] 10-10-10 C Grant, *chsd ldrs,
pushed alng aftr 11th, sn wknd, tld off*
.............................(13 to 2 op 9 to 2 tchd 7 to 1) 3
758* SIR PETER LELY [111] 6-10-4 P Niven, *led till hdd 5th, cl
up, pushed alng whn f 4 out.*
.............................(13 to 8 fav op 7 to 4 tchd 2 to 1) f
STEPFASTER [110] 8-10-3 C Llewellyn, *sn beh, tld off whn
pld up bef 4 out.*...................(12 to 1 op 8 to 1) pu
921[2] SCOLE [113] 8-9-13 (7*) P Murphy, *drpd rear aftr 6th, tld
off whn pld up bef 4 out.*...........(7 to 2 op 5 to 2) pu
Dist: 2½l, dist. 5m 5.10s. a 8.60s (6 Ran).
SR: 32/42/-/ (R W L Bowden), J H Johnson

1030 Tote West Yorkshire Hurdle Grade 2 (4-y-o and up) £9,240 3m 1f.... (1:55)

736[3] DEB'S BALL 7-10-9 D J Moffatt, *beh, hdwy appr 3 out, led
and mstk nxt, styd on wnl pres, all out.*
.............................(9 to 1 op 8 to 1 tchd 10 to 1) 1
SWEET DUKE (Fr) 6-11-7 C Llewellyn, *led till hdd 2 out,
kpt on wl frm last.*......(4 to 1 op 11 to 4 tchd 9 to 2) 2
BURGOYNE 7-11-4 P Niven, *cl up, pushed alng hfwy,
outpcd appr 3 out, no dngr aftr. (2 to 1 fav op 5 to 2)* 3
FLAKEY DOVE 7-11-2 B Powell, *trkd ldrs gng wl, chlgd 3
out, sn rdn and wknd. (11 to 4 op 5 to 2)* 4
759* COUNTORUS 7-11-0 A Maguire, *beh, hdwy up hfwy, ev ch
whn blun 3 out, sn wknd, behind when pld up bef last.*
.............................(8 to 1 op 10 to 1) pu
CARDINAL RED 6-11-4 M Dwyer, *ran in snatches, in tch
till lost pl quickly aftr 7th, wl tld off whn pld up bef 3
out.*.............................(6 to 1) pu
Dist: 2l, 6l, 8l. 6m 2.10s. a 7.10s (6 Ran).
SR: 60/70/61/51/-/-/ (J Calvert), D Moffatt

1031 Charlie Hall Chase (Grade 2) (5-y-o and up) £15,440 3m 110yds..... (2:25)

BARTON BANK 7-11-2 A Maguire, *made all, hit 9th, styd
on wl frm 3 out.*...................(12 to 1 tchd 14 to 1) 1
CAB ON TARGET 7-11-2 P Niven, *hld up, hdwy appr 4
out, chsd wnr frm nxt, kpt on wl approaching last, no
imprsn.*.............................(2 to 1 fav op 7 to 4) 2
866[2] GARRISON SAVANNAH (bl) 10-11-2 B Powell, *chsd wnr
most of way, rdn and wknd frm 3 out.*
.............................(6 to 1 tchd 7 to 1) 3
PAT'S JESTER 10-11-10 B Storey, *in tch till grad wknd
aftr 14th.*.............................(8 to 1) 4
828[2] SIBTON ABBEY 8-11-10 G McCourt, *in tch, sn pushed
alng, wknd rdn aftr 14th, soon wl beh.*
.............................(14 to 1 op 10 to 1) 5
JODAMI 8-11-10 M Dwyer, *trkd ldrs, cl up and ev ch whn
f 4 out.*.............................(9 to 4 op 2 to 1 tchd 5 to 2) f
866[3] TIPPING TIM 8-11-10 C Llewellyn, *mstk and lost tch frm
12th (water), tld off whn pld up bef 4 out.*
.............................(14 to 1 op 10 to 1) pu
Dist: 2l, 20l, 12l, 11l. 6m 10.30s. a 4.30s (7 Ran).
SR: 82/80/60/56/54/-/-/ (Mrs J Mould), D Nicholson

1032 Wensleydale Juvenile Hurdle (Grade 2) (3-y-o) £6,340 2m........... (2:55)

784* BURNT IMP (USA) 11-2 J Callaghan, *trkd ldrs gng wl, led
appr 3 out, quickened betw last 2, ran on well.*
.............................(5 to 2 tchd 9 to 4 and 11 to 4) 1
MARROS MILL 10-7 A Maguire, *hld up, hit 5th, hdwy and
ev ch appr 3 out, sn rdn, kpt on same pace.*
.............................(3 to 1 op 4 to 1 tchd 9 to 2) 2
851[2] LA VILLA ROSE (Fr) 10-7 C Llewellyn, *in tch, hdwy appr 3
out, mstk nxt, kpt on same pace...*(14 to 1 op 9 to 1) 3
830[3] SIR THOMAS BEECHAM 10-12 P Niven, *dsptd ld till appr
3rd, cl up, chalg whn mstk 3 out, grad wknd.*
.............................(5 to 1 op 4 to 1) 4
872* ERZADJAN (Ire) 11-2 G McCourt, *not fluent, dsptd ld till
appr 3rd, cl up, pushed alng aftr 6th, wknd frm 3 out.*
.............................(13 to 8 fav op 2 to 1 tchd 9 to 4) 5
872[4] SALLY OF THE ALLEY 10-7 Gary Lyons, *in tch till wknd
appr 3 out.*.............................(50 to 1 op 33 to 1) 6
870* SEASIDE DREAMER 10-12 Mr A Hambly, *pld hrd, led appr
3rd till hdd approaching 3 out, wknd quickly, tld off
whn f last.*.............................(16 to 1 op 12 to 1) f
Dist: 5l, 2½l, 2l, 5l, 15l. 3m 54.50s. a 13.50s (7 Ran).

(N B Mason (Farms) Ltd), G M Moore

1033 Arthur Stephenson Novices' Chase (5-y-o and up) £6,970 3m 110yds... (3:30)

874 BRACKENFIELD 7-11-4 P Niven, *trkd ldrs, mstk tenth,
slight ld 3 out, hrd pressed whn lft clr last.*
.............................(11 to 10 on op 5 to 4 on tchd Evens) 1
874 ARTHUR'S MINSTREL 6-10-12 C Grant, *chsd ldrs, ev ch 3
out, wknd nxt, btn whn hmpd last.*
.............................(4 to 1 tchd 9 to 2 and 7 to 2) 2
756* VELEDA II (Fr) 6-11-4 J Burke, *led till hdd 3 out, wknd nxt,
btn whn hmpd last...*(11 to 1 op 10 to 1 tchd 12 to 1) 3
874[3] SUPPOSIN 5-10-12 Gary Lyons, *in tch, hdwy to track ldrs
hfwy, mstk and lost pl tenth, wl beh frm 4 out.*
.............................(33 to 1 op 25 to 1) 4
874* SANDY ANDY 7-11-4 T Reed, *trkd ldrs till blun and lost
pl 14th, sn rdn and wknd.*.......(14 to 1 op 20 to 1) 5
ABNEGATION 8-10-12 G McCourt, *hld up, smooth hdwy
whn mstk 4 out, chlgd 2 out, disputing ld and ev ch
when f last.*.............................(7 to 1 op 6 to 1 tchd 8 to 1) f
649[3] BABIL 8-10-12 C Llewellyn, *wth ldr, till pld up lme bef
7th.*.............................(7 to 1 op 8 to 1 tchd 9 to 1) pu
Dist: 10l, 8l, 25l, 15l. 6m 27.30s. a 21.30s (7 Ran).
(Guy Faber), Mrs M Reveley

1034 Pickering Handicap Hurdle (0-135 4-y-o and up) £2,758 2m......... (4:05)

TOOGOOD TO BE TRUE [100] 5-10-0 L Wyer, *made all, clr
whn mstk 3 out, ran on strly frm nxt.*
.............................(11 to 4 fav op 5 to 1) 1
ARCOT [122] 5-11-8 M Ahern, *hld up in tch, hdwy gng wl
aftr 3 out, mstk nxt, rdn appr last, ran on well, not tch
wnr.*.............................(4 to 1 op 7 to 2) 2
729[3] SPACE CAPTAIN [110] 6-10-7 (3*) N Bentley, *in tch, pushed
alng aftr 6th, chsd wnr frm 3 out, no extr appr last.*
.............................(12 to 1 tchd 14 to 1) 3
HOME COUNTIES (Ire) [123] 4-11-6 (3*) D J Moffatt, *hld up,
hdwy appr 3 out, one pace frm nxt. (10 to 1 op 7 to 1)* 4
898[5] KADI (Ger) [128] 4-12-0 A Maguire, *prmnt till wknd 2 out.*
.............................(7 to 2 op 4 to 1 tchd 5 to 1) 5
KANNDABIL [116] (bl) 6-11-2 G McCourt, *prmnt, effrt appr
3 out, wknd.*.............................(10 to 1 op 12 to 1) 6
GYMCRAK STARDOM [124] 7-11-10 M Dwyer, *nvr dngrs.*
.............................(10 to 1) 7
EXPLORATION (USA) [100] 6-10-0 A S Smith, *prmnt till
wknd appr 3 out.*.............................(33 to 1 op 25 to 1) 8
LIABILITY ORDER [106] 4-10-6 C Grant, *chsd ldrs, rdn
appr 3 out, sn wknd.*.............................(7 to 1 op 5 to 1) 9
STARSTREAK [115] 6-11-1 P Niven, *al beh, lost tch appr 3
out.*.............................(6 to 1 op 5 to 1) 10
Dist: 6l, 5l, 1½l, ¾l, 10l, 5l, 10l, 12l. 3m 50.50s. a 9.50s (10 Ran).
SR: 9/25/8/19/23/1/4/-/-/ (Jim McGrath), M H Easterby

CLONMEL (IRE) (good)
Monday November 1st

1035 Aer Lingus Captain Christy Novice Chase (5-y-o and up) £2,760 2½m
.............................(2:15)

941 NUAFFE 8-11-12 S H O'Donovan,............(5 to 2 fav) 1
857[9] ANOTHER GROUSE 6-10-9 (7*) J P Broderick,...(14 to 1) 2
941[3] ANOTHER EXCUSE (Ire) 5-11-2 (7*) Mr W M O'Sullivan,
.............................(3 to 1) 3
989[9] BALLAGH COUNTESS 6-11-2 K F O'Brien,.....(8 to 1) 4
807[7] KINGS HILL 11-11-0 (7*) J Butler,.............(8 to 1) 5
905 TAKE IT EASY KID (Ire) 5-10-10 P P Kinane,...(12 to 1) 6
857[5] RUSSIAN GALE (Ire) 5-10-10 J Collins,.......(12 to 1) 7
CARRIGEEN GALA 6-11-2 A Powell,............(10 to 1) 8
690[8] WAR OFFICE 6-11-2 J Jones,...................(20 to 1) 9
WADI RUM 7-11-7 J A White,.....................(20 to 1) 10
989[7] COOLADERRA LADY 7-11-2 J P Banahan,.....(20 to 1) 11
689 NANCYS LAD 6-11-7 H Rogers,...............(14 to 1) 12
857 SEANS SHOON 6-11-2 A J O'Brien,..............(25 to 1) 13
989 HARLANE (Ire) 5-11-1 F Woods,................(20 to 1) 14
941 THREE BROWNIES 6-11-12 T Horgan,..........(4 to 1) f
Dist: 3½l, dist, 10l. 5m 11.00s. (15 Ran).
(John G Doyle), P A Fahy

1036 Cork Gateway Maiden Hurdle (4-y-o) £2,243 2m.................... (2:45)

925[4] JUPITER JIMMY 10-11 (5*) C O'Brien,.....(3 to 1 jt-fav) 1
854 VON CARTY (Ire) 11-2 K F O'Brien,.............(8 to 1) 2
671[6] NORA ANN (Ire) 10-11 (5*) M A Davey,........(13 to 2) 3
ALVATUR (Ire) 10-9 (7*) K C Hartnett,...........(16 to 1) 4
925[7] KEEPHERGOING (Ire) 10-4 (7*) J P Broderick,....(8 to 1) 5
23 ARDFALLON (Ire) 10-11 H Rogers,...............(20 to 1) 6
MARYVILLE LADY (Ire) 10-11 G M O'Neill,......(33 to 1) 7
939[6] AN MAINEACH (Ire) 11-2 C F Swan,....(3 to 1 jt-fav) 8
925* CHANCERY QUEEN (Ire) 10-9 (7*) K P Gaule,......(8 to 1) 9
925[8] OZEYCAZEY (Ire) 10-11 (5*) S A Finn,........(12 to 1) 10
ALBERTA ROSE (Ire) 11-2 M Duffy,...............(8 to 1) 11
902 MIDDLE SUSIE (Ire) 10-6 (5*) T P Treacy,.......(33 to 1) 12

671	REASON TO BELIEVE (Ire) 10-11 F Woods, ...(25 to 1)	13
555	YOUR UNCLE STANLEY (Ire) 11-2 A J O'Brien, ... (25 to 1)	14
	RAISE THE LIMIT (Ire) 10-6 (5") J R Barry, ... (12 to 1)	15
393⁸	PADDY'S RAMBO (Ire) 11-2 P McWilliams, ... (33 to 1)	16
803	LOVE FOR LYDIA (Ire) 10-4 (7") F Byrne, ...(20 to 1)	17
	WOLVER ROSIE (Ire) 10-4 (7") L A Hurley, ...(33 to 1)	18
	THE DEFENDER (Ire) 11-2 P L Malone, ...(14 to 1)	19

Dist: 5l, 7l, 2l, 1l. 4m 8.70s. (19 Ran).

(James F Murphy), J E Kiely

1037 British Airways Handicap Hurdle (0-123 4-y-o and up) £2,760 3m. . (3:15)

938⁴	UNCLE BART (Ire) [-] 5-11-1 (7") R A Hennessy, ... (4 to 1)	1
708⁴	TUG OF PEACE [-] 6-11-10 (3") C O'Brien, ... (100 to 30)	2
	PRINCE OLE (Ire) [-] 5-11-5 (5") J R Barry, ...(5 to 2 fav)	3
134	REHEY LADY [-] 7-9-5 (5") T J O'Sullivan, ... (14 to 1)	4
904³	BELEEK CASTLE [-] 7-11-2 T Horgan, ... (7 to 1)	5
903²	CLOSUTTON EXPRESS [-] 7-9-13 C F Swan, ... (4 to 1)	6
857⁶	LADY GALE BRIDGE [-] 6-9-11 F Woods, ...(20 to 1)	7
	ROSSI NOVAE [-] 10-9-13 A J O'Brien, ...(20 to 1)	8
1017⁵	MARBLE CITY GIRL [-] (bl) 8-9-8 (5") P A Roche, . . .(10 to 1)	f
904	THE MAD MONK [-] 8-10-6 (7") Mr D K Budds, ...(16 to 1)	ur

Dist: 2½l, 25l, 7l, 8l. 6m 9.90s. (10 Ran).

(W Hennessy), Anthony Mullins

1038 Ryanair Handicap Hurdle (0-109 4-y-o and up) £2,760 2m. . . . .(3:45)

904	BROOK COTTAGE (Ire) [-] 5-11-13 (6ex) K F O'Brien,	
	. . . .(15 to 8 fav)	1
967⁷	JIMMY THE JACKDAW [-] (bl) 6-10-10 P Carberry, . .(5 to 2)	2
805⁵	BALLINDERRY GLEN [-] 7-10-8 (5") M G Cleary, . . .(6 to 1)	3
	TARA'S TRIBE [-] 6-10-9 M Duffy, ...(10 to 1)	4
797⁷	CLASSY MACHINE (Ire) [-] 5-10-7 P M Verling, ...(10 to 1)	5
528	HERE IT IS [-] 6-11-4 (7") M Kelly, ...(13 to 2)	6
	LADY HA HA [-] 6-9-11 (7") J Butler, ... (20 to 1)	7
	JAMES GIRL [-] 9-9-12 (7") B Bowens, ...(12 to 1)	8
362	ARDLEA HOUSE (Ire) [-] 4-10-0 (7") R A Hennessy, (14 to 1)	9

Dist: Sht-hd, 5½l, nk, 9l. 4m 11.10s. (9 Ran).

(T A O'Doherty), Michael Hourigan

1039 Cork Airport Duty Free INH Flat Race (4-y-o) £2,760 2m. . . . .(4:15)

709²	GREAT SVENGALI (Ire) 11-2 (7") Mr K Nolan, ... (7 to 4 on)	1
907	SIOBHAIN DUBH (Ire) 10-11 (7") Mr G R Ryan, . . .(14 to 1)	2
709⁸	BROWNRATH KING (Ire) 11-2 (7") Mr D K Budds, (14 to 1)	3
692⁴	DUN OENGUS (Ire) 10-11 (7") Mr K Whelan, ... (8 to 1)	4
902⁹	HAVE A BRANDY (Ire) (bl) 11-9 Mr D M Bradley, . . .(10 to 1)	5
638⁷	LEISURE CENTRE (Ire) 10-11 (7") Mr R P Cody, . . . (20 to 1)	6
692⁶	UNSINKABLE BOXER (Ire) 11-2 (7") Mr W M O'Sullivan,	
	. . . .(12 to 1)	7
	CUL RUA CREEK (Ire) 10-11 (7") Mr E Sheehy, ...(7 to 1)	8
907⁸	CASTLE CLUB (Ire) 11-1 (3") Mr R O'Neill, ...(14 to 1)	9
923⁵	WALNEY ISLAND 11-9 Mr P Fenton, ...(10 to 1)	10
638³	KESS (Ire) 10-13 (5") Mr H F Cleary, ...(12 to 1)	11
908⁵	LARRYS PENNY (Ire) 10-11 (7") Mr P English, ...(25 to 1)	12
	VAIN PRINCESS (Ire) 11-4 Mr M Phillips, ... (33 to 1)	13
	NOSEABIT (Ire) 11-9 Mr P J Healy, ... (20 to 1)	14

Dist: 1½l, 1l, 3l, 9l. 4m 4.00s. (14 Ran).

(Michael W J Smurfit), Patrick Joseph Flynn

PLUMPTON (good to firm)
Monday November 1st
Going Correction: MINUS 0.05 sec. per fur.

1040 Autumn Novices' Hurdle (4-y-o and up) £1,772 2m 1f. . . . . (1:40)

	DOMINANT FORCE 4-11-0 D Murphy, trkd ldrs, prog aproaching 3 out, led 2 out, clr last, cmftbly.	
	. . . . (10 to 1 tchd 11 to 2)	1
765⁵	GLENCARRIG GALE (Ire) 5-11-0 Peter Hobbs, mstks, middiv, effrt 3 out, ran on to chase wnr appr last, no imprsn. . . . .(12 to 1 tchd 14 to 1)	2
883⁹	MAKING TIME 6-10-9 A Tory, cl up till lost pl aftr 6th., ran on aftr 3 out, nrst finish.	
	. . . .(33 to 1 op 20 to 1 tchd 50 to 1)	3
666⁷	PRIVATE JET (Ire) 4-11-0 N Williamson, al prmnt, rdn 3 out, one pace. . . . .(25 to 1 op 20 to 1 tchd 33 to 1)	4
885²	MASNUN (USA) 8-10-11 (3") D O'Sullivan, cl up till outpcd 3 out, no prog aftr. . . .(11 to 8 fav op Evens tchd 6 to 4)	5
	NAGOBELIA 11-10-9 J McLaughlin, trkd ldrs, prog to ld aftr 7th, hdd and wknd 2 out.	
	. . . .(10 to 1 op 12 to 1 tchd 20 to 1 and 8 to 1)	6
862	BISHOPS TRUTH 7-11-0 D Morris, rear, lost tch aftr 7th, no dngr aftr. . . . .(66 to 1 op 33 to 1)	7
864ᵇ	GAMEFULL GOLD 4-11-0 H Davies, hld up, lost tch 7th. nvr nr to chal. . . . .(33 to 1)	8
888⁸	COUNT BARACHOIS (USA) 5-11-0 N Mann, led till aftr 7th, rdn and wknd aftr. . . . .(16 to 1 op 33 to 1)	9
	BLUE TAIL 5-10-2 (7") S Arnold, rdn on ev 6th, al beh. . . . .(66 to 1 op 33 to 1)	10
864	LISSADELL LADY 4-10-9 Leesa Long, mstk 7th, al beh. . . . .(66 to 1 op 50 to 1)	11

HELLEBORUS 5-10-9 E Murphy, strted slwly, al wl beh,
tld off frm 7th. . . . .(66 to 1 op 33 to 1) | 12
844³ DAUPHIN BLEU (Fr) 7-11-0 Dr P Pritchard, prmnt till wknd
3 out, no dhn f last.
. . . .(20 to 1 op 12 to 1 tchd 25 to 1) f
ROYAL BATTLE 5-10-4 (5") P Hide, prmnt till pld up aftr
3rd, sddl slpd. . . . .(66 to 1 op 33 to 1) pu
Dist: 3l, 4l, 2½l, 5l, 1l, 1½l, 3l, 2½l, 12l, 10l. 4m 9.60s. 4 17.60s (14 Ran).

(Mrs P Jubert), R Hannon

1041 Ringmer Handicap Chase (0-120 5-y-o and up) £2,343 2m 5f. . . . . (2:10)

860*	LITTLE TOM [100] 8-11-1 A Maguire, jmpd wl, led 5th to 7th and frm tenth, pushed clr aftr 3 out, eased r-in.	
	. . . .(6 to 5 fav op 5 to 4 tchd 6 to 4)	1
	RICHVILLE [112] 7-11-13 N Williamson, hld up in tch, prog and ev ch 13th, no extr aftr nxt.	
	. . . .(5 to 2 op 11 to 4 tchd 3 to 1)	2
850²	LOVE ANEW (USA) [103] 8-11-4 D Murphy, in tch, ev ch 13th, sn shaken up and found nil. . . .(5 to 1 op 4 to 1)	3
	HOMME D'AFFAIRE [103] 10-11-1 (3") D O'Sullivan, hld up, lost tch 8th, sn wl beh, styd on ag'n appr last.	
	. . . .(8 to 1 op 5 to 1 tchd 9 to 1)	4
	ON YOUR WAY [95] 11-10-10 R Dunwoody, mstks, led to 5th and 7th to tenth, wknd aftr 12th.	
	. . . .(12 to 1 op 7 to 1)	5
847⁴	SMOOTH DEAL [85] 8-9-9 (5") D Leahy, last till blun and uns rdr 3rd, dead. . . . .(33 to 1 tchd 50 to 1)	ur

Dist: 5l, 3l, 3½l, 15l. 5m 9.60s. a 4.60s (6 Ran).
SR: 31/38/21/17/-/-/

(Mark O'Connor), J S King

1042 Balcombe Selling Handicap Hurdle (4-y-o and up) £1,646 2m 1f. . . . . . . (2:40)

839	ALOSAILI [89] 6-10-5 (7") M Stevens, hld up, prog 5th, led 3 out, clr whn hit nxt, easily.	
	. . . .(8 to 1 op 6 to 1 tchd 5 to 1 and 9 to 1)	1
859⁵	OH SO HANDY [77] 5-10-0 D Morris, pckd second, wl beh till rapid prog frm 7th, rdn 2 out, styd on, no ch wnr. . . . .(33 to 1 op 20 to 1 tchd 50 to 1)	2
861	HANDSOME NED [90] 7-10-13 J Railton, with ldr till led 3rd, clr 6th, hdd and hrd rdn 3 out, wknd nxt.	
	. . . .(6 to 1 op 4 to 1 tchd 13 to 2)	3
922	GREAT HAND [77] (bl) 7-9-11² (5") C Burnett-Wells, chsd ldrs, prog 5th, rdn and no imprsn frm 3 out.	
	. . . .(13 to 2 op 25 to 1 tchd 50 to 1)	4
748³	AT PEACE [90] 7-10-13 A Maguire, chsd ldg pair, cld 6th, hrd rdn and ev ch 3 out, sn wknd. (2 to 1 tchd 13 to 8)	5
	SOLENT LAD [77] 10-10-0 W McFarland, rear, prog and in tch 6th, sn wknd, tld off 3 out.	
	. . . .(66 to 1 op 33 to 1 tchd 100 to 1)	6
748	L'ENCHERE [84] 8-10-7⁴ (7") Paul McEntee, al beh, tld off frm 7th. . . . .(50 to 1 op 25 to 1)	7
861³	MANHATTAN BOY [105] 11-12-0 R Dunwoody, chsd ldrs. prog and cld whn f 6th.	
	. . . .(7 to 4 fav op 2 to 1 tchd 9 to 4)	f
916	GOLDEN SICKLE (USA) [77] 4-9-7 (7") J Neaves, led to 3rd, wknd rpdly 5th, pld up bef 7th. . (100 to 1 op 66 to 1)	pu
932⁶	DON'T FORSAKE ME [77] 4-10-0 J Osborne, hld up, prog whn blun 5th, hmpd nxt, not reco'r, pld up bef 7th.	
	. . . .(8 to 1 op 7 to 1 tchd 12 to 1)	pu

Dist: 10l, 5l, 8l, 2½l, 20l, 10l. 4m 9.30s. a 17.30s (10 Ran).

(Red House Racing), B Stevens

1043 Lewes Novices' Chase (5-y-o and up) £1,608 3m 1f 110yds. . . . .(3:10)

862*	IMPERIAL BRUSH 9-11-5 A Maguire, hld up beh, mstk 11th, prog 14th, mistake 3 out, ev ch nxt, swtchd rght and hrd rdn last, sn led, all out.	
	. . . .(2 to 1 op 7 to 4 tchd 6 to 4 and 9 to 4)	1
763⁴	GALLANT EFFORT (Ire) 5-10-12 H Davies, jmpd slwly early and reminders 6th, prog 14th, mstk nxt, led 2 out, hdd and no extr aftr last. . . . .(7 to 1 op 5 to 1 tchd 9 to 1)	2
917*	PARDON ME MUM (bl) 8-11-5 N Williamson, chsd clr ldr, cld tenth, led 15th, hdd and wknd 2 out.	
	. . . .(5 to 4 fav op Evens tchd 11 to 8)	3
892⁵	TRAIN ROBBER 8-11-0 W Irvine, chsd ldrs, pushed alng 13th, rdn and ev ch 17th, sn wknd. (25 to 1 op 14 to 1)	4
868⁴	THEO'S FELLA 9-11-5 S Hodgson, mstk 8th, clr ldr till hdd 15th, ev ch appr 3 out, btn whn mistake nxt.	
	. . . .(5 to 1 op 7 to 1)	5

Dist: ½l, 20l, 1½l, 2½l. 6m 24.40s. a 12.40s (5 Ran).

(D Baxter), J White

1044 Cuckfield Handicap Chase (0-125 4-y-o and up) £1,882 2m. . . . .(3:40)

	BELMOREDEAN [105] 8-11-7 (3") D O'Sullivan, hld up in tch, prog aftr 8th, mstks nxt 2, rnwd effrt to ld two out, rdn out r-in. . . . .(11 to 2 op 9 to 2 tchd 13 to 2)	1
761²	KISU KALI [99] 6-11-4 S Burrough, chsd ldrs, prog and wth wnr 2 out, hrd rdn appr last, al hld.	
	. . . .(9 to 2 op 7 to 2 tchd 7 to 1)	2
810	COTAPAXI [89] 8-10-8 A Tory, led till 2 out, ev ch appr last, unbl to quicken. . . . .(20 to 1 op 14 to 1)	3

665³ MR FELIX [99] 7-11-4 A Maguire, *led into strt, pressed ldr, ev ch 2 out, sn btn*. (11 to 4 fav op 3 to 1 tchd 5 to 2) 4
946* WICKFIELD LAD [82] 10-10-1 (6ex) S Earle, *in tch till oupaced and mstk tenth, no dngr aftr*.
.......................(3 to 1 tchd 4 to 1) 5
931⁴ STRIDING EDGE [87] 8-10-6 D Murphy, *second*.
.......................(9 to 2 op 4 to 1 tchd 11 to 2) f
FRED SPLENDID [95] 10-11-0 R Dunwoody, *f 1st*.
.......................(8 to 1 op 6 to 1 tchd 9 to 1) f
Dist: 1l, 3½l, 4l, 7l. 3m 56.50s. a 6.50s (7 Ran).
SR: 23/16/2/8/ (Fred Honour), R J O'Sullivan

1045 Chailey Handicap Hurdle (0-125 4-y-o and up) £1,764 2½m..........(4:10)

CAVO GRECO (USA) [83] 4-10-10 D Skyrme, *trkd ldrs, mstk 6th and lost pl, prog to ld aftr 3 out, sn clr, cmftbly*.
.......................(2 to 1 fav op 5 to 2 tchd 11 to 4) 1
861⁷ THUHOOL [96] 5-11-4 (5*) C Burnett-Wells, *settled last, outpcd aftr 3 out, ran on frm nxt, nvr plcd to chal*.
.......................(11 to 4 op 2 to 1 tchd 3 to 1) 2
849⁷ SANTA PONSA BAY [97] 6-11-10 A Maguire, *pressed ldr till led 9th, hdd aftr nxt, one pace*.
.......................(4 to 1 op 5 to 2 tchd 9 to 2) 3
887⁸ KALAMOSS [82] 4-10-2 (7*) Miss S Mitchell, *led to 9th, pushed alng and outpcd aftr nxt, no dngr aftr*.
.......................(9 to 4 op 5 to 2 tchd 7 to 4) 4
Dist: 7l, ¾l, ½l. 4m 55.30s. a 18.30s (4 Ran).

(Jack Joseph), J Joseph

EXETER (firm (races 1,2,4,6), good to firm (3,5))
Tuesday November 2nd
Going Correction: PLUS 0.10 sec. per fur.

1046 Normans Retail Novices' Hurdle (4-y-o and up) £1,954 2¼m.......(1:00)

894⁴ MUSTAHIL (Ire) 4-11-7 R Dunwoody, *hld up early, hdwy to track ldrs frm 3rd, led appr last, rdn clr*.
.......................(3 to 1 tchd 4 to 1) 1
664⁵ DUNDEE PRINCE (NZ) 5-11-0 N Williamson, *led to second, not fluent 4th, led ag'n appr 2 out, hdd bef last, one pace*.......................2
MOAT GARDEN (USA) 5-11-0 B Powell, *pld hrd, led second, clr whn jmpd rght nxt, mstk 4th, wknd and hdd appr 2 out*.......................(6 to 4 fav tchd 7 to 4) 3
795* VIOLET'S BOY 6-11-7 C Maude, *al prmnt, rdn aftr 3 out, sn btn*.......................(5 to 1 op 7 to 2 tchd 11 to 2) 4
RIVER STREAM 6-10-9 M A FitzGerald, *trkd ldrs, ev ch 3 out, sn rdn, wknd quickly*.......................(13 to 1 op 20 to 1) 5
952⁴ JENNYELLEN (Ire) 4-10-9 M Foster, *hld up wl in rear, some late prog, nvr dngrs*.......................(14 to 1 op 10 to 1) 6
952 MENDIP MIST 5-10-9 N Mann, *al wl beh, tld off*.
.......................(100 to 1 op 33 to 1) 7
BRIDGE STREET BOY 4-11-0 M Bosley, *al beh, tld off whn pld up bef 2 out*.......................(100 to 1 op 33 to 1) pu
551 TELMAR SYSTEMS 4-11-0 M Richards, *prmnt to second, wl off whn pld up bef 2 out*.......................(66 to 1 op 33 to 1) pu
MALTESE FLAME 4-10-9 R Greene, *al beh, tld off whn pld up bef 2 out*.......................(100 to 1 op 33 to 1) pu
Dist: 10l, 8l, 15l, 6l, 2½l, dist. 4m 8.80s. a 8.80s (10 Ran).
SR: 23/6/-/-/-/-/ (Unity Farm Holiday Centre Ltd), R J Hodges

1047 Brixham Co-operative Novices' Handicap Hurdle (0-100 4-y-o and up) £1,998 2¼m.................(1:30)

889² HANDY LASS [78] 4-10-3 (7*) D Matthews, *trkd ldr, slight mstk 4th, chlgd 2 out, rdn and ran on to ld cl hme*.
.......................(6 to 4 fav op 5 to 2) 1
891¹ GILBERT (Ire) [68] 5-10-0 Lorna Vincent, *led, rdn r-in, hdd cl hme*.......................(11 to 2 op 4 to 1 tchd 6 to 1) 2
MR ZIEGFELD (USA) [74] (bl) 4-10-6 L Harvey, *pld hrd, ev ch 3 out, wknd whn mstk nxt*.......................(9 to 1 op 5 to 1) 3
EMALLEN (Ire) [82] 5-11-0 A Maguire, *hld up in rear, rdn appr 3 out, sn tld off*.......................(8 to 1 op 6 to 1) 4
959⁹ FITNESS FANATIC [99] 5-11-10 (7*,7ex) J J Brown, *wtd wth in tch, mstk 4th, hit 3 out, wknd appr nxt, btn fourth whn f last*.......................(2 to 1 op 7 to 4 tchd 5 to 2) f
Dist: ½l, 12l, dist. 4m 13.70s. a 13.70s (5 Ran).

(G W Hackling), Mrs A Knight

1048 Plymouth Gin Haldon Gold Challenge Cup Chase (Grade 2) (5-y-o and up) £15,925 2¼m.................(2:00)

TRAVADO 7-11-0 J Osborne, *hld up, al gng wl, trkd ldr frm 6th, jmpd into ld 4 out, clr appr 2 out, easily*.
.......................(11 to 10 fav op 5 to 4) 1
DEEP SENSATION 8-11-6 D Murphy, *hld up, wnt second appr 2 out, no ch wth wnr*.
.......................(4 to 1 op 3 to 1 tchd 5 to 1) 2
931³ AL HASHIMI 9-11-0 R Dunwoody, *led, mstk 7th, hdd 4 out, sn outpcd*.......................(20 to 1 tchd 25 to 1) 3

WELSH BARD 9-11-0 G Bradley, *hld up in rear, hdwy appr 5th, mstk 8th, sn wl beh, tld off*.
WATERLOO BOY 10-11-6 A Maguire, *trkd ldr till mstk 3rd, hit nxt, in tch till pld up bef 4th*....(2 to 1 tchd 9 to 1) pu
Dist: 20l, 4l, 30l. 4m 13.80s. a 2.80s (5 Ran).
SR: 76/62/52/22/-/ (Mrs Michael Ennever), N J Henderson

1049 Plymouth And South Devon Co-operative Juvenile Selling Hurdle (3-y-o) £1,880 2¼m...............(2:30)

851⁴ CONVOY (bl) 10-12 G McCourt, *hld up, hdwy appr 3 out, hrd rdn frm nxt, led r-in, all out*....(6 to 1 op 4 to 1) 1
890⁴ VELVET HEART (Ire) 10-7 S Burrough, *trkd ldr, led 4th, rdn appr last, hdd r-in, one pace*. (5 to 1 op 4 to 1 tchd 11 to 2) 2
760¹ OCTOBER BREW (USA) (bl) 11-8 R Dunwoody, *trkd ldrs, rdn 2 out, one pace*.......................(3 to 1 fav op 4 to 1 tchd 5 to 1) 3
793⁶ NANQUIDNO 10-7 B Clifford, *trkd ldrs, ev ch 3 out, wknd nxt*.......................(33 to 1 op 16 to 1) 4
870⁷ STAR MINSTREL (Ire) 10-12 M Perrett, *hld up in rear, hdwy appr 3rd, rdn and wknd approaching 2 out*.
.......................(9 to 1 op 5 to 1) 5
793³ MUSICAL PHONE 10-12 B Powell, *prmnt, rdn and wknd appr 2 out*.......................(20 to 1 op 12 to 1) 6
642² BOHEMIAN QUEEN 10-7 A Maguire, *in tch to 5th, wknd aftr nxt*.......................(5 to 1 op 7 to 2) 7
LADY RELKO 10-7 A Tory, *mid-div, rdn 5th, sn beh*.
.......................(33 to 1 tchd 50 to 1) 8
793⁴ IVORY HUTCH (bl) 10-12 A Charlton, *mid-div till wknd 3 out*.......................(33 to 1 op 16 to 1) 9
THREEOFUS (v) 10-12 M Richards, *hld up, hdwy and rdn 5th, wkng whn hit 2 out*.
.......................(33 to 1 op 16 to 1 tchd 50 to 1) 10
193⁶ KENNINGTON PROTON 10-7 T Wall, *al beh, tld off*.
.......................(66 to 1 op 33 to 1) 11
896 PARIS ROBBER 10-5 (7*) P Moore, *hld up in rear, nvr on terms, tld off*.......................(66 to 1 op 33 to 1) 12
JUST FOR A LARK 10-7 W Knox, *al beh, tld off*.
.......................(50 to 1 op 33 to 1) 13
702⁴ MAASTRICHT 10-12 D J Burchell, *prmnt till wknd rpdly appr 3 out, pld up bef nxt*.......(7 to 1 op 4 to 1) pu
793⁵ OUR NIKKI 10-7 M A FitzGerald, *pld hrd, led till mstk and hdd 4th, sn wknd, pulled up bef 2 out*.
.......................(66 to 1 op 33 to 1) pu
Dist: 1l, 6l, 12l, 3l, 1l, 12l, 2½l, 1½l, 5l, 15l. 4m 11.10s. a 11.10s (15 Ran).
(The Lavender Cottage Partnership), C J Mann

1050 Whitbread Handicap Chase (0-145 5-y-o and up) £5,744 2m 7f 110yds. . (3:00)

CLEVER SHEPHERD [111] 8-10-12 Peter Hobbs, *hld up in tch, al gng wl, led 4 out, rdn 2 out, styd on*.
.......................(7 to 1 op 5 to 1) 1
935* STUNNING STUFF [123] 8-11-10 N Williamson, *hld up, gd hdwy 5 out, outpcd appr nxt, styd on to go second aftr 2 out*.......(11 to 4 fav op 9 to 4 tchd 3 to 1) 2
COOLE DODGER [113] 8-11-0 R Dunwoody, *led till hdd 4 out, one pace frm nxt*....(7 to 2 op 4 to 1 tchd 9 to 2) 3
THE WIDGET MAN [119] 7-11-6 D Murphy, *hld up in rear, rdn 5 out, one pace aftr*.
.......................(11 to 1 op 8 to 1 tchd 12 to 1) 4
886³ DANDY MINSTREL [112] 9-10-13 D Bridgwater, *beh, hdwy appr tenth, lft second nxt, rdn and wknd quickly approaching 4 out*.......................(8 to 1 op 12 to 1) 5
986⁴ DOONLOUGHAN [106] 8-10-7 A Maguire, *trkd ldr till f 11th*.......................(9 to 2 op 11 to 4) f
842² DRAGONS DEN [107] 7-10-8 J Osborne, *hmpd second, sn trkd ldrs, hit 9th, brght dwn 11th*....(4 to 1 op 3 to 1) bd
FURRY KNOWE [107] 8-10-8 G Bradley, *prmnt whn blun badly second, sn pld up*.
.......................(12 to 1 op 10 to 1 tchd 14 to 1) pu
Dist: 2l, 3½l, 20l, 2½l. 5m 44.00s. a 9.00s (8 Ran).
SR: 18/28/14/-/-/ (M T Lockyer), P J Hobbs

1051 St Austell Brewery Handicap Hurdle (0-140 4-y-o and up) £2,259 2¼m (3:30)

936 NORTHERN SADDLER [97] 6-10-5 G McCourt, *led to 4th, led ag'n 3 out, rdn frm nxt, kpt on gmely*.
.......................(7 to 1 op 5 to 1) 1
894⁵ TRUST DEED (USA) [92] (bl) 5-10-0 L Harvey, *trkd wnr, led 4th to 3 out, al dwn mstk 2 out, rallied and ran on strly to go second r-in*.
.......................(8 to 1 op 7 to 1 tchd 10 to 1 and 12 to 1) 2
HIGHLAND SPIRIT [120] 5-12-0 R Dunwoody, *hld up, hdwy to go second appr 2 out, hrd rdn approaching last, no extr r-in*.......................(13 to 8 fav op 6 to 4 tchd 9 to 4) 3
FAR TOO LOUD [101] 6-10-9 M A FitzGerald, *trkd ldrs, outpcd 3 out, rallied frm nxt, ran on strly r-in*.
.......................(3 to 1 tchd 11 to 4) 4
ALDAHE [92] 8-10-0 C Maude, *in rear, effrt on outsd aftr 3 out, sn btn, tld off*.......(33 to 1 op 20 to 1) 5
887⁴ CAROMANDOO (Ire) [92] (v) 5-10-0 A Maguire, *hld up in tch, wknd and pld up bef 3 out*.
.......................(7 to 2 op 3 to 1 tchd 4 to 1) pu
Dist: ¾l, 3l, nk, 30l. 4m 15.50s. a 15.50s (6 Ran).

(Richard J Evans), R J Hodges

CURRAGH (IRE) (Good to yielding)
Wednesday November 3rd

1052 Potentials INH Flat Race (4-y-o and up) £3,105 2m...............(4:00)

COQ HARDI AFFAIR (Ire) 5-11-9 (5*) Mr B F Murphy, (4 to 1) 1
908⁴ GREAT ADVENTURE (Ire) 5-11-11 (3*) Mr D Marnane,
....(15 to 2) 2
MINIGIRLS NIECE (Ire) 5-11-12 (7*) Mr A Doherty, ... (6 to 1) 3
ANOTHER FROSTY 6-12-0 Mr R Hurley, ... (8 to 1) 4
36 WISE STATEMENT (Ire) 4-11-9 Mr A P O'Brien, ... (9 to 4) 5
THE PERISHER (Ire) 4-11-4 (5*) Mr J A Nash, ...(6 to 4 fav) 6
BELLEW GLEN (Ire) 5-11-2 (7*) Mrs D McDonogh, (20 to 1) 7
METROLAMP (Ire) 5-11-9 (5*) Mrs A M O'Brien, ... (7 to 1) 8
Dist: 20l, 6l, 2l, 6l. 3m 46.60s. (8 Ran).

(Mrs Catherine Howard), Noel Meade

HAYDOCK (Good)
Wednesday November 3rd
Going Correction: PLUS 0.25 sec. per fur. (races 1,3,-5,7), PLUS 0.20 (2,4,6)

1053 Birchfield Novices' Hurdle (4-y-o and up) £2,092 2m................(1:00)

TIME FOR A FLUTTER 4-10-9 M A FitzGerald, al hndy, led
aftr 4 out till appr 2 out, rallied to ld last 50 yards, drvn
out.......................(33 to 1 op 20 to 1) 1
915 COL BUCKMORE (Ire) 5-11-6 N Doughty, patiently rdn,
improved to ld appr 2 out, hit last two, hdd last 50
yards, no extr.......................(9 to 2 op 7 to 2) 2
BOLD BOSTONIAN (Fr) 5-11-0 M Hourigan, nvr far away,
ev ch and drvn alng 3 out, outpcd frm betw last 2.
.................................(12 to 1 op 16 to 1) 3
AAL EL AAL 6-11-0 Peter Hobbs, took keen hold, steady
hdwy to chal 3 out, rdn and not quicken frm betw last
2.................................(3 to 1 tchd 5 to 2) 4
743⁶ LACURVA (Ire) 5-10-7 (7*) P Ward, co'red up in midfield,
feeling pace and drvn alng appr 3 out, styd on, nvr able
to chal.......................(33 to 1) 5
FOURTH IN LINE (Ire) 5-11-0 W Knox, trkd ldg bunch, rdn
appr 3 out, sn struggling.........(16 to 1 op 12 to 1) 6
MALVERN MADAM 6-10-9 Richard Guest, chsd ldg bunch,
struggling to keep up appr 3 out, tld off.......(33 to 1) 7
NORMAN WARRIOR 4-11-0 N Mann, in tch, rdn aftr 4 out,
tld off.........................(16 to 1 op 14 to 1) 8
CROFTON LAKE 5-10-9 (5*) N Leach, settled midfield,
struggling aftr 4 out, tld off frm nxt.........(33 to 1) 9
915 MISTRESS BEE (USA) 4-10-9 A S Smith, pressed ldrs till
wknd quickly 4 out, tld off...... (33 to 1 tchd 25 to 1) 10
CHIEF MALE (USA) 8-10-9 (5*) Mr D McCain, took keen
hold, lost pl quickly and pld up appr 4 out.
.................................(20 to 1 op 14 to 1) pu
RUST PROOF 6-11-0 I Lawrence, beh and drvn alng
hfwy, lost tch 3 out, puled up bef nxt.
.................................(50 to 1 op 33 to 1) pu
NEVER IN THE RED 5-11-0 C Grant, struggling to keep up
hfwy, tld off whn pld up bef 2 out. (20 to 1 op 14 to 1) pu
IN NO DOUBT 4-11-0 M Dwyer, trkd ldrs till pld up appr
3rd....................(20 to 1 op 5 to 1 tchd 11 to 2) pu
916 BALTIC EXCHANGE (Can) 4-11-0 J Osborne, led till hdd
aftr 4 out, lost tch quickly and pld up betw last 2.
.................(11 to 4 fav op 5 to 2 tchd 3 to 1) pu
Dist: 1½l, 7l, nk, ½l, 2l, 25l, nk, hd. 3m 50.50s. a 10.50s (15 Ran).

SR: 16/25/12/11/-/-/ (C James), C James

1054 Bolton Novices' Chase (5-y-o and up) £3,355 3m.....................(1:30)

686² EARTH SUMMIT 5-11-0 C Llewellyn, trkd ldr, drawing
level whn lft alone 6 out.
.......................(100 to 30 op 3 to 1 tchd 7 to 2) 1
751* HOWARYAFXD 6-11-6 J Osborne, dictated pace, not fluent 8th, slight ld whn f 6 out.
.......................(11 to 10 op 5 to 4 on) f
843² FROZEN DROP 6-11-2 Richard Guest, cl 4th whn f second.
.......................(5 to 2 op 5 to 1 tchd 100 to 30) f
CHALIE RICHARDS 6-11-2 C Grant, trkd ldg pair, mstk
tenth (water), effrt whn almost brght dwn 6 out, pld up
lme.................................(10 to 1 op 8 to 1) pu
Dist: 6m 36.30s. a 30.30s (4 Ran).

(Nigel Payne), N A Twiston-Davies

1055 Warrington Handicap Hurdle (0-140 5-y-o and up) £2,716 2m.......(2:00)

781² RED INDIAN [112] 7-10-13 D Byrne, patiently rdn,
improved on bit 2 out, faltered last, rallied to ld last 100
yards, ran on.......................(5 to 2 tchd 2 to 1) 1

459⁵ NIKITAS [115] 8-10-11 (5*) J A McCarthy, wth ldr, led
briefly second, hit 3 out, rallied frm last, edgd lft cl
hme.......................(3 to 1 op 5 to 2) 2
972 WAKE UP [104] 6-10-5 M Dwyer, made most, hdd briefly
second, quickened appr 3 out, headed and no extr last
100 yards.......................(10 to 1 op 8 to 1) 3
873⁵ DAGOBERTIN (Fr) [114] 7-11-1 L Wyer, nvr far away, drvn
alng whn pace lifted frm 3 out, one pace from betw last
2.................................(6 to 4 fav tchd 2 to 1) 4
913 ONE FOR THE POT [127] 8-11-9 (5*) T Jenks, tucked away
on ins, ev ch 2 out, rdn and outpcd r-in.
.................................(10 to 1 op 8 to 1) 5
Dist: ¾l, 1½l, 2l, 6l. 3m 59.20s. a 19.20s (5 Ran).

(Dave Marshall), W W Haigh

1056 Gamekeepers Handicap Chase (0-145 5-y-o and up) £4,026 2m........(2:30)

913⁴ GOOD FOR A LAUGH [115] 9-9-7 (7*) Mr D Parker, patiently
rdn, steadied and a lot to do appr 3 out, shaken up
betw last 2, str run to ld last strd.... (8 to 1 op 7 to 1) 1
780⁴ LAST 'O' THE BUNCH [143] 9-12-0 N Doughty, wth ldr, led
4th (water), mstk and hdd 2 out, rallied to ld r-in, hdd
last strd.........................(11 to 1av op 5 to 4) 2
752* TRIMLOUGH [128] 8-10-13 N Mann, cricker off side,
mstks, led to 4th (water), nosed ahead 2 out, hdd and
no extr r-in.........(11 to 8 op 5 to 4 tchd 6 to 4) 3
963⁴ GOLD ROAD (USA) [115] 7-11-9 (3*) W Marston, in tch, hit
6th, outpcd aftr 4 out, styd on frm betw last 2, nrst
finish.................................(25 to 1) 4
913 CIRCULATION [115] 7-9-9 (5*) D Walsh, nvr far away,
struggling to keep up aftr 3 out, sn btn.
.................................(12 to 1 op 10 to 1) 5
Dist: Hd, 2l, 6l, 12l. 4m 5.90s. a 6.90s (5 Ran).

SR: 35/63/46/-/-/ (Mrs S A Bramall), Mrs S A Bramall

1057 Preston Conditional Jockeys' Hand-icap Hurdle (0-125 4-y-o and up) £2,215 2m 7f 110yds........(3:00)

FORTUNES WOOD [107] 7-11-3 (7*) D Meade, confidently
rdn, improved on bit to ld aftr 3 out, styd on strly frm
last.........................(14 to 1 op 10 to 1 tchd 16 to 1) 1
ASWAMEDH [94] 5-10-11 M Hourigan, wtd wth, improved
to join issue 3 out, effrt and hit last, rallied, flank wl.
.................................(8 to 1 op 5 to 1 tchd 10 to 1) 2
KINTARO [83] 5-10-0 A Procter, patiently rdn, improved
gng wl to draw level 4 out, ridden and mstk last, one
pace.........................(25 to 1 op 20 to 1) 3
873⁶ CHIEF RAIDER (Ire) [104] 5-11-0 (7*) D Ryan, al hndy, led 5
out till aftr 3 out, rdn and btn betw last 2.
.................................(8 to 1 tchd 10 to 1) 4
867⁶ NICKLE JOE [105] 7-11-8 W Marston, nvr far away, feeling pace and bustled alng aftr 3 out, no extr... (8 to 1) 5
914⁸ CELTIC BREEZE [101] (v) 10-11-4 T Jenks, slight ld to 3rd,
struggling to hold pl fnl circuit, kpt on strly frm 2 out.
.................................(14 to 1 op 12 to 1) 6
424² BRIDGE PLAYER [90] 6-10-7 D J Moffatt, settled off the
pace, steady hdwy fnl circuit, rdn and no imprsn frm 2
out.........................(10 to 1 op 7 to 1 and 5 to 1) 7
LINKSIDE [99] 8-11-2 S Lyons, trkd ldg bunch, effrt and
bustled alng appr 3 out, sn outpcd.
.................................(5 to 1 fav op 8 to 1 tchd 9 to 1) 8
605³ KNIGHTLY ARGUS [96] 6-10-13 J McCarthy, wth ldrs, led
3rd, hit 6th, quickened nxt, hdd 5 out, fdd last 2.
.................................(7 to 1 op 4 to 1) 9
SWILLY EXPRESS [102] 7-11-5 D Leahy, co'red up in midfield, effrt and drvn alng whn badly baulked bend
appr 3 out, not rcvr.................(10 to 1 op 8 to 1) 10
767* INTEGRITY BOY [92] (bl) 6-10-2 (7*) K Davies, trkd ldrs for
o'r a circuit, rdn and outpcd frm 3 out.
.................................(7 to 1 op 6 to 1) 11
AL SAHIL (USA) [90] (bl) 8-10-0 (7*) P McLoughlin, patiently
rdn, drvn alng whn pace lifted fnl circuit, no imprsn
frm 3 out.........(10 to 1 op 12 to 1 tchd 14 to 1) 12
819² SWEET CITY [101] 8-10-11 (7*) B Harding, settled off the
pace, pushed alng fnl circuit, nvr nr to chal.
.................................(7 to 1 op 6 to 1) 13
955⁶ PROVERBS GIRL [88] 8-10-5 R Davis, nvr far away, ev ch
3 out, wknd quickly, tld off.... (10 to 1 op 16 to 1) 14
935 WINABUCK [100] 10-11-3 D Meredith, dsptd ld to 3rd,
struggling to keep up fnl circuit, tld off last 3. (20 to 1) 15
Dist: 1½l, 8l, 6l, 3l, ¾l, 1½l, hd, 12l, 20l, 2l. 5m 57.20s. a 26.20s (15 Ran).

(Mrs C A Morrison), T Thomson Jones

1058 Island Novices' Handicap Chase (5-y-o and up) £3,322 2½m........(3:30)

974⁷ ABLE PLAYER (USA) [94] 6-11-1 (5*) J Burke, not fluent,
nrly f 3rd, rallied to ld r-in, veered lft last 50 yards, hld
on to dead-heat for 1st, plcd third... (7 to 1 op 6 to 1) 1D
633² VALIANT WARRIOR [102] 5-12-0 C Grant, nvr far away,
rdn whn hit 3 out, str run frm last, dead-heated for 1st.
.................................(11 to 8 fav op 6 to 4 tchd 13 to 8) 1D

813 WEST BAY [85] 7-10-11 S Smith Eccles, *jmpd wl, led aftr second, hrd pressed frm 3 out, hdd r-in, crowded last 50 yards, no extr, fnshd 3rd, plcd second.*
.... (11 to 2 op 4 to 1 tchd 6 to 1) 2
984² REAL PROGRESS (Ire) [93] (bl) 5-11-5 Peter Hobbs, *al hndy, ev ch and rdn aftr 3 out, ridden and outpcd frm last.* .... (9 to 4 op 2 to 1) 4
710⁴ KING'S RARITY [80] 7-10-6 M A FitzGerald, *led till aftr second, styd hndy, ev ch till blun 2 out, wknd quickly.*
.... (9 to 1 op 8 to 1 tchd 10 to 1) 5
GALLANTRY BANK [74] 8-10-0 A Jones, *not fluent, ran in snatches, rallied and f 7 out.* ....(20 to 1 op 16 to 1) f
Dist: Dd-ht, 2l, 5l, 25l. 5m 23.10s. a 25.10s (6 Ran).
(P Sellars), M D Hammond

1059 Levy Board Novices' Handicap Hurdle (3-y-o and up) £2,820 2m...... (4:00)

934⁷ KYTTON CASTLE [74] 6-9-11 (3*) D Meredith, *confidently rdn, smooth hdwy entering strt, led last, sn clr, easily.*
.... (6 to 1 op 12 to 1) 1
830⁶ QUICK SILVER BOY [86] 3-10-12 D J Burchell, *led aftr second, clr bef nxt, blun 4th, hdd last, no extr und pres.*
.... (8 to 1 op 6 to 1) 2
695⁸ BARELY BLACK [74] 5-10-0 W Humphreys, *cl up in chasing grp, effrt and rdn appr 2 out, ev ch last, fdd...*(16 to 1) 3
658* MOZEMO [100] 6-11-12 J Osborne, *led till hdd aftr second, chsd clr ldr, drvn alng after 3 out, wknd betw last.* ....(5 to 4 fav op Evens tchd 11 to 8) 4
922³ THE GREYSMITH [75] 6-10-1 M A FitzGerald, *patiently rdn, smooth hdwy aftr 4 out, shaken up whn hit 2 out, sn btn.* ....(2 to 1 tchd 7 to 4 and 9 to 4) 5
732² SHARP SENSATION [74] 3-10-0 C Grant, *prmnt in chasing grp, feeling pace and rdn bef 3 out, no extr last 2.*
.... (11 to 2 op 5 to 1) 6
ABELONI [83] 4-10-9 M Dwyer, *al beh, lost tch hfwy, tld off whn pld up 2 out.* (10 to 1 op 12 to 1 tchd 14 to 1) pu
Dist: 7l, 2l, 4l, 3½l, 5l. 3m 50.40s. a 10.40s (7 Ran).
SR: 8/13/-/21/
(Joint Partnership), R Dickin

KELSO (good (races 1,2,3,4,6), good to soft (5,7))
Wednesday November 3rd
Going Correction: PLUS 0.90 sec. per fur. (races 1,3,-5,7), PLUS 0.55 (2,4,6)

1060 Radio Borders Amateur Riders' Maiden Hurdle (4-y-o and up) £2,092 2 ¾m 110yds................... (1:10)

656⁸ ARIADLER (re) 5-11-0 (7*) Mr T Byrne, *hld up, steady hdwy 4 out, chlgd last, rdn to ld flt, ran on.*
.... (33 to 1 op 20 to 1) 1
823³⁵ COQUI LANE 6-11-7 Mr J M Dun, *led, rdn and jnd last, hdd flt, no extr nr finish.*...........(9 to 1 op 7 to 1) 2
725³ FARMER'S CROSS 9-11-4 (3*) Mrs A Farrell, *mid-div, hdwy 8th, rdn 3 out, one pace appr last....*(5 to 1 op 3 to 1) 3
717⁶ MR ROYAL 7-11-0 (7*) Mr C Bonner, *cl up, effrt and ev ch 3 out, sn rdn and wknd nxt.*
.... (9 to 2 op 4 to 1 tchd 7 to 2 and 5 to 1) 4
THE WHIRLIE WEEVIL 5-10-9 (7*) Mr R Hale, *in tch, rdn alng aftr 4 out, sn one pace.*
.... (7 to 1 op 6 to 1 tchd 8 to 1) 5
770² KILMINFOYLE 6-11-2 (5*) Mr M Buckley, *prmnt, effrt and rdn 3 out, wknd nxt............*(3 to 1 fav tchd 4 to 1) 6
823⁶ JENDEE (Ire) 5-11-7 Mr S Swiers, *hld up, effrt and hdwy 4 out, sn rdn and wknd... (6 to 1 op 5 to 1 tchd 8 to 1)* 7
785⁶ IT'S DAY HARDLY 6-11-0 (7*) Mr S Brisby, *al rear.*
.... (200 to 1 op 100 to 1) 8
823³ SARANNPOUR (Ire) (bl) 4-11-2 (3*) Mrs P Nash, *prmnt till rdn and wknd 3 out....*(9 to 2 op 9 to 2 tchd 6 to 1) 9
819 FIRST EVER (Ire) 4-11-0 (7*) Mr A Manners, *in tch, lost pl and beh frm hfwy.*...........(50 to 1 op 20 to 1) 10
GYMCRAK CYRANO (Ire) 4-10-9 (7*) Miss C Metcalfe, *chsd ldrs, lost pl hfwy, beh whn f 4 out.*
.... (40 to 1 op 33 to 1 tchd 50 to 1) f
820 HIGHRYMER 9-10-9 (7*) Miss J Thurlow, *blun and uns rdr 1st.*...................(50 to 1 op 25 to 1) ur
FINE OAK 6-10-9 (7*) Mr S Johnson, *mstks, sn beh, tld off whn pld up bef 7th...............*(200 to 1 op 100 to 1) pu
STONEY BROOK 5-11-0 (7*) Mr A Parker, *chsd ldrs, blun 7th and sn lost pl, tld off whn pld up bef last.*
.... (25 to 1 op 16 to 1) pu
Dist: 1l, 12l, 15l, 3l, 2l, 5l, 7l, nk, sht-hd. 5m 37.60s. a 26.60s (14 Ran).
SR: 28/27/15/-/-/-/
(J A Stephenson), P Cheesbrough

1061 Glengoyne Highland Malt Tamerosia Series Qualifier Novices' Chase (5-y-o and up) £2,737 2¾m 110yds.....(1:40)

CEILIDH BOY 7-11-0 B Storey, *trkd ldr, led tenth, rdn clr appr last, easily.*.........(11 to 10 fav op 5 to 4 on) 1
542⁵ COUNT SURVEYOR 6-11-0 K Johnson, *led till hdd and mstk tenth, rdn and wknd 4 out, blun badly 2 out, styd on frm last.*...........(6 to 1 op 7 to 1 tchd 8 to 1) 2

820* CELTIC SONG 6-10-13 T Reed, *hld up, hdwy and mstk 12th, effrt and ch 3 out, rdn nxt, sn one pace.*
.... (7 to 4 op 2 to 1) 3
786* BENNAN MARCH 6-11-1 (3*) A Dobbin, *mstks, rdn and hdwy 4 out, hrd drvn 2 out, sn wknd.*
.... (13 to 2 op 8 to 1 tchd 9 to 1) 4
Dist: 4l, nk, 15l. 6m 1.30s. a 34.30s (4 Ran).
(Mrs J D Goodfellow), Mrs J D Goodfellow

1062 Middlemas Of Kelso Scottish Borders Trophy Juvenile Novices' Hurdle (3-y-o) £3,420 2m 110yds........(2:10)

971* REGAL AURA (Ire) 11-2 J Callaghan, *trkd ldrs, hdwy 3 out, effrt to ld last, drvn out flt...* (2 to 1 jt-fav op 3 to 1) 1
790* RED MARAUDER 10-9 (7*) J Supple, *cl up, led 3rd, hdd and lost pl appr last, rdn and styd on strly flt.*
.... (2 to 1 jt-fav op 9 to 4) 2
652* PRINCIPAL PLAYER (USA) 10-13 (3*) A Dobbin, *hld up, hdwy 3 out, effrt appr last, ev ch flt, no extr und pres nr finish.*...................(3 to 1 tchd 7 to 2) 3
652³ HYDE'S HAPPY HOUR 10-12 G McCourt, *set slow pace, hdd 3rd, hit nxt, effrt to chal 3 out, ev ch till rdn and wknd appr last.*...............(8 to 1 op 6 to 1) 4
766³ SUMMERS DREAM 10-7 C Hawkins, *hld up, effrt and hdwy 4 out, sn btn...*(33 to 1 op 25 to 1 tchd 50 to 1) 5
872³ BONUS POINT 11-2 P Niven, *trkd ldrs, hit 3rd and 5th, rdn nxt, sn btn...................*(10 to 1 op 7 to 1) 6
GREAT EASEBY (Ire) 10-12 K Johnson, *in tch, lost pl 4 out, sn btn...................* (50 to 1 op 33 to 1) 7
Dist: ½l, ½l, 7l, ½l, 15l, 3½l. 4m 5.10s. a 22.10s (7 Ran).
SR: 15/14/13/2/
(D J Bushell), G M Moore

1063 Pat de Clermont Challenge Cup Handicap Chase For Scott Briggs Memorial Trophy (0-135 5-y-o and up) £5,121 3m 1f...................................(2:40)

655⁵ WHAAT FETTLE [120] 8-11-6 M Moloney, *chsd ldrs, mstk 8th, hdwy 4 out, blun 2 out, rdn and hit last, styd on to ld flt.*...................(4 to 1 op 7 to 2) 1
822³ PINK GIN [106] 6-10-0 B Storey, *in tch, hit 7th, hdwy tenth, hit and rdn 4 out, styd on und pres last, led briefly flt, no extr nr finish...................*(16 to 1) 2
822⁴ BLUFF KNOLL [125] 10-11-5 K Johnson, *chsd ldrs 12th and reminders, outpcd 5 out, styd on und pres frm last...................*(7 to 2 tchd 4 to 1) 3
655* OFF THE BRU [111] (v) 8-10-5 Mr J Bradburne, *chsd ldr, rdn and ev ch 2 out, no extr flt.........*(7 to 1 tchd 8 to 1) 4
ROSS VENTURE [130] 8-11-10 T Reed, *led, rdn 2 out, hdd and wknd flt...................*(5 to 1 tchd 33 to 1) 5
822* PADAVENTURE [122] 8-11-2 P Niven, *in tch, hit 11th, hdwy nxt and sn pushed alng, beh frm 4 out.*
.... (5 to 4 fav op 6 to 4 tchd 7 to 4) 6
PLENTY CRACK [133] 10-11-13 A Merrigan, *not fluent, pushed alng tenth and sn lost pl, tld off frm 6 out.*
.... (5 to 1 op 25 to 1) 7
Dist: ½l, 1½l, 1l, 3l, 30l, 6l. 6m 28.60s. a 26.60s (7 Ran).
(The Edinburgh Woollen Mill Ltd), G Richards

1064 Scottishpower Handicap Hurdle (0-120 4-y-o and up) £2,337 2m 110yds...........................(3:10)

972 SEON [109] 7-11-7 (3*) N Bentley, *chsd clr ldr, pushed alng and hdwy 2 out, rdn flt, led last 50 yards, styd on wl.*...................(13 to 2 op 8 to 1 tchd 9 to 1 and 10 to 1) 1
824* MASTER OF TROY [95] 5-10-3 (7*) Mr A Parker, *beh, hit 8th, hdwy 3 out, rdn and hit last, styd on flt.*
.... (2 to 1 fav op 13 to 8) 2
824⁴ ASTURIAS [88] 10-10-0 (3*) A Larnach, *led and sn clr, rdn 2 out, hdd and wknd last 50 yards.*
.... (7 to 1 op 6 to 1 tchd 8 to 1) 3
818* KALKO [103] 4-10-13 (5*) D Bentley, *in tch, rdn 4 out, kpt on one pace.....................*(6 to 1 op 5 to 1) 4
GLINDIGO (Ire) [101] 5-10-13 (3*) A Dobbin, *beh, effrt and rdn 4 out, nvr dngrs............*(16 to 1 tchd 20 to 1) 5
918³ ALL WELCOME [100] 6-11-1 P Niven, *in tch, rdn 4 out, no hdwy...................*(9 to 4 op 3 to 1) 6
282⁴ BLACKDOWN [86] 6-10-1 P Harley, *beh, some hdwy 4 out, sn rdn and wknd...................*(20 to 1) 7
Dist: 3l, 6l, 10l, 10l, 15l. 4m 3.10s. a 20.10s (7 Ran).
SR: 43/26/19/28/16/5/-/
(C F Hunter Ltd), W Bentley

1065 Scottish Borders Enterprise Handicap Chase (6-y-o and up) £3,396 2m 1f...................................(3:40)

819³ SIMPLE PLEASURE [114] 8-10-2² A Orkney, *outpcd and beh frm 5th, rdn and hdwy 4 out, blun 2 out, styd on und pres appr last, led flt, ran on.*
.... (7 to 1 op 8 to 1 tchd 9 to 1) 1
738* CLAY COUNTY [140] 8-12-0 B Storey, *chsd ldr, led 8th, lft 20 ls clr 3 out, rdn and hdd flt, found nil.*
.... (6 to 5 on op 5 to 4 on) 2

NATIONAL HUNT RESULTS 1993-94

1001³ MAUDLINS CROSS [120] 8-10-8 P Niven, *hit 5th and sn outpcd, effrt and rdn 4 out, no hdwy.*
..............................(7 to 2 op 3 to 1 tchd 4 to 1) 3
769⁵ BORO SMACKEROO [135] 8-11-9 G McCourt, *led, hit 7th, hdd and hit nxt, blun 9th, 5 ls second whn f 3 out.*
..............................(9 to 2 op 4 to 1) f
Dist: 2l, 20l. 4m 19.20s. a 13.20s (4 Ran).
SR: 36/60/20/-/ (Mrs M Stirk), Mrs M Stirk

1066 Levy Board Handicap Hurdle (0-135 4-y-o and up) £2,407 2¾m 110yds
..............................(4:10)

819⁶ LEADING PROSPECT [105] 6-10-10 B Storey, *chsd clr ldr, rdn 3 out, styd on appr last, ran on wl und pres to ld flt.*
..............................(11 to 2 op 6 to 1 tchd 13 to 2) 1
837⁷ NODFORM WONDER [118] 6-11-9 G McCourt, *led and sn clr, rdn and wndrd appr last, hdd and wknd flt.*
..............................(11 to 8 fav tchd 13 to 8 and 5 to 4) 2
972⁴ MASTER OF THE ROCK [95] 4-10-0 C Hawkins, *beh, gd hdwy 6th, rdn alng 4 out, kpt on one pace.*
..............................(11 to 1 op 8 to 1 tchd 12 to 1) 3
914² HAZEL LEAF [99] 7-9-13 (5*) P Waggott, *chsd ldrs till rdn alng and outpcd 5th, styd on und pres frm 2 out.*
..............................(4 to 1 tchd 9 to 2) 4
914⁵ HUDSON BAY TRADER (USA) [123] 6-11-7 (7*) G Tormey, *prmnt, lost pl and beh frm 6th.....*(6 to 1 op 5 to 1) 5
755⁷ SPEEDY SIOUX [95] (bl) 4-9-9 (5*) D Bentley, *al rear, tld off hfwy.*..............................(200 to 1 op 100 to 1) 6
757⁹ MAKE ME PROUD (Ire) [97] (v) 4-9-9 (7*) S Taylor, *chsd ldrs, rdn and hit 7th, sn beh.*
..............................(12 to 1 op 14 to 1 tchd 16 to 1) 7
767⁵ THE GREEN FOOL [100] 6-9-12 (7*) F Perratt, *in tch whn f second.*..............................(14 to 1 op 16 to 1) f
ASTON EXPRESS [116] 10-11-4 (3*) N Bentley, *al beh, tld off whn pld up bef 3 out.*..............................(33 to 1) pu
Dist: 3½l, 3l, 12l, 20l, 10l, 8l. 5m 40.50s. a 29.50s (9 Ran).
(J D Goodfellow), Mrs J D Goodfellow

UTTOXETER (good)
Wednesday November 3rd
Going Correction: PLUS 0.35 sec. per fur. (races 1,2,-4,6), MINUS 0.10 (3,5)

1067 Pallas Leasing Group Novices' Hurdle (4-y-o and up) £2,295 3m 110yds (1:20)

934² ULURU (Ire) 5-10-11 R Dunwoody, *hld up, steady hdwy frm 8th, chlgd 2 out, pushed out to ld r-in.*
..............................(11 to 4 fav op 9 to 4 tchd 7 to 2) 1
OLD FATHER TIME 6-10-11 N Williamson, *trkd ldrs, led appr 4 out, rdn approaching last, hdd r-in.*
..............................(5 to 1 op 4 to 1) 2
CRANK SHAFT 6-10-11 D Gallagher, *hld up, hdwy appr 8th, ev ch 3 out, one pace frm nxt....*(7 to 1 op 6 to 1) 3
664² NEEDWOOD POPPY 5-10-12 B Clifford, *hld up in tch, gd hdwy frm 8th, ev ch 3 out, wknd nxt.*(7 to 2 op 3 to 1) 4
869⁶ OUTFIELD 7-10-12 R Bellamy, *led till aftr second, prmnt till rdn and wknd appr 4 out.*
..............................(14 to 1 op 12 to 1 tchd 16 to 1) 5
737⁴ JALORE 4-10-4 R Greene, *pld hrd, prmnt to 5th, tld off whn f 2 out.*..............................(20 to 1 op 14 to 1) f
773⁴ SPUR BAY 6-10-11 B Powell, *al beh, mstk 5th, tld off frm 8th, pld up bef 3 out.*(14 to 1 op 12 to 1 tchd 16 to 1) pu
545* EXARCH (USA) (bl) 4-11-2 D Bridgwater, *led aftr second, hdd and wknd quickly appr 4 out, pld up bef 2 out.*
..............................(9 to 2 op 7 to 2 tchd 5 to 1) pu
Dist: 1l, 6l, 1l, dist. 5m 58.50s. a 19.50s (8 Ran).
(P J Morgan), C T Nash

1068 Sentinel Water Treatment Claiming Hurdle (4-y-o and up) £2,473 2m (1:50)

859* MISS MARIGOLD (bl) 4-11-7 R Dunwoody, *hld up in tch, smooth hdwy to ld sn aftr 4 out, clr nxt, not extended.*
..............................(13 to 2 op 6 to 1) 1
818² SRIVIJAYA 6-11-12 R Hodge, *hld up, hdwy frm 5th, hmpd on bend aftr nxt, reco'red to chase wnr from 2 out.*
..............................(7 to 4 fav op 9 to 4 tchd 5 to 2) 2
887 SANDRO (bl) 4-11-4 L Harvey, *chsd ldrs, led briefly 4 out, sn outpcd.*..............................(33 to 1) 3
846⁵ WE'RE IN THE MONEY (bl) 5-10-8 D Dalton, *hld up in mid-div, hdwy 5th, one pace frm 3 out.*......(33 to 1) 4
918⁷ ENFANT DU PARADIS (Ire) 5-10-7 A Maguire, *led till aftr 4th, prmnt till outpcd appr 3 out....*(5 to 1 op 9 to 1) 5
951³ BURN BRIDGE (USA) (v) 7-11-0 Peter Caldwell, *mid-div, hdwy 5th, btn whn hmpd 3 out....*(16 to 1 op 14 to 1) 6
936 HOSTETLER 4-11-6 D Bridgwater, *chsd ldrs, rdn frm 5th, no hdwy from 3 out.*......(16 to 1 op 14 to 1) 7
658 NONCOMMITAL 6-10-12 B Powell, *in rear till hdwy 5th, nvr nr to chal.*..............................(16 to 1 op 14 to 1) 8
PANT LLIN 7-11-4 R Hodge, *al beh.* (25 to 1 op 20 to 1) 9
PRIORY PIPER 4-10-11 (5*) T Eley, *nvr on terms, tld off.*
..............................(50 to 1) 10

---

934 SPRING SPIRIT (Ire) (bl) 4-11-2 N Williamson, *trkd ldr, led aftr 4th, wknd and hdd four out, sn beh, tld off.*
..............................(16 to 1 op 14 to 1) 11
GLOSSY 6-11-4 T Wall, *al towards rear, tld off.*
..............................(25 to 1 op 20 to 1 tchd 33 to 1) 12
POLK (Fr) 4-11-8 J Lower, *al beh, tld off.*
..............................(7 to 1 op 3 to 1) 13
MATTS BOY 5-10-11 S Turner, *al beh, tld off.*
..............................(33 to 1 op 50 to 1) 14
SOLO CORNET 8-11-4 W Humphreys, *al beh, tld off.*
..............................(50 to 1) 15
SHIKARI KID 6-10-11 (7*) Mr J L Llewellyn, *al beh, tld off frm 5th....*(12 to 1 op 20 to 1 tchd 25 to 1) 16
BASSIO (Bel) (h) 4-10-10 J McLaughlin, *mid-div, hdwy 4th, wkng whn f 3 out.*..............................(33 to 1 op 25 to 1) f
552 ARTHURS STONE 7-11-0 R Greene, *chsd ldrs, wkng whn jmpd slwly 4 out, pld up bef 3 out.* (33 to 1 op 16 to 1) pu
Dist: 8l, 5l, sht-hd, 15l, 1l, ½l, 6l, 3l, 10l, 3l. 3m 51.90s. a 12.90s (18 Ran).
SR: 20/17/4/-/-/-/ (Mrs Angela Fayers), R J Hodges

1069 Tussac Construction Handicap Chase (0-135 5-y-o and up) £3,647 2m 5f (2:20)

811* CORRARDER [108] 9-10-11 Mr J Smyth-Osbourne, *hld up, al gng wl, hdwy frm 9th, lft second 2 out, quickened well r-in to ld nr finish.*............(5 to 1 op 7 to 2) 1
THE MASTER GUNNER [103] 9-10-6 N Williamson, *trkd ldr, led appr 3 out, hrd rdn r-in, hdd nr finish.*
..............................(9 to 2 op 7 to 2) 2
CATCH THE CROSS [125] (v) 7-12-0 R Dunwoody, *in tch, mstk 5th, outpcd frm 4 out...*(9 to 2 op 4 to 1) 3
SNITTON LANE [116] 7-11-5 D Bridgwater, *chsd ldrs, rdn appr 4 out, sn btn......*(5 to 1 op 11 to 2 tchd 6 to 1) 4
RIVER BOUNTY [125] 7-12-0 R Supple, *jmpd slwly 1st, in tch till wknd appr 4 out....*(12 to 1 op 8 to 1) 5
663⁴ WIGTOWN BAY [97] 10-10-8 B Powell, *hld up, hdwy frm 8th, sn prmnt, wknd quickly appr 4 out.*
..............................(7 to 1 op 10 to 1) 6
BISHOPS ISLAND [124] 7-11-13 A Maguire, *led, sn clr, mstks, hdd appr 3 out, second and ev ch whn f nxt.*
..............................(4 to 1 fav op 7 to 2) f
931⁵ ORCHIPEDZO [97] 8-9-10³ (7*) Judy Davies, *mstk second, al beh, tld off frm 9th, pld up bef 2 out.......*(50 to 1) pu
Dist: ¾l, 12l, 6l, 5l, 15l. 5m 17.40s. a 17.40s (8 Ran).
(Mrs E T Smyth-Osbourne), J A B Old

1070 Peningar Developments Novices' Handicap Hurdle (3-y-o and up) £2,655 2m (2:50)

863⁴ FRANK RICH [85] 6-11-2 G Upton, *hld up in tch, hdwy 3 out, lft second last, sn led, drvn out.*
..............................(6 to 1 op 4 to 1 tchd 13 to 2) 1
953³ KELLY'S DARLING [73] 7-10-4 D Gallagher, *hld up, hdwy appr 3 out, rdn and lft in ld last, sn hdd, one pace r-in.*
..............................(8 to 1 op 7 to 1) 2
891⁴ NAJEB (USA) [69] (v) 4-10-0 R Dunwoody, *trkd ldr till wknd 2 out........*(11 to 2 op 5 to 1 tchd 6 to 1) 3
849³ NORTHERN TRIAL (USA) [93] 5-11-10 R Supple, *hld up in rear, hdwy 5th, rdn appr 3 out, btn whn hmpd r-in.*
..............................(13 to 2 op 5 to 1) 4
456² STERLING BUCK (USA) [75] 6-10-6 W McFarland, *al abt same pl, no hdwy frm 3 out.......*(20 to 1 op 16 to 1) 5
809⁶ JON'S CHOICE [70] (bl) 5-10-1 T Wall, *hld up in rear, rdn hfwy, beh frm 3 out........*(8 to 1 op 7 to 1) 6
814⁵ ENCHANTED FLYER [69] 6-10-0 N Williamson, *prmnt till wknd quickly appr 2 out.*
..............................(5 to 1 op 20 to 1 tchd 33 to 1) 7
RAMSTAR [80] 5-10-4 (7*) Mr G Hogan, *al beh.*
..............................(16 to 1 op 12 to 1 tchd 20 to 1) 8
DAN DE LYON [87] 5-11-4 A Maguire, *trkd ldrs till wknd appr 3 out.*
..............................(100 to 30 fav op 7 to 2 tchd 9 to 2 and 3 to 1) 9
814³ GOLDEN MADJAMBO [69] 7-9-7 (7*) M Doyle, *led, und pres whn ducked lft and ran out last.....*(8 to 1 op 7 to 1) ro
724* SUMMER FLOWER [69] 3-9-9 (5*) T Eley, *pld hrd, mstk 5th, wknd quickly 4 out, pulled up bef nxt.*
..............................(7 to 1 op 8 to 1) pu
Dist: 2½l, 6l, 3½l, 8l, 3l, 6l, 3l, 6l. 3m 53.30s. a 14.30s (11 Ran).
SR: 1/-/-/-/-/-/ (The F R Syndicate), S E Sherwood

1071 Giltor Holdings Plc Novices' Chase (5-y-o and up) £3,165 2m......(3:20)

BAYDON STAR 6-10-12 A Maguire, *trkd ldr al gng wl, led 2 out, hrd hld.* (15 to 8 on op 9 to 4 on tchd 7 to 4 on) 1
933³ SAN LORENZO (USA) (bl) 5-10-9 N Williamson, *led, hit 1st and 3rd, hdd 2 out, kpt on one pace.*
..............................(4 to 1 tchd 9 to 2) 2
COUNTRY LAD (Ire) 5-10-10 D Murphy, *nvr nr to chal, chsd 1st 2 frm 5 out......*(8 to 1 op 7 to 1 tchd 9 to 1) 3
794⁷ CORRIN HILL 6-10-12 R Dunwoody, *chsd 1st 2 to 5 out, nvr nr to chal....*(11 to 1 op 6 to 1) 4
998⁵ HOWGILL 7-10-9 (3*) S Wynne, *mstks, sn beh, tld off.*
..............................(66 to 1 op 50 to 1) 5
549 KEY DEAR (Fr) 6-10-12 T Wall, *pld hrd early, al in rear, tld off 7th, pulled up bef 4 out.......*(66 to 1 op 50 to 1) pu

140

Dist: 2l, 12l, 8l, 4l. 3m 52.20s. a 3.20s (6 Ran).
SR: 36/32/20/14/10/-/ (Mrs Shirley Robins), D Nicholson

1072 Tussac Construction Handicap Hurdle (0-125 4-y-o and up) £3,022 2½m 110yds. . . . . (3:50)

839^{2} JAMESTOWN BOY [88] (bl) 5-10-8 T Wall, *mid-div, rdn frm hfwy, gd hdwy from 2 out to ld r-in.* . . . .(7 to 1 op 8 to 1 tchd 9 to 1) 1
698^{7} HIDDEN OATS [98] 6-11-4 B Powell, *al prmnt, led 3 out till hdd r-in*. . . . .(14 to 1 tchd 16 to 1) 2
936^{8} COUTURE STOCKINGS [94] 9-11-0 N Williamson, *hld up, gd hdwy 4 out, ev ch 2 out till wknd r-in.* . . . . (11 to 2 op 6 to 1) 3
949* MUNIR (USA) [98] 4-11-4 (6ex) J A Harris, *sn pushed alng, beh till hdwy hfwy, kpt on one pace frm 3 out.* . . . .(7 to 1 op 6 to 1) 4
HIGH GRADE [94] 5-11-0 H Davies, *chsd ldrs, one pace frm 3 out*. . . . .(16 to 1 op 14 to 1) 5
912^{6} THE HIDDEN CITY [91] 7-10-11 B Clifford, *chsd ldrs till rdn and wknd appr 2 out.* . . . . (16 to 1 op 14 to 1 tchd 18 to 1) 6
949^{5} TEMPORALE [80] 7-10-0 R Supple, *hld up in rear, hdwy 4 out, nvr nr to chal*. . . . .(20 to 1) 7
PLAYFUL JULIET (Can) [82] 5-10-2^{2} Pat Caldwell, *in tch till rdn and wknd appr 3 out, tld off*. . . . .(50 to 1) 8
936^{2} DRIVING FORCE [102] 7-11-8 D Gallagher, *mid-div, wknd appr 3 out, tld off*. . . . . (13 to 2 op 5 to 1) 9
CAPTAIN MY CAPTAIN (Ire) [93] 5-10-13 Diane Clay, *in rear, nvr nr to chal, tld off*. . . . .(10 to 1 op 8 to 1) 10
951 BRIGHT SAPPHIRE [80] 7-9-7 (7*) A Flannigan, *led, mstk second, hdd 6th, wknd appr 3 out, tld off*. . . . . (20 to 1) 11
FLUTTER MONEY [83] 9-10-3^{3} G Upton, *in tch till wknd 4 out, tld off*. . . . . (50 to 1) 12
OAK PARK (Ire) [104] 5-11-5 (5*) T Eley, *in tch till wknd 4 out, tld off*. . . . .(14 to 1 op 12 to 1) 13
845 BENTLEY MANOR [80] 4-10-0 D Bridgwater, *prmnt, led 6th till hdd 3 out, wknd quickly, tld off.* . . . . (25 to 1 op 33 to 1) 14
623^{2} PINISI [87] 8-10-7 A Maguire, *trkd ldrs, rdn hfwy, beh frm 4 out, tld off*. . . . .(9 to 2 fav op 7 to 2) 15
Dist: 3½l, 1½l, 7l, 2l, 2½l, 7l, 15l, 4l, 1l, 1½l. 5m 0.00s. a 17.00s (15 Ran).
(R A Jones), B Preece

GOWRAN PARK (IRE) (good to yielding)
Thursday November 4th

1073 Bennettsbridge Chase (5-y-o and up) £2,760 2¼m. . . . . (2:20)

807^{5} NILOUSHA 6-10-11 C O'Dwyer, ...(10 to 1) 1
799 CHIC AND ELITE 6-10-11 P P Kinane, ... (25 to 1) 2
929* COMMANCHE NELL (Ire) 5-10-12 G M O'Neill, ...(2 to 1) 3
965* CHIRKPAR 6-11-9 K F O'Brien, ...(11 to 8 on) 4
CASTALINO 7-10-11 F Woods, ...(12 to 1) 5
929 SANTAMORE 6-10-6 (5*) P A Roche, ... (20 to 1) 6
904 SPEAKING TOUR (USA) 5-10-13 D H O'Connor, . . (25 to 1) 7
Dist: Sht-hd, 2½l, ½l, 3l. 4m 36.60s. (7 Ran).
(Midland Racing Syndicate), Victor Bowens

1074 I.N.H. Stallion Owners Hurdle Qualifier (5-y-o and up) £3,450 2¾m. . (2:50)

939^{2} PANDA (Ire) 5-11-4 (5*) T P Treacy, ...(5 to 4 fav) 1
903^{3} LUMINOUS LIGHT 6-10-12 (3*) Mr M Phillips, ...(7 to 2) 2
903^{6} FAMBO LAD (Ire) 5-11-6 Mr J A Berry, ... (10 to 1) 3
927^{2} AMARI QUEEN 6-11-9 C F Swan, ... (9 to 2) 4
638 BOB MONEY (Ire) 5-11-6 D H O'Connor, ... (20 to 1) 5
926^{7} MASTER CRUSADER 7-12-0 K F O'Brien, ...(8 to 1) 6
COMICALITY 5-11-6 T J Taaffe, ... (8 to 1) 7
MAN OF IRON 6-11-6 F Woods, ... (20 to 1) 8
RIVER WATER 6-11-1 L P Cusack, ... (20 to 1) 9
877 BETTER WAY (Ire) 5-11-6 B Sheridan, ... (20 to 1) 10
CHORA'S DREAM (Ire) 5-10-12 (3*) C O'Brien, ... (50 to 1) 11
Dist: 1l, 4½l, 3½l, 1½l. 5m 48.00s. (11 Ran).
(Giles Clarke), P Mullins

1075 Wexford Opportunity Handicap Hurdle (0-123 4-y-o and up) £2,760 2m 1f (3:20)

924^{2} WATERLOO LADY [-] 6-10-7 (2*) D P Murphy, . . (4 to 1 fav) 1
ARCTIC WEATHER (Ire) [-] 4-11-7 (4*) D Finnegan, . .(6 to 1) 2
157^{8} TURALITY (Ire) [-] 4-9-5 (2*) T P Treacy, ...(33 to 1) 3
673^{7} SHIRWAN (Ire) [-] 4-10-4 (2*) M A Davey, ... (6 to 1) 4
60^{6} RUNAWAY GOLD [-] 6-9-11 (4*) R A Hennessy, ... (12 to 1) 5
967* CUBAN QUESTION [-] 6-10-10 (2*,6ex) M G Cleary, (5 to 1) 6
ALWAYS IN TROUBLE [-] 6-11-4 C O'Brien, ... (11 to 2) 7
831^{6} PLUMBOB (Ire) [-] 4-11-1 (2*) T F Lacy Jnr, ... (10 to 1) 8
805 THE BOURDA [-] 7-9-10 (4*) P J Stafford, ... (12 to 1) 9
967^{6} ROSEPERRIE (Ire) [-] 5-9-9 (2*) D T Evans, ...(12 to 1) 10
803^{9} FREEWAY HALO (Ire) [-] 4-9-7 D Bromley, ... (20 to 1) f
967^{5} BOLERO DANCER (Ire) [-] 5-10-6 T J Mitchell, ... (10 to 1) bd
Dist: 15l, 1½l, 8l, hd. 4m 17.00s. (12 Ran).
(John Philip Kelly), James Joseph Mangan

1076 Thomastown Maiden Hurdle (4-y-o and up) £2,760 2m. . . . .(3:50)

NIGHTMAN 4-11-9 C O'Dwyer, ...(6 to 1) 1
HOTEL MINELLA 6-12-0 T Horgan, ...(3 to 1) 2
LEGAL PROFESSION (Ire) 5-12-0 J F Titley, ... (10 to 1) 3
993^{3} FAIRYHILL RUN (Ire) 5-11-1 B Sheridan, ... (14 to 1) 4
801* GLENGARRA PRINCESS 6-11-2 (7*) Mr D K Budds, ...(16 to 1) 5+
877^{4} DEEP THYNE (Ire) 5-11-2 (7*) Mr K F O'Donnell, . . .(12 to 1) 5+
476* KILADANTE (Ire) 4-10-11 (7*) K P Gaule, ... (10 to 1) 7
STEEL DAWN 6-12-0 F Woods, ... (10 to 1) 8
804^{6} AMBER RULER 7-12-0 K F O'Brien, ... (14 to 1) 9
832^{2} HEIST 4-11-9 C F Swan, ...(6 to 4 fav) 10
BLACK DOG (Ire) 5-11-1 (5*) D T Evans, ...(20 to 1) 11
689^{9} THE COBH GALE 6-11-1 H Rogers, ... (25 to 1) 12
804^{7} SAGASTINI (USA) 6-12-0 P L Malone, ... (16 to 1) 13
THE TOASTER 6-11-1 (5*) M G Cleary, ...(33 to 1) 14
877 RUBDAN (USA) 6-11-3 (3*) C O'Brien, ... (50 to 1) 15
877 TREMEIRCHION 7-11-6 M Duffy, ...(50 to 1) 16
877 WITH DIAMONDS 10-10-10 (5*) D P Murphy, ... (50 to 1) 17
LANCANA (Ire) 4-10-13 C N Bowens, ...(25 to 1) f
Dist: 1½l, nk, 3½l, 3l, dd-ht. 4m 9.80s. (18 Ran).
(Mrs A Manning), Charles O'Brien

1077 Irish National Bookmakers INH Flat Race (4-y-o) £3,450 2m 1f. . . . . . (4:20)

KLAIRON DAVIS (Fr) 11-2 (7*) Mr H Murphy, ...(6 to 4 fav) 1
907^{3} MARYJO (Ire) 10-13 (5*) Mr J A Nash, ... (8 to 1) 2
1020^{3} PLASSY BOY (Ire) 11-9 Mr J A Berry, ... (9 to 2) 3
SAM VAUGHAN (Ire) 11-2 (7*) Mr W M O'Sullivan, (12 to 1) 4
530 FATHER RECTOR (Ire) 11-6 (3*) Mrs M Mullins, ...(2 to 1) 5
692^{7} TWO HILLS FOLLY (Ire) 11-4 Mr P Fenton, ... (10 to 1) 6
MICKEY TRICKY (Ire) 10-13 (5*) Mr G J Harford, . . (12 to 1) 7
1020^{9} COOL ROSE (Ire) 11-4 Mr S R Murphy, ...(10 to 1) 8
Dist: 11l, 6l, 1l, 5l. 4m 24.00s. (8 Ran).
(C Jones), A L T Moore

UTTOXETER (good)
Thursday November 4th

Going Correction: PLUS 0.45 sec. per fur. (races 1,2,-5,7), PLUS 0.40 (3,4,6)

1078 EBF 'National Hunt' Novices' Hurdle Qualifier (4,5,6-y-o) £2,494 2m. . (1:10)

SCOBIE BOY (Ire) 5-11-0 J Osborne, *trkd ldr, led appr 3 out, drw clr frm nxt, cmftbly.* . . . .(9 to 2 op 3 to 1 tchd 5 to 1) 1
MARSHALL SPARKS 6-11-0 R Dunwoody, *al prmnt, chsd wnr frm 3 out*. . . . .(3 to 1 tchd 4 to 1) 2
CUNNINGHAMS FORD (Ire) 5-10-7 (7*) Mr A Harvey, *al prmnt, not pace to chal frm 3 out*. . . . (5 to 1 op 3 to 1) 3
809^{2} BALLYHAMAGE (Ire) 5-11-0 A Maguire, *hld up, hdwy frm 5th, one pace from 3 out.* . . . .(9 to 4 fav op 5 to 2 tchd 2 to 1) 4
FROG HOLLOW (Ire) 5-11-0 C Llewellyn, *in tch, rdn 3 out, one pace aftr*. . . . .(25 to 1 op 16 to 1) 5
934 BIRCHALL BOY 5-11-0 G McCourt, *beh, styd on frm 3 out, nvr nrr*. . . . . (50 to 1 op 33 to 1) 6
NEEDWOOD NATIVE 5-11-0 L Harvey, *hld up, hdwy frm 4 out, wknd appr 2 out*. . . . . (20 to 1) 7
EDEN STREAM 6-11-0 B Clifford, *al beh, tld off.* . . . . (50 to 1 op 25 to 1) 8
GEORGE LANE 5-11-0 R Supple, *mid-div whn mstk 4 out, sn beh, tld off*. . . . .(16 to 1 op 12 to 1) 9
983 CURRAGH PETER 6-11-0 R Greene, *al beh, tld off.* . . . . (33 to 1 op 20 to 1) 10
815 COME ON LUCY 4-10-9 A O'Hagan, *pld hrd, led till hdd appr 3 out, wknd quickly, tld off*. . . . .(50 to 1) 11
BOSSYMOSS (Ire) 4-11-0 Susan Kersey, *al beh, tld off frm hfwy*. . . . . (50 to 1 op 33 to 1) 12
TIMELLS BROOK 5-11-0 J Frost, *al beh, tld off frm 5th, pld up bef 2 out*. . . . .(33 to 1) pu
SARGEANTS CHOICE (v) 4-10-9 (5*) T Eley, *in tch to 4 out, wknd whn jmpd rght nxt, pld up bef last*. . . . .(50 to 1) pu
549 ROCKY TYRONE 6-11-0 J Railton, *chsd ldrs till wknd quickly appr 3 out, pld up bef nxt.* (25 to 1 op 20 to 1) pu
Dist: 5l, 3½l, ¾l, 2l, 8l, 2l, 20l, 1l, 1½l, 6l. 3m 52.10s. a 13.10s (15 Ran).
SR: 27/22/18/17/15/7/5/-/-/ (R V Shaw), C R Egerton

1079 Houghton Vaughan Selling Hurdle (4 & 5-y-o) £1,864 2m. . . . . (1:40)

885^{9} DARINGLY 4-10-12 R Bellamy, *hld up wl in rear, steady hdwy appr 3 out, styd on und pres to ld r-in.* . . . . (33 to 1 op 25 to 1) 1
137^{4} ABSOLUTLEY FOXED 4-10-7 T Wall, *al prmnt, led sn aftr 2 out, rdn and hdd r-in*. . . . .(33 to 1) 2
932^{2} PEARLY WHITE 4-10-7 R Dunwoody, *hld up in rear, hdwy appr 3 out, ev ch last, wknd r-in.* . . . .(7 to 1 op 6 to 1 tchd 8 to 1) 3

932⁵ PORT IN A STORM 4-10-12 G McCourt, *wtd wth, in tch, hdwy frm 5th, chlgd 2 out, ev ch till wknd r-in.*
................................(11 to 2 fav op 6 to 1) 4
891³ DANCING DANCER 4-10-7 J Frost, *hld up, hdwy appr 3 out, wknd approaching last.........*(9 to 1 op 8 to 1) 5
994⁶ URSHI-JADE 5-10-0 (7*) P McLoughlin, *beh, rdn and hdwy appr 3 out, styd on, nvr nrr.....................*(14 to 1) 6
ALDINGTON PEACH 4-11-0 J Osborne, *led till wknd and hdd an aftr 2 out.........*(13 to 2 op 6 to 1 tchd 7 to 1) 7
NORTHERN OPTIMIST 5-10-7 (7*) Mr J L Llewellyn, *trkd ldr to 3 out, sn btn....................*(6 to 1 op 4 to 1) 8
837² WINGED WHISPER (USA) 4-10-12 N Williamson, *prmnt till wknd 3 out...................................*(8 to 1) 9
724⁶ NORDIC BEAT (Ire) 4-10-12 Diane Clay, *mid-div, rdn 4 out, sn btn...........................*(9 to 1 op 6 to 1) 10
ROLY WALLACE 4-10-7 (5*) T Eley, *mid-div, hdwy 5th, rdn and wknd appr 3 out......................*(20 to 1) 11
126⁸ MONTAGNE 4-10-7 A O'Hagan, *chsd ldrs till wknd 4 out.*
....(33 to 1) 12
988 DOTTEREL (Ire) 5-10-12 W Humphreys, *al beh.*
......................................(33 to 1 op 20 to 1) 13
ICE WALK 4-10-7 L Harvey, *al beh...*(14 to 1 op 12 to 1) 14
LOXLEY RANGE (Ire) (v) 5-11-5 A Maguire, *mid-div whn mstk 5th, sn wknd, tld off.*
................(11 to 1 op 10 to 1 tchd 12 to 1) 15
PRINCESS OF ORANGE 4-10-7 C Llewellyn, *pld hrd early, hdwy 3rd, wknd quickly 4 out, tld off.*
......................................(14 to 1 op 20 to 1) 16
666 EASY TOWNY (v) 5-10-12 S Smith Eccles, *al towards rear, tld off whn pld up bef 2 out.* (16 to 1 op 12 to 1) pu
Dist: 1½l, 3½l, 3l, 2½l, 1½l, ½l, ½l, ½l, 5l. 3m 53.80s. a 14.80s (17 Ran).
SR: 8/1/-/-/-/-/ (Albury Racing Limited), J C McConnochie

1080 Bowmer & Kirkland Novices' Chase (5-y-o and up) £3,126 3¼m......(2:10)

996 FIVELEIGH FIRST (Ire) 5-10-12 R Supple, *hld up, took clr order 5 out, pressing ldr whn virtually f 2 out, rdr styd on, reco'red and poor second when lft clr last.*
....(100 to 30 op 3 to 1) 1
SENEGALAIS (Fr) 9-11-0 J Frost, *chsd ldrs, mstk 5 out, sn beh, lft second last.................*(25 to 1 op 20 to 1) 2
948⁴ POLLERTON'S PRIDE 6-10-9 A Maguire, *in tch, blun 13th, wknd appr 4 out...........................*(7 to 1) 3
962⁵ HALF A MO 8-10-6 (3*) W Marston, *chsd ldr till wknd 5 out.............................*(25 to 1 op 20 to 1) 4
947 SEA BREAKER (Ire) 5-10-12 E Murphy, *al beh, lost tch 5 out..........................*(14 to 1 op 12 to 1) 5
843 FARDROSS 7-11-6 N Williamson, *hld up, steady hdwy to ld appr 4 out, slight advantage whn f 2 out.*
...............(5 to 4 fav tchd 6 to 4 and 13 to 8) f
COMEDY SPY 9-11-0 R Bellamy, *led till hdd appr 4 out, hld in 3rd pl whn lft clr 2 out, blun and uns rdr last.*
....(14 to 1) ur
867⁸ BANOUR (USA) (bl) 5-10-12 C Llewellyn, *blun and uns rdr second....................*(8 to 1 op 7 to 1 tchd 10 to 1) ur
BEN THE BOMBER 8-10-7 (7*) Judy Davies, *in tch to 13th.*
......................................(33 to 1)
984 DEBT OF HONOR 5-10-12 R Greene, *al towards rear, losing tch whn blun badly 4 out, pld up.*
......................................(12 to 1 op 8 to 1) pu
Dist: 50l, 7l, 6l, ½l. 6m 50.20s. a 34.20s (10 Ran).
(The Equus Club), John R Upson

1081 Invest In East Staffordshire Novices' Handicap Chase (5-y-o and up) £3,452 2m 5f........................(2:40)

741³ BOLL WEEVIL [93] 7-11-5 J Osborne, *al frnt rnk, led 3rd to 8th, led ag'n nxt, kpt on und pres whn chlgd frm 3 out.*
.................................(3 to 1 op 11 to 4 tchd 7 to 2) 1
954⁴ GLENSHANE LAD [102] 7-12-0 N Williamson, *hld up in tch, chalg whn pckd on landing 2 out, styd on one pace.*
....(9 to 2 op 7 to 2) 2
882² PRINCE'S COURT [89] 10-10-8 (7*) D Fortt, *hit 1st, sn trkd ldrs, not al fluent, chalg whn mstk 2 out, one pace aftr.*
................(2 to 1 fav tchd 9 to 4 and 5 to 2) 3
899⁷ TITUS GOLD [91] 8-11-3 C Llewellyn, *al prmnt, ev ch 4 out, one pace frm nxt.........*(9 to 1 op 8 to 1 tchd 10 to 1) 4
957⁴ GENEROUS SCOT [74] 9-10-0 R Bellamy, *led to 3rd, led 8th to 9th, wknd whn hit 2 out..................*(25 to 1) 5
WENRISC [74] 6-10-0 A Maguire, *sn beh, lost tch frm hfwy, tld off.................*(16 to 1 op 14 to 1) 6
THE YOKEL [74] 7-10-0 K Johnson, *mid-div till lost tch appr 5 out, tld off.........................*(25 to 1) 7
862 MR GEE [87] (bl) 8-10-13 J Duggan, *al beh, tld off.* (16 to 1) 8
MO ICHI DO [81] (bl) 7-10-2 (5*) T Eley, *sn rdn alng, lost tch frm 9th, tld off.........*(12 to 1 op 10 to 1 tchd 14 to 1) 9
948⁶ VOLCANIC DANCER (USA) [74] 7-10-0 N Mann, *slwly away, al beh, tld off whn pld up bef 4 out.* f
VISION OF WONDER [74] 9-10-0 R Dunwoody, *not fluent, al beh, tld off whn pld up bef 2 out........*(14 to 1) pu
Dist: 3l, 4l, 4l, 5l, dist, nk, 8l, 1½l. 5m 14.30s. a 14.30s (11 Ran).
SR: 32/38/21/19/-/-/ (John Bolsover), O Sherwood

1082 St Modwen Classic Novices' Hurdle (Grade 2) (4-y-o and up) £6,490 2½m

110yds........................(3:10)

888² BERTONE (Ire) 4-11-0 N Williamson, *hld up in rear, hdwy to cl on ldrs frm 6th, cruised into ld appr 2 out, sn clr, hrd held..............*(9 to 1 op 6 to 1 tchd 10 to 1) 1
983* BELL STAFFBOY (Ire) 4-11-0 W Marston, *hld up, making rapid hdwy and second whn blun 6th, lost pl aftr nxt, reco'red to go second appr last, no ch wth wnr.*
..................................(3 to 1 op 9 to 4 tchd 2 to 1) 2
869³ CLOGHANS BAY (Ire) 4-11-4 R Dunwoody, *hld up in tch, hdwy to go second appr 4 out, rdn and one pace aftr nxt.........................*(7 to 2 tchd 9 to 2) 3
772* KING'S TREASURE (USA) 4-11-0 J Frost, *pld hrd early, lft in ld aftr 3rd, hdd appr 2 out, sn btn.*
......................................(2 to 1 fav tchd 9 to 4) 4
885* AUBURN CASTLE 4-11-0 J Osborne, *led till pld up lme aftr 3rd.......*(4 to 1 tchd 5 to 1 and 7 to 2) pu
MY ROSSINI 4-11-0 T Wall, *trkd ldrs, mstk, wknd quickly appr 4 out, tld off whn pld up bef 2 out.*
......................................(12 to 1 tchd 14 to 1) pu
Dist: 4l, 8l, 12l. 4m 56.20s. a 13.20s (6 Ran).
SR: 46/42/38/22/-/-/ (Mrs Harry J Duffey), K C Bailey

1083 Mason Richards Handicap Chase For Tom Curran Memorial Trophy (0-130 5-y-o and up) £3,772 3¼m......(3:40)

MASTER OATS [107] 7-10-11 N Williamson, *hld up, hdwy 12th, led sn aftr 3 out, drw clr r-in, broke blood vessel.*
......................................(6 to 1 op 9 to 2) 1
MANDER'S WAY [107] 8-10-11 G Upton, *hld up, in tch, hdwy 12th, led 4 out, hdd sn aftr nxt, ev ch till outpcd r-in.........................*(10 to 1 op 7 to 1) 2
865⁴ LAUDERDALE LAD [99] 11-10-3 A Maguire, *led to 4 out, one pace aftr...........................*(5 to 1 op 4 to 1) 3
947² TRIBAL RULER [103] 8-8-7³ G McCourt, *hld up in rear, hdwy 5 out, one pace frm nxt.*
...........................(5 to 1 op 4 to 1 tchd 11 to 2) 4
921⁴ STAY ON TRACKS [124] 11-11-7 (7*) Mr N King, *prmnt, trkd ldr 6th till wknd 14th...*(8 to 1 op 7 to 1 tchd 10 to 1) 5
865³ TAMMY'S FRIEND [103] 6-10-7 I Lawrence, *hld up, steady hdwy to go second 14th, rdn and wknd appr 3 out.*
...............................(11 to 8 fav op 7 to 4) 6
661³ KILLBANON [115] 11-11-5 B Clifford, *mstk second, trkd ldr to 6th, lost tch 5 out.* (25 to 1 op 20 to 1 tchd 33 to 1) 7
Dist: 3½l, 15l, 3½l, 2½l, 1½l, 12l. 6m 37.70s. a 21.70s (7 Ran).
(P A Matthews), K C Bailey

1084 William Hill 'Golden Oldies' Stakes-round 1 In aid of the Injured Jockeys Fund (4-y-o and up) £1,551 1½m (4:10)

MY SWAN SONG 8-12-0 Peter Smith, *wl in rear till hdwy 4 fs out, kpt on to ld appr fnl furlong.*
...............................(20 to 1 op 16 to 1) 1
631² SPACE FAIR 10-11-10 Peter Scudamore, *led 1st furlong, styd prmnt, ev ch ins fnl 2 fs, no extr nr finish.*
......................................(7 to 2 op 5 to 2) 2
952⁶ MISSY-S (Ire) 4-11-9 Jonjo O'Neill, *hld up early, hdwy to go second 6 fs out, led 4 out, rdn and hdd appr fnl furlong, one pace........................*(8 to 1 op 6 to 1) 3
NAVAL BATTLE 6-11-10 Jeff King, *hld up, hdwy hfwy, ev ch 2 fs out, wknd whn hld ins last.* (8 to 1 op 6 to 1) 4
916 LEXUS (Ire) 5-12-11 Bob Davies, *in tch till wknd o'r 2 fs out........................*(4 to 1 op 3 to 1 tchd 5 to 1) 5
WALKING THE PLANK (b) 4-12-3 Nigel Tinkler, *chsd ldrs till wknd o'r 2 fs out.........*(2 to 1 fav op 7 to 4) 6
DEADLY CHARM (USA) 7-11-5 Ron Barry, *hld up, hdwy 5 fs out, wknd 3 out........*(10 to 1 op 6 to 1 tchd 14 to 1) 7
ALAN BALL (bl) 7-11-10 Sue Wilton, *pld hrd, led aftr one furlong, sn clr, hdd 4 out, wknd quickly, tld off.*
....(8 to 1 op 7 to 1) 8
ARDORAN 7-12-0 Mike Gallemore, *in tch to hfwy, tld off.*
......................................(33 to 1) 9
NOBLE BID 9-12-0 Graham Thorner, *al beh, tld off.*
......................................(25 to 1 op 14 to 1) 10
787 ELISSA (v) 7-11-12³ Michael Caulfield, *al beh, tld off.*
......................................(33 to 1) 11
KING CREOLE (Ire) 4-11-10 Jack Berry, *unruly strt, ran out and crashed through rls aftr 100 yards.*
...............(12 to 1 op 6 to 1 tchd 14 to 1) ro
Dist: 1½l, hd, 10l, 6l, ½l, 3l, dist, 7l, sht-hd, 10l. 2m 56.30s. (12 Ran).
(Brian McGowan), J P Smith

WINCANTON (firm)
Thursday November 4th
Going Correction: MINUS 0.15 sec. per fur. (races 1,3,6), NIL (2,4,5)

1085 U.W.E.S.U. Still Standing Novices' Hurdle (4-y-o and up) £2,180 2m (1:20)

888³ MULCIBER 5-10-12 M Perrett, *hld up, cld on ldrs aftr 5th, led last, rdn out........*(11 to 2 op 5 to 1 tchd 6 to 1) 1

964³ KHALIDI (Ire) 4-11-4 P Holley, *led til aftr second, led ag'n 3rd until hdd last, rallied and kpt on r-in.*
.... (5 to 2 tchd 3 to 1 and 9 to 4) 2
PAY HOMAGE 5-10-12 B Powell, *trkd ldrs, wnt second 4th, ev ch whn swtchd 2 out, wknd appr last, not quicken r-in.......* (11 to 10 fav op Evens tchd 5 to 4) 3
885³ SINGERS IMAGE (v) 4-10-12 Richard Guest, *hld up, pushed alng aftr 5th, cl up nxt, rdn and wknd after 3 out, sthn whn mstk next.*
.... (7 to 1 op 6 to 1 tchd 15 to 2) 4
WYJUME (Ire) 4-10-7 D Murphy, *not fluent, mstk 1st, chsd ldrs til wknd quickly 3 out.*...... (20 to 1 op 12 to 1) 5
715⁷ LUCKMAN DREAMER 5-10-12 G Morgan, *sluly away, pld hrd, led aftr second til ran very wide and hdd appr nxt, wknd quickly 4 out, tld off.......* (40 to 1 op 20 to 1) 6
Dist: 1l, 1½l, 10l, 12l, dist. 4m 0.00s. a 23.00s (6 Ran).
(Mrs Penny Treadwell), G Harwood

1086 **Tattersalls Mares Only Novices' Chase Qualifier (5-y-o and up) £2,924 2m 5f.........................(1:50)**

MARTOMICK 6-10-10 G Bradley, *jmpd lft, led second, mstk tenth, stdly drw clr frm 6 out, unchlgd.*
...........(Evens fav tchd 11 to 10 and 11 to 10 on) 1
843⁴ RINANNA BAY 6-10-3 (7") P Carey, *trkd ldrs, wnt second aftr 8th, chsd lder, moderate second whn blun 3 out, no imprsn.*...............(9 to 2 tchd 5 to 1 and 7 to 2) 2
892⁶ PAPER STAR 6-10-10 Richard Guest, *led to second, chsd ldr til outpcd aftr 11th, styd on one pace frm 4 out.*
.... (25 to 1 op 12 to 1) 3
948⁵ PRUDENT PEGGY 6-10-10 B Powell, *prmnt til lost pl aftr 8th, mstk 11th, no ch frm 5 out......*(8 to 1 op 6 to 1) 4
SHAMARPHIL 7-10-10 Peter Hobbs, *hld up, cld up 6th, wnt 3rd tenth, third and rdn whn blun and uns rdr 5 out.*...................... (7 to 1 op 6 to 1 tchd 9 to 1) ur
683 SHOREHAM LADY 8-10-10 Lorna Vincent, *al last, mstks, tld off 8th, pld up bef 3 out.......* (66 to 1 op 33 to 1) pu
796 COOMBESBURY LANE (bl) 7-10-10 M Richards, *hld up and beh, not fluent, some hdwy aftr tenth, sn wknd, 6th and no ch whn pld up bef 5 out....*(25 to 1 op 16 to 1) pu
Dist: 20l, 10l, 8l. 5m 16.20s. a 10.20s (7 Ran).
(Richard Shaw), K C Bailey

1087 **South-West Racecourses Amateur Riders' Series - Round 3 Handicap Hurdle (0-120 4-y-o and up) £2,280 2m ....(2:20)**

977* CABIN HILL [90] 7-11-1 (3") Mr J Durkan, *trkd ldr, led 5th, made rst, cmftbly.*
.... (13 to 8 fav op 7 to 4 tchd 2 to 1 and 6 to 4) 1
DAMIER BLANC (Fr) [95] (bl) 4-11-2 (7") Mr N Moore, *hld up, wnt 3rd out, second 2 out, rdn and no imprsn betw last two........*(8 to 1 op 7 to 1 tchd 10 to 1) 2
887⁷ SMILING CHIEF (Ire) [91] 5-10-12 (7") Miss S Cobden, *hld up and beh, hdwy 3 out, wnt 4th appr nxt, rdn to take 3rd pl aftr last, no imprsn...* (9 to 2 op 4 to 1 tchd 5 to 1) 3
955 DESERT PALM [86] 8-10-7 (7") Mr N Miles, *hld up, trkd ldrs frm 4th, wnt 3rd nxt, pushed alng and no imprsn appr 2 out.*......................(8 to 1 op 7 to 1) 4
713³ PHILIP'S WOODY [96] 5-11-3 (7") Mr C Vigors, *led to 5th, pressed ldr, 3rd and btn whn mstk 2 out, wknd betw last two........*....(5 to 2 op 9 to 4 tchd 11 to 4) 5
KILTONGA [79] 6-10-0 (7") Miss L Horsey, *al last, tld off aftr second.*......................(50 to 1 op 25 to 1) 6
Dist: 4l, 3½l, 7l, 7l, dist. 3m 39.90s. a 2.90s (6 Ran).
SR: 37/38/30/18/21/-/ (The Kinnersley Crew), S Christian

1088 **Badger Beer Chase Limited Handicap (5-y-o and up) £10,335 3m 1f 110yds ....(2:50)**

884* PANTO PRINCE [127] 12-11-10 B Powell, *led to 4th, trkd ldr til led and lft clr 6 out, rdn and styd on wl frm 2 out.*
.... (5 to 2 jt-fav op 7 to 4) 1
886* BONSAI BUD [123] 10-11-6 D Gallagher, *hld up, pushed alng aftr 14th, lft second 6 out, rdn after 4 out, kpt on frm 2 out, not quicken.......*... (5 to 2 jt-fav tchd 3 to 1) 2
630⁵ WELKNOWN CHARACTER [117] 11-11-0 G Bradley, *hld up, wnt 3rd 6th, chsd ldg pair, lft third six out, rdn and styd on frm 2 out, not quicken.*
.... (13 to 2 op 7 to 1 tchd 8 to 1) 3
921 RU VALENTINO [110] (bl) 9-10-7 D Bridgwater, *led 4th til hdd and f 6 out.....*............... (11 to 2 op 9 to 2) f
828 ROCKTOR (NZ) [127] 8-11-10 H Davies, *hld up, lost tch and nvr gng pace aftr 4th, tld off last whn pld after 13th.*......................(4 to 1 op 7 to 2) pu
Dist: 2l, ¾l. 6m 19.80s. a 3.80s (5 Ran).
SR: 58/52/45/-/-/ (Mrs L M Warren), C L Popham

1089 **Silver Buck Handicap Chase (0-135 5-y-o and up) £5,742 2m 5f.....(3:20)**

900⁵ BIBENDUM [120] 7-11-10 Peter Hobbs, *pld hrd, trkd ldr, cl up and ev ch 6 out, second whn mstk 3 out, rdn to ld aftr last, drvn out.*..................(2 to 1 op 7 to 4) 1

884⁴ SMARTIE EXPRESS [119] 11-11-9 M A FitzGerald, *led, rdn aftr 2 out, hdd after last, not quicken nr finish.*
...............(11 to 10 fav op Evens tchd 11 to 10 on) 2
935² ARDCRONEY CHIEF [104] 7-10-8 P Holley, *not fluent, trkd ldr, rdn and rallied appr 3 out, wknd aftr nxt.*
......................(100 to 30 op 4 to 1) 3
Dist: ¾l, 20l. 5m 10.70s. a 4.70s (3 Ran).
SR: 49/47/12/ (Robert Waley-Cohen), R Waley-Cohen

1090 **Mendip 'National Hunt' Novices' Hurdle (4-y-o and up) £2,145 2¾m. . (3:50)**

616³ SOUND CARRIER (USA) 5-10-12 M Richards, *led to 4th, led ag'n 6th, drw clr appr last, styd on wl.*
.... (6 to 5 fav op 7 to 4 tchd 11 to 10) 1
869⁵ WELSH COTTAGE 6-10-12 D Murphy, *al hndy, wnt second aftr 4 out, ev ch whn mstk 2 out, sn rdn and not quicken..................*(7 to 2 op 6 to 4 tchd 9 to 2) 2
CANNING'S COLLEGE 7-10-7 Lorna Vincent, *hld up, hdwy 7th, wnt 3rd aftr 3 out, rdn and kpt on one pace.*
.... (20 to 1 op 10 to 1) 3
772⁴ OATS N BARLEY 4-10-12 I Shoemark, *hld up, mstk 6th, hdwy nxt, wnt 3rd appr 2 out, mistakes last two, sn btn....................*........ (14 to 1 op 8 to 1) 4
955* MAYFIELD PARK 8-10-11 (7") Mr G Hogan, *trkd ldrs, mstk 4th, rdn alng aftr four out, no ch appr 2 out.*
.... (5 to 1 tchd 7 to 1) 5
946⁶ PABREY (bl) 7-10-5 (7") Miss S Mitchell, *led 4th til jmpd sluly and hdd 6th, chsd ldr until rdn and wknd aftr four out.*...................... (25 to 1 op 14 to 1) 6
STORMY SUNSET 6-10-0 (7") Mr N Moore, *rcd wide, hld up, hdwy 6th, cl up whn mstk nxt, wknd 3 out.*
.... (33 to 1 op 16 to 1) 7
901 MR GREY FELLOW (Ire) 5-10-12 A Tory, *trkd ldrs, pushed alng aftr 5th, wknd quickly 7th, tld off 3 out.*
.... (40 to 1 op 20 to 1) 8
541* TWIST 'N' SCU 5-11-4 D Bridgwater, *hld up, mstk 5th, hdwy to chase ldr 5 out, wknd aftr 3 out, beh whn pld bef last......*........ (7 to 1 op 5 to 1 tchd 15 to 2) pu
901 AFTICA 6-10-12 A Charlton, *drpd rear 5th, lost tch 7th, tld off whn pld up bef 2 out.........*(100 to 1 op 33 to 1) pu
Dist: 10l, 15l, 2l, 10l, 2½l, 10l, dist. 5m 13.50s. a 7.50s (10 Ran).
(M L Oberstein), O Sherwood

HEXHAM (good to soft)
Friday November 5th
Going Correction: PLUS 1.15 sec. per fur.

1091 **Federation Brewery Sporting Club Novices' Chase (5-y-o and up) £2,138 3m 1f...........................(1:20)**

LO STREGONE 7-11-0 M Dwyer, *al prmnt, led 13th to 15th, rdn to ld appr last, styd on wl.*
.... (6 to 4 fav op 5 to 4 tchd 13 to 8) 1
TALLYWAGGER 6-11-0 J Callaghan, *al prmnt, led 15th till rdn and hdd appr last, kpt on.......* (4 to 1 op 5 to 2) 2
974⁴ INVERINATE 8-11-0 T Reed, *al prmnt, chsd ldg pair frm 5 out, rdn and one pace last.*
.... (10 to 1 op 16 to 1 tchd 8 to 1) 3
1002 AMADEUS (Fr) 5-10-12 C Grant, *hit 3rd and beh, hdwy tenth, chsd ldrs 4 out, sn rdn and one pace frm nxt.*
.... (33 to 1 op 14 to 1) 4
756⁴ IRISH GENT 7-11-0 K Johnson, *mstks, al rear.*
.... (12 to 1 op 7 to 1) 5
874⁵ EBRO (bl) 7-11-0 A Merrigan, *led to 11th, sn wknd and beh frm 15th.....................*...... (50 to 1 op 33 to 1) 6
786² SANDEDGE 6-10-9 B Storey, *hld up, not fluent, mstk 4th, blun 11th and sn wl beh...........*(16 to 1 op 12 to 1) 7
733³ SCOTTISH GOLD 9-11-7 A Maguire, *prmnt, led 11th to 13th, rdn and blun 5 out, sn wknd and hit nxt, beh whn blunded and uns rdr 3 out...........*(4 to 1 tchd 9 to 2) ur
957⁷ RUSTINO 7-11-0 R Hodge, *mid-div till blun and uns rdr 9th........................*.... (10 to 1 op 16 to 1) ur
LADY BE BRAVE 10-10-9 M Moloney, *al rear, hit 7th, beh whn hit 5 out and pld up bef nxt.*
.... (16 to 1 op 33 to 1 tchd 50 to 1) pu
Dist: 2½l, 1½l, 6l, dist, 15l, sht-hd. 6m 45.50s. a 40.50s (10 Ran).
(Mrs Sylvia Clegg), T P Tate

1092 **North East Racing Club Novices' Handicap Hurdle (3-y-o and up) £1,763 2m...........................(1:50)**

717 TIGHTER BUDGET (USA) [65] 6-10-3 M Moloney, *al prmnt, led briefly 2 out, rdn to chal last, sn led, styd on wl.*
.... (33 to 1 op 25 to 1) 1
818³ STINGRAY CITY (USA) [86] 4-11-3 (7") F Perratt, *led to 3rd, led aftr nxt till jmpd sluly and hdd 3 out, led after 2 out, rdn last, headed and no extr last.*
.... (9 to 4 fav tchd 2 to 1 op 6 to 4) 2
BORING (USA) [82] 4-11-6 K Johnson, *mid-div, hdwy 3 out, chsd ldg pair nxt, sn one pace.*
.... (8 to 1 op 14 to 1 tchd 7 to 1) 3

785[2] BACK BEFORE DAWN [80] 6-11-1 (3*) A Dobbin, *hld up, gd hdwy 5th, led briefly 3 out, rdn and wknd 2 out.* ....(9 to 2 op 6 to 1) 4
KING'S GUEST (Ire) [84] 4-11-8 J Callaghan, *hld up and beh, hdwy 5th, sn rdn and one pace bef 2 out.* ....(8 to 1 op 6 to 1) 5
BARAHIN (Ire) [76] 4-10-11 (3*) D O'Sullivan, *not jump wl, cl up till led 3rd, ran wide and hdd aftr nxt, wknd bef 2 out.*........(5 to 1 op 2 to 1) 6
RALLYING CRY (Ire) [80] 5-11-4 B Storey, *in tch, rdn appr 3 out, sn beh.*........(14 to 1 op 10 to 1) 7
JUST EVE [62] 6-9-10[1] (5*) P Williams, *al rear, tld off 3 out.* ....(20 to 1 op 16 to 1) 8
785[5] DE JORDAAN [85] 6-11-9 A Merrigan, *al rear, tld off aftr 3 out.*........(25 to 1 op 16 to 1) 9
640[3] JIM'S WISH (Ire) [76] (bl) 5-10-7 (7*) Carol Cuthbert, *al rear, mstks 4th and 5th, sn tld off.*........(6 to 1 op 5 to 1) 10
BEACH PATROL (Ire) [62] 5-10-0 D Byrne, *chsd ldrs, rdn 3 out, wknd nxt.*........(33 to 1 op 25 to 1) 11
PANTO LADY [62] 7-9-7 (7*) Miss S Lamb, *al rear, tld off 3 out.*........(33 to 1 op 25 to 1) 12

Dist: 1½l, 15l, 2l, ¾l, 1½l, nk, 15l, 2½l, hd, 2l. 4m 15.80s. a 25.80s (12 Ran).
SR: 1/20/1/-/-/-/ (A Slack), Mrs E Slack

1093 'Pirates' Novices' Handicap Chase (4-y-o and up) £2,025 2m 110yds...(2:20)

820 SEMINOFF (Fr) [75] 7-10-4 (3*) A Dobbin, *led to 3rd, chsd clr ldr till led aftr 8th, hit 3 out, rdn and hld on wl flt.* ....(9 to 2 op 5 to 1 tchd 6 to 1) 1
768[2] CLARE LAD [92] 10-11-10 B Storey, *chsd ldrs, effrt and rdn appr 2 out, styd on flt.*.....(3 to 1 tchd 100 to 30) 2
960 MILLIES OWN [85] 6-11-3 M Perrett, *in tch, blun 4th, effrt and rdn 3 out, kpt on appr last.* ....(11 to 4 fav op 5 to 2 tchd 9 to 4) 3
729 DELPIOMBO [85] 7-11-3 M Dwyer, *hld up, hdwy 9th, chsd wnr 3 out, blun nxt, wknd last.* ....(3 to 1 op 7 to 4 tchd 100 to 30) 4
820[6] MASTER MISCHIEF [84] (bl) 6-11-2 K Johnson, *chsd ldrs till lost pl and beh frm hfwy.* ....(13 to 2 op 5 to 1 tchd 7 to 1) 5
821 AYIA NAPA [69] 6-10-1 Mr J Bradburne, *pld hrd, rapid prog to ld 3rd and sn clr, hit 7th, hdd aftr nxt and soon beh, tld off whn pulled up bef last.*.....(20 to 1 op 16 to 1) pu

Dist: 2l, ½l, 10l, ½l. 4m 26.70s. a 28.70s (6 Ran).
(Guthrie Robertson), P Monteith

1094 Patrick Haslam Racing Club Selling Hurdle (3 - 6-y-o) £1,822 2m.....(2:50)

784[9] RAGGERTY (Ire) 3-10-2 (3*) N Bentley, *in tch, hdwy 3 out, rdn to ld appr last, hrd drvn and styd on gmely flt.* ....(7 to 1 op 5 to 1) 1
861[5] REGAL ROMPER (Ire) 5-11-10 Richard Guest, *chsd ldrs, hdwy to ld 3 out, rdn and hdd appr last, rallied und pres and ev ch flt, no extr nr finish.* ....(9 to 4 fav op 5 to 2) 2
DUNBAR 3-10-5 D Wilkinson, *chsd ldrs, rdn appr 2 out, kpt on one pace.*.......(7 to 1 op 8 to 1 tchd 10 to 1) 3
AL FORUM (Ire) 3-10-5 Mr R McGrath, *al prmnt, led 3 out, rdn and hdd appr nxt, sn one pace.* ....(16 to 1 op 20 to 1) 4
970 STATION EXPRESS (Ire) 5-11-8 (7*) S Mason, *in tch till rdn and one pace aftr 3 out.*........(12 to 1 op 10 to 1) 5
818[8] FELL WARDEN 5-11-2 (3*) A Larnach, *chsd ldrs till rdn and outpcd aftr 3 out.*........(10 to 1 op 8 to 1) 6
DENTICULATA 5-11-5 B Storey, *led to 4th, cl up till rdn and wknd aftr 3 out.*........(33 to 1) 7
588[4] CANNY LAD 3-10-5 M Dwyer, *in tch, effrt and hdwy 3 out, rdn nxt, sn wknd*...(7 to 1 op 6 to 1 tchd 8 to 1) 8
724 SEA-AYR (Ire) 3-10-1[1] A Orkney, *al rear.* ....(20 to 1 op 12 to 1) 9
787[7] LUGER (Ire) 5-11-5 A Merrigan, *in tch till lost pl and beh frm 3 out.*........(20 to 1 op 16 to 1) 10
732[6] DUSKY DUCHESS (Ire) 3-10-0 A Maguire, *cl up, hit 3rd, led nxt, hdd 5th, sn wknd.*........(14 to 1 op 10 to 1) 11
DOT'S JESTER 4-11-5 J Callaghan, *al beh, tld off 5th, pld up bef last.*........(33 to 1) pu
824 ARAGON AYR 5-11-7 (3*) A Dobbin, *in tch till blun 4th, sn lost pl, tld off 3 out, pld up bef last.* (4 to 1 op 3 to 1) pu

Dist: 1l, 12l, 4l, 8l, 1½l, 1½l, 12l, 5l, dist, 2½l. 4m 16.70s. a 26.70s (13 Ran).
SR: -/12/-/-/-/-/ (N Honeyman), G M Moore

1095 Elite Racing Club Handicap Chase (0-125 4-y-o and up) £2,406 2½m 110yds........(3:20)

663[7] PERSIAN HOUSE [113] 6-12-0 A Maguire, *hld up in tch, hdwy and hit tenth, effrt and rdn to ld appr last, ran on wl flt.*........(5 to 2 fav op 3 to 1 tchd 7 to 2) 1
973[6] MOSS BEE [95] 6-10-10[6] T Reed, *in tch, gd hdwy tenth, hit 2 out, rdn to ld briefly appr last, kpt on.* ....(7 to 1 op 6 to 1) 2
FUNNY OLD GAME [101] 6-10-11 (5*) P Waggott, *cl up, led 5th, rdn 2 out, hdd and wknd appr last.* ....(9 to 1 op 8 to 1 tchd 10 to 1) 3
624[3] MOUNTEBOR [94] (bl) 9-10-9 J Callaghan, *in tch, hdwy tenth, hit 4 out, wknd nxt.*........(3 to 1 tchd 7 to 2) 4
780 CHOICE CHALLANGE [103] (v) 10-11-4 C Grant, *pld hrd, led aftr 1st to 5th, prmnt till rdn and wknd 4 out.* ....(5 to 1 tchd 11 to 2) 5
CLONROCHE DRILLER [98] 8-10-6 (7*) Mr D Parker, *chsd ldrs, rdn and wknd 8th, beh frm 4 out.* ....(9 to 1 op 8 to 1) 6
876[5] WHEELIES NEWMEMBER [95] 10-10-10 K Johnson, *led till aftr 1st, in tch till hit 7th and sn beh.* ....(33 to 1 op 25 to 1) 7
973[5] CLASSIC MINSTREL [92] 9-10-2 (5*) P Williams, *in rear till f 5th.*........(7 to 1 tchd 8 to 1) f
913[5] SINGING SAM [90] 8-10-5 A Merrigan, *al rear, mstk 7th, tld off 4 out, pld up bef last.*........(33 to 1 op 25 to 1) pu

Dist: 6l, 8l, 6l, 1½l, 12l, dist. 5m 29.80s. a 28.80s (9 Ran).
SR: 48/24/22/9/16/-/ (Mrs M Guthrie), J M Jefferson

1096 Borcovicus Novices' Hurdle (4-y-o and up) £1,484 2½m 110yds.....(3:50)

823* FOUR DEEP (Ire) 5-11-7 A Maguire, *made all, pushed out flt, readily.*........ (6 to 4 fav op 7 to 4 tchd 15 to 8) 1
DOUBLE SHERRY 4-10-9 D Byrne, *hld up and beh, gd hdwy appr 3 out, chal and ev ch approaching last, hrd rdn and not pace of wnr flt.*.......(20 to 1 op 16 to 1) 2
910[5] TREVVEETHAN (Ire) 4-11-0 D Wilkinson, *hld up, steady hdwy 4 out, rdn appr 2 out, kpt on one pace.* ....(7 to 1 op 5 to 1) 3
875 POLITICAL TOWER 6-10-11 (3*) A Dobbin, *in tch, hdwy 6th, rdn appr 2 out, sn one pace.* ....(3 to 1 op 5 to 2 tchd 100 to 30) 4
MANWELL 6-10-9 (5*) D Bentley, *nvr rchd ldrs.* ....(50 to 1 op 33 to 1) 5
STRONG DEEL (Ire) 5-11-0 T Reed, *al rear.* ....(25 to 1 op 20 to 1) 6
DIG DEEPER 6-11-0 M Dwyer, *cl up, rdn 3 out, wknd nxt.* ....(10 to 1 op 6 to 1) 7
656[9] CARROLLS MARC (Ire) 5-11-0 J Callaghan, *prmnt till rdn and wknd bef 3 out.*........(6 to 1 op 5 to 1) 8
785[3] ROYAL SURPRISE 6-11-0 K Johnson, *in rear, reminders hfwy and some hdwy, wknd quickly 3 out.* ....(10 to 1 op 8 to 1) 9
BALLYBELL 8-10-9 (5*) P Williams, *cl up till lost pl 5th, sn tld off.*........(50 to 1 op 33 to 1) 10
771 CHERYL'S GIRL 7-10-6 (3*) A Larnach, *rear whn f 6th.* ....(50 to 1 op 33 to 1) f
770[7] BLUEBELL TRACK (bl) 7-10-2 (7*) F Perratt, *in tch, hit 5th and lost pl, brght dwn nxt.*........(33 to 1 op 25 to 1) bd
779[9] HAUT-BRION (Ire) 4-11-0 N Doughty, *chsd ldrs, hit 5th, wknd appr 3 out, tld off whn pld up bef last.* ....(20 to 1 op 16 to 1) pu
875[7] MITTON SPRINGS 4-11-0 Richard Guest, *in rear whn pld up bef 3rd, broke leg, dead.*....... (50 to 1 op 33 to 1) pu
717 POCKETPICKER (Ire) 5-11-0 A Merrigan, *al rear, blun 6th and nxt, tld off whn pld up aftr 3 out.* ....(50 to 1 op 33 to 1) pu

Dist: ½l, 10l, 8l, 3l, 3½l, dist, ¾l, 2½l, dist. 5m 21.70s. a 28.70s (15 Ran).
SR: 40/27/22/14/11/7/ (The Braw Partnership), J H Johnson

MARKET RASEN (good)
Friday November 5th
Going Correction: PLUS 0.40 sec. per fur.

1097 'Rocket' Selling Hurdle (3 & 4-y-o) £1,959 2m 1f 110yds............(1:10)

890[5] GROGFRYN 3-10-0 R Dunwoody, *led aftr 3rd, rdn whn mstk 2 out, kpt on wl r-in.*........(7 to 1 op 5 to 1) 1
890[6] RECORD LOVER (Ire) (bl) 3-10-5 J Osborne, *al prmnt, ev ch 3 out, kpt on one pace.*........(5 to 1 op 7 to 2) 2
760[2] MISTER BLAKE (v) 3-10-5 R Campbell, *al prmnt, ev ch whn mstk 2 out, not quicken*.....(9 to 2 fav op 3 to 1) 3
760[3] OMIDJOY (Ire) 3-10-0 N Williamson, *mstk 4th, sn prmnt, rdn appr 2 out, no imprsn.*........(11 to 2 op 9 to 2) 4
766[5] MONASTIC FLIGHT (Ire) 3-9-12 (7*) G Cahill, *al prmnt, rdn 3 out, no hdwy.*........(14 to 1 op 10 to 1) 5
915[7] MANILA RUN (Ire) 4-11-7 L Wyer, *hld up in mid-div, hdwy 6th, chsd ldrs, wknd 2 out.*........(10 to 1 op 6 to 1) 6
912 HIGHCLIFFE JESTER 4-11-7 C Hawkins, *nvr nrr.* ....(33 to 1 op 20 to 1) 7
711[6] TIME OF GRACE (Ire) 3-10-5 R Bellamy, *wl beh till rdn and styd on one pace frm 3 out.*........(16 to 1 op 12 to 1) 8
DANCING BOAT 4-11-0 (7*) P Ward, *in tch to 5th, wknd quickly*........(33 to 1 op 25 to 1) 9
ROYAL EXECUTIVE (Ire) 3-10-5 D Bridgwater, *jmpd slwly 1st, in tch to 5th, sn wknd.*........(12 to 1 op 14 to 1) 10
724[4] BIG GEM 3-10-5 G Lee, *lft in ld 1st, hdd aftr 3rd, wknd 5th, sn beh.*........(14 to 1 tchd 16 to 1) 11
724[3] TINSTONE 3-10-2[2] R Garritty, *chsd ldrs till wknd 3 out.* ....(8 to 1 op 6 to 1) 12
724[7] ALIZARI (USA) 4-11-7 M Robinson, *beh whn reminders and pushed alng aftr 3rd, nvr dngrs.*........ (33 to 1) 13
724 SOUNDS RISKY 3-9-9 (5*) T Eley, *prmnt to 5th, wknd quickly*........(33 to 1) 14

912⁹ JUMPING CACTUS 4-11-7 Miss T Waggott, *lost tch frm 4th, sn beh*....................(20 to 1 tchd 25 to 1) 15
912 ACE REPORTER 4-10-11 (5*) P Midgley, *al beh, tld off whn pld up bef 2 out*...........................(33 to 1) pu
UNINSURED 4-11-2 D Murphy, *beh frm 3rd, tld off whn pld up bef 2 out*...................(20 to 1 op 12 to 1) pu
Dist: 4l, ½l, 5l, 4l, 6l, 7l, 8l, 6l, ¾l, 1½l. 4m 16.00s. a 14.00s (17 Ran).
SR: 3/4/3/-/-/4/   (Mrs S J Popham), C L Popham

1098 Tripleprint Handicap Chase (0-135 4-y-o and up) £4,012 2m 1f 110yds
......................................(1:40)

JUST FRANKIE [111] 9-10-4¹ P Niven, *led aftr second, made rst, lft clr last, styd on wl*......(6 to 1 op 9 to 2) 1
913* BOSTON ROVER [120] 6-10-13 M Brennan, *hld up, wnt 3rd 8th, ev ch appr 3 out, no imprsn, lft moderate second last*...(85 to 40 fav op 9 to 4 tchd 5 to 2 and 11 to 4) 2
825⁴ CAMPSEA-ASH [125] 9-10-11 (7*) P Murphy, *hld up, pushed alng aftr 9th, no imprsn frm 4 out, lft moderate 3rd last*.................................(14 to 1) 3
834³ RUPPLES [107] 6-10-0 W Worthington, *beh frm 6th, tld off aftr 8th, lft poor 4th last*......................(33 to 1) 4
840 VAIN PRINCE [117] (bl) 6-10-10 G McCourt, *hld up, rdn frm 8th, 5th whn f nxt*......................(7 to 1 op 13 to 2) f
850* GOLD HAVEN [110] 9-9-10 (7*) D Fortt, *trkd ldrs, mstk 3rd, ev ch 4 out, sn rdn, second and btn whn f last*.
...............................(7 to 2 op 3 to 1 tchd 4 to 1) f
850⁴ SPREE CROSS [120] 7-10-13 D Murphy, *led to second, mstk nxt, second whn f 8th*.........(7 to 1 op 6 to 1) f
VALIANT BOY [135] 7-12-0 R Garritty, *hld up, blun and uns rdr 3rd*.......................(7 to 1 tchd 8 to 1) ur
Dist: 20l, 25l, dist. 4m 30.30s. a 16.30s (8 Ran).
                              (Lady Susan Watson), Mrs M Reveley

1099 'Penny Banger' 'National Hunt' Novices' Hurdle (4-y-o and up) £2,483 2m 3f 110yds.....................(2:10)

821⁴ LOCH SCAVAIG (Ire) 4-10-4 (3*) D J Moffatt, *hld up and beh, hdwy aftr 4 out, led 2 out, drvn out r-in*.
.................................(7 to 1 op 6 to 1 tchd 8 to 1) 1
869² KENILWORTH LAD 5-10-12 P Niven, *hld up, trkd ldrs frm 6th, rdn 2 out, not fluent last, styd on one pace*.
................................(6 to 4 on op 11 to 8 on) 2
863⁵ FIVE FLAGS (Ire) 5-10-12 Gary Lyons, *al chasing ldrs, ev ch appr 2 out, one pace last two*.(40 to 1 op 25 to 1) 3
910³ CALL ME EARLY 8-10-12 M Brennan, *hld up, wnt 3rd 6th, led aftr 3 out, hdd nxt, wknd betw last 2*.
..................................(10 to 1 tchd 8 to 1) 4
725² SQUIRES TALE (Ire) 5-10-12 L Wyer, *led till hdd aftr 3 out, sn wknd*..............(7 to 1 op 5 to 1 tchd 8 to 1) 5
915⁵ CZAR NICHOLAS 4-10-7 (5*) S Lyons, *hld up, drvn alng aftr 7th, no imprsn*......................(7 to 1) 6
627³ NOBLE BRONZE 5-10-7 R Dunwoody, *hld up, wnt second 6th, chsd ldr till wknd aftr 3 out*..(20 to 1 op 12 to 1) 7
920 FINKLE STREET (Ire) 5-10-5 (7*) P Murphy, *pressed ldr till wknd aftr 6th, sn rdn, beh frm 3 out*.
.................................(50 to 1 op 33 to 1) 8
DOLLY PRICES 8-10-2 (5*) R Farrant, *mid-div, drvn alng sn wknd*......................(33 to 1 tchd 66 to 1) 9
622⁴ MY TATA (v) 7-10-12 J Corkell, *trkd ldrs till wknd aftr 7th, sn beh*......................(40 to 1 op 25 to 1) 10
Dist: 7l, 3½l, 2l, sht-hd, 7l, 12l, 15l, nk, 3½l. 4m 51.20s. a 18.20s (10 Ran).
                              (Mrs G A Turnbull), D Moffatt

1100 Levy Board Novices' Hurdle (4-y-o and up) £2,477 2m 1f 110yds....(2:40)

922* SOUTHOLT (Ire) 5-10-12 (7*) P Murphy, *trkd ldrs, cl up and ev ch 3 out, slight ld nxt, rdn our r-in, styd on strly*.
...............................(3 to 1 fav tchd 100 to 30) 1
CUMBRIAN CHALLENGE (Ire) 4-10-12 L Wyer, *hld up, hdwy aftr 5th, cl up and ev ch appr 2 out, chlgd last, not quicken r-in*..........(7 to 2 op 2 to 1 tchd 4 to 1) 2
915² GORTEERA 7-10-12 M Brennan, *hld up and beh, hdwy 3 out, rdn and styd on betw last 2, one pace r-in*.
.................................(7 to 2 op 4 to 1 tchd 3 to 1) 3
950* WORDY'S WONDER 5-10-9 (5*) R Farrant, *al prmnt, cl up and ev ch 3 out, led appr nxt, sn hdd and unbl to quicken*..........................(14 to 1 op 12 to 1) 4
728⁴ SAFARI PARK 4-11-0 R Dunwoody, *led till hdd 5th, rdn and rallied aftr 2 out, unbl to quicken*.
..............................(12 to 1 op 10 to 1 tchd 14 to 1) 5
915⁶ MAJAL (Ire) 4-10-8¹ (5*) P Midgley, *hld up, beh 3rd, hdwy aftr 5th, wnt 4th appr 2 out, sn no imprsn*.
...................................(14 to 1 op 10 to 1) 6
915 TIBBS INN 4-10-12 M Ranger, *hld up in tch, no hdwy aftr 3 out*...................(16 to 1 tchd 20 to 1) 7
GLENSTAL PRIORY 6-10-7 Miss R Judge, *chsd ldrs to 5th, one pace frm 3 out*.................(50 to 1 op 33 to 1) 8
RUSSIAN CASTLE (Ire) 4-10-12 K Jones, *trkd ldg pair, wnt second 4th, led nxt till hdd aftr 3 out, sn wknd*.
.................................(33 to 1 op 25 to 1) 9
MRS NORMAN 4-10-7 N Williamson, *hld up, trkd ldrs aftr 3rd, in tch till wknd quickly 3 out*. (50 to 1 op 33 to 1) 10

BATTERY FIRED 4-10-5 (7*) J Supple, *chsd ldrs frm 5th till wknd appr 2 out*............(20 to 1 op 14 to 1) 11
DIAMOND INTHE DARK (USA) (v) 5-10-12 P Niven, *in tch to 4th, sn rdn and lost pl, tld off aftr 3 out*.
.................................(33 to 1 op 25 to 1) 12
THE CAN CAN MAN 6-10-12 M Robinson, *pressed ldr, mstk and rdr lost iron second, rdn and wknd 5th, tld off 3 out*......................(10 to 1 op 8 to 1) 13
766⁸ MILO 7-10-12 G McCourt, *beh 3rd, nvr rch ldrs, tld off 3 out*................................(33 to 1 op 25 to 1) 14
WE'RE IN 6-10-7 B Dalton, *al last, tld off 3rd, pld up bef last*......................(50 to 1 op 33 to 1) pu
Dist: 4l, 3½l, 4l, 1l, 1½l, 6l, 2½l, 6l, 12l, 6l. 4m 15.10s. a 13.10s (15 Ran).
SR: 30/19/15/13/12/8/2/-/-/   (G A Hubbard), F Murphy

1101 'Catherine Wheel' Handicap Hurdle (0-135 4-y-o and up) £3,158 2m 1f 110yds.....................(3:10)

918* MRS MAYHEW (Ire) [88] 5-9-11 (7*) P Murphy, *al hndy, cl up and ev ch 5th, led nxt, rdn and styd on wl whn chlgd last, ridden out*.................(6 to 4 fav op 5 to 2) 1
739⁴ MY LINDIANNE [84] 6-10-0 R Dunwoody, *trkd ldr, ev ch 3 out, chlgd last, rdn and unbl to quicken r-in*.
.................................(13 to 2 op 5 to 1) 2
918⁵ EASBY MANDRINA [86] 6-10-2² R Garritty, *hld up, hdwy appr 2 out, styd on to take 3rd pl aftr last, not trble 1st two*.................(7 to 1 op 6 to 1 tchd 8 to 1) 3
936* FROMTHEGETGO (Ire) [108] 4-11-3 (7*) G Cahill, *pushed alng aftr 3rd, chsd ldrs frm 3 out, one pace appr nxt*.
...................................(9 to 2 op 3 to 1) 4
MRS JAWLEYFORD (USA) [106] 5-11-8 M Ranger, *hld up, wnt 3rd 3 out, chsd 1st 2, sn rdn and unbl to quicken*.
.................................(8 to 1 op 7 to 1 tchd 17 to 2) 5
TRISTAN'S COMET [84] 6-10-0 B Dalton, *led till hdd 3 out, sn wknd*......................(20 to 1 tchd 25 to 1) 6
RATIFY [101] 6-11-3 A S Smith, *hld up in last pl, came wide into strt, beh whn f 2 out*...(12 to 1 tchd 14 to 1) f
781⁴ IN TRUTH [106] 5-11-3 (5*) S Lyons, *blun and uns rdr 1st*.
.................................(11 to 2 op 9 to 2) ur
Dist: 2½l, 15l, 1½l, ½l, hd. 4m 18.50s. a 16.50s (8 Ran).
                              (G A Hubbard), F Murphy

1102 Fireworks Novices' Chase (4-y-o and up) £2,976 2½m...............(3:40)

MR WOODCOCK 8-11-5 P Niven, *jmpd wl, trkd ldr, led 7th, hdd briefly 3 out, lft clr nxt, styd on well*.
.................................(15 to 8 op 2 to 1) 1
729 BUSTINELLO (Ire) 5-11-2 (7*) P Murphy, *hld up, wnt 3rd 8th, went second appr 3 out, led three out, blun and hdd nxt, not reco'r*......(4 to 1 op 7 to 2 tchd 9 to 2) 2
593⁴ STAPLEFORD LADY 5-10-5 (7*) A Flannigan, *trkd ldg pair, wnt second 8th, ev ch 6 out, rdn and wknd aftr 4 out, lft moderate 3rd last*....................(33 to 1) 3
ON CUE 6-11-5 W Worthington, *mstk 7th, lost pl aftr 8th, sn beh, lft poor 4th 3 out*.........(50 to 1 op 33 to 1) 4
550 CANTGETOUT 7-11-0 Mr A Pickering, *not fluent, sn last, tld off aftr 8th, lft poor 5th 3 out*..(20 to 1 op 14 to 1) 5
909* BANK VIEW 8-11-11 L Wyer, *hld up, rdn and hdwy 6 out, 3rd and ev ch whn f 3 out*.
.................................(6 to 5 fav op 5 to 4) f
763 CAIRNEYMOUNT 7-11-5 R Dunwoody, *led till hdd 7th, jmpd slwly tenth, sn beh, no ch whn blun badly 3 out, pld up*.................................(20 to 1) pu
Dist: 15l, 10l, 15l, 12l. 5m 11.70s. a 19.70s (7 Ran).
                              (P A Tylor), Mrs M Reveley

1103 Grunwick Stakes National Hunt Flat Race (4,5,6-y-o) £1,702 1m 5f 110yds
.................................(4:10)

STRONG FLAME (Ire) 4-10-9 (5*) S Lyons, *led aftr 2 fs, drw clr o'r two furlongs out, styd on wl*.
.................................(5 to 1 op 9 to 2 tchd 11 to 2) 1
BARNEY'S GIFT (Ire) 5-10-7 (7*) R Moore, *hld up, hdwy aftr 6 fs, rdn and styd on to take second plcd ins last, not trble any*.................(16 to 1 op 12 to 1) 2
815⁴ ROSEBERRY TOPPING 4-10-9 (5*) M W Buckley, *hld up and beh, hdwy o'r 6 fs out, wnt second ins fnl 2 furlongs, wknd final furlong*......(7 to 4 fav tchd 5 to 2) 3
SWORDKING (Ire) 4-11-0 Mr I McLelland, *hld up and beh, hdwy o'r 3 fs out, styd on ins last*.
.................................(10 to 1 tchd 12 to 1) 4
976³ PHILDAN (Ire) 4-10-11 (3*) D J Moffatt, *hld up, hdwy aftr hfuvy, 4th strt, wknd ins fnl 2 fs*.
.................................(10 to 1 op 8 to 1) 5
GARLAND OF GOLD 4-10-7 (7*) J Supple, *chsd ldrs aftr one m, no imprsn o'r 3 fs out*......(16 to 1 op 14 to 1) 6
HOLD YOUR HAT ON 4-11-0 (7*) S Taylor, *trkd ldg pair, second strt, sn rdn and wknd 2 fs out*.
.................................(4 to 1 op 5 to 2) 7
976 LUCKY WEDSONG (v) 4-10-9 (5*) R Farrant, *prmnt aftr 5 fs, 3rd strt, wknd ins fnl 2 furlongs*..(25 to 1 op 16 to 1) 8
723⁷ RELENTED 4-10-6 (3*) W Marston, *hld up, trkd ldrs aftr 6 fs, wknd o'r 4 furlongs out*.
.................................(8 to 1 op 7 to 1 tchd 9 to 1) 9

145

FINAL DILEMMA 4-10-9 (5*) J McCarthy, *led for 2 fs, chsd*
ldr, wknd 3 furlongs out.......... (16 to 1 op 12 to 1) 10
DYNAMITE DAN (Ire) 5-10-9 (5*) W Dwan, *beh aftr 2 fs, nvr*
rch ldrs............................ (10 to 1 op 7 to 1) 11
Dist: 5l, 3½l, 3½l, hd, ½l, 5l, 5l, 1½l, 6l, 1½l. 3m 21.10s. (11 Ran).
(Trevor Hemmings), M D Hammond

CHEPSTOW (good)
Saturday November 6th
Going Correction: PLUS 0.50 sec. per fur.

1104
Carling Black Label Hurdle Handicap (4-y-o) £3,542 2m 110yds....... (1:05)

569 ATHAR (Ire) [108] 10-0 L Harvey, *lft second second, quick-*
ened to led sn aftr 2 out, hit last, ran on.
.................................(7 to 1 op 5 to 1) 1
SCRUTINEER (USA) [125] 11-3 A Maguire, *set slow pace,*
rdn 2 out, sn hdd, hit last, one pace. (7 to 2 op 5 to 1) 2
827⁴ CULTURED [132] 11-10 M Dwyer, *rstrained in rear, slight*
mstk 3rd, ev ch whn hit 2 out, one pace.......(7 to 4 jt-
fav op 5 to 4) 3
841³ WHEELER'S WONDER (Ire) [108] 9-9² (7*) Mr J L Llewellyn,
pld hrd, trkd ldr till hit and uns rdr second. (7 to 4 jt-
fav) ur
Dist: 1½l, 2½l. 4m 12.80s. a 26.80s (4 Ran).
(J W Buxton), J A Baker

1105
Swalec Chase Handicap (4-y-o and up) £6,987 2m 110yds......... (1:35)

931² DR ROCKET [115] 8-9-11 (3*) D Meredith, *hld up in rear, gd*
hdwy 4 out, led 2 out, sn hdd, jmpd into ld ag'n last,
rdn out............................ (13 to 2 op 6 to 1 tchd 7 to 1) 1
919³ THE GREEN STUFF [115] 8-10-0 R Supple, *hld up, hdwy 5*
out, led sn aftr 2 out, not fluent and hdd last, one pace.
.... (11 to 2 op 7 to 1) 2
987² DRUMSTICK [126] 7-10-11 J Osborne, *jmpd rght, led till*
hdd 2 out, rdn and kpt on one pace.
.... (3 to 1 fav tchd 7 to 2) 3
897 FREELINE FINISHING [139] 9-11-10 R Dunwoody, *trkd ldrs,*
wnt second 5th, hit 7th, losing pl whn f 5 out.
.... (100 to 30 op 11 to 4) f
WHATEVER YOU LIKE [127] 8-10-12 G Bradley, *trkd ldr to*
5th, rdn and ev ch whn f 2 out.....(11 to 2 op 9 to 2) f
1009³ SETTER COUNTRY [125] 9-10-10 W Irvine, *wtd wth, hdwy*
to go second appr 5 out, dsptd ld nxt, fdg whn mstk and
brght dwn 2 out.................... (7 to 2 op 3 to 1) bd
Dist: 3½l, 3l. 4m 12.60s. a 13.60s (6 Ran).
SR: 19/15/23/
(The Rocketeers), R Dickin

1106
Tote Silver Trophy H'cap Hurdle (4-y-o and up) £16,633 2½m 110yds....(2:05)

TRIPLE WITCHING [124] 7-10-10 A Maguire, *al travelling*
wl beh ldrs, steady hdwy 7th, moved clr to ld sn aftr 3
out, pushed out, cmftbly.
..........(17 to 2 op 11 to 2 tchd 9 to 1 and 10 to 1) 1
AVRO ANSON [134] 5-11-6 D Byrne, *nvr far away, led*
appr 3 out, hdd sn aftr, rdn, no imprsn.
.........................(6 to 1 fav op 7 to 1 tchd 8 to 1) 2
1005* TAROUDANT [123] 6-10-9 (3ex) P Niven, *mid-div, gd hdwy*
appr 4 out, rdn and ev ch whn hit 2 out, one pace aftr.
.... (8 to 1 tchd 9 to 1) 3
827* LAND AFAR [135] 6-11-4 (3*,5ex) W Marston, *al prmnt, rdn*
and ev ch 2 out, wknd appr last. (10 to 1 tchd 12 to 1) 4
MAAMUR (USA) [133] 5-11-5 R Dunwoody, *wtd wth in tch,*
hdwy frm 5th, one pace from 2 out.
.....................(12 to 1 tchd 14 to 1 and 16 to 1) 5
FAIRFIELDS CONE [114] 10-9-11 (3*) D Meredith, *hld up,*
steady hdwy appr 4 out, one pace frm nxt.....(50 to 1) 6
873³ WILLIE SPARKLE [117] 7-10-0² (5*) P Williams, *in tch till*
wknd 3 out............................ (33 to 1) 7
762⁵ FOTOEXPRESS [116] 5-9-11 (5*) C Burnett-Wells, *hld up,*
hdwy 6th, ev ch 4 out, one pace nxt.
.... (50 to 1 op 40 to 1) 8
240³ WELSHMAN [129] 7-11-1 D Gallagher, *prmnt, led 4 out, sn*
hdd, wknd aftr nxt.......................(16 to 1) 9
ANDREW'S FIRST [127] 6-10-13 S Earle, *hld up in rear,*
hdwy appr 4 out, outpcd frm nxt...........(20 to 1) 10
900³ GIVENTIME [138] 5-11-10 L Harvey, *in rear, hdwy appr 4*
out, wknd nxt.....................(14 to 1 op 12 to 1) 11
348* FAIRWAYS ON TARGET [125] 7-10-11 R Hodge, *not fluent,*
prmnt till wknd 4 out.............(16 to 1 op 14 to 1) 12
NIJMEGEN [120] 5-10-6 M Dwyer, *al beh.*
.... (20 to 1 op 16 to 1) 13
JOPANINI [118] 8-11-8 G Bradley, *led to 8th, led ag'n 6th,*
wknd and hdd four out.............(33 to 1 op 25 to 1) 14
894* HIGH BARON [139] 6-11-11 (3ex) M Hourigan, *al beh, hld*
off frm 4 out.......(7 to 1 tchd 15 to 2 and 8 to 1) 15
1005⁴ ABBOT OF FURNESS [136] 9-11-8 M Moloney, *prmnt till*
wknd 4 out, tld off..............(33 to 1 op 25 to 1) 16
898⁴ ZAMIRAH (Ire) [127] 4-10-13 C Llewellyn, *led 4th to 6th,*
wknd quickly appr four out, tld off.
..................(33 to 1 op 40 to 1 tchd 16 to 1) 17
1005⁷ ANDERMATT [119] 6-10-5 B Powell, *al beh, tld off.*
.................................(33 to 1) 18

SAYFAR'S LAD [133] 9-11-5 M Perrett, *hld up in rear, pld*
up appr 3 out..........................(66 to 1) pu
Dist: 3l, 5l, nk, ½l, 2l, 10l, 5l, nk, nk, sht-hd. 4m 53.30s. a 12.30s (19 Ran).
SR: 62/69/53/64/61/40/33/27/39/
(Mrs Shirley Robins), D Nicholson

1107
November Novices' Chase (5-y-o and up) £2,672 3m.................(2:35)

GRANVILLE GUEST 7-11-2 G Bradley, *jmpd wl, led second*
to 7th, led tenth, styd on frm 3 out.............(9 to 2) 1
957² JUDGES FANCY 9-11-2 C Llewellyn, *hld up, gd hdwy to go*
second 5 out, sprawled on landing nxt, reco'red and
ran on whn mstk 2 out, rdr lost iron, no imprsn.
...........................(4 to 1 jt-fav op 3 to 1) 2
EBONY GALE 7-11-2 B Powell, *wtd wth, mstk 7th, hdwy*
appr 5 out, wknd approaching 3 out.........(4 to 1 jt-
fav op 3 to 1) 3
PROVING 9-11-2 E Murphy, *al beh, tld off frm 13th.*
.... (25 to 1 op 20 to 1) 4
957 NEVER EVER 8-10-9 (7*) Mr G Lewis, *4th whn f 3rd.*
....(50 to 1) f
763³ THE GOLFING CURATE 8-11-2 H Davies, *led to second, 3rd*
whn f 6th..........................(5 to 1 op 9 to 2) f
MARTELL BOY (NZ) 6-11-2 J Frost, *4th whn f 6th.*
...........................(11 to 2 op 5 to 1) f
933⁵ SHARP ANSWER 6-11-2 L Lawrence, *beh whn hmpd and*
uns rdr 3rd.......................(16 to 1 op 14 to 1) ur
847 NEVER OR NOT 7-11-2 L Harvey, *hld up in rear, badly*
hmpd 3rd, tld off whn pld up bef 12th.
...........................(11 to 2 op 5 to 1 tchd 6 to 1) pu
GENERAL BRANDY 7-10-11 (5*) P Hide, *prmnt, led 7th to*
tenth, jmpd slwly 13th, wkng whn mstk 4 out, blun nxt,
pld up bef last........................(25 to 1 op 20 to 1) pu
774⁶ KEMMY DARLING 6-10-5¹ (7*) D Matthews, *al beh, tld off*
whn pld up bef 11th.......................(50 to 1) pu
Dist: 4l, 30l. dist. 6m 20.00s. a 30.00s (11 Ran).
(Paul K Barber), P F Nicholls

1108
Stayers Novices' Hurdle (4-y-o and up) £1,989 3m.................(3:05)

743* LE GINNO (Fr) 6-11-0 G Bradley, *al prmnt, trkd ldr aftr*
5th, led nxt, shaken up appr last, drvn out.
...........................(5 to 4 fav op 5 to 4) 1
869⁴ ARCTIC COURSE (Ire) 5-11-0 A Maguire, *hld up in tch, gd*
hdwy to go second 4 out, outpcd, rallied appr last, ran
on strly r-in..........(11 to 4 op 3 to 1 tchd 7 to 2) 2
883⁶ VERY LITTLE (Ire) 5-10-2 (7*) Mr P Henley, *hld up, hdwy*
7th, rdn appr 4 out, wknd nxt......(25 to 1 op 16 to 1) 3
MAD THYME 6-11-0 M Perrett, *hld up, steady hdwy aftr*
mstk 5th, wknd appr 2 out.
..........................(5 to 1 op 3 to 1 tchd 6 to 1) 4
BUCKSHOT (Ire) 5-10-9 (5*) P Hide, *chsd ldrs till wknd 4*
out..............................(50 to 1 op 33 to 1) 5
883⁴ FILM LIGHTING GIRL 7-10-2 (7*) P Ward, *prmnt, hit 4th,*
wknd appr 3 out.........................(25 to 1) 6
864⁶ CARRIGLAWN 8-11-0 E Murphy, *prmnt, wnt second*
briefly aftr 8th, rdn and wknd nxt, tld off.
...........................(40 to 1 op 33 to 1) 7
778 PARSON'S WAY 6-11-0 G Upton, *chsd ldrs till wknd appr*
4 out, tld off................(66 to 1 op 50 to 1) 8
BETTIVILLE 6-10-11 (3*) W Marston, *prmnt till wknd 8th,*
tld off...........................(33 to 1 op 25 to 1) 9
628⁵ SANDMOOR PRINCE 10-11-0 Dr P Pritchard, *prmnt till*
wknd 8th, pld up bef 4 out.......(66 to 1 op 50 to 1) pu
DEEP IN GREEK 7-11-0 R Dunwoody, *prmnt till wknd*
appr 4 out, pld up bef nxt...........(40 to 1 op 33 to 1) pu
616 SNOWSHILL SHAKER 4-10-13 C Llewellyn, *al beh, tld off*
frm 5th, pld up aftr 8th......................(20 to 1) pu
TRIMAGE (Ire) 5-11-0 B Powell, *chsd ldrs till wknd 8th, tld*
off whn pld up bef 3 out...........(33 to 1 op 20 to 1) pu
901 ROYAL GAIT (NZ) 5-10-9 (5*) R Davis, *mstk 1st, tld off whn*
pld up bef 3 out...........(20 to 1 op 16 to 1) pu
THE CARROT MAN 5-11-0 J Railton, *led to 6th, wknd*
quickly appr 4 out, pld up bef nxt.
...........................(16 to 1 tchd 20 to 1) pu
901 KING RUST 5-10-7 (7*) Mr J L Llewellyn, *beh, pld up bef*
mstk 7th..........................(33 to 1 op 25 to 1) pu
TYRO DOMANI 7-11-0 M Crosse, *sn tld off, pld up aftr*
8th..................................(50 to 1) pu
Dist: Nk, 30l, 1½l, 2l, ¾l, 10l, 20l, 12l. 6m 18.50s. a 40.50s (17 Ran).
(Irish World Partnership), C P E Brooks

1109
EBF 'National Hunt' Novices' Hurdle Qualifier (Div I) (4,5,6-y-o) £1,877 2m 110yds........................ (3:40)

HAWAIIAN YOUTH (Ire) 5-11-0 H Davies, *wtd wth, hdwy to*
track ldrs 4th, rdn to ld sn aftr 2 out, styd on and drvn
clr r-in.................(15 to 8 fav op 5 to 2 tchd 11 to 4) 1
753 SENIOR STEWARD 5-11-0 A Maguire, *al prmnt, led appr 4*
out, hdd sn aftr 2 out, ev ch till edgd lft and no extr
r-in...............(7 to 2 tchd 11 to 2 and 8 to 1) 2
PUNDAY CLUMP 4-11-0 C Llewellyn, *in rear, making*
hdwy whn hmpd 4 out, styd on frm 2 out, nvr nrr.
...........................(8 to 1 op 4 to 1) 3

MONKTON (Ire) 5-11-0 B Powell, *hld up in rear, making hdwy whn hmpd 4 out, styd on frm nxt, nvr dngrs.*
.................................(8 to 1 op 5 to 1) 4
RUSTIC FLIGHT 6-11-0 D Gallagher, *beh till hdwy appr 4 out, wknd nxt.*.................................(33 to 1) 5
LIBERTY JAMES 6-11-0 W McFarland, *slwly away, some late hdwy, nvr nr to chal.*....(50 to 1 op 33 to 1) 6
RIFFLE 6-11-0 E Murphy, *prmnt, ev ch 4 out, wknd aftr nxt.*.................................(9 to 1 op 5 to 1) 7
716⁹ JUNIPER LODGE 5-11-0 I Lawrence, *slwly away, al beh.*
.................................(25 to 1 op 8 to 1) 8
LAY IT OFF (Ire) 4-10-9 S Smith Eccles, *al beh.*
.................................(20 to 1 op 33 to 1) 9
988 MAGGOTS GREEN 6-10-2 (7") Mr G Lewis, *al beh, tld off frm 4 out.*.................(12 to 1 op 14 to 1) 10
SUPER SHARP (NZ) 5-11-0 Jacqui Oliver, *led till wknd aftr 4th, f nxt.*.................(10 to 1 op 5 to 1) f
REFERRAL FEE 6-11-0 S Earle, *prmnt, wknd whn blun and uns rdr 4 out.*...........(10 to 1 op 6 to 1) ur
SIXTH IN LINE (Ire) 5-10-7 (7") M Appleby, *pld hrd, dsptd ld appr second, wknd rpdly and pulled up bef 4 out.*
.................................(33 to 1) pu
Dist: 4l, 7l, 8l, 3½l, ½l, 2l, 3½l, 4l, 20l. 4m 11.60s. a 25.60s (13 Ran).
(G Redford), R Rowe

1110 EBF 'National Hunt' Novices' Hurdle Qualifier (Div II) (4,5,6-y-o) £1,877 2m 110yds...................... (4:10)

764² PRINCESS HOTPOT (Ire) 5-10-9 M Perrett, *nvr far away, smooth hdwy to ld aftr 3 out, rdn clr r-in.*
.................(100 to 30 op 4 to 1 tchd 3 to 1) 1
GOLDEN SPINNER 6-11-0 R Dunwoody, *trkd ldr, led 4 out, hdd nxt, rallied appr last, kpt on one pace r-in.*
.................................(7 to 4 fav op 11 to 8) 2
BOND JNR 4-11-0 G Bradley, *hld up, hdwy 4th, ev ch 3 out, swtchd lft aftr nxt, held whn mstk last.*
.................................(3 to 1 op 7 to 2) 3
GENERAL WOLFE 4-11-0 C Llewellyn, *chsd ldrs, no hdwy frm 2 out.*.....................(10 to 1 op 8 to 1) 4
753⁵ GLENFINN PRINCESS 5-10-9 D Bridgwater, *beh till hdwy 4 out, wknd approaching 2 out.*
.................(10 to 1 op 12 to 1 tchd 14 to 1) 5
901 FERAL BAY (Ire) 4-11-0 J Railton, *led to 4 out, led ag'n briefly nxt, wknd quickly.*......(12 to 1 op 10 to 1) 6
772⁶ DUNNICKS VIEW 4-11-0 C Maude, *prmnt till wknd appr 4 out.*.................................(50 to 1) 7
NOBLE AUK (NZ) 5-10-9 (5") R Davis, *al beh, tld off frm 4 out.*.................(33 to 1 op 16 to 1) 8
COUNTRY FLING 5-10-9 R Supple, *al beh, tld off frm 4 out.*.................................(25 to 1 op 14 to 1) 9
FILE VESTRY (Ire) 5-11-0 B Powell, *chsd ldrs till wknd quickly appr 4 out, tld off.*...(12 to 1 tchd 14 to 1) 10
952⁷ SKYE DUCK 4-10-9 L Harvey, *mstk 1st, al beh, tld off.*
.................................(33 to 1) 11
844 CAMPDEN AGAIN 6-10-6 (3") D Meredith, *al beh, tld off whn pld up bef 3 out.*.........(50 to 1 op 33 to 1) pu
TRADESMARK 5-10-9 M Hourigan, *beh whn jmpd lft second, sn tld off, pld up bef 4 out.*...(50 to 1 op 33 to 1) pu
Dist: 4l, ½l, 6l, 4l, 4l, 15l, 4l, 3½l, 6l, 10l. 4m 5.00s. a 24.50s (13 Ran).
(Mrs Shirley Brasher), Miss H C Knight

LEOPARDSTOWN (IRE) (good to yielding)
Saturday November 6th

1111 Howth Juvenile Hurdle (3-y-o) £4,140 2m...................... (1:15)

706¹ LUSTRINO (USA) (bl) 10-8 (5") Mr J A Nash, ...(5 to 1) 1
968⁷ TEMPLEMARY BOY (Ire) 11-2 T Horgan, ...(5 to 2 jt-fav) 2
290² CALL MY GUEST (Ire) 10-9 J Shortt, ...(9 to 1) 3
391¹ ASSERT STAR 11-2 C F Swan, ...(5 to 2 jt-fav) 4
968⁴ BIZANA (Ire) 11-2 P Carberry, ...(5 to 1) 5
968⁵ PRINTOUT (Ire) 10-4 H Rogers, ...(12 to 1) 6
MYSTICAL CITY 10-4 K F O'Brien, ...(33 to 1) 7
LOUGHMOGUE (Ire) 10-4 F J Flood, ...(9 to 2) 8
NO POSSIBLE DOUBT (Ire) 10-4 F Woods, ...(50 to 1) 9
BENE MERENTI (Ire) 10-9 C O'Dwyer, ...(12 to 1) 10
Dist: 1l, 2½l, ½l, 4l. 3m 49.50s. a 1.50s (10 Ran).
SR: 30/32/28/24/-/ (Mrs Michael Watt), D K Weld

1112 Commology Chase (4-y-o and up) £4,140 2¾m................. (2:45)

707¹ WILL PHONE 7-10-12 (5") Mr D Valentine, ...(7 to 2) 1
856² BORN DEEP 7-11-8 T Horgan, ...(5 to 1) 2
799¹ BELVEDERIAN 6-11-8 C F Swan, ...(5 to 4 on) 3
965³ NORTHERN HIDE 7-11-11 T J Taaffe, ...(7 to 1) 4
879⁴ THE HEARTY CARD (Ire) 5-11-1 D H O'Connor, ...(20 to 1) 5
929⁷ CARRIGEEN KERRIA (Ire) 5-10-10 Mr P J Healy, ...(33 to 1) 6
Dist: 3½l, 11l, 2½l, 6l. 5m 43.80s. a 13.80s (6 Ran).
(Miss G Maher), M J P O'Brien

1113 Kilbarrack I.N.H. Flat Race (4-y-o and up) £3,105 2m................. (4:15)

CHATEAU ROUX 5-12-0 Mr J A Berry, ...(100 to 30) 1
571² THE DASHER DOYLE (Ire) 5-12-0 Mr P J Healy, ...(5 to 1) 2
993⁵ POLLYKENDU (Ire) 5-11-11 (3") Mr D Marnane, ...(8 to 1) 3
1016⁷ CONQUINN (Ire) 4-11-9 Mr P F Graffin, ...(8 to 1) 4
TRICKLE LAD (Ire) 4-11-9 Mr A P O'Brien, ...(5 to 1) 5
923⁴ TAITS CLOCK (Ire) 4-11-9 (5") Mr G J Harford, ...(4 to 1) 6
FORTY ONE (Ire) 5-11-6 (3") Mr D Valentine, ...(3 to 1 fav) 7
945⁷ DOWN THE BACK 6-11-9 Mr J P Dempsey, ...(16 to 1) 8
DEAR BUCK 7-11-9 (5") Mr J A Nash, ...(7 to 1) 9
BIGCANYON (Ire) 5-11-13⁶ (7") Mr J F Brennan, ...(50 to 1) 10
Dist: 3l, 3l, sht-hd, 4l. 3m 45.20s. (10 Ran).
(P M Berry), P M Berry

NEWCASTLE (good)
Saturday November 6th
Going Correction: MINUS 0.05 sec. per fur.

1114 Robin Conditional Jockeys' Novices' Hurdle (4-y-o and up) £1,917 2m 110yds...................... (1:20)

821² RELUCTANT SUITOR 4-11-0 D Bentley, *made all, quickened appr hfwy, clr last 2, drvn out.*
.................................(6 to 5 on op 5 to 4) 1
ABBEYLANDS (Ire) 5-10-11 (3") J Lonergan, *patiently rdn, improved gng wl appr 3 out, kpt on frm last, prmsg.*
.................................(12 to 1 op 6 to 1) 2
910⁶ ASTRALEON (Ire) 5-10-7 (7") S Melrose, *utd wth, steady hdwy, ev ch betw last 2, one pace.*
.................(11 to 1 op 7 to 1 tchd 12 to 1) 3
524⁶ DANCING DOVE (Ire) 5-10-11 (3") B Harding, *tucked away in midfield, effrt aftr 4 out, not quicken last 2.*
.................(9 to 1 op 7 to 1 tchd 10 to 1) 4
821 FLASH OF REALM (Fr) 7-11-0 D J Moffatt, *nvr far away, wnt second appr 3 out, btn betw last 2.*
.................................(33 to 1 tchd 100 to 1) 5
821⁶ BELIEVE IT 4-11-0 P Waggott, *settled midfield, struggling to hold pl 4 out, sn btn.*...........(33 to 1 op 20 to 1) 6
1003⁷ BALISTEROS (Fr) 4-10-11 (3") W Fry, *wl plcd to 3rd, lost grnd and hit nxt, sn tld off.*......(20 to 1 op 16 to 1) 7
915³ JALMUSIQUE 7-11-0 A Larnach, *settled gng wl, ev ch aftr 4 out, wknd quickly nxt, broke blood vessel.*
.................................(3 to 1 op 9 to 4) 8
BIT OF LIGHT 6-11-0 J Burke, *trkd ldrs, struggling to keep up aftr 4 out, tld off.*...(100 to 1 op 33 to 1) 9
976 SKIDDAW CALYPSO 4-10-9 A Dobbin, *not fluent, struggling to keep up 4 out, tld off whn blun and uns rdr 2 out.*....(66 to 1 op 33 to 1 tchd 100 to 1) ur
Dist: 3½l, 7l, 5l, 2l, 10l, 3l, dist, dist. 4m 7.90s. a 14.90s (10 Ran).
(Joe Buzzeo), M D Hammond

1115 Top Of The North Novices' Chase (5-y-o and up) £2,900 3m......... (1:45)

974⁹ ROAD BY THE RIVER (Ire) 5-10-12 C Grant, *nvr far away, drw level 6 out, led 2 out, styd on strly to go clr last.*
.................................(7 to 4 op 2 to 1) 1
LADY'S ISLAND (Ire) 5-10-7 B Storey, *settled gng wl, led 5th, hit 11th and 4 out, hdd 2 out, one pace.*
.................................(6 to 4 fav op 11 to 10) 2
786³ EBORNEEZER'S DREAM (v) 10-11-0 D Telfer, *led till hdd 5th, mstks and lost tch fnl circuit, tld off last 4.*
.................................(11 to 4 op 9 to 4) 3
Dist: 20l, 10l. 6m 17.20s. a 27.20s (3 Ran).
(T P M McDonagh Ltd), P Cheesbrough

1116 Ekbalco Hurdle Limited Handicap (4-y-o and up) £7,050 2m 110yds...(2:15)

873¹ BATABANOO [137] 4-10-7 B Storey, *settled gng wl, quickened up to nose ahead appr last, sprinted clr.*
.................................(11 to 4 op 9 to 4) 1
827³ SATIN LOVER [137] 5-10-7 G McCourt, *patiently rdn, smooth hdwy to chal betw last 2, one pace r-in.*
.................(5 to 4 fav op 13 to 8 tchd 7 to 4) 2
873² BEAUCADEAU [137] 4-10-7 A Dobbin, *set str pace, hdd and rdn appr last, one pace.*
.................(9 to 1 op 10 to 1 tchd 11 to 1 and 7 to 1) 3
BEAUCHAMP GRACE [138] 4-10-3 (5") J Burke, *nvr far away, effrt and drvn alng aftr 3 out, outpcd betw last 2.*.................................(14 to 1 op 12 to 1) 4
1064¹ SEON [137] 7-10-4 (3") N Bentley, *trkd ldrs, effrt 4 out, feeling pace aftr nxt, no extr.*......(50 to 1 op 33 to 1) 5
JINXY JACK [154] 9-11-10 N Doughty, *trkd ldr, drvn alng and lost grnd appr 2 out, better for race.*
.................................(13 to 2 op 9 to 2) 6
726 PEANUTS PET [137] 8-10-7 R Garritty, *trkd ldrs, struggling to hold pl bef 3 out, fdd.*......(33 to 1 op 25 to 1) 7
898⁶ DOMINANT SERENADE [137] 4-10-7 C Grant, *struggling to keep up 3rd, lost tch frm hfwy.*......(14 to 1 op 12 to 1) 8
Dist: 8l, nk, 7l, 3l, 4l, nk, 7l. 3m 53.50s. a 0.50s (8 Ran).
SR: 66/58/57/51/47/60/42/35/ (P D Savill), Mrs M Reveley

1117 Swift Novices' Chase (5-y-o and up) £2,884 2m 110yds.............. (2:45)

1002 COULTON 6-11-6 L Wyer, *jmpd wl, made all, gd leap to go clr last, smoothly*............(5 to 1 on op 4 to 1 on) 1
FULL O'PRAISE (NZ) 6-11-0 T Reed, *pld very hrd, trkd wnr thrght, ev ch 3 out, outpcd r-in.*(4 to 1 op 3 to 1) 2
821 SUPER SANDY 6-10-9 B Storey, *trkd ldg pair till f 4th.* ....(33 to 1 op 20 to 1) f
Dist: 3½l. 4m 19.00s. a 18.00s (3 Ran).

(G E Shouler), M W Easterby

1118 Peaty Sandy Handicap Chase (5-y-o and up) £2,742 3¾m............(3:15)

MISTER ED [133] 10-11-10 D Morris, *settled gng wl, pushed up to chal whn lft in ld 4 out, stumbled bend bef nxt, styd on strly frm 2 out.*........(10 to 4 op 2 to 1) 1
SHOON WIND [129] 10-11-6 C Grant, *not fluent, nvr far away, rdn alng fnl circuit, rallied last 3, kpt on.* ....(7 to 4 fav op 2 to 1 tchd 9 to 4) 2
975² FOSBURY [109] 8-10-0 J Callaghan, *jmpd big and bold, tried to make all, blun and almost f 4 out, rdr lost irons, rallied.*................(11 to 4 op 5 to 2 tchd 3 to 1) 3
975³ GATHERING TIME [116] 7-10-7⁷ G McCourt, *not fluent, ran in snatches, struggling whn nrly f 4 out, sn lost tch.*....................(9 to 1 op 10 to 1 tchd 8 to 1) 4
FORTH AND TAY [109] 11-10-0 A Orkney, *pressed ldrs, struggling to hold pl fnl circuit, lost tch frm 4 out.* ....(9 to 1 op 8 to 1 tchd 10 to 1) 5
Dist: 1½l, 5l, 7l, 10l. 7m 56.80s. a 31.80s (5 Ran).

(The Talking Horse Partnership), R Curtis

1119 Jackdaw Handicap Hurdle (0-135 4-y-o and up) £2,950 3m............(3:45)

1030 COUNTORUS [101] 7-10-8 G McCourt, *al gng wl, quickened to ld 2 out, clr last, styd on well.* ....(5 to 4 fav op 6 to 4) 1
POLISHING [117] 6-11-5 (5*) S Lyons, *wl plcd till outpcd and lost grnd hfwy, rallied frm 2 out, fnshd fst.* ....(33 to 1 op 20 to 1) 2
985* MYSTIC MEMORY [103] 4-10-10 L Wyer, *patiently in, nrly f 7th, reco'red to join issue 3 out, ridden and one pace frm last.*....................(4 to 1 op 3 to 1) 3
654⁴ CHARLOTTE'S EMMA [105] 6-10-12 B Storey, *nvr far away, feeling pace and rdn appr 3 out, kpt on same pace.*........................(8 to 1 op 10 to 1) 4
819 HARDIHERO [93] 7-9-10¹ (5*) P Waggott, *al hndy, drvn alng whn pace quickened 3 out, no extr.* ....(33 to 1 op 20 to 1) 5
HELIOPSIS [115] 5-11-8 C Grant, *nvr far away, drvn alng whn pace quickened 3 out, btn nxt.* (9 to 1 op 7 to 1) 6
1005³ NORTHUMBRIAN KING [111] 7-11-4 J Callaghan, *trkd ldrs, hrd at work aftr 3 out, fdd.* ....(11 to 1 op 12 to 1 tchd 14 to 1) 7
822 EASTERN OASIS [114] 10-11-4 (3*) A Dobbin, *made most till hdd 2 out, fdd betw last two.* ....(10 to 1 op 7 to 1 tchd 12 to 1) 8
750² RIDWAN [103] 6-10-10⁴ A S Smith, *trkd ldg bunch, struggling to keep up appr 3 out, fdd....*(7 to 1 tchd 6 to 1) 9
Dist: 3½l, 4l, 1½l, ½l, 2l, 2l, 5l, 8l. 5m 53.20s. a 11.20s (9 Ran).

(D Gill), J H Johnson

SANDOWN (good to firm)
Saturday November 6th
Going Correction: PLUS 0.30 sec. per fur. (races 1,3,-6,7), MINUS 0.10 (2,4,5)

1120 November Conditional Jockeys' Handicap Hurdle (0-135 4-y-o and up) £3,295 2¾m..................(12:45)

632 NORTHERN VILLAGE [115] 6-11-0 A Dicken, *trkd ldrs, wnt 3rd 6th, mstk nxt, pushed alng 4 out, sstnd run to ld nr finish, all out.*....................(5 to 1 tchd 13 to 2) 1
1006* DE BA LAINE (Fr) [129] 7-12-0 J MacCarthy, *led, rdn 2 out, ct nr finish.*..............(100 to 30 fav op 9 to 4) 2
895² EMERALD SUNSET [109] 8-10-8 A Procter, *mstks, hld up in last pl, hdwy to chase ldrs aftr 4 out, kpt on one pace betw last 2.*........................(7 to 2 op 3 to 1) 3
1004⁶ DERRING VALLEY [106] (bl) 8-10-5 R Farrant, *hld up, cl up aftr 5th, hrd rdn 3 out, no imprsn frm nxt.* ....(12 to 1 op 10 to 1) 4
750⁴ STAR QUEST [103] 6-9-13 (3*) D Fortt, *trkd ldg pair, wnt second 6th, pushed alng 4 out, no imprsn betw last 2.* ....(5 to 1 tchd 11 to 2) 5
762⁶ MAJOR INQUIRY (USA) [120] 7-10-12 (7*) J J Brown, *trkd ldr, wnt 3rd 5th, drpd rear 4 out, tld off appr 2 out.* ....(14 to 1 op 10 to 1) 6
ROYAL PIPER (NZ) [110] 6-10-9 R Greene, *hld up, mstk 3rd, hdwy and gng wl 5 out, wnt second nxt, slightly hmpd whn wkng 3 out, tld off.* ....(7 to 2 op 5 to 1 tchd 11 to 2) 7
Dist: Hd, 10l, 2½l, hd, 30l, 5l. 5m 17.20s. a 11.20s (7 Ran).
SR: 40/54/24/18/15/2/-/ (Visual Identity Ltd-Design Studio), S Dow

1121 Gunpowder Plot Handicap Chase (5-y-o and up) £5,187 3m 110yds...(1:15)

886⁴ FAR SENIOR [135] 7-11-10 Mr M Armytage, *led 8th to nxt, trkd ldr, led 6 out, clr last, styd on wl.* ....(15 to 8 op 6 to 4 tchd 7 to 4) 1
935² NEVADA GOLD [122] 7-11-10 Richard Guest, *hld up, trkd ldrs frm 13th, ev ch 3 out, not quicken appr last.* .....(6 to 5 fav op 5 to 4 tchd 11 to 8 and 11 to 10) 2
884⁵ SIRRAH JAY [112] 13-9-10 (5*) T Jenks, *led 9th till 6 out, ev ch 2 out, wknd appr last.* ....(10 to 1 op 6 to 1 tchd 11 to 1) 3
921³ ROSCOE HARVEY [113] (bl) 11-10-2² M A FitzGerald, *led, mstk 6th, hdd nxt, mistake 13th, sn wknd, last whn pld up aftr 7 out.*............(5 to 1 op 6 to 1) pu
Dist: 6l, 3l. 6m 15.20s. a 16.20s (4 Ran).

(Mrs Harry J Duffey), K C Bailey

1122 Mars and Pedigree Handicap Hurdle (4-y-o and up) £4,084 2m 110yds (1:50)

STATAJACK (Ire) [112] 5-10-7 P Holley, *led to 5th, mstk 2 out, chlgd last, rdn to ld r-in.* ....(10 to 1 op 7 to 1 tchd 11 to 1) 1
900⁴ MARTHA'S SON [130] 6-11-8 (5*) R Farrant, *hld up, cld aftr 5th, ev ch 3 out, led nxt, hdd and not quicken r-in.* ....(9 to 2 tchd 5 to 1 and 4 to 1) 2
887⁷ EL VOLADOR [105] 6-10-0 M Richards, *hld up, cld on ldrs 3 out, ev ch whn mstk nxt, wknd appr last.* ....(5 to 4 fav op 6 to 4) 3
648² BO KNOWS BEST (Ire) [130] 4-11-11 M A FitzGerald, *hld up, hdwy and ev ch 3 out, sn pushed alng, no imprsn frm nxt.*................(13 to 2 op 4 to 1 tchd 7 to 1) 4
841² ALBEMINE (USA) [115] 4-10-10 T Kent, *hit second, led 5th to 2 out, wknd.*............(3 to 1 tchd 7 to 2) 5
JIMMY THE GILLIE [113] 7-11-9 (5*) D Leahy, *trkd ldg pair till wknd quickly aftr 3 out.*........(20 to 1 op 12 to 1) 6
Dist: 1½l, 7l, 2l, 20l, ½l. 3m 57.50s. a 10.50s (6 Ran).
SR: 24/40/8/31/-/13/ (Mrs M E Slade), D R C Elsworth

1123 City Link Handicap Chase (5-y-o and up) £4,893 2½m 110yds.......(2:25)

919⁴ ARDBRIN [128] 10-11-0 D Murphy, *made all, styd on wl frm 2 out.*................(2 to 1 op 7 to 4 tchd 9 to 4) 1
897⁴ CALAPAEZ [137] 9-11-9 M Richards, *trkd ldr, pckd 6 out, rdn 4 out, rallied and pecked 3 out, lft second nxt, no imprsn on wnr.*.....(11 to 8 fav op 5 to 4 tchd 6 to 4) 2
FLASHTHECASH [138] 7-11-10 Richard Guest, *hld up in last pl, wnt second tenth, second and gng wl whn f 2 out.*........................(2 to 1 op 7 to 4 tchd 9 to 4) f
Dist: 6l. 5m 13.30s. a 13.80s (3 Ran).

(Mrs M L Stewart-Brown), T P Tate

1124 Bonfire Party Novices' Chase (5-y-o and up) £4,045 2m................(2:55)

ONE MORE DREAM 6-11-0 Richard Guest, *hld up, mstk 4th, cld on ldrs nxt, led aftr 7th, styd on wl frm 2 out.* ....(7 to 2 tchd 4 to 1) 1
FRENCH CHARMER 8-11-0 D Murphy, *trkd ldrs, ev ch 4 out, lft second nxt, rdn and styd on one pace.* ....(11 to 2 op 9 to 4 tchd 6 to 1) 2
603⁴ PARBOLD HILL 5-11-2 J Duggan, *led till hdd aftr 7th, wknd 4 out, lft poor 3rd 2 out.* ....(16 to 1 op 12 to 1 tchd 20 to 1) 3
916⁴ BUSTLING AROUND 6-10-9 M Bosley, *hld up, mstks, lost tch aftr 6th, tld off 5 out, lft poor 4th 2 out.* ....(50 to 1 op 25 to 1 tchd 66 to 1) 4
899* AMTRAK EXPRESS 6-11-7 M A FitzGerald, *trkd ldr, ev ch 5 out, mstk nxt, second and rdn whn f 2 out.* ....(2 to 1 on op 9 to 4 on tchd 7 to 4 on) f
981³ PRESENT TIMES 7-11-0 J Clarke, *not jump wl, lost tch aftr 6th, sn tld off, pld up bef 2 out.* ....(50 to 1 op 25 to 1 tchd 66 to 1) pu
Dist: 3½l, 30l, 25l. 3m 51.60s. a 3.10s (6 Ran).
SR: 39/35/7/ (Michael Jackson Bloodstock Ltd), G B Baldin

1125 Firework Night Juvenile Novices' Hurdle (3-y-o) £3,387 2m 110yds....(3:30)

830⁵ RICH LIFE (Ire) 11-0 Peter Hobbs, *hld up, hdwy aftr 5th, led 2 out, hdd last, rdn to ld ag'n nr finish, all out.* ....(7 to 2 op 4 to 1 tchd 3 to 1) 1
DOCTOOR (USA) 10-11 (3*) D O'Sullivan, *hld up, trkd ldr frm 5th, ev ch appr 2 out, led last, hdd nr finish.* ....(5 to 2 op 5 to 1 tchd 8 to 1) 2
STAY WITH ME BABY 10-9 P Holley, *led, jmpd lft second, clr whn jumped slwly 3rd, hdd 2 out, btn when mstk last.*....................(4 to 1 op 7 to 2 tchd 9 to 2) 3
MR BEAN 10-9 J Duggan, *hld up, trkd ldrs frm 4th. cl up aftr 3 out, rdn and one pace appr nxt.* ....(16 to 1 tchd 25 to 1) 4
870* MR GENEALOGY (USA) (bl) 11-7 D Murphy, *chsd ldr, rdn alng aftr 3 out, no imprsn appr nxt.* ....(2 to 1 fav op 6 to 4 tchd 9 to 4) 5

507⁷ IS SHE QUICK 10-9 N Dawe, *mid-div 4th, sn rdn alng, no hdwy appr 2 out*.................. (25 to 1 op 16 to 1) 6
LOCHORE 11-0 M A FitzGerald, *hdwy 3rd, wnt third 3 out, wknd appr nxt*............... (16 to 1 op 9 to 1) 7
830⁷ WONDERFUL YEARS (USA) 11-0 M Richards, *beh frm 3rd, lost tch aftr 5th*.................. (50 to 1 op 20 to 1) 8
BACKSTABBER 11-0 M Ahern, *lost tch aftr 4th, tld off whn pld up bef 2 out*............. (25 to 1 op 12 to 1) pu
959 KARIB (bl) 10-9 Leesa Long, *pld hrd, beh whn mstk 3rd, sn tld off, pulled up bef 2 out*......(66 to 1 op 33 to 1) pu
890 MY SET PEACE 10-9 Richard Guest, *rear 4th, losing tch whn mstk nxt, sn beh, tld off when pld up bef 2 out*.
.................................(66 to 1 op 33 to 1) pu
Dist: ½l, 12l, 3l, 7l, 8l, sht-hd, 1l. 3m 59.30s. a 12.30s (11 Ran).
SR: 13/12/-/-/-/-/ *(Mrs Susan Gay), C Weedon*

1126 EBF National Hunt Flat Race (4,5,6-y-o) £2,092 2m 110yds.........(4:05)

SPRINTFAYRE 5-11-0 Mr M Armytage, *led, rdn clr o'r 2 fs out, styd on wl fnl furlong*........ (14 to 1 op 10 to 1) 1
DUTCH MONARCH 6-10-9 (5*) A Dicken, *hld up, wl beh til rdn and styd on ins fnl 2 fs, kpt on to take second pl nr finish*....................................(25 to 1 op 14 to 1) 2
THE CAUMRUE (Ire) 5-10-7 (7*) N Collum, *hld up and beh, hdwy o'r 2 fs out, styd on wl ins fnl furlong.*
.................................(8 to 1 op 5 to 1) 3
CREAG DHUBH 4-10-7 (7*) T Dascombe, *hld up, hdwy hfwy, 6th strt, styd on ins fnl 2 fs*...(10 to 1 op 4 to 1) 4
901⁴ DEAR DO 6-10-7 (7*) Pat Thompson, *mid-div, rdn and styd on o'r 2 fs out, one pace fnl furlong.*
.................................(4 to 1 op 2 to 1) 5
ROMANY BLUES 4-10-2 (7*) Mr C Vigors, *beh, hdwy to track ldg grp aftr one m, one pace fnl 2 fs.*
.................................(20 to 1 op 12 to 1 tchd 25 to 1) 6
901 ASLAR (Ire) 4-10-9 (5*) B Murphy, *hld up and beh, styd on ins fnl 2 fs, nvr nrr*...............(33 to 1 op 16 to 1) 7
NO DEBT 5-10-4 (5*) J McCarthy, *chsd ldg grp frm hfwy, no hdwy 2 fs out*....................(33 to 1 op 16 to 1) 8
WORLDLY PROSPECT (USA) 5-10-4 (5*) R Farrant, *hld up, hdwy aftr one m, 7th strt, wknd ins fnl 2 fs.*
.................................(33 to 1 op 20 to 1) 9
KINDLE'S DELIGHT 5-11-0 Mr J M Pritchard, *trkd ldr, 5th strt, wknd quickly fnl 2 fs.*
.................................(6 to 1 op 4 to 1 tchd 13 to 2) 10
CAIPIRINHA (Ire) 5-10-4 (5*) T Jenks, *trkd ldr, second strt, wknd fnl 2 fs*....................(1 op 7 to 1 tchd 8 to 1) 11
LICENCE TO KILL (Fr) 4-10-9 (5*) S Curran, *trkd ldr, 4th strt, wknd fnl 2 fs*.................(9 to 2 op 16 to 1 tchd 25 to 1) 12
901 TREENS FOLLY 4-10-7 (7*) L Dace, *chsd ldr, 3rd strt, wknd quickly fnl 2 fs.*..............(33 to 1 op 20 to 1) 13
BARGIN BOY 4-10-9 (5*) A Procter, *hld up, hdwy to chase ldr aftr 5 fs, wknd o'r 3 furlongs out.*
.................................(33 to 1 op 16 to 1) 14
FIVEPERCENT 5-10-7 (7*) Mr G Hogan, *trkd ldr till wknd 4 fs out, tld off*....................(25 to 1 op 16 to 1) 15
CHILDSWAY 5-10-9 (5*) D Leahy, *hld up, hdwy o'r 6 fs out, ran very wide trng into strt, beh whn pld up ins fnl furlong*..........(5 to 2 fav op 4 to 1 tchd 5 to 1) pu
Dist: 4l, nk, 5l, 1l, sht-hd, 2l, sht-hd, ½l, 6l, 4l. 3m 58.00s. (16 Ran).
(Peter J Colman), R Simpson

CARLISLE (good to firm)
Monday November 8th
Going Correction: MINUS 0.25 sec. per fur.

1127 Edenhall Services Flat-v-Jump Jockeys Challenge Handicap Hurdle (0-115 5-y-o and up) £1,593 2m 1f
.................................(12:50)

1101³ EASBY MANDRINA [82] 6-10-13 N Doughty, *nvr far away, chlgd 2 out, led appr last, drvn out.*
.................................(7 to 2 op 3 to 1 tchd 4 to 1) 1
580² SUNSET REINS FREE [90] 8-11-0 (7*) J Carroll, *al hndy, led appr 2 out, hdd bef last, not quicken.*
.................................(4 to 1 tchd 9 to 2) 2
657⁶ COMSTOCK [93] 6-11-3 (7*) L Charnock, *hld up in tch, rdn 3 out, styd on same pace frm nxt*...(10 to 1 op 8 to 1) 3
972⁸ MAGIC BLOOM [90] 7-11-7 C Grant, *hld up, hdwy 3 out, ev ch nxt, one pace*..........(2 to 1 fav tchd 5 to 2) 4
418² ITS ALL OVER NOW [76] 9-10-7 M Dwyer, *trkd ldr, rdn 3 out, sn btn*...................(9 to 1 op 8 to 1) 5
912 LADY KHADIJA [69] 7-9-7 (7*) A Mackay, *rcd wide, led till hdd appr 3 out, wknd quickly*...(200 to 1 op 100 to 1) 6
824⁹ INVERTIEL [88] (bl) 9-10-12 (7*) J Fortune, *trkd ldrs, led appr 3 out, hdd sn aftr flight, wknd 2 out.*
.................................(9 to 2 op 3 to 1) 7
1084 ELISSA [69] 7-10-0 B Storey, *al struggling, tld off frm 3rd, pld up bef 2 out*..........(200 to 1 op 100 to 1) pu
Dist: 2l, ½l, nk, 20l, 7l, hd. 4m 16.60s. a 9.60s (8 Ran).
(A Williams), S E Kettlewell

1128 Greenalls Inns Novices' Chase (5-y-o and up) £2,976 2m.............(1:20)

819⁷ GLEMOT (Ire) 5-11-0 A Maguire, *in tch, trkd ldrs hfwy, dsptd ld 4 out, slight lead 2 out, pushed clr r-in.*
.................................(4 to 1 op 7 to 2) 1
998* SHREWD JOHN 7-11-7 R Garritty, *al prmnt, cld up 4 out, ev ch last, no extr r-in.*
.................................(13 to 8 fav op 2 to 1 tchd 6 to 4) 2
1002* KEEP SHARP 7-11-12 Richard Guest, *led, mstk 4th (water), hdd 2 out, kpt on one pace. (6 to 1 op 5 to 1) 3
873⁴ FLOWING RIVER (USA) 7-11-2 B Storey, *hld up rear, prog to join ldrs 4 out, dsptd ld 2 out, wknd appr last.*
.................................(3 to 1 op 5 to 4 tchd 100 to 30) 4
788³ WILD ATLANTIC 10-11-7 K Jones, *hld up beh ldr, dsptd ld 6th to 7th, ev ch till wknd 2 out*...(10 to 1 op 8 to 1) 5
TIMANFAYA 6-11-2 T Reed, *beh frm 5th.*
.................................(16 to 1 tchd 20 to 1) 6
Dist: 3l, 5l, 1½l, 5l, 15l. 4m 4.20s. a 5.20s (6 Ran).
(Kevin McCormick), J H Johnson

1129 T M S Maiden Hurdle (4-y-o and up) £2,072 2½m 110yds...........(1:50)

1028² ANOTHER NICK 7-10-9 (5*) P Williams, *hld up to hfwy, prog to dispute ld frm 7th, slight lead 2 out, shaken up and rdn out r-in.*
.................................(7 to 4 on op 2 to 1 on tchd 6 to 4 on) 1
915⁸ KINDA GROOVY 4-11-0 N Smith, *hld up beh ldrs, dsptd ld on ins 7th, cld on clast, kpt on r-in....* (8 to 1 op 7 to 1) 2
STRONG TRACE (Ire) 4-11-0 C Grant, *prmnt, dsptd ld 7th to 3 out, rdn appr nxt, sn wknd.* (12 to 1 tchd 14 to 1) 3
SKI LADY 5-10-9 B Storey, *in tch, cld up to track ldrs 7th, wknd 3 out.*....................(8 to 1 op 7 to 1) 4
916⁵ SCALP'EM (Ire) 5-11-0 A Maguire, *led or dsptd ld till 3 out, wknd appr nxt*...............(7 to 2) 5
TOLL BOOTH 4-10-2 (7*) J Supple, *in tch in rear till wknd appr 3 out, sddl slpd*............(250 to 1 op 100 to 1) 6
Dist: 1l, 15l, 4l, 20l, 5l. 5m 6.10s. a 13.10s (6 Ran).
(Mrs J M Davenport), J M Jefferson

1130 Lucius Challenge Cup Handicap Chase (0-130 5-y-o and up) £3,590 3¼m...........................(2:20)

1004⁵ ZAM BEE [107] 7-11-0 T Reed, *led or dsptd ld till clr advantage 4 out, pushed alng frm 2 out, kpt on und pres r-in.*.................................(9 to 2) 1
986* BUDDY HOLLY (NZ) [103] 8-10-10 Peter Hobbs, *made most till outpcd frm 4 out, prog from 2 out, rnwd effrt and ev ch r-in, no extr.* (11 to 8 fav tchd 6 to 4 and 5 to 4) 2
CAROUSEL CALYPSO [103] 7-10-10 C Grant, *trkd ldrs, cld up 6 out, kpt on one pace frm 3 out. (5 to 2 op 9 to 4) 3
975 BOREEN OWEN [117] 9-11-10 A Maguire, *trkd ldrs, cld up 13th, wknd 3 out, virtually pld up r-in.*
.................................(9 to 2 op 4 to 1) 4
Dist: ¾l, 3½l, dist. 6m 51.30s. a 21.30s (4 Ran).
(J N Anthony), W G Reed

1131 Bowness Novices' Hurdle (4-y-o and up) £1,810 3m 110yds.........(2:50)

1028³ DURHAM SUNSET 6-10-13 A Maguire, *trkd ldr, led appr 2 out, rdn aftr nxt, pushed out r-in.*
.................................(2 to 1 on op 5 to 2 on tchd 7 to 4 on) 1
875* SHAWWELL 6-11-4 B Storey, *trkd ldrs, cld up 3 out, dsptd ld nxt, sn rdn, kpt on one pace.*
.................................(7 to 4 op 3 to 1 tchd 4 to 1) 2
SELF IMPORTANT (USA) 8-10-12 C Grant, *trkd ldrs, effrt appr 3 out, sn btn*..................(200 to 1 op 100 to 1) 3
970⁶ JUBILATA (USA) 5-10-7 C Dennis, *led till appr 3 out, sn wknd*....................(20 to 1 op 16 to 1) 4
910⁷ BECK COTTAGE 5-10-12 P Niven, *hld up rear, in tch and prog whn f 8th*...............(6 to 1 op 7 to 1) f
DEEPLY ROYAL 6-10-7 K Johnson, *unruly in paddock, swrvd and uns rdr 1st*.............(66 to 1 op 50 to 1) ur
Dist: 2½l, 15l, 12l. 6m 4.30s. a 11.30s (6 Ran).
(W M G Black), J H Johnson

1132 T M S Handicap Chase (0-130 5-y-o and up) £3,172 2m.............(3:20)

946⁴ ISLAND JETSETTER [100] 7-11-9 Richard Guest, *jmpd wl, led, clr 3rd, pushed out r-in.*
.................................(12 to 1 op 8 to 1 tchd 14 to 1) 1
722² DOLIKOS [104] 6-11-13 M Dwyer, *in tch, prog 3 out, chsd ldr nxt, no imprsn r-in.*
.................................(9 to 2 op 4 to 1) 2
769² SONSIE MO [103] 8-11-7 (5*) P Williams, *trkd ldrs, pushed alng 8th, kpt on one pace 3 out.*
.................................(11 to 4 op 9 to 4 tchd 3 to 1) 3
735 BOARDING SCHOOL [103] 6-11-12 B Storey, *in tch, chsd ldr 4 out, no extr one pace.*............(7 to 2) 4
550³ CLEVER FOLLY [104] 13-11-13 N Doughty, *dsptd ld to 3rd, cld ldr aftr, wknd 8th, tld off 3 out*..(12 to 1) 5
913² PIMS GUNNER (Ire) [103] 5-11-12 C Grant, *al rear, rdn 8th, tld off r-in.*...................(5 to 1 op 4 to 1) 6
Dist: 7l, 3½l, 2½l, 10l, 6l. 4m 1.60s. a 2.60s (6 Ran).
SR: 29/26/21/18/9/2/ *(N Wilby), Mrs S J Smith*

1133 Cross Fell Stakes National Hunt Flat Race (4,5,6-y-o) £1,339 2m 1f. . . .(3:50)

KENMORE-SPEED 6-11-4 Mr C Mulhall, *prog to press ldr frm hfwy, led wl o'r 2 fs out, pushed clr appr fnl furlong, cmftbly*..................(20 to 1 op 33 to 1) 1
HEDLEY MILL 5-10-6 (7*) Mr A Parker, *led 3 fs, led ag'n 7 furlongs out till wl o'r 2 out, kpt on one pace.*
....(9 to 2 op 5 to 1) 2
SCRABBLE 4-10-4 (7*) R Wilkinson, *trkd ldrs, ev ch 3 fs out, rdn and wknd o'r 2 out.*........ (4 to 1 op 7 to 2) 3
BOLANEY GIRL (Ire) 4-10-4 (7*) Miss Sue Nichol, *rear, cl up hfwy, ev ch 3 fs out, kpt on one pace.*
....(16 to 1 tchd 20 to 1) 4
CUDDER OR SHUDDER (Ire) 4-10-8 (3*) D J Moffatt, *rear, cld up hfwy, rdn and wknd o'r 3 fs out.*........(7 to 1) 5
778[6] BIBBY BEAR 4-10-4 (7*) D Matthews, *in tch till wknd 4 fs out.*........................(3 to 1 fav tchd 7 to 2) 6
MR FLUORINE (Ire) 4-10-13 (3*) A Thornton, *cl up, led aftr 3 fs til 7 furlongs out, wknd quickly 5 out, tld off.*
....(4 to 1 op 7 to 1) 7
976 ROKER LAD (Ire) 4-10-9 (7*) J Supple, *steadied strt, track ldrs 6 fs, beh frm hfwy, tld off*....(16 to 1 op 12 to 1) 8
Dist: 6l, ½l, 7l, 4l, 20l. 4m 13.80s. (8 Ran).

(K M Dacker), Mrs S J Smith

COMPIEGNE (FR) (heavy)
Monday November 8th

1134 Prix de la Forte (Hurdle) (4-y-o) £5,974 2m 1f 110yds.................(1:00)

RAIDER (Fr) 10-1 L Gerard, ... 1
SARAG (Fr) 10-3 L Metais, ... 2
ROI DE MONTAIGU (Fr) 10-10 P Bigot, ... 3
776[2] ROC COLOR (Fr) 10-10 G Bradley, *in tch till one pace strt.* 4
Dist: 6l, 10l, 2½l, 8l. 4m 24.40s. (18 Ran).

1135 Prix du Carnois (Hurdle) (5-y-o and up) £5,376 2m 1f 110yds....... (2:00)

MAN TO MAN (NZ) 6-9-13 A Kondrat, *made all, unchlgd.*
....(4 to 1) 1
MICK DE CARMONT (Fr) 8-10-4 J Y Artu, ... 2
GLEAM REDERIE (Fr) 5-10-4 J Mercier, ... 3
936 MACEDONAS 5-10-6 G Bradley, *mid-div back strt, outpcd till run on straight.*........................ 5
Dist: 8l, 10l, 5l, 6l, 4l, 6l, hd, 1½l, 10l. 4m 20.20s. (13 Ran).

(S W Clarke), F Doumen

FONTWELL (firm)
Tuesday November 9th
Going Correction: PLUS 0.10 sec. per fur. (races 1,3,5), NIL (2,4,6)

1136 'Nickel Coin' Challenge Cup Novices' Chase (5-y-o and up) £2,082 3¼m 110yds......................... (1:10)

868[3] OCEAN LINK 9-11-6 S Earle, *made all, kicked on frm 16th, ran on wl from last.*
............(2 to 1 on op 7 to 4 on tchd 13 to 8 on) 1
899 CAPSIZE 7-11-0 B Powell, *not fluent early, trkd wnr frm 8th, ev ch r-in, no extr und pres*..... (4 to 1 op 5 to 2) 2
957[3] IVYCHURCH (USA) 7-11-0 J Frost, *in tch, cld and ev ch 3 out, one pace appr nxt.* (9 to 2 op 4 to 1 tchd 5 to 1) 3
962 LOWICK LAD 6-11-0 D Morris, *mstk last, cl up whn hit 6th and uns rdr*......................(50 to 1 op 25 to 1) ur
Dist: ¾l, 15l. 6m 51.20s. a 21.20s (4 Ran).

(N H S New), R H Alner

1137 Oving Novices' Selling Hurdle (4-y-o and up) £1,807 2¾m............(1:40)

553[3] SAKIL (Ire) 5-11-5 H Davies, *hld up in cl tch, quickened to ld appr last, sn hrd rdn, all out.*
..........................(7 to 4 on tchd 6 to 4 on) 1
859[3] BETALONGABILL (v) 4-10-12 R Dunwoody, *chsd ldr, led briefly aftr 7th, rdn appr 2 out, ran on wl und pres frm last, jst fld.*..........(11 to 4 op 3 to 1 tchd 9 to 2) 2
SAGART AROON (bl) 13-10-12 Peter Hobbs, *trkd ldrs, led 4 out till appr last, one pace.*
..........................(20 to 1 op 10 to 1 tchd 25 to 1) 3
964 FREDWILL 6-10-5 (7*) K Goble, *jmpd rght, rcd freely, led to 4 out, fourth and wkng whn f nxt.*
..........................(33 to 1 op 20 to 1 tchd 50 to 1) f
920[6] PATROCLUS 8-10-12 A Tory, *tld off 4th, pld up aftr 7th.*
..........................(33 to 1 op 20 to 1 tchd 50 to 1) pu
1040 LISSADELL LADY 4-10-7 D Morris, *not fluent, lost tch 5th, pld up aftr 4 out.*..................(66 to 1 op 25 to 1) pu
Dist: Hd, 7l. 5m 26.70s. a 17.70s (6 Ran).

(Mrs M Devine), S Dow

1138 Harry Duffey Challenge Trophy Handicap Chase (0-130 4-y-o and up) £3,460 2¼m......................... (2:10)

1105[3] DRUMSTICK [126] 7-12-0 J Railton, *hld up, cld aftr 4 out, jnd ldr 2 out, led last, drvn out.*...... (3 to 1 op 2 to 1) 1
964[4] ST ATHANS LAD [125] (bl) 8-11-13 D Morris, *strted slwly, led second, mstks 5th and 9th, jnd 2 out, hdd last, no extr, eased nr finish.*......... (13 to 8 fav tchd 7 to 4) 2
963* COURT RAPIER [98] 11-9-7 (7*) P Carey, *led to second, cl up, mstk 6th, one pace 3 out.*
..........................(4 to 1 op 5 to 1 tchd 7 to 2) 3
1044[2] KISU KALI [99] 6-10-1 M Richards, *trkd ldrs, pushed alng and outpcd aftr 4 out, wknd quickly, tld off.*
..........................(9 to 2 op 7 to 2 tchd 5 to 1) 4
700[5] CHANCERY BUCK [98] 10-10-0[7] (7*) R Darke, *lost tch 8th, tld off*..............(14 to 1 op 12 to 1 tchd 20 to 1) 5
Dist: 2l, 1½l, dist, 1½l. 4m 27.40s. a 7.40s (5 Ran).
SR: 44/41/12/-/-/   (Sarah Lady Allendale), K C Bailey

1139 Langstone Conservative Club Handicap Hurdle (0-135 4-y-o and up) £2,057 2¾m.................. (2:40)

985[3] MENEBUCK [125] 7-11-11 E Murphy, *beh, reminders aftr 7th, hdwy appr 2 out, led last, drifted rght, ran on und pres.*..................(100 to 30 op 9 to 4 tchd 7 to 2) 1
955[7] NICK THE DREAMER [105] 8-10-5 R Dunwoody, *chsd ldr, led briefly aftr 7th, ev ch last, kpt on und pres.*
..........................(7 to 2 op 3 to 1 tchd 4 to 1) 2
985[2] STRONG MEDICINE [119] 6-11-0 (5*) J McCarthy, *cl up, slpd on bend aftr 3rd, led 4 out to last, kpt on.*
..........................(9 to 4 fav op 5 to 2 tchd 9 to 4) 3
887 BEN ZABEEDY [100] 8-10-0 D Bridgwater, *cl up, niggled alng 4 out, ev ch 2 out, one pace appr last.*
..........................(9 to 2 op 5 to 1 tchd 11 to 2) 4
701[5] LASTING MEMORY [106] 7-10-6[9] J Frost, *sn beh.*
..........................(12 to 1 op 8 to 1) 5
RABA RIBA [114] 8-10-11 (3*) W Marston, *not fluent and jmpd rght, led till aftr 7th, wknd after 3 out.*
..........................(10 to 1 op 12 to 1 tchd 7 to 1) 6
Dist: ¾l, 1½l, 8l, 8l, 6l. 5m 13.80s. a 4.80s (6 Ran).
SR: 49/28/40/13/11/3/   (Lady Sarah Clutton), Lady Herries

1140 Panmure Gordon Handicap Chase (0-135 5-y-o and up) £3,882 3¼m 110yds................... (3:10)

1026 RIO HAINA [107] (bl) 8-11-2 B Powell, *several poss, mstk 5 out, reminders, cld appr last, styd on to ld r-in.*
..........................(6 to 1 op 5 to 1 tchd 13 to 2) 1
1050 DOONLOUGHAN [100] 8-10-9 Richard Guest, *nvr far away, chalg whn lft in ld 3 out, blun last, hdd r-in, no extr*..................(5 to 1 op 9 to 2 tchd 11 to 2) 2
962* ISLAND FOREST (USA) [94] 7-10-3[2] G Bradley, *hld up, mstk 3rd, blun 13th, hdwy 17th, mistake 2 out, one pace.*
..........................(13 to 8 fav op 11 to 8 tchd 7 to 4) 3
886 LITTLE GENERAL [97] 10-10-6 H Davies, *led 5th to 11th, wth ldr till wknd 15th, tld off.*
..........................(9 to 2 op 6 to 1 tchd 4 to 1) 4
COE [115] (bl) 7-11-10 R Dunwoody, *led to 5th, mstks 9th and tenth, sn lost pl and rdn alng, tld off.*
..........................(100 to 30 op 3 to 1 tchd 4 to 1) 5
897 BE SURPRISED [91] 7-9-11[7] (7*) J Clarke, *prmnt, led 11th till hit 3 out and uns rdr.*
..........................(33 to 1 op 20 to 1 tchd 50 to 1) ur
Dist: 8l, 7l, 20l, dist. 6m 44.60s. a 14.60s (6 Ran).

(Lady Pilkington), Capt T A Forster

1141 Ford Novices' Hurdle (4-y-o and up) £1,475 2¼m.................. (3:40)

1010[7] MAMALAMA 5-10-4 (3*) D O'Sullivan, *made all, pushed alng appr 2 out, ran on wl.*
..........................(3 to 1 tchd 5 to 2 and 100 to 30) 1
795[7] JOVIAL MAN (Ire) 4-10-12 M Perrett, *trkd ldr gng wl, ev ch whn mstk last, sn rallied, ran on wl, jst fld.*
..........................(9 to 4 op 7 to 4 tchd 6 to 4) 2
JUMPING JUDGE 6-10-5 (7*) D Meade, *hld up, cld 3 out, ev ch nxt, kpt on frm last.*......(20 to 1 tchd 33 to 1) 3
AITCH N'BEE 10-10-12 E Murphy, *keen hold, trkd ldg pair, one pace appr last.*
..........................(7 to 4 fav op 6 to 4 tchd 5 to 2) 4
SCOTTISH BALL 4-10-7 M Crosse, *hld up rear, tld off 5th.*
..........................(33 to 1 op 20 to 1 tchd 50 to 1) 5
TINAS LASS 4-10-7 D Morris, *hld up rear, clsg whn f last.*
..........................(33 to 1 op 20 to 1 tchd 50 to 1) f
Dist: Hd, 1½l, 5l, dist. 4m 29.50s. a 19.50s (6 Ran).

(J J Bridger), J J Bridger

SEDGEFIELD (good to soft)
Tuesday November 9th
Going Correction: PLUS 1.10 sec. per fur. (races 1,2,-6,7), PLUS 1.20 (3,4,5)

1142 John Wade Haulage Selling Hurdle (3-y-o and up) £1,719 2m 5f 110yds (1:00)

1060³ FARMER'S CROSS 9-11-8 Mrs A Farrell, *al prmnt, led 3 out, clr nxt, mstk last, rdn out.* (9 to 4 jt-fav op 7 to 4) 1
970³ FREE TRANSFER (Ire) 4-11-10 (3*) N Bentley, *hld up, prog to track ldrs 4 out, rdn nxt, effrt appr last, kpt on one pace.*...............(9 to 4 jt-fav op 7 to 4 tchd 5 to 2) 2
659* OK RECORDS 6-11-13 N Mann, *hld up gng wl, prog hfwy, effrt frm 3 out, hng rght aftr nxt, sn btn.*
.....................(5 to 1 op 9 to 2 tchd 11 to 2) 3
639⁸ OVER THE ODDS (Ire) 4-11-1 (7*) D Ryan, *led second till hdd 3 out, sn wknd.*..........................(25 to 1) 4
970⁴ SUNTAN (Fr) 4-11-1 (7*) K Davies, *led to second, remained cl up, rdn 4 out, wknd aftr nxt.....*(8 to 1 tchd 9 to 1) 5
909 RISEUPWILLIEREILLY 7-11-8 N Smith, *in tch till wknd 4 out, sn tld off.*..................(25 to 1 tchd 33 to 1) 6
ANONA 7-11-3 A Merrigan, *in tch till blun 4th, beh aftr, tld off whn pld up aftr 6th.*......(50 to 1 op 20 to 1) pu
1060⁹ SARANNPOUR (Ire) (bl) 4-11-8 G McCourt, *hld up, lost tch 4 out, pld up bef last.*..............(6 to 1 op 4 to 1) pu
1003 FARM TRACK 4-11-3 B Storey, *cl up to second, wknd 4th, tld off whn pld up aftr 6th.*........(33 to 1 op 25 to 1) pu
Dist: 3½l, 8l, 2½l, 8l, dist. 5m 27.30s. a 36.30s (9 Ran).

(P A Farrell), P Beaumont

1143 Wolviston Handicap Hurdle (0-125 4-y-o and up) £1,917 2m 1f 110yds.. (1:30)

972² HALLO MAM (Ire) [94] 4-11-0 M Brennan, *prmnt, smooth prog to track ldrs 3 out, led nxt, rdn and tired r-in, jst hld on.*...................(9 to 2 op 4 to 1 tchd 5 to 1) 1
972* NOTABLE EXCEPTION [96] 4-11-2 P Niven, *hld up rear, prog aftr 5th, chsd ldrs frm 3 out, ran on strly after last, jst fld.*............................(6 to 4 fav tchd 7 to 2) 2
972⁷ STAGS FELL [84] 8-10-1 (3*) N Bentley, *prmnt, cld up 5th, led 3 out, hdd nxt, kpt on one pace.*
.........................(12 to 1 op 10 to 1 tchd 16 to 1) 3
SHAHGRAM (Ire) [108] 5-12-0 Mrs A Farrell, *prmnt, cl up frm 5th, wknd appr 2 out.*......................(16 to 1) 4
757² A GENTLEMAN TWO [86] 7-10-6 S Turner, *made most till 3 out, sn wknd.*........................(8 to 1 op 7 to 1) 5
912* HYPNOTIST [97] 6-11-3 L Wyer, *wth ldr till 3 out, sn rdn, wknd nxt.*.............................(6 to 1 op 5 to 1) 6
719 STARLIGHT WONDER [81] 7-10-11 N Smith, *hld up beh, outpcd frm 5th, styd on one pace frm 2 out.*
............................(50 to 1 op 33 to 1) 7
912⁵ JOHN NAMAN (Ire) [89] 4-10-4 (5*) P Waggott, *pckd badly second, cl up till wknd aftr 3 out..* (8 to 1 op 7 to 1) 8
HIGHFIELD PRINCE [92] 7-10-12 M Dwyer, *trkd ldr to hfwy, wknd and beh aftr 5th.....*(16 to 1 op 14 to 1) 9
LOCHEART LADY [80] 6-10-0 M Moloney, *lost tch 5th, tld off frm nxt.*..........................(33 to 1 op 25 to 1) 10
Dist: Nk, 2½l, 8l, 1½l, nk, dist, dist, 25l, nk. 4m 20.00s. a 25.00s (10 Ran).
SR: 29/30/15/31/7/18/

(O Brennan), O Brennan

1144 Persimmon Homes Handicap Chase (0-130 4-y-o and up) £2,635 2m 5f (2:00)

INVASION [94] (v) 9-10-0 M Brennan, *al prmnt, cld up 4 out, led nxt, pushed clr frm 2 out, readily.*
.........................(10 to 1 op 8 to 1) 1
ROCKET LAUNCHER [103] 7-10-9 M Moloney, *led till 3 out, one pace frm nxt.*....................(7 to 2 tchd 4 to 1) 2
973* NIGHT GUEST [102] 11-10-8 B Storey, *trkd ldrs, rdn 4 out, no imprsn frm nxt.*..................(9 to 4 op 7 to 4) 3
1001⁴ LOGAMIMO [122] 7-11-11 (3*) A Larnach, *not fluent, hld up beh, niggled alng frm hfwy, not gd sn aftr.*
.........................(7 to 4 fav op 6 to 4 tchd 15 to 8) 4
1069¹ WIGTOWN BAY [99] 10-10-5 P Niven, *pressed ldr till wknd quickly 4 out.*.......................(9 to 1 op 8 to 1) 5
Dist: 8l, 3l, 7l, nk. 5m 38.40s. a 34.40s (5 Ran).

(Lady Anne Bentinck), O Brennan

1145 Dick Brewitt Memorial Handicap Chase (0-115 4-y-o and up) £2,709 3m 3f............................(2:30)

921⁷ HIGH PADRE [108] 7-12-0 M Dwyer, *led 8th, drw clr frm 3 out, eased r-in.*..........(11 to 4 op 5 to 2 tchd 3 to 1) 1
479² MILITARY SECRET [101] 7-11-7 G McCourt, *in tch, cld up hfwy, rdn and kpt on one pace frm 3 out.*
...........................(7 to 2 tchd 3 to 1) 2
911³ RADICAL LADY [107] 9-11-6 (7*) J Supple, *led to 8th, trkd ldr aftr, mstk 15th, no imprsn frm 3 out.*
.........................(9 to 4 op 3 to 1) 3
911* CAPITAL PUNISHMENT [99] 7-11-5 C Grant, *hld up beh ldrs, wknd quickly 5 out, tld off.*
.........................(7 to 4 fav op 2 to 1 tchd 9 to 4) 4
789 SANTELLA BOBKES (USA) [88] 8-10-3 (5*) P Waggott, *mstks, beh and pushed alng aftr 6th, tld off frm hfwy.*
.........................(25 to 1 op 20 to 1) 5
911 SPEECH [91] 10-10-11 T Reed, *prmnt, reminders 12th, wknd 15th, tld off.*.................(12 to 1 op 10 to 1) 6
Dist: 5l, 2½l, dist, 4l, 25l. 7m 16.90s. a 37.90s (6 Ran).
SR: 45/33/36/

(J S Murdoch), J G FitzGerald

1146 John Hellens Novices' Chase (4-y-o and up) £2,173 2m 5f........... (3:00)

948² SHEILAS HILLCREST 7-11-0 (7*) J Supple, *made all, clr 11th, pckd last, pushed out..........*(9 to 4 op 2 to 1) 1
1058 ABLE PLAYER (USA) (bl) 6-11-9 (5*) J Burke, *rcd in 3rd, reminder aftr 7th, chsd alng frm hfwy, tld off 11th, took second pl cl hme..............*(100 to 30 op 3 to 1) 2
974³ VAYRUA (Fr) 8-11-4 (3*) A Larnach, *pressed ldr, mstks tenth and 11th, struggling and beh aftr, lost second pl cl hme...............*(11 to 10 on tchd 5 to 4 on) 3
Dist: 6l, 5l. 5m 38.60s. a 34.60s (3 Ran).

(N B Mason), N B Mason

1147 Great North Road Juvenile Novices' Hurdle (3-y-o) £1,483 2m 1f 110yds ....(3:30)

285⁷ ROSCOMMON JOE (Ire) 11-0 M Dwyer, *al prmnt, smooth prog to join ldrs 3 out, slight ld nxt, pushed clr r-in, cmftbly...........................*(7 to 1 op 5 to 1) 1
872² THE PREMIER EXPRES 11-0 C Grant, *pld hrd early, cl up, led aftr 3 out till nxt, kpt on one pace.*
.........................(Evens fav op 5 to 4 tchd 6 to 4) 2
VAIGLY SUNTHYME 11-0 N Smith, *al prmnt, cld up 3 out, rdn nxt, kpt on und pres.*
.........................(7 to 1 op 4 to 1 tchd 8 to 1) 3
MHEMEANLES 11-0 L Wyer, *beh, gd prog aftr 5th, trkd ldrs 3 out, no imprsn frm nxt.*
.........................(7 to 1 op 4 to 1 tchd 8 to 1) 4
ATHERTON GREEN (Ire) 11-0 M Ahern, *pld hrd, cl up, dsptd ld 3 out, rdn and wknd appr nxt.*
.........................(5 to 1 op 7 to 2) 5
622² GOLDMIRE 10-9 S Turner, *in tch, prog to track ldrs 3 out, no imprsn frm nxt...............*(12 to 1 op 8 to 1) 6
971⁵ NATIVE WORTH 10-9 (5*) P Williams, *cl up, ev ch 3 out, sn rdn and wknd........................*(16 to 1 op 12 to 1) 7
578⁵ BELFORTON 10-6 (3*) N Bentley, *rear to 5th, kpt on one pace frm 2 out....................*(12 to 1 op 10 to 1) 8
GERMAN LEGEND 11-0 A Merrigan, *prmnt, wknd aftr 3 out........................*(50 to 1 op 33 to 1) 9
DIXIE HIGHWAY 10-9 K Johnson, *al rear.*
.........................(33 to 1 op 50 to 1 tchd 25 to 1) 10
971⁶ GOLDEN SAVANNAH 10-7 (7*) J Driscoll, *led till slpd and sprawled badly 3 out, no ch aftr....*(10 to 1 op 8 to 1) 11
PINE CLASSIC (Ire) 11-0 A Orkney, *in tch to 5th, sn wknd tld off........................*(25 to 1 op 20 to 1) 12
TODDEN 10-11 (3*) A Larnach, *in tch to 5th, sn wknd, tld off.........................*(33 to 1 op 20 to 1) 13
MARIBELLA 10-9 M Brennan, *mstk second, in tch till wknd 5th, tld off......................*(25 to 1 op 20 to 1) 14
Dist: 3l, 5l, 4l, 5l, 3½l, nk, 1l, nk, ½l, 10l. 4m 26.30s. a 33.30s (14 Ran).

(Mrs Carmel Sweeney), J J O'Neill

1148 Levy Board Handicap Hurdle (0-125 4-y-o and up) £2,364 2m 5f 110yds ....(4:00)

867⁵ BONANZA [115] 6-12-0 R Hodge, *trkd ldrs, rdn frm 3 out, dsptd ld last 2, forged ahead r-in.*
.........................(8 to 1 op 10 to 1 tchd 11 to 1) 1
970² DAWAAM [88] 7-10-1 A Merrigan, *al prmnt, trkd ldrs gng wl frm hfwy, dsptd ld last 2, not quicken r-in.*
.........................(7 to 1 op 6 to 1 tchd 8 to 1) 2
914⁶ IF YOU SAY SO [88] 7-10-1 A Mulholland, *trkd ldr, led 6th, wknd appr 2 out................*(7 to 2 tchd 9 to 2) 3
767⁴ MYTHICAL STORM [91] 6-10-4¹ P Niven, *rear till hfwy, gd prog to track ldrs 7th, rdn and wknd appr 2 out.*
.........................(Evens fav op 9 to 4 tchd 13 to 8) 4
JUPITER MOON [87] 4-10-0 B Storey, *in tch, wknd 8th.*
.........................(16 to 1 op 14 to 1) 5
914⁹ TOP VILLAIN [93] 7-10-6 Mr S Bell, *prmnt, lost pl and beh hfwy, prog to track ldrs 3 out, sn rdn and btn.*
.........................(12 to 1 op 10 to 1) 6
972⁹ CURTAIN FACTORY [87] 4-10-0 L Wyer, *prmnt, pressed ldr frm hfwy, wknd appr 2 out.*......(4 to 1 op 5 to 1) 7
759⁸ ONE FOR LUCK (Ire) [90] 5-10-3 M Dwyer, *al rear, wl beh.*.........................(12 to 1 op 10 to 1) 8
974 CONCERT PAPER [89] (bl) 9-10-2 C Grant, *led to 6th, sn wknd, tld off frm 8th........................*(20 to 1) 9
Dist: 1l, 10l, 2½l, 6l, 4l, 1l, 25l. 5m 20.90s. a 29.90s (9 Ran).
SR: 38/10/-/-/-/-/

(D Needham & Partners), Mrs M Reveley

SOUTHWELL (good)
Tuesday November 9th
Going Correction: PLUS 0.40 sec. per fur.

1149 Nottingham Life Managers' Circle Novices' Chase (5-y-o and up) £1,508 2m..................................(2:20)

446³ DONOSTI 9-11-0 R Greene, *hld up, hdwy 7th, rdn alng and chsd ldr 5 out, lft wl clr nxt, unchlgd.*
.........................(7 to 2 op 2 to 1) 1

151

1071 KEY DEAR (Fr) 6-11-0 T Wall, *hit 1st, in tch till lost pl 6th, lft remote 3rd and tried to refuse 4 out, hit nxt, kpt on appr last*..........................(25 to 1 op 20 to 1) 2

SHADING 9-11-0 R Supple, *led and sn clr, hdd 8th, hit nxt and soon wknd, lft remote second 4 out, blun last 3*. ....(12 to 1 op 10 to 1) 3

SKELETOR 10-11-0 D Murphy, *chsd clr ldr, hdwy 7th, led nxt, wl clear whn f 4 out*. (9 to 2 op 4 to 1 tchd 5 to 1) f

848^{2} ILEWIN 6-11-0 A Maguire, *in tch whn f 6th*. ....(7 to 4 fav op 3 to 1) f

1094^{2} REGAL ROMPER (Ire) 5-11-0 Gary Lyons, *in tch whn blun and uns rdr 3rd*.....................(5 to 1 op 4 to 1) ur

998 MR HAPPY FEET (bl) 6-11-0 R Bellamy, *chsd ldrs, wknd and beh 6th, tld off whn refused and uns rdr 4 out*. ....(40 to 1 op 25 to 1) ref

Dist: Dist, dist. 4m 20.40s. a 21.40s (7 Ran).

(R L C Hartley), R Lee

1150 Jessica Stone's Birthday Novices' Chase (5-y-o and up) £1,528 3m 110yds........................(2:50)

BALLOO HOUSE 8-11-0 A Carroll, *prmnt, hit 5th, hit 9th, hdwy 11th, lft in ld 4 out, sn rdn, styd on gmely*. ....(9 to 4 op 6 to 4 tchd 5 to 2) 1

974^{8} FLASS VALE 5-11-0 R Garritty, *al prmnt, cl up 11th, rdn 3 out and ev ch till no extr last*......(20 to 1 op 16 to 1) 2

948 SILENT CHANT (bl) 9-10-7 (7*) Mr R Griffiths, *prmnt and mstks, rdn alng and wknd tenth, f nxt*. ....(8 to 1 tchd 10 to 1) f

996* SANDAIG (bl) 7-11-5 (3*) A Thornton, *hld up, smooth hdwy tenth, led and f 4 out*. ....(11 to 10 on op 11 to 8 on tchd Evens) f

CALDECOTT 7-11-0 Gary Lyons, *led till hdd 4 out, wknd quickly and remote 3rd, whn blun and pld up 3 out*. ....(10 to 1 op 12 to 1) pu

Dist: 2½l. 6m 53.90s. a 55.90s (5 Ran).

(R Brazier), Mrs P Sly

1151 Southwell Handicap Chase (0-115 5-y-o and up) £1,590 3m 110yds.....(3:20)

947* SANDYBRAES [115] 8-12-0 A Maguire, *trkd ldrs, led tenth, pushed clr appr 2 out, easily*. ....(7 to 4 on tchd 11 to 8 on) 1

RED COLUMBIA [90] 12-10-3 R Supple, *in tch, hdwy 11th, rdn alng and styd on frm 4 out, no ch wth wnr*. ....(16 to 1 op 14 to 1) 2

SINGLESOLE [114] 8-11-13 A Carroll, *led and clr, hit 7th, hdd tenth, chsd wnr and rdn alng 4 out, blun 3 out and wknd*.................(11 to 4 op 2 to 1 tchd 3 to 1) 3

911 SOONER STILL [108] (v) 9-11-0 (7*) Judy Davies, *chsd ldrs till f 9th*.............................(8 to 1 op 7 to 1) f

931 RAHEEN ROVER [87] 9-9-9 (5*) D Leahy, *rear, blun 8th, sn tld off, f 3 out*..................(20 to 1 tchd 25 to 1) f

Dist: 6l, 2½l. 6m 50.10s. a 52.10s (5 Ran).

(Mrs Stewart Catherwood), D Nicholson

SOUTHWELL (A.W) (std)
Tuesday November 9th
Going Correction: PLUS 0.70 sec. per fur.

1152 Edingley Novices' Hurdle (4-y-o and up) £1,492 2½m................(1:20)

CLIFTON CHASE 4-11-0 J A Harris, *al prmnt, effrt to join ldr 3 out, rdn to ld appr last, ran on flt*. ....(8 to 1 op 4 to 1 tchd 9 to 1) 1

916* BLAZON OF TROY 4-11-8 S Smith Eccles, *hld up in tch, gd hdwy 7th, led nxt, jnd 3 out, rdn and hdd appr last, no extr*......................(9 to 4 op 7 to 2 tchd 2 to 1) 2

368* EMERALD VENTURE 6-11-7 Peter Caldwell, *trkd ldrs, hdwy to ld 7th, hdd nxt, rdn and wknd 3 out*. ....(8 to 1 op 6 to 1) 3

821^{7} TAKE BY STORM (Ire) 4-11-0 J Callaghan, *jmpd slwly and beh, hdwy to join ldrs 8th, rdn 3 out, sn btn*. ....(13 to 8 fav op 11 to 10 tchd 2 to 1) 4

823 LAFANTA (Ire) 4-11-0 K Jones, *prmnt till rdn and wknd 4 out*...............................(50 to 1 op 33 to 1) 5

WALDORF T BEAGLE 7-11-2 R Supple, *led to 4th, led aftr 6th to nxt, wknd bef four out*......(33 to 1 op 25 to 1) 6

934 MAKE A LINE 5-11-2 A Maguire, *jmpd slwly second, hdwy to ld 4th, hdd and reminders aftr 6th, sn lost pl, tld off whn pld up bef 3 out*................(9 to 1 op 5 to 1) pu

Dist: 2½l, 12l, 3l, dist, dist. 5m 11.80s. a 30.80s (7 Ran).

(David Cahal), J L Harris

1153 Mansfield Conditional Jockeys' Claiming Hurdle (4-y-o and up) £1,292 2m............................(1:50)

950^{6} GREEN'S SEAGO (USA) 5-11-5 A Thornton, *trkd ldrs, hdwy to chase ldr 4 out, led nxt, sn rdn, hit 2 out, drvn out*..................(12 to 1 op 10 to 1 tchd 14 to 1) 1

950^{4} GRUBBY 4-10-7 S Wynne, *led, rdn and hdd 3 out, hit nxt, plugged on und pres*. ....(15 to 2 op 12 to 1 tchd 7 to 1) 2

681* BONDAID 9-11-10 (5*) P McLoughlin, *in tch, hit 5th and sn rdn alng, drvn up to chal 3 out, soon one pace*. ....(11 to 10 fav op 5 to 4 on tchd 11 to 8) 3

632^{6} FROSTY RECEPTION (bl) 8-11-11 V Slattery, *chsd ldr, hit 4th, rdn and wknd aftr four out, blun 2 out*. ....(11 to 4 op 6 to 4 tchd 100 to 30) 4

520 TAX THE DEVIL (v) 5-11-2 A Dicken, *in tch, hit second, rdn and wknd 5 out*...............(14 to 1 op 10 to 1) 5

950^{3} WILL BONNY (NZ) 6-10-11 (7*) T Murphy, *in tch till f 6th*. ....(10 to 1 op 12 to 1) f

GARTH 5-11-2 M Hourigan, *strted slwly, al beh, tld off whn pld up bef 6th*...............(25 to 1 op 20 to 1) pu

Dist: 2½l, 4l, 4l, 30l. 4m 15.40s. a 29.40s (7 Ran).

(R Atkinson), J L Harris

1154 Fisherton Handicap Hurdle (0-115 4-y-o and up) £1,548 2m............(3:50)

972^{3} TIP IT IN [88] 4-11-0 D Murphy, *trkd ldrs, gd hdwy 5th, led aftr nxt, quickened clr appr 2 out, cmftbly*. ....(4 to 1 op 7 to 2 tchd 3 to 1) 1

949^{3} NORTHERN NATION [95] 5-11-7 Diane Clay, *in tch till blun and lost pl 4th, hdwy appr 3 out and sn ev ch, rdn bef nxt, kpt on one pace*. (3 to 1 fav op 9 to 4 tchd 7 to 2) 2

1068^{3} SANDRO [74] (bl) 4-10-0 L Harvey, *chsd ldrs, led 5th till aftr nxt, rdn 3 out and sn wknd*..............(8 to 1) 3

WHIPPERS DELIGHT (Ire) [100] 5-11-9 (3*) D Meredith, *led to 4th, cl up till rdn and wknd appr 3 out*. ....(20 to 1 op 14 to 1) 4

838* HAVE A NIGHTCAP [102] 4-12-0 J A Harris, *chsd ldrs till rdn alng and lost pl 5th, sn beh*. ....(4 to 1 op 7 to 2 tchd 5 to 1) 5

949^{4} LOCAL FLYER [91] 4-11-3 S Keightley, *in tch, rdn alng 4 out, sn wknd*.....................(7 to 2 tchd 4 to 1) 6

PEACOCK FEATHER [83] 5-10-9 R Supple, *cl up, led 4th, blun and hdd nxt, rdn and wknd four out, beh whn pld up bef next*........................(12 to 1 op 8 to 1) pu

Dist: 10l, 4l, 2l, 15l, 10l. 4m 2.90s. a 16.90s (7 Ran).

SR: 29/26/1/25/12/-/-/ (Mrs M Dunning), A Smith

DOWNPATRICK (IRE) (yielding)
Wednesday November 10th

1155 Bishopscourt Maiden Hurdle (4-y-o) £1,380 2m 1f 172yds............(1:30)

803^{3} SHAWAR (Ire) 11-9 K F O'Brien,..................(5 to 2) 1

GRECIAN LADY (Ire) 10-13 P L Malone,..........(12 to 1) 2

1036^{3} NORA ANN (Ire) 10-13 (5*) M A Davey,.........(2 to 1 fav) 3

902^{7} JO JO BOY (Ire) 11-4 F J Flood,..................(5 to 1) 4

902 KNOCNAGORE (Ire) 11-4 B Sheridan,............(10 to 1) 5

803^{6} COUNTESS PAHLEN (Ire) 10-8 (5*) Mr J A Nash,..(10 to 1) 6

1015^{2} JODONLEE (Ire) 10-10 (3*) T J Mitchell,..........(11 to 2) 7

255 FLIP THE LID (Ire) 10-8 (5*) L Flynn,..............(25 to 1) 8

Dist: 2l, 1½l, 1½l, ½l. (Time not taken) (8 Ran).

(Sean Macklin), J H Scott

1156 Drumcullen Maiden Hurdle (5-y-o and up) £1,380 2½m................(2:00)

745^{6} GARYS GIRL 6-11-2 (7*) J M McCormack,.........(7 to 2) 1

672^{6} RATHCORE 6-12-0 C O'Dwyer,...............(100 to 30) 2

903^{9} LE BRAVE 7-12-0 K F O'Brien,...............(2 to 1 fav) 3

1075^{5} RUNAWAY GOLD 6-11-6 F Woods,..............(5 to 1) 4

907^{6} MULLAGHMEEN 7-10-10 (5*) D P Murphy,........(8 to 1) 5

1016 CELIA'S PET (Ire) 5-11-1 P L Malone,............(33 to 1) 6

SANDEMALL 6-11-1 (5*) Mr B R Hamilton,.......(25 to 1) 7

1014 AVOWIN 11-11-1 F J Flood,.....................(50 to 1) pu

Dist: 2l, nk, sht-hd, 3½l. (Time not taken) (8 Ran).

(S Thompson), D Carroll

1157 North Down Marquees Handicap Hurdle (0-102 4-y-o and up) £1,380 2½m ....(2:30)

CASTLE RANGER [-] 6-12-0 C N Bowens,.........(5 to 1) 1

746* LOAVES AND FISHES [-] 5-11-7 (5*) H Taylor,.. (2 to 1 fav) 2

503* KAITLIN (Ire) [-] 4-11-2 P L Malone,..............(3 to 1) 3

904^{6} ONABUNDA [-] 7-10-2 (7*) F Byrne,...............(8 to 1) 4

808^{6} GLENSHANE PASS [-] 6-11-4 P McWilliams,.......(8 to 1) 5

PROSPECT LADY (Ire) [-] 5-10-10 (3*) Mr P McMahon, ...(10 to 1) 6

555 MR GERAN (Ire) [-] 4-11-0 J Shortt,..............(10 to 1) 7

60 MISS SPLENDOUR (Ire) [-] 5-10-11 (3*) T J Mitchell, ...(14 to 1) 8

SUTTON CENTENARY (Ire) [-] 5-10-11 H Rogers, (20 to 1) 9

MISS MARIPOSA [-] 9-10-5 (5*) L Flynn,..........(20 to 1) 10

Dist: 1½l, 7l, 7l, 1½l. (Time not taken) (10 Ran).

(Mrs M T Quinn), Victor Bowens

1158 Sullome Voe Handicap Chase (0-102 4-y-o and up) £1,380 2½m...... (3:00)

966^6 HO FRETTA [-] 7-10-5 (5*) C O'Brien, ... (5 to 2 jt-fav) 1

1014^6 LA-GREINE [-] 6-11-2 (3*) Mr P McMahon, ... (11 to 4) 2

691 LA CERISE [-] (bl) 10-10-1 F J Flood, ...(6 to 1) 3

1014^4 JOEY KELLY [-] 8-11-13 C O'Dwyer, ...(5 to 2 jt-fav) 4

904 SYLVIA'S SAFFRON [-] (bl) 6-10-9 P McWilliams, . .(12 to 1) 5

966^9 SLAVOMER [-] 8-11-2 (7*) P Stafford, ... (10 to 1) 6

Dist: 7l, 2½l, 7l, 4½l. (Time not taken) (6 Ran).

(Derek Bell), Cecil Mahon

1159 Viking Chase (4-y-o and up) £1,380 2½m. . . . . (3:30)

966^7 HURRICANE TOMMY (bl) 6-11-8 T J Taaffe, ... (4 to 1) 1

1013 MUST DO 7-11-5 (3*) T J Mitchell, ... (9 to 4 fav) 2

1017^6 GOLA LADY 6-10-13 C N Bowens, ... (8 to 1) 3

RAMBLING LORD (Ire) 5-11-1 P Carberry, ...(16 to 1) 4

746^9 REDELVA 6-10-10 (3*) Mr P McMahon, ...(12 to 1) 5

1013^2 WICKET KEEPER 8-11-4 J Shortt, ...(5 to 1) 6

KITES HARDWICKE 6-11-4 F J Flood, ... (8 to 1) 7

744^2 SALINA BAY 7-10-6 (7*) A Wall, ... (16 to 1) f

LARNACA 6-11-4 C O'Dwyer, ... (4 to 1) pu

Dist: 4½l, 7l, 1½l, 1½l. (Time not taken) (9 Ran).

(Seamus Maccrosain), Michael Cunningham

1160 Toal Bookmakers INH Flat Race (4-y-o and up) £1,380 2m 1f 172yds. . . . (4:00)

1113^4 CONQUINN (Ire) 4-10-13 (7*) Mr C Rae, ...(7 to 2) 1

236 KARA'S DREAM (Ire) 5-11-6 Mr S R Murphy, ...(10 to 1) 2

1016^3 COTTON CALL (Ire) 4-10-10 (5*) Mr B R Hamilton, ... (5 to 2 fav) 3

TRENCH HILL LASS (Ire) 4-10-8 (7*) Mr I Buchanan, (8 to 1) 4

945^6 JIMMY GORDON 6-11-11 (7*) Mr M Brennan, . . (100 to 30) 5

OVER THE MALLARD (Ire) 4-11-1 (5*) Mr P J Casey, (8 to 1) 6

MIRASEL 6-11-6 (7*) Mr R I Arthur, ... (10 to 1) 7

IF YOU BELIEVE (Ire) 4-10-13 (7*) Mr R Byrne, ... (33 to 1) 8

926^9 FANCY DISH 7-11-6 Mr J A Berry, ...(8 to 1) 9

1015 DECEMBER BRIDE (Ire) 5-10-13 (7*) Mr L J Gracey, (12 to 1) 10

747^7 KEEP THEM KEEN (Ire) 5-11-4 (7*) Mr L Madine, . . (16 to 1) 11

969 SHABRA SOCKS 7-11-4 (7*) Mr D A Harney, ...(33 to 1) 12

BALLISTIC BLAZE 6-11-11 Mr J P Dempsey, ... (33 to 1) pu

Dist: 4l, 11l, 11l, ½l. (Time not taken) (13 Ran).

(P F Graffin), P F Graffin

NEWBURY (good)
Wednesday November 10th
Going Correction: PLUS 0.65 sec. per fur.

1161 EBF 'National Hunt' Novices' Hurdle Qualifier (4,5,6-y-o) £3,728 2m 110yds . . . . (1:20)

863* OLD BRIDGE (Ire) 5-11-3 (7*) D Fortt, *al frnt rnk, chlgd 3 out, led nxt, styd on wl.* (4 to 1 op 7 to 2 tchd 3 to 1) 1

DANTE'S NEPHEW 6-11-0 D Gallagher, *pressed ldrs, led aftr 4th to 2 out, ev ch whn hit lst, kpt on same pace.* . . . .(5 to 1 op 7 to 2) 2

952 MUSKORA (Ire) 4-11-5 Peter Hobbs, *trkd ldrs, ev ch 3 out, outpcd frm nxt.* . . . . (11 to 4 fav op 7 to 2 tchd 4 to 1) 3

952^5 BELL ONE (USA) (bl) 4-11-0 C Maude, *chsd ldrs, rdn and outpcd frm 3 out.* . . . .(14 to 1 tchd 16 to 1) 4

THE FROG PRINCE (Ire) 5-11-0 R Supple, *beh, kpt on frm 5th, nrst finish.* . . . .(16 to 1 op 8 to 1 tchd 20 to 1) 5

1027^8 PHIL'S DREAM 5-11-0 B Powell, *hdwy 4th, lost pl 5th, styd on frm 2 out.* . . . .(9 to 2 op 5 to 1 tchd 4 to 1) 6

844^5 GAVASKAR (Ire) 4-11-0 J Frost, *made most till aftr 4th, wknd 3 out.* . . . .(8 to 1 op 6 to 1) 7

SO AUDACIOUS 5-11-0 M Richards, *beh, nvr rch ldrs.* . . . . (25 to 1 op 20 to 1 tchd 33 to 1) 8

764^9 THE MINISTER (Ire) 4-10-11 (3*) A Thornton, *effrt 5th, sn btn.* . . . .(33 to 1) 9

901 POLICEMANS PRIDE (Fr) 4-10-7 (7*) J Clarke, *prmnt to 5th.* . . . . (33 to 1) 10

CANCALE (Ire) 5-11-0 E Murphy, *beh 3rd.* . . . . (33 to 1 op 20 to 1) 11

901 LOYAL GAIT (NZ) 5-11-0 B Clifford, *not fluent, al beh.* . . . . (33 to 1 op 20 to 1) 12

MASTER BAVARD (Ire) 5-11-0 V Slattery, *mstks second and 3rd, sn beh.* . . . .(16 to 1 op 12 to 1) 13

FIFTH IN LINE (Ire) 5-11-0 S Earle, *sn beh.* . . . .(33 to 1) 14

Dist: 4l, 3½l, 25l, 2½l, 1½l, 2½l, 6l, sht-hd, 12l, 1½l. 4m 7.50s. a 18.50s (14 Ran).

SR: 18/4/5/-/-/-/ (K C B Mackenzie), Andrew Turnell

1162 Lionel Vick Memorial Handicap Chase (0-145 5-y-o and up) £4,600 3m. . (1:50)

DUBLIN FLYER [119] 7-10-2 B Powell, *jmpd wl, made all, clr 4th, imprsv.* . . . . .(2 to 1 fav op 7 to 4 tchd 85 to 40) 1

COGENT [145] 9-11-7 (7*) D Fortt, *in tch, chsd wnr frm 6th, no imprsn whn mstk 2 out, not fluent last.* . . . . (6 to 1 op 5 to 1 tchd 13 to 2) 2

842^5 KENTISH PIPER [118] 8-10-1 R Supple, *chsd ldrs, wknd 4 out, 3rd and no ch whn f last.* . . . . (11 to 2 op 5 to 1 tchd 6 to 1) f

1050 FURRY KNOWE [117] 8-10-0 D Gallagher, *chsd wnr to 6th, blun tenth and 11th, mstk and uns rdr nxt.* . . . .(14 to 1 op 16 to 1 tchd 20 to 1 and 12 to 1) ur

897^2 GREEN ISLAND (USA) [119] 7-10-2 Peter Hobbs, *brief effrt 14th, sn wknd, no ch whn refused last.* . . . .(9 to 2 op 4 to 1 tchd 5 to 1) ref

935 BUCKSHEE BOY [117] (bl) 11-10-0 D Bridgwater, *beh, lost tch 11th, tld off whn pld up bef 14th.* . . . . (33 to 1) pu

AVONBURN (NZ) [118] 9-10-1 M Richards, *beh, brief effrt 14th, sn wknd, no ch whn pld up bef 2 out.* . . . .(7 to 2 tchd 4 to 1) pu

Dist: 25l. 6m 5.40s. a 17.40s (7 Ran).

SR: 56/57/-/-/ (J B Sumner), Capt T A Forster

1163 Tom Masson Trophy Hurdle (4-y-o and up) £3,444 2m 5f. . . . . (2:20)

829* CASTLE COURAGEOUS 6-11-4 E Murphy, *led till aftr 5th, mstk nxt, chlgd 4 out, not fluent 2 out, ran on gmely r-in to ld cl hme.* . . . . (5 to 4 on tchd 11 to 10 on and 11 to 8 on) 1

900^7 WINTER SQUALL (Ire) 5-11-5 (3*) W Marston, *hld up, hdwy 4 out, led nxt, rdn r-in, kpt on, ct cl hme.* . . . .(4 to 1 op 2 to 1) 2

764^3 BILLY BORU 5-10-9 M Hourigan, *chsd ldr 3rd, led aftr 5th to 3 out, outpcd nxt.* . . . .(12 to 1 tchd 8 to 1) 3

GLAISDALE (Ire) 4-10-7 B Powell, *chsd ldrs, pushed alng and styd on same pace frm 3 out.* . . . .(7 to 2 op 3 to 1 tchd 4 to 1) 4

1079* DARINGLY 4-10-7 R Bellamy, *beh, str hold, hdwy 4 out, wknd nxt.* . . . .(66 to 1 op 33 to 1 tchd 100 to 1) 5

SURE PRIDE (USA) 5-10-11 (7*) J Clarke, *chsd ldrs till wknd 4 out.* . . . . (33 to 1 op 20 to 1 tchd 50 to 1) 6

CORACO 6-11-4 D Bridgwater, *beh, jmpd slwly 5th, rdn 7th, wknd 4 out.* . . . . (33 to 1 op 25 to 1) 7

Dist: ¾l, 10l, 2l, 15l, 6l, 6l. 5m 17.60s. a 24.60s (7 Ran).

(Lady Mary Mumford), Lady Herries

1164 Hallowe'en Novices' Chase (5-y-o and up) £3,626 2½m. . . . . (2:50)

1024* CRYSTAL SPIRIT 6-11-5 J Frost, *made virtually all, wnt clr 3 out, cmftbly.* (11 to 10 fav op 5 to 4 tchd 7 to 4) 1

JUDGED LUCKY (Fr) 6-11-0 R Bellamy, *prmnt, hit 3rd, lost pl tenth, hdwy 12th, styd on to take second r-in, no ch wth wnr.* . . . .(66 to 1 op 33 to 1 tchd 100 to 1) 2

894^3 MUNKA 7-11-0 Peter Hobbs, *prmnt to 12th, rdn 3 out, styd on r-in.* . . . .(13 to 2 op 6 to 1) 3

FANTUS 6-11-0 C Maude, *in tch, chsd wnr 9th, chlgd 11th, ev ch 4 out, sn one pace, wknd r-in.* . . . .(11 to 4 op 5 to 2 tchd 2 to 1 and 3 to 1) 4

1008 STAUNCH RIVAL (USA) 6-11-0 D Bridgwater, *beh, effrt 12th, sn wknd.* . . . . . . (16 to 1 op 14 to 1 tchd 20 to 1) 5

VICTORY GATE (USA) 8-10-7 (7*) J Clarke, *beh 5th, tld off 8th, pld up bef 2 out.* (50 to 1 op 33 to 1 tchd 66 to 1) pu

899^3 PARDON ME SIR 9-11-0 S Hodgson, *hdwy to chase ldrs 6th, wknd 12th, tld off whn pld up bef 2 out.* . . . . (6 to 1 op 5 to 1 tchd 13 to 2) pu

SEDGE WARBLER 6-10-9 M Richards, *hdwy tenth, wknd 12th, tld off whn pld up bef 3 out.* . . . . (14 to 1) pu

Dist: 12l, 3½l, 1l, 20l. 5m 15.60s. a 25.60s (8 Ran).

(Paul Mellon), I A Balding

1165 Winterbourne Handicap Chase (0-140 5-y-o and up) £4,240 2m 1f. . . . . . (3:20)

893* IAMA ZULU [107] 8-10-5 M Hourigan, *chsd ldr to 8th, steadied and confidently rdn, quickened to ld aftr 2 out, wnt lft and hit last, readily.* . . . . (5 to 4 fav tchd 11 to 8 and 11 to 10) 1

1022^7 LUCKY AGAIN [102] 6-10-0 C Maude, *hdwy 4th, chsd ldr 8th, led appr nxt, hit four out, hdd aftr 2 out, wnt lft and mstk last, sn outpcd.* . . . . (12 to 1 tchd 14 to 1) 2

GREEN WILLOW [119] 11-11-3 E Murphy, *led till appr 9th, kpt on one pace.* . . . . (7 to 1 op 6 to 1 tchd 8 to 1) 3

573* PATS MINSTREL [115] (bl) 8-10-13 B Powell, *beh most of way.* . . . . (11 to 4 op 9 to 4) 4

1048^4 WELSH BARD [126] (bl) 9-11-10 M Richards, *beh 3rd, hdwy 9th, wknd aftr 2 out.* . . . .(9 to 2 op 4 to 1 tchd 5 to 1) 5

Dist: 5l, 7l, 12l, 2l. 4m 17.60s. a 16.60s (5 Ran).

SR: 21/11/21/5/14/ (Mrs Anona Taylor), P J Hobbs

1166 Cold Ash Juvenile Novices' Hurdle (3-y-o) £2,872 2m 110yds. . . . . (3:50)

896^2 GRAND APPLAUSE (Ire) 10-12 D Bridgwater, *beh, mstk second, hdwy 4 out, chlgd nxt, drvn to ld appr last, all out.* . . . .(15 to 8 fav op 5 to 4 tchd 2 to 1) 1

HOSTILE WITNESS (Ire) (v) 10-12 M Richards, *chsd ldrs 3rd, chlgd nxt till led 4 out, rdn appr 2 out, hdd approaching last, one pace und pres.* . . . .(9 to 2 op 7 to 1 tchd 8 to 1) 2

HABASHA (Ire) (bl) 10-7 J Lower, *led till jmpd slwly and hdd 3rd, led 4th to four out, wknd nxt, tld off.* . . . . (11 to 4 op 7 to 4 tchd 3 to 1) 3

BUNDERBURG (USA) 10-12 D Skyrme, *chsd ldrs, led 3rd to nxt, wknd approching 4 out, tld off.* . . . . (15 to 2 op 5 to 1 tchd 8 to 1) 4

997* PYRRHIC DANCE 11-8 B Powell, *chsd ldrs to 4th, sn wknd, tld off whn pld up bef 2 out.* (10 to 1 op 6 to 1) pu
1007³ MOHAYA (USA) 10-12 R Bellamy, *in tch till wknd rpdly and pld up 4 out, broke leg, destroyed.*
.......................(7 to 1 op 5 to 1 tchd 8 to 1) pu
Dist: 2½l, dist, 20l. 4m 5.30s. a 16.30s (6 Ran).
SR: 28/25/-/ (M J Lewin), R Simpson

WORCESTER (soft)
Wednesday November 10th
Going Correction: PLUS 1.25 sec. per fur. (races 1,3,- 6,7), PLUS 1.00 (2,4,5)

1167
Rayburn Royal Novices' Hurdle (4-y-o and up) £1,480 2m 5f 110yds.... (1:00)

WORLD WITHOUT END (USA) 4-11-0 Diane Clay, *jmpd rght, led aftr 1st, rdn 3 out, hdd briefly last, rallied, jst hld on.*.................(8 to 1 op 5 to 1 tchd 9 to 1) 1
983 NED THE HALL (Ire) 5-11-0 N Williamson, *hld up, smooth hdwy 6th, pressed wnr 3 out, led briefly last, kpt on und pres, jst fld.*....(21 to 20 fav op Evens tchd 5 to 4) 2
TALBOT 7-11-0 J Osborne, *led till aftr 1st, outpcd appr 3 out, rallied sn after, ev ch till last strds.*
..................(25 to 1 op 33 to 1 tchd 66 to 1) 3
743² GALES CAVALIER (Ire) 5-11-0 R Dunwoody, *hld up, hdwy 4 out, ev ch 2 out, wknd r-in.*
..................(11 to 2 op 7 to 2 tchd 6 to 1) 4
901⁶ GOSPEL (Ire) 4-10-9 C Llewellyn, *hld up in tch, mstk 6th, lost touch aftr nxt, tld off.*
..................(10 to 1 op 8 to 1 tchd 12 to 1) 5
988⁹ MAPLE BAY (Ire) 4-11-0 G McCourt, *al beh, tld off.*
..................(66 to 1 op 50 to 1) 6
983⁹ ANDRATH (Ire) 5-11-0 W Humphreys, *trkd ldrs till wknd 4 out, tld off.*..................(66 to 1 op 50 to 1) 7
FALSIDE 9-10-7 (7*) M Trott, *al beh, tld off frm 5th.*
..................(66 to 1 op 33 to 1) 8
891² LAW FACULTY (Ire) 4-11-0 S Mackey, *trkd ldrs, rdn whn jmpd slwly 5th, sn tld off.*......(33 to 1 op 20 to 1) 9
FIRST CENTURY (Ire) 4-10-7 (7*) Mr J L Llewellyn, *pld hrd, chsd ldrs till wknd rpdly 4 out, tld off.*
..................(40 to 1 op 20 to 1) 10
DARKBROOK 6-11-0 P Holley, *al beh, tld off whn pld up bef 3 out.*.................(10 to 1 op 5 to 1) pu
1023 RED NEST 5-10-9 T Wall, *al beh, tld off whn pld up bef 3 out.*..................(66 to 1 op 50 to 1) pu
RONEO (USA) 5-10-9 (5*) S Curran, *prmnt to 4th, tld off whn pld up bef 3 out.*..........(66 to 1 op 50 to 1) pu
ANDALUCIAN SUN (Ire) 5-11-0 Richard Guest, *beh frm 6th, tld off whn pld up bef 3 out.*.......(14 to 1 op 8 to 1) pu
Dist: Sht-hd, sht-hd, 10l, dist, 5l, 3½l, 2l, ½l, 6l. 5m 27.00s. a 33.00s (14 Ran).
SR: 25/25/15/-/-/ (B A S Limited), W Clay

1168
Kohlangaz Handicap Chase (0-120 4-y-o and up) £3,080 2m....... (1:30)

1022⁴ SAILORS LUCK [97] 8-10-5 M Dwyer, *jmpd wl, al frnt rnk, led appr 4 out, drw clr 2 out, eased r-in.* .....(9 to 2 jt-fav op 4 to 1 tchd 5 to 1) 1
987 TERRIBLE GEL (Fr) [105] 8-10-13 P Niven, *hld up in rear, hdwy frm 4 out, kpt on r-in.*......(7 to 1 op 6 to 1) 2
840* THATS THE LIFE [120] 8-12-0 M A FitzGerald, *led till aftr 3rd, led 6th till appr 4 out, one pace after.*
..................(8 to 1 op 7 to 1) 3
1044 FRED SPLENDID [95] 10-10-3 R Dunwoody, *trkd ldrs, ev ch 4 out, wknd aftr nxt.*..................(8 to 1) 4
TURKISH STAR [92] 8-10-0 S McNeill, *not jump wl, al beh, tld off.*..................(20 to 1 op 10 to 1) 5
999⁴ EDWARD SEYMOUR (USA) T Jenks, [92] 6-9-10¹ (5*) *wl beh whn blun 5th, tld off.*......(25 to 1 op 20 to 1) 6
OVER THE POLE [108] 6-11-2 D Murphy, *trkd ldrs, not fluent, wknd aftr mstks 6th and 7, btn whn f 3 out.*
..................(9 to 2 jt-fav op 7 to 2) f
DARE SAY [100] 10-10-8 G Upton, *tld off 4th, blun 7th, sn pld up.*..................(8 to 1 op 5 to 1) pu
500⁵ TINAS LAD [105] 10-10-13 N Williamson, *chsd ldrs, wknd rpdly 4 out, blun 2 out, sn pld up.*(12 to 1 op 8 to 1) pu
MAJOR EFFORT [92] 8-9-10³ (7*) Mr N Bradley, *beh whn pld up bef 4th.*..................(50 to 1 op 33 to 1) pu
1084⁸ ALAN BALL [104] (bl) 7-10-12 H Davies, *pld hrd, led aftr 3rd, hdd 6th, wknd rpdly 5 out, pulled up bef nxt.*
..................(8 to 1 op 7 to 1) pu
Dist: 5l, 3½l, 7l, 25l, 15l. 4m 10.30s. a 21.30s (11 Ran).
SR: 24/27/38/6/-/-/ (Geoffrey C Greenwood), P G Murphy

1169
Rayburn Nouvelle 'National Hunt' Novices' Hurdle (4-y-o and up) £1,480 3m..........................(2:00)

RAMPOLDI (USA) 6-10-12 G Bradley, *hld up, moved clr frm 7th, led last, rdn out.*............ (7 to 1 op 4 to 1) 1
SOUTHERLY GALE 6-10-12 R Dunwoody, *hld up in rear, hdwy 4 out, chlgd last, one pace r-in.*
..................(12 to 1 op 10 to 1) 2

YES MAN (Ire) 4-10-11 J Osborne, *hld up, hdwy to go second hfwy, led aftr 7th, rdn and hdd last, one pace r-in.*..................(5 to 2 fav op 9 to 4 tchd 3 to 1) 3
770³ SUASANAN SIOSANA 8-10-7 (5*) Mr T Byrne, *mid-div, hdwy 7th, rdn appr 3 out, sn btn, tld off.*
..................(10 to 1 op 16 to 1) 4
1023⁷ WANDERLINE 6-10-12 Peter Caldwell, *beh whn mstk 7th, tld off aftr.*..................(50 to 1 op 33 to 1) 5
CARAGH BRIDGE 6-10-12 N Williamson, *hld up, hdwy hfwy, wknd quickly 3 out, tld off.*
..................(5 to 1 op 8 to 1 tchd 9 to 1) 6
NICHOLAS JAMES (Ire) 5-10-12 Richard Guest, *f 5th, dead.*..................(12 to 1 tchd 14 to 1) f
982⁶ ROCKCLIFFE LAD 4-10-11 C Llewellyn, *in tch till wknd 4 out, tld off whn f last.*..........(14 to 1 op 10 to 1) f
QUEENS WALK 5-10-7 (7*) D Matthews, *broke leg and f second, destroyed.*...(40 to 1 op 33 to 1 tchd 50 to 1) f
814⁷ DOCTOR DUNKLIN (USA) 4-10-6 (5*) R Davis, *bright dwn second.*..................(50 to 1) bd
862 LIZZIES LASS 8-10-7 M Crosse, *pld hrd, led aftr 1st, hdd 4th, wknd rpdly after 6th, pulled up bef nxt.*
..................(100 to 1 op 50 to 1) pu
934⁹ ZACTOO 7-10-12 T Wall, *beh whn mstk 8th, pld up bef nxt.*..........(66 to 1 op 50 to 1 tchd 100 to 1) pu
PUSHY PARSON 7-10-12 Mr R Armson, *sn tld off, pld up bef 7th.*..................(100 to 1 op 33 to 1) pu
1000² ADMIRAL VILLENEUVE 5-10-12 J Railton, *led till aftr 1st, styd prmnt, ev ch 3 out, pld up lme bef nxt.*
..................(4 to 1 op 5 to 2) pu
743 MISTY GREY 4-10-4 (7*) S Lycett, *sn trkd ldr, led 4th, hdd aftr 7th, wknd quickly nxt, tld off whn pld up bef 2 out.*..................(100 to 1 op 50 to 1) pu
901 ITS GRAND 4-10-4 (7*) A Flannigan, *sn beh, tld off whn pld up bef 8th.*..................(100 to 1 op 50 to 1) pu
864⁸ BALLYGRIFFIN LAD (Ire) 4-10-11 W McFarland, *tld off frm hfwy, pld up bef 2 out.*.....(66 to 1 op 50 to 1) pu
ZODIAC STAR 4-10-6 S Mackey, *sn wl beh, pld up bef 7th.*..................(66 to 1 op 50 to 1) pu
Dist: 1½l, 1½l, dist, 1½l, dist. 6m 18.50s. a 42.50s (18 Ran).
(Paul K Barber), P F Nicholls

1170
Aga Worcester Novices' Chase Grade 2 (5-y-o and up) £7,608 2m 7f.... (2:30)

933* SEE MORE INDIANS 6-11-5 G Bradley, *trkd ldr frm 6th, lft in ld 4 out, sn drw clr.*..................(7 to 2 op 5 to 2) 1
1008 RUN UP THE FLAG 6-11-1 D Murphy, *trkd ldrs, lft cl second 4 out, sn wknd, eased r-in.*
..................(9 to 1 op 8 to 1 tchd 10 to 1) 2
CRAIGSTOWN (Ire) 5-10-13 R Davis, *al beh, kpt on one pace frm 4 out.*..................(100 to 1) 3
PRIME DISPLAY (USA) 7-11-1 J Osborne, *trkd ldr to 6th, wknd tenth, tld off.*...(12 to 1 op 7 to 1 tchd 14 to 1) 4
ASK FOR MORE 8-11-1 N Williamson, *beh, hit 8th, tld off frm 11th.*..................(33 to 1 op 20 to 1) 5
CANAVER 7-11-1 G McCourt, *hit second, blun badly 5th, sn tld off, came hme in own time.*
..................(33 to 1 tchd 40 to 1) 6
868* GAELSTROM 6-10-10 C Llewellyn, *led, in command whn f 4 out.*..................(7 to 4 on op 6 to 4 on) f
ONE MORE RUN 6-11-1 Richard Guest, *wl beh whn blun tenth, pld up bef 4 out.*..................(33 to 1) pu
Dist: 30l, 15l, 12l, 7l, ½l. 6m 16.40s. a 32.40s (8 Ran).
(Paul K Barber), P F Nicholls

1171
Glynwed Handicap Chase (0-135 5-y-o and up) £3,392 2m 7f.......... (3:00)

DO BE BRIEF [113] (bl) 8-10-12 I Lawrence, *trkd ldr, led 6th, hit tenth and 11th, hrd rdn r-in, all out.*
..................(11 to 1 op 9 to 2 tchd 12 to 1) 1
DUBACILLA [126] 7-11-11 J Osborne, *wtd wth in tch, blun 6th, trkd wnr frm 11th, mstks 2 out, rdn appr last, ran on und pres.*.........(6 to 1 op 5 to 1 tchd 7 to 1) 2
BERESFORDS GIRL [106] 8-10-5 M Dwyer, *hld up in rear, hit tenth, hdwy 13th, nvr nr to chal.*
..................(14 to 1 op 10 to 1) 3
647 THATCHER ROCK (NZ) [110] 8-10-9 G Bradley, *hld up in rear, making gd hdwy whn jmpd rght 13th, rdn appr 3 out, sn btn.*........(11 to 8 fav op 6 to 4 tchd 13 to 8) 4
MONUMENTAL LAD [123] 10-11-8 G McCourt, *hld up, gd hdwy hfwy, prmnt till wknd quickly appr 3 out, tld off.*..................(5 to 1 op 4 to 1) 5
BOWL OF OATS [109] 7-10-8 S McNeill, *trkd ldrs till mstk 9th, sn beh, tld off.*..........(7 to 1 tchd 6 to 1) 6
860 GLENGRIFFIN [101] 8-9-12³ (5*) P Hide, *in tch till mstk tenth, sn beh, tld off.*..................(33 to 1 op 20 to 1) 7
946³ WINGSPAN (USA) [122] 9-11-7 N Mann, *led to 6th, wknd 11th, tld off whn pld up bef 4 out.*(20 to 1 tchd 25 to 1) pu
LAKE TEEREEN [121] 8-11-6 T Grantham, *beh, effrt tenth, wknd 12th, tld off whn pld up bef 4 out.*
..................(7 to 1 tchd 8 to 1) pu
GLEN CHERRY [108] 7-10-7 C Llewellyn, *prmnt till wknd 11th, tld off whn pld up bef 4 out.* (16 to 1 op 14 to 1) pu
737⁷ MAJOR KINSMAN [117] 8-11-2 L Harvey, *beh, lost tch 11th, tld off whn pld up bef 4 out.*
..................(14 to 1 op 12 to 1 tchd 20 to 1) pu

Dist: ½l, 25l, 2½l, 25l, 12l, ¾l. 6m 11.70s. a 27.70s (11 Ran).
SR: 37/49/4/5/-/-/ (Errol Brown), Mrs J Pitman

1172 Coalbrookdale Handicap Hurdle (0-145 4-y-o and up) £3,492 2¼m (3:30)

1012^{2} CHANGE THE ACT [124] (bl) 8-11-10 J Osborne, *trkd ldrs, led 5th, clr 2 out, idled appr last, pushed out r-in.* ....(3 to 1 op 2 to 1) 1
ALBERTITO (Fr) [115] 6-10-12 (3*) S Wynne, *hld up, gd hdwy 4 out, chlgd nxt, wknd and one pace aftr.* ....(5 to 1 op 9 to 2) 2
1025 MOUNTSHANNON [103] (bl) 7-10-3^{3} Peter Caldwell, *pld hrd, dsptd ld second and 3rd, rdn 5th, wknd appr 3 out, tld off*........ (33 to 1 op 25 to 1 tchd 50 to 1) 3
KAHER (USA) [108] 6-10-8 C Llewellyn, *al beh, lost tch 4 out, tld off*........ (6 to 1 op 4 to 1) 4
ROVULENKA [108] 5-10-8 R Dunwoody, *made most to 5th, wknd quickly, tld off.* ....(6 to 4 on op 5 to 4 tchd 6 to 4) 5
932^{8} SHOW THE FLAG [100] 5-10-0 T Wall, *tld off 4th, pld up bef 3 out*........ (100 to 1 op 50 to 1) pu
Dist: 7l, dist, 30l, 15l. 4m 40.30s. a 32.30s (6 Ran).
(Christopher Heath), O Sherwood

1173 Levy Board Novices' Handicap Hurdle (4-y-o and up) £2,742 2m....... (4:00)

988^{3} SAINT CIEL (USA) [75] 5-10-7 M A FitzGerald, *hld up in tch, drvn to ld appr last, rdn out*........ (4 to 1 op 5 to 1) 1
1068^{8} NONCOMMITAL [68] 6-10-0 N Williamson, *hld up in mid-div, hdwy 5th, led briefly sn aftr 2 out, rdn and one pace r-in*........ (12 to 1 op 7 to 1) 2
KLINGON (Ire) [84] 4-10-11 (5*) R Farrant, *trkd ldr, led 4 out, rdn and hdd sn aftr 2 out, no extr.* .... (14 to 1 op 6 to 1) 3
983^{8} MR POPPLETON [69] 4-10-1^{1} D J Burchell, *mid-div, hdwy 4th, in tch whn mstk 3 out, no imprsn aftr.* .... (20 to 1 op 20 to 1) 4
889^{4} TALLAND STREAM [78] 6-10-10 C Llewellyn, *trkd ldrs till wknd quickly appr 2 out.* ....(2 to 1 fav op 5 to 2 tchd 7 to 2) 5
988^{8} NOTHINGBUTTROUBLE [68] 9-10-0 L Harvey, *al towards rear*........ (20 to 1 op 16 to 1 tchd 25 to 1) 6
650^{4} MARINERS COVE [80] 5-10-12 W Humphreys, *mid-div, lost tch appr 3 out*........ (6 to 1 op 7 to 1 tchd 5 to 1) 7
794 GRAND RAPIDS (USA) [92] 6-11-3 (7*) Mr J Llewellyn, *trkd ldrs, wknd appr 3 out*........ (20 to 1 op 10 to 1) 8
773^{5} LUCAYAN GOLD [68] 9-10-0 R Greene, *led till hdd 4 out, wknd quickly*........ (12 to 1 op 8 to 1) 9
ALTISHAR (Ire) [70] 5-10-2 P Holley, *al in rear.* .... (10 to 1 op 6 to 1) 10
659 FAIR BABE [68] 7-9-10^{3} (7*) Mr N Bradley, *tld off 4th, pld up bef nxt*........ (50 to 1 op 33 to 1) pu
THE JET SET [86] 6-11-4 W McFarland, *in tch, mstks, wknd 5th, tld off whn pld up bef 2 out.* .... (14 to 1 op 10 to 1 tchd 16 to 1) pu
GENERAL SHOT [82] 8-11-0 Diane Clay, *al beh, tld off whn pld up bef 2 out*........ (16 to 1 op 14 to 1) pu
704^{6} KAYRUZ [68] 5-9-7 (7*) Mr G Lewis, *al beh, tld off whn pld up bef 2 out*........ (25 to 1 op 20 to 1) pu
Dist: 4l, 5l, 4l, 12l, ½l, ¾l, 1l, 6l, 2½l. 4m 6.70s. a 25.70s (14 Ran).
SR: 22/11/22/3/-/-/-/11/-/ (Tam Racing), F Jordan

CLONMEL (IRE) (soft) Thursday November 11th

1174 Cashel Maiden Hurdle (5-y-o and up) £2,243 2m.................... (1:00)

942* WILD FANTASY (Ire) 5-11-2 (7*) K P Gaule, ...(7 to 4 fav) 1
993^{6} SEA GALE (Ire) 5-11-1 C F Swan, ...(7 to 2) 2
942^{2} BEGLAWELLA 6-11-9 K F O'Brien, ...(6 to 1) 3
KNOCKAVERRY (Ire) 5-11-2 (7*) Mr M Budds, ... (14 to 1) 4
877 CALDARO 6-11-6 L P Cusack, ...(16 to 1) 5
969^{4} FINNEGANS WAKE 6-11-6 T Horgan, ...(12 to 1) 6
798 BEAU GRANDE (Ire) 5-12-0 P L Malone, ... (12 to 1) 7
1076 THE COBH GALE 6-11-1 H Rogers, ... (20 to 1) 8
907 ASHTON'S VENTURE (Ire) 5-10-8 (7*) M Kelly, ... (20 to 1) 9
ALBONA 5-11-9 D H O'Connor, ...(25 to 1) 10
877^{6} HANG A RIGHT 6-11-9 (5*) T P Treacy, ...(7 to 1) 11
675* BETTYS THE BOSS (Ire) 5-11-9 F J Flood, ...(8 to 1) 12
1074^{6} MASTER CRUSADER 7-12-0 J Shortt, ... (12 to 1) 13
TOMMY'S RUN 6-11-9 (5*) D T Evans, ... (12 to 1) 14
FESTIVAL LIGHT (Ire) 5-11-6 A J O'Brien, ... (33 to 1) 15
SNUGLET (Ire) 5-11-6 M Duffy, ...(33 to 1) 16
CORRIB HAVEN (Ire) 5-10-13 (7*) J P Broderick, .. (25 to 1) 17
49 NORDIC RACE 6-11-1 (5*) P A Roche, ... (20 to 1) 18
305^{5} JO-SU-KI 6-11-6 G Bradley, ... (12 to 1) 19
853 SWEET DEMOND 8-10-13 (7*) J M Donnelly, ... (50 to 1) 20
Dist: 1l, 6l, hd, 5½l. 4m 15.30s. (20 Ran).
(L F Curtin), A P O'Brien

1175 Irish National Hunt Novice Hurdle (4-y-o and up) £4,140 2m.......... (1:30)

672^{2} PADASHPAN (USA) 4-11-1 C F Swan, ...(7 to 4) 1
937* PADRE MIO (Ire) 5-12-0 G Bradley, ... (11 to 10 fav) 2
798* MISS LIME 6-10-10 (5*) P A Roche, ...(11 to 2) 3
1075* WATERLOO LADY 6-11-0 (5*) D P Murphy, ... (10 to 1) 4
937^{5} GREEN GLEN (USA) (bl) 4-11-1 B Sheridan, ... (10 to 1) 5
Dist: 9l, 6l, 7l, 10l. 4m 12.30s. (5 Ran).
(William Brennan), W P Mullins

1176 Templemore Handicap Hurdle (0-116 4-y-o and up) £2,243 2m........ (2:00)

880^{6} VICOSA (Ire) [-] 4-10-9 (5*) Mr A E Lacy, ... (12 to 1) 1
1038^{2} JIMMY THE JACKDAW [-] (bl) 6-10-6 P Carberry, ... (9 to 4 fav) 2
991^{3} SO PINK (Ire) [-] 5-11-5 (5*) T P Treacy, ...(5 to 2) 3
854 NISHIKI (USA) [-] 4-10-7 G M O'Neill, ... (12 to 1) 4
528^{5} ANOTHER COURSE (Ire) [-] 5-10-3 (7*) Mr P M Cloke, ...(14 to 1) 5
925 MOSCOW DUKE (Ire) [-] 4-10-3 J Jones, ...(16 to 1) 6
928^{4} QUIET CITY [-] 6-10-11 (7*) J P Broderick, ...(8 to 1) 7
DARCY'S THATCHER [-] 9-11-4 (5*) C P Dunne, ...(8 to 1) 8
967 CRAZY LADY [-] 7-9-8 (7*) J M Donnelly, ... (25 to 1) 9
902* BALLYHYLAND (Ire) [-] 4-11-5 S H O'Donovan, ...(6 to 1) ro
RAMINA (Ire) [-] 5-9-13 J K Kinane, ... (33 to 1) pu
Dist: 3½l, 1l, 5½l, 1l. 4m 18.20s. (11 Ran).
(T F Lacy), T F Lacy

1177 Merck Sharp & Dohme Eqvalan Chase (5-y-o and up) £3,623 2¼m......(2:30)

ROYAL MOUNTBROWNE 5-11-4 J F Titley, ... (14 to 1) 1
1073^{2} CHIC AND ELITE 6-11-2 P P Kinane, ... (8 to 1) 2
674^{4} DORAN'S TOWN LAD 6-12-0 G Bradley, ... (3 to 1) 3
1035^{6} TAKE IT EASY KID (Ire) 5-10-8 (5*) D P Murphy, ... (16 to 1) 4
965^{3} LADY OLEIN (Ire) 5-10-13 C F Swan, ...(7 to 4 fav) 5
FAIR LISSELAN (Ire) 5-10-13 G M O'Neill, ... (10 to 1) 6
941^{8} THE WEST'S ASLEEP 8-11-4 (3*) C O'Brien, ...(16 to 1) 7
941^{4} DANNIGALE 7-11-7 Mr M Phillips, ...(16 to 1) 8
929 NORTHERN ACE (bl) 7-11-7 A Powell, ...(16 to 1) 9
1035^{4} BALLAGH COUNTESS 6-11-2 K F O'Brien, ...(14 to 1) 10
799^{9} AMERICAN EYRE 8-12-0 C O'Dwyer, ...(10 to 1) 11
1035 HARLANE (Ire) 5-11-4 F Woods, ...(50 to 1) 12
MONEY MADE 6-11-0 (7*) Mr W J Gleeson, ... (40 to 1) 13
1035 SEANS SHOON 6-11-2 A J O'Brien, ...(33 to 1) 14
929^{6} HAVE TO THINK 5-10-13 (5*) T P Rudd, ... (8 to 1) f
Dist: 1l, 9l, 2½l, 1l. 4m 43.60s. (15 Ran).
(Mrs J O'Kane), Patrick G Kelly

1178 Powerstown Handicap Hurdle (4-y-o and up) £2,243 2½m............(3:00)

903* RICH TRADITION (Ire) [-] 5-10-8 C O'Dwyer, ... (7 to 4 fav) 1
854^{8} DOONEGA (Ire) [-] 5-10-8 (3*) C O'Brien, ... (12 to 1) 2
991^{6} CHELSEA NATIVE [-] 6-10-12 (5*) Susan A Finn, ...(8 to 1) 3
858^{4} KING OF THE WORLD (Ire) [-] 5-9-2 (5*) T J O'Sullivan, ...(10 to 1) 4
MRS BARTON (Ire) [-] 5-10-1 M Duffy, ...(8 to 1) 5
1038^{3} BALLINDERRY GLEN [-] 7-9-10 J Collins, ... (10 to 1) 6
904^{8} MYSTIC GALE (Ire) [-] 5-9-11 P McWilliams, ... (12 to 1) 7
880^{9} NUALA'S PET [-] 8-10-9 C F Swan, ...(7 to 2) 8
KING OF THE GLEN [-] 7-10-7 T Horgan, ...(8 to 1) 9
1037^{8} ROSSI NOVAE [-] 10-9-7 P Carberry, ... (16 to 1) 10
1037 MARBLE CITY GIRL [-] (bl) 8-9-0 (7*) J P Broderick, (12 to 1) 11
1017^{7} VINCERO [-] 8-10-3 (5*) M G Cleary, ...(16 to 1) 12
413^{7} CARA DEILISH [-] (bl) 7-10-3 F Woods, ...(16 to 1) 13
PARSONS BRIG [-] 7-10-13 K F O'Brien, ... (12 to 1) 14
DHARKOUM [-] 6-9-7^{7} (7*) Mr R White, ... (16 to 1) I
Dist: Sht-hd, 1½l, 1l, 25l. 5m 13.40s. (15 Ran).
(D R Killian), Anthony Mullins

1179 Kilsheelan Handicap Chase (0-102 5-y-o and up) £2,243 2½m..... (3:30)

966^{3} BOB DEVANI [-] 7-11-5 P Carberry, ... (7 to 2 fav) 1
928^{6} VINEYARD SPECIAL [-] 7-11-11 K F O'Brien, ... (12 to 1) 2
928* MAKE ME AN ISLAND [-] 8-11-5 J F Titley, ...(15 to 2) 3
691^{4} BOG LEAF VI [-] (bl) 10-9-5 (3*) C O'Brien, ...(14 to 1) 4
332^{8} MERLYNS CHOICE [-] 9-10-8 C F Swan, ...(14 to 1) 5
878^{7} LADY EILY [-] 8-11-3 F Woods, ...(6 to 1) 6
800^{7} HURRYUP [-] 6-11-6 (3*) T J Mitchell, ...(12 to 1) 7
928^{7} NOBLE CLANSMAN (USA) [-] 12-11-10 Mr P J Healy, ...(20 to 1) 8
1035^{7} RUSSIAN GALE (Ire) [-] 5-10-8 J Collins, ... (20 to 1) 9
905^{5} MCMAHON'S RIVER [-] 6-11-1 D H O'Connor, ...(12 to 1) 10
806^{7} BENS DILEMMA [-] 8-10-2 (7*) J P Broderick, ...(10 to 1) 11
573 BALLYHEIGUE [-] 7-11-4 G Bradley, ...(10 to 1) 12
905^{6} SHUIL LE CHEILE [-] 6-10-8 W T Slattery Jnr, ...(16 to 1) 13
THE PHOENO [-] 7-9-10 (7*) P P Curran, ... (25 to 1) 14
1035 WADI RUM [-] 7-10-7 (7*) Mr J White, ...(20 to 1) 15
691^{6} CROW RUN [-] 11-10-1 C O'Dwyer, ...(20 to 1) 16
928^{2} DEL MONTE BOY [-] 8-11-4 G M O'Neill, ...(7 to 1) f
906 JOHNJOES PRIDE [-] (bl) 9-10-8 T Horgan, ...(14 to 1) pu
905 CLONEENVERB [-] 9-10-3^{1} (5*) D P Murphy, ...(20 to 1) pu
989^{4} BALLYBRIKEN CASTLE [-] 6-9-12 (5*) T J O'Sullivan, ...(16 to 1) pu
Dist: 3½l, sht-hd, 7l, sht-hd. 5m 24.00s. (20 Ran).
(John O'Meara), Noel Meade

1180 Cahir INH Flat Race (4-y-o) £2,243 2m
.............................(4:00)

ARIES GIRL 10-9 (7") Mr E Norris, ...(Evens fav) 1
THE REAL ARTICLE (Ire) 11-0 (7") Mr T J Murphy, (14 to 1) 2
1039⁶ LEISURE CENTRE (Ire) 10-9 (7") Mr P Cody, ...(20 to 1) 3
1039² SIOBHAILIN DUBH (Ire) 10-9 (7") Mr G F Ryan, ...(5 to 1) 4
CREATIVE BLAZE (Ire) 10-9 (7") Mr D A Harney, ... (12 to 1) 5
1077⁴ SAM VAUGHAN (Ire) 11-0 (7") Mr W M O'Sullivan, (10 to 1) 6
1036 OZEYCAZEY (Ire) 11-2 (5") Mr J A Nash, ... (12 to 1) 7
1039³ BROWNRATH KING (Ire) 11-0 (7") Mr D K Budds, ...(8 to 1) 8
1039⁵ CASTLE CLUB (Ire) 10-13 (3") Mr R O'Neill, ...(20 to 1) 9
ANDROS GALE (Ire) 11-0 (7") Mr M Cahill, ...(10 to 1) 10
930³ WASHINGTON HEIGHTS (USA) 11-0 (7") Mr M Brennan,
....(12 to 1) 11
1052⁵ WISE STATEMENT (Ire) 11-7 Mr A P O'Brien, ... (12 to 1) 12
990 PEGUS PRINCE (Ire) 11-0 (7") Mr J T McNamara, .. (25 to 1) 13
SHANNON AMBER (Ire) 10-9 (7") Mr P Henley, ... (16 to 1) 14
MASALA (Ire) 10-9 (7") Mr R Neylon, ... (25 to 1) 15
NOT A BID (Ire) 10-9 (7") Mr R White, ... (25 to 1) 16
LANCASTER LADY (Ire) 10-13 (3") Miss M Olivefalk,
....(25 to 1) 17
1039 VAIN PRINCESS (Ire) 11-2 Mr M Phillips, ... (50 to 1) 18
Dist: 8l, 2l, 3½l, hd. 4m 15.30s. (18 Ran).

(W E Sturt), P J Flynn

KELSO (good)
Thursday November 11th
Going Correction: PLUS 0.95 sec. per fur. (races 1,3,6), PLUS 0.70 (2,4,5)

1181 Scottish Sports Aid Foundation 'National Hunt' Novices' Hurdle (4-y-o and up) £2,145 2¾m 110yds.....(1:10)

770* LARAPINTA (Ire) 5-11-2 (3") D J Moffatt, patiently rdn,
improved into midfield hfwy, led betw last 2, styd on
wl...(6 to 1 tchd 7 to 1) 1
728 MAJORITY MAJOR (Ire) 4-10-12 K Johnson, settled wth
chasing grp, effrt and drvn alng aftr 3 out, styd on
r-in..............................(10 to 1 op 8 to 1 tchd 11 to 1) 2
DALUSMAN (Ire) 5-10-12 B Storey, settled midfield,
improved fnl circuit, effrt and rdn betw last 2, styd on
same pace.......................................(33 to 1) 3
1028⁸ MASTER BOSTON (Ire) 5-10-12 R Garritty, wtd wth,
improved into midfield fnl circuit, drvn alng last 2, one
pace r-in...(33 to 1) 4
RUN PET RUN 8-10-2 (5") T Jenks, led 3rd, sn clr, hdd and
pushed alng betw last 2, no extr r-in. (9 to 1 op 7 to 1) 5
577⁷ TWIN STATES 4-10-5 (7") W Fry, beh and pushed alng 1st
circuit, styd on frm 3 out, nrst finish.
.... (33 to 1 op 25 to 1) 6
JUST A LIGHT (Ire) 5-10-5 (7") F Perratt, settled off the
pace, improve fnl circuit, kpt on, nvr nrr.
.... (33 to 1 op 20 to 1) 7
1099³ FIVE FLAGS (Ire) 5-10-12 Gary Lyons, settled wth chasing
grp, feeling pace aftr 3 out, fdd.
.... (13 to 2 op 5 to 1 tchd 7 to 1) 8
1000⁸ NAWRIK (Ire) 4-10-12 T Reed, narrow ld to 3rd, hndy till
fdd 3 out............................(20 to 1 op 14 to 1) 9
BUSY BOY 6-10-12 A Merrigan, chsd ldrs, feeling pace
whn hmpd by faller 5 out, sn lost tch.
.............................(10 to 1 op 16 to 1 tchd 8 to 1) 10
1092⁸ JUST EVE 6-10-2 (5") P Williams, chsd alng to keep up aftr
one circuit, sn lost tch.................... (66 to 1 op 50 to 1) 11
723⁵ THE WEATHERMAN 5-10-9 (3") N Bentley, wth chasing grp
for o'r one circuit, fdd 3 out........... (16 to 1 op 14 to 1) 12
731⁹ BE AMBITIOUS (Ire) 5-10-12 K Jones, struggling aftr one
circuit, tld off................(50 to 1 tchd 66 to 1) 13
JUST MOLLY 6-10-7 M Dwyer, blun and almost uns rdr
1st, struggling aftr one circuit, tld off.
....(6 to 1 op 4 to 1) 14
STEPDAUGHTER 7-10-7 C Dennis, struggling aftr one
circuit, tld off................................(100 to 1) 15
WHO SIR 7-10-12 C Grant, beh and drvn alng aftr one
circuit, tld off................(20 to 1 op 16 to 1) 16
MASTER CAVERS (Ire) 5-10-12 J Supple, struggling and
reminders hfwy, tld off..........(33 to 1 op 66 to 1) 17
NINFA (Ire) 5-10-8¹ N Doughty, settled gng wl, second and
clsg whn f 5 out................(11 to 4 fav op 7 to 2) f
Dist: 3½l, 1½l, hd, 1½l, 12l, ½l, 8l, 3l, 3l, 6l. 5m 42.50s. a 31.50s (18 Ran).

(Thomas Harty), J H Johnson

1182 Border Fine Arts Novices' Handicap Chase (5-y-o and up) £2,737 2m 1f
.............................(1:40)

OLD EROS [93] 9-11-8 P Niven, not fluent, led till
rstrained 4th, led four out, styd on to go clr appr last.
.......................(6 to 1 5 fav op 11 to 10 tchd 5 to 4) 1
MARLINGFORD [99] 6-12-0 C Hawkins, chsd ldg pair,
struggling hfwy, styd on frm betw last 2, no imprsn.
.............................(14 to 1 op 10 to 1) 2

820² ZARBANO [83] 7-10-12 A Merrigan, chsd alng to go pace
hfwy, improved und pres aftr 3 out, not pace to chal.
.............................(8 to 1 op 7 to 1 tchd 9 to 1) 3
818 CARDENDEN (Ire) [72] 5-10-11 S Turner, struggling to keep
up hfwy, some hdwy frm 3 out, nvr dngrs.
.............................(66 to 1 op 33 to 1) 4
1093* SEMINOFF (Fr) [81] 7-10-10 (6ex) A Orkney, not fluent, led
4th till blun and hdd four out, fdd betw last 2.
.............................(5 to 1 tchd 6 to 1) 5
909 NORTHERN VISION [74] 6-10-3 K Johnson, beh and struggling aftr 3 out, tld off...........(20 to 1 op 14 to 1) 6
1061³ CELTIC SONG [90] 6-11-5 T Reed, blun and nrly uns rdr
3rd, not reco'r, tld off whn pld up betw last 2.
.............................(3 to 1 op 11 to 4) pu
Dist: 10l, 4l, 5l, 3l, dist. 4m 23.80s. a 17.80s (7 Ran).
SR: 35/31/11/-/1/-/-/ (T S Child), Mrs M Reveley

1183 Langholm Dyeing Company Novices' Handicap Hurdle (4-y-o and up) £2,302 2m 110yds...................(2:10)

CARNETTO [72] 6-10-10 K Johnson, nvr far away, drvn
ahead betw last 2, styd on und pres r-in.
.............................(6 to 1 op 5 to 1) 1
734⁴ FLING IN SPRING [83] 7-11-2 (5") P Williams, tucked away
in midfield, chlgd 2 out, hrd drvn frm last, one pace.
.............................(5 to 1 tchd 6 to 1) 2
1092² STINGRAY CITY (USA) [86] 4-11-3 (7") F Perratt, lft in ld aftr
1st, quickened appr 3 out, hdd betweeen last 2, no extr.
.............................(11 to 10 1av op 5 to 4) 3
779⁸ JUKE BOX BILLY (Ire) [70] 5-10-5 (3") A Larnach, ran in
snatches, outpcd and lost grnd 3 out, styd on und pres
r-in.............................(7 to 2 op 6 to 1 tchd 7 to 1) 4
1099⁹ DOLLY PRICES [62] 8-9-7 (7") S Taylor, last and hld up,
effrt hfwy, rdn and outpcd aftr 3 out.
.............................(10 to 1 op 16 to 1 tchd 25 to 1) 5
1092⁷ RALLYING CRY (Ire) [80] 5-11-4 B Storey, wth ldr, drvn
alng aftr 3 out, btn betw last 2.....(16 to 1 op 14 to 1) 6
CHOIR'S IMAGE [78] 6-11-2 A Mulholland, settled midfield,
ev ch aftr 4 out, fdd nxt.........................(20 to 1) 7
BIN LID (Ire) [73] 4-10-4 (7") B Harding, nvr far away, effrt
hfwy, outpcd 3 out...............(16 to 1 op 14 to 1) 8
818 EMPEROR ALEXANDER (Ire) [78] 5-11-2 S Turner, in tch,
effrt hfwy, feeling pace whn blun 3 out, pld up bef nxt.
.............................(33 to 1) pu
821 CLEAR FOUNTAIN [65] 6-9-12 (5") T Jenks, led till pld up
lme aftr 1st...............(14 to 1 op 10 to 1) pu
Dist: 4l, 2½l, 1½l, 7l, 8l, 15l, 6l. 4m 5.00s. a 22.00s (10 Ran).
SR: 19/26/26/9/-/4/ (Mrs R Brewis), R Brewis

1184 Edinburgh Woollen Mills Reg Tweedie Novices' Chase (5-y-o and up) £3,452 3m 1f.........................(2:40)

1091³ INVERINATE (bl) 8-11-2 T Reed, al hndy, led and hit 2 out,
styd on und pres to go clr last, kpt on.
.............................(5 to 1 tchd 6 to 1 and 9 to 2) 1
1061 CEILIDH BOY 7-11-6 B Storey, wtd wth, blun 8th, led
briefly 5 out and 3 out, drvn alng betw last 2, styd on
r-in.............................(5 to 4 fav op 6 to 4 tchd 13 to 8) 2
1033³ VELEDA II (Fr) 6-11-1 (5") J Burke, settled gng wl, level last
4, rdn and fdd r-in...............(7 to 2 tchd 4 to 1) 3
996³ CROWN EYEGLASS (bl) 7-11-2 R Garritty, trkd ldrs, effrt
whn blun 13th, outpcd appr 3 out, sn lost tch.
.............................(20 to 1 tchd 16 to 1) 4
UNGUIDED MISSILE (Ire) 5-11-0 N Doughty, mstks, al wth
ldrs, led 4 out to nxt, eased whn btn. (7 to 1 op 3 to 1) 5
1033⁴ SUPPOSIN 5-11-0 Gary Lyons, prerssed ldrs, struggling
fnl circuit, tld off 14th...........(66 to 1 op 50 to 1) 6
KING OF STEEL 7-11-2 C Grant, led, hesitated 7th, hdd 5
out, wknd quickly and pld up bef last 2.
.............................(10 to 1 op 8 to 1 tchd 11 to 1) pu
1093⁵ MASTER MISCHIEF (bl) 6-11-2 K Johnson, in tch 1st circuit, tld off and pld up betw last 2. (66 to 1 op 50 to 1) pu
Dist: 2l, 10l, 30l, ¾l, 8l. 6m 27.20s. a 25.20s (8 Ran).
SR: 11/13/3/-/-/ (C J Ewart), L Lungo

1185 R. P. Adam Handicap Chase (0-135 5-y-o and up) £3,420 2¾m 110yds
.............................(3:10)

1063⁷ WHAAT FETTLE [126] 8-11-7 (6ex) M Moloney, wth ldr, led
briefly 5th, led 4 out, hld on gmely r-in.
.............................(11 to 10 op 5 to 4 on tchd Evens) 1
973⁴ PIPER O'DRUMMOND [105] 6-9-7 (7") Mr D Parker, early
mstks, hpind fnl circuit, str run frm last, jst fld. (7 to 1) 2
1004⁴ BALTIC BROWN [108] 8-10-3 Gary Lyons, made most, hit
second, hdd briefly 5th, hrd drvn and headed 4 out,
rallied...............(15 to 8 op 7 to 4 tchd 2 to 1) 3
1063⁷ PLENTY CRACK [133] 10-12-0 L Wyer, trkd ldrs, feeling
pace and rdn alng 5 out, sn btn. (16 to 1 tchd 20 to 1) 4
911⁵ LAURIE-O [105] 9-10-0 A Merrigan, in tch, reminders aftr
one circuit, sn tld off...........(25 to 1 tchd 33 to 1) 5
Dist: Nk, 2l, 15l, dist. 5m 50.70s. a 23.70s (5 Ran).
SR: 13/-/-/2/-/ (The Edinburgh Woollen Mill Ltd), G Richards

1186 Glenmuir Sportswear Handicap Hurdle (0-130 3-y-o and up) £2,635 2¼m
·····························(3:40)

1034* TOOGOOD TO BE TRUE [107] 5-11-6 L Wyer, *made most, quickened 3 out, hit nxt, drvn out r-in.*
·····················(9 to 4 op Evens tchd 6 to 5) 1
1057 SWEET CITY [101] 8-10-7 (7*) Mr R Hale, *patiently rdn, improved frm 3 out, styd on wl r-in.*
·····················(16 to 1 op 12 to 1) 2
1034 STARSTREAK [107] 6-11-6 P Niven, *led early, styd hndy, ev ch till rdn and outpcd 2 out.....(20 to 1 op 14 to 1)* 3
DUAL IMAGE [100] 6-10-13 M Dwyer, *settled gng wl, ev ch 3 out, wknd betw last 2, better for race.*
·····················(100 to 30 op 3 to 1 tchd 7 to 2) 4
1064² MASTER OF TROY [96] 5-10-2 (7*) Mr A Parker, *nvr far away, ev ch hfwy, rdn and one pace 3 out.*
·····················(7 to 2 tchd 4 to 1) 5
1066⁷ MAKE ME PROUD (Ire) [97] (v) 4-10-7 (3*) N Bentley, *pressed ldrs, feeling pace and reminders hfwy, sn lost tch.*
·····················(33 to 1 op 20 to 1) 6
JESTERS PROSPECT [112] 9-11-4 (7*) J Supple, *chsd ldrs, struggling hfwy, sn outpcd.......(66 to 1 op 50 to 1)* 7
Dist: 1½l, 8l, 2½l, 2l, 12l, 8l. 4m 28.80s. a 21.80s (7 Ran).
SR: 45/37/35/25/19/8/15/ (Jim McGrath), M H Easterby

TAUNTON (good to firm)
Thursday November 11th
Going Correction: PLUS 0.40 sec. per fur.

1187 Henlade Claiming Hurdle (4-y-o and up) £1,784 2m 1f...............(1:20)

RUSTY ROC 12-10-13 Mr N Miles, *led to second, led ag'n 4th, mstk nxt and reminders, hld on gmely frm 2 out.*
·····················(7 to 2 fav op 5 to 2 tchd 4 to 1) 1
297⁵ LOCH DUICH 7-10-11 W McFarland, *midfield, hdwy 5th, ran on appr last, kpt on und pres r-in.*
·····················(8 to 1 op 7 to 1 tchd 9 to 1) 2
670⁵ SPARKLER GEBE (bl) 7-10-10 (3*) D O'Sullivan, *trkd ldrs, ev ch 2 out, no extr last.........(10 to 1 op 8 to 1)* 3
LAABAS 10-11-4 R Rowell, *rdn alng and struggling 4th, styd on wl frm 2 out, nvr nrr.*
·····················(33 to 1 op 25 to 1 tchd 50 to 1) 4
RUSTY MUSIC 7-10-4 (7*) A Flannigan, *beh till some hdwy 5th, ran on one pace frm 2 out.....(33 to 1 op 25 to 1)* 5
748⁹ HATS HIGH (bl) 8-11-0 M Crosse, *midfield, ev ch appr 5th, not quicken appr 2 out.........(16 to 1 op 10 to 1)* 6
994⁴ RUTHS PRIDE 8-9-11 (7*) Mr G Lewis, *drpd last 4th, tld off.............................(12 to 1 tchd 14 to 1)* 7
1046 BRIDGE STREET BOY 4-10-13 M Bosley, *al beh, tld off.*
·····················(66 to 1 op 50 to 1) 8
SOUTH SANDS 7-11-1 Mrs C Wonnacott, *beh whn mstk 4th, no ch when f 2 out.*
·····················(14 to 1 op 12 to 1 tchd 16 to 1) f
BALLERINA ROSE 6-10-10 D J Burchell, *hld up, in tch gng wl, smooth hdwy 6th, 3rd and rdn whn f last.*
·····················(6 to 1 op 5 to 1 tchd 13 to 2) f
WAVERLEY BOY 11-10-13 Richard Guest, *trkd ldrs till lost pl 5th, tld off whn pld up bef 2 out...(9 to 1 op 6 to 1)* pu
988 INDIAN MAESTRO 7-10-9 M A FitzGerald, *al beh, tld off whn pld up bef 2 out.........(50 to 1 op 25 to 1)* pu
FRENDLY FELLOW (bl) 9-11-1 D Bridgwater, *beh early, some hdwy 5th, rdn nxt, sn wknd, behind whn pld up bef last............(16 to 1 op 12 to 1 tchd 20 to 1)* pu
796 MOUNTAIN RETREAT (v) 7-11-1 N Mann, *led second to 4th, wknd quickly bef nxt, tld off whn pld up before 6th.*
·····················(7 to 1 op 8 to 1 tchd 9 to 1) pu
1027 CREDIT CALL (Ire) 5-10-9 W Humphreys, *al beh, tld off whn pld up bef 2 out.........(66 to 1 op 33 to 1)* pu
1068 POLK (Fr) (bl) 4-11-5 J Lower, *chsd ldrs, smooth hdwy appr 5th and sn ev ch, rdn and wknd quickly aftr 3 out, pld up bef nxt........(14 to 1 op 12 to 1 tchd 16 to 1)* pu
Dist: 1½l, 1½l, 4l, 2l, 2½l, dist, nk. 4m 2.30s. a 15.30s (16 Ran).
(M W Davies), G W Davies

1188 Orchard Portman Selling Handicap Hurdle (3,4,5-y-o) £1,700 2m 1f..(1:50)

1097² RECORD LOVER (Ire) [71] 3-10-7 J Osborne, *patiently rdn, steady hdwy frm 6th, led last, shaken up and kpt on.*
·····················(7 to 2 jt-fav op 3 to 1 tchd 5 to 1) 1
791 SAAHI (USA) [87] 4-10-11 Peter Hobbs, *hld up, hdwy frm 5th, ev ch 2 out, kpt on r-in......(16 to 1 tchd 20 to 1)* 2
889³ DISTANT MEMORY [76] (bl) 4-10-5 (7*) N Parker, *wth ldrs, led 6th, hdd last and no extr...(7 to 2 jt-fav op 3 to 1)* 3
CHANDIGARH [73] 5-10-9 M A FitzGerald, *trkd ldrs gng wl, ev ch 6th, mstk 2 out, no extr.......(10 to 1 op 7 to 1)* 4
791 COOCHIE [69] (bl) 4-10-5 B Clifford, *hld up, some hdwy frm 3 out, nvr nr to chal....................(12 to 1)* 5
826⁶ MADRAJ (Ire) [88] 5-11-10 W McFarland, *midfield and reminders appr 5th, sn no hdwy..............(7 to 1)* 6
486⁵ FEELING FOOLISH (Ire) [68] (bl) 4-10-4 I Shoemark, *trkd ldrs till wknd appr 6th.........(12 to 1 tchd 14 to 1)* 7

953 BEAM ME UP SCOTTY (Ire) [72] 4-10-8 R Greene, *mstk second, sn beh.................(12 to 1 op 8 to 1)* 8
587³ NORTHERN RAINBOW [66] 5-10-2 R Campbell, *al prmnt, ev ch 6th, sn rdn and wknd nxt......(9 to 2 op 4 to 1)* 9
791⁶ HULLO MARY DOLL [68] 4-10-4 M Perrett, *al beh.*
·····················(25 to 1 op 20 to 1 tchd 33 to 1) 10
994 BROTHERLYAFFECTION [64] 4-10-0 B Powell, *jmpd rght, led till ran out 3rd...............(33 to 1 op 20 to 1)* ro
1049⁵ STAR MINSTREL (Ire) [67] 3-10-3 D Bridgwater, *lft in ld 3rd, hdd 6th, sn rdn and wknd quickly, pld up bef 2 out.*
·····················(12 to 1 op 8 to 1 tchd 14 to 1) pu
1049³ IVORY HUTCH [76] (v) 3-10-12 A Charlton, *al beh, tld off whn pld up bef 6th...............(50 to 1 op 25 to 1)* pu
Dist: 2l, 4l, 5l, 12l, 12l, 2½l, 15l, 1l, 8l. 4m 1.30s. a 14.30s (13 Ran).
SR: 4/-/3/-/-/-/ (Alan Mann), S E Sherwood

1189 Connaught Novices' Handicap Chase (5-y-o and up) £3,582 2m 3f.....(2:20)

813² GOLDEN FARE [87] 8-10-9 R Greene, *trkd ldrs, rdn to chal appr last, sn led, jst hld on.*
·····················(4 to 1 op 7 to 2 tchd 9 to 2) 1
984* ABU MUSLAB [102] (bl) 9-11-10 M A FitzGerald, *sn led, rdn and jnd appr last, soon hdd, ran on.*
·····················(11 to 2 op 5 to 1) 2
1022⁶ BUMPTIOUS BOY [83] (v) 9-10-5 D Bridgwater, *trkd ldrs till rdn and wknd appr 3 out...........(8 to 1 op 7 to 1)* 3
1044⁵ WICKFIELD LAD [82] 10-10-4 C Maude, *hdwy 7th, sn in tch, no imprsn appr 3 out..........(16 to 1 op 12 to 1)* 4
SHAAB TURBO [106] 7-12-0 S Burrough, *hld up in tch, hdwy 9th, mstk 11th, no extr appr 3 out, btn whn blun last, improve................(33 to 1 op 20 to 1)* 5
TEMPORARY [85] 8-10-7 J Frost, *in tch to 5th, sn beh.*
·····················(25 to 1 op 20 to 1) 6
882 DEVIOSITY (USA) [78] (bl) 6-9-7 (7*) Mr G Lewis, *nvr a dngr, tld off..........................(66 to 1 op 50 to 1)* 7
ERIC'S TRAIN [86] 7-10-8 Richard Guest, *tracking ldr whn blun and uns rdr second.*
·····················(7 to 1 op 7 to 2 tchd 8 to 1) ur
STEEPLE JACK [88] 6-10-10 B Powell, *blun and uns rdr second.................(12 to 1 op 16 to 1 tchd 20 to 1)* ur
1008⁵ LAVALIGHT [81] 6-10-3 W Irvine, *trkd ldrs, mstk 9th, 4th and btn whn blun and uns rdr 3 out.*
·····················(11 to 1 op 10 to 1 tchd 12 to 1) ur
1058² WEST BAY [85] 7-10-7 S Smith Eccles, *ran out second.*
·····················(9 to 4 fav op 7 to 2 tchd 4 to 1) ro
882⁶ TARMON (Ire) [78] (v) 5-10-0 M Hourigan, *not jump wl and sn tld off, pld up bef 9th..........(50 to 1 op 25 to 1)* pu
Dist: ½l, 12l, ¾l, 2½l, 25l, 12l. 4m 52.50s. a 18.50s (12 Ran).
(N J Barrowclough), R Lee

1190 South-West Racecourses Amateur Riders' Series - Round 4 Handicap Hurdle (0-125 4-y-o and up) £1,913 2m 3f 110yds....................(2:50)

955² CELCIUS [92] (bl) 9-10-5 (7*) Mr N Moore, *hld up gng wl, hdwy on bit to ld 2 out, quickened clr r-in.*
·····················(11 to 2 op 5 to 1) 1
LORD'S FINAL [87] 6-10-0 (7*) Mr G Hogan, *al hndy, ev ch 2 out, not pace of wnr..(14 to 1 op 10 to 1 tchd 16 to 1)* 2
1087⁴ DESERT PALM [87] 8-10-0 (7*) Mr N Miles, *al tracking ldrs, ran on appr 2 out, kpt on same pace r-in.*
·····················(16 to 1 op 10 to 1) 3
955⁴ AMPHIGORY [87] (bl) 5-10-0 (7*) Miss S Cobden, *beh early, effrt 7th, nvr able to chal.*
·····················(12 to 1 op 6 to 1 tchd 14 to 1) 4
958⁷ EMERALD MOON [87] 6-10-0 (7*) Mr J Culloty, *hld up, smooth hdwy appr 7th, ev ch 2 out, sn btn.*
·····················(14 to 1 op 6 to 1) 5
976⁹ SILVER AGE (USA) [88] 7-10-1 (7*) Mr G Lewis, *al hndy, led 7th, hdd 2 out, sn wknd.*
·····················(10 to 1 op 6 to 1 tchd 11 to 1) 6
979 TROJAN ENVOY [87] 5-10-0 (7*) Mr W Henderson, *last at hfwy, some late hdwy, no dngr...(66 to 1 op 20 to 1)* 7
1087⁷ CABIN HILL [102] 7-11-5 (3*,5ex) Mr J Durkan, *trkd ldr, ev ch 2 out, rdn and wknd quickly appr last.*
·····················(5 to 4 on op Evens tchd 11 to 10 tchd 11 to 8 on) 8
1072 BRIGHT SAPPHIRE [87] 7-10-2 (5*) Mrs P Nash, *led to 7th, wkng whn mstk nxt. (40 to 1 op 14 to 1 tchd 33 to 1)* 9
712 JOYFUL NOISE [115] 10-12-0 (7*) Miss S Barraclough, *in tch till wknd 7th.....(10 to 1 op 20 to 1 tchd 33 to 1)* 10
955⁵ COXANN [87] (bl) 7-10-0 (7*) Mr E Tolhurst, *trkd ldg bunch till wknd 7th...........................(20 to 1)* 11
MARIOLINO [103] 6-11-2 (7*) Miss J Southcombe, *hld up in last pl whn f second..................(25 to 1 op 14 to 1)* f
Dist: 8l, 3½l, ½l, 2½l, 10l, 5l, 1½l, ½l, ½l, 6l. 4m 40.40s. a 19.40s (12 Ran).
(Martin Pipe Racing Club), M C Pipe

1191 Haygrass Handicap Chase (0-125 5-y-o and up) £2,598 3m............(3:20)

956³ NAUGHTY NICKY [87] 9-10-0 R Greene, *trkd ldr frm 6th, lft in ld 14th, sn rdn alng, styd on wl frm 3 out.*
·····················(9 to 2 op 5 to 1 tchd 11 to 2) 1
OBIE'S TRAIN [111] (bl) 7-11-10 J Lower, *nvr far away, ev ch 16th, sn rdn and ran on one pace.(9 to 2 op 3 to 1)* 2

712⁴ POWDER BOY [92] 8-10-5 N Dawe, *patiently rdn, mstk tenth, hdwy aftr nxt, hmpd 14th, blun 16th, kpt on frm 2 out*..........................(100 to 30 fav op 7 to 2) 3
665⁵ UNEX-PLAINED [91] 10-10-4 Lorna Vincent, *mstks 6th and 7th, beh hfwy, tld off*
..........................(20 to 1 op 14 to 1 tchd 25 to 1) 4
712⁸ KARAKTER REFERENCE [115] 11-11-11 (3") D O'Sullivan, *al beh, tld off*........................(8 to 1 op 5 to 1) 5
842⁶ SHANNON GLEN [104] (bl) 7-11-3 B Powell, *led, clr 7th, mstk 9th, f 14th*..................(7 to 2 tchd 4 to 1) f
947 GENTLEMAN ANGLER [97] (bl) 10-10-10 J Osborne, *in tch till reminders appr tenth, sn wknd, tld off whn pld up bef 15th*..................(7 to 1 tchd 8 to 1) pu
Dist: 8l, 2½l, dist, ½l. 6m 10.70s. a 23.70s (7 Ran).

(K Bishop), K Bishop

1192 Shoreditch Novices' Hurdle (4-y-o and up) £2,050 2m 1f.............. (3:50)

839⁷ MATHAL (USA) 4-10-3 (7") D Matthews, *trkd ldr, led 6th, unchlgd*.........(7 to 4 fav op 6 to 4 tchd 9 to 4) 1
795⁸ NORTHERN CREST 7-10-10 Peter Hobbs, *beh till some hdwy 6th, styd on frm 2 out, nrst finish*.
..........................(16 to 1 op 12 to 1) 2
NOBLELY (USA) 6-10-10 B Powell, *midfield, hdwy appr 2 out, styd on r-in, nrst finish*.
..........................(14 to 1 op 10 to 1 tchd 16 to 1) 3
SPORTS VIEW 4-10-10 M Hourigan, *pld hrd, led till hdd 6th, wknd appr 2 out*..(13 to 2 op 6 to 1) 4
885 ROUTING 5-10-10 (7") Mr G Lewis, *trkd ldg bunch, rdn and ran on appr 2 out, second and btn last, wknd r-in*.
..........................(12 to 1 tchd 14 to 1) 5
1047² GILBERT (Ire) 5-11-3 Lorna Vincent, *trkd ldr till lost pl frm 6th*..........................(14 to 1 op 10 to 1) 6
FORGETFUL 4-10-5 Mr N Miles, *trkd ldrs till wknd appr 7th*..........................(16 to 1 op 10 to 1) 7
RAFTERS 4-10-10 D Bridgwater, *in tch, mstk 5th and 6th, sn wknd*..........(6 to 1 op 7 to 1 tchd 9 to 2) 8
778 BUSH POWDER (NZ) 5-10-5 (5") R Farrant, *al rear div*.
..........................(20 to 1 op 14 to 1) 9
716⁸ EARLY STAR 4-10-10 R Greene, *wl beh frm hfwy*.
..........................(25 to 1 op 14 to 1 tchd 33 to 1) 10
952 NEARLY HONEST 5-10-5 A Tory, *al struggling*.
..........................(33 to 1 op 20 to 1 tchd 50 to 1) 11
715⁴ WONDERFULLY POLLY (Ire) 5-10-5 M A FitzGerald, *midfield, smooth hdwy appr 7th, second and rdn whn f 2 out*.
CHEREN BOY 4-10-10 I Shoemark, *sn beh, tld off whn pld up bef 2 out*..........(40 to 1 op 33 to 1) pu
Dist: 10l, sht-hd, 2l, sht-hd, 25l, 5l, 12l, 3l, 1½l, ¾l. 4m 2.30s. a 15.30s (13 Ran).

(Alan G Craddock), N M Babbage

TOWCESTER (good)
Thursday November 11th
Going Correction: PLUS 0.55 sec. per fur. (races 1,4,6), PLUS 0.65 (2,3,5)

1193 Mrs Raverty Novices' Hurdle (4-y-o and up) £1,480 2m.............(1:00)

1010⁴ MOVE A MINUTE (USA) 4-10-7 (5") P Hide, *hld up, steady hdwy to ld 3 out, styd on wl, cmftbly.* (7 to 1 op 4 to 1) 1
1070⁸ RAMSTAR 5-10-5 (7") M Keighley, *hld up in rear, hdwy appr 5th, wnt second sn aftr 2 out, no ch wth wnr.*
..........................(25 to 1 op 12 to 1) 2
1010 NADJATI (USA) 4-10-12 P Holley, *hld up in mid-div, wnt second 3 out till hit nxt, kpt on one pace.*
..........................(13 to 8 fav op 6 to 4 tchd 7 to 4) 3
NIGEL'S LUCKY GIRL 5-10-7 J McLaughlin, *pld hrd, led second till jmpd badly lft and hdd nxt, lost pl till styd on frm 3 out, btn whn blun last*..(33 to 1 op 20 to 1) 4
922⁵ UP ALL NIGHT 4-10-0 (7") G Crone, *mid-div, nvr on terms*.
..........................(20 to 1 op 16 to 1) 5
BIGWHEEL BILL (Ire) 4-10-12 C Llewellyn, *al towards rear*.
..........................(8 to 1 op 6 to 1 tchd 10 to 1) 6
PER QUOD (USA) 8-10-12 R Dunwoody, *led to second, lft in ld nxt, blun badly 4th, sn btn*.
..........................(9 to 4 op 7 to 2 and 9 to 4) 7
DAMCADA (Ire) 5-10-9 (3") W Marston, *al beh*.
..........................(50 to 1 op 33 to 1) 8
SKIMMER HAWK 4-10-12 V Smith, *al beh*.
..........................(33 to 1 op 20 to 1) 9
FORTUNES COURSE (Ire) 4-10-7 N Williamson, *trkd ldrs, led 4th, hdd 3 out, wknd rpdly, tld off*.
..........................(15 to 1 op 12 to 1) 10
MARINE DIVER 7-10-12 V Slattery, *pld hrd, making rapid hdwy and prmnt whn hmpd 3rd, sn reco'red, dsptd ld till wknd 5th, pulled up bef 2 out*...(9 to 1 op 8 to 1) pu
795 ALWAYS ALLIED (Ire) 5-10-12 D Skyrme, *al beh, tld off whn pld up bef 2 out*.........(50 to 1 op 33 to 1) pu
TOOMUCH TOOSOON (Ire) 4-10-7 (5") S Curran, *chsd ldrs to 4th, sn beh, tld off whn pld up bef 2 out*.
..........................(33 to 1 op 16 to 1) pu
Dist: 10l, 2l, 7l, 5l, ½l, 1½l, 3l, 1½l, 25l. 3m 56.50s. a 13.50s (13 Ran).

SR: 37/27/25/13/8/12/10/7/5/ (Mrs T Brown), J T Gifford

1194 Irish RM Novices' Chase (5-y-o and up) £2,695 3m 1f.............. (1:30)

843* OLD BRIG (bl) 7-11-7 R Dunwoody, *led, hdd briefly 14th, headed 3 out, led sn aftr nxt, styd on und pres.*
..........................(2 to 1 fav op 9 to 4) 1
843⁵ BARLEY MOW 7-11-0 P Holley, *not fluent but sd prmnt, hit 7th, styd on to go second r-in*............(50 to 1) 2
917⁵ LOOSE WHEELS (v) 7-11-0 A Carroll, *pressed wnr, led briefly 14th, led ag'n 3 out, hdd sn aftr nxt, hrd rdn, wknd r-in*.........................(10 to 1 op 8 to 1) 3
1043⁵ THEO'S FELLA 9-11-0 S Hodgson, *chsd ldrs, no hdwy frm 3 out*.........(8 to 1 op 6 to 1 tchd 9 to 1) 4
TAREESH 6-10-9 N Williamson, *jmpd slwly 1st 2, beh till gd hdwy 9th, wknd 3 out*.........(7 to 2 op 3 to 1) 5
1058 GALLANTRY BANK 8-11-0 D Skyrme, *beh, tld off 9th, uns rdr 11th*...........(16 to 1 tchd 20 to 1) ur
WELSH COMMANDER 10-11-0 R Supple, *hld up in tch, hdwy 11th, wknd aftr nxt, pld up bef 2 out*.
..........................(9 to 1 op 7 to 1) pu
HUNTING DIARY 7-11-0 S Earle, *in tch till 11th, wkng whn blun 13th, tld off whn pld up bef 2 out.* (33 to 1) pu
920⁵ DOROBO (NZ) 5-10-12 S McNeill, *al beh, tld off whn jmpd badly lft 3 out, pld up bef 2 out*...(6 to 1 op 4 to 1) pu
664⁸ LONG REACH 5-10-12 C Llewellyn, *hld up, hit 3rd, hdwy 9th, wknd 12th, tld off whn pld up bef 4 out*.
..........................(10 to 1 op 6 to 1) pu
Dist: 6l, hd, 7l, 15l. 6m 43.50s. a 28.50s (10 Ran).

(David Jenks), M C Pipe

1195 Flurry Knox Handicap Chase (0-135 4-y-o and up) £3,460 2m 110yds (2:00)

761* HOLTERMANN (USA) [108] 9-11-2 M Richards, *lft second 4th, lost tch 8th, rallied appr 3 out, led nxt, rdn clr.*
..........................(3 to 1 op 5 to 2 tchd 7 to 2) 1
840 AROUND THE HORN [109] 6-11-3 S McNeill, *trkd ldr till jmpd badly lft 4th, wnt second ag'n nxt, led aftr 3 out, jumped left and hdd next, no extr.*
..........................(6 to 4 fav op 11 to 8 tchd 13 to 8) 2
987⁵ BLUE BUCCANEER [98] 10-10-6 L Harvey, *hld up in rear, lost tch 8th, hdwy 3 out, nvr dngrs*.
..........................(100 to 30 op 4 to 1 tchd 5 to 1) 3
893³ ACRE HILL [117] 9-11-11 R Dunwoody, *made most till hdd appr 2 out, wknd rpdly, virtually pld up r-in.*
..........................(100 to 30 op 5 to 2 tchd 7 to 2) 4
Dist: 6l, 2l, dist. 4m 21.50s. a 19.50s (4 Ran).

(V & T Ass), Mrs L Richards

1196 Moonlighter 'National Hunt' Novices' Hurdle (4-y-o and up) £1,480 2m (2:30)

BRIEF GALE 6-10-7 D Murphy, *trkd ldrs, hmpd 4th, sn reco'red, led on bit 3 out, styd on wl.*
..........................(5 to 4 fav op Evens tchd 11 to 8 and 6 to 4) 1
1100³ GORTEENA 7-10-12 M Brennan, *hld up, gd hdwy appr 4th, jnd ldrs 3 out, kpt on one pace frm nxt.*
..........................(2 to 1 tchd 7 to 4) 2
SPREAD YOUR WINGS (Ire) 5-10-7 P Holley, *hld up, hdwy 5th, styd on frm 2 out.*
..........................(14 to 1 op 10 to 1 tchd 20 to 1) 3
G'IME A BUZZ 5-10-7 R Dunwoody, *led second till mstk 4th, sn led ag'n, hdd 3 out, rdn and wknd aftr nxt.*
..........................(9 to 2 op 5 to 1 tchd 11 to 2) 4
PLATINUM SPRINGS 6-10-7 N Williamson, *beh, styd on one pace frm 3 out*........(33 to 1 op 20 to 1) 5
983 ROSEN THE BEAU (Ire) 5-10-12 C Llewellyn, *led to second, prmnt till beh 5th*.............(50 to 1 op 33 to 1) 6
HARDLY ARKENFIELD (Ire) 5-10-12 R Supple, *beh, no ch frm 5th*.........(16 to 1 op 20 to 1 tchd 33 to 1) 7
778 EMBLEY BUOY 5-10-12 S Earle, *trkd ldrs, stdly wknd aftr 4th, tld off*............(50 to 1 op 33 to 1) 8
KATIEM'LU 7-10-11 (7") Mr B Pollock, *al beh, tld off.*
..........................(66 to 1 op 33 to 1) 9
Dist: 6l, 6l, 5l, 6l, 5l, 2l, 30l, 30l. 4m 0.10s. a 17.50s (9 Ran).

(Miss Carrie Zetter), J T Gifford

1197 Tommy Bullit Memorial Handicap Chase (0-125 5-y-o and up) £4,854 2 ¾m.............. (3:00)

POSTMAN'S PATH [98] 7-10-10 H Davies, *nvr far away, rdn appr 2 out, styd on to ld sn aftr last*.
..........................(13 to 2 op 6 to 1 tchd 7 to 1) 1
CITY KID [109] 8-11-2 (5") P Hide, *hld up in tch, cld on ldrs 9th, wnt second 4 out, led 2 out, hdd and hdd sn aftr last, kpt on*................(14 to 1 op 12 to 1) 2
714² TIPP MARINER [97] 8-10-9 R Dunwoody, *hld up in rear, hdwy frm 9th, ev ch 3 out, no extr appr last.*
..........................(9 to 2 op 5 to 1) 3
865⁸ SUNBEAM TALBOT [112] 12-11-10 N Williamson, *in rear, sn pushed alng, styd on frm 4 out, nvr dngrs.*
..........................(14 to 1 op 10 to 1) 4
956² JIMSTER [92] 11-10-4 R Dunwoody, *trkd ldrs, led 9th, hrd rdn 3 out, hdd nxt, sn btn*..........(5 to 1 op 9 to 2) 5

FIDDLERS THREE [108] 10-11-6 L Harvey, *al mid-div, styd on frm 4 out, nvr dngrs*............(14 to 1 op 12 to 1) 6
684⁴ CAMDEN BELLE [94] 11-10-6 S Hodgson, *al towards rear.*
....(33 to 1 op 20 to 1) 7
TOCHENKA [105] 9-11-3 C Llewellyn, *led second to 4th, mstks nxt 2, sn lost tch*........(8 to 1 op 7 to 1) 8
899⁵ SOCIAL CLIMBER [95] 9-10-7 S McNeill, *prmnt whn blun 9th, wknd 11th*....................(13 to 2 op 8 to 1) 9
935⁷ WARNER'S END [94] (bl) 12-10-6 R Bellamy, *led to second, led 4th to 9th, wknd quickly four out.*
....(33 to 1 op 20 to 1) 10
CATCHAPENNY [102] (bl) 8-11-0 S Earle, *al beh, struggling frm 6th*........................(12 to 1 op 14 to 1) 11
607³ TITUS ANDRONICUS [92] (bl) 6-10-4 R Supple, *jmpd badly in rear, wl beh frm 8th*....................(10 to 1) 12
MOZE TIDY [91] 8-9-12 (5*) C Burnett-Wells, *mid-div till lost tch tenth*..................................(20 to 1) 13
SHEEPHAVEN [106] 9-11-4 M Richards, *al beh, tld off whn pld up bef 2 out*................(20 to 1 op 14 to 1) pu
ist: 1l, 4l, 6l, nk, 15l, 12l, 2l, 2l, ¾l, 5l. 5m 44.70s. a 18.70s (14 Ran).
R: 38/48/32/41/20/21/-/4/-/ (Mrs A Reid Scott), Capt T A Forster

1198 Slipper Handicap Hurdle (0-125 4-y-o and up) £3,418 2m 5f.......... (3:30)

FAIR BROTHER [98] 7-10-7 (5*) R Davis, *hld up in rear, steady hdwy frm 7th, led on bit appr 2 out, pushed out r-in*....................................(12 to 1 op 9 to 1) 1
PAMBER PRIORY [110] 10-11-10 G Rowe, *trkd ldr, lft in ld aftr 3rd, hdd nxt, styd prmnt, led 3 out, sn headed, kpt on one pace*.......................(20 to 1 op 14 to 1) 2
814⁴ PRINCE OF SALERNO [86] 6-10-0 R Supple, *hld up in rear, hdwy 7th, ev ch 3 out, one pace frm nxt.*
....(25 to 1 op 20 to 1 tchd 33 to 1) 3
849⁴ TAYLORS PRINCE [92] (v) 6-10-6 V Smith, *hld up in rear, styd on frm 3 out, nvr dngrs.*
....(3 to 1 fav op 4 to 1 tchd 11 to 4) 4
1025* SMITH TOO (Ire) [107] 5-11-7 I Lawrence, *hld up in tch, led 4 out, hdd nxt, one pace aftr.*
....(100 to 30 op 5 to 2 tchd 7 to 2) 5
CAMBO (USA) [92] 7-10-6 D Skyrme, *in tch till one pace frm 3 out*..............(15 to 2 op 8 to 1 tchd 10 to 1) 6
BUCKINGHAM GATE [97] 7-10-11 P Holley, *trkd ldrs, no hdwy frm 4 out*.........(16 to 1 op 10 to 1 tchd 20 to 1) 7
861³⁴ ACCESS SUN [98] 6-10-12 N Williamson, *prmnt, led appr 6th, hit and hdd 4 out, wknd, tld off.*
....(7 to 1 tchd 15 to 2) 8
796⁶ GREENWINE (USA) [86] 7-10-0 M Richards, *al towards rear, lost tch appr 3 out, tld off*....(33 to 1 op 20 to 1) 9
796³ SAILOR BLUE [102] (bl) 6-11-2 L Harvey, *trkd ldrs, led 4th, hdd appr 6th, wknd frm four out, tld off*
....(9 to 2 op 4 to 1) 10
STORYBOOK (NZ) [94] 8-10-8 R Dunwoody, *led till pld up aftr 3rd, dismounted, lme.*
....(11 to 1 op 10 to 1 tchd 12 to 1) pu
1072⁸ PLAYFUL JULIET (Can) [87] 5-10-11 Pat Caldwell, *in rear, lost tch 7th, tld off whn pld up bef last*........(50 to 1) pu
st: 2l, 3½l, 5l, 1l, hd, 2½l, 25l, ¾l, 10l. 5m 17.40s. a 18.40s (12 Ran).
R: 16/26/-/-/13/-/ (Mrs S Watts), G B Balding

AYR (good)
Friday November 12th
Going Correction: MINUS 0.10 sec. per fur.

1199 EBF 'National Hunt' Novices' Hurdle Qualifier (4,5,6-y-o) £2,379 2m.. (1:00)

717⁴ LINNGATE 4-10-9 T Reed, *tongue-tied, al travelling wl, led on bit betw last 2, smoothly.*
....(11 to 8 on op 5 to 4 on tchd 6 to 4 on) 1
976⁷ IVY HOUSE (Ire) 5-11-0 M Dwyer, *settled gng wl, ev ch frm 3 out, styd on, prmsg*..................(16 to 1 op 12 to 1) 2
114³ ASTRALEON (Ire) 5-11-0 B Storey, *tucked away in midfield, improved to ld appr 3 out, hdd betw last 2, kpt on same pace*..........................(5 to 2 op 9 to 4) 3
910 SPIDERS DELIGHT 5-11-0 A Merrigan, *led and sn clr, wknd and hdd appr 3 out, fdd*....(10 to 1 op 8 to 1) 4
731⁷ MARCO-PIERRE (Ire) 4-11-5 B Storey, *took keen hold, settled wth chasing grp, ev ch appr 3 out, fdd*....(25 to 1) 5
EMRAL MISS 5-10-9 N Doughty, *co'red up in midfield, effrt and shaken up appr 3 out, btn nxt*......(33 to 1) 6
EMERALD CHARM (Ire) 5-10-9 K Johnson, *patiently rdn, effrt aftr 4 out, fdd frm nxt*........(16 to 1 op 10 to 1) 7
092⁴ BACK BEFORE DAWN 6-11-0 A Dobbin, *not jump wl, drvn up frm midfield to chal appr 3 out, 4th and btn whn f last*............................(12 to 1 op 8 to 1) f
1060 FINE OAK 6-11-4⁹ Mr D Robertson, *in tch to hfwy, reminders 4 out, tld off whn pld up bef nxt*..(500 to 1) pu
MAGENTA BOY 5-10-11 (3*) N Bentley, *in tch to hfwy, struggling whn nrly f 2 out, pld up bef last.*
....(20 to 1 op 14 to 1) pu
RHYMING THOMAS 5-11-0 C Grant, *struggling to keep up hfwy, tld off whn pld up bef 3 out.*(50 to 1 op 33 to 1) pu
976 THYMON THE HORTH 4-11-0 C Hawkins, *not jump wl, struggling frm hfwy, tld off whn pld up bef 3 out.*
....(100 to 1) pu

Dist: 2½l, 2½l, 12l, 2l, 2½l, 5l. 3m 46.20s. a 9.20s (12 Ran).
(J Nelson), L Lungo

1200 Plasticisers Charisma Novices' Chase (5-y-o and up) £2,424 3m 1f
....(1:30)

ONE MAN (Ire) 5-10-12 N Doughty, *jmpd boldly, trkd ldr till led 8 out, blun 4 out, sn reco'red, imprsv.*
....(3 to 1 on tchd 10 to 3 on) 1
1061⁴ BENNAN MARCH 6-11-7 A Dobbin, *some mstks, al wl plcd, led 8th to 8 out, not pace of wnr last 3.*
....(20 to 1 op 16 to 1) 2
821 RUSHING BURN 7-10-9 B Storey, *beh and bustled alng hfwy, plodded round, nvr dngrs.*(100 to 1 op 50 to 1) 3
LAUDER SQUARE 5-10-12 T Reed, *chsd alng and struggling aftr one circuit, tld off*......(100 to 1 op 33 to 1) 4
KNOCK RANK 8-11-0 P Niven, *struggling to keep up aftr one circuit, tld off*...................(7 to 2 op 3 to 1) 5
786⁵ ALIAS GRAY 6-11-0 K Johnson, *made most to 8th, cl 3rd whn blun and uns rdr nxt*...................(100 to 1) ur
DUCHESS OF TUBBER (Ire) 5-10-4 (3*) A Thornton, *chsd clr ldg pair frm hfwy, no imprsn whn blun and uns rdr 5 out*..(14 to 1) ur

Dist: 20l, 15l, 5l, sht-hd. 6m 22.90s. a 22.90s (7 Ran).
(J Hales), G Richards

1201 Lang Whang Handicap Hurdle (0-120 4-y-o and up) £2,814 3m 110yds (2:05)

1057⁸ LINKSIDE [99] 8-11-3 L Wyer, *patiently rdn, improved to join issue fnl circuit, styd on grimly to ld r-in.*
....(3 to 1 op 5 to 2 tchd 7 to 2) 1
819⁵ TRONCHETTO (Ire) [94] (bl) 4-10-12 M Dwyer, *al handy, led and quickened 7th, drvn alng 2 out, hit last, hdd and no extr r-in*.............(3 to 1 op 9 to 4 tchd 100 to 30) 2
1091 RUSTINO [95] 7-10-13 P Niven, *not fluent, led to 7th, styd hndy, hrd at work appr 3 out, sn btn.*
....(12 to 1 op 10 to 1) 3
1017* SECRET SCEPTRE [105] 6-11-9 C Grant, *took keen hold early, struggling and reminders hfwy, no further dngr.*
....(2 to 1 fav op 5 to 2) 4
759⁴ SHELTON ABBEY [106] 7-11-7 (3*) A Larnach, *wth ldrs to hfwy, struggling fnl circuit, tld off.*(5 to 1 op 4 to 1) 5
972 PANDESSA [103] 6-11-7 A Merrigan, *chsd alng to go pace hfwy, tld off fnl circuit*................(33 to 1 op 20 to 1) 6

Dist: 5l, 3½l, 4l, 10l. 5m 49.00s. a 3.00s (6 Ran).
SR: 35/26/2/4/1/-/ (Linkside Fabrications (L'pool) Ltd), M G Meagher

1202 Galloway Hills Maiden Hurdle (4-y-o and up) £1,997 2m..............(2:40)

SURREY DANCER 5-10-12 P Niven, *confidently rdn, al cruising, led appr 3 out, easily.*
....(Evens fav op 11 to 10 tchd 5 to 4) 1
1000⁶ CLEAR IDEA (Ire) 5-10-12 N Doughty, *pld hrd, led to second, styd hndy till led ag'n briefly appr 3 out, kpt on, prmsg*..........................(5 to 1 op 9 to 2 tchd 6 to 1) 2
COOL LUKE (Ire) 4-10-9 (3*) N Bentley, *settled off the pace, hit 3 out, styd on last 3, can improve.* (4 to 1 op 3 to 1) 3
DOUBLE STANDARDS (Ire) 5-10-12 B Storey, *nvr far away, chsd alng whn pace lifted appr 3 out, one pace.*
....(66 to 1 op 33 to 1) 4
922² TROOPING (Ire) 4-10-12 L Wyer, *in tch, improved frm midfield appr 3 out, no imprsn frm nxt.*
....(9 to 2 op 4 to 1) 5
SCARF (Ire) 5-10-12 M Dwyer, *patiently rdn, improved appr 3 out, not pace of ldrs frm nxt.*
....(16 to 1 op 12 to 1) 6
KUMMEL KING 5-10-12 M Moloney, *shwd up wth chasing grp till grad wknd appr 3 out*......(33 to 1 op 25 to 1) 7
ROYAL FIFE 7-10-2 (5*) P Williams, *chsd ldg bunch, feeling pace appr 3 out, sn btn*................(100 to 1) 8
1003⁴ HICKSONS CHOICE (Ire) 5-10-12 K Jones, *kicked strt, chsd ldrs, hrd at work 3 out, fdd*..(25 to 1 op 16 to 1) 9
KHALLOOF (Ire) 4-10-7 (5*) P Waggott, *led second till hdd and fdd appr 3 out*........(50 to 1 op 33 to 1) 10
EMERALD SEA (USA) 6-10-12 S Turner, *trkd ldg bunch, hrd at work 3 out, sn lost tch.*
....(1 tchd 200 to 1) 11

Dist: 5l, 3½l, 7l, nk, ½l, 7l, 4l, ¾l, 15l, 4l. 3m 48.90s. a 11.90s (11 Ran).
(Laurel (Leisure) Limited), Mrs M Reveley

1203 Mossblown Conditional Jockeys' Handicap Chase (0-115 5-y-o and up) £2,598 2m....................(3:15)

1022⁵ POSITIVE ACTION [100] 7-10-13 A Dobbin, *patiently rdn, steady hdwy hfwy, led and blun 2 out, drvn out r-in.*
....(5 to 2 jt-fav op 9 to 4) 1
913 PRESSURE GAME [87] 10-9-7 (7*) F Perratt, *jmpd wl, tried to make all, hdd and rdn 2 out, kpt on same pace.*
....(25 to 1 tchd 33 to 1) 2
722* ABSAILOR [95] 9-10-8 P Williams, *al chasing ldrs, struggling to go pace hfwy, styd on grimly frm 3 out, nrst finish.*............................(5 to 2 jt-fav op 9 to 4) 3

769⁴ CLARES OWN [100] 9-10-13 D Bentley, *chsd clr ldg pair hfwy, struggling 5 out, styd on ag'n last 2*.
.............................(10 to 1 op 8 to 1)   4
1095 SINGING SAM [90] 8-10-3 A Larnach, *struggling to keep up hfwy, no imprsn frm 5 out*......(50 to 1 op 33 to 1)   5
PURA MONEY [100] 11-10-13 B Harding, *beh and drvn alng hfwy, nvr a factor*..........(16 to 1 op 12 to 1)   6
BELDINE [103] 8-11-2 A Thornton, *midfield whn f 3rd*.
.............................(10 to 1 tchd 14 to 1)   f
735* PINEMARTIN [114] 10-11-13 N Leach, *f 1st*.
.............................(7 to 2 tchd 4 to 1)   f
GREY MINSTREL [100] 9-10-13 P Waggott, *chasing ldrs whn f second*..................(12 to 1 tchd 14 to 1)   f
Dist: 4l, 4l, 5l, 15l, 4l. 4m 0.20s. a 12.20s (9 Ran).

(G Campbell), M A Barnes

1204 Fiveways Novices' Handicap Hurdle (4-y-o and up) £2,326 2½m......(3:45)

1000* SHAFFIC (Fr) [101] 6-11-10 P Niven, *patiently rdn, niggled alng to join issue aftr 4 out, led and hng lft nxt, hdd betw last 2, got up last strd*.....(Evens fav op 11 to 10)   1
1114⁴ DANCING DOVE (Ire) [90] 5-10-6 (7*) B Harding, *settled gng wl, drvn ahead betw last 2, ran on, jst ct*.
.............................(8 to 1 op 6 to 1)   2
1000⁴ JOHNS THE BOY [100] 7-11-4 (5*) J Supple, *al hndy, led hfwy till 3 out, kpt on same pace*. (11 to 1 op 12 to 1)   3
1096⁷ DIG DEEPER [95] 6-11-4 M Dwyer, *settled gng wl, chlgd on bit appr 3 out, rdn and no extr betw last 2*.
.............................(12 to 1 op 10 to 1)   4
734⁶ BELLS HILL LAD [80] 6-10-3 S Turner, *settled midfield, reminders hfwy, struggling frm 4 out*..........(6 to 1)   5
821⁸ RED TEMPEST (Ire) [77] 5-9-7 (7*) F Perratt, *in tch, improved to fltter appr 3 out, fdd nxt*.
.............................(11 to 1 op 12 to 1 tchd 14 to 1)   6
731⁸ CORSTON RACER [76] 5-10-16 (5*) P Williams, *settled off the pace, steady hdwy hfwy, fdd appr 3 out...*(14 to 1)   7
DENBY HOUSE LAD (Can) [81] 6-9-11 (7*) Mr D Parker, *co'red up in midfield, drvn alng whn pace lifted aftr 4 out, sn btn*..........(10 to 1 op 12 to 1 tchd 14 to 1)   8
THE POD'S REVENGE [78] 8-10-11 M Moloney, *trkd ldg bunch, struggling 4 out, sn lost tch*..........(66 to 1)   9
726 SCOTTISH REFORM [85] 6-10-8 L Wyer, *chsd ldg bunch, hit 8th, sn struggling*..........(14 to 1 tchd 16 to 1)   10
823 THE PATTERS MAGIC [78] 6-10-11 C Grant, *led till hdd hfwy, tld off last 3*................(33 to 1 op 16 to 1)   11
Dist: Hd, 2l, 1l, 5l, 2½l, 6l, ½l, 8l. 4m 57.30s. a 18.30s (11 Ran).

(P Davidson-Brown), Mrs M Reveley

CHELTENHAM (good)
Friday November 12th
Going Correction: PLUS 0.55 sec. per fur. (races 1,3,4), PLUS 0.50 (2,5,6)

1205 Coln Valley Fish And Game Company Amateur Riders' Novices' C (5-y-o and up) £4,164 3m 1f...............(1:20)

917² SQUIRE JIM 9-11-6 Mr M Rimell, *chsd ldr frm 8th till lft in ld 9th, slpd 3 out but left clr, cmftbly*.
.............................(9 to 2 op 5 to 1 tchd 6 to 1)   1
1054 HOWARYAFXD 6-11-12 Mr J M Pritchard, *chsd ldrs till drpd rear 6th, pckd 13th (water), lft second 3 out, no imprsn*........................(6 to 1 op 9 to 2)   2
954* ALEGBYE 7-11-12 Mr N Moore, *led till f 9th*.
.............................(7 to 1 op 6 to 1 tchd 8 to 1)   f
686* DON'T LIGHT UP (v) 7-11-12 Mr A Farrant, *rear 3rd but in tch whn f 9th*..........(9 to 2 op 3 to 1 tchd 5 to 1)   f
774² LUSTY LIGHT 7-11-12 Mr M Armytage, *with wnr 11th to 14th, blun 4 out, second and still gng wl whn f 3 out*.
.............................(5 to 2 fav tchd 7 to 2)   f
FLORIDA SKY 6-11-6 Mr T Byrne, *beh till blun and uns rdr 5th*..........................(4 to 1 op 7 to 2)   ur
Dist: 25l. 6m 33.50s. a 27.50s (6 Ran).

(R P Hiorns), N A Twiston-Davies

1206 Morison Stoneham Challenge Conditional Jockeys' Handicap Hurdle (0-135 4-y-o and up) £2,981 2m 5f (1:55)

1106⁶ FAIRFIELDS CONE [110] 10-10-13 D Meredith, *hld up in rear, steady hdwy 6th, trkd ldrs frm 3 out, chlgd last, quickened to ld r-in, readily*........(5 to 1 op 7 to 2)   1
887⁶ NIGHT WIND [98] 6-9-10 (5*) D Fortt, *sn prmnt, slight ld 3 out till hdd r-in, one pace cl hme....*(8 to 1 op 5 to 1)   2
979* KANO WARRIOR [106] 6-10-9 F Jenks, *chsd ldrs, chlgd frm 3 out, str chal last, not quicken r-in*.
.............................(4 to 1 fav tchd 9 to 2)   3
MAILCOM [118] 7-11-2 (5*) L O'Hare, *mid-div, rdn and hit 6th, styd on frm 4 out, not pace to rch ldrs r-in*.
.............................(11 to 1 op 16 to 1)   4
SEA BUCK [113] 7-11-2 S Fox, *drpd rear 4th, kpt on frm 2 out*..........................(14 to 1 tchd 16 to 1)   5

750⁵ MEDITATOR [105] (bl) 9-10-8 S Curran, *beh, reminders aftr 4th and drvn alng, ran on und pres r-in, fnshd wl*.
.............................(12 to 1 op 10 to 1 tchd 14 to 1)   1
985 ASK THE GOVERNOR [113] 7-11-2 R Davis, *beh, some prog frm 3 out, not a dngr*.(11 to 1 op 10 to 1 tchd 12 to 1)   1
1025² MIDFIELDER [121] 7-11-10 M Hourigan, *prmnt till wknd 4 out*....................(11 to 1 op 8 to 1 tchd 12 to 1)   1
519³ STORMHEAD [115] 5-11-4 J McCarthy, *led till hdd 3 out, sn btn*...............(8 to 1 op 7 to 1 tchd 9 to 1)   1
MEDIANE (USA) [116] 8-11-0 (5*) M P FitzGerald, *al beh*.
.............................(33 to 1)   1
COME HOME ALONE [97] 5-9-9 (5*) W Currie, *chsd ldrs till wknd 4 out*.................(40 to 1 op 33 to 1)   1
1041⁵ ON YOUR WAY [97] 11-9-9 (5*) P McLoughlin, *chsd ldrs till drpd rear 6th*............(50 to 1 op 66 to 1)   1
ZEALOUS KITTEN (USA) [103] 5-10-6 R Greene, *beh 4th, hdwy 6th, rdn four out, hld whn blun and uns rdr 3 out*....................(12 to 1)   1
LANDED GENTRY (USA) [109] 4-10-7 (5*) A Flannigan, *chsd ldrs, still in tch whn mstk and uns rdr 3 out...*(20 to 1)   1
1108⁷ CARRIGLAWN [97] 8-9-9 (5*) J J Brown, *beh till ran out 5th*........................(66 to 1 op 50 to 1)   1
Dist: 2l, 1½l, 4l, 5l, 1½l, 1l, 5l, nk, 3½l, 15l. 5m 15.40s. a 16.40s (15 Ran).
SR: 26/12/18/26/16/6/13/16/9/   (Mrs Cheryl Hooker), R Dick

1207 Taylors Estate Agents Chase Handicap (5-y-o and up) £5,868 2m...(2:30)

1001* KING OF THE LOT [150] 10-11-7 A Maguire, *led 5th, made rst, came clr frm 2 out*.
.............................(11 to 8 on op 5 to 4 on tchd 6 to 5 on and 6 to 4 on)   1
1009² YOUNG SNUGFIT [157] 9-12-0 J Osborne, *led to 5th, styd in second, shaken up 2 out, no imprsn*.
.............................(5 to 2 op 2 to 1)   2
1048³ AL HASHIMI [129] 9-10-0 M Hourigan, *sn wl beh, mstk 4th, tld off*...............(9 to 2 op 4 to 1 tchd 6 to 1)   3
Dist: 10l, dist. 4m 2.90s. a 9.90s (3 Ran).
SR: 82/79/-/   (Mrs G M Brisbane), D Nicholson

# 1208 Steel Plate And Sections Young Chasers Championship Final Limited Handicap (5 - 8-y-o) £13,420 3m 1f
............................(3:05)

714⁴ LIGHT VENEER [118] 8-10-5 M A FitzGerald, *beh, hdwy and hit 14th, str chal frm 2 out till hrd drvn to ld r-in, all out*.............(10 to 1 op 12 to 1 tchd 14 to 1)   1
956 INDIAN TONIC [118] 7-10-5 C Maude, *led, clr 11th, rdn 2 out, hdd r-in, styd on same pace*.
.............................(10 to 1 op 14 to 1 tchd 20 to 1)   2
935³ MUSTHAVEASWIG [123] 7-10-10 A Maguire, *prmnt, hit 6th, chsd ldr 15th, hit 2 out, one pace appr last*.
.............................(6 to 1 tchd 7 to 1)   3
995² WASHINGTONCROSSING [127] 7-11-0 S McNeill, *al chasing ldrs, drvn alng frm 3 out, no imprsn....*(7 to 2 jt-fav tchd 4 to 1)   4
SUPERIOR FINISH [139] 7-11-12 B Powell, *prmnt, shaken up 4 out, wknd 3 out*.....(12 to 1 tchd 14 to 1)   5
NATIVE PRIDE [120] 6-10-7 N Williamson, *beh, blun badly 8th, hdwy 15th, rdn 3 out, wknd appr last*.
.............................(4 to 1 op 3 to 1)   6
921⁵ MR JAMBOREE [118] 7-10-5 D Murphy, *chsd ldr till wknd 15th*.................(12 to 1 op 14 to 1 tchd 16 to 1)   7
1143 FLASHTHECASH [118] 7-11-11 Richard Guest, *al beh, lost tch 14th, tld off whn pld up bef 3 out*. ....(7 to 2 jt-fav op 3 to 1)   pu
Dist: 4l, 5l, 2½l, 6l, 1l, dist. 6m 23.10s. a 17.10s (8 Ran).
SR: 44/40/40/41/47/27/-/-/   (Louis Jones), Mrs Merrita Jones

1209 ASW Hurdle (4 & 5-y-o) £5,475 2m 110yds........................(3:40)

STAUNCH FRIEND (USA) 5-11-7 D Murphy, *hld up, hdwy 2 out, chlgd last, shaken up to ld cl hme, cleverly*.
.............................(6 to 5 fav op 11 to 8 tchd 11 to 10)   1
ARABIAN BOLD (Ire) 5-11-0 M A FitzGerald, *led, clr second, rdn aftr 2 out, hdn on gmely r-in, hdd cl hme*.
.............................(6 to 1 op 4 to 1)   2
AMAZON EXPRESS 4-11-7 J Osborne, *chsd ldr, hit 3 out, sn rdn, outpcd frm nxt*............(2 to 1 tchd 5 to 2)   3
1034⁵ KADI (Ger) 4-11-3 A Maguire, *chsd ldr, lost tch frm 3 out*.
.............................(11 to 1 op 10 to 1 tchd 12 to 1)   4
898² NATIVE CHIEFTAN 4-11-0 H Davies, *hld up, shaken up and wknd 3 out*......(11 to 1 op 7 to 1 tchd 12 to 1)   5
Dist: ½l, 8l, 6l, 15l. 4m 1.60s. a 10.60s (5 Ran).
SR: 70/62/61/51/33/   (B Schmidt-Bodner), M H Tompkins

1210 Capital Ventures Novices' Hurdle (4-y-o and up) £2,737 3¼m.......(4:10)

869* FUZZY LOGIC (Ire) 5-11-4 C Llewellyn, *made all, pushed alng and styd on wl frm 2 out*.
.............................(15 to 8 on op 7 to 2 on tchd 7 to 4 on)   1
DOLLY OATS 7-10-9 M A FitzGerald, *prmnt, chsd wnr 7th, ev ch whn blun 2 out, not reco'r*.
.............................(7 to 1 op 10 to 1 tchd 12 to 1)   2

160

LAUGHING GAS (Ire) 4-10-13 R Supple, *beh, styd on frm 3 out to take 3rd r-in, not a dngr.*
.... (20 to 1 op 12 to 1 tchd 25 to 1) 3
OLD STEINE 5-11-0 M Hourigan, *pld hrd, chsd wnr to 7th, rdn 3 out, sn btn, wknd r-in.*
.... (100 to 30 op 3 to 1 tchd 4 to 1 and 5 to 2) 4
1109⁶ LIBERTY JAMES 6-11-0 W McFarland, *al beh, tld off whn pld up bef 3 out.* .... (33 to 1 tchd 40 to 1) pu
Dist: 3l, 10l, 2½l. 6m 52.80s. (5 Ran).

(Cheltenham Racing Ltd), N A Twiston-Davies

HUNTINGDON (good)
Friday November 12th
Going Correction: PLUS 0.60 sec. per fur. (races 1,3,5), PLUS 0.25 (2,4,6)

1211 Kimbolton 'National Hunt' Novices' Claiming Hurdle (4-y-o and up) £1,480 2m 5f 110yds............... (12:45)

1153⁵ TAX THE DEVIL (v) 5-9-13¹ (5*) A Dicken, *took keen hold, led appr 3rd, sn wl clr, mstk last, rdn and wndrd und pres, ran on.*...................... (10 to 1 op 7 to 1) 1
889⁶ BOXING MATCH 6-10-2 (7*) G Lewis, *led chasing grp 5th, cld on wnr appr 2 out, rdn approaching last, no imprsn.*............ (13 to 8 fav op 6 to 4 tchd 2 to 1) 2
889⁸ WEST MONKTON 7-10-4 R Dunwoody, *wtd wth, hdwy 4 out, no imprsn whn mstk 2 out.*
.... (9 to 2 op 3 to 1 tchd 11 to 2) 3
1023 SEMINOLE PRINCESS 5-10-6 M Bosley, *cl up in chasing grp, outpcd frm 6th.*............... (25 to 1 op 12 to 1) 4
976⁶ CLERIC ON BROADWAY (Ire) 5-11-2 R Garritty, *hld up, outpcd aftr 6th, tld off.*............. (5 to 2 op 5 to 4) 5
953⁵ WHAT A RATTLE 4-10-3 Peter Hobbs, *pld up aftr second.*
.... (16 to 1 op 14 to 1 tchd 20 to 1) pu
1126 BARGIN BOY 4-10-7 A Charlton, *jmpd slwly, led to 3rd, lost tch 6th, tld off whn blun 3 out, pld up bef nxt.*
.... (10 to 1 op 7 to 1) pu
Dist: 3l, 15l, 20l, 20l. 5m 25.60s. a 30.60s (7 Ran).

(Mrs Heather Chakko), S Dow

1212 Macer Gifford Handicap Chase (0-140 5-y-o and up) £2,846 2½m 110yds...................... (1:15)

712⁶ CHAMPAGNE LAD [122] 7-11-4 (5*) P Hide, *trkd ldrs, hdwy to ld aftr 3 out, all out.* (11 to 4 op 9 to 4 tchd 3 to 1) 1
1098 SPREE CROSS [120] 7-11-7 G Bradley, *cl up, led 12th till hdd aftr 3 out, sn rdn, rallied after last.*
.... (10 to 1 op 8 to 1) 2
897⁶ CASTLE KING [122] 6-11-9 R Dunwoody, *hld up, hdwy tenth, cld on ldrs frm 4 out, one pace from 2 out.*
.... (5 to 1 op 9 to 2 tchd 11 to 2) 3
919⁶ EMSEE-H [123] (bl) 8-11-3 (7*) P Murphy, *led, clr 5th, mstk 9th, hdd 12th, sn wknd.* (11 to 2 op 5 to 1 tchd 6 to 1) 4
PLAT REAY [113] 9-11-0 C Llewellyn, *al beh, pushed alng 8th, lost tch frm 12th.* (10 to 1 op 8 to 1 tchd 12 to 1) 5
GRANVILLEWATERFORD [120] 8-11-7 G Upton, *wtd wth, outpcd 5 out, sn lost tch.*........ (6 to 4 fav op 9 to 4) 6
Dist: 1½l, 8l, 8l, 12l, 8l. 5m 9.70s. a 14.70s (6 Ran).

(P G James), J T Gifford

1213 Ermine Street Handicap Hurdle (0-125 4-y-o and up) £2,075 2m 110yds (1:45)

812* KABAYIL [103] 4-11-2 J Railton, *trkd ldrs, pushed alng appr 2 out, led last, ran on wl.*
.... (7 to 2 op 5 to 2 tchd 4 to 1) 1
SASKIA'S HERO [90] 6-10-3 D Byrne, *led chasing grp, led briefly 2 out, ev ch last, kpt on one pace.*
.... (16 to 1 tchd 20 to 1) 2
887² MONDAY CLUB [108] 9-11-7 M Richards, *hld up in rear, gd hdwy 3 out, rdn and ev ch whn hmpd by faller last, not reco'r.*............... (8 to 1 op 7 to 1 tchd 9 to 1) 3
1101* MRS MAYHEW (Ire) [95] 5-10-1 (7*,7ex) P Murphy, *trkd ldrs, niggled alng 5th, drvn and lost pl aftr 3 out, fnshd wl.*
.... (5 to 1 op 4 to 1 tchd 6 to 1) 4
MANEREE [93] 6-10-6 R Campbell, *hld up towards rear, hdwy appr last, styd on.*.......... (12 to 1 op 6 to 1) 5
918² FATHER DAN (Ire) [92] 4-10-5 R Dunwoody, *hld up, hdwy 3 out, outpcd after nxt.*........... (7 to 1 op 8 to 1) 6
1085* MULCIBER [87] 5-10-0 (7ex) M Perrett, *hld up in mid-div, niggled alng 3 out, no response.*
.... (9 to 4 fav tchd 5 to 2 and 3 to 1) 7
812⁹ PALACE WOLF (NZ) [115] 9-12-0 R Marley, *hld up, al beh.*
.... (33 to 1 op 25 to 1) 8
841⁵ STAY AWAKE [115] 7-12-0 G Bradley, *al beh.*
.... (16 to 1 op 10 to 1) 9
FIERCE [105] 5-11-4 S Smith Eccles, *trkd ldrs, pushed alng 4th, led aftr 3 till hdd nxt, cl up and ev ch whn f last.*..................... (14 to 1 tchd 16 to 1) f
849⁵ SALMAN (USA) [99] 7-10-12 D Bridgwater, *led, sn clr, hdd aftr 3 out, wknd rpdly, pld up bef last.*
.... (25 to 1 op 16 to 1) pu
Dist: 3l, 3l, 1l, 1½l, 1½l, 3½l, 15l, 3l. 4m 1.40s. a 14.40s (11 Ran).

SR: 43/27/42/28/24/21/12/25/22/ (Elite Racing Club), C R Egerton

1214 Peter Crossman Novices' Chase (5-y-o and up) £2,487 2½m 110yds (2:20)

JUMBEAU 8-10-9 (5*) P Hide, *al prmnt, mstk 8th, led aftr 11th, made rst, mistake 2 out, ran on wl.*
.... (9 to 2 op 11 to 4) 1
603² SQUEEZE PLAY (bl) 8-11-0 Peter Hobbs, *hld up, hdwy 3 out, mstk last, rallied und pres to take second r-in.*
.... (11 to 2 op 7 to 1 tchd 5 to 1) 2
934⁵ ROAD TO FAME 6-11-0 P Holley, *cl up, led 8th till hdd aftr 11th, one pace frm 2 out.*............. (8 to 1 op 7 to 1) 3
MANDIKA 5-10-13 G Bradley, *trkd ldrs, chsd wnr appr 2 out, rdn and one pace aft last, better for race.*
.... (13 to 2 op 6 to 1 tchd 7 to 1) 4
1080⁵ SEA BREAKER (Ire) 5-10-13 E Murphy, *al beh, tld off.*
.... (14 to 1 op 10 to 1) 5
984³ STAGE PLAYER 7-10-9 (5*) T Eley, *chsd ldrs, mstk tenth, rdn and btn 12th, tld off.*......... (9 to 1 op 7 to 2) 6
1102⁵ CANTGETOUT 7-10-9 Mr A Pickering, *pushed alng thrght, al beh, f 9th.*.................... (33 to 1 op 25 to 1) f
RUNNING SANDS 9-10-9 (5*) C Burnett-Wells, *led to 8th, lost tch 4 out, tld off whn pld up bef nxt.*
.... (15 to 2 op 8 to 1 tchd 9 to 1) pu
974² NORTHERN SQUIRE 5-10-13 R Dunwoody, *trkd ldrs, drpd rear 8th, blun nxt and pld up.*
.... (3 to 1 fav op 7 to 2 tchd 4 to 1) pu
Dist: 1½l, 1½l, 3½l, 25l, 15l. 5m 5.20s. a 10.20s (9 Ran).

SR: 35/33/32/27/2/-/ (Pell-Mell Partners), J T Gifford

1215 John Evans Mares Only Novices' Hurdle (4-y-o and up) £1,480 2m 110yds...................... (2:50)

AFFA 4-10-10 S Smith Eccles, *hld up in mid-div, mstk 4th, hdwy 3 out, lft in ld nxt, ran on wl.* (8 to 1 op 8 to 1) 1
SAIL BY THE STARS 4-10-5 (5*) R Farrant, *trkd ldrs, ev ch 2 out, hrd rdn and veered lft r-in, no extr.*
.... (20 to 1 op 12 to 1) 2
1110⁵ GLENFINN PRINCESS 5-10-10 D Bridgwater, *led till ran wide and hdd aftr 3rd, cld on wl chst, one pace.*
.... (12 to 1 op 10 to 1) 3
1040⁸ GAMEFULL GOLD 4-10-12 (5*) A Dicken, *hld up in rear, steady hdwy frm o'r 2 out, hit last, styd on, nvr nrr.*
.... (14 to 1 op 7 to 1) 4
MAZATA (USA) 4-10-10 G Upton, *al beh, tld off.*
.... (14 to 1 op 10 to 1) 5
HINTON LADY 4-10-10 J Railton, *trkd ldrs till wknd quickly 3 out, tld off.*............. (20 to 1 tchd 33 to 1) 6
725⁴ SALLY SOHAM (Ire) 5-10-3 (7*) P Murphy, *trkd ldrs, led 4th till hdd 3 out, sn wknd, tld off.*.....(20 to 1 op 16 to 1) 7
779² POWLEYVALE 6-11-3 R Dunwoody, *trkd ldrs, led 3 out, hit nxt and uns rdr.*
...(5 to 4 op 6 to 4 on tchd 11 to 10 on and Evens) ur
909 PASSAGE TO FREEDOM 11-10-10 D Telfer, *pushed alng in rear, tld off whn pld up lme aftr 5th.*
.... (50 to 1 op 25 to 1) pu
MATUSADONA 6-10-10 J A Harris, *cl up, lost pl appr 5th, tld off whn pld up bef 3 out.*..... (50 to 1 op 25 to 1) pu
975⁵ INDIAN ORCHID 6-10-10 G Bradley, *lft strt, al beh, tld off whn pld up bef 3 out.*... (11 to 2 op 9 to 2 tchd 6 to 1) pu
1040 ROYAL BATTLE 5-10-5 (5*) P Hide, *al beh, tld off whn pld up bef 3 out.*................ (50 to 1 op 33 to 1) pu
Dist: 1½l, 1½l, 1½l, 30l, 3l, 8l. 4m 5.80s. a 18.80s (12 Ran).

(G Oliver), T Thomson Jones

1216 Bedford Conditional Jockeys' Handicap Chase (0-115 5-y-o and up) £2,553 3m...................... (3:20)

LOCH BLUE [107] 11-11-6 A Dicken, *hld up, hdwy to cl on ldrs o'r 2 out, quickened to ld r-in.* (16 to 1 op 10 to 1) 1
847² DUO DROM [99] 8-10-12 W Marston, *chsd ldrs, trkd lder frm 14th, led last, hrd rdn and hdd r-in, no extr.*
.... (5 to 2 fav tchd 3 to 1) 2
COOL AND EASY [97] 7-10-10 P Hide, *mid-div till drpd rear 11th, hdwy 15th, kpt on frm 2 out, ran on aftr last.*
.... (11 to 4 op 7 to 2) 3
984⁴ RYTON GUARD [89] 8-10-2 V Slattery, *led to 4th, cl up in ld 11th, hdd last, one pace.*.... (6 to 1 op 6 to 1) 4
MATERIAL GIRL [113] 7-11-12 A Procter, *trkd ldrs, alng 12th, struggling 3 out, sn hrd ridden and wknd, tld off.*.................. (6 to 1 op 5 to 1 tchd 7 to 1) 5
810² BARTONDALE [87] 8-10-0 R Farrant, *trkd ldrs, pushed alng aftr 12th, hrd rdn and wknd after 3 out, tld off.*
.... (6 to 1 op 5 to 1 tchd 7 to 1) 6
ROCKMOUNT ROSE [87] 8-10-0 C Burnett-Wells, *trkd ldrs till lost pl 15th, tld off.* (9 to 1 op 7 to 1 tchd 10 to 1) 7
978⁵ NOTARY-NOWELL [87] (bl) 7-9-9 (5*) P Murphy, *pushed alng in rear 11th, sn tld off.*.......... (10 to 1 op 7 to 1) 8
700⁶ SOCKS DOWNE [87] 14-9-9 (5*) D Meade, *led 4th till f 11th.*
.... (16 to 1 op 14 to 1) f
Dist: 1l, 2l, 2½l, 20l, 25l, 2l, 25l. 6m 7.20s. a 19.20s (9 Ran).

(S Dow), S Dow

161

AYR (good)
Saturday November 13th
Going Correction: PLUS 0.30 sec. per fur. (races 1,3,-5,7), PLUS 0.50 (2,4,6)

1217 Harcros Scottish Juvenile Novices' Championship Hurdle Qualifier (3-y-o) £2,200 2m. . . . . (12:40)

1062² RED MARAUDER 10-13 (5*) J Supple, *patiently rdn, drw level 3 out, ridden to nose ahead last, drew clr.*
. . . . (11 to 10 fav op Evens tchd 6 to 5) 1
1062³ PRINCIPAL PLAYER (USA) 11-4 A Dobbin, *settled gng wl, chalg whn lft in narrow ld 3 out, hdd when almost f last, not reco'r* . . . . (9 to 4 op 5 to 2) 2
872 DEVILRY 10-12 J Callaghan, *chsd ldg pair, effrt appr 3 out, sn rdn and outpcd.*
. . . . (5 to 1 op 4 to 1 tchd 11 to 2) 3
SUIVEZ 10-3 (5*) D Bentley, *al chasing ldrs, rdn appr 3 out, no imprsn.* . . . . (8 to 1 op 5 to 1) 4
FUNNY FEELINGS 10-8 A Orkney, *beh and bustled alng hfwy, nvr a factor* . . . . (66 to 1 op 50 to 1) 5
REBEL KING 10-7 (5*) P Waggott, *wtd wth, improved to ld appr 4 out, stumbled and f nxt.*
732⁵ . . . . (66 to 1 op 50 to 1) f
561 TAYBRIDGE TOSH 10-12 P Harley, *struggling to keep up hfwy, tld off whn pld up bef 3 out.*
. . . . (150 to 1 op 100 to 1) pu
Dist: 10l, 12l, 1½l, 15l. 3m 50.00s. a 13.00s (9 Ran).
SR: 8/-/-/-/-/ (N B Mason), N B Mason

1218 Glengoyne Highland Malt Tamerosia Series Qualifier Novices' Chase (5-y-o and up) £2,406 2½m. . . . . (1:10)

974* CLASSIC CONTACT 7-10-13 (5*) J Supple, *not fluent, made all, hrd pressed last 4, styd on strly.*
. . . . (5 to 4 fav op 11 to 10 tchd 11 to 8) 1
RIVER PEARL 8-10-9 M Moloney, *nvr far away, jnd issue fnl circuit, rdn last, kpt on.*
. . . . (7 to 1 op 3 to 1 tchd 4 to 1) 2
CAITHNESS PRINCE 7-11-0 B Storey, *al tracking ldrs, effrt appr 4 out, styd on one pace frm betw last 2.*
. . . . (50 to 1 op 20 to 1) 3
GREENFIELD MANOR 6-11-0 A Merrigan, *settled gng wl, ev ch appr 4 out, styd on one pace frm last.* (100 to 1) 4
729* DEEP DECISION 7-11-8 K Johnson, *nvr far away, ev ch whn mstks fnl circuit, rdn and fdd 2 out.*
. . . . (6 to 1 op 9 to 2) 5
1034⁷ GYMCRAK STARDOM 7-11-0 L Wyer, *settled midfield, ev ch appr 4 out, wknd quickly betw last 2.*
. . . . (5 to 1 op 7 to 2) 6
874⁵ MONAUGHTY MAN 7-10-9 (5*) P Williams, *pressed ldrs till grad wknd appr 3 out.* . . . . (50 to 1) 7
DEEP HAVEN 8-11-0 K Jones, *sn struggling to keep up, plodded round fnl circuit.* . . . . (33 to 1) 8
874 VULPIN DE LAUGERE (Fr) 6-10-7 (7*) Mr D Parker, *ran in snatches, lost tch fnl circuit, tld off* . . . . (200 to 1) 9
CASTLEFERGUS 6-11-0 J Callaghan, *in tch, not fluent and lost grnd fnl circuit, pld up betw last 2.*
. . . . (16 to 1 op 10 to 1) pu
Dist: ½l, 7l, 1l, 8l, 3½l, 4l, 15l, 6l. 5m 10.80s. a 23.80s (10 Ran).
(N B Mason), N B Mason

1219 Tennents Lager Handicap Hurdle (0-135 4-y-o and up) £2,584 2½m (1:40)

TRUMP [95] 4-10-0 B Storey, *nvr far away, drw level 3 out, sn led, forged clr r-in* . . . . (9 to 1 op 8 to 1) 1
972⁵ ONLY A ROSE [97] 4-10-2 D Wilkinson, *nvr far away, drvn alng whn pace quickened 3 out, rallied aftr nxt, styd on* . . . . (5 to 2 jt-fav op 9 to 4 tchd 11 to 4) 2
1106⁷ WILLIE SPARKLE [117] 7-11-3 (5*) P Williams, *al wl plcd, niggled alng whn pace quickened 3 out, kpt on same pace frm betw last 2* . . . . (5 to 2 jt-fav tchd 11 to 4) 3
736⁵ BAY TERN (USA) [115] 7-11-6 P Harley, *tried to make all, hdd and rdn 3 out, no extr.*
. . . . (7 to 1 op 6 to 1 tchd 8 to 1) 4
1034³ SPACE CAPTAIN [108] 6-10-10 (3*) N Bentley, *al tracking ldrs, led briefly 3 out, wknd quickly betw last 2, virtually pld up r-in* . . . . . . (7 to 2 op 3 to 1 tchd 4 to 1) 5
ATTADALE [123] 5-12-0 T Reed, *nvr gng wl, sn tld off, pld up bef 3 out.* . . . . (7 to 1 op 6 to 1) pu
Dist: 4l, 3l, 10l, 8l. 4m 52.60s. a 13.60s (6 Ran).
SR: -/-/11/ (Raymond Anderson Green), C Parker

1220 Tennents Special Chase Handicap (5-y-o and up) £6,850 2½m. . . . . (2:10)

WHISPERING STEEL [140] 7-11-10 L Wyer, *jmpd boldly, nvr far away, led and quickened appr 4 out, drvn and ran on strly frm last.* . . . . (6 to 4 fav op 11 to 10) 1

822⁵ KUSHBALOO [120] 8-10-4 B Storey, *al hndy, led briefly 5 out, rallied und pres last 2, kpt on.* (11 to 2 op 4 to 1) 2
1063⁵ ROSS VENTURE [128] 8-10-12 T Reed, *tried to make all, hdd 5 out, rdn and outpcd last 3...* (9 to 4 tchd 5 to 2) 3
RIFLE RANGE [125] 10-10-9 C Grant, *trkd ldrs, hit 7th, feeling pace 6 out, struggling last 4.*
. . . . (5 to 1 tchd 11 to 2) 4
871⁴ CORNET [127] (v) 7-10-6 (5*) P Waggott, *in tch, feeling pace and reminders hfwy, jmpd badly rght, blun and uns rdr 7 out* . . . . (16 to 1 op 10 to 1) ur
Dist: 2½l, 12l, 20l. 5m 0.60s. a 13.60s (5 Ran).
SR: 60/37/33/10/-/ (J Michael Gillow), G Richards

1221 Montgomerie Handicap Hurdle (0-135 4-y-o and up) £2,242 2m. . . . . . (2:40)

654⁶ WEE WIZARD (Ire) [96] 4-10-0 A Dobbin, *al hndy, drw level 3 out, rdn nxt, rallied to ld last 100 yards.*
. . . . (4 to 1 tchd 9 to 2) 1
1034⁴ HOME COUNTIES (Ire) [120] (v) 4-11-7 (3*) D J Moffatt, *patiently rdn, improved on bit to nose ahead aftr last, hdd and no extr last 100 yards* . . . . . . (9 to 2 op 7 to 2) 2
1064⁶ ALL WELCOME [99] 6-9-10 (7*) D Ryan, *made most, quickened aftr 4 out, rdn last 2, hdd after last, kpt on same pace.* . . . . (11 to 2 op 6 to 1) 3
654⁷ SPANISH FAIR (Ire) [96] 5-9-7 (7*) Mr D Parker, *nvr far away, ev ch 3 out, rdn nxt, styd on same pace.*
. . . . (20 to 1 op 16 to 1) 4
562³ PERSUASIVE [123] 6-11-8 (5*) Mr M Buckley, *wtd wth, improved to join issue 3 out, rdn and one pace frm betw last 2.* . . . . (9 to 4 fav op 10 to 1) 5
1064⁵ GLINDIGO (Ire) [97] 5-9-10 (5*) T Jenks, *trkd ldrs, drw level 3 out, eased whn btn betw last 2.* . . . (9 to 1 op 8 to 1) 6
543⁵ GOLDEN ISLE [114] 9-11-4 B Storey, *nvr far away, rdn whn pace quickened appr 3 out, sn btn.*
. . . . (10 to 1 op 8 to 1) 7
Dist: ½l, 3l, 2l, 1½l, nk, 15l. 3m 46.60s. a 9.60s (7 Ran).
SR: 24/47/23/18/43/16/18/ (Armstrong/Greenwell), M A Barnes

1222 Joan Mackay Handicap Chase (0-120 5-y-o and up) £3,192 3m 1f. . . . . . (3:10)

789⁴ ON THE HOOCH [99] 8-10-7 Mr J Bradburne, *nvr far away, jmpd ahead 11th, styd on strly frm 3 out.*
. . . . (10 to 10 to 1 tchd 12 to 1) 1
735² DEEP DAWN [108] 10-11-2 C Grant, *patiently rdn, took clr order fnl circuit, ev ch last 3, styd on.* (9 to 2 op 4 to 1) 2
1095⁴ MOUNTEBOR [92] 9-10-0 J Callaghan, *al hndy, ev ch aftr 5 out, hrd rdn bef nxt, kpt on one pace frm betw last 2* . . . . (12 to 1 op 10 to 1 tchd 14 to 1) 3
1119⁸ EASTERN OASIS [103] 10-10-6 (5*) P Williams, *settled off the pace, drvn alng to improve frm 4 out, styd on, nvr nrr.* . . . . (5 to 1 op 4 to 1) 4
1095³ FUNNY OLD GAME [101] 6-10-9 K Johnson, *settled midfield, improved to track ldrs aftr 5 out, rdn bef nxt, no imprsn.* . . . . (5 to 1 op 7 to 2) 5
1095⁶ CLONROCHE DRILLER [98] 8-9-13 (7*) Mr D Parker, *wth ldrs, struggling to hold pl appr 6 out, lost tch frm nxt.* . . . . (16 to 1 op 14 to 1) 6
MUTUAL TRUST [116] 9-11-10 M Moloney, *trkd ldrs, lost grnd fnl circuit, fdd 5 out.*
. . . . (5 to 2 fav op 4 to 1 tchd 9 to 2) 7
LUPY MINSTREL [102] 8-10-10 B Storey, *in tch, reminders fnl circuitm lost touch frm 5 out.*
. . . . (11 to 1 op 10 to 1 tchd 12 to 1) 8
740 BISHOPDALE [120] 12-12-0 A Merrigan, *chsd ldrs, niggled alng fnl circuit, lost tch frm 6 out.* (66 to 1 op 50 to 1) 9
874 CELTIC WATERS [92] 8-10-7 C Dennis, *chsd ldg bunch, drvn alng whn f 7 out.* . . . . (66 to 1) f
1095 CLASSIC MINSTREL [99] 9-10-7 T Reed, *patiently rdn, some hdwy whn brght dwn 7 out.* (20 to 1 op 16 to 1) bd
BALLINROSTIG [102] 10-10-10 L Wyer, *chsd ldrs for o'r a circuit, tld off whn pld up bef 3 out.*
. . . . (14 to 1 op 12 to 1) pu
Dist: 3½l, 2½l, ½l, 6l, 15l, 6l, ¾l, 4l. 6m 23.50s. a 23.50s (12 Ran).
(Geoffrey Solman), Mrs S C Bradburne

1223 Grunwick Stakes National Hunt Flat Race (4,5,6-y-o) £1,752 2m. . . . . . (3:40)

THE GREY MONK 5-10-12 (7*) B Harding, *al gng wl, nosed ahead aftr 6 fs out, quickened clr last 3 furlongs, easily.* . . . . (5 to 1 co-fav op 7 to 3) 1
DOMINIE (Ire) 5-11-0 (5*) T Jenks, *patiently rdn, improved gng wl entering strt, styd on, not pace of wnr.*
. . . . (5 to 1 co-fav op 3 to 1) 2
GLANDALANE LADY 4-10-7 (7*) R McGrath, *tucked away in midfield, improved entering strt, styd on und pres last 3 fs.* . . . . (5 to 1 op 16 to 1) 3
NAUGHTY FUTURE 4-10-12 (7*) Miss Sue Nichol, *wtd wth, steady hdwy in strt, rng on finish.* (33 to 1 op 25 to 1) 4
JOLIVER (Ire) 5-11-0 (5*) N Leach, *settled off the pace, steady hdwy last 3 fs, nrst finish.* (20 to 1 op 12 to 1) 5
747³ EXCUSE ME (Ire) 4-11-0 (7*) E Husband, *trkd ldrs, jnd issue appr strt, outpcd last 3 fs....* (8 to 1 op 7 to 1) 6
976⁴ OAKLEY 4-11-0 (5*) P Waggott, *nvr far away, ev ch appr strt, fdd last 3 fs...* . . . . (6 to 1 tchd 7 to 1) 7

815 HECTOR MARIO 5-10-12 (7*) Mr G Hogan, *trkd ldr, ev ch till fdd 3 fs out*....................(10 to 1 op 12 to 1) 8

CARIBBEAN SURFER (USA) 4-11-0 (5*) Mr M Buckley, *patiently rdn, improved to join issue entering strt, ridden and btn 3 fs out*......... (5 to 1 co-fav op 14 to 1) 9

THE PIPE FITTER (Ire) 5-11-2 (3*) N Bentley, *al hndy, ev ch entering strt, fdd o'r 2 fs out.* (5 to 1 co-fav op 7 to 2) 10

1133^{5} CUDDER OR SHUDDER (Ire) 4-10-11 (3*) D J Moffatt, *trkd ldg pair till fdd entering strt*......(16 to 1 op 12 to 1) 11

LA DOUTELLE 6-10-9 (5*) P Williams, *nvr far away, effrt appr strt, fdd 3 fs out*.........................(50 to 1) 12

NOBLE MONARCH (Ire) 4-11-2 (3*) A Larnach, *trkd ldrs, feeling pace appr strt, tld off*..................(33 to 1) 13

DERWENT LAD 4-11-5 A Dobbin, *in tch for o'r a m, tld off.* .... (10 to 1 op 8 to 1) 14

976 SCOTTISH GAMBLER 4-11-0 (5*) D Bentley, *led till hdd o'r 6 fs out, sn tld off*............................(10 to 1) 15

CORNISH BAY 5-11-0 Mr D Mactaggart, *al beh, tld off last 6 fs*.............................. (100 to 1 op 50 to 1) 16

ist: 12l, hd, 6l, 3l, 4l, 8l, 12l, hd, 3l, 1½l. 3m 40.20s. (16 Ran).

(Alistair Duff), G Richards

CHELTENHAM (soft)
Saturday November 13th

ioing Correction: PLUS 0.88 sec. per fur. (races 1,3,5), PLUS 0.80 (2,4,6)

1224 Flowers Original Handicap Chase (5-y-o and up) £7,132 3m 3f 110yds (12:50)

1011^{5} ROYAL ATHLETE [161] 10-12-0 G Bradley, *hld up, hdwy 15th, str run to ld last, styd on wl*...(11 to 1 op 8 to 1) 1

740^{3} WHATS THE CRACK [133] 10-10-0 A Maguire, *led to second, styd hndy, ev ch 2 out, one pace r-in.* .... (12 to 1 op 10 to 1) 2

1011^{4} DAKYNS BOY [144] 8-10-11 C Llewellyn, *ran in snatches, hld up in tch, lost pl 11th, hit 14th, 5th whn mstk 2 out, kpt on r-in*...... (9 to 2 co-fav op 4 to 1 tchd 5 to 1) 3

1031^{3} GARRISON SAVANNAH [150] (bl) 10-11-3 B Powell, *tucked in hndy, jnd issue 17th, led nxt, rdn and hdd last, wknd r-in*................. (9 to 2 co-fav tchd 5 to 1) 4

ZETA'S LAD [155] 10-11-8 R Supple, *hld up, effrt appr 3 out, rdn and no extr frm nxt*........(6 to 1 op 5 to 1) 5

1026* PARSONS GREEN [135] (bl) 9-10-2 R Dunwoody, *led second till hdd and blun 18th, not reco'r, tld off.* ....(5 to 1 tchd 11 to 2) 6

1031^{5} SIBTON ABBEY [159] 8-11-5 (7*) P Murphy, *handily plcd till wknd frm 16th, tld off*........ (11 to 1 op 10 to 1) 7

1011^{2} SPRINGALEAK [140] 8-10-7 J Osborne, *trkd ldrs, reminders 12th and rdn nxt, beh frm 16th and pld up bef 18th*.....................(9 to 2 co-fav tchd 5 to 1) pu

st: 3l, 3½l, 1½l, 8l, dist, dist. 7m 19.20s. a 32.20s (8 Ran).

R: 20/-/-/-/-/ (G & L Johnson), Mrs J Pitman

1225 Murphy's Handicap Hurdle (4-y-o and up) £13,550 2m 110yds......... (1:25)

629* LEOTARD [132] 6-12-0 J Osborne, *made virtually all, jnd 3 out, rdn clr r-in*.... (3 to 1 op 9 to 4 tchd 100 to 30) 1

006^{2} NAHAR [124] 8-11-1 (5*) A Dicken, *wth ldr, chlgd 3 out, not quicken last*........(15 to 2 op 6 to 1 tchd 8 to 1) 2

025^{3} JEASSU [129] 10-11-11 A Maguire, *trkd ldrs, rdn 2 out, styd on one pace r-in*...(15 to 2 op 7 to 1 tchd 8 to 1) 3

046* MUSTAHIL (Ire) [105] 4-10-11¹ R Dunwoody, *trkd ldrs till niggled alng 3rd, wknd 5th*........(14 to 1 op 12 to 1) 4

898* MIDDLE MARKER (Ire) [122] 4-11-4 Diane Clay, *hld up till rdn and lost tch appr 3 out.* .... (5 to 1 op 4 to 1 tchd 11 to 2) 5

034^{2} ARCOT [122] 5-11-4 D Murphy, *wtd wth, effrt frm 3 out, 4th and clsg whn f nxt.* ....(2 to 1 fav tchd 9 to 4 and 5 to 2) f

005^{8} CLURICAN (Ire) [123] 4-11-5 G Bradley, *sn beh, mstk 5th, tld off whn pld up bef 3 out*....... (20 to 1 op 16 to 1) pu

st: 5l, hd, 25l, 2l. 4m 7.90s. a 16.90s (7 Ran).

: 63/50/55/6/21/-/-/ (Christopher Heath), O Sherwood

1226 Mackeson Gold Cup Handicap Chase Grade 3 (5-y-o and up) £32,143 2½m 110yds....................... (2:00)

866* BRADBURY STAR [154] 8-11-8 D Murphy, *al hndy gng wl, slight mstk 4 out, chlgd frm 2 out, led r-in, rdn clr.* .... (13 to 2 op 6 to 1 tchd 7 to 1) 1

987* EGYPT MILL PRINCE [135] (bl) 7-10-3 J Osborne, *rcd keenly, led aftr 3rd, rdn appr last, hdd and no extr r-in*..................(9 to 1 op 10 to 1 tchd 12 to 1) 2

001^{2} GENERAL PERSHING [143] 7-10-11 N Doughty, *al prmnt till rdn and one pace appr 2 out.* (11 to 2 fav op 4 to 1) 3

009* STORM ALERT [152] 7-11-6 S McNeill, *chsd ldrs, ev ch 3 out, sn no extr*......... (13 to 2 op 8 to 1 tchd 6 to 1) 4

069^{5} RIVER BOUNTY [132] 7-10-0 R Supple, *hld up and beh till styd on frm 2 out, not rch ldrs*............... (50 to 1) 5

084^{2} SPACE FAIR [149] 10-11-3 L Harvey, *hld up in midfield, no hdwy frm tenth*.....(28 to 1 op 25 to 1 tchd 33 to 1) 6

871^{2} ARMAGRET [143] 8-10-11 D Byrne, *beh 5th, some hdwy frm 2 out, no dngr*................(16 to 1 op 20 to 1) 7

871^{3} SWORD BEACH [135] 9-10-3³ P Niven, *midfield till wknd tenth*................(22 to 1 op 16 to 1 tchd 25 to 1) 8

MORLEY STREET [159] 9-11-13 Richard Guest, *hld up and wl beh, some hdwy 11th, nvr nr to chal.* ....(20 to 1 tchd 22 to 1) 9

119* GENERAL IDEA [156] 8-11-10 R Dunwoody, *hld up in tch till wknd 9th, tld off*....................(8 to 1 op 7 to 1) 10

584* SECOND SCHEDUAL [152] 8-11-6 A Maguire, *hld up in tch, took clr order tenth, second and pushed alng whn f 3 out*............................(6 to 1 tchd 7 to 1) f

897* GUIBURN'S NEPHEW [135] 11-10-3 C Maude, *led till aftr 3rd, styd hndy, 6th and rdn whn blun and uns rdr 4 out*..................(18 to 1 op 16 to 1 tchd 20 to 1) ur

897 BRANDESTON [132] 8-9-7 (7*) P Murphy, *mstk and uns rdr 1st*...............................(40 to 1 op 33 to 1) ur

1031 TIPPING TIM [153] 8-11-7 C Llewellyn, *beh 4th, rdn 7th, sn lost tch, tld off whn pld up bef 3 out.* ....(22 to 1 op 20 to 1 tchd 25 to 1) pu

943* BISHOPS HALL [143] 7-10-11 G Bradley, *in tch, wkng whn blun tenth, beh when pld up bef 4 out.* ....(12 to 1 tchd 14 to 1 and 11 to 1) pu

Dist: 7l, 4l, 2½l, ½l, 12l, 3½l, 5l, 20l, dist. 5m 18.80s. a 18.80s (15 Ran).

SR: 86/60/64/70/49/54/44/31/35/ (James Campbell), J T Gifford

1227 Whitbread White Label Handicap Hurdle (4-y-o and up) £6,937 3¼m.. (2:35)

SILLARS STALKER (Ire) [127] 5-9-11 (3*) W Marston, *took keen hold, hld up gng wl, hdwy appr 8th, wnt second aftr 2 out, led on bit r-in, sn quickened clr.* ....(13 to 8 fav op 11 to 10 tchd 7 to 4) 1

867^{2} NEWTON POINT [127] 4-10-0 A Maguire, *trkd ldr, rdn to chal appr 2 out, led bef last, hdd and no extr r-in.* ....(9 to 1 op 10 to 1 tchd 14 to 1) 2

1030^{3} BURGOYNE [152] 7-11-11 P Niven, *led till hdd bef last, sn wknd*................(9 to 4 tchd 5 to 2 and 2 to 1) 3

914^{4} ARR EFF BEE [127] (bl) 6-10-0 B Powell, *in tch, slight mstk 3rd, wknd appr 9th, tld off*........ (66 to 1 op 33 to 1) 4

1120* NORTHERN VILLAGE [127] 6-9-11² (5*) A Dicken, *patiently rdn, niggled alng appr 9th, wnt second nxt, cl up whn mstk and uns rdr 3 out*............. (5 to 1 op 7 to 1) ur

1030 CARDINAL RED [148] 6-11-7 J Osborne, *tucked in hndy, rdn and tried to pull up aftr 7th, refused to race frm nxt and pld up after 4 out*... (8 to 1 op 7 to 1 tchd 9 to 1) pu

Dist: 6l, dist, dist. 6m 52.70s. a 33.70s (6 Ran).

(Sillars Civil Engineering), Mrs J R Ramsden

1228 Coventry Novices' Chase (5-y-o and up) £6,840 2m.................(3:10)

1071* BAYDON STAR 6-11-6 A Maguire, *trkd ldr, hit 3rd, chlgd appr 3 out, quickened to ld on ins approaching last, sn clr, readily*... (6 to 4 on op 7 to 4 on tchd 11 to 8 on) 1

1008* GHIA GNEUIAGH 7-11-2 C Llewellyn, *led till hdd aftr 2 out, second and one pace whn hit last, no extr.* ....(11 to 4 op 9 to 4) 2

1071^{3} COUNTRY LAD (Ire) 5-11-2 S McNeill, *hld up in tch, mstk 8th, cl 3rd whn slpd on landing 3 out, not reco'r.* .... (10 to 1 op 16 to 1) 3

1008^{2} GANDOUGE GLEN 6-11-2 E Murphy, *not fluent, drpd last 5th, blun 8th, sn in rear, tld off.* ....(6 to 1 op 5 to 1 tchd 7 to 1) 4

Dist: 8l, 7l, dist. 4m 11.80s. a 18.80s (4 Ran).

SR: 45/33/26/-/ (Mrs Shirley Robins), D Nicholson

1229 Flowers Fine Ales Three Yrs Old Hurdle £3,649 2m 110yds...........(3:45)

SPRING MARATHON (USA) 10-12 P Holley, *trkd ldrs, rdn aftr 2 out, ran on gmely to ld r-in*....(9 to 2 op 7 to 2) 1

830* WINGS COVE 11-2 E Murphy, *led appr 3rd, jnd gng to last, rdn and hdd r-in, not quicken.* ....(13 to 8 fav op 5 to 4 tchd 2 to 1) 2

LOVE YOU MADLY (Ire) 10-7 J Lower, *hld up, took clr order aftr 4th, rdn to chal betw last 2, wknd r-in.* .... (10 to 1 op 6 to 1) 3

1021^{6} TACTICAL TOMMY 10-12 C Llewellyn, *led till hdd appr 3rd, styd hndy, rdn 2 out, wknd bef last.* ....(15 to 2 op 11 to 1 tchd 7 to 1) 4

1021 ONE MORE POUND 10-12 P Niven, *hld up, shrtlvd effrt 5th, wknd bef nxt*................(20 to 1 op 33 to 1) 5

NANCY (Ire) 10-4 (3*) W Marston, *hld up, rdn and moderate hdwy aftr 3 out, nvr able to chal*......... (50 to 1) 6

HUBERT 10-5 (7*) A Flannigan, *jmpd rght and uns rdr 1st.* ....(50 to 1 op 33 to 1 tchd 66 to 1) ur

LAMBAST 10-7 A Maguire, *mstk 3rd, sn lost pl and pld up bef nxt*................(7 to 2 op 4 to 1 tchd 11 to 4) pu

HENRIETTA BOO BOO 10-7 Richard Guest, *chsd ldrs till lost pl 5th, beh whn pld up bef last.* ....(12 to 1 op 20 to 1 tchd 33 to 1) pu

Dist: 2½l, 5l, 8l, 2l, 15l. 4m 19.40s. a 28.40s (9 Ran).

(Mrs Nerys Dutfield), Mrs P N Dutfield

NAAS (IRE) (soft)

Saturday November 13th

1230 Kilwarden Maiden Hurdle (4-y-o) £3,105 2m. (12:50)

YUKON GOLD (Ire) (bl) 11-12 C O'Dwyer, ...(3 to 1) 1
803[2] EALING COURT 11-12 A Powell, ...(5 to 1) 2
1020* BUTCHES BOY (Ire) 11-12 S H O'Donovan, ...(8 to 1) 3
990[5] MR SNAGGLE (Ire) 11-4 (3*) C O'Brien, ... (16 to 1) 4
FERRYCARRIG HOTEL (Ire) 11-7 (5*) T F Lacy Jnr, . .(5 to 1) 5
1036 MIDDLE SUSIE (Ire) 10-11 (5*) T P Treacy, ... (25 to 1) 6
832[5] LINDEN'S LOTTO (Ire) 11-4 (3*) Mr A R Coonan, . . (20 to 1) 7
939[3] ALOHA (Ire) 11-2 M Duffy, ... (7 to 1) 8
LUCK OF A LADY (Ire) 10-9 (7*) C McCormack, . . . (33 to 1) 9
JULEIT JONES (Ire) 10-13 (3*) T J Mitchell, ... (16 to 1) 10
MIDNIGHT HOUR (Ire) 11-2 (5*) M G Cleary, ... (14 to 1) 11
832* THE SUBBIE (Ire) 11-12 K F O'Brien, ...(7 to 4 fav) 12
1036[7] MARYVILLE LADY (Ire) 10-11 (5*) T J O'Sullivan, . . (20 to 1) 13
DAMODAR 11-7 F J Flood, ... (20 to 1) 14
1076 LANCANA (Ire) 10-9 (7*) B Bowens, ...(20 to 1) 15
OVER THE JORDAN (Ire) 11-7 P M Verling, ... (20 to 1) 16
1020 SWIFT GLIDER (Ire) 10-9 (7*) K P Gaule, ...(25 to 1) 17
95[8] CLASS OF NINETYTWO (Ire) 11-7 H Rogers, ... (20 to 1) 18
PEACE TRIBUTE (Ire) 11-0 (7*) K D Maher, ...(25 to 1) 19
803 LONG GUE (Fr) 11-2 (5*) D P Geoghegan, ... (20 to 1) 20
RAVEN'S ROCK (Ire) 11-0 (7*) Mr C A Leavy, ...(20 to 1) 21
FOURTWOONEAGAIN (Ire) 10-11 (5*) T P Rudd, . . (16 to 1) 22
990[9] SYLVANER (Ire) 10-11 (5*) P A Roche, ...(14 to 1) 23
990 BON VIVEUR 11-7 T J Taaffe, ... (14 to 1) 24

Dist: 1l, 15l, hd, 4½l. 4m 0.10s. (24 Ran).

(A J O'Reilly), Charles O'Brien

1231 Paddy Cox Handicap Chase (4-y-o and up) £3,795 2m 3f. . . . . (1:20)

799[3] COMMERCIAL ARTIST [-] 7-10-7 C O'Dwyer, . . (5 to 2 fav) 1
943[4] JOE WHITE [-] 7-10-3 P Carberry, ... (6 to 1) 2
928[5] LADY BAR [-] 6-9-7 P M Verling, ... (14 to 1) 3
938[7] HAKI SAKI [-] 7-10-13 T Horgan, ... (12 to 1) 4
966[4] CAPE SPY [-] 7-9-9[1] H Rogers, ... (8 to 1) 5
FERROMYN [-] 8-9-11 C F Swan, ... (10 to 1) 6
GOLD OPTIONS [-] (bl) 11-12-0 Mr E Bolger, ...(10 to 1) 7
878 FRIENDLY ARGUMENT [-] 8-9-4 (3*) C O'Brien, . . . (12 to 1) 8
TENNESSEE PASS [-] 13-9-0 (7*) J Butler, ... (25 to 1) 9
943[5] GUESSWORK [-] 7-10-4 A Powell, ... (10 to 1) 10
MASS APPEAL [-] 8-10-11 B Sheridan, ...(8 to 1) 11
800 CAPTAIN BRANDY [-] 8-10-10 F J Flood, ...(10 to 1) f
119 MAPLE DANCER [-] 7-10-0 F Woods, ...(16 to 1) ur
SOLAR SYMPHONY [-] 7-9-11 J Jones, ...(12 to 1) bd
TARTAN TAILOR [-] 12-9-13[5] (5*) S Lyons, ...(12 to 1) pu
EBONY STAR [-] 10-10-12 K F O'Brien, ... (10 to 1) pu

Dist: 6l, 3l, 7l, 5½l. 5m 9.50s. (16 Ran).

(Michael J O'Neill), Victor Bowens

1232 Clane Handicap Hurdle (0-109 4-y-o and up) £3,105 2m. . . . .(1:50)

804[3] PERSIAN HALO (Ire) [-] 5-12-0 D H O'Connor, ...(8 to 1) 1
1075[4] SHIRWAN (Ire) [-] 4-10-12 (5*) M A Davey, ... (7 to 1) 2
991[5] DANGEROUS REEF (Ire) [-] 5-10-9 (5*) T P Rudd, (12 to 1) 3
117[6] CASTLE KNIGHT [-] 7-11-4 W T Slattery Jnr, ...(20 to 1) 4
CHARLIE MINGUS [-] 6-11-0 J Shortt, ... (14 to 1) 5
UNCLE BABY (Ire) [-] 5-10-7 (7*) K P Gaule, ... (12 to 1) 6
991[2] CASH CHASE (Ire) [-] 5-10-13 (3*) L P Cusack, (4 to 1 jt-fav) 7
COIN MACHINE (Ire) [-] 4-11-8 T Horgan, ...(10 to 1) 8
WINTERBOURNE ABBAS (Ire) [-] 4-11-11 B Sheridan, ...(10 to 1) 9
967[2] CELTIC SAILS (Ire) [-] (bl) 5-11-11 K F O'Brien, ... (9 to 2) 10
COOLAHEARAC [-] 7-11-3 P P Kinane, ... (16 to 1) 11
708[8] ROWAN REX [-] 8-11-11 J F Titley, ... (7 to 1) pu
967[4] PYR FOUR [-] 6-11-3 C O'Dwyer, ... (4 to 1 jt-fav) pu

Dist: ½l, 7l, 9l, 5l. 4m 6.00s. (13 Ran).

(Tematron Racing Club), Michael Kauntze

1233 Quinns Of Baltinglass Chase (5-y-o and up) £6,900 2m. . . . .(2:25)

ITS A CRACKER 9-10-11 (5*) D P Murphy, ...(8 to 1) 1
1019* FURRY STAR 7-11-9 J Jones, ...(6 to 1) 2
807* OPERA HAT (Ire) 5-10-12 A Powell, ...(3 to 1) 3
941[2] TAWNEY FLAME 7-11-2 J Magee, ...(8 to 1) 4
FRANK BE LUCKY 7-11-2 K F O'Brien, ... (5 to 1) 5
1035 NANCYS LAD 6-11-2 H Rogers, ...(33 to 1) 6
HAPPY PERCY 8-11-2 C O'Dwyer, ... (8 to 1) 7
804[8] GONE LIKE THE WIND 6-10-11 (5*) L Flynn, ... (66 to 1) 8
879* VISIBLE DIFFERENCE 7-11-9 C F Swan, ... (5 to 2 fav) f
BALLINABOOLA GROVE 6-11-2 T J Taaffe, ... (14 to 1) ur

Dist: 11l, ¾l, 25l, 2½l. 4m 18.30s. (10 Ran).

(J P Berry), J A Berry

1234 Sean Graham Brown Lad Hurdle (Listed Race - Grade 3) (4-y-o and up) £6,900 2m 3f. (3:00)

1018* MINELLA LAD [-] 7-10-11 T Horgan, *wl plcd, led aftr 3 out, styd on strly strt, hld on*. . . . . (9 to 2) 1
938* DERRYMOYLE (Ire) [-] 4-9-12 (6ex) C F Swan, *mid-div, prog 3 out, ev ch appr last, rdn and no extr r-in*. . . . . (9 to 2)
1037[2] TUG OF PEACE [-] 6-10-7 (3*) C O'Brien, *mid-div, prog appr 3 out, ev ch nxt, wknd approaching last*. (6 to 1)
TOUT VA BIEN [-] 5-9-9 P Carberry, *led or dsptd ld till aftr 3 out, rdn, kpt on one pace*. . . . . (16 to 1)
1014* ST DONAVINT [-] 6-10-1 (3ex) C N Bowens, *dsptd ld till aftr 3 out, rdn, wknd after nxt*. . . . . (10 to 1)
1075[7] ALWAYS IN TROUBLE [-] (bl) 6-10-2 J F Titley, *hld up, prog 3 out, sn rdn, no extr and wknd aftr nxt*. . . . . . . (8 to 1)
123[9] KEPPOLS PRINCE [-] 6-10-6 H Rogers, *wl plcd, rdn 3 out, wknd bef nxt*. . . . . (20 to 1)
707[4] MERAPI [-] 7-10-0 (7*) D J Kavanagh, *mid-div, rdn appr 3 out, kpt on one pace*. . . . . (14 to 1)
GAMARA (Ire) [-] 5-10-11 J P Banahan, *trkd ldrs, rdn 3 out, sn wknd*. . . . .(20 to 1)
904[9] HI MILLIE [-] 7-9-7 F Woods, *al rear*. . . . . (33 to 1)
904 CEDAR COURT (Ire) [-] (bl) 5-10-4 (5*) T J O'Sullivan, *mid-div, rdn and wknd appr 3 out*. . . . .(33 to 1)
533[2] LOSHIAN (Ire) [-] 4-11-0 (7*) K P Gaule, *mid-div, rdn appr 3 out, wknd nxt*. . . . . (100 to 30 fav)
944[5] SHARP INVITE [-] 6-11-2 (7*) M Kelly, *al rear, rdn and wknd aftr 3 out*. . . . .(14 to 1)
831[2] PRETTY NICE (Ire) [-] 5-10-6 P L Malone, *al rear*. (20 to 1)
1037* UNCLE BART (Ire) [-] 5-10-2 (7*,4ex) R A Hennessy, *hld up, prog 4 out, f nxt, dead*. . . . . (9 to 1)
LINVAR [-] 10-11-6 C O'Dwyer, *al rear, tld off whn pld up bef 2 out*. . . . .(40 to 1)

Dist: Nk, dist, 7l, 1½l. 4m 49.50s. (16 Ran).

(John J Nallen), A P O'Bri

1235 Brennans Bread Hurdle (5-y-o and u £3,795 2m 3f. . . . . (3:3

LAW BRIDGE 6-11-8 C F Swan, ...(Evens fav)
904[2] TEMPLEROAN PRINCE 6-12-0 C N Bowens, ... (8 to 1)
939* COOL CHARACTER (Ire) 5-12-0 J F Titley, ...(4 to 1)
938[5] KERFONTAINE 8-11-4 (5*) T P Treacy, ... (8 to 1)
708 SUPER MIDGE 6-12-0 P P Kinane, ... (8 to 1)
BUCKBOARD BOUNCE 7-12-0 C O'Dwyer, ... (8 to 1)
THE PARISH PUMP (Ire) 5-11-8 F Woods, ... (20 to 1)
MOONCAPER 7-11-8 T Horgan, ...(7 to 1)
SOME BRIDGE 6-11-3 S H O'Donovan, ...(50 to 1)
AUSSIE BREEZE (Ire) 5-11-0 (3*) C O'Brien, ... (33 to 1)

Dist: ½l, 13l, 3l, dist. 4m 58.30s. (10 Ran).

(Mrs Ann O'Brien), M J P O'Bri

1236 Tipper Road I.N.H. Flat Race (4-y- and up) £3,105 2m. . . . .(4:0

365* BAY MISCHIEF (Ire) 4-11-6 (7*) Mr J Connolly, ... (6 to 1)
1052* COQ HARDI AFFAIR (Ire) 5-11-13 (5*) Mr B F Murphy, ... (3 to 1 fav)
DROICHEAD LAPEEN 6-11-11 (7*) Mr T J Beattie, (10 to 1)
CASTLEKELLY CROSS 7-12-4 Mr E Bolger, ... (7 to 2)
DAN PATCH 7-11-4 (7*) Mr G T Cuthbert, ...(14 to 1)
857* TRIMMER WONDER (Ire) 5-11-10 (3*) Mrs J M Mullins, ...(7 to 1)
ROUBABAY (Ire) 5-12-4 Mr T Mullins, ...(9 to 2)
858[5] QUEENIES CHILD 6-11-8 (5*) Mr H F Cleary, ...(12 to 1)
YOUR THE MAN 7-11-4 (7*) Mr M Brennan, ... (12 to 1)
SARAKAYA 8-10-13 (7*) Mr E Byrne, ...(33 to 1)
PARKBOY LASS 6-11-8 (5*) Mr G J Harford, ...(14 to 1)
FAITHFULL FELLOW 6-11-8 (3*) Miss C Hutchinson, ...(12 to 1)
LEAP (Ire) 4-11-3 (3*) Mr A R Coonan, ...(25 to 1)
675 SAFRANE 5-11-4 (7*) Mr H Murphy, ...(20 to 1)
DASDILEMMA (Ire) 5-11-1 (5*) Mr D McGoona, . . . (20 to 1)
620* GORYTUS SALA (Ity) 4-11-10 (3*) Mr A E Lacy, . . . (10 to 1)

Dist: 2l, 2½l, 7l, 3l. 4m 3.90s. (16 Ran).

(T Harty), P Bu

NOTTINGHAM (good (races 1,2), good soft (3,4,5,6,7))

Saturday November 13th

Going Correction: PLUS 1.15 sec. per fur. (races 1,2 3,4,7), PLUS 1.00 (5,6)

1237 Ton Up Selling Hurdle (3,4,5-y- £1,841 2m. (12:4

1064[4] KALKO 4-11-10 (7*) Mr C Bonner, *pld hrd, rstrained in rear, hdwy 5th, quickened to ld sn aftr 2 out, ran on wl*. . . . . (11 to 4 op 5 to 2 tchd 3 to 1)
1079[4] PORT IN A STORM 4-11-7 G McCourt, *hld up rear, hdwy 4 out, pressed wnr 2 out till one pace r-in*. . . . .(6 to 1 op 5 to 1)
1007[7] LA POSADA 3-9-9 (7*) P Moore, *led second to 5th, prmnt, ev ch whn mstk 2 out, wknd*. . . . . . .(10 to 1 op 16 to 1)
APRIL CITY 4-11-2 M Dwyer, *hld up, hdwy 4 out, ev ch 2 out, sn btn*. . . . .(14 to 1 op 12 to 1)
1094[3] DUNBAR 3-10-7 R Garritty, *mid-div, hdwy 5th, led appr 3 out till sn aftr nxt, wknd quickly*. . . (11 to 2 op 5 to 1)

NATIONAL HUNT RESULTS 1993-94

997² SWISS MOUNTAIN (v) 3-9-11 (5*) T Eley, *hld up rear, effrt 5th, wknd appr 2 out, tld off.*
..................(9 to 4 fav op 6 to 4 tchd 5 to 2) 6
705⁵ LITTLE PORKY 3-10-7 V Slattery, *led to second, not jump wl, wknd appr 3 out, tld off.......* (16 to 1 op 6 to 1) 7
1021 YOSHAARIK (Ire) 3-10-7 Mr K Green, *prmnt, mstk second, led 5th till appr 3 out, wknd quickly, tld off.*
..................(33 to 1 op 25 to 1) 8
702 ANIL AMIT (bl) 3-10-7 M Hourigan, *al beh, tld off 4 out.*
..................(33 to 1 op 25 to 1) 9
608 MY BOOKS ARE BEST (Ire) 4-11-2 Leesa Long, *pld hrd, mstks, prmnt till wknd 5th, tld off.* (33 to 1 op 25 to 1) 10
BLUE TRUMPET 3-10-7 W Knox, *pld hrd, prmnt till wknd quickly 5th, tld off.....* (9 to 1 op 6 to 1 tchd 10 to 1) 11
Dist: 3l, 10l, 10l, 3l, 20l, 10l, 4l, 25l, 15l, 20l. 4m 9.90s. a 25.90s (11 Ran).
SR: 28/15/-/-/-/-/ (M J Willan), M D Hammond

1238 Tote Lady Riders' Handicap Hurdle (0-115 4-y-o and up) £1,887 2m 5f 110yds......................(1:15)

819* PURITAN (Can) [100] 4-10-9 (5*) Mrs P Nash, *hld up rear, hdwy hfwy, led 3 out, mstk last, hrd held.*
..................(Evens fav op 11 to 10) 1
970* HUNMANBY GAP [86] 8-10-0 Mrs A Farrell, *hld up, rdn and hdwy appr 3 out, chalg whn pckd last, no imprsn r-in.*
..................(7 to 1 op 5 to 1) 2
730⁸ ASTRABEE [90] 8-9-13² (7*) Judy Davies, *hld up, some hdwy hfwy, nvr nr to chal.................*(12 to 1) 3
632² THE MRS [90] 7-10-4 Gee Armytage, *hld up rear, hdwy to go second 4 out, wknd aftr mstk nxt, tld off.*
..................(11 to 4 op 3 to 1) 4
MISS CAPULET [88] 6-10-2 Ann Stokell, *mid-div, lost tch 4 out, tld off.................*(33 to 1) 5
ITALIAN TOUR [86] 13-10-0 Mrs F Needham, *prmnt whn hit 4th, lost tch 7th, tld off.................*(33 to 1) 6
662⁷ WINDWARD ARIOM [94] 7-10-8 Jacqui Oliver, *chsd ldrs, led 7th, mstk 4 out, hdd nxt, wknd quickly, tld off.*
..................(12 to 1 op 10 to 1) 7
367 ANOTHER CORNER [86] (bl) 10-9-7 (7*) Miss S Mitchell, *trkd ldrs till wknd hfwy, tld off.................*(25 to 1) 8
961⁵ DIRECTORS' CHOICE [88] 8-10-2 Susan Kersey, *hld up mid-div, hdwy and 3rd whn blun and uns rdr 7th.*
..................(25 to 1 op 16 to 1) ur
1100⁸ GLENSTAL PRIORY [86] 6-10-0 Miss R Judge, *led to 7th, wknd quickly nxt, tld off whn pld up bef 2 out.*
..................(40 to 1 op 33 to 1 tchd 50 to 1) pu
EDDIE WALSHE [90] 8-10-4 Leesa Long, *pld hrd, prmnt till wknd rpdly hfwy, tld off whn pulled up bef 3 out.*
..................(25 to 1 op 20 to 1) pu
Dist: 1l, 20l, 25l, 5l, 10l, 2½l, dist. 5m 38.50s. a 36.50s (11 Ran).
(J Parks), N Tinkler

1239 Alice Corbett Memorial Conditional Jockeys' Novices' Handicap Hurdle (0-100 4-y-o and up) £1,810 2m 5f 110yds......................(1:45)

844⁴ FATHER FORTUNE [78] (bl) 5-11-8 J McCarthy, *led, mstk 6th, hdd appr last, led sn aftr last, ran on wl.*
..................(5 to 1 co-fav op 9 to 2) 1
1100⁵ SAFARI PARK [77] 4-11-2 (5*) G Cahill, *pld hrd, trkd wnr till hit 5th, rallied 3 out, led and mstk last, sn hdd, one pace.................*(5 to 1 co-fav op 9 to 2) 2
1023⁵ PRINCETHORPE [62] 6-10-6 D Meredith, *hld up in tch, ev ch whn stumbled 3 out, hrd rdn and one pace r-in.*
..................(16 to 1) 3
1053⁷ MALVERN MADAM [70] 6-10-9 (5*) R Wilkinson, *hld up rear, hdwy 4 out, rdn and one pace 2 out.*
..................(9 to 2 tchd 4 to 1) 4
949⁶ VAZON EXPRESS [68] 7-10-5 (7*) D Winter, *chsd ldrs till wknd appr 3 out......* (11 to 1 op 8 to 1 tchd 12 to 1) 5
1000⁵ TITIAN GIRL [80] (bl) 4-11-10 R Davis, *hld up, hdwy to track ldrs hfwy, wknd 4 out, tld off.*
..................(10 to 1 tchd 12 to 1) 6
883⁵ MUTUAL AGREEMENT [72] 6-10-13 (3*) R Darke, *chsd ldrs, wknd 8th, tld off..........* (11 to 2 op 9 to 2) 7
770⁸ MAUREEN'S FANCY [68] 8-10-12 M Hourigan, *hld up, heaway 5th, 3rd whn blun and uns rdr 6th.*
..................(6 to 1 op 7 to 1) ur
1084⁹ ARDORAN [56] 7-10-7 T Eley, *in tch till rdn aftr 6th, sn tld off, pld up bef 3 out.................*(33 to 1) pu
1109⁵ RUSTIC FLIGHT [66] 6-10-10 R Farrant, *al beh, mstk 6th, tld off whn pld up bef 3 out.* (5 to 1 co-fav) pu
950⁷ LEARNER DRIVER [57] (bl) 6-9-10 (5*) N Juckes, *mid-div, wknd hfwy, tld off whn pld up bef 3 out......* (14 to 1) pu
Dist: 2l, 2½l, 4l, 12l, 25l, dist. 5m 45.30s. a 43.30s (11 Ran).
(R B Holt), O Sherwood

1240 Lily Slack Memorial Handicap Hurdle (0-135 4-y-o and up) £1,975 2m..(2:20)

936³ FRONT STREET [86] 6-10-4 G Upton, *trkd ldrs, al gng wl, cld 4 out, led betw last 2, pushed clr r-in, cmftbly.*
..................(11 to 10 on op Evens tchd 5 to 4 and 5 to 4 on) 1
ARANY [95] 6-10-13 R Campbell, *led till betw last 2, hit last, one pace.................*(2 to 1 tchd 13 to 8) 2

1042* ALOSAILI [94] 6-10-5 (7*) M Stevens, *whipped round strt, mstk 1st, beh till hdwy appr 3 out, wknd nxt.*
..................(13 to 2 op 4 to 1) 3
1101 IN TRUTH [106] 5-11-10 M Dwyer, *trkd ldr, rdn appr 3 out, wknd quickly nxt.................*(6 to 1 op 5 to 1) 4
FEASIBLE [92] 9-10-10 Miss R Judge, *slwly away, lost tch 4th, tld off.................*(33 to 1 op 25 to 1 tchd 50 to 1) 5
Dist: 6l, 10l, 30l, dist. 4m 9.30s. a 25.30s (5 Ran).
SR: 7/10/ (Mrs Jean R Bishop), S E Sherwood

1241 Andy And Tracy's Wedding Day Novices' Chase (5-y-o and up) £2,251 2m ....(2:50)

NATIVE MISSION 6-11-0 M Dwyer, *led second to 4th, led 5 out, drw clr 3 out, easily.................*(Evens jt-fav) 1
RODEO STAR (USA) 7-11-0 G McCourt, *blun 4th, hld up, hdwy to go second appr 3 out, no ch wth wnr.* (Evens jt-fav tchd 11 to 10) 2
868 TOI MARINE 8-11-0 Mr A Hambly, *led to fourth, led 4th, mstk 8th, hdd nxt, wknd appr 2 out, btn whn blun last.................*(50 to 1 op 33 to 1 tchd 66 to 1) 3
909⁷ PHALAROPE (Ire) (v) 5-11-0 Mr A Walton, *al beh, tld off 7th.*
..................(16 to 1 tchd 20 to 1) 4
794 BLAKE'S TREASURE (v) 6-10-7 (7*) D Meade, *mstks in rear, lost tch 5th, tld off whn pld up bef 4 out.*
..................(40 to 1 op 33 to 1 tchd 50 to 1) pu
Dist: 15l, 15l, dist. 4m 10.30s. a 19.30s (5 Ran).
SR: 53/38/23/-/-/ (G E Shouler), J G FitzGerald

1242 Colwick Park Handicap Chase (0-125 5-y-o and up) £2,880 3m 110yds (3:20)

986³ ARD T'MATCH [95] (v) 8-10-2² Gary Lyons, *hld up in tch, led 5 out, screwed lft last, styd on.*
..................(100 to 30 op 5 to 1) 1
1082² MANDER'S WAY [107] 8-11-0 M Dwyer, *trkd ldrs, hit tenth, rdn and lost pl appr 4 out, styd on to go second r-in.................*(9 to 4) 2
986⁵ JIMMY O'DEA [93] (v) G-9-0 (6*) T Eley, *led 3rd to 5th, led aftr 9th to 11th, dsptd ld 13th, ev ch till one pace r-in.*
..................(14 to 1 op 12 to 1) 3
895⁴ PHAROAH'S LAEN [117] 12-11-5 (5*) R Farrant, *led to 3rd, led 5th till aftr 9th, led 11th to 13th, wknd rpdly appr 4 out, tld off......* (11 to 1 op 16 to 1 tchd 10 to 1) 4
THE TARTAN SPARTAN [93] 9-9-10³ (7*) P Ward, *al beh, lost tch sn aftr hfwy, tld off.*
..................(11 to 1 op 16 to 1 tchd 10 to 1) 5
1050 DRAGONS DEN [107] 7-11-0 G Upton, *hld up, f 5th.*
..................(7 to 4 fav op 11 to 8) f
Dist: 3½l, 1½l, dist, 2½l. 6m 34.80s. a 39.80s (6 Ran).
(J Rackliff), A L Forbes

1243 River Trent Juvenile Novices' Hurdle (3-y-o) £1,887 2m..............(3:50)

1062⁴ HYDE'S HAPPY HOUR 11-0 M McCourt, *hld up, hdwy 4 out, led 2 out, hit last, rdn clr.*
..................(11 to 4 fav op 7 to 4 tchd 3 to 1) 1
HEATHYARDS BOY 10-11 (3*) S Wynne, *pushed alng in rear, hdwy 4 out, ev ch 2 out, mstk last, no imprsn aftr.*
..................(6 to 1 op 9 to 2) 2
WAMDHA (Ire) 10-9 A S Smith, *hld up, hdwy 5th, led appr 3 out, hdd nxt, wknd r-in.*
..................(8 to 1 tchd 10 to 1 and 7 to 1) 3
1032⁶ SALLY OF THE ALLEY 10-9 Gary Lyons, *prmnt till rdn and wknd appr 2 out.................*(16 to 1 tchd 20 to 1) 4
851⁷ BOLD ACRE 10-9 (5*) R Davis, *pld hrd, led appr 5th till approaching 3 out, wknd rpdly approaching nxt.*
..................(9 to 2 tchd 4 to 1) 5
802⁸ TORC MOUNTAIN (Ire) 10-9 (5*) R Farrant, *mid-div, no hdwy frm 3 out.................*(16 to 1 op 10 to 1) 6
1032 SEASIDE DREAMER 11-0 Mr A Hambly, *beh whn blun and uns rdr 4th.................*(6 to 1) ur
1021 FREE DANCER 10-9 M Hourigan, *al beh, lost tch 4 out, tld off whn pld up bef last............* (16 to 1 op 12 to 1) pu
1021⁷ BARTON ROYAL (Ire) 11-0 A Charlton, *chsd ldrs till wknd quickly 4 out, tld off whn pld up bef 2 out.*
..................(14 to 1 op 16 to 1 tchd 20 to 1) pu
1007⁴ STORM FALCON (USA) 11-0 M Dwyer, *hld up, tld appr 4th, wknd rpdly four out, tld off whn pld up bef 2 out.*
..................(10 to 1 tchd 7 to 1) pu
Dist: 6l, 15l, 5l, 1½l, 2l. 4m 14.70s. a 30.70s (10 Ran).
(Travellers T Time Club), N Tinkler

WINDSOR (good)
Saturday November 13th
Going Correction: PLUS 0.55 sec. per fur. (races 1,4,6), MINUS 0.05 (2,3,5)

1244 Mill Stream Juvenile Novices' Hurdle (3-y-o) £1,480 2m..............(1:05)

BAJAN AFFAIR 10-4 (3*) A Thornton, *al prmnt, rdn to chal appr last, styd on to ld last 50 yards.........* (20 to 1) 1

668³ CHIAPPUCCI (Ire) (bl) 11-5 N Williamson, *hld up in mid-div, prog 5th, led appr 2 out, hrd rdn aftr last, hdd fnl 50 yards*.............. (5 to 2 fav op 2 to 1 tchd 11 to 4) 2
1125⁷ LOCHORE 10-12 M A FitzGerald, *hld up in mid-div, prog appr 3 out, styd on one pace frm nxt*. (8 to 1 op 9 to 2) 3
MY HARVINSKI 10-12 M Richards, *prmnt till wknd aftr 2 out*.............................. (11 to 4 op 9 to 2) 4
570⁸ SHARED GOLD 10-12 M Bosley, *pld hrd, trkd ldrs, effrt aftr 5th, wknd after 2 out*........ (33 to 1 op 20 to 1) 5
890³ APACHEE FLOWER 10-7 J Frost, *prmnt till wknd appr 2 out*................ (8 to 1 tchd 12 to 1 and 14 to 1) 6
AMILLIONMEMORIES 10-12 N Mann, *jmpd slwly 3rd, prmnt, mstk 3 out, sn rdn and btn*............(20 to 1) 7
JACKSONS BAY 10-12 T Grantham, *hld up last, steady prog frm 5th, nvr plcd to chal*..... (33 to 1 op 20 to 1) 8+
SACHA STAR 10-7 R Greene, *beh, rdn frm 3rd, nvr rchd ldrs*.............................(33 to 1 op 20 to 1) 8+
391⁴ ANY MINUTE NOW (Ire) 10-12 D Bridgwater, *led to second and aftr 5th to appr 2 out, sn wknd*. (8 to 1 op 7 to 2) 10
EL GRANDO 10-12 D O'Sullivan, *mid-div, rdn and no prog 2 out*..........................(25 to 1 op 20 to 1) 11
FINDON ACADEMY (Ire) 10-12 H Jenkins, *mid-div, prog 5th, chasing ldrs whn blun 2 out, no dngr aftr*. .... (25 to 1 op 16 to 1) 12
NIGHTMARE LADY 10-7 J McLaughlin, *chsd ldg grp till wknd 3 out*...................... (33 to 1 op 20 to 1) 13
TREBLE LASS 10-7 J Leech, *led second till aftr 5th, wknd 2 out*............................(16 to 1 op 10 to 1) 14
HOBBS (Ire) 10-12 H Davies, *mstk second, beh aftr*. .... (14 to 1 op 12 to 1) 15
TOP GUNNER (Ire) 10-12 R Rowell, *prmnt to 5th, sn wknd*. ....(20 to 1 tchd 33 to 1) 16
HERETICAL MISS 10-7 B Clifford, *strted slwly, mstk 3rd, al beh*...........................(20 to 1 op 12 to 1) 17
NATASHA NORTH 10-7 J Railton, *slwly into strd, al beh*. .... (33 to 1 op 20 to 1) 18
MORAN BRIG 10-12 S Hodgson, *blun badly 1st, al beh*. .... (20 to 1 op 12 to 1) 19
CONBRIO STAR 10-12 S Smith Eccles, *jmpd badly, sn beh, tld off*..........................(25 to 1 op 20 to 1) 20
MISS COPYFORCE 10-7 W McFarland, *slwly into strd, beh till effrt 5th, sn wknd, pld up bef 2 out*. .... (20 to 1 op 16 to 1) pu

Dist: 1½l, 12l, 1½l, 3l, 6l, 1½l, 3½l, dd-ht, 2l, ¾l. 4m 0.40s. a 15.40s (21 Ran).
SR: 13/23/4/2/-/-/ (Miss L C Siddall), Miss L C Siddall

1245 Eton Wick Novices' Chase (5-y-o and up) £2,485 2m.................(1:40)

826³ EASY BUCK 6-11-0 J Frost, *lft in ld appr 4th, made rst, clr last, cmftbly*........ (11 to 4 op 2 to 1 tchd 3 to 1) 1
1071² SAN LORENZO (USA) (bl) 5-11-0 N Williamson, *led and blun second, hdd aftr 3rd and crrd wide on bend, reco'red to chase wnr 9th, mstk 3 out, no imprsn*. .... (11 to 10 fav op 6 to 4 tchd 13 to 8) 2
848⁴ CHAPEL HILL (Ire) 5-10-2 (7*) D Fortt, *prmnt, chsd wnr 7th to 9th, rdn and wknd 3 out*.......... (9 to 1 op 6 to 1) 3
892 STORM FLIGHT 7-11-0 Peter Hobbs, *prmnt, rdn 8th, btn frm nxt*.......................... (33 to 1 op 25 to 1) 4
WAYWARD WIND 9-11-0 M A FitzGerald, *prmnt, rdn 6th, wknd 9th*........... (14 to 1 op 25 to 1 tchd 33 to 1) 5
705⁷ PALM SWIFT 7-10-9 A Tory, *prmnt till wknd rpdly aftr 9th*.................................. (33 to 1 op 25 to 1) 6
601⁶ SING THE BLUES 9-11-0 D Morris, *led to second, crrd wide bend appr 4th, not reco'r*... (20 to 1 tchd 33 to 1) 7
961² MASROUG 6-10-7 (7*) J Clarke, *al rear, lost tch aftr 8th*. .... (12 to 1 op 10 to 1 tchd 14 to 1) 8
954 IMPERIAL FLIGHT 8-10-11 (3*) A Thornton, *prmnt, rdn alng whn blun 7th, sn beh, tld off*. .... (25 to 1 op 20 to 1 tchd 33 to 1) 9
982⁹ ALLIED'S TEAM 6-10-9 D Skyrme, *sn wl beh, tld off whn uns rdr 4th*...................................... (33 to 1) ur
VAIGLY BLAZED 9-11-0 B Clifford, *al beh, tld off and pld up bef 9th*........... (25 to 1 op 20 to 1 tchd 33 to 1) pu
LUCKY BLUE 6-11-0 I Lawrence, *al beh, tld off and pld up bef 9th*..................................(25 to 1 op 20 to 1) pu
1124³ PARBOLD HILL 5-11-6 J Duggan, *beh frm 4th, tld off and pld up bef 9th*......................(14 to 1 op 10 to 1) pu
HELL OF A GUY 6-11-0 H Jenkins, *pld very hrd, led aftr 3rd till tried to run out bend appr nxt, pulled up bef 5th*................................ (33 to 1 op 25 to 1) pu

Dist: 10l, 15l, 8l, 12l, 2½l, 3l, ½l, dist. 3m 59.40s. a 3.40s (14 Ran).
SR: 44/34/14/11/-/-/ (The Burford Laundry Company Ltd), N A Gaselee

1246 Royal Berkshire Handicap Chase (0-130 5-y-o and up) £2,820 3m..(2:10)

UNDER OFFER [95] (bl) 12-10-1¹ M A FitzGerald, *made all, rdn 3 out, hld on gmely r-in*........(7 to 2 tchd 4 to 1) 1
956* CHANNELS GATE [117] 9-11-9 N Williamson, *hld up in cl tch, wnt second 11th, jnd wnr 3 out, hrd rdn appr last, unbl to quicken*. ....(11 to 4 on op 7 to 2 on tchd 5 to 2 on) 2
1029 STEPFASTER [110] 8-10-13 (3*) A Thornton, *trkd wnr to 11th, wknd rpdly aftr 3 out*......... (9 to 2 tchd 5 to 1) 3

Dist: Hd, dist. 6m 12.80s. a 17.80s (3 Ran).
(Miss S Douglas-Pennant), J S King

1247 Marina Novices' Hurdle (4-y-o and up) £1,480 2¾m 110yds............ (2:45)

BEYOND OUR REACH 5-10-12 H Davies, *trkd ldrs, effrt 3 out, led last, rdn clr*.... (5 to 2 op 2 to 1 tchd 11 to 4) 1
FOREST FEATHER (Ire) 5-10-12 Peter Hobbs, *trkd ldrs gng easily, led 3 out, rdn and hdd last, wknd r-in*. .... (10 to 1 op 8 to 1) 2
920² URBAN COWBOY 6-10-12 M A FitzGerald, *in tch till lost pl appr 3 out, ran on ag'n frm 2 out, nrst finish*. ....(5 to 2 op 9 to 4 tchd 3 to 1) 3
843 COAL NOT DOLE (Ire) 5-10-7 (5*) Mr T Byrne, *mid-div, prog 6th, ev ch 3 out till wknd appr last*. (25 to 1 op 14 to 1) 4
650 OUR WIZZER (Ire) 4-10-12 S Earle, *prmnt, led 8th to 3 out, sn wknd*.......................... (33 to 1 op 25 to 1) 5
ANOTHER LOAN 6-10-2 (5*) A Procter, *beh, rdn aftr 5th, tld off frm 3 out*...... (16 to 1 op 10 to 1 tchd 20 to 1) 6
916⁹ SWING LUCKY 8-10-12 M Richards, *prog frm rear 7th, rdn and wknd aftr nxt, sn tld off*. .... (25 to 1 op 20 to 1 tchd 33 to 1) 7
1040 BLUE TAIL 5-10-0 (7*) S Arnold, *al rear, pushed alng 5th, tld off frm 3 out*.................. (33 to 1 op 20 to 1) 8
GREEN'S TRILOGY (USA) 5-10-12 M Ahern, *prmnt, led aftr 5th to 8th, wknd rpdly, sn tld off*. (33 to 1 op 25 to 1) 9
346 SHAURNI GIRL 5-10-7 J McLaughlin, *led till aftr 5th, mstk nxt and wknd, pld up bef 8th*......(33 to 1 op 25 to 1) pu
815⁵ SHERWOOD BOY 4-10-12 N Williamson, *pld hrd and hld up, prog and in tch 3 out, wknd rpdly nxt, pulled up bef last*............(7 to 4 fav op 11 to 8 tchd 9 to 4) pu

Dist: 5l, hd, 4l, 20l, 25l, 4l, 10l, dist. 5m 39.40s. a 20.40s (11 Ran).
SR: 4/-/-/-/-/-/ (Hunt & Co (Bournemouth) Ltd), R J Hodges

1248 Saxon House Novices' Chase (5-y-o and up) £2,968 2m 5f........... (3:15)

HILLWALK 7-11-0 D Morris, *wtd wth, prog to chase ldr tenth, led aftr 12th, sn wl clr, blun last, easily*. .... (5 to 2 op 3 to 1 tchd 4 to 1 and 9 to 2) 1
UNHOLY ALLIANCE 6-11-0 N Williamson, *led into strt, pld into ld second, sn clr, hdd aftr 12th, wkng whn hit 2 out*.................... (11 to 4 op 7 to 4 tchd 3 to 1) 2
998 BATHWICK BOBBIE 6-10-7 (7*) D Fortt, *chsd ldrs, wnt 3rd but outpcd 11th, kpt on*. .... (11 to 1 op 6 to 1 tchd 12 to 1) 3
933 POWER HAPPY 8-10-9 B Clifford, *sn wl beh, styd on frm 3 out, nvr nr to chal*............... (25 to 1 op 20 to 1) 4
1043⁴ TRAIN ROBBER 8-11-0 W Irvine, *led to second, pushed alng 7th, wknd tenth*. .... (16 to 1 op 14 to 1 tchd 20 to 1) 5
959⁴ TAPESTRY DANCER 5-10-13 D Skyrme, *slwly into strd, al beh, tld off frm 11th*............... (25 to 1 op 20 to 1) 6
862 MUTUAL BENEFIT (v) 6-10-11 (3*) A Thornton, *rcd freely, prmnt till wknd tenth, tld off*......(33 to 1 op 20 to 1) 7
932⁴ VIAGGIO 5-10-13 J Railton, *uns rdr 1st*. .... (16 to 1 op 14 to 1) ur
1081 VISION OF WONDER 9-11-0 S Smith Eccles, *in tch to 4th, beh whn blun 7th, pld up bef 11th*. (20 to 1 op 14 to 1) pu
978 CONGREGATION 7-11-6 H Davies, *prmnt in chasing grp till wknd tenth, pld up bef 3 out*. (2 to 1 fav op 5 to 2) pu
869 POLYNOGAN 7-11-0 Peter Hobbs, *mstks, al beh, blun tenth, pld up aftr nxt*..............................(33 to 1) pu

Dist: 20l, 1½l, 20l, 1l, 20l. 5m 35.70s. a 24.70s (11 Ran).
(M L Shone), R Curtis

1249 Sandford Dene Handicap Hurdle (0-130 4-y-o and up) £3,132 2m..(3:45)

887⁵ EASTHORPE [93] 5-10-1¹ M A FitzGerald, *made all, clr 3 out, pushed out r-in, cmftbly*................(7 to 2 jt-fav op 3 to 1 tchd 9 to 2) 1
977² SOLEIL DANCER (Ire) [101] 5-10-9 Peter Hobbs, *mid-div, prog appr 3 out, chsd wnr aftr nxt, ran on one pace*. ....(5 to 1 op 7 to 1) 2
887³ VA UTU [95] 5-10-3 Lorna Vincent, *chsd wnr to 5th and ag'n 3 out till aftr nxt, one pace*. .... (5 to 1 tchd 13 to 2 and 9 to 2) 3
CHEEKY FOX [95] 7-10-3³ M Bosley, *prmnt till outpcd 3 out, kpt on ag'n appr last*........ (20 to 1 op 16 to 1) 4
MISTER ODDY [102] 7-10-10 S Smith Eccles, *prmnt, chsd wnr frm 5th till 3 out, sn wknd*.... (12 to 1 op 14 to 1) 5
WILL JAMES [92] (bl) 7-10-0 D Bridgwater, *cl up till lost pl aftr 5th, no prog frm nxt*.......... (20 to 1 op 14 to 1) 6
1104 WHEELER'S WONDER (Ire) [108] 4-10-9 (7*) Mr J L Llewellyn, *prog to join ldrs 5th, wknd rpdly aftr 3 out*.. .(7 to 2 jt-fav op 4 to 1 tchd 5 to 1) 7
936 FRONT PAGE [102] 6-10-10 J Railton, *hld up beh, lost tch aftr 5th, sn tld off*..................... (7 to 1 op 6 to 1) 8
1124 PRESENT TIMES [92] 7-9-11⁴ (7*) J Clarke, *lost pl 3rd, tld off frm 3 out*.......................... (33 to 1 op 20 to 1) 9
662² LE METAYER (Fr) [116] 5-11-10 N Williamson, *hld up beh, pld up bef 4th, lme*...... (4 to 1 op 3 to 1 tchd 9 to 2) pu

Dist: 6l, 3½l, 2½l, 20l, 15l, 5l, 15l, 10l. 3m 59.50s. a 14.50s (10 Ran).
SR: 16/18/8/5/-/-/ (Martin Broughton), Miss H C Knight

AUTEUIL (FR) (heavy)

Sunday November 14th

1250 Prix La Haye Jousselin Chase (5-y-o and up) £71,685 3m 3f 110yds... (2:00)

ALCAPONE II (Fr) 5-10-8 J Y Beaurain,	1
816* UCELLO II (Fr) 8-11-1 C Aubert,	2
816 THE FELLOW (Fr) 8-10-4 A Kondrat,	3
16⁴ SIRTA (Fr) 9-9-11 J-J Manceau,	4

Dist: 5l, 6l, dist. 7m 33.00s. (4 Ran).

LEICESTER (soft (races 1,2,3,6,7), good to soft (4,5))
Monday November 15th
Going Correction: PLUS 0.55 sec. per fur.

1251 Stoughton 'National Hunt' Novices' Hurdle (4-y-o and up) £1,949 2m
....(12:45)

MR WOODLARK 6-10-10 J Frost, *hld up, hdwy 4 out, led r-in, styd on strly*.......(7 to 1 op 4 to 1 tchd 8 to 1)   1
MISS MONZA 5-10-5 D Bridgwater, *ldg grp, led 3 out till rdn and hdd r-in, not quicken*......(20 to 1 op 12 to 1)   2
GRIFFINS BAR 5-10-10 A Carroll, *led till hdd 3 out, ev ch last, no extr*.....................(50 to 1 op 33 to 1)   3
IN FOR A POUND (Ire) 4-10-10 S Smith Eccles, *chsd ldrs, rdn and one pace appr 2 out.*
.......................(5 to 1 tchd 7 to 1 and 9 to 2)   4
TWO JOHN'S (Ire) 4-10-10 G Bradley, *hld up, hdwy 5th, rdn and btn in fifth pl whn blun last.*
.......................(6 to 4 fav op 5 to 4 tchd 7 to 4)   5
MR PICKPOCKET (Ire) 5-10-10 L Harvey, *hdwy and mstk 5th, outpcd frm 3 out...*(11 to 2 op 7 to 2 tchd 6 to 1)   6
1084⁴ NAVAL BATTLE 6-10-10 M A FitzGerald, *hld up, not fluent 4th, hdwy nxt, ev ch 3 out, sn btn.*
.......................(8 to 1 op 5 to 1 tchd 9 to 1)   7
THE CHANGELING (Ire) 4-10-10 R J Beggan, *chsd ldr til wknd aftr 4 out, btn whn blun 2 out.*
.......................(11 to 1 op 5 to 1)   8
UNEXIS 8-10-10 M Perrett, *al beh, lost tch frm 5th, pld up bef 3 out*............(20 to 1 tchd 25 to 1)   pu
983⁷ THAT'S SPECIAL 4-10-10 A Maguire, *wl plcd til wknd 4 out, pld up bef 2 out.* (14 to 1 op 10 to 1 tchd 16 to 1)   pu

Dist: 3½l, ½l, 8l, 7l, 3l, 1½l, ½l. 4m 3.30s. a 20.30s (10 Ran).

(P A Tylor), R G Frost

1252 Desborough Mares' Only Novices' Handicap Hurdle (4-y-o and up) £1,856 2½m 110yds....................(1:15)

1059* KYTTON CASTLE [80] 6-11-3 (3") D Meredith, *hld up, hdwy and pushed alng 3 out, led last, styd on wl.*
.......................(11 to 4 fav op 11 to 4)   1
RUSSINSKY [84] 6-11-10 R J Beggan, *wl plcd, led 6th till rdn and hdd last, kpt on gmely.*
.......................(9 to 1 op 7 to 1 tchd 10 to 1)   2
1215⁴ GAMEFULL GOLD [81] 4-11-2 (5") A Dicken, *hld up, pressed ldrs and ev ch frm 4 out, one pace appr last.*
.......................(9 to 2 op 5 to 1 tchd 5 to 1)   3
883³ KICKING BIRD [75] 6-11-1 S McNeill, *hld up till improved 5th, ev ch whn pckd badly 3 out, lost pos, no extr betw last 2 flights.*......................(8 to 1 op 9 to 1)   4
863³ POLLY MINOR [78] 6-11-4 M Perrett, *hld up, effrt appr 4 out, not quicken frm nxt.*............(16 to 1 op 20 to 1)   5
795 COUNTRY MISTRESS [74] 6-11-0 A Maguire, *prog 5th, rdn and wknd appr 3 out, tld off.*
.......................(14 to 1 op 16 to 1 tchd 20 to 1)   6
OH SO WINDY [75] 6-11-1 R Dunwoody, *cl up, led 5th to nxt, wknd appr 4 out, tld off.*
.......................(20 to 1 op 16 to 1 tchd 25 to 1)   7
1086⁴ PRUDENT PEGGY [82] 6-11-8 J Frost, *led to 3rd, wknd 7th, tld off.*...........(11 to 1 op 10 to 1 tchd 14 to 1)   8
MILLIE (USA) [65] 5-10-5 M Robinson, *trkd ldrs till wknd 7th, tld off whn pld up bef 2 out.*...(33 to 1 op 25 to 1)   pu
1079² ABSOLUTLEY FOXED [70] 4-10-10 T Wall, *wl in tch, rdn and wknd 6th, tld off whn pld up bef 3 out.*   pu
964⁷ MISS SOUTER [80] 4-10-13 (7") G Lewis, *cl up, led 3rd to 5th, wknd 7th, tld off whn pld up bef 2 out.*
.......................(20 to 1 op 14 to 1)   pu

Dist: 2½l, 4l, 2½l, 6l, 25l, 4l, 30l. 5m 19.40s. a 31.40s (11 Ran).

(Joint Partnership), R Dickin

1253 Junior Selling Hurdle (3 & 4-y-o) £1,980 2m....................(1:45)

742⁴ MY BALLYBOY 3-10-7 N Mann, *mid-div, cld on ldr 4 out, led 2 out, clr last.*.......(5 to 1 op 4 to 1 tchd 11 to 2)   1
DOUALAGO (Fr) 3-10-12 R Dunwoody, *led, hit 3 out, rdn and hdd nxt, sn outpcd.*
.......................(6 to 4 fav op Evens tchd 7 to 4)   2

1094⁴ AL FORUM (Ire) 3-10-7 A Maguire, *steady hdwy frm 5th, ev ch 4 out, one pace from 3 out.*.......(10 to 1 op 8 to 1)   3
1070 SUMMER FLOWER (bl) 3-10-2 (5") Eley, *wth ldr frm 5th til wknd aftr 4 out.*...............(11 to 1 op 8 to 1)   4
SHARE A MOMENT (Can) 3-10-4 (3") S Wynne, *sn beh, effrt 5th, no imprsn on ldrs frm 4 out.*...(10 to 1 op 7 to 1)   5
711² CREAGMHOR 3-10-0 (7") Mr J L Llewellyn, *hld up in mid-div, rdn and no extr appr 4 out.*.....(8 to 1 op 10 to 1)   6
DAJAM 3-10-2 L Harvey, *pressed ldrs till wknd 4 out.*
.......................(25 to 1 tchd 33 to 1)   7
851 MAJOR TRIUMPH (Ire) 3-10-2 R J Beggan, *al beh.*
.......................(12 to 1 op 10 to 1 tchd 14 to 1)   8
1079⁵ DANCING DANCER (Ire) 3-10-7 A Frost, *beh till moderate effrt 5th, no hdwy frm 4 out.*............(8 to 1 op 20 to 1)   9
932 ALIF (Ire) (bl) 4-10-9 Diane Clay, *al beh, tld off whn pld up bef 2 out.*........................(33 to 1 op 20 to 1)   pu
702³ DOCTOR-J (Ire) 3-10-7 S Keightley, *trkd ldrs till wknd frm 6th, pld up bef 2 out.* (12 to 1 op 10 to 1 tchd 14 to 1)   pu
588 LARKSPUR LEGEND 3-10-7 M A FitzGerald, *wl plcd till rdn and lost pos frm 6th, pld up bef 2 out.*
.......................(33 to 1 op 20 to 1 tchd 50 to 1)   pu

Dist: 10l, 2½l, 25l, 12l, 20l, 2l, 3l, 3l. 4m 0.20s. a 17.20s (12 Ran).

(A Bailey), A Bailey

1254 Midland Handicap Chase (0-125 5-y-o and up) £2,978 3m.............(2:15)

696⁷ TORT [111] 9-10-11 (3") W Marston, *made all, mstk 1st, rdn clr frm last.*......................(11 to 8 fav op 5 to 4)   1
1069³ CATCH THE CROSS [125] (v) 7-12-0 M Foster, *hld up in 3rd pl till pressed wnr aftr 13th, ev ch betw last 2 fences, outpcd r-in.*...............(6 to 4 tchd 11 to 8)   2
947⁶ VIVA BELLA (Fr) [97] (bl) 6-9-7 (7") Mr D Parker, *beh and not fluent, lost tch 8th, styd on into 3rd pl 2 out, no ch wth wnr.*.......................(8 to 1 op 6 to 1)   3
JIMSTRO [101] 8-10-4 M Ahern, *chsd wnr till aftr 13th, sn rdn, lost tch appr 3 out.*......(8 to 1 op 4 to 1)   4

Dist: 8l, dist, dist. 6m 18.00s. a 26.00s (4 Ran).

(R A H Perkins), P T Dalton

1255 Leicester Novices' Chase (5-y-o and up) £2,266 2m 1f.............. (2:45)

899² WHAT'S IN ORBIT 8-10-12 G Bradley, *made all, pushed wl clr frm last.*
.......................(11 to 8 on op 5 to 4 on tchd 11 to 10 on)   1
THE FLYING FOOTMAN 7-10-12 A Maguire, *hld up, ev ch frm 3 out till rdn and btn appr last.*
.......................(9 to 2 op 3 to 1 tchd 5 to 1)   2
1081⁴ TITUS GOLD (bl) 8-10-12 M A FitzGerald, *hld up in rear, wnt 3rd 4 out, rdn and outpcd frm nxt.*
.......................(3 to 1 tchd 11 to 4)   3
TINA'S MISSILE 6-10-12 R Greene, *cl up till drpd rear 4 out, sn lost tch, tld off whn blun last.*
.......................(12 to 1 op 10 to 1 tchd 14 to 1)   4

Dist: 12l, 2l, dist. 4m 27.90s. a 18.90s (4 Ran).

(Paul K Barber), P F Nicholls

1256 Thorpe Satchville Hurdle (4-y-o and up) £4,191 2m.................(3:15)

1104³ CULTURED 4-11-3 D Murphy, *hld up gng wl, slight ld last, quickened and pushed clr r-in.*
.......................(9 to 2 op 4 to 1 tchd 5 to 1)   1
SIMPSON 8-11-7 T Grantham, *hld up, hdwy 4 out, led 2 out, hdd last, eased whn btn r-in...*(12 to 1 op 8 to 1)   2
KIVETON TYCOON (Ire) 4-10-8 M Dwyer, *hld up, cld on ldrs 4 out, ev ch nxt, one pace frm 2 out.*
.......................(9 to 2 op 7 to 2)   3
827² ROYAL DERBI 8-11-12 A Maguire, *clr ldr to 4th, rdn and hdd 2 out, sn btn.*
.......................(Evens fav op 11 to 8 on tchd 11 to 10)   4
1116² BEAUCHAMP GRACE 4-10-12 R Dunwoody, *trkd ldr, ev ch whn mstk 4 out, wknd appr 2 out.*
.......................(11 to 2 op 5 to 1 tchd 6 to 1)   5
1108 DEEP IN GREEK 7-10-12 M A FitzGerald, *sn wl outpcd, tld off frm hfwy, pld up bef last...* (500 to 1 op 100 to 1)   pu

Dist: 4l, 2½l, 8l, ¾l. 3m 56.40s. a 13.40s (6 Ran).

SR: 43/43/27/37/22/-/

(B Whitehorn), J White

1257 Levy Board Handicap Hurdle (0-125 4-y-o and up) £3,236 2½m 110yds
....(3:45)

861⁶ DARK HONEY [100] 8-10-11 (5") A Dicken, *wl plcd, led and lft well clr 4 out, hit last, unchlgd...* (3 to 1 op 7 to 4)   1
MR FLUTTS [98] 7-11-0 S McNeill, *beh and outpcd appr 7th, chsd wnr frm 3 out, no imprsn.*
.......................(9 to 1 op 7 to 1 tchd 10 to 1)   2
AUTONOMOUS [84] 8-10-0 D Bridgwater, *hld up beh, hdwy 7th, outpcd appr 4 out.*
.......................(10 to 1 op 12 to 1 tchd 14 to 1)   3
SUPER RITCHART [108] 5-11-10 R Dunwoody, *led to 6th, rdn and outpcd appr 4 out, tld off.*.......(11 to 4 jt-fav op 5 to 2 tchd 7 to 2)   4

1025⁴ SECRET SUMMIT (USA) [95] 7-10-6 (5*) T Eley, *wl plcd till rdn and outpcd 7th, tld off*.
.... (8 to 1 op 10 to 1 tchd 11 to 1) 5
651* ARRAN VIEW [92] 7-10-1 (7*) Mr J L Llewellyn, *trkd ldr, led 6th till jst hdd and f 4 out*. ....(11 to 4 jt-fav op 7 to 4 tchd 3 to 1) f
Dist: Dist, 8l, 20l, 20l. 5m 4.30s. a 16.30s (6 Ran).
SR: 38/-/-/

(Roger Sayer), S Dow

PLUMPTON (good)
Monday November 15th
Going Correction: PLUS 0.65 sec. per fur. (races 1,3,5), PLUS 1.10 (2,4,6)

1258 Jolly Tanners At Staplefield Novices' Chase (4-y-o and up) £1,931 2m (1:00)

794² KALANSKI 7-11-10 J Osborne, *led and mstk 5th, made rst, clr appr 2 out, easily...* (6 to 1 on tchd 11 to 2 on) 1
979⁷ JOKER JACK 8-11-0 (5*) A Procter, *led to 5th, rdn 7th, mstk nxt, no ch wth wnr aftr 3 out*.
.... (11 to 2 op 4 to 1 tchd 6 to 1) 2
TINKER DAN 5-11-5 W McFarland, *last whn mstk 4th, prog to chase wnr 9th, wknd rpdly aftr 3 out*.
.... (50 to 1 op 20 to 1) 3
1042⁷ L'ENCHERE 8-10-7 (7*) G Crone, *blun 5th and 7th, in tch to 8th, sn wknd*...............(50 to 1 op 20 to 1) 4
Dist: 7l, 30l, 2½l. 4m 9.90s. a 19.90s (4 Ran).
SR: 1/

(I Kerman), C R Egerton

1259 Stanmer Conditional Jockeys' Selling Handicap Hurdle (4,5,6-y-o) £1,572 2m 1f............................... (1:30)

859² MECADO [79] 6-11-9 M Hourigan, *trkd ldrs, pushed alng and outpcd 7th, ran on aftr 3 out, led last, rdn out*.
.... (6 to 5 fav op 5 to 4 tchd 11 to 8) 1
666³ ROGER'S PAL [80] 6-11-7 (3*) J Clarke, *set steady pace till quickened 7th, rdn appr 2 out, hdd and mstk last, unbl to quicken*................ (7 to 2 op 3 to 1 tchd 9 to 2) 2
522⁴ TRENDY AUCTIONEER (Ire) [71] (v) 5-11-1 R Davis, *hld up, prog to chase ldr 7th, rdn and not quicken aftr 2 out*.
.... (4 to 1 op 7 to 2 tchd 9 to 2) 3
859⁶ SLICK CHERRY [75] 6-11-5 D O'Sullivan, *in tch till outpcd aftr 7th, no prog after*.
.... (14 to 1 op 10 to 1 tchd 16 to 1) 4
953⁷ GREAT IMPOSTOR [73] (bl) 5-11-0 (3*) T Thompson, *mstk 1st, chsd ldr till lost pl 7th, btn whn blun nxt*.
.... (13 to 2 op 7 to 2 tchd 7 to 1) 5
Dist: 2½l, 2½l, 12l, 6l. 4m 28.60s. a 36.60s (5 Ran).

(Maltsword Ltd), F J Yardley

1260 George Ripley Memorial Challenge Trophy Handicap Chase (0-130 4-y-o and up) £2,175 2m.............(2:00)

1044³ COTAPAXI [87] 8-10-3¹ A Tory, *led till 2 out, sn hrd rdn, styd on to ld ag'n r-in, all out*.
.... (4 to 1 op 3 to 1 tchd 9 to 2) 1
1168⁴ FRED SPLENDID [95] 10-10-11 W Irvine, *settled 3rd till lft second at 8th, led 2 out, sn hrd rdn, not run on and hdd r-in*................................. (11 to 8 on op Evens) 2
1138⁴ KISU KALI [99] 6-11-1 N Williamson, *trkd ldr till blun 8th, lost tch frm tenth*........(2 to 1 op 7 to 4 tchd 9 to 4) 3
Dist: ¾l, 20l. 4m 28.50s. a 38.50s (3 Ran).

(Mrs Barbara Lock), R J Hodges

1261 November Three Yrs Old Novices' Hurdle £1,475 2m 1f........... (2:30)

JULIASDARKINVADER (bl) 10-3 (7*) J Clarke, *settled mid-div gng easily, prog 6th, led aftr 3 out, sn wl clr, unchlgd*...................................(20 to 1) 1
790⁵ BAYRAK (USA) (bl) 10-10 J Osborne, *led aftr second and set str pace, hdd aftr 3 out, sn btn, fnshd tired*.
.... (11 to 4 op 5 to 2) 2
VINEY (USA) 10-10 Peter Hobbs, *hld up, prog and cl up 6th, outpcd and pushed alng aftr nxt, no ch after*.
.... (10 to 1 op 6 to 1 tchd 11 to 1) 3
1049⁸ LADY RELKO 10-5 A Tory, *prmnt, chsd ldr 5th till rdn and wknd aftr 7th*................... (50 to 1 tchd 100 to 1) 4
ANILAFFED 10-10 N Williamson, *tld off whn mstk second, nvr any dngr*.................... (50 to 1 op 20 to 1) 5
1125² DOCTOOR (USA) 10-10 D O'Sullivan, *trkd ldrs, pushed alng aftr 7th, sn wknd, tld off*.
.... (6 to 4 on op 11 to 8 on tchd 5 to 4 on) 6
760⁴ DO BE WARE 10-7 (3*) A Thornton, *rear and rdn 4th, sn tld off*......................... (20 to 1 op 8 to 1) 7
CATEMPO (Ire) 10-10 H Davies, *f 1st*.
.... (33 to 1 op 20 to 1 tchd 25 to 1) f
1021 SHADES OF CROFT (bl) 10-10 E Murphy, *led tll aftr second, rdn and wknd 5th, tld off and pld up bef 2 out*.
.... (20 to 1 op 10 to 1 tchd 25 to 1) pu

YARDLEY COURT 10-3 (7*) Mr Matthew J Jones, *bolted gng to strt, tld off frm second till pld up aftr 7th*.
.... (50 to 1 op 33 to 1 tchd 100 to 1) pu
OVERNIGHT SUCCESS (Ire) 10-5 B Clifford, *rear, reminder 5th, lost tch 7th, tld off and pld up bef 2 out*...(50 to 1) pu
Dist: 30l, 8l, 12l, 12l, 5l, 6l. 4m 16.50s. a 24.50s (11 Ran).
SR: 24/-/-/-/-/-/

(Mike Culling), A Moore

1262 Haywards Heath United Services Club Handicap Chase (0-120 5-y-o and up) £2,343 3m 1f 110yds...........(3:00)

860³ PURBECK DOVE [87] 8-10-8 S Earle, *wtd wth, prog frm 15th, led appr 3 out, clr nxt, easily*.
.... (6 to 1 op 5 to 1 tchd 13 to 2) 1
1081² GLENSHANE LAD [102] 7-11-9 N Williamson, *hld up, prog 15th, chsd wnr 3 out, rdn and no imprsn nxt*.
......................................(7 to 2 op 3 to 1 tchd 4 to 1) 2
SHASTON [101] (bl) 8-11-8 P Holley, *pressed ldr till rdn and wknd appr 3 out*............. (5 to 1 tchd 11 to 2) 3
SECRET RITE [87] 10-10-8 Peter Hobbs, *led till appr 3 out, wknd rpdly*...................... (25 to 1 op 20 to 1) 4
1041⁴ HOMME D'AFFAIRE [103] 10-11-10 D O'Sullivan, *trkd ldrs, 3rd and in tch whn f 15th*.
.... (10 to 1 op 7 to 1 tchd 12 to 1) f
593 STAR OF OUGHTERARD [99] (bl) 8-11-6 W McFarland, *jmpd rght, in tch, mstk 8th, wknd 13th, tld off and pld up bef 16th*................... (12 to 1 op 10 to 1 tchd 14 to 1) pu
HEYFLEET [97] (bl) 10-11-4 I Lawrence, *chsd ldrs, rdn alng frm 7th, wknd 15th, tld off and pld up bef 2 out*.
.... (6 to 1 op 5 to 1 tchd 13 to 2) pu
EXTRA GRAND [101] 7-11-8 J Osborne, *trkd ldrs gng eas-ily till lost pl aftr 14th, hmpd nxt, tld off and pld up bef 2 out*.................... (9 to 4 fav op 5 to 2 tchd 3 to 1) pu
Dist: 15l, 15l, 15l. 6m 33.60s. a 21.60s (8 Ran).
SR: 30/30/14/-/-/

(H V Perry), R H Alner

1263 Jevington 'National Hunt' Novices' Hurdle (4-y-o and up) £1,475 2½m ....(3:30)

1078⁷ SCOBIE BOY (Ire) 5-11-6 J Osborne, *made all, quickened clr r-in, easily*............... (5 to 4 on op Evens) 1
864³ THE WHIP 6-11-0 Peter Hobbs, *al prmnt, chsd wnr appr 3 out, ran on one pace*. (12 to 1 op 7 to 1 tchd 14 to 1) 2
863² ARCTIC LIFE 4-11-0 Mr P Graffin, *rear, rdn and no prog 7th, kpt on und pres to take poor 3rd nr finish*.
.... (11 to 4 op 3 to 1 tchd 7 to 2) 3
CURLY SULLIVAN (Ire) 5-10-2 (7*) S Ryan, *not fluent early, in tch till rdn and outpcd aftr 8th, no dngr after*.
.... (12 to 1 op 16 to 1 tchd 20 to 1) 4
791⁶ THE MINE CAPTAIN 6-11-0 E Murphy, *chsd wnr till appr 3 out, stdly wknd*........(10 to 1 op 8 to 1 tchd 12 to 1) 5
COUNTRY STYLE 4-10-9 S Earle, *lost tch 8th, sn wl beh*.
.... (66 to 1 op 14 to 1) 6
1040³ MAKING TIME 6-10-9 A Tory, *trkd ldrs, pushed alng 8th, sn beh*........................(12 to 1 op 7 to 1) 7
Dist: 5l, 30l, nk, ½l, 2l, 15l. 5m 6.30s. a 29.30s (7 Ran).
SR: 19/8/-/-/

(R V Shaw), C R Egerton

FAIRYHOUSE (IRE) (good to yielding)
Tuesday November 16th

1264 Ward Juvenile Hurdle (3-y-o) £3,105 2m........................(12:45)

MAGIC FEELING (Ire) 10-5 C F Swan, ... (5 to 1) 1
1111³ CALL MY GUEST (Ire) 10-10 J Shortt, ... (6 to 4 fav) 2
SERANERA (Ire) 10-0 (5*) M G Cleary, ...(12 to 1) 3
802* JAZZY REFRAIN (Ire) 10-11 P Carberry, ... (5 to 1) 4
228* THE BERUKI (Ire) 10-6 (5*) T P Treacy, ... (11 to 2) 5
DAHLIA'S BEST (USA) 10-3 (7*) J M Sullivan, ... (8 to 1) 6
1111⁷ MYSTICAL CITY (Ire) 10-5 K F O'Brien, ...(20 to 1) 7
470⁶ TOP DIVER (Ire) (bl) 10-10 A J O'Brien, ...(25 to 1) 8
MAN OF ARRAN (Ire) 10-5 (5*) T J O'Sullivan, ..(12 to 1) 9
802 ANNADOT (Ire) 10-5 F J Flood, ...(16 to 1) 10
1111 BENE MERENTI (Ire) 10-10 B Sheridan, ...(16 to 1) 11
706 SLAINTA (Ire) 10-3 (7*) J P Broderick, ...(50 to 1) 12
Dist: ½l, 20l, 1½l, 2½l. 4m 1.00s. (12 Ran).

(Mrs J M Ryan), A P O'Brien

1265 Curragha Maiden Hurdle (5-y-o) £3,105 2½m. .... (1:15)

DANOLI (Ire) 12-0 C F Swan, ... (6 to 4 on) 1
1074³ FAMBO LAD (Ire) 11-6 A J Berry, ...(10 to 1) 2
926² BEAT THE SECOND (Ire) 11-6 C O'Dwyer, ...(10 to 1) 3
AERODROME FIELD (Ire) 11-6 B Sheridan, ...(14 to 1) 4
1113⁷ FORTY ONE (Ire) 11-1 A Powell, ...(10 to 1) 5
857² WILD VENTURE (Ire) 11-1 D P Fagan, ...(10 to 1) 6
708 BUMBO HALL VI (Ire) 11-6 F J Flood, ...(10 to 1) 7
1076⁵ DEEP THYNE (Ire) 11-2 (7*) Mr K F O'Donnell, ..(5 to 1) 8
1052⁷ BELLEW GLEN (Ire) 11-1 H Rogers, ...(33 to 1) 9
HELENS LOVE (Ire) 10-12 (3*) D Bromley, ...(25 to 1) 10
RIVERLAND (Ire) 11-3 (3*) D P Murphy, ...(25 to 1) 11
1018 RATHNURE LADY (Ire) 10-10 (5*) P A Roche, ...(33 to 1) 12

930⁷ CARRIGKEM (Ire) 11-1 T Horgan, ...(33 to 1) 13
ORDONNANT (Fr) 11-1 (5*) T P Rudd, ...(16 to 1) 14
747⁹ STAR FLYER (Ire) 10-12 (3*) Mr P McMahon, ...(50 to 1) 15
Dist: 4½l, 2l, 8l, 3l. 5m 9.60s. (15 Ran).

(D J O'Neill), Thomas Foley

1266 Mulhuddart EBF Chase (5-y-o and up) £4,140 2¾m. . . . . (1:45)

1112³ BELVEDERIAN 6-11-11 N Williamson, ...(100 to 30) 1
856² SULLANE RIVER (Ire) 5-11-6 D H O'Connor, . . (11 to 4 fav) 2
690⁴ FRIENDS OF GERALD 7-11-11 C F Swan, ...(100 to 30) 3
941⁵ WALLS COURT 6-11-7 P L Malone, ...(33 to 1) 4
941 SHEILA NA GIG 7-11-2 A Powell, ...(14 to 1) 5
1233⁶ NANCYS LAD 6-11-7 H Rogers, ...(33 to 1) 6
1112² BORN DEEP 7-11-11 T Horgan, ...(9 to 2) f
MERRY GALE (Ire) 5-11-4 K F O'Brien, ...(9 to 2) ur
856⁸ AQUAFLAME 6-11-7 J Shortt, ...(33 to 1) pu
Dist: 6l, 15l, 15l, 6l. 5m 32.40s. (9 Ran).

(A J O'Reilly), M F Morris

1267 Kilbride Hurdle (4 & 5-y-o) £3,105 2m . . . .(2:15)

PHARFETCHED 4-11-4 C F Swan, ...(6 to 4 fav) 1
1075² ARCTIC WEATHER (Ire) 4-11-2 (7*) D J Finnigan, . . (9 to 4) 2
LORD NOBLE (Ire) 5-11-11 K F O'Brien, ...(5 to 2) 3
MALIHABAD (Ire) 4-11-2 F J Flood, ... (10 to 1) 4
1015³ SUTR-MAKE (Ire) 4-11-2 J P Byrne, ...(33 to 1) 5
1052⁶ THE PERISHER 4-11-2 J Shortt, ... (12 to 1) 6
1155⁷ JODONLEE (Ire) 4-10-8 (3*) T J Mitchell, ...(33 to 1) 7
Dist: Nk, 10l, 7l, 15l. 4m 11.70s. (7 Ran).

(James Shanahan), A P O'Brien

1268 Donoughmore Handicap Chase (0-109 5-y-o and up) £3,105 2¼m. . . . . . (2:45)

800⁹ WINNING CHARLIE [-] 7-11-7 K F O'Brien, ...(8 to 1) 1
1019 MAGIC MILLION [-] 7-11-9 J P Banahan, ...(7 to 2 fav) 2
906⁴ FAIRY PARK [-] (bl) 8-11-2 F Woods, ...(8 to 1) 3
1231⁵ CAPE SPY [-] 7-11-13 H Rogers, ...(8 to 1) 4
878⁸ BLENHEIM PALACE (USA) [-] 6-9-12 (3*) T J Mitchell,
. . . .(14 to 1) 5
CARTON [-] 6-11-11 T Horgan, ...(14 to 1) 6
674⁶ PINEWOOD LAD [-] 6-10-12 C C O'Dwyer, ...(14 to 1) 7
940⁵ LA MODE LADY [-] 8-10-5 A J O'Brien, ...(10 to 1) 8
941 DEEP ISLE [-] 7-10-9 N Williamson, ...(20 to 1) 9
1158⁷ HO FRETTA [-] 7-10-3 (3*,6ex) C O'Brien, ...(5 to 1) f
966⁷ TURBULENT WIND [-] 6-11-10 C F Swan, ...(14 to 1) f
1179⁴ BOG LEAF VI [-] 10-9-0 (7*) J P Broderick, ...(14 to 1) ur
Dist: ¾l, 15l, 9l, 5l. 4m 40.30s. (12 Ran).

(Mrs D Reddan), Desmond McDonogh

1269 Warrenstown Handicap Hurdle (4-y-o and up) £3,105 2m. . . . .(3:15)

991⁵ BROCKLEY COURT [-] 6-11-6 J P Banahan, ...(5 to 2 fav) 1
880⁴ FINAL FAVOUR (Ire) [-] 4-11-4 (5*) H Taylor, ... (11 to 2) 2
ROMAN FORUM (Ire) [-] 5-10-7 (3*) Mr A E Lacy, . .(14 to 1) 3
1075⁸ PLUMBOB (Ire) [-] 4-10-2 (5*) T P Rudd, ...(20 to 1) 4
831⁸ HEAD OF CHAMBERS (Ire) [-] 5-11-2 P McWilliams,
. . . .(20 to 1) 5
880² ENQLAAB (USA) [-] 5-10-4 K F O'Brien, ...(7 to 1) 6
1176² JIMMY THE JACKDAW [-] (bl) 6-9-7 P Carberry, ...(7 to 1) 7
1232 CELTIC SAILS (Ire) [-] 5-10-6 B Sheridan, ...(12 to 1) 8
161⁶ JUST ONE CANALETTO [-] 5-9-11 N Williamson, . . (14 to 1) 9
BASIE NOBLE [-] 4-9-11 P L Malone, ...(20 to 1) 10
NATASHA'S RUN (Ire) [-] 5-9-8 C F Swan, ...(20 to 1) 11
THE EARL OF CONG [-] 9-10-3 C O'Dwyer, ...(40 to 1) 12
471 HIS WAY (Ire) [-] 4-10-8 J Shortt, ...(14 to 1) 13
RAINBOW VALLEY (Ire) [-] 4-9-13 (7*) R A Hennessy,
. . . .(25 to 1) 14
1015⁴ PYLON SPARKS [-] (bl) 8-10-9 F J Flood, ...(25 to 1) 15
131 PRIDE OF ERIN [-] 9-10-8 L P Cusack, ...(20 to 1) 16
967³ BELLECARA [-] 6-9-8¹ F Woods, ...(12 to 1) 17
1178 CARA DEILISH [-] (bl) 7-9-6 (7*) J P Broderick, ...(33 to 1) 18
804⁹ TOP RUN (Ire) [-] 5-9-10³ H Rogers, ...(50 to 1) 19
473 CLOGS [-] (bl) 9-9-4 (3*) C O'Brien, ...(50 to 1) 20
806 MAYE FANE [-] 9-11-2 (3*) G Kilfeather, ...(50 to 1) 21
831⁵ DEEP INAGH [-] 7-11-8 D P Fagan, ...(8 to 1) pu
Dist: ¾l, 4½l, 2½l, 15l. 3m 59.50s. (22 Ran).

(C Cronin), Mrs John Harrington

1270 Drumree Flat Race (5-y-o and up) £3,105 2¼m. . . . . (3:45)

PIMBERLEY PLACE (Ire) 5-12-0 Mr T Mullins, . . (6 to 4 fav) 1
124⁸ ICED HONEY 6-12-0 Mr A J Martin, ...(9 to 1) 2
801² GOLDEN NUGGET 6-11-7 (7*) Mr H Murphy, ...(6 to 1) 3
945⁸ CLOGEROON BOY (Ire) 5-11-9 (5*) Mr P J Casey, . .(25 to 1) 4
CALMOS 6-11-7 (7*) Mr G R Ryan, ...(7 to 1) 5
969³ BIT OF A CHARACTER 6-11-7 (7*) Mr P M Cloke, . . (5 to 1) 6
907² SIMPLY SARAH 7-11-9 Mr M McNulty, ...(8 to 1) 7
907⁹ DRUMCILL LASS 5-11-9 Mr S R Murphy, ...(10 to 1) 8
DUEONE (Ire) 5-11-10³ (7*) Mr M A James, ...(5 to 1) 9
CROSSABEG ROSE (Ire) 5-11-4 (6*) Mr H F Cleary, .(25 to 1) 10
969⁸ CARRIG BELLE 7-11-2 (7*) Mr L Hambidge, ...(33 to 1) 11
969⁵ BOLD BARNEY (NZ) 7-11-11 (3*) Mr D Marnane, . .(10 to 1) 12

WAPITI 6-11-9 (5*) Mr S Harford, ...(25 to 1) 13
675 TYPHOON JOE (Ire) 5-11-11 (3*) Mrs J M Mullins, (16 to 1) 14
1113⁹ DEAR BUCK 7-11-11 (3*) Mr A R Coonan, ...(14 to 1) 15
BANNOW ISLAND (Ire) 5-11-7 (7*) Mr R White, ...(14 to 1) 16
RUSSIAN SAINT 7-11-7 (7*) Miss C O'Connell, ...(12 to 1) 17
CLASSY MISTRESS 7-11-2 (7*) Mr A Daly, ...(20 to 1) 18
Dist: 6l, 5½l, 2½l, sht-hd. 4m 30.70s. (18 Ran).

(Thomas Mullins), P Mullins

NEWTON ABBOT (soft)
Tuesday November 16th
Going Correction: PLUS 1.15 sec. per fur. (races 1,2,-4,7), PLUS 0.80 (3,5,6)

1271 South West Racing Club Juvenile Novices' Hurdle (3-y-o) £2,242 2m 1f . . . .(12:45)

1049² VELVET HEART (Ire) 10-7 S Burrough, al prmnt, led 3 out, rdn appr last, ran on. . .(9 to 2 op 5 to 1 tchd 4 to 1) 1
570 LOVE IN THE MIST (USA) 10-7 M Foster, rcd in tch, gd hdwy 3 out, ev ch nxt, sn rdn, one pace.
. . . .(12 to 1 op 7 to 1) 2
1021* BUGLET 10-13 R Dunwoody, al frnt rnk, rdn 3 out, no extr appr last. . . . .(5 to 4 fav op 5 to 4 on) 3
KOA 10-12 C Llewellyn, hdwy 3rd, wnt second 3 out, sn rdn, wknd appr last. . .(11 to 1 op 7 to 1 tchd 12 to 1) 4
896⁵ ACROSS THE BOW (USA) 10-12 Peter Hobbs, hld up in tch, effrt 5th, lost frm nxt. . .(33 to 1 op 20 to 1) 5
TAKE THE MICK 10-12 M Perrett, in tch till wknd appr 5th. . . . .(20 to 1 tchd 12 to 1 op 25 to 1) 6
1097* GROGFRYN 10-13 D Morris, led till hdd 3 out, wknd quickly. . . . .(12 to 1 op 6 to 1) 7
SHE KNEW THE RULES (Ire) 10-7 Lorna Vincent, mstks in rear, tld off frm 3rd. . . . .(25 to 1 op 12 to 1) 8
570 STANFORD AVENUE 10-7 M Richards, sn beh, tld off whn pld up bef 5th. . . . .(66 to 1 op 33 to 1) pu
1021 GLOWING PATH (bl) 11-4 H Davies, pld hrd, chsd ldrs till wknd 3 out, pulled up bef nxt. (6 to 1 op 4 to 1) pu
1007⁶ FRANK KNOWS 10-12 C Maude, in tch till rdn and lost pl appr 5th, pld up bef 2 out.
. . . .(40 to 1 op 20 to 1 tchd 50 to 1) pu
SET-EM-ALIGHT 10-12 J Frost, hld up in rear, wkng whn mstk 5th, tld off when pld up bef 2 out.
. . . .(33 to 1 op 20 to 1) pu
Dist: 5l, 1l, 5l, 15l, 12l, 5l, dist. 4m 15.40s. a 25.40s (12 Ran).
SR: 20/15/20/14/-/-/

(Fred Camis), Mrs A Knight

1272 Dartmouth Selling Hurdle (4-y-o and up) £1,939 2m 1f. . . . . (1:15)

994* RULING DYNASTY (bl) 9-11-12 H Davies, hld up in rear, steady hdwy frm 5th, led appr 2 out, sn clr, easily.
. . . .(6 to 5 fav op 5 to 4 on tchd 5 to 4) 1
144³ SEE NOW 8-11-9 S Burrough, hld up in mid-div, gd hdwy to go second frm 5th, ev ch 2 out, held whn mstk last.
. . . .(14 to 1 op 8 to 1) 2
1154 PEACOCK FEATHER 5-11-1 R Dunwoody, al prmnt, led 3rd, mstk nxt, rdn and hdd appr 2 out, sn btn.
. . . .(7 to 1 op 6 to 1) 3
953* FANATICAL (USA) (bl) 7-11-6 L Harvey, hld up in rear, gd hdwy 5th, rdn and wknd appr 2 out. (7 to 1 op 9 to 2) 4
946 BILL QUILL 9-10-7 (7*) R Darke, trkd ldrs till wknd appr 2 out. . . . .(9 to 1 tchd 16 to 1 and 8 to 1) 5
775⁴ MOLLETROIS 5-10-9 Peter Hobbs, chsd ldrs, no hdwy frm 3 out. . . . .(25 to 1 op 20 to 1 tchd 33 to 1) 6
953⁴ REALLY NEAT 7-10-2 (7*) D Matthews, led to second, prmnt till wknd appr 3 out. . . . .(16 to 1 op 12 to 1) 7
SPIRIT LEVEL 5-10-11⁹ (7*) M R Payne, led second to 3rd, outpcd frm 5th. . . . .(50 to 1 op 20 to 1) 8
BAYLORD PRINCE (Ire) 5-11-0 M Hoad, mstks, lost tch 5th. . . . .(50 to 1 op 33 to 1 tchd 66 to 1) 9
CHARMED LIFE 4-11-0 N Dawe, al beh, lost tch appr 5th. . . . .(12 to 1 op 7 to 1 tchd 14 to 1) 10
JANET SCIBS 7-10-2 (7*) Guy Lewis, al towards rear, wknd 5th. . . . .(25 to 1 op 16 to 1) 11
SOUTH SANDS (bl) 7-11-12 Mrs C Wonnacott, mstks in rear, tld off when pld up bef 5th. . .(10 to 1 op 8 to 1) pu
1187 COLONEL GAY 8-11-6 S Mackey, beh whn rdn appr 5th, sn tld off, pld up bef 2 out. . . . . .(50 to 1 op 20 to 1) pu
Dist: 12l, 1½l, 15l, 2l, sht-hd, 1½l, 2l, 5l, 1½l, 6l. 4m 17.60s. a 27.60s (13 Ran).
SR: 17/2/-/-/-/-/

(Midweek Racing), M D I Usher

1273 Claude Whitley Memorial Challenge Cup Handicap Chase (0-130 5-y-o and up) £3,485 3¼m 110yds. . . . .(1:45)

MIDNIGHT CALLER [114] 7-11-10 M Richards, made all, hit 14th, rdn mstk 2 out, ridden and styd on.
. . . .(5 to 4 op 7 to 4 tchd 11 to 10) 1
1205 DON'T LIGHT UP [100] (v) 7-10-10 R Dunwoody, sn trkd wnr, rdn 4 out, ev ch nxt, no imprsn r-in.
. . . .(5 to 1 op 7 to 2) 2
POP SONG [91] 9-10-1¹ P Holley, trkd ldrs, mstk 9th, wknd 14th, lft poor 3rd appr 2 out. (10 to 1 op 8 to 1) 3

SADDLER'S CHOICE [101] 8-10-6 (5*) T Jenks, *al beh, lost tch frm 13th, tld off...* (11 to 1 op 6 to 1 tchd 12 to 1) 4
HOPE DIAMOND [91] (bl) 10-10-11 W McFarland, *beh whn pld up lme bef 11th*...............(33 to 1 op 20 to 1) pu
956⁴ TRUSTY FRIEND [100] (bl) 11-10-10 D Morris, *al beh, tld off whn pld up bef 2 out*.............(12 to 1 op 10 to 1) pu
947 NATIVE SCOT [90] 7-9-11 (3*) W Marston, *trkd ldrs, rdn 15th, wkng 3rd whn pld up bef 2 out, collapsed, dead.*
.... (33 to 1 op 16 to 1) pu
1088 RU VALENTINO [110] (bl) 9-11-6 C Llewellyn, *prmnt, mstk 4th, rdn 13th, sn beh, tld off whn pld up bef four out.*
.................................(5 to 1 op 4 to 1 tchd 6 to 1) pu
1080² SENEGALAIS (Fr) [97] 9-10-77 J Frost, *jmpd badly in rear, tld off whn blun 11th, sn pld up....* (16 to 1 op 7 to 1) pu
HILL TRIX [100] 7-10-10 A Tory, *lost tch frm 11th, tld off whn pld up bef 4 out*...........(10 to 1 tchd 12 to 1) pu
Dist: 1½sl, dist, ¾sl. 6m 46.70s. a 26.70s (10 Ran).
SR: 41/25/-/-/-/-/ (M Worcester), S E Sherwood

1274 William Hill Handicap Hurdle (4-y-o and up) £5,732 2¾m...........(2:15)

1051⁴ FAR TOO LOUD [106] 6-10-0 B Clifford, *al prmnt, led appr 2 out, ran on wl und pres r-in.*
.... (7 to 1 op 5 to 1 tchd 15 to 2) 1
JAILBREAKER [113] 6-10-2 (5*) D Salter, *sn trkd ldrs, pressed wnr 2 out, no extr nr finish.*
....................(20 to 1 op 16 to 1 tchd 25 to 1) 2
GOLDEN MOSS [100] 8-10-0 M Richards, *nvr far away, rdn and ev ch 2 out, no extr cl hme.* (50 to 1 op 20 to 1) 3
MARDOOD [119] 8-10-13 H Davies, *prmnt early, lost pl 4th, hdwy 3 out, ev ch nxt, no extr r-in.*
...................(9 to 2 op 7 to 2 tchd 5 to 1) 4
149³ CARFAX [112] 8-10-6⁶ M Hoad, *hld up, steady hdwy frm 6th, one pace from 2 out*.............(10 to 1 op 8 to 1) 5
1206⁷ FAIRFIELDS CONE [112] 10-10-3 (3*) D Meredith, *hld up, making gd hdwy whn short of room 2 out, one pace aftr*................ (9 to 4 fav op 3 to 1 tchd 2 to 1) 6
955 FREEMANTLE [107] 8-10-1¹ Peter Hobbs, *hld up in rear, hdwy 3 out, kpt on, nvr nrr*........ (66 to 1 op 33 to 1) 7
APARECIDA (Fr) [106] 7-9-7 (7*) N Isaac, *hld up, took clr order frm 6th, wknd appr 2 out*...(150 to 1 op 50 to 1) 8
VADO VIA [121] 5-10-12 (3*) W Marston, *hld up in rear, some hdwy 3 out, nvr dngrs.*
..........................(4 to 1 op 3 to 1 tchd 11 to 2) 9
CAPTAIN DOLFORD [112] 6-10-6 P Holley, *chsd ldr till wknd aftr 3 out*...................(16 to 1 op 10 to 1) 10
1106 SAYFAR'S LAD [125] 9-11-5 R Dunwoody, *led till hdd appr 2 out, wknd quickly, eased.*
.... (14 to 1 op 10 to 1 tchd 16 to 1) 11
HOLY JOE [134] 11-11-7 (7*) K Brown, *hld up, mstk 5th, no hdwy frm 4 out*...............(25 to 1 op 12 to 1) 12
867* SPECIAL ACCOUNT [108] 7-10-2 N Mann, *prmnt to 6th, sn beh, tld off*........... (7 to 1 tchd 6 to 1 and 15 to 2) 13
1051² TRUST DEED (USA) [106] (bl) 5-10-0 L Harvey, *al beh, lost tch appr 4 out, tld off*...........(33 to 1 op 14 to 1) 14
FIGHT TO WIN (USA) [113] 5-10-7 J Frost, *hld up in tch, wknd 4 out, tld off*..............(33 to 1 op 16 to 1) 15
1087⁶ KILTONGA [106] 6-10-0 C Maude, *tld off frm 3rd, pld up aftr 8th*...............(150 to 1 op 50 to 1) pu
Dist: 1l, nk, ¾l, 4l, 1l, 1½l, sht-hd, 1½l, ½l, 1l. 5m 35.30s. a 36.30s (16 Ran).
(Russell Dennis), Mrs J G Retter

1275 Paignton Handicap Chase (0-135 5-y-o and up) £3,003 2m 110yds......(2:45)

MULBANK [109] 7-10-12 C Maude, *3rd whn hit third, gd hdwy to go second 8th, led 4 out, clr nxt, eased r-in.*
.... (11 to 8 on op 5 to 4) 1
1207³ AL HASHIMI [125] 9-12-0 R Dunwoody, *led till hdd 4 out, sn btn*........(11 to 10 on op 5 to 4 tchd 6 to 4) 2
946⁵ RATHER SHARP [97] 7-10-0 D Morris, *trkd ldr till jmpd slwly 8th, sn btn, tld off*.......(12 to 1 tchd 10 to 1) 3
HOLY FOLEY [116] 11-10-9 Peter Hobbs, *not fluent in rear, sn outpcd, tld off frm 6th*........(8 to 1 op 6 to 1) 4
HIGH IMP [103] 13-10-6⁶ H Davies, *al beh, tld off frm 6th, pld up bef 4 out*.................(25 to 1 op 16 to 1) pu
Dist: 10l, 20l, 25l. 4m 14.20s. a 17.20s (5 Ran).
SR: 44/50/2/-/-/ (I L Shaw), P J Hobbs

1276 Stoke Gabriel Novices' Handicap Chase (5-y-o and up) £2,801 2m 110yds......................(3:15)

682* BARONESS ORKZY [77] 7-10-7 R Greene, *made all, clr frm 3 out, unchlgd.*..............(11 to 2 op 5 to 1) 1
FATHER RALPH [83] 7-10-13 P Holley, *nvr far away, cl on ldrs 8th, hit nxt, close 3rd whn blun 3 out, mstk nxt, lft second last*....................(4 to 1 tchd 9 to 2) 2
485⁵ NEEDS MUST [84] 6-11-0 J Frost, *wtd wth, hdwy 6th, btn 4 out, lft 3rd last*...... (14 to 1 op 10 to 1 tchd 16 to 1) 3
PUNCHBAG (USA) [85] 7-11-1 C Maude, *hld up, blun 8th, styd on frm 3 out, nvr nrr*.........(7 to 1 tchd 9 to 1) 4
1071⁴ CORRIN HILL [98] 6-12-0 R Dunwoody, *trkd wnr till blun badly 8th, rdn and wknd appr 3 out.*
.... (4 to 1 op 11 to 4 tchd 9 to 2) 5

794⁸ VERSATILE [71] 9-10-1¹ Peter Hobbs, *trkd ldrs, mstk 7th, wnt second nxt, btn whn f last....* (25 to 1 op 14 to 1) f
899⁴ DURRINGTON [81] 7-10-11 Richard Guest, *f 3rd.*
.................................(9 to 1 op 6 to 1) f
892⁷ FINAL SOUND [70] (bl) 8-10-0 L Harvey, *hit 1st, beh whn pld up lme bef 6th*...............(20 to 1 op 10 to 1) pu
883⁷ NEW PROBLEM [70] 6-9-7 (7*) A Flannigan, *hmpd 3rd, sn beh, tld off whn pld up bef 4 out.*...(50 to 1 op 20 to 1) pu
BEANLEY BROOK [74] 5-10-1 (3*) A Thornton, *al beh, tld off whn pld up bef 4 out.*
.................................(7 to 2 fav op 4 to 1 tchd 9 to 2) pu
Dist: 12l, 10l, 1l, 3½l. 4m 17.50s. a 20.50s (10 Ran).
SR: 6/-/-/-/-/-/ (C I A Paterson), P F Nicholls

1277 Truro National Hunt Flat Race (4,5,6-y-o) £1,736 2m 1f...............(3:45)

UPHAM SURPRISE 5-10-10 (7*) Pat Thompson, *hld up in rear, gd hdwy to ld 4 fs out, rdn clr.*
.....................(10 to 1 tchd 8 to 1 and 12 to 1) 1
HARBOUR OF LOVE (Ire) 4-11-3 R Greene, *hld up, hdwy 5 fs out, chsd wnr fnl 3*..................(9 to 1 op 8 to 1) 2
778² SEE ENOUGH 5-10-10 (7*) N Parker, *hld up in tch, kpt on one pace fnl 4 fs*.........(5 to 1 op 4 to 1 tchd 11 to 2) 3
PRINCE TEETON 4-11-0 (3*) W Marston, *chsd ldrs, one pace fnl 3 fs.*...................(14 to 1 op 10 to 1) 4
778⁹ PENNYMOOR PRINCE 4-10-10 (7*) R Darke, *hld up in rear, styd on fnl 3 fs, nvr dnagerous....* (25 to 1 op 12 to 1) 5
1126 CHILDSWAY 5-11-3 Mr J Durkan, *pld hrd, hdwy hfwy, wknd 3 fs out*..........(3 to 1 fav tchd 7 to 2) 6
LUCKY DAWN (Ire) 4-11-3 V Slattery, *led 1st 4 fs, prmnt till rdn and wknd o'r 3 out.*
.........................(13 to 2 op 6 to 1 tchd 8 to 1) 7
OLYMPIC WAY 4-10-5 (7*) T Murphy, *led aftr 4 fs, hdd four out, sn btn.*....................(8 to 1 op 6 to 1) 8
778⁴ FERNY BALL (Ire) 5-11-0 (3*) R Davis, *chsd ldrs, rdn 5 fs out, sn btn.*....................(9 to 1 op 5 to 1) 9
CORPORAL CHARLIE 4-11-0 (3*) A Thornton, *in tch till wknd o'r 4 fs out*..............(16 to 1 op 10 to 1) 10
MR WENDYL 5-10-10 (7*) D Matthews, *chsd ldrs, wknd quickly 5 fs out.*................(16 to 1 op 10 to 1) 11
LITTLE WISHFUL 5-11-0 (3*) D Meredith, *al beh.*
.................................(14 to 1 op 6 to 1) 12
BARON RUSH 5-10-10 (7*) D Hobbs, *al beh.*
.........................(12 to 1 op 10 to 1 tchd 20 to 1) 13
BETTY'S MATCH 4-10-5 (7*) Mr G Shenkin, *al beh, tld off.*
....................(25 to 1 op 14 to 1) 14
TUDOR BLUES 6-10-5 (7*) D Fortt, *pld hrd, prmnt till wknd hfwy, sn tld off.*
.........................(25 to 1 op 20 to 1 tchd 33 to 1) 15
Dist: 10l, 12l, 5l, 3l, 6l, 4l, 6l, 12l, ½l, 3½l. 4m 10.60s. (15 Ran).
(J A B Old), J A B Old

WARWICK (good to soft)
Tuesday November 16th
Going Correction: MINUS 0.05 sec. per fur. (races 1,3,6), PLUS 0.10 (2,4,5)

1278 Ufton Handicap Hurdle (0-130 4-y-o and up) £3,444 2m............(1:10)

BOTTLES (USA) [115] 6-11-10 S Keightley, *hld up in cl tch, pushed alng appr 2 out, quickened to ld r-in, cmftbly.*
...........................(11 to 2 op 4 to 1) 1
812³ MOVING OUT [94] 5-10-3 J Osborne, *led, shaken up r-in, sn hdd and no extr.* (5 to 4 on op Evens tchd 11 to 10) 2
248⁶ ROSGILL [115] 7-11-10 A Maguire, *trkd ldr till rdn and hdd appr last*........(7 to 2 op 5 to 2 tchd 4 to 1) 3
739³ EASTERN MAGIC [97] 5-10-1 (5*) A Procter, *hld up in cl tch, pushed alng 4 out, wknd aftr nxt.*
...........................(11 to 2 op 7 to 2) 4
Dist: 1½l, 8l, 13l. 3m 43.30s. a 3.30s (4 Ran).
SR: 55/32/45/12/ (R C Taylor), J E Banks

1279 Shirley Novices' Chase (5-y-o and up) £3,756 2m................(1:40)

931 PERSIAN SWORD 7-10-12 A Maguire, *trkd ldrs, lft second 3 out, rallied appr last, ran on und pres to ld last strds.*
...........................(10 to 1 op 5 to 1) 1
848* PEACEMAN 7-11-4 D Murphy, *jmpd soundly, led, sn clr, tired r-in, soon hrd rdn, ct last strds.*
...........................(12 to 1 op 8 to 1) 2
933⁴ GALAXY HIGH 6-10-12 M A FitzGerald, *in tch, rdn and one pace frm 3 out*..................(11 to 2 op 5 to 1) 3
998 PLAYING TRUANT 6-10-12 J Osborne, *trkd ldrs, no hdwy frm 4 out, styd on aftr last.*...........(8 to 1 op 7 to 1) 4
679³ SECRET LIASON (bl) 7-10-12 D Bridgwater, *al beh, tld off.*...........(25 to 1 op 16 to 1) 5
MARY O'REILLY 8-10-7 R Supple, *al beh, tld off frm 5th.*
.........................(66 to 1 op 25 to 1) 6
SUN SURFER (Fr) 5-10-12 B Powell, *cl up, chsd clr ldr frm 6th, clear second whn f 3 out.*
.........................(6 to 4 fav tchd 13 to 8 and 7 to 4) f
MARCH LANE 6-10-12 R Bellamy, *pld hrd, tracking ldrs whn f 6th.*..........(100 to 1 op 33 to 1) f

Dist: Hd, 7l, 5l, dist, dist. 3m 58.40s. a 6.40s (8 Ran).
SR: 36/42/29/24/-/ (Peter Hepworth), D Nicholson

1280 Harbury Claiming Hurdle (4 & 5-y-o) £1,751 2½m 110yds............ (2:10)

OUR SLIMBRIDGE 5-11-10 A Carroll, *hld up in rear, hdwy 7th, ran on und pres to ld cl hme.* .... (2 to 1 fav op 7 to 2 tchd 4 to 1 and 15 to 8) 1
SO DISCREET (USA) 5-11-4 A Maguire, *hld up, hdwy o'r 5 out, led 3 out, hdd r-in, ran on und pres.* ....(5 to 1 op 5 to 2) 2
1072[5] HIGH GRADE 5-10-12 B Powell, *trkd ldrs, cld 5 out, ev ch last, one pace and whished tail und pres.* .... (12 to 1 op 8 to 1) 3
VALIANTHE (USA) 5-11-9 J Lower, *hld up, hdwy 7th, outpcd frm 3 out*..............(7 to 1 op 7 to 2) 4
1038* BROOK COTTAGE (Ire) 5-11-12 M Hourigan, *hld up in mid-div, no prog frm 3 out*............... (7 to 2 op 6 to 4) 5
932[7] NORDROSS 5-10-3 R Bellamy, *hld up in rear, nvr nr to chal*..................................... (50 to 1 op 25 to 1) 6
775[5] THANKSFORTHEOFFER 5-10-11 (5*) A Procter, *wth ldrs till wknd aftr 7th*.......................(50 to 1 op 33 to 1) 7
592[4] WEDNESDAYS AUCTION (Ire) 5-10-12 I Shoemark, *mid-div, pushed alng appr 7th, sn btn*......(25 to 1 op 20 to 1) 8
1079[8] NORTHERN OPTIMIST 5-10-0 (7*) Mr J L Llewellyn, *led till hdd 3 out, sn wknd*.................(12 to 1 op 8 to 1) 9
425[4] WAR BEAT 5-10-11 (7*) G Robertson, *pld hrd, wth ldr, ev ch 4 out, sn wknd*................. (50 to 1 op 33 to 1) 10
996[6] CRAZY HORSE DANCER (USA) (bl) 5-11-0 R Supple, *mid-div, rdn alng aftr 6th, sn btn*...... (25 to 1 op 14 to 1) 11
PIERRE BLANCO (USA) 4-11-8 G Bradley, *chsd ldrs till wknd appr 7th, sn beh, tld off*..... (16 to 1 op 12 to 1) 12
Dist: Hd, ¾l, 15l, 2½l, 8l, 2l, nk, ½l, ½l, 8l. 5m 1.90s. a 14.40s (12 Ran).
(Mrs S Foster), C N Williams

1281 Shipston Handicap Chase (0-145 5-y-o and up) £4,302 3¼m............(2:40)

980* MERE CLASS [125] 7-11-4 G Bradley, *cl up, led 14th, clr 3 out, mstk nxt, cmftbly.* ....(6 to 5 fav op 5 to 4 tchd 11 to 8) 1
WILLSFORD [132] (bl) 10-11-11 A Maguire, *hld up in tch, hdwy to ld 11th, hdd 14th, outpcd nxt, styd on frm appr 2 out*...............................(11 to 2 op 9 to 2) 2
765[2] CYTHERE [116] 9-10-6 (3*) P Hide, *in cl tch, mstk 4th, outpcd frm 14th, styd on from o'r four out.* ....(8 to 1 op 7 to 1) 3
986[2] SMOOTH ESCORT [111] (v) 9-10-4 D Murphy, *led till hdd tenth, cl up, chsd wnr frm 15th, wknd appr 2 out, lost 3rd r-in*............................ (6 to 1 op 9 to 2) 4
DIAMOND FORT [109] 8-10-2[2] S McNeill, *in tch, outpcd 14th, styd on frm o'r 4 out, no extr from 2 out.* ....(8 to 1 op 6 to 1) 5
FIDDLERS PIKE [133] 12-11-12 Mrs R Henderson, *strted slwly, trkd ldrs frm 4th, drpd rear 13th, tld off.* .... (11 to 1 op 10 to 1) 6
DIRECT [119] 10-10-12 J Osborne, *cl up, led briefly tenth, drpd rear 13th, tld off*............(14 to 1 op 10 to 1) 7
Dist: 5l, 7l, 3l, ½l, dist, ½l. 6m 30.50s. a 16.50s (7 Ran).
(Miss M Talbot), C P E Brooks

1282 Varley Hibbs Handicap Chase (0-130 5-y-o and up) £4,250 2½m 110yds ....(3:10)

SHEER ABILITY [102] 7-10-8 A Maguire, *chsd clr ldr, mstk and outpcd 3 out, sn rallied, led aftr last, drvn out.* ....(100 to 30 op 3 to 1 tchd 7 to 2) 1
1022[3] L'UOMO PIU [96] 9-10-2[2] M A FitzGerald, *led, sn clr, hdd aftr last, no extr*..... (13 to 2 op 7 to 1 tchd 10 to 1) 2
777[2] SARTORIUS [112] 7-11-4 B Powell, *jmpd wl, hld up, hdwy to chase ldr 13th, wknd appr last.* .... (11 to 4 op 3 to 1 tchd 7 to 2) 3
1105[2] THE GREEN STUFF [111] 8-11-3 R Supple, *in tch till rdn and wknd aftr 3 out*..............................(9 to 4 fav) 4
ANNIO CHILONE [118] 7-11-7 (3*) P Hide, *chsd clr ldr, drpd rear aftr 11th, sn tld off*............. (8 to 1 op 4 to 1) 5
Dist: 3l, 20l, 15l, 3½l. 5m 4.30s. a 9.30s (5 Ran).
SR: 8/-/ (Michael Devlin), C J Mann

1283 Ashorne Novices' Hurdle (4-y-o and up) £1,473 2m..................(3:40)

964* WINNOWING (Ire) 5-11-0 J Osborne, *al prmnt, hrd rdn to get up nr line*...........................(5 to 1 op 4 to 1) 1
791* FATACK 4-11-0 (5*) S Curran, *led, hrd rdn aftr last, hdd nr line*....................(11 to 2 op 6 to 1 tchd 13 to 2) 2
EMPIRE BLUE 10-10-12 M Bosley, *hld up, not clr run aftr 3 out, hdwy 2 out, hrd rdn and hng lft und pres after last, ran on cl hme*................ (33 to 1 op 20 to 1) 3
753[2] SIMPLY (Ire) 4-10-12 D Bridgwater, *al prmnt, ev ch 2 out, one pace und pres appr last*.......(8 to 1 tchd 10 to 1) 4
MILLION IN MIND (Ire) 4-10-12 R Supple, *trkd ldrs, pushed alng 4 out, kpt on one pace frm 2 out.* ....(3 to 1 fav op 4 to 1) 5
1010 ARMATEUR (Fr) 5-10-12 R Bellamy, *prmnt till lost pl 4th, styd on frm 2 out*.................................. (33 to 1) 6
540[2] GENERAL TONIC 6-10-12 S McNeill, *hld up in mid-div, no hdwy frm o'r 2 out*................ (20 to 1 op 14 to 1) 7
AMAZE 4-10-12 E Murphy, *hld up, steady hdwy frm 3 out, wknd nxt*.........................(11 to 2 op 3 to 1) 8
SECRETARY OF STATE 7-10-12 J Railton, *trkd ldrs, hrd rdn appr 2 out, sn outpcd.* ....(8 to 1 op 12 to 1 tchd 16 to 1) 9
1085[3] PAY HOMAGE 5-10-12 G Bradley, *mid-div, cld on ldrs aftr 3rd, wknd after 3 out*..............(11 to 2 op 7 to 2) 10
ROCA MURADA (Ire) 4-10-12 A Maguire, *hld up in rear, steady hdwy aftr 3 out, eased whn held appr last.* ....(12 to 1) 11
NASHAAT (USA) 5-10-12 B Powell, *hld up, al beh.* (33 to 1) 12
ALTERMEERA 5-10-12 G Morgan, *hld up in rear, hdwy to track ldrs aftr 3rd, ev ch 4 out, wknd nxt*......(33 to 1) 13
ROSEATE LODGE 7-10-12 M A FitzGerald, *mid-div till mstk and drpd rear 3 out*..........(25 to 1 op 20 to 1) 14
1167 FIRST CENTURY (Ire) 4-10-5 (7*) Mr J L Llewellyn, *pld hrd, prmnt till wknd appr 3 out*...................(50 to 1) 15
WOODLANDS LEGEND 4-10-12 W Irvine, *al beh.* ....(100 to 1 op 50 to 1) 16
WORLD OF TOMORROW 4-10-12 Leesa Long, *pld hrd in mid-div, sn beh, pulled up bef 2 out.* ....(100 to 1 op 50 to 1) pu
FORGIVE THE FOLLY 5-10-12 M Hourigan, *sn pushed alng in rear, tld off whn pld up bef 2 out*...........(33 to 1) pu
Dist: Sht-hd, hd, 4l, 2½l, hd, 7l, 1½l, 1½l, 5l, sht-hd. 3m 46.80s. a 6.80s (18 Ran).
SR: 10/15/8/4/1/1/ (Mrs Basil Samuel), O Sherwood

WETHERBY (good to soft)
Tuesday November 16th

Going Correction: PLUS 0.35 sec. per fur. (races 1,4,6), PLUS 0.70 (2,3,5)

1284 John Gosden Owners Juvenile Novices' Hurdle (3-y-o) £1,987 2m.. (1:00)

1147 GOLDEN SAVANNAH 10-5 (7*) J Driscoll, *led to 2 out, sn rdn, lft in ld last, kpt on und pres.* (14 to 1 op 12 to 1) 1
STREPHON (Ire) 10-12 M Dwyer, *al chasing wnr, chlgd 2 out, ev ch aftr last, no extr und pres.* (9 to 1 op 7 to 1) 2
1032[3] LA VILLA ROSE (Fr) 10-7 J Callaghan, *in tch, headay to chase ldrs 5th, drvn alng aftr nxt, kpt on same pace.* ....(5 to 2 tchd 9 to 4) 3
971[7] NEGD (USA) 10-12 R Garritty, *in tch, wknd aftr 6th.* ....(33 to 1) 4
BARSAL (Ire) 10-12 N Smith, *chsd ldrs till wknd aftr 6th.* ....(33 to 1) 5
1062[5] SUMMERS DREAM 10-7 C Hawkins, *in tch, hdwy to chase ldrs appr 6th, sn pushed alng, wknd approaching 3 out*.................... (9 to 1 op 12 to 1 tchd 8 to 1) 6
ALMAMZAR (USA) 10-12 G McCourt, *hld up, hdwy aftr 5th, wknd quickly appr 3 out, eased whn btn.* ....(9 to 4 fav tchd 5 to 2) 7
971 ROSSCOYNE 10-7 P Niven, *al beh, f 2 out.* ....(16 to 1 op 14 to 1) f
1147[4] MHEMEANLES 10-12 L Wyer, *in tch, hdwy to ld 2 out, two ls clr whn blun and uns rdr last*....(7 to 2 tchd 3 to 1) ur
971 KEEP BATTLING 10-12 A Orkney, *in tch till wknd aftr 5th, wl beh whn pld up bef 3 out*....... (50 to 1 op 33 to 1) pu
Dist: 1½l, 10l, 6l, 7l, 10l, sht-hd. 4m 4.50s. a 23.50s (10 Ran).
(Mrs Christine Oxtoby), M W Easterby

1285 Jimmy FitzGerald Owners Handicap Chase (0-140 5-y-o and up) £3,522 2m ....(1:30)

1098* JUST FRANKIE [116] 9-10-4 P Niven, *trkd ldrs, led aftr 6th, almost took wrong course after 8th, styd on wl frm 4 out*.............. (15 to 8 fav op 6 to 4 tchd 2 to 1) 1
1098[3] CAMPSEA-ASH [115] 9-9-10 (7*) P Murphy, *in tch, chsd wnr aftr 4 out, kpt on, no imprsn.* ....(16 to 1 tchd 20 to 1) 2
1009 BOUTZDAROFF [140] 11-12-0 M Dwyer, *hld up in tch, effrt appr 4 out, rdn betw last 2, kpt on same pace.* ....(9 to 2 op 7 to 2 tchd 5 to 1) 3
1132* ISLAND JETSETTER [114] 7-10-2[2] (6ex) Gary Lyons, *cl up till wknd quickly appr 3 out.* .... (11 to 2 op 5 to 1 tchd 6 to 1) 4
1065 BORO SMACKEROO [130] 8-11-4 G McCourt, *mstks, made most till aftr 6th, wknd*..............(5 to 1 op 7 to 1) 5
1055[5] ONE FOR THE POT [113] 8-10-1[1] A Orkney, *hld up in tch, ch whn f 4 out*........................(9 to 2 op 5 to 1) f
Dist: 4l, 7l, 12l, 15l. 4m 5.70s. a 13.70s (6 Ran).
SR: 51/46/64/26/27/-/ (Lady Susan Watson), Mrs M Reveley

1286 Malton And District Trainers Handicap Chase (0-145 5-y-o and up) £3,340 2½m 110yds................... (2:00)

995* BETTER TIMES AHEAD [130] 7-12-0 N Doughty, *sn wth ldr, led tenth, styd on wl frm 2 out.* (9 to 4 jt-fav op 2 to 1) 1

CANDY TUFF [114] 7-10-12 L Wyer, *hld up, hdwy to track wnr 11th, shaken up aftr 3 out, kpt on, no imprsn.*
.......................(9 to 2 op 7 to 2 tchd 5 to 1) 2
1029 SIR PETER LELY [111] 6-10-9 C Grant, *slight ld to tenth, rdn and outpcd aftr nxt.*
.......................(11 to 2 op 5 to 1 tchd 6 to 1) 3
1065* SIMPLE PLEASURE [115] 5-10-11 A Larnach, *chsd ldrs till outpcd alng and outpcd aftr 11th, no dngr after.......* (7 to 1) 4
THE MOTCOMBE OAK [105] 7-10-3 P Niven, *pld hrd early, chsd ldrs 6th, no imprsn aftr 4 out, wknd quickly appr last......................* (9 to 4 jt-fav op 3 to 1) 5
Dist: 3½l, 15l, 3l, 1½l. 5m 20.70s. a 24.20s (5 Ran).

SR: 2/-/ (E Briggs), G Richards

1287 Jacky Mills Conditional Jockeys' Novices' Handicap Hurdle (4-y-o and up) £2,733 2½m 110yds............ (2:30)

639 SWEET NOBLE (Ire) [80] 4-10-7 (7*) F Leahy, *trkd ldrs gng wl, led 4 out, sn clr, styd on well, easily.*
.......................(10 to 1 op 7 to 1) 1
1239 MAUREEN'S FANCY [68] 8-10-2 A Dobbin, *in tch, rdn and outpcd aftr 4 out, styd on wl frm nxt, no ch wth wnr.*
.......................(14 to 1 op 12 to 1) 2
1060⁷ JENDEE (Ire) [77] 5-10-11 A Larnach, *chsd ldrs till outpcd hfwy, styd on frm 3 out.............* (16 to 1 op 10 to 1) 3
1096* FOUR DEEP (Ire) [88] 5-11-8 D J Moffatt, *cl up, hit 4th, sn led, hdd four out, soon btn and no imprsn, wknd appr last..................* (5 to 4 on tchd 11 to 10 on) 4
1169 DOCTOR DUNKLIN (USA) [66] 4-10-0 D Bentley, *trkd ldrs, ev ch 4 out, sn pushed alng, wknd nxt.......* (33 to 1) 5
1092* TIGHTER BUDGET (USA) [70] 6-9-13 (5*) N Leach, *trkd ldrs, effrt aftr 4 out, wknd appr nxt.....* (6 to 1 tchd 7 to 1) 6
1096 HAUT-BRION (Ire) [66] 4-9-11 (3*) J Supple, *chsd ldrs, sn pushed alng, wknd appr 4 out.....* (33 to 1 op 25 to 1) 7
737³ RIDDLEMEROO [66] 8-9-11 (3*) T Eley, *hld up, some hdwy whn hit 6th, sn btn..................* (20 to 1 op 16 to 1) 8
QUIXALL CROSSETT [66] 8-10-0³ (3*) P Williams, *al beh.*
.......................(50 to 1 op 33 to 1) 9
HUNTING COUNTRY [69] 9-9-12 (5*) B Harding, *al beh.*
.......................(20 to 1 op 14 to 1) 10
SPLIT SECOND [75] 4-10-4 (5*) C Woodall, *al beh, tld off whn pld up bef 2 out..............* (16 to 1 op 14 to 1) pu
917 STRONG JOHN (Ire) [90] 5-11-5 (5*) P Murphy, *led till aftr 4th, wknd quickly after four out, beh whn pld up bef nxt...............................* (20 to 1 op 14 to 1) pu
Dist: 15l, 1l, 2l, 20l, 5l, 8l, 3l, 10l. 5m 5.10s. a 18.10s (12 Ran).

(Bezwell Fixings Limited), J G FitzGerald

1288 Middleham Trainers' Association Second To None Novices' Chase (5-y-o and up) £2,872 3m 110yds... (3:00)

1091* LO STREGONE 7-11-6 M Dwyer, *sn wth ldr, led 4 out, canter........* (Evens fav op 11 to 10 on tchd 11 to 10) 1
1218⁷ MONAUGHTY MAN 7-10-9 (5*) P Williams, *led to 4 out, kpt on, no ch wth wnr................................*(66 to 1) 2
1200⁵ KNOCK RANK 8-11-0 P Niven, *in tch till outpcd aftr 14th, no dngr after..............*(14 to 1 op 12 to 1 tchd 16 to 1) 3
TWELFTH MAN 6-11-0 L Wyer, *blundd 4th, sn beh, outpcd aftr 14th.....................*(14 to 1 op 12 to 1 tchd 16 to 1) 4
1033 ABNEGATION 8-11-0 G McCourt, *hld up, hdwy to track ldrs whn f 11th....................*(11 to 10 op 5 to 4) f
Dist: 6l, 6l, 2½l. 6m 47.70s. a 41.70s (5 Ran).

(Mrs Sylvia Clegg), T P Tate

1289 Coolmore Novices' Hurdle (4-y-o and up) £2,320 2m.................(3:30)

MORCELI (Ire) 5-10-9 (3*) D J Moffatt, *made all, styd on strly frm 2 out.......................*(5 to 1 op 4 to 1) 1
100* SOUTHOLT (Ire) 5-11-3 (7*) P Murphy, *trkd ldrs, chsd wnr frm 3 out, kpt on, no imprsn.*
.......................(9 to 2 op 4 to 1 tchd 5 to 1) 2
ADMIRALS SEAT 5-10-12 Mr S Swiers, *hld up in tch, hdwy appr 3 out, kpt on same pace frm nxt.*
.......................(14 to 1 op 10 to 1) 3
VANART 4-10-12 D Byrne, *in tch, effrt aftr 7th, kpt on frm 3 out............................*(33 to 1) 4
ALJADEEN (USA) 4-10-12 R Garritty, *trkd ldrs, effrt appr 3 out, sn btn............*(15 to 2 op 6 to 1 tchd 8 to 1) 5
1100 BATTERY FIRED 4-10-7 (5*) J Supple, *mstk 1st, in tch, no hdwy frm 3 out.....................*(33 to 1) 6
771⁶ MARCHWOOD 6-10-12 K Johnson, *mid-div, effrt appr 3 out, no hdwy................................*(20 to 1) 7
1100² CUMBRIAN CHALLENGE (Ire) 4-10-12 L Wyer, *prmnt, rdn aftr 3 out, hng rght, wknd.*
.......................(9 to 2 op 4 to 1 tchd 5 to 1) 8
ROBERTY LEA 5-10-12 P Niven, *chsd wnr till wknd aftr 3 out................*(11 to 4 fav op 7 to 2 tchd 5 to 2) 9
1143⁴ SHAHGRAM (Ire) 5-10-12 Mrs A Farrell, *in tch till wknd appr 3 out.......* (17 to 2 op 8 to 1 tchd 9 to 1) 10
INAN (USA) 4-10-12 M Dwyer, *nvr dngrs.*
.......................(20 to 1 op 16 to 1) 11
81³ SCRABO VIEW (Ire) 5-10-12 C Grant, *sn beh.....*(25 to 1) 12
WSOM (Ire) 5-10-12 N Smith, *sn beh, blun 4 out.* (33 to 1) 13

723⁴ MISCHIEVOUS GIRL 5-10-7 Mrs F Needham, *sn beh.*
.......................(16 to 1 op 14 to 1) 14
743⁹ WESTCOURT FLYER 4-10-5 (7*) J Driscoll, *nvr better than mid-div.....................................*(33 to 1) 15
640 PRICELESS HOLLY 5-10-12 Mr S Brisby, *beh most of way.*
.......................(33 to 1) 16
1000 TOLLS CHOICE (Ire) 4-10-12 T Reed, *beh most of way.*
.......................(33 to 1) 17
Dist: 12l, 1½l, 15l, ¾l, 3½l, 2½l, 10l, 1l, 4l. 3m 51.60s. a 24.60s (17 Ran).
SR: 34/34/20/5/4/-/ (Mrs J M Corbett), J H Johnson

HAYDOCK (good to soft)
Wednesday November 17th
Going Correction: PLUS 1.00 sec. per fur. (races 1,3,-6,7), PLUS 0.63 (2,4,5)

1290 Newton-le-Willows Police Juvenile Novices' Hurdle (3-y-o) £1,952 2m
....(12:50)

745⁵ DIWALI DANCER 10-12 N Mann, *trkd ldrs, effrt aftr 3 out, styd on wl to ld r-in, hld on und pres.*
.......................(9 to 2 op 4 to 1 tchd 5 to 1) 1
1032⁵ ERZADJAN (Ire) 11-1 G McCourt, *cl up, pushed alng to ld appr 3 out, rdn betw last 2, hdd r-in, kpt on und pres.*
.......................(Evens fav op 5 to 4 tchd 11 to 10 on) 2
830⁸ COEUR BATTANT (Fr) 10-5 (7*) E Husband, *led till appr 3 out, styd cl-up, ev ch betw last 2, wknd r-in.*
.......................(14 to 1 op 12 to 1) 3
DAYADAN (Ire) 10-12 M Dwyer, *prmnt, ev ch 2 out, sn rdn and wknd.......*(4 to 1 op 3 to 1 tchd 9 to 2) 4
LITTLE GUNNER 10-12 P Niven, *in tch, effrt aftr 5th, grad wknd.......................*(14 to 1 op 7 to 1) 5
570 MERCH FACH (Ire) 10-7 M Richards, *in tch, effrt aftr 3 out, wknd quickly, beh whn pld up bef nxt.*
.......................(50 to 1 op 33 to 1) pu
ULTRAKAY (Ire) 10-12 C Hawkins, *lost tch aftr 5th, tld off whn pld up after 3 out..............* (50 to 1 op 33 to 1) pu
BOLD STREET (Ire) 10-12 C Grant, *sn beh, tld off whn pld up bef last.......................*(7 to 1 op 4 to 1) pu
HAPPY DAYS BLANCHE 10-12 A S Smith, *sn beh, tld off whn pld up bef 3 out...........* (33 to 1 op 20 to 1) pu
Dist: Nk, 12l, ½l, 5l. 4m 2.40s. a 22.40s (9 Ran).
SR: 20/22/7/5/-/-/ (Mrs Ann Case), A Bailey

1291 Earlestown Novices' Chase (5-y-o and up) £3,371 2½m................(1:20)

1200* ONE MAN (Ire) 5-11-4 N Doughty, *jmpd wl, wth ldr gng well, led appr 3 out, cmftbly.* (15 to 8 on op 7 to 4 on) 1
MONSIEUR LE CURE 7-11-7 N Doughty, *led till appr 3 out, chsd wnr aftr, kpt on, no imprsn....* (3 to 1 op 5 to 2) 2
FRONT LINE 6-11-1 M Dwyer, *sn tracking ldrs, effrt appr 4 out, grad lost tch......................*(12 to 1 op 8 to 1) 3
820³ REVE DE VALSE (USA) 6-10-10 (5*) P Waggott, *reminders aftr 5th, sn beh, tld off tenth.*
.......................(11 to 1 op 8 to 1 tchd 12 to 1) 4
Dist: 10l, 20l, dist. 5m 17.80s. a 19.80s (4 Ran).
SR: 18/5/-/-/ (J Hales), G Richards

1292 Liverpool Handicap Hurdle (0-125 4-y-o and up) £2,940 2m.............(1:50)

SUNSET ROCK [94] 6-10-8 M Dwyer, *cl up, led second to 2 out, hrd rdn to ld aftr last, all out.*
.......................(6 to 4 fav tchd 13 to 8) 1
1143² NOTABLE EXCEPTION [96] 4-10-10 P Niven, *trkd ldrs, jnd wnr aftr 5th, rdn betw last 2, ev ch till no extr r-in.*
.......................(13 to 8 op 6 to 4) 2
841* SAYMORE [102] 7-10-13 (3*) S Wynne, *hld up in tch, effrt aftr 3 out, led and mstk nxt, hdd after last, no extr.*
.......................(100 to 30 op 11 to 4 tchd 7 to 2) 3
MONTIFIORE AVENUE [110] 7-11-10 L Wyer, *led to second, cl up till outpcd appr 3 out, hld on.*
.......................(16 to 1 op 12 to 1 tchd 20 to 1) 4
Dist: 1½l, ½l, 30l. 4m 4.10s. a 24.10s (4 Ran).
SR: -/-/4/-/ (G E Shouler), J G FitzGerald

1293 Edward Hanmer Memorial Chase Limited Handicap (5-y-o and up) £10,740 3m.................(2:20)

1031 JODAMI [175] 8-12-0 M Dwyer, *jmpd wl, made all, hrd pressed frm 2 out, drvn out r-in, hld on well.....*(5 to 4) 1
1031² ON CARGO TARGET [160] 7-10-13 P Niven, *jmpd wl, sn tracking wnr, shaken up to chal 2 out, switchd r-in, drvn and kpt on well.......................*(5 to 1 op 9 to 2) 2
1056⁴ OLD ROAD (USA) [154] 7-10-7 C Grant, *lost tch 6th, sn tld off...................*(66 to 1 tchd 100 to 1) 3
Dist: ¾l, dist. 6m 27.80s. a 21.80s (3 Ran).
SR: 33/17/-/ (J N Yeadon), P Beaumont

1294 Wargrave Handicap Chase (5-y-o and up) £4,380 2m.................(2:50)

1056* GOOD FOR A LAUGH [116] 9-9-7 (7*) Mr D Parker, *in tch, hdwy to join ldr 8th, led nxt, shaken up aftr last, styd on wl*................................(6 to 1 op 4 to 1) 1
1056² LAST 'O' THE BUNCH [140] 9-11-10 N Doughty, *jmpd wl, led 5th to 9th, styd cl up, rdn aftr last, no imprsn*.
............................(6 to 4 on op 11 to 10 on) 2
897³ DIS TRAIN [130] 9-11-0 M Richards, *led to 5th, lost tch 9th, tld off*...............................(2 to 1 op 6 to 4) 3
Dist: 5l, dist. 4m 11.90s. a 12.90s (3 Ran).

SR: 44/63/-/ (Mrs S A Bramall), Mrs S A Bramall

1295 Hindley Green Novices' Hurdle (4-y-o and up) £1,987 2¾m.....(3:20)

779⁵ SPARROW HALL 6-10-12 M Dwyer, *chsd ldrs, led aftr 9th, hrd pressed frm 2 out, rdn and styd on wl r-in*.
............................(11 to 10 fav op 6 to 4) 1
BRIGADIER DAVIS (Fr) 6-10-12 R Garritty, *in tch, wnt clr wth wnr appr 3 out, chalg whn hit nxt, rdn aftr last, kpt on, no imprsn*....................(12 to 1 op 10 to 1) 2
GRAY'S ELLERGY 7-10-7 P Holley, *beh, effrt aftr 9th, hdwy 3 out, wnt 3rd appr last, not rch ldrs*.
............................(6 to 1 op 10 to 1) 3
1181⁹ NAWRIK (Ire) 4-10-12 T Reed, *in tch, pushed alng aftr 5th, effrt after 9th, kpt on same pace*.........(20 to 1) 4
728⁵ HENRY VILL (Ire) 5-10-7 (5*) T Jenks, *cl up till wknd appr 3 out*...........................(8 to 1 op 7 to 1) 5
1181 WHO SIR 7-10-12 L Wyer, *in tch till wknd aftr 9th*.
............................(16 to 1 op 12 to 1) 6
753⁴ SOUND AND FURY 9-10-12 T Grantham, *slptd till hdd aftr 9th, sn wknd*....(100 to 30 op 2 to 1 tchd 7 to 2) 7
1131 BECK COTTAGE 5-10-12 P Niven, *al beh, effrt aftr 9th, sn btn*.....................(9 to 1 op 8 to 1 tchd 10 to 1) 8
SALINGER 5-10-12 C Grant, *beh, some hdwy 7th, rdn aftr 9th, wknd quickly, tld off whn pld up bef 3 out*.
............................(6 to 1 op 16 to 1) pu
Dist: ¾l, 6l, 8l, 3l, 15l, ½l, nk. 5m 42.60s. a 34.60s (9 Ran).

(Peter Hall), J G FitzGerald

1296 Levy Board Handicap Hurdle (0-135 4-y-o and up) £2,819 2½m......(3:50)

1148⁴ MYTHICAL STORM [93] 6-9-10¹ (5*) Mr M Buckley, *al cl up, led 3 out, pushed clr betw last 2, eased nr finish, cmftbly*...................(15 to 8 tchd 9 to 4) 1
1172² ALBERTITO (Fr) [115] 6-11-5 (3*) S Wynne, *hld up beh, effrt aftr 3 out, hdwy to chase wnr betw last 2, no imprsn after last*.................(2 to 1 op 4 to 1) 2
SOLID FUEL [95] 7-10-0¹ (3*) D J Moffatt, *made most to 5th, outpcd aftr 7th*..................(14 to 1 op 12 to 1) 3
1005⁶ NESSFIELD [117] 7-11-10 A S Smith, *trkd ldrs, led 5th to 3 out, sn wknd*...................(14 to 1 op 10 to 1) 4
DARI SOUND (Ire) [115] 5-11-8 M Dwyer, *trkd ldrs till pld up lme aftr 3 out*.......(5 to 2 op 9 to 4 tchd 11 to 4) pu
Dist: 3l, 15l, 3½l. 5m 13.40s. a 34.90s (5 Ran).

(C C Buckley), Mrs M Reveley

HEREFORD (good)
Wednesday November 17th
Going Correction: PLUS 0.50 sec. per fur. (races 1,3,-5,7,8), PLUS 0.35 (2,4,6)

1297 Wyedean Juvenile Novices' Hurdle (3-y-o) £1,766 2m 1f.............(12:35)

1166³ HABASHA (Ire) 10-7 R Dunwoody, *trkd ldrs, wnt second 4th, led sn aftr four out, clr whn hit last 2*.
............................(13 to 2 op 4 to 1 tchd 7 to 1) 1
1059² QUICK SILVER BOY 10-12 W Knox, *led till hdd sn aftr 6th (4 out), kpt on one pace*.
............................(6 to 5 on op Evens tchd 11 to 10 and 5 to 4 on) 2
997⁴ GUNNER SUE 10-7 D Bridgwater, *prmnt, wknd appr 3 out*.......................(7 to 1 op 6 to 1) 3
1021 DANGER BABY 10-9 (3*) D Meredith, *trkd ldr to 4th, lost tch appr 3 out*..............(20 to 1 op 16 to 1) 4
WITHOUT A FLAG (USA) 10-12 M A FitzGerald, *hld up in rear, lost tch aftr 5th*.
............................(3 to 1 op 5 to 2 tchd 100 to 30) 5
PIPERS REEL 10-7 Mr N Miles, *al beh*.
............................(25 to 1 op 50 to 1) 6
1021 LEGAL RISK (v) 10-7 L Harvey, *prmnt whn mstk second, wknd aftr 4th, tld off*.....(25 to 1 op 50 to 1) 7
1021 STAR MARKET 10-5 (7*) Mr S Joynes, *beh frm strt, tld off 4th*..........................(25 to 1 op 14 to 1) 8
1021⁸ POCONO KNIGHT 10-12 G Upton, *al beh, hit 3rd, tld off 5th, pld up bef 3 out*...................(20 to 1) pu
ADMIRED 10-7 E Murphy, *chsd ldrs till wknd 4th, tld off whn pld up bef 3 out*..........(50 to 1 op 12 to 1) pu
SR: 24/14/-/-/-/-/ (M C Pipe), M C Pipe

1298 Allensmore Novices' Chase (5-y-o and up) £2,424 2m.............(1:05)

TUDOR FABLE (Ire) 5-11-0 R Dunwoody, *trkd ldr, led 3rd, pushed alng frm 3 out, in command whn lft clr last*.
............................(5 to 1 op 7 to 2) 1
958⁵ JAMES THE FIRST 5-11-0 M A FitzGerald, *hld up, hdwy 6th, rdn appr 2 out, lft second last*...(6 to 1 op 9 to 2) 2
954⁶ CRYSTAL BEAR (NZ) 8-11-0 D Bridgwater, *wtd wth, hdwy whn jmpd slwly 5th, ev ch 3 out, sn btn, lft 3rd last*.
............................(5 to 1 op 3 to 1 tchd 11 to 2) 3
981² POPPETS PET 6-11-0 S Earle, *led second till hit nxt, rdn 4 out, wknd bef next*...(10 to 1 op 12 to 1 tchd 14 to 1) 4
PYRO PENNANT 8-11-0 W Knox, *mstk 4th, in tch till wknd four out, tld off*............(20 to 1 op 33 to 1) 5
998 KING'S SHILLING (USA) 6-11-0 Jacqui Oliver, *al prmnt, trkd wnr frm 8th, chlgd 3 out, mstk nxt, tld whn when last*.........(9 to 4 fav op 5 to 2 tchd 2 to 1) f
RUN OF WELD 10-11-0 B Clifford, *led to second, wknd 7th, tld off whn pld up bef 3 out*.
............................(40 to 1 op 20 to 1 tchd 50 to 1) pu
1107 NEVER EVER 8-10-7 (7*) Guy Lewis, *sn beh, tld off whn pld up bef 7th*....................(50 to 1) pu
246 BRYNHILL ALERT 7-11-0 L Harvey, *al beh, tld off whn hit 3 out, pld up bef nxt*.......(33 to 1 tchd 40 to 1) pu
SUPER SPELL 7-11-0 C Maude, *al beh, tld off whn pld up bef 3 out*........................(7 to 1 op 8 to 1) pu
Dist: 10l, 6l, 15l, 30l. 3m 58.90s. a 9.90s (10 Ran).

SR: 43/33/27/12/-/-/ (J E H Collins), N J Henderson

1299 Fownhope Selling Handicap Hurdle (4-y-o and up) £1,805 3¼m.....(1:35)

GORT [82] 5-10-11 J Leech, *wtd wth, hdwy 5th, led 9th, wnt clr frm nxt, very easily*.........(5 to 1 jt-fav) 1
POLECROFT [83] 10-10-12 Mr N Miles, *hld up, gd hdwy 9th, second whn hit 3 out, no ch frm nxt*.
............................(14 to 1 op 20 to 1) 2
859³⁸ IT'S NOT MY FAULT (Ire) [77] 5-10-6 P McDermott, *trkd ldrs, kpt on one pace 3 out*.....(10 to 1 op 8 to 1) 3
437 GRACE MOORE [78] 9-10-7 R Dunwoody, *al prmnt, led 8th to 9th, rdn and wknd 3 out*....(16 to 1 op 14 to 1) 4
994⁷ GROTIUS [84] 9-10-13 C Maude, *in rear, mstk 4th, hdwy four out, nvr dngrs*. (11 to 1 op 14 to 1 tchd 10 to 1) 5
1187⁵ RUSTY MUSIC [80] 7-10-2 (7*) A Flannigan, *hld up in rear, hdwy 7th, one pace frm 4 out*.
............................(9 to 1 op 14 to 1 tchd 8 to 1) 6
MISTRESS ROSS [80] 10-10-9 D Bridgwater, *in tch till wknd 8th, tld off*..........(12 to 1 op 20 to 1) 7
1072⁶ THE HIDDEN CITY [89] 7-11-4 B Clifford, *hld up, hdwy 7th, rdn and wknd 4 out, tld off*....(10 to 1 op 8 to 1) 8
970⁵ INVITE D'HONNEUR [82] 9-11-10 Jacqui Oliver, *hld up, hdwy 6th, wknd rpdly 4 out, tld off*.....(5 to 1 jt-fav op 3 to 1 tchd 9 to 2) 9
312⁴ SMARTIE LEE [95] 6-11-3 (7*) P McLoughlin, *mid-div, lost tch 7th, tld off whn blun and uns rdr last*.........ur
1187⁴ LAABAS [79] 10-10-8 R Rowell, *prmnt, 3rd whn mstk 9th and when blun nxt (4 out), wknd quickly, pld up bef last*........................(10 to 1 op 9 to 1) pu
CREDIT CUT [77] 11-10-3 (3*) R Davis, *pld hrd, dsptd ld second to 4th, wknd rpdly 7th, pulled up bef nxt*.
.... pu
1081⁹ MO ICHI DO [81] (bl) 7-10-10 M A FitzGerald, *prmnt till wknd 8th, tld off whn pld up bef 2 out*.
............................(14 to 1 op 12 to 1) pu
1068 SHIKARI KID [83] 6-10-5 (7*) Mr J L Llewellyn, *al beh, tld off whn pld up bef 3 out*...........(14 to 1 op 10 to 1) pu
CORINTHIAN GIRL [77] 6-10-3 (3*) D Meredith, *prmnt to 7th, sn beh, pld up bef 9th*........(33 to 1) pu
1025⁸ STANE STREET (Ire) [83] 5-10-12 J Railton, *made most to 8th, wknd quickly, tld off whn pld up bef last*.
............................(12 to 1 op 8 to 1 tchd 14 to 1) pu
Dist: 15l, 4l, ¾l, ¾l, 5l, 15l, 7l, 10l. 6m 33.50s. a 33.50s (16 Ran).

(F D Allison), Miss K S Allison

1300 Hereford Hugh Sumner Challenge Bowl Handicap Chase (0-140 5-y-o and up) £3,342 2m 3f........(2:05)

1105 FREELINE FINISHING [139] (bl) 9-12-0 R Dunwoody, *made all, drawing clr whn hit 2 out, unchlgd*.
............................(7 to 4 op 5 to 4) 1
PITHY [111] 11-9-7 (7*) Guy Lewis, *lft second at 1st, rdn appr 4 out, no imprsn frm nxt*.......(9 to 2 op 3 to 1) 2
1041² RICHVILLE [112] 7-10-1 M A FitzGerald, *screwed badly lft and uns rdr 1st*.....(11 to 10 on op Evens tchd 5 to 4) ur
Dist: 10l. 4m 49.50s. a 19.50s (3 Ran).

(Irving Struel), N J Henderson

1301 EBF 'National Hunt' Novices' Hurdle Qualifier (4,5,6-y-o) £2,029 2m 1f (2:35)

778³ RAMALLAH 4-11-0 W McFarland, *hld up in tch, hdwy frm 4th, rdn to ld sn aftr 2 out, drvn out r-in*.
............................(4 to 1 tchd 9 to 2) 1
KELLING 6-11-0 M A FitzGerald, *hld up, steady hdwy frm 5th, outpcd 3 out, rdn to go second appr last, styd on und pres*....(6 to 5 on op 11 to 10 on tchd 5 to 4 on) 2

FIRST COMMAND (NZ) 6-11-0 D Bridgwater, *al prmnt, led 4 out, hdd sn aftr 2 out, one pace*.....(8 to 1 op 5 to 1) 3
1109 REFERRAL FEE 6-11-0 S Earle, *trkd ldrs, outpcd appr 3 out, styd on frm nxt.* (12 to 1 op 10 to 1 tchd 14 to 1) 4
1110[7] DUNNICKS VIEW 4-11-0 C Maude, *prmnt till wknd 4 out.* ....(33 to 1) 5
ALIAS SILVER 6-10-7 (7") Mr N Bradley, *chsd ldrs, lost tch frm 5th*.............(33 to 1 op 20 to 1 tchd 40 to 1) 6
1090[7] STORMY SUNSET 6-10-2 (7") Mr N Moore, *slwly away, nvr on terms*.............(25 to 1 op 16 to 1 tchd 33 to 1) 7
COZZI (Fr) 5-10-7 (7") Guy Lewis, *mid-div till wknd 4 out.* ....(33 to 1 op 25 to 1) 8
1161 CANCALE (Ire) 5-11-0 R Dunwoody, *pld hrd, trkd ldrs till wknd quickly appr 3 out, tld off..*(10 to 1 op 6 to 1) 9
1109 MAGGOTS GREEN 6-10-9 L Harvey, *led till hdd 4 out, wknd rpdly, tld off*...............(25 to 1 tchd 33 to 1) 10
315 MAJESTIC GOLD 5-11-0 B Clifford, *beh whn blun second, tld off frm 4th, pld up bef 2 out.*
........................(25 to 1 op 20 to 1 tchd 33 to 1) pu
1109 SIXTH IN LINE (Ire) 5-11-0 W Knox, *sn beh, tld off whn pld up bef 5th*...................(66 to 1 op 50 to 1) pu
RAIN SHADOW 4-10-4 (5") D Salter, *al beh, tld off whn pld up bef 2 out.*...........(50 to 1 op 33 to 1 tchd 66 to 1) pu
1110 TRADESMARK 5-10-6 (3") R Davis, *sn beh, tld off 4th, pld up bef 3 out.*..................(100 to 1 op 50 to 1) pu
Dist: 2l, 8l, 2½l, 12l, 1l, ¾l, ¾l, 15l, 2½l. 4m 7.20s. a 21.20s (14 Ran).
(Maidens Green Acres), J White

1302 Pontrilas Handicap Chase (0-115 5-y-o and up) £2,948 3m 1f 110yds.... (3:05)

MAN OF MYSTERY [92] 7-10-11 D Bridgwater, *made virtually all, strly rdn frm 3 out, mstks last 2, ran on gmely.*...........................(9 to 2 op 4 to 1) 1
SUNLEY BAY [102] (bl) 7-11-7 R Dunwoody, *trkd wnr frm 8th, ev ch 3 out, rdn and no imprsn appr last.*
......................(11 to 4 fav op 2 to 1 tchd 3 to 1) 2
947[3] MISS FERN [94] 8-10-10 (3") D Meredith, *trkd ldrs, ev ch appr 3 out, one pace aftr.*........(3 to 1 op 5 to 2) 3
1026[4] KINGFISHER BAY [97] 8-11-2 M A FitzGerald, *beh, hdwy tenth, nvr nr to chal*...................(7 to 1 op 8 to 1) 4
1194 HUNTING DIARY [85] 7-10-4 S Earle, *al beh, nvr on terms*. ....(33 to 1) 5
986[6] WOODLANDS GENHIRE [90] 8-10-6 (3") R Davis, *trkd ldrs, took clr order tenth, rdn and wknd 4 out*.
........................(12 to 1 op 14 to 1 tchd 16 to 1) 6
1216 SOCKS DOWNE [83] 14-10-2 W McFarland, *prmnt whn hit 7th, wkng whn blun 14th, tld off*............(20 to 1) 7
947[5] SAMSUN [81] (bl) 11-10-0 C Maude, *al beh, tld off 8th, pld up bef 12th*................(20 to 1 op 16 to 1) pu
1197[7] CAMDEN BELLE [94] 11-10-13 S Hodgson, *dsptd ld early, 3rd whn hit 9th, blun 11th, sn beh, pld up bef 4 out.*
......................(16 to 1 op 14 to 1) pu
1087 KILLBANNON [108] 11-11-13 B Clifford, *hld up, lost tch 11th, tld off whn pld up bef 4 out.* (20 to 1 op 16 to 1) pu
525 MILK QUOTA [81] 10-10-0 D Morris, *beh whn hit 8th, tld off whn pld up bef 12th*.....................(33 to 1) pu
Dist: 2l, 15l, 20l, 4l, 2½l. 30l. 6m 28.40s. a 16.40s (11 Ran).
SR: 8/16/-/-/-/-/ (PCJF Bloodstock), N A Twiston-Davies

1303 Lugwardine Novices' Handicap Hurdle (4-y-o and up) £1,836 2m 3f 110yds ....(3:35)

1047* HANDY LASS [81] 4-10-9 (7") D Matthews, *nvr far away, wnt second 4 out, led appr 2 out, sn clr, easily.*
......................(7 to 1 op 5 to 1) 1
922[8] JUDGE AND JURY [70] (bl) 4-11-0 (5") J McCarthy, *trkd ldr, led sn aftr 6th, wnt clr, rdn and hdd appr 2 out, wl btn whn hit last*...................(4 to 1 fav op 5 to 1) 2
MALAMUTE SALOON (USA) [78] (bl) 7-10-13 R Dunwoody, *chsd ldrs, rdn and wnt second 7th, one pace frm 4 out.*
......................(11 to 2 op 5 to 1) 3
COLETTE'S CHOICE (Ire) [89] 4-11-3 (7") R Darke, *beh, styd on frm 4 out, nvr nrr*.......................(20 to 1) 4
1042[2] OH SO HANDY [74] 5-10-9 D Morris, *al beh.*
......................(12 to 1 op 10 to 1) 5
1173[9] LUCAYAN GOLD [65] 9-10-0 C Maude, *in tch to 6th, tld off*....................(20 to 1 op 16 to 1 tchd 14 to 1) 6
PRINCE VALMY (Fr) [65] 8-10-2 M Foster, *al beh, tld off.*
......................(20 to 1 op 14 to 1) 7
1173[3] KLINGON (Ire) [84] 4-11-2 (3") R Davis, *in tch till wknd 7th, tld off*..................(6 to 1 op 5 to 1) 8
SHARPSIDE [65] 6-9-7 (7") Guy Lewis, *f 3rd.*
......................(7 to 1 op 6 to 1 tchd 8 to 1) f
1173 THE JET SET [86] (bl) 6-11-7 J Lawrence, *bght dwn 3rd.* ....(16 to 1 op 10 to 1) bd
1070 GOLDEN MADJAMBO [69] 7-10-4 M A FitzGerald, *prmnt till wknd 6th, tld off whn pld up bef 2 out.*
......................(8 to 1 op 6 to 1 tchd 9 to 1) pu
IRISH TAN [70] 6-9-12 (7") J Clarke, *al beh, tld off whn pld up bef 3 out.*.................(12 to 1 op 10 to 1) pu
1047[3] MR ZIEGFELD (USA) [72] (bl) 4-10-7 L Harvey, *hmpd 3rd, tld off 6th, pld up bef 4 out*...........(16 to 1 op 10 to 1) pu
CROOKED DEALER (NZ) [76] 6-10-11 G Upton, *al beh, tld off whn pld up bef 2 out.*..........(14 to 1 op 10 to 1) pu

988[6] HERLIN [80] 5-11-1 D Bridgwater, *al beh, tld off whn pld up bef 3 out.*........................(7 to 1 op 5 to 1) pu
988[7] MASTER MURPHY [65] 4-10-0 E Murphy, *led till hdd sn aftr 6th, wknd quickly, tld off whn pld up.*
......................(12 to 1 op 10 to 1) pu
Dist: 15l, 3½l, 8l, 4l, 7l, 10l, 1l. 4m 51.50s. a 30.50s (16 Ran).
(G W Hackling), Mrs A Knight

1304 William Hill 'Golden Oldies' Stakesround 2 In aid of the Injured Jockeys Fund (4-y-o and up) £1,586 1m 5f (4:05)

1084[3] MISSY-S (Ire) 4-11-9 Peter Scudamore, *al prmnt, led o'r 3 fs out, sn clr, very easily...* (11 to 10 fav op 5 to 4 on) 1
1084* MY SWAN SONG 8-12-0 Peter Smith, *hld up, hdwy 4 fs out, chsd wnr fnl 2*...................(9 to 4 op 2 to 1) 2
EMPERORS WARRIOR 7-11-10 Tony Biddlecombe, *al beh, hrd, chsd ldrs fnl 5 fs*...............(10 to 1 op 8 to 1) 3
1173[8] GRAND RAPIDS (USA) 6-11-10 Miss S J Wilton, *prmnt, led hfwy, hdd o'r 3 fs out, sn btn..*. (14 to 1 tchd 16 to 1) 4
CASTELLANI (v) 8-11-10 Jeff King, *led to hfwy, sn outpcd.*
......................(12 to 1 tchd 14 to 1 tchd 16 to 1) 5
1173 KAYRUZ 5-11-10 Rod Millman, *al beh*...........(33 to 1) 6
PHILLIMAY 7-11-5 Richard Linley, *pld hrd, effrt hfwy, sn btn*...........................(8 to 1 op 5 to 1) 7
JORURI 8-12-3[3] Michael Scudamore, *beh, lost tch hfwy*.
......................(20 to 1 op 12 to 1) 8
CASHTAL RUNNER 4-11-12[2] Steve Coathup, *prmnt till wknd hfwy*........................(50 to 1 op 25 to 1) 9
Dist: 7l, 10l, 7l, 10l, 2½l, 1½l, 1½l, 2½l. 3m 9.10s. (9 Ran).
(B J Llewellyn), B J Llewellyn

KEMPTON (good)
Wednesday November 17th
Going Correction: PLUS 0.30 sec. per fur. (races 1,5,6), PLUS 0.40 (2,3,4)

1305 Sunbury Juvenile Novices' Hurdle (3-y-o) £2,238 2m................(1:00)

MYSILV 10-7 A Maguire, *dsptd ld, wnt on 3 out, clr last, easily*...............(13 to 8 fav op 11 to 10 tchd 7 to 4) 1
1021[2] DESTINY CALLS 10-12 C Llewellyn, *dsptd ld till hdd 3 out, hld whn blun nxt, sn outpcd.*
......................(9 to 4 op 2 to 1 tchd 11 to 4) 2
BAG OF TRICKS (Ire) 10-12 N Davies, *hld up beh, wnt poor 3rd aftr 3 out, tld off whn blun last.*
......................(5 to 8 op 2 to 1 tchd 9 to 4) 3
SHOPTILLYOUDROP 10-7 H Jenkins, *not jump wl, al beh, tld off frm 5th, pld up bef 2 out...* (66 to 1 op 20 to 1) pu
870 DIDACTE (Fr) (bl) 10-12 S Smith Eccles, *chsd clr ldrs, hit 3 out, tld off whn pld up bef nxt...* (50 to 1 op 20 to 1) pu
Dist: 30l, 15l. 3m 55.20s. a 15.20s (5 Ran).
(Million In Mind Partnership (3)), D Nicholson

1306 Southern Hero Novices' Chase (5-y-o and up) £3,492 3m..................(1:30)

1086* MARTOMICK 6-11-7 N Williamson, *cld to track ldr frm 8th, led 14th to 4 out, led ag'n appr nxt, jmpd lft last 3, easily.*..............(2 to 1 fav op 7 to 4 tchd 9 to 4) 1
978* SOME DAY SOON 8-11-6 G Bradley, *led till hdd 14th, led ag'n 4 out till appr nxt, sn outpcd.*
......................(11 to 4 op 2 to 1 tchd 9 to 4) 2
YORKSHIRE GALE 7-11-2 D Murphy, *hld up, lft modest 3rd at 8th, nvr nr to chal*.......(7 to 2 tchd 4 to 1) 3
1043[2] GALLANT EFFORT (Ire) 5-11-0 H Davies, *al beh, tld off frm 9th*...................(8 to 1 op 5 to 1 tchd 9 to 1) 4
1107[2] JUDGES FANCY 9-11-2 C Llewellyn, *jmpd awkwardly 1st 2, sn beh, tld off and no ch whn f 4 out.*
......................(5 to 1 op 9 to 2 tchd 11 to 2) f
1107[4] PROVING 9-10-13 (3") P Hide, *chsd ldr, 3rd whn f 8th.*
......................(20 to 1 tchd 33 to 1 and 16 to 1) f
917 PHILIPINTOWN LAD 10-10-11 (5") T Eley, *mstk 3rd, beh whn pld up bef 13th*............(100 to 1 op 66 to 1) pu
Dist: 15l, 15l, 25l. 6m 6.20s. a 17.20s (7 Ran).
SR: 11/1/-/-/ (Richard Shaw), K C Bailey

1307 Limber Hill Handicap Chase (0-145 5-y-o and up) £4,890 2½m 110yds ....(2:00)

1089* BIBENDUM [122] 7-10-12 Peter Hobbs, *in cl tch, quickened to ld aftr 4 out, sn clr, easily.*
......................(7 to 4 fav op 2 to 1 tchd 9 to 4) 1
FIGHTING WORDS [134] 7-11-10 D Murphy, *cl up, wnt second appr 3 out, styd on, no ch wth wnr.*
......................(9 to 1 op 6 to 1 tchd 10 to 1) 2
WELL WRAPPED [134] 9-11-10 J Osborne, *led, clipped twelfth, hdd aftr 4 out, sn wknd.*
......................(100 to 30 op 9 to 4 tchd 7 to 2) 3
1084[7] DEADLY CHARM (USA) [115] 7-10-5 A Maguire, *hld up, blun twelfth, no dngr aftr, tld off.*
......................(100 to 30 op 11 to 4 tchd 7 to 2) 4

1009⁴ ATLAAL [125] 8-11-1 S Smith Eccles, *nvr gng wl, al beh, blun 13th, tld off whn pld up bef 3 out.*
....(6 to 1 op 5 to 1 tchd 7 to 1) pu
Dist: 6l, 25l, 7l. 5m 11.10s. a 18.10s (5 Ran).
(Robert Waley-Cohen), R Waley-Cohen

1308 Nissan Fleet Novices' Chase (5-y-o and up) £3,460 2m.............(2:30)

COONAWARA 7-11-0 B Powell, *jmpd soundly, made all, clr 7th, unchlgd*.....(5 to 4 fav op Evens tchd 11 to 8) 1
981* LACKENDARA 6-11-10 J Osborne, *chsd wnr, akward 6th, outpcd frm nxt*...................(7 to 4 tchd 2 to 1) 2
988⁴ TURF RUN 6-11-0 S McNeill, *hld up, modest 3rd whn f heavily 8th*.........................(16 to 1 op 12 to 1) f
1228⁴ GANDOUGE GLEN 6-10-11 (3*) P Hide, *not jump wl, out-pcd 7th, 3rd and no ch whn f 3 out.*
.............................(7 to 2 op 9 to 4 tchd 4 to 1) f
Dist: 12l. 3m 57.50s. a 10.50s (4 Ran).
SR: 45/43/-/-/
(Simon Sainsbury), Capt T A Forster

1309 Fairview New Homes 'National Hunt' Novices' Hurdle (4-y-o and up) £2,637 2m.........................(3:00)

764* RIVER LOSSIE 4-11-7 J Osborne, *made all, ran on wl frm 2 out,*...................(2 to 1 fav tchd 3 to 1) 1
KONVEKTA KING (Ire) 5-11-0 A Maguire, *chsd ldrs, cld appr 2 out, sn rdn, one pace whn lft second at last.*
.............................(13 to 2 op 6 to 1 tchd 7 to 1) 2
901³ GOOD INSIGHT (Ire) 5-11-0 G Bradley, *keen hold early, in cl tch, pushed alng aftr 3 out, one pace nxt.*
.................................(9 to 1 op 5 to 1 tchd 10 to 1) 3
ARFER MOLE (Ire) 5-11-0 C Llewellyn, *prmnt, outpcd and lost pl aftr 3 out, hmpd last, kpt on wl.*
.................................(7 to 1 tchd 8 to 1 and 6 to 1) 4
1010⁶ SQUIRE SILK 4-11-0 Peter Hobbs, *hld up rear, hdwy aftr 3 out, no imprsn nxt...(10 to 1 op 7 to 1 tchd 12 to 1) 5
HALL END LADY (Ire) 5-10-9 Richard Guest, *al rear, tld off 3 out.*........................(33 to 1 op 20 to 1) 6
JYMJAM JOHNNY (Ire) 4-11-0 N Williamson, *al beh, tld off.*
.............................(33 to 1 op 20 to 1) 7
844⁶ MAC'S LEAP 5-11-0 D Skyrme, *trkd ldrs, sn lost pl, beh 5th, tld off*......................(33 to 1 op 25 to 1) 8
MY WIZARD 6-10-11 (3*) P Hide, *chsd ldrs, outpcd appr 2 out, hdwy and staying on in second whn f last.*
.............................(33 to 1 op 16 to 1) f
FINE THYNE (Ire) 4-11-0 M Perrett, *cl up, ev ch whn f 2 out.*
.............(6 to 1 op 3 to 1 tchd 13 to 2 and 7 to 1) f
ROSE KING 6-11-0 D Murphy, *mid-div, cld on ldrs aftr 4th, one pace whn brght dwn 2 out.*
.................(5 to 1 op 7 to 2 tchd 11 to 2) bd
634⁸ BALLYMGYR (Ire) 4-10-9 (5*) A Procter, *al beh, tld off whn pld up bef 2 out.*......................(33 to 1) pu
Dist: 3½l, 4l, hd, 4l, dist, 2½l, 30l. 3m 50.00s. a 10.00s (12 Ran).
SR: 41/30/26/26/22/-/
(Chris Brasher), C R Egerton

1310 Wimbledon Handicap Hurdle (4 & 5-y-o) £3,362 2m 5f...............(3:30)

PEATSWOOD [124] 5-12-0 Lorna Vincent, *cl up, drpd rear 6th, hdwy aftr 3 out, led appr last, styd on wl.*
.................................(14 to 1 op 6 to 1 tchd 16 to 1) 1
WINGS OF FREEDOM (Ire) [101] 5-10-5 J Osborne, *hld up, cld on bit and ev ch 3 out, sn outpcd, ran on frm last.*
.............................(7 to 1 op 9 to 2 tchd 8 to 1) 2
CASTIGLIERO (Fr) [114] (v) 5-11-4 G Bradley, *led, quick-ened 6th, jnd 3 out, sn pushed alng to go clr nxt, hdd appr last, no extr.*....................(5 to 2 op 3 to 1) 3
829⁴ MR MATT (Ire) [115] 5-11-5 Peter Hobbs, *cl up, awkward 5th, pushed alng 4 out, btn 2 out.*
.................................(3 to 1 op 5 to 2 tchd 100 to 30) 4
979² JAWANI (Ire) [104] 5-10-8 A Carroll, *hld up, pushed alng to cl 6th, rdn and ev ch 3 out, sn btn, tld off.*
.................(15 to 8 fav op 7 to 4 tchd 6 to 4 and 2 to 1) 5
Dist: 1½l, 3l, 5l, dist. 5m 7.00s. a 14.00s (5 Ran).
SR: 23/-/8/4/-/
(Peter Taplin), M R Channon

SOUTHWELL (good to soft)
Wednesday November 17th
Going Correction: PLUS 1.00 sec. per fur.

1311 Witham Novices' Chase (5-y-o and up) £1,370 3m 110yds.............(2:40)

PETTY BRIDGE 9-11-0 (3*) W Marston, *trkd ldrs, hdwy 13th, chlgd 3 out, led nxt, rdn out.*
.............................(4 to 1 op 3 to 1 tchd 9 to 2) 1
1081* BOLL WEEVIL 7-11-10 Mr J Durkan, *led, rdn and hdd 2 out, hit last, no extr.*
.........................(Evens fav op 5 to 4 tchd 11 to 10) 2
954³ WALLISTARO 6-11-3 R Supple, *al prmnt, hit 14th, ev ch whn mstk 3 out, wknd nxt.*................(7 to 1 op 10 to 1) 3
TEE QU 8-11-3 R Bellamy, *cl up, mstk 13th, pushed alng, f 6 out.*........................(16 to 1 op 12 to 1) f
1081⁷ THE YOKEL 7-11-3 K Johnson, *f 3rd.*(9 to 1 op 7 to 1) f

---

1150² FLASS VALE (v) 5-11-0 J Callaghan, *f second.*
....(16 to 1 op 12 to 1) f
1080³ POLLERTON'S PRIDE 6-10-12 Diane Clay, *hmpd second, rear whn brght dwn nxt*..........(6 to 1 op 4 to 1) bd
1080 BANOUR (USA) 6-11-0 W Humphreys, *rear whn hmpd second and 3rd, beh till pld up bef 6th.*
.............................(12 to 1 op 10 to 1 tchd 14 to 1) pu
Dist: 4l, 20l. 6m 52.40s. a 54.40s (8 Ran).
(C T & R G Bouston), A P James

1312 Beck Handicap Chase (0-115 5-y-o and up) £1,456 2m.................(3:10)

913³ BARKISLAND [94] 9-10-11 J Callaghan, *made all, lft clr 3 out.*........................(13 to 8 jt-fav op 5 to 4) 1
834² BOSSBURG [90] (bl) 6-10-7 D Gallagher, *not fluent, chsd ldg pair, blun 6th, sn rdn alng, hit 9th, wl beh, lft poor second 3 out.*...............(6 to 1 op 4 to 1 tchd 7 to 1) 2
1034⁶ KANNDABIL [101] (bl) 6-11-4 G McCourt, *chsd wnr, hit 3rd, mstks 7th and 8th, rdn and 2 ls second whn f 3 out.*
.................................(5 to 2 tchd 3 to 1) f
Dist: 20l. 4m 20.60s. a 21.60s (3 Ran).
SR: 27/3/-/
(John Veitch), P Beaumont

SOUTHWELL (A.W) (std)
Wednesday November 17th
Going Correction: PLUS 0.45 sec. per fur.

1313 Greet Claiming Hurdle (4-y-o and up) £1,303 2m.....................(1:10)

DONIA (USA) 4-10-12 J A Harris, *trkd ldrs, hdwy to ld 6th, sn clr, easily*.........(2 to 1 fav op 5 to 4 tchd 5 to 2) 1
1068 BASSIO (Bel) (h) 4-10-5 J McLaughlin, *in tch, hdwy to chase wnr 4 out, sn rdn and no imprsn.*
.................................(9 to 1 op 6 to 1) 2
1153 WILL BONNY (NZ) 6-10-10 (7*) T Murphy, *hld up, hdwy 5th, sn rdn alng, kpt on one pace frm 4 out.*
.................................(9 to 1 op 8 to 1 tchd 5 to 1) 3
1142⁶ RISEUPWILLIEREILLY (bl) 7-10-5 N Smith, *led aftr 1st to 6th, sn drvn alng, wknd appr 3 out, blun nxt.*
.................................(25 to 1 op 20 to 1) 4
1068 GLOSSY 6-11-9 T Wall, *chsd ldrs, mstk second, rdn appr 4 out, sn struggling.*..............(9 to 1 op 8 to 1) 5
1068⁴ WE'RE IN THE MONEY (bl) 9-11-2 B Dalton, *in tch, effrt 5th, sn drvn alng, beh appr 4 out.*
.............................(100 to 30 op 5 to 1 tchd 7 to 2) 6
1068 MATTS BOY 5-10-5 S Turner, *chsd ldrs, rdn and lost pl 5th, sn beh.*.........................(20 to 1) 7
950 CHAGHATAI (USA) 7-10-13 Diane Clay, *beh 5th.*
.................................(16 to 1 op 14 to 1) 8
1143 LOCHEART LADY 6-11-4 M Moloney, *led till aftr 1st, cl up till lost pl quickly after 4th, beh whn f nxt.*
.................................(8 to 1 op 6 to 1) f
Dist: 15l, 20l, 12l, 3l, 1½l, 5l, 3l. 3m 59.50s. a 13.50s (9 Ran).
SR: 21/-/-/-/-/-/
(J L Harris), J L Harris

1314 Fleet Conditional Jockeys' Handicap Hurdle (0-130 4-y-o and up) £1,244 3m
.............................(1:40)

553² RED CARDINAL [98] 7-11-9 (5*) D Meade, *made all, rdn 2 out, kpt on, fnshd lme...*(9 to 4 op 2 to 1 tchd 5 to 2) 1
951² VALATCH [71] 5-10-1 A Thornton, *trkd wnr, chlgd 3 out, sn rdn, not quicken appr last.*......(3 to 1 tchd 100 to 30) 2
951* FETTLE UP [81] (bl) 5-10-11 M Hourigan, *cl up, pushed alng tenth, reminders nxt, rdn and wknd 3 out.*
.................................(6 to 4 fav op 11 to 8 tchd 13 to 8) 3
951⁴ HAWWAR (USA) [75] 6-10-5 W Marston, *hld up in tch, reminders 9th, sn lost pl, tld off 5 out.*(6 to 1 op 4 to 1) 4
Dist: 6l, 8l, dist. 6m 9.80s. a 32.80s (4 Ran).
(Harry Sibley), T Thomson Jones

1315 Henry Boot Northern Limited Novices' Selling Hurdle (4,5,6-y-o) £1,303 2½m
.............................(2:10)

1156* GARYS GIRL 6-10-11 (3*) S Curran, *in tch, hdwy 7th, chlgd 3 out, sn led, rdn clr appr last, ran on.*
.................................(13 to 8 fav op Evens tchd 7 to 4) 1
1097⁶ MANILA RUN (Ire) 4-10-9 (5*) W Dwan, *chsd ldr, led appr 7th, rdn 3 out, sn hdd, hrd drvn and one pace approaching last...*(100 to 30 op 5 to 1 tchd 6 to 1) 2
TESEKKUREDERIM 6-11-0 Diane Clay, *al prmnt, effrt and ev ch 4 out, rdn and wknd nxt.......*(7 to 2 op 5 to 2) 3
932 SEA PRODIGY 4-11-0 D Gallagher, *chsd ldrs, rdn and wknd whn hit 4 out, sn beh........*(10 to 1 op 7 to 1) 4
869 STAN CARTER (v) 5-11-0 M Ranger, *al rear, tld off 8th.*
.................................(20 to 1) 5
287⁶ WHATCOMESNATURALLY (USA) 4-10-9 S D Williams, *in tch till f 6th.*..........................(8 to 1 op 6 to 1) f
1094 DOT'S JESTER 4-11-0 M Moloney, *sn clr, hit 3rd, hdd and wknd quickly appr 7th, tld off whn pld up bef 3 out.*
.................................(25 to 1 op 20 to 1) pu
1211 WHAT A RATTLE 4-11-0 R J Beggan, *mstks, al beh, tld off whn pld up bef 7th.*................(14 to 1 op 10 to 1) pu

Dist: 6l, dist, 20l, 15l. 5m 12.60s. a 31.60s (8 Ran).
(S Thompson), D Carroll

1316 Barnby Novices' Handicap Hurdle (0-100 4-y-o and up) £1,280 2m. . (3:40)

1093^{3} MILLIES OWN [67] 6-9-9 (7*) D Fortt, *made all, rdn 2 out, ran on wl*.......(4 to 1 tchd 9 to 2) 1
1100^{4} WORDY'S WONDER [77] 5-10-5 (7*) D Meade, *trkd ldrs, hit 4th, hdwy to chase wnr 5 out, effrt and ev ch 2 out, sn hrd rdn, one pace*... (11 to 8 fav op Evens tchd 6 to 4) 2
1153* GREEN'S SEAGO (USA) [66] 5-10-1^{4} (3*) A Thornton, *chsd wnr, hit 5th, rdn appr 4 out, sn btn*.......(4 to 1 op 3 to 1 tchd 9 to 2) 3
705^{3} EARLY DRINKER [89] 5-11-10 Mr J Durkan, *hld up in tch, hdwy 6th, effrt and rdn 4 out, sn wknd*.......(4 to 1 op 3 to 1) 4
731 THISONESFORALICE [65] 5-10-0 J Callaghan, *strted slwly, beh, hdwy and in tch 4th, rdn and wknd 5 out*.......(10 to 1 tchd 12 to 1) 5

Dist: 12l, 15l, 1½l, 15l. 4m 2.60s. a 16.60s (5 Ran).
(Mrs Millie Mullen), S Mellor

HAYDOCK (good to soft) Thursday November 18th

Going Correction: PLUS 1.05 sec. per fur. (races 1,4,6), PLUS 0.53 (2,3,5)

1317 Hoofprint Junior Hurdle (3-y-o) £2,217 2½m.......................(1:10)

1032^{2} MARROS MILL 10-9 A Maguire, *cl up, drw clr wth ldr appr 3 out, led betw last 2, rdn aftr last, styd on wl*.......(5 to 2 on tchd 9 to 4 on) 1
1243^{2} HEATHYARDS BOY 10-11 (3*) S Wynne, *cl up, led 6th till betw last 2, rdn aftr last, no imprsn*. (9 to 2 op 4 to 1) 2
1188* RECORD LOVER (Ire) 11-0 W Worthington, *hld up in tch, effrt appr 3 out, sn wknd*.......(10 to 1 op 8 to 1) 3
1021^{3} SOLOMAN SPRINGS (USA) (bl) 11-0 N Doughty, *led to 6th, cl up till wknd appr 3 out*.......(7 to 1 op 6 to 1) 4

Dist: 5l, 20l, 12l. 5m 5.20s. a 26.70s (4 Ran).
SR: 24/24/4/-/ (Mrs Claire Smith), D Nicholson

1318 Rainford Conditional Jockeys' Handicap Chase (0-120 5-y-o and up) £3,078 2½m.......................(1:40)

1069^{2} THE MASTER GUNNER [105] 9-11-2 R Davis, *made all, clr last, pushed out*.......(5 to 4 fav op Evens) 1
1095* PERSIAN HOUSE [115] 6-11-12 P Williams, *hld up in tch, effrt aftr 3 out, mstk nxt, sn chasing wnr, mistake last, no imprsn*.......(7 to 2 op 5 to 2) 2
1203 PINEMARTIN [114] 10-11-8 (3*) N Leach, *prmnt, trkd wnr frm 11th, pushed alng appr 3 out, wknd betw last 2*.......(5 to 1 op 7 to 2) 3
963^{3} ACHILTIBUIE [89] 9-10-0 D Bentley, *cl up till wknd 11th*.......(20 to 1 op 16 to 1) 4
1185^{2} PIPER O'DRUMMOND [100] 6-10-8 (3*) J Burke, *hld up in tch, f 9th*.......(5 to 1 tchd 11 to 2) f

Dist: 5l, 15l, 12l. 5m 24.70s. a 26.70s (5 Ran).
(Major-Gen R L T Burges), K C Bailey

1319 Tim Molony Memorial Chase Handicap (5-y-o and up) £4,810 3½m 110yds.......................(2:10)

1063^{6} PADAVENTURE [122] 8-11-0 P Niven, *al prmnt, led 4 out till betw last 2, rallied und pres to ld r-in, all out*.......(11 to 4 op 3 to 1) 1
783^{3} ALL JEFF (Fr) [129] 9-11-7 G Bradley, *hld up, effrt aftr 4 out, led betw last 2, rdn after last, hdd and no extr*.......(13 to 8 fav op 5 to 4 tchd 7 to 4) 2
1145^{2} MILITARY SECRET [108] 7-10-0 C Grant, *in tch, pushed alng aftr 4 out, ch nxt, sn rdn and wknd*.......(4 to 1 op 3 to 1) 3
HOTPLATE [120] 10-10-12 N Doughty, *led 4th to four out, sn wknd*.......(5 to 1 tchd 6 to 1) 4
1118^{5} FORTH AND TAY [108] 11-10-0^{5} (5*) P Williams, *hld up, pushed alng aftr 13th, lost tch 17th*.......(12 to 1 op 10 to 1) 5
789^{2} ABERCROMBY CHIEF [108] (v) 8-10-0 A Orkney, *mstks, led to 4th, prmnt till wknd 16th, tld off whn pld up bef 2 out*.......(14 to 1 op 12 to 1) pu

Dist: 1½l, 30l, 10l, 2l. 7m 41.30s. a 25.30s (6 Ran).
(Mrs J G Fulton), Mrs M Reveley

1320 White Lodge Novices' Hurdle (4-y-o and up) £2,092 2½m...........(2:40)

1215 POWLEYVALE 6-11-1 L Wyer, *trkd ldrs, led appr 7th, rdn betw last 2, mstk last, jnd r-in, found extr und pres*.......(4 to 1 op 7 to 2) 1
WHITE WILLOW 4-11-0 P Niven, *not fluent, hld up in tch, jmpd slwly 5th, hdwy aftr nxt, sn chasing wnr, rdn to chal r-in, no extr*.......(11 to 10 on op 5 to 4 on tchd Evens) 2
SAVOY 6-11-0 N Doughty, *in tch, styd on wl frm 3 out, nvr nr to chal*.......(10 to 1 op 8 to 1) 3
CORSTON RAMBO 6-11-0 T Reed, *beh till styd on frm 3 out, nvr dngrs*.......(33 to 1 op 20 to 1) 4
1059^{4} MOZEMO 6-11-6 M Richards, *hld up beh, some hdwy aftr 6th, rdn after 3 out, no headway*.... (7 to 1 op 6 to 1) 5
GREY TRIX (Ire) 5-11-0 R Garritty, *in tch till wknd aftr 7th*.......(20 to 1 op 14 to 1) 6
BOLD AMBITION 6-11-0 Susan Kersey, *prmnt, led 5th till appr 7th, wknd*...... (12 to 1 op 10 to 1 tchd 14 to 1) 7
743^{4} STEEL FABRICATOR 6-11-0 M Dwyer, *chsd ldrs, ch appr 3 out, sn wknd*.......(12 to 1 op 16 to 1) 8
CILERNA'S LAD 8-10-9 (5*) Mr D McCain, *led to 5th, sn wknd, tld off whn pld up bef 3 out*. (33 to 1 op 20 to 1) pu
1078^{6} BIRCHALL BOY 5-11-0 G Bradley, *prmnt till wknd appr 7th, tld off whn pld up bef 2 out*.......(16 to 1 op 14 to 1 tchd 20 to 1) pu

Dist: 1½l, 8l, 10l, 5l, hd, hd, 12l. 5m 5.00s. a 26.50s (10 Ran).
SR: 32/29/21/11/12/6/6/-/-/ (M G St Quinton), B S Rothwell

1321 Makerfield Novices' Chase (5-y-o and up) £3,322 2m..................(3:10)

ROXTON HILL 8-10-12 G Bradley, *made most, drvn out r-in*.......(6 to 5 fav op 5 to 4 tchd 11 to 8) 1
1117^{2} FULL O'PRAISE (NZ) 6-10-12 T Reed, *jmpd lft, cl up, drw clr wth wnr hfwy, ev ch last, rdn and no imprsn*.......(5 to 4 op Evens) 2
909^{5} HEIR OF EXCITEMENT 8-10-12 J Callaghan, *chsd ldrs till lost tch hfwy, tld off*.......(6 to 1 op 4 to 1) 3
1204^{9} THE POD'S REVENGE 8-10-12 M Moloney, *sn tld off*.......(25 to 1 op 20 to 1) 4

Dist: 2l, dist, 15l. 4m 12.20s. a 13.20s (4 Ran).
SR: 37/35/-/-/ (Mrs B Mead), C P E Brooks

1322 Haydock Gold Card Hurdle Handicap (4-y-o and up) £2,999 2¾m......(3:40)

1148* BONANZA [119] 6-10-3 (4ex) R Hodge, *mid-div, pushed alng aftr 8th, hdwy betw last 2, styd on wl und pres to ld nr finish*.......(5 to 1 tchd 11 to 2) 1
1005^{2} BOLLIN WILLIAM [140] 5-11-10 L Wyer, *wth ldr, led appr 9th, kpt on wl frm 2 out, hdd and no extr nr finish*.......(4 to 1 op 7 to 2) 2
1116^{8} DOMINANT SERENADE [129] 4-10-8 (5*) D Bentley, *in tch, pushed alng aftr 8th, hdwy after 2 out, styd on wl r-in*.......(14 to 1 op 12 to 1) 3
1119* COUNTORUS [116] 7-9-12^{1} (3*) D J Moffatt, *hld up in tch, chlgd 2 out, ev ch last, wknd nr finish*.......(11 to 4 fav op 5 to 2) 4
1057^{6} CELTIC BREEZE [116] (v) 10-10-0 A Dobbin, *mid-div, pushed alng 8th, styd on frm 3 out, not trble ldrs*.......(25 to 1) 5
1057* FORTUNES WOOD [116] 7-9-7 (7*) D Meade, *mid-div, hdwy to chase ldr aftr 9th, wknd appr 2 out*.......(4 to 1 tchd 9 to 2) 6
1116^{7} PEANUTS PET [130] 8-11-0 M Dwyer, *trkd ldrs, effrt appr 3 out, wknd*.......(14 to 1) 7
914* TROODOS [116] 7-10-0 D Wilkinson, *al beh, lost tch 3 out*.......(10 to 1 op 8 to 1) 8
SPROWSTON BOY [125] 10-10-9 W Worthington, *made most till appr 9th, wknd*.......(16 to 1 op 14 to 1 tchd 20 to 1) 9
730^{4} BALAAT (USA) [116] 5-10-0 A Orkney, *al beh, lost tch appr 3 out*.......(33 to 1 op 25 to 1) 10
AMBLESIDE HARVEST [116] 6-9-7 (7*) B Harding, *prmnt till wknd aftr 8th, tld off 3 out*.......(14 to 1 op 12 to 1 tchd 16 to 1) 11

Dist: ½l, 1½l, ½l, 6l, 5l, 1½l, 15l, 8l, nk, dist. 5m 40.30s. a 32.30s (11 Ran).
SR: -/3/-/-/-/-/ (D Needham & Partners), Mrs M Reveley

LUDLOW (good to firm) Thursday November 18th

Going Correction: PLUS 0.15 sec. per fur. (races 1,3,5,7), PLUS 0.45 (2,4,6)

1323 Norton Novices' Claiming Handicap Hurdle (4 & 5-y-o) £1,480 2m...(12:50)

1188^{3} DISTANT MEMORY [76] (bl) 4-11-7 (7*) N Parker, *hld up, hdwy to track ldg grp aftr 5th, cl up and hit 2 out, rdn to ld r-in, drvn out*.......(15 to 2 op 5 to 1) 1
1188^{2} SAAHI (USA) [59] 4-10-11 J Osborne, *hld up and beh, steady hdwy aftr 5th, cld on ldrs appr 2 out, ev ch last, rdn and not quicken r-in*.......(11 to 8 fav op 5 to 4 tchd 6 to 5 and 6 to 4) 2
1079 MONTAGNE [49] 4-10-1 N Williamson, *led to second, led ag'n nxt, hdd aftr last, rdn and kpt on*.......(20 to 1 op 25 to 1 tchd 33 to 1) 3
748^{2} FULL SHILLING (USA) [70] 4-11-1 (7*) N Juckes, *hld up, hdwy to track ldrs aftr 5th, ev ch appr 2 out, rdn and wknd after last*.......(7 to 1 op 5 to 1) 4
567^{7} ALTO PRINCESS [63] 4-10-12 (3*) D Meredith, *hld up, rdn alng aftr 5th, styd on one pace after 2 out*.......(20 to 1 op 14 to 1) 5

1070[6] JON'S CHOICE [67] (bl) 5-11-5 T Wall, *hld up, hdwy 4th, dsptd ld appr 2 out, sn rdn and wknd.*
.................................(9 to 1 op 8 to 1 tchd 10 to 1) 6
238[4] THEM TIMES (Ire) [58] 4-10-10 R Supple, *beh, rdn alng aftr 5th, no hdwy appr 2 out.*
.................................(10 to 1 op 14 to 1 tchd 8 to 1) 7
1053 MISTRESS BEE (USA) [55] 4-10-7 A S Smith, *chsd ldr til rdn and wknd quickly appr 2 out.*
.........(20 to 1 op 14 to 1 tchd 25 to 1 and 33 to 1) 8
EXCELLED (Ire) [53] 4-10-5 D Bridgwater, *hld up, drpd rear and rdn alng aftr 4th, sn beh.*
.................................(20 to 1 op 25 to 1 tchd 40 to 1) 9
567[5] MISTY VIEW [76] 4-11-7 (7*) P McLoughlin, *hld up, wnt 3rd 4th, chsd ldg pair, wknd appr 2 out, 8th and btn whn f last.*..................(10 to 1 op 6 to 1 tchd 11 to 1) f
SUPER HEIGHTS [76] 5-11-9 (5*) T Jenks, *not fluent, wkng whn jmpd slwly 5th, sn beh, tld off and pld up bef last.*
.................................(200 to 1 op 50 to 1) pu
148[8] WRETS [62] 4-11-0 L Harvey, *hld up, lost tch aftr 4th, sn tld off whn pld up bef last.....*(14 to 1 op 8 to 1) pu
Dist: 3l, 3½l, 10l, 5l, 2l, 5l, 15l. 3m 47.00s. a 10.00s (12 Ran).
SR: 24/4/-/1/-/-/ (Mrs Ann Weston), P J Hobbs

1324 Sidney Phillips Novices' Chase (5-y-o and up) £2,671 2½m.............(1:20)

1022[2] HEARTS ARE WILD 6-11-0 J Osborne, *hld up, trkd ldrs frm 3rd, led 9th, jmpd lft last 3, left clr last, cmftbly.*
.................................(6 to 4 on tchd 11 to 8 on) 1
996[2] CWM ARCTIC 6-10-9 Mr M Jackson, *lost pl aftr 8th, hdwy to track ldrs after 11th, rdn appr 3 out, no imprsn, ridden to take 2nd place after last.* (20 to 1 op 10 to 1) 2
998[3] GOOD FOR A LOAN 6-11-0 L Harvey, *mstks 1st 2, hld up, hdwy 9th, ev ch appr 3 out, sn rdn and no imprsn.*
.................................(5 to 2 op 9 to 4) 3
1081[5] GENEROUS SCOT 9-11-0 R Bellamy, *led to 4th, led ag'n nxt til hdd 9th, trkd ldr, ev ch appr 3 out, one pace.*
.................................(25 to 1 op 20 to 1) 4
931[6] BALLAD RULER 7-11-0 W Marston, *drpd rear 8th, lost tch tenth, tld off.........*(16 to 1 op 10 to 1 tchd 20 to 1) 5
1248 VISION OF WONDER 9-11-0 D Bridgwater, *chsd ldrs, led briefly aftr 4th, wknd quickly after tenth, tld off whn mstk 2 out......................*(33 to 1 op 20 to 1) 6
1024[2] RICH AND RED 7-10-9 N Williamson, *mstks, hld up, hdwy to chase ldr aftr 11th, ev ch 3 out, second but und pres whn f last.....................*(10 to 1 tchd 14 to 1) f
BILLHEAD 7-10-9 (5*) T Eley, *hld up, hdwy to chase ldrs aftr 11th, wknd after 4 out, tld off whn pld up bef last.*
.................................(50 to 1 op 33 to 1) pu
889 BARE FISTED 5-10-9 (5*) Mrs P Nash, *prmnt, led and mstk 4th, sn hdd, lost tch 9th, soon tld off, pld up bef 3 out.*
.................................(50 to 1 op 33 to 1) pu
Dist: 15l, sht-hd, 3l, dist, 30l. 5m 4.60s. a 13.60s (9 Ran).
SR: 40/20/25/22/-/-/ (T F F Nixon), Capt T A Forster

1325 Craven Arms Selling Hurdle (4-y-o and up) £1,763 2m.............(1:50)

1070[2] KELLY'S DARLING 7-11-0 D Gallagher, *hld up gng wl, trkd ldg grp aftr 5th, led on bit after last, shaken up r-in, cmftbly.........................*(7 to 2 jt-fav tchd 4 to 1) 1
994[5] TAUNTING (Ire) 5-11-0 M Hourigan, *hld up, chsd ldrs frm 4th, ev ch appr 2 out, no imprsn..............*(16 to 1) 2
693[2] FUSSY LADY 6-10-13 L Harvey, *hld up and beh, hdwy to chase ldg grp aftr 3 out, kpt on one pace.*
.................................(11 to 2 op 5 to 1 tchd 6 to 1) 3
260[3] IMMORTAL IRISH 8-11-4 B Clifford, *hld up, hdwy aftr 5th, pckd nxt, led 2 out, jmpd rght last, hdd r-in, not quicken..................................*(12 to 1) 4
1070[3] NAJEB (USA) (bl) 4-11-0 N Williamson, *chsd ldr, ev ch 3 out, cl up whn mstk nxt, wknd appr last.*
.................................(8 to 1 op 4 to 1) 5
1168[6] EDWARD SEYMOUR (USA) 6-10-9 (5*) T Jenks, *hld up, hdwy to chase ldg grp aftr 5th, ev ch appr 2 out, sn rdn and btn............................*(7 to 2 jt-fav op 5 to 2) 6
1068[9] PANT LLIN (bl) 7-11-8 R Supple, *hld up, hdwy aftr 5th, rdn and in tch appr 2 out, sn btn....*(20 to 1 op 16 to 1) 7
BEAUFAN 6-11-4 Gary Lyons, *hld up, hdwy to track ldrs aftr 5th, ev ch appr 2 out, sn rdn and wknd...* (33 to 1) 8
ROYAL ACCLAIM (v) 8-10-9 (5*) R Farrant, *hld up, drvn alng aftr 4th, no hdwy frm 3 out....*(12 to 1 op 6 to 1) 9
812[8] SENSEI 6-11-4 T Wall, *led, hdd and hit nxt, hrd rdn aftr 3rd, chsd ldrs til wknd quickly 2 out.*
.................................(33 to 1 op 16 to 1) 10
953 WESSEX MILORD 8-11-0 D Bridgwater, *hld up and beh, lost tch aftr 4th, nvr dngrs.........*(50 to 1 op 33 to 1) 11
SHIFNAL (v) 8-11-0 J Osborne, *chsd second till hdd appr 2 out, sn wknd...............*(7 to 1 tchd 10 to 1) 12
350[7] WOODLANDS CROWN (bl) 10-10-7 (7*) J Neaves, *hld up, drvn alng aftr 4th, sn lost tch, tld off whn pld up bef 2 out..........................*(50 to 1 op 33 to 1) pu
INDIAN SHOT 13-11-4 R Bellamy, *lost tch aftr 4th, tld off whn pld up and dismounted after 3 out, lme.*
.................................(50 to 1) pu
1187[8] BRIDGE STREET BOY 4-11-0 M Bosley, *hld up, lost tch aftr 4th, tld off whn pld up bef 2 out.*
.................................(50 to 1 op 33 to 1) pu

Dist: 5l, 1½l, 3l, 1½l, 1½l, 7l, 2½l, 8l, 12l, nk. 3m 47.00s. a 10.00s (15 Ran).
SR: 10/5/2/4/-/-/ (D Roderick), F J Yardley

1326 Their Royal Highnesses Prince And Princess Of Wales Challenge Trophy Amateur Riders Handicap Chase (5-y-o and up) £3,127 3m..........(2:20)

1151* SANDYBRAES [121] 8-11-9 (7*,6ex) Mr G Hogan, *hld up, hdwy 6th, led 12th, hdd nxt, led 3 out, jmpd rght next, cmftbly....................*(15 to 8 fav op 5 to 4 tchd 2 to 1) 1
865[9] IMPECCABLE TIMING [91] 10-9-10[3] (7*) Mr A Mitchell, *hld up, hdwy 12th, wnt moderate 3rd 5 out, styd on to take second pl aftr last, not trble nwr.* (50 to 1 op 20 to 1) 2
995[3] COMEDY ROAD [101] 9-10-10 Mr M Armytage, *hld up, cld led 13th to 3 out, wknd appr last, lost second pl r-in..............................*(4 to 1 op 3 to 1) 3
1083[3] LAUDERDALE LAD [97] 11-10-1 (5*) Mrs P Nash, *trkd ldr, led 6th, sn hdd, led 9th to 12th, mstk 14th, soon wknd.*
.................................(5 to 1 op 7 to 2) 4
980[3] TOMPET [103] 7-10-5 (7*) Mr M Rimell, *lost pl aftr tenth, sn rdn alng, no ch frm 6 out............*(2 to 1 op 5 to 2) 5
NEW HALEN [107] 12-10-13 (3*) Mr J Durkan, *led to 6th, led ag'n nxt till mstk and hdd 9th, wknd 7 out.*
.................................(16 to 1 op 10 to 1 tchd 20 to 1) 6
Dist: 7l, 1l, 6l, 15l, 8l. 6m 6.20s. a 17.20s (6 Ran).
SR: 38/1/10/ (Mrs Stewart Catherwood), D Nicholson

1327 Elton 'National Hunt' Novices' Hurdle (4-y-o and up) £1,480 2m 5f 110yds ....(2:50)

1027* NIRVANA PRINCE 4-11-0 T Wall, *hld up in last pl, wnt 4th aftr 6th, trkd ldr, led 2 out, drw clr r-in, styd on wl.*
.................................(11 to 2 op 3 to 1 tchd 9 to 2) 1
KONVEKTA CONTROL 6-11-0 J Osborne, *led til hdd 2 out, rdn, hng lft r-in, no imprsn................*(9 to 4 co-fav tchd 11 to 4) 2
1003[3] EMPEROR BUCK (Ire) 5-11-0 A Maguire, *trkd ldg pair, cl up and ev ch 3 out, blun nxt, rdn and no imprsn r-in.*
.................................(9 to 4 co-fav tchd 5 to 2 and 3 to 1) 3
MAKES ME GOOSEY (Ire) 5-11-0 L Harvey, *mid-div, outpcd aftr 6th, styd on frm 3 out, nvr nrr.* (50 to 1 op 33 to 1) 4
1078[2] MARSHALL SPARKS 6-11-0 M Foster, *trkd ldr in second pl, rdn and ev ch 4 out, wknd 3 out, tld off.*(9 to 4 co-fav op 7 to 2) 5
1169 MISTY GREY 4-10-7 (7*) S Lycett, *hld up, hdwy 6th, outpcd aftr 6th, tld off four out.....*(150 to 1 op 50 to 1) 6
ARBEE TWENTY 7-11-0 I Lawrence, *mid-div, hdwy aftr 6th, tld off...............*(40 to 1 op 20 to 1) 7
743[8] MAYINA 4-10-9 D Bridgwater, *hld up, mstk 3rd, sn rdn alng and lost tch, tld off aftr 6th.* (25 to 1 op 12 to 1) 8
Dist: 10l, 2l, 25l, 30l, 3½l, 15l. 5m 10.50s. a 13.50s (8 Ran).
(D Portman), B Preece

1328 Oldfield Handicap Chase (0-130 5-y-o and up) £2,766 2m.............(3:20)

1168 TINAS LAD [105] 10-11-8 N Williamson, *trkd ldrs, wnt second 6th, led aftr 4 out, rdn and hld on r-in.*
.................................(12 to 1 op 10 to 1 tchd 8 to 1) 1
987[4] CHAIN SHOT [109] 8-11-12 R Bellamy, *hld up, wnt 3rd 6th, chsd ldr, pckd 2 out, rdn and rallied r-in, kpt on nr finish......................*(16 to 1 op 14 to 1 tchd 20 to 1) 2
946 SAILOR'S DELIGHT [90] 9-10-0 (7*) Mr S Joynes, *hld up, hdwy 6th, chsd ldr frm 5 out, wknd aftr 3 out, btn whn jmpd rght and bumped last..........*(50 to 1) 3
1022[8] MURPHY [109] 9-11-12 J Osborne, *led, hdd aftr second, lft in ld nxt, headed after 4 out, wknd after 2 out, btn whn hmpd last, eased r-in,tld off.*
.................................(9 to 2 op 4 to 1 tchd 6 to 1) 4
322* MARKET LEADER [86] 13-10-3 L Harvey, *hld up, hdwy aftr 6th, cl up whn f 4 out.............*(10 to 1 op 5 to 1) f
987[3] STAR OF THE GLEN [111] 7-12-0 A Maguire, *hld up, f 3rd.*
.................................(5 to 4 fav tchd 6 to 5) f
1165[2] LUCKY AGAIN [91] 6-10-8 I Lawrence, *f 1st.*
.................................(100 to 1 op 33 to 1 tchd 7 to 2) f
1168 ALAN BALL [104] (bl) 7-11-7 H Davies, *led, blun and uns rdr 3rd........................*(14 to 1 op 12 to 1) ur
Dist: 1½l, 8l, 30l. 4m 5.50s. a 13.50s (8 Ran).
SR: 31/33/6/-/-/ (Geoffrey Johnson), J A C Edwards

1329 Grunwick Stakes National Hunt Flat Race (4,5,6-y-o) £1,402 2m.....(3:50)

815* CAPTAIN KHEDIVE 5-11-10 M Hourigan, *took str hold, trkd ldr, 3rd strt, rdn to ld ins fnl furlong, ridden out.*
.................................(5 to 4 on tchd 11 to 10 on) 1
815[8] KINGS CHARIOT 6-10-12 (5*) J McCarthy, *hld up, hdwy 5 fs out, 5th strt, led 2 out, hdd ins fnl furlong, not quicken nr finish............*(5 to 1 op 7 to 1 tchd 8 to 1) 2
SEBASTOPOL 4-10-9 (7*) D Hobbs, *hld up and beh, hdwy o'r 4 fs out, styd on ins fnl 2 furlongs, not rch 1st two.*
.................................(10 to 1 op 6 to 1) 3
PETER POINTER 5-10-10 (7*) P Ward, *pld hrd, led aftr one furlong, hdd 2 out, kpt on same pace.*
.................................(20 to 1 op 14 to 1) 4

NUNS CONE 5-10-12 (5") R Farrant, *trkd ldr, 7th strt,*
wknd ins fnl 2 fs.................(33 to 1 op 16 to 1)   5
MEGAMUNCH (Ire) 5-10-10 (7") N Juckes, *hld up and beh,*
steady hdwy o'r 4 fs out, kpt on ins fnl quarter-m, nvr
nrr...................................(14 to 1 op 7 to 1)   6
BIG ARTHUR (Ire) 4-11-2 W Marston, *in tch early, beh aftr*
one m, styd on o'r 3 fs out, nrst finish.
....(7 to 1 op 7 to 2)   7
COME ON CHARLIE 4-10-13 (3") D Meredith, *pld hrd, trkd*
ldr, 6th strt, wknd ins fnl 2 fs.....(20 to 1 op 14 to 1)   8
743 GAYTON RUN (Ire) 4-10-11 (5") A Procter, *led for one fur-*
long, trkd ldr, second strt, wknd 2 fs out.
....(50 to 1 op 33 to 1)   9
CHARLIE BEE 4-11-2 Mr J Durkan, *hld up, hdwy aftr 7 fs,*
wknd 4 out..........................(20 to 1 op 16 to 1)   10
1027 FOXY LASS 4-10-11 Mr J Cambidge, *trkd ldr to hfwy,*
wknd 4 fs out.......................(50 to 1 op 33 to 1)   11
LILIAN MAY GREEN 4-10-4 (7") Guy Lewis, *beh aftr 4 fs,*
nvr rchd ldrs.......................(50 to 1 op 33 to 1)   12
OLD TICKLERTON 4-10-11 (5") D Walsh, *hld up, chsd ldr*
aftr 6 fs, wknd 4 out......................(33 to 1)   13
ALTHREY POET 5-10-10 (7") P McLoughlin, *al beh, tld off*
half way............................(50 to 1 op 33 to 1)   14
Dist: Nk, 10l, 10l, nk, 6l, ½l, ½l, 5l, 6l, ½l. 3m 43.30s. (14 Ran).

(Khedive Partnership), P J Hobbs

TIPPERARY (IRE) (soft)
Thursday November 18th

1330 November Maiden Hurdle (Div 1) (5-y-o and up) £2,760 2m........(12:15)

1174³ BEGLAWELLA 6-11-4 (5") T P Treacy, ...(4 to 1)   1
CHANCE COFFEY 8-10-13 (7") Mr W T O'Donnell, (10 to 1)   2
877⁵ LISCAHILL HIGHWAY 6-11-3 (3") D P Murphy, ..(16 to 1)   3
990⁸ MINSTREL FIRE (Ire) 5-11-6 J Magee, ...(16 to 1)   4
1018³ TOT EM UP 6-11-9 Mr M Phillips, ...(10 to 1)   5
990 OLD ABBEY (Ire) 5-11-3 (3") T Townend, ...(50 to 1)   6
466⁸ HIGHLAND MINSTREL 6-11-1 L P Cusack, ...(20 to 1)   7
BOB NELSON 6-11-6 M Duffy, ...(33 to 1)   8
945² ATOURS (USA) 5-12-0 T J Taaffe, ...(6 to 4 on)   9
1018⁵ CALLERBANN 6-11-1 K F O'Brien, ...(10 to 1)   10
QUEEN OF THE ROCK 5-11-1 C F Swan, ...(12 to 1)   11
939⁵ SAMANTHA'S FLUTTER 7-12-0 T Horgan, ...(10 to 1)   12
1160⁵ JIMMY GORDON 6-12-0 J Shortt, ...(16 to 1)   13
990 MOLLIE WOOTTON (Ire) 5-11-1 H Rogers, ...(33 to 1)   14
926 DUNHILL IDOL 6-11-6 Mr P J Healy, ...(50 to 1)   15
571 DELIGHTFUL CHOICE 5-11-1 A Powell, ...(50 to 1)   16
990 THE REAL GAEL 5-10-12 (3") C O'Brien, ...(50 to 1)   17
BORO DOLLAR 9-11-7 (7") Mr G F Ryan, ...(14 to 1)   pu
Dist: 1½l, 15l, 7l, 1l. 4m 5.50s. (18 Ran).

(Thomas Keane), Thomas Foley

1331 Knocklong Hurdle (4-y-o and up) £2,760 2m.................(12:45)

942³ IF YOU SAY YES (Ire) 5-10-13 K F O'Brien, ...(5 to 1)   1
925* MISTER DRUM (Ire) 4-10-10 (7") Mr J T McNamara, .. 2
209⁴ ROSE APPEAL 7-11-8 C F Swan, ...(7 to 4 fav)   3
MICK O'DWYER 6-11-4 F J Flood, ...(10 to 1)   4
856 MORNING DREAM 6-11-11 J F Titley, ...(8 to 1)   5
689 ABBEY EMERALD 7-10-8 (5") T P Treacy, ...(33 to 1)   6
1175³ MISS LIME 6-10-12 (5") P A Roche, ...(2 to 1)   f
Dist: 1½l, 3½l, 9l, ½l. 4m 6.60s. (7 Ran).

(J Doran), W P Mullins

1332 November Maiden Hurdle (Div 2) (5-y-o and up) £2,760 2m........(1:15)

708⁶ IDIOTS VENTURE 6-12-0 B Sheridan, ...(9 to 2)   1
1174² SEA GALE (Ire) 5-11-1 C F Swan, ...(5 to 4 fav)   2
853⁴ LEGAL ADVISER 6-11-7 (7") C Eyre, ...(4 to 1)   3
636⁶ GRAND TOUR (NZ) 5-12-0 L P Cusack, ...(7 to 1)   4
1074² LUMINOUS LIGHT 6-11-1 Mr M Phillips, ...(7 to 1)   5
1174 CORRIB HAVEN (Ire) 5-10-13 (7") J P Broderick, ..(33 to 1)   6
534⁹ ZORIA (Ire) 5-11-1 P Carberry, ...(10 to 1)   7
993 PAT'S VALENTINE (Ire) 5-11-1 F Woods, ...(33 to 1)   8
1174 FESTIVAL LIGHT (Ire) 5-11-6 A J O'Brien, ...(50 to 1)   9
993 LISNABOY PRINCE 5-11-3 (3") C O'Brien, ...(33 to 1)   10
JUST A BROWNIE (Ire) 5-11-1 T Horgan, ...(20 to 1)   11
857³ BALLINGOWAN STAR 6-10-8 (7") Mr S O'Donnell, (14 to 1)   12
HIGHWAY LASS 7-11-1 S H O'Donovan, ...(25 to 1)   13
926 CHERISHED PRINCESS (Ire) 5-10-10 (5") P A Roche,
....(50 to 1)   14
NOBLE KNIGHT (Ire) 5-11-6 W T Slattery Jnr, ...(33 to 1)   15
ERADA (Ire) 5-11-1 H Rogers, ...(25 to 1)   16
BROTHER BRANSTON (Ire) 5-11-6 C O'Dwyer, ..(33 to 1)   pu
Dist: 4l, 3½l, 2½l, 8l. 4m 2.70s. (17 Ran).

(Blackwater Racing Syndicate), A P O'Brien

1333 Clonoulty Maiden Hurdle (4-y-o) £2,760 2m................(1:45)

907* STRONG SERENADE (Ire) 10-13 (5") T P Treacy, ...(6 to 1)   1
1036⁵ KEEPHERGOING (Ire) 10-6 (7") K F O'Brien, ...(12 to 1)   2
HEMISPHERE (Ire) 11-4 C F Swan, ...(4 to 1)   3

1036⁹ CHANCERY QUEEN (Ire) 11-4 T Horgan, ...(7 to 2 fav)   4
902³ CASTLE CELEBRITY (Ire) 10-6 (7") J P Broderick, (10 to 1)   5
1075³ TURALITY (Ire) 11-4 S H O'Donovan, ...(14 to 1)   6
990⁶ BOHEMIAN CASTLE (Ire) 11-4 F Woods, ...(20 to 1)   7
1113⁶ TAITS CLOCK (Ire) 11-4 P Carberry, ...(12 to 1)   8
1036 ALBERTA ROSE (Ire) 11-4 M Duffy, ...(12 to 1)   9
1036² VON CARTY (Ire) 11-4 J F Titley, ...(4 to 1)   10
ROBERTOLOMY (USA) 11-9 P L Malone, ...(10 to 1)   11
1180³ LEISURE CENTRE (Ire) 10-8² (7") Mr R P Cody, ..(12 to 1)   12
1230 MARYVILLE LADY (Ire) 10-13 B Sheridan, ...(20 to 1)   13
925 LEADING TIME (Fr) 11-4 (5") M G Cleary, ...(20 to 1)   14
1039⁴ DUN OENGUS (Ire) 10-13 J Magee, ...(12 to 1)   15
1020 ELLENOR LAD (Ire) 10-13 (5") T P Rudd, ...(50 to 1)   16
SAHEL SAND (Ire) 10-13 J A White, ...(20 to 1)   17
ORDOG MOR (Ire) 11-1 (3") C O'Brien, ...(20 to 1)   18
469 AMOROUS HUG (Ire) 10-8 (7") Mr J Gleeson, ...(25 to 1)   19
LAURETTA BLUE (Ire) 10-13 H Rogers, ...(20 to 1)   20
Dist: Nk, hd, ¾l, 6l. 4m 14.00s. (20 Ran).

(J R Kidd), Thomas Foley

1334 WinElectric Novice Chase (5-y-o and up) £6,900 2m...........(2:15)

1233 VISIBLE DIFFERENCE 7-11-8 C F Swan, ...(5 to 4 fav)   1
1073³ COMMANCHE NELL (Ire) 5-10-12 T Horgan, ...(2 to 1)   2
ALL THE ACES 6-11-2 T J Taaffe, ...(6 to 1)   3
1177⁷ THE WEST'S ASLEEP 8-10-13 (3") C O'Brien, ..(20 to 1)   4
989³ NOBODYS FLAME (Ire) 10-13 J Magee, ...(8 to 1)   5
1177 MONEY MADE 6-10-9 (7") Mr W J Gleeson, ...(66 to 1)   6
1233⁷ HAPPY PERCY 8-11-2 C O'Dwyer, ...(8 to 1)   f
Dist: 3½l, 2½l, 10l, 25l. 4m 2.00s. (7 Ran).

(Patrick Heffernan), Patrick Heffernan

1335 Tipperary Handicap Hurdle (4-y-o and up) £2,760 2½m.............(2:45)

1234³ TUG OF PEACE [-] 6-10-10 C F Swan, ...(4 to 1 co-fav)   1
BORO EIGHT [-] 7-12-0 Mr T Mullins, ...(4 to 1 co-fav)   2
1176 BALLYHYLAND (Ire) [-] 4-9-10 S H O'Donovan, ..(8 to 1)   3
880³ SIMPLY SWIFT [-] 6-10-12 (5") T P Treacy, ...(13 to 2)   4
1178³ CHELSEA NATIVE [-] 6-9-13 (5") Susan A Finn, (4 to 1 co-
                                                        fav)   5
926* GOOLDS GOLD [-] 7-9-3¹ (5") P A Roche, ...(10 to 1)   6
798 SILENTBROOK [-] 8-9-0 (7") A O'Shea, ...(50 to 1)   7
1157⁴ ONABUNDA [-] 7-9-0 (7") F Byrne, ...(16 to 1)   8
DEEP HERITAGE [-] 7-10-11 (5") T P Rudd, ...(10 to 1)   9
939⁸ BALLYMOE BOY (Ire) [-] 5-9-0 (7") K P Gaule, ..(33 to 1)   10
1178⁷ MYSTIC GALE (Ire) [-] 5-9-7 P McWilliams, ...(14 to 1)   11
1038⁴ TARA'S TRIBE [-] 6-9-7 M Duffy, ...(16 to 1)   12
ARRIGLE PRINCE [-] (bl) 8-9-0 (7") H Rogers, ...(16 to 1)   13
SHANNON KNOCK [-] 8-9-5 (3") C O'Brien, ...(14 to 1)   14
1178 DHARKOUM [-] 6-9-11 J A White, ...(33 to 1)   15
WHISTLING MICK [-] 8-9-7 T Horgan, ...(20 to 1)   16
Dist: 1½l, sht-hd, 8l, 1½l. 5m 5.30s. (16 Ran).

(W J Austin), W J Austin

1336 J.P. McManus Chase (5-y-o and up) £6,900 2m..................(3:15)

FORCE SEVEN 6-11-3 T Horgan, ...(Evens fav)   1
992⁶ LASATA 8-11-5 (3") C O'Brien, ...(3 to 1)   2
940⁶ BLITZKREIG 10-10-12 C F Swan, ...(5 to 2)   3
991 ANOTHER RUSTLE 10-10-12 W T Slattery Jnr, ..(33 to 1)   4
GARAMYCIN 11-11-12 B Sheridan, ...(4 to 1)   5
Dist: 2½l, 2l, 2l, 3l. 4m 1.00s. (5 Ran).

(Mrs C A Moore), P Mullins

1337 Oola INH Flat Race (4-y-o) £2,760 2m ....(3:45)

BELLS LIFE (Ire) 11-9 Mr J E Kiely, ...(7 to 1)   1
BELGARRO (Ire) 11-2 (7") Mr E Norris, ...(Evens fav)   2
1077² MARYJO (Ire) 10-11 (7") Mr P English, ...(12 to 1)   3
WEJEM (Ire) 11-9 Mr S R Murphy, ...(20 to 1)   4
1180⁷ OZEYCAZEY (Ire) 11-4 (5") Mr J A Nash, ...(14 to 1)   5
1180 SHANNON AMBER (Ire) 10-11 (7") Mr B Moran, ..(20 to 1)   6
530³ NINE O THREE (Ire) 11-2 (7") Mr R P Burns, ...(10 to 1)   7
ALLARACKET (Ire) 10-11 (7") Mr D Fogarty, ...(20 to 1)   8
START SINGING (Ire) 11-1 (3") Mrs M Mullins, ...(8 to 1)   9
1180⁵ CREATIVE BLAZE (Ire) 10-11 (7") Mr D A Harney, ..(8 to 1)   10
939 CALL ME HENRY 11-2 (7") Mr J T McNamara, ...(25 to 1)   11
ICANTELYA (Ire) 11-9 Mr T Mullins, ...(25 to 1)   12
RALLYING BEACH (Ire) 10-11 (7") Mr W J Gleeson, (33 to 1)   13
1180 WISE STATEMENT (Ire) 11-9 Mr A P O'Brien, ...(16 to 1)   14
SPANKERS HILL (Ire) 11-9 Mr P Fenton, ...(7 to 1)   15
DIGACRE (Ire) 11-2 (7") Mr G Caplis, ...(25 to 1)   16
MAURA MILISH (Ire) 10-13 (5") Mr H F Cleary, ...(25 to 1)   17
LACKABEG (Ire) 11-1 (3") Mr D Marnane, ...(25 to 1)   18
9⁶ LADY FONTAINE (Ire) 11-4 Mr A J Martin, ...(20 to 1)   19
Dist: Hd, hd, sht-hd, 15l. 4m 1.50s. (19 Ran).

(D L O'Byrne), David A Kiely

WINCANTON (good to firm)
Thursday November 18th
Going Correction: PLUS 0.05 sec. per fur. (races 1,4,5), PLUS 0.25 (2,3,6)

1338 Colin Chaloner Memorial Claiming Hurdle (3-y-o) £1,917 2m.......(1:00)

1049* CONVOY (bl) 11-6 R Dunwoody, *al hndy gng wl, led betw last 2, awkward last, pushed out.*
...................(5 to 4 on op 5 to 4 on tchd 5 to 4) 1
851 MARAT (USA) (v) 10-13 G McCourt, *hld up in tch, rdn appr 2 out, kpt on r-in.*........(8 to 1 op 5 to 1 tchd 9 to 1) 2
1125⁶ IS SHE QUICK 10-6 N Dawe, *prmnt, jmpd slwly 3rd, rdn and ev ch 2 out, sn one pace.*...... (4 to 1 tchd 3 to 1) 3
1049⁶ MUSICAL PHONE 10-9 M A FitzGerald, *led till rdn and hdd betw last 2, wknd.*
...................(10 to 1 op 5 to 1 tchd 11 to 1) 4
793* MY SISTER LUCY 10-4 (7") G McGrath, *hld up in tch, rdn and effrt appr 2 out, sn wknd.*
.... (7 to 1 op 7 to 2 tchd 15 to 2) 5
DIXIE DIAMOND 10-5¹ G Upton, *pld hrd, prmnt till wknd quickly aftr 3 out, tld off.*..........(20 to 1 op 8 to 1) 6
WEST END 10-12 W Irvine, *sn beh, tld off frm 3rd, pld up bef 2 out.*........................(66 to 1 op 33 to 1) pu
Dist: 2½l, 6l, 1l, 10l, dist. 3m 50.00s. a 13.00s (7 Ran).
(The Lavender Cottage Partnership), C J Mann

1339 Ave SpA Complimenti Novices' Chase (5-y-o and up) £3,302 2m 5f. .... (1:30)

948³ DEXTRA DOVE 6-11-1 S Earle, *made all, jnd whn lft clr 3 out, fnshd tired...* (2 to 1 fav op 5 to 2 tchd 11 to 4) 1
1189 STEEPLE JACK 6-11-1 B Powell, *in tch, slightly hmpd 8th, wknd 11th, blun 13th, lft second 3 out, one pace.*
...................(12 to 1 op 10 to 1) 2
GREY ADMIRAL (v) 8-11-1 Mr S Stickland, *in tch, hmpd 8th, mstk nxt, sn struggling, lft remote 3rd 3 out, tld off.*
.... (66 to 1 op 50 to 1) 3
TYRONE BRIDGE 7-11-1 R Dunwoody, *trkd ldrs, mstk 5th, cl 3rd whn f 8th.*..........(9 to 4 op 6 to 4 tchd 5 to 2) f
1025⁷ CANOSCAN 8-11-1 E Murphy, *trkd ldr, reminder aftr 4 out, upsides whn f nxt.*
...................(100 to 30 op 4 to 1 tchd 3 to 1) f
1189 ERIC'S TRAIN 7-11-1 J Railton, *hld up and beh, mstk 7th, lost tch frm tenth, f 13th, broke leg, destroyed.*
.... (7 to 1 op 6 to 1 tchd 15 to 2) f
Dist: 6l, dist. 5m 20.00s. a 46.00s (6 Ran).
(Dextra Lighting Systems), R H Alner

1340 Hamilton Litestat Anniversary Handicap Chase (0-140 5-y-o and up) £5,085 3m 1f 110yds.................. (2:00)

SOLIDASAROCK [122] 11-11-6 G McCourt, *al hndy, blun 7th, led 15th, hdd last, hrd rdn and rallied gmely to ld nr finish.*...................(7 to 1 op 5 to 1) 1
1050* CLEVER SHEPHERD [114] 8-10-12 Peter Hobbs, *hld up tracking ldrs, effrt 4 out and sn ev ch, led last, hrd rdn and hdd nr finish.*......(11 to 4 op 5 to 2 tchd 3 to 1) 2
1088³ WELKNOWN CHARACTER [116] 11-11-0 M A FitzGerald, *hld led 9th till hdd 15th, sn pushed alng, styd on one pace frm 3 out....* (9 to 4 tchd 5 to 2 and 11 to 4) 3
LE PICCOLAGE [129] 9-11-13 R Dunwoody, *led till hdd 9th, styd hndy till lost pl frm 16th, sn wknd.*
...................(2 to 1 fav op 2 to 1) 4
980 EASTSHAW [125] 11-11-9 C Llewellyn, *hld up, mstk 4th, beh whn mistake 13th, no hdwy when blun and uns rdr 16th.*......(10 to 1 op 12 to 1 tchd 14 to 1 and 8 to 1) ur
Dist: Nk, 4l, 15l. 6m 31.00s. a 15.00s (5 Ran).
SR: 6/-/ (Les Randall), R Akehurst

1341 Vale Motors Great Western Novices' Hurdle (4-y-o and up) £3,571 2¾m .... (2:30)

1078³ CUNNINGHAMS FORD (Ire) 5-10-7 (7") Mr A Harvey, *led till hdd aftr 3rd, led ag'n 5th, made rst, drw clr appr last, ran on strly...*.............. (7 to 2 op 2 to 1 tchd 4 to 1) 1
1070* FRANK RICH 6-11-4 G Upton, *handily plcd, took clr order 8th, chsd wnr gng wl frm nxt, rdn and no imprsn appr last.*...................(7 to 1 op 4 to 1 tchd 8 to 1) 2
883* ANNA VALLEY 7-10-13 Richard Guest, *hld up, took clr order 8th, awkward nxt, sn btn.*
...................(9 to 2 op 7 to 2 tchd 5 to 1) 3
1023³ MONKSANDER 7-11-0 A Charlton, *chsd ldrs, niggled aftr 6th, wknd 9th.*......(12 to 1 op 10 to 1 tchd 14 to 1) 4
1067* ULURU (Ire) 5-11-4 R Dunwoody, *hld up early, lost tch frm 8th, tld off....*.....(12 to 1 op 11 to 1 tchd 16 to 1) 5
1085² KHALIDI (Ire) 4-11-4 P Holley, *took keen hold, led aftr 3rd till hdd 5th, mstk 7th, wknd nxt, beh whn pld up bef 3 out.*...................(4 to 1 op 5 to 2 tchd 9 to 2) pu
Dist: 15l, 25l, 6l, 25l. 5m 13.90s. a 7.90s (6 Ran).
SR: 18/7/-/ (Edward Harvey), O Sherwood

1342 Frascio Silver Handicap Hurdle (0-130 4-y-o and up) £3,392 2m....... (3:00)

SAND-DOLLAR [106] 10-11-10 S McNeill, *hld up in tch, rdn appr 2 out, styd on to ld r-in, all out.*
.... (100 to 30 op 9 to 2 tchd 11 to 2) 1

---

887 ALWAYS REMEMBER [95] 6-10-13 Peter Hobbs, *led, mstk 6th, rdn appr nxt, hdd r-in, rallied nr finish.*
...................(7 to 2 op 5 to 2 tchd 4 to 1) 2
958² WOLVER GOLD [92] 6-10-10 C Maude, *trkd ldrs, chlgd 2 out, no extr last...........*(7 to 2 op 3 to 1 tchd 4 to 1) 3
SUNSET AGAIN [97] 8-11-1 Richard Guest, *sn beh, lost tch frm 4th, tld off...........*(50 to 1 op 20 to 1) 4
977³ TOP WAVE [105] 5-11-9 M A FitzGerald, *hld up in tch, cl 4th whn f 2 out.........*(10 to 1 op 7 to 1 tchd 11 to 1) f
1087³ SMILING CHIEF (Ire) [91] 5-10-9 R Dunwoody, *wth ldr, rdn aftr 6th, 4th and wkng whn f last.*
...................(2 to 1 fav op 5 to 2 tchd 11 to 4) f
Dist: ¾l, 3½l, dist. 3m 43.40s. a 6.40s (6 Ran).
SR: 40/28/21/ (R P Fry), J A B Old

1343 Nightingale Handicap Chase (0125 5-y-o and up) £3,548 2m 5f...... (3:30)

1171⁴ THATCHER ROCK (NZ) [110] 8-11-2 C Maude, *hld up, mstk 3rd, hdwy 12th, hit 4 out, lft in ld nxt, styd on wl.*
...................(7 to 2 op 9 to 4 tchd 4 to 1) 1
1089² SMARTIE EXPRESS [119] 11-11-11 M A FitzGerald, *led to second, styd hndy, led 9th, hdd appr 3 out, lft second aftr nxt, kpt on....*(2 to 1 fav op 5 to 2 tchd 11 to 4) 2
978³ WELL BRIEFED [94] 6-10-0 B Powell, *al hndy, effrt to go second 4 out, ev ch whn hmpd 3 out, not reco'r.*
...................(20 to 1 op 12 to 1) 3
1050³ COOLE DODGER [113] 8-11-5 R Dunwoody, *al hndy, led 6th till hdd 9th, rdn and wknd 4 out.*
...................(5 to 4 op 5 to 2 tchd 3 to 1) 4
1246³ STEPFASTER [110] 8-10-13 (3") A Thornton, *last and niggled alng 8th, no hdwy frm 12th...*(20 to 1 op 12 to 1) 5
1171 GLEN CHERRY [108] (bl) 7-11-0 C Llewellyn, *led second, hit 5th, hdd nxt, niggled alng 11th, sn no imprsn.*
...................(16 to 1 op 12 to 1 tchd 20 to 1) 6
GREENHILL RAFFLES [111] 7-11-3 Peter Hobbs, *al cl up, led and f 3 out.*..........(4 to 1 op 7 to 2 tchd 9 to 2) f
Dist: 10l, 3l, ¾l, 20l, 12l. 5m 15.90s. a 9.90s (7 Ran).
SR: 42/41/13/31/8/-/-/ (Miss Gina Hunter), P F Nicholls

ASCOT (good)
Friday November 19th
Going Correction: PLUS 0.23 sec. per fur.

1344 Bingley Novices' Hurdle (4-y-o and up) £2,918 2½m................ (1:00)

983² TOP SPIN 4-11-4 A Maguire, *cl up, niggled alng 6th, led nxt, pld clr frm 2 out, unchlgd...............*(5 to 2 jt-fav op 7 to 2 tchd 9 to 4) 1
1110² GOLDEN SPINNER 6-11-0 R Dunwoody, *trkd ldr, slpd bend appr 7th, reco'red to go second nxt, rdn and no imprsn on wnr approaching 2 out.*
...................(100 to 30 op 5 to 2 tchd 7 to 2) 2
1010⁵ ROSS GRAHAM 5-11-0 P Holley, *hld up, cld aftr 6th, sn ev ch, wknd 2 out....*(33 to 1 op 20 to 1 tchd 50 to 1) 3
889 KING UBAD (USA) 4-11-4 Richard Guest, *led to 7th, sn wknd, tld off.........*(33 to 1 op 14 to 1 tchd 50 to 1) 4
TIME ENOUGH (Ire) 4-11-0 R Supple, *wtd wth, pushed alng aftr 6th, sn wknd, tld off.*
...................(12 to 1 op 10 to 1 tchd 14 to 1) 5
Dist: 20l, 30l, dist, 30l. 4m 55.00s. a 14.00s (5 Ran).
(J M Long), J R Jenkins

1345 Punch Bowl Amateur Riders' Handicap Chase (5-y-o and up) £4,290 3m 110yds..................... (1:35)

1083⁵ STAY ON TRACKS [120] 11-10-8⁶ (7") Mr N King, *led to 16th, led 3 out, styd on wl...*(5 to 1 op 4 to 1 tchd 11 to 2) 1
865² TRI FOLENE (Fr) [122] (bl) 7-10-11 Mr Anthony Martin, *hld up last, rdn 17th, ran on appr 2 out, kpt on one pace.*
..(6 to 5 fav op 11 to 10 tchd 5 to 4 and 11 to 10 on) 2
KEEP TALKING [135] 8-11-10 Mr M Armytage, *wth ldr, led 16th till jmpd slwly and hdd 3 out, sn rdn alng, wknd nxt, virtually pld up r-in.........*(11 to 8 op 5 to 4 on) 3
Dist: 7l, dist. 6m 19.50s. a 16.00s (3 Ran).
(R Oliver Smith), Mrs D Haine

1346 Charles Davis Novices' Handicap Chase (5-y-o and up) £7,667 3m 110yds..................... (2:10)

SPIKEY (NZ) [86] 7-11-0 A Maguire, *handily plcd, led 8th, jnd appr 2 out, styd on wl.*
...................(11 to 2 op 9 to 2 tchd 6 to 1) 1
1080* FIVELEIGH FIRST (Ire) [91] 5-11-5 R Supple, *hld up, hdwy 15th, chlgd appr 2 out, ev ch whn hit last, ran on.*
...................(11 to 2 op 9 to 2 tchd 6 to 1) 2
978⁴ FESTIVAL DREAMS [97] 8-11-11 P Holley, *keen hold, al hndy, lft second 13th, rdn appr 2 out, sn no extr.*
...................(12 to 1 op 6 to 1 tchd 14 to 1) 3
1194⁴ THEO'S FELLA [90] 9-11-4 S Hodgson, *trkd ldrs, lost pl 12th, rdn 14th, shrtlvd effrt aftr nxt, wknd.*
...................(10 to 1 op 10 to 1 tchd 25 to 1) 4

1164³ MUNKA [93] 7-11-7 M Hourigan, *not fluent, hld up till hdwy 7th, lost pl 11th, ran on 15th, wkng whn mstk 3 out*..................(100 to 30 op 3 to 1 tchd 7 to 2) 5
1054* EARTH SUMMIT [96] 5-11-10 C Llewellyn, *ran in snatches, trkd ldrs till lost pl 7th, niggled alng tenth, rnwd effrt nxt, wknd 16th*.....(11 to 4 fav op 9 to 4 tchd 3 to 1) 6
917⁴ DEEPENDABLE [91] 6-11-5 M A FitzGerald, *led, jmpd slwly 5th, sn hdd, styd hndy, second and ev ch whn mstk and uns rdr 13th*.......(6 to 1 op 5 to 1 tchd 13 to 2) ur
Dist: ¾l, 15l, 12l, 2l, ½l. 6m 20.30s. a 16.80s (7 Ran).

(S Powell), J R Jenkins

1347 Coopers & Lybrand Ascot Hurdle Grade 2 (4-y-o and up) £13,329 2½m
.............................(2:40)

KING CREDO 8-11-0 A Maguire, *patiently rdn, mstk 4th, hdwy aftr 7th, led appr 2 out, pushed out, cmftbly*.
.......................(5 to 2 fav op 7 to 4 tchd 11 to 4) 1
1030² SWEET DUKE (Fr) 6-11-5 C Llewellyn, *led, mstk 4th, sn hdd, styd hndy, outpcd appr 3 out, rallied nxt, kpt on one pace*........................(4 to 1 tchd 9 to 2) 2
1030⁴ FLAKEY DOVE 7-11-0 J Osborne, *in tch, lost pl appr 3 out, ran on 2 out, sn not quicken*.
.......................(4 to 1 op 5 to 2 tchd 11 to 2) 3
GRANVILLE AGAIN 7-11-10 R Dunwoody, *hld up, hdwy aftr 7th, ev ch appr 2 out, sn wknd*.
.......................(3 to 1 op 7 to 4 tchd 100 to 30) 4
1106 HIGH BARON 6-11-0 M Hourigan, *nvr far away, led 4th, rdn and hdd appr 2 out, no extr*.
.......................(16 to 1 op 25 to 1 tchd 33 to 1) 5
1163* CASTLE COURAGEOUS 6-11-0 E Murphy, *trkd ldrs, pushed alng appr 3 out, sn lost pl, wknd*.
.......................(6 to 1 op 8 to 1 tchd 11 to 2) 6
Dist: 3½l, nk, 25l, 15l, 7l. 4m 46.30s. a 5.30s (6 Ran).
SR: 79/80/74/59/34/27/ (G Gornall), S Woodman

1348 Hurst Park Novices' Chase Grade 2 (5-y-o and up) £9,195 2m. . . (3:10)

1228* BAYDON STAR 6-11-7 A Maguire, *trkd ldrs, puhed alng briefly 3 out, led appr nxt, sn clr, easily*.
.............(13 to 8 on op 9 to 4 on tchd 6 to 4 on) 1
612² STRONG VIEWS 6-11-0 M A FitzGerald, *hld up, mstk 5th, hdwy 8th, chsd wnr appr 2 out, sn no imprsn*.
.......................(11 to 1 op 10 to 1 tchd 12 to 1) 2
1245* EASY BUCK 6-11-0 C Maude, *hld up in tch, rdn appr 3 out, styd on frm last, nvr able to chal*.
.......................(5 to 1 op 4 to 1 tchd 11 to 2) 3
1228² GHIA GNEUIAGH 7-11-0 C Llewellyn, *wth ldr, led 7th to 3 out, sn wknd, btn whn blun last*.
.......................(5 to 1 op 9 to 2 tchd 11 to 2) 4
KIBREET 6-11-0 S Earle, *made most to 7th, led 3 out, sn hdd, wknd*.......................(33 to 1 tchd 50 to 1) 5
1128³ KEEP SHARP 7-11-4 Richard Guest, *handily plcd, mstk 4th, wknd 7th, beh whn pld up bef 3 out*.
.......................(33 to 1 op 25 to 1 tchd 50 to 1) pu
Dist: 10l, 2½l, 12l, 7l. 3m 55.10s. a 7.60s (6 Ran).
SR: 54/37/34/22/15/-/ (Mrs Shirley Robins), D Nicholson

1349 Lion Gate Handicap Hurdle (4-y-o and up) £4,879 3m. . . . .(3:40)

1106 JOPANINI [136] 8-12-0 M A FitzGerald, *made all, drw clr appr 2 out, rdn out*..(12 to 1 op 10 to 1 tchd 14 to 1) 1
762³ PIPERS COPSE [131] 11-11-9 G Bradley, *hld up, niggled alng appr 8th, ran on frm 3 out, not quicken betw last 2*.......................(5 to 1 op 9 to 2) 2
1120² BAS DE LAINE (Fr) [133] 7-11-6 (5*) J McCarthy, *nvr far away, ev ch 3 out, sn rdn alng, styd on one pace*.
.......................(100 to 30 op 11 to 4 tchd 7 to 2) 3
979³ CAIRNCASTLE [114] 8-10-6 N Mann, *hld up in tch, rdn appr 3 out, not quicken*. (7 to 2 op 4 to 1 tchd 9 to 2) 4
882⁴ SENDAI [129] 7-11-7 D Murphy, *al hndy, ev ch gng wl 3 out, outpcd appr nxt*..(13 to 2 op 5 to 1 tchd 7 to 1) 5
1190⁷ TROJAN ENVOY [108] 5-10-0 M W Henderson, *mstks second and 3rd, sn last, nvr a dngr*.
.......................(100 to 1 tchd 150 to 1) 6
1274* FAR TOO LOUD [108] 6-10-0 (4ex) B Clifford, *trkd ldr early, lost pl 6th, wknd 3 out, tld off*.
.......................(3 to 1 fav op 5 to 2 tchd 100 to 30) 7
Dist: 4l, sht-hd, 6l, 1½l, 20l, 25l. 5m 50.00s. a 17.00s (7 Ran).
(J B A (Consultants) Ltd), N J Henderson

LEICESTER (good to soft (races 1,4,5,6), good (2,3))
Friday November 19th
Going Correction: PLUS 0.57 sec. per fur.

1350 Beginners' Juvenile Novices' Hurdle (3-y-o) £1,764 2m. . . . . (12:45)

406⁷ PYRAMIS PRINCE (Ire) 10-12 N Williamson, *made all, ran on gmely und pres frm 2 out*........(5 to 1 op 4 to 1) 1

851³ O SO NEET 10-12 B Powell, *nvr far away, wnt second appr 3 out, chlgd nxt, mstk last, rallied und pres*.
.......................(15 to 8 fav op 7 to 4 tchd 2 to 1) 2
1021⁵ ALYVAIR 10-7 J Ryan, *hld up, hdwy frm 4th, kpt on one pace frm 3 out, no ch wth 1st 2*.
.......................(11 to 2 op 9 to 2 tchd 7 to 1) 3
ELECTROLITE 10-12 M Richards, *trkd wnr till wknd sn aftr 4 out, tld off*...................(5 to 1 op 4 to 1) 4
1125⁴ MR BEAN 10-12 J Duggan, *hld up in tch, hdwy 5th, wknd appr 3 out, tld off*....(5 to 1 op 7 to 2) 5
448⁴ THE SECRET SEVEN 10-12 (3*) R Davis, *in rear frm hfwy, no ch from 4 out, tld off*..........(12 to 1 op 10 to 1) 6
BOLD STAR 10-9 (3*) S Wynne, *hld up in rear, losing tch whn blun and uns rdr 4 out*.................(25 to 1) ur
PRUSSILUSKAN 10-7 J McLaughlin, *mstks, beginning to tail off whn pld up 4 out*.......................(33 to 1) pu
Dist: Hd, dist, 20l, 8l, 1½l. 3m 58.90s. a 15.90s (8 Ran).
SR: 16/16/-/-/-/ (John Kelsey-Fry), Miss H C Knight

1351 John O'Gaunt Novices' Chase (5-y-o and up) £2,528 3m. . . . .(1:15)

1080 FARDROSS 7-11-6 N Williamson, *hld up, not al fluent, hdwy to go second 5 out, hit nxt, led 3 out, drw clr appr last, eased nr finish*.................(Evens fav op 6 to 4) 1
1107³ EBONY GALE 7-11-0 B Powell, *trkd ldr, led 13th, hdd 3 out, sn rdn, ev ch till wknd appr last*.
.......................(9 to 4 op 7 to 4 tchd 5 to 2) 2
WOODLANDS BOY (Ire) 5-10-12 G McCourt, *hld up, hdwy tenth, rdn and wknd aftr 4 out, tld off*.
.......................(7 to 1 op 4 to 1) 3
411 NO WORD 6-11-0 W McFarland, *led to 13th, wknd appr 4 out, tld off*.........(8 to 1 op 9 to 2 tchd 9 to 1) 4
1081⁸ MR GEE (bl) 8-11-0 S McNeill, *chsd ldrs till blun badly 11th, sn btn, tld off*.......................(33 to 1) 5
GUTE NACHT 10-10-9 (5*) S Lyons, *sn struggling in rear, tld off 8th, pld up bef 4 out*.......................(33 to 1) pu
Dist: 1½l, dist, 10l, 20l. 6m 16.80s. a 24.80s (6 Ran).
(I M S Racing), K C Bailey

1352 Silver Bell Handicap Chase (0-120 5-y-o and up) £2,703 2½m 110yds. . . (1:45)

ZAMIL (USA) [106] 8-11-5 N Williamson, *trkd ldr 5th, hit 7th, outpcd 4 out, hrd rdn appr last, drvn out to ld r-in*.
.......................(7 to 1 op 7 to 2) 1
917³ SPIRIT OF KIBRIS [93] 8-10-6 B Powell, *led, clr 4 out, tired appr last, hdd r-in, rallied and one pace*.
.......................(2 to 1 op 9 to 4 tchd 15 to 8) 2
1069* CORRARDER [111] 9-11-10 Mr J Smyth-Osbourne, *hld up in rear, hdwy appr 6th, hit nxt, wnt second 11th, ev ch last, no extr r-in, eased*.
.......................(11 to 10 on op 5 to 4 on tchd Evens) 3
1222⁶ CLONROCHE DRILLER [98] 8-10-4 (7*) Mr D Parker, *trkd ldr to 5th, last frm nxt, lost tch 5 out*....(8 to 1 op 6 to 1) 4
Dist: 6l, 8l, 15l. 5m 22.10s. a 19.10s (4 Ran).
SR: 17/3/15/-/ (P Sweeting), K R Burke

1353 Barkby Novices' Claiming Hurdle (4-y-o and up) £1,841 2m. . . . . (2:15)

ARMASHOCKER 5-10-13 V Smith, *hld up in rear, gd hdwy 4 out, quickened appr last, led sn aftr, wnt clr*.
.......................(4 to 1 co-fav tchd 5 to 1) 1
1040⁴ PRIVATE JET (Ire) 4-10-7 M Richards, *mid-div, hdwy to ld 5th, hit 3 out, rdn and hdd sn aftr last, one pace*.
.......................(10 to 1 op 12 to 1) 2
1070⁴ NORTHERN TRIAL (USA) 5-11-3 (5*) T Jenks, *hld up in mid-div, hdwy 5th, ev ch 2 out till wknd r-in*.
.......................(4 to 1 co-fav op 2 to 1) 3
959² RUTH'S GAMBLE 5-10-12 (3*) R Davis, *al prmnt, ev ch 2 out, rdn and wknd appr last*.
.......................(4 to 1 co-fav op 3 to 1) 4
BORRETO 9-10-3 (7*) Mr E James, *chsd ldrs till wknd appr 2 out*......................(16 to 1 op 12 to 1) 5
1068 PRIORY PIPER 4-10-13 (3*) A Thornton, *chsd ldr to 5th, rdn and wknd appr 3 out*....(40 to 1 op 33 to 1) 6
1079 ROLY WALLACE (v) 4-10-5 (5*) T Eley, *chsd ldrs till wknd appr last*.......................(50 to 1) 7
1053⁸ NORMAN WARRIOR 4-11-2 H Davies, *mid-div whn jmpd slwly 3rd, wknd 4 out*...................(14 to 1) 8
1173² NONCOMMITAL 6-10-10 N Williamson, *hld up in rear, no hdwy frm 5th*.........(4 to 1 co-fav op 3 to 1) 9
898⁹ ROCKY BAY 4-10-4 (7*) Mr J L Llewellyn, *prmnt, wkng whn blun 3 out*...................(5 to 1 op 7 to 2) 10
LIZZIE DRIPPIN (Can) 4-10-5 W McFarland, *mstks in rear, tld off aftr hit 4th and ffith*..................(33 to 1) 11
1042⁴ GREAT HAND (bl) 7-10-2 (5*) C Burnett-Wells, *in tch to 5th, beh whn hit 3 out, virtually pld up r-in, tld off*.
.......................(25 to 1 op 20 to 1) 12
1193 ALWAYS ALLIED (Ire) (v) 5-10-7 D Skyrme, *led to 5th, wknd rpdly, tld off whn pld up 4 out*.(20 to 1 op 25 to 1) pu
Dist: 3½l, 7l, 4l, 8l, 5l, 5l, 5l, 10l, 2½l, dist. 4m 2.90s. a 19.90s (13 Ran).
(Shock Racing), Bob Jones

1354 Knighton Novices' Hurdle (4-y-o and up) £2,072 2m. . . . .(2:45)

JAZILAH (Fr) 5-10-12 G McCourt, *hld up, al gng wl, hdwy to track ldrs 5th, led 2 out, sn clr, very easily.*
..........................(Evens fav op 2 to 1 on)   1
TAKE THE BUCKSKIN 6-10-12 S Smith Eccles, *trkd ldrs, rcd wide, wnt second 5th, rdn appr 2 out, wknt outpcd.*
....................................(5 to 2 op 7 to 2 tchd 4 to 1)   2
922⁶ TIGER SHOOT (bl) 6-10-12 S Keightley, *led till hdd and wknd 2 out.*........................(8 to 1 op 6 to 1)   3
1108 THE CARROT MAN 5-10-12 J Railton, *hld up in rear, styd on frm 4 out, nvr dngrs.*.....................(20 to 1)   4
JIMLIL 5-10-7 L Harvey, *al abt same pl, no hdwy frm 3 out.*....................................(8 to 1 op 5 to 1)   5
JOLIZAL 5-10-7 H Davies, *al mid-div, no hdwy frm 3 out.*
....(33 to 1)   6
KHAKI LIGHT 5-10-12 M Sharratt, *trkd ldr till wknd 5th.*
....(50 to 1)   7
YOUNG BALDRIC 6-10-5 (7*) D Bohan, *prmnt till wknd appr 5th.*........................(16 to 1 op 12 to 1)   8
MOON MONKEY (Ire) 5-10-12 S McNeill, *al beh, tld off.*
...................................(20 to 1 op 14 to 1)   9
BALZAON KNIGHT 4-10-12 N Williamson, *hld up, some hdwy 5th, wl btn whn f last.*.......(33 to 1 op 20 to 1)   f
864 BIG CHANCE 4-10-12 M Richards, *beh whn mstk 3rd, sn lost tch, tld off when pld up bef 3 out.*..........(50 to 1)   pu
Dist: 12l, 7l, 6l, 12l, 20l, 3l, 10l, dist. 3m 56.80s. a 13.80s (11 Ran).
SR: 37/25/18/12/-/-/   (S Aitken), R Akehurst

1355 Waltham Conditional Jockeys' Handicap Hurdle (0-120 4-y-o and up) £1,970 2m..................(3:15)

CARDINAL BIRD (USA) [82] (bl) 6-10-0 (5*) Christopher Webb, *swtchd off in rear, wl beh till hdwy 3 out, ran on to ld r-in.*........................(10 to 1 tchd 12 to 1)   1
1101² MY LINDIANNE [84] 6-10-7 A Thornton, *trkd ldrs, wnt second 5th, led 3 out, rdn and hdd r-in.*
......................(7 to 4 fav op 9 to 4 tchd 11 to 4)   2
BABY ASHLEY [86] 7-10-9 D Meredith, *led till hdd 3 out, wknd aftr nxt.*........................(8 to 1 op 7 to 1)   3
838² ALREEF [105] 7-12-0 D Meade, *pressed ldr to 5th, rdn and wknd 3 out.*........(11 to 4 op 2 to 1 tchd 7 to 2)   4
BARCHAM [78] 6-10-1 R Farrant, *al beh, tld off 5th, f 2 out.*..........................(11 to 2 op 3 to 1)   f
748⁵ ALL PRESENT (Ire) [85] 5-10-8 W Marston, *al beh, tld off 5th, pld up lme bef 2 out.*
......................(11 to 2 op 6 to 1 tchd 5 to 1)   pu
Dist: ½l, 15l, 5l. 4m 3.90s. a 20.90s (6 Ran).
(John Fane), S Mellor

SEDGEFIELD (good)
Friday November 19th
Going Correction: PLUS 0.70 sec. per fur. (races 1,2,-6,7), PLUS 0.55 (3,4,5)

1356 John Wade Hino Truck Novices' Selling Handicap Hurdle (3-y-o and up) £1,763 2m 1f 110yds...........(12:25)

1114⁵ FLASH OF REALM (Fr) [84] 7-12-0 A Dobbin, *trkd ldrs, hdwy to ld 3 out, rdn clr nxt, hit last, kpt on.*
......................(11 to 2 op 7 to 2 tchd 6 to 1)   1
971³ PEEDIE PEAT [69] 3-10-13 M Dwyer, *led, hdd 3 out, rdn nxt and sn one pace.*...............(3 to 1 op 2 to 1)   2
1183² FLING IN SPRING [83] 7-11-8 (5*) P Williams, *chsd ldrs, rdn appr 2 out, sn one pace.*
......................(9 to 4 fav op 5 to 2 tchd 3 to 1)   3
912⁸ WELLSY LAD (USA) [73] 6-11-3 R Garritty, *hld up, hdwy 5th, rdn 3 out, no imprsn.*.......(10 to 1 op 9 to 1)   4
1183⁵ DOLLY PRICES [56] 8-9-12¹ (3*) N Bentley, *mid-div, effrt and hdwy 5th, sn rdn and one pace.*
......................................(14 to 1 op 10 to 1)   5
912 WAWEEWAWOO (Ire) [56] 5-10-3³ (3*) D J Moffatt, *sn pushed alng, beh frm 4th.*...............(33 to 1)   6
LEADER SAL [56] 4-10-0 D Morris, *in tch, rdn and wknd 5th, sn beh.*.................(50 to 1 op 33 to 1)   7
970 SHAYNA MAIDEL [66] 4-10-10 L O'Hara, *cl up, rdn 3 out, wknd quickly.*..........................(12 to 1)   8
1181 JUST EVE [58] 6-10-2 B Storey, *mid-div, hit 4th, sn wl beh.*........................(33 to 1 op 25 to 1)   9
970 LITTLE CONKER [66] 5-10-10 S Turner, *al prmnt, effrt 3 out, rdn nxt and sn wknd, 4th whn f last.*
......................................(14 to 1 op 12 to 1)   f
1099 MY TATA [60] (v) 7-10-4 J Corkell, *sn beh, tld off bef 3rd, pld up before 3 out.*.............(16 to 1 tchd 20 to 1)   pu
Dist: 3l, 6l, 7l, 3l, 3½l, 2l, 15l. 4m 15.40s. a 20.40s (11 Ran).
SR: 19/1/9/-/-/-/   (P Monteith), P Monteith

1357 Hathaway's Lady Jockeys' Handicap Hurdle (0-115 4-y-o and up) £1,719 2m 1f 110yds.............(12:55)

912³ COOL DUDE [99] 7-11-9 (5*) Mrs P Nash, *trkd ldrs, hdwy 2 out, led appr last and sn clr, ran on.*
......................(100 to 30 fav op 3 to 1 tchd 7 to 2)   1

1127³ COMSTOCK [93] 6-11-8 Lorna Vincent, *beh, hdwy appr 2 out, rdn approaching last, ran on und pres r-in.*
......................................(7 to 2 op 11 to 4)   2
1094⁵ STATION EXPRESS (Ire) [71] 5-10-0 Mrs J Speight, *in tch, smooth hdwy 5th, led nxt, rdn aftr 2 out, hdd and wknd appr last.*..................(8 to 1 op 10 to 1)   3
812 SKOLERN [94] 9-11-9 Gee Armytage, *led till 4th, cl up till rdn appr last, one pace.* (8 to 1 op 6 to 1 tchd 9 to 1)   4
912⁴ J P MORGAN [92] (v) 5-11-7 Mrs A Farrell, *always prmnt, hit 5th, rdn nxt, sn one paced.*...........(9 to 2 op 7 to 2)   5
TAURIAN PRINCESS [73] 4-10-2 Diane Clay, *chsd ldrs, hdwy 4th, ev ch 3 out, sn rdn and wknd.*
......................................(8 to 1 op 12 to 1)   6
972 CAPTAIN TANCRED (Ire) [81] 5-10-10 Jacqui Oliver, *pld hrd, cl up, led 4th, hdd 3 out, grad wknd.*.........(12 to 1)   7
479⁴ NEWMARKET SAUSAGE [71] 12-10-0 Susan Kersey, *in tch till mstk 5th, sn beh.*...................(50 to 1)   8
1143⁹ HIGHFIELD PRINCE [92] 7-11-0 (7*) Judy Davies, *wl beh frm hfwy.*..........................(33 to 1)   9
1092 PANTO LADY [71] 7-9-7 (7*) Miss S Lamb, *al rear, wl beh frm hfwy.*.................(66 to 1 op 50 to 1)   10
Dist: 1½l, 6l, 2½l, 1l, 1½l, ½l, 25l, nk, 2l. 4m 16.00s. a 21.00s (10 Ran).
SR: 13/5/-/-/-/-/   (Maurice Hutchinson), J H Johnson

1358 W. A. Stephenson Memorial Novices' Chase (5-y-o and up) £3,668 2m 5f..................(1:25)

741* BEACHY HEAD 5-11-4 M Dwyer, *led to second, led 5th, hit tenth, hdd nxt, led 4 out, headed last, shaken up to ld r-in, cleverly.*..................(2 to 1 on tchd 7 to 4 on)   1
1182² MARLINGFORD 6-10-12 D Morris, *cl up, led second to 5th, led 11th to 4 out, hrd rdn and rallied to ld last, hdd and not quicken r-in.*..................(9 to 1 op 8 to 1)   2
1146* SHEILAS HILLCREST 7-11-0 (5*) J Supple, *chsd ldrs, hit 5th, outpcd frm 4 out.*..................(7 to 1 op 6 to 1)   3
909⁴ REEF LARK 8-10-12 C Grant, *chsd ldrs, sn pushed alng, hdwy and rdn 8th, one pace frm 4 out.*
......................................(20 to 1 op 16 to 1)   4
ISSYIN 6-10-12 R Bellamy, *sn in tch, steady hdwy 5 out, ch whn hit 3 out, wknd nxt.*......(12 to 1 op 8 to 1)   5
768 EDEN SUNSET 7-10-12 Mr Chris Wilson, *al rear, tld off 12th.*..........................(25 to 1 op 33 to 1)   6
1091⁶ EBRO [9] 7-10-12 A Merrigan, *sn beh, tld off hfwy.*
......................................(50 to 1 op 33 to 1)   7
718² BUCKWHEAT LAD (Ire) 5-10-11 K Johnson, *al rear, tld off 12th.*..........................(50 to 1 op 33 to 1)   8
Dist: ¾l, 25l, 2½l, sht-hd, dist, 15l, 25l. 5m 20.60s. a 16.60s (8 Ran).
SR: 38/31/13/3/3/   (M Tabor), J J O'Neill

1359 Colin MacAndrew Memorial Chase Amateur Riders (5-y-o and up) £2,269 3m 3f..................(1:55)

1118⁴ GATHERING TIME 7-11-7 (5*) Mrs P Nash, *al prmnt, mstks, hit 9th, mistake 15th, rdn appr 2 out, styd on to ld last, ran on wl r-in.*..................(11 to 4 op 9 to 4)   1
1130⁴ BOREEN OWEN 9-12-2 Mr S Swiers, *al prmnt, hit 9th and 14th, led 4 out, hit 2 out, sn rdn, hdd last, no extr r-in.*......................................(11 to 4 op 3 to 1)   2
847² MOYODE REGENT 9-11-10 (7*) Mr A Manners, *trkd ldrs gng wl, hit 16th and rdn alng, hdwy to dispute ld whn hit 4 out, sn one pace.*..................(16 to 1 op 10 to 1)   3
1130³ CAROUSEL CALYPSO 7-11-9 (7*) Mr C Bonner, *cl up, hit 12th and 14th, ev ch 4 out, sn rdn and one paced nxt.*......................................(6 to 4 fav op 5 to 4)   4
BRADWALL 9-12-16 (7*) Mr J G R Barlow, *led, hit 16th, hdd 4 out, sn wknd, pld up bef last.*....(25 to 1 op 16 to 1)   pu
823⁹ BUCKLE IT UP (bl) 8-11-9 (3*) Mrs A Farrell, *hit 9th and sn beh, blun 12th, tld off whn pld up bef 14th.*
......................................(14 to 1 op 10 to 1 tchd 16 to 1)   pu
Dist: 4l, 3½l, 1l. 7m 21.70s. a 42.70s (6 Ran).
(Mrs Dorothy Tulloch), J H Johnson

1360 Crawleas Handicap Chase (0-120 4-y-o and up) £2,733 2m 1f..................(2:30)

1065³ MAUDLINS CROSS [115] 8-12-0 P Niven, *in tch, hdwy 4 out, effrt to ld 2 out, rdn last, hld on r-in.*
......................................(85 to 40 fav op 2 to 1 tchd 9 to 4)   1
1203² PRESSURE GAME [87] 10-9-7 (7*) F Perratt, *led, hit 4 out, hdd 2 out, rdn last and styd on r-in.*
......................................(5 to 1 op 4 to 1 tchd 11 to 2)   2
TRESIDDER [111] 11-11-10 R Garritty, *hld up, hdwy 4 out, rdn appr last, styd on pres r-in.*(5 to 1 op 4 to 1)   3
1203 BELDINE [103] 8-11-2 A Dobbin, *chsd ldr, effrt and hit 8th, rdn and hit 3 out, sn wknd.*.....(5 to 1 op 4 to 1)   4
SILVER HAZE [94] 9-10-7 K Jones, *in tch, hdwy 8th, rdn 4 out, sn wknd.*..................(9 to 1 op 10 to 1 tchd 12 to 1)   5
MILITARY HONOUR [90] 8-10-3 J Callaghan, *al beh.*
......................................(14 to 1 op 10 to 1)   6
1203⁵ SINGING SAM [88] 8-10-1¹ A Merrigan, *in tch till lost pl hfwy, tld off whn pld up bef 3 out.*...........(33 to 1)   pu
Dist: 1½l, nk, 12l, ¾l, 7l. 4m 21.00s. a 16.00s (7 Ran).
SR: 34/4/27/7/   (David Bell), Mrs M Reveley

1361 Sedgefield Paddock Bookmakers Handicap Hurdle (0-125 4-y-o and up) £1,970 2m 5f 110yds...........(3:00)

755² FIRM PRICE [121] 12-12-0 P Niven, *al prmnt, dsptd ld frm 4th, led appr last, hrd drvn r-in, hld on wl.*
.................................(3 to 1 fav op 7 to 2 tchd 4 to 1) 1
1066³ MASTER OF THE ROCK [95] 4-10-2 C Hawkins, *in tch, hdwy 3 out, rdn last, styd on and ev ch r-in, no extr nr finish.*...........(5 to 1 op 6 to 1 tchd 9 to 2) 2
1201² TRONCHETTO (Ire) [95] (bl) 4-10-2¹ M Dwyer, *prmnt, dsptd ld 4th, rdn appr last, wnt rght and wknd r-in.*
.................................(7 to 2 op 11 to 4) 3
1057 INTEGRITY BOY [93] (bl) 6-10-0 L Wyer, *prmnt, rdn 3 out, sn wknd.*.................(7 to 1 op 6 to 1) 4
1143⁷ STARLIGHT WONDER [93] 7-10-0 N Smith, *in tch, rdn and wknd appr 3 out.*..........(66 to 1 op 33 to 1) 5
767⁸ SKIRCOAT GREEN [95] 8-10-2 Mrs A Farrell, *led to 4th, blun nxt, sn beh.*.......(5 to 1 op 4 to 1 tchd 11 to 2) 6
1057⁴ CHIEF RAIDER (Ire) [105] 5-10-7 (5") D Bentley, *prmnt whn blun badly second, rdr lost irons, tld off when uns rider bend aftr nxt.*.................................(9 to 2) ur

Dist: Nk, 3l, 25l, 5l, 2l. 5m 12.10s. a 21.10s (7 Ran).
SR: 39/12/9-/ (Mrs Susan McDonald), Mrs M Reveley

1362 Harpington Novices' Hurdle (4-y-o and up) £1,484 3m 3f 110yds.......(3:30)

1028⁷ PORTONIA 9-10-9 P Niven, *made all, clr 3 out, styd on.*
.................................(4 to 1 op 3 to 1) 1
1067³ CRANK SHAFT 6-11-0 D Gallagher, *chsd ldrs, hit 3rd, hit 7th and lost pl, hdwy 4 out, styd on frm nxt, not rch wnr.*.................(7 to 2 op 3 to 1 tchd 11 to 4) 2
1813³ DALUSMAN (Ire) 5-11-0 B Storey, *chsd wnr, effrt and rdn 3 out, sn one pace.*.................(3 to 1 op 14 to 1) 3
1099⁷ NOBLE BRONZE 5-10-2 (7") C Woodall, *in tch, effrt and rdn 4 out and wknd.*.................(20 to 1 op 14 to 1) 4
1114² ABBEYLANDS (Ire) 5-10-11 (3") D J Moffatt, *hld up and beh, steady hdwy appr 4 out, rdn nxt, sn btn.*
.................................(7 to 4 fav op 11 to 8 tchd 2 to 1) 5
1142⁴ OVER THE ODDS (Ire) 4-10-7 (7") D Ryan, *chsd ldrs, hit 7th, rdn and wknd appr 3 out, tld off whn pld up bef last.*
.................................(33 to 1 op 25 to 1) pu
1129³ STRONG TRACE (Ire) 4-11-0 C Grant, *in tch, wknd 8th, tld off 4 out, pld up bef 2 out.*...........(12 to 1 op 8 to 1) pu
1181⁶ TWIN STATES 4-10-7 (7") W Fry, *al beh, tld off 4 out, pld up bef last.*.................(16 to 1 op 20 to 1) pu
(W H Strawson), Mrs M Reveley

AINTREE (good)
Saturday November 20th
Going Correction: PLUS 0.80 sec. per fur. (races 1,3), PLUS 0.40 (2,4,7), PLUS 0.65 (5,6)

1363 John Parrett Memorial Handicap Chase (0-145 5-y-o and up) £6,907 2m 1f 110yds.................(12:30)

1203³ ABSAILOR [111] (v) 9-10-0⁵ (5") P Williams, *trkd ldg 4, bustled alng to keep up 6th (Becher's), rallied to ld 2 out, lft clr, drvn out.*..............(16 to 1 op 14 to 1) 1
1168³ THATS THE LIFE [117] 8-10-6 S McNeill, *nvr far away, blun 4th, feeling pace and drvn alng 3 out, rallied und pres r-in.*.................(6 to 1 op 5 to 1) 2
GOLDEN FREEZE [120] 11-10-9 C Grant, *pressed ldr, drw level and f 6th (Becher's).*......(4 to 1 op 3 to 1) f
871* HOWE STREET [135] 10-11-10 A Maguire, *led and jmpd wl, quickened 6th (Becher's), tiring whn hdd and f 2 out.*
.................................(6 to 4 fav op 13 to 8 tchd 7 to 4) f
1041* LITTLE TOM [112] 8-10-11 M A FitzGerald, *f 1st.*
.................................(4 to 1 tchd 5 to 2 and 7 to 2) f
1056⁵ CIRCULATION [111] 7-9-9 (5") D Walsh, *pressed ldg pair, blun 5 out and 3 out, 4th and btn whn f nxt...*(25 to 1) f
BEL COURSE [111] 11-10-0 R Bellamy, *not jump wl, struggling in rear whn almost refused 8th (Canal Turn), pld up bef nxt.*.................................(25 to 1) pu

Dist: 3l. 4m 25.90s. (7 Ran).
(Lady Harris), Mrs S C Bradburne

1364 Stanley Leisure Children In Need Handicap Hurdle (0-135 4-y-o and up) £8,481 2m 110yds.............(1:00)

1221⁵ PERSUASIVE [123] 6-10-13 (5") Mr M Buckley, *settled gng wl, hdwy to ld appr 2 out, wnt clr.* (11 to 1 op 8 to 1) 1
1055² NIKITAS [115] 8-10-10 S McNeill, *in tch, jnd ldrs 4 out, styd on same btw last 2....*(7 to 1 op 6 to 1) 2
1106⁹ WELSHMAN [129] 7-11-10 D Gallagher, *settled wth chasing grp, improved to ld appr 3 out, hdd nxt, kpt on same pace.*.................(8 to 1 op 7 to 1 tchd 9 to 1) 3
1292³ SAYMORE [105] 7-9-11 (3") S Wynne, *settled wth chasing grp, mstks 4th and 5th, led briefly 3 out, outpcd betw last 2.*.................(11 to 1 op 8 to 1) 4

1186* TOOGOOD TO BE TRUE [113] 5-10-8 L Wyer, *chsd clr ldr frm 3rd, niggled alng to hold pl aftr 4 out, btn nxt.*
.................................(11 to 4 fav op 2 to 1) 5
1055⁷ RED INDIAN [116] 7-10-11 D Byrne, *patiently rdn, improved frm off the pace aftr 4 out, ridden nxt, sn btn.*
.................................(5 to 1 op 9 to 2) 6
ANTI MATTER [115] 8-10-10 B Clifford, *in tch, effrt hfwy, struggling aftr 4 out, tld off......* (10 to 1 op 12 to 1) 7
1066² NODFORM WONDER [123] 6-11-4 A Maguire, *set str pace, clr ldr to hfwy, hdd bef 3 out, sn lost tch.*
.................................(9 to 2 tchd 5 to 1) 8

Dist: 5l, hd, 6l, 12l, 3l, 4l, 3½l. 3m 58.60s. a 10.60s (8 Ran).
SR: 50/37/51/21/17/17/12/16/ (W G McHarg), Miss L A Perratt

1365 Crowther Homes Becher Handicap Chase (6-y-o and up) £18,729 3m 3f 30yds.........................(1:35)

1208² INDIAN TONIC [120] 7-10-6 C Maude, *jmpd boldly, made all, hrd pressed whn lft clr 2 out, styd on gmely r-in.*
.................................(4 to 1 op 7 to 2 tchd 9 to 2) 1
1029³ SOUTHERN MINSTREL [115] 10-10-1 C Grant, *trkd ldrs, feeling pace and lost grnd 13th (Becher's), styd on frm 3 out, nrst finish.*.................(12 to 1) 2
1118* MISTER ED [134] 10-11-6 D Morris, *settled midfield, wnt 3rd and drvn alng 14th (Becher's), styd on last 3, nvr nrr.*.................(15 to 2 op 6 to 1 tchd 8 to 1) 3
1121³ SIRRAH JAY [115] 13-10-11 S McNeill, *pressed ldrs, rdn and lost grnd aftr 14th (Becher's), styd on frm 3 out, nrst finish.*.................(20 to 1 op 16 to 1) 4
995⁴ HEY COTTAGE [115] 8-10-1 R Dunwoody, *patiently rdn, cld hfwy, outpcd 16th (Canal Turn), no imprsn frm 3 out.*.................(16 to 1 op 33 to 1) 5
1222* ON THE HOOCH [117] 8-10-3³ Mr J Bradburne, *jmpd wl, struggling to go pace hfwy, lost tch 14th (Becher's).*
.................................(50 to 1 op 33 to 1) 6
1011⁷ WONT BE GONE LONG [130] (bl) 11-11-2 M A FitzGerald, *nvr far away, 3rd and niggled alng whn f 12th.*
.................................(14 to 1 op 12 to 1) f
MERANO (Fr) [130] 10-11-2 L Wyer, *settled midfield, struggling fnl circuit, beh whn f 5 out, broke neck, dead.*
.................................(13 to 2 op 6 to 1 tchd 7 to 1) f
1029* USHERS ISLAND [125] 7-10-11 A Maguire, *nvr far away, trkd wnr fnl circuit, hit 3 out, chalg whn f nxt.*
.................................(5 to 2 fav tchd 11 to 4) f
986 GOLD CAP (Fr) [115] 8-10-1 M Hourigan, *trkd ldrs, feeling pace 14th (Becher's), fdg whn blun and uns rdr 4 out.*
.................................(20 to 1 tchd 25 to 1) ur
1121* FAR SENIOR [138] 7-11-10 N Williamson, *chsd ldg 4, struggling to hold pl fnl circuit, lost tch 6 out, pld up bef last.*.................(13 to 2 op 5 to 1) pu

Dist: 6l, 3½l, 4l, 15l, dist. 7m 8.70s. a 24.70s (11 Ran).
SR: 49/38/53/30/15/-/ (Mrs Joanne Richards), N A Twiston-Davies

1366 Liverpool Novices' Handicap Hurdle (4-y-o and up) £3,622 2½m......(2:10)

1252* KYTTON CASTLE [85] 6-9-12 (3",5ex) D Meredith, *confidently rdn, cruised up to chal 3 out, lft clr aftr last, pushed out.*.................(7 to 2 op 3 to 1) 1
983³ BRODESSA [112] 7-11-9 (5") Mr M Buckley, *pld hrd, settled hfwy, led bef 6th, blun last, sn hdd, not reco'r.*
.................................(11 to 2 op 5 to 1) 2
999* WESTHOLME (USA) [112] 5-12-0 L Wyer, *patiently rdn, improved to join ldrs hfwy, niggled alng aftr 3 out, fdd betw last 2.*.................(7 to 4 fav tchd 15 to 8) 3
1193² RAMSTAR [85] 5-10-1 R Bellamy, *tucked away on ins, ev ch aftr 4 out, fdd und pres frm nxt.*(4 to 1 tchd 9 to 2) 4
1303² JUDGE AND JURY [84] (bl) 4-9-9 (5") J McCarthy, *nvr far away, ev ch appr 3 out, rdn and btn betw last 2.*
.................................(12 to 1 op 10 to 1 tchd 14 to 1) 5
605 PERFORATE [84] (bl) 4-10-0 B Clifford, *led till appr 6th, struggling aftr nxt, sn tld off...*(16 to 1 op 12 to 1) 6
1167⁹ LAW FACULTY (Ire) [84] 7-10-0 S Mackey, *trkd ldr, reminders to keep up 5th, tld off nxt..........*(33 to 1) 7

Dist: 7l, 12l, 3l, 8l, 15l, 25l. 4m 54.70s. a 16.70s (7 Ran).
SR: -/6/-/-/ (Joint Partnership), R Dickin

1367 Aldiscon International Novices' Chase (5-y-o and up) £4,045 3m 1f ....(2:45)

1306* MARTOMICK 6-11-5 (3ex) N Williamson, *jmpd soundly, made all, fiddled 5 out, sn clr ag'n, eased r-in.*
.................................(13 to 8 on tchd 6 to 4 on) 1
1164² JUDGED LUCKY (Fr) 6-11-0 R Bellamy, *patiently rdn, jnd wnr fnl circuit, struggling whn blun 3 out, sn btn.*
.................................(11 to 2 op 7 to 2) 2
MASTER JOLSON 5-10-12 R Dunwoody, *mstks, pressed wnr till reminders 11th, lost tch fnl circuit.*
.................................(9 to 4 op 11 to 8) 3

Dist: 15l, dist. 6m 26.90s. a 21.90s (3 Ran).
SR: 35/15/-/ (Richard Shaw), K C Bailey

1368 Tote Bookmakers Novices' Chase (5-y-o and up) £7,995 2½m........(3:20)

1117* COULTON 6-11-7 L Wyer, *mstks, trkd ldg pair, quickened to ld appr 2 out, readily*.
.................(9 to 4 on op 5 to 2 on tchd 2 to 1 on) 1
1348 KEEP SHARP 7-11-7 Richard Guest, *trkd ldr, effrt and drvn alng whn blun 3 out, no ch wth wnr*.
.................(9 to 1 op 10 to 1 tchd 11 to 1) 2
1093 AYIA NAPA 6-11-0 Mr J Bradburne, *set modest pace, hit 6 out and 3 out, sn hdd and btn...* (33 to 1 tchd 50 to 1) 3
Dist: 15l, 5l. 5m 20.50s. a 30.50s (3 Ran).

(G E Shouler), M W Easterby

1369 EBF 'National Hunt' Novices' Hurdle Qualifier (4,5,6-y-o) £2,843 2m 1f 110yds
.................................(3:50)

SHARP PERFORMER (Ire) 4-11-0 N Williamson, *patiently rdn, improved to chal whn hit 2 out, led r-in, hld on gmely und pres*.
.................(8 to 1 op 6 to 1) 1
1003⁶ BASILICUS (Fr) 4-11-0 Gary Lyons, *led tll 3rd, styd hndy, led bef 3 out, hit last, hdd r-in, rallied*.
.................(8 to 1 op 6 to 1) 2
1070⁹ DAN DE LYON 5-11-0 R Dunwoody, *nvr far away, rdn whn pace quickened appr 3 out, no extr*.
.................(3 to 1 tchd 100 to 30) 3
1103* STRONG FLAME (Ire) 4-11-0 C Grant, *not fluent, led and quickened 3rd, hit 5th and 6th, hdd bef 3 out, sn btn*.
.................(6 to 4 fav op 7 to 4 tchd 15 to 8) 4
Dist: Sht-hd, 12l, 3l. 4m 9.80s. a 21.80s (4 Ran).

(Mrs S C Ellen), K C Bailey

MARKET RASEN (good to soft)
Saturday November 20th
Going Correction: PLUS 1.05 sec. per fur.

1370 High Sheriff Selling Handicap Hurdle (4 & 5-y-o) £1,632 2m 1f 110yds (12:40)

1237² PORT IN A STORM [80] 4-11-8 G McCourt, *hld up in tch, steady hdwy 3 out, led last, drvn out*.
.......(15 to 8 fav op 2 to 1 tchd 9 to 4 and 7 to 4) 1
959³ JOLI'S GREAT [86] (bl) 5-12-0 J Ryan, *al prmnt, led appr 3 out, rdn nxt, hdd and hit last, not quicken r-in*.
.................(4 to 1 op 3 to 1 tchd 9 to 2) 2
664 MILL BURN [69] 4-10-11 R Campbell, *hld up in tch, hdwy 4 out and sn ev ch, rdn and hit 3 out, soon wknd*.
.................(6 to 1 op 4 to 1) 3
1097 ALIZARI (USA) [58] (bl) 4-10-0 M Robinson, *prmnt, sn rdn alng, reminders hfwy, hrd drvn and wknd 3 out*.
.................(33 to 1 op 20 to 1) 4
837³ RAAWI [65] 5-10-7 J Frost, *al rear*. (16 to 1 tchd 20 to 1) 5
912⁷ RICHMOND (Ire) [86] (bl) 5-11-7 (7*) G Tormey, *chsd ldrs, rdn alng hfwy, wknd appr 3 out, sn beh*.
.................(11 to 2 op 9 to 2) 6
LARA'S BABY (Ire) [79] (v) 5-11-7 P Niven, *led, rdn and hdd appr 3 out, wknd quickly and tld off whn pld up bef 2 out*.
.................(11 to 2 op 5 to 1 tchd 13 to 2) pu
Dist: 4l, 15l, 2½l, 3l, 10l. 4m 30.60s. a 28.60s (7 Ran).

(S A Barningham), N Tinkler

1371 H. L. Foods Novices' Hurdle (4-y-o and up) £2,427 3m
.................................(1:10)

1067⁴ NEEDWOOD POPPY 5-11-5 J Frost, *trkd ldrs, hdwy and hit 7th, led 4 out, rdn clr betw last 2, ran on strly*.
.................(9 to 2 op 7 to 2) 1D
IRISH STAMP (Ire) 4-10-13 M Dwyer, *trkd ldrs, hdwy 4 out, rdn 2 out, sn wknd, hit last*.
.................(Evens fav op 11 to 10 tchd 11 to 8) 1
1099⁶ CZAR NICHOLAS 4-10-13 P Niven, *hld up and beh, hdwy 4 out, rdn appr 2 out and sn one pace*.
.................(15 to 2 op 6 to 1 tchd 8 to 1) 2
1099⁵ SQUIRES TALE (Ire) 5-11-0 G McCourt, *prmnt, hdwy 8th and ev ch, hit 4 out, rdn and wknd quickly nxt*.
.................(3 to 1 op 4 to 1 tchd 11 to 4) 3
1252 MILLIE (USA) 5-10-9 M Robinson, *led and sn clr, wknd 8th and soon hdd, tld off 3 out*.....(50 to 1 op 33 to 1) 4
1000⁹ EASY RHYTHM 6-10-7 (7*) G Tormey, *in tch till lost pl and beh frm 8th*...........(50 to 1 op 33 to 1) 5
HYDEONIAN 6-11-0 Susan Kersey, *f 1st*.
.................(66 to 1 op 50 to 1) f
920 BE THE BEST 5-10-11 (3*) R Davis, *in tch till lost pl 8th, tld off whn pld up bef 2 out*..........(40 to 1 op 25 to 1) pu
1315 WHATCOMESNATURALLY (USA) 4-10-8 S D Williams, *al rear, tld off whn pld up bef 3 out*...........(20 to 1) pu
Dist: 12l, 8l, dist, dist, 2l. 6m 19.00s. a 37.00s (9 Ran).

(P O'Donnell), J Pearce

1372 Clugston Novices' Chase (5-y-o and up) £3,556 2½m
.................................(1:40)

1102* MR WOODCOCK 8-11-4 P Niven, *led to 4th, led 6 out, very easily*........(5 to 1 on tchd 6 to 1) 1
DARK OAK 7-10-12 L O'Hara, *in tch, hdwy 6 out, chsd wnr frm nxt, kpt on*..........(20 to 1 op 12 to 1) 2
1024 ON CUE 6-10-12 W Worthington, *beh, styd on frm 4 out, nvr dngrs*.........................(25 to 1 op 20 to 1) 3

848⁵ DALLISTON (NZ) 7-10-12 A Carroll, *cl up, led 4th and sn clr, wknd 9th, hdd and hit 6 out, soon weakened and tld off whn f 2 out*.........(11 to 2 op 9 to 2) f
COCK SPARROW 9-10-9 (3*) A Thornton, *beh frm hfwy, tld off whn pld up bef 3 out*.
.................(16 to 1 op 14 to 1 tchd 20 to 1) pu
Dist: 8l, 25l. 5m 19.30s. a 27.30s (5 Ran).
SR: 27/13/   (P A Tylor), Mrs M Reveley

1373 Tattersalls Mares' Only Novices' Chase Qualifier (5-y-o and up) £3,146 2m 1f 110yds
.................................(2:10)

357² NORSTOCK 6-11-6 M Dwyer, *made virtually all, lft wl clr 3 out*....................(4 to 1 op 9 to 2 tchd 5 to 1) 1
MAYWORK 6-10-10 P Niven, *sn beh, lft remote second 3 out, blun nxt*..........(10 to 1 op 5 to 1) 2
998⁴ MENAGHI 6-11-1 G McCourt, *al prmnt, dsptd ld 4 out till f nxt, rmntd*..........(8 to 1 op 7 to 1 tchd 9 to 1) 3
1127* EASBY MANDRINA 6-10-10 R Garritty, *hit 1st, in tch till f 5th*..........(9 to 2 op 5 to 1 tchd 11 to 2) f
1133² HEDLEY MILL 5-10-3 (7*) Mr A Parker, *strted slwly, sn in tch, cl up 5 out, 4 ls 3rd whn f 3 out*.(11 to 2 op 5 to 1) f
933² CHICHELL'S HURST 7-10-10 S Smith Eccles, *al prmnt, cl second whn slightly hmpd and uns rdr 8th*.
.................(11 to 8 fav op 5 to 4) ur
Dist: Dist, dist. 4m 51.40s. a 37.40s (6 Ran).   (Nick Quesnel), J White

1374 Clugston Novices' Hurdle (4-y-o and up) £2,679 2m 1f 110yds
.......(2:45)

1046³ MOAT GARDEN (USA) 5-11-0 J Frost, *made all, clr aftr 3 out, rdn appr last, hld on gmely r-in*. (4 to 1 op 9 to 1) 1
1084⁵ LEXUS (Ire) 5-11-0 S Smith Eccles, *in tch, hdwy 3 out, effrt nxt, rdn to chal last, ev ch till no extr nr finish*.
.................(9 to 1 op 6 to 1) 2
ARTIC WINGS (Ire) 5-10-9 M Brennan, *hld up and beh, steady hdwy 4 out, chsd wnr appr 2 out, sn rdn and one pace*..........(20 to 1 tchd 25 to 1 and 16 to 1) 3
1040⁶ NAGOBELIA 5-11-0 M McLaughlin, *in tch, rdn aftr 3 out, styd on appr last*.....(14 to 1 op 12 to 1 tchd 16 to 1) 4
910* SILVER SAMURAI 4-11-0 (7*) C Woodall, *hld up, hdwy 3 out, sn rdn nxt, no imprsn, hit last*.
.................(7 to 4 fav op 3 to 1 tchd 7 to 2 and 6 to 1) 5
VASILIEV (v) 5-11-0 M Dwyer, *in tch, hdwy whn hmpd aftr 3 out, sn rdn and one pace nxt*.
.................(7 to 1 op 6 to 1 tchd 8 to 1) 6
BRESIL (USA) 4-11-0 T Jarvis, *prmnt, rdn 3 out, sn wknd*.
.................(9 to 1 op 10 to 1) 7
MILTON ROOMS (Ire) 4-10-7 (7*) K Davies, *chsd ldrs till wknd 4 out, sn beh*...........(33 to 1 op 25 to 1) 8
DON'T DROP BOMBS (USA) 4-11-0 G Upton, *cl up till rdn and appr 3 out*.
.................(16 to 1 tchd 20 to 1 and 14 to 1) 9
EXCLUSION 4-11-0 P Niven, *al rear*.
.................(10 to 1 op 8 to 1 tchd 12 to 1) 10
1215 MATUSADONA 6-10-9 J A Harris, *chsd ldrs to 4th, sn lost pl, tld off whn pld up bef 2 out*... (66 to 1 op 33 to 1) pu
TAHITIAN 4-11-0 G McCourt, *hld up and beh, some hdwy 3 out, sn wknd and behind whn pld up bef last*.
.................(8 to 1 op 4 to 1) pu
GOLDEN SUPREME 7-11-0 R Garritty, *al rear, tld off whn pld up bef 2 out*...........................(33 to 1) pu
LADY QUAKER 5-10-2 (7*) G Cahill, *al rear, tld off whn pld up bef 2 out*.....................(33 to 1 op 25 to 1) pu
1010 WATERBEACH VILLAGE (Ire) 5-10-7 (7*) Mr M Gingell, *cl up to 3rd, beh nxt, tld off whn pld up bef 5th*.
.................(40 to 1 op 33 to 1 tchd 50 to 1) pu
1078 BOSSYMOSS (Ire) 4-10-11 (3*) A Thornton, *sn wl beh, tld off 4th, pld up bef 2 out*..... (66 to 1 op 33 to 1) pu
Dist: 1l, 12l, 2½l, ½l, 1l, dist, 1½l, hd, 7l. 4m 26.00s. a 24.00s (16 Ran).
SR: 30/29/12/14/20/12/   (Queen Elizabeth), I A Balding

1375 Cotswold Gold Handicap Chase (0-120 5-y-o and up) £3,743 3m 1f
.....(3:20)

YOUNG MINER [93] 7-10-5 G Upton, *made virtually all, rdn appr 2 out, styd on gmely und pres r-in*.
.................(12 to 1 op 10 to 1) 1
1144* INVASION [99] (v) 9-10-11 M Brennan, *cl up, effrt to chal 4 out, rdn and hit nxt, hrd drvn, hit last, no extr nr finish*......................(11 to 4 op 3 to 1 tchd 9 to 4) 2
911⁴ LAPIAFFE [100] 9-10-12 G McCourt, *cl up, effrt and dsptd ld whn blun 4 out, not reco'r*......(7 to 1 op 5 to 1) 3
1145* HIGH PADRE [113] 7-11-11 M Dwyer, *cl up, hit 9th, rdn alng and lost pl 5 out, sn beh*.
.................(5 to 4 on tchd 11 to 10 on) 4
Dist: ¾l, dist, 10l. 6m 48.50s. a 47.50s (4 Ran).
(Mrs T J McInnes Skinner), Mrs T J McInnes Skinner

1376 Market Rasen National Hunt Flat Race (4,5,6-y-o) £1,872 1m 5f 110yds. .(3:50)

SOUNDS FYNE (Ire) 4-10-7 (7*) G Tormey, *chsd ldrs, effrt and rdn o'r 2 fs out, styd on to ld wl ins last*.
.................(7 to 2 op 3 to 1 tchd 4 to 1) 1

1103³ ROSEBERRY TOPPING 4-10-7 (7") M Herrington, *pld hrd,*
sn chasing ldr, led 3 fs out, rdn 2 furlongs out, hdd and
no extr wl ins last... (5 to 2 fav op 7 to 2 tchd 4 to 1) ... 2
1103⁴ SWORDKING (Ire) 4-11-0 Mr I McLelland, *in tch, effrt and*
rdn 4 fs out, styd on und pres ins last.
.............................(7 to 1 op 6 to 1 tchd 8 to 1) ... 3
CHINO'S DELIGHT 4-10-2 (7") Guy Lewis, *chsd ldrs, effrt*
and ev ch 3 fs out, rdn and one pace fnl 2 furlongs.
.............................(7 to 1 op 6 to 1 tchd 8 to 1) ... 4
1103⁶ GARLAND OF GOLD 4-10-9 (5") J Supple, *led, rdn and hdd*
3 fs out, grad wknd.........................(12 to 1) ... 5
EMERALD QUEEN 4-10-2 (7") R Moore, *beh till styd on fnl*
3 fs, nvr dngrs..........................(12 to 1 op 10 to 1) ... 6
BAGARIDE 4-11-5⁵ Mr D Barlow, *mid-div, rdn alng 4 fs*
out, no imprsn....................(25 to 1 op 16 to 1) ... 7
MY BILLY BOY 4-10-7 (7") S Mason, *hld up and beh, effrt*
and some hdwy on outer hfwy, rdn 4 fs out and sn btn.
.............................(8 to 1 op 7 to 2) ... 8
743 TOUGH DEAL (Ire) 5-11-0 Mr B Leavy, *chsd ldrs, rdn o'r 4 fs*
out and sn wknd..................(50 to 1 op 33 to 1) ... 9
TWICE IN ONE NIGHT 4-10-9 (5") S Lyons, *al rear.*
.............................(25 to 1 op 20 to 1) ... 10
GOLDEN RECORD 5-10-7 (7") E Husband, *beh, hdwy*
hfwy, sn rdn and wknd 4 fs out... (50 to 1 op 33 to 1) ... 11
KNOCKREIGH CROSS (Ire) 4-10-2 (7") G Cahill, *chsd ldrs*
till hmpd and lost pl aftr 3 fs, effrt 5 furlongs out, no
hdwy.............................(10 to 1 op 16 to 1) ... 12
1027 GOOD FEELING 4-10-7 (7") N Juckes, *al beh.*
.............................(20 to 1 op 16 to 1) ... 13
ANOTHER TRYP 5-10-2 (7") G McGrath, *al beh.*
.............................(25 to 1 op 20 to 1) ... 14
SKIDDER 4-11-0 Mr K Green, *pld hrd, cl up till wknd*
quickly aftr 4 fs, sn tld off.................(33 to 1) ... 15
Dist: 3½l, ½l, 4l, 2½l, 6l, 1l, 8l, nk, ½l, 1l. 3m 29.10s. (15 Ran).
(J G FitzGerald), J G FitzGerald

NAVAN (IRE) (Good)
Saturday November 20th

1377 Tara Three Year Old Hurdle £3,105 2m
.............................(12:40)

GLENSTAL FLAGSHIP (Ire) 10-7 (7") K P Gaule, ... (4 to 1) ... 1
NANNAKA (USA) 10-4 (5") T P Treacy, ...(10 to 1) ... 2
FRIENDLY FLYER (Ire) 10-9 K F O'Brien, ...(12 to 1) ... 3
968³ GLOWING VALUE (Ire) 11-0 B Sheridan, ...(6 to 4 fav) ... 4
968 SPORTSTYLE (Ire) 11-0 T J Taaffe, ...(14 to 1) ... 5
ISLAND VISION (Ire) 11-0 J Shortt, ...(8 to 1) ... 6
968 AULD STOCK (Ire) 10-9 G Bradley, ...(10 to 1) ... 7
WHITECRAITS (Ire) 10-9 P Carberry, ...(12 to 1) ... 8
802⁹ RUNNING SLIPPER (Ire) 11-0 L P Cusack, ...(25 to 1) ... 9
BOBADIL (Ire) 10-6 (3") Mr A E Lacy, ...(14 to 1) ... 10
968 FURIETO (Ire) 11-0 C F Swan, ...(10 to 1) ... 11
RIYADH DANCER (Ire) 11-0 M Duffy, ...(10 to 1) ... 12
1111⁶ PRINTOUT (Ire) 10-9 H Rogers, ...(10 to 1) ... 13
SAMOT (Ire) 10-9 (5") J R Barry, ...(10 to 1) ... 14
968 GLAS AGUS OR (Ire) (bl) 10-9 J F Titley, ...(10 to 1) ... 15
THE SALTY FROG (Ire) 11-0 C O'Dwyer, ...(20 to 1) ... 16
688⁷ CHRISTY MOORE (Ire) (bl) 11-0 F Woods, ...(20 to 1) ... 17
KING BRIAN (Ire) 11-0 W T Slattery Jnr, ...(25 to 1) ... 18
LIMAHEIGHTS (Ire) 10-9 A Powell, ...(25 to 1) ... 19
688⁹ RED ROOSTER (Ire) 10-9 (5") M A Davey, ...(33 to 1) ... 20
BOTANIC VERSES (Ire) 10-6 (3") C O'Brien, ...(50 to 1) ... 21
LITTLE TINCTURE (Ire) 10-9 (5") T P Rudd, ...(16 to 1) ... f
Dist: 4½l, 7l, 2l, 6l. 4m 6.20s. (22 Ran).
(Joseph Crowley), A P O'Brien

1378 Killeen Hurdle (4-y-o and up) £3,105 2m 5f.
.............................(1:10)

853² GIMME FIVE 6-11-4 C F Swan, ...(10 to 9 on) ... 1
1235⁶ LAW BRIDGE 6-11-3 (5") Mr D Valentine, ...(13 to 8) ... 2
877² BUMBLY BROOK 6-10-11 (7") J M McCormack, ..(12 to 1) ... 3
558⁵ WOLF WINTER 8-10-13 (5") P A Roche, ...(9 to 1) ... 4
939⁹ DRINK UP DAN 6-11-4 P Carberry, ...(33 to 1) ... 5
1235⁸ MOONCAPER 7-11-4 T Horgan, ...(10 to 1) ... 6
1236⁶ TRIMMER WONDER (Ire) 5-10-13 K F O'Brien, ..(10 to 1) ... 7
SEA BRIGHT (Ire) 5-10-10 (3") D Bromley, ...(66 to 1) ... 8
Dist: 2l, 5½l, 1l, 8l. 5m 13.40s. (8 Ran).
(John P McManus), E J O'Grady

1379 Crossakiel Maiden Hurdle (5-y-o and up) £3,105 2m.
.............................(1:40)

SOUND MAN (Ire) 5-12-0 C F Swan, ...(2 to 1 on) ... 1
1174⁶ FINNEGANS WAKE 6-10-13 (7") K P Gaule, ...(10 to 1) ... 2
1236⁷ ROUBABAY (Ire) 5-12-0 G Bradley, ...(5 to 1) ... 3
1174 HANG A RIGHT 6-11-9 (7") T P Treacy, ...(12 to 1) ... 4
WINDOVER (Ire) 5-11-3 (3") D Bromley, ...(50 to 1) ... 5
NICE PROSPECT (Ire) 5-11-6 T J Taaffe, ...(14 to 1) ... 6
CORRIBLOUGH (Ire) 5-11-6 C O'Dwyer, ...(50 to 1) ... 7
NO BETTER BUACHAIL (Ire) 5-11-6 F J Flood, ...(20 to 1) ... 8
881⁵ I IS 6-11-1 (5") M G Cleary, ...(14 to 1) ... 9
1174 TOMMY'S RUN 6-11-9 (5") D T Evans, ...(14 to 1) ... 10
1160⁷ MIRASEL 6-11-9 P McWilliams, ...(25 to 1) ... 11
JEMMA'S GOLD (Ire) 5-11-1 J P Banahan, ...(50 to 1) ... 12

708⁵ DIRECT RUN 6-12-0 J F Titley, ...(8 to 1) ... 13
1174 ALBONA 5-11-9 D H O'Connor, ...(25 to 1) ... 14
DICK'S CABIN 6-11-6 H Rogers, ...(20 to 1) ... 15
Dist: 8l, 1l, hd, 2l. 4m 13.80s. (15 Ran).
(David Lloyd), E J O'Grady

1380 Dunsany Handicap Hurdle (4-y-o and up) £3,105 3m.
.............................(2:10)

1235² TEMPLEROAN PRINCE [-] 6-10-1 C N Bowens, (2 to 1 fav) ... 1
938⁶ TITIAN BLONDE [-] 5-10-2 C F Swan, ...(8 to 1) ... 2
1178² DOONEGA (Ire) [-] 5-9-10 (3") C O'Brien, ...(6 to 1) ... 3
1335⁶ GOOLDS GOLD [-] 7-9-5³ (5") P A Roche, ...(14 to 1) ... 4
GOLDEN OPAL [-] 8-9-0 (7") J P Broderick, ...(14 to 1) ... 5
1017³ RISING WATERS (Ire) [-] 5-11-1 K F O'Brien, ...(7 to 1) ... 6
938⁸ IL TROVATORE (USA) [-] 7-9-12 P Carberry, ...(14 to 1) ... 7
941 COUMEENOOLE LADY [-] 6-9-5 (7") J M Donnelly, (20 to 1) ... 8
1037 THE MAD MONK [-] 8-9-8 T Horgan, ...(25 to 1) ... 9
1018 FRIGID COUNTESS [-] 6-9-3³ (7") Mr L A Hurley, ..(33 to 1) ... 10
557⁶ THE CRAZY BISHOP (Ire) [-] 5-10-6 S H O'Donovan, (8 to 1) ... 11
VANTON [-] 9-10-4 (7") D J Finnegan, ...(8 to 1) ... 12
BARRONSTOWN BOY [-] 9-9-4² (3") Miss M Olivefalk,
.............................(20 to 1) ... 13
MCCONNELL GOLD [-] 8-9-9² H Rogers, ...(33 to 1) ... 14
1178 VINCERO [-] (bl) 8-9-3 (5") M G Cleary, ...(33 to 1) ... 15
LACKEN BEAU [-] 9-11-5 (5") T P Treacy, ...(20 to 1) ... 16
1235⁴ KERFONTAINE [-] 8-10-3² G Bradley, ...(8 to 1) ... pu
803 SIRAJAO (Ire) [-] 4-9-8⁶ (5") T P Rudd, ...(50 to 1) ... pu
Dist: 1½l, 6l, sht-hd, 2l. 5m 44.80s. (18 Ran).
(E J Donegan), Victor Bowens

1381 Troytown Handicap Chase (Listed - Grade 2) (4-y-o and up) £8,625 3m
.............................(2:40)

855⁴ KING OF THE GALES [-] 6-11-12 C F Swan, *hld up, prog 3*
out, hdwy to ld appr last, styd on strly... (7 to 2 jt-fav) ... 1
539 FISSURE SEAL [-] 7-12-0 G Bradley, *hld up, rear and rdn 3*
out, styd on strly frm nxt, no ch wth wnr...... (6 to 1) ... 2
1231² JOE WHITE [-] 7-11-2 P Carberry, *mid-div, prog 5 out, trkd*
ldr appr 2 out, rdn and no extr approaching last, kpt
on.............................(11 to 2) ... 3
1268⁴ WINNING CHARLIE [-] 7-10-6 (4ex) K F O'Brien, *rear, prog 4*
out, ev ch 2 out, rdn and no extr appr last, kpt on.
....
1233⁷ ITS A CRACKER [-] 9-11-0 (3ex) D P Murphy, *dsptd ld, led 3*
out, rdn and hdd appr last, sn wknd.... (7 to 2 jt-fav) ... 5
992⁷ NEW MILL HOUSE [-] 10-11-9 T J Taaffe, *mid-div, prog 9th,*
rdn and lost pl appr 4 out, kpt on pace....(14 to 1) ... 6
DYSART LASS [-] 8-10-13 M G Cleary, *trkd ldrs, prog 9th..*
ev ch 2 out, sn rdn and wknd.................(16 to 1) ... 7
806⁶ MR HOY [-] 10-10-8 D Bromley, *mid-div, rdn 5 out, wknd*
appr 3 out.............................(33 to 1) ... 8
906 MARKET MOVER [-] (bl) 7-11-3 T Horgan, *dsptd ld to 5th,*
rdn and lost pl 5 out........................(20 to 1) ... 9
992⁵ LAURA'S BEAU [-] 9-12-0 C O'Dwyer, *mid-div, rdn 4 out,*
no extr and wknd aftr nxt....................(10 to 1) ... 10
966⁵ KNOCKNACARRA LAD [-] 8-10-2 F Woods, *f 1st.* (20 to 1) ... f
1231 SOLAR SYMPHONY [-] 7-10-12 J Shortt, *wl plcd, dsptd ld 4*
out to nxt, wknd quickly, pld up.............(10 to 1) ... pu
Dist: 4l, 1½l, hd, 6l. 6m 15.00s. (12 Ran).
(E P King), J E Kiely

1382 Fortria EBF Handicap Chase (Listed - Grade 3) (4-y-o and up) £6,900 2m
.............................(3:10)

1268² MAGIC MILLION [-] 7-9-7 P McWilliams, *mid-div, prog 3*
out, led aftr nxt, rdn, styd on strly frm last..... (7 to 1) ... 1
992³ GALE AGAIN [-] 6-12-0 C P Dunne, *trkd ldrs, ev ch 2 out,*
rdn and no extr appr last, kpt on..........(2 to 1 fav) ... 2
878⁴ RANDOM PRINCE [-] 9-9-7 P Carberry, *hld up, prog 5th..*
trkd ldr 3 out, rdn appr last, wknd r-in....... (20 to 1) ... 3
1336² LASATA [-] 8-10-10 G Bradley, *led or dsptd ld, led aftr 4th*
till appr 3 out, rdn, no extr and wknd last, eased.
.............................(4 to 1) ... 4
MAD TOM [-] 8-10-11 J P Banahan, *rear, prog 3 out, kpt on*
frm nxt, not rch ldrs........................(14 to 1) ... 5
940² KINGS ENGLISH [-] 7-10-8 T J Taaffe, *wl plcd, ev ch appr 2*
out, sn rdn and wknd........................(7 to 2) ... 6
878² FRANTESA [-] (bl) 7-9-7 T Horgan, *mid-div, rdn 3 out,*
wknd nxt.............................(16 to 1) ... 7
940³ KILLINEY GRADUATE [-] 7-10-6 K F O'Brien, *mid-div, beh*
and lost pl 4th, mistake four out, tld off whn pld up bef
2 out.............................(7 to 1) ... pu
1231 MAPLE DANCER [-] 7-10-3 C O'Dwyer, *mid-div, rdn and*
wknd 3 out, pld up..........................(10 to 1) ... pu
Dist: 3l, sht-hd, 8l, 4½l. 4m 19.30s. (9 Ran).
(P J Donohoe), M A O'Toole

1383 Navan Races Golf Classic (C & G) INH Flat Race (4 & 5-y-o) £3,105 2m (3:40)

BUCK THE TIDE (Ire) 4-11-9 Mr T Mullins, ...(7 to 2) ... 1
CAFE PRINCE (Ire) 4-11-2 (7") Miss A O'Brien, ...(9 to 2) ... 2
939⁷ CABLE BEACH (Ire) 4-11-4 (5") Mr G J Harford, ...(5 to 1) ... 3
NO WHEN TO RUN (Ire) 5-12-0 Mr P Fenton, (11 to 10 fav) ... 4

942⁵ LOUGH CULTRA DRIVE (Ire) 5-11-9 (5*) Mr J A Nash,
....(12 to 1) 5
DENNETT VALLEY (Ire) 4-11-2 (7*) Mrs D McDonogh,
....(16 to 1) 6
M T POCKETS (Ire) 5-11-11 (3*) Mrs J M Mullins, ...(9 to 1) 7
SPECTACULAR STAR (Ire) 4-11-9 Mr A J Martin, ..(16 to 1) 8
105⁶ STRAWTALDI (Ire) 5-11-7 (7*) Mr J D O'Connell, ...(20 to 1) 9
1223⁶ EXCUSE ME (Ire) 4-11-2 (7*) Mr P English, ...(16 to 1) 10
BIG JIM 5-11-9 (5*) Mr H F Cleary, ...(14 to 1) 11
Dist: 3l, 2l, 3l, 4l. 4m 10.50s. (11 Ran).

(Mrs Rionda Braga), P Mullins

HUNTINGDON (good to soft)
Tuesday November 23rd
Going Correction: PLUS 1.10 sec. per fur. (races 1,3,6), PLUS 0.62 (2,4,5)

1384 Captain Threadneedle Selling Hurdle (3,4,5-y-o) £1,611 2m 110yds.... (1:00)

1211* TAX THE DEVIL (v) 5-11-7 (5*) A Dicken, led second, jnd 2
out, hdd r-in, rallied to ld cl hme.
....(4 to 1 op 3 to 1 tchd 9 to 2) 1
551⁷ HIGHLAND FLAME 4-11-7 D Murphy, al prmnt, trkd wnr
frm 4th, dsptd ld 2 out, led r-in till cl cl hme.
....(11 to 4 op 5 to 2 tchd 3 to 1) 2
1097³ MISTER BLAKE 3-10-9 R Campbell, led to second, cl up till
wknd 3 out................(2 to 1 fav op 9 to 4 tchd 7 to 4) 3
CHILTERN HUNDREDS (USA) 3-10-9 G McCourt, hld up,
hdwy 4th, not pace to chal.
....................................(11 to 1 op 7 to 1 tchd 12 to 1) 4
1244 TOP GUNNER (Ire) 3-10-9 N Williamson, al beh, tld off whn
pld up bef 2 out......(16 to 1 op 20 to 1 tchd 25 to 1) pu
RUE BALZAC (Ire) 5-11-7 R Dunwoody, al beh, tld off whn
pld up bef 2 out........(7 to 2 op 3 to 1 tchd 4 to 1) pu
PLUM LINE 4-11-7 D Bridgwater, sn tld off, pld up aftr
3rd...(33 to 1 op 20 to 1) pu
857 CLASHREAGH (Ire) 5-10-9 (7*) S Arnold, prmnt till wknd
quickly 4th, tld off whn pld up bef nxt.
......................................(33 to 1 op 20 to 1) pu
Dist: ½l, 12l, 12l. 4m 12.80s. a 25.80s (8 Ran).
SR: 22/16/-/-/-/ (Mrs Heather Chakko), S Dow

1385 Young Telegraph Novices' Chase (4-y-o and up) £2,089 2m 5f (1:30)

1248² UNHOLY ALLIANCE 6-11-5 N Williamson, jmpd soundly,
made virtually all, hrd rdn and ran on wl frm last.
.................(7 to 4 fav op 6 to 4 tchd 9 to 4) 1
BOLLINGER 7-11-5 D Murphy, trkd ldg trio, rdn and
swtchd rght r-in, ran on.
..........................(2 to 1 op 9 to 4 tchd 7 to 4) 2+
SPOONHILL WOOD 7-11-0 R Dunwoody, cl up, ev ch last,
ran on one pace and pres.
.......................(11 to 1 op 7 to 1 tchd 12 to 1) 2+
1081³ PRINCE'S COURT (bl) 10-11-7 (7*) D Fortt, cl up, mstks 3rd
and 9th, ev ch 2 out, mistake last, one pace.
....(7 to 1 op 5 to 1) 4
933 BLACK CHURCH 7-11-5 H Davies, not jump wl, al beh, tld
off..........................(20 to 1 op 12 to 1) 5
1194 WELSH COMMANDER 10-11-5 D Bridgwater, blun 4th, sn
beh, tld off.........................(16 to 1 op 12 to 1) 6
WHAT A NOBLE 7-11-5 G McCourt, hld up rear, reminders
8th, mstk tenth, blun 12th, pld up.. (9 to 1 op 6 to 1) pu
Dist: Nk, dd-ht, 2l, dist, 5l. 5m 18.50s. a 23.50s (7 Ran).

(Mrs S C York), K C Bailey

1386 Hoechst Panacur EBF Mares 'National Hunt' Novices' Hurdle Qualifier (4-y-o and up) £2,089 2m 5f 110yds.... (2:00)

CARLINGFORD LAKES 5-10-12 S Smith Eccles, made
all, kicked clr 4 out, hit 2 out, ran on wl.
..........................(12 to 1 op 8 to 1 tchd 14 to 1) 1
791⁸ WELSH LUSTRE (Ire) 4-10-5 (7*) Mr G Hogan, hld up beh
ldrs, hrd rdn appr 2 out, kpt on.....(10 to 1 op 6 to 1) 2
1110* PRINCESS HOTPOT (Ire) 5-11-5 J Osborne, wth ldr till
outpcd 3 out.
..........................(15 to 8 on op 11 to 8 on tchd 6 to 4) 3
GREEN WALK 6-10-12 T Grantham, hld up rear, outpcd 4
out.............................(33 to 1 op 20 to 1) 4
1085⁵ WYJUME (Ire) 4-10-12 D Murphy, hld up, nvr on terms.
....(6 to 1 op 3 to 1) 5
1110³ COUNTRY FLING 5-10-12 R Supple, wtd wth, rdn alng
and outpcd 4 out.......(25 to 1 op 16 to 1 tchd 33 to 1) 6
1027⁶ FLAPPING FREDA (Ire) 5-10-12 R Dunwoody, hld up rear,
al beh, tld off.........................(10 to 1 op 6 to 1) 7
GREENHILL GO ON 8-10-12 R Rowell, hrd ldg pair till
wknd quickly aftr 4th, tld off whn pld up bef 3 out.
....(50 to 1 op 25 to 1) pu
Dist: ½l, 5l, 12l, 6l, 2l, 20l. 5m 26.00s. a 31.00s (8 Ran).
SR: 11/10/12/-/-/ (T Thomson Jones), T Thomson Jones

1387 Peterborough Column Chase Grade 2 (5-y-o and up) £11,088 2½m 110yds

.... (2:30)

1048* TRAVADO 7-11-9 J Osborne, trkd ldr, led 4th, slpd 8th,
pckd 3 out, hdd briefly nxt, quickened r-in, cmftbly.
...........(13 to 8 on tchd 6 to 4 on and 15 to 8 on) 1
1048² DEEP SENSATION 8-11-9 D Murphy, led to 4th, trkd wnr,
led briefly 2 out, not quicken frm last.
..................................(2 to 1 op 7 to 4 tchd 9 to 4) 2
1226 BRANDESTON 8-11-1 P Murphy, hld up in tch, outpcd o'r
4 out, tld off..........(25 to 1 op 16 to 1 tchd 33 to 1) 3
VERY VERY ORDINARY 7-11-1 R Supple, hld up in tch,
outpcd 4 out, tld off....(9 to 1 op 5 to 1 tchd 10 to 1) 4
Dist: 7l, dist, 3l. 5m 8.50s. a 13.50s (4 Ran).
SR: 87/80/-/-/ (Mrs Michael Ennever), N J Henderson

1388 Telegraph Sport Handicap Chase (0-125 5-y-o and up) £2,684 3m. . (3:00)

1197⁵ JIMSTER [91] 11-10-1 R Dunwoody, wth ldr, blun 9th, led
appr 3 out, styd on wl....................(4 to 1 op 7 to 2) 1
1140⁴ LITTLE GENERAL [94] 10-10-4⁴ H Davies, hld up in tch, cld
on ldrs 3 out, styd on one pace........(7 to 1 op 8 to 1) 2
1171* DO BE BRIEF [118] (bl) 8-12-0 I Lawrence, not fluent, led to
second, cl up, hrd rdn frm 3 out, ev ch nxt, one pace.
....(7 to 4 fav tchd 15 to 8) 3
1050⁵ DANDY MINSTREL [109] 9-11-5 D Bridgwater, hld up, cld
12th, hrd rdn and lost pl 15th, tld off whn mstk last.
....(7 to 1 op 8 to 1) 4
1151³ SINGLESOLE [114] (bl) 8-11-10 R Marley, not jump wl, al
beh, tld off whn pld up aftr 3 out.............(5 to 1) pu
714³ DELGANY RUN [101] 9-10-11 J Osborne, led second till
appr 3 out, disputing 3rd and btn whn blun 2 out, pld
up bef last.............................(4 to 1 op 7 to 2) pu
Dist: 5l, 1l, dist. 6m 18.40s. a 30.40s (6 Ran).

(Mrs S Nash), C T Nash

1389 Weekend Telegraph Handicap Hurdle (0-135 4-y-o and up) £2,022 2m 110yds
.... (3:30)

1213⁵ MANEREE [93] 6-10-11 R Campbell, keen hold beh ldrs,
cld 3 out, sn led, ran on wl.
......................................(5 to 2 fav op 7 to 4 tchd 11 to 4) 1
1101 RATIFY [98] 6-11-2 A S Smith, hld up, cld 3 out, ev ch last,
one pace...................................(10 to 1 op 6 to 1) 2
1342 TOP WAVE [105] 5-11-9 M A FitzGerald, hld up in tch, jnd
ldrs 3 out, sn rdn, ev ch appr last, no extr.
....(5 to 1 op 3 to 1) 3
1072⁹ DRIVING FORCE [100] (bl) 7-11-4 G McCourt, cl up, rdn
and ev ch appr 2 out, one pace.
....(7 to 1 op 6 to 1 tchd 8 to 1) 4
1213⁴ MRS MAYHEW [94] 5-10-5 (7*) P Murphy, set steady
pace, hdd aftr 3 out, no extr...........(4 to 1 op 3 to 1) 5
SOLID (Ire) [86] 5-9-13 (5*) D Walsh, hld up, lost tch 5th, no
dngr aftr.........................(25 to 1 op 14 to 1) 6
CREEAGER [106] 11-11-10 B Dalton, trkd ldrs, mstk 3rd,
wknd 3 out........(20 to 1 op 14 to 1 tchd 25 to 1) 7
1213 FIERCE [105] 5-11-9 S Smith Eccles, cl up, rdn and lost pl
quickly 3 out, pld up lme bef nxt.
....................................(100 to 30 op 7 to 2 tchd 4 to 1) pu
Dist: 1l, 4l, 2l, 5l, 2l, 7l. 4m 14.90s. a 27.90s (8 Ran).

(M Tabor), N A Callaghan

WINDSOR (good to firm)
Wednesday November 24th
Going Correction: PLUS 0.13 sec. per fur.

1390 River Thames Novices' Hurdle (4-y-o and up) £2,086 2m............ (12:20)

809⁴ CHAPEL OF BARRAS (Ire) 4-10-12 M Hourigan, beh, steady
hdwy frm 5th, edgd lft, rght and led last, pushed out.
.....................................(4 to 1 op 7 to 2 tchd 9 to 2) 1
ARFEY (Ire) 4-10-12 S Smith Eccles, chsd ldrs till led sn
aftr 5th, hdd last, styd on one pace. (10 to 1 op 6 to 1) 2
SHAARID (USA) 5-10-12 B Powell, led hld sn aftr 5th,
chlgd 3 out, one pace appr last.
....(100 to 30 op 9 to 4 tchd 7 to 2) 3
658² MILZIG (USA) 5-10-12 D O'Sullivan, trkd ldrs, effrt frm
3 out, btn appr last. (7 to 4 fav op 5 to 4 tchd 2 to 1) 4
1303 MASTER MURPHY 4-10-12 E Murphy, beh, some prog frm
3 out.........................(25 to 1 op 16 to 1 tchd 33 to 1) 5
ROAD TO AU BON (USA) 5-10-12 L Harvey, nvr rch ldrs.
...............................(20 to 1 op 16 to 1 tchd 25 to 1) 6
1283 WOODLANDS LEGEND 4-10-12 G McCourt, hdwy 5th,
wknd sn aftr 3 out...............(33 to 1 op 25 to 1) 7
1161⁸ SO AUDACIOUS 5-10-12 C Llewellyn, nvr rch ldrs.
.................................(20 to 1 op 12 to 1 tchd 25 to 1) 8
JOHNS JOY 8-10-7 (5*) A Dicken, beh, effrt 5th, sn wknd.
.................................(14 to 1 op 10 to 1 tchd 16 to 1) 9
1247⁹ GREEN'S TRILOGY (USA) (bl) 5-10-12 M Ahern, wth ldr to
5th, sn rdn and wknd...........................(33 to 1) 10
AUTUMN LEAF 5-10-7 R Rowell, chsd ldrs, hit 4th, wknd
quickly aftr 5th...................................(50 to 1) 11
DOUNHURST 6-10-7 T Grantham, al beh.........(50 to 1) 12

185

COLONIAL BEAUTY (Fr) 4-10-7 M Richards, *al beh.*
....(50 to 1) 13
PRINCE ROONEY (Ire) 5-10-12 N Williamson, *al beh.*
.... (10 to 1 op 5 to 1) 14
TARTAR TERTIUS 9-10-12 B Clifford, *beh whn mstk 3rd, pld up bef nxt*..........................(33 to 1) pu
Dist: 2½l, 3l, 10l, 20l, 5l, 3l, 3l, 15l, 12l, ¾l. 3m 54.40s. a 9.40s (15 Ran).
SR: 11/8/5/-/-/-/ (Hawkridge Farmhouse Cheese Limited), P J Hobbs

1391 Russell Handicap Chase (0-130 4-y-o and up) £3,525 2m........... (12:50)

CROOKED COUNSEL [90] 7-10-0 N Williamson, *made all, sn clr, not fluent, hit 3rd, 6th and 4 out, blun last, styd on wl*.....................(7 to 2 tchd 11 to 4 and 4 to 1) 1
HOLTERMANN (USA) [114] 9-11-10 M Richards, *hld up, hit 3rd, steady hdwy frm 8th, staying on whn blun 3 out, no imprsn aftr*...... (11 to 8 fav op Evens tchd 6 to 4) 2
FRED SPLENDID [92] 10-10-2 R Dunwoody, *chsd wnr frm 3rd, rdn and one pace from 3 out.*
..........................(2 to 1 op 9 to 4 tchd 3 to 1) 3
BRIGGS BUILDERS [108] 9-11-4 Richard Guest, *chsd wnr to 3rd, sn beh.*............(13 to 2 op 5 to 1 tchd 7 to 1) 4
Dist: 6l, 1l, 25l. 4m 5.40s. a 9.40s (4 Ran).
SR: -/17/-/-/ (I R Scott & D J Macfarlane), K C Bailey

1392 Royal Borough 'National Hunt' Novices' Hurdle (4-y-o and up) £1,925 2¾m 110yds.................... (1:20)

NEFARIOUS 7-10-12 M Richards, *steady hdwy 7th, chlgd 3 out, led nxt, drvn clr r-in.*........(12 to 1 op 12 to 1) 1
FOREST FEATHER (Ire) 5-10-12 A Maguire, *sn tracking ldrs, led 8th, hdd 2 out, btn whn screwed last.*
...............(9 to 4 on op 2 to 1 on tchd 15 to 8 on) 2
DOWRY SQUARE (Ire) 5-10-12 E Murphy, *beh 6th, shaken up and hdwy 3 out, styd on same pace.*........ (33 to 1) 3
ROSEN THE BEAU (Ire) 5-10-12 C Llewellyn, *led to 2nd, pushed alng frm 6th, hrd drvn to chase ldrs 8th, wknd 3 out.*..........................(15 to 2 op 5 to 1 tchd 9 to 1) 4
CARRIGLAWN 8-10-12 D Murphy, *pressed ldrs, chlgd 6th, led 7th, hdd nxt, wknd 3 out.*
.........................(20 to 1 op 12 to 1 tchd 25 to 1) 5
POLICEMANS PRIDE (Fr) 4-10-4 (7') J Clarke, *al beh, lost tch frm 8th*.............(16 to 1 op 25 to 1 tchd 14 to 1) 6
TREASSOWE MARINER 5-10-12 H Davies, *mid-div to 7th, wknd nxt*...........(20 to 1 op 12 to 1 tchd 25 to 1) 7
MASTER BAVARD (Ire) 5-10-12 V Slattery, *pressed ldrs till led 3rd, hdd 7th, sn wknd.*
.............................(11 to 1 op 6 to 1 tchd 12 to 1) 8
Dist: 8l, 10l, 6l, 20l, 2l, 10l, 20l. 5m 35.00s. a 16.00s (8 Ran).
(Mrs Richard Kleinwort), Mark Campion

1393 All Or Nothing At All Novices' Chase (5-y-o and up) £3,210 2m 5f..... (1:50)

THE GLOW (Ire) 5-10-10 P Holley, *hld up, steady hdwy to chase ldrs tenth, chlgd 3 out, slight ld whn lft clr nxt, readily*...............(3 to 1 op 5 to 2 tchd 100 to 30) 1
WANDERWEG (Fr) 5-10-10 H Davies, *al tracking ldrs, kpt on same pace frm 3 out.*
.............................(14 to 1 op 10 to 1 tchd 16 to 1) 2
TAREESH 6-10-6 N Williamson, *prmnt, led tenth, hdd 4 out, sn one pace*...... (10 to 1 op 8 to 1 tchd 14 to 1) 3
LEGAL BEAGLE 6-10-11 G Bradley, *prmnt till drpd rear 8th, kpt on ag'n frm 4 out*.........(14 to 1 op 10 to 1) 4
VIAGGIO 5-10-10 L Harvey, *nvr rch ldrs.*
.............................(20 to 1 op 14 to 1) 5
GENERAL BRANDY 7-10-8 (3') P Hide, *made most till hdd tenth, wknd rpdly*............(20 to 1 tchd 25 to 1) 6
HURRICANE BLAKE (bl) 5-10-10 J Railton, *beh, hit 3rd and 9th, no ch and jmpd lft fnl 4.*
..........................(100 to 30 op 7 to 2 tchd 4 to 1) 7
POWER HAPPY 8-10-6 B Clifford, *hit 1st, chsd ldrs till mstk and uns rdr 7th*...............(33 to 1 op 20 to 1) ur
HILLWALK 7-11-4 D Morris, *sn in tch, led 4 out, narrowly hdd whn blun badly and uns rdr 2 out.*
...........................(6 to 5 fav op 5 to 4 tchd 11 to 8) ur
FLYING FINISH 8-10-11 J Akehurst, *hit 1st, tld off 7th, pld up bef 4 out.*............(33 to 1 op 20 to 1) pu
Dist: 7l, 7l, 3l, 12l, 20l, 6l. 5m 19.80s. a 8.80s (10 Ran).
SR: 21/14/3/5/-/-/ (Mrs T Brown), D R C Elsworth

1394 Masterdrive Handicap Chase (0-130 5-y-o and up) £3,655 3m........ (2:20)

TOUCHING STAR [95] 8-10-4 M Hourigan, *beh, steady hdwy 14th, chlgd 3 out, led nxt, drvn out.*
...............................(5 to 1 op 9 to 2 tchd 6 to 1) 1
SANDAIG [91] 7-10-0 N Williamson, *beh, hdwy appr 4 out, chlgd 2 out, styd on und pres r-in.*
...................(11 to 4 fav tchd 3 to 1 and 5 to 2) 2
SHASTON [101] 8-11-10 P Holley, *chsd ldrs, led 5th, hit tenth, clr 12th, hit 13th and 14th, hdd 2 out, ev ch last, one pace*..........................(7 to 1 tchd 8 to 1) 3

1246* UNDER OFFER [93] (bl) 12-10-2 M A FitzGerald, *led to 3rd, led aftr 4th to 5th, rdn after 14th, wknd four out.*
....................................(5 to 1 op 9 to 2 tchd 6 to 1) 4
1208⁷ MR JAMBOREE [118] 7-11-13 D Murphy, *led 3rd to 4th, wknd 11th*..............................(9 to 1 op 6 to 1) 5
1191² OBIE'S TRAIN [111] (bl) 7-11-6 R Dunwoody, *chsd ldrs, wknq whn hit 12th*......(15 to 2 op 6 to 1 tchd 10 to 1) 6
1343² SMARTIE EXPRESS [119] 11-12-0 G McCourt, *beh till hdwy 13th, 4th and wknq whn pld up bef 3 out.*
..............................(4 to 1 op 5 to 2 tchd 9 to 2) pu
Dist: ½l, ¾l, 25l, 15l, 15l. 6m 3.20s. a 8.20s (7 Ran).
SR: 25/20/29/-/6/-/-/ (P J Hobbs), P J Hobbs

1395 White Hart Conditional Jockeys' Handicap Hurdle (0-125 4-y-o and up) £2,005 2m.................... (2:50)

1213³ MONDAY CLUB [108] 9-11-5 (5') D Meade, *steady hdwy 5th, chlgd 3 out, sn led.*............(7 to 2 op 11 to 4) 1
796* SPRING TO GLORY [97] 6-10-13 A Procter, *chsd ldrs, led appr 3 out, sn hdd, kpt on same pace frm 2 out.*
.............................(7 to 2 op 9 to 2 tchd 6 to 1) 2
1249² SOLEIL DANCER (Ire) [101] 5-11-0 (3') D Fortt, *chsd ldrs 4th, led 5th, hdd appr 3 out, sn led ag'n, headed aftr three out, soon outpcd.*.............(4 to 1 op 3 to 1) 3
1154³ SANDRO [84] (bl) 4-10-0 V Slattery, *chsd ldrs 4th, hdd 5th, wknd aftr 3 out.* (16 to 1 op 14 to 1 tchd 20 to 1) 4
1006 DERISBAY (Ire) [85] (bl) 5-10-1 A Dicken, *led to 3rd, styd prmnt till wknd 3 out.*..........................(33 to 1) 5
1249⁵ MISTER ODDY [97] 7-10-13 J McCarthy, *nvr gng pace to ldrs.*.........................(12 to 1 tchd 14 to 1) 6
1172⁴ KAHER (USA) [105] 6-11-7 T Jenks, *nvr better than mid-div.*..........................(14 to 1 op 12 to 1) 7
1240² ARANY [95] 6-10-6 (5') P Smith Eccles, *prmnt, lost pos 4th, rdn to chase ldrs nxt, sn wknd.*
............................(3 to 1 fav op 11 to 4 tchd 7 to 2) 8
MAD CASANOVA [103] (bl) 8-11-5 D O'Sullivan, *drpd rear 4th, rallied and effrt nxt, sn wknd, tld off whn pld up bef last*..........(11 to 2 op 7 to 1 tchd 9 to 1) pu
Dist: 5l, 7l, 2½l, 10l, 6l, 8l, 10l. 3m 59.40s. a 14.40s (9 Ran).
(J C Tuck), J C Tuck

1396 Levy Board Seventh Handicap Hurdle (0-135 4-y-o and up) £2,127 2¾m 110yds........................ (3:20)

1139² NICK THE DREAMER [107] 8-10-2 R Dunwoody, *trkd ldrs, chlgd 3 out, sn led, pushed out.* ....(4 to 1 jt-fav tchd 5 to 1) 1
1206⁶ MEDITATOR [105] 9-9-9 (5') S Curran, *hdwy 7th, ev ch 3 out, rdn appr last, rallied r-in.*
.............................(7 to 1 op 8 to 1 tchd 7 to 1) 2
701* HUGLI [106] (bl) 6-10-1 M Richards, *prmnt till rdn alng frm 4th, hrd drvn from 3 out, styd on r-in.*
.............................(13 to 2 op 6 to 1 tchd 7 to 1) 3
1139¹ MENEBUCK [129] 7-11-10 E Murphy, *beh 5th, hdwy to track ldrs 8th, one pace frm 3 out.*
.........................(5 to 1 op 4 to 1 tchd 11 to 2) 4
WICK POUND [115] (bl) 7-10-10 T Grantham, *led 3rd to 6th, led ag'n 8th, hdd aftr 3 out, sn wknd*........(4 to 1 jt-fav op 9 to 4 tchd 9 to 2) 5
1006⁴ CHILD OF THE MIST [116] 7-10-11 A Maguire, *led second to 3rd, led 6th to 8th, rdn and wknd 3 out.*
.............................(8 to 1 tchd 7 to 1) 6
979⁵ STORM DRUM [112] 4-10-7 N Williamson, *beh frm 5th.*
...................(10 to 1 op 7 to 1 tchd 12 to 1) 7
DUNCAN IDAHO [107] 10-10-2 M A FitzGerald, *al in rear.*.........................(14 to 1 op 12 to 1 tchd 16 to 1) 8
HAPPY HORSE (NZ) [108] 6-10-3³ A Tory, *chsd ldrs to 8th.*
............................(16 to 1 op 14 to 1 tchd 20 to 1) 9
1072 FLUTTER MONEY [108] 9-10-3³ G Upton, *with ldrs 5th, wknd quickly nxt.*....................(66 to 1) 10
GHOFAR [125] (bl) 10-11-6 P Holley, *al beh, tld off whn pld up bef last*....(20 to 1 op 16 to 1 tchd 25 to 1) pu
Dist: ¾l, 12l, sht-hd, 3½l, 20l, 1½l, dist. 5m 26.20s. a 7.20s (11 Ran).
SR: 31/28/17/40/22/3/ (A K Holbrook), W G M Turner

NAAS (IRE) (soft)
Thursday November 25th

1397 Town Maiden Hurdle (4-y-o) £3,105 2m
....(12:45)

1077* KLAIRON DAVIS (Fr) 11-9 T J Taaffe, ...(5 to 2) 1
902⁴ THE ODD TIME (Ire) 11-1 (3') C O'Brien, ...(12 to 1) 2
1230⁴ MR SNAGGLE (Ire) 10-13 (5') T J O'Sullivan, ...(12 to 1) 3
DOWHATYOULIKE (Ire) 10-13 P Carberry, ...(10 to 1) 4
1036⁸ AN MAINEACH (Ire) 11-4 C F Swan, ...(14 to 1) 5
WOODVILLE STAR (Ire) 10-13 T Horgan, ...(14 to 1) 6
DIVINITY RUN (Ire) 10-13 (5') T P Rudd, ...(8 to 1) 7
1180⁶ SAM VAUGHAN (Ire) 10-11 (7') Mr W M O'Sullivan, (14 to 1) 8
1333 MARYVILLE LADY (Ire) 10-8 K F O'Brien, ...(25 to 1) 9
MAXWELTON BRAES (Ire) 11-4 (5') M G Cleary, ..(25 to 1) 10
923* GALE TOI (Ire) 11-9 G Bradley, ...(6 to 4 fav) 11
902⁶ PEPPERONI EXPRESS (Ire) 11-9 J P Banahan, ...(10 to 1) 12
HAWAIIAN TASCA (Ire) 11-2 (7') J P Broderick, ...(10 to 1) 13

1077³ PLASSY BOY (Ire) 11-4 L P Cusack, ...(12 to 1)   14
FAYS FOLLY (Ire) 10-6 (7") D J Kavanagh, ...(25 to 1)   15
1075 FREEWAY HALO (Ire) 10-10 (3") T J Mitchell, ...(25 to 1)   16
255* KING WAH GLORY (Ire) 11-4 (7") C O'Dwyer, ...(11 to 2)   17
798 THE CRIOSRA (Ire) 11-4 S H O'Donovan, ...(50 to 1)   18
1230 LANCANA (Ire) 10-13 C N Bownes, ...(25 to 1)   19
1230 SWIFT GLIDER (Ire) 10-6 (7") K P Gaule, ...(50 to 1)   20
SHARP CIRCUIT 10-11 (7") E G Callaghan, ...(25 to 1)   21
STEVIES DEN 11-4 K F O'Brien, ...(16 to 1)   22
1333 AMOROUS HUG (Ire) 10-8 (5") C P Dunne, ...(50 to 1)   23
1267⁵ SUTR-MAKE (Ire) 11-9 J P Byrne, ...(12 to 1)   pu
1036⁴ ALVATUR (Ire) 10-11 (7") K C Hartnett, ...(12 to 1)   pu
Dist: 12l, hd, 4l, 1½l. 4m 2.10s. (25 Ran).

(C Jones), A L T Moore

1398 Poplar Square Chase (5-y-o and up) £3,105 2½m. . . . . (1:15)

FLASHING STEEL 8-12-0 K F O'Brien, ...(5 to 4)   1
1231* COMMERCIAL ARTIST 7-11-11 C O'Dwyer, ...(5 to 4 on)   2
940⁴ GOOD TEAM 8-12-0 T J Taaffe, ...(7 to 1)   3
IPANEMA 6-10-6 (5") Mr P M Kelly, ...(33 to 1)   f
Dist: 20l, dist. 5m 27.00s. (4 Ran).

(C J Haughey), J E Mulhern

1399 Kildare Novice Chase (4-y-o and up) £3,450 2m 3f. . . . . (1:45)

ATONE 6-11-8 C F Swan, ... (4 to 1 jt-fav)   1
1019² INCA CHIEF 9-11-3 (5") D P Geoghegan, ...(10 to 1)   2
1035³ ANOTHER EXCUSE (Ire) 5-10-12 (7") Mr W M O'Sullivan,
. . . .(8 to 1)   3
690⁶ FEATHERED GALE 6-11-8 T J Taaffe, ...(11 to 2)   4
1334⁴ THE WEST'S ASLEEP 8-11-5 (3") C O'Brien, ...(16 to 1)   5
929³ STRONG CHERRY 7-10-10 (7") Mr K Taylor, ...(33 to 1)   6
1178 PARSONS BRIG 7-11-8 K F O'Brien, ...(14 to 1)   7
1331⁵ MORNING DREAM 6-11-8 J F Titley, ...(14 to 1)   8
941 MINSTREL SAM 7-11-8 A J Martin, ...(33 to 1)   9
807³ SHEAMY'S DREAM (Ire) (bl) 5-11-5 J Shortt, ...(9 to 1)   10
941 BALLINASEEN BRIDGE 6-11-1 (7") Mr W J Gleeson,
. . . .(25 to 1)   11
969 MR BARNEY 6-11-8 A Powell, ...(33 to 1)   12
674 SUITS ME FINE 10-11-1 (7") Miss M Holohan, ...(20 to 1)   f
BART OWEN 8-11-8 G Bradley, ...(10 to 1)   f
1037⁵ BELEEK CASTLE 7-11-8 T Horgan, ...(14 to 1)   f
RIGHT COOL 7-11-8 S H O'Donovan, ...(33 to 1)   f
BUCKS-CHOICE 6-11-3 (5") T P Treacy, ...(4 to 1 jt-fav)   f
554 MONKS AIRE 6-11-3 L P Cusack, ...(33 to 1)   f
Dist: 1½l, 2½l, ¾l, 13l. 5m 16.60s. (18 Ran).

(Robert Sinclair), J R Cox

1400 Newbridge Handicap Hurdle (4-y-o and up) £3,105 2m. . . . .(2:15)

1036* JUPITER JIMMY [-] 4-10-3 C F Swan, ...(5 to 2 fav)   1
1269⁸ CELTIC SAILS (Ire) [-] (bl) 5-10-7 (5") Mr P J Casey, (12 to 1)   2
805* DARCARI ROSE (Ire) [-] 4-9-1 (7") T Martin, ...(10 to 1)   3
854³ THATCH AND GOLD (Ire) [-] 5-10-12 (5") J R Barry, (8 to 1)   4
1269⁴ PLUMBOB (Ire) [-] 4-10-5 (5") T P Rudd, ...(7 to 1)   5
1269 HIS WAY (Ire) [-] 4-11-0 J Shortt, ...(14 to 1)   6
34³ BANAIYKA (Ire) [-] 4-10-9 (5") T P Treacy, ...(6 to 1)   7
1232⁸ COIN MACHINE (Ire) [-] 4-10-7 T Horgan, ...(8 to 1)   8
1176⁹ CRAZY LADY [-] 7-9-3³ (7") J M Donnelly, ...(33 to 1)   9
1269³ ROMAN FORUM (Ire) [-] 5-10-13 (3") Mr A E Lacy, . .(5 to 1)   10
PARLIAMENT HALL [-] 7-11-13 K F O'Brien, ...(10 to 1)   11
1075⁹ THE BOURDA [-] 7-9-9 F Woods, ...(20 to 1)   12
689 ASHBORO (Ire) [-] 4-9-5 (7") Mr J Williss, ...(20 to 1)   13
1230 PEACE TRIBUTE (Ire) [-] 4-9-3 (7") K D Maher, ...(25 to 1)   14
1036 REASON TO BELIEVE (Ire) [-] 4-9-0 (7") J P Broderick,
. . . .(33 to 1)   15
46⁷ PARTNERS IN CRIME [-] 5-10-5 (7") B Bowens, ...(8 to 1)   ur
Dist: 2½l, 1½l, 1l, 3l. 4m 16.50s. (16 Ran).

(James F Murphy), J E Kiely

1401 INH Stallion Owners N'vce Hurdle Qualifier (5-y-o and up) £3,795 2½m . . . .(2:45)

WINTER BELLE (USA) 5-12-0 J Shortt, ...(2 to 1 fav)   1
937² COURT MELODY (Ire) 5-11-7 (7") J P Broderick, . .(11 to 4)   2
1074⁸ MAN OF IRON 6-11-6 F Woods, ...(33 to 1)   3
1265² FAMBO LAD (Ire) 5-11-6 Mr J A Berry, ...(7 to 1)   4
1332⁵ LUMINOUS LIGHT 6-11-1 Mr M Phillips, ...(8 to 1)   5
1265⁶ WILD VENTURE (Ire) 5-11-1 A Powell, ...(10 to 1)   6
1330³ LISCAHILL HIGHWAY 6-11-3 (3") D P Murphy, ...(14 to 1)   7
IAMWHATIAM 7-11-6 S H O'Donovan, ...(14 to 1)   8
DIFFERENT TUNE 5-11-1 M Duffy, ...(20 to 1)   9
1378⁴ WOLF WINTER 8-11-9 (5") P A Roche, ...(7 to 1)   10
1270⁵ CALMOS 5-10-13 (7") K P Gaule, ...(20 to 1)   11
853⁸ COOLREE (Ire) 5-11-2 O K F O'Brien, ...(12 to 1)   12
689 GALES JEWEL 7-10-10 (5") M G Cleary, ...(14 to 1)   13
JIMS CHOICE 6-11-5 (7") D T Evans, ...(33 to 1)   14
1018⁴ COUNTERBALANCE 6-11-1 B Sheridan, ...(14 to 1)   15
1265 HELENS LOVE (Ire) 5-10-12 (3") D Bromley, ...(25 to 1)   16
GLITTERING PAN 7-10-12 (3") C O'Brien, ...(33 to 1)   17
1074⁷ COMICALITY 5-11-6 T J Taaffe, ...(14 to 1)   18
GOLDEN PLAN (Ire) 5-11-6 C N Bowens, ...(33 to 1)   19

1052² GREAT ADVENTURE (Ire) 5-10-13 (7") Mr P M Cloke,
. . . .(16 to 1)   20
PRANKSTER 7-12-0 C F Swan, ...(12 to 1)   21
1265 RIVERLAND (Ire) 5-11-6 D H O'Connor, ...(20 to 1)   f
1235 AUSSIE BREEZE (Ire) 5-11-1 T Horgan, ...(50 to 1)   pu
Dist: Sht-hd, 25l, 1½l, 1½l. 5m 12.60s. (23 Ran).

(John Muldoon), Patrick Prendergast

1402 Rathcoole Handicap Chase (0-110 4-y-o and up) £3,105 3m. . . . .(3:15)

806 MARKET SURVEY [-] (bl) 12-9-8 T Horgan, ...(25 to 1)   1
1035⁵ KINGS HILL [-] 11-9-9 (7") J Butler, ...(14 to 1)   2
1268 BOG LEAF VI [-] 10-9-0 (7") J P Broderick, ...(10 to 1)   3
1707 GERTIES PRIDE [-] 9-10-13 (3") C O'Brien, ...(14 to 1)   4
1158³ LA CERISE [-] (bl) 10-9-4 (3") D Bromley, ...(14 to 1)   5
905⁸ CAPINCUR EILE [-] 7-10-13 (7") Mr N C Kelleher, . . .(16 to 1)   6
992⁴ OPRYLAND [-] 8-11-2 G Bradley, ...(10 to 1)   7
1158⁵ SYLVIA'S SAFFRON [-] (bl) 6-9-10 (3") T J Mitchell, (20 to 1)   8
1268³ FAIRY PARK [-] (bl) 8-11-2 F Woods, ...(11 to 2 jt-fav)   9
941⁹ WYLDE HIDE [-] 6-9-11 (5") T P Rudd, ...(16 to 1)   10
691⁵ BUNNINADDEN [-] 10-9-12 W T Slattery Jnr, ...(14 to 1)   11
800 WATERLOO ANDY [-] 7-10-9 P L Malone, ...(14 to 1)   f
1179⁹ RUSSIAN GALE (Ire) [-] 5-9-11¹ J Jones, ...(25 to 1)   f
1159³ GOLA LADY [-] 6-10-9 C N Bowens, ...(10 to 1)   ur
SET YOUR SIGHTS [-] 10-11-6 T J Taaffe, ...(8 to 1)   pu
1178 ROSSI NOVAE [-] (bl) 10-12-0 Mr S R Murphy, ...(20 to 1)   pu
966² MALACHYS BAR [-] 9-11-5 J F Titley, ...(6 to 1)   pu
1179 DEL MONTE BOY [-] 8-10-8 G M O'Neill, ...(33 to 1)   pu
941 QUIET MONEY [-] 6-10-4 (5") D P Geoghegan, ...(20 to 1)   pu
1159* HURRICANE TOMMY [-] (bl) 6-10-12 (5",4ex) Mr G J Harford,
. . . .(11 to 2 jt-fav)   pu
1231⁸ FRIENDLY ARGUMENT [-] 8-11-4 J Magee, ...(12 to 1)   pu
1035⁸ CARRIGEEN GALA [-] 6-10-5 A Powell, ...(16 to 1)   12
Dist: 4½l, 1l, 3l, hd. 6m 45.00s. (22 Ran).

(Racing Management Services), V T O'Brien

1403 Celbridge Flat Race (5-y-o) £3,105 2m . . . .(3:45)

MUCKLEMEG (Ire) 11-2 (7") Mr M Kavanagh, ...(4 to 1)   1
926⁸ COURT MASTER (Ire) 11-7 (7") Mr B Moran, ...(10 to 1)   2
808⁴ CAILIN RUA (Ire) 11-6 (3") Mr A E Lacy, ...(10 to 1)   3
MOONSHEE (Ire) 11-6 (3") Miss M Olivefalk, ...(14 to 1)   4
RUN BAVARD (Ire) 11-11 (3") Mrs M Mullins, ...(8 to 1)   5
1160² KARA'S DREAM (Ire) 11-9 Mr S R Murphy, ...(12 to 1)   6
YOU'VE DONE WHAT (Ire) 11-11 (3") Mr D Valentine,
. . . .(9 to 4 fav)   7
CASH IT IN (Ire) 11-4 (5") Mr J P Berry, ...(12 to 1)   8
SOUTH WESTERLY (Ire) 11-7 (7") Mr E Norris, ...(5 to 1)   9
993² NO TAG (Ire) 12-0 Mr E Bolger, ...(9 to 2)   10
TUDOR THYNE (Ire) 11-6 (3") Mr P McMahon, ...(10 to 1)   11
857⁸ PERSPEX GALE (Ire) 11-4 (5") Mr J A Nash, ...(14 to 1)   12
1236 DASDILEMMA (Ire) 11-4 (5") Mr D McGoona, ...(16 to 1)   13
993⁸ CARRIG DANCER (Ire) 11-2 (7") Mr K Whelan, ...(25 to 1)   14
FARNAN (Ire) 12-0 Mr J Queally, ...(12 to 1)   15
1383⁹ STRAWTALDI (Ire) (bl) 11-7 (7") Mr J D O'Connell, . .(20 to 1)   16
LADY MARILYN (Ire) 11-9 Mr A J Martin, ...(12 to 1)   17
PARSONS BELLE (Ire) 11-2 (7") Mr P English, ...(16 to 1)   18
ANOTHER ROLLO (Ire) 12-0 Mr P Fenton, ...(20 to 1)   19
3⁶ PILS INVADER (Ire) 11-9 Mr M McNulty, ...(12 to 1)   20
DOCTOR SHODDY (Ire) 11-11 (3") Mr A R Coonan, . .(12 to 1)   21
MONALEE GALE (Ire) 11-9 (5") Mr H F Cleary, ...(14 to 1)   pu
Dist: 14l, 15l, 1l, 2l. 3m 59.30s. (22 Ran).

(A Kavanagh), S J Treacy

NOTTINGHAM (good to soft)
Thursday November 25th
Going Correction: PLUS 1.20 sec. per fur.

1404 Kegworth Selling Hurdle (3 & 4-y-o) £2,041 2m. . . . .(1:10)

1338² MARAT (USA) (v) 3-10-7 G McCourt, *pushed alng in mid-field, improved appr 3 out, led bef nxt, styd on grimly r-in*. . . . . (7 to 2 fav op 5 to 2 tchd 4 to 1)   1
193⁸ KUTAN (Ire) 3-10-7 E Byrne, *nvr far away, drvn up to join issue 3 out, bumped nxt, kpt on same pace r-in*. (33 to 1)   2
793² MISSED THE BOAT (Ire) 3-10-7 H Davies, *patiently rdn. improved on outsd to join ldrs appr 3 out, ridden and one pace betw last 2*. . . . .(33 to 1)   3
1092⁵ KING'S GUEST (Ire) 4-11-9 J Callaghan, *al wl plcd, ev ch appr 3 out, stumbled nxt, fdd betw last 2*.
. . . .(8 to 1 op 7 to 1)   4
1217⁷ GROGFRYN 3-10-7 A Maguire, *trkd ldr, led appr 3 out till bef nxt, wknd and pres betw last 2*. .(5 to 1 op 4 to 1)   5
851 WATER DIVINER 3-10-7 J Ryan, *settled midfield, drvn up to join issue appr 3 out, fdd und pres r-in*.(50 to 1)   6
1252 ABSOLUTLEY FOXED 4-11-4 T Wall, *pressed ldrs, ev ch appr 3 out, wknd quickly nxt*. . . .(14 to 1 op 12 to 1)   7
1271⁶ TAKE THE MICK (bl) 3-10-7 C Llewellyn, *tucked away on ins, effrt appr 3 out, blun nxt, sn lost tch*.
. . . .(8 to 1 op 7 to 1)   8
BOOGIE BOPPER (v) 4-12-0 J Lower, *nvr far away, hrd at work whn pace lifted appr 3 out, found little*.
. . . .(6 to 1 op 4 to 1)   9

1244 TREBLE LASS 3-10-2 J Leech, *trkd ldrs, ev ch aftr 4 out,
wknd und pres nxt*..............(10 to 1 op 20 to 1) 10
1253 LARKSPUR LEGEND 3-10-2 (5") T Eley, *settled midfield,
pushed alng to keep up appr 4 out, btn nxt*....(33 to 1) 11
1237⁵ DUNBAR 3-10-7 D Wilkinson, *not fluent, beh and struggling hfwy, nvr a factor*..........(14 to 1 op 12 to 1) 12
1079 ICE WALK 4-10-11 (7") P Ward, *beh and struggling hfwy,
tld off*.......................................(25 to 1) 13
1042 GOLDEN SICKLE (USA) 4-11-9 A Coogan, *al al last, tld
off*...(50 to 1) 14
622⁸ PREMIER ENVELOPE (Ire) 4-11-9 C Hawkins, *in tch to
hfwy, tld off whn pld up appr 3 out, dismounted, broke
dwn*..(33 to 1) ur
1244 NIGHTMARE LADY 3-10-2 J McLaughlin, *al in rear, tld off
pld up bef 3 out*...............................(33 to 1) pu
PORTWAY PRINCESS 3-10-2 W Marston, *chsd ldg bunch
to hfwy, tld off whn pld up bef 3 out.*
...................................(16 to 1 op 25 to 1) pu
1187 POLK (Fr) 4-12-0 M Foster, *led till hdd and wknd quickly
aftr 4 out, pld up bef nxt*......................(20 to 1) pu
Dist: 6l, 2l, 5l, 12l, 5l, ½l, 5l, 3½l, 3½l, dist. 4m 13.30s. a 29.30s (18 Ran).

(H E Shepherd), J R Jenkins

1405 Bingham Novices' Chase (5-y-o and up) £2,346 2m 5f 110yds....... (1:40)

MUDAHIM 7-10-12 W Marston, *jmpd rght, dsptd early ld,
chsd clr ldr fnl circuit, drw level 2 out, led and lft clear
last*..............(7 to 4 fav op 5 to 4 tchd 2 to 1) 1
LOBRIC 8-10-12 S Smith Eccles, *chsd ldrs, feeling pace
and struggling fnl circuit, styd on grimly frm 3 out, nvr
able to chal*....................(20 to 1 op 16 to 1) 2
948⁷ FEARSOME 7-10-12 R Supple, *mstks, outpcd whn
slightly hmpd 9th, rallied fnl circuit, one pace last 3.*
...................................(25 to 1 op 20 to 1) 3
1067⁵ OUTFIELD 7-10-7 R Bellamy, *last and niggled alng hfwy,
nvr able to rch chalg pos*....................(33 to 1) 4
1324⁵ BALLAD RULER 7-10-12 A Maguire, *chsd ldrs, not fluent
9th, struggling fnl circuit, nvr a factor.*
...................................(20 to 1 op 12 to 1) 5
SACROSANCT 9-10-12 J Osborne, *set modest pace till
hdd appr 7th, pushed alng whn f 9th.*
...................................(9 to 4 tchd 5 to 2) f
DUHALLOW LODGE 6-10-12 Richard Guest, *mstks, nrly
uns rdr 3rd, led and quickened appr 7th, sn clr, fnd 2
out, hdd and f last.*.................(11 to 4 op 9 to 4) f
984⁵ PICKETSTONE (bl) 6-10-12 G McCourt, *patiently rdn,
steady hdwy to chase clr ldg pair fnl circuit, lost tch
and pld up bef 3 out*.............(14 to 1 op 20 to 1) pu
Dist: 25l, 1l, 12l, dist. 5m 47.00s. a 34.00s (8 Ran).

SR: 2/-/-/-/-/ (K W Bell), C D Broad

1406 Rainworth Novices' Hurdle (4-y-o and up) £1,872 2m 5f 110yds....... (2:10)

1167² NED THE HALL (Ire) 5-10-12 A Maguire, *tucked away on
ins, improved to nose ahead aftr 4 out, clr last, drvn
out*.................(11 to 10 fav op Evens tchd 6 to 4) 1
KENILWORTH (Ire) 5-10-12 M Dwyer, *patiently rdn,
smooth hdwy whn almost cmd out by loose horse 5 out,
drw level last 3, ridden and wnt lft r-in, no extr.*
...................................(11 to 2 op 7 to 2 tchd 6 to 1) 2
LIE DETECTOR 5-10-12 J Osborne, *steadied into midfield
hfwy, jnd ldg pair appr 3 out, one pace frm betw last 2.*
...................................(11 to 4 op 3 to 1) 3
1173⁷ MARINERS COVE 5-10-12 W Humphreys, *nvr far away,
pressed ldg trio 4 out, rdn and outpcd aftr.*
...................................(25 to 1 op 20 to 1) 4
GOD SPEED YOU (Ire) 4-10-12 W Marston, *pressed ldrs,
bustled alng whn pace lifted 4 out, sn lost tch, tld off.*
...................................(25 to 1 op 20 to 1 tchd 33 to 1) 5
1108⁵ PARSON'S WAY 6-10-12 G Upton, *in tch, struggling whn
pace quickened fnl circuit, tld off frm 5 out.* (100 to 1) 6
1301⁶ ALIAS SILVER 6-10-5 (7") Mr N Bradley, *ran in snatches,
struggling to go pace hfwy, sn tld off.*
...................................(33 to 1 op 25 to 1) 7
1169⁶ CARAGH BRIDGE 6-10-12 R Supple, *led till hdd aftr 3rd,
styd hndy till lost tch quickly 4 out, tld off.*
...................................(6 to 1 op 20 to 1) 8
1199² IVY HOUSE (Ire) 5-10-12 L Wyer, *tucked away in midfield,
ev ch whn blun and uns rdr 7th*...... (6 to 1 op 5 to 1) ur
1304⁴ GRAND RAPIDS (USA) 6-11-5 H Davies, *pressed ldrs, drvn
alng whn pace lifted 8th, sn lost tch, pld up bef 2 out.*
...................................(25 to 1 op 16 to 1 tchd 33 to 1) pu
COOL PARADE (USA) 5-10-12 P Niven, *pressed ldr, led aftr
3rd till after 4 out, lost tch quickly and pld up bef nxt.*
...................................(50 to 1) pu
MOYHILL (Ire) 4-10-12 R Garritty, *pressed ldrs for o'r a
circuit, lost tch appr 4 out, tld off whn pld up bef nxt.*
...................................(50 to 1 op 33 to 1) pu
Dist: 4l, 7l, dist, 10l, 8l, 15l, dist. 5m 43.10s. a 41.10s (12 Ran).

(Martyn Booth), K C Bailey

1407 Wollaton Handicap Chase (0-120 5-y-o and up) £2,726 2m 5f 110yds.... (2:40)

1089³ ARDCRONEY CHIEF [102] 7-10-13 P Holley, *made all, clr
fnl circuit, jnd last 2, rallied to go clear ag'n r-in.*
...................................(9 to 2 op 3 to 1) 1
1216² DUO DROM [99] 8-10-10 D Murphy, *hit second, given time
to reco'r, steady hdwy to chase wnr 5 out, drw level last
2, found little r-in.* (13 to 8 fav op 7 to 4 tchd 2 to 1) 2
1144⁵ WIGTOWN BAY [94] 10-10-5 P Niven, *patiently rdn,
improved to chase wnr fnl circuit, drvn alng 4 out, btn
whn hit 2 out*...................(10 to 1 op 8 to 1) 3
1352* ZAMIL (USA) [113] 8-11-10 (7ex) R Supple, *al tracking ldrs,
effrt hfwy, feeling pace 6 out, sn lost tch.*
...................................(5 to 2 op 2 to 1 tchd 11 to 4) 4
1212⁵ PLAT REAY [113] (bl) 9-11-10 C Llewellyn, *pressed wnr,
struggling to hold pl fnl circuit, tired and jmpd rght
last 4, tld off*...................(5 to 1 op 6 to 1) 5
NICKNAVAR [90] 8-10-11 T Grantham, *wth ldrs till pld up
lme bef 4th*.......................(33 to 1 op 25 to 1) pu
Dist: 7l, 10l, 15l, 12l. 5m 47.30s. a 34.30s (6 Ran).

(W H Dore), D R Gandolfo

1408 Merit Three Year Old Hurdle £2,532 2m................... (3:10)

1253* MY BALLYBOY 10-7 (5") A Procter, *al hndy, led appr 2 out,
hrd pressed frm betw last two, kpt on grimly r-in.*
...................................(12 to 1 op 10 to 1 tchd 14 to 1) 1
1166² HOSTILE WITNESS (Ire) (v) 10-12 M Richards, *patiently
rdn, steady hdwy to join ldg trio hfwy, ev ch whn wnt
lft betw last 2, kpt on.*
...................................(9 to 4 fav op 5 to 2 tchd 11 to 4) 2
1062* REGAL AURA (Ire) 11-5 J Callaghan, *nvr far away, ev ch
appr 3 out, rdn and outpcd frm betw last 2.*
...................................(5 to 1 tchd 7 to 2) 3
IJAB (Can) 10-12 N Smith, *patiently rdn, smooth hdwy to
track ldrs appr 3 out, not quicken frm nxt, can
improve*.........................(33 to 1) 4
1243 SEASIDE DREAMER 10-12 Mr A Hambly, *co'red up beh ldg
bunch, steady hdwy appr 3 out, kpt on same pace frm
nxt*............................(33 to 1 op 25 to 1) 5
1284² STREPHON (Ire) 10-12 M Dwyer, *led aftr 3rd to 5th, led
ag'n after 4 out till appr 2 out, no extr.*
...................................(5 to 1 op 4 to 1) 6
790⁸ JASPER ONE 10-12 R Garritty, *nvr far away, ev ch and
niggled alng appr 3 out, wknd quickly aftr nxt.*
...................................(50 to 1) 7
1147² THE PREMIER EXPRES 10-9 (3") N Bentley, *al hndy, led
5th till aftr 4 out, wkng whn blun 2 out.*
...................................(7 to 1 op 5 to 1) 8
851 BITRAN 10-12 A S Smith, *led till aftr 3rd, drvn alng to
hold pl 4 out, sn btn off*..........(7 to 1 op 5 to 1) 9
1244⁵ SHARED GOLD 10-12 M Bosley, *tracking ldrs whn blun
4th, sn lost pl, no further dngr.*....(33 to 1 op 25 to 1) 10
TIMOTHY CASEY 10-12 A Maguire, *last and hld up,
smooth hdwy appr 3 out, wknd and eased bef nxt,
better for race.......(16 to 1 op 20 to 1 tchd 14 to 1) 11
997⁵ WORDSMITH (Ire) 11-5 W Marston, *co'red up beh ldg
bunch, effrt hfwy, fdd appr 3 out...(10 to 1 op 8 to 1) 12
1147 TODDEN 10-9 (3") A Larnach, *beh most of way, tld off frm
4 out.*..........................(50 to 1 op 33 to 1) 13
Dist: 1l, 20l, 5l, 7l, 5l, 8l, 4l, 3l, 12l, 1l. 4m 9.30s. a 25.30s (13 Ran).

SR: 23/22/9/-/-/-/ (A Bailey), A Bailey

1409 Bulwell Handicap Chase (0-115 5-y-o and up) £2,678 2m............. (3:40)

1279* PERSIAN SWORD [89] 7-10-8 (7ex) A Maguire, *nvr far
away, jmpd ahead 3 out, lft clr nxt, kpt on wl r-in.*
...................................(9 to 4 op Evens) 1
1285⁴ ISLAND JETSETTER [105] 7-11-10 Richard Guest, *made
most till hdd 3 out, rdn frm betw last 2, styd on und pres
r-in*...........................(10 to 1 op 5 to 1) 2
1312* BARKISLAND [101] 9-11-6 (7ex) J Callaghan, *wth ldr, led
briefly 5th to nxt, feeling pace 3 out, kpt on ag'n r-in.*
...................................(8 to 1 op 7 to 1) 3
1328 ALAN BALL [104] 7-11-9 H Davies, *patiently rdn, improg
whn blun badly and lost grnd 6 out, rallied frm 2 out,
fnshd wl*........................(16 to 1 op 14 to 1) 4
1360⁵ SILVER HAZE [94] 9-10-13 D Murphy, *settled wth chasing
bunch, effrt appr 5 out, rdn and one pace last 3.*
...................................(12 to 1) 5
1203⁴ CLARES OWN [95] 9-11-0 K Jones, *pressed ldg pair, feeling pace and rdn aftr 6 out, fdd.*
...................................(10 to 1 op 8 to 1 tchd 12 to 1) 6
1168 MAJOR EFFORT [92] 8-10-4 (7") Mr N Bradley, *chsd alng to
go pace whn blun and uns rdr 5th*............(33 to 1) ur
1168² TERRIBLE GEL (Fr) [105] 8-11-10 P Niven, *patiently rdn,
steady hdwy frm 4 out, chalg whn blun and uns rdr 2
out*.............(5 to 1 op 3 to 1 tchd 11 to 2) ur
Dist: 12l, 3l, 4l, 1l, 15l. 4m 15.10s. a 24.10s (8 Ran).

SR: 31/35/28/27/16/2/-/-/ (Peter Hepworth), D Nicholson

TAUNTON (good)
Thursday November 25th
Going Correction: PLUS 0.50 sec. per fur. (races 1,3,-5,6), PLUS 1.00 (2,4)

NATIONAL HUNT RESULTS 1993-94

1410 WPA Somerset Juvenile Selling Hurdle (3-y-o) £1,731 2m 1f........(1:00)

1253³ AL FORUM (Ire) 10-12 D O'Sullivan, *wtd wth in midfield, smooth hdwy aftr 7th to ld appr last, pushed out readily*...............(9 to 4 fav op 5 to 2 tchd 3 to 1) 1
1297 POCONO KNIGHT 10-12 D Bridgwater, *trkd ldrs, led 6th till hdd appr last, sn rdn and not pace of wnr.*
.......................(14 to 1 op 16 to 1 tchd 33 to 1) 2
SYLVAN STARLIGHT 10-2 (5") R Farrant, *pld hrd, hld up in tch, hdwy 7th, cl 3rd whn stumbled 2 out, not reco'r.*
.......................(11 to 1 op 6 to 1 tchd 12 to 1) 3
1338³ IS SHE QUICK 10-7 N Dawe, *midfield, gd hdwy aftr 7th and sn chasing ldrs, not quicken....* (6 to 1 op 7 to 2) 4
1237³ LA POSADA 10-0 (7") P Moore, *hld up in tch, effrt aftr 7th, sn rdn and wknd nxt.*
.......................(4 to 1 op 5 to 2 tchd 9 to 2) 5
1049 OUR NIKKI 10-7 I Shoemark, *prmnt, led 3rd till hdd 6th, btn frm nxt.*...................(66 to 1 op 33 to 1) 6
1338⁴ MUSICAL PHONE 10-12 M A FitzGerald, *led to 3rd, styd hndy and ev ch 7th, wknd appr nxt.*
.......................(10 to 1 op 11 to 2) 7
HOHNE GARRISON 10-12 N Williamson, *beh, rdn 6th, no imprsn.*.................(6 to 1 op 8 to 1 tchd 5 to 1) 8
ESTHAL (Ire) 10-12 R Dunwoody, *trkd ldrs till hrd rdn 7th, wknd quickly*......................(7 to 1 op 5 to 1) 9
1243 BARTON ROYAL (Ire) 10-12 A Charlton, *trkd ldr, mstk 4th, wkng quickly whn hmpd bend aftr 7th, tld off.*
.......................(16 to 1 op 20 to 1 tchd 33 to 1) 10
352⁴ VENTURE PRINTS 10-12 Lorna Vincent, *jmpd slwly 1st and second, beh till hdwy aftr 4th, mstk and uns rdr nxt.*.....................(25 to 1 op 16 to 1) ur
NITA'S CHOICE 10-7 M Hourigan, *slwly into strd, sn beh and not jump wl, tld off whn pld up bef 5th.*
.......................(50 to 1 op 33 to 1) pu
Dist: 6l, 2l, sht-hd, 25l, 10l, ¾l, 20l, 8l, 30l. 4m 7.20s. a 20.20s (8 Ran).

(Martin Hickey), R Ingram

1411 Western Provident Novices' Handicap Chase (5-y-o and up) £4,377 3m (1:30)

962³ LUCKY LANE [87] (bl) 9-11-0 C Maude, *slightly hmpd second, sn prmnt, led 6th to 9th, led ag'n 16th, soon clr, unchlgd.*...................(6 to 1 op 9 to 2) 1
1303⁶ LUCAYAN GOLD [73] 9-10-0 L Harvey, *lft in ld second, hdd 6th, jmpd slwly nxt and sn lost pl, ran on ag'n to chase wnr appr 3 out, no imprsn.*.........(25 to 1 op 16 to 1) 2
954² HAND OUT [86] 9-10-13 B Powell, *hld up, hdwy 9th, 3rd whn blun 16th, sn one pace.*
.......................(15 to 2 op 7 to 1 tchd 8 to 1) 3
1054 FROZEN DROP [95] 6-11-8 J Railton, *trkd ldrs till outpcd 11th, sn rdn alng and unbl to chal.* (11 to 2 op 9 to 1) 4
957⁶ JUDYS LINE [73] 9-9-9 (5") D Salter, *al beh.*
.......................(33 to 1 op 50 to 1 tchd 25 to 1) 5
1140³ ISLAND FOREST (USA) [92] 7-11-5 M A FitzGerald, *in tch, chsd ldr frm 12th, blun 14th, lft in ld nxt, hdd and wknd from 16th.*.................(5 to 1 op 4 to 1) 6
TIJUCA [73] 14-9-7 (7") Mr N Moore, *f 1st.*
.......................(66 to 1 op 25 to 1) f
1189³ BUMPTIOUS BOY [80] (v) 9-10-7 D Bridgwater, *al hndy, led 9th till f 15th.*.............(14 to 1 op 16 to 1 tchd 12 to 1) f
220* MR TITTLE TATTLE [97] (bl) 7-11-10 N Williamson, *led till f second.*.........(5 to 2 fav op 11 to 4 tchd 100 to 30) f
1189 LAVALIGHT [81] 6-10-8 R Dunwoody, *midfield till wknd frm 12th, rdn and wl btn whn f 2 out.*
.......................(14 to 1 op 12 to 1) f
1194² BARLEY MOW [83] 7-10-10 N Williamson, *struggling frm hfwy, tld off whn pld up bef 2 out.*..........(12 to 1 op 10 to 1) pu
1189⁷ DEVIOSITY (USA) [73] 6-10-0 W McFarland, *beh frm 8th, tld off whn pld up bef 3 out.*..........(66 to 1 op 33 to 1) pu
Dist: 15l, 8l, 2½l, 5l, ½l. 6m 20.80s. a 33.80s (12 Ran).

(Rod Hamilton), P J Hobbs

1412 WPA Biiba Mares' Only Handicap Hurdle (0-135 4-y-o and up) £3,550 2m 3f 110yds........................(2:00)

1068* MISS MARIGOLD [100] (bl) 4-11-0 R Dunwoody, *hld up in tch, rdn and effrt aftr 7th, sn ev ch, sstnd chal frm 2 out to ld r-in, drvn out.* (2 to 1 fav op 9 to 4 tchd 7 to 4) 1
1342³ WOLVER GOLD [92] 6-10-6 C Maude, *led till hdd r-in, no extr.*...................(13 to 2 op 9 to 2) 2
982⁵ CRACKLING ANGELS [86] 6-10-0 B Powell, *chsd ldrs, rdn appr 7th, lft 3rd 2 out, styd on r-in.* (11 to 1 op 6 to 1) 3
1025⁵ REVE EN ROSE [90] 7-10-4 M A FitzGerald, *wth ldr till lost pl appr 6th, sn rdn no real imprsn.*
.......................(9 to 2 op 7 to 2) 4
1045⁴ KALAMOSS [86] 4-9-7 (7") Miss S Mitchell, *beh and struggling 5th, some hdwy 7th, nvr a dngr.*
.......................(20 to 1 op 10 to 1) 5
WELSH SIREN [110] 7-11-10 N Williamson, *al tracking ldrs, cl 3rd and rdn whn f 2 out.......*(11 to 4 op 5 to 1) f
STRAIGHT GOLD [86] 8-10-0 W McFarland, *midfield till niggled alng and lost pl hfwy, tld off whn pld up bef 8th.*..................(50 to 1 op 20 to 1 tchd 66 to 1) pu

MILLY BLACK (Ire) [93] 5-10-7 L Harvey, *beh and niggled alng hfwy, tld off whn pld up bef 8th.*
.......................(14 to 1 op 7 to 1) pu
Dist: 2½l, 1l, 20l, 3l. 4m 43.20s. a 22.20s (8 Ran).

(Mrs Angela Fayers), R J Hodges

1413 WPA Novices' Chase (5-y-o and up) £4,084 2m 3f..................(2:30)

1245² SAN LORENZO (USA) [85] 5-11-0 N Williamson, *not fluent, al hndy, led 3 out, clr whn blun last, ran on.*
.......................(13 to 8 op 2 to 1 tchd 7 to 4) 1
1298* TUDOR FABLE (Ire) 5-11-4 R Dunwoody, *al prmnt, led tenth, awkward and hdd 3 out, unbl to quicken.*
.......................(6 to 5 on op 5 to 4 on tchd Evens) 2
1245⁴ STORM FLIGHT 7-11-8 B Powell, *made most to 9th, styd hndy, rdn and no extr appr 3 out, collapsed and died*
.......................(18 to 1 op 12 to 1 tchd 20 to 1) 3
1301 MAGGOTS GREEN 6-10-10 R Farrant, *in tch, led briefly 9th, wknd 11th, tld off.*.......(50 to 1 op 20 to 1) 4
892⁸ JHAL FREZI 5-11-0 A Thornton, *prmnt, jmpd slwly tenth, cl 4th whn blun and uns rdr 12th.* (100 to 1 op 33 to 1) ur
960⁴ CHARLIE JOHNSON 9-11-5 M A FitzGerald, *hld up in tch, niggled alng 6th, lost touch frm 8th, tld off whn pld up bef 12th.*......................(12 to 1 op 8 to 1) pu
1102 CAIRNEYMOUNT 7-11-1 S McNeill, *al struggling, tld off whn pld up bef tenth.*.........(50 to 1 op 20 to 1) pu
Dist: 8l, 3l, dist. 4m 57.30s. a 23.30s (7 Ran).
SR: 42/38/32/-/ (James D Greig), K C Bailey

1414 WPA Blackbrook Novices' Hurdle (4-y-o and up) £3,810 2m 1f.......(3:00)

1192³ NOBLELY (USA) 6-10-12 N Williamson, *made all, rdn clr appr last, styd on wl...* (9 to 1 op 7 to 1 tchd 10 to 1) 1
1010³ HIGH MIND (Fr) 4-10-8 (3") A Thornton, *trkd ldr, hit 5th, ev ch appr 2 out, sn rdn and styd on same pace.*
.......................(5 to 1 op 4 to 1) 2
1053⁴ AAL EL AAL 6-10-12 M Hourigan, *settled midfield, smooth hdwy aftr 6th till rdn and not quicken appr 2 out.*
.......................(6 to 5 on op 7 to 4) 3
982² TOUR LEADER (NZ) 4-10-11 B Powell, *in tch, rdn 7th, styd on same pace.*.................(5 to 1 op 7 to 2) 4
IT'S DELICIOUS 7-10-7 D Bridgwater, *midfield, sn alng 5th, some late hdwy.*....................(33 to 1) 5
1027 PRINCE RUBEN 6-10-12 M A FitzGerald, *beh and reminders 4th, ran on frm nxt till no further hdwy aftr 7th.*...............(25 to 1 op 16 to 1 tchd 33 to 1) 6
MAI PEN RAI 5-10-12 R Dunwoody, *chsd ldrs to 6th, sn wknd, tld off....* (14 to 1 op 10 to 1 tchd 16 to 1) 7
QUINTA ROYALE 6-10-12 L Harvey, *in tch to hfwy, tld off.*
.......................(33 to 1 op 20 to 1) 8
ALICE SPRINGS 4-10-10⁸ Mr T Greed, *al beh, tld off.*
.......................(66 to 1 op 33 to 1 tchd 100 to 1) 9
ROXY RIVER 4-10-12 (7") Mr M Rimell, *effrt 4th and sn prmnt, second and ev ch whn stumbled and uns rdr 2 out.*.......................(50 to 1 op 20 to 1) ur
MERLIN ROCKET 5-10-12 C Maude, *mstk and uns rdr second.*..................(50 to 1 op 20 to 1) ur
1046⁷ MENDIP MIST 5-10-7 W McFarland, *nvr gng pace, tld off whn pld up bef 4th.*.............(200 to 1 op 50 to 1) pu
953 FORTUNE STAR (Ire) 4-10-11 D O'Sullivan, *al beh, tld off whn pld up bef 4th.*.....(100 to 1 op 66 to 1) pu
Dist: 8l, 5l, 1½l, 6l, hd, dist, 30l, dist. 4m 0.50s. a 13.50s (13 Ran).
SR: 34/25/21/18/8/13/ (D H Cowgill), N J H Walker

1415 Providential Novices' Handicap Hurdle (4-y-o and up) £3,550 2m 1f..(3:30)

988⁵ FRANKUS [74] 4-10-4 N Mann, *trkd ldr, led 4th, wndrd appr last, styd on...*(11 to 2 tchd 6 to 1 and 5 to 1) 1
1059⁵ THE GREYSMITH [75] 6-10-5 D Bridgwater, *hld up, gd hdwy appr 7th, sn chasing wnr, not quicken betw last 2....*.......................(9 to 1 op 8 to 1) 2
IN THE GAME (Ire) [70] 4-9-9 (5") R Farrant, *hld up in tch, lost pl and hit 5th, rnwd effrt 7th, styd on und pres r-in....*..............(20 to 1 op 16 to 1 tchd 25 to 1) 3
1185⁵ COOCHIE [70] (bl) 4-10-0 L Harvey, *hld up in tch, gd hdwy 6th and sn ev ch, rdn appr 2 out, not quicken.*
.......................(10 to 1 op 8 to 1) 4
1192² NORTHERN CREST [75] 7-10-5 S McNeill, *handily plcd, wnt second appr 5th, sn rdn alng, no extr approaching 2 out....*................(2 to 1 fav tchd 100 to 30) 5
MANOR MAN [82] 6-10-5 (7") R Dunwoody, *prmnt till wknd frm 7th.*..................(20 to 1 op 12 to 1) 6
1108 RUSTIC FLIGHT [70] 6-10-0 D Gallagher, *beh frm second, nvr able to chal.*.................(25 to 1 op 14 to 1) 7
1108 SANDMOOR PRINCE [70] 10-10-0 Dr P Pritchard, *niggled alng aftr 4th, sn in rear....*...........(50 to 1 op 20 to 1) 8
ALMOST A PRINCESS [72] 5-10-2 M A FitzGerald, *in tch till lost pl appr 7th, sn btn....*.........(16 to 1 op 10 to 1) 9
1141* MAMALAMA [83] 5-10-13 D O'Sullivan, *led to 4th, styd hndy till rdn and wknd appr 2 out.*(10 to 2 tchd 8 to 1) 10
Dist: 2½l, 1½l, 4l, 2½l, 12l, nk, 2½l, hd, 3l. 4m 7.10s. a 20.10s (10 Ran).
(H C S Group), S Mellor

BANGOR (good)

189

Friday November 26th
Going Correction: PLUS 0.50 sec. per fur. (races 1,3,6), PLUS 1.08 (2,4,5)

1416 Crosemere Selling Hurdle (3 & 4-y-o) £1,833 2m 1f.................. (1:20)

DON'T FORGET MARIE (Ire) 3-10-2 N Mann, *patiently rdn, hdwy to ld 3 out, hdd nxt, rallied to lead r-in.* .... (10 to 1 op 8 to 1) 1
994[2] BAND SARGEANT (Ire) 4-11-7 N Doughty, *settled gng wl, led on bit 2 out, hdd aftr last, rdn and no extr.* ....(5 to 4 fav op 6 to 4 tchd 15 to 8) 2
658 BUSMAN (Ire) 4-11-7 M A FitzGerald, *trkd ldrs, effrt and drvn alng appr 3 out, outpcd betw last 2.* ....(5 to 1 op 7 to 2) 3
486 SHAMROCK DANCER (Ire) 3-10-2 L Harvey, *chsd ldrs, feeling pace and drvn alng aftr 4 out, no imprsn nxt.* .... (33 to 1 op 25 to 1) 4
1237[6] SWISS MOUNTAIN (bl) 3-9-11 (5*) T Eley, *co'red up in midfield, effrt and reminders appr 3 out, wknd quickly nxt.*................................(8 to 1 op 6 to 1) 5
1338[5] MY SISTER LUCY 3-10-6 T Jarvis, *wth ldrs, led appr 4 out to nxt, rdn and no extr approaching 2 out.* .... (12 to 1 op 8 to 1) 6
1059 ABELONI 4-11-7 A S Smith, *led till appr 4 out, fdd und pres aftr nxt.*.....................(20 to 1 op 16 to 1) 7
FERDIA (Ire) 4-11-7 M Dwyer, *wth ldrs, rdn and lost grnd appr 3 out, sn lost tch..*.............. (6 to 1 op 5 to 1) 8
453 KINCADE 3-10-7 Mr J Cambidge, *beh and struggling till f 3 out.*............................(66 to 1 op 50 to 1) f
1290 ULTRAKAY (Ire) 3-10-7 C Hawkins, *not jump wl, struggling in rear whn almost f 4 out, pld up bef nxt.....* (50 to 1) pu

Dist: 1½l, 10l, 7l, 6l, 4l, 10l, 10l. 4m 12.30s. a 22.30s (10 Ran).
(Gordon Mytton), A Bailey

1417 Classic Racing Books Novices' Handicap Chase (4-y-o and up) £2,853 2½m 110yds........................ (1:50)

1214* JUMBEAU [93] 8-11-0 (3*) P Hide, *jmpd boldly, made all, quickened clr last 4, styd on wl r-in.* ....(11 to 10 fav op 11 to 8) 1
727 SQUIRES PRIVILEGE (Ire) [87] 5-10-11 M Dwyer, *patiently rdn, blun and almost uns rdr 7th, jmpd rght nxt, rallied to chase wnr last 3, no imprsn.* ....(8 to 1 op 7 to 1 tchd 9 to 1) 2
1255[3] TITUS GOLD [88] 8-10-12 M A FitzGerald, *mstks, reminders 6th, effrt and drvn alng aftr 4 out, no imprsn whn hmpd by faller last.*...............(14 to 1 op 12 to 1) 3
1182* OLD EROS [100] 9-11-10 P Niven, *not jump wl, awkward and lost grnd quickly 8th, struggling aftr, tld off.* ....(3 to 1 op 5 to 2 tchd 7 to 2) 4
1107 READY OR NOT [96] (bl) 7-10-13 (7*) D Fortt, *trkd wnr, struggling to keep up aftr 4 out, disputing second and tired whn f last.*...............................(16 to 1) f
1298 SUPER SPELL [88] 7-10-12 B Powell, *f 1st.* .... (14 to 1 op 12 to 1) f
1189 WEST BAY [85] 7-10-9 S Smith Eccles, *chsd ldg trio, rdn aftr 6 out, poor 5th whn jmpd slwly and uns rdr 2 out.* ....(8 to 1 tchd 9 to 1) ur

Dist: 10l, 6l, dist. 5m 18.20s. a 27.20s (7 Ran).
SR: 38/22/17/-/ (Pell-Mell Partners), J T Gifford

1418 EBF 'National Hunt' Novices' Hurdle Qualifier (4,5,6-y-o) £2,556 2m 1f (2:20)

ARCTIC KINSMAN 5-10-12 D Bridgwater, *jmpd wl, made all, quickened clr aftr 3 out, imprsv.* ....(7 to 4 fav op 6 to 4 tchd 2 to 1) 1
1167[4] GALES CAVALIER (Ire) 5-10-12 J Railton, *tucked away beh ldrs, chsd wnr frm 3 out, styd on r-in.* ....(8 to 1 tchd 9 to 1) 2
1053[2] COL BUCKMORE (Ire) 5-11-3 N Doughty, *nvr far away, hit 4th, hmpd nxt, rallied, eased whn btn 2 out.* .... (11 to 4 op 7 to 2 tchd 4 to 1) 3
1027[2] BLACK OPAL (Ire) 4-10-12 B Powell, *pressed ldrs, effrt and shaken up aftr 4 out, outpcd nxt.* ....(9 to 2 op 3 to 1 tchd 5 to 1) 4
1202[6] SCARF (Ire) 5-10-12 M Dwyer, *patiently rdn, improved frm off the pace 3 out, styd on, nvr able to chal.* .... (14 to 1 op 7 to 1) 5
1078[5] FROG HOLLOW (Ire) 5-10-12 M A FitzGerald, *pressed ldg pair, struggling to hold pl aftr 4 out, fdd.* .... (14 to 1 op 10 to 1) 6
MERRY SCORPION 4-10-9 (3*) A Thornton, *pushed alng in midfield, no imprsn frm 4 out*................ (33 to 1) 7
NICSAMLYN 6-10-7 P Niven, *struggling to keep up hfwy, sn lost tch*.................................(33 to 1) 8
1141[3] JUMPING JUDGE 6-10-12 S Smith Eccles, *chsd wnr, blun 5th, wknd quickly aftr nxt, tld off.* (16 to 1 op 12 to 1) 9
1277 CORPORAL CHARLIE 4-10-12 L Harvey, *chsd ldrs, struggling to stay in tch 4 out, tld off...* (66 to 1 op 50 to 1) 10
MUCH 6-10-12 Mr M Jackson, *al beh, tld off 4 out.* ....(50 to 1) 11
1078 SARGEANTS CHOICE (bl) 4-10-7 (5*) T Eley, *al beh, tld off whn pld up bef 2 out.*............. (66 to 1 op 50 to 1) pu

Dist: 4l, 15l, 15l, nk, 10l, 2l, ¾l, sht-hd, 12l, 1½l. 4m 3.70s. a 13.70s (12 Ran).
SR: 32/28/18/-/-/-/ (Mrs R E Hambro), N A Twiston-Davies

1419 Builder Center Handicap Chase (0-135 4-y-o and up) £3,355 2½m 110yds .... (2:50)

1124[2] FRENCH CHARMER [97] 8-10-2 (3*) P Hide, *al hndy, led and blun 5 out, sn reco'red, ran on strly frm betw last 2.* ....(9 to 4 op 5 to 2) 1
1286[2] CANDY TUFF [114] 7-11-8 P Niven, *mstks, dsptd ld, led aftr 7th to 5 out, rallied, hit 2 out, kpt on same pace.* ....(Evens fav tchd 5 to 4) 2
1069[4] SNITTON LANE [116] 7-11-10 M A FitzGerald, *nvr far away, ev ch and niggled alng aftr 3 out, hit last, styd on same pace..*........................(8 to 1 op 7 to 1) 3
1222[7] MUTUAL TRUST [116] 9-11-10 N Doughty, *led till aftr 7th, wknd after 4 out, eased.*.............(6 to 1 op 9 to 2) 4
BARKIN [104] 10-10-12 M Moloney, *settled off the pace, lost tch frm 6 out.*............................ (20 to 1) 5

Dist: 3½l, 2l, dist, 15l. 5m 27.00s. a 36.00s (5 Ran).
(H T Pelham), J T Gifford

1420 Reach Recruitment Novices' Chase (5-y-o and up) £3,204 3m 110yds (3:20)

MR FLANAGAN 7-11-0 J Railton, *al hndy, led appr 6 out, clr 2 out, kpt on strly, eased nr finish.* .... (11 to 4 op 5 to 2 tchd 3 to 1) 1
1080 COMEDY SPY 9-11-0 M A FitzGerald, *patiently rdn, improved aftr 4 out, effrt and hit last, styd on strly.* .... (10 to 1 op 8 to 1) 2
FINCH'S GEM 5-10-12 N Doughty, *nvr far away, ev ch 3 out, not quicken nxt, improve.....* (16 to 1 op 12 to 1) 3
1170[5] ASK FOR MORE 8-11-0 P Niven, *al wl plcd, ev ch whn hmpd 5 out, rdn and no extr 3 out..*...........(20 to 1) 4
1276[4] PUNCHBAG (USA) 7-11-0 D Bridgwater, *wth ldr, lost pl hfwy, rallied fnl circuit, outpcd 4 out.* .... (14 to 1 op 12 to 1) 5
1071[5] HOWGILL 7-10-11 (3*) S Wynne, *settled to track ldrs, effrt fnl circuit, rdn 5 out, sn lost tch...* (33 to 1 op 25 to 1) 6
1170[2] RUN UP THE FLAG 6-10-11 (3*) P Hide, *patiently rdn, 5th and clsg whn f 9th.* ....(11 to 8 fav tchd 13 to 8 and 5 to 4) f
843 GABRIELLA MIA 8-10-9 T Jarvis, *niggled alng to stay in tch aftr one fircuit, brght dwn 9th.* (10 to 1 op 12 to 1) bd
ONLY ME 5-10-12 M Dwyer, *shaped wl till wknd aftr 4 out, almost f 2 out, pld up bef last.* ....(13 to 2 op 5 to 1 tchd 7 to 1) pu

Dist: 1½l, 12l, 2½l, nk, 15l. 6m 31.50s. a 41.50s (9 Ran).
(Mrs Richard Stanley), C P E Brooks

1421 Blakemere Novices' Hurdle (4-y-o and up) £2,347 2m 7f 110yds........ (3:50)

1295[3] GRAY'S ELLERGY 7-10-7 J Railton, *al hndy, led 8th, quickened clr last 3, easily.* ....(7 to 4 fav op 6 to 4 tchd 15 to 8) 1
1204[3] JOHNS THE BOY 7-11-0 (5*) J Supple, *al wl plcd, ev ch 4 out, rdn and kpt on same pace aftr nxt.* .... (3 to 1 op 11 to 4) 2
920[4] BROWNHALL 5-10-12 (7*) Mr B Pollock, *nvr far away, hit 1st, ev ch appr 3 out, not quicken nxt.* ....(7 to 1 tchd 8 to 1) 3
1320[8] STEEL FABRICATOR 6-10-12 M Dwyer, *settled midfield, effrt and pushed alng 4 out, rdn and no extr nxt.* ....(9 to 1 op 7 to 1) 4
1108[6] FILM LIGHTING GIRL 7-10-0 (7*) P Ward, *chsd ldrs, struggling to hold pl 4 out, fdd*.....................(14 to 1) 5
875 SON OF IRIS 5-10-12 P Niven, *pressed ldrs, effrt hfwy, drvn alng appr 4 out, sn btn.*........(5 to 1 op 4 to 1) 6
ANGEL FALLING 5-10-7 R Bellamy, *sn beh, taiiled off whn pld up bef 3 out..*.................. (33 to 1 op 25 to 1) pu
CARLSAN 7-10-12 Mr M Jackson, *struggling hfwy, tld off whn pld up bef 2 out.*............ (66 to 1 op 50 to 1) pu
DUSKOMI 7-10-12 B Powell, *struggling to keep up hfwy, tld off whn pld up bef 7th.*...................(33 to 1) pu
1323[8] MISTRESS BEE (USA) 4-10-6 A S Smith, *led to 8th, lost pl quickly, pld up bef 2 out.*.....................(33 to 1) pu

Dist: 10l, 1½l, 7l, sht-hd, dist. 5m 56.70s. a 24.70s (10 Ran).
(W H Dore), D R Gandolfo

SOUTHWELL (soft)
Friday November 26th
Going Correction: PLUS 1.50 sec. per fur.

1422 Hawthorn Novices' Chase (5-y-o and up) £2,223 2m.................(1:40)

1149 SKELETOR 10-11-3 R Garritty, *cl up, led aftr 3rd, clr 6 out, unchlgd.*...........(11 to 8 fav op 6 to 4 tchd 6 to 5) 1
1002[2] EXPLOSIVE SPEED (USA) 5-11-9 C Grant, *led till aftr 3rd, hit nxt, chsd wnr, blun 7th and not jump wl after, sn one pace.*.........................(11 to 4 op 5 to 2) 2

703 FLUIDITY (USA) 5-11-3 R Supple, *hld up in tch, hit 4th, effrt and hdwy whn hit 8th, sn rdn alng and plugged on one pace*........................(12 to 1 op 8 to 1) 3
1247[7] SWING LUCKY 8-11-3 R Campbell, *prmnt, hdwy to chase ldr and 6 ls second whn f 5 out*................(25 to 1) f
1298 KING'S SHILLING (USA) 6-11-3 Jacqui Oliver, *hld up in tch, f second*................(5 to 2 op 2 to 1 tchd 11 to 4) f
Dist: 25l, 7l. 4m 29.00s. a 30.00s (5 Ran).
SR: 29/10/ (T P Tate), T P Tate

1423 Willow Amateur Riders' Handicap Chase (0-120 5-y-o and up) £2,409 3m 110yds........................(2:40)

1345* STAY ON TRACKS [127] 11-12-0 (7*,7ex) Mr N King, *led to 6th, led 8th, blun 5 out, pushed clr 3 out, hit nxt, unchlgd*................(3 to 1 op 5 to 2 tchd 7 to 2) 1
1138[5] CHANCERY BUCK [92] 10-9-7 (7*) Mr N Moore, *al prmnt, hit 13th, chsd wnr 15th, rdn 3 out, sn one pace.* ....(11 to 1 op 7 to 1 tchd 12 to 1) 2
1388* JIMSTER [98] 11-9-13 (7*,7ex) Mr C Hancock, *cl up, led 6th to 8th, prmnt and hit 12th, blun 14th and nxt, sn rdn and one pace appr 3 out.* ....(6 to 5 fav op 6 to 4 tchd Evens) 3
911[5] CHOCTAW [97] 9-10-2 (3*) Mrs A Farrell, *prmnt till rdn and lost pl 13th, sn hrd ridden and beh.* ....(5 to 1 op 7 to 2 tchd 11 to 2) 4
1151[2] RED COLUMBIA [92] 12-9-7 (7*) Mrs G Adkin, *prmnt till lost pl and beh 6th, pushed alng and some hdwy 13th, f 5 out*...................... (6 to 1 op 9 to 2 tchd 7 to 2) f
1326[2] IMPECCABLE TIMING [92] 10-9-9[2] (7*) Mr A Mitchell, *hld up in tch, hdwy 13th, effrt to chase wnr whn blun and uns rdr 5 out*..........................(16 to 1 op 12 to 1) ur
Dist: 20l, 2l, 6l. 7m 3.40s. a 65.40s (6 Ran).
(R Oliver Smith), Mrs D Haine

SOUTHWELL (A.W) (std)
Friday November 26th
Going Correction: PLUS 0.60 sec. per fur.

1424 Conifer Novices' Hurdle (4-y-o and up) £1,689 2m.................... (12:40)

1152* CLIFTON CHASE 4-11-5 J A Harris, *trkd ldrs, hdwy to ld 3 out, rdn last, ran on wl flt.* .... (11 to 10 fav op 5 to 4 tchd 11 to 8) 1
1152[2] BLAZON OF TROY 4-11-3 (7*) D Meade, *trkd ldrs, hdwy and ev ch whn hit 3 out, hit nxt, drvn and rallied last, no extr flt*..........................(11 to 8 op 5 to 4) 2
1313[2] BASSIO (Bel) (h) 4-11-0 J McLaughlin, *hld up in tch, gd hdwy appr 3 out, sn rdn and one pace.* ....(12 to 1 op 7 to 1) 3
466[5] GILT DIMENSION 6-11-0 R Supple, *cl up, led 5 out, rdn and hdd appr 3 out, one pace*......(7 to 1 tchd 8 to 1) 4
1169 ZACTOO 7-11-0 T Wall, *led, hdd 5 out, wknd aftr nxt.* ....(50 to 1 op 33 to 1) 5
RITA'S RISK 4-11-0 J Ryan, *al rear, tld off 4 out.* ....(33 to 1 op 20 to 1) 6
Dist: 1½l, 5l, 20l, 10l, 30l. 4m 1.70s. a 15.70s (6 Ran).
SR: 30/33/18/ (David Cahal), J L Harris

1425 Sycamore Novices' Claiming Hurdle (4-y-o and up) £1,631 2½m......(1:10)

1272[5] BILL QUILL 9-10-4 (7*) R Darke, *made all, clr 3 out, rdn appr last, kpt on gmely flt*....... (3 to 1 fav op 5 to 2) 1
1152[5] LAFANTA (Ire) 4-10-8 K Jones, *al prmnt, effrt 3 out, sn rdn, ch whn blun last, no extr flt*.... (5 to 1 op 7 to 1) 2
974[6] CAPTAIN CUTE 8-10-11 D Byrne, *in tch, hit 1st and second, hmpd and beh 5th, styd on und pres frm 3 out, nvr dngrs*..............................(4 to 1 op 7 to 2) 3
1238 GLENSTAL PRIORY 6-10-6 Miss R Judge, *beh, hmpd 5th, rdn 4 out and nvr dngrs*............(6 to 1 op 5 to 1) 4
1374 MATUSADONA 6-10-12 J A Harris, *prmnt, chsd wnr 6th till rdn and wkng whn blun badly 3 out, sn wknd.* ....(14 to 1 op 12 to 1) 5
THE LOVING MARTIAL 9-11-0 R Supple, *hld up, effrt 7th, rdn nxt and sn beh*......(7 to 1 op 6 to 1 tchd 8 to 1) 6
1313[8] CHAGHATAI (USA) 7-10-8 Diane Clay, *prmnt, hit 1st and 3rd, f 5th*............................(8 to 1 op 7 to 1) f
1079 EASY TOOMEY 5-10-8 C Grant, *prmnt till lost pl 4th, tld off 6th, pld up bef nxt*........................ (10 to 1) pu
1167 RONEO (USA) 5-11-1 (5*) S Curran, *rear whn hmpd 5th, sn wl beh and tld off when pld up bef 3 out.* ....(7 to 1 op 5 to 1) pu
Dist: 2l, 12l, 15l, 4l, 8l. 5m 16.50s. a 35.50s (9 Ran).
(Mrs D F Bowden), R G Frost

1426 Oak Handicap Hurdle (0-120 4-y-o and up) £1,828 2½m................(2:10)

553[4] COURT CIRCULAR [97] 4-11-5 M Brennan, *hld up, hdwy 4th, chsd ldr four out, led nxt, rdn clr 2 out.* (6 to 1 co-fav op 5 to 1) 1
1314[3] FETTLE UP [81] (bl) 5-10-3 B Dalton, *led, rdn and hdd 3 out, hit nxt and sn wknd*....(6 to 1 co-fav tchd 7 to 1) 2
1154[5] HAVE A NIGHTCAP [102] 4-11-10 J A Harris, *prmnt, rdn alng and outpcd appr 4 out, styd on und pres approaching last*............(6 to 1 co-fav op 5 to 1) 3
1025[6] FOR HEAVEN'S SAKE (Fr) [89] 8-10-11 T Wall, *hld up, hit second and 3rd, hdwy to chase ldr 7th, rdn 4 out and wknd appr nxt.* (6 to 1 co-fav op 5 to 1 tchd 13 to 2) 4
949[2] SPANISH WHISPER [83] 6-10-5 D Byrne, *prmnt, rdn appr 4 out, sn one pace*........(13 to 2 op 6 to 1 tchd 7 to 1) 5
RAGTIME COWBOY JOE [84] 8-9-13 (7*) Mr N Bradley, *blun 3rd and beh, rdn alng and hit 6th, nvr a factor.* ....(10 to 1 op 8 to 1) 6
1101[6] TRISTAN'S COMET [78] 6-10-0 W McFarland, *chsd ldrs, mstk 8th, sn rdn and wknd 4 out*. ....(6 to 1 co-fav op 8 to 1) 7
846[7] AUVILLAR (USA) [90] (v) 5-10-12 W Knox, *chsd ldrs, hit 7th, sn rdn alng, wknd appr 4 out.* ....(9 to 1 op 7 to 1 tchd 10 to 1) 8
1150 SILENT CHANT [86] (v) 9-10-1 (7*) Mr R Griffiths, *hit 3rd and 4th, sn lost pl and tld off aftr 6th.* (25 to 1 op 20 to 1) 9
1257[3] AUTONOMOUS [84] 8-10-6 W Humphreys, *chsd ldrs, hit 4th and 6th, lost pl 8th and beh whn pld up bef 3 out.* ....(6 to 1 co-fav op 5 to 1 tchd 7 to 1) pu
Dist: 10l, 4l, 1½l, ½l, 4l, sht-hd, 15l, dist. 5m 3.50s. a 22.50s (10 Ran).
(B A S Limited), W Clay

1427 Beech Handicap Hurdle (0-125 4-y-o and up) £1,731 3m..............(3:10)

1139[6] RABA RIBA [111] 8-11-13 V Slattery, *led, rdn 3 out, hdd appr nxt, 4 ls second and btn whn lft clr last.* ....(4 to 1 op 3 to 1) 1
COSMIC DANCER [112] 6-11-7 (7*) Guy Lewis, *hld up, steady hdwy 5 out, rdn to chal 3 out, sn wknd.* ....(7 to 2 op 2 to 1) 2
1279[5] SECRET LIASON [88] (bl) 7-9-13 (5*) T Jenks, *chsd wnr, hrd rdn and wknd appr 3 out.* ....(7 to 1 op 10 to 1 tchd 12 to 1 and 16 to 1) 3
1149[2] KEY DEAR (Fr) [84] 6-10-0 T Wall, *prmnt till rdn and lost pl tenth, sn wl beh*..................(20 to 1 op 12 to 1) 4
1072[4] MUNIR (USA) [97] 4-10-13 J A Harris, *al prmnt, hdwy 4 out, effrt to ld appr 2 out, four ls clr whn f last, broke neck, dead*......(11 to 10 on op Evens tchd 5 to 4 on) f
1274 KILTONGA [84] 6-10-0 M Brennan, *al rear, tld off 8th, pld up bef 11th*........................(33 to 1 op 25 to 1) pu
Dist: 2½l, dist, 6l. 6m 7.10s. a 30.10s (6 Ran).
(Mrs L A Marsh), J L Spearing

1428 Silver Birch National Hunt Flat Race (4,5,6-y-o) £1,234 2m........... (3:40)

815[9] BATTY'S ISLAND 4-10-7 (7*) E Husband, *made all, rdn appr fnl furlong, ran on*.......... (14 to 1 op 10 to 1) 1
1376[3] SWORDKING (Ire) 4-11-0 Mr I McLelland, *chsd ldrs, effrt o'r 2 fs out, sn rdn and hng badly lft, hrd drvn and ev ch ins last, no extr nr finish*......(7 to 4 fav op 2 to 1) 2
COILED SPRING 6-10-9 (5*) T Jenks, *pld hrd, trkd ldrs, hdwy to join wnr hfwy, ev ch 2 fs out, sn rdn and one pace appr last*......................(7 to 1 op 6 to 1) 3
BROAD STEANE 4-10-9 (5*) S Curran, *prmnt, pushed alng and outpcd hfwy, styd on fnl 2 fs. nvr dngrs.* ....(9 to 2 op 5 to 1 tchd 6 to 1 and 4 to 1) 4
1277[8] OLYMPIC WAY 4-10-2 (7*) R Darke, *pld hrd and chsd ldrs, sddl slpd aftr 4 fs, hdwy 6 furlongs out, rdn 3 out and sn one pace*....................... (10 to 1 op 7 to 1) 5
KNOW-NO-NO 4-10-9 (5*) D Bentley, *hld up, hdwy 6 fs out, hrd rdn 3 out and sn btn*........(5 to 1 op 3 to 1) 6
PARAMOUNT 4-10-7 (7*) D Meade, *al rear, beh frm hfwy.* ....(5 to 1 op 3 to 1) 7
SWEET FRIENDSHIP 5-10-4 (5*) J McCarthy, *hld up, hdwy 6 fs out, rdn 4 out and sn wknd*....(12 to 1 op 16 to 1) 8
WHYFOR 5-10-7 (7*) Mr N Moore, *prmnt till wknd hfwy, sn wl beh, tld off fnl 5 fs*..........(12 to 1 op 10 to 1) 9
Dist: 1½l, 6l, 2½l, 6l, 6l, ¾l, 30l, dist. 3m 55.10s. (9 Ran).
(Mrs Mary Price), B Preece

FAIRYHOUSE (IRE) (yielding)
Saturday November 27th

1429 J.C.'s Red Meat Hurdle (4 & 5-y-o) £4,140 2¼m.................. (12:45)

1230* YUKON GOLD (Ire) (bl) 4-11-3 C O'Dwyer,......(5 to 4 on) 1
1267* PHARFETCHED 4-11-4 C F Swan,................ (7 to 4) 2
534[2] RISZARD (USA) 4-10-13 K F O'Brien,.............(7 to 2) 3
1230[8] ALOHA (Ire) 4-10-8 M Duffy,.....................(20 to 1) 4
1155[2] GRECIAN LADY (Ire) 4-10-8 P L Malone,.........(33 to 1) 5
1156[6] CELIA'S PET (Ire) 5-10-13 F Woods,............(100 to 1) 6
Dist: 5½l, sht-hd, 9l, 2l. 4m 28.90s. (6 Ran).
(A J O'Reilly), Charles O'Brien

1430 Drinmore Chase (Listed Race - Grade 3) (5-y-o and up) £5,520 2½m... (1:15)

1334* VISIBLE DIFFERENCE 7-12-0 C F Swan, *setled in 3rd, prog 6th, trkd ldr 5 out, lft in ld aftr 3 out, eased after last.* ....(5 to 1) 1

1334³ ALL THE ACES 6-11-4 T J Taaffe, *rear, tld off 6 out, styd on frm 3 out, nrst finish*.......................(5 to 1) 2
1233³ OPERA HAT (Ire) 5-11-0 A Powell, *trkd ldr, rdn and lost pl 6 out, btn whn mstk 4 out*........................(8 to 1) 3
944² MUBADIR (USA) 5-11-1 P Carberry, *hld up, mstk and f 8th, mntd to finish 4th*.........................(6 to 4 fav) 4
1112* WILL PHONE 7-11-6 J F Titley, *led, jmpd sl, 2-l ld whn f 3 out*...(9 to 4) f

Dist: 6l, 25l, dist. 5m 13.50s. (5 Ran).

(Patrick Heffernan), Patrick Heffernan

1431 Kepak Handicap Hurdle (Listed Race - Grade 3) (4-y-o and up) £11,500 2m ....(1:45)

1269* BROCKLEY COURT [-] 6-11-3 (6ex) J P Banahan, *wl plcd, prog 3 out, lft in ld aftr nxt, hdd r-in, rallied to lead on line*..(8 to 1) 1
1267² ARCTIC WEATHER (Ire) [-] 4-10-6 J F Titley, *mid-div, prog appr 2 out, led r-in, hdd on line*....................(7 to 1) 2
TIME FOR A RUN [-] 6-11-4 C F Swan, *mid-div, prog 2 out, sn rdn, styd on one pace*...................(5 to 2 fav) 3
944⁴ FAMILY WAY [-] 6-10-0 F Woods, *wl plcd, ev ch 2 out, sn rdn, no extr frm last*........................(16 to 1) 4
GAELIC MYTH (USA) [-] 6-11-6 C P Dunne, *hld up, prog 3 out, kpt on one pace after nxt*............(14 to 1) 5
1269² FINAL FAVOUR (Ire) [-] 4-11-0 B Sheridan, *mid-div, prog out, rdn aftr nxt, no extr and wknd r-in*......(10 to 1) 6
1267³ LORD NOBLE (Ire) [-] 5-10-10 K F O'Brien, *sn led, jmpd slwly second, jnd 4 out, hdd nxt, rdn and no extr appr 2 out*..(16 to 1) 7
556* CAMDEN BUZZ (Ire) [-] 5-11-8 T P Treacy, *hld up, prog aftr 3 out, rdn and no extr appr last*..............(9 to 2) 8
1335² BORO EIGHT [-] 7-11-13 J Shortt, *wl plcd, prog to dispute ld 4 out, led aftr nxt, mstk and hdd 2 out, eased*. (8 to 1) 9
294* DUHARRA (Ire) [-] (bl) 5-11-7 A Powell, *trkd ldr, lost pl and wknd quickly aftr 4 out*...........................(12 to 1) 10
GLENCLOUD (Ire) [-] 5-11-8 P Carberry, *rear, prog 4 out, rdn and wknd 2 out*....................................(20 to 1) 11
NOVELLO ALLEGRO (USA) [-] 5-12-0 G M O'Neill, *al rear, mstks, rdn 4 out, wknd aftr nxt*............................(8 to 1) 12
BITOFABANTER [-] 6-11-8 T J Taaffe, *mid-div, rdn appr 2 out, staying on whn f last. dead*..................(7 to 1) f
969* SHEER MIRTH [-] 8-10-0 T Horgan, *mid-div, pld up aftr mstk 1st, lme*..pu

Dist: Sht-hd, 2½l, 1l, 3½l. 3m 50.70s. (14 Ran).

(C Cronin), Mrs John Harrington

1432 Ashbourne Maiden Hurdle (3-y-o) £3,105 2m....................(2:15)

MY KERRY DANCER (USA) 10-9 (5*) T P Treacy, ...(11 to 10 fav) 1
1264³ SERANERA (Ire) 10-9 (5*) M G Cleary, ...(14 to 1) 2
LADY NOBLE (Ire) 10-9 M Duffy, ...(12 to 1) 3
WICKLOW WAY (Ire) 10-2 (7*) J M Sullivan, ...(10 to 1) 4
1264⁶ DAHLIA'S BEST (USA) 11-0 J Shortt, ...(14 to 1) 5
1377 RIYADH DANCER (Ire) 10-9 (5*) J R Barry, ...(12 to 1) 6
1264⁹ MAN OF ARRAN (Ire) 10-9 (5*) T J O'Sullivan, ...(25 to 1) 7
1377⁶ ISLAND VISION (Ire) 10-9 B J Walsh, ...(8 to 1) 8
1377⁸ WHITECRAITS (Ire) 10-9 P Carberry, ...(10 to 1) 9
1377⁵ SPORTSTYLE (Ire) 11-0 B Sheridan, ...(8 to 1) 10
1377 LIMAHEIGHTS (Ire) 10-9 A Powell, ...(33 to 1) 11
BLACK PIPER (Ire) 10-9 F Woods, ...(12 to 1) 12
1377 FURIETTO (Ire) 11-0 C F Swan, ...(10 to 1) 13
SAINT HILDA (Ire) 10-2 (7*) K P Gaule, ...(12 to 1) 14
1377 GLAS AGUS OR (Ire) (bl) 10-9 J F Titley, ...(16 to 1) 15
802⁴ MISS MURPHY (Ire) 10-2 (7*) J P Broderick, ...(16 to 1) 16
688² DANCING VISION (Ire) 11-0 G M O'Neill, ...(5 to 1) 17
LAKE CHARLES (Ire) 11-0 K F O'Brien, ...(33 to 1) 18
SIMPLE DANCER (Ire) 10-7 (7*) J J McKeon, ...(20 to 1) 19
HAWTHORN ROSE (Ire) 10-2 (7*) J Butler, ...(33 to 1) 20
PAKED (Ire) 10-9 (5*) D T Evans, ...(33 to 1) f
1264 ANNADOT (Ire) 10-9 F J Flood, ...(50 to 1) ur
391 NURSE MAID (Ire) 10-9 J Jones, ...(20 to 1) pu

Dist: 3½l, 4½l, ½l, 4l. 3m 56.40s. (23 Ran).

(Hudson Valley Equine Inc), P Mullins

1433 Cottage Handicap Chase (4-y-o and up) £3,105 2¼m................(2:45)

1268⁴ CAPE SPY [-] (bl) 7-9-8 H Rogers, ...(8 to 1) 1
1231² GOLD OPTIONS [-] (bl) 11-12-0 K F O'Brien, ...(9 to 2) 2
1382* MAGIC MILLION [-] 7-9-9 (5ex) C F Swan, ...(6 to 4 fav) 3
NORTON VILLE [-] 7-10-12 B Sheridan, ...(7 to 2) 4
1382³ RANDOM PRINCE [-] 9-9-7 P Carberry, ...(3 to 1) 5

Dist: 1l, 5l, 11l, 7l. 4m 46.40s. (5 Ran).

(C Hanley), J R H Fowler

1434 Herbertstown Hurdle (5-y-o and up) £3,105 3m.................(3:15)

1234* MINELLA LAD 7-12-0 T Horgan, ...(2 to 1) 1
853* MUILEAR OIRGE 6-11-8 J F Titley, ...(4 to 1) 2
926⁴ FINE TUNING (Ire) 5-11-4 T J Taaffe, ...(14 to 1) 3
1074⁵ BOB MONEY (Ire) 5-11-4 D H O'Connor, ...(25 to 1) 4
1037⁶ CLOSUTTON EXPRESS 7-11-4 C F Swan, ...(10 to 1) 5

1178* RICH TRADITION (Ire) 5-11-11 C O'Dwyer, ...(6 to 1) 6
538 HEROIC MYTH 8-11-4 P L Malone, ...(33 to 1) 7
1378⁸ SEA BRIGHT (Ire) 5-10-10 (3*) D Bromley, ...(66 to 1) 8
1074 BETTER WAY (Ire) 5-11-4 B Sheridan, ...(66 to 1) 9

Dist: 5½l, 10l, 4½l, dist. 5m 56.60s. (9 Ran).

(John J Nallen), A P O'Brien

1435 Irish National Bookmakers INH Flat Race (4-y-o and up) £3,795 2m. . (3:40)

1236⁴ CASTLEKELLY CROSS 7-11-11 (7*) Mr B Moran, (2 to 1 jt-fav) 1
1270² ICED HONEY 6-11-11 Mr A J Martin, ...(8 to 1) 2
1236² COQ HARDI AFFAIR (Ire) 5-11-13 (5*) Mr B F Murphy, ...(2 to 1 jt-fav) 3
LOVELY RUN 6-11-10 (3*) Miss C Hutchinson, ...(14 to 1) 4
908* THATS A SECRET 5-11-11 (7*) Mr P English, ...(6 to 1) 5
923² HAUNTING ANGLE (Ire) 4-11-3 (5*) Mr G J Harford, (8 to 1) 6
1236⁹ YOUR THE MAN 7-11-4 (7*) Mr M Brennan, ...(25 to 1) 7
540 COMERAGH MOUNTAIN 6-11-11 Mr P Fenton, ...(20 to 1) 8
MAZAME (USA) 4-11-3 (3*) Mr A R Coonan, ...(9 to 1) 9
1236⁵ DAN PATCH 7-11-6 (5*) Mr H Kirk, ...(9 to 1) 10
1337 WISE STATEMENT (Ire) 4-10-13 (7*) M G Cowman, (20 to 1) 11
1270 RUSSIAN SAINT 7-11-4 (7*) Miss C O'Connell, ...(33 to 1) 12
1160 KEEP THEM KEEN (Ire) 5-11-4 (7*) Mr L Madine, ..(50 to 1) 13

Dist: 2l, ½l, hd, 4l. 3m 51.50s. (13 Ran).

(Mrs M O'Dwyer), Michael Hourigan

NEWBURY (good)
Saturday November 27th

Going Correction: PLUS 0.16 sec. per fur. (races 1,4,- 5,6), PLUS 0.10 (2,3,7)

1436 Jacky Upton Handicap Chase (5-y-o and up) £4,542 2½m...........(12:00)

1226² EGYPT MILL PRINCE [135] (bl) 7-10-7 R Dunwoody, *led aftr 1st, rcd freely to 6th, shaken up t2 out, ran on wl r-in*. ....(15 to 8 fav op 2 to 1 tchd 9 to 4) 1
1226 GUIBURN'S NEPHEW [135] 11-10-7 C Maude, *led till aftr 1st, chsd wnr thrght, chlgd 3 out till 2 out, outpcd appr last*........................(13 to 2 op 6 to 1 tchd 7 to 1) 2
1171² DUBACILLA [129] 7-10-1 D Gallagher, *beh, outpcd 12th, rdn 4 out, styd on frm 2 out, nrst finish*. ....(7 to 2 op 3 to 1 tchd 4 to 1) 3
897⁵ MR ENTERTAINER [133] 10-10-5 C Llewellyn, *headaway 7th, styd on one pace frm 4 out*. ....(20 to 1 op 14 to 1 tchd 25 to 1) 4
884³ KINGS FOUNTAIN [150] 10-11-8 J Osborne, *drpd rear 6th, lost tch 12, rallied frm 2 out, kpt on*. ....(15 to 2 op 7 to 1 tchd 8 to 1) 5
COOL GROUND [150] 11-11-8 P Holley, *beh 6th, nvr dngrs aftr, no ch whn hit 2 out*..........(33 to 1 op 25 to 1) 6
1208 FLASHTHECASH [138] 7-10-10 D Murphy, *effrt 5th and ag'n appr 12th, sn wknd, no ch whn hit 4 out*. ....(8 to 1 op 7 to 1 tchd 9 to 1) 7
ANOTHER CORAL [156] 10-12-0 A Maguire, *drpd rear early, lost tch and pld up bef 8th*. ....(15 to 2 op 5 to 1 tchd 8 to 1) pu

Dist: 4l, 10l, 4l, hd, 10l, 30l. 4m 59.70s. a 9.70s (8 Ran).
SR: 14/10/-/-/11/1/-/-/

(S R Webb), Mrs J Pitman

1437 Bonusprint Gerry Feilden Hurdle Grade 2 (4-y-o and up) £10,760 2m 110yds.......................(12:30)

BOLD BOSS 4-11-3 R Dunwoody, *trkd ldr second, chlgd on bit 2 out, led last, pushed out*. ....(11 to 4 op 5 to 2 tchd 3 to 1) 1
1163² WINTER SQUALL (Ire) 5-11-6 A Maguire, *clr and hit 1st, steadied second, rdn aftr 2 out, hdd last, styd on one pace*.................(2 to 1 fav op 7 to 4 tchd 9 to 4) 2
1116² SATIN LOVER 5-11-3 G McCourt, *chsd ldr to second, rcd in 3rd aftr, chlgd 2 out, rdn whn mstk last, not quicken*. ....(3 to 1 op 5 to 2 tchd 10 to 4) 3
2093 AMAZON EXPRESS 4-11-6 J Osborne, *hdwy 5th, chsd ldrs 3 out, sn outpcd*..(11 to 2 op 4 to 1 tchd 6 to 1) 4
1225⁵ MIDDLE MARKER (Ire) 4-11-0 M Dwyer, *beh, hit 4th, lost tch and pld up bef 5th*..........(20 to 1 tchd 25 to 1) pu

Dist: 5l, 3½l, 12l. 3m 57.70s. a 8.70s (5 Ran).
SR: 19/17/10/1/-/

(John Robson), M C Pipe

1438 Akzo Long Distance Hurdle Grade 2 (4-y-o and up) £11,000 3m 110yds ....(1:00)

1106* TRIPLE WITCHING 7-11-0 A Maguire, *in tch, trkd ldr 3 out, led last, drvn out*......................(2 to 1 fav tchd 9 to 4) 1
1347² SWEET DUKE (Fr) 6-11-7 C Llewellyn, *led till hdd last, styd on same pace and pres*................(2 to 1 tchd 9 to 4) 2
2227³ BURGOYNE 7-11-4 R Dunwoody, *chsd ldr to 3 out, sn rdn and one pace*........(9 to 1 op 7 to 1 tchd 10 to 1) 3
1030* DEB'S BALL 7-10-13 D J Moffatt, *beh, lost tch 6th, rdn and styd on one pace frm 3 out*. ....(11 to 2 op 5 to 1 tchd 6 to 1) 4

LORNA-GAIL 7-10-9 S Earle, *beh, gd hdwy 4 out, chlgd 3 out, wknd quickly nxt*..........(33 to 1 tchd 40 to 1) 5
1256^{2} SIMPSON 8-11-0 T Grantham, *jmpd rght thrght, effrt to chase ldrs 4 out, sn wknd.*
......................(6 to 1 op 5 to 1 tchd 13 to 2) 6
1274 HOLY JOE 11-11-0 J Osborne, *chsd ldrs till wknd quickly appr 4 out*.......................(33 to 1 op 20 to 1) 7
Dist: 6l, 1½l, 8l, 3l, 30l, 6l. 5m 59.90s. a 10.90s (7 Ran).
SR: 2/3/-/-/ (Mrs Shirley Robins), D Nicholson

1439 Hennessy Cognac Gold Cup Handicap Chase Grade 3 (5-y-o and up) £35,152 3¼m 110yds...................(1:35)

1162^{2} COGENT [145] 9-10-1 (7*) D Fortt, *al in tch, led and mstk 3 out, rdn and ran on wl appr last.*
.....................(10 to 1 op 12 to 1 tchd 14 to 1) 1
943^{2} CAHERVILLAHOW [151] 9-11-0 A Maguire, *beh, hit 12th and 14th, rdn and hdwy appr 17th, chlgd and hit 3 out, styd on, not rch wnr.* (7 to 1 tchd 15 to 2 and 13 to 2) 2
828* BLACK HUMOUR [151] 9-11-0 G Bradley, *steady hdwy 16th, tracking ldrs whn blun badly 17th, rallied frm 4 out, rdn 2 out, wnt lft and one pace from last.*
..............................(7 to 2 fav op 3 to 1 tchd 4 to 1) 3
1224^{5} ZETA'S LAD [155] 10-11-4 R Supple, *hit 9th, gd hdwy 17th chlgd 2 out, wknd appr last.*
......................(11 to 2 op 6 to 1 tchd 5 to 1) 4
1220* WHISPERING STEEL [141] 7-10-4[1] N Doughty, *chsd ldr frm 3rd till led aftr 16th, hdd 3 out, wknd nxt.*
....(4 to 1 op 7 to 2) 5
1004^{2} MERRY MASTER [137] 9-10-0 Gee Armytage, *lft in ld 3rd, sn clr, hit 4th and 5th, hit 15th, hit 16th, soon hdd and wknd*..........................(20 to 1 op 16 to 1) 6
1224^{4} GARRISON SAVANNAH [150] (bl) 10-10-13 B Powell, *chsd ldrs till wknd 15th*................(16 to 1 op 20 to 1) 7
1224* ROYAL ATHLETE [161] 10-11-10 J Osborne, *beh till f 13th.*
....(7 to 1 tchd 8 to 1) f
ROLLING BALL (Fr) [140] 10-10-3 R Dunwoody, *led till f 3rd.*
......................(13 to 2 op 5 to 1 tchd 7 to 1) f
Dist: 2½l, 3l, 6l, 10l, 8l, 30l. 6m 33.10s. a 5.10s (9 Ran).
SR: 71/74/71/69/45/33/16/-/-/ (Pell-Mell Partners), Andrew Turnell

1440 North Street Handicap Chase (5-y-o and up) £5,785 2m 1f...........(2:10)

1207^{2} YOUNG SNUGFIT [152] 9-11-2 J Osborne, *made all, gng wl appr last, rdn r-in, ran on well*......(7 to 2 op 5 to 2) 1
WONDER MAN (Fr) [155] 8-11-5 A Maguire, *chsd wnr to 4th, chlgd frm 9th, still gng wl last, rdn r-in, not pace of winner*..............(2 to 1 fav op 7 to 4 tchd 9 to 4) 2
1285^{3} BOUTZDAROFF [140] 11-10-4 M Dwyer, *hdwy to chal frm 8th, still ev ch 4 out, wknd from nxt.*
......................(8 to 1 op 10 to 1 tchd 7 to 1) 3
KATABATIC [164] 10-12-0 S McNeill, *in tch till f 5th.*
.........................(7 to 2 op 4 to 1 tchd 9 to 2) f
1226^{6} SPACE FAIR [149] 10-10-13 L Harvey, *chsd wnr 4th till hit 9th, 3rd but wl in tch whn ran out four out.*
....(7 to 2 op 3 to 1) ro
Dist: ½l, 20l. 4m 6.20s. a 5.20s (5 Ran).
SR: 63/65/30/-/-/ (M L Oberstein), O Sherwood

1441 Fulke Walwyn Chase (5-y-o and up) £5,863 2½m..................(2:45)

1352^{2} SPIRIT OF KIBRIS 8-11-0 J Osborne, *led, clr 4th, still clear last, wknd r-in, jst hld on und pres.* (3 to 1 op 9 to 4) 1
1164^{4} FANTUS 6-11-0 G Bradley, *prmnt, chsd wnr frm 11th, staying on and hit 4 out, rallied appr last, fnshd wl, jst fld*...............(13 to 8 fav op 6 to 4 tchd 15 to 8) 2
1086^{3} PAPER STAR 6-10-9 R Dunwoody, *chsd wnr frm 4th to 11th, sn wknd*.......(25 to 1 op 20 to 1 tchd 33 to 1) 3
1298^{4} POPPETS PET 6-11-0 S Earle, *f 1st*...(12 to 1 op 20 to 1) f
KIWI VELOCITY (NZ) 6-10-9 M Hourigan, *beh 8th, tld off whn blun and uns rdr 3 out*.........(7 to 2 op 3 to 1) ur
1385^{6} WELSH COMMANDER 10-11-0 G McCourt, *sn beh, hit 9th and 11th, tld off whn pld up bef 12th.*
..............................(20 to 1 tchd 25 to 1) pu
LOS BUCCANEROS 10-11-0 G Upton, *al beh, tld off whn pld up bef 8th*.........(15 to 2 op 6 to 1 tchd 8 to 1) pu
Dist: Hd, 30l. 5m 7.30s. a 17.30s (7 Ran).
(Mrs David Laing), Mrs J Pitman

1442 Speen Novices' Hurdle (4-y-o and up) £4,435 2m 110yds.............(3:15)

1010^{2} LARGE ACTION (Ire) 5-11-0 J Osborne, *in tch till lost pos appr 5th, smooth hdwy frm 3 out, chlgd last, sn led, quickened clr*.......(7 to 4 fav op 2 to 1 tchd 9 to 4) 1
1283^{2} FATACK 4-11-1 (5*) S Curran, *led, sn clr, hdd soon aftr last, styd on one pace.*
......................(14 to 1 op 10 to 1 tchd 16 to 1) 2
BOOK OF MUSIC (Ire) 5-11-0 D Murphy, *al in tch, chsd ldrs 3 out till outpcd frm 2 out.*
......................(10 to 1 op 7 to 1 tchd 12 to 1) 3
FLIGHT LIEUTENANT (USA) 4-11-0 A Maguire, *chsd ldrs till outpcd frm 2 out*.......(7 to 2 op 4 to 1 tchd 5 to 1) 4
BRANDON PRINCE (Ire) 5-11-0 J Frost, *al prmnt, no imprsn frm 3 out*......(13 to 2 op 7 to 1 tchd 8 to 1) 5
BARNA BOY (Ire) 5-11-0 R Dunwoody, *beh, mstk 3 out, styd on wl appr last, prmsg.*
....................(12 to 1 op 10 to 1 tchd 14 to 1) 6
BRAVE HIGHLANDER (Ire) 5-10-11 (3*) P Hide, *al in tch, rdn to chase ldrs 3 out, no prog frm nxt.*
..................................(20 to 1 op 16 to 1) 7
809^{8} ORUJO (Ire) 5-11-0 R Marley, *mid-div, hdwy appr 3 out, fdd nxt*.............(25 to 1 op 33 to 1 tchd 50 to 1) 8
1010^{8} IVOR'S FLUTTER 4-11-0 P Holley, *beh till some hdwy frm 2 out*..........................(14 to 1 tchd 16 to 1) 9
1192^{8} RAFTERS 4-10-9 (5*) R Farrant, *hit 3rd, rdn and hit 5th, nvr dngrs aftr*..............................(33 to 1) 10
1010* TEXAN TYCOON 5-11-6 G McCourt, *chsd ldrs till wknd 2 out*....................(9 to 2 op 7 to 2 tchd 5 to 1) 11
SOUND REVEILLE 5-11-0 G Bradley, *sprawled badly and beh second, hmpd 3rd, not reco'r.*
....................(25 to 1 op 14 to 1 tchd 33 to 1) 12
MEADOW COTTAGE 7-10-7 (7*) J J Brown, *al beh.*
..................................(50 to 1 op 33 to 1) 13
1046^{2} DUNDEE PRINCE (NZ) 5-10-11 (3*) A Thornton, *chsd ldr till appr 5th, sn wknd*................(20 to 1 op 14 to 1) 14
1283 ALTERMEERA (bl) 5-11-0 G Morgan, *al beh.*
...............................(66 to 1 op 100 to 1) 15
1237 MY BOOKS ARE BEST (Ire) 4-10-9 Leesa Long, *al beh.*
....(100 to 1) 16
EXECUTION ONLY (Ire) 5-11-0 S Burrough, *prmnt to 4th, tld off*.........................(100 to 1 op 66 to 1) 17
LORD GLENVARA (Ire) 5-11-0 L Harvey, *beh whn f 3rd.*
....(33 to 1) f
1196^{8} EMBLEY BUOY 5-11-0 S Earle, *sn beh, tld off whn pld up bef 3 out*...............................(100 to 1) pu
Dist: 4l, 8l, 1½l, 4l, ½l, 4l, 6l, 2½l, ½l, 3l. 3m 54.20s. a 5.20s (19 Ran).
SR: 50/52/38/36/32/31/27/21/18/ (B T Stewart-Brown), O Sherwood

WARWICK (good)
Saturday November 27th
Going Correction: PLUS 0.10 sec. per fur. (races 1,3,6), PLUS 0.35 (2,4,5)

1443 Quinton Hurdle (4-y-o and up) £3,782 2m..........................(12:45)

1209^{2} ARABIAN BOLD (Ire) 5-11-0 M A FitzGerald, *made all, shaken up appr 2 out, drvn out r-in.*
..............(2 to 1 on op 6 to 4 on tchd 5 to 4 on) 1
WINNIE THE WITCH 9-10-4 D Bridgwater, *trkd wnr, cld frm 5th, hrd rdn appr 2 out, no imprsn r-in.*
......................(7 to 2 tchd 3 to 1 and 4 to 1) 2
SHU FLY (NZ) 9-11-0 Jacqui Oliver, *hld up, hdwy to track ldrs 4th, rdn appr 2 out, kpt on one pace.*
..................................(8 to 1 op 4 to 1) 3
ISLAND JEWEL 5-11-0 M Bosley, *trkd ldrs, outpcd 4th, no dngr aftr*.....................(200 to 1 op 100 to 1) 4
UNCLE ERNIE 8-10-9 W Dwan, *al last, effrt appr 2 out, eased r-in*...........(10 to 1 op 6 to 1 tchd 11 to 1) 5
Dist: 3½l, 8l, ¾l, 10l. 3m 45.80s. a 5.80s (5 Ran).
SR: 44/30/32/31/16/ (Sheikh Amin Dahlawi), N J Henderson

1444 Tower Novices' Chase (4-y-o and up) £3,860 2m.....................(1:20)

1241^{2} RODEO STAR (USA) 7-11-5 D Murphy, *hld up, hdwy to go second 6th, jnd ldr 2 out, pushed out to ld r-in.*
....................(11 to 10 op 5 to 4 tchd 6 to 4) 1
960 MIDNIGHT STORY 8-11-5 D Gallagher, *led second, rdn appr 2 out, hdd r-in, kpt on one pace.*
...................................(12 to 1 op 7 to 1) 2
1149^{3} SHADING 9-11-5 M Brennan, *led to second, outpcd whn blun 8th, tld off*................(66 to 1 op 50 to 1) 3
PEATY GLEN 8-11-5 R Campbell, *jmpd rght, hit 5th, outpcd nxt, tld off*..................(50 to 1 op 33 to 1) 4
1279 SUN SURFER (Fr) 5-11-5 M A FitzGerald, *hld up, hdwy 5th, second whn jmpd slwly 6th, cl 3rd when f 3 out.*
...............(Evens fav op 5 to 4 on tchd 11 to 10) f
Dist: 2l, dist, nk. 4m 9.30s. a 17.30s (5 Ran).
(J C Bradbury), N Tinkler

1445 Warwickshire College Of Agriculture Handicap Hurdle (0-145 4-y-o and up) £3,990 2½m 110yds............ (1:50)

1225^{3} JEASSU [127] 10-11-8 (5*) T Jenks, *steadied in rear, hdwy 4 out, led 2 out, all out.* (9 to 2 op 7 to 2 tchd 5 to 1) 1
1163^{4} GLAISDALE (Ire) [120] 4-11-6 D Murphy, *al prmnt, led 3 out to nxt, rallied und pres, no extr cl hme.*
.........(2 to 1 fav op 9 to 4 tchd 5 to 2 and 7 to 4) 2
948^{9} FOX CHAPEL [114] 6-11-0 W Dwan, *al prmnt, ev ch 2 out, hrd rdn and no extr nr finish*.....(14 to 1 op 10 to 1) 3
1257^{4} SUPER RITCHART [108] 5-10-8 M A FitzGerald, *led to 3 out, rallied last, one pace r-in*.........(14 to 1 op 12 to 1) 4
ONEUPMANSHIP [128] 8-11-7 (7*) S Fox, *prmnt, wnt second 4th, rdn appr 2 out, ev ch till one pace r-in.*
..............................(10 to 1 tchd 12 to 1) 5

1163[7] CORACO [108] 6-10-8 D Bridgwater, *hld up, hdwy 6th,*
rdn and wknd appr 2 out............(12 to 1 op 10 to 1)   6
STAR PLAYER [114] 7-11-0 N Mann, *hld up rear, effrt 7th,*
wknd appr 2 out...........(5 to 1 op 9 to 2 tchd 6 to 1)   7
1120[5] STAR QUEST [102] 6-10-2 D Gallagher, *hld up mid-div, rdn*
whn mstk 3 out, sn btn.............(9 to 1 op 7 to 1)   8
1206 COME HOME ALONE [100] (bl) 5-10-0 M Richards, *al beh,*
lost tch aftr 7th....................(33 to 1 op 20 to 1)   9
1006 DUKE DE VENDOME [106] 10-10-6 E Murphy, *trkd ldr to*
4th, outpcd appr 3 out, tld off.
....................(25 to 1 op 20 to 1 tchd 33 to 1) 10
ROSITARY (Fr) [126] 10-11-5 (7*) Mr G Cosgrove, *al beh, lost*
tch 6th, tld off....................(50 to 1 op 33 to 1) 11
Dist: ½l, sht-hd, 3½l, sht-hd, 10l, 12l, 6l, 3½l, 15l, 20l. 5m 3.60s. a 16.10s (11 Ran).

(Mrs R H Y Mills), A J Wilson

1446 Brandon Handicap Chase (0-135 5-y-o and up) £4,468 2m.............(2:25)

1168* SAILORS LUCK [102] 8-10-0 E Murphy, *led to 3rd, led 3*
out, in command frm nxt.....(11 to 8 fav op 13 to 8)   1
1056[3] TRIMLOUGH [125] 8-11-9 W Marston, *led 3rd, hit 3 out*
and hdd, no imprsn nxt.
....................(15 to 8 op 7 to 4 tchd 2 to 1)   2
665* ALKINOR REX [130] 8-12-0 M Perrett, *disputing ld whn*
mstk 1st, not jump wl aftr, no ch frm 5th.
.........................(9 to 4 op 7 to 4)   3
Dist: 3½l, 25l. 4m 1.80s. a 9.80s (3 Ran).
SR: 30/49/29/   (Geoffrey C Greenwood), P G Murphy

1447 Tiltyard Bridge Handicap Chase (0-145 5-y-o and up) £5,134 3¼m (3:00)

1208* LIGHT VENEER [125] 8-10-10 M Perrett, *patiently rdn,*
hdwy to go second 14th, led last, quickened clr.
.........................(3 to 1 tchd 7 to 2 and 5 to 2)   1
MOORCROFT BOY [119] 8-10-4 W Marston, *hld up, hdwy*
to go second 12th, outpcd 14th, rallied appr 2 out, wnt
second r-in.........................(16 to 1 op 8 to 1)   2
1162* DUBLIN FLYER [125] 7-10-10 C Llewellyn, *led, mstk 8th, hit*
3 out, hrd rdn and hdd last, wknd r-in.....(5 to 1 op 7 to 1)   3
1208[5] SUPERIOR FINISH [139] 7-11-10 B Powell, *prmnt, outpcd*
15th, kpt on frm 3 out, btn whn hit last.
.........................(8 to 1 tchd 9 to 1)   4
WINDY WAYS [130] 8-11-1 M A FitzGerald, *trkd ldr to 12th,*
outpcd 14th, rdn 3 out, sn btn........(5 to 1 op 8 to 1)   5
1088[2] BONSAI BUD [123] 10-10-8 D Gallagher, *hld up, hit 7th, sn*
pld up bef 11th.......................(10 to 1 op 8 to 1) pu
TAGMOUN CHAUFOUR (Fr) [115] 8-10-0 N Mann, *tld off*
pld up bef 11th.............(200 to 1 op 100 to 1) pu
Dist: 5l, ½l, 5l, 20l. 6m 30.20s. a 16.20s (7 Ran).
SR: 11/-/5/14/   (Louis Jones), Mrs Merrita Jones

1448 University Of Warwick Novices' Handicap Hurdle (0-100 3-y-o and up) £1,473 2m.....................(3:30)

GOTTA BE JOKING [82] 5-11-1 M A FitzGerald, *in tch, rdn*
to ld appr last, drw clr r-in........(10 to 1 op 7 to 1)   1
1173[4] MR POPPLETON [67] 4-10-0 D Bridgwater, *led till appr*
last, no extr r-in.............(9 to 2 fav op 14 to 1)   2
1252[3] GAMEFULL GOLD [88] 4-11-2 (5*) A Dicken, *hld up rear,*
hdwy appr 2 out, ran on, nvr nrr....(8 to 1 op 7 to 1)   3
1010 BOLD STREET BLUES [84] 6-11-3 J Railton, *hld up, hdwy*
appr 2 out, ran on, nvr nrr.......(12 to 1 op 10 to 1)   4
1173* SAINT CIEL (USA) [80] 5-10-13 R Supple, *in tch, hit 3 out,*
one pace nxt.......................(5 to 1 op 4 to 1)   5
1068 SOLO CORNET [67] 8-10-0 W Humphreys, *mid-div, hdwy*
to go second 3 out, hrd rdn and wknd nxt....(14 to 1 op 12 to 1)   6
1152[3] EMERALD VENTURE [85] (v) 6-11-4 Peter Caldwell, *prmnt,*
wnt second 4th, wknd aftr 3 out....(14 to 1 op 12 to 1)   7
1239[3] PRINCETHORPE [67] 6-10-0 N Mann, *hld up, hdwy 4th,*
and wknd 3 out........(25 to 1 op 14 to 1 tchd 33 to 1)   8
MORSHOT [84] 6-11-3 C Maude, *hld up, hdwy 3rd, rdn*
and wknd 3 out.....................(6 to 1 op 5 to 1)   9
SIMON JOSEPH [91] 6-11-10 C Llewellyn, *chsd ldrs till*
wknd aftr 3 out.......................(9 to 1 op 7 to 1) 10
COOL SOCIETY (USA) [75] 4-10-3 (5*) A Bates, *hld up,*
hdwy appr 3 out, wknd appr 3 out...(14 to 1 op 8 to 1) 11
1193[8] DAMCADA (Ire) [73] 5-10-6 W Marston, *al beh.*
.........................(33 to 1 op 20 to 1) 12
988 SMART DEBUTANTE (Ire) [78] 4-10-4 (7*) Mr S Joynes, *al*
beh.........................(14 to 1 op 10 to 1) 13
1283 ROSEATE LODGE [78] 7-10-11 D Gallagher, *in tch till*
wknd 5th, tld off.....................(6 to 1 op 10 to 1) 14
COME ON DANCER (Ire) [91] 5-11-10 W McFarland, *prmnt*
till wknd quickly 3 out, tld off...(14 to 1 tchd 16 to 1) 15
ALDINGTON MILLPOND [69] 5-10-0* (3*) R Davis, *sn beh,*
tld off 4th, pld up bef last.
....................(25 to 1 op 20 to 1 tchd 33 to 1) pu
Dist: 5l, 1l, 1½l, 1½l, 2l, 1½l, 1l, ½l, 3l, 7l. 3m 50.30s. a 10.30s (16 Ran).
(Mrs P Scott-Dunn), Miss H C Knight

FAIRYHOUSE (IRE) (good to yielding)
Sunday November 28th

1449 River Hurdle (5-y-o and up) £3,105 2m ....(12:45)

1332* IDIOTS VENTURE 6-11-8 B Sheridan, ...(Evens fav)   1
MONALEE RIVER (Ire) 5-11-4 C F Swan, ...(2 to 1)   2
804[4] HACKETTS CROSS (Ire) 5-11-4 A Powell, ...(8 to 1)   3
1379 ALBONA 5-10-13 H Rogers, ...(33 to 1)   4
1330[9] ATOURS (USA) 5-10-11 (7*) Mr H Murphy, ...(9 to 2)   5
1076 SAGASTINI (USA) 6-11-4 P L Malone, ...(16 to 1)   6
Dist: 1½l, 10l, 15l, 8l. 4m 3.00s. (6 Ran).
(Blackwater Racing Syndicate), A P O'Brien

1450 Strand Handicap Hurdle (4-y-o and up) £3,105 2m.....................(1:15)

1400[3] DARCARI ROSE (Ire) [-] 4-9-0 (7*) T Martin, ...(10 to 1)   1
1400 THE BOURDA [-] 7-9-7 F Woods, ...(25 to 1)   2
SUPER FLAME (Can) [-] 6-10-7 C F Swan, ...(8 to 1)   3
967[8] FAMOUS DANCER [-] 5-9-0 (7*) B Bowens, ...(16 to 1)   4
1269 BELLECARA [-] 6-9-4 (3*) D Bromley, ...(10 to 1)   5
1335[4] SIMPLY SWIFT [-] 6-11-9 G Bradley, ...(5 to 1)   6
265* RATHBRIDES (Ire) [-] 4-10-4 B Sheridan, ...(7 to 1)   7
1232[9] WINTERBOURNE ABBAS (Ire) [-] (bl) 4-10-4 B Sheridan,
.........................(20 to 1)   8
1269[9] JUST ONE CANALETTO [-] 5-9-6 (5*) M G Cleary, (16 to 1)   9
1234[8] MERAPI [-] 7-10-6 (7*) D J Kavanagh, ...(10 to 1) 10
SIMENON [-] 7-11-12 J Short, ...(20 to 1) 11
1155[5] KNOCNAGORE (Ire) [-] 4-9-7 H Rogers, ...(20 to 1) 12
1157* CASTLE RANGER [-] 6-11-0 (6ex) C N Bowens, ...(5 to 1) 13
1269 MAYE FANE [-] 9-10-13 (7*) Mr C A Leavy, ...(33 to 1) 14
HARVEYSLAND [-] 10-11-7 C O'Dwyer, ...(14 to 1) 15
APPELLATE COURT [-] 5-10-13 D H O'Connor, ...(16 to 1) 16
1269[6] ENQELAAB (USA) [-] (bl) 5-10-4 J P Banahan, ..(3 to 1 fav) 17
1397 HAWAIAN TASCA (Ire) [-] 4-9-0 (7*) Mrs K Walsh, ..(25 to 1) 18
Dist: 3l, 15l, 1l, sht-hd. 3m 54.20s. (18 Ran).
(Mrs G Pennicott), F W Pennicott

1451 Bambury Bookmakers Novice Chase (5-y-o and up) £4,140 2¾m....(1:45)

941[6] SPUR OF THE MOMENT 6-11-9 J P Banahan, ...(12 to 1)   1
929[2] SCRIBBLER 7-12-0 L P Cusack, ...(7 to 2)   2
1177 HAVE TO THINK 5-11-6 (5*) T P Rudd, ...(14 to 1)   3
929 FARNEY GLEN 6-12-0 P P Kinane, ...(16 to 1)   4
807 BACK BAR (Ire) 5-11-3 T J Taaffe, ...(50 to 1)   5
1234* TAWNEY FLAME 7-12-0 M Dwyer, ...(6 to 4 fav)   6
1157[8] MISS SPLENDOUR (Ire) 5-11-3 (3*) T J Mitchell, ..(25 to 1)   7
AUTUMN RIDE (Ire) 5-11-3 F Woods, ...(40 to 1)   8
CHOSEN SON 5-10-12 (5*) D P Geoghegan, ...(50 to 1)   9
1266[5] SHEILA NA GIG 7-11-9 A Powell, ...(12 to 1) 10
1035 THREE BROWNIES 6-12-0 G Bradley, ...(7 to 1) 11
1035[2] ANOTHER GROUSE 6-10-11 (7*) J P Broderick, ..(10 to 1) 12
THE COOPER 6-11-9 J F Titley, ...(33 to 1) 13
BEAU BABILLARD 6-12-0 C F Swan, ...(6 to 1)   f
1035[9] WAR OFFICE 6-11-4 J Jones, ...(33 to 1)   f
OLD MONEY 7-12-0 P Carberry, ...(12 to 1) ref
Dist: Hd, 3½l, 3½l, dist. 5m 40.40s. (16 Ran).
(C J McNally), J P Kavanagh

1452 Porterstown Handicap Chase (Listed Race - Grade 3) (5-y-o and up) £6,900 3m 1f.............................(2:15)

943[3] SON OF WAR [-] 6-11-3 F Woods, *led till aftr 4th, wl plcd,*
led appr four out, sn clr, easily................(7 to 2)   1
1381[2] FISSURE SEAL [-] 7-11-4 G Bradley, *rear, mstk 8th, nig-*
gled alng tenth, styd on frm 3 out, not rch wnr. (5 to 2)   2
1381[3] JOE WHITE [-] 7-10-7 P Carberry, *led 5th till rdn and hdd*
appr 4 out, sn btn.......................(7 to 1)   3
1231 MASS APPEAL [-] 8-11-2 B Sheridan, *rear, rdn and lost*
tch 12th.........................(20 to 1)   4
855[4] FOR WILLIAM [-] 7-11-3 K F O'Brien, *tracking ldrs whn f*
12th..........................   f
992* DEEP BRAMBLE [-] 6-12-0 P Niven, *tracking ldrs whn*
brght dwn 12th.............(5 to 4 fav) bd
Dist: 15l, dist, dist. 6m 35.02s. (6 Ran).
(Mrs V O'Brien), Peter McCreery

1453 Glascairn Handicap Hurdle (4-y-o and up) £3,105 2¾m...............(2:45)

1074* PANDA (Ire) [-] 5-10-2 (5*) T P Treacy, ...(9 to 1)   1
938[2] BAVARD DIEU (Ire) [-] 5-10-7 C F Swan, ...(5 to 2 fav)   2
1380[8] COUMEENOOLE LADY [-] 6-10-6 (7*) J M Donnelly,
.........................(20 to 1)   3
1234[5] ST DONAVINT [-] 6-11-0 C N Bowens, ...(8 to 1)   4
1380[2] TITIAN BLONDE [-] 5-11-2 F Woods, ...(4 to 1)   5
708 HORNER WATER (Ire) [-] 5-9-11 (7*) J P Broderick, (14 to 1)   6
1380[9] THE MAD MONK [-] 8-10-6 B Sheridan, ...(25 to 1)   7
1380 FRIGID COUNTESS [-] 6-9-0 (7*) L A Hurley, ...(20 to 1)   8
1157[2] LOAVES AND FISHES [-] 5-10-2 (5*) H Taylor, ..(12 to 1)   9
1232 COOLAHEARAC [-] 7-9-2 P P Kinane, ...(20 to 1) 10
PEBBLE LANE [-] 7-11-1 H Rogers, ...(20 to 1) 11
689[2] CARRON HILL [-] 6-10-0 F Woods, ...(10 to 1) 12
1234[4] TOUT VA BIEN [-] 5-10-7 P Carberry, ...(9 to 1) 13
1380 VINCERO [-] (bl) 8-10-3 (5*) M G Cleary, ...(25 to 1) 14
877* REGALING (Ire) [-] 5-10-8 (5*) T P Rudd, ...(9 to 1) 15

1269 PRIDE OF ERIN [-] 9-11-0 L P Cusack, ...(20 to 1) pu
1178⁸ NUALA'S PET [-] 8-10-11 M Dwyer, ...(12 to 1) pu
    BRINDLEY HOUSE [-] 6-11-4 R Dunwoody, ... (14 to 1) pu
Dist: 2l, 3l, 7l, ½l. 5m 24.00s. (18 Ran).

(Giles Clarke), P Mullins

1454 Juvenile Hurdle (Listed Race - Grade 3) (3-y-o) £5,520 2m...........(3:15)

1264⁵ THE BERUKI (Ire) 10-3 (5") T P Treacy, mid-div, prog appr
    5th, led bef 3 out, jnd last, rallied r-in.........(12 to 1) 1
1264' MAGIC FEELING (Ire) 10-8 C F Swan, prog frm mid-div aftr
    4 out, chsd wnr nxt, chlgd last, wknd cl hme... (5 to 2) 2
1264² CALL MY GUEST (Ire) 10-9 M Dwyer, wl plcd, rdn to go 3rd
    aftr 2 out, wknd appr last...................... (6 to 1) 3
1111² TEMPLEMARY BOY (Ire) 11-2 T Horgan, prog frm mid-div 3
    out, rdn and kpt on one pace strt............(9 to 4 fav) 4
    LAKE OF LOUGHREA (Ire) 10-9 J Shortt, rear, styd on frm 3
    out, not rch ldrs.............................(20 to 1) 5
1111⁵ BIZANA (Ire) 11-2 P Carberry, mid-div, rdn 3 out, no
    imprsn nxt...................................(12 to 1) 6
1111⁴ ASSERT STAR 11-2 R Dunwoody, wl plcd, led appr 4 out
    till bef nxt, sn wknd............................(7 to 1) 7
    DIFFERENT TIMES (Ire) 10-9 C O'Dwyer, prog frm rear 4
    out, trkd ldrs nxt, sn rdn and wknd..............(6 to 1) 8
1377⁴ GLOWING VALUE (Ire) [bl] 10-9 B Sheridan, shrtlvd effrt
    frm rear 4 out, sn btn.........................(10 to 1) 9
968⁹ LEOS LITTLE BIT (Ire) [bl] 9-13 (5") T J O'Sullivan, led till hdd
    and wknd appr 4 out...........................(20 to 1) 10
    STATE PRINCESS (Ire) 9-13 (5") M G Cleary, al rear.
    ....(12 to 1) 11
Dist: 1½l, 3½l, 9l, 4½l. 3m 58.00s. (11 Ran).

(Mrs Geraldine Treacy), S J Treacy

1455 Narrow Neck I.N.H. Flat Race (4 & 5-y-o) £3,105 2m..................(3:40)

    MILTONFIELD 4-11-6 (3") Miss C Hutchinson, ...(7 to 1) 1
    THE BLUEBELL POLKA (Ire) 4-11-4 (5") Mr H F Cleary,
    ....(9 to 4 fav) 2
1020² CLOWATER LADY (Ire) 4-10-11 (7") Mr P English, ..(6 to 1) 3
    GLEN TEN (Ire) 4-11-1 (3") Mrs J M Mullins, ...(6 to 1) 4
    DUN CARRAIG (Ire) 5-11-2 (7") Mr M O'Connor, ...(25 to 1) 5
    SKY VISION (Ire) 4-10-12¹ (7") Mr K F O'Donnell, ..(20 to 1) 6
    BUCKLEUP (Ire) 4-11-2 (7") Mr D A Harney, ...(7 to 1) 7
576⁶ REGAL DAUGHTER (Ire) 4-11-4 Mr A P O'Brien,...(10 to 1) 8
1230⁹ LUCK OF A LADY (Ire) 4-11-10 (7") Mr B M Cash, (14 to 1) 9
1236 LEAP (Ire) 4-11-4 (5") Mr G J Harford, ...(20 to 1) 10
1155⁸ FLIP THE LID (Ire) 4-11-4 (7") Miss H McCourt, ...(50 to 1) 11
620 RAHAN BRIDGE (Ire) 4-11-1 (3") Mr A R Coonan, ..(10 to 1) 12
    BURNHILL LAD (Ire) 4-11-4 (5") Mr B Hamilton, (14 to 1) 13
    HAWTHORN'S WAY (Ire) 5-11-9 Mr A J Martin, ... (20 to 1) 14
1270 CROSSABEG ROSE (Ire) 5-11-2 (7") Mr M McGrath,
    ....(16 to 1) 15
1016⁵ ARCTIC TREASURE (Ire) 4-10-13 (5") Mr C T G Kinane,
    ....(14 to 1) 16
675 FRIENDLY BID (Ire) 5-11-2 (7") Mr N Moran, ...(50 to 1) 17
1113 BIGCANYON (Ire) 5-11-12⁵ (7") Mr J F Brennan, ...(50 to 1) 18
1337⁷ NINE O THREE (Ire) 4-11-2 (7") Mr B Moran, ...(8 to 1) 19
Dist: 2l, 7l, 9l, 12l. 3m 52.10s. (19 Ran).

(J P Savage), J E Mulhern

WORCESTER (good)
Monday November 29th
Going Correction: PLUS 1.12 sec. per fur.

# 1456 Spetchley Novices' Claiming Hurdle (4-y-o and up) £1,961 2m 5f 110yds
..................................(12:30)

889⁵ SIR PAGEANT 4-11-4 D Bridgwater, nvr far away, led
    appr 3 out, drw clr nxt, eased r-in... (5 to 1 op 5 to 1) 1
1142³ OK RECORDS 6-10-12 N Mann, patiently rdn, improved
    appr 3 out, styd on frm betw last 2, nvr finish.
    ....(8 to 1 tchd 10 to 1 and 7 to 1) 2
1325² TAUNTING (Ire) 5-10-10 D Gallagher, settled midfield,
    improved appr 3 out, styd on one pace frm between
    last 2.........................(10 to 1 tchd 12 to 1) 3
1136³ IVYCHURCH (USA) 7-10-10 J Frost, ran in snatches, drvn
    up to chge 3 out, rdn and no extr betw last 2.
    ....(33 to 1 op 20 to 1) 4
    LAFHEEN (Ire) 5-10-6 D Morris, al wl plcd, lft in ld 5th,
    hdd appr 3 out, btn nxt.......................(40 to 1) 5
1353⁵ BORRETO 9-10-2¹ (7") Mr E James, wth ldrs, led 3rd till
    aftr nxt, cl second whn hmpd by faller 5th, sn lost tch,
    no ch frm 4 out................(20 to 1 op 16 to 1) 6
    HEPBURN (Ire) 5-10-11 W Humphreys, beh to hfwy, hdwy
    frm 3 out, nvr dngrs............................(50 to 1) 7
1280⁴ VALIANTHE (USA) 5-11-7 R Dunwoody, wtd wth, improved
    frm midfield appr 3 out, rdn and btn nxt.
    ....(7 to 4 fav op 3 to 1) 8
953⁹ MALLYAN 6-10-0² (3") R Davis, in tch, struggling to go
    pace aftr 4 out, sn btn.........(20 to 1 tchd 25 to 1) 9
1173⁵ TALLAND STREAM 6-11-4 C Llewellyn, in tch, drvn alng in
    midfield hfwy, btn 4 out............(10 to 1 op 6 to 1) 10

1079⁹ WINGED WHISPER (USA) 4-10-5 (5") T Eley, chsd ldrs,
    feeling pace 4 out, sn lost tch......(33 to 1 op 25 to 1) 11
1173 GENERAL SHOT 8-11-0 M A FitzGerald, facing wrong way
    strt, lost many ls, nvr able to reco'r.
    ....(20 to 1 op 33 to 1) 12
1272⁶ MOLLETROIS 5-9-10 (5") T Jenks, slwly away, al wl beh.
    ....(33 to 1 op 20 to 1) 13
    MAORI ICEMAN (NZ) 6-11-6 M Hourigan, chsd ldrs to
    hfwy, lost tch 4 out, tld off whn pld up bef nxt. 14
1090⁵ MAYFIELD PARK 8-10-3 (7") Mr G Hogan, al hndy, led aftr
    4th till f nxt...................................f
    JUST BALLYTOO [bl] 6-10-12 W McFarland, chsd ldrs,
    struggling appr 4 out, tld off whn pld up bef nxt.
    ....(50 to 1) pu
699 WASTEOFTIME 6-10-5 W Marston, led to 3rd, wknd
    quickly aftr nxt, pld up aftr 5th............(100 to 1) pu
747² LONG'S EXPRESS (Ire) 5-10-13 J Osborne, wth ldrs, strug-
    gling whn pace quickened 4 out, tld off whn pld up bef
    nxt............................(7 to 1 op 4 to 1 tchd 8 to 1) pu
1315 WHAT A RATTLE [bl] 4-10-6 C Maude, wth ldrs, struggling
    4 out, lost tch and pld up bef 2 out..............(50 to 1) pu
Dist: 5l, ½l, ¾l, 8l, 15l, 5l, 1½l, 2l, 3½l, 3½l. 5m 40.40s. a 36.40s (19 Ran).

(The Dirty Dozen), K S Bridgwater

1457 Stock Green Novices' Handicap Chase (5-y-o and up) £2,968 2½m 110yds......................(1:00)

1441 POPPETS PET [76] 6-10-2 S Earle, led till aftr second, led
    7th, jnd and hit 3 out, styd on strly r-in.
    ....(14 to 1 op 10 to 1) 1
    HOWARYADOON [98] 7-11-5 (5") C Burnett-Wells, al hndy,
    drw level last 3, styd on und pres r-in.
    ....(16 to 1 op 12 to 1) 2
    RUBINS BOY [81] 7-10-7 M Richards, patiently rdn, jnd
    ldrs hfwy, pushed alng frm 3 out, one pace.
    ....(12 to 1 op 8 to 1) 3
1248³ BATHWICK BOBBIE [81] 6-10-7 S McNeill, nvr far away,
    ev ch and pushed alng whn blun 2 out, not reco'r.
    ....(9 to 2 op 4 to 1 tchd 5 to 1) 4
    FINO [98] 7-11-10 R Dunwoody, trkd ldrs, ev ch and drvn
    alng appr 4 out, outpcd nxt.
    ....(5 to 1 op 7 to 2 tchd 3 to 1) 5
1339² STEEPLE JACK [88] 6-11-0 R Greene, settled to track ldrs,
    hdwy appr 4 out, kpt on same pace nxt.
    ....(10 to 1 op 8 to 1) 6
    UFANO (Fr) [74] 7-10-0 B Powell, led aftr second to 7th,
    hndy till wknd aftr 4 out........(25 to 1 op 14 to 1) 7
1279³ GALAXY HIGH [90] 6-11-2 M A FitzGerald, settled midfield,
    effrt and pushed alng appr 4 out, kpt on same pace.
    ....(9 to 1 op 4 to 1 tchd 5 to 1) 8
1276² FATHER RALPH [83] 7-10-9 P Holley, in tch, pushed alng
    to keep up whn f 8th.................(10 to 1 tchd 8 to 1) f
    FREDS MELODY [77] 8-10-3 C Maude, chsd ldrs, strug-
    gling whn hmpd and uns rdr 2 out.
    ....(14 to 1 op 16 to 1 tchd 20 to 1) ur
    GOLDFINGER [87] 10-10-13 Richard Guest, not fluent,
    struggling hfwy, tld off whn pld up bef 4 out.
    ....(25 to 1 op 20 to 1 tchd 33 to 1) pu
1024 MARTRAJAN [81] 6-10-7 J Osborne, mstks, patiently rdn,
    ev ch whn blun 6 out, rallied, losing tch when tried to
    refuse 2 out, pld up..............(11 to 1 op 7 to 1) pu
    NICKLUP [85] 6-10-11 H Davies, settled midfield, strug-
    gling hfwy, tld off whn pld up bef 4 out.
    ....(10 to 1 op 7 to 1) pu
Dist: 2l, 6l, 3l, 1½l, 2l, nk, 2½l. 5m 32.10s. a 29.10s (13 Ran).
SR: 13/33/10/7/22/10/-/8/-/-

(D J Line), J W Mullins

1458 River Severn Handicap Hurdle (0-135 4-y-o and up) £2,763 3m.......(1:30)

1341⁵ ULURU (Ire) [104] 5-10-0 R Dunwoody, settled gng wl, drw
    level 4 out, led aftr nxt, blun and almost uns rdr 2 out,
    sn hdd, rallied to ld r-in.
    ....(9 to 1 op 10 to 1 tchd 14 to 1) 1
1274⁴ MARDOOD [119] [bl] 8-11-11 H Davies, patiently rdn, jnd
    ldrs 4 out, lft in ld aftr 2 out, hdd r-in, ridden and one
    pace........................(9 to 2 op 5 to 2 tchd 4 to 1) 2
1267⁷ ASK THE GOVERNOR [112] 7-10-2¹ (7") S Fox, wtd wth,
    hdwy fnl circuit, effrt betw last 2, styd on same pace.
    ....(10 to 1 op 7 to 1) 3
1206³ KANO WARRIOR [108] 6-10-4 C Llewellyn, led till aftr 1st,
    led aftr 4th till aftr 3 out, no extr betw last 2.
    ....(4 to 1 op 100 to 30 tchd 9 to 2) 4
1170⁴ PRIME DISPLAY (USA) [132] 7-11-9 (5") J McCarthy, wth
    ldrs, ev ch fnl circuit, rdn and outpcd 3 out.
    ....(10 to 1 op 7 to 1 tchd 11 to 2) 5
1274⁸ APARECIDA (Fr) [104] 7-10-0 D Morris, nvr far away, ev ch
    4 out, rdn aftr nxt, sn btn........(33 to 1 tchd 50 to 1) 6
1322⁵ CELTIC BREEZE [104] [v] 10-10-0 A Dobbin, settled mid-
    field, jnd ldrs fnl circuit, rdn and outpcd 3 out. (7 to 1) 7
1057 WINABUCK [104] 10-9-11 (3") D Meredith, al hndy, ev ch
    aftr 4 out, fdd nxt........(35 to 1 op 20 to 1 tchd 40 to 1) 8
1190 COXANN [104] 7-9-7 (7") E Tolhurst, trkd ldrs, effrt fnl
    circuit, fdd nxt.................(40 to 1 op 33 to 1 tchd 50 to 1) 9

1310² WINGS OF FREEDOM (Ire) [105] 5-10-1 J Osborne, *pressed ldrs till fdd und pres aftr 4 out.* .... (13 to 2 op 6 to 1 tchd 7 to 1) 10
845⁸ BRORA ROSE (Ire) [104] 5-10-0 I Shoemark, *in tch for o'r one circuit, rdn and btn 4 out*.... (100 to 1 op 66 to 1) 11
1322 AMBLESIDE HARVEST [111] 6-10-0 (7*) B Harding, *wth ldrs for o'r one circuit, fdg whn f 4 out.* (14 to 1 op 12 to 1) f
1042⁶ SOLENT LAD [107] 10-10-3¹⁰ (7*) M Stevens, *struggling aftr one circuit, tld off whn pld up bef 3 out.* .... (100 to 1 op 66 to 1) pu
1296⁴ NESSFIELD [110] 7-10-6 A S Smith, *trkd ldrs, struggling appr 4 out, pld up bef nxt*......... (16 to 1 op 14 to 1) pu
CADFORD GIRL [107] 9-10-3³ P Holley, *in tch for o'r one circuit, tailing off whn pld up bef 2 out.* ....(33 to 1 tchd 50 to 1) pu
1363 BEL COURSE [104] (bl) 11-10-0 W Marston, *slwly away, reco'red to ld aftr 1st, sn clr, hdd and reminders after 4th, tld off whn pld up after 7th*... (33 to 1 op 50 to 1) pu
Dist: 5l, 3l, 2l, 2l, 3l, 4l, 8l, dist. 6m 12.60s. a 36.60s (16 Ran).
(P J Morgan), C T Nash

1459 Malvern Handicap Chase (0-120 4-y-o and up) £3,132 2m 7f........... (2:00)

WARNER FOR WINNERS [99] 7-10-13 G McCourt, *patiently rdn, improved fnl circuit, led bef 2 out, blun last, styd on wl*........ (11 to 2 op 5 to 1 tchd 6 to 1) 1
956⁵ RED AMBER [91] (v) 7-10-5 J Osborne, *al hndy, reminders hfwy, rallied to ld 11th, hdd 4 out, led briefly nxt, styd on one pace r-in.* .... (12 to 1 op 10 to 1) 2
1302³ MISS FERN [91] 8-10-2 (3*) D Meredith, *trkd ldrs, led 4 out to nxt, sn drvn alng, fdd betw last 2.* (6 to 1 op 10 to 1) 3
1162 FURRY KNOWE [107] 8-11-7 S McNeill, *tucked away in midfield, ev ch appr 4 out, rdn and outpcd nxt.* .... (16 to 1 op 14 to 1) 4
1197⁶ FIDDLERS THREE [108] 10-11-8 C Llewellyn, *not fluent, wth ldrs, led aftr 9th till blun and hdd 11th, struggling nxt*........................ (12 to 1 op 10 to 1) 5
1151 SOONER STILL [108] (v) 9-11-1 (7*) Judy Davies, *trkd ldrs for o'r one circuit, lost tch quickly and pld up bef 6 out.* ....(25 to 1) pu
NOUGAT RUSSE [104] 12-11-4 D Bridgwater, *struggling to keep up aftr one circuit, tailing off whn pld up bef 6 out*.............................. (14 to 1 op 10 to 1) pu
1191* NAUGHTY NICKY [89] 9-10-3 R Greene, *struggling to go pace aftr one circuit, tld off whn pld up bef 4 out.* .... (10 to 1 op 9 to 1) pu
1262* PURBECK DOVE [94] 8-10-8 S Earle, *settled midfield, pushed alng fnl circuit, poor 4th and tired whn pld up bef last*...........(2 to 1 fav tchd 9 to 4 and 15 to 8) pu
1026² VIRIDIAN [106] (bl) 8-11-6 R Supple, *led till aftr 9th, wknd rpdly and pld up bef 6 out*.........(10 to 1 op 8 to 1) pu
1098 GOLD HAVEN [110] 9-11-3 (7*) D Fortt, *chsd ldrs for o'r one circuit, lost tch and pld up bef 12th.* .... (15 to 2 op 6 to 1 tchd 8 to 1) pu
Dist: 2½l, 20l, 8l, dist. 6m 15.50s. a 31.50s (11 Ran).
SR: 28/17/-/5/-/-/ (Terry Warner Sports), P J Hobbs

1460 Rushock Novices' Hurdle (4-y-o and up) £1,480 2m..................(2:30)

TISSISAT (USA) 4-10-12 J Frost, *settled gng wl, improved appr 4 out, drw level last, sn led, ran on well.* .... (13 to 2 op 11 to 4 tchd 7 to 1) 1
1053* TIME FOR A FLUTTER 4-11-0 S McNeill, *nvr far away, led 3 out, jnd last, sn hdd, one pace*...(14 to 1 op 10 to 1) 2
KEEP ME IN MIND (Ire) 4-10-12 D Skyrme, *wtd wth, improved hfwy, chlgd last 3, kpt on same pace r-in.* ....(50 to 1 op 33 to 1 tchd 100 to 1) 3
1283³ EMPIRE BLUE 10-10-12 M Bosley, *settled midfield, jnd ldrs 4 out, rdn aftr nxt, no extr.* ....(7 to 2 op 3 to 1 tchd 4 to 1) 4
1354⁵ JIMLIL 5-10-7 R Dunwoody, *settled wth chasing grp, improved 4 out, rdn and kpt on same pace last 2.* .... (33 to 1 op 16 to 1) 5
1141⁵ SCOTTISH BALL 4-10-7 M Crosse, *chsd ldrs, hdwy aftr 4 out, styd on, nvr able to chal*....(100 to 1 op 66 to 1) 6
1053³ BOLD BOSTONIAN (Fr) 5-10-12 M Hourigan, *co'red up in midfield, effrt hfwy, drvn alng appr 3 out, sn lost tch.* .... (12 to 1 op 7 to 1) 7
GRECIAN SAILOR 8-10-5 (7*) R Darke, *in tch, drvn alng whn pace quickened appr 4 out, sn tld off.* ....(100 to 1 op 66 to 1) 8
COURAGEOUS KNIGHT 4-10-7 (5*) R Farrant, *settled to chase ldrs, struggling 4 out, tld off.* ....(33 to 1 op 25 to 1) 9
952* BUTLER'S TWITCH 6-11-5 J Osborne, *trkd clr ldr, led 4th, jnd four out, hdd 3 out, wkng quickly whn hit nxt.* ....(11 to 10 on op 5 to 4 tchd 5 to 4 on) 10
SHELLHOUSE (Ire) 5-10-12 M A FitzGerald, *slwly away, improved into midfield hfwy, tld off appr 3 out.* .... (25 to 1 op 10 to 1) 11
932* DOUBLE THE STAKES (USA) 4-11-5 V Slattery, *in tch, struggling to keep up 4 out, tld off nxt.* .... (25 to 1 op 14 to 1) 12
DEVIL'S CORNER 5-10-12 B Powell, *beh and drvn alng hfwy, tld off*....................(100 to 1 op 50 to 1) 13
1078 COME ON LUCY 4-10-4 (3*) R Davis, *struggling hfwy, tld off*..............................(100 to 1 op 50 to 1) 14
634 MARINERS MEMORY 5-10-12 W Humphreys, *struggling hfwy, sn tld off*.................. (100 to 1 op 66 to 1) 15
CALIFORNIA DREAMIN 4-10-7 J Ryan, *wth ldrs early, last and struggling whn blun and uns rdr 4th.* .... (100 to 1 op 50 to 1) ur
1193⁴ NIGEL'S LUCKY GIRL 5-10-7 J McLaughlin, *sn clr, hdd 4th, fdd four out, pld up bef nxt*.....(25 to 1 tchd 33 to 1) pu
DISTANT MILL (Ire) 5-10-9 (3*) D Meredith, *beh and drvn alng hfwy, tld off whn pld up betweeen last 2.* .... (100 to 1 op 33 to 1) pu
Dist: 2l, ¾l, 6l, nk, 1l, dist, 2½l, ¾l, 2l, 4l. 4m 3.60s. a 22.60s (18 Ran).
SR: 37/37/34/28/22/21/ (Urs E Schwarzenbach), I A Balding

1461 Kempsey Handicap Chase (0-120 4-y-o and up) £2,794 2m............(3:00)

1260* COTAPAXI [92] 8-10-0 R Dunwoody, *jmpd wl, made all, hrd pressed frm 4 out, styd on gmely from last.* .... (11 to 1 op 8 to 1 tchd 12 to 1) 1
1285 ONE FOR THE POT [110] 8-11-4 A Dobbin, *al hndy, drw level 4 out, blun 2 out, kpt on same pace r-in.* .... (5 to 2 op 11 to 4 tchd 3 to 1) 2
NORTHERN JINKS [120] 10-11-11 (3*) D Meredith, *al wl plcd, feeling pace and rdn 5 out, rallied to chal nxt, wknd quickly bef 2 out*.............(11 to 4 op 9 to 2) 3
1446* SAILORS LUCK [109] 8-11-3 (7ex) E Murphy, *nvr far away, joining wnr whn blun and uns rdr 5th.* .... (5 to 4 fav op 5 to 4 on tchd 11 to 8) ur
1409 MAJOR EFFORT [92] 8-9-9² (7*) Mr N Bradley, *nvr gng wl, tailing off whn pld up bef 6th.* .... (40 to 1 op 33 to 1 tchd 50 to 1) pu
Dist: 3l, 30l. 4m 18.60s. a 29.60s (5 Ran).
(Mrs Barbara Lock), R J Hodges

1462 Levy Board Handicap Hurdle (0-125 4-y-o and up) £2,442 2m 5f 110yds ....(3:30)

1209⁴ KADI (Ger) [125] 4-12-0 W Marston, *patiently rdn, jnd ldrs appr 3 out, led last, drvn out*..... (12 to 1 op 10 to 1) 1
HEATHFIELD GALE [103] 6-10-6 R Dunwoody, *wtd wth, jnd ldrs appr 3 out, led nxt, hdd last, one pace*...(4 to 1 jt-fav op 3 to 1) 2
1198* FAIR BROTHER [104] 7-10-4 (3*) R Davis, *patiently rdn, hdwy to chal 3 out, kpt on one pace frm last.* (4 to 1 jt-fav op 5 to 1 tchd 11 to 2) 3
936⁶ IMA DELIGHT [97] 6-9-7 (7*) Lorna Brand, *settled midfield, improved frm 3 out, styd on r-in*... (25 to 1 op 16 to 1) 4
BROUGHTON'S TANGO (Ire) [97] 4-10-0 S Keightley, *settled off the pace, improved appr 3 out, styd on frm last.* ....(7 to 1 op 5 to 1 tchd 8 to 1) 5
CAPPUCCINO GIRL [99] 6-10-2² M Crosse, *settled off the pace, squeezed and hit rail on bend aftr 4th, styd on wl frm 3 out, nrst finish*............. (20 to 1 op 16 to 1) 6
1274⁹ VADO VIA [117] 5-10-13 (7*) K Brown, *trkd ldrs, struggling and wl beh hfwy, styd on well frm 3 out, nrst finish.* .... (7 to 1 op 9 to 1 tchd 10 to 1) 7
1190⁶ SILVER AGE (USA) [97] 7-9-9 (5*) R Farrant, *al hndy, led 6th till appr 3 out, rdn and no extr*...............(20 to 1) 8
ISABEAU [102] 6-10-5 A S Smith, *wth ldrs, led 3rd to 6th, fdd 3 out*..........................(16 to 1 op 12 to 1) 9
1280³ HIGH GRADE [97] 5-10-0 B Powell, *nvr far away, feeling pace appr 3 out, no extr*.......... (14 to 1 op 10 to 1) 10
1190⁴ AMPHIGORY [100] (bl) 5-10-3³ M A FitzGerald, *tucked away beh ldrs, chsd alng whn pace quickened appr 3 out, no imprsn*.................. (25 to 1 op 33 to 1) 11
1187 FRENDLY FELLOW [97] (bl) 9-10-0 R Supple, *chsd ldrs till fdd appr 3 out*..... (50 to 1 op 66 to 1 tchd 100 to 1) 12
TILT TECH FLYER [105] 8-10-8 C Llewellyn, *trkd ldrs, led appr 3 out, quickened clr, hdd nxt, sn btn.* ....(20 to 1 tchd 16 to 1) 13
1198⁷ BUCKINGHAM GATE [99] 7-10-2² P Holley, *slight ld to 3rd, lost grnd whn pace quickened appr 3 out, sn btn.* .... (8 to 1 op 14 to 1) 14
PERCY SMOLLETT [98] 5-10-1¹ S McNeill, *chsd ldrs to 4 out, fdd*..........................(50 to 1 op 33 to 1) 15
BALLYLORD [97] 9-9-10³ (7*) B Harding, *wth ldrs, drvn alng aftr 4 out, sn lost tch.* .... (20 to 1 op 16 to 1 tchd 25 to 1) 16
1187 WAVERLEY BOY [97] 11-10-0 M Hourigan, *unruly strt, beh and drvn alng hfwy, pld up bef 3 out.* .... (100 to 1 op 50 to 1) pu
MARCH ABOVE [100] 7-10-3¹⁰ (7*) M Stevens, *trkd ldrs, squeezed and hit rail on bend aftr 4th, lost tch hfwy, pld up bef 3 out*.....(66 to 1 op 33 to 1 tchd 100 to 1) pu
Dist: 2l, 2l, nk, 6l, 4l, 4l, 2½l, hd, 1l, ½l. 5m 27.50s. a 33.50s (18 Ran).
SR: 6/-/-/-/-/-/ (Sheikh Ahmed Bin Saeed Al Maktoum), D Nicholson

FONTWELL (good)
Tuesday November 30th
Going Correction: PLUS 1.05 sec. per fur.

1463 Coomes Conditional Jockeys' Selling Chase (5-y-o and up) £2,264 2¼m
. . . .(1:10)

963² FIGHTING DAYS (USA) (bl) 7-10-13 (3*) J Clarke, *made virtually all, jnd 5th, clr appr 9th, mstk nxt, styd on wl.*
. . . . (5 to 4 fav op 11 to 10 tchd 13 to 8)   1
1189⁴ WICKFIELD LAD 10-11-2 T Jenks, *mstk second, led chasing grp, chsd wnr aftr 9th, hrd rdn after 2 out, kpt on one pace.* . . . . (5 to 1 op 9 to 4 tchd 11 to 2)   2
1318⁴ ACHILTIBUIE 9-11-6 M Hourigan, *hld up, mstk second, hdwy 8th, rdn alng aftr 4 out, one pace.*
. . . .(10 to 1 tchd 12 to 1)   3
1393⁵ VIAGGIO 5-10-12 J McCarthy, *mid-div, hit 4th and 8th, styd on one pace frm o'r four out.*
. . . . (7 to 1 tchd 8 to 1 and 6 to 1)   4
1206 ON YOUR WAY 11-11-6 D Meredith, *prmnt till drpd rear 6th, tld off.* . . . .(14 to 1 op 10 to 1 tchd 16 to 1)   5
1411 DEVIOSITY (USA) 6-10-12 Guy Lewis, *al beh, lost tch 5th, tld off.* . . . .(50 to 1 op 25 to 1)   6
1189⁶ TEMPORARY 8-10-9 (3*) R Darke, *mstk 3rd, sn beh, tld off.*
. . . .(12 to 1 op 10 to 1 tchd 14 to 1)   7
1275³ RATHER SHARP 7-11-2 R Farrant, *cl up, wth wnr frm 5th till wknd appr 9th, mstk 11th, tld off.* (8 to 1 op 5 to 1)   8
957 MAJOR ELSTON 8-10-12 P Hide, *al beh, hrd rdn aftr 8th, blun 11th, tld off whn pld up bef 3 out.*
. . . .(50 to 1 op 33 to 1)   pu
Dist: 4l, 12l, 1½l, 12l, 25l, sht-hd, 30l. 4m 50.90s. a 30.90s (9 Ran).

(F L Hill), A Moore

1464 Blackheath Juvenile Novices' Hurdle (3-y-o) £1,475 2¼m . . . . (1:40)

1125* RICH LIFE (Ire) 11-4 M Perrett, *hld up, hdwy 4 out, second and held whn lft clr last.*
. . . .(5 to 2 fav op 2 to 1 tchd 11 to 4)   1
1244 HERETICAL MISS 10-7 D Gallagher, *hld up in rear, hdwy aftr 3 out, styd on to take modest second r-in.*
. . . . (66 to 1 op 33 to 1)   2
1271* VELVET HEART (Ire) 10-13 S Burrough, *chsd ldrs, led briefly aftr 5th, btn whn blun 2 out.*
. . . . (7 to 2 tchd 5 to 1)   3
1244 MORAN BRIG 10-12 S Hodgson, *cl up till lost pl 5th, styd on frm 2 out.* . . . .(66 to 1 op 33 to 1)   4
494* BENGALI (Ire) 10-11 (7*) D Fortt, *mstk second and lost grnd, cld 5th, prmnt till wknd 2 out.* (10 to 1 op 6 to 1)   5
1261⁷ DO BE WARE 10-12 N Williamson, *chsd ldrs till rdn and wknd appr 3 out.* . . .(50 to 1 op 33 to 1 tchd 66 to 1)   6
1244⁴ MY HARVINSKI (bl) 10-12 M Richards, *hld up rear, hdwy 3 out, sn hrd rdn and btn.* (9 to 2 op 5 to 2 tchd 5 to 1)   7
1244 EL GRANDO 10-12 M Hourigan, *led till aftr 3rd, prmnt till wknd after 5th.* . . . .(50 to 1 op 33 to 1)   8
ORCHESTON 10-4 (3*) P Hide, *chsd ldrs till wknd 4 out.*
. . . . (50 to 1 op 20 to 1)   9
1244 CONBRIO STAR (bl) 10-12 R Dunwoody, *pld hrd, cl up, ev ch 4 out, hard rdn and wknd aftr nxt.*
. . . .(50 to 1 op 33 to 1 tchd 66 to 1)   10
FATHER'S JOY 10-7 G Rowe, *strted slwly, rapid hdwy to ld aftr 3rd, wide and hdd after 5th, sn wknd.*
. . . . (66 to 1 op 33 to 1)   11
SMART DAISY 10-7 M McFarland, *pld hrd, nvr rch ldrs.*
. . . .(16 to 1 op 10 to 1 tchd 20 to 1)   12
CHIEF'S SONG 10-7 (5*) A Dicken, *mid-div, cld 5th, led 3 out and quickened, ran wide appr nxt, clr whn f last.*
. . . .(7 to 2 op 5 to 1 tchd 6 to 1)   f
1384 TOP GUNNER (Ire) 10-5 (7*) G Crone, *drpd rear 5th, tld off whn pld up bef 2 out.*
. . . .(66 to 1 op 50 to 1 tchd 100 to 1)   pu
793 SUNBEAM CHARLIE 10-5 (7*) J Clarke, *al beh, tld off whn pld up bef 2 out.* . . . . .(50 to 1 op 14 to 1 tchd 66 to 1)   pu
Dist: 20l, 6l, 3l, 10l, 10l, nk, nk, 2l, 12l, 10l. 4m 38.30s. a 28.30s (15 Ran).

(Mrs Susan Gay), C Weedon

1465 Coomes Handicap Hurdle (0-145 4-y-o and up) £4,308 2¼m. . . . .(2:10)

1225² NAHAR [124] 8-10-13 (5*) A Dicken, *trkd ldrs, led 3 out, clr nxt, ran on wl, jst hld on.*
. . . .(9 to 2 tchd 5 to 1 and 4 to 1)   1
1172* CHANGE THE ACT [130] 8-11-5 (5*) J McCarthy, *trkd ldrs till lost pl aftr 3rd, sn prmnt, outpcd 3 out, rallied und pres and ran on wl frm last.* . . . .(6 to 1 op 4 to 1)   2
979⁴ CABOCHON [129] 6-11-9 J Frost, *led till hdd 3 out, one pace.* . . . .(6 to 1 op 9 to 2 tchd 7 to 1)   3
VAGADOR (Can) [127] 10-11-7 M Perrett, *beh, cld o'r 3 out, one pace.* . . . .(25 to 1 op 16 to 1 tchd 33 to 1)   4
1364³ WELSHMAN [129] 7-11-9 D Gallagher, *trkd ldrs, reminders aftr 5th, ch 3 out, outpcd appr nxt.* (4 to 1 tchd 7 to 2)   5
MASAI MARA (USA) [115] 5-10-9 B Powell, *hld up in tch, cld o'r 3 out, sn outpcd.*
. . . .(16 to 1 tchd 14 to 1 and 20 to 1)   6
776* HYMNE D'AMOUR (USA) [109] 5-10-3 J Osborne, *hld up, nvr gng wl, reminders aftr 4th, cld o'r 3 out, sn btn.*
. . . .(15 to 8 fav op 5 to 2 tchd 7 to 4)   7

1466 Wally Coomes Handicap Chase (0-130 4-y-o and up) £2,898 2¼m. . . . . . (2:40)

1300 RICHVILLE [112] 7-12-0 N Williamson, *led and hit 1st, nvr far away, jnd ldr 4 out, led aftr 2 out, styd on und pres.*
. . . .(7 to 4 fav op 5 to 4)   1
1260³ KISU KALI [96] 6-10-12 M Richards, *outpcd, cld aftr tenth, styd on one pace frm 3 out.*
. . . .(8 to 1 op 5 to 1 tchd 9 to 1)   2
UNIQUE NEW YORK [90] (v) 10-10-6 R Dunwoody, *cl up, mstk 9th, led 11th, jnd 4 out, hdd aftr 2 out, btn whn mistake last.* . . . .(8 to 1 op 5 to 1 tchd 9 to 2)   3
825² GENERAL JAMES [104] 10-11-6 D Murphy, *in tch, pushed alng aftr 8th, outpcd appr 5 out....* (5 to 2 op 7 to 2)   4
1197 MOZE TIDY [91] (bl) 8-10-2 (5*) C Burnett-Wells, *sn led, mstk 3rd, hdd and hit 11th, soon wknd, pld up bef last.*
. . . .(14 to 1 op 10 to 1 tchd 16 to 1)   pu
412⁴ RUSTIC GENT (Ire) [87] 5-9-12² (7*) S Fox, *mstks 3rd and 5th (water), outpcd, tld off whn pld up bef 2 out.*
. . . .(11 to 1 op 6 to 1 tchd 12 to 1)   pu
Dist: 10l, 8l, 12l. 4m 53.10s. a 33.10s (6 Ran).

(Major-Gen R L T Burges), K C Bailey

1467 Coomes Senior Citizens Novices' Chase (5-y-o and up) £2,270 3¼m 110yds. . . . . (3:10)

1351² EBONY GALE (bl) 7-11-0 J Osborne, *led second, hit 4th, sn hdd, led ag'n 5 out, clr nxt, easily.*
. . . .(15 to 8 fav op 6 to 4)   1
1107 THE GOLFING CURATE 8-10-5 (5*) C Burnett-Wells, *not jump wl, al beh, styd on frm 2 out, ran on to snatch second cl hme.* . . . .(9 to 2 op 4 to 1 tchd 5 to 1)   2
1194* OLD BRIG (bl) 7-11-7 R Dunwoody, *led to second, trkd ldrs, outpcd 5 out, lost poor second cl hme.*
. . . .(5 to 2 tchd 11 to 4 and 9 to 4)   3
1136² CAPSIZE 7-11-0 B Powell, *al beh, lost tch 16th, tld off.*
. . . .(14 to 1 op 10 to 1)   4
1136* OCEAN LINK 9-11-7 S Earle, *cl up, led aftr 4th, clr 11th, hdd 5 out, sn outpcd, disputing second whn mstk last, virtually pld up.* . . . .(8 to 1 op 6 to 1)   5
WILD FORTUNE 11-10-10 Mr G Johnson Houghton, *hit second and uns rdr.* (25 to 1 op 20 to 1 tchd 33 to 1)   ur
1262 STAR OF OUGHTERARD (bl) 8-11-7 W McFarland, *al beh, jmpd rght, pld up aftr 8th.*
. . . .(14 to 1 op 8 to 1 tchd 16 to 1)   pu
962 SPARTAN FLAPJACK 7-10-10 I Lawrence, *in tch, outpcd aftr 8th and pld up.* . . .(50 to 1 op 33 to 1 tchd 66 to 1)   pu
Dist: 25l, ½l, 5l, 3l. 7m 21.80s. a 51.80s (8 Ran).

(Pat Whelan), Mrs J Pitman

1468 Greenwich 'National Hunt' Novices' Hurdle (4-y-o and up) £1,475 2¾m . . . .(3:40)

CALL HOME (Ire) 5-10-12 D Murphy, *hld up, hdwy o'r 4 out, led aftr 2 out, shaken up, cmftbly.*
. . . .(2 to 1 on op 9 to 4 on tchd 13 to 8 on)   1
1283⁶ ARMATEUR (Fr) 5-10-12 R Bellamy, *cl up, led briefly 5th, led 7th, jnd whn hit 2 out, sn hdd, kpt on one pace.*
. . . .(7 to 4 tchd 2 to 1)   2
CADOLIVE 5-10-7 B Powell, *wth ldrs till outpcd aftr 3 out.* . . . .(50 to 1 op 33 to 1)   3
1272 JANET SCIBS 7-10-0 (7*) Guy Lewis, *hld up in tch, rdn and outpcd 4 out.* . . . .(100 to 1)   4
1263⁶ COUNTRY STYLE 4-10-7 S Earle, *hld up, al beh, lost tch o'r 4 out.* . . . .(20 to 1 tchd 33 to 1)   5
PIONEER PETE 6-10-12 J Frost, *made most till mstk and hdd 7th, wknd nxt.* . . . .(10 to 1 op 25 to 1)   6
Dist: 5l, 12l, 10l, sht-hd, 3½l. 5m 53.90s. a 44.90s (6 Ran).

(Maurice E Pinto), J T Gifford

LEICESTER (good to soft (races 1,2,3), soft (4,5,6))
Tuesday November 30th
Going Correction: PLUS 1.33 sec. per fur. (races 1,2,3), PLUS 1.15 (4,5,6)

1469 Spruce Novices' Chase (5-y-o and up) £1,618 2½m 110yds. . . . . (12:50)

1339 CANOSCAN 8-11-0 E Murphy, *jmpd wl, al gng well, led aftr 7th, quickened clr appr 3 out, eased finish.*
. . . .(5 to 4 on tchd 7 to 4 on)   1
SUFFOLK ROAD 6-11-0 C Llewellyn, *nvr far away, lost grnd whn wnr quickened appr 3 out, styd on ag'n frm betw last 2, prmsg.* . . . .(8 to 1 op 5 to 1)   2

HANGOVER 7-11-0 R Greene, *patiently rdn, steady hdwy fnl circuit, styd on frm 3 out, nrst finish.*
................................(9 to 2 op 11 to 4 tchd 5 to 1) 3
1023² RIVER MANDATE 6-11-0 H Davies, *settled midfield, stdly lost grnd fnl circuit, eased whn btn last 3.*
.........(7 to 4 fav op 6 to 4 tchd 2 to 1 and 9 to 4) 4
1214 NORTHERN SQUIRE 5-11-0 M A FitzGerald, *wnt lft strt, improved into midfield aftr one circuit, struggling 6 out, sn lost tch.*....................(10 to 1 op 7 to 1)
ROMANY SPLIT 8-10-7 (7') Mr G Hogan, *led, jmpd lft 7th, sn hdd, wknd quickly appr 4 out, tld off.*
...................................(25 to 1 op 20 to 1) 6
1341⁴ MONKSANDER 7-11-0 Richard Guest, *in tch, struggling fnl circuit, tld off whn pld up bef 6 out.*
...................................(20 to 1 op 14 to 1) pu
1295⁸ BECK COTTAGE 5-10-11 (3') A Thornton, *trkd ldrs, struggling to keep up fnl circuit, tld off whn pld up betw last 2.*........................(33 to 1 op 20 to 1) pu
KINGLY LOOK 6-11-0 R Marley, *chsd ldrs, struggling and lost grnd fnl circuit, tld off whn pld up bef 6 out.*
...................................(33 to 1) pu
Dist: 7l, 1½l, 25l, 20l, 15l. 5m 36.00s. a 33.00s (9 Ran).
SR: 29/22/20/-/-/-/ (Nigel Clutton), Lady Herries

1470 Oak Optional Claiming Chase (5-y-o and up) £2,040 2m 1f.......... (1:20)

1312 KANNDABIL (bl) 6-11-7 M A FitzGerald, *in tch, rdn alng thrght, outpcd 5 out, rallied to ld betw last 2, styd on.*
........................(3 to 1 op 9 to 4 tchd 7 to 2) 1
1105 WHATEVER YOU LIKE 9-12-7 C Maude, *trkd ldr, led aftr 5 out, outpcd clr, jmpd badly lft 3 out and nxt, sn hdd, one pace.*..............(11 to 10 fav op 5 to 4 on) 2
CEDAR RUN 10-10-0 (7') D Meade, *trkd ldg quartet, lost grnd whn pace quickened aftr 4 out, rallied, styd on same pace frm last.*......................(20 to 1) 3
1273 HOPE DIAMOND (bl) 10-10-7 Peter Caldwell, *trkd ldg trio, struggling to keep up 5 out, some hdwy frm 3 out, no imprsn.*..........................(20 to 1 op 14 to 1) 4
1293³ OLD ROAD (USA) 7-11-7 D Bridgwater, *clr ldr till hdd aftr 5 out, wknd bdly till fdd und pres last 2, tld off.*
..............................(3 to 1 op 7 to 2) 5
920 HICKELTON HOUSE 9-10-2 (5') A Bates, *chasing ldrs whn f 1st.*......................(33 to 1 op 25 to 1) f
1245⁶ PALM SWIFT 7-10-2 A Tory, *in tch to hfwy, sn struggling, wl beh whn pld up bef last.*...........(10 to 1 op 20 to 1) pu
Dist: 7l, 15l, 6l, dist. 4m 44.70s. a 35.70s (7 Ran).
(Neil McAndrews), N Tinkler

1471 Sycamore Handicap Chase (0-120 5-y-o and up) £2,162 3m........... (1:50)

1318 PIPER O'DRUMMOND [102] 6-10-4 (7') Mr D Parker, *niggled alng to keep up 1st circuit, relentless prog frm 5 out, led betw last 2, ran on wl.*............(11 to 1 op 8 to 1) 1
1171⁶ BOWL OF OATS [109] (bl) 7-11-4 S McNeill, *nvr far away, nosed ahead 7 out, rdn and hdd betw last 2, kpt on same pace.*............(11 to 2 op 5 to 1 tchd 6 to 1) 2
1216⁷ ROCKMOUNT ROSE [91] 8-9-7 (7') L Dace, *settled midfield, edged up to draw level 4 out, styd on same pace frm last.*......................(20 to 1) 3
1171³ BERESFORDS GIRL [106] 8-11-1 E Murphy, *co'red up in midfield, feeling pace and reminders 6 out, hit 4 out, rallied, not quicken frm last 2.* (7 to 2 fav tchd 4 to 1) 4
ASKINFARNEY [108] 6-11-3 R Supple, *wtd wth, improved into midfield fnl circuit, effrt and drvn alng appr 3 out, no imprsn.*.......................(4 to 1 op 3 to 1) 5
1216⁵ MATERIAL GIRL [113] 7-11-3 (5') A Procter, *trkd ldg pair, led 9th till hdd 7 out, rdn appr 3 out, no extr.*
.............................(10 to 1 tchd 11 to 1) 6
THE FORTIES [99] 8-10-8 J Railton, *jmpd wl, led to 9th, rdn 5 out, sn outpcd.*...........(33 to 1 op 25 to 1) 7
GLOVE PUPPET [103] 8-10-12 Richard Guest, *trkd ldrs, rdn and pace quickened 5 out, struggling last 3.*
...................................(12 to 1 op 10 to 1) 8
1242³ JIMMY O'DEA [92] (v) 6-9-10 (5') T Eley, *wth ldr for o'r a circuit, drvn alng frm 4 out, lost tch frm nxt.*
...................................(12 to 1 op 10 to 1) 9
1359² BOREEN OWEN [115] 9-11-10 M A FitzGerald, *struggling and reminders aftr one circuit, tld off whn pld up bef 3 out.*..................(11 to 2 op 6 to 1 tchd 5 to 1) pu
Dist: 2l, 1½l, 6l, 3l, 2l, 2l, nk, 12l. 6m 29.50s. a 37.50s (10 Ran).
SR: 27/32/12/21/19/17/ (Mrs S A Bramall), Mrs S A Bramall

1472 Chestnut Conditional Jockeys' Selling Hurdle (4-y-o) £1,182 2m....... (2:20)

1370* PORT IN A STORM 11-6 E Husband, *patiently rdn, improved gng wl 4 out, led bef 2 out, clr last.*
..................(5 to 4 on op 6 to 4 on tchd Evens) 1
TYNRON DOON 11-0 R Davis, *settled gng wl, quickened to ld 4 out, hdd bef 2 out, kpt on same pace.*
...................................(11 to 4 op 2 to 1 tchd 3 to 1) 2
1416⁷ ABELONI 11-0 R Greene, *slwly into strd, hdwy to join ldrs appr 4 out, kpt on same pace frm betw last 2.*
.............................(6 to 1 op 4 to 1 tchd 7 to 1) 3

1353⁶ PRIORY PIPER 11-0 A Thornton, *led, hit second, clr nxt, hdd and reminders 4 out, lost tch next.*
...................................(14 to 1 op 10 to 1) 4
1215⁶ HINTON LADY 10-9 A Procter, *settled midfield, ev ch appr 4 out, wknd und pres nxt.*.........(14 to 1 op 10 to 1) 5
1280 PIERRE BLANCO (USA) 10-9 (5') M P FitzGerald, *nvr far away, ev ch appr 4 out, lost tch nxt, tld off.*
...................................(14 to 1 op 12 to 1) 6
1304⁹ CASHTAL RUNNER 11-0 P McLoughlin, *slwly away, improved hfwy, ev ch 4 out, sn wknd, tld off whn pld up bef last.*.......................(33 to 1 op 20 to 1) pu
1353⁷ ROLY WALLACE (v) 11-0 T Eley, *trkd ldrs, effrt appr 4 out, wknd quickly nxt, tld off whn pld up bef 2 out.*
...................................(14 to 1 op 12 to 1) pu
1384 PLUM LINE 11-0 A Bates, *not jump wl, lost tch quickly 4th, tld off whn pld up bef four out.*
...................................(50 to 1 op 33 to 1) pu
Dist: 5l, 3l, 25l, 1½l, dist. 4m 15.00s. a 32.00s (9 Ran).
(S A Barningham), N Tinkler

1473 Ash Juvenile Novices' Hurdle (3-y-o) £1,674 2m.................... (2:50)

NAWAR (Fr) 10-10 J Railton, *al hndy, led 4 out, wnt clr frm nxt, readily.*.................(5 to 2 fav op 4 to 1) 1
MOORISH 10-10 M A FitzGerald, *patiently rdn, steady hdwy aftr 4 out, styd on wl r-in, prmsg.*
.............................(4 to 1 op 2 to 1) 2
1147³ ROSCOMMON JOE (Ire) 11-2 C Maude, *wtd wth, improved into midfield 4 out, styd on frm betw last 2.*
.............................(4 to 1 op 5 to 1) 3
1317⁴ SOLOMAN SPRINGS (USA) 10-7 (3') R Davis, *al tracking ldrs, effrt and pushed alng appr 4 out, outpcd aftr nxt.*
...................................(16 to 1 op 12 to 1) 4
1147⁷ NATIVE WORTH 10-10 S McNeill, *al wl plcd, slight ld 4th till appr four out, grad wknd frm nxt.*........(20 to 1) 5
1290⁵ LITTLE GUNNER 10-10 Richard Guest, *made most to 4th, styd hndy till fdd frm four out.*...(20 to 1 op 16 to 1) 6
1290* DIWALI DANCER 11-2 N Mann, *co'red up in midfield, rdn appr 4 out, sn btn.*......(50 to 1 op 5 to 1 tchd 7 to 1) 7
1229 HUBERT 10-3 (7') A Flannigan, *tucked away in midfield, jnd ldrs appr 4 out, wknd aftr nxt.* (50 to 1 op 33 to 1) 8
1229 LAMBAST 10-5 W Marston, *last and hld up, feeling pace appr 4 out, sn btn.*..................(9 to 1 op 14 to 1) 9
1271⁴ KOA 10-10 C Llewellyn, *chsd ldg bunch till wknd quickly appr 4 out.*..................(12 to 1 op 7 to 1) 10
1229⁶ NANCY (Ire) 10-5 P McDermott, *wtd wth, effrt hfwy, feeling pace appr 4 out, sn btn.*....(20 to 1 op 14 to 1) 11
ANUSHA 10-5 H Davies, *rcd wide, nvr far away, nosed ahead appr 4 out, blun, 3rd and btn whn f last.*
.............................(8 to 1 tchd 12 to 1) f
890⁹ NO SHOW (Ire) 10-10 W Humphreys, *chsd ldg bunch to hfwy, lost tch and pld up bef 2 out.* (50 to 1 op 33 to 1) pu
WILBURY WONDER 10-5 D Bridgwater, *in tch to hfwy, tld off whn pld up bef 4 out.*................(33 to 1) pu
Dist: 8l, 8l, 15l, nk, 2l, 12l, ½l, 10l, 10l, hd. 4m 6.80s. a 23.80s (14 Ran).
SR: 28/20/18/-/-/-/ (J M Long), J R Jenkins

1474 Birch Handicap Hurdle (0-120 4-y-o and up) £1,968 2½m 110yds..... (3:20)

BICKERMAN [89] 10-10-0 W Marston, *al gng wl, led 4 out, clr frm nxt, readily.*.................(25 to 1) 1
1238⁴ THE MRS [89] 7-10-0 L Harvey, *mstks, patiently rdn, improved to chase wnr last 3, styd on r-in.*
.............................(14 to 1 tchd 16 to 1) 2
1257² MR FLUTTS [98] 7-10-9 S McNeill, *settled midfield, bustled alng to improve aftr 4 out, sn one pace frm betw last 2.*......................(14 to 1 op 12 to 1) 3
1249⁴ CHEEKY FOX [92] 10-7-3³ M Bosley, *nvr far away, pushed alng whn pace quickened frm 3 out, no extr.*
.............................(14 to 1 op 8 to 1) 4
1072³ COUTURE STOCKINGS [94] 9-10-5 R Supple, *co'red up beh ldrs, drvn alng to improve aftr 4 out, not pace to chal.*..............(10 to 1 op 8 to 1 tchd 12 to 1) 5
730² LITTLE BIG [89] 6-10-0 C Llewellyn, *beh, improved appr 4 out, nvr able to rch ldrs.*.......(12 to 1 op 9 to 1) 6
TEMPLE GARTH [105] 4-10-13 (3') A Thornton, *led, hit 3rd, hdd 4 out, wknd.*......................(14 to 1) 7
1172³ MOUNTSHANNON [92] (bl) 7-10-3³ Peter Caldwell, *trkd ldrs, drvn alng in midfield appr 4 out, sn btn.* (33 to 1) 8
1205⁵ SEA BUCK [113] 7-11-7 (3') R Davis, *co'red up beh ldrs, chsd alng whn pace quickened appr 4 out, sn btn.*
...................................(10 to 1 op 8 to 1) 9
1238⁷ WINDWARD ARIOM [89] 7-10-0 R Marley, *in tch to hfwy, drvn alng appr 4 out, no imprsn.*.........(33 to 1) 10
ORIEL DREAM [113] 6-11-10 H Davies, *co'red up in midfield, wknd and eased frm 3 out.*
...................................(10 to 1 op 5 to 1 tchd 10 to 1) 11
MR TAYLOR [103] 8-11-0 V Smith, *beh and pushed alng hfwy, nvr trble ldrs.*.................(12 to 1) 12
955³ BLASKET HERO [92] (bl) 5-10-3³ M A FitzGerald, *in tch till wknd quickly appr 4 out.*..............(16 to 1) 13
1361² MASTER OF THE ROCK [98] (v) 4-10-9 C Hawkins, *shwd up wl till wknd quickly appr 4 out.* (8 to 1 fav op 7 to 1) 14
1389⁶ SOLID (Ire) [89] 5-9-9 (5') D Walsh, *chsd ldrs till wknd appr 4 out.*....................(20 to 1) 15

1206 ZEALOUS KITTEN (USA) [103] 5-11-0 N Mann, *tld off hfwy*. ....(9 to 1 op 8 to 1 tchd 10 to 1) 16
860 MIAMI BEAR [110] 7-11-7 P Harley, *in tch to hfwy, tld off*. ....(25 to 1 tchd 33 to 1) 17
RELTIC [89] 6-9-9² (7*) A Flannigan, *al beh, mstk and uns rdr 4 out*..(33 to 1) ur
SOUTHOVER LAD (NZ) [111] 10-11-8 C Maude, *al beh, pld up aftr 6th*..(33 to 1) pu
SYLVIA BEACH [90] 7-10-1 E Murphy, *chsd ldrs to hfwy, lost tch and pld up bef 4 out*.......(10 to 1 op 14 to 1) pu
1045³ SANTA PONSA BAY [94] 6-10-5 Richard Guest, *co'red up in midfield, struggling hfwy, tld off whn pld up bef 4 out*. ....(20 to 1 op 16 to 1) pu
1045* CAVO GRECO (USA) [89] 4-10-0 D Skyrme, *pressed ldrs to hfwy, tld off whn pld up bef 3 out*. (10 to 1 op 8 to 1) pu
Dist: 6l, 10l, 1l, 10l, 5l, 12l, 5l, 1½l, 1½l, 15l. 5m 15.50s. a 27.50s (22 Ran).
SR: 33/27/26/19/11/1/5/-/6/ (B Dowling), J L Spearing

NEWCASTLE (good to soft)
Tuesday November 30th
Going Correction: PLUS 0.65 sec. per fur. (races 1,2,4,6,7), PLUS 0.47 (3,5)

1475 'A Study In Scarlet' Novices' Hurdle (Div I) (4-y-o and up) £2,057 2½m ....(12:30)

873⁸ GREAT MAX (Ire) 4-11-0 B Storey, *trkd ldrs, led 2 out, styd on wl*..............................(5 to 1 op 7 to 2) 1
1183* CARNETTO 6-11-2 K Johnson, *trkd ldrs, pushed alng aftr 3 out, styd on wl frm nxt, no ch wth wnr*. ....(13 to 2 op 6 to 1 tchd 7 to 1) 2
1096⁶ STRONG DEEL (Ire) 5-11-0 T Reed, *made most to 2 out, sn rdn and one pace*..............(20 to 1 op 16 to 1) 3
1181⁷ JUST A LIGHT (Ire) 5-10-7 (7*) F Perratt, *trkd ldrs, ch 2 out, sn rdn and one pace*..............(16 to 1 tchd 20 to 1) 4
1142* FARMER'S CROSS 9-11-0 (7*) B D Grattan, *wth ldr, ch 2 out, wknd*.........................(16 to 1 op 10 to 1) 5
1103 DYNAMITE DAN (Ire) 5-11-0 M Dwyer, *hld up in tch, hdwy to track ldrs aftr 3 out, fdd after nxt*. ....(33 to 1 op 20 to 1) 6
LUVLY BUBBLY 5-11-0 C Grant, *al beh, lost tch appr 3 out, tld off*.........................(33 to 1 op 20 to 1) 7
WEST AUCKLAND 4-11-0 A Merrigan, *lost tch hfwy, tld off*..............................(300 to 1 op 100 to 1) 8
875³ DASHMAR 6-11-0 C Dennis, *chsd ldrs, ev ch whn f 2 out*. ....(16 to 1 op 12 to 1) f
1096² DOUBLE SHERRY 4-10-9 D Byrne, *in tch, effrt aftr 6th, no hdwy, wknd and pld up bef 3 out*. ....(9 to 2 op 7 to 2 tchd 5 to 1) pu
1181 NINFA (Ire) 5-10-9 N Doughty, *trkd ldrs, wknd quickly and pld up bef 3 out*..............(2 to 1 fav op 11 to 8) pu
FINNOW QUAY (Ire) 4-11-0 A Orkney, *mstks, prmnt till wknd appr 3 out, tld off whn pld up bef last*. ....(33 to 1 op 25 to 1) pu
ROYAL HOFSA 6-10-9 A Dobbin, *lost tch hfwy, tld off whn pld up bef 2 out*..............................(100 to 1) pu
Dist: 8l, 5l, 2½l, ¾l, 15l, dist, dist. 5m 12.40s. a 29.40s (13 Ran).
(Raymond Anderson Green), C Parker

1476 'The Sign Of Four' Optional Juvenile Claiming Hurdle (3-y-o) £1,987 2m 110yds........................(1:00)

1094* RAGGERTY (Ire) 10-10 (3*) N Bentley, *hld up in tch, hdwy to ld appr 2 out, hrd pressed frm last, found extr nr finish*..................(7 to 2 op 6 to 1 tchd 7 to 1) 1
1062⁷ GREAT EASEBY (Ire) 10-9 K Johnson, *chsd ldrs, outpcd appr 3 out, rallied und pres approaching last, styd on wl*..................................(25 to 1 op 20 to 1) 2
1290³ COEUR BATTANT (Fr) 11-0 G McCourt, *trkd ldrs, chlgd 2 out, dsptd ld r-in, no extr nr finish*. ....(3 to 1 jt-fav op 5 to 2) 3
1284⁴ NEGD (USA) 10-11 R Garritty, *chsd ldrs, ch last, kpt on wl*. ....(10 to 1 op 6 to 1) 4
MR ABBOT 10-8 P Niven, *hld up in tch, hdwy aftr 3 out, kpt on same pace frm nxt*.........(12 to 1 op 10 to 1) 5
1217⁵ FUNNY FEELINGS 10-9 A Orkney, *nvr trble ldrs*. (100 to 1) 6
1147⁸ BELFORTON 10-5 J Callaghan, *trkd ldrs till wknd appr 2 out*..................................(14 to 1 op 12 to 1) 7
RAVENSPUR (Ire) 10-7 N Smith, *chsd ldrs till wknd betw last 2*..................................(33 to 1 op 25 to 1) 8
1284⁵ BARSAL (Ire) 10-12 M Dwyer, *prmnt till wknd betw last 2*. ....(16 to 1 tchd 20 to 1) 9
PANIC BUTTON (Ire) 10-3 L Wyer, *hld up, mstk 4th, hdwy to join ldrs appr 2 out, sn wknd*......(9 to 1 op 5 to 1) 10
971² ASTRAC TRIO (USA) 11-0 A Dobbin, *made most till appr 2 out, fdd, btn whn blun last*..............(3 to 1 jt-fav op 5 to 2 tchd 9 to 4) 11
ERBIL (Ire) 11-7 T Reed, *beh most of way, pld up bef last*. ....(16 to 1 op 8 to 1 tchd 20 to 1) pu
Dist: ½l, sht-hd, 1½l, 2½l, 8l, 2l, 1½l, ½l, 2½l, ½l. 4m 14.90s. a 21.90s (12 Ran).
(N Honeyman), G M Moore

1477 'The Valley Of Fear' Novices' Chase (5-y-o and up) £2,922 3m....... (1:30)

1033² ARTHUR'S MINSTREL 6-11-0 G McCourt, *cl up, mstk 13th, led nxt, lft clr 2 out, styd on und pres*. ....(7 to 2 op 9 to 2) 1
1184² CEILIDH BOY 7-11-7 B Storey, *cl up, led 9th to 14th, blun 3 out, kpt on same pace*...........(6 to 1 tchd 7 to 1) 2
1358⁶ EDEN SUNSET 7-11-0 Mr Chris Wilson, *hld up, hdwy hfwy, ch whn blun 3 out, not reco'r*..........(50 to 1) 3
1358⁴ REEF LARK 8-11-0 K Johnson, *in tch till wknd aftr 4 out*. ....(33 to 1 op 25 to 1) 4
1184* INVERINATE (bl) 8-11-7 T Reed, *chsd ldrs till wknd appr 3 out*..........................(13 to 2 op 5 to 1 tchd 7 to 1) 5
1091⁷ SANDEDGE 6-10-4 (5*) P Waggott, *mstks, led 3rd to 9th, sn beh, hmpd and uns rdr last, rmntd*..........(100 to 1) 6
EQUINOCTIAL 8-10-11 (3*) A Larnach, *beh whn f tenth*. ....(25 to 1) f
MOW CREEK 9-10-9 (5*) P Williams, *cl up till f 11th*. ....(100 to 1) f
1091² TALLYWAGGER 6-11-0 J Callaghan, *cl up, pushed alng appr 3 out, second and ch whn f nxt*. ....(100 to 30 fav op 5 to 2 tchd 7 to 2) f
1291³ FRONT LINE 6-11-0 L Wyer, *beh, hdwy appr 3 out, second and staying on strly whn f last*.....(12 to 1 op 8 to 1) f
1184⁴ CROWN EYEGLASS 7-11-0 R Garritty, *in tch, effrt aftr 4 out, 3rd and btn whn brght dwn last*. ....(40 to 1 op 33 to 1) bd
GRANYTE PALACE 9-11-0 C Grant, *al beh, tld off whn pld up bef 13th*..(33 to 1) pu
ROUGHSIDE 8-11-0 Mr D Mactaggart, *in tch, blun 9th, sn wknd, tld off whn pld up bef 3 out*..........(100 to 1) pu
I'M TOBY 6-11-0 M Dwyer, *in tch, hmpd 11th, wknd and pld up bef 3 out*.....................(7 to 1 op 4 to 1) pu
1288³ KNOCK RANK 8-11-0 P Niven, *in tch, mstk tenth, sn beh, tld off whn pld up bef 3 out*....... (25 to 1 op 20 to 1) pu
1033⁵ SANDY ANDY 7-11-7 A Orkney, *led till blun 3rd, beh hfwy, tld off whn pld up bef 3 out*............(25 to 1) pu
Dist: 3½l, sht-hd, 10l, 6l, dist. 6m 19.10s. a 29.10s (16 Ran).
(Bernard Hathaway), P Cheesbrough

1478 'The Hound Of The Baskervilles' Novices' Hurdle (4-y-o and up) £2,285 2m 110yds........................ (2:00)

1289⁷ MARCHWOOD 6-11-0 K Johnson, *chsd ldrs, chlgd 2 out, kpt on wl und pres to ld r-in*. ....(14 to 1 op 10 to 1 tchd 16 to 1) 1
1202* SURREY DANCER 5-11-7 P Niven, *hld up in tch, hdwy appr 3 out, slight ld nxt, hdd r-in, no extr und pres*. ....(15 to 8 on op 13 to 8 on) 2
1289 SHAHGRAM (Ire) 5-11-0 Mrs A Farrell, *pld hrd, prmnt, led 3 out to nxt, one pace*..............(10 to 1 op 12 to 1) 3
MAJOR BELL 5-11-0 M Moloney, *cl up till outpcd aftr 3 out, styd on appr last*... (8 to 1 op 5 to 1 tchd 9 to 1) 4
1289 SCRABO VIEW (Ire) 5-11-0 L O'Hara, *in tch, hdwy appr 3 out, wknd nxt*..(200 to 1) 5
HIP HOP (Ire) 4-10-9 (5*) J Burke, *mid-div, kpt on same pace frm 3 out*.................. (100 to 1 op 50 to 1) 6
673³ FORTUNE'S GIRL 5-10-9 C Grant, *nvr dngrs*. ....(17 to 2 op 5 to 1 tchd 9 to 1) 7
1374 TAHITIAN 4-11-0 G McCourt, *nvr dngrs*. ....(20 to 1 op 12 to 1) 8
CAMDEN GROVE 5-10-9 R Hodge, *mid-div, effrt aftr 3 out, no hdwy*..........................(50 to 1 op 33 to 1) 9
1204⁷ CORSTON RACER 5-11-0 M Dwyer, *trkd ldrs till wknd appr 2 out*..(25 to 1) 10
LORD ADVOCATE (v) 5-10-11 (3*) D J Moffatt, *nvr better than mid-div*..........................(50 to 1 op 33 to 1) 11
MONTRAVE 4-11-0 B Storey, *in tch till wknd appr 3 out*. ....(33 to 1 op 20 to 1) 12
BLAYNEYS PRIVILEGE 6-11-0 R Garritty, *hld up, hdwy aftr 3 out, hit nxt, sn btn*........(100 to 1 op 50 to 1) 13
THE MAJOR GENERAL 6-11-0 N Doughty, *trkd ldrs till wknd aftr 3 out*.......................(33 to 1 op 20 to 1) 14
HECKLEY SPARK 5-10-9 T Reed, *nvr better than mid-div*. ....(100 to 1 op 50 to 1) 15
STRONG SILVER (USA) 8-11-0 Miss P Robson, *nvr better than mid-div*..(66 to 1) 16
FIDDLER'S DRUM 6-10-7 (7*) B Harding, *led to 3 out, wknd quickly*..........................(20 to 1 op 14 to 1) 17
1096 CHERYL'S GIRL 7-10-6 (3*) A Larnach, *in tch till wknd appr 3 out*..(100 to 1) 18
304⁹ DESPERADO 5-10-7 (7*) Mr A Parker, *prmnt to hfwy*. ....(66 to 1) 19
Dist: 3l, 12l, 2½l, 3l, 5l, 4l, 1½l, sht-hd, 1l, 8l. 4m 9.20s. a 16.20s (19 Ran).
SR: 31/35/16/13/10/5/ (J A Stephenson), P Cheesbrough

1479 'Silver Blaze' Handicap Chase (5-y-o and up) £2,898 2m 110yds...... (2:30)

1065² CLAY COUNTY [137] 8-11-10 B Storey, *made all, mstk 6th, pushed out frm last*................(2 to 1 tchd 9 to 4) 1
919⁵ ANTONIN (Fr) [135] 5-11-3 (5*) J Burke, *cl up, ev ch 3 out, sn rdn, kpt on, no imprsn*...........(9 to 4 op 7 to 4) 2

1285* JUST FRANKIE [122] 9-10-9 P Niven, *mstks, chsd ldrs, outpcd appr 4 out, no dngr aftr.* (13 to 8 fav op 6 to 4) 3
1360⁴ BELDINE [113] 8-10-0 A Dobbin, *beh, mstk 9th, sn lost tch.*
.... (16 to 1 op 10 to 1) 4
Dist: 2½l, 10l, 10l. 4m 11.80s. a 10.80s (4 Ran).
SR: 66/61/38/19/ (M C Boyd), R Allan

1480 'A Study In Scarlet' Novices' Hurdle (Div II) (4-y-o and up) £2,057 2½m
.... (3:00)

1181⁴ MASTER BOSTON (Ire) 5-10-7 (7*) J Driscoll, *beh, hdwy aftr 6th, rdn appr 2 out, styd on wl to ld r-in.*
.... (16 to 1 op 14 to 1) 1
1204* SHAFFIC (Fr) 6-11-10 P Niven, *hld up, hdwy to track ldrs 6th, rdn to ld betw last 2, hng lft, hdd and no extr r-in.*
.... (11 to 8 fav op 11 to 10 tchd 7 to 4) 2
823⁴ PIRATE HOOK 5-11-0 B Storey, *prmnt till outpcd aftr 3 out, styd on appr last...* (4 to 1 op 9 to 2 tchd 5 to 1) 3
1204⁵ DIG DEEPER 6-11-0 M Dwyer, *made most till appr 2 out, wknd approaching last............* (7 to 1 op 9 to 2) 4
1142⁹ FREE TRANSFER (Ire) 4-11-7 A Dobbin, *prmnt, led appr 2 out, sn hdd and one pace........* (33 to 1 op 25 to 1) 5
1287³ JENDEE (Ire) 5-10-11 (3*) A Larnach, *chsd ldrs till outpcd aftr 3 out, no dngr after............* (14 to 1 op 16 to 1) 6
1003⁵ STRONG MEASURE (Ire) 5-11-0 K Johnson, *chsd ldrs till wknd aftr 3 out..................* (13 to 2 op 8 to 1) 7
1181⁸ FIVE FLAGS (Ire) 5-11-0 Gary Lyons, *chsd ldrs till wknd aftr 7th..........................* (20 to 1) 8
1289⁶ BATTERY FIRED 4-10-9 (5*) J Supple, *trkd ldrs, effrt and mstk 3 out, sn wknd.....* (8 to 1 op 9 to 1 tchd 9 to 1) 9
BOWLAND CONNECTION 6-11-0 A Mulholland, *cl up early, in tch till wknd appr 3 out.* (25 to 1 op 20 to 1) 10
1181 MASTER CAVERS (Ire) 5-11-0 A Merrigan, *al beh, tld off till out...............................* (100 to 1) 11
MANOR RANGER 7-11-0 R Garritty, *in tch, effrt aftr 5th, wknd appr 3 out, beh whn pld up bef last....* (100 to 1) pu
CHORUS LINE (Ire) 4-10-9 Mrs A Farrell, *al beh, tld off whn pld up bef last.......* (12 to 1 op 8 to 1 tchd 5 to 1) pu
Dist: 3l, 5l, nk, 3l, 1½l, 10l, 12l, 1l, 4l. 3m 5m 10.70s. a 27.70s (13 Ran).
(M K Oldham), R D E Woodhouse

1481 'The Final Problem' Handicap Hurdle (0-130 4-y-o and up) £2,406 2m 110yds
.... (3:30)

1292² NOTABLE EXCEPTION [97] 4-9-7 (7*) S Mason, *hld up in tch, hdwy hfwy, effrt appr 2 out, styd on wl to ld approaching last, all out.*
.... (5 to 1 op 4 to 1 tchd 6 to 1) 1
PALACEGATE KING [101] 4-10-4 M Moloney, *led till appr last, rallied and hng lft r-in, hld whn faltered nr fin-ish................................* (13 to 2 op 6 to 1) 2
BOLLIN MAGDALENE [106] 5-10-9 L Wyer, *trkd ldrs, pushed alng appr 2 out, styd on wl aftr last.*
.... (12 to 1 op 8 to 1) 3
1116⁶ SEON [114] 7-11-0 (3*) N Bentley, *prmnt till outpcd aftr 3 out, kpt on frm nxt.* (7 to 4 fav op 5 to 2 tchd 11 to 4) 4
1184² DUAL IMAGE [100] 6-10-3 M Dwyer, *in tch, hdwy appr 3 out, rdn aftr nxt, sn btn..........* (3 to 1 op 5 to 2) 5
819 HERE COMES TIBBY [97] 6-10-0 Mrs A Farrell, *beh hfwy, some late hdwy..................* (100 to 1 op 66 to 1) 6
BRAMBLEBERRY [103] 4-10-6 Gary Lyons, *trkd ldrs, ev ch 2 out, sn wknd.....................* (12 to 1 op 8 to 1) 7
MIDLAND EXPRESS [98] 10-10-11 C Grant, *beh hfwy..........* (50 to 1) 8
1291⁴ REVE DE VALSE (USA) [125] 6-11-9 (5*) P Waggott, *in tch, pushed alng hfwy, wknd 3 out...........* (20 to 1) 9
NORTH PRIDE (USA) [101] 8-10-4⁴ K Jones, *tld off 5th.*
.... (100 to 1 op 66 to 1) 10
1292⁴ MONTIFIORE AVENUE [105] 7-10-8 P Niven, *al beh, tld off whn pld up bef last.....................* (20 to 1) pu
Dist: 3l, ½l, 4l, 5l, 6l, hd, 7l, 2½l, dist. 4m 8.50s. a 15.50s (11 Ran).
SR: 24/25/29/33/14/5/11/-/23/ (Andrews & Wilson), Mrs M Reveley

CATTERICK (good)
Wednesday December 1st
Going Correction: PLUS 0.40 sec. per fur.

1482 Streetlam 'National Hunt' Novices' Hurdle Amateur Riders (4-y-o and up) £1,475 2m
.... (12:50)

663⁵ MEGA BLUE 8-10-10¹ Mr S Swiers, *trkd ldr, led aftr 3 out, quickened clr nxt, very easily.* (7 to 4 on op 6 to 4) 1
1003 STAGGERING (Ire) 4-10-3¹ (7*) Mr J Beardsall, *in tch, effrt aftr 3 out, rdn betw last 2, kpt on towards finish.*
.... (14 to 1 op 12 to 1 tchd 16 to 1) 2
GOODHEAVENS MRTONY 6-10-7 (7*) Mr A Manners, *led till hdd aftr 3 out, rdn appr nxt.* (200 to 1 op 100 to 1) 3
1376² ROSEBERRY TOPPING 4-10-9 (5*) Mr M Buckley, *chsd ldrs frm 4th, rdn alng and ch aftr 3 out, sn outpcd.*
.... (2 to 1 op 6 to 4) 4
LITTLE FREDDIE 4-10-7 (7*) Mr D Parker, *beh frm 4th, tld off.................................* (33 to 1 op 25 to 1) 5

COOL DYNASTY 6-10-2 (7*) Miss V Bevan, *pld hrd early and sn tracking ldrs, losing tch whn blun 4th, wl tld off................................* (66 to 1 op 50 to 1) 6
Dist: 30l, hd, 1l, dist, 30l. 3m 57.00s. a 16.00s (6 Ran).
(Tony Yates), Mrs V A Aconley

1483 Ellerton Juvenile Novices' Hurdle (3-y-o) £1,475 2m
.... (1:20)

1147⁵ ATHERTON GREEN (Ire) 10-12 T Reed, *hld up and beh, dd hdwy aftr 3 out, rdn appr nxt, kpt on und pres to ld cl hme...............* (8 to 1 tchd 9 to 1) 1
OUTSET (Ire) 10-5 (7*) Mr C Bonner, *trkd ldrs, effrt appr last, kpt on und pres r-in, jst fld...* (33 to 1 op 25 to 1) 2
1408⁸ THE PREMIER EXPRES 10-12 L Wyer, *cl up, slight ld frm 4th till hdd and no extr nr finish....* (5 to 1 op 8 to 1) 3
TIGERSONG (USA) 10-12 N Williamson, *cl up, wth ldr frm 4th, mstk 2 out, dsptd ld r-in till no extr nr finish.*
.... (9 to 4 fav op 5 to 4 tchd 5 to 2) 4
1147³ VAIGLY SUNTHYME 10-12 N Smith, *in tch, hdwy to chase ldrs appr 3 out, kpt on same pace frm nxt.*
.... (9 to 1 op 8 to 1) 5
652⁹ MISTROY 10-7 C Grant, *in tch, some hdwy aftr 3 out, not trble ldrs...............................* (16 to 1) 6
QUEEN OF THE QUORN 10-4 (3*) N Bentley, *nvr nr to chal.*
.... (12 to 1 op 10 to 1) 7
1147 DIXIE HIGHWAY 10-7 K Johnson, *prmnt till grad wknd appr 3 out.........* (33 to 1) 8
272* MOONSHINE DANCER 11-5 P Niven, *nvr nr ldrs.*
.... (9 to 1 op 8 to 1) 9
1147 MARIBELLA 10-7 A Dobbin, *chsd ldrs, blun 3rd, wknd 5th.........................* (500 to 1 op 100 to 1) 10
1217⁴ SUIVEZ 10-5 (7*) S Taylor, *led till hdd 4th, wknd quickly appr 3 out.....................* (12 to 1) 11
1408⁴ IJAB (Can) 10-12 B Storey, *in tch whn f 4th.*
.... (10 to 1 tchd 9 to 1 and 12 to 1) f
DEAD CALM 10-12 N Doughty, *al beh, pld up bef 2 out.*
.... (20 to 1 op 16 to 1) pu
INDIAN SECRET (Ire) 10-5 (7*) Mark Roberts, *sn pushed alng and beh, tld off whn pld up bef 2 out.*
.... (10 to 1 op 50 to 1) pu
971 NEWGATESKY 10-0 (7*) F Leahy, *sn beh, pld up bef last.*
.... (100 to 1 op 66 to 1) pu
SOPHIE'S BOY 10-12 R Garritty, *sn beh, pld up bef 2 out.*
.... (33 to 1 op 25 to 1) pu
Dist: Hd, hd, hd, 5l, 20l, 3l, 8l, 1½l, 5l, 8l. 3m 54.10s. a 13.10s (16 Ran).
SR: 17/17/17/17/12/-/ (Atherton And Green), J A Glover

1484 Bobby Faulkner Memorial Challenge Trophy Novices' Chase (4-y-o and up) £2,626 2m
.... (1:50)

FRICKLEY 7-11-4 N Doughty, *sn cl up, led aftr 7th, ran on wl frm 2 out, cmftbly.*
.... (11 to 4 on op 7 to 2 on tchd 5 to 2 on) 1
1096⁴ POLITICAL TOWER 6-11-4 A Dobbin, *sn cl up, jnd wnr 9th, outpcd frm 2 out.............* (8 to 1 op 7 to 1) 2
948⁶ GRAZEMBER 6-11-4 L Wyer, *led till hdd aftr 7th, no imprsn on 1st 2 whn hit 3 out.....* (7 to 1 op 6 to 1) 3
1128⁶ TIMANFAYA 6-11-4 T Reed, *lost tch frm 5th.*
.... (14 to 1 op 12 to 1) 4
1092⁹ DE JORDAAN 6-11-4 A Merrigan, *prmnt early, lost tch frm 5th...........................* (25 to 1 op 16 to 1) 5
912 NOBBY 7-11-4 A Mulholland, *lost tch frm 5th...* (100 to 1) 6
1368³ AYIA NAPA 6-11-4 Mr J Bradburne, *f 3rd.*
.... (20 to 1 op 16 to 1) f
JADE SHOON 8-11-4 B Storey, *tld off whn pld up bef 7th.*
.... (40 to 1 op 33 to 1) pu
Dist: 5l, 12l, dist, 12l, 5l. 4m 1.10s. a 12.10s (8 Ran).
SR: 33/28/16/-/-/ (Robert Ogden), G Richards

1485 Kiplin Selling Handicap Hurdle (4-y-o and up) £1,880 2m 3f
.... (2:20)

1143³ STAGS FELL [84] 8-11-1 (3*) N Bentley, *in tch, gd hdwy aftr 4th, led 6th, ran on wl frm 2 out.........* (9 to 2 jt-fav op 4 to 1 tchd 5 to 1) 1
1426⁵ SPANISH WHISPER [83] 6-11-3 D Byrne, *prmnt, dsptd ld 6th, slightly outpcd appr 2 out, kpt on und pres frm last.....................* (9 to 1 op 8 to 1) 2
1280 WAR BEAT [72] 5-9-13 (7*) G Robertson, *trkd ldrs, chlgd appr 2 out, sn rdn and one paced.*
.... (20 to 1 tchd 25 to 1) 3
1356 LITTLE CONKER [66] 5-10-0 S Turner, *al chasing ldrs, kpt on same pace frm 2 out.....* (20 to 1 op 16 to 1) 4
GREENACRES LAD [71] 10-10-5 A Mulholland, *trkd ldrs, effrt appr 2 out, kpt on same pace.* (50 to 1 op 33 to 1) 5
1357⁵ J P MORGAN [90] (v) 5-11-10 A Dobbin, *prmnt, outpcd appr 2 out.................* (9 to 1 op 8 to 1) 6
1186⁶ MAKE ME PROUD (Ire) [90] 4-11-10 L Wyer, *beh, blun 5th, nvr trbld ldrs...................* (20 to 1 op 16 to 1) 7
1198 PLAYFUL JULIET (Can) [71] 5-10-4 Pat Caldwell, *cl up, led 4 till hdd 6th, wknd appr 3 out.* (33 to 1 op 25 to 1) 8
1068⁶ BURN BRIDGE (USA) [84] (v) 7-11-4 Peter Caldwell, *nvr dngrs....................* (12 to 1 op 10 to 1) 9
1091 LADY BE BRAVE [69] 10-10-3 K Johnson, *nvr dngrs.*
.... (12 to 1 op 8 to 1 tchd 10 to 1) 10

1143⁵ A GENTLEMAN TWO [84] 7-11-4 P Niven, *led till hdd 4th,*
wknd aftr nxt............(8 to 1 op 7 to 1 tchd 9 to 1) 11
1204 THE PATTERS MAGIC [67] 6-10-11⁴ C Grant, *in tch, hdwy to*
track ldrs 6th, wknd appr 2 out....(12 to 1 op 10 to 1) 12
1143⁶ HYPNOTIST [94] 6-11-7 (7ᵉ) S Taylor, *mstk second, prmnt,*
pushed alng appr 3 out, wknd approaching nxt.
..................(11 to 1 op 10 to 1 tchd 12 to 1) 13
PONDERED BID [74] 9-10-8 N Williamson, *sn beh.*
..........................(16 to 1 op 14 to 1) 14
1238⁶ ITALIAN TOUR [68] 13-10-2 Mrs A Farrell, *sn beh.* (25 to 1) 15
719⁴ COLORADO INSIGHT [73] 5-10-7 J Callaghan, *sn beh.*
..........................(6 to 1 tchd 7 to 1) 16
970⁸ ELDER PRINCE [70] 7-10-4 R Garritty, *mid-div, pushed*
alng hfwy, sn btn. (9 to 2 jt-fav op 7 to 1 tchd 4 to 1) 17
1190⁹ BRIGHT SAPPHIRE [73] (bl) 7-10-4 (3ᵉ) R Davis, *prmnt till*
wknd appr 5th...................(16 to 1 op 14 to 1) 18
970 TAYLORMADE BOY [89] 10-11-4 (5ᵉ) P Waggott, *mid-div till*
wknd appr 3 out, wl beh whn virtually pld up r-in.
..................(12 to 1 tchd 14 to 1) 19
1068 ARTHURS STONE [74] 7-10-8 B Dalton, *sn beh, tld off whn*
pld up bef 2 out..................(33 to 1 op 20 to 1) pu
Dist: 2l, ½l, 2½l, 1½l, 10l, 2l, ½l, 1½l, 4l, 2½l. 4m 41.70s. (20 Ran).
SR: 14/11/-/-/-/2/ (Richard Johnson), G M Moore

1486 **Charles Vickery Memorial Cup Handicap Chase (0-120 5-y-o and up) £3,002 3m 1f 110yds.................(2:50)**

NO MORE TRIX [107] 7-11-1 R Garritty, *jmpd wl, trkd ldrs*
frm hfwy, led 15th, clr 3 out, cmftbly.
..................(7 to 1 tchd 8 to 1) 1
1365⁶ ON THE HOOCH [101] 8-10-9 Mr J Bradburne, *prmnt, led*
9th till hdd 13th, outpcd aftr 4 out, styd on wl frm 2 out.
..................(11 to 1 op 10 to 1) 2
1262² GLENSHANE LAD [102] 7-10-10 N Williamson, *in tch till*
blun badly 7th, sn wl beh, cld up 11th, hdwy to chase
wnr aftr 3 out, no imprsn.... (5 to 1 jt-fav op 9 to 2) 3
1222³ MOUNTEBOR [92] 9-10-0 J Callaghan, *prmnt, led 13th to*
15th, grad wknd appr 3 out...................(14 to 1) 4
911² TRUELY ROYAL [95] 9-10-3 B Storey, *cl up, mstk and lost*
pl 3rd, chsd ldrs frm tenth till grad wknd aftr 4 out.
..................(5 to 1 jt-fav op 9 to 2) 5
DUBIOUS JAKE [102] 10-10-10 N Doughty, *lost tch frm*
13th...................(20 to 1 op 16 to 1) 6
1254³ VIVA BELLA (Fr) [92] (bl) 6-9-7 (7ᵉ) Mr D Parker, *beh most of*
way...................(33 to 1) 7
1222⁹ BISHOPDALE [114] 12-11-8 A Merrigan, *lost tch frm 12th.*
..................(66 to 1 op 50 to 1) 8
POLAR REGION [119] 7-11-13 P Niven, *led 4th to 6th, lost*
pl hfwy, wl beh whn f 14th.
..................(11 to 1 op 10 to 1 tchd 12 to 1) f
1145³ RADICAL LADY [103] 9-10-6 (5ᵉ) J Supple, *chsd ldrs till*
blun and uns rdr 14th. (9 to 1 op 8 to 1 tchd 10 to 1) ur
1359⁴ CAROUSEL CALYPSO [101] 7-10-9 C Grant, *in tch, mstk*
11th, sn pushed alng, wknd 13th, tld off whn pld up bef
2 out..................(6 to 1 op 11 to 2) pu
1222 BALLINROSTIG [102] 10-10-10 L Wyer, *prmnt, led 6th to*
9th, wknd aftr 11th, wl beh whn pld up bef 13th.
..................(16 to 1) pu
1130* ZAM BEE [108] 7-11-2 T Reed, *led to 4th, cl up till wknd*
aftr 12th, tld off whn pld up bef 2 out..........(11 to 2) pu
Dist: 8l, 1½l, 10l, 5l, 7l, ¾l, 15l. 6m 43.60s. a 28.60s (12 Ran).
(The Roses Syndicate), T P Tate

1487 **Brompton Handicap Hurdle (0-120 4-y-o and up) £2,110 2m...........(3:20)**

1154* TIP IT IN [96] 4-10-10 S Turner, *mid-div, steady hdwy to ld*
appr 2 out, drvn out frm last...................(7 to 1) 1
TAPATCH (Ire) [110] 5-11-10 J Callaghan, *hld up in tch,*
hdwy to chase wnr aftr 3 out, mstk nxt, kpt on, no
imprsn...................(16 to 1 op 12 to 1 tchd 20 to 1) 2
999² ADMIRALTY WAY [106] 7-11-6 N Williamson, *chsd ldrs,*
slightly outpcd aftr 3 out, styd on wl frm nxt.
..................(8 to 1 op 12 to 1) 3
1148⁷ CURTAIN FACTORY [86] 4-10-0 L Wyer, *in tch, effrt aftr 3*
out, nvr real hdwy till styd on nr fin.
..................(10 to 1 op 8 to 1) 4
1213² SASKIA'S HERO [92] 6-10-6 D Byrne, *in tch, effrt aftr 3*
out, kpt on same pace.........(4 to 1 fav tchd 9 to 2) 5
GYMCRAK SOVEREIGN [103] 5-11-3 R Garritty, *cl up, led 3*
out, sn hdd, grad wknd...........(25 to 1 op 20 to 1) 6
1221³ ALL WELCOME [82] 6-10-12 P Niven, *chsd ldrs, ev ch appr*
2 out, grad wknd, btn whn hit last...(8 to 1 op 7 to 1) 7
818⁴ SAOIRSE (Ire) [86] 5-10-0³ (3ᵉ) J Moffatt, *nvr dngrs.*
..................(25 to 1 op 20 to 1) 8
ANY DREAM WOULD DO [87] 4-10-1 C Hawkins, *prmnt till*
wknd appr 2 out...................(25 to 1 op 20 to 1) 9
1357² COMSTOCK [93] 6-10-0 (7ᵉ) E Husband, *led to second, cl*
up till wknd appr 2 out.
..................(14 to 1 tchd 12 to 1 and 9 to 1) 10
1202² CLEAR IDEA (Ire) [89] 5-9-10 (7ᵉ) B Harding, *led second till*
hdd 3 out, sn lost pl....(10 to 1 op 9 to 2 tchd 6 to 1) 11
1127² SUNSET REINS FREE [90] 8-10-4 K Jones, *chsd ldrs till*
wknd appr 3 out...................(10 to 1) 12
1143⁸ JOHN NAMAN (Ire) [86] 4-10-0 A Dobbin, *beh frm 5th.*
..................(33 to 1) 13

1355² MY LINDIANNE [86] 6-10-0 N Mann, *sn tld off.*
..................(8 to 1 op 10 to 1 tchd 7 to 1) 14
MASTER GLEN [110] 5-11-5 (5ᵉ) P Midgley, *lost tch and pld*
up aftr 4th...................(50 to 1) pu
Dist: 1½l, nk, 8l, 1½l, 1l, hd, 3l, 1l, 1l, 10l. 3m 52.80s. a 1.80s (15 Ran).
SR: 28/40/35/7/11/21/16/1/1/ (Mrs M Dunning), A Smith

HUNTINGDON (good to soft)
Wednesday December 1st
Going Correction: PLUS 0.87 sec. per fur. (races 1,3,-5,7), PLUS 0.70 (2,4,6)

1488 **Montagu Conditional Jockeys' Selling Hurdle (3-y-o and up) £1,939 2m 110yds.....................(12:30)**

1374⁴ NAGOBELIA 5-11-4 P Hide, *chsd ldrs, led 3 out, edgd lft*
aftr last, drvn out.....(10 to 1 op 7 to 1 tchd 12 to 1) 1
1272* RULING DYNASTY (bl) 9-11-13 M Hourigan, *hld up, hdwy*
aftr 4th, chsd wnr appr 2 out, kpt on.
..................(Evens fav op 5 to 4 tchd 6 to 4) 2
918³ ELEGANT FRIEND 5-11-13 W Marston, *trkd ldrs, outpcd 3*
out, no imprsn whn hit nxt.........(7 to 1 op 5 to 1) 3
COBB GATE 5-11-5 (4ᵉ) M Stevens, *took keen hold, hld up*
in mid-div, outpcd 5th, effrt 3 out, styd on.
..................(50 to 1 op 20 to 1) 4
1289 WESTCOURT FLYER 4-11-0 (4ᵉ) J Driscoll, *beh til styd on*
frm 2 out, nrst finish...................(50 to 1 op 33 to 1) 5
1299⁸ THE HIDDEN CITY 7-11-13 A Thornton, *wtd wth in mid-div, outpcd 4 out, drvn and no imprsn frm 2 out.*
..................(14 to 1 op 12 to 1 tchd 16 to 1) 6
1384* TAX THE DEVIL (v) 5-11-13 A Dicken, *strted slwly, sn*
reco'red to ld second, clr 4th, hdd 3 out, wknd quickly.
..................(12 to 1 op 6 to 1) 7
1097⁸ TIME OF GRACE (Ire) 3-10-0 (7ᵉ) E Tolhurst, *al beh.*
..................(50 to 1 op 25 to 1) 8
MAJORITY HOLDING 8-11-5 (4ᵉ) P McLoughlin, *chsd ldrs*
till outpcd 4 out...................(14 to 1 op 9 to 1) 9
959⁵ MABTHUL (USA) 5-11-5 (4ᵉ) N Juckes, *al beh.*
..................(16 to 1 op 10 to 1) 10
1353⁸ NORMAN WARRIOR (bl) 4-11-4 D Meredith, *trkd ldrs, hrd*
rdn aftr 4 out, sn wknd...........(50 to 1 op 25 to 1) 11
1139⁴ BEN ZABEEN 8-11-9 (4ᵉ) S Ryan, *chsd ldrs till reminders*
and drpd rear aftr 3rd. (13 to 2 op 4 to 1 tchd 7 to 1) 12
1406⁵ WATER DIVINER (bl) 3-10-7 R Farrant, *cl up till rdn and*
lost pl 4 out, tld off...................(50 to 1 op 33 to 1) 13
1374 WATERBEACH VILLAGE (Ire) 5-11-4 A Procter, *al beh, tld*
off...................(50 to 1 op 25 to 1) 14
725 BROWN MYSTIQUE 7-10-9 (4ᵉ) A Flannigan, *cl up till wknd*
appr 4th, tld off whn pld up bef 3 out.
..................(100 to 1 op 33 to 1) pu
Dist: 1½l, dist, ¾l, ¾l, 1l, 5l, 8l, 12l, 2½l, 12l. 4m 14.60s. a 27.60s (15 Ran).
(T L Buxton), J Pearce

1489 **Long Sutton Handicap Chase (0-125 4-y-o and up) £3,003 2½m 110yds**
..................(1:00)

1132² DOLIKOS [102] 6-10-6 M Dwyer, *trkd ldrs, cld on lder o'r 2*
out, led last, ran on...................(10 to 1 op 8 to 1) 1
1212² SPREE CROSS [120] 7-11-10 D Murphy, *cl up, led 6th, clr 4*
out, hit nxt, hdd last, no extr.
..................(8 to 1 op 6 to 1 tchd 9 to 1) 2
CHIASSO FORTE (Ity) [104] 10-10-8 M Hourigan, *chsd ldrs,*
pushed alng tenth, sn outpcd, styd on appr 2 out, one
pace whn jmpd rght last...........(5 to 1 op 11 to 2) 3
1214 RUNNING SANDS [96] 9-9-11² (5ᵉ) C Burnett-Wells, *led til*
hdd 6th, cl up till outpcd frm 4 out.(20 to 1 op 16 to 1) 4
MONTALINO [105] 10-10-9 A Tory, *trkd ldrs early, drpd*
rear 9th, modest prog frm 2 out, tld off.
..................(16 to 1 op 12 to 1 tchd 20 to 1) 5
1363 LITTLE TOM [106] 8-10-10 A Maguire, *cl up, rdn 4 out, sn*
wknd, tld off...................(4 to 1 fav op 7 to 2) 6
1165³ GREEN WILLOW [114] 11-11-4 R Dunwoody, *chsd ldrs till*
wknd 12th, tld off whn pld up bef 2 out.
..................(10 to 1 op 7 to 1) pu
YAHEEB (USA) [101] 9-10-5 G McCourt, *nvr gng wl, al beh,*
tld off whn pld up bef 11th, broke blood vessel.
..................(50 to 1 op 33 to 1) pu
1285² CAMPSEA-ASH [115] 9-10-12 (7ᵉ) P Murphy, *trkd ldrs till*
drpd rear 11th, tld off whn pld up bef 2 out.
..................(8 to 1 op 6 to 1) pu
CASINO MAGIC [96] 9-10-0 W Marston, *al beh, tld off 12th,*
pld up bef 2 out...................(33 to 1 op 20 to 1) pu
BOBBY SOCKS [110] 7-11-0 L Harvey, *mstk 1st, beh, rdn*
11th, sn tld off, pld up bef 2 out.....(8 to 1 op 7 to 1) pu
Dist: 5l, 2l, 10l, 20l, 5l. 5m 13.20s. a 18.20s (11 Ran).
SR: 40/53/35/17/6/2/ (Mrs M Guthrie), J M Jefferson

1490 **EBF 'National Hunt' Novices' Hurdle Qualifier (4,5,6-y-o) £1,980 2m 110yds**
..................(1:30)

1309² KONVEKTA KING (Ire) 5-11-0 A Maguire, *hld up, cld 4th, quickened to ld aftr 3 out, sn clr, easily.*
.................................(7 to 4 fav op 2 to 1 tchd 9 to 4)   1
1010⁹ MR JERVIS (Ire) 4-11-0 D Murphy, *nvr far away, cld on ldrs 4th, chsd wnr frm 2 out, one pace.*
.................................(14 to 1 op 8 to 1)   2
1354² TAKE THE BUCKSKIN 6-11-0 G McCourt, *trkd ldrs,led 5th till hdd aftr 3 out, hrd rdn and no extr.*
.................................(9 to 2 op 7 to 2 tchd 5 to 1)   3
901⁴ JUNGLE RITES (Ire) 5-11-0 M Dwyer, *chsd ldrs, ch 3 out, btn whn blun last.....(10 to 1 op 4 to 1 tchd 12 to 1)   4
ESSDOUBLEYOU (NZ) 5-11-0 H Davies, *mid-div, hdwy 4 out, sn outpcd, styd on appr last.*
.................................(14 to 1 op 20 to 1 tchd 33 to 1)   5
1251⁸ THE CHANGELING (Ire) 4-11-0 R J Beggan, *hld up, hdwy 3 out, styd on wl.*.................(33 to 1)   6
1028⁶ TOPPING TOM (Ire) 4-11-0 C Llewellyn, *jmpd badly lft thrght, led briefly 3rd, prmnt till outpcd 4 out, ran on frm last.*.....................(16 to 1 op 14 to 1)   7
MYRTILLA 4-10-9 L Harvey, *beh, hdwy appr 2 out, nrst finish.*.....................(14 to 1 op 10 to 1)   8
1161⁶ PHIL'S DREAM 5-11-0 R Dunwoody, *mid-div, cld on ldrs 4th, outpcd nxt.*.......................(10 to 1)   9
LOCAL MANOR 6-11-0 M Richards, *trkd ldrs till lost pl aftr 4th.*.....................(14 to 1 op 10 to 1) 10
1193 FORTUNES COURSE (Ire) 4-10-9 S Smith Eccles, *chsd ldrs, hmpd 4 out, sn lost pl.*
.................................(50 to 1 op 20 to 1) 11
SCEPTICAL 5-11-0 S McNeill, *al beh.* (50 to 1 op 20 to 1) 12
SPANISH BLAZE (Ire) 5-11-0 M A FitzGerald, *nvr dngrs.*
.................................(16 to 1 op 8 to 1) 13
1126 KINDLE'S DELIGHT 5-11-0 J Osborne, *cl up, led briefly 4th, sn outpcd.........(7 to 1 op 5 to 1 tchd 16 to 1) 14
TRADER TYE (Ire) 5-10-7 (7*) P Murphy, *hld up, al beh.*
.................................(50 to 1 op 25 to 1) 15
WEE WINDY (Ire) 4-11-0 E Murphy, *al beh.*
.................................(20 to 1 op 14 to 1) 16
1251² MISS MONZA 5-10-9 D Bridgwater, *al prmnt, tracking ldrs whn f heavily 4 out.........(10 to 1 tchd 12 to 1)   f
HERESY (Ire) 4-10-9 W Humphreys, *strted slwly, al beh, tld off whn pld up bef 2 out.*.....(100 to 1 op 50 to 1)   pu
1090⁸ MR GREY FELLOW (Ire) 5-11-0 A Tory, *led to 3rd, cl up till lost pl 4th, tld off whn pld up bef last.*
.................................(100 to 1 op 50 to 1)   pu
1329 LILIAN MAY GREEN 4-10-9 Ann Stokell, *mid-div till drpd rear 4th, tld off whn pld up bef last.*
.................................(100 to 1 op 50 to 1)   pu
Dist: 10l, 3½l, 8l, 3l, sht-hd, 2l, ½l, 10l, 1l, 1l. 4m 10.90s. a 23.90s (20 Ran).
(Konvekta Ltd), D Nicholson

1491 **Crowland Novices' Chase (5-y-o and up) £2,487 3m...............(2:00)**

1206⁴ MAILCOM 7-10-12 J Osborne, *hit 1st, jmpd lft but soundly aftr, made all, clr appr 2 out, styd on wl.*
.................................(7 to 4 fav op 2 to 1)   1
1171⁷ GLENGRIFFIN 8-10-9 (3*) P Hide, *second, cl up, outpcd appr 2 out, kpt on.......(20 to 1 op 16 to 1)   2
829⁶ ROYAL SQUARE (Can) 7-10-12 M Perrett, *hld up, cld tenth, outpcd 14th, styd on appr last.*
.................................(7 to 1 op 5 to 1)   3
981 KEV'S LASS (Ire) 5-10-0 (7*) P Murphy, *cl up, ev ch 3 out, sn outpcd................(12 to 1 op 10 to 1)   4
1311* PETTY BRIDGE 9-11-3 R Bellamy, *al beh, pckd 5th, tld off.*
.................................(11 to 4 op 5 to 2 tchd 3 to 1)   5
SILVER STICK 6-10-12 G McCourt, *hld up beh, mstk 3rd, hdwy 12th, outpcd frm 4 out, tld off.*......(10 to 1)   6
1306⁴ GALLANT EFFORT (Ire) 5-10-12 H Davies, *chsd ldrs, 5th whn blun badly 13th, no dngr aftr, tld off.*
.................................(12 to 1 op 9 to 1)   7
HEATHVIEW 6-10-12 M Dwyer, *in tch, blun 7th, f tenth.*
.................................(10 to 1 op 8 to 1)   f
1008 GIVEITAGO 7-10-12 S McNeill, *in tch till blun 16th and nxt, tld off whn pld up bef 2 out.....(7 to 1 op 9 to 2)   pu
Dist: 12l, 6l, 2½l, 15l, 20l, 12l. 6m 29.40s. a 41.40s (9 Ran).
(Mailcom Plc), Mrs J Pitman

1492 **Tetworth Handicap Hurdle (0-125 4-y-o and up) £2,145 2m 110yds.....(2:30)**

CHUCK CURLEY (USA) [100] 5-10-7 D Murphy, *hld up in rear, steady hdwy frm 4th, led on bit 2 out, ran on wl.*
.................................(7 to 2 op 2 to 1)   1
1389* MANEREE [99] 6-10-6 (6ex) R Campbell, *hld up in mid-div, cld and jmpd slwly 4th, led briefly appr 2 out, kpt on one pace..........................(9 to 2 op 3 to 1)   2
1249* EASTHORPE [100] 5-10-7 J Osborne, *led til hdd and mstk 2 out, rallied r-in....(5 to 2 fav op 4 to 1 tchd 9 to 4)   3
1396⁶ CHILD OF THE MIST [116] 7-11-9 A Maguire, *trkd ldrs, outpcd 3 out, kpt on frm last...(8 to 1 op 6 to 1)   4
1198⁶ CAMBO (USA) [93] 7-10-0 D Skyrme, *chsd ldrs to 4th, sn hrd rdn and outpcd, tld off..........(9 to 2 op 7 to 1)   5
1045² THUHOOL [94] 5-9-11 (5*) C Burnett-Wells, *cl up til outpcd appr 4 out, tld off..........(9 to 2 op 4 to 1)   6
MIZYAN [121] 5-12-0 S Keightley, *hld up in rear, al beh, tld off.........(16 to 1 op 12 to 1 tchd 20 to 1)   7

1240³ ALOSAILI [95] 6-10-2⁹ (7*) M Stevens, *al beh, tld off.*
.................................(25 to 1 op 16 to 1)   8
1034⁸ EXPLORATION (USA) [93] 6-10-0 A S Smith, *chsd ldrs to 4th, sn drpd rear, tld off..........(25 to 1 op 20 to 1)   9
PINECONE PETER [93] 6-10-0 M Brennan, *mid-div whn f 5th.....................(25 to 1 tchd 33 to 1)   f
MOTTRAM'S GOLD [93] 8-9-13⁴ (5*) A Dicken, *sn tld off, pld up bef 3 out................(33 to 1 tchd 25 to 1)   pu
1395⁶ MISTER ODDY [99] 7-10-6⁴ S Smith Eccles, *cl up, mstk 4 out, sn lost pl, pld up bef 2 out....(25 to 1 op 20 to 1)   pu
HAVE A PARTY [95] 6-10-2 S McNeill, *mid-div till outpcd whn pld up bef 2 out....(50 to 1 op 25 to 1)   pu
Dist: 1l, sht-hd, 2l, 30l, 2l, 2l, 10l, 15l. 4m 5.80s. a 18.80s (13 Ran).
SR: 35/33/34/48/-/-/19/-/-/   (P Byrne), B J Curley

1493 **Bishops Stortford Novices' Handicap Chase (4-y-o and up) £2,225 2m 110yds......................(3:00)**

1255² THE FLYING FOOTMAN [87] 7-11-11 A Maguire, *cl up, led 2 out, jmpd rght last, sn clr........(6 to 4 fav op 7 to 4)   1
SUNDAY PUNCH [90] 7-12-0 E Murphy, *hld up beh, cld 8th, lost pl aftr 3 out, mstk nxt, ran on frm last.*
.................................(10 to 1 op 5 to 1)   2
1245⁵ WAYWARD WIND [73] 9-10-11 W McFarland, *led to 3rd, cl up, ev ch 3 out, wknd and lost second r-in.... (14 to 1)   3
1093⁴ DELPIOMBO [78] 7-11-2 D Murphy, *hld up, cld and hit 8th, one pace frm 3 out. (6 to 1 op 7 to 1 tchd 8 to 1)   4
PETMER [77] 6-11-1 M A FitzGerald, *trkd ldrs, led 3rd till hdd 4 out, hrd rdn aftr nxt, wknd appr last.*
.................................(5 to 1 op 7 to 2)   5
1245³ CHAPEL HILL (Ire) [83] 5-11-0 (7*) D Fortt, *wth ldr, led 4 out to nxt, sn outpcd...........(5 to 1 op 7 to 2)   6
1256 DEEP IN GREEK [70] 7-10-8 R Dunwoody, *beh, cld 7th, sn outpcd.................(25 to 1 op 33 to 1 tchd 50 to 1)   7
751 MIDDAY SHOW (USA) [70] 6-10-8 J Osborne, *beh frm 5th, tld off................(16 to 1 op 14 to 1 tchd 20 to 1)   8
1255⁴ TINA'S MISSILE [80] 6-11-4 R Greene, *hmpd 5th, al beh, tld off.....................(16 to 1 op 14 to 1)   9
1276 VERSATILE [70] 9-10-8 S McNeill, *f 5th.*
.................................(6 to 1 op 7 to 1 tchd 8 to 1)   f
DOVEHILL [70] 7-10-8 Mr P Bull, *blun and uns rdr 5th.*
.................................(20 to 1 op 8 to 1)   ur
Dist: 15l, 3l, 2½l, ½l, ¾l, 3l, 30l, 10l. 4m 22.00s. a 24.00s (11 Ran).
(Mrs James West), D Nicholson

1494 **Grunwick Stakes National Hunt Flat Race (4,5,6-y-o) £1,951 2m 110yds ....(3:30)**

LEAD VOCALIST (Ire) 4-10-9 (5*) C Burnett-Wells, *hld up beh ldrs, cld 4 fs out, led ins last, drvn out.*
.................................(14 to 1 op 9 to 1)   1
AUTO PILOT (NZ) 5-11-3 R Greene, *beh, hdwy 3 fs out, led o'r one out till hdd ins last, ran on.(16 to 1 op 12 to 1)   2
RELKEEL 4-10-7 (7*) M Keighley, *trkd ldrs, ev ch 2 fs out, one pace.....................(10 to 1 tchd 12 to 1)   3
LYME GOLD (Ire) 4-10-9 (5*) J McCarthy, *mid-div, hdwy o'r 3 fs out, ev ch 2 out, one pace.*
.................................(7 to 2 fav op 4 to 1 tchd 4 to 1 and 6 to 1)   4
1223² DOMINIE (Ire) 5-10-12 (5*) T Jenks, *mid-div, rapid hdwy o'r 4 fs out, ev ch 2 out, one pace over one out.*
.................................(5 to 1 op 2 to 1)   5
1103² BARNEY'S GIFT (Ire) 5-10-10 (7*) R Moore, *trkd ldrs, pushed alng 3 fs out, wknd o'r one out.*
.................................(5 to 1 op 8 to 1)   6
RAISIN TURF (Ire) 4-10-2 (7*) R Massey, *cl up, led o'r 6 fs out, hdd over one out, wknd.*
.................................(9 to 2 op 5 to 1 tchd 8 to 1)   7
THREE OF CLUBS (Ire) 4-11-0 Mr J M Pritchard, *chsd ldrs till wknd 3 fs out.......(10 to 1 op 6 to 1 tchd 12 to 1)   8
RUTH'S BOY (Ire) 4-10-7 (7*) J Driscoll, *mid-div, prog to chase ldrs aftr 6 fs, wknd 3 out....(25 to 1 op 16 to 1)   9
TWISTALL (Ire) 5-10-10 (7*) P Murphy, *nvr better than mid-div.....................(14 to 1 op 10 to 1) 10
1329⁶ MEGAMUNCH (Ire) 5-10-10 (7*) N Juckes, *prmnt till wknd quickly o'r 2 fs out...............(7 to 1 op 16 to 1) 11
QUEEN'S AWARD (Ire) 4-10-11 (3*) P Hide, *hld up, nvr better than mid-div................(15 to 1 op 20 to 1) 12
CAST ADRIFT 6-10-5 (7*) M Berry, *nvr dngrs.*
.................................(14 to 1 op 12 to 1) 13
INGLETONIAN 4-10-9 (5*) D Bentley, *mid-div, sn pushed alng, beh hfwy....................(20 to 1 op 16 to 1) 14
JUST MAID IT 4-10-2 (7*) Pat Thompson, *strted slwly, al beh.....................(8 to 1 op 6 to 1 tchd 12 to 1) 15
CUMBERLAND BLUES (Ire) 4-10-9 (5*) S Lyons, *trkd ldrs till wknd quickly 4 fs out..........(8 to 1 op 5 to 1) 16
GAY MUSE 4-10-2 (7*) Guy Lewis, *al beh.*
.................................(12 to 1 op 6 to 1 tchd 14 to 1) 17
KELLSBORO KATE 6-10-12 M Hourigan, *cl up til wknd quickly o'r 4 fs out.............(12 to 1 op 7 to 1) 18
WOODBRIDGE (Ire) 4-10-7 (7*) Mr F Cashman, *strted slwly, al beh, tld off..................(25 to 1 op 20 to 1) 19
WHATAPICKLE (Ire) 4-11-0 V Slattery, *led til hdd o'r 6 fs out, wknd quickly..............(25 to 1 op 14 to 1) 20
CEREAL GEM 5-10-12 W Dwan, *chsd ldrs till wknd quickly hfwy, pld up, sddl slpd....(25 to 1 op 16 to 1)   pu

DESTINY ANGEL 4-10-3^{1} (7*) Mr R Griffiths, *al beh, pld up hfwy*..(25 to 1) pu
Dist: Nk, 5l, 2l, nk, 10l, 1l, 4l, 2l, 4l, nk. 4m 4.70s. (22 Ran).
(Capt A Pratt), R Rowe

THURLES (IRE) (soft)
Thursday December 2nd

1495 Littleton Opportunity Handicap Hurdle (0-116 4-y-o and up) £2,760 2¼m ....(12:30)

234^{8} PERCY BRENNAN [-] 6-9-8 (4*) J M Donnelly,.....(50 to 1) 1
DECENT LUKE (Ire) [-] 5-9-13 D Bromley,.........(50 to 1) 2
1074^{4} AMARI QUEEN [-] 6-10-2 (2*) M G Cleary,.........(10 to 1) 3
904 EYREFIELD ROSE [-] 7-9-7 (4*) P P Curran,.......(20 to 1) 4
1038^{6} HERE IT IS [-] 6-10-13 (4*) M Kelly,..............(12 to 1) 5
1178^{6} BALLINDERRY GLEN [-] 7-10-4 (2*) D T Evans,....(12 to 1) 6
1331 MISS LIME [-] 6-11-9 (4*) C McCormack,..........(4 to 1) 7
1176^{4} NISHIKI (USA) [-] 4-10-0 (4*) D J Kavanagh,.......(12 to 1) 8
FOGELBERG (USA) [-] 5-12-0 T J Mitchell,.......(20 to 1) 9
1178^{4} KING OF THE WORLD (Ire) [-] 5-10-1 (2*) T J O'Sullivan, ...(8 to 1) 10
1397^{9} MARYVILLE LADY (Ire) [-] (bl) 4-9-11 (2*) P A Roche, ...(20 to 1) 11
1400 PEACE TRIBUTE (Ire) [-] 4-9-13 (4*) K D Maher,... (25 to 1) 12
123 PRINCE TAUFAN (Ire) [-] 4-10-0 (2*) Susan A Finn, (14 to 1) 13
1335 SHANNON KNOCK [-] 8-11-1 C O'Brien,..........(16 to 1) 14
1330^{7} HIGHLAND MINSTREL [-] 6-9-13 (2*) D P Geoghegan, ...(16 to 1) 15
1400 ASHBORO (Ire) [-] 4-10-3 (4*) J M Willis,..........(25 to 1) 16
1178^{5} MRS BARTON (Ire) [-] 5-10-9 (2*) J R Barry, (100 to 30 fav) f
1333^{6} TURALITY (Ire) [-] 4-9-10 C Everard,............(8 to 1) f
GOLDEN AMBITION [-] 7-10-13 (4*) K P Gaule,... (10 to 1) pu
555 CARBON FIVE (Ire) [-] 4-9-5 (4*) R A Hennessy,... (25 to 1) pu
636^{4} BOLEREE (Ire) [-] 5-9-13 (2*) T P Treacy,...........(6 to 1) pu
1333^{5} CASTLE CELEBRITY (Ire) [-] 4-9-13 (4*) J P Broderick, ...(10 to 1) pu
Dist: 1½l, ¾l, 6l, 4l. 4m 38.30s. (22 Ran).
(Mrs W Larkin), Capt D G Swan

1496 Holycross Hurdle (5-y-o and up) £2,243 2¾m 110yds............ (1:00)

1378* GIMME FIVE 6-11-6 C F Swan,................(3 to 1 on) 1
536* BAMANYAR (Ire) 5-10-9 (7*) Mr J J Murphy,.......(14 to 1) 2
1330^{5} TOT EM UP 6-10-6 (5*) P A Roche,...............(14 to 1) 3
991^{4} BLAZING COMET 7-10-11 F Woods,.............(25 to 1) 4
23* ANMACA (Ire) 5-10-11 M Duffy,..................(12 to 1) 5
853^{6} TROPICAL TIMES 7-10-11 Mr P J Healy,.........(16 to 1) 6
1335 ARRIGLE PRINCE (bl) 8-11-2 H Rogers,........ (100 to 1) 7
1378^{5} DRINK UP DAN 6-11-2 P Carberry,.............. (20 to 1) 8
1378^{6} MOONCAPER 7-11-2 T Horgan,.................. (14 to 1) 9
1403 CARRIG DANCER (Ire) 5-10-4 (7*) J P Broderick, (100 to 1) 10
1330 BORO DOLLAR 9-10-9 (7*) Mr G F Ryan,.........(33 to 1) 11
877^{3} OLYMPIC D'OR (Ire) 5-11-2 J F Titley,...........(14 to 1) 12
907 BETTY BALFOUR 7-10-4 (7*) J Butler,........... (100 to 1) 13
1378^{7} TRIMMER WONDER (Ire) 5-10-4 (7*) P Morris,.... (14 to 1) 14
990^{3} ROYAL OAK LADY (Ire) 5-10-6 (5*) Susan A Finn,..(20 to 1) 15
1332 HIGHWAY LASS 7-10-11 S H O'Donovan,........(100 to 1) 16
HOLY FOX (Ire) 5-11-2 C O'Dwyer,.............(20 to 1) 17
1018^{9} MISGIVINGS (Ire) 5-10-8 (3*) Miss M Olivefalk,.... (33 to 1) 18
1331^{6} ABBEY EMERALD 7-10-6 (5*) T P Treacy,....... (100 to 1) 19
1174 SWEET DEMOND 8-10-9 (7*) J M Donnelly,..... (100 to 1) 20
1401 PRANKSTER 7-10-11 (5*) M G Cleary,........... (33 to 1) 21
853 MRS HEGARTY 7-10-11 A Powell,.............. (25 to 1) pu
Dist: 1½l, 14l, 7l, ¾l. 5m 42.40s. (22 Ran).
(John P McManus), E J O'Grady

1497 Leugh Chase (5-y-o and up) £2,243 2 ¾m............................ (1:30)

1399 BART OWEN 8-11-1 (3*) T J Mitchell,.............(7 to 1) 1
1035* NUAFFE 8-11-8 S H O'Donovan,.................(6 to 1) 2
1399^{7} PARSONS BRIG 7-10-11 (7*) J P Broderick,...... (16 to 1) 3
1266 BORN DEEP 7-11-8 T Horgan,............... (5 to 4 fav) 4
856^{5} NEW CO (Ire) 4-11-2 C O'Dwyer,................ (10 to 1) 5
941* MERCIFUL HOUR 6-11-8 T J Taaffe,..............(6 to 1) 6
1451 THE COOPER 6-10-13 (5*) C O'Brien,........... (50 to 1) 7
CLEAKILE 7-11-4 F Woods,.................... (25 to 1) 8
1334^{2} COMMANCHE NELL (Ire) 5-11-1 G M O'Neill,......(5 to 1) f
Dist: 4½l, 3½l, dist, 1½l. 5m 41.50s. (9 Ran).
(Mrs Sandra McCarthy), P Mullins

1498 Seskin Novice Chase (5-y-o and up) £2,243 2m..................... (2:00)

881^{4} SORRY ABOUT THAT 7-12-0 P Carberry,..........(4 to 1) 1
1073^{7} SPEAKING TOUR (USA) 5-11-12 D H O'Connor,.. (20 to 1) 2
1177^{2} CHIC AND ELITE 6-11-9 P P Kinane,............. (11 to 2) 3
1232^{4} CASTLE KNIGHT 7-12-0 W T Slattery Jnr,........(14 to 1) 4
1177^{5} LADY OLEIN (Ire) 5-11-7 C F Swan,..........(7 to 2 fav) 5
PROGRAMMED TO WIN 6-12-0 S H O'Donovan, (10 to 1) 6
1178^{9} KING OF THE GLEN 7-11-11 (3*) C O'Brien,......(12 to 1) 7
536^{9} JOHNNY SCATTERCASH 11-11-9 F Woods,..... (16 to 1) 8
1235^{5} SUPER MIDGE 6-12-0 J Magee,................ (10 to 1) 9
1177^{6} FAIR LISSELAN (Ire) 5-11-7 G M O'Neill,.......... (7 to 1) 10
BROGUESTOWN 8-12-0 F J Flood,.............. (14 to 1) 11
CROSSHUE CROSS 6-11-9 C O'Dwyer,......... (10 to 1) 12
DOZING STAR 7-11-2 (7*) J P Broderick,..........(6 to 1) 13
MAMMY'S FRIEND 9-11-9 T Horgan,............(14 to 1) 14
1399 BELEEK CASTLE 7-11-11 (3*) D P Murphy,.......(12 to 1) 15
1177 HARLANE (Ire) 5-11-4 J P Banahan,..............(50 to 1) 16
Dist: 1½l, 1l, ½l, 3½l. 4m 18.90s. (16 Ran).
(D Mulvihill), Thomas Carberry

1499 Molony Cup (0-120 4-y-o and up) £2,243 3m.................... (2:30)

MINISTER FOR FUN (Ire) [-] 5-9-13 C F Swan,..(5 to 2 fav) 1
1231^{3} LADY BAR [-] 6-11-1 P M Verling,................ (5 to 1) 2
1266^{4} WALLS COURT [-] 6-9-13 P L Malone,............(12 to 1) 3
1402^{4} GERTIES PRIDE [-] 9-10-2 (3*) C O'Brien,......... (9 to 1) 4
1179^{5} MERLYNS CHOICE [-] 9-9-7 T Horgan,............(7 to 1) 5
WRECKLESS MAN [-] 6-10-11 (5*) P A Roche,.... (12 to 1) 6
690 KIL KIL CASTLE [-] 6-9-0 (7*) Mr A O'Shea,.......(33 to 1) 7
364^{4} KINGSTON WAY [-] 7-11-0 A J O'Brien,...........(10 to 1) 8
1402^{6} CAPINCUR EILE [-] (bl) 7-10-9 P Carberry,........(10 to 1) 9
855 PROPUNT [-] 8-11-7 J F Titley,..................(10 to 1) 10
1179^{6} LADY EILY [-] 8-9-9 S H O'Donovan,.............(12 to 1) 11
IFFEEE [-] 6-10-7 C O'Dwyer,...................(14 to 1) 12
GOLDEN CARRUTH (Ire) [-] 5-9-6 (7*) J P Broderick, ...(16 to 1) 13
1179 JOHNJOES PRIDE [-] (bl) 9-9-7 W T Slattery Jnr,.. (25 to 1) 14
1402^{9} FAIRY PARK [-] (bl) 8-10-5 F Woods,.............(10 to 1) 15
906^{5} ALTNABROCKY [-] 9-9-7 H Rogers,...............(33 to 1) ur
TIRRY'S FRIEND [-] 11-9-7 M Duffy,............. (20 to 1) pu
799 CASTLE BRANDON [-] 7-10-13 F J Flood,........(16 to 1) pu
Dist: 5½l, 7l, 5½l, ¾l. 6m 23.40s. (18 Ran).
(John P McManus), E J O'Grady

1500 Horse And Jockey INH Flat Race (4-y-o and up) £2,243 2m......... (3:00)

1180* ARIES GIRL 4-11-1 (7*) Mr E Norris,........... (Evens fav) 1
1230^{3} BUTCHES BOY (Ire) 4-11-6 (7*) Mr M P Dunne,.... (6 to 1) 2
1397^{7} DIVINITY RUN (Ire) 4-11-5 (3*) Mr A E Lacy,........(8 to 1) 3
1379^{3} ROUBABAY (Ire) 5-12-4 Mr T Mullins,..............(5 to 2) 4
969^{7} NOBLE MINISTER 6-11-11 Mr D M O'Brien,......(14 to 1) 5
1236 PARKBOY LASS 6-11-10 (3*) Miss M Olivefalk,... (20 to 1) 6
COOL MOSS 7-11-11 (7*) Mrs C Doyle,.......... (25 to 1) 7
45^{6} PUNTERS BAR 6-11-13 (5*) Mr H F Cleary,.......(16 to 1) 8
1236 SARAKAYA 8-10-13 (7*) Mr E Byrne,.............(25 to 1) 9
TORONTO TELEGRAM 7-11-1 (5*) Mr J P Berry,.. (12 to 1) 10
1270 WAPITI 6-11-11 Mr J A Flynn,....................(33 to 1) 11
Dist: 2½l, 5½l, 12l, 7l. 4m 5.10s. (11 Ran).
(W E Sturt), P J Flynn

1501 Toboradora INH Flat Race (4 & 5-y-o) £2,243 2m..................... (3:30)

1337^{2} BELGARRO (Ire) 4-10-13 (7*) Mr E Norris,... (11 to 10 fav) 1
MISS MUPPET (Ire) 4-10-12 (3*) Mrs M Mullins,.... (8 to 1) 2
1403^{2} COURT MASTER (Ire) 5-11-4 (7*) Mr B Moran,..... (6 to 1) 3
1180^{4} SIOBHAILIN DUBH (Ire) 4-10-8 (7*) Mr G F Ryan,..(10 to 1) 4
AMEEN (Ire) 5-11-6 (5*) Mr J A Nash,............ (20 to 1) 5
DONBOLINO (Ire) 5-10-13 (7*) Mr P Cody,........ (10 to 1) 6
469^{7} RAHEEN FLOWER (Ire) 5-11-6 Mr D M O'Brien,... (16 to 1) 7
1180^{9} CASTLE CLUB (Ire) 4-10-12 (3*) Mr R O'Neill,..... (20 to 1) 8
1020^{4} MY SUNNY WAY (Ire) 4-10-13 (7*) Mr D K Budds, (14 to 1) 9
1265 RATHNURE LADY (Ire) 5-11-1^{2} (7*) Mr P J O'Gorman, ...(33 to 1) 10
SWIFT SAILER (Ire) 4-10-13 (7*) Mr M A Cahill,.... (10 to 1) 11
993^{4} TULLOVIN (Ire) 5-11-11 Mr J A Berry,.............(7 to 1) 12
TOMMY THE DUKE (Ire) 5-11-6^{2} (7*) Mr M Kelleher, (16 to 1) 13
CABBERY ROSE (Ire) 5-11-6 Mr J A Flynn,......... (8 to 1) 14
908^{6} SAMMIES DOZER (Ire) 5-10-13 (7*) Mr P English, (20 to 1) 15
1270 TYPHOON JOE (Ire) 5-11-8 (3*) Mrs J M Mullins,.. (20 to 1) 16
1403 DASDILEMMA (Ire) 5-10-13 (7*) Mr J Keville,......(20 to 1) 17
BAUNFAUN RUN (Ire) 5-11-1^{2} (7*) Mr P M Crowe, (20 to 1) 18
RESERVOIR BOY (Ire) 4-10-13 (7*) Mr J A Collins, (14 to 1) 19
DOONEAL HERO (Ire) 5-11-4 (7*) Mr N C Kelleher, (16 to 1) 20
1337 MAURA MILISH (Ire) 4-10-10 (5*) Mr H F Cleary,...(20 to 1) 21
Dist: 1l, ½l, 2½l, nk. 4m 6.50s. (21 Ran).
(F O Hannon), Patrick Joseph Flynn

UTTOXETER (good)
Thursday December 2nd

Going Correction: PLUS 0.35 sec. per fur. (races 1,3,-5,7), PLUS 0.75 (2,4,6)

1502 Antique Wine Company Novices' Hurdle (4-y-o and up) £2,081 2m... (12:30)

CORROUGE (USA) 4-10-12 C Llewellyn, *al gng wl, led to 3rd, led bef 4 out, drw clr, easily.* .... (11 to 8 fav op 11 to 10 tchd 6 to 4) 1
1283^{7} GENERAL TONIC 6-10-12 S McNeill, *al hndy, ev ch 4 out, styd on same pace frm betw last 2.* (12 to 1 op 10 to 1) 2
SWIFT ROMANCE (Ire) 5-10-7 (5*) R Farrant, *tucked away in midfield, improved appr 4 out, rdn aftr nxt, kpt on same pace*...(50 to 1) 3

MADAM PICASSO (Ire) 4-10-0 (7*) Miss S Mitchell, *trkd ldg 4, ev ch appr four out, rdn and no extr nxt.* .... (33 to 1 op 25 to 1) 4
1421 ANGEL FALLING 5-10-4 (3*) A Thornton, *patiently rdn, hdwy frm 4 out, kpt on from betw last 2*....... (33 to 1) 5
FIRST LESSON (NZ) 7-10-5 (7*) Guy Lewis, *dsptd ld, led 3rd till bef 4 out, rdn and no extr nxt.* .... (10 to 1 op 8 to 1 tchd 11 to 1) 6
1099[4] CALL ME EARLY 8-10-12 M Brennan, *trkd ldrs, feeling pace appr 4 out, nvr able to chal.* .... (12 to 1 op 10 to 1 tchd 14 to 1) 7
1406 IVY HOUSE (Ire) 5-10-12 M Dwyer, *settled midfield, lost grnd quickly appr 4 out, no dngr aftr.* ....(5 to 1 tchd 9 to 2) 8
1163[5] DARINGLY 4-11-4 R Bellamy, *beh and feeling pace hfwy, nvr trble ldrs*.........(14 to 1 op 12 to 1 tchd 20 to 1) 9
1078[8] EDEN STREAM 6-10-12 J Railton, *co'red up in midfield, outpcd whn ldrs quickened appr 4 out, sn btn.* (50 to 1) 10
NO ASHES 6-10-9 (3*) R Davis, *struggling to stay in tch hfwy, sn btn*................................ (50 to 1) 11
1353* ARMASHOCKER 5-11-4 V Smith, *in tch, feeling pace hfwy, tld off 4 out*...................(8 to 1 op 5 to 1) 12
1283 NASHAAT (USA) 5-10-12 R Dunwoody, *chsd ldrs to hfwy, tld off 4 out*...................... (33 to 1 op 20 to 1) 13
1283 ROCA MURADA (Ire) 4-10-12 A Maguire, *in tch to hfwy, tld off 4 out*............................(5 to 1 op 5 to 2) 14

Dist: 6l, 7l, 2½l, 3½l, 2½l, 8l, 4l, 4l, 1½l, nk. 3m 52.80s. a 13.80s (14 Ran).
SR: 2/-/-/-/-/-/ (Michael Gates), N A Twiston-Davies

1503 North Derbyshire Newspapers Handicap Chase (0-125 5-y-o and up) £2,827 2m 7f..........................(1:00)

1388[3] DO BE BRIEF [118] (bl) 8-11-7 I Lawrence, *al wl plcd, led 5 out, styd on strly last 2, clr r-in*......(6 to 1 op 5 to 1) 1
740[2] CAMELOT KNIGHT [114] (bl) 7-11-3 C Llewellyn, *al hndy, led second to 5 out, drvn alng nxt, styd on same pace.* .... (11 to 2 op 4 to 1 tchd 6 to 1) 2
1273[2] DON'T LIGHT UP [100] (v) 7-10-3 R Dunwoody, *al wl plcd, drvn alng frm 4 out, styd on und pres r-in.* ....(3 to 1 fav op 9 to 4) 3
1208[3] MUSTHAVEASWIG [123] 7-11-12 A Maguire, *nvr far away, ev ch till not jump wl frm 4 out, fdd r-in.* .... (100 to 30 op 3 to 1 tchd 7 to 2) 4
BROMPTON ROAD [114] 10-11-3 R Greene, *chsd ldrs, lost grnd quickly fnl circuit, styd on frm 3 out, nvr nrr.* ....(16 to 1) 5
1407[3] WIGTOWN BAY [97] 10-10-0 W Marston, *beh aftr one circuit, styd on frm 3 out, nvr nrr*.... (25 to 1 op 20 to 1) 6
947[4] OVERHEREOVERTHERE [104] 10-10-7 R Supple, *chsd ldrs, struggling to keep up fnl circuit, tld off 6 out.* ....(10 to 1 tchd 14 to 1) 7
1220[4] RIFLE RANGE [125] 10-12-0 M Dwyer, *slight ld to second, wl plcd whn f nxt*................ (16 to 1 op 12 to 1) f
1359 BRADWALL [97] 9-10-0 D Gallagher, *wth ldrs, lost grnd quickly aftr one circuit, tld off whn pld up bef 4 out.* .... (50 to 1 op 33 to 1) pu
1365[5] HEY COTTAGE [115] 8-11-4 C Grant, *struggling aftr one circuit, tld off whn pld up bef 4 out.* .... (10 to 1 op 12 to 1) pu
NINE BROTHERS [97] 9-10-0 Mr K Green, *lost tch quickly aftr one circuit, tld off whn pld up bef 2 out.* .... (66 to 1 op 50 to 1) pu

Dist: 12l, 3l, ½l, 2l, 2½l, dist. 5m 56.00s. a 26.00s (11 Ran).
SR: 6/-/-/-/-/-/ (Errol Brown), Mrs J Pitman

1504 Rocester F.C. Three Year Old Novices' Hurdle £1,945 2½m 110yds (1:30)

PONDERING (v) 10-12 R Dunwoody, *al wl plcd, led bef 3 out, styd on well to go clr betw last 2.* .... (100 to 30 op 4 to 1 tchd 3 to 1) 1
1317* MARROS MILL 10-13 A Maguire, *al hndy, led appr 4 out till bef nxt, rdn 3 out, outpcd betw last 2.* ....(15 to 8 fav op 5 to 4 tchd 2 to 1) 2
1290[2] ERZADJAN (Ire) (bl) 11-4 L Wyer, *nvr far away, led briefly appr 3 out, sn drvn alng, fdd betw last 2.* ....(8 to 1 op 5 to 1 tchd 9 to 1) 3
1317[2] HEATHYARDS BOY 10-9 (3*) S Wynne, *settled midfield, outpcd whn ldrs quickened hfwy, some hdwy 3 out, nvr dngrs*................................ (7 to 1 op 5 to 1) 4
1297[4] DANGER BABY 10-9 (3*) D Meredith, *chsd ldrs, struggling to keep up hfwy, tld off 4 out*.... (33 to 1 tchd 40 to 1) 5
1244[6] APACHEE FLOWER 10-0 (7*) Guy Lewis, *chsd ldrs, feeling pace and lost grnd hfwy, tld off 4 out.* ....(25 to 1 op 20 to 1 tchd 33 to 1) 6
PAPER DAYS 10-7 (5*) D Matthews, *trkd ldrs, drvn alng to keep up hfwy, tld off 4 out*........ (33 to 1 op 20 to 1) 7
1408[5] SEASIDE DREAMER 10-12 Mr A Hambly, *patiently rdn, hdwy appr 4 out, eased whn btn nxt.* .... (33 to 1 op 25 to 1) 8
IMAD (USA) 10-12 C Grant, *chsd alng in midfield hfwy, lost tch 4 out, tld off*..................(8 to 1 op 9 to 2) 9
1408[6] STREPHON (Ire) 10-12 P Niven, *led till appr 4 out, sn lost pl, tld off*........................ (16 to 1 op 14 to 1) 10
1237[8] YOSHAARIK (Ire) 10-7 (5*) T Eley, *in tch to hfwy, sn tld off, pld up bef 3 out*................................(50 to 1) pu
SANTA STELLAR 10-8[6] (5*) P Midgley, *struggling 4th, tailing off whn pld up aftr nxt*...... (33 to 1 tchd 50 to 1) pu
1290[4] DAYADAN (Ire) 10-12 C Llewellyn, *nvr gng wl, tld off whn pld up aftr 5th*.................... (12 to 1 op 10 to 1) pu
1244[8] SACHA STAR 10-7 R Greene, *struggling hfwy, tld off whn pld up bef 3 out*..........................(50 to 1) pu

Dist: 12l, 15l, 15l, 7l, 12l, 1½l, 3l, ½l, 3l. 4m 54.50s. a 11.50s (14 Ran).
SR: 40/29/19/-/-/-/ (M C Pipe), M C Pipe

1505 Douglas Concrete Novices' Chase (5-y-o and up) £2,729 2m.........(2:00)

1228[3] COUNTRY LAD (Ire) 5-10-12 S McNeill, *wth ldr, led appr 6 out, hrd pressed last 3, styd on gmely r-in.* .... (6 to 4 on tchd 11 to 8 on) 1
1298[2] JAMES THE FIRST 5-10-12 C Maude, *patiently rdn, hdwy whn lft second 5 out, drw level last 3, ridden and no extr r-in*.................................(9 to 2 op 7 to 2) 2
OSTURA 8-10-12 A Maguire, *last and hld up, pushed alng to improve aftr 5 out, styd on, no imprsn 3 out.* .... (10 to 1 op 8 to 1 tchd 12 to 1) 3
MR OPTIMISTIC 6-10-12 P Niven, *chsd ldg 4, effrt and pushed alng hfwy, struggling aftr 5 out, no imprsn.* ....(8 to 1 op 7 to 1) 4
998[6] LINGER HILL 6-10-12 R Bellamy, *chsd ldrs, feeling pace and drvn alng hfwy, tld off whn almost uns rdr 4 out.* ....(33 to 1) 5
848[3] HIGHLAND POACHER 6-10-12 C Grant, *beh whn blun 5th, struggling aftr, tld off 6 out*........ (12 to 1 op 8 to 1) 6
MISAAFF 10-10-12 R Dunwoody, *wtd wth, improved to go second whn f 5 out*................ (25 to 1 op 20 to 1) f
1298 RUN OF WELD 10-10-12 T Wall, *led till aftr 6th, wl plcd whn blun and uns rdr six out*..... (50 to 1 op 33 to 1) ur

Dist: 1½l, 15l, 15l, 25l, dist. 4m 6.30s. a 17.30s (8 Ran).
SR: 31/29/14/-/-/ (S A Douch), Mrs S D Williams

1506 Derbyshire Property Guide Selling Handicap Hurdle (3,4,5-y-o) £1,626 2m ....(2:30)

1426[8] AUVILLAR (USA) [90] (v) 5-12-0 A Maguire, *wth ldr, led 5th, hdd briefly and rdn 3 out, drvn clr betw last 2, all out.* .... (6 to 1 op 5 to 1 tchd 13 to 2) 1
1079 LOXLEY RANGE (Ire) [70] 5-10-1 (7*) N Juckes, *wtd wth, improved to ld briefly 3 out, rdr drpd whip, styd on same pace r-in*.................... (12 to 1 op 8 to 1) 2
1079[7] ALDINGTON PEACH [78] 4-11-2 L Wyer, *led to 5th, styd hndy, rdn alng appr 3 out, kpt on same pace.* ....(3 to 1 tchd 7 to 2) 3
1272[3] PEACOCK FEATHER [80] 5-11-4 R Dunwoody, *nvr far away, feeling pace and rdn alng appr 3 out, outpcd nxt*.................................(4 to 1 op 3 to 1) 4
1416[5] SWISS MOUNTAIN [70] (bl) 3-10-3 (5*) T Eley, *chsd ldg pair, struggling to keep up aftr 4 out, sn lost tch*.....(8 to 1) 5
1188[8] BEAM ME UP SCOTTY (Ire) [68] 4-10-6 S McNeill, *sn tld off, some hdwy 3 out, nvr dngrs*..................(16 to 1) 6
836[3] ALDINGTON CHAPPLE [62] (bl) 5-9-9 (5*) T Jenks, *struggling hfwy, sn lost tch.* .... (16 to 1 op 12 to 1 tchd 20 to 1) 7
1357[3] STATION EXPRESS (Ire) [67] 5-10-5 C Llewellyn, *nvr gng wl, tld off 3 out*......................(5 to 2 fav op 2 to 1) 8

Dist: 5l, 8l, 5l, 12l, ½l, 4l, 8l. 3m 58.60s. a 19.60s (8 Ran).
(Mrs J M Snape), D Burchell

1507 Barry D. Trentham Challenge Bowl Handicap Chase (0-140 5-y-o and up) £3,468 2m 5f...................(3:00)

1121[2] NEVADA GOLD [122] 7-10-11 D Gallagher, *slwly away, wl beh, prog fnl circuit, led 2 out, kpt on strly r-in.* ....(9 to 2 op 4 to 1 tchd 5 to 1) 1
1343* THATCHER ROCK (NZ) [115] 8-10-4 C Maude, *nvr far away, drw level 2 out, rdn and swtchd r-in, kpt on.* ....(3 to 1 jt-fav tchd 5 to 2 and 7 to 2) 2
1069 BISHOPS ISLAND [124] 7-10-13 A Maguire, *led, clr aftr one circuit, jnd 4 out, hdd 2 out, kpt on same pace.* ....(7 to 1 op 5 to 1) 3
1254[2] CATCH THE CROSS [125] (bl) 7-11-0 M Foster, *slwly away, bustled alng to improve aftr one circuit, effrt 5 out, rdn and outpcd last 3*..............(10 to 1 op 8 to 1) 4
1300* FREELINE FINISHING [139] (bl) 9-12-0 R Dunwoody, *settled gng wl, hit 6th, drw level 4 out, hit nxt, fdd.* ....(8 to 1 op 7 to 1 tchd 9 to 1) 5
ROUGH QUEST [132] 7-11-7 M Richards, *slwly away, struggling 3 out, tld off fnl circuit.* ....(14 to 1 op 10 to 1 tchd 16 to 1) 6
1318* THE MASTER GUNNER [111] 9-9-13[2] (3*) R Davis, *chsd ldg pair aftr one circuit, feeling pace appr 5 out, tld off.* .... (3 to 1 jt-fav tchd 7 to 2) 7
GOLDEN CELTIC [135] 9-11-10 P Niven, *wth ldrs till wknd quickly 7th, pld up bef 9th*....... (33 to 1 op 14 to 1) pu

Dist: 1½l, nk, 15l, 2½l, dist, dist. 5m 26.70s. a 26.70s (8 Ran).
(Maltsword Ltd), F J Yardley

1508 Abacus Lighting Handicap Hurdle (0-130 4-y-o and up) £2,666 2m..(3:30)

1135⁵ MACEDONAS [112] 5-11-6 S McNeill, *patiently rdn, drw level 3 out, sn led, all out.*
.................(5 to 2 fav op 2 to 1 tchd 11 to 4) 1
RICHARDSON [100] 6-10-8 L Wyer, *not fluent, settled off the pace, shaken up and hdwy frm 3 out, str run aftr last, fnshd wl.*...................(6 to 1) 2
SILIAN [102] 11-10-7 (3*) S Wynne, *settled midfield, chlgd appr 2 out, rdn and one pace last.* (25 to 1 op 20 to 1) 3
1198⁸ ACCESS SUN [95] 6-10-3 A Maguire, *led second to 5th, hndy till fdd und pres 2 out.*
.................(8 to 1 op 7 to 1 tchd 9 to 1) 4
1325⁶ EDWARD SEYMOUR (USA) [92] 6-9-9 (5*) T Jenks, *nvr far away, drvn alng appr 3 out, rallied, one pace betw last 2.*...............(12 to 1 op 16 to 1 tchd 20 to 1) 5
1249⁷ WHEELER'S WONDER (Ire) [105] 4-10-6 (7*) Mr J L Llewellyn, *last and chsd alng hfwy, hdwy whn not much room appr 3 out, styd on one pace nxt.*
.................(6 to 1 op 9 to 2 tchd 13 to 2) 6
ELEMENTARY [120] 10-12-0 R Dunwoody, *al hndy, led 5th, rdn nxt, hdd appr 2 out, fdd.*...............(10 to 1) 7
1187 BALLERINA ROSE [92] 6-10-0 V Slattery, *trkd ldg 4, chsd alng aftr four out, sn lost tch.......*(10 to 1 op 8 to 1) 8
1072 OAK PARK (Ire) [104] 5-10-7 (5*) T Eley, *struggling in rear whn f 4 out.*.........(14 to 1 op 10 to 1 tchd 16 to 1) f
1154⁴ WHIPPERS DELIGHT (Ire) [98] 5-9-13 (7*) D Meade, *led to second, hndy till stumbled and pld up aftr 4th.*
.................(5 to 1 op 3 to 2 tchd 11 to 2) pu
Dist: ½l, 4l, 1½l, 1¼l, 4l, 12l. 8l. 3m 51.50s. a 12.50s (10 Ran).
SR: 23/10/8/-/-/3/6/-/-/   (Jim McCarthy), C P E Brooks

WINDSOR (good)
Thursday December 2nd
Going Correction: PLUS 0.30 sec. per fur. (races 1,2,-5,7), PLUS 0.35 (3,4,6)

1509 Oakley Green Novices' Hurdle (Div I) (4-y-o and up) £1,851 2m...... (12:20)

1354* JAZILAH (Fr) 5-11-7 G McCourt, *al prmnt, led appr 2 out, clr whn mstk last.*
.............(5 to 2 op 7 to 4 on tchd 13 to 8 on) 1
BALLET ROYAL (USA) 4-11-0 M Perrett, *hld up in mid-div, hdwy 5th, ev ch appr 2 out, kpt on to go second r-in.*
.................(10 to 1 op 6 to 1 tchd 11 to 1) 2
SURE HAVEN (Ire) 4-11-0 W McFarland, *nvr far away, led 3 out, rdn hdd, btn whn hit last......*(16 to 1 op 10 to 1) 3
COLTRANE 5-11-0 J Lower, *hld up in rear, styd on frm 3 out, nvr dngrs.*....................(8 to 1 op 7 to 2) 4
BARDOLPH (USA) 6-11-0 J Osborne, *trkd ldrs, led sn aftr 5th, hit 3 out and hdd, soon btn.*
.................(13 to 2 op 3 to 1 tchd 7 to 1) 5
1384² HIGHLAND FLAME 4-11-0 D Bridgwater, *hld up, hdwy appr 3 out, wknd quickly bef nxt, tld off.*
.................(33 to 1 op 16 to 1) 6
1309 BALLYMGYR (Ire) 4-10-9 (5*) A Procter, *al in rear, tld off.*
.................(40 to 1 op 20 to 1) 7
1047 FITNESS FANATIC 5-11-7 D Murphy, *led briefly 5th, fdd nxt, tld off.*..................(14 to 1 op 8 to 1) 8
1374³⁸ DON'T DROP BOMBS (USA) 4-11-0 G Upton, *beh, effrt 3rd, tld off frm 3 out.*...............(25 to 1 op 16 to 1) 9
TITIAN MIST 7-10-9 L Harvey, *trkd ldr to 3rd, wknd quickly aftr nxt, tld off whn pld up bef 3 out.*
.................(50 to 1 op 25 to 1) pu
1193 TOOMUCH TOOSOON (Ire) 5-10-9 (5*) S Curran, *beh frm second, tld off whn pld up bef 2 out.*
.................(50 to 1 op 25 to 1) pu
1040⁹ COUNT BARACHOIS (USA) 5-11-0 N Mann, *beh, tld off whn pld up bef 2 out.*............(40 to 1 op 20 to 1) pu
922⁹ WORTHY MEMORIES 4-10-9 J McLaughlin, *led till hdd 5th, wknd quickly, pld up bef 2 out.*
.................(50 to 1 op 25 to 1) pu
SWEET SCIMITAR 4-10-9 B Powell, *in tch whn jmpd slwly 3rd, tld off whn pld up bef 2 out.*
.................(50 to 1 op 25 to 1) pu
Dist: 6l, ½l, 15l, nk, 25l, 6l, 1l, dist. 3m 55.00s. a 10.00s (14 Ran).
SR: 41/28/27/12/11/-/   (S Aitken), R Akehurst

1510 Pangbourne Juvenile Novices' Hurdle (3-y-o) £1,807 2m............ (12:50)

ADMIRAL'S WELL (Ire) 10-12 G McCourt, *wtd wth in tch, not fluent 4th and 5th, led and hit last, drvn out.*
.................(100 to 30 op 9 to 4 tchd 7 to 2) 1
SUPREME MASTER 10-12 D Murphy, *mstk second, nvr far away, led 3 out till hdd last, one pace r-in.*
.................(9 to 2 op 7 to 2 tchd 7 to 1) 2
RUNAWAY PETE (USA) 10-12 N Williamson, *al prmnt, dsptd ld 2 out, btn whn blun last.*
.................(9 to 1 op 7 to 1 tchd 10 to 1) 3
GROUND NUT 10-12 J Osborne, *trkd ldr till one pace frm 3 out.*............(12 to 1 op 8 to 1 tchd 14 to 1) 4
DUVEEN (Ire) 10-12 D Bridgwater, *hld up, hdwy 5th, rdn appr 2 out, one pace.* (5 to 2 fav op 7 to 2 tchd 4 to 1) 5
SUMMER WIND (Ire) 10-7 P Holley, *led till hdd 3 out, sn btn.*....................(5 to 1 op 4 to 1 tchd 7 to 1) 6

1243³ WAMDHA (Ire) 10-7 A S Smith, *slwly away, hdwy frm 5th, wknd appr 2 out.....* (20 to 1 op 14 to 1 tchd 25 to 1) 7
1271 GLOWING PATH 11-5 W McFarland, *mid-div, beh frm 5th.*
.................(25 to 1 op 16 to 1) 8
WOLLBOLL 10-12 Richard Guest, *al beh, lost tch 5th.*
.................(50 to 1 op 33 to 1) 9
ECU DE FRANCE (Ire) 10-12 M Perrett, *prmnt till hit 5th, sn beh.*....................(20 to 1 op 16 to 1) 10
830⁹ AMAZING AIR (USA) 10-12 A McCabe, *al beh, tld off.*
.................(33 to 1 op 20 to 1 tchd 40 to 1) 11
KISMETIM 10-12 B Powell, *al beh, tld off.*
.................(14 to 1 op 8 to 1 tchd 16 to 1) 12
WARSPITE 10-12 D Skyrme, *chsd ldrs to 5th, wknd rpdly, pld up bef nxt.*...................(50 to 1 op 33 to 1) pu
BARNIEMEBOY 10-12 W Elderfield, *beh whn blun second, tld off frm 4th, pld up bef 2 out.* (50 to 1 op 33 to 1) pu
Dist: 5l, 3l, 3½l, 6l, 12l, 3l, 10l, 3l, 2l, 12l. 3m 57.30s. a 12.30s (14 Ran).
SR: 9/4/1/-/-/-/   (A D Spence), R Akehurst

1511 Woodside Novices' Handicap Chase (4-y-o and up) £2,407 2m 5f..... (1:20)

960² EMERALD STORM [83] 6-10-9 M A FitzGerald, *hld up in tch, hdwy 7th, led 3 out, drvn out r-in.*
.................(9 to 2 op 7 to 2 tchd 5 to 1) 1
1343³ WELL BRIEFED [91] 6-11-3 B Powell, *al prmnt, led 11th till hdd 3 out, ev ch till no imprsn und pres r-in.*
.................(7 to 2 fav op 4 to 1 tchd 9 to 2) 2
CHRISTMAS GORSE [78] 7-10-4⁴ J Frost, *beh, styd on frm 4 out, nvr nr to chal.*...........(25 to 1 op 16 to 1) 3
1426⁹ SILENT CHANT [81] (v) 9-10-7⁷ G McCourt, *mid-div, hdwy appr 4 out, one pace nxt.*
.................(25 to 1 op 20 to 1 tchd 14 to 1) 4
1086² RINANNA BAY [76] 6-10-2 S Earle, *hld up in rear, gd hdwy appr 4 out, wknd nxt.*
.................(12 to 1 op 10 to 1 tchd 14 to 1) 5
1214² SQUEEZE PLAY [86] 8-10-5 (7*) D Fortt, *trkd ldrs, mstk 3rd, outpcd 11th, kpt on one pace frm 3 out.*
.................(11 to 2 op 5 to 1 tchd 13 to 2) 6
1311² BOLL WEEVIL [98] 7-11-10 J Osborne, *prmnt till rdn and wknd appr 3 out.*.................(11 to 2 op 9 to 2) 7
1405 SACROSANCT [100] 9-11-12 N Williamson, *led till mstk and hdd 6th, led 9th to 11th, wkng whn jmpd badly lft 2 out.*....................(7 to 1 tchd 8 to 1) 8
1248⁵ TRAIN ROBBER [74] 8-10-0 M Hourigan, *mid-div, lost tch 11th.*...............(10 to 1 op 14 to 1 tchd 16 to 1) 9
1194 DOROBO (NZ) [81] 5-10-7 M Perrett, *al beh.*
.................(20 to 1 op 14 to 1) 10
1342⁴ SUNSET AGAIN [80] 8-10-6 Richard Guest, *mstk 7th, al beh.*....................(33 to 1) 11
1313³ WALLISTRANO [85] 6-10-6 (5*) Mr T Byrne, *beh, tld off.*....................(14 to 1) 12
1258⁴ L'ENCHERE [74] 8-9-7 (7*) G Crone, *in tch to 7th, sn beh.*....................(66 to 1 op 50 to 1) 13
SALVAGER [76] 9-10-2² R Rowell, *trkd ldr, led and mstk 6th, hdd 9th, wkng whn blun 11th, tld off when pld up bef 4 out.*....................(66 to 1) pu
1058⁵ KING'S RARITY [74] 7-10-0 D Bridgwater, *beh whn pld up aftr 6th.*...............(20 to 1 op 16 to 1 tchd 25 to 1) pu
Dist: 2l, 6l, 5l, 2½l, 1l, 1½l, 10l, 8l, 6l, 3½l. 5m 24.90s. a 13.90s (15 Ran).
SR: 16/22/3/1/-/2/12/4/-/   (Ed McGrath), N J Henderson

1512 Eton Handicap Chase (0-125 5-y-o and up) £3,785 3m................ (1:50)

1394* TOUCHING STAR [102] 8-10-6 (7ex) M Hourigan, *hld up, gd hdwy frm 5 out, led 2 out, pushed clr.*
.................(6 to 1 op 9 to 2 tchd 13 to 2) 1
1197³ TIPP MARINER [98] 8-10-2¹ G Upton, *al prmnt, led and mstk 12th, hdd 2 out, one pace aftr......*(100 to 30 jt-fav op 9 to 2 tchd 5 to 1 and 3 to 1) 2
1326* SANDYBRAES [121] 8-11-4 (7*) M G Hogan, *hld up, mstk 9th, steady hdwy frm nxt, rdn and one pace from 3 out.*....................(7 to 2 op 2 to 1) 3
1242* ARD T'MATCH [98] (v) 8-10-2² Gary Lyons, *mstks early, sn prmnt, dsptd ld 4 out, wknd aftr nxt.*
.................(14 to 1 op 12 to 1 tchd 16 to 1) 4
1138³ COURT RAPIER [97] 11-9-9¹ (7*) P Carey, *led to 5th, led 9th to 12th, lost tch 4 out.............*(16 to 1 op 14 to 1) 5
1273⁴ SADDLER'S CHOICE [101] 8-10-5 M A FitzGerald, *prmnt, led 5th to 9th, sn pushed alng, wknd appr 4 out.*
.................(12 to 1 op 14 to 1) 6
1388² LITTLE GENERAL [99] 10-10-3³ H Davies, *prmnt till lost tch appr 5 out.*....................(8 to 1 op 12 to 1) 7
1191⁴ UNEX-PLAINED [99] 8-9-7 (7*) C Wright, *tld off frm 5th, made some late hdwy.*....................(33 to 1) 8
1050² STUNNING STUFF [124] 8-12-0 N Williamson, *hld up in tch, f 5 out.*.................(100 to 30 jt-fav op 3 to 1 tchd 5 to 2 and 7 to 2) f
Dist: 3l, 10l, 1l, 12l, 3l, 3l, 4l. 6m 11.20s. a 16.20s (9 Ran).
SR: -/-/6/-/-/-/   (P J Hobbs), P J Hobbs

1513 Stoy Hayward Recovery Handicap Hurdle (0-135 4-y-o and up) £2,637 2m .... (2:20)

1104* ATHAR (Ire) [108] 4-10-3 L Harvey, *hld up in rear, hdwy appr 3 out, led and hit last, edgd lft r-in, drvn out, fnshd 1st, plcd second*.............. (4 to 1 tchd 9 to 2) 1D
HERE HE COMES [130] 7-11-11 G McCourt, *hld up, hdwy 4th, led 2 out, wndrd and hdd last, crrd lft, swtchd rght, one pace, fnshd second, plcd 1st.*
................................(7 to 2 op 3 to 1 tchd 4 to 1) 1
PROPAGANDA [112] 5-10-7 M A FitzGerald, *al prmnt, rdn and no hdwy frm 2 out.* (6 to 1 op 5 to 1 tchd 13 to 2) 3
1122* STATAJACK (Ire) [116] (bl) 5-10-11 P Holley, *mstk 3rd, made most till hdd 2 out, sn wknd.*
................................(3 to 1 fav op 9 to 4 tchd 100 to 30) 4
1395² SPRING TO GLORY [105] 6-9-9 (5*) A Procter, *trkd ldr, dsptd ld 4th, wknd appr 2 out* ..... (8 to 1 op 6 to 1) 5
KETTI [128] 8-11-2 (7*) Mr G Hogan, *chsd ldrs, beh frm 4th.*
................................(16 to 1 op 14 to 1 tchd 20 to 1) 6
861 MY SENOR [105] 4-10-0 M Perrett, *beh frm 3rd.*
................................(33 to 1 op 25 to 1 tchd 40 to 1) 7
RIVER ISLAND (USA) [115] 5-10-10 T Grantham, *hld up, hdwy 4th, hrd rdn 3 out, wknd nxt.*
................................(11 to 2 op 5 to 1 tchd 6 to 1) 8
1190 MARIOLINO [106] 6-10-11 S Hodgson, *al beh.*
................................(25 to 1 op 20 to 1 tchd 33 to 1) 9
Dist: 1½l, 3½l, 4l, 1l, 25l, ½l, 2½l. 3m 56.60s. a 11.60s (9 Ran).
SR: 7/27/5/5/-/-/   (E Harrington), R Akehurst

1514 Dorney Handicap Chase (0-125 5-y-o and up) £3,622 2m............ (2:50)

1389⁴ DRIVING FORCE [108] (bl) 7-10-13 G McCourt, *lft in ld second, made rst, clr whn mstk 3 out, kpt up to work aftr*....................(3 to 1 op 7 to 2 tchd 4 to 1) 1
1168 DARE SAY [100] 10-10-5 S Earle, *hld up, hdwy 5 out, chsd wnr frm nxt.*....................(10 to 1 op 6 to 1) 2
1409⁴ ALAN BALL [104] 7-10-9 H Davies, *rstrained in rear, some hdwy appr 4 out, one pace.*
................................(5 to 1 op 6 to 1 tchd 7 to 1 and 9 to 2) 3
1105 SETTER COUNTRY [123] 9-12-0 W Irvine, *mstk 6th, chsd wnr sixth to 4 out, sn btn*............(4 to 1 op 9 to 4) 4
1342² ALWAYS REMEMBER [95] 6-10-0 M Hourigan, *led till hit second, stumbled on landing, uns rdr.*
................................(2 to 1 fav op 5 to 2 tchd 7 to 4) ur
1195⁴ ACRE HILL [110] 9-11-1 M A FitzGerald, *chsd wnr second till hit 6th, beh frm nxt, tld off whn pld up bef 2 out.*
................................(10 to 1 op 5 to 1) pu
Dist: 10l, 1l, 3l. 4m 7.00s. a 11.00s (6 Ran).
SR: 31/13/16/32/-/-/   (B J Reid), Mrs M McCourt

1515 Oakley Green Novices' Hurdle (Div II) (4-y-o and up) £1,851 2m...... (3:20)

SPIRIT IN THE NITE (Ire) 4-11-0 D Murphy, *chsd ldrs, hdwy to ld appr 2 out, all out*..............(9 to 1 op 6 to 1) 1
SYLVAN SABRE (Ire) 4-11-0 J Osborne, *hld up, hdwy appr 3 out, ev ch frm nxt, no imprsn cl hme.*
................................(14 to 1 op 12 to 1) 2
DAWN FLIGHT 4-11-0 E Murphy, *hld up in tch, led 5th til appr 2 out, wknd*....(10 to 1 op 6 to 1 tchd 11 to 1) 3
BITTER ALOE 4-11-0 M Perrett, *beh, rdn hfwy, hdwy appr 3 out, styd on frm nxt.*
................................(12 to 1 op 8 to 1 tchd 14 to 1) 4
DUCKEY FUZZ 5-11-0 D Bridgwater, *wl in rear till gd hdwy appr 3 out, wknd aftr nxt.*
................................(5 to 1 op 3 to 1 tchd 6 to 1) 5
1390⁴ MILZIG (USA) (bl) 4-11-0 J Frost, *led to 5th, prmnt till wknd appr 2 out.*....................(4 to 1 tchd 6 to 1) 6
DURSHAN (USA) 4-11-0 S Smith Eccles, *chsd ldrs till wknd appr 3 out, tld off.*
................................(2 to 1 fav op 9 to 4 tchd 7 to 2) 7
SPEAKER'S HOUSE (USA) 4-11-0 B Powell, *trkd ldr to 5th, wknd bef nxt, tld off.* (10 to 1 op 6 to 1 tchd 14 to 1) 8
BALLYHAYS (Ire) 4-11-0 G McCourt, *mstk 3rd, sn beh, tld off.*.................................(12 to 1 op 6 to 1) 9
772⁵ SNICKERSNEE 5-11-0 S Hodgson, *prmnt to 4th, sn beh, tld off.*....................(33 to 1 op 25 to 1) 10
1390 AUTUMN LEAF 5-10-9 R Rowell, *al in rear, tld off.*
................................(33 to 1) 11
DIME BAG 4-10-9 N Williamson, *f 1st.*
................................(8 to 1 op 6 to 1 tchd 14 to 1) f
1141 TINAS LASS 4-10-9 D Morris, *beh till f 5th*.......(33 to 1) f
885⁴ ANDARE 4-11-0 S Earle, *al beh, tld off whn pld up bef 3 out.*................................(33 to 1) pu
Dist: ½l, 10l, 5l, 3l, ¾l, dist, 10l, 20l. 4m 0.50s. a 15.50s (14 Ran).
                                  (Mrs Timothy Pilkington), J T Gifford

EXETER (good)
Friday December 3rd
Going Correction: PLUS 0.70 sec. per fur.

1516 Woolea Old For New Conditional Jockeys' Novices' Handicap Hurdle (4-y-o and up) £1,822 2¼m......(12:50)

JUMP START [85] 6-11-4 A Dicken, *hld up, steady hdwy frm 3rd, led 2 out, hit last, rdn out.*
................................(6 to 1 op 1 tchd 13 to 2) 1

1303* HANDY LASS [86] 4-11-5 D Matthews, *al prmnt, rdn appr 2 out, kpt on one pace.*
................................(13 to 8 fav op 7 to 4 tchd 2 to 1) 2
1193⁵ UP ALL NIGHT [67] 4-9-11 (3*) G Crone, *beh till hdwy aftr 3 out, styd on, nvr nrr*................(10 to 1 op 6 to 1) 3
982³ STYLE AND CLASS [95] 4-11-11 (3*) L Dace, *led 3 out, rdn and one pace aftr.* (7 to 2 op 11 to 4 tchd 9 to 4) 4
1415⁶ MANOR MAN [82] 6-10-9 (6*) T Murphy, *sn in tch, wknd frm 3rd*.....(16 to 1 op 10 to 1 tchd 20 to 1) 5
1303⁷ PRINCE VALMY (Fr) [67] 8-9-11 (3*) L Reynolds, *chsd ldrs till wknd 5th.*........(16 to 1 op 10 to 1 tchd 20 to 1) 6
1252 MISS SOUTER [75] 4-10-5 (3*) R Darke, *chsd ldr to 3rd, sn rear.*....................................(16 to 1 op 10 to 1) 7
1272⁷ REALLY NEAT [67] 7-9-8 (6*) J Fordham, *beh whn blun and uns rdr 3rd.*.................(33 to 1 op 20 to 1) ur
CORPUS [67] 4-9-11 (3*) T Thompson, *sddld slpd, ran out second.*............(33 to 1 op 16 to 1 tchd 50 to 1) ro
1303 MR ZIEGFELD (USA) [72] (bl) 4-10-5 D Salter, *prmnt till wknd 5th, tld off whn pld up bef 2 out.*
................................(25 to 1 op 16 to 1 tchd 33 to 1) pu
1303 SHARPSIDE [67] 6-10-0 Guy Lewis, *prmnt, rdn 4th, sn beh, tld off whn pld up bef last.*
................................(7 to 2 op 8 to 1 tchd 3 to 1) pu
Dist: 4l, 5l, 1l, 25l, 5l, hd. 4m 19.90s. a 19.90s (11 Ran).
SR: 17/14/-/17/-/-/   (Stewart Pike), S Pike

1517 Woolea Part Exchange Juvenile Hurdle (3-y-o) £1,910 2¼m......... (1:20)

1408* MY BALLYBOY 11-5 N Mann, *trkd ldrs, led 5th, rdn whn tired appr last, rallied r-in.*
................................(6 to 5 on op 5 to 4 on tchd 6 to 4 on and Evens) 1
1271³ BUGLET 11-0 R Dunwoody, *trkd ldr, hrd rdn to chal last, ev ch till no extr cl hme*...........(7 to 4 op 9 to 4) 2
YOUNG TESS 10-7 S Burrough, *hld up rear, hdwy to go 3rd appr 2 out, kpt on one pace*.....(10 to 1 op 6 to 1) 3
MALWOOD CASTLE (Ire) 10-12 B Powell, *outpcd early, styd on frm 2 out.*................(33 to 1 op 12 to 1) 4
793⁷ IRISH DOMINION 10-5 (7*) Guy Lewis, *pld hrd, outpcd 4th.*
................................(50 to 1 op 20 to 1) 5
830 RAGAZZO (Ire) (bl) 10-12 Richard Guest, *chsd ldrs till wknd 3 out, wl beh whn hit last...* (20 to 1 op 10 to 1) 6
1271⁵ ACROSS THE BOW (USA) 10-12 C Maude, *led to 5th, wknd quickly.*..........................(14 to 1 tchd 33 to 1) 7
Dist: Nk, 10l, 6l, 20l, 2½l, 8l. 4m 24.30s. a 24.30s (7 Ran).
                                              (A Bailey), A Bailey

1518 Woolea Retail Of Street & Wells Novices' Chase (5-y-o and up) £4,719 2¼m
................................(1:50)

1012³ BIG BEAT (USA) 5-11-0 P Holley, *made all, jmpd wl, clr 6th, unchlgd.*.............(5 to 4 fav op 11 to 8) 1
1298³ CRYSTAL BEAR (NZ) 8-11-2 B Powell, *hld up, not fluent, wnt second 8th, no ch whn wnr.*
................................(6 to 1 op 4 to 1 tchd 7 to 1) 2
BUSH HILL 8-11-2 N Mann, *chsd ldrs, outpcd frm 4th, tld off.*................(12 to 1 tchd 20 to 1) 3
1168⁵ TURKISH STAR 8-10-11 C Maude, *outpcd, beh whn blun and uns rdr 4th....*(12 to 1 op 14 to 1 tchd 20 to 1) ur
892* IN THE NAVY 7-11-7 R Dunwoody, *pckd 1st, trkd wnr, jmpd slwly 7th, wknd rpdly, tld off whn pld up bef 4 out.*..............................(5 to 4 op Evens) pu
Dist: Dist, dist. 4m 26.80s. a 15.80s (5 Ran).
SR: 54/-/   (Ray Richards), D R C Elsworth

1519 Woolea Retail Of Street & Wells Selling Hurdle (4,5,6-y-o) £1,792 2¼m
................................(2:20)

795³ CHICKABIDDY 5-10-9 G Upton, *hld up, hdwy appr 3 out, led 2 out, pushed clr.* (5 to 1 fav op 5 to 2 tchd 7 to 4) 1
1303⁵ OH SO HANDY 5-10-7 (7*) G Crone, *hld up rear, hdwy 3 out, ran on, nvr nrr*.............(12 to 1 op 8 to 1) 2
932³ LEGAL WIN (USA) 5-11-0 (7*) Mr G Shenkin, *mid-div, styd on aftr 3 out, nvr nrr.*...........(16 to 1 op 8 to 1) 3
1404 POLK (Fr) 4-11-0 (7*) L Reynolds, *led 1st, rdn and hdd 2 out, one pace aftr*...........(16 to 1 op 14 to 1) 4
1280⁹ NORTHERN OPTIMIST 5-10-9 (7*) Mr J L Llewellyn, *prmnt till wknd quickly appr 2 out.*
................................(11 to 2 op 4 to 1 tchd 6 to 1) 5
1252⁸ PRUDENT PEGGY 6-10-9 B Powell, *led to 1st, in tch till wknd 3 out.*............(7 to 1 op 5 to 1 tchd 8 to 1) 6
1259⁴ SLICK CHERRY 6-11-2 Richard Guest, *mid-div, no hdwy frm 3 out.*.............(12 to 1 op 8 to 1 tchd 14 to 1) 7
1272⁸ SPIRIT LEVEL 5-10-10⁸ (7*) Mr R Payne, *al rear.*
................................(25 to 1 op 20 to 1 tchd 33 to 1) 8
1189 TARMON (Ire) (bl) 5-11-7 W Irvine, *in tch to 3rd, sn beh, tld off.*....................(33 to 1 op 14 to 1) 9
MARY'S MUSIC 5-10-9 C Maude, *in tch till wknd appr 5th, tld off*...........(16 to 1 op 14 to 1 tchd 20 to 1) 10
BUCK COMTESS (USA) 4-10-9 R Dunwoody, *tld off second*.................(33 to 1 op 16 to 1 tchd 12 to 1) 11
859⁷ MILDRED SOPHIA 6-10-9 (7*) Miss S Mitchell, *prmnt, chsd ldr second till wknd 3 out, no ch whn f nxt.*
................................(16 to 1 op 25 to 1 tchd 33 to 1) f

QUALITAIR IDOL 4-10-9 S Burrough, *beh whn f 3rd.*
.... (25 to 1 op 12 to 1 tchd 33 to 1) f
VITAL TYCOON 5-10-2 (7*) J Neaves, *mid-div, effrt 4th, sn
wknd, pld up bef 2 out* .... (33 to 1 op 20 to 1) pu
Dist: 6l, 8l, 1½l, 7l, 5l, 2l, 20l, 2l, dist. 4m 22.40s. a 22.40s (14 Ran).

(G F Edwards), G F Edwards

1520 Woolea Retail Of Street & Wells Handicap Chase (0-135 5-y-o and up) £5,127 2m 7f 110yds. .... (2:50)

1171 LAKE TEEREEN [121] 8-11-6 R Dunwoody, *trkd ldr, led 7th
to tenth, styd prmnt, rdn to ld last, all out.*
.... (9 to 4 tchd 9 to 1) 1
1396 GHOFAR [125] (bl) 10-11-10 P Holley, *trkd ldrs, wnt second
5 out, led nxt, rdn and hdd last, edgd rght and one pace
r-in* .... (14 to 1 op 12 to 1 tchd 20 to 1) 2
1274² JAILBREAKER [111] 6-10-5 (5*) D Salter, *al prmnt, trkd ldr
7th, led tenth, pckd and hdd 4 out, sn btn.*
.... (9 to 2 op 7 to 2) 3
956 MASTER GLEASON [101] 10-10-0 M Foster, *beh, hdwy
tenth, rdn 13th, no headway 4 out.* (16 to 1 op 12 to 1) 4
JUST SO [124] (bl) 10-11-9 S Burrough, *beh, plugged on
one pace frm 4 out, nvr dngrs* ..... (20 to 1 op 16 to 1) 5
1340² CLEVER SHEPHERD [116] 8-10-8 (7*) Guy Lewis, *hld up,
making hdwy whn hit tenth, mstks, btn 5 out.*
.... (11 to 10 fav 11 to 10 on tchd 6 to 5) 6
RAFIKI [105] 8-10-4 Richard Guest, *f 6th.*
.... (10 to 1 op 8 to 1) f
LOCAL WHISPER [119] 9-11-4 B Powell, *led, hit 3rd, hdd
7th, wknd 9th, pld up bef 11th.* .... (14 to 1 op 12 to 1) pu
Dist: ¾l, 15l, 3l, 5l, 12l. 5m 59.30s. a 24.30s (8 Ran).
SR: 13/16/-/-/-/ (Mrs A T Grantham), R Rowe

1521 Woolea Retail Of Street & Wells Handicap Hurdle (0-125 4-y-o and up) £2,721 2¼m. .... (3:20)

ABSALOM'S LADY [122] 5-12-0 P Holley, *hld up, hdwy
appr 3rd, wnt second approaching 2 out, led and lft clr
last.* ....(3 to 1 jt-fav tchd 5 to 1) 1
1443⁴ ISLAND JEWEL [94] 5-10-0 W Irvine, *beh and feeling pace
5th, hdwy and pres aftr nxt, styd on to go second r-in.*
....(14 to 1 op 10 to 1) 2
1240* FRONT STREET [96] 6-10-2² G Upton, *hld up in rear, gd
hdwy frm 5th, ev ch 2 out till wknd r-in.* .....(3 to 1 jt-
fav op 9 to 4 tchd 100 to 30) 3
1051* NORTHERN SADDLER [100] 6-10-6 M Richards, *in tch, rdn
appr 2 out, kpt on one pace.* .... (8 to 1 op 5 to 1) 4
FAUX PAVILLON [97] 9-10-3³ Richard Guest, *trkd ldrs, wnt
second 3 out, rdn and wknd bef nxt.*
.... (7 to 1 op 14 to 1 tchd 10 to 1) 5
1274⁷ FREEMANTLE [94] 8-10-0 B Powell, *beh, some late hdwy.*
.... (12 to 1 op 14 to 1 tchd 16 to 1) 6
1355⁴ ALREEF [101] 7-10-0 (7*) D Meade, *prmnt, hrd rdn appr 2
out, sn btn.* ....(12 to 1 op 8 to 1 tchd 14 to 1) 7
1274 TRUST DEED (USA) [94] 5-9-7 (7*) Guy Lewis, *prmnt till
wknd 3 out.* ....(14 to 1 tchd 12 to 1) 8
1395⁴ SANDRO [94] 4-10-0 N Mann, *prmnt till wknd 5th.*
.... (25 to 1 op 12 to 1) 9
1190⁵ EMERALD MOON [96] 6-10-2² S Burrough, *beh, lost tch
5th.* ....(16 to 1 op 12 to 1) 10
1087² DAMIER BLANC (Fr) [95] (bl) 4-10-1 R Dunwoody, *hld up in
tch, hdwy aftr second, led appr 3 out, und pres and jst
hdd whn f last* ....(11 to 2 op 4 to 1 tchd 9 to 2) f
1272 COLONEL GAY [94] 8-9-13⁶ (7*) Mr Richard White, *in tch to
3rd, pld up bef 5th.* ....(50 to 1 op 25 to 1) pu
1492 HAVE A PARTY [95] 6-10-1 C Maude, *led till appr 3 out,
wknd rpdly, tld off whn pld up bef last.*
.... (33 to 1 op 25 to 1) pu
Dist: 5l, hd, 4l, 5l, ¾l, 4l, 15l, 12l, 8l. 4m 16.20s. a 16.20s (13 Ran).
SR: 64/31/33/33/25/21/24/2/-/ (Whitcombe Manor Racing Stables Limited),
D R C Elsworth

HEREFORD (good to soft)
Friday December 3rd
Going Correction: PLUS 0.80 sec. per fur. (races 1,3,-5,7), PLUS 0.50 (2,4,6)

1522 Tupsley Juvenile Claiming Hurdle (3-y-o) £1,938 2m 1f. .... (12:40)

1416* DON'T FORGET MARIE (Ire) 9-13 (5*) A Procter, *hld up,
hdwy to track ldrs aftr 4th, ev ch 3 out, led after nxt,
hit last, drvn out.*
.... (13 to 8 fav op 2 to 1 tchd 9 to 4 and 6 to 4) 1
260 SABEEL 9-13 (5*) T Jenks, *hdwy 4th, led four out till hdd
aftr 2 out, rallied appr last, one pace r-in.* ..... (33 to 1) 2
1253² DOUALAGO (Fr) 10-13 J Lower, *hld up, wnt 3rd 5th, chsd
ldr, sn rdn and found nothing, no imprsn aftr 3 out.*
...........................(2 to 1 op 5 to 4 tchd 9 to 4) 3
1253⁶ CREAGMHOR 10-10 (3*) R Davis, *chsd ldg grp frm 5th,
rdn alng aftr nxt, wknd aftr 3 out.*
.... (16 to 1 tchd 20 to 1) 4

1350 BOLD STAR 10-10 (3*) S Wynne, *al chasing ldrs, hit 3rd,
ev ch 4 out, wknd aftr nxt.*
................................(33 to 1 op 20 to 1 tchd 40 to 1) 5
MANON LESCAUT 10-12 W McFarland, *beh whn mstk 4th,
lost tch aftr 3 out.* ....(9 to 2 op 5 to 1) 6
SAXON MAGIC 10-4 R Greene, *beh 3rd, styd on aftr 3 out,
nvr dngrs.* ....(33 to 1 op 25 to 1) 7
1271⁸ SHE KNEW THE RULES (Ire) 10-4 Lorna Vincent, *beh frm
3rd, nvr rchd ldrs.* ....(33 to 1 op 20 to 1) 8
1244 NATASHA NORTH 10-4 P Harley, *chsd ldrs till wknd
quickly aftr 5th* ....(33 to 1 op 25 to 1) 9
1049 KENNINGTON PROTON (bl) 10-6 Gary Lyons, *led till hdd
and mstk 6th, rdn and wknd rpdly, tld off whn pld up
bef last.* ....(33 to 1 op 25 to 1) pu
SCOTTISH TEMPTRESS 10-0 D Bridgwater, *lost tch aftr
4th, sn tld off, tld off whn pld up bef 3 out.* ...(33 to 1) pu
ROBRO 10-13 T Wall, *lost tch aftr 3rd, tld off whn pld up
after 5th.* ....(33 to 1) pu
1257⁷ DAJAM 10-0 L Harvey, *chsd ldrs, reminder aftr 4th, lost
tch after nxt, tld off whn pld up bef 3 out.* ....(33 to 1) pu
1049 JUST FOR A LARK 10-5⁵ Mr S Blackwell, *tld off aftr 4th,
pld up bef 3 out.* ....(33 to 1 op 20 to 1) pu
Dist: 4l, 8l, 2l, 5l, 20l, 4l, 1½l, 1½l. 4m 5.40s. a 19.40s (14 Ran).
SR: 18/14/15/13/8/-/ (Gordon Mytton), A Bailey

1523 Bacton Handicap Chase (0-135 5-y-o and up) £2,878 2m 3f. .... (1:10)

1302* MAN OF MYSTERY [99] 7-10-0 D Bridgwater, *made all, rdn
and styd on wl frm 2 out* ....(9 to 4 op 7 to 4) 1
1171⁸ MONUMENTAL LAD [123] 10-11-10 L Harvey, *wnt second
6th, ev ch 4 out, rdn and no imprsn aftr 2 out.*
.... (9 to 1 op 7 to 1 tchd 10 to 1) 2
1300² PITHY [103] 11-10-1 (3*) R Davis, *cld up 6th, chsd ldr, rdn
and no imprsn frm 3 out.* ....(9 to 1 op 12 to 1) 3
1326⁶ NEW HALEN [107] 12-10-8 R Bellamy, *chsd ldr till lost pl
9th, rallied and ev ch 4 out, 3rd whn mstk 2 out, sn one
pace.* ....(16 to 1 op 12 to 1) 4
1343 GREENHILL RAFFLES [111] 7-10-12 S Earle, *trkd ldr, hrd
rdn aftr 5 out, wknd quickly after nxt, tld off 3 out.*
.... (Evens fav tchd 6 to 5 and 11 to 10 on) 5
Dist: 4l, 2l, 1½l, 25l. 4m 48.90s. a 18.90s (5 Ran).
(PCJF Bloodstock), N A Twiston-Davies

1524 Ballingham Novices' Hurdle (4-y-o and up) £1,850 3¼m. .... (1:40)

934⁶ TEXAN BABY (Bel) 4-11-2 D Bridgwater, *made all, hrd rdn
aftr 3 out, styd on strly whn chlgd 2 out, all out.*
.... (4 to 1 op 5 to 2 tchd 9 to 2) 1
1421* GRAY'S ELLERGY 7-10-6 (5*) Mrs P Nash, *trkd ldr, jnd
wnr 2 out, rdn and kpt on aftr last, not quicken nr
finish.* ....(5 to 2 fav op 3 to 1 tchd 7 to 2) 2
1371* NEEDWOOD POPPY 5-11-3 L Harvey, *chsd ldrs, pushed
alng and outpcd 5 out, styd on to take 3rd pl appr last,
not trble last 2.* ....(4 to 1 op 5 to 2) 3
1108³ VERY LITTLE (Ire) 5-9-12 (7*) Mr P Henley, *pushed alng frm
7th, outpcd 5 out, styd on aftr 2 out, no imprsn.*
.... (9 to 1 op 7 to 1 tchd 10 to 1) 4
1277 LUCKY DAWN (Ire) 4-10-0 V Slattery, *hld up, wnt 3rd 7th,
ev ch 4 out, rdn and wknd aftr 3 out.*
.... (25 to 1 tchd 33 to 1) 5
NODDYS EXPRESS 8-10-10 W Marston, *hld up, chsd ldrs
frm 7th till rdn and wknd aftr 5 out, tld off.*.. (33 to 1) 6
WARFIELD 6-10-10 R Greene, *hld up, hdwy 7th, chsd ldr
seventh and wkng whn f 4 out.*
................................(4 to 1 op 7 to 2 tchd 9 to 2) ur
PRINCE OF BARODA 9-10-10 Mr M Jackson, *chsd ldr till
wknd quickly aftr 8th, tld off whn pld up bef 4 out.*
.... (150 to 1 op 50 to 1) pu
1151 RAHEEN ROVER 9-10-10 W McFarland, *chsd ldr till wknd
7th, tld off whn pld up bef 5 out.* .... (33 to 1) pu
NESSELNITE 7-10-5 S Earle, *beh frm 4th, tld off whn pld
up bef 5 out.*............................(33 to 1 op 20 to 1) pu
1169⁵ WANDERLINE 6-10-10 Peter Caldwell, *al beh, lost tch aftr
7th, tld off whn pld up bef 5 out...* (50 to 1 op 33 to 1) pu
1196⁹ KATIEM'LU 7-9-12 (7*) Mr B Pollock, *lost pl aftr 5th, beh
frm 7th, tld off whn pld up bef 5 out.*
.... (100 to 1 op 50 to 1) pu
CRUISER TOO 6-10-10 R Bellamy, *lost tch 7th, tld off whn
pld up bef 5 out.* ....(100 to 1 op 50 to 1) pu
Dist: ¾l, 5l, 20l, ¾l, dist. 6m 31.80s. a 31.80s (13 Ran).
(John McKenna), N A Twiston-Davies

1525 Golden Valley Inns Novices' Chase (5-y-o and up) £2,554 2m. .... (2:10)

1348⁵ KIBREET 6-11-0 S Earle, *trkd ldrs, led 3 out, drw clr aftr
nxt, styd on wl...* (5 to 4 fav op 6 to 4 tchd 11 to 10) 1
1324⁴ GENEROUS SCOT 9-11-0 R Bellamy, *led till hdd 6th, mstk
cl up, ev ch 3 out, second and btn whn blun last.*
......................(3 to 1 op 5 to 2 tchd 11 to 4) 2
1272⁴ FANATICAL (USA) (bl) 7-11-0 L Harvey, *hld up, hdwy whn
mstk 7th, styd on frm 4 out, 3rd and btn when mistake
last.* ....(6 to 1 op 5 to 1) 3

207

1413⁴ MAGGOTS GREEN 6-10-4 (5*) R Farrant, *hld up in mid-div, wnt 3rd aftr 4 out, mstks last 3, styd on one pace.*
....(33 to 1 tchd 40 to 1)   4
703⁷ PECCAVI 9-10-8¹ (7*) Mr C Campbell, *al prmnt, led 7th to 3 out, wknd nxt.*...........................(25 to 1 op 16 to 1)   5
SPINNING STEEL 6-11-0 S Hodgson, *hld up and beh, styd on one pace frm 4 out.*..........(25 to 1 op 16 to 1)   6
APRIL'S MODEL LADY 7-10-9 D Bridgwater, *al rear, no ch aftr 6th.*................(7 to 1 op 6 to 1 tchd 8 to 1)   7
441⁴ ALICE SMITH 6-10-2 (7*) Mr L Jefford, *rear whn blun and uns rdr second.*...................(14 to 1 op 12 to 1)   ur
1470 PALM SWIFT 7-10-9 W Marston, *pld hrd, prmnt, led 6th, hdd nxt, sn rdn and wknd quickly aftr 5 out, tld off whn pulled up bef 2 out.*.....................(50 to 1 op 33 to 1)   pu
EIGHTY EIGHT 8-11-0 V Slattery, *mstks, lost tch aftr 4th, tld off whn pld up bef 2 out.* ......(50 to 1 op 33 to 1)   pu
Dist: 7l, 2l, 8l, 15l, 10l, 5l. 4m 3.10s. a 14.10s (10 Ran).
SR: 25/18/16/3/-/-/   (Derek Simester), R H Alner

1526 Pencoed Novices' Selling Hurdle (4,5,6-y-o) £1,480 2m 1f........(2:40)

PROJECT'S MATE 6-10-7 (7*) P McLoughlin, *chsd ldrs, led appr 3 out, blun last, all out.*........(33 to 1)   1
1188⁴ CHANDIGARH 5-11-0 L Harvey, *slwly away, pld hrd, hld up, hdwy to track ldrs aftr 5th, wnt second after 3 out, rdn and no imprsn.*.................(9 to 2 op 7 to 2)   2
1192⁷ FORGETFUL 4-10-9 W Knox, *pld hrd, al prmnt, ev ch 3 out, wknd rdn and no imprsn.*.......(5 to 1 op 7 to 1)   3
1315³ TESEKKUREDERIM 6-11-0 D Bridgwater, *chsd ldrs, ev ch 3 out, rdn, eased whn btn aftr 2 out.* ....(4 to 1 jt-fav op 3 to 1 tchd 9 to 2)   4
1245 LUCKY BLUE (bl) 6-11-0 S Earle, *chsd ldrs, ev ch 3 out, rdn and wknd nxt.* (4 to 1 jt-fav op 7 to 2 tchd 9 to 2)   5
1167 RED NEST 5-10-9 T Wall, *hld up, hdwy to track ldrs aftr 5th, wknd after 4 out.*....................(33 to 1)   6
HITCHIN A RIDE 6-11-0 M Ahern, *prmnt till rdn and wknd quickly aftr 4 out.*......................(33 to 1)   7
704⁷ BLUE LYZANDER 4-10-9 V Slattery, *mid-div, hrd rdn aftr 5th, sn wknd.*......................(20 to 1 tchd 25 to 1)   8
1153 GARTH 5-11-0 W Marston, *rdn and hdwy aftr 4th, sn wknd.*.....................................(33 to 1)   9
775⁶ FORGED PUNT 6-11-0 S Hodgson, *tld off aftr 3rd.*
....(33 to 1 op 20 to 1)   10
WALKING SAINT 6-10-9 R Bellamy, *drpd rear aftr 3rd, sn tld off, pld up bef 3 out.*..........(25 to 1 op 20 to 1)   pu
1211² BOXING MATCH 6-11-3 (3*) R Davis, *drpd rear aftr 4th, sn beh, tld off whn pld up bef 3 out.*.....(7 to 1 op 7 to 2)   pu
1192⁶ GILBERT (Ire) 5-11-6 Lorna Vincent, *led to 5th, sn rdn, wknd quickly, tld off whn pld up bef 2 out.*
....(6 to 1 tchd 13 to 2)   pu
1110 CAMPDEN AGAIN 6-10-6 (3*) D Meredith, *prmnt till lost pl and wknd rpdly aftr 5th, tld off whn pld up bef 3 out.*
....(25 to 1 op 20 to 1)   pu
Dist: 3l, 8l, 15l, 10l, 2½l, 5l, 15l, ½l, dist. 4m 7.50s. a 21.50s (14 Ran).
SR: 7/4/-/-/-/-/   (R L Brown), R L Brown

1527 Kings Caple Novices' Handicap Chase (5-y-o and up) £2,554 3m 1f 110yds.........................(3:10)

VISAGA [86] 7-10-13 D Bridgwater, *made all, rdn 4 out, drw clr aftr 2 out, eased r-in.*
...........................(5 to 1 op 4 to 1 tchd 11 to 2)   1
962⁶ MAJOR CUT [74] 7-10-1 W Marston, *mstk 1st, pressed ldr, cl up and ev ch 5 out, rdn and wknd aftr 2 out, styd on ag'n, not trble wnr.*............(25 to 1 op 16 to 1)   2
996 LASTOFTHEVIKINGS [75] 8-9-13 (3*) R Davis, *hld up, hdwy 13th, wnt 3rd 4 out, mstk nxt, styd on one pace.*
....(14 to 1 op 8 to 1)   3
1411 MR TITTLE TATTLE [97] (bl) 7-11-7 (3*) A Thornton, *hld up, wnt 3rd 6th, third whn blun 11th, sn reco'red, chsd ldr till drvn alng and wknd aftr 3 out.*
....(3 to 1 fav op 7 to 4)   4
1324² CWM ARCTIC [77] 6-10-4 Mr M Jackson, *jmpd slwly 3rd, beh till hdwy 13th, wknd 5 out, tld off.*
.....................................(100 to 30 op 7 to 2 tchd 4 to 1)   5
1081⁶ WENRISC [74] 6-10-1⁸ (7*) Mr G Hogan, *hld up, lost tch tenth, tld off.*.................(25 to 1 op 20 to 1)   6
1298⁵ PYRO PENNANT [73] 8-9-11 (3*) D Meredith, *hld up, hdwy 9th, wnt 4th 12th, wkng whn f four out.*
....(25 to 1 op 20 to 1)   f
1107 KEMMY DARLING [73] 6-10-0 S Hodgson, *prmnt whn mstk 7th, chsd ldrs frm 12th, wknd 5 out, 5th and btn when f last.*................................(33 to 1)   f
1327⁷ ARBEE TWENTY [73] 7-9-7 (7*) L O'Hare, *mstk 1st and rdr lost irons, pld up bef next.*.............(33 to 1)   pu
1170⁶ CANAVER [87] 7-11-0 R Bellamy, *prmnt, 5th whn blun tenth, chsd ldr till wknd 14th, beh when pld up bef 3 out.*.....................(9 to 2 op 4 to 1 tchd 11 to 2)   pu
SAM PEPPER [79] 7-10-6 S Mackey, *pushed alng and reminders aftr tenth, tld off whn pld up bef 6 out.*
....(25 to 1 op 16 to 1)   pu
1302⁵ HUNTING DIARY [82] 7-10-9 S Earle, *lost tch tenth, sn beh, tld off whn pld up bef 6 out.*.....(16 to 1 op 12 to 1)   pu
Dist: 1½l, 4l, 15l, dist, 3l. 6m 33.50s. a 21.50s (12 Ran).
    (L Hellstenius), N A Twiston-Davies

1528 Bogmarsh Conditional Jockeys' Novices' Handicap Hurdle (4-y-o and up) £1,480 2m 3f 110yds...........(3:40)

889* EDIMBOURG [91] 7-11-6 D Meredith, *led, drw clr aftr 4 out, hit last, unchlgd.*
.........................(Evens fav op 11 to 10 on tchd 11 to 10)   1
889 DERRYMOSS [71] (v) 7-9-9 (5*) T Dascombe, *al chasing ldr, second whn mstk 5 out, no imprsn aftr 4 out, kpt on one pace.*..............................(16 to 1 tchd 25 to 1)   2
1047⁴ EMALLEN (Ire) [75] 5-10-4 S Fox, *wl beh 6th, rdn and styd on to take poor 3rd aftr 3 out, no imprsn on 1st 2, tld off.*
....(33 to 1 op 20 to 1)   3
1303 THE JET SET [75] (bl) 6-10-1 (3*) L O'Hare, *mstks, al chasing ldr, rdn alng 5 out, sn wknd, tld off.*
....(16 to 1 op 10 to 1)   4
1301⁸ COZZI (Fr) [71] 5-10-0 A Thornton, *hld up, hdwy to chase ldr aftr 5th, wknd after 5 out, tld off aftr 3 out.*
....(10 to 1 op 33 to 1)   5
CARLINGFORD BELLE [82] 7-10-8 (3*) P McLoughlin, *hdwy 6th, chsd ldr, btn 4th whn f 2 out.* (33 to 1 op 25 to 1)   f
1167⁶ MAPLE BAY (Ire) [75] 4-10-4 H Davis, *mstks and sn last, tld off aftr 6th, pld up bef 3 out.*......(25 to 1 op 16 to 1)   pu
1448 SMART DEBUTANTE (Ire) [78] 4-10-7 T Jenks, *rdn alng all the way, tld off aftr 6th, pld up bef 3 out.*
....(16 to 1 op 14 to 1)   pu
1415⁷ RUSTIC FLIGHT [71] (v) 6-10-0 W Marston, *mstk 3rd, chsd ldr, mistakes 5 out and nxt, wknd quickly, tld off whn pld up bef last.*.................(33 to 1 op 25 to 1)   pu
1301² KELLING [95] 6-11-10 R Greene, *pushed alng aftr 5th, some hdwy after 4 out, sn wknd, tld off whn pld up bef last.*.................................(7 to 4 tchd 2 to 1)   pu
Dist: 15l, dist, 2l, dist. 4m 52.90s. a 31.90s (10 Ran).
    (Mrs Iva Winton), Miss H C Knight

NOTTINGHAM (good to soft (races 1,4,5,7), good (2,3,6))
Friday December 3rd
Going Correction: PLUS 1.43 sec. per fur. (races 1,4,-5,7), PLUS 1.10 (2,3,6)

1529 Lake Selling Hurdle (3,4,5-y-o) £1,618 2m.....................(12:35)

1237⁴ APRIL CITY 4-11-4 S Keightley, *hld up in tch, hdwy 6th, led nxt, rdn clr, ran on flt.*.......(12 to 1 op 6 to 1)   1
1097⁴ OMIDJOY (Ire) 3-10-2 M Brennan, *hld up, hdwy 6th, ev ch nxt, sn rdn and one pace.*........(8 to 1 op 6 to 1)   2
1410* AL FORUM (Ire) 3-11-0 D O'Sullivan, *led second till hdd and hit 3 out, sn rdn and one pace.*
...........................(6 to 5 on op 11 to 8 on tchd Evens)   3
1384³ MISTER BLAKE (v) 3-10-7 R Campbell, *chsd ldg pair, blun 6th and sn rdn, wknd 3 out, beh whn hit 2 out.*
....(6 to 1 op 9 to 2 tchd 13 to 2)   4
1356² PEEDIE PEAT (bl) 3-10-7 B Storey, *in tch, rdn alng hfwy, wknd aftr 6th and sn beh.*
....(9 to 4 op 7 to 4 tchd 5 to 2)   5
1097 SOUNDS RISKY 3-9-11 (5*) T Eley, *led to second, cl up till rdn and wknd 6th, beh whn pld up bef 3 out.*
....(33 to 1 op 20 to 1)   pu
Dist: 4l, 1½l, 15l, 15l. 4m 20.60s. a 36.60s (6 Ran).
    (Michael P Holmes), M J Heaton-Ellis

1530 EBF Mares Only Novices' Handicap Chase (5-y-o and up) £2,076 2m 5f 110yds.........................(1:05)

1313⁶ WE'RE IN THE MONEY [70] (bl) 9-10-11 B Dalton, *chsd ldrs, hdwy 4 out, sn rdn, second and hld whn lft clr last.*
....(10 to 1)   1
1115² LADY'S ISLAND (Ire) [77] 5-11-4 B Storey, *in tch, hit 3rd, blun 12th, sn one pace, lft poor second at last.*.................................(2 to 1 op 9 to 4)   2
1385² SPOONHILL WOOD [87] 7-12-0 J Railton, *led, hdd briefly 9th and 12th, rdn and headed appr 3 out, sn drvn alng, wknd.*...........................(6 to 4 fav op Evens)   3
1102³ STAPLEFORD LADY [75] 5-10-9 (7*) A Flannigan, *cl up, led briefly 9th and 12th, wknd 4 out.*
....(5 to 1 tchd 7 to 1 and 8 to 1)   4
MISTRESS MCKENZIE [70] 7-10-11 R Marley, *in tch, rdn alng and lost pl tenth, tld off 12th.* (16 to 1 op 12 to 1)   5
1457 NICKLUP [85] 6-11-12 G McCourt, *hld up, hit 5th, hdwy 12th, led appr 3 out, clr whn f last.* (7 to 2 op 11 to 4)   f
Dist: 20l, 5l, 6l, dist. 5m 51.10s. a 38.10s (6 Ran).
    (Agate, Evans & Morley), J Wharton

1531 Sherwood Forest Novices' Chase (5-y-o and up) £2,271 2m.........(1:35)

1122² MARTHA'S SON 6-10-7 (5*) R Farrant, *trkd ldrs, hit 5 out and nxt, effrt 2 out, chlgd last, quickened to ld flt.*
....(11 to 8 op 5 to 4 tchd 6 to 4)   1

1444* RODEO STAR (USA) 7-11-4 G McCourt, chsd ldr, hdwy 5
out, led nxt, rdn 2 out, hdd and not quicken flt.
.............(5 to 4 on op 6 to 4 on tchd 6 to 5 on) 2
1197⁹ SOCIAL CLIMBER 9-11-4 S McNeill, led, rdn and hdd 4
out, wkng whn hit 2 out........ (8 to 1 tchd 10 to 1) 3
1324 BILLHEAD 7-10-7 (5*) T Eley, trkd ldrs, hit 5th, effrt 4 out,
rdn nxt and sn wknd......................(33 to 1) 4
Dist: 3½l, 15l, 8l. 4m 13.50s. a 22.50s (4 Ran).
SR: 35/37/22/8/ (M Ward-Thomas), Capt T A Forster

1532 Colwick Juvenile Novices' Claiming Hurdle (3-y-o) £1,702 2m.......(2:05)

870⁹ TOUCH SILVER 10-7³ (7*) M Appleby, pld hrd, hld up,
hdwy aftr 4 out, led 2 out, styd on wl.
.............(16 to 1 tchd 16 to 1 and 20 to 1) 1
1261² BAYRAK (USA) (bl) 11-5 J Railton, chsd ldr, led appr 4th,
sn wl clr, pushed alng 3 out, hdd nxt, soon btn.
.............(11 to 10 fav op Evens tchd 5 to 4) 2
1408⁹ BITRAN 11-1 A S Smith, led till appr 4th, chsd ldr till rdn
and btn approaching 3 out.........(12 to 1 op 8 to 1) 3
1243⁴ SALLY OF THE ALLEY 9-13 (7*) D Towler, in tch, rdn alng
and outpcd frm 4 out...(5 to 1 op 11 to 4 tchd 7 to 2) 4
EVE'S TREASURE 10-5 (5*) S Lyons, f 1st.
.............(16 to 1 op 8 to 1 tchd 20 to 1) f
1097 ROYAL EXECUTIVE (Ire) 10-13 W Humphreys, brght dwn
1st........................(16 to 1 op 14 to 1) bd
NANNY MARGARET (Ire) 10-7 (5*) A Bates, chsd ldrs, blun
4th, sn lost pl, tld off whn pld up bef 2 out.
.............(9 to 2 op 3 to 1 tchd 5 to 1) pu
Dist: 10l, 12l, 15l. 4m 16.00s. a 32.00s (7 Ran).
(H J Manners), H J Manners

1533 Tyne Handicap Hurdle (0-115 4-y-o and up) £1,940 3½m...........(2:35)

861 LESBET [92] 8-10-6 D Morris, prmnt, led 4th, rdn clr and
hit 3 out, blun last, jst hld on.
.............(9 to 1 op 7 to 1 tchd 10 to 1) 1
948 JEFFERBY [92] 6-10-6 T Reed, hdwy to chase wnr appr 3
out, hrd drvn last, styd on wl flt, jst fld.
.............(14 to 1 op 12 to 1) 2
1206 MEDIANE (USA) [112] 8-11-5 (7*) M P FitzGerald, hld up
and beh, hdwy 4 out, rdn nxt, styd on same pace.
.............(10 to 1 op 8 to 1) 3
1148³ IF YOU SAY SO [88] 7-10-2 A Mulholland, al prmnt, effrt
appr 3 out, sn rdn and one pace, blun last.
.............(11 to 2 fav op 5 to 1) 4
UNDERWYCHWOOD (Ire) [90] 5-9-13 (5*) R Farrant, hld up,
hdwy 9th, hrd rdn aftr 3 out and sn wknd.
.............(14 to 1 op 10 to 1) 5
1458⁹ COXANN [86] 7-9-7 (7*) E Tolhurst, prmnt to 6th, sn lost pl
and rdn alng, nvr dngrs.........(25 to 1 op 20 to 1) 6
1238⁵ MISS CAPULET [86] (bl) 6-9-9 (5*) T Eley, prominent, rdn 4
out and grad wknd.... (9 to 1 op 8 to 1 tchd 10 to 1) 7
424⁴ SMILES AHEAD [86] 5-10-0 M Brennan, led till jmpd slwly
and hdd 4th, lost pl 6th, rdn alng and hdwy four out,
wknd nxt.....................(7 to 1 op 6 to 1) 8
1210³ LAUGHING GAS (Ire) [86] 4-10-0 R Supple, hld up in mid-
div, effrt and some hdwy appr 4 out, sn rdn and no
imprsn.....................(10 to 1 tchd 12 to 1) 9
1351 BLAKNOT [86] 10-10-0⁵ (5*) S Lyons, hld up and beh,
hdwy 5 out, rdn and wknd................(66 to 1) 10
1119⁹ RIDWAN [95] 6-10-9 A S Smith, prmnt, rdn 4 out, wknd
appr nxt and sn beh.............(8 to 1 op 5 to 1) 11
1274⁵ CARFAX [99] 8-10-13 M Hoad, in tch till lost pl and beh
frm tenth, pld up aftr 4 out.
.............(6 to 1 op 5 to 1 tchd 13 to 2) pu
1245 VAIGLY BLAZED [86] 9-10-0 D Gallagher, hld up, hdwy 9th,
sn rdn and wknd, tld off whn pld up bef 3 out.
.............(66 to 1 op 50 to 1) pu
1287 HUNTING COUNTRY [86] 9-10-0 B Storey, mid-div, effrt
and some hdwy tenth, rdn 4 out and sn wknd, pld up
bef 2 out.....................(20 to 1) pu
1296³ SOLID FUEL [89] 7-9-12 (5*) D J Moffatt, hld up, al beh, tld
off whn pld up bef 3 out...........(7 to 1 op 6 to 1) pu
Dist: ½l, 12l, 7l, ½l, 20l, ½l, 2½l, 4l, 12l, dist. 7m 24.90s. a 44.90s (15 Ran).
SR: 28/27/35/4/5/-/ (Mrs L W Carlson), R Curtis

1534 Gedling Handicap Chase (0-120 5-y-o and up) £2,301 2m 5f 110yds.... (3:05)

1343⁶ GLEN CHERRY [103] (bl) 7-11-10 G McCourt, made all, hit
twelfth, blun 4 out, rdn nxt and styd on strly.
.............(4 to 5 fav op 8 to 15 tchd 2 to 1) 1
1216⁴ RYTON GUARD [85] 8-10-6 T Reed, chsd ldg pair, hit
tenth, effrt and hit 5 out, rdn nxt, one pace 3 out.
.............(6 to 5 fav op 5 to 4 on tchd 5 to 4) 2
1328³ SAILOR'S DELIGHT [87] 9-10-1 (7*) Mr S Joynes, al chasing
wnr, rdn 4 out and one paced frm nxt.
.............(7 to 2 op 5 to 2) 3
1357⁸ NEWMARKET SAUSAGE [85] 12-10-6 J Callaghan, lost pl
and beh twelfth, kpt on appr last, nvr dngrs.
.............(25 to 1 op 14 to 1 tchd 33 to 1) 4
Dist: 12l, 8l, 1½l. 5m 50.60s. a 37.60s (4 Ran).
(G J Phillips), Capt T A Forster

1535 Ruddington Novices' Handicap Hurdle (4-y-o and up) £1,748 2m...... (3:35)

1215³ GLENFINN PRINCESS [80] 5-11-4 G McCourt, hld up, gd
hdwy appr 3 out, effrt to chal nxt, rdn to ld approaching last, drvn clr flt......................(4 to 1 co-
fav op 5 to 1 tchd 11 to 2) 1
1374³ ARTIC WINGS (Ire) [77] 5-11-1 M Brennan, in tch, hdwy
appr 3 out and sn ev ch, rdn approaching last, kpt on
one pace flt.......(4 to 1 co-fav op 3 to 1 tchd 9 to 2) 2
1316* MILLIES OWN [75] 6-10-13 J Railton, led, hdd 4th, cl up till
led 3 out, sn rdn, headed and one pace appr last.
.............(5 to 1 op 6 to 1) 3
1325* KELLY'S DARLING [84] 7-11-10 D Gallagher, hld up, gd
hdwy appr 3 out and sn ev ch, rdn approaching last,
sutchd lft flt, kpt on one pace.....(9 to 1 op 6 to 1) 4
1366⁵ JUDGE AND JURY [70] (bl) 4-10-3 (5*) J McCarthy, in tch,
effrt and hdwy 3 out, rdn nxt, styd on one pace and
pres...........(4 to 1 co-fav op 3 to 1 tchd 9 to 2) 5
SCARBA [70] 5-10-1 (7*) K Davies, in tch, effrt and rdn 3
out, sn btn....................(16 to 1 op 20 to 1) 6
1092⁶ BARAHIN (Ire) [74] 4-10-12 D O'Sullivan, chsd ldrs, rdn 4
out and wkng whn blun nxt........(12 to 1 op 8 to 1) 7
1070⁷ ENCHANTED FLYER [62] (bl) 6-9-9 (5*) T Eley, hdwy and ev
ch 3 out, sn rdn and wknd....... (25 to 1 op 20 to 1) 8
1183⁷ CHOIR'S IMAGE [76] 6-11-0 A Mulholland, chsd ldr, led 4th
till rdn and hdd appr 3 out, sn wknd.
.............(20 to 1 op 14 to 1) 9
1320 BIRCHALL BOY [75] 5-10-13 S McNeill, al rear.
.............(16 to 1 tchd 20 to 1) 10
1353⁹ NONCOMMITAL [68] 6-10-6 R Supple, hld up, effrt and
hdwy appr 3 out, sn rdn and wknd.
.............(8 to 1 op 6 to 1) 11
Dist: 8l, hd, sht-hd, nk, 12l, 4l, 2½l, 12l, ¾l, 7l. 4m 13.90s. a 29.90s (11 Ran).
SR: 20/9/7/18/1/-/ (Patrick McGinty), K S Bridgwater

SANDOWN (good to soft (races 1,4,6), good (2,3,5))
Friday December 3rd
Going Correction: PLUS 0.63 sec. per fur.

1536 Sandown 'National Hunt' Novices' Hurdle (4-y-o and up) £3,772 2m 110yds.......................(12:55)

1309 MY WIZARD 6-10-11 (3*) P Hide, hld up in mid-div, al gng
wl, cld 3 out, led aftr last, styd on strly.
.............(14 to 1 op 8 to 1 tchd 16 to 1) 1
1196* BRIEF GALE 6-10-13 D Murphy, led to second, led 4 out to
nxt, led 2 out till aftr last, kpt on und pres.
.............(11 to 10 fav op 7 to 4 tchd Evens) 2
1161* OLD BRIDGE (Ire) 5-11-1 (7*) D Fortt, nvr far away, lost pl 3
out, hdwy and ev ch nxt, one pace whn mstk last.
.............(5 to 1 op 7 to 2 tchd 11 to 2) 3
1309⁴ ARFER MOLE (Ire) 5-11-0 T Grantham, trkd ldrs, outpcd
aftr 3 out, hrd drvn and kpt on appr last.
.............(10 to 1 op 8 to 1) 4
ANTARCTIC CALL 6-11-0 J Osborne, cl up, led briefly
second, one pace 3 out........(10 to 1 op 8 to 1) 5
1109* HAWAIIAN YOUTH (Ire) 5-11-4 N Davies, trkd ldrs, ev ch 2
out, sn outpcd.........(12 to 1 op 8 to 1 tchd 14 to 1) 6
GILPA VALU 4-11-0 J Lawrence, chsd ldrs, led briefly 3
out, sn outpcd....................(50 to 1 op 20 to 1) 7
MARROB 6-11-0 M Perrett, hld up, hdwy frm 2 out, nvr
plcd to chal.....................(50 to 1 op 20 to 1) 8
605⁸ RAGTIME BOY 5-11-0 L Wyer, mid-div, lost pl aftr 5th, no
dngr after.....................(50 to 1 op 33 to 1) 9
1109² SENIOR STEWARD 5-11-0 J Frost, hld up in tch, cld 3 out,
rdn appr nxt, wknd............(14 to 1 op 8 to 1) 10
VICAR OF BRAY 4-10-7 (7*) N Collum, chsd ldrs, lost pl aftr
4th.........................(50 to 1 op 33 to 1) 11
CREDON 5-11-0 A Maguire, hld up, jmpd slwly 3rd, nvr
on terms.....................(10 to 1 op 14 to 1) 12
1263⁷ MAKING TIME 6-10-9 A Tory, cl up, ev ch 3 out, sn rdn and
lost pl.........(50 to 1 op 33 to 1 tchd 66 to 1) 13
764⁴ RELATIVE OCTAVE 4-11-0 M Hourigan, nvr better than
mid-div.......(20 to 1 op 10 to 1 tchd 25 to 1) 14
1161⁵ THE FROG PRINCE 5-11-0 C Llewellyn, trkd ldrs,
wknd o'r 4 out....................(50 to 1 op 33 to 1) 15
1247⁵ OUR WIZZER (Ire) 4-11-0 P Niven, al beh.
.............(50 to 1 op 33 to 1) 16
1126⁶ ROMANY BLUES 4-10-9 G Grant, al beh.
.............(50 to 1 op 33 to 1) 17
1126⁸ NO DEBT 5-10-9 M Murphy, trkd ldrs till lost pl aftr 3rd.
.............(50 to 1 op 20 to 1) 18
CAPTAIN BERT 4-11-0 N Williamson, jmpd slwly 1st, al
beh.........................(50 to 1 op 33 to 1) 19
1167 ANDALUCIAN SUN (Ire) 5-11-0 R J Beggan, trkd ldrs, lost
pl appr 3rd, tld off...................(50 to 1 op 20 to 1) 20
1110⁶ FERAL BAY (Ire) 4-11-0 M A FitzGerald, al beh, tld off.
.............(50 to 1 op 33 to 1) 21
Dist: 3l, 4l, 1½l, 2½l, 1½l, 10l, 3l, 1l, 1½l, 2½l. 4m 6.80s. a 19.80s (21 Ran).
(Mrs Angela Brodie), J T Gifford

1537 Pond Novices' Chase (5-y-o and up) £4,123 3m 110yds............. (1:25)

1306⁶ YORKSHIRE GALE 7-10-12 D Murphy, *led briefly 1st, hld up, drpd rear 12th, hdwy 16th, shaken up to ld aftr last, drvn out*..........(6 to 1 op 5 to 1 tchd 13 to 2) 1
1346* SPIKEY (NZ) 7-11-5 A Maguire, *cl up, lft in ld 11th, blun nxt, pckd 4 out, hdd aftr last, kpt on.*
.......................(11 to 2 op 7 to 1 tchd 5 to 1) 2
1033* BRACKENFIELD 7-11-5 P Niven, *hld up, cld 11th, pckd and lost pl 17th, rallied 3 out, kpt on one pace.*
..................(Evens fav op 5 to 4 on tchd 11 to 10) 3
1346 DEEPENDABLE 6-10-12 M A FitzGerald, *led second till aftr 4th, outpcd 5 out, rallied and hrd drvn 2 out, one pace.*
.......................(20 to 1 op 14 to 1 tchd 25 to 1) 4
1205* SQUIRE JIM 9-11-5 C Llewellyn, *not fluent in rear, rallied 4 out, outpcd nxt.*....................(5 to 1 op 4 to 1) 5
1411* LUCKY LANE (bl) 9-11-5 M Hourigan, *led aftr 4th till hit 11th and uns rdr*..................(12 to 1 op 8 to 1) ur
Dist: 2½l, nk, 8l, 4l. 6m 30.80s. a 31.80s (6 Ran).

(Bill Naylor), J T Gifford

1538 Crowngap Construction Handicap Chase (0-145 5-y-o and up) £4,924 2½m 110yds................... (2:00)

1307⁴ DEADLY CHARM (USA) [115] 7-10-11 A Maguire, *cl up, led 3 out, clr nxt, easily.....* (13 to 2 op 9 to 2 tchd 7 to 1) 1
1123* ARDBRIN [128] 10-11-10 P Niven, *led to 3 out, one pace.*
.......................(4 to 1 op 7 to 2 tchd 9 to 2) 2
BUCK WILLOW [119] 9-11-1 D Murphy, *hld up rear, outpcd 11th, styd on appr last.*
.......................(12 to 1 op 8 to 1 tchd 14 to 1) 3
1165* IAMA ZULU [108] 8-10-4 M Hourigan, *cl up, closed on ldr 11th, outpcd appr 2 out.*
.......................(5 to 2 op 2 to 1 tchd 11 to 4) 4
1307 BIBENDUM [128] 7-11-10 J Osborne, *keen hold early, hld up in tch, blun and uns rdr 7th.*
.......................(6 to 4 fav op 13 to 8 tchd 15 to 8) ur
Dist: 12l, 3½l, ¾l. 5m 18.00s. a 18.50s (5 Ran).
SR: 27/28/15/3/-/   (J B R Morris), D Nicholson

1539 Crowngap Winter Novices' Hurdle Grade 2 (4-y-o and up) £9,780 2¾m .... (2:30)

1344* TOP SPIN 4-11-4 A Maguire, *hld up beh ldrs, hdwy 4 out, pushed alng aftr nxt, led appr 2 out, drvn out.*
.......................(11 to 2 op 4 to 1 tchd 6 to 1) 1
1263* SCOBIE BOY (Ire) 5-11-0 J Osborne, *al prmnt, ev ch 2 out, no extr und pres.*.........(7 to 1 op 5 to 1 tchd 8 to 1) 2
1108⁴ MAD THYME 6-11-0 M Perrett, *stried ldrs, hdwy in rear, cld aftr 3 out, kpt on frm last.*(50 to 1 op 25 to 1) 3
1082* BERTONE (Ire) 4-11-7 N Williamson, *settld wth, mstk 3rd, steady hdwy frm 4 out, shaken up appr 2 out, found little.*..................(5 to 1 op 9 to 2 tchd 11 to 2) 4
1082⁴ KING'S TREASURE (USA) 4-11-0 J Frost, *hld up in rear, steady hdwy frm 4 out, wknd aftr 2 out.*
.......................(9 to 1 op 8 to 1 tchd 12 to 1) 5
1418* ARCTIC KINSMAN 5-11-4 C Llewellyn, *led till appr 2 out, wknd quickly and pres.*
.......................(9 to 4 fav tchd 5 to 2 and 2 to 1) 6
1341* CUNNINGHAMS FORD (Ire) 5-11-4 Mr A Harvey, *trkd ldrs till lost pl appr 6th, tld off.*
.......................(11 to 1 op 8 to 1 tchd 12 to 1) 7
982* JULIUS GENIUS 6-11-0 D Murphy, *trkd ldrs, cld 6th, wknd quickly aftr 3 out, tld up bef last.*
....................................(9 to 1 op 7 to 1) pu
1309³ GOOD INSIGHT (Ire) 5-11-0 M A FitzGerald, *trkd ldrs till lost pl 6th, pld up bef 2 out.*
.......................(14 to 1 op 20 to 1 tchd 12 to 1) pu
Dist: 3l, nk, 12l, 2½l, 20l, 15l. 5m 23.90s. a 17.90s (9 Ran).
SR: 50/43/42/37/27/11/   (J M Long), J R Jenkins

1540 P & O Handicap Chase (5-y-o and up) £4,947 3m 5f 110yds........... (3:00)

1319* PADAVENTURE [123] 8-10-0 L Wyer, *wtd wth, cld 12th, mstks 14th and 18th (water), led nxt, clr 2 out, styd on wl.*.......................(7 to 2 tchd 4 to 1) 1
1224² WHATS THE CRACK [133] 10-10-10 A Maguire, *trkd ldrs, lost pl 6th, reminders 11th, cld 14th, one pace frm 3 out.*
.......(5 to 2 fav op 9 to 4 tchd 2 to 1 and 11 to 4) 2
1285⁵ ANNIO CHILONE [123] 7-9-12¹ (3*) P Hide, *led 5th to 19th, ev ch 3 out, one pace.*...........(14 to 1 op 12 to 1) 3
1011* LATENT TALENT [144] 9-11-7 J Osborne, *hld up, lost pl 14th, jmpd slwly 16th, cld 4 out, btn nxt, virtually pld up r-in.*.............(5 to 1 tchd to 1 op 6 to 1) 4
1118² SHOON WIND [129] (v) 10-10-6 C Grant, *not jump wl, led to 5th, lost tch 14th, tld off.*...........(9 to 1 tchd 10 to 1) 5
1340³ WELKNOWN CHARACTER [123] 11-9-9² (7*) D Fortt, *in cl tch whn f 19th.*.............(10 to 1 op 8 to 1 tchd 9 to 1) f
1224⁶ PARSONS GREEN [135] (bl) 9-10-12 M A FitzGerald, *trkd ldrs, hrd drvn 17th, wknd quickly, pld up aftr 4 out.*
.......................(7 to 1 op 5 to 1 tchd 15 to 2) pu

1365 GOLD CAP (Fr) [123] 8-10-0 M Hourigan, *beh, lost tch 5th, tld off whn pld up bef 9th.*............(33 to 1 op 20 to 1) pu
Dist: 7l, 3½l, 20l, 20l. 7m 41.60s. a 28.60s (8 Ran).
(Mrs J G Fulton), Mrs M Reveley

1541 Surrey Racing Three Year Old Novices' Hurdle £3,343 2m 110yds.. (3:30)

BAGALINO (USA) 11-0 M Perrett, *trkd ldg pair, led appr last, rdn and ran on wl.*
.......................(9 to 4 op 7 to 4 tchd 100 to 30) 1
1229² WINGS COVE 11-7 E Murphy, *trkd ldr, led 3 out till appr last, ran on....*(11 to 10 on op Evens tchd 11 to 8 on) 2
1125³ STAY WITH ME BABY 10-9 J Osborne, *led to 3 out, ev ch nxt, sn outpcd.*.........(7 to 1 op 6 to 1 tchd 8 to 1) 3
1244 HOBBS (Ire) 11-0 S Smith Eccles, *al beh, mstk second, tried to run out 3 out, tld off.*
.......................(40 to 1 op 33 to 1 tchd 50 to 1) 4
1244⁷ AMILLIONMEMORIES 11-0 A Maguire, *jmpd slwly 1st, al beh, tld off appr 3 out.*...........(50 to 1 op 16 to 1) 5
EXHIBIT AIR (Ire) 10-9 D Murphy, *hld up, effrt 5th, outpcd aftr 3 out, wknd quickly, tld off....*(8 to 1 tchd 9 to 1) 6
Dist: ¾l, 15l, 25l, ¾l, 25l. 4m 7.10s. a 20.10s (6 Ran).
(Sir Eric Parker), G Harwood

CHEPSTOW (soft (races 1,3,5,7), good to soft (2,4,6))
Saturday December 4th
Going Correction: PLUS 1.75 sec. per fur.

1542 ANC 'National Hunt' Novices' Hurdle (4-y-o and up) £3,564 2m 110yds ....(12:30)

1110³ BOND JNR (Ire) 4-11-0 R Dunwoody, *al prmnt, chlgd 2 out, rdn to ld last, pushed out.*
.......................(100 to 30 fav op 9 to 4 tchd 7 to 2) 1
1163³ BILLY BORU 5-11-5 M Hourigan, *led aftr 1st, rdn and hdd whn slight mstk last, ran on one pace.*
.......................(5 to 1 op 7 to 2 tchd 11 to 2) 2
SPUFFINGTON 5-11-0 E Murphy, *led till aftr 1st, styd prmnt, one pace frm 2 out, styd on.*
.......................(9 to 1 op 7 to 1 tchd 10 to 1) 3
HOLD YOUR RANKS 6-10-7 (7*) R Darke, *mid-div, hdwy appr 4 out, kpt on one pace frm nxt.*
.......................(66 to 1 op 33 to 1) 4
A N C EXPRESS 5-11-0 R Greene, *mid-div, styd on frm 3 out, nvr nrr.*.............(50 to 1 op 20 to 1) 5
FUN MONEY 6-11-0 M Dwyer, *mid-div, no hdwy frm 3 out.*.......................(16 to 1 op 10 to 1) 6
901² CONEY ROAD 4-11-0 P Holley, *in rear till hdwy 4th, wknd appr 3 out.*.................(4 to 1 tchd 9 to 2) 7
795⁵ MR WILBUR 7-11-0 J Frost, *al beh...*(20 to 1 op 14 to 1) 8
483⁶ PECTORUS (Ire) (bl) 5-11-0 M Foster, *mid-div till wknd appr 4 out.*....................(10 to 1 op 8 to 1) 9
787 SOLO GENT 4-11-0 G Upton, *mstk 1st, sn beh, tld off.*
.......................(50 to 1 op 33 to 1) 10
ROYAL GARDEN 4-11-0 J Railton, *al beh, tld off.*
.......................(16 to 1 op 10 to 1) 11
1414⁹ ALICE SPRINGS 4-10-9 Mr T Greed, *beh whn f second.*
.......................(50 to 1 op 33 to 1) f
212³ GAYLOIRE (Ire) 4-10-8¹ (7*) Mr A Harvey, *trkd ldrs, second and gng wl whn f 4 out.*..........(10 to 1 op 7 to 1) f
1251 UNEXIS 8-10-11 (3*) A Thornton, *al beh, tld off whn pld up bef 4 out.*.............(50 to 1 op 33 to 1) pu
1301⁷ STORMY SUNSET 6-10-2 (7*) Mr N Moore, *in tch till wknd appr 4 out, pld up bef nxt.*...........(50 to 1 op 25 to 1) pu
BOX OF DELIGHTS 5-11-0 W Humphreys, *al beh, tld off whn pld up bef last.*...........(50 to 1 op 33 to 1) pu
1169 ITS GRAND 4-10-7 (7*) A Flannigan, *prmnt till mstk second, sn beh, tld off whn pld up bef four out.*
.......................(66 to 1 op 33 to 1) pu
1277⁹ FERNY BALL (Ire) 5-11-0 C Maude, *chsd ldrs till wknd 4th, tld off whn pld up bef four out.*
.......................(25 to 1 op 20 to 1 tchd 33 to 1) pu
1247⁶ ANOTHER LOAN 6-10-4 (5*) A Procter, *mid-div, rdn 4th, sn beh, tld off whn pld up bef four out.*
.......................(50 to 1 op 25 to 1) pu
Dist: 1½l, 3½l, 3½l, 8l, 6l, 10l, 4l, 7l, 10l, 15l. 4m 24.60s. a 38.60s (19 Ran).
(Paul K Barber), P F Nicholls

1543 Jack Brown Bookmaker Handicap Chase (0-140 5-y-o and up) £4,500 3¼m 110yds.............. (1:00)

1281⁷ DIRECT [119] 10-10-7 (3*) R Davis, *al prmnt, wnt second 13th, led 16th, styd on wl frm 3 out.*............(12 to 1) 1
1281³ CYTHERE [113] 9-10-4 E Murphy, *hld up rear, hdwy appr 5 out, chsd wnr frm nxt, rdn 2 out, eased whn held r-in.*
.......................(9 to 1 op 8 to 1 tchd 10 to 1) 2
1302² SUNLEY BAY [109] (bl) 7-10-0 R Greene, *jmpd slwly and wl beh till hdwy 12th, wnt second appr 5 out, wknd nxt.*
.......................(7 to 1 op 6 to 1) 3
1281² WILLSFORD [132] (bl) 10-11-9 C Llewellyn, *wl in rear and struggling frm hfwy, styd on frm 4 out, nvr in race.*
.......................(9 to 2 op 5 to 1 tchd 11 to 2) 4

1242⁴ PHAROAH'S LAEN [115] 12-10-1 (5°) R Farrant, *led to 16th,*
wknd appr 5 out, virtually pld up r-in.
..................................(66 to 1 op 33 to 1)   5
1197⁷ SUNBEAM TALBOT [113] 12-10-4² G Upton, *wl beh till*
hdwy appr 12th, hld in 3rd pl whn f 3 out.
..................................(14 to 1 op 12 to 1)   f
STIRRUP CUP [131] 9-11-8 J Railton, *trkd ldr early, still in*
tch whn f tenth.........................(7 to 1 op 6 to 1)   f
1281° MERE CLASS [130] 7-11-7 M Dwyer, *hld up in tch till blun*
and uns rdr 13th..................(7 to 4 fav op 11 to 8)   ur
CUSHINSTOWN [137] 10-12-0 R Dunwoody, *in trck ldr,*
wknd frm 13th, tld off whn pld up bef 4 out.
..................................(11 to 1 op 14 to 1 tchd 16 to 1)   pu

Dist: 7l, 15l, 7l, 7l. 7m 35.20s. a 60.20s (9 Ran).

(H Kaye), J A C Edwards

1544 Ginsters Handicap Hurdle (0-145 4-y-o and up) £3,715 2½m 110yds.....(1:30)

1396² MEDITATOR [107] 9-9-12 (5°) S Curran, *hld up, gd hdwy to*
go second 7th, led 4 out, wl clr whn hit 2 out, unchlgd.
..................................(7 to 1 op 6 to 1)   1
1445⁵ ONEUPMANSHIP [128] 8-11-3 (7°) S Fox, *al in tch, led*
appr 6th, hdd 4 out, sn rdn, lft beh frm nxt.
..................................(11 to 2 op 7 to 1 tchd 8 to 1 and 5 to 1)   2
GRENAGH [120] 12-10-9 (7°) P McLoughlin, *hld up in rear,*
some hdwy appr 4 out, no ch with 1st 2.
..................................(10 to 1 op 10 to 1 tchd 12 to 1 and 8 to 1)   3
1169⁷ RAMPOLDI (USA) [106] 6-10-2 R Dunwoody, *hld up, lost*
tch appr 4 out........(2 to 1 fav op 9 to 4 tchd 11 to 4)   4
IRISH BAY [118] 7-11-0 J Railton, *trkd ldr to 5th, rdn and*
wknd aftr 7th....................(7 to 1 op 5 to 1)   5
JOSIE SMITH [104] 9-9-9 (5°) D Matthews, *prmnt till wknd*
quickly 5th, tld off whn pld up bef 4 out.
..................................(100 to 1 op 66 to 1)   pu
1445⁴ SUPER RITCHART [108] 5-10-4 C Llewellyn, *led till appr*
6th, wknd quickly, tld off whn pld up bef 4 out.
..................................(10 to 1 op 7 to 1)   pu
CARIBOO GOLD (USA) [123] 4-11-5 M Dwyer, *hld up in*
rear, hdwy 6th, wknd and pld up bef 4 out.
..................................(7 to 2 op 9 to 4)   pu

Dist: 25l, 3l, 12l, nk. 5m 20.60s. a 39.60s (8 Ran).
SR: 38/34/23/-/8/   (Miss Jacqueline S Doyle), Miss Jacqueline S Doyle

1545 Rehearsal Chase Limited Handicap Grade 2 (5-y-o and up) £15,970 3m
....................................(2:05)

PARTY POLITICS [158] 9-10-9 C Llewellyn, *hld up in tch,*
gd hdwy appr 5 out, led 3 out, drw clr frm nxt.
..................................(11 to 2 op 4 to 1)   1
RIVERSIDE BOY [156] 10-10-7 R Dunwoody, *led till rdn*
and hdd 3 out, no imprsn frm nxt.(8 to 1 tchd 12 to 1)   2
1293⁴ JODAMI [177] 8-12-0 M Dwyer, *hld up, cld on ldrs 8th,*
wnt second 13th, ev ch whn blun 3 out, lost pl, no extr
aftr..........(7 to 2 on op 4 to 1 on tchd 3 to 1 op)   3
1281⁶ FIDDLERS PIKE [156] 12-10-7 Mrs R Henderson, *prmnt till*
wknd appr 8th, tld off frm 13th.....(28 to 1 op 25 to 1)   4
1282° SHEER ABILITY [156] 7-10-7 J Railton, *in cl tch till wknd*
appr 5 out, tld off whn f 3 out.
..................................(33 to 1 op 50 to 1 tchd 66 to 1)   f

Dist: 5l, 7l, dist. 6m 32.60s. a 42.60s (5 Ran).
SR: 75/68/82/-/-/   (Mrs David Thompson), N A Gaselee

1546 Good Luck Selling Hurdle (4-y-o) £1,702 2½m 110yds...........(2:35)

1416³ BUSMAN (Ire) 11-0 M Hourigan, *hld up, steady hdwy frm*
6th, led 3 out, edgd lft appr last and r-in, rdn out.
..................................(11 to 4 op 5 to 2)   1
1371³ CZAR NICHOLAS 11-0 M Dwyer, *wtd with, gd hdwy appr 4*
out, ev ch 2 out, rdn and ran on r-in.
..................................(9 to 4 fav op 3 to 1 tchd 2 to 1)   2
795⁶ SOUL TRADER 10-9 S Burrough, *al prmnt, wnt second*
appr 4 out, outpcd frm nxt.
..................................(9 to 4 op 7 to 4 tchd 15 to 2)   3
1404⁹ BOOGIE BOPPER (Ire) 11-5 R Dunwoody, *al prmnt, led aftr*
4th, rdn and hdd 3 out, sn btn.
..................................(9 to 2 tchd 5 to 1 and 4 to 1)   4
1253⁹ DANCING DANCER 10-9 J Frost, *chsd ldrs, ev ch 4 out,*
wknd nxt................(12 to 1 op 8 to 1 tchd 14 to 1)   5
1366⁷ LAW FACULTY (Ire) 11-0 P Holley, *led till aftr 4th, jmpd*
slwly nxt, wknd appr four out.
..................................(12 to 1 op 8 to 1 tchd 14 to 1)   6
LAGGARD'S QUEST 11-0 Upton, *sn tld off, pld up aftr*
4th...................................(33 to 1 op 20 to 1)   pu
1272 CHARMED LIFE 11-0 N Dawe, *al beh, tld off whn jmpd*
slwly 6th, sn pld up...........(20 to 1 op 14 to 1)   pu
1169 ZODIAC STAR 10-9 S Mackey, *in tch to 6th, sn beh, tld off*
whn pld up bef 4 out...........(33 to 1 op 20 to 1)   pu

Dist: 1l, 8l, 8l, 12l, 15l. 5m 41.70s. a 60.70s (9 Ran).

(Mrs M T O'Shea), J G M O'Shea

1547 Flurry Knox Novices' Chase (5-y-o and up) £2,942 2m 3f 110yds.... (3:05)

1405° MUDAHIM 7-11-2 C Llewellyn, *trkd ldr, led tenth, in com-*
mand whn lft clr 3 out, eased r-in, unchlgd.
..................................(11 to 8 op Evens tchd 6 to 4)   1
1057⁵ NICKLE JOE 7-10-12 R Bellamy, *in tch to 6th, lft remote*
second 3 out...............(10 to 1 tchd 11 to 1)   2
1291² MONSIEUR LE CURE 7-10-12 R Dunwoody, *led to tenth,*
tired and hld whn f 3 out.
..................................(7 to 1 op 6 to 1)   f
1339³ GREY ADMIRAL (v) 8-11-0² Mr S Stickland, *beh whn jmpd*
slwly 7th, pld up bef nxt........(50 to 1 op 33 to 1)   pu
STRIDE ALONG 10-10-5 (7°) M Darke, *mstks and outpcd in*
rear, tld off whn pld up bef tenth.
..................................(40 to 1 op 33 to 1 tchd 50 to 1)   pu
IT'S AFTER TIME 8-10-12 R Greene, *beh till hdwy 6th,*
wknd tenth, tld off whn pld up bef 5 out.
..................................(40 to 1 op 33 to 1)   pu
1298 NEVER EVER 8-10-5 (7°) Guy Lewis, *in tch whn hit 4th, sn*
beh, tld off whn pld up bef 8th. (100 to 1 op 50 to 1)   pu

Dist: 20l. 5m 32.20s. a 45.20s (7 Ran).

(K W Bell), C D Broad

1548 Grunwick 'Championship' Stakes National Hunt Flat Race (4,5,6-y-o) £4,532 2m 110yds..............(3:40)

1277³ SEE ENOUGH 5-11-0 N Parker, *hld up, gd hdwy 5 fs out,*
led wl o'r 2 out, rdn out........... (25 to 1 op 20 to 1)   1
1133* KENMORE-SPEED 6-11-4 Mr C Mulhall, *mid-div, hdwy*
hfwy, led 6 fs out, came wide into strt and rcd alone,
hdd to o'r 2 out, no extr pres..(12 to 1 op 8 to 1)   2
1329* CAPTAIN KHEDIVE 5-11-7 M Hourigan, *hld up, hdwy*
hfwy, dsptd ld 4 fs out, sn hrd rdn, wknd 2 out.
..................................(5 to 1 op 4 to 1 tchd 6 to 1)   3
MR CLANCY (Ire) 5-11-0 A Thornton, *hld up, hdwy 6 fs*
out, lft beh fnl 3...........(5 to 1 op 4 to 1 tchd 6 to 1)   4
A FORTIORI (Ire) 5-11-4 T Dascombe, *dsptd ld early,*
prmnt till wknd 5 fs out, sn tld off.
..................................(11 to 2 op 6 to 1 tchd 8 to 1)   5
PRECIOUS JUNO (Ire) 4-10-13 L O'Hare, *chsd ldrs till rdn*
and wknd 5 fs out, tld off......(9 to 4 fav tchd 5 to 2)   6
1277⁴ PRINCE TEETON 4-11-0 Mr P Henley, *chsd ldrs till wknd*
o'r 5 fs out, tld off...........(33 to 1 op 20 to 1)   7
1126* SPRINTFAYRE 5-11-4 Mr M Armytage, *pld hrd, made most*
to 6 fs out, wknd quickly, tld off.....(8 to 1 op 5 to 1)   8
SLIPMATIC 4-10-9 Guy Lewis, *prmnt till rdn 5 fs out, sn*
wknd, tld off.......................(20 to 1 op 14 to 1)   9
MERTON MISTRESS 6-10-9 Mr G Cosgrove, *in tch to*
hfwy, tld off...............(33 to 1 op 25 to 1)   10
1329³ SEBASTOPOL 4-11-0 R Greene, *al beh, tld off.*
..................................(9 to 1 op 6 to 1)   11

Dist: ¾l, 25l, 12l, 15l, 8l, 12l, 5l, 8l, 5l, ¾l. 4m 21.80s. (11 Ran).

(J A G Meaden), R H Buckler

PUNCHESTOWN (IRE) (soft) Saturday December 4th

1549 Elverstown Maiden Hurdle (5-y-o and up) £3,105 2m...............(12:30)

1401² COURT MELODY (Ire) 5-11-7 (7°) J P Broderick,
..................................(11 to 8 on)   1
1379⁵ WINDOVER (Ire) 5-11-3 (3°) D Bromley, ...(14 to 1)   2
KAWA-KAWA 6-10-10 (5°) T J O'Sullivan, ...(20 to 1)   3
926³ SUPER TACTICS (Ire) 5-11-6 F Woods, ...(8 to 1)   4
1265° DEEP THYNE (Ire) 5-11-2 (7°) Mr K F O'Donnell, ...(8 to 1)   5
1403 FARNAN (Ire) 5-11-6 M Duffy, ...(16 to 1)   6
930° JIMMY O'GOBLIN 6-11-6 B Sheridan, ...(12 to 1)   7
WANOVOWERS (Ire) 5-12-0 A Powell, ...(16 to 1)   8
1174 BETTYS THE BOSS (Ire) 5-11-9 F J Flood, ...(10 to 1)   9
1174 NORDIC RACE 6-11-1 (5°) P A Roche, ...(33 to 1)   10
1174⁷ BEAU GRANDE (Ire) 5-12-0 L P Cusack, ...(12 to 1)   11
1330 MOLLIE WOOTTON (Ire) 5-11-1 W T Slattery Jnr, ..(50 to 1)   12
RATHFARDON (Ire) 5-11-3 (3°) C O'Brien, ...(50 to 1)   13
LORD DIAMOND 7-12-0 K F O'Brien, ...(10 to 1)   14
1379⁷ CORRIBLOUGH (Ire) 5-11-6 C O'Dwyer, ...(20 to 1)   15
1076⁴ FAIRYHILL RUN (Ire) 5-11-1 C F Swan, ...(7 to 1)   16
1401 GOLDEN PLAN (Ire) 5-11-6 C N Bowens, ...(33 to 1)   17
MARBLE FONTAINE 6-10-8 (7°) J M Donnelly, ...(50 to 1)   18
1265 STAR FLYER (Ire) (bl) 5-10-12 (3°) Mr P McMahon, ..(50 to 1)   19
211 IM OK (Ire) 5-10-12 (3°) T J Mitchell, ...(50 to 1)   20
FINAWAY BOY (Ire) 5-11-6 J P Banahan, ...(33 to 1)   21
BEST INTEREST (Ire) 5-11-6 J Shortt, ...(25 to 1)   22
SLEMISH MIST 6-11-1 P L Malone, ...(50 to 1)   23
1379 DICK'S CABIN 6-11-6 H Rogers, ...(25 to 1)   24
SLEAVEEN HILL 6-11-1 D H O'Connor, ...(50 to 1)   25

Dist: 5l, 7l, nk, 1l. 4m 2.60s. (25 Ran).

(P P Johnson), Michael Hourigan

1550 Narraghmore Handicap Chase (0-102 5-y-o and up) £3,105 2m..... (1:00)

1179* BOB DEVANI [-] 7-11-7 P Carberry, ...(9 to 4 jt-fav)   1
BLUE RING [-] 9-10-10 F Woods, ...(12 to 1)   2
1402³ BOG LEAF VI [-] 10-9-0 (7°) J P Broderick, ...(8 to 1)   3
1381⁴ WINNING CHARLIE [-] 7-12-6 (6ex) K F O'Brien, .. (5 to 1)   4
806 ALL A QUIVER [-] 6-11-6 C N Bowens, ...(14 to 1)   5

1402 FRIENDLY ARGUMENT [-] 8-11-11 J Magee, ... (14 to 1) 6
1179 BALLYHEIGUE [-] 7-10-13 T Horgan, ... (14 to 1) 7
1268 HO FRETTA [-] 7-10-10 (3") C O'Brien, ... (6 to 1) 8
878⁵ CHARMING EXCUSE [-] 9-11-6 (5") C P Dunne, . . (12 to 1) 9
1399² INCA CHIEF [-] 9-11-4 (5") D P Geoghegan, . . (9 to 4 jt-fav) 0
Dist: 2½l, 5½l, 7l, 1l. 4m 20.00s. (10 Ran).

(John O'Meara), Noel Meade

1551 Burtown Wood Handicap Hurdle (0-116 4-y-o and up) £3,105 2m. . (1:30)

1232* PERSIAN HALO (Ire) [-] 5-11-10 D H O'Connor, ... (6 to 1) 1
1453* PANDA (Ire) [-] 5-11-2 (5",6ex) T P Treacy, ... (4 to 1) 2
1450* DARCARI ROSE (Ire) [-] 4-10-1 (7",6ex) T Martin, . . . (5 to 1) 3
1232⁶ UNCLE BABY [-] 5-10-0 (7") K P Gaule, ... (12 to 1) 4
MR BOAL (Ire) [-] 4-11-10 C F Swan, ... (7 to 2 fav) 5
123 BALLYCANN [-] 6-11-4 (7") P J Mulligan, ... (14 to 1) 6
LAWYER'S BRIEF (Fr) [-] 6-10-10 L P Cusack, ... (7 to 1) 7
1450⁴ FAMOUS DANCER [-] 5-10-4 C N Bowens, ... (12 to 1) 8
1400 PARTNERS IN CRIME [-] 5-10-13 (7") B Bowens, . . .(8 to 1) 9
1495 PRINCE TAUFAN (Ire) [-] 4-10-1 J Magee, ... (25 to 1) 10
TARA MILL (Ire) [-] 4-11-7 K F O'Brien, ... (12 to 1) 11
ROCHE MELODY (Ire) [-] 5-10-4 P Carberry, ... (25 to 1) 12
BLAZING ACE [-] 7-10-0 J P Banahan, ... (50 to 1) 13
1400 REASON TO BELIEVE (Ire) [-] 4-9-2 (7") J P Broderick,
. . . . (50 to 1) 14
Dist: 2l, 4l, hd, 1½l. 3m 58.50s. (14 Ran).

(Tematron Racing Club), Michael Kauntze

1552 Irish Field Chase (5-y-o and up) £6,930 2m. . . . . (2:00)

1335⁹ DEEP HERITAGE 7-11-8 T J Taaffe, ... (100 to 30) 1
992³ DESERT LORD 7-11-6 C F Swan, ... (5 to 1) 2
1382 KILLINEY GRADUATE 7-10-9 (7") J P Broderick, . . (8 to 1) 3
HOW'S THE BOSS 7-11-12 C O'Dwyer, ... (5 to 4 fav) 4
SARAEMMA 7-11-7 J F Titley, ... (12 to 1) 5
WHO'S TO SAY 7-11-6 T Horgan, ... (7 to 1) 6
831 THIRD QUARTER 8-11-6 K F O'Brien, ... (12 to 1) 7
1398³ GOOD TEAM 8-11-8 F Woods, ... (12 to 1) f
Dist: 2½l, 3l, 5l, hd. 4m 18.60s. (8 Ran).

(J P McManus), A L T Moore

1553 Conyngham Cup Handicap Chase (5-y-o and up) £4,190 3¼m. . . . . . (2:30)

1402⁷ OPRYLAND [-] 8-10-1 (3") Mr A R Coonan, ... (14 to 1) 1
1381⁵ ITS A CRACKER [-] 9-11-4 Mr J A Berry, ... (3 to 1) 2
966⁸ JOHNEEN [-] 7-9-11 (7") Miss L Townsley, ... (14 to 1) 3
1266³ FRIENDS OF GERALD [-] 7-11-2 Mr J A Flynn, ... (4 to 1) 4
1231⁶ FERROMYN [-] 8-11-2 Mr P Fenton, ... (5 to 2 fav) 5
1381 LAURA'S BEAU [-] 9-11-13 (5") Mr G J Harford, . . . (14 to 1) 6
1336⁴ ANOTHER RUSTLE [-] 10-10-4 Mr M Phillips, ... (14 to 1) 7
1402⁸ SYLVIA'S SAFFRON [-] (bl) 6-9-13 (5",1ex) Mr P M Kelly,
. . . . (50 to 1) f
906³ MID-DAY GAMBLE [-] 9-9-12¹ (7") Mr P English, . . (10 to 1) su
1381⁹ MARKET MOVER [-] (bl) 7-11-7 Mr S R Murphy, . . . (14 to 1) pu
1231 CAPTAIN BRANDY [-] 8-11-10 (5") Mr H F Cleary, . . (8 to 1) pu
1381⁸ MR HOY [-] 10-10-6¹ (7") Mr J Bright, ... (20 to 1) pu
Dist: 6l, 3l, 1l, 2l. 7m 4.40s. (12 Ran).

(F Lennon), F Lennon

1554 Morgiana Hurdle (Listed) (4-y-o and up) £6,900 2¼m. . . . . (3:00)

1175* PADASHPAN (USA) 4-10-9 (7") P Morris, mid-div, prog 4th,
dsptd ld 3 out, led appr last, styd on strly. . . . . (4 to 1) 1
SHUIL AR AGHAIDH 7-11-9 B Sheridan, rear, some prog 4
out, rdn aftr nxt, styd on wl frm 2 out, nrst finish.
. . . . (8 to 1) 2
SHAWIYA (Ire) 4-11-4 C F Swan, wl plcd, dsptd ld 3 out,
rdn and hdd appr last, mstk and wknd. . . . . . (5 to 4 out) 3
1380* TEMPLEROAN PRINCE 6-11-7 C N Bowens, mid-div, rdn 3
out, kpt on one pace frm nxt, not rch ldrs. . . . . . (10 to 1) 4
1431 NOVELLO ALLEGRO (USA) 5-11-4 P Carberry, mid-div,
prog 3 out, sn rdn, no extr and wknd aftr nxt. . (6 to 1) 5
831⁷ STORM FRONT (Ire) 5-10-13 F Woods, trkd ldr, rdn and
lost pl 3 out, no extr and wknd appr last. . . . . . (14 to 1) 6
1450⁶ SIMPLY SWIFT 6-10-8 (5") T P Treacy, mid-div, rdn and
wknd 3 out. . . . . (14 to 1) 7
1269 DEEP INAGH 7-11-2 D P Fagan, led, jnd 3 out, hdd bef
nxt, wknd. . . . . (16 to 1) 8
1450 SIMENON 7-11-4 J P Banahan, al rear. . . . . (25 to 1) 9
1234 LINVAR 10-10-11 (7") D J Kavanagh, al rear. . . . . . (50 to 1) 10
TORANFIELD 9-11-4 K F O'Brien, trkd ldrs, rdn and lost pl
appr 4 out. . . . . (20 to 1) 11
GLAMOROUS GALE 9-10-13 J Magee, al rear. . . . . (20 to 1) 12
Dist: 1½l, 2l, 8l, 4l. 4m 30.50s. (12 Ran).

(William Brennan), W P Mullins

1555 Baron's Bog I N H Flat Race (5-y-o) £3,105 2m. (3:30)

990² DOONANDORAS (Ire) 12-0 Mr J E Kiely, ... (6 to 4 fav) 1
585 LEGATISSIMO (Ire) 11-11 (3") T J Mitchell, ... (5 to 2) 2
TAXSON (Ire) 12-0 Mr J P Durkan, ... (10 to 1) 3
ARCHER (Ire) 12-0 Mr A J Martin, ... (7 to 1) 4
1018⁸ THATS MY BOY (Ire) 11-7 (7") B Bowens, ...(8 to 1) 5

1383⁵ LOUGH CULTRA DRIVE (Ire) 11-9 (5") Mr J A Nash, (14 to 1) 6
1383⁷ M T POCKETS (Ire) 11-11 (3") Mrs J M Mullins, ...(7 to 1) 7
FEARLESS HUNTER (Ire) 11-7 (7") Mr P O'Reilly, . . (33 to 1) 8
1403³ CAILIN RUA (Ire) 11-6 (3") Mr A E Lacy, ... (10 to 1) 9
7⁷ TWO IN TUNE (Ire) 11-7 (7") Miss L Gough, ... (25 to 1) 10
DIOCESE (Ire) 11-11 (3") Mr A R Coonan, ... (14 to 1) 11
MONGARD (Ire) 11-7 (7") Mr M G Wiseman, ... (33 to 1) 12
GROUP HAT (Ire) 11-7 (7") Mr G A Kingston, ... (12 to 1) 13
1269 TOP RUN (Ire) 11-7 (7") Mr C O'Neill, ... (33 to 1) 14
1403 LADY MARILYN (Ire) 11-6⁴ (7") Mr D L Doyle, ... (20 to 1) 15
1383 BIG JIM 11-9 (5") Mr H F Cleary, ... (14 to 1) 16
IRISH LIGHT (Ire) 11-7 (7") Mr N C Kelleher, ... (16 to 1) 17
BRAMBLE RUN (Ire) 11-9 (5") T J O'Sullivan, ... (20 to 1) 18
DEEP PERK (Ire) 11-6 (5") Mr D Marnane, ... (16 to 1) 19
THE HAW LANTERN 11-4 (5") Mr P M Kelly, ... (33 to 1) 20
Dist: 1l, 8l, 3l, 2l. 3m 57.50s. (20 Ran).

(E P King), J E Kiely

SANDOWN (good (races 1,3,5), good to soft (2,4,6))
Saturday December 4th
Going Correction: PLUS 0.82 sec. per fur. (races 1,3,5), PLUS 0.97 (2,4,6)

1556 Ewell Chase (5-y-o and up) £6,170 3m 110yds. . . . . (12:50)

1031* BARTON BANK 7-11-10 A Maguire, made all, clr frm 14th,
blun 18th, unchlgd.
. . . . (10 to on op 5 to 4 on tchd 21 to 20 on) 1
1293² CAB ON TARGET 7-11-10 P Niven, not fluent, lost tch frm
14th. . . . . (Evens op 11 to 10 on) 2
Won by 20l. 6m 29.00s. a 30.00s (2 Ran).
SR: -/-/

(Mrs J Mould), D Nicholson

1557 Esher Novices' Handicap Hurdle (4-y-o and up) £6,035 2m 110yds. . . (1:20)

988* SUPER COIN [92] 5-11-5 A Maguire, nvr far away, hdwy
to ld appr 2 out, sn clr, rdn out. 1
1040* DOMINANT FORCE [92] 4-11-5 J Osborne, chsd ldrs, lost
pl appr 3rd, ran on betw last 2, hit last, not quicken.
. . . . (9 to 1 op 8 to 1 tchd 10 to 1) 2
1343³ ROSS GRAHAM [82] 5-10-9 G Morgan, hld up, rdn and
ran on aftr 3 out, styd on one pace frm nxt.
. . . . (11 to 1 op 10 to 1 tchd 14 to 1) 3
1366* KYTTON CASTLE [95] 6-11-5 (3") D Meredith, hld up and
beh, some hdwy 2 out, not rch ldrs.
. . . . (9 to 2 op 4 to 1 tchd 5 to 1) 4
1213⁷ MULCIBER [94] 5-11-7 M Perrett, hld up in midfield, some
hdwy 3 out, wknd appr last. . . . . . (20 to 1 op 12 to 1) 5
1515* FRANKUS [80] 4-10-7 N Mann, led till appr 2 out, sn
wknd. . . . . (16 to 1 op 12 to 1) 6
1161³ MUSKORA (Ire) [97] 4-11-10 P Niven, not fluent, reminders
3rd, effrt nxt, sn chasing ldrs, wknd 3 out.
. . . . (10 to 1 op 8 to 1) 7
836* SWIFT CONVEYANCE (Ire) [85] 4-10-12 S McNeill, trkd ldrs,
pushed alng aftr 3 out, sn wknd. . . . . (10 to 1 op 8 to 1) 8
1412³ CRACKLING ANGELS [86] 6-10-13 M A FitzGerald, trkd ldr,
rdn 6th, sn wknd. . . . . (33 to 1 op 20 to 1 tchd 50 to 1) 9
1193* MOVE A MINUTE (USA) [97] 4-11-10 D Murphy, pld hrd and
rstrained early, hdwy 5th, wknd appr 2 out.
. . . . (4 to 1 fav op 5 to 1) 10
1448³ GAMEFULL GOLD [89] 4-11-2 H Davies, midfield early,
drpd last 5th, sn rdn and no imprsn.
. . . . (12 to 1 op 8 to 1) 11
Dist: 6l, 7l, nk, 15l, 2½l, 2½l, 12l, 2l, sht-hd, 12l. 4m 7.70s. a 20.70s (11 Ran).
SR: 44/38/21/33/17/-/14/-/-/

(George Brookes), R Lee

1558 Westminster-Motor Taxi Insurance Henry VIII Novices' Chase Grade 2 (5-y-o and up) £9,150 2m. . . . . (1:50)

1348* BAYDON STAR 6-11-7 A Maguire, trkd ldr, led 6th, shaken
up and quickened aftr 3 out, readily.
. . . . (2 to 1 on tchd 15 to 8 on) 1
1124* ONE MORE DREAM 6-11-4 Richard Guest, hld up, effrt
7th, mstk nxt, chlgd appr 3 out, not pace of wnr.
. . . . (3 to 1 op 11 to 4 tchd 100 to 30) 2
1348² STRONG VIEWS 6-11-0 M A FitzGerald, hld up in tch, cld
appr 3 out, outpcd bef nxt, rdn and put head in air
r-in, no imprsn. . . . .(10 to 1 op 6 to 1) 3
1358² MARLINGFORD 6-11-0 D Morris, led to 6th, styd hndy till
rdn and wknd appr 3 out. . . . . (14 to 1 op 10 to 1) 4
Dist: 6l, 2l, 12l. 4m 9.90s. a 21.40s (4 Ran).
SR: 10/1/-/-/

(Mrs Shirley Robins), D Nicholson

1559 William Hill Handicap Hurdle Grade 3 (4-y-o and up) £20,750 2m 110yds
. . . . (2:25)

1106⁴ LAND AFAR [137] 6-11-2 W Marston, al in tch, wnt second
aftr 5th, led appr last, hld on gmely.
. . . . (13 to 2 op 9 to 2 tchd 7 to 1) 1

212

HIGHBROOK (USA) [124] 5-10-3 D Murphy, *patiently rdn, beh till smooth hdwy appr 2 out, chlgd frm last, jst hld.*
.....................................(8 to 1 tchd 10 to 1)   2

1347⁵ HIGH BARON [138] 6-11-3 S Earle, *midfield early, hdwy 3rd and sn chasing ldrs, ev ch appr 2 out, ran on one pace.*......................(16 to 1 op 20 to 1)   3

1106⁵ MAAMUR (USA) [134] 5-10-13 A Maguire, *trkd ldrs, rdn appr 2 out, kpt on r-in...*(8 to 1 op 6 to 1 tchd 9 to 1)   4

1106³ TAROUDANT [128] 6-10-7 P Niven, *hld up early, hdwy 4th, ev ch whn mstk 3 out, ran on ag'n aftr nxt, no extr last.*.....................(10 to 1 tchd 12 to 1)   5

KILCASH (Ire) [145] 5-11-10 M Richards, *hld up and beh, hdwy appr 2 out, btn whn hit last.* (20 to 1 op 33 to 1)   6

1443* ARABIAN BOLD (Ire) [130] 5-10-9 M A FitzGerald, *led till rdn and hdd appr last, sn btn......*(5 to 1 tchd 6 to 1)   7

1106 ZAMIRAH (Ire) [122] 4-9-10 (5*) T Jenks, *prmnt till ran on 3 out, sn wknd......*(50 to 1 op 33 to 1 tchd 66 to 1)   8

1012* SUNSET AND VINE [123] 6-10-2² H Davies, *hld up and beh, some hdwy aftr 3 out, hrd rdn betw last 2, sn wknd.....................* (15 to 2 op 7 to 1 tchd 8 to 1)   9

898³ EDEN'S CLOSE [122] (v) 4-10-1 M Perrett, *nvr better than mid-div...................* (25 to 1 tchd 33 to 1) 10

1122⁶ JIMMY THE GILLIE [131] 7-10-5 (5*) M McCarthy, *chsd ldg bunch till rdn and lost pl frm 3 out.*
.................................(50 to 1 tchd 66 to 1) 11

1225* LEOTARD [136] 6-11-1 (4ex) J Osborne, *chsd ldr, mstk 4th, rdn and wknd quickly appr 2 out.*
.....................(9 to 4 fav op 5 to 2 tchd 3 to 1) 12

Dist: Nk, 2l, 1l, 3½l, 4l, 1l, 6l, 2l. 4m 4.80s. a 17.80s (12 Ran).
SR: 70/56/68/53/56/69/50/41/36/   (T J Ford), J Webber

1560 Mitsubishi Shogun Tingle Creek Trophy Limited Handicap Chase Grade 2 (5-y-o and up) £15,550 2m..... (2:55)

SYBILLIN [159] 7-11-9 P Niven, *hld up early, hdwy 8th and sn ev ch, led 2 out, hdd r-in, rallied to ld last 100 yards..................* (6 to 1 op 8 to 1 tchd 9 to 1)   1

1387² DEEP SENSATION [154] 8-11-4 D Murphy, *al prmnt, led 3rd to 5th, led 9th to 3 out, led r-in, hdd last 100 yards.*
......................(100 to 30 op 3 to 1 tchd 7 to 2)   2

1048 WATERLOO BOY [162] 10-11-12 A Maguire, *al prmnt, led 6th to 9th, led briefly 3 out, no extr betw last 2.*
......................(10 to 1 op 12 to 1 tchd 14 to 1)   3

1387* TRAVADO [164] 7-12-0 J Osborne, *hld up in tch, mstk 4 out, outpcd appr nxt, kpt on r-in...*(5 to 2 op 9 to 4)   4

1226⁴ STORM ALERT [150] 7-11-0 S McNeill, *set slow early pace, hdd and pckd 3rd, led 5th to nxt, mstk 4 out, sn lost pl and rdn alng, kpt on appr last.*
.....................(9 to 4 fav op 2 to 1 tchd 5 to 2)   5

1098 VALIANT BOY [143] 7-10-2 (5*) S Lyons, *hld up, cld 7th, blun 9th, not reco'r.* (50 to 1 op 33 to 1 tchd 66 to 1)   6

CYPHRATE (USA) [150] 7-11-0 M Perrett, *hld up and beh, awkward 5th, blun 8th, nvr able to chal.*
..........................(20 to 1 op 14 to 1)   7

Dist: 1½l, 4l, 3½l, nk, 7l, 7l. 4m 2.20s. a 13.70s (7 Ran).
SR: 89/82/84/69/55/55/   (Marquesa de Moratalla), J G FitzGerald

1561 Doug Barrott Handicap Hurdle (4-y-o and up) £4,968 2¾m...........(3:30)

1257* DARK HONEY [112] 8-10-3 (5*) A Dicken, *keen hold, nvr away, led appr 2 out, hdd, hrd rdn betw last two, rallied to ld r-in......* (9 to 2 op 5 to 1 tchd 4 to 1)   1

1396⁵ WICK POUND [115] (bl) 7-10-11 T Grantham, *hld up early, hdwy 6th and sn in tch, led 2 out, hdd betw last two, kpt on und pres.................*(14 to 1 tchd 16 to 1)   2

RIVA (NZ) [116] 6-10-12 H Davies, *patiently rdn, hdwy frm 7th, led appr last, veered lft and hdd r-in, not reco'r.*
.....................................(11 to 2 op 9 to 2)   3

1247* BEYOND OUR REACH [104] 5-10-0 J Osborne, *beh, some hdwy 3 out, styd on appr last, nvr nrr.*
.........................(8 to 1 op 11 to 1 tchd 12 to 1)   4

THE DECENT THING [118] 10-10-11 (3*) R Davis, *last early, some hdwy 8th, kpt on one pace frm 2 out, nvr able to chal.................*(25 to 1 op 20 to 1 tchd 33 to 1)   5

1274³ GOLDEN MOSS [105] 8-10-1 M Richards, *chsd ldg bunch, rdn aftr 8th, sn unbl to quicken...* (25 to 1 op 20 to 1)   6

1120³ EMERALD SUNSET [108] 8-10-4 D Gallagher, *with ldrs, ev ch appr 2 out, sn rdn and wknd.* (16 to 1 tchd 20 to 1)   7

1349² PIPERS COPSE [131] 11-11-13 M Perrett, *led, hit 5th, hdd aftr 3 out, sn wknd......*(8 to 1 tchd 10 to 1 and 7 to 1)   8

1119² POLISHING [117] 6-10-13 P Niven, *chsd ldg bunch, pushed alng 3 out, sn btn.*
....................................(10 to 1 op 10 to 1 tchd 12 to 1)   9

1163⁶ SURE PRIDE (USA) [104] 5-9-9² (7*) J Clarke, *midfield, rdn alng aftr 3 out, no dngr............*(33 to 1 op 20 to 1) 10

1322* BONANZA [121] 6-11-6 R Hodge, *hld up and beh, bustled alng and some hdwy 8th, nvr able to chal.*
.....................................(16 to 1 op 10 to 1) 11

CASH IS KING [125] 9-11-7 M A FitzGerald, *beh till shrtlvd effrt 7th, sn no imprsn.......................*(33 to 1 op 20 to 1) 12

1278³ ROSGILL [110] 7-10-6 Richard Guest, *chsd ldrs 4 out and wknd aftr 3 out.....................*(20 to 1) 13

1412 WELSH SIREN [110] 7-10-6 S McNeill, *tucked away in midfield till drpd rear frm 7th.*
...................................(10 to 1 op 8 to 1 tchd 11 to 1) 14

1438⁷ HOLY JOE [130] 11-11-12 A Maguire, *trkd ldrs till rdn nd wknd aftr 3 out, beh whn pld up bef last.*   pu

1349⁵ SENDAI [127] 7-11-9 D Murphy, *trkd ldr till wknd quickly 7th, wl beh bef last...* (8 to 1 tchd 9 to 1)   pu

Dist: 2l, 4l, 6l, 8l, 10l, 4l, 3½l, sht-hd, 1l, 2l. 5m 32.80s. a 26.80s (16 Ran).
SR: 25/26/23/5/11/-/-/6/-/   (Roger Curzon), S Dow

TOWCESTER (Soft)
Saturday December 4th
Going Correction: PLUS 1.00 sec. per fur. (races 1,3,-6,7), PLUS 1.25 (2,4,5)

1562 Blue Rosette Selling Handicap Hurdle (4,5,6-y-o) £1,793 2m.........(12:35)

861⁸ ALICE'S MIRROR [81] (v) 4-10-6 W McFarland, *hdwy 4th, wth ldr 3 out, led appr last, drvn out.*
.....................(9 to 1 op 7 to 1 tchd 10 to 1)   1

1325³ FUSSY LADY [77] 6-10-2 L Harvey, *hld up, hdwy 4th, wnt second nxt, led 3 out, hdd appr last, sn rdn, one pace.*
....................(7 to 4 fav op 9 to 4 tchd 5 to 2)   2

659⁸ BAYBEEJAY [75] 6-10-0 D Bridgwater, *hld up, hdwy 5th, chsd ldg pair, sn rdn and one pace, btn whn blun last.*   3

861 WILTOSKI [78] 5-10-3 Mrs N Ledger, *wl beh 3rd, styd on aftr 3 out, kpt on betw last 2, nvr nrr.*
.....................................(16 to 1 op 10 to 1)   4

1404⁷ ABSOLUTLEY FOXED [75] 4-10-0 T Wall, *chsd ldr, lost tch aftr 5th, one pace frm 3 out........*(12 to 1 op 7 to 1)   5

59³ SOMERSET DANCER (USA) [107] 6-12-4 D O'Sullivan, *hld up, rdn and effrt 5th, one pace frm 3 out.*
.....................(11 to 1 op 4 to 1 tchd 9 to 1)   6

RED JACK (Ire) [90] 4-11-1 R Supple, *hld up, rdn alng and lost pl aftr 4th, tld off 3 out.*
.................................(4 to 1 op 3 to 1 tchd 9 to 2)   7

1474 SOLID (Ire) [85] (bl) 5-10-5 (5*) D Walsh, *pld hrd, led 4th til hdd 3 out, wknd rpdly, tld off.*
.....................(10 to 1 op 7 to 1 tchd 11 to 1 and 12 to 1)   8

1188 BROTHERLYAFFECTION [77] 4-10-2² Gary Lyons, *led, hit second, hdd 4th, wknd rpdly, sn tld off, pld up bef 2 out.......................*(33 to 1 op 20 to 1)   pu

1392⁷ TREASSOWE MARINER [75] (bl) 5-9-9² (7*) J Clarke, *chsd ldr till wknd quickly 5th, sn tld off, pld up bef 2 out.*
.....................(25 to 1 op 12 to 1)   pu

Dist: 5l, 10l, 1½l, ¾l, 7l, 30l, 2l, 8l. 4m 5.30s. a 22.30s (10 Ran).
SR: 15/6/-/-/-/20/   (T P McGovern), T P McGovern

1563 Barnsdale Country Club Novices' Chase (5-y-o and up) £3,210 3m 1f ....(1:05)

1306 JUDGES FANCY (bl) 9-11-0 D Bridgwater, *hld up, mstk 1st, hdwy 7th, trkd ldrs til led 3 out, drw clr aftr nxt, styd on wl.................*(4 to 1 op 7 to 2 tchd 9 to 2)   1

1351* FARDROSS 7-11-12 N Williamson, *hld up, hdwy to chase ldrs 12th, ev ch 5 out, sn rdn and unbl to quicken, eased whn btn aftr last...* (13 to 8 fav op 6 to 4 tchd 7 to 4)   2

1372² DARK OAK 7-11-0 L O'Hara, *hld to second, led ag'n 12th to 3 out, one pace..........* (8 to 1 op 5 to 1 tchd 10 to 1)   3

1205 FLORIDA SKY 6-11-0 R Supple, *mstks, beh 11th, styd on frm 3 out, nvr nrr.............................*(4 to 1 op 2 to 1)   4

1194³ LOOSE WHEELS (v) 7-11-0 R Marley, *led second, mstk 9th, sn wknd...............*(8 to 1 op 7 to 1)   5

1170³ CRAIGSTOWN (Ire) 5-10-13 S Hodgson, *hld up, hdwy 6th, in tch whn mstk 11th, wknd aftr nxt.*
...................................(16 to 1 op 10 to 1 tchd 20 to 1)   6

1386 GREENHILL GO 8-10-9 R Rowell, *f 1st.*
.....................................(40 to 1 op 33 to 1)   F

1311 TEE QU 8-10-7 (7*) Mr G Hogan, *al beh, mstk 5 out, tld off whn pld up bef 2 out.* (40 to 1 op 33 to 1 tchd 50 to 1)   pu

1306 PROVING 9-10-9 (5*) C Burnett-Wells, *hdwy 4th, pressed ldr til wknd 12th, beh whn pld up bef 2 out.*
.....................................(20 to 1 op 12 to 1)   pu

1444² PEATY GLEN 8-11-0 R Campbell, *mstks, blun tenth, beh whn pld up bef nxt.......................*(33 to 1 op 14 to 1)   pu

BLAKEINGTON 7-11-0 A Tory, *beh frm 12th, tld off whn pld up bef 2 out..................*(50 to 1 op 33 to 1)   pu

Dist: 10l, 10l, 5l, 7l, 12l. 6m 55.00s. a 40.00s (11 Ran).
SR: -/1/-/-/-/-/   (Mrs S A Scott), N A Twiston-Davies

1564 Anthony Simpson, M.E.P., Blue Rosette Novices' Hurdle (4-y-o and up) £2,041 2m 5f.................(1:35)

1110⁴ GENERAL WOLFE 4-10-12 B Powell, *trkd ldg grp, mstk 4th, rdn aftr four out, styd on to ld appr last, drvn out.*
.................................(7 to 2 op 5 to 2 tchd 4 to 1)   1

1406* NED THE HALL (Ire) 5-11-5 N Williamson, *hld up, trkd ldr gng wl 5 out, wnt second 3 out, led nxt, hdd appr last, unbl to quicken...* (6 to 4 fav op 11 to 10 tchd 2 to 1)   2

SUNY BAY (Ire) 4-10-12 R Supple, *trkd ldr, cl up and ev ch 4 out, blun 2 out, wknd betw last two.*
.....................................(16 to 1 op 8 to 1)   3

1173^{6} NOTHINGBUTTROUBLE 9-10-12 V Slattery, *mstk second, chsd ldr till wknd 4 out*........................(50 to 1) 4
1252^{2} RUSSINSKY 6-10-7 R J Beggan, *hld up, hdwy 5th, led nxt, hdd 2 out, wknd quickly.*
..........................(2 to 1 op 7 to 4 tchd 9 to 4) 5
1196^{5} PLATINUM SPRINGS 6-10-7 L Harvey, *hld up, hdwy 4th, lost pl aftr 6th, sn beh, tld off whn pld up bef 2 out.*
.....................(20 to 1 op 16 to 1 tchd 33 to 1) pu
605 GUITING GIRL 4-10-7 D Bridgwater, *led to 6th, wknd quickly, tld off whn pld up bef 4 out.*
....................(16 to 1 tchd 20 to 1 and 25 to 1) pu
Dist: 1½l, 15l, 15l, 7l. 5m 31.90s. a 32.90s (7 Ran).
(G S Beccle), Capt T A Forster

1565 'Well To Do' Challenge Cup Handicap Chase (0-135 5-y-o and up) £5,970 3m 1f..............................(2:10)

1375^{2} INVASION [101] (v) 9-10-0 M Brennan, *hmpd and lost pl 9th, hdwy to chase ldrs 12th, styd on frm 2 out, hrd rdn to ld r-in, all out*.......(7 to 1 op 6 to 1 tchd 10 to 1) 1
1197* POSTMAN'S PATH [102] 7-10-1 B Powell, *hld up in tch, cl up and ev ch 4 out, slight ld 2 out, rdn and hdd r-in, unbl to quicken*......(9 to 4 fav op 2 to 1 tchd 5 to 2) 2
1226^{5} RIVER BOUNTY [125] 7-11-10 R Supple, *hld up, rdn and hdwy 4 out, cl up and ev ch 2 out, ridden and unbl to quicken r-in*........... (5 to 1 op 3 to 1 tchd 11 to 2) 3
1281^{4} SMOOTH ESCORT [108] (v) 9-10-7 D Bridgwater, *lft in ld 1st, jmpd slwly nxt, hdd 11th, led ag'n 13th to 2 out, rdn and kpt on*............(12 to 1 op 8 to 1 tchd 14 to 1) 4
1302^{6} WOODLANDS GENHIRE [101] 8-9-9^{2} (7*) D Fortt, *mstk 6th, beh and pushed alng tenth, styd on one pace frm 3 out.*
......................(33 to 1 op 25 to 1 tchd 40 to 1) 5
1083^{6} TAMMY'S FRIEND [101] 6-10-0 I Lawrence, *prmnt, led 11th to 13th, wknd aftr 4 out.* (8 to 1 op 6 to 1 tchd 9 to 1) 6
LEAGAUNE [101] 11-10-0 P Harley, *rdn alng 9th, beh frm 12th*.................(25 to 1 op 16 to 1 tchd 33 to 1) 7
865^{5} GUILDWAY [101] 10-10-0^{7} (7*) Mr M Rimell, *al beh, no ch frm 6 out*...........................(20 to 1 tchd 25 to 1) 8
1254* TORT [116] 9-11-1 L Harvey, *led and f 1st.*
..................................(7 to 1 op 5 to 1 tchd 8 to 1) f
1063^{2} PINK GIN [104] 6-10-3 N Williamson, *hdwy tenth, chsd ldrs, in tch whn f 4 out.* (7 to 1 op 5 to 1 tchd 8 to 1) f
Dist: 1½l, 1½l, 2l, 12l, 1l, 10l, 1½l. 6m 55.00s. a 40.00s (10 Ran).
SR: -/-/5/-/-/-/ (Lady Anne Bentinck), O Brennan

1566 Berkeley Burke Handicap Chase (0-130 5-y-o and up) £3,557 2m 110yds..............................(2:40)

REJOINUS [106] 8-10-11 N Williamson, *trkd ldr till led aftr 5th, rdn and styd on wl whn chlgd 2 out, pushed clr r-in*..................................(5 to 1 op 4 to 1) 1
1098^{2} BOSTON ROVER [115] 8-11-6 M Brennan, *hld up, hdwy to chase ldg pair aftr 6th, rdn to join wnr 2 out, swtchd appr last, one pace*.............(2 to 1 fav tchd 5 to 2) 2
1282^{4} THE GREEN STUFF [110] 8-11-1 R Supple, *hld up and beh, hdwy to chase ldr aftr 8th, pushed alng 4 out, no imprsn*.................(7 to 2 op 3 to 1 tchd 4 to 1) 3
FILE CONCORD [123] 9-12-0 I Lawrence, *led till aftr 5th, pressed ldr till wknd 4 out.*
.........................(7 to 1 op 6 to 1 tchd 15 to 2) 4
JIM VALENTINE [102] 7-10-7 P McDermott, *hld up, nvr gng pace, styd on frm 3 out.* (9 to 1 op 6 to 1 tchd 10 to 1) 5
1195^{3} BLUE BUCCANEER [96] 10-10-1 L Harvey, *nvr gng pace, lost tch aftr 3rd, tld off after 8th, pld up bef 2 out.*
....(7 to 1 op 5 to 1) pu
Dist: 5l, 6l, 3½l, 6l. 4m 26.80s. a 24.80s (6 Ran).
SR: 41/45/34/43/16/-/ (C R Galloway), A P Stringer

1567 Penman 'National Hunt' Novices' Hurdle (Div I) (4-y-o and up) £1,980 2m 5f..............................(3:10)

1003^{8} OTTOMAN EMPIRE 6-10-12 M Brennan, *hld up, steady hdwy to track ldr aftr 6th, cl up and ev ch 4 out, led after 3 out, hit last 2, cmftbly.*
......................(14 to 1 op 7 to 1 tchd 16 to 1) 1
920* OCEAN LEADER 6-11-5 D Bridgwater, *hld up, hdwy aftr 4 out, chsd wnr frm 2 out, no imprsn.*
...........................(7 to 1 op 6 to 1 tchd 8 to 1) 2
CATS RUN (Ire) 5-10-12 R Supple, *hld up, hdwy aftr 6th, cl up and ev ch 4 out, one pace frm 2 out.*
..................................(33 to 1 tchd 50 to 1) 3
1167^{3} TALBOT 7-10-7 (5*) A Procter, *led til hdd appr 2 out, rdn and styd on betw last two.*
...........................(9 to 2 op 5 to 2 tchd 5 to 1) 4
1392^{2} FOREST FEATHER (Ire) 5-10-7 (5*) C Burnett-Wells, *hld up, hdwy 6th, wnt second nxt, trkd ldr til wknd aftr 3 out.*
...........................(8 to 1 op 5 to 1 tchd 9 to 1) 5
1301^{4} REFERRAL FEE 6-10-12 L Harvey, *hld up, chsd ldg grp frm 5 out, wknd aftr 3 out.* (14 to 1 op 7 to 1 tchd 16 to 1) 6
1108 TRIMAGE (Ire) 5-10-7 (5*) R Farrant, *hld up and beh, hdwy aftr 3 out, styd on one pace, nvr nrr.*
.......................(25 to 1 op 16 to 1 tchd 33 to 1) 7
1169^{3} YES MAN (Ire) 4-10-12 N Williamson, *in tch, trkd ldr frm 5 out, rdn and wknd 3 out*........(15 to 8 fav op 5 to 2) 8
1090^{4} OATS N BARLEY 4-10-12 I Shoemark, *hld up, hdwy to chase ldr aftr 7th, in tch til wknd quickly 3 out.*
..................................(33 to 1 op 20 to 1) 9
1109^{4} MONKTON (Ire) 5-10-12 B Powell, *hld up, pushed alng aftr 6th, sn lost tch, tld off whn pld up bef 2 out.*
...................................(6 to 1 op 5 to 1) pu
1161 FIFTH IN LINE (Ire) 5-10-6^{1} (7*) Mr C Vigors, *pressed ldr til wknd quickly 4 out, beh whn pld up bef 2 out.* (50 to 1) pu
ROMANY CREEK (Ire) 4-10-12 S Hodgson, *lost pl aftr 5th, tld off whn pld up bef 2 out*....... (20 to 1 op 10 to 1) pu
1263^{4} CURLY SULLIVAN (Ire) 5-10-7 R J Beggan, *beh frm 5th, pushed alng from nxt, sn tld off, pld up bef 3 out.*
.....................(20 to 1 op 14 to 1 tchd 25 to 1) pu
CHENOATS 5-10-12 L O'Hara, *lost tch aftr 6th, tld off whn pld up bef 3 out*..........................(50 to 1) pu
Dist: 5l, 4l, 1½l, 10l, 2½l, 2½l, 1½l, 20l. 5m 32.40s. a 33.40s (14 Ran).
(Lady Anne Bentinck), O Brennan

1568 Penman 'National Hunt' Novices' Hurdle (Div II) (4-y-o and up) £1,964 2m 5f..............................(3:40)

888 TOTHEWOODS 5-10-12 D Bridgwater, *hld up, hdwy 5th, led on bit appr 2 out, sn clr, cmftbly.*
.....................(12 to 1 op 10 to 1 tchd 16 to 1) 1
NICK THE BEAK (Ire) 4-10-12 R Supple, *hld up, trkd ldrs frm 5th, ev ch whn mstk 3 out, kpt on betw last 2, not trble wnr*...............(9 to 1 op 8 to 1 tchd 10 to 1) 2
1108^{5} BUCKSHOT (Ire) 5-10-12 E Murphy, *al prmnt, ev ch 3 out, rdn and one pace aftr three out*....(5 to 1 tchd 6 to 1) 3
COUNTRY STORE 4-10-7 W McFarland, *hld up, hit 7th, styd on aftr 3 out, nvr nrr*.........(33 to 1 op 20 to 1) 4
EASTERN RIVER 7-10-12 B Powell, *hld up in tch, cl up and ev ch 3 out, sn rdn, eased whn btn betw last 2.*
.... (13 to 2 op 4 to 1 tchd 7 to 1) 5
HECTOR'S RETURN 5-10-12 V Slattery, *al prmnt, cl up and ev ch aftr 3 out, wknd appr nxt.*
..................................(25 to 1 op 16 to 1) 6
1109^{9} LAY IT OFF (Ire) 4-10-7 L Harvey, *hld up and beh, kpt on one pace frm 3 out*............. (33 to 1 op 25 to 1) 7
DIVINE CHANCE (Ire) 5-10-12 I Lawrence, *lost pl aftr 4th, styd on one pace frm 3 out*.........(20 to 1 op 10 to 1) 8
TOP BRASS (Ire) 5-10-12 N Williamson, *led 3rd till appr 2 out, wknd quickly.*
.... (5 to 4 on op Evens tchd 5 to 4 and 11 to 8) 9
ROCK DIAMOND 7-10-12 E Leonard, *al beh.*
..................................(20 to 1 op 14 to 1) 10
658 STORMING RUN (Ire) 5-10-12 R Marley, *led to 3rd, pressed ldr till wknd quickly 3 out*.........(33 to 1 op 25 to 1) 11
1283 FORGIVE THE FOLLY 5-10-7 (5*) R Farrant, *al beh, tld off aftr 6th*.......................................(33 to 1) 12
GREEN'S GAME 5-10-12 D Skyrme, *al beh, tld off aftr 6th.*
....(33 to 1) 13
SWINGING SONG 6-10-12 B Dalton, *beh whn slpd up bend aftr 4th*........ (25 to 1 op 20 to 1 tchd 33 to 1) su
Dist: 5l, 7l, 3½l, 2l, 4l, ½l, 7l, 2½l, 5l, 5l. 5m 36.60s. a 37.60s (14 Ran).
(Robert Cooper), N A Twiston-Davies

WETHERBY (good)
Saturday December 4th
Going Correction: PLUS 0.45 sec. per fur. (races 1,3,6), PLUS 0.80 (2,4,5)

1569 Thorp Arch Juvenile Novices' Hurdle (3-y-o) £2,057 2m............. (12:45)

1243* HYDE'S HAPPY HOUR 11-4 G McCourt, *prmnt, rdn to ld appr 3 out, kpt on wl und pres frm last, jst hld on.*
......................(5 to 1 tchd 11 to 2 and 9 to 2) 1
784^{6} GENSERIC (Fr) 10-12 R Garritty, *hld up, steady hdwy aftr 5th, chsd wnr frm 2 out, styd on wl und pres from last, jst fld*...............(14 to 1 op 10 to 1 tchd 20 to 1) 2
1350^{2} O SO NEET 10-12 S Smith Eccles, *chsd ldr, rdn appr 3 out, kpt on same pace und pres.*
...........................(7 to 2 op 3 to 1 tchd 4 to 1) 3
1284 MHEMEANLES 10-12 L Wyer, *chsd ldrs, rdn aftr 3 out, sn btn*..........................(5 to 4 fav tchd 11 to 8) 4
1284* GOLDEN SAVANNAH 10-11 (7*) J Driscoll, *led till hdd appr 3 out, grad wknd*..................(10 to 1 op 8 to 1) 5
1284^{7} ALMAMZAR (USA) 10-5 (7*) E Husband, *beh, hdwy aftr 5th, wknd appr 3 out*..............(20 to 1 op 10 to 1) 6
ZAAHEYAH (USA) 10-7 C Grant, *beh frm 5th.*
..................................(25 to 1 op 14 to 1) 7
HO-JOE (Ire) 10-12 N Smith, *al beh, lost tch frm 6th.*
..................................(20 to 1 op 16 to 1) 8
1217 ADMISSION (Ire) 10-12 A Merrigan, *in tch till wknd appr 6th, tld off*........................(66 to 1 op 50 to 1) 9
872^{5} JUMBO STAR 10-5 (7*) Mr R Hale, *beh frm 4th, tld off whn pld up bef 3 out*..................(50 to 1 op 25 to 1) pu
Dist: Nk, 12l, 2½l, 6l, 10l, 12l, nk, dist. 4m 1.40s. a 20.40s (10 Ran).
(Travellers T Time Club), N Tinkler

1570 Dick Warden Novices' Chase (5-y-o and up) £4,370 2½m 110yds.....(1:15)

1420 RUN UP THE FLAG 6-11-0 P Hide, *cl up, led tenth, styd on*
wl frm 2 out......... (13 to 8 fav op 5 to 4 tchd 7 to 4)   1
1218⁵ DEEP DECISION 7-11-10 K Johnson, *hld up, hdwy appr 4*
out, chsd wnr frm nxt, btn whn slight mstk last, kpt on.
....(8 to 1)   2
PRECIPICE RUN 8-11-0 N Doughty, *led till hdd tenth, lost*
pl aftr 3 out, kpt on frm last.......... (4 to 1 op 7 to 2)   3
BIG MAC 6-11-0 C Grant, *hld up in tch, pushed alng and*
outpcd aftr 7th, no dngr after.... (20 to 1 op 16 to 1)   4
1148⁹ CONCERT PAPER 9-11-0 K Davies, *prmnt, en ch 4 out, sn*
rdn, grad wknd..................(25 to 1 op 16 to 1)   5
FATHER TIME 9-11-0 S Smith Eccles, *mstk second, prmnt*
till wknd appr 4 out.................(4 to 1 op 7 to 2)   6
1146² ABLE PLAYER (USA) (bl) 6-11-6 J Burke, *hld up in tch, effrt*
aftr 4 out, sn wknd..................(8 to 1 op 7 to 1)   7
Dist: 5l, 6l, 1½l, sht-hd, 12l, nk. 5m 23.40s. a 26.90s (7 Ran).

(Pell-Mell Partners), J T Gifford

1571 ATS Handicap Hurdle (4-y-o and up) £3,236 2m.....................(1:45)

MAJED (Ire) [133] 5-11-4 (5") Mr M Buckley, *hld up, hdwy*
gng wl aftr 6th, led on bit 2 out, stumbled and hdd after
last, quickened and styd on strly to ld nr finish.
....(4 to 1 op 9 to 4)   1
1225 ARCOT [122] 5-10-12 G McCourt, *hld up, hdwy gng wl*
appr 3 out, chlgd nxt, quickened to ld aftr last, hdd
and no extr nr finish.
.... (2 to 1 fav op 3 to 1 tchd 100 to 30)   2
1364⁵ TOOGOOD TO BE TRUE [113] 5-10-3 L Wyer, *made most*
till hdd 3 out, styd on same pace.
.... (7 to 1 tchd 8 to 1 and 13 to 2)   3
1364⁷ PERSUASIVE [130] 6-10-13 (7") S Mason, *hld up, steady*
hdwy aftr 5th, slight ld 3 out, hdd nxt, one pace.
....(7 to 1 op 6 to 1)   4
1116³ BEAUCADEAU [134] 7-11-10 A Dobbin, *prmnt, chlgd 3*
out, sn rdn and btn............. (12 to 1 op 9 to 1)   5
1443⁵ UNCLE ERNIE [130] 8-10-13 (7") F Leahy, *in tch, chlgd 3*
out, sn rdn and btn............... (20 to 1 op 14 to 1)   6
LOCH GARANNE [117] 5-10-7 D Byrne, *hld up, effrt aftr*
6th, kpt on frm 2 out, nt trble ldrs.
....(12 to 1 op 10 to 1)   7
1225 CLURICAN (Ire) [120] 4-10-3 (7") E Husband, *chsd ldrs till*
outpcd appr 6th, no dngr aftr.... (40 to 1 op 25 to 1)   8
1481⁴ SEON [114] 7-10-1 (3") N Bentley, *prmnt, dsptd ld 6th, sn*
wknd......................(11 to 1 op 9 to 1 tchd 12 to 1)   9
1320⁷ BOLD AMBITION [110] 6-10-0 J Callaghan, *chsd ldr till*
wknd aftr 6th........................(40 to 1 op 33 to 1)   10
DIZZY (USA) [125] 5-10-8 (7") F Perratt, *in tch till wknd aftr*
6th................................... (20 to 1 op 14 to 1)   11
1055³ WAKE UP [110] 6-10-0 C Grant, *prmnt early, beh frm 6th.*
....(25 to 1 op 20 to 1)   12
Dist: ¾l, 12l, 1l, 7l, 3½l, 2l, 6l, 3½l, 1½l, 3l. 3m 51.00s. a 10.00s (12 Ran).

SR: 67/55/34/50/47/39/24/21/11/   (Laurel (Leisure) Limited), Mrs M Reveley

1572 Wharfe Handicap Chase (0-140 5-y-o and up) £7,351 3m 110yds......(2:15)

1004⁵ MR BOSTON [130] 8-11-11 L Wyer, *in tch, pushed alng*
and slightly outpcd aftr 14th, rallied appr 4 out, lft in
ld aftr nxt, clr whn hit last.... (15 to 8 fav op 2 to 1)   1
1365² SOUTHERN MINSTREL [115] 10-10-10 G McCourt, *in tch,*
trkd ldrs frm hfwy, chlgd 14th, kpt on same pace from 4
out....................... (13 to 2 op 6 to 1 tchd 7 to 1)   2
1181⁵ RUN PET RUN [107] 8-10-2 A Dobbin, *cl up, led 9th till hdd*
4 out, one pace.....................(11 to 1 op 10 to 1)   3
1197² CITY KID [112] 8-10-4 (3") P Hide, *hld up in tch, effrt appr*
4 out, sn rdn and wknd quickly, tld off.
....(4 to 1 op 7 to 2)   f
1503 RIFLE RANGE [125] 10-11-6 R Garritty, *jmpd sluly 1st, sn*
led, f 6th............................(14 to 1 op 12 to 1)   f
1222² DEEP DAWN [107] 10-10-2 C Grant, *led till aftr 1st, in tch*
whn f 9th.........................(12 to 1 op 8 to 1)   f
CAROUSEL ROCKET [108] 10-9-12 (5") D Bentley, *bright*
dwn 6th.................................(33 to 1 op 20 to 1)   bd
1286* BETTER TIMES AHEAD [133] 7-12-0 N Doughty, *cl up, lft in*
ld 6th, hdd 9th, led ag'n 4 out, jst in frnt whn pld up
lme aftr..................(7 to 2 op 3 to 1 tchd 4 to 1)   pu
Dist: 6l, 1l, dist. 6m 34.00s. a 28.00s (8 Ran).

SR: 13/-/-/-/-/   (M K Oldham), Mrs M Reveley

1573 'Emmerdale' Handicap Chase (5-y-o and up) £3,548 2½m 110yds.....(2:45)

YOUNG BENZ [140] 9-11-11 L Wyer, *in tch, hdwy on bit*
appr 11th, led approaching 3 out, jmpd lft last 2, cmft-
bly..............................(14 to 1 op 8 to 1)   1
1479² ANTONIN (Fr) [135] 5-11-1 (5") J Burke, *with Ed, led*
11th till hdd appr 3 out, kpt on, no ch with wnr.
....(8 to 1 tchd 9 to 1)   2
1307² FIGHTING WORDS [134] 7-11-2 (3") P Hide, *in tch, pushed*
alng aftr 8th, kpt on frm 3 out, nvr dngrs.
....(7 to 2 tchd 4 to 1)   3
1226³ GENERAL PERSHING [143] 7-12-0 N Doughty, *led, mstk*
3rd, hdd aftr 11th, grad lost pl. (Evens fav op 11 to 10)   4

1226⁸ SWORD BEACH [129] 9-11-0 G McCourt, *sn tracking ldrs,*
chlgd appr 4 out, soon rdn and btn.
.... (7 to 1 op 13 to 2 tchd 8 to 1)   5
1226⁷ ARMAGRET [140] 8-11-11 D Byrne, *lost tch and pld up bef*
7th....................................(7 to 1 op 6 to 1)   pu
Dist: 6l, 1½l, 5l, 20l. 5m 15.90s. a 19.40s (6 Ran).

SR: 67/56/53/57/23/-/   (T H Bennett), M H Easterby

1574 Walshford 'National Hunt' Novices' Hurdle (4-y-o and up) £2,145 3m 1f ....(3:15)

1320³ SAVOY 6-10-12 N Doughty, *trkd ldrs, led 3 out, kpt on*
und pres frm last......................(5 to 4 fav tchd 6 to 4)   1
1060² COQUI LANE 6-10-12 B Storey, *led till hdd aftr 9th, out-*
pcd appr 3 out, rallied und pres to chase wnr betw last
2, no imprsn r-in...... (9 to 2 op 6 to 1 tchd 5 to 1)   2
SCOTTON BANKS (Ire) 4-10-12 L Wyer, *hld up gng wl,*
hdwy aftr 8th, effrt appr 3 out, kpt on same pace.
....(14 to 1 op 10 to 1)   3
1295* SPARROW HALL 6-10-11 (7") G Tormey, *prmnt, mstk 5th,*
slight ld aftr 9th till hdd 3 out, one pace.
................................(4 to 1 op 3 to 1 tchd 9 to 2)   4
ASK TOM (Ire) 4-10-12 R Garritty, *hld up in tch, effrt aftr*
9th, sn btn...........(11 to 1 op 8 to 1 tchd 12 to 1)   5
1129² KINDA GROOVY 4-10-12 N Smith, *chsd ldrs till wknd aftr*
8th.......................................(12 to 1 op 8 to 1)   6
1181² MAJORITY MAJOR (Ire) 4-10-12 K Johnson, *chsd ldrs till*
wknd appr 8th......................(8 to 1 op 6 to 1)   7
1287⁹ QUIXALL CROSSETT 8-10-7 (5") J Supple, *lost tch frm*
hfwy, tld off....................................(100 to 1)   8
Dist: 1½l, 6l, 1l, 15l, 20l, 2½l, dist. 6m 24.30s. a 29.30s (8 Ran).

(Robert Ogden), G Richards

PUNCHESTOWN (IRE) (yielding)
Sunday December 5th

1575 Cappagh (C & G) Hurdle (3-y-o) £3,105 2m.........................(12:30)

1377* GLENSTAL FLAGSHIP (Ire) 10-11 (7") K P Gaule, ..(5 to 2)   1
1432* MY KERRY DANCER (USA) 10-13 (5") T P Treacy,
....(11 to 10 fav)   2
1432⁶ RIYADH DANCER (Ire) 10-12 M Duffy, ...(20 to 1)   3
1432⁵ DAHLIA'S BEST (USA) 10-12 J Shortt, ...(14 to 1)   4
1377 THE SALTY FROG (Ire) 10-12 M Flynn, ...(50 to 1)   5
BALLYSPARKLE (Ire) 10-12 L P Cusack, ...(25 to 1)   6
1377 KING BRIAN (Ire) 10-12 W Slattery Jnr, ...(100 to 1)   7
TENCA (Ire) 10-12 M Dwyer, ...(33 to 1)   8
1377 LITTLE TINCTURE (Ire) 10-12 T J Taaffe, ...(50 to 1)   9
MOUNT OVAL (Ire) 10-5 (7") J Pearse, ...(100 to 1)   10
BAEZA 10-7 (5") C P Dunne, ...(33 to 1)   11
1454⁸ DIFFERENT TIMES (Ire) 10-12 C O'Dwyer, ...(12 to 1)   12
SHEREGORI (Ire) 10-12 C F Swan, ...(4 to 1)   f
Dist: 13l, 7l, 5l, 2l. 3m 58.30s. (13 Ran).

(Joseph Crowley), A P O'Brien

1576 Ballycaghan Hurdle (4-y-o and up) £3,105 2m.....................(1:00)

1265* DANOLI (Ire) 5-11-1 (5") T P Treacy, ...(11 to 8 on)   1
881* WHAT A QUESTION (Ire) 5-11-1 N Williamson, ...(8 to 1)   2
DIPLOMATIC 4-10-11 J P Banahan, ...(12 to 1)   3
1076³ LEGAL PROFESSION (Ire) 6-11-2 C F Swan, ...(4 to 1)   4
1331* IF YOU SAY YES 5-11-1 K F O'Brien, ...(8 to 1)   5
1331⁴ MICK O'DWYER 6-11-2 F J Flood, ...(14 to 1)   6
924⁴ EAGLE ROCK (USA) 5-11-2 C O'Brien, ...(12 to 1)   7
1331³ ROSE APPEAL 7-11-3 (3") T J Mitchell, ...(12 to 1)   8
1236⁸ QUEENIES CHILD 6-10-11 A Powell, ...(33 to 1)   9
EMPEROR GLEN (Ire) 5-11-2 M Dwyer, ...(20 to 1)   10
THOMOND PARK (Ire) 5-11-2 J Shortt, ...(50 to 1)   11
1330 JIMMY GORDON 6-11-2 A Maguire, ...(33 to 1)   12
TWIN RAINBOW 6-11-2 L P Cusack, ...(16 to 1)   13
DRUMREAGH LAD (Ire) 5-11-2 H Rogers, ...(66 to 1)   14
SHANDONAGH BRIDGE 6-11-2 C O'Dwyer, ...(50 to 1)   15
1230 SYLVANER (Ire) 4-10-1 (5") P A Roche, ...(100 to 1)   16
Dist: 4l, 11l, ½l, 10l. 3m 58.60s. (16 Ran).

(D J O'Neill), Thomas Foley

1577 Frank Ward & Co. Sols Cross Country Chase (5-y-o and up) £3,795 4m 1f ....(1:30)

MILLER'S CHAP 6-10-11 (7") Miss L Townsley, ...(10 to 1)   1
TEL D'OR 8-10-11 (7") Mr P J Millington, ...(20 to 1)   2
WATERLOO KING 6-11-9 Mr M Phillips, ...(14 to 1)   3
584⁹ HAVE A BARNEY 12-11-9 Mr A J Martin, ...(15 to 8 fav)   4
969 TORSTAR 8-11-12¹ (7") Mr M Ewing, ...(25 to 1)   5
CROSS THE FLOOR 12-10-12¹ (7") Mr W T O'Donnell,
....(10 to 1)   6
926⁵ FAIR GO 7-10-11 (7") Miss C A Harrison, ...(16 to 1)   7
1268⁵ BLENHEIM PALACE (USA) 6-11-4 (5") Mr G J Harford,
....(12 to 1)   ur
HAZY STORM (Ire) 5-10-12 Mr R Hurley, ...(5 to 1)   ur
BIANCONI 7-11-2 (7") Capt W S Hayes, ...(6 to 1)   ro
BUCK ME UP 10-11-7³ Mr E Bolger, ...(7 to 2)   pu

SIOBHAN MARIE 7-10-10 (3°) Mr D Valentine, ... (20 to 1)   pu
THE DANCING PARSON 6-10-10 (3°) Mr A R Coonan,
. . . .(20 to 1)   pu
Dist: 2½l, 2½l, 3l, 4l. 10m 3.50s. (13 Ran).

(Ms R Rooney), Ms Rosemary Rooney

1578 Durkan Bros International Punchestown Chase (Listed) (5-y-o and up) £11,700 2m 5f. . . . . (2:00)

1439² CAHERVILLAHOW 9-11-4 N Williamson, *led till aftr 5th,
led 7th to nxt, led 3 out, rdn appr last, styd on strly.
. . . .(3 to 1)   1
1226 GENERAL IDEA 8-12-0 A Maguire, *trkd ldrs, chsd wnr frm
3 out, rdn and wknd appr last.* . . . . (11 to 4 fav)   2
1231⁴ HAKI SAKI 7-11-8 G M O'Neill, *trkd ldrs, lost pl tenth,
styd on wl in strt.* . . . .(25 to 1)   3
1380 VANTON 9-11-4 J F Titley, *led aftr 5th to nxt, led 8th till
mstk and hdd 3 out, sn btn.*. . . . .(8 to 1)   4
1433⁴ NORTON VILLE 7-11-8 K F O'Brien, *rear, nvr trble ldrs.*
. . . .(20 to 1)   5
FOURTH OF JULY 9-11-4 J P Banahan, *prog frm rear to
track ldrs 8th, 4th four out, rdn and btn nxt.* (16 to 1)   6
1336³ BLITZKREIG 10-11-4 C F Swan, *mid-div, rdn and weeakened 4 out.* . . . .(12 to 1)   7
1336° FORCE SEVEN 6-11-9 T Horgan, *mid-div, prog to track
ldrs 7th, f tenth.* . . . .(5 to 1)   f
1398² COMMERCIAL ARTIST 7-11-4 C O'Dwyer, *f 1st.* . . (12 to 1)   f
1433² GOLD OPTIONS (bl) 11-12-0 M Dwyer, *tracking ldrs whn
uns rdr 7th.* . . . .(6 to 1)   ur
1336⁵ GARAMYCIN 11-11-8 B Sheridan, *brght dwn 1st.* (10 to 1)   bd
Dist: 9l, 3½l, 12l, 2l. 5m 30.00s. (11 Ran).

(Mrs Miles Valentine), M F Morris

1579 ESB WinElectric Chase (5-y-o and up) £6,900 2¼m. . . . .(2:30)

1266 MERRY GALE (Ire) 5-11-0 K F O'Brien, ...(13 to 8 fav)   1
1399° ATONE 6-11-6 C F Swan, ...(2 to 1)   2
1430 WILL PHONE 7-11-5 J F Titley, ...(3 to 1)   3
1177³ DORAN'S TOWN LAD 6-11-8 A Maguire, ...(12 to 1)   4
1233² FURRY STAR 7-11-10 J Jones, ...(10 to 1)   5
1159° WICKET KEEPER 6-9-10 (7°) Mr L J Gracey, ...(50 to 1)   ur
1450 CASTLE RANGER 6-11-2 A Powell, ...(20 to 1)   ur
Dist: 5l, 7l, nk, 2l. 4m 39.90s. (7 Ran).

(Herb M Stanley), J T R Dreaper

1580 Longtown Handicap Hurdle (4-y-o and up) £3,105 2½m. . . . .(3:00)

1234² DERRYMOYLE (Ire) [-] 4-11-5 C F Swan, ...(5 to 4 on)   1
1174 MASTER CRUSADER [-] 7-9-13 N Williamson, . . .(20 to 1)   2
MONKEY AGO [-] 6-11-7 J J Taaffe, ...(14 to 1)   3
1335° TUG OF PEACE [-] 6-11-7 (7°,3ex) J P Broderick, . .(6 to 1)   4
1400⁷ BANAIYKA (Ire) [-] 4-11-2 (3°) T P Treacy, ...(9 to 2)   5
1380 KERFONTAINE [-] 8-11-3 A Maguire, ...(8 to 1)   6
1234 HI MILLIE [-] (bl) 7-10-6 P L Malone, ...(16 to 1)   7
SWIFT RUN [-] 6-10-8 F Woods, ...(12 to 1)   8
SLANG [-] 7-9-8¹ T Horgan, ...(50 to 1)   9
1434° RICH TRADITION (Ire) [-] 5-10-11 (7°) R A Hennessy,
. . . .(10 to 1)   ur
COOL CARLING [-] 6-9-10 J Magee, ...(33 to 1)   pu
Dist: ½l, 20l, 2½l, 3l. 5m 38.00s. (11 Ran).

(Herb M Stanley), Michael Cunningham

1581 Bawnogues I N H Flat Race (4-y-o) £3,105 2m. . . . .(3:30)

GALLOWS HILL (Ire) 11-6 (3°) Mrs J M Mullins, ...(6 to 1)   1
CAREFORMENOW (USA) (bl) 11-2 (7°) Mr E Norris, (3 to 1)   2
1337³ MARYJO (Ire) 11-1 (3°) Mr A E Lacy, ...(14 to 1)   3
1337 ICANTELYA (Ire) 11-3 Mr T Mullins, ...(16 to 1)   4
1383⁵ CABLE BEACH (Ire) 11-4 (5°) Mr G J Harford, . . (5 to 2 fav)   5
1455³ CLOWATER LADY (Ire) 11-1 (3°) Mr A R Coonan, . . (6 to 1)   6
FINAWAY EXPRESS (Ire) 11-4 (5°) Mr D McGoona, (20 to 1)   7
1455° SKY VISION (Ire) 10-8 (7°) Mr K F O'Donnell, ...(25 to 1)   8
1337⁴ WEJEM (Ire) 11-9 Mr S R Murphy, ...(6 to 1)   9
1383⁸ SPECTACULAR STAR (Ire) 11-9 Mr A J Martin, . .(16 to 1)   10
STRUGGLING LASS (Ire) 11-4 Mr A J Flynn, ...(20 to 1)   11
1714 THE BRIDGE TAVERN (Ire) 11-2 (7°) Miss C M Duggan,
. . . .(8 to 1)   12
832   TREANAREE (Ire) 11-2 (7°) Mr D K Budds, ...(20 to 1)   13
1016² DOCS DILEMMA (Ire) 11-2 (7°) Mr N Brennan, . . .(14 to 1)   14
211² DROP THE HAMMER (Ire) 11-3¹ (7°) Mr R Pugh, . .(14 to 1)   15
MANANKHALI (Ire) 11-2 (7°) Mr D L Cullen, ...(25 to 1)   16
C'MURRA (Ire) 11-2 (7°) Miss A T Green, ...(25 to 1)   17
FAIRY STRIKE (Ire) 11-9 Mr J A Berry, ...(12 to 1)   18
333⁴ BEAU CINQ (Ire) 11-6 (3°) Miss E Hutchinson, ...(66 to 1)   19
VALTORUS (Ire) 11-2 (7°) Mr T J Murphy, ...(16 to 1)   20
1267° THE PERISHER (Ire) 11-4 (5°) Mr J A Nash, ...(8 to 1)   21
1337 DIGACRE (Ire) 11-2 (7°) Mr R G Caplis, ...(33 to 1)   22
RELISHING 11-1 (3°) Mr D Marnane, ...(25 to 1)   23
BARNISH ROSE (Ire) 10-11 (7°) Mr S Kerr, ...(25 to 1)   24
1397 STEVIES DEN (Ire) 11-2 (7°) Mr P Burns, ...(25 to 1)   25
Dist: Nk, 4l, 2l, 10l. 3m 56.30s. (25 Ran).

(John J Brennan), W P Mullins

EDINBURGH (Good to firm)
Monday December 6th
Going Correction: MINUS 0.30 sec. per fur. (races 1,3,5,7), MINUS 0.45 (2,4,6)

1582 EBF 'National Hunt' Novices' Hurdle Qualifier (4,5,6-y-o) £2,036 2m (12:15)

1114° RELUCTANT SUITOR 4-11-0 C Grant, *led second, made
rst, drvn out.* . . . .(5 to 2 op 7 to 4)   1
1199° LINNGATE 4-11-5 T Reed, *hld up, steady hdwy whn
badly hmpd 3 out, rdn to chase wnr betw last 2, ch last,
kpt on, no imprsn.* (11 to 8 fav op 5 to 4 tchd 6 to 4)   2
1199³ ASTRALEON (Ire) 5-11-0 B Storey, *trkd ldrs, effrt aftr 3
out, kpt on same pace frm nxt.* . . . .(14 to 1 op 10 to 1)   3
547° THREE STRONG (Ire) 4-10-11 (3°) D J Moffatt, *hld up, gd
hdwy aftr 4th, chsd wnr 3 out till wknd betw last 2.*
. . . . (15 to 2 op 6 to 1 tchd 8 to 1)   4
1237² OAKLEY 4-10-9 (5°) P Waggott, *in tch, effrt and ch aftr 3
out, one pace frm nxt.* . . . .(66 to 1)   5
723³ ORD GALLERY (Ire) 4-11-0 P Harley, *chsd ldrs till outpcd
aftr 3 out, no dngr after.* . . . .(33 to 1 op 25 to 1)   6
INDIAN RIVER (Ire) 5-11-0 M Dwyer, *nvr nr to chal.*
. . . .(6 to 1 tchd 7 to 1)   7
734⁸ LONDON HILL 5-11-0 C Dennis, *chsd ldrs till wknd appr 2
out.* . . . .(200 to 1)   8
1369² BASILICUS (Fr) 4-11-0 Richard Guest, *prmnt, rdn whn
blun 3 out, sn wknd.* . . . .(11 to 1 op 7 to 1)   9
1114 SKIDDAW CALYPSO 4-10-9 A Dobbin, *prmnt to hfwy.*
. . . .(100 to 1)   10
FOLLY FURLONG 6-10-2 (7°) Mr R Hale, *sn beh.* (200 to 1)   11
KIRKCALDY (Ire) 4-11-0 Mr J Bradburne, *led to second,
prmnt till wknd appr 3 out.* . . . .(100 to 1)   12
1003 THE ADJUTANT (Ire) 5-11-0 (7°) B Harding, *sn tracking
ldrs, effrt aftr 3 out, soon btn.* . . . .(33 to 1)   13
PLUM DUFF 6-11-0 K Johnson, *beh most of way.*
. . . .(100 to 1)   14
SIRRONS DEAL 4-10-9 K Jones, *sn beh, tld off.* (200 to 1)   15
Dist: 3½l, 7l, 1l, 10l, 1l, 1½l, 1½l, 15l, 2½l, 1½l. 3m 58.70s. a 0.70s (15 Ran).
SR: 31/32/20/19/9/8/6/4/-/   (Joe Buzzeo), M D Hammond

1583 Musselburgh Claiming Chase (5-y-o and up) £2,635 2m. . . . .(12:45)

1132³ SONSIE MO 8-10-12 T Reed, *in tch, hdwy to chase ldr
7th, lft clr 4 out, styd on strly.* . . . . . .(5 to 2 op 7 to 4)   1
1357⁴ SKOLERN 9-10-6 B Storey, *beh, mstk 3rd, gd hdwy to
chase wnr 3 out, blun nxt, no imprsn.*
. . . .(6 to 1)   2
1409⁵ SILVER HAZE 9-11-0 K Jones, *chsd ldrs till wknd appr 4
out.* . . . .(12 to 1 op 8 to 1)   3
RAHINANE 10-10-12 A Orkney, *sn beh.*
. . . . (16 to 1 op 10 to 1)   4
1360² PRESSURE GAME 10-10-10 A Merrigan, *chsd ldr till wknd
appr 8th, sn beh, tld off.* . . . .(7 to 1 op 6 to 1)   5
1409² ISLAND JETSETTER 7-10-12 Richard Guest, *led, 3 ls clr
and gng wl whn f 4 out.* . . . .(Evens fav op 5 to 4)   f
KIRSTENBOSCH 6-10-5 (7°) F Perratt, *al beh, pld up bef
8th.* . . . .(16 to 1 op 10 to 1 tchd 20 to 1)   pu
Dist: 20l, 12l, ½l, 30l. 3m 48.10s. b 1.90s (7 Ran).
SR: 31/5/1/-/   (Timothy Hardie), Mrs S C Bradburne

1584 Harcros Scottish Juvenile Championship Qualifier Three Years Old Novices' Hurdle £1,924 2m. . . . .(1:15)

1476 ERBIL (Ire) 10-12 T Reed, *hld up and beh, effrt betw last
2, quickened to ld towards finish, cleverly.*
. . . .(50 to 1 tchd 66 to 1)   1
1473³ ROSCOMMON JOE (Ire) 11-4 M Dwyer, *trkd ldrs gng wl,
led last till hdd and no extr towards finish, broke blood
vessel.* . . . .(Evens fav op 5 to 4 tchd 6 to 4)   2
ERICOLIN (Ire) 10-8 G McCourt, *in tch, hdwy aftr 3 out,
slight ld betw last 2, blun and hdd last, no extr.*
. . . .(2 to 1 op 5 to 4)   3
652° COPABELLA 10-2 (5°) P Waggott, *in tch, ev ch 2 out, rdn
appr last, one pace.* . . . . . .(7 to 1 op 6 to 1 tchd 8 to 1)   4
1476 ASTRAC TRIO (USA) 11-4 A Dobbin, *led till hdd betw last
2, fdd.* . . . .(8 to 1 op 6 to 1)   5
SHARP AT SIX (Ire) 10-8 P Harley, *hld up, effrt aftr 3 out,
no hdwy.* . . . .(40 to 1 op 16 to 1 tchd 50 to 1)   6
DIGNIFIED (Ire) 9-10 (7°) A Linton, *chsd ldrs till wknd 2 out.*
. . . .(40 to 1 op 25 to 1 tchd 50 to 1)   7
1483 INDIAN SECRET (Ire) (bl) 10-12 C Grant, *chsd ldr, rdn appr
2 out, sn wknd, tld off.* . . . .(33 to 1 op 16 to 1)   8
Dist: 1l, 1½l, 2l, 2½l, 12l, sht-hd, 30l. 3m 46.20s. a 8.20s (8 Ran).

(Bill Fraser), L Lungo

1585 Wee Jimmy Mitchell Handicap Chase (0-125 5-y-o and up) £2,762 3m. .(1:45)

1095⁵ CHOICE CHALLANGE [98] 10-10-1¹ C Grant, *cl up, led aftr
tenth, styd on wl frm 2 out.* . . . . . . (14 to 1 op 10 to 1)   1

1132⁴ BOARDING SCHOOL [102] 6-10-5 B Storey, *in tch, trkd ldrs frm 11th, chlgd 3 out, ev ch nxt, no extr appr last.*
....(6 to 1 op 5 to 1) 2
1220 CORNET [125] 7-12-0 M Dwyer, *in tch, effrt appr 4 out, ev ch nxt, kpt on same pace.........*(6 to 1 tchd 7 to 1) 3
1222 CLASSIC MINSTREL [104] 9-10-7⁷ T Reed, *mstks early, hld up and beh, styd on wl frm 3 out, nrst finish.*
....(14 to 1 op 12 to 1) 4
876 OVER THE DEEL [112] 7-11-1 A Orkney, *prmnt, effrt appr 4 out, one pace....................*(7 to 2 tchd 4 to 1) 5
1185³ BALTIC BROWN [105] 8-10-8 Richard Guest, *trkd ldrs, ev ch 4 out, grad wknd, btn whn hit 2 out.*
....(5 to 2 fav tchd 11 to 4) 6
1095² MOSS BEE [97] 6-10-0 R Hodge, *beh, hdwy hfwy, wknd appr 4 out...................................*(10 to 1) 7
1093² CLARE LAD [97] 10-9-9 (5*) D Bentley, *chsd ldrs till outpcd aftr 11th, no dngr after..........*(12 to 1 op 10 to 1) 8
1145⁶ SPEECH [97] 10-9-7 (7*) F Perratt, *led till hdd aftr tenth, wknd appr 14th, tld off..................*(100 to 1) 9
RAWYARDS BRIG [97] 10-10-0 A Dobbin, *beh frm hfwy, wl tld off...*(66 to 1) 10
1186⁷ JESTERS PROSPECT [108] 9-10-11 M Moloney, *al beh, tld off whn pld up bef 13th..........* (33 to 1 op 25 to 1) pu
Dist: 3l, 1½l, 4l, 6l, 1½l, 8l, 8l, 20l. 5m 52.60s. a 2.60s (11 Ran).

(D F Sills), M D Hammond

1586 Gorebridge Conditional Jockeys' Handicap Hurdle (0-120 4-y-o and up) £1,987 2m....................(2:15)

LEGITIM [76] 4-9-11 (3*) G Tormey, *in tch, hdwy aftr 3 out, led appr last, ran on wl........................*(25 to 1) 1
972⁶ CHEEKY POT [92] 5-11-2 P Waggott, *in tch, outpcd aftr 3 out, styd on wl frm nxt................*(8 to 1 op 6 to 1) 2
1153³ BONDAID [83] 9-10-4 (3*) P McLoughlin, *in tch, led appr 2 out, hdd approaching last, no extr............*(6 to 1) 3
824⁵ RAPID MOVER [80] 6-10-4 W Dwan, *in tch, effrt appr nxt, kpt on same pace frm nxt.....*(6 to 1 op 5 to 1) 4
1066 THE GREEN FOOL [100] 6-11-10 D Bentley, *in tch, effrt appr 2 out, kpt on same pace.....*(11 to 1 op 10 to 1) 5
ASHDREN [88] 6-10-12 T Jenks, *chsd ldrs, ev ch 2 out, sn rdn and one pace..........................*(8 to 1) 6
FAMILY LINE [104] 5-12-0 F Perratt, *beh, styd on frm 2 out, nvr nr to chal........................*(11 to 1 op 10 to 1) 7
CHARLYCIA [80] 5-10-1⁴ (7*) M Clarke, *dsptd ld till wknd appr 2 out.....................................*(20 to 1) 8
1487 JOHN NAMAN (Ire) [83] 4-10-7 A Dobbin, *in tch, effrt aftr 3 out, no hdwy......................*(16 to 1 op 14 to 1) 9
914³ SERAPHIM (Fr) [103] 4-11-10 (3*) S Taylor, *sn beh, some late hdwy, nvr dngrs..............*(14 to 1 op 10 to 1) 10
1487 CLEAR IDEA (Ire) [89] 5-10-10 (3*) B Harding, *led or dsptd ld till hdd appr 2 out, sn btn...............*(10 to 1) 11
1127⁷ INVERTIEL [84] (bl) 9-10-1 (7*) S Melrose, *in tch till wknd appr 2 out....................*(25 to 1 op 20 to 1) 12
1357* COOL DUDE [101] 7-11-11 D J Moffatt, *sn beh.*
....(5 to 1 fav tchd 6 to 1) 13
GOLDEN REVERIE (USA) 7-9-5 10-3 S Mason, *sn beh.*
....(33 to 1 op 25 to 1 tchd 40 to 1) 14
Dist: 2½l, ½l, 2l, 1½l, 2l, nk, 3l, 1l, 1½l, 1½l. 3m 39.10s. a 11.10s (14 Ran).
SR: 13/26/16/11/29/15/30/3/5/

(John Donald), J M Jefferson

1587 Lasswade Maiden Chase (5-y-o and up) £2,479 2½m...............(2:45)

1484⁴ TIMANFAYA 6-11-5 B Storey, *beh, hdwy to chase ldr hfwy, slightly outpcd aftr 12th, styd on wl und prs to ld aftr last out...*(50 to 1 op 66 to 1) 1
1218⁹ VULPIN DE LAUGERE (Fr) 6-11-0 (5*) J Burke, *prmnt, reminders aftr 9th, chsd ldr aftr 12th, wndrd betw last 2, chlgd last, no extr........................*(50 to 1) 2
1351⁴ NO WORD 6-11-5 W McFarland, *led 3rd till hdd and no extr aftr last......* (11 to 8 fav op 7 to 4 tchd 2 to 1) 3
1182⁴ CARDENDEN (Ire) 5-11-5 S Turner, *chsd ldrs till blun and lost pl 8th, sn beh....* (25 to 1 op 20 to 1 tchd 33 to 1) 4
1356³ FLING IN SPRING 7-11-5 A Orkney, *al beh.*
....(7 to 1 tchd 8 to 1) 5
1061² COUNT SURVEYOR 6-11-5 C Grant, *outpcd and reminders aftr 8th, sn lost tch.......* (7 to 4 op 5 to 4) 6
1358⁷ EBRO (bl) 7-11-5 K Jones, *al beh, lost tch hfwy, tld off.*
....(100 to 1) 7
THE LORRYMAN (Ire) 5-11-5 T Reed, *chsd ldrs till wknd aftr 9th, sn lost tch, tld off.....................*(50 to 1) 8
641⁴ JUNIORS CHOICE 10-11-5 A Merrigan, *jmpd lft, led to 3rd, chsd ldrs till wknd quickly appr 12th, tld off.*
....(12 to 1 op 10 to 1 tchd 14 to 1) 9
JINGLIN' GEORDIE (Ire) 5-11-5 K Johnson, *in tch whn f 7th..*(50 to 1 op 33 to 1) f
1150 CALDECOTT 7-11-5 Richard Guest, *stumbled badly and uns rdr 6th..*(14 to 1 op 10 to 1) ur
Dist: 2½l, 2l, 20l, nk, 1½l, 20l, 2½l, 4l. 5m 1.40s. a 11.40s (11 Ran).

(Mrs D F Culham), W G Reed

1588 Levy Board Novices' Handicap Hurdle (4-y-o and up) £1,882 2½m......(3:15)

1183⁴ JUKE BOX BILLY (Ire) [70] 5-10-1 (3*) A Larnach, *cl up, led 4th to 6th, dsptd ld till led aftr 3 out, clr betw last 2, styd on............................*(9 to 4 op 5 to 2 tchd 11 to 4) 1
1204⁶ RED TEMPEST (Ire) [70] 5-9-11 (7*) F Perratt, *led to 4th, chsd clr ldrs till outpcd appr 3 out, rallied nxt, staying on strly whn blun last...............*(12 to 1 op 10 to 1) 2
1287* SWEET NOBLE (Ire) [90] 4-11-3 (7*) F Leahy, *cl up, led or dsptd ld frm 6th till hdd aftr 3 out, kpt on same pace.*
....(11 to 10 fav op 5 to 4 tchd Evens) 3
1183³ BIN LID (Ire) [68] 4-9-9 (7*) B Harding, *hld up, hdwy appr 3 out, effrt aftr last...........................*(16 to 1 op 14 to 1) 4
1183⁵ RALLYING CRY (Ire) [72] 5-10-6 B Storey, *in tch, outpcd aftr 7th, no dngr after.....................*(16 to 1 op 12 to 1) 5
1181 STEPDAUGHTER [70] 7-10-0 C Dennis, *in tch till outpcd aftr 7th, no dngr after...........................*(100 to 1) 6
577⁴ DENIM BLUE [82] 4-11-2 T Reed, *lost tch aftr 7th, no dngr after..*(7 to 1 tchd 8 to 1) 7
DAVARA [68] 7-9-9 (7*) Mr D Parker, *in tch till outpcd aftr 7th, tld off whn pld up lme bef 3 out..........*(25 to 1) pu
HIGHLAND FRIEND [67] 5-10-1 K Johnson, *tld off frm 7th, pld up bef 2 out...................................*(50 to 1) pu
Dist: 5l, 5l, 12l, 3½l, 2l, ¾l. 4m 43.30s. a 5.30s (9 Ran).

(Tom Patterson), J H Johnson

LUDLOW (good to firm)
Monday December 6th
Going Correction: PLUS 0.33 sec. per fur.

1589 Wistanstow Novices' Selling Hurdle (4-y-o and up) £1,480 2m.....(12:30)

1211³ WEST MONKTON 7-11-0 R Dunwoody, *ldg grp, led briefly appr 2 out, rallied und pres to ld nr finish.*
....(6 to 1 op 4 to 1) 1
1448⁶ SOLO CORNET 8-11-0 W Humphreys, *hdwy 5th, slight ld 2 out till rdn and hdd nr finish.*
....(6 to 1 op 5 to 1 tchd 10 to 1) 2
934 ICE MAGIC 6-11-0 D Gallagher, *trkd ldrs, ev ch 2 out till hit last, one pace aftr..................*(7 to 1 op 10 to 1) 3
SILK DYNASTY 7-10-11 (3*) S Wynne, *hld up, ran on frm 6th, styd on one pace aftr last......*(14 to 1 op 10 to 1) 4
232⁹ CAOIMSEACH (Ire) 5-11-0 B Powell, *hld up, hdwy 6th, rdn and no extr frm 2 out...............*(7 to 2 fav op 5 to 2) 5
1188 HULLO MARY DOLL 4-10-2 (7*) Chris Webb, *beh, ran on appr 2 out, nvr dngrs................*(20 to 1 tchd 25 to 1) 6
TEA-LADY (Ire) 5-10-9 S McNeill, *handily plcd, rdn and no extr betw last 2.*
....(8 to 1 op 7 to 1 tchd 10 to 1 and 14 to 1) 7
1473² ABELONI 4-11-0 R Greene, *hld up, improved appr 2 out, no imprsn approaching last.*
....(8 to 1 op 5 to 1 tchd 10 to 1) 8
CLEAR LIGHT 6-11-0 Mr T Stephenson, *wl plcd, wknd appr 2 out, tld off.....................*(16 to 1 op 8 to 1) 9
1472 CASHTAL RUNNER 4-11-0 Pat Caldwell, *led 3rd till appr 2 out, sn wknd, tld off.....................*(50 to 1) 10
1173 FAIR BABE 7-10-7 (7*) Mr N Bradley, *not fluent, rdn alng in rear 4th, tld off......................*(50 to 1) 11
323 PRECISION RACER 5-10-9 C Llewellyn, *wl plcd till lost pos quickly 5th, tld off.........*(50 to 1 op 33 to 1) 12
AKIMBO 6-11-0 A Maguire, *led to 3rd, wknd 5th, tld off nxt....................................*(8 to 1 tchd 10 to 1) 13
ROYAL ACCLAIM 8-10-11 (3*) R Farrant, *beh aftr 4th, pld up bef 6th...................................*(16 to 1 op 8 to 1) pu
Dist: 1½l, 2½l, 6l, sht-hd, hd, hd, 1½l, dist, 8l, dist. 3m 50.20s. a 13.20s (14 Ran).
SR: 7/5/2/-/-/-/

(Mrs B Hobbs), C T Nash

1590 Temeside Novices' Handicap Chase (5-y-o and up) £2,762 3m......(1:00)

1367³ MASTER JOLSON [92] 5-11-10 A Maguire, *handily plcd, led 13th, wnt clr 2 out, eased nr finish.*
....(5 to 2 op 9 to 4) 1
1462⁸ SILVER AGE (USA) [79] 7-10-8 (3*) R Farrant, *ran on frm rear 9th, styd on chase appr 3 out.*
....(14 to 1 op 10 to 1) 2
1080 DEBT OF HONOR [74] 5-10-6 R Greene, *drpd rear 4th, ran on appr 3 out, nrst finish..........*(14 to 1 op 8 to 1) 3
1086 COOMBESBURY LANE [70] (bl) 7-10-2 W Marston, *cld on ldrs tenth, chsd wnr appr 3 out, wknd 2 out.*
....(25 to 1 op 16 to 1) 4
1276 NEW PROBLEM [70] 6-9-10¹ (7*) A Flannigan, *in tch in mid-div, blun 15th, not reco'r, tld off......*(33 to 1 op 33 to 1) 5
1306 PHILIPINTOWN LAD [70] 10-9-11 (5*) T Eley, *led second to 11th, wknd 15th, tld off......*(50 to 1 op 33 to 1) 6
1394² SANDAIG [92] (bl) 7-11-10 N Williamson, *hld up in tch, blun and drpd rear 9th, mstk 13th, tld off nxt.*
....(Evens fav op 11 to 10 on tchd 11 to 10) 7
1527 ARBEE TWENTY [70] 7-10-2 I Lawrence, *led to second, led 11th to 13th, wknd 15th, tld off...........*(16 to 1 op 12 to 1) 8
1325⁷ PANT LLIN [80] 7-10-12 R Supple, *mid-div, hdwy 15th, 4th and btn whn f 2 out.................*(14 to 1 op 10 to 1) f
Dist: 8l, 3½l, 4l, 25l, ½l, 3l, 15l. 6m 9.10s. a 20.10s (9 Ran).

(Mrs E Roberts), D Nicholson

217

1591 Hugh Sumner Handicap Chase (0-130 5-y-o and up) £3,095 2m....... (1:30)

1443³ SHU FLY (NZ) [125] 9-12-0 Jacqui Oliver, trkd ldg pair, led 8th, clr aftr nxt, unchlgd........ (2 to 1 fav op 9 to 4) 1
1098⁴ RUPPLES [97] 6-10-0 W Worthington, outpcd in rear till styd on 3 out, chsd wnr appr last, no imprsn.
.................................(25 to 1 op 20 to 1) 2
1312² BOSSBURG [97] 6-10-0 D Gallagher, outpcd in rear till styd on frm 2 out, nrst finish......(16 to 1 op 12 to 1) 3
1132⁵ CLEVER FOLLY [104] 13-10-7¹ N Doughty, outpcd frm 5th.
.................................(7 to 1 op 6 to 1) 4
1328 MARKET LEADER [97] 13-10-0 L Harvey, al beh.
.................................(14 to 1 op 12 to 1 tchd 16 to 1) 5
1328² CHAIN SHOT [109] 8-10-12 A Maguire, led, hit 1st, hdd 8th, outpcd last.................(9 to 4 tchd 5 to 2) 6
1328* TINAS LAD [109] 10-10-12 N Williamson, wth ldr to 8th, chsd wnr aftr nxt till wknd after 2 out, tld off.
.................................(5 to 1 op 5 to 2) 7
Dist: 7l, 12l, 7l, 2l, 2l, 20l. 4m 2.10s. a 10.10s (7 Ran).
SR: 52/17/5/5/-/6/-/ (Severn First Partnership), C D Broad

1592 Culmington Claiming Hurdle (4-y-o and up) £1,987 2m 5f 110yds.... (2:00)

1190* CELCIUS (bl) 9-11-11 R Dunwoody, hld up rear, cld on ldrs frm 8th, led last, quickened clr.
.................................(15 to 8 fav op 9 to 4 tchd 7 to 4) 1
1325⁵ NAJEB (USA) (v) 4-10-5 N Williamson, hld up rear, ran on 2 out, styd on wl r-in..(11 to 1 op 7 to 1 tchd 12 to 1) 2
936 PEAK DISTRICT 7-10-13 A Maguire, in tch, ev ch 2 out till rdn and no extr r-in...(11 to 1 op 8 to 1 tchd 12 to 1) 3
1426 AUTONOMOUS 8-11-3 W Humphreys, hld up rear, jnd ldrs 8th, not quicken 2 out.........(14 to 1 op 12 to 1) 4
1299⁷ MISTRESS ROSS 10-10-8 D Bridgwater, led 2 out, wknd frm last.........................(14 to 1 op 16 to 1) 5
1187⁷ RUTHS PRIDE 8-9-13² (3*) R Davis, hdwy frm rear 8th, led 2 out, hdd and no extr last........(14 to 1 op 10 to 1) 6
1458 CADFORD GIRL 9-10-8 P Holley, trkd ldrs till no extr 2 out.................................(12 to 1) 7
1485³ WAR BEAT 5-11-0 (7*) G Robertson, ldg grp till rdn and lost pl appr 2 out......(11 to 1 op 7 to 1 tchd 12 to 1) 8
1462 FRENDLY FELLOW (bl) 9-10-5 R Supple, hadway 6th, wknd appr 2 out....(12 to 1 op 10 to 1 tchd 14 to 1) 9
1458 BRORA ROSE (Ire) 5-10-12 I Shoemark, nvr better than mid-div, lost tch 8th, tld off...(33 to 1 op 25 to 1) 10
1425⁶ THE LOVING MARTIAL 9-11-3 J Railton, at rear, lost tch 8th, tld off.........................(20 to 1) 11
1299⁶ RUSTY MUSIC 7-10-5 M Hourigan, ldg grp till wknd 8th, tld off.................(8 to 1 tchd 10 to 1) 12
HARPLEY (bl) 6-10-7 V Slattery, pressed ldr till wknd 8th, tld off.................(14 to 1 op 12 to 1 tchd 16 to 1) 13
1127⁵ ITS ALL OVER NOW (v) 9-10-11 S McNeill, wl plcd till drpd rear 8th, tld off.........(12 to 1 op 8 to 1) 14
CATHS FOLLY 6-10-10 R Bellamy, chsd ldrs to 6th, tld off 8th, pld up bef 2 out.............(50 to 1 op 33 to 1) pu
1460 COME ON LUCY 4-10-9 (3*) A Thornton, prmnt till jmpd slwly 6th, pld up bef nxt.........(33 to 1 tchd 40 to 1) pu
Dist: 8l, ¾l, 6l, ½l, ½l, 7l, ¾l, 3l, 20l, 6l. 5m 16.20s. a 19.20s (16 Ran).
(Martin Pipe Racing Club), M C Pipe

1593 Stokesay Novices' Chase (5-y-o and up) £2,515 2m................(2:30)

1324³ GOOD FOR A LOAN 6-11-0 L Harvey, wth ldr, led 7th to 8th, lft clr nxt, styd on und pres frm last.
.................................(4 to 1 op 5 to 1 tchd 3 to 1) 1
HIDDEN PLEASURE 7-11-0 G Upton, wl plcd, lft in second pl 9th, mstk 2 out, no extr frm last.
.................................(12 to 1 op 8 to 1 tchd 3 to 1) 2
JAY JAY'S VOYAGE 10-10-7 (7*) Mr B Pollock, in tch till outpcd 9th.................(66 to 1 op 50 to 1) 3
BALLY PARSON 7-11-0 N Williamson, mstk 5th, outpcd 9th.................................(25 to 1 op 14 to 1) 4
1478 FIDDLER'S DRUM 6-11-0 N Doughty, al beh, no ch whn blun 3 out and nxt.............(12 to 1 op 7 to 1) 5
1372³ ON CUE 6-11-0 W Worthington, al struggling, outpcd 9th.
.................................(33 to 1 op 25 to 1) 6
1413 JHAL FREZI 5-10-11 (3*) A Thornton, wl plcd till mstk 7th, wknd 8th, hmpd nxt, no dngr aftr. (25 to 1 op 14 to 1) 7
1328 STAR OF THE GLEN 7-11-0 A Maguire, led to 7th, led 8th till f nxt.........(7 to 4 on tchd 11 to 8 on) f
Dist: 2l, 20l, 2l, 7l, hd, 1½l. 4m 3.30s. a 11.30s (8 Ran).
SR: 26/24/4/2/-/ (Racing Investments), R Lee

1594 Bircher Novices' Hurdle (4-y-o and up) £1,480 2m 5f 110yds...........(3:00)

1327* NIRVANA PRINCE 4-11-6 T Wall, rstrained in rear and not fluent, hdwy 8th, led 2 out, clr whn hit last, easily.
.................................(11 to 8 fav op 6 to 4 tchd 5 to 4) 1
1386² WELSH LUSTRE (Ire) 4-10-9 A Maguire, ldg grp, rdn and not quicken appr 2 out, styd on one pace frm last.
.................................(7 to 2 op 9 to 4 tchd 4 to 1) 2
1247³ URBAN COWBOY 6-11-0 S McNeill, hld up rear, improved appr 2 out, sn rdn and one pace.....(6 to 1 op 7 to 2) 3

TIME WON'T WAIT (Ire) 4-11-0 J Railton, hld up in mid-div, led aftr 8th to 2 out, wndrd und pres betw last two.
.................................(33 to 1 op 14 to 1) 4
1406⁷ ALIAS SILVER 6-10-7 (7*) Mr N Bradley, led to second, led 7th to nxt, outpcd 2 out.
.................................(25 to 1 op 33 to 1 tchd 50 to 1) 5
RIVERSIDE MOSS (Ire) 5-10-9 (5*) T Eley, wl plcd till rdn and no hdwy appr 2 out..........(66 to 1 op 50 to 1) 6
STORMY SWAN 7-11-0 W Humphreys, in tch till drpd rear 8th.............................(66 to 1 op 50 to 1) 7
1301³ FIRST COMMAND (NZ) 6-11-0 D Bridgwater, hld up, ran on 8th, wknd approaching last..(6 to 1 op 4 to 1) 8
CELTIC BRIDGE 5-10-9 W Marston, nvr plcd to chal.
.................................(50 to 1 op 33 to 1) 9
1215⁵ MAZATA (USA) 4-10-9 J Osborne, trkd ldrs till wknd aftr 8th.........................(10 to 1 tchd 12 to 1) 10
1078 CURRAGH PETER 6-11-0 R Greene, led second to 7th, led briefly nxt, sn wknd, f last........(66 to 1 op 33 to 1) f
1414 MERLIN ROCKET 5-11-0 C Maude, beh till pld up aftr 7th.
.................................(33 to 1) pu
Dist: 7l, 4l, 3l, 25l, ½l, 12l, 5l, 20l, ½l. 5m 15.30s. a 18.30s (12 Ran).
(D Portman), B Preece

PLUMPTON (soft)
Tuesday December 7th
Going Correction: PLUS 1.20 sec. per fur. (races 1,3,-5,7), PLUS 1.05 (2,4,6)

1595 Ditchling Novices' Hurdle (4-y-o and up) £1,475 2½m..............(12:45)

SEEKIN CASH (USA) 4-11-0 J Osborne, al prmnt, led appr 2 out, ran on strly r-in. (7 to 2 op 4 to 1 tchd 9 to 4) 1
1283⁴ SIMPLY (Ire) 4-11-0 G McCourt, trkd ldrs gng easily, chsd wnr aftr 2 out, no imprsn r-in.
.................................(2 to 1 fav tchd 7 to 4 and 9 to 4) 2
ESPRIT DE FEMME (Fr) 7-10-9 J Akehurst, prmnt till outpcd aftr 3 out, kpt on ag'n after last.
.................................(14 to 1 op 6 to 1) 3
1414* NORELEY (USA) 6-11-6 N Williamson, led till appr 2 out, weakened rpdly......(9 to 4 op 5 to 2 tchd 11 to 4) 4
1109⁸ JUNIPER LODGE 5-11-0 S Earle, cl up to 6th, wl beh frm 2 out.........(50 to 1 op 20 to 1 tchd 66 to 1) 5
1344⁵ TIME ENOUGH (Ire) 4-11-0 R Supple, cl to 6th, sn wl beh, tld off..........(25 to 1 op 16 to 1 tchd 33 to 1) 6
1460⁵ JIMLIL 5-10-9 M A FitzGerald, prmnt till wknd aftr 6th, sn tld off........(10 to 1 op 6 to 1 tchd 12 to 1) 7
CASPIAN GATES 9-11-0 D Skyrme, beh frm 4th, tld off and pld up bef 3 out..(25 to 1 op 12 to 1 tchd 33 to 1) pu
1456⁵ LAFHEEN (Ire) 5-11-0 W Humphreys, cl up till rdn and wknd aftr 5th, pld up bef 3 out.
.................................(50 to 1 op 33 to 1 tchd 66 to 1) pu
PETER MARTIN TWO 4-11-0 D O'Sullivan, beh frm 3rd, tld off whn pld up bef 3 out.
.................................(50 to 1 op 33 to 1 tchd 100 to 1) pu
TOO CLEVER BY HALF 5-11-0 Mr G Johnson Houghton, tld off frm second till pld up bef 3 out.
.................................(50 to 1 op 25 to 1 tchd 66 to 1) pu
BALLISTRADE 6-10-7 (7*) M Stevens, lft strt, tld off till pld up bef 5th.........(50 to 1 op 25 to 1) pu
Dist: 12l, 30l, 2½l, 20l, dist, 6l. 5m 5.70s. a 28.70s (12 Ran).
SR: 39/27/-/-/-/-/ (Sheikh Ahmed Bin Saeed Al Maktoum), C R Egerton

1596 Galleano Challenge Cup (Handicap Chase) (0-125 4-y-o and up) £2,238 2m ....(1:15)

1339⁷ DEXTRA DOVE [95] 6-10-11 S Earle, led to second and frm nxt, made rst, drvn out r-in.
.................................(6 to 4 fav op 11 to 10 tchd 13 to 8) 1
1391³ FRED SPLENDID [92] 10-10-8 R Dunwoody, mstk 1st, pressed wnr frm 4th, ev ch last, hrd rdn and not run-on.................................(5 to 2 op 7 to 4 tchd 11 to 4) 2
NATHIR (USA) [96] 7-10-12 M A FitzGerald, hld up, jmpd rght 3rd, prog 7th, rdn and held whn blun last.
.................................(3 to 1 op 4 to 1 tchd 11 to 4) 3
1391⁴ BRIGGS BUILDERS [108] (v) 9-11-10 Richard Guest, blun 1st, led second to 3rd, wknd 7th, sn tld off.
.................................(9 to 2 op 5 to 1 tchd 8 to 1) 4
Dist: 8l, 3½l, dist. 4m 12.20s. a 22.20s (4 Ran).
SR: 29/18/18/-/ (Dextra Lighting Systems), R H Alner

1597 Henfield Conditional Jockeys' Selling Handicap Hurdle (4-y-o and up) £1,836 2m 1f...........................(1:45)

1395⁵ DERISBAY (Ire) [83] (bl) 5-10-6² D O'Sullivan, led to 5th and ag'n 2 out, rdn appr last, hld on wl nr finish.
.................................(15 to 2 op 16 to 1) 1
1042 MANHATTAN BOY [105] 11-12-0 A Thornton, trkd ldrs till outpcd aftr 5th, rallied 2 out, styd on gmely frm last, nvr nrr.................................(2 to 1 op 5 to 2) 2
QUALITAIR MEMORY (Ire) [77] 4-10-0 M Hourigan, prmnt, led 5th to 2 out, wth wnr aftr till rdn and wknd last.
.................................(3 to 1 fav op 5 to 1) 3

218

1198⁹ GREENWINE (USA) [82] (bl) 7-10-5 J McCarthy, *mid-div,
outpcd aftr 5th, sn wl beh, styd on ag'n after last.*
............................(7 to 1 op 5 to 1)   4
1187² LOCH DUICH [78] 7-10-1 T Jenks, *trkd ldrs till rdn and
struggling aftr 3 out.................*(7 to 2 op 5 to 2)   5
1259² ROGER'S PAL [86] 6-10-9 J Clarke, *hld up, lost tch aftr
5th, sn tld off.........................* (8 to 1 op 6 to 1)   6
1488⁴ COBB GATE [79] 5-10-2² M Stevens, *mstk 4th, al rear, rdn
5th, sn tld off.......* (14 to 1 op 10 to 1 tchd 16 to 1)   7
1241 BLAKE'S TREASURE [77] (bl) 6-10-0 D Meade, *prmnt till
wknd aftr 3 out, virtually pld up r-in.*
....................(25 to 1 tchd 16 to 1 and 50 to 1)   8
YAAFOOR (USA) [78] 4-10-1 L Dace, *cl till f 5th.*
................................(33 to 1 op 14 to 1)   f
1415⁹ ALMOST A PRINCESS [77] (bl) 5-10-0 R Davis, *cl up to 5th,
sn wknd, tld off and pld up bef last.*
...............(33 to 1 op 16 to 1 tchd 50 to 1)   pu
1474 SANTA PONSA BAY [94] 6-11-3 D Meredith, *al rear, hrd
rdn and no prog aftr 4th, hmpd nxt, sn pld up.*
....................(16 to 1 op 12 to 1 tchd 20 to 1)   pu
Dist: 2l, 6l, 8l, 15l, 20l, 5l, 2l. 4m 28.50s. a 36.50s (11 Ran).
(Miss Julie Self), J J Bridger

1598 Scotts Restaurant Novices' Chase (4-y-o and up) £2,214 2m......... (2:15)

1134⁴ ROC COLOR (Fr) 4-10-7 G Bradley, *mstk 1st, settled off
pace, wnt poor 3rd aftr 7th, shaken up last, ran on
strly r-in to ld nr finish.....................*(6 to 4 jt-
fav tchd 5 to 4 and 13 to 8)   1
1457⁸ GALAXY HIGH (bl) 6-11-4 M A FitzGerald, *led second to 3rd
and frm 6th, drvn clr aftr last, hdd nr finish.*
.....................(9 to 2 op 4 to 1 tchd 5 to 1)   2
1258* KALANSKI 7-12-0 J Osborne, *led to second, jnd ldr 6th, ev
ch aftr till wknd last...........* (6 to 4 jt-fav op 11 to 8)   3
1252⁶ COUNTRY MISTRESS 6-10-13 T Grantham, *reminder 5th,
al rear, lost tch aftr 6th.*
....................(14 to 1 op 16 to 1 tchd 20 to 1)   4
1248⁶ TAPESTRY DANCER 5-11-4 D Skyrme, *al rear, pushed
alng 6th, sn beh frm nxt...........*(33 to 1 op 20 to 1)   5
1492 MOTTRAM'S GOLD 8-11-4 H Davies, *al rear, rdn 6th, wl
beh frm nxt..........*(33 to 1 op 20 to 1 tchd 50 to 1)   6
DAWN CHANCE 7-11-4 R Dunwoody, *led 3rd to 6th, wknd
rpdly, tld off...........*(33 to 1 op 20 to 1 tchd 50 to 1)   7
Dist: 3½l, 15l, 15l, 15l, sht-hd, 30l. 4m 12.00s. a 22.00s (7 Ran).
SR: 27/34/29/-/ (Mrs Susan McCarthy), C P E Brooks

1599 Midland Bank Handicap Hurdle (0-125 4-y-o and up) £2,511 2m 1f..... (2:45)

1213* KABAYIL [113] 4-11-10 J Osborne, *cl up, trkd ldr 2 out,
chlgd aftr last, hrd rdn to ld nr finish.*
....................................(6 to 5 on op Evens)   1
1042³ HANDSOME NED [92] (bl) 7-10-3³ J Railton, *pressed ldr till
led aftr 5th, rdn after last, hdd and no extr nr finish.*
............................(13 to 2 op 8 to 1 tchd 9 to 1)   2
1492⁸ ALOSAIL [92] 6-10-3⁷ (7*) M Stevens, *hld up, mstk second,
effrt aftr 5th, one pace.*
...............(16 to 1 op 7 to 1 tchd 20 to 1)   3
DJEBEL PRINCE [101] 6-10-7 (5*) A Procter, *hld up, lost pl
aftr 5th, styd on frm 2 out, nvr nr to chal.*
............................(8 to 1 op 1 tchd 10 to 1)   4
1412² WOLVER GOLD [92] 6-10-3 C Maude, *led till aftr 5th,
wknd 2 out..............*(4 to 1 op 11 to 4 tchd 9 to 2)   5
PERSIAN LUCK [95] 7-9-13 (7*) P McLoughlin, *prmnt till
lost pl aftr 5th, styd on ag'n 2 out, disputing 3rd and no
ch whn f last..........* (20 to 1 op 12 to 1 tchd 25 to 1)   f
TIPP DOWN [92] 10-10-3 L Harvey, *rdn and lost tch aftr
4th, tld off and pld up bef last..* (16 to 1 tchd 20 to 1)   pu
CLEVER DICK [95] 8-9-13 (7*) J Clarke, *pushed alng and
lost tch 5th, tld off and pld up bef last.*
............................(20 to 1 op 14 to 1)   pu
Dist: 1l, 15l, ½l, 20l. 4m 26.70s. a 34.70s (8 Ran).
(Elite Racing Club), C R Egerton

1600 Keymer Handicap Chase (0-130 5-y-o and up) £2,427 3m 1f 110yds.... (3:15)

1459³ MISS FERN [91] 8-10-1 (3*) D Meredith, *trkd ldrs till outpcd aftr 13th, ran on frm 3 out, led r-in, drvn out.*
.............................(6 to 1 op 7 to 2)   1
956 RUFUS [109] 7-11-8 B Powell, *ran in snatches, led to
second, rdn 12th, rallied 2 out, ev ch r-in, ran on.*
...............(15 to 2 op 7 to 1 tchd 10 to 1)   2
1191³ POWDER BOY [91] 8-10-4 R Dunwoody, *led second to 6th
and ag'n 14th, clr 3 out, shaken up aftr last, wknd and
hdd r-in................* (11 to 2 op 5 to 1 tchd 7 to 1)   3
1334³ SHASTON [101] (bl) 8-11-0 P Holley, *prmnt, led 6th till hdd
and mstk 14th, blun nxt, wkng whn hit 2 out.*
.............................(5 to 2 tchd 11 to 4)   4
1216* LOCH BLUE [111] 8-11-5 (5*) A Dicken, *hld up, lost tch
aftr 13th, effrt after last, nvr on terms.*
.............................(9 to 4 fav op 7 to 4 tchd 5 to 4)   5
1197 SHEEPHAVEN [106] 9-11-5 G McCourt, *mstks 3rd and 9th,
rdn 11th, wknd nxt, sn tld off....* (12 to 1 op 10 to 1)   6
MACHO MAN [97] 8-10-10 M A FitzGerald, *sn beh frm 7th, tld
off aftr 12th.........*(20 to 1 op 14 to 1 tchd 25 to 1)   7

1458 SOLENT LAD [90] (bl) 10-10-3¹0 (7*) M Stevens, *tld off 7th,
clambered o'r nxt, pld up bef 11th.*
....................(50 to 1 op 33 to 1 tchd 66 to 1)   pu
Dist: 2l, 2½l, 8l, 4l, 25l, 1l. 6m 47.00s. a 35.00s (8 Ran).
SR: -/10/-/-/-/ (Phipps, Duane & Company), R Dickin

1601 Eastbourne Novices' Handicap Hurdle (3-y-o and up) £2,385 2m 1f..... (3:45)

1141² JOVIAL MAN (Ire) [87] 4-11-11 M Perrett, *hld up, mstk 5th,
pushed alng and prog aftr 3 out, rdn to ld r-in, ran on
wl...............................*(13 to 8 fav op 6 to 4)   1
KOBYRUN [83] 7-11-7 J Railton, *trkd ldr till led appr last,
hdd and one pace r-in.* (6 to 1 op 4 to 1 tchd 13 to 2)   2
CASTLE ORCHARD [65] 9-9-12 (5*) A Procter, *prog to track
ldrs 5th, rdn aftr 3 out, kpt on one pace.*
.....................(20 to 1 op 33 to 1 tchd 16 to 1)   3
GOLD GLEN (Ire) [90] (bl) 5-12-0 Richard Guest, *set steady
pace till quickened aftr 3 out, hdd and wknd appr last.*
....................................(4 to 1 tchd 6 to 1)   4
1137* SAKIL (Ire) [80] 5-10-13 (5*) A Dicken, *trkd ldrs, rdn and
outpcd aftr 3 out..................* (5 to 2 op 6 to 4)   5
1390⁹ JOHNS JOY [84] 8-11-8 D O'Sullivan, *lost tch 5th, sn tld
off...............................*(20 to 1 op 12 to 1)   6
Dist: 7l, 3½l, 15l, ½l, 25l. 4m 34.80s. a 42.80s (6 Ran).
(Mrs Jenny Ells), G Harwood

SEDGEFIELD (good to soft)
Tuesday December 7th
Going Correction: PLUS 1.15 sec. per fur. (races 1,2,6), PLUS 0.85 (3,4,5)

1602 John Wade Hino Truck Novices' Selling Hurdle (3-y-o and up) £1,742 2m 5f 110yds...................... (12:30)

1448 DAMCADA (Ire) 5-11-8 W Marston, *made most, styd on wl
und pres frm last..............*(5 to 1 op 4 to 1)   1
1362 OVER THE ODDS (Ire) 4-11-8 A Maguire, *cl up, effrt appr 2
out, kpt on wl und pres frm last, no imprsn on wnr.*
.............................(7 to 1 tchd 8 to 1)   2
1311⁴ JUBILATA (USA) 5-11-3 C Dennis, *chsd ldrs, rdn alng aftr
3 out, kpt on same pace.............*(8 to 1 op 7 to 1)   3
1097⁴ DENTICULATA 5-11-8 B Storey, *in tch, hdwy aftr 3 out,
rdn appr nxt, one pace............*(33 to 1 op 25 to 1)   4
1476* RAGGERTY (Ire) 3-10-11 (3*) N Bentley, *in tch, pushed alng
and hdwy aftr 6th, outpcd appr 3 out, rallied
approaching nxt, one paced.*
....................(5 to 4 fav op Evens tchd 11 to 8)   5
1456 GENERAL SHOT 8-11-8 M Brennan, *trkd ldrs till wknd
appr 2 out............*(15 to 2 op 6 to 1 tchd 8 to 1)   6
1096 BALLYBELL 8-11-8 T Reed, *wth wnr till wknd aftr 6th,
tld off........................*(66 to 1 op 50 to 1)   7
1476* BELFORTON 3-10-3 J Callaghan, *chsd ldrs till wknd appr
3 out, tld off..............* (14 to 1 op 12 to 1)   8
1371 HYDEONIAN 6-11-1 (7*) D Waters, *tld off frm hfwy, pld up
bef 3 out....................................*(66 to 1)   pu
1356⁶ WAWEEWAWOO (Ire) 5-11-0 (3*) D J Moffatt, *in tch till
wknd appr 3 out, tld off whn pld up bef last.*
.....................(25 to 1 op 20 to 1)   pu
137⁷ REACH FOR GLORY 4-11-8 S Turner, *trkd ldrs till wknd
aftr 7th, tld off whn pld up bef 2 out.*
.............................(12 to 1 op 10 to 1)   pu
1060⁸ I'D SAY HARDLY 6-11-8 Mr S Brisby, *al beh, lost tch frm
6th, tld off whn pld up bef last..* (33 to 1 op 25 to 1)   pu
Dist: 1½l, 8l, sht-hd, 10l, 1½l, 25l, 12l. 5m 27.50s. a 36.50s (12 Ran).
(E4 Racing), D J Wintle

1603 Dickie Dods Memorial Handicap Hurdle (0-125 4-y-o and up) £2,022 3m 3f 110yds...................... (1:00)

1480⁶ JENDEE (Ire) [77] 5-10-1 (3*) A Larnach, *mid-div, steady
hdwy to ld 9th, clr 2 out, styd on wl.............*(8 to 1)   1
1091 SCOTTISH GOLD [93] 9-11-6 A Maguire, *in tch till lost pl
and beh aftr 5th, some strong effrt frm 3 out, not trble wnr.*
.............................(6 to 1 op 5 to 1)   2
ST VILLE [100] 7-11-6 (7*) S Mason, *in tch, hdwy frm nxt,
aftr 3 out, no imprsn, wknd appr last......*(10 to 1)   3
1119⁵ HARDIHERO [90] 7-11-3 B Storey, *led 3rd till hdd 9th, one
paced frm 3 out....................*(5 to 1 op 7 to 2)   4
1148⁵ JUPITER MOON [84] 4-10-11 M Dwyer, *mid-div, ev ch appr
3 out, kpt on same pace............*(15 to 2 op 5 to 1)   5
1481⁶ HERE COMES TIBBY [81] 6-10-8⁴ T Reed, *mid-div, effrt
aftr tenth, grad wknd.........* (16 to 1 tchd 20 to 1)   6
1201³ RUSTINO [91] 7-11-4 P Niven, *mid-div, effrt aftr tenth, ev
ch 3 out, wknd appr nxt.*
.............................(12 to 1 op 14 to 1 tchd 10 to 1)   7
SHELTON ABBEY [91] 7-12-0 C Grant, *trkd ldrs, rdn
alng aftr tenth, grad wknd.........*(7 to 1 op 6 to 1)   8
MR FENWICK [86] 9-10-13 A Mulholland, *led to 3rd, prmnt
till wknd aftr tenth....................*(33 to 1)   9
1299³ IT'S NOT MY FAULT (Ire) [78] 5-10-5 P McDermott, *cl up till
wknd aftr 9th.................*(10 to 1)   10

1152⁶ WALDORF T BEAGLE [78] 7-10-5 Mrs G Adkin, *rcd wide,
*chsd ldrs till wknd aftr 8th....................... (33 to 1) 11

845⁵ BADASTAN (Ire) [94] 4-11-0 (7*) W Fry, *beh, hmpd 8th, no
*ch aftr......................(13 to 2 op 11 to 2) 12

1148² DAWAAM [93] 7-11-6 A Merrigan, *hld up, steady hdwy
whn f 8th.......... (11 to 2 fav op 5 to 1 tchd 6 to 1) f

972 DUTCH BLUES [82] 6-10-9 D Wilkinson, *sn beh, tld off whn
pld up bef 2 out.................. (25 to 1 op 20 to 1) pu

1066⁶ SPEEDY SIOUX [73] (bl) 4-10-0 A Dobbin, *prmnt till wknd
quickly aftr 8th, tld off whn pld up aftr nxt.
....(66 to 1 op 33 to 1) pu

Dist: 7l, 8l, 6l, hd, 15l, 2½l, 6l, 12l, 4l, ¾l. 7m 4.00s. a 38.00s (15 Ran).
SR: 12/21/20/4/-/-/ (The Avenue Racing Partnership), J A Hellens

1604 Hardwick Arms Novices' Handicap Chase (4-y-o and up) £2,154 2m 1f

....(1:30)

974⁵ DOWN THE ROAD [97] 6-11-5 A Maguire, *hld up, gd hdwy
aftr 8th, led appr 2 out, sn clr, easily. (7 to 1 op 5 to 1) 1

1146³ VAYRUA (Fr) [92] (bl) 8-10-11 (3*) A Larnach, *cl up, pushed
alng and outpcd aftr 3 out, kpt on appr last.
....(8 to 1 op 6 to 1) 2

1182⁵ SEMINOFF (Fr) [78] 7-10-0 A Dobbin, *cl up, led 9th till hdd
appr 2 out, jmpd lft last, wknd r-in. (8 to 1 op 7 to 1) 3

1128⁵ WILD ATLANTIC [89] 10-10-11 K Jones, *prmnt till wknd
aftr 7th.......................... (14 to 1 op 10 to 1) 4

1321³ HEIR OF EXCITEMENT [79] 8-10-1 J Callaghan, *prmnt till
wknd aftr 7th...................... (9 to 1 op 7 to 1) 5

1422* SKELETOR [106] 10-12-0 M Dwyer, *cl up, led 4th till hdd
*9th, wknd aftr nxt, fourth and btn whn blun and uns
rdr 2 out.................... (Evens fav op 5 to 4) ur

1480 MANOR RANGER [78] 7-10-0 L O'Hara, *mstk second, beh
whn blun and unseateed rdr 6th. (66 to 1 op 40 to 1) ur

718⁴ WEST WITH THE WIND [94] 6-11-2 T Reed, *al beh, lost tch
aftr 7th, pld up bef last.
....(13 to 2 op 5 to 1 tchd 7 to 1) pu

SUPREME BLUSHER [78] 6-10-0 E McKinley, *sn tld off, pld
up aftr 6th................... (100 to 1 op 33 to 1) pu

Dist: 5l, 7l, 12l, 7l. 4m 25.40s. a 20.40s (9 Ran).
SR: 32/22/1/-/-/-/ (R J Crake), J H Johnson

1605 Black Lion Mares Only Novices' Chase (5-y-o and up) £2,185 2m 5f

....(2:00)

1182 CELTIC SONG 6-11-1 T Reed, *made all, blun 4th, clr frm
hfwy, rdn aftr 2 out, styd on wl..... (8 to 1 op 6 to 1) 1

1131* DURHAM SUNSET 6-10-10 A Maguire, *in tch, chsd wnr
frm hfwy, rdn from 2 out, no imprsn.
....(11 to 10 fav op 11 to 8) 2

1117 SUPER SANDY 6-10-10 A Orkney, *al wl beh, tld off whn
hmpd 2 out, styd on frm last....... (66 to 1 op 33 to 1) 3

1485 LADY BE BRAVE 10-10-10 K Johnson, *chsd wnr till out-
pcd hfwy, tld off................. (50 to 1 op 33 to 1) 4

1357 PANTO LADY 7-10-3 (7*) Miss S Lamb, *tld off frm hfwy,
f 12th.......................... (100 to 1 op 66 to 1)

BELLAGROVE (Ire) 5-10-3 (7*) G Cahill, *in tch till outpcd
hfwy, tld off whn f 3 out......... (25 to 1 op 20 to 1)

1373 CHICHELL'S HURST 7-10-10 A Carroll, *in tch whn f 8th.*

1477⁶ SANDEDGE 6-10-10 B Storey, *chsd ldrs till outpcd hfwy,
tld off whn f 2 out............... (25 to 1 op 16 to 1) pu

Dist: 6l, dist, hd. 5m 34.00s. a 30.00s (8 Ran).
(Miss Rosemary Jeffreys), W G Reed

1606 Hope Inn Handicap Chase (0-120 4-y-o and up) £2,684 2m 5f

....(2:30)

1222⁸ LUPY MINSTREL [102] 8-11-1 B Storey, *made most, hrd
pressed frm 2 out, styd on wl, all out.
....(7 to 1 tchd 10 to 1) 1

1144³ NIGHT GUEST [99] 11-10-12 A Dobbin, *trkd ldrs, rdn to
chal 2 out, ev ch till no extr towards finish.
....(7 to 4 fav tchd 15 to 8) 2

1225 FUNNY OLD GAME [98] 6-10-11 K Johnson, *trkd ldrs, ev
ch 3 out, grad wknd............ (7 to 2 op 3 to 1) 3

1203 GREY MINSTREL [100] 9-10-8 (5*) P Waggott, *prmnt till
wknd aftr 3 out.................... (20 to 1) 4

1423 RED COLUMBIA [87] 12-10-0 Mrs G Adkin, *prmnt till wknd
aftr hfwy, no dngr after......... (20 to 1) 5

BAD TRADE [115] 11-12-0 C Grant, *in tch, ev ch 3 out, rdn
and btn appr last............... (10 to 1 tchd 12 to 1) 6

MERITMOORE [97] 10-10-10 J Callaghan, *prmnt till wknd
hfwy, tld off.................. (6 to 1 tchd 13 to 2) 7

Dist: ½l, 15l, 2½l, 5l, 8l, dist. 5m 35.30s. a 31.30s (7 Ran).
(Raymond Anderson Green), C Parker

1607 Nags Head Novices' Handicap Hurdle (0-100 4-y-o and up) £1,689 2m 1f 110yds.

....(3:00)

1356* FLASH OF REALM (Fr) [91] 7-11-10 A Dobbin, *cl up, drw clr
whn ldr aftr 5th, outpcd betw last 2, lft clear last.
....(100 to 30 op 5 to 2 tchd 7 to 2) 1

1096⁵ MANWELL [67] 6-9-9 (5*) D Bentley, *chsd ldrs, outpcd aftr
5th, no dngr after............. (10 to 1) 2

1289 INAN (USA) [89] 4-11-8 M Dwyer, *hld up, hdwy hfwy,
wknd aftr 3 out........... (4 to 1 op 5 to 1) 3

1100 MRS NORMAN [68] 4-10-11 C Grant, *nvr on terms.*
....(33 to 1) 4

1092³ BORING (USA) [80] 4-10-13 K Johnson, *f 3rd.*
....(6 to 1 tchd 13 to 2) f

1181* LARAPINTA (Ire) [95] 5-12-0 A Maguire, *made all, 8 ls clr
whn f last, dead. (5 to 4 fav op 11 to 10 tchd 11 to 8) f

1374 GOLDEN SUPREME [67] 7-10-0 L O'Hara, *lost tch hfwy,
tld off whn pld up bef last....... (100 to 1 op 66 to 1) pu

823 DOUGAL'S BIRTHDAY [67] 7-9-11² (5*) J Supple, *lost tch
hfwy, tld off whn pld up bef last. (100 to 1 op 66 to 1) pu

Dist: 15l, 5l, 1½l. 4m 22.40s. a 27.40s (8 Ran).
SR: 23/-/1/-/-/ (Allan W Melville), P Monteith

CLONMEL (IRE) (heavy) Wednesday December 8th

1608 Winter Mares Maiden Hurdle (4-y-o and up) £2,243 2m............. (12:30)

1332² SEA GALE (Ire) 5-11-6 C F Swan, ...(5 to 4 fav) 1
797³ HURRICANE EDEN 6-11-1 (5*) M A Davey, ...(12 to 1) 2
1397⁴ DOWHATYOULIKE (Ire) 4-11-4 P Carberry, ...(7 to 1) 3
1265⁵ FORTY ONE (Ire) 5-10-13 (7*) D J Kavanagh, ...(12 to 1) 4
1333² KEEPHERGOING (Ire) 4-11-4 F O'Brien, ...(7 to 1) 5
1156⁵ MULLAGHMEEN 7-11-3 (3*) D P Murphy, ...(16 to 1) 6
1333 VON CARTY (Ire) 4-11-4 Mr J T McNamara, ..(12 to 1) 7
1496 HIGHWAY LASS 7-11-6 S H O'Donovan, ...(50 to 1) 8
1333⁴ CHANCERY QUEEN (Ire) 4-11-9 T Horgan, ...(7 to 4) 9
TARA'S SERENADE (Ire) 4-11-4 A J O'Brien, ...(16 to 1) 10
JOES NIGHTMARE 6-10-13 (7*) D M Drewitt, ...(50 to 1) 11
6 SMOOTH COUP 7-10-13 (7*) Mr D K Budds, ...(50 to 1) 12
FAIR ADELINE 6-11-6 P M Verling, ...(33 to 1) 13
SHIMMERETTO 7-10-13 (7*) J M Donnelly, ...(50 to 1) 14
1333 SAHEL SAND (Ire) 4-11-4 J A White, ...(33 to 1) 15
431⁸ SHUILNAMON (Ire) 4-11-4 B Sheridan, ...(12 to 1) 16
CALL ME COOL 7-10-13 (7*) Mr F P Cahill, ...(50 to 1) 17
1160⁹ FANCY DISH 7-11-6 Mr J A Berry, ...(25 to 1) 18
KAREN HONEY 6-11-1 (5*) M G Cleary, ...(25 to 1) 19
LISNAGREE PRINCESS (Ire) 5-11-6 L P Cusack, ..(50 to 1) pu

Dist: 2½l, 2½l, 15l, 7l. 4m 23.80s. (20 Ran).
(Mrs E J O'Grady), E J O'Grady

1609 Wilderness Handicap Hurdle (0-116 4-y-o and up) £2,415 2½m...... (1:00)

1156² RATHCORE [-] 6-10-10 L P Cusack, ...(8 to 1) 1
1176³ SO PINK (Ire) [-] 5-11-5 (3*) T P Treacy, ...(9 to 2) 2
1380 BARRONSTOWN BOY [-] 9-10-4 C F Swan, ...(7 to 1) 3
1380⁵ GOLDEN OPAL [-] 8-11-4 A J O'Brien, ...(6 to 1) 4
1380³ DOONEGA (Ire) [-] 5-11-6 (3*) C O'Brien, ...(7 to 4 fav) 5
1495 SHANNON KNOCK [-] 8-10-13 T Horgan, ...(16 to 1) 6
JACINTA'S BOY [-] 6-10-8 J Shortt, ...(12 to 1) 7
1555 MONGARD (Ire) [-] 5-10-1 P Carberry, ...(25 to 1) 8
1496⁷ ARRIGLE PRINCE [-] (bl) 8-9-13 H Rogers, ...(66 to 1) 9
1180 PEGUS PRINCE (Ire) [-] 4-9-12 F Woods, ...(33 to 1) 10
1176⁶ MOSCOW DUKE (Ire) [-] (bl) 4-9-12 J Jones, ...(12 to 1) 11
1453⁶ HORNER WATER (Ire) [-] 5-10-6 (7*) J P Broderick, (9 to 2) f
1335 MYSTIC GALE [-] 5-9-13 (7*) M P M Cloke, ...(12 to 1) su
1230⁶ MIDDLE SUSIE (Ire) [-] 4-9-12 (3*) T J Mitchell, ..(12 to 1) pu

Dist: 6l, hd, 4½l, ½l. 5m 36.50s. (14 Ran).
(Michael Kiernan), Michael Kiernan

1610 Cahir Maiden Hurdle (4-y-o) £2,243 2m

....(1:30)

1397⁸ SAM VAUGHAN (Ire) 10-11 (7*) Mr W M O'Sullivan, (8 to 1) 1
1397⁶ WOODVILLE STAR (Ire) 10-13 T Horgan, ...(5 to 2) 2
1333³ HEMISPHERE (Ire) 11-4 C F Swan, ...(6 to 4 fav) 3
TELLTALK (Ire) 10-13 (5*) J R Barry, ...(12 to 1) 4
1337 BOHEMIAN CASTLE (Ire) 11-4 F Woods, ...(12 to 1) 5
530⁹ KING'S DECREE (Ire) 11-4 J P Banahan, ...(20 to 1) 6
1501⁹ MY SUNNY WAY (Ire) 10-11 (7*) Mr D K Budds, ..(10 to 1) 7
1337⁵ OZEYCAZEY (Ire) 10-13 (5*) Susan A Finn, ...(10 to 1) 8
1337⁶ SHANNON AMBER (Ire) 10-6 (7*) J P Broderick, ..(14 to 1) 9
MAJBOOR (Ire) 11-2 (7*) Mr A G Kearns, ...(14 to 1) 10
1180 NOT A BID (Ire) 10-13 J A White, ...(33 to 1) 11
1435 WISE STATEMENT (Ire) 10-11 (7*) Mr F McGirr, ..(20 to 1) 12
1180 ANDROS GALE (Ire) 11-4 N Williamson, ...(14 to 1) 13
1397 FAYS FOLLY (Ire) 10-6 (7*) D J Kavanagh, ...(14 to 1) 14
PROPHET'S THUMB (Ire) 10-11 (7*) Mr A Hickey, ..(33 to 1) 15
1333 LAURETTA BLUE (Ire) (bl) 10-13 H Rogers, ...(50 to 1) 16
MURPHY'S LADY (Ire) 10-10 (3*) C O'Brien, ...(33 to 1) 17
925 RED VERONA 10-13 J Jones, ...(33 to 1) 18
GENIE MACK (Ire) 11-4 A J O'Brien, ...(25 to 1) pu
1333 LEISURE CENTRE (Ire) 10-8 (5*) K P Gaule, ...(12 to 1) pu

Dist: ½l, 2½l, 6l, 1½l. 4m 34.90s. (20 Ran).
(M O'Sullivan), Eugene M O'Sullivan

1611 Morris Oil Chase (5-y-o and up) £5,520 3m.............................(2:00)

1381* KING OF THE GALES 6-11-7 C F Swan, ...(5 to 4 on) 1
1578³ HAKI SAKI 7-11-7 G M O'Neill, ...(100 to 30) 2
1499² LADY BAR 6-11-2 P M Verling, ...(11 to 1) 3

1553⁶ LAURA'S BEAU 9-12-0 B Sheridan, ...(8 to 1) 4
EBONY JANE 8-11-9 F J Flood, ...(4 to 1) su
Dist: 1½l, 20l, 4l. 6m 57.70s. (5 Ran).
(E P King), J E Kiely

1612 Clonmel E.B.F. Chase (5-y-o and up) £2,760 3m. . . . . (2:30)

1399³ ANOTHER EXCUSE (Ire) 5-10-11 (7*) Mr W M O'Sullivan,
. . . .(9 to 4 fav) 1
1451 BEAU BABILLARD 6-11-6 C F Swan, ...(7 to 2) 2
1451 THREE BROWNIES 6-11-6 T Horgan, ...(12 to 1) 3
1498⁶ PROGRAMMED TO WIN 6-11-6 S H O'Donovan, . . .(8 to 1) 4
1177⁸ DANNIGALE 7-11-6 Mr M Phillips, ...(14 to 1) 5
1399⁹ MINSTREL SAM 7-11-6 A J O'Brien, ... 0
1497⁵ NEW CO (Ire) 4-11-4 N Williamson, ... (5 to 2) f
1159² MUST DO 7-11-7 (3*) T J Mitchell, ...(10 to 1) su
1179 WADI RUM 7-11-6 J A White, ...(20 to 1) pu
1112⁵ THE HEARTY CARD (Ire) 5-11-4 D H O'Connor, ... (8 to 1) pu
1379⁸ NO BETTER BUACHAIL (Ire) 5-11-4 A Powell, ... (20 to 1) pu
1399⁶ STRONG CHERRY 7-10-8 (7*) Mr K Taylor, ... (20 to 1) pu
Dist: 7l, 7l, dist, 12l. 6m 52.80s. (11 Ran).
(Kilshannig Racing Syndicate), Eugene M O'Sullivan

HAYDOCK (soft)
Wednesday December 8th
Going Correction: PLUS 1.83 sec. per fur.

1613 Ashton Novices' Hurdle (4-y-o and up) £2,127 2m. . . . . (12:20)

1374⁶ VASILIEV (v) 5-11-0 C Grant, tucked away in midfield,
improved 3 out, chlgd last, led r-in, styd on.
. . . .(10 to 1 tchd 12 to 1) 1
1289⁵ ALJADEER (USA) 4-11-0 M Dwyer, patiently rdn,
improved 3 out, drvn and ch last, styd on same pace.
. . . .(9 to 2 op 5 to 1 tchd 6 to 1) 2
1289⁶ CUMBRIAN CHALLENGE (Ire) 4-11-0 L Wyer, wtd wth,
hdwy 3 out, effrt betw last 2, kpt on r-in.
. . . .(9 to 1 op 6 to 1) 3
1023³ COOL LUKE (Ire) 4-10-11 (3*) N Bentley, nvr far away, led 4
out, rdn and hdd aftr last, wknd quickly.
. . . .(7 to 2 op 3 to 1) 4
1289⁴ VANART 4-11-0 D Byrne, patiently rdn, drvn alng whn pace
quickened out, one pace nxt. . . . .(10 to 1) 5
MEDIA MESSENGER 4-10-9 (5*) P Waggott, trkd ldrs,
struggling to hold pl appr out, wknd quickly nxt.
. . . .(20 to 1 op 14 to 1) 6
910⁸ JOMOVE 4-11-0 P Niven, wl beh hfwy, nvr a factor.
. . . .(9 to 1 op 5 to 1) 7
SIE AMATO (Ire) 4-11-0 A Maguire, pressed ldr to hfwy, lost
pl quickly aftr 4 out, tld off. . . . .(20 to 1 op 14 to 1) 8
1502⁵ ANGEL FALLING 5-10-6 (3*) A Thornton, trkd ldrs till aftr 4
out, sn lost tch, tld off. . . . . (33 to 1 op 20 to 1) 9
1289 TOLLS CHOICE (Ire) 4-10-7 (7*) J Driscoll, settled midfield,
struggling to hold pl 3 out, no ch whn f last.
. . . .(50 to 1 op 25 to 1) f
821 LAZY RHYTHM (USA) 7-11-0 S Turner, al struggling, tld off
whn pld up bef 2 out. . . . .(50 to 1 op 25 to 1) pu
CLAUDIA MISS 6-10-9 S D Williams, struggling to keep up
hfwy, tld off whn pld up bef last. (25 to 1 op 16 to 1) pu
1374⁸ MOAT GARDEN (USA) 5-11-6 J Frost, keen hold, rcd wide,
led till jmpd rght and hdd 4 out, tld off whn pld up bef 2
out. . . . .(5 to 2 fav op 7 to 4 tchd 11 to 4) pu
731³ THISTLE PRINCESS 4-10-10¹ N Doughty, settled midfield,
lost pl quickly aftr 4 out, tld off whn pld up bef last.
. . . .(15 to 2 op 5 to 1 tchd 8 to 1) pu
Dist: 2l, 2½l, 8l, 2½l, 10l, 8l, hd, 6l. 4m 15.00s. a 35.00s (14 Ran).
SR: 29/27/24/16/13/3/1/-/-/ (R L Houlton), M D Hammond

1614 Beeches Farm Conditional Jockeys' Handicap Hurdle (0-125 4-y-o and up) £2,022 2m. . . . . (12:50)

IT'S THE PITS [97] 6-10-6 (3*) F Perratt, patiently rdn,
hdwy on ins 4 out, led on bit last, drvn clr. . . (10 to 1) 1
1221⁴ WEE WIZARD (Ire) [98] 4-10-10 A Dobbin, al hndy, rdn to
draw level appr 2 out, kpt on same pace r-in.
. . . .(4 to 1 op 6 to 1) 2
TIMUR'S KING [88] 6-9-11 (3*) D Fortt, led to 3rd, hndy till
drvn alng aftr 3 out, one pace nxt. . . . .(16 to 1) 3
STYLUS [116] 4-11-9 (5*) R Massey, al wl plcd, led 3rd, jnd
appr 2 out, mstk and hdd last, fdd. . .(7 to 1 op 6 to 1) 4
PERSONAL HAZARD [104] 4-10-11 (5*) J Driscoll, tucked
away in midfield, drvn alng 3 out, sn wknd, eased
betw last 2. . . . .(8 to 1) 5
1508² RICHARDSON [100] 6-10-7 (5*) G Tormey, wtd wth,
improved into midfield hfwy, rdn alng aftr 4 out, sn
lost tch. . . . .(9 to 4 fav op 7 to 4) 6
824 RINGLAND (USA) [94] 5-10-1 (5*) Carol Cuthbert, settled off
the pace, struggling to keep up aftr 4 out, sn tld off.
. . . .(10 to 1 op 20 to 1) 7
1204² DANCING DOVE (Ire) [94] 5-10-1 (5*) B Harding, trkd ldrs,
feeling pace and rdn appr 3 out, sn lost tch.
. . . . (10 to 1 op 6 to 1) 8

1240⁴ IN TRUTH [96] 5-10-8 D Bentley, trkd ldrs, struggling to
keep up 4 out, tld off nxt. . . . . . . (16 to 1 tchd 20 to 1) 9
1280⁵ BROOK COTTAGE (Ire) [112] 5-11-10 M Hourigan, chsd
aloong to keep up hfwy, tld off 4 out.
. . . . (14 to 1 op 12 to 1) 10
1237* KALKO [100] 4-10-9 (3*) J Supple, keen hold, trkd ldrs till
appr 3 out, poor 5th whn f nxt. . . . . . .(7 to 1 op 6 to 1) f
Dist: 6l, 3l, ½l, 20l, hd, 15l, 4l, 5l, 5l. 4m 13.70s. a 33.70s (11 Ran).
SR: 37/32/19/46/14/10/ (Currie Group), L Lungo

1615 Tony Dickinson Memorial Novices' Chase (5-y-o and up) £3,355 3m (1:20)

1291* ONE MAN (Ire) 5-11-2 N Doughty, jmpd wl, al gng well,
made most, pckd 3 out, imprsv.
. . . . (6 to 5 on op 6 to 4 on tchd 11 to 10 on) 1
1288* LO STREGONE 7-11-2 M Dwyer, settled gng wl, jnd wnr
hfwy, ev ch last 3, outpcd r-in. . . . . .(11 to 10 op 5 to 4) 2
1477 CROWN EYEGLASS 7-10-12 R Garritty, trkd ldrs, struggling aftr pace lifted appr 3 out, sn lost tch. . . (33 to 1) 3
1511 KING'S RARITY 7-10-12 T Reed, wth wnr to hfwy,
reminders 5 out, lost tch 3 out. . . . .(33 to 1) 4
Dist: 3½l, dist, 2l. 6m 55.00s. a 49.00s (4 Ran).
SR: 37/33/-/-/ (J Hales), G Richards

1616 Tommy Whittle Chase (5-y-o and up) £10,042 3m. . . . . (1:50)

GAMBLING ROYAL 10-10-12 A Maguire, nvr far away, hit
3 out, slight ld nxt, lft clr last.
. . . .(7 to 2 op 9 to 4 tchd 4 to 1) 1
1185⁴ PLENTY CRACK 10-11-2 B Storey, mstks, wth ldr, feeling
pace and lost grnd aftr 4 out, lft poor second at last.
. . . .(33 to 1 op 25 to 1) 2
1387⁴ VERY VERY ORDINARY 7-10-12 R Supple, wtd wth,
improved hfwy, lft in ld 4 out, hmpd by loose horse and
hdd 2 out, ev ch whn crowded and f last, remounte
. . . .(9 to 2 op 3 to 1) 3
1439⁵ WHISPERING STEEL 7-11-0 N Doughty, jmpd rght, made
most till blun and uns rdr 4 out.
. . . .(15 to 8 on op 6 to 4 on) ur
Dist: 12l, dist. 7m 5.00s. a 59.00s (4 Ran).
(Roach Foods Limited), D Nicholson

1617 Waterloo Hurdle Grade 2 (4-y-o and up) £9,330 2½m. . . . . (2:20)

1322² BOLLIN WILLIAM 5-11-0 L Wyer, led aftr 1st, sn clr, styd
on stly frm 3 out, unchlgd.
. . . .(13 to 8 fav op 7 to 4 tchd 6 to 4) 1
1438⁴ DEB'S BALL 7-10-13 D J Moffatt, led till aftr 1st, ran in
snatches, staying on but no imprsn whn blun last.
. . . .(5 to 1) 2
1116⁶ JINXY JACK 9-11-4 M Dwyer, patiently rdn, hdwy hfwy,
chsd wnr 3 out, ridden and no imprsn betw last 2.
. . . .(9 to 2 op 4 to 1 tchd 5 to 1) 3
PRECIOUS BOY 7-11-0 N Doughty, settled gng wl, ev ch
hfwy, lost pl appr 3 out, eased nxt. . . (8 to 1 op 7 to 1) 4
1443² WINNIE THE WITCH 9-10-9 D Bridgwater, not fluent, chsd
wnr hfwy to 3 out, sn tld off. . . . . (5 to 1) 5
1006³ HIGH ALLTITUDE (Ire) 5-11-2 C Grant, trkd ldrs, almost f
4th, not reco'r, tld off whn pld up bef 2 out. . . . .(5 to 1) pu
Dist: 20l, ½l, 30l, dist. 5m 24.40s. a 45.90s (6 Ran).
(Sir Neil Westbrook), M H Easterby

1618 Leigh Handicap Chase (5-y-o and up) £5,034 2m. . . . . (2:50)

1294² LAST 'O' THE BUNCH [140] 9-11-3 N Doughty, jmpd wl,
made all, styd on stly frm last. . .(Evens tchd 11 to 10) 1
VIKING FLAGSHIP [147] 6-11-10 A Maguire, al hndy, slpd
bend appr 3 out, ch nxt, hit last, kpt on same pace.
. . . .(6 to 5 on op 5 to 4 on tchd 11 to 10 on) 2
Won by 3l. 4m 30.90s. a 31.90s (2 Ran).
SR: 63/67/ (G Middlebrook), G Richards

1619 Levy Board Handicap Hurdle (0-140 4-y-o and up) £2,840 2m 7f 110yds
. . . . (3:20)

1201* LINKSIDE [105] 8-10-6 A Maguire, nvr far away, led appr 3
out, jnd nxt, hdd r-in, rallied to ld last strd.
. . . .(5 to 1 op 4 to 1) 1
NORTHANTS [107] 7-10-8 R Hodge, settled gng wl,
improved frm midfield to draw level 2 out, led r-in, ct
last strd. . . . .(10 to 1 op 14 to 1) 2
1322² PEANUTS PET [126] 8-11-13 R Garritty, trkd ldrs, rdn aft-
field, pushed alng to improve frm 3 out, styd on r-in.
. . . .(14 to 1 tchd 16 to 1 and 12 to 1) 3
1119⁶ HELIOPSIS [113] 5-11-0 C Grant, tucked away in midfield, drvn alng whn pace quickened 3 out, fdd nxt.
. . . .(6 to 1) 4
THE DEMON BARBER [127] 11-12-0 N Doughty, led aftr 1st
till aftr nxt, styd hndy, feeling pace and rdn appr 3
out, fdd. . . . .(6 to 1) 5
1296* MYTHICAL STORM [99] 6-9-10¹ (5*) Mr M Buckley, co'red
up beh ldrs, struggling to keep up appr 3 out, tld off.
. . . .(6 to 1) 6

1072 CAPTAIN MY CAPTAIN (Ire) [99] 5-10-0 D Bridgwater, in tch, chsd alng fnl circuit, no ch whn almost f 3 out.
............................(33 to 1 op 25 to 1) 7
1219* TRUMP [101] 4-10-2 B Storey, wtd wth, improved on ins to track ldrs appr 3 out, fdd und pres bef nxt, tld off.
...............................(6 to 1) 8
1219² ONLY A ROSE [99] 4-10-0 D Wilkinson, led till aftr 1st, styd hndy, led appr 4 out till bef nxt, fourth and fdg whn f 2 out...................(7 to 1 op 6 to 1) f
WISHING GATE (USA) [108] 5-10-9 M Dwyer, pressed ldrs, ev chnnce 4 out, fdd und pres and pld up betw last 2.
......................(10 to 1) pu
1481³ BOLLIN MAGDALENE [106] 5-10-7 L Wyer, chsd ldrs, hit 9th, struggling appr 3 out, pld up betw last 2.
.................(4 fav op 3 to 1 tchd 5 to 2) pu
1474 ORIEL DREAM [113] 6-11-0 P Niven, wtd wth, improved on ins appr 3 out, wknd quickly nxt, pld up betw last 2.
.................(9 to 1 op 7 to 1 tchd 10 to 1) pu
NODDLE (USA) [99] 5-9-7 (7") F Perratt, led aftr second, sddl slpd, sn clr, hdd and wknd appr 4 out, tld off whn pld up bef nxt................(33 to 1) pu
Dist: Sht-hd, 4l, 15l, 20l, 2½l, 15l. dist. 6m 41.50s. a 70.50s (13 Ran).
(M R Johnson), M G Meagher

WORCESTER (heavy)
Wednesday December 8th
Going Correction: PLUS 1.60 sec. per fur.

1620 Champagne Selling Hurdle (4-y-o) £1,779 2¼m.................(12:30)

1353 ROCKY BAY 10-2 (7") Mr J L Llewellyn, in tch, mstk 4th, hrd drvn to chal frm 3 out till led last, all out.
..............(100 to 30 op 7 to 2 tchd 4 to 1) 1
1546* BUSMAN (Ire) 11-7 (7ex) M A FitzGerald, chsd ldr second to 5th, gng wl 3 out, hrd rdn aftr 2 out, hdd last, sn btn.
..............(15 to 8 on op 5 to 2 on tchd 6 to 4) 2
1472⁵ HINTON LADY (bl) 10-9 J Osborne, led till hdd 5th, sn btn, tld off.............(5 to 1 op 7 to 2) 3
1472 PLUM LINE (v) 10-9 (5") A Bates, tld off frm 5th, no ch whn blun badly last...............(66 to 1 op 33 to 1) 4
CUPID'S COURAGE (Ire) 10-6 (3") D Meredith, tld off aftr 3rd, jmpd very slwly and pld up aftr nxt.
..................(66 to 1 op 25 to 1) pu
Dist: 3l, dist, dist. 4m 59.10s. a 51.10s (Flag start) (5 Ran).
(Lodge Cross Partnership), B J Llewellyn

1621 Mistletoe Novices' Chase (5-y-o and up) £3,059 2½m 110yds........(1:00)

1059³ BARELY BLACK 5-10-12 W Humphreys, in tch, styd on frm 3 out, chlgd last, drvn to ld nr finish.
...................(50 to 1 op 33 to 1) 1
687⁵ TEKLA (Fr) 8-10-12 A Tory, prmnt, styd on frm 3 out, slight ld last, hdd r-in, no extr...................(33 to 1) 2
1279² PEACEMAN 7-11-3 E Murphy, led, sn clr, still clear 3 out, wknd aftr 2 out, hdd last, soon btn.
..................(3 to 1 op 5 to 2 tchd 7 to 2) 3
1106 ANDREW'S FIRST 6-10-12 S Earle, chsd ldrs 4th, wknd 3 out.............(11 to 4 fav op 5 to 2 tchd 9 to 4) 4
LEESWOOD 6-10-12 L Harvey, al beh.
..................(16 to 1 op 10 to 1) 5
1505⁴ MR OPTIMISTIC 6-10-12 R Dunwoody, in tch to tenth.
...............(5 to 1 op 6 to 1 tchd 10 to 1) 6
1405³ FEARSOME 7-10-12 M A FitzGerald, prmnt to 8th, no ch whn f last............(14 to 1 op 16 to 1 tchd 12 to 1) f
BUCKELIGHT (Ire) 5-10-12 B Powell, lost pos 6th, hdwy 8th, chasing ldrs whn f 9th.
..................(10 to 1 op 8 to 1 tchd 16 to 1) f
1372 COCK SPARROW 9-10-12 W Marston, prmnt to 9th, tld off whn pld up bef 2 out..........(33 to 1 tchd 40 to 1) pu
1311 THE YOKEL 7-10-12 T Wall, al beh, blun 9th, tld off whn pld up bef tenth.............(66 to 1 op 33 to 1) pu
ISIPINGO 6-10-9 (3") R Davis, tld off whn pld up bef 5th.
.................(66 to 1 op 33 to 1) pu
1287⁸ RIDDLEMEROO 8-10-7 (5") T Eley, al beh, tld off whn pld up bef 7th................(66 to 1 op 33 to 1) pu
PUNCH'S HOTEL 8-10-12 T Grantham, beh frm hfwy, tld off whn pld up bef 2 out.
..................(11 to 1 op 5 to 1 tchd 10 to 1) pu
1211⁴ SEMINOLE PRINCESS 5-10-7 M Bosley, al beh, tld off whn pld up bef 9th...............(66 to 1 op 33 to 1) pu
PAKENHAM 7-10-12 M Moloney, beh and blun 7th, tld off whn pld up bef 3 out.........(12 to 1 op 8 to 1) pu
1090 TWIST 'N' SCU 5-10-12 C Llewellyn, beh frm 6th, tld off whn puled up bef 2 out.......(16 to 1 op 8 to 1) pu
CROPREDY LAD 6-10-12 R Bellamy, in tch to 9th, tld off whn pld up bef 2 out. (14 to 1 op 8 to 1 tchd 16 to 1) pu
1406⁶ PARSON'S WAY 6-10-12 G Upton, beh 6th, tld off whn pld up bef 3 out...........(66 to 1 op 33 to 1) pu
Dist: 1½l, 10l, 2½l, dist, 3l. 5m 41.60s. a 38.60s (18 Ran).
SR: 26/24/19/11/-/-/ (John Cantrill), N M Babbage

1622 Turkey Novices' Hurdle (4-y-o and up) £1,480 2m.................(1:30)

1490⁷ TOPPING TOM (Ire) 4-10-12 C Llewellyn, hld up, steady hdwy 5th, chlgd and mstk 2 out, sn led, clr r-in.
..............(11 to 4 fav op 5 to 1) 1
CASTLE COURT (Ire) 5-10-12 B Powell, prmnt, led aftr 5th, hdd sn after 2 out, kpt on same pace. (4 to 1 op 7 to 4) 2
1303⁸ KLINGON (Ire) 4-10-9 (3") R Farrant, al prmnt, styd on same pace frm 3 out...............(11 to 2 op 8 to 1) 3
898 DUSTY SERGEANT (Ire) 4-10-12 M Ahern, in tch 3rd, lost pl 5th, ran on ag'n frm 2 out..................(50 to 1) 4
1283 FIRST CENTURY (Ire) 4-10-5 (7") Mr J L Llewellyn, hdwy to track ldrs 3rd, pressed lders 3 out, wknd nxt.
..................(25 to 1 op 50 to 1) 5
1418⁸ NICSAMLYN 6-10-7 Mr T Stephenson, beh till gd hdwy 5th, wth ldrs 3 out, sn wknd........(20 to 1 op 33 to 1) 6
1442 RAFTERS 4-10-12 M A FitzGerald, nvr rch ldrs.
.................(7 to 1 op 6 to 1) 7
1456⁷ HEPBURN (Ire) 5-10-7 W Humphreys, al beh.
..................(20 to 1 tchd 25 to 1) 8
SARAZAR (Ire) 4-10-12 R Dunwoody, prmnt whn hmpd second, wknd aftr 5th..........(5 to 1 op 3 to 1) 9
EAGLES LAIR (bl) 7-10-7 (5") J McCarthy, chsd ldrs 3rd, wknd aftr 5th..............(25 to 1 op 16 to 1) 10
GLASGOW (bl) 4-10-12 H Davies, took str hold, led and sn clr, hdd and wknd quickly aftr 5th...........(33 to 1) 11
844 IN DEEP FRIENDSHIP (Ire) 5-10-12 J Osborne, mid-div, hdwy 5th, chsd ldrs 3 out, wknd quickly aftr 2 out.
..................(11 to 1 op 5 to 1 tchd 12 to 1) 12
IT'S CONFIDENTIAL (NZ) 6-10-9 (3") R Davis, pld hrd, wth ldrs, wnt badly rght second, rear 4th, tld off whn pulled up bef 3 out....................(33 to 1 op 25 to 1) pu
DISTANT MILL (Ire) 5-10-9 (3") D Meredith, beh frm 4th, tld off whn pld up bef 3 out............(50 to 1 op 33 to 1) pu
Dist: 8l, 5l, 2½l, 2l, 2½l, 12l, 2½l, 10l, 5l, dist. 4m 13.00s. a 32.00s (14 Ran).
SR: 20/12/7/4/2/-/ (Mrs J Mould), N A Twiston-Davies

1623 Billy Love Memorial Handicap Chase (0-120 5-y-o and up) £3,201 2m.. (2:00)

1044⁴ MR FELIX [96] 7-10-4 B Powell, made virtually all, shaken up and kpt on wl r-in.............(9 to 2 op 7 to 1) 1
3047 PHILLIMAY [92] 7-10-0 L Harvey, hdwy to chase ldrs 4th, hit 6th, ev ch whn hit last, styd on one pace.
...................(16 to 1 op 33 to 1) 2
1409* PERSIAN SWORD [98] 7-11-6 W Marston, beh, reminders aftr 7th, rdn frm 3 out, staying on whn hit last, rallied nr finish......(Evens fav tchd 11 to 10 and 11 to 10 on) 3
1461* COTAPAXI [92] 8-10-0 (6ex) R Dunwoody, wth wnr to 3rd, styd prmnt, hit 7th, ev ch 3 out, wknd nxt.
...................(4 to 1 op 7 to 2) 4
1461³ NORTHERN JINKS [120] 10-11-11 (3") D Meredith, chsd ldrs till lost pl 5th, rallied ag'n 3 out, sn wknd, tld off.
..................(6 to 1 op 7 to 2) 5
Dist: 2l, 1½l, 15l, dist. 4m 24.20s. a 35.20s (5 Ran).
(Felix Rosenstiel's Widow & Son), R Champion

1624 Cranberry Novices' Hurdle (4-y-o and up) £1,480 2m 5f 110yds.......(2:30)

1108² ARCTIC COURSE (Ire) 5-10-12 W Marston, confidently rdn, hdwy to track ldrs 7th, led aftr 3 out, cmftbly.
..................(11 to 8 on op 7 to 4 on tchd 5 to 4 on) 1
SMITH'S BAND (Ire) 5-10-12 R Dunwoody, mstk 1st, hdwy 7th, styd on to chase wnr frm 2 out, not quicken r-in.
..................(14 to 1 op 10 to 1 tchd 16 to 1) 2
CALLEROSE 6-10-12 B Powell, in tch whn mstk and lost pl 7th, rallied and ran on ag'n frm 2 out.
..................(12 to 1 op 7 to 1) 3
1354⁴ THE CARROT MAN 5-10-12 J Osborne, hdwy 6th, rdn aftr 3 out, sn one paced. (10 to 1 op 12 to 1 tchd 14 to 1) 4
1251⁷ NAVAL BATTLE 6-10-12 M A FitzGerald, led till hdd aftr 7th, wknd 2 out, tld off.
..................(14 to 1 op 12 to 1 tchd 20 to 1) 5
1491 GIVEITAGO (bl) 7-10-12 S McNeill, prmnt, chlgd 6th, led aftr nxt, hdd sn after 3 out, wknd quickly.
..................(5 to 2 op 9 to 2 tchd 8 to 1) 6
639 ASSEMBLY DANCER 6-10-9 (3") R Davis, al beh.
..................(66 to 1 op 33 to 1) 7
869 PHAROAH'S SON 7-10-12 S Earle, beh frm 4th, tld off.
..................(100 to 1 op 33 to 1) 8
THE SHAW TRADER 4-10-12 C Llewellyn, chsd ldrs 4th, wknd aftr 7th........(20 to 1 op 10 to 1 tchd 25 to 1) 9
934⁴ TALENT SPOTTER 6-10-5 (7") A Shakespeare, chsd ldrs to 7th..................(16 to 1 op 10 to 1) 10
1239 ARDORAN 7-10-7 (5") T Eley, effrt 5th, sn wknd, tld off whn pld up bef 3 out........(100 to 1 op 33 to 1) pu
KING TASMAN (NZ) 6-10-12 H Davies, beh frm 5th, tld off whn pld up bef 3 out............(50 to 1 op 25 to 1) pu
1108⁹ BETTIVILLE 6-10-12 A Carroll, beh frm 4th, tld off whn pld up bef 7th................(66 to 1 op 25 to 1) pu
ON THE BOOK 4-10-7 A Tory, prmnt to 5th, tld off whn pld pld up bef 3 out...........(100 to 1 op 33 to 1) pu
Dist: 1½l, 10l, 25l, 4l, 1½l, dist, 4l, 1½l, dist. 5m 40.70s. a 46.70s (14 Ran).
(Mrs Shirley Robins), D Nicholson

1625 Saint Nicholas Handicap Chase (0-130 5-y-o and up) £3,327 2m 7f......(3:00)

1273* MIDNIGHT CALLER [119] 7-12-0 J Osborne, *al frnt rnk, led tenth to 12th, led ag'n 3 out, quickened wl whn chlgd frm last, readily*....(2 to 1 jt-fav op Evens tchd 9 to 4) 1
1503² CAMELOT KNIGHT [114] (bl) 7-11-9 C Llewellyn, *led to 7th, chlgd 11th, led nxt, hdd 3 out, str chal and wnt lft last, outpcd*.......... (2 to 1 jt-fav op 5 to 2 tchd 11 to 4) 2
THAMESDOWN TOOTSIE [94] 8-10-3³ G Upton, *hmpd second, hit 4th and 5th, styd chasing ldrs till outpcd frm 11th*.......... (12 to 1 op 14 to 1 tchd 16 to 1) 3
SIDE OF HILL [116] 8-11-11 R Dunwoody, *prmnt, led 7th to tenth, wknd appr 3 out, no ch whn blun 2 out.*
.......................(9 to 2 op 7 to 2 tchd 5 to 1) 4
1419⁴ MUTUAL TRUST [116] 9-11-11 M Moloney, *chsd ldrs 8th, hit tenth and wknd, virtually pld up r-in.*
..........................(6 to 1 op 4 to 1 tchd 13 to 2) 5
1262 HEYFLEET [97] (bl) 10-10-6 I Lawrence, *f second.*
.......................(16 to 1 op 20 to 1 tchd 14 to 1) f
FATHER JOHN [91] 9-10-0 W Irvine, *beh 8th, refused tenth.*
......................(66 to 1 op 50 to 1 tchd 100 to 1) ref
GADBROOK [91] (v) 11-10-0 L Harvey, *hit 4th, tld off 5th, pld up bef 9th.*......................(25 to 1 op 20 to 1) pu
Dist: 2l, dist, sht-hd, dist. 6m 29.40s. a 45.40s (8 Ran).

SR: 14/7/-/-/-/ (M Worcester), S E Sherwood

1626 Grunwick Stakes National Hunt Flat Race (4,5,6-y-o) £1,869 2m.......(3:30)

RED PARADE (NZ) 5-11-4 (3*) R Davis, *hdwy to chase ldrs 7 fs out, led ins fnl 2, pushed clr.*
.....................(13 to 2 op 4 to 1 tchd 7 to 1) 1
ST MELLION FAIRWAY (Ire) 4-10-12 (7*) Pat Thompson, *al prmnt, led 5 fs out, hdd ins fnl 2, kpt on same pace.*
.......................(20 to 1 op 14 to 1) 2
DUQUES 6-10-9 (7*) L Dace, *hdwy 4 fs out, kpt on same pace frm o'r 2 out.*......................(20 to 1) 3
CHAPRASSI (Ire) 4-10-12 (7*) T Dascombe, *hdwy hfwy, rdn 3 fs out, ran green and one pace frm o'r 2 out.*
..........................(8 to 1 op 4 to 1) 4
THE BARGEMAN (NZ) 5-11-4 (3*) A Thornton, *sn prmnt, no prog fnl 4 fs.*.........(4 to 1 fav op 9 to 2 tchd 5 to 1) 5
SHIMBA HILLS 5-11-7 Mrs J Retter, *beh, hdwy 6 fs out, styd on fnl 2 furlongs.*............ (6 to 1 op 20 to 1) 6
COUNTRYWIDE LAD 4-11-0 (5*) C Burnett-Wells, *nvr rch ldrs.*..........................(20 to 1) 7
MOORE BONES 5-11-0 (7*) A Dowling, *beh till some prog fnl 3 fs.*..........................(10 to 1 op 8 to 1) 8
BECKFORD 4-11-5 Mr P Macewan, *nvr dngrs.*
..........................(14 to 1 op 12 to 1) 9
KING SCORPIO (Ire) 4-11-0 (5*) A Procter, *hdwy 7 fs out, wknd 3 out.*..........................(10 to 1 op 4 to 1) 10
CAPO CASTANUM 4-11-5 Mr J M Pritchard, *made most till hdd 5 fs out, wknd quickly.*........(7 to 1 op 9 to 1) 11
ST MELLION GREEN (Ire) 4-11-5 R Greene, *al beh.*
..........................(25 to 1 op 20 to 1) 12
MAGGIE TEE 5-10-11 (5*) S Curran, *pressed ldrs till wknd 5 fs out.*..........................(25 to 1 op 20 to 1) 13
SUZY BLUE 4-10-9 (5*) T Jenks, *al beh.*.......... (33 to 1) 14
WHITELOCK QUEST 5-11-0 (7*) Miss C Spearing, *prmnt 11 fs.*..........(6 to 1 op 16 to 1 tchd 5 to 1) 15
FINWAG 6-11-2 (5*) T Eley, *chsd ldrs 11 fs.*........(50 to 1) 16
ROSENTHAL 5-10-9 (7*) T Murphy, *al beh.*........(25 to 1) 17
CASTLE WARRIOR 6-11-0 (7*) N Juckes, *sn beh.* (33 to 1) 18
COMIC TURN 4-11-2 (3*) R Farrant, *prmnt till wknd 5 fs out.*..........(12 to 1 op 8 to 1 tchd 9 to 1) 19
MY LITTLE SECRET 5-11-0 (7*) Mr N Bradley, *prmnt ten fs.*..........................(33 to 1 op 20 to 1) 20
EL KHAMSIN (Ire) 5-10-9 (7*) Paul McEntee, *al beh.*
..........................(50 to 1) 21
Dist: 3l, 10l, 2½l, 4l, 20l, 3l, 6l, 2½l, 10l, 3l. 4m 6.50s. (21 Ran).
(Russell J Peake), D H Barons

FAKENHAM (good)
Thursday December 9th
Going Correction: PLUS 0.70 sec. per fur.

1627 Fitzwilliam Selling Handicap Hurdle (4-y-o and up) £1,976 2m 110yds
.......................(12:30)

846⁹ WEEKDAY CROSS (Ire) [84] 5-10-11 J Railton, *mid-div, hdwy 5th, led aftr 2 out, sn clr*......(7 to 1 op 5 to 1) 1
1492 PINECONE PETER [93] 6-11-6 M Brennan, *ran on frm rear appr 3 out, one pace betw last 2*......(7 to 1 op 6 to 1) 2
1426⁷ TRISTAN'S COMET [76] 6-10-3 B Dalton, *led to second, wth ldrs, no extr frm 3 out*......(10 to 1 op 12 to 1) 3
EARLY BREEZE [80] 7-10-0 (7*) Leanne Eldredge, *in tch, effrt approching 2 out, not quicken betw last two.*
..........................(9 to 1 op 8 to 1) 4
1353⁴ RUTH'S GAMBLE [73] (v) 5-9-11² (5*) T Jenks, *ldg grp, led 7th till aftr 2 out, sn outpcd*....... (5 to 1 op 8 to 1) 5
846⁸ STYLISH GENT [73] 6-10-0 I Lawrence, *handily plcd, led 6th to nxt, btn 2 out.* (25 to 1 op 20 to 1 tchd 50 to 1) 6
1418⁶ RARFY'S DREAM [100] 5-11-13 S Keightley, *nvr nr to chal.*.......................(15 to 2 op 8 to 1 tchd 7 to 1) 7

1424³ BASSIO (Bel) [82] (h) 4-10-9 J Ryan, *mid-div, rdn and lost tch aftr 5th.*..........................(6 to 1 tchd 7 to 1) 8
1390 GREEN'S TRILOGY (USA) [73] 5-10-0 M Ahern, *nvr on terms, tld off 5th.*.................(33 to 1 op 25 to 1) 9
950⁸ HADLEIGHS CHOICE [73] 6-10-0 M Robinson, *in tch whn uns rdr 3rd.*.................(33 to 1 op 25 to 1) ur
693⁵ SINGING GOLD [73] 7-10-0³ (3*) R Davis, *al rear, pld up bef 2 out.*.......................(33 to 1 op 25 to 1) pu
1355 BARCHAM [73] 6-10-0 D Murphy, *chsd ldrs to 5th, sn wknd, pld up r-in...* (2 to 1 fav op 3 to 1 tchd 4 to 1) pu
1372 DALLISTON (NZ) [98] 7-11-11 A Carroll, *wl plcd till wknd 5th, tld off whn pld up r-in...*.....(7 to 1 op 5 to 1) pu
1370³ MILL BURN [75] (bl) 4-10-2² R Campbell, *led second till aftr 5th, wknd quickly, pld up bef 2 out.*
..........................(16 to 1 op 14 to 1) pu
Dist: 6l, 1l, 3l, 4l, 1l, 10l, 12l, dist. 4m 10.60s. a 20.60s (14 Ran).
(M Desmond FitzGerald), J R Jenkins

1628 Eastern Daily Press Novices' Handicap Hurdle (4-y-o and up) £1,819 2m 5f
..........................(1:00)

1196² GORTEERA [92] 7-11-5 M Brennan, *hld up, ran on frm 8th, led 3 out, quickened clr aftr nxt, eased nr finish.*
..........................(5 to 4 on op 6 to 4 on) 1
1488* NAGOBELIA [101] 5-12-0 D Murphy, *hld up, chsd wnr frm 3 out, outpcd betw last 2*............(2 to 1 op 6 to 4) 2
1371⁵ MILLIE (USA) [73] 5-10-0 M Robinson, *clr ldr till wknd and hdd aftr 8th, sn lost pl, styd on appr last.*
..........................(20 to 1 op 14 to 1) 3
1528³ EMALLEN (Ire) [75] 5-10-2 N Williamson, *chsd ldr, led aftr 8th to 3 out, wknd appr nxt.*
..........................(13 to 2 op 8 to 1 tchd 6 to 1) 4
1215 ROYAL BATTLE [73] 5-10-0³ (3*) R Davis, *al rear, rdn and outpcd appr 3 out, pld up bef nxt.* (50 to 1 op 25 to 1) pu
Dist: 20l, 3l, 7l. 5m 26.00s. a 33.00s (5 Ran).
(Miss P Harding), O Brennan

1629 Stephenson Smart Handicap Chase (0-130 5-y-o and up) £3,371 3m.. (1:30)

1216³ COOL AND EASY [97] 7-10-0 D Murphy, *pressed ldr, led 14th, reminders to quicken clr appr last, easily.*
..........................(15 to 8 fav op 9 to 4 tchd 7 to 4) 1
1407² DUO DROM [99] (v) 8-10-2 N Williamson, *sn settled in 3rd pl, cld on ldrs 14th, ev ch 2 out, rdn and no extr appr last.*..........................(3 to 1 op 9 to 4) 2
1423* STAY ON TRACKS [125] 11-11-7 (7*) Mr N King, *led to 14th, mstks nxt 2, sn btn.*..........(2 to 1 op 11 to 8) 3
1502⁷ CALL ME EARLY [97] 8-10-0 M Brennan, *al beh, tld off tenth.*..........(8 to 1 op 6 to 1 tchd 10 to 1) 4
1388 SINGLESOLE [114] 8-11-3 A Carroll, *not jump wl, beh and lost tch 7th, tld off whn pld up bef tenth.*
..........................(10 to 1 op 6 to 1) pu
Dist: 15l, ¾l, dist. 6m 23.10s. a 31.10s (5 Ran).
(H T Pelham), J T Gifford

1630 L. L. Firth Memorial Handicap Chase (0-115 5-y-o and up) £3,355 2m 110yds
..........................(2:00)

1514* DRIVING FORCE [112] (bl) 7-11-8 (3*,4ex) R Davis, *hld up in tch, jnd ldr 7th, led aftr 2 out, sn clr.* (7 to 4 op 5 to 1) 1
1391* CROOKED COUNSEL [97] 7-10-10 N Williamson, *led 3rd to 5th, led 8th, blun 2 out, sn hdd and outpcd.*
..........................(11 to 8 fav op 6 to 4 tchd 13 to 8) 2
1493⁵ PETMER [87] 6-9-10¹ (5*) T Jenks, *hld up, pckd 6th, hdwy 9th, no imprsn on ldrs frm 2 out.*
.......................(10 to 1 op 8 to 1 tchd 12 to 1) 3
1394⁵ MR JAMBOREE [115] 7-12-0 D Murphy, *led to 3rd, led 5th to 8th, wknd tenth.*........(7 to 2 tchd 4 to 1) 4
1415⁸ SANDMOOR PRINCE [90] 10-10-3 Dr P Pritchard, *outpcd.*..........................(25 to 1 op 20 to 1) 5
1466 RUSTIC GENT (Ire) [88] 5-10-11 S Hodgson, *in tch, mstks 3rd, 4th and 5th, struggling 7th, tld off.*
..........................(14 to 1 op 12 to 1) 6
Dist: 12l, 2l, 10l, 2½l, dist. 4m 14.10s. a 17.10s (6 Ran).
SR: 41/14/2/20/-/-/ (B J Reid), Mrs M McCourt

1631 Cottesmore Novices' Chase (5-y-o and up) £2,396 2m 5f 110yds.... (2:30)

1385² BOLLINGER 7-11-2 D Murphy, *pressed ldr, not fluent and lost pl 3 out, rallied appr last, hrd drvn to ld last strd.*
..........................(13 to 8 on op 7 to 4 on tchd 6 to 4 on) 1
1385* UNHOLY ALLIANCE 6-11-10 N Williamson, *cld on ldrs tenth, led 2 out till hrd drvn and hdd last strd.*
..........................(15 to 8 op 11 to 8 tchd 2 to 1) 2
1491⁴ KEV'S LASS (Ire) 5-10-4 (7*) P Murphy, *made most till blun and hdd 2 out, sn btn.* (13 to 2 op 8 to 1 tchd 7 to 1) 3
1470 HICKELTON HOUSE 9-10-11 (5*) A Bates, *trkd ldg pair, cld 11th, ev ch whn blun 4 out, not reco'r.*
..........................(33 to 1 op 20 to 1) 4
970⁷ STROKED AGAIN 8-10-11 D Telfer, *rear whn blun 4th, lost tch, mstk 11th, tld off.*.... (50 to 1 op 33 to 1) 5
Dist: Sht-hd, 15l, 15l, dist. 5m 43.20s. a 31.20s (5 Ran).
(R F Eliot), J T Gifford

1632 Fakenham Racecourse Caravan Site Handicap Hurdle (0-125 4-y-o and up) £2,640 2m 110yds.............. (3:00)

1355* CARDINAL BIRD (USA) [86] (bl) 6-9-7 (7*) Chris Webb, *hld up rear, cld on ldrs 3 out, led betw last 2, pushed out.* ....(6 to 1 op 5 to 1) 1
1492[4] CHILD OF THE MIST [114] 7-12-0 N Williamson, *mid-div, jnd ldrs 3 out, ev ch frm nxt, not quicken aftr last.* .... (11 to 4 fav op 3 to 1 tchd 100 to 30) 2
1149 ILEWIN [95] 6-10-9 M Ahern, *wl plcd, slight ld appr 2 out, hdd and outpcd betw last two*...... (6 to 1 op 10 to 1) 3
1395[8] ARANY [93] 6-10-7 D Murphy, *led till appr 2 out, sn btn, fnshd 4th, collapsed, dead*..........(5 to 1 op 7 to 2) 4
1154[6] LOCAL FLYER [89] 4-10-3 S Keightley, *hld up in tch, hmpd and lost pl 6th, styd on frm 2 out*...(8 to 1 tchd 9 to 1) 5
1353[3] NORTHERN TRIAL (USA) [88] (v) 5-9-11 (5*) T Jenks, *settled rear, outpcd and lost tch 6th.* ....(6 to 1 op 5 to 1 tchd 7 to 1) 6
REGGAE BEAT [108] 8-11-8 R Campbell, *hld up rear, improved 4th, mstk and lost pl 6th.* ....(9 to 2 op 5 to 1 tchd 7 to 1) 7
VICTORY ANTHEM [96] 7-10-10 I Lawrence, *chsd ldr till wknd appr 6th*...................(14 to 1 op 10 to 1) 8
1355[3] BABY ASHLEY [86] 7-10-0[3] (3*) R Davis, *hdwy frm rear 4th, wknd 2 out, virtually pld up aftr last.* ....(20 to 1 op 14 to 1) 9

Dist: Nk, 15l, 8l, 4l, 8l, 1l, 2l, dist. 4m 7.30s. a 17.30s (9 Ran).
SR: 14/41/7/-/-/-/ (John Fane), S Mellor

HAYDOCK (heavy)
Thursday December 9th

Going Correction: PLUS 2.30 sec. per fur. (races 1,2,-4,7), PLUS 2.05 (3,5,6)

1633 Widnes Claiming Hurdle (4,5,6-y-o) £2,215 2½m.................. (12:20)

1462 HIGH GRADE 5-10-10 H Davies, *patiently rdn, improved frm midfield aftr 3 out, styd on to ld r-in, swshd tail, ridden out*....................................(8 to 1) 1
1485[7] MAKE ME PROUD (Ire) 4-10-5 L Wyer, *dsptd ld, led briefly hfwy, lost grnd and drvn alng 3 out, rallied frm betw last 2*...(14 to 1) 2
1445[3] FOX CHAPEL 6-11-2 M Dwyer, *led, quickened hfwy, jnd last 2, hdd and no extr r-in*.........(9 to 4 op 2 to 1) 3
1259* MECADO (v) 6-10-9 A Maguire, *al hndy, drvn to chal betw last 2, one pace r-in*...........................(7 to 1) 4
1487 COMSTOCK 6-9-13 (7*) E Husband, *wtd wth, improved into midfield appr 3 out, effrt and rdn nxt, no imprsn.* ....(9 to 1 op 8 to 1 tchd 10 to 1) 5
324[2] THE BLACK MONK (Ire) (v) 5-11-0 M Foster, *tucked away gng wl, effrt appr 4 out, rdn and found little nxt.* ....(11 to 8 fav op 6 to 4) 6
1201[6] PANDESSA 6-10-7 P Niven, *nvr far away, drvn alng appr 3 out, fdd*....................................(14 to 1) 7
1241[4] PHALAROPE (Ire) 5-10-3 (7*) R Moore, *trkd ldrs, pushed up to draw level appr 3 out, fdd nxt*..........(33 to 1) 8
1487[8] SAOIRSE (Ire) 5-10-4 (3*) D J Moffatt, *settled rear, drvn alng whn pace lifted hfwy, btn 4 out*.........(12 to 1) 9
SECRET CASTLE 5-11-2 T Wall, *al last, reminders 3 out, tld off whn pld up bef last*..................(20 to 1) pu

Dist: 8l, 1l, ¾l, 4l, 6l, 3½l, 4l, 8l. 5m 30.60s. a 52.10s (10 Ran).
SR: 21/8/18/10/3/5/ (Under Orders Racing III), Miss S J Wilton

1634 Southport Juvenile Novices' Hurdle (3-y-o) £2,162 2m............. (12:50)

GIORDANO (Ire) 10-12 Gary Lyons, *nvr far away, rdn to chal betw last 2, styd on gmely to ld cl hme.* ....(11 to 1 op 10 to 1 tchd 12 to 1) 1
1483[3] THE PREMIER EXPRES 10-12 L Wyer, *led, quickened hfwy, clr aftr 3 out, rdn and ct cl hme.* ....(9 to 2 op 5 to 1 tchd 4 to 1) 2
1473[6] LITTLE GUNNER 10-12 A Maguire, *tucked away in midfield, rdn to chal 2 out, kpt on same pace frm last.* ....(11 to 1 op 12 to 1 tchd 10 to 1) 3
1229[3] LOVE YOU MADLY (Ire) 10-7 M Foster, *patiently rdn, improved 3 out, outpcd betw last 2, rallied.* ....(11 to 8 fav op 5 to 4 tchd 6 to 4) 4
ANORAK (USA) 10-12 J Callaghan, *trkd ldrs, drvn alng appr 3 out, styd on same pace frm betw last 2.* .... (12 to 1 op 10 to 1) 5
742[3] DEMILUNE (USA) 10-12 C Llewellyn, *al hndy, drvn whn pace quickened 3 out, no extr*.......(7 to 2 op 11 to 4) 6
561[4] ON GOLDEN POND (Ire) 10-10 (3*) N Bentley, *trkd ldrs, feeling pace and scrubbed alng appr 3 out, sn btn.* ....(15 to 2 op 7 to 1 tchd 8 to 1) 7
PUBLIC WAY (Ire) 10-12 T Reed, *ran in snatches, effrt appr 4 out, lost tch quickly and pld up betw last 2.* ....(16 to 1 op 12 to 1) pu
742 TARGET LINE 10-7 (5*) Mr D McCain, *beh frm 3rd, tld off whn pld up bef 2 out*.........................(33 to 1) pu

KEEN AND CLEAN (Ire) 10-4 (3*) D J Moffatt, *not fluent, al struggling, tld off whn pld up bef 2 out.* ....(20 to 1 op 16 to 1) pu

Dist: ¾l, 3½l, hd, sht-hd, 8l, 15l. 4m 24.30s. a 44.30s (10 Ran).
SR: 9/8/4/-/4/-/ (J D Garrattley), P D Evans

1635 Ronnie Johnston Memorial Trophy Handicap Chase (5-y-o and up) £5,628 4m 110yds....................(1:20)

1319[2] ALL JEFF (Fr) [128] 9-11-7 G Bradley, *beh one circuit, improved hfwy, hit 15th and 7 out, led 2 out till hdd and hit last, rallied to ld last 100 yards.* ....(2 to 1 tchd 15 to 8) 1
1447[2] MOORCROFT BOY [119] 8-10-12 A Maguire, *settled travelling wl, led on bit aftr 3 out to nxt, slight ld frm last till hdd and one pace last 100 yards.* ....(13 to 8 fav op 6 to 4 tchd 7 to 4) 2
1520[5] JUST SO [124] (bl) 10-11-3 S Burrough, *al hndy, led briefly 3rd, led 17th till aftr 3 out, one pace*...........(8 to 1) 3
1572 CAROUSEL ROCKET [108] 10-10-1 C Grant, *wtd wth, improved fnl circuit, effrt and rdn appr 3 out, sn btn.* ....(12 to 1 tchd 14 to 1) 4
1352[4] CLONROCHE DRILLER [107] 8-9-7 (7*) Mr D Parker, *led 4th to 17th, lost grnd aftr 6 out, rallied, btn after 3 out.* ....(25 to 1 tchd 33 to 1) 5
1471 BOREEN OWEN [115] 9-10-8 P Niven, *slight ld to 3rd, styd hndy till outpcd aftr 6 out, rallied, fdd after 3 out, virtually pld up*..................(12 to 1 tchd 14 to 1) 6
865* MAYORAN (NZ) [107] 9-10-0 C Maude, *mstks, nvr gng wl, tld off till pld up bef 17th (water).* (7 to 2 tchd 4 to 1) pu

Dist: 2½l, 15l, 20l, 15l, dist. 9m 34.30s. a 74.30s (7 Ran).
SR: 16/4/-/-/ (Lady Joseph), C P E Brooks

1636 EBF 'National Hunt' Novices' Hurdle Qualifier (4,5,6-y-o) £2,145 2m.. (1:50)

WITH IMPUNITY 4-11-0 C Llewellyn, *made most, hdd and rdn aftr last, bumped and hit rls, rallied to ld last 75 yards*..........................(10 to 1 op 8 to 1) 1
1490* KONVEKTA KING (Ire) 5-11-5 A Maguire, *patiently rdn, improved into narrow ld aftr last, hng lft, hdd and no extr last 75 yards*..........(7 to 2 on tchd 10 to 3 on) 2
COMEDIMAN 5-10-7 (7*) Mr G Hogan, *nvr far away, effrt whn blun and rdr lost reins 2 out, not reco'r.* ....(25 to 1 op 20 to 1) 3
FULL OF FIRE 6-11-0 N Doughty, *led briefly second, effrt appr 2 out, rdn and fdd betw last two.* ....(4 to 1 op 7 to 2 tchd 9 to 2) 4
FLINTERS 6-11-0 M Moloney, *blun 1st, reco'red to track ldrs, effrt appr 2 out, eased whn btn r-in.* .... (25 to 1 op 20 to 1) 5

Dist: 2½l, 12l, 1½l, 12l. 4m 25.30s. a 45.30s (5 Ran).
SR: 1/3/ (Guest Leasing & Bloodstock Co Ltd), N A Twiston-Davies

1637 Dry Blackthorn Cider Novices' Chase (6-y-o and up) £3,428 2½m......(2:20)

1348[3] EASY BUCK 6-11-4 C Maude, *made most, jnd 7th, clr 3 out, kpt on gmely r-in*.............(11 to 8 op 5 to 4) 1
1393[2] WANDERWEG (Fr) 5-11-0 H Davies, *wtd wth, lft second 4 out, effrt und pres betw last 2, styd on same pace.* ....(7 to 1 tchd 15 to 2) 2
1218[4] GREENFIELD MANOR 6-11-0 T Reed, *trkd ldrs, struggling to hold pl fnl circuit, rdn 6 out, plodded round.* .... (16 to 1 op 14 to 1) 3
COULDNT BE BETTER 6-11-0 G Bradley, *patiently rdn, last but in tch whn f 7 out*....(5 to 4 fav tchd 11 to 8) f
1054 CHALIE RICHARDS 6-11-0 C Llewellyn, *wth ldr, led briefly 7th, second and hndy whn f 4 out.* (20 to 1 op 16 to 1) f

Dist: 3l, dist. 5m 44.40s. a 46.40s (5 Ran).
SR: 36/29/ (The Burford Laundry Company Ltd), N A Gaselee

1638 Boston Pit Veterans Handicap Chase (0-140) £4,104 2½m.............(2:50)

684[2] WIDE BOY [125] 11-11-10 A Maguire, *jmpd wl, made all, given breather 3 out, kpt on strly frm betw last 2.* ....(7 to 4 op 6 to 4) 1
THE MALTKILN [103] (v) 10-10-2 C Grant, *nvr far away, feeling pace and drvn alng appr 3 out, styd on frm betw last 2*.................. (9 to 1 op 12 to 1 tchd 8 to 1) 2
1294* GOOD FOR A LAUGH [120] 9-10-12 (7*) Mr D Parker, *patiently rdn, mstk 7th, blun 4 out, rallied, eased whn btn r-in*...................... (11 to 10 fav op 5 to 4) 3
1318[3] PINEMARTIN [109] 10-10-3 (5*) N Leach, *trkd wnr, struggling to hold pl appr 3 out, tld off*....(5 to 1 op 9 to 2) 4

Dist: 4l, 30l, 30l. 5m 49.30s. a 51.30s (4 Ran).
(M Popham), P J Hobbs

1639 William Hill 'Golden Oldies' Stakes (Round 3) (4-y-o and up) £1,551 1½m ....(3:20)

1304* MISSY-S (Ire) 4-11-9 Peter Scudamore, *nvr far away, led entering strt, hrd pressed and rdn o'r 2 fs out, styd on gmely to go clr fnl furlong.*
.... (5 to 4 on tchd Evens and 11 to 8 on) 1
1304² MY SWAN SONG 8-12-0 Peter Smith, *co'red up in midfield, reminder entering strt, ev ch over 2 fs out, wndrd, one pace*.................... (5 to 1 op 7 to 2) 2
1299 MO ICHI DO 7-11-13³ Mike Gallemore, *ran in snatches, lost gd pos and last strt, ran on last 2 fs, fnshd wl, disqualified*..................... (33 to 1 op 25 to 1) 3D
BIRD WATCHER 4-11-10 Nigel Tinkler, *patiently rdn, improved frm midfield entering strt, shaken up o'r 2 fs out, nvr plcd to chal, fnshd 4th, pld 3rd.*
.... (7 to 1 op 4 to 1) 3
767⁷ MILL DE LEASE 8-12-4⁴ Bob Davies, *settled midfield, lost grnd quickly appr strt, styd on last 2 fs, fnshd 5th, plcd 4th*.................... (33 to 1 op 25 to 1) 4
SAFE ARRIVAL (USA) 5-11-5 Charles Fawcus, *nvr far away, led 7 fs out till entering strt, lost tch o'r 2 out, fnshd 6th, plcd 5th.*............... (14 to 1 op 12 to 1) 5
1456³ TAUNTING (Ire) 5-12-0 Steven Coatup, *led 5 fs, rcd alone far side in strt, fdd und pres 2 out, fnshd 7th, plcd 6th.*
.... (7 to 1 tchd 8 to 1) 6
1329⁸ COME ON CHARLIE 4-11-10 Phil Tuck, *tucked away, feeling pace and pushed alng appr strt, lost tch o'r 2 fs out.*
.... (16 to 1) 8
LEOLENE POKEY 4-11-10 Ron Barry, *chsd ldrs, bustled alng hfwy, btn entering strt*....... (33 to 1 op 25 to 1) 9
1406 GRAND RAPIDS (USA) 6-11-10 Sue Wilton, *chsd ldrs to strt, sn lost tch*.................... (10 to 1) 10
NELTEGRITY 4-12-4⁴ Michael Scudamore, *sddl slpd sn aftr strt, pld up after 3 fs.*............. (8 to 1 op 7 to 1) pu
⁻ist: 6l, 5l, 7l, 8l, 1½l, 1l, 8l, 1½l, nk. 3m 3.00s. (11 Ran).
(B J Llewellyn), B J Llewellyn

TAUNTON (good to soft)
Thursday December 9th
ioing Correction: PLUS 0.78 sec. per fur. (races 1,3,-4,6,7), PLUS 1.02 (2,5)

1640
Chard Selling Hurdle (3 & 4-y-o) £1,784 2m 1f.................. **(12:40)**

1323² SAAHI (USA) 4-11-5 J Osborne, *al prmnt, lft in ld 2 out, rdn clr*.............. (100 to 30 op 3 to 1 tchd 9 to 2) 1
1049⁴ NANQUIDNO 3-10-0 B Clifford, *al prmnt, lft cl second 2 out, outpcd*.................... (12 to 1 op 5 to 1) 2
WHATEVER'S RIGHT (Ire) 4-11-5 B Powell, *hld up in rear, hdwy 5th, kpt on one pace frm 2 out.*
.... (12 to 1 op 6 to 1) 3
1253⁵ SHARE A MOMENT (Can) 3-10-2 (3*) S Wynne, *mid-div, hdwy 5th, rdn and ev ch appr 2 out, kpt on one pace.*
.... (12 to 1 op 7 to 1) 4
1410⁴ IS SHE QUICK 3-10-0 P Holley, *al prmnt, rdn whn hit 2 out, no extr*..................... (8 to 1) 5
1353² PRIVATE JET (Ire) (bl) 4-11-5 M Richards, *al prmnt, led and mstk 5th, hdd and wknd appr 2 out.*
.... (11 to 4 fav op 4 to 1 tchd 5 to 2) 6
1517⁵ IRISH DOMINION 3-9-12 (7*) Guy Lewis, *beh, effrt 5th, wknd 3 out*................... (33 to 1 op 25 to 1) 7
1410 VENTURE PRINTS 3-10-5 R Bellamy, *al beh, lost tch 6th.*
.... (25 to 1 op 16 to 1) 8
JOGORAN 3-10-5 M A FitzGerald, *al beh, tld off frm 5th.*
.... (33 to 1 op 16 to 1) 9
1188⁷ FEELING FOOLISH (Ire) (bl) 4-11-5 I Shoemark, *al beh, tld off frm 5th.*.................... (9 to 1 op 16 to 1) 10
NYMPH ERRANT 3-9-7 (7*) Mr M Moore, *f second.*(33 to 1) f
1410³ SYLVAN STARLIGHT 3-9-11 (3*) R Farrant, *hld up in rear, steady hdwy frm 5th, took ld and gng wl whn f 2 out.*
.... (9 to 2 op 5 to 1 tchd 11 to 2) f
1410 NITA'S CHOICE 3-10-1⁸ (7*) R Darke, *jmpd badly lft 1st, refused and uns rdr second*.......... (66 to 1 op 33 to 1) ur
1297 ADMIRED 3-9-10¹ (5*) D Matthews, *made most to 5th, mstk nxt, sn beh, tld off whn pld up bef 2 out.*
.... (50 to 1 op 20 to 1) pu
st: 10l, 2l, nk, 2l, 1½l, 7l, 8l, 20l, 12l. 4m 12.80s. a 25.80s (14 Ran).
(Martin N Peters), C Weedon

1641
Dunster Handicap Chase (0-125 5-y-o and up) £2,775 2m 3f.......... **(1:10)**

1394 SMARTIE EXPRESS [119] 11-12-0 M A FitzGerald, *hld up, gd hdwy 9th, second whn lft clr 3 out, unchlgd.*
.... (9 to 1 op 7 to 1) 1
1419* FRENCH CHARMER [102] 8-10-8 (3*) P Hide, *wtd wth, hdwy to dispute second 9th till aftr 4 out, lft second nxt*.................... (5 to 4 fav tchd 11 to 8) 2
1489⁵ MONTALINO [105] 10-11-0 A Tory, *trkd ldrs, wkng whn mstk 11th, lft poor 3rd 3 out*........ (12 to 1 op 10 to 1) 3
J J JIMMY [99] 9-10-8 G Upton, *al beh, tld off frm 8th.*
.... (14 to 1 op 12 to 1) 4
1489 CASINO MAGIC [92] 9-10-1 W Marston, *in tch to 9th, sn beh, tld off.*.................... (25 to 1 op 20 to 1) 5
1191 SHANNON GLEN [104] (bl) 7-10-13 J Osborne, *led to 1st, led 6th till f 3 out*.................. (9 to 1 op 7 to 1) f

PASTORAL PRIDE (USA) [108] 9-11-3 R Dunwoody, *led 1st to 6th, wknd quickly appr 9th, tld off whn pld up bef 11th*..................... (7 to 2 tchd 4 to 1) pu
1364⁷ ANTI MATTER [115] 8-11-10 Richard Guest, *mstks in rear, tld off 8th, pld up bef 11th*.......(14 to 1 op 10 to 1) pu
Dist: 15l, 25l, dist, 7l. 4m 59.90s. a 25.90s (8 Ran).
SR: 35/3/-/-/-/ (S J Norman), R J Hodges

1642
Mendip Plywood Novices' Hurdle (Div I) (4-y-o and up) £2,064 2m 1f... (1:40)

1192* MATHAL (USA) 4-11-3 (5*) D Matthews, *made all, clr whn hit last, unchlgd*........ (11 to 4 op 2 to 1 tchd 3 to 1) 1
1192⁵ ROUTING 5-10-5 (7*) Guy Lewis, *hld up, steady hdwy frm 5th, wnt second appr 2 out, no ch wth wnr.*
.... (25 to 1 op 14 to 1) 2
1390² ARFEY (Ire) 4-10-12 S Smith Eccles, *chsd wnr till wknd aftr 3 out, mstk nxt, rallied r-in.*
.... (7 to 4 fav op 5 to 1 tchd 9 to 4) 3
THE MILLWRIGHT 6-10-12 M Perrett, *hld up in rear, styd on frm 3 out, nvr dngrs*...........(14 to 1 op 10 to 1) 4
934⁸ GROG (Ire) 4-10-12 G Upton, *rcd keenly, mstk 4th, in tch till outpcd frm 3 out*... (9 to 1 op 8 to 1 tchd 10 to 1) 5
983 BRIMPTON BERTIE 4-10-12 B Powell, *beh, some hdwy frm 6th, nvr dngrs*.................... (14 to 1 op 20 to 1) 6
1456⁸ VALIANTHE (USA) 5-10-12 R Dunwoody, *in tch to 5th, rdn and sn beh*................ (9 to 1 op 5 to 1 tchd 10 to 1) 7
773 DAVES DELIGHT 7-10-0 (7*) Mr G Shenkin, *al beh, tld off.*
.... (40 to 1 op 20 to 1 tchd 50 to 1) 8
983⁶ SHIRLEY'S TRAIN (USA) 4-10-12 M Hourigan, *pld hrd, prmnt to 5th, sn beh, tld off.*
.... (6 to 1 op 5 to 1 tchd 7 to 1) 9
BANDMASTER (USA) 4-10-12 M Richards, *chsd ldrs till wknd 5th, tld off*....(14 to 1 op 12 to 1 tchd 16 to 1) 10
TRUSTINO 5-10-7 W Marston, *prmnt till wknd 5th, tld off*.................... (50 to 1 op 25 to 1) 11
VERRO (USA) 6-10-12 R Greene, *prmnt till wknd 3rd, tld off whn pld up bef 3 out*.......... (50 to 1 op 33 to 1) pu
1442 EXECUTION ONLY (Ire) 5-10-12 Richard Guest, *al beh, tld up bef four out.*.......... (50 to 1 op 20 to 1) pu
1301 TRADESPARK 5-10-7 D Gallagher, *al beh, tld off 4th, pld up bef four out*........ (100 to 1 op 50 to 1) pu
Dist: 12l, ¾l, 4l, 4l, 5l, 2½l, 3l, 20l, ¾l, dist. 4m 5.30s. a 28.30s (14 Ran).
SR: 40/22/21/17/13/8/5/-/-/ (Alan G Craddock), N M Babbage

1643
Gay Sheppard Memorial Challenge Trophy Handicap Hurdle (0-125 4-y-o and up) £3,631 3m 110yds...... (2:10)

1396⁸ DUNCAN IDAHO [102] 10-11-1 W McFarland, *hld up in rear, hdwy appr 4 out, led bef 2 out, drvn out.*
.... (11 to 2 op 5 to 1 tchd 6 to 1) 1
1342 SMILING CHIEF (Ire) [89] 5-10-2 R Dunwoody, *hld up, hdwy 8th, lft in ld 3 out, hdd bef nxt, rallied to press wnr r-in.*
.... (12 to 1 tchd 14 to 1) 2
1474³ MR FLUTTS [98] 7-10-11 S McNeill, *hld up, rdn and hdwy 3 out, styd on und pres r-in.*... (4 to 1 fav op 9 to 2) 3
1458⁸ WINABUCK [94] 10-10-4 (3*) D Meredith, *hld up in rear, mstk 3rd, hdwy 4 out, hrd rdn and ran on, r-in.*
.... (12 to 1 op 11 to 1 tchd 14 to 1) 4
1349⁶ TROJAN ENVOY [87] 5-10-0 Mr W Henderson, *pld hrd, prmnt till lost pl 5th, rdn 4 out, styd on wl frm 2 out.*
.... (66 to 1 op 33 to 1 tchd 100 to 1) 5
1299⁵ GROTIUS [87] (bl) 9-10-0 R Bellamy, *prmnt whn hit 5th, in tch till wknd aftr 4 out.*
.... (20 to 1 op 16 to 1 tchd 25 to 1) 6
1274 SPECIAL ACCOUNT [105] 7-11-4 N Mann, *mid-div, lost tch 4 out, tld off*.............. (5 to 1 tchd 6 to 1) 7
SWEET GEORGE [88] 6-10-1 M A FitzGerald, *chsd ldrs till wknd rpdly appr 2 out, virtually pld up r-in, tld off.*
.... (14 to 1 op 11 to 1) 8
1322⁶ FORTUNES WOOD [114] 7-11-6 (7*) D Meade, *prmnt, hit 7th, led appr 4 out, blun badly and lost all ch nxt, tld off*.................... (7 to 1 op 6 to 1) 9
1273³ POP SONG [87] 9-10-0 P Holley, *led till hdd appr 4 out, wknd rpdly, pld up bef 2 out.*
.... (20 to 1 op 16 to 1 tchd 25 to 1) pu
1349⁷ FAR TOO LOUD [106] 6-11-5 B Clifford, *prmnt till wknd quickly 3 out, pld up bef nxt*.......(7 to 1 op 6 to 1) pu
Dist: ¾l, 1½l, hd, ½l, 10l, 20l, 15l, ¾l. 6m 7.90s. a 33.40s (11 Ran).
(R Callow), R Callow

1644
Stoke St Mary Novices' Handicap Chase (5-y-o and up) £2,879 3m (2:40)

1164⁵ STAUNCH RIVAL (USA) [85] 6-10-13 J Frost, *hld up, steady hdwy 13th, led last, drvn clr.*
.... (12 to 1 op 10 to 1 tchd 14 to 1) 1
1214³ ROAD TO FAME [85] 9-10-13 P Holley, *al prmnt, led 7th to 8th, led ag'n 9th, mstk 2 out, hdd last, no extr.*
.... (12 to 1 op 10 to 1) 2
1411⁴ FROZEN DROP [92] 6-10-13 (7*) S Fox, *in tch till lost pl tenth, making hdwy whn hit 5 out, plugged on one pace.*................... (14 to 1 op 10 to 1) 3
1511⁵ RINANNA BAY [76] 6-9-11 (7*) P Carey, *beh till hdwy tenth, wknd 5 out.*......... (16 to 1 op 14 to 1 tchd 20 to 1) 4

ALL FOR LUCK [92] 8-11-6 R Dunwoody, *prmnt, led 6th to 7th and 8th to 9th, disputing ld whn hit 3 out, rdn and sn btn*...........(100 to 30 fav op 5 to 1 tchd 3 to 1)   5

1411³ HAND OUT [83] 9-10-11 B Powell, *al in rear.*
.....................(10 to 1 op 8 to 1 tchd 12 to 1)   6

1420⁵ PUNCHBAG (USA) [85] 7-10-13 M Hourigan, *led second to 6th, wknd 12th, tld off*...........(20 to 1 op 14 to 1)   7

1457³ RUBINS BOY [81] 7-10-9 M Richards, *in rear whn f 8th.*
....(7 to 1)   f

1411 BUMPTIOUS BOY [80] (v) 9-10-8 D Bridgwater, *jmpd badly in rear, pld up bef 11th.* (15 to 2 op 8 to 1 tchd 7 to 1) pu

1393⁴ LEGAL BEAGLE [90] (bl) 6-11-4 M Perrett, *prmnt, led to second, wkng whn blun badly 14th, not reco'r, pld up bef 4 out*.............(10 to 1 op 12 to 1 tchd 14 to 1) pu

1511⁹ TRAIN ROBBER [74] 8-10-2 W Irvine, *beh whn hit 14th, tld off when blun 2 out, pld up bef last.*
.................................(25 to 1 op 16 to 1) pu

867 MICKEEN [93] 6-11-7 M A FitzGerald, *prmnt till wknd 9th, tld off whn pld up bef 13th.*
.....................(20 to 1 op 12 to 1 tchd 25 to 1) pu

1393³ TAREESH [86] 6-11-0 S McNeill, *not jump wl, in tch till wknd quickly 11th, tld off whn pld up bef 14th.*
..............................(9 to 1 op 8 to 1) pu

Dist: 10l, 25l, 4l, 2l, 10l, 20l. 6m 17.30s. a 30.30s (13 Ran).

SR: 27/17/-/-/-/   (C Humphry), G Thorner

1645 Bicknoller Novices' Handicap Hurdle (0-100 4-y-o and up) £1,742 3m 110yds
....(3:10)

1299* GORT [92] 5-11-11 J Leech, *hld up in tch, dsptd ld 7th, pushed alng frm nxt, wl in touch whn hit 2 out, rdn to lead r-in*......................(8 to 1 op 6 to 1)   1

1525 ALICE SMITH [68] 6-10-1 W McFarland, *led to second, led 6th till rdn and hdd r-in*..........(33 to 1 op 20 to 1)   2

1414⁵ IT'S DELICIOUS [77] 7-10-10 D Bridgwater, *hld up, hdwy 8th, outpcd appr 2 out*...........(20 to 1 op 16 to 1)   3

1458⁶ APARECIDA (Fr) [76] 7-10-1 (7*) N Isaac, *hld up, hdwy appr one pace frm 3 out*............(3 to 1 fav op 7 to 2)   4
LANSDOWNE [78] 5-10-11 B Powell, *trkd ldrs till rdn and wknd 3 out*...........(12 to 1 op 10 to 1 tchd 9 to 1)   5

354³ PLAYPEN [88] 9-11-7 J Frost, *sn prmnt, wknd 4 out.*
.................................(25 to 1 op 20 to 1)   6

1456⁶ BORRETO [74] 9-10-1¹ (7*) Mr E James, *prmnt, rdn 5th, beh frm 7th*.................(16 to 1 op 14 to 1)   7
APSIMORE [81] 6-11-0 S McNeill, *hld up, hdwy appr 5th, wknd 4 out*................(9 to 1 op 7 to 1 tchd 10 to 1)   8

1406⁴ MARINERS COVE [71] 5-10-4 W Humphreys, *al beh, tld off.*
.................(16 to 1 op 14 to 1 tchd 20 to 1)   9

814* OSMOSIS [84] 7-11-3 D Gallagher, *al beh, mstk 4th, brief effrt appr four out, eased aftr nxt, tld off.*
.............................(9 to 2 op 7 to 2) 10

1252⁷ OH SO WINDY [74] 6-10-7 R Dunwoody, *hld up, effrt 7th, drpd out quickly 4 out, tld off.*
................(14 to 1 op 12 to 1 tchd 16 to 1) 11

1313⁵ WOODLANDS BOY (Ire) [81] 5-10-11 (3*) A Thornton, *prmnt to 5th, rdn 7th, tld off.*
.................(10 to 1 op 12 to 1 tchd 14 to 1) 12

1456² OK RECORDS [86] 6-11-5 N Mann, *al beh, tld off whn pld up bef 4 out*...............(12 to 1 op 10 to 1) pu

1046⁵ RIVER STREAM [76] 6-10-9 M A FitzGerald, *led second to 6th, wknd rpdly nxt, tld off whn pld up bef 4 out.*
.................................(50 to 1 op 33 to 1) pu

Dist: 2½l, 12l, 1½l, 12l, ¾l, 6l, 5l, 15l, 10l, 10l. 6m 7.20s. a 32.70s (14 Ran).

    (F D Allison), Miss K S Allison

1646 Mendip Plywood Novices' Hurdle (Div II) (4-y-o and up) £2,064 2m 1f..(3:40)

FRIENDLY FELLOW 4-10-12 P Holley, *hld up, hdwy appr 4 out, lft second and plenty to do 2 out, rdn to ld sn aftr last*............................(5 to 2 jt-fav op 3 to 1)   1
WILKINS 4-10-12 M A FitzGerald, *led to second, led 5th, mstk last, sn hdd and outpcd.*
....................(4 to 1 op 5 to 2 tchd 9 to 2)   2

1460⁹ COURAGEOUS KNIGHT 4-10-5 (7*) Guy Lewis, *chsd ldrs, lft beh appr 2 out*.................(20 to 1 op 14 to 1)   3

1390³ SHAARID (USA) 5-10-12 B Powell, *pld hrd, al prmnt, wknd on bend aftr 3 out*....................(5 to 2 jt-fav tchd 3 to 1 and 9 to 4)   4

ACHIEVED AMBITION (Ire) 5-10-12 N Mann, *hld up in rear, hdwy 4 out, nvr nr to chal.*
.................(50 to 1 op 33 to 1 tchd 66 to 1)   5

640⁵ NOEL (Ire) 4-10-12 M Hourigan, *hld up, nvr got into race.*
.................(25 to 1 op 20 to 1 tchd 33 to 1)   6

1390⁸ SO AUDACIOUS 5-10-12 R Supple, *al beh.*
.................................(50 to 1 op 33 to 1)   7

1390⁶ ROAD TO AU BON (USA) 5-10-12 L Harvey, *mid-div, effrt 5th, wknd 3 out*.........(33 to 1 op 25 to 1 tchd 14 to 1)   8

1516 CORPUS 4-10-12 R Dunwoody, *mid-div, losing tch whn mstk 6th*....................(66 to 1 op 50 to 1)   9

1460 DEVIL'S CORNER 5-10-12 M Bosley, *tld off frm 6th.*
.................................(100 to 1 op 66 to 1) 10

1414 ROXY RIVER 4-10-0 (7*) Mr M Rimell, *al frnt rnk, chalg whn blun and uns rdr 2 out.*
.................(5 to 1 op 7 to 1 tchd 8 to 1) ur

UNCERTAIN 5-10-5 (7*) L Reynolds, *led second till mstk 5th, sn btn, tld off whn pld up bef 2 out.*
.................(50 to 1 op 33 to 1 tchd 66 to 1) pu

MYSTICAL MISTRAL 6-10-7 D Gallagher, *al beh, tld off whn pld up bef 4 out*...........(100 to 1 op 66 to 1) pu

Dist: 6l, 12l, 3½l, 15l, 4l, 12l, 4l, 10l, 1l. 4m 10.80s. a 23.80s (13 Ran).

    (The Radio Three), D R C Elsworth

CHELTENHAM (good)
Friday December 10th
Going Correction: PLUS 0.60 sec. per fur. (races 1,2,- 4,7), PLUS 0.72 (3,5,6)

1647 Charlton Kings Three Yrs Old Novices' Hurdle £2,948 2m 1f.....(12:00)

1305* MYSILV 10-12 A Maguire, *made all, jmpd wl, quickened clr r-in, readily.*
.................(11 to 10 on tchd 11 to 10 and 5 to 4) 1

1510⁴ GROUND NUT (Ire) 11-0 J Osborne, *chsd wnr, effrt appr last, kpt on one pace.* (11 to 1 op 8 to 1 tchd 12 to 1) 2

1229⁷ SPRING MARATHON (USA) 11-7 P Holley, *beh, hdwy to go 3rd 3 out, rdn and no imprsn on ldrs appr nxt.*
.................(7 to 2 op 9 to 2 tchd 5 to 1) 3

1244* BAJAN AFFAIR 10-9 (3*) A Thornton, *prmnt till wknd 3 out, tld off.*..................(20 to 1 op 16 to 1) 3
ELBURG (Ire) 11-0 M Hoad, *prmnt, blun 4th, wknd 6th, tld off*.......................(16 to 1 op 14 to 1) 5

FOREVER SHINEING 10-9 M Perrett, *al beh, tld off 5th.*
.................(50 to 1 op 33 to 1) 6

320² WHO'S THE BEST (Ire) 11-0 T Jarvis, *beh till f 3rd.*
.................(25 to 1 op 20 to 1 tchd 33 to 1) f

1517* MY BALLYBOY 11-3 N Mann, *hdwy 6th, 4th whn f nxt.*
.................(12 to 1 op 10 to 1 tchd 14 to 1) f

1510⁵ DUVEEN (Ire) 11-0 C Llewellyn, *chsd ldrs to 5th, sn wknd, fifth and tld off whn f last.*
.................(9 to 1 op 7 to 1 tchd 10 to 1) f
TONY'S MIST 10-11 (3*) R Farrant, *al beh, hit 4th, brght dwn 7th*....................(50 to 1 op 20 to 1) bd

Dist: 8l, 25l, dist, 2½l, 6l. 4m 9.40s. a 14.90s (10 Ran).

SR: 37/31/13/-/-/   (Million In Mind Partnership (3)), D Nicholson

1648 Bristol Novices' Hurdle (4-y-o and up) £2,997 2½m.................(12:35)

1442³ BOOK OF MUSIC (Ire) 5-11-0 D Murphy, *hld up nr, hdwy 3 out, chlgd last, sn led, drvn out.*
.................(2 to 1 fav tchd 5 to 2) 1

1557⁴ KYTTON CASTLE 6-10-13 (3*) D Meredith, *beh, hdwy 7th, chlgd last, led briefly, kpt on, not pace of wnr.*
.................(6 to 1 tchd 8 to 1) 2

1442⁹ IVOR'S FLUTTER (bl) 4-11-0 P Holley, *beh, hdwy 3 out, hrd drvn appr last, ran on r-in*........(4 to 1 op 5 to 1) 3

1344² GOLDEN SPINNER 6-11-0 R Dunwoody, *in tch, hit 4th, led 6th to nxt, led 2 out till sn aftr last, one pace.*
.................................(7 to 5 op 5 to 2) 4

650³ GRAHAM GOOCH 7-11-0 J Frost, *hld up, hdwy 2 out, styd on same pace appr last*......(16 to 1 op 12 to 1) 5

1539 JULIOS GENIUS 6-11-4 A Maguire, *chsd ldrs, led 7th, hdd and pckd 2 out, wknd quickly appr last.*
.................................(9 to 1 op 6 to 1) 6

1161 LOYAL GAIT (NZ) 5-11-0 L Harvey, *in tch till wknd 3 out, tld off*....................(66 to 1 op 33 to 1) 7

1460 MARINERS MEMORY 5-11-0 W Humphreys, *beh 4th, tld off*.........................(100 to 1 op 33 to 1) 8
MARANO 5-11-0 M Bosley, *made most to 6th, sn wknd, tld off*......................(100 to 1 op 33 to 1) 9
MISS CRUISE 6-10-9 S Earle, *beh 5th, tld off.*
.................(25 to 1 op 20 to 1 tchd 33 to 1) 10

409* SKEOUGH (Ire) 5-11-7 R Bellamy, *wth ldr to 4th, wknd 8th, tld off*................(14 to 1 op 10 to 1) 11

Dist: 1l, 1l, 1½l, 2l, 25l, dist, 1l, 6l, 10l, 3l. 5m 10.30s. (11 Ran).

    (Mrs D Lousada), J T Gifford

1649 Kineton Conditional Jockeys' Handicap Chase (0-140 5-y-o and up) £3,98? 2m 110yds.....................(1:10)

1275* MULBANK [115] 7-11-2 M Hourigan, *made most to 6th, styd wth ldr, led 9th, hdd briefly 3 out, ran on wl whn chlgd frm 2 out*.................(11 to 10 on tchd 5 to 4) 1

1105* DR ROCKET [113] 8-11-0 D Meredith, *wnd 3rd 8th, hdwy 3 out, chlgd nxt, rdn and str chal appr last, outpcd r-in.*
.................................(5 to 2 op 9 to 4) 2

1165⁴ PATS MINSTREL [110] (bl) 8-10-11 A Thornton, *wth wnr, led 6th to 9th, chlgd nxt, led briefly 3 out, btn next.*
.................(4 to 1 op 7 to 2 tchd 9 to 2) 3

1470² WHATEVER YOU LIKE [127] 9-11-9 (5*) D Hobbs, *drpd rear 8th, no dngr aftr*............(9 to 1 op 6 to 1) 4

Dist: 3l, 15l, 10l. 4m 17.30s. a 21.30s (4 Ran).

    (I L Shaw), P J Hobb?

1650 Annie At Everyman Handicap Hurdle (0-135 4-y-o and up) £4,890 2m 1f (1:45)

1342* SAND-DOLLAR [110] 10-10-10 S McNeill, *hld up, hdwy 3 out, chlgd last, sn led, drvn out...* (13 to 2 op 11 to 2) 1

1465* NAHAR [130] 8-11-11 (5*,6ex) A Dicken, *wth ldr, led aftr second, hdd last, rallied, not pace of wnr.* ....(7 to 1 op 6 to 1) 2

1395* MONDAY CLUB [113] 9-10-6 (7*) D Meade, *hld up, hdwy 6th, led last, sn hdd, rdn and wknd.* ....(5 to 1 op 4 to 1 tchd 6 to 1) 3

1513⁴ STATAJACK (Ire) [116] (bl) 5-11-2 P Holley, *led till aftr second, prmnt, rdn frm 2 out, one pace.* ....(15 to 2 op 6 to 1 tchd 8 to 1) 4

1296² ALBERTITO (Fr) [111] 6-10-11 A Maguire, *lost tch 3 out, hrd drvn nxt, styd on r-in.* ....(3 to 1 jt-fav op 11 to 4 tchd 100 to 30) 5

1513³ PROPAGANDA [112] 5-10-12 M A FitzGerald, *chsd ldrs till outpcd 3 out.*..................(3 to 1 jt-fav op 5 to 2) 6

1422 KING'S SHILLING (USA) [115] 6-11-1 Jacqui Oliver, *hdwy to track ldrs 5th, wknd aftr 2 out.* ....(14 to 1 op 12 to 1 tchd 16 to 1) 7

Dist: 1½l, 5l, 3½l, ¾l, 1l, 20l. 4m 12.10s. a 17.60s (7 Ran).
SR: 8/26/4/3/ (R P Fry), J A B Old

1651 Allied Dunbar Novices' Chase (5-y-o and up) £4,833 3m 1f 110yds.... (2:20)

1170* SEE MORE INDIANS 6-11-6 G Bradley, *led second to 3rd, led 4th to 7th, led 11th to 13th, led 16th, shaken up r-in, cmftbly.* (5 to 2 op 11 to 4 on tchd 3 to 1 on and 9 to 4 on) 1

1346⁶ EARTH SUMMIT (bl) 5-11-6 C Llewellyn, *chlgd 5th, led 7th to 11th, led 13th to 16th, pressed wnr till outpcd r-in.* ....(4 to 1 op 5 to 2) 2

1467 WILD FORTUNE 10-10-12 M A FitzGerald, *wnt 3rd 11th, no dngr aftr.*....................(20 to 1 op 33 to 1) 3

1420 GABRIELLA MIA 8-10-7 T Jarvis, *blun 4th, beh 7th.* ....(10 to 1 tchd 11 to 1) 4

1467 SPARTAN FLAPJACK 7-11-0² Miss L Blackford, *led to second, led 3rd to 4th, sn beh, hit 9th, tenth and 12th, tld off 14th.*.......................................(66 to 1) 5

Dist: 2½l, dist, dist, dist. 6m 44.40s. a 28.40s (5 Ran).
(Paul K Barber), P F Nicholls

1652 Food Brokers Fisherman's Friend Chase Handicap (5-y-o and up) £10,357 3m 1f 110yds.......... (2:55)

1398* FLASHING STEEL [147] 8-11-2 R Dunwoody, *in tch, chsd ldr 13th, led 17th to 4 out, led 2 out, ran on wl.* (4 to 1 jt-fav op 9 to 2 tchd 7 to 2) 1

1365 USHERS ISLAND [131] 7-10-0 N Williamson, *in tch, mstk same pace.*....................(5 to 1 op 4 to 1) 2

1011³ TOPSHAM BAY [155] 10-11-10 J Frost, *chsd ldrs, drvn and styd on same pace frm 3 out.* ....(16 to 1 op 12 to 1 tchd 20 to 1) 3

1447* LIGHT VENEER [132] 8-10-11 M A FitzGerald, *beh, outpcd and rdn alng 15th, styd on same pace und pres frm 3 out.*.................(4 to 1 jt-fav tchd 9 to 2 and 7 to 2) 4

1447⁴ SUPERIOR FINISH [134] 7-10-3 J Osborne, *chsd ldr to 13th, mstk nxt, wknd 4 out.* ....(9 to 2 op 4 to 1 tchd 5 to 1) 5

1365* INDIAN TONIC [131] 7-10-0 C Maude, *led to 17th, sn wknd.* ....(8 to 1 op 7 to 1 tchd 9 to 1) 6

1436⁷ FLASHTHECASH [136] 7-10-5 D Murphy, *al beh, shaken up 4 out, no response.*........(11 to 1 op 14 to 1) 7

1467 DUNTREE [132] 8-10-1 A Maguire, *hit 4th, lost tch nxt, rallied 11th, wknd 15th.*................(9 to 1 op 6 to 1) 8

Dist: 5l, 3l, ½l, 15l, 10l, 8l, 8l. 6m 35.60s. a 19.60s (8 Ran).
SR: 76/55/76/52/39/26/23/11/ (C J Haughey), J E Mulhern

1653 ASW Bill Love Memorial Gold Card Hurdle Handicap (4-y-o and up) £5,186 3m 110yds.................... (3:30)

1227² NEWTON POINT [115] 4-10-6 (5*) T Jenks, *led to 3rd, led 5th till appr last, rallied gmely und pres to ld cl hme.* ....(11 to 1 op 10 to 1 tchd 12 to 1) 1

1227* SILLARS STALKER (Ire) [128] 5-11-10 W Marston, *hld up, hdwy frm 3 out, led appr last, rdn r-in, not quicken and ct cl hme.*......... (11 to 2 op 4 to 1 tchd 7 to 2) 2

1445⁶ CORACO [107] 6-10-3 D Bridgwater, *in tch, chlgd 3 out, rdn nxt, outpcd appr last.*..........(12 to 1 op 8 to 1) 3

1322⁴ CONTORUS [118] 7-11-0 R Dunwoody, *hdwy to track ldrs 7th, rdn 2 out, sn outpcd.* ....(9 to 2 op 5 to 1 tchd 8 to 1) 4

845⁴ ELEGANT KING (Ire) [104] 4-10-0 T Jarvis, *chsd ldrs till outpcd 3 out, styd on appr last.*....(33 to 1 op 25 to 1) 5

FLYER'S NAP [105] 7-10-1 S Earle, *chsd ldrs, chlgd 3 out, wknd aftr nxt.*....................(10 to 1 op 16 to 1) 6

1198² HARMER PRIORY [112] 10-10-8 G Rowe, *chsd ldrs, rdn 3 out, sn wknd.* 7

1465⁸ LYPHENTO (USA) [127] 9-11-6 (3*) P Hide, *wth wnr, led 3rd to 5th, wknd appr 2 out.*......(50 to 1 op 33 to 1) 8

895* AAHSAYLAD [128] 7-11-10 A Maguire, *beh, jmpd slwly 8th, sn rdn and no response.* ....(11 to 4 fav op 5 to 2 tchd 7 to 2) 9

METAL OISEAU (Ire) [120] (bl) 5-11-2 A Charlton, *al beh, lost tch 8th.*.......................(16 to 1 tchd 20 to 1) 10

1561* DARK HONEY [120] 8-10-11 (5*,8ex) A Dicken, *mid-div, hdwy 7th, 4th and gng wl whn f 2 out.* f

TAXI LAD [104] 9-10-0 W Humphreys, *al beh, tld off 7th, pld up aftr 3 out.*.............(200 to 1 op 100 to 1) pu

Dist: 1l, 15l, 2l, 3½l, 6l, 30l, 3l, ½l, 8l. 5m 59.20s. a 19.20s (12 Ran).
SR: 38/50/14/23/5/-/ (PPS Racing Partnership), T R George

DONCASTER (Good)
Friday December 10th
Going Correction: PLUS 0.50 sec. per fur. (races 1,2,-5,7), PLUS 0.35 (3,4,6)

1654 Saucy Kit Novices' Hurdle (4-y-o and up) £2,129 2½m............... (12:15)

1320* POWLEYVALE 6-11-5 L Wyer, *in tch, led 6th, drw clr 3 out, easily.*....................(13 to 8 fav op 7 to 4) 1

1129* ANOTHER NICK 7-10-13 (5*) P Williams, *mid-div, hdwy 7th, chsd wnr frm 2 out, no imprsn.* ....(5 to 1 op 9 to 2 tchd 11 to 2) 2

1239⁶ TITIAN GIRL (bl) 4-10-7 P Niven, *prmnt, outpcd and lost pl hfwy, styd on frm 3 out.*....................(16 to 1) 3

1096³ TREVVEETHAN (Ire) 4-10-12 D Wilkinson, *chsd ldrs, ev ch appr 3 out, kpt on same pace.*......(10 to 1 op 8 to 1) 4

1392⁸ MASTER BAVARD (Ire) (bl) 5-10-12 V Slattery, *in tch, chsd ldrs frm 6th, one pace appr 3 out.* (20 to 1 op 16 to 1) 5

1000⁷ MUST BE MAGICAL (USA) 5-10-12 R Supple, *beh, hdwy whn mstk 2 out, nvr dngrs.* ....(14 to 1 op 10 to 1 tchd 16 to 1) 6

RAKES OF MALLOW 6-10-7 (5*) T Eley, *nvr on terms.* ....(50 to 1) 7

AURORA LAD 6-10-12 Richard Guest, *hld up, hdwy aftr 5th, wknd appr 3 out.*.....(16 to 1 tchd 20 to 1) 8

1167⁷ ANDRAITH (Ire) 5-10-5 (7*) Mr G Hogan, *in tch, chsd ldrs aftr 6th till wknd appr 3 out.*................(33 to 1) 9

1567⁷ OTTOMAN EMPIRE 6-11-4 M Brennan, *hld up, hmpd 6th, chsd wnr appr 3 out, wknd aftr nxt, 5th and btn whn blun last, virtually pld up.* ....(11 to 4 op 9 to 4 tchd 3 to 1) 10

1251³ GRIFFINS BAR 5-10-12 A Carroll, *led to 6th, wknd quickly aftr nxt, beh whn pld up bef 3 out.* ....(9 to 1 op 7 to 1 tchd 10 to 1) pu

Dist: 6l, 2½l, 6l, 8l, 2½l, 12l, 1½l, 3l, 15l. 5m 1.90s. (M G St Quinton), B S Rothwell

1655 Glasgow Paddocks Selling Hurdle (3 & 4-y-o) £1,841 2m 110yds..... (12:45)

1529³ AL FORUM (Ire) 3-11-0 D O'Sullivan, *in tch gng wl, led 2 out, pushed clr aftr last.* ....(5 to 2 fav tchd 11 to 2) 1

1284⁶ SUMMERS DREAM 3-10-3 C Hawkins, *in tch, hdwy appr 3 out, chlgd on bit nxt, rdn aftr last, no imprsn.*.......................................(6 to 1) 2

1193⁹ SKIMMER HAWK 4-11-8 V Smith, *chsd clr ldr, led appr 3 out, hdd nxt, no extr approaching last.* ....(14 to 1 op 12 to 1) 3

1476⁵ MR ABBOT 3-10-8 P Niven, *beh, hdwy appr 3 out, ev ch betw last 2, sn rdn and no extr.* ....(9 to 2 op 7 to 2 tchd 5 to 1) 4

MARY MACBLAIN 4-11-3 B Dalton, *in tch, hdwy appr 3 out, rdn and wknd approaching last.* ....(16 to 1 op 14 to 1) 5

SPRAY OF ORCHIDS 4-11-3 P Harley, *beh, styd on frm 3 out, nvr trble ldrs.*................(16 to 1 op 14 to 1) 6

1472* PORT IN A STORM 4-11-7 (7*) E Husband, *hld up, hdwy aftr 5th, rdn appr 3 out, sn btn...*(5 to 2 fav op 9 to 4) 7

1374⁸ MILTON ROOMS (Ire) 4-11-1 (7*) K Davies, *mid-div till wknd 3 out.*........................(12 to 1 tchd 14 to 1) 8

971 RYTHMIC RYMER 3-10-3 M Dwyer, *chsd ldrs, wknd aftr 5th.*.......................................(33 to 1) 9

1097 BIG GEM 3-10-8 W Worthington, *led, clr second, hdd appr 3 out, wknd quickly.*........................(33 to 1) 10

1476⁸ RAVENSPUR (Ire) 3-10-8 N Smith, *mid-div till wknd approaching 3 out.*.......(16 to 1 op 14 to 1) 11

THATCHED (Ire) 3-10-8⁵ (5*) P Midgley, *in tch, ch appr 3 out, sn wknd.*......................(25 to 1) 12

1404³ MISSED THE BOAT (Ire) 3-10-8 H Davies, *sn beh.* ....(5 to 1 op 4 to 1) 13

1483 MARIBELLA 3-10-3 A Dobbin, *in tch, no hdwy whn f 3 out.*...................................(50 to 1 op 33 to 1) f

1532 EVE'S TREASURE 3-9-13¹ (5*) S Lyons, *mid-div, wkng whn hmpd 3 out, pld up.*.........(33 to 1 op 25 to 1) pu

Dist: 5l, 8l, 1l, 10l, 8l, 1½l, ½l, 2½l, 3l, nk. 4m 8.80s. a 18.30s (15 Ran).
(Martin Hickey), R Ingram

1656 Vulrory's Clown Handicap Chase (0-130 5-y-o and up) £3,947 2m 3f 110yds........................ (1:20)

GNOME'S TYCOON [115] 7-11-10 J Railton, *trkd ldrs, led 4 out, sn wl clr, very easily.*.........(7 to 2 op 11 to 4) 1

1242 DRAGONS DEN [107] (bl) 7-11-2 G Upton, trkd ldr, led aftr 8th, jmpd slwly and hdd 4 out, sn outpcd.
...... (11 to 8 fav op 5 to 4 tchd 6 to 5 and 6 to 4) 2
946[2] VULRORY'S CLOWN [91] 15-10-0 M Brennan, led till hdd aftr 8th, outpcd frm 4 out............ (12 to 1 op 10 to 1) 3
1503[6] WIGTOWN BAY [91] 10-10-0 R Supple, al beh, lost tch frm 8th...................................(7 to 1 op 8 to 1) 4
1132[6] PIMS GUNNER (Ire) [99] 5-10-8 C Grant, not jump wl, sn pushed alng and beh, lost tch frm 8th.
....(7 to 2 op 3 to 1) 5
Dist: 15l, 10l, 12l, 15l. 4m 57.30s. a 11.30s (5 Ran).
SR: 50/27/1/-/-/ (Irvin S Naylor), R T Phillips

1657 Norec Novices' Chase (5-y-o and up) £3,002 3m.....................(1:55)

1184[3] VELEDA II (Fr) 6-10-12 (5") J Burke, cl up, led aftr 4 out, clr and rdn appr 2 out, all out.........(5 to 1 tchd 7 to 2) 1
996[4] THE LIGHTER SIDE 7-10-5 (7") Judy Davies, in tch, chsd wnr frm 2 out, kpt on from last..... (14 to 1 op 12 to 1) 2
WESTWELL BOY 7-10-12 C Hawkins, cl up till outpcd appr 4 out, styd on ag'n approaching last.
.... (20 to 1 op 14 to 1) 3
1477 I'M TOBY 6-10-12 M Dwyer, chsd ldrs, till outpcd aftr 11th...(4 to 1 tchd 9 to 2) 4
1441* SPIRIT OF KIBRIS 8-11-3 I Lawrence, made most till hdd aftr 4 out, wknd quickly appr 2 out. (11 to 4 op 9 to 4) 5
1405 DUHALLOW LODGE 6-10-12 Richard Guest, in tch till outpcd aftr 8th, jmpd slwly and pld up after tenth.
....(7 to 4 fav op 2 to 1) pu
SOPHINI 5-10-5 D Byrne, jmpd very slwly and sn tld off, pld up aftr 4th..................................(50 to 1) pu
Dist: 2½l, hd, 15l, nk. 6m 21.20s. a 27.20s (7 Ran).
(L H Froomes), Mrs S A Bramall

1658 Doorknocker Novices' Handicap Hurdle (3-y-o and up) £2,110 2m 110yds
....(2:30)

890[2] ALLEGATION [85] (v) 3-11-5 M Foster, chsd ldr, led aftr 5th, clr whn jmpd lft and blun 2 out, jumped left last, styd on...................................... (5 to 1 op 7 to 2) 1
1535[7] BARAHIN (Ire) [74] 4-10-8 D O'Sullivan, in tch, hdwy aftr 5th, chsd wnr frm 2 out, kpt on, no imprsn.
....(13 to 2 op 14 to 1 tchd 6 to 1) 2
1406[8] CARAGH BRIDGE [66] 6-10-0 R Supple, beh, hdwy aftr 5th, kpt on frm 3 out, nrst finish...(16 to 1 op 12 to 1) 3
1535[2] ARTIC WINGS (Ire) [77] 5-10-11 M Brennan, hld up, hdwy aftr 5th, chsd wnr 3 out till wknd nxt.
....(9 to 4 op 4 to 1) 4
1097[5] MONASTIC FLIGHT (Ire) [66] 3-9-7 (7") G Cahill, in tch, effrt aftr 5th, kpt on same pace frm 3 out.
....(20 to 1 op 14 to 1) 5
1448* GOTTA BE JOKING [90] 5-11-10 P Niven, chsd ldrs till wknd aftr 5th................. (5 to 4 fav op 11 to 10) 6
1303 CROOKED DEALER (NZ) [73] (bl) 6-10-7 G Upton, led till 5th, wknd appr 3 out......... (16 to 1 op 12 to 1) 7
1356[4] WELLSY LAD (USA) [72] 6-10-6 R Garritty, chsd ldrs till wknd appr 3 out................. (16 to 1 op 12 to 1) 8
1425[5] MATUSADONA [66] 6-10-0 B Dalton, chsd ldrs till wknd appr 3 out.................................(25 to 1) 9
LEARNED STAR [67] 8-10-1 A Mulholland, in tch, reminders hfwy, sn beh, pld up bef 2 out...... (33 to 1) pu
1406 COOL PARADE (USA) [66] (bl) 5-9-7 (7") W Fry, sn beh, tld off whn pld up bef 3 out.
.... (40 to 1 op 33 to 1 tchd 50 to 1) pu
STRATHBOGIE MIST (Ire) [66] 5-10-0 N Smith, beh, hfwy, pld up bef 2 out.........................(33 to 1 op 25 to 1) pu
Dist: 4l, 5l, 1½l, 5l, 20l, 2½l, 1l, 10l. 4m 4.50s. a 14.00s (12 Ran).
SR: 34/19/6/15/-/3/ (Southern Depots), M C Pipe

1659 Lottery Conditional Jockeys' Handicap Chase (0-120 5-y-o and up) £2,872 2m 110yds........................(3:00)

1195[2] AROUND THE HORN [109] 6-11-5 (3") D Fortt, trkd ldrs, led appr 2 out, kpt on wl frm last.
.............................(7 to 4 op 13 to 8 tchd 15 to 8) 1
1482* MEGA BLUE [115] 8-11-9 (5") C Woodall, led till hdd appr 2 out, rallied aftr last, no extr und pres towards finish.
....(6 to 4 fav op 13 to 8) 2
1463[2] WICKFIELD LAD [87] 10-9-11 (3") Guy Lewis, cl up till wknd appr 3 out..................... (12 to 1 op 10 to 1) 3
1363* ABSAILOR [100] (v) 9-10-13 P Williams, sn beh, lost tch aftr 7th, tld off.......... (11 to 4 op 5 to 2 tchd 3 to 1) 4
Dist: 1½l, 25l, 20l. 4m 7.00s. a 12.00s (4 Ran).
SR: 32/36/-/-/ (Pell-Mell Partners), Andrew Turnell

1660 Past Glories National Hunt Flat Race (4,5,6-y-o) £1,674 2m 110yds....(3:30)

DUNNOHALM 4-11-0 Mr S Swiers, hld up and beh, gd hdwy o'r 4 fs out, led over one out, pushed out.
....................(5 to 1 op 4 to 1 tchd 7 to 1) 1
SKIDDAW SAMBA 4-10-7 (7") M Herrington, hld up, hdwy 6 out, slight ld 3 out, hdd o'r one out, no extr.
..............................(8 to 1 op 3 to 1 tchd 10 to 1) 2

1376[4] CHINO'S DELIGHT 4-10-7 (7") Guy Lewis, trkd ldrs, dsptd ld 3 fs out, no extr entering fnl furlong.
....(6 to 1 tchd 11 to 2) 3
CORN BOW 4-10-7 (7") Mr G Hogan, mid-div, effrt and hdwy o'r 4 fs out, kpt on same pace fnl 3 furlongs.
....(16 to 1 op 14 to 1) 4
LEXY LADY 4-10-7 (7") Mr E James, led till hdd aftr 6 fs, led ag'n o'r 4 out, headed 3 out, kpt on.
....(10 to 1 op 5 to 2) 5
1494 CEREAL GEM 5-11-0 W Dwan, chsd ldrs, outpcd o'r 4 fs out, styd on und pres fnl 3 furlongs.
....(25 to 1 op 16 to 1) 6
1223[3] GLANDALANE LADY 4-10-7 (7") R McGrath, prmnt, ev ch 4 fs out, kpt on same pace.......... (7 to 2 fav op 5 to 1) 7
CATCH THE PIGEON 4-10-9 (5") P Midgley, in tch, effrt and hdwy o'r 4 fs out, wknd over 3 out. (33 to 1 op 25 to 1) 8
815 CAPTIVA BAY 4-10-11 (3") S Wynne, nvr dngrs... (33 to 1) 9
1376[6] EMERALD QUEEN 4-10-7 (7") R Moore, nvr dngrs.
....(12 to 1 op 10 to 1) 10
GAY'S GAMBIT 4-10-7 (7") J Driscoll, nvr dngrs.
....(14 to 1 op 12 to 1) 11
APACHE GOLD 6-11-0 V Slattery, in tch, effrt and ev ch 4 fs out, sn wknd...............................(14 to 1) 12
BREAD OF HEAVEN 4-10-11 (3") R Davis, nvr dngrs.
....(25 to 1 op 20 to 1) 13
MISS PALEFACE 5-10-7 (7") J Railton, prmnt till wknd quickly 5 fs out, tld off........(6 to 1 op 5 to 1) 14
ANNE CARTER 4-10-7 (7") S Mason, in tch till wknd quickly 4 fs out, tld off.........................(20 to 1) 15
1133[4] BOLANEY GIRL (Ire) 4-10-7 (7") Miss Sue Nichol, cl up, led aftr 6 fs till hdd o'r 4 out, wknd quickly, tld off.
....(14 to 1 op 8 to 1) 16
ARLEY GALE 5-10-9 (5") Mr D McCain, sddl slpd, prmnt till lost pl 5 fs out, tld off...... (20 to 1 op 16 to 1) 17
Dist: 2l, sht-hd, 3l, 2l, 1½l, 2l, 7l, 1½l, 1l, 4m 11.20s. (17 Ran).
(Mrs Joan Smith (Lincoln)), Mrs J R Ramsden

CHELTENHAM (good)
Saturday December 11th
Going Correction: PLUS 0.62 sec. per fur. (races 1,3,-5,7), PLUS 0.55 (2,4,6)

1661 Laurels Novices' Hurdle Grade 2 (4-y-o and up) £6,460 2m 1f......(12:15)

1442* LARGE ACTION (Ire) 5-11-7 J Osborne, in tch, outpcd appr 3 out, effrt and mstk 2 out, smooth hdwy to ld approaching last, quickened clr, imprsv....(7 to 2 co-fav op 3 to 1) 1
1442[2] FATACK 4-11-0 S Curran, led to second, led 3rd to 6th, led ag'n 3 out, hdd appr last, kpt on, not pace of wnr.
....(8 to 1 op 7 to 1) 2
1289* MORCELI (Ire) 5-11-0 R Dunwoody, chsd ldr till led 6th to 3 out, styd pressing for ld till outpcd appr last.
.......................(7 to 2 co-fav op 3 to 1 tchd 4 to 1) 3
1513 ATHAR (Ire) 4-10-13 Richard Guest, chsd ldrs till wknd 3 out...................(16 to 1 op 12 to 1 tchd 20 to 1) 4
695* LINPAC WEST 7-11-0 A Maguire, al beh, lost tch frm 5th, tld off.........................(4 to 1 op 7 to 2) 5
1502* CORROUGE (USA) 4-11-0 C Llewellyn, led second to 3rd, styd chasing ldrs till rdn 2 out, disputing third but hld whn f last...................(7 to 2 co-fav op 3 to 1) f
1515[7] DURSHAN (USA) 4-11-0 D Murphy, al beh, tld off whn pld up bef 2 out....................(66 to 1 op 50 to 1) pu
Dist: 8l, 4l, dist, dist. 4m 7.90s. a 13.40s (7 Ran).
SR: 64/49/45/-/ (B T Stewart-Brown), O Sherwood

1662 Bonusprint Novices' Chase (5-y-o and up) £10,211 2m 5f............(12:45)

1164* CRYSTAL SPIRIT 6-11-6 J Frost, led to second, led ag'n 3rd to 4th, styd chasing ldrs, rdn frm 3 out, led r-in, drvn out.............................(15 to 8 fav op 6 to 4) 1
1368* COULTON 6-11-10 J Osborne, trkd ldrs till led 5th, clr nxt, steadied 8th, hit 4 out and next, not fluent last, sn hdd, hng rght, styd on.................... (9 to 4 op 6 to 4) 2
1393* THE GLOW (Ire) 5-11-5 P Holley, al chasing ldrs, stumbled aftr 9th (water), rdn 2 out, styd on r-in.
.......................(9 to 1 op 7 to 1 tchd 10 to 1) 3
1547* MADAHIM 7-11-6 W Marston, led second to 3rd, led 4th to 5th, styd frnt rnk, rdn 13th, chlgd and hit four out, wknd nxt....................(11 to 4 op 7 to 2 tchd 3 to 1) 4
1346[3] FESTIVAL DREAMS 8-11-6 A Maguire, sn beh, lost tch frm 8th, tld off.............(16 to 1 op 14 to 1 tchd 33 to 1) 5
Dist: 1½l, sht-hd, 10l, dist. 5m 20.70s. a 16.70s (5 Ran).
SR: 41/43/38/29/-/ (Paul Mellon), I A Balding

1663 Bula Hurdle Grade 2 (4-y-o and up) £21,560 2m 1f.................(1:20)

1209* STAUNCH FRIEND (USA) 5-11-8 D Murphy, hld up in rear, steady hdwy 2 out, quickened to ld r-in, cmftbly.
....(6 to 1 op 5 to 1) 1
HALKOPOUS 7-11-8 G McCourt, prmnt, chsd ldr 3 out till led aftr 2 out, rdn last, hdd r-in, not quicken.
.......................(3 to 1 tchd 11 to 4 and 7 to 2) 2

MUSE 6-11-8 P Holley, *led, clr 3rd, hdd aftr 2 out, styd on same pace*..........................(14 to 1 op 16 to 1) 3
1347³ FLAKEY DOVE 7-10-13 J Osborne, *hit 3rd, chsd ldr to 3 out, rdn 2 out, sn btn*. ....(14 to 1 op 16 to 1 tchd 12 to 1) 4
1256⁴ ROYAL DERBI 8-11-8 W Marston, *hdwy 3 out, effrt 2 out, sn rdn and wknd*..................(16 to 1 op 25 to 1) 5
1347* KING CREDO 8-11-4 A Maguire, *hld up in rear till f 4th*. ....(2 to 1 fav op 7 to 4) f
1347⁴ GRANVILLE AGAIN 7-11-8 R Dunwoody, *hld up in rear till f 4th*...................(13 to 2 op 9 to 2 tchd 7 to 1) f

Dist: 5l, 1l, 6l, 3l. 4m 6.10s. a 11.60s (7 Ran).
SR: 83/78/77/62/68/-/-/ (B Schmidt-Bodner), M H Tompkins

1664 Tripleprint Gold Cup Handicap Chase Grade 3 (5-y-o and up) £31,215 2m 5f ....(1:55)

FRAGRANT DAWN [137] 9-10-2 D Murphy, *hld up, steady hdwy frm 12th, quickened to ld r-in, kpt on*. ....(14 to 1 tchd 16 to 1) 1
884² YOUNG HUSTLER [150] 6-11-1 C Llewellyn, *prmnt, led 12th to 13th, rdn and led ag'n aftr 3 out, hrd drvn and hdd r-in, one pace*..... (11 to 2 op 9 to 2 tchd 6 to 1) 2
1507⁵ FREELINE FINISHING [139] (bl) 9-10-4 J Osborne, *hld up in rear, steady hdwy whn blun 4 out, ran on frm 2 out, not pace to rch ldrs*..........................(20 to 1) 3
1512 STUNNING STUFF [135] 8-10-0 S McNeill, *beh 7th, hdwy 13th, no imprsn frm 3 out*.........(16 to 1 op 20 to 1) 4
1226 SECOND SCHEDUAL [152] 8-11-3 A Maguire, *chsd ldrs, hit 11th, led 13th, hdd aftr 3 out, wknd 2 out*. ....(4 to 1 op 3 to 1 tchd 9 to 2) 5
1573⁴ GENERAL PERSHING [143] 7-10-8 N Doughty, *wth ldr to 3rd, blun 8th and 9th, wknd 13th*... (10 to 1 op 8 to 1) 6
1226⁹ MORLEY STREET [159] 9-11-10 J Frost, *mstk 8th, al beh*. .... (14 to 1 op 16 to 1) 7
1573 ARMAGRET [140] 8-10-5 L O'Hara, *chsd ldrs till wknd 13th*...(33 to 1) 8
1436* EGYPT MILL PRINCE [139] (bl) 7-10-4 R Dunwoody, *led, not fluent and hdd 12th, wknd quickly appr 2 out, no ch whn blun last, virtually pld up bef finish*. ....(5 to 2 fav op 3 to 1) 9
1436 ANOTHER CORAL [156] 10-11-7 W Marston, *effrt 8th, hit tenth, sn wknd, tld off*............. (11 to 1 op 8 to 1) 10
1387³ BRANDESTON [135] 8-9-7 (7*) P Murphy, *chsd ldrs to 11th, tld off whn pld up bef 3 out*....... (50 to 1 op 33 to 1) pu

Dist: 3l, ¾l, 20l, nk, 1½l, 30l, 1½l, dist, 8l. 5m 16.20s. a 12.20s (11 Ran).
SR: 68/78/66/42/58/47/33/12/-/ (D & S Mercer), M C Pipe

1665 Lonesome Glory Hurdle for the Sport of Kings Challenge (4-y-o and up) £9,085 2½m.................. (2:30)

755* DANCE OF WORDS (Ire) 4-10-4 W Marston, *in tch, rdn aftr 3 out, outpcd frm 2 out, styd on ag'n r-in to ld cl hme*. ....(8 to 1 op 11 to 1) 1
1437³ SATIN LOVER 5-11-8 G McCourt, *hld up, steady hdwy 3 out, led last, rdn r-in, ct nr finish*. ....(3 to 1 op 11 to 4 tchd 100 to 30) 2
1462* KADI (Ger) 4-10-9 A Maguire, *hdwy 6th, chlgd 2 out, ev ch last, rdn and not quicken r-in*. ....(5 to 2 fav op 9 to 4 tchd 11 to 4) 3
MOTORCADE (USA) 4-11-7 R Dunwoody, *prmnt, chsd ldr 6th till led 2 out, rdn and hdd appr last, sn one pace*. ....(10 to 1) 4
1227 CARDINAL RED (bl) 6-11-8 J Osborne, *led, sn wl clr, hdd 2 out, styd in tch till wknd appr last*. ....(14 to 1 tchd 16 to 1) 5
1559⁸ ZAMIRAH (Ire) 4-10-4 C Llewellyn, *chsd ldr to 6th, sn rdn and not a dngr aftr*..................(7 to 1 op 5 to 1) 6
1468* CALL HOME (Ire) 5-11-0 D Murphy, *al beh, lost tch frm 6th*. ....(9 to 2 op 4 to 1 tchd 5 to 1) 7

Dist: 3l, ¾l, 6l, 2½l, 8l, dist. 4m 59.70s. (7 Ran).
(J Howard Johnson), J H Johnson

1666 George Stevens Handicap Chase (4-y-o and up) £5,460 2m 110yds...(3:05)

1440 KATABATIC [164] 10-12-0 S McNeill, *rcd in 3rd, awkward second, hit 4 out, styd on frm 3 out, chlgd from nxt till stayed on to ld r-in*............ (7 to 4 jt-fav op 6 to 4) 1
1363 HOWE STREET [136] 10-10-0 R Dunwoody, *led, rdn frm 3 out, drvn and ct r-in, no extr*. ....(9 to 4 op 5 to 2 tchd 3 to 1) 2
1440 SPACE FAIR [145] 10-10-9 A Maguire, *chsd ldr, chlgd tenth to 3 out, wknd quickly appr 2 out, tld off*. ....(7 to 4 jt-fav op 6 to 4) 3

Dist: ¾l, dist. 4m 11.00s. a 15.00s (3 Ran).
SR: 41/12/-/ (Pell-Mell Partners), Andrew Turnell

1667 Newent Handicap Hurdle (4-y-o and up) £4,952 2½m................(3:40)

1544* MEDITATOR [115] 9-10-2 (5*) S Curran, *led sn clr, rdn and ran on wl appr last*..................(11 to 4 op 2 to 1) 1
1445² GLAISDALE (Ire) [124] 4-11-2 D Murphy, *chsd wnr to 6th, rallied appr last, no extr r-in*...(5 to 2 fav tchd 9 to 4) 2
1445* JEASSU [132] 10-11-5 (5*) T Jenks, *hld up, took str hold, hdwy to chase wnr 6th, rdn appr last, one pace*. ....(7 to 2 op 3 to 1) 3
1445⁷ STAR PLAYER [113] 7-10-5 N Mann, *hld up, took str hold, gd hdwy frm 3 out, rdn and styd on same pace appr last*...................(6 to 1 op 11 to 2 tchd 13 to 2) 4
1513⁶ KETTI [128] (bl) 8-11-6 R Dunwoody, *al beh, lost tch frm 2 out*................... (13 to 2 op 7 to 1 tchd 15 to 2) 5

Dist: 2½l, 1½l, hd, 30l. 5m 18.20s. (5 Ran).
(Miss Jacqueline S Doyle), Miss Jacqueline S Doyle

DONCASTER (good)
Saturday December 11th
Going Correction: PLUS 0.70 sec. per fur. (races 1,4,5,7), PLUS 0.58 (2,3,6)

1668 St Leger Banqueting Suite Novices' Hurdle (4-y-o and up) £2,250 2m 110yds.......................(12:40)

1366³ WESTHOLME (USA) 5-11-7 L Wyer, *led to 3rd, trkd ldr, led on bit appr 2 out, drw clr, very easily*. ....(5 to 4 on op 11 to 10 on) 1
1557⁸ SWIFT CONVEYANCE (Ire) 4-10-9 (7*) S McDougall, *cl up, led 3rd till hdd appr 2 out, kpt on, no ch wth wnr*. ....(12 to 1 op 10 to 1) 2
1193⁶ BIGWHEEL BILL (Ire) 4-11-0 S Smith Eccles, *chsd ldrs, pushed alng aftr 5th, kpt on same pace frm 3 out*. .... (11 to 1 op 14 to 1 tchd 10 to 1) 3
1490⁴ JUNGLE RITES (Ire) 5-11-0 M Dwyer, *chsd ldrs, kpt on same pace frm 3 out*................ (7 to 1 op 5 to 1) 4
1374⁵ SILVER SAMURAI 4-11-4 W McFarland, *chsd ldrs, pushed alng aftr 5th, wknd appr 3 out*.......(5 to 1 op 4 to 1) 5
1478⁸ TAHITIAN 4-10-7 (7*) E Husband, *nvr on terms*. .... (16 to 1 op 10 to 1) 6
FLOATING LINE 5-11-0 R Garritty, *hld up, hdwy to chase clr ldrs 3 out, no imprsn, wkng whn blun badly last*. .... (20 to 1 op 14 to 1) 7
DHARAMSHALA (Ire) 5-11-0 M Brennan, *in tch till wknd aftr 5th*.......................... (25 to 1 op 16 to 1) 8
PITCH BLACK (Ire) 4-10-7 (7*) F Leahy, *in tch till wknd aftr 5th, tld off*......................... (33 to 1 op 25 to 1) 9
FUTURE FAME (USA) 4-11-0 D Wilkinson, *beh, lost tch aftr 5th, pld up bef 3 out*.............................. (33 to 1) pu
1129⁶ TOLL BOOTH 4-10-4 (5*) J Supple, *not jump wl, tld off frm hfwy, pld up bef 3 out*...................... (100 to 1) pu

Dist: 12l, 15l, sht-hd, 6l, 7l, 4l, 8l, dist. 4m 6.40s. a 15.90s (11 Ran).
SR: 49/32/15/15/13/2/ (T H Bennett), M H Easterby

1669 Forgive'n Forget Novices' Chase (4-y-o and up) £2,794 2m 3f 110yds (1:10)

1484* FRICKLEY 7-11-8 M Dwyer, *cl up, mstk 6th, led aftr 8th, clr after 2 out, cmftbly*..... (2 to 1 on tchd 15 to 8 on) 1
1214⁶ STAGE PLAYER 7-10-13 (5*) T Eley, *in tch, hdwy to chase wnr tenth, rdn aftr 3 out, no imprsn*. .... (14 to 1 op 12 to 1) 2
ISLAND GALE 8-11-1 (3*) A Thornton, *chsd ldrs, mstk 6th, outpcd appr 4 out, kpt on und pres frm 2 out*. .... (25 to 1 op 20 to 1) 3
1558⁴ MARLINGFORD 6-11-4 C Hawkins, *made most till hdd aftr 8th, mstk 11th, sn wknd*.........(4 to 1 op 3 to 1) 4
BALLYDOUGAN (Ire) 5-11-4 S Smith Eccles, *sn beh*. .... (25 to 1 op 20 to 1) 5
1417³ TITUS GOLD (v) 8-11-4 B Powell, *wth ldr, reminder aftr 8th, wknd appr 11th*.............(12 to 1 tchd 14 to 1) 6
1605 BELLAGROVE (Ire) 5-10-6 (7*) G Cahill, *sn beh, tld off whn pld up bef 9th*........(40 to 1 op 33 to 1 tchd 50 to 1) pu

Dist: 3½l, 3½l, 15l, 12l, 1l. 5m 5.30s. a 19.30s (7 Ran).
SR: 14/6/2/-/ (Robert Ogden), G Richards

1670 Constant Security Handicap Chase (5-y-o and up) £5,637 3¼m........ (1:40)

921* CARBISDALE [140] 7-10-0 L Wyer, *jmpd wl, in tch, led 4 out, clr aftr 2 out, pushed out r-in*. .... (15 to 8 op 2 to 1 tchd 9 to 4) 1
1447³ DUBLIN FLYER [140] 7-10-0 B Powell, *jmpd wl, led till hdd 4 out, styd on well frm last*......(13 to 8 fav op 5 to 4) 2
DOCKLANDS EXPRESS [168] 11-12-0 M Dwyer, *in tch, pushed alng aftr 12th, ch 3 out, grad wknd*. .... (11 to 4 op 9 to 4) 3
1486 POLAR REGION [140] 7-9-7 (7*) F Leahy, *in tch, mstk 12th, sn wknd tld off*.................. (16 to 1 op 12 to 1) 4

Dist: 1½l, 12l, dist. 6m 35.20s. a 16.20s (4 Ran).
SR: 61/59/75/-/ (Mrs M Williams), Mrs M Reveley

1671 Steelphalt Handicap Hurdle (4-y-o and up) £3,760 2½m................ (2:10)

1238* PURITAN (Can) [112] 4-11-5 (5*) Miss P Jones, *in tch, hdwy to chase ldr 2 out, rdn and quickened to ld r-in*. .... (2 to 1 fav tchd 9 to 4) 1
1389⁷ CREEAGER [101] 11-10-13 B Dalton, *cl up, led 3rd, clr 2 out, hdd and no extr r-in*...................... (12 to 1) 2

1221⁴ SPANISH FAIR (Ire) [91] 5-9-10 (7*) Mr D Parker, *trkd ldrs, ch 3 out, sn rdn and one pace*.......(5 to 1 tchd 11 to 2) 3
1028⁴ ROYAL VACATION [109] 4-11-4 (3*) N Bentley, *hld up, reminder aftr 7th, styd on same pace frm 3 out.*
1426* CLOUT CIRCULAR [104] 4-11-2 M Brennan, *chsd ldrs till wknd aftr 3 out*....................(4 to 1 tchd 9 to 2) 4
1445 DUKE DE VENDOME [98] 10-10-3 (7*) Mr G Haine, *prmnt, ev ch appr 3 out, grad wknd*...................(9 to 2 op 4 to 1) 5
1571 WAKE UP [103] 6-11-1 L Wyer, *led to 3rd, cl up till wknd appr 3 out, tld off*..............(25 to 1) 6
 ....(10 to 1 tchd 12 to 1) 7
Dist: 2½l, 6l, 3l, 7l, 6l, 15l. 4m 57.70s. (7 Ran).

(J Parks), N Tinkler

1672 Sea Pigeon Handicap Hurdle (0-145 4-y-o and up) £3,201 2m (2:40)

STRATH ROYAL [115] 7-12-0 M Brennan, *trkd ldrs gng wl, led 3 out, clr whn blun last, drvn out.*(4 to 1 op 7 to 2) 1
1481⁵ CAMALOU (Ire) [112] 6-10-12 M Dwyer, *led to 5th, trkd ldrs aftr, effrt after 2 out, kpt on frm last.*
 ....(100 to 30 fav op 7 to 2 tchd 3 to 1) 2
1364² NIKITAS [115] 8-11-11 (3*) R Farrant, *cl up, led 5th till hdd 3 out, kpt on same pace*..............(7 to 2 op 3 to 1) 3
1571⁸ CLURICAN (Ire) [115] 4-11-7 (7*) E Husband, *hld up, effrt aftr beh, effrt aftr 3 out, styd on, not trble ldrs*....(20 to 1) 4
1487³ ADMIRALTY WAY [107] 7-11-6 B Powell, *hld up, effrt appr 3 out, sn wknd*....................(9 to 5 tchd 5 to 1) 5
1487² TAPATCH (Ire) [112] 5-11-8 (3*) N Bentley, *trkd ldrs, ev ch 3 out, sn wknd*....................(7 to 2 op 3 to 1) 6
Dist: 2l, ¾l, 3½l, 3l, 7l. 4m 11.70s. a 21.20s (6 Ran).
SR: 4/-/1/ (Lady Anne Bentinck), O Brennan

1673 Freebooter Novices' Chase (4-y-o and up) £2,924 2m 110yds......... (3:10)

1241* NATIVE MISSION 6-11-8 M Dwyer, *cl up, led 4 out, clr 2 out, eased towards finish, cmftbly.*
 ....(3 to 1 on op 7 to 2 on tchd 11 to 4 on) 1
1241³ TOI MARINE 8-11-4 Mr A Hambly, *led till hdd 4 out, chsd wnr aftr, no imprsn*...................(25 to 1) 2
1366⁴ RAMSTAR 5-10-11 (7*) G Hogan, *trkd ldrs, effrt appr 4 out, one pace*...................(4 to 1 op 7 to 2) 3
1593⁶ ON CUE 6-11-4 W Worthington, *in tch till outpcd and beh 6th, kpt on frm 2 out*....................(33 to 1) 4
1531⁴ BILLHEAD 7-10-13 (5*) T Eley, *beh, hdwy to track ldrs 6th, wknd quickly aftr 3 out*.........(25 to 1 tchd 33 to 1) 5
1373 HEDLEY MILL 5-10-8 (5*) J Supple, *beh, hmpd 4th, lost tch 6th, tld off*................(14 to 1 op 16 to 1) 6
Dist: 1½l, ½l, 7l, 8l, 12l. 4m 13.40s. a 18.40s (6 Ran).
SR: 6/-/-/ (G E Shouler), J G FitzGerald

1674 Louella Stud 'Nomadic Way' National Hunt Flat Race (4,5,6-y-o) £1,800 2m 110yds..................... (3:40)

1428³ COILED SPRING 6-10-11 (3*) A Thornton, *made all, ran on wl, cmftbly*....................(8 to 1 tchd 10 to 1) 1
 VALERIOS KING (Ire) 4-11-0 V Slattery, *in tch, hdwy 5 out, kpt on wl fnl 2 fs, no imprsn on wnr*..........(10 to 1) 2
 FED ON OATS 5-10-7 (7*) Mr G Haine, *in tch, pushed alng and hdwy 5 out, chsd wnr 3 out, no imprsn.*
 ....(9 to 2 op 4 to 1) 3
 EVEN BLUE (Ire) 5-10-9 (5*) Mr D McCain, *mid-div, hdwy 6 out, kpt on same pace frm 4 out*.............(25 to 1) 4
 TOO BRAVE (Ire) 4-10-7 (7*) J Driscoll, *chsd wnr till grad wknd frm 4 out*................(11 to 2 op 9 to 2) 5
 SEATWIST 4-10-7 (7*) P McLoughlin, *mid-div, effrt 5 out, kpt on same pace*...................(25 to 1 op 20 to 1) 6
 D'ARBLAY STREET (Ire) 4-10-7 (7*) S McDougall, *beh, reminder hfwy, kpt on fnl 3 fs, not rch ldrs*...(25 to 1) 7
 SOUNDS GOLDEN 5-11-0 M Hourigan, *prmnt, chsd wnr 4 out till wknd 3 out*....................(10 to 1) 8
 SPA KELLY 5-11-8⁸ Mr J Holt, *nvr dngrs.*
 ....(25 to 1 op 20 to 1) 9
 SPEARHEAD AGAIN (Ire) 4-10-9 (5*) J McCarthy, *nvr on terms*...................(7 to 2 jt-fav op 5 to 1) 10
 BALLYROVERS 4-10-7 (7*) P Johnson, *chsd ldrs, pushed alng 6 out, wknd o'r 4 out*........(14 to 1 op 12 to 1) 11
 BANOFFI 4-10-7 (7*) G Tormey, *sn pushed alng, nvr on terms*...................(7 to 2 jt-fav op 9 to 4) 12
 MIGHTY EXPRESS 4-10-9 (5*) J Supple, *nvr better than mid-div*...................(20 to 1 op 14 to 1) 13
 WHOCOMESNATURALLY 4-10-9 (5*) T Eley, *nvr better than mid-div*...................(25 to 1 op 20 to 1) 14
1376 GOLDEN RECORD 5-10-7 (7*) E Husband, *chsd ldrs till wknd o'r 4 out*....................(25 to 1) 15
 HELP YOURSELF (Ire) 4-10-7 (7*) P Carr, *al beh, tld off.*
 ....(20 to 1 op 16 to 1) 16
 AHBEJAYBUS (Ire) 4-10-7 (7*) Mr G Hogan, *prmnt early, beh frm hfwy, wl tld off*....................(50 to 1) 17
Dist: 3l, 2½l, 8l, 5l, 1l, 1½l, ¾l, 1½l, ½l, 5l. 4m 0.60s. (17 Ran).
(A Vergette), G M Vergette

EDINBURGH (good to firm)
Saturday December 11th

Going Correction: MINUS 0.05 sec. per fur. (races 1,3,6), MINUS 0.25 (2,4,5)

1675 Charlotte Square Novices' Hurdle (4-y-o and up) £1,997 2m........ (12:50)

821³ AMERICAN HERO 5-11-4 B Storey, *jmpd quick and cleanly, made all, ran on strly frm betw last 2.*
 ....(11 to 8 fav op 6 to 4) 1
731⁴ IMPERIAL BID (Fr) 5-10-7 (5*) P Waggott, *settled midfield, improved to join ldrs aftr 3 out, effrt appr last, one pace*...................(6 to 1 op 4 to 1) 2
809* LADY DONOGHUE (USA) 4-10-13 P Niven, *al hndy, ev ch aftr 3 out, rdn and no extr betw last 2.*
 ....(3 to 1 op 5 to 2 tchd 100 to 30) 3
 CLEEVAUN (Ire) 5-10-7 (5*) P Williams, *chsd alng to keep up hfwy, styd on grimly frm 3 out, nrst finish.*
 ....(16 to 1 op 10 to 1) 4
626³ ROAD TO THE WEIR 6-10-7 (5*) J Burke, *nvr far away, rdn whn pace quickened appr 2 out, no extr.*
 ....(33 to 1 op 25 to 1) 5
1199 BACK BEFORE DAWN 6-10-12 A Dobbin, *pressed ldg quartet, feeling pace whn hit 3 out, no imprsn frm nxt.*
 ....(25 to 1 op 16 to 1) 6
1084⁶ WALKING THE PLANK (bl) 4-10-12 D Byrne, *last and pushed alng whn blun 3rd, sn lost tch, tld off.*
 ....(3 to 1 tchd 4 to 1) 7
 BREEZE AWAY 4-10-7 C Grant, *struggling to go pace hfwy, tld off whn pld up betw last 2.*
 ....(25 to 1 op 20 to 1 tchd 33 to 1) pu
Dist: 5l, 8l, 8l, 5l, 10l, 30l. 3m 42.20s. a 4.20s (8 Ran).
SR: 40/29/22/13/8/ (David S Leggate), R Allan

1676 Rusty Nail Novices' Handicap Chase (5-y-o and up) £2,425 3m...... (1:20)

1477⁵ INVERINATE [96] (bl) 8-12-0 T Reed, *slight ld to 4th, styd hndy, drvn alng whn lft in lead last, rdn out.*
 ....(7 to 2 op 3 to 1) 1
1359³ MOYODE REGENT [89] 9-11-2 (5*) J Burke, *settled mid-field, drvn alng fnl circuit, ev ch 3 out, styd on one pace r-in.*...................(6 to 1 op 9 to 2) 2
1585⁸ CLARE LAD [92] 10-11-10 B Storey, *blun 1st, struggling to go pace aftr one circuit, rallied frm 3 out, nrst finish.*
 ....(10 to 1 tchd 8 to 1) 3
1184 MASTER MISCHIEF [77] 6-10-9 R Hodge, *trkd ldg bunch, lost grnd whn pace quickened 6 out, styd on wl frm betw last 2*...................(33 to 1 op 16 to 1) 4
1200³ RUSHING BURN [74] 7-10-6³ P Niven, *chasing ldrs whn f second*...................(14 to 1 op 10 to 1) f
1587⁴ CARDENDEN (Ire) [70] 5-10-2 S Turner, *wth ldrs, led hfwy till f 7 out*...................(16 to 1 op 14 to 1) f
1587⁹ JUNIORS CHOICE [73] 10-10-0² (7*) M Parker, *wth ldrs, nosed ahead 4th to hfwy, lft in ld 7 out, 3 ls clr whn blun and uns rdr last*...........(50 to 1 op 25 to 1) ur
1603² SCOTTISH GOLD [93] 9-11-6 (5*) P Williams, *in tch, chsd alng to hold pl whn hmpd by faller 7 out, sn lost touch, pld up bef 4 out.*
 ....(11 to 4 fav op 3 to 1 tchd 5 to 2 and 100 to 30) pu
1311 FLASS VALE [70] 5-10-2 A Orkney, *jmpd stickily in rear, pld up aftr 5th.*...................(8 to 1 op 7 to 1) pu
1587* TIMANFAYA [87] 6-11-5 (6ex) C Grant, *trkd ldrs, blun 9th and nxt, still hndy whn pld up bef 7 out.*
 ....(6 to 1 op 9 to 2) pu
Dist: 3½l, 7l, 2l. 6m 9.20s. a 19.20s (10 Ran).
(C J Ewart), L Lungo

1677 Edinburgh University Turf Club Maiden Hurdle (4-y-o and up) £1,955 3m........................... (1:50)

1478⁴ MAJOR BELL 5-11-0 M Moloney, *patiently rdn, steady hdwy to join issue fnl circuit, led appr 4 out, clr betw last 2, readily*..........(9 to 4 op 7 to 4 tchd 5 to 2) 1
547⁶ WEY I MAN (Ire) 4-11-0 P Niven, *tucked away in midfield, drvn up to take clr order appr 2 out, kpt on, no imprsn.*
 ....(33 to 1 op 100 to 1) 2
1371² IRISH STAMP (Ire) 4-11-0 C Grant, *settled to track ldrs, led briefly 5 out, niggled alng aftr, outpcd frm betw last 2*...................(11 to 10 on op 11 to 8) 3
1475 DASHMAR 6-11-0 C Dennis, *wth ldrs, led 4th to 6th, struggling to hold pl appr 3 out, wknd.*
 ....(5 to 1 op 4 to 1) 4
1060 HIGHRYMER 9-10-9 A Dobbin, *wth ldrs, led 6th to 5 out, drvn alng aftr nxt, sn outpcd*........(33 to 1 op 25 to 1) 5
1202⁸ ROYAL FIFE 7-10-4 (5*) P Williams, *trkd ldg bunch, feeling pace aftr one circuit, struggling frm 4 out.*
 ....(25 to 1 op 16 to 1) 6
1478 LORD ADVOCATE (v) 5-10-11 (3*) D J Moffatt, *struggling and tld off aftr 3rd, not a factor*.............(33 to 1) 7
1587⁸ THE LORRYMAN (Ire) 5-11-0 T Reed, *slight ld to 4th, styd hndy till drvn alng fnl circuit, lost tch four out.*
 ....(50 to 1 op 66 to 1) 8
1223 LA DOUTELLE (USA) 4-11-0 Mr J Bradburne, *in tch, struggling to keep up fnl circuit, tld off*......(50 to 1 op 33 to 1) 9
Dist: 5l, 5l, 8l, 2½l, 12l, 12l, 12l, 15l. 5m 50.10s. a 10.10s (9 Ran).
(A C Whillans), A C Whillans

1678 I Want To Be Rich Handicap Chase
(0-135 5-y-o and up) £3,081 2m . . (2:20)

1583* SONSIE MO [108] 8-10-8 (5*,6ex) P Williams, al hndy, feeling pace appr 5 out, rallied, staying on whn lft in ld 2 out, sn clr . . . .(9 to 2 op 4 to 1 tchd 5 to 1) 1
1360¹ MAUDLINS CROSS [115] 8-11-6 P Niven, made most to hfwy, pushed alng whn blun 4 out, lft second and hmpd by faller 2 out, one pace.
. . . .(100 to 30 op 3 to 1 tchd 7 to 2) 2
973² CROSS CANNON [118] 7-11-6 (3*) A Larnach, dashed up to ld briefly aftr 4th, styd hndy till rdn appr four out, sn outpcd . . . .(6 to 1 op 5 to 1) 3
1144² ROCKET LAUNCHER [103] 7-10-8 M Moloney, al hndy, led hfwy, jmpd lft, quickened 5 out, jumped badly left and f 2 out. (85 to 40 fav op 9 to 4 tchd 5 to 2 and 2 to 1) f
1220² KUSHBALOO [119] 8-11-10 B Storey, blun and uns rdr 1st.
. . . .(7 to 2 op 3 to 1) ur
Dist: 10l, 12l. 3m 50.90s. a 0.90s (5 Ran).
SR: 36/33/24/-/-/ (Timothy Hardie), Mrs S C Bradburne

1679 Princes Street Claiming Chase (5-y-o and up) £2,603 2½m . . . .(2:50)

1375³ LAPIAFFE 9-11-2 B Storey, patiently rdn, improved to ld 6 out, styd on wl frm betw last 2.
. . . .(2 to 1 on tchd 15 to 8 on) 1
1585⁹ SPEECH 10-10-13 (5*) F Perratt, led, clr 3rd, hit 5th and 7th, hdd 6 out, rallied, one pace frm betw last 2.
. . . .(10 to 1 op 7 to 1) 2
1477 MOW CREEK 9-10-9 (5*) P Williams, nvr far away, effrt and drvn alng aftr 6 out, reminders 4 out, outpcd frm nxt. . . . .(5 to 1 op 9 to 2) 3
1095⁷ WHEELIES NEWMEMBER 10-11-0 T Reed, jmpd lft thrght, struggling aftr 6th, tld off whn ran out through wing 3 out . . . .(5 to 1 op 9 to 2) ro
Dist: 7l, 7l. 5m 7.50s. a 17.50s (4 Ran).
(Mrs B Ramsden), A Harrison

1680 Ladbrokes On-course Amateur Riders' Handicap Hurdle (0-125 4-y-o and up) £2,295 2½m . . . .(3:20)

1119³ MYSTIC MEMORY [103] 4-11-5 (5*) Mr M Buckley, patiently rdn, improved aftr 3 out, styd on strly to ld r-in.
. . . .(11 to 8 on op 13 to 8 on tchd 5 to 4 on) 1
1586⁴ RAPID MOVER [80] (bl) 6-9-8 (7*) Mr L Donnelly, made most till hdd aftr 6th, rallied to ld ag'n 2 out, headed and rdn r-in, one pace . . . .(4 to 1 tchd 7 to 2) 2
1485 A GENTLEMAN TWO [80] 7-9-12⁴ (7*) Mr A Manners, trkd ldg trio, drvn alng whn pace quickened 3 out, rallied, one pace frm betw last 2 . . . .(14 to 1 op 12 to 1) 3
1586 SERAPHIM (Fr) [103] 4-11-10 Mr S Swiers, al hndy, ev ch and drvn alng aftr 2 out, no extr . .(4 to 1 tchd 9 to 2) 4
644⁵ HAMANAKA (USA) [90] 4-10-4 (7*) Mr S Love, wth ldr, led aftr 6th, clumsy 4 out, hdd 2 out, wknd quickly.
. . . .(20 to 1 op 14 to 1) 5
1199 FINE OAK [79] 6-9-12⁵ (7*) Mr S Johnson, chsd ldrs, struggling hfwy, tld off frm 4 out . . . .(50 to 1 op 33 to 1) 6
Dist: 1½l, 4l, 7l, 10l, dist. 4m 47.00s. a 9.00s (6 Ran).
(Carnoustie Racing Club Ltd), Mrs M Reveley

FAIRYHOUSE (IRE) (yielding to soft)
Saturday December 11th

1681 Thomastown Maiden Hurdle (4 & 5-y-o) £3,105 2m . . . .(12:30)

1267⁴ MALIHABAD (Ire) 4-11-9 F J Flood, ...(15 to 2 fav) 1
1500⁴ ROUBABAY (Ire) 5-11-11 (3*) T P Treacy, ...(2 to 1) 2
1379⁶ NICE PROSPECT (Ire) 5-11-6 T J Taaffe, ...(8 to 1) 3
1230 MIDNIGHT HOUR (Ire) 4-11-4 C F Swan, ...(14 to 1) 4
1265³ BEAT THE SECOND (Ire) 5-11-6 G M O'Neill, ...(8 to 1) 5
STRALDI (Ire) 5-11-7 (7*) E G Callaghan, ...(14 to 1) 6
1333⁸ TAITS CLOCK (Ire) 4-11-4 P Carberry, ...(12 to 1) 7
TIME IT RIGHT (Ire) 4-11-9 K F O'Brien, ...(8 to 1) 8
1435⁶ HAUNTING ANGLE (Ire) 4-10-11 (7*) T Martin, ...(12 to 1) 9
UNA'S CHOICE (Ire) 5-11-6 A Powell, ...(20 to 1) 10
1429⁵ GRECIAN LADY (Ire) 4-10-13 P L Malone, ...(12 to 1) 11
1332⁶ CORRIB HAVEN (Ire) 5-10-13 (7*) J P Broderick, . . .(20 to 1) 12
MORNING IN MAY (Ire) 5-11-6 J Shortt, ...(20 to 1) 13
STEEL GEM (Ire) 4-11-4 F Woods, ...(16 to 1) 14
747⁵ AMME ENAEK (Ire) 4-10-10 (3*) K B Walsh, ...(20 to 1) 15
HIGH TONE (Ire) 4-11-1 (3*) D Bromley, ...(25 to 1) 16
1020⁸ NORA'S ERROR (Ire) 4-11-4 J P Banahan, ...(25 to 1) 17
1455 ARCTIC TREASURE (Ire) 4-10-10 (3*) T J Mitchell, . .(20 to 1) 18
1333 LEADING TIME (Fr) 4-11-4 (5*) M G Cleary, ...(20 to 1) 19
803 LOOK NONCHALANT (Ire) 4-10-6 (7*) Mr T J Beattie,
. . . .(33 to 1) 20
SHINETHYME (Ire) 4-10-10 (3*) C O'Brien, ...(20 to 1) 21
NO ONE KNOWS (Ire) 5-11-1 H Rogers, ...(20 to 1) 22
1230 CLASS OF NINETYTWO (Ire) 4-11-4 B Sheridan, . . .(33 to 1) 23
ST AIDAN (Ire) 5-11-1 (5*) L Flynn, ...(33 to 1) 24
1230 FOURTWOONEAGAIN (Ire) 4-10-13 J F Titley, ...(33 to 1) 25

DERRAVARAGH GALE (Ire) 4-10-6 (7*) D J Kavanagh,
. . . .(20 to 1) 26
Dist: 6l, 8l, 4½l, 4l. 4m 2.80s. (26 Ran).
(R P Behan), F Flood

1682 Brooklyn Handicap Chase (4-y-o and up) £3,105 2m . . . .(1:00)

1552⁵ SARAEMMA [-] 7-11-2 C F Swan, ...(7 to 1) 1
1382⁴ LASATA [-] 8-10-11 (3*) C O'Brien, ...(5 to 2 fav) 2
1550⁴ WINNING CHARLIE [-] 7-10-1 K F O'Brien, ...(7 to 2) 3
1382⁷ FRANTESA [-] (bl) 7-9-11 T Horgan, ...(7 to 1) 4
1433⁵ RANDOM PRINCE [-] 9-9-12 P Carberry, ...(6 to 1) 5
1552⁶ WHO'S TO SAY [-] 7-10-9 (3*) T J Mitchell, ...(4 to 1) ur
Dist: ¾l, 6l, nk, 15l. 4m 14.20s. (6 Ran).
(D Cox), J H Scott

1683 Sillogue Hurdle (4-y-o and up) £3,105 2¾m . . . . (1:30)

1449* IDIOTS VENTURE 6-11-11 B Sheridan, ...(9 to 4) 1
1378² LAW BRIDGE 6-11-8 C F Swan, ...(7 to 4 fav) 2
1434² MUILEAR OIRGE 6-11-8 J F Titley, ...(7 to 2) 3
1378³ BUMBLY BROOK 6-10-11 (7*) J M McCormack, . . .(10 to 1) 4
COMMAND 'N CONTROL 4-10-10 (3*) T J Mitchell, (20 to 1) 5
1576⁵ IF YOU SAY YES (Ire) 5-11-3 K F O'Brien, ...(9 to 1) 6
1235⁷ THE PARISH PUMP (Ire) 5-11-4 F Woods, ...(20 to 1) 7
1401⁶ WILD VENTURE (Ire) 5-10-13 A Powell, ...(20 to 1) 8
LANIGANS WINE 11-11-4 T Horgan, ...(20 to 1) 9
1496 PRANKSTER (bl) 7-10-13 (5*) M G Cleary, ...(33 to 1) 10
1581 BEAU CING (Ire) 4-10-6 (7*) D W Cullen, ...(100 to 1) f
1160 SHABRA SOCKS 7-11-4 G M O'Neill, ...(50 to 1) pu
Dist: 5l, ¾l, 2½l. 5m 48.40s. (12 Ran).
(Blackwater Racing Syndicate), A P O'Brien

1684 Harristown Novice Chase (4-y-o and up) £3,450 2¼m . . . . (2:00)

1431* BROCKLEY COURT 6-12-0 J P Banahan, . . .(11 to 10 fav) 1
1401 COOLREE (Ire) 5-11-5 (7*) J P Broderick, ...(14 to 1) 2
1430² ALL THE ACES 6-12-0 T J Taaffe, ...(7 to 4) 3
1498 BROGUESTOWN 8-12-0 F J Flood, ...(20 to 1) 4
ATHY SPIRIT 8-12-0 K F O'Brien, ...(10 to 1) 5
1451⁴ FARNEY GLEN 6-12-0 C F Swan, ...(5 to 1) 6
1159⁴ RAMBLING LORD (Ire) 5-11-12 P Carberry, ...(16 to 1) 7
1018⁷ OXFORD QUILL 6-12-0 L P Cusack, ...(14 to 1) 8
969⁹ FOUR ZEROS 6-12-0 A Powell, ...(33 to 1) 9
1156⁴ RUNAWAY GOLD 6-12-0 F Woods, ...(20 to 1) f
Dist: 7l, 5l, 8l, 4l. 4m 50.60s. (10 Ran).
(C Cronin), Mrs John Harrington

1685 Snail Box Handicap Hurdle (0-130 4-y-o and up) £3,105 3m . . . .(2:30)

1234⁶ ALWAYS IN TROUBLE [-] 6-10-13 J F Titley, ...(7 to 1) 1
1380 MCCONNELL GOLD [-] 8-9-7 H Rogers, ...(50 to 1) 2
1453 CARRON HILL [-] 6-9-13 T Horgan, ...(20 to 1) 3
1335⁵ CHELSEA NATIVE [-] 6-10-11 (5*) Susan A Finn, . . .(7 to 1) 4
1453² BAVARD DIEU (Ire) [-] 5-10-8 C F Swan, ...(4 to 1 fav) 5
1380⁷ IL TROVATORE (USA) [-] (bl) 7-10-8 P Carberry, . .(14 to 1) 6
1453³ COUMEENOOLE LADY [-] 6-10-8 (3*) Miss M Olivefalk,
. . . .(12 to 1) 7
1453⁵ TITIAN BLONDE (Ire) [-] 5-11-3 F Woods, ...(6 to 1) 8
937⁴ DANCING COURSE (Ire) [-] 5-10-0 (5*) P A Roche, . .(20 to 1) 9
1315* GARYS GIRL [-] 6-9-6 (7*) J M McCormack, ...(10 to 1) 10
1380⁶ RISING WATERS (Ire) [-] 5-11-7 (7*) J P Broderick, .(10 to 1) 11
940¹ FINAL TUB [-] 10-10-3 B Sheridan, ...(10 to 1) 12
1497³ PARSONS BRIG [-] 7-11-0 K F O'Brien, ...(14 to 1) 13
RUST NEVER SLEEPS [-] 9-11-1 (3*) C O'Brien, . . .(20 to 1) pu
1453 PRIDE OF ERIN [-] 9-10-11 L P Cusack, ...(33 to 1) pu
GOLDEN SHINE [-] 7-10-10 (7*) B Bowens, ...(20 to 1) pu
HIGHLAND BRIDGE [-] 5-9-4 (7*) D J Kavanagh,
. . . .(33 to 1) pu
Dist: 3l, sht-hd, 1l, ¾l. 6m 18.20s. (17 Ran).
(Mrs M O'Rourke), M J P O'Brien

1686 Kilshane Handicap Hurdle (4-y-o and up) £6,900 2m . . . .(3:00)

1431⁴ FAMILY WAY [-] 6-9-11 F Woods, ...(7 to 4 fav) 1
1429² PHARFETCHED [-] 4-10-4 C F Swan, ...(4 to 1) 2
1453 PEBBLE LANE [-] 7-9-12 H Rogers, ...(16 to 1) 3
1295⁵ HEAD OF CHAMBERS [-] 5-10-3 J P Banahan, . . .(14 to 1) 4
1400 PARLIAMENT HALL [-] 7-10-3 (7*) J P Broderick, . .(14 to 1) 5
1431 GLENCLOUD [-] 5-11-6 P Carberry, ...(12 to 1) 6
1576⁸ ROSE APPEAL [-] 7-9-13 (3*) T P Treacy, ...(12 to 1) 7
1431² ARCTIC WEATHER [-] 4-10-2 (5*) K L O'Brien, . . .(3 to 1) 8
DASHING ROSE [-] 5-9-7 P M Duffy, ...(20 to 1) 9
1431 DUHARRA (Ire) [-] (bl) 5-11-0 (5*) Mr J A Nash, . . .(12 to 1) 10
Dist: 2½l, 1½l, ¾l, 6l. 4m 7.60s. (10 Ran).
(John P McManus), A L T Moore

1687 Fort William Flat Race (5-y-o and up) £3,105 2¼m . . . .(3:30)

1435⁷ YOUR THE MAN 7-11-7 (7*) Mr M Brennan, ...(12 to 1) 1
1270⁴ CLOGRECON BOY (Ire) 5-11-9 (5*) Mr P J Casey, . .(20 to 1) 2
1401 CALMOS 6-12-0 Mr A P O'Brien, ...(16 to 1) 3

1455² THE BLUEBELL POLKA (Ire) 4-11-4 (5*) Mr H F Cleary,
....(Evens fav) 4
1435 DAN PATCH 7-11-7 (7*) Mr G Cuthbert, ...(20 to 1) 5
1403 TUDOR THYNE (Ire) 5-11-6 (3*) Mr P McMahon, ..(16 to 1) 6
1555⁵ THATS MY BOY (Ire) 5-11-9 (5*) Mr J A Nash, ...(5 to 1) 7
1379⁹ I IS 6-12-0 Mr S R Murphy, ...(12 to 1) 8
1403⁵ RUN BAVARD (Ire) 5-11-11 (3*) Mrs M Mullins, ...(8 to 1) 9
1330 QUEEN OF THE ROCK (Ire) 5-11-9 Mr J E Kiely, ..(10 to 1) 10
1555 LADY MARILYN 5-11-9 Mr A J Martin, ...(25 to 1) 11
1401⁷ LISCAHILL HIGHWAY 6-11-7 (7*) Mr P Carey, ...(33 to 1) 12
SECRET MISSILE 6-11-11 (3*) Mrs J M Mullins, ...(4 to 1) 13
1403⁷ YOU'VE DONE WHAT (Ire) 5-11-7 (7*) Miss A O'Brien,
....(7 to 1) 14
1435⁸ COMERAGH MOUNTAIN 6-12-0 Mr P Fenton, ...(25 to 1) 15
1435 RUSSIAN SAINT 7-11-7 (7*) Miss C O'Connell, ...(25 to 1) 16
DEEP WAVE 6-11-9 (5*) Mr C T G Kinane, ...(20 to 1) 17
1403 PERSPEX GALE (Ire) 5-11-6 (3*) Mr D Marnane, ..(16 to 1) 18
993 MASTER EYRE (Ire) 5-11-7 (7*) Mr M J Bowe, ...(33 to 1) 19
1403 PILS INVADER (Ire) 5-11-6 (3*) Mr R Neylon, ...(33 to 1) 20
675 VALMAR (Ire) 5-11-7 (7*) Mr A K Wyse, ...(33 to 1) 21
1500 WAPITI (bl) 6-11-9 (5*) Mr G J Harford, ...(33 to 1) 22
LEGAL APPEAL 6-11-7 (7*) Mr R Byrne, ...(50 to 1) 23
KNOCKNAMEAL 6-11-7 (7*) Mr D A Harney, ...(12 to 1) 24
MASTER NIALL 7-11-9 (5*) Mr B R Hamilton, ...(33 to 1) 25
DOONEEN MIST (Ire) 5-11-2 (7*) Mr D P Daly, ...(25 to 1) 26
Dist: 6l, 6l, hd, 6l. 4m 38.50s. (27 Ran).

(Oliver Lehane) J H Scott

LINGFIELD (good to soft)
Saturday December 11th
Going Correction: PLUS 0.55 sec. per fur. (races 1,3,-5,7), PLUS 0.95 (2,4,6)

1688 Downs 'National Hunt' Novices' Hurdle (4-y-o and up) £2,234 2m 110yds
....(12:30)

SPARKLING SUNSET (Ire) 5-10-12 M A FitzGerald, hld up in tch, second whn mstk 2 out, rdn and chalg when lft clr last, cmftbly..........(6 to 4 fav op 5 to 4 tchd 7 to 4) 1
1309⁵ SQUIRE SILK 4-10-5 (7*) D Fortt, hld up, hdwy appr 3 out, rdn and lft second last, no ch wth wnr.
....(7 to 2 op 6 to 1) 2
753³ THE BUD CLUB (Ire) 5-10-12 N Williamson, trkd ldr frm second, one pace appr 2 out.
....(5 to 1 op 4 to 1 tchd 7 to 2) 3
1126⁹ WORLDLY PROSPECT (USA) 5-10-0 (7*) D Meade, hld up, hdwy 3 out, nvr nr to chal........(100 to 1 op 50 to 1) 4
1309⁶ HALL END LADY (Ire) 5-10-7 B Clifford, al beh.
....(50 to 1 op 20 to 1) 5
METROPOLIS 6-10-12 R Supple, in tch till outpcd frm 6th......................................(9 to 1 op 20 to 1) 6
1442 MEADOW COTTAGE 7-10-9 (3*) P Hide, trkd ldr to second, wknd 5th......................(16 to 1 op 8 to 1 tchd 20 to 1) 7
1442 MY BOOKS ARE BEST (Ire) 4-10-7 Leesa Long, in tch to 5th, tld off......................(100 to 1 op 33 to 1) 8
1542² BILLY BORU 5-11-5 D Gallagher, led till f last.
....(5 to 1 op 3 to 1) f
LUCKY LORENZO 5-10-12 M Richards, beh, lost tch 5th, tld off whn pld up bef 2 out......(50 to 1 op 25 to 1) pu
Dist: 7l, 2l, 12l, 5l, 2l, 5l, 12l. 4m 4.10s. a 13.10s (10 Ran).
SR: 44/37/35/18/13/16/11/-/-/ (Richard Shaw), N J Henderson

1689 Peak Handicap Chase (0-135 5-y-o and up) £2,682 2½m 110yds.........(1:00)

1466* RICHVILLE [118] 7-11-10 N Williamson, hld up, jmpd slwly 6th, wnt second briefly 4 out, led nxt, jumped lft last, sn clr, eased.
....(7 to 4 fav op 5 to 4 tchd 2 to 1 and 9 to 4) 1
860 SCOTONI [109] 7-11-1 D O'Sullivan, led till hdd 3 out, outpcd appr last.....................(3 to 1 op 11 to 4) 2
1407⁴ ZAMIL (USA) [107] 8-10-13 M A FitzGerald, trkd ldr till mstk 9th, rdn appr 3 out, kpt on one pace.
....(2 to 1 op 11 to 10) 3
1466² KISU KALI [96] 6-10-2 M Richards, rcd 3rd, hit 8th, second whn mstk 4 out, wknd aftr nxt.
....(11 to 2 op 5 to 1 tchd 6 to 1) 4
Dist: 3½l, hd, 30l. 5m 25.50s. a 24.50s (4 Ran).
SR: 45/32/30/-/ (Major-Gen R L T Burges) K C Bailey

1690 TJH Group Handicap Hurdle (0-140 4-y-o and up) £3,436 2m 110yds (1:30)

1513* HERE HE COMES [134] 7-11-6 (7*) S Ryan, rcd in 3rd pl, gd hdwy to led 3 out, quickened and pushed clr frm nxt, cmftbly..........(15 to 8 fav op 11 to 8 tchd 7 to 4) 1
1508 WHIPPERS DELIGHT (Ire) [107] 5-9-7 (7*) D Meade, led to 1st, rdn and lost pl 3 out, rallied and styd on to go second r-in..............(20 to 1 op 14 to 1) 2
944¹ BIG MATT (Ire) [135] 5-12-0 M A FitzGerald, hld up, cld on ldrs appr 5th, wnt second approaching 2 out, rdn and wknd r-in..............(5 to 2 op 7 to 4 tchd 11 to 4) 3

KAYTAK (Fr) [109] 6-10-2 N Williamson, outpcd in rear, making hdwy whn jmpd lft 5th, outpaced appr 2 out.
....(7 to 2 op 3 to 1 tchd 4 to 1) 4
1465⁶ MASAI MARA (USA) [112] 5-10-5 J Railton, led 1st till hdd 3 out, sn btn......................(12 to 1 tchd 14 to 1) 5
BUONARROTI [125] 6-11-4 T Grantham, outpcd in rear, hdwy appr 3 out, wknd bef nxt.....(11 to 2 op 9 to 2) 6
Dist: 4l, 2½l, 2½l, 2½l, 2l. 4m 7.40s. a 16.40s (6 Ran).
SR: 26/-/20/-/-/2/ (E Harrington), R Akehurst

1691 Lowndes Lambert December Novices' Chase Grade 2 (5-y-o and up) £9,375 3m.........................(2:00)

1367* MARTOMICK 6-10-13 N Williamson, hld up, making hdwy whn hit tenth, wnt second 5 out, led appr 3 out, pckd on landing and hdd last, led cl hme.
....(6 to 4 op 6 to 4 on tchd Evens) 1
1346² FIVELEIGH FIRST (Ire) 5-10-13 R Supple, hld up in rear, gd hdwy 4 out, led last, rdn and hdd cl .
....(8 to 1 op 7 to 1 tchd 9 to 1) 2
1393 HILLWALK 7-11-0 D Morris, hld up, hit 7th, hdwy 9th, ev ch 3 out, wknd whn hit last.
....(4 to 1 tchd 7 to 2 and 9 to 2) 3
1348⁴ GHIA GNEUIAGH 7-11-0 D Bridgwater, led to 3rd, hit nxt, led 12th till hdd appr 3 out, wknd bef next, eased.
....(11 to 4 tchd 100 to 30) 4
1385⁵ BLACK CHURCH 7-11-0 H Davies, led 3rd to 12th, sn beh, tld off whn pld up bef 3 out......(50 to 1 op 33 to 1) pu
Dist: Nk, 20l, 30l. 6m 24.80s. a 31.80s (5 Ran).
(Richard Shaw), K C Bailey

1692 Wetton Cleaning Summit Junior Hurdle Grade 2 (3-y-o) £6,640 2m 110yds
....(2:35)

1510* ADMIRAL'S WELL (Ire) 10-12 M A FitzGerald, hld up, cld on ldrs 5th, led sn aftr 2 out, blun and wnt rght last, rallied, jst held on...(100 to 30 op 3 to 1 tchd 7 to 2) 1
1473* NAWAR (Fr) 10-12 J Railton, al frnt rnk, led appr 2 out, hdd sn aftr, hrd rdn and hit last, ran on cl hme.
....(5 to 4 fav op 6 to 4 tchd 13 to 8) 2
1166* GRAND APPLAUSE (Ire) 11-2 D Gallagher, al prmnt on outsd, hrd rdn appr 2 out, styd on wl r-in.
....(14 to 1 op 12 to 1 tchd 16 to 1) 3
1032* BURNT IMP (USA) 11-2 J Callaghan, al prmnt, trkd ldr frm 3rd, led 5th, hdd appr 2 out, wknd bef last.
....(5 to 1 op 5 to 1 tchd 13 to 2) 4
1408² HOSTILE WITNESS (Ire) (bl) 10-12 M Richards, beh, gd hdwy 5th, ev ch 2 out, sn wknd.
....(12 to 1 op 14 to 1 tchd 16 to 1) 5
1541* BAGALINO (USA) 11-2 M Perrett, hld up in tch, rdn and wknd aftr 3 out..........(4 to 1 op 7 to 2 tchd 9 to 2) 6
KARAR (Ire) 10-12 H Davies, al beh, lost tch aftr hit 5th.
....(25 to 1 op 14 to 1) 7
1229⁴ TACTICAL TOMMY 10-12 D Bridgwater, not jump wl, made most till hdd 5th, wknd quickly, tld off whn pld up bef last........................(50 to 1 op 25 to 1) pu
Dist: Nk, ¾l, 6l, 8l, 12l, 3½l. 4m 6.90s. a 15.90s (8 Ran).
SR: 16/15/18/15/-/ (A D Spence), R Akehurst

1693 Lingfield Park Perpetual Challenge Trophy Handicap Chase (5-y-o and up) £7,148 3m.....................(3:10)

1050⁴ THE WIDGET MAN [119] 7-11-10 (3*) P Hide, hld up, hdwy 6th, wnt second 3 out, hrd rdn to ld cl hme.
....(9 to 2 op 4 to 1 tchd 5 to 1) 1
1162 AVONBURN (NZ) [118] 9-11-3 M Richards, jmpd wl, rstrained in rear, wnt second tenth, led appr 3 out, rdn and hdd cl hme..........(7 to 1 op 8 to 1 tchd 10 to 1) 2
1543 MERE CLASS [130] 7-11-11 G Bradley, trkd ldrs to tenth, outpcd 5 out, rallied nxt, btn 3rd whn mstk 2 out.
....(6 to 5 on op 5 to 4 on tchd 11 to 10 on) 3
1520* LAKE TEEREEN [123] 8-11-4 T Grantham, led till hdd appr 3 out, jump slwly, sn wknd..........(7 to 2 op 5 to 2) 4
Dist: Nk, 12l, 30l. 6m 26.10s. a 33.10s (4 Ran).
(A Ilsley), J T Gifford

1694 Levy Board Handicap Hurdle (0-130 4-y-o and up) £2,640 2m 3f 110yds
....(3:45)

1492² MANEREE [102] 6-10-0 R Campbell, hld up, al gng wl, trkd ldr frm 6th, led appr 3 out, clr whn hit last.
....(9 to 4 op 11 to 10 tchd 6 to 4) 1
1462⁵ BROUGHTON'S TANGO (Ire) [102] 4-10-0 S Keightley, hld up in rear, rdn and hdwy 3 out, styd on to go second last......................(6 to 1 op 4 to 1 tchd 3 to 1) 2
1396⁷ STORM DRUM [108] 4-10-6 N Williamson, led till hdd appr 3 out, outpcd frm nxt...(13 to 2 op 3 to 1 tchd 7 to 1) 3
YOUR WELL [130] 7-12-0 B Clifford, nvr far away, outpcd frm 2 out....................(25 to 1 op 12 to 1 tchd 14 to 1) 4
RAMBLE (USA) [102] 6-10-0 T Grantham, in tch till wknd appr 2 out..............(7 to 1 op 8 to 1 tchd 10 to 1) 5
1307 ATLAAL [130] 8-12-0 J Railton, prmnt till wknd sn aftr 3 out........................(6 to 1 op 8 to 1 tchd 10 to 1) 6

NUT TREE [102] 8-10-0 D Bridgwater, *trkd ldr to 3rd,*
struggling in rear frm 6th.
.... (25 to 1 op 14 to 1 tchd 33 to 1)   7
Dist: 3l, 8l, 8l, 4l, 3l, 15l. 5m 8.40s. a 34.40s (7 Ran).
(M Tabor), N A Callaghan

NEWTON ABBOT (soft)
Monday December 13th
Going Correction: PLUS 1.78 sec. per fur. (races 1,3,-
5,7), PLUS 1.70 (2,4,6)

1695 Plympton Novices' Hurdle (4-y-o and up) £1,931 2m 1f............. (12:15)

BOLD STROKE 4-11-0 R Dunwoody, *trkd ldrs, led gng wl*
appr 2 out, drvn approaching last, kpt on well.
.... (11 to 10 fav op Evens tchd 6 to 4)   1
1460[3] KEEP ME IN MIND (Ire) 4-11-0 D Skyrme, *in tch, rdn 2 out,*
chlgd last, kpt on same pace.........(8 to 1 op 4 to 1)   2
1460[4] EMPIRE BLUE 10-11-0 M Bosley, *beh, hdwy 5th, rdn frm 3*
out, one pace.....................(7 to 1 op 4 to 1)   3
1542* BOND JNR (Ire) 4-11-6 G Bradley, *in tch, outpcd 3 out,*
drvn and hdwy on rls to chal appr 2 out, sn outpaced.
.... (2 to 1 op 7 to 4 tchd 13 to 8)   4
FENGARI 4-11-0 N Williamson, *beh, steady hdwy 5th,*
pressed ldrs 3 out, wknd 2 out.....(33 to 1 op 12 to 1)   5
1642[8] DAVES DELIGHT 7-10-2 (7") Mr G Shenkin, *led to second,*
styd wth ldr to 5th, wknd aftr 3 out.
.... (33 to 1 op 12 to 1)   6
TENAYESTELIGN 5-10-4 (5") J McCarthy, *beh 4th, hdwy*
5th, wknd aftr 3 out..............(33 to 1 op 14 to 1)   7
BROWN ROBBER 5-11-0 Mr W Henderson, *prmnt, drpd*
rear 4th, nvr dngrs aftr.......... (100 to 1 op 50 to 1)   8
1010 MEDINAS SWAN SONG 5-11-0 G McCourt, *wnt prmnt 3rd,*
led 4th, hdd and wknd quickly appr 2 out.
.... (100 to 1 op 20 to 1)   9
1568 GREEN'S GAME 5-11-0 C Maude, *led second to 4th, wknd*
5th................................ (100 to 1 op 25 to 1)   10
778[5] KRAKATOA 4-10-9 R Greene, *beh, hdwy and jmpd slwly*
5th, no ch whn blun nxt, tld off. (100 to 1 op 20 to 1)   11
1428[9] WHYFOR 5-10-7 (7") Mr N Moore, *chsd ldrs to 5th, wknd*
quickly 3 out.....................(100 to 1 op 25 to 1)   12
SHADOWLAND (Ire) 5-11-0 V Slattery, *hdwy 5th, wknd*
quickly, tld off..................(100 to 1 op 20 to 1)   13
1509 TITIAN MIST 7-10-9 N Mann, *tld off frm 5th.*
.... (100 to 1 op 25 to 1)   14
Dist: 2l, 5l, 5l, hd, 3½l, 12l, 10l, 5l, ½l, dist. 4m 25.30s. a 35.30s (14 Ran).
SR: 36/34/29/30/24/15/3/-/-/   (Mrs David Thompson), M C Pipe

1696 Tattersalls Mares Only Novices' Chase Qualifier (5-y-o and up) £2,762 2m 5f........................(12:45)

1519[6] PRUDENT PEGGY 6-10-10 J Frost, *chsd ldr to 4th, styd*
prmnt till led four out, sn clr, readily.
.... (14 to 1 op 10 to 1)   1
1644[6] HAND OUT 9-10-3 (7") Mr G Hogan, *jmpd slwly second, in*
tch and not fluent 6th, chsd wnr frm 3 out, no imprsn.
.... (8 to 1 op 5 to 1)   2
1276* BARONESS ORKZY 7-11-1 R Greene, *led to 9th, pressing*
ldr whn lft in ld 11th, sn hdd and btn.
.... (7 to 2 op 9 to 4)   3
1524 KATIEM'LU 7-10-3 (7") Mr B Pollock, *tld off frm 9th.*
.... (50 to 1 op 33 to 1)   4
1474[2] THE MRS 7-10-10 S Earle, *took str hold in rear till f 7th.*
.... (9 to 2 op 3 to 1)   f
FANTASY WORLD 7-10-10 E Murphy, *f 1st.*
.... (3 to 1 tchd 7 to 2)   f
1530 WILLOW GALE 6-10-10 B Powell, *chsd ldr frm 4th, led 9th, still*
slight ld whn bumped and f 11th. (5 to 2 fav op 7 to 4)   f
Dist: 12l, 25l, 30l. 5m 44.90s. a 44.90s (7 Ran).
(Mrs J McCormack), R G Frost

1697 South-West Racecourses Series Amateur Riders' Hurdle Championship Final Handicap (0-125 4-y-o and up) £2,200 2¾m.................. (1:15)

1592* CELCIUS [97] (bl) 9-9-9 (7",5ex) Mr N Moore, *hld up,*
smooth hdwy to chal 2 out, sn led, cmftbly.
.... (6 to 4 on tchd 5 to 4 on)   1
1462 AMPHIGORY [95] (bl) 5-9-7 (7") Miss S Cobden, *dsptd moderate pace to 3rd, led 5th, hdd appr 7th, led ag'n aftr 3 out, headed sn after 2 out, not quicken.*
.... (12 to 1 op 6 to 1 tchd 14 to 1)   2
1643 FAR TOO LOUD [105] 6-10-3 (7") Mr J Culloty, *dsptd moderate pace to 3rd, styd in tch, outpcd 7th, gd hdwy appr 2 out, sn outpaced...............*(11 to 2 op 3 to 1)   3
DECIDED (Can) [104] 10-9-12 (7") Miss P Jones, *set modest pace to 3rd, led ag'n appr 7th, hdd aftr 3 out, sn btn.*
.... (10 to 1 op 5 to 1 tchd 12 to 1)   4
1521[6] FREEMANTLE [95] 8-9-13[6] (7") Mr G Hogan, *led 3rd to 5th, styd prmnt till wknd 3 out.*
.... (9 to 2 op 5 to 2 tchd 5 to 1)   5
Dist: 2l, 5l, 6l, 15l. 6m 7.90s. a 68.90s (5 Ran).

(Martin Pipe Racing Club), M C Pipe

1698 Tom Holt And Reality Handicap Chase (5-y-o and up) £3,380 2m 5f..... (1:45)

1507[2] THATCHER ROCK (NZ) [115] 8-10-7 G Bradley, *rcd in 3rd till hdwy to chase ldr 11th, slight ld 2 out, rdn appr last, all out..............*(Evens fav op 11 to 10 on)   1
1282[2] L'UOMO PIU [108] 9-10-0 N Williamson, *rcd in 4th till rapid hdwy tenth, led 11th, hdd 2 out, rallied to chal last, no extr cl hme.............*(10 to 1 op 8 to 1)   2
1436[2] GUIBURN'S NEPHEW [132] 11-11-10 C Maude, *led till mstk and hdd 11th, sn outpcd.......* (6 to 4 op 5 to 4)   3
1275[4] HOLY FOLEY [108] 11-9-7 (7") Guy Lewis, *chsd ldr, reminders 6th, rdn 9th, wknd nxt, tld off whn pld up bef 2 out.............*(12 to 1 op 10 to 1 tchd 14 to 1)   pu
Dist: Hd, 8l. 5m 40.60s. a 40.60s (4 Ran).
SR: 30/23/39/-/   (Miss Gina Hunter), P F Nicholls

1699 Parracombe Selling Handicap Hurdle (4,5,6-y-o) £1,813 2m 1f........ (2:15)

1519 MILDRED SOPHIA [60] 6-9-7 (7") Miss S Mitchell, *beh, hdwy 5th, sn outpcd, plenty to do aftr 3 out, styd on frm 2 out, led soon after last, ran on wl.*
.... (9 to 1 op 10 to 1 tchd 6 to 4)   1
JOKERS PATCH [64] 6-10-4 N Mann, *beh, rdn appr 5th, chlgd 3 out, led last, sn hdd and one pace.*
.... (9 to 1 op 12 to 1 tchd 14 to 1)   2
1562[3] BAYBEEJAY [75] 6-11-1 G McCourt, *chsd ldrs, rdn and wknd 3 out, styd on ag'n frm 2 out. ....*(4 to 1 co-
fav op 3 to 1 tchd 9 to 2)   3
1506[2] LOXLEY RANGE (Ire) [66] 5-9-13 (7") N Juckes, *hdwy 5th, wknd appr 2 out..................*(4 to 1 co-
fav op 4 to 1 tchd 9 to 2)   4
1546[4] BOOGIE BOPPER (Ire) [88] (bl) 4-12-0 R Dunwoody, *chsd ldrs till wknd quickly 5th...........*(11 to 2 op 3 to 1)   5
1506[4] PEACOCK FEATHER [74] 5-11-0 N Williamson, *led till hdd 2 out, 3rd and hld whn f last........*(4 to 1 co-
fav op 5 to 1 tchd 11 to 2)   f
1325[8] BEAUFAN [68] 6-10-8 Gary Lyons, *chsd ldrs, rdn to ld 2 out, hdd last, 3rd and hld whn veered rght and uns rdr r-in.................*(8 to 1 op 12 to 1 tchd 14 to 1)   ur
1259[5] GREAT IMPOSTOR [70] (bl) 5-10-10 I Lawrence, *prmnt, rdn appr 5th, sn wknd, tld off whn pld up bef 2 out.*
.... (9 to 1 op 5 to 1 tchd 10 to 1)   pu
(N R Mitchell), N R Mitchell

1700 Torpoint Novices' Chase (5-y-o and up) £3,103 3¼m 110yds........(2:45)

1503[3] DON'T LIGHT UP (v) 7-11-5 G Bradley, *pressed ldr frm 6th, slight ld 2 out, hrd drvn r-in, jst hld on.*
.... (5 to 4 on op 6 to 4 on)   1
1537 LUCKY LANE (bl) 9-11-5 C Maude, *led till narrowly hdd 2 out, styd pressing wnr, hrd rdn r-in, jst fld.*
.... (3 to 1 op 7 to 4)   2
1644[2] PUNCHBAG (USA) 7-11-0 B Powell, *prmnt, chlgd 12th, outpcd frm 16th.................*(5 to 1 op 6 to 1)   3
1086 SHOREHAM LADY 8-10-9 Lorna Vincent, *jmpd slwly 1st and second and beh, hit 9th, nvr dngrs.*
.... (33 to 1 op 20 to 1)   4
1527 KEMMY DARLING 6-10-9 M Ahern, *f second.*
.... (9 to 1 op 7 to 1)   f
1411[5] JUDYS LINE 9-10-4 (5") D Salter, *al beh, tld off whn pld up bef 2 out............*(11 to 1 op 10 to 1 tchd 12 to 1)   pu
Dist: ¾l, 30l, 15l. 7m 28.60s. a 68.60s (6 Ran).
(Geoffrey Solman), P F Nicholls

1701 Plymouth Handicap Hurdle (0-120 4-y-o and up) £2,575 2m 1f........(3:15)

1521[4] NORTHERN SADDLER [100] 6-10-8 G McCourt, *made all, drvn and styd on frm 3 out....*(7 to 4 fav tchd 9 to 4)   1
300[6] NOVA SPIRIT [92] 5-10-0 B Powell, *chsd wnr frm 5th, no imprsn appr 2 out..........*(5 to 1 op 7 to 2)   2
1502[4] MADAM PICASSO (Ire) [92] 4-9-7 (7") Miss S Mitchell, *mid-div, outpcd 5th, styd on frm 3 out, no imprsn aftr nxt.*
.... (7 to 1 op 8 to 1 tchd 10 to 1)   3
1521 HAVE A PARTY [92] 6-10-0 N Mann, *chsd wnr to 5th, one pace frm 3 out.................*(33 to 1 op 20 to 1)   4
1276[5] CORRIN HILL [120] 6-12-0 R Dunwoody, *hld up in rear, nvr dngrs.............*(13 to 2 op 5 to 1 tchd 7 to 1)   5
VILLA RECOS [116] 8-11-10 N Williamson, *chsd ldrs to 5th, sn wknd................*(12 to 1 op 8 to 1)   6
COMEDY RIVER [92] 6-10-0 V Slattery, *hld up, hdwy 5th, sn wknd.....................*(9 to 1 op 5 to 1)   7
1508[6] WHEELER'S WONDER (Ire) [103] 4-10-4 (7") Mr J L Llewellyn, *chsd ldrs to 5th, tld off whn pld up bef 2 out.*
.... (5 to 1 op 3 to 1 tchd 10 to 1)   pu
Dist: 12l, 4l, 2½l, 10l, 15l, 15l. 4m 28.50s. a 38.50s (8 Ran).
(Richard J Evans), R J Hodges

WARWICK (soft)
Monday December 13th

233

NATIONAL HUNT RESULTS 1993-94

Going Correction: PLUS 0.80 sec. per fur. (races 1,2,-4,6,7), PLUS 0.75 (3,5)

1702 Youngsters Conditional Jockeys' Novices' Selling Hurdle (3 & 4-y-o) £1,473 2m............................(12:30)

497* SOUTHAMPTON 3-10-2 (7") N Collum, *hld up, gd hdwy to chase ldr frm 5th, led 2 out, sn clr...*(6 to 1 op 4 to 1) 1
1526³ FORGETFUL 4-10-9 (3") P McLoughlin, *trkd ldr, led appr 4th, hdd 2 out, fnshd tired....................*(6 to 1) 2
1522⁵ BOLD STAR 3-10-5 S Wynne, *hld up in rear, hdwy appr 4th, nvr nrr........*(7 to 1 op 8 to 1 tchd 9 to 1) 3
GALACTIC FURY 3-10-11 (5") M Stevens, *beh till hdwy 4th, styd on, nvr nrr.........*(8 to 1 op 6 to 1 tchd 10 to 1) 4
1404⁵ GROGFRYN 3-10-4 R Farrant, *chsd ldrs, wnt second briefly 4th, wknd aftr nxt..........*(7 to 1 tchd 8 to 1) 5
1410⁵ LA POSADA 3-9-11² (5") P Moore, *beh, some hdwy 4th, nvr nr to chal.....................*(12 to 1 op 10 to 1) 6
1416⁶ MY SISTER LUCY 3-9-13 (5") G McGrath, *prmnt till wknd appr 4th..........................*(12 to 1) 7
OOZLEM (Ire) (bl) 4-11-3 M Hourigan, *al beh.* ....(12 to 1 op 14 to 1) 8
JOSEPH'S WINE (Ire) 4-11-3 H Bastiman, *al beh.* (20 to 1) 9
724 SOLAR KNIGHT 3-10-0 W Marston, *chsd ldrs till wknd appr 4th, tld off.....................*(12 to 1) 10
1490 LILIAN MAY GREEN 4-10-5 (7") M Keighley, *prmnt till wknd aftr 3rd, tld off.....................*(33 to 1) 11
1532* TOUCH SILVER 3-10-7³ (5") M Appleby, *mstks 1st 2, wl in rear till hdwy appr 4th, btn whn sddl slpd and uns rdr approaching two out........*(11 to 2 fav op 4 to 1) ur
1640 ADMIRED (bl) 3-10-2 D Matthews, *led till hdd appr 4th, drpd out quickly. tld off whn pld up bef 2 out.* (33 to 1) pu
Dist: 12l, 8l, sht-hd, 12l, 2l, 15l, 2½l, 4l, dist, dist. 3m 58.50s (13 Ran).
SR: 24/15/-/-/-/-/ (Highflyers), G B Balding

1703 Ettington Handicap Hurdle (0-135 4-y-o and up) £3,742 2½m 110yds... (1:00)

1462³ FAIR BROTHER [104] 7-9-13² (3") R Davis, *hld up in rear, hdwy appr 7th, led approaching 2 out, hit last, all out.* ....(5 to 2 fav op 3 to 1 tchd 4 to 1) 1
1492⁷ MIZYAN (Ire) [120] 5-11-2 S Keightley, *hld up in tch, hdwy 3 out, mstk nxt, swtchd lft and ev ch last, hng left run in, no extr cl hme........*(5 to 1 op 8 to 1 tchd 11 to 2) 2
900⁶ BALLY CLOVER [128] 6-11-10 M A FitzGerald, *al frnt rnk, led 4 out, hdd appr 2 out, one pace.* ....(9 to 1 op 6 to 1 tchd 10 to 1) 3
1561 SENDAI [126] 7-11-8 D Murphy, *led second till hdd 4 out, one pace appr 2 out..........................*(10 to 1) 4
SUPER MALT (Ire) [113] 5-10-9 A Maguire, *trkd ldrs, rdn 3 out, one pace aftr.......*(7 to 1 op 5 to 1 tchd 8 to 1) 5
1417 SUPER SPELL [113] 7-10-9 J Osborne, *led to second, prmnt till one pace appr 2 out....*(12 to 1 op 6 to 1) 6
1559⁹ SUNSET AND VINE [120] 6-11-2 H Davies, *hld up in tch, ev ch appr 2 out, wknd approaching last.* ....(7 to 2 op 3 to 1) 7
1474 MR TAYLOR [104] 8-10-0 V Smith, *beh till hdwy appr 7th, lost tch nxt, tld off.....................*(50 to 1) 8
NOBLE YEOMAN [104] 9-9-11 (3") D Meredith, *beh, outpcd frm 7th, tld off whn pld up bef last.*(16 to 1 op 10 to 1) pu
Dist: ¾l, 8l, hd, ¾l, 1½l, nk, dist. 5m 14.70s. a 27.20s (9 Ran).
(Mrs S Watts), G B Balding

1704 Budbrooke Novices' Chase (5-y-o and up) £3,678 3¼m...............(1:30)

1491* MAILCOM 7-11-4 J Osborne, *led frm 7th, wth ldr whn hit 5 out, led nxt, drawing clr when blun last.* ....(6 to 5 on op 6 to 4 on) 1
1563⁴ FLORIDA SKY 6-11-0 R Supple, *led 7th to 4 out, no extr frm 2 out..........*(7 to 2 op 9 to 2 tchd 100 to 30) 2
1405² LOBRIC 8-11-0 A Maguire, *wl beh 9th, some hdwy to go 3rd 7 out, no ch wth 1st 2.............*(8 to 1 op 7 to 1) 3
1491³ ROYAL SQUARE (Can) 7-11-0 M Perrett, *in tch whn hit tenth, rdn to go 3rd 13th, lost touch frm nxt, tld off.* ....(7 to 1 op 6 to 1) 4
WAYWARD SAILOR 7-11-0 W Marston, *in tch till wknd 11th, tld off whn pld up bef 6 out............*(50 to 1) pu
JUST A SECOND 8-10-9 M A FitzGerald, *al beh, lost tch hfwy, tld off whn pld up bef 5 out.*(40 to 1 op 33 to 1) pu
1420 ONLY ME 5-11-0 M Dwyer, *prmnt to tenth, sn rdn and beh, tld off whn pld up bef 7 out.*.....................................(8 to 1 op 7 to 1 tchd 9 to 1) pu
Dist: 15l, dist, 4l. 6m 47.50s. a 33.50s (7 Ran).
(Mailcom Plc), Mrs J Pitman

1705 Hampton Juvenile Novices' Hurdle (3-y-o) £1,473 2m...............(2:00)

1510⁹ WOLLBOLL 10-12 Richard Guest, *mid-div, hdwy 5th, rdn 2 out, led r-in...........................*(25 to 1) 1
PHROSE 10-12 D O'Sullivan, *al prmnt, led appr 2 out, rdn and hdd r-in..................*(12 to 1 op 8 to 1) 2
LODESTONE LAD (Ire) 10-9 (3") D Meredith, *nvr far away, styd on frm 2 out..........................*(33 to 1) 3

NORTHERN JUDY (Ire) 10-4 (3") S Wynne, *prmnt whn hit 4th and lost pl, rallied appr 2 out, one pace...* (33 to 1) 4
1473⁹ LAMBAST 10-7 W Marston, *hld up, hdwy 5th, nvr nr to chal.....................*(12 to 1 op 5 to 1) 5
SECRET FORMULA 10-9 (3") R Davis, *hld up, hdwy appr 4th, one pace frm 2 out...........*(20 to 1 op 16 to 1) 6
1410² POCONO KNIGHT 10-12 G Upton, *prmnt, led 3 out, sn hdd and wknd...................*(12 to 1 op 10 to 1) 7
1517² BUGLET 11-0 D Murphy, *led till hdd appr 5th, rdn and sn btn......*(7 to 4 fav op 2 to 1 tchd 5 to 2 and 3 to 1) 8
1473⁸ HUBERT 10-12 M A FitzGerald, *al towards rear.* 9
LEEWA (Ire) 10-12 M Richards, *prmnt till rdn 3 out, sn btn.* ....(12 to 1 op 8 to 1) 10
LANZAMAR 10-7 J Railton, *al beh....*(20 to 1 op 16 to 1) 11
1410⁸ HOHNE GARRISON 10-5 (7") P McLoughlin, *al rear.* ....(33 to 1) 12
1350⁶ THE SECRET SEVEN 10-7 B Clifford, *in tch to 3th, sn rear.* ....(20 to 1) 13
CHAIRMANS CHOICE 10-12 T Jarvis, *al beh, tld off whn f last, rmntd...........*(50 to 1 op 33 to 1) 14
1464⁴ MORAN BRIG (bl) 10-12 S Hodgson, *prmnt, led appr 5th, hdd nxt, rdn and hld whn f 2 out.*
RUMPUS (Ire) 10-7 A Maguire, *chsd ldrs till blun and uns rdr 5th...............*(7 to 2 op 2 to 1 tchd 4 to 1) ur
1261 CATEMPO (Ire) 10-12 H Davies, *beh whn blun and uns rdr 4th.....................*(50 to 1 op 33 to 1) ur
1473 WILBURY WONDER 10-7 D Bridgwater, *al beh, tld off whn pld up bef 2 out........*(50 to 1 op 33 to 1) pu
POSSOM PICKER 10-12 S Burrough, *prmnt to 3rd, beh whn pld up bef 2 out...........*(50 to 1 op 33 to 1) pu
Dist: 1½l, 2l, 6l, 10l, nk, 2½l, 5l, 6l, ½l, sht-hd. 4m 6.70s. a 26.70s (19 Ran).
(Mike Weaver), P J Makin

1706 Stoneleigh Handicap Chase (0-135 5-y-o and up) £4,146 2½m 110yds ....(2:30)

1396⁴ MENEBUCK [110] 7-10-4 D Murphy, *wtd wth, hdwy 8th, wnt second 7 out, jnd ldr 2 out, led sn aftr last, pushed out.......*(7 to 2 tchd 4 to 1) 1
1507³ BISHOPS ISLAND [124] 7-11-4 A Maguire, *led 1st, hrd rdn 2 out, hdd sn aftr last, no extr.* ....(7 to 4 fav tchd 2 to 1 and 13 to 8) 2
1419³ SNITTON LANE [115] 7-10-9 M A FitzGerald, *hld up, hdwy to go 3rd 7 out, no ch wth 1st 2.* ....(9 to 2 op 4 to 1 tchd 5 to 1) 3
1436⁴ MR ENTERTAINER [126] 10-11-6 C Llewellyn, *hit second, in tch till lost pl 9th, nvr on terms aftr.* (6 to 1 tchd 4 to 1) 4
1307³ WELL WRAPPED [134] 9-12-0 J Osborne, *in tch till wknd 7 out.................................*(9 to 2 op 3 to 1) 5
1197 WARNER'S END [106] (bl) 12-10-0 R Bellamy, *led to 1st, wknd appr 7 out, tld off..........*(66 to 1 op 50 to 1) 6
Dist: 2½l, dist, 20l, ¾l, dist. 5m 14.50s. a 19.50s (6 Ran).
SR: 34/45/-/ (Lady Sarah Clutton), Lady Herries

1707 Hoechst Panacur EBF Mares 'National Hunt' Novices' Hurdle Qualifier (4-y-o and up) £2,679 2½m 110yds.....(3:00)

1594² WELSH LUSTRE (Ire) 4-10-12 A Maguire, *hld up in mid-div, steady hdwy frm 6th, led appr 2 out, rdn clr.* ....(6 to 4 fav op 7 to 4 tchd 2 to 1 and 9 to 4) 1
1524² GRAY'S ELLERGY 7-11-5 P Holley, *nvr far away, wnt second appr 7th, led briefly on bend aftr 3 out, kpt on one pace........*(5 to 2 op 7 to 4 tchd 11 to 4) 2
1167⁵ GOSPEL (Ire) 4-10-12 C Llewellyn, *mid-div, hit 3rd, hdwy frm 3 out, styd on, nvr nrr.........*(14 to 1 op 10 to 1) 3
1210² DOLLY OATS 7-10-12 D Gallagher, *led till hdd sn aftr 3 out, one pace........*(5 to 1 op 8 to 1 tchd 10 to 1) 4
BLACK H'PENNY 5-10-12 T Grantham, *hld up, hdwy 7th, wknd appr 2 out............*(33 to 1 op 25 to 1) 5
1027² SOLO GIRL (Ire) 5-10-12 G Upton, *in rear till hdwy 7th, nvr nr to chal...................*(20 to 1 op 16 to 1) 6
DAWN CALL 6-10-5 (7") Mr N Bradley, *beh till hdwy 4 out, nvr nr to chal.....................*(20 to 1 op 33 to 1) 7
1386⁵ WYJUME (Ire) 4-10-12 D Murphy, *nvr on terms.* ....(12 to 1 op 6 to 1) 8
1027⁵ HOT 'N ROSIE 4-10-12 S McNeill, *slwly away, mstks in rear, al beh......................*(16 to 1 op 10 to 1) 9
1536 NO DEBT 5-10-12 M Dwyer, *prmnt till wknd 4 out.* ....(20 to 1) 10
DEBBIGENE 7-10-12 R Supple, *al beh..........*(50 to 1) 11
864⁸ MISS NOSEY OATS 5-10-12 M A FitzGerald, *chsd ldrs till wknd 7th......................*(16 to 1 op 14 to 1) 12
1468⁴ JANET SCIBS 7-10-12 W McFarland, *al beh, tld off.* ....(50 to 1 op 33 to 1) 13
MANDY LOUISE 5-10-12 T Jarvis, *prmnt till wknd aftr 6th, ran out nxt........................*(33 to 1) ro
ESSEN AITCH 4-10-12 Richard Guest, *beh, rdn appr 7th, pld up bef 3 out.....................*(50 to 1) pu
POP FESTIVAL 4-10-12 W Marston, *prmnt to 6th, beh whn pld up bef nxt.....................*(50 to 1) pu
1129⁴ SKI LADY 5-10-12 B Storey, *al beh, tld off whn pld up bef 4 out...................*(20 to 1 op 16 to 1) pu
Dist: 6l, 10l, 5l, 8l, 3l, 4l, 8l, 3l, 10l, 10l. 5m 17.90s. a 30.40s (17 Ran).

234

1708 Temple Grafton Novices' Handicap Hurdle (0-100 4-y-o and up) £1,793 2m
................................(3:30)

1526* PROJECT'S MATE [81] 6-10-11 (7*) P McLoughlin, *nvr far
away, wnt second appr 4th, led 3 out, hdd nxt, rallied
to ld ag'n r-in.
....................(15 to 2 op 7 to 1 tchd 6 to 1 and 8 to 1) 1
1173 ALTISHAR (Ire) [68] 5-10-5 P Holley, *hld up in rear, hdwy 3
out, led last, sn hdd, kpt on*........ (10 to 1 op 6 to 1) 2
1502³ SWIFT ROMANCE (Ire) [82] 5-11-5 A Maguire, *hld up in
rear, hdwy 4th, ev ch 2 out, rdn and no imprsn r-in.*
...................(5 to 2 fav tchd 3 to 1 and 7 to 2) 3
1070⁵ STERLING BUCK (USA) [72] 6-10-9 W McFarland, *al prmnt,
ev ch appr 2 out, kpt on one pace.* (14 to 1 op 10 to 1) 4
1542 UNEXIS [65] 8-9-9 (7*) Chris Webb, *wl beh till gd hdwy frm
3 out, ran on, nvr nrr*......................(33 to 1) 5
1536 VICAR OF BRAY [87] 6-11-10 S Hodgson, *mid-div, hdwy
4th, one pace frm 2 out.* (8 to 1 op 5 to 1 tchd 10 to 1) 6
1589² SOLO CORNET [65] 8-10-2 W Humphreys, *hld up in rear,
hdwy 5th, led 2 out, rdn and hdd last, wknd r-in.*
...................................(7 to 2 op 9 to 2) 7
1415³ IN THE GAME (Ire) [71] 4-10-8 S McNeill, *chsd ldrs till
wknd sn aftr 3 out*.................(11 to 2 op 6 to 1) 8
ORTON HOUSE [70] 6-10-7 B Storey, *led till hdd 3 out,
wknd quickly*.........(8 to 1 tchd 7 to 1 and 10 to 1) 9
454* RED INK [78] 4-10-8 (7*) W Walsh, *al beh.*
....................................(10 to 1 op 6 to 1) 10
ARTIC MISSILE [65] 6-10-2 A Stokell, *prmnt whn mstk
3rd, outpcd frm nxt*.............. (50 to 1 op 33 to 1) 11
ODYSSEUS [71] 7-10-8¹ M A FitzGerald, *hld up, making
hdwy whn f 3 out*.................(33 to 1 op 16 to 1) f
LETTS GREEN (Ire) [65] 5-10-2 D Morris, *prmnt to 3rd, tld
off whn pld up bef last*......................(33 to 1) pu
Dist: ¾l, 1½l, 1l, ¾l, 1½l, 1l, 12l, nk, 6l, 7l. 4m 9.40s. a 29.40s (13 Ran).
(R L Brown), R L Brown

FOLKESTONE (soft (races 1,2,3,7), good to soft (4,5,6))
Tuesday December 14th
Going Correction: PLUS 0.80 sec. per fur. (races 1,2,-3,7), PLUS 0.75 (4,5,6)

1709 Levy Board Handicap Hurdle (0-125 4-y-o and up) £2,238 2m 1f 110yds
................................(12:15)

1389³ TOP WAVE [105] 5-11-10 M A FitzGerald, *trkd ldrs, led
betw last 2, sn clr, unchlgd*.... (2 to 1 jt-fav op Evens) 1
1395³ SOLEIL DANCER (Ire) [101] 5-11-6 Peter Hobbs, *keen hold,
trkd ldrs, outpcd and not clr run appr last, styd on
ag'n r-in*........... (2 to 1 jt-fav op 6 to 4 tchd 5 to 2) 2
1513⁷ MY SENOR [95] 4-11-0 R Dunwoody, *led aftr second, rdn
and hdd betw last 2, sn btn.*
...............(14 to 1 op 10 to 1 tchd 16 to 1) 3
NORDANSK [90] 4-10-9 A Maguire, *hld up in tch, effrt and
rdn to chase wnr appr last, no imprsn, wknd r-in.*
.............(7 to 1 op 5 to 1) pu
JALINGO [104] 6-11-9 Richard Guest, *led till aftr second,
pressed ldr till wknd rpdly after 2 out, pld up bef last.*
.........(7 to 2 op 8 to 1 tchd 3 to 1) pu
Dist: 15l, 1l, 1½l. 4m 22.50s. a 25.50s (5 Ran).
(A K Collins), N J Henderson

1710 Stanford Juvenile Novices' Hurdle (3-y-o) £1,475 2m 1f 110yds......(12:45)

1504² PONDERING (v) 11-5 R Dunwoody, *trkd ldrs, rdn betw last
2, led sn aftr last, ran on strly.*
.. (11 to 8 on op 5 to 4 on tchd 5 to 4 and 6 to 4 on) 1
1464 CHIEF'S SONG 10-12 H Davies, *wtd wth, prog 4th, led
betw last 2, hdd aftr last, unbl to quicken.*
....................(9 to 4 op 3 to 1 tchd 7 to 2) 2
MUHTASHIM (Ire) 10-12 A Maguire, *mid-div, prog aftr 5th,
ev ch betw last 2, wknd appr last.*
.............................(20 to 1 tchd 25 to 1) 3
1244 ANY MINUTE NOW (Ire) 10-12 D Bridgwater, *led 3rd till rdn
and hdd betw last 2, wknd*....... (50 to 1 op 20 to 1) 4
SILVER STANDARD 10-12 B Powell, *chsd ldg grp, outpcd
aftr 5th, kpt on appr last*...........(25 to 1 op 10 to 1) 5
1510³ RUNAWAY PETE (USA) (bl) 10-12 J Osborne, *prmnt till
wknd betw last 2*........(6 to 1 op 5 to 1 tchd 7 to 1) 6
1510⁶ SUMMER WIND (Ire) 10-7 P Holley, *led to 3rd, wkng whn
mstk 3 out*...............(12 to 1 op 5 to 1 tchd 14 to 1) 7
1464² HERETICAL MISS 10-7 D Gallagher, *hld up beh, nvr plcd
to chal*.........................(5 to 1 op 14 to 1) 8
SMUGGLER'S POINT (USA) 10-12 D O'Sullivan, *hld up beh,
nvr nr to chal*........(25 to 1 op 8 to 1 tchd 33 to 1) 9
1229⁵ ONE MORE POUND 10-12 D Murphy, *prmnt till rdn and
wknd aftr 4th*.................(25 to 1 tchd 33 to 1) 10
TOP PET (Ire) 10-12 G McCourt, *hld up, prog to chase ldg
grp 2 out, wknd rpdly.*
....................(25 to 1 op 10 to 1 tchd 33 to 1) 11

1711 Sellindge Handicap Hurdle (0-110 4-y-o and up) £2,532 2¾m 110yds... (1:15)

1396⁹ HAPPY HORSE (NZ) [92] 6-10-13 A Tory, *keen hold, trkd
ldrs, led appr last, sn clr, easily*... (10 to 1 op 8 to 1) 1
1462 BUCKINGHAM GATE [95] 7-11-2 R Dunwoody, *led to 5th,
outpcd 3 out, ran on ag'n appr last, no ch wth wnr.*
....(14 to 1 op 12 to 1) 2
BRIGHTLING BOY [92] 8-10-13 Peter Hobbs, *mid-div,
pushed alng 7th, prog nxt, outpcd 2 out, styd on to
chase wnr appr last, one pace*....(12 to 1 op 20 to 1) 3
845³ PRIZE MATCH [91] 4-10-12 R Supple, *hld up, prog 3 out,
cld on ldrs betw last 2, sn btn.*
...................(4 to 1 fav op 5 to 1 tchd 11 to 2) 4
1474⁴ CHEEKY FOX [88] (bl) 7-10-9 M Bosley, *prmnt, led 7th to 3
out, rdn and ev ch appr last, wknd.* (5 to 1 op 10 to 1) 5
1057 AL SAHIL (USA) [90] (bl) 8-10-11 N Williamson, *nvr nrr.*
.................................(16 to 1 op 10 to 1 tchd 9 to 1) 6
1601⁵ SAKIL (Ire) [80] 5-10-0⁴ D'A Dicken, *mid-div, no prog frm
3 out*..................(12 to 1 op 14 to 1 tchd 16 to 1) 7
750⁶ DONT TELL THE WIFE [100] 7-11-7 D Murphy, *hld up beh,
prog 3 out, cld on ldrs betw last 2, sn wknd.*
......................................(8 to 1 op 6 to 1) 8
1474 RELTIC [79] 6-10-0 W Marston, *prmnt, led 5th to 7th and 3
out till appr last, wknd rpdly.*
.................(15 to 2 op 7 to 1 tchd 8 to 1) 9
646 KNIGHTON COOMBE (NZ) [92] 7-10-13 I Shoemark, *mid-div, wknd aftr 8th*.......................(33 to 1) 10
1462 MARCH ABOVE [92] (bl) 7-10-6 (7*) M Stevens, *prmnt till
rdn and wknd 8th.*........................(33 to 1) 11
1533 CARFAX [95] 8-11-2 M Hoad, *hld up rear, lost tch aftr 8th,
sn beh*..................(10 to 1 op 8 to 1 tchd 12 to 1) 12
1627⁶ STYLISH GENT [79] 6-10-0 I Lawrence, *al beh, virtually
pld up r-in*.........(16 to 1 op 10 to 1 tchd 20 to 1) pu
1533 VAIGLY BLAZED [79] 9-10-0 B Clifford, *al beh, lost tch 8th,
tld off whn pld up bef 2 out*....(50 to 1 tchd 100 to 1) pu
1187³ SPARKLER GEBE [90] (bl) 7-10-11 D O'Sullivan, *prmnt,
mstk 7th, wknd nxt, wl beh whn pld up bef last.*
.............(14 to 1 op 10 to 1 tchd 16 to 1) pu
TROPICAL ACE [80] 6-10-1 J Osborne, *last frm 4th, tld off
from 7th pld up bef 3 out*.................(20 to 1) pu
1562* ALICE'S MIRROR [87] (v) 4-10-8 W McFarland, *hld up, prog
6th, rdn and wknd 3 out, wl beh whn pld up bef last.*
.........(20 to 1) pu
Dist: 6l, 5l, 7l, 6l, 4l, 1l, 12l, 4l, 1½l, 2l. 5m 43.50s. a 29.50s (17 Ran).
(Major Ian Manning), Mrs J Renfree-Barons

1712 Folkestone Novices' Chase (Div I) (5-y-o and up) £2,134 2m 5f.......(1:45)

1469* CANOSCAN 8-11-7 E Murphy, *cl up, rdn to chase ldr 3
out, led and lft clr last...* (6 to 5 op Evens tchd 5 to 4) 1
STAR ACTOR 7-11-2 R Dunwoody, *jmpd lft and not fluent, led to 9th, btn aftr 3 out, left second last.*
.............(13 to 2 op 5 to 1 tchd 7 to 1) 2
1493⁸ MIDDAY SHOW (USA) (bl) 6-11-2 A Maguire, *keen hold,
prmnt to 7th, no ch whn hmpd 3 out, lft poor 3rd last.*
.............(33 to 1 op 16 to 1 tchd 50 to 1) 3
1396 FLUTTER MONEY 9-11-2 G Upton, *chsd ldrs, mstk 8th,
4th and no ch whn f 3 out*........(10 to 1 op 33 to 1) f
1393 FLYING FINISH 8-11-2 J Akehurst, *al beh, tld off whn f 3
out*........(66 to 1 op 20 to 1 tchd 100 to 1) f
1417⁴ JUMBEAU 8-11-9 (3*) P Hide, *trkd ldrs, led 9th till hdd
and f last*.........(10 to 1 fav op Evens tchd 5 to 4) f
1511 SALVAGER 9-11-2 R Rowell, *mstks, in tch till wknd 7th,
tld off and pld up bef 11th*........(100 to 1 op 33 to 1) pu
1493 DOVEHILL 7-11-2 Mr P Bull, *al beh, tld off and pld up bef
3 out*..................(100 to 1 op 33 to 1) pu
Dist: 12l, dist. 5m 31.10s. a 21.10s (8 Ran).
SR: 39/22/-/-/-/ (Nigel Clutton), Lady Herries

1713 Heathfield Handicap Chase (0-130 5-y-o and up) £3,590 3¼m......... (2:15)

1507⁴ CATCH THE CROSS [125] (bl) 7-12-0 R Dunwoody, *hld up
in tch, trkd ldr 2 out, led last, ran on wl.*
.............................(5 to 1 op 3 to 1) 1
1540³ ANNIO CHILONE [118] 7-11-4 (3*) P Hide, *led till last, unbl
to quicken*.................(9 to 4 on op 5 to 4) 2
1520² GHOFAR [123] (bl) 10-11-12 P Holley, *trkd ldr till 2 out, hrd
rdn and found nil*....................(5 to 1 op 6 to 1) 3
921⁶ SAM SHORROCK [97] (bl) 11-10-0 D Bridgwater, *lost tch
aftr mstk 8th, sn tld off.*
...............(14 to 1 op 10 to 1 tchd 33 to 1) 4
1467² THE GOLFING CURATE [97] 8-10-0 A Maguire, *mstks 1st
and second, blun 3rd and pld up.*
..............(9 to 1 op 12 to 1 tchd 8 to 1) pu

1464⁹ ORCHESTON 10-4 (3*) P Hide, *mid-div till wknd aftr 4th,
sn wl beh*........................(50 to 1 op 25 to 1) 12
JULY BRIDE 10-7 J Akehurst, *al beh, tld off and pld up bef
last*.............(50 to 1 op 33 to 1 tchd 100 to 1) pu
1464 SMART DAISY 10-7 Richard Guest, *jmpd badly, beh frm
4th, pld up bef 2 out.*
....................(50 to 1 op 33 to 1 tchd 100 to 1) pu
Dist: 6l, 20l, 4l, 6l, ¾l, 6l, 6l, ½l, 10l, 25l. 4m 16.00s. a 19.00s (14 Ran).
SR: 41/28/8/4/-/-/ (M C Pipe), M C Pipe

235

Dist: 2½l, 10l, dist. 7m 1.10s. a 49.10s (5 Ran).

(D A Beswick), M C Pipe

1714 Folkestone Novices' Chase (Div II) (5-y-o and up) £2,115 2m 5f. . . . .(2:45)

1491⁷ GALLANT EFFORT (Ire) 5-11-2 H Davies, *set slow pace to 5th, led ag'n 8th, quickened 11th, drvn clr appr 2 out, unchlgd.* . . . .(11 to 2 op 7 to 2 tchd 6 to 1) 1
1444 SUN SURFER (Fr) 5-11-2 B Powell, *trkd ldrs, mstks tenth and 11th, sn outpcd, lft second 2 out, no imprsn.*
. . . .(5 to 4 on op 11 to 10 tchd 6 to 4 on) 2
1276 DURRINGTON 7-11-2 Richard Guest, *in tch, chsd wnr 9th till hrd rdn and wknd aftr 3 out...*(20 to 1 op 10 to 1) 3
REAL HARMONY 7-11-2 D O'Sullivan, *lost tch frm tenth, sn tld off.* . . . .(40 to 1 op 16 to 1 tchd 50 to 1) 4
1308 GANDOUGE GLEN 6-11-2 D Murphy, *trkd ldrs, rdn and outpcd 3 out, second and btn whn f nxt.*
. . . .(2 to 1 op 7 to 4 tchd 5 to 2) f
HIGH HAGBERG 7-11-2 Mrs K Hills, *pld hrd, hld up, led 5th to 8th, wknd rpdly, pulled up bef 12th.*
. . . .(50 to 1 op 20 to 1) pu
Dist: 10l, 15l, dist. 5m 36.60s. a 26.60s (6 Ran).

(T M J Keep), S Dow

1715 Dover 'National Hunt' Novices' Hurdle (4-y-o and up) £2,110 2¾m 110yds . . . .(3:15)

1392* NEFARIOUS 7-11-6 M Richards, *hld up, prog 6th, led betw last 2, rdn appr last, styd on wl.*
. . . .(9 to 2 op 3 to 1 tchd 5 to 1) 1
1169² SOUTHERLY GALE 6-11-0 R Dunwoody, *hld up, prog 7th, gng easily betw last 2, ev ch appr last, sn hrd rdn and not quicken.* . . . .(Evens fav op 5 to 4 on tchd 6 to 4) 2
1198³ PRINCE OF SALERNO 6-11-0 R Supple, *hld up, prog hfwy, pushed alng and outpcd aftr 2 out, styd on ag'n appr last.* . . . .(4 to 1 op 5 to 1 tchd 6 to 1) 3
1263² THE WHIP 6-11-0 Peter Hobbs, *trkd ldr frm 4th till led 3 out, rdn and hdd betw last 2, wknd.*
. . . .(11 to 2 op 7 to 2 tchd 6 to 1) 4
864³ WALTON THORNS (bl) 5-11-0 J Osborne, *mstks, set gd pace till 3 out, wknd rpdly.*
. . . .(12 to 1 op 8 to 1 tchd 14 to 1) 5
MUSCLETON 8-11-0 P Holley, *hld up, effrt to chase ldg grp 8th, nvr on terms, wl beh whn pld up bef last.*
. . . .(8 to 1 tchd 12 to 1) pu
CRUISE CONTROL 7-11-0 E Murphy, *beh frm 4th, tld off whn pld up bef 8th.* . . . .(33 to 1 op 20 to 1) pu
1563 GREENHILL GO ON 8-10-9 R Rowell, *prmnt, rdn and wknd 7th, tld off whn pld up bef 3 out.*
. . . .(66 to 1 op 33 to 1 tchd 100 to 1) pu
1567 MONKTON (Ire) 5-11-0 B Powell, *sn rdn alng, struggling frm hfwy, pld up bef 8th.* . . . . . .(25 to 1 op 12 to 1) pu
1169 BALLYGRIFFIN LAD (Ire) 4-10-12 W McFarland, *al rear, rdn and lost tch 7th, tld off whn pld up bef last.*
. . . .(66 to 1 op 33 to 1 tchd 100 to 1) pu
Dist: 5l, nk, 7l, dist. 5m 48.50s. a 34.50s (10 Ran).

(Mrs Richard Kleinwort), Mark Campion

EXETER (heavy)
Wednesday December 15th
Going Correction: PLUS 1.30 sec. per fur. (races 1,2,- 4,6), PLUS 1.25 (3,5)

1716 Herald Express Mares' Only Novices' Handicap Hurdle (4-y-o and up) £2,219 2¼m. . . . .(12:40)

1516² HANDY LASS [86] 4-10-11 (5*) D Matthews, *hdwy 4th, led aftr 2 out, cmftbly...*(5 to 4 on op 3 to 1 tchd 7 to 2) 1
1535* GLENFINN PRINCESS [88] 5-11-4 D Bridgwater, *hdwy 4th, led aftr 3 out, hdd aftr 2 out, styd on same pace.*
. . . .(3 to 1 op 5 to 2 tchd 7 to 2) 2
1516³ UP ALL NIGHT [70] 4-9-7 (7*) G Crone, *in tch, pushed alng frm 4th, styd on frm 2 out...*(16 to 1 op 10 to 1) 3
1460¹² TIME FOR A FLUTTER [98] 4-11-7 (7*) Mr E James, *prmnt, led 3rd to 4th, one pace frm 3 out...*(13 to 2 op 4 to 1) 4
CHERYLS PET (Ire) [72] 5-10-2 B Powell, *led to 3rd, led ag'n 4th till hdd aftr 3 out, sn outpcd.*
. . . .(11 to 1 op 6 to 1 tchd 12 to 1) 5
1057 PROVERBS GIRL [84] 8-11-0 E Leonard, *beh and rdn 5th, some prog frm 2 out...*. . . . .(10 to 1 op 8 to 1) 6
1526¹¹ BLUE LYZANDER [70] 4-9-10¹ (5*) T Jenks, *beh frm 5th.*
. . . .(33 to 1 op 25 to 1) 7
1468³ CADOLIVE [70] 5-10-0 I Lawrence, *prmnt to 5th, sn wknd.*
. . . .(10 to 1 op 8 to 1) 8
1516 REALLY NEAT [70] 7-10-0 S Keightley, *prmnt to 5th.*
. . . .(40 to 1 op 25 to 1) 9
953 ELEGANT TOUCH [70] (bl) 4-9-7 (7*) Mr M Burrows, *beh, rapid hdwy 3rd, wknd 5th.*. . . . . . .(25 to 1 op 14 to 1) 10
LIRELLA [70] 6-9-7 (7*) T Thompson, *al beh.*
. . . .(50 to 1 op 33 to 1) 11

1303⁴ COLETTE'S CHOICE (Ire) [88] 4-11-4 S Mackey, *chlgd 4th, chald ag'n frm 3 out, 3rd and rdn whn f 2 out.*
. . . .(12 to 1 op 8 to 1 tchd 16 to 1) f
1519⁸ SPIRIT LEVEL [81] 5-10-11¹⁸ (7*) Mr R Payne, *tld off 3rd, pld up bef 2 out.* . . . .(66 to 1 op 33 to 1) pu
Dist: 7l, 1l, 2½l, 2l, 10l, ¾l, 20l, 4l, 12l. 4m 32.30s. a 32.30s (13 Ran).

(G W Hackling), Mrs A Knight

1717 Devonair Radio Novices' Claiming Hurdle (4-y-o and up) £2,013 2¼m . . . .(1:10)

1528² DERRYMOSS (v) 7-10-4 (7*) T Dascombe, *gd hdwy 3rd, led 3 out, hrd rdn frm 2 out, jst hld on.*
. . . .(10 to 1 op 7 to 1 tchd 11 to 1) 1
1519* CHICKABIDDY 5-10-10 M A FitzGerald, *mid-div, steady hdwy frm 5th, chlgd last, ev ch r-in, hng badly rght and not quicken nr finish.*
. . . .(11 to 10 fav op 2 to 1 tchd Evens) 2
1546³ SOUL TRADER 4-10-6 S Burrough, *al chasing ldrs, outpcd frm 2 out.* . . . .(12 to 1 op 7 to 1) 3
1528⁴ THE JET SET (bl) 6-11-1 I Lawrence, *hdwy 4th, stumbled bend aftr 3 out, sn btn...*. . . . .(20 to 1 op 12 to 1) 4
ROYAL SEGOS 4-10-13 N Dawe, *chsd ldr till led 3rd, hdwy 3 out, wknd aftr 2 out, no ch whn blun last.*
. . . .(13 to 2 op 20 to 1 tchd 25 to 1) 5
BIDDLESTONE BOY (NZ) 6-11-6 (3*) R Davis, *in tch, rdn 3 out, sn btn...*. . . . .(20 to 1 op 14 to 1 tchd 25 to 1) 6
PIRATE OF PENZANCE 5-10-13 Mrs C Wonnacott, *hdwy 5th, wknd aftr 3 out...*. . . . . . .(50 to 1 op 33 to 1) 7
1425* BILL QUILL 9-10-4 (7*) R Darke, *led to 3rd, wknd quickly 3 out.* . . . .(10 to 1 op 6 to 1) 8
1642⁷ VALIANTHE (USA) (bl) 5-11-5 R Dunwoody, *beh and rdn whn f 4th...*. . . . . . .(9 to 2 op 7 to 2 tchd 5 to 1) f
1526 FORGED PUNT 6-11-1 S Hodgson, *f second.*
. . . .(50 to 1 op 33 to 1) f
POLDEN PRIDE 5-11-4 Richard Guest, *mstk 1st, f second.*
. . . .(14 to 1 op 6 to 1 tchd 16 to 1) f
1353 LIZZIE DRIPPIN (Can) 4-10-5² H Davies, *some hdwy 3 out, rdn and no ch wth ldrs whn blun and uns rdr last.*
. . . .(33 to 1 op 25 to 1) ur
DYNAVON 7-10-2 L Harvey, *beh frm 4th, tld off whn pld up bef 2 out...*. . . . . . .(25 to 1 op 14 to 1) pu
953⁸ GENERALLY JUST 8-10-13 Mr S Stickland, *chsd ldrs to 5th, tld off whn pld up bef 2 out...*(66 to 1 op 50 to 1) pu
KINGS BROMPTON 7-10-11³ (7*) Mr R Payne, *al beh, tld off whn pld up bef 2 out...*. . . . . .(66 to 1 op 50 to 1) pu
1301 RAIN SHADOW (bl) 4-10-2 (5*) D Salter, *beh frm 4th, tld off whn pld up bef 2 out...*. . . . . .(50 to 1 op 25 to 1) pu
1468⁵ COUNTRY STYLE 4-11-0 S Earle, *prmnt to 4th, tld off whn pld up bef 2 out...*. . . . . . .(20 to 1 op 12 to 1) pu
Dist: Nk, 15l, 1½l, 10l, 6l, 3l, 5l, 21l. 4m 37.70s. a 31.70s (17 Ran).

(Mrs J K L Watts), M C Pipe

1718 BBC Radio Devon Novices' Claiming Chase (5-y-o and up) £3,226 2¼m . . . .(1:40)

1525⁴ MAGGOTS GREEN 6-10-6 (3*) R Farrant, *hdwy to track ldr 6th, led 2 out, cmftbly.*. . . . . . .(12 to 1 op 10 to 1) 1
1518² CRYSTAL BEAR (NZ) (bl) 8-11-12 B Powell, *drvn alng and 1st, mstk and lost pl 8th, rallied to chal 4 out, one pace frm nxt.*. . . . .(4 to 1 op 3 to 1) 2
1644 MICKEEN 6-11-4 M A FitzGerald, *pressed ldr till led 8th, hdd 2 out, sn rdn and btn.*
. . . .(9 to 1 op 5 to 1 tchd 10 to 1) 3
1463⁴ VIAGGIO 5-10-8 L Harvey, *hdwy 5th, chlgd 8th, styd on same pace frm 3 out...*(6 to 1 op 5 to 1 tchd 10 to 1) 4
1456⁴ IVYCHURCH (USA) 7-10-12 J Frost, *hdwy to chase ldrs 5th, rdn and no ch aftr nxt...*(10 to 1 op 8 to 1) 5
1493⁶ CHAPEL HILL (Ire) 5-10-0 (7*) D Fortt, *chsd ldrs, lost pos appr 5th, rdn and hit 7th, sn wknd, tld off.*
. . . .(5 to 4 fav op 2 to 1 tchd 5 to 2) 6
1518 TURKISH STAR 8-10-13 S McNeill, *in tch, hit 4th, uns rdr 6th...*. . . . .(8 to 1 op 10 to 1 tchd 7 to 1) ur
1245⁹ IMPERIAL FLIGHT 8-10-10 R Greene, *led till hdd 8th, wkng whn blun and uns rdr 4 out.*(12 to 1 op 10 to 1) ur
1516⁶ PRINCE VALMY (Fr) 8-11-4 M Foster, *al beh, tld off whn pld up bef 4 out...*. . . . . . .(33 to 1 op 25 to 1) pu
1516⁵ MANOR MAN 6-11-2 R Dunwoody, *in tch whn blun 7th, sn wknd, tld off whn pld up bef 4 out.*(11 to 1 op 8 to 1) pu
CREDIT NOTE 7-11-0 S Earle, *al beh, tld off whn pld up bef 4 out...*. . . . . . .(33 to 1 op 16 to 1) pu
Dist: 4l, 3l, 1½l, 10l, dist. 4m 40.50s. a 29.50s (11 Ran).
SR: 11/24/13/1/-/-/ (E A Hayward), J M Bradley

1719 Western Morning News Selling Handicap Hurdle (4-y-o and up) £1,910 2¼m . . . .(2:10)

1521⁹ SANDRO [74] (bl) 4-10-11 L Harvey, *led 3rd, made rst, rdn aftr 2 out, ran on...*. . . . . . .(8 to 1 op 7 to 1) 1
1603 IT'S NOT MY FAULT (Ire) [78] 5-11-1 P McDermott, *hdwy 4th, chsd wnr aftr 2 out, no imprsn.*
. . . .(12 to 1 op 10 to 1 tchd 14 to 1) 2

CORLY SPECIAL [72] 6-10-9 N Williamson, *chasing ldrs whn blun badly 3 out, rdn and styd on ag'n frm 2 out.*
.... (16 to 1 op 12 to 1 tchd 20 to 1) 3

889⁹ MOBILE MESSENGER (NZ) [82] 5-11-5 J Frost, *hdwy 4th, rdn 2 out, sn one pace.*
.... (3 to 1 fav op 7 to 2 tchd 5 to 1) 4

1627⁴ EARLY BREEZE [80] 7-11-3 B Clifford, *led to 3rd, styd chasing wnr till wknd aftr 2 out.*
.... (13 to 2 op 4 to 1 tchd 7 to 1) 5

1051⁵ ALDAHE [70] 8-10-2 (5⁴) D Salter, *nvr rch ldrs.*
.... (16 to 1 op 10 to 1) 6

1299 LAABAS [74] 10-10-11 R Rowell, *beh, hdwy 3rd, rdn 4th, wknd appr 2 out.......* (6 to 1 op 7 to 1 tchd 9 to 1) 7

1187⁶ HATS HIGH [80] (bl) 8-11-3 M Crosse, *nvr rch ldrs.*
.... (10 to 1 op 6 to 1) 8

ONE TO NOTE [91] 9-12-0 R Dunwoody, *prmnt, rdn 3 out, sn wknd................* (7 to 1 op 5 to 1 tchd 8 to 1) 9

1699⁵ BOOGIE BOPPER (Ire) [88] (bl) 4-11-4 (7⁴) O Burrows, *sn beh....................* (20 to 1 op 10 to 1) 10

1592 BRORA ROSE (Ire) [74] (bl) 5-10-11 I Shoemark, *chsd ldrs to 4th, sn wknd..............* (16 to 1 op 12 to 1) 11

1699⁴ MILDRED SOPHIA [65] 6-9-9 (7⁴,7ex) Miss S Mitchell, *rn rear till styd up appr 3rd....* (8 to 1 op 5 to 1 tchd 10 to 1) su

1462 WAVERLEY BOY [77] 11-11-0 Richard Guest, *al beh, tld off whn pld up bef last....................* (33 to 1 op 16 to 1) pu

592 DRAW LOTS [63] 9-9-11² (5⁴) D Matthews, *sn beh, tld off whn pld up bef 2 out........* (33 to 1 op 20 to 1) pu

1272² SEE NOW [76] 8-10-13 S Burrough, *chsd ldrs to 5th, sn wknd, tld off whn pld up bef last...* (8 to 1 op 6 to 1) pu
Dist: 4l, 8l, 3½l, 2l, 15l, 1½l, ¾l, 15l, hd, ¾l. 4m 33.20s. a 33.20s (15 Ran).
(Mrs Merrilyn Rowe), R J Baker

1720 Weatherbys 'Newcomers' Series Handicap Chase (0-125 5-y-o and up) £4,485 2m 7f 110yds...........(2:40)

1545 SHEER ABILITY [105] 7-10-9 R Dunwoody, *al tracking ldrs, rdn 4 out, led last, drvn out.*
.... (9 to 4 fav op 3 to 1 tchd 7 to 2) 1

1459⁴ FURRY KNOWE [100] 8-10-4 S McNeill, *chsd ldrs, led appr 4 out, hdd last, styd on und pres.*
.... (16 to 1 op 14 to 1 tchd 20 to 1) 2

1459 PADBROOK DOVE [96] 8-10-0 S Earle, *al in tch, rdn and outpcd appr 4 out..............* (12 to 1 tchd 14 to 1) 3

1471³ ROCKMOUNT ROSE [96] 8-9-7 (7⁴) L Dace, *chsd ldrs till wknd appr 4 out................* (16 to 1 op 8 to 1) 4

1512⁴ TOUCHING STAR [107] 8-10-11 M Hourigan, *al beh, rdn no imprsn...* (15 to 2 op 5 to 1 tchd 9 to 1) 5

1302 CAMDEN BELLE [96] 11-10-0 S Hodgson, *chsd ldrs 6th, beh frm 11th....................* (66 to 1 op 33 to 1) 6

1459² RED AMBER [96] (bl) 7-10-0 M Richards, *led till appr second, led ag'n 9th till hdd and wknd quickly appr 4 out.*
.... (11 to 1 op 8 to 1 tchd 12 to 1) 7

1394⁴ UNDER OFFER [96] (bl) 12-10-0 A Maguire, *beh frm 8th.*
.... (16 to 1 op 12 to 1) 8

1471⁴ BERESFORDS GIRL [104] 8-10-8 E Murphy, *hdwy tenth, rdn and wkng whn f 4 out.........* (9 to 2 tchd 5 to 1) f

1471⁸ GLOVE PUPPET [103] 8-10-7 Richard Guest, *mstk and uns rdr 3rd....................* (11 to 2 op 8 to 1) ur

ROYAL BATTERY (NZ) [120] 10-11-7 (3⁴) R Davis, *prmnt to 11th, tld off whn pld up bef 4 out.* (20 to 1 op 12 to 1) pu

1625 HEYFLEET [97] (bl) 10-10-1 I Lawrence, *al beh, tld off whn pld up bef tenth..................* (33 to 1 op 20 to 1) pu

1388 HONEYBEER MEAD [100] 11-10-4 M Mann, *beh till pld up bef 9th....................* (33 to 1 op 16 to 1) pu

1388 DELGANY RUN [101] 9-10-5 J Osborne, *led aftr second, hit 6th, hdd 9th, wknd 11th, tld off whn pld up bef 13th.*
.... (12 to 1 op 8 to 1) pu

1520 RAFIKI [105] 8-10-9 M A FitzGerald, *beh most of way, tld off whn pld up bef last.*
.... (11 to 1 op 12 to 1 tchd 14 to 1) pu
Dist: ½l, 10l, 15l, 12l, 6l, 10l, 15l. 6m 12.30s. a 37.30s (15 Ran).
SR: 2/-/-/-/-/-/ (Michael Devlin), C J Mann

1721 Express & Echo Handicap Hurdle (0-125 5-y-o and up) £2,529 2¼m (3:10)

1528⁴ EDIMBOURG [105] 7-11-0 J Osborne, *made all, clr 4th, imprsv.*
(11 to 10 on op 6 to 5 on tchd Evens and 11 to 8 on) 1

1521² ISLAND JEWEL [94] 5-10-3 M Bosley, *prmnt, chsd wnr appr 2 out, no imprsn.*
.... (9 to 4 op 3 to 1 tchd 100 to 30) 2

1508⁴ ACCESS SUN [94] 6-10-3 A Maguire, *chsd wnr till appr 2 out, sn outpcd..................* (5 to 1 tchd 6 to 1) 3

1474 SYLVIA BEACH [91] 7-10-0 E Murphy, *chsd ldrs to 3rd, nvr dngrs aftr.* (9 to 1 op 8 to 1 tchd 6 to 1 and 11 to 1) 4

1513⁹ MARIOLINO [100] 6-10-9 S Hodgson, *al beh.*
.... (25 to 1 op 16 to 1) 5

1474 WINDWARD ARIOM [91] 7-10-0 N Williamson, *in tch to 4th.*
.... (33 to 1 op 20 to 1) 6

1544 JOSIE SMITH [91] 9-9-12³ (5⁴) D Matthews, *sn beh.*
.... (66 to 1 op 20 to 1) 7

BOOTSCRAPER [75] 6-11-3 (7⁴) N Downs, *lost tch frm second, tld off whn pld up bef 3 out.* (33 to 1 op 8 to 1) pu

ODSTONE PEAR [96] 8-10-5¹ H Davies, *tld off frm second, pld up bef last......* (20 to 1 op 14 to 1 tchd 25 to 1) pu

---

Dist: 4l, 8l, 15l, 10l, 12l, 10l. 4m 27.30s. a 27.30s (9 Ran).
SR: 47/32/24/6/5/-/ (Mrs Iva Winton), Miss H C Knight

KELSO (soft)
Thursday December 16th
Going Correction: PLUS 1.50 sec. per fur. (races 1,3,-5,7), PLUS 1.40 (2,4,6)

1722 Philip Wilson 'National Hunt' Novices' Hurdle (Div I) (4-y-o and up) £2,407 2 ¾m 110yds..................(12:10)

1480⁴ DIG DEEPER 6-10-12 P Niven, *made all, clr aftr 2 out, styd on wl................* (3 to 1 tchd 11 to 4 and 7 to 2) 1

18⁹ PAR-BAR (Ire) 5-10-7 L Wyer, *in tch till outpcd and reminders hfwy, styd on strly frm 3 out to chase wnr appr last............* (16 to 1 op 14 to 1 tchd 20 to 1) 2

BARNEY RUBBLE 8-10-12 M Moloney, *chsd ldrs, pushed alng aftr 4 out, kpt on same pace frm nxt......* (25 to 1) 3

1060⁴ ARIADLER (Ire) 5-11-5 C Grant, *mid-div, pushed alng aftr 6th, mstk 4 out, no hdwy aftr.*
.... (6 to 5 fav op 11 to 10 on tchd 5 to 4) 4

MOSSIMAN (Ire) 5-10-12 S Turner, *in tch, pushed alng aftr 4th, wknd appr 3 out..................* (100 to 1) 5

1199 RHYMING THOMAS 5-10-12 J Railton, *in tch, wknd aftr 7th........................* (50 to 1) 6

1602² OVER THE ODDS (Ire) 4-10-5 (7⁴) D Ryan, *chsd wnr, 3rd and wkng whn f last.......................* (20 to 1) f

1588⁵ RALLYING CRY (Ire) 5-10-12 B Storey, *lost tch aftr 7th, wl beh whn pld up bef last.* (20 to 1 op 16 to 1) pu

1582 FULLY FURLONG 6-10-0 (7⁴) Mr D Parker, *lost tch aftr 6th, wl beh whn pld up bef last..................* (100 to 1) pu

1475 FINNOW QUAY (Ire) 4-10-7 (5⁴) F Perratt, *in tch to 7th, wl beh whn pld up bef last.* (66 to 1 op 50 to 1) pu

1475³ STRONG DEEL (Ire) 5-10-12 T Reed, *chsd ldrs till wknd aftr 7th, wl beh whn pld up bef last.* (7 to 2 op 5 to 2) pu

RUSTY BLADE 4-10-12 R Hodge, *jmpd slwly and sn wl beh, pld up bef 6th...........................* (100 to 1) pu
Dist: 2½l, 20l, 4l, 6l, 15l. 5m 54.80s. a 43.80s (12 Ran).
(Ian G M Dalgleish), J J O'Neill

1723 Queens Head, Kelso Novices' Chase (5-y-o and up) £3,013 2¾m 110yds ....(12:40)

CLYDE RANGER 6-11-0 C Grant, *led to 4th, cl up, led 3 out, styd on strly frm last......* (7 to 2 fav tchd 4 to 1) 1

1477⁴ ARTHUR'S MINSTREL 6-11-7 P Niven, *cl up, led 8th, hdd 3 out, ev ch till no extr r-in...........* (9 to 2 op 7 to 2) 2

1119⁴ CHARLOTTE'S EMMA 6-10-9 B Storey, *al prmnt, ev ch last, wknd r-in................* (6 to 1 op 5 to 1) 3

THISTLE MONARCH 8-11-0 N Doughty, *prmnt till wknd appr 3 out................* (4 to 1 tchd 9 to 2) 4

1218⁸ DEEP HAVEN 8-11-0 R Hodge, *tld off frm 12th.*
.... (66 to 1 op 50 to 1) 5

GARCALL 7-11-0 M Moloney, *led 4th to 8th, chasing ldrs whn f 12th.................* (20 to 1 op 12 to 1) f

CLARE COAST 7-11-0 K Jones, *f second, dead.*
.... (66 to 1 op 16 to 1) f

1587 JINGLIN' GEORDIE (Ire) 5-11-0 L O'Hara, *f 1st.... (66 to 1) f

KILCOLGAN 6-11-0 A Orkney, *brght dwn 1st.....* (50 to 1) bd

MAN OF MOREEF 6-10-9 (5⁴) F Perratt, *brght dwn 1st.*
.... (66 to 1 op 50 to 1) bd

1602⁷ BALLYBELL 8-10-9 (5⁴) P Williams, *beh whn pld up aftr 11th...........................* (200 to 1) pu

REDHALL ROYALE 9-10-9 Miss P Robson, *beh till pld up aftr 11th.................* (66 to 1 op 50 to 1) pu

LOTHIAN PILOT 6-11-0 T Reed, *beh whn pld up aftr 11th.*
.... (16 to 1 op 12 to 1) pu

DASTARDLY DALE 7-11-0 J Railton, *in tch whn pld up aftr 11th........................* (66 to 1 op 50 to 1) pu

EASTER OATS 6-10-6 (3⁴) A Larnach, *beh whn pld up aftr 11th..........................* (25 to 1 op 20 to 1) pu

1477 FRONT LINE 6-11-0 L Wyer, *beh whn pld up aftr 11th.*
.... (4 to 1 op 3 to 1 tchd 9 to 2) pu
Dist: 6m 4.10s. a 37.10s (16 Ran). Race declared void.
SR: 30/-/-/-/-/-/ (I Bray), M D Hammond

1724 Percy Arms Novices' Hurdle (4-y-o and up) £2,180 2m 110yds......(1:10)

1582² LINNGATE 4-11-0 T Reed, *hld up, hdwy to track wnr 5th, led on bit last, hrd held.*
.... (5 to 4 on op 6 to 4 on tchd 11 to 10 on) 1

CHIEF MINISTER (Ire) 4-10-12 P Harley, *in tch, hdwy appr 3 out, led aftr nxt, hdd last. rdn and kpt on wl, no ch wth wnr.....................* (7 to 4 op 6 to 4) 2

1060⁶ THE WHIRLIE WEEVIL 5-10-7 M Moloney, *beh till styd on frm 3 out, not trble ldrs...........* (33 to 1 op 25 to 1) 3

1478 MONTRAVE 4-10-12 B Storey, *in tch, hdwy appr 3 out, kpt on same pace frm nxt.........* (14 to 1 op 8 to 1) 4

1582⁸ LONDON HILL 5-10-12 C Dennis, *prmnt, outpcd aftr 3 out, kpt on frm nxt.................* (50 to 1 op 25 to 1) 5

1478 CORSTON RACER 5-10-7 (5⁴) P Williams, *led 3rd, clr 5th, hdd aftr 2 out, sn btn..................* (50 to 1) 6

1199^{5} MARCO-PIERRE (Ire) 4-10-12 S Turner, *prmnt till wknd aftr 3 out*........................ (33 to 1 op 25 to 1) 7
1060 STONEY BROOK 5-10-5 (7*) Mr A Parker, *led to 3rd, prmnt till wknd aftr 3 out*...............(33 to 1 op 25 to 1) 8
779 TICO GOLD 5-10-12 C Grant, *sn beh.* (33 to 1 op 25 to 1) 9
HIGHLANDMAN 7-10-12 A Orkney, *nvr dngrs.* .... (50 to 1 op 25 to 1) 10
CALL THE SHOTS (Ire) 4-10-12 K Jones, *in tch till wknd aftr 5th*.. (100 to 1) 11
CLAN REEL 4-10-9 (3*) A Larnach, *sn beh, tld off.* ....(100 to 1) 12
TAUVALERA 6-10-7 Mr D Swindlehurst, *al beh, tld off whn pld up bef 2 out*........................(66 to 1 op 100 to 1) pu
1478^{9} CAMDEN GROVE 5-10-7 R Hodge, *in tch till wknd appr 3 out, wl beh whn pld up bef last*.............. (50 to 1) pu
1582 SKIDDAW CALYPSO 4-10-7 A Dobbin, *in tch till wknd aftr 5th, wl beh whn pld up bef last*....(50 to 1 op 33 to 1) pu
Dist: 2l, 15l, sht-hd, nk, 8l, 8l, ¾l, 5l, 12l, 2l. 4m 12.60s. a 29.60s (15 Ran).
SR: 37/33/13/18/17/9/1/-/-/ (J Nelson), L Lungo

1725 Glassedin Securities Handicap Chase (0-135 5-y-o and up) £3,436 3½m (1:40)

1616^{2} PLENTY CRACK [128] 10-11-10 B Storey, *cl up, led 5th till hdd 4 out, led ag'n aftr last, styd on wl.* ....(7 to 2 tchd 4 to 1) 1
1572^{3} RUN PET RUN [107] 8-10-3 A Dobbin, *trkd ldrs, led 4 out, hdd aftr last, no extr und pres...* (2 to 1 fav op 9 to 4) 2
1585^{5} OVER THE DEEL [112] 7-10-8 A Orkney, *in tch, chsd ldrs frm 16th, no imprsn*..... (6 to 1 op 5 to 1 tchd 7 to 1) 3
1565 PINK GIN [105] 6-10-1[1] C Grant, *mstks, sn beh, lost tch aftr 15th*.............(5 to 1 op 9 to 2 tchd 11 to 2) 4
1063^{4} OFF THE BRU [109] (v) 8-10-5 Mr J Bradburne, *led to 5th, outpcd aftr 15th*........(13 to 2 op 6 to 1 tchd 7 to 1) 5
TARTAN TYRANT [113] 7-10-9 N Doughty, *wth ldrs till f 11th*.................. (9 to 1 op 8 to 1 tchd 10 to 1) f
1319 ABERCROMBY CHIEF [113] 8-10-9[9] T Reed, *sn beh, blun 14th, tld off aftr, pld up bef last*..............(25 to 1) pu
Dist: 6l, 6l, 15l, 15l. 7m 37.90s. a 47.90s (7 Ran).
SR: 9/-/-/-/ (B Mactaggart), B Mactaggart

1726 Philip Wilson 'National Hunt' Novices' Hurdle (Div II) (4-y-o and up) £2,407 2 ¾m 110yds.................... (2:10)

1204^{5} BELLS HILL LAD 6-10-12 A Dobbin, *cl up, slight ld frm 5th, hrd pressed from 2 out, kpt on wl und pres, all out.* .... (9 to 1 op 10 to 1 tchd 14 to 1) 1
1574^{3} SCOTTON BANKS (Ire) 4-10-12 L Wyer, *cl up, jnd wnr 2 out, rdn aftr last, ev ch till no extr close hme.* .... (6 to 4 on op 5 to 4 on tchd 11 to 10 on) 2
1421^{6} SON OF IRIS 5-10-12 P Niven, *in tch, outpcd appr 3 out, no dngr aftr*...................... (14 to 1 op 10 to 1) 3
KIRKTON GREY 6-10-12 B Storey, *beh, hdwy to chase ldrs hfwy, outpcd appr 3 out, no dngr aftr.* .... (10 to 1 op 8 to 1) 4
1100^{9} RUSSIAN CASTLE (Ire) 4-10-12 K Jones, *prmnt, blun 8th, sn wknd*......................... (14 to 1 op 10 to 1) 5
PADDY MORRISSEY 6-10-12 A Orkney, *prmnt till wknd aftr 6th*......................................(33 to 1) 6
1096^{9} ROYAL SURPRISE 6-10-12 Miss P Robson, *in tch till outpcd hfwy, tld off*..................(33 to 1 op 25 to 1) 7
HOWCLEUCH 6-10-2 (5*) F Perratt, *led till hdd 5th, wknd appr 7th, tld off whn pld up bef 3 out.* .... (16 to 1 op 14 to 1) pu
1131^{2} SHAWWELL 6-11-2 (3*) D J Moffatt, *hit 4th, lost tch 6th, tld off whn pld up aftr nxt.* ....(3 to 1 op 9 to 4 tchd 7 to 2) pu
Dist: Nk, 30l, 6l, 3½l, 10l, 20l. 6m 0.70s. a 49.70s (9 Ran).
(Mrs Kathryn Collins), J Barclay

1727 Bert McElrath Memorial Handicap Chase (0-130 5-y-o and up) £3,338 2m 1f.............................. (2:40)

1409 TERRIBLE GEL (Fr) [105] 8-11-10 P Niven, *led second, clr aftr 2 out, cmftbly*............................ (6 to 4) 1
1203^{*} POSITIVE ACTION [101] 7-11-6 A Dobbin, *in tch, chsd wnr frm 8th, rdn aftr 3 out, no imprsn.* ....(5 to 4 fav op 11 to 10) 2
1583^{3} SILVER HAZE [91] 9-10-10 K Jones, *led to second, cl up, mstk 8th, grad wknd*.............. (25 to 1 op 20 to 1) 3
1203^{6} PURA MONEY [100] 11-11-5 N Doughty, *beh, hmpd 9th, sn lost tch*.......................... (14 to 1 op 10 to 1) 4
1479^{4} BELDINE [100] 8-11-5 A Orkney, *in tch, mstk 4th, f 9th.* ....(7 to 1 op 6 to 1) f
Dist: 12l, 8l, 7l. 4m 38.30s. a 32.30s (5 Ran).
SR: 11/-/ (R C Watts), Mrs M Reveley

1728 Tweeddale Press Group Conditional Jockeys' Handicap Hurdle (0-125 4-y-o and up) £2,442 2m 110yds...... (3:10)

1094 ARAGON AYR [89] 5-10-0 D J Moffatt, *in tch, rdn and hdwy aftr 3 out, led r-in, styd on wl*......... (33 to 1) 1
1614^{2} WEE WIZARD (Ire) [98] 4-10-9 A Dobbin, *al prmnt, led last, sn hdd, kpt on*..................... (6 to 1 op 5 to 1) 2
1614^{*} IT'S THE PITS [103] 6-11-0 (6ex) F Perratt, *beh, hdwy whn mstk 5th, rdn and kpt on frm 2 out, nrst finish.* ....(7 to 4 fav tchd 15 to 8) 3
1481^{2} PALACEGATE KING [102] 4-10-13 D Bentley, *chsd ldrs, ev ch last, one paced*.................. (9 to 2 op 7 to 2) 4
1219^{4} BAY TERN (USA) [113] 7-11-6 (4*) A Linton, *led till hdd last, no extr*...........................(14 to 1 op 12 to 1) 5
1614^{5} PERSONAL HAZARD [104] 4-10-11 (4*) J Driscoll, *in tch till grad wknd frm 3 out.* (16 to 1 op 14 to 1 tchd 20 to 1) 6
1586^{2} CHEEKY POT [92] (v) 5-10-3 P Waggott, *chsd ldrs, pushed alng hfwy, wknd appr 2 out*.......(10 to 1 op 8 to 1) 7
1186^{2} SWEET CITY [102] 8-10-9 (4*) B Harding, *lost pl and beh aftr 3rd, no dngr after...*(5 to 1 op 6 to 1 tchd 7 to 1) 8
MANGROVE MIST (Ire) [97] 5-10-8 A Larnach, *al beh, lost tch aftr 3rd*...................... (50 to 1 op 33 to 1) 9
Dist: 1½l, ¾l, 3½l, 2l, 7l, 10l, 5l, 3½l. 4m 14.10s. a 31.10s (9 Ran).
SR: 8/15/19/14/23/7/ (Lt-Col W L Monteith), P Monteith

TOWCESTER (heavy)
Thursday December 16th
Going Correction: PLUS 0.95 sec. per fur. (races 1,3,6), PLUS 1.20 (2,4,5)

1729 Christmas Pudding Novices' Hurdle (4-y-o and up) £1,983 2m...... (12:30)

1494^{3} RELKEEL 4-10-12 A Maguire, *in tch, chsd ldr aftr 3 out, chlgd 2 out, sn led, all out*........... (7 to 1 op 6 to 1) 1
650^{6} TRYING AGAIN 5-10-12 P Holley, *led, sn clr, rdn aftr 3 out, hdd after 2 out, rallied last, no extr nr finish.* .... (12 to 1 op 6 to 1 tchd 14 to 1) 2
1628^{*} GORTEERA 7-11-5 M Brennan, *hdwy 5th, chsd ldrs 3 out, outpcd frm 2 out*...... (4 to 1 op 5 to 1 tchd 11 to 2) 3
1509^{2} BALLET ROYAL (USA) 4-10-12 M Perrett, *chsd ldr to 3 out, sn rdn, one pace frm 2 out.* ....(6 to 4 fav op 2 to 1 tchd 11 to 8) 4
1327^{4} MAKES ME GOOSEY (Ire) 5-10-12 L Harvey, *some hdwy frm 3 out, nrst finish*.............. (33 to 1 op 8 to 1) 5
THE PORTSOY LOON 6-10-12 D Bridgwater, *beh 3rd, some prog frm 3 out*.........................(50 to 1 op 12 to 1) 6
1548^{4} MR CLANCY (Ire) 5-10-12 N Williamson, *chsd ldrs till wknd 5th*.................. (12 to 1 op 5 to 1 tchd 14 to 1) 7
LE BARON PERCHE (Fr) 4-10-12 S McNeill, *chsd ldrs to 5th, sn wknd*......................(33 to 1 op 20 to 1) 8
ISLAND BLADE (Ire) 4-10-12 G McCourt, *chsd ldrs to 5th, sn wknd*............... (8 to 1 op 7 to 2 tchd 9 to 1) 9
1490 SPANISH BLAZE (Ire) 5-10-12 M A FitzGerald, *al beh.* .... (16 to 1 op 12 to 1 tchd 20 to 1) 10
THE GREY TEXAN 4-10-12 Richard Guest, *al beh.* .... (50 to 1 op 20 to 1) 11
BENNYS SPECIAL 6-11-3[5] Mr A Sansome, *tld off frm 3rd.* .... (50 to 1 op 16 to 1) 12
1263^{3} ARCTIC LIFE (Ire) 4-10-5 (7*) W J Walsh, *bolted bef strt, chsd ldr to 4th, wkng whn f 3 out.* (20 to 1 op 10 to 1) f
BRIC LANE (USA) 6-10-12 Leesa Long, *prmnt to 5th, tld off whn pld up bef 2 out*..........(50 to 1 op 20 to 1) pu
1642 BANDMASTER (USA) 4-10-12 E Murphy, *hdwy 4th, sn wknd, tld off whn pld up bef 2 out.* (50 to 1 op 33 to 1) pu
Dist: 1½l, 6l, 2l, 15l, 10l, 3l, 3½l, 1½l, 5l, ½l. 4m 4.10s. a 21.10s (15 Ran).
SR: 25/23/24/15/-/-/ (Brig C B Harvey), D Nicholson

1730 Mistletoe Novices' Chase (5-y-o and up) £3,210 2¾m................ (1:00)

1457^{5} FINO 7-11-0 A Maguire, *chsd ldrs 6th, led 9th, wnt lft aftr 2 out, drvn appr last, all out*...... (5 to 1 tchd 6 to 1) 1
1469^{4} RIVER MANDATE 6-11-0 B Powell, *al frnt rnk, dsptd ld frm 4 out, slightly hmpd and wnt rght aftr 2 out, rallied r-in, no extr nr finish*...............(6 to 1 op 5 to 1) 2
1563^{*} JUDGES FANCY (bl) 9-11-7 C Llewellyn, *hdwy to track ldrs 12th, rdn and one pace frm 3 out.* ....(5 to 2 fav op 2 to 1 tchd 11 to 4) 3
1570^{3} PRECIPICE RUN 8-11-0 R Dunwoody, *in tch till wknd 12th, tld off*.......................... (7 to 2 op 3 to 1) 4
1530^{5} MISTRESS MCKENZIE 7-10-9 R Greene, *led to second, wknd aftr 8th, mstk 9th, wl beh whn f 12th*....(33 to 1) f
VITAL SCORE 7-11-0 S Smith Eccles, *led second to 9th, disputing ld whn f tenth*......................(33 to 1) f
1170 ONE MORE RUN 6-11-0 Richard Guest, *blun 4th, chsd ldrs 7th, wl beh whn blunded and uns rdr 12th.* .... (20 to 1 op 14 to 1) ur
1493^{7} DEEP IN GREEK 7-10-11 (3*) R Davis, *beh frm 7th, tld off whn pld up bef 2 out*............. (50 to 1 op 33 to 1) pu
1469^{2} SUFFOLK ROAD 6-11-0 H Davies, *beh frm 8th, tld off whn pld up bef 4 out*...... (3 to 1 tchd 7 to 2 and 11 to 4) pu
NO LIGHT 6-11-0 L Harvey, *beh, mstk 1st, blun 4th, hit 6th, lost tch aftr 8th, tld off whn pld up bef 2 out.* .... (20 to 1 op 14 to 1) pu
Dist: Nk, 8l, dist. 6m 5.00s. a 39.00s (10 Ran).
(Mrs Shirley Robins), D Nicholson

1731 Turkey And Ham Conditional Jockeys' Selling Hurdle (4-y-o) £1,631 2m (1:30)

1655⁷ PORT IN A STORM 11-8 E Husband, *beh, lost pos 5th, gd hdwy 3 out, styd on frm 2 out, led last, drvn out.
....(11 to 4 op 2 to 1) 1

1640⁶ PRIVATE JET (Ire) 10-12 A Thornton, *chsd ldrs, slight ld 2 out, hdd last, styd on one pace.*
....(4 to 1 op 3 to 1 tchd 9 to 2) 2

1079 NORDIC BEAT (Ire) 10-12 R Farrant, *chsd ldrs, chlgd 3 out, ev ch 2 out, wknd appr last*......(12 to 1 op 8 to 1) 3

1472² TYNRON DOON 10-12 R Davis, *dsptd ld till slight advantage 3 out, hdd and wknd 2 out.* (9 to 4 fav op 5 to 2) 4

1079³ PEARLY WHITE 10-7 M Hourigan, *tld off frm 5th.*
....(6 to 1 op 5 to 1 tchd 10 to 1) 5

1562⁵ ABSOLUTLEY FOXED 10-7 A Procter, *dsptd ld till f 3 out.*
....(8 to 1 op 7 to 1) f

CAPTAIN TANDY (Ire) 10-12 W Marston, *beh most of way, tld off whn pld up bef 2 out.*..... (12 to 1 op 10 to 1) pu

Dist: 5l, 6l, 4l, dist. 4m 14.80s. a 31.80s (7 Ran).

(S A Barningham), N Tinkler

1732 Chris Thornton Silver Fox Handicap Chase (0-130 5-y-o and up) £5,605 3m 1f............................(2:00)

1503² DO BE BRIEF [122] (bl) 8-11-3 (7*) L O'Hare, *made all, rdn 2 out, all out, jst hld on*........... (3 to 1 fav op 2 to 1) 1

1543² CYTHERE [113] 9-10-12 (3*) P Hide, *in tch, hit tenth, sn drvn alng, plenty to do frm 3 out, styd on from 2 out, jst fld*...................(7 to 2 op 4 to 1 tchd 9 to 2) 2

1565* INVASION [104] (v) 9-10-6 M Brennan, *ran in snatches, pushed alng 8th, rallied 9th, hit 12th, no imprsn frm 4 out*...................(9 to 2 op 7 to 2 tchd 6 to 1) 3

1503⁵ BROMPTON ROAD [114] 10-11-2 A Maguire, *wnt prmnt 7th, chsd wnr appr tenth, chlgd 3 out, sn wknd.*
....(6 to 1 tchd 7 to 1) 4

BIT OF A CLOWN [115] 10-11-3 L Harvey, *beh, pushed alng 8th, wkng whn hit 13th, tld off.*
....(9 to 1 op 6 to 1 tchd 10 to 1) 5

1365⁴ SIRRAH JAY [111] 13-10-8 (5*) T Jenks, *chsd wnr till wknd aftr 8th, wkng quickly whn f 9th.*
....(16 to 1 op 12 to 1 tchd 20 to 1) f

1471² BOWL OF OATS [109] (bl) 7-10-11 S McNeill, *in tch, chsd wnr aftr 8th till appr tenth, wknd 4 out, tld off whn pld up bef last.* (7 to 2 op 3 to 1 tchd 11 to 4 and 5 to 1) pu

Dist: ¾l, 10l, 5l, dist. 6m 52.60s. a 37.60s (7 Ran).

SR: 20/10/-/-/

(Errol Brown), Mrs J Pitman

1733 Champagne Handicap Chase (0-130 5-y-o and up) £3,525 2m 110yds (2:30)

THREEOUTOFFOUR [108] 8-10-12 M Brennan, *hit 4th, rdn 7th, rapid hdwy to chase ldrs 3 out, chlgd 2 out, sn led, drvn out*...............(11 to 2 op 4 to 1 tchd 6 to 1) 1

1489* DOLIKOS [106] 6-10-10 M Dwyer, *made most to 3rd, styd chasing ldr, chlgd 2 out, sn hdd, hrd drvn r-in, no extr cl hme*....................(7 to 4 op 2 to 1) 2

1489² SPREE CROSS [120] 7-11-10 D Murphy, *pressed ldr till led 3rd, hdd 5th, led ag'n 8th, headed 2 out, sn btn.*
....(4 to 1 op 3 to 1) 3

1566* REJOINUS [109] 8-10-13 R Garritty, *chsd ldrs, led 5th, mstk and hdd 8th, sn wknd.*
....(6 to 4 fav tchd 5 to 4 and 11 to 8) 4

MASTER COMEDY [96] (bl) 9-10-0 N Williamson, *al beh, tld off 6th.*...............(33 to 1 op 20 to 1 tchd 50 to 1) 5

Dist: 2l, 12l, 3l, dist. 4m 26.00s. a 24.00s (5 Ran).

SR: 42/38/40/26/-/

(Miss Cindy Brennan), O Brennan

1734 Christmas Cracker Mares' Only Novices' Hurdle (4-y-o and up) £1,866 2m ....(3:00)

916³ CARPET SLIPPERS 7-10-10 D Murphy, *rear 3rd, gd hdwy 4th, led 5th, came clr frm 2 out, cmftbly.*
....(6 to 1 op 4 to 1) 1

1475 NINFA (Ire) 5-10-10 R Dunwoody, *prmnt, chsd wnr aftr 3 out, rdn and no imprsn frm 2 out.*
....(7 to 2 op 5 to 2 tchd 5 to 1) 2

1478⁷ FORTUNE'S GIRL 5-10-10 A Maguire, *in tch, rdn to chase ldrs 2 out, wknd 2 out.*
....(to 4 fav tchd 2 to 1 and 9 to 4) 3

1536 MAKING TIME 6-10-10 A Tory, *chsd ldrs till rdn and wknd appr 2 out.*........................ 4

PLACE STEPHANIE (Ire) 5-10-10 H Davies, *wth ldr to 4th, wknd and mstk 3 out.*........(11 to 2 op 7 to 2) 5

1386⁷ FLAPPING FREDA 6-10-10 G McCourt, *nvr rch ldrs.*
....(33 to 1 op 20 to 1) 6

1252⁵ POLLY MINOR 6-10-10 M Perrett, *in tch till mstk and wknd 4th.*........................(14 to 1 op 33 to 1) 7

ROMANY TRAVELLER 5-10-10 W McFarland, *mstk 4th, beh most of way.*.........................(33 to 1) 8

1126 CAIPIRINHA (Ire) 5-10-10 G Upton, *al beh.*
....(20 to 1 op 14 to 1) 9

WHAT DO YOU THINK 5-10-10 C Llewellyn, *made most to 5th, wknd quickly aftr 3 out.*
....(6 to 1 op 7 to 1 tchd 8 to 1) 10

81 OZONE LASS (Ire) 5-10-10 M Brennan, *beh, hdwy to chase ldrs 4th, wknd rpdly aftr 3 out, tld off whn pld up bef 2 out.*...................(25 to 1 op 20 to 1) pu

Dist: 6l, 6l, 5l, 1½l, ½l, 12l, 2l, 10l, 1l. 4m 10.50s. a 27.50s (11 Ran).

(Mrs Diana Haine), Mrs D Haine

CATTERICK (good to soft)
Friday December 17th
Going Correction: PLUS 0.60 sec. per fur.

1735 Glebe House Novices' Chase (5-y-o and up) £2,286 2m...........(12:50)

1484² POLITICAL TOWER 6-11-0 A Dobbin, *cl up, led 6th, rdn aftr 2 out, styd on wl*.................(5 to 1 op 9 to 2) 1

1358⁵ ISSYIN 6-11-0 R Garritty, *jmpd rght 1st, led till hdd 6th, wth wnr till no extr betw last 2*...... (7 to 1 op 6 to 1) 2

1364⁶ RED INDIAN 7-11-0 D Byrne, *beh, effrt whn mstk 6th, not trble ldrs*........................(10 to 1 op 7 to 1) 3

1221⁷ GOLDEN ISLE 9-11-0 B Storey, *nvr on terms.*
....(16 to 1 op 14 to 1) 4

1149 REGAL ROMPER (Ire) 5-11-0 Richard Guest, *chsd ldrs till wknd appr 3 out, tld off*..........(25 to 1 op 16 to 1) 5

1484⁵ DE JORDAAN 6-11-0 P Niven, *al beh, tld off frm 4 out.*
....(100 to 1) 6

1669* FRICKLEY 7-12-0 N Doughty, *hmpd, mstk and uns rdr 1st.*
....(7 to 4 on op 5 to 4 on) ur

Dist: 6l, 12l, 6l, dist, 8l. 4m 5.20s. a 16.20s (7 Ran).

SR: 20/14/2/-/

(G R S Nixon), M A Barnes

1736 Glebe 'National Hunt' Novices' Hurdle (4-y-o and up) £1,480 2m...... (1:20)

1548² KENMORE-SPEED 6-10-12 Richard Guest, *made virtually all, ran on strly frm last.* (9 to 4 op 5 to 2 tchd 2 to 1) 1

1418³ COL BUCKMORE (Ire) 5-11-4 N Doughty, *hld up, badly hmpd second, steady hdwy to track wnr 3 out, chlgd nxt, no extr appr last.*
....(11 to 8 fav op 6 to 4 on tchd 11 to 10) 2

1478⁵ SCRABO VIEW (Ire) 5-10-12 L O'Hara, *in tch, outpcd aftr 3 out, kpt on frm nxt.*...............(10 to 1 op 8 to 1) 3

1320⁶ GREY TRIX (Ire) 5-10-12 R Garritty, *in tch till outpcd aftr 3 out, no dngr aftr.*....... (7 to 1 op 6 to 1 tchd 8 to 1) 4

1494 INGLETONIAN 4-10-7 (5*) D Bentley, *prmnt till wknd appr 2 out*......................(50 to 1 op 33 to 1) 5

ISLAND RIVER (Ire) 5-10-12 C Dennis, *lost tch frm hfwy, tld off*..........................(50 to 1 op 33 to 1) 6

645⁶ AMBER HOLLY 4-10-0 (7*) Mr R Hale, *prmnt, mstk 3 out, sn wknd, tld off*..................(50 to 1 op 33 to 1) 7

1376 KNOCKREIGH CROSS (Ire) 4-10-0 (7*) G Cahill, *lost tch frm hfwy, tld off*...................(50 to 1 op 33 to 1) 8

ZIN ZAN (Ire) 5-10-9 (3*) D J Moffatt, *f second.*
....(7 to 1 op 12 to 1 tchd 14 to 1) f

SOLAR NOVA 5-10-7 J Callaghan, *mstk 1st, f second.*
....(20 to 1 op 12 to 1) f

1199⁷ EMERALD CHARM (Ire) 5-10-7 B Storey, *sn beh, tld off whn pld up bef 2 out.*..........(14 to 1 op 12 to 1) pu

Dist: 8l, 7l, 6l, 3l, 25l, 8l, 1½l. 3m 59.60s. a 18.60s (11 Ran).

(K M Dacker), Mrs S J Smith

1737 Cleveland Medical Laboratories Ltd Handicap Chase (0-125 4-y-o and up) £2,684 2m...................(1:50)

1360³ TRESIDDER [111] 11-11-2 R Garritty, *hld up, hdwy aftr 4 out, chsd wnr after nxt, rdn to ld r-in.*
....(5 to 1 op 7 to 2) 1

HAPPY BREED [98] 10-10-3 J Callaghan, *prmnt, led appr 3 out till hdd and no extr r-in.*........(25 to 1 op 16 to 1) 2

1566² BOSTON ROVER [115] 8-11-6 M Brennan, *in tch, blun badly and lost touch 4 out, hmpd nxt, not reco'r.*
....(5 to 2 op 2 to 1 tchd 11 to 4) 3

KAMART [95] 5-10-0 A Dobbin, *sn beh, tld off appr 3 out.*
....(14 to 1 op 10 to 1 tchd 16 to 1) 4

1285³ BORO SMACKEROO [123] 8-12-0 A Orkney, *led, blun 4 out, sn hdd, 3rd and btn whn f 2 out.*
....(10 to 1 op 7 to 1) f

1678 ROCKET LAUNCHER [103] 7-10-8 M Moloney, *chsd ldrs, effrt aftr 4 out, disputing second whn f nxt, dead.*
....(5 to 4 fav tchd 6 to 4) f

Dist: 3l, 15l, 12l. 4m 3.40s. a 14.40s (6 Ran).

SR: 40/24/26/

(S H J Brewer), M W Easterby

1738 Burn House Claiming Hurdle (4-y-o and up) £2,072 2m.............(2:20)

1485⁵ GREENACRES LAD 10-10-10 A Mulholland, *trkd ldrs, rdn betw last 2, led r-in, ran on und pres.*
....(50 to 1 op 33 to 1) 1

1187* RUSTY ROC 12-10-10 Mr N Miles, *led, rdn betw last 2, hdd r-in, no extr*.................(3 to 1 jt-fav op 2 to 1) 2

1404⁴ KING'S GUEST (Ire) 4-11-0 J Callaghan, *chsd ldr, chlgd 2 out, no extr appr last.*...... (16 to 1 op 20 to 1) 3

MISTIC GLEN (Ire) 4-10-4 (7*) S Mason, *beh till styd on und pres frm appr 2 out, nrst finish*... (16 to 1 op 12 to 1) 4

1416² BAND SARGEANT (Ire) 4-11-0 N Doughty, *prmnt, ev ch 3 out, grad wknd appr nxt*.......... (4 to 1 op 7 to 2) 5

NORTINO 5-10-6 B Storey, *in tch, outpcd aftr 3 out, no dngr after*.......................(14 to 1 op 12 to 1) 6

1739 — Abraham Transport Handicap Chase (0-120 5-y-o and up) £2,684 3m 1f 110yds. (2:50)

1262⁴ SECRET RITE [94] 10-10-3³ Peter Hobbs, *cl up, led 14th, rdn appr 3 out, styd on wl und pres frm last.*
....(7 to 1 op 9 to 2) 1
1486⁵ TRUELY ROYAL [93] 9-10-2 B Storey, *led till hdd 14th, chsd wnr aftr, styd on wl frm last, no imprsn.*
................................(100 to 30 op 11 to 4 tchd 7 to 2) 2
973 MOULTON BULL [91] 7-10-0 J Callaghan, *in tch, slightly hmpd 14th, sn lost pl, styd on wl frm 3 out, not rch ldrs.*
....(12 to 1 op 10 to 1) 3
HEAVENLY CITIZEN (Ire) [94] 5-10-3³ R Garritty, *in tch till outpcd aftr 14th, no dngr after.*....... (6 to 1 op 9 to 2) 4
1115³ EBORNEEZER'S DREAM [95] 10-10-4⁴ D Telfer, *in tch, wknd aftr 14th, tld off.*
................................(40 to 1 op 33 to 1 tchd 50 to 1) 5
1319⁴ HOTPLATE [119] 10-12-0 N Doughty, *prmnt till wknd aftr 14th, tld off.*....................(8 to 1 op 7 to 1) 6
1359* GATHERING TIME [102] 7-10-11 Richard Guest, *in tch, reminders aftr tenth, chalg whn f 14th.*
....(3 to 1 fav op 5 to 2) f
1486 ZAM BEE [108] 7-11-3 T Reed, *in tch, slightly hmpd 14th, sn wknd, tld off whn pld up bef last.* (7 to 1 op 6 to 1) pu
Dist: 1½l, 10l, 10l, 30l, 8l. 6m 52.90s. a 37.90s (8 Ran).
(Miss Carrie Zetter), C Weedon

1740 — Hutton Wandesley Handicap Hurdle (0-115 4-y-o and up) £2,143 3m 1f 110yds. (3:20)

1619 NODDLE (USA) [87] 5-10-11 T Reed, *made all, mstk 4th, styd on strly frm 2 out, cmftbly...* (11 to 2 tchd 5 to 1) 1
1633² MAKE ME PROUD (Ire) [86] 4-10-5 (5*) F Perratt, *beh, hdwy aftr 8th, styd on wl to chase wnr betw last 2, no imprsn.*
................................(10 to 1 op 9 to 1 tchd 12 to 1) 2
1533² JEFFERBY [98] 6-11-8 Richard Guest, *chsd wnr most of way, pushed alng hfwy, kpt on same pace frm 2 out.*
....(7 to 1 op 6 to 1) 3
1533⁴ IF YOU SAY SO [87] 7-10-11 A Mulholland, *trkd ldrs, ev ch 3 out, grad wknd appr nxt.*............(50 to 1) 4
FURRY BABY [97] 6-11-7 R Garritty, *in tch, hdwy hfwy, ev ch 3 out, grad wknd.*............(12 to 1 op 10 to 1) 5
THIS NETTLE DANGER [95] 9-11-5 M Brennan, *hld up, hdwy hfwy, ev ch 3 out, sn wknd.*............(12 to 1) 6
1603 DAWAAM [93] 7-11-3 P Niven, *hld up, hdwy hfwy, chsd wnr appr 2 out, sn wknd, btn whn blun last, eased r-in.*
....(5 to 1 fav op 7 to 2) 7
1603⁴ HARDIHERO [90] 7-11-0 B Storey, *in tch till outpcd hfwy, no dngr after.*........................(7 to 1 op 6 to 1) 8
TIM SOLDIER (Fr) [93] 6-11-3 S McNeill, *mid-div till wknd appr 3 out.*..(33 to 1) 9
1603⁵ JUPITER MOON [84] 4-10-8 B Powell, *chsd ldrs till wknd appr 3 out.*............................(10 to 1) 10
819²⁹ AS D'EBOLI (Fr) [89] 6-10-6 (7*) S Hogg, *sn beh.*
................................(33 to 1 op 20 to 1) 11
TRAVEL BOUND [78] 8-10-2 W McFarland, *beh frm hfwy.*
....(33 to 1) 12
1474 MASTER OF THE ROCK [96] 4-11-6 C Hawkins, *in tch till wknd aftr 8th.*....................(11 to 1 op 10 to 1) 13
1639⁴ MILL DE LEASE [76] 8-9-9 (5*) D Bentley, *in tch, pushed alng whn f 3 out.*................(12 to 1 op 50 to 1) f
1299² POLECROFT [86] 10-10-10 Mr N Miles, *prmnt to hfwy, tld off whn pld up bef 2 out.*......................(8 to 1) pu
YACHT CLUB [91] 11-11-1 S Turner, *beh frm hfwy, tld off whn pld up bef 3 out.*......................(50 to 1) pu
Dist: 5l, 1½l, 10l, 2l, 5l, 15l, 3l, 1½l, nk, nk. 6m 31.60s. a 30.60s (16 Ran).
(J C Galbraith), L Lungo

MARKET RASEN (soft)
Friday December 17th
Going Correction: PLUS 1.00 sec. per fur. (races 1,5,6), PLUS 1.40 (2,3,4)

1741 — Pre Christmas Novices' Selling Handicap Hurdle (3 & 4-y-o) £1,749 2m 1f 110yds. (12:40)

1602⁵ RAGGERTY (Ire) [71] 3-11-0 (3*) N Bentley, *hld up, pushed alng hfwy, hdwy 3 out, rdn and hng rght appr 2 out, led last, drvn out.*................(11 to 4 fav op 9 to 4) 1
1532³ BITRAN [58] 3-10-4 A S Smith, *made most till rdn and hdd last, kpt on und pres last.*
................................(7 to 1 op 10 to 1 tchd 12 to 1) 2
1456 WINGED WHISPER (USA) [60] 4-10-6 N Williamson, *trkd ldrs, hdwy to dispute ld 4th, rdn and hmpd appr 2 out, hit last two and one pace.*................(7 to 1 op 5 to 1) 3
1448 COOL SOCIETY (USA) [72] 4-11-4 D Murphy, *chsd ldrs rdn and hit 3 out, sn one pace.*..........(5 to 1 op 7 to 2) 4
1597 YAAFOOR (USA) [78] 4-11-10 M Richards, *hld up, hdwy hfwy, rdn 3 out, hit nxt and sn beh.* (6 to 1 op 6 to 1) 5
1370⁴ ALIZARI (USA) [54] (bl) 4-10-0 M Robinson, *prmnt, reminders 3rd, wknd 3 out.*............(25 to 1 op 20 to 1) 6
1404 DUNBAR [65] (bl) 3-10-11 D Wilkinson, *in tch till rdn and wknd bef 3 out, sn beh.*
................................(14 to 1 op 10 to 1 tchd 16 to 1) 7
1708 RED INK [78] 4-11-10 G McCourt, *hld up, effrt and rdn 3 out, sn wknd and beh...* (9 to 2 op 3 to 1 tchd 5 to 1) 8
Dist: 1½l, 8l, 10l, 1l, sht-hd, 10l, 15l. 4m 26.80s. a 24.80s (8 Ran).
SR: 16/1/-/-/2/ (N Honeyman), G M Moore

1742 — Clugston Novices' Handicap Chase (4-y-o and up) £3,041 2½m. (1:10)

ASTINGS (Fr) [85] 5-12-0 M Dwyer, *led to 4th, trackced ldrs till hdwy 3 out, led appr last and lft clr.*
................................(13 to 8 fav op 6 to 4 tchd 7 to 4 and 15 to 8) 1
1712³ MIDDAY SHOW (USA) [70] (bl) 6-10-9 M McCourt, *not fluent, blun 4th and 9th, beh frm tenth, lft poor second last.*................................(14 to 1 op 12 to 1) 2
1533 HUNTING COUNTRY [70] 9-10-13 N Williamson, *trkd ldrs, rdn alng and hdd 4 out, cl 3rd whn blun badly 3 out, blunded last 2, fnshd very tired......(7 to 1 op 8 to 1) 3
1530* WE'RE IN THE MONEY [70] (bl) 9-10-13 B Dalton, *prmnt, led 4th, jnd 3 out, hdd appr last and 2 ls seconds whn f last, rmntd.*......................(4 to 1 op 7 to 2 tchd 9 to 2) 4
1287² MAUREEN'S FANCY [70] 8-10-13 N Smith, *hit 1st, f second.*......................(7 to 1 op 6 to 1 tchd 9 to 2) f
1358⁸ BUCKWHEAT LAD (Ire) [83] 5-11-12 C Grant, *not jump wl, beh and reminders 7th, tld off frm 9th, pld up bef 3 out.*................................(5 to 1 op 7 to 2) pu
Dist: 12l, 10l, dist. 5m 27.20s. a 35.20s (6 Ran).
SR: 28/1/-/ (W A A Farrell), J G FitzGerald

1743 — Newark Storage Novices' Chase (4-y-o and up) £4,175 2m 1f 110yds (1:40)

1598* ROC COLOR (Fr) 4-10-11 G Bradley, *al cl up, effrt to ld 3 out, rdn last and quickened flt.*
................................(9 to 4 op 7 to 4 tchd 5 to 2) 1
782² BELLTON 5-11-2 M Dwyer, *cl up, led second, hdd 3 out, rdn last, ev ch, not quicken flt.*
................................(6 to 4 on tchd 5 to 4 on) 2
1218⁶ GYMCRAK STARDOM 7-11-2 L Wyer, *trkd ldrs, hdwy and hit 4 out, ev ch whn hit nxt, rdn 2 out wkng when hit last.*................................(6 to 1 op 5 to 1) 3
HIGHLY DECORATED 8-11-2 Gary Lyons, *cl up till rdn and wknd 3 out.*........................(33 to 1 op 20 to 1) 4
CONSTRUCTION 8-11-2 R Supple, *led till f second.*
................................(33 to 1 op 16 to 1) f
Dist: 4l, 12l, 3½l. 4m 49.40s. a 35.40s (5 Ran).
(Mrs Susan McCarthy), C P E Brooks

1744 — Hugh Bourn Developments Handicap Chase (0-135 6-y-o and up) £4,305 3m 1f. (2:10)

MATT REID [107] 9-10-6 M Dwyer, *hld up, took clr order 13th, led aftr 4 out, clr 2 out......(7 to 4 tchd 6 to 4) 1
1572 RIFLE RANGE [125] 10-11-10 N Williamson, *trkd ldr till lft in ld 11th, jnd 13th, hdd aftr 4 out, wkng whn blun 2 out.*................................(9 to 4 tchd 5 to 2) 2
1375* YOUNG MINER [103] 7-10-2² G Upton, *led till blun and uns rdr 13th......(6 to 4 fav op 5 to 4 tchd 13 to 8) ur
Dist: 6m 48.80s. a 47.80s (3 Ran).
(W G N Morgan), J P Leigh

1745 — Roseland 'National Hunt' Novices' Hurdle (4-y-o and up) £2,477 3m (2:40)

1502⁸ IVY HOUSE (Ire) 5-10-12 N Williamson, *hld up and beh, steady hdwy 4 out, effrt to chal 2 out, led and hit last, rdn and ran on flt.*..........................(12 to 1) 1
1574⁷ MAJORITY MAJOR (Ire) 4-10-12 C Grant, *prmnt, effrt and ev ch 2 out, led briefly appr last, sn rdn and no extr flt.*................................(14 to 1 op 10 to 1) 2
1295⁵ HENRY VILL (Ire) 5-10-12 D Bridgwater, *chsd ldrs, effrt and hdwy 3 out, rdn and hit 2 out, kpt on one pace appr last.*................................(11 to 1 op 6 to 1) 3

1485 HYPNOTIST 6-10-9 (5*) D Bentley, *chsd ldrs, outpcd aftr 3 out, no dngr after.*................(10 to 1 tchd 11 to 1) 7
1485* STAGS FELL 8-10-11 (7*) N Stocks, *hld up, effrt aftr 3 out, no real hdwy........*(10 to 1 op 12 to 1 tchd 8 to 1) 8
WHAT IF 9-10-7 M Brennan, *hld up, hdwy to track ldrs hfwy, pushed alng aftr 3 out, wknd quickly after nxt, eased whn btn...............*(3 to 1 jt-fav tchd 7 to 2) 9
BOLD MOOD 4-10-10 L O'Hara, *nvr better than mid-div.*
................................(33 to 1) 10
SCARABEN 5-11-12 R Garritty, *al beh*...........(12 to 1) 11
1488⁵ WESTCOURT FLYER 4-10-7 (7*) J Driscoll, *al beh.*
................................(25 to 1 op 20 to 1) 12
NEPAL STAR (USA) 4-10-7 (7*) G Tormey, *sn tracking ldrs, wknd aftr 5th, tld off......*(50 to 1 op 33 to 1) 13
RESOLUTE BAY 7-11-0 S Turner, *mid-div till wknd aftr 5th, tld off.......................*(20 to 1 op 16 to 1) 14
1702 LILIAN MAY GREEN 4-10-3 Ann Stokell, *sn beh, tld off whn pld up aftr 3 out.................*(100 to 1 op 66 to 1) pu
Dist: 3l, 3½l, sht-hd, 6l, 1l, 1l, 1½l, ¾l, 15l, 4l. 3m 56.90s. a 15.90s (15 Ran).
SR: 19/18/16/13/12/1/8/10/-/ (Miss Angela Bennett), J L Eyre

1533 GUTE NACHT 10-10-7 (5*) S Lyons, beh, steady hdwy 3
out, sn rdn, styd on frm 2 out......(50 to 1 op 33 to 1)   4
1469⁵ NORTHERN SQUIRE 5-10-7 (5*) P Williams, chsd ldrs, hit 4
out, rdn nxt, one pace appr 2 out. (33 to 1 op 25 to 1)   5
SPARKLING FLAME 9-10-12 M A FitzGerald, mid-div,
steady hdwy hfwy, effrt to ld 2 out, sn rdn, hdd and
wknd appr last.........(3 to 1 tchd 4 to 1 and 9 to 2)   6
1181 JUST MOLLY 6-10-7 M Dwyer, cl up, led 4 out, rdn and
hdd 2 out, grad wknd................(10 to 1 op 10 to 1)   7
1568 SWINGING SONG 6-10-12 B Dalton, led, hdd 4 out, grad
wknd.................................(50 to 1 op 40 to 1)   8
1108* LE GINNO (Fr) 6-11-4 G Bradley, not fluent, cl up, effrt to
chal and hit 4 out, sn rdn and wknd rpdly nxt, pld aftr
after.......................(11 to 8 on op 13 to 8 on)   pu
1657 SOPHINI 5-10-0 (7*) C Woodall, hit 1st, in tch till lost pl
and hit 7th, sn beh and pld up bef 2 out,
...............................(66 to 1 op 33 to 1)   pu
Dist: 2l, 4l, 4l, 3½l, 2½l, 6l, dist. 6m 22.30s. a 40.30s (10 Ran).
(Mrs L R Joughin), J J O'Neill

1746 Consort Travel Handicap Hurdle (0-125 4-y-o and up) £2,427 2m 1f 110yds....................... (3:10)

1487⁶ GYMCRAK SOVEREIGN [103] 5-10-12 R Marley, made virtually all, hit 3rd, rdn clr 2 out, hit last, kpt on wl.
......................(9 to 1 op 10 to 1 tchd 8 to 1)   1
1672⁴ CLURICAN (Ire) [115] 4-11-10 G McCourt, trkd ldrs, hdwy 3
out, effrt and hit 2 out, sn hrd drvn and styd on.
...............................(6 to 1 op 7 to 1)   2
1481⁷ BRAMBLEBERRY [103] 4-10-12 Gary Lyons, al chasing
wnr, rdn appr 2 out and one pace. (12 to 1 op 10 to 1)   3
1485 ELDER PRINCE [91] 7-10-0 R Supple, beh, pushed alng
and hdwy hfwy, hrd rdn appr 2 out and no imprsn.
.............................(50 to 1 op 33 to 1 tchd 66 to 1)   4
1219⁵ SPACE CAPTAIN [106] 6-10-12 (3*) N Bentley, hld up and
beh, hdwy hfwy, rdn appr 2 out and no imprsn.
....................................(12 to 1 op 10 to 1)   5
1389² RATIFY [101] 6-10-10 A S Smith, hld up, hit 3rd, gd hdwy
aftr 4 out, rdn appr 2 out and sn btn.
.................................(9 to 2 op 4 to 1 tchd 5 to 1)   6
DORADUS [96] 5-10-5 M Dwyer, prmnt, rdn 3 out and
grad wknd.....................(8 to 1 op 6 to 1)   7
KEEP HOPE ALIVE [97] 9-10-6 E Murphy, chsd ldrs on
outer, rdn alng 3 out and sn wknd...(8 to 1 op 5 to 1)   8
EMERALD GEM [91] 7-10-0 S Keightley, al beh.
...............................(16 to 1 op 20 to 1 tchd 33 to 1)   9
7813 SEAGULL HOLLOW (Ire) [100] 4-10-9 L Wyer, in tch, effrt
appr 3 out, sn rdn and wknd.
...................................(7 to 2 fav op 9 to 2 tchd 4 to 1)   10
1127⁴ MAGIC BLOOM [91] 7-9-11 (3*) A Larnach, prmnt to 4th, sn
lost pl and beh......................(11 to 1 op 10 to 1)   11
1487 MY LINDIANNE [91] 6-10-0 W Worthington, al rear, tld off
frm 3 out.............................(14 to 1 tchd 16 to 1)   12
Dist: 3l, 6l, 10l, ½l, 3l, 1½l, 4l, 2l, 20l, 5l. 4m 25.90s. a 23.90s (12 Ran).
SR: 20/29/11/-/3/-/   (The Gymcrak Thoroughbred Racing Club), G Holmes

UTTOXETER (heavy)
Friday December 17th
Going Correction: PLUS 0.40 sec. per fur. (races 1,3,-
5,7), PLUS 1.15 (2,4,6)

1747 St Modwen Novices' Hurdle (4-y-o and up) £2,463 2½m 110yds.......(12:30)

MAN TO MAN (NZ) 6-11-5 A Kondrat, jmpd wl, made all,
quickened away frm 3 out, fluffed last 2, easily.
..............(11 to 4 on op 3 to 1 on tchd 9 to 4 on)   1
1542⁶ FUN MONEY 6-10-12 A Maguire, tucked away in midfield, improved to chase wnr aftr 3 out, styd on, no
imprsn...................(8 to 1 op 7 to 1 tchd 9 to 1)   2
1524 WARFIELD 6-10-12 R Dunwoody, nvr far away, drvn to go
second appr 3 out and outpcd frm betw last 2.
......................................(14 to 1 op 10 to 1)   3
1624⁴ PHAROAH'S SON 7-10-12 S Earle, al wl plcd, feeling pace
and drvn alng appr 3 out, no extr frm nxt.
....(150 to 1 op 100 to 1)   4
BOWLAND GIRL (Ire) 4-10-4 (3*) S Wynne, chsd ldg bunch,
improved und pres appr 4 out, no imprsn frm nxt.
...................................(50 to 1 op 50 to 1)   5
1448⁸ PRINCETHORPE 6-10-9 (3*) D Meredith, trkd ldg quartet,
hrd at work whn pace lifted aftr 4 out, struggling frm
nxt........................(50 to 1 op 33 to 1)   6
HIT THE FAN 4-10-12 C Llewellyn, chsd ldg bunch, chased
alng to hold pl appr 4 out, fdd frm nxt.
...................................(9 to 1 op 8 to 1)   7
GREAT ORME (NZ) 6-10-5 (7*) Mr G Shenkin, trkd ldg 6, hrd
at work aftr 4 out, sn lost tch.....(66 to 1 op 50 to 1)   8
SENNA BLUE 8-10-12 V Slattery, nvr far away, chsd alng
and lost grnd aftr 4 out, sn btn....(66 to 1 op 50 to 1)   9
864 THE OVERTRUMPER 6-10-12 R Greene, chsd alng to keep
up hfwy, lost tch frm 4 out......(150 to 1 op 100 to 1)   10
1460⁸ GRECIAN SAILOR 8-10-12 J Frost, in tch, chsd alng to
keep up hfwy, tld off frm 4 out. (150 to 1 op 100 to 1)   11

1329 FOXY LASS 4-10-7 Mr J Cambidge, in tch, drvn alng to
keep up hfwy, tld off frm 4 out. (150 to 1 op 100 to 1)   12
1602 HYDEONIAN 6-10-12 M Hourigan, struggling frm 3rd, tld
off whn pld up bef 6th.........(150 to 1 op 100 to 1)   pu
1108 ROYAL GAIT (NZ) 5-10-9 (3*) R Davis, chsd ldrs, beh,
struggling and lost grnd appr 4 out, tld off whn pld up
bef 2 out........................(50 to 1 op 33 to 1)   pu
Dist: 20l, 20l, 6l, 3l, 25l, 4l, 1½l, 7l, 12l, 3½l. 5m 6.20s. a 23.20s (14 Ran).
(Stanley Clarke), F Doumen

1748 Octagon Conditional Jockeys' Handicap Chase (0-120 5-y-o and up) £2,571 2m 5f..........................(1:00)

1639 MO ICHI DO [82] 7-10-0 T Eley, nvr far away, led and
stumbled 4 out, styd on grimly frm betw last 2.
...............................(14 to 1 op 20 to 1)   1
THE LAUGHING LORD [106] 7-11-10 A Thornton, patiently
rdn, imprvg whn jmpd lft 3 out, effrt and ridden nxt,
styd on same pace r-in............(5 to 2 fav op 6 to 1)   2
1471* PIPER O'DRUMMOND [104] 6-11-8 J Burke, wtd wth,
steady hdwy frm off the pace 5 out, effrt betw last 2,
ran on same pace......(11 to 4 op 5 to 2 tchd 3 to 1)   3
1470³ CEDAR RUN [82] 10-10-0 D Meade, not fluent, drvn alng
in midfield fnl circuit, blun and lost grnd 5 out, some
hdwy last 2, nvr dngrs.............(25 to 1 op 20 to 1)   4
1534⁴ NEWMARKET SAUSAGE [82] 12-10-0 M Hourigan, tried to
make all, hdd 4 out, grad wknd...............(50 to 1)   5
1423² CHANCERY BUCK [88] 10-10-1 (5*) R Darke, trkd ldg
bunch, bustled alng to hold pl fnl curcuit, lost tch frm 6
out.......................................(9 to 1 op 7 to 1)   6
1238⁶ ANOTHER CORNER [87] (bl) 10-10-0 (5*) P McLoughlin,
dsptd ld, drvn alng to hold pl appr 4 out, lost tch bef
nxt...(50 to 1)   7
SOME OBLIGATION [106] 8-11-5 (5*) D Winter, nvr far
away, feeling pace and rdn 6 out, tld off frm 4 out.
....(6 to 1 tchd 8 to 1)   8
1388⁴ DANDY MINSTREL [108] 9-11-12 W Marston, trkd ldrs, hit
4th, ev ch whn crrd lft 3 out, disputing 3rd and hld
when f nxt.............(6 to 1 op 11 to 2 tchd 13 to 2)   f
Dist: 3½l, ½l, dist, 8l, 8l, 2l, dist. 5m 40.80s. a 40.80s (9 Ran).
(Miss Sue Wilton), Miss S J Wilton

1749 Wintertons Selling Hurdle (3 - 6-y-o) £1,721 2m.................... (1:30)

1408 SHARED GOLD 3-10-5 M Bosley, patiently rdn, chsd alng
to improve 3 out, led betw last 2, drvn clr.
...............................(10 to 1 op 7 to 1 tchd 12 to 1)   1
1522³ DOUALAGO (Fr) (bl) 3-10-13 R Dunwoody, made most to
5th, rallied frm 3 out to nose ahead briefly aftr nxt,
outpcd r-in.....(5 to 4 on op 6 to 4 on tchd 11 to 10)   2
1313⁵ GLOSSY 6-11-4 (7*) G Robertson, wth ldr, led 5th till rdn
and hdd aftr 2 out, wknd quickly. (20 to 1 op 14 to 1)   3
526⁶ BAND OF HOPE (USA) 6-11-10 Diane Clay, chsd ldg bunch,
struggling to keep up aftr 4 out, lost tch frm nxt.
.................(7 to 2 op 3 to 1 tchd 4 to 1)   4
1522⁴ CREAGMHOR 3-9-12 (7*) Mr J L Llewellyn, chsd clr ldg trio,
hrd at work frm hfwy, tld off aftr 4 out.
...............................(8 to 1 op 6 to 1)   5
TRENTSIDE MIST 5-11-7 M Ranger, struggling in midfield
thrght, tld off frm 4 out........(16 to 1 op 8 to 1)   6
ANTE UP (Ire) (bl) 5-11-7 L Harvey, reluctant to race, tld off
till pld up bef 4th.............(33 to 1 op 20 to 1)   pu
1519 QUALITAIR IDOL 4-11-2 S Burrough, sn outpcd and beh,
tld off whn pld up betw last 2.... (50 to 1 op 20 to 1)   pu
448⁶ MAD MYTTON 3-10-5 N Mann, al struggling, tld off whn
pld up bef 3 out.................(10 to 1 op 7 to 2)   pu
1522 SCOTTISH TEMPTRESS 3-10-0 T Wall, flt out the whole
way, tld off whn pld up bef 2 out. (50 to 1 op 20 to 1)   pu
SWEETWATER MOON 3-10-0 A Maguire, wth ldg pair,
struggling and reminders hfwy, tld off whn pld up bef 3
out..................(25 to 1 op 12 to 1 tchd 33 to 1)   pu
Dist: 10l, 20l, ¾l, dist, 12l. 3m 52.00s. a 13.00s (11 Ran).
SR: 11/9/1/-/-/-/   (P A Deal), J R Bosley

1750 Orbital Centre Novices' Chase (5-y-o and up) £2,905 2m 7f.......... (2:00)

1485⁸ PLAYFUL JULIET (Can) (v) 5-10-7 Pat Caldwell, patiently
rdn, steady hdwy to join issue appr 4 out, led nxt, gng
clr whn blun last, styd on....................(100 to 1)   1
1107 MARTELL BOY (NZ) 6-10-12 J Frost, settled midfield,
improved to chal appr 4 out, drw level 2 out, outpcd frm
last.........................(9 to 1 op 5 to 1 tchd 7 to 1)   2
1527* VISAGA 7-11-4 C Llewellyn, jmpd wl, tried to make all,
jnd fnl circuit, hdd 3 out, fdd.
...................................(100 to 30 op 3 to 1 tchd 7 to 2)   3
955⁸ MOUNTAIN MASTER 7-10-12 Mr J M Pritchard, struggling
thrght, tld off fnl circuit, plodded round.
......................................(33 to 1 op 20 to 1)   4
1420* MR FLANAGAN 7-11-4 J Railton, al hndy, ev ch appr 4
out, disputing 3rd but looked btn whn f 2 out.
.................(11 to 10 on op Evens tchd 6 to 4)   f
1420³ FINCH'S GEM 5-10-12 R Dunwoody, wth ldr, ev ch appr 4
out, disputing 3rd but looked btn whn f 2 out.
...............................(11 to 2 op 4 to 1)   f

1657² THE LIGHTER SIDE 7-10-5 (7") Judy Davies, *al chasing
ldrs, struggling fnl circuit, tld off whn pld up aftr 4
out*..................................(14 to 1) pu
Dist: 8l, 15l, dist. 6m 9.40s. a 39.40s (7 Ran).

(Brian Brennan), T H Caldwell

1751 Levy Board Novices' Handicap Hurdle (3-y-o and up) £2,284 2m...... (2:30)

1504⁴ HEATHYARDS BOY [81] 3-11-10 R Dunwoody, *slight ld to
3rd, styd hndy till nosed ahead 3 out, hit nxt, forged
clr*..........................(100 to 30 op 5 to 2 tchd 7 to 2) 1
1448⁵ SAINT CIEL (USA) [80] 5-11-9 A Maguire, *patiently rdn,
improved to draw level 3 out, ridden betw last 2, no
extr*...........................(5 to 2 fav tchd 11 to 4) 2
MAHONG [65] 5-10-8 V Slattery, *nvr far away, drw level
last 2, rdn and outpcd r-in.*
..........................(3 to 1 op 11 to 4 tchd 100 to 30) 3
934 KADARI [70] 4-10-13 Diane Clay, *slight ld frm 3rd till appr
3 out, wknd quickly from nxt*...........(8 to 1 tchd 9 to 1) 4
1535⁸ ENCHANTED FLYER [60] (bl) 6-9-12 (5") T Eley, *dsptd ld frm
3rd till appr 3 out, sn tld off*.................(25 to 1) 5
1588⁴ BIN LID (Ire) [68] 4-10-4 (7") B Harding, *last but in tch, lost
grnd frm 4 out, tld off last 3.*
..........................(11 to 2 op 7 to 2 tchd 6 to 1) 6
Dist: 6l, hd, 12l, dist, dist. 3m 53.00s. a 14.00s (6 Ran).
SR: 20/13/-/ (L A Morgan), R Hollinshead

1752 Sheer Brilliance Handicap Chase (0-145 5-y-o and up) £3,412 2m.. (3:00)

1446² TRIMLOUGH [123] 8-11-10 W Marston, *jmpd wl, made all,
ran on strly frm 3 out, readily.*
..........................(5 to 4 fav op 6 to 4 tchd 7 to 4) 1
1461² ONE FOR THE POT [108] 8-10-9 A Maguire, *al hndy, effrt
and drvn alng last 4, not quicken r-in.*
..........................(7 to 2 op 4 to 1) 2
ITS NEARLY TIME [122] 10-11-9 R Dunwoody, *trkd wnr
most of way, ev ch 4 out, wknd quickly aftr nxt.*
..........................(11 to 4 op 9 to 4 tchd 10 to 1) 3
1514⁴ SETTER COUNTRY [117] 9-11-4 W Irvine, *tracking ldr whn
blun and uns rdr second.*
..........................(7 to 2 op 5 to 1) ur
Dist: 6l, dist. 4m 12.30s. a 23.30s (4 Ran).
SR: 47/26/-/-/ (R A H Perkins), P T Dalton

1753 Festival Park Handicap Hurdle (0-135 4-y-o and up) £2,827 2m....... (3:30)

1639 NELTEGRITY [106] 4-10-1¹ Peter Caldwell, *patiently rdn,
improved frm 3 out, styd on grimly to ld r-in.*
..........................(25 to 1 op 20 to 1 tchd 33 to 1) 1
1106 ABBOT OF FURNESS [133] 9-12-0 R Dunwoody, *tried to
make all, drvn alng appr last, hdd and no extr r-in.*
..........................(13 to 2 op 4 to 1) 2
1614⁴ STYLUS [116] 4-10-11 A Maguire, *wtd wth, improved to
join issue 3 out, rdn and no extr betw last 2.*
..........................(6 to 4 fav op Evens) 3
1690² WHIPPERS DELIGHT (Ire) [105] 5-9-7 (7") D Meade, *nvr far
away, ev ch appr 3 out, rdn and one pace frm nxt.*
..........................(6 to 1 op 4 to 1 tchd 7 to 1) 4
1508³ SILLIAN [105] 11-9-11 (3") S Wynne, *al tracking ldrs, effrt
appr 3 out, rdn and no imprsn frm nxt.*
..........................(14 to 1 tchd 16 to 1) 5
CELTIC BOB [105] 13-9-7 (7") P Maddock, *chsd ldg bunch,
feeling pace appr 3 out, sn btn*...............(33 to 1) 6
EMERALD RULER [105] 6-10-0 W Marston, *trkd ldr, hrd at
work appr 3 out, fdd*................(8 to 1 op 6 to 1) 7
1586⁷ FAMILY LINE [105] 5-10-0 M Hourigan, *trkd ldg trio, effrt
appr 3 out, sn rdn and btn.*
..........................(9 to 2 op 7 to 2 tchd 6 to 1) 8
Dist: 1½l, 4l, 4l, 1½l, 15l, 4l, 8l. 3m 51.40s. a 12.40s (8 Ran).
SR: 13/38/17/2/-/ (R S G Jones), T H Caldwell

ASCOT (good to soft)
Saturday December 18th
Going Correction: PLUS 0.73 sec. per fur. (races 1,4,5), PLUS 0.78 (2,3,6)

1754 Noel Novices' Chase Grade 2 (5-y-o and up) £8,918 2m 3f 110yds... (12:15)

1637⁸ EASY BUCK 6-11-3 C Maude, *trkd ldrs, cld appr 11th, led
3 out, lft clr nxt, eased r-in*........(3 to 1 tchd 9 to 1) 1
1558³ BAYDON STAR 6-11-10 A Maguire, *hld up in tch, mstk
5th, hdwy appr 11th, rdn aftr nxt, rallying whn blun 2
out, not reco'r*.
..........................(13 to 8 on op 7 to 4 on tchd 6 to 4 on) 2
1457² POPPETS PET 6-11-3 S Hodgson, *wth ldr early, mstk 7th,
sn lost pl, ran on frm 2 out.*
..........................(9 to 1 op 33 to 1 tchd 100 to 1) 3
1547 MONSIEUR LE CURE 7-11-3 P Niven, *chsd ldrs, mstk 9th,
effrt 12th, drvn whn blun 2 out, not reco'r*.
..........................(14 to 1 op 12 to 1 tchd 16 to 1) 4
1489⁴ RUNNING SANDS 9-11-3 G McCourt, *beh, some hdwy frm
2 out, nvr a dngr*.....(66 to 1 op 50 to 1 tchd 100 to 1) 5

1518* BIG BEAT (USA) 5-11-7 P Holley, *led, clr 4th till hdd and
blun 3 out, sn wknd*..................(7 to 2 op 3 to 1) 6
1288² MONAUGHTY MAN 7-11-3 P Williams, *al beh, tld off.*
..........................(100 to 1 op 50 to 1) 7
1637² WANDERWEG (Fr) 5-11-3 H Davies, *not jump wl, sn last,
tld off whn pld up aftr 6th.*
..........................(20 to 1 op 16 to 1 tchd 25 to 1) pu
Dist: 15l, 3½l, 2l, 3l, 4l, 20l. 5m 0.40s. a 18.90s (8 Ran).
SR: 42/34/23/21/18/18/-/-/ (The Burford Laundry Company Ltd), N A Gaselee

1755 Knights Royal Hurdle (4 & 5-y-o) £5,524 2m 110yds............. (12:50)

1521* ABSALOM'S LADY 5-10-7 P Holley, *hld up, hdwy frm 5th,
sn tracking ldrs, led aftr last, quickened clr.*
..........................(13 to 8 fav op 6 to 4 tchd 7 to 4) 1
1665² SATIN LOVER 5-11-5 G McCourt, *tucked in hndy, led
appr 2 out, hdd aftr last, not pace of wnr.*
..........................(11 to 2 op 6 to 1 tchd 13 to 2) 2
1559⁶ KILCASH (Ire) (bl) 5-11-5 M Richards, *wth ldr, led aftr 3rd
till appr 2 out, sn rdn, kpt on one pace.*
..........................(9 to 2 tchd 5 to 1) 3
1559² HIGHBROOK (USA) 5-10-7 D Murphy, *wtd wth, hdwy frm
5th, shaken up aftr 2 out, sn btn.....(3 to 1 op 5 to 2) 4
898⁸ MAJOR BUGLER (Ire) 4-11-5 R Dunwoody, *trkd ldrs, ev ch
3 out, wknd bef nxt.*.(20 to 1 op 16 to 1 tchd 25 to 1) 5
PONTYNYSWEN 5-10-12 A Maguire, *led till aftr 3rd, hndy
till wknd 5th*........(14 to 1 op 12 to 1 tchd 16 to 1) 6
SHARRIBA 4-10-7 C Llewellyn, *hld up, rdn 3 out, sn no
imprsn*.............(66 to 1 op 33 to 1 tchd 100 to 1) 7
1442 SOUND REVEILLE 5-10-12 M A FitzGerald, *blun 1st, struggling frm 5th*......(66 to 1 op 33 to 1 tchd 100 to 1) 8
Dist: 5l, 7l, 1½l, 10l, 15l, 15l, 5l. 4m 0.80s. a 14.80s (8 Ran).
SR: 60/67/60/46/48/26/6/6/ (Whitcombe Manor Racing Stables Limited), D R C Elsworth

1756 Long Walk Hurdle Grade 1 (4-y-o and up) £25,372 3m 1f 110yds... (1:20)

1438² SWEET DUKE (Fr) 6-11-7 C Llewellyn, *wth ldr, led 7th, rdn
frm 2 out, styd on wl*...............(7 to 2 tchd 4 to 1) 1
1438³ BURGOYNE 7-11-7 P Niven, *led to 7th, sn rdn alng,
rallied aftr last*......(16 to 1 op 14 to 1 tchd 20 to 1) 2
1106² AVRO ANSON 5-11-7 D Byrne, *trkd ldrs, wnt second appr
2 out, btn whn mstk last*.............(10 to 1 op 8 to 1) 3
BALASANI (Fr) 7-11-7 R Dunwoody, *patiently rdn, hdwy
9th, ridden appr 2 out, sn no extr...(7 to 1 op 5 to 1) 4
1617* BOLLIN WILLIAM 5-11-7 L Wyer, *pld hrd, handily plcd, ev
ch 3 out, wknd betw last 2.*
..........................(10 to 1 op 12 to 1 tchd 14 to 1) 5
1310* PEATSWOOD 5-11-7 Lorna Vincent, *in tch till wknd 8th.*
..........................(50 to 1 tchd 66 to 1) 6
1438* TRIPLE WITCHING 7-11-7 A Maguire, *hld up in midfield,
effrt 8th, rdn appr 3 out, sn wknd, tld off whn virtually
pld up r-in*.......(11 to 4 jt-fav op 9 to 4 tchd 3 to 1) 7
1554² SHUIL AR AGHAIDH 7-11-2 C Swan, *hld up in last pl till f
6th*.................(11 to 4 jt-fav op 9 to 4 tchd 3 to 1) f
1458² MARDOOD 8-11-7 H Davies, *al beh, tld off whn pld up bef
2 out*.............................(50 to 1 tchd 66 to 1) pu
Dist: 2l, 3l, 7l, 4l, 15l, dist. 6m 22.30s. a 23.30s (9 Ran).
SR: 59/57/54/47/43/28/ (Andy Mavrou), N A Twiston-Davies

1757 Betterware Cup Handicap Chase (5-y-o and up) £23,206 3m 110yds..(1:55)

1664² YOUNG HUSTLER [150] 6-11-10 C Llewellyn, *led to 4 out,
led appr 2 out, sn clr, easily.*
..........................(9 to 8 fav tchd 5 to 4 and 6 to 4) 1
1540⁴ LATENT TALENT [144] (bl) 9-11-4 M Richards, *hld up in
midfield, hdwy 6p second hfwy, led 4 out till appr 2
out, sn no extr*...................(14 to 1 tchd 16 to 1) 2
1573⁸ FIGHTING WORDS [134] 7-10-8 D Murphy, *midfield,
reminders 12th, hdwy appr 15th, styd on one pace.*
..........................(8 to 1 op 10 to 1) 3
1447⁵ WINDY WAYS [130] 8-10-4 M A FitzGerald, *al hndy, rdn
and outpcd 16th, no further imprsn.*
..........................(12 to 1 op 16 to 1 tchd 20 to 1) 4
1616³ VERY VERY ORDINARY [145] 7-11-5 R Supple, *hld up beh,
reminders and shrtlvd effrt 15th, nvr able to chal.*
..........................(9 to 2 op 7 to 2 tchd 5 to 1) 5
1365³ MISTER ED [136] 10-10-8 D Morris, *trkd ldrs, stumbled
bend aftr 8th, lost pl 12th, sn rear.*
..........................(20 to 1 op 16 to 1 tchd 25 to 1) 6
CAPABILITY BROWN [145] 6-11-5 R Dunwoody, *cl up till
wknd appr 4 out, beh whn pld up bef 2 out.*
..........................(5 to 1 op 4 to 1 tchd 11 to 2) pu
1652² FLASHTHECASH [138] 7-10-12 A Maguire, *al beh, tld off
whn pld up bef 2 out*..........(14 to 1 tchd 16 to 1) pu
Dist: 6l, 13l, 4l, 2½l, 7l, dist. 6m 22.70s. a 19.20s (8 Ran).
SR: 83/71/49/41/53/41/-/-/ (G M MacEchern), N A Twiston-Davies

1758 Frogmore Handicap Chase (5-y-o and up) £9,530 2m............(2:30)

1009⁵ BILLY BATHGATE [130] 7-10-3 M A FitzGerald, *hld up gng
wl, rapid hdwy to ld 2 out, sn clr, easily.*
..........................(7 to 1 op 8 to 1 tchd 9 to 1) 1

1440[2] WONDER MAN (Fr) [155] 8-12-0 A Maguire, *trkd ldr, chlgd 8th, led nxt, hdd 2 out, sn btn.* .... (5 to 4 fav op 11 to 10 tchd 11 to 8) 2

1571[6] UNCLE ERNIE [148] 8-11-7 M Dwyer, *nvr far away, rdn 9th, ev ch nxt, sn no extr.* .... (11 to 4 op 5 to 2 tchd 3 to 1) 3

1440* YOUNG SNUGFIT [153] 9-11-7 (5*) J McCarthy, *led to 9th, ev ch nxt, sn rdn and wknd.* .... (100 to 30 op 5 to 2 tchd 7 to 2) 4

1328 LUCKY AGAIN [129] 6-10-2[2] R Dunwoody, *cl 3rd whn f third*.......................... (66 to 1 tchd 100 to 1) f

Dist: 15l, 2½l, 8l. 4m 0.60s. a 13.10s (5 Ran).
SR: 61/71/61/58/-/ (Michael Buckley), N J Henderson

1759 Hampton Court Handicap Hurdle Amateur Riders (0-145 4-y-o and up) £2,892 2½m.................. (3:00)

BELLEZZA [117] 6-9-12[5] (7*) Mr T McCarthy, *midfield, hdwy on ins to ld appr 2 out, sn rdn, hld on gmely r-in.* .... (6 to 1 op 5 to 1) 1

1474[9] SEA BUCK [117] 7-9-11[4] (7*) Mr Raymond White, *hld up, hdwy frm 7th, chlgd r-in, not quicken last 100 yards.* .... (10 to 1 op 7 to 1) 2

1458* ULURU (Ire) [117] 5-9-10[3] (7*) Mr C Hancock, *chsd ldr, outpcd 3 out, ran on frm last.* ....(4 to 1 op 3 to 1 tchd 9 to 2) 3

EVERALDO (Fr) [152] 9-12-0 (7*) Mr J O'Shaughnessy, *midfield, effrt 6th, ev ch appr 2 out, wknd last.* .... (10 to 1 op 7 to 1) 4

1274 CAPTAIN DOLFORD [117] 6-9-9 (5*) Miss P Jones, *midfield, lost pl 7th, kpt on one pace frm 2 out.* ....(7 to 1 op 6 to 1 tchd 8 to 1) 5

1565[3] RIVER BOUNTY [124] 7-10-3[1] (5*) Mr T Byrne, *midfield, rdn alng 3 out, styd on same pace*......(6 to 1 tchd 7 to 1) 6

1641 SHANNON GLEN [128] (bl) 7-10-6[2] (7*) Mr A Wyse, *sn clr, wknd and hdd appr 2 out, soon btn.* (6 to 1 op 8 to 1) 7

1561[5] THE DECENT THING [118] 10-9-12[4] (7*) Mr G Hogan, *hld up beh, rdn appr 8th, no imprsn.* ....(11 to 4 fav op 3 to 1 tchd 7 to 2) 8

1671[6] DUKE DE VENDOME [117] 10-9-7 (7*) Mr G Haine, *last early, nvr a threat*............... (66 to 1 op 50 to 1) 9

1466 MOZE TIDY [117] (bl) 8-9-10[3] (7*) Mr A Mitchell, *midfield, mstk 4th, effrt 6th, wknd nxt, tld off.* .... (50 to 1 op 33 to 1) 10

1445 ROSITARY (Fr) [118] 10-10-1[8] (7*) Mr G Cosgrove, *midfield, lost pl 5th, sn rear, tld off*.......(20 to 1 tchd 25 to 1) 11

936 WILTSHIRE YEOMAN [117] 13-9-7 (7*) Miss S White, *chsd ldr, lost pl 4th, sn rear, tld off*.................(66 to 1) 12

Dist: 1l, 6l, 3½l, 10l, 4l, 15l, 2½l, hd, 10l, 20l. 5m 4.90s. a 23.90s (12 Ran).
(K Higson), A Moore

NAVAN (IRE) (soft)
Saturday December 18th

1760 Sherry Maiden Hurdle (5-y-o and up) £3,105 2¼m.................. (12:30)

HARCON (Ire) 5-12-0 K F O'Brien, ... (4 to 1) 1
1549[2] WINDOVER (Ire) 5-11-3 (3*) D Bromley, ... (3 to 1 fav) 2
1052[3] MINIGIRLS NIECE (Ire) 5-11-1 A Powell, ...(8 to 1) 3
993 ISN'T THAT NICE (Ire) 5-11-6 J Shortt, ... (10 to 1) 4
1379[2] FINNEGANS WAKE 6-11-1 (5*) K P Gaule, ...(4 to 1) 5
BARRAFONA (Ire) 5-11-1 (5*) P A Roche, ...(14 to 1) 6
I AM 5-12-0 T Horgan, ... (10 to 1) 7
1401 COMICALITY 5-11-6 T J Taaffe, ... (12 to 1) 8
1549 BEAU GRANDE (Ire) 5-12-0 L P Cusack, ... (10 to 1) 9
1549 FINAWAY BOY (Ire) 5-11-6 J P Banahan, ... (20 to 1) 10
1549 GOLDEN PLAN (Ire) 5-11-6 C N Bowens, ...(25 to 1) 11
1549 LORD DIAMOND 7-12-0 H Rogers, ...(10 to 1) 12
1496 BETTY BALFOUR 7-10-8 (7*) J Butler, ... (33 to 1) 13
MAMBO KING 6-11-6 P Carberry, ... (10 to 1) 14
1270[3] GOLDEN NUGGET 6-11-6 F Woods, ...(7 to 1) 15
1500[6] PARKBOY LASS 6-11-9 D H O'Connor, ... (16 to 1) 16
CAILIN GEAL (Ire) 5-11-1 Mr S R Murphy, ... (20 to 1) 17
1549[7] JIMMY O'GOBLIN 6-11-6 B Sheridan, ... (8 to 1) 18
1379 JEMMA'S GOLD (Ire) 5-11-1 C O'Dwyer, ... (25 to 1) 19
COURSING GLEN (Ire) 5-11-6 M Duffy, ... (14 to 1) 20
1681 ST AIDAN (Ire) 5-11-1 (5*) L Flynn, ... (33 to 1) 21
POOR MOTHER (Ire) 5-11-1 F J Flood, ...(25 to 1) f
RAREABILITY (Ire) 5-10-10 (5*) H Taylor, ...(25 to 1) pu
ORCHARD POSER (Ire) 5-11-7 (7*) J P Broderick, (16 to 1) pu
Dist: 13l, 6l, 1½l, 1l. 4m 44.30s. (24 Ran).
(Mrs P J Conway), J T R Dreaper

1761 Mince Pie Handicap Chase (4-y-o and up) £3,105 2m..................(1:00)

1550* BOB DEVANI [-] 7-10-1 (6ex) P Carberry, ...(10 to 9 on) 1
1382[5] MAD TOM [-] 8-11-8 J P Banahan, ... (7 to 1) 2
1179[3] MAKE ME AN ISLAND [-] 8-9-0 (7*) J P Broderick, ..(7 to 1) 3
1682[4] FRANTESA [-] 7-10-3 T Horgan, ...(10 to 1) 4
1682 WHO'S TO SAY [-] 7-11-1 (3*) T J Mitchell, ... (9 to 1) 5
1433* CAPE SPY [-] (bl) 7-10-10 H Rogers, ... (100 to 30) pu
Dist: 2½l, 4l, 15l, 3l. 4m 35.50s. (6 Ran).
(John O'Meara), Noel Meade

1762 Carol Maiden Hurdle (4-y-o) £3,105 2m ....(1:30)

1076 HEIST 11-9 P Carberry, ... (Evens fav) 1
1610[4] TELLTALK (Ire) 10-13 (5*) J R Barry, ... (7 to 1) 2
925[2] SENSE OF VALUE 11-4 B Sheridan, ... (4 to 1) 3
1581[7] FINAWAY EXPRESS (Ire) 10-11 (7*) P J Mulligan, .. (12 to 1) 4
BANNER GALE (Ire) 11-4 C O'Dwyer, ... (20 to 1) 5
1397 MAXWELTON BRAES (Ire) 11-4 (5*) M G Cleary, ... (25 to 1) 6
1016* WHAT IT IS (Ire) 11-4 J Shortt, ...(6 to 1) 7
1333 ROBERTOLOMY (USA) 11-9 P L Malone, ... (12 to 1) 8
292[5] REMAINDER LASS (Ire) 10-8 (5*) M J Holbrook, ... (8 to 1) 9
1581 FAIRY STRIKE (Ire) 11-4 K F O'Brien, ... (20 to 1) 10
INAUGURATION (Ire) 11-4 A Powell, ... (16 to 1) 11
39[4] KEY WEST (Ire) 11-4 P Mooney, ...(20 to 1) 12
1077[7] MICKEY TRICKY (Ire) 10-13 T Horgan, ... (16 to 1) 13
MORBIDELLI (Ire) 11-4 M Flynn, ...(12 to 1) 14
MANTEGNA (Ire) 11-4 J P Banahan, ... (16 to 1) 15
Dist: 2½l, nk, 4l, 9l. 4m 21.80s. (15 Ran).
(Mrs G Mathews), Noel Meade

1763 Navan E.B.F. Chase (5-y-o and up) £4,140 2½m.................. (2:00)

1177* ROYAL MOUNTBROWNE 5-11-11 J F Titley, ... (5 to 1) 1
1553[2] ITS A CRACKER 9-11-13 Mr J A Berry, ... (5 to 4 fav) 2
BERMUDA BUCK 7-11-9 F Woods, ...(9 to 2) 3
1684[6] FARNEY GLEN 6-11-2 (7*) Mr D A Harney, ...(7 to 1) 4
1233 BALLINABOOLA GROVE 6-11-9 T J Taaffe, ... (12 to 1) 5
1684 RUNAWAY GOLD 6-11-6 (3*) C O'Brien, ... (16 to 1) 6
TALK TO YOU LATER 7-11-9 H Rogers, ... (14 to 1) 7
BUY A DREAM (Fr) 7-11-2 (7*) J P Broderick, ... (14 to 1) pu
1451[8] AUTUMN RIDE (Ire) 5-11-7 K F O'Brien, ... (25 to 1) pu
Dist: 7l, 20l, ½l, dist. 5m 29.80s. (9 Ran).
(Mrs J O'Kane), Patrick G Kelly

1764 Roast Turkey Handicap Hurdle (0-109 4-y-o and up) £3,105 2¼m...... (2:30)

803* STEEL MIRROR [-] 4-11-8 J Shortt, ...(6 to 1) 1
1335 BALLYMOE BOY (Ire) [-] 5-10-7 (5*) K P Gaule, ...(16 to 1) 2
1453 TOUT VA BIEN [-] 5-11-6 P Carberry, ...(3 to 1 fav) 3
1551[3] DARCARI ROSE (Ire) [-] 4-10-9 (7*) T Martin, ... (4 to 1) 4
SADDLESTOWN GLEN [-] 8-11-3 (3*) T J Mitchell, (20 to 1) 5
1495[4] EYREFIELD ROSE [-] 7-9-10 (7*) P P Curran, ...(7 to 1) 6
11[6] GOODNIGHT IRENE (Ire) [-] 4-10-1 (5*) M J Holbrook, ...(16 to 1) 7
1038[7] LADY HA HA [-] 6-9-10 (7*) J Butler, ... (16 to 1) 8
1155[6] COUNTESS PAHLEN (Ire) [-] 4-10-3 A Powell, ... (12 to 1) 9
1609[7] JACINTA'S BOY [-] 6-11-0 K F O'Brien, ... (14 to 1) 10
1157[5] GLENSHANE PASS [-] 6-10-10 F Woods, ... (14 to 1) 11
NATINA (Ire) [-] 4-10-9 P Mooney, ... (20 to 1) 12
1579 CASTLE RANGER [-] 6-12-0 C N Bowens, ...(10 to 1) 13
1551 ROCHE MELODY (Ire) [-] 5-10-8 (3*) C O'Brien, ... (16 to 1) 14
1609 MIDDLE SUSIE (Ire) [-] (bl) 4-10-4 (3*) T P Treacy, ..(20 to 1) 15
1400[9] CRAZY LADY [-] 7-9-9 (7*) J M Donnelly, ... (25 to 1) pu
1551 BLAZING ACE [-] 7-10-7 J P Banahan, ...(33 to 1) pu
1609[8] MONGARD (Ire) [-] 5-10-7 H Rogers, ...(14 to 1) pu
1495 HIGHLAND MINSTREL [-] 6-10-7 L P Cusack, ... (10 to 1) pu
Dist: 8l, ¾l, 6l, dist. 4m 47.90s. (19 Ran).
(Quarrywell Syndicate), M Halford

1765 Christmas Pudding Handicap Hurdle (4-y-o and up) £6,900 2m....... (3:00)

1554[8] DEEP INAGH [-] 7-10-11 D P Fagan, ...(6 to 1) 1
1580* DERRYMOYLE (Ire) [-] 4-10-8 (8ex) K F O'Brien, (10 to 9 on) 2
1234[7] KEPPOLS PRINCE [-] 6-9-12 H Rogers, ...(10 to 1) 3
1400[2] CELTIC SAILS (Ire) [-] (bl) 5-9-7 (3*) D Bromley, ...(7 to 1) 4
1686[4] HEAD OF CHAMBERS (Ire) [-] 5-10-3 J P Banahan, (5 to 1) 5
1400 ROMAN FORUM (Ire) [-] 5-9-13 C N Bowens, ...(10 to 1) 6
1551[9] PARTNERS IN CRIME [-] 5-9-2 (7*) B Bowens, ... (14 to 1) 7
SOCIETY BAY (USA) [-] 7-10-1 (7*) R A Hennessy, (12 to 1) 8
VISIONS PRIDE [-] 6-11-1 P Carberry, ... (12 to 1) 9
Dist: 1½l, 20l, 2½l, 1l. 4m 15.30s. (9 Ran).
(Noel McMullan), J R H Fowler

1766 E.B.F. Mares Flat Race (4,5,6-y-o) £3,455 2m.................... (3:30)

1500[3] DIVINITY RUN (Ire) 4-11-10 (3*) Mr A E Lacy, ...(4 to 1) 1
1687[4] THE BLUEBELL POLKA (Ire) 4-11-6 (5*) Mr H F Cleary, ...(4 to 1) 2
1435[4] LOVELY RUN 6-12-1 (3*) Miss C Hutchinson, ... (4 to 1) 3
ACKLE BACKLE 6-12-4 Mr T Mullins, ...(8 to 1) 4
1576[9] QUEENIES CHILD 6-11-13 (5*) Mr G J Harford, ... (10 to 1) 5
1455 RAHAN BRIDGE (Ire) 4-10-13 (7*) Miss W Fox, ... (10 to 1) 6
1403[8] CASH IT IN (Ire) 5-11-11 Mr J P Berry, ... (16 to 1) 7
638* WATERLOO BALL (Ire) 4-11-13 Mr A P O'Brien, (7 to 2 fav) 8
540 DALUA RIVER (Ire) 5-11-8 (3*) Mrs M Mullins, ... (12 to 1) 9
67 SUIL AWAIN (Ire) 4-10-13 (7*) Mr S J Mahon, ... (25 to 1) 10
THE KINGS SEAL (Ire) 5-11-4 (7*) Mr E Gibney, ... (20 to 1) 11
SERIOUS NOTE (Ire) 5-11-6 (5*) Mr B R Hamilton, (12 to 1) 12
1403 PARSONS BELLE (Ire) 5-11-11 Miss M Olivefalk, .. (20 to 1) 13
MACS MISS (Ire) 4-11-3 (3*) Mr P McMahon, ... (16 to 1) 14
292 RIYASHA (Ire) 5-11-4 (7*) Miss S Taaffe, ... (25 to 1) 15

RADICAL NURSE (Ire) 4-10-13 (7") Mr M McLoughney,
....(16 to 1) 16
RATHER AINNIS (Ire) 4-10-13 (7") Miss L E A Doyle, (16 to 1) pu
Dist: 3l, 2½l, 2½l, hd. 4m 14.90s. (17 Ran).

(Mrs M McCrudden), F J Lacy

NOTTINGHAM (good to soft)
Saturday December 18th
Going Correction: PLUS 1.25 sec. per fur. (races 1,2,6), PLUS 1.45 (3,4,5)

1767 Tollerton Juvenile Novices' Hurdle (3-y-o) £2,182 2m.............(12:45)

KADASTROF (Fr) 10-12 W Humphreys, *hit 1st, al prmnt, lft in ld 4 out, rdn clr appr last, styd on wl......*(9 to 2 jt-fav op 7 to 1) 1
1634* GIORDANO (Ire) 11-5 Gary Lyons, *trkd ldrs, effrt and hit 3 out, rdn nxt, kpt on one pace and pres.*
.....................................(11 to 2 op 5 to 1 tchd 6 to 1) 2
HEART OF SPAIN 10-12 T Wall, *al prmnt, ev ch 2 out, sn rdn and one paced.*....................(14 to 1 op 10 to 1) 3
1483⁶ MISTROY 10-7 C Grant, *hld up, steady hdwy 4 out, rdn 2 out and sn one paced.*...............(16 to 1 tchd 20 to 1) 4
FINE SIR 10-12 W Marston, *in tch, hit 4th, hdwy appr 3 out, sn rdn and wknd bef 2 out....*(16 to 1 op 10 to 1) 5
LYFORD CAY (Ire) (bl) 10-12 J Osborne, *trkd ldrs, hmpd and lost pl 4 out, hdwy on inner nxt, rdn 2 out and sn btn*.................(9 to 2 jt-fav op 5 to 1 tchd 4 to 1) 6
STRICTLY PERSONAL (USA) 10-5 (7") P Ward, *nvr rch ldrs.*
......................(14 to 1 op 8 to 1 tchd 16 to 1) 7
GYMCRAK TIGER (Ire) 10-12 R Marley, *al beh.*
.....................................(25 to 1 op 33 to 1) 8
1483* ATHERTON GREEN (Ire) 11-5 T Reed, *beh, some hdwy 3 out, sn rdn and wknd.* (9 to 1 op 5 to 1 tchd 10 to 1) 9
1297³ GUNNER SUE 10-7 R Bellamy, *prmnt, wknd aftr 4 out.*
.....................................(20 to 1 op 16 to 1) 10
1408⁷ JASPER ONE 10-12 R Garritty, *al beh.*
.....................................(50 to 1 op 33 to 1) 11
MR CUBE (Ire) 10-7 (5") D Matthews, *hld up in tch, hdwy 4 out, rdn and wknd nxt.*....................(33 to 1) 12
1473 ANUSHA 10-7 G Bradley, *hld up in tch, hdwy appr 3 out, sn rdn and wknd.*......(15 to 2 op 5 to 1 tchd 8 to 1) 13
SOLO CHARTER 10-12 S Earle, *led till 4 out.*....(33 to 1) f
RED LEADER (Ire) 10-5 (7") D Meade, *al beh, tld off whn f last.*......................................(33 to 1) f
GREEN'S FAIR (Ire) 10-12 S Mackey, *in tch, hdwy appr 3 out, rdn and wknd nxt, f last.*.................(33 to 1) f
ALBERSTAN 10-12 W Worthington, *beh, sddl slpd and uns rdr 2 out.*...................................(33 to 1) ur
1410⁷ MUSICAL PHONE 10-12 R Greene, *mid-div, rdn 4 out, beh whn pld up bef 3 out.*..................(33 to 1) pu
1640 SYLVAN STARLIGHT 10-0 (7") Guy Lewis, *in tch, blun 5th and sn lost pl, beh whn pld up bef last.*
.......................(14 to 1 tchd 16 to 1) pu
DYAB (USA) 10-12 A Carroll, *sn outpcd and beh, blun 4th and tld off, pld up bef last.*......(14 to 1 op 12 to 1) pu
TANGO IN PARIS (Arg) 10-12 Richard Guest, *in rear, beh whn pld up bef 2 out.*.......................(33 to 1) pu
Dist: 12l, 7l, 2½l, 20l, sht-hd, 2½l, 5l, 1½l, hd, 15l. 4m 8.70s. (21 Ran).

SR: 37/32/18/10/-/-/ (A P Paton), R Dickin

1768 Plumtree 'National Hunt' Novices' Hurdle (4-y-o and up) £2,343 2m (1:15)

1309 FINE THYNE (Ire) 4-10-12 M Perrett, *trkd ldrs, hdwy appr 3 out, led approaching nxt, clr last.*
.........................(Evens fav tchd 6 to 4) 1
QUARRY HOUSE (Ire) 5-10-12 J Railton, *mid-div, steady hdwy appr 3 out, rdn 2 out, styd on frm last, no ch with wnr.*.....................(12 to 1 op 8 to 1) 2
1003⁹ DISTINCTIVE (Ire) 4-10-5 (7") P Ward, *mid-div, hdwy 4 out, rdn appr 2 out, kpt on one pace...*(20 to 1 op 16 to 1) 3
CELTIC LAIRD 5-10-12 I Lawrence, *al prmnt, led appr 3 out, hdd approaching nxt, btn whn hit last.*
.......................(12 to 1 op 10 to 1) 4
ANNIE KELLY 5-10-0 (7") B Dalton, *mid-div, steady hdwy 3 out, hit nxt, sn rdn and one paced.*(50 to 1 op 25 to 1) 5
1478 BLAYNEYS PRIVILEGE 6-10-12 R Garritty, *beh, some late hdwy, nvr a factor.*..................(50 to 1 op 33 to 1) 6
1027 OUR ARNOLD 6-10-5 (7") P Maddock, *beh and hit 3rd, some hdwy frm 3 out, nvr dngrs...*(50 to 1 op 33 to 1) 7
FALCONBRIDGE BAY 6-10-12 J Osborne, *prmnt, effrt and ch appr 3 out, sn rdn, wknd bef nxt.* (8 to 1 op 9 to 2) 8
1528 KELLING 6-10-12 G Bradley, *cl up, led 3rd to 4th, rdn 3 out, wknd appr 2 out.*...........(9 to 1 op 5 to 1) 9
1658 STRATHBOGIE MIST (Ire) 5-10-12 N Smith, *al rear.*
.....................................(50 to 1 op 33 to 1) 10
GO UNIVERSAL (Ire) 5-10-12 C Grant, *hld up and beh, gd hdwy 4 out, rdn and wknd appr 2 out.*
.......................(16 to 1 op 20 to 1) 11
1428⁴ BROAD STEANE 4-10-12 A Carroll, *al beh.*
......................(16 to 1 op 14 to 1 tchd 20 to 1) 12

1133³ SCRABBLE 4-10-7 Richard Guest, *prmnt, wknd 5th and sn beh.*.........(16 to 1 op 20 to 1 tchd 25 to 1) 13
836 PRINCE OF PREY 5-10-12 Peter Hobbs, *chsd ldrs, pushed alng 5th and sn lost pl.*............(14 to 1 op 10 to 1) 14
1528⁵ COZZI (Fr) 5-10-5 (7") Guy Lewis, *led to 3rd, led 5th till aftr off*.................(33 to 1 op 25 to 1) 15
1329⁷ BIG ARTHUR (Ire) 4-10-12 W Marston, *beh frm hfwy, tld off*.........(5 to 1 op 7 to 1 tchd 8 to 1 and 9 to 2) 16
MANDYS LAD 4-10-12 W Humphreys, *mid-div, blun and uns rdr 4th.*...................(16 to 1 op 10 to 1) ur
1078 ROCKY TYRONE 6-10-7 (5") D Walsh, *cl up, led 4th till nxt, rdn and wknd quickly four out, pld up bef 2 out.*
.......................(50 to 1 op 33 to 1) pu
1376 ANOTHER TRYP 5-10-7 G Upton, *al rear, tld off whn pld up bef 2 out.*.........(50 to 1 op 25 to 1) pu
Dist: 10l, 2½l, 2½l, 12l, 3l, 5l, 4l, 3l, 1½l, 5l. 4m 10.70s. a 26.70s (19 Ran).
SR: 17/7/4/1/-/-/ (Peter Wiegand), G Harwood

1769 Stan Mellor Handicap Chase (0-115 5-y-o and up) £3,176 3m 3f 110yds ....(1:45)

1242⁵ THE TARTAN SPARTAN [89] 9-10-1 (7") P Ward, *prmnt, led 5th, clr 6 out, blun 4 out, styd on wl.......*(20 to 1) 1
1512⁷ LITTLE GENERAL [94] 10-10-13 Peter Hobbs, *al prmnt, hit 15th, rdn nxt, kpt on frm 3 out, no ch with wnr.*
.....................................(16 to 1 op 10 to 1) 2
1565⁵ WOODLANDS GENHIRE [87] (v) 8-10-3 (3") R Davis, *al prmnt, rdn 6 out, sn one pace......*(8 to 1 tchd 10 to 1) 3
1486⁶ DUBIOUS JAKE [102] 10-11-7 R Garritty, *hld up, gd hdwy 13th, hit 16th, rdn nxt, sn one pace.*
.....................................(11 to 1 op 10 to 1) 4
1543³ SUNLEY BAY [105] (bl) 7-11-10 G Bradley, *in tch, hit 8th, beh whn blun 13th, tld off frm 6 out.*
.......................(9 to 2 op 4 to 1 tchd 5 to 1) 5
1273 TRUSTY FRIEND [95] 11-11-0 R Greene, *cl up, rdn alng and lost pl 13th, tld off frm 6 out.* (14 to 1 op 12 to 1) 6
1512⁴ ARD T'MATCH [96] (v) 8-11-1 Gary Lyons, *hld up, steady hdwy 14th, chsd wnr 5 out, rdn and wknd 3 out, pld up lme r-in........*(8 to 1 op 7 to 1 tchd 10 to 1) pu
1512⁶ SADDLER'S CHOICE [99] (bl) 8-11-4 C Grant, *blun badly 1st and pld up......*(8 to 1 op 10 to 1 tchd 10 to 1) pu
1471⁹ JIMMY O'DEA [87] (v) 6-10-1 (5") T Eley, *made most to 5th, prmnt till lost pl 13th, beh whn blun 15th, sn pld up.*
.......................(20 to 1 op 16 to 1 tchd 25 to 1) pu
1565² POSTMAN'S PATH [102] 7-11-7 J Osborne, *trkd ldrs, blun badly 5th and sn beh, last whn tried to run out, pld up bef......*(9 to 4 fav op 7 to 4) pu
Dist: 20l, 2l, 12l, 8l, 20l. 7m 38.10s. a 50.10s (10 Ran).

(Mrs Delyth Batchelor), M J Wilkinson

1770 Maguire And Batty Novices' Chase (5-y-o and up) £2,547 3m 110yds...(2:15)

1205 LUSTY LIGHT 7-11-7 I Lawrence, *hld up, hdwy hfwy, led 6 out, hdd nxt, rdn to chal 2 out, steadied last, hrd drvn and styd on r-in to ld nr finish.*
.......................(11 to 4 fav op 5 to 4 tchd 3 to 1) 1
1184⁶ SUPPOSIN 5-11-0 Richard Guest, *in tch, hdwy tenth, led 11th to nxt, led 5 out, pckd 2 out, rdn and clr advantage r-in, hdd and no ext nr finish....* (25 to 1 op 16 to 1) 2
1544⁴ RAMPOLDI (USA) 6-11-2 G Bradley, *prmnt, blun 7th, rdn alng 5 out and sn one paced.....*(13 to 2 op 11 to 2) 3
1563³ DARK OAK 7-11-2 R Garritty, *in tch, hdwy 8th, led briefly tenth, rdn 5 out and sn one paced.*
.......................(6 to 1 op 11 to 2 tchd 8 to 1) 4
1457² HOWARYADOON 7-10-11 (5") C Burnett-Wells, *mstks, in tch, blun tenth, blunded 13th, rdn nxt, wknd 5 out.*
.......................(3 to 1 op 9 to 4) 5
957* CROFT MILL 7-11-7 J Osborne, *prmnt till f 4th...* (7 to 2) f
833 BILDAK 6-11-15 (5") T Eley, *prmnt, led 3rd to tenth, blun and uns rdr nxt.*....................(33 to 1 op 25 to 1) ur
1469⁶ ROMANY SPLIT 8-10-9 (7") P Ward, *led to 3rd, lost pl and beh frm tenth, pld up bef 3 out.*...............(25 to 1) pu
Dist: ¾l, 25l, 1½l, 12l. 6m 37.30s. a 42.30s (8 Ran).
SR: 25/17/-/-/-/ (B R H Burrough), Mrs J Pitman

1771 Colwick Intermediate Chase (5-y-o and up) £2,678 2m.............(2:45)

998² THUMBS UP 7-11-0 J Osborne, *led, hdd aftr 5 out, effrt to chal 2 out, led last, cleverly.*
..............(11 to 10 on op 5 to 4 on tchd Evens) 1
1591* SHU FLY (NZ) 9-11-10 Jacqui Oliver, *trkd wnr, hdwy to ld aftr 5 out, hit 2 out, rdn and hdd last, not quicken r-in.*
.....................................(11 to 10 op Evens) 2
1591³ BOSSBURG 6-11-1 G Bradley, *in tch, hit 9th and outpcd aftr........*(11 to 2 op 4 to 1 tchd 6 to 1) 3
SANDY-BRANDY 8-10-7 (7") P Murphy, *cl up, blun badly 5th and sn tld off, blunded 2 out...*(50 to 1 op 20 to 1) 4
Dist: 2l, dist, 25l. 4m 21.80s. a 30.80s (4 Ran).
SR: 10/18/-/-/ (Michael Buckley), N J Henderson

1772 Clifton Conditional Jockeys' Handicap Hurdle (0-115 4-y-o and up) £2,302 2m 5f 110yds....................(3:15)

NATIONAL HUNT RESULTS 1993-94

1474⁵ COUTURE STOCKINGS [94] 9-11-0 T Eley, *al prmnt, effrt 2 out, rdn to ld r-in, ran on strly.*
....(5 to 1 op 9 to 2 tchd 4 to 1) **1**
1458 WINGS OF FREEDOM (Ire) [104] (v) 5-11-7 (3⁵) D Fortt, *hld up, gd hdwy on inner aftr 4 out, rdn on bit appr 2 out, rdn last, sn hdd and one pace r-in...* (7 to 1 op 5 to 1) **2**
1480⁴ MASTER BOSTON (Ire) [95] 5-10-12 (3⁵) J Driscoll, *hld up, hdwy 3 out, effrt nxt, sn rdn and one pace.*
....(9 to 2 op 3 to 1) **3**
WICKET [92] 8-10-7 (5⁵) P Ward, *hld up, hdwy 3 out, rdn nxt and sn btn.*........ (9 to 1 op 10 to 1 tchd 8 to 1) **4**
1533⁶ COXANN [80] 7-9-7 (7⁵) E Tolhurst, *prmnt, rdn alng 7th and lost pl, beh frm 4 out*........(20 to 1 op 16 to 1) **5**
1462⁴ IMA DELIGHT [96] 6-10-9 (7⁵) Lorna Brand, *trkd ldrs, lost pl 7th, hdwy appr 3 out, wknd btn nxt.*
....(3 to 1 fav tchd 7 to 2) **6**
1653⁵ ELEGANT KING (Ire) [100] 4-11-1 (5⁵) G McGrath, *cl up, lft in ld 9th, hdd and wknd appr 2 out.* (7 to 1 op 8 to 1) **7**
1239⁴ MALVERN MADAM [80] 6-9-9 (5⁵) R Wilkinson, *al prmnt, effrt and ev ch 2 out, rdn and wkng whn blun badly last.*........................(14 to 1 op 10 to 1) **8**
1238 DIRECTORS' CHOICE [86] 8-10-6 A Dicken, *mid-div, smooth hdwy 4 out, ev ch nxt, sn rdn and wknd quickly.*........................(20 to 1 op 16 to 1) **9**
JARRWAH [91] 5-10-11 V Slattery, *led till f 9th.*
....(9 to 1 op 8 to 1 tchd 10 to 1) **f**
Dist: 6l, 15l, 3l, 2l, ½l, nk, 2l. 5m 42.60s. a 40.60s (10 Ran).
(Couture Marketing Ltd), J Mackie

UTTOXETER (heavy)
Saturday December 18th
Going Correction: PLUS 0.35 sec. per fur. (races 1,3,- 5,7), PLUS 1.00 (2,4,6)

1773
Technical High School Past Pupils Novices' Hurdle (4-y-o and up) £2,008 2m.........................(12:30)

SHUJAN (USA) 4-11-0 D Bridgwater, *took keen hold, led aftr second, hit nxt, given a breather 3 out, clr last.*
....(13 to 8 fav op 6 to 4 tchd 7 to 4) **1**
1622⁷ RAFTERS 4-10-11 (3⁵) R Farrant, *trkd ldrs, improved frm 3 out, styd on, no ch wth wnr*........(20 to 1 op 16 to 1) **2**
ROUSITTO 5-10-11 (3⁵) S Wynne, *al chasing ldrs, improved aftr 3 out, styd on one pace frm nxt.*
....(14 to 1 op 10 to 1) **3**
LYPHANTASIC (USA) 4-11-0 B Powell, *patiently rdn, steady hdwy frm midfield appr 3 out, kpt on, prmsg.*
....(12 to 1 op 7 to 1) **4**
1542 GAYLOIRE (Ire) 4-10-9² (7⁵) Mr A Harvey, *chsd ldg trio, feeling pace 4 out, struggling frm nxt.*
....(2 to 1 op 7 to 4 tchd 9 to 4) **5**
PICKLES 5-11-0 L Harvey, *sn last and pushed alng, drvn into midfield hfwy, nvr nr to chal.*
....(16 to 1 op 14 to 1 tchd 20 to 1) **6**
EULOGY (Fr) 6-11-0 N Williamson, *slight ld till aftr second, styd hndy till rdn and outpcd frm 3 out.*
....(12 to 1 op 7 to 1) **7**
TEST MATCH 6-11-0 Diane Clay, *beh and drvn alng hfwy, nvr nr to chal.*........................(12 to 1 op 10 to 1) **8**
1295 SALINGER 5-11-0 V Smith, *wth ldr till aftr second, styd hndy till fdd appr 3 out.*........(50 to 1 op 33 to 1) **9**
1376⁹ TOUGH DEAL (Ire) 5-11-0 Mr B Leavy, *bustled alng in midfield, struggling 4 out, tld off.* (100 to 1 op 50 to 1) **10**
SYLVAN (Ire) 4-10-6 (3⁵) N Bentley, *chsd ldg quartet, struggling appr 4 out, tld off.*.......... (20 to 1 op 12 to 1) **11**
Dist: 10l, 10l, 2l, 12l, 1½l, ¾l, sht-hd, 10l, dist, 8l. 3m 50.10s. a 11.10s (11 Ran).
SR: 31/21/11/9/-/-/ (Sir Eric Parker), R Akehurst

1774
Steve Lilley Racing Novices' Chase (5-y-o and up) £2,814 2m......(1:00)

1308* COONAWARA 7-11-6 B Powell, *jmpd fluently, made all, hrd pressed appr 4 out, styd on strly to go clr betw last 2.*........(9 to 4 on tchd 5 to 2 on and 85 to 40 on) **1**
1505* COUNTRY LAD (Ire) 5-11-6 S McNeill, *al hndy, pressed wnr appr 4 out, rdn betw last 2, stumbled last, one pace.*........................(85 to 40 op 2 to 1 tchd 9 to 4) **2**
1505⁶ HIGHLAND POACHER 6-11-0 D Gallagher, *not fluent, struggling to keep up hfwy, plodded round.*
....(25 to 1 op 20 to 1) **3**
GIPSY RAMBLER 8-10-9 (5⁵) J Supple, *struggling and beh frm 4th, tld off.*................(100 to 1 op 66 to 1) **4**
998⁸ THE WOODEN HUT (v) 10-11-0 Mr M Jackson, *chsd wnr till hit 4th, mstk nxt, sn lost tch, tld off whn f 3 out.*
....(100 to 1 op 50 to 1) **f**
Dist: 5l, dist, 15l. 4m 9.40s. a 20.40s (5 Ran).
SR: 48/43/ (Simon Sainsbury), Capt T A Forster

1775
Bob Jacobs Memorial Novices' Handicap Hurdle (4-y-o and up) £2,113 3m 110yds.....................(1:30)

1524⁴ VERY LITTLE (Ire) [80] 5-10-5 W McFarland, *led till aftr second, led 6th till after 9th, rallied to ld r-in.*
....(8 to 1 op 7 to 1) **1**
1362² CRANK SHAFT [99] 6-11-10 D Gallagher, *settled midfield, improved hfwy, outpcd and rdn 3 out, rallied r-in.*
....(8 to 1 op 6 to 1) **2**
1645⁶ PLAYPEN [86] 9-10-11 J Frost, *led aftr second till after 6th, led after 9th till hdd and no extr r-in.*
....(14 to 1 op 12 to 1) **3**
1645⁵ LANSDOWNE [78] 5-10-3 B Powell, *al hndy, feeling pace and drvn alng 3 out, rallied frm last.*....... (8 to 1) **4**
1524³ NEEDWOOD POPPY [95] 5-11-6 L Harvey, *nvr far away, ev ch and rdn 3 out, kpt on same pace frm betw last 2.*
....(3 to 1 fav tchd 7 to 2) **5**
1169⁴ SUASANAN SIOSANA [75] 8-9-7 (7⁵) D Winter, *in tch, struggling to go pace hfwy, rallied und pres frm 3 out, nrst finish.*........................(20 to 1) **6**
1456* SIR PAGEANT [97] 4-11-8 D Bridgwater, *co'red up in midfield, improved to join ldrs bef 3 out, rdn nxt, sn btn.*
....(11 to 2 op 4 to 1 tchd 6 to 1) **7**
1448⁹ MORSHOT [82] 6-10-7 S McNeill, *in tch, struggling to keep up appr 4 out, tld off frm nxt...* (8 to 1 op 6 to 1) **8**
1607² MANWELL [75] 6-9-9 (5⁵) D Bentley, *outpcd and lost pl hfwy, tld off frm 4 out........................*(33 to 1) **9**
1295⁶ WHO SIR [76] 7-10-1 N Williamson, *wl plcd on ins, ev ch till wknd aftr 4 out, eased whn btn.*
....(16 to 1 op 14 to 1) **10**
755³ FAUGHAN LODGE [90] 6-11-1 Diane Clay, *tracking ldrs whn hit 5th, broke leg and pld up, destroyed.*
....(9 to 1 op 7 to 1) **pu**
1533⁹ LAUGHING GAS (Ire) [82] 4-10-0 (7⁵) J James, *in tch whn sddl slpd and pld up aftr second...*(12 to 1 op 10 to 1) **pu**
Dist: 2l, nk, sht-hd, 1½l, 5l, 12l, 20l, 20l, 10l. 6m 19.50s. a 40.50s (12 Ran).
(Plumber Purns Partnership), R H Alner

1776
Manny Bernstein Novices' Handicap Chase (5-y-o and up) £3,126 3¼m ....(2:05)

1511 DOROBO (NZ) [75] (bl) 5-10-6 (3⁵) R Farrant, *nvr far away, dsptd ld frm 2 out, kpt on grimly to lead r-in.*
....(14 to 1 op 12 to 1) **1**
1590² SILVER AGE (USA) [79] 7-10-13 L Harvey, *settled midfield, improved to ld 7 out, hdd 4 out, nosed ahead 2 out, headed and one pace r-in....*..........(6 to 1 op 5 to 1) **2**
1417² SQUIRES PRIVILEGE (Ire) [87] 5-11-7 N Williamson, *patiently rdn, jnd issue fnl circuit, led 4 out, hdd and slpd 2 out, one pace.*..............(5 to 1 op 7 to 2) **3**
1511³ CHRISTMAS GORSE [72] 7-10-6 J Frost, *settled midfield, niggled alng fnl circuit, blun 6 out, no imprsn frm nxt.*
....(7 to 4 fav tchd 2 to 1) **4**
1457³ UFANO (Fr) [74] 7-10-8 B Powell, *trkd ldg trio, effrt and rdn 6 out, lost tch last 4.*............(9 to 1 op 8 to 1) **5**
1570⁵ CONCERT PAPER [88] 9-11-1 (7⁵) K Davies, *co'red up in midfield, struggling bef 5 out, sn lost tch.*
....(9 to 1 op 7 to 1) **6**
1637 CHALIE RICHARDS [90] 6-11-5 (5⁵) Mr D McCain, *al in tch, rdn fnl circuit, tld off frm 4 out....* (8 to 1 tchd 9 to 1) **7**
1321⁴ THE POD'S REVENGE [70] 8-10-4 M Moloney, *wth ldrs for o'r a circuit, tld off whn pld up bef 4 out*....(20 to 1) **pu**
1503 NINE BROTHERS [75] 9-10-9 Mr K Green, *wth ldrs, led 5th till hdd 7 out, wknd quickly and pld up bef 3 out.*
....(50 to 1) **pu**
1651⁵ SPARTAN FLAPJACK [70] 7-10-4² (7⁵) Mr Richard White, *struggling to go pace hfwy, tld off whn pld up bef 7 out.*
....(50 to 1) **pu**
Dist: 6l, 25l, 7l, 4l, dist, 4l. 7m 17.00s. a 61.00s (10 Ran).
(Lady Lewinton), Capt T A Forster

1777
Queensway China Challenge Trophy Handicap Hurdle (0-125 4-y-o and up) £2,866 2½m 110yds............(2:35)

1474* BICKERMAN [101] 10-10-2 (7⁵) Miss T Spearing, *made most aftr second, jnd and rdn 3 out, jmpd rght nxt, styd on r-in.*........(4 to 1 op 3 to 1 tchd 9 to 2) **1**
1106 ANDERMATT [114] 6-11-8 N Williamson, *patiently rdn, improved to join issue 3 out, bumped nxt, swtchd aftr last, one pace...........*......(7 to 2 fav op 4 to 1) **2**
1139⁵ LASTING MEMORY [98] 7-10-6⁶ J Frost, *settled midfield, improved appr 3 out, styd on, nvr nrr.*
....(12 to 1 op 14 to 1) **3**
NEEDWOOD MUPPET [116] 6-11-10 L Harvey, *chsd clr ldg pair, ev ch aftr 4 out, rdn and one pace last 2.*
....(10 to 1 op 8 to 1) **4**
895 CHIEF CELT [106] 7-11-0 B Powell, *settled wth chasing bunch, outpcd 4 out, no imprsn....*(13 to 2 op 6 to 1) **5**
1671² WAKE UP [94] 6-9-9 (7⁵) K Davies, *settled off the pace, effrt hfwy, struggling frm 4 out...*(12 to 1 op 14 to 1) **6**
1667⁴ STAR PLAYER [113] 7-11-7 N Mann, *settled off the pace, drvn alng appr 4 out, no imprsn.* (9 to 2 op 4 to 1) **7**
1458⁷ CELTIC BREEZE [101] (v) 10-10-9 A Dobbin, *led till aftr second, styd hndy and drvn alng, hit 4 out, sn btn.*
....(12 to 1 op 14 to 1) **8**
1025 FIRST CRACK [93] 8-10-1 D Bridgwater, *beh and bustled alng hfwy, nvr able to trble ldrs...* (14 to 1 op 12 to 1) **9**
Dist: 4l, 8l, 3½l, 4l, 8l, 25l, 3l, 1½l. 5m 12.50s. a 29.50s (9 Ran).

(B Dowling), J L Spearing

1778 Heathyards Engineering Handicap Chase (0-145 5-y-o and up) £3,338 2m 7f............................(3:05)

1436³ DUBACILLA [126] 7-11-7 D Gallagher, *patiently rdn, improved to ld 4 out, drw clr, kpt on strly frm last.*
......................(6 to 4 fav tchd 7 to 4 and 11 to 8) 1
GAY RUFFIAN [133] 7-12-0 J Lower, *nvr far away, effrt whn mstk and swshd tail 5 out, rallied last 3, not rch unr*......................(4 to 1) 2
1689³ ZAMIL (USA) [106] 8-10-1 N Williamson, *wth ldr, led 5th till hdd 4 out, rdn and one pace frm nxt.*
......................(8 to 1 tchd 12 to 1) 3
560* GRANGE BRAKE [120] (bl) 7-11-1 D Bridgwater, *slight ld to 5th, rdn aftr 5 out, tld off*........(11 to 4 op 9 to 4) 4
MR SETASIDE [111] 8-10-6 B Powell, *hit second, struggling hfwy, tld off whn pld up bef 5 out.*
......................(8 to 1 op 5 to 1) pu
Dist: 3l, 1½l, dist. 6m 11.20s. a 41.20s (5 Ran).

(Mrs Veronica Cole), H T Cole

1779 Levy Board Stakes National Hunt Flat Race (4,5,6-y-o) £2,123 2m......(3:35)

THERMAL WARRIOR 5-10-9 (7*) Pat Thompson, *wtd wth, improved entering strt, styd on grimly to ld ins fnl furlong*......................(10 to 1 op 8 to 1) 1
LANDSKER PRYDE 4-10-4 (7*) T Dascombe, *hld up, improved hfwy, led 2 fs out, hdd and no extr ins fnl furlong*......................(7 to 1 op 7 to 2) 2
CHIEF RAGER 4-10-9 (7*) Mr S Joynes, *patiently rdn, improved entering strt, styd on last 2 fs, nrst finish.*
......................(12 to 1 op 6 to 1) 3
1084 KING CREOLE (Ire) 4-10-9 (7*) S Haworth, *made most till hdd 2 fs out, kpt on same pace*.....(12 to 1 op 10 to 1) 4
BETTER BYTHE GLASS (Ire) 4-10-9 (7*) Mr M Rimell, *chsd ldg bunch, effrt and drvn alng o'r 3 fs out, one pace.*
......................(10 to 1 op 8 to 1) 5
KEEP POPPING 5-10-11 (5*) D Salter, *nvr far away, drvn alng whn pace lifted o'r 2 fs out, one pace.*
......................(16 to 1 op 25 to 1) 6
1223 THE PIPE FITTER (Ire) 5-10-9 (7*) R McGrath, *co'red up in midfield, effrt hfwy, rdn 3 fs out, fdd.*
......................(8 to 1 op 5 to 1 tchd 9 to 1) 7
CELTIC EMERALD 5-10-4 (7*) P McLoughlin, *wth ldrs for o'r a m, fdd entering strt*........(25 to 1 op 20 to 1) 8
1626 FINWAG 6-10-13 (3*) S Wynne, *settled off the pace, shaken up to improve appr strt, nvr able to chal.*
......................(33 to 1) 9
1674⁸ SOUNDS GOLDEN 5-10-13 (3*) A Thornton, *frnt rnk till fdd entering strt*........(14 to 1 op 10 to 1) 10
1626* RED PARADE (USA) 5-11-6 (3*) R Davis, *pressed ldrs, struggling appr strt, sn lost tch*........(6 to 4 fav op 5 to 2) 11
LEENEY 4-11-2 Mrs S Bosley, *settled midfield, bustled alng appr strt, fdd*........(33 to 1 op 20 to 1) 12
LLANTHONY ABBEY (Ire) 5-10-4 (7*) R Coles, *struggling to keep up hfwy, sn lost tch*........(11 to 1 op 7 to 1) 13
GUSHKA 6-10-9 (7*) D Meade, *settled wth ldg grp, drvn alng o'r 5 fs out, tld off*........(20 to 1) 14
1329⁵ NUNS CONE 5-10-13 (3*) R Farrant, *wl plcd for o'r a m, sn lost tch*........(14 to 1) 15
1329⁵ GAYTON RUN (Ire) 4-10-11 (5*) A Procter, *tld off frm hfwy, pld up 3 fs out*........(50 to 1) pu
Dist: 2½l, 1½l, ½l, 1l, hd, 12l, ¾l, 7l, 3l, hd. 3m 50.10s. (16 Ran).

(C J Oakley), J A B Old

NAVAN (IRE) (heavy)
Sunday December 19th

1780 Reindeer Handicap Hurdle (0-130 4-y-o and up) £3,105 2m...........(12:30)

1551⁵ MR BOAL (Ire) [-] 4-10-12 C F Swan,.........(3 to 1) 1
1450⁸ WINTERBOURNE ABBAS (Ire) [-] (bl) 4-10-4 B Sheridan,
......................(14 to 1) 2
1580³ MONKEY AGO [-] 6-11-0 T J Taaffe,........(7 to 4 fav) 3
1551* PERSIAN HALO (Ire) [-] 5-11-4 (6ex) D H O'Connor, (4 to 1) 4
1400⁵ PLUMBOB (Ire) [-] 4-10-11 (5*) M G Cleary,......(8 to 1) 5
1551⁶ BALLYCANN [-] 6-10-6 (7*) P J Mulligan,......(12 to 1) 6
1400⁸ COIN MACHINE (Ire) [-] 4-10-1 T Horgan,......(8 to 1) f
CLOUGHTANEY [-] 12-11-2 C O'Dwyer,........(33 to 1) pu
1269 RAINBOW VALLEY (Ire) [-] 4-10-6 H Rogers,......(20 to 1) pu
1269 BASIE NOBLE [-] 4-9-11 P L Malone,........(14 to 1) pu
1038⁹ ARDLEA HOUSE (Ire) [-] 4-9-0⁶ (7*) R A Hennessy, (20 to 1) pu
Dist: 4½l, 9l, 2l, 1½l. 4m 27.70s. (11 Ran).

(David Prentice), J H Scott

1781 Irish National Hunt Novice Hurdle (4-y-o and up) £4,140 2m.........(1:00)

1397* KLAIRON DAVIS (Fr) 4-11-1 T J Taaffe,........(9 to 4 on) 1
1576⁴ LEGAL PROFESSION (Ire) 5-11-2 C F Swan,.......(7 to 2) 2
1576 EMPEROR GLEN (Ire) 5-11-2 T Horgan,........(25 to 1) 3
1230 JULEIT JONES (Ire) 4-10-3 (3*) T J Mitchell,......(25 to 1) 4

1333* STRONG SERENADE (Ire) 4-10-7 (3*) T P Treacy, ...(5 to 1) pu
Dist: 6l, dist, 4l. 4m 26.70s. (5 Ran).

(C Jones), A L T Moore

1782 Christmas Presents Handicap Hurdle (4-y-o and up) £3,105 3m.......(1:30)

1580² MASTER CRUSADER [-] 7-9-9 C F Swan,........(5 to 1) 1
1685⁶ IL TROVATORE (USA) [-] (bl) 7-10-8 P Carberry, ..(8 to 1) 2
1685³ CARRON HILL [-] 6-9-13 T Horgan,................(9 to 2) 3
1609* RATHCORE [-] 6-10-4 (4ex) L P Cusack,........(13 to 2) 4
1685⁴ CHELSEA NATIVE [-] 6-10-11 (5*) Susan A Finn, ...(8 to 1) 5
1544 TEMPLEROAN PRINCE [-] 6-11-5 C N Bowens, (4 to 1 fav) 6
1201⁴ SECRET SCEPTRE [-] 6-10-3 F Woods,..........(10 to 1) 7
1437 THE MAD MONK [-] 8-10-3 M Flynn,..........(20 to 1) 8
1580⁵ BANAIYKA (Ire) [-] 4-10-11 (3*) T P Treacy, ...(12 to 1) 9
1400⁶ HIS WAY (Ire) [-] 4-10-12 J Shortt,..........(16 to 1) 10
1496⁸ DRINK UP DAN [-] 6-9-9 (3*) C O'Brien, ...(20 to 1) 11
1453 COOLAHEARAC [-] 7-9-12 P P Kinane,..........(50 to 1) 12
TAUWETTER [-] 7-9-7 P Mooney,................(50 to 1) 13
1075 ROSEPERRIE (Ire) [-] (bl) 5-9-2⁵ (5*) D T Evans,...(25 to 1) 14
1580⁹ SLANG [-] (bl) 7-9-7 H Rogers,................(66 to 1) 15
1179 BENS DILEMMA [-] 8-9-6 (7*) J P Broderick,......(25 to 1) pu
Dist: 6l, 5½l, 2½l, 1l. 6m 21.20s. (16 Ran).

(Kilkea Castle Racing Syndicate), J H Scott

1783 Lismullen Hurdle (4-y-o and up) £3,450 2½m........................(2:00)

1554⁵ NOVELLO ALLEGRO (USA) 5-11-7 P Carberry, (9 to 4 on) 1
1330* BEGLAWELLA 6-11-0 (3*) T P Treacy,............(7 to 2) 2
1500⁸ PUNTERS BAR 6-11-2 C O'Dwyer,..............(20 to 1) 3
FINAL ISSUE 6-11-9 (5*) H Taylor,..........(14 to 1) 4
1685 GOLDEN SHINE 7-11-1 (7*) B Bowens,..........(16 to 1) 5
BOOM TIME 8-10-9 (7*) Mr G A Kingston,......(9 to 1) 6
Dist: 2l, 5½l, 1½l, dist. 5m 35.20s. (6 Ran).

(Mrs Rita Polly), Noel Meade

1784 Santa Claus Handicap Chase (4-y-o and up) £6,900 3m............(2:30)

1497² NUAFFE [-] 8-9-8 S H O'Donovan,..............(15 to 2) 1
1553⁵ FERROMYN [-] 8-10-4 C F Swan,............(11 to 4 fav) 2
1553* OPRYLAND [-] 8-9-1 (7*,8ex) J P Broderick,......(6 to 1) 3
1499⁵ MERLYNS CHOICE [-] 9-9-2 (5*) K P Gaule,......(14 to 1) 4
HIGH PEAK [-] 9-10-12 B Sheridan,..........(14 to 1) 5
GREEN TIMES [-] 8-9-11 P L Malone,..........(20 to 1) 6
1452³ JOE WHITE [-] 7-10-8 P Carberry,..............(6 to 1) 7
1553 MID-DAY GAMBLE [-] 9-9-7 F Woods,..........(14 to 1) 8
1553 MARKET MOVER [-] 8-10-7 (7*) K F O'Brien, ...(20 to 1) 9
1380 LACKEN BEAU [-] 9-10-11 J Shortt,..........(20 to 1) 10
1683⁹ LANIGANS WINE [-] 11-10-2 T Horgan,..........(20 to 1) 11
CALLMECHA [-] 8-10-4 G M O'Neill,..........(16 to 1) 12
1685 RUST NEVER SLEEPS [-] 9-11-11 (3*) C O'Brien, ..(20 to 1) 13
1578⁴ VANTON [-] 9-11-8 (3*) Mr D Valentine,........(7 to 2) 14
Dist: 12l, 1½l, 20l, 15l. 6m 38.40s. (14 Ran).

(John G Doyle), P A Fahy

1785 Tattersalls Mares Novice Chase (5-y-o and up) £3,450 2½m............(3:00)

GYPSY LASS 6-12-0 T Horgan,................(9 to 1) 1
1550² BLUE RING 9-11-9 F Woods,................(9 to 2) 2
PRINCESS CASILIA 8-12-0 B Sheridan, ...(6 to 4 fav) 3
1179 SHUIL LE CHEILE 6-11-6 (3*) C O'Brien, ...(20 to 1) 4
410 PEJAWI 6-11-9 J P Banahan,..............(20 to 1) 5
1451 SHEILA NA GIG 7-12-0 A Powell,..............(3 to 1) f
MOUNTAIN STAGE (Ire) 5-11-12 C F Swan,......(9 to 2) f
507⁸ YVONNES PRINCESS 6-11-9 K F O'Brien,......(10 to 1) pu
Dist: 6l, 15l, 9l. 5m 42.60s. (8 Ran).

(Mrs Riona Molony), W Harney

1786 Irish National Bookmakers Flat Race (4 & 5-y-o) £3,795 2m......(3:30)

1455⁴ GLEN TEN (Ire) 4-11-1 (3*) Mrs J M Mullins, ...(5 to 2) 1
SHERE (Ire) 5-11-7 (7*) Mr M Brennan,..........(11 to 2) 2
1555⁴ ARCHER (Ire) 5-12-0 Mr A J Martin,..........(11 to 8 on) 3
1549 CORRIBLOUGH (Ire) 5-11-9 (5*) Mr G J Harford, ..(16 to 1) 4
1383⁶ DENNETT VALLEY (Ire) 4-11-2 (7*) Mrs D McDonogh,
......................(10 to 1) 5
1581 DROP THE HAMMER (Ire) 4-11-2 (7*) Mr R Pugh, ..(8 to 1) 6
1555 GROUP HAT (Ire) 5-11-9 (5*) Mr J A Nash, ...(16 to 1) 7
MAJOR BERT (Ire) 5-11-7 (7*) Mr J Lombard, ...(20 to 1) 8
OUR SON (Ire) 4-11-2 (7*) Mr T M Finnegan,......(33 to 1) 9
TUSCANY HIGHWAY (Ire) 4-11-9 Mr M Phillips, ...(14 to 1) 10
MILENKEH (Ire) 4-11-2 (7*) Miss H E McNamara, ..(20 to 1) 11
157 CIARRAI (Ire) 4-11-2 (7*) Mr P A Brosnan, ...(20 to 1) su
Dist: ½l, 6l, 5l, 3½l. 4m 22.70s. (12 Ran).

(Hugh McCann), W P Mullins

EDINBURGH (good)
Monday December 20th
Going Correction: MINUS 0.25 sec. per fur.

1787 Buchan Automotive Maiden Hurdle (3-y-o and up) £2,110 2½m...... (12:15)

1675² IMPERIAL BID (Fr) 5-11-3 (5") P Waggott, *hld up in tch, hdwy hfwy, led gng wl appr last, rdn and ran on.*
..................(5 to 2 fav op 2 to 1 tchd 3 to 1) 1
1583² ASTRALEON (Ire) 5-11-8 B Storey, *hld up in tch, hdwy gng wl appr 2 out, ev ch last, no extr.*
..................(5 to 1 op 6 to 1 tchd 8 to 1) 2
BERING ISLAND (USA) 3-10-5 (3") N Bentley, *in tch, effrt aftr 3 out, hdwy to chal last, sn rdn, one pace.* (50 to 1) 3
1476² GREAT EASEBY (Ire) 3-10-8 R Hodge, *beh, reminders aftr 8th, hdwy and ch betw last 2, btn whn mstk last.*
..................(12 to 1 tchd 14 to 1) 4
1675⁴ CLEEVAUN (Ire) 5-11-3 (5") P Williams, *prmnt, led 2 out till appr last, sn btn........* (7 to 1 op 5 to 1 tchd 8 to 1) 5
1202⁹ HICKSONS CHOICE (Ire) 5-11-8 A Maguire, *chsd ldrs till wknd aftr 2 out.*................................(14 to 1) 6
1369⁴ STRONG FLAME (Ire) 4-11-8 C Grant, *not jump wl, led to 2 out, wknd.*..........................(5 to 1 op 3 to 1) 7
1478⁶ HIP HOP (Ire) 4-11-3 (5") J Burke, *mid-div till wknd appr 2 out.*......................(9 to 1 op 8 to 1 tchd 10 to 1) 8
PESIDANAMICH (Ire) 5-11-8 M Moloney, *nvr nr to chal.*
..................(40 to 1 op 33 to 1 tchd 50 to 1) 9
1584² DIGNIFIED (Ire) 3-9-10 (7") A Linton, *chsd ldrs till wknd appr 2 out.*...................................(50 to 1) 10
1724⁵ LONDON HILL 5-11-8 C Dennis, *chsd ldrs till wknd appr 2 out.*..................................(12 to 1) 11
BOWLANDS HIMSELF (Ire) 5-11-1 (7") Mr A Parker, *mid-div till wknd quickly and lost tch aftr 3 out.*
..................(66 to 1 op 50 to 1) 12
1147 PINE CLASSIC (Ire) 3-10-8 G McCourt, *al beh, tld off 9th.*
..................................(50 to 1) 13
821 CHALKIEFORT 4-11-8 K Jones, *cl up to hfwy, wknd quickly, tld off 9th.*...............(100 to 1 op 66 to 1) 14

Dist: 3l, hd, 7l, sht-hd, 5l, 3l, 5l, 1½l, 8l, 15l. 4m 44.30s. a 6.30s (14 Ran).
(Lord Durham), Denys Smith

1788 Fred Wilson And Partners Selling Handicap Hurdle (3-y-o and up) £1,955 2m.......................... (12:45)

1655* AL FORUM (Ire) [80] 3-10-13 D O'Sullivan, *in tch, quickened to ld betw last 2, ran on wl.*............(3 to 1 jt-fav op 5 to 2) 1
1589³ JOHN NAMAN (Ire) [78] 4-10-11 A Dobbin, *chsd ldrs, reminders aftr 4th, styd on wl frm 2 out, no ch wth wnr.*
..................(15 to 2 op 7 to 1 tchd 8 to 1) 2
1738⁷ HYPNOTIST [90] 6-11-4 (5") D Bentley, *prmnt, led appr 5th till betw last 2, kpt on same pace...* (10 to 1 op 8 to 1) 3
BEND SABLE (Ire) [81] 3-11-0 J Callaghan, *beh, styd on wl appr 2 out, nrst finish.*.......................(20 to 1) 4
1526² CHANDIGARH [77] 5-10-10 A Maguire, *in tch, hdwy to track ldrs 3 out, ev ch till fdd nxt.*............(3 to 1 jt-fav op 4 to 1 tchd 9 to 2) 5
1586⁸ CHARLYCIA [80] (v) 5-10-13 A Orkney, *led till appr 5th, sn lost pl.*................(7 to 1 op 6 to 1 tchd 8 to 1) 6
1680⁵ HAMANAKA (USA) [81] 4-11-0 Mr S Love, *mid-div, effrt appr 2 out, no hdwy, blun last....* (16 to 1 op 12 to 1) 7
1680³ A GENTLEMAN TWO [82] 7-11-1 P Niven, *prmnt till wknd appr 2 out.*....................(7 to 1 op 6 to 1) 8
1583² SKOLERN [91] 9-11-10 B Storey, *nvr dngrs.*
..................(20 to 1 op 16 to 1) 9
HELLO GEORGIE [85] (bl) 10-11-4 R Garritty, *nvr dngrs.*
..................(40 to 1 op 33 to 1 tchd 50 to 1) 10
824⁸ JUST PULHAM [76] 8-10-9 K Jones, *al beh.*
..................(16 to 1 op 14 to 1) 11
1183 EMPEROR ALEXANDER (Ire) [68] 5-10-1 S Turner, *nvr better than mid-div.*...........................(33 to 1) 12
1047 BLACKDOWN [81] 6-11-0 P Harley, *chsd ldrs, chlgd 5th, wknd quickly appr 2 out, virtually pld up nr finish, lme.*...............(14 to 1 op 12 to 1 tchd 16 to 1) 13

Dist: 5l, 2l, hd, 2l, 1l, hd, 1½l, 1l, 2l, hd. 3m 41.70s. a 3.70s (13 Ran).
SR: 8/1/11/2/-/-/-/3/
(Martin Hickey), R Ingram

1789 Glassedin Securiies Handicap Chase (0-130 5-y-o and up) £3,096 2½m (1:15)

1286³ SIR PETER LELY [109] (bl) 6-11-3 C Grant, *wth ldr, led 8th, clr aftr 3 out, styd on wl.*.........(5 to 1 tchd 11 to 2) 1
1585³ CORNET [120] 7-10-4 M Dwyer, *in tch, pushed alng aftr tenth, chsd wnr aftr 3 out, no imprsn.*
..................(5 to 1 op 5 to 1 tchd 4 to 1) 2
1585⁴ CLASSIC MINSTREL [99] 9-10-7⁶ T Reed, *hld up beh, lost tch hfwy, styd on strly frm 3 out, nrst finish...* (8 to 1) 3
1679* LAPIAFFE [98] 9-10-6³ G McCourt, *in tch, hdwy aftr 12th, chasing wnr whn blun 3 out, not reco'r.*
..................(7 to 1 op 9 to 2 tchd 8 to 1) 4
1678 KUSHBALOO [119] 8-11-13 B Storey, *hld up, hdwy hfwy, one pace 4 out.*.......................(9 to 2 op 7 to 2) 5
1591⁴ CLEVER FOLLY [92] 13-10-0 M Moloney, *in tch, no hdwy frm 4 out.*.....................(16 to 1 op 12 to 1) 6
1679² SPEECH [93] 10-10-1⁴ (3") A Thornton, *led to 8th, cl up, rdn aftr 12th, wknd, btn whn blun 2 out.*
..................(66 to 1 op 25 to 1) 7

1486² ON THE HOOCH [101] 8-10-9 Mr J Bradburne, *al beh, lost tch hfwy.*.........................(8 to 1 tchd 9 to 1) 8
1326³ COMEDY ROAD [97] 9-10-5 A Maguire, *prmnt till wknd aftr 11th...........* (7 to 2 fav op 4 to 1 tchd 11 to 2) 9
KILDIMO [120] 13-12-0 Gary Lyons, *chsd ldrs till wknd aftr 11th, pld up lme bef 4 out....*(16 to 1 tchd 20 to 1) pu

Dist: 4l, hd, 4l, sht-hd, 20l, nk, 6l, 12l. 4m 53.00s. a 3.00s (10 Ran).
SR: 9/16/-/-/11/-/ (John Doyle Construction Limited), M D Hammond

1790 Swarland Grain Driers Novices' Chase (5-y-o and up) £2,549 2½m
..................................(1:45)

1587⁷ EBRO 7-11-0 A Dobbin, *cl up, led appr 4 out, rdn aftr nxt, styd on wl.*........................(33 to 1) 1
1604⁴ WILD ATLANTIC 10-11-7 K Jones, *made most till appr 4 out, rallied betw last 2, no extr frm last.*
..................................(6 to 1 op 5 to 1) 2
1477⁴ REEF LARK 8-10-11 (3") A Thornton, *in tch, effrt appr 4 out, kpt on same pace, mstk last....* (7 to 2 op 11 to 4) 3
1676 JUNIORS CHOICE 10-10-7 (7") Mr A Parker, *in tch, effrt appr 4 out, no hdwy, btn whn mstk last....*(11 to 4 jt-fav op 5 to 2 tchd 3 to 1) 4
1587 CALDECOTT 7-11-0 Gary Lyons, *wth ldr till blun and lost pl 11th, beh whn blundered 2 out.*
..................(6 to 1 op 5 to 1 tchd 13 to 2) 5
1677⁶ ROYAL FIFE 7-10-4 (5") P Williams, *f second.*
..................(25 to 1 op 33 to 1) f
1605 PANTO LADY 7-10-2 (7") Miss S Lamb, *sn tld off, pld up bef tenth.*..................(100 to 1 op 66 to 1) pu
1637³ GREENFIELD MANOR 6-11-0 T Reed, *outpcd and lost tch hfwy, tld off whn pld up bef 12th...........*(11 to 4 jt-fav op 9 to 4) pu

Dist: 2½l, 2l, 5l, dist. 5m 0.90s. a 10.90s (8 Ran).
(Mrs F A Veasey), V Thompson

1791 Philip Wilson Corn Factors Novices' Handicap Hurdle (3-y-o and up) £2,305 2m.......................... (2:15)

1408³ REGAL AURA (Ire) [90] 3-11-10 J Callaghan, *trkd ldrs, led betw last 2, ran on wl und pres.*
..................(7 to 1 op 11 to 2 tchd 8 to 1) 1
1668⁶ TAHITIAN [75] 4-10-9 G McCourt, *in tch, rdn aftr 2 out, ev ch last, no extr und pres....* (5 to 2 fav tchd 11 to 4) 2
1092 BEACH PATROL (Ire) [66] 5-10-0 D Byrne, *led till 3 out, styd cl up, ev ch last, no extr und pres.*
..................(66 to 1 op 200 to 1) 3
1586* LEGITIM [79] 4-10-6 (7") G Tormey, *hld up in tch, rdn aftr 2 out, ev ch whn not clr run appr last, kpt on und pres.*
..................(13 to 2 op 11 to 2 tchd 7 to 1) 4
1584² ERBIL (Ire) [81] 3-11-1 T Reed, *hld up, effrt betw last 2, sn rdn, no hdwy.*......................(4 to 1 op 7 to 2) 5
1586 CLEAR IDEA (Ire) [85] 5-11-5 N Doughty, *cl up, slight ld aftr 3 out, hdd betw last 2, edgd lft appr last, no extr und pres.*...........................(14 to 1 op 8 to 1) 6
1607 BORING (USA) [80] 4-11-0 R Hodge, *in tch, effrt appr 2 out, sn wknd.*............(9 to 1 op 7 to 1 tchd 10 to 1) 7
1658² BARAHIN (Ire) [76] 4-10-10 D O'Sullivan, *cl up till wknd quickly aftr 2 out.*.................(4 to 1 op 3 to 1) 8
1060 GYMCRAK CYRANO (Ire) [77] 4-10-11 R Garritty, *pld up aftr second, iron broke.*...........(25 to 1 tchd 33 to 1) pu

Dist: 1l, hd, sht-hd, 2l, nk, 8l, 12l. 3m 49.70s. a 11.70s (9 Ran).
(D J Bushell), G M Moore

1792 Cobb McCallum & Company Novices' Chase (4-y-o and up) £2,455 2m (2:45)

1128* GLEMOT (Ire) 5-11-10 A Maguire, *chsd ldrs, led and lft clr 4 out, pushed out frm last.*
..................(15 to 8 fav op 5 to 4 tchd 7 to 4) 1
1669⁴ MARLINGFORD 6-11-5 D Morris, *led to 5th, outpcd aftr 7th, styd on wl frm 3 out.* (9 to 2 op 4 to 1 tchd 5 to 1) 2
1673⁶ HEDLEY MILL 5-10-7 (7") Mr A Parker, *beh, styd on wl frm 4 out, nrst finish...................*(16 to 1 op 14 to 1) 3
1735² REGAL ROMPER (Ire) 5-11-5 Gary Lyons, *in tch, no hdwy frm 8th, btn whn mstks last 2....*(33 to 1 op 20 to 1) 4
QUALITY ASSURED 8-11-5 T Reed, *sn beh, nvr dngrs.*
..................(150 to 1 op 100 to 1 tchd 200 to 1) 5
1604³ SEMINOFF (Fr) 7-11-10 A Dobbin, *in tch, hit 5th, wknd aftr 8th.*............(14 to 1 op 10 to 1) 6
1571⁹ SEON 7-11-2 (3") N Bentley, *al beh, tld off.*
..................(9 to 2 op 4 to 1 tchd 5 to 1) 7
1604 SUPREME BLUSHER 6-11-0 K Jones, *sn beh, tld off.*
..................(100 to 1 op 66 to 1) 8
1284² FLOWING RIVER (USA) 7-11-5 B Storey, *in tch, hdwy aftr 7th, 3rd and ev ch whn f 4 out.*......(9 to 2 op 7 to 2) f
1675⁵ ROAD TO THE WEIR 6-11-0 (5") J Burke, *cl up, led 5th till hdd and f 4 out.*................(66 to 1 op 33 to 1) f
1484 AYIA NAPA 6-11-5 Mr J Bradburne, *cl up, led 4th to nxt, wknd quickly aftr 7th, beh whn pld up bef four out.*
..................(50 to 1 op 33 to 1) pu

Dist: 3l, nk, 20l, 2½l, 15l, dist, 8l. 3m 52.90s. a 2.90s (11 Ran).
SR: 27/19/13/-/-/-/ (Ken McCormick), J H Johnson

1793 Christmas Present Handicap Hurdle (0-120 4-y-o and up) £2,200 3m.. (3:15)

1586⁵ THE GREEN FOOL [97] 6-10-6 A Dobbin, *in tch, pushed alng aftr 3 out, rdn to ld appr last, styd on wl.*
.........................(10 to 1 tchd 12 to 1) 1
1361³ TRONCHETTO (Ire) [94] (bl) 4-10-3 P Niven, *made most, hdd appr last, no extr.*.... (4 to 1 op 5 to 1 tchd 11 to 2) 2
1619 WISHING GATE (USA) [105] 5-11-0 M Dwyer, *trkd ldrs, ev ch 2 out, sn rdn, one pace.*
.........................(11 to 4 fav op 5 to 2 tchd 3 to 1) 3
MINGUS (USA) [91] 6-10-0³ (3") A Thornton, *hld up, hdwy appr 3 out, styd on same pace frm nxt.*........(12 to 1) 4
1066* LEADING PROSPECT [112] 6-11-7 B Storey, *in tch, outpcd aftr 3 out, kpt on frm nxt.*..........(9 to 1 tchd 10 to 1) 5
1656⁵ PIMS GUNNER (Ire) [98] 5-10-2 (5") D Bentley, *nvr trble ldrs.*
.........................(50 to 1 op 33 to 1) 6
1588² RED TEMPEST (Ire) [91] 5-9-3 (5") F Perratt, *prmnt, wknd frm 2 out.*........................(33 to 1) 7
1481⁹ REVE DE VALSE (USA) [119] 6-11-9 (5") P Waggott, *in tch till wknd appr 2 out.*...................(25 to 1) 8
1562⁶ SOMERSET DANCER (USA) [107] 6-11-2 D O'Sullivan, *chsd ldrs till wknd aftr 3 out.*.....................(7 to 1) 9
1637 PANDESSA [91] 6-9-7 (7") S Mason, *mid-div till wknd aftr 3 out.*.........................(33 to 1) 10
1680² RAPID MOVER [93] (bl) 6-10-2² C Grant, *hld up, hdwy aftr 7th, wknd after 3 out.*...................(20 to 1) 11
1680⁴ SERAPHIM (Fr) [97] 4-10-6² G McCourt, *cl up till wknd aftr 3 out.*....................(8 to 1 op 7 to 1 tchd 9 to 1) 12
975⁵ CHARMING GALE [92] 6-10-1⁶ (5") P Williams, *mid-div till wknd aftr 3 out.*...................(14 to 1) 13
767⁹ NO SID NO STARS (USA) [95] 5-10-4 A Maguire, *in tch till wknd aftr 9th, tld off 3 out.*....(20 to 1 op 16 to 1) 14
Dist: 2l, ½l, 2½l, 8l, 2l, 3l, 3½l, 1½l, ¾l, 7l. 5m 43.50s. a 3.50s (14 Ran).
(Mrs B Kirke), V Thompson

HEREFORD (heavy)
Tuesday December 21st
Going Correction: PLUS 1.32 sec. per fur. (races 1,4,6), PLUS 1.02 (2,3,5)

1794 Cowslip Conditional Jockeys' Nov- ices' Selling Hurdle (4-y-o and up) £1,480 2m 1f.................(12:45)

1717* DERRYMOSS (v) 7-11-0 (5") T Dascombe, *sn trkd ldr, led appr last, drw clr, cmftbly.*
.........(11 to 8 fav op 5 to 4 tchd 11 to 10 and 6 to 4) 1
1702² FORGETFUL 4-10-6 (3") P McLoughlin, *pld hrd, led till appr last, one pace.*......(6 to 1 op 5 to 1 tchd 7 to 1) 2
MINI FETE (Fr) 4-10-4 (5") N Juckes, *al prmnt, rdn 2 out, one pace.*.....................(50 to 1 op 33 to 1) 3
TENDRESSE (Ire) 5-10-9 M Hourigan, *hld up, hdwy 5th, nvr nrr.*........................(7 to 2 op 5 to 2) 4
1589³ ICE MAGIC 6-11-0 A Thornton, *mid-div, lost tch 5th.*
.........................(16 to 1 tchd 12 to 1) 5
GIVE ME HOPE (Ire) 5-10-9 Guy Lewis, *hld up, hdwy appr 4th, wknd bef 2 out.*..................(12 to 1 op 7 to 1) 6
1589⁴ SILK DYNASTY 7-11-0 S Wynne, *beh, hdwy 4th, wknd appr 2 out.*.....................(16 to 1 op 10 to 1) 7
1695 SHADOWLAND (Ire) 5-11-0 V Slattery, *rear, hdwy 3rd, wknd nxt, tld off.*................(50 to 1 op 33 to 1) 8
LAST APPEARANCE 4-10-9 R Farrant, *al beh, tld off.*
.........................(50 to 1 op 20 to 1) 9
OURPALWENTY 6-10-9 (5") Pat Thompson, *chsd ldrs till wknd 4th, tld off.*................(50 to 1 op 20 to 1) 10
1354 BALZAON KNIGHT 6-11-0 S Curran, *prmnt till wknd appr 4th, tld off whn pld up bef last.*
.........................(11 to 1 op 12 to 1 tchd 14 to 1 and 10 to 1) pu
OSCILANTE 5-10-9 (5") L Reynolds, *in tch till wknd quickly appr 4th, tld off whn pld up bef 2 out.*
.........................(20 to 1 op 12 to 1) pu
1589⁸ ABELONI 4-11-0 R Greene, *sn beh, blun 3rd, tld off whn pld up bef last.*.......(12 to 1 op 16 to 1 tchd 20 to 1) pu
Dist: 5l, 5l, 2½l, 15l, 7l, 3l, 30l, ½l, 20l. 4m 18.50s. a 32.50s (13 Ran).
(Mrs J K L Watts), M C Pipe

1795 Caraway Novices' Handicap Chase (5- y-o and up) £2,424 2m.........(1:15)

1718* MAGGOTS GREEN [76] 6-10-8 (3",6ex) R Farrant, *hld up, gng wl, hdwy 6th, sent second nxt, led last, ran on well.*.........................(7 to 1) 1
1598⁷ DAWN CHANCE [70] 7-10-5 R Dunwoody, *led to last, not pace of unr.*......................(20 to 1 op 10 to 1) 2
1527² MAJOR CUT [74] 7-10-9 B Powell, *trkd ldr to 7th, kpt on one pace frm 2 out.*................(8 to 1 tchd 10 to 1) 3
1518³ BUSH HILL [74] 8-10-9 S McNeill, *in tch till wknd nxt, sn hdwy frm 7th.*................(25 to 1 op 20 to 1) 4
1696 THE MRS [83] 7-11-4 S Earle, *beh, nvr rchd 1ft 3rd, nvr on terms.*.........................(5 to 1 op 7 to 2) 5
1505³ OSTURA [88] 8-11-9 A Maguire, *prmnt, ev ch whn jmpd slwly 3 out, sn rdn, btn 3rd when mstk last, wknd.*
.........................(9 to 4 fav op 5 to 2 tchd 2 to 1) 6
887⁹ KNIGHT IN SIDE [71] 7-10-6 C Maude, *in tch, wkng whn blun 3 out, tld off.*.............(4 to 1 op 9 to 4) 7
Dist: 5l, 3½l, 7l, 1l, 3l, dist. 4m 11.50s. a 22.50s (7 Ran).
SR: 21/10/10/3/11/13/-/   (E A Hayward), J M Bradley

1796 Comfrey Handicap Chase (0-130 5-y-o and up) £2,724 3m 1f 110yds.... (1:45)

1523* MAN OF MYSTERY [107] 7-10-10 D Bridgwater, *made all, mstk 12th, tired aftr last, rallied und pres, ran on fnl 100 yards.*.........(6 to 4 fav op 5 to 4 tchd 2 to 1) 1
1197 CATCHAPENNY [102] (bl) 8-10-5 S Earle, *al prmnt, rdn appr 2 out, chlgd aftr last, no imprsn fnl 100 yards.*
.........................(4 to 1 tchd 9 to 2) 2
1302⁴ KINGFISHER BAY [97] 8-10-0 A Maguire, *wl beh 6th, blun 3 out, styd on past btn horses frm nxt.*
.........................(9 to 1 op 5 to 1 tchd 10 to 1) 3
1459* WARNER FOR WINNERS [104] 7-10-7 Peter Hobbs, *wtd wth, pushed alng hfwy, hdwy to go second appr 3 out, blun nxt, rdn and wknd r-in.*
.........................(9 to 4 op 7 to 4 tchd 5 to 2) 4
1600³ POWDER BOY [97] 8-10-0 R Dunwoody, *chsd wnr till wknd appr 3 out.*.............(8 to 1 tchd 9 to 1) 5
1776 SPARTAN FLAPJACK [112] 7-11-1⁵ Miss L Blackford, *mstk 1st, sn wl beh, tld off whn blun 7th, pld up aftr nxt.*
.........................(500 to 1 op 66 to 1 tchd 1000 to 1) pu
Dist: 2½l, 10l, ½l, 20l. 6m 44.60s. a 32.60s (6 Ran).
SR: 16/8/-/   (PCJF Bloodstock), N A Twiston-Davies

1797 Thyme Mares Only Novices' Hurdle (4-y-o and up) £1,515 2m 1f..... (2:15)

ELAINE TULLY (Ire) 5-10-12 Peter Hobbs, *al prmnt, hit 4th, cld on ldr appr 2 out, rdn to ld 150 yards out.*
.........................(7 to 2 op 9 to 4) 1
815² TOO SHARP 5-10-12 J Osborne, *led, rdn aftr last, hdd 150 yards out, one pace.*
.........................(13 to 8 fav op 6 to 4 tchd 7 to 4) 2
1622⁶ NICSAMLYN 6-10-12 Mr T Stephenson, *trkd ldr, wknd quickly appr 2 out.*..........(12 to 1 op 8 to 1) 3
SAMS QUEEN 4-10-12 R Supple, *mstk second, hdwy 4th, nvr on terms.*...............(25 to 1 op 7 to 1) 4
1626 ROSENTHAL 5-10-12 R Dunwoody, *chsd ldrs, lost tch aftr 4th.*........................(20 to 1 op 12 to 1) 5
MISTRESS MINX 4-10-7² (7") M M Rimell, *in tch till outpcd 3rd.*.........................(50 to 1 op 33 to 1) 6
1594⁹ CELTIC BRIDGE 5-10-12 W Marston, *al beh, lost tch 3rd.*
.........................(14 to 1 op 20 to 1 tchd 12 to 1) 7
1421 MISTRESS BEE (USA) 4-10-12 A S Smith, *al beh, rdn appr 4th, tld off.*................(33 to 1 op 25 to 1) 8
1660 ARLEY GALE 5-10-12 G Bradley, *beh 3rd, pld up bef 3 out.*.........................(20 to 1 tchd 25 to 1) pu
RHYMING PROSE 5-10-12 T Grantham, *beh, hdwy 3rd, blun nxt, pld up bef 3 out.*
.........................(4 to 1 op 7 to 2 tchd 9 to 2) pu
Dist: 3l, 25l, 15l, 5l, 1½l, ¾l, dist. 4m 19.00s. a 33.00s (10 Ran).
(Mrs P G Wilkins), P J Hobbs

1798 Cloves Handicap Chase (0-130 5-y-o and up) £2,570 2m............. (2:45)

GALAGAMES (USA) [90] 6-10-5 B Powell, *made all, clr to 3rd, steadied 2 out, drvn clear frm last.*
.........................(14 to 1 op 8 to 1) 1
1523³ PITHY [100] 11-10-8 (7") Guy Lewis, *al prmnt, wnt second 6th, chlgd 2 out, no imprsn r-in.*......(5 to 2 op 9 to 2) 2
1649² DR ROCKET [113] 8-11-11 (3") D Meredith, *hld up, hdwy 6th, wn ch 2 out, rdn and wknd r-in.* (5 to 2 op 2 to 1) 3
1623² PHILLIMAY [92] 7-10-7 A Maguire, *hld up, hdwy 4th, wknd appr 2 out, btn whn stumbled last.*
.........................(15 to 8 fav op 7 to 4 tchd 2 to 1) 4
1596² FRED SPLENDID [92] 10-10-7 R Dunwoody, *chsd wnr to 6th, wkng whn blun 2 out, tld off.*
.........................(5 to 1 op 4 to 1 tchd 6 to 1) 5
Dist: 3½l, 7l, 12l, dist. 4m 13.10s. a 24.10s (5 Ran).
SR: -/5/11/-/-/   (S J Norman), R H Buckler

1799 Rosemary Handicap Hurdle (0-115 4-y-o and up) £2,239 2m 1f..... (3:15)

1721* EDIMBOURG [112] 7-11-13 (7ex) J Osborne, *made all, pushed clr appr last, cmftbly.*
.........(13 to 8 on op 6 to 4 on tchd 11 to 8 on and 7 to 4 on) 1
1599⁴ DJEBEL PRINCE [100] 6-10-10 (5") A Procter, *al prmnt, trkd wnr frm 3rd, one pace 2 out.*
.........................(4 to 1 op 5 to 1 tchd 11 to 2) 2
GOLDINGO [88] 6-10-0 (3") R Davis, *hld up, hdwy to track ldrs 4th, rdn appr 2 out, wkng whn hng lft bef last.*
.........................(13 to 2 op 10 to 1 tchd 6 to 1) 3
1633⁴ MECADO [94] 6-10-9 D Gallagher, *ran in snatches, styd on frm last.*................(20 to 1 op 14 to 1) 4
DONNA'S TOKEN [85] 6-10-0 (7") P McLoughlin, *trkd wnr to 3rd, wknd aftr nxt.*...(16 to 1 op 14 to 1 tchd 20 to 1) 5
GARDA'S GOLD [89] 10-10-1 (3") D Meredith, *al beh.*
.........................(33 to 1 op 25 to 1) 6
1650⁷ KING'S SHILLING (USA) [111] 6-11-5 (7") Mr M Rimell, *beh, hdwy 3rd, wknd aftr nxt.*............(16 to 1 op 12 to 1) 7
1701⁴ HAVE A PARTY [90] 6-10-5 S McNeill, *al beh, tld off whn f 2 out.*.......................(33 to 1 op 25 to 1) f
Dist: 8l, 7l, 2½l, 8l, 10l, hd. 4m 13.30s. a 27.30s (8 Ran).

SR: 50/30/11/14/-/-/13/-/   (Mrs Iva Winton), Miss H C Knight

LUDLOW (soft)
Wednesday December 22nd
Going Correction: PLUS 0.87 sec. per fur. (races 1,2,-5,7), PLUS 1.23 (3,4,6)

1800   **Tanners Manzanilla 'National Hunt' Novices' Hurdle (4-y-o and up) £1,913 2m**. . . . .**(12:40)**

1636[2]	KONVEKTA KING (Ire) 5-11-4 A Maguire, *hld up in tch, hdwy 5th, led appr 2 out, clr whn jmpd lft last, ran on.* . . . . . . (6 to 5 fav op 5 to 4 tchd 11 to 8 and 11 to 10)	1
	CAWARRA BOY 5-10-5 (7*) Mr E James, *nvr far away, hdwy 3 out, chsd wnr frm nxt.* . . . . (66 to 1)	2
1490[3]	TAKE THE BUCKSKIN 6-10-12 S Smith Eccles, *al prmnt, wnt second 5th, led briefly aftr nxt, hld whn hit last.* . . . . (6 to 1 op 5 to 1)	3
1542[7]	CONEY ROAD 4-10-12 P Holley, *chsd ldrs, lost pl 5th, styd on frm 2 out.* . . . . (7 to 2 op 6 to 1)	4
	GLENTOWER (Ire) 5-10-12 R Dunwoody, *hld up, hdwy whn hmpd on bend appr 2 out, one pace aftr.* . . . . (14 to 1 op 7 to 1)	5
	ROCKY PARK 7-10-12 J Frost, *hld up, hdwy 3 out, not pace to chal.* . . . . (14 to 1 op 10 to 1)	6
	FOUR HEARTS (Ire) 4-10-12 B Powell, *mid-division, nvr rch ldrs.* . . . . (33 to 1 op 20 to 1)	7
1109	SUPER SHARP (NZ) 5-10-12 Jacqui Oliver, *pld hrd, chsd ldrs, rdn and wkng whn hit 2 out.* (14 to 1 op 10 to 1)	8
	FORT RANK 6-10-11 (7*) R Darke, *beh, hdwy 3 out, nvr dngrs.* . . . . (33 to 1 op 25 to 1)	9
	MARINER'S AIR 6-10-7 W Marston, *al rear.* . . . . . . (33 to 1)	10
1636[3]	COMEDIMAN 5-10-5 (7*) Mr G Hogan, *pld hrd, mstk second, prmnt till wknd appr 2 out.* . . . (10 to 1 op 7 to 1)	11
1414[6]	PRINCE RUBEN 6-10-9 (3*) R Farrant, *mid-div, no hdwy frm 3 out.* . . . . (33 to 1 op 25 to 1)	12
1624[9]	THE SHAW TRADER 4-10-12 C Llewellyn, *trkd ldr, led 4th till aftr 3 out, wknd quickly.* . . . . (20 to 1 op 14 to 1)	13
	PEBBLE ROCK 4-10-12 N Williamson, *beh 4th.* . . . . (33 to 1 op 20 to 1)	14
1108	KING RUST 5-10-12 M Hourigan, *beh, tld off 5th.* . . . . (100 to 1 op 66 to 1)	15
1639[8]	COME ON CHARLIE 4-10-12 A O'Hagan, *al beh, tld off.* . . . . (100 to 1)	16
1542	BOX OF DELIGHTS (v,e/c,e/s) 5-10-9 (3*) D Meredith, *led till pckd and beh 4th, sn drpd back, tld off.* . . . (100 to 1)	17

Dist: 12l, 1¼l, ½l, 3l, 4l, 3l, 4l, 5l, ½l, 4l, ½l. 3m 55.80s. a 18.80s (17 Ran).
SR: 41/23/21/20/17/13/10/5/-/   (Konvekta Ltd), D Nicholson

1801   **Tanners Sauvignon Conditional Jockeys' Selling Handicap Hurdle (3-y-o and up) £1,836 2m 5f 110yds (1:10)**

1426[4]	FOR HEAVEN'S SAKE (Fr) [85] 8-11-5 M Hourigan, *led second, wnt clr 7th, rdn appr 2 out, plugged on gmely.* . . . . (13 to 2 op 6 to 1 tchd 7 to 1)	1
1719[2]	IT'S NOT MY FAULT (Ire) [73] 5-10-7 W Marston, *hdwy appr 3rd, poushed alng frm nxt, hrd rdn to chase wnr aftr 2 out.* . . . . (4 to 1 op 5 to 1 tchd 3 to 1)	2
1716[6]	PROVERBS GIRL [84] 8-11-4 S Fox, *beh till hdwy 6th, kpt on pace frm 2 out.* . . . . (14 to 1)	3
260[4]	MISS EQUILIA (USA) [90] 7-11-10 T Dascombe, *hld up rear, hdwy 6th, wnt second aftr nxt, wknd appr 2 out, one pace.* . . . . (13 to 2 op 9 to 2)	4
1485[2]	SPANISH WHISPER [78] 6-10-12 J Twomey, *prmnt till wknd aftr 3 out.* . . . . (15 to 2 op 6 to 1 tchd 8 to 1)	5
1072[7]	TEMPORALE [75] 7-10-9 N Juckes, *hit 4th, nvr nr to chal.* . . . . (12 to 1 op 10 to 1)	6
1529[2]	OMIDJOY (Ire) [66] 3-10-0 L Dace, *sn beh, tld off 6th.* . . . . (12 to 1 op 7 to 1)	7
1592[2]	NAJEB (USA) [75] (bl) 4-10-4 (5*) Mark Brown, *al beh, tld off.* . . . . (9 to 1 op 8 to 1 tchd 10 to 1)	8
1655	BIG GEM [67] 3-10-11 S Lycett, *prmnt, wknd 5th, tld off.* . . . . (66 to 1 op 33 to 1)	9
1592[9]	FRENDLY FELLOW [72] (bl) 9-10-6 D O'Sullivan, *al beh, tld off whn pld up bef 2 out.* . . (20 to 1 op 16 to 1)	pu
1592[7]	CADFORD GIRL [75] 9-10-9 R Darke, *pld up lme aftr second.* . . . . (10 to 1 op 25 to 1)	pu
1719[5]	EARLY BREEZE [80] 7-11-0 Leanne Eldredge, *mid-div, wknd 5th, tld off whn pld up bef 2 out.* . . . . (25 to 1 op 16 to 1)	pu
1370	LARA'S BABY (Ire) [72] (v) 5-10-6 D Meredith, *prmnt till wknd 4th, tld off whn pld up bef 7th.* . . . . (16 to 1 op 10 to 1)	pu
	ROYAL CIRCUS [84] 4-11-4 P Ward, *chsd ldrs till wknd 6th, tld off whn pld up bef 2 out.* . (25 to 1 op 20 to 1)	pu
1280[7]	THANKSFORTHEOFFER [66] 5-10-0 Guy Lewis, *hdwy second, wkng whn mstk 4th, tld off bef nxt.* . . . . (16 to 1)	pu
891[5]	NEW STATESMAN [67] 5-10-1 R Greene, *led, mstk 1st, hdd nxt, wknd appr 5th, tld off whn pld up bef 2 out.* . . . . (9 to 1 op 10 to 1 tchd 8 to 1)	pu

Dist: 5l, 4l, 3l, 15l, 15l, 3½l, 20l, dist. 5m 42.70s. a 45.70s (16 Ran).
(M Ephgrave), B Preece

1802   **Tanners Champagne Handicap Chase (0-125 5-y-o and up) £2,968 2½m (1:40)**

1511[2]	WELL BRIEFED [91] 6-10-9 B Powell, *hit second, trkd ldr frm 4th, chlgd 3 out, sn led, ran on.* . . . . (100 to 30 op 7 to 4 tchd 7 to 2)	1
1523[4]	NEW HALEN [102] 12-11-6 R Bellamy, *jmpd wl, led till sn aftr 3 out, one pace.* . . . . . (8 to 2 op 4 to 1 tchd 5 to 1)	2
1698[2]	L'UOMO PIU [92] 9-10-10 N Williamson, *hld up, hdwy whn hit tenth, mstk nxt, effrt appr 3 out, one pace.* . . . . (5 to 4 fav op 11 to 10 tchd 11 to 8)	3
1591[2]	RUPPLES [87] 6-10-5 W Worthington, *al beh, outpcd and mstks tenth and 11th, sn tld off.* . . . . (12 to 1 op 8 to 1)	4
1407[5]	PLAT REAY [106] (bl) 9-11-10 C Llewellyn, *ran in snatches, jmpd rght, mstk 3rd, struggling tenth, tld off whn pld up bef 3 out.* . . . . (4 to 1 op 7 to 2 tchd 9 to 2)	pu

Dist: 10l, 5l, dist. 5m 20.60s. a 29.60s (5 Ran).
SR: 31/32/17/-/-/   (Peter Jones), R H Buckler

1803   **Tanners Wines Novices' Chase (5-y-o and up) £3,558 2m**. . . . .**(2:10)**

1413*	SAN LORENZO (USA) 5-11-10 N Williamson, *trkd ldr, led 8th, lft clr last, unchlgd.* (9 to 4 op 2 to 1 tchd 5 to 2)	1
1525[7]	APRIL'S MODEL LADY 7-10-9 D Bridgwater, *jmpd poorly in rear, tld off 6th, styd on aftr blun 3 out, wnt second r-in.* . . . . (25 to 1 op 16 to 1 tchd 40 to 1)	2
1593	STAR OF THE GLEN 7-11-0 A Maguire, *rcd in 3rd pl, mstk 4th, hit four out, sn wknd, lft poor second at last.* . . . . (11 to 8 fav op 5 to 4)	3
1413[2]	TUDOR FABLE (Ire) 5-11-6 R Dunwoody, *led to 8th, ev ch 3 out, hld whn f last.* . . . . (9 to 4 op 7 to 4)	f

Dist: 30l, 15l. 4m 26.30s. a 34.30s (4 Ran).
(James D Greig), K C Bailey

1804   **Tanners Claret Novices' Handicap Hurdle (0-100 4-y-o and up) £1,480 2m 5f 110yds**. . . . .**(2:40)**

1645[2]	ALICE SMITH [73] 6-9-13[3] (5*) D Matthews, *made all, ran on wl frm 2 out.* . . . . (7 to 1 op 6 to 1)	1
1658[3]	CARAGH BRIDGE [72] 6-10-0 R Supple, *hld up, hdwy to go 3rd 3 out, rdn and hit nxt, wnt second r-in, no ch wth wnr.* . . . . (8 to 1 op 10 to 1)	2
1708[4]	STERLING BUCK (USA) [72] 6-10-0 W McFarland, *chsd wnr frm second, hit 5th, wknd r-in, fnshd tired.* . . . . (11 to 1 op 8 to 1)	3
1594[7]	STORMY SWAN [73] 7-10-1 W Humphreys, *chsd ldrs till outpcd 6th, kpt on one pace frm 2 out.* . . . . (50 to 1 op 33 to 1)	4
1414*	TOUR LEADER (NZ) [87] 4-11-1 B Powell, *hld up, hdwy 4th, wnt 3rd nxt, wknd appr 2 out.* . . . . (11 to 2 op 5 to 1 tchd 6 to 1)	5
	LEINTHALL PRINCESS [72] 7-10-0 N Williamson, *rear, some hdwy frm 3 out, nvr dngrs.* . . . . (10 to 1)	6
	MARINE SOCIETY [76] 5-10-4 R Greene, *beh, some hdwy appr 3 out, nvr dngrs.* . . . . (20 to 1 op 16 to 1)	7
1526	CAMPDEN AGAIN [72] 6-9-11 (3*) D Meredith, *al beh.* . . . . (100 to 1 op 50 to 1)	8
1708[6]	VICAR OF BRAY [87] 6-11-1 S Hodgson, *beh, rdn 5th, sn tld off.* . . . . (9 to 2 fav op 5 to 1 tchd 4 to 1)	9
	MAESTROSO (Ire) [100] (bl) 4-12-0 A Maguire, *pld hrd, hld up in tch, hit 3 out, wknd quickly, eased, tld off.* . . . . (14 to 1 op 8 to 1)	10
1567[6]	REFERRAL FEE [79] 6-10-7 S Earle, *prmnt till wknd 6th, f 3 out.* . . . . (20 to 1 op 16 to 1)	f
	ELITE LEO [74] 8-10-2 Peter Hobbs, *rear whn blun and uns rdr 3rd.* . . . . (9 to 1 op 11 to 2)	ur
1708[2]	ALTISHAR (Ire) [72] 5-10-0 P Holley, *hld up rear, hdwy 6th, wknd quickly 3 out, pld up bef nxt.* .(7 to 1 op 6 to 1)	pu
	BILBERRY [83] 4-10-11 R Dunwoody, *prmnt till wknd 4th, pld up bef 6th.* . . . . (20 to 1 op 12 to 1)	pu
402	CROSULA [72] 5-9-7 (7*) Guy Lewis, *prmnt till rdn and wknd aftr 4th, pld up bef 6th.* . . . . (100 to 1)	pu
1287[5]	DOCTOR DUNKLIN (USA) [72] 4-10-0[3] (3*) R Davis, *al beh, tld off whn pld up bef 2 out.* . . . . (50 to 1)	pu

Dist: 10l, 6l, sht-hd, 2l, 1½l, 7l, 5l, 20l, 2½l. 5m 37.80s. a 40.80s (16 Ran).
(Mrs J H E Eckley), B J Eckley

1805   **Tanners Chardonnay Novices' Handicap Chase (5-y-o and up) £2,996 3m**. . . . .**(3:10)**

	JOLLY JAUNT [82] 8-10-3[2] (7*) P Ward, *patiently rdn, hdwy 12th, ridden 3 out, lft second at last, styd on to ld fnl 100 yards.* . . . . (10 to 1 op 12 to 1 tchd 25 to 1)	1
1590*	MASTER JOLSON [102] 5-12-0 A Maguire, *hld up, hdwy 11th, led briefly 4 out, ev ch whn lft in ld last, rdn and hdd fnl 100 yards.* . . . . (11 to 8 fav tchd 7 to 4)	2
1547	IT'S AFTER TIME [74] 8-9-7 (7*) Guy Lewis, *al prmnt, hit 14th, rallied aftr nxt, no hdwy 3 out.* . . . . (25 to 1 op 33 to 1)	3
1593[4]	BALLY PARSON [84] 7-10-10 H Davies, *ran in snatches, prmnt most of way, no hdwy appr 3 out.* . . . . (12 to 1 op 8 to 1)	4

1527[4] MR TITTLE TATTLE [97] (bl) 7-11-9 N Williamson, *in tch whn blun tenth, wknd 4 out*............(12 to 1 op 7 to 1) 5
1058[4] REAL PROGRESS (Ire) [92] 5-11-4 Peter Hobbs, *prmnt, led 8th to 12th, wknd 4 out*.............(9 to 1 op 7 to 1) 6
1590 PANT LLIN [80] 7-10-6 R Supple, *rear whn mstk 3rd, hdwy 12th, wknd 4 out*..................(25 to 1 op 16 to 1) 7
PHYL'S LEGACY [74] 8-10-0 D Bridgwater, *al beh.*
..............................(100 to 1 op 66 to 1) 8
1527[3] LASTOFTHEVIKINGS [74] 8-10-0[3] (3[*]) R Davis, *rear till f 8th*.........................(14 to 1 op 10 to 1) f
1644 RUBINS BOY [81] 7-10-7 M Richards, *prmnt, jmpd slwly 3rd, led 12th to 4 out, sn led ag'n, refused last.*
...........................(7 to 1 op 9 to 2) ref
1530[4] STAPLEFORD LADY [74] 5-10-0 W McFarland, *prmnt to hfwy, tld off whn pld up bef 4 out.* (66 to 1 op 20 to 1) pu
1590[5] NEW PROBLEM [74] 6-10-0 C Maude, *hld up, lost tch 12th, pld up bef 3 out*...........(50 to 1 op 33 to 1) pu
1590[3] DEBT OF HONOR [74] (v) 5-10-0 R Greene, *led to 8th, jmpd slwly 11th, sn rdn and beh, tld off whn pld up bef 4 out.*
.................................(7 to 1 op 5 to 1) pu
Dist: 2½l, 20l, 2½l, 15l, ½l, nk, 6l. 6m 29.90s. a 40.90s (13 Ran).
(Mrs Jessie F Hayward), M J Wilkinson

1806 Tanners Cava Stakes National Hunt Flat Race (4,5,6-y-o) £1,308 2m. .(3:40)

1494[2] AUTO PILOT (NZ) 5-10-9 (7[*]) S Fox, *chsd ldrs, led o'r 4 fs out to 3 out, led over one out, edgd lft, cmftbly.*
..................(6 to 4 fav tchd 5 to 4 and 13 to 8) 1
BIG STRAND (Ire) 4-10-9 (7[*]) T Dascombe, *survd rght strt, sn in tch, led 3 fs out till appr last, kpt on.*
..............................(7 to 2 op 3 to 1 tchd 4 to 1) 2
1674[4] EVEN BLUE (Ire) 5-10-11 (5[*]) Mr D McCain, *rear, rcd wide, hdwy hfwy, kpt on one pace fnl 2 fs.*
..............................(14 to 1 op 8 to 1) 3
FLAPJACK LAD 4-10-9 (7[*]) Mr M Rimell, *al prmnt, ev ch o'r 2 fs out, one pace*................(10 to 1 op 5 to 1) 4
ORSWELL LAD 4-10-9 (7[*]) C Quinlan, *hld up, hdwy 5 fs out, rdn 3 out, one pace*..........(10 to 1 op 5 to 1) 5
MAXXUM EXPRESS (Ire) 5-10-13 (3[*]) R Davis, *hmpd strt, beh till hdwy 5 fs out, one pace 3 out.* (8 to 1 op 4 to 1) 6
KNOTTED 4-10-9 (7[*]) L O'Hare, *hld up, hdwy hfwy, no imprsn fnl 2 fs*..............(8 to 1 op 5 to 1 tchd 9 to 1) 7
SHINING LIGHT (Ire) 4-10-9 (7[*]) M Keighley, *prmnt till wknd 2 fs out*.....................(10 to 1 op 6 to 1) 8
SPRINGFIELD-BARON 4-10-9 (7[*]) Guy Lewis, *prmnt on outsd, rdn 4 fs out, sn btn*.......(33 to 1 op 20 to 1) 9
CLOSE OF PLAY 4-10-9 (7[*]) Mr G Hogan, *prmnt till weak-end o'r 5 fs out*..................(50 to 1 op 20 to 1) 10
BIG BAD WOLF (Ire) 5-11-2 Mr J Durkan, *prmnt till wknd 6 fs out*..........................(14 to 1 op 8 to 1) 11
BOURNEL 5-10-4 (7[*]) Mr Richard White, *hmpd strt, al beh.*
.................................(50 to 1 op 20 to 1) 12
FORBURIES (Ire) 4-10-11 W Marston, *led aftr 6 fs till o'r 4 out, wknd quickly*...............(33 to 1 op 20 to 1) 13
1779 NUNS CONE 5-10-13 (3[*]) R Farrant, *al prd, hrd, lost tch hfwy, tld off*....................(33 to 1 op 20 to 1) 14
1660 MISS PALEFACE 5-10-4 (7[*]) R Darke, *led 6 fs, wknd hfwy, tld off*...................(25 to 1 op 20 to 1) 15
LANLAU (Ire) 4-10-9 (7[*]) Mr C Vigors, *al beh, tld off.*
.................................(50 to 1 op 20 to 1) 16
WATERROW 5-10-11 M Hourigan, *al beh, slpd up o'r 2 fs out*.....................(33 to 1 op 20 to 1) su
Dist: 2½l, 2½l, 1½l, 1½l, 2½l, sht-hd, 2l, 12l, 2½l, ½l. 3m 59.50s. (17 Ran).
(C Cowley), Mrs J Renfree-Barons

SOUTHWELL (heavy)
Wednesday December 22nd
Going Correction: PLUS 2.30 sec. per fur.

1807 Hastings Novices' Chase (5-y-o and up) £2,136 3m 110yds......... (1:30)

1402 QUIET MONEY 6-11-0 C Grant, *prmnt, led 11th, lft wl clr 6 out*......................(11 to 1 op 9 to 1) 1
1080 BEN THE BOMBER 8-10-7 (7[*]) Judy Davies, *al rear, lft remote second 6 out, f 2 out, rmntd*...........(33 to 1) 2
1537[4] DEEPENDABLE 6-11-0 M A FitzGerald, *in tch, hit 5th, f 8th*...................(5 to 4 fav op 6 to 4) f
LADY BLAKENEY 7-10-9 L Wyer, *hld up, f 5th.*
.................................(5 to 1 op 4 to 1) f
1218[7] CLASSIC CONTACT 7-11-5 (5[*]) J Supple, *mstks, trkd ldr, blun 6th, hit nxt, blunded and uns rdr 8th.*
..............................(11 to 8 op 5 to 4 on) ur
GOLDEN SHOON 9-11-0 D Gallagher, *led, f tenth, hdd nxt, 6 ls second and very tired whn pld up bef six out.*
.................................(25 to 1) pu
Dist: Dist. 7m 24.00s. a 86.00s (6 Ran).
(Ecudawn), M D Hammond

1808 F. G. Construction Handicap Chase (0-125 5-y-o and up) £2,342 2½m 110yds....................... (2:00)

1585[6] BALTIC BROWN [103] 8-11-4 Gary Lyons, *led aftr second, pushed clr 2 out and styd on strly.* (2 to 1 op 11 to 8) 1

1420[6] HOWGILL [85] 7-9-11 (3[*]) S Wynne, *led till aftr second, chsd wnr, rdn 3 out, blun nxt and wknd.*
.................................(14 to 1 tchd 16 to 1) 2
RADICAL REQUEST [91] 10-10-6 D Gallagher, *in tch, hdwy 6 out, effrt and ev ch whn blun badly 3 out, no chance aftr*.........................(6 to 1 tchd 7 to 1) 3
1286[4] SIMPLE PLEASURE [113] 8-11-9 (5[*]) J Supple, *in tch, hit 5th and 8th, sn rdn alng and beh, tld off whn blun 6 out*.....................(7 to 4 fav op 2 to 1) 4
1641[5] CASINO MAGIC [88] 9-10-3 D Murphy, *in tch whn wknd 5 out, beh whn pld up bef 3 out*.....(5 to 1 tchd 6 to 1) pu
Dist: 15l, 30l, dist. 5m 59.60s. a 56.60s (5 Ran).
(Mrs S Smith), Mrs S J Smith

SOUTHWELL (A.W) (Std)
Wednesday December 22nd
Going Correction: PLUS 0.25 sec. per fur.

1809 Agincourt 'National Hunt' Novices' Handicap Hurdle (4-y-o and up) £1,689 2½m....................... (12:30)

1425[2] LAFANTA (Ire) [64] 4-10-9 K Jones, *al prmnt, led aftr 4 out, rdn 2 out and ran on*....(6 to 1 op 5 to 1 tchd 7 to 1) 1
1535[3] MILLIES OWN [75] 6-10-13 (7[*]) D Fox, *al prmnt, rdn 3 out, kpt on one pace*....(15 to 8 fav op 7 to 4 tchd 2 to 1) 2
1658[7] CROOKED DEALER (NZ) [65] 6-10-11 J Osborne, *cl up, led second to 3rd, hit 4th and lost pl, pushed alng 6th, styd on und pres frm 3 out, one pace appr last.*
..............................(15 to 2 op 6 to 1 tchd 8 to 1) 3
MEKSHARP [59] (bl) 9-10-2 M A FitzGerald, *al chasing ldrs, hit 5 out and sn rdn, wknd 3 out*.......(10 to 1 op 12 to 1) 4
1239[5] VAZON EXPRESS [67] 7-10-12 M A FitzGerald, *prmnt, rdn 5 out, wknd 3 out*...........(10 to 1 op 9 to 1) 5
1594[5] ALIAS SILVER [66] 6-10-4 (7[*]) Mr N Bradley, *hld up, hit 7th, sn rdn and beh whn pld up bef 3 out.*
..............................(11 to 2 op 5 to 1 tchd 6 to 1) pu
1630[6] RUSTIC GENT (Ire) [76] (v) 5-11-7 Richard Guest, *prmnt, led 3rd till aftr 4 out, sn rdn, wknd quickly and pld up bef 3 out*........................(14 to 1 op 12 to 1) pu
1546[2] CZAR NICHOLAS [83] 4-12-0 P Niven, *hld up and beh, hdwy 6th, rdn and hit nxt, sn behind and pld up bef 3 out*........................(4 to 1 op 11 to 4 tchd 9 to 2) pu
1620[4] PLUM LINE [55] (v) 4-10-8 B Clifford, *hit 1st and second, wknd quickly nxt and pld up bef 4th*.........(33 to 1) pu
1488 WATERBEACH VILLAGE (Ire) [55] 5-9-9 (5[*]) A Procter, *pld hrd, led till hdd and hit second, sn lost pl and tld off hfwy, pulled up bef 4 out.*
.................................(25 to 1 op 16 to 1 tchd 33 to 1) pu
Dist: 1½l, sht-hd, 15l, ½l. 5m 1.20s. a 20.20s (10 Ran).
(John Wade), J Wade

1810 Marston Moor Selling Hurdle (4-y-o and up) £1,969 2m............. (1:00)

SAYANT 8-12-0 Diane Clay, *in tch, hdwy appr 3 out, rdn nxt, styd on r-in to ld nr finish*......(8 to 1 op 5 to 1) 1
1632[8] BABY ASHLEY 7-11-9 N Mann, *al prmnt, hdwy to ld aftr 4 out, rdn 2 out, hdd and no extr nr finish.*
..............................(8 to 1 op 9 to 2) 2
1508[8] BALLERINA ROSE 6-10-11 (5[*]) A Procter, *al prmnt, effrt 4 out, chlgd nxt, sn rdn and one pace appr last.*
.................................(6 to 1 op 9 to 2) 3
1627[5] RUTH'S GAMBLE (v) 5-11-7 Richard Guest, *al prmnt, rdn bef 3 out, one pace*..................(12 to 1) 4
950[2] BAHER (USA) 4-11-0 B Clifford, *prmnt, rdn 4 out, sn wknd*.........................(8 to 1 op 7 to 1) 5
YUVRAJ 9-11-7 S Keightley, *hld up, hdwy appr 3 out, sn rdn and one pace...*(20 to 1 op 16 to 1 tchd 25 to 1) 6
PHARGOLD (Ire) 4-11-7 D Gallagher, *led, rdn and hdd aftr 4 out, wkng whn blun nxt.*
..............................(9 to 1 op 12 to 1 tchd 8 to 1) 7
1483[8] ELEGANT FRIEND 5-12-0 D Murphy, *hld up, some hdwy 5 out, rdn and btn appr 3 out.*
.................................(6 to 1 op 9 to 2 tchd 7 to 1) 8
1040 DAUPHIN BLEU (Fr) 7-11-0 Dr P Pritchard, *al rear.*
.................................(12 to 1 op 10 to 1) 9
1589[9] CLEAR LIGHT 6-11-0 Mr T Stephenson, *al rear.*
.................................(20 to 1 op 16 to 1) 10
1488 MARTHUL (USA) 5-11-7 J Osborne, *in tch, rdn and wknd 4 out*........................(14 to 1 op 10 to 1) 11
1562[8] SOLID (Ire) (bl) 5-11-2 (5[*]) D Walsh, *al rear, f last.*
.................................(12 to 1 op 7 to 1) 12
1655[6] SPRAY OF ORCHIDS 4-10-9 P Niven, *mid-div whn f second, broke neck, dead.*
..............................(4 to 1 fav op 9 to 2 tchd 5 to 1) f
1371 WHATCOMESNATURALLY (USA) (bl) 4-10-4 (5[*]) T Eley, *mid-div whn f 2 out*......................(10 to 1 op 20 to 1) f
SOL ROUGE (Ire) 4-10-9 Mr I McLelland, *al rear, tld off whn f 2 out*......................(10 to 1) f
369[3] MAJOR RISK 4-11-0 S D Williams, *in tch, rdn alng and blun badly 4 out, beh whn pld up bef nxt.* (16 to 1 op 14 to 1) pu
731 TIME PIECE (Ire) 5-10-9 (5[*]) J Supple, *bolted bef strt, pld hrd and prmnt to 3rd, sn lost pl, tld off, pulled up before 3 out*........................(20 to 1 op 14 to 1) pu

Dist: ¾l, 1½l, 6l, 7l, 4l, 3l, 1l, 5l, 3½l, 4l. 3m 57.30s. a 11.30s (17 Ran).
SR: 27/21/12/11/-/-/-/3/-/   (T Walker), W Clay

1811 Trafalgar Novices' Hurdle (4-y-o and up) £1,704 2m................(2:30)

1100[6]	MAJAL (Ire) 4-10-11 (5*) P Midgley, *hld up, hdwy 5th, led 4 out, quickened 2 out, ran on wl r-in.* ....(15 to 2 op 6 to 1 tchd 8 to 1)	1
1424*	CLIFTON CHASE 4-11-5 (7*) D Fortt, *trkd ldrs, hdwy 3 out, pushed alng nxt, rdn last, kpt on r-in, not rch wnr.* ....(7 to 4 on tchd 6 to 4 on)	2
1460	DOUBLE THE STAKES (USA) 4-11-0 (7*) P McLoughlin, *in tch, hdwy to chase wnr 4 out, ev ch nxt, sn rdn and one pace appr last*.........(13 to 2 op 5 to 1 tchd 7 to 1)	3
1655[5]	MARY MACBLAIN 4-10-11 B Dalton, *beh, hdwy 5th, rdn aftr 4 out, sn one pace*..........(12 to 1 tchd 14 to 1)	4
1630[5]	SANDMOOR PRINCE 10-11-2 Dr P Pritchard, *led, hdd 4 out, grad wknd.*...................(20 to 1)	5
1646[6]	NOEL (Ire) 4-11-2 M A FitzGerald, *in tch, rdn and wknd bef 4 out.*............(15 to 2 op 7 to 1 tchd 8 to 1)	6
	SALMON DANCER (Ire) 4-11-2 S Keightley, *chsd ldr, lost pl 5th and sn beh, pld up bef 2 out.*.......(25 to 1)	pu

Dist: 2l, ¾l, 8l, 8l, 15l. 3m 59.30s. a 13.30s (7 Ran).
SR: -/3/-/-/   (Mrs P Wake), J S Wainwright

1812 Waterloo Handicap Hurdle (0-125 4-y-o and up) £1,925 3m...........(3:00)

1427*	RABA RIBA [112] 8-12-0 V Slattery, *prmnt, led appr tenth, rdn approaching 2 out, hit last, styd on gmely und pres r-in.*...............(15 to 2 op 6 to 1 tchd 8 to 1)	1
1426[3]	WAIN A NIGHTCAP [99] 4-11-1 D Gallagher, *in tch, hdwy 5 out, rdn alng to chase wnr 3 out, hrd drvn appr last, ran on wl r-in.*...........(6 to 1 op 5 to 1 tchd 9 to 2)	2
1533[8]	SMILES AHEAD [85] 5-10-1[1] J Osborne, *prmnt, rdn aftr 4 out, one pace frm 3 out.*...................(6 to 1 op 5 to 1)	3
1671[5]	COURT CIRCULAR [101] 4-11-3 Diane Clay, *hld up and beh, hdwy, hit 5 out, rdn and kpt on one pace appr 3 out.*....................(4 to 1 fav tchd 9 to 2)	4
1426[2]	FETTLE UP [84] (bl) 5-9-9 (5*) J Supple, *led, hit 7th, hdd appr tenth, rdn and wknd 3 out.*....(8 to 1 op 7 to 1)	5
1314[2]	VALATCH [84] 5-9-7 (7*) P McLoughlin, *prmnt, rdn appr 4 out, plugged on one pace frm nxt.*...........(16 to 1)	6
1426[6]	RAGTIME COWBOY JOE [84] 8-9-7 (7*) Mr N Bradley, *nvr rch ldrs.*.....................(10 to 1)	7
1620[2]	BUSMAN (Ire) [89] 4-10-5[2] M A FitzGerald, *al beh.* ....(10 to 1 op 6 to 1)	8
1485	ITALIAN TOUR [84] 13-10-0 L Wyer, *in tch, f 9th.* (50 to 1)	f
	DODGER DICKINS [95] 6-10-8 (3*) S Wynne, *beh till f 7th.* ....(12 to 1 op 10 to 1 tchd f 7th.)	f
1628[3]	MILLIE (USA) [84] 5-10-0 M Robinson, *prmnt till uns rdr 8th.*.....................(50 to 1)	ur
970	SAFARI KEEPER [84] (v) 7-9-7 (7*) W Fry, *al beh, pld up bef 3 out.*.....................(33 to 1)	pu
1562[2]	FUSSY LADY [84] 6-10-0 L Harvey, *in tch, rdn and wknd appr 4 out, beh and pld up bef nxt.*...........(14 to 1)	pu
1597	SANTA ROSA BAY [87] (v) 6-10-3[1] Richard Guest, *mid-div, hmpd 9th, hdwy nxt, rdn and wknd 4 out, pld up bef 3 out.*...................(16 to 1)	pu
1614	BROOK COTTAGE (Ire) [98] 5-11-0 Peter Caldwell, *al beh, pld up bef 3 out.*...........(14 to 1 tchd 16 to 1)	pu

Dist: Nk, 15l, 5l, 1½l, 7l, 1½l, 30l. 5m 57.00s. a 20.00s (15 Ran).
         (Mrs L A Marsh), J L Spearing

1813 Armada National Hunt Flat Race (4,5,6-y-o) £1,456 2m..........(3:30)

1428*	BATTY'S ISLAND 4-11-3 (5*) E Husband, *al cl up, led o'r 4 fs out, ran on strly.*..........(11 to 8 fav op 6 to 4)	1
	SEAHAWK RETRIEVER 4-10-9 (7*) F Leahy, *al hndy, effrt o'r 3 fs out, styd on, no ch with wnr.* ....(7 to 2 op 5 to 2 tchd 4 to 1)	2
	ANYTHINGYOULIKE 4-11-2 Mr T Stephenson, *rcd wide, beh till hdwy hfwy, sn prmnt, styd on fnl 3 fs, no imprsn.*....................(8 to 1 op 14 to 1)	3
	ST BRAD (Ire) 5-10-11 (5*) D Walsh, *led appr one furlong till o'r 4 out, wknd fnl 2 and a half fs.* ....(12 to 1 tchd 14 to 1)	4
	STEVE FORD 4-10-11 (5*) A Procter, *prmnt till outpcd o'r 4 fs out, sn btn.*...................(14 to 1)	5
1329[4]	PETER POINTER 5-10-9 (7*) D Meade, *slwly into strd, hdwy aftr 6 fs, rdn 7 out, nvr dngrs after.* ....(11 to 2 op 9 to 2)	6
1103[9]	RELENTED 4-10-4 (7*) P McLoughlin, *al rear div.* ....(16 to 1 op 12 to 1)	7
1103[8]	LUCKY WEDSONG (v) 4-10-9 (7*) S Taylor, *chsd ldrs till hfwy.*.....................(14 to 1)	8
1027	ALTESSE ROXANNE 4-10-4 (7*) Mr B Pollock, *lost tch frm hfwy.*.....................(20 to 1)	9
	WHAT'S THE JOKE 4-10-6 (5*) J McCarthy, *wl beh frm hfwy.*...............(10 to 1 op 8 to 1)	10
1376	MISTI MAC (Ire) 5-10-13 (3*) S Wynne, *sn wl beh.* (25 to 1)	11
	SKIDDER 4-11-2 Mr K Green, *led one furlong, lost pl aftr 6 fs, pld up hfwy.*...................(25 to 1)	pu

Dist: 20l, 8l, 1l, 25l, 5l, 4l, 1½l, 1l, 12l, 7l. 3m 50.70s. (12 Ran).
         (Mrs Mary Price), B Preece

LEOPARDSTOWN (IRE) (soft)
Sunday December 26th
Going Correction: PLUS 0.75 sec. per fur. (races 1,2,-3,5,7), PLUS 0.50 (4,6)

1814 Ballyfree Maiden Hurdle (5-y-o and up) £4,140 2¼m..............(12:25)

1435[3]	COQ HARDI AFFAIR (Ire) 5-12-0 P Carberry, (100 to 30 fav)	1
1766[3]	LOVELY RUN 6-11-9 H Rogers, ...(10 to 1)	2
1681[6]	STRALDI (Ire) 5-12-0 C F Swan, ...(9 to 2)	3
1555[2]	LEGATISSIMO (Ire) 5-11-6 F Woods, ...(7 to 2)	4
1401	RIVERLAND (Ire) 5-11-3 (3*) D P Murphy, ...(25 to 1)	5
1435[2]	ICED HONEY 6-11-6 Mr A J Martin, ...(10 to 1)	6
1332[3]	LEGAL ADVISER 6-12-0 N Williamson, ...(4 to 1)	7
1496	HOLY FOX (Ire) 5-11-6 C O'Dwyer, ...(20 to 1)	8
1576	THOMOND PARK (Ire) 5-11-6 J Shortt, ...(20 to 1)	9
1760	GOLDEN PLAN (Ire) 5-11-6 C N Bowens, ...(33 to 1)	10
1576	DRUMREAGH LAD (Ire) 5-11-3 (3*) Mr P McMahon, (33 to 1)	11
111	STRONG PLATINUM (Ire) 5-10-13 (7*) Mr J Connolly, (7 to 1)	12
	BUCK'S DELIGHT (Ire) 5-11-6 G Bradley, ...(16 to 1)	13
1549	IM OK (Ire) 5-10-8 (7*) T Martin, ...(100 to 1)	14
1576	JIMMY GORDON 6-11-7 (7*) Mr M Brennan, ...(100 to 1)	15
1687	LADY MARILYN (Ire) 5-11-1 T Horgan, ...(100 to 1)	16
	FLYING COLUMN 6-11-6 A Powell, ...(33 to 1)	17
1760	LORD DIAMOND 7-12-0 K F O'Brien, ...(16 to 1)	18
	CRACKLING FROST (Ire) 5-11-6 T J Taaffe, ...(16 to 1)	19
1496	BORO DOLLAR 9-12-0 R Dunwoody, ...(14 to 1)	20
1687[7]	THATS MY BOY (Ire) 5-10-13 (7*) B Bowens, ...(10 to 1)	pu

Dist: 4½l, 1l, 2½l, 5½l. 4m 35.20s. a 19.20s (21 Ran).
SR: 43/33/37/26/20/-/   (Mrs Catherine Howard), Noel Meade

1815 S.M. Morris Maiden Hurdle (4-y-o) £4,140 2m..................(12:55)

1576[3]	DIPLOMATIC 11-7 J P Banahan, ...(5 to 4 fav)	1
	SAIBOT (USA) 11-7 B Sheridan, ...(4 to 1)	2
1762[6]	MAXWELTON BRAES (Ire) (bl) 11-7 R Hughes, ...(20 to 1)	3
1020	WEST BROGUE (Ire) 11-2 J Shortt, ...(14 to 1)	4
1501	SWIFT SAILER (Ire) 11-2 G Bradley, ...(8 to 1)	5
1397	KING WAH GLORY (Ire) 11-0 (7*) Mr J Connolly, (12 to 1)	6
1681	HIGH TONE (Ire) 10-13 (3*) D Bromley, ...(25 to 1)	7
1762[8]	ROBERTOLOMY (USA) 11-7 P Malone, ...(20 to 1)	8
1683[5]	COMMAND 'N CONTROL 11-7 K F O'Brien, ...(9 to 1)	9
1681[9]	HAUNTING ANGLE (Ire) 10-9 (7*) T Martin, ...(12 to 1)	10
1230	RAVEN'S ROCK (Ire) 10-9 (7*) Mr C A Leavy, ...(33 to 1)	11
	FATHER GREGORY (Ire) 11-2 C F Swan, ...(20 to 1)	12
1397	GALE TOI (Ire) 11-4 (3*) T P Treacy, ...(5 to 2)	13
1020	LADY IMELDA (Ire) 10-11 A Powell, ...(50 to 1)	14
1762	MORBIDELLI (Ire) 11-2 M Flynn, ...(50 to 1)	15
1681	LOOK NONCHALANT (Ire) 10-4 (7*) Mr T J Beattie, (50 to 1)	f
	LOTTOVER (Ire) 10-8 (3*) D P Murphy, ...(16 to 1)	ur

Dist: 6l, 1l, 3½l, 3l. 4m 9.00s. a 21.00s (17 Ran).
SR: 3/-/-/-/-/   (Mrs J Keeling), M A O'Toole

1816 Dennys Juvenile Hurdle (Listed) (3-y-o) £8,280 2m................(1:30)

	SHIRLEY'S DELIGHT (Ire) 10-4 P Carberry, *mid-div, mstk 5th, prog appr 2 out, hdwy to ld approaching last, cmftbly.*....................(15 to 8 fav)	1
1454*	THE BERUKI (Ire) 10-6 (3*) T P Treacy, *ul plcd, led appr 2 out, sn rdn, hdd and no extr approaching last, wknd.* ....(4 to 1)	2
1454[2]	MAGIC FEELING (Ire) 10-4 C F Swan, *mid-div, prog appr 2 out, rdn and no extr approaching last, wknd.* (9 to 4)	3
	SKIPO (USA) 10-9 B Sheridan, *hld up, some prog 2 out, kpt on one pace.*..................(5 to 1)	4
1454[4]	TEMPLEMARY BOY (Ire) 11-0 T Horgan, *hld up, prog 2 out, sn rdn, no extr approaching last*..............(10 to 1)	5
802	CREHELP EXPRESS (Ire) 10-4 C N Bowens, *mid-div and wknd aftr 3 out.*...................(33 to 1)	6
1454[7]	ASSERT STAR 10-9 (5*) M J Halbrook, *sn led, hdd 5th, rdn and hdd bef 2 out.*...................(14 to 1)	7
1432[7]	MAN OF ARRAN (Ire) 10-9 H Rogers, *trkd ldr, dsptd ld to 5th, rdn and wknd quickly appr 2 out.*......(33 to 1)	8
	LEGAL FLAIR (Ire) 10-9 P L Malone, *al rear, lost tch 3 out, tld off wln pld up bef 2 out.*..........(12 to 1)	pu

Dist: 4l, 2l, 10l, 5½l. 4m 10.50s. a 22.50s (9 Ran).
         (Liam Doherty), Noel Meade

1817 Dennys Gold Medal Chase (Listed) (4-y-o and up) £11,500 2m 1f......(2:05)

1073[4]	CHIRKPAR 6-11-11 R Dunwoody, *mid-div, rdn 4 out, rdn nxt, no imprsn appr last, styd on strly to ld r-in.* ....(3 to 1)	1
1684[1]	BROCKLEY COURT 6-11-8 J P Banahan, *hld up, dispute ld 2 out, lft in lead last, no extr and hdd r-in.* ....(Evens fav)	2
1019[4]	FABRICATOR 7-11-8 K F O'Brien, *trkd ldr, dsptd ld 5th till aftr 2 out, no extr and wknd appr last.* ....(16 to 1)	3
1498[3]	CHIC AND ELITE 6-10-13 N Williamson, *hld, jnd 5th, hdd appr 2 out, wknd quickly.*..........(20 to 1)	4

1430* VISIBLE DIFFERENCE 7-12-0 C F Swan, *mid-div, prog 3*
  out, rdn and wknd quickly aftr nxt. . . . .(9 to 2) 5
1430⁴ MUBADIR (USA) 5-11-2 P Carberry, *hld up, prog to dis-*
  pute ld appr 2 out, quickened to lead approaching last,
  mstk and 2 . . . .(7 to 1) f
Dist: 2½l, 2½l, 2l, 10l. 4m 26.70s. a 11.70s (6 Ran).
SR: 65/59/56/45/50/-/   (Michael W J Smurfit), J S Bolger

1818 Low Low Handicap Hurdle (4-y-o and up) £6,900 2¼m. . . . . (2:40)

1175² PADRE MIO (Ire) [-] 5-11-7 G Bradley, ...(7 to 2) 1
1764* STEEL MIRROR [-] 4-10-0 (5ex) N Williamson, ...(9 to 2) 2
1686³ PEBBLE LANE [-] 7-10-1 H Rogers, ...(5 to 1) 3
1686⁶ GLENCLOUD (Ire) [-] 5-11-10 P Carberry, ...(16 to 1) 4
1765⁸ SOCIETY BAY (USA) [-] 7-10-6 (7*) R A Hennessy, (20 to 1) 5
1450 APPELLATE COURT [-] 5-10-7 A Powell, ...(50 to 1) 6
1782 HIS WAY (Ire) [-] 4-9-10 (5*) B J Walsh, ...(20 to 1) 7
1782⁹ BANAIYKA (Ire) [-] 4-10-0 (3*) T P Treacy, ...(14 to 1) 8
1765⁵ HEAD OF CHAMBERS (Ire) [-] 5-10-8 J P Banahan, (12 to 1) 9
  THE ILLIAD [-] 12-12-0 K F O'Brien, ...(7 to 1) 10
1765⁶ ROMAN FORUM (Ire) [-] 5-10-4 C N Bowens, ...(14 to 1) 11
1765⁹ VISIONS PRIDE [-] 6-11-6 F Woods, ...(33 to 1) 12
1686² PHARFETCHED [-] 4-10-9 R Dunwoody, ...(9 to 2) 13
1554⁷ SIMPLY SWIFT [-] 6-11-1 C O'Dwyer, ...(16 to 1) 14
1780* MR BOAL (Ire) [-] 4-10-10 (6ex) C F Swan, ... (11 to 4 fav) pu
Dist: 3½l, 9l, 10l, 3l. 4m 36.40s. a 20.40s (15 Ran).
SR: 24/-/-/4/-/-/   (Paddy Fennelly), Anthony Mullins

1819 Paddy Power Handicap Chase (0-116 4-y-o and up) £4,140 2m 5f. . . . . .(3:10)

1550⁶ FRIENDLY ARGUMENT [-] 8-10-8 F Woods, ...(14 to 1) 1
  GALLEY GALE [-] 7-10-4 C F Swan, ...(8 to 1) 2
823 ARDUBH [-] 6-9-11 N Williamson, ...(8 to 1) 3
635⁵ BACK DOOR JOHNNY [-] 7-11-2 J Shortt, ...(4 to 1) 4
1268⁹ DEEP ISLE [-] 7-9-9 P Carberry, ...(20 to 1) 5
1268⁶ CARTON [-] 6-10-5 K F O'Brien, ...(12 to 1) 6
1579⁴ DORAN'S TOWN LAD [-] 6-11-8 G Bradley, ...(9 to 4 fav) f
1499³ WALLS COURT [-] 6-10-3 P L Malone, ...(8 to 1) ur
1550⁵ ALL A QUIVER [-] 6-10-4 C N Bowens, ...(12 to 1) su
  TRIAURUM [-] 11-9-8 T Horgan, ...(25 to 1) pu
1019³ PARGALE [-] 7-11-4 T J Taaffe, ...(20 to 1) pu
Dist: 6l, sht-hd, hd, 10l. 5m 50.50s. a 36.50s (11 Ran).
                                               (F Warren), F Warren

1820 Ballyfree Flat Race (4-y-o) £4,140 2m . . . . (3:40)

OMAR (Ire) 4-11-6 Mr J P Dempsey, ...(14 to 1) 1
1581² CAREFORMENOW (USA) (bl) 10-13 (7*) Mr E Norris, (7 to 4) 2
  MOYGANNON COURT (Ire) 11-1 (5*) Mr H F Cleary, (11 to 2) 3
  DUDDON SANDS (Ire) 11-3 (3*) Mr D Marnane, ...(16 to 1) 4
1762⁴ FINAWAY EXPRESS (Ire) 11-1 (5*) Mr G J Harford, (10 to 1) 5
1039⁵ HAVE A BRANDY (Ire) 11-6 Mr D M O'Brien, ...(12 to 1) 6
1581 TREANAREE (Ire) 10-13 (7*) Mr D K Budds, ...(33 to 1) 7
  THE BOBTAIL FOX (Ire) 11-6 Mr J P Durkan, ...(Evens fav) 8
1786⁵ DENNETT VALLEY (Ire) 11-6 Mr A J Martin, ...(14 to 1) 9
1581 THE BRIDGE TAVERN (Ire) 10-13 (7*) Miss C Duggan,
  . . . .(14 to 1) 10
692⁸ BRIDGE PEARL (Ire) 11-6 Mr T S Costello, ...(14 to 1) 11
1581 THE PERISHER (Ire) 10-13 (7*) Mr J Connolly, ...(16 to 1) 12
1020 LAURA GALE (Ire) 10-10 (5*) Mr P M Kelly, ...(33 to 1) 13
  THE PUNTERS PAL (Ire) 10-13 (7*) Mr K McGrath, (25 to 1) 14
1766 MACS MISS (Ire) 10-8 (7*) Mr M Brennan, ...(66 to 1) 15
Dist: 3l, nk, 4l, 5l. 4m 5.50s. (15 Ran).
                                          (E O'Leary), M Halford

LIMERICK (IRE) (heavy)
Sunday December 26th

1821 Westward Ho & Souths Pubs Maiden Hurdle (Div 1) (4-y-o) £3,450 2m (12:35)

1397³ MR SNAGGLE (Ire) 10-13 (3*) C O'Brien, ... (100 to 30) 1
1610⁵ BOHEMIAN CASTLE (Ire) 10-9 (7*) Mr J T McNamara,
  . . . .(6 to 1) 2
1581⁹ WEJEM (Ire) 11-2 S R Murphy, ...(8 to 1) 3
1551 PRINCE TAUFAN (Ire) 11-2 J Magee, ...(10 to 1) 4
1762² TELLTALK (Ire) 10-11 (5*) J R Barry, ...(10 to 9 on) 5
  DONNASOO (Ire) 10-9 (7*) Mr M J Spillane, ...(14 to 1) 6
1608 TARA'S SERENADE (Ire) 10-11 A J O'Brien, ...(10 to 1) 7
1581 SPECTACULAR STAR (Ire) 11-2 L P Cusack, ...(12 to 1) 8
  ISLAND ROW (Ire) 10-9 (7*) J P Broderick, ...(16 to 1) 9
1610 GENIE MACK (Ire) 11-2 D H O'Connor, ...(20 to 1) 10
1681 FOURTWOONEAGAIN (Ire) 10-11 J F Titley, ...(14 to 1) 11
1501 MAURA MILISH (Ire) 10-11 F J Flood, ...(12 to 1) 12
  ORMOND BEACH (Ire) 11-2 J Jones, ...(14 to 1) 13
1581 VALTORUS (Ire) 11-2 M P Hourigan, ...(12 to 1) ur
Dist: 2½l, hd, 1½l, 2½l. 4m 25.30s. (14 Ran).
                                          (Mrs W H Young), L Young

1822 Westward Ho & Souths Pubs Maiden Hurdle (Div 2) (4-y-o) £3,450 2m (1:05)

1608³ DOWHATYOULIKE (Ire) 10-11 P M Verling, ...(7 to 4 fav) 1

1681 STEEL GEM (Ire) 10-9 (7*) K D Maher, ...(12 to 1) 2
1610⁹ SHANNON AMBER (Ire) 10-4 (7*) J P Broderick, . .(10 to 1) 3
1230 OVER THE JORDAN (Ire) 11-2 D H O'Connor, ...(9 to 4) 4
  ELIADE (Ire) 11-2 M A Davey, ...(7 to 1) 5
  KYLE HOUSE VI (Ire) 10-4 (7*) J M Donnelly, ...(14 to 1) 6
1455 NINE O THREE (Ire) 11-2 L P Cusack, ...(7 to 1) 7
  HAZY ROSE (Ire) 11-2 J F Titley, ...(9 to 2) 8
1397 THE CRIOSRA (Ire) 11-2 S H O'Donovan, ...(20 to 1) 9
  NOT AN INCH (Ire) 11-2 J Jones, ...(20 to 1) 10
1036 THE DEFENDER (Ire) 11-2 J Magee, ...(14 to 1) 11
469 BRIGADIER SUPREME (Ire) 10-13 (3*) G Kilfeather, (20 to 1) 12
1581 STRUGGLING LASS (Ire) 10-11 A J O'Brien, ...(12 to 1) f
Dist: 4l, 6l, 5l, 2½l. (Time not taken) (13 Ran).
                                          (Patrick J Casey), K Riordan

1823 Ciaran Skelly Bookmaker Handicap Hurdle (0-109 4-y-o and up) £3,450 2 ½m. . . . . (1:35)

9277 SHREWD MOVE [-] (bl) 4-10-5 J Jones, ...(14 to 1) 1
1782⁴ RATHCORE [-] 6-11-10 (6ex) L P Cusack, ...(5 to 1) 2
1608⁵ KEEPHERGOING (Ire) [-] 4-10-7 (7*) Mr R P Byrnes, (14 to 1) 3
1609 HORNER WATER (Ire) [-] 5-11-0 (7*) Mr P Moran, . .(3 to 1) 4
1685⁹ DANCING COURSE (Ire) [-] 5-11-4 (5*) P A Roche, (14 to 1) 5
1463³ TOT EM UP [-] 6-10-9 Mr M Phillips, ...(8 to 1) 6
  MANTAS MELODY (Ire) [-] 5-10-12 (3*) C O'Brien, (14 to 1) 7
1609³ BARRONSTOWN BOY [-] 9-10-9 (3*) Miss M Olivefalk,
  . . . .(8 to 1) 8
864 DEGO DANCER [-] 6-10-6 (7*) J P Broderick, ...(14 to 1) 9
1609⁸ ARRIGLE PRINCE [-] (bl) 8-10-7² J F Titley, ...(25 to 1) 10
1609⁶ SHANNON KNOCK [-] 8-11-7 S H O'Donovan, ...(10 to 1) 11
1335⁷ SILENTBROOK [-] 8-9-13 (7*) Mr A O'Shea, ...(20 to 1) 12
1496 ABBEY EMERALD [-] 7-9-13 (5*) T J O'Sullivan, ...(20 to 1) 13
1462² BAMANYAR (Ire) [-] 5-10-7 (7*) Mr J Murphy, ...(14 to 1) 14
1609 PEGUS PRINCE (Ire) [-] (bl) 4-10-1² (7*) Mr D P Daly,
  . . . .(20 to 1) 15
1038⁵ CLASSY MACHINE (Ire) [-] 5-10-6 P M Verling, ...(16 to 1) 16
1495⁸ NISHIKI (USA) [-] 4-10-11 G M O'Neill, ...(14 to 1) 17
472* BALLYBROWN FLASH (Ire) [-] 5-10-3 (5*) R Gaule,
  . . . .(20 to 1) 18
1764 HIGHLAND MINSTREL [-] 6-10-2 (5*) M G Cleary, (16 to 1) pu
Dist: 3l, 3l, hd, 2l. 5m 48.00s. (19 Ran).
                                          (James McNamara), E McNamara

1824 Coopers & Lybrand Hurdle (5-y-o and up) £3,450 2m . . . .(2:10)

1549* COURT MELODY (Ire) 5-10-11 (7*) J P Broderick, . .(2 to 1) 1
1431⁵ GAELIC MYTH (USA) 6-10-13 (5*) C P Dunne, . .(Evens fav) 2
1495⁷ MISS LIME 6-10-7² (7*) Mr M J Bowe, ...(8 to 1) 3
1330² CHANCE COFFEY 8-11-0 G M O'Neill, ...(8 to 1) 4
1765⁴ CELTIC SAILS (Ire) (bl) 5-10-8 (5*) Mr P J Casey, . .(12 to 1) 5
1686⁷ ROSE APPEAL 7-11-4 S H O'Donovan, ...(8 to 1) 6
Dist: 6l, sht-hd, 25l, 7l. 4m 19.30s. (6 Ran).
                                          (P P Johnson), Michael Hourigan

1825 Murphys Irish Stout Chase (Listed) (5-y-o and up) £6,900 2½m. . . . . . . (2:45)

1266² SULLANE RIVER (Ire) 5-11-0 D H O'Connor, *mid-div, prog*
  to track ldrs 9th, led aftr 2 out, ran on strly. 1
1763* ROYAL MOUNTBROWNE 5-11-5 J F Titley, *led till appr*
  5th, lft in ld 7th, hdd aftr 2 out, kpt on und pres.
  . . . .(5 to 2) 2
1685 PARSONS BRIG 7-10-9 (7*) J P Broderick, *rear, rdn 9th, tld*
  off frm 4 out. . . . .(14 to 1) 3
1785³ PRINCESS CASILIA 8-10-8 (3*) T J Mitchell, *mstks, rdn 9th,*
  sn wknd, tld off. 4
905* WINDS OF WAR 8-11-5 S R Murphy, *mid-div whn f 7th.*
  . . . .(7 to 1) f
1784* NUAFFE 8-11-7 S H O'Donovan, *led appr 5th till f 7th.*
  . . . . f
1498⁷ KING OF THE GLEN 7-10-13 (3*) C O'Brien, *wl plcd, rdn in*
  3rd whn uns rdr 2 out. . . . .(10 to 1) ur
1177 AMERICAN EYRE 8-11-5 J Jones, *al rear, pld up bef*
  tenth. . . . .(20 to 1) pu
Dist: 5½l, dist, dist. 5m 23.70s. (8 Ran).
                                          (S Lucey), David J McGrath

1826 Holmes O'Malley & Sexton Handicap Chase (0-109 4-y-o and up) £3,450 2 ¾m. . . . . (3:20)

1612* ANOTHER EXCUSE (Ire) [-] 5-10-11 (7*,4ex) Mr W M O'Sul-
  livan, ... (5 to 4 fav) 1
1784⁴ MERLYNS CHOICE [-] 9-9-6 (5*) K P Gaule, ...(7 to 1) 2
1499 GOLDEN CARRUTH (Ire) [-] 5-10-2 (7*) J P Broderick,
  . . . .(10 to 1) 3
1268⁷ PINEWOOD LAD [-] 6-10-4 (5*) C P Dunne, ...(14 to 1) 4
1761³ MAKE ME AN ISLAND [-] 8-10-9 J F Titley, ...(9 to 2) 5
1499 LADY EILY [-] (bl) 8-10-3 (3*) T J Mitchell, ...(14 to 1) 6
1498² SPEAKING TOUR (USA) [-] 5-11-10 D H O'Connor, (12 to 1) 7
332 CHILDPOUR [-] 6-10-10 (5*) P A Roche, ...(14 to 1) 8
1553⁷ ANOTHER RUSTLE [-] 10-10-11 W T Slattery Jnr, . .(20 to 1) 9
1499⁴ GERTIES PRIDE [-] 9-10-12 (3*) C O'Brien, ...(8 to 1) 10
1577³ WATERLOO KING [-] 6-11-7 Mr M Phillips, ...(10 to 1) 11

1402 WATERLOO ANDY [-] 7-10-7 S H O'Donovan, ... (14 to 1) 12
1179⁸ NOBLE CLANSMAN (USA) [-] 12-10-11 Mr P J Healy,
. . . . (20 to 1) 13
1399 BALLINAHEEN BRIDGE [-] 6-9-5¹ (5*) M A Davey, . (25 to 1) 14
1334⁶ MONEY MADE [-] 6-9-2 (5*) M G Cleary, ... (50 to 1) 15
1499⁹ CAPINCUR EILE [-] 7-11-2 L P Cusack, ... (12 to 1) ur
989 SQUIRRELLSDAUGHTER [-] (bl) 6-9-11 J Collins, . (25 to 1) ur
1402 DEL MONTE BOY [-] 8-10-8 G M O'Neill, ... (14 to 1) pu
1550³ BOG LEAF VI [-] 10-9-7³ S R Murphy, ... (8 to 1) pu
1402 RUSSIAN GALE (Ire) [-] 5-9-10 J Jones, ... (16 to 1) pu
Dist: 6l, 8l, sht-hd, 4l. 5m 58.50s. (20 Ran).

(Kilshannig Racing Syndicate), Eugene M O'Sullivan

1827 Craig Gardner Price Waterhouse Flat Race (4-y-o and up) £3,450 2m. . (3:50)

JOHNNY KELLY 6-12-0 Mr J A Berry, ... (5 to 4 fav) 1
1397⁵ AN MAINEACH (Ire) 4-11-6 (3*) Miss M Olivefalk, . .(11 to 2) 2
EUROPA POINT 8-11-9 (5*) Mrs C Robinson, ... (12 to 1) 3
BALLYBODEN 6-11-7 (7*) Mr B Moran, ...(5 to 2) 4
1337⁸ ALLARACKET (Ire) 4-10-11 (7*) Mr D M Fogarty, ...(6 to 1) 5
993⁷ MIGHTY HAGGIS 6-11-7 (7*) Mr N C Kelleher, ... (16 to 1) 6
536³ FIFI'S MAN 7-11-7 (7*) Mr D P Carey, ... (7 to 1) 7
1501⁵ AMEEN (Ire) 5-11-9 (5*) Mr J A Nash, ... (5 to 1) 8
DOUGLAS PYNE (Ire) 4-11-2 (7*) Mr W Ewing, . . . (12 to 1) 9
SALTY SNACKS (Ire) 4-11-9 Mr P Fenton, ...(8 to 1) 10
1687 DEEP WAVE 6-11-9 (5*) Mr C T G Kinane, ... (12 to 1) 11
DAVE FLECK (Ire) 5-11-8¹ (7*) Mr M Kiernan, ... (14 to 1) 12
1687 LISCAHILL HIGHWAY 6-11-7 (7*) Mr P Carey, ... (16 to 1) 13
CARRAIG-AN-OIR (Ire) 4-11-9 Mr M Phillips, ... (12 to 1) 14
WINNIE WUMPKINS (Ire) 4-10-11 (7*) Mr T N Cloke,
. . . . (20 to 1) 15
ALLY LLOYD (Ire) 4-11-2 (7*) Mrs K Walsh, ... (16 to 1) 16
COLCANON 7-11-7 (7*) Mr J Lombard, ... (33 to 1) 17
1332⁹ FESTIVAL LIGHT 5-11-9 (5*) Mr J P O'Brien, . .(20 to 1) 18
930⁹ CAPTAIN CHARLES (Ire) 5-11-7 (7*) Mr P O'Connor,
. . . . (16 to 1) 19
ELTON'S SON 7-11-7 (7*) Mr K Whelan, ... (12 to 1) 20
Dist: 1l, 11l, 3l, 4m 19.00s. (20 Ran).

(P M Berry), P M Berry

DOWN ROYAL (IRE) (heavy)
Monday December 27th

1828 Sportsman's Opportunity Handicap Hdle (0-116 4-y-o and up) £1,207 2½m
. . . . (1:00)

ROSIN THE BOW [-] 4-9-11 (4*) P Morris, ...(20 to 1) 1
1685⁵ BAVARD DIEU (Ire) [-] (bl) 5-11-5 (2*) M G Cleary, . .(5 to 2) 2
1782⁷ SECRET SCEPTRE [-] 6-10-11 (4*) H Taylor, ... (6 to 1) 3
FURRY WOOD LADY [-] 5-10-0 (4*) T Martin, ...(7 to 1) 4
1764⁵ SLADESTOWN GLEN [-] (bl) 8-11-2 D Bromley, . .(10 to 1) 5
1782⁷ MASTER CRUSADER [-] 7-11-3 (6ex) T J Mitchell,
. . . . (11 to 10 fav) 6
798 JUNGLE STAR (Ire) [-] 5-10-4 (4*) E Stafford, ... (14 to 1) 7
1397 PEPPERONI EXPRESS (Ire) [-] 4-10-11 (4*) M Kelly, (10 to 1) 8
Dist: 2l, 2l, 3l, 13l. (Time not taken) (8 Ran).

(W Crangle), David McBratney

1829 Bet With The Tote E.B.F Maiden Hurdle (5-y-o and up) £1,380 3m. . . . (1:30)

1265⁷ BUMBO HALL VI (Ire) 5-11-6 F J Flood, ... (6 to 1) 1
RED THUNDER 6-11-1 D P Fagan, ... (7 to 1) 2
1156³ LE BRAVE 7-11-11 (3*) T J Mitchell, ... (4 to 1) 3
1401³ MAN OF IRON 6-11-6 Mr P F Graffin, ... (9 to 2) 4
1401 JIMS CHOICE 6-11-1 (5*) Mr R J Patton, ... (6 to 1) 5
1685² MCCONNELL GOLD 8-11-1 H Rogers, ...(2 to 1 fav) 6
1434⁵ CLOSUTTON EXPRESS 7-12-0 Mr W P Mullins, . . .(5 to 2) 8
1156⁷ SANDEMALL (bf) 6-11-6 D Fisher, ... (20 to 1) pu
1782 TAUWETTER 7-11-1 P Mooney, ... (20 to 1) 9
Dist: Hd, 7l, 7l, 4½l. (Time not taken) (9 Ran).

(Mrs F Flood), F Flood

1830 Harp Lager E.B.F. Handicap Chase (0-102 4-y-o and up) £1,380 2½m (2:00)

806⁹ HARRY'S BOREEN [-] 6-10-6 (3*) T J Mitchell, ... (7 to 1) 1
1013³ EDENAKILL LAD [-] 6-10-1 (3*) D Bromley, ... (6 to 1) 2
1402 GOLA LADY [-] 6-11-4 Mr A J Martin, ... (5 to 2 fav) 3
1158² LA-GREINE [-] 6-11-2 (3*) Mr P McMahon, ... (3 to 1) 4
1266⁶ NANCYS LAD [-] 6-10-7 H Rogers, ... (8 to 1) 5
1159⁷ KITES HARDWICKE [-] 6-10-12 F J Flood, ... (6 to 1) 6
1550⁸ HO FRETTA [-] 7-10-11 (5*) M A Davey, ... (12 to 1) 7
Dist: Hd, 3l, 4l, dist. (Time not taken) (7 Ran).

(Mrs K Malone), J T R Dreaper

1831 Jim Rea Memorial Chase (4-y-o and up) £1,207 2½m. . . . . (2:30)

989² NORDIC SUN (Ire) 8-11-4 Mr A J Martin, ... (6 to 4 fav) 1
1402 HURRICANE TOMMY (bl) 6-11-6 (5*) Mr G J Harford,
. . . .(5 to 2) 2
1159⁵ REDELVA 6-10-10 (3*) Mr P McMahon, ... (14 to 1) 3
1684⁷ RAMBLING LORD (Ire) 5-11-2 H Rogers, ... (6 to 1) 4

1579 WICKET KEEPER 8-10-11 (7*) Mr L J Gracey, ... (6 to 1) f
1612 MUST DO 7-11-5 (3*) T J Mitchell, ... (4 to 1) f
805 SHABRA CONNECTION 6-11-1 (3*) D Bromley, . . (25 to 1) pu
1159 SALINA BAY 7-10-8 (5*) M G Cleary, ...(16 to 1) pu
Dist: 1l, 15l, dist. (Time not taken) (8 Ran).

(Rom Racing Syndicate), A J Martin

1832 Calor Gas (Mares) QR Ladies INH Flat Race (4-y-o and up) £1,380 2m. . (3: 0)

1762⁹ REMAINDER LASS 4-11-6 (3*) Mrs J M Mullins, . (5 to 1) 1
1687⁶ TUDOR THYNE (Ire) 5-11-7 (7*) Miss S Kelly, ... (9 to 2) 2
1270⁷ SIMPLY SARAH 7-11-7 (7*) Miss S Kauntze, ... (7 to 2) 3
1016 PRINCESS DILLY (Ire) 4-11-2 (7*) Mrs A O'Brien, . . (7 to 1) 4+
AMAKANE LADY 4-11-6 (3*) Miss C Hutchinson,
. . . . (7 to 1) 4+
MILLHAVEN PRINCESS 7-11-7 (7*) Miss E Hymdman,
. . . . (33 to 1) 6
1766 SERIOUS NOTE (Ire) 5-11-7 (7*) Miss M Savage, . . (18 to 1) 7
KINROSS 6-11-7 (7*) Miss S D Blair, ... (6 to 1) 8
1337⁹ START SINGING (Ire) 4-11-6 (3*) Mrs S McCarthy,
. . . . (6 to 4 fav) 9
1401 HELENS LOVE (Ire) 5-11-7 (7*) Miss J Cox, ... (14 to 1) 10
BANJO BELLE 8-11-7 (7*) Miss A Brady, ... (20 to 1) 11
FIDSPRIT 6-12-0 Mrs A Ferris, ... (20 to 1) 12
FOYLE BOREEN 6-11-7 (7*) Miss C Gordon, ... (14 to 1) 13
1766 RIYASHA (Ire) 5-11-7 (7*) Miss C Rogers, ... (25 to 1) 14
1455 FRIENDLY BID (Ire) 5-11-7 (7*) Miss G Ferris, . . . (12 to 1) 15
Dist: 1l, 11l, 11l, dd-ht. (Time not taken) (15 Ran).

(John G Gardiner), P A Fahy

1833 Down Royal Bookmakers (C&G) INH Flat Race (4-y-o and up) £1,207 2m
. . . . (3:30)

1020⁶ ABAVARD (Ire) 4-11-2 (7*) Mr M P Dunne, ... (12 to 1) 1
1760² WINDOVER (Ire) 5-11-9 (5*) Mr G J Harford, ...(6 to 4 fav) 2
1160⁸ IF YOU BELIEVE (Ire) 4-11-2 (7*) Mr R Byrne, ... (20 to 1) 3
A MONKEY FOR DICK (Ire) 4-11-2 (7*) Mr E Magee, (20 to 1) 4
SIR MOSS 6-12-0 Mr J A Quinn, ... (6 to 1) 5
747⁶ NO DOZING (Ire) 4-11-4 (5*) Mr B R Hamilton, ...(8 to 1) 6
FIVE FROM HOME (Ire) 5-12-0 Mr A J Martin, ... (16 to 1) 7
881⁸ SAME DIFFERENCE (Ire) 5-11-9 (5*) Mr G A Kingston,
. . . . (8 to 1) 8
1687⁵ DAN PATCH 7-11-9 (5*) Mr H Kirk, ...(11 to 4) 9
1160⁶ OVER THE MALLARD (Ire) 4-11-2 (7*) Mr P Purfield,
. . . . (10 to 1) 10
1687⁸ I IS 6-11-7 (7*) Mr L J Gracey, ... (12 to 1) 11
1681 MORNING IN MAY (Ire) 5-11-7 (7*) Mr P J Baker, . . (14 to 1) 12
1760⁴ INST THAT NICE (Ire) 5-11-7 (7*) Mr M Brennan, . . (5 to 1) 13
1555 TOP RUN (Ire) 5-12-0 Mr P F Graffin, ... (16 to 1) 14
1455 LEAP (Ire) 4-11-6 (3*) Mr A R Coonan, ... (20 to 1) 15
THE THIRD MAN (Ire) 4-11-9 Mr D M Christie, . . . (20 to 1) 16
1435 KEEP THEM KEEN (Ire) 5-11-7 (7*) Mr L Madine, . (16 to 1) 17
MONARROW (Ire) 5-11-7 (7*) Mr J Bright, ... (33 to 1) 18
Dist: Hd, 7l, hd, ½l. (Time not taken) (18 Ran).

(Mrs N Smyth), P A Fahy

HUNTINGDON (soft (races 1,3,5), heavy (2,4,6))
Monday December 27th
Going Correction: PLUS 1.15 sec. per fur.

1834 Aegon Financial Services Novices' Handicap Chase (4-y-o and up) £2,626 2m 110yds. . . . . (12:30)

WATERFORD CASTLE [84] 6-10-13 B Powell, chsd ldrs,
styd on til ld r-in, pushed out. . . . . (7 to 1) 1
1531³ SOCIAL CLIMBER [95] 9-11-10 S McNeill, led til last, no
extr r-in. 2
1598² GALAXY HIGH [90] (bl) 6-11-5 M A FitzGerald, trkd ldr, ev
ch 2 out, btn nxt, found little und pres.
. . . . (5 to 4 fav op 5 to 4 on) 3
1530³ SPOONHILL WOOD [87] (bl) 7-11-2 B Dalton, chsd ldr, wnt
second at 6th, no extr frm 2 out. . . (5 to 1 tchd 11 to 2) 4
1708⁵ UNEXIS [71] 8-9-7 (7*) Chris Webb, chsd ldr, blun and uns
rdr 9th. . . . . (14 to 1 op 16 to 1 tchd 25 to 1) ur
1287 STRONG JOHN (Ire) [81] 5-10-3 (7*) P Murphy, slow jump in
rear at 1st, mstk, jump lft second and jmpd left and uns
rdr 3rd. . . . . (10 to 1) ur
Dist: 5l, 3l, 25l. 4m 23.30s. a 25.30s (6 Ran).
SR: 22/28/20/

(Sybil Lady Joseph), Andrew Turnell

1835 Aegon Financial Services Novices' Hurdle (4-y-o and up) £2,042 2m 5f 110yds. . . . . (1:00)

1568² NICK THE BEAK (Ire) 4-10-7 (5*) Mr T Byrne, trkd ldrs, gd
prog to ld aftr 3 out, pushed out.
. . . . (9 to 4 fav op 7 to 4 tchd 5 to 2) 1
FINESSE THE KING (Ire) 5-10-12 D Bridgwater, hld up, took
clr order hfwy, styd on aftr 2 out, no imprsn on wnr.
. . . . (9 to 2 op 4 to 1 tchd 5 to 1) 2

253

1542 SOLO GENT 4-10-12 S McNeill, *chsd ldr, styd on one pace*
frm 2 out..................................(33 to 1 op 25 to 1) 3
MALENOIR (USA) 5-10-12 M A FitzGerald, *chsd ldr, led*
briefly bef 3 out, no extr frm nxt...(16 to 1 op 14 to 1) 4
1028⁵ MAN O MINE (Ire) 4-10-5 (7*) P Murphy, *rcd wide in tch, no*
hdwy frm 3 out......................(12 to 1 op 10 to 1) 5
RASTA MAN 5-10-12 T Kent, *hld up, hdwy 5th, wknd*
appr 3 out..............................(10 to 1 op 10 to 1) 6
1626 KING SCORPIO (Ire) 4-10-12 B Wright, *wth ldr to 7th, sn*
wknd......................................(14 to 1 op 10 to 1) 7
1424⁶ RITA'S RISK 4-10-12 J Ryan, *led til 7th, wknd quickly, pld*
up bef 2 out.......................(9 to 1 op 33 to 1) pu
1568⁵ EASTERN RIVER 7-10-12 B Powell, *chsd ldr, wknd and*
pld up bef 3 out.............(9 to 2 op 5 to 2 tchd 5 to 1) pu
LORD NASKRA (USA) 4-10-12 R Campbell, *lost tch frm*
5th, tld off and pld up bef 3 out....(20 to 1 op 14 to 1) pu
Dist: 8l, 5l, 2½l, 3l, 12l, 30l. 5m 28.70s. a 33.70s (10 Ran).
(Sir Nicholas Wilson), John R Upson

1836 Aegon Financial Services Handicap Chase (0-120 5-y-o and up) £3,042 2½m 110yds.....................(1:30)

1808³ RADICAL REQUEST [91] 10-11-0 M A FitzGerald, *hld up in*
rear, took clr order bef 5 out, led before 2 out, pushed
clr......................................(9 to 2 op 7 to 2) 1
1748* MO ICHI DO [86] 7-10-9 B Powell, *chsd ldr, styd on to take*
second pl cl hme...............................(2 to 1 jt-
fav op 9 to 4 tchd 5 to 2 and 7 to 4) 2
1631³ KEV'S LASS (Ire) [83] 5-9-13 (7*) P Murphy, *chsd ldr, lft in ld*
4 out, hdd aftr nxt, no extr run in...........(2 to 1 jt-
fav op 6 to 4 tchd 9 to 4) 3
1457⁴ BATHWICK BOBBIE [81] (bl) 6-10-4 S McNeill, *made rng til*
blun and uns rdr 4 out..........(9 to 4 op 7 to 1) ur
Dist: 6l, hd. 5m 32.80s. a 37.80s (4 Ran).
(Mrs Elaine M Burke), K R Burke

1837 Aegon Novices' Hurdle (4-y-o and up) £1,763 3¼m.....................(2:00)

1564² NED THE HALL (Ire) 5-11-2 (3*) A Thornton, *trkd ldrs,*
smooth prog to ld 2 out, hng lft aftr last, drvn clr.
......................................(5 to 1 op 4 to 1) 1
1624³ CALLEROSE 6-10-12 B Powell, *led 7th to 2 out, no extr*.
..................(100 to 30 op 3 to 1 tchd 11 to 4 and 7 to 2) 2
1567² OCEAN LEADER 6-11-5 M A FitzGerald, *trkd ldr, took clr*
order bef 3 out, one pace frm nxt... (5 to 1 tchd 6 to 1) 3
1775⁶ SUASANA SIOSANA 8-10-7 (5*) Mr T Byrne, *hld up in*
rear, effrt frm 3 out, kpt on same pace.
......................................(16 to 1 op 12 to 1) 4
1745³ HENRY VILL (Ire) 5-10-12 D Bridgwater, *trkd ldr, wknd frm*
3 out...................................(5 to 2 fav op 5 to 2) 5
920³ LITTLE THYNE 8-10-12 Dr P Pritchard, *led till 7th, sn*
wknd...............................(20 to 1 op 14 to 1) 6
1707² GRAY'S ELLERGY 7-10-9 (5*) Miss P Jones, *in rear whn f*
7th....(4 to 1 op 3 to 1 tchd 100 to 30 and 9 to 2) f
1747 THE OVERTRUMPER 6-10-12 T Kent, *mid-div, lost pl 8th,*
tld off and pld up bef 2 out.......(50 to 1 op 33 to 1) pu
1090 AFTICA (bl) 6-10-5 (7*) P Moore, *beh whn pld up aftr 7th*.
.......................(33 to 1 op 20 to 1) pu
Dist: 8l, 1½l, 4l, 30l, 12l. 6m 47.40s. a 46.40s (9 Ran).
(Martyn Booth), K C Bailey

1838 Aegon Handicap Chase (0-120 5-y-o and up) £3,236 3m.............(2:30)

1083* MASTER OATS [114] 7-11-11 (3*) A Thornton, *hld up, cld*
readily to have ev ch 2 out, led last, drvn clr.(3 to 1 jt-
fav tchd 7 to 2) 1
1748 DANDY MINSTREL [108] 9-11-8 D Bridgwater, *dsptd ld,*
took clr advantage bef 4 out, ev ch 2 out, one pace aftr.
......................................(6 to 1) 2
1565⁷ LEAGAUNE [96] 11-10-10 E Byrne, *prmnt til pushed alng*
frm 15th, no extr...................(10 to 1 op 7 to 1) 3
1732 BOWL OF OATS [109] (bl) 7-11-9 S McNeill, *prmnt, led*
briefly 11th, wknd 3 out.............(9 to 2 op 4 to 1) 4
1625³ THAMESDOWN TOOTSIE [91] 8-11-5 B Powell, *mstk 1st,*
chsd ldrs till 12th.......................(9 to 1 op 10 to 1) 5
1423³ JIMSTER [95] 11-10-9 M A FitzGerald, *sn beh, no imprsn*.
.............(3 to 1 jt-fav op 5 to 2 tchd 100 to 30) 6
1487 ANOTHER CORNER [86] (bl) 10-10-0 B Dalton, *dsptd ld til*
11th, hit 13th, sn wknd.............(33 to 1 op 25 to 1) 7
1029 SCOLE [113] 8-11-6 (7*) P Murphy, *al beh, tld off whn pld*
up aftr 11th.............................(7 to 1 op 8 to 1) pu
Dist: 12l, 25l, 5l, 2l, ½l, dist. 6m 28.10s. a 40.10s (8 Ran).
(P A Matthews), K C Bailey

1839 Aegon Financial Services Handicap Hurdle (0-120 4-y-o and up) £2,511 2m 110yds.....................(3:00)

1665⁶ ZAMIRAH (Ire) [117] 4-11-12 D Bridgwater, *dsptd ld, quick-*
ened aftr 5th, und threat last, styd on wl to go clr ag'n
r-in...........(9 to 4 op 7 to 4 tchd 5 to 2 and 3 to 1) 1
1709* TOP WAVE [114] 5-11-9 M A FitzGerald, *trkd ldrs in 3rd pl,*
wnt second aftr 3 out, chlgd last, unbl to quicken r-in.
......................(2 to 1 fav op 7 to 4 tchd 9 to 4) 2

1389⁵ MRS MAYHEW (Ire) [94] 5-9-10 (7*) P Murphy, *dsptd ld,*
outpcd frm 3 out, no extr.............(7 to 2 op 5 to 2) 3
1206² NIGHT WIND [103] 6-10-12 B Powell, *trkd ldrs gng wl till*
3 out, no extr.........(5 to 2 op 2 to 1 tchd 11 to 4) 4
Dist: 6l, 4l, 8l. 4m 11.50s. a 24.50s (4 Ran).
SR: 43/34/10/11/ (N A Twiston-Davies), N A Twiston-Davies

KEMPTON (good)
Monday December 27th
Going Correction: PLUS 0.55 sec. per fur. (races 1,3,6), PLUS 0.45 (2,4,5)

1840 Bonusphoto Novices' Hurdle (4-y-o and up) £5,845 2m.............(12:45)

1773* SHUJAN (USA) 4-11-0 G McCourt, *led to 3 out, sn led ag'n,*
clr nxt...........(100 to 30 fav op 7 to 2 tchd 4 to 1) 1
1661 CORROUGE (USA) 4-11-0 C Llewellyn, *in tch, styd on to*
chase wnr appr 2 out, one pace frm last.
......................................(10 to 1 op 6 to 1) 2
1536* MY WIZARD 6-11-5 D Murphy, *hdwy 5th, rdn and one*
pace appr 2 out......................(12 to 1 op 8 to 1) 3
1747* MAN TO MAN (NZ) 6-11-5 A Kondrat, *sn tracking wnr, led*
briefly 3 out, wknd appr nxt........(9 to 2 op 7 to 2) 4
DUKE OF EUROLINK 4-11-0 R Dunwoody, *not fluent 3rd,*
moderate prog 3 out, no ch wth wnr.
.......................(11 to 2 op 7 to 1 tchd 5 to 1) 5
1209⁵ NATIVE CHIEFTAN 4-11-0 H Davies, *outpcd 5th*.
..................(16 to 1 tchd 20 to 1 and 14 to 1) 6
885⁴ VITAL WONDER 5-11-0 P Holley, *beh whn mstk 4th, not*
trble ldrs aftr......(66 to 1 op 33 to 1 tchd 100 to 1) 7
1688 BILLY BORU 5-11-0 D Gallagher, *settled mid-div, effrt 5th,*
sn rdn and btn......(33 to 1 op 25 to 1 tchd 20 to 1) 8
1557² DOMINANT FORCE 4-11-0 M Perrett, *rear whn mstk 4th,*
no hdwy nxt.........................(25 to 1 op 16 to 1) 9
1442⁴ FLIGHT LIEUTENANT (USA) 4-11-0 G Bradley, *wl plcd till*
wknd and jmpd lft 2 out.(6 to 1 op 8 to 1 tchd 9 to 1) 10
1460* TISSISAT (USA) 4-11-0 J Frost, *hld up rear, jmpd slwly*
5th, sn rdn and no prog.
.................(10 to 1 op 8 to 1 tchd 11 to 1) 11
1502 ROCA MURADA (Ire) 4-11-0 A Maguire, *al rear*.
.......................(66 to 1 op 33 to 1) 12
1515² SYLVAN SABRE (Ire) (v) 4-11-0 J Osborne, *pld hrd, in tch*
till aftr 4th, btn whn mstk 3 out, pulled up bef nxt.
......................(50 to 1 op 25 to 1) pu
Dist: 8l, 8l, 1½l, 12l, 2½l, ½l, 10l, 2½l, 1½l, 12l. 3m 53.60s. a 12.10s (13 Ran).
SR: 53/45/42/40/23/20/19/9/6/ (Sir Eric Parker), R Akehurst

1841 Tripleprint Feltham Novices' Chase Grade 1 (5-y-o and up) £19,140 3m ....(1:15)

1651* SEE MORE INDIANS 6-11-7 G Bradley, *led 4th, mstk tenth,*
hdd nxt, jnd ldr 3 out, hit next, led and blun last, rdn
out................................(7 to 2 tchd 4 to 1) 1
1662* CRYSTAL SPIRIT 6-11-7 J Frost, *led to 4th, led 11th till*
hdd and blun last, kpt on gmely.
......................(6 to 4 fav tchd 5 to 4) 2
1537² SPIKEY (NZ) 7-11-7 A Maguire, *chsd ldrs till beh and*
outpcd 11th, tld off................(10 to 1 op 12 to 1) 3
1189* GOLDEN FARE 8-11-7 R Greene, *mstk 1st, in tch whn*
mistake 6th, beh and outpcd frm tenth, tld off.
..............(50 to 1 op 25 to 1 tchd 66 to 1) 4
1662² COULTON 6-11-7 R Dunwoody, *hld up, mstk 11th, cl 4th*
whn f 13th...........(2 to 1 op 7 to 4 tchd 9 to 4) f
1730 ONE MORE RUN 6-11-7 P Holley, *mstk 4th, rear whn blun*
and uns rdr 9th.....................(100 to 1 op 50 to 1) ur
1621⁴ ANDREW'S FIRST 6-11-7 C Llewellyn, *hdwy appr 13th, cl*
3rd whn pld up lme bef 15th, destroyed.
.............(16 to 1 op 14 to 1 tchd 20 to 1) pu
Dist: 2½l, dist, 4l. 6m 8.60s. a 19.60s (7 Ran).
SR: 5/2/-/-/ (Paul K Barber), P F Nicholls

1842 Bonusprint Handicap Hurdle (4-y-o and up) £4,402 2m.............(1:45)

1632² CHILD OF THE MIST [117] 7-10-2 A Maguire, *wl plcd, led*
appr 2 out, rdn clr, kpt on nr finish.
...............(5 to 1 op 6 to 1 tchd 13 to 2) 1
1755³ KILCASH (Ire) [143] (bl) 5-12-0 M Richards, *hld up in rear,*
hmpd 5th, rdn and ran on frm 2 out, styd on wl nr
finish............(9 to 2 jt-fav op 5 to 1 tchd 4 to 1) 2
1746² CLURICAN (Ire) [115] 4-10-0 D Murphy, *wl plcd, hrd rdn*
aftr 3 out, no imprsn on wnr frm nxt........(9 to 2 jt-
fav op 7 to 2 tchd 5 to 1) 3
1559² ARABIAN BOLD (Ire) [152] 5-11-3 N Williamson, *led to 4th,*
led 6th till appr 2 out, sn rdn and btn.
..............(13 to 2 op 6 to 1 tchd 7 to 1) 4
1701⁵ CORRIN HILL [117] 6-10-2 D Gallagher, *in tch, mstk 5th,*
l... .l. nd mistake nxt, no further prog.
......................(25 to 1 op 20 to 1) 5
HONEST WORD [137] 8-11-8 R Dunwoody, *led 4th to 6th,*
sn wknd und pres....(6 to 1 op 4 to 1 tchd 13 to 2) 6
1650³ MONDAY CLUB [115] 9-9-7 (7*) D Meade, *beh, improved*
aftr 4th, rdn and outpcd frm 3 out.(8 to 1 tchd 9 to 1) 7

1755[7] SHARRIBA [120] 4-10-5 C Llewellyn, *al beh, tld off.* ....(25 to 1 op 20 to 1 tchd 33 to 1) 8

1437[4] AMAZON EXPRESS [135] 4-11-6 J Osborne, *hld up mid-div till f 5th*..........(13 to 2 op 7 to 1 tchd 6 to 1) f

Dist: 2l, 10l, 7l, 1½l, ¾l, ¾l, 25l. 3m 52.30s. a 12.30s (9 Ran).

SR: 39/63/25/35/18/37/14/-/-/ (John Whyte), John Whyte

1843 King George VI Tripleprint Chase Grade 1 (5-y-o and up) £51,780 3m ....(2:20)

1556* BARTON BANK 7-11-10 A Maguire, *led to second, led 8th, blun 4 out, drvn out frm last, kpt on gmely.* ....(9 to 2 op 5 to 1 tchd 11 to 2) 1

1226* BRADBURY STAR 8-11-10 D Murphy, *hld up mid-div, hdwy 13th, ev ch frm 3 out, not quicken r-in.* ....(5 to 1 tchd 11 to 2) 2

1250[3] THE FELLOW (Fr) (bl) 8-11-10 A Kondrat, *hld up in tch, ev ch 2 out, mstk last, no extr.* ....(7 to 2 fav op 3 to 1 tchd 4 to 1) 3

1757* YOUNG HUSTLER 6-11-10 C Llewellyn, *led second to 5th, ldg grp, ev ch 3 out till wknd appr last.* ....(9 to 2 op 3 to 1 tchd 5 to 1) 4

1439[4] ZETA'S LAD 10-11-10 R Supple, *hld up rear, hdwy 4 out, ev ch whn not fluent nxt, mstk 2 out, sn wknd.* ....(20 to 1 tchd 25 to 1) 5

1507* NEVADA GOLD 7-11-10 D Gallagher, *not fluent 4th, rear whn blun 9th, no imprsn on ldrs appr 3 out.* ....(66 to 1 op 50 to 1 tchd 100 to 1) 6

1670[3] DOCKLANDS EXPRESS 11-11-10 N Williamson, *cld frm rear 12th, rdn alng and hit 4 out, mstk nxt, sn btn.* ....(14 to 1 op 16 to 1) 7

1560[4] TRAVADO 7-11-10 J Osborne, *hld up, hit 5th, in tch in 4th pl whn f 13th*..................(8 to 1 op 10 to 1) f

1439 ROLLING BALL (Fr) 10-11-10 R Dunwoody, *pressed ldrs, led 5th to 8th, hit nxt, wknd quickly tenth, pld up bef 14th*.................(14 to 1 op 16 to 1 tchd 20 to 1) pu

1439[3] BLACK HUMOUR 9-11-10 G Bradley, *hld up rear, lost tch 14th, pld up bef 2 out, broke blood vessel.* ....(6 to 1 tchd 7 to 1) pu

Dist: Hd, 10l, 10l, hd, 15l, 15l. 6m 0.40s. a 11.40s (10 Ran).

SR: 90/90/80/70/70/55/40/-/-/ (Mrs J Mould), D Nicholson

1844 Bonusfilm Wayward Lad Novices' Chase (5-y-o and up) £8,364 2½m 110yds.......................(2:50)

1349[3] BAS DE LAINE (Fr) 7-11-0 M Richards, *wl plcd, led tenth, mstk and hdd last, rallied to ld nr finish.* ....(5 to 2 tchd 11 to 4) 1

1754[4] MONSIEUR LE CURE 7-11-0 N Williamson, *ldg grp, hit 5th, mstk 12th, pressed ldr frm 3 out, led last, hdd und pres nr finish*...............(7 to 1 op 6 to 1 tchd 8 to 1) 2

1754[3] POPPETS PET 6-11-4 S Hodgson, *led to tenth, wknd 12th, sn lost tch*..................(20 to 1 op 16 to 1) 3

1469[3] HANGOVER 7-11-0 A Maguire, *sn pushed alng in rear, lost tch 11th, tld off*................. (7 to 1 op 8 to 1) 4

1691[4] GHIA GNEUIAGH 7-11-4 C Llewellyn, *pressed ldrs, cl second whn f 13th*..................(7 to 1 tchd 8 to 1) f

75[6] MUSIC SCORE 7-11-0 Mr M Armytage, *beh till f 13th.* ....(50 to 1 op 33 to 1 tchd 66 to 1) f

1161[2] DANTE'S NEPHEW 6-11-0 R Dunwoody, *slwly into strd, mid-div whn f 8th, destroyed*......(10 to 1 op 12 to 1) f

1662[3] THE GLOW (Ire) 5-11-4 P Holley, *mstk 5th, rear whn hmpd and uns rdr 8th*.... (7 to 4 fav op 5 to 4 tchd 15 to 8) ur

Dist: Sht-hd, dist, 15l. 5m 11.10s. a 18.10s (8 Ran).

(R K Bids Ltd), O Sherwood

1845 Tripleprint Handicap Hurdle (4-y-o and up) £4,402 3m 110yds...... (3:20)

1756[6] PEATSWOOD [129] 5-11-12 Lorna Vincent, *hld up, prog 4 out, quickened frm last to ld fnl 50 yards.* ....(6 to 1 tchd 13 to 2) 1

1561[4] BEYOND OUR REACH [104] 5-10-1 R Dunwoody, *handily plcd, led appr 2 out, sn clr, rdn and hdd fnl 50 yards.* ....(2 to 1 fav op 7 to 4 tchd 9 to 4) 2

1458[5] PRIME DISPLAY (USA) [131] 7-12-0 M Richards, *led till appr 2 out, sn wknd*..............(9 to 1 op 8 to 1) 3

1561[8] PIPERS COPSE [130] 11-11-13 M Perrett, *hld up rear, styd on appr 2 out, no imprsn on ldrs.* ....(10 to 1 op 8 to 1 tchd 12 to 1) 4

1349[4] CAIRNCASTLE [111] 8-10-8 A Maguire, *ldg grp till rdn and wknd appr 2 out*..................(5 to 1 tchd 11 to 2) 5

1561 CASH IS KING [122] (bl) 9-11-5 G Bradley, *hld up rear, hit second, shrtlvd effrt appr 2 out, no extr.* ....(20 to 1 tchd 25 to 1) 6

1393[7] HURRICANE BLAKE [114] (bl) 5-10-11 N Williamson, *hld up in tch, rdn alng 4 out, wknd nxt.* ....(12 to 1 op 7 to 1 tchd 14 to 1) 7

1653[7] PAMBER PRIORY [110] 10-10-7 G Rowe, *ldg grp, mstk 6th, blun 3 out, sn lost pl, tld off.* ....(10 to 1 op 8 to 1 tchd 12 to 1) 8

1561[7] EMERALD SUNSET [107] 8-10-4 D Gallagher, *al rear, tld off whn pld up bef 9th.* ....(14 to 1 op 12 to 1 tchd 16 to 1) pu

1653 METAL OISEAU (Ire) [117] (bl) 5-11-0 A Charlton, *beh till pld up bef 4th*.............(15 to 2 op 8 to 1 tchd 9 to 1) pu

Dist: 1½l, 15l, 2l, ¾l, nk, 2½l, dist. 6m 6.40s. a 19.40s (10 Ran).

SR: 39/12/24/21/1/11/ (Peter Taplin), M R Channon

LEOPARDSTOWN (IRE) (soft) Monday December 27th

Going Correction: PLUS 1.25 sec. per fur. (races 1,3,-4,6,7), PLUS 0.45 (2,5)

1846 Tote Investors Ltd Festival Hurdle (3-y-o) £4,140 2m................(12:25)

1454[9] GLOWING VALUE (Ire) (bl) 10-7 B Sheridan,.......(8 to 1) 1

1377[2] NANNAKA (USA) 9-13 (3*) T P Treacy,.............(2 to 1) 2

MAYASTA (Ire) 9-9 (7*) D J Kavanagh,........ (13 to 8 fav) 3

1377[3] FRIENDLY FLYER (Ire) 10-2 K F O'Brien,...........(9 to 2) 4

FLORA WOOD (Ire) 10-7 P Carberry,..................... 5

1454 STATE PRINCESS (Ire) 10-2 R Hughes,............(7 to 1) 6

1575[8] TENCA (Ire) 10-7 C F Swan,...................(12 to 1) 7

1432[8] ISLAND VISION (Ire) 10-0 (7*) J M Sullivan,.......(12 to 1) 8

FALCARRAGH (Ire) 10-7 C O'Dwyer,.............(14 to 1) 9

1575[9] LITTLE TINCTURE (Ire) 10-7 P L Malone,.........(25 to 1) 10

1432 PAKED (Ire) 9-11 (5*) D T Evans,.................(33 to 1) 11

1111[9] NO POSSIBLE DOUBT (Ire) 10-2 F Woods,.......(33 to 1) 12

MANGANS HILL (Ire) 10-2 P M Verling,...........(20 to 1) pu

Dist: Nk, sht-hd, 5½l, 7l. 4m 22.20s. a 34.20s (13 Ran).

(F Dunne), F Dunne

1847 McCain Handicap Chase (5-y-o and up) £5,520 2m 1f............. (12:55)

1682[2] LASATA [-] 8-10-12 C O'Dwyer,...................(6 to 1) 1

1682* SARAEMMA [-] 7-11-4 (4ex) J F Titley,............ (5 to 1) 2

1761* BOB DEVANI [-] 7-10-4 (8ex) P Carberry,..... (13 to 8 fav) 3

1578[7] BLITZKREIG [-] 10-11-7 C F Swan,...............(12 to 1) 4

1231 EBONY STAR [-] 10-11-5 K F O'Brien,...........(16 to 1) 5

1552[3] KILLINEY GRADUATE [-] 7-10-4 (3*) C O'Brien,.... (8 to 1) f

1579[5] FURRY STAR [-] 7-10-0 J Jones,................(12 to 1) f

1382[6] KINGS ENGLISH [-] 7-10-12 T Horgan,............(6 to 1) f

879[2] OH SO GRUMPY [-] 5-10-4 J P Banahan,........ (12 to 1) f

Dist: ¾l, 7l, 20l, 13l. 4m 26.50s. a 11.50s (9 Ran).

SR: 46/51/30/27/12/-/ (A J O'Reilly), M F Morris

1848 Goat Dublin Sporting Pub Maiden Hurdle (4-y-o) £4,140 2m........... (1:30)

1230[5] FERRYCARRIG HOTEL (Ire) 11-7 D H O'Connor,... (5 to 1) 1

1337* BELLS LIFE (Ire) 11-7 C F Swan,..............(5 to 4 fav) 2

ANGAREB (Ire) 11-7 J Shortt,...................(16 to 1) 3

1681[8] TIME IT RIGHT (Ire) 11-7 K F O'Brien,.............(7 to 1) 4

1762[3] SENSE OF VALUE 11-2 B Sheridan,................(9 to 2) 5

1397 PLASSY BOY (Ire) 11-2 P Carberry,..............(14 to 1) 6

1230 DAMODAR 11-2 P L Malone,.....................(25 to 1) 7

1681[4] MIDNIGHT HOUR (Ire) 11-2 R Hughes,............(6 to 1) 8

1610 ANDROS GALE (Ire) 11-2 C O'Dwyer,............(16 to 1) 9

ARISTODEMUS 11-2 T J Taaffe,.................(16 to 1) 10

STORMPROOF (Ire) 11-2 J Magee,...............(20 to 1) 11

1762 INAUGURATION (Ire) 11-2 A Powell,.............(25 to 1) 12

555 JUST FOUR (Ire) 10-4 (7*) Mr C M Healy,.........(33 to 1) 13

1681 ARCTIC TREASURE (Ire) 10-11 F Woods,........ (33 to 1) 14

KEEP EM GUESSIN (Ire) 11-2 T Horgan,..........(12 to 1) pu

Dist: 1½l, sht-hd, 3½l, 2½l. 4m 12.90s. a 24.90s (15 Ran).

SR: 44/42/42/38/30/-/ (J C Lacy), James Joseph O'Connor

1849 The 1st Choice Novice Hurdle (4-y-o and up) £6,900 2¼m............(2:00)

1401* WINTER BELLE (USA) 5-11-8 J Shortt,............(3 to 1) 1

1434* MINELLA LAD 7-12-0 T Horgan,..................(3 to 1) 2

1576* DANOLI (Ire) 5-11-8 (3*) T P Treacy,............(5 to 4 on) 3

1429[3] RISZARD (USA) 4-10-13 K F O'Brien,.............(7 to 1) 4

924* COCKNEY LAD (Ire) 4-11-6 C F Swan,..............(9 to 1) 5

1549 FAIRYHILL RUN (Ire) 5-10-6 (7*) J M Donnelly,.... (66 to 1) 6

Dist: 2l, ½l, 2l, 8l. 4m 46.80s. a 30.80s (6 Ran).

SR: 11/15/11/ (John Muldoon), Patrick Prendergast

1850 Findus Handicap Chase (Listed) (4-y-o and up) £20,625 3m............ (2:35)

1611* KING OF THE GALES [-] 6-11-11 (3ex) C O'Brien, *hld up, prog 3 out, rdn to ld aftr last, styd on wl und pres.* ....(7 to 2) 1

1784[2] FERROMYN [-] 8-10-0 C F Swan, *trkd ldr, dsptd ld aftr 9th, led entering strt, hdd after last, kpt on*.... (8 to 1) 2

1552* DEEP HERITAGE [-] 7-11-2 T J Taaffe, *mid-div, prog 5 out, ev ch 2 out, rdn and no extr appr last*.........(7 to 1) 3

1552[2] DESERT LORD [-] 7-10-8 J F Titley, *trkd ldr, dsptd ld aftr 9th, hdd entering strt, wknd*..................(9 to 1) 4

1578[6] FOURTH OF JULY [-] 9-10-12 J P Banahan, *hld up, prog 3 out, rdn aftr nxt, wknd*......................(7 to 1) 5

1611 EBONY JANE [-] 8-12-0 K F O'Brien, *wl plcd, prog 4 out, rdn appr 2 out, sn wknd*......................(8 to 1) 6

1381[6] NEW MILL HOUSE [-] 10-10-9 T Horgan, *wl plcd, rdn 4 out, wknd aftr nxt*..............................(16 to 1) 7

1452* SON OF WAR [-] 6-11-8 F Woods, *led, mstk and lost pl 9th,*
trkd ldrs at nxt, rdn and wknd aftr 5 out ... (3 to 1 fav) 8
1611⁴ LAURA'S BEAU [-] (bl) 9-11-1 C O'Dwyer, *mid-div, prog to*
tenth, rdn and wknd 3 out .... (16 to 1) 9
1682³ WINNING CHARLIE [-] 7-10-0 P Carberry, *rear, prog tenth,*
rdn and wknd aftr 4 out .... (14 to 1) 10
1452⁴ MASS APPEAL [-] 8-10-12 B Sheridan, *al rear, rdn and*
lost tch aftr 5 out .... (25 to 1) 11
1685 FINAL TUB [-] 10-10-12 A Powell, *al rear, rdn and wknd*
appr 3 out .... (12 to 1) 12
119 KINDLY KING [-] 9-10-0 J Magee, *mid-div, bad mstk and*
uns rdr 5 out .... (50 to 1) ur
Dist: ¾l, 11l, 10l, 3½l. 6m 32.20s. a 20.20s (13 Ran).
SR: 3/-/-/-/-/-/   (E P King), J E Kiely

1851
Cheltenham Gold Card Handicap Hurdle Qualifier (Listed) (4-y-o and up) £5,520 3m .... (3:10)

1076⁸ STEEL DAWN [-] 6-9-4 (3*) C O'Brien, *rear, steady hdwy to*
track ldrs 5 out, led appr last, slight mstk, styd on strly.
.... (25 to 1) 1
1612² BEAU BABILLARD [-] 6-11-1 C F Swan, *mid-div, prog 3*
out, ev ch aftr nxt, rdn and no extr appr last, kpt on.
.... (8 to 1) 2
1174* WILD FANTASY (Ire) [-] 5-10-1 (5*) K P Gaule, *trkd ldr, dsptd*
ld 3 out, led bef nxt, rdn and hdd before last, kpt on.
.... (8 to 1) 3
1017² LOVE AND PORTER (Ire) [-] 5-10-9 D H O'Connor, *hld up, gd*
prog 3 out, trkd ldr aftr nxt, rdn and no extr appr last.
.... (8 to 1) 4
1782⁵ CHELSEA NATIVE [-] 6-10-3 (5*) Susan A Finn, *wl plcd, rdn*
and lost pl appr 3 out, kpt on ag'n strt. .... (10 to 1) 5
1580⁶ KERFONTAINE [-] 8-10-4 T Horgan, *wl plcd, rdn and wknd*
appr 3 out .... (16 to 1) 6
1430³ OPERA HAT (Ire) [-] 5-10-5 A Powell, *hld up, prog to track*
ldrs 3 out, rdn and no extr aftr nxt, wknd ...... (10 to 1) 7
1685* ALWAYS IN TROUBLE [-] 6-10-13 (Bex) J F Titley, *mid-div,*
prog 3 out, sn rdn, wknd aftr nxt .... (9 to 4 fav) 8
881³ PRINCIPLE MUSIC (USA) [-] 5-10-11 B Sheridan, *hld up,*
prog to track ldrs 3 out, rdn and wknd nxt ...... (10 to 1) 9
1782² IL TROVATORE (USA) [-] (bl) 7-10-0 P Carberry, *led, 6 ls clr*
at second, reduced advantage 4 out, hdd nxt, wknd
quickly .... (11 to 2) 10
1685 RISING WATERS (Ire) [-] 5-11-6 K F O'Brien, *mid-div, rdn*
and wknd aftr 4 out .... (16 to 1) 11
1499⁶ WRECKLESS MAN [-] 6-9-13 J Magee, *mid-div, rdn and*
wknd 3 out .... (33 to 1) 12
MURAHIN (USA) [-] 4-10-8 C O'Dwyer, *wl plcd, prog to*
dispute ld 3 out, sn rdn, wknd at nxt, pld up bef last.
.... (14 to 1) pu
1551² PANDA (Ire) [-] 5-10-3 (3*) T P Treacy, *mid-div, rdn and lost*
pl appr 4 out, tld off and pld up bef 2 out ..... (13 to 2) pu
Dist: 4l, nk, nk, 15l. 6m 32.00s. a 50.00s (14 Ran).
                        (Ronald Curran), Ronald Curran

1852
Yuletide I N H Flat Race (4-y-o and up) £4,140 2m .... (3:40)

709³ WHATTABOB (Ire) 4-10-13 (7*) Mr P J Kelly, ... (5 to 2) 1
1270* PIMBERLEY PLACE (Ire) 5-12-4 Mr T Mullins, ...(Evens fav) 2
1039* GREAT SVENGALI (Ire) 4-11-6 (7*) Mr E Norris, ... (2 to 1) 3
BOWLING CHERRY (Ire) 5-11-4 (7*) Mr D Harley, .. (33 to 1) 4
MARTINS PARTY 8-11-11²⁴ (7*) Mr W T Murphy, .. (50 to 1) 5
Dist: ½l, 8l, dist, 6l. 4m 6.06s. (5 Ran).
                    (Mrs Mairead Higgins), Francis Berry

LIMERICK (IRE) (heavy)
Monday December 27th

1853
Mellon Stud Maiden Hurdle (3-y-o) £3,450 2m .... (12:35)

1575⁵ THE SALTY FROG (Ire) 10-11 M Flynn, ... (9 to 2) 1
968⁸ CARHUE STAR (Ire) 10-1 (5*) T J O'Sullivan, ... (8 to 1) 2
DARK SWAN (Ire) 10-6 (5*) C P Dunne, ... (12 to 1) 3
1432 DANCING VISION (Ire) 10-11 M O'Neill, ... (6 to 1) 4
1432 SAINT HILDA (Ire) 10-9²⁰ (7*) Mr G F Ryan, ... (12 to 1) 5
1377 BOBADIL (Ire) 10-6 S R Murphy, ... (12 to 1) 6
1432 NURSE MAID (Ire) 10-6 J Collins, ... (14 to 1) 7
802⁶ TOUCHING MOMENT (Ire) 10-4 (7*) Mr H Murphy, .. (6 to 1) 8
1377⁷ AULD STOCK (Ire) 10-6 M Duffy, ... (4 to 1) 9
PERSIAN GEM (Ire) 9-13 (7*) Miss L Townsley, ... (7 to 1) 10
1432 BLACK PIPER (Ire) 9-13 (7*) Mr B M Cash, ... (12 to 1) 11
1575⁷ KING BRIAN (Ire) 10-11 W T Slattery Jnr, ... (14 to 1) 12
1377 CHRISTY MOORE (Ire) 10-11 L P Cusack, ... (20 to 1) 13
1432 MISS MURPHY (Ire) 10-9²⁰ (7*) Mr B Moran, ... (8 to 1) 14
QUENIE TWO (Ire) 10-6 S H O'Donovan, ... (14 to 1) 15
1575 BAEZA 10-6 (5*) P A Roche, ... (20 to 1) 16
1432 HAWTHORN ROSE (Ire) 9-13 (7*) J Butler, ... (20 to 1) 17
TANHONEY (Ire) 10-1 (5*) M J Holbrook, ... (14 to 1) 18
STRATEGIC TIMING (Ire) 10-1 (5*) J R Barry, ... (6 to 1) 19
968⁸ MUSCOVY DUCK (Ire) 9-13 (7*) J P Broderick, ... (7 to 2 fav) f
Dist: ½l, nk, sht-hd, 4l. 4m 17.10s. (20 Ran).
                    (Mrs Tina Carmody), Thomas Carmody

1854
Bank Of Ireland Hurdle (5-y-o and up) £3,450 2½m .... (1:05)

1037³ PRINCE OLE (Ire) 5-12-0 M Duffy, ... (7 to 4 on) 1
BALLINASCREENA 7-11-0 (7*) J P Broderick, ...(5 to 2) 2
536 RHINESTALL 6-10-13 (3*) Mr A E Lacy, ...(7 to 1) 3
BOY BLUE 6-11-2 (5*) T J O'Sullivan, ...(8 to 1) 4
LEAVE IT TO JUDGE 6-11-0 (7*) Mr W J Gleeson, (14 to 1) 5
BUCKHILL 6-11-7 A J O'Brien, ...(14 to 1) 6
Dist: 3½l, 6l, 8l, 15l. 6m 44.00s. (6 Ran).
                    (Mrs Patrick Flynn), Patrick Joseph Flynn

1855
Bank Of Ireland Handicap Hurdle (4-y-o and up) £3,450 2m .... (1:35)

533⁸ IMPERIAL CALL (Ire) [-] 4-11-3 G M O'Neill, ... (100 to 30) 1
1686⁵ PARLIAMENT HALL [-] 7-11-7 (7*) J P Broderick, (9 to 4 fav) 2
1551⁴ UNCLE BABY (Ire) [-] 5-9-9 (5*) J R Barry, ... (6 to 1) 3
REPLACEMENT [-] 6-9-10 (5*) P A Roche, ... (20 to 1) 4
1175⁴ WATERLOO LADY [-] 6-10-12 (3*) D P Murphy, ...(5 to 1) 5
991⁸ PREMIER LEAP [-] 4-9-11 (5*) T J O'Sullivan, ... (8 to 1) 6
294 MARIAN YEAR [-] 7-10-11 J Collins, ...(10 to 1) 7
1176* VICOSA (Ire) [-] 4-10-9 L P Cusack, ...(6 to 1) 8
1495 BOLEREE (Ire) [-] 5-9-8² S H O'Donovan, ... (10 to 1) 9
Dist: 1l, 2½l, 10l, 3l. 4m 14.40s. (9 Ran).
                    (Lisselan Farms Ltd), Fergus Sutherland

1856
James McMahon Group Handicap Chase (5-y-o and up) £3,450 2½m .... (2:10)

539³ LIFE OF A LORD [-] 7-10-12 M Flynn, ... (5 to 2) 1
1176⁷ QUIET CITY [-] 6-9-3 (5*) T J O'Sullivan, ... (5 to 1) 2
BLAZING DAWN [-] 6-10-11 S H O'Donovan, ... (6 to 1) 3
1611² HAKI SAKI [-] 7-11-10 G M O'Neill, ... (6 to 4 on) ro
Dist: Nk, dist. 5m 42.40s. (4 Ran).
                            (M J Clancy), T Costello

1857
Tattersalls Mares Novice Chase (5-y-o and up) £3,105 2½m .... (2:45)

DUSKY LADY 7-12-0 G M O'Neill, ... (7 to 1) 1
1451 ANOTHER GROUSE 6-11-7 (7*) J P Broderick, ...(5 to 1) 2
72⁵ BALADINE 6-12-0 W T Slattery Jnr, ...(16 to 1) 3
929⁸ DOORSLAMMER 8-12-0 S R Murphy, ...(13 to 2) 4
1785⁵ PEJAWI 6-11-9 (5*) T J O'Sullivan, ...(12 to 1) 5
1608⁸ HIGHWAY LASS 7-12-0 A J O'Brien, ...(25 to 1) 6
1785 YVONNES PRINCESS 6-11-11 (3*) Mr T Lombard, (10 to 1) 7
1612 STRONG CHERRY 7-11-7 (7*) Mr K Taylor, ...(10 to 1) 8
554² HIGHBABS 7-11-11 (3*) D P Murphy, ...(6 to 1) 9
1785 MOUNTAIN STAGE 5-11-12 S H O'Donovan,
.... (9 to 4 fav) 10
989 GODFREYS CROSS (Ire) 5-11-12 P P Kinane, ... (33 to 1) 11
1073⁶ SANTAMORE 6-11-9 (5*) P A Roche, ...(8 to 1) f
1495⁶ BALLINDERRY GLEN 7-12-0 J Collins, ...(10 to 1) ur
1399 MONKS AIR 6-12-0 L P Cusack, ...(33 to 1) ur
1177 SEANS SHOON 6-11-7 (7*) Mr K Whelan, ...(33 to 1) pu
MELDRUM MISS (Ire) 5-11-7 (5*) C P Dunne, ...(20 to 1) pu
Dist: Nk, 11l, 4½l, 9l. 5m 41.00s. (16 Ran).
                    (Lisselan Farms Ltd), Fergus Sutherland

1858
Punchs Pub & Restaurant Mares Flat Race (4 & 5-y-o) £3,450 2m ..... (3:20)

MIDNIGHT AT MAY'S (Ire) 5-11-7 (7*) Mr B Hassett, (7 to 1) 1
SISTER ALICE (Ire) 5-12-0 Mr P Fenton, ...(4 to 1) 2
1581³ MARYJO (Ire) 4-11-4 (5*) Mr J A Nash, ...(2 to 1 fav) 3
1501⁶ DONBOLINO (Ire) 5-11-7 (7*) Mr P Cody, ... (8 to 1) 4
DAWN ADAMS (Ire) 5-11-9 (5*) Mr H F Cleary, ...(6 to 1) 5
1501⁸ CASTLE CLUB (Ire) 4-11-2 (7*) Miss C O'Neill, .. (16 to 1) 6
1608 SHUILNAMON (Ire) 4-11-2 (7*) Mr D J McGrath, ..(14 to 1) 7
1766⁷ CASH IT IN (Ire) 5-11-9 (5*) Mr J P Berry, ... (8 to 1) 8
907 ANOTHER STAR (Ire) 4-11-2 (7*) Mr D K Budds, ..(20 to 1) 9
RAMBLE ALONG (Ire) 4-11-2 (7*) Mr D Kenneally, (14 to 1) 10
1333 DUN OENGUS (Ire) 4-11-9 Mr K Whelan, ... (6 to 1) 11
LA MAJA (Ire) 4-11-6 (3*) Miss M Olivefalk, ...(12 to 1) 12
LISNAGAR LADY (Ire) 4-11-9 Mr J A Flynn, ...(16 to 1) 13
JENNYS GROVE (Ire) 5-11-7 (7*) Mr D Deacon, ...(14 to 1) 14
A WOMAN'S HEART (Ire) 4-11-2 (7*) Mr M A Cahill, (8 to 1) 15
BUNNINADDEN PHIL (Ire) 5-11-7 (7*) Mr B Walsh, (14 to 1) 16
1077⁶ TWO HILLS FOLLY (Ire) 4-11-2 (7*) Mr E Gallagher, (14 to 1) 17
Dist: Hd, 8l, ½l, 6l. 4m 17.08s. (17 Ran).
                        (G M Mungovan), Donal Hassett

1859
Joe Donnelly Bookmaker I N H Flat Race (5-y-o) £3,450 2½m .... (3:50)

1555⁶ LOUGH CULTRA DRIVE (Ire) 11-6 (5*) Mr J A Nash, (5 to 2) 1
1687 QUEEN OF THE ROCK (Ire) 11-6 Mr J E Kiely, ... (11 to 2) 2
1995⁵ AMACA (Ire) 11-13 Mr P Fenton, ...(13 to 8 fav) 3
1403* MOONSHEE (Ire) 11-3 (3*) Miss M Olivefalk, ... (8 to 1) 4
1681 CORRIB HAVEN (Ire) 11-11 Mr E Bolger, ...(9 to 1) 5
172⁶ D'S FANCY (Ire) 12-4 Mr A P O'Brien, ... (6 to 1) 6
1555 TWO IN TUNE (Ire) 11-4 (7*) Miss L Gough, ... (20 to 1) 7
MARGURITES PET (Ire) 11-13 (3*) Mr R O'Neill, .. (8 to 1) pu
1687 DOONEEN MIST (Ire) 10-13 (7*) Mr D P Daly, ...(20 to 1) pu
Dist: 1½l, 1½l, 25l, dist. 5m 45.08s. (9 Ran).

256

(S C Hennelly), V T O'Brien

MARKET RASEN (soft)
Monday December 27th
Going Correction: PLUS 0.60 sec. per fur. (races 1,4,6), PLUS 1.35 (2,3,5)

1860 BBC Radio Lincolnshire Selling Handicap Hurdle (4-y-o and up) £2,026 2m 1f 110yds...................... (12:55)

1719[3] CORLY SPECIAL [72] 6-10-6 A Carroll, *trkd ldrs, rdn to ld betw last 2, styd on strly*.......... (11 to 2 op 5 to 1) 1
POINT TAKEN (USA) [66] 6-10-0 A S Smith, *led till hdd betw last 2, no extr*.................... (33 to 1 op 25 to 1) 2
1462 BALLYLORD [90] 9-11-10 S Smith Eccles, *prmnt till pushed alng and lost pl aftr 4th, hdwy appr 2 out, styd on*.............................(7 to 2 jt-fav op 5 to 1) 3
1746[4] ELDER PRINCE [70] (bl) 7-10-4 W Worthington, *mid-div, styd on appr 2 out, wknd last*..... (5 to 1 op 11 to 2) 4
1738[9] WHAT IF [90] 9-11-10 M Brennan, *hld up towards rear, cld appr 3 out, sn ev ch, wknd and pres frm nxt*. .... (13 to 2 op 6 to 1 tchd 7 to 1) 5
1633[8] PHALAROPE (Ire) [75] 5-10-9 Mr A Walton, *trkd ldrs, pushed alng aftr 3rd, mstk and lost pl 3 out*. .... (20 to 1 op 14 to 1) 6
1738* GREENACRES LAD [80] 10-11-0 A Mulholland, *nvr better than mid-div*.................... (7 to 2 jt-fav op 3 to 1) 7
693[6] HELLO VANOS [66] 5-10-0 Mr K Green, *al towards rear*. .... (33 to 1 op 20 to 1) 8
1325[4] IMMORTAL IRISH [81] 8-11-1 Gary Lyons, *cl up till wknd quickly aftr 3 out*.................... (14 to 1 op 12 to 1) 9
1741[6] ALIZARI (USA) [66] (bl) 4-10-0 M Robinson, *sn rdn alng in rear, al beh*...................... (33 to 1 op 33 to 1) 10
1627 HADLEIGHS CHOICE [66] 6-10-0 Miss R Judge, *al beh, tld off frm 4th*...................... (50 to 1 op 33 to 1) 11
1701[7] COMEDY RIVER [85] 6-11-5 D Byrne, *hld up in rear, pld up bef 5th*.................................. (8 to 1) pu
Dist: 7l, 1l, 3l, ½l, 1½l, 5l, 10l, 2l, 12l, 12l. 4m 20.60s. a 18.60s (12 Ran).
SR: -/-/7/-/3/-/ (P A Brazier), K R Burke

1861 General Security Development Novices' Chase (4-y-o and up) £2,974 2½m .... (1:30)

1358[3] SHEILAS HILLCREST 7-11-6 (5*) J Supple, *cl up, led 6th, pressed frm tenth, all out, fnshd tired*. ....(5 to 2 op 7 to 2) 1
1743[4] HIGHLY DECORATED 8-11-5 Gary Lyons, *al prmnt, pressed wnr frm tenth, ev ch last, no extr*. .... (13 to 2 op 6 to 1) 2
1730[4] PRECIPICE RUN 8-11-5 S Smith Eccles, *led till hdd 6th, second whn f nxt*. (13 to 8 fav op 11 to 8 tchd 7 to 4) f
1544[5] IRISH BAY 7-11-5 D Byrne, *hld up, awkward 8th (water), pushed alng 4 out, mstk nxt, staying on in 3rd whn blun and uns rdr last*...............(5 to 2 op 2 to 1) ur
1469 KINGLY LOOK 6-11-5 Mr K Green, *not fluent, lost tch 9th, blun and uns rdr nxt*........................ (50 to 1) ur
SOLO BUCK 7-10-7 (7*) C Woodall, *wtd wth in tch, ev ch 5 out, outpcd appr 3 out, refused nxt*. ....(16 to 1 tchd 20 to 1) ref
Dist: 1½l. 5m 26.10s. a 34.10s (6 Ran).
SR: 26/18/-/ (N B Mason), N B Mason

1862 Bruce Carr Memorial Trophy Novices' Handicap Chase (5-y-o and up) £3,065 3m 1f.........................(2:00)

1214 CANTGETOUT [78] 7-10-0 Mr A Pickering, *hld up towards rear, hdwy 14th, styd on frm last to ld fnl strds*. .... (25 to 1 op 16 to 1) 1
1750* PLAYFUL JULIET (Can) [92] (v) 5-11-0 Pat Caldwell, *hld up in rear, hdwy 14th, outpcd aftr 4 out, styd on appr 2 out, lft in ld last till hdd fnl strds*. .... (11 to 4 op 2 to 1 tchd 3 to 1) 2
1770[2] SUPPOSIN [88] 5-10-10 Gary Lyons, *cl up, ev ch appr 3 out, one pace frm nxt*...............(5 to 2 op 9 to 4) 3
1570[4] BIG MAC [88] 6-10-10 S Smith Eccles, *led, awkward 3rd, shaken up appr 3 out, narrow advantage whn blun and uns rdr last*.............. (7 to 4 fav tchd 2 to 1) ur
1745[4] GUTE NACHT [80] 10-10-0[3] (5*) S Lyons, *not jump wl, sn beh, pld up bef 14th*. (12 to 1 op 10 to 1 tchd 16 to 1) pu
1091[5] IRISH GENT [86] 7-10-8 M Brennan, *cl up till wknd 13th, pld up bef 4 out*......... (4 to 1 op 6 to 1 tchd 7 to 1) pu
Dist: Hd, 4l. 7m 1.00s. a 60.00s (6 Ran).
(Mrs C W Pinney), C W Pinney

1863 Kilvington Handicap Hurdle (0-140 4-y-o and up) £3,626 2m 3f 110yds ....(2:30)

1462[9] ISABEAU [102] 6-10-8 A S Smith, *cl up, led aftr 5th, hrd pressed frm 3 out, ran on gmely*... (10 to 1 op 12 to 1) 1
1633[3] FOX CHAPEL [114] 6-10-13 (7*) G Tormey, *chsd ldrs, chlgd 2 out, ev ch r-in, ran on*............ (7 to 1 op 6 to 1) 2
1703[2] MIZYAN (Ire) [120] 5-11-7 (5*) J Twomey, *hld up beh ldrs, cld 4th, lost pl four out, styd on frm 2 out*. ....(4 to 1 op 7 to 2 tchd 9 to 2) 3
1746* GYMCRAK SOVEREIGN [109] 5-11-1 R Marley, *led till hdd aftr 5th, cl up, rallied appr 2 out, wknd approaching last*..................................(4 to 1 op 7 to 2) 4
1728[6] PERSONAL HAZARD [99] (bl) 4-10-5 R Garritty, *cl up, ev ch 3 out, pushed alng and wknd appr nxt*........(8 to 1) 5
1322 BALAAT (USA) [94] 5-10-0 W Worthington, *hld up towards rear, nvr nr to chal*.............(10 to 1 tchd 12 to 1) 6
1753* NELTEGRITY [108] 4-11-0 Peter Caldwell, *hld up in rear, hdwy und pres aftr 3 out, btn nxt*. (11 to 2 tchd 6 to 1) 7
1034[9] LIABILITY ORDER [103] 4-10-9 S Smith Eccles, *hld up in rear, al beh*.....................................(8 to 1) 8
1571[7] LOCH GARANNE [114] 5-11-6 M Brennan, *hld up in mid-div, cld 4 out, hrd rdn nxt, sn btn*. .... (100 to 30 fav op 3 to 1 tchd 4 to 1) 9
1812 MILLIE (USA) [94] 5-10-0 M Robinson, *cl up till wknd aftr 3rd, tld off after 5th*..............(40 to 1 op 50 to 1) 10
Dist: Nk, 15l, nk, 15l, ¾l, 20l, nk, ½l, 15l. 4m 49.80s. a 16.80s (10 Ran).
SR: 29/40/31/19/-/-/ (T R Pryke), K A Morgan

1864 Lincolnshire National Handicap Chase (0-140 5-y-o and up) £7,262 4m 1f.............................. (3:05)

1281[5] DIAMOND FORT [109] 8-10-0 M Brennan, *hld up, cld 17th, led nxt, clr 4 out, blun last, styd on wl*. .... (9 to 1 op 8 to 1 tchd 10 to 1) 1
1732[4] BROMPTON ROAD [109] 10-10-0 A S Smith, *hld up, cld o'r 4 out, sn chsd wnr, blun last, ran on*. .... (11 to 2 op 5 to 1 tchd 6 to 1) 2
1635* ALL JEFF (Fr) [130] 9-11-7 S Smith Eccles, *hld up, cld 16th, lost pl aftr nxt, hdwy 5 out, styd on wl frm 2 out*. ....(7 to 4 fav op 6 to 4 tchd 15 to 8) 3
1362* PORTONIA [122] 9-10-8 (5*) Mr M Buckley, *jmpd lft through out, made most till hdd 18th, outpcd frm 4 out*. ....(4 to 1 op 7 to 2 tchd 3 to 1) 4
1670[4] POLAR REGION [119] 7-10-3 (7*) G Tormey, *cl up, mstk 13th and lost pl, sn reco'red to take closer order, wknd 5 out*...................................(8 to 1 op 7 to 1) 5
1769[4] DUBIOUS JAKE [109] 10-9-9 (5*) C Burnett-Wells, *in tch, mstk 15th, lost touch nxt, tld off*...(10 to 1 op 14 to 1) 6
1776 NINE BROTHERS [109] 9-10-0 Mr K Green, *wth ldr till drpd rear 17th, beh whn f 4 out*.............. (50 to 1) f
1419[5] BARKIN [109] 10-10-0 M Moloney, *trkd ldrs, pushed alng 17th, sn wknd, pld up bef 2 out*................(6 to 1) pu
Dist: 1½l, 1l, 25l, 8l, 20l. 9m 12.10s. a 66.10s (8 Ran).
(Mrs R E Stocks), J C McConnochie

1865 Lincs FM Novices' Hurdle (3-y-o and up) £2,652 2m 1f 110yds........ (3:35)

1510[7] WAMDHA (Ire) 3-10-1 A S Smith, *hld up towards rear, hdwy gng wl 3 out, led betw last 2, ran on strly*. ....(4 to 1 op 3 to 1) 1
1655 EVE'S TREASURE 3-9-10 (5*) S Lyons, *led aftr 1st, hdd betw last 2, kpt on wl*............ (25 to 1 op 20 to 1) 2
1317[3] RECORD LOVER (Ire) 3-10-12 W Worthington, *hld up beh ldrs, kpt on one pace frm 2 out*... (100 to 30 op 3 to 1) 3
1607[4] MRS NORMAN 4-11-1 L O'Hara, *mid-div, styd on frm 2 out*..............................(20 to 1 tchd 25 to 1) 4
1529* APRIL CITY 4-11-7 M Ranger, *chsd ldrs till wknd aftr 3 out*..................................(4 to 1 op 5 to 1) 5
1639[3] BIRD WATCHER 4-11-6 S Smith Eccles, *al beh*. ....(4 to 1 tchd 9 to 2) 6
1582[7] INDIAN RIVER (Ire) 5-10-13 (7*) G Tormey, *al beh*. .... (3 to 1 fav tchd 7 to 2) 7
1658 LEARNED STAR 8-11-6 A Mulholland, *cl up, ev ch 3 out, wknd*.............................(25 to 1 op 20 to 1) 8
1613 LAZY RHYTHM (USA) 7-11-6 R Garritty, *led till hdd aftr 1st, prmnt till wknd 4 out*.................... (16 to 1) 9
TIP NAP 5-11-6 Gary Lyons, *hld up in rear, hdwy to cl on ldrs appr 3 out, weakend quickly nxt, tld off*. .... (25 to 1 op 16 to 1) 10
Dist: 1½l, 3½l, 6l, 10l, 4l, 6l, ½l, 1½l, 20l. 4m 24.80s. a 22.80s (10 Ran).
(T R Pryke), K A Morgan

NEWTON ABBOT (heavy)
Monday December 27th
Going Correction: PLUS 1.90 sec. per fur.

1866 Mid Devon Novices' Chase (5-y-o and up) £2,501 2m 5f.............. (12:45)

1598[3] KALANSKI 7-11-8 J Railton, *al cl up, mstk second, disputing ld whn blun 2 out, led last, ran on*. .... (5 to 1 op 3 to 1 tchd 11 to 2) 1
1441 KIWI VELOCITY (NZ) 6-10-9 L Harvey, *trkd ldr, led aftr 3 out, hdd last, no extr*. ....(3 to 1 fav op 7 to 2 tchd 5 to 1) 2
1621* BARELY BLACK 5-11-4 W Humphreys, *trkd ldrs, jmpd slwly 4th, beh frm 3 out*. (9 to 2 op 4 to 1 tchd 5 to 1) 3
1511[7] BOLL WEEVIL 7-11-4 Mr J Durkan, *led till hdd sn aftr 3 out, soon btn*........................(9 to 2 op 4 to 1) 4

1458³ ASK THE GOVERNOR 7-11-0 Craig Thornton, *beh, effrt 6th, wkng whn hit 3 out*............(4 to 1 op 3 to 1) 5
1696* PRUDENT PEGGY 6-10-6 (7*) R Darke, *prmnt whn blun badly second, nvr on terms aftr, tld off.*
.... (11 to 2 op 4 to 1 tchd 6 to 1) 6
1718 PRINCE VALMY (Fr) 8-11-0 M Foster, *mid-div, wknd aftr 6th, tld off whn pld up bef 3 out...*(50 to 1 op 33 to 1) pu
1621 PARSON'S WAY (bl) 6-11-0 G Upton, *al beh, tld off whn pld up bef 7th....................*(50 to 1 op 33 to 1) pu
Dist: 2½l, 25l, 7l, ¾l, dist. 5m 44.80s. a 44.80s (8 Ran).
SR: 45/29/13/6/1/   (I Kerman), C R Egerton

1867   Christmas Selling Handicap Hurdle (4,5,6-y-o) £1,847 2m 1f........(1:15)

1719 MILDRED SOPHIA [66] 6-9-7 (7*) Miss S Mitchell, *hld up in rear, gd hdwy frm 3 out, led nxt, drvn out......*(5 to 1) 1
1519³ LEGAL WIN (USA) [74] 5-10-1 (7*) Mr G Shenkin, *hld up in rear, hdwy aftr 4th, hrd rdn 2 out, kpt on one pace.*
............................(7 to 1 op 6 to 1) 2
1799⁴ MECADO [94] 6-11-7 (7*) P McLoughlin, *hld up, hdwy 5th, hrd rdn whn swrvd rght and stumbled appr 2 out, rallied bef last, one pace............*(6 to 1 op 5 to 1) 3
1719* SANDRO [84] (bl) 4-11-4 L Harvey, *led till hdd 2 out, no extr...................*(6 to 2 jt-fav tchd 11 to 4) 4
1717² PIRATE OF PENZANCE [66] 5-10-0 Mrs C Wonnacott, *beh, hdwy 5th, one pace frm 2 out........*(33 to 1 op 20 to 1) 5
1719 BOOGIE BOPPER (Ire) [80] (v) 4-10-7 (7*) L Reynolds, *trkd ldr, hrd rdn appr 2 out, not run on.*
............................(6 to 1 tchd 10 to 1) 6
1716 SPIRIT LEVEL [75] 5-10-9¹⁶ (7*) Mr R Payne, *chsd ldrs, one pace frm 5th...................*(40 to 1 op 33 to 1) 7
1751³ MAHONG [66] (bl) 5-10-0 V Slattery, *prmnt, wkng whn bumped appr 2 out, not reco'r.* (5 to 2 jt-fav op 2 to 1) 8
1642 VERRO (USA) [66] 6-10-0 I Shoemark, *beh, hdwy 5th, wknd 3 out, f last................*(40 to 1 op 20 to 1) f
CHARLAFRIVOLA [70] 5-10-4 W Humphreys, *in tch to 4th, wkng whn blun and uns rdr 3 out.*
........................(12 to 1 op 14 to 1 tchd 16 to 1) ur
Dist: ¾l, 2½l, 3½l, 1½l, 1½l, hd, 7l. 4m 31.40s. a 41.40s (10 Ran).
SR: -/-/5/-/-/-/   (N R Mitchell), N R Mitchell

1868   Thurlestone Hotel Handicap Hurdle (0-135 4-y-o and up) £2,587 2m 1f (1:45)

1701* NORTHERN SADDLER [105] 6-10-10 W Irvine, *led to second, styd in tch, led aftr 3 out, drvn out nxt.*
............................(9 to 4 fav op 2 to 1 tchd 5 to 2) 1
999³ MOHANA [123] 4-11-7 (7*) Mr N Moore, *made most frm second, hdd sn aftr 3 out, rallied nxt, ev ch last, no imprsn cl hme...........*(3 to 1 op 4 to 1 tchd 7 to 2) 2
1701² NOVA SPIRIT [95] 5-9-9² (7*) Guy Lewis, *hld up in rear, gd hdwy 5th, rdn and outpcd appr 2 out.*
............................(11 to 2 op 4 to 1) 3
1700³ PUNCHBAG (USA) [99] 7-10-4⁴ G Upton, *in tch, reminders and lost pl appr 5th, drvn 2 out, one pace.*
............................(7 to 2 op 5 to 1) 4
1661⁴ ATHAR (Ire) [111] 4-11-2 L Harvey, *hld up, nvr gng wl frm 4th, al beh...........*(5 to 2 op 2 to 1) 5
Dist: ¾l, 10l, 2½l, 15l. 4m 26.70s. a 36.70s (5 Ran).
SR: 38/55/17/18/15/   (Richard J Evans), R J Hodges

1869   Royal Castle Hotel Novices' Handicap Hurdle (4-y-o and up) £2,220 2¾m ....(2:15)

1695⁶ DAVES DELIGHT [74] 7-10-1 (7*) Mr G Shenkin, *hld up, gd hdwy aftr 6th, led wl bef 2 out, rdn out.*
............................(12 to 1 op 9 to 1) 1
1624⁴ THE CARROT MAN [69] 5-10-3 J Railton, *nvr far away, led 3 out, sn hdd, one pace..............*(5 to 1 op 7 to 2) 2
1775⁴ LANSDOWNE [79] 5-10-13 S Mackey, *hld up, gd hdwy appr 6th, outpcd bef 2 out..............*(5 to 1 op 4 to 1) 3
1715³ PRINCE OF SALERNO [83] 6-11-3 L Harvey, *trkd ldrs, hmpd badly and lost pl appr 3rd, styd on frm 3 out, nvr dngrs..............*(100 to 30 op 11 to 4 tchd 7 to 2) 4
1563 BLAKEINGTON [66] (bl) 7-9-7 (7*) Miss S Mitchell, *led aftr 4th, hdd 3 out, wknd quickly......*(50 to 1 op 33 to 1) 5
1716³ UP ALL NIGHT [68] 4-9-9 (7*) G Crone, *hmpd on bend appr 3rd, effrt 6th, nvr dngrs.*
............................(13 to 2 op 8 to 1 tchd 9 to 1 and 5 to 1) 6
1716* HANDY LASS [94] 4-11-9 (5*) D Matthews, *hld up, pushed alng frm 6th, no hdwy frm 3 out.*
............................(3 to 1 fav op 11 to 4 tchd 100 to 30) 7
1645 RIVER STREAM [68] 6-10-2 Mr N Harris, *beh, hdwy 6th, wknd 3 out...................*(50 to 1 op 25 to 1) 8
1602* DAMCADA (Ire) [74] 5-10-8 M Foster, *led till aftr 4th, wknd rpdly 7th, pld up bef 2 out..........*(7 to 2 op 9 to 1) pu
1463⁷ TEMPORARY [72] 8-10-3⁴ (7*) R Darke, *prmnt till wknd 4th, pld up bef four out............*(50 to 1 op 25 to 1) pu
SHERWOOD FOX [66] 6-10-0 Mrs C Wonnacott, *tld off frm 3rd, pld up appr 4 out............*(50 to 1 op 20 to 1) pu
1707 ESSEN AITCH [66] 4-10-0 V Slattery, *al beh, tld off whn pld up aftr 6th............*(50 to 1 op 20 to 1) pu
Dist: 1½l, 8l, 7l, 1l, 2l, hd, 8l. 5m 56.80s. a 57.80s (12 Ran).
      (Miss S Waterman), Miss S Waterman

1870   Langstone Cliff Hotel Handicap Chase (0-135 6-y-o and up) £3,477 3¼m 110yds........................(2:45)

1713* CATCH THE CROSS [128] (bl) 7-11-11 M Foster, *trkd ldrs, wnt second tenth, led bef 2 out, sn clr........*(6 to 4 jt-fav tchd 11 to 8) 1
1520³ JAILBREAKER [104] 6-9-10 (5*) D Salter, *hld up in rear, gd hdwy tenth, wnt second 3 out, hld whn blun nxt, hld last............*(6 to 4 jt-fav op 5 to 4 tchd 13 to 8) 2
1769⁶ TRUSTY FRIEND [107] 11-10-4⁴ S Burrough, *led second, mstk 9th, hdd nxt, wknd 3 out.*
............................(10 to 1 tchd 11 to 1 and 9 to 1) 3
1543 SUNBEAM TALBOT [111] 12-10-8 G Upton, *drpd out quickly aftr blun tenth, tld off whn pld up bef 2 out......................*(7 to 2 op 5 to 2) pu
Dist: 15l, 6l. 7m 36.80s. a 76.80s (4 Ran).
      (D A Beswick), M C Pipe

1871   EBF 'National Hunt' Novices' Hurdle Qualifier (4,5,6-y-o) £2,249 2m 1f (3:15)

1542⁴ HOLD YOUR RANKS 6-11-0 (7*) R Darke, *wtd wth, gd hdwy 5th, led aftr 2 out, sn clr.*
............................(12 to 1 fav op 5 to 2 tchd 3 to 1) 1
1542 STORMY SUNSET 6-10-2 (7*) Mr N Moore, *al frnt rnk, lft in ld aftr 5th, hdd aftr 2 out, one pace.*
............................(25 to 1 op 33 to 1 tchd 20 to 1) 2
1717⁶ BIDDLESTONE BOY (NZ) 6-10-7 (7*) Mr G Shenkin, *hld up, rdn 4th, outpcd frm 3 out......*(8 to 1 tchd 10 to 1) 3
1622 IT'S CONFIDENTIAL (NZ) 6-11-0 Mrs C Wonnacott, *hld up in rear, some hdwy 5th, nvr dngrs.* (25 to 1 op 14 to 1) 4
1617 GAVASKAR (Ire) 4-11-0 E Leonard, *in tch till wknd 5th.*
............................(9 to 2 op 11 to 1) 5
1695⁸ BROWN ROBBER 5-11-0 Mr W Henderson, *hld up, nvr on terms................*(12 to 1 op 10 to 1 tchd 11 to 1) 6
1210 LIBERTY JAMES 6-10-11⁴ (7*) Mr R Payne, *very slwly away, in tch frm second, beh from 4th.*
............................(25 to 1 op 33 to 1) 7
1707⁶ SOLO GIRL (Ire) 5-10-9 G Upton, *prmnt till rdn and wknd rpdly appr 5th, tld off.*
............................(4 to 1 op 5 to 1 tchd 6 to 1 and 3 to 1) 8
KING'S MAVERICK (Ire) 5-11-0 M Foster, *pld hrd early, settled in ld, stumbled on landing and uns rdr aftr 5th.*
............................(9 to 4 op 2 to 1 tchd 5 to 2) ur
Dist: 7l, 15l, 4l, 4l, 3l, 4l, 15l. 4m 29.50s. a 39.50s (9 Ran).
SR: 14/2/-/-/-/-/   (R G Frost), R G Frost

WETHERBY (soft)
Monday December 27th
Going Correction: PLUS 0.95 sec. per fur. (races 1,3,6), PLUS 1.35 (2,4,5)

1872   Christmas Novices' Hurdle (4-y-o and up) £2,250 2m................(1:00)

1613³ CUMBRIAN CHALLENGE (Ire) 4-11-0 L Wyer, *patiently rdn, led 3 out, gd jump to go clr last, ran on.*
............................(11 to 1 op 10 to 1) 1
1613² ALJADEER (USA) 4-11-0 N Doughty, *nvr far away, led briefly appr 3 out, ev ch betw last 2, one pace r-in.*
............................(5 to 1 op 9 to 2 tchd 11 to 2) 2
STOPROVERITATE 4-10-9 D Wilkinson, *wtd wth, improved appr 3 out, rdn and one pace frm nxt.*
............................(20 to 1 op 25 to 1) 3
1320² WHITE WILLOW 4-11-0 P Niven, *patiently rdn, improved 4 out, ridden bef nxt, no imprsn.*
............................(2 to 1 fav op 7 to 4 tchd 9 to 4) 4
1736* KENMORE-SPEED 6-11-7 Richard Guest, *keen hold, led till second, styd hndy till fdd und pres frm 3 out.*
............................(3 to 1 op 9 to 2 tchd 4 to 1) 5
GOLDEN TORQUE 6-10-9 (5*) H Bastiman, *wtd wth, hdwy appr 3 out, styd on finish.............*(25 to 1) 6
1613* VASILIEV (v) 5-11-7 C Grant, *reluctant to strt, improved into midfield hfwy, no imprsn frm 3 out.*
............................(10 to 1 tchd 11 to 1) 7
BANCHORY 4-10-7 (7*) J Driscoll, *trkd ldg grp till wknd frm 4 out................*(50 to 1 op 33 to 1) 8
WESTFIELD MOVES (Ire) 5-11-0 V Smith, *chsd ldg pair, feeling pace and lost grnd aftr 4 out, sn lost tch.*
............................(10 to 1 tchd 14 to 1) 9
PERFECT LIGHT 4-11-0 A Jones, *red wide and pld hrd, led second till appr 3 out, sn beh...*(66 to 1 op 50 to 1) 10
1199 MAGENTA BOY 5-10-11 (3*) N Bentley, *chsd ldg trio till fdd und pres frm 4 out...........*(66 to 1 op 50 to 1) 11
TALOS (Ire) 5-11-0 S Turner, *chsd ldg grp, bustled alng whn f 4 out..............*(25 to 1 op 33 to 1) f
1406 MOYHILL (Ire) 4-10-7 (7*) D Fortt, *beh and drvn alng whn baulked by faller and uns rdr 4 out........*(100 to 1) ur
1675⁷ WALKING THE PLANK (bl) 4-10-9 (5*) E Husband, *beh and drvn alng whn brght dwn 4 out..* (20 to 1 op 16 to 1) bd
ZAFARRANCHO (Ire) 4-11-0 M Dwyer, *trkd ldrs till wknd and pld up bef 3 out...............*(20 to 1 op 16 to 1) pu
Dist: 4l, 6l, 2l, ½l, 4l, ¾l, 3½l, 1½l, 15l, dist. 4m 1.20s. a 20.20s (15 Ran).

SR: 36/32/21/24/30/19/25/14/12/ (Cumbrian Industrials Ltd), M H Easterby

1873 Boroughbridge Novices' Chase (5-y-o and up) £2,976 3m 110yds...... (1:30)

1615* ONE MAN (Ire) 5-11-7 N Doughty, *jmpd wl, confidently rdn, led appr 6th, quickened hfwy, smoothly.*
..................(2 to 1 on op 9 to 4 on) 1
1723* CLYDE RANGER 6-11-0 C Grant, *led till appr 6th, styd hndy, ev ch and rdn last 4, one pace.* (7 to 2 op 3 to 1) 2
1570² DEEP DECISION 7-11-8 M Dwyer, *chsd ldg pair thrght, drvn alng and some hdwy 4 out, nvr on terms.*
..................(11 to 2 op 5 to 1 tchd 5 to 1) 3
1477³ EDEN SUNSET 7-11-0 Mr Chris Wilson, *last and struggling aftr one circuit, no ch whn blun 4 out.*
..................(22 to 1 op 25 to 1 tchd 20 to 1) 4
Dist: 3½l, dist, 8l. 6m 47.20s. a 41.20s (4 Ran).
SR: 12/1/-/-/ (J Hales), G Richards

1874 St John Ambulance Handicap Hurdle (0-140 4-y-o and up) £2,560 2m.. (2:00)

1668* WESTHOLME (USA) [112] 5-10-0 L Wyer, *al hndy, rdn to draw level 3 out, styd on to ld r-in.*
..................(5 to 4 fav op 13 to 8 tchd 7 to 4 and 15 to 8) 1
1221² HOME COUNTIES (Ire) [121] (v) 4-10-6 (3*) D J Moffatt, *patiently rdn, improved appr 3 out, nosed ahead bef nxt, hdd r-in, ridden and found little.*
..................(7 to 1 op 6 to 1) 2
1753² ABBOT OF FURNESS [133] 8-11-7 N Doughty, *quickened to ld appr 4th, clr aftr nxt, hdd after 3 out, one pace.*
..................(13 to 2 op 6 to 1) 3
1256³ KIVETON TYCOON (Ire) [126] (bl) 4-11-0 M Dwyer, *settled gng wl, ev ch appr 3 out, rdn nxt, btn whn blun last.*
..................(4 to 1) 4
1676 FLASS VALE [112] 5-10-0 D Wilkinson, *led aftr second till appr 4th, feeling pace four out, sn btn.*
..................(66 to 1 op 50 to 1) 5
1122⁴ BO KNOWS BEST (Ire) [128] 4-11-2 P Niven, *trkd ldrs, rdn 4 out, sn lost tch.*..................(13 to 2 op 6 to 1) 6
1470* KANNDABIL [114] (bl) 6-10-2 C Grant, *last and struggling frm hfwy, sn lost tch.*..................(14 to 1) 7
1617⁴ PRECIOUS BOY [140] 7-12-0 Richard Guest, *slight ld till aftr second, settled wth chasing grp till wknd frm 3 out, f last.*..................(9 to 1 op 8 to 1 tchd 10 to 1) f
Dist: Nk, 6l, 7l, 12l, 5l, hd. 4m 0.20s. a 19.20s (8 Ran).
SR: 32/40/46/32/6/17/3/-/ (T H Bennett), M H Easterby

1875 Rowland Meyrick Handicap Chase (5-y-o and up) £13,630 3m 110yds.. (2:30)

1664⁶ GENERAL PERSHING [140] 7-10-13 N Doughty, *jmpd boldly, made all, jnd 3 out, kpt on strly to draw clr r-in.*
..................(3 to 1 op 7 to 2 tchd 4 to 1) 1
1572* MR BOSTON [135] 8-10-8 P Niven, *trkd wnr, rdn to draw level 3 out, outpcd frm last.*..........(9 to 4 fav op 6 to 4) 2
1664 ANOTHER CORAL [155] 10-12-0 W Marston, *mstks, in tch, reminders 6 out, lost touch frm nxt, tld off.*
..................(11 to 1 op 10 to 1) 3
1573* YOUNG BENZ [144] 9-11-3 L Wyer, *trkd ldrs, hit 4th and tenth, 3rd and chalg whn f four out.* (3 to 1 op 7 to 2) f
1670* CARBISDALE [134] 10-11-7 M Dwyer, *last but hndy whn pld up aftr 9th, dismounted.*
..................(100 to 30 op 7 to 1 tchd 9 to 1) pu
Dist: 5l, dist. 6m 40.50s. a 34.50s (5 Ran).
SR: 71/61/ (J E Potter), G Richards

1876 Supermaster Handicap Chase (5-y-o and up) £3,695 2½m 110yds..... (3:00)

1758³ UNCLE ERNIE [147] 8-12-0 M Dwyer, *patiently rdn, jmpd ahead 3 out, clr betw last 2, ridden out.*
..................(7 to 4 op 5 to 4) 1
1572 DEEP DAWN [120] 10-10-1* C Grant, *al hndy, lft in ld 6th till 3 out, rdn and one pace betw last 2.*
1618* LAST 'O' THE BUNCH [141] 9-11-8 N Doughty, *led till f 6th, broke shoulder, destroyed.*
..................(11 to 8 on op 11 to 10 on tchd Evens) f
Dist: 1½l. 5m 34.10s. a 37.60s (3 Ran).
SR: 1/-/-/ (J G FitzGerald), J G FitzGerald

1877 Boxing Day Novices' Handicap Hurdle (4-y-o and up) £2,022 2m...... (3:30)

1659² MEGA BLUE [90] 8-11-10 P Niven, *jmpd wl, made all, drw clr frm 2 out, easily.* (7 to 4 fav op 6 to 4 tchd 2 to 1) 1
1582⁹ BASILICUS (Fr) [88] 4-11-1 (7*) D Towler, *al hndy, drvn alng whn wnr quickened frm 3 out, styd on same pace.*
..................(11 to 2 op 5 to 1) 2
GYMCRAK DAWN [70] 8-10-4 P Harley, *wtd wth, took clr order appr 3 out, rdn and one pace frm nxt.*
..................(10 to 1 op 20 to 1) 3
1768 STRATHBOGIE MIST (Ire) [70] 5-10-1 (3*) D J Moffatt, *last and wl beh hfwy, styd on well frm 3 out, nrst finish.*
..................(16 to 1 op 20 to 1) 4

1480⁷ STRONG MEASURE (Ire) [84] 5-11-4 C Grant, *nvr far away, effrt and rdn alng appr 3 out, outpcd frm nxt.*
..................(6 to 1 op 5 to 1) 5
PESSOA [76] 6-10-3 (7*) R Wilkinson, *settled midfield, effrt 4 out, rdn nxt, fdd.*..................(16 to 1 tchd 20 to 1) 6
STEEL RIVER [66] 6-10-0 V Smith, *pressed ldrs till fdd und pres appr 3 out, tld off.*
..................(8 to 1 op 10 to 1 tchd 12 to 1) 7
1791² TAHITIAN [75] 4-10-9 M Dwyer, *trkd ldg trio, reminders 5th, wknd quickly and pld up bef 3 out.*
..................(5 to 2 op 2 to 1 tchd 11 to 4) pu
Dist: 8l, 1½l, 8l, 8l, 5l, 15l. 4m 3.40s. a 22.40s (8 Ran).
SR: 24/14/-/-/-/ (Tony Yates), Mrs V A Aconley

CHEPSTOW (heavy)
Tuesday December 28th
Going Correction: PLUS 2.12 sec. per fur. (races 1,3,-5,7), PLUS 2.37 (2,4,6)

1878 Levy Board Novices' Hurdle (4-y-o and up) £2,792 2½m 110yds....(12:20)

1236⁷ BAY MISCHIEF (Ire) 4-11-0 C Llewellyn, *not fluent early, pressed ldr till led 4th, shaken up 2 out, styd on wl.*
..................(9 to 4 fav op 2 to 1 tchd 5 to 2) 1
1648² KYTTON CASTLE 6-11-0 (3*) D Meredith, *rcd freely in tch, chsd wnr frm 4 out, rdn appr last, one pace.*
..................(5 to 1 tchd 6 to 1) 2
1539³ MAD THYME 6-11-0 M Perrett, *took str hold, steadied in rear, kpt on frm 2 out, not rch ldrs.*
..................(7 to 1 op 5 to 1 tchd 11 to 2) 3
1442⁵ BRANDON PRINCE (Ire) 5-11-0 J Frost, *chsd ldrs, rdn 3 out, sn one pace.*..................(4 to 1 op 5 to 1) 4
1548* SEE ENOUGH 5-11-0 B Powell, *beh, mstk 5th, steady hdwy to chase wnr appr 4 out, wknd frm 3 out.*
..................(10 to 1 op 8 to 1 tchd 12 to 1) 5
CHEMIN LE ROI 6-11-0 I Lawrence, *beh, hdwy 7th, ch 3 out, wknd 2 out.*..................(10 to 1 op 20 to 1) 6
THE QUAKER 7-10-9 D Bridgwater, *beh, some prog appr 4 out, wknd aftr 3 out.*..................(100 to 1 op 33 to 1) 7
LETS RUMBLE (Ire) 4-11-0 S Earle, *chsd ldrs till wknd aftr 4 out.*..................(25 to 1 op 14 to 1 tchd 33 to 1) 8
1536 OUR WIZZER (Ire) 4-11-0 S Hodgson, *in tch till wknd 4 out.*..................(66 to 1 op 50 to 1) 9
1648⁸ MARANO 5-11-0 M Bosley, *made most to 4th, wknd appr 10 out.*..................(66 to 1 op 50 to 1) 10
1768⁷ OUR ARNOLD 6-10-7 (7*) P Maddock, *took str hold, steadied in rear, some prog appr 4 out, wknd frm f nxt.*
..................(66 to 1 op 50 to 1) f
1620* ROCKY BAY 4-10-6 (7*) Mr J L Llewellyn, *chsd ldrs till jmpd slwly and wknd 7th, tld off whn pld up aftr 4 out.*
..................(25 to 1 op 20 to 1 tchd 33 to 1) pu
1528 RUSTIC FLIGHT 6-11-0 D Gallagher, *beh, mstk 4th, rdn 6th, tld off whn pld up bef four out.*
..................(66 to 1 op 33 to 1) pu
1536 SENIOR STEWARD 5-11-0 J Railton, *in tch, wknd quickly and pld up bef 4 out.*..................(20 to 1 op 10 to 1) pu
Dist: 3l, 15l, ½l, 12l, 2½l, 2l, 2l, dist. 5m 29.40s. a 48.40s (14 Ran).
SR: 37/37/19/18/6/3/ (J R Featherstone), N A Twiston-Davies

1879 Festive Spirit Novices' Chase (4-y-o and up) £3,098 3m........... (12:50)

1651² EARTH SUMMIT (bl) 5-11-9 C Llewellyn, *made all, clr 7th, blun 11th, hit 12th, came clear frm 4 out.*
..................(2 to 1 fav op 7 to 4 tchd 9 to 4) 1
1730 SUFFOLK ROAD 6-11-5 J Railton, *chsd wnr frm 7th, effrt 12th, wknd from 4 out, fnshd tired.* (14 to 1 op 16 to 1) 2
YOUNG BRAVE 7-11-5 S Earle, *beh till f 5th.*
..................(14 to 1 op 12 to 1 tchd 16 to 1) f
1527 SAM PEPPER 7-11-5 S Mackey, *chsd wnr to 7th, sn wknd, blun 11th and tld off, distant 3rd whn refused 2 out.*..................(66 to 1 op 50 to 1) ref
1467* EBONY GALE (bl) 7-11-10 I Lawrence, *in tch till rdn and lost pl aftr 6th, mstk tenth, tld off whn pld up bef 11th.*
..................(9 to 4 op 5 to 2) pu
1691² FIVELEIGH FIRST (Ire) 5-11-9 R Supple, *not fluent, beh, tld off whn pld up aftr 9th.*..................(9 to 4) pu
1696² HAND OUT 9-11-0 B Powell, *lost tch 7th, tld off whn pld up bef 12th.*..................(20 to 1 op 16 to 1) pu
Dist: 20l. 7m 0.00s. a 70.00s (7 Ran).
(Nigel Payne), N A Twiston-Davies

1880 Finale Junior Hurdle Grade 1 (3-y-o) £15,892 2m 110yds........... (1:20)

1647* MYSILV 10-9 A Maguire, *made all, came clr appr 2 out, cmftbly.*..........(10 to 1 fav op 5 to 4 tchd Evens) 1
1692⁴ BURNT IMP (USA) 11-0 J Callaghan, *in tch, hdwy to track ldrs 4 out, chasing wnr whn mstk 2 out, no imprsn.*
..................(14 to 1 op 12 to 1) 2
1767* KADASTROF 11-0 D Meredith, *chsd wnr frm 3rd to aftr 3 out, blun 2 out, btn whn hit last...* (6 to 1 op 7 to 1) 3
1692² NAWAR (Fr) 11-0 J Railton, *hdwy 4th, wknd four out.*
..................(11 to 2 tchd 6 to 1 and 5 to 1) 4

259

1647³ SPRING MARATHON (USA) 11-0 P Holley, *al in rear, struggling.....................................*(25 to 1 op 16 to 1)   5
1767² GIORDANO (Ire) (bl) 11-0 Gary Lyons, *chsd ldrs to 4th,
wknd quickly, tld off whn pld up bef 3 out.*
....(25 to 1 op 16 to 1)   pu
1692³ GRAND APPLAUSE (Ire) 11-0 D Gallagher, *beh, lost tch 4th,
tld off whn pld up bef 3 out.........*(8 to 1 tchd 10 to 1)   pu
    JUST YOU DARE (Ire) 11-0 R Dunwoody, *chsd wnr 1st to
3rd, wknd aftr 4 out, tld off whn pld up bef 3 out.*
....(10 to 1 tchd 9 to 1)   pu
1767 SOLO CHARTER 11-0 S Earle, *tld off second, pld up bef 4
out..*(100 to 1 op 66 to 1)   pu
1751* HEATHYARDS BOY 11-0 J Frost, *tld off 4th, pld up bef
four out..*(20 to 1)   pu
1692* ADMIRAL'S WELL (Ire) 11-0 D Bridgwater, *mstk second,
blun 3rd, pld up bef nxt.* (4 to 1 op 7 to 2 tchd 9 to 2)   pu
1305 DIDACTE (Fr) 11-0 R Bellamy, *tld off 4th, pld up bef four
out..*(100 to 1)   pu
Dist: 8l, 12l, 1l, 4l. 4m 25.40s. a 39.40s (12 Ran).
SR: 37/34/22/21/17/-/   (Million In Mind Partnership (3)), D Nicholson

1881
**Coral Welsh National Handicap Chase
Grade 3 (5-y-o and up) £24,492 3m 5f
110yds........................... (1:55)**

1545² RIVERSIDE BOY [137] 10-10-0 R Dunwoody, *made all,
steadied pace aftr 15th, came clr ag'n frm 4 out,
readily.............*(6 to 4 fav op 7 to 4 tchd 15 to 8)   1
1545⁴ FIDDLERS PIKE [137] 12-10-0 Mrs R Henderson, *chsd wnr
till aftr tenth, mstk and lost pos 15th, rallied 16th,
chased winner frm imprsn frm 3 out.*
....(20 to 1 tchd 25 to 1)   2
1436⁶ COOL GROUND [150] 11-10-13 P Holley, *prmnt, chsd wnr
aftr tenth, rdn 16th, wknd 3 out, wl btn whn hit last.*
....(9 to 4 tchd 5 to 2)   3
1543⁴ WILLSFORD [137] (bl) 10-10-0 D Bridgwater, *rdn to stay in
tch appr tenth, chsd ldrs 11th, lost pl 15th, rallied
approaching 16th, wknd 4 out.*
....(7 to 1 op 8 to 1 tchd 9 to 1)   4
1600² RUFUS [137] (v) 7-10-0 B Powell, *lost tch 13th, blun 14th
(water), rallied appr 16th, sn wknd.*
....(25 to 1 op 50 to 1 tchd 66 to 1)   5
1439⁶ MERRY MASTER [137] 9-10-0 Gee Armytage, *beh, mstk
6th, hit 9th, rdn alng aftr tenth, f 11th.*
....(9 to 1 op 8 to 1 tchd 10 to 1)   f
1652⁶ INDIAN TONIC [137] 7-10-0 C Maude, *stumbled, slpd and
uns rdr bend aftr strt..........*(9 to 2 op 4 to 1)   ur
1224⁷ SIBTON ABBEY [157] 8-11-6 S Smith Eccles, *beh, tld off
whn pld up bef 11th..........*(10 to 1 op 9 to 1)   pu
Dist: 20l, 8l, 5l, ½l. 8m 44.90s. a 78.90s (8 Ran).
    (Bisgrove Partnership), M C Pipe

1882
**Sport Of Kings Hurdle (4-y-o and up)
£6,742 2m 110yds............... (2:25)**

1536³ OLD BRIDGE (Ire) 5-10-9 S McNeill, *rcd in 3rd till hdwy to
chase ldr 4 out, led appr 3 out, rdn approaching last,
jst hld on.......................................*(7 to 1 op 8 to 2 to 4)   1
1559⁴ MAAMUR (USA) 5-10-9 R Dunwoody, *led, rdn appr 4 out,
hdd approaching 3 out, rallied und pres to chal last,
hrd drvn r-in, jst fld..........*(5 to 4 on op 5 to 2 on)   2
1502⁹ DARINGLY 4-10-9 R Bellamy, *rcd in last pl till styd on to
take poor 3rd frm 4 out.*
....(13 to 1 op 20 to 1 tchd 25 to 1 and 12 to 1)   3
1622⁵ FIRST CENTURY (Ire) 4-10-9 Mr J L Llewellyn, *chsd ldr till
chlgd 3rd to 4th, rdn and wknd appr four out.*
....(13 to 1 op 20 to 1 tchd 25 to 1 and 12 to 1)   4
Dist: Sht-hd, 30l, 12l. 4m 30.00s. a 44.00s (4 Ran).
    (K C B Mackenzie), Andrew Turnell

1883
**Christmas Cracker Handicap Chase
(0-140 5-y-o and up) £2,765 2m 3f
110yds........................... (3:00)**

1625² CAMELOT KNIGHT [114] (bl) 7-10-9 C Llewellyn, *led second
to 4th, hit 7th, chsd ldr appr 11th, styd on to ld 2 out,
wnt lft last, all out........................*(11 to 8 jt-
    fav op Evens tchd 6 to 4)   1
1720 RAFIKI [108] 8-10-3³ S Burrough, *led second to 4th, led
6th, rdn 11th, hdd 2 out, rallied and ev ch last, kpt on.*
....(9 to 1 op 6 to 1 tchd 10 to 1)   2
1638* WIDE BOY [129] 11-11-10 A Maguire, *led to second, led 4th
to 6th, mstk 9th (water), wknd four out, no ch whn
mistake 2 out.....................*(11 to 8 jt-fav op 6 to 4)   3
1649⁴ WHATEVER YOU LIKE [119] 9-11-0 R Dunwoody, *al in 4th
till lost tch tenth and reminders, tld off whn pld up bef
four out..*(9 to 2 op 5 to 1 tchd 6 to 1)   pu
Dist: 1½l, dist. 5m 38.30s. a 51.30s (4 Ran).
SR: 30/22/-/-/   (Michael Gates), N A Twiston-Davies

1884
**Yuletide Conditional Jockeys' Hand-
icap Hurdle (0-120 4-y-o and up)
£1,975 2½m 110yds.......... (3:30)**

1721⁴ SYLVIA BEACH [92] 7-10-0 D Matthews, *in tch, hdwy 6th,
led 4 out, ran on wl frm 2 out......*(12 to 1 op 10 to 1)   1

1544³ GRENAGH [118] 12-11-12 W Marston, *al prmnt, rdn and
kpt on frm 2 out, styd on r-in, not rch wnr.*
....(4 to 1 op 7 to 2 tchd 9 to 2)   2
1462² HEATHFIELD GALE [107] 6-10-11 (4*) T Dascombe, *beh,
steady hdwy 7th, chsd ldrs 4 out, outpcd frm nxt.*
....(13 to 8 fav op 5 to 4 tchd 7 to 4)   3
    CHIAROSCURO [92] 7-9-10 (4*) N Parker, *al in tch, chlgd 4
out, rdn 3 out, sn wknd............*(11 to 1 op 8 to 1)   4
1697⁴ DECIDED (Can) [99] 10-10-3 (4*) P McLoughlin, *sn in tch,
rdn and wknd aftr 4 out.........*(16 to 1 op 14 to 1)   5
1198 SAILOR BLUE [98] (bl) 6-10-6 P Hide, *led second to 4 out,
sn wknd...............................*(7 to 6 to 1 tchd 8 to 1)   6
1216⁸ NOTARY-NOWELL [110] 7-11-0 (4*) P Murphy, *led to second, wknd 5th, sn tld off.......*(20 to 1 op 14 to 1)   7
    SURCOAT [95] 6-10-3 R Farrant, *in tch, pressed ldrs 4 out,
chsd wnr frm 3 out, second and hld whn f last.*
....(11 to 1 op 8 to 1 tchd 12 to 1)   f
    LEAVENWORTH [114] 9-11-1 (7*) J Fordham, *al beh, no ch
whn mstk and uns rdr 3 out........*(16 to 1 op 14 to 1)   ur
1643⁶ GROTIUS [92] (bl) 9-10-0 R Davis, *prmnt, rdn 5th, tld off
whn pld up bef 3 out.............*(25 to 1 op 14 to 1)   pu
    NOBLE EYRE [92] 12-9-7 (7*) A Dowling, *tld off 5th, pld up
bef 2 out...*(33 to 1)   pu
1711⁴ PRIZE MATCH [92] 4-9-8¹ (7*) W Currie, *prmnt, chlgd 6th to
7th, wknd quickly appr 4 out, pld up bef nxt.*
....(5 to 1 tchd 7 to 1)   pu
Dist: 3l, 15l, 12l, 12l, 20l, dist. 5m 29.60s. a 48.60s (12 Ran).
SR: 21/44/18/-/-/-/   (Geoffrey C Greenwood), P G Murphy

KEMPTON (good to soft)
Tuesday December 28th
**Going Correction: PLUS 1.05 sec. per fur. (races
1,4,6), PLUS 1.13 (2,3,5)**

1885
**Bonusprint Juvenile Novices' Hurdle
(3-y-o) £3,752 2m 5f........... (12:45)**

1541² WINGS COVE 11-0 E Murphy, *made all, styd on gmely
whn chlgd last...* (13 to 8 jt-fav op 6 to 4 tchd 7 to 4)   1
1692⁷ KARAR (Ire) 10-9 N Williamson, *hld up in rear, gd hdwy
7th, wnt second appr 2 out, chlgd last, kpt on gmely.*
....(12 to 1 tchd 14 to 1)   2
1710² CHIEF'S SONG 10-9 H Davies, *al prmnt, tchd wnr frm
6th, wknd appr 2 out...................*(13 to 8 jt-
    fav op 11 to 8 tchd 7 to 4)   3
1464* RICH LIFE (Ire) 11-0 Peter Hobbs, *hld up in rear, hdwy frm
6th, ev ch 3 out, sn wknd bef nxt.......*(6 to 1 tchd 7 to 1)   4
1261⁵ ANILAFFED 10-9 Richard Guest, *mstks in rear, styd on
one pace frm 3 out..............*(100 to 1 op 33 to 1)   5
2967 ROWLANDSONS GOLD (Ire) 10-4 Lorna Vincent, *al in rear.*
....(100 to 1 op 50 to 1)   6
1706 RUNAWAY PETE (USA) 10-9 J Osborne, *in rear, hdwy to
go 3rd 7th, wknd nxt................*(16 to 1 op 12 to 1)   7
1125⁸ WONDERFUL YEARS (USA) 10-6 (3*) A Thornton, *prmnt till
wknd appr 7th, tld off............*(66 to 1 op 50 to 1)   8
1248⁸ JACKSONS BAY 10-9 T Grantham, *trkd wnr to 6th, sn
wknd, pld up bef 2 out............*(20 to 1 op 14 to 1)   pu
Dist: Nk, 25l, 15l, 5l, ½l, 10l, dist. 5m 26.40s. a 33.40s (9 Ran).
    (Edwin N Cohen), Lady Herries

1886
**Bonusfilm Novices' Chase (5-y-o and
up) £8,052 2m.................(1:15)**

1803* SAN LORENZO (USA) 5-11-0 N Williamson, *made all, jmpd
wl, drw clr 3 out, eased to walk r-in.*
....(3 to 1 op 11 to 4 tchd 100 to 30)   1
1771* THUMBS UP 7-11-0 M A FitzGerald, *rcd in 3rd pl, mstk
6th, hit 9th, wnt second appr 3 out, rdn and sn btn.*
....(5 to 4 fav tchd 11 to 8)   2
1696 FANTASY WORLD 7-10-9 D Murphy, *trkd wnr till appr 3
out, one pace aftr...*(20 to 1 op 16 to 1 tchd 25 to 1)   3
1558² ONE MORE DREAM 6-11-0 Richard Guest, *last whn blun
second, pld up bef 5th.........*(2 to 1 op 13 to 8)   pu
Dist: 2½l, ¾l. 4m 9.50s. a 22.50s (4 Ran).
SR: 41/38/32/-/   (James D Greig), K C Bailey

1887
**Tripleprint Handicap Chase (5-y-o and
up) £13,680 2½m 110yds.......(1:45)**

1689* RICHVILLE [125] 7-11-0 N Williamson, *hld up, al gng wl,
hdwy frm tenth, cl second whn lft clr 3 out.*
....(2 to 1 fav op 5 to 2 tchd 11 to 4)   1
1641* SMARTIE EXPRESS [124] 11-10-13 M A FitzGerald, *mid-
div, outpcd 11th, styd on to go second appr 2 out, no ch
wth wnr...............................*(9 to 1 op 5 to 2 tchd 11 to 2)   2
1538³ BUCK WILLOW [119] 9-10-8 D Murphy, *mstk second, in
rear till gd hdwy frm 7th, ev ch till wknd appr 3 out.*
....(5 to 1 op 4 to 1 tchd 11 to 2)   3
1641³ MONTALINO [114] 10-10-3³ Peter Hobbs, *wl in rear, styd
on frm 3 out, nvr nrr.* (50 to 1 op 33 to 1 tchd 66 to 1)   4
    LAUNDRYMAN [116] 10-10-5¹ Richard Guest, *jmpd wl, led
appr 5th, wknd and hdd 4 out, sn btn.*
....(11 to 4 op 9 to 2 to 20 to 1)   5
1573² ANTONIN (Fr) [135] 5-11-5 (5*) J Burke, *trkd ldr, wnt second 7th, mstk 12th, led 4 out, narrow ld whn stumbled
and uns rdr nxt....................*(11 to 2 op 9 to 2)   ur

260

MIGHTY FALCON [119] 8-10-8 M Richards, *al beh, lost tch
tenth, tld off whn pld up bef 3 out.*
.................................(20 to 1 op 16 to 1 tchd 25 to 1) pu
1538² ARDBRIN [128] 10-11-3 J Osborne, *led till hdd appr 5th,
sn beh, tld off whn pld up bef 3 out.*
.................................(5 to 1 op 9 to 2 tchd 11 to 2) pu
Dist: 10l, 12l, 1½l, 8l. 5m 23.70s. a 30.70s (8 Ran).
SR: 11/-/-/-/-/ (Major-Gen R L T Burges), K C Bailey

1888 Bonusprint Christmas Hurdle Grade 1 (4-y-o and up) £33,960 2m...... (2:20)

1663³ MUSE 6-11-7 M Richards, *made all, ran on strly to go clr
appr last.*.....................(3 to 1 op 7 to 2 tchd 4 to 1) 1
1559³ HIGH BARON 6-11-7 M Hourigan, *trkd wnr, ev ch 2 out,
rdn and kpt on gmely r-in.......*(33 to 1 tchd 50 to 1) 2
1755* ABSALOM'S LADY 5-11-2 D Murphy, *hld up in tch, cld on
ldrs 3 out, hrd rdn and kpt on one pace frm nxt.*
.................................(4 to 1 op 5 to 1) 3
1663² HALKOPOUS 7-11-7 G McCourt, *trkd ldrs, mstk and lost
pl 3 out, rdn and sn rallied, no imprsn r-in.*
.................................(7 to 4 fav op 6 to 4 tchd 15 to 8) 4
1663 KING CREDO 8-11-7 J Osborne, *hld up in rear, not al
fluent, pushed alng 3 out, no hdwy and eased whn btn
appr last, virtually pld up r-in.*
.................................(11 to 4 op 2 to 1 tchd 3 to 1) 5
Dist: 5l, ¾l, ¾l, dist. 3m 58.10s. a 18.10s (5 Ran).
SR: 80/75/69/73/-/ (White Horse Racing Ltd), D R C Elsworth

1889 Bonusprint Handicap Chase (0-145 5-y-o and up) £5,905 3m....... (2:50)

1757³ FIGHTING WORDS [133] 7-11-13 D Murphy, *trkd ldr frm
5th, took narrow ld 14th, tired whn steadied last,
nudged out r-in.*................(5 to 1 op 4 to 1) 1
1670² DUBLIN FLYER [125] 7-11-5 G McCourt, *led second to 14th,
ev ch 3 out, swtchd lft appr nxt, no imprsn r-in, fnshd
tired.*...........................(7 to 4 fav op 2 to 1) 2
1664⁴ STUNNING STUFF [124] 8-11-4 N Williamson, *hld up in
rear, hit 9th, hdwy 11th, cld on ldrs 4 out, no extr frm
nxt.*.............................(4 to 1 op 3 to 1 tchd 9 to 2) 3
1340⁴ LE PICCOLAGE [129] 9-11-9 M A FitzGerald, *led to second,
trkd ldr till hit 5th, losing tch whn pmpd slwly 13th, tld
off when f 4 out.*..................(7 to 2 op 4 to 1) f
1720⁵ TERMINATOR STAR [107] 8-10-1 M Hourigan, *hld up in rear,
not jump ul aftr mstk 3rd, tld off tenth, pld up bef 12th.*
.................................(9 to 1 op 6 to 1 tchd 10 to 1) pu
Dist: 3½l, 4l. 6m 20.00s. a 31.00s (5 Ran).
SR: 60/48/43/-/-/ (Pell-Mell Partners), J T Gifford

1890 Bonusphoto Handicap Hurdle (4-y-o and up) £4,425 2m 5f.......... (3:20)

1667³ JEASSU [132] 10-11-5 B Clifford, *hld up in rear, rcd on
outsd, hmpd 6th, sn made hdwy, led 2 out, pushed out
r-in.*............................(4 to 1 op 7 to 2 tchd 9 to 2) 1
961³ LUSTY LAD [117] 8-10-4⁴ H Davies, *led till hdd 2 out,
rallied r-in, styd on.* (20 to 1 op 14 to 1 tchd 25 to 1) 2
1465² CHANGE THE ACT [137] 8-11-10 J Osborne, *al prmnt, trkd
ldr frm 6th, one pace from 2 out.* (100 to 30 op 11 to 4) 3
1703³ BALLY CLOVER [124] 6-10-11 M A FitzGerald, *trkd ldr to
6th, styd in cl tch till rdn appr 2 out, one pace.*
.................................(3 to 1 jt-fav op 11 to 4 tchd 100 to 30) 4
1462 TILT TECH FLYER [113] 8-10-0 N Williamson, *hld up in
rear, hdwy 3 out, rdn and wknd nxt.*
.................................(14 to 1 op 12 to 1) 5
1759* BELLEZZA [123] 6-10-3 (7*) Mr T McCarthy, *hld up in tch,
rdn 3 out, btn whn f last.*...........(3 to 1 jt-
fav op 11 to 4 tchd 100 to 30) f
COWORTH PARK [118] 8-10-2 D Murphy, *rcd in tch on
outsd, hit 6th, pld up, broke leg, destroyed.*
.................................(10 to 1 op 16 to 1) pu
Dist: 2½l, 10l, 1½l, nk. 5m 31.00s. a 38.00s (7 Ran).
(Mrs R H Y Mills), A J Wilson

LEOPARDSTOWN (IRE) (soft) Tuesday December 28th
Going Correction: PLUS 0.60 sec. per fur. (races 1,2,-4,6,7), PLUS 1.70 (3,5)

1891 Christmas Hurdle (4-y-o and up) £4,200 2¾m................. (12:25)

1576² WHAT A QUESTION (Ire) 5-10-12 G Bradley, ...(6 to 1) 1
583 DEE ELL 7-11-10 T J Taaffe,....................(8 to 1) 2
1783⁴ FINAL ISSUE 6-10-9 (5*) H Taylor,..............(25 to 1) 3
1756 SHUIL AR AGHAIDH 7-11-5 C F Swan, ...(11 to 8 on) f
MUIR STATION (USA) (bl) 5-11-3 K F O'Brien,......(5 to 1) bd
Dist: 9l, dist. 5m 58.70s. a 46.70s (5 Ran).
(Mrs Miles Valentine), M F Morris

1892 Tote Investment (Ireland) Ltd Killiney Maiden Hurdle (5-y-o and up) £4,140 2 ½m...................... (12:55)

1576⁶ MICK O'DWYER 6-12-0 F J Flood, ...(6 to 4 fav) 1

43³ DADDY LONG LEGGS 6-11-6 K F O'Brien, ...(10 to 1) 2
1760⁷ I AM 5-12-0 T Horgan,.......................(5 to 1) 3
1687³ CALMOS 6-11-6 C F Swan,....................(7 to 1) 4
1113² THE DASHER DOYLE (Ire) 5-11-6 Mr P J Healy, ...(13 to 2) 5
675⁴ CUCHULLAINS GOLD (Ire) 5-11-6 C O'Dwyer, ...(16 to 1) 6
1549 MOLLIE WOOTTON (Ire) 5-11-1 W T Slattery Jnr, ..(33 to 1) 7
ROYAL SEER 7-11-6 T J Taaffe,................(7 to 1) 8
ST CRISTOPH 6-11-9 Mr W P Mullins, ...(5 to 1) 9
1549 RATHFARDON (Ire) 5-11-6 A Powell,............(33 to 1) 10
I DON'T KNOW 9-11-6 G Bradley,..............(12 to 1) pu
Dist: 1½l, 6l, 1½l, dist. 5m 26.80s. a 41.80s (11 Ran).
(Mrs P J Whelan), F Flood

1893 William Neville & Sons Chase (5-y-o and up) £6,900 2¾m........... (1:30)

1266* BELVEDERIAN 6-11-11 G Bradley,............(7 to 4 on) 1
1451* SPUR OF THE MOMENT 6-11-3 J P Banahan, ...(12 to 1) 2
1785* GYPSY LASS 6-11-3 T Horgan,...............(6 to 1) 3
1825 NUAFFE 8-11-11 S H O'Donovan,..............(9 to 2) 4
1399⁴ FEATHERED GALE 6-11-4 T J Taaffe,...........(8 to 1) ur
Dist: 25l, 3½l, 7l. 6m 17.60s. a 47.60s (5 Ran).
(A J O'Reilly), M F Morris

1894 R.T.E. Handicap Hurdle (4-y-o and up) £6,900 2m.................... (2:00)

1400* JUPITER JIMMY [-] 4-9-7 C F Swan, ...(5 to 2 fav) 1
1400⁴ THATCH AND GOLD (Ire) [-] 5-9-13 F Woods, ...(10 to 1) 2
1579² ATONE [-] 6-11-5 K F O'Brien,................(9 to 2) 3
533* LIFE SAVER (Ire) [-] 4-10-11 P Carberry, ...(4 to 1) 4
533⁴ JUDICIAL FIELD (Ire) [-] 4-10-10 B Sheridan, ...(7 to 1) 5
1780³ MONKEY AGO [-] 6-9-12 (3*) T Treacy,.........(10 to 1) 6
1780⁵ PLUMBOB (Ire) [-] 4-9-2 (5*) M G Cleary, ...(14 to 1) 7
1765³ KEPPOLS PRINCE [-] 6-9-12 H Rogers, ...(14 to 1) 8
1495⁹ FOGELBERG (USA) [-] 5-9-13 (3*) T J Mitchell, ...(33 to 1) 9
1757 PARTNERS IN CRIME [-] 5-9-2 (7*) B Bowens, ...(50 to 1) 10
1765* DEEP INAGH (USA) [-] 10-10-2 C O'Dwyer,.......(7 to 1) 11
MASTER SWORDSMAN (USA) [-] 10-10-2 C O'Dwyer,
.................................(20 to 1) 12
Dist: 5l, ½l, 3l, 11l. 3m 59.60s. a 11.60s (12 Ran).
SR: 45/46/65/54/42/-/ (James F Murphy), J E Kiely

1895 Ericsson Chase (Listed Race - Grade I) (5-y-o and up) £29,750 3m..... (2:35)

1452 DEEP BRAMBLE 6-11-11 P Niven, *trkd ldr, dsptd ld 11th,
hdd 2 out, rdn, rallied to lead ag'n r-in.*.......(9 to 1) 1
1652* FLASHING STEEL 8-11-11 K F O'Brien, *mid-div, prog 3
out, rdn appr last, kpt on strly und pres r-in, jst fld.*
.................................(11 to 4 jt-fav) 2
1578 FORCE SEVEN 6-11-6 T Horgan, *hld up, gd prog 4 out,
dsptd ld aftr nxt, led 2 out, hdd r-in, kpt on....*(9 to 1) 3
1578² GENERAL IDEA 8-12-0 B Sheridan, *hld up, prog 4 out, rdn
aftr 2 out, no extr after last....*..............(5 to 1) 4
1763² ITS A CRACKER 9-11-11 Mr J A Berry, *wl plcd, rdn 3 out,
wknd aftr nxt...*.....................(33 to 1) 5
1578* CAHERVILLAHOW 9-12-0 G Bradley, *led, jmd 11th, hdd
aftr 3 out, headed appr 2 out, btn whn mstk last.*
.................................(11 to 4 jt-fav) 6
1226 BISHOPS HALL 7-12-0 C O'Dwyer, *al rear, rdn 4 out,
wknd aftr nxt.....*....................(16 to 1) 7
1578 GOLD OPTIONS (bl) 11-12-0 M Dwyer, *wl plcd, rdn and
lost pl 4 out, wknd aftr nxt, virtually pld up r-in.*
.................................(12 to 1) 8
1578 GARAMYCIN 11-12-0 C F Swan, *mid-div, mstk and lost pl
4 out, wknd aftr nxt, pld up bef last......*....(14 to 1) pu
Dist: Hd, nk, 6l, 20l. 6m 55.10s. a 43.10s (9 Ran).
SR: 75/75/69/71/48/-/ (J F Mernagh), Michael Hourigan

1896 Orchard Inns Rathfarnham and Stillorgan Hurdle (4-y-o and up) £4,140 2 ½m..................... (3:10)

TIANANMEN SQUARE (Ire) 5-11-10 C F Swan, (2 to 1 on) 1
798² DORANS PRIDE (Ire) 4-11-12 K F O'Brien, ...(8 to 1) 2
1683² LAW BRIDGE (bl) 6-11-2 (5*) K L O'Brien, ...(3 to 1) 3
1818⁹ HEAD OF CHAMBERS (Ire) 5-11-3 (7*) D J Kavanagh,
.................................(14 to 1) 4
1783² REGLAWELLA 6-10-13 (3*) T P Treacy,............(4 to 1) ur
Dist: 1l, dist, 10l. 5m 18.30s. a 33.30s (5 Ran).
(Mrs J Magnier), Noel Meade

1897 P.B. Bumper INH Flat Race (5-y-o and up) £8,280 2½m............ (3:40)

1681 UNA'S CHOICE (Ire) 5-11-2 (5*) Mr H F Cleary, ...(7 to 1) 1
1786³ ARCHER (Ire) 5-11-7 Mr J A Nash, ...(6 to 1) 2
1687* YOUR THE MAN 7-11-7 (7*) Mr M Brennan, ...(7 to 2) 3
1401⁸ IAMWHATIAM 7-11-7 Mr P Fenton,............(12 to 1) 4
1829⁸ CLOSUTTON EXPRESS 7-12-0 Mr W P Mullins, ...(14 to 1) 5
1576 TWIN RAINBOW 6-11-7 (5*) Mr A Kinane, ..(9 to 4 fav) 6
1236 FAITHFULL FELLOW 6-11-7 Mr A J Martin, ...(6 to 1) 7
1555 DIOCESE (Ire) 5-11-4 (3*) Mr A R Coonan, ...(33 to 1) 8
1766⁴ ACKLE BACKLE 6-11-9 Mr T Mullins,............(11 to 2) 9
1555⁷ M T POCKETS (Ire) 5-11-4 (3*) Mrs J M Mullins, .(10 to 1) 10
1496⁹ MOONCAPER 7-12-0 Mr A P O'Brien,...........(10 to 1) 11
1814 BORO DOLLAR 9-11-7 (7*) Mr R P Cody, ...(25 to 1) 12

NATIONAL HUNT RESULTS 1993-94

PRINCE THEO 6-11-0 (7*) Mr D Carey, ... (33 to 1)   13
Dist: 13l, ¾l, 7l, 9l. 5m 15.10s. (13 Ran).

(Fish & Poultry Portions Ltd), F Flood

LIMERICK (IRE) (heavy)
Tuesday December 28th

1898 I.N.H. Stallion Owners Novice Hurdle (5-y-o and up) £3,450 2m 5f. . . . . (1:20)

1401⁴	FAMBO LAD (Ire) 5-11-6 D H O'Connor, ... (7 to 4 fav)	1
1681⁵	BEAT THE SECOND (Ire) 5-11-6 G M O'Neill, ... (9 to 4)	2
1496	MISGIVINGS (Ire) 5-10-8 (7*) J M Donnelly, ... (20 to 1)	3
1401	COUNTERBALANCE 6-11-1 L P Cusack, ... (10 to 1)	4
1859³	ANMACA (Ire) 5-11-4 (5*) J R Barry, ... (5 to 1)	5
1332	BALLINGOWAN STAR 6-10-8 (7*) Mr S O'Donnell, (10 to 1)	6
	TRINITY GALE (Ire) 5-10-12 (3*) D P Murphy, . . . (14 to 1)	7
1608	FAIR ADELINE 6-11-1 P M Verling, ... (20 to 1)	8
1760	PARKBOY LASS 6-11-9 R Hughes, ... (14 to 1)	9
1330	THE REAL GAEL (Ire) 5-10-10 (5*) C P Dunne, . . . (20 to 1)	10
1330	DUNHILL IDOL 6-11-6 J F Titley, ... (20 to 1)	11
	APPROACH THE WEST 7-11-3 (3*) C O'Brien, . . . (10 to 1)	12
	MONEY SAVED 9-10-13 (7*) Mr W J Gleeson, . . . (16 to 1)	13
857	SARAKIN (Ire) 5-10-8 (7*) J P Broderick, ... (20 to 1)	14
1403⁹	SOUTH WESTERLY (Ire) 5-11-6 M Duffy, ... (8 to 1)	f

Dist: 3l, 4½l, 3½l, 15l. 6m 1.90s. (15 Ran).

(J A Berry), J A Berry

1899 MacDonagh Boland Cullen Duggan Handicap Hurdle (4-y-o and up) £3,450 2½m . . . . (1:50)

1401⁵	LUMINOUS LIGHT [-] 6-9-0 (7*) M D Murphy, ... (8 to 1)	1
1576⁷	EAGLE ROCK (USA) [-] 6-11-3 C O'Brien, ... (5 to 1)	2
	IM MELODY (Ire) [-] 5-9-13 (7*) J P Broderick, . . . (5 to 2 fav)	3
410⁴	AEGEAN FANFARE (Ire) [-] 4-10-9 R Hughes, ... (9 to 1)	4
1580⁴	TUG OF PEACE [-] 6-11-5 J F Titley, ... (11 to 2)	5
1609²	SO PINK (Ire) [-] 5-10-8 P L Malone, ... (9 to 2)	6
1855⁷	MARIAN YEAR [-] 7-10-5 J Collins, ... (12 to 1)	7
1495	MRS BARTON (Ire) [-] 5-9-11 M Duffy, ... (3 to 1)	8

Dist: 15l, 2l, 1½l, 12l. 5m 41.50s. (8 Ran).

(B A Gaynor), Michael O'Connor

1900 Lucey Feeds Group Novice Chase (4-y-o and up) £3,450 2½m . . . . (2:20)

1399	BUCKS-CHOICE 6-12-0 J F Titley, ... (5 to 4 fav)	1
1684³	ALL THE ACES 6-12-0 L P Cusack, ... (7 to 4)	2
1609⁵	DOONEGA (Ire) 5-11-9 (3*) C O'Brien, ... (9 to 2)	3
1612⁵	DANNIGALE 7-12-0 M A Phillips, ... (14 to 1)	4
1612	MINSTREL SAM 7-12-0 A J O'Brien, ... (14 to 1)	5
411	MOBILE MAN 6-12-0 M Flynn, ... (7 to 1)	6
1497⁷	THE COOPER (bl) 6-12-0 J Jones, ... (33 to 1)	7
1498	MAMMY'S FRIEND 9-11-6 (3*) D P Murphy, ... (14 to 1)	f
1399	MR BARNEY 6-12-0 J K Kinane, ... (20 to 1)	f

Dist: Sht-hd, 9l, 15l, dist. 5m 34.60s. (9 Ran).

(Hudson Valley Equine Inc), P Mullins

1901 McMahon Group (F. Spaight & Sons Ltd) Handicap Chase (5-y-o and up) £3,450 3m. (2:50)

1826⁷	SPEAKING OUT (USA) [-] 5-10-1 D H O'Connor, . . (8 to 1)	1
1784	CALLMECHA [-] (bl) 8-10-8 G M O'Neill, ... (7 to 1)	2
1826	GERTIES PRIDE [-] 9-9-4 (3*) C O'Brien, ... (9 to 2)	3
	CONNA RAMBLER [-] 10-9-4³ (5*) P A Roche, ... (6 to 1)	4
1578⁵	NORTON VILLE [-] 7-11-8 M Flynn, ... (6 to 4 fav)	5
1784	LANIGANS WINE [-] 11-9-13 (7*) J P Broderick, . . . (7 to 1)	6
1499	PROPUNT [-] 8-10-8 J F Titley, ... (7 to 2)	7

Dist: 2½l, 20l, 7l, dist. 6m 38.60s. (7 Ran).

(E O'Dwyer), James Joseph O'Connor

1902 Woodlands House Mares INH Flat Race (6-y-o and up) £3,450 2½m (3:20)

1453⁸	FRIGID COUNTESS 6-11-7 (7*) Mrs K Walsh, ... (8 to 1)	1
1760	BETTY BALFOUR 7-11-7 (7*) Miss F M Crowley, . . (14 to 1)	2
1113⁸	DOWN THE BACK 6-11-11 (3*) Miss M Olivefalk, . . (8 to 1)	3
	LISALEAN RIVER 6-11-11 (3*) Mrs M Mullins, . . (7 to 4 fav)	4
1549	SLEMISH MIST 6-11-7 (7*) Miss A Sloane, ... (20 to 1)	5
	ARDCARN GIRL 6-11-11 (3*) Miss C Hutchinson, . . (2 to 1)	6
1580	COOL CARLING 6-11-11 (3*) Mrs S McCarthy, . . (16 to 1)	7
	ATH DARA 6-11-7 (7*) Mrs S Bolger, ... (12 to 1)	8
857	FIALADY 8-11-7 (7*) Miss A Dawson, ... (20 to 1)	9
30	THE PLEDGER 6-11-7 (7*) Miss L Gough, ... (20 to 1)	10
490³	ALLOON BAWN 7-11-7 (7*) Miss C Rogers, ... (8 to 1)	11
229⁶	MILLER'S CROSSING 6-11-7 (7*) Mrs C Doyle, . . . (6 to 1)	12
	ON DRAUGHT 6-11-7 (7*) Miss S Kauntze, ... (12 to 1)	pu

Dist: 2½l, 3l, 4l, 4l. 5m 46.80s. (13 Ran).

(W Dooly), W Dooly

1903 Pegus Gold INH Flat Race (4-y-o) £3,450 2m. (3:50)

1500*	ARIES GIRL 11-4 (7*) Mr E Norris, ... (6 to 4 on)	1
	REDEEMYOURSELF (Ire) 11-6 Mr M Phillips, ... (16 to 1)	2

1076⁷ KILADANTE (Ire) 11-4 (7*) Mr G F Ryan, ... (7 to 2)   3
1500² BUTCHES BOY (Ire) 11-6 (7*) Mr M P Dunne, ... (9 to 4)   4
Dist: ½l, 1½l, 1½l. 4m 34.90s. (4 Ran).

(W E Sturt), P J Flynn

LEOPARDSTOWN (IRE) (soft (races 1,2), heavy (3,4,5,6,7))
Wednesday December 29th
Going Correction: PLUS 1.25 sec. per fur. (races 1,3,- 4,5,7), PLUS 1.05 (2,6)

1904 David Power Maiden Hurdle (5-y-o and up) £4,140 2m. . . . . (12:40)

1781²	LEGAL PROFESSION (Ire) 5-11-9 (5*) K L O'Brien, . . (2 to 1)	1
1555*	DOONANDORAS (Ire) 5-12-0 C F Swan, ... (6 to 4 on)	2
1760³	MINIGIRLS NIECE (Ire) 5-11-1 A Powell, ... (10 to 1)	3
1760⁵	FINNEGANS WAKE 6-11-6 K P Gaule, ... (10 to 1)	4
939	VISTAGE (Ire) 5-12-0 B Sheridan, ... (12 to 1)	5
1549⁵	DEEP THYNE (Ire) 5-11-2 (7*) Mr R O'Donnell, . . (10 to 1)	6

Dist: Nk, 4l, 6l, 10l. 4m 23.00s. a 35.00s (6 Ran).

(Kevin Norton), M J P O'Brien

1905 Kevin McManus Chase (4-y-o and up) £4,140 2m 3f. . . . . (1:10)

1553⁴	FRIENDS OF GERALD 7-11-8 C F Swan, ... (2 to 1 fav)	1
1552⁷	THIRD QUARTER 8-11-11 K F O'Brien, ... (11 to 2)	2
1761⁵	WHO'S TO SAY 7-11-5 (3*) T J Mitchell, ... (8 to 1)	3
1612⁴	PROGRAMMED TO WIN 6-11-2 T Horgan, ... (25 to 1)	4
1678³	BLUE RING 9-10-11 F Woods, ... (8 to 1)	5
1552	GOOD TEAM 8-11-7 (7*) Mr H Murphy, ... (6 to 1)	6
	TABLE ROCK 7-12-0 G Bradley, ... (9 to 4)	f
1763	BUY A DREAM (Fr) 7-10-9 (7*) J P Broderick, ... (25 to 1)	pu
1684⁴	BROGUESTOWN 8-11-2 F J Flood, ... (16 to 1)	pu

Dist: 11l, 15l, ½l, 15l. 5m 8.20s. a 25.20s (9 Ran).
SR: 42/34/16/9/-/-/

(R Sheehan), J E Kiely

1906 Bookmakers Hurdle (Listed Race - Grade I) (4-y-o and up) £14,375 2m . . . . (1:40)

	FORTUNE AND FAME 6-12-0 B Sheridan, hld up, prog aftr 3 out to track ldrs, hdwy to ld last, drvn clr. (2 to 1 fav)	1
1554*	PADASHPAN (USA) 4-11-2 C F Swan, trkd ldr, dsptd ld 2 out, sn led, mstk and hdd last, no extr . . . . . (3 to 1)	2
1663⁵	ROYAL DERBI 8-12-0 D Murphy, led, jnd 3 out, hdd aftr nxt, wknd appr last . . . . (3 to 1)	3
	DESTRIERO 7-12-0 K F O'Brien, wl plcd, dsptd ld 3 out till aftr nxt, wknd appr last . . . . (8 to 1)	4
1617³	JINXY JACK 9-11-7 G Bradley, hld up, prog to track ldrs 4th, rdn aftr 3 out, sn wknd. . . . . (7 to 1)	5
1783*	NOVELLO ALLEGRO (USA) 5-12-0 P Carberry, mid-div, rdn and lost pl aftr 3 out, eased when hit aftr nxt. (7 to 1)	6
1554²	SIMENON (bl) 7-11-7 J P Banahan, al rear, wknd appr 3 out, tld off aftr nxt. . . . . (33 to 1)	7

Dist: 2l, 4l, 4½l, 10l. 4m 10.00s. a 22.00s (7 Ran).
SR: 80/66/74/69/52/-/-/

(Michael W J Smurfit), D K Weld

1907 Seamus Mulvaney Handicap Hurdle (4-y-o and up) £4,140 2m. . . . . . . (2:10)

1332⁴	GRAND TOUR (NZ) [-] 5-9-13 L P Cusack, ... (4 to 1)	1
1232	PYR FOAT [-] 6-9-1 (7*) D A McLaughlin, ... (10 to 1)	2
1780⁴	PERSIAN HALO (Ire) [-] 5-11-0 D H O'Connor, . . (9 to 4 fav)	3
	STARK CONTRAST (USA) [-] 4-9-9 R Hughes, . . (11 to 2)	4
1399⁸	MORNING DREAM [-] 6-9-1 (7*) J P Broderick, . . . (7 to 1)	5
106	TOUCHDOWN [-] 5-9-9 R Hughes, ... (4 to 1)	6
1764	BLAZING ACE [-] 7-9-2 (5*) M G Cleary, ... (33 to 1)	7

Dist: Hd, 15l, ½l. 4m 11.70s. a 23.70s (7 Ran).
SR: 34/29/34/18/2/-/-/

(D W Samuel), Michael Robinson

1908 Joe Donnelly I.N.H. Flat Race (4-y-o and up) £4,140 2m. . . . . (2:40)

1455*	MILTONFIELD 4-11-13 Mr A J Martin, ... (9 to 4 fav)	1
1681²	ROUBABAY (Ire) 5-12-4 Mr T Mullins, ... (5 to 2)	2
1449⁵	ATOURS (USA) 5-11-11 (7*) Mr H Murphy, ... (7 to 2)	3
1766*	DIVINITY RUN (Ire) 4-11-8 (3*) Mr A E Lacy, ... (3 to 1)	4
942⁴	RHABDOMANCY (Ire) 5-11-6 (7*) Mr A Daly, ... (10 to 1)	5
1762⁷	WHAT IT IS (Ire) 4-11-4 (7*) Mr M Brennan, ... (10 to 1)	6

Dist: 3l, 5l, 8l, 15l. 4m 11.90s. (6 Ran).

(J P Savage), J E Mulhern

1909 Noel Cummins Handicap Chase (0-116 4-y-o and up) £4,140 3m. . . . . . . (3:10)

1553³	JOHNEEN [-] 7-10-5 C O'Dwyer, ... (6 to 1)	1
1830³	GOLA LADY [-] 6-10-1 K F O'Brien, ... (10 to 1)	2
1784³	OPRYLAND [-] 7-11-7 (7*) J P Broderick, ... (7 to 2)	3
1612	THE HEARTY CARD (Ire) [-] 5-10-7 D H O'Connor, (12 to 1)	4
1763⁵	BALLINABOOLA GROVE [-] 6-10-5 P Carberry, . . . (6 to 1)	5
1499*	MINISTER FOR FUN (Ire) [-] 5-10-13 C F Swan, (5 to 4 on)	6
1499	ALTNABROCKY [-] 9-9-9 H Rogers, ... (25 to 1)	7
1783⁶	BOOM TIME [-] 8-11-4 J P Banahan, ... (7 to 1)	8

Dist: 2½l, 12l, 2l, dist. 7m 2.90s. a 50.90s (8 Ran).
(Mrs M K Moore), Ms Rosemary Rooney

Dist: 10l, ½l, 4l, 1½l. 5m 45.30s. (9 Ran).
(A J McNamara), A J McNamara

1910 Pat O'Hare I.N.H. Flat Race (4-y-o and up) £4,140 2m. . . . .(3:40)

1786²	SHERE (Ire) 5-11-7 (7") Mr M Brennan, ...(5 to 4 on)	1
	DAENIS (Ire) 5-12-0 Mr P Fenton, ... (11 to 2)	2
1786⁷	GROUP HAT 5-11-9 (5") Mr J A Nash, ...(14 to 1)	3
832⁸	DOONAGLERAGH (Ire) 4-10-11 (7") Mr A Daly, ...(10 to 1)	4
	TREACYS CROSS 7-11-7 (7") Mr D P Carey, ...(10 to 1)	5
	RICHIE'S GIRL (Ire) 5-11-2 (7") Mr C J Stafford, . . (14 to 1)	6
969	YOUR SHOUT 7-12-0 Mr A J Martin, ...(10 to 1)	7
	ROSDEMON (Ire) 5-12-0 Mr M McNulty, ...(6 to 1)	8
	TUL NA GCARN 8-11-7 (7") Ms V Charlton, ...(12 to 1)	9
	PURRIT THERE 7-11-7 (7") Miss M Tullet, ...(25 to 1)	10
	NOPADDLE 9-11-11 (3") Mrs J M Mullins, ...(6 to 1)	11
	PLEASURE SHARED (Ire) 5-12-0 Mr A P O'Brien, . . .(8 to 1)	12
	JOHNNYS GIRL 6-11-8⁶ (7") Mr B Deegan, ...(33 to 1)	13

Dist: 2l, 7l, 2l, 3½l. 4m 18.70s. (13 Ran).
(Hugh Tunney), J H Scott

LIMERICK (IRE) (heavy)
Wednesday December 29th

1911 Croom House Stud Hurdle (3-y-o) £3,450 2m. . . . . (1:20)

	BISSTAMI (Ire) 10-10 G M O'Neill, ...(11 to 4)	1
1575³	RIYADH DANCER (Ire) 10-10 M Duffy, ... (6 to 4 fav)	2
617²	MILLERS MILL (Ire) 11-1 J Jones, ...(7 to 4)	3
1454	LEOS LITTLE BIT (Ire) (bl) 10-0 (5") T J O'Sullivan, (10 to 1)	4

Dist: 4½l, 15l, 15l. 4m 18.10s. (4 Ran).
(Lisselan Farms Ltd), Fergus Sutherland

1912 Lydon House Catering Maiden Hurdle (5-y-o) £3,450 2m. . . . .(1:50)

1549⁴	SUPER TACTICS (Ire) 11-1 (5") P A Roche, ...(5 to 4 fav)	1
1855³	UNCLE BABY (Ire) 11-1 (5") J R Barry, ...(5 to 1)	2
	MALMSEY (USA) 11-11 (3") C O'Brien, ...(100 to 30)	3
1330⁴	MINSTREL FIRE (Ire) 11-6 J Magee, ...(7 to 1)	4
1330⁶	OLD ABBEY (Ire) 11-3 (3") T Townend, ...(8 to 1)	4
939	EXILE RUN (Ire) (bl) 11-6 S H Murphy, ...(14 to 1)	6
	CARIBEAN ROSE (Ire) 10-10 (5") C P Dunne, ...(10 to 1)	7
	ARABIAN SPRITE (Ire) 11-1 Mr P J Healy, ...(10 to 1)	8
1555	BIG JIM 11-6 S H O'Donovan, ...(10 to 1)	9
	PHARELLA 11-9 Mr M J Quaid, ...(8 to 1)	10
	CLONE (Ire) 10-13 (7") J M Donnelly, ...(14 to 1)	11
	THREE SISTERS (Ire) 11-1 P P Kinane, ...(14 to 1)	pu
	SARVO (Ire) 11-1 (5") T J O'Sullivan, ...(12 to 1)	pu

Dist: 3½l, 13l, 1½l. dd-ht. 4m 20.90s. (13 Ran).
(F P Taaffe), C Kinane

1913 J.J. O'Toole (Packaging) Handicap Hurdle (4-y-o and up) £3,450 3m (2:20)

1496	OLYMPIC D'OR (Ire) [-] 5-9-7 S R Murphy, ...(8 to 1)	1
1380⁴	GOOLDS GOLD [-] 7-9-8 (5") P A Roche, ...(9 to 2)	2
1609	MYSTIC GALE (Ire) [-] 5-9-2 (5") T J O'Sullivan, ...(10 to 1)	3
1782³	CARRON HILL [-] 5-9-6 (3") C O'Brien, ...(9 to 1)	4
1685⁷	COUMEENHOLE LADY [-] 6-10-5 (3") Miss M Olivefalk,	
	. . . .(7 to 2)	5
1823⁶	TOT EM UP [-] 6-9-11 (7") M M Murphy, ...(6 to 1)	6
1453	BRINDLEY HOUSE [-] 6-10-13 J Shortt, ...(7 to 1)	7
1782	COOLAHEARAC [-] 7-9-1 (7") J Butler, ...(16 to 1)	8
1823	ARRIGLE PRINCE [-] (bl) 8-9-10³ J Jones, ...(16 to 1)	9
1782⁸	THE MAD MONK [-] 8-9-6 (7") Miss C Rogers, ...(12 to 1)	10

Dist: 1½l, 3½l, nk, 10l. 6m 46.90s. (10 Ran).
(Mrs Dorine Reihill), M F Morris

1914 Limerick Racing Club Novice Chase (4-y-o and up) £3,450 2m. . . . . . .(2:50)

1498⁴	CASTLE KNIGHT 7-12-0 W T Slattery Jnr, ...(4 to 1)	1
929	BLACKPOOL BRIDGE 8-11-9 S H O'Donovan, ...(4 to 1)	2
1550⁶	CHARMING EXCUSE 9-11-9 (5") C P Dunne, ...(6 to 1)	3
1857	SANTAMORE 6-11-4 (5") P A Roche, ...(6 to 1)	4
1498	FAIR LISSELAN (Ire) 5-11-7 G M O'Neill, ...(2 to 1 fav)	5
1826	BALLINAVEEN BRIDGE 6-11-4 (5") M A Davey, ...(16 to 1)	6
1498	BELEEK CASTLE 7-12-0 J Shortt, ...(8 to 1)	7
1498⁹	SUPER MIDGE 6-12-0 J Magee, ...(3 to 1)	f

Dist: Nk, 7l, 3l, 7l. 4m 33.00s. (8 Ran).
(W Trehy), W Trehy

1915 Gain Handicap Chase (0-108 5-y-o and up) £3,450 2½m. . . . .(3:20)

1550⁷	BALLYHEIGUE [-] 7-10-11 (3") D P Murphy, ...(13 to 2)	1
1399⁵	THE WEST'S ASLEEP [-] 8-10-8 J Magee, ...(11 to 2)	2
1785⁴	SHUIL LE CHEILE [-] 6-9-7 (3") C O'Brien, ...(5 to 1)	3
1826³	GOLDEN CARRUTH (Ire) [-] 5-10-9 A J O'Brien, (6 to 4 fav)	4
1826	RUSSIAN GALE (Ire) [-] 5-9-10 J Jones, ...(12 to 1)	5
1499	THIRSTY FRIEND [-] 11-10-0 M Duffy, ...(12 to 1)	6
1826	MONEY MADE [-] 6-9-7 W T Slattery Jnr, ...(20 to 1)	ur
119	CITIZEN LEVEE [-] 7-11-4 (5") Mr W M O'Sullivan, . .(4 to 1)	pu
1498	HARLANE [-] 5-9-8 J Collins, ...(20 to 1)	pu

1916 Irish National Bookmakers INH Flat Race (4-y-o and up) £3,450 2m. . (3:50)

1786⁴	CORRIBLOUGH (Ire) 5-11-6 (5") Mr G J Harford, ...(9 to 2)	1
	CONQUERING LEADER (Ire) 4-10-8 (7") Mr S O'Brien,	
	. . . .(20 to 1)	2
1270⁹	DUEONE (Ire) 5-11-6 (5") Mr H F Cleary, ...(7 to 2)	3
	PRINCESS BAVARD 8-11-13 Mr M Phillips, ...(9 to 2)	4
1501*	BELGARRO (Ire) 4-11-6 (7") Mr F Norris, ...(5 to 4 on)	5
	MONKSLAND 8-11-4 (7") Mr L Mannerings, ...(10 to 1)	6
	WAKEUP LITTLESUSIE 6-10-13 (7") Mr G K Keegan,	
	. . . .(16 to 1)	7

Dist: 3½l, 7l, 20l, 20l. 4m 18.10s. (7 Ran).
(Patrick Molloy), V T O'Brien

NEWCASTLE (heavy)
Wednesday December 29th
Going Correction: PLUS 1.00 sec. per fur. (races 1,3,5), PLUS 1.25 (2,4,6)

1917 Grouse Handicap Chase (0-135 5-y-o and up) £3,492 3m. . . . .(1:00)

1723²	ARTHUR'S MINSTREL [102] 6-10-1 L Wyer, chsd ldr, hit 4 out, led appr nxt, sn clr, cmftbly.	
	. . . .(11 to 4 op 9 to 4 tchd 3 to 1)	1
1725²	RUN PET RUN [107] 8-10-6 A Dobbin, led, clr hfwy, mstk 11th, hdd appr 3 out, kpt on, no ch wth wnr.	
	. . . .(11 to 1 op 12 to 1 tchd 11 to 4)	2
1185*	WHAAT FETTLE [125] 8-11-10 M Moloney, in tch, effrt appr 3 out, no hdwy. . . . .(9 to 2 op 5 to 2 tchd 5 to 1)	3
1748³	PIPER O'DRUMMOND [104] 6-9-10 (7") Mr D Parker, hld up in tch, hdwy whn blun 3 out, no ch aftr.	
	. . . .(3 to 1 tchd 11 to 4)	4

Dist: 12l, 12l, 15l. 6m 24.30s. a 34.30s (4 Ran).
(Bernard Hathaway), P Cheesbrough

1918 Woodcock Novices' Hurdle (4-y-o and up) £3,600 2½m. . . . .(1:30)

1661³	MORCELI (Ire) 5-11-0 (3") D J Moffatt, led aftr 1st, mstk 3 out, rdn betw last 2, styd on und pres, all out.	
	. . . .(6 to 4 op 5 to 4 on)	1
1574*	SAVOY 6-11-3 N Doughty, prmnt, chsd wnr frm 3 out, rdn betw last 2, kpt on, no imprsn. . . . .(13 to 2 op 4 to 1)	2
1475²	CARNETTO 6-11-0 (5") F Leahy, in tch, sn pushed alng, styd on frm 3 out, not rch ldrs.	
	. . . .(12 to 1 op 10 to 1 tchd 16 to 1)	3
1724²	CHIEF MINISTER (Ire) 4-11-0 P Harley, chsd wnr till wknd aftr 3 out. . . . .(6 to 1 op 4 to 1 tchd 13 to 2)	4
1722	STRONG DEEL 5-11-0 T Reed, beh, styd on frm 3 out, nvr trbld ldrs. . . . .(33 to 1)	5
627⁵	DUNREIDY BAY (Ire) 5-10-9 (5") P Williams, in tch, no hdwy frm 7th. . . . .(10 to 1)	6
	TRAVELLING LIGHT 7-11-0 Mr S Swiers, in tch, hdwy hfwy, wknd 3 out. . . . .(16 to 1 op 12 to 1)	7
1675⁶	BACK BEFORE DAWN 6-11-0 A Dobbin, nvr dngrs.	
	. . . .(50 to 1 op 33 to 1)	8
1722*	DIG DEEPER 6-11-3 P Niven, led till aftr 1st, prmnt till wknd appr 3 out. . . . .(10 to 1)	9
1475⁷	LUVLY BUBBLY 5-11-0 C Grant, beh hfwy. . . . . .(100 to 1)	10
875²	KAUSAR (USA) 6-11-0 J Callaghan, prmnt to 4th, sn wknd, tld off whn pld up bef 2 out. . . . .(200 to 1)	pu
	GRAAL LEGEND 8-11-0 M Brennan, sn beh, tld off whn pld up bef 2 out. . . . .(200 to 1)	pu
	WOODSTOCK LODGE (USA) 5-10-7 (7") Mr Carr, sn beh, tld off whn pld up bef 2 out. . . . .(100 to 1)	pu
1356⁷	LEADER SAL (Ire) 4-10-7 (7") D Ryan, in tch to hfwy, tld off whn pld up bef 2 out. . . . .(200 to 1)	pu
	MANOR COURT (Ire) 5-10-9 (5") J Burke, al beh, tld off whn pld up bef 7th. . . . .(100 to 1 tchd 500 to 1)	pu
1478	HECKLEY SPARK 5-10-9 A Orkney, al beh, tld off whn pld up bef 2 out. . . . .(200 to 1)	pu
	SAMS-THE-MAN 5-11-0 C Hawkins, al beh, tld off whn pld up bef 7th. . . . .(200 to 1)	pu

Dist: 2l, 15l, 4l, 12l, 12l, ½l, 10l, 3l, 2l. 5m 19.10s. a 36.10s (17 Ran).
(Mrs J M Corbett), J H Johnson

1919 Northumberland Gold Cup Novices' Chase Grade 1 (4-y-o and up) £15,515 2m 110yds. . . . .(2:00)

1673*	NATIVE MISSION 6-11-7 M Dwyer, trkd ldrs, led 3 out, pushed clr betw last 2, cmftbly.	
	. . . .(11 to 10 on op 5 to 4 on tchd Evens)	1
1743²	BELLTON 5-11-7 B Storey, cl up, hit 9th, outpcd aftr 3 out, styd on appr last, no ch wth wnr.	
	. . . .(13 to 2 op 7 to 1 tchd 6 to 1)	2
1774²	COUNTRY LAD (Ire) 5-11-7 S McNeill, in tch, hit 6th, reminder aftr 8th, rdn appr 3 out, ev ch nxt, one pace.	
	. . . .(3 to 1 op 7 to 2)	3

1792* GLEMOT (Ire) 5-11-7 A Orkney, *not fluent, hld up beh, effrt appr 3 out, kpt on frm last, nvr dngrs.*
....(7 to 1 tchd 8 to 1)   4
1605* CELTIC SONG 6-11-2 T Reed, *led to 3 out, wknd appr last.*.................................(16 to 1 op 14 to 1)   5
1676⁴ MASTER MISCHIEF (bl) 6-11-7 R Hodge, *in tch, pushed alng aftr 5th, f 8th.*..............................(100 to 1)   f
Dist: 5l, 1l, 1½l, 7l. 4m 22.80s. a 21.80s (6 Ran).
SR: 40/35/34/32/20/-/   (G E Shouler), J G FitzGerald

1920 Partridge Juvenile Novices' Hurdle (3-y-o) £3,980 2m 110yds.........(2:30)

1473⁵ NATIVE WORTH 10-7 (5") P Williams, *made virtually all, styd on wl frm last.*..............................(25 to 1)   1
1217* RED MARAUDER 11-3 (5") J Supple, *mid-div, hdwy appr 3 out, chlgd last, swrvd lft and no extr r-in.*
...............................(7 to 1 op 5 to 1 tchd 8 to 1)   2
1483² OUTSET (Ire) 10-5 (7") Mr C Bonner, *pld hrd, dsptd ld till outpcd appr 2 out, styd on appr last.*
...............................(7 to 1 op 5 to 1 tchd 8 to 1)   3
1569⁴ MHEMEANLES 10-12 L Wyer, *prmnt, ev ch appr 2 out, kpt on same pace.*.......................(7 to 1 op 6 to 1)   4
BALLON 10-8¹ T Reed, *beh, styd on strly frm 2 out, fnshd wl.*..............................(50 to 1 op 33 to 1)   5
THALEROS 10-12 J Callaghan, *trkd ldrs, ev ch 2 out, sn wknd....* (100 to 30 op 7 to 2 tchd 3 to 1 and 4 to 1)   6
1147⁹ GERMAN LEGEND 10-7 (5") J Burke, *prmnt, chlgd 2 out, sn wknd.*.....................(100 to 1 op 50 to 1)   7
1483 IJAB (Can) 10-12 M Dwyer, *chsd ldrs till wknd appr 2 out.*...............................(14 to 1 op 10 to 1)   8
FRET (USA) 10-9 (3") N Bentley, *nvr on terms.*
...............................(10 to 1 op 6 to 1)   9
1787⁴ GREAT EASEBY (Ire) 10-12 R Hodge, *mid-div, pushed alng aftr 4th, no hdwy.*.................(20 to 1 op 16 to 1)   10
1569⁸ HO-JOE (Ire) 10-12 N Smith, *nvr on terms.*
...............................(50 to 1 op 25 to 1)   11
CIVIL LAW (Ire) 10-12 P Niven, *in tch till weeakened aftr 3 out.*...............................(12 to 1 op 14 to 1)   12
1787 DIGNIFIED (Ire) 10-0 (7") A Linton, *al beh.*.........(66 to 1)   13
1476⁶ FUNNY FEELINGS 10-12 A Dobbin, *beh, hdwy aftr 5th, wknd quickly appr 2 out.*....................(66 to 1)   14
RED FAN (Ire) 10-12 B Storey, *in tch to hfwy, tld off whn pld up bef 2 out.*.......................(50 to 1 op 33 to 1)   pu
ADMISSION (Ire) 10-12 C Grant, *lost tch appr 3 out, tld off whn pld up bef nxt.*...........................(100 to 1)   pu
FRIENDLY KNIGHT 10-12 A Orkney, *sn beh, tld off whn pld up bef 2 out.*.............................(100 to 1)   pu
Dist: 1½l, 12l, 8l, 1l, 1½l, 3l, 1l, 1½l, 6l, 10l. 4m 20.10s. a 27.10s (17 Ran).
SR: 19/27/5/-/-/-/   (Mrs M Barker), J M Jefferson

1921 Gamebird Handicap Chase (5-y-o and up) £3,492 2½m...............(3:00)

1664⁸ ARMAGRET [135] 8-12-0 L O'Hara, *made all, steadied aftr 4th, quickened appr 3 out, styd on wl.*
...............................(2 to 1 fav op 7 to 4 tchd 9 to 4)   1
1752² ONE FOR THE POT [108] 8-10-1 L Wyer, *hld up, hdwy to chase wnr appr 2 out, ch whn hit last, no extr.*
...............................(5 to 2 op 9 to 4 tchd 9 to 4)   2
1606⁶ BAD TRADE [112] 11-10-5 C Grant, *cl up, chsd wnr appr 3 out till wknd approaching nxt.*
...............................(6 to 1 op 5 to 1 tchd 7 to 1)   3
1606² NIGHT GUEST [107] 11-10-0 A Dobbin, *trkd wnr till rdn and wknd appr 3 out.*...............(11 to 4 op 3 to 1)   4
1583⁴ RAHINANE [108] 10-10-1¹ A Orkney, *pld up aftr 1st, lme.*
...............................(25 to 1 op 16 to 1)   pu
Dist: 2½l, 15l, ¾l. 5m 37.40s. a 46.40s (5 Ran).
(Mrs R M Wilkinson), B E Wilkinson

1922 Pheasant Handicap Hurdle (0-140 4-y-o and up) £3,850 2½m.........(3:30)

1619² NORTHANTS [111] 7-10-4 R Hodge, *hld up, hdwy to join ldr 3 out, led nxt, styd on wl frm last.*
...............................(5 to 4 fav op 7 to 4 tchd 11 to 10)   1
1322³ DOMINANT SERENADE [131] 4-11-5 (5") D Bentley, *cl up, mstk 4th, chalg whn blun 3 out, chsd wnr nxt, swshd tail, no imprsn.*...............................(9 to 2 op 4 to 1)   2
1728⁴ PALACEGATE KING [107] 4-10-0 M Moloney, *hld up, hdwy appr 2 out, rdn aftr last, kpt on same pace.*
...............................(11 to 1 op 10 to 1 tchd 12 to 1)   3
TINDARI (Fr) [119] 5-10-7 (5") P Williams, *prmnt, mstk 5th, outpcd aftr 3 out.......*(11 to 1 op 9 to 1 tchd 12 to 1)   4
1728⁵ BAY TERN (USA) [110] 7-10-3 P Harley, *led to 2 out, sn wknd.*...............................(13 to 2 op 5 to 1)   5
1617 HIGH ALLTITUDE (Ire) [135] 5-11-11 (3") N Bentley, *in tch, pushed alng aftr 8th, reminders appr 3 out, sn wknd.*...............................(14 to 1 op 10 to 1)   6
1101⁴ FROMTHEGETGO (Ire) [107] 4-10-0 L Wyer, *hld up, effrt aftr 3 out, sn wknd, tld off.*
...............................(11 to 1 op 7 to 1 tchd 12 to 1)   7
Dist: 10l, 12l, 4l, 4l, 15l, dist. 5m 22.30s. a 39.30s (7 Ran).
(C B Rennison), W Storey

SOUTHWELL (heavy)

Wednesday December 29th
Going Correction: PLUS 1.90 sec. per fur.

1923 Medieval Conditional Jockeys' Claiming Chase (5-y-o and up) £1,641 2m ....(1:15)

1463⁸ RATHER SHARP 7-10-12 R Farrant, *made most to 7th, effrt to ld 3 out, sn clr, styd on wl.*
...............................(7 to 2 op 4 to 1 tchd 9 to 2)   1
JAMES MY BOY 13-10-12 R Davis, *al prmnt, led 7th, hdd and hit 3 out, sn wknd, blun badly last, fnshd very tired.*...............................(5 to 1 op 4 to 1 tchd 2 to 1)   2
1484⁶ NOBBY (bl) 7-10-6 A Larnach, *hld up, hdwy 3 out, rdn nxt, kpt on.*......................(20 to 1 op 16 to 1)   3
1727³ SILVER HAZE 9-11-1 R Greene, *cl up, hit 7th and 8th, lost pl 4 out, beh whn f 3 out.*
...............................(11 to 8 fav op 6 to 4 tchd 5 to 4)   f
1127⁶ LADY KHADIJA 7-10-8 (5") C Woodall, *pld hrd, cl up whn uns rdr 1st.*...............................(33 to 1)   ur
Dist: 15l, sht-hd. 4m 36.30s. a 37.30s (5 Ran).
SR: 15/-/   (C L Popham), C L Popham

1924 British Coal Novices' Chase (5-y-o and up) £1,785 2½m 110yds.....(1:45)

1214⁴ MANDIKA 5-11-2 Richard Guest, *led to 3rd, in tch till hdwy 6 out, led 3 out, blun nxt, rdn last and ran on wl flt.*...............................(2 to 1 op 7 to 4 tchd 13 to 8)   1
1564³ RUSSINSKY 6-10-11 R J Beggan, *prmnt, led tenth, hdd 3 out, effrt and rdn nxt, ev ch whn hit last, kpt on.*
...............................(4 to 1 op 7 to 2 tchd 9 to 2)   2
RAIDO 8-11-2 Gary Lyons, *cl up, led 3rd, hit 7th, hdd tenth, wknd 5 out.*................(6/l to 1 op 20 to 1)   3
MAC RAMBLER 6-11-2 N Garritty, *in tch till f 3rd.*
...............................(16 to 1 op 14 to 1 tchd 20 to 1)   f
MARIDADI 7-10-9 (7") P Ward, *in tch, hit 1st, f 3rd.*
...............................(8 to 1 op 14 to 1)   f
1623³ PERSIAN SWORD 7-11-12 W Marston, *al prmnt, jmpd slwly 4th, hit 6 out and sn rdn alng, und pres whn blun and uns rdr 3 out...* (13 to 8 fav op 6 to 4 tchd 7 to 4)   ur
Dist: 1½l, dist. 6m 0.70s. a 57.70s (6 Ran).
(R L Capon), M A Jarvis

1925 Georgian Handicap Chase (0-115 5-y-o and up) £1,987 3m 110yds.....(2:15)

1769* THE TARTAN SPARTAN [94] 9-10-3 (7") P Ward, *trkd ldrs, hit 3rd, lft in ld 7th, hit 8th and 11th, hdd 13th, hit 15th, led 4 out, clr appr 2 out.* (11 to 4 op 2 to 1 tchd 3 to 1)   1
1565⁸ GUILDWAY [92] 10-10-2¹ (7") Mr M Rimell, *in tch, blun 12th, hdwy to ld nxt, hdd 4 out, rdn and wkng whn blunded 3 out.*......................(8 to 1 tchd 10 to 1)   2
1606³ FUNNY OLD GAME [95] 6-10-8 (3") A Thornton, *trkd ldrs, blun badly tenth and beh, struggling frm 5 out, blunded badly 3 out and last.*..............(9 to 2 op 4 to 1)   3
TRUBLION (Fr) [97] 8-10-13 Richard Guest, *led till f 7th.*
...............................(11 to 1 op 8 to 1 tchd 12 to 1)   f
1471⁶ MATERIAL GIRL [108] 7-11-5 (5") A Procter, *cl up till blun and uns rdr 3rd....*......(5 to 1 op 9 to 2 tchd 6 to 1)   ur
1778³ ZAMIL (USA) [106] 8-11-8 D Gallagher, *cl up whn blun badly second, hit 4th and sn pld up.*
...............................(5 to 2 fav op 9 to 4 tchd 11 to 4)   pu
Dist: 20l, dist. 7m 13.10s. a 75.10s (6 Ran).
(Mrs Delyth Batchelor), M J Wilkinson

SOUTHWELL (A.W) (std)
Wednesday December 29th
Going Correction: PLUS 0.05 sec. per fur.

1926 Victorian Novices' Handicap Hurdle (4-y-o and up) £1,604 2m..... (12:45)

1316³ GREEN'S SEAGO (USA) [63] 5-10-4 D Gallagher, *hld up in mid-div, steady hdwy 4 out, led 3 out, clr aftr nxt.*
...............................(9 to 2 op 11 to 1)   1
1589⁶ HULLO MARY DOLL [62] 4-9-10 (7") Chris Webb, *al prmnt, led rdn 2 out, kpt on flt.*........(14 to 1 op 8 to 1)   2
1809* LAFANTA (Ire) [71] 4-10-12 (7ex) K Jones, *cl up, led 3rd to 5th, led nxt to 3 out, sn hrd rdn, btn whn hit last.*
...............................(9 to 4 fav op 5 to 2)   3
1658³ MATUSADONA [59] 6-10-0 B Dalton, *hld up and beh, steady hdwy appr 4 out, ev ch nxt, sn rdn and crsd pace...*...............................(5 to 1 op 20 to 1 tchd 33 to 1)   4
1152 MAKE A LINE [77] 5-11-4 G Upton, *in tch, hdwy to chase ldr 4 out, rdn nxt and sn btn.........(11 to 1 tchd 12 to 1)   5
1812⁸ BUSMAN (Ire) [87] 4-11-11 (3") R Davis, *hld up and beh, effrt and some hdwy appr 3 out, nvr a factor.*
...............................(12 to 1 op 6 to 1)   6
1747⁵ BOWLAND GIRL (Ire) [69] 4-10-7 (3") S Wynne, *al rear, tld off frm hfwy.*.....................(6 to 1 tchd 8 to 1)   7
1770 ROMANY SPLIT [60] 8-10-1 W Marston, *led to 3rd, led 5th till hdd and hit nxt, sn rdn and wknd, tld off 3 out.*
...............................(6 to 1)   8

1811[6] NOEL (Ire) [75] (bl) 4-10-9 (7*) P McLoughlin, *cl up till blun badly 4 out and sn beh*..................(12 to 1 op 10 to 1)   9
1527 PYRO PENNANT [62] 8-9-12 (5*) A Procter, *chsd ldrs, hit 4th and lost pl, stumbled and f aftr four out.*
....(20 to 1 op 12 to 1)   f
Dist: 7l, nd, 3l, 2l, 8l, 20l, 1l, 15l. 4m 1.10s. a 15.10s (10 Ran).

(Bob Welch), J L Harris

1927 Elizabethan Juvenile Novices' Hurdle (3-y-o) £1,674 2m..............(2:45)

1297[2] QUICK SILVER BOY 10-5 (5*) A Procter, *led and sn clr, rdn 2 out, styd on wl frm last.*
......................................(7 to 4 fav op 5 to 4 tchd 2 to 1)   1
1532[2] BAYRAK (USA) 10-10 J Railton, *in tch, hdwy to chase wnr 4 out, effrt and ev ch 2 out, sn hrd rdn and not quicken last.*...........................(6 to 1 op 5 to 1 tchd 7 to 1)   2
1705 LEEWA (Ire) 10-10 D Gallagher, *in tch, hdwy 4 out, effrt nxt, rdn and hit last, not quicken flt.*
..................................(12 to 1 op 14 to 1 tchd 10 to 1)   3
1504[8] SEASIDE DREAMER 10-10 S D Williams, *beh till styd on frm 4 out, nvr dngrs.*....................(7 to 1 tchd 9 to 1)   4
1350[4] ELECTROLYTE (v) 10-10 R Greene, *chsd ldrs, rdn 4 out and sn one pace........*(9 to 1 op 8 to 1 tchd 10 to 1)   5
1702[5] GROGFRYN 10-7 (3*) R Farrant, *prmnt till rdn and wknd 4 out.*..............................(12 to 1 op 8 to 1)   6
FATAL SHOCK 10-5 J Ryan, *mid-div, effrt and some hdwy 6th, wknd 4 out.*........................(20 to 1 op 16 to 1)   7
1705[4] NORTHERN JUDY (Ire) 10-2 (3*) S Wynne, *at rear, tld off 5 out, always rear........*(4 to 1 tchd 5 to 1)   8
GREEN MILL 10-10 B Dalton, *at rear, tld off 4 out.*
....(25 to 1 op 16 to 1)   9
1527 SAXON MAGIC (bl) 10-5 L Harvey, *chsd ldr, rdn 6th, wknd nxt and sn beh, pld up bef 2 out..*(25 to 1 op 16 to 1)   pu
JOYCE & JACKSON 10-6[1] Richard Guest, *strted slwly, al beh, tld off whn pld up bef 5th....*(25 to 1 op 16 to 1)   pu
Dist: 13½l, nk, 30l, 7l, 5l, 2½l, 6l, ½l. 3m 52.40s. a 6.40s (11 Ran).

SR: 26/22/21/-/-/-/   (David Burchell), D Burchell

1928 Edwardian Handicap Hurdle (0-120 4-y-o and up) £1,718 3m........ (3:15)

1812[4] COURT CIRCULAR [101] (v) 4-11-10 Diane Clay, *pld hrd, made virtually all, quickened clr 3 out, unchlgd.*
......................................(3 to 1 jt-fav tchd 4 to 1)   1
FLYAWAY (Fr) [91] 8-11-0 D Gallagher, *hld up in tch, hit 8th, hdwy 5 out, chsd wnr 3 out, sn rdn and one pace.*
......................................(3 to 1 jt-fav tchd 5 to 2)   2
1812[7] RAGTIME COWBOY JOE [79] 8-9-9 (7*) Mr N Bradley, *hld up in tch, hdwy 5 out, rdn and outpcd 3 out, kpt on appr last...*..............................(8 to 1 op 7 to 1)   3
1603[8] SHELTON ABBEY [97] 7-11-6 Richard Guest, *cl up, rdn alng tenth, hit nxt, hrd drvn and wknd appr 3 out.*
......................................(7 to 1 op 6 to 1 tchd 8 to 1)   4
ANGELICA PARK [93] 7-11-2 B Dalton, *trkd ldrs, effrt and hdwy 3 out, second and no ch wth wnr whn f last.*
....(13 to 2 op 9 to 2)   f
1694[3] STORM DRUM [105] (bl) 4-11-11 (3*) A Thornton, *cl up till rdn 5 out, hit nxt and sn wknd, rear whn f 3 out.*
..................................(4 to 1 op 100 to 30 tchd 9 to 2)   f
Dist: 5l, ¾l, 30l. 6m 10.20s. a 33.20s (6 Ran).

(B A S Limited), W Clay

STRATFORD (good to soft)
Wednesday December 29th
Going Correction: PLUS 1.03 sec. per fur. (races 1,2,- 3,7), PLUS 1.38 (4,5,6)

1929 Auld Lang Syne Novices' Hurdle (Div I) (4-y-o and up) £1,912 2m 110yds ....(12:40)

1646 ROXY RIVER 4-10-7 D Bridgwater, *jmpd rght, led till rdn and hdd 3 out, sn hrd drvn to ld ag'n nxt, headed last, rallied und pres to lead r-in.*
......................................(9 to 4 op 3 to 1 tchd 2 to 1)   1
SMART IN SABLE 6-10-7 M Richards, *hdwy to track ldrs 4th, led 3 out, hdd 2 out, slight ld last, sn headed, one pace.*......................................(14 to 1 op 9 to 1)   2
1695[7] TENAYESTELIGN 5-10-2 (5*) J McCarthy, *hdwy 4th, chsd ldr briefly aftr 2 out, 3rd and rdn whn mstk last.*
......................................(7 to 1 op 10 to 1 tchd 12 to 1)   3
MASTER TUCK 7-10-12 R Bellamy, *wl beh till styd on frm 2 out, nrst finish.*..............(50 to 1 op 33 to 1)   4
SINCLAIR BOY 7-10-12 E Byrne, *in tch, rdn 5th, wknd 3 out.*..............................(25 to 1 op 20 to 1)   5
1810[9] DAUPHIN BLEU (Fr) 7-10-12 Dr P Pritchard, *prmnt till wknd 3 out.*.............................(25 to 1 op 20 to 1)   6
PRINCE RODNEY 4-10-7 A Dunwoody, *chsd ldrs till rdn and hdwy quickly appr 2 out.....*(8 to 1 op 5 to 1)   7
CRU EXCEPTIONNEL 5-10-12 A Maguire, *al beh.*
......................(85 to 40 fav op 5 to 4 tchd 9 to 4 and 5 to 2)   8
ROBENKO (USA) 4-10-5 (7*) D Meade, *chsd ldrs, still in tch whn f 4th.*....................(10 to 1 op 8 to 1)   f

---

GANESHAYA 4-10-5 (7*) Mr N Bradley, *al beh, tld off whn pld up bef 3 out.................*(50 to 1 op 33 to 1)   pu
KIMBOLTON KRACKER 6-10-7 A Carroll, *sn tld off, pld up bef 5th....................*(50 to 1 op 33 to 1)   pu
1442 EMBLEY BUOY 5-10-12 S Earle, *chsd ldrs to 3 out, wknd 2 out, pld up bef last....................*(50 to 1)   pu
Dist: 2l, 8l, nk, 20l, 4l, 15l, 25l. 4m 18.10s. a 29.10s (12 Ran).

(Mrs M R T Rimell), J L Spearing

1930 Auld Lang Syne Novices' Hurdle (Div II) (4-y-o and up) £1,912 2m 110yds ....(1:10)

1460 BUTLER'S TWITCH 6-11-5 J Osborne, *led, shaken up appr last, hdd r-in, rallied und pres to ld ag'n cl hme.*
..................................(11 to 4 op 5 to 2 tchd 3 to 1)   1
1695[2] KEEP ME IN MIND (Ire) 4-10-12 D Skyrme, *beh till steady hdwy frm 3 out, chlgd last, sn rdn, found no extr and hdd cl hme.*........................(7 to 1 tchd 8 to 1)   2
1509[3] SURE HAVEN (Ire) 4-10-12 R Dunwoody, *al in tch, chsd ldrs frm 3 out, not fluent nxt, sn oupaced.*
......................................(3 to 1 op 7 to 2 tchd 4 to 1)   3
1800 MARINER'S AIR 6-10-7 N Williamson, *hdwy 5th, styd on one pace frm 2 out..........*(25 to 1 op 16 to 1)   4
JURA 5-10-12 S Smith Eccles, *in tch, chsd ldrs and not fluent 3 out, ev ch 2 out, sn wknd....*(9 to 2 op 5 to 2)   5
983[5] GESNERA 5-10-7 A Maguire, *hdwy to chase ldrs 5th, wknd appr 2 out, tld off.*
..................................(11 to 1 op 12 to 1 tchd 10 to 1)   6
1509[6] HIGHLAND FLAME 4-10-12 D Bridgwater, *nvr rch ldrs, tld off..........................*(66 to 1 op 50 to 1)   7
MUZO (USA) 6-10-12 W Humphreys, *prmnt to 4th, tld off.*......................(100 to 1 op 50 to 1)   8
1773[9] SALINGER 5-10-12 V Smith, *al off whn pld up bef last....................*(100 to 1 op 50 to 1)   pu
AMYS DELIGHT 5-10-7 B Powell, *al beh, tld off whn pld up bef 2 out....................*(100 to 1 op 50 to 1)   pu
1460 SHELLHOUSE (Ire) 5-10-12 M A FitzGerald, *prmnt, chlgd 4th, wknd frm 3 out, tld off whn pld up bef last.*
..................................(25 to 1 op 20 to 1)   pu
1768 MANDYS LAD 4-10-12 C Llewellyn, *chsd ldrs to 5th, wknd quickly, tld off whn pld up bef 3 out.*
..................................(20 to 1 op 14 to 1)   pu
Dist: ½l, 20l, sht-hd, 1½l, dist, 2l, 15l. 4m 10.90s. a 21.90s (12 Ran).

SR: 24/34/19/12/-/   (Christopher Heath), O Sherwood

1931 Bran Tub Selling Handicap Hurdle (3 & 4-y-o) £1,800 2m 110yds....... (1:40)

1297[8] STAR MARKET [63] 3-10-2 T Wall, *chsd ldrs frm 4th, drvn to ld 2 out, edgd and hrd driven appr last, all out.*
......................................(11 to 1 op 8 to 1 tchd 12 to 1)   1
1702[3] BOLD STAR [67] 3-10-6 J Osborne, *beh, ran on frm 3 out, chsd wnr aftr 2 out, no imprsn last.* (5 to 1 op 7 to 2)   2
1749[2] DOUALAGO (Fr) [80] (v) 3-11-5 R Dunwoody, *led to 5th, rdn 3 out, sn 8th..........*(9 to 4 to 1 tchd 2 to 1)   3
1741[5] YAAFOOR (USA) [71] (v) 4-10-10 M Richards, *prmnt, chlgd 4th, led nxt, hdd and btn 2 out.*
......................................(7 to 1 op 5 to 1 tchd 8 to 1 and 9 to 1)   4
1562[7] RED JACK (Ire) [89] 4-12-0 A Maguire, *in tch till wknd appr 5th.................*(15 to 2 op 6 to 1 tchd 8 to 1)   5
1801[8] NAJEB (USA) [75] (bl) 4-11-0 N Williamson, *mstk second, al beh, tld off....................*(15 to 2 op 10 to 1)   6
1528 SMART DEBUTANTE (Ire) [75] 4-10-7 (7*) Mr S Joynes, *in tch till appr 5th, tld off....................*(12 to 1 op 10 to 1)   7
1749[5] CREAGMHOR [70] 3-10-9 V Slattery, *beh frm 4th, tld off.*
..................................(14 to 1 op 10 to 1)   8
1794 ABELONI [66] (bl) 4-10-5 B Powell, *uns rdr and bolted bef strt, rdn and beh frm 4th, pld up before 2 out.*
..................................(16 to 1 op 12 to 1)   pu
1640[7] IRISH DOMINION [65] 3-10-4 H Davies, *al beh, tld off, pld up bef 2 out....................*(20 to 1 op 16 to 1 tchd 25 to 1)   pu
Dist: 10l, 20l, 5l, nk, dist, 8l, 25l. 4m 18.50s. a 29.50s (11 Ran).

(Midland Markets Ltd), Mrs P M Joynes

1932 J. H. Rowe Challenge Trophy Handicap Chase (0-135 5-y-o and up) £3,649 3m..............................(2:10)

1345[2] TRI FOLENE (Fr) [82] 7-11-7 R Dunwoody, *in tch, chsd ldr frm 12th, rdn aftr 3 out, second and wl hld whn lft clr 2 out.....................*(4 to 1 jt-fav tchd 2 to 1)   1
1802[2] NEW HALEN [102] 12-10-1 R Bellamy, *chsd ldr frm 4th, hit 7th, chlgd frm 9th till led 11th, hdd and hit 3 out, sn wknd.........................*(4 to 1 op 7 to 2)   2
SIKERA SPY [125] 11-11-10 B Powell, *led to 11th, wknd 13th, tld off..........*(15 to 2 op 6 to 1 tchd 8 to 1)   3
1732 SIRRAH JAY [110] 13-10-4 (5*) T Jenks, *beh frm 7th, tld off.*......................(12 to 1 op 8 to 1)   4
1486[3] GLENSHANE LAD [102] 7-10-1 N Williamson, *mstk 8th, hdwy 13th, chlgd and hit 4 out, led 3 out, in command whn f 2 out.....................*(7 to 4 jt-fav)   f
Dist: 10l, dist, 3l. 6m 24.80s. a 37.80s (5 Ran).

SR: 46/16/   (David L'Estrange), M C Pipe

1933 Vivian Street Handicap Chase Amateur Riders (0-125 5-y-o and up) £2,635

2m 1f 110yds................. (2:40)

1752³ ITS NEARLY TIME [122] 10-11-7 (7*) Miss J Brackenbury,
hdwy 7th, chsd ldr 8th till led sn aftr 3 out, readily.
.... (9 to 2 tchd 4 to 1 and 5 to 1) 1
1591⁶ CHAIN SHOT [105] 8-10-4 (7*) Mr G Hogan, *led, hit 3rd,*
hdd appr 4th, styd in tch, chsd wnr approaching 2 out,
no imprsn....................(6 to 1 op 4 to 1) 2
1275² AL HASHIMI [121] 9-11-6 (7*) Major G Wheeler, *chlgd 3rd,*
led appr nxt, hdd sn aftr 3 out, wknd quickly.
.... (11 to 2 op 5 to 1) 3
1630* DRIVING FORCE [115] (bl) 7-11-4 (3*) Mr J Durkan, *hld up,*
hdwy 9th, drvn to chase ldrs whn hit 4 out, sn rdn and
not reco'r...........(Evens fav op 11 to 10 tchd 5 to 4) 4
1811⁵ SANDMOOR PRINCE [94] 10-9-12⁵ (7*) Dr P Pritchard, *beh*
7th, hit nxt, no ch whn blun last. (33 to 1 op 25 to 1) 5
AIR COMMANDER [101] 8-10-3³ (7*) Mr S Joynes, *chsd ldrs*
6th, wknd 9th........(14 to 1 op 12 to 1 tchd 16 to 1) 6
Dist: 6l, 15l, 3½l, 10l, 2½l. 4m 33.60s. a 29.60s (6 Ran).

SR: 45/22/23/13/-/-/   (Mrs R Brackenbury), Mrs R Brackenbury

1934 Yarnolds Of Stratford Novices' Handicap Chase (5-y-o and up) £3,192 2m 5f 110yds................. (3:10)

1441² FANTUS [92] 6-11-10 R Dunwoody, *in tch, jmpd slwly 3rd,*
led aftr 12th, came clr frm 3 out.
.... (11 to 10 fav op 5 to 4 tchd 11 to 8) 1
984 MAJOR BAY [92] (bl) 9-11-10 J Osborne, *prmnt, chlgd 4th,*
led 5th to nxt, slight ld 8th, mstk 12th, sn hdd, styd on
but no ch wth wnr....... (8 to 1 op 5 to 1 tchd 9 to 1) 2
FREE JUSTICE [77] 9-10-9 C Llewellyn, *al chasing ldrs,*
lost tch frm 4 out....................(7 to 1 op 5 to 1) 3
PEGMARINE (USA) [82] 10-10-9 (5*) J McCarthy, *mid-div,*
hit 9th, al beh, tld off........................(50 to 1) 4
1776⁶ CONCERT PAPER [84] 9 10 9 (7*) K Davies, *in tch whn slpd*
up bend bef 7th.................(10 to 1 op 16 to 1) su
1511⁴ SILENT CHANT [71] (v) 9-10-3 D Bridgwater, *al beh, tld off*
whn pld up bef 4 out...........(10 to 1 tchd 12 to 1) pu
1194 GALLANTRY BANK [74] 8-10-6 W McFarland, *beh 7th, tld*
off whn pld up bef 12th............(33 to 1 op 25 to 1) pu
1718³ MICKEEN [85] (bl) 6-11-3 M A FitzGerald, *led to 5th, led*
ag'n 6th to 8th, styd wth ldr to 11th, sn wknd, blun 4
out, tld off whn pld up bef 2 out..... (6 to 1 op 9 to 1) pu
1621 BUCKELIGHT (Ire) [87] 5-11-5 B Powell, *mstks, al beh, tld*
off whn pld up bef 4 out...........(15 to 2 op 7 to 1) pu
Dist: 10l, 2½l, dist. 5m 46.20s. a 43.20s (9 Ran).

(Hunt & Co (Bournemouth) Ltd), P F Nicholls

1935 Good Resolutions 'National Hunt' Novices' Hurdle (4-y-o and up) £2,178 2¾m 110yds................. (3:40)

1707* WELSH LUSTRE (Ire) 4-10-13 A Maguire, *in tch, hdwy 6th,*
led appr 3 out, drvn out r-in.
.................(2 to 1 fav op 9 to 4 tchd 5 to 2) 1
LOVING AROUND (Ire) 5-10-7 M A FitzGerald, *hdwy and*
hit 6th, reco'red 6th, styd on to chase wnr appr last, no
extr r-in.......................(20 to 1 op 10 to 1) 2
1729⁷ MR CLANCY (Ire) 5-10-12 N Williamson, *prmnt, chsd wnr*
appr 2 out, rdn and wknd approaching last.
.........................(20 to 1 op 10 to 1) 3
1053⁵ LACURVA (Ire) 5-10-12 S Earle, *chsd ldrs 6th, rdn 7th, styd*
on und pres frm 2 out.......... (14 to 1 op 25 to 1) 4
DESERT RUN (Ire) 5-10-12 R Dunwoody, *prmnt, chsd wnr 3*
out, rdn nxt, wknd quickly appr last.
......................(9 to 1 op 5 to 1) 5
1567³ CATS RUN (Ire) 5-10-12 R Supple, *hdwy 5th, wknd aftr 3*
out........................(10 to 1 op 8 to 1) 6
MY DEAR GOOD MAN (Ire) 5-10-12 T Grantham, *beh 5th,*
hrd drvn to on ldg grp appr 2 out, wknd approaching
last............................(16 to 1 op 12 to 1) 7
1392³ DOWRY SQUARE (Ire) 5-10-12 E Murphy, *pressed ldr till*
led 5th, hdd aftr 7th, wknd 3 out. (25 to 1 op 20 to 1) 8
ARDSCUD 6-10-12 P Holley, *beh, effrt 6th, wknd aftr 7th.*
.........................(20 to 1 op 14 to 1) 9
1490⁵ ESSDOUBLEYOU (NZ) 5-10-12 H Davies, *took str hold, in*
tch 4th, chsd ldrs 3 out, wknd quickly nxt.
...........................(5 to 2 tchd 3 to 1) 10
1568 ROCK DIAMOND 7-10-12 E Leonard, *beh frm 6th.* (33 to 1) 11
1648 MISS CRUISE 6-10-7 D Bridgwater, *beh frm 6th.* (50 to 1) 12
1327² KONVEKTA CONTROL 6-10-12 J Osborne, *made most to*
5th, styd wth ldr till wknd quickly appr 3 out.
..........................(5 to 2 tchd 3 to 1) 13
1626 CASTLE WARRIOR 6-10-12 T Wall, *al beh, tld off whn pld*
up aftr 7th.................(100 to 1 op 66 to 1) pu
LADY ROMANCE (Ire) 5-10-0 (7*) Mr J L Llewellyn, *prmnt*
early, beh frm 6th, tld off whn pld up aftr 7th.
....................(66 to 1 tchd 100 to 1) pu
1648⁸ MARINERS MEMORY 5-10-12 W Humphreys, *sn beh, tld*
off whn pld up bef 3 out.................(66 to 1) pu
901⁹ HURRICANE HANKS 4-10-12 C Llewellyn, *hit second, beh*
in tch till wknd 7th, tld off whn pld up bef 2 out.
.........................(20 to 1 op 14 to 1) pu
Dist: 2½l, 20l, ½l, 12l, 5l, 2l, 2l, 3l, nk, 12l. 5m 57.10s. a 45.10s (17 Ran).
(Mrs L R Lovell), D Nicholson

CARLISLE (soft)
Thursday December 30th
Going Correction: PLUS 0.95 sec. per fur.

1936 Bells Field Selling Handicap Hurdle (4-y-o and up) £1,688 3m 110yds
...........................(12:50)

1602³ JUBILATA (USA) [64] 5-10-0 C Dennis, *nvr far away, drvn*
to ld betw last 2, hld on und pres cl hme. ..(11 to 2 jt-
fav op 5 to 1 tchd 6 to 1) 1
SANSOOL [92] 7-11-9 (5*) P Williams, *patiently rdn, hdwy*
appr 3 out, effrt and ridden betw last 2, ran on. jst fld.
..........................(7 to 1 op 7 to 2) 2
1699⁴ LOXLEY RANGE (Ire) [65] (v) 5-9-9¹ (7*) N Juckes, *last and*
hld up, improved appr 3 out, effrt betw last 2, one pace
und pres..................(6 to 1 op 5 to 1) 3
1775⁹ MANWELL [64] 6-9-10¹ (5*) D Bentley, *led to 3rd, hndy till*
outpcd appr 4 out, kpt on frm last. (8 to 1 tchd 10 to 1) 4
1603⁹ MR FENWICK [82] 9-11-4 A Mulholland, *wth ldr, led 3rd,*
jnd hfwy, hdd appr 4 out, rdn and no extr nxt.
............................(6 to 1 op 5 to 1) 5
1602⁴ DENTICULATA [67] 5-10-3 B Storey, *wtd wth, chlgd appr 3*
out, rdn and no extr aftr nxt. ....(11 to 2 jt-
fav op 5 to 1 tchd 6 to 1) 6
1788⁷ HAMANAKA (USA) [81] 4-11-3 Mr S Love, *trkd ldrs till pace*
quickened aftr 4 out, sn struggling.
....................(14 to 1 op 12 to 1) 7
1788 HELLO GEORGIE [85] (bl) 10-11-7 R Garritty, *patiently rdn,*
hdwy to ld appr 4 out, hdd betw last 2, wknd quickly.
.................(13 to 2 op 5 to 1) 8
1788 EMPEROR ALEXANDER (Ire) [68] 5-10-4 S Turnor, *wth ldrs,*
drvn alng appr 4 out, lost tch frm nxt........(33 to 1) 9
914 JUSTICE LEA [70] 13-9-13 (7*) Carol Cuthbert, *struggling*
aftr second, tld off fnl circuit......(14 to 1 op 12 to 1) 10
1145⁵ SANTELLA BOBKES (USA) [88] (bl) 8-11-10 A Dobbin, *dsptd*
ld, lost grnd quickly hfwy, tld off fnl circuit.
..................(16 to 1 op 14 to 1 tchd 20 to 1) 11
Dist: Sht-hd, 6l, 4l, 1½l, ½l, 12l, 10l, 3l, 10l, 4l. 6m 27.40s. a 34.40s (11 Ran).
(Mrs Karen S Pratt), Martyn Wane

1937 Tattersalls Mares Only Novices' Chase Qualifier (5-y-o and up) £2,581 3m................. (1:20)

1605² DURHAM SUNSET 6-10-10 N Doughty, *led to 7th, 1ft in ld*
11th, hrd pressed 2 out, styd on strly to go clr r-in.
.................(11 to 8 jt-fav op 5 to 4 tchd 6 to 4) 1
1723³ CHARLOTTE'S EMMA 6-10-10 B Storey, *al wl plcd, led*
7th, blun and hdd 11th, rallied last 4, one pace r-in.
.................(11 to 8 jt-fav op 5 to 4 tchd 6 to 4) 2
1530² LADY'S ISLAND (Ire) 5-10-10 J Callaghan, *patiently rdn,*
niggled alng to improve fnl circuit, outpcd appr 4 out,
tld off........................(9 to 1 op 12 to 1 tchd 8 to 1) 3
1605³ SUPER SANDY 6-10-10 A Orkney, *in tch, bustled alng to*
keep up fnl circuit, lost touch frm 5 out, tld off.
.........................(33 to 1 op 20 to 1) 4
1723 REDHALL ROYALE 9-10-10 Miss P Robson, *trkd ldg trio,*
almost uns rdr second, reminders aftr nxt, tld off fnl
circuit.........................(100 to 1 op 50 to 1) 5
1603⁶ HERE COMES TIBBY 6-10-10 T Reed, *settled midfield,*
pressed ldg pair appr 5 out, lost tch nxt, tld off.
....................(14 to 1 op 12 to 1) 6
1200 DUCHESS OF TUBBER (Ire) 5-10-7 (3*) A Thornton, *wth*
ldrs, second and ev ch whn blun and uns rdr 6 out.
.................(25 to 1 op 20 to 1) ur
Dist: 10l, 25l, 2l, 15l, 2l. 6m 43.10s. a 44.10s (7 Ran).
(W M G Black), J H Johnson

1938 Gossip Holme Novices' Hurdle (4-y-o and up) £1,982 2½m 110yds.....(1:50)

1745⁵ NORTHERN SQUIRE 5-11-0 T Reed, *led aftr 4th, jnd 3*
out, styd on strly to go clr r-in.... (16 to 1 op 14 to 1) 1
ASLAN (Ire) 5-11-0 M Dwyer, *patiently rdn, hdwy gng wl*
appr 3 out, sn ridden, no imprsn approaching last.
.............(6 to 5 fav op 6 to 4 tchd 13 to 8 and 11 to 10) 2
EASBY JOKER 5-11-0 R Garritty, *settled midfield, drw*
level 3 out, rdn whn pckd last, no extr.
...........................(6 to 1 tchd 5 to 1) 3
1099* LOCH SCAVAIG (Ire) 4-10-13 (3*) D J Moffatt, *wtd wth,*
imprvg into midfield whn blun 6th, styd on frm 3 out,
nrst finish.....................(5 to 1 op 4 to 1) 4
1722³ BARNEY RUBBLE 8-11-0 M Moloney, *nvr far away, ev ch*
appr 3 out, fdd nxt...........................(7 to 1 op 5 to 1) 5
1287⁴ FOUR DEEP (Ire) 5-12-0 J Callaghan, *keen hold, led till*
aftr 4th, hndy till wknd quickly 2 out.
.........................(10 to 1 op 8 to 1) 6
1726⁴ KIRKTON GREY 6-11-0 B Storey, *settled off the pace,*
hdwy frm 4 out, nvr plcd to chal...(16 to 1 op 14 to 1) 7
1736⁶ ISLAND RIVER (Ire) 5-11-0 C Dennis, *tucked away in mid-*
field, effrt hfwy, fdd 4 out........(66 to 1 op 50 to 1) 8
1113* CHATEAU ROUX 5-11-0 P Niven, *shaped wl till grad*
wknd frm 4 out, improve..........(7 to 1 tchd 8 to 1) 9

1736⁸ KNOCKREIGH CROSS (Ire) 4-10-2 (7*) G Cahill, *beh and pushed alng hfwy, not rch ldrs*.............. (100 to 1) 10
1722⁵ MOSSIMAN (Ire) 5-11-0 S Turner, *pressed ldrs, feeling pace and lost grnd 4 out, sn btn*....... (50 to 1 op 33 to 1) 11
1722 RUSTY BLADE 4-11-0 R Hodge, *trkd ldrs, pushed alng whn pace quickened 4 out, sn lost tch*.......(100 to 1) 12
HOWARD'S POST 4-10-7 (7*) M Malloy, *chsd ldrs, struggling to hold pl 4 out, tld off*..................(33 to 1) 13
1779⁷ THE PIPE FITTER (Ire) 5-11-0 C Grant, *trkd ldrs, lost pl appr 4 out, tld off nxt*............ (40 to 1 op 33 to 1) 14
MISS TINO 5-10-4 (5*) P Williams, *blun and uns rdr 1st*.
....(500 to 1) ur
LADYSIBELOU 5-10-9 A Dobbin, *struggling hfwy, tld off whn pld up betw last 2*......................(100 to 1) pu
Dist: 5l, ¾l, 10l, 4l, 12l, hd, hd, 1½l, 3½l, 5l. 5m 17.90s. a 24.90s (16 Ran).
SR: 32/27/26/18/12/14/   (Mrs J M Davenport), J M Jefferson

1939 Todd Hills Handicap Chase (0-135 5-y-o and up) £3,655 3¼m......... (2:20)

1725 TARTAN TYRANT [113] 7-10-11 N Doughty, *jmpd wl, confidently rdn, improved on bit 4 out, led betw last 2, readily*..................(9 to 4 op 7 to 2 tchd 2 to 1) 1
1725³ OVER THE DEEL [110] 7-10-8 A Dobbin, *jmpd wl, al well plcd, led 12th, clr 5 out, hdd betw last 2, one pace*.
......................................(4 to 1 op 3 to 1) 2
1739⁶ HOTPLATE [113] 10-10-11 M Moloney, *al hndy, ev ch and drvn alng 4 out, rdn and mstk 2 out, no extr*.
...............................(25 to 1 op 14 to 1) 3
1319⁵ FORTH AND TAY [104] 11-10-2⁷ (5*) P Williams, *wtd wth, improved fnl circuit, drvn alng aftr 5 out, no imprsn*.
...............................(16 to 1 op 14 to 1) 4
1725⁴ PLENTY CRACK [130] 10-12-0 B Storey, *not fluent, wth ldrs, led tenth to 12th, hit 6 out, sn struggling*.
.................................(2 to 1 fav op 6 to 4) 5
1359 BUCKLE IT UP [108] 9-10-6 Mr D Mactaggart, *made most to 6th, drvn alng whn pace quickened appr six out, sn tld off*...........................(40 to 1 op 33 to 1) 6
1635⁶ BOREEN OWEN [110] 9-10-8 P Niven, *dsptd ld, led 6th to tenth, hit six out, blun nxt, not reco'r, pld up bef 4 out*.
.................................(8 to 1 op 7 to 1) pu
Dist: 12l, 3½l, 7l, 8l, 30l. 7m 12.50s. a 42.50s (7 Ran).
(The Edinburgh Woollen Mill Ltd), G Richards

1940 Mary Brow Handicap Hurdle (0-125 4-y-o and up) £2,551 (2:50)

1728⁸ SWEET CITY [100] 8-10-0³ (7*) Mr R Hale, *settled midfield, pushed alng to improve frm 4 out, styd on wl to ld r-in*.
.................................(4 to 1 tchd 9 to 2) 1
1186⁵ MASTER OF TROY [96] 5-9-12⁵ (7*) Mr A Parker, *patiently rdn, led aftr 4 out, ridden whn hit last, hdd and no extr r-in*..................(9 to 2 op 4 to 1) 2
1728² WEE WIZARD (Ire) [98] 4-10-2 A Dobbin, *nvr far away, ev ch and drvn alng frm 3 out, not quicken betw last 2*.
..................(7 to 4 fav op 6 to 4 tchd 2 to 1) 3
1489 YAHEEB (USA) [120] 9-11-10 Mr S Swiers, *steadied strt, hdwy appr 3 out, nvr able to chal*. (12 to 1 op 10 to 1) 4
1586 GOLDEN REVERIE (USA) [97] 5-10-1¹ B Storey, *chsd ldrs, bustled alng to stay in tch aftr 4 out, no imprsn nxt*.
.................................(50 to 1 op 33 to 1) 5
1571 DIZZY (USA) [124] 5-12-0 A Orkney, *made most till aftr 4 out, wknd quickly last 2, eased r-in*. (9 to 1 op 7 to 1) 6
GREY MERLIN [96] 6-9-10¹ (5*) D Bentley, *wth ldrs, struggling to hold pl appr 4 out, tld off*. (50 to 1 op 33 to 1) 7
1669 BELLAGROVE (Ire) [96] 5-9-7 (7*) G Cahill, *wth ldr, reminders 4th, lost tch 5 out, tld off*.
.................................(50 to 1 op 33 to 1) 8
LOGICAL FUN [105] 5-10-6 (3*) D J Moffatt, *in tch, chsd alng hfwy, tld off whn pld up betw last 2*.
..................(13 to 2 op 16 to 1 tchd 6 to 1) pu
Dist: 2l, 4l, 12l, 15l, 1l, 4l, ½l. 4m 27.00s. a 20.00s (9 Ran).
SR: 37/31/29/39/1/27/   (W J Peacock), G Richards

1941 Hoary Tom Amateur Riders' Handicap Chase (0-120 5-y-o and up) £2,782 2½m 110yds................... (3:20)

1486⁷ VIVA BELLA (Fr) [87] (bl) 6-10-1 (7*) M D Parker, *al wl plcd, drvn to ld bef 3 out, kpt on und pres frm last*.
...............................(14 to 1 tchd 16 to 1) 1
1669³ ISLAND GALE [88] 8-10-2 (7*) Miss P Robson, *settled midfield, improved hfwy, rdn alng frm 6 out, styd on r-in*.
.................................(6 to 1 op 5 to 1) 2
1789⁸ ON THE HOOCH [101] 8-11-5 (3*) Mr J Bradburne, *led till appr 3 out, drvn alng nxt, one pace*.
..................(11 to 2 op 5 to 1 tchd 33 to 1) 3
1638⁴ PINEMARTIN [103] 10-11-3 (7*) Mr R Hale, *nvr far away, effrt 6 out, rdn nxt, no extr*.......(10 to 1 tchd 12 to 1) 4
1676² MOYODE REGENT [86] 9-10-0 (7*) Mr A Manners, *wtd wth, jnd ldrs appr 6 out, rdn and outpcd 4 out*.
.................................(9 to 2 op 4 to 1) 5
1606⁷ MERITMOORE [94] (bl) 10-11-1 Mr S Swiers, *wth ldr, pushed alng and lost grnd hfwy, fdd 6 out*.
.................................(10 to 1 op 4 to 1) 6

1218³ CAITHNESS PRINCE [90] 7-10-6 (5*) Mr M Buckley, *chsd ldrs, effrt hfwy, struggling 6 out, tld off*.
..........(3 to 1 fav op 7 to 2 tchd 4 to 1 and 11 to 4) 7
KAMBALDA RAMBLER [98] 9-10-12 (7*) Mr A Parker, *mstks, reminders 9th, tld off whn pld up bef 2 out*.
.................................(8 to 1 op 7 to 1) pu
Dist: 2½l, 12l, 5l, 8l, 10l, nk. 5m 34.30s. a 31.30s (8 Ran).
(L H Froomes), Mrs S A Bramall

FONTWELL (heavy)
Thursday December 30th
Going Correction: PLUS 2.50 sec. per fur.

1942 Tortington Selling Hurdle (4,5,6-y-o) £1,704 2¼m.................. (1:15)

1699 PEACOCK FEATHER 5-11-6 M A FitzGerald, *made all, drw clr aftr 3 out, very easily*...........(11 to 2 op 7 to 1) 1
1412 MILLY BLACK (Ire) 5-11-6 D Gallagher, *prmnt till rdn and lost pl aftr 5th, sn al beh, styd on frm 2 out, took second nr finish*....................(13 to 2 op 10 to 1) 2
1597⁵ COBB GATE (bl) 5-11-5 M Stevens, *hld up beh, steady prog frm 6th, chsd wnr appr last, no imprsn, fnshd tired*.................................(8 to 1 op 10 to 1) 3
1655³ SKIMMER HAWK 4-11-5 V Smith, *prmnt, rdn to chase wnr aftr 6th, wknd after 2 out*.........(100 to 30 op 5 to 2) 4
1711⁷ SAKIL (Ire) 5-11-12 (5*) A Dicken, *hld up, no prog aftr 5th, fnshd tired*.........................(10 to 1 op 7 to 1) 5
WHATMORECANIASKFOR (Ire) 5-10-7 (7*) D Meade, *sn rdn alng, al beh, tld off 5th*..........(33 to 1 op 20 to 1) 6
1245⁸ MASROUG 6-11-4 (7*) J Clarke, *prmnt, chsd wnr 5th till aftr nxt, sn rdn, wknd rpdly*.
..................(5 to 2 fav op 9 to 4 tchd 11 to 4) 7
JULFAAR (USA) 6-11-0 (5*) J Twomey, *hld up, prog 5th, 4th whn blun nxt, sn wknd. pld up bef 2 out*.
..................(12 to 1 op 5 to 1 tchd 14 to 1) pu
1598⁵ TAPESTRY DANCER 5-11-11 D Skyrme, *hld up, lost tch 6th, tld off whn pld up bef 2 out*.
.................................(20 to 1 op 16 to 1 tchd 25 to 1) pu
EL PERSA (USA) 5-11-5 H Davies, *al beh, tld off 5th till pld up bef 2 out*..........(20 to 1 op 14 to 1) pu
Dist: 15l, 5l, 12l, 30l, 1½l, 15l. 5m 8.00s. a 58.00s (10 Ran).
(Mrs J Smith), K R Burke

1943 Brighton Handicap Chase (0-115 5-y-o and up) £2,551 3¼m 110yds.....(1:45)

1565⁶ TAMMY'S FRIEND [98] (bl) 6-11-2 I Lawrence, *trkd ldrs gng wl, led 9th, clr 2 out, easily*. (2 to 1 co-fav tchd 9 to 4) 1
SILVERINO [98] 7-11-2 M Richards, *jmpd slwly second, prmnt, pushed alng aftr 15th, chsd wnr appr 3 out, no imprsn*.......(2 to 1 co-fav tchd 7 to 4 and 9 to 4) 2
1600⁴ SHASTON [100] (bl) 8-11-4 M A FitzGerald, *mstks, prmnt, chsd wnr tenth till wknd appr 3 out*.......(2 to 1 co-fav tchd 5 to 2) 3
1607⁷ MACHO MAN [97] 8-10-12 (3*) P Hide, *made most to 9th, rdn and wknd 14th, pld up bef 17th*.
..................(20 to 1 op 10 to 1 tchd 14 to 1) pu
1463⁵ ON YOUR WAY [83] 11-10-1¹ W McFarland, *beh, effrt aftr 15th, sn wknd, tld off whn pld up bef 3 out*.
..................(25 to 1 op 12 to 1 tchd 33 to 1) pu
Dist: 12l, 15l. 7m 52.60s. a 82.60s (5 Ran).
(Mrs Elizabeth Hitchins), Mrs J Pitman

1944 Whitelaw Challenge Cup Handicap Chase (0-130 4-y-o and up) £3,614 2m 3f............................ (2:15)

1572⁴ CITY KID [112] 8-10-12 (3*) P Hide, *made all, clr 3 out, ran on wl aftr last*.................(13 to 8 fav op 11 to 10) 1
1248 CONGREGATION [102] 7-10-5¹ H Davies, *hld up beh, prog 11th, ran on strly frm 2 out, not rch wnr*.
..................(14 to 1 op 9 to 2) 2
1733⁵ MASTER COMEDY [97] (bl) 9-10-0 D Gallagher, *chsd ldg pair, mstk 11th, sn wknd*.
...............................(25 to 1 op 16 to 1 tchd 33 to 1) 3
1446³ ALKINOR REX [125] 8-12-0 M Perrett, *wnr wnr to 6th, reminder aftr 8th, blun 11th, disputing second whn blunded and uns rdr last*.
..................(2 to 1 op 7 to 4 tchd 5 to 2) ur
MASTER SOUTH LAD [97] 9-10-0 D Skyrme, *hld up, struggling 9th, tld off whn pld up bef 2 out*.
..................(14 to 1 op 10 to 1 tchd 16 to 1) pu
Dist: 1½l, dist. 5m 31.80s. a 56.80s (5 Ran).
(Pell-Mell Partners), J T Gifford

1945 Worthing Handicap Hurdle (0-130 4-y-o and up) £2,092 2¼m......... (2:45)

1753⁴ WHIPPERS DELIGHT (Ire) [100] 5-10-5 (7*) D Meade, *made all, drw clr frm 6th, eased r-in, unchlgd*.
..................(11 to 2 op 5 to 1) 1
1597* DERISBAY (Ire) [88] (bl) 5-9-13⁴ (5*) A Dicken, *al chasing wnr, outpcd frm 6th, rdn and kpt on r-in*.
..................(7 to 1 op 5 to 1 tchd 8 to 1) 2

1561 SURE PRIDE (USA) [102] 5-10-7 (7*) J Clarke, *chsd ldg pair, rdn to go second briefly aftr last, no imprsn.*

.... (10 to 1 op 6 to 1) 3

1709² SOLEIL DANCER (Ire) [99] 5-10-11 J Railton, *hld up middiv, prog gng easily 5th, outpcd nxt, no ch whn blun last.*........... (5 to 1 op 4 to 1 tchd 11 to 2) 4

1599³ ALOSAILI [94] 6-10-6² M Stevens, *sn last and beh, styd on frm 2 out, nvr nr to chal.*..........(14 to 1 op 10 to 1) 5

1709³ MY SENOR [92] 4-10-4 M A FitzGerald, *chsd ldrs till rdn and wknd aftr 5th.*................. (6 to 1 op 10 to 1) 6

1772⁹ DIRECTORS' CHOICE [80] (bl) 8-10-1¹ W McFarland, *prog 5th, rdn bef nxt, sn btn.*..........(25 to 1 tchd 33 to 1) 7

1601* JOVIAL MAN (Ire) [93] 4-10-5 M Perrett, *beh frm 4th.*

.... (5 to 2 fav op 11 to 4 tchd 100 to 30) 8

L'ORAGE (Ire) [113] 5-11-4 (7*) N Collum, *al beh, tld off 6th.*

.... (25 to 1 op 20 to 1) 9

1249⁸ FRONT PAGE [100] 6-10-12 D Murphy, *chsd ldrs till wknd 6th, tld off whn pld up bef 2 out.*..... (9 to 2 op 5 to 1) pu

Dist: 15l, 2½l, 10l, 8l, 20l, sht-hd. 5m 1.60s. a 51.60s (10 Ran).

SR: 18/-/2/-/-/-/ (S P Tindall), G F H Charles-Jones

TAUNTON (Soft)
Thursday December 30th
Going Correction: PLUS 1.47 sec. per fur.

1946
Holly Tree Novices' Hurdle (Div I) (4-y-o and up) £1,742 2m 1f.......(1:00)

1729² TRYING AGAIN 5-10-10 P Holley, *led, drw clr appr 2 out, styd on strly.*...................(4 to 1 tchd 11 to 2) 1

1695³ EMPIRE BLUE 10-10-10 M Bosley, *hld up, beh 4th, hdwy to chase ldr aftr 5th, pushed alng 3 out, styd on betw last 2, not trble wnr.*..(10 to 1 op 7 to 1 tchd 11 to 1) 2

SESAME SEED (Ire) 5-10-10 B Powell, *hld up, beh 4th, hdwy aftr nxt, pushed alng 3 out, fourth whn mstk next, styd on r-in....* (14 to 1 op 12 to 1 tchd 16 to 1) 3

1695* BOLD STROKE 4-11-3 R Dunwoody, *not fluent 1st 2, trkd ldr frm 4th, wnt second 6th, rdn alng from nxt, wknd appr last.*....................(5 to 4 on op 11 to 10) 4

1636* WITH IMPUNITY 4-11-3 D Bridgwater, *trkd ldr in second pl, rdn alng aftr 6th, wknd quickly after 3 out.*

.................................(7 to 2 op 9 to 4) 5

MAHATMACOAT 6-10-10 S Burrough, *trkd ldg pair, niggled alng aftr 5th, wknd after 4 out, tld off.*

.................................(40 to 1 op 33 to 1) 6

1717 POLDEN PRIDE 6-10-10 Richard Guest, *hld up, beh 4th, last whn mstk nxt, sn tld off.*......(50 to 1 op 33 to 1) 7

1456 LONG'S EXPRESS (Ire) 5-10-5 N Williamson, *lost tch aftr 3rd, tld off after nxt.*.............(40 to 1 op 20 to 1) 8

1622 EAGLES LAIR 7-10-5 (5*) J McCarthy, *hld up, beh 4th, lost tch aftr nxt, tld off whn pld up bef 2 out.*

.................................(100 to 1 op 50 to 1) pu

Dist: 10l, 3l, 2l, 25l, 20l, 3½l, 15l. 4m 17.00s. a 30.00s (9 Ran).

SR: 32/22/19/24/-/-/ (W H Dore), D R Gandolfo

1947
Reindeer Novices' Chase £2,593 2m 110yds....................... (1:30)

1525* KIBREET 6-11-4 S Earle, *led aftr second, hdd 6th, trkd ldr till led ag'n 5 out, drw clr after 3 out, unchlgd.*

.................................(100 to 30 op 5 to 2) 1

1701⁶ VILLA RECOS 8-11-0 N Williamson, *hld up, hdwy aftr 8, wnt second 4 out, btn whn blun nxt, no imprsn.*

.... CAOIMSEACH (Ire) .... (12 to 1 op 20 to 1 tchd 25 to 1) 2

1525 PALM SWIFT 7-10-9 A Tory, *led till aftr second, led ag'n 6th till hdd 5 out, sn wknd.*...... (50 to 1 op 25 to 1) 3

1008⁴ MINE'S AN ACE (NZ) 6-11-4 J Frost, *hld up, hmpd 4th, hdwy aftr 8th, moderate fourth whn f nxt.*

.................................(4 to 1 op 3 to 1) f

1505 MISAAFF 10-11-0 R Dunwoody, *in tch whn stumbled and uns rdr 4th.*.................... (7 to 1 op 6 to 1) ur

1505² JAMES THE FIRST 5-11-0 G Bradley, *hld up, mstk 5th, hdwy aftr nxt, 3rd whn blun and uns rdr 8th.*

.................................(5 to 2 fav op 11 to 4 tchd 3 to 1) ur

BALLINAMOE 8-11-0 W Marston, *beh, rdn 6th, rear whn blun and uns rdr 8th.*..........(66 to 1 op 33 to 1) ur

1667⁵ KETTI 8-10-6 (3*) R Davis, *al struggling, tld off aftr 6th, pld up bef 9th.*....................(7 to 1 op 5 to 1) pu

1708⁷ SOLO CORNET 8-11-0 Gary Lyons, *beh 6th, tld off whn pld up bef 5 out.*..... (25 to 1 op 20 to 1 tchd 33 to 1) pu

Dist: 20l, 20l. 4m 39.20s. a 41.20s (9 Ran).

(Derek Simester), R H Alner

1948
Hangover Novices' Selling Handicap Hurdle (4,5,6-y-o) £1,658 3m 110yds ....(2:00)

1719⁴ MOBILE MESSENGER (NZ) [82] 5-11-7 (7*) Mr G Shenkin, *hld up and beh, hdwy aftr 8th, wnt second after 3 out, led after last, drvn out.* (5 to 1 op 3 to 1 tchd 11 to 2) 1

1716⁷ BLUE LYZANDER [60] 4-10-6 D Bridgwater, *hld up, trkd ldrs frm 5th, led aftr 8th, sn clr, rdn and wknd appr last, hdd r-in, one pace.*

.................................(11 to 1 op 10 to 1 tchd 12 to 1) 2

1463⁶ DEVIOSITY (USA) [63] 6-10-9 B Powell, *lost pl aftr 6th, hdwy 4 out, 3rd whn mstk 2 out, no imprsn.*

.... (20 to 1 op 10 to 1) 3

1717³ SOUL TRADER [72] 4-11-4 S Burrough, *lost pl and rdn alng aftr 5th, hdwy after 7th, second whn jmpd lft 3 out, ridden and no imprsn....* (5 to 2 fav tchd 11 to 4) 4

1801 THANKSFORTHEOFFER [63] (bl) 5-10-9 P McDermott, *prmnt whn mstk 5th, chsd ldr till wknd aftr 4 out.*

.... (11 to 1 op 8 to 1) 5

1699 GREAT IMPOSTOR [62] 5-10-8 R Dunwoody, *hld up, chsd ldr frm 6th till wknd 3 out, tld off....*(7 to 1 op 3 to 1) 6

KEMALS DELIGHT [70] 6-11-2 Jacqui Oliver, *hld up, lost tch aftr 7th, tld off 3 out.*

.... (5 to 1 tchd 6 to 1 and 9 to 2) 7

1624⁷ ASSEMBLY DANCER [54] 6-10-0 Gee Armytage, *chsd ldr, led aftr 7th, hdd and pckd nxt, sn wknd, beh whn pld up bef 9th.*...................(12 to 1 op 5 to 1) pu

1716 LIRELLA [60] 6-10-6 I Shoemark, *led till hdd aftr 7th, wknd rpdly, tld off whn pld up after 8th.*

.... (25 to 1 op 20 to 1) pu

1280⁶ NORDROSS [59] 5-10-5 T Wall, *pld hrd, hld up, hdwy aftr 5th, led 8th, sn hdd, wknd quickly, beh whn pulled up bef 9th.*..........................(5 to 1 op 7 to 2) pu

1495 JUST BALLYTOO [62] (bl) 6-10-8 W Marston, *hld up, hdwy 3rd, lost pl aftr 7th, tld off whn pld up bef 9th.*

.................................(16 to 1 tchd 20 to 1) pu

Dist: 4l, 2½l, 8l, 20l, dist, 6l. 6m 42.00s. a 67.50s (11 Ran).

(J B Wilcox), D H Barons

1949
Christmas Pudding Conditional Jockeys' Handicap Hurdle (0-120 3-y-o and up) £1,700 2m 1f.......... (3:00)

1632* CARDINAL BIRD (USA) [88] (bl) 6-10-6 (5*) Chris Webb, *hld up in last pl, hdwy aftr 4th, cld on ldrs after 2 out, led last, drvn clr r-in.*.............. (7 to 4 fav op 5 to 4) 1

1703 NOBLE YEOMAN [95] 9-11-4 D Meredith, *hld up, hdwy aftr 4th, ev ch appr last, not quicken r-in.*

.... (6 to 1 op 14 to 1) 2

1697* CELCIUS [101] (bl) 9-11-10 T Dascombe, *wnt second 4th, trkd ldr, led aftr 2 out, hdd last, rdn and not quicken.*

.... (15 to 8 op 5 to 4) 3

EXACT ANALYSIS (USA) [88] 7-10-11 S Curran, *led till hdd aftr 2 out, rdn and styd on one pace.*

.... (13 to 2 op 6 to 1 tchd 5 to 1) 4

1510⁸ GLOWING PATH [80] 3-10-3 R Davis, *trkd ldrs, ev ch 3 out, rdn and wknd aftr nxt.*

.................................(12 to 1 op 10 to 1 tchd 14 to 1) 5

1493 VERSATILE [77] 9-10-0 D Matthews, *drpd rear 4th, sn pushed alng, no ch aftr 3 out.*

.................................(16 to 1 op 20 to 1 tchd 25 to 1 and 14 to 1) 6

OUNAVARRA MILL [80] 7-10-3 V Slattery, *pressed ldr till drvn alng and lost pl appr 4th, sn beh.*

.................................(25 to 1 op 20 to 1 tchd 33 to 1) 7

Dist: 8l, 2l, 12l, 6l, 20l, 5l. 4m 32.40s. a 45.40s (7 Ran).

(John Fane), S Mellor

1950
Holly Tree Novices' Hurdle (Div II) (4-y-o and up) £1,742 2m 1f.....(4:00)

1613 MOAT GARDEN (USA) 5-11-3 J Frost, *made all, drw clr appr last, cmftbly....*(5 to 4 fav op Evens tchd 6 to 4) 1

1519 MARY'S MUSIC 5-10-5 C Maude, *hld up and beh, hdwy aftr 4th, wnt 3rd appr last, styd on r-in, not rch wnr.*

.................................(14 to 1 op 12 to 1 tchd 16 to 1) 2

1589⁵ CAOIMSEACH (Ire) 5-10-10 S Mackey, *hld up in tch, chsd ldr aftr 4th, styd on appr last, one pace.*

.... (10 to 1 op 7 to 1) 3

1794⁴ TENDRESSE (Ire) 5-10-5 R Dunwoody, *trkd ldr, wnt second aftr 5th, ev ch after 2 out, rdn and wknd appr last.*

.... (5 to 2 tchd 3 to 1 and 9 to 4) 4

1695 GREEN'S GAME 5-10-10 G Upton, *hld up, rdn alng aftr 4th, kept one pace after 2 out....*(14 to 1 op 12 to 1) 5

1716⁹ REALLY NEAT 7-10-11 (5*) D Matthews, *hld up, hdwy 4th, ev ch 2 out, rdn and wknd appr last.*

.................................(50 to 1 op 25 to 1) 6

1515 SNICKERSNEE 5-10-10 S Hodgson, *trkd ldr till wknd quickly 2 out, btn whn mstk last, tld off.*

.................................(14 to 1 op 25 to 1) 7

1301⁹ CANCALE (Ire) 5-10-10 P Holley, *hld up in tch, drvn alng aftr 4th, sn wknd, tld off after 2 out.*

.................................(16 to 1 op 12 to 1 tchd 20 to 1) 8

1797 RHYMING PROSE 5-10-5 T Grantham, *hld up, effrt aftr 4th, sn wknd, mstk 2 out, tld off....* (9 to 1 op 9 to 2) 9

Dist: 10l, 7l, 8l, 4l, 3l, 30l, 20l, 2l. 4m 33.40s. a 46.40s (9 Ran).

(Queen Elizabeth), I A Balding

WARWICK (heavy (races 1,3,4,5,7), soft (2,6))
Thursday December 30th
Going Correction: PLUS 1.00 sec. per fur.

1951
Bob Cratchit Novices' Hurdle (4-y-o and up) £1,473 2m........... (12:40)

1622* TOPPING TOM (Ire) 4-11-7 C Llewellyn, *led 3rd, hit 2 out, edgd lft aftr last, styd on wl.*
.... (2 to 1 tchd 9 to 4 and 7 to 4) 1
1536 THE FROG PRINCE (Ire) 5-11-0 R Supple, *hdwy frm 4th, sstnd chal from 2 out, ran on wl nr finish.*
.... (20 to 1 op 14 to 1) 2
1202⁵ TROOPING (Ire) 4-11-0 L Wyer, *led to 3rd, pressed ldrs, ev ch and not quicken betw last 2 flights.*
.... (16 to 1 op 8 to 1) 3
1661⁵ LINPAC WEST 7-11-7 A Maguire, *cld on wnr frm 4th, mstk 6th, no extr und pres appr 2 out.*
.... (6 to 4 on op 7 to 4 on tchd 5 to 4 on) 4
NO BATTERY NEEDED 6-10-9 (5*) J Supple, *beh frm 5th.*
.... (100 to 1 op 50 to 1) 5
PEACE FORMULA (Ire) 4-11-0 R Bellamy, *al towards rear, tld off aftr 4th.......* (33 to 1 op 20 to 1 tchd 50 to 1) 6
1773⁵ ROUSITTO 5-10-11 (3*) S Wynne, *in tch in mid-div, wknd frm 4th, f last................* (14 to 1 op 8 to 1 tchd 16 to 1) f
CELTIC BLOOM 6-10-9 R J Beggan, *al beh, tld off frm 4th, pld up bef 2 out....................* (66 to 1 op 33 to 1) pu
Dist: 1½l, 4l, 5l, dist, 5l. 4m 3.80s. a 23.80s (8 Ran).
SR: 15/6/2/4/-/ (Mrs J Mould), N A Twiston-Davies

1952 Charlie Johnson Payne Novices' Handicap Chase (4-y-o and up) £3,756 3¼m. . . . . (1:10)

1657* VELEDA II (Fr) [96] 6-11-5 (5*) J Burke, *pressed ldrs, led 5th to 11th, led 17th to 2 out, rallied und pres to ld r-in, all out......................* (7 to 1 op 4 to 1) 1
1776* DOROBO (NZ) [81] (bl) 5-10-6 (3*) R Farrant, *ldg grp, led 15th to 17th, led 2 out, hrd rdn and hdd r-in, all out.*
.... (3 to 1 tchd 7 to 2) 2
1805 LASTOFTHEVIKINGS [74] 8-10-2 R Supple, *blun 3rd, hdwy frm rear 12th, took third pl aftr last.* (14 to 1 op 10 to 1) 3
1776 THE POD'S REVENGE [72] 8-9-9 (5*) A Procter, *wl plcd, led 11th to 15th, mstk 3 out, wknd nxt.* (25 to 1 op 10 to 1) 4
1505⁵ LINGER HILL [72] 6-10-0 R Bellamy, *cl up till hit 6th, lost pl, rear frm tenth, tld off 14th.*
.... (12 to 1 op 10 to 1 tchd 14 to 1) 5
1776² SILVER AGE (USA) [80] 7-10-8 A Maguire, *hld up in tch till f 11th................................* (3 to 1) f
1770 CROFT MILL [85] 7-10-13 J Osborne, *led to 5th, lost pl aftr tenth, hmpd nxt, tld off wkn bld up bef 3 out.*
.... (9 to 4 fav op 7 to 4 tchd 5 to 2) pu
Dist: Hd, 10l, 2½l, dist. 7m 3.10s. a 49.10s (7 Ran).
(L H Froomes), Mrs S A Bramall

1953 Tiny Tim Novices' Hurdle (4-y-o and up) £1,473 2½m 110yds. . . . . (1:40)

1622² CASTLE COURT (Ire) 5-11-0 C Llewellyn, *made virtually all, hit last, hld on und pres cl hme.*
.... (3 to 1 tchd 7 to 2 and 11 to 4) 1
1283* WINNOWING (Ire) 5-11-7 J Osborne, *hld up wl in tch, ev ch whn not fluent 2 out, rallied und pres frm last, jst fld....................* (11 to 10 fav op Evens tchd 5 to 4) 2
1448 SIMON JOSEPH 6-11-0 A Maguire, *hld up towards rear, prog 7th, rdn and hit 2 out, no extr appr last.*
.... (3 to 1 op 5 to 1) 3
1773² RAFTERS 4-11-0 B Clifford, *not fluent 3rd, hdwy frm rear 8th, styd on one pace appr 2 out....* (8 to 1 op 5 to 1) 4
RAKAIA RIVER (NZ) 6-10-11 (3*) R Farrant, *prog frm rear appr 7th, wknd from 3 out, tld off.* (25 to 1 op 14 to 1) 5
1645⁹ MARINERS COVE 5-11-0 W Humphreys, *prmnt til wknd 7th, tld off.....................* (10 to 1 op 33 to 1) 6
PETRADARE 6-10-4 (5*) T Eley, *mid-div til lost pl aftr 5th, tld off frm 7th......................* (66 to 1 op 50 to 1) 7
1668³ BIGWHEEL BILL (Ire) 4-11-0 S Smith Eccles, *ldg grp til wknd 3 out, tld off.............* (14 to 1 op 10 to 1) 8
EMERALD WATERS 6-10-9 R Marley, *wl plcd til wknd frm 7th, pld up aftr 3 out.........* (40 to 1 op 20 to 1) pu
1624⁵ NAVAL BATTLE 6-10-9 (5*) A Procter, *hld up, effrt 7th, wknd 3 out, mstk nxt, pld up bef last.*
.... (33 to 1 op 20 to 1) pu
Dist: Hd, 8l, 8l, dist, ½l, ¾l, 15l. 5m 23.10s. a 35.60s (10 Ran).
(Mrs David Thompson), N A Gaselee

1954 Blackmore Amateur Riders' Handicap Chase (0-130 5-y-o and up) £4,552 2½m 110yds. . . . . (2:10)

1798² PITHY [100] 11-10-10 (7*) Mr G Hogan, *chsd ldr frm 11th, rdn to get up nr finish.* (15 to 8 op 7 to 4 tchd 2 to 1) 1
1489³ CHIASSO FORTE (Ity) [104] 10-11-4 (3*) Mr J Durkan, *sn led, clr 7th, jnd appr last, hdd und pres nr line.*
.... (9 to 4 fav op 6 to 4) 2
1407* ARDCRONEY CHIEF [107] 7-11-5 (5*) Miss P Jones, *jmpd slwly early stages, chsd ldr to 11th, outpcd frm 4 out.*
.... (9 to 4 op 7 to 4 tchd 5 to 2) 3
Dist: Nk, 30l. 5m 25.50s. a 30.50s (3 Ran).
(B Owen), R J Price

1955 Mintexdon Handicap Hurdle (0-135 4-y-o and up) £3,600 2m. . . . . (2:40)

1868* NORTHERN SADDLER [111] 6-12-0 (6ex) G McCourt, *made all, rdn clr frm last.....* (6 to 1 op 9 to 2 tchd 13 to 2) 1
1474 ZEALOUS KITTEN (USA) [100] 5-11-3 J Osborne, *lost pl 3rd, styd on appr 2 out, took second place und pres r-in.*
.... (5 to 1 tchd 4 to 1) 2
SOCIETY GUEST [101] 7-11-4 S McNeill, *cl up, rdn alng and ev ch appr 2 out, one pace frm last.*
.... (14 to 1 op 8 to 1) 3
1364⁴ SAYMORE [102] 7-11-2 (3*) S Wynne, *hld up in rear, pushed alng 3 out, no imprsn on ldrs frm nxt.*
.... (11 to 2 op 3 to 1) 4
1703⁶ SUPER SPELL [107] 7-11-10 C Llewellyn, *chsd ldrs til wknd appr 5th, tld off.* (13 to 2 op 8 to 1 tchd 6 to 1) 5
1292* SUNSET ROCK [98] 6-11-1 A Maguire, *pressed wnr frm 4th til rdn and lost pl whn f 2 out.*
.... (Evens fav op 5 to 4 tchd 11 to 8) f
Dist: 3½l, 1½l, 8l, dist. 4m 1.50s. a 21.50s (6 Ran).
SR: 45/30/29/22/-/-/ (Richard J Evans), R J Hodges

1956 Walter Charles Challenge Trophy Novices' Chase (4-y-o and up) £3,822 2m. . . . . (3:10)

1493* THE FLYING FOOTMAN 7-11-10 A Maguire, *pressed ldr, led appr 6th to 8th, blun 9th, dsptd ld frm 3 out til definite advantage last 100 yards, rcd clr.*
.... (13 to 8 on tchd 11 to 8 on) 1
1492 MISTER ODDY 7-11-4 S Smith Eccles, *trkd ldrs, led 8th, dsptd ld frm 3 out til hdd and one pace last 100 yards.*
.... (14 to 1 op 10 to 1 tchd 16 to 1) 2
1737 EMERALD RULER 6-11-4 G McCourt, *hit 5th, prog nxt, outpcd frm 9th.....................* (9 to 2 op 7 to 2) 3
1709 JALINGO 6-11-4 B Clifford, *not jump wl, sn beh, blun 5th, pld up bef nxt.....................* (10 to 1 op 8 to 1) pu
1795² DAWN CHANCE 7-11-4 C Llewellyn, *led till appr 6th, sn wknd, pld up bef 8th...* (6 to 1 op 7 to 1 tchd 11 to 2) pu
Dist: 5l, 20l. 4m 15.40s. a 23.40s (5 Ran).
SR: 22/11/ (Mrs James West), D Nicholson

1957 Christmas Present National Hunt Flat Race (4,5,6-y-o) £2,087 2m. . . . . . (3:40)

BEATSON (Ire) 4-10-9 (5*) T Jenks, *al wl plcd, rdn to join ldr 5 out, led o'r 2 out, drvn out.....* (6 to 1 op 3 to 1) 1
1806⁴ FLAPJACK LAD 4-10-7 (7*) Mr M Rimell, *led til hdd o'r 2 out, kpt on same pace fnl furlong.*
.... (7 to 1 tchd 9 to 2 and 5 to 1) 2
1027³ BASS ROCK 5-10-7 (7*) R Darke, *hld up, steady prog o'r 4 out, rdn and one pace fnl furlong.* (7 to 4 fav tchd 9 to 4) 3
HENRY'S SISTER 6-10-2 (7*) P Ward, *hld up, hdwy o'r 2 fs out, styd on one pace fnl furlong.* (16 to 1 op 14 to 1) 4
COUNTRY PARSON (Ire) 4-10-7 (7*) E Tolhurst, *hld up, improved 5 out, not quicken ins last 2 fs.*
.... (33 to 1 op 20 to 1) 5
1027 DREAMLINE 4-10-2 (7*) M P FitzGerald, *beh til styd on last 3 fs.....................* (50 to 1) 6
THE MEXICANS GONE 5-10-9 (5*) Mr T Byrne, *improved frm rear aftr hfwy, no extr ins last 2 fs.*
.... (33 to 1 op 25 to 1) 7
UNCERTAIN TIMES 6-11-0 Mrs M Grantham, *beh til moderate prog last 3 fs...............* (10 to 1 op 7 to 1) 8
1674⁶ SEATWIST 4-10-7 (7*) P McLoughlin, *ldg grp til rdn and wknd o'r one furlong out.*
.... (16 to 1 op 20 to 1 tchd 25 to 1) 9
1674⁹ SPA KELLY 5-10-9 (5*) T Eley, *hdwy 4 fs out, not rch frnt rnk.........................* (20 to 1 op 25 to 1) 10
1428⁷ PARAMOUNT 4-11-0 Mr J Durkan, *in tch in mid-div, no imprsn fnl 4 fs..................* (20 to 1 op 14 to 1) 11
1660 BREAD OF HEAVEN 4-10-2 (7*) D Fortt, *prmsg effrt on outsd hfwy, wknd last 3 fs........* (33 to 1 op 16 to 1) 12
1779⁹ FINWAG 6-10-11 (3*) S Wynne, *in tch for 12 fs...* (50 to 1) 13
RECTORY GARDEN (Ire) 4-10-11 (3*) R Farrant, *nvr nr to chal.........................* (10 to 1 op 8 to 1) 14
LONE WOLF 5-10-2 (7*) A Shakespeare, *chsd ldrs till wknd o'r 4 fs out....................* (50 to 1 op 33 to 1) 15
ZUB ZUB 6-10-2 (7*) G Crone, *took clr order on outsd hfwy, wknd last 4 fs.................* (50 to 1) 16
1660 ANNE CARTER 4-10-4 (5*) A Procter, *cl up til wknd 7 fs out...................................* (33 to 1) 17
NOREN (Ire) 4-10-7 (7*) T Thompson, *in tch to hfwy.*
.... (33 to 1 op 20 to 1) 18
LADY ORWELL (Ire) 4-10-2 (7*) A Flannigan, *ldg grp for 11 fs...........................* (25 to 1 op 20 to 1) 19
MARINERS DANCE 5-10-2 (7*) Mr G Hogan, *al beh, tld off.*
.... (33 to 1) 20
GREENHAM COMMON 4-10-7 (7*) J Bond, *al beh, tld off appr hfwy....................* (33 to 1 op 20 to 1) 21
Dist: 4l, 2½l, 1½l, 6l, ½l, 2½l, 6l, 2½l, 2½l, ¾l. 3m 58.20s. (21 Ran).
(Mrs E B Gardiner), N A Twiston-Davies

CATTERICK (soft)
Friday December 31st
Going Correction: PLUS 1.10 sec. per fur. (races 1,3,5), PLUS 0.80 (2,4,6)

1958 Camp Novices' Chase (5-y-o and up) £1,488 2m................. (12:30)

1735*	POLITICAL TOWER 6-11-7 A Dobbin, *wth ldr, led 6th, lft clr 8th, blun last, easily*............(7 to 2 tchd 4 to 1)	1
1735⁴	GOLDEN ISLE 9-11-0 B Storey, *in tch till outpcd aftr 6th, chsd wnr frm 8th, no imprsn*.....(14 to 1 tchd 20 to 1)	2
1743³	GYMCRAK STARDOM 7-11-0 L Wyer, *in tch till outpcd aftr 6th, tld off*............(9 to 2 op 7 to 2)	3
1735	FRICKLEY 7-11-10 N Doughty, *slight ld to 6th, chasing wnr whn f 8th*...........(13 to 8 on tchd 6 to 4 on)	f

Dist: 20l, dist. 4m 12.40s. a 23.40s (4 Ran).
SR: 35/8/-/-/ (G R S Nixon), M A Barnes

1959 Stand 'National Hunt' Novices' Hurdle (4-y-o and up) £1,030 2m...... (1:00)

	HILLTOWN (Ire) 5-11-0 G McCourt, *hld up, smooth hdwy appr 2 out, led last, rdn and ran on wl*. ....(20 to 1 op 14 to 1 tchd 25 to 1)	1
910²	VAE DE RAMA (Ire) 4-10-9 (5*) P Waggott, *mstks. made most frm aftr 1st till hdd last, kpt on und pres*. ....(9 to 1 op 12 to 1 tchd 8 to 1)	2
1003*	AUBURN BOY 6-11-7 L Wyer, *trkd ldrs, ev ch 2 out, sn rdn and one pace*......(Evens fav op 5 to 4 tchd 11 to 8)	3
1736²	COL BUCKMORE (Ire) 5-11-7 N Doughty, *trkd ldrs, rdn aftr 2 out, one pace*.........(3 to 1 op 2 to 1)	4
	DON'T TELL JUDY (Ire) 5-11-0 P Niven, *prmnt, led briefly aftr 3 out, grad wknd frm nxt*... (500 to 1 op 200 to 1)	5
1103⁵	PHILDAN (Ire) 4-10-11 (3*) D J Moffatt, *pld hrd, in tch till lost pl aftr 3 out, no dngr after*. ....(25 to 1 op 14 to 1 tchd 33 to 1)	6
	TIDERUNNER (Ire) 5-11-0 T Reed, *slightly hmpd 1st, nvr nr ldrs*.........(50 to 1 op 14 to 1)	7
	SHATRAVIV 5-10-9 B Storey, *in tch, effrt aftr 3 out, hit nxt, sn btn*.........(50 to 1 op 25 to 1)	8
1674	BALLYROVERS 4-11-0 R Garritty, *nvr on terms*. ....(100 to 1 op 50 to 1)	9
1482²	STAGGERING (Ire) 4-10-9 A Dobbin, *in tch till wknd aftr 3 out*.........(50 to 1 op 25 to 1)	10
1736⁵	INGLETONIAN 4-10-9 (5*) D Bentley, *mstks, prmnt till blun and lost pl 3 out*.........(33 to 1 op 16 to 1)	11
1362	STRONG TRACE (Ire) 4-11-0 C Grant, *chsd ldrs till wknd aftr 3 out*.........(16 to 1)	12
1660	GAY'S GAMBIT 4-10-31 (7*) J Driscoll, *slightly hmpd 1st, sn chasing ldrs, wknd aftr 3 out*. (100 to 1 op 50 to 1)	13
1736⁷	AMBER HOLLY 4-10-9 L O'Hara, *al beh*. ....(200 to 1 op 100 to 1)	14
1494	CUMBERLAND BLUES (Ire) 4-10-9 (5*) S Lyons, *chsd ldrs till wknd aftr 3 out*...........(100 to 1 op 50 to 1)	15
1660⁶	CEREAL GEM 5-10-9 D Byrne, *f 1st*. (20 to 1 op 33 to 1)	f
1872	MAGENTA BOY 5-10-11 (3*) N Bentley, *led till mstk 1st, rdr lost irons, sn pld up*.........(100 to 1 op 50 to 1)	pu

Dist: 3l, 2½l, ½l, 5l, 7l, 1½l, 2l, 2l, 10l, 5l. 4m 4.20s. a 23.20s (17 Ran).
(J Howard Johnson), J H Johnson

1960 Zetland Novices' Handicap Chase (5-y-o and up) £1,708 2m 3f....... (1:30)

1735²	ISSYIN [88] 6-10-13 R Garritty, *jmpd rght, hld up, hdwy to track ldrs 7th, led aftr 3 out, drvn out*. ....(7 to 2 op 4 to 1 tchd 9 to 2)	1
1604*	DOWN THE ROAD [103] 6-12-0 Richard Guest, *led to second, chsd wnr aftr 7th, drw clr wth wnr after 4 out, blun nxt, sn hdd, eased whn btn r-in*. ....(5 to 2 fav op 2 to 1 tchd 11 to 4)	2
	PREOBLAKENSKY [92] 6-11-3 N Doughty, *hld up, some hdwy frm 4 out, nvr nr ldrs*........(4 to 1 tchd 3 to 1)	3
1774⁴	GIPSY RAMBLER [75] 8-9-9 (5*) J Supple, *trkd ldrs till outpcd appr 4 out*.........(10 to 1 op 33 to 1)	4
1423³	HUNTING COUNTRY [76] 9-10-1¹ C Grant, *sn beh*. ....(16 to 1 op 12 to 1 tchd 20 to 1)	5
	CAROUSEL CROSSETT [75] 12-9-9² (7*) K Davies, *in tch till wknd aftr 9th*.........(100 to 1 op 50 to 1)	6
1790³	REEF LARK [80] 8-10-0 (5*) P Waggott, *mstks, sn beh*. ....(13 to 2 op 6 to 1 tchd 7 to 1)	7
1417⁴	OLD EROS [100] 9-11-11 P Niven, *led second, blun 5th, hdd aftr 7th, wknd quickly after tenth, wl beh whn pld up bef 2 out*.........(6 to 1 op 11 to 2 tchd 7 to 1)	pu

Dist: 25l, 4l, 4l, 20l, 4l, 12l. 5m 0.50s. (8 Ran).
(Mrs H Brown), M W Easterby

1961 Fingall Selling Hurdle (4 & 5-y-o) £977 2m.................. (2:00)

1731*	PORT IN A STORM 4-11-6 G McCourt, *hld up, smooth hdwy aftr 3 out, led last, drvn out*. ....(Evens fav tchd 6 to 5 and 5 to 4)	1
1485⁶	J P MORGAN (v) 5-11-6 A Dobbin, *led second, reminders hfwy, hdd last, kpt on*. (13 to 2 op 8 to 1 tchd 10 to 1)	2
1788⁶	CHARLYCIA 5-10-8 (7*) M Clarke, *prmnt, effrt aftr 3 out, one pace*.........(9 to 1 op 12 to 1)	3
1633⁹	SEAORSE (Ire) 5-11-2 (3*) D J Moffatt, *chsd ldrs till outpcd aftr 3 out*.........(9 to 1 op 7 to 1 tchd 10 to 1)	4
1773	TOUGH DEAL (Ire) 5-11-0 Mr B Leavy, *in tch, some hdwy aftr 3 out, sn rdn and btn*..................(100 to 1)	5

	INTREPID FORT (bl) 4-11-0 W Dwan, *in tch, pushed alng hfwy, sn beh*.........(33 to 1 op 25 to 1)	6
	SERIOUS TIME 5-11-0 K Jones, *tld off frm 5th*. ....(25 to 1 op 16 to 1)	7
1791	GYMCRAK CYRANO (Ire) 4-10-6 (3*) N Bentley, *mstk and uns rdr 1st*..............(20 to 1 op 25 to 1)	ur
	GASCOIGNE WOOD 5-11-0 Mrs F Needham, *led, hmpd and uns rdr second*.................(100 to 1)	ur
1675	BREEZE AWAY 4-10-9 P Niven, *refused to race, took no part*.......................(33 to 1)	ref
1738³	KING'S GUEST (Ire) 4-11-0 J Callaghan, *led to second, cl up, wknd quickly aftr 3 out, beh whn pld up bef three out*.........(100 to 30 op 9 to 4 tchd 7 to 2)	pu
875	SONIC BELLE 4-10-4 (5*) P Waggott, *chsd ldrs till wknd appr 2 out, beh whn pld up bef last*. ....(50 to 1 op 33 to 1)	pu

Dist: 2½l, 15l, 15l, 8l, 15l. 8l. 4m 0.70s. a 19.70s (12 Ran).
SR: 22/19/-/-/-/-/ (S A Barningham), N Tinkler

1962 Neville Crump Handicap Chase (0-115 5-y-o and up) £2,406 3m 1f 110yds .... (2:30)

1739⁴	HEAVENLY CITIZEN (Ire) [88] 5-10-4 R Garritty, *hld up, steady hdwy frm 13th, led aftr last, drvn out*. ....(5 to 1 op 7 to 1)	1
1739²	TRUELY ROYAL [92] 9-10-8 B Storey, *cl up, drw clr wth ldr frm 12th, ev ch 2 out, kpt on*... (11 to 4 fav op 3 to 1)	2
1808*	BALTIC BROWN [108] 8-11-10 Richard Guest, *cl up, jnd ldr 10th, led aftr nxt, mstk last, sn hdd and wknd*. ....(9 to 2 op 4 to 1)	3
	HOUXTY LAD [85] 7-10-1¹ J Callaghan, *beh, some hdwy whn blun 4 out, no ch aftr, tld off*............(33 to 1)	4
1739⁵	EBORNEEZER'S DREAM [88] 10-10-4¹ D Telfor, *al beh, wl tld off*.........(50 to 1 op 33 to 1)	5
1486	CAROUSEL CALYPSO [101] 7-11-3 P Niven, *beh frm 12th, wl tld off*...........(7 to 1 op 6 to 1)	6
	TRES AMIGOS [104] 6-11-3 (3*) A Larnach, *in tch whn f 7th*...........(13 to 2 op 6 to 1 tchd 7 to 1)	f
1676*	INVERINATE [96] (bl) 8-10-12 T Reed, *sn pushed alng, led till hdd aftr 11th, grad wknd, tld off whn pld up bef last*.........(9 to 2 op 4 to 1)	pu

Dist: 1½l, 8l, dist, 3l, dist. 6m 52.60s. a 37.60s (8 Ran).
(Mrs J Young), T P Tate

1963 Barton Handicap Hurdle (0-115 4-y-o and up) £1,604 3m 1f 110yds.... (3:00)

1740*	NODDLE (USA) [99] 5-11-9 T Reed, *made all, rdn betw last 2, styd on wl*..... (11 to 8 fav op 6 to 4 tchd 13 to 8)	1
1740⁵	FURRY BABY [97] 6-11-7 R Garritty, *sn tracking wnr, effrt appr 2 out, styd on, no imprsn*........(9 to 2 op 7 to 2)	2
1740⁶	THIS NETTLE DANGER [95] 9-11-5 M Brennan, *hld up, hdwy to track ldrs 8th, pushed alng aftr 3 out, sn btn*. ....(6 to 1 op 7 to 1)	3
1603*	JENDEE (Ire) [89] 5-10-10 (3*) A Larnach, *in tch, outpcd aftr 8th, no dngr after*. (11 to 2 op 7 to 1 tchd 5 to 1)	4
1740²	MAKE ME PROUD (Ire) [91] 4-11-1 L Wyer, *chsd ldrs, outpcd aftr 8th, no dngr after*........(8 to 1 op 13 to 2)	5
1740⁸	HARDIHERO [88] 7-10-12 B Storey, *prmnt till wknd aftr 8th, tld off*...................(20 to 1)	6
1740	AS D'EBOLI (Fr) [85] 6-10-2 (7*) Kate Sellars, *sn lost tch, tld off*.............(25 to 1 tchd 33 to 1)	7
	SUREST DANCER (USA) [77] 7-10-1¹ R Marley, *chsd ldrs till wknd aftr 8th, tld off*.................(100 to 1)	8
1485	PONDERED BID [76] 9-9-9 (5*) D Bentley, *sn lost tch, wl tld off*.........................(50 to 1)	9
	PALM HOUSE [100] 8-11-3 (7*) N Stocks, *sn lost tch, tld off whn pld up bef 2 out*............(40 to 1 op 33 to 1)	pu
1740	YACHT CLUB [80] 11-10-4 A Mulholland, *mstks, beh frm 7th, tld off whn pld up bef 2 out*..(66 to 1 op 50 to 1)	pu

Dist: 8l, 12l, 2½l, 1l, 30l, 25l, 1l, dist. 6m 34.90s. a 33.90s (11 Ran).
(J C Galbraith), L Lungo

LEICESTER (heavy (races 1,2,6), soft (3,4,5))
Friday December 31st
Going Correction: PLUS 1.82 sec. per fur. (races 1,2,6), PLUS 1.78 (3,4,5)

1964 Hancock Handicap Hurdle (0-120 4-y-o and up) £2,595 2½m 110yds.... (12:50)

	FIRED EARTH (Ire) [93] 5-10-9 A Maguire, *hld up in tch, styd on to ld 2 out, tired but clr whn jmpd lft and mstk last*..............(3 to 1 op 9 to 4 tchd 7 to 2)	1
1492⁵	CAMBO (USA) [90] 7-10-6 D Skyrme, *al frnt rnk, led 4 out, hdd 2 out, one pace*................(6 to 1 op 9 to 2)	2
1533*	LESBET [100] 8-11-2 D Morris, *led till hdd 4 out, kpt on one pace aftr*............(9 to 1 op 7 to 1)	3
1057	SWILLY EXPRESS [98] 7-11-0 M Dwyer, *hld up, hdwy 7th, nvr nr to chal*..................(16 to 1)	4
1614³	TIMUR'S KING [88] 6-10-4 S Earle, *prmnt till rdn and wknd 3 out*..................(11 to 4 fav op 3 to 1)	5

1703⁸ MR TAYLOR [97] 8-10-13 V Smith, *al beh.*
.................................(16 to 1 op 12 to 1) 6
1619⁷ CAPTAIN MY CAPTAIN (Ire) [90] 5-10-6 Diane Clay, *al in rear*.................(14 to 1 op 20 to 1 tchd 12 to 1) 7
1621 FEARSOME [97] 7-10-13 N Williamson, *trkd ldrs till wknd appr 4 out, pld up bef nxt*..........(12 to 1 op 8 to 1) pu
1427² COSMIC DANCER [112] 6-12-0 A Carroll, *beh whn hit 5th, tld off when pld up bef 4 out*......(16 to 1 op 14 to 1) pu
1072 BENTLEY MANOR [84] 4-10-0 D Bridgwater, *in tch till wknd rpdly appr 4 out, pld up bef 2 out.*
.................................(16 to 1 op 25 to 1 tchd 33 to 1) pu
Dist: 8l, 8l, 8l, 1l, 7l, 15l. 5m 29.70s. a 41.70s (10 Ran).
SR: 37/26/28/18/7/9/   (Mrs J Fanshawe), J R Fanshawe

1965 Hoby Selling Hurdle (3 & 4-y-o) £1,918 2m.............................(1:25)

1702 TOUCH SILVER 3-10-5 (7*) Mr Richard White, *hld up in tch, led sn aftr 3 out, wnt clr appr last.* (11 to 2 op 5 to 1) 1
1731⁴ TYNRON DOON (bl) 4-11-7 A Maguire, *hld up, trkd ldr aftr 5th, led 3 out, sn hdd, one pace.*
.................................(3 to 1 fav op 5 to 2 tchd 100 to 30) 2
1472⁴ PRIORY PIPER 4-11-2 (5*) T Eley, *led till hdd 3 out, sn btn.*
.................................(25 to 1 op 20 to 1) 3
MARSHALL PINDARI 3-10-7 D Bridgwater, *hld up in rear, hdwy 4 out, nvr nr to chal.*................(33 to 1) 4
BONAR BRIDGE (USA) 3-10-7 N Williamson, *hld up in rear, hdwy 4th, wknd appr 3 out.*......(5 to 1 op 5 to 2) 5
THE COUNTRY DANCER 3-10-3¹ M Dwyer, *hld up in rear, wknd appr 4 out, wknd nxt.*.......(12 to 1 op 8 to 1) 6
1404² KUTAN (Ire) 3-10-7 E Byrne, *in tch till outpcd 5th, tld off.*
.................................(4 to 1 op 4 to 1 tchd 9 to 2) 7
1068⁷ HOSTETLER 4-11-7 (5*) T Jenks, *al beh, tld off whn pld up bef 2 out.*................(20 to 1 op 25 to 1 tchd 33 to 1) pu
GYPSY LEGEND 3-10-2 R Dunwoody, *prmnt till wknd appr 4 out, tld off whn pld up bef last.*
.................................(20 to 1 op 25 to 1 tchd 33 to 1) pu
1705 LANZAMAR 3-10-2 J Railton, *hld up in mid-div, gd hdwy 5th, wknd appr 3 out, pld up bef last.*
.................................(12 to 1 tchd 14 to 1) pu
1640⁹ JOGORAN (bl) 3-10-7 R Greene, *trkd ldr till wknd aftr 5th, tld off whn pld up bef 3 out.*...........(33 to 1) pu
Dist: 15l, 10l, 4l, 12l, 4l, 25l. 4m 20.70s. a 37.70s (11 Ran).
(H J Manners), H J Manners

1966 Leicestershire Silver Fox Handicap Chase (0-135 5-y-o and up) £6,108 2½m 110yds....................(1:55)

1720* SHEER ABILITY [107] 7-10-10 R Dunwoody, *trkd ldr, led 7th, quickened clr appr last, cmftbly.*
.................................(Evens fav op 6 to 5 tchd 11 to 10 on) 1
1566⁴ FILE CONCORD [121] (bl) 9-11-10 J Lawrence, *hld up, cld on ldrs 7th, wnt second tenth, jnd wnr 3 out, outpcd and held whn hit last...* (9 to 2 op 7 to 2 tchd 5 to 1) 2
1733² DOLIKOS [106] 6-10-9 M Dwyer, *hld up in tch till blun and lost pl 7th, kpt on one pace 3 out, no ch wth 1st 2.*
.................................(2 to 1 op 6 to 4) 3
1706⁶ WARNER'S END [97] (bl) 12-10-0 R Bellamy, *led to 7th, hit tenth, stdly wknd.*................(33 to 1 op 25 to 1) 4
Dist: 7l, 20l, 20l. 5m 43.60s. a 40.60s (4 Ran).
SR: 41/48/13/-/   (Michael Devlin), C J Mann

1967 Quorn Novices' Claiming Chase (5-y-o and up) £2,205 2m 1f...............(2:25)

1718⁴ VIAGGIO (v) 5-10-8 (5*) T Eley, *nvr far away, rdn appr 2 out, led sn aftr, drvn out........*(4 to 1 jt-fav op 7 to 2) 1
1699 BEAUFAN 6-11-2 Gary Lyons, *trkd ldrs, mstk 6th, ev ch 2 out, hrd rdn and no imprsn r-in...*(14 to 1 op 10 to 1) 2
1742² MIDDAY SHOW (USA) (bl) 6-11-5 A Maguire, *trkd ldr, led 5th to 4 out, led briefly ag'n 2 out, rdn and one pace.*
.................................(9 to 2 op 5 to 1 tchd 6 to 1) 3
1631⁴ HICKELTON HOUSE 9-10-7 M Dwyer, *hld up in rear, gd hdwy appr 3 out, ev ch nxt, wknd approaching last.*
.................................(4 to 1 jt-fav op 3 to 1) 4
1712 FLUTTER MONEY 9-10-13 C Maude, *hld up in tch, hdwy 3rd, led 4 out, hdd 2 out, no extr...*(12 to 1 op 16 to 1) 5
1673⁵ BILLHEAD 7-10-10 N Williamson, *led till hdwy 4 out, wknd quickly aftr nxt, eased, tld off.* (8 to 9 op 3 to 1) 6
1717⁴ THE JET SET (bl) 6-11-12 Lawrence, *blun and uns rdr 1st.*
.................................(5 to 1 op 7 to 2) ur
1624 ARDORAN 7-10-13¹ T Wall, *led to 5th, wkng whn beh whn hit 4 out, pld up bef nxt.*..........(33 to 1) pu
Dist: 3l, 3½l, 2½l, nk, dist. 4m 50.30s. a 41.30s (8 Ran).
(Tony Forbes), A L Forbes

1968 Gallowtree Novices' Chase (5-y-o and up) £2,438 3m.................(2:55)

BINKLEY (Fr) 7-10-12 D Bridgwater, *made all, jmpd rght, lft clr 4 out, tired and wndrd in frnt frm 2 out, all out.*
.................................(7 to 2 op 5 to 2) 1
1533⁶ UNDERWYCHWOOD (Ire) 5-10-12 A Maguire, *trkd ldr to tenth, lft poor second 4 out, tried to cl frm nxt, swtchd rght r-in, fnshd tired.*................(5 to 1 op 6 to 1) 2

1590⁷ SANDAIG (bl) 7-11-5 N Williamson, *hld up, mstk 1st, hit 5th, hdwy nxt, wnt second tenth, f 4 out, rmntd.*
.................................(11 to 4 op 2 to 1 tchd 3 to 1) 3
1879 EBONY GALE (bl) 7-11-2 I Lawrence, *last whn hit 7th, mstk 9th, sn beh, tld off when pld up bef 5 out.*
.................................(5 to 4 fav op 6 to 4) pu
Dist: 7l, dist. 6m 47.70s. a 55.70s (4 Ran).
(R Rainbow), N A Twiston-Davies

1969 Pytchley 'National Hunt' Novices' Hurdle (4-y-o and up) £1,903 2m....(3:30)

1729* RELKEEL 4-11-4 A Maguire, *hld up in tch, wnt second 4 out, sn led, went clr 2 out, canter.*
.................................(7 to 2 on op 11 to 4 on tchd 5 to 2 on) 1
1568⁵ DIVINE CHANCE (Ire) 5-10-12 J Frost, *hld up, mstk 4th, rdn 3 out, second whn hit last, no ch wth wnr.*
.................................(7 to 1 op 6 to 1) 2
1729 ARCTIC LIFE (Ire) 4-10-12 N Williamson, *trkd ldr, led 5th, hdd sn aftr 4 out, rdn and wknd soon after last.*
.................................(7 to 1 op 6 to 1) 3
1654 GRIFFINS BAR 5-10-12 A Carroll, *led to 5th, ev ch 4 out, wknd quickly, tld off..............*(10 to 1 op 8 to 1) 4
Dist: 6l, 12l, dist. 4m 19.30s. a 36.30s (4 Ran).
SR: 18/6/-/-/   (Brig C B Harvey), D Nicholson

NEWBURY (heavy)
Friday December 31st
Going Correction: PLUS 1.25 sec. per fur. (races 1,4,6), PLUS 1.42 (2,3,5)

1970 Wantage Novices' Chase (5-y-o and up) £3,652 2m 1f..............(1:05)

1690³ BIG MATT (Ire) 5-11-0 M A FitzGerald, *jmpd rght, hdwy and hit 4th, led 5th, made rest, drvn out.*
.................................(11 to 10 fav op Evens tchd 5 to 4 on) 1
1521³ FRONT STREET 6-11-0 G Upton, *hld up, hdwy 8th, ev ch frm 4 out till rdn and not quicken r-in.*
.................................(3 to 1 tchd 7 to 2) 2
JOHNNY WILL (bl) 8-11-0 J Osborne, *mstks, dsptd ld to 3rd, hit 5th and 6th, chasing ldrs whn blun 9th, rallied, wknd appr last........*(3 to 1 op 5 to 2 tchd 7 to 4) 3
NICKSLINE 7-11-0 D Murphy, *hit 6th, lost tch 9th, tld off.*
.................................(14 to 1 tchd 20 to 1) 4
1417 WEST BAY 7-11-0 B Powell, *dsptd ld to 3rd, led 4th, hit 5th and 6th, wknd 3 out, no ch whn fourth and no chance when refused last......*(20 to 1 op 16 to 1) ref
1730 DEEP IN GREEK (bl) 7-10-11 (3*) R Davis, *led 3rd, hdd 4th, hit 8th, sn wknd, tld off whn pld up bef last.*
.................................(66 to 1 op 50 to 1 tchd 80 to 1) pu
Dist: 1½l, 15l, dist. 4m 27.60s. a 26.60s (6 Ran).
SR: 32/30/15/   (Richard Shaw), N J Henderson

1971 Weyhill Handicap Hurdle (0-145 5-y-o and up) £4,337 2m 5f..........(1:35)

1690⁴ KAYTAK (Fr) [109] (v) 6-10-0 D Murphy, *hld up, hdwy frm 3 out, led last, shaken up and styd on r-in.*
.................................(100 to 30 op 3 to 1) 1
1650⁵ ALBERTITO (Fr) [109] 6-9-11 (3*) S Wynne, *chsd ldr to 6th, chased lder ag'n 8th till led aftr 2 out, hdd last, sn outpcd..............*(5 to 2 fav op 11 to 4) 2
1759² SEA BUCK [118] 7-10-6 (3*) R Davis, *beh, tld off 7th, ran on und pres frm 3 out, nrst finish....*(3 to 1 op 9 to 4) 3
COKENNY BOY [133] 8-11-10 J Osborne, *hdwy 4th, chsd ldr 6th, mstk 7th, wknd aftr 8th.*
.................................(7 to 1 op 5 to 1 tchd 8 to 1) 4
SABAKI RIVER [129] 9-11-6 M A FitzGerald, *led, clr 3rd, hdd aftr 2 out, wknd quickly, virtually pld up nr finish, tld off........*(5 to 1 tchd 11 to 2) 5
Dist: 8l, 1l, 20l, dist. 5m 30.30s. a 37.30s (5 Ran).
(T J Myles & Co (Contractors) Ltd), J R Jenkins

1972 Abingdon Conditional Jockeys' Handicap Hurdle (0-140 5-y-o and up) £2,900 3m 110yds............(2:05)

1759⁵ CAPTAIN DOLFORD [109] 6-11-1 J McCarthy, *chsd ldr till led 6th, jmpd rght 9th, mstk 2 out, hrd drvn and not fluent last, styd on wl.* (5 to 1 op 7 to 2 tchd 11 to 2) 1
MONTAGNARD [118] 9-11-5 (5*) M P FitzGerald, *led to 6th, styd prmnt till outpcd 2 out, rallied and ran on ag'n r-in, not rch wnr...................*(12 to 1 op 8 to 1) 2
1772⁴ WICKET [94] 8-10-0 W Marston, *hdwy 8th, ev ch 2 out, rdn appr last, sn one pace...* (6 to 1 op 8 to 1 tchd 9 to 1) 3
1703⁵ SUPER MALT (Ire) [113] 5-11-2 (3*) D Fortt, *al chasing ldrs, rdn and styd on one pace frm 2 out.*
.................................(5 to 2 fav op 11 to 4 tchd 3 to 1) 4
1703* FAIR BROTHER [108] 7-11-0 R Davis, *hld up, steady hdwy 3 out, ev ch 2 out, rdn last, sn btn.............* (3 to 1 jt-fav op 5 to 2 tchd 100 to 30) 5
CRABBY BILL [101] 6-10-7 A Dicken, *hdwy to chase ldrs 9th, rdn aftr 3 out, sn wknd.*
.................................(25 to 1 op 20 to 1 tchd 33 to 1) 6

1057^{2} ASWAMEDH [99] 5-10-0 (5*) N Parker, *chsd ldrs till rdn and wknd 3 out, tld off, broke blood vessel*...(3 to 1 jt-fav op 5 to 2 tchd 100 to 30) 7
BLACK SAPPHIRE [117] 6-11-6 (3*) S Curran, *beh 6th, tld off 9th, pld up bef 3 out*.......... (33 to 1 op 25 to 1) pu
Dist: 5l, 5l, 2½l, 2l, 5l, dist. 6m 29.70s. a 40.70s (8 Ran).
SR: 28/32/3/19/12/ (R E Brinkworth), D R Gandolfo

1973 Elcot Park Novices' Chase (5-y-o and up) £3,678 3m..................(2:35)

1662^{4} MUDAHIM 7-11-8 W Marston, *prmnt, chlgd 7th, led 8th, hdd 12th, led ag'n nxt, rdn and styd on wl frm 2 out*. ....(11 to 8 fav op 5 to 4 tchd 6 to 4) 1
1704* MAILCOM 7-11-8 J Osborne, *led, hit 3rd, hdd 8th, led ag'n tenth, headed 12th, rdn 3 out, rallied frm 2 out, no extr cl hme*...........(13 to 8 op 11 to 8 tchd 7 to 4) 2
1730^{2} RIVER MANDATE 6-11-0 B Powell, *prmnt, led 12th to 13th, hit 14th, wknd 4 out*. (100 to 30 op 7 to 2 tchd 4 to 1) 3
SAYYURE (USA) 7-11-0 C Llewellyn, *prmnt till hit 5th and drpd rear, lost tch 12th, tld off*.....(10 to 1 op 8 to 1) 4
1730 VITAL SCORE 7-11-0 S Smith Eccles, *beh till f 13th*. ....(33 to 1 op 25 to 1) f
WILLOW GALE 6-10-9 M A FitzGerald, *hit 3rd, al beh, tld off whn pld up bef 4 out*...........(33 to 1 op 20 to 1) pu
Dist: 1½l, 30l, dist. 6m 23.30s. a 35.30s (6 Ran).
SR: 41/39/1/ (K W Bell), C D Broad

1974 Ramsbury Hurdle (4-y-o) £4,224 2m 5f ....(3:05)

1667^{2} GLAISDALE (Ire) 10-12 D Murphy, *hld up, not much room bend appr 3 out, chlgd 2 out, led r-in, drvn out*. ....(5 to 4 fav op Evens tchd 11 to 8) 1
1082^{2} BELL STAFFBOY (Ire) 10-12 W Marston, *hld up, hdwy 7th, led 3 out, hdd r-in, styd on, not pace of wnr*. ....(4 to 1 op 7 to 2 tchd 9 to 2) 2
1568^{7} LAY IT OFF (Ire) 10-7 L Harvey, *wnt prmnt 4th, wknd 3 out*. ....(66 to 1 op 33 to 1 tchd 100 to 1) 3
1747^{7} HIT THE FAN 10-12 C Llewellyn, *mstk 1st, prmnt, rdn and wknd 3 out*.......... (16 to 1 op 12 to 1 tchd 20 to 1) 4
1406^{5} GOD SPEED YOU (Ire) 10-12 M A FitzGerald, *prmnt, lft in ld appr 6th, hdd 7th, wknd approaching 3 out*. ....(100 to 1 op 50 to 1) 5
1309* RIVER LOSSIE 11-3 J Osborne, *led till ran badly wide and lost many ls bend aftr 5th, led ag'n 7th, hdd 3 out, 3rd and no ch wth ldrs whn f last*....(6 to 4 op 7 to 4) f
SAIF AL ADIL (Ire) 10-12 R Campbell, *al beh, tld off whn pld up bef 4 out*..................(100 to 1 op 50 to 1) pu
Dist: ½l, 25l, 20l, 20l. 5m 27.00s. a 34.00s (7 Ran).
SR: 42/41/11/-/ (Oceala Limited), M H Tompkins

1975 Old Year Handicap Chase (0-145 5-y-o and up) £4,175 2m 1f........... (3:35)

1733^{3} SPREE CROSS [116] 7-11-5 G Bradley, *chsd ldr, chlgd 8th, led 9th, came clr frm 4 out*........... (5 to 1 op 4 to 1) 1
1638^{3} GOOD FOR A LAUGH [120] 9-11-4 (5*) J Burke, *very slwly away, hit 5th, wl beh 6th, ran on und pres frm 3 out, took distant second r-in*. ....(5 to 1 op 9 to 2 tchd 11 to 2) 2
1694^{6} ATLAAL [125] (bl) 8-12-0 S Smith Eccles, *hit 4th, beh, styd on frm 9th, chsd wnr aftr four out, wknd quickly r-in*. ....(10 to 1 op 8 to 1) 3
1282^{3} SARTORIUS [108] 7-10-11 B Powell, *slwly into strd, al beh*...................(5 to 1 op 9 to 2 tchd 11 to 2) 4
1461 SAILORS LUCK [107] 8-10-10 D Murphy, *effrt 6th, sn btn*. ....(2 to 1 fav op 11 to 4) 5
825 TILDARG [119] 9-11-8 J Osborne, *led to 9th, wknd 4 out, no ch whn blun last*.....(7 to 1 op 5 to 1 tchd 8 to 1) 6
1623^{5} NORTHERN JINKS [119] 10-11-5 (3*) D Meredith, *hit 1st, prmnt till wknd 9th*... (14 to 1 op 8 to 1 tchd 16 to 1) 7
Dist: 20l, 5l, ¾l, 15l, 15l. 4m 27.10s. a 26.10s (7 Ran).
SR: 42/26/26/8/ (P L Mason), Mrs D Haine

PUNCHESTOWN (IRE) (heavy) Friday December 31st

1976 Dunlavin Opportunity Handicap Hurdle (4-y-o and up) £3,450 2m...(12:45)

1823^{9} DEGO DANCER [-] 6-9-6 (4*) J P Broderick,....... (8 to 1) 1
880 HEADBANGER [-] 6-10-12 (4*) Mr C A Leavy,...... (7 to 1) 2
1174^{5} CALDARO [-] 6-9-6^{4} (2*) K L O'Brien,............. (9 to 2) 3
1549^{9} BETTYS THE BOSS (Ire) [-] 5-9-10 T J Mitchell,.... (7 to 1) 4
1855^{5} WATERLOO LADY [-] 6-11-0 D P Murphy,......... (9 to 2) 5
1780 BASIE NOBLE [-] 4-9-11 (4*) J Pearse,..........(12 to 1) 6
937^{3} FABULIST (Ire) [-] 4-10-11 T P Treacy,....... (3 to 1 jt-fav) 7
1833 TOP RUN (Ire) [-] 5-9-3 (4*) P Morris,.............(25 to 1) 8
1686^{9} DASHING ROSE [-] 5-10-8 (2*) M G Cleary,.. (3 to 1 jt-fav) f
Dist: 9l, 8l, ¾l, 2l. 4m 10.10s. (9 Ran).
(Mrs Ann McAllen), Patrick McAllen

1977 Harristown Hurdle (4-y-o and up) £3,330 2½m................... (1:15)

1453^{9} LOAVES AND FISHES 5-10-11 (7*) B D Murtagh,..(10 to 1) 1D
1683* IDIOTS VENTURE 6-11-10 B Sheridan,........ (3 to 1 on) 1
1824^{3} MISS LIME 6-10-6^{1} (7*) Mr M J Bowe,......... (100 to 30) 2
Dist: Dist, dist. 6m 2.60s. (3 Ran).
(Blackwater Racing Syndicate), A P O'Brien

1978 Dunstown Wood Maiden Hurdle (5 & 6-y-o) £3,105 2m................ (1:45)

1760 FINAWAY BOY (Ire) 5-11-6 J P Banahan,.........(14 to 1) 1
1608^{4} FORTY ONE (Ire) 5-10-8 (7*) D J Kavanagh,........(9 to 2) 2
1379 TOMMY'S RUN 6-11-9 (5*) D T Evans,............(9 to 2) 3
1549^{3} KAWA-KAWA 6-10-10 (5*) T J O'Sullivan,..........(7 to 2) 4
1814 STRONG PLATINUM (Ire) 5-11-6 C O'Dwyer,...(6 to 4 fav) 5
1760 ST AIDAN (Ire) 5-10-13 (7*) Mr A Wall,............(33 to 1) 6
TAGANINI (Ire) 5-11-7 (7*) C McCormack,........ (14 to 1) 7
NOBLE MADAME (Ire) 5-11-1 K F O'Brien,....... (10 to 1) 8
1549 SLEAVEEN HILL 6-11-1 H Rogers,.............. (50 to 1) 9
DEEP DOVE (Ire) 5-11-3 (3*) G Kilfeather,.........(14 to 1) 10
Dist: 2½l, 20l, 2l, 20l. 4m 16.80s. (10 Ran).
(B Maguire), Michael Cunningham

1979 Tom Byrne Handicap Chase (4-y-o and up) £3,795 3m 1f........... (2:15)

1784^{6} GREEN TIMES [-] 8-10-7 P L Malone,.............(9 to 4) 1
1611^{3} LADY BAR [-] 6-10-11 P M Verling,.............(6 to 4 fav) 2
1784 LACKEN BEAU [-] 9-11-0 (7*) J P Broderick,....... (7 to 1) 3
1784^{7} JOE WHITE [-] 7-11-4 P Carberry,................ (5 to 2) 4
1553 SYLVIA'S SAFFRON [-] (bl) 6-9-4^{2} (3*) T J Mitchell, (33 to 1) pu
Dist: 2l, 20l, dist. 7m 4.60s. (5 Ran).
(Noel McGrady), Michael Cunningham

1980 Brannockstown Handicap Hurdle (4-y-o and up) £3,105 2½m........ (2:45)

1495^{3} AMARI QUEEN [-] 6-9-12 R Hughes,...............(5 to 1) 1
1823^{8} BARRONSTOWN BOY [-] 9-9-10 C F Swan,...... (13 to 2) 2
1828^{5} SADDLESTOWN GLEN [-] (bl) 8-10-8 F Woods,... (14 to 1) 3
1554 LINVAR [-] (bl) 10-11-2 (7*) D J Kavanagh,........ (12 to 1) 4
1851^{6} KERFONTAINE [-] 8-11-2 J F Titley,................(5 to 1) 5
1782 ROSEPERRIE (Ire) [-] (bl) 5-9-2^{6} (5*) D T Evans,... (20 to 1) 6
306 QUAYSIDE BUOY [-] 10-11-3 T Horgan,...........(12 to 1) 7
1764^{7} GOODNIGHT IRENE (Ire) [-] 4-9-5 (3*) C O'Brien,..(14 to 1) 8
1580 RICH TRADITION (Ire) [-] 5-11-4 C O'Dwyer,.... (Evens fav) f
Dist: 2l, 25l, 5½l, 5l. 5m 49.00s. (9 Ran).
(M Ward-Thomas), D T Hughes

1981 Dollardstown Novice Chase (5-y-o and up) £3,105 2m..................(3:15)

1451^{3} HAVE TO THINK 5-11-7 (5*) T P Rudd,............(2 to 1) 1
1684^{8} OXFORD QUILL 6-12-0 T J Taaffe,................(5 to 1) 2
1450 ENQELAAB (USA) 5-11-12 J P Banahan,...........(5 to 1) 3
ALTEREZZA (USA) 6-12-0 B Sheridan,........ (7 to 4 fav) 4
1398 IPANEMA 6-11-2 (7*) P P Kelly,..................(12 to 1) f
1763 AUTUMN RIDE (Ire) (bl) 5-11-12 F Woods,........(20 to 1) f
1233^{8} GONE LIKE THE WIND 6-11-9 (5*) L Flynn,....... (20 to 1) bd
Dist: 2½l, 1½l, 11l. 4m 32.80s. (7 Ran).
(Peter M Law), A L T Moore

1982 Mullaboden I N H Flat Race (4-y-o) £3,105 2m..................... (3:45)

1337 CREATIVE BLAZE (Ire) 10-13 (5*) Mr J A Nash,..... (6 to 1) 1
1230^{7} LINDEN'S LOTTO (Ire) 11-6 (3*) Mr A R Coonan,....(7 to 4) 2
1762^{5} BANNER GALE (Ire) 11-2 (7*) Mr P G Kelly,.....(5 to 4 fav) 3
1820^{6} HAVE A BRANDY (Ire) 11-9 Mr D M O'Brien,........(6 to 1) 4
I'LL FLY AWAY (Ire) 11-4 (5*) Mr G J Harford,.......(25 to 1) 5
LIFFEYSIDE LADY (Ire) 10-11 (7*) Mr J P Geoghegan, ...(25 to 1) 6
LIME LADY (Ire) 10-11 (7*) Mr M J Bowe,..........(14 to 1) 7
BACKTOWN JOHNNY (Ire) 11-2 (7*) Mr S O'Donnell, ...(14 to 1) 8
1766 RADICAL NURSE (Ire) 10-11 (7*) Mr M McLoughney, ...(50 to 1) ur
Dist: 3l, 7l, 20l, 9l. 4m 9.30s. (9 Ran).
(W J Austin), W J Austin

NAAS (IRE) (soft)
Saturday January 1st

1983 Barrow Maiden Hurdle (4-y-o) £3,105 2m........................(12:45)

1846^{2} NANNAKA (USA) 10-1 (3*) T P Treacy, ...(9 to 4 fav) 1
1853^{2} CARHUE STAR (Ire) 9-13 (5*) T J O'Sullivan, ...(10 to 1) 2
1816^{4} SKIPO (USA) 11-0 B Sheridan, ...(3 to 1) 3
1432^{2} SERANERA (Ire) 9-13 (5*) M G Cleary, ...(7 to 1) 4
TINERANA (Ire) 11-0 C F Swan, ...(3 to 1) 5
1816^{6} CREHELP EXPRESS (Ire) 10-4 K F O'Brien, ...(16 to 1) 6
REASILVIA (Ire) 10-4 R Hughes, ...(20 to 1) 7
SCHMEICHEL (Ire) 10-9 H Rogers, ...(16 to 1) 8
BOTHSIDESNOW (Ire) 11-0 P Carberry, ...(10 to 1) 9
1454^{5} LAKE OF LOUGHREA (Ire) 11-0 J Shortt, ...(10 to 1) 10
1432 ANNADOT (Ire) 10-4 F J Flood, ...(50 to 1) 11
1846^{9} FALCARRAGH (Ire) 10-9 C O'Dwyer, ...(20 to 1) 12
1846 PAKED (Ire) 9-13 (5*) D T Evans, ...(50 to 1) 13
Dist: 2½l, 3l, 2l, 2l. 4m 6.80s. (13 Ran).
(Mrs P Mullins), P Mullins

1984 Slaney E.B.F. Hurdle (Listed) (5-y-o and up) £6,900 2m 3f........... (1:15)

1849^{2} MINELLA LAD 8-12-1 T Horgan, *led till aftr 1st, trkd ldr till rdn to chal 2 out, led appr last, ran on.* (11 to 8 on) 1
1824* COURT MELODY (Ire) 6-11-5 (7*) J P Broderick, *led aftr 1st, mstk nxt, quickened 6th, rdn after 2 out, hdd appr last, mistake, no extr*.............................(6 to 4) 2
1896 BEGLAWELLA 7-11-1 (3*) T P Treacy, *trkd ldr in 3rd, rdn and btn aftr 3 out*..............................(8 to 1) 3
1978^{2} FORTY ONE (Ire) 6-10-7 (7*) D J Kavanagh, *al rear, lost tch 7th*...(25 to 1) 4
Dist: 3½l, 20l, 8l. 5m 1.40s. (4 Ran).
(John J Nallen), A P O'Brien

1985 Boyne Handicap Chase (5-y-o and up) £6,900 2m 3f..................(1:45)

1761^{2} MAD TOM [-] 9-11-2 (7*) J P Broderick, ...(5 to 1) 1
1905^{2} THIRD QUARTER [-] 9-11-4 K F O'Brien, ...(5 to 1) 2
1819^{2} GALLEY GALE [-] 8-9-4 (3*) C O'Brien, ...(10 to 1) 3
1498* SORRY ABOUT THAT [-] 8-10-7 P Carberry, ...(15 to 2) 4
1268 TURBULENT WIND [-] 7-10-6 C F Swan, ...(6 to 1) 5
SATULA [-] 10-10-7 T Horgan, ...(7 to 2) f
1850^{5} FOURTH OF JULY [-] 10-11-10 J P Banahan, .. (3 to 1 fav) pu
VALRODIAN (NZ) [-] 11-11-8 L P Cusack, ...(20 to 1) pu
Dist: 10l, 15l, nk, 2½l. 5m 23.90s. (8 Ran).
(Anne Duchess Of Westminster), J T R Dreaper

1986 Liffey Hurdle (5-y-o and up) £3,105 2m 3f.............................(2:15)

1814* COQ HARDI AFFAIR (Ire) 6-12-0 P Carberry, ...(13 to 8) 1
1815* DIPLOMATIC 5-11-10 J P Banahan, ...(Evens fav) 2
1823^{3} KEEPHERGOING (Ire) 5-10-12 K F O'Brien, ...(14 to 1) 3
1766^{5} QUEENIES CHILD 7-11-2 J Shortt, ...(14 to 1) 4
1848^{4} TIME IT RIGHT (Ire) 5-11-3 F Woods, ... (6 to 1) 5
ROCK POOL 5-11-3 F J Flood, ...(20 to 1) 6
PELEUS (USA) 9-11-11 S R Murphy, ...(14 to 1) 7
Dist: 3l, 9l, 15l, 13l. 4m 52.70s. (7 Ran).
(Mrs Catherine Howard), Noel Meade

1987 Slate Handicap Hurdle (0-123 4-y-o and up) £3,105 2m..............(2:45)

1822^{3} SHANNON AMBER (Ire) [-] 5-9-7 (7*) J P Broderick, (8 to 1) 1
1824^{5} CELTIC SAILS (Ire) [-] 6-11-2 (5*) Mr P J Casey, ... (9 to 2) 2
1894^{7} PLUMBOB (Ire) [-] 5-11-1 (3*) Mr A E Lacy, ... (8 to 1) 3
1764 JACINTA'S BOY [-] 7-10-7 J Shortt, ...(14 to 1) 4
499^{8} FARAGHAN (Ire) [-] 5-9-10 P Carberry, ...(12 to 1) 5
1780^{2} WINTERBOURNE ABBAS (Ire) [-] (bl) 5-11-2 B Sheridan, ... (6 to 4 fav) 6
MONTE FIGO [-] 7-11-7 T J Taaffe, ...(9 to 1) 7
854 ENERGANCE (Ire) [-] 6-11-5 F J Flood, ...(10 to 1) 8
Dist: 1½l, 4½l, 3l, 15l. 4m 8.30s. (8 Ran).
(J B FitzGerald), Michael Hourigan

1988 Craddoxtown Chase (5-y-o and up) £3,450 2m 3f..................(3:15)

1451^{2} SCRIBBLER 8-11-7 L P Cusack, ...(5 to 2) 1
1763^{3} BERMUDA BUCK 8-11-7 F Woods, ...(7 to 4 fav) 2
1764^{3} TOUT VA BIEN 6-11-7 P Carberry, ...(7 to 1) 3
1612 NEW CO (Ire) 5-11-7 C O'Dwyer, ...(7 to 1) 4
1612 NO BETTER BUACHAIL (Ire) 6-11-7 F J Flood, ...(20 to 1) 5
1831 SHABRA CONNECTION 7-11-4 (3*) D Bromley, ... (66 to 1) 6
1550 INCA CHIEF 10-11-7 T J Taaffe, ...(3 to 1) pu
1902^{8} ATH DARA 7-11-2 K F O'Brien, ...(20 to 1) pu
Dist: 2½l, 4½l, ¾l, sht-hd. 5m 27.40s. (8 Ran).
(Mrs H T Murphy), A L T Moore

1989 Dodder Flat Race (5-y-o and up) £3,105 2m.................... (3:45)

PRODIGAL PRINCE 6-12-0 Mr A J Martin, ...(5 to 2 fav) 1
1180^{2} THE REAL ARTICLE (Ire) 5-11-3 (7*) Mr T J Murphy, (7 to 2) 2
LACKEN CROSS (Ire) 6-12-0 Mr A P O'Brien, ...(6 to 1) 3
GLEN SALGIUS (Ity) 5-11-10 Mr T Mullins, ... (10 to 1) 4
1832^{3} SIMPLY SARAH 8-11-2 (7*) Miss S Kauntze, ...(10 to 1) 5
331 COOMACHEO (Ire) 5-11-3 (7*) Mr D A Harney, ... (14 to 1) 6
1016^{6} COLLIERS HILL (Ire) 6-11-9 (5*) Mr P J Casey, ... (8 to 1) 7
801^{7} MISS POLLERTON (Ire) 6-11-2 (7*) Mr M J Bowe, (14 to 1) 8
1916^{6} MONKSLAND 9-11-7 (7*) Mr L Mannerings, ... (50 to 1) 9
709^{4} CORYMANDEL (Ire) 5-11-10 Mr P Fenton, ...(3 to 1) ro
Dist: 5l, sht-hd, 7l, 4½l. 4m 3.70s. (10 Ran).
(Miss Louise Wood), J R H Fowler

NEWBURY (soft)
Saturday January 1st
Going Correction: PLUS 1.15 sec. per fur. (races 1,2,-3,5,7), PLUS 1.00 (4,6)

1990 Wickham Novices' Hurdle (4-y-o) £3,324 2m 110yds............. (12:40)

WINTER FOREST (USA) 11-0 A Maguire, *hld up, hdwy to chal 3 out, slight ld 2 out, shaken up whn lft clr last.* ....(3 to 1 op 9 to 4 tchd 100 to 30) 1
MARIUS (Ire) 11-0 D Murphy, *prmnt, ev ch 3 out, outpcd frm nxt*...............(10 to 1 op 7 to 1 tchd 12 to 1) 2
1647 DUVEEN (Ire) 11-0 C Llewellyn, *beh till steady hdwy 5th, chlgd 3 out, sn led, hdd 2 out, one pace.* ....(10 to 1 op 7 to 1 tchd 12 to 1) 3
VOLUNTEER POINT (Ire) 10-9 (5*) J Burke, *led to 3 out, sn rdn and wknd*....... (33 to 1 op 20 to 1 tchd 50 to 1) 4
DESERT CHALLENGER (Ire) 11-0 S Smith Eccles, *str hold, chsd ldrs 5th, ev ch 3 out, sn wknd.* (25 to 1 op 16 to 1) 5
MONAZITE 11-0 R Bellamy, *prmnt till wknd appr 3 out.* .... (50 to 1 op 20 to 1 tchd 66 to 1) 6
IF IT SUITS 11-0 G McCourt, *prmnt, pressed ldrs 4th, ev ch appr 3 out, sn wknd*..............(20 to 1 op 16 to 1) 7
UPWARD SURGE (Ire) 11-0 N Williamson, *blun 3rd, effrt appr 3 out, sn btn*.....(12 to 1 op 7 to 1 tchd 14 to 1) 8
1705^{2} PHROSE 11-0 Peter Hobbs, *prmnt, hit 1st, ch 3 out, 4th and btn whn f last*................. (10 to 1 op 8 to 1) f
1510^{2} SUPREME MASTER 11-0 R Dunwoody, *hld up, hdwy to chal frm 3 out till blun and uns rdr last.* ....(7 to 4 fav op 9 to 4 tchd 5 to 2) ur
DEE RAFT (USA) 11-0 J Osborne, *chsd ldr to 5th, sn wknd, pld up bef 2 out*.................... (9 to 1 op 6 to 1) pu
GREENHILL WONDER (bl) 10-9 B Powell, *whipped round strt, sn reco'red, tld off 3rd, pld up bef 5th.* .... (66 to 1 op 33 to 1) pu
Dist: 6l, 3l, 25l, 8l, 3l, 3½l, 1½l. 4m 15.30s. a 26.30s (12 Ran).
SR: 14/8/5/-/-/-/ (Sheikh Ahmed Bin Saeed Al Maktoum), D Nicholson

1991 Rocking Horse Nursery Handicap Hurdle (0-145 4-y-o and up) £7,304 2m 110yds........................ (1:10)

1672^{3} NIKITAS [115] 9-10-2 A Maguire, *chsd ldr, led 2 out, drvn out r-in*...............(5 to 2 op 2 to 1 tchd 11 to 4) 1
1690* HERE HE COMES [138] 8-11-11 G McCourt, *hld up, gd hdwy to chal 3 out, continued str challenge to last, not quicken r-in*........(15 to 8 fav op 2 to 1 tchd 9 to 4) 2
MIAMI SPLASH [120] 7-10-7 M Hourigan, *led to 2 out, outpcd appr last*....... (4 to 1 op 5 to 1 tchd 11 to 2) 3
HOLY WANDERER (USA) [126] 5-10-13 G Upton, *str hold, hld up, hdwy 3 out, hit nxt, sn rdn and btn.* ....(7 to 2 op 5 to 2 tchd 4 to 1) 4
IVEAGH HOUSE [121] 8-10-8 S McNeill, *chsd ldrs, ev ch 3 out till wknd aftr nxt*............ (20 to 1 op 14 to 1) 5
Dist: 3l, 7l, ¾l, 10l. 4m 10.90s. a 21.90s (5 Ran).
SR: 45/65/40/45/30/ (Miss A Whitfield), Miss A J Whitfield

1992 Challow Hurdle Grade 1 (4-y-o and up) £17,075 2m 5f.................. (1:40)

1661* LARGE ACTION (Ire) 6-11-7 J Osborne, *in tch, chlgd 3 out, led nxt, idled r-in, shaken up and sn clr, readily.* .... (5 to 4 on op 6 to 4 on tchd 11 to 10 on) 1
1840^{2} CORROUGE (USA) 5-11-7 C Llewellyn, *in tch, lost pos 8th, rallied and ev ch 3 out till outpcd r-in.* ....(5 to 1 op 7 to 1 tchd 9 to 2) 2
1539* TOP SPIN 5-11-7 N Williamson, *hdwy 7th, led 3 out to nxt, sn outpcd*.............(11 to 2 op 5 to 1 tchd 6 to 1) 3
1624* ARCTIC COURSE (Ire) 6-11-7 A Maguire, *led to second, styd in tch, led 8th to 3 out, sn wknd.* ....(9 to 1 op 6 to 1 tchd 10 to 1) 4
1648^{3} IVOR'S FLUTTER 5-11-7 P Holley, *drpd rear 5th, lost tch 7th*..............................(14 to 1 tchd 16 to 1) 5
1654* POWLEYVALE 7-11-2 R Dunwoody, *led second, clr 5th, hdd 8th, sn btn*..... (14 to 1 op 12 to 1 tchd 16 to 1) 6
1648* BOOK OF MUSIC (Ire) 6-11-7 D Murphy, *chsd ldrs, chlgd 8th, wknd 3 out, tld off whn pld up bef last.* ....(10 to 1 op 8 to 1 tchd 12 to 1) pu
Dist: 3½l, 12l, 10l, 15l, dist. 5m 20.70s. a 27.70s (7 Ran).
SR: 58/54/42/32/17/-/-/ (B T Stewart-Brown), O Sherwood

1993 — Ladbroke Gold Cup Handicap Chase (0-145 6-y-o and up) £17,587 3¼m 110yds..................(2:15)

1887 ANTONIN (Fr) [135] 6-11-1 (5*) J Burke, *mid-div, hdwy 13th to chase ldr nxt, chlgd 3 out, sn led, ran on wl.*
...........................(25 to 1 op 20 to 1) 1
886² RATHVINDEN HOUSE (USA) [115] 7-10-0 B Powell, *led, mstk 3 out, sn hdd, styd on same pace.*
...........................(12 to 1 op 10 to 1 tchd 14 to 1) 2
1778⁴ GRANGE BRAKE [117] (bl) 8-10-2 C Llewellyn, *hit 6th, chsd ldrs, rdn alng aftr 11th, styd on same pace frm 4 out.*
...........................(12 to 1 op 10 to 1 tchd 14 to 1) 3
935⁵ AUCTION LAW (NZ) [120] 10-10-5 R Dunwoody, *chsd ldrs, blun 16th, wknd.*............(25 to 1 op 20 to 1) 4
1732* DO BE BRIEF [123] (bl) 9-10-8 I Lawrence, *in tch, blun 12th, hit 14th, rdn nxt, sn btn.*
...........................(4 to 1 op 9 to 2 tchd 7 to 2) 5
1625* MIDNIGHT CALLER [124] 8-10-9 J Osborne, *hmpd and f second.*............(5 to 2 fav op 3 to 1 tchd 7 to 2) f
1616* GAMBLING ROYAL [142] 11-11-13 A Maguire, *blun 4th, hdwy 13th, hit nxt, wknd 16th, tld off whn pld up bef four out.*............(6 to 1 op 9 to 2 tchd 7 to 1) pu
1713² ANNIO CHILONE [118] 8-10-0 (3*) P Hide, *chsd ldr to 14th, blun 16th, sn wknd, tld off whn pld up bef last.*
...........................(10 to 1 tchd 12 to 1) pu
1543 STIRRUP CUP [131] 10-11-2 G Bradley, *hit 5th, lost tch nxt, tld off whn pld up bef 16th....* (8 to 1 tchd 9 to 1) pu
1208⁶ NATIVE PRIDE [120] 7-10-5 N Williamson, *hdwy 11th, wknd nxt, tld off whn pld up bef 4 out.*
...........................(7 to 1 op 5 to 1) pu
Dist: 12l, 25l, 6l, 7l. 6m 57.10s. a 29.10s (10 Ran).
SR: 66/34/11/8/4/-/ (M Stanners), Mrs S A Bramall

1994 — Newbury Racecourse Conference And Exhibition Centre Novices' Hurdle (5-y-o and up) £3,285 3m 110yds...(2:45)

1595* SEEKIN CASH (USA) 5-11-4 J Osborne, *in tch, chlgd 9th, led 2 out, wnt clr r-in.*
...........................(7 to 4 fav op 2 to 1 tchd 9 to 4) 1
1568* TOTHEWOODS 6-11-4 C Llewellyn, *beh 6th, hdwy 9th, effrt 2 out, hld whn hit last.*
...........................(3 to 1 op 5 to 2 tchd 100 to 30) 2
1747² FUN MONEY 7-11-0 A Maguire, *mid-div, chlgd 9th, led tenth to 2 out, sn outpcd.*........(6 to 1 tchd 5 to 1) 3
1564³ SUNY BAY (Ire) 5-11-0 R Supple, *prmnt to 7th.*
...........................(16 to 1 op 12 to 1) 4
1648⁴ GOLDEN SPINNER 7-11-0 R Dunwoody, *led to tenth, sn wknd, no........* (5 to 1 op 9 to 2 tchd 6 to 1) 5
1707⁴ DOLLY OATS 8-10-9 D Gallagher, *prmnt early, beh 6th.*
...........................(16 to 1 tchd 20 to 1) 6
1648⁷ LOYAL GAIT (NZ) 6-11-0 B Powell, *beh 6th.*
...........................(66 to 1 op 33 to 1) 7
1645* GORT 6-11-4 J Leech, *al beh, tld off.*
...........................(11 to 2 op 5 to 1 tchd 6 to 1) 8
1536 ROMANY BLUES 5-10-9 N Williamson, *beh till mstk and uns rdr 5th.*.................(16 to 1 op 33 to 1) ur
1469 MONKSANDER 8-11-0 B Clifford, *prmnt early, tld off whn pld up bef tenth.*.................(16 to 1 op 33 to 1) pu
1747⁴ PHAROAH'S SON 8-11-0 S Earle, *chsd ldrs to 8th, wknd tenth, tld off whn pld up....*.......(50 to 1 op 33 to 1 tchd 66 to 1) pu
1747⁸ GREAT ORME (NZ) 7-11-0 J Frost, *prmnt early, beh 6th, tld off whn pld up 2 out....*. (66 to 1 op 33 to 1) pu
1747 ROYAL GAIT (NZ) (bl) 6-10-11 (3*) R Davis, *al beh, tld off whn pld up bef 2 out.*.............(66 to 1 op 33 to 1) pu
Dist: 12l, 8l, 20l, hd, 15l, dist, 3l. 6m 23.50s. a 34.50s (13 Ran).
SR: 27/15/3/-/-/-/ (Sheikh Ahmed Bin Saeed Al Maktoum), C R Egerton

1995 — Hungerford Handicap Chase (6-y-o and up) £5,486 2½m...........(3:15)

1656* GNOME'S TYCOON [122] 8-10-1¹ J Railton, *made all, qng clr whn hit 2 out, styd on wl.*
......(5 to 4 fav op 6 to 4 tchd 13 to 8 and 11 to 10) 1
1618² VIKING FLAGSHIP [147] 7-11-12 A Maguire, *in tch, chlgd 11th, outpcd frm 3 out.*............(2 to 1 op 6 to 4) 2
1653⁸ LYPHENTO (USA) [121] 10-10-0 D Murphy, *chsd wnr, chlgd tenth till wknd appr 4 out.........*(12 to 1 op 8 to 1) 3
1698* THATCHER ROCK (NZ) [121] 9-9-7 (7*) Guy Lewis, *in tch, chlgd 11th, 3rd and no ch whn pld up bef last.*
...........................(3 to 1 op 11 to 4 tchd 100 to 30) pu
Dist: 15l, 30l. 5m 20.90s. a 30.90s (4 Ran).
(Irvin S Naylor), R T Phillips

1996 — Open National Hunt Flat Race (4,5,6-y-o) £1,856 2m 110yds.........(3:45)

1626² ST MELLION FAIRWAY (Ire) 5-10-12 (7*) Pat Thompson, *hdwy 7 fs out, led 2 out, drvn and styd on wl frm o'r one out.*...........(4 to 1 op 5 to 2 tchd 9 to 2) 1
1494* LEAD VOCALIST (Ire) 5-11-7 C Burnett-Wells, *beh, hdwy 6 fs out, chsd wnr 2 out, not rch wnr.*
...........................(5 to 1 op 7 to 4 tchd 11 to 4) 2

ACE PLAYER (NZ) 6-10-12 (7*) S Fox, *prmnt, led 7 fs out to 4 out, ev ch till not quicken ins last.*
...........................(5 to 1 op 10 to 1 tchd 14 to 1) 3
NAHTHEN LAD (Ire) 5-10-12 (7*) L O'Hare, *in tch, rdn and styd on one pace fnl 2 fs...........*(11 to 2 op 8 to 1) 4
HOPE THATCH (NZ) 6-11-2 (3*) R Davis, *prmnt, led 4 fs out to 2 out, sn one pace.* (14 to 1 op 8 to 1 tchd 16 to 1) 5
LINTON ROCKS 5-11-5 S Smith Eccles, *chsd ldrs, ev ch 4 out fs out till wknd ins fnl 2.*
...........................(12 to 1 op 8 to 1 tchd 14 to 1) 6
MISTER SPECTATOR (Ire) 5-11-0 (7*) M Keighley, *prmnt, ev ch 4 fs out, wknd o'r 2 out.*
...........................(12 to 1 op 10 to 1 tchd 20 to 1) 7
1779⁵ BETTER BYTHE GLASS (Ire) 5-11-5 C Llewellyn, *chsd ldrs, rdn 3 fs out, sn wknd....*(5 to 1 op 4 to 1 tchd 6 to 1) 8
GOTT TO BE JOKING 6-11-5 S Burrough, *beh, effrt 4 fs out, sn fdd.*...........................(33 to 1 op 20 to 1) 9
WOODLAND CUTTING 6-11-5 W Humphreys, *al beh.*
...........................(33 to 1 op 20 to 1) 10
NORTHERN SINGER 4-10-7 G McCourt, *beh, nvr rch ldrs.*
...........................(14 to 1 op 10 to 1) 11
OLYMPIC ROSE (Ire) 5-11-0 Peter Hobbs, *mid-div, hdwy to chase ldrs 4 fs out, wknd quickly.* (33 to 1 op 20 to 1) 12
1428⁶ SWEET FRIENDSHIP 6-11-0 R Supple, *al beh.*
...........................(33 to 1 op 20 to 1) 13
CAPITAIN 5-11-5 N Williamson, *led for o'r 9 fs, sn wknd.*
...........................(33 to 1 op 20 to 1) 14
Dist: 1½l, 1½l, ¾l, 7l, ¾l, 5l, 6l, 4l, 2½l, 10l. 4m 15.80s. (14 Ran).
(St Mellion Estates Ltd), J A B Old

NOTTINGHAM (soft)
Saturday January 1st
Going Correction: PLUS 1.50 sec. per fur. (races 1,3,5), PLUS 1.23 (2,4,6)

1997 — Hogmanay Conditional Jockeys' Handicap Chase (0-100 5-y-o and up) £2,633 2m 5f 110yds...........(1:00)

1486⁴ MOUNTEBOR [88] 10-11-10 S Taylor, *keen hold, led aftr 9th, hld on gmely r-in............*(5 to 1 op 3 to 1) 1
1423 IMPECCABLE TIMING [77] 11-10-6 (7*) P Maddock, *not jump wl, ran in snatches, rallied und pres r-in, jst hld.*
...........................(7 to 2 op 5 to 1) 2
1739³ MOULTON BULL [86] 8-11-8 A Thornton, *jmpd wl, slight ld 4th till aftr 9th, drw level appr 2 out, one pace r-in.*
...........................(5 to 4 fav op 5 to 4) 3
1748⁵ NEWMARKET SAUSAGE [66] 13-10-2 P McLoughlin, *nvr far away, mstk 6 out, reminders nxt, wknd 3 out, tld off.*................(10 to 1 tchd 12 to 1 and 9 to 1) 4
MARTIN'S FRIEND [87] 11-11-9 R Greene, *wth ldrs whn f 3rd....*........................(7 to 1 op 5 to 1) f
ANOTHER STRIPLIGHT [86] 11-11-8 W Marston, *slight ld to 4th, reminders to hold pl hfwy, tld off whn pld up bef 2 out.*...........................(33 to 1 tchd 50 to 1) pu
Dist: ½l, 8l, dist. 5m 54.30s. a 41.30s (6 Ran).
SR: 6/-/-/ (Mrs Jean Turpin), P C Haslam

1998 — 'Come Racing In 1994' Novices' Hurdle (4-y-o and up) £2,061 2m 5f 110yds...........................(1:30)

1654 OTTOMAN EMPIRE 7-12-0 M Brennan, *settled gng wl, led aftr 7th, blun and hdd briefly 4 out, styd on und pres frm last............*(13 to 8 fav op 6 to 4 tchd 7 to 4) 1
1729⁵ MAKES ME GOOSEY (Ire) 6-11-7 L Harvey, *nvr far away, led briefly 4 out, rdn last 3, kpt on.*
...........................(100 to 30 op 3 to 1 tchd 7 to 2) 2
1473⁴ SOLOMAN SPRINGS (USA) 4-10-5 (3*) A Thornton, *al hndy, drw level 3 out, one pace.*
...........................(7 to 2 op 3 to 1) 3
1767 ALBERSTAN 4-10-8 W Worthington, *in tch, rdn alng hfwy, wknd rpdly bef 4 out, tld off....*..........(50 to 1) 4
1571 BOLD AMBITION 7-11-7 Susan Kersey, *pressing ldrs whn f second....................*(4 to 1 op 11 to 2 tchd 6 to 1) f
GRANNY'S LAD 7-11-7 W Marston, *set modest pace, clr 3rd, jmpd right 4th, 5th and 6th, hdd and wknd nxt, tld off whn pld up bef 3 out...........*(50 to 1 op 33 to 1) pu
Dist: 2l, 2½l, dist. 5m 48.70s. a 46.70s (6 Ran).
(Lady Anne Bentinck), O Brennan

1999 — 'Auld Lang Syne' Novices' Chase (5-y-o and up) £2,499 2m 5f 110yds (2:00)

1547² NICKLE JOE 8-11-5 W Marston, *made most to 3 out, rallied gmely to ld r-in.*
...........................(13 to 8 fav op 7 to 4 tchd 2 to 1) 1
1711⁸ BRIGHT THE WIFE 8-11-5 D Bridgwater, *nvr far away, jmpd ahead 3 out, rdn last, hdd and one pace r-in.*
...........................(15 to 8 op 7 to 4 tchd 2 to 1) 2
1669² STAGE PLAYER 8-11-0 (5*) T Eley, *dsptd ld, niggled alng 7 out, hit nxt, tiring rpdly whn f 4 out.*
...........................(11 to 4 op 2 to 1) f
1730 NO LIGHT 7-11-5 L Harvey, *not jump wl, improved fnl circuit, led briefly 5 out, tired whn f 2 out.*
...........................(10 to 1 op 6 to 1) f

Dist: 1½l. 5m 51.80s. a 38.80s (4 Ran).
SR: 26/24/-/-/   (Mrs E Tate), M Tate

2000   Good Resolutions Novices' Handicap Hurdle (0-100 4-y-o) £1,722 2m. . (2:30)

1749*	SHARED GOLD [77] 10-13 M Bosley, *nvr far away, rdn to ld last, hld on gmely und pres*..... (13 to 2 op 11 to 2)	1
1504ᴬ	DANGER BABY [65] 9-12 (3*) D Meredith, *led, hrd pressed frm 3 out, hdd last, rallied*..........(8 to 1 op 6 to 1)	2
1476⁴	NEGD (USA) [67] 10-3 M Brennan, *settled off the pace, rdn to cl 3 out, ridden and one pace nxt.*	
	....(5 to 1 tchd 6 to 1)	3
1880	HEATHYARDS BOY [88] 11-7 (3*) S Wynne, *al hndy, rdn 3 out, sn btn*.................(6 to 1 op 5 to 1 tchd 13 to 2)	4
497	CASHABLE [68] 10-4 M A FitzGerald, *pressed ldrs, rdn whn pace lifted 3 out, sn lost tch.* (14 to 1 op 10 to 1)	5
1476³	COEUR BATTANT (Fr) [75] 10-6 (5*) E Husband, *trkd ldr, led briefly 4 out, rdn and wknd quickly nxt.*	
	..................................(7 to 1 op 6 to 1)	6
1702*	SOUTHAMPTON [88] 11-3 (7*) N Collum, *chsd ldrs, effrt hfwy, struggling appr 3 out, tld off.* (9 to 2 op 7 to 2)	7
1767⁴	MISTROY [73] 10-4 (5*) D Bentley, *trkd ldrs, struggling to keep up appr 3 out, tld off.*	
	............................(4 to 1 fav op 5 to 1 tchd 7 to 2)	8

Dist: 1l, 15l, ½l, 12l, 1½l, 10l, 20l. 4m 13.00s. a 29.00s (8 Ran).
                  (P A Deal), J R Bosley

2001   New Year Handicap Chase (0-115 5-y-o and up) £3,052 3m 3f 110yds. . (3:05)

	SHRADEN LEADER [102] 9-11-4 A Tory, *nvr far away, led 7 out, clr 3 out, styd on strly r-in*.... (10 to 1 op 7 to 1)	1
1720²	FURRY KNOWE [100] 9-11-2 M A FitzGerald, *trkd ldg 4, effrt and drvn alng four out, styd on one pace frm betw last 2*....................................(5 to 2 fav op 2 to 1)	2
1720⁸	UNDER OFFER [90] (bl) 13-9-13 (7*) M Hancock, *al hndy, led 8 out to nxt, rallied 4 out, lft 3rd at last.*	
	......................................(14 to 1 op 12 to 1)	3
1471⁷	THE FORTIES [99] 9-10-12 (3*) A Thornton, *settled midfield, effrt fnl circuit, rdn whn pace quickened aftr 5 out, sn btn*....................(14 to 1 op 16 to 1 tchd 20 to 1)	4
1769³	WOODLANDS GENHIRE [84] (v) 9-10-0 W Marston, *made most to 8 out, wknd quickly aftr nxt, tld off.*	
	..........................(9 to 1 op 8 to 1 tchd 10 to 1)	5
1635⁴	CAROUSEL ROCKET [101] 11-11-3 C Grant, *trkd ldrs, reminders aftr one circuit, lost tch frm 8 out, tld off.*	
	....(9 to 2 op 4 to 1)	6
1838²	DANDY MINSTREL [108] 10-11-10 D Bridgwater, *patiently rdn, jnd ldrs fnl circuit, ev ch 4 out, 3rd and hld whn f last.*........................(9 to 2 op 4 to 1 tchd 5 to 1)	f
1796³	KINGFISHER BAY [94] (bl) 9-10-10 W McFarland, *chsd ldrs, reminders to hold pl aftr one circuit, tld off whn pld up bef 5 out*......................(13 to 2 op 6 to 1)	pu

Dist: 10l, 20l, 6l, sht-hd, dist. 7m 41.00s. a 53.00s (8 Ran).
                (W R J Everall), K C Bailey

2002   'First Footing' Handicap Hurdle (0-120 4-y-o and up) £2,226 2m....... (3:35)

1492³	EASTHORPE [105] 6-10-13 M A FitzGerald, *jmpd wl, made all, jnd 3 out, quickened away last, easily.*	
	......................................(4 to 1 op 5 to 2)	1
1672*	STRATH ROYAL [120] 8-12-0 M Brennan, *settled gng wl, ev ch 3 out, rdn and outpcd frm betw last 2.*	
	..........................(9 to 4 tchd 5 to 2 and 11 to 4)	2
1753⁶	CELTIC BOB [97] 14-9-12 (7*) P Maddock, *last and hld up, feeling pace and lost grnd 4 out, styd on frm betw last 2, no imprsn*.......................(33 to 1 op 16 to 1)	3
1569*	HYDE'S HAPPY HOUR [94] 4-10-2² M Dwyer, *trkd wnr till aftr 4 out, btn whn hmpd 2 out, eased r-in.*	
	........................(1 to 1 fav op 6 to 4)	4
1357⁶	TAURIAN PRINCESS [93] 5-10-11¹ Diane Clay, *chsd ldrs, struggling whn pace lifted hfwy, tld off 4 out.*	
	................................(33 to 1 op 20 to 1)	5
1198⁴	TAYLORS PRINCE [92] (v) 7-10-0 V Smith, *wtd wth, cld 4 out, 3rd and drvn alng whn f 2 out.* (4 to 1 tchd 5 to 1)	f

Dist: 5l, 25l, 6l, 1l. 4m 7.70s. a 23.70s (6 Ran).
SR: 45/55/7/   (Martin Broughton), Miss H C Knight

AYR (good to soft)
Monday January 3rd
Going Correction: PLUS 0.50 sec. per fur. (races 1,3,6), PLUS 0.70 (2,4,5)

2003   Dalrymple Novices' Hurdle (4-y-o and up) £2,134 2m................(12:50)

1217³	DEVILRY 4-10-7 J Callaghan, *mid-div, gd hdwy to ld appr 3 out, hmpd three out, styd on wl frm last.*	
	......................................(14 to 1 op 12 to 1)	1
779*	MERRY NUTKIN 8-12-0 P Niven, *mid-div, steady hdwy to ld appr 3 out, sn hdd, ev ch betw last 2, no extr.*	
	.................(11 to 10 fav tchd Evens and 5 to 4)	2
1613⁶	MEDIA MESSENGER 5-11-0 (5*) P Waggott, *chsd ldrs, rdn appr 3 out, kpt on, no imprsn*.... (16 to 1 op 14 to 1)	3

1504³	ERZADJAN (Ire) (bl) 4-10-13 G McCourt, *hmpd 1st, chsd ldrs, pushed alng aftr 6th, kpt on same pace.*	
	............................(3 to 1 op 7 to 2 tchd 4 to 1)	4
1724⁸	STONEY BROOK 6-11-5 B Storey, *in tch, effrt aftr 6th, kpt on same pace.*..........................(50 to 1)	5
1768⁶	BLAYNEYS PRIVILEGE 7-11-5 R Garritty, *cl up, led 5th till hdd appr 3 out, wknd.*......................(50 to 1)	6
1726	HOWCLEUCH 7-11-0 T Reed, *in tch, no hdwy frm 6th.*	
	.............................(50 to 1 op 33 to 1)	7
1724³	THE WHIRLIE WEEVIL 6-11-0 M Moloney, *trkd ldrs, effrt aftr 6th, grad wknd..* (8 to 1 op 10 to 1 tchd 9 to 1)	8
	FLOATER (USA) 11-11-2 (3*) D J Moffatt, *nvr dngrs.*	
	....(500 to 1)	9
1535⁹	CHOIR'S IMAGE 7-11-0 A Mulholland, *led 1st till hdd 5th, grad wknd.*..........................(100 to 1)	10
1787⁹	PESIDANAMICH (Ire) 6-11-5 N Doughty, *in tch till grad lost pl aftr 5th.*...................(25 to 1 op 16 to 1)	11
1223	DERWENT LAD 5-11-5 A Dobbin, *al beh*.........(200 to 1)	12
1724	TAUVALERA 7-11-0 Mr D Swindlehurst, *prmnt till wknd aftr 6th.*..................................(500 to 1)	13
1053⁹	CROFTON LAKE 6-11-0 (5*) Mr H Hale, *badly hmpd 1st, sn beh, tld off.*.........................(200 to 1)	14
1677⁹	LA DOUTELLE 7-11-0 Mr J Bradburne, *al beh, tld off.*	
	...................(200 to 1 tchd 250 to 1)	15
1680⁶	FINE OAK 7-11-4⁴ Mr D Robertson, *beh whn blun 5th, tld off.*..	16
	FIVE TO SEVEN (USA) 5-11-5 D Wilkinson, *led till f 1st.*	
	..................................(6 to 1 op 5 to 1)	f
	LAWNSWOOD QUAY 4-10-7 C Grant, *dsptd ld till wknd aftr 5th, tld off whn pld up bef 3 out.*	
	............................(66 to 1 op 100 to 1)	pu
	LOMOND SPRINGS (Ire) 5-11-5 S Turner, *al beh, tld off whn pld up bef 3 out*....................(100 to 1)	pu

Dist: 2½l, 4l, 10l, 1l, 1½l, 2½l, 4l, 3l, hd. 3m 50.80s. a 13.80s (19 Ran).
SR: 21/39/24/8/12/11/4/1/2/   (Miss V Foster), G M Moore

2004   Culroy Novices' Chase (5-y-o and up) £2,879 3m 1f...................(1:20)

1723	LOTHIAN PILOT 7-11-5 T Reed, *trkd ldrs gng wl, led 3 out, styd on well.*........................(4 to 1 op 5 to 2)	1
1754⁷	MONAUGHTY MAN 8-11-0 (5*) P Williams, *led till mstk and hdd 3 out, kpt on wl.*............(14 to 1 tchd 12 to 1)	2
1723⁵	DEEP HAVEN 9-11-5 K Jones, *in tch till wknd aftr 14th, tld off.*.............................(33 to 1 op 25 to 1)	3
	BOWLANDS WAY 10-11-5 A Mulholland, *beh, lost tch aftr 14th, tld off.*..........................(33 to 1 op 25 to 1)	4
1477²	CEILIDH BOY 8-11-11 B Storey, *trkd ldrs, pushed alng aftr 15th, 3rd and no ch whn f 2 out.*	
	..............................(Evens fav op 5 to 4 on)	f
1726⁶	PADDY MORRISSEY 7-11-5 A Dobbin, *in tch, pushed alng hfwy, f 13th*..........................(50 to 1)	f
1723	GARCALL 8-11-5 M Moloney, *prmnt, hit 15th, wkng whn blun and uns rdr 4 out.*..........(4 to 1 op 3 to 1)	ur
1218	CASTLEFERGUS 7-11-5 J Callaghan, *beh, lost tch aftr 14th, tld off whn pld up bef 4 out.*	
	....................(12 to 1 op 14 to 1 tchd 16 to 1)	pu
1677⁸	THE LORRYMAN (Ire) 6-11-0 (5*) F Perratt, *mstks, wl beh whn pld up bef tenth.*......................(100 to 1)	pu

Dist: 2½l, dist, 6l. 6m 40.70s. a 40.70s (9 Ran).
             (Crawford, Wares & Hamilton), L Lungo

2005   Ayr New Year Handicap Hurdle (0-140 4-y-o and up) £2,867 2m....... (1:50)

1874*	WESTHOLME (USA) [116] 6-10-11 (4ex) R Garritty, *dsptd ld, rdn aftr 2 out, jmpd rght last, sn led, kpt on und pres.*	
	............(6 to 4 fav op 5 to 4 tchd 13 to 8 and 7 to 4)	1
1728*	ARAGON AYR [105] 6-10-0 A Dobbin, *trkd ldrs, effrt appr 3 out, kpt on wl frm nxt*..........(10 to 1 tchd 12 to 1)	2
1487⁷	ALL WELCOME [105] 7-9-7 (7*) D Ryan, *led or dsptd ld till bumped and hdd last, no extr*..... (12 to 1 op 10 to 1)	3
1793⁸	REVE DE VALSE (USA) [114] 7-10-4 (3*) P Waggott, *in tch, struggling aftr 3 out, not rch ldrs*..........(14 to 1)	4
1874³	ABBOT OF FURNESS [133] 10-12-0 N Doughty, *trkd ldrs till grad lost pl aftr 6th*................(7 to 2 op 3 to 1)	5
1571⁴	PERSUASIVE [129] 7-11-5 (5*) Mr M Buckley, *hld up, hdwy aftr 6th, no imprsn frm 3 out*......... (7 to 2 tchd 4 to 1)	6
	ELGIN [105] 5-10-1⁴ (3*) D J Moffatt, *outpcd and lost tch hfwy, nvr dngrs*.......................(66 to 1)	7
1614⁷	RINGLAND (USA) [105] 6-9-7 (7*) Carol Cuthbert, *beh, some hdwy hfwy, wknd aftr 6th*........(33 to 1 op 50 to 1)	8
1863⁸	LIABILITY ORDER [106] 5-10-11 C Grant, *in tch, pushed alng aftr 6th, sn wknd*............(20 to 1 tchd 25 to 1)	9
	DANCING STREET [106] 6-10-11 C Hawkins, *trkd ldrs till wknd appr 6th*...............(200 to 1 op 100 to 1)	10
	PIT PONY [105] 10-10-0 L O'Hara, *in tch till wknd appr 6th*..................................(200 to 1)	11

Dist: 2l, 1½l, 2l, 5l, 8l, 8l, 3½l, 1½l, 4l, 3½l. 3m 53.60s. a 16.60s (11 Ran).
             (T H Bennett), M H Easterby

2006   McAlpine Challenge Cup Handicap Chase (0-140 5-y-o and up) £3,403 2 ½m...........................(2:20)

| 1876² | DEEP DAWN [106] 11-10-6 C Grant, *made virtually all, rdn clr betw last 2, styd on wl.* (5 to 4 fav tchd 11 to 8) | 1 |

NATIONAL HUNT RESULTS 1993-94

1739 ZAM BEE [108] 8-10-8 T Reed, *in tch, ch 4 out, rdn aftr 2 out, kpt on same pace.* (8 to 1 op 7 to 1 tchd 10 to 1) 2
1941⁴ PINEMARTIN [103] 11-9-12 (5*) N Leach, *trkd ldrs, effrt aftr 4 out, ch 2 out, one pace.*
.... (7 to 2 tchd 4 to 1 and 5 to 1) 3
550 RED UNDER THE BED [100] 7-10-0 J Callaghan, *cl up, hit 13th, sn wknd, tld off.*...................(3 to 1 op 9 to 4) 4
IDA'S DELIGHT [124] 15-11-10 B Storey, *lost tch 9th, tld off whn pld up bef 3 out.*............... (12 to 1 op 7 to 1) pu
Dist: 5l, 1½l, dist. 5m 24.20s. a 37.20s (5 Ran).

(Stuart Thomas Brankin), M D Hammond

2007 Hurlford Novices' Chase (5-y-o and up) £2,554 2m...................(2:50)

1531² RODEO STAR (USA) 8-11-9 G McCourt, *cl up, led 5th, clr betw last 2, ran on wl.*
.... (7 to 4 fav op Evens tchd 15 to 8) 1
GALLATEEN 6-11-3 N Doughty, *trkd ldrs, effrt appr 2 out, kpt on same pace.*.......(9 to 4 op 2 to 1 tchd 11 to 4) 2
1671³ SPANISH FAIR (Ire) 6-10-12 (5*) J Burke, *trkd ldrs, chsd 1st 2 frm 4 out, no imprsn.*
.........(15 to 2 op 10 to 1 tchd 11 to 1 and 12 to 1) 3
BULA NUDAY 9-11-3 T Reed, *beh, styd on wl frm 4 out, nvr trbld ldrs.*........ (25 to 1 op 20 to 1 tchd 33 to 1) 4
1724 HIGHLANDMAN 8-11-3 B Storey, *in tch till grad wknd aftr 8th.*..................................(100 to 1) 5
1587⁵ FLING IN SPRING 8-10-12 (5*) P Williams, *beh frm 5th.*
..................................(33 to 1 tchd 50 to 1) 6
1181 BE AMBITIOUS (Ire) 6-11-3 K Jones, *chsd ldrs till wknd aftr 8th, wl beh whn blun 3 out.*................(50 to 1) 7
1958² POLITICAL TOWER 7-12-1 (6ex) A Dobbin, *mstks, prmnt, effrt and ev ch whn f 4 out.*
.................(9 to 2 op 4 to 1 tchd 5 to 1 and 11 to 1) f
1792 AYIA NAPA 7-11-3 Mr J Bradburne, *led till hdd 5th, blun and uns rdr nxt.*................................(200 to 1) ur
1792⁶ SEMINOFF (Fr) 8-11-9 C Grant, *al beh, tld off whn pld up bef 4 out.*...................(33 to 1 tchd 50 to 1) pu
1723 FRONT LINE 7-11-3 P Niven, *al beh, tld off whn pld up bef 4 out.*.............(7 to 1 op 6 to 1 tchd 8 to 1) pu
Dist: 3l, 8l, 15l, nk, 20l, 1½l. 4m 4.20s. a 16.20s (11 Ran).

SR: 45/36/28/13/12/-/ (J C Bradbury), N Tinkler

2008 Coylton 'National Hunt' Novices' Handicap Hurdle (5-y-o and up) £1,966 2¾m........................(3:20)

1745* IVY HOUSE (Ire) [95] 6-11-9 C Grant, *hld up, hdwy hfwy, rdn to ld aftr last, styd on wl.*
....................(5 to 1 op 9 to 2 tchd 6 to 1) 1
1677⁶ MAJOR BELL [90] 6-11-4 M Moloney, *settled midfield, gd hdwy to ld aftr 9th, mstk last, sn hdd and no extr.*
....................(7 to 1 op 5 to 1 tchd 8 to 1) 2
1772³ MASTER BOSTON (Ire) [96] 6-11-3 (7*) J Driscoll, *prmnt, rdn to chase ldr appr 3 out, ev ch till no extr frm last.*
....................(16 to 1 op 12 to 1) 3
1295⁴ NAWRIK (Ire) [80] 5-10-8¹ T Reed, *prmnt, slightly outpcd aftr 3 out, rallied betw last 2, no extr frm last.*
....................(8 to 1 tchd 7 to 1 and 10 to 1) 4
1726* BELLS HILL LAD [95] 7-11-9 A Dobbin, *chsd ldrs till outpcd aftr 9th, no dngr after.*........ (12 to 1 op 10 to 1) 5
1734² NINFA (Ire) [90] 6-11-4 N Doughty, *prmnt till outpcd aftr 9th, no dngr after.*.......(4 to 1 op 5 to 1 tchd 9 to 1) 6
1588* JUKE BOX BILLY (Ire) [82] 6-10-7 (3*) D J Moffatt, *led till hdd 9th, sn wknd.*
.................(9 to 4 fav op 3 to 1 tchd 7 to 1 and 7 to 2) 7
1677⁴ DASHMAR [81] 7-10-9 C Dennis, *beh most of way.*
.................(25 to 1 op 16 to 1) 8
1708⁹ ORTON HOUSE [72] 7-10-0 J Callaghan, *al beh.*
.................(50 to 1 op 33 to 1) 9
1724⁶ CORSTON RACER [73] 6-10-1⁶ (5*) P Williams, *beh, some hdwy aftr 7th, wknd after 9th.*.....(25 to 1 op 16 to 1) 10
1588⁶ STEPDAUGHTER [78] 8-10-6¹3 (7*) P Kennedy, *sn beh, blun 7th.*.......................(66 to 1 tchd 100 to 1) 11
CARSON CITY [86] 7-11-0 P Niven, *beh most of way, pld up bef 3 out.*...............(12 to 1 tchd 14 to 1) pu
1480³ PIRATE HOOK [93] 6-11-7 B Storey, *chsd ldrs till wknd quickly appr 9th, beh whn pld up bef 2 out.*
.................(11 to 1 op 8 to 1) pu
1723 JINGLIN' GEORDIE (Ire) [100] 6-12-0 K Jones, *sn beh, tld off whn pld up bef 2 out.*.................(500 to 1) pu
Dist: 2l, 2l, 1l, 15l, 8l, 1½l, 10l, 1l, 4l, 4l. 5m 44.60s. a 34.60s (14 Ran).

(Mrs L R Joughin), J J O'Neill

CHELTENHAM (soft)
Monday January 3rd
Going Correction: PLUS 1.80 sec. per fur. (races 1,4,6), PLUS 1.90 (2,3,5)

2009 Cheltenham Sponsorship Club Handicap Hurdle (4-y-o and up) £5,056 2m 5f 110yds....................(12:40)

1571³ TOOGOOD TO BE TRUE [112] 6-10-5 L Wyer, *hld up beh ldrs, cld frm 4 out, led appr last, styd on wl.*
....................(7 to 1 op 6 to 1) 1
1665³ KADI (Ger) [130] 5-11-9 A Maguire, *chsd ldrs, led aftr 2 out till appr last, no extr.*............. (6 to 1 tchd 11 to 2) 2
1690⁶ BUONARROTI [125] 7-11-4 T Grantham, *beh, cld 6th, ev ch 2 out, outpcd appr last, kpt on r-in.*
....................(15 to 2 op 13 to 2) 3
1759³ ULURU (Ire) [115] 6-10-8 R Dunwoody, *cl up, led 3 out till aftr nxt, wknd.*....................(6 to 1) 4
1653 DARK HONEY [120] 9-10-8 (5*) A Dicken, *beh, effrt frm 4 out, outpcd aftr nxt.*...........(4 to 1 fav tchd 9 to 2) 5
1561 HOLY JOE [124] 12-10-12 (5*) T Jenks, *trkd ldrs to 4th, in tch till wknd 3 out.*....................(33 to 1) 6
1845³ PRIME DISPLAY (USA) [131] 8-11-5 J McCarthy, *led till aftr 3rd, wknd 5th, tld off 2 out.* (14 to 1 tchd 12 to 1) 7
1777² ANDERMATT [115] 7-10-8 M Dwyer, *al beh, tld off.*
....................(13 to 2 op 6 to 1) 8
1839* ZAMIRAH (Ire) [121] (bl) 5-11-0 (4ex) C Llewellyn, *trkd ldr, led aftr 3rd, mstk and hdd 3 out, sn wknd, tld off.*
....................(7 to 1 op 6 to 1) 9
1759⁸ THE DECENT THING [114] 11-10-4 (3*) R Davis, *al beh, pushed alng 5th, tld off 8th, pld up bef last.*
....................(16 to 1 op 14 to 1) pu
Dist: 5l, ¾l, 15l, 6l, 15l, 20l, 1½l, 5l. 5m 44.30s. a 42.80s (10 Ran).
SR: 36/49/43/18/17/6/ (Jim McGrath), M H Easterby

2010 Steel Plate And Sections Young Chasers Qualifier Novices' (5 - 8-y-o) £4,742 2m 5f...................(1:15)

1879* EARTH SUMMIT (bl) 6-11-12 C Llewellyn, *wth ldr, led tenth, ran on strly frm 2 out.*
....................(9 to 4 op 13 to 8 tchd 5 to 2) 1
1615² LO STREGONE 8-11-12 M Dwyer, *in cl tch, pushed alng 12th, reminders nxt, ev ch und pres appr 2 out, sn one pace.*...........(11 to 10 fav op 6 to 4 tchd 13 to 8) 2
1772² WINGS OF FREEDOM (Ire) (v) 6-11-4 A Maguire, *wtd wth, cld 3 out, styd on one pace.*
....................(10 to 1 op 7 to 1 tchd 12 to 1) 3
1802* WELL BRIEFED 7-11-8 R Dunwoody, *led till not fluent and hdd tenth, ev ch 3 out, wknd appr nxt.*
....................(8 to 1 op 6 to 1 tchd 17 to 2) 4
1750² MARTELL BOY (NZ) 7-11-4 J Frost, *wtd wth in tch, outpcd 4 out.*...........(17 to 2 op 5 to 1 tchd 9 to 1) 5
Dist: 8l, 3½l, 5l, 3½l. 5m 49.20s. a 45.20s (5 Ran).
SR: 45/37/25/24/16/ (R I Sims), N A Twiston-Davies

2011 A. S. W. Handicap Chase (5-y-o and up) £7,067 4m 1f...............(1:50)

1635² MOORCROFT BOY [131] 9-10-0 A Maguire, *hld up, al gng wl, cld 20th, led aftr 3 out, sn clr, cmftbly.*
....................(7 to 2 fav op 4 to 1) 1
1653³ JUST SO [133] (bl) 11-10-2² S Burrough, *hld up beh, lost tch 21st, hdwy und pres 2 out, styd on to take second r-in.*...................(11 to 1 op 14 to 1) 2
1757⁶ MISTER ED [133] 11-10-2 D Morris, *in tch, drpd rear tenth, lost touch 21st, styd on und pres appr last.*
....................(4 to 1 op 7 to 3 tchd 9 to 2) 3
1838³ LEAGAUNE [131] 12-10-0 E Byrne, *in tch, drpd rear 19th, tld off 21st, took 4th r-in.*...............(100 to 1) 4
1881 INDIAN TONIC [131] 8-10-0 C Maude, *led second to 4th, led 6th till aftr 3 out, wknd quickly, fnshd tired.*
....................(4 to 1 tchd 7 to 2 and 9 to 2) 5
1732⁵ BIT OF A CLOWN [131] 11-9-7 (7*) P Ward, *sn pushed alng in rear, hdwy 17th, lost tch 23rd...* (33 to 1 op 20 to 1) 6
1543* DIRECT [131] 11-9-13² R Davis, *cl up, mstk 4 out, ev ch whn blun and uns rdr nxt.*
....................(5 to 1 op 9 to 2 tchd 11 to 2) ur
1564* SMOOTH ESCORT [131] (v) 10-10-0 C Llewellyn, *led 4th to 6th, cl up whn blun and uns rdr 12th.*
....................(33 to 1 op 20 to 1) ur
1652³ TOPSHAM BAY [155] 11-11-10 J Frost, *led to second, trkd ldrs, mstk 22nd, lost pl, pld up bef 4 out.*
....................(13 to 2 op 11 to 2) pu
Dist: 15l, 3½l, 7l, 3½l, dist. 9m 23.30s. a 66.30s (9 Ran).
SR: 36/23/19/10/6/-/ (K G Manley), D Nicholson

2012 Unicoin Homes Spa Hurdle (5-y-o and up) £5,507 2m 5f 110yds........(2:25)

1756* SWEET DUKE (Fr) 7-11-12 C Llewellyn, *made all, wnt clr aftr 2 out, rdn out.*
.................(6 to 5 on 11 to 10 on tchd Evens) 1
1765⁵ BOLLIN WILLIAM 6-11-8 L Wyer, *trkd wnr, ev ch 2 out, sn outpcd, no extr whn hit last.*
....................(7 to 2 op 5 to 2 tchd 4 to 1) 2
1845* PEATSWOOD 6-11-0 Lorna Vincent, *in tch, outpcd appr 2 out, styd on approaching last.*
....................(17 to 2 op 8 to 1 tchd 10 to 1) 3
1759⁴ EVERALDO (Fr) 10-11-0 R Dunwoody, *hld up in tch, outpcd aftr 3 out, tld off...* (9 to 2 op 4 to 1 tchd 11 to 2) 4
BRABAZON (USA) 9-11-0 M Dwyer, *wtd wth in tch, tld off 6th.*.......................(33 to 1 op 20 to 1) 5
1665⁵ CARDINAL RED (bl) 7-11-8 A Maguire, *in tch till drpd rear 5th, pld up appr 4 out.* (14 to 1 op 10 to 1 tchd 16 to 1) pu

276

Dist: 10l, 3l, 4l, dist. 5m 41.50s. a 40.00s (6 Ran).
SR: 85/71/60/56/-/-/ (Andy Mavrou), N A Twiston-Davies

2013 World Promotions Handicap Chase (5-y-o and up) £5,656 2m 5f........(2:55)

1572² SOUTHERN MINSTREL [115] 11-10-6 A Maguire, *lft in ld 4th, made rst, clr appr 2 out, ran on wl.* ....(9 to 4 op 2 to 1 tchd 5 to 2) 1
1693⁴ LAKE TEEREEN [121] 9-10-12 T Grantham, *lft second at 4th, pressed wnr aftr, reminders 13th, ev ch 3 out, outpcd appr nxt.*.........(5 to 1 tchd 6 to 1) 2
1778² GAY RUFFIAN [133] 8-11-10 R Dunwoody, *led till f 4th.* ....(7 to 4 fav op 6 to 4) f
1212* CHAMPAGNE LAD [125] 8-10-13 (3*) P Hide, *in cl tch whn hmpd and uns rdr 4th.* ....(100 to 30 op 3 to 1 tchd 7 to 2) ur
Dist: 3l. 5m 52.20s. a 48.20s (4 Ran).
(Bernard Hathaway), P Cheesbrough

2014 World Promotions Novices' Hurdle (4-y-o and up) £3,257 2m 1f........(3:25)

1536⁴ ARFER MOLE (Ire) 6-11-5 T Grantham, *chsd ldrs, outpcd appr 2 out, hdwy und pres approaching last, styd on wl to ld cl hme.*..........(5 to 1 tchd 11 to 2) 1
1329² KINGS CHARIOT 7-11-0 (5*) J McCarthy, *hld up rear, hdwy aftr 5th, hrd rdn appr last, kpt on wl.* ....(16 to 1 op 12 to 1) 2
1442⁶ BARNA BOY (Ire) 6-11-5 R Dunwoody, *trkd ldrs, led betw last 2, edgd lft und pres, hdd cl hme.* ....(6 to 4 fav op 11 to 8 tchd 13 to 8) 3
1504⁷ PAPER DAYS 4-10-7 E Murphy, *prmnt till outpcd appr 2 out, kpt on wl und pres frm last.*..........(50 to 1) 4
1707³ GOSPEL (Ire) 5-11-0 C Llewellyn, *prmnt, pushed alng 2 out, one pace.*..........(11 to 1 op 10 to 1) 5
1478* MARCHWOOD 7-11-9 A Maguire, *prmnt, outpcd aftr 2 out.*..........(11 to 2 op 4 to 1) 6
1301⁵ DUNNICKS VIEW 5-11-5 C Maude, *hld up rear, hdwy 2 out, styd on appr last, nvr nrr.*..........(50 to 1) 7
THE BRUD 6-11-5 G Upton, *mid-div till outpcd aftr 3 out, tld off.*..........(8 to 1 op 7 to 1 tchd 10 to 1) 8
1078⁹ GEORGE LANE 6-11-5 J Frost, *al beh, tld off.* ....(50 to 1 op 33 to 1) 9
IVORLINE 7-11-5 V Slattery, *mid-div, mstk and drpd rear 3rd, tld off.*..........(50 to 1) 10
1729 SPANISH BLAZE (Ire) 6-10-12 (7*) Pat Thompson, *mstk 1st, mid-div till drpd rear 5th, tld off.*..........(33 to 1) 11
1813⁶ PETER POINTER 6-11-5 D Skyrme, *keen hold, mid-div to hfwy, tld off appr 3 out.*..........(50 to 1) 12
1646² WILKINS 5-11-5 M Dwyer, *led till betw last 2, btn whn f last.*..........(7 to 1 op 6 to 1) f
GOLDEN FELLOW (Ire) 6-11-5 L Wyer, *hld up, al beh, taile off whn pld up bef last.*..........(50 to 1) pu
Dist: Hd, 2l, 1½l, 4l, ¾l, ¾l, 20l, dist, dist, ¾l. 4m 31.30s. a 36.80s (14 Ran).
SR: 29/29/27/13/16/24/19/-/-/ (W E Sturt), J A B Old

EXETER (heavy)
Monday January 3rd
Going Correction: PLUS 1.67 sec. per fur.

2015 Deep Wealth Novices' Handicap Hurdle (0-100 5-y-o and up) £1,948 2¼m ....(1:05)

1794* DERRYMOSS [84] (v) 8-10-9 (7*) T Dascombe, *led sn aftr second, jmpd rght nxt 2, rdn appr last, all out.* ....(4 to 1 op 5 to 1 tchd 13 to 2) 1
1716⁵ CHERYLS PET (Ire) [72] 6-10-4 S Earle, *hld up in tch, hdwy 3 out, jnd wnr r-in, jst fld.* ....(17 to 2 op 10 to 1 tchd 7 to 1) 2
864² NAZZARO [85] 5-10-10 (7*) R Darke, *al prmnt, chsd wnr into strt, hit last, no extr r-in.*.....(16 to 1 op 10 to 1) 3
1516* JUMP START [89] 7-11-4 (3*) A Thornton, *mid-div, hdwy 5th, ev ch 2 out, sn btn.*..........(9 to 4 fav op 3 to 1) 4
1717² CHICKABIDDY [83] 6-11-1 G Upton, *hld up in rear, hdwy 3 out, nvr nr to chal.*..........(8 to 1 op 6 to 1) 5
1804 ELITE LEO [74] 9-10-6 Peter Hobbs, *nvr far away, ev ch 3 out, wknd nxt.*..........(7 to 1 op 12 to 1 tchd 14 to 1) 6
1768 COZZI (Fr) [68] 6-9-7 (7*) P McLoughlin, *prmnt till wknd 3 out.*..........(66 to 1 op 40 to 1) 7
1747³ WARFIELD [77] (bl) 7-10-9 G Bradley, *hld up, hdwy appr 3rd, rdn and wknd aftr 3 out.*..........(8 to 1 op 10 to 1) 8
1867 CHARLAFRIVOLA [70] 6-10-2 W Humphreys, *al beh.* ....(66 to 1 op 33 to 1) 9
1594⁸ FIRST COMMAND (NZ) [88] (bl) 7-11-6 B Powell, *prmnt till wknd quickly 3 out.* (14 to 1 op 10 to 1 tchd 16 to 1) 10
1624⁶ GIVEITAGO [90] (bl) 8-11-8 L Harvey, *mid-div, lost tch 4th.* ....(14 to 1 op 10 to 1) 11
1516⁷ MISS SOUTER [75] 5-10-0 (7*) Guy Lewis, *beh frm 3rd, tld off.*..........(50 to 1 op 33 to 1 tchd 66 to 1) 12
1800⁶ ROCKY PARK [92] 8-11-10 Craig Thornton, *led till jst aftr second, f 4th.*..........(16 to 1 op 10 to 1 tchd 20 to 1) f
1869* DAVES DELIGHT [81] 8-10-6 (7*,7ex) Mr G Shenkin, *mid-div whn brght dwn 4th.*..........(14 to 1 op 10 to 1) bd
1869⁸ RIVER STREAM [68] 7-10-0 Mr N Harris, *brght dwn 4th.* ....(66 to 1 op 50 to 1) bd
RUFFINSWICK [72] 8-10-4² J Railton, *al beh, tld off whn pld up 3 out.*..........(66 to 1 op 50 to 1) pu
Dist: Sht-hd, ¾l, 20l, 1½l, 10l, 2½l, 12l, 2½l, 1½l, 5l. 4m 36.40s. a 36.40s (16 Ran).
SR: 26/14/26/10/2/-/ (Mrs J K L Watts), M C Pipe

2016 Thurlestone Hotel Novices' Hurdle (4-y-o) £1,801 2¼m..........(1:35)

1634⁴ LOVE YOU MADLY (Ire) 10-7 J Lower, *rcd in mid-div, hdwy appr 2 out, drvn to go second last, flashed tail, led last strd.*..........(6 to 4 on op Evens tchd 5 to 4) 1
1464³ VELVET HEART (Ire) 10-9 (5*) D Matthews, *tried to make all, hit 4th, clr appr 2 out, tired bef last, rallied, ct on line.* ....(11 to 2 op 5 to 1) 2
1710⁵ SILVER STANDARD 10-12 B Powell, *chsd ldr till rdn and wknd appr last.*..........(11 to 2 op 4 to 1) 3
1705 MORAN BRIG 10-12 S Hodgson, *prmnt till lost pl 5th, rallied appr 2 out, kpt on one pace.* ....(14 to 1 op 10 to 1) 4
1767 GUNNER SUE 10-7 R Bellamy, *hld up in rear, hdwy frm 3rd, rdn and wknd appr 2 out.*.....(16 to 1 op 12 to 1) 5
WISHFUL PRINCESS 10-7 D Bridgwater, *last whn mstk 3rd, tried to cl frm 3 out, wknd nxt.* (66 to 1 op 33 to 1) 6
HONEY GUIDE 10-12 L Harvey, *prmnt till wknd 3 out.* ....(16 to 1 tchd 20 to 1) 7
BORROWED AND BLUE 10-7 Peter Hobbs, *beh, making hdwy whn mstk 3rd, wknd quickly 3 out, tld off.* ....(20 to 1 op 10 to 1) 8
1705⁶ SECRET FORMULA 10-12 E Leonard, *pld hrd in rear, tld off frm 5th.*..........(11 to 1 op 7 to 1 tchd 12 to 1) 9
Dist: Hd, 5l, 1½l, 20l, 5l, 2½l, 15l, 12l. 4m 39.30s. a 39.30s (9 Ran).
(Mrs Alison C Farrant), M C Pipe

2017 David Garrett Memorial Gold Challenge Trophy Novices' Chase (6-y-o and up) £6,986 2m 7f 110yds.... (2:05)

1866* KALANSKI 8-11-10 J Railton, *not fluent but nvr far away, wnt second 5 out, jmpd slwly nxt, led last, ran on.* ....(11 to 2 op 4 to 1) 1
1700² LUCKY LANE (bl) 10-11-7 Guy Lewis, *trkd ldr, led 7th, rdn and hdd last, one pace r-in.*..........(10 to 1 op 7 to 1) 2
1770³ RAMPOLDI (USA) (bl) 7-11-0 G Bradley, *beh, hdwy 6th, lost pl 8th, rallied appr 4 out, rdn and no imprsn frm 2 out.* ....(12 to 1 op 8 to 1) 3
1750³ VISAGA 8-11-7 D Bridgwater, *led to second, in tch till wknd quickly appr 4 out, tld off.*....(12 to 1 op 8 to 1) 4
1866² KIWI VELOCITY (NZ) 7-10-9 Peter Hobbs, *in tch whn f 7th.* ....(9 to 2 op 7 to 2 tchd 5 to 1) f
MELDON 7-11-0 D Salter, *in tch till wknd 9th, wl beh whn f 2 out.*..........(33 to 1 op 25 to 1) f
HOPS AND POPS 7-10-9 S Earle, *led second to 7th, in tch till wknd quickly 5 out, eased, pld up bef nxt.* ....(5 to 4 fav op 9 to 4) pu
1806⁶ MAXXUM EXPRESS (Ire) 6-11-0 Richard Guest, *beh, lost tch 7th, pld up bef nxt.* ....(25 to 1 op 16 to 1 tchd 33 to 1) pu
Dist: 2½l, 6l, dist. 6m 20.40s. a 45.40s (8 Ran).
SR: 34/28/15/-/-/ (I Kerman), C R Egerton

2018 Upton Pyne Novices' Selling Hurdle (4 & 5-y-o) £1,759 2¼m.......... (2:35)

1049³ OCTOBER BREW (USA) (bl) 4-10-8 J Lower, *hld up in tch, hdwy to ld 5th, came wide on turn into strt, clr 2 out, eased r-in.*......(21 to 20 on op 6 to 4 on tchd Evens) 1
1640² NANQUIDNO 4-10-3 Richard Guest, *led till appr second, led 4th to 5th, wknd approaching 2 out, fnshd tired.* ....(6 to 1 op 9 to 2 tchd 13 to 2) 2
1542 ALICE SPRINGS 5-11-1 Mr T Greed, *wl beh, some hdwy frm 2 out, nvr dngrs.* (16 to 1 op 25 to 1 tchd 33 to 1) 3
1695 KRAKATOA 5-11-1 R Greene, *second whn blun 1st, sn reco'red, rdn and wknd quickly 4th, tld off.* ....(10 to 1 op 12 to 1 tchd 16 to 1) 4
1878 ROCKY BAY 5-11-1 (7*) Mr J L Llewellyn, *led appr second, hdd 4th, wknd quickly, tld off.* ....(9 to 2 op 4 to 1 tchd 11 to 2) 5
1640³ WHATEVER'S RIGHT (Ire) 5-11-6 B Powell, *al beh, tld off whn pld up bef 2 out.*..........(13 to 2 op 9 to 2) pu
1640 NITA'S CHOICE 4-10-3³ (3*) A Thornton, *beh, jmpd badly in rear, tld off whn pld up bef 3 out.* ....(66 to 1 op 50 to 1 tchd 100 to 1) pu
Dist: 25l, 7l, 15l, dist. 4m 44.90s. a 44.90s (7 Ran).
(Martin Pipe Racing Club), M C Pipe

2019 Haldon Sunday Market Handicap Hurdle (0-135 4-y-o and up) £2,458 2¼m ....(3:05)

1868² MOHANA [123] 5-11-10 J Lower, *made all, reminders 4th, rdn whn chal 2 out, ran on gmely.* ....(5 to 4 fav op 2 to 1 tchd 5 to 2) 1

1694² BROUGHTON'S TANGO (Ire) [99] 5-10-0 S Keightley, *hld up,*
hdwy second, wnt second 3th, ev ch 2 out, tiring whn
mstk last..............(95 to 40 op 6 to 4 tchd 5 to 2) 2
KALOGY [121] 7-11-8 Richard Guest, *rcd wide, al prmnt,*
trkd wnr second to 5th, lost tch wth 1st 2 bef two out,
one pace.....................(9 to 2 op 4 to 1 tchd 5 to 1) 3
1697² AMPHIGORY [99] 6-9-12³ (5*) D Matthews, *in tch till wknd*
aftr 3 out.................................(16 to 1 op 12 to 1) 4
1842⁵ CORRIN HILL [117] 7-11-4 B Powell, *prmnt till wknd 3 out.*
.............................(15 to 2 op 7 to 1 tchd 8 to 1) 5
1721 BOOTSCRAPER [110] 7-10-4 (7*) N Downs, *beh frm sec-*
ond, tld off.......................(25 to 1 op 20 to 1) 6
MISS PURBECK [99] 7-9-8¹ (7*) Mr J Culloty, *struggling*
appr 3rd, sn tld off, pld up r-in.
...............................(11 to 1 op 10 to 1 tchd 12 to 1) pu
Dist: 12l, 10l, 2l, hd, dist. 4m 38.30s. a 38.30s (7 Ran).
SR: 14/-/-/-/   (Martin Pipe Racing Club), M C Pipe

2020 Thurlestone Hotel Claiming Chase (5-y-o and up) £2,818 2¼m....... (3:35)

1718² CRYSTAL BEAR (NZ) (bl) 9-11-8 B Powell, *sn rdn, mstk*
second, hdwy appr 3rd, made most frm nxt, drw clr 4
out.........................(11 to 4 op 5 to 2 tchd 3 to 1) 1
1954² CHIASSO FORTE (Ity) 11-11-2 L Harvey, *led second to 4th,*
jmpd badly rght four out, sn btn.
.................(13 to 8 fav op 5 to 4 tchd 7 to 4) 2
1644³ FROZEN DROP 7-11-4 Richard Guest, *led second to 4th, in*
tch till wknd appr four out.
..................(12 to 1 op 8 to 1 tchd 10 to 1) 3
1925 MATERIAL GIRL 8-11-0 (3*) A Procter, *prmnt, led briefly 5*
out, btn whn hmpd and blun nxt, fnshd tired.
...............................(9 to 2 op 5 to 2) 4
1748⁶ CHANCERY BUCK 11-10-5 (7*) R Darke, *beh frm 4th, sn tld*
off..........................(16 to 1 op 10 to 1) 5
1302⁷ SOCKS DOWNE 15-10-12 G Bradley, *led to second, beh*
4th, tld off whn pld up 5 out.
.......................(14 to 1 op 16 to 1 tchd 20 to 1) pu
1275 HIGH IMP 14-10-8 S Earle, *sn struggling in rear, tld off*
whn pld up bef 5th...............(50 to 1 op 20 to 1) pu
1748⁴ CEDAR RUN 11-10-3 (7*) D Meade, *al beh, tld off whn pld*
up bef 5th.......................(16 to 1 op 10 to 1) pu
Dist: 15l, 30l, 10l, dist. 4m 47.70s. a 36.70s (8 Ran).
SR: 28/7/-/-/-/   (Lady Knutsford), Capt T A Forster

2021 Exeter National Hunt Flat Race (4,5,6-y-o) £1,896 2¼m.............. (4:05)

KARICLEIGH BOY 6-10-12 (7*) Mr J Culloty, *in tch till rdn*
and lost touch 6 fs out, rallied 3 out, swtchd rght and
ran on to ld ins last...................(16 to 1 op 10 to 1) 1
TAP SHOES (Ire) 4-10-4 (3*) A Thornton, *hdwy hfwy, led w*
o'r one furlong out, rdn and hdd ins last.
....(14 to 1 op 10 to 1) 2
1806 BOURNEL 6-10-7 (7*) Mr Richard White, *in rear, hdwy o'r 3*
fs out, styd on, nvr nrr.............(33 to 1 op 25 to 1) 3
1806⁵ ORSWELL LAD 5-10-12 (7*) C Quinlan, *al prmnt, led o'r 4 fs*
out, hrd rdn and hdd over 2 out, one pace.
..............................(8 to 1 op 4 to 1) 4
778* HENRYS NO PUSHOVER 5-11-7 (5*) D Salter, *hld up, hdwy*
hfwy, led on bit o'r 2 fs out, sn rdn, hdd wl over one
furlong out, wknd.
....(11 to 4 fav op 3 to 1 tchd 100 to 30 and 5 to 2) 5
TANGO'S DELIGHT 6-10-12 (7*) N Willmington, *beh till*
hdwy hfwy, wknd o'r 2 fs out.
...............................(7 to 2 op 5 to 2 tchd 4 to 1) 6
1626⁶ SHIMBA HILLS 6-11-5 Mrs J Retter, *rcd in tch, no hdwy*
fnl 3 fs................................(7 to 2 op 4 to 1) 7
IVE CALLED TIME 6-10-12 (7*) Guy Lewis, *in tch, led 6 fs*
out, hdd o'r 4 out, no further hdwy.
....................................(25 to 1 op 20 to 1) 8
1133⁶ BIBBY BEAR 5-10-7 (7*) Mr G Shenkin, *prmnt early, lost*
tch hfwy, tld off.....................(20 to 1 op 12 to 1) 9
DUNLIR 4-10-0 (7*) Miss S Cobden, *mid-div, hdwy o'r one*
m out, dsptd ld 6 fs out, sn wknd, tld off.
.............................(33 to 1 op 20 to 1) 10
FRIENDLY VIKING 4-10-7 Miss S Young, *in frnt rnk till*
wknd 6 fs out, tld off.............(50 to 1 op 25 to 1) 11
BESSIE BOSSY BOOTS 4-10-2 R Greene, *swshd tld frm*
strt, al struggling in rear, tailed off.
................................(5 to 1 op 14 to 1) 12
SOLDIER-B 4-10-0 (7*) M Isaac, *led till hdd 6 fs out, wknd*
stdly, tld off.........................(33 to 1 op 20 to 1) 13
INDERRING ROSE 4-10-0 (7*) D Meade, *prmnt to hfwy, tld*
off......................................(20 to 1 op 12 to 1) 14
HENGIST 6-11-0 (5*) D Matthews, *sn beh, tld off fnl 6 fs.*
....(10 to 1 op 8 to 1) 15
Dist: 1½l, 8l, 1l, nk, 12l, 1½l, 20l. 4m 38.30s. (15 Ran).
(E C Eveleigh), Mrs J G Retter

FAIRYHOUSE (IRE) (heavy)
Monday January 3rd

2022 WinElectric Chase (5-y-o and up) £8,200 2¼m................. (12:45)

1763⁷ TALK TO YOU LATER 8-11-2 H Rogers,..........(6 to 4) 1
1823⁴ HORNER WATER (Ire) 6-10-11 K F O'Brien, *f and rmntd to*
finish second................................(7 to 4 on) 2
Won by Dist. 5m 22.60s. (2 Ran).
SR: -/-/   (Michael Bailey), Thomas O'Neill

2023 First Crack Hurdle (5-y-o and up) £3,105 2m.................... (1:15)

1977* IDIOTS VENTURE 7-12-0 B Sheridan,.........(6 to 4 on) 1
1449³ HACKETTS CROSS (Ire) 6-11-4 A Powell,.......(10 to 1) 2
1904* LEGAL PROFESSION (Ire) 6-11-8 C F Swan,.......(6 to 4) 3
1016⁴ JATINGA (Ire) 6-11-4 K F O'Brien,...........(25 to 1) 4
Dist: 9l, 9l, 2½l. 4m 21.60s. (4 Ran).
(Blackwater Racing Syndicate), A P O'Brien

2024 New Year Maiden Hurdle (4-y-o and up) £3,105 2m...................(1:45)

BE MY HOPE (Ire) 5-11-5 P Carberry,..............(5 to 2) 1
1833⁵ SIR MOSS 7-11-6 J F Titley,....................(10 to 1) 2
1551⁷ LAWYER'S BRIEF (Fr) 7-11-6 L P Cusack,.......(7 to 1) 3
1904⁴ FINNEGANS WAKE 7-11-6 C F Swan,.............(7 to 1) 4
1681³ NICE PROSPECT (Ire) 6-11-6 T J Taaffe,......(9 to 4 fav) 5
BARNAGEERA BOY (Ire) 5-11-2 P L Malone,.....(14 to 1) 6
FREE THYNE (Ire) 5-10-11 (5*) M G Cleary,.....(20 to 1) 7
1549 DICK'S CABIN 7-11-1 (5*) H Taylor,............(20 to 1) 8
1814 DRUMREAGH LAD (Ire) 6-11-6 H Rogers,.......(20 to 1) 9
1848 INAUGURATION (Ire) 5-11-2 A Powell,.........(20 to 1) 10
BERESFORD LADY (Ire) 4-10-4 F Woods,........(10 to 1) 11
1762 KEY WEST (Ire) 5-11-2² P Mooney,.............(20 to 1) 12
1821 VALTORUS (Ire) 5-11-2 K F O'Brien,...........(16 to 1) 13
CONQUEST OF LIGHT (Ire) 5-11-2 R Hughes,.....(20 to 1) 14
1912³ MALMSEY (USA) 6-11-11 (3*) C O'Brien,........(14 to 1) 15
BOBS LADY (Ire) 5-10-8 (3*) D Bromley,........(25 to 1) 16
EARLY RISER (Ire) 6-11-1 S R Murphy,.........(25 to 1) 17
1762 FAIRY STRIKE (Ire) 5-11-2 J Shortt,............(25 to 1) su
Dist: 1l, 2l, 6l, 6l. 4m 19.90s. (18 Ran).
(Mrs John Magnier), Noel Meade

2025 Father Time Handicap Chase (0-109 5-y-o and up) £3,105 3m 1f..... (2:15)

1402 WYLDE HIDE [-] 7-9-10 F Woods,............(100 to 30) 1
1826² MERLYNS CHOICE [-] (bl) 10-9-11 C F Swan,..(5 to 2 fav) 2
1819 WALLS COURT [-] 7-10-10 P L Malone,..........(7 to 1) 3
1179 THE PHOENO [-] 8-9-4 (3*) C O'Brien,..........(20 to 1) 4
1819³ ARDUBH [-] (bl) 7-10-4 B Sheridan,.............(6 to 1) 5
1402* MARKET SURVEY [-] (bl) 13-9-13 T Horgan,.....(13 to 2) f
1831 MUST DO [-] 8-10-12 J Shortt,...................(8 to 1) f
1850 KINDLY KING [-] 10-12-0 L P Cusack,...........(8 to 1) pu
364 LIGHT THE WICK [-] 8-10-13 (5*) M G Cleary,...(14 to 1) pu
1819 ALL A QUIVER [-] 7-10-11 K F O'Brien,..........(14 to 1) pu
Dist: 6l, 7l, 15l, 10l. 7m 15.60s. (10 Ran).
(Mrs A L T Moore), A L T Moore

2026 Fairyhouse Handicap Hurdle (5-y-o and up) £6,900 2¼m............(2:45)

1818³ PEBBLE LANE [-] 8-10-9 H Rogers,...........(5 to 2 fav) 1
1818⁵ SOCIETY BAY (USA) [-] 8-10-12 (7*) R A Hennessy, (8 to 1) 2
1431⁶ FINAL FAVOUR (Ire) [-] 5-11-7 (5*) H Taylor,.....(3 to 1) 3
1610³ HEMISPHERE (Ire) [-] 5-9-8 R Hughes,..........(7 to 1) 4
1818 MR BOAL (Ire) [-] 7-11-3 (6ex) C F Swan,.......(7 to 2) 5
880 MR FIVE WOOD (Ire) [-] 6-9-12 S R Murphy,....(10 to 1) 6
1682⁵ RANDOM PRINCE [-] 10-12-0 P Carberry,........(12 to 1) 7
1453 REGALING (Ire) [-] 6-9-11 (5*) T P Rudd,..........(9 to 2) pu
Dist: 7l, ¾l, 4½l, 7l. 4m 48.30s. (8 Ran).
(B O'Hare), Bernard Jones

2027 Ballymacoll Maiden Hurdle (5-y-o and up) £3,105 2¾m................(3:15)

1902* FRIGID COUNTESS 7-11-2 (7*) L A Hurley,......(11 to 1) 1
1892⁴ CALMOS 7-11-6 C F Swan,.......................(6 to 1) 2
1849⁴ RISZARD (USA) 5-11-10 K F O'Brien,......(5 to 4 on) 3
1814⁵ RIVERLAND (Ire) 6-11-1 (5*) M G Cleary,.......(10 to 1) 4
1829² RED THUNDER 7-11-1 D P Fagan,..............(10 to 1) 5
1608 JOES NIGHTMARE 7-10-8 (7*) D M Drewett,.....(20 to 1) 6
1898* BEAT THE SECOND (Ire) 6-11-8 J F Titley,......(20 to 1) 7
1764 NATINA (Ire) 5-10-11 P Mooney,................(25 to 1) 8
1760⁶ BARRAFON (Ire) 6-11-6 P Carberry,.............(8 to 1) 9
1555⁹ CAILIN RUA (Ire) 6-11-1 A Powell,..............(14 to 1) 10
1265⁴ AERODROME FIELD (Ire) 6-11-6 B Sheridan,....(14 to 1) 11
1760 CAILIN GEAL (Ire) 6-11-1 J P Banahan,.........(33 to 1) 12
1683 BEAU CINQ (Ire) 5-10-9 (7*) Mr D W Cullen,....(33 to 1) 13
1898 SOUTH WESTERLY (Ire) 6-11-6 M Duffy,.......(14 to 1) su
DIAMOND BUCK (Ire) 6-11-6 H Rogers,........(25 to 1) su
Dist: 4½l, 20l, ½l, 8l. 5m 59.70s. (15 Ran).
(W Dooly), W Dooly

2028 Corinthian I N H Flat Race (5-y-o and up) £3,105 2m.................(3:45)

1555³ TAXSON (Ire) 6-11-4 (7*) Mr D A Harney,........(2 to 1) 1
1766² THE BLUEBELL POLKA (Ire) 5-11-1 (5*) Mr H F Cleary,
....(10 to 9 on) 2

PUNTER'S SYMPHONY (Ire) 6-11-11 (7") Miss H McCourt,
....(9 to 2)   3

(H V Perry), R H Alner

1814 JIMMY GORDON 7-11-11 (7") Mr M Brennan, ...(12 to 1)   4
PATS FAREWELL (Ire) 6-11-11 Mr P F Graffin, ...(16 to 1)   5
REMO GROVE (Ire) 6-11-4 (7") Mr L J Gracey, ...(25 to 1)   6
Dist: 2l, 6l, 3l, 3l. 4m 18.70s. (6 Ran).

(O R Cantwell), Noel Meade

LEICESTER (heavy (races 1,5,6), soft (2,3,4))
Monday January 3rd
Going Correction: PLUS 2.25 sec. per fur. (races 1,5,6), PLUS 2.20 (2,3,4)

2029 Humberstone Novices' Hurdle (4-y-o and up) £1,618 2m.............(1:00)

1251⁶ MR PICKPOCKET (Ire) 6-11-5 R Supple, led til aftr second, lost bl appr 4 out, styd on nxt, rdn to ld last 100 yards.
....(9 to 2 tchd 11 to 2)   1
1196³ SPREAD YOUR WINGS (Ire) 6-11-0 W McFarland, wl ldrs, led appr 2 out, hit last, hdd fnl 100 yards, rallied cl hme...............(11 to 8 fav to 11 to 8 on)   2
FORMAL AFFAIR 4-10-2 W Marston, prog 5th, ev ch whn mstk 2 out, wknd btn appr last....(4 to 1 op 9 to 4)   3
1773⁸ TEST MATCH 7-11-5 Diane Clay, led aftr second, hdd appr 2 out, eased whn btn approaching last.
....(6 to 1 op 9 to 2)   4
1646³ COURAGEOUS KNIGHT 5-11-2 (3") R Farrant, sn towards rear, jmpd slwly 3rd, hdwy aftr nxt, wknd appr 4 out, tld off.........................(8 to 1 op 5 to 1)   5
1027 CUMREWS NEPHEW 6-11-0 (5") P Midgley, sn wl beh, tld off frm 8th..............................(33 to 1)   6
NORTH HOLLOW 9-11-0 (5") Mr D McCain, al wl beh, tld off whn pld up bef 4 out....................(50 to 1)   pu
Dist: Sht-hd, 7l, 7l, dist, 12l. 4m 25.60s. a 42.60s (7 Ran).
SR: 25/20/1/11/

(John Holmes), J Akehurst

2030 New Year Novices' Handicap Chase (5-y-o and up) £2,115 2m 1f..... (1:30)

1673³ RAMSTAR [86] 6-11-10 W Marston, trkd ldrs, led aftr 2 out, shaken up to draw clr run in....(5 to 1 op 7 to 2)   1
1490 LOCAL MANOR [75] 7-10-13 Mr J Durkan, led 3rd, hdd aftr 2 out, one pace frm last............(8 to 1 op 5 to 1)   2
1744³ HIGHLAND POACHER [76] 7-10-9 (5") D Walsh, hld up, hdwy and blun badly 6th, effrt 3 out, wknd frm nxt.
....(14 to 1 op 10 to 1)   3
1795* MAGGOTS GREEN [83] 7-11-4 (3") R Farrant, in tch, hmpd 6th, effrt 4 out, wknd aftr nxt.
....(13 to 8 fav tchd 7 to 4 and 2 to 1)   4
1502⁶ FIRST LESSON (NZ) [78] 8-11-2 M Hourigan, led to 3rd, wth ldrs whn f 6th.........................(5 to 1 op 3 to 1)   f
1598⁴ COUNTRY MISTRESS [66] 7-10-4 R Supple, beh whn f 4th.
....(16 to 1 op 14 to 1)   f
1621⁶ MR OPTIMISTIC [77] 7-11-1 D Byrne, in tch till uns rdr 4th...........................(9 to 2 op 7 to 2)   ur
Dist: 5l, dist, 20l. 4m 55.50s. a 46.50s (7 Ran).
SR: 5/-/-/-/

(U K Home Computers), D Nicholson

2031 Ford Novices' Chase (5-y-o and up) £2,134 2½m 110yds........... (2:00)

1604² VAYRUA (Fr) 9-11-5 M Hourigan, hld up in tch, sstnd run frm 4 out, led aftr 2 out, rdn out....(4 to 1 op 5 to 1)   1
1605 CHICHELL'S HURST 8-11-0 R Marley, hld up, mstk 4th, prog 8th, led appr 3 out, hdd aftr nxt, ran on same pace..............................(13 to 8 fav op 11 to 10)   2
1644⁴ RINANNA BAY 7-10-7 (7") P Carey, chsd ldrs till lost pl tenth, kpt on ag'n frm 3 out......(12 to 1 op 10 to 1)   3
1776⁷ CHALIE RICHARDS 7-11-0 (5") Mr D McCain, ldg grp, mstk 4 out, wknd nxt............(10 to 1 tchd 12 to 1)   4
BUCKS SURPRISE 6-11-5 W Marston, in tch, rdn and wknd appr 3 out..................(11 to 1 op 10 to 1)   5
1621² TEKLA (Fr) 9-11-5 A Tory, mstk 4th, wl in tch til wknd 11th, pld up bef 2 out..............(7 to 2 tchd 4 to 1)   pu
1770 RIDAKA 7-11-0 (5") T Eley, led till hdd appr 3 out, sn wknd, pld up bef 2 out..................(8 to 1 op 5 to 1)   pu
Dist: 2l, dist, 8l, 25l. 5m 54.30s. a 51.30s (7 Ran).
SR: 29/22/-/-/

(J A Hellens), J A Hellens

2032 Wigston Handicap Chase (0-100 5-y-o and up) £2,175 2m 1f.......... (2:30)

1514² DARE SAY [98] 11-12-0 W McFarland, cl up, jmpd slwly 3rd, led 7th, drw wl clr frm 3 out, eased r-in.
....(2 to 1 op 7 to 4)   1
1470⁵ OLD ROAD (USA) [86] 8-11-2 W Marston, pressed ldrs til drpd rear 8th, styd on ag'n into second pl frm 2 out.
....(11 to 4 op 2 to 1 tchd 3 to 1)   2
1933⁵ SANDMOOR PRINCE [83] 11-10-13 Dr P Pritchard, led til hdd 7th, wknd frm 3 out.........(6 to 1 op 5 to 1)   3
1771³ BOSSBURG [85] (bl) 7-11-0 (5") Mr D McCain, wl in tch, ev ch 4 out, wknd nxt..........(15 to 8 fav op 7 to 4)   4
Dist: 20l, 8l, 10l. 5m 1.40s. a 52.40s (4 Ran).

2033 Parsley Novices' Claiming Hurdle (5-y-o and up) £1,520 2½m 110yds (3:00)

1837⁶ LITTLE THYNE 9-10-12 Dr P Pritchard, chsd ldr, rdn alng 6th, led 4 out, clr 2 out, styd on, easily.
....(4 to 1 op 3 to 1)   1
1645⁷ BORRETO 10-10-4³ (7") Mr E James, hld up, hdwy 7th, ran on frm 3 out, no imprsn on wnr appr last.
....(7 to 2 op 5 to 2)   2
1749⁶ TRENTSIDE MIST 6-10-12 M Ranger, in tch, rdn to chase wnr 4 out, one pace frm 2 out........(10 to 1 op 6 to 1)   3
1589 CASHTAL RUNNER 5-11-2 Pat Caldwell, clr ldr to 6th, hdd and mstk 4 out, pld up bef 2 out.
....(16 to 1 op 12 to 1 tchd 20 to 1)   pu
1731³ NORDIC BEAT (Ire) (bl) 5-11-2 Diane Clay, in tch in mid-div, mstk and wknd 7th, pld up bef 4 out........(11 to 4 jt-fav op 2 to 1)   pu
1626⁷ COUNTRYWIDE LAD 5-11-6 M Hourigan, effrt frm rear 6th, lost tch nxt, pld up bef 3 out. ....(11 to 4 jt-fav op 5 to 2 tchd 4 to 1 and 9 to 2)   pu
Dist: 12l, 5l. 5m 54.00s. a 66.00s (6 Ran).

(Mrs T Pritchard), Dr P Pritchard

2034 Glebe Handicap Hurdle (0-115 5-y-o and up) £2,127 3m.............(3:30)

1918⁰ DIG DEEPER [100] 7-11-5 W Marston, made all, rdn clr 2 out, styd on strly....................(7 to 1 op 6 to 1)   1
1653⁶ FLYER'S NAP [104] 8-11-9 W McFarland, wl plcd, chsd wnr frm 9th, hit 3 out, one pace from nxt.......(11 to 4 jt-fav op 3 to 1 tchd 7 to 2 and 4 to 1)   2
1711⁹ RELTIC [81] 7-9-7 (7") A Flannigan, wl plcd, lost pos 8th, rdn and ran on ag'n 3 out, wnt pres whn blun last.
....(14 to 1 op 8 to 1)   3
1711* HAPPY HORSE (NZ) [102] 7-11-7 A Tory, wl in tch, rdn and one pace appr 4 out, wknd nxt.........(11 to 4 jt-fav tchd 7 to 2)   4
1775 LAUGHING GAS (Ire) [82] 5-10-1 R Supple, al beh, lost tch frm 7th, tld off.........(14 to 1 op 12 to 1)   5
FOUR STAR LINE [89] 9-11-5 (3") R Farrant, f at 3rd.
....(16 to 1 op 14 to 1)   f
1651⁴ GABRIELLA MIA [98] 9-11-3 D Byrne, drpd rear and lost tch 7th, pld up bef 4 out.....(8 to 1 op 6 to 1)   pu
RIMOUSKI [99] 6-11-4 Mr J Cambidge, al beh, lost tch 7th, pld up bef 4 out......(13 to 2 op 6 to 1 tchd 7 to 1)   pu
1488⁶ THE HIDDEN CITY [84] 8-10-3 M Hourigan, chsd wnr till aftr 7th, pld up bef 4 out... (16 to 1 op 12 to 1)   pu
1172⁵ ROVULENKA [108] 6-11-13 M Foster, wth ldrs, chsd wnr aftr 7th till wknd 9th, pld up bef 4 out.
....(8 to 1 op 5 to 1)   pu
Dist: 10l, 5l, 20l, dist. 6m 49.60s. a 62.60s (10 Ran).
SR: 5/-/-/-/-/-/

(Ian G M Dalgleish), J J O'Neill

TRAMORE (IRE) (heavy)
Monday January 3rd

2035 Dunmore East Mares Novice Chase (5-y-o and up) £2,243 2m...... (12:50)

1914⁵ FAIR LISSELAN (Ire) 6-11-9 G M O'Neill, ...(5 to 2)   1
1501 RATHNURE LADY (Ire) 6-11-4 (5") P A Roche, ...(12 to 1)   2
1857⁸ STRONG CHERRY 8-11-2 (7") Mr K Taylor, ...(10 to 1)   3
1330 DELIGHTFUL CHOICE (Ire) 6-11-2 (7") J P Broderick,
....(20 to 1)   4
534 RAINBOW ALLIANCE (Ire) 6-11-4 (5") C P Dunne, (20 to 1)   5
1857⁷ YVONNES PRINCESS (bl) 7-11-6 (3") Mr T Lombard, (8 to 1)   6
1610 FAYS FOLLY (Ire) 5-11-0 J Magee, ...(14 to 1)   7
1608 FANCY DISH 8-11-6 (3") D P Murphy, ...(12 to 1)   8
1857⁵ PEJAWI 7-11-6 (3") T J Mitchell, ...(8 to 1)   9
1818 SIMPLY SWIFT (bl) 7-11-9 C O'Dwyer, ...(6 to 1 fav)   f
Dist: 4½l, 1½l, 1l, 2½l. 4m 30.80s. (10 Ran).

(Lisselan Farms Ltd), Fergus Sutherland

2036 Fenor Opportunity Handicap Chase (0-102 5-y-o and up) £2,657 2½m (1:20)

1826⁴ PINEWOOD LAD [-] 7-11-1 (2") C P Dunne, ...(11 to 2)   1
1826 BOG LEAF VI [-] 11-9-5 (2") T J O'Sullivan, ...(7 to 1)   2
1915* BALLYHEIGUE [-] 8-11-0 D P Murphy, ...(3 to 1 fav)   3
1830⁶ KITES HARDWICKE [-] 7-10-6 (4") J P Broderick, ..(10 to 1)   4
1402² KINGS HILL [-] 12-10-6 (4") J Butler, ...(9 to 1)   5
1830⁵ NANCYS LAD [-] 7-10-3 (2") J R Barry, ...(16 to 1)   6
1826⁸ CHILIPOUR [-] 7-11-7 (2") P A Roche, ...(7 to 1)   7
1857⁹ HIGHBABS [-] 8-10-12 (2") J Mitchell, ...(7 to 1)   8
ITS A SNIP [-] 9-9-10 (2") M A Davey, ...(8 to 1)   9
1826 SQUIRRELSDAUGHTER (-) (bl) 9-10-5 T P Treacy, (25 to 1)   10
1914² BLACKPOOL BRIDGE [-] 9-10-3 (2") D T Evans, ...(7 to 1)   f
Dist: 3l, 1l, 4l, 5l. 5m 25.10s. (11 Ran).

(Pinewood Laboratories Ltd), C Kinane

2037 Waterford Crystal Chase (5-y-o and up) £3,618 2¾m.............(1:50)

1901² CALLMECHA (bl) 9-11-9 G M O'Neill, ...(4 to 1 jt-fav)   1

1857[2] ANOTHER GROUSE 7-10-2 (7*) J P Broderick, ...(7 to 1) 2
1554 GLAMOROUS GALE 10-11-0 J Magee, ...(4 to 1 jt-fav) 3
1851 WRECKLESS MAN 7-11-10 (5*) P A Roche, ...(11 to 2) 4
1901* SPEAKING TOUR (USA) 6-11-12 D H O'Connor, ... (5 to 1) ur
1784 RUST NEVER SLEEPS 10-11-10 (5*) Mr G J Harford, (5 to 1) pu
1901[3] GERTIES PRIDE (bl) 10-10-9 (5*) T J O'Sullivan, ...(9 to 1) pu
1499 IFFEEE 7-11-9 C O'Dwyer, ...(8 to 1) pu
Dist: 4l, 15l, 2l. 6m 3.20s. (8 Ran).
(T P O'Sullivan), Augustine Leahy

2038 Benvoy Ladies Q.R. Maiden Hurdle (6-y-o and up) £2,243 2½m. .... (2:20)

SLANEY LAMB (Ire) 6-11-0 (7*) Miss L E A Doyle, ...(7 to 2) 1
1496[4] BLAZING COMET 8-10-1 (7*) Miss L Townsley, ...(7 to 1) 2
1783[3] PUNTERS BAR 7-11-4 (3*) Miss C Hutchinson, (5 to 4 fav) 3
1608[6] MULLAGHMEEN 8-10-1 (7*) Miss A Sloane, ...(8 to 1) 4
1608 SHIMMERETTO 8-10-1 (7*) Miss W Fox, ... (33 to 1) 5
158 LADY BUDD (Ire) 6-10-1 (7*) Miss M Horgan, ...(8 to 1) 6
1498 DOZING STAR 8-11-0 (7*) Miss M Flynn, ... (8 to 1) 7
LADY CHLORIS 8-10-1 (7*) Mrs K Walsh, ... (10 to 1) 8
1859[4] MOONSHEE (Ire) 6-10-5 (3*) Miss M Olivefalk, ... (10 to 1) 9
1823 ABBEY EMERALD 8-10-3[2] (7*) Miss A Dawson, ... (33 to 1) ur
1902[7] COOL CARLING 7-10-1 (7*) Miss C Rogers, ... (14 to 1) ur
Dist: ½l, 6l, 1l, 20l. 5m 20.10s. (11 Ran).
(Slaney Cooked Meats), P J P Doyle

2039 Kilfarassy Maiden Hurdle (5-y-o) £2,243 2m. .... (2:50)

1155[4] JO JO BOY (Ire) 11-6 F J Flood, ...(4 to 1) 1
1822[2] STEEL GEM (Ire) 10-13 (7*) K D Maher, ... (3 to 1 fav) 2
1495 TURALITY (Ire) 11-6 S H O'Donovan, ... (7 to 1) 3
1608[7] VON CARTY (Ire) 11-2 (7*) Mr J T McNamara, ...(4 to 1) 4
1821[7] TARA'S SERENADE (Ire) 11-1 A J O'Brien, ...(13 to 2) 5
1822[6] KYLE HOUSE VI (Ire) 10-8 (7*) J M Donnelly, ...(14 to 1) 6
1681 AMME ENAEK (Ire) 10-12 (3*) K B Walsh, ...(14 to 1) 7
1610 PROPHET'S THUMB (Ire) 11-6 W T Slattery Jnr, ...(20 to 1) 8
1495 MARYVILLE LADY (Ire) 11-1 G M O'Neill, ...(14 to 1) 9
1821 GENIE MACK (Ire) (bl) 10-13 (7*) Mr J Lombard, ...(20 to 1) 10
1821[4] PRINCE TAUFAN (Ire) 11-6 J Magee, ...(9 to 2) 11
1822 THE DEFENDER (Ire) (bl) 11-6 J Collins, ...(25 to 1) 12
LANCASTER COURT (Ire) 10-12 (3*) D P Murphy, (20 to 1) 13
Dist: 20l, nk, 20l, 5½l. 4m 21.20s. (13 Ran).
(Raymond McConn), F Flood

2040 Tramore Q.R. Handicap Hurdle (0-116 4-y-o and up) £2,243 2m. .... (3:20)

1176[5] ANOTHER COURSE (Ire) [-] 6-10-4 (7*) Mr P M Cloke,
....(5 to 1) 1
1823* SHREWD MOVE [-] (bl) 5-9-13 (7*,4ex) Mrs K Walsh, (7 to 2) 2
1855[6] PREMIER LEAP (Ire) [-] 5-11-1 Mr P Fenton, ... (5 to 1) 3
1828[8] PEPPERONI EXPRESS (Ire) [-] 5-10-11 (7*) Mr G A Kingston,
....(12 to 1) 4
1823 SHANNON KNOCK [-] 9-10-13 (3*) Mr A E Lacy, ... (5 to 1) 5
1495 ASHBORO (Ire) [-] 5-10-2 (7*) Mrs F A O'Sullivan, ..(12 to 1) 6
1816[5] TEMPLEMARY BOY (Ire) [-] 4-11-6 (7*) Mr M H Naughton,
.... (5 to 2 fav) 7
Dist: 12l, 7l, ¾l, 5½l. 4m 22.80s. (7 Ran).
(Patrick Heffernan), Patrick Heffernan

2041 Irish National Bookmakers I N H Flat Race (5-y-o and up) £2,933 2m.. (3:50)

FIONANS FLUTTER (Ire) 6-11-7 (7*) Mr M Hartrey, .. (7 to 1) 1
1827[7] FIFI'S MAN 8-12-0 Mr P Fenton, ... (7 to 2) 2
1496 CARRIG DANCER (Ire) 6-11-2 (7*) Mr K Whelan, .. (20 to 1) 3
1501[7] RAHEEN FLOWER (Ire) 6-11-9 Mr D M O'Brien, ... (12 to 1) 4
1403 ANOTHER ROLLO (Ire) 6-11-7 (7*) Mr N Stokes, .. (20 to 1) 5
1858[8] CASH IT IN (Ire) 6-11-9 Mr J A Berry, ...(8 to 1) 6
SLANEY AGAIN (Ire) 6-11-7 (7*) Miss L E A Doyle, .. (8 to 1) 7
1910 NOPADDLE 10-11-11 (3*) Mrs J M Mullins, ...(5 to 2 fav) 8
1500[5] NOBLE MINISTER 7-11-9 (5*) Mr J P O'Brien, ...(7 to 1) 9
1858[6] CASTLE CLUB (Ire) 5-11-2 (3*) Mr R O'Neill, ... (8 to 1) 10
1401 GREAT ADVENTURE (Ire) 6-11-11 (3*) Mr D Marnane,
....(5 to 1) 11
1827 SALTY SNACKS (Ire) 5-11-5 (5*) Mr G J Harford, .. (12 to 1) 12
PALLASTOWN BREEZE 7-11-9 Mr W P Mullins, ...(7 to 1) 13
KAVS DREAM (Ire) 6-11-2 (7*) Mr E Norris, ...(25 to 1) pu
1766[9] DALUA RIVER (Ire) 6-11-6 (3*) Mrs M Mullins, ... (8 to 1) pu
Dist: 12l, 4l, 5½l, sht-hd. 42m 17.00s. (15 Ran).
(S Crowley), Donal Hassett

WINDSOR (soft)
Monday January 3rd
Going Correction: PLUS 1.35 sec. per fur. (races 1,3,-5,7), PLUS 0.95 (2,4,6)

2042 Gran Alba 'National Hunt' Novices' Hurdle (Div I) (4-y-o and up) £1,961 2m ....(12:40)

901* MISTER NOVA 5-11-5 M A FitzGerald, *hld up, prog 5th, led aftr 3 out, clr whn mstk nxt, easily.*
.... (11 to 8 fav op Evens tchd 6 to 4) 1
1536[6] HAWAIIAN YOUTH (Ire) 6-11-12 H Davies, *prmnt, ev ch 3 out, sn rdn and kpt on one pace.*
........................(4 to 1 op 7 to 2 tchd 9 to 2) 2
1309[7] JYMJAM JOHNNY (Ire) 5-11-5 D Gallagher, *pld hrd, prmnt, outpcd 3 out, kpt on und pres frm last.*
.... (50 to 1 op 33 to 1) 3
1797[2] TOO SHARP 6-11-0 J Osborne, *prmnt, led aftr 5th till after 3 out, wknd last...* (7 to 2 op 4 to 1 tchd 9 to 2) 4
1695[9] MEDINAS SWAN SONG 6-11-5 S McNeill, *led till tried to run out bend aftr second, rapid prog to ld ag'n nxt, hdd after 5th, wknd 2 out.*
.................(50 to 1 op 33 to 1 tchd 66 to 1) 5
1536 CREDON 6-11-5 M Richards, *hld up, prog 5th, no imprsn on ldrs frm nxt*..................(16 to 1 op 6 to 1) 6
1110 FILE VESTRY (Ire) 6-11-5 I Lawrence, *hld up, prog to chase ldrs 5th, btn frm 3 out*............(50 to 1 op 20 to 1) 7
TITAN EMPRESS 5-11-0 M Perrett, *hld up, effrt 5th, nvr on terms*...........................(50 to 1 op 20 to 1) 8
BONE SETTER (Ire) 4-10-0 (7*) Chris Webb, *mstk 1st, al beh*.................................(50 to 1 op 33 to 1) 9
1040[7] BISHOPS TRUTH 8-10-12 (7*) G Crone, *hld up, al beh.*
................................(50 to 1 op 25 to 1) 10
1252[4] KICKING BIRD 7-11-0 N Williamson, *lft in ld bend aftr second, hdd nxt, wknd 5th, beh whn pld up bef 2 out.*
......................(14 to 1 op 8 to 1 tchd 16 to 1) pu
1688[5] HALL END LADY (Ire) 6-11-0 B Clifford, *al beh, tld off and pld up bef 5th*.....................(50 to 1 op 20 to 1) pu
AXEL 7-11-5 D Murphy, *chsd ldrs till mstk and wknd 4th, tld off whn pld up bef 2 out*....... (33 to 1 op 14 to 1) pu
1494 QUEEN'S AWARD (Ire) 5-11-5 S Smith Eccles, *prmnt till mstk 3rd, sn beh, tld off and pld up bef 2 out.*
....................(66 to 1 op 33 to 1 tchd 100 to 1) pu
Dist: 7l, 3l, 2l, 6l, 3l, 1½l, 12l, 2l, 12l. 4m 15.90s. a 30.90s (14 Ran).
(Lord Matthews), N J Henderson

2043 Scottish Reel Novices' Handicap Chase (5-y-o and up) £2,918 2m (1:10)

1632[3] ILEWIN [90] 7-10-5 M Ahern, *not fluent, al prmnt, led appr last, drw clr r-in, easily.*
......................(10 to 1 op 8 to 1 tchd 12 to 1) 1
1630[2] CROOKED COUNSEL [97] 8-10-12 N Williamson, *led to 3rd and frm 4th, mstk 2 out, hrd rdn and hdd appr last, unbl to quicken*..................(9 to 2 op 7 to 2) 2
QUENTIN DURWOOD [94] 8-10-9 S McNeill, *prmnt, chsd ldr 7th till 9th, wknd aftr 2 out.*
..........................(6 to 1 op 7 to 1 tchd 8 to 1) 3
1444[2] MIDNIGHT STORY [89] 9-10-4 D Gallagher, *trkd ldrs till no prog frm 8th, collapsed aftr race, dead.*
.... (3 to 1 fav op 2 to 1 tchd 100 to 30) 4
RICH NEPHEW [88] 9-10-3 H Davies, *jinked strt and lost several ls, rear till effrt 8th, not rch ldrs, no ch whn mstk 2 out*..........................(6 to 1 op 5 to 1) 5
1120[6] MAJOR INQUIRY (USA) [101] 8-11-2 D Murphy, *prmnt till lost tch frm 8th, no ch whn mstk last.*
......................(10 to 1 op 8 to 1 tchd 12 to 1) 6
1714[3] DURRINGTON [85] 8-10-0 B Clifford, *in tch till 5th, sn struggling*....................................(14 to 1) 7
1621 SEMINOLE PRINCESS [88] 6-10-3[3] M Bosley, *sn pushed alng, al beh, tld off frm 8th*.......(100 to 1 op 50 to 1) 8
1627[9] GREEN'S TRILOGY (USA) [85] 6-9-13[6] (7*) Mr G Hogan, *mstk 1st, al beh, tld off frm 8th*... (100 to 1 op 50 to 1) 9
1558[3] STRONG VIEWS [113] 7-12-0 M A FitzGerald, *led 3rd to 4th, wknd rpdly aftr 8th, pld up bef 3 out.* (4 to 1 op 7 to 2) pu
Dist: 6l, 10l, 5l, 3½l, 10l, 2½l, 10l, 7l. 4m 16.70s. a 20.70s (10 Ran).
SR: 22/23/10/-/-/-/ (Middx Packaging Ltd), M P Muggeridge

2044 Tote Credit Handicap Hurdle (0-130 5-y-o and up) £3,810 2¾m 110yds ....(1:40)

1711[3] BRIGHTLING BOY [93] 9-10-1 D Gallagher, *rear, prog 6th, rdn to ld 2 out, drvn out r-in.*
......................(12 to 1 op 8 to 1 tchd 14 to 1) 1
1777[5] CHIEF CELT [104] 8-10-12 S Smith Eccles, *al prmnt, hrd rdn appr 2 out, ev ch approaching last, unbl to quicken*..............(10 to 1 op 8 to 1 tchd 12 to 1) 2
1643[7] SPECIAL ACCOUNT [104] 8-10-12 M A FitzGerald, *prmnt till lost pl and mstk 8th, rallied aftr 3 out, ran on r-in.*
...............................(14 to 1 tchd 16 to 1) 3
1721[2] ISLAND JEWEL [98] 6-10-6 M Bosley, *trkd ldrs, rdn whn squeezed out appr 2 out, ran on one pace frm last.*
..........(100 to 30 op 4 to 1 tchd 5 to 1 and 3 to 1) 4
1713 THE GOLFING CURATE [92] 9-9-9 (5*) C Burnett-Wells, *hld up beh, mstk 4th, prog to join ldrs 7th, wknd 2 out.*
...............................(25 to 1 tchd 33 to 1) 5
1643[4] WINABUCK [93] 11-9-12 (3*) D Meredith, *led till rdn and hdd 2 out, wknd*................. (16 to 1 op 12 to 1) 6
1845[2] BEYOND OUR REACH [104] 6-10-12 H Davies, *hld up, prog 6th, pushed alng 8th, wknd 3 out, eased.*
.................................(2 to 1 fav op 5 to 2) 7
1759[7] SHANNON GLEN [120] (bl) 8-11-7 (7*) L O'Hare, *cl up, pushed alng 5th, mstk 7th and hrd rdn, wknd 3 out.*
.......................(20 to 1 op 16 to 1 tchd 25 to 1) 8
1740[9] TIM SOLDIER (Fr) [93] 7-10-1 M Perrett, *in tch till wknd 8th*..(33 to 1) 9

NATIONAL HUNT RESULTS 1993-94

1561 WELSH SIREN [107] 8-11-1 N Williamson, *rear, effrt 6th,
wknd nxt, tld off and pld up bef 2 out.*
........................(12 to 1 tchd 16 to 1) pu
SALMON PRINCE [92] 8-10-0 N Mann, *hld up rear, wknd
7th, tld off and pld up bef 2 out....*(33 to 1 op 25 to 1) pu
BALLYSTATE [108] 6-11-2 S McNeill, *prmnt till wknd
rpdly 6th, tld off whn pld up bef 2 out.*
........................(16 to 1 op 14 to 1) pu
1599* KABAYIL [115] 5-11-9 J Osborne, *trkd ldrs gng easily till
wknd 3 out, pld up bef nxt .*
.......................(9 to 1 op 7 to 2 tchd 11 to 2) pu
Dist: 2½l, hd, 2½l, 15l, 5l, 7l, 10l. 5m 54.80s. a 35.80s (13 Ran).
SR: 20/28/28/19/-/-/-/4/-/ (M Hayden), D M Grissell

2045 Thompson Investments Novices' Chase (6-y-o and up) £2,931 2m 5f ....(2:10)

1844 THE GLOW (Ire) 6-11-7 P Holley, *hld up, prog to join ldrs
whn blun 4 out, led 2 out, clr last, styd on.*
........................(5 to 4 on tchd 5 to 4) 1
134⁸ VAVASIR 8-11-0 N Williamson, *led till aftr 11th, hrd rdn
and ev ch 2 out, btn whn mstk last...*(7 to 1 op 4 to 1) 2
1694⁴ YOUR WELL 8-11-0 B Clifford, *prmnt, led appr 4 out, rdn
and hdd 2 out, btn whn mstk last.*
........................(100 to 30 op 3 to 1 tchd 5 to 2 and 7 to 2) 3
1385⁴ PRINCE'S COURT (bl) 11-11-0 (7*) D Fortt, *prmnt till mstk
11th, sn tld off........*(14 to 1 op 8 to 1 tchd 16 to 1) 4
HERMES HARVEST 6-10-7 (7*) Mr G Hogan, *mstk 3rd, prog
tenth, led briefly aftr nxt, cl 4th whn f four out.*
........................(66 to 1 op 33 to 1 tchd 100 to 1) f
1341² FRANK RICH 7-11-0 M Richards, *mstk 5th, effrt 8th, wknd
11th, btn whn hmpd 4 out, refused nxt.*
........................(7 to 1 op 4 to 1 tchd 15 to 2) ref
1669⁵ BALLYDOUGAN (Ire) 6-11-0 N Mann, *al beh, tld off 9th, pld
up bef 4 out........*(33 to 1 op 16 to 1) pu
Dist: 7l, ½l, dist. 5m 48.90s. a 37.90s (7 Ran).
(Mrs T Brown), D R C Elsworth

2046 Cheveley Park Stud New Year's Day Hurdle Limited Handicap (4-y-o and up) £8,169 2m..................(2:40)

1888³ ABSALOM'S LADY [143] 6-11-10 P Holley, *hld up, gd prog
5th, led aftr 3 out, sn clr, hit last, drvn out.*
........................(5 to 2 fav op 9 to 4 tchd 3 to 1) 1
1663⁴ FLAKEY DOVE [147] 8-12-0 N Williamson, *hld up, prog 5th,
rdn to chase wnr 2 out, ran on one pace.*
........................(11 to 2 op 9 to 2) 2
1559 LEOTARD [141] 7-11-8 J Osborne, *led till 5th, wknd rpdly
3 out........................*(11 to 4 op 5 to 2 tchd 3 to 1) 3
1842 AMAZON EXPRESS [135] 5-11-2 M Richards, *al rear, rdn
and lost tch 5th.......*(8 to 1 op 10 to 1 tchd 11 to 1) 4
DANCING PADDY [130] 6-10-11 D O'Sullivan, *trkd ldrs till
wknd aftr 5th........*(10 to 1 op 7 to 2 tchd 9 to 2) 5
1755⁴ HIGHBROOK (USA) [130] 6-10-11 O Murphy, *pressed ldr till
led 5th, hdd aftr 3 out, 3rd and btn whn f nxt.*
........................(4 to 1 op 7 to 2 tchd 9 to 2) f
Dist: 6l, 30l, 5l, 3½l. 4m 11.70s. a 26.70s (6 Ran).
SR: 45/43/7/ (Whitcombe Manor Racing Stables Limited), D R C Elsworth

2047 Party Politics Handicap Chase (0-125 5-y-o and up) £3,875 3m........(3:10)

1693² AVONBURN (NZ) [118] 10-11-10 M Richards, *hld up, prog
9th, rdn 14th, led aftr 4 out, all out.*
........................(2 to 1 fav op 9 to 4) 1
1796⁴ WARNER FOR WINNERS [104] (bl) 8-10-10 J Osborne, *led
till aftr 4 out, blun nxt, rallied appr last, not quicken
nr finish...................*(9 to 1 op 8 to 1 tchd 10 to 1) 2
1621 PUNCH'S HOTEL [94] 9-9-9 (5*) C Burnett-Wells, *wtd wth,
mstk 8th, prog 13th, chalg whn mistake 2 out and last,
no extr r-in....................*(14 to 1 tchd 16 to 1) 3
1932 GLENSHANE LAD [102] 8-10-8 N Williamson, *prmnt, blun
13th, wknd 4 out...*(100 to 30 op 7 to 2 tchd 5 to 1) 4
1600* MISS FERN [94] 9-9-11 (3*) D Meredith, *prmnt till wknd
rpdly aftr 4 out.......*(7 to 1 op 8 to 1 tchd 9 to 1) 5
1641⁴ J J JIMMY [99] 10-10-5 P Holley, *rear but in tch till f 9th.*
........................(16 to 1 op 12 to 1 tchd 20 to 1) f
663⁸ FALSE ECONOMY [114] 9-11-6 D Gallagher, *prmnt, wth ldr
14th, wknd and mstk nxt, 6th and tld off whn refused
last...................*(16 to 1 op 14 to 1 tchd 20 to 1) ref
1925 ZAMIL (USA) [106] 9-10-12 J P Banahan, *prmnt till wknd
and mstk 13th, beh whn pld up bef 2 out.*
........................(10 to 1 op 8 to 1) pu
1759 ROSITARY (Fr) [102] 7-11-10-8 M Perrett, *rear till hmpd 9th,
beh aftr till pld up bef twelfth.*
........................(40 to 1 op 33 to 1 tchd 50 to 1) pu
934 HICKELTON LAD [94] 10-9-13⁶ (7*) Mr G Hogan, *rear, effrt
13th, mstk and wknd nxt, pld up bef 4 out.*
........................(100 to 1 op 66 to 1) pu
1796⁵ POWDER BOY [94] 9-10-0 I Lawrence, *prmnt till blun
twelfth, not reco'r, tld off and pld up bef 4 out.*
........................(9 to 1 op 20 to 1 tchd 33 to 1) pu
NEARCO BAY (NZ) [122] 10-12-0 M A FitzGerald, *prmnt,
wkng whn blun 14th, pld up bef nxt.*
........................(25 to 1 op 16 to 1) pu

Dist: 1l, 2½l, 30l, 30l. 6m 31.10s. a 36.10s (12 Ran).
(Howard Spooner), P R Hedger

2048 Gran Alba 'National Hunt' Novices' Hurdle (Div II) (4-y-o and up) £1,947 2m ....(3:40)

1688² SQUIRE SILK 5-11-5 S McNeill, *hld up, prog aftr 5th, led
gng easily appr 2 out, hrd rdn and ran on wl r-in.*
........................(5 to 1 op 4 to 1 tchd 11 to 2 and 6 to 1) 1
OLDHILL WOOD (Ire) 4-10-0 (7*) Chris Webb, *mid-div, gd
prog 5th, ev ch appr 2 out, styd on one pace.*
........................(33 to 1 op 25 to 1 tchd 40 to 1) 2
1646* FRIENDLY FELLOW 5-11-12 P Holley, *hld up, prog 4th,
rdn aftr nxt, ev ch 3 out, one pace.*
........................(2 to 1 op 6 to 4 tchd 9 to 4) 3
1126² DUTCH MONARCH 7-11-0 (5*) A Dicken, *mid-div, mstk
and lost pl 4th, ran on frm 2 out, fnshd wl.*
........................(12 to 1 op 7 to 1) 4
1536⁸ MARROB 7-11-5 M Perrett, *trkd ldrs, prog and pushed
alng aftr 5th, rdn to chal appr 2 out, wknd last.*
........................(7 to 4 fav op 5 to 2) 5
1392⁶ POLICEMANS PRIDE (Fr) 5-10-12 (7*) J Clarke, *led till aftr
5th, wknd appr 2 out.......*(66 to 1 tchd 100 to 1) 6
1490 FORTUNES COURSE (Ire) 5-11-0 S Smith Eccles, *prmnt,
mstk 5th, sn led, hdd and wknd appr 2 out.*
........................(33 to 1 op 16 to 1) 7
MORIARTY 7-11-5 J Osborne, *prmnt till wknd 3 out.*
........................(50 to 1 tchd 66 to 1) 8
1548 MERTON MISTRESS 7-11-0 D O'Sullivan, *al beh.*
........................(66 to 1 op 50 to 1) 9
1688 LUCKY LORENZO 6-11-5 M Richards, *al beh.*
........................(66 to 1 tchd 100 to 1) 10
1768⁸ FALCONBRIDGE BAY 7-11-5 M A FitzGerald, *mid-div till
wknd 4th........................*(33 to 1 op 14 to 1) 11
PRETTY BOY GEORGE 5-11-5 M Ahern, *prmnt to 4th, sn
wknd...................*(66 to 1 tchd 100 to 1) 12
1768⁴ CELTIC LAIRD 6-11-5 I Lawrence, *in tch till wknd aftr 5th,
pld up bef 2 out........*(50 to 1 op 33 to 1 tchd 66 to 1) pu
883 STATE LADY (Ire) 5-11-0 N Williamson, *in tch to 4th, tld off
whn pld up bef 2 out.* (50 to 1 op 33 to 1 tchd 66 to 1) pu
Dist: 5l, 1l, 1l, 4l, 15l, 2l, 15l, sht-hd, 10l, 2½l. 4m 18.40s. a 33.40s (14 Ran).
(Robert Ogden), Andrew Turnell

CAGNES-SUR-MER (FR) (good)
Wednesday January 5th

2049 Prix des Amandiers (Hurdle) (5-y-o and up) £6,857 2m 110yds...... (2:45)

SHANGOL DE PERSE (Fr) 5-10-1 P Chevalier, ... 1
TEXASIAN (USA) 7-10-5 W Fournier, ... 2
TIP TOP BOY (Fr) 5-10-1 T Berthelot, ... 3
1570⁷ ABLE PLAYER (USA) 7-10-5 S Jaunet, *nvr dngrs.*.......... 0
1256⁵ BEAUCHAMP GRACE 5-10-1 D Parker, *in tch for o'r ten fs.*
Dist: 1½l, 1l, 4l, 2½l, 3l, ½l, dist. 3m 51.10s. (13 Ran).
(Mme C Chauby), L Audon

PUNCHESTOWN (IRE) (heavy)
Wednesday January 5th

2050 Punchestown Mares Maiden Hurdle (5 & 6-y-o) £3,105 2½m.......... (12:45)

1683⁸ WILD VENTURE (Ire) 6-11-6 A Powell, ...(6 to 4 fav) 1
1898³ MISGIVINGS (Ire) 6-11-6 C F Swan, ...(7 to 2) 2
FURRY DUCK (Ire) 6-12-0 B Sheridan, ...(10 to 1) 3
1912⁷ CARIBEAN ROSE (Ire) 6-11-6 K F O'Brien, ...(12 to 1) 4
1760 POOR MOTHER (Ire) 6-11-3 (3*) T J Mitchell, ...(14 to 1) 5
1980⁶ ROSEPERRIE (Ire) (bl) 6-11-1 (5*) D T Evans, ...(10 to 1) 6
1858* MIDNIGHT AT MAY'S (Ire) 6-11-7 (7*) J P Broderick, (12 to 2) 7
1832² TUDOR THYNE (Ire) 6-11-3 (3*) Mr P McMahon, ...(5 to 1) 8
1898² TRINITY GALE (Ire) 6-11-3 (3*) D P Murphy, ...(12 to 1) 9
1610 NOT A BID (Ire) 5-11-2 J A White, ...(33 to 1) 10
803 BELLE O' THE BAY (Ire) 5-10-13 (3*) D Bromley, ...(12 to 1) 11
1766 PARSONS BELLE (Ire) 6-11-1 (5*) T P Rudd, ...(33 to 1) 12
1681 SHINETHYME (Ire) 5-11-2 J P Banahan, ...(33 to 1) 13
1898 THE REAL GAEL (Ire) 6-11-3 (3*) C O'Brien, ...(20 to 1) 14
1332 JUST A BROWNIE (Ire) 6-11-6 T Horgan, ...(20 to 1) pu
Dist: 1l, 12l, 5½l, 25l. 5m 56.50s. (15 Ran).
(Lady J Fowler), J R H Fowler

2051 Tattersalls Mares Novice Chase (6-y-o and up) £3,450 2m............(1:15)

CHARLIES UNYOKE 8-11-11 (3*) D P Murphy, ...(10 to 1) 1
1685⁸ TITIAN BLONDE (Ire) 6-12-0 C F Swan, ...(100 to 30) 2
1905⁵ BLUE RING 10-11-9 P Woods, ...(100 to 30) 3
1857⁴ DOORSLAMMER 9-12-0 S R Murphy, ...(11 to 2) 4
1857 BALLINDERRY GLEN 8-11-9 (5*) M G Cleary, ...(10 to 1) 5
1825⁴ PRINCESS CASILIA 9-12-0 B Sheridan, ...(5 to 2 fav) 6
2035⁵ RAINBOW ALLIANCE (Ire) 6-11-9 J F Titley, ...(14 to 1) 7
Dist: 3l, 2½l, 6l, 14l. 4m 33.00s. (7 Ran).
(Real Unyoke Syndicate), W P Mullins

281

NATIONAL HUNT RESULTS 1993-94

2052 Irish National Stud Novice Hurdle (6-y-o and up) £3,795 2½m....... (1:45)

1760*	HARCON (Ire) 6-11-12 K F O'Brien, ...(5 to 2 on)	1
1824⁴	CHANCE COFFEY 9-11-6 G M O'Neill, ...(8 to 1)	2
1894⁶	MONKEY AGO 7-11-12 C F Swan, ...(11 to 2)	3
1892³	I AM 6-11-6 T Horgan,........................(8 to 1)	4
1897⁵	CLOSUTTON EXPRESS 8-11-6 Mr W P Mullins, ..(14 to 1)	5
1760	JIMMY O'GOBLIN 7-11-6 B Sheridan, ...(25 to 1)	6
1829⁴	MAN OF IRON 7-11-6 F Woods,................(20 to 1)	7
	EXTRA MILE 7-10-10² (7ᵇ) Mr B Lennon, ...(25 to 1)	8

Dist: 2l, 12l, 7l, 15l. 5m 55.50s. (8 Ran).

(Mrs P J Conway), J T R Dreaper

2053 Carrick Hill Handicap Chase (0-109 5-y-o and up) £3,105 2m 5f..... (2:15)

1830²	EDENAKILL LAD [-] 7-9-8 C F Swan, ...(5 to 2 fav)	1
1830⁴	LA-GREINE [-] 7-10-6 (3ᵇ) Mr P McMahon, ...(8 to 1)	2
1819*	FRIENDLY ARGUMENT [-] 9-11-5 (4ex) F Woods, .. (7 to 2)	3
1819⁶	CARTON [-] 7-10-12 K F O'Brien, ...(7 to 1)	4
1819⁵	DEEP ISLE [-] 8-10-2 P Carberry, ...(8 to 1)	5
1782	BENS DILEMMA [-] 9-9-6 (7ᵇ) J P Broderick, ...(8 to 1)	f
1402	SET YOUR SIGHTS [-] 11-11-3 T J Taaffe, ...(5 to 1)	pu
1819	TRIAURUM [-] 12-10-1 T Horgan, ...(20 to 1)	pu

Dist: 3l, 15l, 7l, 6l. 5m 48.70s. (8 Ran).

(J R Cox), J R Cox

2054 Fairyland Handicap Hurdle (0-123 5-y-o and up) £3,105 2m...........(2:45)

1818⁶	APPELLATE COURT [-] (bl) 6-11-6 A Powell, ...(8 to 1)	1
1907*	GRAND TOUR (NZ) [-] 6-10-12 (4ex) L P Cusack, ...(7 to 2)	2
1987²	CELTIC SAILS (Ire) [-] 6-10-9 (5ᵇ) Mr P J Casey, ...(4 to 1)	3
1551	TARA MILL (Ire) [-] 5-10-7 (7ᵇ) J P Broderick, ...(8 to 1)	4
1976	DASHING ROSE [-] 6-10-11 P Carberry, ...(7 to 4 fav)	5
1976²	HEADBANGER [-] 7-11-3 C O'Dwyer, ...(6 to 1)	6

Dist: Nk, 15l, 3l, 4½l. 4m 17.60s. (6 Ran).

(James Dunne), James Dunne

2055 Mullacash Novice Chase (5-y-o and up) £3,105 3m..................(3:15)

1825	KING OF THE GLEN 8-11-11 (3ᵇ) C O'Brien, ...(5 to 2)	1
1892²	DADDY LONG LEGGS 7-11-9 K F O'Brien, ..(9 to 4 fav)	2
1687	DEER TRIX 9-11-1 (3ᵇ) D Bromley, ...(25 to 1)	3
1451⁹	CHOSEN SON 6-11-4 (5ᵇ) T P Rudd,...............(14 to 1)	4
1683	PRANKSTER 8-11-9 S R Murphy, ...(14 to 1)	5
1900⁶	MOBILE MAN 7-12-0 T Horgan, ...(7 to 1)	6
	THE MIGHTY BUCK 11-11-9 J F Titley, ...(12 to 1)	ur
1900	MR BARNEY 7-11-9 J K Kinane, ...(20 to 1)	pu
1577²	TEL D'OR 9-11-2 (7ᵇ) Mr P J Millington, ...(6 to 1)	pu
1684⁹	FOUR ZEROS 7-11-9 A Powell, ...(20 to 1)	pu
1760⁸	COMICALITY 6-11-9 T J Taaffe, ...(6 to 1)	pu

Dist: Sht-hd, dist, 15l, 25l. 6m 57.20s. (11 Ran).

(Michael J Walshe), A J McNamara

2056 Martinstown INH Flat Race (5-y-o) £3,105 2m..................(3:45)

	TOURIST ATTRACTION (Ire) 11-2 (3ᵇ) Mrs J M Mullins, ...(7 to 1)	1
1820³	MOYGANNON COURT (Ire) 11-5 (5ᵇ) Mr H F Cleary, (7 to 4)	2
1848⁸	MIDNIGHT HOUR (Ire) 11-3 (7ᵇ) Mr D A Harney, ...(6 to 1)	3
	ARDSHUIL 11-10 Mr A J Martin, ...(to 4 fav)	4
1766⁶	RAHAN BRIDGE (Ire) 11-2 A Condon, ...(8 to 1)	5
1820	LAURA GALE (Ire) 11-0 (5ᵇ) Mr P M Kelly, ...(16 to 1)	6
747	THE BREAK (Ire) 11-2 (3ᵇ) Mr D Marnane, ...(14 to 1)	7
1786	TUSCANY HIGHWAY (Ire) 11-10 Mr M Phillips, ...(33 to 1)	8
292	FURTHER APPRAISAL (Ire) 11-6⁶ (5ᵇ) Mr P J Dreeling, ...(14 to 1)	pu

Dist: 9l, 11l, 20l, 11l. 4m 4.10s. (9 Ran).

(North Kildare Racing Club), W P Mullins

SOUTHWELL (A.W) (Std)
Wednesday January 5th
Going Correction: PLUS 0.10 sec. per fur.

2057 Camembert Novices' Hurdle (4-y-o and up) £1,553 2m.............(1:20)

851⁵	TEEN JAY 4-10-8 J Osborne, patiently rdn, improved appr 3 out, ran on und pres to ld last 50 yards. ....(3 to 1 fav op 7 to 2 tchd 9 to 2)	1
138³	YAAKUM 5-11-1 (5ᵇ) J Twomey, settled midfield, drw level aftr 3 out, led betw last 2, hdd and no extr last 50 yards. ....(11 to 1 op 10 to 1 tchd 12 to 1)	2
1927³	LEEWA (Ire) 4-10-8 M Richards, led till aftr 4 out, rallied to ld nxt, hdd betw last 2, no extr.......(4 to 1 op 7 to 2)	3
1628²	NAGOBELIA 6-11-6 N Williamson, nvr far away, ev ch and rdn aftr 3 out, btn whn then last. ....(5 to 1 op 3 to 1 tchd 11 to 2)	4
1811*	MAJAL (Ire) 5-11-7 (5*) P Midgley, wtd wth, improved frm midfield to ld aftr 4 out, hdd and rdn nxt, fdd betw last 2.............................(7 to 1 op 5 to 1)	5

2058 Wensleydale Selling Hurdle (4-y-o and up) £1,722 2¾m............(1:50)

1801²	IT'S NOT MY FAULT (Ire) 6-11-12 P McDermott, al hndy, feeling pace whn jmpd rght 3 out, no imprsn on ldr whn lft clr last....................(3 to 1 op 6 to 4)	1
1526⁴	TESEKKUREDERIM 7-11-6 Diane Clay, nvr far away, effrt and pushed alng fnl circuit, staying on same pace whn lft second last...........................(6 to 1)	2
1425³	CAPTAIN CUTE 9-11-1 (5*) P Midgley, trkd ldrs, effrt and drvn alng fnl circuit, no imprsn frm 3 out. ....(9 to 1 op 8 to 1)	3
1592	RUSTY MUSIC 8-11-5 (7*) A Flannigan, al hndy, chalg whn f 8th...........................(6 to 1 op 8 to 1)	f
1931³	DOUALAGO (Fr) (bl) 4-11-5 R Dunwoody, led, quickened appr 3 out, clr whn f last. ....(7 to 4 fav op 2 to 1 tchd 5 to 2)	f
1967⁴	HICKELTON HOUSE 10-11-6 N Williamson, patiently rdn, gng wl whn hmpd and uns rdr 8th...(5 to 1 op 7 to 2)	ur
935	CASTLE WARRIOR 7-11-6 T Wall, struggling to keep up hfwy, lost tch fnl circuit, tld off whn pld up bef 3 out. ....(33 to 1 op 25 to 1)	pu

Dist: 4l, 25l. 5m 42.60s. a 33.60s (7 Ran).

(R J Peake), D J Wintle

2059 Brie Novices' Handicap Hurdle (0-100 4-y-o and up) £1,553 2½m....(2:20)

1718⁶	CHAPEL HILL (Ire) [81] 6-11-11 (3*) A Procter, trkd ldr, led aftr 6th, quickened 3 out, rdn clr betw last 2. ....(7 to 2 op 3 to 1 tchd 4 to 1)	1
1809³	CROOKED DEALER (NZ) [67] 7-11-0 J Osborne, led, jnd hfwy, hdd aftr 6th, rallied, rdn and one pace betw last 2..................................(9 to 4 jt-fav op 6 to 4)	2
	CARLINGFORD LIGHTS (Ire) [60] 6-10-7 G Bradley, settled gng wl, improved on bit to chal 3 out, rdn and found little betw last 2................(9 to 4 jt-fav op 5 to 2)	3
2000³	NEGD (USA) [67] (bl) 4-11-0 R Garritty, nvr far away, lost grnd whn pace quickened appr 3 out, styd on r-in. ....(5 to 2 tchd 3 to 1)	4

Dist: 7l, ¾l, 5l. 5m 7.20s. a 26.20s (4 Ran).

(Eamonn O'Malley), D Burchell

2060 Cheddar Handicap Hurdle (0-115 4-y-o and up) £1,825 2½m...........(2:50)

594⁸	ARCTIC OATS [101] 9-11-13 D Byrne, nvr far away, led 2 out, kpet on wl frm last. ....(10 to 1 op 7 to 1 tchd 12 to 1)	1
1928²	FLYAWAY (Fr) [91] 9-11-3 R Dunwoody, led, jnd hfwy, rdn and hdd 2 out, not extr r-in.(2 to 1 fav op 5 to 2)	2
1799⁵	DONNA'S TOKEN [82] 9-10-1 (7*) A Flannigan, wth ldr, ev ch whn hit 3 out, no extr betw last 2. (6 to 1 op 8 to 1)	3
1793⁶	PIMS GUNNER (Ire) [93] 6-11-0 (5*) D Bentley, trkd ldrs, reminders aftr 7th, outpcd 3 out. ....(11 to 2 op 7 to 2 tchd 6 to 1)	4
1812²	HAVE A NIGHTCAP [102] 5-12-0 D Gallagher, tracking ldrs whn f second..............(3 to 1 op 2 to 1 tchd 7 to 2)	f
	DANCING DAYS [80] (bl) 8-11-6 N Smith, struggling hfwy, tld off whn pld up betw last 2.................(10 to 1)	pu
1749⁴	BAND OF HOPE (USA) [84] (bl) 7-10-10 Diane Clay, rdn alng to keep up hfwy, lost tch bef 4 out, tld off whn pld up betw last 2.....................(8 to 1 op 7 to 1)	pu

Dist: 3l, 8l, 6l. 5m 2.40s. a 21.40s (7 Ran).

(R P Dineen), W W Haigh

2061 Stilton Conditional Jockeys' Claiming Hurdle (4-y-o and up) £1,799 2¼m ....(3:20)

1749³	GLOSSY 7-11-1 (5*) G Robertson, made most, hit 4 out and nxt, hdd briefly r-in, rallied. ....(9 to 2 op 5 to 1 tchd 6 to 1)	1

1926 PYRO PENNANT 9-11-3 (3*) A Procter, pressed ldrs, rdn appr 3 out, fdd...................(33 to 1 op 20 to 1) — 6

1251⁴	IN FOR A POUND (Ire) 5-11-6 S Smith Eccles, trkd ldrs, drvn alng aftr 4 out, fdd nxt......(5 to 1 tchd 6 to 1)	7
1926⁴	MATUSADONA 7-11-1 B Dalton, co'red up in midfield, struggling to keep up whn almost f 4 out, tld off. ....(20 to 1)	8
	QUINBERRY 6-11-1 V Slattery, chsd ldrs, struggling appr 4 out, no ch whn f last.....................(50 to 1)	f
1797⁶	MISTRESS MINX 5-11-1 S D Williams, pressed ldrs, struggling hfwy, lost tch and pld up bef 4 out.....(33 to 1)	pu
1813⁵	STEVE FORD 5-11-6 T Wall, blun second, not reco'r, pld up aftr 4th..............................(25 to 1)	pu
896³	CRIMINAL RECORD (USA) (bl) 4-10-8 Diane Clay, bustled alng to keep in tch hfwy, jmpd slwly aftr, tld off whn pld up bef 3 out................................(25 to 1)	pu
1229	HENRIETTA BOO BOO 4-9-13³ (7*) A Flannigan, dsptd ld, drvn alng and lost grnd aftr 4 out, tld off whn pld up bef nxt................(16 to 1 op 10 to 1 tchd 20 to 1)	pu
1504	SACHA STAR 4-10-3 R Greene, blun second, sn lost tch, tld off whn pld up bef 3 out.............(33 to 1)	pu

Dist: ¾l, 3l, 1½l, 15l, 25l, dist. 3m 53.70s. a 7.70s (14 Ran).
SR: 19/30/13/22/26/5/

(F J Bush), S E Sherwood

282

2002³ CELTIC BOB 14-10-11 (5*) P Maddock, *patiently rdn, improved to join ldrs 3 out, led briefly r-in, no extr cl hme*................(7 to 2 fav op 4 to 1 tchd 3 to 1) 2
1810⁷ PHARGOLD (Ire) 5-10-13 (5*) P Ward, *nvr far away, rdn and ev ch 3 out, blun and rdr lost irons nxt, not reco'r, one pace r-in*...........(9 to 2 op 5 to 2 tchd 5 to 1) 3
RAIN-N-SUN 8-11-6 A Procter, *pressed ldr, hrd rdn whn pace quickened appr 3 out, sn lost tch.*
....................................(7 to 1 op 5 to 1) 4
1794⁷ SILK DYNASTY 8-11-2 S Wynne, *pressed ldg trio, struggling to keep up appr 4 out, sn tld off.*
....................................(4 to 1 op 3 to 1) 5
1942 JULFAAR (USA) 7-11-4 J Twomey, *chsd ldrs to hfwy, tld off whn pld up bef 2 out.* (8 to 1 op 7 to 1 tchd 9 to 1) pu
1810 SOL ROUGE (Ire) 5-11-3 M Hourigan, *pressed ldrs to 4th, lost tch hfwy, tld off whn pld up bef 3 out.*
..................................(12 to 1 op 10 to 1) pu
Dist: Hd, 4l, 30l, 25l. 4m 27.30s. a 15.30s (7 Ran).

(Ed Weetman (Haulage & Storage) Ltd), B A McMahon

2062 Cheshire Handicap Hurdle (0-105 4-y-o and up) £1,909 2m............(3:50)

1627³ TRISTAN'S COMET [75] 7-10-0 B Dalton, *made all, pushed clr aftr 3 out, hit last, styd on wl.* (5 to 1 tchd 11 to 2) 1
1810² BABY ASHLEY [87] 8-10-12 N Mann, *al hndy, effrt whn squeezed for room aftr 4 out, rallied nxt, rdn and one pace betw last 2*..................(7 to 2 tchd 9 to 2) 2
1654⁹ ANDRATH (Ire) [75] 6-10-0 W Humphreys, *mstks, pressed ldrs, feeling pace appr 3 out, styd on one pace betw last 2*..................... (14 to 1 op 16 to 1 tchd 12 to 1) 3
1701 WHEELER'S WONDER (Ire) [103] 5-11-7 (7*) Mr J L Llewellyn, *al hndy, ev ch aftr 4 out, rdn and outpcd nxt.*
.... (10 to 1 op 5 to 1) 4
1154² NORTHERN NATION [94] 6-11-5 Diane Clay, *trkd ldrs, niggled alng hfwy, reminders 4 out, sn btn.*
.... (11 to 10 on tchd 5 to 4 on and Evens) 5
1633 SECRET CASTLE [93] 6-11-4 T Wall, *last and hld up, pushed alng aftr 4 out, 5th and no ch whn f 2 out.*
.... (16 to 1 op 12 to 1 tchd 20 to 1) f
Dist: 3l, 3½l, 4l, 10l. 3m 57.70s. a 11.70s (6 Ran).

(D Wilcox), J L Harris

LINGFIELD (A.W) (std)
Thursday January 6th
Going Correction: NIL

2063 Bad Penny Maiden Hurdle (4-y-o and up) £1,814 2½m................(1:00)

CALOGAN 7-11-7 C Llewellyn, *beh, hdwy 7th, chsd ldr 2 out, str chal last, sn led, ran on wl.*
.... (10 to 1 op 5 to 1 tchd 12 to 1) 1
1767 MUSICAL PHONE 4-10-8 M A FitzGerald, *chsd ldr, led 4 out, hit nxt, hdd sn aftr last, one pace und pres.*
.... (16 to 1 op 10 to 1 tchd 20 to 1) 2
1464⁶ DO BE WARE 4-10-5 (3*) A Thornton, *chsd ldrs, rdn alng 8th, no imprsn on lders.*
.... (14 to 1 op 12 to 1 tchd 16 to 1) 3
1248⁷ MUTUAL BENEFIT (bl) 7-11-7 Lorna Vincent, *hit 3rd, beh 5th, moderate prog frm 3 out.*
.... (16 to 1 op 12 to 1 tchd 20 to 1) 4
1587³ NO WORD 7-11-7 W McFarland, *led to 4 out, wknd aftr nxt, tld off*...........(5 to 2 op 7 to 4 tchd 11 to 4) 5
MRS TWEED 8-11-2 E Byrne, *chsd ldrs 5th, hit 8th, sn weekened, no ch whn mstk 2 out, tld off.*
.... (14 to 1 op 20 to 1 tchd 33 to 1) 6
FAIR ROWANNA 6-10-9 (7*) P McLoughlin, *mstk second, al beh, tld off*......................(33 to 1 op 20 to 1) 7
1595 PETER MARTIN TWO 5-11-7 D O'Sullivan, *beh 8th, tld off.*
.... (20 to 1 op 12 to 1) 8
CHRISTIAN SOLDIER 7-11-7 W Elderfield, *al beh, lost tch 5th, tld off*..........(33 to 1 op 25 to 1 tchd 50 to 1) 9
1557⁹ CRACKLING ANGELS 7-11-2 B Powell, *pld up aftr 1st, broke leg, destroyed.*
.... (Evens fav op 11 to 10 tchd 5 to 4) pu
Dist: 2l, 20l, 8l, 3½l, 25l, 20l, 4l, 1½l. 4m 53.10s. a 22.10s (10 Ran).

(K H Burks), B Smart

2064 Stitch In Time Claiming Hurdle (5-y-o and up) £1,922 2½m............(1:30)

1488 BEN ZABEEDY 9-11-4 G McCourt, *prmnt, chlgd 4 out, drvn alng to chase ldrs nxt, styd on und str pres to ld nr finish*............ (4 to 1 jt-fav op 3 to 1 tchd 9 to 2) 1
1711 SPARKLER GEBE (bl) 8-11-8 D O'Sullivan, *pressed ldrs, led tenth to 4 out, led nxt, rdn r-in, ct nr finish.*
.... (11 to 2 op 7 to 2 tchd 6 to 1) 2
1642⁵ GROG (Ire) 5-11-4 J Osborne, *hld up in tch, chsd ldrs frm 2 out, ran on und pres r-in.*
.... (5 to 1 tchd 9 to 2 and 11 to 2) 3
1942⁵ SAKIL (Ire) 6-11-1 (5*) A Dicken, *blun second, hdwy 8th, chsd ldrs tenth, outpcd 3 out.*
.... (12 to 1 op 8 to 1 tchd 14 to 1) 4

1153⁴ FROSTY RECEPTION (bl) 9-11-10 L Harvey, *led 6th to tenth, led 4 out to nxt, sn wknd.*
.........................(7 to 1 op 6 to 1 tchd 8 to 1) 5
1592⁸ WAR BEAT 6-11-3 (7*) G Robertson, *hdwy tenth, rdn and mstk 3 out, sn wknd.* (20 to 1 op 16 to 1 tchd 25 to 1) 6
1759 MOZE TIDY 9-11-8 H Davies, *nvr rch ldrs.*
................................(14 to 1 tchd 16 to 1) 7
1789⁴ LAPIAFFE 10-11-9 (5*) T Jenks, *led to second, wth ldr 6th to 8th, wknd aftr 4 out*............ (10 to 1 op 6 to 1) 8
1719 BRORA ROSE (Ire) 6-11-3 I Shoemark, *al beh, lost tch 5th.*
.... (50 to 1 op 33 to 1) 9
1272⁹ BAYLORD PRINCE (Ire) 6-10-12 M Hoad, *mstk second, al beh*............................ (50 to 1 op 25 to 1) 10
1370² JOLI'S GREAT (bl) 6-11-3 D Gallagher, *prmnt, chlgd 4 out, sn rdn and btn*.... (4 to 1 jt-fav op 5 to 2 tchd 9 to 2) 11
1714 HIGH HAGBERG 8-10-10 Mrs K Hills, *jmpd big 1st 2, led second to 6th, wknd quickly, tld off.*
.... (66 to 1 op 50 to 1 tchd 100 to 1) 12
Dist: Nk, ¾l, 15l, 3½l, 4l, 10l, 7l, 3½l, ¾l, 5l. 4m 48.30s. a 17.30s (12 Ran).

(Richard Armstrong), R Akehurst

2065 Too Many Cooks Handicap Hurdle (0-110 4-y-o and up) £1,830 2m..(2:00)

1801 ROYAL CIRCUS [79] 5-10-8 D Bridgwater, *led 4th till aftr nxt, led 6th till after 2 out, rallied und prressure to ld last, all out*.......... (12 to 1 op 8 to 1 tchd 14 to 1) 1
1627⁷ RARFY'S DREAM [96] 6-11-6 (5*) J Twomey, *in tch whn hit 4th, chlgd 3 out, led aftr nxt, hdd last, rdn and no extr.*
.... (100 to 30 fav op 4 to 1 tchd 9 to 2) 2
LAKE DOMINION [92] 5-11-7 D Skyrme, *chsd ldrs, chlgd 3 out, wknd aftr nxt*..... (6 to 1 op 5 to 1 tchd 7 to 1) 3
1632⁸ VICTORY ANTHEM [92] 8-11-7 I Lawrence, *hdwy 7th, chlgd 3 out to nxt, wknd appr last.*
.... (9 to 1 op 7 to 1 tchd 10 to 1) 4
979⁶ TEL E THON [96] (v) 7-11-11 R Dunwoody, *led to 4th, led aftr 5th to nxt, wknd 2 out.*
.... (14 to 1 op 10 to 1 tchd 16 to 1) 5
1627 MILL BURN [74] 5-10-3³ R Campbell, *rear till styd on frm 3 out, not a dngr*..... (33 to 1 op 20 to 1 tchd 40 to 1) 6
1711 STYLISH GENT [71] 7-9-7 (7*) T Dascombe, *prmnt, rdn aftr 5th, wknd 4 out*..... (25 to 1 op 33 to 1 tchd 20 to 1) 7
1525³ FANATICAL (USA) [79] (bl) 8-10-8 L Harvey, *beh, hdwy 7th, wknd 3 out*.....................(10 to 1 tchd 12 to 1) 8
1422³ FLUIDITY (USA) [90] 6-11-5 W Marston, *beh 5th.*
.... (20 to 1 op 14 to 1) 9
1810⁴ RUTH'S GAMBLE [72] (bl) 6-10-1¹ Richard Guest, *rdn aftr 1st, prmnt till wknd 6th.*
.... (12 to 1 op 8 to 1 tchd 14 to 1) 10
1597⁴ GREENWINE (USA) [80] 8-10-9 M Richards, *al beh, tld off.*
.... (20 to 1 op 14 to 1) 11
1586³ BONDAID [83] 10-10-12 N Williamson, *mid-div, drpd rear 5th, lost tch nxt*.................... (7 to 1 op 5 to 1) 12
1586⁶ ASHDREN [88] 7-10-12 (5*) T Jenks, *drpd rear 5th, tld off whn pld up bef 4 out*.... (6 to 1 op 4 to 1 tchd 7 to 1) pu
Dist: 2½l, 7l, ¾l, hd, 2½l, 12l, 10l, 10l, hd, 25l. 3m 39.10s. a 6.10s (13 Ran).
SR: 19/33/22/21/25/-/ (P W Hiatt), P W Hiatt

2066 Rolling Stone Novices' Handicap Hurdle (0-100 4-y-o and up) £1,753 2½m ....(2:30)

1640* SAAHI (USA) [71] 5-11-1 J Osborne, *hld up, led aftr 9th, quickened clr 3 out, easily.*
..................(5 to 4 on op 7 to 4 on tchd Evens) 1
1926⁶ BUSMAN (Ire) [81] 5-11-4 (7*) P McLoughlin, *mstk 1st, prmnt, chsd wnr frm 3 out, no imprsn.*
.... (9 to 4 tchd 2 to 1 and 5 to 2) 2
1192 NEARLY HONEST [58] 6-10-2² A Tory, *dsptd ld to second, styd prominent, chlgd 8th, outpcd 4 out.*
.... (20 to 1 op 25 to 1 tchd 33 to 1) 3
RADAR KNIGHT [84] 6-11-7 (7*) L O'Hare, *made most till aftr 9th, wknd 3 out.* (16 to 1 op 12 to 1 tchd 20 to 1) 4
1646⁸ ROAD TO AU BON (USA) [70] 6-11-0 L Harvey, *beh, rdn 4 out, no imprsn*.................. (8 to 1 tchd 10 to 1) 5
1628⁴ EMALLEN (Ire) [67] 6-10-11 N Williamson, *prmnt, chlgd 5th to 6th, rdn 9th, sn wknd.*
.... (14 to 1 op 10 to 1 tchd 16 to 1) 6
1948 JUST BALLYTOO [62] (v) 7-10-6 I Lawrence, *beh 6th, rdn nxt, chsd ldrs 8th, sn wknd, tld off whn pld up bef 2 out*..............................(25 to 1 tchd 33 to 1) pu
Dist: 12l, 2½l, 12l, 5l, 15l. 4m 51.00s. a 20.00s (7 Ran).

(Martin N Peters), C Weedon

2067 Bird In The Hand Handicap Hurdle (0-115 4-y-o and up) £1,784 2¾m (3:00)

1772 JARRWAH [91] 6-11-4 W Marston, *made all, rdn and styd on wl frm last*... (5 to 1 co-fav op 4 to 1 tchd 11 to 2) 1
1597³ QUALITAIR MEMORY (Ire) [76] 5-10-3 R Dunwoody, *chsd wnr most of way, hrd drvn r-in, no imprsn.* (5 to 1 co-fav tchd 11 to 2) 2
1521⁷ ALREEF [97] 8-11-3 (7*) Guy Lewis, *chsd ldrs, rdn and one pace 3 out*....... (5 to 1 co-fav op 4 to 1 tchd 11 to 2) 3
JADIDH [95] 6-11-3 (5*) D Salter, *hdwy 9th, styd on frm 3 out*..............................(12 to 1 tchd 14 to 1) 4

1711 CARFAX [91] 9-11-4 M Hoad, *some prog frm 3 out.*
.... (13 to 2 op 5 to 1 tchd 7 to 1) 5
1972⁶ CRABBY BILL [101] 7-11-9 (5") A Dicken, *mstk 1st, beh, hrd drvn aftr 9th, hit nxt, nvr dngrs....*(10 to 1 op 7 to 1) 6
SHIMMERING SCARLET (Ire) [98] 6-11-11 B Powell, *hdwy 6th, rdn 4 out, sn wknd.*
.... (9 to 1 op 7 to 1 tchd 10 to 1) 7
1373* NORSTOCK [98] 7-11-4 (7") P McLoughlin, *prmnt, hit 8th, rdn and hit tenth, sn wknd........*(6 to 1 tchd 7 to 1) 8
1719⁷ LAABAS [76] (bl) 11-10-3³ R Rowell, *prmnt, wkng whn mstk 11th, f 4 out...............* (25 to 1 tchd 33 to 1) f
1412⁵ KALAMOSS [73] 5-9-7 (7") Miss S Mitchell, *beh till f 11th.*
.... (14 to 1) f
1793 SERAPHIM (Fr) [92] 5-11-0 (5") T Jenks, *al beh, tld off whn mstk and uns rdr last..*(10 to 1 op 7 to 1 tchd 12 to 1) ur
MILTON BRYAN [73] 9-10-0 D Gallagher, *sn beh, tld off whn pld up bef 3 out.*(50 to 1 op 33 to 1 tchd 66 to 1) pu
1562⁴ WILTOSKI [76] 6-10-3 Mrs N Ledger, *beh frm 9th, tld off whn pld up bef last.* (20 to 1 op 16 to 1 tchd 25 to 1) pu
Dist: ¾l, 15l, 8l, 3½l, ½l, 2l, 10l. 5m 12.00s. a 13.00s (13 Ran).
(Alan C Cadoret), J L Spearing

EDINBURGH (Good)
Friday January 7th
Going Correction: MINUS 0.10 sec. per fur. (races 1,3,5,7), PLUS 0.05 (2,4,6)

2068 Lothians Racing Syndicate Maiden Hurdle (4-y-o and up) £2,029 2½m
.... (12:30)

1920³ OUTSET (Ire) 4-10-4 (7") Mr C Bonner, *made all, clr betw last 2, ran on wl....................*(5 to 1 op 3 to 1) 1
1654³ TITIAN GIRL (bl) 5-11-2 (3") A Thornton, *chsd wnr frm hfwy, rdn aftr 2 out, kpt on, no imprsn.*
.... (8 to 1 tchd 10 to 1) 2
1582⁵ OAKLEY 5-11-5 (5") P Waggott, *pld hrd early, sn tracking ldrs, effrt appr 2 out, kpt on same pace.*
.... (25 to 1 op 20 to 1) 3
1582⁴ THREE STRONG (Ire) 5-11-10 A Maguire, *hld up, hdwy appr 3 out, rdn aftr nxt, one pace.*
.... (7 to 4 fav op 2 to 1 tchd 11 to 4) 4
SUNKALA SHINE 6-11-10 M Dwyer, *hld up in tch, outpcd aftr 3 out, styd on frm nxt.*
.... (4 to 1 op 9 to 2 tchd 5 to 1) 5
MUFID (USA) 5-11-10 P Niven, *prmnt, effrt appr 3 out, one pace......................* (33 to 1 tchd 50 to 1) 6
1202⁴ DOUBLE STANDARDS (Ire) 6-11-10 C Grant, *trkd ldrs till wknd appr 3 out....*(16 to 1 op 14 to 1 tchd 20 to 1) 7
1793⁷ RED TEMPEST (Ire) 6-11-5 (5") F Perratt, *chsd ldrs till wknd appr 2 out..................* (20 to 1 op 16 to 1) 8
RAGING THUNDER 4-10-11 T Reed, *beh most of way.*
.... (25 to 1 op 20 to 1) 9
1938 LADYSBELOU 6-11-5 A Dobbin, *sn beh, tld off.*(200 to 1) 10
1655 RAVENSPUR (Ire) (bl) 4-10-11 N Smith, *in tch till wknd appr 3 out.............................*(50 to 1) 11
1787 CHALKIEFORT 5-11-10 K Jones, *sn beh, tld off.* (100 to 1) 12
1938 MISS TINO 6-11-0 (5") P Williams, *beh frm hfwy, tld off.*
.... (200 to 1) 13
1787² ASTRALEON (Ire) 6-11-10 B Storey, *settled midfield, slpd up and f aftr 6th........* (9 to 2 op 4 to 1 tchd 5 to 1) su
1114⁹ BIT OF LIGHT 7-11-5 (5") J Burke, *al beh, tld off whn pld up bef 2 out.................................*(100 to 1) pu
Dist: 10l, 5l, ½l, 1½l, ½l, 20l, 1l, 1l. 4m 47.10s. a 9.10s (15 Ran).
(Mark Kilner), M D Hammond

2069 Glengoyne Highland Malt Tamerosia Series Novices' Chase Qualifier (5-y-o and up) £2,411 2½m. (1:00)

1807 CLASSIC CONTACT 8-12-0 J Callaghan, *made all, hrd pressed frm 4 out, pushed out r-in.*
.... (5 to 4 fav op 6 to 4 and 11 to 10) 1
OVER THE ISLAND (Ire) 6-11-1 A Maguire, *cl up, chalg whn hit 4 out, ev ch last, rdn and no extr.*
.... (11 to 4 op 5 to 2 tchd 3 to 1) 2
1145⁴ CAPITAL PUNISHMENT 8-12-0 C Grant, *chsd ldrs, rdn alng aftr 9th, tld off frm 4 out.......* (7 to 2 op 5 to 2) 3
1200 ALGAIS GRAY 7-11-1 (5") D Bentley, *cl up till grad wknd aftr 12th, tld off...................................*(50 to 1) 4
1679³ MOW CREEK 10-11-1 (5") P Williams, *lost tch hfwy, wl tld off......................................* (33 to 1) 5
1792⁵ QUALITY ASSURED 9-11-6 T Reed, *chsd ldrs till wknd aftr 12th, no ch whn blun and uns rdr 3 out.*
.... (10 to 1 op 66 to 1) ur
1677⁵ HIGHRYMER 10-10-8 (7") Mr A Parker, *lost tch frm hfwy, tld off whn pld up bef 12th................*(33 to 1) pu
1792⁸ SUPREME BLUSHER 7-11-1 K Jones, *lost tch hfwy, tld off whn pld up bef 4 out.....................* (9 to 1) pu
Dist: 1½l, 30l, ½l, 25l. 5m 5.20s. a 15.20s (8 Ran).
(N B Mason), N B Mason

2070 Broughton Handicap Hurdle (0-110 4-y-o and up) £2,305 2m. (1:30)

1582* RELUCTANT SUITOR [103] 5-11-2 (5") D Bentley, *made all, hit 2 out, ran on wl.* (3 to 1 fav op 7 to 2 tchd 4 to 1) 1
1961² J P MORGAN [86] (v) 6-9-13 (5") T Jenks, *al cl up, kpt on wl frm 2 out, no imprsn.................*(8 to 1 op 5 to 1) 2
1728⁷ CHEEKY POT [90] (bl) 6-10-3 (5") P Waggott, *mid-div, sn pushed alng, styd on wl frm 2 out.*(12 to 1 op 10 to 1) 3
1672⁶ TAPATCH (Ire) [110] 6-12-0 J Callaghan, *hld up, hdwy appr 3 out, kpt on same pace frm nxt...* (12 to 1 op 10 to 1) 4
1753⁸ FAMILY LINE [103] 6-11-7 A Maguire, *hld up in tch, effrt whn not much room 2 out, no hdwy frm nxt.*
.... (25 to 1 tchd 10 to 1) 5
1487⁴ CURTAIN FACTORY [84] (bl) 5-10-2 L Wyer, *prmnt till wknd aftr 2 out...................* (6 to 1 op 5 to 1) 6
1961⁴ SAOIRSE (Ire) [84] 6-9-13 (3") D J Moffatt, *lost tch aftr second, styd on wl frm 2 out, nvr dngrs.......* (50 to 1) 7
1614⁶ RICHARDSON [102] 7-11-6 M Dwyer, *lost tch aftr second, nvr dngrs................* (8 to 1 op 6 to 1 tchd 10 to 1) 8
1788² JOHN NAMAN (Ire) [82] 5-10-0 A Dobbin, *chsd ldrs till wknd aftr 3 out.................*(16 to 1 op 14 to 1) 9
1788³ HYPNOTIST [90] 7-10-5 (3") N Bentley, *chsd ldrs till wknd appr 2 out...........* (20 to 1 op 16 to 1) 10
1068² GRIVIJAYA [110] 7-12-0 P Niven, *trkd ldrs, ev ch appr 2 out, sn wknd, eased whn btn.*
.... (15 to 2 op 8 to 1 tchd 10 to 1) 11
1791⁴ LEGITIM [82] 5-9-7 (7") G Tormey, *in tch, effrt aftr 3 out, ch whn blun and uns rdr last.*
.... (8 to 1 op 6 to 1 tchd 9 to 1) ur
1791³ BEACH PATROL (Ire) [82] 6-10-0 D Byrne, *lost tch aftr second, tld off whn pld up bef 2 out..........* (50 to 1) pu
Dist: 2l, 11½l, 5l, 8l, 9l, ¾l, nk, 3½l, 2l, 2½l. 3m 42.00s. a 4.00s (13 Ran).
SR: 37/18/20/35/23/-/-/12/-/ (Joe Buzzeo), M D Hammond

2071 Auchengray Novices' Handicap Chase (5-y-o and up) £2,320 3m (2:00)

910 DONEGAL STYLE (Ire) [69] 6-10-7 A Maguire, *hld up in tch, hdwy aftr 12th, chlgd last, led r-in, drvn out.*
.... (7 to 1 op 6 to 1 tchd 8 to 1) 1
1952 SILVER AGE (USA) [80] 8-11-1 (3") R Farrant, *al prmnt, lft in ld 4 out, hdd r-in, no extr.*
.... (9 to 4 fav op 5 to 2 tchd 3 to 1) 2
1790⁴ JUNIORS CHOICE [73] 11-10-4 (7") Mr A Parker, *rcd wide, prmnt, lost pl aftr tenth, hdwy and ev ch approachiang 4 out, kpt on same pace.*
.... (4 to 1 op 5 to 1 tchd 11 to 2) 3
1740 TRAVEL BOUND [78] 9-11-2 A Dobbin, *cl up, led 11th till hdd 14th, grad wknd...............*(20 to 1 op 16 to 1) 4
1676 RUSHING BURN [71] 8-10-9 B Storey, *beh till styd on frm 14th, not tch ldrs......................*(20 to 1 op 12 to 1) 5
1919 MASTER MISCHIEF [72] (bl) 7-10-10 R Hodge, *sn beh, tld off..............* (8 to 1 op 7 to 1 tchd 10 to 1) 6
2004 THE LORRYMAN (Ire) [90] 6-12-0 T Reed, *led till hdd 11th, sn wknd, tld off..............*(150 to 1 op 200 to 1) 7
1807* QUIET MONEY [86] 7-11-10 C Grant, *prmnt, rdn to ld 14th, slight lead whn f 4 out...........*(5 to 1 op 3 to 1) f
FIRST LORD [85] 8-11-9 P Niven, *prmnt till wknd quickly hfwy, tld off whn pld up bef 13th.*
.... (5 to 1 op 7 to 2 tchd 6 to 1) pu
1790 PANTO LADY [62] 8-9-7 (7") Miss S Lamb, *sn beh, tld off whn pld up bef 13th.........................* (200 to 1) pu
1742 MAUREEN'S FANCY [70] 9-10-8 N Smith, *sn beh, tld off whn pld up bef 13th................*(20 to 1 op 16 to 1) pu
Dist: 2½l, 8l, 3½l, ¾l, 30l, 1½l. 6m 6.40s. a 16.40s (11 Ran).
(Mrs A Taylor (Co Durham)), J H Johnson

2072 Harcros Scottish Juvenile Hurdle Qualifier (4-y-o) £2,295 2m. (2:30)

1569² GENSERIC (Fr) 11-0 R Garritty, *trkd ldrs, outpcd aftr 3 out, styd on wl appr last, led last strds.*
.... (11 to 8 fav op 5 to 4 tchd 6 to 4) 1
1791* REGAL AURA (Ire) 11-0 J Callaghan, *trkd ldrs, led betw last 2, ran on wl frm last, ct last strds.*
.... (7 to 6 op 6 to 4 tchd 2 to 1) 2
1788⁴ BEND SABLE (Ire) 11-0 B Storey, *led aftr second till hdd betw last 2, ch last, one paced.*
.... (9 to 1 op 10 to 1 tchd 11 to 1) 3
1584⁴ CORNFLAKE 10-4 (5") P Waggott, *al prmnt, ev ch betw last 2, wknd last..........*(10 to 1 op 8 to 1) 4
1767 SYLVAN STARLIGHT 10-6 (3") R Farrant, *in tch till wknd aftr 3 out....................* (12 to 1 op 16 to 1) 5
1483⁸ DIXIE HIGHWAY 10-4 (5") N Leach, *led till aftr second, wknd appr 3 out............*(100 to 1 op 50 to 1) 6
1634 KEEN AND CLEAN (Ire) 10-6 (3") D J Moffatt, *sn beh.*
.... (33 to 1) 7
320⁵ COMMANCHE CREEK 11-0 C Grant, *sn beh.*
.... (16 to 1 op 12 to 1 tchd 20 to 1) 8
Dist: Hd, 6l, 1l, 12l, 3½l, 12l, 8l. 3m 54.50s. a 16.50s (8 Ran).
(Mrs S L Worthington), T P Tate

2073 Pathead Conditional Jockeys' Handicap Chase (0-125 5-y-o and up) £2,262 2m. (3:00)

1921² ONE FOR THE POT [108] 9-11-7 T Jenks, *hld up, smooth hdwy to chase ldr 8th, led 4 out, drvn out.*
.... (3 to 1 fav tchd 7 to 2) 1

1678* SONSIE MO [108] 9-11-7 P Williams, *chsd ldr till slightly outpcd aftr 8th, styd on wl frm 4 out.* ....(100 to 30 op 3 to 1 tchd 7 to 2) 2
1678² MAUDLINS CROSS [115] 9-12-0 G Lee, *prmnt till outpcd aftr 8th, no dngr after*...(9 to 2 op 4 to 1 tchd 5 to 1) 3
1737⁴ KAMART [88] 6-10-1 A Dobbin, *chsd ldrs till wknd aftr 8th*..........(12 to 1 op 8 to 1) 4
1583⁵ PRESSURE GAME [87] 11-10-0 F Perratt, *led till hdd 4 out, wknd quickly nxt*..........(16 to 1 op 14 to 1) 5
1737² HAPPY BREED [98] 11-10-11 A Thornton, *in tch till f 7th.* ....(7 to 2 op 3 to 1 tchd 4 to 1) f
COSMIC RAY [88] 9-10-1 C Woodall, *beh whn hmpd and uns rdr 7th*..........(16 to 1 op 10 to 1) ur
Dist: 1½l, 12l, 6l, 1½l. 3m 56.30s. a 6.30s (7 Ran).
SR: 38/36/31/-/ (Philip Davies), M P Naughton

2074 'First Of Many' Stakes National Hunt Flat Race (4,5,6-y-o) £1,722 2m. .(3:30)

CALL EQUINAME 4-10-9 (5*) F Perratt, *led 5 fs, cl up, led 6 out, drw clr frm 4 out, very easily.* (5 to 1 tchd 7 to 1) 1
BENBEATH 4-10-9 (5*) D Bentley, *hld up, hdwy 5 out, styd on wl fnl 2 fs, no ch wth wnr*...... (20 to 1 op 10 to 1) 2
SLAUGHT SON (Ire) 6-11-7 (3*) A Thornton, *trkd ldrs, effrt 4 out, kpt on same pace*... (9 to 2 op 3 to 1 tchd 5 to 1) 3
1779⁴ KING CREOLE (Ire) 5-11-3 (7*) S Haworth, *cl up, led aftr 5 fs, hdd 6 out, one pace fnl 4 furlongs.* ....(5 to 1 tchd 6 to 1) 4
1223⁹ CARIBBEAN SURFER (USA) 5-11-10 A Dobbin, *trkd ldrs frm hfwy, ev ch 4 out, grad wknd.* ....(13 to 2 op 4 to 1 tchd 7 to 1) 5
MANETTIA (Ire) 5-11-5 (7*) M Herrington, *hld up and beh, effrt hfwy, no real hdwy*......(4 to 1 fav op 5 to 2) 6
ONE LAST CHANCE 5-10-12 (7*) S Melrose, *beh till some late hdwy, nvr dngrs*..........(16 to 1) 7
BISHOPS CASTLE (Ire) 6-11-3 (7*) M Clarke, *chsd ldrs till wknd 4 out*..........(10 to 1 tchd 14 to 1) 8
1813² SEAHAWK RETRIEVER 5-11-3 (7*) G Tormey, *mid-div till wknd 4 out*..........(12 to 1 op 8 to 1) 9
1674 HELP YOURSELF (Ire) 5-11-3 (7*) P Carr, *chsd ldrs till wknd 4 out*..........(100 to 1) 10
SHILDON (Ire) 6-11-5 (5*) P Waggott, *trkd ldrs, rdn 4 out, sn wknd*..........(20 to 1 op 16 to 1) 11
TRUE TALENT 4-10-2 (7*) Mr C Bonner, *sn beh, tld off.* ....(33 to 1 op 16 to 1) 12
BILLY BUOYANT 5-11-10 Mr A Robson, *sn beh, tld off.* ....(50 to 1) 13
RIGHT TERM (Ire) 5-11-3 (7*) M Molloy, *beh most of way, f one furlong out*..........(12 to 1 op 5 to 1) f
Dist: 15l, 4l, nk, 8l, ¾l, 7l, 7l, 4l, 10l, 3l. 3m 38.90s. (14 Ran).
(Mrs Karen McLintock), D Eddy

LEOPARDSTOWN (IRE) (soft (races 1,2,4,-5,6,7), heavy (3))
Saturday January 8th
Going Correction: PLUS 1.60 sec. per fur. (races 1,3), PLUS 1.15 (2,4,5,6,7)

2075 Fitzpatricks Hotel Group Chase (5-y-o and up) £4,140 2m 1f.......... (12:35)

1817³ FABRICATOR 8-11-8 K F O'Brien,..........(11 to 4) 1
1985⁴ SORRY ABOUT THAT 8-11-8 P Carberry,..........(8 to 1) 2
1817* CHIRKPAR 7-12-0 Declan Murphy,..........(6 to 4 fav) 3
1847 OH SO GRUMPY 6-11-8 J P Banahan,..........(3 to 1) 4
1847 FURRY STAR 8-11-11 J Jones,..........(9 to 1) 5
1988 INCA CHIEF 10-11-4 T J Taaffe,..........(14 to 1) 6
Dist: 7l, 7l, 1l, 11l. 4m 45.80s. a 30.80s (6 Ran).
SR: 58/51/50/43/35/-/ (Mrs C Marks), J T R Dreaper

2076 Fitzpatricks Castle Hurdle (5-y-o and up) £5,520 2m..................(1:05)

1762* HEIST 5-11-4 P Carberry,..........(Evens fav) 1
1814³ STRALDI (Ire) 6-10-11 (7*) E G Callaghan,..........(13 to 2) 2
1908² ROUBABAY (Ire) 6-11-4 G Bradley,..........(2 to 1) 3
1848³ ANGAREB (Ire) 5-11-0 J Shortt,..........(8 to 1) 4
MANHATTAN CASTLE (Ire) 5-11-0 T J Taaffe,..........(14 to 1) 5
Dist: ¾l, 9l, 2½l, 1½l. 4m 10.40s. a 22.40s (5 Ran).
SR: 50/49/40/33/31/ (Mrs G Mathews), Noel Meade

2077 Tedcastles Oil Handicap Chase (Listed Race - Grade III) (5-y-o and up) £8,280 2m 5f.................. (1:35)

1235⁶ BUCKBOARD BOUNCE [-] 8-10-6 A Maguire, *dsptd ld 1st till led tenth, clr aftr 2 out, pushed out r-in, easily.* ....(6 to 1) 1
1819⁴ BACK DOOR JOHNNY [-] 8-9-7 F Woods, *rear, lost tch 9th, styd on und pres to go poor second appr last, no ch wth wnr*..........(14 to 1) 2
1850⁴ DESERT LORD [-] 8-9-13 C F Swan, *led or dsptd ld 1st till hdd tenth, rdn aftr 3 out, wknd and btn nxt*... (5 to 2) 3
1895 GARAMYCIN [-] 12-12-0 B Sheridan, *rear, tld off tenth.* ....(10 to 1) 4
1850³ DEEP HERITAGE [-] 8-10-7 N Williamson, *led chasing grp till cld on ldrs tenth, rdn aftr 3 out, 3rd and btn whn f last*..........(11 to 8 fav) f
1847² SARAEMMA [-] 8-10-6 J F Titley, *mid-div, prog to track ldrs tenth, uns rdr nxt*..........(9 to 2) ur
Dist: 10l, 15l, dist. 6m 10.70s. a 56.70s (6 Ran).
(J E Mulhern), J E Mulhern

2078 Long Distance Handicap Hurdle (0-150 4-y-o and up) £3,450 3m........ (2:05)

1609⁴ GOLDEN OPAL [-] 9-9-13 (7*) J P Broderick,..........(7 to 1) 1
1854* PRINCE OLE (Ire) [-] 6-11-7 A Maguire,..........(4 to 1) 2
2038⁴ MULLAGHMEEN [-] 8-9-4 (3*) C O'Brien,..........(25 to 1) 3
1828³ SECRET SCEPTRE [-] 7-10-7 F Woods,..........(10 to 1) 4
1899⁴ AEGEAN FANFARE (Ire) [-] 5-11-3 R Hughes,..........(10 to 1) 5
1913⁵ COUMEENOOLE LADY [-] (bl) 7-10-8 (7*) J M Donnelly, ...(12 to 1) 6
1892* MICK O'DWYER [-] 7-11-4 (3ex) F J Flood,..........(7 to 2 fav) 7
1980⁵ KERFONTAINE [-] 9-11-2 G Bradley,..........(12 to 1) 8
2026 REGALING (Ire) [-] 6-10-11 T J Taaffe,..........(9 to 2) 9
1828⁶ MASTER CRUSADER [-] 8-10-6 (3ex) C F Swan,... (4 to 1) 10
Dist: 3l, 14l, 5½l, 6l. 6m 22.30s. a 40.30s (10 Ran).
(Mrs A M Kennelly), Michael Hourigan

2079 The Ladbroke Handicap Hurdle (Listed Race - Grade I) (4-y-o and up) £34,700 2m.................... (2:40)

1894³ ATONE [-] 7-10-8 K F O'Brien, *rear, prog on outsd into mid-div 3 out, smooth hdwy to track ldrs nxt, led bef last, ran on wl*..........(10 to 1) 1
1686⁸ ARCTIC WEATHER (Ire) [-] 5-10-0 T Horgan, *rear of mid-div to hfwy, prog to track ldrs 2 out, styd on r-in.* (25 to 1) 2
1894⁵ JUDICIAL FIELD (Ire) [-] (bl) 5-10-0 A Maguire, *wl-plcd, kpt on und pres strt*..........(10 to 1) 3
1765² DERRYMOYLE (Ire) [-] 5-10-0 P L Malone, *wl-plcd, second aftr 3 out, rdn and no extr appr last, kpt on one pace r-in*..........(16 to 1) 4
1431³ TIME FOR A RUN [-] 7-10-7 C F Swan, *prog frm mid-div to track ldrs 3 out, rdn and btn bef last*..........(5 to 1) 5
1894² THATCH AND GOLD (Ire) [-] 6-10-0 M Duffy, *mid-div, rdn and styd on strt without rching ldrs*..........(66 to 1) 6
COCK COCKBURN [-] 8-10-6 S R Murphy, *prog frm rear into 9th pl 3 out, rdn and no imprsn r-in*..... (33 to 1) 7
1552⁴ HOW'S THE BOSS [-] 8-10-10 M Dwyer, *prog frm mid-div to track ldrs 2 out, ev ch entering strt, rdn and no extr appr last*..........(20 to 1) 8
1849⁵ COCKNEY LAD (Ire) [-] 5-10-0 M P Hourigan, *nvr better than mid-div*..........(40 to 1) 9
1559* LAND AFAR [-] 7-11-3 W Marston, *wl-plcd, led 5th till hdd and wknd bef last*..........(16 to 1) 10
1894⁴ LIFE SAVER (Ire) [-] 5-10-0 P Carberry, *nvr better than mid-div*..........(12 to 1) 11
1465⁵ WELSHMAN [-] 8-10-0 D Gallagher, *wl-plcd till rdn and lost pl 5th*..........(40 to 1) 12
1824² GAELIC MYTH (USA) [-] 7-10-7 Declan Murphy, *rdn in mid-div 3 out, nvr rch ldrs*..........(9 to 1) 13
1234 SHARP INVITE [-] 7-10-7 N Williamson, *rear, nvr rch ldrs.* ....(25 to 1) 14
1755² SATIN LOVER [-] 6-10-9 G McCourt, *prog frm mid-div to track ldrs 5th, 3rd and rdn 2 out, sn btn*.... (4 to 1 fav) 15
831* AIYBAK (Ire) [-] (bl) 6-10-8 B Sheridan, *rear, rdn and no imprsn frm 3 out*..........(25 to 1) 16
1818⁴ GLENCLOUD (Ire) [-] (bl) 6-10-8 G M O'Neill, *al rear.* ....(20 to 1) 17
1906⁶ NOVELLO ALLEGRO (USA) [-] (bl) 6-10-13 R Hughes, *mid-div, rdn and wknd aftr 3 out*..........(40 to 1) 18
1818 THE ILLIAD [-] 13-10-10 F Woods, *trkd ldrs, prog into second 3 out, rdn and btn nxt*..........(10 to 1) 19
1842² KILCASH (Ire) [-] (bl) 6-11-2 M Richards, *wl-plcd till rdn and wknd aftr 3 out, fnshd lme*..........(6 to 1) 20
1906³ ROYAL DERBI [-] 9-11-12 G Bradley, *al rear*...... (33 to 1) 21
CONDOR PAN [-] 11-10-12 T J Taaffe, *al rear*.....(50 to 1) 22
1894⁸ KEPPOLS PRINCE [-] 7-10-0 H Rogers, *led 1st till hdd bef 4th, wknd nxt*..........(66 to 1) 23
1650² NAHAR [-] 9-10-0 A Dicken, *wl-plcd, rdn in 7th pl 3 out, sn btn*..........(16 to 1) 24
1906⁷ SIMENON [-] 8-10-0 C O'Dwyer, *wl-plcd, led 4th till hdd bef nxt, sn rdn and wknd*..........(50 to 1) 25
Dist: 4½l, 1l, 2l, 4½l. 4m 9.70s. a 21.70s (25 Ran).
SR: 47/34/33/31/33/-/ (Robert Sinclair), J R Cox

2080 Ashford INH Flat Race (5-y-o and up) £4,140 2m.................... (3:10)

1903³ KILADANTE (Ire) 5-11-12 Mr A P O'Brien,..........(7 to 1) 1
POWER PACK (Ire) 6-11-6 (5*) Mr B R Hamilton,.. (14 to 1) 2
1852² PIMBERLEY PLACE (Ire) 6-12-4 Mr T Mullins,.. (7 to 4 fav) 3
1581* GALLOWS HILL (Ire) 5-11-11 (3*) Mrs J M Mullins,..(2 to 1) 4
1910* SHERE (Ire) 6-12-1 (3*) Mr J A Nash,..........(11 to 4) 5
JOHNY BELINDA (Ire) 6-11-6 Mr J P Dempsey,... (25 to 1) 6
1897⁷ FAITHFULL FELLOW 7-11-11 Mr A J Martin,..........(6 to 1) 7
Dist: 1l, 6l, 7l, 9l. 4m 16.50s. (7 Ran).
(William Feighery), A P O'Brien

2081 Taney INH Flat Race (4-y-o) £3,105 2m
....(3:40)

RANAGAR (Ire) 11-2 (5") Mr H F Cleary, ...(7 to 2) 1
GRAPHIC IMAGE (Ire) 11-7 Mr A P O'Brien, ...(5 to 2 fav) 2
FEATHER SONG 10-13 (3") Mr R Neylon, ...(9 to 2) 3
ROYAL RANK (USA) 11-4 (3") Miss M Olivefalk, ...(12 to 1) 4
KULIKOVA (Ire) 11-4 (3") Mr J A Nash, ...(5 to 1) 5
WHAT THE HELL (Ire) (bl) 10-9 (7") Mr D A Harney, ..(9 to 2) 6
TIFASI (Ire) 11-4 (3") Mr D Marnane, ...(8 to 1) 7
KITZBUHEL (Ire) 10-13 (3") Mr A R Coonan, ...(8 to 1) 8
CNOC AN RIOG (Ire) 11-4 (3") Mr A E Lacy, ...(12 to 1) 9
Dist: ¾l, 1l, 11l. 4m 28.60s. (9 Ran).

(Mrs V M Khaleq), M Phelan

WARWICK (soft)
Saturday January 8th
Going Correction: PLUS 0.95 sec. per fur. (races 1,2,- 5,7), PLUS 0.82 (3,4,6)

2082 Sherbourne Conditional Jockeys' Handicap Hurdle (0-115 4-y-o and up) £2,469 2m.....................(12:40)

1772[6] IMA DELIGHT [93] 7-10-4 (7") Lorna Brand, chsd ldrs till led
3 out, hdd aftr 2 out, styd on ag'n r-in to ld chme.
................................(15 to 2 op 6 to 1 tchd 8 to 1) 1
1799[2] DJEBEL PRINCE [100] 7-11-4 A Procter, mid-div, hdwy
5th, chlgd 2 out, sn led, rdn r-in, ct cl hme.
..............................(2 to 1 fav tchd 9 to 4 and 7 to 4) 2
1949[2] NOBLE YEOMAN [94] 10-10-12 D Meredith, slwly into strd,
rcd wide, hdwy to chase ldrs 4th, ev ch 2 out, wnt lft
and wknd last.......... (4 to 1 op 7 to 2 tchd 9 to 2) 3
1884* SYLVIA BEACH [97] 8-11-1 D Matthews, dsptd ld till led
3rd, hdd 3 out, sn outpcd...........(7 to 2 op 3 to 1) 4
1799[6] GARDA'S GOLD [84] 11-9-9 (7") W Turton, hdwy and hit
4th, nvr rchd ldrs..................................(25 to 1) 5
LAND OF THE FREE [103] 5-11-7 A Thornton, chsd ldrs till
wknd frm 3 out.......(11 to 1 op 10 to 1 tchd 12 to 1) 6
1868[4] PUNCHBAG (USA) [90] 8-10-8 R Davis, dsptd ld to 3rd,
wknd aftr 3 out......................(8 to 1 tchd 9 to 1) 7
1945[9] L'ORAGE (Ire) [110] 6-11-10 (4") N Collum, rdn appr 3rd, al
beh....................(25 to 1 op 20 to 1 tchd 33 to 1) 8
1599 TIPP DOWN [87] 11-10-5 S Curran, prmnt to 4th, tld off
whn pld up bef 2 out...........................(33 to 1) pu
Dist: Nk, 8l, 6l, 3l, 5l, hd, 5l. 4m 1.90s. a 21.90s (9 Ran).

SR: 16/22/8/5/-/3/-/5/-/ (Mrs P Sly), Mrs P Sly

2083 Leasowes Novices' Hurdle (4-y-o) £1,542 2m.....................(1:10)

453[2] PREROGATIVE (v) 10-12 R Dunwoody, led till hdd briefly
4th, sn led ag'n, rdn and ran on wl frm 2 out.
..............................(2 to 1 fav tchd 11 to 4) 1
1767 JASPER ONE 10-5 (7") R Gantly, chsd ldrs, chlgd 3 out,
styd on one pace frm 2 out.....................(50 to 1) 2
ABSOLUTELY AVERAGE (Ire) 10-12 R Supple, beh, hdwy
5th, styd on frm 3 out, mstk last, not quicken. (33 to 1) 3
1767 GREEN'S FAIR (Ire) 10-12 P Holley, beh till ran on frm 3
out, one pace from 2 out.
................................(14 to 1 op 16 to 1 tchd 20 to 1) 4
1710[4] ANY MINUTE NOW (Ire) 10-12 D Bridgwater, prmnt, led
briefly 4th, wknd 3 out.............(10 to 1 op 5 to 1) 5
DARING PAST 10-12 C Grant, some hdwy frm 3 out, no
headway from nxt....................(9 to 1 op 6 to 1) 6
1990 PHROSE 10-12 D O'Sullivan, pld hrd, prmnt till wknd
aftr 3 out.......................(6 to 1 op 4 to 1) 7
2016[4] MORAN BRIG (v) 10-12 S Hodgson, hdwy to track ldrs
3rd, wknd 3 out.........................(9 to 1 op 8 to 1) 8
1920 HO-JOE (Ire) 10-12 N Smith, al beh....(25 to 1 op 20 to 1) 9
1927[8] NORTHERN JUDY (Ire) 10-4 (3") S Wynne, nvr dngrs.
................................(16 to 1 op 14 to 1) 10
PLAIN SAILING (Fr) 10-12 M A FitzGerald, chsd ldrs to 5th.
................................(33 to 1 op 20 to 1) 11
1705[2] LODESTONE LAD (Ire) 10-9 (3") D Meredith, al beh.
...............................(4 to 1 tchd 9 to 2) 12
FORMAESTRE (Ire) 10-7 A Tory, al beh.............(25 to 1) 13
NEVER SO LOST 10-12 W McFarland, in tch to 5th.
................................(33 to 1 op 25 to 1) 14
TAKE A FLYER (Ire) 10-12 I Lawrence, beh frm 4th, tld off
whn pld up bef 3 out.......................(33 to 1) pu
Dist: 4l, 1½l, 12l, 1l, nk, 4l, 1½l, 3½l, 3½l, ¾l. 4m 1.00s. a 21.00s (15 Ran).

SR: 26/22/20/8/7/6/2/-/-/ (D A Johnson), M C Pipe

2084 Burton Hill Novices' Chase (6-y-o and up) £3,590 2½m 110yds........(1:40)

1842[6] HONEST WORD 9-10-12 R Dunwoody, led second to 3rd,
styd pressing ldr till led aftr tenth, came clr frm 4 out.
..............................(2 to 1 fav tchd 5 to 2 and 7 to 4) 1
1420[2] COMEDY SPY 10-10-12 M A FitzGerald, beh 7th, hdwy
11th, ran on frm 3 out, no ch whn wnr.
...............................(8 to 1 op 5 to 1) 2

KNAVE OF CLUBS 7-10-12 D Bridgwater, beh 7th, hdwy
aftr tenth, styd on frm 3 out, no ch wth wnr.
................................(14 to 1 op 10 to 1) 3
1346[5] MUNKA 8-10-12 C Maude, not fluent, beh frm 7th, some
hdwy from 4 out.......(9 to 1 op 6 to 1 tchd 10 to 1) 4
1947[2] VILLA RECOS 9-10-12 B Powell, led 3rd to 4th, styd chasing ldrs till mstk and wknd four out.
................................(16 to 1 op 20 to 1 tchd 25 to 1) 5
933[6] WILLIE MCGARR (USA) 9-10-12 Richard Guest, prmnt,
mstk 8th, wknd tenth..............(25 to 1 op 20 to 1) 6
1770[5] HOWARYADOON 8-10-12 H Davies, beh frm tenth.
................................(8 to 1 tchd 7 to 1 and 10 to 1) 7
1934[3] FREE JUSTICE 10-10-12 C Llewellyn, led to second, styd
in tch till wknd 12th, broke blood vessel.
................................(11 to 2 op 5 to 1 tchd 7 to 1) 8
1493[2] SUNDAY PUNCH 8-10-12 E Murphy, led 4th to 6th, led
ag'n 7th till aftr tenth, wkng whn f four out.
................................(11 to 2 op 5 to 1) f
1776[4] CHRISTMAS GORSE 8-10-12 J Frost, hdwy 11th, no
imprsn whn brght dwn 4 out......(12 to 1 op 8 to 1) bd
1474[8] MOUNTSHANNON 8-10-12 B Clifford, beh frm 5th, tld off
whn pld up bef 4 out........................(50 to 1) pu
Dist: 3l, nk, 12l, 1l, 20l, 15l. 5m 19.80s. a 24.80s (11 Ran).

SR: 4/1/-/-/-/-/ (Mrs H J Clarke), M C Pipe

2085 Warwick Premier Chase (6-y-o and up) £4,777 3¼m..............(2:10)

2013 GAY RUFFIAN 8-11-3 R Dunwoody, jmpd slwly 5th, chsd
ldr 9th till lft clr 14th....(6 to 5 op Evens tchd 5 to 4) 1
1881[5] RUFUS 8-11-3 B Powell, not jump wl, rdn aftr tenth, wnt
poor second appr 14th.
................................(10 to 1 op 12 to 1 tchd 14 to 1) 2
1273 RU VALENTINO 10-11-3 C Llewellyn, chsd ldr till wknd
appr 14th, tld off................(16 to 1 op 12 to 1) 3
1993 MIDNIGHT CALLER 8-11-10 J Osborne, led and jmpd wl
till f 14th.......................(11 to 10 fav tchd 11 to 8) f
Dist: dist, dist. 6m 53.80s. a 39.80s (4 Ran).

(Frank Jones), M C Pipe

2086 Whitnash Handicap Hurdle (0-135 4-y-o and up) £3,817 2½m 110yds...(2:40)

1619 BOLLIN MAGDALENE [104] 6-10-0 L Wyer, trkd ldrs, jmpd
rght 4th, chlgd 6th, led 7th, clr frm 2 out, easily.
................................(4 to 1 op 3 to 1) 1
1884 SURCOAT [104] 7-10-0 L Harvey, in tch, hdwy 6th, chsd
wnr aftr 3 out, no imprsn........(6 to 1 op 9 to 2) 2
1955[2] ZEALOUS KITTEN (USA) [104] 6-10-0 J Osborne, chsd ldrs
till lost pos 7th, sn rdn, styd on one pace frm 2 out.
................................(15 to 8 fav op 11 to 4 tchd 7 to 4) 3
SEA PATROL [104] (bl) 7-10-0 R Dunwoody, led to 7th,
wknd 2 out.......................(6 to 1 op 9 to 2) 4
WHY RUN [106] 9-10-2[2] G Rowe, in tch till wknd aftr 3
out.......................(33 to 1 op 20 to 1) 5
1643[2] SMILING CHIEF (Ire) [104] 6-9-7 (7") T Dascombe, hdwy to
chase ldrs 7th, wknd frm 3 out.
................................(17 to 2 op 8 to 1 tchd 10 to 1) 6
1971[4] COKENNY BOY [132] 9-11-7 (7") L O'Hare, al beh.
................................(5 to 1 op 6 to 1 tchd 13 to 2) 7
Dist: 3½l, 2l, 5l, 1l, 8l, 20l. 5m 16.90s. a 29.40s (7 Ran).

(Sir Neil Westbrook), M H Easterby

2087 Bear Handicap Chase (0-140 5-y-o and up) £4,825 2m................(3:10)

1802[3] L'UOMO PIU [93] 10-10-0 B Powell, led second till appr
6th, led ag'n 3 out, drvn out........(7 to 1 op 6 to 1) 1
1798[3] DR ROCKET [113] 9-11-3 (3") D Meredith, hdwy to chase
ldrs 6th, rdn and no imprsn frm 2 out.
................................(13 to 2 op 5 to 1) 2
1947* KIBREET [109] 7-11-2 S Earle, prmnt till outpcd 6th, ran
on ag'n und pres frm 3 out.........(7 to 2 op 3 to 1) 3
1933[3] AL HASHIMI [121] 10-12-0 R Dunwoody, rear 7th, nvr
dngrs aftr............(14 to 1 op 10 to 1 tchd 16 to 1) 4
1877* MEGA BLUE [115] 9-11-8 P Niven, led to second, lost pos
appr 6th, nvr dngrs aftr.
................................(2 to 1 fav op 5 to 2 tchd 3 to 1) 5
1925 TRUBLION [97] 9-10-4 Richard Guest, prmnt till led
appr 6th, hdd 3 out, sn wknd.....(12 to 1 op 16 to 1) 6
1737[3] BOSTON ROVER [115] 9-11-8 M Brennan, beh till hdwy
8th, sn wknd.......................(13 to 2 op 5 to 1) 7
1363 GOLDEN FREEZE [120] 12-11-13 M A FitzGerald, beh till
refused 5th.......................(10 to 1 op 7 to 1) ref
Dist: 7l, 3l, hd, 12l, 3½l, 20l. 4m 10.00s. a 18.00s (8 Ran).

SR: 24/37/30/42/24/2/-/-/ (C J Spencer), A Barrow

2088 Hampton Hill Novices' Handicap Hurdle (0-100 5-y-o and up) £2,059 2m
....(3:40)

1747[6] PRINCETHORPE [63] 7-9-11 (3") D Meredith, prmnt, led 3
out, drvn out.......................(14 to 1 op 20 to 1) 1
1390[5] MASTER MURPHY [63] 5-10-8 B Powell, beh, steady hdwy
frm 5th, not fluent last, one pace.. (13 to 2 op 6 to 1) 2
1877[2] BASILICUS (Fr) [86] 5-11-9 Richard Guest, al frnt rnk, rdn
and one pace frm 2 out.............(6 to 1 op 4 to 1) 3

1969² DIVINE CHANCE (Ire) [87] 6-11-10 C Llewellyn, *sn wl th, rdn and styd on same pace appr 2 out....(7 to 1 op 6 to 1)* 4
1926⁷ BOWLAND GIRL (Ire) [63] 5-9-11 (3*) S Wynne, *drpd rear 3rd, hdwy 2 out, styd on r-in......* (14 to 1 op 10 to 1) 5
1951³ TROOPING (Ire) [83] 5-11-6 L Wyer, *led to 3 out, rdn 2 out, sn wknd...............* (7 to 2 fav tchd 4 to 1) 6
1708* PROJECT'S MATE [83] 7-10-13 (7*) P McLoughlin, *chsd ldrs 3rd, wknd appr 2 out.............* (10 to 1) 7
1794⁶ GIVE ME HOPE (Ire) [64] 6-9-8 (7*) Guy Lewis, *chsd ldrs 3rd, wknd appr 2 out.....* (9 to 1 op 10 to 1 tchd 16 to 1) 8
1515 ANDARE [72] 5-10-9 S Earle, *nvr dngrs.........* (33 to 1) 9
1950³ CAOIMSEACH (Ire) [73] 6-10-10 S Mackey, *beh frm 4th.* ....* (10 to 1 op 7 to 1) 10
956 MINT-MASTER [70] 9-10-0 (7*) K Brown, *chsd ldrs to 4th.* ....* (33 to 1) 11
1804 ALTISHAR (Ire) [68] 6-10-5 P Holley, *hdwy whn mstk and uns rdr 5th........................* (7 to 1 op 13 to 1) ur
Dist: 1l, 3l, ¾l, 5l, 2l, 1l, 4l, 10l, nk, 20l. 4m 1.70s. a 21.70s (12 Ran).
SR: 7/6/26/26/-/15/14/-/-/ (G A Farndon), B R Cambidge

SOUTHWELL (A.W) (std)
Monday January 10th
Going Correction: PLUS 0.40 sec. per fur.

2089 **Fibresand Handicap Hurdle (0-130 4-y-o and up) £1,691 2½m..... (12:45)**

1928* COURT CIRCULAR [104] (v) 5-11-0 Diane Clay, *al hndy, led 5th to hfwy, rallied, drw level last, led and ran on r-in.* ....* (11 to 4 op 9 to 4) 1
1863³ MIZYAN (Ire) [118] 6-11-9 (5*) J Twomey, *al wl plcd, led hfwy, hit 8th, hdd aftr nxt, rallied und pres to draw level nxt 3, kpt on.* ...... (15 to 8 fav op 2 to 1 tchd 9 to 4 and 7 to 4) 2
2060 HAVE A NIGHTCAP [105] 5-11-1 D Gallagher, *led to 5th, rallied to rgn ld aftr 4 out, hdd and no extr r-in.* ....* (11 to 2 op 7 to 2) 3
2034 RIMOUSKI [99] 6-10-9 Mr J Cambidge, *hit 1st, trkd ldrs till lost grnd quickly frm 7th, tld off.* (12 to 1 tchd 16 to 1) 4
1949³ CELCIUS [99] (bl) 10-10-9 R Dunwoody, *patiently rdn, effrt and reminders 5 out, tld off last 3.* ....* (3 to 1 op 2 to 1 tchd 100 to 30) 5
Dist: ½l, 1l, dist, 4l. 4m 57.60s. a 16.60s (5 Ran).
SR: -/13/ (B A S Limited), W Clay

2090 **All Weather Handicap Hurdle (0-120 4-y-o and up) £1,722 2m....... (1:15)**

1792⁴ REGAL ROMPER (Ire) [88] 6-10-3 Richard Guest, *settled gng wl, improved 3 out, drvn ahead betw last 2, ran on.* ....* (5 to 1 op 6 to 1 tchd 7 to 1) 1
1422² EXPLOSIVE SPEED (USA) [113] 6-11-9 (5*) D Bentley, *jmpd rght most of way, led till hdd briefly appr 3 out, rdn and headed betw last 2. one pace.* ....* (4 to 1 op 3 to 1 tchd 9 to 2) 2
1487⁵ SASKIA'S HERO [92] 7-10-7 D Byrne, *nvr far away, mstk and rdn 4 out, rallied and hit 2 out, one pace.* ....* (7 to 4 tchd 15 to 8) 3
1101⁵ MRS JAWLEYFORD (USA) [105] 6-11-6 M Ranger, *trkd ldrs, led briefly appr 3 out, rdn and blun nxt, sn lost tch.* ....* (13 to 8 fav op 7 to 4) 4
Dist: 2l, 10l, 12l. 3m 58.60s. a 12.60s (4 Ran).
SR: 13/36/5/6/ (Mrs S Smith), Mrs S J Smith

2091 **Dam Busters Novices' Handicap Hurdle (4-y-o and up) £1,784 2m.... (1:45)**

2018* OCTOBER BREW (USA) [97] (bl) 4-11-13 (7ex) R Dunwoody, *al hndy, hit second, jnd ldr hfwy, definite advantage bef 2 out, clr whn hit last, ran on.* ....* (11 to 8 op Evens tchd 6 to 4) 1
1125⁵ MR GENEALOGY (USA) [98] (bl) 4-12-0 A Maguire, *trkd ldg pair, reminders and struggling 5 out, rallied und pres frm betw last 2.* ....* (11 to 10 fav op 6 to 4 on tchd 6 to 4) 2
1877⁶ PESSOA [73] 7-10-3 Richard Guest, *tried to make all, jnd hfwy, hdd and rdn appr 2 out, one pace.* ....* (9 to 2 op 7 to 2 tchd 5 to 1) 3
Dist: 2½l, 3l. 4m 6.20s. a 20.20s (3 Ran).
(Martin Pipe Racing Club), M C Pipe

2092 **Submerged Novices' Hurdle (4-y-o and up) £1,698 2¾m............ (2:15)**

1658* ALLEGATION (v) 4-10-13 R Dunwoody, *not fluent, made all, quickened clr frm 8th, won easing dwn.* ....* (6 to 1 on op 8 to 1 on tchd 4 to 1 on) 1
1473 NO SHOW (Ire) (bl) 4-10-7 W Humphreys, *took keen hold, wth wnr till lost tch frm 6 out, nrly f 4 out, tld off.* ....* (25 to 1 op 16 to 1) 2
2058 HICKELTON HOUSE 10-11-4 A Maguire, *patiently rdn, improved to track wnr 9th. fdd aftr nxt, pld up lme bef 3 out.* ....* pu
Dist: Dist. 5m 42.00s. a 33.00s (3 Ran).
(Southern Depots), M C Pipe

2093 **Bookmaker's Delight Maiden Hurdle (4-y-o and up) £1,938 2¼m....(2:45)**

2057² YAAKUM 5-11-0 (5*) J Twomey, *tucked away, improved on bit to nose ahead bef 4 out, gng wl whn lft clr 2 out.* ....* (11 to 10 on tchd 5 to 4 on and Evens) 1
1969³ ARCTIC LIFE (Ire) 5-11-5 A Maguire, *led, clr to hfwy, hdd bef 4 out, lost pl nxt, rallied und pres r-in.* ....* (4 to 1 op 9 to 4) 2
1053 BALTIC EXCHANGE (Can) 5-11-5 R Dunwoody, *settled gng wl, hit 5th, improved to draw level 3 out, niggled alng whn nrly uns rdr nxt, not reco'r.* ....* (7 to 2 op 3 to 1 tchd 9 to 2) 3
1673⁴ ON CUE (bl) 7-11-5 W Worthington, *trkd ldrs, struggling to hold pl appr 4 out, tld off........* (25 to 1 op 12 to 1) 4
1835 RITA'S RISK 5-11-5 J Ryan, *wl on terms till fdd und pres bef strt, tld off........* (50 to 1 op 33 to 1 tchd 66 to 1) 5
1731 ABSOLUTLEY FOXED 5-11-0 T Wall, *trkd ldr to hfwy, sn rdn and lost tch, tld off whn pld up bef 3 out.* ....* (11 to 1 op 10 to 1 tchd 14 to 1) pu
Dist: 8l, 1l, 20l, 8l. 4m 26.50s. a 14.50s (6 Ran).
SR: 18/10/9/ (S Whittle), J E Banks

2094 **Noah's Ark Selling Hurdle (4-y-o and up) £1,799 2¾m.............(3:15)**

2058 DOUALAGO (Fr) (bl) 4-11-7 R Dunwoody, *made all, quickened clr aftr 4 out, drvn out frm last.* ....* (5 to 4 fav op 6 to 4 tchd 2 to 1) 1
1931² BOLD STAR (bl) 4-10-7 J Osborne, *al hndy, effrt aftr 4 out, drvn alng frm nxt, styd on r-in.* ....* (4 to 1 op 11 to 4 tchd 9 to 2) 2
1519⁵ NORTHERN OPTIMIST 4-10-13 (7*) Mr J L Llewellyn, *nvr far away, ev ch 4 out, drvn alng bef nxt, sn outpcd.* ....* (14 to 1) 3
1299 SMARTIE LEE 7-10-13 (7*) P McLoughlin, *ran in snatches, drvn up to chal appr 4 out, fdg und pres whn blun badly 2 out.....................* (8 to 1 op 5 to 1) 4
1421⁵ FILM LIGHTING GIRL 8-10-13 A Maguire, *steadied strt, improved 4th, struggling fnl circuit, tld off frm 5 out.* ....* (6 to 1 op 9 to 2) 5
1965⁵ BONAR BRIDGE (USA) (h) 4-10-7 N Williamson, *tracking ldr whn f 6th............* (9 to 1 op 3 to 1 tchd 10 to 1) f
1948⁵ THANKSFORTHEOFFER (v) 6-11-4 P McDermott, *chsd ldg bunch, struggling to keep up hfwy, poor 5th whn blun and uns rdr 3 out.............* (20 to 1 tchd 25 to 1) ur
MALAQUETTE 12-10-13 P Harley, *rdn alng to hold pl 5th, sn tld off, pld up aftr 4 out.................* (50 to 1) pu
1287⁷ HAUT-BRION (Ire) 5-11-4 Richard Guest, *trkd ldrs, effrt fnl circuit, in tch whn pld up lme bef 4 out.* ....* (25 to 1 op 20 to 1) pu
Dist: 3l, 25l, 1½l, dist. 5m 37.60s. a 28.60s (9 Ran).
(Martin Pipe Racing Club), M C Pipe

2095 **Seventh National Hunt Flat Race (4,5,6-y-o) £1,784 2m............ (3:45)**

HANDMAIDEN 4-9-13 (7*) S Mason, *al gng best, led o'r 2 fs out, clr ins last, readily.* (5 to 1 op 3 to 1 tchd 6 to 1) 1
NORMAN'S CONVINCED 4-10-4 (7*) L Reynolds, *nvr far away, led 7 fs out till hdd o'r 2 out, no ch wth wnr.* ....* (5 to 1 op 6 to 1 tchd 7 to 2) 2
CREST 4-10-4 (7*) C Woodall, *red freely in clr ld till hdd 7 fs out, rallied and kpt on same pace fnl furlong.* ....* (6 to 1 op 10 to 1) 3
1126⁴ CREAG DHUBH 5-11-0 (7*) T Dascombe, *settled off the pace, bustled alng to improve appr strt, nvr on terms.* ....* (9 to 4 fav op 11 to 10 on) 4
DANCING BAREFOOT 5-10-9 (7*) P McLoughlin, *settled wth chasing bunch, struggling 7 fs out, tld off.* ....* (16 to 1 op 14 to 1) 5
STANLEY HOUSE (Ire) 4-11-7 Mr Chris Wilson, *chsd ldg bunch for a m, sn tld off...........* (12 to 1 op 8 to 1) 6
1376⁵ GARLAND OF GOLD 5-11-4 (3*) R Davis, *chsd clr ldg trio for a m, sn tld off..............* (12 to 1 tchd 14 to 1) 7
SCOTCH 'N IRISH (Ire) 5-11-0 (7*) D Towler, *settled off the pace, lost tch hfwy, tld off.* ....* (14 to 1 op 12 to 1) 8
BENS BIG BROTHER 4-10-4 (7*) N Juckes, *tld off aftr 6 fs, pld up 5 furlongs out, found to have bkn down.* ....* (12 to 1 op 16 to 1) pu
RAJAH'S FANDANGO (bl) 5-11-7 Mr B Leavy, *settled in rear, broke nr fore aftr 6 fs, pld up, destroyed.* ....* (20 to 1 op 16 to 1) pu
Dist: 10l, hd, dist, dist, 2l, 1½l, dist. 3m 45.50s. (10 Ran).
(R Fenwick-Gibson), M J Camacho

THURLES (IRE) (heavy)
Monday January 10th

2096 **Cashel Hurdle (5-y-o) £2,243 2¼m ....(12:45)**

1610* SAM VAUGHAN (Ire) 11-4 (5*) Mr W M O'Sullivan, .. (6 to 1) 1
1822⁴ OVER THE JORDAN (Ire) 11-5 C O'Dwyer, ...(10 to 1) 2
1815³ MAXWELTON BRAES (Ire) 11-5 R Hughes, ... (11 to 2) 3

1681* MALIHABAD (Ire) 11-9 F J Flood, ...(5 to 4 on)   4
1821³ WEJEM (Ire) 11-5 S R Murphy, ...(7 to 1)   5
1821* MR SNAGGLE (Ire) 11-6 (3°) C O'Brien, ...(5 to 1)   6
1821⁶ DONNASOO (Ire) 10-9² (7°) Mr M J Spillane, ...(25 to 1)   7
1821 ORMOND BEACH (Ire) 11-5 James Jones, ...(100 to 1)   8
1815⁵ SWIFT SAILER (Ire) 11-5 G Bradley, ...(10 to 1)   pu
Dist: 8l, 3l, 2l, 4l. 4m 49.40s. (9 Ran).

(E J O'Sullivan), Eugene M O'Sullivan

2097 Irish National Hunt Novice Hurdle Series (5-y-o and up) £4,140 2m (1:15)

1781* KLAIRON DAVIS (Fr) 5-11-6 T J Taaffe, ...(11 to 4 on)   1
1899² EAGLE ROCK (USA) 6-11-5 (3°) C O'Brien, ...(4 to 1)   2
1822⁵ ELIADE (Ire) 5-10-7 G Bradley, ...(12 to 1)   3
1814 BUCK'S DELIGHT (Ire) 6-11-2 C O'Dwyer, ...(20 to 1)   4
1824⁶ ROSE APPEAL 8-11-6 C F Swan, ...(7 to 1)   f
Dist: 3l, 6l, dist. 4m 14.90s. (5 Ran).

(C Jones), A L T Moore

2098 Holiday Opportunity Handicap Hurdle (0-116 4-y-o and up) £2,657 2¼m (1:45)

1911² RIYADH DANCER (Ire) [-] 4-10-6 (2°) J R Barry, ...(9 to 1)   1
1823² RATHCORE [-] 7-11-3 C O'Brien, ...(7 to 2 jt-fav)   2
1851 PANDA (Ire) [-] 6-11-12 T P Treacy, ...(7 to 1)   3
1495* PERCY BRENNAN [-] 7-10-0 (4°) J M Donnelly, ...(6 to 1)   4
1823⁷ MANTAS MELODY (Ire) [-] 6-10-7 (2°) T J O'Sullivan,
. . . .(12 to 1)   5
1987⁴ JACINTA'S BOY [-] 7-10-10 T J Mitchell, ...(12 to 1)   6
1980* AMARI QUEEN [-] 7-10-8 (2°,4ex) M G Cleary, (7 to 2 jt-fav)   7
1500⁷ COOL MOSS [-] 8-10-12 (2°) P A Roche, ...(16 to 1)   8
1232³ DANGEROUS REEF (Ire) [-] 6-10-8 (2°) T P Rudd, . .(8 to 1)   9
1853 CHRISTY MOORE (Ire) [-] 4-9-13 (2°) R Dolan, ...(25 to 1)   10
1823 NIKISH (USA) [-] 5-10-1 (4°) B M Duggan, ...(14 to 1)   11
1912⁶ EXILE RUN (Ire) [-] (bl) 6-9-13 (2°) M A Davey, ...(10 to 1)   12
Dist: 1½l, 8l, 2l, 1l. 4m 44.30s. (12 Ran).

(Miss C M Coady), Patrick Joseph Flynn

2099 Killinan Hurdle (4-y-o) £2,243 2m
. . . .(2:15)

1983* NANNAKA (USA) 10-8 G Bradley, ...(10 to 9 on)   1
1853⁴ DANCING VISION (Ire) 10-9 C F Swan, ...(7 to 2)   2
1816⁸ MAN OF ARRAN (Ire) 10-4 (5°) T J O'Sullivan, ...(14 to 1)   3
1853⁷ NURSE MAID (Ire) 10-4 James Jones, ...(20 to 1)   4
1853⁶ SAINT HILDA (Ire) 9-13 (5°) K P Gaule, ...(12 to 1)   5
1853 PERSIAN GEM (Ire) 10-4 C O'Dwyer, ...(12 to 1)   6
1846⁵ FLORA WOOD (Ire) 9-11 (7°) J M Sullivan, ...(9 to 1)   7
1846⁸ STATE PRINCESS (Ire) 10-4 R Hughes, ...(7 to 1)   8
1846⁷ TENCA (Ire) 10-9 S R Murphy, ...(14 to 1)   9
1983 LAKE OF LOUGHREA (Ire) 10-9 J Shortt, ...(10 to 1)   10
1853 BAEZA 10-2 (7°) Mr K Whelan, ...(40 to 1)   11
1377 RED ROOSTER (Ire) (bl) 10-9 L P Cusack, ...(50 to 1)   pu
Dist: 2l, ½l, 8l, 5½l. 4m 9.70s. (12 Ran).

(Mrs P Mullins), P Mullins

2100 Horse And Jockey Handicap Chase (0-102 5-y-o and up) £2,243 3m. . (2:45)

1826* ANOTHER EXCUSE (Ire) [-] 6-11-12 (5°,8ex) Mr W M O'Sul-
livan, ...(7 to 4 fav)   1
1826 DE MONTE BOY [-] 9-10-8 (7°) M D Murphy, ...(14 to 1)   2
2025² MERLYNS CHOICE [-] (bl) 10-10-4 C F Swan, ...(4 to 1)   3
1826⁹ ANOTHER RUSTLE [-] 11-11-4 W T Slattery Jnr, . .(14 to 1)   4
1499⁷ KIL KIL CASTLE [-] 7-9-13 (7°) Mr A O'Shea, ...(25 to 1)   5
1857* DUSKY LADY [-] 8-11-6 (3ex) G M O'Neill, ...(8 to 1)   6
2025⁴ THE PHOENO [-] (bl) 8-9-13 S R Murphy, ...(14 to 1)   7
1901⁴ CONNA RAMBLER [-] 11-11-6 (3°) D P Murphy, . . .(16 to 1)   8
1915³ SHUIL LE CHEILE [-] 7-10-0 (3°) C O'Brien, ...(9 to 1)   9
941⁷ PALMROCK DONNA [-] 7-10-2 (5°) P A Roche, ...(20 to 1)   f
1915 MONEY MADE [-] (bl) 7-9-5 (7°) J P Broderick, ...(50 to 1)   f
1979 SYLVIA'S SAFFRON [-] (bl) 8-10-7 I F Woods, ...(33 to 1)   pu
2036² BOG LEAF VI [-] 11-9-2 (5°) T J O'Sullivan, ...(8 to 1)   pu
1832 BANJO BELLE [-] 9-9-4 (3°) D Bromley, ...(50 to 1)   pu
2025 MUST DO [-] 8-11-5 J Shortt, ...(14 to 1)   pu
WHAT A MINSTREL [-] 8-10-0 C O'Dwyer, ...(50 to 1)   pu
Dist: 2l, 1½l, 20l, 5l. 6m 43.90s. (16 Ran).

(Kilshannig Racing Syndicate), Eugene M O'Sullivan

2101 Phil Sweeney Memorial Chase (5-y-o and up) £2,760 2¾m 110yds. . . . .(3:15)

1763⁴ FARNEY GLEN 7-11-7 C F Swan, ...(9 to 2)   1
1988⁴ NEW CO (Ire) 5-11-7 C O'Dwyer, ...(5 to 1)   2
1893² SPUR OF THE MOMENT 7-11-6 J P Banahan, (2 to 1 fav)   3
1915² THE WEST'S ASLEEP 9-11-7 J Magee, ...(10 to 1)   4
1913² GOOLDS GOLD 8-11-4 (3°) D P Murphy, ...(7 to 1)   5
1856³ BLAZING DAWN 7-12-0 S H O'Donovan, ...(8 to 1)   6
1900³ DOONEGA (Ire) 6-11-4 (3°) C O'Brien, ...(9 to 1)   f
Dist: 6l, 3½l, 2½l, 10l. 6m 31.40s. (7 Ran).

(M Harney), W Harney

2102 Archerstown I N H Flat Race (5 & 6-y-o) £2,243 2m. . . . .(3:45)

1903² REDEEMYOURSELF (Ire) 5- M Phillips, ...(2 to 1 fav)   1

KELSO (soft (races 1,3,5), heavy (2,4,6)) Wednesday January 12th
Going Correction: PLUS 1.75 sec. per fur. (races 1,3,5), PLUS 1.82 (2,4,6)

2103 Bet With The Tote Novices' Chase Qualifier (6-y-o and up) £2,948 3m 1f
. . . .(1:10)

2004* LOTHIAN PILOT 7-11-3 T Reed, led to 3rd, steadied, hdwy
aftr 12th, led last, styd on wl . . .(7 to 4 fav tchd 2 to 1)   1
2004 PADDY MORRISSEY 7-10-10 A Dobbin, in tch, rdn alng
aftr 12th, styd on frm 4 out, not trble wnr.
. . . .(66 to 1 op 25 to 1)   2
1115* ROAD BY THE RIVER (Ire) 6-11-3 M Dwyer, wth ldrs, mstk
15th, one pace 2 out. . . . .(12 to 1 op 10 to 1)   3
1723 KILCOLGAN 7-10-10 B Storey, beh, hmpd 7th, hdwy to
track ldrs hfwy, kpt on same pace frm 4 out.
. . . .(20 to 1 tchd 33 to 1)   4
1750 FINCH'S GEM 6-10-10 N Doughty, led 3rd to 7th, prmnt
till wknd 15th. . . . .(8 to 1 op 7 to 1)   5
1862 BIG MAC 7-10-10 G Grant, cl up, led tenth to last, wknd.
. . . .(11 to 2 op 5 to 1)   6
1605⁴ LADY BE BRAVE 11-10-5 R Hodge, beh most of way.
. . . .(50 to 1 op 33 to 1 tchd 66 to 1)   7
1477 TALLYWAGGER 7-10-10 J Callaghan, mstks, beh 14th.
. . . .(5 to 2 op 2 to 1)   8
2004³ DEEP HAVEN 9-10-10 K Jones, led 7th to tenth, wknd aftr
13th. . . . .(50 to 1 op 33 to 1)   9
1918 GRAAL LEGEND 9-10-10 P Niven, f 7th.
. . . .(66 to 1 op 33 to 1)   f
1477 ROUGHSIDE 9-10-10 Mr D Mactaggart, lost tch and pld up
aftr 14th. . . . .(66 to 1 op 25 to 1)   pu
Dist: 7l, 1½l, 2l, nk, 11½l, 12l, 6l, 15l. 7m 0.30s. a 58.30s (11 Ran).

(Crawford, Wares & Hamilton), L Lungo

2104 Oswald Hughes Novices' Hurdle (4-y-o and up) £2,127 2¾m 110yds (1:40)

MISS PLUM 5-11-1 P Niven, hld up, hdwy to track ldrs
hfwy, led last, pushed clr.
. . . .(5 to 1 op 3 tchd 6 to 1)   1
1918² SAVOY 7-11-12 N Doughty, cl up, slight ld frm 7th to last,
no extr. (13 to 8 on op 6 to 4 tchd 7 to 4 on and 5 to 4 on)   2
1745² MAJORITY MAJOR (Ire) 5-11-6 C Grant, in tch, effrt 8th,
chlgd 2 out, wknd appr last. . . . .(10 to 1 op 7 to 1)   3
2008⁵ BELLS HILL LAD 7-11-12 A Dobbin, cl up till wknd aftr
8th. . . . .(20 to 1 op 14 to 1)   4
1722² PAR-BAR (Ire) 6-11-1 D Byrne, made most to 7th, wknd
aftr nxt. . . . .(5 to 1 op 9 to 2 tchd 6 to 1)   5
1320⁴ CORSTON RAMBO 7-11-6 T Reed, in tch, jnd ldrs 8th,
wknd quickly appr 2 out, virtually pld up r-in.
. . . .(10 to 1 op 8 to 1 tchd 12 to 1)   6
1131 DEEPLY ROYAL 7-10-8 (7°) Mr A Manners, refused 1st.
. . . .(100 to 1)   ref
1938 MOSSIMAN (Ire) 6-11-6 S Turner, chsd ldrs, mstk 7th, sn
beh, tld off whn pld up bef last. . . . .(100 to 1)   pu
1582 KIRKCALDY (Ire) 5-11-1 (5°) P Williams, mstk 1st, sn beh,
lost tch hfwy, tld off whn pld up bef 2 out . . . .(66 to 1)   pu
Dist: 7l, 5l, 10l, nk, dist. 6m 4.80s. a 53.80s (9 Ran).

(Lucayan Stud), Mrs M Reveley

2105 Farewell To Law Handicap Chase for the Stewart Wight Memorial Trophy (0-130 5-y-o and up) £3,452 3m 1f (2:10)

1941² ISLAND GALE [98] 9-10-1⁴ (3°) A Thornton, prmnt, jnd ldrs
12th, outpcd aftr 2 out, styd on wl frm last to ld nr
finish. . . . .(9 to 1 op 16 to 1)   1
1917² RUN PET RUN [107] 9-10-10 A Dobbin, al cl up, led aftr
last, wknd and ct nr finish.
. . . .(9 to 4 fav op 5 to 2 tchd 11 to 4)   2
1939⁴ FORTH AND TAY [98] 12-10-1⁶ (5°) P Williams, beh, effrt
aftr 15th, styd on wl frm 2 out, nrst finish.
. . . .(14 to 1 op 12 to 1)   3
1285⁵ THE MOTCOMBE OAK [103] 8-10-6 P Niven, trkd ldrs, led 2
out, hdd and wknd aftr last.
. . . .(5 to 2 op 9 to 4 tchd 11 to 4)   4

288

1917³ WHAAT FETTLE [125] 9-12-0 N Doughty, *cl up, led 9th to 2
out, sn btn*..................(12 to 1 op 6 to 1) 5
1585 RAWYARDS BRIG [104] 11-10-7⁷ Mr D Mactaggart, *mstks,
led to 9th, sn lost pl, f 13th*......(100 to 1 op 66 to 1) f
2004 CEILIDH BOY [98] 8-10-1¹ B Storey, *in tch till wknd aftr
15th, no ch whn blun and uns rdr 2 out*.
...................(9 to 2 op 4 to 1 tchd 11 to 2) ur
BOLD SPARTAN [99] 11-9-11 (5*) F Perratt, *al beh, tld off
whn pld up bef 2 out*. (12 to 1 op 10 to 1 tchd 14 to 1) pu
2006² ZAM BEE [108] 8-10-11 T Reed, *cl up till wknd quickly
aftr 13th, tld off whn pld up bef 3 out*.
....................(12 to 1 op 10 to 1) pu
Dist: 2l, 2¹/₂l, 7l, 1¹/₂l. 60.40s. a 48.40s (9 Ran).
SR: 27/34/22/20/40/-/ (John McCune), D McCune

2106 Cheviot Rentals Modular Marquees 'National Hunt' Novices' Hurdle (4-y-o and up) £2,110 2m 110yds...... (2:40)

1918³ CARNETTO 7-10-13 (7*) F Leahy, *settled in chasing grp,
led aftr 4th till appr 3 out, led betw last 2, kpt on wl frm
last*......................(5 to 1 tchd 7 to 1) 1
1099² KENILWORTH LAD 6-11-5 P Niven, *hld up in tch, hdwy
hfwy, chlgd last, kpt on, no imprsn*.
...................(4 to 1 tchd 5 to 1) 2
1223* THE GREY MONK (Ire) 6-11-5 N Doughty, *chsd clr ldr, led
appr 3 out till betw last 2, sn btn*.
...................(11 to 4 op 9 to 4 tchd 3 to 1) 3
CALLERNOY (Ire) 4-10-0 (7*) Mr A Manners, *beh till styd on
frm 3 out, nvr dngrs*....................(100 to 1) 4
1418⁵ SCARF (Ire) 6-11-5 M Dwyer, *in tch, no hdwy frm 5th*.
...................(12 to 1 op 10 to 1) 5
RALLEGIO 5-11-5 A Dobbin, *nvr on terms*......(50 to 1) 6
1959⁵ DON'T TELL JUDY (Ire) 6-11-5 B Storey, *beh hfwy*.
...................(25 to 1 op 20 to 1 tchd 33 to 1) 7
1938³ EASBY JOKER 6-11-5 R Garritty, *settled in chasing grp,
trkd ldrs hfwy till wknd quickly appr 2 out*.
...................(9 to 4 fav op 7 to 4) 8
2003 FINE OAK 7-11-1¹ Mr D Robertson, *sn beh, tld off*.
....................(500 to 1) 9
ROMAN SWORD 6-10-7 (7*) Mr A Parker, *in tch whn mstk
and uns rdr 4th*......................(100 to 1) ur
1810 TIME PIECE (Ire) 6-11-0 (5*) J Supple, *keen hold, led and
sn clr, hdd aftr 4th, wknd quickly, tld off whn pld up
bef 2 out*......................(100 to 1) pu
1918 SAMS-THE-MAN 6-11-5 C Hawkins, *sn beh, tld off whn
pld up bef 2 out*. (200 to 1 op 500 to 1 tchd 1000 to 1) pu
PRINCE BALTASAR 5-11-5 C Grant, *sn beh, tld off whn pld
up bef 2 out*......................(100 to 1) pu
Dist: 1¹/₂l, 12l, 10l, 3l, 4l, 15l, 10l, dist. 4m 18.70s. a 35.70s (13 Ran).
SR: 35/32/20/-/7/3/ (Mrs R Brewis), R Brewis

2107 Wilfred & Patricia Crawford Memorial Handicap Chase (0-135 5-y-o and up) £3,322 2m 1f................. (3:10)

1727 BELDINE [94] 9-10-8 T Reed, *hld up in tch, effrt whn hit 3
out and nxt, stumbled betw last 2, led last, sn clr*.
...................(8 to 1 op 7 to 1 tchd 9 to 1) 1
2006³ PINEMARTIN [101] 11-10-10 (5*) N Leach, *cl up, led 5th, hit
3 out, hdd last, kpt on same pace*.
...................(10 to 1 tchd 12 to 1) 2
1659¹ ABSAILOR [100] (v) 10-10-9 (5*) P Williams, *led to 5th,
outpcd aftr 8th, kpt on frm 2 out*.
...................(10 to 1 tchd 10 to 1) 3
1727² POSITIVE ACTION [101] 8-11-1 A Dobbin, *cl up, rdn appr 3
out, sn btn*......................(3 to 1) 4
1727¹ TERRIBLE GEL (Fr) [110] 9-11-10 P Niven, *hld up in tch, f
5th*......................(10 to 1 tchd 12 to 1) f
Dist: 7l, 2l, 12l. 4m 41.40s. a 35.40s (5 Ran).
SR: 24/24/21/10/-/ (Lt-Col W L Monteith), P Monteith

2108 Peter & Gillian Allan Conditional Jockeys' Handicap Hurdle (0-110 4-y-o and up) £2,460 2¹/₄m........... (3:40)

2005² ARAGON AYR [90] 6-10-13 A Dobbin, *hld up in tch, hdwy
to ld 2 out, kpt on und pres*.
...................(13 to 8 fav op 5 to 4 tchd 7 to 4) 1
1936² SANSOOL [98] 8-11-4 (3*) B Harding, *led to second, prmnt,
outpcd aftr 3 out, styd on wl frm nxt*.
...................(12 to 1 op 8 to 1) 2
1860³ BALLYLORD [91] 10-11-0 P Williams, *led betw appr 2 out,
one pace*......................(9 to 2 op 5 to 1 tchd 11 to 2) 3
1940⁵ GOLDEN REVERIE (USA) [77] 6-10-0 F Perratt, *prmnt, mstk
6th, outpcd aftr 3 out, sn on frm last*.
...................(12 to 1 op 10 to 1) 4
2005⁷ ELGIN [82] 5-10-5 D J Moffatt, *nvr nr to chal*.
...................(16 to 1 tchd 20 to 1) 5
1961* IN A STORM [94] 5-11-3 E Husband, *hld up, effrt
aftr 3 out, no real hdwy*. (7 to 2 op 4 to 1 tchd 9 to 2) 6
1738 BOLD MOOD [80] 5-10-3 D Bentley, *chsd ldrs, led appr 2
out, sn hdd and wknd*......................(33 to 1) 7
2005 PIT PONY [77] 10-10-0 N Leach, *al beh*.......(50 to 1) 8
LOVING OMEN [79] (bl) 7-10-2⁴ A Thornton, *chsd ldrs till
wknd aftr 6th*......................(25 to 1) 9

1924 MAC RAMBLER [78] 7-9-12 (3*) G Tormey, *in tch, effrt appr
3 out, sn wknd*......................(33 to 1) 10
1357⁷ CAPTAIN TANCRED (Ire) [78] 6-10-1 N Bentley, *refused to
race*...................(14 to 1 op 16 to 1 tchd 12 to 1) l
Dist: 2¹/₂l, 15l, nk, 8l, hd, ³/₄l, 15l, nk, sht-hd. 4m 49.40s. a 42.40s (11 Ran).
(Lt-Col W L Monteith), P Monteith

LINGFIELD (A.W) (std)
Wednesday January 12th
Going Correction: PLUS 0.10 sec. per fur.

2109 Indian Handicap Hurdle (0-130 4-y-o and up) £1,630 2¹/₂m............(1:15)

1689² SCOTONI [104] 8-11-0 D O'Sullivan, *trkd ldr, led tenth,
rdn frm 3 out, hld on gmely*............(7 to 2 op 9 to 1) 1
2089² MIZYAN (Ire) [118] 6-12-0 A Maguire, *hld up in tch, mstk
5th, rdn appr 3 out, rallied last, kpt on*.
...................(11 to 10 on 11 to 10 tchd 5 to 4) 2
1890² LUSTY LAD [114] 9-11-10 H Davies, *led till hdd tenth, styd
hndy, still ev ch last, no extr and eased whn btn*.
...................(5 to 2 op 2 to 1) 3
1964 COSMIC DANCER [108] (bl) 7-11-4 A Carroll, *hld up, niggled alng hfwy, stdly lost tch, tld off*. (8 to 1 op 9 to 2) 4
Dist: ¹/₂l, 2¹/₂l, dist. 4m 58.10s. a 27.10s (4 Ran).
(D G & D J Robinson), R J O'Sullivan

2110 Pacific Handicap Hurdle (0-120 4-y-o and up) £1,645 2m.............(1:45)

2065² RARFY'S DREAM [96] 6-10-13 A Maguire, *al hndy, led 3
out, clr frm nxt, cmftbly*.
...................(6 to 4 on op 5 to 4 on tchd 13 to 8 on) 1
1945* WHIPPERS DELIGHT (Ire) [107] 6-11-10 D Meade, *wth ldr,
rdn frm 3 out, no same pace*.
...................(5 to 2 op 9 to 4 tchd 11 to 4) 2
1328⁴ MURPHY [102] 10-11-5 M Richards, *jmpd wl, sn led, hdd 3
out, wknd frm nxt....*. (10 to 1 op 6 to 1 tchd 11 to 1) 3
FORGE [95] 6-10-12 Richard Guest, *hld up in tch till
outpcd appr 3 out*......(13 to 2 op 9 to 2 tchd 8 to 1) 4
1526⁵ LUCKY BLUE [83] 7-9-7 (7*) T Thompson, *not jump wl, sn
in rear, tld off*....................(50 to 1 op 33 to 1) 5
Dist: 4l, 20l, 25l, dist. 3m 39.80s. a 6.80s (5 Ran).
SR: 33/40/15/-/-/ (J A Bianchi), J E Banks

2111 Atlantic Novices' Handicap Hurdle (4-y-o and up) £1,660 2m......... (2:15)

2066³ NEARLY HONEST [55] 6-10-4 A Tory, *led frm second, jnd 3
out, rdn and ran on wl frm nxt*............(6 to 4 jt-
fav op 11 to 8) 1
870 ERLKING (Ire) [75] 4-11-3 (7*) D Fortt, *al hndy, effrt 8th, sn
chalg, no extr appr last*....................(6 to 4 jt-
fav op 11 to 8 tchd 13 to 8) 2
1414⁸ QUINTA ROYALE [62] 7-10-11 Mrs J Gault, *beh 4th, rnwd
effrt 8th, one pace frm nxt*........(10 to 1 op 8 to 1) 3
1597⁸ BLAKE'S TREASURE [60] 7-10-2 (7*) Guy Lewis, *led to second, styd hndy, rdn 7th, wknd frm nxt*.
...................(6 to 1 op 4 to 1 tchd 7 to 1) 4
KINGSFOLD PET [79] 5-12-0 H Davies, *al beh*.
...................(16 to 1 op 10 to 1) 5
Dist: 5l, 20l, 25l, 15l. 3m 47.20s. a 14.20s (5 Ran).
(Jock Cullen), R J Hodges

2112 Baltic Maiden Hurdle (4-y-o and up) £1,830 2¹/₄m (2:45)

964² WILD STRAWBERRY 5-11-0 M Richards, *led frm second,
clr tenth, shaken up betw last 2, eased r-in*.
...................(6 to 4 on op 11 to 8 on tchd 5 to 4 on) 1
1515⁶ MILZIG (USA) 5-11-5 D O'Sullivan, *hld up, steady hdwy
frm 7th, chsd wnr appr 3 out, no further imprsn betw
last 2*....................(11 to 2 op 7 to 2 tchd 6 to 1) 2
2063² MUSICAL PHONE 4-10-9 P Holley, *chsd ldr till rdn aftr
tenth, sn unbl to quicken*.
...................(14 to 1 op 8 to 1 tchd 16 to 1) 3
1707 NO DEBT 6-11-0 B Powell, *wl beh till moderate late
hdwy, nvr a dngr*....................(50 to 1 op 25 to 1) 4
1710³ MUHTASHIM (Ire) 4-10-9 A Maguire, *in tch, reminders 7th,
wknd frm 9th*....................(11 to 4 op 2 to 1) 5
1522⁹ NATASHA NORTH 4-10-4 E Byrne, *prmnt till wknd frm
7th*...................(10 to 1 op 33 to 1) 6
1880 SOLO CHARTER 4-10-9 S Earle, *al beh*.
...................(14 to 1 op 12 to 1 tchd 16 to 1) 7
1472⁶ PIERRE BLANCO (USA) 5-11-5 Richard Guest, *mstk 5th,
shrtlvd effrt 8th, sn wknd*......(50 to 1 op 20 to 1) 8
RUMBELOW 5-11-5 S McNeill, *led till aftr 1st, sn lost pl
and struggling frm 6th, tld off*....(50 to 1 op 20 to 1) 9
Dist: 5l, 25l, 20l, 5l, 15l, 1¹/₂l, dist. 4m 12.00s. a 11.00s (9 Ran).
(Copyforce Ltd), Miss B Sanders

2113 North Selling Hurdle (4-y-o and up) £1,645 2³/₄m................. (3:15)

2065 GREENWINE (USA) 8-11-1 M Richards, *made all, clr 12th,
unchlgd*......................(7 to 4 fav op 6 to 4) 1

NATIONAL HUNT RESULTS 1993-94

2063⁴ MUTUAL BENEFIT (bl) 7-11-4 Lorna Vincent, *in tch till lost pl 6th, ran on ag'n appr 3 out, sn chasing wnr, no further imprsn betw last 2.*
.........................(9 to 2 op 7 to 2 tchd 5 to 1)   2
2063³ DO BE WARE (v) 4-10-7 A Maguire, *wth ldr, mstks tenth and 11th, sn rdn and wknd.........*(9 to 4 op 5 to 4)   3
LADY POLY 6-11-13 Leesa Long, *al beh, tld off.*
.........................(12 to 1 tchd 14 to 1)   4
ALL ELECTRIC 9-11-4 P Holley, *in tch, mstk 5th, rdn tenth, sn wknd, beh whn pld up bef last.*
.........................(4 to 1 op 6 to 1)   pu
Dist: 12l, 25l, dist. 5m 17.80s. a 18.80s (5 Ran).
(Tony Clay), Mrs L Richards

2114 Biscay National Hunt Flat Race (4,5,6-y-o) £1,660 2m.............(3:45)

1996⁶ LINTON ROCKS 5-11-2 (5*) A Dicken, *made all, rdn 3 fs out, styd on wl.* (Evens fav op 5 to 4 on tchd 11 to 10)   1
1126⁷ ASLAR (Ire) 5-11-0 (7*) P Moore, *wth ldr thrght, rdn 2 fs out, unbl to quicken.* (100 to 30 op 2 to 1 tchd 7 to 2)   2
LITTLE BERTHA 5-10-9 (7*) Guy Lewis, *in tch till rdn o'r 4 fs out, sn btn..........*(4 to 1 op 5 to 1 tchd 11 to 2)   3
RUSTIC ROMANCE 6-10-9 (7*) T Thompson, *prmnt till rdn 5 fs out, wknd...............*(20 to 1 op 10 to 1)   4
1126 TREENS FOLLY 5-11-0 (7*) L Dace, *beh, niggled alng hfwy, sn tld off......*(12 to 1 op 10 to 1 tchd 16 to 1)   5
BELMORE CLOUD 5-11-2 D O'Sullivan, *beh, pushed alng o'r 5 fs out, wknd quickly.*
.........................(11 to 2 op 4 to 1 tchd 6 to 1)   6
Dist: 2½l, 25l, 8l, 8l, 20l. 3m 37.10s. (6 Ran).
(Mrs C A Morrison), T Thomson Jones

SOUTHWELL (A.W) (std)
Wednesday January 12th
Going Correction: PLUS 0.35 sec. per fur.

2115 Tempest Juvenile Novices' Hurdle (4-y-o) £1,553 2m.............(1:00)

PRIDWELL 10-12 R Dunwoody, *settled gng wl, nosed ahead on bit bef 2 out, quickened clr last.*
.........................(11 to 2 op 11 to 4)   1
1767⁷ STRICTLY PERSONAL (USA) 10-12 L Harvey, *nvr far away, chlgd appr 2 out, crowded and one pace betw last two.*
.........................(11 to 2 op 8 to 1)   2
1767⁶ LYFORD CAY (Ire) (bl) 10-12 J Osborne, *trkd ldrs gng wl, led on bit appr 3 out, hdd bef nxt, edgd lft betw last 2, not keen.*
.........(13 to 8 fav op 6 to 4 tchd 7 to 4 and 9 to 4)   3
QAFFAL (USA) 10-12 J Railton, *tried to make all, hdd appr 3 out, fdd nxt.................*(14 to 1)   4
1767⁵ FINE SIR 10-12 S Smith Eccles, *pressed ldrs, effrt and bustled alng 4 out, fdd frm nxt......*(13 to 1)   5
1767 TANGO IN PARIS (Arg) 10-12 G McCourt, *beh and reminders 4th, tld off frm hfwy...............*(33 to 1)   6
DOC SPOT 10-12 D Gallagher, *struggling frm 4th, sn tld off................................*(20 to 1 op 16 to 1)   7
1647 TONY'S MIST 10-9 (3*) R Farrant, *struggling and beh 4th, tld off..............................*(14 to 1 op 10 to 1)   8
2000⁴ HEATHYARDS BOY 11-5 D Murphy, *ran in snatches, lost grnd quickly hfwy, tld off whn pld up bef 3 out.*
.........................(5 to 1 op 4 to 1)   pu
Dist: 15l, 3½l, 5l, 2l, 20l, 20l, 15l. 3m 57.30s. a 11.30s (9 Ran).
SR: 27/12/8/3/1/-/   (Pond House Racing), M C Pipe

2116 King Lear Selling Hurdle (4-y-o and up) £1,845 2½m.............(1:30)

1395⁷ KAHER (USA) 7-11-13 (5*) T Jenks, *led till appr 1st, styd hndy till led ag'n hfwy, driver clr last 3.*
......(3 to 1 fav op 5 to 2 tchd 100 to 30 and 7 to 2)   1
1532 NANNY MARGARET (Ire) 4-9-11 (5*) A Bates, *nvr far away, blun 5 out, chsd wnr aftr nxt, one pace......*(12 to 1)   2
1801⁷ OMIDJOY (Ire) 4-10-2 R Dunwoody, *settled midfield, drvn to improve 4 out, no imprsn on ldg pair frm nxt.*
.........................(4 to 1 op 11 to 4)   3
2058² TESEKKUREDERIM 7-11-6 Diane Clay, *sn beh, blun 4th, drvn alng and tld off hfwy, styd on frm 3 out, nvr nrr.*
.........................(7 to 2 op 5 to 2)   4
1534³ SAILOR'S DELIGHT 10-10-13 (7*) Mr S Joynes, *trkd ldrs, feeling pace and many reminds frm hfwy, tld off appr 3 out.........*(10 to 1 op 8 to 1 tchd 11 to 1)   5
1931⁸ CREAGMHOR (bl) 4-10-0 (7*) Mr J L Llewellyn, *chsd ldrs, struggling fnl circuit, tld off frm 4 out.*
.........................(12 to 1 op 5 to 1)   6
1613⁸ SIE AMATO (Ire) 5-11-6 D Gallagher, *drvn up frm midfield hfwy, struggling appr 4 out, tld off bef nxt.*
.........................(7 to 1 op 5 to 1)   7
1927⁷ FATAL SHOCK 4-10-2 J Ryan, *struggling hfwy, sn tld off.*
.........................(12 to 1 tchd 14 to 1)   8
2033 CASHTAL RUNNER 5-11-6 Pat Caldwell, *led appr 1st till hdd hfwy, blun 7th, sn tld off....*(25 to 1 op 20 to 1)   9
Dist: 10l, 15l, 8l, 10l, 8l, 6l, 20l. 5m 4.30s. a 23.30s (9 Ran).
(F J Mills), N A Twiston-Davies

2117 As You Like It 'National Hunt' Novices' Hurdle (5-y-o and up) £1,784 2¾m.............(2:00)

197² CREWS CASTLE 7-10-5 (7*) W J Walsh, *nvr far away, led on bit, drvn clr betw last 2, styd on.*
.........................(7 to 2 op 9 to 4)   1
1809⁴ MEKSHARP 7-10-7 (5*) T Eley, *improved off the pace to join issue fnl circuit, ev ch and rdn 3 out, hdd nxt, rallied...................................*(16 to 1)   2
2015⁷ COZZI (Fr) 6-10-9 (5*) R Farrant, *patiently rdn, took clr order fnl circuit, ridden appr 3 out, sn outpcd.*
.........................(25 to 1 op 20 to 1)   3
1588 HIGHLAND FRIEND (bl) 6-10-12 M A FitzGerald, *in tch, drvn up into midfield fnl circuit struggling aftr 4 out, sn btn...................*(20 to 1 op 50 to 1)   4
1813⁹ ALTESSE ROXANNE 5-10-0 (7*) Mr B Pollock, *al struggling in rear, plodded round fnl circuit............*(33 to 1)   5
1809² MILLIES OWN 7-10-11 (7*) Chris Webb, *tracking ldrs and uns rdr 1st.........*(9 to 4 fav op 2 to 1 tchd 5 to 2)   ur
1813⁴ ST BRAD (Ire) 6-10-12 D Murphy, *struggling to keep in tch and reminders 8th, pld up bef nxt.* (10 to 1 op 8 to 1)   pu
1707 POP FESTIVAL 5-10-7 W Marston, *al struggling, tld off whn pld up aftr 8th...........*(25 to 1 op 20 to 1)   pu
OHCUMGACHE 6-10-7 R Dunwoody, *trkd ldr, led aftr second till aftr 4 out, wknd quickly and pld up betw last 2.........................*(6 to 1 op 4 to 1)   pu
1715⁵ WALTON THORNS (bl) 6-10-12 J Osborne, *led aftr second, styd hndy, hit 8th, blun and lost grnd 5 out, pld up bef 3 out...................*(20 to 1 op 14 to 1)   pu
1797⁵ ROSENTHAL 6-10-0 (7*) T Murphy, *chsd ldg bunch, struggling fnl circuit, tld off whn pld up bef 2 out.*
.........................(20 to 1 op 16 to 1)   pu
Dist: 3½l, dist, nk, dist. 5m 40.00s. a 31.00s (11 Ran).
(Mrs T McCoubrey), J R Jenkins

2118 Shakespeare Novices' Handicap Hurdle (0-100 4-y-o and up) £1,553 2m.............(2:30)

1931* STAR MARKET [72] 4-10-0 T Wall, *al hndy, drvn alng frm 3 out, kpt on grimly to ld last strd...* (8 to 1 op 5 to 1)   1
216² MERLINS WISH (USA) [100] 5-12-0 R Dunwoody, *al wl plcd, led aftr 5th, hrd pressed and hit 3 out, kpt on und pres, jst ct....*(7 to 4 fav op 6 to 4 tchd 9 to 4 and 5 to 2)   2
1926⁵ GREEN'S SEAGO (USA) [76] 6-10-0 D Gallagher, *drvn alng to keep in tch 4th, relentless prog to chal 3 out, kpt on one pace frm betw last 2.*
.........................(13 to 2 op 5 to 1 tchd 7 to 1)   3
1927² BAYRAK (USA) [80] 4-10-8 J Osborne, *unruly strt, improved frm off the pace to chal frm 3 out, rdn and no extr nxt..............*(7 to 2 op 3 to 1 tchd 4 to 1)   4
BALADIYA [72] 7-10-0 N Mann, *settled gng wl, imprvg whn hit 5th, blun and lost pl 4 out, rallied and hit nxt, no extr........................*(10 to 1 op 8 to 1)   5
1809 RUSTIC GENT (Ire) [72] (v) 6-10-0 M Hourigan, *chsd ldg bunch, drvn up to chal appr 3 out, fdg und pres whn nrly uns rdr nxt.......................*(20 to 1)   6
1794² FORGETFUL [79] 5-10-7 D J Burchell, *rcd keenly in ld, hdd 4th, struggling appr four out, tld off.*
.........................(6 to 1 op 5 to 1 tchd 7 to 1)   7
1948⁷ KEMALS DELIGHT [72] 7-10-0 Jacqui Oliver, *not fluent, tld off frm 8th, plodded round........*(20 to 1 op 14 to 1)   8
1153² GRUBBY [72] 5-9-11 (3*) S Wynne, *trkd ldrs, led briefly 4th till aftr nxt, lost tch bef four out, tld off.*
.........................(20 to 1 tchd 33 to 1)   9
Dist: Hd, 1½l, 12l, ½l, 25l, 1½l, 8l, 1½l. 3m 57.30s. a 11.30s (9 Ran).
SR: 15/43/13/9/-/-/   (Midland Markets Ltd), Mrs P M Joynes

2119 Macbeth Handicap Hurdle (0-115 4-y-o and up) £1,993 2m.............(3:00)

2062* TRISTAN'S COMET [84] 7-10-0 (6ex) B Dalton, *trkd ldg 5, improved to ld 4 out, quickened away betw last 2, easily....................*(6 to 1 tchd 13 to 2)   1
1278⁴ EASTERN MAGIC [92] 6-10-1 (7*) Chris Webb, *nvr far away, effrt and bustled alng 3 out, styd on, not pace of wnr.................................*(7 to 1)   2
3082⁷ HOWGILL [84] 8-9-11 (3*) S Wynne, *al hndy, bustled alng whn ldr quickened 3 out, kpt on same pace frm nxt.*
.........................(14 to 1 op 8 to 1)   3
1947 MISAAFF [85] 11-10-1 R Dunwoody, *trkd ldg pair, nosed ahead hfwy, hdd 4 out, one pace last 3.*
.........................(9 to 1 op 10 to 1)   4
1863⁴ GYMCRAK SOVEREIGN [108] 6-11-10 L Wyer, *made most to hfwy, styd hndy till rdn and no extr frm 3 out.*
.........................(9 to 4 fav op 2 to 1 tchd 5 to 2)   5
1812 SANTA PONSA BAY [84] (v) 7-10-0 M Hourigan, *last and pushed alng, lost tch frm hfwy, tld off.*
.........................(14 to 1 op 20 to 1)   6
1535⁴ KELLY'S DARLING [86] 8-9-11 (5*) S Curran, *in tch, improved into midfield hfwy, grad wknd appr 3 out.*
.........................(12 to 1 op 8 to 1)   7
1627 DALLISTON (NZ) [89] 8-10-5 R Marley, *chsd ldg bunch, struggling to keep up whn bad mstk 5th, reminders nxt, sn tld off..................*(12 to 1 op 8 to 1)   8

290

1719 SEE NOW [88] 9-10-4⁴ M A FitzGerald, *trkd ldg quartet,*
rdn and lost pl appr 4 out, tld off whn pld up bef nxt.
....(20 to 1) pu
Dist: 8l, 3½l, 4l, 1l, 20l, 6l, 2½l. 3m 56.80s. a 10.80s (9 Ran).
SR: 20/20/8/5/27/-/   (D Wilcox), J L Harris

2120 Hamlet Handicap Hurdle (0-105 4-y-o and up) £1,943 2½m . . . . (3:30)

1772⁷ ELEGANT KING (Ire) [96] 5-11-6 M A FitzGerald, *al wl plcd,*
led appr 3 out, sn clr, styd on well frm last.
...................................(6 to 1 op 4 to 1) 1
2060² FLYAWAY (Fr) [88] 9-10-12 D Gallagher, *patiently rdn,*
improved to chase war frm 3 out, ridden and kpt on
same pace from betw last 2.
...............................(10 to 1 op 8 fav op 7 to 4 tchd 9 to 4) 2
1603³ ST VILLE [100] 8-11-3 (7*) S Mason, *settled off the pace,*
improved appr 3 out, styd on same pace aftr nxt.
...................................(9 to 2 op 3 to 1) 3
1810³ BALLERINA ROSE [79] 7-10-0 (3*) A Procter, *al hndy, led*
aftr 6th, hdd and drvn alng appr 3 out, fdd frm nxt.
...................................(5 to 1 op 9 to 2) 4
1485⁹ BURN BRIDGE (USA) [82] (v) 8-10-6² Peter Caldwell, *trkd*
ldg bunch, hit 3rd, pushed alng hfwy, struggling aftr 4
out...............................(10 to 1 op 8 to 1) 5
1740 JUPITER MOON [81] 5-10-5 D Murphy, *led till appr 1st,*
chsd alng to hold pl hfwy, tld off approaching 3 out.
...............................(17 to 2 op 12 to 1 tchd 8 to 1) 6
1933⁶ AIR COMMANDER [98] 9-11-1 (7*) Mr S Joynes, *led bef 1st,*
hdd aftr 6th, lost tch frm 4 out, tld off.
...................................(20 to 1 op 14 to 1) 7
1721⁷ JOSIE SMITH [76] 10-10-0⁵ (5*) D Matthews, *struggling to*
keep up hfwy, sn tld off...........(40 to 1 op 33 to 1) 8
Dist: 3l, 3l, 12l, 3½l, 15l, dist, 3½l. 4m 58.70s. a 17.70s (8 Ran).
                                            (L Fust), A P Jarvis

CAGNES-SUR-MER (FR) (good) Thursday January 13th

2121 Grande Course de Haies de Cagnes (Hurdle) (5-y-o and up) £22,857 2½m . . . . (1:00)

LE ROI THIBAULT (Fr) 5-10-8 J-Y Beaurain, ... 1
PREDILECTION (Fr) 7-10-8 P Havas, ... 2
GAMBELLAN (Fr) 6-10-1 E Duverger, ... 3
2049 ABLE PLAYER (USA) 7-9-11 D Parker, *nvr dngrs.* 8
Dist: Dist, 2½l, 7½l, 1l, dist, dist, dist. 4m 57.40s. (10 Ran).
                                    (Haras Du Reuilly), G Doleuze

GOWRAN PARK (IRE) (soft) Thursday January 13th

2122 Eircell Maiden Hurdle (4-y-o) £3,105 2m. . . . . (1:10)

BALAWHAR (Ire) 11-0 C F Swan, ...(11 to 10 op) 1
1983² CARHUE STAR (Ire) 9-13 (5*) T J O'Sullivan, ... (4 to 1) 2
1983⁴ SERANERA (Ire) 9-13 (5*) M G Cleary, ... (8 to 1) 3
      HUNCHEON CHANCE 10-2 (7*) J P Broderick, ...(50 to 1) 4
706 SHANGANOIR (Ire) 10-4 P Carberry, ...(12 to 1) 5
1853⁸ TOUCHING MOMENT (Ire) 11-0¹ T J Taaffe, ... (12 to 1) 6
1846 MANGANS HILL (Ire) 10-9 P M Verling, ...(33 to 1) 7
1846⁴ FRIENDLY FLYER (Ire) 10-4 K F O'Brien, ... (8 to 1) 8
      HOME PARK (Ire) 10-2 (7*) Mr G Kearns, ...(33 to 1) 9
1983 FALCARRAGH (Ire) 10-9 J Shortt, ...(33 to 1) 10
1983⁹ BOTHSIDESNOW (Ire) 11-0 H Rogers, ...(14 to 1) 11
2099⁶ PERSIAN GEM (Ire) 10-4 C O'Dwyer, ...(14 to 1) 12
      RISKY GALORE 10-4 (5*) K P Gaule, ...(16 to 1) 13
1846 LITTLE TINCTURE (Ire) 10-4 (7*) T P Rudd, ...(33 to 1) 14
      NOELS DANCER (Ire) 10-9 P L Malone, ...(33 to 1) 15
      LIBRAN ROCK (Ire) 10-9 J A White, ...(16 to 1) 16
1432 SIMPLE DANCER (Ire) 10-9 S R Murphy, ... (20 to 1) 17
      ONODI (Ire) 9-11 (7*) Mr M Hyland, ... (66 to 1) 18
Dist: 2l, 11l, ¾l, ¾l. 4m 11.90s. (18 Ran).
                                      (Michael Tabor), E J O'Grady

2123 I.S.D.N. Maiden Hurdle (5-y-o and up) £3,105 2m. . . . . (1:40)

1912² UNCLE BABY (Ire) 6-11-1 (5*) K P Gaule, ... (8 to 1) 1
1903⁴ BUTCHES BOY 5-11-10 S H O'Donovan, . . (7 to 4 fav) 2
2038³ PUNTERS BAR 7-11-9 (5*) P A Roche, ...(12 to 1) 3
1978⁴ KAWA-KAWA 7-10-10 (5*) T J O'Sullivan, ... (10 to 1) 4
1982* CREATIVE BLAZE (Ire) 5-11-5 C F Swan, ... (8 to 1) 5
2038⁷ DOZING STAR (Ibl) 8-11-7 (7*) J P Broderick, ...(12 to 1) 6
1827⁴ BALLYBODEN 7-11-6 K F O'Brien, ...(14 to 1) 7
1897⁶ TWIN RAINBOW 7-12-0 L P Cusack, ... (9 to 2) 8
1496 TRIMMER WONDER (Ire) 6-11-2 (7*) M Kelly, ... (20 to 1) 9
2038 ABBEY EMERALD 8-10-12 (3*) T P Treacy, ... (50 to 1) 10
1760 COURSING GLEN (Ire) 6-11-6 M Duffy, ...(20 to 1) 11
      ANNIE FOX 7-10-10 (5*) M M Treacy, ...(33 to 1) 12
2041 GREAT ADVENTURE (Ire) 6-10-13 (7*) Mr P M Cloke,
....(20 to 1) 13
1815 FATHER GREGORY (Ire) 5-10-13 (3*) T J Mitchell, (50 to 1) 14

1892 RATHFARDON (Ire) 6-11-6 A Powell, ...(50 to 1) 15
      SUMMING UP 7-11-6 P M Verling, ... (25 to 1) 16
2038⁵ SHIMMERETTO 8-10-10 (5*) T P Rudd, ...(33 to 1) 17
1849⁶ FAIRYHILL RUN (Ire) 6-11-1 B Sheridan, ... (10 to 1) 18
2041⁶ CASH IT IN (Ire) 6-10-12 (3*) D P Murphy, ...(16 to 1) 19
1892⁹ ST CRISTOPH 7-11-9 Mr W P Mullins, ... (8 to 1) su
Dist: 2½l, 2l, hd, ½l. 4m 13.90s. (20 Ran).
                                    (N P Doyle), Patrick Joseph Flynn

2124 Chargecard Handicap Hurdle (0-130 4-y-o and up) £3,795 2m 1f. . . . . . (2:10)

1855* IMPERIAL CALL (Ire) [-] 5-11-9 (4ex) G M O'Neill, . . .(5 to 1) 1
1912* SUPER TACTICS (Ire) [-] 6-10-3 (5*,3ex) P A Roche,
....(3 to 1 fav) 2
1855² PARLIAMENT HALL [-] 8-11-7 (7*) J P Broderick, . .(13 to 2) 3
1232⁷ CASH CHASE (Ire) [-] 6-10-5 L P Cusack, ...(12 to 1) 4
1980 RICH TRADITION (Ire) [-] 6-11-3 G Bradley, ... (6 to 1) 5
1907⁴ STARK CONTRAST (USA) [-] 5-11-6 H Rogers, ...(14 to 1) 6
1764² BALLYMOE BOY (Ire) [-] 6-9-9 (5*) K P Gaule, ...(14 to 1) 7
1832* REMAINDER LASS (Ire) [-] 5-9-11 S H O'Donovan, (12 to 1) 8
      THE SHAUGHRAUN [-] 8-11-5 T Horgan, ...(10 to 1) 9
2054* APPELLATE COURT [-] (bl) 6-11-10 (3ex) A Powell, (10 to 1) 10
1681 NORA'S ERROR (Ire) [-] 5-9-2 (5*) M G Cleary, . . . (33 to 1) 11
1450⁷ RATHBRIDES JOY [-] 7-11-1 C F Swan, ...(10 to 1) 12
1851 MURAHIN (USA) [-] 5-11-6 C O'Dwyer, ... (20 to 1) pu
Dist: 1l, 1½l, 11l, 7l. 4m 27.60s. (13 Ran).
                                    (Lisselan Farms Ltd), Fergus Sutherland

2125 Telecom Eireann Thyestes Handicap Chase (Listed - Grade II) (5-y-o and up) £14,375 3¼m 70yds. . . . . . . (2:40)

1893⁴ NUAFFE [-] 9-10-12 S H O'Donovan, *led 1st, mstks 7th and 11th, hdd aftr 3 out, lft in frnt nxt, ran on und pres.*
....(10 to 1) 1
2037* CALLMECHA [-] (bl) 9-11-4 (3ex) G M O'Neill, *rear, prog into mid-div 11th, rdn 3 out, lft poor second 2 out, kpt on.*
....(10 to 1) 2
1553 CAPTAIN BRANDY [-] 9-11-12 K F O'Brien, *mid-div, rdn in 4th 3 out, styd on r-in.*......... (33 to 1) 3
2037* WRECKLESS MAN [-] 7-10-11 P A Roche, *prog into mid-div tenth, kpt on und pres strt.*........ (25 to 1) 4
1909* JOHNEEN [-] 8-10-0 (4ex) C O'Dwyer, *wl plcd till rdn and wknd 3 out, wknd.*.................... (8 to 1) 5
1979² LADY BAR [-] 7-10-12 P M Verling, *prog to track ldrs 11th, rdn and wknd appr 3 out.*......... (14 to 1) 6
1909³ OPRYLAND [-] 9-10-5 F Woods, *mid-div, mstk 6th, rdn and no imprsn frm 3 out.*.............. (10 to 1) 7
1979* GREEN TIMES [-] (bl) 9-10-10 (2ex) P L Malone, *rear.*
....(8 to 1) 8
1864² BROMPTON ROAD [-] (bl) 11-10-8 T Horgan, *wl plcd, mstk 4 out, sn wknd.*.................... (8 to 1) 9
1979³ LACKEN BEAU [-] 10-11-6 J Shortt, *mid-div, rdn and no imprsn frm 4 out.*.................. (20 to 1) 10
1901⁶ LANIGANS WINE [-] 12-10-10 A Powell, *mid-div, lost tch 12th.*.......................... (33 to 1) 11
1497* BART OWEN [-] 9-10-11 G Bradley, *wl plcd whn f 7th.*
....(6 to 1) f
1784⁵ HIGH PEAK [-] 10-11-9 C F Swan, *wl plcd, mstk 11th, led aftr 3 out, f nxt.*................ (5 to 1) f
1895⁵ ITS A CRACKER [-] 10-11-2 Mr J A Berry, *rear whn f 7th.*
....(15 to 2) f
1825* SULLANE RIVER (Ire) [-] 6-11-7 (5ex) D H O'Connor, *trkd ldrs, 3rd and ev ch whn f 3 out.*...... (4 to 1 fav) f
Dist: 8l, 7l, 2l, 9l. 7m 16.90s. (15 Ran).
                                            (John G Doyle), P A Fahy

2126 Freefone Handicap Chase (0-116 5-y-o and up) £3,105 2½m. . . . . (3:10)

1612³ THREE BROWNIES [-] 7-10-7 C O'Dwyer, ... (7 to 2) 1
1985³ GALLEY GALE [-] 8-10-7 C F Swan, ... (9 to 2) 2
2037 SPEAKING TOUR (USA) [-] 6-11-8 (5ex) D H O'Connor,
....(6 to 1) 3
1830* HARRY'S BOREEN [-] 7-9-10 (3*,4ex) T J Mitchell,
....(5 to 2 fav) 4
1914⁴ SANTAMORE [-] (bl) 7-10-5 T Horgan, ... (10 to 1) 5
2053⁵ DEEP ISLE [-] 8-9-5 (7*) J P Broderick, ...(12 to 1) f
2036⁶ NANCYS LAD [-] 7-9-2¹ (5*) J R Barry, ... (33 to 1) f
1907⁵ MORNING DREAM [-] 7-10-5 J F Titley, ... (8 to 1) f
2051⁴ DOORSLAMMER [-] 9-10-6 S R Murphy, ... (10 to 1) ur
2100 PADKNOCK DONNA [-] 7-9-5² (5*) P A Roche, ... (14 to 1) bd
Dist: 2½l, 8l, 20l, dist. 5m 40.30s. (10 Ran).
                                            (Mrs A M Daly), M F Morris

2127 Phoneplus Peter McCreery Memorial INH Flat Race (4-y-o and up) £3,105 2m . . . . (3:40)

1852³ GREAT SVENGALI (Ire) 5-11-7 (7*) Mr E Norris, ...(5 to 2) 1
1897⁴ IAMWHATIAM 8-11-4 (7*) Mr P English, ...(8 to 1) 2
1833* ABAVARD (Ire) 5-11-7 (7*) Mr M P Dunne, ... (10 to 1) 3
1781⁴ JULEIT JONES (Ire) 5-10-11 (5*) Mr H F Cleary, ... (6 to 1) 4
1916⁴ PRINCESS BAVARD 9-11-13 Mr M Phillips, ...(14 to 1) 5
1859 MARGURITES PET (Ire) 6-11-6 (7*) Miss C O'Neill, (20 to 1) 6
1501² MISS MUPPET (Ire) 5-10-13 (3*) Mrs M Mullins, (5 to 4 on) ur

Dist: 15l, 8l, hd, 9l. 4m 15.80s. (7 Ran).
(Michael W J Smurfit), Patrick Joseph Flynn

2128 Weatherline INH Flat Race (5-y-o and up) £3,105 2¼m. . . . . (4:10)

1858⁴	DONBOLINO (Ire) 6-11-9 Mr A P O'Brien, ... (7 to 1)	1
1681⁷	TITLE CLOCK (Ire) 5-11-5 (5*) Mr H F Cleary, ... (8 to 1)	2
	SOFT WINTER (Ire) 6-11-11 (3*) Mrs M Mullins, (10 to 9 on)	3
2102⁸	SKY VISION (Ire) 5-10-12² (7*) Mr K F O'Donnell, . . (14 to 1)	4
2041²	FIFI'S MAN 8-12-0 Mr P Fenton, ... (8 to 1)	5
1910⁹	TUL NA GCARN 9-11-7 (7*) Mr P English, ... (20 to 1)	6
1910³	GROUP HAT (Ire) 6-11-11 (3*) Mr J A Nash, ... (6 to 1)	7
1858	RAMBLE ALONG (Ire) 5-10-12 (7*) Mr D Kenneally, . (33 to 1)	8
1827	DEEP WAVE 7-11-9 (5*) Mr C T G Kinane, ... (20 to 1)	9
1827⁹	DOUGLAS PYNE (Ire) 5-11-10 Mr J A Berry, ... (14 to 1)	10
1827	CARRAIG-AN-OIR (Ire) 5-11-10 Mr M Phillips, ... (20 to 1)	11
1989⁴	GLEN SALGIUS (Ity) 5-11-7 (3*) Mrs J M Mullins, . . . (7 to 1)	12
1786⁸	MAJOR BERT 6-11-9 (5*) Mr T Lombard, ... (33 to 1)	13
1916⁷	WAKEUP LITTLESUSIE 7-11-2⁵ (7*) Mr B Deegan, (33 to 1)	14
2041	CASTLE CLUB (Ire) 5-11-2 (3*) Mr R O'Neill, ... (20 to 1)	15
1989⁶	COOMACHEO (Ire) 5-11-3 (7*) Mr D A Harney, ... (14 to 1)	16
1910	PURRIT THERE 8-11-7 (7*) Mr E Norris, ... (33 to 1)	17
1822	NOT AN INCH (Ire) 5-11-3 (7*) Mr K Whelan, ... (33 to 1)	18
	DISADVANTAGED 7-11-7 (7*) Mr F Cooper, ... (20 to 1)	19

Dist: 3½l, ½l, 15l, 3½l. 4m 43.10s. (19 Ran).
(Walter James Purcell), A P O'Brien

LINGFIELD (A.W) (std)
Thursday January 13th
Going Correction: PLUS 0.10 sec. per fur.

2129 Quentin Durward Novices' Hurdle (4-y-o and up) £1,768 2¼m. . . . . . . (1:30)

1595⁴	NOBLELY (USA) 7-11-8 R Marley, made all, hit 2 out, sn quickened clr, not extended.	
	. . . .(7 to 4 fav op 11 to 8 tchd 5 to 2)	1
2064³	GROG (Ire) 5-11-2 J Osborne, al prmnt, trkd wnr frm 5th, ev ch 3 out, hit nxt, outpcd. . . . . (2 to 1 op 3 to 1)	2
1788*	AL FORUM (Ire) 4-11-9 D O'Sullivan, al hndy, chsd ldr, chased pair frm 7th wknd appr 3 out.	
	. . . . (11 to 4 op 9 to 4 tchd 3 to 1)	3
1929⁵	SINCLAIR BOY 8-11-2 E Byrne, trkd ldrs, outpcd frm 7th, tld off. . . . .(14 to 1 op 8 to 1)	4
1418⁹	JUMPING JUDGE 7-11-2 D Meade, in tch, outpcd 7th, tld off. . . . .(14 to 1 op 16 to 1)	5
1464	TOP GUNNER (Ire) 4-9-12 (7*) G Crone, al beh, tld off whn pld bef 3 out. . . . . (100 to 1 op 50 to 1)	pu
	O K EALY 4-10-5 M Richards, hld up beh, tld off 7th, pld up bef 3 out. . . . . (50 to 1 op 20 to 1)	pu
1137	FREDWILL (bl) 7-10-9 (7*) J Clarke, trkd wnr till hit 5th, wknd quickly, pld up bef 4 out. . (100 to 1 op 33 to 1)	pu

Dist: 6l, 30l, 20l, 6l. 4m 10.50s. a 9.50s (8 Ran).
SR: 17/5/-/-/-/ (D H Cowgill), N J H Walker

2130 Guy Mannering Claiming Hurdle (4-y-o and up) £1,907 2m. . . . . (2:00)

2064*	BEN ZABEEDY 9-11-4 J Osborne, al prmnt, outpcd o'r 3 out, cld aftr nxt, ran on wl and squeezed through ins to ld close hme. . . . . (7 to 1 fav op 7 to 4 tchd 9 to 4)	1
1942⁷	MASROUG 7-11-2 M Richards, hld up beh ldrs, rdn to ld aftr 4 out, hdd cl hme. . . . . (8 to 1 op 7 to 1)	2
1410	BARTON ROYAL (Ire) (v) 4-10-3 (7*) S Fox, led 3rd till hdd 4 out, kpt on. . . . . (50 to 1 op 25 to 1)	3
2065⁶	MILL BURN 5-11-4 R Campbell, hld up in rear, hdway 6th, blun 2 out, ran on and pres frm last. (10 to 1 op 5 to 1)	4
1408	WORDSMITH (Ire) (v) 4-11-2 D J Burchell, al prmnt, wknd aftr 2 out. . . . .(7 to 2 op 3 to 1)	5
1835	LORD NASKRA (USA) 5-11-5 (5*) J Twomey, hld up in rear, hdway 3 out, outpcd frm nxt, styd on.	
	. . . . (33 to 1 op 20 to 1)	6
1261⁴	LADY RELKO 4-10-11 A Tory, led to 3rd, wth ldr will wknd aftr 3 out. . . . . (50 to 1 op 33 to 1)	7
1404⁸	TAKE THE MICK (bl) 4-10-7 (3*) A Procter, trkd ldr, mstk 3rd, rdn 4 out, wknd. (20 to 1 op 14 to 1 tchd 33 to 1)	8
1640	NYMPH ERRANT 4-9-9 (7*) Mr N Moore, chsd ldrs, cld 7th, outpcd seventh, wknd quickly. . . . .(50 to 1 op 33 to 1)	9
1801	EARLY BREEZE 8-10-9 (7*) Leanne Eldredge, nvr a factor.	
	. . . . (16 to 1 op 14 to 1)	10
1965⁷	KUTAN (Ire) 4-10-10 E Byrne, al beh. (14 to 1 op 10 to 1)	11
1793⁹	SOMERSET DANCER (USA) 7-12-0 D O'Sullivan, al, beh, tld off. . . . . (5 to 1 tchd 7 to 1)	12
1885⁹	WONDERFUL YEARS (USA) 4-10-3 (3*) A Thornton, mid-div till drpd rear 4 out, tld off. . . . . . (8 to 1 op 6 to 1)	13
1415⁴	COOCHIE (bl) 5-10-13 L Harvey, mid-div, slightly hmpd 3rd, sn beh, tld off whn pld up bef 2 out.	
	. . . . (12 to 1 op 10 to 1)	pu
1965	GYPSY LEGEND 4-10-0² (7*) R Darke, al beh, mstk 5th, tld off whn pld up bef 2 out. . . . . (50 to 1 op 33 to 1)	pu

Dist: Hd, 1l, 2l, 10l, 1½l, 4l, 2½l, 3½l, 10l, hd. 3m 44.70s. a 11.70s (15 Ran).
(Richard Armstrong), R Akehurst

2131 Waverley Handicap Hurdle (0-115 4-y-

o and up) £1,814 3m. . . . . (2:30)

1474	BLASKET HERO [86] (bl) 6-11-1 J Osborne, hld up in rear, hdwy 12th, led aftr 3 out, ran on wl.	
	. . . . (9 to 1 op 7 to 1 tchd 10 to 1)	1
2067*	JARRWAH [97] 6-11-12 (6ex) W Marston, led till mstk 3 out, sn hdd, one pace. . . . . (7 to 4 fav op 5 to 4 tchd 2 to 1)	2
2067⁴	JADDIH [95] 6-11-5 (5*) D Salter, sn prmnt, rdn aftr 4 out, outpcd. . . . . (11 to 2 op 5 to 1 tchd 6 to 1)	3
1511	SUNSET AGAIN [85] 9-10-7 (7*) S Fox, chase ldrs, drpd rear 7th, no dngr aftr. . . . . (33 to 1)	4
1805	RUBINS BOY [88] 8-11-3 M Richards, beh, cld 7th, wknd 11th, tld off. . . . . (3 to 1 tchd 9 to 2)	5
2067⁵	CARFAX [91] (bl) 9-11-6 M Hoad, al prmnt, reminders 11th, ev ch 4 out, wknd quickly, tld off.	
	. . . . (4 to 1 tchd 7 to 2 and 9 to 2)	6
1715	CRUISE CONTROL [71] 8-9-12³ (5*) C Burnett-Wells, beh, cld 11th, outpcd aftr 4 out, tld off. (14 to 1 op 20 to 1)	7
1719	WAVERLEY BOY [72] 12-10-1 V Smith, in tch to hfwy, tld off whn pld up bef 3 out. . . . . (33 to 1)	pu
1485	BRIGHT SAPPHIRE [71] 8-9-13⁴ (5*) D Matthews, cl up till wknd 13th, tld off whn pld up bef 3 out.	
	. . . . (33 to 1 op 25 to 1)	pu
2034	FOUR STAR LINE [89] 9-10-11 (7*) R Darke, nvr on terms, tld off whn pld up bef 2 out. . . . . . (20 to 1 op 16 to 1)	pu
1136	LOWICK LAD [71] 7-10-0 S Keightley, tld off second, pld up bef 3 out. . . . .(100 to 1)	pu

Dist: 5l, 20l, 3l, 2l, 20l, 20l. 5m 36.10s. a 9.10s (11 Ran).
SR: 20/26/4/-/-/-/ (D C Coard), Mrs S D Williams

2132 Weatherbys 'Newcomers' Series Handicap Hurdle (0-100 4-y-o and up) £1,830 2¼m. . . . . (3:00)

2066*	SAAHI (USA) [77] 5-10-6 (6ex) J Osborne, hld up in cl tch, al gng wl, quickened to ld 3 out, hit nxt, sn clr, very easily. . . . . (6 to 4 on op 5 to 4 on)	1
1970	WEST BAY [77] 8-10-6 S Smith Eccles, beh, cld 4 out, styd on und pres to take second r-in, no ch wth wnr.	
	. . . . (16 to 1 op 10 to 1 tchd 20 to 1)	2
1245⁷	SING THE BLUES [85] 10-11-0 D Morris, trkd ldr, led 8th till hdd 3 out, one pace. . . . . (10 to 1 tchd 12 to 1)	3
1087⁵	PHILIP'S WOODY [95] 6-11-3 (7*) Pat Thompson, prmnt, mstk 7th, sn pushed alng, outpcd 4 out.	
	. . . . (5 to 1 op 4 to 1 tchd 11 to 2)	4
1867⁴	SANDRO [84] (bl) 5-10-13 L Harvey, trkd ldrs, hrd rdn aftr 4 out, wknd. . . . .(12 to 1 op 10 to 1)	5
1801⁶	TEMPORALE [71] 8-10-0 R Marley, al beh.	
	. . . .(12 to 1 tchd 14 to 1)	6
1810⁶	YUVRAJ [78] 10-10-7 S Keightley, al beh.	
	. . . . (14 to 1 op 12 to 1 tchd 16 to 1)	7
1963⁷	AS D'EBOLI (Fr) [78] 7-10-0 (7*) Kate Sellars, sn tld off.	
	. . . . (20 to 1 op 12 to 1 tchd 25 to 1)	8
670	TOUCHING TIMES [77] 6-10-1 (5*) C Burnett-Wells, al beh, tld off. . . . . (9 to 1 op 6 to 1 tchd 10 to 1)	9
	JAN-RE [99] 10-11-7 (7*) P Murphy, led till hdd 8th, prmnt whn broke leg appr 3 out, pld up bef nxt, dead.	
	. . . . (20 to 1 op 14 to 1)	pu

Dist: 10l, 2½l, 8l, 5l, 2l, ¾l, 10l, 4l. 4m 11.40s. a 10.40s (10 Ran).
(Martin N Peters), C Weedon

2133 Ivanhoe Mares' Novices' Handicap Hurdle (4-y-o and up) £1,630 2½m . . . . (3:30)

1801³	PROVERBS GIRL [83] 9-11-7 (7*) S Fox, hld up, wnt second 4 out, rdn appr last, styd on to ld r-in.	
	. . . . (11 to 8 op 5 to 1)	1
1926²	HULLO MARY DOLL [62] 5-10-4 (3*) A Procter, hld up, led 4 out till hdd r-in. . . . . (Evens fav op 5 to 4 on)	2
1734⁷	POLLY MINOR [78] 7-11-4 (5*) A Dicken, led, clr 6th, hit 5 out, hdd nxt, wknd quickly, tld off. (9 to 2 op 7 to 1)	3

Dist: 3l, dist. 4m 53.30s. a 22.30s (3 Ran).
(J G Thatcher), G B Balding

2134 Red Gauntlet National Hunt Flat Race (4,5,6-y-o) £1,548 2m. . . . . (4:00)

	COLOSSUS OF ROADS 5-11-0 (7*) Guy Lewis, hld up in tch, smooth hdwy to ld o'r one furlong out, shaken up and ran on strly. . . . . (6 to 4 on op Evens)	1
	MIGHTY MAURICE (Ire) 5-11-2 (5*) J McCarthy, hld up in tch, hdwy 2 fs out, styd on und pres.	
	. . . . (4 to 1 tchd 5 to 1)	2
	FAWLEY FLYER 5-11-0 (7*) R Darke, cl up, led o'r 2 fs till hdd over one out, one pace, tld off. . . . . . . (33 to 1)	3
	ESPERER 4-10-4 (5*) A Dicken, led till hdd o'r 2 fs out, wknd. . . . . (20 to 1 op 14 to 1)	4
	RATAKINS 5-11-0 (7*) Mr R McGrath, hld up in last pl, effrt 4 fs out, unbl to chal. . . . . (12 to 1 op 10 to 1)	5
	DUPAD 4-10-4 (5*) C Burnett-Wells, cl up till wknd 4 fs out, sn tld off. . . . . (8 to 1 op 9 to 1)	6
	JOYFUL JENNY 5-10-13 (3*) A Thornton, stumbled and uns rdr sn aftr strt. . . . . (10 to 1 op 9 to 1)	u

Dist: 7l, 1l, 10l, 3l, 20l. 3m 41.20s. (7 Ran).
(David F Wilson), T Thomson Jones

WETHERBY (soft)
Thursday January 13th
Going Correction: PLUS 1.40 sec. per fur. (races 1,4,6), PLUS 1.95 (2,3,5)

2135 Healaugh Novices' Hurdle (4-y-o) £2,373 2m. . . . . (1:10)

1920*	NATIVE WORTH 11-0 (5*) P Williams, *made all, hrd pressed frm 3 out, styd on wl und pres.*	
	. . . .(9 to 4 op 2 to 1 tchd 5 to 2)	1
	NETHERBY SAID 10-12 C Dennis, *in tch, chsd ldrs frm 6th, ev ch last, no extr*. . . . .(33 to 1 op 25 to 1)	2
	SHARKASHKA (Ire) 10-7 L Wyer, *al prmnt, rdn to chal 2 out, ev ch last, no extr*. . . . .(7 to 1 op 5 to 1)	3
1575⁶	BALLYSPARKLE (Ire) 10-12 A Mulholland, *chsd wnr till outpcd aftr 6th, styd on frm 2 out.* (12 to 1 op 20 to 1)	4
2003³	DEVILRY 11-5 J Callaghan, *trkd ldrs, pushed alng appr 3 out, sn btn*. . . . .(13 to 8 fav op 2 to 1 tchd 9 to 4)	5
784⁵	MALAWI 10-12 B Storey, *trkd ldrs till lost pl aftr 3rd, no dngr after*. . . . .(16 to 1)	6
2083⁹	HO-JOE (Ire) 10-12 N Smith, *hld up, steady hdwy frm 6th, nvr nr to chal*. . . . .(33 to 1)	7
1920⁸	IJAB (Can) 10-12 C Grant, *beh most of way.* . . . .(20 to 1 op 16 to 1)	8
1787³	BERING ISLAND (USA) 10-9 (3*) N Bentley, *chsd ldrs till wknd quickly and pld up bef 3 out.* . . . .(13 to 2 op 7 to 1 tchd 6 to 1)	pu
	MURPHY'S HOPE (Ire) 10-5 (7*) W Fry, *beh frm 5th, tld off whn pld up bef 3 out*. . . . .(33 to 1 op 20 to 1)	pu
754⁴	DANCE FEVER (Ire) 10-12 M Dwyer, *jmpd rght, beh most of way, tld off whn pld up bef 3 out.* (14 to 1 op 12 to 1)	pu

Dist: 1½l, ½l, 7l, 6l, 4l, 3l, 12l. 4m 14.90s. a 33.90s (11 Ran).
(Mrs M Barker), J M Jefferson

2136 Wike Conditional Jockeys' Handicap Chase (0-125 6-y-o and up) £3,590 2 ½m 110yds. . . . . (1:40)

1934	CONCERT PAPER [97] (v) 10-9-9² (7*) K Davies, *made all, clr 3 out, styd on wl*. . . . .(16 to 1)	1
1759⁶	RIVER BOUNTY [125] 8-11-7 (7*) D Winter, *sn beh, hit 8th, effrt aftr tenth, styd on to go second 3 out, no imprsn on wnr*. . . . .(9 to 4 tchd 11 to 4)	2
1678³	CROSS CANNON [114] 8-11-3 P Waggott, *sn chasing wnr, effrt whn blun 4 out, soon btn*. . . . . (7 to 2 tchd 4 to 1)	3
1638²	THE MALTKILN [103] (v) 11-10-6 D Bentley, *prmnt till wknd appr 11th, wl beh whn badly hmpd 3 out, tld off*.	
	. . . .(15 to 8 fav op 13 to 8 tchd 2 to 1)	4
1025⁸	FAST CRUISE [97] 9-10-0 A Dobbin, *prmnt, mstk 8th, sn outpcd, no ch whn f 3 out*. . . . .(12 to 1)	f
1360⁶	MILITARY HONOUR [97] (bl) 9-10-0 N Bentley, *mstk and uns rdr 3rd*. . . . .(17 to 2 op 8 to 1 tchd 9 to 1)	ur
1960⁶	CAROUSEL CROSSETT [97] 13-10-0 P Williams, *sn beh, lost tch aftr 6th, wl tld off whn pld up bef 4 out.* . . . .(50 to 1 tchd 66 to 1)	pu

Dist: 25l, 2½l, 30l. 5m 42.00s. a 45.50s (7 Ran).
SR: 17/20/6/-/ (Steve Hammond), R O'Leary

2137 Collingham Novices' Chase (5-y-o and up) £3,850 3m 110yds. . . . . (2:10)

1873²	CLYDE RANGER 7-11-5 C Grant, *trkd ldr, led 13th, lft wl clr 2 out, easily.*	
	. . . .(Evens fav op 11 to 10 tchd 11 to 10 on)	1
1928⁴	SHELTON ABBEY 8-11-5 T Reed, *in tch, some hdwy aftr 11th, wknd after 14th*. . . . .(20 to 1 op 16 to 1)	2
2004²	MONAUGHTY MAN 8-11-0 (5*) P Williams, *led till mstk and hdd 13th, wknd aftr nxt*. . . . .(14 to 1 op 12 to 1)	3
	DEVONGALE 8-11-5 R Garritty, *in tch, steady hdwy to chase wnr aftr 14th, no imprsn whn f 2 out, rmntd.*	
	. . . .(16 to 1 op 14 to 1)	4
1862*	CANTGETOUT 8-11-6 Mr A Pickering, *sn wl beh, tld off.* . . . .(25 to 1)	5
2004⁴	BOWLANDS WAY 10-11-5 A Mulholland, *chsd ldrs, no imprsn whn f 11th*. . . . .(50 to 1)	f
1862²	PLAYFUL JULIET (Can) (v) 6-11-6 Pat Caldwell, *beh whn f 9th*. . . . .(20 to 1)	f
1742	BUCKWHEAT LAD (Ire) 6-11-5 L Wyer, *beh whn f 8th.* . . . .(20 to 1)	f
1537³	BRACKENFIELD 8-12-3 P Niven, *cl up whn blun and uns rdr 6th*. . . . .(9 to 4 tchd 11 to 4)	ur
	EXTRA SPECIAL 9-11-5 N Doughty, *sn beh, tld off whn pld up bef tenth*. . . . .(33 to 1 op 20 to 1)	pu

Dist: 30l, ½l, dist, 12l. 7m 10.00s. a 64.00s (10 Ran).
(I Bray), M D Hammond

2138 Cowthorpe Handicap Hurdle (0-125 4-y-o and up) £3,132 2m. . . . . . . (2:40)

	GREY POWER [110] 7-10-13 P Niven, *hld up, steady hdwy hfwy, led appr 2 out, ran on strly*. . .(5 to 1 op 4 to 1)	1
1874²	HOME COUNTIES (Ire) [121] (v) 5-11-7 (3*) D J Moffatt, *hld up in tch, hdwy aftr 5th, ev ch appr 2 out, kpt on same pace*. . . . .(5 to 2 fav op 9 to 4)	2

(continued top of next column)

1874⁷	KANNDABIL [108] (bl) 7-10-6 (5*) E Husband, *chsd ldrs till outpcd aftr 6th, styd on strly frm 2 out.*	
	. . . .(14 to 1 op 12 to 1 tchd 16 to 1)	3
1863⁵	PERSONAL HAZARD [97] (bl) 5-10-0 L Wyer, *trkd ldr, led appr 3 out, hdd approaching nxt, btn whn mstk last.* . . . .(5 to 1 op 13 to 2)	4
1746⁷	DORADUS [97] 6-9-7 (7*) F Leahy, *chsd ldrs till wknd aftr 3 out*. . . . .(10 to 1 op 8 to 1)	5
1874⁶	BO KNOWS BEST (Ire) [125] 5-12-0 M Dwyer, *in tch till wknd appr 6th*. . . . .(9 to 1 op 7 to 1)	6
1627²	PINECONE PETER [97] 7-10-0 M Brennan, *al beh.*	
	. . . .(9 to 1 op 8 to 1 tchd 10 to 1)	7
1777⁶	WAKE UP [97] 7-9-9² (7*) K Davies, *al beh.*	
	. . . .(20 to 1 op 16 to 1)	8
2070⁵	FAMILY LINE [103] 6-10-1 (5*) F Perratt, *led till hdd appr 3 out, wknd quickly*. . . . .(8 to 1 op 7 to 1)	9
	CANDID LAD [97] 7-10-0 C Dennis, *in tch till wknd appr 6th*. . . . .(25 to 1 op 20 to 1)	10
	HUSO [97] 6-9-7 (7*) S Taylor, *al beh, pld up and dismounted bef 2 out*. . . . .(20 to 1 op 16 to 1)	pu

Dist: 10l, 1l, 6l, 3l, 15l, 2½l, 1½l, 15l, ¾l. 4m 7.50s. a 26.50s (11 Ran).
SR: 44/45/31/14/11/24/ (A Frame), Mrs M Reveley

2139 Keswick Handicap Chase (0-145 5-y-o and up) £4,305 3m 110yds. . . . . . (3:10)

1733*	THREEOUTOFFOUR [116] 9-10-1¹ M Brennan, *in tch, hdwy to track ldr 13th, led 4 out, drw clr, cmftbly.*	
	. . . .(3 to 1 jt-fav op 5 to 2)	1
1881	MERRY MASTER [135] 10-11-6 Gee Armytage, *led till hdd 4 out, kpt on same pace*. . . . .(11 to 2 op 9 to 2)	2
1744*	MATT REID [115] 10-10-0 J Callaghan, *chsd ldrs, ev ch appr 4 out, 3rd and wkng whn blun nxt.*	
	. . . .(5 to 1 op 11 to 2)	3
	DEEP COLONIST [121] 12-10-6 M Dwyer, *chsd ldrs till wknd appr 14th, tld off*. . . . .(16 to 1 op 14 to 1)	4
1419²	CANDY TUFF [115] 8-10-0 L Wyer, *prmnt, jinked lft appr 4 out, wknd quickly, tld off*. . .(3 to 1 jt-fav tchd 5 to 1)	5
1144⁴	LOGAMIMO [122] 8-10-7 T Reed, *in tch whn f 11th, dead.* . . . .(12 to 1 op 10 to 1)	f
1778	MR SETASIDE [115] 9-10-0 B Storey, *lost tch aftr 12th, tld off whn pld up bef 4 out*. . . . .(16 to 1)	pu
1757⁵	VERY VERY ORDINARY [143] 8-12-0 R Supple, *in tch till effrt aftr 12th, tld off whn pld up bef 4 out.* . . . .(13 to 2 op 10 to 1)	pu

Dist: 12l, 7l, 25l, 7l. 7m 4.60s. a 58.60s (8 Ran).
(Miss Cindy Brennan), O Brennan

2140 Whixley 'National Hunt' Novices' Hurdle (5-y-o and up) £2,486 2½m 110yds . . . . (3:40)

1726²	SCOTTON BANKS (Ire) 5-11-0 L Wyer, *trkd ldr, led aftr 7th, clr 3 out, easily.* (7 to 4 fav op 9 to 4 tchd 3 to 1)	1
734²	ALI'S ALIBI 7-11-0 P Niven, *mid-div, hdwy hfwy, chsd wnr frm 3 out, no imprsn.*	
	. . . .(11 to 4 op 7 to 2 tchd 4 to 1 and 9 to 4)	2
1677²	WEY I MAN (Ire) 5-11-0 J Callaghan, *in tch, hdwy to track ldrs aftr 6th, kpt on same pace frm nxt.*	
	. . . .(10 to 1 op 8 to 1)	3
1574⁵	ASK TOM (Ire) 5-11-0 R Garritty, *led till hdd aftr 7th, sn btn*. . . . .(9 to 1)	4
	LAST REFUGE (Ire) 5-11-0 B Storey, *mid-div, kpt on same pace frm 7th*. . . . .(33 to 1 op 20 to 1)	5
1959⁷	TIDERUNNER (Ire) 6-11-0 T Reed, *chsd ldrs, grad wknd frm 7th*. . . . .(9 to 1 op 7 to 1)	6
1959	CEREAL GEM 6-10-9 D Byrne, *mid-div, effrt appr 7th, sn wknd*. . . . .(33 to 1 op 20 to 1)	7
	MARKS REFRAIN 10-10-9 (5*) Mr R Hale, *mid-div till wknd appr 7th*. . . . .(33 to 1)	8
	MERRY PANTO (Ire) 5-11-0 R Supple, *chsd ldrs till wknd aftr 7th*. . . . .(16 to 1 op 12 to 1)	9
1215	INDIAN ORCHID 7-10-2 (7*) J Lonergan, *al beh.*	
	. . . .(16 to 1 op 12 to 1 tchd 20 to 1)	10
2003⁶	BLAYNEYS PRIVILEGE 7-11-0 N Doughty, *nvr on terms, wl beh whn pld up bef 3 out*. . . . . . .(20 to 1 op 16 to 1)	pu
	HAZEL CREST 7-11-0 M Dwyer, *in tch till wknd aftr 6th, wl beh whn pld up bef 3 out*. . . . .(12 to 1 op 8 to 1)	pu
	YOUNG PARSON 8-11-0 A Dobbin, *chsd ldrs till wknd aftr 6th, wl beh whn pld up bef 3 out.*	
	. . . .(5 to 1 op 20 to 1)	pu
	YOUNG GUS 7-11-0 R Hodge, *nvr on terms, wl beh whn pld up bef 3 out*. . . . .(14 to 1 op 12 to 1)	pu
1103	FINAL DILEMMA 5-11-0 A S Smith, *chsd ldrs till wknd aftr 6th, wl beh whn pld up bef 3 out.* (33 to 1 op 20 to 1)	pu
1779	SOUNDS GOLDEN 6-11-0 C Grant, *sn wl beh, tld off whn pld up bef 3 out*. . . . .(25 to 1)	pu
1957	ANNE CARTER 5-10-9 M Ranger, *sn wl beh, pld up bef 3 out*. . . . .(10 to 1 op 50 to 1)	pu
1959⁹	BALLYROVERS 5-11-0 Mr S Swiers, *al beh, tld off whn pld up bef 3 out*. . . . .(50 to 1)	pu

Dist: 20l, 2½l, 15l, 1½l, 5l, 8l, 15l, 12l, 10l. 5m 25.10s. a 38.10s (18 Ran).
(I Bray), M H Easterby

WINCANTON (good to soft)
Thursday January 13th

Going Correction: PLUS 0.75 sec. per fur. (races 1,2,-4,7), PLUS 1.03 (3,5,6)

2141 Corscombe Novices' Hurdle (Div I) (4-y-o and up) £2,285 2¾m....... (12:50)

1568[9] TOP BRASS (Ire) 6-11-6 N Williamson, *hld up, hdwy 7th, chlgd 2 out, led aftr last, ran on und pres.* ....(8 to 1 op 6 to 1) 1
1745[6] SPARKLING FLAME 10-11-6 M A FitzGerald, *chsd ldrs, led 3 out till aftr last, one pace*..........(8 to 1 op 6 to 1) 2
1734[5] PLACE STEPHANIE (Ire) 6-10-8 (7*) L Dace, *hdwy 6th, rdn and kpt on frm 2 out.* (50 to 1 op 20 to 1 tchd 66 to 1) 3
1564* GENERAL WOLFE 5-11-12 B Powell, *in tch, lost pl 5th, sn rdn, styd on frm 2 out*..............(6 to 1 op 7 to 2) 4
1327[3] EMPEROR BUCK (Ire) 6-11-6 A Maguire, *hdwy 7th, chsd ldrs 2 out, sn wknd*.....(11 to 2 op 7 to 2 tchd 6 to 1) 5
1715[2] SOUTHERLY GALE 7-11-6 R Dunwoody, *hld up in tch, ev ch 2 out, sn rdn and wknd*..... (5 to 2 fav tchd 4 to 1) 6
1716 COLETTE'S CHOICE (Ire) 5-11-1 S Mackey, *sn in tch, rdn and wknd appr 2 out*...........(10 to 1 tchd 20 to 1) 7
1885[5] ANILAFFED (v) 4-10-7 D Bridgwater, *mstk second, sn beh, some prog frm 3 out*............... (50 to 1 op 33 to 1) 8
1935 ROCK DIAMOND 8-11-6 E Leonard, *beh till ran on frm 3 out, not a dngr*...... (50 to 1 op 16 to 1 tchd 66 to 1) 9
1567[7] TRIMAGE (Ire) 6-11-6 C Llewellyn, *nvr better than mid-div*.................. (40 to 1 op 33 to 1 tchd 50 to 1) 10
PENLEA LADY 7-11-1 D Gallagher, *in tch till wknd aftr 7th*................................ (100 to 1 op 50 to 1) 11
1948[3] DEVIOSITY (USA) 7-11-6 W McFarland, *prmnt, rdn 6th, sn wknd*............................(66 to 1 op 33 to 1) 12
1953[5] RAKAIA RIVER (NZ) 7-11-3 (3*) R Farrant, *in tch to 7th.* .... (25 to 1 op 16 to 1 tchd 33 to 1) 13
SHOCK TACTICS 7-11-6 S McNeill, *prmnt to 7th.* .... (33 to 1 op 25 to 1) 14
1935[9] ARDSCUD 7-11-6 G Upton, *beh, hdwy 5th, chlgd 6th to 7th, wknd 3 out*.................. (25 to 1 op 33 to 1) 15
1878[8] LETS RUMBLE (Ire) 5-11-6 S Earle, *prmnt, not fluent early, led 6th to 3 out, sn wknd.* .... (25 to 1 op 20 to 1 tchd 16 to 1) 16
1779 GUSHKA 7-11-6 G McCourt, *al beh.* (66 to 1 op 16 to 1) 17
778[8] QUAGO 6-11-1 J Railton, *prmnt to 7th.* .... (66 to 1 op 20 to 1) 18
2029[2] SPREAD YOUR WINGS (Ire) 6-11-1 P Holley, *mid-div whn slpd and uns rdr bend aftr 5th.* ....(7 to 2 op 4 to 1 tchd 5 to 1) ur
1716[8] CADOLIVE 6-11-1 C Maude, *prmnt to 6th, sn wknd, tld off whn pld up bef 2 out*...........(50 to 1 op 20 to 1) pu
111[9] SARACEN'S BOY (Ire) 6-10-13 (7*) Mr B Pollock, *prmnt, led 4th to 6th, sn wknd, tld off whn pld up bef 2 out.* .... (66 to 1 op 50 to 1 tchd 100 to 1) pu
1595 BALUSTRADE 7-11-6 M Stevens, *led to 4th, sn wknd, tld off whn pld up aftr 7th*..........(100 to 1 op 50 to 1) pu

Dist: 1½l, 10l, 4l, 2½l, 8l, 8l, 5l, hd, 1½l, 3l. 5m 33.70s. a 27.70s (22 Ran).

(Top Brass Partnership), K C Bailey

2142 Jamboree Conditional Jockeys' Handicap Hurdle (0-105 4-y-o and up) £2,616 2m..................... (1:20)

1801[4] MISS EQUILIA (USA) [89] 8-10-13 (3*) L Reynolds, *hld up, nudged alng aftr 3rd, hdwy appr 2 out, rdn and quickened r-in to ld nr finish*..........(6 to 1 tchd 13 to 2) 1
1516[4] STYLE AND CLASS [92] 5-11-2 (3*) L Dace, *beh, hdwy appr 2 out, ran on wl r-in, not rch wnr*....(6 to 1 op 5 to 1) 2
1945[5] ALOSAILI [89] 7-10-13 (3*) M Stevens, *hdwy 5th, led aftr 2 out, rdn r-in, wknd and ct nr finish.* .... (20 to 1 op 16 to 1) 3
1949* CARDINAL BIRD (USA) [95] (bl) 7-11-5 (3*) Chris Webb, *sn wl beh, rdn alng frm 3rd, styd on from 2 out, not rch ldrs.* .... (7 to 2 fav tchd 4 to 1) 4
2110[5] LUCKY BLUE [73] 7-9-11 (3*) T Thompson, *chsd ldrs, strly rdn and one pace aftr 3 out*...... (50 to 1 op 33 to 1) 5
1884 GROTIUS [81] (bl) 10-10-8 R Davis, *in tch, hdwy 4th, led sn aftr 3 out, hdd and wknd after nxt.* .... (33 to 1 op 20 to 1) 6
1699[3] BAYBEEJAY [75] 7-9-13 (3*) T Dascombe, *nvr rch ldrs.* .... (20 to 1 op 14 to 1) 7
1884[4] CHIAROSCURO [88] 8-10-12 (3*) N Parker, *prmnt, hit 5th, chlgd 3 out, sn btn*..... (13 to 2 op 5 to 1 tchd 7 to 1) 8
1721[5] MARIOLINO [95] 7-11-5 (3*) M Moran, *beh, mid-div whn blun 3 out*.......... (40 to 1 op 25 to 1 tchd 50 to 1) 9
1057[3] KINTARO [85] 6-10-12 T Jenks, *al beh.* (11 to 1 op 9 to 1) 10
COURT APPEAL [73] 12-9-11 (3*) P McLoughlin, *chsd ldrs to 3 out*......................................(50 to 1) 11
1949[4] EXACT ANALYSIS (USA) [83] 8-10-10 S Curran, *chsd ldrs, led 5th, mstk 3 out, sn hdd and wknd.* .... (10 to 1 op 12 to 1) 12
1955[3] SOCIETY GUEST [101] 8-12-0 D Fortt, *mid-div whn mstk and uns rdr 3rd*......... (4 to 1 op 7 to 2 tchd 9 to 2) ur
1882[3] DARINGLY [76] 5-9-11 (6*) E Tolhurst, *led to 5th, sn wknd, tld off whn pld up bef 2 out*...... (14 to 1 op 10 to 1) pu

Dist: Nk, 2l, 8l, 2½l, ¾l, 3½l, 8l, 2½l, 1½l, 7l. 3m 55.00s. a 18.00s (14 Ran).

SR: 28/30/25/23/-/5/-/-/4/ (Martin Pipe Racing Club), M C Pipe

2143 Lillo Lumb Challenge Cup Handicap Chase (0-130 5-y-o and up) £3,938 3m 1f 110yds...................... (1:50)

1993[4] AUCTION LAW (NZ) [115] 10-11-1 J Frost, *chsd ldrs, led 6th to 7th, led 16th to nxt, led 2 out, ran on wl.* .... (10 to 1 op 6 to 1) 1
1838* MASTER OATS [121] 8-11-7 N Williamson, *in tch, hit 11th, led 17th, gng wl 3 out, hdd 2 out, rdn last, not quicken.* .....(11 to 4 fav op 100 to 30 tchd 7 to 2 and 5 to 2) 2
1769[5] SUNLEY BAY [102] 8-10-2 A Maguire, *beh, mstk 4th, hdwy 15th, chlgd four out, wknd appr 2 out.* .... (10 to 1 op 8 to 1) 3
1629* COOL AND EASY [100] 8-10-0 D Murphy, *in tch, chsd ldrs 9th, rdn and no imprsn 4 out*........ (9 to 2 op 7 to 2) 4
1883[2] RAFIKI [105] 9-10-5 M A FitzGerald, *hit 3rd, beh 12th, no dngr aftr*..............................(12 to 1 op 8 to 1) 5
1943[3] SHASTON [100] (bl) 9-10-0 R Greene, *led 4th, jmpd slwly and hdd 6th, led 7th to 16th, mstk 17th, wknd appr 3 out*..(16 to 1) 6
GLENBROOK D'OR [116] 10-11-2 B Clifford, *hit 12th, al beh*......................................(20 to 1 op 14 to 1) 7
2047[2] WARNER FOR WINNERS [107] (bl) 8-10-7[3] G McCourt, *in tch to 15th*............................ (10 to 1 op 8 to 1) 8
1870* CATCH THE CROSS [128] (bl) 8-12-0 R Dunwoody, *hdwy 8th, chsd ldrs till mstk and wknd 15th.* ....(5 to 1 tchd 13 to 2) 9
1447 TAGMOUN CHAUFOUR (Fr) [100] 9-10-0 B Powell, *led second to 4th, wknd 16th*............(66 to 1 op 100 to 1) 10
1966[2] FILE CONCORD [120] (bl) 10-11-6 I Lawrence, *hdwy to chase ldrs 12th, rdn 17th, wknd aftr 4 out, eased r-in.* ....(11 to 1 op 9 to 1 tchd 12 to 1) 11
1845[8] PAMBER PRIORY [118] 11-11-4 G Rowe, *not fluent, hdwy and hit 9th, tld off whn pld up bef 16th.* .... (20 to 1 op 14 to 1) pu
1887 MIGHTY FALCON [119] (bl) 9-11-5 P Holley, *effrt 13th, wknd 16th, tld off whn pld up bef last.* ....(16 to 1 tchd 14 to 1) pu
2047 FALSE ECONOMY [114] 9-11-0 D Gallagher, *led to second, prmnt till wknd 13th, tld off whn pld up bef 4 out.* .... (33 to 1 op 20 to 1) pu

Dist: ¾l, 10l, 15l, 5l, 4l, 12l, 6l, 7l, 4l, 3l. 6m 46.40s. a 30.40s (14 Ran).

SR: 46/51/22/5/5/-/ (Mrs Brenda Gittins), D H Barons

2144 Corscombe Novices' Hurdle (Div II) (4-y-o and up) £2,285 2¾m........ (2:20)

1797* ELAINE TULLY (Ire) 6-11-7 M Hourigan, *chsd ldrs, styd on to ld last, ran on wl*................. (7 to 1 op 5 to 1) 1
1567[4] TALBOT 8-11-6 J Railton, *chsd lea ders, led 6th to 7th, chlgd 3 out, styd on frm nxt*........ (13 to 2 op 5 to 1) 2
1800[5] GLENTOWER (Ire) 6-11-6 R Dunwoody, *in tch, shaken up appr 2 out, styd on wl r-in*...........(7 to 1 op 5 to 1) 3
1542[3] SPUFFINGTON 6-11-6 D Murphy, *prmnt, led 3 out to last, wknd r-in*.............................(3 to 1 op 7 to 2) 4
1935[7] MY DEAR GOOD MAN (Ire) 6-11-6 T Grantham, *chsd ldrs, led 7th to 3 out, wknd aftr nxt, tld off.* .... (16 to 1 op 12 to 1 tchd 20 to 1) 5
1542[8] MR WILBUR 8-11-6 J Frost, *beh, some hdwy frm 3 out, tld off*..(33 to 1) 6
1953[3] SIMON JOSEPH 7-11-6 A Maguire, *beh, hdwy to track ldrs 6th, rdn aftr 3 out, sn wknd, tld off.* ....(7 to 1 op 5 to 1) 7
MAJOR MINER (Ire) 6-11-6 E Leonard, *beh 5th, tld off.* .... (33 to 1 op 20 to 1) 8
1835[3] SOLO GENT 5-11-6 S McNeill, *in tch to 7th, tld off.* .... (20 to 1 op 14 to 1) 9
1835 EASTERN RIVER 8-11-6 B Powell, *beh 6th, tld off.* .... (14 to 1 op 12 to 1) 10
1624[2] SMITH'S BAND (Ire) 6-11-6 I Lawrence, *in tch, hdwy 7th, ran wide and wknd aftr 3 out, tld off.* ....(9 to 4 fav op 5 to 2 tchd 2 to 1) 11
1946[6] MAHATMACOAT 7-11-6 M A FitzGerald, *chsd ldrs to 6th, tld off*..............................(50 to 1 op 20 to 1) 12
1646[5] ACHIEVED AMBITION (Ire) 6-11-6 N Mann, *beh 5th, tld off.* .... (16 to 1 op 20 to 1 tchd 33 to 1) 13
1935 MISS CRUISE 7-11-1 W Humphreys, *in tch 5th, sn wknd, tld off*..............................(50 to 1 op 33 to 1) 14
MISS PARKES 5-10-8 (7*) T Dascombe, *in tch to 5th, tld off*.......................................(50 to 1 op 33 to 1) 15
1950[5] GREEN'S GAME 6-11-6 G Upton, *sn beh, tld off.* .... (50 to 1 op 33 to 1) 16
BEACHY GLEN 7-11-6 S Mackey, *led to 6th, wkng whn slpd up bend appr 7th*............(50 to 1 op 33 to 1) su
1994 PHAROAH'S SON 8-11-6 S Earle, *chsd ldrs, wknd and pld up bef 2 out, dismounted.* .... (33 to 1 op 25 to 1 tchd 50 to 1) pu
1871[4] IT'S CONFIDENTIAL (NZ) 7-11-6 Mrs C Wonnacott, *sn beh, tld off whn pld up bef 2 out*...... (50 to 1 op 25 to 1) pu
1654[5] MASTER BAVARD (Ire) (bl) 6-11-6 V Slattery, *in tch to 6th, tld off whn pld up bef 2 out*....... (50 to 1 op 20 to 1) pu
1594 MERLIN ROCKET 6-11-6 C Maude, *beh 5th, tld off whn pld up bef 7th*........(33 to 1 op 25 to 1 tchd 50 to 1) pu
2029[6] CUMREWS NEPHEW 6-11-6 D Bridgwater, *sn tld off, pld up bef 6th*..........................(50 to 1 op 33 to 1) pu

Dist: 1½l, ½l, 1l, dist, 2½l, 2l, 12l, 1½l, 3l, 2l. 5m 37.50s. a 31.50s (22 Ran).

(Mrs P G Wilkins), P J Hobbs

2145 John Bull Chase (5-y-o and up) £5,182
2m 5f. . . . . (2:50)

1560² DEEP SENSATION 9-11-10 D Murphy, *hld up, cld 4 out, led
appr nxt, idled r-in, shaken up close hme.*
. . . . (9 to 4 on op 5 to 2 on tchd 2 to 1 on) 1
ELFAST 11-11-10 G McCourt, *drpd rear 8th, ran on to
track ldrs 4 out, ev ch nxt, rdn and styd on r-in, not
pace of wnr.* . . . . (10 to 1 op 8 to 1) 2
TOBY TOBIAS 12-11-6 R Dunwoody, *hdwy 7th, jmpd
slwly 13th, pressed ldrs 4 out till aftr nxt, shaken up
and kpt on r-in.* . . . . (4 to 1 op 7 to 2) 3
2047 HICKELTON LAD 10-11-2 M A FitzGerald, *chsd ldr, led 9th
till appr 3 out, wknd.* . . . . (66 to 1 op 50 to 1) 4
1844⁵ POPPETS PET 7-11-2 S Earle, *jmpd slwly second, hit 5th,
drpd rear nxt, hit 8th, chlgd tenth to 13th, sn wknd.*
. . . . (12 to 1 op 10 to 1) 5
RUSSELL ROVER 9-11-2 B Powell, *led, mstk and hdd 9th,
tld off whn pld up bef 11th.* . . . . (66 to 1 op 33 to 1) pu
Dist: ½l, ½l, 30l, ¾l. 5m 37.90s. a 31.90s (6 Ran).

(R F Eliot), J T Gifford

2146 EBF Blackmore Vale Mares' Novices'
Handicap Chase (5-y-o and up) £3,002
2m. . . . . (3:20)

1696 NICKLUP [85] 7-11-0 B Powell, *in tch, chlgd 4 out, sn led,
kpt on wl appr last.* (4 to 1 fav op 7 to 2 tchd 9 to 2) 1
1866⁶ PRUDENT PEGGY [85] 7-11-0 J Frost, *rcd wide, hdwy 7th,
chlgd 3 out, shaken up and not quicken appr last.*
. . . . (10 to 1 op 6 to 1) 2
389⁴ WEST LODGE LADY [74] 9-10-3³ P Holley, *hdwy 8th, styd
on same pace appr 3 out.* . . . . (50 to 1 op 25 to 1) 3
2030⁴ MAGGOTS GREEN [83] 7-10-9 (3*) R Farrant, *hdwy 8th,
rdn and hld whn blun 3 out, not fluent last 2.*
. . . . (5 to 1 op 9 to 2) 4
1947 KETTI [90] 9-11-5 R Dunwoody, *prmnt till rdn and no
imprsn 4 out.* . . . . (12 to 1 op 10 to 1) 5
1879 HAND OUT [79] 10-10-8 S Earle, *led to second, in tch to
9th.* . . . . (14 to 1 op 12 to 1) 6
1886³ FANTASY WORLD [99] 8-12-0 D Murphy, *in tch to 8th.*
. . . . (11 to 2 op 7 to 2) 7
1947³ PALM SWIFT [73] 8-10-2² S McNeill, *led second, clr 4th,
pckd nxt, hdd aftr four out, wknd rpdly.*
. . . . (33 to 1 op 25 to 1) 8
1564 PLATINUM SPRINGS [71] 7-10-0 N Williamson, *beh 6th.*
. . . . (50 to 1 op 33 to 1) 9
1718 TURKISH STAR [80] 9-10-9 S Mackey, *beh whn blun 7th,
tld off when pld up bef 4 out.* . . . (25 to 1 op 14 to 1) pu
BAGS [71] 10-10-0 I Lawrence, *tld off 6th, pld up bef 9th.*
. . . . (50 to 1 op 33 to 1) pu
2017 KIWI VELOCITY (NZ) [95] 7-11-10 M Hourigan, *not jump wl,
beh whn blun 8th, tld off when pld up bef 2 out.*
. . . . (5 to 1 op 4 to 1 tchd 11 to 2) pu
GLADYS EMMANUEL [72] 7-10-1¹ C Maude, *mstk 4th, beh,
tld off whn pld up bef four out.* . . (10 to 1 op 20 to 1) pu
1696³ BARONESS ORKZY [87] 8-11-2 R Greene, *in tch whn mstk
5th, sn beh, tld off when pld up bef 3 out.*
. . . . (13 to 2 op 6 to 1 tchd 7 to 1) pu
Dist: 5l, 10l, 2½l, 10l, 20l, 1½l, dist. 4m 13.00s. a 22.00s (14 Ran).
SR: 30/25/4/10/8/-/ (Lord Cadogan), Capt T A Forster

2147 Spetisbury 'National Hunt' Novices'
Hurdle (4-y-o and up) £2,495 2m (3:50)

1418² GALES CAVALIER (Ire) 6-11-5 R Dunwoody, *chsd ldrs, led
4th, shaken up and wnt clr appr 2 out.*
. . . . (11 to 4 fav op 7 to 2 tchd 4 to 1 and 5 to 2) 1
1935⁵ DESERT RUN (Ire) 6-11-5 A Maguire, *hdwy 4th, styd on
frm 2 out, no imprsn on wnr.* . . . . . . (5 to 1 op 3 to 1) 2
1800⁴ CONEY ROAD 5-11-5 A McCabe, *beh, ran on frm 3 out,
kpt on same pace appr last.* . . . . . . (14 to 1 op 10 to 1) 3
1442⁷ BRAVE HIGHLANDER (Ire) 6-11-5 D Murphy, *hld up, hdwy
to track ldrs aftr 3 out, shaken up aftr nxt, wknd last.*
. . . . (5 to 1 op 3 to 1) 4
ILE DE SOO 8-11-5 H Davies, *hdwy frm 4th, one pace
appr 2 out.* . . . . (12 to 1 op 20 to 1) 5
1548⁷ PRINCE TEETON 5-11-5 S Earle, *hdwy to chase ldrs 5th,
wknd appr 2 out.* . . . . (50 to 1 op 33 to 1) 6
1871⁹ BIDDLESTONE BOY (NZ) 7-11-2 (3*) R Davis, *beh, hdwy to
chase ldrs aftr nxt, wknd after nxt.*
. . . . (5 to 1 op 20 to 1) 7
2048³ FRIENDLY FELLOW 5-11-11 P Holley, *nvr rch ldrs.*
. . . . (5 to 2 op 5 to 1 tchd 4 to 1) 8
RIVAGE BLEU 7-10-12 (7*) Mr E James, *prmnt, chsd ldrs
5th till wknd appr 2 out.* . . . . (100 to 1 op 50 to 1) 9
1626 MAGGIE TEE 6-11-0 G Upton, *beh, hdwy 5th, wknd aftr 3
out.* . . . . (100 to 1 op 50 to 1) 10
1800⁷ FOUR HEARTS (Ire) 5-11-5 B Powell, *chsd ldrs to 4th.*
. . . . (16 to 1 op 14 to 1 tchd 20 to 1) 11
GREENHIL TARE AWAY 6-11-5 M Hourigan, *beh hfwy.*
. . . . (20 to 1 op 12 to 1) 12
1494⁸ THREE OF CLUBS (Ire) 5-11-5 N Williamson, *effrt 5th,
wknd 3 out.* . . . . (33 to 1 op 16 to 1) 13

1800 COMEDIMAN 6-11-5 R Bellamy, *beh hfwy.*
. . . . (25 to 1 op 14 to 1) 14
JOURNEYS FRIEND (Ire) 6-11-5 M A FitzGerald, *beh till ran
out 3rd.* . . . . (20 to 1 op 10 to 1) ro
MAMES BOY 7-11-5 E Murphy, *beh, hmpd 3rd, pld up
aftr.* . . . . (33 to 1 op 12 to 1) pu
1567 FIFTH IN LINE (Ire) 6-11-5 C Maude, *beh 5th, tld off whn
pld up bef 2 out.* . . . . . . (20 to 1 op 50 to 1 tchd 66 to 1) pu
2014 GOLDEN FELLOW (Ire) 6-11-5 J Railton, *prmnt to 4th, sn
wknd, tld off whn pld up bef last.* . . . . (50 to 1) pu
1021 CORNELIUS O'DEA (Ire) 4-10-7 W Irvine, *led to 4th, wknd
quickly, tld off whn pld up bef 2 out.*
. . . . (66 to 1 op 50 to 1) pu
1646 MYSTICAL MISTRAL 7-11-0 D Gallagher, *sn beh, tld off
whn pld up bef 2 out.* . . . . (100 to 1 op 50 to 1) pu
Dist: 4l, hd, 1½l, 7l, 6l, 1½l, 6l, 2½l, nk, 7l. 3m 58.90s. a 21.90s (20 Ran).
(T J Whitley), D R Gandolfo

EDINBURGH (good)
Friday January 14th
Going Correction: NIL

2148 Dyewater Maiden Hurdle (Div I) (4-y-o
and up) £1,945 2m. . . . . (12:45)

LEGION OF HONOUR 6-11-4 (5*) T Jenks, *traacked ldrs,
led gng wl afer 2 out, quickened appr last, easily.*
. . . . (5 to 2 op 6 to 1 tchd 8 to 1) 1
1613⁴ COOL LUKE (Ire) 5-11-6 (3*) N Bentley, *hld up in tch, hdwy
to chal 2 out, sn rdn, kpt on, no imprsn.*
. . . . (Evens fav op 11 to 10 tchd 5 to 4) 2
1724⁴ MONTRAVE 5-11-9 B Storey, *hld up, hdwy aftr 3 out,
styd on frm nxt, nrst finish.* . . . . . . (10 to 1 tchd 8 to 1) 3
DANCE ON SIXPENCE 6-11-9 A Maguire, *hld up, hdwy
aftr 3 out, rdn after nxt, kpt on same pace.*
. . . . (11 to 1 op 8 to 1) 4
2003³ MEDIA MESSENGER 5-11-4 (5*) P Waggott, *mid-div, ch
appr 2 out, kpt on same pace.*
. . . . (9 to 2 op 5 to 1 tchd 8 to 1) 5
2003 CHOIR'S IMAGE 7-11-4 A Mulholland, *led second till aftr 2
out, wknd.* . . . . (50 to 1 op 33 to 1) 6
PRIMO FIGLIO (bl) 4-10-8 (3*) A Thornton, *chsd ldrs, wknd
aftr 2 out.* . . . . (9 to 1 op 7 to 1 tchd 10 to 1) 7
2003 PESIDANAMICH (Ire) 6-11-9 C Grant, *led to second, prmnt
till wknd aftr 3 out.* . . . . (33 to 1 op 25 to 1) 8
1959⁸ SHATRAVIV 6-11-4 R Dunwoody, *trkd ldrs, ev ch 2 out,
wknd quickly.* . . . . (25 to 1 op 20 to 1) 9
UNSUSPICIOUS (Ire) 4-10-11 P McDermott, *sn beh, some
late hdwy, nvr dngrs.*
. . . . (25 to 1 op 14 to 1 tchd 33 to 1) 10
2068⁶ MUFID (USA) 5-11-9 P Niven, *chsd ldrs till wknd aftr 3
out.* . . . . (14 to 1 op 12 to 1 tchd 16 to 1) 11
SUPREME SOVIET 4-10-6 (5*) J Supple, *in tch till wknd
aftr 3 out.* . . . . (100 to 1) 12
GOLDEN CAIRN (Ire) 5-11-9 T Reed, *sn beh, tld off whn
pld up bef 2 out.* . . . . (50 to 1 op 33 to 1) pu
Dist: 8l, ¾l, nk, 1½l, 6l, 3½l, 1½l, sht-hd, 6l, 4l. 3m 46.40s. a 8.40s (13 Ran).
SR: 11/3/2/1/-/-/ (Robson/Pattinson Partnership), M P Naughton

2149 Hopeswater Novices' Claiming Chase
(6-y-o and up) £2,203 3m. . . . . . . (1:15)

1807 LADY BLAKENEY 8-11-1 R Dunwoody, *cl up, led 4th, styd
on wl frm 2 out.* . . . . . (11 to 1 op 8 to 1 tchd 12 to 1) 1
2071⁴ TRAVEL BOUND 9-11-2 A Maguire, *chsd ldrs, slightly
outpcd aftr 3 out, sn on wl und pres frm 2 out.*
. . . . (13 to 2 op 5 to 1 tchd 7 to 1) 2
1790* EBRO 8-11-6 A Dobbin, *sn tracking ldrs, jnd wnr 13th,
rdn appr 3 out, wknd.* . . . . (10 to 1 op 6 to 1) 3
2007⁶ FLING IN SPRING (v) 8-10-5 (5*) P Williams, *hld up, hdwy
to track ldrs 11th, ev ch 4 out, kpt on same pace.*
. . . . (16 to 1 op 12 to 1) 4
1676³ CLARE LAD 11-10-12 B Storey, *nvr trble ldrs. .* . . (3 to 1 jt-
fav op 11 to 4) 5
2069³ CAPITAL PUNISHMENT 8-11-6 C Grant, *in tch, pushed
alng appr 11th, sn beh.* . . . . (3 to 1 jt-fav op 5 to 1) 6
1605 SANDEDGE 7-10-4 (5*) P Waggott, *in tch whn blun 8th
and tenth, sn beh.* . . . . (33 to 1) 7
1923³ NOBBY (bl) 8-10-6 A Mulholland, *blun 3rd, al beh, f 14th.*
. . . . (20 to 1 op 16 to 1) f
1723 BALLYBELL 9-10-8² T Reed, *led, mstk 3rd, hdd nxt, wth
wnr till wknd, blun and uns rdr 13th.*
. . . . (60 to 1 op 33 to 1) ur
2071 QUIET MONEY 7-11-6 P Niven, *trkd ldrs till wknd hfwy,
lost tch and pld up 8th.* . . . . (5 to 1 op 4 to 1) pu
Dist: 2½l, 4l, ½l, 15l, 20l, hd. 6m 8.60s. a 18.60s (10 Ran).
(J B Young), B S Rothwell

2150 Whitewater Novices' Handicap Hurdle
(4-y-o and up) £2,008 2m. . . . . . . (1:45)

2070 LEGITIM [81] 5-10-11 (5*) P Williams, *trkd ldrs, l/t clr 2 out,
styd on wl.* . . . . (5 to 1 co-fav tchd 6 to 1) 1
1734³ FORTUNE'S GIRL [88] 6-11-4 (5*) D Bentley, *in tch, hit
second, hdwy aftr 3 out, chsd wnr nxt, no imprsn.*
. . . . (8 to 1 op 6 to 1 tchd 10 to 1) 2

1613[7] JOMOVE [89] 5-11-10 R Dunwoody, *in tch, hdwy aftr 3 out, kpt on same pace frm nxt*.....(20 to 1 op 12 to 1) 3
1865* WAMDHA (Ire) [76] 4-10-11 A S Smith, *hld up, hdwy on outsd aftr 3 out, hmpd nxt, no ch after*. ....(5 to 1 co-fav op 6 to 1 tchd 7 to 1) 4
1722 RALLYING CRY (Ire) [67] (v) 6-10-2 B Storey, *chsd ldrs, effrt appr 3 out, no hdwy*................(33 to 1 op 20 to 1) 5
988 AVISHAYES (USA) [73] 7-10-8 P Niven, *beh, some late hdwy, nvr dngrs*......(12 to 1 op 8 to 1 tchd 14 to 1) 6
1877 TAHITIAN [77] 5-10-12 G McCourt, *chsd ldrs, sn pushed alng, wknd appr 2 out*................(7 to 1 tchd 8 to 1) 7
2068[8] RED TEMPEST (Ire) [77] 6-10-12 L O'Hara, *al beh*.
....(33 to 1 op 25 to 1) 8
2005 DANCING STREET [74] 6-10-9 C Hawkins, *in tch till wknd appr 2 out*.........(40 to 1 op 33 to 1 tchd 50 to 1) 9
1959 STAGGERING (Ire) [65] 5-9-11[2] (5*) T Jenks, *beh, hdwy appr 3 out, hmpd nxt, sn wknd*..............(50 to 1) 10
1791[5] ERBIL (Ire) [81] 4-10-11 (5*) F Perratt, *prmnt till wknd appr 2 out*.....................(5 to 1 co-fav tchd 6 to 1) 11
1791[7] BORING (USA) [77] 5-10-12 A Maguire, *led, hrd pressed whn f 2 out*....................(14 to 1 op 12 to 1) f
1668[2] SWIFT CONVEYANCE (Ire) [82] 5-10-10 (7*) S McDougall, *al cl up, rdn whn f 2 out*. (11 to 2 op 5 to 1 tchd 6 to 1) f
1865[8] LEARNED STAR (Ire) [66] 9-10-1[6] (5*) S Lyons, *sn beh, tld off whn pld up bef 2 out*....................(50 to 1) pu
1647[4] BAJAN AFFAIR [83] 4-11-3 (3*) A Thornton, *chsd ldrs to hfwy, sn wknd, tld off whn pld up bef 2 out*.
....(10 to 1 op 8 to 1) pu
Dist: 3½l, 10l, 10l, 4l, 1l, ¾l, 3½l, sht-hd, 4l, 3l. 3m 44.50s. a 6.50s (15 Ran).
SR: 23/26/17/-/-/-/ (John Donald), J M Jefferson

2151 Whiteadder Handicap Chase (0-110 5-y-o and up) £2,801 2½m..... (2:15)

1486[8] BISHOPDALE [104] 13-11-8 A Dobbin, *mid-div, pushed alng hfwy, reminders aftr tenth, chlgd 3 out, led last, all out*.................................(50 to 1) 1
2064[8] LAPIAFFE [95] 10-10-13 R Dunwoody, *al cl up, chlgd 4 out, dsptd ld last, no extr*..............(14 to 1 op 12 to 1) 2
2073* ONE FOR THE POT [107] 9-11-6 (5*) T Jenks, *hld up, hdwy aftr tenth, led 3 out to nxt, no extr*.
....(5 to 2 fav op 7 to 2) 3
591[9] KIND'A SMART [106] 9-11-10 A S Smith, *mid-div, kpt on frm 3 out, not rch ldrs*.........(14 to 1 tchd 16 to 1) 4
973[3] CENTENARY STAR [102] 9-11-6 P Niven, *hld up, hdwy to track ldrs hfwy, lost pl appr 4 out*...(8 to 1 op 7 to 1) 5
1222[4] EASTERN OASIS [101] 11-11-5 G McCourt, *beh, styd on frm 4 out, nvr nr to chal*...........(9 to 1 op 8 to 1) 6
1789[3] CLASSIC MINSTREL [97] 10-11-1 T Reed, *trkd ldrs, blun 8th, one pace 4 out*.........(11 to 2 op 6 to 1) 7
1585[7] MOSS BEE [89] 7-10-7 R Hodge, *sn cl up, lft in ld tenth, hdd 3 out, soon wknd*.......(16 to 1 op 14 to 1) 8
1343[5] STEPFASTER [107] 9-11-8 (3*) A Thornton, *beh hfwy*.
....(25 to 1 op 20 to 1 tchd 33 to 1) 9
1585* CHOICE CHALLANGE [98] 11-11-2 C Grant, *cl up, lft in ld aftr 6th till f tenth*....(5 to 1 op 4 to 1 tchd 11 to 2) f
2073[2] SONSIE MO [108] 9-11-7 (5*) P Williams, *led till pld up lme aftr 6th*.................(7 to 1 op 5 to 1) pu
Dist: 2l, 1½l, 2½l, 1½l, 1l, nk, 8l, 15l. 5m 4.30s. a 14.30s (11 Ran).
(S Chadwick), S G Chadwick

2152 Fasery Conditional Jockeys' Claiming Hurdle (5-y-o and up) £2,050 2½m
....(2:45)

1361* FIRM PRICE 13-11-7 (5*) G Lee, *sn tracking ldrs, led last, pushed clr, cmftbly*.
....(11 to 8 on op 6 to 4 on tchd 5 to 4 on) 1
VALIANT DASH 8-10-9 (5*) Mark Roberts, *prmnt, jnd ldr hfwy, sn pushed alng, ev ch appr last, kpt on nr finish*.
....(5 to 1 op 4 to 1) 2
1788[8] A GENTLEMAN TWO 8-10-10 S Lyons, *led to last, btn whn eased nr finish*..................(14 to 1 tchd 16 to 1) 3
1788[9] SKOLERN (v) 10-10-9 A Thornton, *trkd ldrs, kpt on same pace frm 3 out*................(10 to 1 op 12 to 1) 4
2070[7] SAOIRSE (Ire) 6-10-8 D J Moffatt, *beh, kpt on frm 3 out, not rch ldrs*..........(9 to 1 op 8 to 1 tchd 10 to 1) 5
818 HOTDIGGITY 6-10-10 A Dobbin, *hld up, hdwy hfwy, chsd ldrs 3 out, wknd appr nxt*....(33 to 1 tchd 50 to 1) 6
1940[8] BELLAGROVE (Ire) (bl) 6-10-8 (5*) G Cahill, *in tch, no hdwy frm 3 out*...............(50 to 1 op 33 to 1) 7
818[9] DOCTOR'S REMEDY 8-10-6 S Taylor, *chsd ldrs to hfwy, sn beh*.......................(33 to 1) 8
1963 PALM HOUSE 9-11-7 (5*) N Stocks, *beh hfwy*.
....(20 to 1 op 16 to 1) 9
2071 MAUREEN'S FANCY 9-10-10 S Mason, *prmnt to hfwy, sn beh*..................(25 to 1 tchd 33 to 1) 10
1096 BLUEBELL TRACK 8-10-8 F Perratt, *outpcd and lost tch hfwy*.................................(50 to 1) 11
1961 GYMCRAK CYRANO (Ire) 5-10-9 D Bentley, *chsd ldrs to hfwy, sn beh*.......(33 to 1 op 25 to 1) 12
JANE'S AFFAIR 6-11-3 S Wynne, *al beh, tld off*.
....(50 to 1 op 33 to 1) 13
Dist: 5l, nd, 6l, 8l, 2l, 4l, 12l, nk, 5l, 10l. 4m 58.60s. a 20.60s (13 Ran).
(Mrs Susan McDonald), Mrs M Reveley

2153 Watch Water Handicap Hurdle (0-115 4-y-o and up) £2,347 3m....... (3:15)

1740[4] IF YOU SAY SO [87] 8-10-1 A Mulholland, *cl up, led 7th, drw clr betw last 2, cmftbly*........(10 to 1 op 8 to 1) 1
1480[2] SHAFFIC (Fr) [110] 7-11-10 P Niven, *jmpd lft, hld up, effrt aftr 3 out, styd on frm nxt, no ch cth wnr*.
....(7 to 2 fav op 4 to 1 tchd 5 to 1) 2
1793* THE GREEN FOOL [108] 7-11-8 A Dobbin, *sn cl up, dsptd ld 7th till no extr betw last 2*.........(8 to 1 op 7 to 1) 3
1793[4] MINGUS (USA) [96] 7-10-7 (3*) A Thornton, *hld up, hdwy aftr 7th, kpt on same pace frm 3 out*..(6 to 1 op 5 to 1) 4
1619[8] TRUMP [96] 5-10-10 B Storey, *hld up, hdwy 8th, kpt on same pace frm 3 out*............(5 to 1 op 4 to 1) 5
2060[4] PIMS GUNNER (Ire) [93] 6-10-2 (5*) D Bentley, *mid-div, no hdwy 3 out*.........(14 to 1 op 10 to 1 tchd 16 to 1) 6
REXY BOY [86] 7-10-0 R Marley, *led to 7th, wknd 9th*.
....(25 to 1 op 33 to 1) 7
1746[5] SPACE CAPTAIN [102] 7-10-13 (3*) N Bentley, *in tch, hdwy to chase ldrs 9th, wknd appr 2 out*.
....(11 to 1 op 12 to 1 tchd 14 to 1) 8
1963[6] HARDIHERO [87] 8-10-1[1] C Hawkins, *beh 8th*.
....(16 to 1 tchd 20 to 1) 9
ROSE TABLEAU [104] 11-11-4 R Dunwoody, *beh 8th*.
....(14 to 1 op 12 to 1) 10
1725[5] OFF THE BRU [103] (v) 9-11-3 Mr J Bradburne, *chsd ldrs till wknd aftr 7th*...................(16 to 1 op 14 to 1) 11
1793[5] LEADING PROSPECT [112] 7-11-5 (7*) Mr A Parker, *beh 9th*.
....(8 to 1 op 10 to 1 tchd 12 to 1) 12
1458 NESSFIELD [104] 8-11-4 A S Smith, *trkd ldrs till wknd aftr tenth*.................................(12 to 1) 13
2071 PANTO LADY [86] 8-9-7 (7*) Miss S Lamb, *sn tld off*.
....(500 to 1) 14
1936[8] HELLO GEORGIE [89] (bl) 11-10-3[3] R Garritty, *beh 8th, pld up bef last*...............(33 to 1 tchd 50 to 1) pu
Dist: 7l, 1½l, ½l, ½l, 6l, 6l, 4l, 8l, 2½l, ½l. 5m 54.60s. a 14.60s (15 Ran).
(S J Smith), J L Eyre

2154 Dyewater Maiden Hurdle (Div II) (4-y-o and up) £1,945 2m.............(3:40)

1920[5] BALLON 4-10-6 T Reed, *hld up beh, hdwy aftr 3 out, led appr last, quickened clr, easily*.
....(13 to 2 op 6 to 1 tchd 7 to 1) 1
PRINCESS MAXINE (Ire) 5-11-4 P Niven, *hld up, hdwy hfwy, led betw last 2, sn hdd, kpt on, no ch cth wnr*.
....(7 to 2 op 3 to 1 tchd 4 to 1) 2
1414[2] HIGH MIND (Fr) 5-11-6 (3*) A Thornton, *chsd ldrs, outpcd aftr 3 out, styd on frm nxt*........(7 to 2 op 6 to 1) 3
KING ATHELSTAN (USA) 6-11-9 A S Smith, *led aftr second till betweeen last 2, sn wknd*.
....(7 to 1 op 5 to 1 tchd 8 to 1) 4
1959[6] PHILDAN (Ire) 5-11-6 (3*) D J Moffatt, *sn tld off, styd on wl frm 2 out, nrst finish*.............(25 to 1 op 20 to 1) 5
1959[2] VAL DE RAMA (Ire) 5-11-4 (5*) P Waggott, *chsd ldrs, ev ch appr 2 out, sn wknd*............(6 to 1 op 5 to 1) 6
1787[7] STRONG FLAME (Ire) 5-11-4 (5*) S Lyons, *cl up till wknd appr 2 out*.................(16 to 1 op 12 to 1) 7
1658[5] MONASTIC FLIGHT (Ire) (v) 4-10-4 (7*) G Cahill, *beh 5th*.
....(50 to 1 op 33 to 1) 8
1655[2] SUMMERS DREAM 4-10-6 C Hawkins, *trkd ldrs, rdn aftr 3 out, sn wknd*................(25 to 1 op 14 to 1) 9
1920[6] THALEROS 4-10-11 J Callaghan, *in tch, hdwy appr 3 out, rdn approaching nxt, sn wknd*...(5 to 2 fav op 6 to 4) 10
BROWN BOMBER 5-11-9 R Garritty, *sn beh, tld off*.
....(100 to 1) 11
2068 CHALKIEFORT 5-11-4 (5*) K Jones, *led till hmpd and hdd aftr second, sn beh, tld off whn pld up bef 2 out*. (500 to 1) pu
Dist: 7l, 10l, 6l, 8l, 1½l, 8l, 1½l, ½l, 7l, 20l. 3m 50.30s. a 12.30s (12 Ran).
(Whitworth Racing), M Dods

PUNCHESTOWN (IRE) (heavy) Saturday January 15th

2155 Brannockstown Maiden Hurdle (5-y-o and up) £3,105 2m.............(1:00)

2024[3] LAWYER'S BRIEF (Fr) 7-11-6 L P Cusack, ...(6 to 4 fav) 1
1815 LOTTOVER (Ire) 5-11-0 C O'Dwyer, ...(14 to 1) 2
2096[3] MAXWELTON BRAES (Ire) 5-11-10 C F Swan, ...(4 to 1) 3
2050[5] POOR MOTHER (Ire) 6-11-1 F J Flood, ...(12 to 1) 4
2024 INAUGURATION (Ire) 5-11-2 A Powell, ...(20 to 1) 5
2052[6] JIMMY O'GOBLIN 7-10-13 (7*) F Byrne, ...(8 to 1) 7
1815[6] KING WAH GLORY (Ire) 5-11-3 (7*) Mr J Connolly, ..(5 to 1) 8
1978[7] TAGANINI (Ire) 6-11-7 (7*) C McCormack, ...(14 to 1) 9
2024 VALTORUS (Ire) 5-11-2 K F O'Brien, ...(14 to 1) 10
GALTIG 6-11-6 H Rogers, ...(20 to 1) 11
1854[5] LEAVE IT TO JUDGE 7-10-13 (7*) J P Broderick, ..(25 to 1) 12
1904[5] VISTAGE (Ire) 6-12-0 B Sheridan, ...(8 to 1) 13
1858[9] ANOTHER STAR (Ire) 5-10-11 M Moran, ...(20 to 1) 14
Dist: Hd, 3½l, 5½l, hd. 4m 19.10s. (14 Ran).
(P D Osborne), P D Osborne

2156 Michael McHugh Memorial Hurdle (4-y-o) £3,450 2m. . . . . (1:30)

1816[3] MAGIC FEELING (Ire) 10-9 C F Swan, ... (5 to 4 jt-fav) 1
1846[3] MAYASTA (Ire) 10-5 C O'Dwyer, ...(5 to 4 jt-fav) 2
1853* THE SALTY FROG (Ire) 11-0 M Flynn, ... (6 to 1) 3
1983[7] REASILVIA (Ire) 10-5 T Horgan, ...(8 to 1) 4
Dist: 7l, 2l, 25l. 4m 14.20s. (4 Ran).
(Mrs J M Ryan), A P O'Brien

2157 Berneys Bar & Restaurant Novice Chase (5-y-o and up) £3,795 2m 5f . . . .(2:00)

1900[2] ALL THE ACES 7-12-0 T J Taaffe, ...(5 to 2 fav) 1
1851[2] BEAU BABILLARD 7-12-0 C F Swan, ... (3 to 1) 2
1988[2] BERMUDA BUCK 8-12-0 F Woods, ...(5 to 1) 3
1451[5] BACK BAR (Ire) 6-11-9 J Shortt, ...(25 to 1) 4
2055 THE MIGHTY BUCK 11-11-9 J F Titley, ... (16 to 1) 5
1981[3] ENQELAAB (USA) 6-12-0 J P Banahan, ... (10 to 1) 6
1914 SUPER MIDGE 7-11-11 (3*) C O'Brien, ...(14 to 1) 7
1829* BUMBO HALL VI (Ire) 6-11-6 (3*) T J Mitchell, ...(12 to 1) 8
1829[3] LE BRAVE 8-11-9 K F O'Brien, ... (12 to 1) 9
1892[8] ROYAL SEER 8-11-4 (5*) T P Rudd, ...(16 to 1) 10
1785 SHEILA NA GIG 8-11-9 A Powell, ...(8 to 1) 11
1981[2] OXFORD QUILL 7-11-9 L P Cusack, ...(10 to 1) 12
1986[7] PELEUS (USA) 9-11-9 (5*) M G Cleary, ... (20 to 1) 13
1897 MOONCAPER 8-11-9 T Horgan, ... (12 to 1) 14
2055[5] PRANKSTER 8-11-9 C O'Dwyer, ... (40 to 1) 15
1451 OLD MONEY 8-12-0 P Carberry, ... (16 to 1) 16
1981 GONE LIKE THE WIND 7-11-4 (5*) L Flynn, ... (66 to 1) 17
1235[9] SOME BRIDGE 7-11-4 S H O'Donovan, ...(66 to 1) f
1905 BROGUESTOWN 9-12-0 F J Flood, ... (16 to 1) pu
Dist: 8l, 14l, 9l, ½l. 6m 4.60s. (19 Ran).
(John P McManus), A L T Moore

2158 Blackhills Hurdle (2-y-o) £3,105 2½m . . . .(2:30)

2098[2] RATHCORE 11-8 L P Cusack, ... (10 to 9 on) 1
KELLYMOUNT 10-9 (7*) P Morris, ... (13 to 2) 2
258[7] PROFIT MOTIVE (Ire) 10-12 C F Swan, ...(6 to 1) 3
2096[6] MR SNAGGLE (Ire) 11-1 (3*) C O'Brien, ...(3 to 1) 4
1898 MONEY SAVED 11-2 W T Slattery Jnr, ... (33 to 1) 5
Dist: 9l, ½l, 2½l, 20l. 6m 8.10s. (5 Ran).
(Michael Kiernan), Michael Kiernan

2159 Ballymore Eustace Handicap Chase (5-y-o and up) £6,900 2¼m. . . . . .(3:00)

1985 SATULA [-] 10-10-0 C O'Dwyer, ... (4 to 1) 1
1985[2] THIRD QUARTER [-] 9-10-11 K F O'Brien, ...(5 to 1) 2
1847[3] BOB DEVANI [-] 8-10-6 P Carberry, ...(100 to 30) 3
1433[3] MAGIC MILLION [-] 8-10-3 J P Banahan, ...(6 to 1) 4
1985* MAD TOM [-] 9-11-1 (7*,6ex) J P Broderick, ...(3 to 1 fav) 5
1847 KINGS ENGLISH [-] 8-11-0 T Horgan, ...(8 to 1) 6
2077 SARAEMMA [-] 8-11-6 C F Swan, ... (5 to 1) 7
Dist: 2½l, 2l, 6l, ¾l. 5m 3.00s. (7 Ran).
(Mrs L Burke), V T O'Brien

2160 Landenstown Handicap Hurdle (0-137 4-y-o and up) £3,105 2¾m. . . . . . (3:30)

2078* GOLDEN OPAL [-] 9-9-13 (7*,4ex) J P Broderick, (2 to 1 fav) 1
1899* LUMINOUS LIGHT [-] 7-9-7 (7*,4ex) M D Murphy, . . (9 to 4) 2
1980[2] BARRONSTOWN BOY [-] 10-9-8 C F Swan, ...(9 to 2) 3
1829[6] MCCONNELL GOLD [-] 9-9-9 H Rogers, ... (10 to 1) 4
2078[5] AEGEAN FANFARE (Ire) [-] 5-10-8 (5*) M G Cleary, (12 to 1) 5
1980[4] LINVAR [-] (bl) 11-10-12 (7*) D J Kavanagh, ... (14 to 1) 6
1980[3] SADDLESTOWN GLEN [-] (bl) 9-10-4 F Woods, . . . (12 to 1) 7
1981 IPANEMA [-] 7-10-3 J P Banahan, ... (25 to 1) 8
1987[6] WINTERBOURNE ABBAS (Ire) [-] (bl) 5-10-8 B Sheridan, ...(10 to 1) f
Dist: 3½l, 2l, 8l, 20l. 6m 20.00s. (9 Ran).
(Mrs A M Kennelly), Michael Hourigan

2161 Greens Gorse Flat Race (5-y-o and up) £3,105 2m. (4:00)

1989[2] THE REAL ARTICLE (Ire) 5-11-3 (7*) Mr T J Murphy, ... (5 to 4 jt-fav) 1
1982[2] LINDEN'S LOTTO (Ire) 5-11-7 (3*) Mr A R Coonan, (5 to 4 jt-fav) 2
2041[8] NOPADDLE 10-11-11 (3*) Mrs J M Mullins, ... (13 to 2) 3
1814 FLYING COLUMN 7-11-9 (5*) Mr H F Cleary, ...(12 to 1) 4
1910[8] ROSDEMON (Ire) 6-12-0 Mr M McNulty, ...(8 to 1) 5
1910 PLEASURE SHARED (Ire) 6-12-0 Mr A P O'Brien, (12 to 1) 6
1982[6] LIFFEYSIDE LADY (Ire) 5-10-12 (7*) Mr J P Geoghegan, ...(14 to 1) 7
Dist: 5l, 3½l, 3l, 2l. 4m 10.90s. (7 Ran).
(William J Brennan), Gerard Stack

SOUTHWELL (A.W) (std)
Saturday January 15th
Going Correction: PLUS 0.60 sec. per fur.

2162 Putter Novices' Handicap Hurdle (4-y-o and up) £1,614 3m. . . . . (1:00)

1877[3] GYMCRAK DAWN [76] 9-10-0 P Harley, *al hndy, jnd ldr hfwy, led aftr 4 out, jmpd rght last 3, ran on.* . . . .(5 to 2 op 2 to 1) 1
1386* CARLINGFORD LAKES (Ire) [104] 6-12-0 S Smith Eccles, *led, hit 6 out, hdd and rdn aftr 4 out, kpt on same pace betw last 2....* (9 to 4 on op 5 to 2 on tchd 2 to 1 on) 2
1302 SAMSUN [81] (bl) 12-10-5[5] D O'Sullivan, *hit 1st, mstk and lost pl 5th, tld off.* . . . .(10 to 1 op 6 to 1) 3
Dist: 6l, dist. 6m 11.10s. a 34.10s (3 Ran).
(F Sanders), J Hetherton

2163 Niblick Claiming Hurdle (4-y-o and up) £1,753 2m. . . . . (1:30)

1810* SAYANT 9-11-4 Diane Clay, *made most frm 3rd, hit 4 out, drvn clr betw last 2, fnshd lme.* . . . . .(85 to 40 on op 7 to 4 on tchd 13 to 8 on and 9 to 4 on) 1
2061[4] RAIN-N-SUN 8-11-2 D Gallagher, *led to 3rd, styd upsides, rdn betw last 2, rallied.* . . . . (10 to 1 op 8 to 1 tchd 11 to 1) 2
1506[8] STATION EXPRESS (Ire) 6-10-9 (7*) S Mason, *trkd ldg pair, reminders to hold pl appr 4 out, styd on ag'n frm betw last 2.* . . . .(5 to 1 op 4 to 1) 3
COSMIC STAR 4-10-9 D O'Sullivan, *settled gng wl, effrt whn hit 6th, lost tch aftr 4 out, tld off.* . . . . (11 to 2 op 3 to 1) 4
Dist: 1½l, 8l, dist. 4m 2.00s. a 16.00s (4 Ran).
SR: 26/22/14/-/ (T Walker), W Clay

2164 Mashie Maiden Hurdle (4-y-o and up) £1,784 2m. (2:00)

1506[7] ALDINGTON CHAPPLE 6-11-5 T Wall, *settled midfield, led and lft clr 3 out, drvn out r-in.* . . . . (25 to 1 op 20 to 1 tchd 33 to 1) 1
1100 THE CAN CAN MAN 7-11-5 M Robinson, *keen hold, al hndy, drvn alng frm 3 out, kpt on same pace r-in.* . . . . (5 to 1 op 4 to 1 tchd 11 to 2) 2
2016[5] GUNNER SUE 4-10-5[1] J Railton, *nvr far away, feeling pace and rdn alng aftr 4 out, rallied and hmpd nxt, styd on r-in.* . . . .(5 to 1 op 5 to 1) 3
1865[6] BIRD WATCHER 5-11-5 C Grant, *settled gng wl, drvn to join ldrs aftr 4 out, rdn and no extr betw last 2.* . . . .(9 to 2 op 4 to 1 tchd 5 to 1) 4
2069 SUPREME BLUSHER 7-10-7 (7*) S McDougall, *hit 1st, improved into midfield hfwy, reminders aftr 5th, sn lost tch, tld off.* . . . .(50 to 1 op 33 to 1) 5
1872 PERFECT LIGHT 5-11-5 Richard Guest, *led, hdd whn f 3 out.* . . . .(10 to 1) f
1613[5] VANART 5-11-5 D Byrne, *settled off the pace, improved aftr 4 out, chalg whn hmpd and uns rdr nxt.* . . . . (11 to 8 fav op 11 to 10 tchd 6 to 4) ur
1768 ANOTHER TRYP 6-10-7 (7*) G McGrath, *pressed ldrs to hfwy, tld off whn blun and uns rdr 3 out.* . . . . (33 to 1 op 25 to 1) ur
Dist: 3l, 1½l, 7l, dist. 4m 3.20s. a 17.20s (8 Ran).
SR: 15/12/-/3/-/ (R J Dawson), B Preece

2165 Cleek Selling Handicap Hurdle (4-y-o and up) £1,737 2½m. . . . .(2:30)

2067[2] QUALITAIR MEMORY (Ire) [80] 5-11-3 D Gallagher, *made most, jnd 3rd, hit 2 out, hld on gmely r-in.* . . . .(7 to 4 fav op 5 to 4 tchd 15 to 8) 1
1801* FOR HEAVEN'S SAKE (Fr) [91] 9-11-9 (5*) E Husband, *dsptd ld thrght, ev ch frm 3 out, rdn last, rallied.* . . . .(3 to 1 op 5 to 2) 2
1801[5] SPANISH WHISPER [75] 7-10-7 (5*) J Twomey, *wtd wth, improved to track ldg pair appr 4 out, rdn alng frm nxt, one pace.* . . . . (3 to 1 op 7 to 2 tchd 11 to 4) 3
1863 MILLIE (USA) [63] 6-10-0 M Robinson, *struggling to keep up aftr 3rd, sn tld off.* . . . .(14 to 1 op 12 to 1) 4
1592 HARPLEY [80] (v) 7-10-10 (7*) N Juckes, *hit 1st, shrtlvd effrt hfwy, lost tch bef 4 out, tld off.* (14 to 1 op 7 to 1) 5
1627 SINGING GOLD [63] 8-9-9 (5*) S Curran, *trkd ldrs, lost pl quickly fnl circuit, tld off whn pld up bef 3 out.* . . . .(14 to 1 tchd 16 to 1) pu
1801[9] BIG GEM [63] 4-10-0 W Worthington, *sn struggling in rear, tld off whn pld up bef 5th.* . . . . (25 to 1 op 16 to 1) pu
Dist: Hd, 5l, dist, dist. 5m 7.10s. a 26.10s (7 Ran).
(Anthony Samuels), J Akehurst

2166 Brassie Handicap Hurdle (0-120 4-y-o and up) £1,707 2¾m. . . . .(3:00)

2089* COURT CIRCULAR [110] (v) 5-11-6 (6ex) Diane Clay, *led to second, led 6th, kpt on gmely r-in.* . . . . (85 to 40 op 7 to 4 tchd 9 to 4) 1
2060* ARCTIC OATS [105] 9-11-1 D Byrne, *patiently rdn, hdwy to join ldr appr 3 out, hit nxt, kpt on same pace frm last.* . . . . (9 to 4 op 2 to 1) 2
2120* ELEGANT KING (Ire) [102] 5-10-5 (7*,6ex) G McGrath, *wtd wth, drw level fnl circuit, rdn whn pace quickened 3 out, no extr.* . . . .(7 to 4 fav tchd 15 to 8) 3

1212⁴ EMSEE-H [116] 9-11-5 (7*) P Murphy, led aftr second to 6th, tld off after nxt, pld up bef 3 out.
.... (10 to 1 op 6 to 1)   pu
Dist: Nk, 12l. 5m 38.70s. a 29.70s (4 Ran).
(B A S Limited), W Clay

2167 Spoon Novices' Hurdle (4-y-o and up) £1,676 2½m.................(3:30)

2115 HEATHYARDS BOY (bl) 4-10-10 (3*) S Wynne, slight ld till quickened clr hfwy, hit 6 out, hld 4 out, rallied to lead cl hme.......(11 to 8 fav op Evens tchd 6 to 4)   1
1834 STRONG JOHN (Ire) 6-11-3 (7*) P Murphy, wtd wth, jnd ldr 6 out, led 4 out, faltered appr last, wknd and jst cr.
.... (11 to 4 op 7 to 4)   2
1837 KING SCORPIO (Ire) 5-11-4 J Railton, ran in snatches, rallied to chal aftr 4 out, rdn nxt, sn btn.
.... (3 to 1 tchd 7 to 2)   3
2048⁹ MERTON MISTRESS 7-10-13 D O'Sullivan, sn struggling. tld off hfwy.
.........(14 to 1 op 10 to 1 tchd 16 to 1 and 20 to 1)   4
1327⁶ MISTY GREY 5-10-11 (7*) S Lycett, dsptd ld till appr hfwy, sn lost pl, tld off.....(12 to 1 op 16 to 1 tchd 20 to 1)   5
Dist: Nk, 25l, 25l, 15l. 5m 7.00s. a 26.00s (5 Ran).
(L A Morgan), R Hollinshead

2168 Driver Handicap Hurdle (0-115 4-y-o and up) £1,737 2¼m...........(3:55)

LAVA FALLS (USA) [85] 8-11-1 D Skyrme, dsptd ld, led 7th, quickened clr aftr 4 out, styd on....(11 to 2 op 7 to 2)   1
1614⁹ IN TRUTH [86] 6-11-2 C Grant, dsptd ld to 7th, rdn alng frm 4 out, styd on same pace from nxt.
.... (5 to 2 op 9 to 4 tchd 11 to 4)   2
1936³ LOXLEY RANGE (Ire) [70] (v) 6-9-9² (7*) N Juckes, wtd wth, chlgd 7th, rdn appr 3 out, fdd bef nxt.
.... (7 to 2 op 3 to 1)   3
1839³ MRS MAYHEW (Ire) [94] 6-11-3 (7*) P Murphy, refused to race..........................(11 to 8 fav tchd 6 to 4)   I
Dist: 4l, 15l. 4m 41.40s. a 29.40s (4 Ran).
(Mrs M C Banks), M C Banks

WARWICK (heavy)
Saturday January 15th
Going Correction: PLUS 1.20 sec. per fur. (races 1,4,-7,8), PLUS 1.10 (2,3,5,6)

2169 Red Rose Four Year Old Hurdle £5,865 2m...........................(12:40)

1880³ KADASTROF (Fr) 11-4 D Meredith, pld hrd early, al prmnt, led aftr 3 out, hit nxt, drvn clr r-in.
.... (9 to 2 op 6 to 1 tchd 4 to 1)   1
1990* WINTER FOREST (USA) 11-6 A Maguire, hld up, making hdwy whn hit 3 out, hrd rdn to chal nxt, no extr r-in.
.... (13 to 8 fav op 7 to 4 tchd 6 to 4)   2
1880³ BURNT IMP (USA) 11-8 J Callaghan, chsd ldrs, rdn appr 3 out, kpt on one pace... (7 to 2 op 3 to 1 tchd 4 to 1)   3
2016² VELVET HEART (Ire) 10-13 M A FitzGerald, led till aftr 3rd, led nxt till sn aftr 3 out, wknd.
.... (16 to 1 op 12 to 1 tchd 20 to 1)   4
1990³ DUVEEN (Ire) 11-0 C Llewellyn, hld up rear, hdwy 4th, wknd appr 2 out.....(12 to 1 op 10 to 1 tchd 16 to 1)   5
1647 MY BALLYBOY 11-6 N Mann, hdwy aftr 3rd, rdn 5th, one pace appr 2 out...............(12 to 1 op 5 to 1)   6
2091² MR GENEAOLOGY (USA) (bl) 11-4 W McFarland, mid-div, hrd rdn 5th, no hdwy frm 3 out.
.... (16 to 1 op 12 to 1 tchd 20 to 1)   7
2000* SHARED GOLD 11-4 M Bosley, prmnt, led aftr 3rd to nxt, wknd quickly, tld off............(16 to 1 op 10 to 1)   8
PRIME OF LIFE (Ire) 11-0 S McNeill, hld up rear, outpcd 5th, tld off..............................(50 to 1)   9
1510 BARNIEMEBOY 11-0 W Elderfield, prmnt to 3rd, sn tld off, pld up bef 3 out.........(200 to 1 op 50 to 1)   pu
Dist: 4l, 8l, 4l, 1½l, ½l, 5l, 30l, 3l. 4m 4.10s. a 24.10s (10 Ran).
SR: 41/39/33/20/19/24/17/-/-/   (A P Paton), R Dickin

2170 Westminster-Motor Taxi Insurance Novices' Chase (5-y-o and up) £3,824 2½m 110yds....................(1:10)

190² CASTLE DIAMOND 7-11-8 R Dunwoody, jmpd wl, al prmnt, led 8th, ran on und pres frm 2 out, jst hld on.
.... (14 to 1 op 8 to 1)   1
2030* RAMSTAR 6-11-4 A Maguire, hld up, hdwy 6th, jnd wnr 7 out, ev ch whn not fluent last 2, hrd rdn and rallied r-in, jst fld............(7 to 2 jt-fav op 11 to 4 tchd 4 to 1)   2
1999² DONT TELL THE WIFE 8-11-4 D Murphy, hld up in tch, hdwy tenth, ev ch 2 out, one pace.
.... (9 to 2 op 5 to 1 tchd 11 to 2)   3
1805* JOLLY JAUNT 9-11-1 (7*) P Ward, nvr far away, outpcd frm 3 out...........(9 to 1 op 6 to 1)   4
DON VALENTINO 9-11-4 G Bradley, mid-div, hdwy tenth, rdn 4 out, wknd nxt.........................(7 to 2 jt-fav op 3 to 1 tchd 4 to 1)   5

1770⁴ DARK OAK 8-11-4 L O'Hara, chsd ldrs, wknd 6 out, tld off.................(14 to 1 op 10 to 1)   6
1527 CANAVER 8-11-4 G McCourt, hld up, hdwy tenth, wknd 6 out, tld off........(25 to 1 op 12 to 1)   7
BALLYKILTY 9-11-4 D Bridgwater, beh till hdwy tenth, wkng whn mstk 4 out, tld off......(25 to 1 op 12 to 1)   8
1967² BEAUFAN 7-11-4 Gary Lyons, al beh, mstk 12th, tld off.
.... (25 to 1 op 14 to 1)   9
1934⁴ PEGMARINE (USA) 11-10-13 (5*) J McCarthy, prmnt till wknd appr 7 out, tld off.........(66 to 1 op 50 to 1) 10
KATY KEYS 10-10-13 J Corkell, prmnt whn mstk 4th, wknd tenth, tld off.................(50 to 1 op 33 to 1) 11
CRUISING ON 7-10-13 W Marston, led aftr 1st to 8th, wkng whn mstk tenth, tld off.....................(50 to 1) 12
JENNY'S GLEN 7-11-4 R Supple, jmpd poorly in rear, tld off......................(20 to 1 op 16 to 1 tchd 33 to 1) 13
GOOSE GREEN 14-10-13 W Elderfield, led till aftr 1st, hit nxt, wknd 8th, blun tenth, tld off, collapsed after race, dead...............(100 to 1 op 66 to 1) 14
1567 ROMANY CREEK (Ire) 5-10-5 (3*) R Davis, f 1st.
.... (20 to 1 op 14 to 1)   f
2137 PLAYFUL JULIET (Can) (v) 6-11-3 Peter Caldwell, al beh, tld off whn blun 3 out, pld up bef last. (12 to 1 op 8 to 1)   pu
Dist: Sht-hd, 12l, 12l, 1½l, 15l, 15l, 15l, 8l, 5l, 1½l. 5m 30.20s. a 35.20s (16 Ran).
(Mrs S Kavanagh), H M Kavanagh

2171 Victor Chandler Handicap Chase Grade 2 (5-y-o and up) £19,328 2m ....(1:40)

1995² VIKING FLAGSHIP [147] 7-10-10 R Dunwoody, trkd ldr, led briefly 5th, rdn appr 2 out, ran on wl und pres to ld r-in....................(3 to 1 op 5 to 2 tchd 100 to 30)   1
1664⁹ EGYPT MILL PRINCE [141] (bl) 8-10-4 J Osborne, jmpd wl, made most till rdn and hdd r-in... (11 to 4 op 3 to 1)   2
1758* BILLY BATHGATE [141] 8-10-4 (4ex) M A FitzGerald, hld up, tried to cl 4 out, wknd nxt, tld off.... (3 to 1 op 9 to 4)   3
1560³ WATERLOO BOY [161] 11-11-10 A Maguire, in tch, rdn and cl 3rd whn mstk 4 out, sn btn and eased, tld off.
.... (5 to 2 fav tchd 11 to 4)   4
Dist: 2l, dist, 2½l. 4m 10.50s. a 18.50s (4 Ran).
SR: 73/65/-/-/   (Roach Foods Limited), D Nicholson

2172 Taxinews Handicap Hurdle Gold Card Qualifier (4-y-o and up) £4,825 2½m 110yds.......................(2:10)

2009* TOOGOOD TO BE TRUE [120] 6-10-13 L Wyer, hld up in tch, outpcd 3 out, hrd rdn and rallied wl nxt, led r-in.
.... (7 to 1 op 8 to 1)   1
1922* NORTHANTS [116] 8-10-9 R Hodge, hld up, hdwy 5 out, led sn aftr 3 out, rdn and hdd r-in.
.... (6 to 1 fav op 5 to 1)   2
1619* LINKSIDE [114] 9-10-7 M A FitzGerald, led to 3rd, ev ch 3 out, rallied appr last, kpt on r-in.
.... (14 to 1 tchd 16 to 1)   3
1863² FOX CHAPEL [117] 7-10-3 (7*) G Tormey, al prmnt, led 4 out to nxt, ev ch appr last, no extr frl 50 yards.
.... (12 to 1 op 10 to 1)   4
1922⁴ TINDARI (Fr) [119] 6-10-7 (5*) P Williams, nvr far away, ev ch 4 out rdn and wknd appr last.
.... (16 to 1 op 20 to 1)   5
1890* JEASSU [135] 11-11-9 (5*) T Jenks, hld up rear, hdwy 5 out, ev ch appr 2 out, wkng whn mstk last.... (16 to 1)   6
2009⁸ ANDERMATT [114] 7-10-7 N Williamson, hld up, hdwy 5 out, ev ch 3 out, one pace nxt.. (20 to 1 tchd 25 to 1)   7
2009² KADI (Ger) [132] 5-11-11 A Maguire, hld up in tch, ev ch 4 out, wknd aftr nxt.............(8 to 1 op 12 to 1)   8
BRAVE BUCCANEER [113] 7-10-6 P Niven, hld up, hdwy 4 out, wknd appr 2 out.. (14 to 1 op 8 to 1 tchd 16 to 1)   9
1972² MONTAGNARD [119] 10-10-12 G Bradley, al in tch, ev ch 3 out, rdn and wknd bef nxt.............(9 to 1 op 10 to 1) 10
2008* IVY HOUSE (Ire) [107] 6-10-0 B Powell, hld up, effrt appr 3 out, sn btn.................(14 to 1 op 12 to 1) 11
1462⁶ CAPPUCCINO GIRL [111] 7-10-4⁴ M Crosse, beh, effrt 4 out, sn btn...........................(66 to 1) 12
613⁴ SIR CRUSTY [107] 12-9-7 (7*) P Maddock, al beh. (66 to 1) 13
1971³ SEA BUCK [117] 8-10-7 (3*) R Davis, in tch till wknd appr 4 out.....................(25 to 1 op 33 to 1) 14
1972⁴ SUPER MALT (Ire) [112] 6-10-5 R Dunwoody, prmnt till wknd 4 out....................(16 to 1 op 25 to 1) 15
1993 STIRRUP CUP [129] 10-11-8 J Osborne, prmnt till wknd 6th..........................(33 to 1) 16
1992⁶ POWLEYVALE [110] 7-10-3 R Supple, al beh..... (25 to 1) 17
1881⁴ WILLSFORD [134] (bl) 11-11-6 (7*) L O'Hare, hld up, hdwy 6th, wknd quickly 3 out, eased, tld off.
.... (20 to 1 op 14 to 1 tchd 25 to 1) 18
1972⁴ MWEENISH [115] 12-10-8 G McCourt, led 3rd to 4th, hit 7th, sn wknd, tld off... (50 to 1 op 66 to 1) 19
DOOLAR (USA) [119] 9-10-9 N Mann, led 4th to 8th, wknd quickly, tld off..............(50 to 1) 20
1974* GLAISDALE (Ire) [129] 5-11-8 D Murphy, in tch, cl on ldrs 5 out, led briefly 3 out, wknd and btn whn f last.
.... (17 to 2 op 10 to 1 tchd 12 to 1)   f
1521 DAMIER BLANC (Fr) [107] (bl) 5-9-7 (7*) M Foster, in tch till f 5th................(12 to 1 op 11 to 1 tchd 14 to 1)   f

2009[9] ZAMIRAH (Ire) [121] 5-11-0 C Llewellyn, *mid-div whn brght dwn 5th*............ (14 to 1 op 10 to 1 tchd 25 to 1) bd
ROCHESTOWN LASS [107] 8-9-11[4] (7*) D Winter, *al beh, tld off whn pld up bef 4 out*..........(20 to 1 op 16 to 1) pu
Dist: ½l, 1½l, sht-hd, 6l, 1l, 4l, ½l, 1½l, 3l, 3½l. 5m 22.50s. a 35.00s (24 Ran).
(Jim McGrath), M H Easterby

2173 Warwick National Handicap Chase (5-y-o and up) £7,727 3m 5f........(2:40)

2011* MOORCROFT BOY [139] 9-10-0 A Maguire, *hld up, hdwy appr 7 out, wnt second 3 out, led bef nxt, styd on strly.* ....(2 to 1 fav op 7 to 2) 1
CHATAM (USA) [163] 10-11-10 R Dunwoody, *nvr far away, cld on ldrs 12th, styd on wl frm 2 out.* (9 to 2 op 7 to 2) 2
INTO THE RED [139] 10-10-0 N Williamson, *hld up, took clr order 7 out, chlgd 2 out, wknd r-in.* (14 to 1 op 12 to 1) 3
KING'S CURATE [139] 10-10-0 M Perrett, *prmnt, led 8th, hdd appr 2 out, one pace*........... (5 to 1 op 4 to 1) 4
1864[3] ALL JEFF (Fr) [142] 10-10-3[3] G Bradley, *beh and not gng wl in rear, some hdwy 12th, outpcd 7 out, styd on frm 3 out, nvr nrr*.......................(11 to 2 op 4 to 1) 5
1881[3] COOL GROUND [145] 12-10-6 P Holley, *trkd ldrs, ev ch whn hit 3 out, sn btn, eased*......... (8 to 1 op 5 to 1) 6
1881[2] FIDDLERS PIKE [139] 13-10-0 Mrs R Henderson, *led 3rd to 8th, wknd 5 out*...................(10 to 1 op 8 to 1) 7
1720[6] CAMDEN BELLE [139] 12-9-12[3] (5*) C Burnett-Wells, *al beh, lost tch 5 out, tld off*............ (200 to 1 op 100 to 1) 8
2011 SMOOTH ESCORT [139] (v) 10-10-0 D Bridgwater, *led to 3rd, wknd 15th, tld off whn pld up bef 3 out*...(50 to 1) pu
Dist: 3l, 4l, 2½l, 1l, 20l, nk, dist. 7m 59.50s. a 50.50s (9 Ran).
(K G Manley), D Nicholson

2174 Tote Trio Handicap Chase for the Edward Courage Cup (0-145 5-y-o and up) £5,182 2½m 110yds.........(3:10)

1887* RICHVILLE [132] 8-11-10 N Williamson, *hld up, hdwy tenth, wnt second 3 out, led on bit nxt, edgd lft and rdn r-in, fnshd 1st, plcd second.* ....(11 to 10 on op Evens tchd 11 to 10) 1D
1162 KENTISH PIPER [118] 9-10-10 C Llewellyn, *dsptd second pl, outpcd 3 out, rallied nxt, short of room and swtchd rght r-in, ran on cl hme, fnshd second, plcd 1st.* ....(10 to 1 op 8 to 1) 1
2087* L'UOMO PIU [108] 10-10-0 B Powell, *led, sn clr, rdn and hdd 2 out, one pace*... (10 to 1 op 8 to 1 tchd 12 to 1) 3
1538* DEADLY CHARM (USA) [121] 8-10-13 A Maguire, *hld up in tch, rdn 5 out, no hdwy*. (9 to 2 op 7 to 2 tchd 5 to 1) 4
2087[2] DR ROCKET [113] 9-10-2 (3*) D Meredith, *in tch, wnt second 7 out, wknd quickly appr 2 out.* (5 to 1 op 7 to 1) 5
1883[3] WIDE BOY [127] 12-11-5 G McCourt, *dsptd second pl till wknd 6 out*.........................(10 to 1 op 7 to 1) 6
1171 MAJOR KINSMAN [117] 9-10-9 L Harvey, *hld up, mstk 7th, wknd tenth, tld off whn pld up bef 2 out.* ....(25 to 1 op 16 to 1 tchd 33 to 1) pu
Dist: ½l, 10l, 15l, 5l, 6l. 5m 31.00s. a 36.00s (7 Ran).
(Mrs Gordon Pepper), N A Gaselee

2175 Warwick Castle Handicap Hurdle (4-y-o and up) £3,720 2m..........(3:40)

SOUTHFAST (USA) [108] 5-10-0 T Grantham, *al prmnt, led appr 2 out, drvn out*................(8 to 1 op 10 to 1) 1
SECOND CALL [108] 5-9-11 (3*) R Farrant, *nvr far away, pressed wnr 2 out, kpt on*.........(16 to 1 op 20 to 1) 2
1106 NIJMEGEN [120] 6-10-12 M Dwyer, *hld up, hdwy appr 4th, ev ch approaching 2 out, rdn and ran on one pace.* ....(9 to 2 op 5 to 1) 3
2005* WESTHOLME (USA) [118] 6-10-10 L Wyer, *prmnt, lft in ld aftr 3rd, hdd appr 2 out, ran on frm last.* ....(7 to 2 fav op 3 to 1) 4
1650[4] STATAJACK (Ire) [114] 6-10-6 P Holley, *hld up rear, hdwy 3rd, wknd aftr 3 out*............. (8 to 1 tchd 9 to 1) 5
1991[3] MIAMI SPLASH [118] 7-10-10 M Hourigan, *in tch till wknd appr 2 out*............................(4 to 1 op 5 to 1) 6
BADRAKHANI (Fr) [130] 8-11-8 R Dunwoody, *in tch, ev ch 4 out, rdn and sn wknd*............. (8 to 1 op 14 to 1) 7
2005[6] PERSUASIVE [128] 7-11-1 (5*) Mr M Buckley, *hld up rear, hdwy 5th, rdn and wknd 3 out*.... (10 to 1 op 8 to 1) 8
1755[5] MAJOR BUGLER (Ire) [132] 5-11-3 (7*) S Fox, *prmnt, jmpd slwly 3rd, rdn and hit nxt, sn beh.* (12 to 1 op 14 to 1) 9
ARCHIE BROWN [121] 7-10-13 G Upton, *hld up, ran in snatches, wknd appr 3 out, tld off*... (7 to 1 op 5 to 1) 10
SOUTH PARADE [125] 10-11-3 G Bradley, *led till pld up lme aftr 3rd*..(33 to 1) pu
Dist: 2½l, 1½l, 2l, 3½l, 2l, 12l, nk, 1½l, 8l. 4m 8.00s. a 28.00s (11 Ran).
(W E Sturt), J A B Old

2176 Warwick Mares National Hunt Flat Race (4,5,6-y-o) £2,122 2m......(4:10)

TIP THE DOVE 5-10-10 (7*) Mr G Hogan, *made all, pushed alng and edgd lft appr fnl furlong, kpt on wl.* ....(11 to 1 op 12 to 1 tchd 10 to 1) 1
IDIOT'S LADY 5-10-10 (7*) D Bohan, *al hndy, wnt second 4 fs out, kpt on same pace frm 2 out*... (8 to 1 op 3 to 1) 2
1779[2] LANDSKER PRYDE 5-10-10 (7*) T Dascombe, *hld up, prog 6 fs out, wknd o'r one out.* ....(2 to 1 fav op 5 to 2 tchd 7 to 2) 3
TARTAN MOSS (Ire) 5-10-10 (7*) N Parker, *wtd wth, improved 4 fs out, ran on strly fnl furlong, nrst finish.* .... (14 to 1 op 8 to 1 tchd 16 to 1) 4
PENNANT COTTAGE (Ire) 6-10-10 (7*) Leanne Eldredge, *pressed ldrs till wknd ins last 2 fs*............. (33 to 1) 5
MRS MONEYPENNY 5-10-10 (7*) P Ward, *chsd ldrs till wknd 2 fs out*........ (12 to 1 tchd 8 to 1 and 14 to 1) 6
CROWTHER HOMES 4-10-0 (7*) S Knott, *nvr rch ldrs.* .... (33 to 1 op 20 to 1) 7
ONLY JESTING 4-10-0 (7*) Lorna Brand, *wl plcd till wknd 3 fs out*............................ (25 to 1 op 20 to 1) 8
CHIEF LADY NICOLA 4-10-0 (7*) E Tolhurst, *cl up, rdn 3 fs out, sn lost pl*....................... (33 to 1 op 20 to 1) 9
PINE VALE 6-10-10 (7*) S Fox, *wl beh till ran on last 3 fs.* .... (20 to 1 op 14 to 1) 10
DO LETS 5-11-0 (3*) R Farrant, *pressed ldrs, rdn alng 6 fs out, wknd o'r 3 out*................................ (33 to 1) 11
MY ADVENTURE (Ire) 4-10-4 (3*) A Thornton, *settled in midfield, prog 4 fs out, wknd ins last 2.* ....(5 to 1 op 7 to 1 tchd 4 to 1) 12
ARCHIE'S SISTER 5-11-0 (3*) D Meredith, *ldg grp, pushed alng 6 fs out, wknd 4 out*........ (20 to 1 op 16 to 1) 13
WINDSOR FOX (Ire) 4-10-0 (7*) L Dace, *wl beh till moderate prog last 3 fs*...................... (10 to 1 op 12 to 1) 14
STRAY HARMONY 4-10-2 (5*) T Jenks, *frnt rnk till wknd 4 fs out*.............................. (6 to 1 op 4 to 1) 15
ORCHESTRATED CHAOS (Ire) 5-11-3 Mr J H Mead, *shrtlvd effrt hfwy, tld off*............ (25 to 1 op 20 to 1) 16
LADY BREYFAX 4-10-0 (7*) G Crone, *wl plcd 6 fs, tld off frm six out*.. (33 to 1) 17
ALLERTON BARGE (Ire) 6-10-12 (5*) T Eley, *tld off.* (33 to 1) 18
DUNNICKS COUNTRY 4-10-0 (7*) Guy Lewis, *al rear, tld off*.. (33 to 1) 19
LEGATA (Ire) 5-10-12 (5*) P Midgley, *al rear, tld off.* ....(33 to 1) 20
PRINCESS FLEUR 4-10-4 (3*) A Procter, *al rear, tld off.* .... (33 to 1 op 25 to 1) 21
LLAMA LADY 5-10-10 (7*) A Dowling, *al rear, tld off.* ....(33 to 1) 22
2134 JOYFUL JENNY 5-11-0 (3*) R Davis, *chsd ldrs to hfwy, tld off*.. (33 to 1) 23
1957 LADY ORWELL (Ire) 5-10-10 (7*) A Flannigan, *hndy to hfwy, tld off*.............................(33 to 1 op 20 to 1) 24
DONEGAL PRINCESS (Ire) 5-10-12 (5*) D Bentley, *pld hrd, al rear, tld off fnl 6 fs*............. (33 to 1 op 20 to 1) 25
Dist: 4l, 12l, 2l, 3½l, 15l, 1½l, nk, 1½l, hd, 6l. 4m 7.00s. (25 Ran).
(Cecil J Price), R J Price

NAVAN (IRE) (soft (races 1,2,4,5,6), heavy (3,7))
Sunday January 16th

2177 Mullacurry Maiden Hurdle (5 & 6-y-o) £3,105 2m...................... (1:00)

2024 FAIRY STRIKE (Ire) 5-11-2 K F O'Brien,........... (16 to 1) 1
WHALE OF A KNIGHT (Ire) 5-10-13[2] (5*) Mr T P Hyde, ...(10 to 1) 2
2028[3] PUNTER'S SYMPHONY (Ire) 6-12-0 H Rogers, (6 to 4 fav) 3
491[2] PENNYBRIDGE (Ire) 5-11-2 J Shortt,............. (13 to 2) 4
1908[5] RHABDOMANCY (Ire) 6-11-6 (3*) G Kilfeather,..... (5 to 1) 5
STRONG HICKS (Ire) 6-11-6 F J Flood,.............(7 to 1) 6
PROFESSOR STRONG (Ire) 6-11-6 L P Cusack,....(7 to 1) 7
CUTTER'S WHARF (Ire) 5-11-2 B Sheridan,........(8 to 1) 8
1814 IM OK (Ire) 6-10-8 (7*) T Martin,.................. (33 to 1) 9
1982 RADICAL NURSE (Ire) 5-10-8 (3*) T J Mitchell,.... (16 to 1) 10
SHELTERED (Ire) 6-11-1 F Woods,.................(4 to 1) 11
Dist: 3l, 14l, 1l, sht-hd. 4m 28.00s. (11 Ran).
(Mrs Denise Reddan), Desmond McDonogh

2178 Navan Hurdle (5-y-o and up) £3,195 2 ¼m.......................... (1:30)

2023* IDIOTS VENTURE 7-12-0 B Sheridan,......... (6 to 4 on) 1
1896[2] DORANS PRIDE (Ire) 5-11-4 K F O'Brien,..........(5 to 4) 2
Won by 4l. 4m 57.40s. (2 Ran).
SR: -/-/ (Blackwater Racing Syndicate), A P O'Brien

2179 WinElectric Chase (5-y-o and up) £7,000 2m.................... (2:00)

1579* MERRY GALE (Ire) 6-11-10 K F O'Brien,....... (4 to 1 on) 1
2075[2] SORRY ABOUT THAT 8-11-6 P Carberry,..........(7 to 2) 2
1831 WICKET KEEPER 9-10-9 (7*) Mr L J Gracey,......(25 to 1) 3
Dist: Dist, 15l. 4m 36.40s. (3 Ran).
(Herb M Stanley), J T R Dreaper

2180 Proudstown Handicap Hurdle (4-y-o and up) £6,900 2¼m............(2:30)

1818[2] STEEL MIRROR [-] 5-10-7 J Shortt,.............(Evens fav) 1
1976* DEGO DANCER [-] 7-9-0 (7*,4ex) J P Broderick,....(8 to 1) 2
1981* HAVE TO THINK [-] 6-9-7 F Woods,...............(10 to 1) 3

2026² SOCIETY BAY (USA) [-] 8-10-11 (7*) R A Hennessy, (11 to 2) 4
2026* PEBBLE LANE [-] 8-10-10 (2ex) H Rogers, ...(5 to 1) 5
1780⁶ BALLYCANN [-] 7-10-2 (7*) P J Mulligan, ...(20 to 1) 6
1683⁶ IF YOU SAY YES (Ire) [-] 6-9-11 (7*) P Morris, ...(9 to 1) 7
Dist: Nk, 1l, 1l, ½l. 4m 44.20s. (7 Ran).
(Quarrywell Syndicate), M Halford

2181 I.N.H. Stallion Owners Novice Hurdle (6-y-o and up) £3,795 3m....... (3:00)

2050* WILD VENTURE (Ire) 6-11-6 A Powell, ...(5 to 1) 1
1898* FAMBO LAD (Ire) 6-11-11 D H O'Connor, ...(3 to 1) 2
1829⁵ JIMS CHOICE 7-11-0 (7*) Mr R J Patton, ...(25 to 1) 3
1913* OLYMPIC D'OR (Ire) 6-11-11 C O'Dwyer, ...(6 to 1) 4
1851³ WILD FANTASY (Ire) 6-11-1 (5*) K P Gaule, ...(Evens fav) f
Dist: 9l, 15l, dist. 6m 33.30s. (5 Ran).
(Lady J Fowler), J R H Fowler

2182 Boyne Flat Race (5-y-o and up) £3,105 2m............................(3:30)

THE LATVIAN LARK (Ire) 6-11-11 (3*) Mr D Marnane, (6 to 4) 1
VENTANA CANYON (Ire) 5-11-10 Mr P Fenton, (5 to 4 fav) 2
1815⁴ WEST BROGUE (Ire) 5-11-10 Mr J P Dempsey, ...(6 to 1) 3
TOTAL CONFUSION 7-11-7 (7*) Mr T J Beattie, ...(7 to 1) 4
1832⁴ AMAKANE LADY (Ire) 5-11-2 (3*) Miss C Hutchinson, ...(10 to 1) 5
1982⁵ I'LL FLY AWAY (Ire) 5-11-5 (5*) Mr G J Harford, ...(25 to 1) 6
1910⁶ RICHIE'S GIRL (Ire) 6-11-2 (7*) Mr C Stafford, ...(10 to 1) 7
1832⁶ MILLHAVEN PRINCESS 8-11-2 (7*) Miss E Hyndman, ...(50 to 1) 8
ONE LAST LOOK 7-12-0 Mr W P Mullins, ...(10 to 1) 9
Dist: ¾l, 12l, nk, dist. 4m 8.30s. (9 Ran).
(Mrs Rosalind Kilpatrick), Noel Meade

2183 Trim Handicap Chase (0-123 5-y-o and up) £3,450 2½m................(4:00)

1499 CASTLE BRANDON [-] 8-10-8 F J Flood, ...(11 to 2) 1
1915⁴ GOLDEN CARRUTH (Ire) [-] 6-9-3 (7*) J P Broderick, ...(7 to 4 fav) 2
1985⁵ TURBULENT WIND [-] 7-10-11 C F Swan, ...(9 to 4) 3
1831² HURRICANE TOMMY [-] (bl) 7-10-3 P L Malone, (100 to 30) 4
MACAMORE GALE [-] 8-11-0 (3*) C O'Brien, ...(11 to 1) 5
Dist: 1½l, 25l, dist, ½l. 5m 42.80s. (5 Ran).
(Corrin Hill Racing Club), F Flood

FONTWELL (soft)
Monday January 17th
Going Correction: PLUS 2.05 sec. per fur.

2184 Houghton Amateur Riders' Handicap Chase (0-115 5-y-o and up) £2,504 3 ¼m 110yds....................(1:30)

1713⁴ SAM SHORROCK [89] (bl) 12-10-1¹ (5*) Mr G Johnson Houghton, *in tch, lost pl 15th, effrt aftr 19th, led 2 out, drvn clr*...........................(10 to 1 op 7 to 1) 1
2011⁴ LEAGAUNE [89] 12-10-0² (7*) Mr G Hogan, *in tch, cld 14th, reminders aftr nxt, styd on appr 2 out, one pace r-in*. ....(100 to 30 op 5 to 2 tchd 7 to 2) 2
2001³ UNDER OFFER [85] (bl) 13-9-9¹ (7*) Mr C Hancock, *led to 15th, led nxt to 17th, led aftr 19th to 2 out, no extr*. ....(7 to 1 op 6 to 1) 3
2047 ROSITARY (Fr) [98] (bl) 11-10-7 (7*) Mr G Cosgrove, *al hndy, mstk 3rd, led 17th till aftr 19th, sn rdn alng, not quicken*....................................(33 to 1) 4
1870 SUNBEAM TALBOT [108] 13-11-5 (5*) Mr S Bush, *beh 3rd, some hdwy appr 3 out, nvr able to chal*. ....(9 to 2 op 4 to 1) 5
2045² VAVASIR [98] 8-10-7 (7*) Mr S Mulcaire, *hld up, mstk 11th, hdwy 15th, rdn alng whn blun 19th, not reco'r, virtually pld up r-in*..............(13 to 8 fav op 7 to 4) 6
CLONROCHE GAZETTE [84] 14-9-9² (7*) Miss S Wallin, *mstk second, sn lost pl, beh whn pld up aftr 15th*. ....(50 to 1 op 33 to 1) pu
HALF BROTHER [97] 12-10-6 (7*) Mr T McCarthy, *trkd ldr, led 15th till appr nxt, wknd quickly, beh whn pld up bef 18th*..........................(10 to 1 op 8 to 1) pu
Dist: 6l, 1½l, ½l, 5l, dist. 7m 38.10s. a 68.10s (8 Ran).
(Keith Ogden), G Thorner

2185 Shopwyke Selling Handicap Hurdle (4,5,6-y-o) £1,707 2¼m......... (2:00)

MOYNSHA HOUSE (Ire) [56] 6-10-0 E Murphy, *hld up in tch gng wl, hdwy 4 out, led appr 2 out, sn clr, easily*. ....(2 to 1 fav) 1
1942² MILLY BLACK (Ire) [79] 6-11-9 D Gallagher, *mstks, sn beh, rdn hfwy, kpt on 2 out, no ch wth wnr*. ....(8 to 1 op 4 to 1 tchd 10 to 1) 2
1711 ALICE'S MIRROR [84] (v) 5-12-0 W McFarland, *chsd ldrs, hit second, niggled alng hfwy, styd on appr 2 out, sn no extr*................(9 to 2 tchd 5 to 1 and 4 to 1) 3
1710 ONE MORE POUND [74] (v) 4-11-4 D Murphy, *sn led, mstk 4th, hdd aftr 3 out, wkng whn f nxt*. ....(5 to 1 op 5 to 2 tchd 6 to 1) f
791⁹ CLEAR COMEDY (Ire) [63] 6-10-7 J Frost, *beh 3rd, tld off whn pld up bef 6th*...(16 to 1 op 10 to 1 tchd 20 to 1) pu
1942* PEACOCK FEATHER [83] 6-11-13 M A FitzGerald, *hndy till rdn 3 out, sn wknd, pld up bef nxt*. ....(9 to 4 op 7 to 4 tchd 5 to 2) pu
Dist: 15l, 2½l. 4m 54.30s. a 44.30s (6 Ran).
SR: -/6/8/ (P Byrne), B J Curley

2186 Peter Duncanson Memorial Challenge Trophy Novices' Chase (5-y-o and up) £3,672 2m 3f.................... (2:30)

1774* COONAWARA 8-12-0 B Powell, *made all, jmpd rght 1st, sn clr, mstk 11th, unchlgd*...(5 to 2 on tchd 9 to 4 on) 1
1970⁴ NICKSLINE 8-11-4 D Murphy, *chsd wnr 5th, sn no imprsn*. ....(20 to 1 op 12 to 1 tchd 25 to 1) 2
1924² RUSSINSKY 7-10-13 R J Beggan, *hld up beh, some hdwy 9th, nvr able to chal*..............(11 to 1 op 7 to 1) 3
1947 BALLINAMOE 9-11-4 W Marston, *second whn uns rdr second*...........(100 to 1 op 50 to 1 tchd 200 to 1) ur
1964 FEARSOME 8-11-4 M A FitzGerald, *al beh, tld off whn pld up bef tenth*....................(50 to 1 op 20 to 1) pu
2010³ WINGS OF FREEDOM (Ire) (v) 6-11-4 A Maguire, *chsd wnr to 5th, sn lost pl, beh whn pld up bef tenth*. ....(100 to 30 op 3 to 1 tchd 5 to 2 and 7 to 2) pu
Dist: 15l, 1l. 5m 20.10s. a 45.10s (6 Ran).
SR: 38/13/7/ (Simon Sainsbury), Capt T A Forster

2187 Hoechst Panacur EBF Mares 'National Hunt' Novices' Hurdle Qualifier (5-y-o and up) £2,553 2¼m............(3:00)

1800⁹ FORT RANK 7-10-12 J Frost, *in tch, effrt appr 6th, wnt second approaching 2 out, rdn to ld r-in, edgd lft, ran on*....................(5 to 1 op 7 to 1 tchd 10 to 1) 1
1568⁴ COUNTRY STORE 5-10-12 W McFarland, *tucked in hndy, wnt second aftr 5th, led appr 2 out, hdd and no extr r-in*.................................(3 to 1 op 2 to 1) 2
1734⁴ MAKING TIME 7-10-12 B Powell, *dsptd ld to 5th, sn niggled alng, rallied to lead briefly 3 out, soon one pace*. ....(12 to 1 op 8 to 1 tchd 14 to 1) 3
1957⁶ DREAMLINE 5-10-5 (7*) M P FitzGerald, *hld up, hit second, mstk 6th, nvr able to chal*. ....(14 to 1 op 8 to 1 tchd 16 to 1) 4
1386³ PRINCESS HOTPOT (Ire) 6-11-0 (5*) J McCarthy, *dsptd ld, led 5th to 3 out, wknd quickly, pld up bef nxt, broke blood vessel*... (5 to 4 on op 6 to 4 on tchd 6 to 5 on) pu
Dist: 2l, 6l, 30l. 5m 0.00s. a 50.00s (5 Ran).
(P A Tylor), R G Frost

2188 Selsey Handicap Chase (0-120 5-y-o and up) £2,508 2¼m............(3:30)

1944* CITY KID [113] 9-11-7 (7*) J J Brown, *led 4th, jnd 3 out, quickened away nxt, easily*......(9 to 4 tchd 11 to 4) 1
1466³ UNIQUE NEW YORK [87] (v) 11-10-2 A Maguire, *in tch, blun tenth, chlgd 3 out, sn rdn and btn, fnshd tired*. ....(4 to 1 op 7 to 2) 2
1754⁵ RUNNING SANDS [91] 10-10-6 R Dunwoody, *led 3rd to 4th, prmnt, mstk 12th, sn wknd*..... (15 to 8 fav op 2 to 1) 3
1836* RADICAL REQUEST [96] 11-10-11 M A FitzGerald, *hld up, blun 7th, nvr a dngr*.....(4 to 1 op 7 to 2 tchd 9 to 2) 4
1944³ MASTER COMEDY [86] (bl) 10-10-1 N Williamson, *led to 3rd, beh hfwy*........(16 to 1 op 14 to 1 tchd 20 to 1) 5
Dist: 15l, 4l, 10l, 6l. 5m 4.90s. a 44.90s (5 Ran).
SR: 20/-/ (Pell-Mell Partners), J T Gifford

2189 Middleton Novices' Hurdle (4-y-o) £1,543 2¼m.................. (4:00)

2016³ SILVER STANDARD 10-12 B Powell, *al prmnt, led 5th till rdn and hdd appr 2 out, rallied to ld last, all out*. ....(12 to 1 op 7 to 1) 1
1885² KARAR (Ire) 10-12 N Williamson, *led second to 5th, led appr 2 out, hrd rdn and hdd last, jst hld*. ....(6 to 5 on op 5 to 4 on) 2
MILLMOUNT (Ire) (v) 10-7 W McFarland, *al hndy, rdn aftr 6th, ev ch appr 2 out, sn wknd*.....(11 to 1 op 10 to 1) 3
1885⁶ ROWLANDSONS GOLD (Ire) 10-7 Lorna Vincent, *beh, moderate late hdwy frm 2 out, nvr a dngr*. ....(33 to 1 op 25 to 1 tchd 40 to 1) 4
1990² MARIUS (Ire) 10-12 D Murphy, *pld hrd, prmnt till rdn aftr 3 out, sn btn*..........................(7 to 4 op 2 to 1) 5
1517⁶ RAGAZZO (Ire) 10-12 A Maguire, *led to second, lost tch hfwy, tld off whn pld up bef 2 out*. ....(40 to 1 op 25 to 1 tchd 50 to 1) pu
1464 FATHER'S JOY 10-7 R Dunwoody, *al beh, tld off whn pld up bef 2 out*........(66 to 1 op 25 to 1 tchd 100 to 1) pu
Dist: Hd, 15l, 10l, 6l. 4m 52.50s. a 42.50s (7 Ran).
SR: 28/28/8/-/ (G W Lugg), Capt T A Forster

FOLKESTONE (heavy (races 1,3,5,7), soft (2,4,6))

Tuesday January 18th
Going Correction: PLUS 1.33 sec. per fur. (races 1,3,-5,7), PLUS 0.80 (2,4,6)

2190 Northiam Novices' Hurdle (4-y-o) £1,543 2m 1f 110yds............(1:00)

FOOLS ERRAND (Ire) 10-12 R Dunwoody, *made all, quickened clr aftr 2 out, very easily.* ....(6 to 5 fav op 6 to 4 tchd 5 to 4 on) 1
516^{6} BILJAN (USA) 10-5 (7*) W J Walsh, *mstks, chsd wnr till aftr 2 out, kpt on ag'n appr last.* ....(11 to 2 op 5 to 1 tchd 7 to 1) 2
1297^{5} WITHOUT A FLAG (USA) 10-12 A Maguire, *hld up, rdn to chase wnr aftr 2 out, no imprsn, wknd and mstk last.* ....(7 to 4 op 6 to 4 tchd 2 to 1) 3
ARAMON 10-12 J Osborne, *hld up in tch, outpcd aftr 2 out, no ch after*.................. (10 to 1 op 4 to 1) 4
BRIGHTON BREEZY 10-12 R Rowell, *mstk 1st, rdn and losing tch whn mistake 4th, sn tld off.* .... (50 to 1 op 12 to 1) 5

Dist: 30l, 2l, 12l, dist. 4m 31.00s. a 34.00s (5 Ran).
(Mrs David Russell), R Hannon

2191 Ted Long Challenge Cup Amateur Riders' Handicap Chase (0-110 5-y-o and up) £2,464 2m 5f........... (1:30)

1838^{4} BOWL OF OATS [107] (bl) 8-11-7 (7*) Mr J Rees, *al prmnt, shaken up to ld last, sn clr, cmftbly.* ....(7 to 2 op 3 to 1 tchd 4 to 1) 1
2032^{2} OLD ROAD (USA) [81] 8-9-13^{4} (7*) Mr G Hogan, *in tch, pushed alng 8th, wnt second 11th, rdn to ld 2 out, hdd and one pace last*...... (11 to 2 op 8 to 1 tchd 9 to 1) 2
600 BETTY HAYES [100] 10-11-4 (3*) Mr J Durkan, *led to second, rdn frm tenth, ev ch whn mstk and lost pl 3 out, styd on ag'n from last*....... (3 to 1 fav op 5 to 2 tchd 7 to 2) 3
1720^{4} ROCKMOUNT ROSE [87] 9-10-2^{1} (7*) Mr J Luck, *jmpd lft, led second till 2 out, sn wknd*........(5 to 1 op 4 to 1) 4
1943 ON YOUR WAY [79] (v) 12-9-12^{5} (7*) Mr B Pollock, *prmnt, rdn and ch whn mstk 2 out, sn btn.* (20 to 1 op 10 to 1) 5
2064^{9} BRORA ROSE (Ire) [79] 6-9-7 (7*) Miss S Cobden, *ran in snatches, lost tch 11th, ran on ag'n frm last.* .... (33 to 1 op 20 to 1) 6
1943 MACHO MAN [93] 9-10-9 (5*) Mr D McCain, *in tch till 8th, sn struggling*....... (12 to 1 op 10 to 1 tchd 14 to 1) 7
1925^{2} GUILDWAY [90] 11-10-4 (7*) Mr M Rimell, *lost pl 5th, reminder 8th, sn beh*.... (7 to 2 op 5 to 2 tchd 4 to 1) 8

Dist: 2½l, 2½l, 4l, ¾l, sht-hd, 10l, 2½l. 5m 46.40s. a 36.40s (8 Ran).
(Mrs Anthony Morley), Andrew Turnell

2192 Robertsbridge Handicap Hurdle (0-135 4-y-o and up) £2,684 2m 1f 110yds......................... (2:00)

1839^{2} TOP WAVE [114] 6-11-10 M A FitzGerald, *trkd ldrs gng easily, led betw last 2, sn clr, rdn out.* ....(7 to 2 op 5 to 2 tchd 4 to 1) 1
1551^{8} FAMOUS DANCER [92] 6-10-2 A Maguire, *hld up last, smooth prog 3 out, rdn to chase wnr appr last, unbl to quicken*............................(6 to 1 op 5 to 1) 2
2082^{2} DJEBEL PRINCE [102] 7-10-12 J Osborne, *trkd ldrs, hrd rdn and not quicken aftr 2 out, kpt on appr last.* ....(6 to 4 fav op 5 to 4 tchd 13 to 8) 3
CARRIKINS [90] 7-10-0 M Richards, *pushed alng, lost tch aftr 5th, sn wl beh, kpt on appr last, no dngr.* .... (33 to 1 op 10 to 1) 4
SCENT OF BATTLE [93] 6-10-3 R Dunwoody, *trkd ldr till led 4th, hdd and wknd rpdly betw last 2.* ....(8 to 1 op 6 to 1) 5
1599^{2} HANDSOME NED [92] (bl) 8-10-2 J Railton, *led to 4th, ev ch 2 out, hrd rdn and wknd rpdly appr last.* ....(4 to 1 op 7 to 2) 6

Dist: 4l, 5l, 6l, ¾l, 8l. 4m 25.90s. a 28.90s (6 Ran).
SR: 40/14/19/1/3/-/ (A K Collins), N J Henderson

2193 Whitelaw Gold Cup Novices' Chase (5-y-o and up) £4,172 3¼m........ (2:30)

1973^{2} MAILCOM 8-12-0 J Osborne, *led till blun and hdd 13th, blunded nxt and lost tch, rallied 3 out, styd on strly to ld last strds*.... (11 to 10 on op 11 to 8 on tchd Evens) 1
1841^{3} SPIKEY (NZ) 8-12-0 A Maguire, *prmnt, led 14th, hrd rdn last, hng lft r-in, hdd last strds, fnshd second, plcd 3rd.* ....(5 to 1 op 6 to 1 tchd 7 to 1) 2D
1631* BOLLINGER 8-11-10 D Murphy, *hld up gng wl, prog 15th, rdn to chal last, hmpd and swtchd rght r-in, not reco'r, fnshd 3rd, plcd second.* (4 to 1 op 9 to 4 tchd 9 to 2) 2
1730^{3} JUDGES FANCY (bl) 10-11-10 C Llewellyn, *jmpd slwly early and beh, prog tenth, cl up aftr till hrd rdn and wknd after 3 out*.......................(5 to 1 tchd 6 to 1) 4
1973^{4} SAYYURE (USA) 8-11-6 G McCourt, *prmnt, pushed alng and lft in ld 13th, hdd nxt, hrd rdn and wknd aftr 3 out*.................. (12 to 1 op 10 to 1 tchd 14 to 1) 5
MISS MUIRE 8-11-1 D Morris, *in tch whn uns rdr 4th.* .... (25 to 1 op 20 to 1 tchd 33 to 1) ur
1013* DUKES SON 7-11-10 G Bradley, *prmnt till mstks 9th and tenth, sn drpd out, tld off and pld up bef 4 out.* .... (11 to 1 op 6 to 1 tchd 12 to 1) pu

Dist: Hd, 2½l, 30l, 15l. 7m 0.20s. a 48.20s (7 Ran).
(Mailcom Plc), Mrs J Pitman

2194 Dan Swinden 'National Hunt' Novices' Hurdle (5-y-o and up) £1,543 2¾m 110yds........................ (3:00)

2015^{3} NAZZARO 5-10-12 R Dunwoody, *chsd ldr, rdn and no imprsn betw last 2, styd on and lft in ld last, drvn out.* .... (9 to 1 op 5 to 1 tchd 10 to 1) 1
1878* BAY MISCHIEF (Ire) 5-11-5 C Llewellyn, *led, drw clr betw last 2, wknd, blun and hdd last, sn btn.* ....(9 to 2 on op 5 to 1 on) 2
2048^{4} DUTCH MONARCH 7-10-12 A Maguire, *hld up, hmpd 4th, not fluent aftr, in tch till rdn and wknd betw last 2.* .... (11 to 2 op 3 to 1 tchd 6 to 1) 3
BOURNE LANE 9-10-12 J Railton, *chsd ldrs till lost tch aftr 6th, sn tld off*...(50 to 1 op 20 to 1 tchd 100 to 1) 4
GRAND COLONIST 7-10-9 (3*) A Procter, *not jump wl, lost tch 6th, pld up bef nxt.* .... (66 to 1 op 33 to 1 tchd 100 to 1) pu
1027 LEWESDON PRINCESS 6-10-7 W McFarland, *al beh, tld off and pld up bef 8th.* .... (66 to 1 op 20 to 1 tchd 100 to 1) pu

Dist: 8l, 12l, dist. 5m 55.10s. a 41.10s (6 Ran).
(A Morrish), W G M Turner

2195 Deal Novices' Chase (5-y-o and up) £2,467 2m..................... (3:30)

2017 HOPS AND POPS 7-10-11 S Earle, *jmpd wl, made all, shaken up appr last, ran on well*.... (3 to 1 op 5 to 1) 1
PROPERO 9-11-2 D Murphy, *chsd wnr, cld aftr 3 out, ev ch whn mstk nxt, sn rdn and one pace.* ....(2 to 1 op 6 to 4) 2
1964^{2} CAMBO (USA) 8-11-2 D Skyrme, *outpcd in mid-div, styd on frm 2 out, no dngr.* (10 to 1 op 7 to 1 tchd 12 to 1) 3
1743* ROC COLOR (Fr) 5-11-4 G Bradley, *chsd ldg pair, rdn and effrt aftr 3 out, sn no imprsn, wknd last.* .... (11 to 8 fav op 5 to 4 on tchd 6 to 4) 4
1712 DOVEHILL 8-11-2 Mr P Bull, *al beh, tld off frm 8th.* .... (66 to 1 op 20 to 1) 5
1948 LIRELLA 7-10-11 I Shoemark, *tld off last till f 6th.* .... (50 to 1 op 33 to 1 tchd 66 to 1) f
1719 DRAW LOTS 10-10-11 (5*) D Matthews, *al beh, tld off and pld up bef 8th*..................... (66 to 1 op 33 to 1) pu

Dist: 4l, 8l, 1½l, dist. 4m 12.80s. a 17.80s (7 Ran).
SR: 33/34/26/26/ (B Dennett), R H Alner

2196 Levy Board Novices' Handicap Hurdle (0-100 5-y-o and up) £1,695 2m 1f 110yds........................ (4:00)

2044^{5} THE GOLFING CURATE [82] 9-10-12 G McCourt, *trkd ldrs, led 3 out, drw wl clr frm nxt, unchlgd.* ....(9 to 2 op 3 to 1) 1
1965^{2} TYNRON DOON [76] (bl) 5-10-6 A Maguire, *led till 3 out, sn drpd out, kpt on ag'n appr last, no ch wth wnr.* ....(3 to 1 op 5 to 1 tchd 7 to 1) 2
1621 TWIST 'N' SCU [83] 6-10-13 C Llewellyn, *pushed alng frm 3rd, hrd rdn and outpcd aftr 3 out, kpt on ag'n appr last, no dngr*............ (7 to 1 op 5 to 1 tchd 8 to 1) 3
1708 LETTS GREEN (Ire) [70] 6-10-0 D Morris, *hld up, prog 5th, chsd wnr aftr nxt, hrd rdn and no imprsn, wknd last.* .... (33 to 1 op 16 to 1) 4
1303 IRISH TAN [70] 7-10-0 N Williamson, *hld up, prog 3 out, rdn aftr nxt, no imprsn, wknd appr last.* ....(11 to 2 op 6 to 1 tchd 8 to 1 and 5 to 1) 5
1193^{7} PER QUOD (USA) [98] 9-12-0 R Dunwoody, *wth ldr till 3 out, wknd rpdly aftr nxt, tld off and pld up bef last.* ....(2 to 1 fav op 6 to 4 tchd 9 to 4) pu
1601^{2} KOBYRUN [83] 8-10-13 J Railton, *chsd ldrs, wknd rpdly aftr 2 out, tld off and pld up bef last.* .... (13 to 2 op 3 to 1 tchd 7 to 1) pu

Dist: Dist, 1½l, 3½l, 20l. 4m 27.40s. a 30.40s (7 Ran).
SR: 13/-/-/-/ (Poem Racing), R Rowe

FAIRYHOUSE (IRE) (soft)
Wednesday January 19th

2197 Fairyhouse EBF Mares Maiden Hurdle (Qualifier) (4-y-o and up) £3,450 2¼m ....(1:10)

1814^{2} LOVELY RUN 7-12-0 H Rogers,............ (11 to 10 fav) 1
1904^{3} MINIGIRLS NIECE (Ire) 6-11-6 A Powell,...........(5 to 1) 2
2123 CASH IT IN (Ire) 6-11-3 (3*) D P Murphy,..........(14 to 1) 3
2050^{3} FURRY DUCK (Ire) 6-12-0 B Sheridan,............ (8 to 1) 4
1986^{4} QUEENIES CHILD 7-12-0 J Shortt,............. (7 to 1) 5
2050 PARSONS BELLE (Ire) 6-11-1 (5*) T P Rudd,...... (50 to 1) 6
1898^{9} PARKBOY LASS 7-12-0 P L Malone,............ (25 to 1) 7
WINNING SALLY (Ire) 4-10-9 K F O'Brien,........ (33 to 1) 8
DUGGERNE ROCK (Ire) 4-10-2^{2} (7*) Mr G W Barry, (33 to 1) 9

1832⁸ KINROSS 7-11-6 C F Swan, ... (12 to 1) 10
1832⁷ SERIOUS NOTE (Ire) 6-11-1 (5⁺) Mr B R Hamilton, (33 to 1) 11
     MAID OF GLENDURAGH (Ire) 6-12-0 T J Taaffe, ...(8 to 1) 12
2027⁶ JOES NIGHTMARE 7-10-13 (7⁺) D M Drewett, ... (25 to 1) pu
Dist: 6l, 9l, 4l, 20l. 4m 39.10s. (13 Ran).

(Kevin A Geraghty), T K Geraghty

2198 G V Malcomson Memorial EBF Chase
(Listed - Grade 3) (5-y-o and up) £5,920
2¼m. . . . . (1:40)

1817 MUBADIR (USA) 6-11-2 P Carberry, hld up, prog to ld appr
     last, eased cl hme, cmftbly. . . . .(9 to 4 on) 1
1905⁶ GOOD TEAM 9-11-10 T J Taaffe, trkd ldr, dsptd ld frm 5th,
     led briefly appr 2 out, rdn and no extr last. . . . (4 to 1) 2
1905³ WHO'S TO SAY 8-11-3 (3⁺) T J Mitchell, led, jnd 5th, blun 6
     out, hdd appr 2 out, rdn, no extr last. . . . .(9 to 2) 3
Dist: 1½l, sht-hd. 5m 4.20s. (3 Ran).

(Liam Keating), Noel Meade

2199 Goosander Maiden Hurdle (5-y-o)
£3,105 2m. (2:10)

1848⁵ SENSE OF VALUE 11-5 B Sheridan, ... (8 to 1) 1
     DARU (USA) 11-10 C F Swan, ... (9 to 4 jt-fav) 2
1848⁷ DAMODAR 11-2 F J Flood, ...(25 to 1) 3
2123² BUTCHES BOY (Ire) 11-5 S H O'Donovan, . . (9 to 4 jt-fav) 4
1815 GALE TOI (Ire) 11-10 Mr W P Mullins, ...(7 to 1) 5
2024⁷ FREE THYNE (Ire) 10-11 (5⁺) M G Cleary, ... (16 to 1) 6
1820⁸ THE BOBTAIL FOX (Ire) 11-2 P Carberry, ...(8 to 1) 7
2123 FATHER GREGORY (Ire) 10-13 (3⁺) T J Mitchell, . . (50 to 1) 8
558² COMMON POLICY (Ire) 11-10 K F O'Brien, ... (10 to 1) 9
1815 RAVEN'S ROCK (Ire) 10-9 (7⁺) C A Leavy, ... (25 to 1) 10
1821⁹ ISLAND ROW (Ire) 10-9 (7⁺) J P Broderick, ... (33 to 1) 11
1986⁶ ROCK POOL 11-2 A Powell, ...(14 to 1) 12
1820⁵ FINAWAY EXPRESS (Ire) 10-9 (7⁺) P Mulligan, . . (14 to 1) 13
469 RHOMAN FUN (Ire) 10-9 (7⁺) D J Kavanagh, ... (33 to 1) pu
907 GALE GRIFFIN (Ire) 10-11 C O'Dwyer, ...(66 to 1) pu
Dist: Hd, 11l, 1l, 7l. 4m 4.00s. (15 Ran).

(F Dunne), F Dunne

2200 Eider Handicap Chase (0-109 5-y-o
and up) £3,105 3m 1f. . . . . (2:40)

2053⁺ EDENAKILL LAD [-] 7-10-3 (3ex) C F Swan, ... (9 to 4 fav) 1
2037² ANOTHER GROUSE [-] 7-10-8 (7⁺) J P Broderick, (11 to 2) 2
2100³ MERLYNS CHOICE [-] 10-10-5 T Horgan, ... (4 to 1) 3
2025³ WALLS COURT [-] 7-10-13 P L Malone, ...(6 to 1) 4
2053 BENS DILEMMA [-] 9-9-12 (5⁺) K P Gaule, ... (12 to 1) 5
2100 MUST DO [-] 8-10-13 (3⁺) T J Mitchell, ... (10 to 1) 6
     MR MYAGI [-] 10-10-8 (3⁺) D Bromley, ... (10 to 1) 7
2100¹⁴ ANOTHER RUSTLE [-] 11-10-11 W T Slattery Jnr, (10 to 1) f
2100 MONEY MADE [-] (bl) 7-9-7³ J Jones, ...(25 to 1) pu
Dist: 4l, 2½l, dist, 15l. 7m 1.70s. (9 Ran).

(Noel MacClancy), J R Cox

2201 Teal Handicap Hurdle (0-123 4-y-o and
up) £3,105 2¼m. . . . . (3:10)

2079⁶ THATCH AND GOLD (Ire) [-] 6-11-8 M Duffy, (11 to 10 fav) 1
2052³ MONKEY AGO [-] 7-11-5 (3⁺) T P Treacy, ...(6 to 1) 2
2026⁴ HEMISPHERE [-] 5-10-5 C F Swan, ... (7 to 2) 3
42 GRANADOS (USA) [-] 6-10-5 P Carberry, ... (12 to 1) 4
1987⁸ ENERGANCE (Ire) [-] 6-10-4 (7⁺) J P Broderick, . . (16 to 1) 5
1828⁺ ROSIN THE BOW (Ire) [-] 5-9-6 (7⁺) M Morris, ... (8 to 1) 6
1495 GOLDEN AMBITION [-] 8-10-8 (5⁺) K P Gaule, ... (8 to 1) 7
Dist: ½l, 1½l, 4l, 20l. 4m 36.30s. (7 Ran).

(Mrs Anna Doyle), Patrick Joseph Flynn

2202 Widgeon Handicap Chase (0-116 5-y-o
and up) £3,105 2¼m. . . . . (3:40)

2053³ FRIENDLY ARGUMENT [-] 9-10-11 F Woods, ... (4 to 1) 1D
2126² GALLEY GALE [-] 8-10-3 K F O'Brien, ... (100 to 30) 1
708 BOLD FLYER [-] 11-11-5 (7⁺) J P Broderick, ... (12 to 1) 2
2126 PALMROCK DONNA [-] 7-9-2⁴ (5⁺) P A Roche, ... (6 to 1) 4
2077² BACK DOOR JOHNNY [-] 8-11-2 J Short, ... (11 to 4 fav) 5
91 OLDIE CRESCENT [-] 8-11-7 C F Swan, ... (12 to 1) 6
2075⁵ FURRY STAR [-] 8-11-6 J Jones, ...(5 to 1) 7
Dist: 2½l, 7l, 11l, 9l. 5m 1.60s. (7 Ran).

(J J Connolly), Daniel O'Connell

2203 Merganser INH Flat Race (5-y-o and
up) £3,105 2m. . . . .(4:10)

2127 MISS MUPPET (Ire) 5-11-2 (3⁺) Mrs M Mullins, . .(5 to 4 fav) 1
     RING THE ALARM (Ire) 6-11-9 (5⁺) Mr G J Harford, (10 to 1) 2
1144 DROMOD POINT (Ire) 5-11-3 (7⁺) Mr E Norris, ... (5 to 2) 3
     BEDFORD RAMBLER (Ire) 5-11-3 (7⁺) Mr D J McAteer,
     . . . . (16 to 1) 4
     CHAINMAIL (Ire) 6-11-11 (3⁺) Mr A R Coonan, ... (8 to 1) 5
     BLAIR HOUSE (Ire) 5-10-12 (7⁺) Mr H Murphy, ... (8 to 1) 6
     REEL HIM IN 6-11-11 (3⁺) Miss M Olivefalk, ... (16 to 1) 7
1332 LISNABOY PRINCE 7-11-7 (7⁺) Mr F McGirr, ... (20 to 1) 8
1852⁴ BOWLING CHERRY (Ire) 6-11-4 (3⁺) Mr J A Nash, (14 to 1) 9
     QUICK RAISE (Fr) 5-11-3 (7⁺) Mr R C Purfield, ... (25 to 1) 10
     BALLYHARRON 7-11-2 (7⁺) Mr J S Cullen, ...(33 to 1) 11
     LITTLE JOE (Ire) 5-11-7² (5⁺) Mr P J Dreeling, ... (10 to 1) 12

MEDIEVAL BEAUTY (Ire) 6-11-2 (7⁺) Mr P E I Newell,
. . . . (33 to 1) 13
     SISTER NORA (Ire) 6-11-2 (7⁺) Mr J Johnston, . . (33 to 1) 14
2102 JENNYS GROVE (Ire) 6-11-2 (7⁺) Mr D Deacon, . . (33 to 1) 15
1786⁹ OUR SON (Ire) 5-11-3 (7⁺) Mr T M Finnegan, ...(50 to 1) 16
Dist: 5l, 3½l, ½l, 5l. 3m 58.70s. (16 Ran).

(Mrs John Magnier), Anthony Mullins

LUDLOW (good)
Wednesday January 19th
Going Correction: PLUS 0.55 sec. per fur. (races 1,4,-
5,7), PLUS 0.62 (2,3,6)

2204 Marshbrook Novices' Hurdle (4-y-o
and up) £1,550 2m. . . . .(1:10)

1800⁺ KONVEKTA KING (Ire) 6-12-0 A Maguire, slwly away,
     hdwy to track ldr 5th, hng and jmpd lft 2 out, edgd left
     r-in, all out, fnshd 1st, plcd second.
     . . . .(5 to 4 on op Evens tchd 11 to 10) 1D
1946² EMPIRE BLUE 11-11-5 M Bosley, hld up, mstk 4th, hdwy 3
     out, chalg whn hmpd nxt, rallied and short of room
     r-in, ran on, fnshd second, awarded race.
     . . . .(6 to 1 op 5 to 1 tchd 7 to 1) 1
997³ SQUIRE YORK 4-10-7 M A FitzGerald, hld up in tch, kpt
     on wl frm 2 out. . . . . . .(10 to 1 op 12 to 1 tchd 8 to 1) 3
1741⁺ RAGGERTY (Ire) 4-10-13 (3⁺) N Bentley, chsd ldrs, no hdwy
     appr 2 out. . . . .(25 to 1 op 16 to 1) 4
1494⁷ SHERRY TUFF (Ire) 5-11-0 W Marston, al prmnt, rdn appr 2
     out, one pace. . . . . (25 to 1 op 16 to 1) 5
1929⁴ MASTER TUCK 8-11-5 M Richards, towards rear, styd on
     frm 2 out, nvr dngrs. . . . .(16 to 1 op 14 to 1) 6
1990⁶ MONAZITE 4-10-7 R Bellamy, prmnt till wknd aftr 3 out.
     . . . .(25 to 1 op 14 to 1) 7
     ACANTHUS (Ire) 4-10-7 B Powell, slwly away, nvr nr to
     chal. . . . .(12 to 1 op 8 to 1) 8
1076⁵ GLENGARRA PRINCESS 7-11-0 P Holley, led, mstk 3 out,
     hdd and wknd quickly bef nxt. . . . .(12 to 1 op 8 to 1) 9
     FONTANAYS (Ire) 6-11-5 G McCourt, slwly away, al beh.
     . . . .(5 to 1 op 12 to 1) 10
     OSSIE 5-11-5 C Llewellyn, prmnt till wknd 3 out, wl beh
     whn blun last. . . . . (20 to 1 op 14 to 1) 11
     KETFORD BRIDGE 7-11-2 (3⁺) D Meredith, al towards rear.
     . . . .(50 to 1) 12
     AUSTRAL JANE 4-10-2 D Bridgwater, al rear.
     . . . . (33 to 1) 13
1695 WHYFOR 6-10-12 (7⁺) Mr N Moore, prmnt to 4th, tld off.
     . . . .(100 to 1 op 66 to 1) 14
1800 COME ON CHARLIE 5-11-5 N Williamson, al beh, tld off.
     . . . .(100 to 1 op 66 to 1) 15
     RANORA (Ire) 4-9-11 (5⁺) T Jenks, al beh, tld off. (33 to 1) 16
1806 CLOSE OF PLAY 5-11-5 W Humphreys, al beh, f last.
     . . . .(100 to 1 op 66 to 1) f
1996 SWEET FRIENDSHIP 6-11-0 R Supple, pld hrd, chsd ldr to
     5th, wkng whn mstk nxt, tld off when pulled up 2 out.
     . . . .(100 to 1 op 50 to 1) pu
Dist: Nk, 5l, 6l, 15l, nk, 2l, 2l, 1½l, 2l, 2l. 3m 51.30s. a 14.30s (18 Ran).
SR: 45/35/18/21/4/8/   (Mrs H M Innes), J R Bosley

2205 Richards Castle Handicap Chase
(0-130 5-y-o and up) £2,769 2½m (1:40)

1649⁺ MULBANK [118] 8-11-5 C Maude, made all, jmpd wl, lft
     clr 2 out. . . . .(7 to 4 fav op 6 to 4) 1
1954⁺ PITHY [100] 12-9-8 (7⁺) Guy Lewis, rcd in 4th pl, rdn 12th,
     lft poor second 2 out. . . . . (4 to 1 op 3 to 1) 2
1933⁺ ITS NEARLY TIME [127] 11-11-7 (7⁺) Miss J Brackenbury, not
     fluent, al last, lost tch tenth, lft remote 3rd 2 out.
     . . . .(7 to 2) 3
1789⁹ COMEDY ROAD [99] 10-10-0 L Harvey, trkd wnr, dsptd ld
     appr 3 out, rdn whn f nxt. . . . . . . (10 to 1 op 8 to 1) f
1924 PERSIAN SWORD [99] 8-10-0 A Maguire, trkd ldrs, hit 6th
     and tenth, rdn and hld in 3rd whn f 2 out.
     . . . .(3 to 1 op 5 to 2) f
Dist: 12l, 12l. 5m 12.90s. a 21.90s (5 Ran).

(I L Shaw), P J Hobbs

2206 Welshpool Novices' Handicap Chase
(5-y-o and up) £2,820 3m. . . . . . (2:10)

1812⁺ RABA RIBA [90] 9-10-13 V Slattery, led, blun and hdd
     tenth, hdwy to ld 5 out, clr 3 out. (12 to 1 op 10 to 1) 1
1805² MASTER JOLSON [102] 6-11-11 A Maguire, al prmnt, lft in
     ld tenth, hdd 13th, rdn appr 3 out, no hdwy.
     . . . .(11 to 2 op 4 to 1) 2
1952⁺ THE POD'S REVENGE [77] 9-9-11 (3⁺) A Procter, hld up,
     hdwy 6th, rdn appr 3 out, one pace.
     . . . .(33 to 1 op 25 to 1) 3
2010⁵ MARTELL BOY (NZ) [89] 7-10-12 J Frost, hld up, hdwy 4
     out, held whn mstk 2 out. . . . .(11 to 2 op 5 to 1) 4
2044² CHIEF CELT [88] 8-10-11 G McCourt, jmpd slwly 3rd, rear
     till hdwy 7th, wknd appr 3 out.
     . . . . (11 to 2 op 4 to 1 tchd 6 to 1) 5
1952³ LASTOFTHEVIKINGS [77] 9-10-0 T Wall, rear, hdwy 4 out,
     btn whn blun nxt 2. . . . .(20 to 1 op 14 to 1) 6

1952[2] DOROBO (NZ) [84] (bl) 6-10-4 (3*) R Farrant, *prmnt, rdn appr 12th, wknd 4 out*..............(10 to 1 op 8 to 1) 7
1805[8] PHYL'S LEGACY [77] 9-9-11[2] (5*) T Jenks, *in tch frm 6th till wknd appr 4 out*..............(100 to 1 op 66 to 1) 8
1644* STAUNCH RIVAL (USA) [92] 7-11-1 D Bridgwater, *hld up, rdn and hdwy appr 12th, wknd quickly 5 out*. ....(3 to 1 fav op 7 to 2) 9
1805[7] PANT LLIN [77] 8-10-0 R Supple, *al beh, tld off*. ....(33 to 1 op 25 to 1) 10
HERE COMES CHARTER [84] 9-10-7 J Lower, *prmnt, led 5 out to nxt, wknd quickly, tld off*....(12 to 1 op 8 to 1) 11
1776[3] SQUIRES PRIVILEGE (Ire) [87] 6-10-10 N Williamson, *not jump wl, prmnt early, lost tch 11th, tld off*. ....(10 to 1 tchd 12 to 1) 12
SOUTH STACK [80] 8-10-3[3] Gary Lyons, *beh 5th, hit 13th, f 4 out*..............................(33 to 1 op 25 to 1) f
1795[3] MAJOR CUT [77] 8-10-0 B Powell, *f 1st*. ....(16 to 1 op 14 to 1) f
1651[3] WILD FORTUNE [80] 12-10-3[3] M A FitzGerald, *prmnt to tenth, rear whn brght dwn 4 out*. (33 to 1 op 25 to 1) bd
Dist: 7l, 4l, nk, 7l, ¾l, 3l, 5l, 8l, 10l, ½l. 6m 9.50s. a 20.50s (15 Ran).
SR: 29/34/5/16/8/-/ (Mrs L A Marsh), J L Spearing

2207 Church Stretton Conditional Jockeys' Selling Hurdle (4,5,6-y-o) £1,696 2m ....(2:40)

1942[3] COBB GATE (bl) 6-11-6 (3*) M Stevens, *rcd keenly, led to second, led appr 2 out, ran on wl*... (10 to 1 op 8 to 1) 1
1794[3] MINI FETE (Fr) 5-10-9 (5*) N Juckes, *trkd ldrs frm 3rd, ev ch 2 out, rdn and no imprsn r-in*.......(7 to 2 op 25 to 2) 2
1738[5] BAND SARGEANT (Ire) 5-11-5 N Leach, *hld up, cld on ldrs 2 out, rdn and no imprsn r-in*. ....(Evens fav tchd 11 to 10 and 11 to 10 on) 3
2083 PLAIN SAILING (Fr) 4-10-7 W Marston, *pld hrd, rdn appr 2 out, one pace*..........................(5 to 1 op 7 to 2) 4
1323[5] ALTO PRINCESS 5-11-0 D Meredith, *hld up, ev ch appr 2 out, rdn and sn btn*............... (12 to 1 op 8 to 1) 5
1965[4] MARSHALL PINDARI 4-10-7 R Davis, *hld up, wknd 3 out*. ....(14 to 1 tchd 16 to 1) 6
997 MANDALIA MELODY 4-10-7 D Walsh, *led second, hit 4th, hdd and wknd quickly appr 2 out*. (33 to 1 op 25 to 1) 7
Dist: 1l, 1½l, 1½l, 6l, 8l, 8l. 4m 10.00s. a 33.00s (7 Ran).
(Red House Racing), B Stevens

2208 Longmynd Novices' Handicap Hurdle (4-y-o and up) £1,938 2m 5f 110yds ....(3:10)

2015[2] CHERYLS PET (Ire) [76] 6-10-10 B Powell, *prmnt till outpcd 5th, hdwy appr 2 out, rdn to ld r-in, ran on*. .... (10 to 1 op 8 to 1) 1
1869[3] LANSDOWNE [79] 6-10-13 A Maguire, *hld up, hdwy 3 out, led briefly sn aftr last, rdn and no extr cl hme*. .... (10 to 1 op 8 to 1) 2
1804* ALICE SMITH [82] 7-11-2 W McFarland, *led, hit 2 out, rdn and hdd sn aftr last, no extr*. ....(6 to 1 op 8 to 1 tchd 9 to 1) 3
1948* MOBILE MESSENGER (NZ) [87] 6-11-7 J Frost, *al prmnt, rdn appr 2 out, kpt on one pace*... (14 to 1 op 12 to 1) 4
1837[5] HENRY VILL (Ire) [87] 6-11-7 C Llewellyn, *nvr far away, ev ch whn rdn appr 2 out, wknd*........(9 to 1 op 8 to 1) 5
2015* DERRYMOSS [89] (v) 8-11-2 (7*) T Dascombe, *hld up, hdwy appr 5th, wknd approaching 2 out*. ....(9 to 1 op 8 to 1 tchd 10 to 1) 6
1729[6] THE PORTSOY LOON [75] 7-10-9 D Bridgwater, *prmnt, rdn aftr 3 out, btn whn hit nxt*..........(8 to 1 op 7 to 1) 7
1998[2] MAKES ME GOOSEY (Ire) [90] 6-11-10 L Harvey, *mstk second, nvr nr to chal*................(16 to 1 op 12 to 1) 8
2142 DARINGLY [76] 5-10-10 R Bellamy, *hld up, hdwy 7th, wknd appr 2 out*..............................(25 to 1) 9
1392[4] ROSEN THE BEAU (Ire) [73] (bl) 6-10-7 R Supple, *prmnt till wknd 3 out*..................................(25 to 1) 10
1930[4] MARINER'S AIR [81] 7-11-1 W Marston, *hld up, hdwy 5th, wknd aftr 3 out*.................(8 to 1 tchd 9 to 1) 11
1654[8] AURORA LAD [82] 7-11-2 Richard Guest, *trkd ldr, dsptd ld 4th to 5th, wknd quickly nxt, tld off*. .... (20 to 1 op 16 to 1) 12
2033* LITTLE THYNE [83] 9-11-3 Dr P Pritchard, *al beh, tld off 5th*..(20 to 1) 13
1528 CARLINGFORD BELLE [76] 8-10-10 R J Beggan, *prmnt early, rear 4th, tld off*....................... (33 to 1) 14
1645 OK RECORDS [80] 7-11-0 N Mann, *al beh, tld off*. (25 to 1) 15
1967 THE JET SET [72] (v) 7-10-6 V Slattery, *jmpd poorly in rear, tld off*...(25 to 1) 16
HIGH BEACON [78] (bl) 7-10-12 N Williamson, *chsd ldr to 4th, wknd quickly aftr nxt, tld off*. ....(11 to 2 fav op 8 to 1 tchd 10 to 1 and 4 to 1) 17
2042[7] FILE VESTRY (Ire) [80] 6-11-0 I Lawrence, *hld up, hdwy 6th, rdn 3 out, btn whn pld up bef nxt*. .... (14 to 1 op 10 to 1) pu
Dist: 2l, 6l, 4l, 8l, sht-hd, 15l, 2l, 10l, 15l, 2½l. 5m 25.20s. a 28.20s (18 Ran).
(Peter Partridge), R H Buckler

2209 Telford Novices' Chase (5-y-o and up) £2,716 2½m.................. (3:40)

1973[3] RIVER MANDATE 7-11-5 B Powell, *mstk second, trkd ldr 9th, led briefly aftr 4 out, rdn and styd on to ld r-in*. .... (3 to 1 op 11 to 4 tchd 7 to 2) 1
2084[3] KNAVE OF CLUBS 7-11-5 D Bridgwater, *hld up, hdwy appr tenth, drvn to ld approaching 3 out, rdn and hdd r-in*.................................. (15 to 8 fav op 5 to 2) 2
1198[5] SMITH TOO (Ire) 6-11-5 I Lawrence, *mstk 4th, hld up in tch, rdn 11th, sn btn*.................(7 to 1 op 5 to 1) 3
1968* BINKLEY (Fr) 8-11-9 C Llewellyn, *led second, hit tenth, hdd sn aftr 4 out, wknd*............ (8 to 1 op 7 to 1) 4
1462 PERCY SMOLLETT 6-11-5 R Bellamy, *al beh, lost tch tenth, tld off*....................(20 to 1 op 16 to 1) 5
2058 CASTLE WARRIOR 7-11-5 T Wall, *sn beh, tld off whn pld up bef 8th*.......................(100 to 1 op 50 to 1) pu
1934 MICKEEN (bl) 7-11-5 M A FitzGerald, *led to second, hit nxt, wkng whn mstk 11th, pld up bef 4 out*. .... (20 to 1 op 14 to 1) pu
978[2] FACTOR TEN (Ire) 6-11-5 J Osborne, *trkd ldrs, wknd 11th, pld up bef 3 out*.................... (3 to 1 op 5 to 2) pu
Dist: 4l, dist, nk, 12l. 5m 10.40s. a 19.40s (8 Ran).
SR: 22/18/-/-/-/ (Anne Duchess Of Westminster), Capt T A Forster

2210 Broome Stakes National Hunt Flat Race (4,5,6-y-o) £1,644 2m......(4:10)

COURTOWN BOY 4-10-3 (7*) Mr G Hogan, *hld up, hdwy hfwy, led wl o'r one furlong out, rdn out*. .... (4 to 1 op 14 to 1) 1
LIGHTENING LAD 6-11-0 (7*) Mr E James, *hld up, hdwy 4 fs out, edgd lft appr last, one pace ins*. .... (16 to 1 op 14 to 1) 2
THE PADRE (Ire) 5-11-2 (5*) J McCarthy, *hld up, hdwy 5 fs out, led o'r 3 out till wl over one out, one pace*. .... (16 to 1 op 14 to 1) 3
SO HOPEFUL (NZ) 5-11-4 (3*) R Davis, *al prmnt, chsd ldr aftr 4 fs, outpcd frm 2 out*..........(5 to 1 op 3 to 1) 4
PONGO WARING (Ire) 5-11-4 (3*) R Farrant, *rear till hdwy 4 fs out, nvr dngrs*................... (8 to 1 op 6 to 1) 5
VILLAINS BRIEF (Ire) 5-11-4 (3*) N Bentley, *hld up in tch, rdn and wknd 3 fs out*............(33 to 1 op 25 to 1) 6
POLAR RHAPSODY (Ire) 5-11-7 Mr J M Pritchard, *hld up, hdwy hfwy, one pace fnl 3 fs*...... (10 to 1 op 8 to 1) 7
CORPORATE IMAGE 4-10-3 (7*) A Flannigan, *led 3 fs, prmnt till wknd three out*...............(33 to 1 op 25 to 1) 8
DIAMOND FLIER (Ire) 5-11-4 (3*) D Meredith, *chsd ldrs till wknd o'r 3 fs out*..................(10 to 1 op 8 to 1) 9
MENDIP SON 4-10-5 (5*) D Matthews, *nvr on terms*. ....(6 to 1 op 7 to 1 tchd 5 to 1) 10
HOODWINKER (Ire) 5-11-7 W Marston, *nvr far away, rdn and wknd 3 fs out*................(14 to 1 op 10 to 1) 11
FUN SPORT (Ire) 5-11-4 (3*) S Wynne, *al beh*..... (25 to 1) 12
DREAM START 4-10-3 (7*) R Wilkinson, *rominent till wknd o'r 4 fs out*..................................(25 to 1) 13
FILTHY REESH 5-11-2 (5*) T Jenks, *led aftr 3 fs till o'r three out, wknd quickly*......... (7 to 2 fav op 5 to 2) 14
PINBER 6-10-9 (7*) Mr S Mulcaire, *slwly away, al beh*. .... (33 to 1 op 25 to 1) 15
SEA SCAMP (Ire) 6-11-0 (7*) Mr G Haine, *al beh, tld off*. .... (33 to 1 op 25 to 1) 16
CARLINGFORD LASS (Ire) 4-9-12 (7*) M Doyle, *prmnt to hfwy, tld off*.....................(33 to 1 op 25 to 1) 17
YULEDUFERMEE (Ire) 5-11-0 (7*) S Knott, *pld hrd, prmnt to hfwy, tld off*..................(10 to 1 op 8 to 1) 18
Dist: 2½l, 5l, 12l, 8l, 2l, hd, 5l, 1l, 4l, ½l. 3m 53.70s. (18 Ran).
(J F Creaton), O O'Neill

SOUTHWELL (A.W) (std)
Wednesday January 19th
Going Correction: PLUS 0.50 sec. per fur.

2211 Tom Brown Juvenile Novices' Hurdle (4-y-o) £1,553 2m...............(1:25)

2115* PRIDWELL 11-5 R Dunwoody, *al gng best, slight ld till aftr 1st, led after 4 out, quickened clr last 2, easily*. ....(13 to 2 on op 6 to 1 on tchd 5 to 1 on) 1
1350[3] ALYVAIR 10-7 J Ryan, *nvr far away, led and hit 5th, hdd aftr 4 out, kpt on, no ch wth wnr*... (12 to 1 op 7 to 1) 2
2072[5] SYLVAN STARLIGHT 10-7 D Gallagher, *al hndy, led briefly aftr 4th, outpcd four out, no imprsn frm nxt*. .... (10 to 1 op 7 to 1 tchd 12 to 1) 3
QUIET CONFIDENCE (Ire) 10-2 (5*) S Curran, *trkd ldrs, rdn and lost grnd 4 out, tld off nxt*....(16 to 1 op 10 to 1) 4
1237 BLUE TRUMPET 10-12 R Greene, *pld hrd, led aftr 1st till after 4th, sn tld off, pulled up bef 3 out*. .... (33 to 1 op 20 to 1) pu
Dist: 3l, 20l, 20l. 4m 2.80s. a 16.80s (5 Ran).
SR: 3/-/ (Pond House Racing), M C Pipe

2212 Oliver Selling Hurdle (4-y-o and up) £1,861 2¾m.................. (1:55)

2094* DOUALAGO (Fr) (bl) 4-11-2 R Dunwoody, *led, rdn and hdd aftr 3 out, rallied to ld r-in, kpt on*. ....(6 to 4 on op 11 to 8 on tchd 5 to 4 on) 1

2061² CELTIC BOB 14-10-12 (7*) P Maddock, *patiently rdn, improved fnl circuit, led aftr 3 out to r-in, no extr.*
.......................(9 to 1 op 8 to 1 tchd 10 to 1) 2
1926³ LAFANTA (Ire) 5-11-10 K Jones, *nvr far away, ev ch and drvn alng 3 out, not quicken betw last 2.*
.......................(10 to 1 op 8 to 1) 3
2067 SERAPHIM (Fr) 5-10-7 (7*) S Taylor, *al hndy, niggled alng frm hfwy, rallied 3 out, no extr betw last 2.*
.......................(11 to 2 op 4 to 1 tchd 6 to 1) 4
646 CLASSIC STATEMENT 8-11-2 (3*) A Thornton, *wth ldr till rdn and lost grnd aftr 8th, tld off whn pld up bef 3 out.*
.......................(16 to 1 tchd 20 to 1) pu
2064 JOLI'S GREAT (bl) 6-11-0 J Ryan, *early mstks, struggling to go pace aftr one circuit, tld off whn pld up bef 3 out.*
.......................(13 to 2 op 5 to 1 tchd 7 to 1) pu
1654⁷ RAKES OF MALLOW 7-11-5 D Gallagher, *chsd ldrs, rdn to keep up aftr one circuit, tld off whn blun 4 out, pld up bef nxt.*
.......................(33 to 1) pu
Dist: ¾l, 6l, 4l. 5m 42.00s. a 33.00s (7 Ran).
(Martin Pipe Racing Club), M C Pipe

2213 Great Expectations Novices' Handicap Hurdle (4-y-o and up) £1,553 2¼m
.......................(2:25)

2065 RUTH'S GAMBLE [69] 6-9-13 (7*) Mr B Pollock, *settled gng wl, jnd ldrs fnl circuit, drw level and hit 2 out, led bef last, wnt clr.*.......................(9 to 1 op 8 to 1 tchd 10 to 1) 1
1736³ SCRABO VIEW (Ire) [87] 6-11-10 L O'Hara, *nvr far away, led aftr 5th, jnd and rdn 3 out, hdd bef last, one pace.*
.......................(7 to 1 tchd 8 to 1) 2
1639 GRAND RAPIDS (USA) [72] 7-10-4 (5*) T Eley, *ran in snatches, effrt and mstks fnl circuit, rdn 3 out, one pace.*.......................(11 to 1 op 14 to 1) 3
2118³ GREEN'S SEAGO (USA) [70] 6-10-7 D Gallagher, *dsptd early ld, lost grnd and rdn hfwy, some hdwy appr 3 out, no imprsn.*.......................(5 to 2 fav op 9 to 4 tchd 3 to 1) 4
2059³ CARLINGFORD LIGHTS (Ire) [63] 6-10-0 J Ryan, *made most, mstk and reminders 4th, hdd aftr nxt, lost tch bef four out, tld off.* (5 to 1 op 11 to 2 tchd 6 to 1 and 9 to 2) 5
1738 WESTCOURT FLYER [65] 5-10-2⁷ (7*) J Driscoll, *hld ldrs, rdn to keep up fnl circuit, tld off bef 4 out.*.....(16 to 1) 6
1869 DAMCADA (Ire) [70] 6-10-7 P McDermott, *chsd ldg grp till blun and uns rdr 5th.*.......................(7 to 1 op 11 to 1) ur
1953⁴ RAFTERS [85] 5-11-8 R Dunwoody, *settled to track ldrs, hit second, lost tch hfwy, tld off whn pld up bef 3 out.*
.......................(3 to 1 op 5 to 2 tchd 7 to 1) pu
Dist: 7l, 7l, 12l, 4l. Dist: 4m 29.00s. a 17.00s (8 Ran).
SR: -/9/-/-/-/   (Mrs A Emanuel), Mrs L C Jewell

2214 Nicholas Nickelby Handicap Hurdle (0-105 4-y-o and up) £1,976 2m. (2:55)

2165³ SPANISH WHISPER [75] 7-10-3 (5*) J Twomey, *al gng wl, drw level hfwy, led aftr 4 out, jnd 2 out, blun last, kpt on.*.......................(6 to 1 op 5 to 1 tchd 9 to 2) 1
1427³ SECRET LIASON [79] 8-10-12 R Dunwoody, *led till aftr second, led 6th till aftr 4 out, drw level last 2, one pace r-in.*.......................(9 to 1 tchd 10 to 1) 2
2119⁶ SANTA PONSA BAY [77] 7-10-10 J Railton, *lost tch and tld off last hfwy, shaken up to improve 3 out, styd on wl frm last.*.......................(20 to 1 op 33 to 1) 3
2119* TRISTAN'S COMET [79] 7-10-12 (6ex) B Dalton, *trkd ldrs, drvn alng to keep up appr hfwy, styd on und pres last 2, nrst finish.*....(11 to 10 on op 6 to 4 on tchd Evens) 4
1506* AUVILLAR (USA) [92] 6-11-11 D J Burchell, *pressed ldg pair, reminders aftr 3rd, struggling frm hfwy, no imprsn last.*.......................(8 to 1 op 5 to 1) 5
2090³ SASKIA'S HERO [92] 7-11-11 D Byrne, *wth ldr, led aftr second till hdd and rdn 4th, rallied aftr nxt, wknd and pld up bef last, dismounted.....(7 to 1 op 6 to 1) pu
1931⁷ SMART DEBUTANTE (Ire) [69] 5-9-11 (5*) T Eley, *reminders to keep up 4th, sn tld off, pld up bef 3 out.*
.......................(12 to 1 op 14 to 1) pu
Dist: 1l, 2½l, 2l, 15l. 4m 0.40s. a 14.40s (8 Ran).
SR: 16/19/14/14/12/-/-/   (The Barton Bendish Partnership), J R Bostock

2215 Scrooge Maiden Claiming Hurdle (4-y-o and up) £1,553 2½m....... (3:25)

TOP PRIZE 6-11-5 (7*) S Mason, *tucked away in midfield, pushed up to ld 8th, rdn alng last 2, styd on r-in.*
.......................(16 to 1 op 14 to 1 tchd 20 to 1) 1
1602⁶ GENERAL SHOT 9-11-8 Diane Clay, *trkd ldg bunch, bustled alng to improve bef 4 out, styd on betw last 2, nrst finish.*.......................(14 to 1 op 16 to 1 tchd 20 to 1) 2
2116³ OMIDJOY (Ire) 4-9-11 (7*) W J Walsh, *nvr far away, rdn and ev ch frm 3 out, kpt on same pace r-in.*
.......................(9 to 1 op 5 to 1 tchd 7 to 1) 3
2059² CROOKED DEALER (NZ) 7-11-10 G Upton, *wth ldrs, dsptd ld hfwy, reminders 4 out, rallied, no extr aftr nxt.*
.......................(20 to 1 op 16 to 1) 4
1938 KNOCKREIGH CROSS (Ire) 5-10-10 (7*) G Cahill, *chsd ldg bunch, feeling pace and struggling appr 4 out, outpcd bef nxt.*.......................(25 to 1) 5
974 GOLDEN BANKER (Ire) 6-11-8 K Jones, *slight ld till 4th, not fluent aftr, lost tch fnl circuit.*.......................(33 to 1) 6

2094 THANKSFORTHEOFFER (v) 6-11-3 (3*) A Thornton, *struggling to keep in tch hfwy, tld off fnl circuit.*
.......................(14 to 1 op 12 to 1) 7
1483 NEWGATESKY 4-10-0 W Dwan, *dsptd ld, made most frm 4th to 8th, wknd appr 3 out, tld off.*.......(50 to 1) 8
1425⁴ GLENSTAL PRIORY 7-11-1 D Gallagher, *struggling to keep up hfwy, tld off whn pld up bef 3 out.*
.......................(14 to 1 op 12 to 1 tchd 16 to 1) pu
2093³ BALTIC EXCHANGE (Can) 5-11-10 R Dunwoody, *co'red up beh ldrs, improved appr 4 out, rdn bef nxt, found little, pld up before 2 out.*.......................(9 to 2 op 5 to 2 on tchd Evens) pu
2130⁹ NYMPH ERRANT 4-10-4¹ S Earle, *in tch for one circuit, lost tch and tld off bef 3 out.*...(33 to 1 tchd 50 to 1) pu
Dist: 1l, 2½l, 15l, 10l, ½l, 3l, 12l. 5m 10.50s. a 29.50s (11 Ran).
(Northgate Lodge Racing Ltd), M Brittain

2216 Jane Eyre Handicap Hurdle (0-110 5-y-o and up) £1,970 3m.........(3:55)

2120³ ST VILLE [100] 8-11-3 (7*) S Mason, *nvr far away, led bef 4 out till appr nxt, led last, hld on gmely.*
.......................(7 to 4 fav op 6 to 4 tchd 2 to 1) 1
2067³ ALREEF [97] (v) 8-11-4 (3*) A Thornton, *settled gng wl, hdwy to ld bef 3 out, sn drvn alng, hdd last, rallied.*
.......................(6 to 1 tchd 7 to 1) 2
2120² FLYAWAY (Fr) [90] 9-11-0 D Gallagher, *wl plcd till outpcd and lost grnd 5 out, rallied nxt, rdn and outpaced frm 3 out.*.......................(3 to 1 op 5 to 2 tchd 100 to 30) 3
1809⁵ VAZON EXPRESS [76] 8-9-7 (7*) D Winter, *sn hndy, led aftr 8th till bef 4 out, soon btn.*......(16 to 1 op 33 to 1) 4
BOREEN JEAN [100] 10-11-10 R Dunwoody, *led till aftr 8th, reminders fnl circuit, tld off bef 4 out.*
.......................(11 to 2 op 5 to 1) 5
2059* CHAPEL HILL (Ire) [87] 6-10-11 D J Burchell, *blun and uns rdr second.*............(11 to 2 op 5 to 1 tchd 6 to 1) ur
Dist: Sht-hd, 25l, 6l, dist. 6m 3.60s. a 26.60s (6 Ran).
(J W P Curtis), J W Curtis

AYR (soft)
Thursday January 20th
Going Correction: PLUS 0.80 sec. per fur. (races 1,4,6), PLUS 0.85 (2,3,5)

2217 Straiton Novices' Hurdle (4-y-o and up) £2,081 2m.................(1:25)

1938² ASLAN (Ire) 6-11-4 M Dwyer, *prmnt, trkd ldr frm 4th, led aftr 6th, mstk last, pushed out.......(5 to 2 op 7 to 4) 1
2003 FIVE TO SEVEN (USA) 5-11-4 D Wilkinson, *led till hdd aftr 6th, chsd wnr after, kpt on wl.*
.......................(5 to 1 op 6 to 1 tchd 7 to 1) 2
1872 TALOS (Ire) 6-11-4 L Wyer, *prmnt, ev ch 6th, grad wknd appr 3 out.*..........(12 to 1 op 10 to 1 tchd 14 to 1) 3
1217 REBEL KING 4-10-7 A Dobbin, *mid-div, effrt appr 6th, kpt on frm 3 out.*................(20 to 1 op 16 to 1) 4
2148* LEGION OF HONOUR 6-11-5 (5*) T Jenks, *mid-div, hdwy to track ldrs hfwy, rdn whn mstk 3 out, sn btn.*
.......................(9 to 2 op 4 to 1 tchd 5 to 1) 5
1787⁵ CLEEVAUN (Ire) 6-10-13 (5*) A Roche, *beh till styd on frm 3 out, not trble ldrs.*...............(25 to 1 op 20 to 1) 6
971 WEAVER GEORGE (Ire) 4-10-2 (5*) J Supple, *beh till styd on frm 3 out.*..............................(20 to 1 op 16 to 1) 7
1202 EMERALD SEA (USA) 7-11-4 S Turner, *nvr dngrs.* (200 to 1) 8
MONT MIRAIL 8-11-4 N Doughty, *mid-div till wknd aftr 6th.*..........(33 to 1 op 20 to 1 tchd 40 to 1) 9
2003⁵ STONEY BROOK 6-11-4 B Storey, *in tch, effrt appr 6th, sn btn.*.......................(20 to 1 op 14 to 1) 10
1918⁴ CHIEF MINISTER (Ire) (bl) 5-11-4 P Niven, *chsd ldr till wknd aftr 6th.*.......(9 to 4 fav op 5 to 2 tchd 3 to 1) 11
19207 GERMAN LEGEND 4-10-7 A Merrigan, *mid-div, effrt appr 6th, sn btn.*........(33 to 1 op 50 to 1 tchd 66 to 1) 12
2003⁹ FLOATER (USA) 11-11-1 (3*) D J Moffatt, *sn beh...(50 to 1) 13
ELVETT BRIDGE (Ire) 6-10-13 (5*) F Perratt, *chsd ldrs till wknd appr 6th.*.......................(100 to 1) 14
2003 TAUVALERA 7-10-13 Mr D Swindlehurst, *chsd ldrs till wknd appr 6th.*.......................(200 to 1) 15
2106⁹ FINE OAK 7-11-11² Mr D Robertson, *sn wl beh, tld off.*
.......................(500 to 1) 16
STREET LADY 4-10-2 N Mann, *sn wl beh, tld off.*
.......................(12 to 1 op 25 to 1) 17
Dist: 3l, 20l, ¾l, 3l, 7l, nk, 1½l, 3l, 1l. 4m 55.00s. a 18.00s (17 Ran).
SR: 38/35/15/3/17/4/-/-/-/   (Raymond Anderson Green), J G FitzGerald

2218 John Brown Memorial Challenge Trophy Novices' Handicap Chase (5-y-o and up) £2,840 2m.............(1:55)

2007 POLITICAL TOWER [101] 7-11-10 A Dobbin, *trkd ldrs frm 4th, led 3 out, pushed clr appr last, cmftbly.*
.......................(5 to 2 op 2 to 1) 1
1182³ ZARBANO [81] 8-10-4 A Merrigan, *cl up, led 4th, hdd 3 out, btn whn mstk last.*..........(14 to 1 op 10 to 1) 2

1960³ PREOBLAKENSKY [92] 7-11-1 N Doughty, *trkd ldrs, outpcd aftr 8th, styd on frm 2 out.*
.................................(9 to 4 fav op 2 to 1 tchd 5 to 2) 3
1960⁴ GIPSY RAMBLER [77] 9-9-9 (5*) J Supple, *in tch, slightly outpcd aftr 8th, styd on frm 3 out.*...........(33 to 1) 4
2007⁷ BE AMBITIOUS (Ire) [82] 6-10-5⁴ K Jones, *cl up, dsptd ld frm 4th till wknd appr four out, 3rd and btn whn blun nxt.*...........................(25 to 1 op 20 to 1) 5
1941⁷ CAITHNESS PRINCE [88] 8-10-11 B Storey, *in tch till grad wknd frm 8th.*......................(10 to 1 op 8 to 1) 6
VESTAL HILLS [96] 8-11-2 (3*) A Thornton, *nvr on terms.*
.................................(20 to 1 tchd 25 to 1) 7
1919⁵ CELTIC SONG [94] 7-11-3 T Reed, *prmnt to hfwy, sn beh.*
.................................(7 to 2 op 4 to 1) 8
2007 SEMINOFF (Fr) [78] 8-9-11¹ (5*) T Jenks, *cl up frm 4th, wknd aftr 8th.*.....................(14 to 1 tchd 16 to 1) 9
2108⁸ PIT PONY [77] 10-10-0 R Hodge, *sn wl beh, f 4 out.*
.................................(66 to 1) f
MACCONACHIE [85] 7-10-8 P Niven, *beh whn blun and uns rdr second.*.................(33 to 1 op 20 to 1) ur
2007 AYIA NAPA [77] 7-10-0⁵ (5*) P Williams, *led to 4th, sn wknd, wl beh whn pld up bef 2 out.*..............(66 to 1) pu
BELLOFAGUS [77] 9-9-10¹ (5*) F Perratt, *nvr on terms, wl beh whn pld up bef 3 out.*............(66 to 1) pu
Dist: 15l, 2l, ¾l, 15l, 1l, 1½l, 5l, 1½l. 4m 7.60s. a 19.60s (13 Ran).
SR: 36/1/10/-/-/-/ (G R S Nixon), M A Barnes

2219 Dunure Claiming Chase (6-y-o and up) £2,598 3m 1f.................(2:25)

2149³ EBRO 8-11-6 A Dobbin, *hld up in tch, hdwy to track ldrs 11th, led 3 out, hrd pressed frm nxt, held on wl.*
.................................(20 to 1 op 12 to 1) 1
2105³ FORTH AND TAY 12-10-7 (5*) P Williams, *beh, hdwy to track ldrs 11th, rdn alng aftr 13th, chlgd 2 out, ev ch till no extr towards finish.*..........(7 to 4 fav tchd 2 to 1) 2
2069⁵ MOW CREEK 10-10-10 Mr J Bradburne, *cl up, led 6th till hdd 3 out, grad wknd.*..........(100 to 1 op 50 to 1) 3
1939⁶ BUCKLE IT UP 9-10-11 Mr D Mactaggart, *lost tch aftr 11th, no dngr after.*......(14 to 1 op 12 to 1 tchd 16 to 1) 4
2149⁷ SANDEDGE 7-10-9 B Storey, *prmnt, ev ch 4 out, wkng whn blun 2 out.*....................(66 to 1 op 33 to 1) 5
1962⁶ CAROUSEL CALYPSO 8-10-12 P Niven, *prmnt whn blun and uns rdr 4th.*................(9 to 2 op 7 to 2) ur
1676 SCOTTISH GOLD 10-11-6 T Reed, *led to 6th, sn lost pl, tld off whn pld up bef tenth.*
.................................(5 to 1 op 9 to 2 tchd 13 to 2) pu
1723 DASTARDLY DALE 8-12-0 J Railton, *cl up, dsptd ld 6th till appr 11th, sn wknd, tld off whn pld up bef 4 out.*
.................................(50 to 1 op 25 to 1 tchd 100 to 1) pu
2151⁷ CLASSIC MINSTREL 10-11-0 C Grant, *mstks, al beh, lost tch and pld up bef 11th.* (9 to 2 op 7 to 2 tchd 5 to 1) pu
Dist: ½l, 15l, 7l, 2l. 6m 58.40s. a 58.40s (9 Ran).
(Mrs F A Veasey), V Thompson

2220 Electric Brae Novices' Hurdle (4-y-o and up) £2,050 2½m..............(2:55)

1574² COQUI LANE 7-11-4 P Niven, *chsd ldr, led 8th, styd on wl.*
.................................(3 to 1 tchd 7 to 2) 1
1938⁴ LOCH SCAVAIG (Ire) 5-11-2 (3*) D J Moffatt, *beh, hdwy aftr 8th, kpt on wl und pres frm last, nvr rch wnr.*
.................................(7 to 2 op 5 to 2) 2
2003⁸ THE WHIRLIE WEEVIL 6-10-13 N Doughty, *prmnt, dsptd ld 8th, wknd aftr 2 out.*............(12 to 1 op 10 to 1) 3
2104⁶ CORSTON RAMBO 7-11-4 T Reed, *in tch till outpcd aftr 8th, no dngr after.*...............(8 to 1 tchd 10 to 1) 4
STOP THE WALLER (Ire) 5-11-4 A Dobbin, *chsd ldrs, ev ch appr 3 out, grad wknd.*................(33 to 1) 5
1918⁷ TRAVELLING LIGHT 8-11-4 Mr S Swiers, *hld up in tch, some hdwy aftr 8th, one pace frm 3 out.*
.................................(9 to 4 fav tchd 3 to 1 and 2 to 1) 6
CAITHNESS CLOUD 6-11-4 B Storey, *led till hdd 8th, grad wknd.*.........................(14 to 1 op 12 to 1) 7
1938 THE PIPE FITTER (Ire) 6-11-4 M Dwyer, *in tch till wknd appr 8th.*..............................(50 to 1) 8
1918 MANOR COURT (Ire) 6-11-4 A Merrigan, *in tch till wknd appr 8th.*..........................(200 to 1) 9
2140⁸ MARKS REFRAIN 10-10-13 (5*) Mr R Hale, *al beh, tld off.*
.................................(66 to 1) 10
1918 WOODSTOCK LODGE (USA) 6-10-11 (7*) P Carr, *sn prmnt, wknd quickly appr 8th, tld off whn pld up bef 3 out.*
.................................(100 to 1) pu
GILMANSCLEUCH (Ire) 6-10-8 (5*) F Perratt, *prmnt to hfwy, tld off whn pld up bef 3 out.*...........(100 to 1) pu
GRAND AS OWT 4-10-4 (3*) A Thornton, *sn beh, wl tld off whn pld up bef 3 out.*............(33 to 1 op 25 to 1) pu
1918⁵ STRONG DEEL (Ire) 6-11-4 C Grant, *sn beh, wl tld off whn pld up bef 3 out.*...(14 to 1 op 16 to 1 tchd 20 to 1) pu
2003 LOMOND SPRINGS (Ire) 5-11-4 S Turner, *wl beh hfwy, well tld off whn pld up bef 3 out.*...........(200 to 1) pu
Dist: 1½l, 10l, 15l, 1l, 1½l, 6l, 6l, 7l, 20l. 5m 14.00s. a 35.00s (15 Ran).
(J M Dun), G R Dun

2221 Maybole Handicap Chase (0-125 5-y-o and up) £3,046 2½m..........(3:25)

1925³ FUNNY OLD GAME [89] 7-10-6 (3*) A Thornton, *trkd ldrs, led 9th, hrd pressed frm 2 out, styd on wl.*
.................................(2 to 1 tchd 5 to 1) 1
1873³ DEEP DECISION [98] 8-11-4 M Dwyer, *hld up in tch, tracking ldrs whn hit 4 out, ch 2 out, sn rdn, no imprsn.*
.................................(5 to 1 op 4 to 1 tchd 11 to 2) 2
2006² DEEP DAWN [108] 11-12-0 C Grant, *cl up, chlgd 13th, sn pushed alng, wknd aftr 3 out.*
.................................(2 to 1 fav op 7 to 4 tchd 9 to 4) 3
1941³ ON THE HOOCH [99] 9-11-5 Mr J Bradburne, *prmnt, dsptd ld 9th till wknd appr 13th.*......(5 to 1 tchd 11 to 2) 4
2137³ MONAUGHTY MAN [86] 8-10-1 (5*) P Williams, *led till hdd 9th, wkng whn mstk 11th, tld off whn pld up bef 3 out.*
.................................(4 to 1 op 9 to 2 tchd 5 to 1) pu
Dist: 1l, 25l, 15l. 5m 33.50s. a 46.50s (5 Ran).
(David McCune), D McCune

2222 Girvan Handicap Hurdle (0-125 4-y-o and up) £2,305 2½m.....(3:55)

2138* GREY POWER [116] 7-11-6 (6ex) P Niven, *hld up, gd hdwy to track ldrs 8th, led 2 out, styd on wl.*
.................................(6 to 4 fav tchd 7 to 4) 1
1458 AMBLESIDE HARVEST [108] 7-10-12 M Dwyer, *mid-div, hdwy aftr 8th, led 3 out, hdd nxt, kpt on wl.*
.................................(10 to 1 op 7 to 1) 2
2005⁴ REVE DE VALSE (USA) [114] 7-10-13 (5*) P Waggott, *mid-div, effrt aftr 8th, kpt on same pace frm 3 out.*
.................................(9 to 1 op 8 to 1 tchd 10 to 1) 3
1940* SWEET CITY [107] 9-10-6 (5*) Mr R Hale, *trkd ldrs, effrt aftr 8th, kpt on same pace.*.........(10 to 1 op 8 to 1) 4
1777⁸ CELTIC BREEZE [96] (v) 11-9-11² (5*) T Jenks, *led to 7th, outpcd aftr nxt, kpt on frm 2 out.* (16 to 1 op 14 to 1) 5
2108⁴ GOLDEN REVERIE (USA) [96] 6-9-9 (5*) F Perratt, *cl up till wknd appr 3 out.*..............(50 to 1 op 33 to 1) 6
1919² BELLTON [124] 6-11-7 (7*) F Leahy, *trkd ldrs, led 7th, hdd 3 out, wkng whn mstk nxt.*
.................................(10 to 1 op 12 to 1 tchd 14 to 1) 7
1789⁵ KUSHBALOO [112] 9-10-9 (7*) Mr D Parker, *prmnt till wknd aftr 8th.*............(16 to 1 op 25 to 1 tchd 20 to 1) 8
519¹⁰ FORWARD GLEN [108] 7-10-12 C Grant, *al beh.*
.................................(33 to 1 op 25 to 1) 9
1940 LOGICAL FUN [100] (bl) 6-11-0 (3*) D J Moffatt, *mid-div till wknd quickly aftr 8th, tld off.*.........(33 to 1) 10
KIR (Ire) [98] 6-10-2 A Dobbin, *trkd ldrs till wknd quickly appr 8th, tld off.*................(50 to 1) 11
1728³ IT'S THE PITS [103] 7-10-7 T Reed, *hld up, hdwy appr 8th, cl 3rd and rdn whn f 2 out.*
.................................f
1619⁵ THE DEMON BARBER [122] 12-11-12 N Doughty, *prmnt, jnd ldrs 6th, wknd quickly and pld up bef 3 out.*
.................................(25 to 1 op 16 to 1) pu
Dist: 3l, 10l, 1l, 5l, 1l, ½l, 1l, 10l. 5m 15.40s. a 36.40s (13 Ran).
(A Frame), Mrs M Reveley

LINGFIELD (heavy)
Thursday January 20th
Going Correction: PLUS 1.95 sec. per fur.

2223 Many Cooks Novices' Chase (5-y-o and up) £2,717 3m.............(2:40)

1393⁶ GENERAL BRANDY 8-11-4 D Murphy, *chsd ldrs, led 3 out, ran on.*................(25 to 1 op 14 to 1 tchd 33 to 1) 1
1704³ LOBRIC (bl) 9-11-4 A Maguire, *chsd ldrs, cld and ev ch whn blun badly last, not reco'r.*
.................................(13 to 2 op 5 to 1 tchd 8 to 1) 2
1714* GALLANT EFFORT (Ire) 6-11-10 M A FitzGerald, *al prmnt, led 4 out to nxt, wknd appr 2 out.*
.................................(9 to 4 fav op 7 to 4 tchd 7 to 2) 3
2023³ FROZEN DROP 7-11-4 Richard Guest, *beh frm tenth, tld off.*.................(7 to 1 op 5 to 1 tchd 10 to 1) 4
1861 IRISH BAY 8-11-4 J Osborne, *trkd ldrs, ev ch whn f 3 out.*
.................................(5 to 1 op 11 to 1) f
FOUR FROM THE EDGE 11-11-4 Dr P Pritchard, *al beh, blun badly and pld up 13th.*.....(20 to 1 tchd 33 to 1) pu
1714⁴ REAL HARMONY 8-11-4 D O'Sullivan, *al struggling in rear, tld off whn pld up bef 2 out.*
.................................(50 to 1 op 20 to 1 tchd 66 to 1) pu
1712⁵ STAR ACTOR 8-11-4 R Dunwoody, *jmpd soundly, led to 4 out, wknd quickly, pld up bef nxt.*.(3 to 1 tchd 7 to 2) pu
2193 MISS MUIRE 8-10-13 D Morris, *mstks, beh, cld hfwy, sn lost pl, tld off whn pld up bef 2 out.*
.................................(25 to 1 op 14 to 1 tchd 33 to 1) pu
Dist: 8l, 25l, 15l. 6m 46.80s. a 53.80s (9 Ran).
SR: 20/12/-/-/-/-/ (Barry Fearn), J T Gifford

LINGFIELD (A.W) (std)
Thursday January 20th
Going Correction: MINUS 0.20 sec. per fur.

2224 Pennywise Maiden Hurdle (4-y-o and up) £1,876 2m.................(1:10)

2112² MILZIG (USA) 5-11-7 D O'Sullivan, *nvr far away, cld aftr 4 out, led appr last, hrd hld.*
.....................(13 to 8 fav op 6 to 4 tchd 7 to 4) 1
MONTY ROYALE (Ire) 5-11-7 N Williamson, *cl up, led 4 out to nxt, pushed alng aftr 2 out, ev ch last, one pace und pres*..........................(7 to 1 op 6 to 1 tchd 8 to 1) 2
2130⁴ MILL BURN 5-11-7 R Campbell, *al prmnt, gng wl 4 out, led nxt tll hdd appr last, one pace...*(6 to 1 op 7 to 2) 3
2130³ BARTON ROYAL (Ire) (v) 4-10-2 (7") S Fox, *al prmnt tll wknd 2 out.*..........................(10 to 1 op 5 to 1) 4
1424⁴ GILT DIMENSION 7-11-7 R Supple, *nvr nr to chal.*
.............(9 to 1 op 8 to 1 tchd 6 to 1 and 10 to 1) 5
1488 WATER DIVINER 4-10-9 J Ryan, *cld on ldrs 4th, wknd four out.*........................(50 to 1 op 33 to 1) 6
1464 SUNBEAM CHARLIE 4-10-2 (7") K Goble, *hld up towards rear, effrt 4 out, sn no imprsn.....* (50 to 1 op 25 to 1) 7
1767 RED LEADER (Ire) 4-10-9 D Meade, *led, sn clr, hdd 4 out and wknd, tld off.*.............(33 to 1 op 20 to 1) 8
2115³ LYFORD CAY (Ire) (bl) 4-10-9 J Osborne, *prmnt to 4th, sn lost pl, tld off.*........................(4 to 1 op 2 to 1) 9
CRASH BANG WALLOP (Ire) 6-11-0 (7") L O'Hare, *hit 6th, beh whn pld up bef 3 out.*
.........................(25 to 1 op 20 to 1 tchd 33 to 1) pu
1729 THE GREY TEXAN 5-11-7 Richard Guest, *al beh, pld up bef 3 out.*........................(14 to 1 op 25 to 1) pu
WOTAWEEK 5-11-2 P Holley, *sn tld off, pld up bef 6th.*
.........................(25 to 1 op 14 to 1) pu
Dist: 4l, 1½l, 15l, ½l, 12l, 10l, 25l, 5l. 3m 42.00s. a 9.00s (12 Ran).

(Jack Joseph), R J O'Sullivan

2225 More Haste Claiming Hurdle (4-y-o and up) £1,768 2¾m............(1:40)

2064² SPARKLER GEBE (bl) 8-11-8 D O'Sullivan, *hld up in tch, hdwy to cl on ldrs 6th, led appr last, rdn out.*
.......(11 to 10 fav op 6 to 4 tchd 13 to 8 and Evens) 1
2067⁶ CRABBY BILL (bl) 7-11-10 A Maguire, *led till hdd appr last, no extr.*.......(7 to 4 tchd 13 to 8 and 2 to 1) 2
2064⁵ FROSTY RECEPTION (bl) 9-11-6 L Harvey, *cl up, hrd rdn appr tenth and ag'n aftr 4 out, styd on one pace.*
.........................(15 to 2 op 6 to 1 tchd 8 to 1) 3
1731⁵ PEARLY WHITE 5-11-1 R Dunwoody, *chsd ldrs till wknd tenth.*.......(12 to 1 op 8 to 1 tchd 14 to 1) 4
2132⁶ TEMPORALE 8-11-6 R Marley, *trkd ldrs till hrd rdn and wknd 11th.*.......(16 to 1 op 10 to 1 tchd 20 to 1) 5
1946⁸ LONG'S EXPRESS (Ire) 6-11-1 N Williamson, *trkd ldrs, drpd rear and reminders aftr 9th, hdwy whn hit nxt, sn outpcd.*........................(20 to 1 op 12 to 1) 6
1929⁶ DAUPHIN BLEU (Fr) 8-11-5 Dr P Pritchard, *prmnt to 9th, sn lost pl, tld off.*........................(20 to 1 op 14 to 1) 7
2113² MUTUAL BENEFIT (bl) 7-11-4 Lorna Vincent, *sn beh, tld off.*
.........................(20 to 1 op 16 to 1) 8
1600 SOLENT LAD 11-11-2 M Stevens, *beh frm 5th, tld off.*
.........................(33 to 1 tchd 50 to 1) 9
Dist: 3½l, 6l, 30l, 1l, 1l, 20l, 25l, 15l. 5m 11.70s. a 12.70s (9 Ran).

(Sparkler Filters (Great Britain) Ltd), R J O'Sullivan

2226 Friend In Need Handicap Hurdle (0-115 4-y-o and up) £1,660 2½m (2:10)

2065⁵ TEL E THON [94] (v) 7-11-0 R Dunwoody, *led to 9th, led ag'n 4 out, rdn appr last, drvn out.*
.........................(7 to 4 fav tchd 2 to 1) 1
AUTHORSHIP (USA) [108] 8-12-0 D Murphy, *strted slwly and beh, cld aftr 4 out, wnt second 2 out, one pace und pres frm last*........................(9 to 4 op 5 to 2) 2
2064⁴ RADAR KNIGHT [83] 6-9-10 (7") L O'Hare, *cld 9th till hdd 4 out, rdn, outpcd aftr nxt.*(14 to 1 op 10 to 1) 3
1278² MOVING OUT [95] 6-11-1 J Osborne, *cl up till lost pl quickly 8th, no dngr aftr.*............(2 to 1 op Evens) 4
2082⁸ L'ORAGE (Ire) [105] 6-11-11 R J Beggan, *sn struggling, tld off whn pld up bef 3 out.*..........(25 to 1 op 20 to 1) pu
Dist: 4l, 8l, 15l. 4m 42.90s. a 11.90s (5 Ran).

(Eddie Wilkinson), P J Jones

2227 New Broom Amateur Riders' Handicap Hurdle (0-120 4-y-o and up) £1,737 2¼m.................(3:10)

1352³ CORRARDER [102] 10-11-3¹ (7") M J Smyth-Osbourne, *hld up in mid-div, hdwy to track ldr aftr 7th, led 3 out, ran on wl*.................(2 to 1 tchd 7 to 4 and 9 to 4) 1
2110² WHIPPERS DELIGHT (Ire) [107] 6-11-7 (7") Mr A Charles-Jones, *led till hdd 3 out, one pace und pres frm last.*........................(5 to 4 fav op Evens tchd 6 to 4) 2
SHAMSHOM AL ARAB (Ire) [81] 6-9-10¹ (7") Miss V Haigh, *blun badly second, beh, hdwy 9th, outpcd frm nxt.*
.........................(6 to 1 op 4 to 1) 3
2133¹ PROVERBS GIRL [89] 9-10-8⁵ (7",6ex) Mr J Thatcher, *beh, hdwy 2 out, nvr nrr...*(11 to 1 op 7 to 1 tchd 12 to 1) 4
1930⁷ HIGHLAND FLAME [79] 5-9-10³ (7") Miss J Davis, *trkd ldrs till wknd aftr 8th.*.........(16 to 1 op 10 to 1) 5
2065⁷ STYLISH GENT [81] 7-10-2⁹ (7") Mr P Clarke, *cl up till wknd 4 out.*.........................(16 to 1 op 10 to 1) 6
2064 BAYLORD PRINCE (Ire) [79] (bl) 6-9-7 (7") Miss J Ewer, *al beh.*.........................(66 to 1 op 50 to 1) 7

1942⁶ WHATMORECANIASKFOR (Ire) [82] (bl) 6-10-3¹⁰ (7") Mr Richard White, *cl up till drpd rear 7th.*
.........................(13 to 8 op 20 to 1) 8
Dist: 5l, 15l, 6l, hd, 2½l, 10l, 7l. 4m 11.90s. a 10.90s (8 Ran).

(Mrs E T Smyth-Osborne), J A B Old

2228 Little Acorns Novices' Handicap Hurdle (4-y-o and up) £1,729 2½m.. (3:40)

2132⁴ SAAHI (USA) [89] 5-10-13 (7ex) J Osborne, *cl up, led 8th to nxt, led ag'n 3 out, sn quickened clr, imprsv.*
.....(15 to 8 on op 7 to 4 on tchd 2 to 1 on and 13 to 8 on) 1
2063⁴ CALOGAN [86] 7-10-10 C Llewellyn, *led till hdd 8th, led ag'n 9th to 4 out, outpcd aftr 2 out.*
.........................(8 to 1 op 4 to 1 tchd 9 to 1) 2
1840⁹ DOMINANT FORCE [100] 5-11-0 D Murphy, *cl up, led 4 out to nxt, wknd quickly aftr 2 out, pld up bef last, lme.*
.........................(2 to 1 tchd 7 to 4) pu
Dist: 15l. 4m 51.50s. a 20.50s (3 Ran).

(Martin N Peters), C Weedon

2229 Caveat Emptor Handicap Hurdle (0-115 4-y-o and up) £1,753 2m.. (4:10)

2129⁷ NOBLELY (USA) [101] 7-12-0 (6ex) R Dunwoody, *set gd pace, made all, rdn appr last, ran on wl.*
.........................(13 to 8 fav op 7 to 4 tchd 2 to 1) 1
2110⁴ RARFY'S DREAM [103] 6-12-2 (6ex) A Maguire, *cl up, ev ch 2 out, sn rdn and one pace appr last, eased nr finish.*
.........................(4 to 1 op 3 to 1 tchd 9 to 2) 2
2130² MASROUG [83] 7-10-10 M Richards, *outpcd, hdwy 3 out, styd on, nvr dngrs.......*(8 to 1 op 5 to 1 tchd 9 to 1) 3
2065⁴ VICTORY ANTHEM [91] 8-10-11 (7") T Dascombe, *trkd ldrs, rdn and outpcd aftr 4 out, no ch whn blun last.*
.........................(5 to 1 tchd 6 to 1) 4
2132³ SING THE BLUES [85] 10-10-12 D Morris, *chsd ldrs till wknd 4 out, tld off.*..............(16 to 1 op 12 to 1) 5
2065¹ ROYAL CIRCUS [83] 5-10-10 D Bridgwater, *trkd ldrs, jmpd slwly 6th and sn lost pl, tld off.*
.........................(3 to 1 op 5 to 2 tchd 7 to 2) 6
2065⁹ FLUIDITY (USA) [86] (bl) 6-10-13 W Marston, *al beh, tld off.*
.........................(33 to 1 tchd 50 to 1) 7
Dist: 3½l, 15l, 3½l, 20l, 15l, ¾l. 3m 35.80s. a 2.80s (7 Ran).
SR: 40/38/3/7/

(D H Cowgill), N J H Walker

TRAMORE (IRE) (heavy)
Thursday January 20th

2230 Fenor Claiming Hurdle (5-y-o and up) £2,243 2m.................(1:15)

2039⁶ KYLE HOUSE VI (Ire) 5-10-5 C F Swan, ...(8 to 1) 1
1157³ KAITLIN (Ire) 5-10-9 P L Malone, ...(3 to 1) 2
1914³ CHARMING EXCUSE 10-10-9 (5") Mr C T G Kinane,
.........................(9 to 4 fav) 3
2128⁵ FIFI'S MAN 8-10-9 (7") P A Roche, ...(5 to 1) 4
BALLAD SONG 11-11-1 (5") Mr G J Harford, ...(6 to 1) 5
2155 GALZIG 6-11-0 H Rogers, ...(20 to 1) 6
804 CURRAGH ROSE 7-9-12 (7") J Butler, ...(9 to 1) 7
Dist: Sht-hd, 2l, nk, 2l. 4m 23.40s. (7 Ran).

(Capt D G Swan), Capt D G Swan

2231 Brownstown Hurdle (5-y-o and up) £2,243 2m.....................(1:45)

1608² HURRICANE EDEN 7-10-11 (5") M A Davey, ...(6 to 1) 1
1899⁸ MRS BARTON (Ire) (bl) 6-10-11 (5") J R Barry, ...(7 to 1) 2
2097³ ELIADE (Ire) 5-10-12 C O'Dwyer, ...(4 to 1) 3
2024⁴ FINNEGANS WAKE 7-11-7 C F Swan, ...(6 to 1) 4
2123³ PUNTERS BAR 7-11-2 P A Roche, ...(8 to 1) 5
2123⁴ KAWA-KAWA 7-10-11 (5") T J O'Sullivan, ...(4 to 1) 6
1858 TWO HILLS FOLLY (Ire) 5-10-12 B Sheridan, ...(20 to 1) 7
2038* SLANEY LAMB (Ire) 6-12-0 D H O'Connor, ...(7 to 2 fav) 8
1337 CALL ME HENRY 5-11-3 F Woods, ...(20 to 1) 9
1978³ TOMMY'S RUN 7-11-2 (5") D T Evans, ...(8 to 1) 10
476⁵ SLANEY FOOD 7-11-4 (3") D P Murphy, ...(10 to 1) 11
1982⁴ HAVE A BRANDY (Ire) 5-11-3 A J O'Brien, ...(14 to 1) 12
689⁵ AWBEG ROVER (Ire) 6-11-1 (3") Mr T Lombard, ..(14 to 1) 13
PORT PRINCESS (Ire) 5-10-9 (3") C O'Brien, ...(16 to 1) 14
2102⁴ THE BRIDGE TAVERN (Ire) 5-10-10 (7") Miss C Duggan,
.........................(12 to 1) f
Dist: ¾l, 4l, 4l, ¾l. 4m 20.60s. (15 Ran).

(M J Tynan), M J Tynan

2232 Lismore Handicap Hurdle (0-109 4-y-o and up) £2,243 2m............(2:15)

2039* JO JO BOY (Ire) [-] 5-11-4 (5ex) F J Flood, ...(9 to 2) 1
2040* ANOTHER COURSE (Ire) [-] 6-10-10 (7",5ex) Mr P M Cloke,
.........................(9 to 2) 2
2039³ TURALITY (Ire) [-] 5-10-2 S H O'Donovan, ...(8 to 1) 3
2050⁶ ROSEPERRIE (Ire) [-] (bl) 6-9-12¹ (5") D T Evans, ..(10 to 1) 4
1549 NORDIC RACE [-] 7-9-7 A J O'Brien, ...(14 to 1) 5
2024⁶ BARNAGEERA BOY (Ire) [-] 5-10-10 H Rogers, ...(10 to 1) 6
2098 CHRISTY MOORE (Ire) [-] (bl) 4-10-5 A Powell, ...(33 to 1) 7
1823 CLASSY MACHINE (Ire) [-] 6-10-3 P M Verling, ...(20 to 1) 8

2124 RATHBRIDES JOY [-] 7-12-0 T Horgan, ... (14 to 1) 9
2098[4] PERCY BRENNAN [-] 7-10-9 C F Swan, ...(10 to 1) 10
1902 MILLER'S CROSSING [-] 7-10-6 (3") C O'Brien, . . (20 to 1) 11
2123* UNCLE BABY (Ire) [-] 6-10-10 (5*,2ex) K P Gaule,
. . . . (9 to 4 fav) f
2040[3] PREMIER LEAP (Ire) [-] 5-10-6 (7") M D Murphy, . .(10 to 1) bd
1983 ANNADOT (Ire) [-] 4-9-13 (3") T J Mitchell, ... (33 to 1) bd
Dist: 4½l, hd, 13l, 1½l. 4m 19.10s. (14 Ran).

(Raymond McConn), F Flood

2233 Waterford (C & G) Novice Chase (5-y-o and up) £2,243 2m. . . . .(2:45)

ALBERT'S FANCY 8-11-7 D H O'Connor, ... (6 to 1) 1
1981[4] ALTEREZZA (USA) 7-11-7 B Sheridan, ... (10 to 9 on) 2
2101[5] GOOLDS GOLD 8-11-7 T Horgan, ... (8 to 1) 3
1760[9] BEAU GRANDE (Ire) 6-11-7 L P Cusack, ... (12 to 1) 4
1335 DHARKOUM 7-11-7 J A White, ... (12 to 1) 5
1988[5] NO BETTER BUACHAIL (Ire) 6-11-7 F J Flood, ...(4 to 1) 6
1814 CRACKLING FROST (Ire) 6-11-7 T J Taaffe, ... (14 to 1) 7
2040[6] ASHBORO (Ire) 5-10-5 (7") J Willis, ... (20 to 1) 8
1854[4] BOY BLUE 7-11-7 G M O'Neill, ... (10 to 1) 9
Dist: 3½l, 1½l, 2l, 15l. 4m 23.20s. (9 Ran).

(Slaney Cooked Meats), P J P Doyle

2234 Tramore Mares Novice Chase (5-y-o and up) £2,243 2m. . . . .(3:15)

2038[2] BLAZING COMET 8-11-7 F Woods, ... (3 to 1 fav) 1
1857[3] BALADINE 7-11-7 S H O'Donovan, ... (5 to 1) 2
2035[2] RATHNURE LADY (Ire) 6-11-2 (5") P A Roche, ... (5 to 1) 3
2035[4] DELIGHTFUL CHOICE (Ire) 6-11-0 (7") J P Broderick,
. . . . (10 to 1) 4
2126[5] SANTAMORE (bl) 7-11-7 T Horgan, ... (4 to 1) 5
2157 SOME BRIDGE 7-11-4 (3") C O'Brien, ... (25 to 1) 6
2038 COOL CARLING 7-11-7 J Magee, ... (14 to 1) 7
2035[3] STRONG CHERRY 8-11-0 (7") Mr K Taylor, ... (8 to 1) f
2051[7] RAINBOW ALLIANCE (Ire) (bl) 6-11-7 J F Titley, . . (12 to 1) f
Dist: ¾l, 15l, 6l, 11l. 4m 25.30s. (9 Ran).

(Miss P M Maher), Miss P M Maher

2235 Dungarvan Handicap Chase (0-102 5-y-o and up) £2,243 2¾m. . . . . . (3:45)

2037 IFFEEE [-] 7-12-0 C O'Dwyer, ... (14 to 1) 1
1826[5] MAKE ME AN ISLAND [-] 9-10-13 (7") J P Broderick, (6 to 1) 2
1851 IL TROVATORE (USA) [-] 8-11-10 P Carberry, ... (7 to 1) 3
2100 WHAT A MINSTREL [-] 8-10-4 T Horgan, ... (16 to 1) 4
2036[5] KINGS HILL [-] 12-10-6 (7") J Butler, ... (10 to 1) 5
2100[2] DEL MONTE BOY [-] 9-10-10 (7") M D Murphy, ...(6 to 1) 6
2036[4] KITES HARDWICKE [-] 7-10-10 F J Flood, ... (7 to 1) 7
2036[9] ITS A SNIP [-] 9-10-1 J Jones, ... (14 to 1) 8
2126 NANCYS LAD [-] 7-10-5 H Rogers, ... (20 to 1) 9
2036[7] CHILIPOUR [-] 7-11-5 (5") P A Roche, ... (8 to 1) 10
2183[4] HURRICANE TOMMY [-] (bl) 7-11-8 (5") Mr G J Harford,
. . . . (8 to 1) 11
2100[8] CONNA RAMBLER [-] 11-11-8 (3") D P Murphy, . . (12 to 1) ur
LISNAVARAGH [-] 8-10-10 J Shortt, ... (20 to 1) pu
2036* PINEWOOD LAD [-] 7-11-5 (5*,5ex) C P Dunne, (9 to 2 fav) pu
Dist: 2½l, 4½l, 1½l, 3½l. 6m 0.20s. (14 Ran).

(Ronald Khoo), Patrick Day

2236 Cappoquin INH Flat Race (6-y-o and up) £2,243 2m. . . . .(4:15)

2161[3] NOPADDLE 10-11-11 (3") Mrs J M Mullins, ... (7 to 1) 1
534 SLANEY FAYRE (Ire) 6-11-7 (7") Miss L E A Doyle, . (8 to 1) 2
1902[5] SLEMISH MIST 7-11-4 (5") Mr G J Harford, ... (14 to 1) 3
1827[6] MIGHTY HAGGIS 7-11-7 (7") Mr N C Kelleher, ... (12 to 1) 4
2102[6] ANOTHER ROLLO (Ire) 6-11-7 (7") Mr N Stokes, . . (12 to 1) 5
2041[4] RAHEEN FLOWER (Ire) 6-11-9 Mr D M O'Brien, . . . (12 to 1) 6
2038[6] LADY BUDD (Ire) 6-11-2 (7") Mr J Fleming, ... (12 to 1) 7
31[5] LITTLE BUCK (Ire) 6-11-7 (7") Mr J S Cullen, ... (12 to 1) 8
ASHPLANT 7-11-11 (3") Mrs M Mullins, ... (6 to 1) 9
2102[3] BLACK AVENUE (Ire) 6-11-4 (5") Mr H F Cleary, to 4 fav) 10
1855[4] REPLACEMENT 7-12-0 Mr A J Martin, ... (8 to 1) 11
1910[5] TREACYS CROSS 8-11-7 (7") Mr D Carey, ...(8 to 1) 12
TIP THE CAN (Ire) 6-11-11 (3") Mr A R Coonan, . . (12 to 1) 13
CROBALLY 7-11-2 (7") Mr K Whelan, ... (20 to 1) 14
DICKS DELIGHT (Ire) 6-11-7 (7") Mr E Sheehy, . . . (20 to 1) pu
Dist: 5½l, 2½l, ½l, 1l. 4m 18.50s. (15 Ran).

(Mrs J M Mullins), W P Mullins

CATTERICK (good to soft)
Friday January 21st
Going Correction: PLUS 0.65 sec. per fur. (races 1,3,-5,7), PLUS 1.00 (2,4,6)

2237 EBF 'National Hunt' Novices' Hurdle Qualifier (Div I) (5,6,7-y-o) £2,364 2m 3f . . . .(12:50)

2008[2] MAJOR BELL 6-11-5 M Moloney, made all, clr whn mstk 2
out, pushed out.
. . . .(13 to 8 on op 7 to 4 on tchd 6 to 4 on) 1

717[5] HIGH PENHOWE 6-10-9 D Byrne, in tch, chsd wnr frm
aftr 3 out, kpt on und pres, no imprsn.
. . . . (9 to 1 op 8 to 1 tchd 10 to 1) 2
1289 MISCHIEVOUS GIRL 6-10-9 Mrs F Needham, wl beh till
styd on frm 3 out, nvr dngrs. . . . .(50 to 1 op 33 to 1) 3
1959 GAY'S GAMBIT 5-10-2 (7") J Driscoll, sn beh, tld off.
. . . .(50 to 1) 4
1582[6] ORD GALLERY (Ire) 5-10-7 (7") A Linton, chsd wnr till wknd
aftr 3 out, 3rd and no ch whn f nxt.
. . . . (10 to 1 op 8 to 1 tchd 12 to 1) f
1736 ZIN ZAN (Ire) 6-11-0 G Upton, cl up till rdn and wknd
quickly aftr 4th, blun nxt, wl beh whn pld up bef 6th.
. . . . (100 to 30 op 3 to 1 tchd 7 to 2) pu
ARTHUR BEE 7-10-9 (5") N Leach, sn wl beh, tld off whn
pld up bef 3 out. . . . .(100 to 1 op 50 to 1) pu
2004 CASTLEFERGUS 7-11-0 J Callaghan, in tch, 4th whn pld
up lme bef 5th. (14 to 1 op 12 to 1) pu
2003 DERWENT LAD 5-11-0 A Dobbin, beh frm hfwy, tld off
whn blun 2 out, pld up bef last. . . (20 to 1 op 16 to 1) pu
1674 GOLDEN RECORD 6-11-0 L O'Hara, sn beh, tld off whn
pld up bef 3 out. . . . . (33 to 1) pu
Dist: 5l, dist, dist. 4m 48.10s. (10 Ran).

(A C Whillans), A C Whillans

2238 Stayers' Novices' Chase (5-y-o and up) £2,734 3m 1f 110yds. . . . . . . (1:20)

1937[2] CHARLOTTE'S EMMA 7-11-0 B Storey, hld up, hdwy
hfwy, chsd ldr frm 4 out, led r-in, all out.
. . . . (9 to 4 fav op 2 to 1 tchd 5 to 2) 1
1793[3] WISHING GATE (USA) 6-11-5 M Dwyer, dsptd ld, mstk 9th,
led 13th, hdd r-in, rallied und pres. . (3 to 1 op 5 to 2) 2
1657[3] WESTWELL BOY 8-11-5 C Hawkins, cl up, led 11th till hdd
13th, en ch till grad wknd aftr 4 out.(10 to 1 op 8 to 1) 3
1066[5] HUDSON BAY TRADER (USA) 7-11-5 Mrs A Farrell, in tch,
pushed alng and outpcd aftr 11th, styd on frm 3 out,
nvr dngrs. . . . .(4 to 1 op 7 to 2) 4
2103[2] PADDY MORRISSEY 7-11-5 A Dobbin, chsd ldrs till wknd
aftr 11th. . . . . (12 to 1 op 14 to 1) 5
1937 DUCHESS OF TUBBER (Ire) 6-10-11 (3") A Thornton, beh
frm hfwy. . . . .(16 to 1 op 14 to 1) 6
1862[3] SUPPOSIN 6-11-5 Richard Guest, mstks, in tch till wknd
aftr 13th, tld off. . . . .(8 to 1) 7
STRONG CHANCE 8-11-5 J Callaghan, beh whn f 5th.
. . . . (66 to 1 op 100 to 1) f
SOLO BUCK 8-11-0 G McCourt, sn beh, tld off whn f 15th.
. . . .(8 to 1) f
2071[7] THE LORRYMAN (6-11-5 T Reed, mstk 3rd, made most
till hdd 11th, sn beh, tld off whn f 2 out.
. . . . (100 to 1 op 50 to 1) f
MERRYDALE FARM 9-11-5 C Grant, sn beh, tld off whn
pld up bef 9th. . . . . (33 to 1) pu
CALMATA 13-11-0 C Dennis, sn beh, tld off whn pld up
bef two[f]th. . . . .(25 to 1 op 20 to 1) pu
1962[5] EBORNEEZER'S DREAM 11-11-5 Telfer, sn beh, tld off
whn pld up bef 14th. . . . .(50 to 1) pu
2103 GRAAL LEGEND 9-11-5 P Niven, sn tld off, pld up bef
14th. . . . .(100 to 1) pu
1790 GREENFIELD MANOR 7-11-5 A Merrigan, trkd ldrs till
wknd aftr 13th, wl beh whn pld up bef 2 out. (25 to 1) pu
Dist: Hd, 20l, 4l, 20l, 3l, dist. 6m 48.50s. a 33.50s (15 Ran).
SR: 6/11/-/-/-/-/ (Mrs J D Goodfellow), Mrs J D Goodfellow

2239 EBF 'National Hunt' Novices' Hurdle Qualifier (Div II) (5,6,7-y-o) £2,343 2m 3f. . . . . (1:50)

1362 TWIN STATES 5-10-7 (7") W Fry, trkd ldrs, led 3 out, drw
clr appr last, styd on wl. . . . .(5 to 1 op 6 to 1) 1
2074[8] BISHOPS CASTLE (Ire) 6-11-0 M Dwyer, trkd ldrs, chlgd
aftr 3 out, ev ch till no extr appr last. . . . .(7 to 1) 2
2106[7] DON'T TELL JUDY (Ire) 6-11-0 L Wyer, led till hdd aftr 4th,
outpcd and sn beh, styd on wl frm 2 out.
. . . .(7 to 2 op 3 to 1 tchd 4 to 1) 3
2140 SOUNDS GOLDEN 6-11-0 R Garritty, chsd ldrs till grad
wknd appr 2 out. . . . .(10 to 1) 4
2140 BALLYROVERS 5-11-0 G McCourt, hld up, reminders aftr
5th, no hdwy. . . . .(5 to 1 op 9 to 1) 5
GINETRICK 5-11-0 T Reed, hld up, effrt appr 3 out, sn
btn. . . . .(10 to 1 tchd 12 to 1) 6
1708 ARTIC MISSILE 7-11-0 Ann Stokell, dsptd ld till wknd aftr
5th, sn beh. . . . .(40 to 1 op 25 to 1 tchd 50 to 1) 7
1959 MAGENTA BOY 6-10-11 (3") N Bentley, cl up, led aftr 4th
till hdd 3 out, sn wknd. . . . . (8 to 1 tchd 10 to 1) 8
1482[4] ROSEBERRY TOPPING 5-11-0 P Niven, hld up in tch till
ran out 3 out, bit slpd.
. . . . (2 to 1 fav op 6 to 4 tchd 5 to 2) ro
Dist: 10l, 6l, ½l, 10l, 3½l, 10l, 12l. 4m 48.00s. (9 Ran).

(J R Turner), J R Turner

2240 Dinsdale Conditional Jockeys' Selling Handicap Chase (5-y-o and up) £2,296 2m. . . . . (2:20)

1923* RATHER SHARP [85] 8-11-6 R Farrant, trkd ldrs gng wl, led
2 out, sn clr, cmftbly. . . . .(2 to 1 fav op 7 to 4) 1

2149 BALLYBELL [65] 9-10-0 P Williams, *blun 1st, sn wl beh,*
blunded 6th, styd on well frm 4 out, not rch wnr.
....(33 to 1) 2
2073⁴ KAMART [84] 6-11-5 A Dobbin, *prmnt, chlgd 2 out, sn*
wknd.................(9 to 4 op 2 to 1 tchd 5 to 2) 3
2058³ CAPTAIN CUTE [85] 9-11-2 (4⁴) K Davies, *chsd ldrs till*
outpcd aftr 5th, no dngr after.....(12 to 1 op 10 to 1) 4
2149⁵ CLARE LAD [89] (bl) 11-11-3 (7⁴) S Melrose, *pushed alng*
thrght, lost tch appr 4 out........................(6 to 1) 5
1360 SINGING SAM [84] 9-11-5 P Waggott, *prmnt, blun 7th and*
8th, sn beh............(25 to 1 op 33 to 1 tchd 50 to 1) 6
2073⁵ PRESSURE GAME [82] 11-11-3 F Perratt, *led, mstk 5th*
(water), jnd whn blun and uns rdr 2 out.
....(9 to 2 op 4 to 1) ur
Dist: 3½l, 15l, 12l, nk, 5l. 4m 12.60s. a 23.60s (7 Ran).
SR: 16/-/-/-/   (M A Long), C L Popham

# 2241   Maltby Novices' Hurdle (4-y-o) £2,215
2m.................................(2:50)

1634² THE PREMIER EXPRES 10-12 M Dwyer, *made most, styd*
on wl frm 2 out, pushed out.
.................................(6 to 1 op 7 to 1 tchd 8 to 1) 1
1473⁷ DIWALI DANCER 11-5 N Mann, *pld hrd early, trkd ldrs,*
chlgd 2 out, kpt on und pres.......(16 to 1 op 12 to 1) 2
971⁴ HASTA LA VISTA 10-12 R Garritty, *al prmnt, ev ch 2 out,*
kpt on und pres.......(14 to 1 op 12 to 1 tchd 16 to 1) 3
STAR RAGE (Ire) 10-5 (7⁴) J Driscoll, *mid-div, hdwy to*
chase ldrs aftr 3 out, kpt on same pace frm nxt.
....(200 to 1) 4
2072³ BEND SABLE (Ire) 10-12 B Storey, *in tch, effrt aftr 3 out,*
kpt on same pace, mstk last.
.........................(14 to 1 op 12 to 1 tchd 16 to 1) 5
2135³ SHARKASHKA (Ire) 10-7 L Wyer, *dsptd ld, led appr 2 out,*
sn hdd, wknd betw last two.
...................(7 to 4 fav op 9 to 4 tchd 5 to 2) 6
ZAJIRA (Ire) 10-8¹ Mr S Swiers, *pld hrd early, hld up in*
tch, kpt on wl frm 2 out, nvr nr to chal.
...................................(12 to 1 op 6 to 1) 7
1569⁶ ALMAZZAR (USA) 10-12 G McCourt, *hld up, effrt aftr 3*
out, no real hdwy.................(16 to 1 op 12 to 1) 8
1920 FRIENDLY KNIGHT 10-12 A Dobbin, *cl up till wknd aftr 3*
out...(200 to 1) 9
1920⁹ FRET (USA) 10-9 (3⁴) N Bentley, *hld up and beh, hdwy aftr*
3 out, nvr nr to chal.................(6 to 1 op 7 to 2) 10
1767³ HEART OF SPAIN 10-12 C Grant, *pld hrd early, trkd ldrs*
till wknd appr 3 out................(5 to 1 op 9 to 2) 11
PANTHER (Ire) 10-12 P Harley, *nvr on terms.*......(14 to 1) 12
1655 THATCHED (Ire) 10-12 N Smith, *cl up till wknd appr 3 out.*
....(100 to 1) 14
1634 PUBLIC WAY (Ire) 10-7 (5⁴) J Supple, *in tch till wknd appr*
3 out........................................(33 to 1) 15
971 SKY WISH 10-12 J Callaghan, *pld hrd early, trkd ldrs till*
mstk 5th, sn wknd...........................(100 to 1) 16
FANFOLD (Ire) 10-7 E McKinley, *al beh.*.............(50 to 1) 17
1920 RED FAN (Ire) 10-12 A Merrigan, *lost tch appr 3 out, tld off.*
....(100 to 1) 18
Dist: 2l, ¾l, 3l, 3l, 1½l, 2½l, ½l, 5l, 4l, 8l. 3m 59.50s. a 18.50s (18 Ran).
SR: 3/8/-/-/-/-/   (Ron Davison), W Bentley

2242   Stokesley Handicap Chase (0-110 5-y-
o and up) £2,820 2m 3f.........(3:20)

2044⁹ TIM SOLDIER (Fr) [93] 7-11-2 R Garritty, *in tch till outpcd*
aftr tenth, hdwy whn slightly hmpd 3 out, styd on wl
und pres to ld towards finish.......(20 to 1 op 16 to 1) 1
1861² HIGHLY DECORATED [81] 9-10-4¹ Richard Guest, *hld up in*
tch, hdwy aftr 4 out, styd on to ld last, hdd and no extr
towards finish.....................(9 to 1 op 9 to 2) 2
2136 MILITARY HONOUR [90] (bl) 9-10-13 M S Swiers, *chsd ldrs,*
led 8th, hdd last, no extr....................(12 to 1) 3
2138³ KANNDABIL [101] (bl) 7-11-10 G McCourt, *in tch till outpcd aftr tenth, no dngr after.*
...................(100 to 30 fav op 7 to 2 tchd 3 to 1) 4
1409³ BARKISLAND [94] 10-11-3 M Dwyer, *led till hdd 8th, cl*
second and pushed alng whn blun badly 2 out, not
reco'r................................(4 to 1 op 7 to 2) 5
1606⁴ GREY MINSTREL [97] 10-11-1 (5⁴) P Waggott, *sn beh, lost*
tch frm tenth....................(6 to 1 op 7 to 1) 6
2145⁴ HICKELTON LAD [89] 10-10-5 (7⁴) Mr G Hogan, *blun and*
uns rdr 4th............................(14 to 1 op 12 to 1) ur
1921³ BAD TRADE [105] 12-12-0 C Grant, *in tch till wknd aftr*
9th, tld off whn pld up bef 3 out.
...................(7 to 1 op 5 to 1 tchd 15 to 2) pu
2151⁸ MOSS BEE [89] 7-10-12 T Reed, *prmnt till wknd aftr*
tenth, tld off whn pld up bef 3 out.(6 to 1 tchd 13 to 2) pu
Dist: 2½l, 1½l, 12l, 6l, 8l. 5m 0.00s. (9 Ran).
                                               (N Jinks), M F Barraclough

2243   Leyburn Handicap Hurdle (0-105 4-y-o
and up) £2,902 2m.............(3:50)

KILGARIFF [104] 8-11-13 P Harley, *in tch, hdwy to chase*
ldrs 5th, styd on wl to ld towards finish.........(33 to 1) 1
2138⁸ WAKE UP [88] 7-10-11 L Wyer, *al chasing ldrs, ev ch last,*
kpt on und pres...................(7 to 1 op 8 to 1) 2

2070² J P MORGAN [88] (v) 6-10-11 T Reed, *cl up, drvn alng to ld*
3 out, hdd aftr nxt, styd on to lead r-in, headed and no
extr towards finish.................(7 to 1 op 5 to 1) 3
1478³ SHAHGRAM (Ire) [88] 6-10-11 M Dwyer, *hld up, steady*
hdwy hfwy, led aftr 2 out, mstk last, sn hdd and no
extr.....................................(6 to 1 op 5 to 1) 4
1746³ BRAMBLEBERRY [101] 5-11-10 Richard Guest, *trkd ldrs*
till grad lost pl frm 2 out..........(8 to 1 tchd 7 to 1) 5
ALL GREEK TO ME (Ire) [105] 6-11-7 (7⁴) F Leahy, *beh till*
styd on frm 3 out, nvr dngrs...................(33 to 1) 6
EUROTWIST [103] 5-11-12 G McCourt, *nvr nr to chal.*
....(9 to 1 op 8 to 1) 7
2065 ASHDREN [88] 7-10-11 B Storey, *in tch, some hdwy whn*
mstk 2 out, nvr dngrs........................(14 to 1) 8
1940² MASTER OF TROY [100] 6-11-2 (7⁴) Mr A Parker, *chsd ldrs*
till outpcd appr 3 out, no dngr aftr. (8 to 1 tchd 9 to 1) 9
2108 CAPTAIN TANCRED (Ire) [78] 6-10-1 E McKinley, *in tch,*
some hdwy whn blun 2 out, no ch aftr.
....................................(25 to 1 op 20 to 1) 10
2005³ ALL WELCOME [100] 7-11-9 P Niven, *slight ld till hdd 3*
out, wknd frm nxt................(5 to 1 fav op 6 to 1) 11
1614 KALKO [98] 5-11-2 (5⁴) P Midgley, *nvr on terms.*
....................................(20 to 1 op 14 to 1) 12
2138 HUSO [96] 6-10-12 (7⁴) S Taylor, *prmnt till wknd appr 3*
out...............................(33 to 1 tchd 50 to 1) 13
1586 COOL DUDE [98] 8-11-2 (5⁴) Miss P Jones, *chsd ldrs till*
wknd frm 3 out...................(9 to 1 op 8 to 1) 14
1738⁴ MISTIC GLEN (Ire) [92] 5-11-1 A Dobbin, *beh frm hfwy.*
....(10 to 1) 15
2073 COSMIC RAY [93] 9-11-2 W McFarland, *beh frm hfwy.*
....(33 to 1) 16
1492⁹ EXPLORATION (USA) [86] 7-10-9 A S Smith, *prmnt till*
wknd quickly hfwy, tld off whn pld up bef 2 out.
....................................(25 to 1 op 20 to 1) pu
Dist: 2½l, sht-hd, 2½l, 10l, 10l, ¾l, 15l, nk, ¾l, ½l. 3m 57.30s. a 16.30s (17
Ran).
SR: 40/21/21/18/21/15/12/-/-/   (B L Parry), R A Fahey

KEMPTON (good to soft)
Friday January 21st
Going Correction: PLUS 1.07 sec. per fur.

2244   Ashford Novices' Hurdle (Div I) (5-y-o
and up) £2,574 2m............(1:00)

1539² SCOBIE BOY (Ire) 6-11-4 J Osborne, *chsd ldr, blun 4th, sn*
reco'red, led appr 3 out, quickened clr last, easily.
....................................(13 to 8 fav op 6 to 4 tchd 15 to 8) 1
1729⁴ BALLET ROYAL (USA) 5-10-12 M Perrett, *hmpd second and*
beh, hdwy 5th, chsd ldrs 2 out, hit last, kpt on, no ch
wth wnr..................(9 to 2 tchd 5 to 1) 2
1289² SOUTHOLT (Ire) 6-11-4 R Dunwoody, *al prmnt, chsd ldr*
aftr 3 out, rdn after nxt, wknd r-in.
........................(11 to 4 op 2 to 1 tchd 3 to 1) 3
869⁸ FLY GUARD (NZ) 7-10-12 J Frost, *prmnt, pushed alng aftr*
3 out, wknd nxt.......................(5 to 1 op 14 to 1) 4
1729⁸ LE BARON PERCHE (Fr) 5-10-12 S McNeill, *hit second, pld*
hrd, in tch till wknd appr 2 out...(66 to 1 op 33 to 1) 5
1929* ROXY RIVER 5-10-0 (7⁴) Mr M Rimell, *mid-div, rdn and*
effrt 3 out, sn wknd................(11 to 2 op 4 to 1) 6
1953 EMERALD WATERS 7-10-7 R Marley, *beh 5th, tld off.*
....(66 to 1 op 33 to 1) 7
747⁸ JOKERS THREE (Ire) 5-10-5 (7⁴) Chris Webb, *al beh, tld off.*
....(66 to 1 op 33 to 1) 8
2042⁵ MEDINAS SWAN SONG 6-10-12 N Williamson, *led till appr*
3 out, beh whn f 2 out..............(66 to 1 op 33 to 1) f
DOMITOR'S LASS 7-10-7 M S Nager, *beh till rapid*
hdwy 5th, pressed ldrs 3 out, wkng in 6th whn f last.
....(66 to 1 op 50 to 1) f
2144 MISS PARKES 5-10-7 I Lawrence, *al beh, tld off whn pld*
up bef 2 out.....................(66 to 1 op 33 to 1) pu
HURRICANE RYAN (Ire) 6-10-12 G Bradley, *hdwy 4th,*
wknd nxt, tld off whn pld up bef 2 out.
....................................(16 to 1 op 12 to 1 tchd 20 to 1) pu
Dist: 7l, 15l, 15l, 12l, 6l, dist, 12l. 4m 1.30s. a 21.30s (12 Ran).
SR: 48/35/26/5/-/-/   (R V Shaw), C R Egerton

# 2245   Walton Novices' Hurdle (4-y-o) £2,784
2m.................................(1:30)

HALHAM TARN (Ire) 10-10 P Holley, *hdwy 4th, led aftr 3*
out, drvn out......(12 to 1 op 8 to 1 tchd 14 to 1) 1
1880 SCENIC (Ire) 10-10 R Dunwoody, *hdwy 4th, rdn*
and chsd ldrs appr 2 out, styd on same pace und pres.
....................................(20 to 1 op 12 to 1) 2
1634⁶ DEMILUNE (USA) 10-10 C Llewellyn, *chsd ldrs, drvn alng*
frm 5th, mstk 2 out, wknd and no pres to take 3rd r-in.
....................................(20 to 1 op 12 to 1) 3
1990 SUPREME MASTER 10-10 G Bradley, *hdwy 4th, chsd ldrs*
3 out, drvn nxt, sn one pace.
....................................(11 to 10 on op 6 to 4 tchd 13 to 8) 4
SHAMSHADAL (Ire) 10-10 A Maguire, *prmnt, chlgd 5th till*
wknd appr 2 out....(100 to 30 op 5 to 2 tchd 9 to 2) 5
2000² DANGER BABY 10-7 (3⁴) D Meredith, *hdwy 5th, wknd aftr*
3 out............................(33 to 1 op 16 to 1) 6

PRINCESS TATEUM (Ire) 10-5 Lorna Vincent, *chsd ldrs, led aftr 4th till after 3 out, sn wknd.*
.........................(12 to 1 op 8 to 1 tchd 14 to 1) 7
ERCKULE 10-10 R Supple, *al beh.*
.........................(20 to 1 op 16 to 1 tchd 25 to 1) 8
CLEAR LOOK 10-5 J Osborne, *effrt 5th, sn fdd, tld off.*
.........................(33 to 1 op 20 to 1 tchd 50 to 1) 9
2083 FORMAESTRE (Ire) 10-5 E Murphy, *al beh, tld off.*
.........................(50 to 1 op 33 to 1) 10
1473 KOA 10-10 D Bridgwater, *al beh, tld off.*
.........................(50 to 1 op 20 to 1) 11
PRAIRIE GROVE 10-10 M A FitzGerald, *prmnt whn blun 3rd, sn beh, tld off.*.........(50 to 1 op 20 to 1) 12
1990⁸ UPWARD SURGE (Ire) 10-10 N Williamson, *al beh, tld off.*
.........................(50 to 1 op 20 to 1) 13
NUTTY BROWN 10-10 M Hourigan, *pld hrd, chlgd 3rd to 4th, wknd rpdly appr nxt, no ch whn f 2 out.*
.........................(50 to 1 op 33 to 1) f
2016⁶ WISHFUL PRINCESS 10-5 S McNeill, *f 1st.*
.........................(50 to 1 op 33 to 1) f
IKHTIRAA (USA) 10-10 D Murphy, *led till aftr 4th, wknd rpdly, tld off whn pld up bef 2 out.* (33 to 1 op 50 to 1) pu
KIMBERLEY BOY 10-10 B Powell, *hmpd 1st, beh, tld off whn pld up bef 2 out.*.........(33 to 1 op 25 to 1) pu
Dist: 7l, 1½l, 1l, 8l, 1l, 10l, 7l, dist, 3l, 6l. 4m 5.50s. a 25.50s (17 Ran).
(Lady Dundas), D R C Elsworth

2246 Hanworth Conditional Jockeys' Handicap Chase (0-135 5-y-o and up) £3,158 3m.........................(2:00)

1796² CATCHAPENNY [107] (bl) 9-10-0 P Ward, *hdwy to chase ldrs 7th, led aftr 4 out, styd on.*......(7 to 1 op 6 to 1) 1
1993 ANNIO CHILONE [118] 8-10-11 P Hide, *chsd ldrs, lost pl 6th, rdn 12th, styd on frm 3 out.*..(8 to 1 tchd 10 to 1) 2
2143* AUCTION LAW (NZ) [119] 10-10-12 (4ex) R Davis, *mstks 1st and second, beh, cld on ldrs 15th, sn one pace.*
.........................(2 to 1 fav tchd 9 to 4 and 7 to 4) 3
1600⁵ LOCH BLUE [108] 12-10-1 A Dicken, *chsd ldrs 8th, wknd aftr 4 out.*.........................(10 to 1 op 8 to 1) 4
1995³ LYPHENTO (USA) [115] 10-10-8 J J Brown, *chsd ldrs, lft in ld 15th, hdd aftr 4 out, sn wknd, no ch whn mstk 2 out.*
.........................(20 to 1) 5
REPEAT THE DOSE [135] 9-12-0 J McCarthy, *chsd ldrs till wknd quickly 13th.*.........(5 to 1 tchd 33 to 1) 6
1796* MAN OF MYSTERY [114] 8-10-7 T Jenks, *led till f 15th.*
.........................(5 to 1 tchd 11 to 2) f
1375⁴ HIGH PADRE [113] 8-10-6 G Tormey, *mid-div whn blun and ran appr 8th.*.........(5 to 1 op 4 to 1) ur
1720 GLOVE PUPPET [107] 9-10-0 S Fox, *al beh, tld off 12th, refused 3 out.*.........(12 to 1 op 10 to 1) ref
ON THE TWIST [125] 12-11-4 P Murphy, *beh, hit 5th, tld off tenth, pld up bef 15th.*.........(33 to 1) pu
Dist: 12l, 5l, 2½l, 20l, 30l. 6m 21.40s. a 32.40s (10 Ran).
SR: 5/4/-/-/-/-/ *(C J Courage),* M J Wilkinson

2247 Royal Mail Handicap Hurdle (0-135 4-y-o and up) £3,106 3m 110yds (2:30)

2009⁵ DARK HONEY [119] 9-11-7 (3*) A Dicken, *al prmnt, led aftr 3 out, wide into strt, all out.*.........(7 to 1 op 6 to 1) 1
1513⁵ SPRING TO GLORY [98] 7-10-3 A Maguire, *beh, hdwy 8th, chlgd 3 out till outpcd appr last.*
.........................(10 to 1 op 6 to 1 tchd 12 to 1) 2
1653* NEWTON POINT [123] 5-11-9 (5*) T Jenks, *chsd ldrs, led 9th till aftr 3 out, styd on one pace...*(8 to 1 op 6 to 1) 3
2044* BRIGHTLING BOY [98] 9-10-3 J Railton, *al chasing ldrs, rdn and kpt on one pace frm 2 out.*
.........................(5 to 1 op 4 to 1 tchd 11 to 2) 4
1721³ ACCESS SUN [95] 7-10-0 N Williamson, *hdwy to chase ldrs 5th, wknd 3 out.*.........(12 to 1 tchd 14 to 1) 5
LING (USA) [100] 9-10-5 R J Beggan, *nvr rch ldrs.*
.........................(20 to 1 op 16 to 1 tchd 25 to 1) 6
1697³ FAR TOO LOUD [100] 7-10-5 M A FitzGerald, *chsd ldrs, wknd 8th.*
.........................(11 to 1 op 12 to 1 tchd 14 to 1 and 10 to 1) 7
1971* KAYTAK (Fr) [113] (v) 7-11-4 D Murphy, *al beh, nvr dngrs.*
.........................(8 to 1 op 7 to 1 tchd 9 to 1) 8
1964³ LESBET [100] 9-10-5 D Morris, *led to 7th, wknd 9th.*
.........................(10 to 1 tchd 12 to 1) 9
PARLEZVOUSFRANCAIS [98] 10-10-3 R Dunwoody, *in tch, pressed ldrs aftr 3 out.* (16 to 1 op 12 to 1) 10
2172 MWEENISH [115] 12-11-6 R Bellamy, *beh most of way.*
.........................(66 to 1 op 50 to 1) 11
2184⁴ ROSITARY (Fr) [101] (bl) 11-10-6 M Perrett, *drpd rear 6th, tld off whn pld up bef 9th.*...(33 to 1 tchd 40 to 1) pu
1945² DERISBAY (Ire) [99] (bl) 6-10-4† D O'Sullivan, *chsd ldrs, chlgd 5th, led 7th to 9th, sn wknd, tld off whn pld up bef 2 out.*.........................(33 to 1 op 25 to 1) pu
1310³ CASTIGLIERO (Fr) [116] (bl) 6-11-7 G Bradley, *hld up, hdwy to chase ldrs 9th, chlgd und pres appr 2 out, sn wknd and pld up.*.........................(7 to 1 op 4 to 1) pu
Dist: 7l, ½l, 4l, 10l, 2½l, 1½l, nd, 10l, dist, dist. 6m 20.70s. a 33.70s (14 Ran).
SR: 21/-/17/-/-/-/ *(Roger Sayer),* S Dow

2248 Easter Hero Handicap Chase (0-140 5-y-o and up) £3,590 2m.........(3:00)

1975⁷ NORTHERN JINKS [115] (bl) 11-10-12 (3*) D Meredith, *made all, kpt on wl frm 3 out.*
.........................(33 to 1 op 25 to 1 tchd 50 to 1) 1
1596⁴ BRIGGS BUILDERS [108] (v) 10-10-8 N Williamson, *prmnt, chsd wnr 8th, no imprsn frm 3 out.*
.........................(14 to 1 op 10 to 1 tchd 16 to 1) 2
1752* TRIMLOUGH [128] 9-12-0 W Marston, *in tch, rdn and no imprsn on ldrs frm 4 out.*
.........................(5 to 2 tchd 9 to 4 and 11 to 4) 3
BROUGHTON MANOR [120] 9-11-6 M A FitzGerald, *chsd wnr, hit 8th, sn wknd.*...(12 to 1 op 7 to 1) 4
2166 EMSEE-H [120] 9-10-13 (7*) P Murphy, *sn wl beh.*
.........................(25 to 1 op 16 to 1 tchd 33 to 1) 5
AMBASSADOR [122] (bl) 11-11-8 R Dunwoody, *hdwy 8th, rdn in 3rd and no ch whn f last.*
.........................(9 to 2 op 7 to 2 tchd 5 to 1) f
1975* SPREE CROSS [121] 8-11-7 D Murphy, *f 3rd.*
1975³ ATLAAL [121] (bl) 9-11-7 J Osborne, *hmpd 3rd, al beh, tld off whn pld up bef 9th.*........(8 to 1 tchd 10 to 1) pu
Dist: 4l, 12l, 20l, 25l. 4m 9.00s. a 22.00s (8 Ran).
SR: 38/27/35/7/-/ *(Mrs E R Smith),* R Dickin

2249 Sunbury Novices' Chase (5-y-o and up) £3,965 2½m 110yds.........(3:30)

1712 JUMBEAU 9-11-7 (3*) P Hide, *prmnt, led 6th to 12th, outpcd 3 out, styd on, lft chalg for ld last, sn led, ran on wl.*.........................(100 to 30 op 3 to 1 tchd 7 to 2) 1
2030² LOCAL MANOR 7-11-4 J Osborne, *led to 6th, chlgd 11th, led nxt to 4 out, lft in narrow ld last, sn hdd and one pace.*.........(12 to 1 op 10 to 1 tchd 14 to 1) 2
1621 CROFTON LAD 7-11-4 R Bellamy, *al wl beh.*
.........................(50 to 1 op 33 to 1) 3
952 COTTAGE WALK (NZ) 7-11-4 J Frost, *jmpd poorly, al beh, tld off whn f 12th.*.........(50 to 1 op 25 to 1) f
1970* BIG MATT (Ire) 6-11-4 M A FitzGerald, *in tch whn mstk and uns rdr 7th.*.........(5 to 4 fav tchd Evens) ur
2045* THE GLOW (Ire) 6-11-10 P Holley, *chsd ldrs, led 4 out, blun 2 out, rdn, wknd and refused last.*
.........................(2 to 1 op 6 to 4 tchd 9 to 4) ref
Dist: 1½l, dist. 5m 30.40s. a 37.40s (6 Ran).
(Pell-Mell Partners), J T Gifford

2250 Ashford Novices' Hurdle (Div II) (5-y-o and up) £2,574 2m.........(4:00)

1539⁶ ARCTIC KINSMAN 6-11-4 C Llewellyn, *led to 3 out, drvn to ld nxt, ran on gmely.*
.........................(13 to 8 fav op 5 to 4 tchd Evens and 7 to 4) 1
1557* SUPER COIN 6-11-4 A Maguire, *chsd ldrs, chlgd 5th, led 3 out to nxt, edgd rght appr last, sn outpcd.*
.........................(4 to 1 tchd 5 to 1) 2
2014² KINGS CHARIOT 7-10-7 (5*) J McCarthy, *styd on frm 3 out, not pace to rch ldrs.*..(13 to 2 op 5 to 1 tchd 7 to 1) 3
1768* FINE THYNE (Ire) 5-11-4 M Perrett, *chsd ldrs till outpcd 3 out.*.........(11 to 4 op 5 to 2 tchd 3 to 1) 4
1800² CAWARRA BOY 6-10-5 (7*) Mr E James, *prmnt, chlgd 4th to nxt, wknd aftr 3 out.*
.........................(20 to 1 op 16 to 1 tchd 25 to 1) 5
PORT SUNLIGHT (Ire) 6-10-12 S McNeill, *beh, effrt appr 3 out, sn wknd.*...(12 to 1 op 8 to 1 tchd 14 to 1) 6
1929 ROBENKO (USA) 5-10-12 D Bridgwater, *al beh.*
.........................(50 to 1 op 33 to 1 tchd 66 to 1) 7
ANLACE 5-10-0 (7*) Chris Webb, *al beh.*
.........................(66 to 1 op 33 to 1) 8
TREGURTHA 8-10-9 (3*) R Davis, *al beh.*
.........................(66 to 1 op 33 to 1) 9
1536 CAPTAIN BERT 5-10-12 N Williamson, *beh, hmpd 3rd, no dngr aftr.*.........(33 to 1 op 20 to 1 tchd 50 to 1) 10
CAP DIAMANT (USA) 6-10-5 (7*) W J Walsh, *mid-div whn f 3rd.*.........................(66 to 1 op 33 to 1) f
COPER CABLE 7-10-12 M Ranger, *beh till pld up bef 5th.*
.........................(66 to 1 op 33 to 1) pu
Dist: 5l, 15l, 1½l, 20l, 15l, 5l, 5l, 15l, 12l. 4m 3.20s. a 23.20s (12 Ran).
SR: 29/24/3/7/-/-/ *(Mrs A T A Twiston-Davies)*

CATTERICK (good)
Saturday January 22nd
Going Correction: PLUS 0.75 sec. per fur. (races 1,3,5), PLUS 0.50 (2,4,6)

2251 Premier Meats Pitching Butcher Novices' Chase (5-y-o and up) £2,519 2m.........(1:10)

1792⁷ SEON 8-11-3 P Niven, *chsd ldrs, rdn to ld 3 out, styd on wl.*.........................(5 to 1 fav op 3 to 1) 1
1958² GOLDEN ISLE 10-11-3 B Storey, *cl up, led 4 out, hdd nxt, kpt on same pace.*.........(5 to 1 op 5 to 1) 2
2146⁵ KETTI 9-10-5 (7*) Mr G Hogan, *in tch, hdwy aftr 4 out, one pace frm nxt.*.........(8 to 1 tchd 10 to 1) 3
1491⁶ SILVER STICK 7-11-3 R Garritty, *led till blun 3rd and lost pl, outpcd aftr 4 out, styd on ag'n frm 2 out.*
.........................(10 to 1 op 5 to 1 tchd 13 to 2) 4

1938[6] FOUR DEEP (Ire) 6-11-3 G Upton, chsd ldrs, mstk 8th, wknd appr 3 out...... (11 to 2 op 4 to 1 tchd 6 to 1) 5
2218 MACCONACHIE 7-11-3 A Merrigan, in tch, slightly hmpd 4 out, sn beh, no ch whn hit 2 out. (16 to 1 op 12 to 1) 6
ROBINS LAD 8-11-3 T Reed, led 4th till hdd 9th, grad lost pl............(33 to 1 op 25 to 1 tchd 50 to 1) 7
1478 STRONG SILVER (USA) (bl) 9-10-12 (5*) P Waggott, f second............(100 to 1 op 50 to 1) f
1947 SOLO CORNET 9-11-3 W Humphreys, f 1st.
.....................(50 to 1 tchd 33 to 1 and 100 to 1) f
2007[5] HIGHLANDMAN 8-11-3 A Dobbin, chsd ldrs till f 4 out.
.........................(12 to 1 op 8 to 1) f
2069[4] ALIAS GRAY 7-10-12 (5*) D Bentley, led 3rd till f nxt.
.........................(33 to 1 op 20 to 1 tchd 50 to 1) f
1872[7] VASILIEV (v) 6-11-3 C Grant, strtd very slwly, tld off whn pld up aftr 4th........ (11 to 2 op 4 to 1 tchd 6 to 1) pu
Dist: 10l, nk, 1½l, 15l, 15l, 12l. 4m 6.30s. a 17.30s (12 Ran).
SR: 36/26/20/23/8/-/ (C F Hunter Ltd), W Bentley

2252 Spending Frenzy Catterick Sunday Market Novices' Hurdle (5-y-o and up) £2,145 3m 1f 110yds. . . . . (1:40)

2140* SCOTTON BANKS (Ire) 5-11-6 R Garritty, made all, quick-ened appr 8th, wl clr whn blun last, easily. ....(11 to 4 op 2 to 1 on) 1
2008[6] NINFA (Ire) 6-10-2 (7*) B Harding, trkd ldrs, chsd wnr frm 8th, no imprsn........ (17 to 2 op 6 to 1 tchd 5 to 1) 2
1654[4] TREVVEETHAN (Ire) 5-11-0 D Wilkinson, hld up, hdwy to track ldrs hfwy, chsd wnr frm 8th, one pace...(14 to 1) 3
771[9] PRECIOUS HENRY 5-11-0 B Storey, in tch till outpcd appr 8th, no dngr aftr.................(25 to 1 op 20 to 1) 4
1114[7] BALISTEROS (Fr) 5-10-7 (7*) W Fry, in tch till outpcd appr 8th, no dngr aftr.................(33 to 1 op 25 to 1) 5
1574[6] KINDA GROOVY 5-11-0 N Smith, in tch till outpcd appr 8th, no dngr aftr.................(12 to 1 op 10 to 1) 6
1963[8] SUREST DANCER (USA) 8-11-0 G Harker, slightly hmpd 1st, outpcd appr 8th.................(50 to 1) 7
1918 LUVLY BUBBLY 6-11-0 C Grant, beh frm hfwy, lost tch appr 8th, wl tld off.................(33 to 1 op 25 to 1) 8
1289 PRICELESS HOLLY 6-10-7 (7*) C Woodall, in tch till outpcd appr 8th, wl tld off..............(100 to 1 op 50 to 1) 9
1060[6] KILMINFOYLE 7-11-0 P Niven, f 1st......(7 to 1 op 5 to 1) f
1582 PLUM DUFF 7-11-0 A Merrigan, lost tch frm hfwy, wl tld off whn pld up bef 2 out...........(100 to 1 op 50 to 1) pu
ANOTHER SHOON 7-11-0 A Dobbin, lost tch aftr 7th, tld off whn pld up aftr 7th.....................(50 to 1) pu
Dist: 25l, 10l, 6l, nk, 1l, 12l, dist, nk. 6m 39.40s. a 38.40s (12 Ran).
(I Bray), M H Easterby

2253 S. R. Hill Catering 'Quality Butty' Handicap Chase (0-105 5-y-o and up) £3,054 3m 1f 110yds. . . . . (2:10)

2136[4] THE MALTKILN [98] (v) 11-11-8 C Grant, in tch till outpcd appr 4 out, styd on wl und pres frm 2 out to ld towards finish.........................(8 to 1 op 7 to 1) 1
2105[4] THE MOTCOMBE OAK [102] 8-11-12 P Niven, hld up in tch, effrt whn blun 14th and 15th, chsd ldr 4 out, led appr last, hdd and no extr towards finish.
.....................(3 to 1 op 5 to 2 tchd 100 to 30) 2
1997[3] MOULTON BULL [83] 8-10-7 J Callaghan, cl up, led 12th, clr aftr 4 out, hdd appr last, kpt on. (5 to 1 op 6 to 1) 3
1962[4] HOUXTY LAD [85] 8-10-9[7] T Reed, dsptd ld, mstk 11th, chsd ldr frm nxt, rdn aftr 4 out, 3rd whn hit 2 out, kpt on.........................(14 to 1 op 20 to 1) 4
1962* HEAVENLY CITIZEN (Ire) [93] 6-11-3 R Garritty, in tch till outpcd appr 4 out, kpt on frm 2 out.
.........................(11 to 4 fav op 3 to 1) 5
1864[6] DUBIOUS JAKE [97] 11-11-0 (7*) C Woodall, in tch till outpcd appr 4 out, kpt on frm 2 out.
.........................(20 to 1 op 16 to 1) 6
2170 KATY KEYS [77] 10-10-1[1] J Corkell, led or dsptd ld till hdd 12th, prmnt till wknd aftr 4 out. (100 to 1 op 66 to 1) 7
1962[2] TRUELY ROYAL [92] 10-11-2 B Storey, in tch till outpcd appr 4 out, no dngr aftr. (9 to 2 op 4 to 1 tchd 5 to 1) 8
MAJIC RAIN [86] 9-10-10 A Merrigan, tld off frm 6th.
.........................(50 to 1 op 33 to 1) 9
1870[3] TRUSTY FRIEND [88] 12-10-12 S Burrough, f second.
.........................(14 to 1) f
1864 BARKIN [104] 11-12-0 M Moloney, blun and uns rdr 5th.
.........................(20 to 1 op 16 to 1) ur
Dist: 2½l, nk, 1l, 2½l, 1½l, 8l, 2½l, dist. 6m 51.70s. a 36.70s (11 Ran).
(M W Horner, H Young, and D S Arnold), M D Hammond

2254 F. Hutchinson 'Fruit & Veg' Outdoor Market Fruit Arada Selling Handicap Hurdle (4-y-o and up) £1,922 2m (2:40)

1505 RUN OF WELD [75] 11-10-6 W McFarland, cl up, led 5th, kpt on wl frm 2 out...(10 to 1 op 12 to 1 tchd 14 to 1) 1
1607* FLASH OF REALM (Fr) [93] 8-11-10 A Dobbin, in tch, hit 5th, drvn alng to chase wnr aftr 3 out, kpt on, no imprsn...........(4 to 1 fav op 7 to 2 tchd 9 to 2) 2
1860[7] GREENACRES LAD [78] 10-11-0-9 A Mulholland, mid-div, hdwy aftr 3 out, ch nxt, kpt on same pace.
.........................(9 to 2 op 7 to 2 tchd 5 to 1) 3

2108[7] BOLD MOOD [76] 5-10-2 (5*) D Bentley, sn beh, styd on wl frm 2 out, nrst finish... (13 to 2 op 6 to 1 tchd 7 to 1) 4
DRU RI'S BRU RI [76] (v) 6-10-2 (5*) P Waggott, mid-div, hdwy to chase ldrs aftr 3 out, kpt on same pace.
.........................(20 to 1 op 16 to 1) 5
1860[2] POINT TAKEN (USA) [71] 7-10-2[1] R Garritty, chsd ldrs till outpcd aftr 5th, styd on frm 2 out.
.........................(11 to 2 op 5 to 1 tchd 6 to 1) 6
SERDARLI [69] 12-10-0 J Ryan, in tch, effrt aftr 3 out, no hdwy.........................(33 to 1) 7
FERRUFINO (Ire) [71] 6-10-2[2] P McDermott, trkd ldrs till appr 2 out, sn wknd.......... (33 to 1 tchd 66 to 1) 8
1961[3] CHARLYCIA [76] 6-10-3 (7*) M Clarke, prmnt, reminders appr 4th, sn beh........(9 to 1 op 8 to 1 tchd 10 to 1) 9
2152 GYMCRAK CYRANO (Ire) [69] 5-10-0 B Storey, beh, some hdwy aftr 5th, wknd appr 2 out... (25 to 1 op 20 to 1) 10
1738[8] STAGS FELL [87] 9-11-1 (3*) N Bentley, hld up in tch, steady hdwy hfwy, ev ch aftr 3 out, wknd after nxt.
.........................(6 to 1 op 5 to 1) 11
1461 MAJOR EFFORT [69] 9-10-0 Ann Stokell, beh frm hfwy.
.........................(50 to 1 op 33 to 1) 12
HILLTOWN BLUES [77] 5-10-1 (7*) A Larnton, cl up till wknd quickly appr 2 out.........(9 to 1 op 8 to 1) 13
ANFIELD SALLY [69] 8-10-0 C Hawkins, led till hdd 5th, sn wknd, tld off.........(33 to 1 op 25 to 1) 14
1961 GASCOIGNE WOOD [70] 6-10-1 Mrs F Needham, chsd ldrs till wknd hfwy, wl beh whn pld up bef 2 out.
.........................(66 to 1 op 50 to 1) pu
Dist: 6l, 3½l, 4l, 2l, 10l, 3l, ¾l, 1½l, sht-hd, nk. 3m 55.80s. a 4.80s (15 Ran).
SR: 10/22/3/-/-/-/ (Graham Parker), F J Yardley

2255 Juicy Hog Roast And Apple Sauce Handicap Chase (0-105 5-y-o and up) £2,898 2m. . . . . (3:10)

2242[3] MILITARY HONOUR [90] (bl) 9-11-7 S Turner, outpcd and lost tch aftr 4th, styd on frm four out, lft in slight ld last, forged clr.........(9 to 2 op 4 to 1 tchd 5 to 1) 1
2107* BELDINE [97] 9-12-0 A Dobbin, prmnt, chsd wnr frm 7th, hit 3 out, lft cl second last, no extr.
.........................(4 to 7 on op 4 to 6 tchd 15 to 8) 2
2240 PRESSURE GAME [82] 11-10-8 (5*) F Perratt, led till hdd 7th, grad wknd.................(8 to 1 op 6 to 1) 3
2240* RATHER SHARP [85] 8-10-13 (3*) R Farrant, trkd ldr, led 7th, mstks 4 out and 2 out, 12 ls clr whn f last, rmntd.
.........................(13 to 8 fav tchd 7 to 4) 4
9374 SUPER SANDY [69] 7-10-0 B Storey, mstks, sn tld off, pld up bef 3 out.........(20 to 1 op 14 to 1 tchd 25 to 1) pu
Dist: 15l, 20l, 25l. 4m 8.60s. a 19.60s (5 Ran).
SR: 17/9/ (J E Swiers), J E Swiers

2256 Cowton Handicap Hurdle (0-105 5-y-o and up) £2,616 3m 1f 110yds. . . . (3:40)

1963* NODDLE (USA) [105] 6-12-0 T Reed, made all, quickened aftr 8th, clr 2 out, eased r-in, cmftbly.
.........................(5 to 4 fav op 6 to 4 tchd 7 to 4) 1
1603[7] RUSTINO [87] 8-10-10 P Niven, in tch, hdwy to chase wnr aftr 3 out, kpt on, no imprsn.....(14 to 1 tchd 16 to 1) 2
INTEGRITY BOY [88] (bl) 7-10-11 J Callaghan, hld up in tch, steady hdwy to chase ldrs 3 out, kpt on same pace frm nxt.........................(14 to 1 op 12 to 1) 3
1533[7] MISS CAPULET [83] (bl) 7-10-3 (3*) D Meredith, chsd ldrs till rdn and grad wknd aftr 3 out.....(20 to 1 op 16 to 1) 4
1862 GUTE NACHT [77] 11-9-11[4] (7*) C Woodall, beh till styd on frm 3 out, nvr dngrs. (25 to 1 tchd 33 to 1) 5
MR FENWICK [80] 10-10-3 A Mulholland, prmnt, chsd wnr 9th till wknd aftr 3 out.................(12 to 1) 6
1963[5] MAKE ME PROUD [99] 8-11-7 N Bentley, beh, sn pushed alng, some hdwy appr 8th, soon btn.
.........................(7 to 1 op 8 to 1 tchd 9 to 1) 7
2153[9] HARDIHERO [77] (bl) 8-10-0 B Storey, chsd wnr till wknd aftr 9th.........................(14 to 1) 8
2103[7] LADY BE BRAVE [77] 11-10-0 A Dobbin, prmnt till wknd appr 8th.........................(33 to 1) 9
1603 BADASTAN (Ire) [89] 5-10-12 R Garritty, in tch till wknd frm 8th.........(7 to 1 op 10 to 1 tchd 16 to 1) 10
1740 MILL DE LEASE [77] 9-9-9 (5*) D Bentley, in tch, some hdwy whn blun 9th, sn btn.................(33 to 1) 11
1964[4] SWILLY EXPRESS [96] 8-11-5 G Upton, beh most of way.
.........................(9 to 2 op 6 to 1 tchd 8 to 1) 12
SERPHIL [77] (bl) 6-9-7 (7*) I Jardine, cl beh, tld off.
.........................(33 to 1 op 25 to 1) 13
1629 SINGLESOLE [97] 9-11-6 A Carroll, sn beh, tld off.
.........................(14 to 1 op 12 to 1) 14
TAP DANCING [77] 8-9-7 (7*) Mr N Bradley, chsd ldrs till wknd aftr 8th, tld off.........(10 to 1 op 33 to 1) 15
1603 DUTCH BLUES [77] 7-10-0 D Wilkinson, beh whn blun and uns rdr 8th.........................(50 to 1) ur
1874[5] FLASS VALE [96] 6-11-5 C Grant, sn beh, tld off frm 8th, pld up befdore 2 out.........(33 to 1 tchd 40 to 1) pu
Dist: 2½l, 2l, 20l, 10l, 2½l, 6l, 5l, 2½l, 2½l, 8l. 6m 32.50s. a 31.50s (17 Ran).
(J C Galbraith), L Lungo

HAYDOCK (soft)
Saturday January 22nd

Going Correction: PLUS 1.62 sec. per fur. (races 1,2,6), PLUS 1.45 (3,4,5)

2257 Premier Long Distance Hurdle Grade 2 (5-y-o and up) £9,680 2m 7f 110yds
....(1:00)

1438[6] SIMPSON 9-11-3 T Grantham, *trkd ldrs, hdwy 3 out, led appr last, sn rdn and ran on wl.* (14 to 1 tchd 20 to 1) 1

1756[3] AVRO ANSON 6-11-3 D Byrne, *hld up, hdwy 7th, hit 4 out, effrt nxt, sn rdn and one pace 2 out.*
....(7 to 2 op 3 to 1) 2

2012* SWEET DUKE (Fr) 7-11-10 C Llewellyn, *led, rdn 2 out, hdd appr last, wknd r-in.*
....(11 to 10 fav op 6 to 4 tchd 13 to 8) 3

1756[2] BURGOYNE (bl) 8-11-3 C Swan, *cl up, pushed alng 7th, sn lost pl, nvr dngrs aftr.*............(6 to 1 op 9 to 2) 4

1665* DANCE OF WORDS (Ire) 5-11-2 W Marston, *prmnt, chsd ldr frm 4th, rdn and wknd four out.*
....(14 to 1 op 12 to 1) 5

2012[6] BRABAZON (USA) 9-11-3 G Bradley, *hld up, rdn alng and beh frm hfwy.*...........................(50 to 1) 6

54 SWEET GLOW (Fr) 7-11-10 R Dunwoody, *al rear, tld off and rdn 4 out.*.......................(8 to 1 op 7 to 1) 7

1653[9] AAHSAYLAD (bl) 8-11-3 M Dwyer, *trkd ldrs, hdwy 7th, effrt and rdn 4 out, sn btn.*.....(8 to 1 tchd 9 to 1) 8

Dist: 3½l, sht-hd, 20l, 3½l, 30l, 4l, 1l. 6m 23.60s. a 52.60s (8 Ran).

(M S Jarvis), J A B Old

2258 Haydock Park Champion Hurdle Trial Grade 2 (5-y-o and up) £9,380 2m
....(1:30)

2046[2] FLAKEY DOVE 8-11-5 R Dunwoody, *trkd ldr, hdwy to ld 3 out, rdn last and ran on wl.*
....(9 to 2 op 5 to 1) 1

1896* TIANANMEN SQUARE (Ire) 6-11-3 C Swan, *hld up, hdwy 4 out, effrt 2 out, sn ev ch, rdn last, soon wknd.*
....(11 to 10 fav op Evens tchd 6 to 5) 2

1560* SYBILLIN 8-11-3 M Dwyer, *hld up, hdwy hfwy, effrt 3 out, sn rdn and wknd quickly nxt.* (11 to 8 op 7 to 4) 3

1755[6] PONTYNYSWEN 6-11-3 D J Burchell, *led, hdd and wknd 3 out.*.....................(33 to 1 op 20 to 1) 4

CELTIC SHOT 12-11-3 G Bradley, *prmnt, lost pl 4th, sn beh.*.....................(33 to 1 op 25 to 1) 5

Dist: 20l, 12l, 1½l, 12l. 4m 7.50s. a 27.50s (5 Ran).
SR: 75/53/41/39/27/ (J T Price), R J Price

2259 Peter Marsh Chase Limited Handicap Grade 2 (5-y-o and up) £15,475 3m
....(2:00)

1843[5] ZETA'S LAD [163] 11-10-10 R Supple, *hld up in tch, smooth hdwy 3 out, chlgd nxt, rdn to ld r-in, held on wl.*.........................(5 to 1 tchd 11 to 2) 1

RUN FOR FREE [167] 10-11-0 M Perrett, *led and sn clr, rdn and hit 3 out, jmpd lft 2 out, hdd r-in and swrvd badly left, ran on nr finish.*.............(5 to 2 op 7 to 4) 2

1545[3] JODAMI [177] 9-11-10 M Dwyer, *al tracking ldrs, effrt 2 out, outpcd appr last, kpt on strly nr finish.*
....(9 to 4 fav tchd 2 to 1) 3

1993* ANTONIN (Fr) [163] 6-10-5 (5*) J Burke, *chsd ldr till hit 5th and lost pl, hdwy and mstk 11th, blun 13th, sn beh.*
....(7 to 1 op 10 to 1) 4

1993 GAMBLING ROYAL [163] 11-10-10 R Dunwoody, *prmnt, rdn 4 out, wknd bef nxt.*.........(16 to 1 tchd 20 to 1) 5

1850* KING OF THE GALES [163] 7-10-10 C Swan, *in tch, not fluent, hit 15th, rdn 14th, sn rdn, wknd 4 out, blunded and uns rdr nxt.*..............(9 to 2 tchd 5 to 1) ur

Dist: Hd, 2l, dist, 4l. 6m 40.60s. a 34.60s (6 Ran).
SR: 80/84/92/ (Andrew L Cohen), John R Upson

2260 Steel Plate And Sections Young Chasers Qualifier Novices' (5 - 8-y-o) £3,387 2½m....................... (2:30)

2045[3] YOUR WELL 8-11-3 B Clifford, *hld up in tch, hdwy and hit 3 out, led last, rdn, ran on r-in.*
....(11 to 4 op 9 to 4 tchd 3 to 1) 1

1999* NICKLE JOE 8-11-7 W Marston, *led to 8th, rdn and led 3 out, blun nxt, hdd and no extr last.* (9 to 2 op 5 to 1) 2

1750 MR FLANAGAN 8-11-7 G Bradley, *hit 1st, cl up till led 8th, hdd 4 out, ev ch 2 out, wknd and btn.*
....(100 to 30 op 3 to 1) 3

2007[3] SPANISH FAIR (Ire) 6-10-12 (5*) J Burke, *al prmnt, led 4 out, hdd nxt and sn rdn, wknd appr last.*
....(6 to 1 tchd 13 to 2) 4

1653[4] COUNTORNIS 8-11-3 R Dunwoody, *f second.*.(9 to 4 fav) f

1964[5] TIMUR'S KING 7-11-3 M Perrett, *in tch, hit 6th, lost pl nxt and beh whn pld up aftr 5 out.*...(12 to 1 op 10 to 1) pu

Dist: 3l, 7l, 10l. 5m 42.60s. a 44.60s (6 Ran).

(D J M Newell), J White

2261 North West Racing Club Handicap Chase (5-y-o and up) £4,866 2m (3:00)

1975[2] GOOD FOR A LAUGH [120] 10-10-3 (5*) J Burke, *hit second, pushed alng and hit 5 out, rdn 3 out, hdwy nxt, led last, drvn out.*..................(6 to 4 op 5 to 4) 1

1479* CLAY COUNTY [140] 9-12-0 R Dunwoody, *led and clr, hit 2 out and sn rdn, hdd last, kpt on und pres r-in.*
....(5 to 4 on op Evens) 2

STRONG APPROACH [118] 9-10-6 C Swan, *chsd ldr till f 3rd.*.......................(6 to 1 op 5 to 1) f

Dist: 1l. 4m 25.90s. a 26.90s (3 Ran).
SR: 43/62/-/ (Mrs S A Bramall), Mrs S A Bramall

2262 Garswood Novices' Hurdle (4-y-o and up) £2,232 2½m.................... (3:30)

1710* PONDERING (v) 4-10-11 R Dunwoody, *cl up, led 3rd, quickened clr 3 out, unchlgd.* (2 to 1 on op 5 to 2 on) 1

2106[2] KENILWORTH LAD 6-11-1 (5*) Mr M Buckley, *trkd ldrs, hdwy to chase wnr 4th, rdn appr 3 out, sn outpcd.*
....(4 to 1 tchd 9 to 2) 2

1957[2] FLAPJACK LAD 5-11-6 C Llewellyn, *led till hdd and hit 3rd, lost pl nxt, sn tld off.*
....(9 to 2 op 4 to 1 tchd 5 to 1) 3

2042 AXEL 7-11-6 M Dwyer, *not fluent in rear, some hdwy 5th, nvr a factor.*......................(25 to 1 op 16 to 1) 4

PROFESSOR LONGHAIR 7-11-6 C Swan, *mstks, al rear, wl tld off frm 5th.*.................(14 to 1 op 12 to 1) 5

Dist: 15l, dist, dist, 20l. 5m 22.90s. a 44.40s (5 Ran).

(M C Pipe), M C Pipe

KEMPTON (good to soft)
Saturday January 22nd
Going Correction: PLUS 1.12 sec. per fur. (races 1,3,-5,7), PLUS 0.65 (2,4,6)

2263 Middlesex Novices' Hurdle (5-y-o and up) £2,973 2m 5f............. (12:45)

1992[2] CORROUGE (USA) 5-11-7 D Bridgwater, *prmnt, chlgd frm 5th till took definite ld appr 3 out, shaken up approaching last, came clr, readily.*
....(6 to 5 on op 5 to 4 on tchd Evens) 1

1992[3] TOP SPIN 5-11-7 A Maguire, *hdwy 6th, chsd wnr frm 3 out, styd on one pace from 2 out.*
....(11 to 2 op 5 to 1 tchd 6 to 1) 2

1878[3] MAD THYME 7-11-0 J Frost, *beh, steady hdwy 7th, shaken up and styd on, one pace from 2 out.*
....(14 to 1 op 10 to 1 tchd 16 to 1) 3

1688* SPARKLING SUNSET (Ire) 6-11-7 M A FitzGerald, *in tch, chsd ldrs frm 3 out, tll outpcd from 2 out.*
....(9 to 2 op 3 to 1) 4

1768 BROAD STEANE 5-11-0 S Earle, *sluly into strd, hdwy 6th, chsd ldrs 3 out, wknd appr 2 out.*
....(66 to 1 op 33 to 1 tchd 100 to 1) 5

1804 MAESTROSO (Ire) (bl) 5-11-0 G McCourt, *beh till hdwy 7th, sn drvn alng, wknd appr 3 out.*
....(25 to 1 op 20 to 1 tchd 33 to 1) 6

DO BE HAVE (Ire) 6-11-0 I Lawrence, *beh, hdwy 7th, fdd 3 out.*...........(33 to 1 op 20 to 1 tchd 50 to 1) 7

1878[7] THE QUAKER 8-10-9 Lorna Vincent, *al prmnt, led 5th till appr 3 out, wknd three out.*.......(100 to 1 op 66 to 1) 8

1536[5] ANTARCTIC CALL 7-11-0 J Osborne, *led to 3rd, continued to dispute ld till wknd aftr 6th.*
....(10 to 1 op 8 to 1 tchd 12 to 1) 9

1515[4] BITTER ALOE 5-11-0 I Shoemark, *chsd ldrs till wknd 7th, tld off.*............................(33 to 1 op 16 to 1) 10

1648 SKEOUGH (Ire) 6-11-7 R Bellamy, *al beh, tld off.*
....(33 to 1 op 16 to 1) 11

1869[5] BLAKEINGTON (bl) 8-10-7 (7*) Miss S Mitchell, *prmnt, led to 5th, wknd quickly aftr 6th, tld off whn pld up bef 2 out.*.................(100 to 1 op 66 to 1) pu

NIGHT FANCY 6-10-9 (5*) J McCarthy, *pld up appr 3rd, dismounted.*.................(100 to 1 op 66 to 1) pu

1973 VITAL SCORE 8-11-0 S Smith Eccles, *al beh, tld off whn pld up bef 2 out.*..........(100 to 1 op 66 to 1) pu

Dist: 4l, 2½l, 2½l, 15l, 12l, 4l, 15l, 1½l, dist, 7l. 5m 20.00s. a 24.00s (14 Ran).
SR: 58/54/44/48/26/14/10/-/-/ (Michael Gates), N A Twiston-Davies

2264 Hampton Novices' Chase (6-y-o and up) £3,785 3m.................(1:15)

1844[2] MONSIEUR LE CURE 8-10-10 N Williamson, *hld up, blun 9th, hdwy to track ldrs 14th, chalg whn blunded 3 out, led nxt, cmftbly...* (11 to 8 fav op 5 to 4 tchd 13 to 8) 1

1844 GHIA GNEUIAGH 8-11-0 D Bridgwater, *hdwy to chase ldrs 9th, led appr 3 out, hdd 2 out, btn whn rdr lost iron briefly r-in.*.........(5 to 1 op 4 to 1 tchd 11 to 2) 2

1533[3] MEDIANE (USA) 9-10-10 P Holley, *prmnt, led 7th to tenth, led ag'n 12th till appr 3 out, sn one pace.*
....(14 to 1 op 16 to 1 tchd 12 to 1) 3

2017[2] LUCKY LANE (bl) 10-11-0 C Maude, *prmnt, led 4th to 6th, chlgd 11th, wknd frm four out, no ch whn blun 2 out.*
....(8 to 1 op 6 to 1) 4

1952* VELEDA II (Fr) 7-10-7 (7*) Mr D Parker, *in tch to 15th, tld off.*.......................(5 to 1 op 9 to 2) 5

1441[3] PAPER STAR (v) 7-10-5 M Ahern, *al beh, hit 3rd and 8th, no ch whn blun and uns rdr 15th.* (66 to 1 op 50 to 1) ur

NATIONAL HUNT RESULTS 1993-94

2117 MILLIES OWN 7-10-3 (7") D Fortt, *prmnt to 13th, wkng whn blun badly 15th, pld up bef nxt.*
.... (33 to 1 op 25 to 1) pu
2045 HERMES HARVEST 6-10-10 B Powell, *beh frm 9th, tld off whn pld up bef 3 out.* (20 to 1 op 16 to 1 tchd 10 to 1) pu
1511* EMERALD STORM 7-11-0 M A FitzGerald, *led to 4th, led ag'n 6th to 7th, led 8th to tenth, wknd nxt, tld off whn pld up bef 2 out.......* (11 to 2 op 9 to 2 tchd 6 to 1) pu
1879 YOUNG BRAVE 8-10-10 S Earle, *chsd ldrs 9th, wknd 13th, tld off whn pld up bef 3 out.*
.... (25 to 1 op 16 to 1 tchd 33 to 1) pu
1563⁶ CRAIGSTOWN (Ire) 6-10-10 A Maguire, *prmnt, led tenth to 12th, wknd rpdly, tld off whn pld up bef 3 out.*
.... (33 to 1 op 50 to 1) pu
Dist: 3l, 15l, 8l, dist. 6m 18.40s. a 29.40s (11 Ran).

(Hector H Brown), J A C Edwards

2265 Bic Lady Shaver Handicap Hurdle (0-145 5-y-o and up) £3,210 2m 5f (1:45)

1667* MEDITATOR [123] 10-10-5 (5") S Curran, *prmnt, drvn to ld 3 out, briefly hdd but sn led ag'n, ran on wl und pres frm 2 out.....................* (7 to 2 fav tchd 4 to 1) 1
2172⁴ FOX CHAPEL [118] 7-9-12 (7") G Tormey, *prmnt, chlgd 6th, led briefly aftr 3 out, sn hdd, rdn 2 out, styd on r-in, not rch wnr.................* (4 to 1 op 7 to 2 tchd 9 to 2) 2
2049⁸ BEAUCHAMP GRACE [133] 5-10-13 (7") Mr D Parker, *gd hdwy 7th, chlgd frm 3 out till wknd aftr 2 out.*
.... (13 to 2 op 7 to 1 tchd 8 to 1) 3
1633* HIGH GRADE [113] 6-10-8 B Powell, *in tch, chlgd 6th, led 7th, hdd 3 out, wknd appr 2 out...* (12 to 1 op 14 to 1) 4
2044 WELSH SIREN [113] 8-9-9 (5") J McCarthy, *beh till effrt 7th, sn wknd............* (16 to 1 op 14 to 1 tchd 20 to 1) 5
1971² ALBERTINO (Fr) [113] 7-9-11 (3") S Wynne, *beh frm 6th.*
.... (9 to 1 op 8 to 1 tchd 10 to 1) 6
1597² MANHATTAN BOY [113] 12-10-0 A Maguire, *led aftr second, hdd 7th, sn wknd.*
.... (20 to 1 op 16 to 1 tchd 25 to 1) 7
1349¹ JOPANINI [141] 9-12-0 M A FitzGerald, *led till aftr second, wknd aftr 6th.........* (5 to 1 op 4 to 1 tchd 11 to 2) 8
PAPERWORK BOY [113] 9-9-7 (7") P McLoughlin, *beh, mstk 5th, tld off whn pld up aftr 3 out.*
.... (66 to 1 op 100 to 1) pu
2046⁴ AMAZON EXPRESS [132] 5-11-5 J Osborne, *drpd rear 6th, tld off whn pld up bef 8th.........* (7 to 1 tchd 6 to 1) pu
Dist: 3½l, ¾l, 8l, 12l, 12l, 4l, 12l. 5m 23.00s. a 30.00s (10 Ran).
SR: 17/8/22/-/-/-/ (Miss Jacqueline S Doyle), Miss Jacqueline S Doyle

2266 Fulwell Handicap Chase (0-150 5-y-o and up) £7,448 2½m 110yds.....(2:15)

UNCLE ELI [126] 11-10-5 S Earle, *in tch, chlgd and hit 3 out and nxt, lft chalg appr last, ran on to ld last strds.*
.... (10 to 1) 1
1507⁶ ROUGH QUEST [125] 8-10-4 G McCourt, *hld up, hdwy 12th, lft in narrow ld last, hrd drvn, ct last strds.*
.... (16 to 1 tchd 20 to 1) 2
1538 BIBENDUM [128] 8-10-7 M A FitzGerald, *hdwy 12th, drvn to chase ldrs 4 out, outpcd frm 3 out.*
.... (9 to 2 fav op 4 to 1) 3
2143 MIGHTY FALCON [121] (bl) 9-10-0 P Holley, *beh and rdn appr 8th, moderate prog approaching 3 out.*
.... (33 to 1 tchd 66 to 1) 4
1921* ARMAGRET [135] 9-11-0 L O'Hara, *prmnt, hmpd 3rd, led 11th to 13th, wknd appr 3 out......* (6 to 1 tchd 7 to 1) 5
CUDDY DALE [128] 11-10-0 (7") P Murphy, *al beh.*
.... (33 to 1 op 25 to 1) 6
1698³ GUIBURN'S NEPHEW [130] 12-10-9 C Maude, *dsptd ld till f 3rd.......................* (6 to 1 tchd 13 to 2) f
RYDE AGAIN [149] 11-12-0 J Osborne, *hmpd 3rd and beh, nvr dngrs aftr, tld off whn pld up bef 3 out.*
.... (10 to 1 op 8 to 1) pu
1887 ARDBRIN [128] 11-10-7 D Murphy, *led to 11th, sn wknd, tld off whn pld up bef 3 out.......* (10 to 1 op 8 to 1) pu
2174⁴ DEADLY CHARM (USA) [121] 8-10-0 A Maguire, *in tch, blun tenth, sn reco'red to chase ldrs, wknd 13th, tld off whn pld up bef last.........* (5 to 1 op 9 to 2 tchd 11 to 2) pu
2013 CHAMPAGNE LAD [125] 8-10-1 (3") P Hide, *chsd ldrs, chlgd 8th to tenth, led 13th, still slight ld whn wnt lme and pld up bef last............* (6 to 1 tchd 11 to 2) pu
Dist: Nk, 25l, 12l, 5l, 10l. 5m 20.30s. a 27.30s (11 Ran).

(James Burley), R H Alner

2267 Bic Razor Lanzarote Handicap Hurdle (4-y-o and up) £16,995 2m......(2:45)

2175³ NIJMEGEN [121] 6-10-6 J Osborne, *hld up in tch, led 2 out, came clr appr last............* (5 to 1 tchd 11 to 2) 1
1888² HIGH BARON [142] 7-11-13 M Hourigan, *chsd ldr 4th, chlgd frm 3 out till outpcd aftr 2 out.........* (4 to 1 jt-fav op 3 to 1 tchd 9 to 2) 2
1661² FATACK [122] 5-10-2 (5") S Curran, *led to second, sn led ag'n, hdd 2 out, soon outpcd.* (4 to 1 jt-fav op 3 to 1 tchd 9 to 2) 3
2172 ZAMIRAH (Ire) [121] 5-10-6 D Bridgwater, *beh, hdwy 5th, styd on same pace frm 2 out.......* (8 to 1 op 14 to 1) 4

2175⁸ PERSUASIVE [128] 7-10-8 (5") J McCarthy, *hmpd 1st, al beh................* (20 to 1 tchd 25 to 1) 5
1955* NORTHERN SADDLER [115] 7-10-0 N Williamson, *effrt 5th, wknd aftr 3 out.......* (9 to 1 op 8 to 1 tchd 10 to 1) 6
1842* CHILD OF THE MIST [120] 8-10-5 A Maguire, *in tch, chlgd 4th to 5th, wknd aftr 3 out.*
.... (5 to 1 op 11 to 2 tchd 6 to 1) 7
2192* TOP WAVE [119] 6-10-4 (5ex) M A FitzGerald, *al beh.*
.... (10 to 1 op 8 to 1 tchd 12 to 1) 8
1165⁵ WELSH BARD [138] (bl) 10-11-9 M Richards, *led second, sn hdd, wknd 4th, tld off whn pld up bef 2 out.*
.... (50 to 1 op 33 to 1 tchd 66 to 1) pu
1842³ CLURICAN (Ire) [115] 5-10-0 D Murphy, *al beh, tld off whn pld up bef 2 out......* (16 to 1 op 14 to 1 tchd 20 to 1) pu
Dist: 5l, 6l, 2½l, 10l, 7l, 15l, 1l. 4m 1.60s. a 21.60s (10 Ran).
SR: 41/57/31/27/24/4/ (W Hancock), J G FitzGerald

2268 Bic Razor Novices' Chase (5-y-o and up) £3,655 2m.................(3:15)

CURRENT EXPRESS 7-11-3 M A FitzGerald, *jmpd wl, chlgd 8th till led 4 out, drvn and styd on well r-in.*
.... (5 to 2 op 9 to 4 tchd 2 to 1 and 11 to 4) 1
1754² BAYDON STAR 7-11-11 A Maguire, *chsd ldr till led 9th, hit 4 out, chalg whn hit 3 out, chlgd and hit last, ran on, jst fld.....................* (5 to 4 on tchd Evens) 2
1754⁶ BIG BEAT (USA) 6-11-11 P Holley, *led to 9th, outpcd frm 3 out........................* (7 to 2 op 3 to 1 tchd 4 to 1) 3
2043⁵ RICH HEMPTON 9-11-3 N Williamson, *effrt 7th, sn wknd.*
.... (33 to 1 op 20 to 1) 4
1731² PRIVATE JET (Ire) 5-10-4 (3") A Thornton, *hit 1st, al beh.*
.... (66 to 1 op 33 to 1 tchd 100 to 1) 5
Dist: Hd, 15l, dist, 6l. 4m 0.80s. a 13.80s (5 Ran).
SR: 55/63/48/-/-/ (Lord Matthews), N J Henderson

2269 Foxhills Open National Hunt Flat Race (4,5,6-y-o) £1,926 2m..........(3:45)

1494⁵ DOMINIE (Ire) 6-11-5 N Williamson, *hdwy to track ldrs hfwy, led ins fnl 2 fs, sn clr.*
.... (16 to 1 op 10 to 1 tchd 20 to 1) 1
1957² BEATSON (Ire) 5-11-7 (5") T Jenks, *made most till hdd o'r 4 fs out, ev ch over 2 out, styd on, no chance wth wnr.*
.... (7 to 1 op 9 to 1 tchd 20 to 1) 2
1957³ BASS ROCK 6-11-5 J Frost, *al pressing ldrs, rdn and styd on same pace fnl 2 fs..............* (14 to 1 op 7 to 1) 3
2021² TAP SHOES (Ire) 4-10-7 L Harvey, *hdwy hfwy, rdn and no imprsn fnl 2 fs......................* (14 to 1 op 7 to 1) 4
1806² BIG STRAND (Ire) 5-11-5 J Lower, *al chasing ldrs, led 4 fs out, hdd o'r 2 furlongs out, wknd fnl furlong.*
.... (11 to 4 op 3 to 1) 5
1996³ ACE PLAYER (NZ) 6-11-5 A Maguire, *beh, hdwy 7th fs, wknd o'r 2 out.*
.... (9 to 1 op 7 to 1 tchd 9 to 4) 6
OUROWNFELLOW (Ire) 5-10-12 (7") G Crone, *chsd ldrs hfwy, chlgd 5 fs out, wknd wl o'r 3 out.*
.... (33 to 1 op 16 to 1 tchd 50 to 1) 7
WOODMANTON 6-10-7 (7") P McLoughlin, *in tch ten fs.*
.... (25 to 1 op 12 to 1 tchd 33 to 1) 8
IVY EDITH 4-10-4² D O'Sullivan, *chsd ldrs 11 fs.*
.... (33 to 1 op 16 to 1) 9
815⁷ CRUNCH TIME (Ire) 5-11-5 D Bridgwater, *prmnt ten fs.*
.... (33 to 1 op 16 to 1) 10
GALAXY ABOUND (NZ) 6-11-5 Craig Thornton, *in tch ten fs.....................* (25 to 1 op 12 to 1 tchd 33 to 1) 11
MAGELLAN BAY (Ire) 6-10-12 (7") D Bohan, *gd hdwy to track ldrs 7 fs out, sn wknd.*
.... (14 to 1 op 12 to 1 tchd 20 to 1) 12
I'M IN CLOVER (Ire) 5-11-5 S Smith Eccles, *al beh.*
.... (25 to 1 op 12 to 1 tchd 33 to 1) 13
1957 NORDEN (Ire) 5-11-5 A Tory, *beh frm hfwy.*
.... (33 to 1 op 16 to 1 tchd 50 to 1) 14
WIN A HAND 4-10-4² M A FitzGerald, *in tch ten fs.*
.... (33 to 1 op 20 to 1) 15
1957 PARAMOUNT 5-11-5 Mr J Durkan, *al beh.*
.... (33 to 1 op 16 to 1) 16
1779 LEENEY 5-11-5 M Bosley, *al beh...* (33 to 1 op 20 to 1) 17
1806⁸ SHINING LIGHT (Ire) 5-10-12 (7") M Keighley, *chsd ldrs o'r ten fs........* (16 to 1 op 10 to 1 tchd 20 to 1) 18
1996 NORTHERN SINGER 4-10-7 G McCourt, *nvr better than mid-div........* (33 to 1 op 14 to 1 tchd 50 to 1) 19
GOOD BLOW (Ire) 6-10-12 (7") K Brown, *al beh.*
.... (33 to 1 op 16 to 1) 20
JOE GILLIS 5-10-12 (7") Pat Thompson, *al beh, collapsed and died ins fnl furlong........* (11 to 2 op 5 to 1) f
JAY EM ESS (NZ) 5-11-2 (3") R Davis, *chsd ldrs ten fs, no ch whn collapsed nr finish.........* (33 to 1 op 12 to 1) f
Dist: 20l, 3l, 1½l, 2l, 1¼l, 5l, 10l, 5l, 15l, 2l. 3m 57.10s. (22 Ran).

(Exors Of The Late Mrs C F Fairbairn), J A C Edwards

MARKET RASEN (soft)
Saturday January 22nd
Going Correction: PLUS 1.20 sec. per fur. (races 1,3,5), PLUS 0.65 (2,4,6,7)

2270 Spalding Amateur Riders' Novices' Chase (6-y-o and up) £2,544 3m 1f ....(1:05)

2084[7] HOWARYADOON 8-11-1 (3*) Mr G Johnson Houghton, *trkd ldrs, ev ch appr 3 out, rdn to ld last, pushed clr r-in, cmftbly*..........................(5 to 2 fav op 3 to 1) 1
1861 PRECIPICE RUN 9-10-13 (5*) Mr R Hale, *led, mstk 6th, rdn and hit 2 out, hdd last, sn btn.* ....(11 to 4 op 2 to 1 tchd 3 to 1) 2
2137 EXTRA SPECIAL 9-10-11 (7*) Mr S Brisby, *hld up, rdn and hdwy aftr 6 out, chsd ldr, kpt on one pace frm 3 out.* ....(25 to 1 op 16 to 1) 3
1834[4] SPOONHILL WOOD (bl) 8-10-13 Mr S Swiers, *trkd ldr, cl up whn jmpd slwly 13th and nxt, ev ch 4 out, hrd rdn aftr next, sn btn*..................(11 to 2 op 9 to 2) 4
1873[4] EDEN SUNSET 8-10-11 (7*) Mr Chris Wilson, *trkd ldr, jmpd slwly 7th, ev ch 4 out, rdn and wknd nxt.* ....(6 to 1 op 7 to 1 tchd 8 to 1) 5
2071 FIRST LORD 8-10-11 (7*) Miss A Deniel, *hld up, jmpd big early, hdwy to chase ldr aftr 5 out, sn wknd.* ....(10 to 1 op 6 to 1) 6
2137 BUCKWHEAT LAD (Ire) 6-10-13 (5*) Mr T Byrne, *hld up, reminder aftr 8th, pushed alng frm 13th, sn beh.* ....(16 to 1 op 12 to 1 tchd 20 to 1) 7
2137[5] CANTGETOUT 8-10-10 (7*) Mr A Pickering, *hld up, mstks, rdn and lost tch 13th, tld off whn pld up and dismounted bef 3 out*..............(12 to 1 tchd 14 to 1) pu
Dist: 15l, hd, 1l, 15l, 6l. 6m 55.60s. a 54.60s (8 Ran).
(Thomas Thompson), R Rowe

2271 Boston Selling Handicap Hurdle (4 & 5-y-o) £1,707 2m 1f 110yds......(1:35)

2093 ABSOLUTLEY FOXED [65] 5-9-13 (7*) G Robertson, *pushed alng aftr 3rd, styd on after 2 out, mstk last, sn reco'red, led r-in, drvn out*...... (11 to 2 op 4 to 1 tchd 6 to 1) 1
1741[2] BITRAN [62] 4-10-3 A S Smith, *led, rdn and wknd appr last, hdd r-in, no extr.* ....(11 to 8 fav op 6 to 4 tchd 7 to 4) 2
1810 WHATCOMESNATURALLY (USA) [59] 5-10-0 L Wyer, *hld up, rdn alng aftr 4th, styd on one pace frm 2 out, no ch wth 1st two*..........................(10 to 1 op 14 to 1) 3
1965[3] PRIORY PIPER [61] 5-9-11 (5*) T Eley, *trkd ldr, rdn alng aftr 5th, ev ch 3 out, sn one pace.* ....(11 to 2 op 5 to 1 tchd 6 to 1) 4
1655[9] RYTHMIC RYMER [60] 4-10-1[6] (5*) P Williams, *trkd ldr, rdn alng aftr 4th, ev ch 3 out, btn whn mstks last 2.* ....(14 to 1 op 12 to 1 tchd 16 to 1) 5
2068 RAVENSPUR (Ire) [59] 4-9-13[2] (3*) D J Moffatt, *hld up, beh and rdn alng aftr 4th, no imprsn.* ....(12 to 1 tchd 14 to 1) 6
2000[5] CASHABLE [66] 4-10-7 J Railton, *hld up, trkd ldr aftr 3rd, hrd rdn after 3 out, sn btn.* ....(11 to 2 op 4 to 1 tchd 6 to 1) 7
1655[8] MILTON ROOMS (Ire) [83] 5-11-3 (7*) K Davies, *hld up, rdn alng aftr 4th, sn beh*.....(8 to 1 op 7 to 1 tchd 9 to 1) 8
Dist: 1½l, 10l, 10l, ¾l, 10l. 4m 23.20s. a 21.20s (8 Ran).
(G C Chipman), B A McMahon

2272 Eric And Lucy Papworth Handicap Chase (0-120 5-y-o and up) £3,571 2m 1f 110yds......................(2:05)

2087[7] BOSTON ROVER [112] 9-11-10 M Brennan, *hld up, mstk 3rd, hdwy 8th, lft third 3 out, second and held whn left clr last*..........................(11 to 2 op 5 to 1) 1
1802[4] RUPPLES [88] 7-10-0 W Worthington, *hld up, lost tch 7th, tld off, lft poor second at last.* ....(11 to 1 op 10 to 1 tchd 14 to 1) 2
FAVOURED VICTOR (USA) [88] 7-10-0 A S Smith, *led, clr 3rd, jmpd lft and hdd 6 out, pressed ldr till wknd aftr 3 out, tld off*............(10 to 1 op 7 to 1 tchd 12 to 1) 3
1514[3] ALAN BALL [101] 8-10-8 (5*) T Eley, *wnt 3rd 6th, trkd ldr, led 3 out, 2 ls clr whn f last.* ....(9 to 2 op 4 to 1 tchd 5 to 1) f
2043[3] QUENTIN DURWOOD [94] 8-10-6 S McNeill, *chsd ldr, cld 6th, led six out till hdd and f 3 out.* ....(5 to 2 op 9 to 4 tchd 3 to 1) f
2107 TERRIBLE GEL (Fr) [110] 9-11-1 (7*) J Lonergan, *jmpd slwly second, mstks, lost pl 5th, hdwy aftr 4 out, lft second nxt, btn 3rd whn blun and uns rdr 2 out.* ....(9 to 4 fav tchd 2 to 1) ur
Dist: 25l, dist. 4m 47.90s. a 33.90s (6 Ran).
(P Stoner), O Brennan

2273 Sleaford Handicap Hurdle (0-135 4-y-o and up) £2,997 3m..............(2:35)

2086* BOLLIN MAGDALENE [107] 6-10-4 L Wyer, *in tch, trkd ldrs frm 6th, led aftr 3 out, styd on strly.* ....(11 to 8 fav op 5 to 4 tchd 6 to 4) 1
1963[2] FURRY BABY [103] 7-10-0 R Marley, *in tch, rdn to chase ldr aftr 3 out, kpt on betw last 2, not quicken.* ....(4 to 1 op 7 to 2 tchd 9 to 2) 2
1863* ISABEAU [106] 7-10-3 A S Smith, *dsptd ld 6th, led aftr 7th till after 3 out, styd on one pace.* ....(5 to 1 op 9 to 2 tchd 11 to 2) 3
2005[5] ABBOT OF FURNESS [131] 10-12-0 N Doughty, *hld up in tch, ev ch 3 out, wkng whn mstk nxt.* (9 to 1 op 8 to 1) 4
1657 DUHALLOW LODGE [115] 7-10-12 Richard Guest, *hld up, hdwy whn stumbled aftr 4 out, sn wknd.* ....(6 to 1 op 11 to 2 tchd 7 to 1) 5
1963[3] THIS NETTLE DANGER [103] 10-10-0 M Brennan, *hld up, hdwy aftr 7th, chsd ldr till wknd quickly 3 out.* ....(12 to 1 op 10 to 1 tchd 14 to 1) 6
1322[9] SPROWSTON BOY [122] 11-11-5 W Worthington, *led, dsptd ld 6th till aftr nxt, wknd quickly, sn beh.* ....(20 to 1 op 16 to 1 tchd 25 to 1) 7
DR MACCARTER (USA) [103] 7-9-9 (5*) T Eley, *hld up, rdn alng aftr 6th, sn lost tch, tld off whn pld up bef 2 out.* ....(25 to 1 op 14 to 1 tchd 33 to 1) pu
HOW DOUDO [105] 7-10-2[2] S McNeill, *hld up, lost tch aftr 6th, sn beh, tld off whn pld up bef last.* ....(33 to 1 op 20 to 1) pu
Dist: 5l, 3½l, 20l, 7l, 12l, 15l. 6m 7.80s. a 25.80s (9 Ran).
(Sir Neil Westbrook), M H Easterby

2274 Stamford Handicap Chase (0-130 5-y-o and up) £3,614 2¾m 110yds.....(3:05)

2139* THREEOUTOFFOUR [120] 9-12-0 M Brennan, *hld up, wnt 3rd 8th, led nxt, clr 2 out, stumbled aftr last, sn reco'red, styd on wl.* (11 to 10 on op 11 to 8 on tchd 6 to 4 on and Evens) 1
1962[3] BALTIC BROWN [105] 9-10-13 Richard Guest, *led 5th, mstk 7th, hdd 9th, outpcd 5 out, rallied to go second aftr 2 out, not rch wnr*........ (7 to 1 op 5 to 1 tchd 8 to 1) 2
1944[2] CONGREGATION [101] 8-10-9 J Railton, *trkd ldr frm 8th, ev ch 4 out, chsd lder till wknd appr last.* ....(3 to 1 op 5 to 1) 3
1962 TRES AMIGOS [104] 7-10-9 (3*) A Larnach, *lost pl aftr 4th, hdwy 8th, sn pushed alng, lost tch 5 out, tld off.* ....(6 to 1 op 5 to 1 tchd 13 to 2) 4
THE LEGGETT [115] 11-11-9 A S Smith, *led to 5th, lost tch tenth, sn tld off*..............................(16 to 1) 5
Dist: 6l, 15l, dist, dist. 6m 0.00s. a 32.00s (5 Ran).
SR: 50/29/10/-/-/ (Miss Cindy Brennan), O Brennan

2275 Grimsby Novices' Hurdle (4-y-o) £2,460 2m 1f 110yds............(3:35)

RUSTY REEL 10-12 R Campbell, *in tch, wnt second 6th, wth ldr whn mstk last, rallied to ld nr finish, all out.* ....(16 to 1 op 14 to 1) 1
851* ABJAR 10-13 (5*) A Bates, *prmnt, hit 3rd, led 6th, mstks last 2, hrd rdn and hdd nr finish.* ....(3 to 1 tchd 100 to 30) 2
2154* BALLON 10-13 L Wyer, *hld up beh, hdwy aftr 5th, rdn and styd on appr 2 out, sn one pace.* .... (11 to 8 on op Evens tchd 11 to 10) 3
1865[2] EVE'S TREASURE 10-2 (5*) S Lyons, *mid-div, rdn alng aftr 5th, styd on one pace frm 2 out.* ....(11 to 1 op 12 to 1 tchd 10 to 1) 4
1767[8] GYMCRAK TIGER (Ire) 10-12 R Marley, *chsd ldr, wknd aftr 4th, lost tch after nxt*................................(20 to 1) 5
1885 JACKSONS BAY 10-7 (5*) C Burnett-Wells, *hld up in last pl, some hdwy aftr 5th, wknd appr 2 out, tld off.* ....(14 to 1 op 8 to 1 tchd 16 to 1) 6
1504 STREPHON (Ire) 10-12 S McNeill, *led to 6th, wknd aftr 3 out, sixth and btn whn f last.* ....(12 to 1 op 8 to 1 tchd 14 to 1) f
INFANTRY GLEN (v) 10-7 (5*) P Midgley, *beh 3rd, lost tch aftr nxt, tld off whn pld up bef 2 out.* ....(25 to 1 op 20 to 1) pu
COUSIN WENDY 10-2 (5*) T Eley, *beh, mstk 4th, sn lost tch, tld off whn pld up bef 2 out*............. (50 to 1) pu
1880 DIDACTE (Fr) (bl) 10-12 J Railton, *pressed ldr, wknd aftr 4th, sn beh, tld off whn pld up bef 2 out.* ....(50 to 1 op 25 to 1) pu
KATIE'S BOY (Ire) 10-12 A S Smith, *beh 3rd, sn lost tch, tld off whn pld up bef last*...........(33 to 1 op 20 to 1) pu
Dist: ½l, 15l, 6l, 12l, dist. 4m 19.50s. a 17.50s (11 Ran).
SR: 23/28/8/-/-/-/ (Ian Campbell), I Campbell

2276 Levy Board Novices' Handicap Hurdle (4-y-o and up) £2,390 2m 5f 110yds ....(4:05)

1775 WHO SIR [69] 8-10-3 (5*) A Roche, *hld up, hdwy 7th, ev ch appr 2 out, rdn to ld r-in, drvn out.* ....(20 to 1 tchd 25 to 1) 1
1938* NORTHERN SQUIRE [85] 6-11-5 (5*) P Williams, *al prmnt, led 6th till aftr 3 out, led appr nxt, hdd and not quicken r-in*............................ (2 to 1 fav op 5 to 2) 2
1877[4] STRATHBOGIE MIST (Ire) [63] 6-9-13 (3*) D J Moffatt, *hld up, hdwy aftr 4 out, rdn and styd on betw last 2, kpt on wl nr finish*......................(10 to 1 op 8 to 1) 3
1865[5] APRIL CITY [68] 5-10-7 M Ranger, *led to 6th, styd cl up, led aftr 3 out till appr nxt, not quicken betw last 2.* .... (16 to 1 op 14 to 1) 4

1726^{7}	ROYAL SURPRISE [63] 7-10-2 Miss P Robson, *rdn and lost pl 6th, hdwy 3 out, styd on aftr nxt, not quicken.*	(33 to 1)	5
1953^{7}	PETRADARE [61] 7-9-9 (5*) T Eley, *jmpd slwly 1st, pressed ldr till no imprsn aftr 3 out*	(50 to 1)	6
1920	GREAT EASEBY (Ire) [78] 4-11-3 N Doughty, *trkd ldrs, ev ch 3 out, kpt on one pace betw last 2.*	(14 to 1 op 12 to 1 tchd 16 to 1)	7
1003	HURRICANE HORACE [81] 7-11-6 R Hodge, *hld up, hdwy aftr 7th, chlgd 2 out, ev ch last, wknd r-in.*	(8 to 1 op 6 to 1)	8
1865^{4}	MRS NORMAN [61] 5-10-0 M Brennan, *hld up, hdwy 7th, chsd ldrs till wknd appr 2 out.*	(9 to 1 op 12 to 1 tchd 8 to 1)	9
2008^{7}	JUKE BOX BILLY (Ire) [80] 6-11-2 (3*) A Larnach, *hld up, effrt aftr 4 out, wknd appr 2 out.*	(6 to 1 op 5 to 1 tchd 13 to 2)	10
2094^{2}	BOLD STAR [71] (bl) 4-10-10 S McNeill, *in tch, pressed ldr 6th till wknd aftr 3 out.*	(11 to 2 op 8 to 1 tchd 11 to 1)	11
1607^{3}	INAN (USA) [84] 5-11-9 L Wyer, *hld up, hdwy 6th, chsd ldr till wknd quickly aftr 3 out*	(10 to 1 op 8 to 1)	12

Dist: 1l, 1l, 4l, 1½l, 1½l, 2l, 2l, 1½l, 20l. 5m 38.80s. a 34.80s (12 Ran).

(Mrs June Doyle), J J O'Neill

NAAS (IRE) (soft)
Saturday January 22nd

2277 Tattersalls Mares Novice Chase (6-y-o and up) £3,450 2m 3f........... (1:15)

2051^{2}	TITIAN BLONDE (Ire) 6-11-2 (7*) F Woods,	(6 to 4 fav)	1
2055^{3}	DEER TRIX 9-11-6 (3*) D Bromley,	(10 to 1)	2
2098^{7}	AMARI QUEEN 7-11-4 (5*) M G Cleary,	(7 to 1)	3
	CROGEEN LASS 7-11-9 H Rogers,	(10 to 1)	4
1909^{2}	GOLA LADY 7-11-9 K F O'Brien,	(3 to 1)	f
1902^{6}	ARDCARN GIRL 7-11-9 A Powell,	(12 to 1)	f
2098^{3}	PANDA (Ire) 6-11-6 (3*) T J Mitchell,	(4 to 1)	bd

Dist: 15l, 20l, 3l. 5m 35.50s. (7 Ran).

(D Harvey), D Harvey

2278 Naas Maiden Hurdle (5-y-o and up) £3,105 2m 3f.................. (1:45)

1827*	JOHNNY KELLY 7-12-0 C O'Dwyer,	(5 to 1)	1
2076^{3}	ROUBABAY (Ire) 6-11-11 (3*) T P Treacy,	(6 to 1)	2
2052^{2}	CHANCE COFFEY 9-11-6 G M O'Neill,	(5 to 1)	3
1902^{3}	DOWN THE BACK 7-10-10 (5*) M G Cleary,	(20 to 1)	4
2027^{2}	CALMOS 7-11-6 T Horgan,	(10 to 1)	5
1897*	UNA'S CHOICE (Ire) 6-12-0 F J Flood,	(7 to 2 fav)	6
2027	SOUTH WESTERLY (Ire) 6-11-6 M Duffy,	(10 to 1)	7
1821^{2}	BOHEMIAN CASTLE (Ire) 5-11-2 F Woods,	(10 to 1)	8
	LEVEL VIBES 5-11-2 P Carberry,	(14 to 1)	9
1683^{4}	BUMBLY BROOK 7-10-13 (7*) J M McCormack,	(8 to 1)	10
1833	ISN'T THAT NICE (Ire) 6-11-6 J Shortt,	(14 to 1)	11
2158^{2}	KELLYMOUNT 8-11-7 (7*) M Kelly,	(7 to 1)	12
1898	SARAKIN (Ire) 6-10-8 (7*) D O'Driscoll,	(100 to 1)	13
1854^{3}	RHINESTALL 7-10-12 (3*) Mr A E Lacy,	(20 to 1)	14
2155^{8}	KING WAH GLORY (Ire) 5-11-3 (7*) Mr J Connolly,	(8 to 1)	15
	KILMOYLER 7-11-3 (3*) Mr D Marnane,	(33 to 1)	16
2052^{8}	EXTRA MILE 7-11-9 S H O'Donovan,	(20 to 1)	17
	JUST DONT CARE 8-10-13 (7*) J P Broderick,	(33 to 1)	18
1912	CLONE (Ire) 6-10-13 (7*) J M Donnelly,	(20 to 1)	19
2155	LEAVE IT TO JUDGE 7-10-13 (7*) Mr W J Gleeson,	(100 to 1)	20
1912	SARVO (Ire) 6-11-3 (3*) C O'Brien,	(100 to 1)	21

Dist: ¾l, 2l, 13l, nk. 4m 52.90s. (21 Ran).

(P M Berry), P M Berry

2279 Brittas Handicap Hurdle (0-130 4-y-o and up) £3,105 2m.............. (2:15)

1984^{4}	FORTY ONE (Ire) [-] 6-9-2 (7*) J P Broderick,	(10 to 1)	1
2026^{5}	MR BOAL (Ire) [-] 5-10-12 (7*) Mr M Brennan,	(6 to 1)	2
1894	DEEP INAGH [-] 8-12-0 D P Fagan,	(6 to 1)	3
1816^{7}	ASSERT STAR [-] 4-10-2 (5*) K P Gaule,	(6 to 1)	4
1232^{2}	SHIRWAN (Ire) [-] 5-9-7 (7*) D J Kavanagh,	(9 to 2)	5
1976^{7}	FABULIST (Ire) [-] 5-10-6 (3*) T P Treacy,	(12 to 1)	6
1987^{7}	MONTE FIGO [-] 7-10-4 (5*) T P Rudd,	(8 to 1)	7
	GREEN MACHINE [-] 7-9-13 F Woods,	(25 to 1)	8
2079	KEPPOLS PRINCE [-] 7-10-10 H Rogers,	(10 to 1)	9
2097^{2}	EAGLE ROCK (USA) [-] 6-11-0 (3*) C O'Brien,	(3 to 1 fav)	10
1855^{8}	VICOSA (Ire) [-] 5-10-5 A Powell,	(10 to 1)	11

Dist: 7l, nk, 5½l, 2l. 3m 58.50s. (11 Ran).

(M W Hickey), M C Hickey

2280 Tassaggart Handicap Chase (5-y-o and up) £6,900 2m.............. (2:45)

1847*	LASATA [-] 9-10-8 P Carberry,	(6 to 1)	1
2159*	SATULA [-] 10-9-7 (4ex) C O'Dwyer,	(2 to 1 fav)	2
2124^{3}	PARLIAMENT HALL [-] 8-9-8 (5*) J P Broderick,	(10 to 1)	3
2079^{8}	HOW'S THE BOSS [-] 8-11-3 J Magee,	(4 to 1)	4
2159^{2}	THIRD QUARTER [-] 9-10-1 K F O'Brien,	(9 to 2)	5
	STIGON [-] 8-10-2 A Powell,	(14 to 1)	6
	THE REAL UNYOKE [-] 9-9-10^{5} (3*) D P Murphy,	(20 to 1)	7
1847^{4}	BLITZKREIG [-] 11-10-8 T Horgan,	(12 to 1)	8
1985	VALRODIAN (NZ) [-] 11-9-13 L P Cusack,	(33 to 1)	9
1856*	LIFE OF A LORD [-] 8-10-3 M Flynn,	(10 to 1)	10
2101^{6}	BLAZING DAWN [-] 7-9-13 S H O'Donovan,	(14 to 1)	11

Dist: 1l, 2l, 10l, 8l. 4m 22.20s. (11 Ran).

(A J O'Reilly), M F Morris

2281 Donadea Hurdle (4-y-o and up) £3,105 2m............................ (3:15)

	SEEK THE FAITH (USA) 5-11-3 B Sheridan,	(3 to 1)	1
1076*	NIGHTMAN 5-11-12 C O'Dwyer,	(5 to 4 on)	2
1331^{2}	MISTER DRUM (Ire) 5-11-5 (7*) Mr J T McNamara,	(11 to 2)	3
1908^{6}	WHAT IT IS (Ire) 5-10-12 J Shortt,	(12 to 1)	4
2122	BOTHSIDESNOW (Ire) 4-10-7 P Carberry,	(16 to 1)	5
2157	PELEUS (USA) 9-11-8 (5*) M G Cleary,	(20 to 1)	6
2155^{9}	TAGANINI (Ire) 6-11-0 (7*) C McCormack,	(25 to 1)	7

Dist: 1l, 3½l, 5l, 1l. 4m 16.80s. (7 Ran).

(M G Hynes), D K Weld

2282 Sherlockstown Chase (5-y-o and up) £3,105 3m..................... (3:45)

2157^{2}	BEAU BABILLARD 7-11-1 T Horgan,	(3 to 1 fav)	1
1988*	SCRIBBLER 8-11-5 L P Cusack,	(4 to 1)	2
2125	BART OWEN 9-11-2 (3*) T J Mitchell,	(9 to 2)	3
1825^{3}	PARSONS BRIG 8-11-1 K F O'Brien,	(12 to 1)	4
1913^{4}	CARRON HILL 7-11-1 F Woods,	(12 to 1)	5
2101^{4}	THE WEST'S ASLEEP (bl) 9-11-1 J Magee,	(20 to 1)	6
2101*	FARNEY GLEN 7-11-2 (3*) C O'Brien,	(7 to 1)	f
2126*	THREE BROWNIES 7-11-5 C O'Dwyer,	(11 to 2)	f
2157^{9}	LE BRAVE (bl) 8-11-1 J Shortt,	(25 to 1)	f
	BALLYFIN BOY 8-10-12 (3*) Miss M Olivefalk,	(33 to 1)	ur
2200	MONEY MADE (bl) 7-10-8 (7*) Mr W J Gleeson,	(66 to 1)	bd

Dist: 2½l, 15l, dist, dist. 6m 58.70s. (11 Ran).

(C P Millikin), E J O'Grady

2283 Irish National Bookmakers Flat Race (4-y-o and up) £3,795 2m 3f..... (4:15)

2127^{2}	IAMWHATIAM 8-11-4 (7*) Mr E Norris,	(12 to 1)	1
1897^{3}	YOUR THE MAN 8-11-11 (7*) Mr M Brennan,	(12 to 1)	2
1989	CORYMANDEL (Ire) 5-11-7 Mr P Fenton,	(9 to 2)	3
1435^{5}	THATS A SECRET 6-11-11 (7*) Mr P English,	(14 to 1)	4
1989*	PRODIGAL PRINCE 6-12-4 Mr A J Martin,	(11 to 8 fav)	5
1859*	LOUGH CULTRA DRIVE (Ire) 6-12-1 (3*) Mr J A Nash,	(10 to 1)	6
	PREMIER COUNTY 8-11-6^{2} (7*) Mr C P McGivern,	(33 to 1)	7
	DORAN'S DELIGHT 7-12-4 Mr J P Dempsey,	(12 to 1)	8
2056*	TOURIST ATTRACTION (Ire) 6-11-6 (3*) Mrs J M Mullins,	(9 to 4)	pu

Dist: 1l, 5l, 20l, 3½l. 4m 48.20s. (9 Ran).

(Seamus O'Farrell), Seamus O'Farrell

LEOPARDSTOWN (IRE) (soft)
Sunday January 23rd

Going Correction: PLUS 1.05 sec. per fur. (races 1,2,-4,6,7), PLUS 1.25 (3,5)

2284 Sandymount Handicap Hurdle (0-123 5-y-o and up) £3,105 2¾m...... (1:10)

2027*	FRIGID COUNTESS [-] 7-10-2 (7*,9ex) L A Hurley,	(5 to 1)	1
	GROUND WAR [-] 7-10-13 R Dunwoody,	(5 to 1)	2
1822*	DOWHATYOULIKE (Ire) [-] 5-10-7 P Carberry,	(7 to 1)	3
2181^{2}	FAMBO LAD (Ire) [-] 6-10-9 Mr J A Berry,	(6 to 1)	4
1851^{7}	OPERA HAT (Ire) [-] 6-11-6 A Powell,	(5 to 1)	5
2124^{4}	CASH CHASE (Ire) [-] 6-10-10 L P Cusack,	(10 to 1)	6
1913^{3}	MYSTIC GALE (Ire) [-] 6-10-3 C F Swan,	(12 to 1)	7
2022^{2}	HORNER WATER (Ire) [-] 6-10-6 (5*) J P Broderick,	(4 to 1 fav)	8
2078^{4}	SECRET SCEPTRE [-] (bl) 7-10-10 F Woods,	(10 to 1)	9
1823^{5}	DANCING COURSE (Ire) [-] 6-10-7 (5*) P A Roche,	(12 to 1)	f
1815^{9}	COMMAND 'N CONTROL [-] 5-10-13 K F O'Brien,	(12 to 1)	pu
2040^{2}	SHREWD MOVE [-] (bl) 5-10-0 J Jones,	(12 to 1)	pu

Dist: ½l, 1l, 7l, 5l. 5m 42.20s. a 30.20s (12 Ran).

SR: 10/13/6/1/7/-/ (W Dooly), W Dooly

2285 Diners Club Stillorgan Hurdle (4-y-o) £4,140 2m..................... (1:40)

2122*	BALAWHAR (Ire) 10-11 C F Swan,	(5 to 4)	1
1816*	SHIRLEY'S DELIGHT (Ire) 10-6 P Carberry,	(10 to 9 on)	2
2122^{4}	HUNCHEON CHANCE 10-2 (5*) J P Broderick,	(20 to 1)	3
2156^{3}	THE SALTY FROG (Ire) 10-11 M Flynn,	(14 to 1)	4
1983^{3}	SKIPO (USA) 10-7 B Sheridan,	(7 to 1)	5
	TEXAS FRIDAY (Ire) 10-2 (5*) T J O'Sullivan,	(25 to 1)	6
2122^{9}	HOME PARK (Ire) 10-7 A Powell,	(33 to 1)	7

Dist: 3l, 15l, 12l, dist. 4m 15.20s. a 27.20s (7 Ran).

(Michael Tabor), E J O'Grady

2286 Baileys Arkle Perpetual Challenge Cup Chase (Listed -Grade 2) (6-y-o and up) £8,280 2m 3f........... (2:10)

2079* ATONE 7-11-6 K F O'Brien, *wtd wth, prog into second appr 2 out, rdn to ld approaching last, ran on.*
.... (9 to 4 fav) 1
1893* BELVEDERIAN 7-12-0 G Bradley, *wl plcd, led appr 2 out till approaching last, styd on*................. (5 to 2) 2
1900* BUCKS-CHOICE 7-11-6 A Maguire, *trkd ldrs, mstks 6th and 3 out, chlgd appr last, kpt on one pace r-in.* (5 to 1) 3
18175 VISIBLE DIFFERENCE 8-12-0 C F Swan, *mid-div, trkd ldrs into strt, 4th last, wknd r-in*................. (16 to 1) 4
2198* MUBADIR (USA) 6-11-10 P Carberry, *hld up, blun 4th, rdn in 5th 3 out, sn btn*.......................... (3 to 1) 5
2075* FABRICATOR 8-12-0 C O'Dwyer, *led till appr 2 out, wknd quickly*..(12 to 1) 6
1893³ GYPSY LASS 7-11-1 T Horgan, *rear, lost tch 8th, pld up entering strt*................................(33 to 1) pu
Dist: 6l, 9l, 25l. 5m 10.40s. a 27.40s (7 Ran).
SR: 56/58/49/48/19/-/-/ (Robert Sinclair), J R Cox

2287 A.I.G. Europe Champion Hurdle (Listed Grade I) (4-y-o and up) £30,250 2m (2:45)

1906* FORTUNE AND FAME 7-11-10 A Maguire, *rear, prog to track ldrs 3 out, led nxt, pushed out r-in, eased cl hme.*
.... (5 to 4 on) 1
1849³ DANOLI (Ire) 6-11-10 C F Swan, *wl plcd, dsptd ld appr 3 out to nxt, rdn and kpt on well strt*............. (12 to 1) 2
1554³ SHAWIYA (Ire) 5-11-1 N Williamson, *wl plcd, dsptd ld appr 3 out to nxt, rdn and wknd bef last*............ (11 to 2) 3
1663 GRANVILLE AGAIN 8-11-10 R Dunwoody, *trkd ldrs, rdn 2 out, no imprsn strt*............................(7 to 2) 4
1906⁴ DESTRIERO 8-11-10 K F O'Brien, *mid-div, rdn in 4th entering strt, not rch ldrs*.......................(11 to 2) 5
1906² PADASHPAN (USA) 5-11-6 P Morris, *rear, rdn and lost tch appr 5th*.......................................(16 to 1) 6
1818* PADRE MIO (Ire) 6-11-10 G Bradley, *led till appr 3 out, sn wknd*.. (16 to 1) 7
Dist: 1½l, 10l, 5l, 3½l. 4m 7.10s. a 19.10s (7 Ran).
SR: 73/71/52/56/52/-/-/ (Michael W J Smurfit), D K Weld

2288 Pierse Leopardstown Chase (Listed) (5-y-o and up) £14,375 3m (3:15)

2125 HIGH PEAK [-] 10-10-0 C F Swan, *mid-div, prog to track ldrs 8th, led appr 2 out, styd on strly*............(7 to 2) 1
2077* BUCKBOARD BOUNCE [-] 8-10-10 (6ex) R Dunwoody, *led 1st till appr 2 out, mstk last, kpt on*............. (11 to 2) 2
1850⁸ SON OF WAR [-] 7-10-11 F Woods, *trkd ldrs, in 5th 3 out, styd on strt*................................ (7 to 1) 3
1850⁶ EBONY JANE [-] 9-11-2 C O'Dwyer, *trkd ldrs, 3rd and ev ch 2 out, rdn and wknd appr last*................ (8 to 1) 4
1895³ FORCE SEVEN [-] 7-11-4 A Maguire, *mid-div, rdn in 4th appr 2 out, sn btn*...............................(6 to 4 fav) 5
1856 HAKI SAKI [-] 8-10-11 G M O'Neill, *mid-div, blun 9th, rdn and lost tch 12th*...........................(10 to 1) 6
1895⁴ GENERAL IDEA [-] 9-12-0 B Sheridan, *al rear*...... (7 to 1) 7
RIVER TARQUIN [-] (bl) 10-11-1 K F O'Brien, *wl plcd till rdn and wknd appr 4 out*......................(14 to 1) 8
1381⁷ DYSART LASS [-] 9-10-0 N Williamson, *wl plcd till rdn, lost tch 9th, pld up aftr 13th*...............(25 to 1) pu
Dist: 7l, 1½l, 2l, 25l. 6m 44.90s. a 32.90s (9 Ran).
SR: 43/46/45/48/25/-/ (J P McManus), E J O'Grady

2289 Sugarloaf I N H Flat Race (5-y-o and up) £3,105 2¼m (3:45)

1383* BUCK THE TIDE (Ire) 5-10-9 Mr T Mullins, ...(13 to 8 fav) 1
GLINT OF EAGLES (Ire) 5-11-0 (7*) Mr S P McCarthy,
.... (10 to 1) 2
2161⁴ FLYING COLUMN 7-11-6 (5*) Mr H F Cleary, ...(10 to 1) 3
1687² CLOGRECON BOY (Ire) 6-11-6 (5*) Mr P J Casey, (12 to 1) 4
1916³ DUEONE (Ire) 6-11-11 Mr A J Martin, ...(14 to 1) 5
1786* GLEN TEN (Ire) 5-11-6 (3*) Mrs J M Mullins, ...(5 to 1) 6
1018 SPEAK OF THE DEVIL 7-11-11 (7*) Mr D McDonnell,
.... (20 to 1) 7
1827² AN MAINEACH (Ire) 5-11-4 (3*) Miss M Olivefalk, ...(7 to 1) 8
2123⁷ BALLYBODEN 7-11-4 (7*) Mr B Moran, ...(10 to 1) 9
1910² DAENIS (Ire) 6-11-4 (7*) Mr M Brennan, ...(5 to 1) 10
1815⁷ HIGH TONE (Ire) 5-11-4 (3*) Mr J A Nash, ...(5 to 2) 11
67⁵ SWANING AROUND (Ire) 5-11-4 (3*) Mr D Marnane,
.... (25 to 1) 12
1833⁴ A MONKEY FOR DICK (Ire) 5-11-0 (7*) Mr E Magee, (20 to 1) 13
FRANCOIS'S CRUMPET (Ire) 6-11-3 (3*) Mr A R Coonan,
.... (14 to 1) 14
Dist: 6l, 1½l, 20l, 1l. 4m 27.80s. (14 Ran).
(Mrs Rionda Braga), P Mullins

2290 Foxrock I N H Flat Race (4-y-o) £3,105 2m (4:15)

SOVEREIGN CHOICE (Ire) 11-2 (3*) Mr J A Nash, (7 to 4 fav) 1
SUBLIME FELLOW (Ire) 11-0 (7*) J P Broderick, ...(8 to 1) 2
SHANES HERO (Ire) 10-12 (7*) Mr B M Cash, ...(10 to 1) 3
MOSES PREY (Ire) 11-3 (3*) Mr H F Cleary, ...(7 to 2) 4
BALLYQUIN BELLE (Ire) 10-7 (7*) Mr E Norris, ...(6 to 1) 5
KIMANICKY (Ire) 10-12 (7*) K D Maher, ...(14 to 1) 6
SHINOUMA 11-2 (3*) Mrs J M Mullins, ...(6 to 1) 7

CONCLAVE (Ire) 10-12 (7*) Miss J Lewis, ...(8 to 1) 8
CASTLEGRACE BOY (Ire) 10-12 (7*) Mr M P Dunne,
.... (12 to 1) 9
LORD BARNARD (Ire) 11-2 (3*) Miss C Hutchinson, (10 to 1) 10
DERRYSHERIDAN 11-5 Mr J A Berry, ...(12 to 1) 11
Dist: Nk, ½l, 6l, 2l. 4m 11.60s. (11 Ran).
(Michael W J Smurfit), D K Weld

LEICESTER (heavy (races 1,2,5,6), good to soft (3,4))
Monday January 24th
Going Correction: PLUS 2.15 sec. per fur. (races 1,2,-5,6), PLUS 1.95 (3,4)

2291 Croxton Park Novices' Hurdle (4-y-o and up) £2,037 2m (1:30)

GOOGLY 5-11-0 A Maguire, *hld up early, hdwy to track ldr frm 4th, led 3 out, hit last, edgd lft, kpt on.*
.... (7 to 4 fav tchd 15 to 8) 1
PARADISE NAVY 5-11-5 R Dunwoody, *led, not fluent, hit 4th, hdd 3 out, kpt on one pace.*
.... (4 to 1 tchd 9 to 2 and 7 to 2) 2
1773⁵ GAYLOIRE (Ire) 5-10-12 (7*) Mr A Harvey, *al prmnt, outpcd 4 out, rallied and styd on frm 2 out.* (5 to 1 op 7 to 2) 3
BENTICO 5-11-5 C Llewellyn, *trkd ldrs, rdn appr 4 out, sn btn, tld off*...................................(14 to 1) 4
2057 MISTRESS MINX 5-10-7 (7*) Mr N Bradley, *al beh, tld off aftr 5th*..(66 to 1) 5
1969⁴ GRIFFINS BAR (v) 6-11-5 A Carroll, *rcd wide in last, hit 5th, wknd appr 4 out*.............................(25 to 1) 6
2029 NORTH HOLLOW 9-11-0 (5*) Mr D McCain, *al beh, tld off frm 4th*..(100 to 1 op 50 to 1) 7
1990⁴ VOLUNTEER POINT (Ire) 4-10-2 (5*) J Burke, *chsd ldrs till wknd appr 5th, tld off*.......................(9 to 1 op 7 to 1) 8
WHAT A MOUNT 11-11-5 R Bellamy, *al beh, tld off whn pld up aftr 4th*..........................(200 to 1 op 100 to 1) pu
WOODYARD 5-11-0 (5*) T Eley, *al beh, tld off whn pld up bef 4 out*..............................(100 to 1) pu
1125 BACKSTABBER 4-10-7 R Greene, *prmnt to 3rd, tld off whn pld up bef 5th*............................(25 to 1 op 33 to 1) pu
1745⁸ SWINGING SONG 7-11-5 B Dalton, *al beh, tld off whn pld up bef 3 out*..(50 to 1) pu
Dist: 2l, 1½l, dist, 10l, 8l, dist, 20l. 4m 22.80s. a 39.80s (12 Ran).
SR: 32/35/33/-/-/-/ (Ms M Horan), J White

2292 Brook Conditional Jockeys' Selling Handicap Hurdle (4 - 7-y-o) £1,764 2m (2:00)

2048⁸ MORIARTY [66] 7-10-0 J McCarthy, *hld up in rear, steady hdwy 5th, led 2 out, clr whn mstk last.*
.... (16 to 1 op 14 to 1 tchd 20 to 1) 1
2204⁴ RAGGERTY (Ire) [76] 4-10-10 N Bentley, *trkd ldr, rdn 5th, led 4 out, hdd 2 out, btn whn hit last.*
.... (7 to 4 op 7 to 4 tchd 9 to 4) 2
1699² JOKERS PATCH [69] 7-10-3 A Thornton, *hld up, hdwy 4th, one pace frm 3 out*......(5 to 1 op 4 to 1 tchd 11 to 2) 3
2142⁷ BAYBEEJAY [70] (bl) 7-10-4 T Dascombe, *hld up, hdwy 5th, rdn and wknd appr 2 out*......(11 to 2 op 4 to 1) 4
2138⁷ PINECONE PETER [89] (v) 7-11-4 (5*) R Moore, *mid-div, effrt 5th, wknd appr 3 out*....................(7 to 1 op 5 to 1) 5
1867³ MECADO [94] (v) 7-11-9 (5*) M Berry, *beh aftr hit 3rd, tld off whn pld up bef 2 out*................(7 to 1 op 6 to 1) pu
970 SATIN LAKE (USA) [72] 7-10-6⁴ P Midgley, *chsd ldrs, rdn and wknd aftr 5th, tld off whn pld up bef last.*
.... (7 to 1 op 5 to 1) pu
2185 PEACOCK FEATHER [83] 6-10-12 (5*) N Juckes, *led, clr 3rd, hdd 4 out, wknd quickly, pld up bef 2 out.*
.... (10 to 1 op 8 to 1) pu
Dist: 10l, 6l, 12l, 1½l. 4m 25.80s. a 42.80s (8 Ran).
(Mrs K Oseman), R J Price

2293 Dick Christian Novices' Chase (6-y-o and up) £2,776 2½m 110yds (2:30)

RAYMYLETTE 7-10-12 R Dunwoody, *pld hrd, hdwy to ld aftr second, drw clr frm 3 out*...............(11 to 4 jt-fav op 7 to 4 tchd 3 to 1) 1
ROUYAN 8-10-12 I Lawrence, *wtd wth, hdwy to track wnr tenth, mstk and wknd 3 out.*
.... (7 to 2 op 9 to 2 tchd 6 to 1) 2
1836³ KEV'S LASS (Ire) 6-10-0 (7*) P Murphy, *al beh, nvr on terms*......................................(16 to 1) 3
2031 RIDAKA 7-10-12 N Williamson, *rcd wide, led ld aftr second, trkd wnr to 5th, mstk 7th, wknd 3 out*
.... (40 to 1 op 33 to 1 tchd 50 to 1) 4
1866⁵ ASK THE GOVERNOR 8-10-12 E Leonard, *towards rear, f 4 out*........................(12 to 1 tchd 14 to 1) f
542⁰ BOOK OF RUNES 8-10-12 C Llewellyn, *trkd ldr, sent second and briefly an jmpd lft 7th, tried to refuse and uns rdr 9th*...................................(20 to 1 op 12 to 1) ur
1812³ SMILES AHEAD 6-10-12 (5*) T Eley, *prmnt, chsd wnr 5th to 7th, second ag'n nxt to tenth, wknd appr 4 out, pld up bef 2 out*..............................(20 to 1 tchd 50 to 1) pu

2031² CHICHELL'S HURST 8-10-7 A Carroll, *mstks in rear, tld off whn pld up bef 8th*.................(11 to 2 op 5 to 1) pu
1834 UNEXIS 9-10-12 S Earle, *in rear, pld up bef 8th*.
.................(33 to 1 op 20 to 1) pu
MAYOR OF LISCARROL 9-10-12 Mr S Brisby, *al beh, tld off whn pld up bef 4 out*.............(66 to 1 op 50 to 1) pu
2170² RAMSTAR 11-4-4 A Maguire, *in tch, hit 5th, wkng whn mstk 4 out, tld off when pld up bef 2 out*...(11 to 4 jt-fav op 7 to 2 tchd 4 to 1) pu
Dist: 30l, 30l, 10l. 5m 46.60s. a 43.60s (11 Ran).
SR: 48/18/-/-/-/-/ (Lady Lloyd Webber), N J Henderson

2294 Rabbit Handicap Chase (0-105 5-y-o and up) £3,340 3m.............(3:00)

2084 CHRISTMAS GORSE [76] 8-10-0 C Llewellyn, *hld up in mid-div, steady hdwy 5 out, led appr 2 out, cmftbly*.
.........................(10 to 1 op 12 to 1) 1
1941* VIVA BELLA (Fr) [90] (bl) 7-10-9 (5*) J Burke, *nvr far away, ev ch 2 out, one pace*.(16 to 1 op 14 to 1 tchd 20 to 1) 2
1423⁴ CHOCTAW [95] 10-11-5 C Hawkins, *al prmnt, led 6th till hdd and wknd appr 2 out*........(25 to 1 op 20 to 1) 3
2136 FAST CRUISE [90] 9-10-11 (3*) A Thornton, *chsd ldrs, no hdwy frm 3 out*...........................(20 to 1) 4
2001⁵ WOODLANDS GENHIRE [77] (v) 9-10-0² (3*) R Davis, *beh till hdwy hfwy, styd on one pace frm 3 out*.
.........................(16 to 1 op 14 to 1 tchd 20 to 1) 5
1925* THE TARTAN SPARTAN [99] 10-11-2 (7*) P Ward, *prmnt, hit 5 out, wknd aftr nxt*........(6 to 1 jt-fav op 5 to 1) 6
1083⁴ TRIBAL RULER [97] 9-11-7 G McCourt, *prmnt till wknd 13th*............................(16 to 1 tchd 20 to 1) 7
1635⁵ CLONROCHE DRILLER [94] 9-10-11 (7*) Mr D Parker, *al towards rear*........................(33 to 1) 8
1600⁶ SHEEPHAVEN [99] 10-11-9 R Supple, *al beh, tld off*.
.........................(16 to 1) 9
2143 TAGMOUN CHAUFOUR (Fr) [84] 9-10-8 B Powell, *al towards rear, tld off*....................(50 to 1) 10
2136* CONCERT PAPER [94] (v) 10-10-11 (7*) K Davies, *led 3rd to 6th, rdn and wknd 12th, tld off*............(8 to 1) 11
1884⁷ NOTARY-NOWELL [83] 8-10-7 A Maguire, *in rear whn blun tenth, tld off*...............(20 to 1 op 16 to 1) 12
2184² LEAGAUNE [89] 12-10-13 R Dunwoody, *in tch till wknd 8th, tld off frm 13th*..................(14 to 1) 13
2001⁴ THE FORTIES [92] 9-11-2 J Railton, *f 5th*.
.........................(14 to 1 op 20 to 1) f
1730 MISTRESS McKENZIE [76] 8-10-8 R Greene, *led to second, wknd tenth, tld off whn f 3 out*..............(100 to 1) f
1720 BERESFORDS GIRL [104] 9-12-0 E Murphy, *blun and uns rdr 1st*.............(14 to 1 op 12 to 1) ur
1625 GADBROOK [88] (v) 12-10-12 L Harvey, *sn beh, tld off whn pld up aftr 8th*......................(33 to 1) pu
2191³ BETTY HAYES [100] 10-11-10 Mr J Durkan, *al beh, blun badly 4 out, sn pld up*........(14 to 1 op 10 to 1) pu
1254⁴ JIMSTRO [101] 9-11-11 M Ahern, *led second to 3rd, tld off whn pld up bef 9th*.......(25 to 1 op 20 to 1) pu
1943² SILVERINO [98] 8-11-8 M Richards, *al beh, tld off whn pld up bef 4 out*..................(14 to 1 tchd 16 to 1) pu
WOODY WILL [99] 8-11-9 J Osborne, *al beh, jmpd badly lft 11th, tld off whn pld up bef 3 out*.........(14 to 1) pu
1943* TAMMY'S FRIEND [103] (bl) 7-11-13 I Lawrence, *chsd ldrs, wkng whn mstk 5 out, pld up bef nxt*.......(6 to 1 jt-fav op 7 to 2 tchd 4 to 1) pu
Dist: 6l, 12l, 7l, 4l, 1l, 2½l, 2½l, 12l, 3l. 6m 46.50s. a 54.50s (22 Ran).
SR: -/3/-/-/-/-/ (D R Stoddart), N A Gaselee

2295 Stonesby Novices' Hurdle (5-y-o and up) £1,989 3m.................(3:30)

1994² TOTHEWOODS 6-11-6 C Llewellyn, *hld up, smooth hdwy 9th, led 3 out, sn clr, eased r-in*.
.........................(11 to 10 on op 5 to 4 on tchd Evens) 1
934* CORNER BOY 7-11-6 A Maguire, *slwly away, settled in rear, hdwy 8th, ev ch 3 out, second and hld whn mstk 2 out, no extr*.........(9 to 4 op 2 to 1 tchd 5 to 2) 2
1704 JUST A SECOND 9-10-9 R Dunwoody, *al frnt rnk, rdn appr 4 out, kpt on one pace*......(25 to 1 op 16 to 1) 3
1775* VERY LITTLE (Ire) 6-11-1 S Earle, *trkd ldrs frm hfwy, ev ch 4 out, wknd aftr nxt*. (10 to 1 op 8 to 1 tchd 14 to 1) 4
1938⁵ BARNEY RUBBLE 9-11-0 M Moloney, *trkd ldrs, led appr 9th, hdd 3 out, wknd*......(25 to 1 op 16 to 1) 5
KILLURA (Ire) 6-11-0 N Williamson, *mid-div, effrt 8th, wknd nxt, tld off*..................(7 to 1 op 5 to 1) 6
1948² BLUE LYZANDER 5-10-9 D Bridgwater, *prmnt till lost pl 6th, hdd 8th, wknd appr 4 out, tld off*.
.........................(33 to 1 op 16 to 1) 7
PHILIPPONNAT (USA) 8-11-0 C Maude, *prmnt to 4th, sn beh, tld off whn pld up aftr 8th*. (100 to 1 op 33 to 1) pu
1747⁹ SENNA BLUE 9-11-0 V Slattery, *prmnt till wknd before quickly appr 4 out, pld up bef nxt*..................(50 to 1) pu
952 ANA BLAKE 7-10-4 (5*) D Matthews, *led, mstk 4th, hdd and wknd quickly appr 9th, pld up sn aftr*.
.........................(100 to 1 op 50 to 1) pu
1951⁵ NO BATTERY NEEDED 7-11-0 R Supple, *in tch till wknd quickly 9th, tld off whn pld up bef 4 out*.
.........................(100 to 1 op 50 to 1) pu
Dist: 3½l, 1½l, ½l, 12l, dist. 6m 53.60s. a 66.60s (11 Ran).
(Robert Cooper), N A Twiston-Davies

2296 Daniel Lambert Handicap Hurdle (0-125 5-y-o and up) £2,721 2½m 110yds........................(4:00)

1206⁹ STORMHEAD [115] 6-11-10 J Osborne, *made all, hit 1st, quickened wl whn chlgd 2 out, rdn out*.
.........................(7 to 1 op 4 to 1) 1
2172 DAMIER BLANC (Fr) [96] (bl) 5-10-4 R Dunwoody, *hld up, gd hdwy to go second 3 out, ev ch nxt, rdn and no imprsn r-in*...............(4 to 1 op 7 to 2) 2
2082⁴ SYLVIA BEACH [96] 8-10-5 E Murphy, *chsd wnr to 3 out, rdn and wknd nxt*...............(7 to 1 op 6 to 1) 3
2086³ ZEALOUS KITTEN (USA) [98] 6-10-2 J McCarthy, *nvr far away, rdn appr 4 out, wknd nxt*.....(5 to 1 op 6 to 1) 4
RED RING [99] 7-10-8 W Marston, *prmnt till wknd appr 2 out*.........................(20 to 1 op 16 to 1) 5
2108² SANSOOL [101] 8-10-10 M Moloney, *chsd ldrs, rdn 7th, sn btn*.........(100 to 30 fav op 3 to 1 tchd 9 to 2) 6
1867* MILDRED SOPHIA [91] 7-9-7 (7*) Miss S Mitchell, *hld up in rear, gd hdwy appr 4 out, wknd quickly aftr nxt*.
.........................(7 to 1 op 4 to 1) 7
1720 HEYFLEET [91] (bl) 11-10-0 I Lawrence, *al beh, tld off frm 5th*...............(25 to 1 tchd 33 to 1) 8
2082* IMA DELIGHT [96] 7-10-5 A Carroll, *beh, hdwy 6th, wknd 4 out, wl behind whn jmpd badly lft 2 out, tld off*.
.........................(11 to 2 op 9 to 2 tchd 6 to 1) 9
2168 MRS MAYHEW (Ire) [94] 6-10-3 A Maguire, *refused to race*.
.........................(12 to 1 op 10 to 1) 10
Dist: 1½l, 15l, 12l, 8l, 3l, 2½l, dist, 10l. 5m 36.30s. a 48.30s (10 Ran).
SR: 54/32/18/8/1/-/ (M L Oberstein), O Sherwood

CHEPSTOW (soft)
Tuesday January 25th
Going Correction: PLUS 2.35 sec. per fur. (races 1,3,5), PLUS 2.15 (2,4,6)

2297 Ralph Morel Handicap Chase (0-140 5-y-o and up) £2,745 2m 3f 110yds
........................(1:20)

2143⁵ RAFIKI [105] 9-10-12 S Burrough, *hit 5th, narrow ld frm 6th, styd on wl from 3 out, all out*.
.........................(100 to 30 op 4 to 1 tchd 3 to 1) 1
1993³ GRANGE BRAKE [117] (bl) 8-11-10 C Llewellyn, *led to 3rd, hit 5th, shaken up tenth, drvn alng 12th, ran on frm last, not rch wnr*........(11 to 4 op 9 to 4 tchd 3 to 1) 2
2170* CASTLE DIAMOND [100] 7-10-7 R Dunwoody, *led 3rd to 6th, wth wnr till outpcd appr last*.
.........................(5 to 4 fav op Evens tchd 6 to 4) 3
2020² CHIASSO FORTE (Ity) [100] 11-10-7 M Hourigan, *not fluent early, jmpd slwly 7th and 8th, hdwy 12th, sn btn*.
.........................(11 to 2 op 4 to 1 tchd 6 to 1) 4
Dist: 1½l, 7l, 25l. 5m 38.40s. a 51.40s (4 Ran).
SR: 28/38/14/-/ (J P Carrington), Mrs J G Retter

2298 Clive Graham Handicap Hurdle (5-y-o and up) £4,406 3m.............(1:50)

1972* CAPTAIN DOLFORD [113] 7-10-6 (5*) J McCarthy, *prmnt, chlgd 4th to 5th, led four out, wnt clr 2 out*.
.........................(11 to 2 op 9 to 2) 1
2034² FLYER'S NAP [105] 8-10-3 S Earle, *in tch, chsd ldrs 7th, chlgd 4 out till outpaced 2 out*...........(4 to 1 co-fav op 11 to 2) 2
MAN FOR ALL SEASON (USA) [102] 8-10-0 M Hourigan, *chsd ldrs, shaken up and styd on frm 2 out*.
.........................(15 to 1 op 25 to 1 tchd 33 to 1 and 16 to 1) 3
2009³ BUONARROTI [126] 7-11-10 T Grantham, *hld up, pushed alng 7th, hdwy 4 out, no imprsn 2 out*......(4 to 1 co-fav op 7 to 2) 4
1884² GRENAGH [118] 13-11-2 W Marston, *hdwy to chase ldrs 6th, one pace 3 out*.....(7 to 1 op 11 to 2 tchd 8 to 1) 5
SNOWY LANE (Ire) [118] (v) 6-11-2 R Dunwoody, *made most to 4 out, sn wknd*...............(12 to 1 op 8 to 1) 6
1884 LEAVENWORTH [106] 10-10-4 S Burrough, *beh, effrt appr 4 out, sn wknd*............(40 to 1 op 20 to 1) 7
2172 STIRRUP CUP [126] 10-11-10 J Railton, *prmnt till drpd rear 6th, pld up bef nxt*...........(33 to 1 op 16 to 1) pu
2172³ LINKSIDE [116] 9-11-0 D Murphy, *prmnt till drpd rear 7th, tld off whn pld up bef 2 out*.............(4 to 1 co-fav op 3 to 1 tchd 9 to 2) pu
1653³ CORACO [106] 7-10-4 D Bridgwater, *beh, rdn 6th, wknd quickly and pld up bef 4 out*.
.........................(10 to 1 op 14 to 1 tchd 9 to 1) pu
Dist: 15l, 6l, 2½l, 1½l, 8l, 25l. 6m 34.20s. a 56.20s (10 Ran).
SR: 37/14/3/24/14/6/ (R E Brinkworth), D R Gandolfo

2299 Aspiring Champions Novices' Chase (5-y-o and up) £3,659 3m...... (2:20)

1973* MUDAHIM 8-11-11 W Marston, *led to second, led 9th, wnt clr frm 14th*.................(6 to 4 on op 5 to 4 on) 1

2010* EARTH SUMMIT (bl) 6-12-0 C Llewellyn, *led second, sn hdd, blun 6th, pushed alng 8th, chlgd 11th to 13th, outpcd nxt*.................(11 to 8 op 5 to 4 tchd 6 to 4) 2

2084⁶ WILLIE MCGARR (USA) 9-11-5 R Dunwoody, *led aftr second, clr 7th, hdd 9th, wknd tenth, hit 13th, no ch frm nxt, blun last*......................(25 to 1 op 20 to 1) 3

2206⁸ PHYL'S LEGACY 9-11-0 D Bridgwater, *beh till f 6th*.
.....................................(120 to 1 op 100 to 1) f

2170 ROMANY CREEK (Ire) 5-10-7 J Frost, *hit second, not fluent, al beh, tld off whn pld up bef 14th*.
....(50 to 1 op 33 to 1) pu

1189⁵ SHAAB TURBO 8-11-5 S Burrough, *hdwy and hit 8th, wknd and mstk nxt, tld off whn pld up bef 4 out*.
....(20 to 1 op 14 to 1) pu

Dist: 25l, 7l. 7m 2.50s. a 72.50s (6 Ran).

(K W Bell), C D Broad

2300 Grouse Juvenile Novices' Hurdle (4-y-o) £1,968 2m 110yds..........(2:50)

DEVILS DEN (Ire) 11-0 R Dunwoody, *str hold early, trkd ldrs, chlgd 4 out, narrow ld nxt, wnt clr 2 out, readily*.
......................................(11 to 8 on op 5 to 4) 1

CYBORGO (Fr) 11-0 M Foster, *chsd ldrs, drvn to ld appr 4 out, hdd nxt, styd on, no ch wth wnr*.
....(3 to 1 op 12 to 1) 2

2016* LOVE YOU MADLY (Ire) 11-1 J Lower, *beh 3rd, effrt appr 4 out, sn wknd*........(14 to 1 op 10 to 1 tchd 16 to 1) 3

1504⁹ IMAD (USA) 11-0 W McFarland, *hdwy to chase ldrs 4th, wknd four out*......(12 to 1 op 6 to 1 tchd 14 to 1) 4

2190* FOOLS ERRAND (Ire) 11-6 D Murphy, *led till hdd and slpd up bend appr 4 out*..(3 to 1 op 9 to 4 tchd 100 to 30) su

1007 POLLY LEACH 10-9 B Powell, *jmpd slwly 1st, str hold, beh 4th, tld off whn pld up bef 4 out*..(66 to 1 op 33 to 1) pu

2014⁴ PAPER DAYS 11-6 E Murphy, *tld off second, pld up bef 4 out*.........(5 to 1 op 11 to 2 tchd 6 to 1 and 4 to 1) pu

2169⁴ VELVET HEART (Ire) 11-1 S Burrough, *chsd ldrs till appr 4 out, sn wknd, tld off whn pld up bef 2 out*.
......................................(14 to 1 tchd 20 to 1) pu

Dist: 8l, 30l, 20l. 4m 31.00s. a 45.00s (8 Ran).

(T Beresford), M C Pipe

2301 Earthstoppers Hunters' Chase (6-y-o and up) £1,548 3m.............(3:20)

DOUBLE SILK 10-11-11 (5*) Mr R Treloggen, *jmpd wl, led second, wnt clr appr 14th, easily*.
....(7 to 4 on op 9 to 4 on) 1

SALCOMBE HARBOUR (Ire) 10-11-3 (7*) Dr P Pritchard, *prmnt, chsd wnr frm 8th, chlgd 12th, sn outpcd*.
....(33 to 1 op 20 to 1) 2

RUSTY BRIDGE 7-11-3 (7*) Mr R Johnson, *mstk 4th, blun 7th, hdwy 12th, no ch whn hit 14th*.
....(9 to 1 op 6 to 1) 3

EASTER FROLIC 12-11-3 (7*) Mr A Phillips, *in tch, effrt 9th, blun tenth, hit 13th, no ch aftr*..(25 to 1 op 14 to 1) 4

DOUBTING DONNA 8-11-8⁷ (7*) Mr V Hughes, *mid-div whn f 6th*.................................(16 to 1 op 12 to 1) f

SPORTING MARINER 12-11-3 (7*) Mr D Bloor, *mstk and uns rdr 5th*...........................(50 to 1 op 20 to 1) ur

PARKBHRIDE 8-11-3 (7*) Mr J A Llewellyn, *beh whn hmpd and uns rdr 6th*....................(10 to 1 op 6 to 1) ur

MAJESTIC BUCK 14-11-5 (5*) Miss P Jones, *led to second, mstk 8th, blun 9th, tld off whn pld up aftr 11th*.
........................(33 to 1 op 25 to 1 tchd 40 to 1) pu

MY MELLOW MAN 11-11-5 (5*) Miss P Curling, *al beh, tld off whn pld up bef 3 out*.
.......................(6 to 1 op 7 to 1 tchd 5 to 1 and 13 to 2) pu

Dist: 25l, 10l, 1½l. 7m 11.20s. a 81.20s (9 Ran).

(R C Wilkins), R C Wilkins

2302 Quail Novices' Handicap Hurdle (0-100 5-y-o and up) £2,108 2m 110yds ....(3:50)

GO MARY [68] 8-10-0 W Marston, *sn in tch, mstk 4th, led appr nxt, clr aftr 3 out, rdn and wnt lft, pushed out*.
....(33 to 1 op 20 to 1 tchd 50 to 1) 1

1946⁵ WITH IMPUNITY [94] 5-11-12 C Llewellyn, *wth ldr, led second till appr 5th, styd on, no ch wth wnr*.
....(5 to 1 tchd 11 to 2) 2

2030 FIRST LESSON (NZ) [68] 8-11-3 M Hourigan, *led to second, str hold, one pace 4 out*..........(9 to 1 op 8 to 1) 3

1953 NAVAL BATTLE [68] 7-10-0 R Dunwoody, *chsd ldrs, mstk second, no prog frm 4 out*.
....(9 to 1 op 8 to 1 tchd 10 to 1) 4

1661 DURSHAN (USA) [76] 5-10-8 D Murphy, *beh and rdn 4th, hdwy appr 5th, sn btn*..(9 to 2 op 7 to 2 tchd 5 to 1) 5

1866 PRINCE VALMY (Fr) [68] (bl) 9-10-0 B Powell, *al beh*.
....(66 to 1 op 33 to 1) 6

1878⁶ CHEMIN LE ROI [90] 7-11-8 I Lawrence, *hdwy to chase ldrs 3rd, rdn aftr nxt, sn wknd*..........(9 to 2 op 7 to 2) 7

1791⁸ BARAHIN (Ire) [76] 5-10-8 D O'Sullivan, *al beh*.
....(14 to 1 op 8 to 1) 8

1804³ STERLING BUCK (USA) [72] 7-10-4 W McFarland, *al beh*.
....(17 to 1 op 8 to 1 tchd 10 to 1) 9

1882⁴ FIRST CENTURY (Ire) [76] 5-10-1 (7*) Mr J L Llewellyn, *in tch, disputing 3rd but no ch wth wnr whn mstk and uns rdr 3 out*.........(12 to 1 op 8 to 1 tchd 14 to 1) ur

HIGHLAND BRAVE [68] 7-10-0 L Harvey, *sn beh, tld off whn pld up bef 4 out*..........(66 to 1 op 33 to 1) pu

2088² MASTER MURPHY [68] 5-10-0 E Murphy, *al beh, tld off whn pld up bef 4 out*.
....(4 to 1 fav op 5 to 1 tchd 11 to 2) pu

2147 FIFTH IN LINE (Ire) [68] (bl) 6-10-0 C Maude, *beh 3rd, tld off whn pld up bef 4 out*.......(50 to 1 op 33 to 1) pu

Dist: 25l, 15l, 1½l, 8l, 10l, 4l, 20l, 25l. 4m 32.30s. a 46.30s (13 Ran).

(Miss C Phillips), Miss C Phillips

NOTTINGHAM (soft)
Tuesday January 25th
Going Correction: PLUS 1.90 sec. per fur. (races 1,4,6), PLUS 1.25 (2,3,5)

2303 Wilford Novices' Hurdle (4-y-o and up) £2,138 2m.....................(1:30)

1473² MOORISH 4-10-6 A Maguire, *keen hold, confidently rdn, hdwy on bit to ld bef last, sn clr*.
..........................(6 to 4 fav op 11 to 8 tchd 7 to 4) 1

1951² THE FROG PRINCE (Ire) 6-11-3 R Supple, *patiently rdn, cld 3 out, kpt on wl, no ch wth wnr*. (8 to 1 op 6 to 1) 2

2251 VASILIEV (v) 6-11-3 C Grant, *trkd ldg bunch, pushed alng and reminders 4 out, rallied last 2, styd on*.
....(14 to 1 op 12 to 1) 3

1872⁶ GOLDEN TORQUE 7-10-12 (5*) H Bastiman, *nvr far away, ev ch frm 3 out, rdn and kpt on same pace r-in*.
....(8 to 1 op 10 to 1 tchd 6 to 1) 4

2029⁴ TEST MATCH 7-11-3 Diane Clay, *al hndy, ev ch 3 out, rdn and one pace nxt*.....................(10 to 1 op 16 to 1) 5

1584³ ERICOLIN (Ire) 4-10-8² G McCourt, *patiently rdn, steady hdwy on outsd appr 3 out, shaken up betw last 2, one pace*................(5 to 1 op 5 to 1 tchd 7 to 1) 6

2245 UPWARD SURGE (Ire) 4-10-6 N Williamson, *led, rdn and hdd appr last, no extr*...................(33 to 1) 7

2130⁶ LORD NASKRA (USA) 5-11-3 R Campbell, *tracked away in midfield, steady hdwy aftr 4 out, hit nxt, eased whn btn*..(25 to 1) 8

1768⁵ ANNIE KELLY 6-10-12 B Dalton, *trkd ldg bunch, effrt aftr 4 out, blun nxt, not reco'r*.........(50 to 1 op 33 to 1) 9

2014 IVORLINE 7-11-3 V Slattery, *co'red up on ins, effrt hfwy, outpcd frm 3 out*.............(50 to 1 op 33 to 1) 10

1768³ DISTINCTIVE (Ire) 5-10-10 (7*) P Ward, *settled beh ldg bunch, effrt appr 3 out, no extr frm nxt*.
....(14 to 1 op 10 to 1) 11

ANAR (Ire) (v) 5-11-3 L O'Hara, *tracked away in midfield, feeling pace appr 3 out, fdd*......(50 to 1 op 25 to 1) 12

1320⁵ MOZEMO (bl) 7-11-10 J Osborne, *frnt rnk till fdd appr 3 out*.................(8 to 1 op 9 to 1 tchd 10 to 1) 13

1335³ BALLYHYLAND (Ire) 5-11-3 R Bellamy, *trkd ldrs, drvn alng appr 3 out, fdd*............(10 to 1 op 7 to 1) 14

WORKINGFORPEANUTS (Ire) 4-10-3² A Carroll, *settled off the pace, tld off frm hfwy*................(33 to 1) 15

2140 YOUNG GUS 7-11-3 P Niven, *settled beh ldg bunch, grad lost tch frm 4 out, eased whn btn*. (16 to 1 op 10 to 1) 16

1475⁶ DYNAMITE DAN (Ire) 6-11-3 M Dwyer, *settled gng wl, effrt appr 3 out, wknd and eased frm nxt*.
....(16 to 1 op 12 to 1) 17

851⁹ MULLED ALE (Ire) 4-10-1 M Richards, *wth ldrs, rdn whn pace quickened appr 3 out, fdd*....(33 to 1 op 20 to 1) 18

497 ARE YOU HAPPY (Ire) 4-9-8 (7*) J James, *settled midfield, drvn alng to hold pl aftr 4 out, sn btn*.
....(50 to 1 op 33 to 1) 19

KRISSOS 7-10-12 (5*) P Waggott, *trkd ldrs, struggling to hold pl aftr 4 out, sn lost tch*......(50 to 1 op 20 to 1) 20

1794 OURPALWENTY 7-10-10 (7*) Pat Thompson, *chsd ldg bunch to hfwy, lost tch quickly and pld up bef 3 out*.
....(50 to 1 op 33 to 1) pu

PERSIAN BUD (Ire) 6-11-3 M Bosley, *struggling to keep in tch hfwy, tailing off whn pld up bef 2 out*.
....(50 to 1 op 33 to 1) pu

Dist: 8l, sht-hd, 2l, 4l, nk, 3l, 10l, ½l, ½l, 2l. 4m 20.00s. a 36.00s (22 Ran).

SR: 22/25/32/23/19/9/4/5/-/   (Adrian Fitzpatrick), J White

2304 Arnold Novices' Chase (5-y-o and up) £2,541 2m.....................(2:00)

NAKIR (Fr) 6-11-3 J Osborne, *trkd clr ldr, drw level gng wl 3 out, hit nxt, led bef last, readily*. (11 to 2 op 9 to 2) 1

2007 FRONT LINE 7-11-3 N Williamson, *patiently rdn, improved frm off the pace 4 out, shaken up last, fnshd wl*..................................(10 to 1 op 7 to 1) 2

NEWLANDS-GENERAL 8-11-3 M Dwyer, *jmpd boldly, sn clr ldr, jnd 3 out, hit nxt, hdd and wknd appr last*.
....(100 to 30 op 5 to 2) 3

1956³ EMERALD RULER 7-11-3 G McCourt, *chsd ldrs, bustled alng to stay in tch hfwy, tld off appr 4 out*.
....(10 to 1 op 8 to 1 tchd 12 to 1) 4

1369³ DAN DE LYON 6-11-3 A Maguire, *tracking ldg pair whn f 4th*.................(10 to 1 op 7 to 1) f

1746⁹ EMERALD GEM 8-11-3 M Brennan, *tucked away, swrvd to avoid faller and uns rdr 4th.*
............................(14 to 1 op 12 to 1 tchd 16 to 1)   ur
1970² FRONT STREET 7-11-3 G Upton, *settled off the pace, steady hdwy whn blun 6 out and nxt, 3rd and one pace when pld up bef 2 out.*........(6 to 4 fav op 5 to 4)   pu
2144 MISS CRUISE 7-10-12 W Humphreys, *struggling to go pace hfwy, tld off whn pld up bef 4 out.*........(50 to 1)   pu
Dist: 4l, 15l, dist. 4m 16.30s. a 25.30s (8 Ran).

SR: 36/32/17/-/-/   (Jim Lewis), S Christian

2305 Ollerton Handicap Chase (0-125 5-y-o and up) £3,114 3m 110yds...... (2:30)

2001* SHRADEN LEADER [109] 9-11-3 A Tory, *patiently rdn, improved to ld 11th, girth extension broke and sddl slpd back frm 3 out, drw clr betw last 2.*
............................(11 to 4 fav op 9 to 4)   1
1744 YOUNG MINER [96] 8-10-4¹ G Upton, *led early, styd hndy, ev ch till rdn and outpcd betw last 2.*
............................(9 to 1 op 8 to 1 tchd 10 to 1)   2
2173 SMOOTH ESCORT [106] (v) 10-11-6 N Williamson, *led ecto 11th, rallied 4 out, not quicken nxt.*
............................(10 to 1 op 12 to 1)   3
2047⁵ MISS FERN [92] 9-9-11 (3*) D Meredith, *wtd wth, improved frm off the pace fnl circuit, ev ch 4 out, wknd from nxt.*
............................(14 to 1 op 10 to 1)   4
1836² MO ICHI DO [92] 8-9-9 (5*) T Eley, *trkd ldrs, drvn alng in midfield whn f 9th.*............... (25 to 1 op 20 to 1)   f
1503 HEY COTTAGE [110] 9-11-4 G McCourt, *trkd ldg bunch, effrt fnl circuit, tiring in 5th whn f 2 out.*
............................(20 to 1 op 25 to 1)   f
URANUS COLLONGES (Fr) [112] 8-11-6 P Niven, *steadied and swrvd strt, jmpd stickily in rear till blun and uns rdr 11th.*....................(8 to 1 op 7 to 1)   ur
1864⁵ POLAR REGION [116] 8-11-10 M Dwyer, *in tch for o'r a circuit, tld off whn pld up bef 3 out.*
............................(12 to 1 op 10 to 1)   pu
PEAJADE [113] 10-11-7 A Maguire, *settled to track ldrs, feeling pace and lost tch aftr 6 out, tld off whn pld up bef 4 out.*...................(8 to 1 op 6 to 1)   pu
2139³ MATT REID [110] 10-11-4 Mr W Morgan, *not fluent, al beh, pld up bef 3 out.*..............(9 to 1 op 8 to 1)   pu
1748² THE LAUGHING LORD [107] 8-10-12 (3*) A Thornton, *trkd ldrs, struggling fnl circuit, lost tch frm 6 out, pld up bef 4 out.*.....................(7 to 1 op 6 to 1)   pu
2047 NEARCO BAY [120] 10-12-0 M A FitzGerald, *wth ldr, blun 6th, struggling to hold pl fnl circuit, tld off whn pld up bef 4 out.*..........(25 to 1 op 16 to 1)   pu
Dist: 15l, sht-hd, 15l. 6m 41.20s. a 46.20s (12 Ran).

(W R J Everall), K C Bailey

2306 Carlton Handicap Hurdle (0-120 4-y-o and up) £2,284 2m............. (3:00)

1190⁸ CABIN HILL [99] 8-11-2 G McCourt, *patiently rdn, improved gng wl to ld aftr 3 out, hit nxt, hrd drvn r-in, kpt on.*........................(15 to 2 op 7 to 1)   1
2044⁴ ISLAND JEWEL [97] 6-11-0 M Bosley, *wtd wth, drvn up frm midfield 3 out, ev ch and hit last, kpt hrd rdn r-in, ran on.*..................(5 to 1 fav op 9 to 2 tchd 11 to 2)   2
2138⁴ PERSONAL HAZARD [93] 5-10-10 L Wyer, *co'red up beh ldrs, niggled alng to improve whn hit 3 out, rallied und pres r-in, no extr cl hme.*
............................(11 to 2 op 5 to 1 tchd 6 to 1)   3
1694⁵ RAMBLE (USA) [93] 7-10-10 A Maguire, *tucked away in midfield, improved to chal aftr 3 out, kpt on same pace frm last.*..................(6 to 1 op 4 to 1)   4
2168² IN TRUTH [85] 6-10-2 C Grant, *al hndy, led 4 out till aftr nxt, fdd betw last 2.*..............(12 to 1 op 10 to 1)   5
1960 OLD EROS [107] 10-11-10 P Niven, *led, clr 3rd, hdd 5th, rallied appr 3 out, wknd quickly aftr nxt.*
............................(9 to 1 op 8 to 1 tchd 10 to 1)   6
1619⁶ MYTHICAL STORM [94] 7-10-6 (5*) M Buckley, *patiently rdn, effrt and drvn alng appr 3 out, struggling nxt, btn, nvr able to chal.*...............(6 to 1 op 4 to 1)   7
1669⁶ TITUS GOLD [106] (v) 9-11-9 Diane Clay, *wth ldr, led 5th to nxt, ev ch till wknd quickly aftr 3 out.*
............................(14 to 1 op 12 to 1)   8
1487 MASTER GLEN [100] 6-10-12 (5*) P Midgley, *trkd ldg bunch, effrt and drvn alng appr 3 out, nvr able to chal.*
............................(50 to 1 op 33 to 1)   9
SODA POPINSKI (USA) [65] 6-10-2 P M Campbell, *settled off the pace, improved gng wl appr 3 out, wknd quickly frm nxt.*...........(25 to 1 op 20 to 1)   10
2142⁴ CARDINAL BIRD (USA) [95] (bl) 7-10-5 (7*) Chris Webb, *slwly away, reluctant to race, tld off whn refused and uns rdr 4 out.*..........................(6 to 1 op 9 to 2)   ref
Dist: 2l, nk, hd, 8l, 15l, 1½l, 5l, 12l, 8l. 4m 20.40s. a 36.40s (11 Ran).

SR: 28/24/19/19/3/10/-/2/-/   (The Kinnersley Crew), S Christian

2307 Bonnington Handicap Chase (0-135 5-y-o and up) £2,710 2m....... (3:30)

2272 ALAN BALL [102] 8-9-9 (5*) T Eley, *nvr far away, led 3 out, clr nxt, rdn out r-in.*..........(11 to 4 jt-fav op 5 to 2)   1

2087⁴ AL HASHIMI [120] 10-11-4 A Maguire, *tubed, al hndy, led 4th to 3 out, rdn and outpcd frm betw last 2.*
............................(4 to 1 tchd 9 to 2)   2
2174⁵ DR ROCKET [113] 9-10-8 (3*) D Meredith, *settled gng wl, ev ch frm 4 out, rdn no extr betw last 2....(11 to 4 jt-fav op 2 to 1)   3
1887⁵ LAUNDRYMAN [115] 11-10-13 G Bradley, *led to 4th, hndy till fdd and pres 2 out.*........(4 to 1 op 9 to 2)   4
GREENHEART [130] 11-12-0 Mr P Bull, *blun 1st, mfy uns rdr nxt, reco'red hfwy, lost tch frm 5 out, pld up betw last 2.*..................(33 to 1 op 25 to 1)   pu
1098 VAIN PRINCE [117] (bl) 7-11-1 G McCourt, *in tch, reminders to keep up hfwy, no response, tld off whn pld up bef 3 out.*................(8 to 1 op 6 to 1)   pu
Dist: 15l, 3½l, 15l. 4m 18.80s. a 27.80s (6 Ran).

(Gilberts Animal Feed Products), Miss S J Wilton

2308 Stop Gap Novices' Handicap Hurdle (0-100 5-y-o and up) £2,030 2m 5f 110yds...................... (4:00)

2088⁴ DIVINE CHANCE (Ire) [87] 6-11-10 J Osborne, *nvr far away, effrt and rdn alng appr 2 out, styd on wl to ld cl hme.*...........................(15 to 2 op 9 to 1)   1
1837 THE OVERTRUMPER [63] 7-9-12³ (5*) T Jenks, *al hndy, rdn to draw level 2 out, sn led, ridden r-in, jst ct.*
............................(100 to 1 op 66 to 1)   2
1804⁶ LEINTHALL PRINCESS [63] 8-10-0 N Williamson, *tucked away beh ldrs, improved frm midfield aftr 4 out, rdn nxt, styd on one pace r-in.*.........(14 to 1 op 16 to 1)   3
2106⁵ SCARF (Ire) [85] 6-11-8 M Dwyer, *patiently rdn, shaken up to join issue 3 out, ridden nxt, one pace.*
............................(13 to 8 fav op 7 to 4 tchd 2 to 1)   4
1516 SHARPSIDE [63] (bl) 7-10-0 A Maguire, *led, rdn and jnd 2 out, sn hdd, fdd......(14 to 1 op 16 to 1 tchd 20 to 1)   5
2196² TYNRON DOON [76] (bl) 5-10-8 (5*) E Husband, *settled midfield, effrt hfwy, feeling pace appr 3 out, sn btn.*
............................(14 to 1 op 10 to 1)   6
1797³ NICSAMLYN [75] 7-10-12 Mr T Stephenson, *settled to track ldg bunch, rdn aftr 4 out, no imprsn.*
............................(16 to 1 op 14 to 1)   7
2208 AURORA LAD [74] 7-10-11 Richard Guest, *wth ldrs, struggling to hold pl appr 3 out, sn btn.*.........(16 to 1)   8
1502 ARMASHOCKER [80] 6-11-3 V Smith, *struggling to keep in tch hfwy, nvr a factor................(11 to 1 op 8 to 1)   9
1511 WALLISTRANO [67] 7-10-4 R Supple, *in tch, chsd alng to go pace appr 4 out, sn lost touch.*......(20 to 1)   10
2239* TWIN STATES [89] 5-11-5 (7*,10ex) W Fry, *wtd wth, improved hfwy, effrt and rdn bef 3 out, btn whn f nxt.*.......................(11 to 1 op 8 to 1)   f
1869⁶ SUN ALIGHT [67] 5-10-4 D Morris, *in tch, improved frm midfield hfwy, rdn 4 out, wknd quickly and pld up bef 2 out....................(12 to 1)   pu
CRYSTAL MINSTREL [64] 8-9-91 (7*) J James, *chsd ldrs, struggling to hold pl 4 out, wknd quickly and pld up bef nxt..........................(33 to 1)   pu
1726³ SON OF IRIS [84] 6-11-7 P Niven, *chsd ldg bunch for o'r a circuit, lost tch frm 4 out, pld up bef nxt.*
............................(11 to 1 op 7 to 1)   pu
Dist: Nk, 6l, 6l, 8l, 6l, 8l, 8l, 4l, 15l. 5m 55.40s. a 53.40s (14 Ran).

(R E Morris-Adams), N A Gaselee

DOWN ROYAL (IRE) (soft)
Wednesday January 26th

2309 Lurgan Maiden Hurdle (5-y-o and up) £1,207 2m.................... (1:45)

2199³ DAMODAR 5-11-2 F J Flood,.................(3 to 1)   1
1833⁷ FIVE FROM HOME (Ire) 6-11-6 F Woods,.........(33 to 1)   2
1833² WINDOVER (Ire) 6-11-6 C F Swan,............(5 to 4 fav)   3
2052⁴ I AM 6-11-9 (5*) K P Gaule,....................(13 to 2)   4
2283⁷ PREMIER COUNTY 8-11-3 (7*) Mr D J McAteer, (33 to 1)   5
2123⁶ DOZING STAR (bl) 8-12-0 K F O'Brien,.........(8 to 1)   6
2028⁶ REMO GROVE (Ire) 6-11-1 (5*) M M Mackin,.....(33 to 1)   7
1833 OVER THE MALLARD (Ire) 5-10-13 (3*) D Bromley, (16 to 1)   8
2024 KEY WEST (Ire) 5-11-2 P Mooney,..............(20 to 1)   9
1833³ IF YOU BELIEVE (Ire) 5-11-2 J Shortt,.........(14 to 1)   10
1833⁶ NO DOZING (Ire) 5-11-2 P Carberry,............(8 to 1)   11
2230⁶ GALZIG 6-11-6 H Rogers,......................(33 to 1)   12
2155 VISTAGE (Ire) 6-12-0 B Sheridan,.............(14 to 1)   13
255⁸ WE PAY MORE (Ire) 5-10-6 (5*) L Flynn,.........(33 to 1)   14
2024 EARLY RISER (Ire) 6-10-8 (7*) Mr G T Morrow,...(14 to 1)   15
Dist: 4½l, 1½l, 2l, ¾l. (Time not taken) (15 Ran).

(Michael Holly), F Flood

2310 Michael Stanley Handicap Hurdle (0-109 5-y-o and up) £1,207 2½m (2:15)

2098⁹ DANGEROUS REEF (Ire) [-] 6-10-9 (5*) T P Rudd, (12 to 1)   1
1157⁶ PROSPECT LADY (Ire) [-] 6-10-1 (3*) Mr B McMahon,
............................(12 to 1)   2
2160⁴ MCCONNELL GOLD [-] 9-10-5 (5*) K P Gaule,....(5 to 1)   3
2050 BELLE O' THE BAY (Ire) [-] 5-9-11 (3*) D Bromley, (25 to 1)   4
2230² KAITLIN (Ire) [-] 5-10-10 P L Malone,.............(6 to 1)   5
2201⁴ GRANADOS (USA) [-] 6-11-1 P Carberry,.........(4 to 1)   6

1764 ROCHE MELODY (Ire) [-] 6-10-5 (3") C O'Brien, ... (20 to 1) 7
2199⁸ FATHER GREGORY (Ire) [-] 5-10-0 (3") T J Mitchell, (25 to 1) 8
2124 NORA'S ERROR (Ire) [-] 5-10-5 J P Banahan, ... (20 to 1) 9
FIDDLERS BOW VI (Ire) [-] 6-10-8 H Rogers, ... (10 to 1) 10
BYE FOR NOW [-] 8-9-13 (7") T Martin, ...(20 to 1) 11
2199* SENSE OF VALUE [-] 5-11-10 (2ex) B Sheridan, (2 to 1 fav) 12
2201⁶ ROSIN THE BOW (Ire) [-] 4-10-5 C F Swan, ...(7 to 1) 13
Dist: 4½l, 8l, 1l, 1½l. (Time not taken) (13 Ran).

(Mrs F P Lalor), B Lalor

2311 Moira Mares Maiden Hurdle (5-y-o and up) £1,207 2½m..................(2:45)

2027⁵ RED THUNDER 7-11-6 D P Fagan, ...(11 to 2) 1
2155⁴ POOR MOTHER (Ire) 6-11-6 F J Flood, ...(7 to 4 fav) 2
2078³ MULLAGHMEEN 8-11-3 (3") C O'Brien, ...(5 to 1) 3
PARSON'S RUN 7-11-9 (5") P A Roche, ...(5 to 1) 4
2203 SISTER NORA (Ire) 6-11-1 (5") M M Mackin, ...(33 to 1) 5
538⁶ KIZZY ROSE 7-11-6 K F O'Brien, ...(10 to 1) 6
2050⁴ CARIBEAN ROSE (Ire) 6-11-6 F Woods, ...(12 to 1) 7
2182⁵ AMAKANE LADY 5-11-2 C F Swan, ...(10 to 1) 8
2197 KINROSS 7-11-6 J Shortt, ...(12 to 1) 9
2123 SHIMMERETTO 8-11-1 (5") T P Rudd, ...(33 to 1) 10
2197 SERIOUS NOTE (Ire) 6-11-1 (5") Mr B R Hamilton, (16 to 1) 11
1848 ARCTIC TREASURE (Ire) 5-11-2 B Sheridan, ...(16 to 1) 12
1832⁴ PRINCESS DILLY (Ire) 5-10-13 (3") Mr P McMahon, (16 to 1) 13
NANCY KISSINGER 6-11-6 P Carberry, ...(12 to 1) 14
1902 ALLOON BAWN 8-11-1 (5") K P Gaule, ...(10 to 1) 15
2024 BOBS LADY (Ire) 5-11-2 H Rogers, ...(33 to 1) 16
BRISCE HILL (Ire) 6-10-13 (7") Mr B M Cash, ... (33 to 1) su
1581 BARNISH ROSE 5-10-9 (7") S Kerr, ...(33 to 1) pu
Dist: 3l, 3½l, 6l, 2½l. (Time not taken) (18 Ran).

(Mrs Dion Egan), J R H Fowler

2312 Jameson Irish National Trial Handicap Chase (0-116 5-y-o and up) £3,105 3m 1f.............................(3:15)

2235³ IL TROVATORE (USA) [-] 8-10-7 P Carberry, ...(5 to 1) 1
2200* EDENAKILL LAD [-] 7-10-0 (7ex) C F Swan, ...(6 to 4 on) 2
2235⁷ KITES HARDWICKE [-] 7-9-4 (3") D Bromley, ...(14 to 1) 3
2183² GOLDEN CARRUTH (Ire) [-] 6-10-2 K F O'Brien, ...(6 to 1) 4
2125⁶ GREEN TIMES [-] 9-11-1 (5") Mr G J Harford, ...(4 to 1) 5
1784⁹ MARKET MOVER [-] 8-11-7 (5") M G Cleary, ...(16 to 1) 6
Dist: 2l, 15l, 7l, 11l. (Time not taken) (6 Ran).

(J Hunt), Noel Meade

2313 Drumbo Novice Chase (5-y-o and up) £1,380 2½m..................(3:45)

2157⁸ BUMBO HALL VI (Ire) 6-12-0 F J Flood, ...(9 to 2) 1
1981 AUTUMN RIDE (Ire) 6-12-0 F Woods, ...(12 to 1) 2
2157 PRANKSTER 8-11-9 (5") M G Cleary, ...(20 to 1) 3
1831⁴ RAMBLING LORD (Ire) 6-12-0 P Carberry, ...(8 to 1) 5
2035⁷ FAYS FOLLY (Ire) 5-11-0 A Powell, ...(20 to 1) 6
1831³ REDELVA 7-11-6 (3") Mr B McMahon, ...(10 to 1) 7
2160* GOLDEN OPAL 9-12-0 K F O'Brien, ...(6 to 4 on) 8
1976³ CALDARO 7-11-0 L P Cusack, ...(7 to 1) pu
Dist: 14l, 5l, 15l, 1½l. (Time not taken) (9 Ran).

(Mrs F Flood), F Flood

2314 Lisburn INH Flat Race (4-y-o and up) £1,207 2m..................(4:15)

2080² POWER PACK (Ire) 6-11-9 (5") Mr B R Hamilton, (5 to 4 on) 1
SARAH BLUE (Ire) 4-10-9⁶ Mr R Hurley, ...(16 to 1) 2
2081³ FEATHER SONG 4-10-6 (3") Mr R Neylon, ...(10 to 1) 3
2028⁵ PATS FAREWELL (Ire) 6-12-0 Mr P F Graffin, ...(10 to 1) 4
2122 NOELS DANCER (Ire) 4-10-9 (5") Mr G J Harford, (14 to 1) 5
2203⁴ BEDFORD RAMBLER (Ire) 5-11-3 (7") Mr D J McAteer,
....(13 to 2) 6
2127⁴ JULEIT JONES (Ire) 5-11-0 (5") Mr H F Cleary, ...(8 to 1) 7
1833 THE THIRD MAN (Ire) 5-11-10 Mr D M Christie, ...(33 to 1) 8
1076 THE TOASTER 7-11-11 (3") Mr J A Nash, ...(9 to 1) 9
1989⁷ COLLIERS HILL (Ire) 6-11-7 (5") Mr P J Casey, ...(10 to 1) 10
SEYMOUR LAD 6-11-7 (7") Mr J McGurgan, ... (25 to 1) 11
491⁵ LITTLE BALLYWOODEN (Ire) 6-11-2 (7") Mr E Magee,
....(33 to 1) 12
THE SHIRALEE 6-11-7 (7") Mrs A Conmey, ... (20 to 1) 13
Dist: 5l, 13l, 4½l, 1½l. (Time not taken) (13 Ran).

(P A D Scouller), J F C Maxwell

LINGFIELD (heavy)
Wednesday January 26th
Going Correction: PLUS 1.30 sec. per fur. (races 1,3,6), PLUS 1.50 (2,4,5)

2315 Holtye 'National Hunt' Novices' Hurdle (4-y-o and up) £1,984 2m 110yds
....(1:50)

2147 MAMES BOY 7-11-5 D Murphy, sn chasing ldrs, cld 5th, led aftr last, ran on wl und pres...(33 to 1 op 20 to 1) 1

2042² HAWAIIAN YOUTH (Ire) 6-11-11 G McCourt, trkd ldrs, hrd rdn appr last, ev ch r-in, kpt on und pres.
.......................(11 to 4 fav op 9 to 4 tchd 3 to 1) 2
1490⁶ THE CHANGELING [-] 5-11-5 R J Beggan, hld up in mid-div, hdwy 5th, led aftr 3 out to r-in, no extr und pres.
...................(14 to 1 op 10 to 1 tchd 16 to 1) 3
2021⁶ TANGO'S DELIGHT 6-11-5 P Holley, hld up rear, cld to mid-div hfwy, hdwy appr 2 out, styd on one pace.
...................................(5 to 1 tchd 7 to 1) 4
1835⁶ RASTA MAN 6-11-5 S Smith Eccles, mid-div, cld 5th, out-
...................................(20 to 1 op 14 to 1) 5
2147² DESERT RUN (Ire) 6-11-5 G Bradley, trkd ldrs till outpcd 3 out....................(100 to 30 op 2 to 1 tchd 7 to 2) 6
2144⁶ MR WILBUR 8-11-5 J Frost, trkd ldrs till wknd quickly 2 out, eased...........................(20 to 1 op 12 to 1) 7
2042⁹ BONE SETTER (Ire) 4-10-7 M Perrett, chsd ldrs till outpcd 3 out...............................(33 to 1 op 25 to 1) 8
1950² MARY'S MUSIC 6-11-0 C Maude, al beh, tld off.
...................(20 to 1 op 14 to 1 tchd 25 to 1) 9
2042⁶ CREDON 6-10-12 (7") Guy Lewis, chsd ldrs till mstk 3 out, sn wknd, tld off....(10 to 1 op 6 to 1 tchd 12 to 1) 10
EXE CRACKER 5-11-5 N Mann, al beh, tld off.
...................................(33 to 1 op 20 to 1) 11
1957⁸ UNCERTAIN TIMES 7-11-5 T Grantham, beh, reminders 4th, tld off..........................(20 to 1 op 10 to 1) 12
1871 KING'S MAVERICK (Ire) 6-11-5 R Dunwoody, wth ldr, led 4th till aftr 3 out, wknd quickly, tld off.
...................(7 to 2 op 9 to 4 tchd 4 to 1) 13
2194 GRAND COLONIST 7-11-5 R Rowell, sn pushed alng in rear, tld off.....(50 to 1 op 33 to 1 tchd 100 to 1) 14
982⁷ BOOTH'S BOUQUET 6-11-5 J Osborne, led to 4th, cl up till wknd quickly aftr 3 out, tld off.
...................(14 to 1 op 12 to 1 tchd 16 to 1) 15
NELLIELLAMAY 8-11-0 Mr P Killick, al beh, mstk second, tld off....................(33 to 1 op 20 to 1 tchd 50 to 1) 16
Dist: Hd, 2l, 12l, 10l, 7l, 2½l, 2½l, 25l, 2½l, ½l. 4m 18.80s. a 27.80s (16 Ran).
SR: 27/33/25/13/3/-/   (Maurice E Pinto), J T Gifford

2316 Edenbridge Claiming Chase (6-y-o and up) £2,588 2½m 110yds.....(2:20)

DERRYMORE BOY 12-9-13 (7") Guy Lewis, nvr far away, al gng wl, led 3 out, ran on well...(5 to 1 tchd 6 to 1) 1
1775³ PLAYPEN 10-11-6 J Frost, cl up, led 4 out to nxt, ev ch last, no extr.......................(5 to 4 on tchd Evens) 2
1470⁴ HOPE DIAMOND (bl) 11-11-0 B Clifford, made most to 4 out, wknd appr nxt, tld off.
...................................(5 to 1 op 4 to 1) 3
2146⁹ PLATINUM SPRINGS (bl) 7-10-7 R Dunwoody, cl up, rdn aftr 8th, outpcd after 4 out, tld off. (10 to 1 op 6 to 1) 4
2188⁵ MASTER COMEDY (bl) 10-11-6 N Williamson, losing tch whn slpd up aftr 6th... (9 to 1 op 6 to 1 tchd 12 to 1) su
COLNE VALLEY KID 9-10-10 J Akehurst, cl up, mstk 6th, outpcd aftr 8th, sn tld off, pld up after 4 out.
...................................(33 to 1 op 20 to 1) pu
1796 SPARTAN FLAPJACK 8-10-5 (7") Mr Richard White, al beh, tld off 7th, pld up aftr 4 out.......(33 to 1 op 20 to 1) pu
Dist: 3l, dist, 30l. 5m 43.90s. a 42.90s (7 Ran).
(Mrs A S Prosser), P F Nicholls

2317 Worth Wood Conditional Jockeys' Selling Handicap Hurdle (4-y-o and up) £1,753 2m 110yds.........(2:50)

2225² CRABBY BILL [98] (v) 7-12-0 A Dicken, trkd ldrs aftr 3rd, chsd clr ldr after 3 out, led r-in, styd on wl.
...............................(4 to 1 op 3 to 1) 1
1042⁵ AT PEACE [85] 8-10-12 (3") P McLoughlin, cl up, led appr 3 out, sn clr, tired and hdd r-in.(7 to 2 co-fav op 5 to 1) 2
1867⁶ BOOGIE BOPPER (Ire) [89] (bl) 5-10-1 (7") O Burrows, beh, styd on appr 2 out, nvr able to chal.
...................(5 to 1 op 5 to 2 tchd 11 to 2) 3
1931⁵ RED JACK (Ire) [87] (bl) 5-11-3 J McCarthy, led till appr 3 out, wknd quickly, tld off...........(7 to 2 co-
fav op 9 to 1 tchd 4 to 1) 4
1945⁶ MY SENOR [86] 5-10-13 (3") J Clarke, in tch till wknd 5th, tld off..............(7 to 2 co-fav op 3 to 1 tchd 5 to 1) 5
2225⁹ SOLENT LAD [70] (bl) 11-10-0³ (3") M Stevens, al beh, tld off.....................(40 to 1 op 16 to 1 tchd 50 to 1) 6
NOTED STRAIN (Ire) [98] 6-11-7 (7") S Arnold, cl up, hit 3rd and lost pl quickly, tld off.
...................(16 to 1 op 12 to 1 tchd 20 to 1) 7
Dist: 4l, 3l, 30l, 5l, 8l, dist. 4m 21.80s. a 30.80s (7 Ran).
SR: 6/-/-/-/   (Financial Trace & Collections), Miss B Sanders

2318 Felcourt Handicap Chase (0-130 5-y-o and up) £3,054 3m.............(3:20)

2143² MASTER OATS [125] 8-12-0 N Williamson, hld up in tch, led 12th, clr whn jmpd lft last, sn eased.
...................................(4 to 1 op 3 to 1) 1
1459⁵ FIDDLERS THREE [101] (bl) 11-11-0 (3") R Farrant, cl up, reminders 11th, ev ch 4 out, outpcd nxt.
...................(9 to 1 op 7 to 1 tchd 14 to 1) 2
2143³ SUNLEY BAY [102] 8-10-5 R Dunwoody, hld up in tch, pushed alng to cl on ldrs 7th, mstk 11th, sn outpcd, styd on frm 2 out..................(9 to 1 op 5 to 1) 3

1732² CYTHERE [113] 10-10-13 (3") P Hide, *beh, mstk 5th, styd on frm 2 out, nrst finish*.
.............................(15 to 2 op 6 to 1 tchd 8 to 1) 4

1262 HOMME D'AFFAIRE [103] 11-10-6 D O'Sullivan, *chsd ldrs till outpcd 11th*...............(20 to 1 tchd 25 to 1) 5

1864* DIAMOND FORT [110] 9-10-13 S McNeill, *hld up rear, keen hold early, reminders and outpcd 9th, tld off*.
.............................(5 to 1 tchd 11 to 2) 6

2085 MIDNIGHT CALLER [124] 8-11-13 J Osborne, *not fluent, led to 12th, sn lost pl, tld off whn pld up bef 3 out*.
.............................(5 to 4 fav op 6 to 4 tchd 7 to 4) pu

Dist: 2l, 2½l, 3½l, 12l, 10l. 6m 42.40s. a 49.40s (7 Ran).

(P A Matthews), K C Bailey

2319 Adventure Novices' Chase (5-y-o and up) £2,535 2m...............(3:50)

1465³ CABOCHON 7-11-4 J Frost, *trkd ldrs, chsd lder aftr 6th, led appr 3 out, clr r-in, eased*...(7 to 4 fav tchd 9 to 4) 1

1621³ PEACEMAN 8-11-9 D Murphy, *led till appr 3 out, ev ch nxt, one pace, eased whn hld*.
.............................(2 to 1 op 9 to 4) 2

1956² MISTER ODDY 8-11-4 R Dunwoody, *trkd ldrs, blun 6th, outpcd aftr 4 out*........(9 to 4 op 4 to 1 tchd 5 to 1) 3

2043⁶ MAJOR INQUIRY (USA) 8-11-1 (3") P Hide, *nvr on terms*.
.............................(10 to 1 op 8 to 1) 4

2043* ILEWIN 7-11-9 M Ahern, *blun second and 3rd, al beh*.
.............................(9 to 2 op 4 to 1 tchd 7 to 2 and 5 to 1) 5

1422 SWING LUCKY 9-11-4 R Campbell, *al beh, mstk 5th, reminders, tld off whn pld up aftr 4 out*.
.............................(25 to 1 op 20 to 1) pu

1525⁶ SPINNING STEEL 7-11-4 S Hodgson, *trkd ldr, lost pl aftr 6th, tld off whn pld up aftr 4 out*. (25 to 1 op 20 to 1) pu

Dist: 10l, 12l, 10l, 8l. 4m 22.80s. a 28.80s (7 Ran).

SR: 42/37/20/10/7/-/-/ (Jack Joseph), R G Frost

2320 Heddon Novices' Handicap Hurdle (0-100 4-y-o and up) £1,876 2m 3f 110yds...................(4:20)

2196* THE GOLFING CURATE [89] 9-11-3 (7ex) G McCourt, *trkd ldrs, led 4 out, awkward nxt, pushed clr appr 2 out, easily*.............(5 to 4 on op Evens tchd 11 to 10) 1

1715⁴ THE WHIP [85] 7-10-13 J Osborne, *cl up, chsd wnr frm 4 out, outpcd appr 2 out*. (11 to 2 op 5 to 1 tchd 6 to 1) 2

1715* NEFARIOUS [100] 8-12-0 D Murphy, *hld up mid-div, cld 4 out, sn outpcd, no dngrs*..........(4 to 1 op 3 to 1) 3

1448⁴ BOLD STREET BLUES [84] 7-10-12 L Harvey, *trkd ldrs till outpcd 4 out*......................(12 to 1 tchd 14 to 1) 4

1595⁵ ESPRIT DE FEMME (Fr) [85] 8-10-13 J Akehurst, *led to 4 out, wknd*..............(10 to 1 op 8 to 1 tchd 14 to 1) 5

2083⁷ PHROSE [84] 4-10-12 D O'Sullivan, *hld up rear, cld appr 6th, sn outpcd*.......(12 to 1 op 7 to 1 tchd 14 to 1) 6

RACK RATE (Ire) [86] 6-11-0 C Maude, *hld up rear, keen hold, no ch whn blun 2 out, pld up bef last*.
.............................(20 to 1 op 12 to 1 tchd 25 to 1) pu

Dist: 7l, 10l, 2l, 7l, 10l. 5m 18.80s. a 44.80s (7 Ran).

(Poem Racing), R Rowe

SEDGEFIELD (good to soft)
Wednesday January 26th
Going Correction: PLUS 0.90 sec. per fur. (races 1,2,6), PLUS 0.73 (3,4,5)

2321 Stonegrave Aggregates Selling Handicap Hurdle (4-y-o and up) £1,907 2m 5f 110yds...................(1:30)

1936⁴ MANWELL [63] 7-10-0 C Grant, *made all, hrd pressed last, styd on wl*.............................(10 to 1) 1

1722 OVER THE ODDS (Ire) [66] 5-10-3 A Maguire, *al cl up, ev ch last, kpt on, no imprsn*..........(2 to 1 fav op 3 to 1) 2

2254⁵ DRU RI'S BRU RI [75] (v) 8-10-7 (5") P Waggott, *trkd ldrs, ev ch last, sn rdn and no extr*........(12 to 1 op 10 to 1) 3

2152⁶ HOTDIGGITY [64] 6-10-1 A Dobbin, *mid-div, pushed alng and hdwy appr 2 out, ch last, one pace*.
.............................(12 to 1 op 8 to 1) 4

2254⁴ BOLD MOOD [76] 5-10-8 (5") D Bentley, *mid-div, hdwy und pres aftr 2 out, ch last, wknd r-in*.
.............................(13 to 2 op 7 to 1 tchd 8 to 1 and 6 to 1) 5

VERY EVIDENT (Ire) [64] 5-10-1¹ J Callaghan, *beh, styd on frm 2 out, nvr rch ldrs*............(20 to 1 op 14 to 1) 6

2168³ LOXLEY RANGE (Ire) [65] 6-9-9 (7") N Juckes, *hld up and beh, hdwy aftr 3 out, ch last, wknd r-in*.
.............................(9 to 1 op 8 to 1) 7

2152²⁹ PALM HOUSE [91] 9-11-7 (7") N Stocks, *pushed alng halfway, nvr dngrs*..............(25 to 1 op 20 to 1) 8

2256 SERPHIL [76] (bl) 6-10-6 (7") I Jardine, *nvr dngrs*. (14 to 1) 9

SHAHMIRAJ [71] 6-10-8 K Jones, *mid-div till wknd aftr 3 out*......................(16 to 1 op 14 to 1) 10

1963 YACHT CLUB [68] 12-10-5 A Mulholland, *prmnt till wknd appr 3 out*......................(33 to 1) 11

2152 MAUREEN'S FANCY [64] 9-10-1 L Wyer, *chsd ldrs till outpcd hfwy, no dngr aftr*.
.............................(10 to 1 op 10 to 1 tchd 14 to 1) 12

2108 MAC RAMBLER [69] 7-10-6 R Garritty, *mid-div till wknd appr 2 out*..............................(25 to 1) 13

2094⁵ FILM LIGHTING GIRL [65] 8-10-2 M Brennan, *trkd ldrs till wknd appr 2 out*..........(14 to 1 op 12 to 1) 14

TIBER RUN [67] 9-10-4¹¹ (7") M Clarke, *chsd ldrs till wknd aftr 3 out*.......................(33 to 1) 15

2152 BLUEBELL TRACK [63] (bl) 8-9-9 (5") F Perratt, *sn beh*.
.............................(33 to 1) 16

1357⁹ HIGHFIELD PRINCE [77] 8-11-0 M Dwyer, *settled midfield till grad wknd aftr 3 out*....(25 to 1 op 33 to 1) 17

2213⁶ WESTCOURT FLYER [65] 5-10-2⁷ (7") J Driscoll, *beh frm 6th, tld off*.........................(16 to 1 op 10 to 1) 18

FOUR ALLS LADY [63] 8-10-0 D Byrne, *lost tch hfwy, tld off whn pld up bef 2 out*........(33 to 1 tchd 50 to 1) pu

Dist: 4l, 2½l, ½l, 6l, sht-hd, 4l, 1½l, 8l, sht-hd. 5m 22.70s. a 31.70s (19 Ran).

(B M Temple), B M Temple

2322 Acropola Handicap Hurdle (0-135 5-y-o and up) £2,217 3m 3f 110yds.. (2:00)

1963⁴ JENDEE (Ire) [86] 6-10-3 (3") A Larnach, *chsd ldrs till outpcd and lost tch aftr 6th, styd on wl frm 2 out to ld r-in*.
.............................(5 to 2 fav tchd 11 to 4) 1

2153 LEADING PROSPECT [107] 7-11-13 B Storey, *hld up in tch, slight ld 2 out till hdd and no extr r-in*.
.............................(8 to 1 op 7 to 1) 2

2153³ THE GREEN FOOL [108] 7-12-0 A Dobbin, *hld up in tch, chlgd and mstk 2 out, dsptd ld till wknd aftr last*.
.............................(15 to 2 op 7 to 1 tchd 8 to 1) 3

2104⁵ PAR-BAR (Ire) [94] 6-11-0 A Maguire, *in tch, effrt appr 2 out, sn wknd*......(6 to 1 op 5 to 1 tchd 13 to 2) 4

2034⁷ DIG DEEPER [106] 7-11-12 M Dwyer, *led till hdd 2 out, wknd quickly*.................(7 to 2 op 5 to 2) 5

1864⁴ PORTONIA [102] 10-11-8 P Niven, *lost tch aftr 6th, sn tld off*.................(3 to 1 tchd 100 to 30) 6

Dist: 2l, 6l, 10l, ½l, dist. 6m 57.90s. a 31.90s (6 Ran).

SR: 7/26/21/-/8/-/ (The Avenue Racing Partnership), J A Hellens

2323 Winter Sports Handicap Chase (0-120 5-y-o and up) £2,768 2m 5f......(2:30)

1358* BEACHY HEAD [108] 6-11-6 M Dwyer, *made all, clr 3 out, easily*.............(6 to 4 fav op 7 to 4 tchd 15 to 8) 1

1997* MOUNTEBOR [89] 9-10-9 (7") S Taylor, *prmnt, chsd wnr frm aftr 11th, no imprsn*..........(9 to 2 tchd 5 to 1) 2

1561 BONANZA [116] 7-12-0 R Hodge, *beh, pushed alng and outpcd hfwy, kpt on frm 2 out*....(5 to 1 op 4 to 1) 3

2242 BAD TRADE [105] 12-11-3 C Grant, *hld up in tch, effrt aftr 12th, one pace*.....................(33 to 1) 4

1732³ INVASION [103] (bl) 10-11-1 M Brennan, *sn pushed alng, wl beh frm tenth till some late hdwy*.
.............................(6 to 1 tchd 7 to 1) 5

1960² DOWN THE ROAD [103] 7-11-1 A Maguire, *prmnt, jnd wnr hfwy, mstk 11th, wknd aftr nxt*.
.............................(6 to 1 tchd 7 to 1) 6

2006⁴ RED UNDER THE BED [98] 7-10-5 (5") J Burke, *in tch till wknd hfwy, sn wl beh*..............(16 to 1 op 14 to 1) 7

Dist: 7l, 4l, 1l, 10l, 6l, 6l. 5m 24.10s. a 20.10s (7 Ran).

SR: 44/18/41/29/17/11/-/ (M Tabor), J J O'Neill

2324 Curling Amateur Riders' Handicap Chase (0-125 5-y-o and up) £2,312 2m 1f...........................(3:00)

2073³ MAUDLINS CROSS [112] 9-11-8 (5") Mr M Buckley, *trkd ldr, led 3 out, ran on wl, cmftbly*.
.............................(2 to 1 op 9 to 4 tchd 9 to 4) 1

1737* TRESIDDER [111] 12-11-12 Mr S Swiers, *trkd ldrs, slightly outpcd aftr 4 out, styd on frm 2 out, nt trble wnr*.
.............................(6 to 5 fav op 5 to 4 tchd 11 to 8 and 11 to 10) 2

1941⁶ MERITMOORE [90] (bl) 11-10-1¹ (5") Mr R Hale, *led till heded 3 out, wknd aftr nxt*.
.............................(11 to 2 op 5 to 1) 3

1739 GATHERING TIME [102] 8-10-10 (7") Miss V Haigh, *mstks, wl beh frm 7th, tld off whn blun last*....(6 to 1 op 5 to 1) 4

Dist: 3l, 15l, dist. 4m 24.40s. a 19.40s (4 Ran).

SR: 29/25/-/-/ (David Bell), Mrs M Reveley

2325 Downhill Novices' Handicap Chase (5-y-o and up) £2,225 3m 3f.......(3:30)

MORGANS HARBOUR [93] 8-11-6 P Niven, *hld up in tch, hdwy aftr 16th, led 2 out, styd on wl*. (5 to 1 op 9 to 2) 1

2137⁴ DEVONGALE [86] 8-10-13 R Garritty, *hld up in tch, ev ch 3 out, sn pushed alng and slightly outpcd, styd on wl frm last*...................(11 to 4 op 3 to 1) 2

2206³ THE POD'S REVENGE [73] 9-9-11 (3") A Procter, *cl up, led 16th till hdd 2 out, kpt on same pace*. (9 to 1 op 7 to 1) 3

660² KILDOWNEY HILL [92] 8-11-5 A Maguire, *led till hdd 16th, grad wknd, no ch whn hmpd 2 out*.
.............................(8 to 1 op 9 to 1 tchd 7 to 1) 4

2137⁷ SHELTON ABBEY [86] 8-10-13 K Jones, *cl up, mstk 15th, wknd aftr nxt*...............(12 to 1 tchd 14 to 1) 5

2219* EBRO [87] 8-11-0 (8ex) A Dobbin, *hld up and beh, lost tch aftr 16th, tld off*................(9 to 1 op 8 to 1) 6

2238 GRAAL LEGEND [73] 9-10-0 B Storey, *mstks, al beh, no ch whn f 17th*.............................. (66 to 1 op 50 to 1)   f
2103* LOTHIAN PILOT [101] 7-12-0 T Reed, *hld up in tch, mstk 15th, rdn aftr 3 out, 4th and btn whn f nxt*.
.... (9 to 4 fav tchd 5 to 2)   f
1960⁵ HUNTING COUNTRY [73] 10-9-9 (5*) A Roche, *mstks, sn beh, tld off whp up bef 2 out*...(25 to 1 op 20 to 1)   f
Dist: 4l, nk, 25l, 25l, 30l. 7m 13.70s. a 34.70s (9 Ran).

(P C W Owen), Mrs M Reveley

2326 Ski-ing Mares 'National Hunt' Novices' Hurdle (4-y-o and up) £1,799 2m 1f 110yds.................... (4:00)

2176 MY ADVENTURE (Ire) 4-10-5 L Wyer, *hld up in tch, gd hdwy aftr 2 out, led last, styd on*... (10 to 1 op 7 to 1)   1
2074⁶ MANETTIA (Ire) 5-11-2 P Niven, *beh, hdwy appr 2 out, styd on wl frm last, not rch wnr*. (2 to 1 fav op 5 to 4)   2
1768 SCRABBLE 5-11-2 Richard Guest, *led till hdd last, kpt on same pace*........................ (16 to 1 op 12 to 1)   3
1658⁴ ARTIC WINGS (Ire) 6-11-2 M Brennan, *trkd ldrs, chlgd 2 out, disputing ld whn wndrd appr last, grad wknd*.
.... (4 to 1 op 7 to 2 tchd 11 to 4)   4
1660⁷ GLANDALANE LADY 5-11-2 M Dwyer, *prmnt till grad wknd appr 2 out*...................... (3 to 1 op 5 to 1)   5
1918 HECKLEY SPARK 6-11-2 T Reed, *in tch, trkd ldrs frm h'fwy, chlgd 2 out, sn wknd*........ (50 to 1 op 33 to 1)   6
1660⁸ CATCH THE PIGEON 5-11-2 N Smith, *in tch till wknd appr 2 out*....................... (33 to 1 op 20 to 1)   7
1480 CHORUS LINE (Ire) 5-11-2 C Hawkins, *pld hrd early, in tch till wknd quickly appr 2 out, tld off*.
.... (25 to 1 op 16 to 1)   8
PAMPERED GEM 6-11-2 B Storey, *lost tch h'fwy, tld off*.
.... (50 to 1 op 25 to 1)   9
1959 AMBER HOLLY 5-11-2 A Maguire, *sn beh, wl tld off*.
.... (50 to 1 op 25 to 1)   10
2237⁴ GAY'S GAMBIT 5-10-9 (7*) J Driscoll, *in tch whn blun and uns rdr 3rd*........................ (50 to 1 op 25 to 1)   ur
Dist: 2½l, 1l, 4l, 10l, 8l, 3l, 30l, dist, dist. 4m 24.50s. a 29.50s (11 Ran).

(Mrs Jean P Connew), M H Easterby

SOUTHWELL (A.W) (std)
Wednesday January 26th
Going Correction: PLUS 0.60 sec. per fur.

2327 Garnet Novices' Hurdle (4-y-o and up) £1,553 2¼m.................... (1:40)

2245 KOA 4-10-7 C Llewellyn, *patiently rdn, improved to join issue h'fwy, led briefly appr 3 out, nosed ahead nxt, drvn out frm last*................... (10 to 1 op 6 to 1)   1
2057⁷ TEEN JAY 4-11-0 M Richards, *settled gng wl, niggled along to chal aftr 4 out, led nxt, hdd 2 out, found little*.
.... (5 to 4 on op Evens tchd 5 to 4)   2
2213² SCRABO VIEW (Ire) 6-11-5 L O'Hara, *nvr far away, ev ch and drvn alng whn squeezed for room beng appr 3 out, rallied nxt, kpt on same pace r-in*................. (5 to 1)   3
599⁴ PIE HATCH (Ire) (bl) 5-11-0 V Smith, *tld bg bunch, hrd rdn to improve aftr 4 out, no imprsn frm nxt*.
.... (14 to 1 op 10 to 1)   4
2115⁶ TANGO IN PARIS (Arg) (bl) 4-10-2 (5*) S Curran, *led till aftr second, rgned ld briefly 4 out, fdd and pres aftr nxt*.
.... (33 to 1)   5
1594⁴ TIME WON'T WAIT (Ire) 5-11-5 J Railton, *tucked away gng wl, smooth hdwy to chal appr 3 out, rdn and found little betw last 2*................ (11 to 2 op 7 to 2)   6
2147 GREENHIL TARE AWAY 6-11-5 M Hourigan, *chsd ldrs to h'fwy, sn struggling, tld off frm 4 out*.
.... (16 to 1 op 10 to 1)   7
2154⁸ MONASTIC FLIGHT (Ire) (bl) 4-10-0 (7*) G Cahill, *led aftr second till hdd 4 out, lost pl quickly and pld up bef 2 out*........................ (20 to 1)   pu
MASTER FRITH 6-11-5 D Bridgwater, *struggling to keep up h'fwy, tld off whn pld up bef 3 out*......... (33 to 1)   pu
1717 RAIN SHADOW 5-11-0 S Keightley, *struggling in rear thrght, tld off whn pld up bef 4 out*....... (50 to 1)   pu
1800 KING RUST 6-11-2 (3*) A Thornton, *jmpd slwly 1st, pressing ldrs whn broke leg and pld up aftr 6th, destroyed*.
.... (50 to 1)   pu
1707 MANDY LOUISE 6-11-0 M A FitzGerald, *chsd ldrs to go pace h'fwy, tld off whn pld up bef 3 out*.
.... (16 to 1 op 20 to 1)   pu
Dist: 2l, 1l, 4l, 8l, 2l, dist. 4m 32.60s. a 20.60s (12 Ran).

(Michael J Arnold), N A Twiston-Davies

2328 Diamond Selling Handicap Hurdle (4-y-o and up) £1,768 2½m........ (2:10)

1964 BENTLEY MANOR [74] 5-10-6 D Bridgwater, *al gng wl, jnd ldr appr 4 out, led nxt, clr betw last 2*.
.... (11 to 2 op 4 to 1)   1
2120⁵ BURN BRIDGE (USA) [78] (v) 8-10-10 Peter Caldwell, *al hndy, led h'fwy till blun and hdd 3 out, hit nxt, no extr und pres*........................ (11 to 2 op 4 to 1)   2

1719⁶ ALDAHE [68] 9-9-10¹ (5*) D Salter, *chsd ldg bunch, drvn alng and blun 6 out, plodded on frm 3 out, no imprsn*.
.... (8 to 1 tchd 10 to 1)   3
1121 ROSCOE HARVEY [92] 12-11-3 (7*) M Berry, *sn disputing ld, chsd alng to hold pl appr 4 out, soon rdn and btn*.
.... (7 to 1 op 4 to 1)   4
2163³ STATION EXPRESS (Ire) [68] 6-9-9 (5*) S Mason, *dsptd ld to h'fwy, sn pushed alng to hold pl, lost tch frm 4 out*.
.... (6 to 1 op 5 to 1)   5
1967⁵ FLUTTER MONEY [76] 10-10-8 G Upton, *in tch, struggling to keep up h'fwy, tld off frm 5 out*. (12 to 1 op 10 to 1)   6
1997 ANOTHER STRIPLIGHT [68] 11-10-0 Mr I McLelland, *tubed, last and detached thrght, pld up bef 3 out*.
.... (33 to 1 op 25 to 1)   pu
2257⁷ DAUPHIN BLEU (Fr) [68] 8-10-0 Dr P Pritchard, *jmpd erratically, made most to h'fwy, sn lost tch, tld off whn pld up bef 3 out*...................... (20 to 1)   pu
2094³ NORTHERN OPTIMIST [74] 6-9-13 (7*) Mr J L Llewellyn, *pressed ldrs to h'fwy, sn lost tch, tld off whn pld up bef 3 out*........................ (7 to 1 op 6 to 1)   pu
2119⁸ DALLISTON (NZ) [78] 8-10-10 A Carroll, *reminders to keep up 3rd, tld off whn pld up bef 5 out*.
.... (16 to 1 op 12 to 1)   pu
2058 RUSTY MUSIC [68] 8-10-0³ (3*) A Thornton, *struggling to keep in contention h'fwy, tld off whn pld up bef 3 out*.
.... (7 to 1 op 5 to 1)   pu
Dist: 5l, 15l, 12l, 1½l, 8l. 5m 3.30s. a 22.30s (11 Ran).

(R Paul Russell), K S Bridgwater

2329 Emerald Handicap Hurdle (0-105 4-y-o and up) £1,976 2m............ (2:40)

2213* RUTH'S GAMBLE [75] 6-10-4 (7*,6ex) Mr B Pollock, *settled gng wl, chalg on bit whn lft clr 3 out, jmpd rght last 2, unchlgd*........................ (9 to 4 fav op 7 to 4)   1
2061³ GLOSSY [75] 7-10-4 (7*) G Robertson, *tried to make all, hdd and rdn aftr 4 out, fourth and btn whn lft second nxt, no imprsn*.................... (9 to 1 op 4 to 1)   2
1799 HAVE A PARTY [78] 7-11-0 M A FitzGerald, *chsd alng to go pace h'fwy, sn lost tch, plodded round, tld off*. (12 to 1)   3
2057⁶ PYRO PENNANT [65] 9-10-1¹ D J Burchell, *al hndy, rdn to nose ahead entering strt, slight advantage whn f 3 out*.
.... (12 to 1 op 10 to 1)   f
2167² STRONG JOHN (Ire) [88] 6-11-10 C Llewellyn, *al hndy, led on bit aftr 4 out till appr nxt, upsides whn brght dwn 3 out*................... (3 to 1 op 9 to 4)   bd
TOP SCALE [87] 8-11-6 (3*) A Thornton, *reminders to keep up 4th, sn tld off, pld up bef 3 out*.
.... (6 to 1 op 5 to 1 tchd 13 to 2)   pu
Dist: 15l, dist. 4m 5.40s. a 19.40s (6 Ran).

(Mrs A Emanuel), Mrs L C Jewell

2330 Ruby Handicap Hurdle (0-115 4-y-o and up) £1,976 2½m.......... (3:10)

2166³ ELEGANT KING (Ire) [102] 5-11-6 M A FitzGerald, *nvr far away, hit 6 out, reco'red to ld 3 out, drw clr betw last 2*........................ (4 to 1 tchd 7 to 2)   1
2216 CHAPEL HILL (Ire) [87] 6-10-5 D J Burchell, *al hndy, led aftr 6th, clr after nxt, hdd 3 out, nrly uns rdr nxt, sn btn*.................... (3 to 1 fav tchd 7 to 2 and 4 to 1)   2
2162* GYMCRAK DAWN [82] 9-10-0 P Harley, *al wl plcd, drvn alng to chase ldr 5 out, struggling frm nxt, sn lost tch*.
.... (7 to 1 op 6 to 1)   3
2119³ HOWGILL [82] 8-9-11 (3*) S Wynne, *wtd wth, hit second, took clr order und pres aftr 4 out, fdg whn blun nxt*.
.... (10 to 1 tchd 11 to 1)   4
2168* LAVA FALLS (USA) [90] 8-10-8 D Skyrme, *chsd ldrs thrght, hrd rdn appr 4 out, sn lost tch*......... (5 to 1 op 9 to 2)   5
2060³ DONNA'S TOKEN [82] 9-10-0³ (3*) A Thornton, *dsptd ld, rdn alng and lost grnd h'fwy, tld off appr 4 out*.
.... (12 to 1 op 10 to 1)   6
2116* KAHER (USA) [103] 7-11-7 C Llewellyn, *made most till aftr 6th, struggling and lost tch bef 4 out, tld off*.
.... (4 to 1 op 3 to 1 tchd 9 to 2)   7
Dist: 15l, 5l, 12l, 12l, 2½l, 20l. 5m 5.30s. a 24.30s (7 Ran).

(L Fust), A P Jarvis

2331 Opal Claiming Hurdle (4-y-o and up) £1,984 2m.................... (3:40)

2062⁴ WHEELER'S WONDER (Ire) 5-11-2 (7*) Mr J L Llewellyn, *nvr far away, pushed ahead appr 3 out, styd on to race clr betw last 2*........................ (5 to 2 fav op 3 to 1)   1
2120³ BALLERINA ROSE 7-10-13 D J Burchell, *patiently rdn, improved to ld aftr 5th, hdd bef 3 out, kpt on same pace*.
.... (4 to 1 op 5 to 2)   2
1931 ABELONI 5-11-5 (3*) S Wynne, *settled in tch, hrd rdn whn ldg pair quickened frm 4 out, styd on, nvr nrr*. (33 to 1)   3
2163² RAIN-N-SUN 8-11-6 D Gallagher, *wth ldrs, led 4th to h'fwy, fdd und pres four out, sn lost tch*.
.... (10 to 1 tchd 12 to 1)   4
1425 CHAGHATAI (USA) 8-11-4 Mr B Leavy, *chsd alng beh ldg bunch, effrt h'fwy, outpcd bef 4 out, no imprsn*.
.... (33 to 1 op 25 to 1)   5

950⁵ SHARP DANCE 5-11-1 B Powell, *jmpd stickily, chsd alng to keep in tch hfwy, struggling bef 4 out, no imprsn*.
....(20 to 1) 6

2061¹³ PHARGOLD (Ire) 5-10-13 (3*) A Thornton, *trkd ldg trio, effrt to go 3rd 4 out, struggling bef nxt, tld off*.
....(9 to 1 op 8 to 1 tchd 10 to 1) 7

1634 TARGET LINE 4-10-8 (5*) Mr D McCain, *settled in rear, drvn alng whn pace lifted bef 4 out, sn lost tch*.
....(33 to 1) 8

2165 SINGING GOLD 8-10-13 (5*) S Curran, *slight ld to 4th, wknd quickly aftr nxt, tld off whn pld up bef 3 out*.
....(33 to 1) pu

2243 KALKO 5-11-9 (5*) P Midgley, *patiently rdn, improved hfwy, wknd quickly aftr 4 out, pld up bef 2 out*.
....(4 to 1 op 5 to 2) pu

1965 HOSTETLER (bl) 5-11-10 D Bridgwater, *chsd ldg bunch, struggling bef 4 out, tld off whn pld up before nxt*.
....(9 to 1 op 12 to 1) pu

1297⁶ PIPERS REEL 4-10-4 Mr N Miles, *trkd ldrs, led briefly hfwy, lost tch quickly, tld off whn pld up bef 3 out*.
....(14 to 1 op 20 to 1 tchd 33 to 1) pu

Dist: 6l, 5l, 15l, sht-hd, 3l, 5l, 6l. 4m 2.30s. a 16.30s (12 Ran).

SR: 28/12/16/-/-/-/ (B J Llewellyn), B J Llewellyn

2332 Amethyst National Hunt Flat Race (4,5,6-y-o) £897 2m..............(4:10)

CERTAIN ANGLE 5-11-3 (7*) N Parker, *patiently rdn, improved gng wl hfwy, styd on well to ld ins fnl furlong, ran on*.............(5 to 1 op 4 to 1 tchd 6 to 1) 1

BORNE 4-10-7 (5*) S Mason, *settled gng wl, led 1 fs out, ran green last 2 furlongs, hdd and one pace ins last*.
....(4 to 1 fav op 5 to 2) 2

2176⁷ CROWTHER HOMES 4-10-0 (7*) S Knott, *nvr far away, bustled alng appr strt, kpt on last 2 fs*........(12 to 1) 3

2081⁷ TIFASI (Ire) 4-10-7 (5*) S Curran, *settled off the pace, rcd wide, improved to draw level o'r one furlong out, no extr last 100 yards*...............(6 to 1 op 4 to 1) 4

2074⁵ CARIBBEAN SURFER (USA) 5-11-3 (7*) F Leahy, *patiently rdn, improved to join issue appr strt, ridden and fdd o'r one furlong out*.
....(5 to 1 op 6 to 1 tchd 7 to 1 and 8 to 1) 5

HOAGY POKEY 4-10-12 W Dwan, *trkd ldrs, feeling pace and drvn alng appr strt, sn lost tch*.
....(13 to 2 op 6 to 1 tchd 7 to 1) 6

1027⁹ HURRICANE SUE 5-10-12 (7*) G McGrath, *chsd ldg bunch, hrd at work last 5 fs, sn tld off*.......(8 to 1 op 6 to 1) 7

HIGHLAND HEIGHTS (Ire) 6-11-0 (5*) T Eley, *chsd ldrs, effrt and drvn alng hfwy, tld off appr strt*.........(10 to 1) 8

ERINS BAR (Ire) 5-11-7 (3*) A Thornton, *led aftr 2 fs till o'r a m out, fdd appr strt, tld off*.........(12 to 1) 9

FORTITUDE STAR 4-10-2 (5*) D Salter, *beh and pushed alng hfwy, sn tld off*.............................(20 to 1) 10

1376 GOOD FEELING 5-11-3 (7*) N Juckes, *pushed alng in midfield hfwy, sn lost tch, tld off*.............(14 to 1) 11

1329 OLD TICKLERTON 5-11-5 (5*) D Walsh, *bustled alng in midfield whn pace quickened hfwy, lost tch, tld off*.
....(33 to 1) 12

VOLCANIC ROC 4-10-12 Mr N Miles, *led for 2 fs, led ag'n o'r a m out to 7 furlongs out, wknd, tld off*...(25 to 1) 13

2176 JOYFUL JENNY 5-11-0 (5*) J Twomey, *struggling in rear hfwy, tld off*...................................(33 to 1) 14

CANADIAN CRUISE 5-11-7 (3*) N Bentley, *chsd ldg bunch to hfwy, tld off appr strt*........(12 to 1 op 10 to 1) 15

Dist: 4l, 1¼l, 3l, dist, 2½l, 1½l, 3l, 5l, 5l. 3m 56.60s. (15 Ran).
(The Plyform Syndicate), P J Hobbs

HUNTINGDON (soft)
Thursday January 27th
Going Correction: PLUS 1.32 sec. per fur.

2333 Offord 'National Hunt' Novices' Hurdle (4-y-o and up) £2,156 2m 110yds (1:25)

2147* GALES CAVALIER (Ire) 6-11-12 R Dunwoody, *lft in ld second, pushed clr 2 out, cmftbly*.
....(2 to 1 on op 11 to 8 on) 1

1301* RAMALLAH 5-11-12 W McFarland, *wth ldrs, rdn and outpcd appr 2 out*........(8 to 1 op 3 to 1 tchd 10 to 1) 2

1548⁹ SLIPMATIC 5-11-0 N Williamson, *in tch, ran on aftr 4th, lost pl and hit 3 out, styd on after nxt*.
....(33 to 1 op 16 to 1 tchd 40 to 1) 3

2057⁴ NAGOBELIA 6-11-5 G McCourt, *in tch, effrt 5th, wknd appr 2 out*..............(9 to 1 op 10 to 1 tchd 12 to 1) 4

1124⁴ BUSTLING AROUND 7-11-0 M Bosley, *beh most of way, tld off*..............................(40 to 1 op 25 to 1) 5

BALNAGOWN 6-11-5 V Smith, *ldg grp till wknd 3 out, tld off*.............................(33 to 1 op 20 to 1) 6

CORNS LITTLE FELLA 6-11-5 R Supple, *tld off 3rd*.
....(50 to 1 op 25 to 1) 7

1996⁷ MISTER SPECTATOR (Ire) 5-11-5 W Marston, *mid-div to 5th, tld off*.............(16 to 1 op 8 to 1 tchd 20 to 1) 8

BLURRED VISION (Ire) 5-11-5 S Mackey, *wl plcd to 4th, no ch whn f 2 out*....................(50 to 1 op 33 to 1) f

1309⁸ MAC'S LEAP 6-11-5 M Hourigan, *f 1st*.
....(40 to 1 op 16 to 1) f

FAR VIEW (Ire) 5-11-5 D Skyrme, *rear 4th, tld off whn hmpd and uns rdr 2 out*.........(50 to 1 op 33 to 1) ur

1490⁸ MYRTILLA 5-11-0 L Harvey, *prmnt whn hmpd and uns rdr second*......(16 to 1 op 7 to 1 tchd 20 to 1) ur

1724 CALL THE SHOTS (Ire) 6-11-5 K Jones, *blun and uns rdr 1st*...................................(40 to 1 op 20 to 1) ur

1957 RECTORY GARDEN (Ire) 5-11-2 (3*) R Farrant, *in tch to 5th, btn in fifth whn blun and uns rdr last*.
....(40 to 1 op 20 to 1) ur

DEVIL'S STING (Ire) 5-11-5 C Llewellyn, *led till hmpd and uns rdr second*.........(9 to 1 op 7 to 1 tchd 10 to 1) ur

1957⁹ SEATWIST 5-11-0 (5*) T Eley, *brght dwn 1st*.
....(50 to 1 op 20 to 1) bd

Dist: 15l, nk, 2l, dist, 2l, 8l, 3l. 4m 14.30s. a 27.30s (16 Ran).
SR: 43/28/15/18/-/-/ (T J Whitley), D R Gandolfo

2334 St Neots Conditional Jockeys' Handicap Chase (0-125 5-y-o and up) £2,840 2½m 110yds................(1:55)

1629² DUO DROM [99] (v) 9-10-6 W Marston, *settled in 3rd, chsd ldr 12th, led 2 out, shaken up to go clr last*.
....(3 to 1 op 5 to 2 tchd 100 to 30) 1

1630⁴ MR JAMBOREE [113] 8-11-6 P Hide, *led to 2 out, ran on same pace*...........................(5 to 1 op 7 to 2) 2

2001 DANDY MINSTREL [108] 10-11-1 T Jenks, *pushed alng in 4th pl frm 5th, hit 8th, lost tch and mstk 11th, tld off*.
....(9 to 4 jt-fav op 7 to 4 tchd 5 to 2) 3

PRIVATE AUDITION [121] 12-11-10 (4*) P Murphy, *sn beh, mstk 3rd, not fluent and lost tch 9th, tld off*.
....(7 to 1 op 10 to 1) 4

1534* GLEN CHERRY [108] (bl) 8-11-1 R Farrant, *pressed ldr to 12th, wkng in 3rd pl whn refused 3 out*......(9 to 1 jt-fav op 2 to 1) ref

Dist: 8l, dist, dist. 5m 27.00s. a 32.00s (5 Ran).
SR: 28/34/ (F J Haggas), Mrs D Haine

2335 Yelling Novices' Hurdle (4-y-o and up) £1,995 2m 110yds..............(2:25)

2204 FONTANAYS (Ire) 6-11-5 G McCourt, *handily plcd, rdn to ld aftr last, drvn out*. (11 to 1 op 6 to 1 tchd 12 to 1) 1

1734* CARPET SLIPPERS 8-11-7 G Bradley, *cl up, led 4th, hit 3 out, hdd r-in, fnshd lme*....................(6 to 1 jt-fav op 5 to 2 tchd 11 to 4) 2

RIO TRUSKY 5-11-5 J Railton, *hld up, hdwy 5th, ev ch 2 out, styd on wl nr finish*.........(33 to 1 op 20 to 1) 3

DEDUCE 5-11-5 N Williamson, *ldg grp, ev ch 2 out, rdn and no extr last 100 yards*............(6 to 1 jt-fav op Evens tchd 5 to 4 on) 4

1929³ TENAYESTELIGN 6-10-9 (5*) J McCarthy, *hld up rear, prog appr 3 out, ev ch last, not quicken*.
....(10 to 1 op 7 to 1 tchd 12 to 1) 5

RAGAMUFFIN ROMEO 5-11-0 (5*) S Curran, *improved hfwy, dsptd ld frm 3 out, ev ch 4th whn hit last, no extr*.
....(33 to 1 op 14 to 1) 6

LLOYDS DREAM 5-11-5 R Supple, *trkd ldrs, rdn and one pace appr 2 out*...................(33 to 1 op 14 to 1) 7

DOCK OF THE BAY (Ire) 4-10-3 (5*) T Jenks, *hdwy 3rd, rdn and btn appr 2 out*...(25 to 1 op 20 to 1 tchd 33 to 1) 8

MERRYHILL MADAM 5-11-0 W Humphreys, *effrt hfwy, wknd aftr 3 out*..........................(33 to 1 op 20 to 1) 9

1460⁶ SCOTTISH BALL 5-11-0 M Crosse, *mstk 1st, effrt and hit 3 out, sn btn, tld off*. (11 to 1 op 10 to 1 tchd 12 to 1) 10

KING'S GOLD 4-10-3 (5*) C Burnett-Wells, *mid-div till lost tch 5th, tld off*..................(33 to 1 op 20 to 1) 11

2169 BARNIEMEBOY (v) 4-10-8 W Elderfield, *cld on ldrs 4th, refused and uns rdr nxt*.................(33 to 1) ref

2144 BEACHY GLEN 7-11-5 S Mackey, *led till aftr 3rd, wknd 5th, pld up bef 3 out*...................(33 to 1 op 20 to 1) pu

2250 CAP DIAMANT (USA) 6-11-5 R Dunwoody, *hmpd and lost tch 5th, pld up bef 3 out*......(16 to 1 op 12 to 1) pu

TEMPLE KNIGHT 5-11-5 S Earle, *chsd ldrs till aftr 5th, wknd quickly, pld up bef 2 out*....(20 to 1 op 14 to 1) pu

2154 CHALKIEFORT 5-10-12 (7*) S McDougall, *led aftr 3rd to nxt, sn wknd, pld up bef 3 out*.....(50 to 1 op 33 to 1) pu

Dist: 1½l, nk, 2½l, ½l, ¾l, 2l, 15l, 10l, 20l, dist. 4m 16.70s. a 29.70s (16 Ran).
SR: 12/12/9/6/-/4/2/-/-/ (Pegasus Racing Partnership), Mrs M McCourt

2336 Bet With The Tote Novices' Chase Qualifier (6-y-o and up) £2,976 3m (2:55)

751 TARAMOSS 7-10-10 N Williamson, *chsd ldr 11th, led appr 2 out, sn clr, unchlgd*..................(fav op 7 to 4 tchd 11 to 4) 1

1392⁵ CARRIGLAWN 9-10-7 (3*) P Hide, *led to second, outpcd 13th, lft poor second 2 out*.......(12 to 1 tchd 16 to 1) 2

1844 MUSIC SCORE 8-10-3 (7*) P Ward, *mstk 1st, beh and lost tch 13th, remote 3rd whn f 2 out*.
....(14 to 1 op 12 to 1 tchd 16 to 1) f

2047³ PUNCH'S HOTEL 9-10-10 R Dunwoody, *chsd ldr, blun and uns rdr 11th*...........(5 to 2 jt-fav op 7 to 4) ur

1645 WOODLANDS BOY (Ire) 6-10-10 G McCourt, *in tch till outpcd 13th, pld up bef 16th*.
....(11 to 2 op 5 to 1 tchd 13 to 2) pu

1869[2] THE CARROT MAN 6-10-10 J Osborne, *led second till hdd and pld up appr 2 out*..............(11 to 4 op 3 to 1) pu
ROYAL EXHIBITION 10-10-10 D Morris, *beh 5th, jmpd slwly and lost tch 7th, tld off whn pld up bef 15th.*
.... (25 to 1 op 16 to 1) pu

Dist: 15l. 6m 37.60s. a 49.60s (7 Ran).

(Howard Parker), J A C Edwards

2337 Eastern Electricity Handicap Chase (0-125 5-y-o and up) £3,465 2m 110yds
.................................(3:25)

1531* MARTHA'S SON [106] 7-10-10 (3*) R Farrant, *chsd ldr 8th, blun 2 out, slight ld last, sn clr.*
......(6 to 5 fav op Evens tchd 5 to 4 on and 5 to 4) 1
2248 SPREE CROSS [121] 8-12-0 G Bradley, *led second, hdd last, outpcd r-in*........(9 to 4 op 2 to 1 tchd 5 to 2) 2
1596* DEXTRA DOVE [102] 7-10-9 S Earle, *hld up, hit 6th, rdn and one pace 2 out*...(100 to 30 op 7 to 2 tchd 9 to 2) 3
2248³ EMSEE-H [120] 9-11-13 R Dunwoody, *led to second, chsd ldr till wknd 8th, sn tld off*........ (9 to 1 op 12 to 1) 4

Dist: 2¹/₂l, 20l, dist. 4m 24.50s. a 26.50s (4 Ran).
SR: 38/50/11/-/

(M Ward-Thomas), Capt T A Forster

2338 Sapley Handicap Hurdle (0-115 5-y-o and up) £2,553 3¹/₄m...........(3:55)

1837 GRAY'S ELLERGY [100] 8-11-6 P Holley, *hld up, hdwy 7th, led nxt, clr appr 2 out, styd on wl.*
.......................(6 to 1 op 13 to 2 tchd 7 to 1) 1
1994⁸ GORT [108] 6-12-0 R Dunwoody, *in tch, chsd wnr appr 2 out, no imprsn frm last.*(15 to 2 op 4 to 1 tchd 8 to 1) 2
2141³ PLACE STEPHANIE (Ire) [94] 6-10-7 (7*) L Dace, *hld up in mid-div, cld on ldrs aftr 8th, styd on one pace frm 2 out.*
.......................(13 to 2 op 5 to 1 tchd 7 to 1) 3
2034³ RELTIC [80] 7-10-0 W Marston, *led 3rd, ldg grp, ev ch 3 out, no extr nxt*........ (8 to 1 tchd 10 to 1 and 6 to 1) 4
2086² SURCOAT [98] 7-11-4 L Harvey, *hld up, prog 8th, no imprsn appr 2 out.* (7 to 2 fav tchd 4 to 1 and 3 to 1) 5
2142⁶ GROTIUS [80] (bl) 10-10-0 R Bellamy, *wl plcd till lost pos 8th, effrt und pres appr 3 out, sn btn.*
.................................(16 to 1 op 33 to 1 tchd 12 to 1) 6
VILLA PARK [85] 12-10-5 M Perrett, *pressed ldrs, led 7th to nxt, wknd 3 out*...................(33 to 1 op 25 to 1) 7
2192⁴ CARRIKINS [88] 7-10-8 J Railton, *mid-div most of way, no extr appr 3 out*......(12 to 1 op 10 to 1 tchd 14 to 1) 8
2172 CAPPUCCINO GIRL [99] 7-11-5 M Crosse, *jnd ldrs 8th, rdn and wknd appr 2 out*...(9 to 1 op 5 to 1 tchd 10 to 1) 9
2223² LOBRIC [96] (bl) 9-11-2 N Williamson, *nvr nr to chal.*
.................................(5 to 1 op 10 to 1 tchd 11 to 1) 10
1759⁸ DUKE DE VENDOME [87] (v) 11-10-0 (7*) Mr G Haine, *trkd ldrs till no hdwy 9th*....................(33 to 1 op 20 to 1) 11
2063⁹ CHRISTIAN SOLDIER [84] 7-10-4⁴ W Elderfield, *ldg grp till uns rdr aftr 5th.*.................................(50 to 1) ur
2064⁷ MOZE TIDY [84] 9-10-4 T Grantham, *cl up, led 3rd to 7th, wknd nxt, pld up bef 2 out.*
.......................(25 to 1 op 20 to 1 tchd 33 to 1) pu

Dist: 6l, 4l, 10l, 12l, 1l, 12l, 2¹/₂l, sht-hd, 15l, 10l. 6m 50.20s. a 49.20s (13 Ran).

(W H Dore), D R Gandolfo

2339 Open National Hunt Flat Race (4,5,6-y-o) £1,898 2m 110yds.........(4:25)

BEAR CLAW 5-10-12 (7*) R Massey, *in tch, rdn to ld o'r 2 fs out, edgd lft over one out, hld on cl hme.*
.................................(20 to 1 op 10 to 1 tchd 25 to 1) 1
KILLONE ABBOT (Ire) 5-11-5 T Grantham, *hld up, hdwy 4 fs out, ev ch not much room o'r one out, not quicken nr finish.*...............(7 to 4 fav op 9 to 4) 2
ARDENT LOVE (Ire) 5-10-7 (7*) R Moore, *hdwy o'r 3 fs out, styd on one pace ins last*.................(33 to 1) 3
WHERE'S WILLIE (Fr) 5-11-0 (5*) T Jenks, *trkd ldrs, cld 5 fs out, led briefly 3 out, sn one pace.*
.........................(9 to 1 op 10 to 1 tchd 16 to 1 and 8 to 1) 4
BILLYGOAT GRUFF 5-10-12 (7*) M Keighley, *hdwy hfwy, rdn alng 2 fs out, not quicken...* (10 to 1 tchd 16 to 1) 5
1806³ EVEN BLUE (Ire) 6-11-0 (5*) Mr D McCain, *made most till o'r 2 fs out, no extr*......(10 to 1 op 6 to 1 tchd 33 to 1) 6
MACKABEE (Ire) 5-10-12 (7*) D Bohan, *improved frm rear 7 fs out, not rch frnt rnk from 3 out.*
.......................(8 to 1 op 7 to 1 tchd 16 to 1) 7
1674⁷ D'ARBLAY STREET (Ire) 5-10-12 (7*) S McDougall, *ldg grp, ev ch o'r 3 fs out, wknd over 2 out.*
.................................(20 to 1 op 25 to 1 tchd 33 to 1) 8
NO MORE NICE GUY (Ire) 5-11-5 M Perrett, *pressed ldrs till lost pl last 3 fs.*........(6 to 1 tchd 8 to 1 and 5 to 1) 9
SUVLA BAY (Ire) 6-11-5 M Brennan, *improved 6 fs out, no imprsn o'r 2 out.*...(20 to 1 op 16 to 1 tchd 33 to 1) 10
WIDE-EYED 4-10-2 V Smith, *wl plcd till lost pos o'r 3 fs out*...................(11 to 1 op 16 to 1) 11
ABSOLUTELYMUSTARD (Ire) 5-11-5 J Osborne, *trkd ldrs till fs*.................................(12 to 1 op 5 to 1) 12
SOBER ISLAND 5-11-5 C Llewellyn, *not plcd to chal frm hfwy*.................(12 to 1 op 6 to 1 tchd 14 to 1) 13
WOODLANDS POWER 6-11-2 (3*) R Davis, *beh most of way*.................................(20 to 1 op 33 to 1) 14
CLOWN AROUND 6-11-0 Mr L Lay, *al rear*.......(33 to 1) 15

BOY BUSTER 5-11-5 M Crosse, *beh appr hfwy, tld off.*
.................................(33 to 1) 16
EDD THE DUCK 4-10-7 M Ranger, *wth ldr till lost pl 7 fs out, tld off*.................(33 to 1) 17
RUN ON FLO (Ire) 6-11-0 N Williamson, *al beh, lost tch aftr 7 fs, tld off*.................(33 to 1) 18

Dist: Sht-hd, 12l, ³/₄l, 2l, sht-hd, 8l, 3¹/₂l, ³/₄l, 2¹/₂l, 12l. 4m 11.50s. (18 Ran).

(Roach Foods Limited), D Nicholson

LINGFIELD (heavy)
Thursday January 27th
Going Correction: PLUS 1.80 sec. per fur.

2340 Attlee Novices' Chase (5-y-o and up) £2,558 2¹/₂m 110yds............(2:40)

2170³ DONT TELL THE WIFE 8-11-4 D Bridgwater, *hld up in rear, cld 7th, led 2 out, pushed alng and ran on wl.*
.......................(3 to 1 op 5 to 2 tchd 4 to 1) 1
1008 GINGER TRISTAN 8-11-4 A Tory, *trkd ldrs, cld 4 out, led nxt, hdd 2 out, one pace*..........(7 to 1 op 5 to 1) 2
2144⁵ MY DEAR GOOD MAN (Ire) 6-11-4 C Maude, *trkd ldrs till outpcd aftr 4 out, styd on frm 2 out.* (12 to 1 op 7 to 1) 3
1385 WHAT A NOBLE 8-11-1 (3*) A Thornton, *wth ldr, led briefly 4 out, one pace frm nxt*...........(12 to 1 op 10 to 1) 4
1697⁵ FREEMANTLE 9-11-4 B Powell, *chsd ldrs, lft in ld 6th, hdd 4 out, wknd nxt.* (12 to 1 op 8 to 1 tchd 14 to 1) 5
2167 FANTASY WORLD 8-10-13 D Murphy, *led til f 6th.*
.................................(14 to 1 op 8 to 1 tchd 16 to 1) f
2195⁵ DOVEHILL 8-11-4 Mr P Bull, *tracking ldrs whn brght dwn 6th*............(66 to 1 op 50 to 1 tchd 100 to 1) bd
1879² SUFFOLK ROAD 7-11-4 M A FitzGerald, *tracking ldg pair whn brght dwn 6th*............(5 to 2 fav tchd 3 to 1) bd
2186 BALLINAMOE 9-11-4 M Richards, *hld up in rear, lost tch and pld up bef 6th.*
.................................(66 to 1 op 50 to 1 tchd 100 to 1) pu

Dist: 2¹/₂l, 8l, 10l, 8l. 5m 45.30s. a 44.30s (9 Ran).
SR: 16/13/5/-/-/-/

(H & K Commissions), Mrs D Haine

LINGFIELD (A.W) (std)
Thursday January 27th
Going Correction: PLUS 0.05 sec. per fur.

2341 Thatcher Maiden Claiming Hurdle (4-y-o and up) £1,722 2¹/₂m.......(1:10)

2083 TAKE A FLYER (Ire) 4-10-7 A Tory, *hld up, jmpd slwly and drpd rear second, pushed alng and hdwy aftr 8th, reminders 3 out, led last, rdn out.* (12 to 1 op 10 to 1) 1
2112⁹ RUMBELOW 5-11-3 M Richards, *hld up, cld appr 9th, led nxt, hdd last, no extr*...........(16 to 1 tchd 20 to 1) 2
2215³ OMIDJOY (Ire) 4-9-11 (7*) W J Walsh, *hld up in mid-div, hdwy 4 out, styd on wl appr last.*
.......................(2 to 1 fav op 6 to 4 tchd 9 to 4) 3
2227⁸ WHATMORECANIASKFOR (Ire) (bl) 6-10-7 (3*) D Meredith, *al prmnt, outpcd appr 3 out*........(6 to 1 tchd 8 to 1) 4
1590⁸ ARBEE TWENTY 8-11-7 I Lawrence, *trkd ldrs, reminders 8th, wknd tenth, tld off.*
.................................(10 to 1 op 7 to 1 tchd 11 to 1) 5
2129⁵ JUMPING JUDGE 7-11-6 (3*) A Dicken, *hld up in rear, outpcd and lost tch tenth, tld off.*
.......................(5 to 2 op 9 to 4 tchd 11 to 4) 6
2225⁶ LONG'S EXPRESS (Ire) (bl) 6-10-11 (3*) A Thornton, *trkd ldrs, led 7th till hdd tenth, sn drvn and wknd, tld off.*
.......................(13 to 2 op 9 to 2 tchd 7 to 1) 7
2141 BALUSTRADE 7-11-3 M Stevens, *made most to 7th, wknd quickly and pld up aftr nxt.*
.......................(20 to 1 op 16 to 1 tchd 25 to 1) pu

Dist: 6l, hd, 1l, 30l, ¹/₂l, 2l. 4m 54.20s. a 23.20s (8 Ran).

(Bull & Bear Racing), R J Hodges

2342 Asquith Conditional Jockeys' Handicap Hurdle (0-105 4-y-o and up) £1,722 2m...........(1:40)

1149* DONOSTI [99] 10-11-11 (3*) D Fortt, *cl up settled wl, led sn aftr 2 out, pushed out.*
.......................(11 to 10 fav op Evens tchd 11 to 8) 1
680² SAFETY (USA) [94] (bl) 7-11-4 (5*) P McLoughlin, *pld hrd, set slow pace, quickened 4 out, hdd sn aftr 2 out, kpt on.*
.......................(6 to 4 tchd 13 to 8) 2
960³ CANDLE KING (Ire) [73] 6-10-2⁶ (5*) M Appleby, *cl up, ev ch 7th, outpcd appr 3 out.*
.......................(11 to 1 op 6 to 1 tchd 12 to 1) 3
1741⁸ RED INK [76] 5-10-0 (5*) W J Walsh, *in cl tch till outpcd 4 out, tld off.*......(11 to 2 op 3 to 1 tchd 6 to 1) 4

Dist: 2¹/₂l, 5l, dist. 4m 55.80s. a 22.80s (4 Ran).

(R L C Hartley), R Lee

2343 Palmerston Novices' Handicap Hurdle (0-100 4-y-o and up) £1,768 2¹/₄m (2:10)

2227⁵ HIGHLAND FLAME [65] 5-10-9 D Gallagher, *trkd ldrs, led 2 out, clr appr last, cmftbly.*
...................................(6 to 1 op 5 to 1 tchd 7 to 1) 1

2133² HULLO MARY DOLL [62] 5-9-13 (7⁰) Chris Webb, *trkd ldrs, ev ch 2 out, one pace appr last.*
.... (8 to 1 op 5 to 1 tchd 10 to 1) 2

2111* NEARLY HONEST [60] 6-10-4 A Tory, *cl up, led 6th to 8th, led ag'n briefly 3 out, ev ch nxt, one pace.*
...........................(8 to 4 op 7 to 4 tchd 5 to 2) 3

2224³ MILL BURN [75] 5-11-5 R Campbell, *hld up in rear, cld 9th, pushed alng aftr 4 out, ch 2 out, sn rdn and no imprsn.* (13 to 8 fav op 7 to 4 tchd 2 to 1 and 6 to 4) 4

2111⁵ KINGSFOLD PET [65] 5-10-9 M Richards, *hld up in rear, cld 8th, ch 2 out, wknd appr last.*
...................(20 to 1 op 8 to 1 tchd 25 to 1) 5

1867 VERRO (USA) [56] 7-10-0 I Shoemark, *beh, mstk and pushed alng aftr 7th, sn lost tch...*(33 to 1 op 25 to 1) 6

2111⁴ BLAKE'S TREASURE [56] (bl) 7-9-7 (7⁰) Guy Lewis, *led til hdd 6th, led ag'n 8th to 3 out, wknd quickly, tld off.*
..........................(20 to 1 op 7 to 1) 7

2224 BARTON ROYAL (Ire) [80] (v) 4-11-10 Richard Guest, *nvr gng wl in rear, reminders 1st and second, rdn 7th, lost tch nxt, tld off....*...(16 to 1 op 8 to 1 tchd 20 to 1) 8
Dist: 5l, 4l, 2½l, nk, 25l, 2l, dist. 4m 13.70s. a 12.70s (8 Ran).

(A G Blackmore), A G Blackmore

2344 Disraeli Novices' Hurdle (4-y-o and up) £1,660 2¾m.............(3:10)

795⁴ DEBACLE (USA) 5-12-4 D Murphy, *hld up in cl trck, quick-ened to ld sn aftr 2 out, sprinted clr.*
.... (6 to 4 on op 5 to 4 on) 1

2228² CALOGAN 7-11-12 B Powell, *chsd ldr, led 8th till hdd sn aftr 2 out, outpcd....*(5 to 4 op 5 to 4 on tchd 11 to 8) 2

1700 KEMMY DARLING 7-11-1 M Ahern, *led til hdd 8th, hrd rdn and ev ch 2 out, wknd appr last.*
.... (33 to 1 op 20 to 1 tchd 50 to 1) 3
Dist: 6l, 8l. 5m 20.80s. a 21.80s (3 Ran).

(Mrs Lisa Olley), B J McMath

2345 Gladstone Novices' Hurdle (4-y-o and up) £1,768 2m.............(3:40)

2112* WILD STRAWBERRY 5-11-7 M Richards, *made all, clr 2 out, not extended.*
...................(11 to 4 on op 2 to 1 on tchd 7 to 4 on) 1

2224* MILZIG (USA) 5-11-12 D O'Sullivan, *trkd ldrs, chsd wnr frm 4 out, no imprsn whn blun last.* (4 to 1 op 11 to 4) 2

1622⁴ DUTY SERGEANT (Ire) 5-11-6 M Ahern, *mstk 3rd, trkd ldrs till rdn and outpcd appr 3 out....*(14 to 1 op 8 to 1) 3

1046 TELMAR SYSTEMS 5-11-6 R Campbell, *took keen hold, trkd ldrs, awkward 6th and nxt, sn lost pl, tld off.*
...................(66 to 1 op 25 to 1) 4

2224⁷ SUNBEAM CHARLIE 4-10-1 (7⁰) K Goble, *hld up beh, cld 6th, rdn and outpcd aftr 4 out, fourth and no ch whn blun and uns rdr nxt.*
...................(66 to 1 op 33 to 1 tchd 100 to 1) ur

MOGWAI (Ire) 5-11-3 (3⁰) A Dicken, *tld off 5th, pld up aftr 4 out.*...............(16 to 1 op 8 to 1 tchd 20 to 1) pu

MINSHAAR 4-10-3 T Wall, *beh whn blun badly 4th, tld off when pld up bef 7th.* (50 to 1 op 25 to 1 tchd 66 to 1) pu
Dist: 7l, 30l, dist. 3m 39.80s. a 6.80s (7 Ran).

SR: 33/31/-/-/ (Copyforce Ltd), Miss B Sanders

2346 Lloyd George Handicap Hurdle (0-110 4-y-o and up) £1,768 2½m......(4:10)

2229⁶ ROYAL CIRCUS [83] 5-10-13 D Bridgwater, *made virtually all, drvn appr last, ran on gmely.*
...................(11 to 2 op 5 to 1 tchd 6 to 1) 1

2132² WEST BAY [77] 8-10-7 S Smith Eccles, *cl up, hrd rdn and ev ch last, no extr r-in.*
...................(9 to 1 op 10 to 1 tchd 11 to 1) 2

2067⁷ SHIMMERING SCARLET (Ire) [98] 6-11-7 (7⁰) Mr C Bonner, *hld up beh, cld 8th, outpcd appr 3 out, styd on frm nxt.*
...................(8 to 1) 3

2113* GREENWINE (USA) [83] 8-10-13 M Richards, *beh, tld off 5th, hdwy frm 2 out, nrst finish...*(14 to 1 op 12 to 1) 4

2110⁴ FORGE [93] 6-11-9 A Charlton, *cl up til stdly lost pl aftr 4 out, tld off.*...........(13 to 2 op 5 to 1 tchd 6 to 1) 5

2165* QUALITAIR MEMORY (Ire) [82] 5-10-12 D Gallagher, *chsd ldrs till wknd 4 out, tld off.........*(5 to 1 op 4 to 1) 6

2019⁴ AMPHIGORY [93] (bl) 6-11-2 (7⁰) Miss S Cobden, *towards rear whn f 8th, dead.*..............(14 to 1 tchd 16 to 1) f

2131* BLASKET HERO [91] (bl) 6-11-7 S McNeill, *hld up, outpcd 8th, hdwy aftr 4 out, staying on but plenty to do in 3rd whn blun and uns rdr 2 out.....*(2 to 1 fav op 6 to 4) ur

1467⁴ CAPSIZE [95] 8-11-11 E Murphy, *trkd ldrs till lost pl aftr 8th, tld off whn pld up bef 2 out.* (8 to 1 tchd 10 to 1) pu
Dist: 1½l, 4l, 5l, 25l, ½l. 4m 42.10s. a 11.10s (9 Ran).

(P W Hiatt), P W Hiatt

TRAMORE (IRE) (heavy)
Thursday January 27th

2347 Dunmore East Opportunity Handicap Hurdle (95-116 5-y-o and up) £2,657 2m.............(1:30)

2231⁵ PUNTERS BAR [-] 7-10-8 (2⁰) P A Roche, ...(8 to 1) 1
2231⁴ FINNEGANS WAKE [-] 7-11-1 (2⁰) K P Gaule, ...(5 to 1) 2
2232² ANOTHER COURSE (Ire) [-] 6-10-10 (2⁰) M G Cleary, (9 to 1) 3
2279* FORTY ONE (Ire) [-] 6-10-10 C O'Brien, ...(2 to 1 fav) 4
2041⁷ SLANEY AGAIN (Ire) [-] 6-10-10 D P Murphy, ...(8 to 1) 5
2201⁵ ENERGANCE (Ire) [-] 6-11-3 T J Mitchell, ...(10 to 1) 6
2054⁴ TARA MILL (Ire) [-] 5-11-4 (4⁰) D J Kavanagh, ...(6 to 1) 7
Dist: 1l, 8l, 3½l, 8l. 4m 13.40s. (7 Ran).

(Cedars Racing Syndicate), Patrick Day

2348 Passage East (C&G) Maiden Hurdle (5-y-o) £2,243 2m.............(2:00)

2199⁶ COMMON POLICY (Ire) 11-5 (5⁰) T J O'Sullivan, (7 to 2 jt-fav) 1
2039² STEEL MAN (Ire) 11-5 J Shortt, ...(6 to 1) 2
2231⁹ CALL ME HENRY 11-5 F Woods, ...(20 to 1) 3
2232³ TURALITY (Ire) 11-0 (5⁰) P A Roche, ...(6 to 1) 4
2096⁵ WELEM (Ire) 11-5 P M Verling, ...(4 to 1) 5
9447 MAGNUM STAR (Ire) 11-5 C F Swan, ...(8 to 1) 6
2096² OVER THE JORDAN (Ire) 11-5 G M O'Neill, .(7 to 2 jt-fav) 7
1610⁷ MY SUNNY WAY (Ire) 10-12 (7⁰) Mr M Budds, ...(10 to 1) 8
GEOFFREY TREVOR (Ire) 11-0 (5⁰) C P Dunne, ..(33 to 1) 9
2199 RAVEN'S ROCK (Ire) 10-12 (7⁰) C A Leavy, ...(14 to 1) 10
2127³ ABAVARD (Ire) 11-10 S H O'Donovan, ...(8 to 1) 11
2039⁸ PROPHET'S THUMB (Ire) 11-5 J Jones, ...(33 to 1) 12
2155 VALTORUS (Ire) 11-5 K F O'Brien, ...(14 to 1) 13
Dist: 4l, 4l, 2½l, ¾l. 4m 12.60s. (13 Ran).

(Patrick O'Leary), Patrick O'Leary

2349 Brownstown (Mares) Maiden Hurdle (4-y-o) £2,243 2m.............(2:30)

2122² CARHUE STAR (Ire) 10-4 (5⁰) T J O'Sullivan, ...(11 to 8 on) 1
2094⁴ NURSE MAID (Ire) 11-0 J Jones, ...(12 to 1) 2
2099⁵ SAINT HILDA (Ire) 11-0 C F Swan, ...(10 to 1) 3
2123³ SERANERA (Ire) (bl) 10-4 (5⁰) M G Cleary, ...(5 to 1) 4
2122 PERSIAN GEM (Ire) (bl) 10-9 G M O'Neill, ...(12 to 1) 5
1983⁶ CREHELP EXPRESS (Ire) 10-9 C N Bowens, ...(8 to 1) 6
DUCHESS AFFAIR (Ire) 10-6 (3⁰) Mr A R Coonan, ..(14 to 1) 7
GENTLE REEF (Ire) 10-12 (5⁰) T J Mitchell, ...(33 to 1) 8
LADYS BID (Ire) 10-2 (7⁰) J M Donnelly, ...(25 to 1) 9
1853 BLACK PIPER (Ire) 10-9 F Woods, ...(20 to 1) 10
MY TRELAWNY (Ire) 11-0 J Collins, ...(6 to 1) 11
WHAT MAGIC (Ire) 10-9 H Rogers, ...(14 to 1) 12
BOSSY PATRICIA (Ire) 10-2 (7⁰) D M Bean, ...(20 to 1) 13
1983 PAKED (Ire) 10-4 (5⁰) D T Evans, ...(33 to 1) 14
MRS SNUGGS (Ire) 11-0 M Duffy, ...(8 to 1) pu
Dist: 1l, 5l, 9l, 12l. 4m 17.40s. (15 Ran).

(Patrick O'Leary), Patrick O'Leary

2350 Woodstown Handicap Chase (0-102 5-y-o and up) £2,243 2½m.... (3:00)

2200² ANOTHER GROUSE [-] 7-11-5 (3⁰) C O'Brien, ...(7 to 2) 1
2235* IFFEEE [-] 7-11-12 (5⁰,3ex) P A Roche, ...(5 to 2 fav) 2
2100 BOG LEAF VI [-] 11-9-10 T Horgan, ...(6 to 1) 3
2036³ BALLYHEIGUE [-] 8-11-4 C F Swan, ...(4 to 1) 4
1179 MCMAHON'S RIVER [-] 7-11-2 D H O'Connor, ...(8 to 1) 5
2235 CONNA RAMBLER [-] 11-11-4 (7⁰) Mr J Lombard, ..(8 to 1) 6
1915 TIRRY'S FRIEND [-] 12-10-11 M Duffy, ...(7 to 1) 7
2234 STRONG CHERRY [-] 8-10-8¹ (7⁰) Mr K Taylor, ...(10 to 1) bd
1915⁵ RUSSIAN GALE (Ire) [-] 4-11-2 A J Jones, ...(16 to 1) su
Dist: 1½l, 6l, nk, 14l. 5m 12.50s. (9 Ran).

(M Kelly), Edward P Mitchell

2351 Metal Man Novice Chase (6-y-o and up) £2,243 2m.............(3:30)

MACAMORE STAR 8-11-4 (3⁰) C O'Brien, ...(4 to 1) 1
2230³ CHARMING EXCUSE 10-11-2 (5⁰) C P Dunne, ...(7 to 1) 2
1899⁶ SO PINK (Ire) 6-10-13 (3⁰) T J Mitchell, ...(7 to 1) 3
1857 MONKS AIR 7-11-2 A J O'Brien, ...(20 to 1) 4
1495⁵ HERE IT IS 7-11-2 C F Swan, ...(7 to 1) 5
905 WHEATSTONE BRIDGE 8-11-2 (5⁰) P A Roche, ...(10 to 1) 6
2232² ALTEREZZA (USA) 7-11-7 B Sheridan, ...(11 to 10 fav) f
2027⁹ BARRAFONA (Ire) 6-11-7 (7⁰) Mr J Lombard, ...(10 to 1) f
2233⁹ BOY BLUE 7-11-7 G M O'Neill, ...(16 to 1) f
2234 RAINBOW ALLIANCE (Ire) (bl) 6-11-2 J F Titley, ...(14 to 1) pu
Dist: 3l, 2l, 20l, ½l. 4m 23.10s. (10 Ran).

(Patrick O'Brien), Thomas Foley

2352 Annstown Hunters' Chase (5-y-o and up) £2,275 2¾m.............(4:00)

30⁶ FAHA GIG (Ire) 5-11-0 Mr P F Graffin, ...(9 to 4 fav) 1
STYLISH STEPPER 9-11-7 (7⁰) Mr A K Wyse, ...(4 to 1) 2
FLAHERTYS BEST VI 7-11-6 (3⁰) Miss M Olivefalk, (20 to 1) 3
BONZER BOB 8-11-7 (7⁰) Mr G R Caplis, ...(9 to 2) 4
169 TROPICAL GABRIEL (Ire) 6-12-0 Mr P J Healy, ...(4 to 1) f
71⁵ AUTHENTICITY (Ire) 6-11-6 (3⁰) Mr T Lombard, ...(10 to 1) ur
ROSLAVAN LAD 10-11-7 (7⁰) Mr K Whelan, ...(6 to 1) pu
Dist: 14l, 20l. 6m 15.80s. (7 Ran).

(P O'Mahony), Gerard Cully

2353 Garrarus Flat Race (5-y-o and up) £2,243 2m.................... (4:30)

1610⁶	KING'S DECREE (Ire) 5-11-3 (7ᵉ) Mr J T McNamara, (7 to 1)	1
1687⁹	RUN BAVARD (Ire) 6-11-7 (7ᵉ) Mr P English, ... (7 to 1)	2
2236⁴	MIGHTY HAGGIS 7-11-7 (7ᵉ) Mr N C Kelleher, ... (7 to 1)	3
2128⁶	TUL NA GCARN 9-11-9 (5ᵉ) Mr G J Harford, ... (8 to 1)	4
1501⁴	SIOBHAILIN DUBH (Ire) 5-11-5 Mr A P O'Brien, (9 to 4 fav)	5
	VENT VERT (Ire) 6-11-2 (7ᵉ) Mr E Norris, ...(5 to 1)	6
1827⁸	AMEEN (Ire) 6-11-11 (3ᵉ) Mr J A Nash, ... (7 to 1)	7
	MATTS DILEMMA (Ire) 6-11-7 (7ᵉ) Miss L E A Doyle, (8 to 1)	8
2128⁸	RAMBLE ALONG (Ire) 5-10-12 (7ᵉ) Mr D Kenneally, (10 to 1)	9
2128	WAKEUP LITTLESUSIE 7-11-2 (7ᵉ) Miss I Lewis, .. (33 to 1)	10
1827	COLCANON 8-11-7 (7ᵉ) Mr J Lombard, ... (33 to 1)	11
	JENAWAY (Ire) 5-10-12 (7ᵉ) Mr E Gallagher, ...(14 to 1)	12
	SILKEN MOSS (Ire) 6-11-7 (7ᵉ) Mr G Kearns, ...(16 to 1)	13
2236⁹	ASHPLANT 7-11-11 (3ᵉ) Mrs M Mullins, ... (8 to 1)	14
1455	CROSSABEG ROSE (Ire) 6-11-4 (5ᵉ) Mr H F Cleary, (20 to 1)	15

Dist: ½l, ½l, 3l, 3½l. 4m 19.30s. (15 Ran).

(Jeremiah Cronin), A J McNamara

DONCASTER (good to soft)
Friday January 28th
Going Correction: PLUS 0.43 sec. per fur.

2354 Selby Conditional Jockeys' Claiming Hurdle (4,5,6-y-o) £1,952 2½m (12:55)

1280²	SO DISCREET (USA) 6-11-7 (3ᵉ) P McLoughlin, trkd ldrs, led gng wl aftr 3 out, sn clr, easily.	
	.... (Evens fav op 11 to 10 tchd 5 to 4)	1
2243	MISTIC GLEN (Ire) 5-11-5 A Dobbin, in tch, led 7th till aftr 3 out, no ch whn blun last.............(5 to 1 op 9 to 2)	2
2212⁴	SERAPHIM (Fr) 5-11-5 S Lyons, led 3rd to 7th, sn outpcd and beh, styd on frm 2 out............... (6 to 1 op 5 to 1)	3
1860⁸	HELLO VANOS 6-11-2 A Thornton, chsd ldrs, mstk 6th, sn pushed alng, kpt on same pace frm 3 out.	
	.... (33 to 1 op 25 to 1)	4
2108⁶	PORT IN A STORM 5-11-10 E Husband, hld up, pushed alng and hdwy aftr 7th, wknd appr 3 out.	
	...........................(4 to 1 op 5 to 2)	5
1787⁸	HIP HOP (Ire) 5-11-12 J Burke, in touch, jnd ldr 7th, wknd quickly appr 3 out...(16 to 1 op 14 to 1 tchd 20 to 1)	6
1640⁴	SHARE A MOMENT (Can) 4-10-7 S Wynne, chsd ldrs till outpcd and lost pl aftr 4th, hdwy aftr 7th, wknd quickly appr 3 out...(12 to 1 op 10 to 1 tchd 14 to 1)	7

Dist: 25l, 12l, 3½l, 15l, 8l, 2½l. 5m 2.40s. a 24.40s (7 Ran).

(Ms M Horan), J White

2355 Sandall Beat Novices' Handicap Chase (5-y-o and up) £3,429 3m (1:30)

2103³	ROAD BY THE RIVER (Ire) [95] 6-11-2 C Grant, cl up, led 14th, mstk and hdd 4 out, led aftr last, all out.	
	......................(7 to 1 op 5 to 1)	1
	FAIR CROSSING [101] 8-11-8 J Osborne, al prmnt, slight ld 4 out, gng best whn slpd aftr last and hdd, rallied und pres...............(9 to 1 op 8 to 1 tchd 10 to 1)	2
2105⁴	ISLAND GALE [98] 9-11-2 (3ᵉ) A Thornton, chsd ldrs, outpcd and rdn alng aftr 11th, hdwy to chase lders 4 out, no imprsn...................(5 to 1 fav tchd 9 to 2)	3
1644	TAREESH [86] 7-10-7 N Williamson, in tch, rdn appr 4 out, no hdwy........................(10 to 1 op 8 to 1)	4
1750	THE LIGHTER SIDE [86] 8-10-0 (7ᵉ) Jacqui Davies, beh 12th.	
	...................................(8 to 1 op 7 to 1)	5
2170⁴	JOLLY JAUNT [85] 9-9-13 (7ᵉ) P Ward, in tch, effrt aftr 12th, wknd appr 4 out.................(11 to 2 op 9 to 2)	6
1491	HEATHVIEW [83] 7-10-4 M Dwyer, settled midfield, blun and lost pl 12th, beh whn blunded and uns rdr 14th.	
	..................................(9 to 1 op 8 to 1)	ur
2238⁴	HUDSON BAY TRADER (USA) [103] 7-11-10 Mrs A Farrell, beh whn blun 6th, sn tld off, pld up bef 4 out.	
	...............(10 to 1 op 12 to 1 tchd 14 to 1)	pu
1420⁴	ASK FOR MORE [86] (bl) 9-10-7 P Niven, led, hit 7th and 9th, blun 14th and hdd, sn wknd, beh whn pld up bef 3 out.......................(8 to 1 op 5 to 1)	pu
1924	MARIDADI [81] 8-10-2 S Earle, sn beh, tld off whn pld up bef 9th........................(20 to 1 tchd 25 to 1)	pu
2149²	LADY BLAKENEY [79] 8-9-7 (7ᵉ) G Cahill, beh 12th, tld off whn pld up bef 3 out........................(7 to 1)	pu

Dist: Hd, 5l, 15l, 2l, 2l. 6m 16.90s. a 22.90s (11 Ran).

(T P M McDonagh Ltd), P Cheesbrough

2356 Rossington Main Novices' Hurdle Grade 2 (4-y-o and up) £6,735 2m 110yds..................... (2:00)

1872*	CUMBRIAN CHALLENGE (Ire) 5-11-5 L Wyer, in tch gng wl, hdwy to ld 2 out, quickened clr, cmftbly.	
	.........................(12 to 1 op 10 to 1)	1
2244*	SCOBIE BOY (Ire) 6-11-5 J Osborne, trkd ldrs, ev ch 2 out, kpt on wl frm last, no chance wth wnr.	
	...................(11 to 10 fav op 7 to 4 tchd Evens)	2

1478²	SURREY DANCER 6-11-5 P Niven, hld up, hdwy to track ldrs aftr 5th, ev ch 2 out, kpt on same pace..... (8 to 1)	3
2250*	ARCTIC KINSMAN 4-11-5 C Llewellyn, prmnt, led appr 3 out to nxt, one pace..................(7 to 2 op 3 to 1)	4
1930*	BUTLER'S TWITCH 7-11-5 M Richards, beh, hdwy aftr 5th, ev ch 3 out, sn rdn and btn.	
	...................(9 to 1 op 8 to 1 tchd 10 to 1)	5
2087⁵	MEGA BLUE 9-11-0 D Byrne, chsd ldrs, outpcd hfwy, kpt on wl frm 3 out....................(25 to 1 op 20 to 1)	6
1918*	MORCELI (Ire) 6-11-9 K O'Brien, prmnt till wknd appr 3 out...........................(5 to 1 tchd 11 to 2)	7
1675*	AMERICAN HERO 6-11-5 B Storey, led till appr 3 out, sn wknd......................(20 to 1 op 16 to 1)	8
2154³	HIGH MIND (Fr) 5-11-5 A Thornton, in tch till wknd hfwy.	
	...........................(50 to 1)	9
922	NATIVE FIELD (Ire) 5-11-5 M Dwyer, jmpd slwly 3rd, beh aftr, tld off.................(14 to 1 op 12 to 1)	10
	SHARP CHALLENGE 7-11-5 K Jones, chsd ldr to 4th, sn wknd, tld off.....................(100 to 1)	11

Dist: 3½l, 6l, 4l, 4l, ½l, 5l, 12l, 12l, dist, 15l. 4m 0.90s. a 10.40s (11 Ran).
SR: 58/54/48/44/40/34/32/38/22/10/ (Cumbrian Industrials Ltd), M H Easterby

2357 Balby Novices' Chase (6-y-o and up) £2,929 2m 110yds.............. (2:35)

1886*	SAN LORENZO (USA) 6-11-10 N Williamson, led, pushed alng and hdd betw last 2, led last, styd on wl.	
	...................(2 to 1 op 6 to 4 on)	1
1960*	ISSYIN 7-11-6 R Garritty, jmpd rght, trkd ldrs 5th, slight ld betw last 2, hdd last, no extr.	
	...................(100 to 30 op 11 to 4 tchd 7 to 2)	2
1792	ROAD TO THE WEIR 7-10-9 (5ᵉ) J Burke, sn tracking ldr, wknd appr 4 out.................(33 to 1 op 16 to 1)	3
2304	EMERALD GEM 8-11-0 M Brennan, lost tch 8th, tld off.	
	...........................(14 to 1 op 12 to 1)	4
1484³	GRAZEMBER 7-11-0 M Dwyer, chasing ldrs whn blun and uns rdr 7th....................(9 to 1 op 6 to 1)	ur

Dist: 1½l, 30l, 12l. 4m 7.50s. a 12.50s (5 Ran).
SR: 42/36/ (James D Greig), K C Bailey

2358 Cusworth Novices' Hurdle (5-y-o and up) £2,110 3m 110yds.......... (3:05)

2104*	MISS PLUM 5-10-13 P Niven, hld up, hdwy aftr 6th, led 2 out, clr whn jmpd lft last.... (11 to 8 on op 5 to 4 on)	1
2144²	TALBOT 8-10-12 J Osborne, led to 2 out, kpt on, no ch wth wnr......................(5 to 1 op 9 to 2 tchd 6 to 1)	2
2074³	SLAUGHT SON (Ire) 6-10-12 G McCourt, trkd ldrs, ev ch appr 3 out, sn outpcd.......................(20 to 1)	3
1935⁴	LACURVA (Ire) 6-10-12 S Earle, tch, wknd aftr 7th, outpcd appr 3 out.................(20 to 1 op 16 to 1)	4
	BECKLEY FOUNTAIN (Ire) 6-10-12 K O'Brien, al beh, tld off.......................(12 to 1 op 14 to 1)	5
1935³	MR CLANCY (Ire) 6-10-12 N Williamson, prmnt, pushed alng aftr 7th, sn wknd, tld off....(20 to 1 op 16 to 1)	6
2252	KILMINFOYLE 7-10-12 L Wyer, chsd ldrs, lost pl aftr 4th, tld off..........................(20 to 1)	7
1583³	SWEET NOBLE (Ire) 5-10-12 R Garritty, cl up till wknd quickly aftr 8th, tld off............(10 to 1 op 8 to 1)	8
2140⁷	CEREAL GEM 6-10-7 D Byrne, beh hfwy, tld off. (50 to 1)	9
1654²	ANOTHER NICK 8-10-13 (5ᵉ) P Williams, chsd ldrs till rdn and wknd quickly appr 3 out, virtually pld up r-in, tld off.......................(14 to 1 op 10 to 1)	10
1998*	OTTOMAN EMPIRE 7-11-10 M Brennan, hld up near, effrt aftr 7th, sn btn, beh whn pld up bef 3 out..... (14 to 1)	pu
1722⁴	ARIADLER (Ire) 6-11-4 C Grant, sn pushed alng and beh, tld off 6th, pld up bef 3 out......(12 to 1 op 10 to 1)	pu

Dist: 8l, 20l, 4l, dist, 1l, 1½l, sht-hd, 8l, dist. 6m 9.10s. a 29.10s (12 Ran).
(Lucayan Stud), Mrs M Reveley

2359 Barnby Moor Handicap Chase (0-135 5-y-o and up) £4,077 2m 3f 110yds ....(3:35)

2007*	RODEO STAR (USA) [110] 8-10-6 G McCourt, jmpd wl, trkd ldrs, led 11th, clr whn mstk 2 out, ran on well.	
	...................(11 to 8 on op 5 to 4 on)	1
2151⁵	CENTENARY STAR [104] 9-9-9 (5ᵉ) Mr M Buckley, made most till aftr 7th, hit tenth, lost pl, styd on wl frm 3 out.	
	...................(11 to 2 op 9 to 2)	2
1242²	MANDER'S WAY [107] 9-10-3 G Upton, wth ldr, led aftr 7th to 11th, kpt on same pace........(8 to 1 op 7 to 1)	3
1706³	SNITTON LANE [115] 8-10-11 N Williamson, hld up in tch, hdwy to chase wnr 4 out, wknd 2 out.	
	...................(8 to 1 tchd 10 to 1)	4
842	LUMBERJACK (USA) [132] (bl) 10-12-0 J Osborne, hld up in tch, effrt 11th, wknd quickly after 4 out.	
	...................(11 to 2 op 9 to 2)	5

Dist: 6l, 5l, 2½l, 12l. 5m 3.30s. a 17.30s (5 Ran).
(J C Bradbury), N Tinkler

2360 Bessacarr Handicap Hurdle (0-135 4-y-o and up) £2,950 2m 110yds (4:05)

2138²	HOME COUNTIES (Ire) [121] (v) 5-10-13 (3ᵉ) D J Moffatt, trkd ldr, led on bit appr 2 out, clr last, easily.	
	...................(100 to 30 op 3 to 1)	1

1940[6] DIZZY (USA) [119] 6-11-0 A Dobbin, *prmnt, rdn aftr 3 out, kpt on frm nxt, no ch wth wnr*..............(3 to 1 jt-fav tchd 100 to 30) 2
1746 SEAGULL HOLLOW (Ire) [105] 5-10-0 L Wyer, *hld up, effrt appr 3 out, kpt on frm nxt, not rch ldrs.*
..........................(7 to 1 tchd 8 to 1) 3
1737 BORO SMACKEROO [133] 9-12-0 K O'Brien, *led till appr 2 out, kpt on same pace*...............(12 to 1 op 10 to 1) 4
1746[6] RATIFY [105] 7-10-0 A S Smith, *in tch, hdwy to chal 2 out, second and btn whn blun and wnt lft last, eased nr finish*...........................(8 to 1 op 7 to 1) 5
1955[4] SAYMORE [105] 8-9-11 (3*) S Wynne, *hld up, effrt appr 3 out, no hdwy*....................(8 to 1 op 7 to 1) 6
1481* NOTABLE EXCEPTION [105] 5-9-9 (5*) Mr M Buckley, *hld up, effrt appr 3 out, sn btn.*.................(3 to 1 jt-fav tchd 100 to 30) 7
IRISH DITTY (USA) [105] 7-9-11 (3*) D Meredith, *refused to race*..............................(20 to 1) l
Dist: 8l, 1½l, 2l, 5l, 2l, 15l. 4m 5.00s. a 14.50s (8 Ran).
SR: 14/4/-/14/-/ (Roxy Cinemas (Dalton) Ltd), D Moffatt

WINCANTON (good to soft)
Friday January 28th
Going Correction: PLUS 0.72 sec. per fur. (races 1,4,6), PLUS 0.95 (2,3,5)

2361 Potters Novices' Handicap Hurdle (5-y-o and up) £2,390 2¾m....... (1:55)

2015[8] WARFIELD [71] 7-9-7 (7*) Guy Lewis, *mid-div, hdwy 5th, led appr 2 out, came clr approaching last, easily.*
....................(10 to 1 tchd 14 to 1 and 9 to 1) 1
1023* ACT OF PARLIAMENT (Ire) [93] 6-11-8 G Bradley, *hld up mid-div, hdwy 6th, chasing wnr whn mstk 2 out, sn rdn and one pace*................(9 to 4 fav tchd 7 to 2) 2
2142[2] STYLE AND CLASS [95] 5-11-10 R Dunwoody, *sn in tch, pushed alng appr 2 out, no imprsn on ldrs.*
...............(9 to 2 op 4 to 1 tchd 7 to 2 and 5 to 1) 3
1415[5] NORTHERN CREST [75] 8-10-4 S McNeill, *beh 5th, drvn and hdwy aftr 3 out, styd on same pace appr last.*
.............................(14 to 1 op 10 to 1) 4
2015[6] ELITE LEO [71] 9-10-0 M Hourigan, *in tch, mstk 7th, led 3 out, hdd appr 2 out, sn btn*.......(14 to 1 op 10 to 1) 5+
2015[5] CHICKABIDDY [83] 6-10-7 D Salter, *hdwy 6th, head-way and weakened aftr 3 out, sn btn.*
....................(10 to 1 op 8 to 1 tchd 12 to 1) 5+
2141[9] ROCK DIAMOND [79] 8-10-8 E Leonard, *beh, hdwy 7th, bumped rail aftr 3 out, kpt on same pace*
..............................(33 to 1 op 20 to 1) 6
1930[8] MUZO (USA) [71] 7-10-0 W Humphreys, *hdwy appr 3 out, rdn and mstk 2 out, sn wknd.*
...............(66 to 1 op 33 to 1 tchd 100 to 1) 7
869[9] TEARFUL PRINCE [71] 10-10-0 D Bridgwater, *nvr rch ldrs.*
..............................(50 to 1 op 33 to 1) 8
1023[6] ROYAL REFRAIN [90] 9-11-2 (3*) R Farrant, *hdwy 7th, rdn and wknd appr 3 out*..........(14 to 1 op 10 to 1) 9
1836 BATHWICK BOBBIE [87] (bl) 7-10-9 (7*) D Fortt, *in tch till wknd frm 3 out*..............(10 to 1 op 6 to 1) 10
2263 BLAKEINGTON [71] (bl) 8-9-7 (7*) Miss S Mitchell, *prmnt, chlgd 7th, beh, hdd 3 out, sn btn.*
..............................(100 to 1 op 33 to 1) 11
1456 MAYFIELD PARK [89] 9-11-4 C Maude, *prmnt, pressed ldrs 6th, wknd 8th*........(16 to 1 op 14 to 1 tchd 20 to 1) 12
HEAR A NIGHTINGALE [77] 7-9-13 (7*) D Hobbs, *f 1st.*
.....................(25 to 1 op 20 to 1 tchd 33 to 1) f
1935[8] DOWRY SQUARE (Ire) [79] 6-10-8 E Murphy, *f 1st.*
.............................(16 to 1 op 10 to 1) f
2146 TURKISH STAR [74] 9-10-3 S Mackey, *prmnt, led aftr 6th, hdd 8th, wknd rpdly, tld off whn pld up bef 2 out.*
.......................(50 to 1 op 25 to 1) pu
953 ENTERPRISE PRINCE [72] 8-10-1¹ D Murphy, *al beh, tld off whn pld up bef 2 out.*
............................(66 to 1 op 33 to 1) pu
1711 TROPICAL ACE [75] 7-10-4 A Tory, *prmnt to 5th, tld off whn pld up bef 2 out.*(20 to 1 op 16 to 1 tchd 25 to 1) pu
2196[5] IRISH TAN [72] 7-10-1¹ Richard Guest, *nvr better than mid-div, tld off whn pld up bef 2 out.*
..............................(20 to 1 op 10 to 1) pu
2066[6] EMALLEN (Ire) [71] 6-9-12⁵ (7*) Mr B Pollock, *led till hdd aftr 6th, sn wknd, tld off whn pld up bef last.*
.............................(50 to 1 op 20 to 1) pu
1950[7] SNICKERSNEE [73] 6-10-2² S Hodgson, *tld off till pld up aftr 5th.*...............(50 to 1 op 33 to 1) pu
2187[3] MAKING TIME [77] 7-10-6 B Powell, *prmnt to 5th, tld off whn pld up bef 2 out.*(10 to 1 op 12 to 1 tchd 20 to 1) pu
Dist: 10l, 10l, 3½l, 2½l, 1½l, 1l, 15l, 2l, 8l, 2½l. 5m 34.60s. a 28.60s (22 Ran).
(Colin Lewis), P F Nicholls

2362 Bet With The Tote Novices' Chase Qualifier (6-y-o and up) £3,314 3m 1f 110yds...................... (2:25)

1570* RUN UP THE FLAG 7-11-3 D Murphy, *hld up, hit 16th, led 3 out, cmftbly*...........(11 to 8 op 7 to 4 tchd 2 to 1) 1

2146 KIWI VELOCITY (NZ) 7-10-5 L Harvey, *not fluent, led 5th to 8th, hit 9th, dsptd ld tenth to 11th, led 13th, hdd and misake 3 out, sn btn.*................(100 to 1 op 50 to 1) 2
2195 DRAW LOTS 10-10-5 (5*) D Matthews, *chsd ldrs till lost tch frm 16th*........................(100 to 1 op 50 to 1) 3
2191[6] BRORA ROSE (Ire) 6-10-5 I Shoemark, *al wl beh, hit 15th, blun 4 out, hit 2 out, tld off*....(66 to 1 op 50 to 1) 4
2144 MAHATMACOAT 7-10-10 S Burrough, *f 1st.*
..............................(100 to 1 op 25 to 1) f
1107* GRANVILLE GUEST 8-11-3 G Bradley, *led till blun badly 4th and lost many ls, hdwy to chase ldrs 12th, wknd appr out, pld up bef nxt...* (Evens fav op 11 to 10 on) pu
2017 MAXXUM EXPRESS (Ire) 6-10-10 Richard Guest, *hmpd 1st, chsd ldrs, lft in ld aftr 4th, hdd 5th, led 8th to 13th, wknd 15th, tld off whn pld up four out.*
..............................(50 to 1 op 25 to 1) pu
Dist: 2l, dist, ½l. 7m 1.40s. a 45.40s (7 Ran).

(Pell-Mell Partners), J T Gifford

2363 Pat Ruthven And Guy Nixon Memorial Vase Handicap Chase For Amateur Riders (0-125 5-y-o and up) £3,704 3m 1f 110yds...................... (2:55)

1197[8] TOCHENKA [105] 10-10-1 (7*) Mr M Rimell, *made virtually all, came clr frm 16th, unchlgd.....* (10 to 1 op 6 to 1) 1
1932[2] NEW HALEN [97] 13-9-10¹ (5*) Miss P Jones, *in tch, chlgd 12th to 14th, outpcd frm 16th.*
..............................(10 to 1 op 6 to 1 tchd 12 to 1) 2
2143[4] COOL AND EASY [100] 8-9-10 (7*) Mr T McCarthy, *wl beh till drvn and styd on frm 3 out to poor 3rd r-in.*
..............(11 to 4 jt-fav op 3 to 1 tchd 7 to 2) 3
2184[3] UNDER OFFER [97] 13-9-7 (7*) Mr C Hancock, *chlgd 5th to 8th, wknd 14th*.................(16 to 1 tchd 20 to 1) 4
1459 NOUGAT RUSSE [104] 13-10-6⁶ (7*) Mr S Joynes, *beh, rdn and hit 11th, sn lost tch.*
..............................(16 to 1 op 10 to 1 tchd 20 to 1) 5
1540 WELKNOWN CHARACTER [116] 12-10-12 (7*) Miss J Brackenbury, *beh, blun 9th, hit 13th, nvr dngrs.*
..............................(7 to 1 op 6 to 1 tchd 10 to 1) 6
1246² CHANNELS GATE [115] 10-11-1 (3*) Mr J Durkan, *prmnt whn blun 6th, effrt and hit 13th, sn btn.....*(11 to 4 jt-fav op 5 to 2 tchd 3 to 1) 7
2184[5] SUNBEAM TALBOT [108] 13-10-8² (5*) Mr S Bush, *wl beh, hit 12th, no ch whn mstk and uns rdr 15th.*
..............(14 to 1 op 12 to 1 tchd 16 to 1) ur
2143[6] SHASTON [97] 9-9-7 (7*) Mr J Rees, *uns rdr 3rd.*
..............................(12 to 1 op 10 to 1) ur
PACO'S BOY [125] (bl) 9-11-7 (7*) Mr N Moore, *jmpd badly and tld off pld up bef 9th.*
..............(12 to 1 op 8 to 1 tchd 14 to 1) pu
2184* SAM SHORROCK [97] (bl) 12-10-0³ (3*,4ex) Mr G Johnson Houghton, *wl beh till pld up bef 4 out.*
..............................(11 to 1 op 7 to 1) pu
Dist: 12l, 30l, 2l, 2½l, 25l, 1½l. 6m 51.00s. a 35.00s (11 Ran).

(R K Minton-Price), N A Twiston-Davies

2364 Sculptors Claiming Hurdle (4-y-o) £1,970 2m...................... (3:25)

2169[7] MR GENEAOLOGY (USA) (bl) 11-12 W McFarland, *al in tch, hrd drvn frm 2 out, edgd lft and led last.*
.............(11 to 10 on op 6 to 4 on tchd 5 to 5 on) 1
2018² NANQUIDNO 10-6 M A FitzGerald, *led, not fluent second and 3rd, hdd but ev ch last, rdr lost whip, not quicken.*
..............................(5 to 1 tchd 4 to 1) 2
2016[7] HONEY GUIDE 11-2 L Harvey, *al in tch, styd on same pace frm 2 out...*(16 to 1 op 12 to 1 tchd 20 to 1) 3
2224[9] LYFORD CAY (Ire) (bl) 11-4 J Railton, *trkd ldrs, shaken up and found nothing frm 2 out...*(7 to 1 op 4 to 1) 4
1049[7] BOHEMIAN QUEEN 10-7 R Dunwoody, *beh, hdwy 4th, wknd aftr 3 out.*.................(7 to 1 op 5 to 1) 5
1464 CONBRIO STAR 10-13 R Bellamy, *al beh.*.......(33 to 1) 6
2163⁴ COSMIC STAR 10-11 C Maude, *beh 4th, hdwy 3 out, sn wknd.*................(20 to 1 op 12 to 1 tchd 33 to 1) 7
1244 FINDON ACADEMY (Ire) 10-10 H Jenkins, *mstk 3rd, hdwy 3 out, sn wknd.*...............(12 to 1 op 8 to 1) 8
2189 RAGAZZO (Ire) 11-12 A Charlton, *in tch 5th, wknd rpdly 3 out, tld off whn pld up bef 2 out.*
..............................(33 to 1 op 20 to 1 tchd 50 to 1) pu
Dist: 6l, ¾l, 10l, 15l, 4l, 12l, 15l. 4m 4.00s. a 27.00s (9 Ran).

(Mrs P A White), J White

2365 Maurice Lister Handicap Chase (0-140 5-y-o and up) £4,134 2m....... (3:55)

2171² EGYPT MILL PRINCE [139] (bl) 8-12-0 G Bradley, *made all, strode clr frm 4 out, easily.*
..............................(11 to 8 on op Evens tchd 5 to 4) 1

1752 SETTER COUNTRY [117] 10-10-6 W Irvine, *hdwy 6th, chsd wnr frm 8th, no imprsn*.............(8 to 1 op 6 to 1) 2
1771² SHU FLY (NZ) [125] 10-11-0 Jacqui Oliver, *beh whn hmpd second, chsd wnr 6th till jmpd slwly 8th, sn btn.*
...................(9 to 2 op 7 to 2 tchd 5 to 1) 3
1975⁵ SAILORS LUCK [111] 9-10-0 E Murphy, *f second.*
...................(14 to 1 op 10 to 1 tchd 16 to 1) f
1255* WHAT'S IN ORBIT [111] 9-10-0 D Murphy, *f second.*
...................(11 to 2 op 6 to 1 tchd 5 to 1) f
2174³ LUOMO PIU [111] 10-10-0 B Powell, *chsd wnr till slpd badly and uns rdr 5th (water)*.....(25 to 1 op 12 to 1) ur
Dist: 8l, 20l. 4m 9.30s. a 18.30s (6 Ran).
SR: 69/39/27/ (S R Webb), Mrs J Pitman

2366 Painters Handicap Hurdle (0-125 4-y-o and up) £2,861 2m.............(4:25)

2015⁴ JUMP START [87] 7-9-12 (3") A Dicken, *hit 1st, steady hdwy appr 2 out, led last, pushed out.*
...................(7 to 2 tchd 4 to 1) 1
1930² KEEP ME IN MIND (Ire) [102] 5-11-2 D Skyrme, *al in tch, chlgd 2 out till outpcd r-in.*........(11 to 2 op 4 to 1) 2
2142 SOCIETY GUEST [101] 8-11-1 S McNeill, *chsd ldrs, led aftr 3 out, hdd last, sn outpcd.*
...................(9 to 4 fav op 4 to 1 tchd 9 to 2) 3
MAESTRO PAUL [104] 8-11-4 D Murphy, *beh, hdwy appr 2 out, kpt on r-in.*.........(25 to 1 op 14 to 1) 4
CHEERFUL TIMES [103] 11-11-3 J Railton, *beh, hdwy appr 2 out, no imprsn last.* (25 to 1 op 14 to 1 tchd 20 to 1) 5
2086⁶ SMILING CHIEF (Ire) [90] 6-10-4 W Irvine, *chsd ldrs till wknd 2 out.*.........(8 to 1 tchd 10 to 1) 6
2142* MISS EQUILIA (USA) [94] 8-10-8 R Dunwoody, *beh, shaken up 3 out, no response...*(7 to 2 op 9 to 2 tchd 4 to 1) 7
ASHFIELD BOY [93] 10-10-7 M A FitzGerald, *pld hrd, led second, hdd aftr 3 out, wknd quickly 2 out.*
...................(16 to 1 op 25 to 1) 8
2082⁶ LAND OF THE FREE [102] 5-11-2 L Harvey, *led to second, wknd 3 out.*......(16 to 1 op 12 to 1 tchd 20 to 1) 9
COASTING 8-10-4 Craig Thornton, *nvr better than mid-div*..........................(50 to 1 op 25 to 1) 10
1641 ANTI MATTER [111] 9-11-4 (7") Mr J Culloty, *beh frm 4th.*
...................(50 to 1 op 25 to 1) 11
Dist: 1½l, 7l, 8l, 1l, 2½l, 25l, 3½l, 7l, 3l, 12l. 3m 53.70s. a 16.70s (11 Ran).
SR: 21/34/26/21/19/3/ (Stewart Pike), S Pike

AYR (soft)
Saturday January 29th
Going Correction: PLUS 0.90 sec. per fur. (races 1,3,-5,7), PLUS 1.05 (2,4,6)

2367 Barr 'National Hunt' Novices' Hurdle (5-y-o and up) £1,955 2¾m......(1:25)

1003² SEVEN TOWERS (Ire) 5-11-0 (5") Mr M Buckley, *patiently rdn, hdwy to join ldrs 3 out, led bef last, drvn clr.*
...................(11 to 8 fav op 5 to 4 tchd 6 to 4) 1
1726⁵ RUSSIAN CASTLE (Ire) 5-10-12 K Jones, *nvr far away, led 4 out to nxt, no ch whn wnr r-in...* (33 to 1 op 25 to 1) 2
2237* MAJOR BELL 6-11-12 M Moloney, *settled gng wl, improved to ld 3 out, rdn and hdd bef last, no extr.*
...................(5 to 1 tchd 6 to 1) 3
2322⁴ PAR-BAR (Ire) (bl) 6-10-7 N Doughty, *trkd ldrs, reminders 3rd, led briefly hfwy, led 5 out to nxt, no extr betw last 2*........................(8 to 1 op 6 to 1) 4
2220³ THE WHIRLIE WEEVIL 6-10-0 (7") B Harding, *al hndy, effrt in midfield hfwy, chlgd 3 out, one pace frm nxt.*
...................(7 to 1 tchd 8 to 1) 5
2008 CARSON CITY 7-10-12 R Hodge, *al hndy, led 7th to nxt, fdd und pres frm 2 out.*...........(25 to 1 op 14 to 1) 6
2104⁴ BELLS HILL LAD 7-11-5 A Dobbin, *tucked away beh ldrs, feeling pace appr 3 out, fdd.*.......(14 to 1 op 12 to 1) 7
PETER 6-10-7 (5") P Williams, *trkd ldrs till aftr 4 out, sn lost tch.*..........................(50 to 1) 8
2008⁴ NAWRIK (Ire) 5-10-12 T Reed, *slight ld to hfwy, fdd und pres appr 3 out.*........(8 to 1 op 7 to 1 tchd 10 to 1) 9
2140⁵ LAST REFUGE (Ire) 5-10-12 L O'Hara, *trkd ldrs till fdd und pres appr 3 out.*....(25 to 1 tchd 33 to 1 and 50 to 1) 10
1938⁷ KIRKTON GREY 7-10-12 B Storey, *wtd wth, improved to join ldrs hfwy, fdd appr 3 out, pld up bef nxt.*
...................(8 to 1 op 7 to 1 tchd 10 to 1 and 11 to 1) pu
2217 FINE OAK 7-11-2ᵃ Mr D Robertson, *lost tch quickly aftr one circuit, pld up bef 5 out.*............(500 to 1) pu
451 BEN RHYDDING 7-10-5 (7") S McDougall, *struggling to keep up hfwy, tld off whn pld up bef 5 out.*.. (200 to 1) pu
PRINCE ROSSINI (Ire) 6-10-7 (5") F Perratt, *chsd alng to keep up fnl circuit, tld off whn pld up bef 5 out.*
...................(40 to 1 op 20 to 1 tchd 50 to 1) pu
Dist: 10l, sht-hd, 1½l, 1½l, 15l, 3½l, 2½l, 1½l, 25l. 5m 47.90s. a 37.90s (14 Ran).
(Mrs E A Murray), Mrs M Reveley

2368 Mason Organisation Pattern Novices' Chase Grade 2 (5-y-o and up) £10,296 3m 1f........................(1:55)

813* KILLULA CHIEF 7-11-5 M Dwyer, *trkd ldr, lft clr bef 13th, blun 4 out, f 2 out, rmntd to ld ag'n, rdr rode wthout irons, gmely.......* (5 to 4 jt-fav op 6 to 5 tchd 11 to 8) 1
2294 CONCERT PAPER 10-11-5 K Davies, *not jump wl, struggling fnl circuit, blun and rdr lost irons 3 out, led briefly aftr nxt, hit last, no extr.....* (6 to 1 op 5 to 1) 2
2069* CLASSIC CONTACT 8-11-5 J Callaghan, *jmpd wl, sn moderest pace, quickened hfwy, broke dwn and pld up bef 13th........................*(5 to 4 jt-fav op 11 to 10) pu
Dist: 2½l. 7m 3.50s. a 63.50s (3 Ran).
(T G K Construction Ltd), J G M O'Shea

2369 Lady Isle Maiden Hurdle (4 & 5-y-o) £2,102 2m....................(2:25)

2217² FIVE TO SEVEN (USA) 5-11-5 D Wilkinson, *made all, clr 3 out, hit last 2, easily.*.....(6 to 4 on op 5 to 4 on) 1
2217⁷ WEAVER GEORGE (Ire) 4-10-4 (5") J Supple, *given time to settle, improved to chase wnr frm 3 out, no imprsn.*
...................(50 to 1 tchd 100 to 1) 2
2217⁴ REBEL KING 4-10-9 A Dobbin, *settled midfield, drvn alng aftr 4 out, one pace.* (16 to 1 tchd 20 to 1 and 25 to 1) 3
2154² PRINCESS MAXINE (Ire) 5-10-9 (5") Mr M Buckley, *bustled alng to chase ldg pair, struggling bef 3 out, sn lost tch.*
...................(4 to 1 op 5 to 1) 4
CROMARTY 4-10-4 M Dwyer, *patiently rdn, improved to chase wnr hfwy, hit 4 out, eased whn btn, prmsg.*
...................(7 to 1 op 6 to 1 tchd 8 to 1) 5
NICHOLAS PLANT 5-11-5 T Reed, *sn beh, tld off frm hfwy........................*(33 to 1 op 25 to 1) 6
WINSOME GRAIN 5-10-9 (5") P Williams, *settled wth chasing bunch, struggling 4 out, tld off.*
...................(33 to 1 op 25 to 1) 7
2333 CALL THE SHOTS (Ire) 5-11-5 K Jones, *wl plcd early, reminders hfwy, tld off frm 4 out*...........(100 to 1) 8
AMERIGUE 4-10-4 M Moloney, *f 1st*..........(33 to 1) f
2241 FANFOLD (Ire) 4-10-4 E McKinley, *sn outpcd, tld off whn pld up bef 3 out.*..........................(66 to 1) pu
1475⁸ WEST AUCKLAND 5-11-5 C Grant, *sn struggling, tld off frm hfwy, pld up bef 3 out.*............(100 to 1) pu
1724⁷ MARCO-PIERRE (Ire) 5-11-5 S Turner, *settled wth chasing bunch, lost tch hfwy, tld off whn pld up bef 3 out.*
...................(33 to 1 op 25 to 1) pu
2135² NETHERBY SAID 4-10-9 C Dennis, *in tch, chsd wnr hfwy, wl plcd wth chasing pair whn pld up bef 3 out.*
...................(15 to 2 op 7 to 1 tchd 8 to 1) pu
Dist: 10l, 20l, 7l, ¾l, 10l, 7l, dist. 3m 56.60s. a 19.60s (13 Ran).
SR: 39/-/-/-/-/ (The Five To Seven Partnership), C W Thornton

2370 Vulmidas Trophy Handicap Chase (0-125 5-y-o and up) £3,566 3m 1f (2:55)

1939* TARTAN TYRANT [118] 8-11-9 N Doughty, *patiently rdn, steady hdwy frm 4 out, led betw last 2, styd on wl.*
...................(2 to 1 op on 7 to 4 on) 1
2242⁶ GREY MINSTREL [95] 10-10-0 B Storey, *wtd wth, improved to track ldr fnl circuit, led 3 out till betw last 2, one pace.*...................(20 to 1 op 14 to 1) 2
1744² RIFLE RANGE [117] 11-11-8 M Dwyer, *led, blun 6 out, blunded and hdd 3 out, no extr.....* (5 to 1 op 9 to 2) 3
1540⁵ SHOON WIND [123] 11-12-0 C Grant, *trkd ldrs, reminders to keep up fnl circuit, outpcd appr 4 out, sn btn.*
...................(5 to 1 op 9 to 2) 4
2001⁶ CAROUSEL ROCKET [95] 11-9-9 (5") D Bentley, *trkd ldr for o'r one circuit, struggling 5 out, lost tch.*
...................(16 to 1 op 12 to 1) 5
Dist: 6l, 12l, 1½l, hd. 6m 37.90s. a 37.90s (5 Ran).
(The Edinburgh Woollen Mill Ltd), G Richards

2371 Skeldon Conditional Jockeys' Handicap Hurdle (0-115 4-y-o and up) £2,326 2m....................(3:25)

2108* ARAGON AYR [100] 6-11-5 A Dobbin, *settled midfield, chlgd 3 out, rdn and outpcd betw last 2, rallied gmely to ld cl hme.*................(7 to 2 op 3 to 1 tchd 4 to 1) 1
2243 HUSO [88] 6-10-7 S Taylor, *patiently rdn, drvn up to join ldrs 3 out, led bef last, ridden and ct cl hme...* (16 to 1) 2
2241* THE PREMIER EXPRES [86] 4-10-5 D J Moffatt, *nvr far away, led 5th till appr 2 out, rallied r-in, one pace cl hme........*(11 to 4 fav op 5 to 2 tchd 3 to 1) 3
2243² WAKE UP [90] 7-10-4 (5") K Davies, *co'red up beh ldrs, outpcd and rdn appr 3 out, styd on wl frm last.*
...................(4 to 1 op 5 to 1 tchd 9 to 2) 4
2243 ALL WELCOME [98] 7-10-12 (5") G Lee, *nvr far away, led bef 2 out, hdd betw last two, no extr r-in.*
...................(8 to 1 op 6 to 1) 5
1922³ PALACEGATE KING [102] 5-11-7 P Williams, *al hndy, led briefly hfwy, rdn appr 3 out, sn btn.* (9 to 2 op 4 to 1) 6
2138 CANDID LAD [93] 7-10-12 D Bentley, *trkd ldg bunch, chsd alng whn pace lifted 4 out, sn btn.*...........(25 to 1) 7
NIGHT OF MADNESS [87] 7-10-3 (3") B Harding, *last and hld up, lost grnd whn pace quickened 4 out, sn btn.*
...................(20 to 1 op 16 to 1) 8
2152² VALIANT DASH [105] 8-11-10 F Perratt, *led till reminders and hdd hfwy, fdd und pres aftr 4 out.*
...................(20 to 1 op 14 to 1) 9

Dist: ¾l, 2l, 1½l, 1½l, 12l, 6l, 4l, ½l. 3m 59.10s. a 22.10s (9 Ran).
SR: 14/1/-/-/5/-/   (Lt-Col W L Monteith), P Monteith

2372 Sorn Novices' Handicap Chase (5-y-o and up) £2,827 2m............(3:55)

2270² PRECIPICE RUN [86] 9-10-13 N Doughty, *led to 4th, styd hndy, led betw last 2, ran on wl.*
.........................(4 to 1 op 9 to 2 tchd 5 to 1) 1
2218⁴ GIPSY RAMBLER [74] 9-10-11 C Grant, *patiently rdn, improved to jump ahead 4 out, hdd betw last 2, one pace.*......................(12 to 1 tchd 14 to 1) 2
2251* SEON [98] 8-11-11 T Reed, *tucked away in midfield, effrt appr 4 out, blun nxt, rdn and one pace.*
.........................(2 to 1 fav op 6 to 4 tchd 9 to 4) 3
1861* SHEILAS HILLCREST [92] 8-11-0 (5*) J Supple, *trkd ldr, led 4th, rdn and hdd four out, fdd frm nxt.*
.........................(5 to 1 op 9 to 2) 4
2218 PIT PONY [73] 10-10-0 R Hodge, *chsd ldrs, feeling pace whn slightly hmpd by faller 6th, lost tch frm 5 out.*
.........................(50 to 1) 5
2218² ZARBANO [81] 8-10-8 A Merrigan, *trkd ldg pair, blun 4th, f 6th.*.........................(12 to 1 op 10 to 1) f
1955 SUNSET ROCK [91] 7-11-4 M Dwyer, *tracking ldrs whn f second, broke off fore, destroyed.*
.........................(11 to 4 op 5 to 2) f
823 BITOFANATTER [75] 6-10-2⁵ (3*) A Larnach, *al struggling, tld off whn pld up bef 2 out.*...(66 to 1 op 50 to 1) pu
Dist: 3½l, 1½l, 12l, 10l. 4m 10.70s. a 22.70s (8 Ran).
SR: 26/10/32/14/-/   (Cumbrian Racing Club), G Richards

2373 Levy Board National Hunt Flat Race (4,5,6-y-o) £1,838 2m..........(4:25)

1223⁴ NAUGHTY FUTURE 5-11-5 (5*) A Roche, *al travelling wl, led on bit 2 fs out, quickened, ran on.*
.........................(13 to 2 op 5 to 1 tchd 7 to 1) 1
WHO IS EQUINAME (Ire) 4-10-9 (5*) D Bentley, *al hndy, led 7 fs out, rdn and hdd 2 out, rallied.*
.........................(13 to 8 fav op 2 to 1 tchd 5 to 2) 2
723² RHOSSILI BAY 6-11-5 (5*) Mr M Buckley, *settled gng wl, drw level 2 fs out, rdn and one pace ins last.*
.........................(11 to 4 op 2 to 1 tchd 3 to 1 and 7 to 2) 3
ADDINGTON BOY (Ire) 6-11-3 (7*) B Harding, *trkd ldg bunch, ev ch entering strt, outpcd last 2 fs.*
.........................(7 to 1 op 4 to 1 tchd 9 to 1) 4
KERNEL GRAIN (Ire) 5-11-7 (3*) D J Moffatt, *trkd ldrs, ev ch and bustled alng entering strt, no extr last 2 fs.*
.........................(14 to 1 op 8 to 1) 5
VAN DER GRASS 5-11-10 A Dobbin, *wtd wth, drvn up to go hndy appr strt, fdd 2 fs out.*.....(25 to 1 op 20 to 1) 6
OAT COUTURE 6-11-5 (5*) F Perratt, *led to 7 fs out, fdd o'r 2 out.*..........(11 to 1 op 10 to 1 tchd 14 to 1) 7
JIMMY WAG 6-11-10 Mr C Ewart, *nvr far away, rdn entering strt, fdd.*......................(33 to 1 op 20 to 1) 8
SEABURN 4-10-9 (5*) J Supple, *chsd ldg bunch till fdd appr strt.*......................(12 to 1 tchd 14 to 1) 9
ANKOR GOLD 6-11-5 (5*) N Leach, *chsd ldg bunch to strt, fdd.*......................(20 to 1 op 16 to 1) 10
CRAIGIE RAMBLER (Ire) 5-11-5 Mr D Robertson, *whipped round strt, reco'red aftr 2 fs, fdd appr strt...* (100 to 1) 11
AFRICAN GOLD 6-11-3 (7*) I Jardine, *prmnt till appr strt, sn lost tch.*......................(25 to 1 tchd 33 to 1) 12
OUR WILMA 5-10-12 (7*) R McGrath, *pressed ldrs for o'r one m, sn lost tch.*......................(50 to 1) 13
TASHREEF 4-10-11 (3*) A Larnach, *struggling aftr one m, tld off.*..............(14 to 1 op 12 to 1 tchd 16 to 1) 14
Dist: 1½l, 2l, 7l, 1½l, 5l, 6l, sht-hd, 4l, 12l, 8l. 3m 56.40s. (14 Ran).
                                             (A K Collins), J J O'Neill

CHELTENHAM (soft)
Saturday January 29th
Going Correction: PLUS 1.50 sec. per fur.

2374 Food Brokers 'Finesse' Four Years Old Hurdle Grade 2 £6,280 2m 1f (1:10)

2211* PRIDWELL 11-0 R Dunwoody, *hld up, steady hdwy to ld last, ran on wl..*
.........................(3 to 1 op 11 to 4 tchd 9 to 4 and 100 to 30) 1
2169⁶ MY BALLYBOY 11-0 S Smith Eccles, *pressed ldrs, led appr 2 out, hdd approaching last, str chal but not quicken r-in.*......................(14 to 1 op 12 to 1 tchd 16 to 1) 2
1880⁴ NAWAR (Fr) 11-0 D Murphy, *hld up, not much room 3 out, chlgd 2 out, led appr last, sn hdd and wknd.*
.........................(2 to 1 fav op 6 to 4 tchd 9 to 4) 3
2245* HALHAM TARN (Ire) 11-0 P Holley, *hdwy and jmpd slwly 3 out, rdn and chsd ldrs appr last, sn btn.*
.........................(9 to 4 tchd 3 to 1) 4
2204⁷ MONAZITE 11-0 R Bellamy, *sn beh, rdn and no prog frm 3 out.*......................(66 to 1 op 50 to 1) 5
2189² KARAR (Ire) (v) 11-0 N Williamson, *rcd freely, pressed ldrs, ev ch 2 out, wknd.*......................(8 to 1 tchd 10 to 1) 6
2245³ DEMILUNE (USA) 11-0 C Llewellyn, *made most till hdd appr 2 out, sn btn.*......................(20 to 1 op 25 to 1) 7
Dist: 3l, 8l, 8l, 2½l, ¾l, 30l. 4m 26.70s. a 32.20s (7 Ran).

SR: 19/16/8/-/   (Pond House Racing), M C Pipe

2375 Timeform Hall Of Fame Chase (6-y-o and up) £10,308 3m 1f 110yds... (1:45)

1778* DUBACILLA 8-10-12 D Gallagher, *hld up, steady hdwy to chal 3 out, led appr 2 out, strode clr, readily.*
.........................(8 to 1 tchd 9 to 1) 1
1843⁴ YOUNG HUSTLER 7-11-6 C Llewellyn, *dsptd ld to second, chlgd aftr 15th, led 4 out, hdd appr 2 out, kpt on one pace.*......................(7 to 4 op 11 to 8 tchd 15 to 8) 2
2259² RUN FOR FREE 10-11-6 M Perrett, *led, hit second, jmpd slwly and hdd 4 out, styd on same pace, hng lft r-in.*
.........................(6 to 5 on op 5 to 4 on tchd 11 to 10 on) 3
1881 SIBTON ABBEY 9-11-10 D Murphy, *lost tch frm 14th, tld off.*......................(20 to 1 tchd 33 to 1) 4
BELMOUNT CAPTAIN 9-11-6 Richard Guest, *hit 3rd, rear 5th, hit tenth, lost tch 12th, tld off whn pld up bef 14th.*
.........................(40 to 1 op 20 to 1) pu
Dist: 6l, 10l, dist. 6m 59.40s. a 43.40s (5 Ran).
SR: 33/35/25/-/-/   (Mrs Veronica Cole), H T Cole

2376 Cleeve Hurdle Grade 1 (4-y-o and up) £25,120 2m 5f 110yds........(2:20)

2258* FLAKEY DOVE 8-11-3 R Dunwoody, *trkd ldrs till quickened to ld last, sn clr, easily.*(4 to 1 co-fav tchd 9 to 2) 1
2257³ SWEET DUKE (Fr) 7-11-8 C Llewellyn, *led, sn clr, hdd last, kpt on, no ch wth wnr.*......................(4 to 1 co-fav op 7 to 2 tchd 9 to 2) 2
MOLE BOARD 12-11-8 T Grantham, *hld up, hdwy to chase ldrs 2 out, rdn and one pace appr last.*
.........................(6 to 1 op 8 to 1) 3
1756⁷ TRIPLE WITCHING 8-11-8 N Williamson, *hdwy 3 out, rdn and no imprsn on ldrs frm 2 out.*
.........................(11 to 2 op 5 to 1 tchd 6 to 1) 4
2257⁷ SWEET GLOW (Fr) 7-11-8 M Foster, *al beh and nvr dngrs.*
.........................(25 to 1 op 20 to 1) 5
2046* ABSALOM'S LADY 6-11-3 P Holley, *took str hold, hdwy 6th, hit 3 out, wknd 2 out...* (4 to 1 co-fav tchd 9 to 2) 6
1888⁵ KING CREDO 9-11-8 D Murphy, *chsd ldrs in 3rd till wknd quickly and pld up aftr 2 out, dismounted.*
.........................(6 to 1 op 5 to 1) pu
Dist: 6l, ½l, 15l, 12l, 3l. 5m 36.70s. a 35.20s (7 Ran).
SR: 59/58/57/42/30/22/-/   (J T Price), R J Price

2377 Lobb Partnership Hall Of Fame Handicap Chase (5-y-o and up) £5,810 2m 5f ....(2:55)

2171⁴ WATERLOO BOY [158] 11-12-0 R Dunwoody, *al in tch, chlgd 3 out, led 2 out, ran on gmely r-in, all out.*
.........................(9 to 1 op 6 to 1 tchd 10 to 1) 1
2174 RICHVILLE [132] 8-10-2 N Williamson, *hld up, hit 8th and lost pos, hdwy and hit 13th, ev ch 2 out, str chal last, jst fld.*......................(6 to 4 fav op 13 to 8 tchd 2 to 1) 2
2013* SOUTHERN MINSTREL [130] 11-10-0 B Powell, *led to 2 out, rallied last, one pace und pres.*
.........................(8 to 1 op 7 to 1 tchd 14 to 1 and 7 to 1) 3
2266 RYDE AGAIN [147] 11-11-3 D Murphy, *in tch till one pace frm 3 out.*......................(8 to 1 op 7 to 1) 4
2174⁶ WIDE BOY [130] 12-9-9 (5*) Guy Lewis, *pressed ldrs till wknd 4 out.*......................(33 to 1) 5
828³ ROMANY KING [149] 10-11-5 Richard Guest, *in tch till wknd 4 out, mstk nxt...*(20 to 1 op 12 to 1) 6
FOR THE GRAIN [142] 10-10-12 M A FitzGerald, *chsd ldrs, 4th and hdd whn unt 9ne and pld up bef 2 out.*
.........................(14 to 1 op 10 to 1 tchd 16 to 1) pu
2145³ TOBY TOBIAS [140] 10-11-0 G Bradley, *in tch, hit 11th, wknd 4 out, pld up bef last.*.......(7 to 2 op 3 to 1) pu
Dist: Hd, 2½l, 12l, 8l, 8l. 5m 42.90s. a 38.90s (8 Ran).
SR: 26/-/-/-/-/   (M R Deeley), D Nicholson

2378 Letheby & Christopher Hall Of Fame Novices' Handicap Chase (5-y-o and up) £4,279 2m 5f..............(3:30)

2264* MONSIEUR LE CURE [120] 8-12-0 N Williamson, *in tch, chlgd tenth, stumbled 11th, led 2 out, ran on wl.*
.........................(5 to 1 tchd 6 to 1 and 9 to 2) 1
2010⁴ WELL BRIEFED [98] 7-10-6 B Powell, *chsd ldrs, led 4 out, hdd 2 out, ev ch last, styd on......*(8 to 1 tchd 9 to 1) 2
2249 THE GLOW (Ire) [120] 6-12-0 P Holley, *hdwy to chase ldrs 4 out, outpcd frm 2 out...*............(10 to 1 op 8 to 1) 3
2195² PROPERO [112] 9-11-3 (3*) P Hide, *chsd ldrs till mstk and outpcd 9th, in tch whn hit 4 out, no imprsn frm nxt.*
.........................(4 to 1 tchd 5 to 1) 4
2145⁵ POPPETS PET [93] 7-10-1 S Hodgson, *made most till mstk and hdd 4 out, sn btn.* (9 to 1 op 7 to 1 tchd 10 to 1) 5
1491⁵ PETTY BRIDGE [96] 10-10-4 R Bellamy, *prmnt till wknd 12th...*......................(16 to 1) 6
1841 ONE MORE RUN [92] 7-10-0 R Supple, *hit 8th, al beh.*
.........................(40 to 1 op 20 to 1) 7
2170⁷ CANAVER [92] 8-10-0 C Maude, *not jump wl, al beh.*
.........................(50 to 1 op 33 to 1) 8
1700⁴ SHOREHAM LADY [96] 9-10-4⁴ M Foster, *not jump wl, al beh, f 3 out.*......................(100 to 1) f

1934* FANTUS [102] 7-10-10 R Dunwoody, *chsd ldrs, chlgd tenth, blun 12th, chald 3 out, rdn and ev ch whn f 2 out*.............................(2 to 1 fav op 13 to 8) f
Dist: 3l, 12l, 1l, 5l, 10l, 8l, 2l. 5m 41.30s. a 37.30s (10 Ran).
SR: 42/17/27/18/-/-/ (Hector H Brown), J A C Edwards

2379 Cheltenham Hall Of Fame Handicap Hurdle (0-145 4-y-o and up) £4,926 2m 1f.............................(4:05)

2046⁵ DANCING PADDY [129] 6-11-12 D O'Sullivan, *chsd ldrs, jmpd slwly 4th, drvn to chlgd last and not fluent, sn led, all out*.........................(15 to 2 op 8 to 1) 1
2267⁶ NORTHERN SADDLER [113] 7-10-10 M A FitzGerald, *led to second, styd chasing ldr till led aftr 2 out, hdd r-in, stayed on same pace*... (9 to 1 op 7 to 1 tchd 10 to 1) 2
1508⁷ ELEMENTARY [120] 11-11-3 D Murphy, *mid-div, hdwy on bit appr 2 out, shaken up and no headway approaching last*............................ (33 to 1 op 16 to 1) 3
LYNCH LAW (Ire) [110] 6-10-7 R Dunwoody, *al chasing ldrs, rdn appr last, sn wknd.*
....................(5 to 2 fav op 2 to 1 tchd 11 to 4) 4
2175⁶ MIAMI SPLASH [118] 7-11-1 M Hourigan, *hld up, hdwy to track ldrs appr last, sn rdn, found little.*
.......................(15 to 2 op 6 to 1 tchd 8 to 1) 5
2227² WHIPPERS DELIGHT (Ire) [107] 6-10-4 D Meade, *led second, hdd aftr 2 out, sn wknd.*
.......................(9 to 1 op 10 to 1 tchd 12 to 1) 6
2175* SOOTHFAST (USA) [115] 5-10-12 T Grantham, *beh till hdwy appr 2 out, rdn and wknd quickly approaching last*...................(11 to 4 tchd 3 to 1 and 9 to 4) 7
2175⁷ BADRAKHANI (Fr) [130] 8-11-13 M Bosley, *mid-div till wknd 3 out*...................(20 to 1 op 14 to 1) 8
NO SIR ROM [108] 8-10-2 (3*) D Meredith, *al beh, lost tch 3 out, tld off whn pld up bef 2 out*...(40 to 1 op 20 to 1) pu
Dist: 7l, ½l, 2l, ¾l, 6l, 3½l, 8l. 4m 23.70s. a 29.20s (Flag start) (9 Ran).
SR: 61/38/44/32/39/22/26/33/-/ (Bychance Racing), K O Cunningham-Brown

2380 Racegoers Club Hall Of Fame Novices' Handicap Hurdle (5-y-o and up) £2,932 2m 1f...................(4:40)

1969* RELKEEL [108] 5-11-10 R Dunwoody, *trkd ldrs, chlgd 3 out, sn led, came clr aftr 2 out.*
.......................(11 to 4 op 9 to 4 tchd 3 to 1) 1
2204* EMPIRE BLUE [96] 11-10-12 M Bosley, *beh 4th, drvn and ran on frm 2 out, styd on, no ch wth wnr.*
.................................(11 to 2 op 6 to 1) 2
1490² MR JERVIS (Ire) [90] 5-10-6 D Murphy, *hld up, hdwy 3 out, chsd wnr appr last, sn rdn and one pace.*
.................................(5 to 2 fav op 5 to 2) 3
1951* TOPPING TOM (Ire) [103] 5-11-5 C Llewellyn, *in tch till lost pos appr 2 out, styd on ag'n approaching last.*
.................................(7 to 2 tchd 4 to 1) 4
2044⁷ BEYOND OUR REACH [105] 6-11-7 M A FitzGerald, *chsd ldrs, chlgd and not fluent 2 out, wknd appr last.*
.................................(7 to 1 tchd 8 to 1) 5
988² WILL'S BOUNTY [84] 11-10-0 N Williamson, *hdwy 5th, wknd 2 out, tld off*................(50 to 1 op 33 to 1) 6
WALKERS POINT [84] 8-10-0 W Humphreys, *led to 3 out, sn hdd, tld off*......................(50 to 1 op 33 to 1) 7
Dist: 8l, 4l, 2½l, ½l, dist, 6l. 4m 27.80s. a 33.30s (7 Ran).
SR: 18/-/-/-/ (Brig C B Harvey), D Nicholson

DONCASTER (good to soft)
Saturday January 29th
Going Correction: PLUS 0.45 sec. per fur. (races 1,2,-5,7), PLUS 0.40 (3,4,6)

2381 Brewers Juvenile Hurdle (4-y-o) £4,224 2m 110yds..............(1:00)

2169² WINTER FOREST (USA) 11-6 W Marston, *mid-div, hdwy 4 out, wide strt, hit 3 out and nxt, led and hit last, hrd rdn and ran on r-in*...........(5 to 4 on op 11 to 10) 1
2115² STRICTLY PERSONAL (USA) 11-0 L Harvey, *mid-div, hdwy 4 out, rdn and chlgd 2 out, hit last, ev ch whn hmpd flt, fnshd 3rd, plcd second*...........................(20 to 1) 2
2241² DIWALI DANCER 11-0 N Mann, *trkd ldrs, led 3 out, rdn, hdd and hit last, ev ch and hng rght r-in, ran on, fnshd second, plcd 3rd*.................(14 to 1 tchd 16 to 1) 3
2148⁷ PRIMO FIGLIO (bl) 10-11 (3*) A Thornton, *chsd ldrs, effrt and ev ch 3 out, rdn and hit nxt, sn one pace.* (33 to 1) 4
MAMARA REEF 10-4 (5*) P Waggott, *hld up, hdwy 4 out, rdn nxt, one pace frm 2 out*.....................(33 to 1) 5
CALIANDAK (Ire) 11-0 G McCourt, *hld up, steady hdwy on outer 4 out, ev ch nxt, grad wknd.*
.................................(10 to 1 tchd 12 to 1) 6
1767 DYAB (USA) 11-0 S Keightley, *led, rdn and hdd 4 out, kpt on one pace frm nxt*........................ (33 to 1) 7
2118* STAR MARKET 11-0 T Wall, *chsd ldrs, rdn alng 4 out, btn nxt*.............................(25 to 1 tchd 33 to 1) 8
1522* DON'T FORGET MARIE (Ire) 10-6 (3*) A Procter, *hld up, pushed alng hfwy, effrt and some hdwy 3 out, sn rdn and btn nxt*......................(16 to 1 op 14 to 1) 9
2072² REGAL AURA (Ire) 11-3 (3*) N Bentley, *in tch, hdwy 4 out, ev ch nxt, sn rdn and wknd.*
..........(15 to 2 op 7 to 1 tchd 13 to 2 and 8 to 1) 10
2204⁸ ACANTHUS (Ire) (bl) 10-9 (5*) T Eley, *in rear, blun 4th and sn beh*..........................(20 to 1 op 16 to 1) 11
TEJANO GOLD (USA) 11-0 W Humphreys, *chsd ldrs till rdn and wknd 4 out*..............................(50 to 1) 12
1767⁹ ATHERTON GREEN (Ire) 11-0 P Niven, *hld up, blun 4th, beh frm four out*................. (14 to 1 op 12 to 1) 13
DON'T JUMP (Ire) 10-9 R Campbell, *prmnt, led 4 out to nxt, sn rdn and wknd*............(20 to 1 op 16 to 1) 14
2204 RANORA (Ire) 10-4 (5*) T Jenks, *cl up till rdn and wknd 4 out*..(50 to 1) 15
2275 INFANTRY GLEN (v) 10-9 (5*) P Midgley, *blun 3rd, al beh.*
....(50 to 1) 16
LIVONIAN 11-0 J Osborne, *not fluent, hld up, beh frm 4 out, pld up aftr nxt, broke blood vessel.*
......................................(4 to 1 tchd 9 to 2) pu
Dist: Hd, 2½l, 12l, 3l, 1l, 1½l, 6l, 4l, 1½l, 1l. 4m 5.80s. a 15.30s (17 Ran).
SR: 13/7/4/-/-/-/ (Sheikh Ahmed Bin Saeed Al Maktoum), D Nicholson

2382 River Don Novices' Hurdle Grade 2 (4-y-o and up) £6,825 2½m........ (1:35)

1994* SEEKIN CASH (USA) 5-11-10 J Osborne, *made all, clr 2 out, styd on strly*......(11 to 4 op 3 to 1 tchd 7 to 2) 1
1594* NIRVANA PRINCE 5-11-6 T Wall, *hld up pulling hrd, not fluent early, hdwy 6th, effrt 3 out and sn rdn, styd on appr last, no ch wth wnr*...........(6 to 1 op 11 to 2) 2
2263* CORROUGE (USA) 5-11-6 D Bridgwater, *hld up in tch, hdwy 7th, effrt to chal and hit 3 out, sn rdn and one pace*.........(11 to 10 fav op 11 to 10 on tchd 5 to 4) 3
2014⁶ MARCHWOOD 7-11-6 G McCourt, *in tch, pushed alng 6th, effrt and rdn appr 3 out, one pace.*
..................................(25 to 1 op 20 to 1) 4
2153² SHAFFIC (Fr) 7-11-6 P Niven, *hld up, effrt and some hdwy 7th, sn rdn and btn nxt*.......... (16 to 1 op 12 to 1) 5
2175⁴ WESTHOLME (USA) 6-11-6 L Wyer, *cld up, ev ch till rdn and wknd quickly aftr 4 out*........(13 to 2 op 5 to 1) 6
2068² TITIAN GIRL (bl) 5-11-1 A Thornton, *cl up to 5th, sn lost pl, tld off frm 3 out*...................(66 to 1 op 50 to 1) 7
BRAVE AND TENDER (Ire) 5-11-6 K O'Brien, *pld hrd, hdwy to join ldrs 4th, rdn and wknd four out, tld off whn pulled up bef 2 out*...........................(33 to 1) pu
Dist: 12l, 4l, 1½l, 25l, 5l, 30l. 4m 50.90s. a 12.90s (8 Ran).
SR: 57/41/37/35/10/5/-/-/ (Sheikh Ahmed Bin Saeed Al Maktoum), C R Egerton

2383 Mansion House Handicap Chase (5-y-o and up) £5,842 2m 110yds...(2:05)

2261* GOOD FOR A LAUGH [124] 10-9-7 (7*) Mr D Parker, *chsd ldrs, blun 5th, hdwy 4 out, effrt to chal 2 out, rdn last, led r-in*................ (9 to 2 op 4 to 1 tchd 5 to 1) 1
1758⁴ YOUNG SNUGFIT [152] 10-12-0 J Osborne, *led, rdn last, hdd and no extr r-in.*
..................(6 to 4 fav tchd 11 to 8 and 13 to 8) 2
1479³ JUST FRANKIE [124] 10-10-0 L Wyer, *hld up, hit 3rd, hdwy 4 out, one pace 2 out, better for race.*
.......................(9 to 2 op 4 to 1 tchd 5 to 1) 3
1666² HOWE STREET [135] 11-10-11 K O'Brien, *wth ldr, effrt and ev ch 5 out, rdn and wknd nxt.*
.......................(9 to 4 op 7 to 4 tchd 5 to 2) 4
Dist: ½l, 20l, dist. 4m 3.90s. a 8.90s (4 Ran).
SR: 49/76/28/-/ (Mrs S A Bramall), Mrs S A Bramall

2384 Great Yorkshire Handicap Chase (0-145 5-y-o and up) £19,008 3m (2:40)

1875 CARBISDALE [134] 8-11-4 P Niven, *hld up, gd hdwy 5 out, led 3 out, clr nxt, hit last, ran on.*
.......................(13 to 2 op 6 to 1 tchd 7 to 1) 1
2047* AVONBURN (NZ) [118] 10-10-2 M Richards, *hld up, hit 4th, hdwy 12th, rdn four out, hit nxt, styd on appr last.*
....(14 to 1) 2
1995* GNOME'S TYCOON [127] 8-10-11 J Railton, *trkd ldrs gng wl, smooth hdwy to ld 5 out, hdd and rdn 3 out, sn one pace*............... (11 to 4 fav op 4 to 1 tchd 9 to 2) 3
1875* GENERAL PERSHING [143] 8-11-13 J Osborne, *led, hdd 5 out, sn rdn and one pace*...........(9 to 1 op 8 to 1) 4
1664* FRAGRANT DAWN [144] 10-12-0 J Lower, *hld up and beh, mstks, hdwy 12th, rdn and hit 3 out, no imprsn.*
................................(11 to 2 op 4 to 1) 5
1889³ STUNNING STUFF [123] 9-10-7 S McNeill, *hit 1st, chsd ldrs to 8th, sn in rear*.....(11 to 1 op 12 to 1 tchd 10 to 1) 6
1486* NO MORE TRIX [117] 8-10-1¹ R Garritty, *hld up, hdwy 8th, rdn and ev ch 4 out, 3rd and held whn f 2 out.*
................................(11 to 2 op 6 to 1) f
1838 SCOLE [116] 9-9-7 (7*) P Murphy, *prmnt till blun and uns rdr 11th*..................................(50 to 1) ur
1652² USHERS ISLAND [132] 8-11-2 K O'Brien, *chsd ldrs, hdwy 11th, dsptd ld nxt, rdn and wknd quickly 13th, beh whn pld up bef 3 out*.............. (15 to 2 op 6 to 1) pu

1503⁴ MUSTHAVEASWIG [121] 8-10-5 W Marston, *mid-div, hdwy
tenth, rdn alng 12th and sn lost pl, beh whn pld up bef
4 out*.............................(10 to 1 op 12 to 1) pu
Dist: 10l, 1½l, 15l, 15l, ¾l. 6m 5.70s. a 11.70s (10 Ran).
SR: 69/43/50/51/37/15/   (Mrs M Williams), Mrs M Reveley

2385 Yorkshire Handicap Hurdle (0-145 4-y-o and up) £3,782 2½m......... (3:10)

2138⁶ BO KNOWS BEST (Ire) [123] 5-10-6 W Marston, *hld up in
mid-div, hdwy 6th, led 2 out, rdn last, styd on wl r-in.*
...........................(7 to 1 op 5 to 1 tchd 8 to 1) 1
1922⁶ HIGH ALLTITUDE (Ire) [131] (bl) 6-11-1 L Wyer, *trkd ldrs,
hdwy to chal 2 out, rdn last, no extr run- in.*
..................................(33 to 1 op 25 to 1) 2
2002² STRATH ROYAL [119] 8-10-2 M Brennan, *hld up and beh.
gd hdwy 4 out, effrt and ev ch nxt, rdn 2 out and sn one
pace.*...........................(4 to 1 jt-fav op 6 to 1) 3
1874⁴ KIVETON TYCOON (Ire) [123] (bl) 5-10-6 G McCourt, *hld up
and beh, steady hdwy appr 4 out, effrt nxt and ev ch,
rdn 2 out and sn btn.*................(8 to 1 op 7 to 1) 4
1361 CHIEF RAIDER (Ire) [117] 6-9-7 (7*) D Ryan, *in tch, hdwy
5th, chsd ldr and blun nxt, led 4 out, hdd appr 2 out
and grad wknd.*...................(66 to 1 op 100 to 1) 5
22737 SPROWSTON BOY [117] 11-10-0 W Worthington, *in tch till
outpcd 4th and beh nxt, styd on frm 3 out, nvr dngrs.*
...........................(40 to 1 op 33 to 1 tchd 50 to 1) 6
1653² SILLARS STALKER (Ire) [134] 6-10-12 (5*) J Twomey, *hld up
and beh, some hdwy appr 3 out, nvr rch ldrs.* (4 to 1 jt-
fav op 9 to 2) 7
1280* OUR SLIMBRIDGE [117] 6-10-0 S Keightley, *hld up and
beh, some hdwy appr 3 out, nvr rch ldrs.*
...................................(12 to 1 op 10 to 1) 8
2222³ REVE DE VALSE (USA) [117] 7-9-9 (5*) P Waggott, *chsd ldrs,
rdn 4 out and sn wknd.*..................(12 to 1) 9
2222 THE DEMON BARBER [118] 12-10-1 J Osborne, *al rear.*
...................................(25 to 1) 10
FETTUCCINE [126] 10-10-6 (3*) A Thornton, *chsd ldrs till
rdn 6th and sn wknd.*...........(25 to 1 op 20 to 1) 11
1474⁷ TEMPLE GARTH [117] 5-9-7 (7*) B Grattan, *prmnt till rdn
and wknd 6th.*........................(50 to 1) 12
1364⁸ NODFORM WONDER [122] 7-10-5 K O'Brien, *led and chsd
hdd 4 out and wknd quickly.*.......(10 to 1 op 8 to 1) 13
VIARDOT (Ire) [129] 5-10-12 P Niven, *hld up, al beh.*
...........................(8 to 1 op 6 to 1) 14
2172 DOOLAR (USA) [117] 7-10-0 N Mann, *chsd clr ldr to 5th, sn
wknd.*..........................(20 to 1 op 25 to 1) 15
AMBUSCADE (USA) [145] 8-12-0 M Richards, *al rear, tld
off whn pld up bef 2 out.*...................(25 to 1) pu
Dist: 4l, 4l, 10l, 5l, 15l, hd, ½l, 2l, sht-hd, 8l. 4m 48.90s. a 10.90s (16 Ran).
SR: 59/63/47/41/30/15/32/14/12/   (Nigel Goldman), Mrs J R Ramsden

2386 Burghwallis Novices' Chase (5-y-o and up) £3,078 2m 3f 110yds.... (3:45)

1372* MR WOODCOCK 9-11-12 P Niven, *wth ldr, hit 5th, led 4
out, rdn nxt, styd on gmely und pres r-in.*
...........................(13 to 8 on op 11 to 8 on) 1
SLIEVENAMON MIST 8-11-4 S McNeill, *al prmnt, effrt to
chal 4 out, rdn nxt, ev ch till no extr r-in.*
...........................(11 to 2 op 9 to 2) 2
2195³ CAMBO (USA) 8-11-4 D Skyrme, *in tch, hit tenth, wknd 5
out.*..........................(7 to 1 op 6 to 1) 3
2260 COUNTORIS 8-11-4 K O'Brien, *led, rdn and hdd 4 out, sn
wknd.*..........................(9 to 2 op 7 to 1) 4
THE PUB 8-11-4 J Corkell, *blun und rn rdr 1st.*
...........................(66 to 1 op 50 to 1) ur
Dist: 6l, 8l, 12l. 5m 6.90s. a 20.90s (5 Ran).
(P A Tylor), Mrs M Reveley

2387 Louella Stud 'Primitive Rising' National Hunt Flat Race (4,5,6-y-o) £2,214 2m 110yds............. (4:15)

LIEN DE FAMILLE (Ire) 4-10-9 (5*) E Husband, *chsd ldrs, rdn
4 fs out, styd on to ld 2 out, ran on wl und pres fnl
furlong.*.........................(4 to 1 op 7 to 2) 1
2074* CALL EQUINAME 4-11-2 (5*) J Burke, *cl up, led 4 fs out,
rdn and pld 2 out, edgd lft and wknd ins last.*
...........................(7 to 4 fav op 5 to 4 to 2) 2
DISSINGTON DENE 5-11-5 (5*) P Midgley, *al prmnt, effrt
and ev ch 4 out, sn rdn and kpt on one pace...(20 to 1) 3
EXCLUSIVE EDITION (Ire) 4-10-9 W Marston, *sn led, rdn
and hdd 4 fs out, grad wknd.*.........(4 to 1 op 8 to 1) 4
GREY SMOKE 4-10-7 (7*) J Driscoll, *chsd ldrs, outpcd 7 fs
out, styd on und pres fnl 3 furlongs, nvr dngrs.*
...........................(14 to 1) 5
CAPENWRAY (Ire) 5-12-0 (3*) A Thornton, *prmnt, ev ch 4 fs
out, sn rdn and wknd 3 furlongs out.*
...........................(10 to 1 op 8 to 1) 6
KING LUCIFER (Ire) 5-11-3 (7*) M Keighley, *hld up and beh,
some hdwy 4 fs out, nvr dngrs.....*(10 to 1 op 7 to 1) 7
MASTER TOBY 4-10-9 (5*) T Jenks, *in tch, effrt and rdn 5
fs out, sn one pace.*.........................(20 to 1) 8
HUTCEL BRIG 5-10-12 (7*) P Johnson, *beh till some hdwy
fnl 3 fs, nvr a factor.*..............(16 to 1 op 14 to 1) 9

LINGCOOL 4-10-4 (5*) P Waggott, *al rear.*
...........................(12 to 1 tchd 10 to 1) 10
GRAND PASHA (Ire) 6-11-3 (7*) W Fry, *nvr a factor.*
...........................(12 to 1 op 10 to 1) 11
MY LISA TOO 5-10-12 (7*) G Tormey, *beh frm hfwy.*
...........................(25 to 1) 12
SPEAKER WEATHERILL (Ire) 5-11-3 (7*) R Moore, *in tch on
outer, rdn o'r 6 fs out and sn lost pl.....*(20 to 1) 13
BLACK STAG (Ire) 5-11-3 (7*) P Ward, *al rear.*
...........................(16 to 1 op 14 to 1) 14
SPY DESSA 6-11-3 (7*) M Clarke, *beh frm hfwy.* (20 to 1) 15
CAPITAL LETTER (Ire) 5-11-10 Mr J Durkan, *beh frm hfwy,
tld off fnl 4 fs...*........................(25 to 1) 16
WARREN HOUSE 6-11-5 (5*) S Lyons, *in tch, lost pl
quickly 7 fs out and sn tld off.....*(12 to 1 op 10 to 1) 17
Dist: 8l, ¾l, 20l, 5l, ¾l, 3½l, 10l, 1½l, 2½l, 20l. 4m 3.00s. (17 Ran).
(Mrs Marie Taylor), J F Bottomley

NAAS (IRE) (heavy)
Saturday January 29th

2388 Sallins Maiden Hurdle (4-y-o) £3,105 2m..........................(1:30)

ANDANTE (Ire) 10-9 C F Swan,................(5 to 2 fav) 1
SOVIET CHOICE (Ire) 10-4 (5*) C P Dunne,.........(9 to 2) 2
2081⁴ ROYAL RANK (USA) 10-2 (7*) J M Donnelly,......(10 to 1) 3
1853³ DARK SWAN (Ire) 11-0 T Horgan,...............(8 to 1) 4
1575 SHEREGORI (Ire) 10-4 (5*) K L O'Brien,.........(5 to 1) 5
2122 RISKY GALORE 10-4 (5*) K P Gaule,.............(12 to 1) 6
2285³ HUNCHEON CHANCE 10-4 (5*) J P Broderick,.....(3 to 1) 7
2122⁵ SHANGANOIR (Ire) 10-4 P Carberry,.............(5 to 1) 8
TRIBAL MEMORIES (Ire) 10-1 (3*) C O'Brien,....(25 to 1) 9
ABEREDW (Ire) 10-4 A Powell,..................(7 to 1) 10
WONDERFUL SONG (USA) (bl) 10-9 H Rogers,...(20 to 1) 11
GLIDING ALONG (Ire) 10-4 L P Cusack,...........(20 to 1) 12
SYLVESTER (Ire) 10-9 J P Banahan,.............(20 to 1) 13
Dist: 7l, 1l, sht-hd, 5l. 4m 16.50s. (13 Ran).
(Patrick O'Leary), Patrick O'Leary

2389 Monread Maiden Hurdle (5-y-o and up) £3,105 2½m...............(2:00)

2278³ CHANCE COFFEY 9-11-6 G M O'Neill,...........(11 to 2) 1
2199² DARU (USA) 5-11-10 C F Swan,..............(5 to 4 on) 2
2199⁴ BUTCHES BOY (Ire) 5-11-10 S H O'Donovan,....(10 to 1) 3
2201³ HEMISPHERE (Ire) (bl) 5-10-11 (5*) M G Cleary,....(10 to 1) 4
JOHNNY SETASIDE (Ire) 5-11-2 P Carberry,.....(20 to 1) 5
2123⁸ TWIN RAINBOW 7-12-0 L P Cusack,.............(14 to 1) 6
2052⁷ MAN OF IRON 7-11-6 T J Taaffe,.............(20 to 1) 7
2283² YOUR THE MAN 8-12-0 J Shortt,..............(10 to 1) 8
555 DHOMSONS BUCK (Ire) 5-10-9 (7*) D J Finnegan,..(20 to 1) 9
2123⁹ TRIMMER WONDER (Ire) 6-11-2 (7*) M Kelly,....(20 to 1) 10
2203⁸ LISNABOY PRINCE 7-11-1 (5*) K P Gaule,.......(33 to 1) 11
555⁴ BAWNROCK (Ire) 5-11-10 T Horgan,............(6 to 1) 12
2278 SARVO (Ire) 6-11-3 (3*) T J O'Sullivan,.....(100 to 1) 13
2050⁹ TRINITY GALE (Ire) 6-10-12 (3*) D P Murphy,...(33 to 1) 14
2231 SLANEY FOOD 7-12-0 D H O'Connor,.............(25 to 1) 15
1916* CORRIBLOUGH (Ire) 6-11-10 (5*) C O'Brien,...(14 to 1) 16
BOBSVILLE (Ire) 6-11-6 C N Bowens,...........(20 to 1) 17
1898⁴ COUNTERBALANCE 7-11-1 J P Banahan,........(20 to 1) 18
2289⁹ BALLYBODEN 7-11-1 (5*) J P Broderick,........(16 to 1) 19
1822⁷ NINE O THREE (Ire) 5-11-2 H Rogers,.........(25 to 1) 20
GARBONI (USA) 5-11-10 B Sheridan,............(12 to 1) 21
1854⁶ BUCKHILL 7-11-6 A J O'Brien,..................(50 to 1) 22
1858⁷ SHUILNAMON (Ire) 5-10-11 F Woods,............(33 to 1) 23
2283⁸ DORAN'S DELIGHT 7-12-0 J F Titley,............(20 to 1) f
MARVELOUS CHOICE (Ire) 6-11-1 A Powell,.....(33 to 1) pu
Dist: Sht-hd, 14l, 1½l, 7l. 5m 20.50s. (25 Ran).
(P J O'Donnell), P F O'Donnell

2390 Naas E.B.F. Chase (5-y-o and up) £4,140 3m....................(2:30)

2100* ANOTHER EXCUSE (Ire) 6-11-9 (5*) Mr W M O'Sullivan,
...........................(5 to 2) 1
2277* TITIAN BLONDE (Ire) 6-11-3 C F Swan,.........(5 to 1) 2
2125 SULLANE RIVER (Ire) 6-11-9 D H O'Connor,...(5 to 4 on) 3
2282 LE BRAVE 8-11-4 J Shortt,...................(20 to 1) 4
1913 THE MAD MONK 9-11-4 M Flynn,................(33 to 1) 5
2101³ SPUR OF THE MOMENT 7-11-3 J P Banahan,......(9 to 1) ur
2201² MONKEY AGO 7-11-1 (3*) J T Mitchell,.........(10 to 1) ur
Dist: 2½l, 3l, dist, 20l. 7m 20.90s. (7 Ran).
(Kilshannig Racing Syndicate), Eugene M O'Sullivan

2391 Naas Supporters Hurdle (4-y-o and up) £4,485 2m.................(3:00)

2097* KLAIRON DAVIS (Fr) 5-11-3 (7*) Mr H Murphy, ..(5 to 4 fav) 1
1984² COURT MELODY (Ire) 6-11-4 (5*) J P Broderick, .. (11 to 8) 2
2096* SAM VAUGHAN (Ire) 5-11-0 (5*) Mr W M O'Sullivan, (6 to 1) 3
2281⁴ WHAT IT IS (Ire) 5-10-7 J Shortt,............(25 to 1) 4
2197³ CASH IT IN (Ire) 6-10-8 (3*) D P Murphy,.......(25 to 1) 5
2156⁴ REASILVIA (Ire) 4-9-11 C F Swan,.............(10 to 1) 6
1978* FINAWAY BOY (Ire) 6-11-9 J P Banahan,.........(14 to 1) 7
Dist: 3l, 2½l, 6l, 3½l. 4m 37.30s. (7 Ran).

(C Jones), A L T Moore

2392 Celbridge Handicap Hurdle (4-y-o and up) £6,900 2m 3f............ (3:30)

2178²	DORANS PRIDE (Ire) [-] 5-10-4 (5²) J P Broderick, . . (6 to 1)	1
2124*	IMPERIAL CALL (Ire) [-] 5-11-0 (6ex) G M O'Neill, . . (8 to 1)	2
1848*	FERRYCARRIG HOTEL (Ire) [-] 5-9-13 D H O'Connor,	
	.........................(7 to 1)	3
2079²	COCK COCKBURN [-] 8-11-5 P Carberry, ... (11 to 2)	4
2283*	IAMWHATIAM [-] 8-9-9 S H O'Donovan, ...(14 to 1)	5
2078²	PRINCE OLE (Ire) [-] 6-10-7 M Duffy, ...(8 to 1)	6
2284²	GROUND WAR [-] 7-9-8 F Woods, ...(11 to 2)	7
2079⁴	DERRYMOYLE (Ire) [-] 5-11-0 C F Swan, ...(9 to 4 fav)	8
2160²	LUMINOUS LIGHT [-] 7-9-1 (7⁴) M D Murphy, ...(12 to 1)	9
2078⁷	MICK O'DWYER [-] 7-10-1 F J Flood, ...(20 to 1)	10
2277	PANDA (Ire) [-] 6-10-0 (3⁴) T P Treacy, ...(20 to 1)	11
2155³	MAXWELTON BRAES (Ire) [-] (bl) 5-9-3 (5⁴) M G Cleary,	
	.........................(33 to 1)	12
413³	SHANKORAK [-] 7-11-7 (7⁴) D J Kavanagh, ...(25 to 1)	13

Dist: Sht-hd, ¾l, sht-hd, 3½l. 4m 59.30s. (13 Ran).

(T J Doran), Michael Hourigan

2393 Cedar Building Handicap Chase (0-123 5-y-o and up) £3,795 3m. . (4:00)

2157³	BERMUDA BUCK [-] 8-10-13 F Woods, ... (7 to 4 fav)	1
2202*	GALLEY GALE [-] 8-10-3 C F Swan, ...(5 to 1)	2
2200³	MERLYNS CHOICE [-] 10-9-3 (5⁴) K P Gaule, ...(11 to 2)	3
2125⁴	WRECKLESS MAN [-] 7-10-13 (5⁴) P A Roche, ...(7 to 1)	4
2235⁴	WHAT A MINSTREL [-] 8-9-7 T Horgan, ...(10 to 1)	5
1850⁷	NEW MILL HOUSE [-] (bl) 11-11-9 (5⁴) T P Rudd, .. (8 to 1)	ur
2183*	CASTLE BRANDON [-] 8-11-4 (4ex) F J Flood, ...(5 to 1)	ur
1915	CITIZEN LEVEE [-] 8-10-11 (5⁴) Mr W M O'Sullivan, (12 to 1)	ref

Dist: 3l, 1l, 15l, 12l. 7m 16.50s. (8 Ran).

(Mrs L Rooney), J T R Dreaper

2394 Maynooth INH Flat Race (5-y-o and up) £3,105 2m.................... (4:30)

	GAILY RUNNING (Ire) 5-11-10 Mr T Mullins, ...(7 to 4 fav)	1
2102²	CAREFORMENOW (Ire) (bl) 5-11-3 (7⁴) Mr E Norris,	
	.........................(5 to 1)	2
2182⁴	TOTAL CONFUSION 7-11-7 (7⁴) Mr J Beattie, ...(10 to 1)	3
1858²	SISTER ALICE (Ire) 6-11-9 Mr P Fenton, ...(8 to 1)	4
1989³	LACKEN CROSS (Ire) 6-12-0 Mr A P O'Brien, ...(9 to 4)	5
2128	COOMACHEO (Ire) 5-11-3 (7⁴) Mr D A Harney, ...(20 to 1)	6
620	THE ROCKING CHAIR (Ire) 6-11-7 (7⁴) Mr S M Hanley,	
	.........................(25 to 1)	7
	LARRY'S LEGACY (Ire) 5-11-5 (5⁴) Mr G J Harford, (8 to 1)	8
1330⁸	BOB NELSON 7-11-7 (7⁴) Mr A A Cahill, ...(50 to 1)	9
	QUEENLIER (Ire) 5-10-12 (7⁴) Miss F M Crowley, ...(12 to 1)	10
	WHOTHATIS 8-11-2 (7⁴) Mr A Doherty, ...(33 to 1)	11
1687	SECRET MISSILE 7-11-11 (3⁴) Mrs J M Mullins, ...(12 to 1)	12
	BORRISMORE FLASH (Ire) 6-11-11 (3⁴) Mr D Marnane,	
	.........................(25 to 1)	13
	DERBY HAVEN 7-11-11 (3⁴) Mr A R Coonan, ...(25 to 1)	14
	GOOD BYE MONEY (Ire) 5-11-0 (5⁴) Mr H F Cleary, (12 to 1)	15
1270⁸	DRUMCILL LASS (Ire) 6-11-2 (7⁴) Mr S Durack, ...(20 to 1)	16
	PRETTY PRETENDER (Ire) 6-11-2 (7⁴) Mr P E I Newell,	
	.........................(25 to 1)	17

Dist: 6l, 5l, ¾l, 7l. 4m 9.90s. (17 Ran).

(Thomas J Farrell), P Mullins

PLUMPTON (good to soft)
Monday January 31st
Going Correction: PLUS 1.75 sec. per fur. (races 1,4,6), PLUS 1.35 (2,3,5)

2395 Poynings Conditional Jockeys' Selling Hurdle (4,5,6-y-o) £1,676 2m 1f. . (1:45)

2129³	AL FORUM (Ire) 4-11-9 D O'Sullivan, nvr far away gng wl, led appr 3 out, shaken up r-in.	
	.........................(7 to 4 op 11 to 10 tchd 13 to 8)	1
849	MAJOR'S LAW (Ire) 7-11-9 M P McLoughlin, took keen hold in tch, wnt second 3 out, sn chalg and rdn alng, not quicken r-in........(6 to 5 fav op 11 to 10 tchd 5 to 4)	2
1702⁴	GALACTIC FURY 4-10-5 (3⁴) M Stevens, gd hdwy, hld up, effrt aftr 3 out, sn rdn alng, no imprsn on 1st 2.	
	.........................(7 to 2 op 4 to 1 tchd 9 to 2)	3
1729	BANDMASTER (USA) 5-11-4 A Thornton, trkd ldr, ev ch appr 3 out, sn rdn and outpcd......(20 to 1 op 14 to 1)	4
2113³	DO BE WARE 4-10-8 R Davis, led till hdd appr 3 out, sn wknd...............(25 to 1 op 10 to 1 tchd 33 to 1)	5

Dist: 1½l, 10l, 8l, 25l. 4m 36.20s. (5 Ran).

(Martin Hickey), W N Guest

2396 Plumpton Handicap Chase (0-130 5-y-o and up) £2,660 2m 5f......... (2:15)

1966*	SHEER ABILITY [113] 8-12-0 R Dunwoody, not fluent early, hld up, reminders aftr 9th, gd hdwy to ld 12th, rdn 2 out, styd on strly...... (11 to 10 fav tchd 6 to 4)	1

2017*	KALANSKI [109] 8-11-10 J Osborne, al tracking ldrs, mstk 5th, led tenth to 12th, ev ch last, jst hld.	
	.......................(9 to 4 op 2 to 1 tchd 7 to 4 and 5 to 2)	2
2191⁴	ROCKMOUNT ROSE [85] 9-9-7 (7⁴) L Dace, nvr far away, led 6th to tenth, ran on one pace.	
	.........................(6 to 1 op 5 to 1 tchd 13 to 2)	3
2188²	UNIQUE NEW YORK [85] (v) 11-10-0 A Maguire, prmnt till wknd 12th...............(7 to 1 op 6 to 1 tchd 5 to 1)	4
2191⁷	MACHO MAN [87] (bl) 9-10-2 N Williamson, sn led, blun second, hdd 6th, stdly lost pl.	
	.........................(33 to 1 op 20 to 1 tchd 50 to 1)	5
2188⁴	RADICAL REQUEST [93] 11-10-8 M A FitzGerald, rdn 8th, lost tch frm tenth.............(20 to 1 op 10 to 1)	6

Dist: ¾l, 12l, 15l, 5l, 10l. 5m 40.50s. a 35.50s (6 Ran).
SR: 29/24/-/ (Michael Devlin), C J Mann

2397 Albourne Handicap Chase (0-115 5-y-o and up) £2,758 2m............ (2:45)

1596³	NATHIR (USA) [96] 8-11-7 M A FitzGerald, hld up, hdwy 9th, awkward 3 out, led last, drvn out.	
	.........................(9 to 1 op 5 to 1)	1
2192⁶	HANDSOME NED [80] 8-10-5 J Railton, led to 4th, led ag'n aftr 7th till hdd 9th, sn lost pl till rallied r-in.	
	.........................(6 to 1 op 5 to 1 tchd 7 to 1)	2
1798⁵	FRED SPLENDID [92] 11-11-3 R Dunwoody, al hndy, blun 8th, led nxt, hdd last, sn no extr.	
	.........................(9 to 1 op 6 to 1 tchd 10 to 1)	3
1623*	MR FELIX [99] 8-11-10 A Maguire, trkd ldr, led 4th till blun and hdd 7th, sn reco'red and ev ch till wknd 2 out.	
	.........................(3 to 1 tchd 7 to 2)	4
1689⁴	KISU KALI [93] 7-11-4 T Wall, mstk 5th, hdwy to ld briefly 7th, rdn 9th, sn wknd and beh whn pld up bef last.	
	.........................(20 to 1 op 12 to 1)	pu
2255⁴	RATHER SHARP [88] (v) 10-10-3 S McNeill, trkd ldrs till wknd quickly appr 9th, pld up bef nxt.	
	.......................(6 to 5 fav op 11 to 8)	pu

Dist: 1½l, 3½l, 10l. 4m 17.80s. a 27.80s (6 Ran).
SR: 31/19/21/18/-/-/ (A J Taaffe), P Butler

2398 Hickstead Novices' Hurdle (4-y-o) £1,543 2m 1f.................... (3:15)

1297*	HABASHA (Ire) 10-13 R Dunwoody, al hndy, flashed tail 6th, led nxt, chlgd frm 2 out, kpt on.	
	.......................(13 to 8 on op Evens)	1
2189³	MILLMOUNT (Ire) (v) 10-7 W McFarland, trkd ldrs, ev ch 7th, sn rdn alng, rallied gmely aftr last.	
	.........................(14 to 1 op 7 to 1 tchd 16 to 1)	2
2112⁵	MUHTASHIM (Ire) 10-12 A Maguire, hld up, mstk 6th, hdwy aftr 7th, rdn appr 2 out, kpt on r-in.	
	.........................(12 to 1 op 8 to 1 tchd 14 to 1)	3
2189*	SILVER STANDARD 11-4 B Powell, trkd ldr till led 4th, hdd 7th, rdn alng appr 2 out, sn rallied, ev ch whn hit last, not reco'r.............(4 to 1 op 7 to 2 tchd 9 to 2)	4
1705*	DON TOCINO 10-12 N Williamson, hld up, effrt 7th, sn rdn, no further imprsn.............(33 to 1 op 14 to 1)	5
1990⁷	WOLLBOLL 11-4 Richard Guest, midfield till effrt 7th, rdn frm nxt, sn beh.................(10 to 1 op 6 to 1)	6
	IF IT SUITS 10-12 G McCourt, jmpd slwly second, in tch till rdn aftr 6th, sn wknd, beh whn pld up bef 2 out.	
	.........................(20 to 1 op 12 to 1 tchd 25 to 1)	pu
	BORDER DREAM 10-5 (7⁴) R Darke, awkward second, mstk 5th, struggling frm hfwy, beh whn pld up bef 2 out.........................(66 to 1 op 33 to 1)	pu
2190²	BILJAN (USA) 10-12 J Osborne, led to 4th, wknd appr 7th, beh whn pld up bef 2 out.	
	.........................(10 to 1 op 12 to 1 tchd 25 to 1)	pu
	CLASSY KAHYASI (Ire) 10-7 M Hourigan, unruly bef strt, sn wl beh, tld off whn pld up before 7th.	
	.........................(16 to 1 op 14 to 1 tchd 33 to 1)	pu

Dist: 1½l, hd, 1½l, 15l, 2½l. 4m 32.80s. a 40.80s (10 Ran).
(Terry Neill), M C Pipe

2399 Sheekeys Restaurant Novices' Chase (5-y-o and up) £2,266 2m...... (3:45)

2195*	HOPS AND POPS 7-11-4 S Earle, made all, sn clr, mstk 3rd, jmpd rght 7th, blun 2 out, unchlgd.	
	.........................(8 to 1 on tchd 7 to 1)	1
1970	DEEP IN GREEK 8-11-3 R Dunwoody, chsd wnr thrght, no imprsn frm hfwy.................(14 to 1 op 12 to 1)	2
2196⁴	LETTS GREEN (Ire) 6-11-3 D Morris, mstks, 3rd and no ch whn blun 8th...........(10 to 1 op 8 to 1 tchd 11 to 1)	3
350⁶	ARCTICFLOW (USA) (bl) 9-11-3 P Holley, jmpd slwly 4th, sn wknd......(20 to 1 op 16 to 1)	4

Dist: 25l, 20l. 4m 19.70s. a 29.70s (4 Ran).
SR: 9/ (B Dennett), R H Alner

2400 Pyecombe Handicap Hurdle (0-115 4-y-o and up) £2,040 2½m...... (4:15)

2296²	DAMIER BLANC [-] (bl) 5-10-8 R Dunwoody, tucked away, took clr order frm hfwy, ev ch 3 out, outpcd betw last 2, rallied to ld r-in, styd on..(7 to 1 op 5 to 1)	1
2034⁴	HAPPY HORSE (NZ) [100] 7-10-13 A Tory, al hndy, led appr 3 out, clr betw last 2 till wknd last, hdd and no extr r-in.................(7 to 1 op 5 to 1 tchd 15 to 2)	2

1310⁴ MR MATT (Ire) [114] 6-11-13 J Railton, *al prmnt, led 4th till hdd appr 3 out, kpt on same pace*..(12 to 1 op 8 to 1) 3
GEORGE BUCKINGHAM [93] (bl) 9-10-6 B Powell, *in tch till rdn and lost pl aftr 7th, styd on ag'n frm 2 out*.
..............................(33 to 1 op 20 to 1) 4
1868³ NOVA SPIRIT [90] 6-10-3 M A FitzGerald, *trkd ldrs, hrd rdn aftr 3 out, sn wknd*......(8 to 1 op 9 to 2 tchd 9 to 1) 5
RED BEAN [88] 6-9-13¹ (3') A Dicken, *hld up and beh, moderate hdwy 8th, nvr able to chal*.
..............................(33 to 1 op 20 to 1) 6
1396* NICK THE DREAMER [110] 9-11-2 (7') R Darke, *led to 4th, wknd frm 8th and sn wl beh*.......(9 to 2 tchd 6 to 1) 7
MORE OF IT [114] 9-11-13 N Williamson, *midfield to hfwy, sn wknd, tld off*......(25 to 1 op 20 to 1 tchd 33 to 1) 8
LUCKY OAK [87] 8-9-7 (7') L Dace, *al beh, tld off*.
..............................(33 to 1 op 20 to 1 tchd 50 to 1) 9
2296⁷ MILDRED SOPHIA [87] 7-9-7 (7') Miss S Mitchell, *hld up, hdwy appr 9th, 5th and no imprsn whn slpd up bend bef 2 out*......................(50 to 1 op 33 to 1) su
2265⁷ MANHATTAN BOY [104] 12-11-3 A Maguire, *hld up in tch, niggled alng aftr 7th, beh whn pld up bef 9th*.
..............................(12 to 1 op 7 to 1) pu
2131 FOUR STAR LINE [87] 9-10-0 R Greene, *prmnt early till rdn alng 5th, sn lost pl, tld off whn pld up bef 3 out*.
..............................(50 to 1 op 33 to 1) pu
Dist: ¾l, 7l, 25l, 2½l, 20l, nk, 12l, 5l. 5m 16.70s. a 39.70s (12 Ran).
SR: 33/37/44/-/-/-/   (Trevor Painting), M C Pipe

NOTTINGHAM (heavy)
Tuesday February 1st
Going Correction: PLUS 2.05 sec. per fur. (races 1,3,-4,5,7), PLUS 1.80 (2,6)

2401 Bradmore Selling Hurdle (4 & 5-y-o) £1,876 2m.....................(1:30)

2308⁶ TYNRON DOON (bl) 5-11-5 N Williamson, *nvr far away, led hfwy, clr bef 2 out, rdn last, styd on wl*.
..............................(7 to 1 op 8 to 1 tchd 10 to 1) 1
MASON DIXON 5-11-5 M Dwyer, *patiently rdn, imprvg whn hit 3 out, ch when blun last, no extr*.
..............................(7 to 1 op 10 to 1 tchd 16 to 1) 2
2303 WORKINGFORPEANUTS (Ire) 4-10-4 D Bridgwater, *settled gng wl, jnd ldrs appr thee out, rdn and no extr nxt*.
..............................(14 to 1 op 12 to 1) 3
1747 FOXY LASS 5-11-0 Mr J Cambidge, *settled rear, improved appr 3 out, rdn and no imprsn nxt*..........(33 to 1) 4
2354⁵ PORT IN A STORM 5-11-8 (5') E Husband, *wtd wth, improved on outsd appr 3 out, rdn and no imprsn nxt*.
..............................(13 to 8 fav op 5 to 4 tchd 2 to 1) 5
ERLEMO 5-11-5 Diane Clay, *trkd ldrs, effrt appr 3 out, sn rdn and btn*...........................(20 to 1) 6
2271* ABSOLUTELY FOXED 5-10-12 (7') G Robertson, *pressed ldrs, drvn alng appr 3 out, fdd*.......(8 to 1 op 5 to 1) 7
LANCASTER PILOT 4-10-9 A Mulholland, *al hndy, ev ch appr 3 out, sn rdn and btn*..........(20 to 1) 8
AIR COMMAND (Bar) 4-10-9 D J Burchell, *nvr far away, ev ch appr 3 out, wknd quickly bef nxt*.
..............................(14 to 1 op 12 to 1) 9
2303 ANAR (Ire) (v) 5-11-5 M Brennan, *in tch, drvn alng to improve hfwy, struggling 4 out, tld off*.
..............................(6 to 1 op 14 to 1) 10
SUMMER EXPRESS 5-10-12 (7') Miss C Spearing, *not fluent, pressed ldrs till fdd und pres 3 out*..........(20 to 1) 11
971⁹ PAAJIB (Ire) 4-10-2 (7') W Fry, *settled midfield, 6th and drvn alng whn f 3 out*.......(16 to 1 op 10 to 1) f
2271¹² BITRAN 4-10-9 A S Smith, *keen hold, disputing ld whn ran out 1st*.......................(5 to 1 tchd 9 to 2) ro
CAPITAL LAD 5-11-5 R Marley, *led to hfwy, wknd rpdly 4 out, pld up bef nxt*....................(25 to 1) pu
Dist: 7l, 15l, 7l, ¾l, 4l, 2l, 15l, ¾l, dist, 4l. 4m 25.50s. a 41.50s (14 Ran).
SR: 4/-/-/-/-/   (G Wiltshire), Mrs N Macauley

2402 Kingston Novices' Chase (5-y-o and up) £2,339 2m.................(2:00)

2372³ SEON 8-11-10 L Wyer, *nvr far away, hit 8th, drvn alng nxt, rallied 3 out, styd on wl to ld r-in*.
..............................(7 to 1 op 5 to 1 tchd 8 to 1) 1
1441 LOS BUCCANEROS 11-11-6 G Upton, *patiently rdn, improved to track ldr 5 out, lft in ld 2 out, hdd and no extr r-in*......................(16 to 1 op 6 to 1) 2
VITAL WITNESS (Can) 7-11-6 A S Smith, *rod hwdy, hit to 6th, rdn aftr nxt, rallied till jmpd lft 3 out, btn next*.
..............................(16 to 1 op 12 to 1 tchd 20 to 1) 3
1418⁶ FROG HOLLOW (Ire) 6-11-6 B Powell, *led to 4th, hndy till hit 7th, fdd 5 out, tld off*...........(20 to 1 op 14 to 1) 4
2254⁷ SERDARLI 12-11-1 L Harvey, *pressed ldrs, struggling to keep up 6 out, sn tld off*........(50 to 1 op 33 to 1) 5
1841 COULTON 7-12-0 M Dwyer, *last and hld up whn f second*.
..............................(13 to 8 on op 7 to 4 on tchd 11 to 8 on) f
2175² SECOND CALL 5-10-2 (3') R Farrant, *with ldrs, led 6th, 2¹s clr and gng wl whn f two out*......(7 to 2 tchd 4 to 1) f
Dist: 3l, 6l, 25l, 8l. 4m 26.40s. a 35.40s (7 Ran).
SR: 30/23/17/-/-/   (C F Hunter Ltd), W Bentley

2403 Nottingham Gold Card Handicap Hurdle Qualifier (4-y-o and up) £4,068 2m 5f 110yds.....................(2:30)

2273* BOLLIN MAGDALENE [115] 6-10-0 L Wyer, *confidently rdn, improved to ld 4 out, clr betw last 2, hld on wl*.
..............................(6 to 1 op 5 to 1 tchd 13 to 2) 1
1703⁴ SENDAI [119] 8-10-4 D Murphy, *al hndy, feeling pace and lost grnd appr 3 out, rallied frm last, ran on*.
..............................(10 to 1 op 8 to 1) 2
2247 CASTIGLIERO (Fr) [120] (bl) 6-10-5⁵ G Bradley, *settled beh ldrs, hdwy frm 3 out, styd on, nrst finish*.
..............................(12 to 1 op 10 to 1) 3
MISTER MAJOR [115] 6-10-0 E Leonard, *settled beh ldrs, improved 3 out, styd on, nrst finish*.........(25 to 1) 4
2172 WILLSFORD [130] (bl) 11-10-8 (7') D Bohan, *chsd ldrs, pushed alng 3 out, kpt on, not pace to chal*.. (20 to 1) 5
2243* KILGARIFF [115] 8-10-0 P Harley, *patiently rdn, improved 3 out, ridden nxt, one pace*..............(14 to 1) 6
2298* CAPTAIN DOLFORD [121] 7-10-1 (5*,8ex) J McCarthy, *settled midfield, pushed alng appr 3 out, not pace of ldrs*.
..............................(5 to 1 op 6 to 1) 7
ACROW LINE [118] 9-10-3 D J Burchell, *chsd ldrs, pushed alng appr 3 out, no imprsn*......(14 to 1 op 12 to 1) 8
2193⁴ JUDGES FANCY [126] (bl) 10-10-11 C Llewellyn, *chsd ldrs, feeling pace appr 3 out, fdd*......(12 to 1 op 10 to 1) 9
1219 ATTADALE [123] 6-10-8 T Reed, *settled off the pace, improved fnl circuit, no imprsn frm 3 out*......(20 to 1) 10
1777* BICKERMAN [115] 11-9-7 (7') Miss T Spearing, *in tch, improved to track ldrs 4 out, rdn and no extr nxt*.
..............................(16 to 1 op 14 to 1) 11
2089⁴ RIMOUSKI [118] 6-10-3² Mr J Cambidge, *settled rear, effrt fnl circuit, nvr on terms*...............(100 to 1) 12
1561⁹ POLISHING [116] 7-9-13³ (5*) S Lyons, *hld up beh ldrs, nvr rch chalg pos*....................(16 to 1 op 20 to 1) 13
2323³ BONANZA [123] 7-10-8 R Hodge, *wtd wth, cld fnl circuit, fdd appr 3 out*....................(14 to 1 op 8 to 1) 14
1496* GIMME FIVE [127] 7-10-12 C Swan, *wtd wth, improved into midfield fnl circuit, rdn and btn 3 out*.
..............................(9 to 2 fav op 7 to 1) 15
2667⁷ CHILD OF THE MIST [119] 8-10-4 R Dunwoody, *trkd ldrs for r'r one circuit, fdd approachiang 3 out*.
..............................(14 to 1 op 12 to 1) 16
1544 CARIBOO GOLD (USA) [119] 5-10-4 N Williamson, *wtd wth, trkd ldrs fnl circuit, wkng whn blun 3 out, eased*.
..............................(14 to 1 op 12 to 1) 17
ERCALL MILLER [115] 7-10-0 A O'Hagan, *al beh, tld off 4 out*........................(100 to 1) 18
2296* STORMHEAD [123] 6-10-8 (8ex) J Osborne, *made most to 4 out, wknd and eased nxt*. 19
556 FLUSTERED (USA) [119] 8-9-11 (7') K Davies, *chsd ldrs one circuit, tld off 4 out*...............(33 to 1) 20
2273⁵ DUHALLOW LODGE [117] 7-10-2² Richard Guest, *settled midfield, improved to press ldrs fnl circuit, wknd quickly 4 out, tld off*.................(20 to 1) 21
2012⁴ EVERALDO (Fr) [139] 10-11-3 (7') Mr J O'Shaughnessy, *ran in snatches, no imprsn on ldrs whn f 2 out*... (20 to 1) f
BRAVO STAR (USA) [115] 9-9-7 (7') M Moran, *wl beh whn pld up bef nxt*...................(33 to 1) pu
1972 BLACK SAPPHIRE [115] 7-10-0 B Powell, *struggling to keep up aftr one circuit, tld off whn pld up betw last 2*.
..............................(50 to 1 op 33 to 1) pu
KNIGHTS (NZ) [115] 8-10-0 Jacqui Oliver, *al struggling, tld off*................(16 to 1 tchd 20 to 1) pu
Dist: ½l, 10l, 15l, 6l, nk, ¾l, sht-hd, ¾l, 1½l, 1½l. 5m 48.10s. a 46.10s (25 Ran).
SR: 52/55/46/26/35/19/24/21/28/   (Sir Neil Westbrook), M H Easterby

2404 Charnwood Maiden Hurdle (4-y-o and up) £2,488 2m 5f 110yds........(3:00)

2300² CYBORGO (Fr) 4-10-9 R Dunwoody, *al hndy, rdn to draw level betw last 2, led r-in, styd on wl*.
..............................(2 to 1 fav tchd 5 to 2) 1
1168 OVER THE POLE 7-11-7 D Murphy, *patiently rdn, improved to ld on bit 3 out, jnd and ridden bef last, hdd and no extr r-in*..................(8 to 1 op 7 to 1) 2
2144³ GLENTOWER (Ire) 6-11-7 M A FitzGerald, *wtd wth, improved into midfield fnl circuit, effrt 3 out, styd on one pace*....................(7 to 1 tchd 8 to 1) 3
1872² ALJADEER (USA) 5-11-7 C Swan, *patiently rdn, jnd ldrs appr 3 out, kpt on same pace nxt*... (4 to 1 op 3 to 1) 4
1994³ FUN MONEY 7-11-7 N Williamson, *tucked away beh ldrs, pushed alng to improve 3 out, no extr nxt*.
..............................(7 to 1 op 10 to 1) 5
2220⁶ TRAVELLING LIGHT 8-11-7 Mr S Swiers, *wtd wth, led 5 out to 3 out, fdd*.................(16 to 1) 6
JURASSIC CLASSIC 7-11-7 D Bridgwater, *settled midfield, wnt hndy 4 out, wknd and eased nxt*.....(50 to 1) 7
2173⁷ TALOS (Ire) 6-11-7 L Wyer, *settled beh ldrs, slight ld hfwy to 5 out, fdd last 3*.....................(33 to 1) 8
2135⁴ BALLYSPARKLE (Ire) 4-10-9 A Mulholland, *chsd ldrs, effrt whn hit 3 out, fdg when almost brght dwn nxt, eased when btn*....................(25 to 1) 9

2144 SMITH'S BAND (Ire) 6-11-7 J Osborne, *pressed ldrs, effrt 4 out, feeling pace bef nxt, fdd.......* (12 to 1 op 8 to 1) 10
17349 CAIPIRINHA (Ire) 6-11-2 G Upton, *chasing ldrs whn f 6th.*
.....................................(100 to 1) f
1674* COILED SPRING 7-11-7 W Marston, *tucked away beh ldrs, effrt whn hmpd 6th, rallied 4 out, 7th and drvn alng when f 2 out................* (8 to 1 op 6 to 1) f
2063⁶ MRS TWEED 8-11-2 E Byrne, *al beh, tld off whn pld up bef 7th..........................*(100 to 1) pu
BROADWOOD LAD 8-11-7 I Lawrence, *al beh, tld off whn pld up bef 3 out..........................*(100 to 1) pu
2204 KETFORD BRIDGE 7-11-4 (3") D Meredith, *chsd ldrs one circuit, tld off whn pld up bef 3 out.........* (100 to 1) pu
2262⁵ PROFESSOR LONGHAIR 7-11-4 (3") R Davis, *trkd ldrs, blun 5th, pld up bef nxt..........* (16 to 1 op 12 to 1) pu
658 TOMASHENKO 5-11-2 (5") T Eley, *pressed ldrs one circuit, lost tch quickly 4 out, pld up bef nxt........* (100 to 1) pu
1568³ BUCKSHOT (Ire) 6-11-4 (3") P Hide, *made most to hfwy, struggling to hold pl bef 4 out, tld off whn pld up before nxt...........................* (16 to 1 op 14 to 1) pu
1800 BOX OF DELIGHTS 6-11-7 W Humphreys, *struggling hfwy, tld off whn pld up bef 5 out..........* (100 to 1) pu
GRUNGE (Ire) 6-11-7 D Gallagher, *in tch, drvn alng fnl circuit, tld off whn pld up bef 2 out...........* (12 to 1) pu
2135⁶ MALAWI 4-10-9 G Bradley, *sn beh, tld off whn pld up bef 3 out..................................*(25 to 1) pu
2176 ORCHESTRATED CHAOS (Ire) 5-11-3¹ Mr J Mead, *struggling hfwy, tld off whn pld up bef 3 out.......*(100 to 1) pu
HENLOW GRANGE 7-11-7 B Powell, *sn struggling to keep up, tld off whn pld up bef 7th...........*(100 to 1) pu
RED BRANCH (Ire) 5-11-7 G McCourt, *in tch, drvn alng to hold pl fnl circuit, tld off whn pld up bef 3 out.*
.....................................(33 to 1 op 50 to 1) pu
Dist: 8l, 6l, 6l, 12l, 5l, 2½l, 8l, 7l, sht-hd. 5m 57.10s. a 55.10s (24 Ran).

(County Stores (Somerset) Holdings Ltd), M C Pipe

2405 Plumtree Novices' Handicap Hurdle
(0-100 4-y-o and up) £1,938 2m. . (3:30)

1535⁶ SCARBA [66] 6-9-11³ (7") K Davies, *settled gng wl, led bef 3 out, wndrd aftr nxt, drvn alng r-in, hld on well.*
.....................................(25 to 1) 1
2088* PRINCETHORPE [67] 7-9-13 (3") D Meredith, *patiently rdn, pushed alng to improve aftr 4 out, ev ch after last, kpt on same pace..................*(5 to 1 op 7 to 1) 2
2208 MARINER'S AIR [76] 7-10-11 N Williamson, *settled midfield, drvn up to chal 3 out, kpt on same pace below last 2..........................*(12 to 1 tchd 14 to 1) 3
2292* MORIARTY [65] 7-9-9 (5") J McCarthy, *wtd wth, improved aftr 4 out, ev ch nxt, one pace r-in.*
.....................................(11 to 4 fav op 3 to 1 tchd 7 to 2) 4
1953⁸ BIGWHEEL BILL (Ire) [80] 5-11-1 S Smith Eccles, *last and pushed alng hfwy, styd on frm 3 out, nvr able to chal.*
.....................................(12 to 1 tchd 14 to 1) 5
2150² FORTUNE'S GIRL [89] 6-11-5 (5") D Bentley, *settled beh ldrs, drvn alng bef 4 out, styd on, nvr able to chal.*
.....................................(5 to 1 op 7 to 1) 6
2241⁸ ALMANZAR (USA) [77] 4-10-12 G McCourt, *patiently rdn, improved gng wl appr 3 out, hit nxt, fdd betw last 2.*
.....................................(100 to 30 op 9 to 4 tchd 7 to 2) 7
1707⁸ WYJUME (Ire) [84] 5-11-5 D Murphy, *settled rear, effrt hfwy, outpcd bef 4 out, tld off....*(16 to 1 op 14 to 1) 8
2196³ TWIST 'N' SCU [81] 6-11-2 C Llewellyn, *wth ldrs, led briefly aftr 3rd, not fluent back strt, lost tch 4 out.*
.....................................(16 to 1 op 14 to 1) 9
ROBINS SON [75] 7-10-10 Richard Guest, *co'red up in midfield, bustled alng hfwy, tld off 4 out......*(33 to 1) 10
1569⁵ GOLDEN SAVANNAH [88] 4-11-9 R Dunwoody, *settled to track ldrs, feeling pace appr 4 out, tld off.*
.....................................(8 to 1 op 6 to 1 tchd 10 to 1) 11
2276 INAN (USA) [83] (bl) 5-11-4 L Wyer, *led to 3rd, led aftr nxt till after 4 out, wknd quickly, f next.*
.....................................(14 to 1 op 12 to 1) f
1923 LADY KHADIJA [65] 8-9-11 (3") R Farrant, *wth ldrs, led briefly 3rd, sn lost tch, tld off whn pld up bef 3 out.*
.....................................(100 to 1) pu
UPTON LASS (Ire) [73] 5-10-8 L Harvey, *pressed ldrs to hfwy, tld off whn pld up bef 3 out...........*(16 to 1) pu
Dist: 2½l, ¾l, 2½l, 10l, 2l, 2l, 25l, 1l, 10l, 8l. 4m 29.60s. a 45.60s (14 Ran).

(Bryan Gordon), D T Garraton

2406 Gotham Handicap Chase (0-105 5-y-o and up) £2,917 3m 110yds...... (4:00)

2274² BALTIC BROWN [105] 9-12-0 Richard Guest, *al hndy, slight ld 3rd to tenth, rallied to lead bef 3 out, styd on wl.............................*(10 to 1 op 8 to 1) 1
2294* CHRISTMAS GORSE [78] 8-10-1 (6ex) C Llewellyn, *patiently rdn, improved gng wl appr 4 out, ev ch and ridden nxt, one pace frm last.*
.............(21 to 20 fav op 11 to 10 tchd 5 to 4 on) 2
2084² COMEDY SPY [100] 10-11-9 M A FitzGerald, *led to 3rd, dsptd ld till rdn appr 4 out, sn outpcd.*
.....................................(6 to 1 op 4 to 1 tchd 7 to 1) 3
1402⁵ LA CERISE [77] (bl) 11-9-7 (7") M Moran, *nvr far away, led 7 out till bef 4 out, fdd und pres.....*(25 to 1 op 20 to 1) 4

1968² UNDERWYCHWOOD (Ire) [83] 6-10-6 I Lawrence, *settled to track ldrs, effrt and drvn alng fnl circuit, outpcd 4 out.*
.....................................(20 to 1) 5
2191² OLD ROAD (USA) [80] 8-10-3 W Marston, *pressed ldrs, mstk and rdn 9th, rallied, outpcd 5 out, tld off.*
.....................................(12 to 1 op 10 to 1) 6
2323⁵ INVASION [103] (v) 10-11-12 M Brennan, *jmpd slwly, lost pl quickly frm 5th, tld off whn pld up bef 4 out.*
.....................................(7 to 1 op 5 to 1 tchd 15 to 2) pu
2305 MO ICHI DO [86] (bl) 8-10-4 (5") T Eley, *settled midfield, niggled alng hfwy, effrt fnl circuit, lost tch and pld up bef 3 out..............*(14 to 1 op 10 to 1) pu
INCONCLUSIVE [87] 7-10-5 (5") J Burke, *settled off the pace, gng wl hfwy, lost tch and pld up bef 4 out.*
.....................................(25 to 1 op 20 to 1) pu
Dist: 2½l, 30l, 2½l, 8l, dist. 6m 53.50s. a 58.50s (9 Ran).

(Mrs Smith), Mrs S J Smith

2407 Levy Board National Hunt Flat Race
(4,5,6-y-o) £2,015 2m.............. (4:30)

1996* ST MELLION FAIRWAY (Ire) 5-11-7 (7") Pat Thompson, *patiently rdn, jnd ldr entering strt, led o'r 2 fs out, drvn out........................* (5 to 2 fav tchd 3 to 1) 1
1674² VALERIOS KING (Ire) 5-11-2 (5") J McCarthy, *settled midfield, improved appr strt, ev ch last 2 fs, kpt on.*
.....................................(4 to 1 op 9 to 2 tchd 5 to 1) 2
2095² NORMAN'S CONVINCED (Ire) 4-10-4 (7") L Reynolds, *led till o'r 2 fs out, rdn and one pace........*(5 to 1 op 4 to 1) 3
MINTY'S FOLLY (Ire) 4-10-11 W Marston, *settled off the pace, improved last 3 fs, nvr dngrs....*(4 to 1 op 3 to 1) 4
DOVETTO 5-11-0 (7") Mr G Hogan, *trkd ldrs, effrt appr strt, sn lost 3 fs.......................*(4 to 1) 5
1957 SPA KELLY 6-11-2 (5") T Eley, *trkd ldr, drvn alng appr strt, sn lost tch..................*(33 to 1) 6
1376⁸ MY BILLY BOY 5-11-0 (7") M Herrington, *settled gng wl, hdwy appr strt, fdd o'r 2 fs out.*
.....................................(9 to 1 op 8 to 1 tchd 10 to 1) 7
SHERWOOD GRANGE (Ire) 6-11-0 (7") R Moore, *wtd wth, pushed up appr strt, wknd quickly o'r 2 fs out.*(20 to 1) 8
1996⁵ HOPE THATCH (NZ) 6-11-4 (3") R Davis, *pressed ldg trio for o'r one m, sn lost tch...* (8 to 1 op 7 to 1 tchd 10 to 1) 9
CACAHWETE 5-10-9 (7") Mr D Parker, *settled beh ldrs, lost tch hfwy, tld off...................*(20 to 1 op 12 to 1) 10
TUESDAYNIGHTMARE 5-10-11 (5") F Perratt, *chsd ldrs one m, sn tld off........................*(14 to 1 op 12 to 1) 11
BEN CONNAN (Ire) 4-10-6 (5") S Curran, *al beh, virtually pld up last 3 fs..................*(33 to 1 op 16 to 1) 12
KENNINGTON KUWAIT 4-10-4 (7") N Juckes, *al rear, virtually pld up strt.........* (50 to 1 op 25 to 1) 13
DARING CREST 4-10-3 (3") D Meredith, *chsd ldrs one m, virtually pld up last 3 fs.....*(20 to 1 op 12 to 1) 14
2269⁷ OUROWNFELLOW (Ire) 5-11-0 (7") G Crone, *prmnt one m, wknd quickly appr strt, virtually pld up.*
.....................................(16 to 1 op 33 to 1) 15
2095⁸ SCOTCH 'N IRISH (Ire) 5-11-0 (7") D Towler, *chsd ldrs one m, virtually pld up strt...............*(33 to 1) 16
Dist: 2l, 8l, dist, sht-hd, 5l, 12l, 15l, 7l, 8l, 4l. 4m 2.20s. (16 Ran).

(St Mellion Estates Ltd), J A B Old

SEDGEFIELD (good to soft)
Tuesday February 1st
Going Correction: PLUS 1.00 sec. per fur. (races 1,2,6), PLUS 0.65 (3,4,5)

2408 John Wade Haulage Selling Handicap Hurdle (4-y-o and up) £1,784 2m 1f 110yds......................... (1:50)

2321⁶ VERY EVIDENT (Ire) [61] 5-10-0 J Callaghan, *hld up, hdwy hfwy, led appr 2 out, pushed clr...........* (4 to 1 jt-fav tchd 9 to 2) 1
2214* SPANISH WHISPER [78] 7-10-12 (5") J Twomey, *trkd ldrs, chlgd 3 out, kpt on same pace frm nxt........*(4 to 1 jt-fav op 7 to 2 tchd 9 to 2) 2
2256 DUTCH BLUES [70] 7-10-9 D Wilkinson, *cl up, led 3 out, hdd appr nxt, kpt on same pace.............*(20 to 1) 3
2317² AT PEACE [85] 8-11-3 (7") P McLoughlin, *chsd ldrs, ev ch appr 2 out, no extr...................*(9 to 2 op 7 to 2) 4
2328⁵ STATION EXPRESS (Ire) [66] 6-10-0³ (3") A Larnach, *hld up, gd hdwy aftr 3 out, one pace frm nxt.*
.....................................(9 to 1 op 7 to 1) 5
2217 ELVETT BRIDGE (Ire) [66] 6-10-5¹ K Jones, *chsd ldrs, pushed alng aftr 3 out, kpt on same pace......*(13 to 2) 6
FIRE 'N' FURY [72] 8-10-11 C Grant, *hld up, hdwy appr 3 out, wknd approaching nxt.*
.....................................(9 to 1 op 20 to 1 tchd 8 to 1) 7
2254 ANFIELD SALLY [62] 8-10-1¹ S Turner, *chsd ldrs till wknd aftr 3 out..........................*(33 to 1) 8
2321³ DRU RI'S BRU RI [75] (v) 8-10-9 (5") P Waggott, *trkd ldrs till wknd aftr 3 out...................*(6 to 1) 9
2321 SHAHMIRAJ [71] 6-10-10 A Dobbin, *prmnt till wknd appr 3 out........................*(14 to 1) 10
2154⁹ SUMMERS DREAM [74] 4-10-13 C Hawkins, *hld up, hdwy hfwy, ev ch 3 out, sn rdn and wknd quickly.....*(8 to 1) 11

333

1485 ARTHURS STONE [65] 8-10-1 (3*) A Thornton, *led till hdd 3 out, wknd quickly, tld off*..................(100 to 1) 12
2106 TIME PIECE (Ire) [61] 6-9-9 (5*) J Supple, *pld very hrd early, lost tch aftr 5th, wl tld off*............(50 to 1) 13
Dist: 5l, 2½l, 3½l, 3l, 2½l, 1½l, 4l, 2l, 10l, 4l. 4m 21.50s. a 26.50s (13 Ran).
(Mrs Susan Moore), G M Moore

2409 Peterlee Novices' Hurdle (4-y-o and up) £1,922 2m 5f 110yds....... (2:20)

2140² ALI'S ALIBI 7-11-4 P Niven, *cl up, led 3rd, hrd pressed frm 3 out, kpt on und pres, all out.*
..........................(3 to 1 op 5 to 2 tchd 7 to 2) 1
2140³ WEY I MAN (Ire) 5-10-11 (7*) P Carr, *trkd ldrs, chlgd 3 out, ev ch nxt, kpt on und pres frm last...*(9 to 1 op 6 to 1) 2
1283⁵ MILLION IN MIND (Ire) 5-11-4 W McFarland, *led to 3rd, prmnt, rdn and slightly outpcd 3 out, kpt on und pres frm nxt.*......(6 to 4 on op 5 to 4 on tchd 7 to 4 on) 3
2308⁸ AURORA LAD 7-11-4 D Byrne, *in tch, outpcd aftr 7th, styd on frm 3 out, nrst finish....*. (33 to 1 op 20 to 1) 4
1918⁶ DUNREIDY BAY (Ire) 6-11-4 K Jones, *beh till styd on frm 3 out, not trble ldrs....*.......... (25 to 1 op 20 to 1) 5
1634⁷ ON GOLDEN POND (Ire) 4-10-8 J Callaghan, *cl up, ev ch 3 out, sn rdn and wknd.*.............(14 to 1 op 12 to 1) 6
2252⁶ KINDA GROOVY 5-11-4 N Smith, *in tch, no hdwy frm 7th.*
..........................(16 to 1 op 12 to 1) 7
1003 HERBALIST 5-11-1 (3*) A Larnach, *prmnt till wknd appr 3 out.*.................................. (14 to 1 op 10 to 1) 8
WHITE DIAMOND 6-11-4 J Railton, *in tch till wknd aftr 7th.*.................................(16 to 1) 9
22373 MISCHIEVOUS GIRL 6-10-13 Mrs F Needham, *in tch till wknd aftr 7th.*............................(50 to 1) 10
2303 KRISSOS 7-10-13 (5*) P Waggott, *beh frm hfwy.* (25 to 1) 11
JUST WOODY 6-11-4 C Grant, *beh frm hfwy.*
..........................(25 to 1 op 20 to 1) 12
1861 KINGLY LOOK 7-11-1 (3*) A Thornton, *prmnt to hfwy, sn wknd, tld off.*.........................(50 to 1) 13
MIDORI 6-10-8 (5*) P Williams, *sn lost tch, wl tld off.*
..........................(100 to 1) 14
JACKS ARMY 8-10-13 (5*) T Jenks, *stumbled and uns rdr strt.*..........................(16 to 1) ur
872 BUZZ-B-BABE 4-10-7 S Turner, *sn wl beh, tld off whn pld up bef 7th.*......................(50 to 1 op 33 to 1) pu
ANDRETTI'S HEIR 8-11-4 C Hawkins, *pld hrd early, prmnt till wknd quickly hfwy, tld off whn pulled up aftr 2 out.*..........................(100 to 1) pu
Dist: ½l, 6l, 2½l, 3½l, 10l, 8l, nk, 3½l, 5l, 7l. 5m 27.80s. a 36.80s (17 Ran).
(Mrs B Kearney), Mrs M Reveley

2410 Ramside Handicap Chase (0-120 5-y-o and up) £2,794 3m 3l.......... (2:50)

2294³ CHOCTAW [95] 10-10-7 C Hawkins, *made all, drw clr aftr 2 out, cmftbly.*..................(5 to 2 fav op 9 to 4) 1
2253⁶ DUBIOUS JAKE [94] 11-9-13 (7*) C Woodall, *prmnt, slightly outpcd appr 2 out, kpt on und pres frm last.*
..........................(3 to 1 op 5 to 2) 2
REGAL ESTATE [112] 10-11-10 R Garritty, *trkd wnr, ev ch appr 2 out, no extr.*..............(9 to 1 op 7 to 1) 3
2253 BARKIN [104] 11-11-2 M Moloney, *al beh, tld off.*
..........................(12 to 1 op 8 to 1) 4
1939 BOREEN OWEN [106] 10-10-13 (5*) A Roche, *al beh, tld off.*..........................(5 to 1 op 4 to 1) 5
2001 KINGFISHER BAY [94] 10-9-6 W McFarland, *mstks, prmnt till outpcd aftr tenth, wl tld off...* (3 to 1 tchd 7 to 2) 6
Dist: 7l, ½l, dist, 6l, 30l. 7m 16.70s. a 37.70s (6 Ran).
(J N Yeadon), P Beaumont

2411 Hetton Novices' Chase (5-y-o and up) £2,649 2m 5f................. (3:20)

2031* VAYRUA (Fr) 9-11-7 (3*) A Larnach, *in tch, chlgd 2 out, led last, styd on und pres.*............. (11 to 4 on op 11 to 4) 1
2251⁴ SILVER STICK 7-11-4 R Garritty, *prmnt, dsptd ld 4 out, slight lead 2 out till slpd aftr last, not reco'r.*
..........................(7 to 2 op 4 to 1) 2
2120⁶ JUPITER MOON 5-10-8 J Railton, *made most till hdd 2 out, grad wknd.*........................(16 to 1) 3
2218³ PREOBLAKENSKY 7-11-4 N Doughty, *prmnt, slight ld 9th, hdd 4 out, wkng whn hmpd nxt.*
..........................(11 to 4 fav op 3 to 1 tchd 7 to 2) 4
2293 MAYOR OF LISCARROL 9-11-4 G Harker, *cl up, wkng whn blun 12th.*..........................(50 to 1) 5
2103⁶ BIG MAC 7-11-4 C Grant, *chsd ldrs, pushed alng hfwy, sn wknd.*.....................(9 to 2 tchd 5 to 1) 6
NORRISMOUNT 8-11-4 M Moloney, *hmpd 6th, al beh.*
..........................(16 to 1 op 12 to 1) 7
2170 JENNY'S GLEN 7-11-4 R Supple, *hmpd 4th, al beh.*
..........................(50 to 1 op 33 to 1) 8
2170⁶ DARK OAK 8-11-4 L O'Hara, *in tch, effrt and ch whn f 3 out.*..........(14 to 1 op 12 to 1 tchd 16 to 1) f
BISHOP'S TIPPLE 8-11-4 B Storey, *in tch whn f 6th, dead.*
..........................(16 to 1 op 14 to 1) f
915⁹ UNCLES-LAD 6-11-1 (3*) N Bentley, *prmnt whn f 4th.*
..........................(50 to 1 op 33 to 1) f
2206 SOUTH STACK 8-11-4 D Byrne, *al beh, tld off whn pld up bef 12th.*..........................(33 to 1 op 25 to 1) pu

1807² BEN THE BOMBER 9-10-11 (7*) Judy Davies, *sn beh, tld off whn pld up bef 8th.*........................(50 to 1) pu
TUKUM 6-10-13 (5*) P Midgley, *sn wl beh, tld off whn pld up and dismounted aftr 9th.*..................(50 to 1) pu
Dist: 4l, 4l, 30l, 25l, 15l, 2½l, 7l. 5m 29.00s. a 25.00s (14 Ran).
(J A Hellens), J A Hellens

2412 Mainsforth Handicap Chase (0-130 5-y-o and up) £2,716 2m 1f..... (3:50)

2255* MILITARY HONOUR [90] (bl) 9-10-5 S Turner, *made most till hdd 7th, blun 9th, rdn to ld appr 3 out, drw clr frm nxt.*
..........................(11 to 2 op 5 to 1 tchd 6 to 1) 1
2324* MAUDLINS CROSS [118] 9-12-0 (5*,6ex) Mr M Buckley, *blun 1st, sn cl up, led 7th till hdd appr 3 out, soon btn.*
..........................(9 to 4 tchd 5 to 2) 2
2324² TRESIDDER [111] 12-11-12 R Garritty, *dsptd ld to 5th, in tch till blun and lost touch 8th, kpt on frm 2 out.*
..........................(5 to 2 op 9 to 4) 3
2151³ ONE FOR THE POT [109] 9-11-5 (5*) T Jenks, *hld up and beh, took clr order 7th, effrt aftr 4 out, sn wknd, tld off.*
..........................(13 to 8 fav op 6 to 4 tchd 7 to 4) 4
Dist: 10l, 1½l, 25l. 4m 21.10s. a 16.10s (4 Ran).
SR: 26/44/35/8/
(J E Swiers), J E Swiers

2413 Boyston Grove Novices' Hurdle (5-y-o and up) £1,845 2m 1f 110yds.... (4:20)

1872⁴ WHITE WILLOW 5-11-0 P Niven, *made all, sn clr, hit 3 out, rdn aftr last, all out.*
..........................(Evens fav op 11 to 8 on tchd 6 to 4 on) 1
2243⁴ SHAHGRAM (Ire) 6-10-10 Mrs A Farrell, *in tch, chsd wnr frm appr 3 out, no imprsn till styd on from nxt, kpt on wl towards finish.......* (7 to 2 op 4 to 1 tchd 9 to 2) 2
1865⁷ INDIAN RIVER (Ire) 6-10-3 (7*) F Leahy, *beh till some late hdwy, nvr on terms.* (12 to 1 op 10 to 1 tchd 14 to 1) 3
2252³ TREVVEETHAN (Ire) 5-10-10 D Wilkinson, *chsd ldrs till outpcd aftr 5th, no dngr after....*(14 to 1 op 12 to 1) 4
TUSKY 6-10-7 (3*) N Bentley, *al beh...*(10 to 1 op 7 to 1) 5
2220 MARKS REFRAIN 10-10-10 Mr R Hale, *sn beh.*
..........................(66 to 1 op 50 to 1) 6
2237 GOLDEN RECORD 6-10-10 L O'Hara, *sn beh, tld off.*
..........................(100 to 1) 7
CARDINAL SINNER (Ire) 5-10-10 K Jones, *sn beh, tld off.*
..........................(33 to 1) 8
1613 TOLLS CHOICE (Ire) 5-10-3 (7*) J Driscoll, *sn beh, tld off whn pld up bef last.*.................(50 to 1) pu
2148² COOL LUKE 5-10-10 J Callaghan, *chsd wnr till wknd quickly appr 3 out, wl beh whn pld up bef last.*
..........................(11 to 2 op 9 to 2) pu
MR WESTCLIFF 6-10-5 (5*) P Waggott, *not jump wl, sn beh, tld off whn pld up...*.......(33 to 1) pu
Dist: 1½l, 30l, ¾l, 20l, 3l, dist. 4m 17.30s. a 22.30s (11 Ran).
SR: 34/32/2/1/-/-/
(Exors Of The Late Mrs H North), Mrs M Reveley

LEICESTER (heavy (races 1,2,5,6), good to soft (3,4))
Wednesday February 2nd
Going Correction: PLUS 2.00 sec. per fur. (races 1,2, 5,6), PLUS 1.87 (3,4)

2414 Burton Lazars Selling Hurdle (4,5,6-y-o) £1,780 2m................. (1:30)

685 PREENKA GIRL (Fr) 5-11-6 R Dunwoody, *made all, drw clr 3 out, very easily.........*(5 to 4 on op 11 to 10 on) 1
2315⁵ RASTA MAN 6-11-6 S Smith Eccles, *hld up, hdwy 5th, staying on whn hit 2 out, sn chsd wnr.*
..........................(2 to 1 op 7 to 4) 2
2207⁶ MARSHALL PINDARI 4-10-10 D Bridgwater, *hld up, hdwy to chase wnr frm 4th, mstk nxt, rdn and wknd 2 out.*
..........................(16 to 1 op 10 to 1) 3
2244⁸ JOKERS THREE (Ire) 5-11-6 J Osborne, *trkd wnr to 4th, wknd four out, btn whn blun last.*
..........................(9 to 1 op 10 to 1 tchd 14 to 1) 4
1867² LEGAL WIN (USA) 6-11-4 (7*) Mr G Shenkin, *pld hrd, prmnt till jmpd slwly 3rd, last whn blun 4 out, pulled up bef nxt.......*(7 to 1 op 5 to 1 tchd 8 to 1 and 10 to 1) pu
KILLSHANDRA (Ire) (bl) 5-11-1 N Mann, *mstk 1st, al beh, tld off whn pld up bef 4 out.........*(50 to 1 op 33 to 1) pu
2275 COUSIN WENDY 4-10-0 (5*) T Eley, *chsd ldrs till wknd 4th, tld off whn pld up bef four out....* (50 to 1 op 33 to 1) pu
Dist: 6l, 8l, 2½l. 4m 31.10s. a 48.10s (7 Ran).
(Martin Pipe Racing Club), M C Pipe

2415 Golden Miller Novices' Hurdle (4-y-o and up) £4,190 2m............. (2:00)

1974 RIVER LOSSIE (bl) 5-11-10 J Osborne, *made all, rcd wide, drw clr appr 3 out, fnshd alone.*
..........................(11 to 8 op Evens tchd 6 to 4) 1
2042¹ MISTER NOVA 5-11-5 M R Fitzgerald, *mstk second, trkd wnr, hit 4 out, rdn and blun nxt, sn tld off, pld up bef last.*..........................(13 to 8 on op 6 to 4 on) pu
4m 19.70s. a 36.70s (2 Ran).

SR: 49/-/   (Chris Brasher), C R Egerton

2416   Marshall Handicap Chase (0-125 5-y-o and up) £2,761 2½m 110yds.....(2:30)

1870² JAILBREAKER [101] 7-10-4 M A FitzGerald, *hld up in tch, trkd ldr frm 9th, jmpd into ld 2 out, sn clr.*
....(7 to 1 op 9 to 2)   1
SARAVILLE [117] 7-11-6 R Dunwoody, *trkd ldr, led 6th, rdn and hdd 2 out, sn btn, eased r-in.* ....(9 to 4 jt-fav op 5 to 2 tchd 2 to 1)   2
2297³ CASTLE DIAMOND [100] 7-9-12² (7ᵉ) S Fox, *hit 1st, not fluent, trkd ldrs, wkng whn blun 4 out, tld off.*
....(4 to 1 op 5 to 2)   3
2246 ON THE TWIST [125] 12-11-7 (7ᵉ) P Murphy, *wl beh frm 4th, tld off whn pld up bef 5 out.*...................(33 to 1)   pu
615³ ICARUS (USA) [122] 8-11-11 Mr A Rebori, *hit second, mstk 6th, tld off 9th, pld up bef 4 out...*(20 to 1 op 12 to 1)   pu
COMPLETE OPTIMIST [101] 10-10-4 J Osborne, *hld up in tch, hdwy 5th, rdn and wknd 9th, pld up bef 4 out.*
.........................(8 to 1 op 6 to 1 tchd 9 to 1 and 10 to 1)   pu
2246 MAN OF MYSTERY [114] 8-11-3 D Bridgwater, *led to 6th, rdn and wknd appr tenth, pld up bef nxt....*(9 to 4 jt-fav op 7 to 4)   pu

Dist: 25l, dist. 5m 46.30s. a 43.30s (7 Ran).
SR: 26/17/-/-/   (Jack-Del-Roy), B R Millman

2417   Silver Bell Novices' Chase (6-y-o and up) £2,498 3m.................(3:00)

2084¹ HONEST WORD 9-11-4 R Dunwoody, *made all, mstk 7th, drw clr frm 4 out, unchlgd.*
.........................(4 to 1 on op 5 to 4 tchd 6 to 1 on)   1
1994⁶ DOLLY OATS 8-10-7 M A FitzGerald, *beh whn mstk 5th, styd on to pass btn horses frm 3 out, wnt second r-in.*
.........................(20 to 1 op 14 to 1)   2
2193⁵ SAYYURE (USA) 8-10-12 J Osborne, *chsd wnr to 7th, mstk 11th, wnt second ag'n 3 out, wknd r-in.*
.........................(8 to 1 op 7 to 1)   3
2293³ KEY'S LASS (Ire) 6-10-0 (7ᵉ) P Murphy, *al prmnt, chsd wnr 7th to 3 out, tired 3rd whn f nxt.*...(9 to 1 op 16 to 1)   f
1411 BARLEY MOW 8-10-12 N Mann, *rcd wide, mstk 8th and sn lost pl, tld off whn pld up bef 5 out.*(20 to 1 op 12 to 1)   pu
STORM ISLAND 9-10-12 D Skyrme, *hit 4th, sn beh, tld off whn pld up bef twelfth.*...........(20 to 1 op 16 to 1)   pu
2293⁴ RIDAKA 7-10-7 (5ᵉ) T Eley, *in tch, pushed alng and 4th whn blun badly twelfth, hit nxt, pld up bef 5 out.*
....(50 to 1)   pu

Dist: 25l, 15l. 6m 43.20s. a 51.20s (7 Ran).
SR: 27/-/-/-/   (Mrs H J Clarke), M C Pipe

2418   Charnwood Claiming Hurdle (4-y-o and up) £1,892 2m.............(3:30)

1561 ROSGILL 8-11-13 D Bridgwater, *hld up, gd hdwy to go second 4 out, hng in beh ldr frm nxt, shaken up, edgd rght and quickened to ld r-in.*
.........................(9 to 4 op 3 to 1 tchd 2 to 1)   1
2214⁵ AUVILLAR (USA) (v) 6-11-7 R Dunwoody, *led till hdd and outpcd r-in.*...........(11 to 2 op 9 to 2 tchd 7 to 1)   2
1860¹ CORLY SPECIAL 7-11-13 R Marley, *prmnt, rdn and wknd appr 4 out, tld off....*(9 to 1 op 14 to 1 tchd 16 to 1)   3
1508 OAK PARK (Ire) 6-11-8 (5ᵉ) T Eley, *hld up, mstk second, hdwy to go second 4th, wkng whn mistake 3 out, tld off......*(12 to 1 op 10 to 1)   4
2208 LITTLE THYNE 9-11-10 Dr P Pritchard, *rdn and lost tch aftr 3rd, tld off....*(20 to 1 op 14 to 1 tchd 25 to 1)   5
SCHWEPPES TONIC 8-11-4 M A FitzGerald, *chsd ldrs, pushed alng whn f 5th.*
.........................(14 to 1 op 12 to 1 tchd 16 to 1)   f
FLYING SPEED (USA) 6-11-12 (7ᵉ) Mr N Moore, *trkd ldr to 4th, rdn and wknd aftr nxt, tld off whn pld up bef 2 out....*.........(15 to 8 fav op Evens tchd 2 to 1)   pu
BROUGHTON'S GOLD (Ire) 6-11-5 N Mann, *al beh, tld off whn pld up bef 3 out.*(40 to 1 op 33 to 1 tchd 50 to 1)   pu
1488 BROWN MYSTIQUE 8-10-10 W Marston, *whipped round strt and reluctant to race, al beh, tld off whn pld up bef 3 out...*...(33 to 1)   pu

Dist: 2l, short-head, 7l, 2l. 4m 24.40s. a 41.40s (9 Ran).
SR: 5/-/-/-/-/   (Brigadier Racing), J White

2419   EBF 'National Hunt' Novices' Hurdle Qualifier (5,6,7-y-o) £2,721 2½m 110yds....................... (4:00)

1779³ CHIEF RAGER 5-11-0 D Bridgwater, *hld up in tch, led aftr 7th, came wide into strt, pushed clr appr last.*
.........................(5 to 4 op 11 to 10 tchd Evens)   1
2308¹ DIVINE CHANCE (Ire) 6-11-10 J Osborne, *al prmnt, led 3rd to aftr nxt, ev ch 3 out till wknd appr last.*
.........................(Evens fav op 11 to 10 tchd 6 to 5)   2
2176⁵ PENNANT COTTAGE (Ire) 6-10-9 R Dunwoody, *al prmnt, led appr 5th, hdd nxt, wknd approaching 3 out, tld off.*
....(9 to 1 op 6 to 1)   3
SWEET MANATTE 7-10-9 C Maude, *led to 3rd, led ag'n 6th, hdd sn aftr nxt, wknd appr 3 out, tld off.*
.........................(3 to 1 op 33 to 1)   4

SLIEVE LEAGUE (Ire) 5-10-9 R Bellamy, *prmnt, led betw 4th and 5th, rdn and wknd aftr 7th, tld off.*
.........................(25 to 1 op 12 to 1)   5
1099⁸ FINKLE STREET (Ire) 6-10-7 (7ᵉ) P Murphy, *al beh, tld off whn pld up bef 4 out...............*(50 to 1)   pu
SEPTEMBER SAND 6-10-6 (3ᵉ) R Davis, *beh, lost tch 6th, tld off whn pld up bef 4 out............*(50 to 1)   pu
1568 FORGIVE THE FOLLY 6-11-0 W Marston, *in rear, hdwy 5th, wknd 7th, tld off whn pld up bef 2 out.*
.........................(33 to 1 op 16 to 1)   pu

Dist: 10l, dist, 2½l, 12l. 5m 45.60s. a 57.60s (8 Ran).
     (James Cheetham), N A Twiston-Davies

SOUTHWELL (A.W) (std)
Wednesday February 2nd
Going Correction: PLUS 0.55 sec. per fur.

2420   Curate Novices' Handicap Hurdle (0-100 4-y-o and up) £1,553 2½m (1:40)

2331³ ABELONI [60] 5-9-11 (3ᵉ) S Wynne, *hld up, gd hdwy to ld 4 out, clr nxt, styd on.*
.........................(5 to 2 fav op 7 to 4 tchd 11 to 4)   1
2329 STRONG JOHN (Ire) [88] 6-12-0 M Hourigan, *trkd ldrs, effrt 4 out, sn rdn and chsd wnr 3 out, no imprsn.*
.........................(7 to 2 op 11 to 4)   2
2329⁴ RUTH'S GAMBLE [82] 6-11-1 (7ᵉ,7ex) Mr B Pollock, *not fluent, trkd ldrs, hit 5 out, effrt nxt, sn rdn and one pace...*.........................(11 to 4 op 2 to 1)   3
2271⁶ RAVENSPUR (Ire) [60] (bl) 4-10-0 A Dobbin, *chsd ldrs, hdwy 7th, led 5 out, hdd nxt, rdn and wknd appr 3 out.*
....(20 to 1)   4
2213 DAMCADA (Ire) [70] 6-10-10 W Marston, *led till hdd and hit second, cl up till led 6th, rdn and headed 5 out, sn wknd...........*.........................(4 to 1 op 10 to 1)   5
1775⁸ MORSHOT [73] (bl) 7-10-13 G Bradley, *cl up, led second, hit 5th, hdd and hit 6th, sn hrd drvn, blun 7th, soon beh, tld off whn pld up bef 3 out....*(8 to 1 op 7 to 1)   pu

Dist: 8l, 8l, 3l, 30l. 5m 7.80s. a 26.80s (6 Ran).
     (J Hardman), R Hollinshead

2421   Priest Selling Handicap Hurdle (4-y-o and up) £1,830 2m.............(2:10)

2328² BURN BRIDGE (USA) [78] (v) 8-11-5 Peter Caldwell, *led aftr 1st, hit 5 out and hdd nxt, effrt and hit 2 out, hrd drvn to chal last, styd on to ld r-in.*
.........................(7 to 2 op 3 to 1 tchd 4 to 1)   1
2164⁴ ALDINGTON CHAPPLE [65] 6-10-6 T Wall, *led till aftr 1st, prmnt, led 4 out, hdd briefly nxt, hrd rdn last, headed and ev ch r-in..............*(5 to 2 op 7 to 4)   2
1811³ DOUBLE THE STAKES (USA) [83] 5-11-10 D J Burchell, *trkd ldrs sng wl, smooth hdwy to chal 4 out, led and hit nxt, sn hdd, hrd drvn and ev ch till wknd last.*
.........................(7 to 4 fav op 9 to 4)   3
2331⁵ CHAGHATAI (USA) [60] (bl) 8-10-1 Mr B Leavy, *prmnt, ev ch 4 out, sn rdn and one pace.*
.........................(12 to 1 op 10 to 1 tchd 14 to 1)   4
2170⁹ BEAUFAN [67] 7-10-5 (3ᵉ) D Meredith, *in tch till rdn 5th and sn lost pl...........*(8 to 1 op 7 to 1)   5
2331 HOSTETLER [73] 5-10-7 (7ᵉ) M Griffiths, *in tch till rdn 5th and sn lost pl......*(10 to 1 op 12 to 1)   6
1707 JANET SCIBS [59] 8-10-1 O Shoemark, *hit second, in tch till rdn and hit 5th, sn wknd.*
.........................(20 to 1 op 16 to 1 tchd 25 to 1)   7
2321 FOUR ALLS LADY [59] (bl) 8-10-0 M Hourigan, *reminders and beh frm 5th, tld off whn pld up bef 3 out.*
.........................(25 to 1 op 20 to 1 tchd 33 to 1)   pu

Dist: 2l, 2½l, 8l, 10l, 8l, dist. 4m 2.10s. a 16.10s (8 Ran).
SR: 18/3/18/-/-/   (T H Caldwell), T H Caldwell

2422   Monseigneur Juvenile Novices' Hurdle (4-y-o) £1,553 2m.......... (2:40)

2241 FRET (USA) 10-9 (3ᵉ) N Bentley, *chsd ldrs, second whn lft clr lder 5th, rdn 3 out, all out.*
.........................(9 to 4 op 5 to 4 tchd 5 to 2)   1
BOZO BAILEY 10-12 R Campbell, *outpcd till hdwy 6th, rdn 3 out, styd on, not rch wnr.* (16 to 1 tchd 20 to 1)   2
VISIMOTION (USA) 10-12 T Kent, *chsd ldrs, lft second 5th, rdn 3 out, hit 2 out, wknd last.......*(9 to 1 op 6 to 1)   3
1476⁹ BARSAL (Ire) 10-12 A Dobbin, *mid-div, hit 6th, sn beh.*
.........................(12 to 1 op 16 to 1)   4
2068⁹ RAGING THUNDER 10-9 (3ᵉ) A Larnach, *al outpcd and beh...........*.........................(9 to 1 op 14 to 1)   5
1927¹ QUICK SILVER BOY 11-5 D J Burchell, *cl up, led 4th, clr whn f nxt............*(11 to 10 fav op 6 to 4)   f
SOVIET EXPRESS (bl) 10-12 G Bradley, *led till hdd and hit 4th, 3rd whn hmpd and uns rdr nxt.* (9 to 1 op 6 to 1)   bd
1710 SMART DAISY 10-4 (3ᵉ) D Meredith, *in tch to 3rd, sn out-pcd and beh, tld off whn pld up bef 4 out......*(33 to 1)   pu
2207⁷ MANDALIA MELODY 10-7 (5ᵉ) D Walsh, *al outpcd and beh, tld off whn pld up bef 4 out..........*(50 to 1)   pu

Dist: 1l, 5l, 15l, 12l. 4m 8.10s. a 22.10s (9 Ran).
     (N Honeyman), G M Moore

2423 Bishop Handicap Hurdle (0-110 5-y-o and up) £1,926 2¼m............(3:10)

2328* BENTLEY MANOR [80] 5-11-5 (6ex) W Humphreys, *hld up off pace, pushed alng 6th, steady hdwy 4 out, led 2 out, quickened clr appr last, cmftbly.* (2 to 1 fav op 6 to 4) 1
2214^{3} SANTA PONSA BAY [77] 7-10-9 (7*) Mr B Pollock, *cl up, led 5 out, rdn and hdd 2 out, btn whn hit last*......(8 to 1) 2
2214^{4} TRISTAN'S COMET [82] 7-11-7 B Dalton, *led, rdn and hdd 5 out, wknd aftr 3 out.* (11 to 4 op 5 to 2 tchd 3 to 1) 3
2062^{3} ANDRATH (Ire) [67] 6-10-6 M Hourigan, *mstks, sn outpcd and beh*................(8 to 1 op 10 to 1 tchd 7 to 1) 4
2215* TOP PRIZE [77] 6-10-11 (5*) S Mason, *cl up, rdn and blun 5 out, sn wknd*........................(9 to 2 op 4 to 1) 5
2306 SODA POPINSKI (USA) [85] 6-11-10 R Campbell, *hld up, f 4th*......................(8 to 1 op 5 to 1 tchd 9 to 1) f
Dist: 4l, 10l, 25l, 12l. 4m 28.70s. a 16.70s (6 Ran).
SR: 23/16/11/ (R Paul Russell), K S Bridgwater

2424 Verger Novices' Claiming Hurdle (5-y-o and up) £1,553 3m..........(3:40)

1606^{5} RED COLUMBIA 13-11-2 Mrs G Adkin, *made all, rdn clr appr 2 out, kpt on*.........................(14 to 1) 1
2141 DEVIOSITY (USA) 7-11-2 I Shoemark, *al prmnt, ev ch whn blun 4 out, sn rdn, styd on to chase wnr nxt, kpt on.* ....(10 to 1) 2
2321 MAUREEN'S FANCY (bl) 9-10-10 A Dobbin, *hld up in tch, hdwy 5 out, ev ch nxt, rdn appr 3 out, sn one paced.* .... (6 to 1 op 5 to 1 tchd 13 to 2) 3
2215^{2} GENERAL SHOT 9-11-2 Diane Clay, *trkd ldrs, effrt 4 out, sn rdn and outpcd*............. (6 to 4 fav tchd 2 to 1) 4
2225^{4} PEARLY WHITE 5-10-2 (7*) Mr G Hogan, *hld up, hdwy 4th, in tch till rdn and wknd bef four out.* ....(7 to 1 op 5 to 1 tchd 8 to 1) 5
2117^{4} HIGHLAND FRIEND (bl) 6-11-2 C Grant, *in rear, hit 4th, sn scrubbed alng and beh, tld off frm 5 out.* .... (7 to 1 op 14 to 1 tchd 16 to 1) 6
2327 MASTER FRITH 6-11-0 W Humphreys, *al rear, tld off frm 5 out*..............................(16 to 1 tchd 20 to 1) 7
2215^{5} KNOCKREIGH CROSS (Ire) 5-10-6 (7*) G Cahill, *in tch, effrt and hdwy 5 out, rdn and wknd bef 3 out*......(16 to 1) 8
2215^{6} GOLDEN BANKER (Ire) 6-11-2 K Jones, *not jump wl, beh frm hfwy, sn tld off*............... (16 to 1 op 33 to 1) 9
2295^{7} BLUE LYZANDER 5-10-11 T Wall, *cl up, rdn alng 9th, hit nxt and sn wknd, pld up bef 11th*.... (5 to 1 op 3 to 1) pu
Dist: 4l, 5l, 8l, 30l, hd, hd, ½l, 5l. 6m 17.80s. a 40.80s (10 Ran).
(F Coton), F Coton

2425 Vicar Handicap Hurdle (0-115 4-y-o and up) £1,943 2¾m............(4:10)

2109^{4} COSMIC DANCER [100] (bl) 7-11-4 A Carroll, *hld up and beh, steady hdwy 8th, chsd ldr 4 out, sn led and clr nxt, easily*............... (9 to 4 fav op 3 to 1 tchd 4 to 1) 1
2166* COURT CIRCULAR [110] (v) 5-12-0 Diane Clay, *beh, rdn alng hfwy, styd on frm 4 out, no ch wth wnr.* ....(5 to 2 op 6 to 4) 2
2165^{2} FOR HEAVEN'S SAKE (Fr) [92] 9-10-10 T Wall, *cl up, led appr 3rd, sn clr, rdn and hdd aftr 4 out, soon one pace.* ....(4 to 1 op 7 to 2 tchd 9 to 2) 3
1643^{8} SWEET GEORGE [83] 7-10-1^{1} D J Burchell, *prmnt, rdn appr 4 out, sn wknd*..................(9 to 1 op 7 to 1) 4
2212 CLASSIC STATEMENT [82] 8-10-0^{3} (3*) A Larnach, *chsd ldrs, lost pl and beh frm hfwy, tld off 5 out.* .... (25 to 1 op 20 to 1) 5
KING OF SHADOWS [94] 7-10-5 (7*) Mr D Parker, *al beh, tld off whn pld up bef 3 out*..................... (33 to 1) pu
1805 DEBT OF HONOR [82] 6-10-0 R Greene, *mstks, sn chasing ldrs, rdn tenth and grad lost pl, tld off whn pld up bef 3 out*.................... (8 to 1 op 6 to 1 tchd 9 to 1) pu
2167* HEATHYARDS BOY [88] 4-10-3 (3*) S Wynne, *led till appr 3rd, prmnt till rdn and wknd bef 4 out, beh whn pld up before 2 out*......................... (6 to 1 op 4 to 1) pu
Dist: 4l, 4l, 8l, 30l. 5m 41.00s. a 32.00s (8 Ran).
(S P C Woods), S P C Woods

WINDSOR (good to soft) Wednesday February 2nd

Going Correction: PLUS 1.52 sec. per fur. (races 1,3,-5,7), PLUS 1.22 (2,4,6)

2426 Brocas 'National Hunt' Novices' Hurdle (4-y-o and up) £2,276 2m.... (1:20)

NO PAIN NO GAIN (Ire) 6-11-3 E Murphy, *in tch whn jmpd slwly 3rd and 4th, hdwy nxt, led appr last, cmftbly.* .... (10 to 1 op 6 to 1 tchd 12 to 1) 1
2263^{7} DO BE HAVE (Ire) 6-11-3 I Lawrence, *chsd ldrs, ev ch 3 out till outpcd appr last*....(8 to 1 op 7 to 1 tchd 10 to 1) 2
2269^{3} BASS ROCK 6-11-3 J Frost, *in tch, pressed ldrs aftr 3 out till outpcd appr last*..... (6 to 1 op 5 to 1 tchd 7 to 1) 3
2048^{2} OLDHILL WOOD (Ire) 4-10-7 S Earle, *beh, hdwy appr 3 out, rdn and one pace nxt.* .... (9 to 2 op 4 to 1 tchd 7 to 2 and 5 to 1) 4
1490 KINDLE'S DELIGHT 6-11-3 N Williamson, *pressed ldr, led 2 out, hdd and wknd appr last*..... (50 to 1 op 25 to 1) 5
2147^{6} PRINCE TEETON 5-11-3 B Powell, *chsd ldrs 3rd, wknd 2 out*............................(20 to 1 tchd 33 to 1) 6
1835^{2} FINESSE THE KING (Ire) 6-11-3 C Llewellyn, *in tch, rdn to chase ldrs appr 3 out, wknd approaching nxt.* ....(7 to 2 fav op 3 to 1) 7
993^{9} BRIDEPARK ROSE (Ire) 6-10-12 M Ahern, *hdwy to press ldrs 4th, wknd aftr 3 out*.....................(33 to 1) 8
1548^{6} PRECIOUS JUNO (Ire) 5-10-12 D Murphy, *beh, hdwy to chase ldrs 4th, wknd 3 out.* .... (11 to 2 op 9 to 2 tchd 6 to 1) 9
1688^{4} WORLDLY PROSPECT (USA) 6-10-9 (3*) R Farrant, *chsd ldrs 4th, wknd aftr 3 out*.....................(16 to 1) 10
2048^{6} POLICEMANS PRIDE (Fr) 5-10-10 (7*) J Clarke, *led to 2 out, wknd quickly*........(33 to 1 op 20 to 1 tchd 50 to 1) 11
GOLDEN DROPS (NZ) 6-11-3 A Tory, *in tch whn blun 3rd, no dngr aftr*....................(14 to 1 tchd 16 to 1) 12
2333 DEVIL'S STING (Ire) 5-10-12 (5*) T Jenks, *chsd ldrs to 5th, sn wknd*.............. (12 to 1 op 7 to 1 tchd 14 to 1) 13
2042^{8} TITAN EMPRESS 5-10-12 M Perrett, *al beh.* .... (14 to 1 op 16 to 1 tchd 20 to 1) 14
WAIPIRO 4-10-7 S McNeill, *chsd ldrs to 5th*.....(33 to 1) 15
2176 LADY BREYFAX 4-9-9 (7*) G Crone, *al beh.* .... (50 to 1 op 33 to 1) 16
1626 SUZY BLUE 5-10-12 C Maude, *al beh*........... (33 to 1) 17
HERES A RONDO 11-10-12 S Burrough, *prmnt early, sn beh*.............................. (33 to 1 op 25 to 1) 18
2147 MAGGIE TEE 6-10-12 G Upton, *beh whn sddl slpd and pld up bef 3rd*.........................(50 to 1 op 33 to 1) pu
Dist: 5l, 2½l, 1½l, 7l, 2l, 1l, ½l, ¾l, ½l, 5l. 4m 14.60s. a 29.60s (19 Ran).
SR: 36/31/28/16/19/17/16/10/9/ (Mrs B J Curley), B J Curley

2427 Oakside Novices' Chase (5-y-o and up) £2,810 3m..................(1:50)

2141 RAKAIA RIVER (NZ) 7-11-5 B Powell, *in tch 9th, chlgd 14th, led 4 out, rdn and hng lft r-in, all out.* .... (25 to 1 op 16 to 1 tchd 33 to 1) 1
NEW GHOST 9-10-12 (7*) Mr S Mulcaire, *prmnt, chlgd 7th to 9th, led 12th to 4 out, ev ch till rdn and not quicken r-in*..............................(33 to 1 op 16 to 1) 2
1973 WILLOW GALE 7-11-0 N Williamson, *beh 5th, hdwy 12th, rdn to chase ldrs 3 out, btn nxt.* .... (20 to 1 op 25 to 1 tchd 33 to 1) 3
FREDDY OWEN 8-11-5 W McFarland, *in tch 9th, wknd aftr 14th*...........................(33 to 1 op 25 to 1) 4
2206^{5} CHIEF CELT 8-11-5 G McCourt, *chsd ldrs, rdn 7th, lost pl tenth, wknd 14th*................. (4 to 1 tchd 9 to 2) 5
2086^{7} COKENNY BOY 9-11-5 D Murphy, *beh till f 8th.* ....(5 to 2 op 2 to 1) f
2209^{4} BINKLEY (Fr) 8-11-11 C Llewellyn, *led to 12th, chlgd 14th, wknd quickly, tld off whn pld up bef 2 out.* .... (9 to 1 op 6 to 1 tchd 10 to 1) pu
2270* HOWARYADOON 8-11-11 J Railton, *jmpd slwly 3rd, blun nxt, no dngr aftr, tld off whn pld up bef 11th.* .... (9 to 4 fav tchd 5 to 2) pu
1167 DARKBROOK 7-11-5 P Holley, *in tch, hit 8th, rear tenth, pld up aftr nxt*........ (13 to 2 op 6 to 1 tchd 7 to 1) pu
2141 SHOCK TACTICS 7-11-5 S McNeill, *chsd ldrs, chlgd 9th, blun nxt 2, tld off whn pld up bef 4 out.* .... (33 to 1 op 16 to 1) pu
2146^{6} HAND OUT 10-11-0 S Earle, *mstks, al beh, tld off whn pld up bef 4 out*......... (20 to 1 op 14 to 1 tchd 25 to 1) pu
2336 WOODLANDS BOY (Ire) (bl) 6-11-2 (3*) A Thornton, *wth ldr, chlgd 9th, hit 13th, wkng whn blun nxt, tld off when pld up bef 4 out*..... (20 to 1 op 16 to 1 tchd 33 to 1) pu
Dist: 1l, 10l, 15l, 10l. 6m 30.50s. a 35.50s (12 Ran).
SR: 29/28/13/3/-/-/ (Mrs J H Meredith), Capt T A Forster

2428 Levy Board Novices' Handicap Hurdle (0-100 4-y-o and up) £1,999 2¾m 110yds........................ (2:20)

2141^{8} ANILAFFED [69] (v) 4-10-5 D Gallagher, *in tch, trkd ldr appr 3 out, led nxt, drvn out*.....(12 to 1 tchd 14 to 1) 1
2293 UNEXIS [65] 9-9-8 (7*) Chris Webb, *beh, hdwy 6th, pushed alng 3 out, styd on to go second r-in, not rch wnr.* .... (14 to 1 op 12 to 1) 2
1869^{4} PRINCE OF SALERNO [82] 7-11-4 R Supple, *in tch, chlgd 5th, led 7th to 2 out, sn rdn and one pace*....(9 to 2 jt-fav op 4 to 1) 3
2308 UP ALL NIGHT [67] 5-10-3 D Morris, *beh, hdwy 7th, styd on same pace frm 3 out*........... (16 to 1 op 14 to 1) 4
1750^{4} MOUNTAIN MASTER [82] 8-10-13 (5*) J McCarthy, *led briefly second, prmnt till wknd 8th.* ....(12 to 1 tchd 14 to 1) 5
2263^{8} THE QUAKER [64] 8-10-0 Lorna Vincent, *led to second, chlgd 6th to 7th, wknd nxt.* .... (6 to 1 op 5 to 1 tchd 13 to 2) 6
1702^{6} LA POSADA [64] (v) 4-10-0 W McFarland, *beh, hdwy 7th, wknd appr 3 out*...................(20 to 1 op 14 to 1) 7
2147^{9} RIVAGE BLEU [68] 7-10-1^{4} (7*) Mr E James, *in tch to 8th.* ....(25 to 1) 8
1304^{3} EMPERORS WARRIOR [76] 8-10-12 A Tory, *hdwy to chase ldrs 6th, wknd 8th*................ (10 to 1 op 12 to 1) 9

2083[8] MORAN BRIG [79] (v) 4-11-1 S Hodgson, *rdn and lost tch*
8th................................(14 to 1 op 12 to 1) 10
2117[*] CREWS CASTLE [88] 7-11-10 G McCourt, *al beh, tld off*
whn pld up bef 3 out... (15 to 2 op 6 to 1 tchd 8 to 1) pu
2014 SPANISH BLAZE (Ire) [73] 6-10-9 N Williamson, *lost tch 6th,*
tld off whn pld up bef 2 out.....................(14 to 1) pu
2208[8] MAKES ME GOOSEY (Ire) [87] (bl) 6-11-9 L Harvey, *led aftr*
second, mstk and hdd 7th, sn wknd, tld off whn pld up
bef 2 out............(11 to 1 op 10 to 1 tchd 12 to 1) pu
2295[4] VERY LITTLE (Ire) [85] 6-11-7 S Earle, *beh 5th, tld off whn*
pld up bef 3 out................(9 to 2 jt-fav op 4 to 1) pu
Dist: 3l, 6l, 15l, 7l, 7l, 1l, 12l, 12l, ½l. 6m 3.60s. a 44.60s (14 Ran).
(Mrs S K McLean), J Akehurst

2429 Boveney Handicap Chase (0-125 5-y-o and up) £2,838 3m..............(2:50)

1713[3] GHOFAR [115] (bl) 11-11-10 P Holley, *chsd ldrs 9th, led*
and hit 2 out, wnt lft last, rdn out... (9 to 2 op 7 to 2) 1
1769[2] LITTLE GENERAL [91] 11-10-0 B Powell, *wth ldr, led 6th to*
nxt, chlgd 12th, led 3 out to next, rallied last, one pace.
......................................(4 to 1 fav tchd 5 to 1) 2
2294 BERESFORDS GIRL [104] 9-10-13 E Murphy, *hit 1st, tld off*
second, styd on frm 4 out, nrst finish.
....(6 to 1 op 5 to 1 tchd 13 to 2) 3
1838[5] THAMESDOWN TOOTSIE [92] 9-10-11 D Murphy, *prmnt,*
chlgd 12th, lost pl 14th, rallied appr 4 out, sn btn.
......................................(7 to 1 op 12 to 1) 4
2143 FALSE ECONOMY [110] (bl) 9-11-5 N Williamson, *led to 6th,*
led nxt to 3 out, sn btn.
......................................(8 to 1 op 12 to 1 tchd 14 to 1) 5
1274 FIGHT TO WIN (USA) [109] (bl) 6-11-4 M Perrett, *hit 1st and*
4th, chsd ldrs 8th, beh tenth.
....................................(14 to 1 op 12 to 1 tchd 16 to 1) 6
2334[3] DANDY MINSTREL [108] 10-11-3 C Llewellyn, *hit 7th, drpd*
rear 9th, no ch whn hit 12th.
......................................(9 to 2 op 4 to 1) 7
1391[2] HOLTERMANN (USA) [114] 10-11-9 M Richards, *slwly*
away, tld off, pld up bef 6th..........(5 to 1 op 11 to 2) pu
Dist: 5l, 6l, 3l, 12l, ¾l, 7l. 6m 33.20s. a 38.20s (8 Ran).
SR: 7/-/-/-/-/ (Sir Hugh Dundas), D R C Elsworth

2430 Burnham Novices' Hurdle (4-y-o and up) £2,076 2m................(3:20)

FIRST AVENUE 10-11-3 J Railton, *wl beh till hdwy frm 3*
out, chlgd last, sn led, ran on well.
......................................(7 to 1 op 8 to 1 tchd 14 to 1) 1
1647[6] FOREVER SHINEING 4-10-2 M Perrett, *hld up, plenty to*
do 3 out, quickened appr last, fnshd wl, not rch wnr.
......................................(33 to 1 op 25 to 1 tchd 40 to 1) 2
1230[2] EALING COURT 5-11-3 V Slattery, *al chasing ldrs, dsptd*
ld 3 out to nxt, one pace r-in..............(2 to 1 jt-
....fav op 5 to 4 tchd 9 to 4) 3
KALAKATE 9-11-3 D O'Sullivan, *in tch, lost pl 5th, rallied*
frm 2 out....................(20 to 1 op 16 to 1 tchd 33 to 1) 4
2154[4] KING ATHELSTAN (USA) 6-11-3 A S Smith, *pld hrd, pressed*
ldrs, chlgd 4th, led aftr nxt 3 out, sn btn.
..........................(5 to 1 op 7 to 2 tchd 11 to 2) 5
2204 AUSTRAL JANE 4-9-13 (3[*]) R Farrant, *hdwy to chase ldrs*
5th, wknd 3 out... (25 to 1 tchd 33 to 1 and 20 to 1) 6
1557 MOVE A MINUTE (USA) 5-11-7 (3[*]) P Hide, *in tch, dsptd ld 3*
out to nxt, sn wknd..........................(2 to 1 jt-
....fav tchd 7 to 4 and 9 to 4) 7
MA BELLA LUNA 5-10-12 A Charlton, *effrt 5th, sn btn.*
......................................(12 to 1 op 10 to 1 tchd 14 to 1) 8
BEE BEAT 6-11-3 M Bosley, *al beh...* (33 to 1 op 20 to 1) 9
2250[7] ROBENKO (USA) (bl) 5-11-3 N Williamson, *wth ldrs, led*
aftr second till after 5th, sn wknd. (20 to 1 op 14 to 1) 10
KITSBEL 6-11-3 W McFarland, *jmpd rght, led till aftr*
second, wknd 4th....................(33 to 1 tchd 50 to 1) 11
379[4] PATONG BEACH 4-10-2 M Ahern, *pressed ldrs to 5th.*
......................................(20 to 1 op 14 to 1) 12
ROYAL GLINT 5-10-12 A Tory, *beh hfwy.*
......................................(14 to 1 op 10 to 1) 13
CASTILLO 7-11-3 B Powell, *beh 4th.* (33 to 1 op 20 to 1) 14
809 GIVE ALL 8-10-10 (7[*]) M Appleby, *al beh, tld off whn pld*
up bef 3 out........................(33 to 1 tchd 50 to 1) pu
Dist: 8l, hd, 8l, ¾l, 12l, 3l, 15l, 7l, 6l. 4m 15.40s. a 30.40s (15 Ran).
SR: 28/5/20/12/11/-/3/-/-/ (C J Drewe), C J Drewe

2431 Holyport Conditional Jockeys' Handicap Chase (0-110 5-y-o and up) £2,819 2m 5f...........................(3:50)

2318[2] FIDDLERS THREE [101] (bl) 11-11-7 R Farrant, *wth ldr, led*
4th, clr 7th, rdn 3 out, styd on gmely........(2 to 1 jt-
....fav op 5 to 4 tchd 9 to 4) 1
1041[3] LOVE ANEW (USA) [101] 9-11-7 Guy Lewis, *al in tch, trkd*
ldr gng wl 3 out, rdn appr last, no extr.
......................................(5 to 1 op 4 to 1) 2
1795[4] BUSH HILL [80] 9-10-0 A Thornton, *led to 4th, chsd wnr,*
rdn 8th, wknd aftr 11th.
......................................(4 to 1 tchd 12 to 1 and 8 to 1) 3
1489 GREEN WILLOW [106] 12-11-12 P Hide, *hdwy to chase*
wnr 11th, hit 4 out and nxt, 3rd and no ch whn f 2 out.
......................................(5 to 1 op 4 to 1) f

2268[4] RICH NEPHEW [88] 9-10-8 C Burnett-Wells, *al beh, hit 4th*
and 11th, tld off whn pld up bef 2 out.......(2 to 1 jt-
....fav op 5 to 2) pu
Dist: 4l, dist. 5m 51.40s. a 40.40s (5 Ran).
(Simon Sainsbury), Capt T A Forster

2432 Copper Horse Handicap Hurdle (0-105 4-y-o and up) £2,490 2m.......(4:20)

2226[3] MOVING OUT [90] 6-11-1 M Perrett, *led aftr second to 3*
out, sn after nxt, drvn out.
..........................(13 to 2 op 5 to 1 tchd 7 to 1) 1
CARIBBEAN PRINCE [86] 6-10-11 S Burrough, *led to sec-*
ond, prmnt, slight ld 3 out till aftr nxt, rdn and one
pace r-in...............(10 to 1 tchd 8 to 1 and 12 to 1) 2
AVERON [75] 14-10-0 Lorna Vincent, *beh, virtually tld off*
3 out, plenty to do appr last, ran on, fnshd wl. (50 to 1) 3
1768[9] KELLING [90] (bl) 7-10-10 (5[*]) Guy Lewis, *hdwy to track*
ldrs 4th, rdn 3 out, no imprsn. (9 to 2 jt-fav op 7 to 1) 4
961 TIP TOP LAD [99] 7-11-10 J Railton, *nvr rch ldrs.*
..........................(14 to 1 op 10 to 1 tchd 16 to 1) 5
2130 SOMERSET DANCER (USA) [90] 7-11-1 D O'Sullivan, *al beh.*
......................................(14 to 1 op 12 to 1 tchd 16 to 1) 6
2003[4] ERZADJAN (Ire) [90] (bl) 4-11-1 G McCourt, *in tch, chlgd*
5th, rdn and btn appr 3 out...................(9 to 2 jt-
....fav op 4 to 1 tchd 5 to 1) 7
2319[5] ILEWIN [90] 7-11-1 M Ahern, *hdwy to track ldrs 4th, wknd*
appr 3 out....................(10 to 1 tchd 11 to 1) 8
HEDGEHOPPER (Ire) [80] 6-10-5 M Richards, *led briefly*
second, wknd 5th..................(16 to 1 op 14 to 1) 9
2243[7] EUROTWIST [103] 5-12-0 W McFarland, *mid-div, wknd*
5th....................................(10 to 1 op 7 to 1) 10
2192[2] FAMOUS DANCER [92] 6-11-3 D Murphy, *hdwy 5th, wknd*
quickly 3 out....................(5 to 1 tchd 11 to 2) 11
2306[9] MASTER GLEN [106] 6-11-6 (5[*]) P Midgley, *prmnt, wknd*
5th, no ch whn jmpd lft 2 out.
..........................(10 to 1 op 14 to 1 tchd 8 to 1) 12
CLOGHRAN LAD [80] 7-10-5 P McDermott, *al beh.*
......................................(16 to 1 op 14 to 1) 13
2142 EXACT ANALYSIS (USA) [80] 8-10-5 G Upton, *prmnt, jmpd*
slwly 3rd, sn beh.......(25 to 1 op 20 to 1) 14
1945 FRONT PAGE [95] 7-11-6 D Gallagher, *prmnt till wknd 5th,*
tld off whn pld up bef 2 out.
......................................(10 to 1 op 8 to 1) pu
2015[9] CHARLAFRIVOLA [75] 6-10-0 B Clifford, *al beh, tld off whn*
pld up bef 2 out........................(66 to 1) pu
Dist: 10l, 10l, nk, 12l, ½l, 4l, nk, sht-hd, ¾l, 1½l. 4m 17.20s. a 32.20s (16 Ran).
SR: 8/-/-/-/-/-/ (Mrs Shirley Brasher), Miss H C Knight

EDINBURGH (good)
Thursday February 3rd
Going Correction: PLUS 0.10 sec. per fur.

2433 Loganlea Claiming Hurdle (4-y-o) £1,871 2m....................(2:00)

2303[6] ERICOLIN (Ire) 11-3 G McCourt, *settled midfield, hdwy to*
chal aftr 2 out, led last, ran on and pres.
......................................(11 to 10 on op Evens) 1
2241[5] BEND SABLE (Ire) 11-7 B Storey, *hld up, hdwy aftr 3 out,*
slight ld gng wl betw last 2, mstk and hdd last, kpt on
und pres..................(3 to 1 op 9 to 4 tchd 7 to 2) 2
1920 DIGNIFIED (Ire) 9-11 (7[*]) A Linton, *chsd ldr, led 2 out, sn*
hdd, kpt on same pace.............(50 to 1 op 25 to 1) 3
1634[5] ANORAK (USA) 11-0 (7[*]) S Taylor, *chsd ldrs, ev ch 2 out, sn*
rdn, one pace....................(5 to 1 op 3 to 1) 4
2148 SUPREME SOVIET 10-2 (5[*]) J Supple, *led, clr to hfwy, hdd*
2 out, wknd........................(50 to 1 op 25 to 1) 5
UNNAB 10-7 (5[*]) P Waggott, *in tch, effrt appr 2 out, no*
hdwy........................(33 to 1 op 20 to 1) 6
2241 THATCHED (Ire) 10-13 N Smith, *in tch, pushed alng aftr 3*
out, sn wknd.........................(100 to 1) 7
1920 FUNNY FEELINGS 10-11 A Dobbin, *blun second, lost tch*
hfwy, tld off....................(16 to 1 op 20 to 1) 8
HOD-MOD (Ire) 10-13 C Grant, *lost tch hfwy, tld off.*
......................................(66 to 1 tchd 100 to 1) 9
2271[5] RYTHMIC RYMER 10-0[1] (5[*]) P Williams, *chsd ldrs, ch 2 out,*
4th and btn whn pld up and dismounted bef last.
......................................(25 to 1) pu
Dist: 1½l, 8l, 2l, 8l, 5l, 5l, 25l, dist. 3m 46.10s. a 8.10s (10 Ran).
SR: 24/26/1/16/-/-/ (Gormley Marble Ltd), N Tinkler

2434 Penicuik Novices' Chase Glengoyne Highland Malt Tamerosia Series Qualifier (5-y-o and up) £2,411 3m ....(2:30)

1805[5] MR TITTLE TATTLE (bl) 8-11-10 N Williamson, *made all,*
blun 12th, clr 4 out, eased r-in.
......................................(4 to 1 op 7 to 2 tchd 9 to 2) 1
2270[3] EXTRA SPECIAL 9-11-4 N Doughty, *in tch, outpcd whn*
hmpd 9th, hdwy to chase wnr 14th, kpt on wl frm last,
no imprsn....................(14 to 1 op 10 to 1) 2
2219 SCOTTISH GOLD (v) 10-11-10 G McCourt, *beh, hdwy frm*
11th, ev ch 14th, sn wknd.......(25 to 1 op 14 to 1) 3

2251[5] FOUR DEEP (Ire) 6-11-4 A Dobbin, *prmnt, chsd wnr aftr
tenth, wknd quickly appr 14th, tld off.*
.... (12 to 1 op 10 to 1 tchd 14 to 1)   4
2238[2] WISHING GATE (USA) 6-11-4 M Dwyer, *prmnt till f 9th,
broke leg, destroyed.*
.... (13 to 8 on op 7 to 4 on tchd 6 to 4 on)   f
2003 LA DOUTELLE 7-10-8 (5*) P Williams, *sn beh, tld off whn f
12th.*...................... (66 to 1)   f
1619 ORIEL DREAM 7-10-10 (3*) A Thornton, *sn tracking wnr,
wknd 11th, beh whn pld up bef 14th.*
.... (14 to 1 op 12 to 1)   pu
2071[5] RUSHING BURN 8-10-13 B Storey, *blun second, sn beh,
tld off whn pld up bef 4 out....* (25 to 1 op 16 to 1)   pu
1587[2] VULPIN DE LAUGERE (Fr) (bl) 7-10-13 (5*) J Burke, *reminder
aftr 5th, hmpd 9th, sn beh, tld off whn pld up bef 4 out.*
.... (20 to 1 op 16 to 1)   pu
Dist: 2l, 15l, 25l. 6m 14.60s. a 24.60s (9 Ran).

(Mrs J K Newton), K C Bailey

2435 Harperrig Maiden Hurdle (4-y-o and up) £1,966 3m ....(3:00)

1688[3] THE BUD CLUB (Ire) 6-11-6 N Williamson, *hld up, hdwy to
track ldrs hfwy, rdn to ld betw last 2, styd on wl.*
.... (11 to 10 on op 6 to 4 on tchd Evens)   1
HOT PUNCH 5-11-1 (5*) P Waggott, *in tch, effrt aftr 3 out,
styd on frm nxt, no imprsn on wnr.* (25 to 1 op 20 to 1)   2
2358[3] SLAUGHT SON (Ire) 6-11-6 G McCourt, *cl up, led tenth till
betw last 2, sn btn......* (7 to 1 op 20 to 1)   3
WHY NOT EQUINAME 6-11-6 A Dobbin, *hld up, hdwy aftr
9th, ev ch appr 2 out, sn wknd.*
.... (16 to 1 op 25 to 1 tchd 33 to 1)   4
1621 PAKENHAM 8-11-6 N Doughty, *led to tenth, sn wknd.*
.... (10 to 1 op 7 to 1 tchd 12 to 1)   5
2153 PANTO LADY 8-10-8 (7*) Miss S Lamb, *trkd ldrs, outpcd
aftr 9th, sn beh...* (200 to 1 op 250 to 1 tchd 500 to 1)   6
1959 CUMBERLAND BLUES (Ire) 5-11-6 C Grant, *beh most of
way, tld off....................* (33 to 1 op 100 to 1)   7
1133[7] MR FLUORINE (Ire) 5-11-3 (3*) A Thornton, *beh hfwy, tld
off whn pld up bef 2 out.*
.... (16 to 1 op 12 to 1 tchd 20 to 1)   pu
Dist: 5l, 8l, 6l, 12l, 3½l, 20l. 6m 3.00s. a 23.00s (8 Ran).

(Bud Flanagan Leukaemia Fund), K C Bailey

2436 Anderson Strathern W. S. Novices' Chase (5-y-o and up) £2,814 2m (3:30)

2386[2] SLIEVENAMON MIST 8-11-4 N Williamson, *trkd ldrs, led
8th, clr aftr 4 out, jmpd lft last 3, kpt on wl.*
.... (7 to 4 fav op 5 to 4 tchd 2 to 1)   1
1219[3] WILLIE SPARKLE 8-10-13 (5*) P Williams, *beh, styd on frm
4 out, crrd lft 2 out, fnshd wl.......* (6 to 1 op 4 to 1)   2
2251[2] GOLDEN ISLE 10-11-4 A Dobbin, *trkd ldrs, chsd wnr 8th,
blun 4 out, kpt on frm nxt, no imprsn.*
.... (8 to 1 op 7 to 1)   3
2243[8] ASHDREN 7-11-4 G McCourt, *hld up, hdwy to track ldrs
8th, kpt on same pace frm 4 out..............* (33 to 1)   4
1321[2] FULL O'PRAISE (NZ) 7-11-4 T Reed, *jmpd lft thrght, led,
almost ran out and hdd 5th, cl up till outpcd aftr 8th,
kpt on frm 3 out.............* (4 to 1 tchd 5 to 1)   5
1792 FLOWING RIVER (USA) 8-11-4 B Storey, *nvr nr to chal.*
.... (6 to 1 op 5 to 1)   6
2218 AYIA NAPA 7-11-4 Mr J Bradbourne, *cl up, lft in ld 5th, hdd
8th, wknd......................* (100 to 1)   7
2240[2] BALLYBELL 9-11-4 Mr R Hale, *sn beh, tld off...* (8 to 1)   8
NATIVE KNIGHT 9-11-1 (3*) A Larnach, *chsd ldrs till wknd
quickly aftr 7th, tld off.*
.... (66 to 1 op 50 to 1 tchd 100 to 1)   9
2108[9] LOVING OMEN 7-11-4 D Byrne, *f 3rd.* (33 to 1 op 25 to 1)   f
2357[3] ROAD TO THE WEIR 7-10-13 (5*) J Burke, *mid-div, no
hdwy whn f 4 out...............* (25 to 1 tchd 33 to 1)   f
2357 GRAZEMBER 7-11-4 Mrs A Farrell, *prmnt, wkng whn
hmpd and uns rdr 4 out..........* (20 to 1 op 16 to 1)   ur
2251[7] ROBINS LAD 8-11-4 C Grant, *al beh, tld off whn pld up
bef 4 out...................* (50 to 1)   pu
1790 ROYAL FIFE 8-10-8 (5*) F Perratt, *al beh, tld off whn pld
up bef 4 out..........* (40 to 1 op 33 to 1 tchd 50 to 1)   pu
Dist: 4l, 2½l, 2l, 5l, 8l, 15l, 20l, 1l. 3m 58.20s. a 8.20s (14 Ran).
SR: 24/20/17/15/10/2/   (I M S Racing), K C Bailey

2437 J. R. McNair Amateur Riders' Handicap Chase (0-120 5-y-o and up) £2,584 2½m......................... (4:00)

1789* SIR PETER LELY [115] (bl) 7-11-2 (7*) Mr C Bonner, *made all,
clr appr 4 out, eased r-in.........* (3 to 1 fav op 9 to 4)   1
DEADLINE [98] (bl) 11-9-7 (7*) Miss J Thurlow, *chsd ldrs, kpt
on wl frm 3 out, no ch wth wnr...* (50 to 1 op 33 to 1)   2
1789[2] CORNET [120] (v) 8-12-0 Mr S Swiers, *in tch, effrt aftr
12th, kpt on same pace...........* (7 to 2 op 3 to 1)   3
2222[4] SWEET CITY [101] 9-10-4 (5*) Mr R Hale, *mstks, beh, some
hdwy frm 4 out, nvr dngrs...........* (9 to 2 op 4 to 1)   4
2107[3] ABSAILOR [96] (v) 10-10-4[5] (3*) Mr J Bradbourne, *chsd ldrs,
reminders aftr 9th, wknd 12th............* (9 to 1 op 11 to 1)   5
2151[2] LAPIAFFE [95] 10-9-10 (7*) Mr D Parker, *chsd wnr, no
imprsn whn hit 4 out, wknd nxt.....* (9 to 1 op 4 to 1)   6

768 DROMINA STAR [97] 13-10-5[12] (7*) Mr M Bradburne, *sn lost
tch, tld off..................* (100 to 1)   7
2162[3] SAMSUN [92] (bl) 12-9-7 (7*) Miss S White, *sn lost tch, tld
off whn f 4 out........* (16 to 1 op 50 to 1 tchd 66 to 1)   f
2242[5] BARKISLAND [94] 10-9-13 (3*) Mrs A Farrell, *in tch whn
blun 8th, sn beh, tld off when pld up bef 4 out.*
.... (9 to 2 op 4 to 1)   pu
Dist: 2½l, 5l, 10l, ½l, nk, dist. 5m 5.20s. a 15.20s (9 Ran).
(John Doyle Construction Limited), M D Hammond

2438 Wallyford Novices' Handicap Hurdle (4-y-o and up) £2,305 2½m......(4:30)

2070* RELUCTANT SUITOR [109] 5-11-9 (5*) D Bentley, *made all,
rdn aftr 2 out, ran on strly, eased nr finish.*
.... (7 to 4 fav tchd 2 to 1)   1
2150* LEGITIM [88] 5-10-2 (5*) P Williams, *prmnt, mstk 7th, chsd
wnr aftr 3 out, rdn and ev ch after nxt, no imprsn.*
.... (9 to 2 op 3 to 1 tchd 3 to 1)   2
2382[7] TITIAN GIRL [82] (bl) 5-10-0[2] (3*) A Thornton, *prmnt, rdn
appr 3 out, sn wknd....* (8 to 1 op 6 to 1 tchd 10 to 1)   3
2072[4] CORNFLAKE [81] 4-9-9 (5*) P Waggott, *prmnt, rdn aftr 3
out, sn wknd...........* (13 to 8 on tchd 11 to 10 on)   4
2276[8] HURRICANE HORACE [81] 7-10-0 R Hodge, *beh, pushed
alng hfwy, tld off 3 out, pld up bef nxt.*
.... (5 to 2 op 6 to 4)   pu
Dist: 2½l, 30l, 10l. 4m 57.10s. a 19.10s (5 Ran).
(Joe Buzzeo), M D Hammond

LINGFIELD (A.W) (std)
Thursday February 3rd
Going Correction: NIL

2439 Quebec Maiden Hurdle (4-y-o and up) £1,953 2m..................... (1:40)

2111[2] ERLKING (Ire) 4-10-3 (7*) Chris Webb, *cl up, led 7th, clr aftr
nxt, lft wl clear last.*
.... (9 to 4 fav op 7 to 4 tchd 5 to 2)   1
2364[6] CONBRIO STAR (bl) 4-10-10 R Dunwoody, *led til hdd 7th,
wknd aftr nxt, no ch whn lft poor second at last.*
.... (20 to 1 op 14 to 1 tchd 25 to 1)   2
1276[3] NEEDS MUST 7-11-6 J Frost, *trkd ldrs till wknd 4 out, lft
poor 3rd at last.....* (14 to 1 op 10 to 1 tchd 16 to 1)   3
2164[2] THE CAN CAN MAN 7-11-6 M Robinson, *trkd ldrs, blun
5th, hmpd 7th and wknd, tld off.*
.... (11 to 4 op 3 to 1 tchd 7 to 2)   4
2043[9] GREEN'S TRILOGY (bl) 6-11-6 M Ahern, *cl up till lost pl
quickly 3rd, tld off...............* (50 to 1)   5
2083 NEVER SO LOST 4-10-10 W McFarland, *beh, lost tch 6th,
tld off.....................* (25 to 1 op 33 to 1)   6
2224[5] GILT DIMENSION 7-11-6 R Supple, *mid-div, hdwy 7th,
chsd wnr aftr 4 out, clr second but no ch whn f last.*
.... (13 to 2 op 5 to 1 tchd 7 to 1)   f
1410[6] OUR NIKKI 4-10-5 I Shoemark, *hld up, f sth......* (33 to 1)   f
2317[7] NOTED STRAIN (Ire) 6-11-3 (7*) S Arnold, *blun and uns
rdr second..........................* (10 to 25 to 1)   ur
2345[4] TELMAR SYSTEMS 5-11-6 H Campbell, *trkd ldrs till blun
and uns rdr 7th..................* (33 to 1)   ur
ALL THE JOLLY 6-11-1 S Earle, *lost tch 6th, tld off whn
pld up bef 3 out.....................* (50 to 1)   pu
RISING WOLF 4-10-10 D O'Sullivan, *blun 3rd and rdr lost
irons, pld up bef nxt................* (3 to 1 op 4 to 1)   pu
Dist: Dist, ½l, 10l, dist, 2l. 3m 38.00s. a 5.00s (12 Ran).
SR: 32/-/-/-/-/-/   (S P Tindall), S Mellor

2440 British Columbia Novices' Hurdle (4-y-o and up) £1,737 2½m....... (2:10)

1595 TOO CLEVER BY HALF 6-11-6 Mr G Johnson Houghton, *hld
up beh ldrs, cld 9th, led appr last, hdd briefly r-in, all
out........................* (50 to 1 op 25 to 1)   1
1489 BOBBY SOCKS 8-11-6 L Harvey, *chsd ldrs, cld 4 out, hrd
rdn appr last, led briefly r-in, no extr und pres.*
.... (16 to 1 op 12 to 1 tchd 20 to 1)   2
2319 SWING LUCKY (bl) 9-11-6 R Campbell, *cl up, led 6th till
hdd appr last, one pace..........* (5 to 1 op 9 to 2)   3
2327[4] PIE HATCH (Ire) (bl) 5-11-1 R J Beggan, *hld up beh ldrs, cld
6th, outpcd and jmpd awkwardly 3 out, one pace und
pres.......................* (7 to 1 tchd 8 to 1)   4
1539[5] KING'S TREASURE (USA) 5-12-4 J Frost, *hld up in rear,
hdwy 6th, outpcd frm 4 out, nvr dngrs.*
.... (11 to 10 fav op 5 to 4)   5
2341* TAKE A FLYER (Ire) 4-11-1 A Tory, *chsd ldrs till wknd
quickly aftr 4 out, tld off.*
.... (14 to 1 op 10 to 1 tchd 16 to 1)   6
2345[2] MILZIG (USA) 5-11-12 D O'Sullivan, *sn detached frm main
grp, al beh, tld off......* (7 to 4 op 13 to 8 tchd 2 to 1)   7
1464[8] EL GRANDO 4-10-9 A Charlton, *al beh, tld off.*
.... (50 to 1 op 33 to 1)   8
ROGEVIC BELLE 6-11-6 D Gallagher, *jmpd deliberately,
led til hdd 6th, sn wknd, pld up bef 4 out.*
.... (50 to 1 op 33 to 1)   pu
GLEN PENNANT 7-11-6 M Richards, *cl up to 5th, mstk nxt
and lost pl, tld off whn pld up bef 3 out.*
.... (50 to 1 op 33 to 1)   pu

Dist: ¾l, 10l, 2½l, 12l, dist, 6l, 25l. 4m 43.70s. a 12.70s (10 Ran).

(Mrs R F Johnson Houghton), R F Johnson Houghton

2441 Newfoundland Claiming Hurdle (4-y-o and up) £1,722 2¼m............(3:10)

2226* TEL E THON (v) 7-11-8 R Dunwoody, *made all, clr 5th to 4 out, shaken up appr last, cmftbly.*
............................(11 to 8 op 5 to 4 on tchd 6 to 4) 1
2225* SPARKLER GEBE (b) 8-11-6 D O'Sullivan, *hld up, chsd wnr aftr 4 out, ev ch nxt, held appr last.*
............................(5 to 4 fav tchd 11 to 8) 2
2292 MECADO (v) 7-11-4 D Gallagher, *wtd wth in last pl, lost tch 7th, styd on frm 3 out, nvr dngrs.*
............................(13 to 2 op 5 to 1 tchd 7 to 1) 3
1931⁴ YAAFOOR (USA) (bl) 5-11-2 M Richards, *chsd wnr to 7th, cl up till outpcd aftr 4 out.*
............................(14 to 1 op 8 to 1 tchd 16 to 1) 4
1942 TAPESTRY DANCER 6-11-2 D Skyrme, *hld up in tch, wnt second at 7th, wknd 4 out, tld off whn pld up bef last.*
............................(25 to 1 op 16 to 1 tchd 33 to 1) pu
Dist: 10l, 12l, 5l. 4m 12.50s. a 11.50s (5 Ran).

(Eddie Wilkinson), P J Jones

2442 Ontario Handicap Hurdle (0-105 4-y-o and up) £1,722 2½m............(3:40)

2228* SAAHI (USA) [90] 5-11-10 J Osborne, *hld up in tch, led aftr 2 out, stumbled after last, easily.*
............................(7 to 2 on op 9 to 2 on) 1
2229⁵ SING THE BLUES [84] 10-11-4 D Morris, *led till aftr 2 out, one pace.*............(8 to 1 op 9 to 2 tchd 9 to 1) 2
1743 CONSTRUCTION [80] 9-11-0 R Supple, *not jump wl, cl up till outpcd aftr 4 out.*............(25 to 1 op 20 to 1) 3
2343³ NEARLY HONEST [67] 6-10-1¹ A Tory, *f 3rd.*
............................(6 to 1 op 5 to 1 tchd 7 to 1) f
Dist: 8l, 15l. 4m 44.20s. a 13.20s (4 Ran).

(Martin N Peters), C Weedon

2443 Manitoba Handicap Hurdle (0-115 4-y-o and up) £1,722 2m............(4:10)

2342* DONOSTI [99] 10-11-2 (7*) D Fortt, *in cl tch, chsd ldr frm 6th, rdn to ld betw last 2, lft clr r-in.*
............................(7 to 4 op 5 to 4 tchd 15 to 8) 1
2229² RARFY'S DREAM [102] 6-11-12 D Gallagher, *hld up in last pl, not fluent, effrt to cl 4 out, sn no imprsn, lft second r-in.*............(7 to 4 on op 6 to 4 on tchd 11 to 8 on) 2
1717⁸ BILL QUILL [76] 10-9-13⁶ (7*) R Darke, *pld hrd early, in cl tch till outpcd 4 out, tld off.*
............................(10 to 1 op 7 to 1 tchd 12 to 1) 3
1238 EDDIE WALSHE [84] 9-10-8 Leesa Long, *rcd freely, led, sn clr, rdn and hdd betw last 2, blun last and uns rdr r-in.*
............................(50 to 1 op 20 to 1) ur
Dist: 8l, dist. 3m 39.10s. a 6.10s (4 Ran).
SR: 34/29/-/-/

(R L C Hartley), R Lee

2444 Alberta National Hunt Flat Race (4,5,6-y-o) £1,604 2m................(4:40)

1548 SEBASTOPOL 5-10-12 (7*) D Hobbs, *pld hrd early, trkd ldrs, led o'r 3 fs out, rdn clr over one out.*
............................(13 to 8 fav op 5 to 1) 1
2269⁹ IVY EDITH 4-10-4 D O'Sullivan, *al prmnt, led appr 4 fs out till hdd o'r 3 out, outpcd over one out.*
............................(6 to 1 tchd 8 to 1) 2
KEEL ROW 4-10-4 D Meade, *sn pushed alng in rear, prog into mid-div aftr 4 fs, styd on frm four out.*
rear, hdwy frm 3 fs out, styd on wl, improve.
............................(16 to 1 op 25 to 1 tchd 33 to 1) 4
2021 DUNLIR 4-10-2 (7*) T Thompson, *beh, effrt 7 fs out, styd on und pres fnl 2.*...(20 to 1 op 25 to 1 tchd 33 to 1) 5
2339 SOBER ISLAND 5-11-0 (5*) T Jenks, *trkd ldrs, led 7 fs out till hdd appr 4 out, rdn and wknd.*
............................(5 to 1 op 3 to 1 tchd 6 to 1) 6
STEEL FAUCON (Ire) 5-11-5 Mr J Durkan, *pld hrd towards rear, nvr on terms.*............(33 to 1 tchd 50 to 1) 7
2134³ FARLEY FLYER 5-10-12 (7*) R Darke, *slwly into strd, hld up in rear, nvr on terms.*...(8 to 1 op 9 to 4) 8
2134⁴ ESPERER 4-10-6 (3*) A Dicken, *sn led til hdd 7 fs out, wknd o'r 4 out.*...(12 to 1 op 10 to 1 tchd 14 to 1) 9
SURGICAL SPIRIT 4-9-11 (7*) S Fox, *al beh, tld off.*
............................(33 to 1 op 20 to 1) 10
CASTLE ROSE 6-10-11 (3*) A Procter, *mid-div till rdn and wknd 5 fs out, tld off.*......(33 to 1 op 25 to 1) 11
TOUGHNUTOCRACK 4-10-2 (7*) S Arnold, *prmnt till lost pl o'r 5 fs out, tld off.*........(33 to 1 tchd 50 to 1) 12
Dist: 15l, 2½l, 12l, 8l, 7l, ½l, 3l, 8l, 20l, 1½l. 3m 32.80s. (12 Ran).

(Derrick Page), P F Nicholls

KELSO (soft)
Friday February 4th
Going Correction: PLUS 1.05 sec. per fur. (races 1,3,5), PLUS 1.20 (2,4,6,7)

2445 Ship Hotel Novices' Hurdle (4-y-o and up) £2,547 2m 110yds.........(1:20)

2356³ SURREY DANCER 6-11-10 P Niven, *hld up, hdwy hfwy, chlgd betw last 2, led aftr last, drvn out.*
............................(6 to 4 on op 7 to 4 on tchd 5 to 4 on) 1
2106⁴ CALLERNOY (Ire) 4-10-1 (7*) Mr A Manners, *trkd ldrs, chlgd 3 out, dsptd ld till shaken up and no extr aftr last.*............................(16 to 1 tchd 20 to 1) 2
2303⁰⁷ UPWARD SURGE (Ire) 4-10-8 N Williamson, *led to second, cl up, led 5th till aftr last, no extr.* (8 to 1 tchd 7 to 1) 3
2217⁸ EMERALD SEA (USA) 7-11-4 S Turner, *prmnt till wknd appr last.*............................(50 to 1) 4
LITTLE BROMLEY 7-10-13 Mr R Hale, *led second to 5th, cl up till wknd appr 2 out.*....(33 to 1 op 25 to 1) 5
2356 SHARP CHALLENGE 7-11-4 K Jones, *chsd ldrs, drvn alng and outpcd hfwy, sn beh.*....................(100 to 1) 6
2252⁴ PRECIOUS HENRY 5-11-4 Mr N Wilson, *nvr dngrs.*
............................(25 to 1 tchd 33 to 1) 7
2068⁴ THREE STRONG (Ire) 5-11-1 (3*) D J Moffatt, *hit 1st, in tch till wknd hfwy.*......(8 to 1 tchd 9 to 1) 8
SALDA 5-11-4 T Reed, *al beh, tld off.*...(12 to 1 op 8 to 1) 9
945³ TEMPLERAINEY (Ire) 6-10-13 (5*) P Williams, *f 3rd.*
............................(10 to 1 tchd 14 to 1) f
JUSTICE IS DONE (Ire) 4-10-1 A Linton, *f second.*
............................(33 to 1) f
827³ KING MELODY 8-11-4 N Doughty, *in tch till wknd quickly appr 4th, tld off whn pld up bef nxt.*
............................(16 to 1 tchd 20 to 1) pu
2303 YOUNG GUS 7-11-4 R Hodge, *hmpd second, al beh, tld off whn pld up bef last.*........(33 to 1 op 25 to 1) pu
Dist: 3l, ½l, 6l, 15l, 20l, 5l, 3l, 6l. 4m 6.40s. a 23.40s (13 Ran).
SR: 35/16/15/19/-/-/

(Laurel (Leisure) Limited), Mrs M Reveley

2446 Tattersalls Mares Only Novices' Chase Qualifier (6-y-o and up) £2,811 2¾m 110yds.................(1:50)

1937³ DURHAM SUNSET 7-11-1 N Doughty, *made all, lft clr 13th, easily.*.............(6 to 4 tchd 7 to 4) 1
1937⁶ HERE COMES TIBBY 7-10-10 Mrs A Farrell, *prmnt, mstk tenth, outpcd aftr nxt, chsd wnr 13th, no imprsn.*
............................(25 to 1 op 20 to 1) 2
STAGSHAW BELLE 10-10-10 Mr J Bradburne, *chsd wnr to tenth, outpcd aftr nxt.*......(25 to 1 op 20 to 1) 3
2238* CHARLOTTE'S EMMA 7-11-1 B Storey, *in tch, chsd wnr frm tenth, cl second whn f 13th.*
............................(6 to 5 on op 11 to 8 on tchd 11 to 10 on) f
2003⁷ HOWCLEUCH 7-10-10 T Reed, *f 3rd.* (14 to 1 op 16 to 1) f
1937⁵ REDHALL ROYALE 10-10-10 Miss P Robson, *prmnt, mstk 9th, outpcd aftr 11th, wkng whn hmpd and uns rdr 13th.*............................(100 to 1) ur
2068 MISS TINO 6-10-10 A Dobbin, *beh whn hmpd 3rd, blun 8th, tld off whn pld up bef 3 out.*.........(100 to 1) pu
Dist: 30l, 15l. 6m 17.50s. a 50.50s (7 Ran).

(W M G Black), J H Johnson

2447 EBF George Macdonald Bookmaker 'National Hunt' Novices' Hurdle Qualifier (5,6,7-y-o) £2,512 2¼m.....(2:20)

2140⁴ ASK TOM (Ire) 5-11-0 R Garritty, *made virtually all, hrd pressed 2 out, styd on wl.*
............................(9 to 1 op 6 to 1 tchd 10 to 1) 1
2262² KENILWORTH LAD 6-11-0 P Niven, *chsd ldrs, chlgd last, dsptd ld till edgd lft and no extr fnl 100 yards.* (5 to 4 jt-
fav tchd 6 to 4) 2
2106* CARNETTO 7-10-12 (7*) F Leahy, *al prmnt, chlgd 2 out, dsptd ld till wknd fnl 100 yards.*.........(5 to 4 jt-
fav op Evens tchd 11 to 8) 3
2106⁶ RALLEGIO 5-11-0 A Dobbin, *in tch, led ldrs 7th, wknd appr 2 out.*...................(14 to 1 op 33 to 1) 4
1722 FINNOW QUAY (Ire) 5-10-11 (3*) D J Moffatt, *beh, lost tch appr 7th.*........................(50 to 1 op 33 to 1) 5
2237 ORD GALLERY (Ire) 5-10-7 (7*) A Linton, *in tch till wknd appr 7th.*............................(50 to 1 op 33 to 1) 6
GOING PUBLIC 7-11-0 K Johnson, *al beh, lost tch appr 7th.*............................(100 to 1) 7
WOLF'S DEN 5-10-9 (5*) F Perratt, *lost tch appr 7th, tld off whn pld up bef 3 out.*...................(100 to 1) pu
2106 ROMAN SWORD 6-10-9 C Hawkins, *lost tch aftr 4th, tld off whn pld up bef 3 out.*.........(100 to 1) pu
Dist: 1½l, 4l, 15l, 20l, 12l, 15l. 4m 39.50s. a 32.50s (9 Ran).

(B T Stewart-Brown), T P Tate

2448 Doncaster Bloodstock 'Ken Oliver's 80th Birthday Celebration' Handicap Chase (0-140 5-y-o and up) £4,318 3½m.........................(2:50)

1939² OVER THE DEEL [114] 8-10-0 A Dobbin, *al prmnt, led last, styd on wl und pres.*............(14 to 1 op 10 to 1) 1
2305* SHRADEN LEADER [115] 9-10-11 (4ex) A Tory, *in tch, hdwy aftr 14th, led appr 3 out, mstk and hdd last, rallied und pres.*............................(5 to 4 fav op Evens tchd 11 to 8) 2

1917* ARTHUR'S MINSTREL [114] 7-10-0 L Wyer, al prmnt, hit
16th, rdn whn mstk 3 out, kpt on same pace frm nxt.
................................(7 to 2 op 4 to 1)   3

2141² SPARKLING FLAME [135] 10-11-7 M A FitzGerald, sn tracking ldr, ev ch 2 out, wknd appr last. (8 to 1 op 7 to 1)   4

2139² MERRY MASTER [130] 10-11-2 Gee Armytage, led till appr
3 out, wknd quickly....(11 to 2 op 5 to 1 tchd 6 to 1)   5

2103⁹ DEEP HAVEN [118] 9-10-4⁴ K Jones, beh hfwy, tld off.
................................(500 to 1)   6

2219² FORTH AND TAY [115] 12-10-11⁷ C Hawkins, f 4th.   f

2139⁴ DEEP COLONIST [116] 12-10-2 R Garritty, lost tch and pld
up bef 16th......................(25 to 1 tchd 33 to 1)   pu

2253⁹ MAJIC RAIN [117] (bl) 9-10-3³ A Merrigan, sn tld off, pld up
bef 14th.............(200 to 1 op 150 to 1)   pu

2323⁷ RED UNDER THE BED [114] 7-9-7 (7*) Mr D Parker, blun
13th, lost tch and pld up bef 16th.
................................(50 to 1 tchd 66 to 1)   pu
Dist: 2½l, 12l, 5l, 20l, dist. 7m 36.20s. a 46.20s (10 Ran).

(George Tobitt), J H Johnson

2449 Jinxy Jack Morebattle Hurdle (4-y-o and up) £6,742 2m 110yds...... (3:20)

2222* GREY POWER 7-11-0 P Niven, beh, hdwy to track ldrs 3
out, rdn to ld r-in, edgd lft, ran on wl und pres.
................................(11 to 8 fav op 5 to 4 tchd 6 to 4)   1

2360² DIZZY (USA) 6-11-0 A Dobbin, beh, cld 5th, led 2 out to
r-in, kpt on.........................(12 to 1 op 10 to 1)   2

1906⁵ JINXY JACK 10-11-9 N Doughty, wth ldr, led 3rd to 4th,
led 5th till blun and hdd 2 out, sn btn.
................................(9 to 4 op 5 to 4 tchd 11 to 4)   3

1617² DEB'S BALL 8-11-4 D J Moffatt, beh, some late hdwy, nvr
dngrs...........................(9 to 2 op 4 to 1)   4

2360⁴ BORO SMACKEROO 9-11-5 N Williamson, made most to
5th, wknd quickly aftr 3 out, tld off.
................................(10 to 1 tchd 12 to 1)   5

2222 KIR (Ire) 6-11-5 M A FitzGerald, beh, tld off.
................................(100 to 1 op 200 to 1)   6
Dist: 6l, 15l, 2l, dist, 2½l. 4m 3.10s. a 20.10s (6 Ran).
SR: 58/52/46/39/-/-/   (A Frame), Mrs M Reveley

2450 Carlsberg Rutherford Handicap Chase (0-145 5-y-o and up) £3,337 2m 1f............................ (3:50)

2151 SONSIE MO [112] 9-10-0 C Hawkins, chsd ldr, hdwy aftr 2
out, led r-in, sn clr, cmftbly.
................................(9 to 2 op 5 to 1 tchd 6 to 1)   1

2261² CLAY COUNTY [140] 9-12-0 B Storey, led, sn clr, hit 8th,
rdn aftr last, hdd r-in, no extr.
................................(6 to 4 on op 13 to 8 on tchd 11 to 10 on)   2

1808⁴ SIMPLE PLEASURE [113] 9-10-1 J Callaghan, in tch,
pushed alng and outpcd appr 3 out, kpt on frm last.
................................(9 to 2 op 4 to 1 tchd 7 to 2)   3

2255² BELDINE [112] 9-10-0 A Dobbin, beh, mstk 6th, some
hdwy whn hit 2 out, sn wknd.
................................(9 to 1 op 7 to 1 tchd 10 to 1)   4
Dist: 10l, 2l, 20l. 4m 29.60s. a 23.60s (4 Ran).
SR: 40/58/29/8/   (Timothy Hardie), Mrs S C Bradburne

2451 Janco Services Cessford Hunters' Chase (5-y-o and up) £1,952 3m 1f .... (4:20)

DAVY BLAKE 7-12-2 (5*) Mr J M Dun, made all, styd on wl.
................................(11 to 10 on op 5 to 4 on tchd Evens)   1

ONCE STUNG 8-12-7 Mr J Greenall, mstk second, sn chasing wnr, ev ch 4 out, kpt on, no imprsn.
................................(13 to 8 op 6 to 4 tchd 7 to 4)   2

WINTER RAMBLE 8-11-7 (7*) Miss Sue Nichol, beh 12th, tld
off..(100 to 1)   3

POLLIBRIG 10-11-11 (5*) Mr M Buckley, chsd ldrs, mstks
13th and 15th, sn wknd, tld off. (20 to 1 tchd 25 to 1)   4

READY STEADY 12-11-7 (7*) Mr R W Green, blun and uns
rdr 1st........................(14 to 1 op 12 to 1)   ur

CALL COLLECT 13-11-7 (7*) Miss J Thurlow, beh 12th, tld
off whn pld up lme aftr last.
................................(10 to 1 op 12 to 1 tchd 14 to 1)   pu

759⁷ IT'S A PRY 13-11-9 (5*) Mr R Hale, blun second, sn beh,
blunded 12th and nxt, soon pld up.
................................(33 to 1 op 25 to 1)   pu
Dist: 5l, dist, dist. 6m 53.00s. a 51.00s (7 Ran).
(T N Dalgetty), T N Dalgetty

LINGFIELD (heavy) Friday February 4th
Going Correction: PLUS 1.52 sec. per fur.

2452 Orpington Novices' Hurdle (4-y-o and up) £1,768 2m 110yds......... (2:00)

2291² PARADISE NAVY 5-11-2 R Dunwoody, led and mstk 1st, sn
hdd, led ag'n aftr second, pushed alng and styd on frm
2 out, all out. (5 to 2 op 9 to 4 on tchd 2 to 1 on)   1

2315* MAMES BOY 7-11-8 D Murphy, chsd wnr frm 4th, rdn
appr 2 out, no imprsn approaching last.
................................(2 to 1 op 6 to 4)   2

AUGUST TWELFTH 6-11-2 Mr Raymond White, led second,
sn hdd, chsd wnr to 4th, lost tch 3 out, tld off.
................................(66 to 1 op 33 to 1)   3

1594 CURRAGH PETER 7-11-2 W McFarland, al beh, rdn and
lost tch aftr 4th, tld off whn pld up aftr 3 out.
................................(28 to 1 op 20 to 1 tchd 33 to 1 and 40 to 1)   pu
Dist: 6l, dist. 4m 23.30s. a 32.30s (4 Ran).
SR: 16/16/-/-/   (W J Gredley), M C Pipe

2453 Phyllis Clayton Handicap Chase (5-y-o and up) £3,106 3m............. (2:30)

2363 SHASTON [97] (bl) 9-11-13 R Dunwoody, made all, shaken
up and hit 3 out, styd on wl.
................................(13 to 2 op 5 to 1 tchd 7 to 1)   1

2294 SILVERINO [98] 8-12-0 M Richards, in tch, hrd drvn frm 4
out, chsd wnr appr 3 out, no imprsn approaching last.
................................(9 to 4 on op 7 to 4 on tchd 8 to 1)   2

2223* GENERAL BRANDY [87] 8-11-3 D Murphy, chsd wnr frm
8th till appr 3 out, sn wknd, fnshd tired.
................................(3 to 1 fav op 2 to 1)   3

1739* WINTER RITE [94] 11-11-10 J Osborne, chsd wnr till jmpd
badly lft 8th, rdn 11th, sn wknd.....(4 to 1 tchd 6 to 1)   4

2294 LEAGAUNE [89] 12-11-5 E Byrne, prmnt early, beh frm
6th, nvr dngrs aftr...........(14 to 1 op 10 to 1)   5

2173⁸ CAMDEN BELLE [89] 12-11-0 (5*) C Burnett-Wells, al beh.
................................(25 to 1 op 20 to 1)   6

FAARIS [85] 13-11-1 J Railton, al beh. (16 to 1 op 12 to 1)   7

GINGER DIP [77] 12-10-4 (3*) R Farrant, al beh.
................................(40 to 1 op 33 to 1)   8

2253 TRUSTY FRIEND [88] 12-11-4 S Burrough, chsd ldrs till
brght dwn 8th.................(8 to 1 op 10 to 1)   bd

2340⁴ WHAT A NOBLE [82] 8-10-12 G McCourt, blun 1st, al beh,
tld off whn pld up bef 3 out..........(8 to 1 op 10 to 1)   pu
Dist: 12l, 25l, 8l, ¾l, 20l, 2l, 3l. 6m 51.90s. a 58.90s (10 Ran).
(Kavanagh Roofing Southern Limited), W G M Turner

2454 Sanderstead Novices' Claiming Hurdle (5-y-o and up) £1,722 2m 3f 110yds .... (3:00)

2066² BUSMAN (Ire) 5-11-2 M Hourigan, beh, hdwy to chase wnr
appr 7th, slight ld frm 2 out, rdn r-in, edgd lft, hld on,
all out.............(9 to 2 op 3 to 1 tchd 5 to 1)   1+

2208⁶ DERRYMOSS (v) 8-11-8 R Dunwoody, led till narrowly
hdd 2 out, rallied und pres last, styd on gmely r-in to
get up last strds.
................................(9 to 4 on op 2 to 1 on tchd 7 to 4 on)   1+

2227⁷ BAYLORD PRINCE (Ire) (bl) 6-10-7 M Hoad, chsd wnr 5th to
6th, sn wknd, tld off...........(100 to 1 op 33 to 1)   3

2033² BORRETO 10-10-2² (7*) Mr E James, beh frm 4th, tld off.
................................(15 to 2 op 5 to 1 tchd 8 to 1)   4

2244 MISS PARKES 5-9-9 (7*) D Fortt, al beh, mstk 6th, tld off.
................................(66 to 1 op 50 to 1)   5

2263 BITTER ALOE 5-12-0 M Perrett, rdn to chase wnr 6th,
wknd 3 out, tld off....(10 to 1 op 8 to 1 tchd 12 to 1)   6

863⁶ OLIVIPET 5-10-5 M Crosse, chsd wnr to 5th, wknd
quickly, tld off whn pld up bef 3 out.
................................(66 to 1 op 50 to 1)   pu
Dist: Dd-ht, dist, 10l, ½l, 30l. 5m 22.50s. a 48.50s (7 Ran).
(Mrs M T O'Shea & Mrs J K L Watts), J G M O'Shea & M C Pipe

2455 Northfleet Cleaning Services Novices' Chase (5-y-o and up) £2,672 2½m 110yds........................ (3:30)

54⁸ LORD RELIC (NZ) 8-11-4 R Dunwoody, made all, sn clr,
unchlgd.....................(9 to 10 on op 4 to 1 on)   1

1714² SUN SURFER (Fr) 6-11-4 B Powell, chsd wnr aftr 5th but
nvr in contention, jmpd slwly 4 out, hit 2 out and last.
................................(6 to 1 op 5 to 1 tchd 7 to 1)   2

ELMORE 7-11-4 J Lower, chsd wnr till aftr 5th, nvr dngrs
after.......................(20 to 1 op 10 to 1)   3

2264 HARNESS HARVEST 6-10-11 (7*) Mr G Hogan, beh 5th, rdn
appr 6th, tld off.................(40 to 1 op 33 to 1)   4

APOLLO VENTURE 6-10-11 (7*) S Arnold, tld off till f 6th.
................................(33 to 1 op 20 to 1)   f

2186² NICKSLINE 8-11-4 D Murphy, lost tch frm 6th, sn tld off,
pld up bef 3 out.........(13 to 2 op 6 to 1 tchd 7 to 1)   pu
Dist: Dist, 2½l, dist. 5m 34.60s. a 33.60s (6 Ran).
SR: 66/-/-/   (Mrs H J Clarke), M C Pipe

2456 R. E. Sassoon Memorial Hunters' Chase (5-y-o and up) £1,192 3m (4:00)

FIFTH AMENDMENT (bl) 9-12-0 (7*) Mr R Ponsonby, made
all, pushed alng and wnt clr frm 3 out.
................................(4 to 1 op 7 to 2)   1

TRYUMPHANT LAD 10-11-7 (7*) Mr S Deasley, hdwy 13th,
styd on und pres frm 3 out, took second r-in, no ch with
wnr.......................(14 to 1 op 10 to 1)   2

MANDRAKI SHUFFLE (bl) 12-12-0 (7*) Mr A Harvey, beh,
hdwy 8th, wknd 4 out, styd on ag'n to take poor 3rd cl
hme.............(3 to 1 jt-fav op 7 to 2 tchd 4 to 1)   3

LE CHAT NOIR 11-12-0 (7*) Mr C Newport, *prmnt, chsd wnr 4 out, hit last, wknd quickly and virtually pld up nr finish*.................................(3 to 1 jt-
..................fav op 5 to 2 tchd 100 to 30 and 7 to 2) 4
KELLY'S HONOR 15-12-2 (5*) Mr J Sharp, *drpd rear 6th, hit 9th, nvr dngrs aftr*................(8 to 1 op 5 to 1) 5
TEAM CHALLENGE 12-12-0 (7*) Mr J Rees, *effrt 8th, wknd tenth*..............................(10 to 1 op 7 to 1) 6
2301 SPORTING MARINER 12-12-0 (7*) Mr D Bloor, *al beh, hit 5th, tld off 8th, pld up aftr 4 out*...(25 to 1 op 20 to 1) pu
JAAEZ 10-11-7 (7*) Mr J Trice-Rolph, *chlgd 4th to 6th, wknd quickly 9th, tld off pld up bef 12th*.
....(16 to 1 op 12 to 1) pu
ROYAL DAY 8-11-9 (5*) Mr R Russell, *hdwy 9th, wknd rpdly and pld up aftr 4 out*.
.................................(5 to 1 op 4 to 1 tchd 11 to 2) pu
Dist: 12l, 25l, sht-hd, 8l, ¾l. 6m 59.90s. a 66.90s (9 Ran).
(Rupert Ponsonby), C J Mann

2457 Three Counties Handicap Hurdle (0-125 4-y-o and up) £2,280 2m 110yds .... (4:30)

2317² CRABBY BILL [98] (v) 7-9-13 (3*) A Dicken, *chsd ldr till led 4th, rdn appr 2 out, hdd approaching last, rallied und pres to ld ag'n nr finish*..............(3 to 1 op 9 to 1) 1
1945⁴ SOLEIL DANCER (Ire) [96] 6-10-0 R Dunwoody, *took str hold early, chsd wnr 3 out, gng best 2 out, led appr last, rdn r-in, found nothing and hdd cl hme*.
...............(5 to 2 op 9 to 4 tchd 11 to 4 and 3 to 1) 2
2306² RAMBLE (USA) [96] 7-10-0 T Grantham, *chsd ldrs till wknd 5th*.................(7 to 4 fav op 5 to 4 tchd 13 to 8) 3
1944 ALKINOR REX [124] 9-12-0 M Perrett, *led to 4th, sn rdn, nvr dngrs aftr*.............(4 to 1 op 7 to 2 tchd 9 to 2) 4
Dist: 1½l, 12l, 7l. 4m 21.80s. a 29.80s (4 Ran).
SR: 17/13/1/22/ (Financial Trace & Collections), Miss B Sanders

CHEPSTOW (soft)
Saturday February 5th
Going Correction: PLUS 2.30 sec. per fur. (races 1,3,5), PLUS 2.20 (2,4,6)

2458 Tony Preston Memorial Novices' Chase (5-y-o and up) £2,843 2m 110yds....................... (1:00)

2186* COONAWARA 8-11-12 B Powell, *led till mstk and hdd 3rd, led 7th, drw clr frm 5 out, unchlgd*.
.........................(11 to 4 on tchd 5 to 2 on) 1
1518 IN THE NAVY 8-11-9 J Lower, *pressed ldr, led 3rd to 7th, no imprsn frm 5 out*... (9 to 2 op 3 to 1 tchd 5 to 1) 2
2251³ KETTI (v) 9-10-5 (7*) Mr G Hogan, *chsd ldrs, effrt 5 out, sn no imprsn*.............(14 to 1 op 10 to 1) 3
2030³ HIGHLAND POACHER 7-11-3 D Gallagher, *sn struggling*.
........................(66 to 1 op 25 to 1 tchd 80 to 1) 4
2204 WHYFOR 6-10-12 (5*) D Salter, *sn wl beh, tld off whn f 4 out*.........................(100 to 1 op 33 to 1) f
2299³ WILLIE MCGARR (USA) 9-11-3 L Harvey, *prmnt early, sn toiling, tld off whn pld up bef 7th*.
........................(25 to 1 op 16 to 1 tchd 33 to 1) pu
2084⁵ VILLA RECOS 9-11-3 M Hourigan, *tld off 4th, pld up bef 5 out*.........................(25 to 1 op 20 to 1) pu
2208 THE JET SET 7-11-3 V Slattery, *jmpd rght, sn toiling, tld off whn pld up bef 5 out*......(100 to 1 op 50 to 1) pu
Dist: 15l, 12l, 6l. 4m 40.20s. a 41.20s (8 Ran).
SR: 65/47/24/23/-/ (Simon Sainsbury), Capt T A Forster

2459 Allbright Bitter Starlet Novices' Staying Hurdle (5-y-o and up) £10,554 3m .... (1:30)

1878⁵ SEE ENOUGH 6-11-0 A Tory, *al cl up, led appr 4 out, rdn out*........................(33 to 1 op 25 to 1) 1
1992 BOOK OF MUSIC (Ire) 6-11-3 P Hide, *keen hold, trkd ldrs frm 4th, ev ch 2 out, one pace*....(16 to 1 op 12 to 1) 2
2338² GRAY'S ELLERGY 8-11-0 J Railton, *hld up in rear, prog 8th, styd on same pace frm 3 out*...(11 to 1 op 8 to 1) 3
2295⁴ TOTHEWOODS 6-11-5 D Bridgwater, *trkd ldrs, chlgd 3 out, wknd appr 2 out*....(5 to 2 op 3 to 1) 4
2144² ELAINE TULLY (Ire) 6-11-0 M Hourigan, *wtd wth, prog 6th, wknd quickly 4 out*.
.............................(10 to 1 op 7 to 1 tchd 12 to 1) 5
1992⁴ ARCTIC COURSE (Ire) 6-11-3 W Marston, *keen hold, cld on ldrs 8th, hrd rdn and wknd appr 4 out, tld off*.
..............................(7 to 1 op 9 to 2) 6
TONGADIN 8-11-0 J Lower, *lost tch hfwy, tld off whn pld up bef 4 out*......................(33 to 1 op 20 to 1) pu
PENIARTH 8-10-9 M Bosley, *chsd ldrs to 5th, sn rdn and beh, tld off whn pld up bef 4 out*. (200 to 1 op 100 to 1) pu
2194² NAZZARO 5-11-3 C Maude, *drpd rear hfwy, tld off whn pld up bef 3 out*......(25 to 1 op 20 to 1 tchd 33 to 1) pu
2208* CHERYLS PET (Ire) 6-10-12 B Powell, *drpd rear and rdn hfwy, sn tld off, pld up bef 3 out*...(33 to 1 op 25 to 1) pu
1775² CRANK SHAFT 7-11-0 D Gallagher, *al in rear, tld off whn pld up bef 4 out*..................(20 to 1 op 14 to 1) pu

2252* SCOTTON BANKS (Ire) 5-11-5 L Wyer, *led till appr 4 out, sn btn, pld up bef 2 out*......(2 to 1 fav tchd 11 to 4) pu
2162² CARLINGFORD LAKES (Ire) 6-10-12 S Smith Eccles, *pressed ldrs, hit 6th, lost pl nxt, tld off whn pld up bef 3 out*..........................(20 to 1 op 16 to 1) pu
Dist: 5l, 6l, 15l, dist, 15l. 6m 34.60s. a 56.60s (13 Ran).
SR: 48/46/37/27/-/-/ (J A G Meaden), R H Buckler

2460 John Hughes Grand National Trial Handicap Chase £8,758 3m 5f 110yds .... (2:00)

2011² JUST SO [123] (bl) 11-10-2² S Burrough, *beh, improved 16th, rdn to go second appr 5 out, mstk 3 out, jmpd slwly nxt, styd on to ld r-in, drvn out*.
..............................(10 to 1 op 8 to 1) 1
2318⁴ CYTHERE [121] 10-9-13² (3*) P Hide, *chsd ldr appr 7th, mstk 13th, led 16th, clr approaching 5 out, rdn betw last 2, hdd and no extr r-in*.
..............(14 to 1 op 12 to 1 tchd 16 to 1) 2
2173⁷ FIDDLERS PIKE [130] 13-10-9 Mrs R Henderson, *sn struggling, tld off frm 7th, lft remote 3rd 3 out*.
..............................(20 to 1 op 14 to 1) 3
1881* RIVERSIDE BOY [145] 11-11-10 J Lower, *chsd ldr till appr 7th, lost pl 13th, 3rd and wkng whn pld up aftr 15th*.
..............................(8 to 1 op 10 to 1 tchd 7 to 2) pu
2173³ INTO THE RED [129] 10-10-8 D Bridgwater, *hld up, prog 5th, rdn and wknd 13th, pld up bef 15th*.
..............................(11 to 10 fav op 6 to 4) pu
2305 PEAJADE [121] 10-10-0 W Marston, *struggling appr 7th, beh whn hrd rdn approaching 11th, tld off when pld up bef 15th*.........(28 to 1 op 16 to 1 tchd 33 to 1) pu
2011⁵ INDIAN TONIC [124] 8-10-3 C Maude, *led to 16th, wknd appr 5 out, poor 3rd whn pld up bef 2 out*.
..............................(11 to 2 op 4 to 1) pu
Dist: 3½l, dist. 8m 37.60s. a 71.60s (7 Ran).
SR: 37/31/-/-/ (H T Cole), H T Cole

2461 Fledgling Conditional Jockeys' Selling Hurdle (4-y-o and up) £2,080 2m 110yds............................. (2:30)

1719⁹ ONE TO NOTE 10-11-0 (5*) M P FitzGerald, *wl plcd till lost pos hfwy, rallied 3 out, not fluent last 2, styd on und pres to ld nr finish*..............(8 to 1 op 6 to 1) 1
1950⁴ TENDRESSE (Ire) 6-10-11 (3*) T Thompson, *patiently rdn, plenty to do whn prog 3 out, ridden appr last, kpt on wl r-in*.......................(9 to 1 op 5 to 1 tchd 10 to 1) 2
2328 NORTHERN OPTIMIST 6-11-1 (5*) D Hobbs, *second till led appr 4 out, sn clr, hdd and no extr nr finish*.
..............................(20 to 1 op 14 to 1 tchd 25 to 1) 3
2212² CELTIC BOB 14-11-0 (5*) P Maddock, *beh till improved und pres hfwy, no extr frm last*......(9 to 1 op 5 to 1) 4
2414* PREENKA GIRL (Fr) 5-11-4 (5*,3ex) L Reynolds, *led till appr 4 out, sn btn, lost pl 2 out*....(2 to 1 on op 6 to 4) 5
NOBLE SOCIETY 6-11-5 P McLoughlin, *prog frm rear 4th, mstk four out, sn wknd*.
..............................(25 to 1 op 16 to 1 tchd 33 to 1) 6
2993 ANA BLAKE 7-11-0 W Marston, *mstk second, tld off frm hfwy*.........(33 to 1 op 50 to 1 tchd 66 to 1) 7
2207² MINI FETE (Fr) 5-10-9 (5*) N Juckes, *cl up, rdn appr 4 out, sn wknd, tld off*.........(8 to 1 op 11 to 2) 8
1338 WEST END 4-10-4 (3*) J Neaves, *beh, shrtlvd effrt aftr 4th, tld off*...................(100 to 1 op 50 to 1) 9
1935 LADY ROMANCE (Ire) 6-10-9 (5*) Chris Webb, *al beh, tld off frm hfwy*......(25 to 1 op 33 to 1 tchd 66 to 1) 10
2361 TURKISH STAR 9-11-0 R Darke, *chsd ldrs till rdn and lost pl aftr 4th, tld off whn pld up bef last*.
..............................(25 to 1 op 20 to 1) pu
Dist: ¾l, sht-hd, 3½l, 10l, 10l, dist, 8l, 2l, ½l. 4m 43.50s. a 57.50s (11 Ran).
(J F Mitchell), M P Muggeridge

2462 Huntsman Handicap Chase (5-y-o and up) £4,082 2m 3f 110yds........ (3:00)

2013² LAKE TEEREEN [121] 9-11-2 C Maude, *al cl up, led 5 out, hld on wl und str pres frm last*......(5 to 1 op 4 to 1) 1
2188* CITY KID [120] 9-10-12 (3*) P Hide, *hld up, went second at 3rd, hit 5th, led 7th to 5 out, chlgd r-in, no extr nr finish*........(7 to 2 op 5 to 2 tchd 4 to 1) 2
2297* RAFIKI [107] 9-10-2 S Burrough, *wtd wth, hit 5th, prog to ld nxt, hdd 7th, rdn and wknd appr 5 out, blun next, tld off*..........(5 to 2 op 2 to 1 tchd 11 to 8) 3
2085* GAY RUFFIAN [133] 8-12-0 J Lower, *hld up, mstk 7th, sn lost pl, rallied 3 out, hrd rdn and cl 3rd whn f nxt*.
..............................f
995 BALDA BOY [124] 10-11-5 B Powell, *led to 6th, wknd 8th, tld off whn pld up bef 5 out*.
..............................(10 to 1 op 8 to 1 tchd 14 to 1) pu
Dist: 2l, dist. 5m 41.40s. a 54.40s (5 Ran).
(Mrs A T Grantham), R Rowe

2463 Gamekeepers Handicap Hurdle (0-140 4-y-o and up) £2,617 2m 110yds (3:30)

1051³ HIGHLAND SPIRIT [120] 6-11-10 J Lower, *hld up, wnt second 4 out, led on bridle last, shaken up und rdn to* ....(9 to 4 tchd 5 to 2) 1
2379⁵ MIAMI SPLASH [116] 7-11-6 M Hourigan, *led, jmpd lft 2 out, hdd last, kpt on wl und pres.* ....(7 to 4 jt-fav op 2 to 1) 2
1753³ STYLUS [114] 5-11-4 W Marston, *chsd ldr to 4 out, hit nxt, rdn and wknd betw last 2* ....(7 to 4 jt-fav) 3
2087 GOLDEN FREEZE [111] 12-11-1 L Harvey, *reluctant to race, refused 1st.....* (16 to 1 op 12 to 1 tchd 20 to 1) ref
Dist: Nk, 15l. 4m 45.70s. (4 Ran).

(T Richmond), M C Pipe

NAVAN (IRE) (heavy)
Saturday February 5th

2464 Dunboyne EBF Mares Maiden Hurdle (Qualifier) (4-y-o and up) £3,450 2m
....................................(1:45)

STRONG DESIRE (Ire) 5-10-12 (5*) Mr B R Hamilton, ...(14 to 1) 1
2123 ANNIE FOX 7-11-3 (3*) T P Treacy, ...(6 to 1) 2
2197² MINIGIRLS NIECE (Ire) 6-11-6 A Powell, ...(11 to 10 fav) 3
BALLYMADUN LASS (Ire) 5-11-0 (3*) T J Mitchell, ..(14 to 1) 4
2039⁷ AMME ENAEK (Ire) 5-11-0 (3*) K B Walsh, ...(16 to 1) 5
2310 BYE FOR NOW 8-10-13 (7*) T Martin, ...(20 to 1) 6
SOLMUS (Ire) 6-11-6 J P Banahan, ...(8 to 1) 7
1549 MARBLE FONTAINE 7-11-6 C F Swan, ...(10 to 1) 8
2177 RADICAL NURSE (Ire) 5-10-10 (7*) P J Mulligan, .(33 to 1) 9
2311⁸ AMAKANE LADY (Ire) 5-10-12 (5*) M G Cleary, ..(12 to 1) 10
2236 BLACK AVENUE (Ire) 6-11-6 F J Flood, ...(5 to 1) 11
LOVELY AFFAIR (Ire) 5-11-3 C O'Dwyer, ...(14 to 1) 12
1610 MURPHY'S LADY (Ire) 5-10-12 (5*) C P Dunne, ..(25 to 1) 13
2197⁸ WINNING SALLY 4-10-11 K F O'Brien, ...(12 to 1) 14
1681 NO ONE KNOWS (Ire) 6-11-6 H Rogers, ...(20 to 1) 15
1687 PILS INVADER (Ire) 6-11-1 (5*) D T Evans, ...(33 to 1) 16
SIMONE STAR (Ire) 5-10-12 (5*) J P Broderick, ...(25 to 1) 17
COMMANCHE LYN (Ire) 4-10-8 (3*) C O'Brien, ...(20 to 1) 18
2197⁹ DUGGERNE ROCK (Ire) 4-10-4 (7*) Mr G W Barry, (20 to 1) pu
Dist: 6l, 4½l, 8l. 4m 26.80s. (19 Ran).

(H Morrison), J F C Maxwell

2465 Duleek Maiden Hurdle (5 & 6-y-o) £3,105 2¼m. ....(2:15)

2278² ROUBABAY (Ire) 6-11-7 (3*) T P Treacy, ...(Evens fav) 1
2309⁴ I AM 6-11-5 (5*) K P Gaule, ...(10 to 1) 2
2102⁹ NO TAG (Ire) 6-11-2 J F Titley, ...(14 to 1) 3
1821⁵ TELLTALK (Ire) 5-10-8 (5*) J R Barry, ...(13 to 2) 4
1076 BLACK DOG (Ire) 5-10-8 D T Evans, ...(16 to 1) 5
1821⁸ SPECTACULAR STAR (Ire) 5-10-13 L P Cusack, ..(20 to 1) 6
2309⁸ OVER THE MALLARD (Ire) 5-10-10 (3*) D Bromley, (20 to 1) 7
1912⁴ OLD ABBEY (Ire) 6-10-11 (5*) P A Roche, ...(14 to 1) 8
2309³ KEY WEST (Ire) 5-10-13 P Mooney, ...(33 to 1) 9
2161² LINDEN'S LOTTO (Ire) 5-10-13 J Shortt, ...(10 to 1) 10
2177⁶ STRONG HICKS (Ire) 6-11-2 F J Flood, ...(10 to 1) 11
2389 GARBONI (USA) 5-11-7 B Sheridan, ...(12 to 1) 12
PARSONS TERM (Ire) 6-10-11 P Carberry, ...(12 to 1) 13
SMALL TALK (Ire) 5-10-8 H Rogers, ...(33 to 1) 14
2309 NO DOZING (Ire) 5-10-13 K F O'Brien, ...(12 to 1) 15
179⁸ TRAP ONE (Ire) 6-10-9 (7*) D J Kavanagh, ...(25 to 1) 16
2024⁵ NICE PROSPECT (Ire) 6-11-2 T J Taaffe, ...(4 to 1) 17
SILVERFONT LAD (Ire) 5-10-8 (5*) T P Rudd, ...(20 to 1) 18
71 COOLGREEN (Ire) 6-11-2 T Horgan, ...(33 to 1) 19
1848 ARISTODEMUS 5-10-6 (7*) D R Thompson, ...(25 to 1) 20
Dist: 6l, hd, 7l, 1l. 5m 1.60s. (20 Ran).

(A D Brennan), P Mullins

2466 Webster Handicap Chase (5-y-o and up) £6,900 2m. ....(2:45)

2230⁵ BALLAD SONG [-] 11-9-9 C F Swan, ...(12 to 1) 1
2159⁶ KINGS ENGLISH [-] 8-11-0 T Horgan, ...(11 to 2) 2
1850 WINNING CHARLIE [-] 8-10-0 K F O'Brien, ...(14 to 1) 3
1554 TORANFIELD [-] 10-11-0 (5*) J P Broderick, ...(9 to 2) 4
2159⁶ MAD TOM [-] 9-11-8 J P Banahan, ...(7 to 2) 5
2280* LASATA [-] 9-11-10 (5ex) C O'Dwyer, ...(5 to 2 fav) 6
2280⁹ VALRODIAN (NZ) [-] 11-10-10 L P Cusack, ...(16 to 1) 7
Dist: 4½l, hd, 2½l, 2l. 4m 47.10s. (7 Ran).

(Seamus MacCrosain), Michael Cunningham

2467 Kepak Boyne EBF Hurdle (Listed) (5-y-o and up) £5,520 2¾m. ....(3:15)

1984* MINELLA LAD 8-11-12 T Horgan, *led 6th to 8th, rdn to chal betw last 2, led appr last, ran on.....*(5 to 1) 1
1782⁶ TEMPLEROAN PRINCE 7-11-7 C N Bowens, *set slow pace till hdd 6th, led 8th to nxt, rdn in 3rd appr last, styd on.* ....(12 to 1) 2
2079 NOVELLO ALLEGRO (USA) (bl) 6-11-7 P Carberry, *wl plcd, led 4 out till hdd and wknd appr last.....*(9 to 2) 3
2079 SHARP INVITE 7-10-11 C F Swan, *wtd rear, effrt appr 2 out, no imprsn.* ....(11 to 4) 4
1236³ DROICHEAD LAPEEN 7-10-9 (7*) Mr T J Beattie, *trkd ldrs, mstk 2 out, sn btn.* ....(20 to 1) 5

Dist: 2½l, 3l, 6l, 2l. 6m 41.70s. (5 Ran).

(John J Nallen), A P O'Brien

2468 Kells Handicap Hurdle (0-130 4-y-o and up) £3,105 3m. ....(3:45)

2284³ DOWHATYOULIKE (Ire) [-] 5-10-3 P Carberry, ...(7 to 1) 1
2278⁵ CALMOS [-] 7-10-0 K F O'Brien, ...(7 to 1) 2
2284* FRIGID COUNTESS [-] 7-10-0 (7*) L A Hurley, ..(4 to 1 fav) 3
2124⁷ BALLYMOE BOY (Ire) [-] 6-9-10 (5*) K P Gaule, ...(25 to 1) 4
2050² MISGIVINGS (Ire) [-] 6-9-11 C F Swan, ...(5 to 1) 5
2181* WILD VENTURE (Ire) [-] 6-10-4 A Powell, ...(5 to 1) 6
1763⁶ RUNAWAY GOLD [-] 7-9-11 F Woods, ...(25 to 1) 7
ZVORNIK [-] 7-10-12 (5*) P A Roche, ...(33 to 1) 8
2310⁷ ROCHE MELODY (Ire) [-] 6-9-7 (3*) C O'Brien, ...(25 to 1) 9
1977 LOAVES AND FISHES [-] 6-10-3 (7*) B D Murtagh, (14 to 1) 10
2313⁸ GOLDEN OPAL [-] 9-10-12 (5*) J P Broderick, ...(7 to 1) 11
291 TERZIA [-] 7-11-13 T Horgan, ...(8 to 1) 12
2311* RED THUNDER [-] 7-9-10 (2ex) D P Fagan, ...(10 to 1) ur
Dist: ¾l, 5½l, ½l, 2½l. 6m 46.80s. (13 Ran).

(Patrick J Casey), K Riordan

2469 Papas Buskins Chase (5-y-o and up) £3,795 2½m. ....(4:15)

1825² ROYAL MOUNTBROWNE 6-12-0 J F Titley, ...(6 to 4) 1
2157* ALL THE ACES 7-11-11 T J Taaffe, ...(11 to 10 fav) 2
JOHNNY'S TURN 9-11-7 B Sheridan, ...(10 to 1) 3
2277² DEER TRIX 9-10-13 (3*) D Bromley, ...(14 to 1) 4
2180⁶ BALLYCANN 7-11-4 (3*) T J Mitchell, ...(20 to 1) 5
2022* TALK TO YOU LATER 8-11-11 H Rogers, ...(14 to 1) ur
1831* NORDIC SUN (Ire) 6-12-0 T Horgan, ...(9 to 1) pu
TOPICAL TIP (Ire) 5-10-12 K F O'Brien, ...(20 to 1) pu
Dist: 20l, 12l, 8l, dist. 5m 38.00s. (8 Ran).

(Mrs J O'Kane), Patrick G Kelly

2470 Navan Flat Race (5-y-o and up) £3,105 2m. ....(4:45)

MARINGO (Ire) 5-11-8 (3*) Mrs J M Mullins, ...(8 to 1) 1
BALLYHIRE LAD (Ire) 5-11-11 Mr A P O'Brien, ..(2 to 1 fav) 2
RUN BAVARD (Ire) 6-11-9 (5*) Mr P M Kelly, ...(7 to 1) 3
1820⁷ TREANAREE (Ire) 5-11-4 (7*) Mr D K Budds, ...(25 to 1) 4
2394² CAREFORMENOW (USA) (bl) 5-11-4 (7*) Mr E Norris, ...(9 to 4) 5
1455⁵ DUN CARRAIG (Ire) 6-11-11 (3*) Mr A R Coonan, ..(12 to 1) 6
SWEET CALLERNISH (Ire) 5-11-4 (7*) Mr J P Dwan, (20 to 1) 7
2314⁶ BEDFORD RAMBLER (Ire) 5-11-4 (7*) Mr D J McAteer, ...(14 to 1) 8
COLLEEN'S BELLE (Ire) 6-11-2 (7*) Miss A O'Brien, (7 to 1) 9
THE ROCKING CHAIR (Ire) 6-12-0 Mr P Fenton, ..(16 to 1) 10
23947 PARADISE ROAD 5-11-11 Mr A J Martin, ...(12 to 1) 11
2314⁴ PATS FAREWELL (Ire) 6-11-7 (7*) Mr C A McCartney, ...(20 to 1) 12
CARMELS DELIGHT (Ire) 5-11-1 (5*) Mr H F Cleary, (8 to 1) 13
SECRET COURSE (Ire) 5-10-13 (7*) Mr J McGuinness, ...(25 to 1) 14
BALLY UPPER (Ire) 6-11-7 (7*) Mr S O'Brien, ...(25 to 1) 15
2236³ SLEMISH MIST 7-11-4 (5*) Mr G J Harford, ...(14 to 1) 16
1988⁶ SHABRA CONNECTION 7-11-9 (5*) Mr B R Hamilton, ...(66 to 1) 17
Dist: 5l, 6l, 6l, 1l. 4m 22.20s. (17 Ran).

(Alexander McCarthy), W P Mullins

SANDOWN (heavy (races 1,3,5,7), soft (2,4,6))
Saturday February 5th
Going Correction: PLUS 1.32 sec. per fur. (races 1,3,-5,7), PLUS 0.93 (2,4,6)

2471 Ripley Four Year Old Hurdle £3,566 2m 110yds. ....(12:50)

2300* DEVILS DEN (Ire) 11-4 R Dunwoody, *mstk 1st, al prmnt, led appr 2 out, sn clr, hit last, pushed out r-in.* ....(2 to 1 on op 7 to 4 on tchd 13 to 8 on) 1
2245⁸ ERCKULE 11-0 C Llewellyn, *al prmnt, rdn and kpt on wl frm last.* ....(33 to 1 op 25 to 1 tchd 40 to 1) 2
2300 PAPER DAYS 11-0 S McNeill, *led till hdd appr 2 out, one pace.....* ....(25 to 1 tchd 33 to 1) 3
1504² MARROS MILL 10-13 M A FitzGerald, *prmnt, rdn aftr 6th, wknd 2 out.....*(15 to 2 op 7 to 1 tchd 13 to 2) 4
2374⁴ HALHAM TARN (Ire) 11-4 P Holley, *not fluent, al abt same pl, one pace appr 2 out.* ....(10 to 1 op 7 to 1 tchd 12 to 1) 5
FRONTIER FLIGHT (USA) 10-10 J Osborne, *ran wl till wknd appr 2 out, should improve.* ....(12 to 1 op 7 to 1 tchd 14 to 1) 6
2275² ABJAR 10-13 (5*) A Bates, *pressed ldrs, wknd 2 out, 4th and no chn whn blun and uns rdr last.* ....(10 to 1 op 7 to 1) ur
2248⁶ RED LEADER (Ire) 11-0 D Meade, *lost tch 6th, pld up bef last.....* ....(40 to 1 op 33 to 1 tchd 50 to 1) pu
HEDGEHOG 10-2 (3*) A Dicken, *mstk 1st, tld off frm nxt, pld up aftr 6th.....* ....(66 to 1 op 50 to 1) pu

HARROW WAY (Ire) 10-10 D Murphy, *lost tch 6th, pld up bef last*............................. (33 to 1 op 20 to 1) pu
Dist: 3½l, 12l, 20l, 2l, 8l. 4m 17.50s. a 30.50s (10 Ran).
SR: 3/-/-/-/-/-/ (T Beresford), M C Pipe

2472 Scilly Isles Novices' Chase Grade 1
(5-y-o and up) £18,450 2½m 110yds
................................(1:20)

2268² BAYDON STAR 7-11-6 R Dunwoody, *hld up, chlgd 3 out, sn led, rdn out r-in.* (6 to 4 fav op 6 to 5 tchd 13 to 8) 1
1841² CRYSTAL SPIRIT (bl) 7-11-6 J Frost, *led till hdd aftr 3 out, kpt on same pace frm last.*
................................(7 to 4 op 9 to 4 tchd 5 to 2) 2
1844* BAS DE LAINE (Fr) 8-11-6 J Osborne, *jmpd slwly second, rear till hdwy tenth, rdn aftr 3 out, sn wknd.*
................................(100 to 30 op 5 to 2 tchd 7 to 2) 3
2264² GHIA GNEUIAGH 8-11-6 C Llewellyn, *f 1st.*
................................(12 to 1 op 10 to 1) f
Dist: 3½l, 20l. 5m 21.50s. a 22.00s (4 Ran).
SR: 63/59/39/-/ (Mrs Shirley Robins), D Nicholson

2473 Sandown Handicap Hurdle (4-y-o and up) £13,520 2¾m................(1:55)

2247* DARK HONEY [134] 9-9-11 (3") A Dicken, *mid-div and rdn alng frm 3 out, styd on r-in to ld nr finish.*
................................(8 to 1 op 12 to 1 tchd 14 to 1) 1
1922² DOMINANT SERENADE [134] 5-9-9 (5") D Bentley, *hdwy 6th, styd on and ev ch r-in, no extr cl hme.*
................................(12 to 1 op 10 to 1 tchd 14 to 1) 2
OLYMPIAN [135] (bl) 7-10-1 R Dunwoody, *led, clr frm 3rd, hit 7th, hdd cl hme.*....(7 to 1 tchd 10 to 1 and 6 to 1) 3
2376² SWEET DUKE (Fr) [158] 7-11-5 (5") T Jenks, *chsd ldr, rdn and ev ch last, one pace r-in.*..........(7 to 1 op 6 to 1) 4
2298⁴ BUONARROTI [134] 7-10-0 T Grantham, *some prog frm 3 out, nvr dngrs.*......................(25 to 1 op 16 to 1) 5
2172⁶ JEASSU [135] 11-10-1 B Clifford, *beh till steady prog frm 3 out, not rch ldrs.*........(7 to 1 op 6 to 1 tchd 8 to 1) 6
2385² HIGH ALLTITUDE (Ire) [134] (bl) 6-10-0 C Llewellyn, *sn prmnt, cl up whn hit 3 out, fdd.*
................................(11 to 2 fav op 6 to 1 tchd 7 to 1) 7
2265* MEDITATOR [134] 10-9-9 (5") S Curran, *nvr rch ldrs.*
................................(10 to 1 op 8 to 1 tchd 12 to 1) 8
2265⁸ JOPANINI [137] 9-10-3 M A FitzGerald, *prmnt till wknd 6th, tld off.*....(12 to 1 op 11 to 1 tchd 14 to 1) 9
BOSCEAN CHIEFTAIN [143] 10-10-9 S McNeill, *in tch till wknd 7th, pld up bef 2 out.*....(20 to 1 tchd 25 to 1) pu
2012³ PEATSWOOD [135] 6-10-1 Lorna Vincent, *mstk 4th, lost tch nxt, tld off whn pld up bef last.*......(9 to 1 op 8 to 1) pu
1438⁵ LORNA-GAIL [134] 8-10-0 S Earle, *rear 5th, hdwy 7th, wknd aftr 3 out, pld up bef nxt.*.....(15 to 2 op 6 to 1) pu
Dist: ½l, 1l, 8l, 3l, ¾l, 30l, 10l. 5m 36.40s. a 30.40s (12 Ran).
SR: 58/57/57/72/45/45/14/4/-/ (Roger Sayer), S Dow

2474 Agfa Diamond Chase Limited Handicap Grade 2 (5-y-o and up) £18,570 3m 110yds....................(2:30)

1664⁵ SECOND SCHEDUAL [150] 9-10-7 R Dunwoody, *wnt second 13th, led 4 out, quickly steadied, led ag'n nxt, styd on strly.*...............(6 to 1 op 5 to 1 tchd 13 to 2) 1
2259* ZETA'S LAD [155] 11-10-12 R Supple, *hld up, effrt 2 out, not quicken r-in.* (5 to 2 jt-fav op 9 to 4 tchd 11 to 4) 2
2375² YOUNG HUSTLER [156] 7-10-13 C Llewellyn, *led, quickened 16th, hdd 4 out, sn rgned ld, headed nxt, rdn and ev ch 2 out, no extr last.*....................(5 to 2 jt-fav op 9 to 4 tchd 11 to 4) 3
1843² BRADBURY STAR [167] 9-11-10 D Murphy, *hld up, blun 4 out, ev ch nxt, rdn and sn btn.*
................................(3 to 1 op 5 to 2 tchd 100 to 30) 4
2173⁴ KING'S CURATE [150] 10-10-7 M Perrett, *chsd ldrs till blun 13th, cl up whn f 17th.*.........(5 to 1 op 8 to 1) f
Dist: 1l, 4l, 20l. 6m 37.60s. a 38.60s (5 Ran).
(Hugh McMahon), D Nicholson

2475 Agfa Hurdle (5-y-o and up) £9,967 2m 110yds.......................(3:05)

1888* MUSE 7-11-10 P Holley, *chsd ldr, led appr 2 out, ran on strly...*(13 to 8 fav op 7 to 4 tchd 2 to 1 and 11 to 8) 1
VALFINET (Fr) 7-11-8 R Dunwoody, *led, hit 4th, hdd appr 2 out, one pace.*............(7 to 2 op 9 to 4 tchd 4 to 1) 2
2376³ MOLE BOARD 12-11-8 T Grantham, *confidently rdn off the pace, effrt aftr 3 out, awkward nxt, sn ridden and no ch.*................(7 to 1 op 4 to 1 tchd 15 to 8) 3
1694* MANEREE 7-10-9 R Campbell, *hld up, wknd appr 2 out.*
................................(20 to 1 tchd 16 to 1) 4
2019³ KALOGY 7-10-4 M A FitzGerald, *lost tch frm 6th.*
................................(12 to 1 op 10 to 1 tchd 14 to 1) 5
Dist: 12l, 8l, 10l, 3½l. 4m 13.00s. a 26.00s (5 Ran).
SR: 54/40/32/9/-/ (White Horse Racing Ltd), D R C Elsworth

2476 Elmbridge Handicap Chase (5-y-o and up) £5,394 2m.................(3:40)

1560⁵ STORM ALERT [148] 8-11-7 S McNeill, *cl up, led 7th to 8th, led ag'n 5 out, strly pressed frm nxt, rdn out and hld on wl from last.*....(7 to 4 op 13 to 8 tchd 15 to 8) 1
1758² WONDER MAN (Fr) [155] 9-12-0 R Dunwoody, *hld up in cl tch, chlgd wnr frm 4 out, ev ch r-in, kpt on und pres.*
................................(6 to 5 fav op 13 to 8 tchd 11 to 10) 2
1887³ BUCK WILLOW [128] 10-10-11 D Murphy, *hld up in cl tch, effrt 4 out, outpcd appr nxt.*
................................(11 to 4 op 7 to 1 tchd 8 to 1) 3
2365 L'UOMO PIU [129] 10-10-2² M FitzGerald, *dsptd ld till wnt on 4th, mstk and hdd 7th, wknd appr nxt, tld off.*
................................(25 to 1 op 20 to 1 tchd 40 to 1) 4
2307² AL HASHIMI [127] 10-10-0 P Holley, *made most to 4th, led ag'n 8th to nxt, ev ch four out, wknd appr next, tld off.*
................................(10 to 1 op 8 to 1 tchd 12 to 1) 5
Dist: Nk, 25l, 5l, 25l. 4m 7.80s. a 19.30s (5 Ran).
SR: 49/55/3/-/-/ (Lt Col W Whetherly), Andrew Turnell

2477 February Novices' Hurdle (5-y-o and up) £2,957 2m 110yds.........(4:10)

1309 ROSE KING 7-11-0 D Murphy, *tracaked ldg pair, al gng easily, led on bit last, hrd hld.*
................................(6 to 4 fav op 7 to 4 tchd 5 to 4) 1
2042³ JYMJAM JOHNNY (Ire) 5-11-0 D Gallagher, *awkward 1st, led till hdd last, no ch wth wnr.*
................................(7 to 2 op 4 to 1 tchd 5 to 1) 2
RAINBOW CASTLE 7-11-0 R Dunwoody, *hld up, rdn and hdwy appr 2 out, wknd and mstk last.*
................................(9 to 1 op 9 to 2 tchd 9 to 1) 3
1835⁴ MALENOIR (USA) 6-11-0 M A FitzGerald, *not jump wl, trkd ldr, rdn rdn aftr 3 out, btn whn blun nxt.*
................................(11 to 2 op 4 to 1 tchd 6 to 1) 4
ROYAL IRISH 10-11-0 J Frost, *hld up in last pl, al beh, tld off frm 8th.*...........(13 to 2 op 4 to 1 tchd 7 to 1) 5
1109⁷ RIFFLE 7-11-0 S McNeill, *beh, effrt aftr 3 out, btn whn blun badly nxt, pld up bef last....* (14 to 1 op 7 to 1) pu
PARLIAMENTARIAN (Ire) 5-11-0 C Llewellyn, *beh frm hfwy, mstk 5th, tld off whn pld up bef last.*
................................(33 to 1 op 20 to 1) pu
Dist: 6l, 12l, 30l, dist. 4m 22.50s. a 35.50s (7 Ran).
(Maurice E Pinto), J T Gifford

STRATFORD (good to soft)
Saturday February 5th
Going Correction: PLUS 1.25 sec. per fur. (races 1,3,6), PLUS 1.45 (2,4,5)

2478 Charlecote Novices' Hurdle (4-y-o) £2,066 2m 110yds.............(1:55)

2083² PREROGATIVE (v) 11-4 M Foster, *made all, drw clr frm 2 out, easily.*......(6 to 4 on op 11 to 10 tchd 5 to 4) 1
2083⁶ DARING PAST 10-12 G Bradley, *al prmnt, pressed wnr 3 out to nxt, sn outpcd.* (10 to 1 op 8 to 1 tchd 11 to 1) 2
2245⁵ SHAMSHADAL (Ire) 10-5 (7") D Fortt, *al in tch, rdn to chal 3 out, mstk nxt, sn btn....*(7 to 1 op 5 to 1 tchd 9 to 1) 3
2381⁸ STAR MARKET 11-3 (7") Pat Thompson, *wtd wth, hdwy 5th, nvr nr to chal.*............(33 to 1 op 25 to 1) 4
2276 BOLD STAR (bl) 10-12 N Mann, *chsd wnr till wknd rpdly appr 5th....*(25 to 1 op 20 to 1 tchd 33 to 1) 5
2245 PRAIRIE GROVE 10-12 R Greene, *prmnt, wnt second appr 5th, wknd quickly bef 2 out....*(10 to 1 op 25 to 1) 6
WAKT 10-7 W McFarland, *prmnt till rdn and wknd aftr 5th, tld off...*................(14 to 1 op 7 to 1) 7
2345 MINSHAAR 10-7 T Wall, *blun and uns rdr 1st.*
................................(66 to 1 op 50 to 1) ur
2148 UNSUSPICIOUS (Ire) 10-12 P McDermott, *al beh, rdn 4th, tld off whn pld up bef last........*(66 to 1 op 50 to 1) pu
2245 FORMAESTRE (Ire) 10-7 E Murphy, *al rear, lost tch 4th, tld off whn pld up bef 2 out...........*(66 to 1 op 50 to 1) pu
ZAYAN (USA) 10-12 M Richards, *slwly away, al beh, tld off whn pld up bef 2 out...*(10 to 1 op 16 to 1 tchd 8 to 1) pu
PACIFIC SPIRIT 10-7 R Bellamy, *al beh, tld off whn pld up bef 2 out...........*(66 to 1 op 50 to 1 tchd 100 to 1) pu
Dist: 7l, 7l, 25l, 8l, 4l, dist. 4m 15.00s. a 26.00s (12 Ran).
SR: 36/23/16/3/-/-/ (D A Johnson), M C Pipe

2479 Bet With The Tote Novices' Chase Qualifier (6-y-o and up) £3,095 3m
................................(2:25)

2293² ROUYAN 8-10-12 I Lawrence, *jmpd wl, al in tch, wnt second 12th, led 4 out, drw clr appr 2 out.*
................................(3 to 1 op 9 to 4) 1
2193² BOLLINGER 8-11-4 E Murphy, *nvr far away, led 11th, hdd and outpcd 4 out, styd on to go second appr last.*
................................(11 to 4 fav op 6 to 4 tchd 9 to 2) 2
2260² NICKLE JOE 8-11-4 R Bellamy, *al prmnt, wnt second 3 out, wknd aftr nxt.....*(5 to 1 op 4 to 1 tchd 11 to 2) 3
SALLY'S GEM 9-10-12 W McFarland, *prmnt, lost tch 5 out.*
................................(11 to 2 op 5 to 1 tchd 9 to 2) 4

2257[6] BRABAZON (USA) 9-10-12 M Richards, *not fluent, ran in snatches, in tch till wknd appr 5 out.*
................................(14 to 1 tchd 16 to 1) 5
2031[5] BUCKS SURPRISE 6-10-12 N Mann, *al beh, tld off tenth.*
................................(33 to 1) 6
2293 BOOK OF RUNES 9-10-12 W Humphreys, *blun 1st, prmnt whn f 9th.*........................(12 to 1 op 7 to 1) f
2263 VITAL SCORE 8-10-12 R Greene, *made most to 11th, wkng whn hit 13th, refused and uns rdr 5 out.*......(50 to 1) ref
1837[2] CALLEROSE 7-10-12 G Bradley, *mstks in rear, hmpd 9th, pld up lme bef nxt.*......................(9 to 1 op 8 to 1) pu
2336 ROYAL EXHIBITION (bl) 10-10-12 D Morris, *chsd ldrs till wknd 6th, tld off whn pld up bef 12th.*........(50 to 1) pu
Dist: 7l, 8l, 15l, 2l, dist. 6m 26.90s. a 39.90s (10 Ran).
SR: 33/32/24/3/1/-/ (Peter Mines), Mrs J Pitman

2480 Avon Handicap Hurdle (0-140 4-y-o and up) £3,532 2m 110yds...... (2:55)

1991[*] NIKITAS [119] 9-10-13 (7") D Fortt, *chsd ldrs, rdn whn hit 3 out, wnt second aftr nxt, in frnt when hit last, all out.*
................................(9 to 4 fav op 2 to 1 tchd 3 to 1) 1
2385[4] KIVETON TYCOON (Ire) [123] (bl) 5-11-10 G Bradley, *rear, styd on one pace frm 2 out, wnt second r-in.*
................................(5 to 1 op 4 to 1) 2
2265[6] ALBERTINO (Fr) [105] 7-10-3 (3") S Wynne, *rear, virtually tld off hfwy, ran on past btn horses appr last.*
................................(100 to 30 op 11 to 4) 3
2360[3] SEAGULL HOLLOW (Ire) [99] 5-10-0 R Marley, *trkd ldrs, led 3 out, clr nxt, wknd quickly and hdd appr last.*
................................(3 to 1 tchd 5 to 2) 4
LE TEMERAIRE [110] 8-10-6 (5") Miss P Jones, *led to 3 out, wknd quickly aftr nxt, eased.*.......(9 to 1 op 10 to 1) 5
2379[8] BADRAKHANI (Fr) [127] 8-11-7 (7") Pat Thompson, *trkd ldr till wknd aftr 4th, tld off.*..........(25 to 1 op 20 to 1) 6
1842[8] SHARRIBA [112] 5-10-10 (3") D Meredith, *trkd ldrs, rdn and wknd aftr 4th, tld off.*......(16 to 1 tchd 20 to 1) 7
Dist: 2½l, 6l, 7l, 3l, 15l, 20l. 4m 18.40s. a 29.40s (7 Ran).
SR: 4/5/-/-/ (Miss A Whitfield), Miss A J Whitfield

2481 Alscot Handicap Chase (0-125 5-y-o and up) £3,629 2m 1f 110yds... (3:25)

2365 SAILORS LUCK [107] 9-11-4 E Murphy, *led to 8th, styd in cl tch, led appr 2 out, drvn out.*....(5 to 1 tchd 6 to 1) 1
2365[2] SETTER COUNTRY [113] 10-11-10 W Irvine, *hld up, wnt 3rd 6th, rdn and styd on to go second appr last, no imprsn r-in.*................(9 to 4 op 3 to 1 tchd 5 to 2) 2
2307[*] ALAN BALL [108] 8-11-0 (5") T Eley, *trkd ldr, mstk 3rd, led 8th, mistake nxt, hdd appr 2 out, wknd.*
................................(2 to 1 fav op 6 to 4) 3
2195[4] ROC COLOR (Fr) [105] 5-11-2 G Bradley, *hld up, last frm 6th, no ch from 4 out, eased, tld off.* (9 to 4 op 2 to 1) 4D
Dist: 8l, 10l, dist. 4m 38.80s. a 34.80s (4 Ran).
(Geoffrey C Greenwood), P G Murphy

2482 Credit Call Cup Hunters' Chase (6-y-o and up) £1,870 2m 5f 110yds... (3:55)

MR MURDOCK 9-12-4 (3") Mr R Alner, *hld up in tch, led 3 out, hdd nxt, rallied to ld last, ran on.*
................................(7 to 4 on op Evens) 1
DUNCAN 9-11-7 (7") Mr B Pollock, *al prmnt, led appr tenth, not fluent and hdd 3 out, led nxt, headed last, no extr.*................................(7 to 1 op 5 to 2) 2
MATSIX 13-11-9 (5") Miss P Jones, *led to 5th, wknd appr 5 out, lft remote 3rd at last.*
................................(7 to 1 op 5 to 1 tchd 10 to 1) 3
PORTER'S SONG 13-11-7 (7") Mr L Lay, *beh, some hdwy hfwy, wkng when mstk 3 out, tld off.*
................................(12 to 1 op 8 to 1 tchd 14 to 1) 4
697[6] CURAHEEN BOY 14-12-0 (7") Miss J Butler, *prmnt till lost tch aftr hfwy, tld off.*......(14 to 1 op 8 to 1) 5
R N COMMANDER 8-11-7 (7") Mr J R Cornwall, *jmpd slwly 3rd, led 6th till appr tenth, wkng whn blun and uns rdr 4 out.*........................(66 to 1 op 50 to 1) ur
2301 DOUBTING DONNA 8-11-5[3] (7") Mr V Hughes, *hld up rear, hdwy 9th, rdn and wknd appr 3 out, poor 3rd whn blun and uns rdr last.*................(25 to 1 op 16 to 1) ur
CLONONY CASTLE 8-11-7 (7") Mr Patrick J Hanly, *last whn blun 8th, sn tld off, pld up bef 12th.*
................................(20 to 1 op 14 to 1) pu
KILLESHIN 8-11-7 (7") Mr G Brown, *trkd ldr, led 5th, jmpd slwly and hdd nxt, drpd out 9th, tld off whn pld up bef 13th.*........................(50 to 1 op 33 to 1) pu
Dist: 2l, dist, 5l, 10l. 5m 52.50s. a 49.50s (9 Ran).
(B Nettley), H Wellstead

2483 Loxley Novices' Handicap Hurdle (0-100 4-y-o and up) £2,108 2¾m 110yds...................... (4:25)

2208[2] LANSDOWNE [82] 6-11-3 (7") D Fortt, *al in tch, led appr 3 out, rdn and styd on strly approaching last.*
................................(9 to 1 op 6 to 1) 1

2361[*] WARFIELD [81] 7-11-4 (5") Guy Lewis, *hld up in tch, wnt second 2 out, rdn and no imprsn.*
................................(5 to 4 fav tchd 11 to 10 and 11 to 8) 2
RACE TO THE RHYTHM [77] 7-11-5 D Bridgwater, *beh, styd on frm 3 out, nvr nrr.*................(6 to 1 op 7 to 1) 3
2276[3] STRATHBOGIE MIST (Ire) [64] 6-10-3 (3") D Meredith, *hld up, hdwy 7th, rdn and wknd appr 2 out.*
................................(7 to 1 op 8 to 1 tchd 10 to 1) 4
2302[3] FIRST LESSON (NZ) [82] 8-11-10 G Bradley, *led to 3rd, outpcd 7th.*........................(14 to 1 op 10 to 1) 5
2308[2] THE OVERTRUMPER [65] 7-10-2 (5") T Jenks, *prmnt, wnt second 3 out, wknd rpdly aftr nxt.* (12 to 1 op 8 to 1) 6
2321[*] MANWELL [68] 7-10-10 R Marley, *trkd ldr, led 3rd till appr 3 out, wknd quickly, tld off.*...(14 to 1 op 8 to 1) 7
1645 OH SO WINDY [69] 7-10-11 W McFarland, *al beh, lost tch 8th, tld off.*........................(33 to 1) 8
1998[3] SOLOMAN SPRINGS (USA) [77] 4-11-2 (3") R Davis, *al beh, lost tch appr 3 out, tld off.*....(20 to 1 op 16 to 1) 9
2276[6] PETRADARE [59] 7-9-10 (5") T Eley, *al beh, tld off whn pld up bef last.*........................(25 to 1 op 50 to 1) pu
2254[8] FERRUFINO (Ire) [62] 6-10-4 P McDermott, *beh, hdwy appr 6th, wknd 8th, tld off whn pld up bef last.*
................................(66 to 1 op 50 to 1) pu
2380[7] WALKERS POINT [73] 8-11-1 W Humphreys, *prmnt till wknd 8th, tld off whn pld up bef last.*
................................(50 to 1 op 33 to 1) pu
2276[4] APRIL CITY [66] 4-11-0 M Ranger, *prmnt, chsd ldr 4th, wknd quickly 3 out, tld off whn pld up bef last.*
................................(33 to 1 op 16 to 1) pu
OAKLANDS WORD [93] 5-12-0 (7") Mr E Williams, *prmnt to 5th, tld off whn pld up 4 out.*(500 to 1 op 100 to 1) pu
2361 DOWRY SQUARE (Ire) [79] 6-11-7 E Murphy, *al beh, tld off whn pld up aftr 7th.*............(20 to 1 op 14 to 1) pu
Dist: 5l, 4l, 15l, 6l, ¾l, 20l, 15l. 5m 58.00s. a 46.00s (15 Ran).
(R F Denmead), G A Ham

WETHERBY (soft)
Saturday February 5th
Going Correction: PLUS 1.50 sec. per fur.

2484 350th Anniversary Hunters' Chase (6-y-o and up) £1,674 3m 110yds...(1:05)

TEAPLANTER 11-11-13 (5") Mr R Russell, *wth ldr, led appr 4 out, blun and hdd nxt, led aftr last, all out.*
................................(11 to 10 fav tchd 5 to 4 and Evens) 1
MINERS MELODY (Ire) 6-11-10 Mr J Greenall, *made most till hdd appr 4 out, led and hit nxt, hit last, sn headed and no extr.*........................(20 to 1 op 14 to 1) 2
1004[3] ON THE OTHER HAND 11-11-11 (7") Capt A Ogden, *al tracking ldrs, effrt appr 4 out, kpt on, no imprsn.*
................................(5 to 2 op 7 to 4) 3
REGAN (USA) 7-11-7[1] (7") Mr S Whitaker, *chsd ldrs till wknd frm hfwy, tld off.*................(8 to 1) 4
HOUGHTON 8-11-11 (7") Major M Watson, *f 1st.*
................................(12 to 1 op 10 to 1 tchd 14 to 1) f
PACIFIC SOUND 11-11-3 (7") Mr P Murray, *sn wl beh, tld off whn pld up bef 14th.*
................................(20 to 1 op 16 to 1 tchd 25 to 1) pu
GUNNER'S FLIGHT 10-10-12 (7") Mr R Wakeham, *not jump wl, sn well beh, tld off whn pld up bef 4 out.*
................................(16 to 1 op 10 to 1) pu
CELTIC HARRY 10-11-3 (7") Mr J G Townson, *al beh, tld off whn pld up bef 3 out.*............(33 to 1) pu
Dist: 2½l, 8l, dist. 6m 58.50s. a 52.50s (8 Ran).
(R G Russell), Miss C Saunders

2485 Fairfax Novices' Hurdle (4-y-o and up) £2,637 2m.................... (1:35)

2213 RAFTERS 5-11-5 N Williamson, *settled midfield, steady hdwy to ld betw last 2, ran on wl.* (10 to 1 tchd 12 to 1) 1
1872[8] BANCHORY 5-11-5 P Niven, *al prmnt, led 3 out, hdd betw last 2, no extr.*................(11 to 2 op 4 to 1) 2
2369[2] WEAVER GEORGE (Ire) 4-10-4 (5") J Supple, *hld up in tch, effrt appr 3 out, kpt on wl frm nxt, nvr able to chal.*
................................(5 to 1 op 9 to 2) 3
2241[7] ZAJIRA (Ire) 4-10-4 S Turner, *in tch, effrt whn mstk 6th, sn pushed alng, ran on frm nxt.*(4 to 4 fav op 6 to 4 tchd 11 to 8) 4
1668[7] FLOATING LINE 6-11-5 R Garritty, *trkd ldrs, effrt and ev ch appr 3 out, kpt on same pace frm nxt.*
................................(12 to 1 op 10 to 1 tchd 14 to 1) 5
1787[6] HICKSONS CHOICE (Ire) 6-11-5 K Jones, *sn chasing ldr, ev ch 3 out, grad wknd.*................(25 to 1) 6
COMBELLINO 4-10-9 C Grant, *in tch, effrt appr 3 out, sn btn.*........................(9 to 1 op 7 to 1 tchd 10 to 1) 7
1724[9] TICO GOLD 6-11-5 K Johnson, *nvr nr to chal.*
................................(25 to 1 op 20 to 1) 8
2091[3] PESSOA 7-11-5 Richard Guest, *led till hdd 3 out, wkng whn blun nxt.*........................(20 to 1) 9
2239[4] SOUNDS GOLDEN 6-11-5 T Reed, *nvr dngrs.*
................................(25 to 1 op 16 to 1) 10
2271[3] WHATCOMESNATURALLY (USA) 5-11-0 W Worthington, *nvr dngrs.*........................(33 to 1 op 25 to 1) 11

344

1738 SCARABEN 6-11-5 N Doughty, *mid-div, mstk 5th, sn*
wknd................................. (25 to 1) 12
ROYAL MANOEVRE 4-10-2 (7*) Mark Roberts, *chsd ldrs till*
wknd aftr 5th................... (33 to 1 op 25 to 1) 13
1567 CHENOATS 6-11-5 L O'Hara, *unruly strt, beh frm 5th.*
.... (50 to 1 op 33 to 1) 14
2369 FANFOLD (Ire) 4-10-4 E McKinley, *prmnt till wknd hfwy,*
tld off......................... (50 to 1 op 33 to 1) 15
664 TRICYCLE (Ire) 5-10-12 (7*) J Driscoll, *in tch to 5th, wl beh*
whn pld up bef last............ (33 to 1 op 25 to 1) pu
GREY SEASON 5-11-5 Mr R Armson, *sn in rear, wl beh*
whn pld up bef last. (50 to 1 op 33 to 1 tchd 100 to 1) pu
RICH ASSET (Ire) 4-10-9 C Hawkins, *mstks, sn beh, tld off*
whn pld up bef 3 out............ (25 to 1 tchd 33 to 1) pu
ABLE MCCLEOD 4-10-9 J Callaghan, *al beh, tld off whn*
pld up bef 3 out................... (50 to 1 op 33 to 1) pu
Dist: 4l, 2½l, 1½l, nk, 12l, 3½l, 5l, 1l, 5l, 15l. 4m 11.40s. a 30.40s (19 Ran).
SR: 27/23/10/3/17/5/ (M B Carver), J M Bradley

2486 EBF Mares' Only Novices' Handicap Chase (5-y-o and up) £3,362 2m (2:10)

2270⁴ SPOONHILL WOOD [79] (bl) 8-10-0 B Dalton, *cl up, led 8th,*
hdd 2 out, rallied to ld last, kpt on wl.
.... (9 to 1 op 8 to 1) 1
1218² RIVER PEARL [94] 9-11-1 T Reed, *led till hdd 8th,*
remained cl up, led ag'n 2 out, headed last, no extr.
.... (9 to 4 fav op 5 to 2 tchd 11 to 4) 2
2069² OVER THE ISLAND (Ire) [90] 6-10-11 A Dobbin, *chsd ldrs,*
chlgd 3 out, wknd aftr nxt.......... (4 to 1 op 3 to 1) 3
2265³ BEAUCHAMP GRACE [114] 5-12-2 (5*) J Burke, *beh,*
pushed alng grdh 4th, outpcd after 7th, no dngr after.
.... (11 to 4 op 5 to 2 tchd 3 to 1) 4
2146⁴ MAGGOTS GREEN [81] 7-10-2 N Williamson, *beh, pushed*
alng and outpcd hfwy, tld off.
.... (7 to 2 op 100 to 30 tchd 4 to 1) 5
Dist: 6l, 20l, 15l, dist. 4m 21.50s. a 29.50s (5 Ran).
SR: 17/26/2/11/-/ (R M Micklethwait), J Wharton

2487 Cromwell Handicap Hurdle (4-y-o and up) £3,236 3m 1f............... (2:40)

2172² NORTHANTS [120] 8-10-2 A Carroll, *hld up, hdwy aftr 7th,*
led and mstk 3 out, styd on wl......... (3 to 1 op 5 to 2) 1
1556² CAB ON TARGET [146] 8-12-0 P Niven, *hld up in tch, chlgd*
3 out, dsptd ld till no extr betw last 2.
.... (13 to 8 fav op 2 to 1 tchd 9 to 4) 2
2172⁵ TINDARI (Fr) [119] 6-10-0⁴ (5*) P Williams, *cl up, led hfwy,*
hdd 3 out, kpt on wl................. (7 to 2 op 3 to 1) 3
1619³ PEANUTS PET [126] 9-10-8 R Garritty, *hld up, effrt aftr 3*
out, kpt on same pace frm nxt.
.... (13 to 2 op 6 to 1 tchd 7 to 1) 4
2385 VIARDOT (Ire) [129] 5-10-11 R Hodge, *hld up, kpt on frm 2*
out, nvr nr to chal............... (20 to 1 op 14 to 1) 5
2385⁶ SPROWSTON BOY [118] 11-10-0 W Worthington, *led to*
hfwy, cl up till grad wknd appr 3 out.
.... (20 to 1 op 14 to 1) 6
2216* ST VILLE [118] 8-9-9 (5*) S Mason, *chsd ldrs, pushed alng*
aftr 8th, wknd appr 3 out.......... (20 to 1 op 14 to 1) 7
LION OF VIENNA [118] 7-10-0 B Storey, *in tch till wknd*
appr 3 out......................... (33 to 1 op 25 to 1) 8
NEGATORY (USA) [119] 7-10-1¹ C Grant, *lost tch frm hfwy,*
tld off whn pld up bef 3 out.... (50 to 1 op 33 to 1) pu
Dist: 2½l, 1½l, 4l, 3½l, 3½l, 15l, 3½l. 6m 47.50s. a 52.50s (9 Ran).
(C B Rennison), W Storey

2488 Marston Moor Chase Limited Handicap Grade 2 (5-y-o and up) £15,996 2 ½m 110yds................... (3:15)

BLAZING WALKER [156] 10-11-10 C Grant, *hld up, effrt*
appr 4 out, led last, ran on wl und pres.
.... (14 to 1 op 12 to 1) 1
1876* UNCLE ERNIE [147] 9-11-1 M Dwyer, *in tch, led gng wl*
aftr 3 out, hdd last, no extr und pres.
.... (6 to 1 tchd 13 to 2 and 7 to 1) 2
1029² DAWSON CITY [139] 7-10-7 R Garritty, *in tch, slightly*
outpcd aftr 9th, rallied after 4 out, kpt on wl und pres,
not rch ldrs....................... (20 to 1 op 14 to 1) 3
2377² RICHVILLE [139] 8-10-7 N Williamson, *in tch, hit 7th, effrt*
after 4 out, wknd appr 2 out..... (100 to 30 op 11 to 4) 4
HAWTHORN BLAZE [145] 8-10-13 G McCourt, *jmpd rght,*
led, blun badly 3rd, clr 8th, hit 11th, blunded badly 3
out, sn hdd and wknd.
.... (13 to 8 fav op 2 to 1 tchd 6 to 4) 5
2266⁵ ARMAGRET [139] 9-10-7 L O'Hara, *lost tch aftr tenth, tld*
off whn blun 3 out and 2 out, pld up bef last.
.... (17 to 2 op 10 to 1) pu
Dist: 1l, 3l, 12l, 20l. 5m 37.60s. a 40.10s (6 Ran).
SR: 2/-/-/ (P Piller), P Cheesbrough

2489 Ironsides Novices' Chase (5-y-o and up) £3,542 2½m 110yds........(3:45)

2238⁷ SUPPOSIN 6-11-2 Richard Guest, *trkd ldrs, lft in ld 7th,*
jmpd left 3 out, sn rdn, blun last, hng left r-in, all out.
.... (5 to 1 tchd 11 to 2) 1

2357² ISSYIN 7-11-8 R Garritty, *hld up and beh, steady hdwy to*
track wnr 11th, crrd lft 3 out, chlgd last, no extr und
pres.........(13 to 8 on op 9 to 4 on tchd 6 to 4 on) 2
799 PRINCE YAZA 7-11-8 L O'Hara, *in tch, pushed alng and*
reminders aftr 6th, grad wknd appr 4 out.
.........................(7 to 1 op 5 to 1) 3
2117³ COZZI (Fr) 6-11-2 N Williamson, *led till 7th.*
.........................(14 to 1 op 20 to 1 tchd 25 to 1) f
MISTER CUMBERS 7-11-2 A Dobbin, *prmnt till stumbled*
badly and uns rdr aftr 9th (water). (10 to 1 op 8 to 1) ur
Dist: ½l, 15l. 5m 52.30s. a 55.80s (5 Ran).
(Mrs S Smith), Mrs S J Smith

2490 Wetherby Bumper National Hunt Flat Race (4,5,6-y-o) £1,884 2m......(4:15)

FEELS LIKE GOLD (Ire) 6-11-0 (7*) T Dascombe, *al prmnt,*
slight ld 3 out, kpt on wl und pres fnl furlong, jst hld
on......................... (10 to 1 op 7 to 1 tchd 11 to 1) 1
976* MAYBE O'GRADY (Ire) 5-11-3 (5*) S Mason, *in tch, effrt 5*
out, styd on wl fnl 2 fs, jst fld...(6 to 4 fav op 11 to 4) 2
SPRING CALL (Ire) 4-10-4 (7*) Mr D Parker, *in tch, hdwy 5*
out, chlgd one out, wknd ins fnl furlong.
.... (11 to 2 op 7 to 1 tchd 8 to 1) 3
GARBO'S BOY 4-10-4 (7*) W Fry, *prmnt, chlgd 3 out, ev ch*
till wknd entering fnl furlong... (33 to 1 tchd 50 to 1) 4
MOREOF A GUNNER 4-10-6 (5*) P Williams, *prmnt, ev ch*
o'r 3 out, kpt on same pace....... (10 to 1 op 5 to 1) 5
1674 BANOFFI (Ire) 5-11-0 (7*) F Leahy, *chsd ldrs, grad wknd*
frm 4 out......................... (12 to 1 op 8 to 1) 6
MONY-GRIT (Ire) 5-11-2 (5*) S Lyons, *hld up, hdwy hfwy,*
grad wknd fnl 3 fs. (14 to 1 tchd 16 to 1 and 12 to 1) 7
SECOND SLIP 5-11-2 (5*) E Husband, *in tch till wknd 5*
out......................... (10 to 1 op 12 to 1 tchd 16 to 1) 8
TERRINGTON 4-10-4 (7*) J Driscoll, *cl up, led hfwy, hdd 3*
out, wknd quickly.................. (25 to 1 op 16 to 1) 9
KILMESSAN JUNCTION (Ire) 5-11-0 (7*) S Taylor, *nvr dngrs.*
.... (10 to 1 op 11 to 2 tchd 12 to 1) 10
2387⁹ HUTCEL BRIG 5-10-9 (7*) P Johnson, *nvr dngrs.*
.... (14 to 1 op 10 to 1) 11
GIVE HIM TIME 5-11-7 W Dwan, *in tch, effrt 6 out, wknd*
o'r 3 out......................... (33 to 1) 12
WHATDIDYOUSAY 6-11-2 (5*) N Leach, *ran very wide*
bend aftr 4 fs, nvr dngrs............ (33 to 1) 13
HALF'N HALF 4-10-4³ (5*) J Supple, *al beh.......* (25 to 1) 14
SKI PATH 5-10-9 (7*) G Tormey, *prmnt to hfwy, sn beh.*
.... (33 to 1 op 25 to 1) 15
2373 TASHREEF (bl) 4-10-4 (7*) B Harding, *sn beh...*(25 to 1) 16
2176 LEGATA (Ire) 5-10-11 (5*) P Midgley, *chsd ldrs till wknd*
hfwy......................... (33 to 1) 17
CITY RHYTHM 4-10-4 (7*) Mr C Bonner, *sn beh...* (20 to 1) 18
BAYLINER 5-10-9 (7*) C Woodall, *sn beh, virtually pld up*
fnl 2 fs, wl tld off............... (33 to 1) 19
2074 RIGHT TERM (Ire) 5-11-0 (7*) M Molloy, *hng rght, led to*
hfwy, sn beh, tld off whn pld up o'r 4 out.
.... (20 to 1 op 14 to 1) pu
Dist: Hd, 1½l, 3l, 10l, 15l, ¾l, 20l, 2½l, 12l, ½l. 4m 8.40s. (20 Ran).
(Independent Twine Manufacturing Co Ltd), M C Pipe

FONTWELL (soft)
Monday February 7th
Going Correction: PLUS 1.80 sec. per fur.

2491 Climping Conditional Jockeys' Handicap Chase (0-125 6-y-o and up) £2,334 2¼m................. (2:00)

1975⁴ SARTORIUS [104] 8-11-10 D Meade, *keen hold, led 4th till*
aftr 5th, led 6th, rdn out r-in.....(5 to 4 fav op 7 to 4) 1
1164 VICTORY GATE (USA) [80] 9-10-0 A Thornton, *prmnt till*
lost pl 7th, kpt on frm 2 out, no dngr.
.........................(16 to 1 op 12 to 1 tchd 20 to 1) 2
GENERAL MERCHANT [92] (bl) 14-10-8 (4*) T Thompson,
hld up, cld hfwy, chsd wnr frm appr 3 out, sn no
imprsn, fnshd tired.....(7 to 2 op 3 to 1 tchd 4 to 1) 3
2396⁴ UNIQUE NEW YORK [84] (v) 11-10-4 Guy Lewis, *in tch till*
wknd appr 3 out, fnshd tired.
.... (20 to 1 op 14 to 1 tchd 25 to 1) 4
1463* FIGHTING DAYS (USA) [94] 8-11-0 J Clarke, *led to 4th, led*
aftr 5th to nxt, sn niggled alng, wknd, wl beh whn pld
up bef last.............. (4 to 1 op 5 to 2 tchd 9 to 2) pu
Dist: 15l, sht-hd, 20l. 5m 3.50s. a 43.50s (5 Ran).
(M Popham), T Thomson Jones

2492 Pagham Selling Hurdle (4-y-o) £1,830 2¼m........................ (2:30)

WITCHWAY NORTH (v) 10-7 V Smith, *chsd ldr, rdn appr 2*
out, sntchd rght to ld r-in, all out. (50 to 1 op 33 to 1) 1
2364² NANQUIDNO 10-7 R Dunwoody, *led, rdn appr 2 out, hdd*
and not quicken r-in.
.... (5 to 4 fav op 13 to 8 on tchd 6 to 4) 2
2189⁴ ROWLANDSONS GOLD (Ire) 10-7 Lorna Vincent, *sn wl beh,*
hdwy 6th, shaken up and ran on strly r-in, too much to
do.................. (7 to 2 op 4 to 1 tchd 6 to 1) 3

1522^{6} MANON LESCAUT 10-7 A Maguire, *hld up midfield, hdwy to chase ldrs hfwy till wknd betw last 2.* .... (10 to 1 op 6 to 1) 4
2335^{8} DOCK OF THE BAY (Ire) 10-12 D Bridgwater, *al beh, tld off.* .... (10 to 1 op 12 to 1) 5
FREEBYJOVE 10-7 M A FitzGerald, *prmnt to 3rd, sn rear, beh whn pld up bef 6th.* .... (50 to 1 op 33 to 1 tchd 66 to 1) pu
MIND THE ROOF (Ire) 10-7 D Murphy, *chsd ldrs, reminders hfwy, sn wknd, tld off whn pld up bef 6th.* ....(9 to 2 op 6 to 1 tchd 7 to 2) pu
2364 RAGAZZO (Ire) (bl) 10-12 A Charlton, *chsd ldrs to hfwy, beh whn pld up bef 2 out*........ (50 to 1 tchd 66 to 1) pu
1305 SHOPTILLYOUDROP 10-7 H Jenkins, *in tch to hfwy, tld off whn pld up bef 2 out*..........(33 to 1 op 20 to 1) pu
CELTIC LILLEY 10-7 M Hoad, *al beh, tld off wehn pld up bef 2 out*.......................... (50 to 1 op 33 to 1) pu
Dist: ½l, 3l, 15l, dist. 4m 55.40s. a 45.40s (10 Ran).
(John Berry), H J Collingridge

2493 Bet With The Tote Novices' Chase Qualifier (6-y-o and up) £2,794 3¼m 110yds.......................... (3:00)

2264^{4} LUCKY LANE 10-11-3 C Maude, *led second, mstk 14th, hld on gmely r-in, all out.* .... (6 to 1 op 9 to 2 tchd 13 to 2) 1
2223 IRISH BAY (bl) 8-10-10 J Osborne, *trkd wnr thrght, hit 15th, mstk 17th, ev ch last, ran on, jst hld.* ....(7 to 2 op 4 to 1) 2
2260^{*} YOUR WELL 8-11-3 B Clifford, *hld up last, mstk 15th, hdwy appr 3 out, styd on one pace r-in.* ....(5 to 4 fav op 7 to 4 tchd 2 to 1) 3
2223 MISS MUIRE 8-10-5 D Morris, *trkd ldrs till wknd 4 out.* .... (20 to 1 op 50 to 1) 4
1537^{*} YORKSHIRE GALE 8-11-3 D Murphy, *trkd ldrs, losing tch whn reminder 18th, sn btn.* .... (11 to 4 op 6 to 4 tchd 3 to 1) 5
Dist: Nk, 2l, 30l, 2l. 7m 32.10s. a 62.10s (5 Ran).
(Rod Hamilton), P J Hobbs

2494 Chichester Novices' Hurdle (4-y-o and up) £1,543 2¼m................ (3:30)

2244^{2} BALLET ROYAL (USA) 5-11-2 M Perrett, *trkd ldrs, led 6th, clr last, shaken up, easily.* .... (11 to 10 on op 11 to 8 on tchd Evens) 1
2407 OUROWNFELLOW (Ire) 5-11-2 D Morris, *hld up midfield, hdwy 6th, sn ev ch, ran on one pace und pres appr last.* .... (50 to 1 op 66 to 1) 2
ZULU PEARL 6-10-11 E Murphy, *hld up midfield, hdwy 5th, outpcd appr 3 out, styd on r-in.* .... (33 to 1 op 25 to 1) 3
2335^{*} FONTANAYS (Ire) 6-11-8 G McCourt, *hld up, hdwy appr 6th, ev ch 2 out, sn btn.* .... (3 to 1 tchd 7 to 2 and 11 to 4) 4
RING CORBITTS 6-11-2 R Dunwoody, *wth ldr, ev ch 6th, sn lost pl, ran on one pace nxt.* .... (14 to 1 op 12 to 1 tchd 20 to 1) 5
2144 GREEN'S GAME 6-11-2 G Upton, *led till rdn alng and hdd 6th, sn lost pl*.......................... (66 to 1) 6
2345^{3} DUTY SERGEANT (Ire) 5-11-2 M Ahern, *chsd ldrs, rdn 3 out, wknd*........................ (25 to 1 op 16 to 1) 7
DENVER BAY 7-11-2 D Murphy, *hld up, some hdwy appr 3 out, nvr nr to chal*............... (25 to 1 op 14 to 1) 8
2335 TEMPLE KNIGHT 5-11-2 S Earle, *trkd ldrs, pushed alng appr 3 out, sn btn*....(33 to 1 op 25 to 1 tchd 50 to 1) 9
863 YELLOW CORN 5-10-11 J Railton, *midfield till wknd appr 6th*....................(7 to 1 op 6 to 1 tchd 8 to 1) 10
MIGAVON 4-10-1 D Gallagher, *al rear*...........(50 to 1) 11
2315 UNCERTAIN TIMES 7-11-2 T Grantham, *al beh.* .... (50 to 1 op 33 to 1) 12
LB'S GIRL 5-10-4 (7*) J Clarke, *f 1st.* (66 to 1 op 50 to 1) f
2244 DOMITOR'S LASS 7-10-11 Mrs N Ledger, *trkd ldrs to hfwy, wkng whn mstk 6th, beh when pld up bef 2 out.* ....(33 to 1) pu
Dist: 12l, 2½l, 3l, 10l, 7l, 1l, 2l, 12l, 1½l, 5l. 4m 47.70s. a 37.70s (14 Ran).
SR: 35/23/15/23/7/-/ (Park Farm Thoroughbreds), G Harwood

2495 Bognor Regis Handicap Chase (0-125 5-y-o and up) £2,508 3¼m 110yds ....(4:00)

1540 GOLD CAP (Fr) [115] 9-11-10 G McCourt, *in tch, mstk 4th, led four out, blun 2 out, sn clr, drvn out.* ....(5 to 1 tchd 13 to 2) 1
2247 ROSITARY (Fr) [91] (bl) 11-10-0 A Maguire, *led till aftr 12th, ev ch appr 2 out, sn no extr.* .... (11 to 2 op 5 to 1 tchd 6 to 1) 2
2206^{7} DOROBO (NZ) [91] (bl) 6-9-11 (3*) R Farrant, *al rdn alng, drpd last 7th, styd on r-in, nvr able to chal.* ....(3 to 1 op 7 to 2 tchd 4 to 1) 3
2294 TAMMY'S FRIEND [103] (bl) 7-10-12 I Lawrence, *trkd ldrs, mstk tenth, led aftr 12th to 4 out, sn rdn and btn.* ....(13 to 8 fav op 6 to 4 tchd 7 to 4) 4

1543^{5} PHAROAH'S LAEN [108] 13-11-3 S Earle, *blun 1st, trkd ldrs to 11th, sn wknd, tld off whn pld up aftr 15th.* .... (25 to 1 op 14 to 1) pu
1140 BE SURPRISED [91] 8-10-0 B Powell, *prmnt early, hit 4th, lost pl 8th, tld off whn pld up bef 13th.* .... (12 to 1 op 8 to 1 tchd 14 to 1) pu
Dist: 15l, 8l, 4l. 7m 35.40s. a 65.40s (6 Ran).
(Poem Racing), P J Hobbs

2496 Arundel Handicap Hurdle (0-110 4-y-o and up) £2,358 2¾m............(4:30)

2400^{2} HAPPY HORSE (NZ) [100] 7-11-4 A Tory, *nvr far away, led appr 2 out, sn clr, hit last, hng rght r-in, eased fnl 100 yards*..........................(4 to 1 fav op 6 to 1) 1
2131^{3} JADIDH [93] 6-10-6 (5*) D Salter, *midfield, hdwy 8th, ev ch appr 2 out, not pace of wnr*........(20 to 1 op 14 to 1) 2
2338^{5} SURCOAT [98] 7-11-2 L Harvey, *hld up, hdwy 5th, sn chasing ldrs, rdn 3 out, styd on same pace.* .... (9 to 1 op 7 to 1 tchd 10 to 1) 3
1690^{5} MASAI MARA (USA) [107] (bl) 6-11-11 B Powell, *rcd wide, led second, clr 8th, hdd appr 2 out, sn wknd.* ....(20 to 1 op 10 to 1 tchd 25 to 1) 4
2338^{7} VILLA PARK [84] 12-10-2 M Perrett, *hld up, hdwy aftr 7th, lost tch nxt*.......................... (50 to 1 op 33 to 1) 5
2400 MILDRED SOPHIA [82] 7-9-7 (7*) Miss S Mitchell, *sn beh, hdwy 8th, nvr able to chal*........ (66 to 1 op 50 to 1) 6
1884 PRIZE MATCH [85] 5-10-3 C Llewellyn, *hld up beh, hdwy 8th, sn btn*............(7 to 1 op 8 to 1 tchd 10 to 1) 7
2338^{8} CARRIKINS [86] 7-10-4 M Richards, *in tch, rdn alng aftr 5th, sn lost pl*........ (25 to 1 op 20 to 1 tchd 33 to 1) 8
2067 WILTOSKI [82] 6-10-0 Mrs N Ledger, *prmnt to 3rd, jmpd slwly nxt, sn wknd*.................(66 to 1 op 50 to 1) 9
2338^{9} CAPPUCCINO GIRL [97] 7-11-1 M Crosse, *nvr better than mid-div*..............(25 to 1 op 20 to 1 tchd 33 to 1) 10
2320^{*} THE GOLFING CURATE [105] 9-11-9 G McCourt, *hld up, shrtlvd effrt 4th, wknd nxt.* ....(9 to 2 op 4 to 1 tchd 7 to 2 and 5 to 1) 11
2212^{*} DOUALAGO (Fr) [88] (bl) 4-10-6 R Dunwoody, *led to second, hndy, sn rdn alng, wknd 7th, tld off.* .... (9 to 1 op 6 to 1 tchd 10 to 1) 12
PODRIDA [89] 8-10-7 D O'Sullivan, *al beh, tld off whn pld up bef last*........................ (50 to 1 op 25 to 1) pu
2247^{5} ACCESS SUN [92] 7-10-10 A Maguire, *prmnt, rdn alng and pld up aftr 7th*..............(10 to 1 tchd 12 to 1) pu
2247^{4} BRIGHTLING BOY [97] 9-11-1 J Railton, *in tch, rdn alng 7th, sn wknd, beh whn pld up bef 3 out.* ....(5 to 1 tchd 7 to 1) pu
1795^{5} THE MRS [90] 8-10-8 S Earle, *al beh, tld off whn pld up bef 2 out*.............(16 to 1 op 12 to 1 tchd 20 to 1) pu
Dist: 12l, 5l, 2l, 3½l, 3½l, ½l, 2½l, 1l, ½l, 5l. 6m 0.00s. a 51.00s (16 Ran).
(Major Ian Manning), Mrs J Renfree-Barons

CARLISLE (soft (races 1,3,5), good to soft (2,4,6))

Tuesday February 8th

Going Correction: PLUS 0.90 sec. per fur. (races 1,3,5), PLUS 0.67 (2,4,6)

2497 Bet With The Tote Novices' Chase Qualifier (6-y-o and up) £3,262 3m ....(1:50)

2010^{2} LO STREGONE 8-11-10 M Dwyer, *al wl-plcd, dsptd ld frm 6th, jmpd ahead 2 out, drvn out r-in.* ....(13 to 8 on op 2 to 1 on tchd 6 to 4 on) 1
2434 VULPIN DE LAUGERE (Fr) 7-10-5 (5*) J Burke, *al hndy, lft in slight ld 6th, hdd 2 out, rallied r-in, prmsg.* .... (33 to 1 op 25 to 1) 2
2434^{2} EXTRA SPECIAL 9-10-10 N Doughty, *led till aftr 1st, styd hndy and ev ch 6 out, rdn and one pace last 4.* ....(7 to 2 tchd 4 to 1) 3
2411^{7} NORRISMOUNT 8-10-10 M Moloney, *blun 1st, rcd wide and mstks, prmsg effrt fnl circuit, can improve.* ....(25 to 1 op 20 to 1 tchd 33 to 1) 4
1862 IRISH GENT 8-10-10 K Johnson, *chsd ldg bunch, effrt and reminders hfwy, hit 11th, feeling pace appr 4 out, sn btn*.............................. (20 to 1 op 14 to 1) 5
2238^{5} PADDY MORRISSEY 7-10-10 A Dobbin, *nvr far away, ev ch 6 out, rdn and outpcd aftr nxt, sn btn.* .... (10 to 1 op 12 to 1) 6
MY PARTNER (Ire) 6-10-10 T Reed, *patiently rdn, hmpd by faller 7th, struggling 6 out, sn btn.* ....(50 to 1 tchd 100 to 1) 7
2325 GRAAL LEGEND 9-10-10 C Grant, *hit 1st, feeling pace and pushed alng hfwy, blun 12th, sn tld off.* .... (66 to 1 op 50 to 1) 8
2238 STRONG CHANCE 8-10-10 B Storey, *settled in rear, hmpd by faller 6th, lost tch fnl circuit, tld off.* .... (66 to 1 op 50 to 1) 9
2270^{7} BUCKWHEAT LAD (Ire) 6-10-7[2] (5*) Mr T Byrne, *trkd ldg bunch, effrt fnl circuit, lost tch bef 6 out, tld off.* .... (33 to 1 op 20 to 1) 10

2325[5] SHELTON ABBEY 8-10-10 K Jones, *trkd ldg bunch, hmpd by faller 6th, lost tch bef six out, tld off.*
.................................(14 to 1 op 12 to 1) 11
2386 THE PUB 8-10-10 J Corkell, *took str hold, led aftr 1st, hit 5th, f nxt.*.......................................(200 to 1) f
974 LORD BERTRAM (Ire) 6-10-7 (3*) A Larnach, *settled mid-field, f 7th.*..(66 to 1) f
2219[3] MOW CREEK 10-10-10 Mr J Bradburne, *in tch, improved to join issue whn mstk tenth, wknd rpdly and pld up bef 4 out.*........................(33 to 1 op 25 to 1) pu
Dist: 1l, 15l, 2½l, 10l, ½l, 15l, 8l, 1½l, 6l, 10l. 6m 36.30s. a 37.30s (14 Ran).
(Mrs Sylvia Clegg), T P Tate

2498 Wetheral Selling Handicap Hurdle (4-y-o and up) £1,861 2m 1f.......(2:20)

2408[3] DUTCH BLUES [71] 7-10-0 D Wilkinson, *nvr far away, drvn ahead aftr 3 out, clr last, ran on wl.*
.................................(5 to 1 op 9 to 2) 1
2254[2] FLASH OF REALM (Fr) [95] 8-11-10 A Dobbin, *settled gng wl, improved to draw level 3 out, rdn and one pace betw last 2.*................(6 to 4 fav op 7 to 4 tchd 2 to 1) 2
MASHUM [88] 8-10-7 K Johnson, *co'red up beh ldg bunch, improved hfwy, rdn and one pace frm 3 out.*
.................................(14 to 1 op 8 to 1) 3
2371[8] NIGHT OF MADNESS [87] 7-11-2 N Doughty, *tucked away in midfield, took clr order hfwy, rdn and no extr frm 3 out.*..........................(13 to 2 op 9 to 2 tchd 7 to 1) 4
1936[7] HAMANAKA (USA) [79] 5-10-8[2] Mr S Love, *wth ldr, led 3rd, clr nxt, hdd and fdd aftr 3 out.*
.................................(7 to 1 op 6 to 1 tchd 8 to 1) 5
2152[3] A GENTLEMAN TWO [86] 8-11-1 O Pears, *al hndy, feeling pace and reminders appr 3 out, fdd.* (5 to 1 op 6 to 1) 6
2321 MAC RAMBLER [71] 7-10-0 N Williamson, *patiently rdn, improved to track ldrs hfwy, ridden and btn 3 out.*
.................................(12 to 1 tchd 14 to 1) 7
1936[9] EMPEROR ALEXANDER (Ire) [71] 6-10-0 S Turner, *slight ld to 3rd, styd hndy till fdd und pres appr 3 out.* (50 to 1) 8
2217 TAUVALERA [71] 7-10-0 B Storey, *pressed ldrs till rdn and lost grnd 4 out, tld off.*...........(33 to 1 op 25 to 1) 9
Dist: 7l, 7l, 1l, nk, 7l, ½l, 20l, 7l. 4m 26.20s. a 19.20s (9 Ran).
SR: -/11/-/-/-/-/   (Scotnorth Racing Ltd), Mrs S M Austin

2499 Stanwix Handicap Chase (0-120 5-y-o and up) £3,655 3m.............(2:50)

2370[5] CAROUSEL ROCKET [91] 11-9-12 (5*) D Bentley, *tucked away in midfield, improved fnl circuit, nosed ahead bef last, styd on wl.*......(8 to 1 op 7 to 1 tchd 10 to 1) 1
2294[2] VIVA BELLA (Fr) [90] (bl) 7-9-9 (7*) Mr D Parker, *ran in snatches, rallied und pres to draw level last, one pace towards finish.*.......(15 to 8 fav op 7 to 4 tchd 2 to 1) 2
2355[3] ISLAND GALE [98] 9-10-7 (3*) A Thornton, *led or dsptd ld for o'r a circuit, rallied frm 3 out, kpt on one pace r-in.*
.................................(5 to 2 op 9 to 4) 3
2410[5] BOREEN OWEN [101] 10-10-8 (5*) A Roche, *led or dsptd ld, definite advantage 11th, clr 3 out, wknd and hdd appr last.*.......................(12 to 1 op 8 to 1 tchd 14 to 1) 4
2294[4] FAST CRUISE [90] 9-10-2 N Williamson, *nvr far away, ev ch fnl circuit, fdd und pres frm 4 out, tld off.*
.................................(7 to 1 op 6 to 1) 5
1939[3] HOTPLATE [112] 11-11-10 N Doughty, *led or dsptd ld for o'r a circuit, wknd quickly 11th, tld off whn pld up bef 6 out.*..........................(11 to 2 op 5 to 1 tchd 6 to 1) pu
2219[4] BUCKLE IT UP [92] 9-10-4[4] Mr D Mactaggart, *in tch, strug-gling to keep up hfwy, tld off whn pld up bef 4 out.*
.................................(25 to 1 op 20 to 1) pu
Dist: ¾l, 1½l, 20l, dist. 6m 33.30s. a 34.30s (7 Ran).
(A Saccomando), M D Hammond

2500 EBF 'National Hunt' Novices' Hurdle Qualifier (5,6,7-y-o) £2,110 2½m 110yds......................(3:20)

2276[2] NORTHERN SQUIRE 6-11-0 (5*) P Williams, *al hndy, led 4th to 6th, led ag'n 3 out, kpt on strly frm betw last 2.*
.................................(11 to 4 op 5 to 2 tchd 3 to 1) 1
2172 IVY HOUSE (Ire) 6-11-10 M Dwyer, *patiently rdn, improved gng wl fnl circuit, chlgd and hit 3 out, ridden and one pace betw last 2.*......(5 to 4 on op 2 to 1 on) 2
2409[9] WHITE DIAMOND 6-11-0 J Railton, *wtd wth, improved frm midfield appr 3 out, styd on from betw last 2.*
.................................(20 to 1 op 16 to 1 tchd 25 to 1) 3
2220[5] STOP THE WALLER (Ire) 5-11-0 A Dobbin, *trkd ldg bunch, pushed alng to improve appr 3 out, one pace betw last 2.*.......................(10 to 1 op 8 to 1) 4
2367 LAST REFUGE (Ire) 5-11-10 N Williamson, *tucked away beh ldrs, effrt fnl circuit, rdn and one pace frm 3 out.*
.................................(16 to 1) 5
2339[6] D'ARBLAY STREET (Ire) 5-10-7 (7*) S McDougall, *settled midfield, took clr order 3 out, one pace frm nxt.*
.................................(40 to 1 op 33 to 1) 6
2321[2] OVER THE ODDS (Ire) 5-10-7 (7*) D Ryan, *wth ldr, led 6th till 3 out, rdn and btn nxt.*......................(20 to 1) 7
2367[8] PETER 6-11-0 M Moloney, *rcd wide, shwd up wl till wknd and eased appr 3 out.*................(25 to 1 op 20 to 1) 8

2220 LOMOND SPRINGS (Ire) 5-11-0 S Turner, *chsd ldg trio, feeling pace and drvn alng appr 3 out, sn btn.*
.................................(200 to 1) 9
1938 RUSTY BLADE 5-11-0 R Hodge, *in tch, struggling and drvn alng fnl circuit, nvr dngrs.*................(100 to 1) 10
CLARET AND GOLD 7-11-0 A Mulholland, *tried to refuse and jmpd very slwly 1st, struggling thrght.*
.................................(40 to 1 op 50 to 1) 11
875[4] JOYFUL IMP 7-10-9 Mr R Hale, *in tch for a circuit, sn tld off.*..(50 to 1) 12
2148[9] SHATRAVIV 6-10-9 B Storey, *trkd ldrs for o'r a circuit, fdd und pres appr 3 out.* (20 to 1 op 16 to 1 tchd 25 to 1) 13
2003 CROFTON LAKE 6-11-0 L O'Hara, *led till hdd 4th, lost tch fnl circuit, tld off.*...........................(100 to 1) 14
CROSS REFERENCE 6-10-9 T Reed, *in tch to hfwy, tld off whn f 5 out.*.............................(100 to 1) f
COMPANY SECRETARY 6-10-2 (7*) A Linton, *unsighted whn hmpd and f 1st.*........................(100 to 1) f
2068 LADYSIBELOU 6-10-9 Miss P Robson, *struggling frm hfwy, tld off whn pld up aftr 5 out.*...........(100 to 1) pu
Dist: 5l, 4l, 5l, sht-hd, 2l, 3l, 10l, 8l, 25l, 2l. 5m 15.40s. a 22.40s (17 Ran).
SR: 4/4/-/-/-/-/   (Mrs J M Davenport), J M Jefferson

2501 Kingmoor Handicap Chase (0-125 5-y-o and up) £3,622 2m............(3:50)

1966[3] DOLIKOS [105] 7-11-8 M Dwyer, *nvr far away, quickened ahead bef 4 out, hrd pressed last 2, styd on wl und pres.*
.................................(2 to 1 op 7 to 4) 1
2372* PRECIPICE RUN [91] 9-10-8 N Doughty, *made most till hdd appr 4 out, hit nxt, rallied last 2, kpt on.*
.................................(11 to 8 fav op 6 to 4) 2
2372 ZARBANO [84] 8-10-1[1] A Merrigan, *trkd ldrs, ev ch 4 out, hit nxt, kpt on same pace frm last.*....(8 to 1 op 7 to 1) 3
2221[4] ON THE HOOCH [99] 9-11-2 Mr J Bradburne, *al hndy, dsptd ld 5th till appr 4 out, fdd.*
.................................(15 to 2 op 7 to 1 tchd 8 to 1) 4
BLACK SPUR [105] 12-11-8 B Storey, *dsptd ld to 6th, wknd quickly, no ch aftr.*............(9 to 1 op 7 to 1) 5
MACKINNON [107] 9-11-10 M Moloney, *drpd out strt, improved hfwy, lost tch quickly and pld up bef 4 out.*
.................................(20 to 1 op 14 to 1) pu
Dist: 1l, 12l, 5l, 25l. 4m 18.90s. a 19.90s (6 Ran).
SR: 39/24/5/15/-/-/   (B Molloy), T H Caldwell

2502 Hethersgill Conditional Jockeys' Handicap Hurdle (0-125 4-y-o and up) £2,469 3m 110yds.............(4:20)

2256[4] MISS CAPULET [81] (bl) 7-10-1 T Eley, *trkd ldr, led aftr 5 out, clr 2 out, kpt on r-in.*.............(8 to 1 op 7 to 1) 1
2256[3] INTEGRITY BOY [88] (bl) 7-10-3 (5*) K Davies, *patiently rdn, steady hdwy appr 3 out, ridden bef nxt, kpt on same pace r-in.*...................(9 to 2 tchd 4 to 1) 2
2256 BADASTAN (Ire) [85] 5-10-2 (3*) W Fry, *settled beh ldg bunch, improved frm 3 out, styd on from last.* (20 to 1) 3
2256[6] MR FENWICK [80] 10-10-0 S Lyons, *al hndy, ev ch 3 out, rdn and no extr betw last 2.*.................(16 to 1) 4
2296[6] SANSOOL [100] 8-11-6 P McLoughlin, *blun and lost gd pos 1st, chsd alng wl fnl circuit, nvr a factor.*
.................................(8 to 1 op 6 to 1) 5
2256[7] MAKE ME PROUD (Ire) [84] 5-10-4 F Perratt, *settled off the pace, effrt fnl circuit, nvr nr to chal.* (8 to 1 op 7 to 1) 6
2295[2] BARNEY RUBBLE [87] 9-10-7 P Williams, *chsd ldrs for a circuit, tld off frm 3 out.*....(16 to 1 op 14 to 1) 7
2273[2] FURRY BABY [104] 7-11-5 (5*) F Leahy, *patiently rdn, improved fnl circuit, ridden bef 4 out, sn btn.*
.................................(2 to 1 fav op 5 to 2 tchd 3 to 1) 8
GYMCRAK GAMBLE [95] 6-10-10 (5*) A Linton, *chsd ldg bunch, effrt fnl circuit, fdd bef 3 out.*
.................................(16 to 1 op 12 to 1) 9
1361[6] SKIRCOAT GREEN [90] 9-10-3 (7*) B Grattan, *led, clr 3rd, mstk and jmpd lft 5th, hdd aftr 5 out, rallied and ch whn blun and uns rdr 2 out.*......(14 to 1 op 12 to 1) ur
2222[9] FORWARD GLEN [104] 7-11-10 A Thornton, *trkd ldg bunch, struggling bef 4 out, tld off whn pld up before last.*....................................(16 to 1) pu
1614[8] DANCING DOVE (Ire) [94] 6-10-11 (3*) B Harding, *settled off the pace, wl beh whn pld up bef last.*
.................................(14 to 1 op 10 to 1) pu
Dist: 4l, 12l, 6l, 10l, 3½l, 20l, 1½l, 15l. 6m 14.50s. a 21.50s (12 Ran).
SR: 22/25/10/-/9/-/   (C I P Racing), T W Donnelly

WARWICK (soft (races 1,3,5,7), good to soft (2,4,6))
Tuesday February 8th
Going Correction: PLUS 1.22 sec. per fur.

2503 Ryton Novices' Hurdle (4-y-o) £1,542 2m.........................(1:30)

1692[5] HOSTILE WITNESS (Ire) (v) 10-12 M Richards, *hld up, steady hdwy 5th, led 3 out, drvn out frm appr last.*
.................................(9 to 4 op 5 to 2 tchd 3 to 1 and 2 to 1) 1

347

2169[9] PRIME OF LIFE (Ire) 10-12 T Kent, *prmnt, led 4th, hdd 3 out, styd on same pace*............(33 to 1 op 20 to 1)
2083 LODESTONE LAD (Ire) 10-9 (3*) D Meredith, *wth ldrs, led appr 4th, hdd sn aftr, rdn and styd on same pace frm 3 out*....................(20 to 1 op 10 to 1) 3
2381[2] STRICTLY PERSONAL (USA) 10-12 L Harvey, *in tch, hdwy 5th, rdn 3 out, staying on same pace whn mstk last.* ....(7 to 4 fav op 11 to 10 tchd 2 to 1) 4
1541[5] AMILLIONMEMORIES 10-12 P Holley, *led aftr 3rd till appr 4th, wkng whn mstk 3 out.* ....(50 to 1 op 25 to 1 tchd 66 to 1) 5
NOBLE RISK 10-12 S McNeill, *rcd freely, led till aftr 3rd, wknd 5th, no ch whn badly hmpd 3 out, tld off.* ....(20 to 1 op 10 to 1) 6
2381 DON'T JUMP (Ire) 10-7 D Murphy, *effrt 4th, beh whn mstk and hmpd 3 out, tld off.* ....(12 to 1 op 6 to 1 tchd 14 to 1) 7
1705 RUMPUS (Ire) 10-7 W Marston, *pressed ldrs to 4th, 5th and wkng whn f 3 out*....................(3 to 1 op 5 to 1) f
WOT NO PERKS 10-12 V Smith, *sn beh, tld off whn pld up aftr 5th.*....................(50 to 1 op 25 to 1) pu
Dist: 4l, 7l, ¾l, 20l, dist, 2l. 4m 4.80s. a 24.80s (9 Ran).

SR: 32/28/21/20/-/-/ (The Pink Panthers), P R Hedger

2504 Princethorpe Novices' Chase (5-y-o and up) £3,610 2½m 110yds.....(2:00)

2293* RAYMYLETTE 7-11-10 R Dunwoody, *rcd keenly early, made all, jmpd rght 9th and tenth, pushed out frm 2 out.*....................(9 to 4 on op 5 to 2 on) 1
2209* RIVER MANDATE 7-11-10 B Powell, *prmnt, chsd wnr frm 8th, chased winner from 8h, jmpd slwly 13th, rdn and one pace from 3 out.*......(5 to 1 op 9 to 2) 2
1934 BUCKELIGHT (Ire) 6-11-2 (3*) R Farrant, *beh till hdwy 12th, styd on same pace frm 4 out.*......(40 to 1 op 33 to 1) 3
1866[3] BARELY BLACK 6-11-10 W Humphreys, *chsd ldrs till hit 12th, wknd aftr nxt.*............(20 to 1 tchd 33 to 1) 4
2186 WINGS OF FREEDOM (Ire) (bl) 6-11-5 A Maguire, *al beh, tld off frm 13th, blun badly last and virtually pld up r-in.* ....(14 to 1 op 10 to 1) 5
2084[8] FREE JUSTICE 10-11-5 C Llewellyn, *chsd wnr till f 8th.* ....(20 to 1 op 14 to 1) f
1525 EIGHTY EIGHT 9-11-5 V Slattery, *beh, hit 7th, hmpd 8th, tld off tenth, pld up bef 11th.*......(100 to 1 op 50 to 1) pu
2340 FANTASY WORLD 8-11-0 D Murphy, *hit 5th, hdwy 8th, hit 12th and wknd, tld off whn pld up bef 3 out.* ....(14 to 1 op 8 to 1) pu
Dist: 6l, 15l, 5l, dist. 5m 26.80s. a 31.80s (8 Ran).

SR: 29/23/3/-/-/ (Lady Lloyd Webber), N J Henderson

2505 EBF 'National Hunt' Novices' Hurdle Qualifier (5,6,7-y-o) £2,910 2½m 110yds......................(2:30)

1539[7] CUNNINGHAMS FORD (Ire) 6-11-3 (7*) Mr A Harvey, *trkd ldrs, led appr 7th, shaken up and styd on wl frm 2 out.* ....(6 to 1 op 4 to 1) 1
2263[3] MAD THYME 7-11-0 J Frost, *hdwy appr 7th, chsd wnr approaching 2 out, ev ch whn hit last, kpt on.* ....(11 to 4 fav op 3 to 1) 2
2144[4] SPUFFINGTON 6-11-0 D Murphy, *in tch, pressed wnr frm 7th till wknd appr 2 out.* (5 to 1 op 6 to 1 tchd 7 to 1) 3
2029* MR PICKPOCKET (Ire) 6-11-5 R Supple, *hld up mid-div, hdwy 7th, rdn and styd on one pace appr 2 out.* ....(7 to 1 op 9 to 1) 4
1542[5] A N C EXPRESS 6-11-0 R Greene, *hit second, beh, hdwy appr 7th, hit 3, wkng and no ch wth ldrs whn mstk 2 out.*............(16 to 1 tchd 20 to 1) 5
1568[6] HECTOR'S RETURN 6-11-0 D Bridgwater, *prmnt, lost pl 7th, hrd drvn and styd on ag'n frm 3 out.* ....(20 to 1 op 14 to 1) 6
2263[3] BROAD STEANE 5-11-0 S Earle, *hdwy to track ldrs frm 7th, wknd 3 out.*............(14 to 1 op 12 to 1) 7
1996[8] BETTER BYTHE GLASS (Ire) 5-11-0 C Llewellyn, *beh frm 5th, nvr rchd ldrs.*............(14 to 1 op 12 to 1) 8
1707[5] BLACK H'PENNY 6-10-9 T Grantham, *beh frm 5th.* ....(12 to 1 op 10 to 1) 9
483 TAKE CHANCES 6-11-0 P Holley, *hdwy to chase ldrs 7th, wknd 3 out.*....................(50 to 1) 10
LADY OF ROME 7-10-4 (5*) J Supple, *not jmpd wl, al beh.*............(33 to 1 op 25 to 1) 11
2187[4] DREAMLINE 5-10-9 M Ahern, *beh frm 5th, tld off, broke blood vessel.*....................(50 to 1) 12
CELESTIAL STREAM 7-10-11 (3*) R Farrant, *led till aftr 6th, wkng whn f 7th.*....................(50 to 1) f
1957[4] HENRY'S SISTER 7-10-2 (7*) P Ward, *f 1st.* ....(20 to 1 op 10 to 1) f
CELTIC ROMPER 7-11-0 R Bellamy, *chsd ldrs to 4th, tld off 6th, pld up bef 2 out.*............(33 to 1 op 25 to 1) pu
2141 GUSHKA 7-11-0 G McCourt, *nvr better than mid-div, tld off whn pld up bef 2 out.*......(100 to 1 op 50 to 1) pu
1813[7] BATTY'S ISLAND 5-11-0 T Wall, *chsd ldrs 6th, wknd aftr 7th, tld off whn pld up aftr 2 out.* ....(9 to 1 op 10 to 1 tchd 7 to 1) pu
1277 BARON RUSH 6-11-0 Tracy Turner, *chsd ldrs to 5th, tld off whn bef 3 out.*............(100 to 1 op 50 to 1) pu

---

2333[7] CORNS LITTLE FELLA 6-11-0 A Maguire, *effrt 5th, wknd appr 7th, tld off whn pld up bef 2 out.*........(50 to 1) pu
WHITE HUNTER (NZ) 6-11-0 C Maude, *steadied strt, pld hrd, tld off whn pulled up bef 7th.* (33 to 1 op 16 to 1) pu
Dist: Nk, 20l, 1l, 1l, 5l, 1½l, hd, 2½l, 20l, 10l. 5m 18.30s. a 30.80s (20 Ran).

SR: 39/28/8/12/6/1/ (Edward Harvey), O Sherwood

2506 George Coney Challenge Cup Handicap Chase (5-y-o and up) £5,020 3m 5f
................................(3:00)

1652[5] SUPERIOR FINISH [130] 8-10-11 J Osborne, *pressed ldrs 7th to tenth, chsd lder frm 16th, led 2 out, hdd last, rallied gmely r-in to lead ag'n last strds.* ....(9 to 4 fav op 2 to 1 tchd 5 to 2) 1
2143[7] GLENBROOK D'OR [119] 10-10-0 B Clifford, *steady hdwy frm 16th, styd on to ld last, rdn r-in, ct last strds.* ....(13 to 2 op 7 to 1) 2
ROC DE PRINCE (Fr) [135] 11-11-2 R Dunwoody, *wth ldr 6th till led 14th, hdd 2 out, sn outpcd.* (7 to 1 op 5 to 1) 3
2143 PAMBER PRIORY [119] 11-10-0 B Powell, *hit 5th, beh 7th, drvn, hdwy and hit 13th, wknd 4 out.* ....(16 to 1 tchd 20 to 1) 4
2375 BELMOUNT CAPTAIN [140] 9-11-7 J Frost, *beh frm 6th.* ....(12 to 1 tchd 16 to 1) 5
2246[2] ANNIO CHILONE [119] 8-10-0[3] (3*) P Hide, *dsptd ld till led 5th, hdd 14th, wknd rpdly, tld off.* ....(4 to 1 op 9 to 2 tchd 5 to 1) 6
1652[8] DUNTREE [132] 9-10-13 A Maguire, *hit 5th, beh nxt, tld off whn pld up bef 14th.*........(8 to 1 op 7 to 1) pu
2294[5] WOODLANDS GENHIRE [121] (v) 9-10-2[5] (3*) R Davis, *beh, hit 6th, tld off whn pld up aftr 15th.*........(100 to 1) pu
1757[4] WINDY WAYS [128] 9-10-9 M A FitzGerald, *dsptd ld to 5th, hit tenth, wknd 15th, tld off whn pld up bef 18th.* ....(6 to 1 op 5 to 1) pu
Dist: Hd, 12l, dist, 25l, 8l. 7m 47.30s. a 38.30s (9 Ran).

SR: 55/44/48/-/-/-/ (Drawact Ltd), Mrs J Pitman

2507 Globe Handicap Hurdle (0-140 4-y-o and up) £3,557 2½m 110yds.....(3:30)

2044[6] SHANNON GLEN [114] (bl) 8-11-3 (7*) D Bohan, *led to 4th, lft in ld ag'n 6th, pushed alng and styd on frm 2 out.* ....(9 to 1 op 12 to 1 tchd 20 to 1 and 8 to 1) 1
2298[7] LEAVENWORTH [100] 10-10-10 M A FitzGerald, *beh 3rd, rdn 3 out, gd hdwy frm 2 out, ran on r-in, not rch wnr.* ....(16 to 1 op 12 to 1) 2
2306[2] ISLAND JEWEL [98] 6-10-8 M Bosley, *prmnt 5th, chsd wnr frm 6th, chlgd 3 out, no imprsn frm 2 out.* (3 to 1 co-fav op 11 to 4) 3
VICTOR BRAVO (NZ) [104] 7-11-0 C Llewellyn, *beh, styd on to chase ldrs 3 out, wnt lft and no imprsn frm 2 out.* ....(10 to 1 op 8 to 1 tchd 11 to 1) 4
2265[4] HIGH GRADE [102] 6-10-12 R Dunwoody, *in tch till rdn and wknd appr 3 out.*........(3 to 1 co-fav op 7 to 2) 5
2385[8] OUR SLIMBRIDGE [115] 6-11-11 A Carroll, *hld up, hdwy 7th, sn rdn and wknd.* ....(3 to 1 co-fav tchd 7 to 2) 6
2044 BALLYSTATE [107] 6-11-3 S McNeill, *prmnt, chlgd 5th, hmpd and lost pos 6th, tld off.*..(20 to 1 op 14 to 1) 7
SPARTAN TIMES [103] 10-10-13 B Powell, *chlgd 3rd, led 4th till f 6th.*....................(16 to 1 op 10 to 1) f
1507 GOLDEN CELTIC [118] 10-12-0 J Osborne, *chsd ldrs till wknd aftr 6th, tld off whn pld up bef 4 out.* ....(25 to 1 op 16 to 1 tchd 33 to 1) pu
Dist: 3l, sht-hd, 30l, 15l, 12l, dist. 5m 21.90s. a 34.40s (9 Ran).

SR: 2/-/-/-/-/ (Mrs Elizabeth Hitchins), Mrs J Pitman

2508 Air Wedding Trophy Hunters' Chase (5-y-o and up) £1,576 2½m 110yds
................................(4:00)

EASTERN DESTINY 16-11-9 (7*) Mr A Griffith, *chsd ldrs 3rd, led 14th, ran on wl frm 3 out...* (10 to 1 op 7 to 1) 1
DARK DAWN 10-12-8 Mr J Greenall, *hdwy to chase ldrs 8th, led aftr tenth, hdd 14th, wknd after 2 out.* ....(7 to 4 on op 2 to 1 on) 2
MAN OF THE WEST 11-11-9 (7*) Mr M Gingell, *drpd rear 8th, nvr dngrs aftr.*....................(33 to 1 op 25 to 1) 3
2301[2] SALCOMBE HARBOUR (NZ) 10-11-9 (7*) Dr P Pritchard, *chsd ldrs till wknd 14th, styd on ag'n frm 2 out.* ....(16 to 1 op 12 to 1) 4
KAMEO STYLE 11-11-9 (7*) Mr B Pollock, *beh frm 5th, tld off.*....................(20 to 1 op 12 to 1) 5
JOLLY ROGER 7-11-9 (7*) Mr Michael J Jones, *led to second, hit 11th, still in tch whn f 12th.* ....(16 to 1 tchd 20 to 1) f
BOLD REPUBLIC (bl) 8-11-9 (7*) Mr R Ridout, *led second to 3rd, wkng whn mstk and uns rdr tenth.*........... ur
WRENS TRIX 10-11-9 (7*) Mr S Blackwell, *hit 9th and beh, tld off whn pld up bef 2 out.*......(100 to 1 op 50 to 1) pu
NO ESCORT 10-12-3 (5*) Mr R. Russell, *led 3rd till aftr tenth, sn wknd, tld off whn pld up bef 2 out.* ....(4 to 1 op 3 to 1 tchd 9 to 2) pu
Dist: 8l, 12l, 1l, dist. 5m 39.50s. a 44.50s (9 Ran).

(E J W Griffith), Mrs J G Griffith

348

2509 EBF Stakes National Hunt Flat Race (4,5,6-y-o) £1,884 2m.......... (4:30)

2339* BEAR CLAW 5-11-7 (7*) R Massey, *mid-div, pushed alng to chase ldrs 5 fs out, rdn frm 2 furlongs out, ran on to ld ins fnl furlong*........(8 to 1 op 6 to 1 tchd 9 to 1) 1
PETE THE PARSON (Ire) 5-11-0 (7*) Pat Thompson, *hdwy hfwy, led ins fnl 3 fs, rdn frm o'r one furlong out, hdd and one pace inside last.*(7 to 1 op 3 to 1 tchd 8 to 1) 2
2210* COURTOWN BOY 4-10-11 (7*) Mr G Hogan, *in tch, gd hdwy to press ldrs frm 4 fs out, rdn 2 furlongs out, one pace*......................(9 to 2 op 7 to 1 tchd 4 to 1) 3
JUNGLE KING (NZ) 5-11-0 (7*) S Fox, *steady hdwy 5 fs out, rdn and no imprsn ins fnl 2 furlongs.*
......................................(14 to 1 op 10 to 1) 4
COUNTRY CONCORDE 4-10-8 (3*) D Meredith, *sn chasing ldrs, one pace frm o'r 2 fs out*................(50 to 1) 5
1626[8] MOORE BONES 6-11-7 W Marston, *prmnt till led aftr 7 fs, hdd ins fnl 3 furlongs, one pace final 2 furlongs.*
....(20 to 1 tchd 25 to 1) 6
1494[4] LYME GOLD (Ire) 5-11-2 (5*) J McCarthy, *hld up mid-div, smooth hdwy frm 5 fs out to chal 3 furlongs out, rdn o'r 2 furlongs out, sn wknd*.........(2 to 1 fav op 2 to 1) 7
2269[2] BEATSON (Ire) 5-11-9 (5*) T Jenks, *led 7 fs, styd frnt rnk till wknd frm 3 furlongs out.*
......................................(8 to 1 op 7 to 1 tchd 9 to 1) 8
1957[5] COUNTRY PARSON (Ire) 5-11-0 (7*) E Tolhurst, *in tch till wknd o'r 3 fs out*...................(33 to 1 op 25 to 1) 9
KING'S COURTIER (Ire) 5-11-0 (7*) T Dascombe, *chsd ldrs till wknd 4 fs out*.................(14 to 1 op 5 to 1) 10
GLENSKI 5-11-0 (7*) N Collum, *nvr rchd ldrs.*
......................................(20 to 1 op 16 to 1) 11
HAILE DERRING 4-10-5[1] (7*) Mr S Joynes, *chsd ldrs till wknd 4 fs out*.................................(50 to 1) 12
GAMBLES LANE 4-10-4 (7*) P Maddock, *al beh...* (50 to 1) 13
2021* KARICLEIGH BOY 6-11-7 (7*) Mr J Culloty, *nvr rchd ldrs.*
......................................(20 to 1 op 14 to 1) 14
JACK DREAMING (Ire) 5-11-4 (3*) R Davis, *nvr better than mid-div*............................(50 to 1 op 33 to 1) 15
GALES OF LAUGHTER 5-11-4 (3*) R Farrant, *in tch till wknd o'r 4 fs out.*......................(20 to 1) 16
2339 WOODLANDS POWER (v) 6-11-0 (7*) Mr M Rimell, *in tch to hfwy*.......................................(50 to 1) 17
815 RELAXED LAD 5-11-0 (7*) J Bond, *beh most of way.*
....(50 to 1) 18
GUNS OF GOLD 4-10-4 (7*) R Walker, *al beh.....* (33 to 1) 19
BONNY BEAU 6-10-11 (5*) Guy Lewis, *al beh, tld off.*
....(50 to 1) 20
Dist: 1½l, 7l, 2l, 6l, sht-hd, 4l, 2½l, 4l, 1½l, 10l. 3m 59.20s. (20 Ran).
(Roach Foods Limited), D Nicholson

ASCOT (heavy (races 1,3,6), soft (2,4,5)) Wednesday February 9th
Going Correction: PLUS 0.70 sec. per fur. (races 1,3,6), PLUS 0.60 (2,4,5)

2510 Fernbank Novices' Hurdle (4-y-o and up) £4,221 2m 110yds........ (1:30)

2356[2] SCOBIE BOY (Ire) 6-11-4 J Osborne, *jmpd wl, made all, jnd appr 2 out, shaken up and quickened approaching last, ran on, cmftbly.*
......................(11 to 8 on op 6 to 4 on tchd 5 to 4 on) 1
1840[3] MY WIZARD 7-11-7 P Hide, *trkd wnr 4 out, ev ch appr 2 out, kpt on one pace...* (7 to 2 op 11 to 4 tchd 4 to 1) 2
1729[3] GORTEERA 8-11-4 M Brennan, *hld up, hdwy 5th, ev ch appr 2 out, sn outpcd*..........(10 to 1 tchd 12 to 1) 3
2014* ARFER MOLE (Ire) 6-11-7 T Grantham, *not fluent, last whn mstk 5th, ran on aftr nxt, sn btn.*
......................................(11 to 2 op 4 to 1 tchd 6 to 1) 4
2303[3] VASILIEV (v) 6-11-4 C Grant, *reminder 1st, effrt 5th, rdn nxt, sn outpcd, ran on frm last.* (16 to 1 tchd 20 to 1) 5
Dist: 1½l, 8l, nk, hd. 4m 6.60s. (5 Ran).
(R V Shaw), C R Egerton

2511 James Capel Novices' Chase (5-y-o and up) £10,065 2m.......... (2:00)

1308[2] LACKENDARA 7-11-8 J Osborne, *jmpd wl, made all, drw clr frm 2 out, easily.*..............(7 to 2 tchd 4 to 1) 1
2357* SAN LORENZO (USA) 6-11-12 N Williamson, *hld up, mstk 4th, hdwy 7th, sn ev ch, hit 2 out, soon btn.*
......................................(2 to 1 fav op 7 to 4 tchd 9 to 4) 2
2087[3] KIBREET 7-11-4 S Earle, *trkd ldrs till wknd 7th, ran on aftr last to take 3rd....* (5 to 1 op 9 to 2 tchd 11 to 2) 3
1919[4] GLEMOT (Ire) 6-11-4 N Doughty, *trkd ldr till wknd appr 3 out*.......................(6 to 1 op 5 to 1 tchd 13 to 2) 4
2365 WHAT'S IN ORBIT 9-11-4 G Bradley, *cl up whn mstk and uns rdr 6th*.................(4 to 1 op 11 to 4) ur
Dist: 10l, 10l, 1½l. 4m 1.90s. a 14.40s (5 Ran).
SR: 46/40/22/20/-/ (Opening Bid Partnership), Miss H C Knight

2512 Stanlake Hurdle Limited Handicap (4-y-o and up) £8,364 3m........ (2:30)

2247[3] NEWTON POINT [123] 5-11-1 (5*) T Jenks, *trkd ldr, led appr 7th till aftr 3 out, rallied to ld r-in.*
......................................(7 to 2 op 4 to 1) 1
2473[5] BUONARROTI [125] 7-11-8 T Grantham, *trkd ldrs, rdn aftr 3 out, sn led, hdd and no extr r-in.*...........(2 to 1 jt-fav op 5 to 2) 2
1845 METAL OISEAU (Ire) [113] (bl) 6-10-10 A Charlton, *hld up in tch, reminders aftr 6th, shrtlvd effrt nxt, sn no imprsn.*
......................................(12 to 1 op 8 to 1 tchd 14 to 1) 3
2172 SIR CRUSTY [107] 12-9-11 (7*) P Maddock, *hld up, hmpd aftr 1st, hdwy 7th, rdn after nxt, sn btn.*
......................................(20 to 1 tchd 25 to 1) 4
2009[7] PRIME DISPLAY (USA) [127] (bl) 8-11-10 J Osborne, *led till appr 7th, wknd nxt, virtually pld up r-in.*
......................................(9 to 1 op 7 to 1 tchd 10 to 1) 5
2403[7] CAPTAIN DOLFORD [119] 7-10-11 (5*) J McCarthy, *slpd up bend aftr 1st.....*(2 to 1 jt-fav op 7 to 4 tchd 9 to 4) su
Dist: 3l, 15l, 4l, dist. 5m 59.30s. a 26.30s (6 Ran).
(PPS Racing Partnership), T R George

2513 Comet Handicap Chase (5-y-o and up) £13,745 3m 110yds........... (3:05)

2375* DUBACILLA [148] 8-12-0 D Gallagher, *al hndy, effrt 14th, led appr 2 out, ran on gmely frm last.*
......................................(11 to 4 op 5 to 2 tchd 3 to 1) 1
2266[2] ROUGH QUEST [130] 8-10-10 G McCourt, *untd wth, hdwy 4 out, str chal betw last 2, not quicken r-in.*
......................................(6 to 1 op 5 to 1 tchd 13 to 2) 2
1693* THE WIDGET MAN [120] 8-9-13[2] (3*) P Hide, *hld up, hdwy 4 out, sn ev ch, wknd betw last 2....*(6 to 1 tchd 11 to 2) 3
2274* THREEOUTOFFOUR [125] 9-10-5 M Brennan, *in tch, jmpd slwly 14th, niggled alng and lost pl nxt, kpt on one pace frm 2 out.....*(2 to 1 fav op 7 to 4 tchd 9 to 4) 4
2266[6] CUDDY DALE [128] 11-10-8 N Williamson, *led till hdd and wknd appr 2 out...*(33 to 1 op 25 to 1 tchd 50 to 1) 5
2297[2] GRANGE BRAKE [120] (bl) 8-10-0 C Llewellyn, *trkd ldr, blun second, reminder tenth, wknd 4 out.*
......................................(10 to 1 tchd 11 to 1) 6
2359[5] LUMBERJACK (USA) [125] (bl) 10-10-5 J Osborne, *handily plcd, niggled alng and wkng whn pckd 4 out, not reco'r, tld off......*(12 to 1 op 10 to 1 tchd 14 to 1) 7
2264[4] MIGHTY FALCON [120] (bl) 9-10-0 P Holley, *keen hold, chsd ldrs till blun and uns rdr 13th.*
......................................(25 to 1 op 16 to 1 tchd 33 to 1) ur
Dist: ½l, 10l, 8l, 4l, 1l, dist. 6m 25.60s. a 22.10s (8 Ran).
SR: 26/7/-/-/-/ (Mrs Veronica Cole), H T Cole

2514 Reynoldstown Novices' Chase Grade 2 (5-y-o and up) £15,029 3m 110yds ....(3:35)

1873* ONE MAN (Ire) 6-11-5 N Doughty, *nvr far away, hit 9th, hdwy nxt, led 12th, clr 2 out, imprsv.*
......................................(1 to 1 fav tchd 9 to 4) 1
2193* MAILCOM 8-11-5 J Osborne, *led to 12th, mstk 4 out, lft second 2 out, styd on wl r-in....*(9 to 2 tchd 5 to 1) 2
2193 SPIKEY (NZ) 8-11-9 N Williamson, *trkd ldrs, rdn alng appr 4 out, lft remote 3rd 2 out, no extr.*
......................................(33 to 1 op 20 to 1 tchd 50 to 1) 3
1770* LUSTY LIGHT 8-11-5 I Lawrence, *hld up in tch, rdn and wknd appr 15th, tld off.*
......................................(33 to 1 op 20 to 1 tchd 50 to 1) 4
2299* MUDAHIM 8-11-5 W Marston, *trkd ldr, hit tenth, rdn appr 3 out, second and no imprsn whn f 2 out.*
......................................(9 to 4 op 2 to 1) f
2137* CLYDE RANGER 7-11-5 C Grant, *wl plcd, second whn blun 8th, mstk and uns rdr nxt.*
......................................(33 to 1 op 20 to 1 tchd 14 to 1) ur
2209[2] KNAVE OF CLUBS (bl) 7-11-5 M Dwyer, *beh whn blun 7th, lost tch 13th, tld off whn pld up bef 4 out.*
......................................(33 to 1 op 20 to 1 tchd 50 to 1) pu
2362 GRANVILLE GUEST 8-11-5 G Bradley, *mstk 3rd, jmpd slwly nxt, drpd last aftr tenth, beh whn pld up bef 15th...........*(14 to 1 op 10 to 1 tchd 16 to 1) pu
2299[2] EARTH SUMMIT (bl) 6-11-9 C Llewellyn, *slwly away, jmpd slowly 6th, rdn alng 9th, lost tch 12th, tld off whn pld up bef 15th..........*(14 to 1 op 10 to 1 tchd 16 to 1) pu
Dist: 3l, 15l, dist. 6m 21.10s. a 17.60s (9 Ran).
SR: 62/59/48/-/-/-/ (J Hales), G Richards

2515 Kilfane Conditional Jockeys' Handicap Hurdle (0-135 5-y-o and up) £3,501 2½m................... (4:05)

1707* SUNSET AND VINE [113] 7-10-10 A Dicken, *al gng wl, in tch, awkward 4th, hdwy 7th, led 2 out, cleverly.*
......................................(3 to 1 op 11 to 4 tchd 7 to 1) 1
2457* CRABBY BILL [103] (v) 7-10-0 A Procter, *chsd ldrs, led appr 3 out to nxt, ran on und pres, no ch whn wnr.*
......................................(13 to 2 op 5 to 1 tchd 7 to 1) 2
1524* TEXAN BABY (Bel) [115] 5-10-12 T Jenks, *wth ldr, led appr 3rd to 6th, hndy and ev ch 3 out, sn btn.*
......................................(5 to 1 op 7 to 2) 3
1972[5] FAIR BROTHER [106] 8-10-3 R Davis, *hld up, hdwy appr 6th, no imprsn frm 3 out.* (4 to 1 op 3 to 1 tchd 9 to 2) 4

2273⁴ ABBOT OF FURNESS [130] 10-11-10 (3") B Harding, *trkd ldrs, led 6th till appr 3 out, wknd.*
.... (6 to 1 op 5 to 1 tchd 13 to 2) 5
2296³ SYLVIA BEACH [104] 8-10-1¹ D Matthews, *hld up in tch, wknd appr 3 out....*(11 to 1 op 10 to 1 tchd 12 to 1) 6
2172 SEA BUCK [114] 8-10-11 S Fox, *hld up, lost tch 6th.*
.... (9 to 1 op 4 to 1 tchd 10 to 1) 7
2296⁵ RED RING [103] 7-10-0 W Marston, *sn beh, nvr a dngr.*
.... (13 to 2 op 8 to 1 tchd 9 to 1 and 6 to 1) 8
2416 ON THE TWIST [103] 12-9-11 (3") P Murphy, *led till appr 3rd, sn lost pl, tld off whn pld up bef 6th, dismounted.*
.... (40 to 1 op 33 to 1 tchd 50 to 1) pu
Dist: ¾l, 15l, 15l, 6l, ¾l, 1l, 7l. 4m 59.60s. a 18.60s (9 Ran).
SR: 36/25/22/-/16/-/ (Sunset & Vine Plc), S Dow

FOLKESTONE (heavy (races 1,4,6), soft (2,3,5))
Wednesday February 9th
Going Correction: PLUS 1.60 sec. per fur. (races 1,4,6), PLUS 1.25 (2,3,5)

2516 Brenzett Novices' Hurdle (4-y-o) £1,691 2m 1f 110yds...........(2:05)

2303¹ MOORISH 11-5 D Murphy, *pld hrd and heavily rstrained in rear, cruised into ld appr last, hard hld.* (6 to 1 on) 1
2439 RISING WOLF 10-12 B Powell, *led, clr second, mstk 2 out, hdd appr last, kpt on one pace....* (12 to 1 op 7 to 1) 2
1990⁵ DESERT CHALLENGER (Ire) 10-12 J Railton, *trkd ldr, hit 3rd, wnt clr 5th, rdn and wkng whn blun last.*
.... (11 to 2 op 4 to 1) 3
Dist: 2½l, 25l. 4m 37.70s. a 40.70s (3 Ran).
(Adrian Fitzpatrick), J White

2517 Brookland Novices' Chase (5-y-o and up) £2,277 2m 5f..............(2:35)

763¹ YELLOW SPRING 9-11-8 J Railton, *made all, jmpd wl apart frm mstk tenth, drw clr from 2 out.*
.... (7 to 2 op 11 to 4) 1
2146* NICKLUP 7-11-3 B Powell, *chsd wnr frm 4th, hit 5 out, outpcd 3 out, wnt second ag'n nxt.*
.... (100 to 30 op 5 to 2) 2
2274³ CONGREGATION 8-11-8 M Perrett, *hld up in rear, rdn 3 out, styd on one pace.....*(7 to 1 op 4 to 1) 3
2427 COKENNY BOY 9-11-2 D Murphy, *trkd ldrs, wnt second 3 out, sn wkng and btn whn hit last.*
SUPER SENSE 9-11-2 C Maude, *hit 3rd, al in rear, jmpd slwly 8th, lost tch frm 9th, tld off.*
.... (100 to 30 op 5 to 2 tchd 7 to 2) 5
2340 DOVEHILL 8-11-2 Mr P Bull, *hit 1st, trkd wnr to 4th, wkng whn jmpd slwly 9th, tld off whn pld up bef 3 out.*
.... (50 to 1 op 20 to 1) pu
Dist: 10l, 4l, 15l, 12l. 5m 41.70s. a 31.70s (6 Ran).
SR: 40/25/26/5/-/-/ (Mrs R Howell), D M Grissell

2518 Dymchurch Handicap Chase (0-105 5-y-o and up) £2,862 3¼m......(3:05)

2453² SILVERINO [98] (bl) 8-11-9 M Richards, *pressed ldr, led 3 out, styd on wl and sn clr.*
.... (4 to 1 op 5 to 1 tchd 11 to 2) 1
2363³ COOL AND EASY [100] 8-11-11 D Murphy, *made most till hdd 3 out, rdn and one pace.*
.... (13 to 2 op 9 to 2 tchd 7 to 1) 2
2294 BETTY HAYES [100] 10-11-4 (7") P Carey, *not fluent but al in tch, rdn 5 out, outpcd frm 3 out.* (16 to 1 op 8 to 1) 3
2294⁶ THE TARTAN SPARTAN [99] 10-11-3 (7") P Ward, *beh, rdn 3 out, nvr dngrs......* (100 to 30 op 7 to 2 tchd 4 to 1) 4
2001² FURRY KNOWE [100] 9-11-11 S McNeill, *trkd ldrs, frequent blunds, rdn 13th and sn wknd, pld up bef 3 out.*
.... (6 to 4 fav op 11 to 8) pu
2336 PUNCH'S HOTEL [90] 9-11-1 M Perrett, *in rear, tld off aftr blun 12th, pld up bef 5 out.....*(9 to 1 op 7 to 1) pu
2427 HOWARYADOON [103] 8-11-9 (5") C Burnett-Wells, *in rear, rdn and lost tch 14th, tld off whn pld up bef 2 out.*
.... (9 to 1 op 6 to 1) pu
Dist: 10l, 4l, 15l. 7m 6.20s. a 54.20s (7 Ran).
(David Humphreys), G L Moore

2519 Lydd Novices' Hurdle (4-y-o and up) £1,896 2¾m 110yds...........(3:40)

2141⁴ GENERAL WOLFE 5-11-12 B Powell, *trkd ldr, led on bend aftr 2 out, styd on grimly, fnshd tired.*
.... (9 to 4 op 7 to 4 tchd 5 to 2) 1
2358² TALBOT 8-11-6 J Railton, *led till hdd on bend aftr 2 out, rdn and no imprsn.* (11 to 8 fav op Evens tchd 6 to 4) 2
2338³ PLACE STEPHANIE (Ire) 6-10-8 (7") L Dace, *trkd ldrs till lost tch 7th, tld off whn pld up bef 2 out.*
.... (13 to 8 tchd 2 to 1) pu
2117⁵ ALTESSE ROXANNE 5-10-8 (7") Honey Pearce, *tld off 5th, pld up bef 2 out..........* (66 to 1 op 25 to 1) pu

1996 CAPITAIN 5-11-6 W McFarland, *tld off 5th, pld up bef 7th.*
.... (66 to 1 op 25 to 1) pu
Dist: 3½l. 5m 56.20s. a 42.20s (5 Ran).
SR: 36/26/ (G S Beccle), Capt T A Forster

2520 Ivychurch Handicap Chase (0-110 5-y-o and up) £2,392 2m 5f.........(4:10)

1641² FRENCH CHARMER [102] 9-11-10 D Murphy, *wtd wth, making hdwy and mstk 1 out, led appr 3 out, sn led, styd on, cmftbly...*(13 to 8 fav op 11 to 8 tchd 7 to 4) 1
2031³ RINANNA BAY [78] 7-9-8¹ (7") P Carey, *trkd ldr, led 9th till hdd aftr 3 out, one pace after.....*(5 to 1 tchd 11 to 2) 2
1795⁶ OSTURA [88] 9-10-10 W McFarland, *hld up, mstks in rear, hdwy 4 out, wnt second last, wknd r-in.*
.... (11 to 4 op 5 to 2 tchd 3 to 1) 3
1511⁶ SQUEEZE PLAY [84] (bl) 9-10-6 J Railton, *led to 9th, wknd 3 out....*.......................... (7 to 2 op 3 to 1) 4
2191⁵ ON YOUR WAY [78] (v) 12-10-0⁷ (7") Mr B Pollock, *trkd ldrs till wknd 9th.........*(14 to 1 op 10 to 1 tchd 16 to 1) 5
2338 MOZE TIDY [88] 9-10-5 (5") C Burnett-Wells, *in tch, wkng whn mstk tenth, blun and uns rdr 3 out.*
.... (20 to 1 op 16 to 1 tchd 25 to 1) ur
Dist: 4l, 2l, 25l, 7l. 5m 44.70s. a 34.70s (6 Ran).
SR: 11/-/-/ (H T Pelham), J T Gifford

2521 Snargate Handicap Hurdle (0-110 4-y-o and up) £2,216 2m 1f 110yds.. (4:40)

RUN HIGH [95] 11-11-10 Mr R Teal, *hld up in tch, cld on ldrs 4th, led 2 out, rdn clr......*(7 to 2 tchd 4 to 1) 1
2002 TAYLORS PRINCE [90] (v) 7-11-5 V Smith, *hld up in rear, hdwy to go second aftr 2 out, no ch whn blun last.*
.... (15 to 8 op 7 to 4 tchd 2 to 1) 2
2192⁵ SCENT OF BATTLE [91] 6-11-6 J Railton, *with ldr, rdn 3 out, no hdwy frm nxt.........*(7 to 4 fav tchd 2 to 1) 3
2432³ AVERON [71] 14-10-0 D Murphy, *hld up in tch, outpcd frm 2 out....................*(8 to 1 tchd 9 to 1) 4
2335⁷ LLOYDS DREAM [81] 5-10-5 (5") J Supple, *pld hrd, led to 2 out, wknd quickly....*(11 to 2 op 7 to 1 tchd 13 to 1) 5
Dist: 10l, 4l, 7l, ½l. 4m 34.30s. a 37.30s (5 Ran).
SR: 3/-/ (Mrs Patricia Mitchell), P Mitchell

LUDLOW (good to soft (races 1,2,4,7), good (3,5,6))
Wednesday February 9th
Going Correction: PLUS 0.50 sec. per fur. (races 1,2,-4,7), PLUS 0.70 (3,5,6)

2522 Bull Ring Maiden Hurdle (4-y-o) £1,550 2m..................(1:50)

2204³ SQUIRE YORK 11-0 M A FitzGerald, *trkd ldrs, led appr 2 out, pushed clr approaching last....* (5 to 1 op 7 to 2) 1
2029³ FORMAL AFFAIR 10-9 A Maguire, *hdwy 5th, chsd ldrs appr 2 out, kpt on, no imprsn on wnr........*(2 to 1 jt-fav op 11 to 4 tchd 3 to 1) 2
MANILA BAY (USA) 11-0 R Greene, *prmnt, chlgd appr 2 out, sn outpcd.....................* (7 to 1 op 7 to 2) 3
2364³ HONEY GUIDE 11-0 L Harvey, *in tch, rdn and hdwy aftr 3 out, btn 2 out...................*(14 to 1) 4
2245⁶ DANGER BABY 10-11 (3") D Meredith, *led to 5th, led ag'n sn aftr 3 out, soon btn.*
.... (10 to 1 op 7 to 1) 5
1705⁷ POCONO KNIGHT 11-0 G Upton, *in tch, rdn to chase ldrs appr 2 out, sn btn...........*(33 to 1 op 25 to 1) 6
2164³ GUNNER SUE 10-9 A Tory, *al beh, no ch whn hit 2 out.*
.... (50 to 1 op 33 to 1) 7
SPICE AND SUGAR 10-9 Mr J Cambidge, *al beh.*
.... (50 to 1 op 33 to 1) 8
2381 TEJANO GOLD (USA) 11-0 W Humphreys, *sn beh, tld off.*
.... (50 to 1 op 33 to 1) 9
MUSICAL HIGH (Fr) 10-9 R Dunwoody, *with ldr, led 5th, jmpd slwly 3 out and sn hdd, wknd rpdly, tld off.*
.... (2 to 1 jt-fav op 5 to 4 tchd 9 to 4) 10
FULL COURT 11-0 R Bellamy, *beh frm 3rd, tld off.*
.... (33 to 1 op 33 to 1) 11
Dist: 5l, 15l, 5l, 2½l, ½l, 12l, 2½l, dist, 2l, 15l. 3m 51.00s. a 14.00s (11 Ran).
SR: 26/16/6/1/-/-/ (J Powell-Tuck), M W Eckley

2523 Neenton Selling Handicap Hurdle (4-7-y-o) £1,759 2m..............(2:20)

2421⁵ BEAUFAN [67] 7-10-9 Gary Lyons, *drvn and hdwy appr 2 out, wnt lft approaching last, chlgd, sn led, all out.*
.... (16 to 1 op 14 to 1) 1
2401 BITRAN [67] 4-10-9 A S Smith, *pressed ldr, hit 3rd, sn lost pl, rallied frm 2 out, edgd rght and ran on r-in.*
.... (7 to 1 op 6 to 1) 2
2423⁴ ANDRATH (Ire) [67] 6-10-9 W Humphreys, *al prmnt, ran on frm 2 out, slight ld last, sn hdd, one pace.*
.... (14 to 1 tchd 16 to 1) 3
2207* COBB GATE [80] (bl) 6-11-8 M Stevens, *led to 3rd, styd in tch, str chal last, outpcd r-in........*(8 to 1 op 6 to 1) 4

2321⁷ LOXLEY RANGE (Ire) [63] (v) 6-9-12 (7*) N Juckes, *led 3rd, clr frm 5th, bumped and narrowly hdd appr last, sn one pace.*......................................(12 to 1) 5

2361 IRISH TAN [82] 7-10-6 M A FitzGerald, *beh, rdn aftr 3 out, moderate prog und pres appr last.*
....(3 to 1 fav op 6 to 1) 6

1418 MUCH [70] 7-10-12 Mr M Jackson, *not fluent, nvr better than mid-div.*...(33 to 1) 7

2317³ BOOGIE BOPPER (Ire) [76] (v) 5-10-11 (7*) O Burrows, *nvr rch ldrs.*............................(8 to 1 op 5 to 1) 8

1804⁷ MARINE SOCIETY [74] 6-11-2 A Maguire, *beh, drvn 3 out, no imprsn on ldrs.*......................(5 to 1 op 4 to 1) 9

2060 BAND OF HOPE (USA) [74] (v) 7-11-2 Diane Clay, *beh 5th, no ch whn blun last.*....................(8 to 1 op 5 to 1) 10

1592 CATHS FOLLY [60] 7-10-2 T Wall, *al beh.*.........(33 to 1) 11

2132⁵ SANDRO [82] (bl) 5-11-10 L Harvey, *chsd ldrs to appr 2 out.*
....(7 to 1 op 6 to 1) 12

1794⁸ SHADOWLAND (Ire) [58] (bl) 6-10-0 V Slattery, *effrt 3 out, sn wknd.*.............(10 to 1 op 33 to 1 tchd 8 to 1) 13

Dist: ½l, 2l, 1l, 2l, 1½l, 3l, 7l, 3½l, ½l, 6l. 3m 57.80s. a 20.80s (13 Ran).
(D Craddock), B R Cambidge

2524 Butts Novices' Handicap Chase (5-y-o and up) £2,840 3m..................(2:50)

1807 DEEPENDABLE [90] (bl) 7-10-9 M A FitzGerald, *prmnt, tracking ldr whn hit 3 out, hrd rdn r-in to ld nr finish.*
....(7 to 1 op 5 to 1) 1

2206* RABA RIBA [102] 9-11-7 V Slattery, *led second, hit 12th, mstk 4 out, wnt rght 2 out, rdn r-in, ct nr finish.*
....(2 to 1 fav op 9 to 1) 2

2206⁶ LASTOFTHEVIKINGS [81] 9-10-0 T Wall, *beh, hit 5th, styd on frm 3 out, not rch ldrs.*..........(20 to 1 op 14 to 1) 3

2378⁶ PETTY BRIDGE [93] 10-10-12 R Bellamy, *beh frm 6th, nvr dngrs.*..................................(7 to 1 tchd 8 to 1) 4

2206 HERE COMES CHARTER [84] 9-10-3 R Dunwoody, *led to second, styd in tch till mstk 13th, sn wknd.*
....(5 to 1 op 7 to 2 tchd 6 to 1) 5

MELEAGRIS [109] 10-12-0 A Maguire, *unruly and reared start, chsd ldr briefly tenth, awkward 11th (water), wknd quickly aftr 4 out.*.................(7 to 2 op 3 to 1) 6

2361 HEAR A NIGHTINGALE [81] 7-9-9 (5*) Guy Lewis, *hit 4th, lost tch frm 13th, tld off whn pld up bef 3 out.*
....(14 to 1 op 12 to 1) pu

2084 MOUNTSHANNON [83] 8-10-2 M Hourigan, *sn beh, tld off whn pld up bef 12th.*......................(20 to 1) pu

2355 MARIDADI [81] 8-10-0 R Supple, *not jump wl, tld off whn pld up bef 12th.*.......................(20 to 1) pu

Dist: 1½l, 12l, 10l, nk, 15l. 6m 11.80s. a 22.80s (9 Ran).
SR: 21/31/-/-/-/-/ (Mrs P Sherwood), N J Henderson

2525 Marshbrook Novices' Hurdle (5-y-o and up) £1,906 2m..............(3:25)

1674³ FED ON OATS 6-11-0 A Maguire, *in tch, hmpd second, chalg whn not much room and hampered 2 out, chlgd and wnt lft last, drvn to ld r-in.*
..............................(6 to 1 op 9 to 2 tchd 13 to 2) 1

2224² MONTY ROYALE (Ire) 5-10-11 (3*) A Thornton, *al in tch, chlgd 2 out, slight ld last, hdd r-in, not quicken.*
....(14 to 1 op 12 to 1) 2

1548³ CAPTAIN KHEDIVE 6-11-0 M Hourigan, *in tch, steadied 4th, mstk 3 out, chsd ldrs frm 2 out, rdn and styd on r-in.*...................................(6 to 1 op 4 to 1) 3

2014 WILKINS 5-11-0 M A FitzGerald, *led, sn clr, rdn 2 out, hdd but ev ch last, styd on same pace.*................. 4

2118² MERLINS WISH (USA) 5-11-7 R Dunwoody, *chsd ldrs, ev ch frm 2 out till rdn and one pace r-in.*
................................(7 to 4 fav op 5 to 2 tchd 3 to 1) 5

BIG PAT 5-11-0 V Slattery, *trkd ldrs 4th, ev ch frm 2 out till wknd r-in.*.................(6 to 1 op 4 to 1 tchd 13 to 2) 6

1421 CARLSAN 8-11-0 Mr M Jackson, *mstk second, al beh.*
....(100 to 1 op 50 to 1) 7

ADMIRAL BYNG (Fr) 7-10-11 (3*) D Meredith, *in tch, styd on to chase ldrs aftr 3 out, wknd appr 2 out.*
....(8 to 1 tchd 6 to 1) 8

BELLE LOCK 6-10-2 (7*) J Neaves, *al beh.*
....(100 to 1 op 50 to 1) 9

1624 ON THE BOOK 5-10-9 S Smith Eccles, *al beh.*
....(66 to 1 op 50 to 1) 10

2404 BROADWOOD LAD (v) 8-11-0 Gary Lyons, *al beh.*
....(100 to 1 op 50 to 1) 11

HIGH BACCARAT 5-11-0 Lorna Vincent, *al beh.*
....(100 to 1 op 50 to 1) 12

RARE PADDY 5-10-9 R Supple, *al beh, tld off.*
....(25 to 1 op 14 to 1) 13

BLUSHING DORA (v) 8-10-9 Gee Armytage, *f 1st.*
....(100 to 1 op 50 to 1) f

OPEN AGENDA (Ire) 5-11-0 T Wall, *al beh, tld off whn pld up bef 2 out.*...........................(66 to 1 op 50 to 1) pu

1930 AMYS DELIGHT (v) 8-10-9 A Tory, *chsd ldr to 5th, tld off whn pld up bef 2 out.*.................(100 to 1 op 50 to 1) pu

2204 SWEET FRIENDSHIP (bl) 6-10-9 R Greene, *al beh, tld off whn pld up bef 2 out.*.......................(50 to 1) pu

2332 OLD TICKLERTON 5-11-0 L Harvey, *blun 3rd and beh, tld off whn pld up bef 2 out.*........(100 to 1 op 50 to 1) pu

Dist: 2½l, ½l, nk, ¾l, 3l, 20l, 10l, 10l, 6l, 1l. 3m 56.40s. a 19.40s (18 Ran).
(John Kottler), D Nicholson

2526 Ashford Carbonell Hunters' Chase (6-y-o and up) £1,637 3m.........(3:55)

BROWN WINDSOR 12-12-4 (3*) Mr J Durkan, *pressed ldr till led aftr 4 out, hrd drvn whn chlgd frm 2 out, all out.*
....(7 to 4 fav op Evens) 1

CAPE COTTAGE 10-11-7 (7*) Mr A Phillips, *hdwy to chase ldrs tenth, ev ch frm 2 out, ran on wl, not quite get up.*
....(5 to 1 op 4 to 1) 2

KNOCKUMSHIN 11-12-2 (5*) Mr T Byrne, *hdwy tenth, chlgd 14th, ev ch frm 2 out, styd on und pres.*
....(3 to 1 tchd 7 to 2) 3

NGERU 8-11-7 (7*) Mr A Edwards, *led to second, led ag'n 3rd, hdd aftr 4 out, ev ch 2 out, sn wknd.*..(33 to 1) 4

MY NOMINEE 6-11-7 (7*) Mr C Stockton, *hdwy to track ldrs 13th, lost tch appr 3 out.*.....(25 to 1 tchd 20 to 1) 5

WALLY WREKIN 11-11-8¹ (7*) Mr R Ford, *beh frm 7th, nvr dngrs.*.....................................(14 to 1 op 12 to 1) 6

DOWNSVIEW LADY 10-11-2 (7*) Mr M Sheppard, *hit 7th and beh, nvr dngrs.*................(9 to 1 op 20 to 1) 7

SPACE PRINCE 13-11-7 (7*) Mr C Campbell, *effrt frm rear 12th, sn wknd.*................................(33 to 1) 8

2301 MAJESTIC BUCK 14-11-9 (5*) Miss J Pones, *chsd ldrs till wknd quickly 12th.*.................(33 to 1 op 25 to 1) 9

GANOON (USA) 11-11-7 (7*) Mr P J Hanly, *lost tch frm 12th.*
....(50 to 1 op 33 to 1) 10

FELLOW'S NIGHT 11-11-7 (7*) Mr M Jackson, *f 1st.*
....(50 to 1) f

LOCHINGALL 9-11-7 (7*) Mr J M Pritchard, *in tch whn f 6th.*.......................................(10 to 1 op 14 to 1) f

366 SOLICITOR'S CHOICE 11-11-7 (7*) Miss S Higgins, *led second till mstk and hdd 3rd, wknd 12th, tld off whn pld up bef 4 out.*..........................(50 to 1) pu

HOLY AWL 9-11-11 (7*) Mr R J Evans, *prmnt, hit 4th, rear 12th, tld off whn pld up bef four out.*.........(50 to 1) pu

Dist: Nk, ½l, 15l, 15l, 3l, 10l, 10l. 6m 24.20s. a 35.20s (14 Ran).
(W Shand Kydd), Miss C Saunders

2527 Tenbury Novices' Chase (5-y-o and up) £2,749 2½m.........(4:25)

1970³ JOHNNY WILL 9-11-5 M A FitzGerald, *chsd ldrs, hit tenth, led 12th, hit 2 out and last, all out.*
.....................................(6 to 4 jt-fav op 6 to 4 tchd 5 to 2) 1

1934² VAZON BAY (bl) 10-11-5 R Dunwoody, *prmnt, led 12th, ev ch 2 out, rdn last, found little.*......(9 to 4 jt-fav tchd 2 to 1) 2

PRIMITIVE SINGER 6-11-0 (5*) T Eley, *hdwy to chase ldrs 4 out, outpcd frm 3 out.*....................(10 to 1 op 10 to 1) 3

1841⁴ GOLDEN FARE 9-11-11 A Maguire, *led, hit 4th, narrowly hdd and f 5th.*..................(5 to 2 op 11 to 4 tchd 3 to 1) f

HAPPY DEAL 8-11-5 L Harvey, *beh till f 5th.*
....(66 to 1 op 50 to 1) f

889 DUNKERY BEACON 8-11-0 (5*) Guy Lewis, *in tch, 4th and rdn whn f four out.*.................(25 to 1 op 20 to 1) f

1869 ESSEN AITCH 5-10-4 V Slattery, *slwly into strd, beh till f 5th.*.......................................(50 to 1) f

1924³ RAIDO 9-11-5 Gary Lyons, *took str hold, prmnt to tenth, tld off whn pld up bef 4 out.*......................... pu

1590⁴ COOMBESBURY LANE (bl) 8-11-0 R Supple, *hit 3rd, wknd frm tenth, tld off whn pld up bef 4 out.*
....(14 to 1 op 12 to 1) pu

Dist: 2½l, 12l. 5m 17.40s. a 26.40s (9 Ran).
(Lord Chelsea), Miss H C Knight

2528 Leominster Handicap Hurdle (0-115 4-y-o and up) £2,400 2m 5f 110yds ....(4:55)

2385⁵ CHIEF RAIDER (Ire) [110] 6-11-12 A Maguire, *led to 5th, led ag'n 3 out, hdd r-in, rallied und pessure to ld again nr finish.*....................(8 to 1 op 7 to 1 tchd 10 to 1) 1

COSMIC FORCE (NZ) [84] 10-10-0 Jacqui Oliver, *trd wide thrght, led 5th, hdd 3 out, chlgd frm 2 out, led r-in, shaken up and ct cl hme.*.........(20 to 1 op 16 to 1) 2

1955⁶ SUPER SPELL [100] 8-11-2 S Mackey, *beh, hit drvn 6th, hdwy to chase ldrs frm 3 out, one pace r-in.*
....(16 to 1 op 14 to 1) 3

JACKSON FLINT [104] 6-11-6 S Smith Eccles, *trkd ldrs, ev ch 2 out, not quicken approachiang last.*
....(10 to 1 op 11 to 1) 4

1884⁵ DECIDED (Can) [95] 11-10-6 (5*) Miss P Jones, *in tch, rdn and styd on same pace frm 2 out.*.........(20 to 1) 5

1474⁶ LITTLE BIG [87] 7-9-10 (7*) N Collum, *beh till ran on frm 3 out, nrst finish.*...............(12 to 1 op 10 to 1) 6

1972³ WICKET [93] 9-10-9 S Earle, *hdwy frm 6th, trkd ldrs aftr 3 out, wknd 2 out.*.....(10 to 1 op 8 to 1 tchd 11 to 1) 7

2247⁶ LING (USA) [94] 9-10-13 R J Beggan, *hld up, hdwy to track ldrs 6th, fdd 2 out.*............(7 to 2 fav op 8 to 1) 8

1865³ RECORD LOVER (Ire) [84] 4-10-0 T Wall, *chsd ldrs 6th, wknd 3 out.*..............................(25 to 1) 9

1863¹ BALAAT (USA) [90] 6-10-6 W Worthington, *nvr rch ldrs.*
....(10 to 1 op 9 to 1) 10

2216[5] BOREEN JEAN [96] 10-10-12 W Humphreys, *nvr nr ldrs*.
..................................(14 to 1 op 12 to 1) 11
2403 BLACK SAPPHIRE [105] 7-11-2 (5") S Curran, *prmnt to 5th*.
..................................(50 to 1) 12
2265[5] WELSH SIREN [100] 8-10-13 (3") A Thornton, *chsd ldrs 5th,*
sn wknd..............(7 to 1 op 6 to 1 tchd 15 to 2) 13
DUCKHAVEN [88] (bl) 11-10-4 W Irvine, *prmnt to 6th*.
..................................(33 to 1) 14
2209 MICKEEN [100] 7-11-2 M A FitzGerald, *chsd ldrs to 6th*.
..................................(20 to 1 op 14 to 1) 15
2273[3] ISABEAU [106] 7-11-8 A S Smith, *chsd ldrs till wknd 6th*.
..................................(5 to 1 tchd 6 to 1) 16
1445[9] COME HOME ALONE [88] (bl) 6-10-4 R Supple, *al beh,*
virtually pld up nr finish........(14 to 1 op 12 to 1) 17
2366[5] CHEERFUL TIMES [100] 11-11-2 R Dunwoody, *al beh*.
..................................(8 to 1 op 7 to 1) 18
2366[9] LAND OF THE FREE [98] 5-11-01 Harvey, *beh, rdn aftr 4th,*
nvr dngrs..............................(16 to 1) 19
Dist: Nk, 3½l, nk, 3½l, 2l, nk, 10l, 2½l, 6l, 1l. 5m 26.70s. a 29.70s (19 Ran).
(John Wade), J Wade

SOUTHWELL (A.W) (std)
Wednesday February 9th
Going Correction: PLUS 0.55 sec. per fur.

2529 Rock Novices' Hurdle (4-y-o and up)
£1,553 2m.....................(2:10)

524[5] DULZURA 6-10-12 D Bridgwater, *made all, clr appr 3 out,*
styd on...........................(10 to 1 op 5 to 1) 1
1460[7] BOLD BOSTONIAN (Fr) 6-11-3 B Clifford, *hld up in tch,*
hdwy to chase wnr aftr 4 out, sn rdn and one pace.
..................................(13 to 8 op 5 to 4 tchd 7 to 4) 2
2420[2] STRONG JOHN (Ire) 6-11-12 (7") P McLoughlin, *chsd wnr,*
rdn aftr 4 out and sn wknd.
..................................(5 to 4 on op Evens tchd 11 to 10) 3
2116[7] SIE AMATO (Ire) 5-11-3 A Dobbin, *chsd wnr, blun badly*
5th, hmpd nxt and sn wl beh.......(12 to 1 op 7 to 1) 4
1865 TIP NAP 6-10-10 (7") D Towler, *not fluent, effrt and hdwy*
5th, cl up whn f nxt................(33 to 1 op 25 to 1) f
Dist: 6l, dist, dist. 4m 1.90s. a 15.90s (5 Ran).
SR: 13/12/
(Mrs D B Brazier), A P Jarvis

2530 Clay Claiming Hurdle (4-y-o and up)
£1,799 2¼m.....................(2:40)

2421* BURN BRIDGE (USA) 4-8-11-1 Peter Caldwell, *chsd ldrs,*
effrt to ld appr 3 out, sn clr, easily.
..................................(7 to 4 fav op 2 to 1 tchd 5 to 2) 1
2303[8] LORD NASKRA (USA) (v) 5-11-2 R Campbell, *in tch, hdwy*
7th, chsd wnr appr 3 out, blun 2 out, no imprsn.
..................................(100 to 30 op 5 to 2 tchd 4 to 1) 2
2058* IT'S NOT MY FAULT (Ire) 6-11-4 P McDermott, *cl up till lost*
pl and beh appr 4 out, styd on und pres approaching
last..........................(5 to 1 op 3 to 1) 3
2331[4] RAIN-N-SUN 8-11-2 D Bridgwater, *prmnt, led 7th till rdn*
and hdd appr 3 out, sn wknd......(12 to 1 op 10 to 1) 4
1007[5] HOT OFF THE PRESS 4-10-11 S Turner, *prmnt, lft in ld*
3rd, hdd 5th, rdn 4 out and sn one pace.
..................................(6 to 1 op 4 to 1) 5
2186 FEARSOME 8-10-11 Mr S Astaire, *prmnt to 4th, sn lost pl*
and beh frm hfwy.................(16 to 1 op 14 to 1) 6
2420[4] RAVENSPUR (Ire) (bl) 4-10-5 A Dobbin, *hld up, steady*
hdwy 7th, ev ch nxt, rdn 4 out and sn wknd...(16 to 1) 7
2148[6] CHOIR'S IMAGE 7-10-13 A Mulholland, *prmnt, blun 4th*
and sn pushed alng, beh frm 7th....(9 to 1 op 10 to 1) 8
1240[5] FEASIBLE 10-11-2 Miss R Judge, *al rear, tld off whn pld*
up bef 6 out........................(14 to 1 tchd 16 to 1) pu
IMPERIAL TOKAY (USA) (v) 4-10-5 S D Williams, *prmnt, led*
5th till appr 7th, sn wknd and beh whn pld up bef 3 out.
..................................(33 to 1) pu
BASKERVILLE BALLAD 4-9-11 (3") R Farrant, *pld hrd, led*
till sddl slpd and pulled up bef 3rd............(33 to 1) pu
Dist: 25l, nk, 10l, 2½l, 20l, 20l, 2½l. 4m 33.30s. a 21.30s (11 Ran).
(T H Caldwell), T H Caldwell

2531 Granite Novices' Hurdle
(0-100 4-y-o and up) £1,553 2¾m (3:15)

2420* ABELONI [72] 5-10-9 (3",7ex) S Wynne, *hld up in tch,*
hdwy on bit 4 out, led appr nxt, sn rdn, kpt on.
..................................(5 to 4 fav op 11 to 10 tchd 6 to 4) 1
2093[2] ARCTIC LIFE (Ire) [84] 5-11-10 S Turner, *made all pace,*
rdn and quickened 4 out, hdd nxt and sn hrd drvn, kpt
on gmely flt......................(3 to 1 op 7 to 2 tchd 4 to 1) 2
2216[4] VAZON EXPRESS [70] 8-10-3 (7") D Winter, *trkd ldr, rdn*
alng 4 out and wknd appr nxt.
..................................(8 to 1 op 10 to 1 tchd 16 to 1) 3
2327* KOA [79] 4-11-5 D Bridgwater, *trkd ldr, hit 8th, effrt to*
chal 5 out, sn rdn and wknd quickly appr 3 out.
..................................(9 to 4 op 11 to 8) 4
Dist: 1l, 30l, dist. 5m 46.10s. a 37.10s (4 Ran).
(J Hardman), R Hollinshead

2532 Chalk Handicap Hurdle (0-125 4-y-o
and up) £1,842 2m..............(3:45)

2164 VANART [84] 5-10-11 R Garritty, *hld up, hdwy appr 3 out,*
sn rdn, styd on flt to ld nr finish. (5 to 2 fav op 9 to 4) 1
2331[2] BALLERINA ROSE [77] 7-10-4 D J Burchell, *cl up gng wl,*
led appr 3 out, sn clr, rdn last, hdd and no extr nr
finish.........................(11 to 4 op 3 to 1) 2
2330[5] LAVA FALLS (USA) [87] 8-11-0 D Skyrme, *chsd ldr, led appr*
4 out, rdn and hdd bef nxt, sn wknd. (6 to 1 op 7 to 1) 3
2213[4] SPEEN'S SEAGO (USA) [73] 6-10-0 D Bridgwater, *prmnt,*
rdn alng aftr 4th, sn lost pl and beh frm hfwy.
..................................(4 to 1 op 7 to 2) 4
1514 ALWAYS REMEMBER [97] 7-11-10 B Clifford, *led, rdn 5 out*
and sn hdd, wknd and pld up bef 3 out, lme.
..................................(3 to 1 op 9 to 4 tchd 7 to 2) pu
Dist: 1l, dist, dist. 4m 0.90s. a 14.90s (5 Ran).
SR: 22/14/
(W W Haigh), W W Haigh

2533 Cheese Conditional Jockeys' Handicap Hurdle (0-115 4-y-o and up)
£1,764 2½m...................(4:15)

2428 CREWS CASTLE [88] 7-10-7 (5") W J Walsh, *trkd ldr till*
hmpd and lft in ld 5th, hdd 7th and cl up, rdn 3 out,
styd on und pres to lead nr line.
..................................(7 to 4 op 2 to 1 tchd 9 to 4) 1
2166[2] ARCTIC OATS [104] 9-12-0 D J Moffatt, *hld up in tch,*
hmpd appr 5th, took slight ld 7th, rdn and rdr lost whip
2 out, hdd nr line.
..................................(Evens fav op 6 to 4 on tchd 11 to 10) 2
1592[4] AUTONOMOUS [78] 9-10-2 S Wynne, *led till pld up lme*
appr 5th................(7 to 2 op 3 to 1 tchd 4 to 1) pu
Dist: Sht-hd. 5m 17.50s. a 36.50s (3 Ran).
(Mrs T McCoubrey), J R Jenkins

2534 Sandy National Hunt Flat Race (4,5,6-
y-o) £897 2m..................(4:45)

2095* HANDMAIDEN 4-10-8 (5") S Mason, *trkd ldrs, smooth*
hdwy 4 fs out, led 2 and a half out, pushed out.
..................................(7 to 4 op 2 to 1 on on tchd 5 to 4 on) 1
HULLBANK 4-10-8 (3") D J Moffatt, *mid-div, hdwy o'r 4 fs*
out, chsd wnr 2 out, kpt on und pres ins last.
..................................(10 to 1 op 7 to 1) 2
MALACHITE GREEN 4-10-8 (3") S Wynne, *in tch, effrt and*
hdwy on outer o'r 3 fs out, sn rdn and one pace fnl 2
furlongs........................(12 to 1 op 7 to 1) 3
ADIB (USA) 4-10-8 (3") N Bentley, *trkd ldrs, pushed alng*
and outpcd 4 fs out, styd on one pace und pres fnl 2
furlongs.........................(6 to 1 op 7 to 1) 4
TELEPHONE 5-11-0 (7") Pat Thompson, *trkd ldrs, gd hdwy*
on inner 4 fs out, rdn 3 out and sn one pace.
..................................(6 to 1 op 4 to 1) 5
2407 SCOTCH 'N IRISH (Ire) 5-11-0 (7") D Towler, *led till hdd and*
wknd 2 and a half fs out.
..................................(25 to 1 op 20 to 1 tchd 33 to 1) 6
MOPHEAD KELLY 5-11-7 Mr B Leavy, *prmnt, rdn 4 fs out,*
sn wknd....................(25 to 1 op 20 to 1 tchd 33 to 1) 7
2490 LEGATA (Ire) 5-10-11 (5") P Midgley, *prmnt, rdn alng 6 fs*
out, wknd quickly o'r 4 out......(25 to 1 op 20 to 1) 8+
STEANARD LAD 6-11-2 (5") S Lyons, *in tch till rdn 4 fs out,*
sn wknd...........................(12 to 1 op 7 to 1) 8+
LINPAC PRESS 4-10-6 (5") D Fortt, *al beh*.
..................................(12 to 1 op 7 to 1) 10
KALAJO 4-10-11 Miss R Judge, *mid-div, effrt and hdwy*
on outer hfwy, rdn and wknd o'r 4 fs out.
..................................(14 to 1 op 12 to 1) 11
Dist: 1½l, 10l, 2l, 12l, 10l, 8l, 15l, dd-ht, sht-hd, dist. 4m 1.00s. (11 Ran).
(R Fenwick-Gibson), M J Camacho

HUNTINGDON (soft)
Thursday February 10th
Going Correction: PLUS 1.25 sec. per fur. (races
1,3,6), PLUS 1.40 (2,4,5)

2535 Glatton Claiming Hurdle (4-y-o and
up) £2,057 2m 5f 110yds.......(2:10)

2354[2] MISTIC GLEN (Ire) 5-11-1 A Dobbin, *hld up, hdwy to ld 2*
out, edgd lft and drvn out r-in, jst held on, fnshd 1st,
plcd second.
..................................(7 to 1 op 12 to 1 tchd 14 to 1 and 16 to 1) 1D
2354* SO DISCREET (USA) 6-11-10 A Maguire, *hld up wl in tch,*
led 3 out, hdd nxt, ev ch whn bumped r-in, styd on und
pres, fnshd second, plcd 1st... (7 to 4 on op 6 to 4 on) 1
THE PAPPARAZI 14-11-0 E Murphy, *hld up, ev ch frm 3 out*
til wknd last 100 yards........(16 to 1 op 14 to 1 tchd 11 to 2) 3
ENBORNE LAD (bl) 10-11-4 M Perrett, *wl plcd, led 7th, hdd*
3 out, sn one pace appr nxt..........(16 to 1 op 8 to 1) 4
2120[8] JOSIE SMITH 10-10-8 (5") D Matthews, *trkd ldrs till wknd*
frm 7th..........................(33 to 1 op 25 to 1) 5
2034 THE HIDDEN CITY 8-11-2 B Powell, *dsptd ld frm second*
till no extr 3 out..................(20 to 1 op 16 to 1) 6
2418 BROUGHTON'S GOLD (Ire) 6-11-1 S Smith Eccles, *trkd ldrs*
till outpcd aftr 3 out...............(33 to 1 op 20 to 1) 7
2354[4] HELLO VANOS 6-10-7 (7") P McLoughlin, *chsd ldrs till*
drpd rear aftr 6th.................(33 to 1) 8

KILMYSHALL 8-11-1 (3*) P Hide, *led and dsptd ld till hdd 7th, sn lost pl*...................... (16 to 1 op 12 to 1) 9
TRY NEXT DOOR 7-11-4 M Brennan, *reminders and beh frm 6th, tld off*..................... (12 to 1 op 6 to 1) 10
KEELBY 9-11-10 M Dwyer, *hld up in mid-div, effrt 7th, wknd 3 out, pld up and dismounted bef nxt.*
.... (10 to 1 op 5 to 1) pu
)ist: Hd, 7l, 20l, 20l, 10l, sht-hd, 20l, 20l. 5m 36.70s. a 41.70s (11 Ran).
(Ms M Horan), J White

2536 Whittlesey Handicap Chase (0-120 5-y-o and up) £3,756 3m....... (2:40)

2406* BALTIC BROWN [110] 9-11-9 (5ex) Richard Guest, *lft in ld 3rd, hdd 11th, led 13th, made rst, rdn out frm last.*
.... (5 to 2 fav op 9 to 4) 1
2246⁴ LOCH BLUE [108] 12-11-4 (3*) A Dicken, *hld up, not fluent 13th, ran on 3 out, lft second and pckd last, edgd left und pres and one pace r-in.*
.... (8 to 1 op 7 to 1 tchd 10 to 1) 2
2386³ CAMBO (USA) [91] 8-10-4 D Skyrme, *hld up towards rear, hit 7th, blun and rdr lost irons 15th, rallied aftr 3 out, no imprsn frm nxt*...................... (10 to 1 op 8 to 1) 3
1769 POSTMAN'S PATH [102] 8-11-1 B Powell, *chsd ldrs till rdn and btn appr 2 out*.................. (4 to 1 op 7 to 2) 4
2384 SCOLE [113] 9-11-12 A Maguire, *wth ldrs, led 11th to 13th, wknd quickly aftr 3 out*................. (7 to 2 op 3 to 1) 5
2340* DONT TELL THE WIFE [92] 8-10-5 D Bridgwater, *hld up, prog 15th, hit 2 out, cl second whn f last.*
.... (7 to 2 op 3 to 1) f
2274⁵ THE LEGGETT [115] (bl) 11-12-0 A S Smith, *led till refused 3rd.*......................... (33 to 1 op 20 to 1) ref
st: 10l, 30l, ½l, dist. 6m 38.60s. a 50.60s (7 Ran).
(Mrs S Smith), Mrs S J Smith

2537 Sidney Banks Memorial Novices' Hurdle (4-y-o and up) £6,872 2m 5f 110yds ....(3:10)

2382* SEEKIN CASH (USA) 5-11-6 J Osborne, *made all, shaken up and quickened clr frm 2 out.*
.... (9 to 4 on op 2 to 1) 1
2380* RELKEEL 5-11-2 A Maguire, *hld up, chsd wnr frm 5th, jnd issue 3 out, outpcd frm nxt.*........ (2 to 1 op 6 to 4) 2
1809 CZAR NICHOLAS 5-11-2 W Worthington, *wnt poor 3rd 6th, sn lost tch, tld off*...(33 to 1 tchd 66 to 1 and 50 to 1) 3
2477⁴ MALENOIR (USA) 6-11-4 Richard Guest, *chsd wnr to 5th, quickly nxt, tld off*...........(33 to 1 op 20 to 1) 4
ist: 10l, dist, dist. 5m 25.30s. a 30.30s (4 Ran).
R: 58/44/-/-/- (Sheikh Ahmed Bin Saeed Al Maktoum), C R Egerton

2538 Croxton Novices' Chase (5-y-o and up) £2,498 2m 110yds............. (3:40)

2244³ SOUTHOLT (Ire) 6-11-3 D Bridgwater, *wl plcd, cld on ldr appr 2 out, rdn to ld nr finish.* ....(11 to 4 jt-fav op 2 to 1 tchd 3 to 1) 1
2304³ NEWLANDS-GENERAL 8-11-3 M Dwyer, *jmpd lft, led till hdd und pres nr finish.*................(11 to 4 jt-fav op 2 to 1) 2
2020* CRYSTAL BEAR (NZ) (bl) 9-11-10 B Powell, *not fluent and drpd rear 4th, reminders nxt, ran on 3 out, hit last, no extr r-in.*.....................(7 to 2 op 5 to 1) 3
2304 DAN DE LYON 6-11-3 A Maguire, *ldg grp, ch 3 out, one pace and hit nxt, sn wknd.*
.... (7 to 1 op 5 to 1 tchd 8 to 1) 4
2272 QUENTIN DURWOOD 8-11-3 J Osborne, *chsd ldrs till wknd appr 2 out*....... (5 to 1 op 6 to 1) 5
♦7413 WINGED WHISPER (USA) 5-10-3 (5*) T Eley, *in tch till wknd 7th, grad lost touch*........(25 to 1 op 20 to 1) 6
2015 FIRST COMMAND (NZ) 7-11-0 (3*) R Farrant, *chsd ldrs till beh frm 6th, tld off*.............(14 to 1 tchd 16 to 1) 7
♦790⁵ CALDECOTT 8-11-3 Richard Guest, *blun and uns rdr 3rd.*......................(20 to 1 tchd 25 to 1) ur
SIMWELL (Ire) 6-10-10 (7*) P Murphy, *al rear, tld off frm 5th, pld up bef 3 out.*............(14 to 1 op 10 to 1) pu
st: 1½l, 8l, 15l, 15l, 12l, 15l. 4m 26.30s. a 28.30s (9 Ran).
R: 37/35/34/12/-/- (G A Hubbard), F Murphy

2539 Farcet Fen Handicap Chase (0-135 5-y-o and up) £2,804 2m 110yds (4:10)

2248 ATLAAL [121] (v) 9-11-10 S Smith Eccles, *trkd ldr, led 2 out, clr last, eased nr line.*
.... (11 to 10 on op 5 to 2 on tchd Evens) 1
2337⁴ EMSEE-H [115] 9-11-4 A Maguire, *led till hdd 2 out, rdn and one pace appr last.*
.............(7 to 4 op 5 to 4 on tchd 11 to 4 and 3 to 1) 2
2334⁴ PRIVATE AUDITION [119] 12-11-1 (7*) P Murphy, *not jump wl, al beh, lost tch 8th, rnwd efrt appr 2 out, btn whn blun and uns rdr last, rmntd.*........(7 to 2 op 5 to 1) 3
st: 5l, dist. 4m 34.40s. a 36.40s (3 Ran).
(O J Donnelly), J R Jenkins

2540 Long Stanton Handicap Hurdle (0-125 5-y-o and up) £2,724 2m 110yds (4:40)

2243⁵ BRAMBLEBERRY [99] 5-10-11 Richard Guest, *handily plcd, led 2 out, rdn clr aftr last, eased nr line.*
...................(7 to 2 co-fav op 5 to 2 tchd 4 to 1) 1
SO PROUD [110] 9-11-8 M Perrett, *led till hdd aftr 3rd, pressed ldrs, styd on one pace frm 2 out.....*(7 to 2 co-fav tchd 4 to 1) 2
2138⁵ DORADUS [92] 6-9-11 (7*) F Leahy, *led aftr 3rd, hdd and hit 2 out, no extr frm last.*...................(7 to 2 co-fav op 3 to 1 tchd 4 to 1) 3
2333⁴ NAGOBELIA [90] 6-10-2 A Maguire, *prog frm rear aftr 4th, cld on ldrs 3 out, rdn and btn appr nxt. .....*(7 to 2 co-fav op 3 to 1) 4
2338 DUKE DE VENDOME [88] (v) 11-9-7 (7*) Mr G Haine, *mid-div, rdn and wknd aftr 4th.*
.... (25 to 1 op 20 to 1 tchd 33 to 1) 5
2403 KNIGHTS (NZ) [108] 8-11-6 Jacqui Oliver, *al beh, tld off frm 4th.*...........................(10 to 1 op 7 to 1) 6
1940⁴ YAHEEB (USA) [110] 5-11-8 G McCourt, *settled towards rear, rdn alng and lost tch frm 5th.*
.... (9 to 2 op 5 to 1 tchd 6 to 1) 7
Dist: 6l, 2l, 12l, 15l, 6l, 10l. 4m 12.70s. a 25.70s (7 Ran).
SR: 32/37/17/3/ (Mrs S Smith), Mrs S J Smith

LINGFIELD (A.W) (std)
Thursday February 10th
Going Correction: MINUS 0.15 sec. per fur.

2541 Forsythia Juvenile Novices' Hurdle (4-y-o) £1,730 2m.................. (1:50)

2275* RUSTY REEL 11-4 R Campbell, *in tch, took clr order frm 7th, led 2 out, awkward last, shaken up and ran on wl.*
.... (6 to 4 jt-fav op Evens) 1
2439⁴ ERLKING (Ire) 10-11 (7*) Chris Webb, *in tch, hndy, led appr 3 out, hdd nxt, rallied last, no extr fnl 100 yards.*
.... (6 to 4 jt-fav tchd 7 to 4 and 2 to 1) 2
2190⁴ ARAMON 10-12 G McCourt, *hld up, hdwy 8th, styd on same pace frm nxt.*...............(20 to 1 op 8 to 1) 3
2422 SOVIET EXPRESS (bl) 10-12 D Gallagher, *took keen hold, handily plcd, jmpd slwly 3rd, effrt 8th, btn whn mstk 2 out.*....................(12 to 1 op 10 to 1 tchd 16 to 1) 4
2439² CONBRIO STAR (bl) 10-7 (5*) D Fortt, *chsd ldr till led 5th, hdd appr 3 out, sn rdn and btn....*(33 to 1 op 16 to 1) 5
2245 NUTTY BROWN 10-12 W McFarland, *pld hrd, led till hdd 5th, wknd 8th.*...................(16 to 1 op 8 to 1) 6
2364⁷ COSMIC STAR 10-7 A Merrigan, *lost tch frm 8th.*
.... (9 to 1 op 10 to 1 tchd 33 to 1) 7
2398 BILJAN (USA) 10-12 Mr G Johnson Houghton, *midfield till wknd 8th.*...........(12 to 1 op 14 to 1 tchd 33 to 1) 8
PAIR OF JACKS (Ire) 10-12 M Richards, *al struggling.*
.... (9 to 1 op 8 to 1) 9
2345 SUNBEAM CHARLIE 10-12 G Upton, *not fluent, rear div, rdn, no dngr*...............(33 to 1 tchd 50 to 1) 10
Dist: 2½l, 15l, 12l, 3½l, 8l, 2l, 3½l, hd, 7l. 3m 38.30s. a 5.30s (10 Ran).
SR: 13/10/-/-/-/-/- (S M Perry), I Campbell

2542 Buddleia Selling Hurdle (4-y-o and up) £1,730 2¼m.................... (2:20)

2440 ROGEVIC BELLE 6-11-4 W McFarland, *jmpd rght thrght, made all, styd on strly frm 2 out.*..(25 to 1 op 20 to 1) 1
2341² RUMBELOW 5-10-13 (5*) D Fortt, *hld up, hdwy tenth and sn chasing ldrs, ran on to take second r-in.*
.... (7 to 1 op 4 to 1) 2
2293³ MASROUG 7-11-10 M Richards, *al hndy, chsd wnr frm 8th, rdn 2 out, no imprsn frm nxt and lost second r-in.*...................(9 to 4 on op 6 to 4) 3
2342⁴ RED INK 5-11-3 (7*) W J Walsh, *in tch, effrt 9th, wknd appr 3 out....*(6 to 1 op 7 to 2 tchd 13 to 2) 4
2113 ALL ELECTRIC 9-11-4 A Merrigan, *in tch, effrt 7th, rdn alng nxt, sn btn.*................(25 to 1 op 14 to 1) 5
2441 TAPESTRY DANCER 6-11-3 (7*) Chris Webb, *wl plcd till wknd tenth.*................(14 to 1 op 12 to 1) 6
2401 SUMMER EXPRESS 5-10-11 (7*) Miss C Spearing, *drpd last 7th, lost tch frm 9th, tld off.*..(20 to 1 op 10 to 1) 7
844 EASY AMANDA 6-10-13 A Tory, *trkd wnr to 5th, drpd out quickly, pld up aftr nxt, lme.*.......(25 to 1 op 16 to 1) pu
Dist: 5l, sht-hd, 12l, 8l, ½l, 25l. 4m 14.20s. a 13.20s (8 Ran).
(Robert Stronge), R M Stronge

2543 Cotoneaster Novices' Handicap Hurdle (0-100 4-y-o and up) £1,722 2¾m (2:50)

2442 NEARLY HONEST [60] 6-10-8 A Tory, *wnt second 8th, led 2 out, readily....*(5 to 4 on tchd 6 to 4 on and Evens) 1
1169 LIZZIES LASS [52] 9-9-7 (7*) G Crone, *led, clr 3rd, reminders aftr 12th, hdd 2 out, rallied last, sn no extr.*
.... (50 to 1 op 33 to 1) 2
2341⁴ WHATMORECANIASKFOR (Ire) [55] (bl) 6-10-0 (3*) D Meredith, *chsd ldr to 8th, hit nxt, sn rdn and wknd.*
.... (4 to 1 op 3 to 1) 3
953⁶ COLONIAL OFFICE (USA) [67] (bl) 10-10-8 (7*) N Juckes, *hmpd 1st, mstk 7th, some hdwy 9th, mistake 11th, sn btn.*...................(14 to 1 op 8 to 1 tchd 16 to 1) 4

NATIONAL HUNT RESULTS 1993-94

2264 PAPER STAR [76] 7-11-3 (7*) M P FitzGerald, *mstk and uns rdr 1st*........(9 to 4 op 2 to 1 tchd 5 to 2 and 11 to 4)   ur
Dist: 2½l, 20l, 10l. 5m 15.20s. a 16.20s (5 Ran).

(Jock Cullen), R J Hodges

2544 Clematis Handicap Hurdle (0-115 4-y-o and up) £1,753 2½m......... (3:20)

2442* SAAHI (USA) [96] 5-11-6 (5*,6ex) J McCarthy, *hld up, niggled alng appr 3 out, ran on aftr nxt, str run to ld r-in*.
.... (6 to 4 fav op Evens tchd 13 to 8)   1
2442³ CONSTRUCTION [73] 9-10-2 D Gallagher, *trkd ldrs, wnt second tenth, led last, hdd and not quicken r-in*.
.... (33 to 1 op 20 to 1)   2
2346* ROYAL CIRCUS [89] 5-11-1 (3*) S Wynne, *led till hdd last, no extr*.................... (5 to 1 tchd 11 to 2)   3
2343⁵ KINGSFOLD PET [71] 5-10-0 M Richards, *sn wl beh, mstk 5th, ran on appr 3 out, no further imprsn nxt*.
.... (12 to 1 op 8 to 1)   4
2185³ ALICE'S MIRROR [82] (v) 5-10-11 W McFarland, *not fluent, in tch till wknd frm 11th*.......... (7 to 1 tchd 10 to 1)   5
2131² JARRWAH [99] 6-12-0 V Slattery, *trkd ldr till pushed alng tenth, sn wknd*................ (9 to 4 tchd 2 to 1)   6
Dist: 1½l, 1½l, 20l, 8l, 3l. 4m 39.00s. a 8.00s (6 Ran).

(Martin N Peters), C Weedon

2545 Japonica Handicap Hurdle (0-115 4-y-o and up) £1,737 2m........... (3:50)

1842⁷ MONDAY CLUB [112] 10-12-0 D Meade, *hld up, hdwy 8th, lft second 3 out, rdn to ld r-in*.
.............(3 to 1 op 5 to 2 tchd 100 to 30 and 7 to 2)   1
2229⁴ VICTORY ANTHEM [87] 8-9-12 (5*) D Fortt, *chsd ldr frm 3rd, lft in ld 3 out, slight mstk last, hdd and no extr r-in*............... (9 to 4 fav tchd 5 to 2 and 11 to 4)   2
2379⁶ WHIPPERS DELIGHT (Ire) [105] 6-11-0 (7*) W J Walsh, *chsd ldr to 3rd, rdn alng 8th, styd on same pace frm nxt*.
.... (3 to 1 op 7 to 2)   3
2342³ CANDLE KING (Ire) [84] 6-9-13¹ (7*) M Appleby, *handily plcd, rdn alng whn lft 3rd 3 out, no extr*.
.............(25 to 1 op 14 to 1 tchd 33 to 1)   4
1415 MAMALAMA [88] 6-10-4⁴ D O'Sullivan, *prmnt till lost pl 3rd, wknd 7th*.................... (12 to 1 op 10 to 1)   5
1708⁸ IN THE GAME (Ire) [84] 5-9-9 (5*) J McCarthy, *jmpd slwly 4th and sn in rear, tld off*........ (33 to 1 op 25 to 1)   6
2443 EDDIE WALSHE [84] 9-10-0 Leesa Long, *sn led, 3 ls clr whn f three out*................. (9 to 1 tchd 7 to 1)   f
730⁵ CYRILL HENRY (Ire) [86] 5-10-2² A Merrigan, *f second*.
.... (20 to 1 op 12 to 1)   f
Dist: 1l, 12l, ¾l, 10l, 30l. 3m 36.20s. a 3.20s (8 Ran).
SR: 44/18/24/2/-/

(J C Tuck), J C Tuck

2546 Wisteria National Hunt Flat Race (4,5,6-y-o) £1,590 1m 5f........ (4:20)

2134* COLOSSUS OF ROADS 5-11-7 (5*) Guy Lewis, *al hndy gng wl, led on bit o'r 3 fs out, idled and shaken up appr fnl furlong, kpt on*.
............(7 to 4 on op 2 to 1 tchd 6 to 4 on)   1
QUEENFORD BELLE 4-10-2 (3*) A Thornton, *midfield till styd on stdly frm 5 fs out, chsd wnr fnl 2 furlongs, ran on*................ (7 to 1 op 3 to 1 tchd 9 to 1)   2
2134² MIGHTY MAURICE (Ire) (bl) 5-11-0 (5*) J McCarthy, *al prmnt, led aftr 4 fs till hdd o'r 3 out, wknd appr last*.
.............(4 to 1 op 9 to 2 tchd 5 to 1)   3
2210⁸ CORPORATE IMAGE 4-10-7 (3*) S Wynne, *beh and rdn alng till styd on same pace fnl 3 fs, nvr a dngr*.
.............(25 to 1 op 16 to 1 tchd 33 to 1)   4
2176 LLAMA LADY 5-10-7 (7*) A Dowling, *in tch to hfwy*.
.... (33 to 1 op 25 to 1)   5
HIZAL 5-10-12 (7*) M Appleby, *sn rdn alng and wl beh, moderate late hdwy, no dngr*.......... (33 to 1)   6
THE LATCHIKO (Ire) 4-10-3 (7*) D Hobbs, *nvr able to chal*.
.... (8 to 1 op 12 to 1)   7
2114⁶ BELMORE CLOUD 5-10-11 (3*) R Davis, *chsd ldrs till wknd o'r 4 fs out*............ (20 to 1 op 14 to 1)   8
2269 NORTHERN SINGER 4-10-7 (3*) D Meredith, *prmnt till rdn and wknd 4 fs out*.............. (8 to 1 op 12 to 1)   9
1277 BETTY'S MATCH 5-10-7 (7*) Mr G Shenkin, *al beh, tld off*.
.... (33 to 1)   10
JOALTO 4-10-3 (7*) Miss T Honeyball, *led 4 fs, wknd quickly an wl tld off*.
............(16 to 1 op 14 to 1 tchd 20 to 1)   11
Dist: 1½l, 15l, 15l, 2½l, 6l, hd, 6l, sht-hd, dist, dist. 2m 54.60s. (11 Ran).

(David F Wilson), T Thomson Jones

THURLES (IRE) (soft (races 1,2,6,7), heavy (3,4,5))
Thursday February 10th

2547 Vista Therm Hurdle (4-y-o) £3,450 2m .... (1:45)

2099¹ NANNAKA (USA) 10-13 (3*) T P Treacy,.......... (6 to 4 fav)   1
1432⁴ WICKLOW WAY (Ire) 10-9 K F O'Brien,........... (10 to 1)   2
2349¹ CARHUE STAR (Ire) 10-10 (3*) T J O'Sullivan,.... (6 to 1)   3

494³ DRESS DANCE (Ire) 11-0 A Powell,.............. (20 to 1)   4
BLAKE'S FABLE (Ire) 9-11 (7*) J M Donnelly,...... (33 to 1)   5
2388³ ROYAL RANK (USA) 11-0 C F Swan,.............. (10 to 1)   6
2388⁹ TRIBAL MEMORIES (Ire) 10-1 (3*) C O'Brien,.... (33 to 1)   7
2349⁸ GENTLE REEF (Ire) 10-6 (3*) T J Mitchell,....... (33 to 1)   8
732 CHALLENGER ROW (Ire) 11-0 C O'Dwyer,........ (20 to 1)   9
BARLEY COURT (Ire) 10-4 (5*) P Dunne,.......... (20 to 1)   10
EMERALD BREFFNI (Ire) 10-9 H Rogers,.......... (33 to 1)   11
1911* BISSTAMI (Ire) 11-4 (7*)...................... (3 to 1)   f
TRES JOUR (Ire) 10-4 P M Verling,.............. (20 to 1)   ur
ONOMATOPOEIA (Ire) 10-9 M Duffy,.............. (8 to 1)   pu
Dist: 2l, 7l, 5l, hd. 4m 3.80s. (14 Ran).

(Mrs P Mullins), P Mullins

2548 I.N.H. Stallion Owners Novice Hurdle (6-y-o and up) £3,450 2¾m 110yds .... (2:15)

798⁶ PRECARIUM (Ire) 6-11-4 C O'Dwyer,............. (5 to 1)   1
2392⁵ IAMWHATIAM 8-11-4 S H O'Donovan,........... (5 to 2)   2
2389 COUNTERBALANCE 7-10-13 B Sheridan,....... (12 to 1)   3
2181 WILD FANTASY (Ire) 6-11-6 C F Swan,....... (11 to 8 on)   4
2389 CORRIBLOUGH (Ire) 6-11-1 (3*) C O'Brien,..... (14 to 1)   5
801⁸ HI-WAY'S GALE 7-10-8 (5*) K P Gaule,.......... (16 to 1)   6
2197⁶ PARSONS BELLE (Ire) 6-10-8 (5*) T P Rudd,.... (25 to 1)   7
2353 ASHPLANT 7-11-4 P Kavanagh,................. (10 to 1)   8
Dist: 2½l, 7l, 7l, ¾l. 5m 45.30s. (8 Ran).

(Mrs Lewis C Murdock), M F Morris

2549 P.Z. Mower E.B.F. Chase (Listed Race - Grade II) (6-y-o and up) £8,280 2½m .... (2:45)

1578 COMMERCIAL ARTIST 8-11-4 C N Bowens, *trkd ldrs, mstk 8th, prog to ld aftr 4 out, rdn betw last 2, styd on r-in*.
.... (3 to 1 fav)   1
2288⁶ HAKI SAKI 8-12-0 T Horgan, *mid-div, niggled alng tenth, prog to chal 3 out, rdn and no extr appr last*... (5 to 1)   2
2125⁶ LADY BAR 7-10-13 P M Verling, *rear, prog into 4th aftr 3 out, kpt on one pace r-in*................... (12 to 1)   3
2280⁴ HOW'S THE BOSS 8-12-0 J Magee, *wtd wth in rear, rdn 3 out, no imprsn r-in*................... (8 to 1)   4
2077 DEEP HERITAGE 8-11-11 T J Taaffe, *trkd ldrs, rdn appr 3 out, wknd*.......................... (10 to 1)   5
2077³ DESERT LORD 8-11-4 C F Swan, *rear, rdn tenth, lost tch frm 4 out*............................ (6 to 1)   6
1819 DORAN'S TOWN LAD 7-11-4 F Woods, *led or dsptd ld to 7th, led appr tenth till aftr 4 out, wkng whn f nxt*.
.... (12 to 1)   f
2159⁷ SARAEMMA 8-11-9 K F O'Brien, *dsptd ld frm 5th, led 7th till appr tenth, rdn and wknd 4 out, btn whn brght dwn nxt*........................... (10 to 1)   bd
Dist: 9l, 8l, 7l, 20l. 5m 31.90s. (8 Ran).

(Michael J O'Neill), Victor Bowens

2550 Tattersalls Mares Chase (Qualifier) (5-y-o and up) £3,105 2¼m...... (3:15)

2286 GYPSY LASS 7-11-9 T Horgan,.................. (3 to 1)   1
1112⁶ CARRIGEEN KERRIA (Ire) 6-11-2 Mr P J Healy,... (10 to 1)   2
1497 COMMANCHE NELL (Ire) 6-11-9 J F Titley,..... (5 to 2 fav)   3
2183³ TURBULENT WIND 7-11-2 C F Swan,........... (7 to 1)   4
2351⁴ MONKS AIR 7-11-2 A J O'Brien,............... (16 to 1)   5
2202⁴ PALMROCK DONNA 7-11-1 (5*) P A Roche,..... (12 to 1)   6
1851⁵ CHELSEA NATIVE 7-10-11 (5*) Susan A Finn,... (10 to 1)   7
2278 EXTRA MILE 7-11-2 S H O'Donovan,........... (12 to 1)   8
2234⁴ DELIGHTFUL CHOICE (Ire) 6-10-11 (5*) J P Broderick,
.... (9 to 1)   9
2392 PANDA (Ire) 8-10-3 (3*) T J Mitchell,.......... (8 to 1)   10
1857 GODFREYS CROSS (Ire) 6-11-2 P M Verling,.... (33 to 1)   11
2036⁸ HIGHBABS 8-11-2 C O'Dwyer,................ (10 to 1)   12
2347 COOL CARLING 7-11-2 J Magee,............... (20 to 1)   ref
DOS ADVENTICA 10-11-12 A Powell,........... (25 to 1)   pu
2277 ARDCARN GIRL 7-11-2 K F O'Brien,........... (16 to 1)   pu
Dist: Sht-hd, 1½l, 15l, 2½l. 5m 5.10s. (15 Ran).

(Mrs Riona Molony), W Harney

2551 Glacial Storm Hunters Chase (5-y-o and up) £3,450 3m............. (3:45)

ELEGANT LORD (Ire) 6-11-9⁵ Mr E Bolger,..... (3 to 1 on)   1
MATTY TYNAN 7-11-4 Mr P Fenton,........... (11 to 2)   2
TASSE DU THE 7-10-13 Mr A J Martin,......... (14 to 1)   3
TOP MINSTREL 11-11-1 (3*) Mr T Lombard,...... (6 to 1)   4
2352 TROPICAL GABRIEL (Ire) 6-11-4 Mr P J Healy,... (14 to 1)   5
LOVELY CITIZEN 11-10-13 (5*) Mr W M O'Sullivan, (12 to 1)   6
GARRYLUCAS 8-10-12¹ (7*) Mr J Lombard,..... (10 to 1)   7
BERRINGS DASHER 7-11-4 Mr P F Graffin,...... (12 to 1)   8
2352³ FLAHERTYS BEST VI 7-10-10 (3*) Miss M Olivefalk,
.... (33 to 1)   9
2352 ROSLAVAN LAD 10-11-0 (7*) Mr K Whelan,.....(20 to 1)   pu
Dist: 5l, 3½l, 15l, 10l. 6m 59.10s. (10 Ran).

(John P McManus), E Bolger

2552 Littleton Handicap Hurdle (0-130 4-y-o and up) £2,760 2m............. (4:15)

354

2232 UNCLE BABY (Ire) [-] 6-10-0 (5ᵒ) K P Gaule, ...(8 to 1) 1
2347² FINNEGANS WAKE [-] 7-10-8 C F Swan, ...(10 to 1) 2
2347ᵖ PUNTERS BAR [-] 7-10-5 (1ex) C O'Dwyer, ...(10 to 1) 3
2391³ SAM VAUGHAN (Ire) [-] 5-11-0 (5ᵒ) Mr W M O'Sullivan,
. . . . (2 to 1 fav) 4
1987ᵉ SHANNON AMBER (Ire) [-] 5-9-10 (5ᵒ) J P Broderick, (8 to 1) 5
2155ᵉ LAWYER'S BRIEF (Fr) [-] 7-10-9 L P Cusack, ...(8 to 1) 6
1977² MISS LIME [-] 7-11-1 (7ᵒ) R A Hennessy, ...(7 to 1) 7
2177ᵉ FAIRY STRIKE (Ire) [-] 5-10-4 K F O'Brien, ...(14 to 1) 8
2279⁵ SHIRWAN (Ire) [-] 5-10-2 (7ᵒ) J Kavanagh, ...(10 to 1) 9
1914 BELEEK CASTLE [-] 8-11-1 J Shortt, ...(20 to 1) 10
1610⁸ OZEYCAZEY (Ire) [-] 5-9-7 (5ᵒ) Susan A Finn, ...(20 to 1) 11
CASTLE CALL [-] 8-9-6 (3ᵒ) C O'Brien, ...(50 to 1) 12
2231ᵉ HURRICANE EDEN [-] 7-10-1 (5ᵒ) M A Davey, ...(10 to 1) f
Dist: ¾l, hd, 7l, ½l. 4m 4.80s. (13 Ran).

(N P Doyle), Patrick Joseph Flynn

2553 Horse And Jockey INH Flat Race (5-y-o and up) £2,760 2m . . . . (4:45)

2389 NINE O THREE (Ire) 5-11-4 (7ᵒ) Mr T J Murphy, ...(14 to 1) 1
RAPHAEL BODINE (Ire) 5-11-8 (3ᵒ) Mrs M Mullins,
. . . . (7 to 4 fav) 2
1986³ KEEPHINGOUGH (Ire) 5-10-13 (7ᵒ) Mr R P Burns, . .(8 to 1) 3
2289³ FLYING COLUMN 7-11-9 (5ᵒ) Mr H F Cleary, ...(7 to 2) 4
NAKURU (Ire) 5-11-6 Mr A P O'Brien, ...(6 to 1) 5
PEGUS GOLD 7-11-2 (7ᵒ) Mr J Connolly, ...(10 to 1) 6
DOUBLE SYMPHONY (Ire) 6-11-2 (7ᵒ) Mr J Dwan, (12 to 1) 7
2102⁷ DAVE FLECK (Ire) 6-11-11 (3ᵒ) Mr D Marnane, ...(12 to 1) 8
2102⁵ ALLARACKET (Ire) 5-10-13 (7ᵒ) Mr D M Fogarty, ...(8 to 1) 9
1982⁷ LIME LADY (Ire) 5-10-13 (7ᵒ) Mr M J Bowe, ...(20 to 1) 10
THE LEFT FOOTER (Ire) 5-11-4 (7ᵒ) Mr J T McNamara,
. . . .(10 to 1) 11
SERGEANT DAN (Ire) 6-11-7 (7ᵒ) Mr P O'Reilly, ...(33 to 1) 12
2203⁶ BLAIR HOUSE (Ire) 5-11-6 Mr A J Martin, ...(8 to 1) 13
MISS BERTAINE (Ire) 5-11-6 Mr P J Healy, ...(14 to 1) 14
2394 WHOTHATIS 8-11-2 (7ᵒ) Mr A F Doherty, ...(14 to 1) 15
1501 BAUNFAUN RUN (Ire) 6-11-4 (5ᵒ) Mr J P Berry, ...(33 to 1) 16
TENPENCE PRINCESS (Ire) 5-11-3 (3ᵒ) Miss M Olivefalk,
. . . .(14 to 1) 17
947ᵖ SNULL SHELL (Ire) 5-11-3 (3ᵒ) Mrs J M Mullins, ...(8 to 1) 18
2039 THE DEFENDER (Ire) 5-11-11⁷ (7ᵒ) Mr J A Waldron, (20 to 1) 19
73⁶ RIGHT AND REASON (Ire) 5-10-13 (7ᵒ) Mr J P Codd,
. . . .(16 to 1) 20
1403 MONALEE GALE (Ire) 6-11-11 (3ᵒ) Mr A R Coonan, (20 to 1) 21
Dist: Nk, hd, 11l, 7l. 4m 3.04s. (21 Ran).

(Michael A Young), Michael Hourigan

WINCANTON (good to soft)
Thursday February 10th
Going Correction: PLUS 0.65 sec. per fur. (races 1,3,-5,7), PLUS 1.25 (2,4,6)

2554 Gillingham Conditional Jockeys' Handicap Hurdle (0-130 4-y-o and up) £2,322 2m . . . . (1:30)

1414³ AAL EL AAL [90] 7-9-10 (4ᵒ) N Parker, in tch, hdwy to track
ldrs 4th, chlgd gng wl 2 out, sn led, cmftbly.
. . . .(4 to 1 op 5 to 1 tchd 11 to 2 and 7 to 2) 1
2366ᵉ JUMP START [94] 7-10-4 A Thornton, hld up, pushed alng
to cl aftr 3 out, hrd rdn nxt, ran on appr last, not rch
wnr . . . .(13 to 8 fav op 7 to 4) 2
2306ᵉ CABIN HILL [103] 8-10-6 (7ᵒ) P Melia, trkd ldrs, slight ld 2
out, sn hdd, one pace . . . .(7 to 2 tchd 4 to 1) 3
2463³ STYLUS [114] 5-11-6 (4ᵒ) R Massey, beh, hdwy to chase
ldrs 3 out, ev ch whn slpd nxt, sn one pace.
. . . .(6 to 1 op 5 to 1 tchd 13 to 2) 4
2019⁵ CORRIN HILL [107] 8-7-11-3 W Marston, led, sn clr, hdd 2
out, soon wknd . . . .(9 to 1 op 7 to 1 tchd 10 to 1) 5
2142⁹ MARIOLINO [90] 7-9-10 (4ᵒ) M Moran, effrt and mstk 3 out,
wknd . . . .(20 to 1 op 16 to 1) 6
ECOSSAIS DANSEUR (USA) [93] (bl) 8-9-13 (4ᵒ) L Reynolds,
chsd ldr to 4th, sn wknd . . . .(50 to 1 op 25 to 1) 7
HOME COUNTY [90] 12-10-0 A Procter, jmpd slwly 1st, al
beh . . . .(100 to 1 op 33 to 1) 8
Dist: 8l, 8l, 2l, 6l, 5l, dist. 2m 53.20s. (8 Ran).
SR: 34/30/31/40/27/5/-/-/

(Mrs Christine Hake), P J Hobbs

2555 Times 'Rising Stars' Hunters' Chase Qualifier (6,7,8-y-o) £1,970 3m 1f 110yds. . . . . (2:00)

SUNNY MOUNT 8-11-12 Mr J Greenall, mstks, in tch, trkd
ldrs tenth, hit 14th, chasing lder whn hit 4 out, mistake
nxt, led 2 out, pushed out . . . . .(11 to 10 fav tchd 5 to 4) 1
MR GOLIGHTLY 7-11-5 (7ᵒ) Miss J Cobden, led to second,
str hold, chlgd 7th, led 9th, hit 3 out, hdd nxt, styd on.
. . . .(7 to 2) 2
UPHAM CLOSE 8-11-0 (7ᵒ) Miss A Turner, beh, lost tch
12th, hdwy 4 out, chasing ldrs whn hit 2 out, not
quicken . . . .(25 to 1 op 12 to 1) 3
ZORRO'S MARK 7-11-5 (7ᵒ) Mr J Dufosee, beh most of
way, lost tch 14th . . . .(25 to 1 op 14 to 1) 4

FLAME O'FRENSI 8-11-0 (7ᵒ) Miss J Cumings, chsd ldrs,
mstk and wknd 15th, hit nxt . . . .(3 to 1 op 4 to 1) 5
SAGARO SUN 8-11-5 (7ᵒ) Miss C Thomas, led second, hit
9th and hdd, chlgd 11th to nxt, hit 17th, wknd, no ch
whn mstk and uns rdr 2 out . . . . . .(66 to 1 op 33 to 1) ur
OVER THE EDGE 8-12-5 (7ᵒ) Mr S Sporborg, lost tch 14th,
no ch whn ran out last . . . .(9 to 2 op 3 to 1) ro
Dist: 2½l, 8l, 20l, 5l. 7m 0.40s. a 44.40s (7 Ran).

(J E Greenall), Miss C Saunders

2556 Premiere 'National Hunt' Auction Novices' Hurdle Guaranteed minimum value £17500 (5,6,7-y-o) £11,200 2m . . . . (2:30)

2014⁵ GOSPEL (Ire) 5-10-10 C Llewellyn, chsd ldrs, rdn to hold pl
2 out, str chal last, ran on wl to ld r-in.
. . . .(11 to 1 op 7 to 1) 1
1695⁴ BOND JNR (Ire) 5-11-2 G Bradley, wth ldr, ev ch 2 out till
outpcd r-in . . . .(7 to 2 op 3 to 1 tchd 4 to 1) 2
2303² THE FROG PRINCE 6-11-1 R Supple, hdwy 5th, ran
on to take narrow ld last, hdd r-in, sn one pace.
. . . .(7 to 1 op 6 to 1) 3
2147³ CONEY ROAD 5-11-10 P Holley, hld up near, hdwy 3 out,
feeling to do appr nxt, rdn and ran on wl approaching
last . . . .(8 to 1 tchd 10 to 1) 4
1882ᵉ OLD BRIDGE (Ire) 5-10-3 S McNeill, trkd ldrs, hit 4th, led 2
out to last, sn btn . . .(6 to 4 fav op 2 to 1 tchd 9 to 4) 5
2315 KING'S MAVERICK (Ire) 6-11-1 R Dunwoody, beh, hit 5th,
in tch appr 2 out, sn btn . . . .(16 to 1 op 8 to 1) 6
1515ᵉ SPIRIT IN THE NITE (Ire) 5-11-7 D Murphy, led to 2 out, cl
5th whn f last . . . .(7 to 1 op 4 to 1) f
1878 RUSTIC FLIGHT 7-10-12 M A Fitzgerald, al beh, rdn and
wknd 3 out, tld off whn pld up bef last.
. . . .(66 to 1 op 33 to 1) pu
Dist: 1½l, 2½l, nk, 2½l, 30l. 3m 58.30s. a 21.30s (8 Ran).

(Miss J K Powell), N A Twiston-Davies

2557 Racing In Wessex Chase (5-y-o and up) £5,247 2m 5f . . . . (3:00)

1439⁷ GARRISON SAVANNAH 11-11-2 G Bradley, led second,
jmpd wl, made rst, ran on well r-in.
. . . .(7 to 2 op 3 to 1 tchd 4 to 1) 1
2377⁴ RYDE AGAIN 11-11-10 D Murphy, 4th till wnt 3rd 13th, hit
four out, chsd wnr frm 2 out, eased whn hld nr finish.
. . . .(4 to 1 op 11 to 4) 2
2377ᵉ WATERLOO BOY 11-12-0 R Dunwoody, led to second, trkd
wnr, chlgd 3 out, rdn and hit nxt, sn btn.
. . . .(9 to 4 on op Evens) 3
1887² SMARTIE EXPRESS 12-11-6 M A FitzGerald, 3rd till wknd
13th . . . .(100 to 1 op 33 to 1 tchd 12 to 1) 4
2406⁴ LA CERISE 11-11-6 M Moran, al tld off.
. . . .(100 to 1 op 50 to 1) 5
Dist: 3l, 5l, 20l, dist. 5m 34.50s. a 28.50s (5 Ran).
SR: 66/71/70/42/-/

(Autofour Engineering), Mrs J Pitman

2558 Hoechst Panacur EBF Mares 'National Hunt' Novices' Hurdle Qualifier (5-y-o and up) £2,784 2¾m . . . . (3:30)

1536² BRIEF GALE 7-11-0 D Murphy, al in tch gng wl, improved
7th, led appr 2 out, easily . . . .(11 to 10 on op Evens) 1
883² CANAL STREET 5-10-7 M Hourigan, mid-div, hdwy 7th,
chsd wnr aftr 2 out, no imprsn.
. . . .(5 to 1 op 6 to 1 tchd 8 to 1) 2
2141 SPREAD YOUR WINGS (Ire) 6-10-7 P Holley, prmnt, led 5th
till appr 2 out, wknd approaching last.
. . . .(9 to 1 op 10 to 1 tchd 14 to 1) 3
FOREST PRIDE (Ire) 5-10-7 N Williamson, beh, hdwy 8th,
rdn and no imprsn appr 2 out.
. . . .(8 to 1 op 10 to 1 tchd 14 to 1) 4
2146 GLADYS EMMANUEL 7-10-7 S Burrough, nvr rch ldrs.
. . . .(100 to 1 op 66 to 1) 5
1974³ LAY IT OFF (Ire) 5-10-7 L Harvey, effrt 6th, sn wknd.
. . . .(25 to 1 op 20 to 1 tchd 33 to 1) 6
2141 QUAGO 6-10-7 J Railton, prmnt to 6th.
. . . .(66 to 1 op 50 to 1) 7
1871⁸ SOLO GIRL (Ire) 5-10-7 S McNeill, al beh.
. . . .(66 to 1 op 33 to 1) 8
2018³ ALICE SPRINGS 5-10-11ᵉ M T Greed, beh most of way.
. . . .(100 to 1 op 50 to 1) 9
2187ᵉ FORT RANK 7-11-0 J Frost, f second. (25 to 1 op 14 to 1) f
2344³ KEMMY DARLING 7-10-7 M Ahern, brght dwn second.
. . . .(100 to 1) bd
LADY CAROTINO 10-10-7 B Clifford, led to 5th, wknd nxt,
pld up bef 7th . . . .(100 to 1) pu
1196⁴ G'IME A BUZZ 6-10-7 R Dunwoody, prmnt till wknd
quickly 7th, tld off whn pld up bef 3 out.
. . . .(10 to 1 op 12 to 1 tchd 14 to 1) pu
CLOUD CUCKOO 6-10-7 G Bradley, al beh, tld off whn
pld up bef 2 out . . . .(33 to 1 op 16 to 1) pu
2204⁵ RAISIN TURF (Ire) 5-10-7 W Marston, prmnt, rdn 7th,
wknd 3 out, tld off whn pld up bef last.
. . . .(20 to 1 op 14 to 1) pu
2419ᵉ SLIEVE LEAGUE (Ire) 5-10-7 R Bellamy, beh 5th, tld off
whn pld up bef 2 out . . . .(66 to 1 op 50 to 1) pu

2404 ORCHESTRATED CHAOS (Ire) 5-10-2 (5*) S Curran, *chsd ldrs to 6th, tld off whn pld up bef 2 out......* (100 to 1) pu
TANDEM 6-10-7 M A FitzGerald, *in tch to 7th, tld off whn pld up bef last....................* (33 to 1 op 20 to 1) pu
Dist: 12l, 15l, 1l, 30l, 1l, 4l, 3½l, ½l. 5m 35.30s. a 29.30s (18 Ran).
(Miss Carrie Zetter), J T Gifford

2559 Weatherbys 'Newcomers' Series Novices' Chase (5-y-o and up) £3,288 3m 1f 110yds.....................(4:00)

2298⁶ SNOWY LANE (Ire) 4-11-4 R Dunwoody, *dsptd ld, led 5th, jmpd slwly 15th, hdd nxt, led 4 out to next, led last, all out....................*(11 to 0 on 5 to 4) 1
2017³ RAMPOLDI (USA) (bl) 7-11-4 G Bradley, *dsptd ld to 5th, chsd wnr, led 16th to 4 out, led 3 out to last, ran on.*
....................(9 to 4 op 7 to 4) 2
2264 YOUNG BRAVE 8-11-4 S Earle, *in tch, mstk tenth, hdwy to track ldrs 13th, lost touch 16th...* (9 to 1 op 10 to 1) 3
2141 TRIMAGE (Ire) 6-11-4 C Llewellyn, *chsd ldrs, mstk 4th, wknd 14th, tld off.....*(10 to 1 op 8 to 1 tchd 12 to 1) 4
2303 OURPALWENTY 7-11-4 W Marston, *f 1st.*
....................(66 to 1 op 50 to 1 tchd 100 to 1) f
2362³ DRAW LOTS 10-10-11 (7*) T Thompson, *mstk and uns rdr*
....................(16 to 1 op 8 to 1) ur
2399⁴ ARCTICFLOW (USA) (bl) 9-11-4 P Holley, *hit second, tld off nxt, mstk 4th, pld up bef next...* (100 to 1 op 50 to 1) pu
2362 MAXXUM EXPRESS (Ire) 6-11-4 M A FitzGerald, *hit second, al beh, lost tch 13th, tld off whn pld up bef 4 out.*
....................(50 to 1 op 25 to 1) pu
Dist: ¾l, dist, dist. 6m 57.90s. a 41.90s (8 Ran).
(M & N Plant Ltd), M C Pipe

2560 Wincanton Open National Hunt Flat Race (4,5,6-y-o) £1,998 2m......(4:30)

SPARKLING CONE 5-11-3 R Dunwoody, *al tracking ldrs, led ins fnl 3 fs, wnt clr frm 2 out.*
....................(8 to 1 op 5 to 1 tchd 9 to 1) 1
2176* TIP THE DOVE 5-10-12 (7*) Mr G Hogan, *led till ins fnl 3 fs, kpt on, no ch wth wnr.*
....................(13 to 8 fav op 3 to 1 tchd 4 to 1) 2
BOYFRIEND 4-10-7 P Holley, *beh, hdwy 6 fs out, one pace 3 out........................* (5 to 1) 3
12775 PENNYMOOR PRINCE 5-10-10 (7*) R Darke, *hdwy 7 fs out, rdn and no imprsn on ldrs frm 3 out.*
....................(25 to 1 op 10 to 1) 4
2176⁴ TARTAN MOSS (Ire) 5-10-5 (7*) N Parker, *chsd ldrs, rdn and hng rght frm o'r 2 fs out.*
....................(6 to 1 op 5 to 1 tchd 13 to 2) 5
2021³ BOURNEL 6-10-5 (7*) Mr Richard White, *in tch, hdwy 6 fs out, rdn and wknd 3 out.............* (25 to 1 op 14 to 1) 6
RIVER LEVEN 5-11-3 J Railton, *prmnt 9 fs.*
....................(25 to 1 op 25 to 1) 7
2339⁴ WHERE'S WILLIE (Fr) 5-10-12 (5*) T Jenks, *hdwy 7 fs out, wknd 4 out.............*(4 to 1 op 7 to 2 tchd 9 to 2) 8
PERSISTENT GUNNER 4-10-2 I Lawrence, *al beh.*
....................(11 to 1 op 20 to 1 tchd 9 to 1) 9
CHANCE DE LA VIE 5-10-10 (7*) Pat Thompson, *rdn and some hdwy 7 fs out, sn wknd......* (50 to 1 op 33 to 1) 10
778 COUNTRY LORD 5-11-3 G Bradley, *beh till steady hdwy 6 fs out, wknd 4 out..............*(12 to 1 op 8 to 1) 11
COUNTRY KEEPER 6-11-3 M A FitzGerald, *chsd ldrs ten fs.*
....................(25 to 1 op 20 to 1) 12
2210⁹ DIAMOND FLIER (Ire) 5-11-3 Mr J M Pritchard, *nvr better than mid-div....................*(20 to 1 op 10 to 1) 13
2176 DUNNICKS COUNTRY 4-10-2 C Maude, *al beh.*
....................(66 to 1 op 33 to 1) 14
PAPRIKA (Ire) 5-10-12 S McNeill, *al beh.*
....................(50 to 1 op 25 to 1) 15
2210 PINBER 6-10-5 (7*) Mr S Mulcaire, *sn beh.*
....................(66 to 1 op 50 to 1) 16
SALTHORSE DELIGHT 6-10-12 W Marston, *pld hrd, chsd ldr 5 fs, wknd rpdly hfwy.........* (50 to 1 op 33 to 1) 17
Dist: 8l, 1½l, 20l, 2l, 7l, 1½l, ¾l, 4l, 5l, 2½l. 3m 46.00s. (17 Ran).
(Mrs M Horton), M C Pipe

CATTERICK (good to soft)
Friday February 11th
Going Correction: PLUS 0.47 sec. per fur.

2561 Great Catterick Racing Game Gamble Novices' Hurdle (5-y-o and up) £2,085 3m 1f 110yds.................(2:15)

2322⁶ PORTONIA 10-10-13 P Niven, *pld hrd, al prmnt, effrt 2 out, rdn to ld appr last, ran on wl.* (12 to 1 op 8 to 1) 1
2220* COQUI LANE 7-11-4 B Storey, *led, rdn appr 2 out, hdd bef last, hit last, kpt on....................*(3 to 1 op 5 to 2) 2
1475⁵ FARMER'S CROSS 10-11-4 Mrs A Farrell, *pld hrd, al prmnt, effrt and ev ch 2 out, sn rdn and wknd appr last....................*(12 to 1 op 16 to 1) 3
2358⁷ KILMINFOYLE 7-10-12 R Hodge, *hld up, hdwy hfwy, effrt to chase ldrs and hit 2 out, sn one pace.*
....................(33 to 1 op 25 to 1) 4

2276⁵ ROYAL SURPRISE 7-10-12 Miss P Robson, *in tch till rdn alng and wknd hfwy, sn wl beh.* (100 to 1 op 33 to 1) 5
1574⁴ SPARROW HALL 7-11-4 M Dwyer, *trkd ldrs, gd hdwy hfwy, cl up whn blun 8th, not reco'r.*
....................(6 to 1 op 11 to 2) 6
2239² BISHOPS CASTLE (Ire) 6-10-12 A Dobbin, *hld up, steady hdwy hfwy, rdn 4 out and sn wknd.*
....................(14 to 1 op 16 to 1 tchd 20 to 1) 7
POLLITTS PRIDE 8-10-7 A Mulholland, *pld hrd, prmnt till wknd hfwy, beh whn f 4 out.....* (100 to 1 op 66 to 1) f
1745 SOPHINI 6-10-7 R Garritty, *al rear, beh whn pld up bef 8th....................*(100 to 1 op 50 to 1) pu
2104² SAVOY 7-11-4 N Doughty, *prmnt till pld up bef 4 out, lme.*
....................(10 to 1 on tchd Evens) pu
2140⁶ TIDERUNNER (Ire) 6-10-12 T Reed, *al rear, wl beh whn pld up bef 2 out....................*(16 to 1 tchd 20 to 1) pu
Dist: 3½l, 10l, 5l, 12l, 10l, 30l. 6m 32.60s. a 31.60s (11 Ran).

2562 Great Value Catterick Club 1994 Handicap Chase (0-105 5-y-o and up) £2,476 3m 1f 110yds.................(2:45)

2410* CHOCTAW [101] 10-11-11 (6ex) C Hawkins, *cl up, led tenth, rdn 3 out, hit nxt, kpt on.*
....................(100 to 30 op 3 to 1 tchd 7 to 2) 1
2253⁵ HEAVENLY CITIZEN (Ire) [90] 6-11-0 R Garritty, *in tch, reminders 11th, rdn alng to chase wnr 5 out, kpt on one pace and pres appr last.........*(5 to 2 fav op 7 to 2) 2
2242* TIM SOLDIER (Fr) [96] 7-11-6 D Murphy, *hld up in tch, effrt and hdwy 3 out and sn ev ch, rdn nxt and one pace.*
....................(9 to 2 op 4 to 1) 3
2151 CHOICE CHALLENGE [98] 11-11-3 (5*) S Lyons, *prmnt, mstks, blun baldy and rdr lost irons 7 out, wnt reco'r.*
....................(11 to 2 op 4 to 1 tchd 6 to 1) 4
2370² GREY MINSTREL [93] 10-11-3 B Storey, *in tch, hdwy 12th, blun 4 out and sn wknd, collapsed aftr race, dead.*
....................(5 to 1 op 4 to 1) 5
WHITWOOD [104] 9-12-0 P Niven, *led, hdd tenth, wknd quickly and pld up bef 12th.*
....................(8 to 1 op 7 to 1 tchd 9 to 1) pu
Dist: 2l, 7l, 10l, 8l. 6m 47.10s. a 32.10s (6 Ran).
(J N Yeadon), P Beaumont

2563 Hawk Handicap Chase (0-110 5-y-o and up) £2,611 2m.............(3:15)

2412* MILITARY HONOUR [96] (bl) 9-11-0 (6ex) Mr S Swiers, *chsd ldr, led aftr 4 out, clr 2 out, styd on wl.*
....................(3 to 1 op 5 to 2) 1
2151⁴ KIND'A SMART [104] 9-11-8 A S Smith, *hld up and beh, gd hdwy appr 3 out, rdn nxt and kpt on.........*(7 to 2) 2
2412³ TRESIDDER [109] 12-11-13 R Garritty, *hld up, gd hdwy hfwy, effrt 3 out, rdn nxt and sn one pace.*
....................(9 to 4 fav op 5 to 2 tchd 11 to 4) 3
1656³ VULRORY'S CLOWN [82] 16-10-0 M Brennan, *led, hdd aftr 4 out, sn one pace.............* (9 to 1 op 7 to 1) 4
2272 TERRIBLE GEL (Fr) [110] 9-12-0 P Niven, *chsd ldrs, hit 5th, sn rdn and beh frm 5 out.*
....................(100 to 30 op 5 to 2 tchd 7 to 2) 5
2436⁸ BAILYBELL [93] 9-10-1* (5*) P Williams, *chsd ldrs, mstk 5th, sn rdn alng and beh........*(50 to 1 op 66 to 1) 6
Dist: 8l, 5l, 10l, 1½l, 7l. 4m 1.40s. a 12.40s (6 Ran).
SR: 37/37/37/-/26/-/
(J E Swiers), J E Swiers

2564 Lightning Novices' Hurdle (4-y-o) £2,249 2m.....................(3:45)

2478² DARING PAST 10-12 P Niven, *chsd ldrs, hdwy to ld 4 out, rdn clr 2 out, cmftbly.........*(5 to 1 op 7 to 2) 1
1454³ CALL MY GUEST (Ire) 10-12 M Dwyer, *in tch, hdwy appr 3 out, chsd wnr frm nxt, sn rdn and no imprsn.*
....................(9 to 2 op 4 to 1 tchd 7 to 2) 2
2241⁴ STAR RAGE (Ire) 10-5 (7*) J Driscoll, *beh, steady hdwy 3 out, rdn and styd on frm nxt......* (12 to 1 op 10 to 1) 3
2381⁴ PRIMO FIGLIO (bl) 10-9 (3*) A Thornton, *led, rdn and hdd 4th, grad wknd frm 3 out.....* (20 to 1 op 25 to 1) 4
2422* FRET (USA) 11-1 (3*) N Bentley, *mid-div, effrt and some hdwy appr 3 out, sn rdn and btn bef nxt.*
....................(9 to 1 op 7 to 1) 5
1920 CIVIL LAW (Ire) 10-12 C Hawkins, *beh till styd on appr 2 out, nvr dngrs..................*(16 to 1) 6
2381⁵ MAMARA REEF 10-2 (5*) P Waggott, *in tch, rdn alng hfwy, one pace 3 out..............* (25 to 1 op 33 to 1) 7
BLUE GROTTO (Ire) 10-12 D Murphy, *cl up pulling hrd, effrt appr 3 out, sn rdn and btn bef nxt.*
....................(9 to 4 fav op 3 to 1 tchd 4 to 1) 8
1569⁷ ZAAHEYAH (USA) 10-2 (5*) S Lyons, *al rear.*
....................(50 to 1 op 25 to 1) 9
1483⁵ VAIGLY SUNTHYME 10-12 N Smith, *cl up, rdn appr 2 out and sn wknd.....................* (25 to 1) 10
2241 PREMIER STAR 10-12 T Reed, *al rear...........*(50 to 1) 11
2241¹⁹ FRIENDLY KNIGHT 10-12 A Dobbin, *cl up, led 4th to nxt, sn rdn and wknd..................*(66 to 1 op 50 to 1) 12
2135 BERING ISLAND (USA) 10-12 L Wyer, *prmnt till rdn and wknd bef 3 out....................*(25 to 1) 13
2405 GOLDEN SAVANNAH 11-4 G Bradley, *jmpd lft, al beh.*
....................(33 to 1 op 25 to 1) 14

2387 LINGCOOL 10-7 R Garritty, *al beh.* (100 to 1 op 50 to 1) 15
2381³ DIWALI DANCER 11-4 N Mann, *mid-div, effrt and rdn alng 3 out, no hdwy and f 2 out*.....(4 to 1 op 5 to 2) f
Dist: 10l, 3l, 4l, 1½l, 6l, 1½l, sht-hd, 5l, ½l, 1½l. 3m 54.20s. a 13.20s (16 Ran).
SR: 27/17/14/10/14/2/ (John A Petty), M D Hammond

2565 Pantha Novices' Chase (5-y-o and up) £2,306 2m 3f................... (4:15)

1477 EQUINOCTIAL 9-11-3 K Jones, *al prmnt, effrt and hdwy to ld appr 3 out, rdn last, ran on wl flt.* ....(6 to 1 op 5 to 1) 1
HAGAR 5-10-7 B Storey, *jmpd slow early and sn wl beh, hdwy 4 out, styd on well appr last, rdn and not rch wnr approaching flt*..................(16 to 1 op 12 to 1) 2
2251 HIGHLANDMAN 8-11-3 A Dobbin, *mid-div, effrt and rdn 4 out, plugged on one pace frm nxt*....(5 to 1 op 7 to 2) 3
768* KEEP BIDDING 8-11-10 T Reed, *cl up, led 9th till appr 3 out, second and btn whn blun 2 out.* ....(13 to 8 fav op 2 to 1 tchd 9 to 4) 4
2357⁴ EMERALD GEM 8-11-3 M Brennan, *not fluent, in tch, effrt and some hdwy hfwy, rdn appr 3 out and sn btn.* ....(9 to 1 op 8 to 1 tchd 10 to 1) 5
2436 GRAZEMBER 7-11-3 L Wyer, *led, hdd 9th, rdn and blun badly 3 out, sn wknd*...............(5 to 1 op 4 to 1) 6
2251⁶ MACCONACHIE 7-11-3 A Merrigan, *hld up, effrt and some hdwy 4 out, sn btn*.................(8 to 1 op 6 to 1) 7
2325⁶ EBRO 8-11-12 (5*) F Perratt, *not jump wl, sn beh and tld off frm hfwy*....................(10 to 1 op 7 to 1) 8
Dist: 3½l, 8l, 5l, 1½l, 3l, 25l, 15l. 4m 59.80s. (8 Ran).
(Norman Miller), N Miller

2566 Cobra Handicap Hurdle (0-120 4-y-o and up) £2,469 2m 3f........... (4:45)

1619 ONLY A ROSE [97] 5-10-11 D Wilkinson, *mid-div, hdwy whn blun badly and lost pl 4 out, sn drvn alng, headway appr last, str run flt, led nr finish.* ....(7 to 1 tchd 8 to 1) 1
2371⁴ WAKE UP [90] 7-10-4 G Bradley, *mstk 1st, sn tracking ldrs, effrt 2 out, rdn to chal last, soon led, hdd and no extr nr finish*...................(5 to 1 tchd 11 to 2) 2
2119⁵ GYMCRAK SOVEREIGN [107] 6-11-7 R Marley, *led to 5th, led ag'n 3 out, rdn nxt, hdd and no extr flt.* ....(9 to 1 op 7 to 1 tchd 10 to 1) 3
2322³ THE GREEN FOOL [108] 7-11-8 A Dobbin, *al prmnt, effrt appr 2 out and ev ch till rdn and no extr approaching last*...(8 to 1) 4
2413² SHAHGRAM (Ire) [88] 6-10-2 Mrs A Farrell, *mid-div, hdwy 4 out, rdn appr 2 out and sn one pace.* ....(15 to 8 fav op 7 to 4 tchd 2 to 1) 5
2371⁷ CANDID LAD [89] 7-10-3 C Dennis, *chsd ldrs, led 5th, hdd 3 out and grad wknd frm nxt*................(25 to 1) 6
2070⁶ CURTAIN FACTORY [86] 5-10-0 L Wyer, *al rear.* ....(20 to 1 op 14 to 1) 7
2385⁹ REVE DE VALSE (USA) [114] 7-11-9 (5*) P Waggott, *cl up, rdn 3 out and sn wknd*..........(12 to 1 tchd 14 to 1) 8
MARSH'S LAW [93] 7-10-7 M Brennan, *chsd ldrs, rdn and mstk 4 out, sn wknd*...(10 to 1 op 8 to 1 tchd 12 to 1) 9
2070⁸ RICHARDSON [100] 7-11-0 M Dwyer, *al rear, scrubbed alng hfwy, no hdwy*..............(6 to 1 op 4 to 1) 10
2254 STAGS FELL [86] 9-9-11 (3*) N Bentley, *in tch, rdn 4 out and sn wknd*.....................(20 to 1 op 16 to 1) 11
Dist: Nk, 2½l, hd, 3l, 12l, ½l, 4l, ¾l. 4m 42.50s. (11 Ran).
(Guy Reed), C W Thornton

NEWBURY (heavy)
Friday February 11th
Going Correction: PLUS 1.40 sec. per fur.

2567 Aldermaston Novices' Chase (5-y-o and up) £3,590 2m 1f........... (2:00)

2319* CABOCHON 7-11-8 J Frost, *mstks, trkd ldr, hit second, led 8th, hdd and hit nxt, quickened to chal last, sn led, all out*....................(6 to 1 on tchd 5 to 1 on) 1
1691 BLACK CHURCH 8-11-4 R Dunwoody, *led to 8th, led nxt, rdn and hdd sn aftr last, pressed wnr to line.* ....(8 to 1 op 6 to 1) 2
GROOMSMAN 8-11-4 W Humphreys, *al last, blun and lost pl 7th, effrt appr 4 out, btn whn blunded 2 out, tld off.* ....(11 to 1 op 6 to 1 tchd 12 to 1) 3
Dist: 1l, dist. 4m 34.30s. a 33.30s (3 Ran).
(Jack Joseph), R G Frost

2568 Stroud Green Hurdle (4-y-o) £4,875 2m 110yds........................ (2:30)

1880* MYSILV 11-0 A Maguire, *made all, drw clr 3 out, eased r-in, canter.* (7 to 1 on op 6 to 1 on tchd 11 to 2 on) 1
2169³ BURNT IMP (USA) 11-5 J Callaghan, *wnt second appr second, ev ch 3 out, rdn and sn btn.* ....(8 to 1 op 4 to 1 tchd 9 to 1) 2
1880 GRAND APPLAUSE (Ire) 11-0 D Gallagher, *trkd wnr till appr second, mstk nxt, rdn and btn whn f 3 out, rmntd to finish*.........................(12 to 1 op 6 to 1) 3
Dist: 7l, dist. 4m 16.00s. a 27.00s (3 Ran).
SR: 46/44/-/ (Million In Mind Partnership (3)), D Nicholson

2569 Arkell Brewery Handicap Chase (0-135 5-y-o and up) £4,012 2m 1f (3:00)

1294³ DIS TRAIN [130] 10-12-0 J Osborne, *jmpd wl, made all, drw clr frm 2 out, cmftbly.* ....(5 to 1 op 4 to 1 tchd 11 to 2) 1
2397⁴ MR FELIX [102] 8-10-0 A Maguire, *rcd keenly, chsd wnr frm 7th to 2 out, rallied to go second ag'n last.* ....(9 to 2 op 5 to 1 tchd 6 to 1 and 4 to 1) 2
2481³ ALAN BALL [108] 8-10-6 M A FitzGerald, *chsd wnr to 7th, sn last, rdn 3 out, kpt on one pace.* ....(6 to 1 op 9 to 2 tchd 13 to 2) 3
2359* RODEO STAR (USA) [120] 8-11-4 G McCourt, *outpcd in rear, hdwy 7th, mstk 3 out, wnt second nxt, rdn and wknd appr last.* ....(13 to 8 on op 9 to 4 on tchd 6 to 4 on) 4
Dist: 5l, 4l, 6l. 4m 32.50s. a 31.50s (4 Ran).
SR: 23/ (M L Oberstein), S E Sherwood

2570 Charles Higgins Memorial Foxhunters' Cup Hunters' Chase (5-y-o and up) £2,304 2½m................ (3:30)

2482² DUNCAN 9-11-13 (7*) Mr B Pollock, *al in tch, wnt second 11th, led 4 out, lft clr last, fnshd tired.* ....(7 to 2 op 3 to 1 tchd 9 to 2) 1
MINSTREL MAN 10-11-13 (7*) Mr T McCarthy, *trkd ldr frm 7th, ev ch 4 out, sn wknd, lft poor second at last.* ....(5 to 1 tchd 6 to 1) 2
ROYAL PAVILION 11-11-9 (7*) Mr C Gordon, *sn trkd ldr, wknd 11th, no ch aftr.* (10 to 1 op 8 to 1 tchd 12 to 1) 3
SONNENDEW 11-11-4 (7*) Mr P Bull, *al beh, tld off 8th.* ....(50 to 1 tchd 66 to 1) 4
WILD ILLUSION 10-11-9 (7*) Mr J Trice-Rolph, *mstks in rear, hdwy 11th, disputing ld whn f 4 out.* ....(6 to 5 on op 11 to 10 tchd 5 to 4 on) f
BEE GARDEN (bl) 13-12-1 (5*) Miss P Curling, *led to 4 out, wkng whn blun nxt, poor second when refused last.* ....(7 to 1 op 5 to 1 tchd 8 to 1) ref
Dist: 25l, 1½l, dist. 5m 53.70s. a 63.70s (6 Ran).
(C R Saunders), Miss C Saunders

2571 Cricklade Handicap Hurdle (5-y-o and up) £3,496 2m 5f............... (4:00)

2475⁴ MANEREE [110] 7-10-11 R Campbell, *trkd ldr, al gng wl, led 2 out, pushed out r-in*..... (2 to 1 fav tchd 9 to 4) 1
594² MYHAMET [103] 7-10-4 A Maguire, *hld up early, sn trkd ldrs, outpcd 2 out, rallied and ran on wl frm last.* ....(100 to 30 op 3 to 1 tchd 4 to 1) 2
ROBINGO (Ire) [126] (bl) 5-11-13 D Gallagher, *hld up rear, hdwy appr 3 out, rdn and ev ch last, kpt on one pace.* ....(10 to 1 op 8 to 1 tchd 12 to 1) 3
2267⁴ ZAMIRAH (Ire) [119] 5-11-6 C Llewellyn, *set steady pace, hit 6th, hdd 2 out, ev ch last, wknd r-in.* ....(4 to 1 op 3 to 1) 4
2247⁸ KAYTAK (Fr) [110] (bl) 7-10-11 M A FitzGerald, *trkd ldrs, hit 4th, lost tch appr 3 out, tld off.* ....(11 to 4 op 3 to 1 tchd 5 to 2) 5
Dist: 2l, 1½l, ½l, 25l. 5m 36.00s. a 43.00s (5 Ran).
(M Tabor), N A Callaghan

2572 February 'National Hunt' Novices' Hurdle (4-y-o and up) £3,470 2m 5f ....(4:30)

2147⁸ FRIENDLY FELLOW 5-11-10 P Holley, *hld up, hdwy aftr 4th, rdn to ld last, ran on wl*.........(8 to 1 op 6 to 1) 1
2327⁷ GREENHIL TARE AWAY 6-11-6 M Hourigan, *chsd ldr, mstk 6th, led 3 out, mistake and hdd last, one pace aftr.* ....(50 to 1 op 33 to 1 tchd 66 to 1) 2
1935* WELSH LUSTRE (Ire) 5-11-9 A Maguire, *hld up, hdwy 6th, ev ch 3 out, rdn and wknd appr last.* ....(13 to 8 op 6 to 4 tchd 15 to 8) 3
1871* HOLD YOUR RANKS 7-11-10 J Frost, *pld hrd, led to 3 out, sn wknd*...............(5 to 1 op 7 to 1 tchd 8 to 1) 4
1509⁷ BALLYMGYR (Ire) 5-11-6 M Perrett, *al beh, tld off whn blun 3 out*...............(50 to 1 op 33 to 1 tchd 66 to 1) 5
1490⁹ PHIL'S DREAM 6-11-6 I Lawrence, *mstks in rear, beh 6th, tld off*..............(14 to 1 op 10 to 1 tchd 16 to 1) 6
1953² WINNOWING (Ire) 6-11-5 J Osborne, *trkd ldrs frm 4th, chalg whn f 2 out.* (11 to 8 fav op 5 to 4 tchd 13 to 8) f
2404 PROFESSOR LONGHAIR 7-11-6 N Williamson, *trkd ldrs, blun 4th, sn beh, tld off whn pld up bef 3 out.* ....(50 to 1 op 25 to 1 tchd 66 to 1) pu
Dist: 3½l, 7l, 30l, 25l, 2½l. 5m 32.60s. a 39.60s (8 Ran).
(The Radio Three), D R C Elsworth

AYR (good to soft)
Saturday February 12th
Going Correction: PLUS 1.05 sec. per fur. (races 1,3,6), PLUS 1.30 (2,4,5)

2573 Martnaham Maiden Hurdle (4-y-o and up) £2,060 2m................(2:20)

2433² BEND SABLE (Ire) 4-10-10 B Storey, *mid-div, hdwy 5th, led 3 out, hit nxt, jmpd rght last, hdwy and edgd right, hld on*...........(9 to 2 co-fav op 7 to 2 tchd 5 to 1) 1
2369⁵ CROMARTY 4-10-0 (5*) A Roche, *hld up, hdwy 4 out, effrt and ev ch whn hmpd last, styd on und pres, jst fld.*
..........................(9 to 2 co-fav tchd 5 to 1) 2
1504 DAYADAN (Ire) 4-10-10 T Reed, *cl up, mstk second, hld 5th, led 4 out to nxt, rdn and one pace appr last.*
..........................(10 to 1 tchd 12 to 1) 3
1428⁶ KNOW-NO-NO (Ire) 5-11-3 (3*) D Bentley, *chsd ldrs, rdn and blun 3 out, sn one pace......*...(16 to 1 tchd 20 to 1) 4
2373⁴ ADDINGTON BOY (Ire) 6-11-6 N Doughty, *in tch, rdn alng appr 3 out, sn one pace*.........(10 to 1 op 8 to 1) 5
2445 TEMPLERAINEY (Ire) 6-11-1 (5*) P Williams, *prmnt, rdn and wknd bef 3 out*........(11 to 2 op 4 to 1 tchd 6 to 1) 6
2447⁴ RALLEGIO 5-11-6 A Dobbin, *mid-div, rdn alng and hdwy 4 out, wknd nxt*.................(8 to 1 tchd 9 to 1) 7
TROY BOY 4-10-10 J Callaghan, *beh, styd on frm 3 out, nvr dngrs.*.......................(20 to 1) 8
2404⁸ TALOS (Ire) 6-11-6 R Hodge, *chsd ldrs, rdn and wknd aftr 4 out.*...............(9 to 2 co-fav op 7 to 1 tchd 9 to 1) 9
976⁹ WANG HOW 6-11-3 (3*) A Thornton, *chsd ldrs, rdn 4 out, sn wknd.*.................(33 to 1) 10
1636⁵ FLINTERS 7-11-6 M Moloney, *prmnt, rdn and wknd 4 out.*
..........................(33 to 1 op 20 to 1) 11
2373⁹ SEABURN 4-10-5 (5*) J Supple, *mstk 1st, al rear.* (33 to 1) 12
2326³ SCRABBLE 5-11-1 Richard Guest, *led till rdn and hdd 4 out, sn wknd*.........(7 to 1 op 5 to 1 tchd 9 to 1) 13
2008 JINGLIN' GEORDIE (Ire) 6-11-6 K Jones, *prmnt, wknd 4th, sn beh, tld off four out.*....................(200 to 1) 14
2373⁵ KERNEL GRAIN 6-11-3 (3*) J Moffatt, *beh hfwy, f 2 out.*..........................(25 to 1 op 20 to 1) f
FINDOGLEN 8-11-3 (3*) A Larnach, *al rear, tld off hfwy, pld up bef 3 out.*....................(200 to 1) pu
2237 DERWENT LAD 5-11-6 A Merrigan, *beh 4th, tld off whn pld up bef 2 out*...............(66 to 1 tchd 100 to 1) pu
Dist: Hd, 7l, 7l, 7l, 7l, 2l, 2l, 1l, hd, hd, 2½l. 3m 59.80s. a 22.80s (17 Ran).
SR: 22/17/15/18/11/9/7/-/6/   (F S Storey), F S Storey

2574 Carsphairn Handicap Chase (0-120 5-y-o and up) £2,668 2½m......(2:50)

2486² RIVER PEARL [94] 9-11-2 T Reed, *hld up in tch, hdwy 5 out, led 3 out, rdn nxt, hit last, styd on.*
..........................(9 to 2 op 4 to 1 tchd 11 to 2) 1
2359² STARTER STAR [99] 9-11-7 B Storey, *led to 6th, cl up, led 11th to 3 out, sn rdn, blun nxt, kpt on one pace.*
..........................(3 to 1 fav tchd 7 to 2) 2
2221² DEEP DECISION [98] 8-11-6 K Johnson, *in tch, effrt and hdwy whn hit 12th, blun nxt, sn one pace.*
..........................(9 to 2 op 4 to 1 tchd 5 to 1) 3
2240³ KAMART [82] 6-10-4 A Dobbin, *in tch, rdn and hit 12th, blun nxt, sn wknd.*............(25 to 1 op 16 to 1) 4
2411* VAYRUA (Fr) [102] 9-11-7 (3*) A Larnach, *in tch till f 8th.*
..........................(9 to 2 op 3 to 1) f
2221* FUNNY OLD GAME [90] 7-10-9 (3*) A Thornton, *cl up, led 6th to 11th, rdn and wknd 4 out, f nxt.*
..........................(5 to 1 op 4 to 1 tchd 11 to 2) f
2323⁴ BAD TRADE [100] 12-11-8 Richard Guest, *beh hfwy, tld off whn pld up bef 4 out*............(12 to 1 op 8 to 1) pu
Dist: 3l, 6l, dist. 5m 19.10s. a 32.10s (7 Ran).
SR: 27/29/22/-/   (Mrs A G Martin), L Lungo

2575 Fisherton Selling Handicap Hurdle (4-y-o and up) £2,580 2½m.......(3:20)

2408* VERY EVIDENT (Ire) [81] 5-10-0 J Callaghan, *hld up beh, hdwy hfwy, led 3 out, rdn last, hdd r-in, rallied to ld nr finish.*..........................(11 to 2 op 5 to 1) 1
2454* BUSMAN (Ire) [82] 5-10-1 Richard Guest, *hld up beh, hdwy 4 out, chsd wnr and hit 3 out, rdn last, led r-in, hdd and no extr nr finish.*
..........................(5 to 2 fav op 3 to 1 tchd 7 to 2) 2
2243⁶ ALL GREEN TO ME (Ire) [105] 6-11-5 S Mason, *hld up, hdwy appr 3 out, rdn nxt, sn one pace.*........(5 to 1) 3
2149⁴ FLING IN SPRING [83] 8-10-14 (5*) P Williams, *trkd ldrs, hdwy 5 out, sn cl up, rdn 3 out, wknd.*
..........................(10 to 1 op 8 to 1) 4
2371⁹ VALIANT DASH [105] 8-11-5 (5*) F Perratt, *prmnt, led 5 out, rdn and pushd along 3 out, kpt on one pace.*
..........................(25 to 1 tchd 33 to 1) 5
1941 KAMBALDA RAMBLER [90] 10-10-9 B Storey, *prmnt, rdn and one pace appr 3 out.*
..........................(25 to 1 op 16 to 1) 6
2321⁴ HOTDIGGITY [81] 6-10-0 A Dobbin, *mid-div, effrt and some hdwy 5 out, rdn nxt, sn wknd.*
..........................(25 to 1 op 16 to 1 tchd 33 to 1) 7
2222⁶ GOLDEN REVERIE (USA) [81] 6-10-0 A Merrigan, *prmnt, rdn and wknd 4 out*............(5 to 1 op 3 to 1) 8
2411⁴ PREOBLAKENSKY [116] (v) 7-12-0 (7*) B Harding, *chsd ldrs, wknd bef 4 out.*......(7 to 1 op 6 to 1 tchd 8 to 1) 9
2321⁵ BOLD MOOD [81] 5-10-0 E McKinley, *led till hdd and blun 5 out, sn wknd*.........(20 to 1 op 14 to 1) 10

2325 HUNTING COUNTRY [81] 10-9-9 (5*) A Roche, *beh hfwy, tld off whn pld up bef 2 out.*
..........................(33 to 1 op 66 to 1 tchd 100 to 1) pu
2369⁷ WINSOME GRAIN [82] 5-10-1⁴ (3*) A Thornton, *hit 3rd, sn beh, pld up bef last, lme*.................(33 to 1) pu
Dist: ½l, 12l, ½l, 2l, 12l, 6l, 7l, 25l. 5m 7.30s. a 28.30s (12 Ran).
SR: -/-/10/-/7/-/   (Mrs Susan Moore), G M Moore

2576 Mellerays Belle Challenge Cup Handicap Chase (5-y-o and up) £3,403 3m 1f ....(3:50)

2368* KILLULA CHIEF [116] 7-10-1¹ Richard Guest, *hld up, hdwy tenth, sn cl up, quickened to ld appr last, soon clr.*
..........................(3 to 1 op 11 to 4) 1
2384⁴ GENERAL PERSHING [143] 8-12-0 N Doughty, *led, hit 8th, blun tenth, rdn alng 3 out, hdd and one pace appr last.*
..........................(9 to 4 on tchd 2 to 1) 2
HE WHO DARES WINS [117] 11-10-2 K Johnson, *hld up, hdwy hfwy, sn cl up, ev ch 3 out, rdn nxt, kpt on one pace.*..........................(10 to 1 op 8 to 1) 3
2219 CAROUSEL CALYPSO [115] 8-9-11 (3*) D Bentley, *chsd ldr, rdn and wknd 13th.*...............(33 to 1 op 25 to 1) 4
2448 FORTH AND TAY [115] 12-10-0⁵ (5*) P Williams, *sn outpcd and beh.*...............(16 to 1 tchd 20 to 1) 5
2448⁶ DEEP HAVEN [119] 9-10-4⁴ K Jones, *chsd ldr, rdn and wknd 13th.*..........................(200 to 1) 6
Dist: 4l, ½l, 20l, nk, 15l. 6m 36.50s. a 36.50s (6 Ran).
SR: 33/56/29/7/6/-/   (T G K Construction Ltd), J G M O'Shea

2577 Carwinshoch Novices' Chase (5-y-o and up) £2,840 2½m..........(4:20)

2007² GALLATEEN 6-11-2 N Doughty, *cl up, led 7th, clr 4 out, unchlgd*.................(11 to 4 on op 10 to 3 on) 1
2411³ JUPITER MOON 5-10-7 Richard Guest, *hld up, hdwy and cl up 11th, lost pl and beh nxt, styd on appr last, no ch with wnr*....................(11 to 2 tchd 6 to 1) 2
2372⁵ PIT PONY 10-11-2 R Hodge, *in tch, scrubbed alng hfwy, ran on one pace frm 4 out.*............(66 to 1) 3
2218⁶ CAITHNESS PRINCE 8-11-2 B Storey, *in tch, hld second and 5th, rdn and wknd 5 out.*..............(12 to 1) 4
2372⁴ SHEILAS HILLCREST 8-11-9 (5*) J Supple, *led till hdd and hit 7th, chsd wnr, rdn 4 out, wknd quickly aftr 2 out.*
..........................(9 to 1 op 8 to 1 tchd 14 to 1) 5
Dist: 15l, 2l, 3½l, 5l. 5m 29.90s. a 42.90s (5 Ran).
                                   (E R Madden), G Richards

2578 Marchburn 'National Hunt' Novices' Handicap Hurdle (4-y-o and up) £2,242 2¾m............ (4:50)

2308⁴ SCARF (Ire) [81] (bl) 6-10-9 (5*) A Roche, *hld up, hdwy 4 out, led 2 out, sn clr.*......................(7 to 2 co-fav op 9 to 2 tchd 5 to 1) 1
2367⁶ CARSON CITY [81] 7-11-0 R Hodge, *al cl up, led 5 out, rdn and hdd 2 out, kpt on one pace und pres....*(7 to 2 co-fav op 3 to 1 tchd 4 to 1) 2
2367² RUSSIAN CASTLE (Ire) [84] 5-11-3 K Jones, *prmnt, ev ch 3 out, sn rdn, kpt on same pace.*............(7 to 2 co-fav op 4 to 1 tchd 9 to 2) 3
2219 CLASSIC MINSTREL [83] 10-10-11 (5*) P Williams, *chsd ldrs, effrt 4 out, dsptd ld nxt, rdn 2 out, sn wknd.*
..........................(12 to 1 op 8 to 1) 4
2367⁵ THE WHIRLIE WEEVIL [87] 6-11-6 N Doughty, *led to 5 out, sn wknd.*........(10 to 1 op 8 to 1 tchd 11 to 1) 5
2367⁷ BELLS HILL LAD [91] 7-11-10 A Dobbin, *prmnt, rdn and wknd 4 out.*..........(14 to 1 op 10 to 1) 6
2483⁴ STRATHBOGIE MIST (Ire) [67] 6-9-12¹ (3*) J Moffatt, *hld up beh, hit 3rd, rdn alng 4 out, no hdwy.*
..........................(8 to 1 op 9 to 1) 7
2088³ BASILICUS (Fr) [86] 5-11-5 Richard Guest, *prmnt, rdn and wknd aftr 4 out.*...........(5 to 1 op 7 to 2) 8
Dist: 2½l, 1½l, 5l, 3l, 10l, 15l, 7l. 5m 52.80s. a 42.80s (8 Ran).
                            (Ian G M Dalgleish), J J O'Neill

CATTERICK (good to soft)
Saturday February 12th
Going Correction: PLUS 0.50 sec. per fur. (races 1,4,6), PLUS 0.40 (2,3,5,7)

2579 Brough Novices' Handicap Chase (5-y-o and up) £2,558 3m 1f 110yds (1:55)

2325² DEVONGALE [86] 8-11-10 R Garritty, *al hndy, took clr order fnl circuit, hit 6 out, effrt and rdn 3 out, ev ch frm nxt, led r-in, kpt on.*
..........................(6 to 5 on op 11 to 10 tchd 6 to 5) 1
2411 DARK OAK [76] 8-11-0 L O'Hara, *nvr far away, lft in ld 5th, rdn alng 2 out, hdd r-in, no extr.*(9 to 2 op 5 to 1) 2
RAIN MAN (NZ) [80] 9-10-11 (7*) Mr C Bonner, *in tch on ins, outpcd fnl circuit, tld off last 3.*.......(10 to 1 op 10 to 1) 3
2270 CANTGETOUT [79] 8-11-3 Mr A Pickering, *sn beh, reminders 9th, struggling to keep up fnl circuit, tld off.*
..........................(14 to 1 op 10 to 1) 4

1745⁷ JUST MOLLY [62] 7-10-0 L Wyer, *patiently rdn, improved to join issue 4th, hit 8th, outpcd 13th, 3rd and hld whn f four out*............................(13 to 2 op 5 to 1) f
2253⁷ KATY KEYS [72] 10-10-10 J Corkell, *led till blun and uns rdr 5th*..............(14 to 1 op 12 to 1 tchd 16 to 1) ur
2489 MISTER CUMBERS [71] 7-10-2 (7") M Molloy, *tracking ldrs whn blun and uns rdr 7th*........(16 to 1 op 10 to 1) ur
823 CASTLE CROSS [62] 7-10-0 W McFarland, *pressed ldg grp, mstks and lost grnd fnl circuit, tld off whn pld up aftr 4 out*........................(33 to 1 op 14 to 1) pu
Dist: 1l, dist, dist. 6m 48.50s. a 33.50s (8 Ran).

(Victor Ogden), M H Easterby

2580 Aske Handicap Hurdle (0-130 4-y-o and up) £2,343 2m............(2:25)

2360⁵ RATIFY [98] 7-11-8 A S Smith, *rcd wide, al hndy, led bef 4th, jmpd lft nxt, hdd briefly 2 out, jumped left last and hng left, ran on gmely*..............(9 to 2 op 7 to 2) 1
2243³ J P MORGAN [90] (v) 6-11-0 R Garritty, *led till hdd bef 4th, styd hndy, outpcd and drvn alng aftr 3 out, rallied betw last 2, kpt on r-in*..........(6 to 1 op 4 to 1) 2
2306³ PERSONAL HAZARD [93] (bl) 5-11-3 L Wyer, *pressed ldg grp, rdn aftr 3 out, chlgd nxt, edgd rght betw last 2, no extr r-in*......................(5 to 1 op 7 to 2) 3
2432 EUROTWIST [98] 5-11-8 W McFarland, *patiently rdn, drvn alng aftr 3 out, chlgd nxt and fdd bef last*..........................(5 to 1 op 7 to 2) 4
1672² DUAL IMAGE [100] 7-11-3 (7") G Tormey, *nvr far away, improved to ld briefly 2 out, not much room and swtchd betw last two, sn btn*..........(11 to 8 fav op 7 to 4) 5
1860⁵ WHAT IF [90] 10-11-0 M Brennan, *hld up, took clr order bef 3 out, rdn and wknd appr nxt*..(12 to 1 tchd 16 to 1) 6
335⁵ MASTER'S CROWN (USA) [95] 6-11-5 W Worthington, *trkd ldrs, rdn alng bef 4th, struggling aftr four out, tld off*..........................(16 to 1 op 12 to 1) 7
Dist: 1¼l, 5l, 5l, 1l, 5l, 10l. 3m 53.80s. a 12.80s (7 Ran).
SR: 30/20/18/18/19/4/-/

(J C Fretwell), K A Morgan

2581 Bridge Selling Hurdle (4-y-o and up) £1,953 2m............(2:55)

2254³ GREENACRES LAD 11-11-9 A Mulholland, *nvr far away, led briefly 3 out, lft clr bef nxt, hit last, ran on und pres*........................(8 to 1 op 7 to 1 tchd 9 to 1) 1
2292⁵ PINECONE PETER (v) 7-11-3 M Brennan, *hld up, relentless prog frm 3 out, kpt on und from last, not rch wnr*..........................(6 to 1 tchd 13 to 2) 2
2408⁹ DRU RI'S BRU RI (v) 8-10-10 (7") S Taylor, *settled midfield, took clr order 5th, effrt and drvn alng aftr nxt, one pace betw last 2*....................(20 to 1 op 14 to 1) 3
2243 COOL DUDE 8-11-6 (3") N Bentley, *al hndy, drvn alng aftr 3 out, one pace frm nxt*. (5 to 1 op 7 to 2 tchd 9 to 2) 4
2405 ROBINS SON 7-11-3 Gary Lyons, *patiently rdn, gd hdwy to chase ldrs frm 5th, drvn alng aftr 3 out, outpcd from nxt*......................(16 to 1 op 14 to 1 tchd 20 to 1) 5
2070 HYPNOTIST 7-11-9 D Wilkinson, *trkd ldg bunch, improved aftr 4 out, drvn alng after nxt, sn outpcd*..........................(10 to 1 op 7 to 1) 6
2254⁶ POINT TAKEN 5-10-10 (7") A Large, *keen hold, cl up, led 3rd, hdd bef nxt, styd hndy, drvn alng 3 out, sn outpcd, btn whn blun last*..........(12 to 1 op 10 to 1) 7
SOME DO NOT 10-11-3 A Carroll, *al beh, lost tch hfwy, tld off*........................(16 to 1 op 12 to 1) 8
2433⁶ UNNAB 4-9-11 (5") P Waggott, *settled midfield, took clr order bef 5th, sn drvn alng, outpcd aftr 3 out, soon tld off*......................(14 to 1 op 12 to 1) 9
DEPUTY TIM 11-10-12 (5") H Bastiman, *beh, struggling frm hfwy, nvr a factor*..........(33 to 1 op 20 to 1) 10
INNOCENT GEORGE 5-11-3 R Garritty, *beh, struggling to keep up hfwy, tld off*....................(25 to 1) 11
2413 MR WESTCLIFF 6-11-3 L O'Hara, *beh, blun second, struggling to keep up fnl circuit, tld off*. (50 to 1 op 25 to 1) 12
2321 TIBER RUN 9-10-10 (7") M Clarke, *in tch, drvn alng bef 5th, sn lost touch, tld off*.......(33 to 1 op 25 to 1) 13
2251 SOLO CORNET 9-11-3 W Humphreys, *beh whn stumbled and f aftr 3rd*................(14 to 1 op 10 to 1) f
2360 IRISH DITTY (USA) 7-11-3 A S Smith, *refused to take part*.......................... ref
2254⁷ RUN OF WELD 11-11-9 W McFarland, *led till hdd 3rd, rgned ld bef nxt, headed briefly 3 out, broke leg and pld up before next, destroyed*........(7 to 2 fav op 5 to 1) pu
2152 JANE'S AFFAIR 6-10-7 (5") S Lyons, *grmant, feeling pace and lost grnd 4th, sn struggling, tld off whn pld up 2 out*........................(50 to 1 op 25 to 1 tchd 100 to 1) pu
SR: 10/2/-/-/-/-/

(Miss Angela Bennett), J L Eyre

2582 Catterick Grand National Trial Handicap Chase (0-135 5-y-o and up) £3,542 3½m 110yds............(3:25)

2253⁸ TRUELY ROYAL [91] 10-9-7 (7") Mr D Parker, *wth ldr, lft in ld appr 6th, hdd 12th, chalg whn slpd bend bef 3 out, chal frm last, led cl hme*...........................(11 to 2 op 5 to 1 tchd 6 to 1) 1

2253⁷ THE MALTKILN [101] (v) 11-10-10 L Wyer, *cl up, led 12th, hrd pressed and rdn fnl 2, hdd close hme*..........................(7 to 2 op 3 to 1) 2
2384 NO MORE TRIX [112] 11-11-7 R Garritty, *trkd ldrs, improved fnl circuit, hit 5 out, ev ch 3 out, swtchd and rnwd chal r-in, no extr cl hme*. (6 to 5 fav op 5 to 4 tchd 11 to 8) 3
2410³ REGAL ESTATE [112] 10-11-7 C Hawkins, *led till ran out appr 6th*............(3 to 1 op 7 to 2 tchd 5 to 2) ro
Dist: Hd, 1l. 7m 47.00s. a 45.00s (4 Ran).

(I H Pearson), J I A Charlton

2583 Gladiator 'National Hunt' Novices' Handicap Hurdle (4-y-o and up) £2,448 2m 3f............(3:55)

2154⁷ STRONG FLAME (Ire) [78] 5-10-7 (5") S Lyons, *led 1st, hdd bef 3rd, lft in ld nxt, made rst, forged clr betw last 2*..........................(14 to 1 op 10 to 1) 1
2409* ALI'S ALIBI [90] 7-11-5 (5") Mr M Buckley, *in tch, rdr lost irons and drpd rear second, sn reco'red, improved to join issue 5th, ev ch bef 2 out, one pace*..........................(7 to 4 fav op 11 to 8) 2
2237² HIGH PENHOWE [75] 6-10-9 W McFarland, *chsd ldrs, effrt and rdn bef 2 out, one pace whn hit last*..........................(7 to 2 op 5 to 1) 3
2485⁹ PESSOA [69] 7-10-3¹ Gary Lyons, *sn beh, took clr order fnl circuit, outpcd aftr 3 out, no imprsn frm nxt*..........................(12 to 1) 4
2409⁷ KINDA GROOVY [90] 6-5-10-13 N Smith, *nvr far away, effrt and drvn alng aftr 3 out, btn appr nxt*..........................(12 to 1 op 10 to 1) 5
2326* MY ADVENTURE (Ire) [77] 4-10-11 L Wyer, *chsd ldg grp, struggling to keep up frm 5th, tld off bef 2 out*..........................(5 to 1 op 9 to 4) 6
2239⁵ BALLYROVERS [74] (bl) 5-10-1 (7") J Driscoll, *jmpd badly, trkd ldrs, struggling to keep up 4 out, sn lost tch, tld off*..........................(16 to 1) 7
CARLA ADAMS [67] 8-10-11 A Carroll, *led to 1st, rgned ld bef 3rd, f nxt*................(16 to 1 op 14 to 1) f
KERRY TO CLARE [68] 8-9-11² (7") Mark Roberts, *sn beh and struggling, tld off whn pld up bef 6th*..........................(33 to 1 op 20 to 1) pu
Dist: 4l, 2l, 2½l, 2½l, dist, dist. 4m 43.90s. (9 Ran).

(Trevor Hemmings), M D Hammond

2584 EBF Novices' Chase (5-y-o and up) £2,390 2m............(4:25)

1958³ GYMCRAK STARDOM 8-11-2 R Marley, *in tch, mstk 5th, improved frm 4 out to ld bef 2 out, sn hrd pressed, styd on gmely r-in*............(6 to 1 op 11 to 2) 1
2402* SEON 8-12-0 L Wyer, *in tch, struggling hfwy, improved 3 out, chlgd nxt, hng lft appr last, rallied*..........................(13 to 8 jt-fav op 7 to 4 on 5 to 4 tchd 2 to 1 and 6 to 4) 2
2538 CALDECOTT 8-11-2 Gary Lyons, *chsd clr ldr, improved to draw level aftr 4 out, lft in ld nxt, hdd bef 2 out, one pace*........................(33 to 1) 3
2409 KRISSOS 7-10-11 (5") P Waggott, *jmpd badly, sn beh, struggling frm hfwy, tld off*..........(33 to 1) 4
2272³ FAVOURED VICTOR (USA) 7-11-2 A S Smith, *led and sn clr, jnd bef 3 out, f three out*..........(7 to 1 op 11 to 2) f
2489² ISSYIN 7-11-8 R Garritty, *in tch whn f second*. (13 to 8 jt-fav op 5 to 4 tchd 7 to 4) f
Dist: ½l, 12l, 30l. 4m 3.20s. a 14.20s (6 Ran).
SR: 26/37/13/

(The Gymcrak Thoroughbred Racing Club), G Holmes

2585 Levy Board Novices' Hurdle (5-y-o and up) £1,922 2m............(4:55)

2369* FIVE TO SEVEN (USA) 5-11-7 D Wilkinson, *wth ldr, led bef 4th, sn clr, unchlgd*..........(11 to 10 on op 5 to 4 tchd 11 to 8) 1
1872³ STOPINOVERITATE 5-10-9 L Wyer, *led till hdd bef 4th, chsd wnr, no imprsn fnl 2*........(4 to 1 tchd 5 to 1) 2
SARTIGILA 5-10-4 (5") S Lyons, *hld up, improved bef 3 out, staying on whn hit nxt, better for race*.. (16 to 1) 3
2068⁵ SUNKALA SHINE 6-10-7 (7") F Leahy, *patiently rdn, steady hdwy 3 out, shaken up bef last, prmsg*..........................(12 to 1 op 8 to 1) 4
2303⁴ GOLDEN TORQUE 7-10-9 (5") H Bastiman, *hld up in rear, shaken up bef 2 out, nvr nr to chal*..........................(7 to 1 op 6 to 1) 5
2485⁵ FLOATING LINE 6-11-0 R Garritty, *in tch, rdn alng 4 out, btn bef 2 out*......................(20 to 1) 6
1787¹ IMPERIAL BID (Fr) 6-11-2 (5") P Waggott, *settled beh ldrs, improved 5th, rdn alng nxt, grad wknd, no ch whn blun last*......................(8 to 1 op 4 to 1) 7
2413⁵ TUSKY 6-10-11 (3") N Bentley, *chsd ldg grp, struggling to keep up aftr 4 out, tld off fnl 2*....(20 to 1 op 14 to 1) 8
2485 CHENOATS 6-11-0 L O'Hara, *reluctant to line up, slwly into strd, al beh and struggling, tld off*...... (100 to 1) 9
2413 TOLLS CHOICE (Ire) 5-10-7 (7") J Driscoll, *patiently rdn, struggling, tld off bef 2 out*........(100 to 1) 10
1959* HILLTOWN (Ire) 6-11-7 A S Smith, *in tch, struggling to keep up aftr 4 out, fdd, tld off*.....(10 to 1 op 6 to 1) 11
REVEL 6-10-7 (7") Mark Roberts, *cl up till wknd quickly bef 4th, tld off whn pld up before 6th*........(100 to 1) pu

Dist: 10l, ½l, 4l, ½l, 1½l, 7l, dist, 15l. 3m 52.00s. a 11.00s (12 Ran).
SR: 47/25/24/25/24/22/22/-/-/ (The Five To Seven Partnership), C W Thornton

FAIRYHOUSE (IRE) (heavy)
Saturday February 12th

2586 Fanmond Maiden Hurdle (5 & 6-y-o) £3,105 2¼m................. (2:00)

CURRENCY BASKET (Ire) 5-11-11 C F Swan, . . (5 to 2 fav)	1
2128²	TAITS CLOCK (Ire) 5-11-3 P Carberry, ... (7 to 1)	2
2465	LINDEN'S LOTTO (Ire) 5-11-3 C O'Dwyer, ... (10 to 1)	3
	JESSIE'S BOY (Ire) 5-10-10 (7*) T Martin, ...(25 to 1)	4
162⁸	IFALLELSEFAILS 6-11-6 Mr A J Martin, ... (9 to 1)	5
2465²	I AM 6-11-9 (5*) K P Gaule, ...(7 to 2)	6
618⁴	STRONG DILEMMA (Ire) 6-11-6 T J Taaffe, ... (7 to 1)	7
2155⁶	BEST INTEREST (Ire) 6-11-3 (3*) D Bromley, ... (12 to 1)	8
2056³	MIDNIGHT HOUR (Ire) 5-10-12 (5*) M G Cleary, ... (8 to 1)	9
2283³	CORYMANDEL (Ire) 5-10-12 (5*) P A Roche, ... (7 to 1)	10
585⁶	MAY GALE (Ire) 6-11-1 S H O'Donovan, ... (10 to 1)	11
1820⁹	DENNETT VALLEY (Ire) 5-10-12 (5*) J P Broderick, (16 to 1)	12
1687	YOU'VE DONE WHAT (Ire) 6-11-1 (5*) K L O'Brien, (10 to 1)	13
1820	THE PERISHER (Ire) 5-11-3 J Shortt, ... (14 to 1)	14
2309²	FIVE FROM HOME (Ire) 6-11-6 F Woods, ... (8 to 1)	15
2389	SARVO (Ire) 6-11-3 (3*) T J O'Sullivan, ... (33 to 1)	16
2353⁵	SIOBHAILIN DUBH (Ire) 5-10-12 T Horgan, ... (14 to 1)	17
1976⁸	TOP RUN (Ire) 6-10-13 (7*) C O'Neill, ... (20 to 1)	18
2311⁵	SISTER NORA (Ire) 6-10-6 (5*) M M Mackin, ... (20 to 1)	19
2465	STRONG HICKS (Ire) 6-11-6 F J Flood, ... (10 to 1)	20
2278	ISN'T THAT NICE (Ire) 6-11-6 C N Bowens, ... (16 to 1)	21
2128⁷	GROUP HAT (Ire) 6-11-6 J P Banahan, ... (12 to 1)	22
2348	VALTORUS 5-11-3 K F O'Brien, ... (25 to 1)	23
2161⁶	PLEASURE SHARED (Ire) 6-11-6 A Powell, ... (25 to 1)	24
	MY HALL DOOR 5-10-12 (5*) D T Evans, ... (33 to 1)	25
2465	TRAP ONE (Ire) 6-10-13 (7*) D J Kavanagh, ... (25 to 1)	26
2161⁷	LIFFEYSIDE LADY (Ire) 5-10-7 (7*) D M Bean, ... (33 to 1)	27
2232⁶	BARNAGEERA BOY (Ire) 5-11-3 H Rogers, ... (14 to 1)	f
2389	BOBSVILLE (Ire) 6-10-13 (7*) B Bowens, ... (25 to 1)	f

Dist: 3l, 2½l, 3l, ½l. 4m 49.40s. (29 Ran).

(P O'Leary), Patrick O'Leary

2587 Irish National Hunt Novice Hurdle (5-y-o and up) £4,140 2¼m....... (2:30)

2392*	DORANS PRIDE 5-11-1 (5*) J P Broderick, ...(3 to 1)	1
1379*	SOUND MAN (Ire) 6-11-6 C F Swan, ...(10 to 9 on)	2
1986²	DIPLOMATIC 5-11-3 J P Banahan, ... (6 to 1)	3
1815	HAUNTING ANGLE (Ire) 5-10-1 (7*) T Martin, ...(20 to 1)	4
2311⁴	PARSON'S RUN 7-10-6 (5*) P A Roche, ... (20 to 1)	5
2197*	LOVELY RUN 7-11-1 H Rogers, ... (12 to 1)	6
1896³	LAW BRIDGE 7-11-1 (5*) K L O'Brien, ... (9 to 1)	7
59*	CABRA TOWERS 7-11-1 (5*) M M Mackin, ... (33 to 1)	8
	DUNFERNE CLASSIC (Ire) 5-10-13 T Horgan, ...(14 to 1)	9
2311⁹	KINROSS 7-10-11 J Shortt, ...(33 to 1)	10

Dist: 1l, 15l, 3½l, 1l. 4m 42.60s. (10 Ran).

(T J Doran), Michael Hourigan

2588 Maxwell House Novice Chase (5-y-o and up) £4,140 2½m............ (3:00)

	BELMONT KING (Ire) 6-11-9 L P Cusack, ... (9 to 1)	1
2079	GLENCLOUD (Ire) 6-12-0 P Carberry, ...(7 to 2 jt-fav)	2
2051³	BLUE RING 10-11-4 F Woods, ... (7 to 1)	3
1905⁴	PROGRAMMED TO WIN 7-12-0 C F Swan, ... (6 to 1)	4
2389⁴	HEMISPHERE (Ire) 5-10-6 (5*) M G Cleary, ... (10 to 1)	5
2469	TOPICAL TIP (Ire) 5-11-0 K F O'Brien, ... (16 to 1)	6
2160	WINTERBOURNE ABBAS (Ire) 5-11-5 B Sheridan, (10 to 1)	7
2233⁵	DHARKOUM 7-11-9 J A White, ... (16 to 1)	8
2282	BALLYFIN BOY 8-11-11 (3*) T J Mitchell, ... (25 to 1)	9
2157⁷	SUPER MIDGE 7-11-11 (3*) C O'Brien, ... (7 to 1)	10
2055⁴	CHOSEN SON 6-11-4 (5*) D P Geoghegan, ... (14 to 1)	11
2157	GONE LIKE THE WIND 7-11-4 (5*) L Flynn, ... (50 to 1)	12
2469⁴	DEER TRIX 9-11-1 (3*) D Bromley, ... f
2390	MONKEY AGO 7-12-0 C O'Dwyer, ... (11 to 2)	f
2233⁷	CRACKLING FROST (Ire) 6-11-9 J Shortt, ... (20 to 1)	f
1905	BUY A DREAM (Fr) 8-11-9 (5*) J P Broderick, ... (20 to 1)	pu
2055	TEL D'OR 9-11-31 (7*) Mr P J Millington, ... (20 to 1)	pu
1235³	COOL CHALLENGE (Ire) 6-12-0 J F Titley, . . . (7 to 2 jt-fav)	pu
2389	LISNABOY PRINCE 7-11-9 T Horgan, ... (20 to 1)	pu

Dist: 7l, ½l, 10l. hd. 5m 28.70s. (19 Ran).

(S J Lambert), S J Lambert

2589 Impudent Barney Handicap Chase (0-109 4-y-o and up) £3,105 2¾m (3:30)

2180³	HAVE TO THINK (-) 6-11-9 (5*) T P Rudd, ...(8 to 1)	1
2312²	EDENAKILL LAD (-) 7-10-13 K F O'Brien, ... (4 to 1)	2
2126	DEEP ISLE (-) 8-9-11 (5*) J P Broderick, ...(7 to 1)	3
2350*	ANOTHER GROUSE (-) 7-11-3 (3*,2ex) C O'Brien, . (6 to 1)	4
2200⁷	MR MYAGI (-) 10-11-0 (3*) D Bromley, ... (14 to 1)	5
2200	ANOTHER RUSTLE (-) 11-10-13 T Horgan, ... (14 to 1)	6
2157	ROYAL SEER (-) 8-11-1 L P Cusack, ...(12 to 1)	7
2350³	BOG LEAF VI (-) 11-9-4 (3*) T J O'Sullivan, ... (14 to 1)	8
2235	PINEWOOD LAD (-) 7-11-0 (5*) C P Dunne, ... (12 to 1)	9
2125⁵	JOHNEEN (-) 8-11-8 C O'Dwyer, ... (13 to 2)	pu

---

2202	FRIENDLY ARGUMENT (-) 9-12-0 F Woods, ... (8 to 1)	pu

Dist: ¾l, 14l, sht-hd, ½l. 6m 1.10s. (11 Ran).

(Peter M Law), A L T Moore

2590 Monaloe Handicap Hurdle (0-137 4-y-o and up) £3,105 2¼m........... (4:00)

2160⁷	SADDLESTOWN GLEN (-) 9-9-7 P Carberry, ... (16 to 1)	1
2279²	MR BOAL (Ire) (-) 5-10-12 C F Swan, ...(7 to 1)	2
2124²	SUPER TACTICS (Ire) (-) 6-9-7 (5*) P A Roche, . .(9 to 4 fav)	3
1780	COIN MACHINE (Ire) (-) 5-9-8 T Horgan, ...(12 to 1)	4
2310	ROSIN THE BOW (Ire) (-) 5-9-7 (7*) P Morris, ... (20 to 1)	5
2280³	PARLIAMENT HALL (-) 8-11-3 K F O'Brien, ... (9 to 2)	6
2158*	RATHCORE (-) 7-9-13 L P Cusack, ... (7 to 2)	7
1498⁵	LADY OLEIN (Ire) (-) 6-12-0 J P Banahan, ... (10 to 1)	8
1377	PRINTOUT (Ire) (-) 4-9-4 (3*) D Bromley, ... (16 to 1)	9
2279⁷	MONTE FIGO (-) 7-9-13 F Woods, ... (12 to 1)	10
59⁶	STAR ROSE (-) 12-9-12 (7*) J Butler, ... (12 to 1)	11
	QUEEN PERSIAN (-) 7-9-0 (7*) R Burke, ... (50 to 1)	12

Dist: 1½l, ¾l, 3l, 6l. 4m 47.90s. (12 Ran).

(J Curran), T G McCourt

2591 Tom Dreaper Handicap Chase (5-y-o and up) £6,900 2½m.........(4:30)

2288²	BUCKBOARD BOUNCE (-) 9-11-9 C F Swan, . .(9 to 4 fav)	1
2549*	COMMERCIAL ARTIST (-) 8-11-5 C N Bowens, ... (7 to 2)	2
2807	THE REAL UNYOKE (-) (bl) 9-9-11 (3*) D P Murphy, (14 to 1)	3
2125³	CAPTAIN BRANDY (-) 9-10-12 F J Flood, ...(8 to 1)	4
2198³	WHO'S TO SAY (-) 8-10-3 S H O'Donovan, ... (10 to 1)	5
44*	PROVERB PRINCE (-) 10-9-7 J Magee, ... (16 to 1)	6
2198²	GOOD TEAM (-) 9-10-8 F Woods, ... (7 to 1)	7
2393	NEW MILL HOUSE (-) 11-10-5 T Horgan, ... (14 to 1)	8
1825	AMERICAN EYRE (-) 9-9-5 (3*) C O'Brien, ... (16 to 1)	9
2202²	BOLD FLYER (-) 11-9-12 (5*) J P Broderick, . . .(12 to 1)	10
1847⁵	EBONY STAR (-) 11-10-12 K F O'Brien, ... (12 to 1)	f
2280²	SATULA (-) 10-10-2 C O'Dwyer, ... (5 to 1)	f
2466³	WINNING CHARLIE (-) 8-9-9 P Carberry, ... (8 to 1)	f

Dist: 2½l, 15l, 3½l, ¾l. 5m 27.30s. (13 Ran).

(J E Mulhern), J E Mulhern

2592 Clonee INH Flat Race (4 & 5-y-o) £3,105 2m.................(5:00)

	EDGE OF NIGHT 5-11-12 (3*) Mr D Marnane, ... (6 to 1)	1
2289⁶	GLEN TEN (Ire) 5-11-7 (3*) Mrs J M Mullins, ...(6 to 1)	2
2081²	GRAPHIC IMAGE (Ire) 4-10-13 Mr A P O'Brien, ...(4 to 1)	3
	HERO STATUS (Ire) 5-11-1 (7*) Mr T J Beattie, . . . (20 to 1)	4
	CLOVER MOR LASS (Ire) 5-11-0 (3*) Mr A R Coonan,	
	. . . .(14 to 1)	5
	PREMIUM BRAND 5-11-5 (3*) Mr R Neylon, ...(20 to 1)	6
	RUN TO GLORY (Ire) 4-10-3 (5*) Mr H F Cleary, . . .(12 to 1)	7
	AUNT ROSE (Ire) 5-10-12 (5*) Mr G J Harford, ...(25 to 1)	8
	DESPERATE DAYS (Ire) 5-11-1 (7*) Mr D A Harney, (14 to 1)	9
2388	GLIDING ALONG (Ire) 4-10-5 (3*) Mr A E Lacy, . . . (20 to 1)	su
	LEGAL DEALINGS (Ire) 5-11-5 (3*) Mr J A Nash, (6 to 4 on)	pu

Dist: 2l, 9l, 7l, 10l. 4m 11.20s. (11 Ran).

(Mrs M O'Toole), M A O'Toole

NEWBURY (soft)
Saturday February 12th
Going Correction: PLUS 1.25 sec. per fur. (races 1,2,-4,6), PLUS 1.05 (3,5,7)

2593 Mandarin Handicap Chase (0-140 6-y-o and up) £7,096 3¼m 110yds...(1:10)

1706²	BISHOPS ISLAND [124] 8-11-3 A Maguire, *prmnt, hit 3rd, chsd ldr frm 8th, hit 9th, slight ld last, drvn out.*	
	. . . .(7 to 2 op 4 to 1 tchd 9 to 2)	1
1993²	RATHVINDEN HOUSE (USA) [115] 7-10-8 B Powell, *led 5th, jmpd slwly 6th, hdd last, styd on one pace.*	
	. . . .(9 to 4 fav op 5 to 2 tchd 11 to 4)	2
2513⁶	GRANGE BRAKE [117] (bl) 8-10-10 C Llewellyn, *led to 5th, hit tenth and 13th, rear and rdn 16th, styd on, nvr a dngr frm 3 out.* . . . .(14 to 1 op 12 to 1)	3
	FIT FOR FIRING (Fr) [119] 10-10-12 P Holley, *drpd rear 7th, hdwy to chase ldrs 12th, outpcd 4 out, wknd 2 out.*	
	. . . . (15 to 2 op 7 to 1 tchd 8 to 1)	4
1088	ROCKTOR (NZ) [127] 9-11-6 J Frost, *jmpd poorly in rear, hmpld 11th, nvr dngrs.* (12 to 1 op 8 to 1 tchd 14 to 1)	5
2246*	CATCHAPENNY [109] (bl) 9-9-9 (7*) P Ward, *mstks and beh, stumbled badly 11th, rdn 12th, blun 14th, nvr dngrs.*	
	. . . .(7 to 2 op 5 to 1 tchd 6 to 1)	6
	STRONG BEAU [122] 9-11-1 W Marston, *nvr in contention, lost tch frm 11th.* (14 to 1 op 8 to 1 tchd 16 to 1)	7

Dist: 7l, 30l, 2l, 2½l, 8l. 7m 13.40s. a 45.40s (7 Ran).

(Lord Vestey), D Nicholson

2594 Mitsubishi Shogun Game Spirit Chase Grade 2 (5-y-o and up) £15,480 2m 1f ....(1:40)

2171*	VIKING FLAGSHIP 7-11-10 A Maguire, *trkd ldr till led 3 out, hit 2 out, ran on gmely r-in....* (3 to 1 op 11 to 4)	1

2476² WONDER MAN (Fr) 9-11-3 J Osborne, *dsptd second pl, ev ch 3 out, hit 2 out and last, swtchd rght and one pace r-in*..............................(4 to 1 op 7 to 2 tchd 9 to 2)   2

2258³ SYBILLIN 8-11-7 M Dwyer, *hld up, chlgd on bit frm 3 out, rdn and found nothing rnn-in.*
..............................(2 to 1 fav tchd 9 to 4)   3

2145* DEEP SENSATION 9-11-10 D Murphy, *hld up, chlgd and slpd 3 out, rdn and held whn mstk last.*
..............................(5 to 1 op 4 to 1 tchd 11 to 2)   4

2365* EGYPT MILL PRINCE (bl) 8-11-3 G Bradley, *led to 3 out, wknd 2 out*............(13 to 2 op 6 to 1 tchd 7 to 1)   5

Dist: 2½l, 3l, 15l, 30l. 4m 23.00s. a 22.00s (5 Ran).
SR: 89/79/80/68/31/   (Roach Foods Limited), D Nicholson

2595 Tote Gold Trophy Handicap Hurdle Grade 3 (4-y-o and up) £33,305 2m 110yds............................(2:15)

1992* LARGE ACTION (Ire) [140] 6-10-8 J Osborne, *pressed ldr till led 4th, hdd 5th, led 2 out, headed r-in, rallied gmely to ld ag'n last strds*........ (9 to 2 op 4 to 1 tchd 5 to 1)   1

OH SO RISKY [160] 7-12-0 P Holley, *missed break, hld up, steady hdwy frm 3 out, chlgd last, led r-in, ct last strds.*
..............................(14 to 1 op 12 to 1)   2

2376* FLAKEY DOVE [147] 8-11-1 N Williamson, *in tch, ev ch frm 3 out, outpcd r-in...*(5 to 2 fav op 3 to 1 tchd 4 to 1)   3

1886² THUMBS UP [136] 8-10-4 M A FitzGerald, *hld up, steady hdwy to chal 2 out, ev ch last, not quicken.*
..............................(9 to 1 op 8 to 1 tchd 10 to 1)   4

2079 LAND AFAR [144] 7-10-12 W Marston, *hdwy to track ldrs 5th, ev ch frm 3 out, outpcd appr last.*
..............................(10 to 1 tchd 11 to 1)   5

HER HONOUR [132] 5-10-0 J Lower, *hdwy 5th, no imprsn frm 3 out*............(16 to 1 op 14 to 1 tchd 20 to 1)   6

2079 WELSHMAN [132] 8-10-0 D Gallagher, *led to 4th, led ag'n 5th to 2 out, sn btn.* (25 to 1 tchd 33 to 1 and 20 to 1)   7

2267* NIJMEGEN [132] 6-10-0 M Dwyer, *in tch, rdn and ev ch 3 out, wknd 2 out*...............(7 to 1 op 6 to 1)   8

2480* NIKITAS [132] 9-10-0 A Maguire, *prmnt to 5th.*
..............................(12 to 1 op 14 to 1 tchd 16 to 1)   9

1617⁵ WINNIE THE WITCH [132] 10-10-0 D Bridgwater, *al beh.*
..............................(50 to 1 op 33 to 1)   10

2267² HIGH BARON [142] 7-10-10 M Hourigan, *hdwy 5th, wknd 2 out, no ch whn refused last.*
..............................(5 to 1 op 9 to 2 tchd 6 to 1)   ref

Dist: Sht-hd, 4l, 2½l, 5l, 7l, 3l, 2l, 10l, 5l. 4m 7.40s. a 18.40s (11 Ran).
SR: 69/89/72/58/61/42/39/37/27/   (B T Stewart-Brown), O Sherwood

2596 Kung Hei Fat Choy Novices' Chase (5-y-o and up) £3,525 2½m........(2:45)

2378³ THE GLOW (Ire) 6-11-12 P Holley, *hld up, hit 8th, steady hdwy to track ldrs 4 out, led r-in, readily.*
..............................(11 to 4 op 2 to 1 tchd 3 to 1)   1

2249* JUMBEAU 9-11-9 (3*) P Hide, *led second, hit 2 out, hdd r-in, outpcd.*........(100 to 30 op 4 to 1 tchd 9 to 1)   2

1691³ HILLWALK 8-11-8 D Morris, *hdwy to track ldrs tenth, outpcd frm 3 out.*......(7 to 2 tchd 3 to 1 and 4 to 1)   3

2458 VILLA RECOS 9-11-4 B Powell, *led to second, styd chasing wnr till wknd frm 3 out.*
..............................(20 to 1 op 14 to 1 tchd 25 to 1)   4

2472 GHIA GNEUIAGH 8-11-8 C Llewellyn, *in tch, chsd ldrs 4 out, rdn and wknd nxt.*
..............................(9 to 4 fav op 2 to 1 tchd 9 to 4)   5

1804⁹ VICAR OF BRAY 7-11-4 E Leonard, *hit 8th and beh, lost tch frm tenth.*........(33 to 1 op 20 to 1 tchd 50 to 1)   6

Dist: 3½l, 15l, 12l, 20l, 10l. 5m 28.70s. a 38.70s (6 Ran).
(Mrs T Brown), D R C Elsworth

2597 Levy Board Handicap Hurdle (0-140 4-y-o and up) £3,655 3m 110yds (3:15)

2172⁹ BRAVE BUCCANEER [113] 7-10-4 P Niven, *mid-div 6th, gd hdwy 7th, chlgd 8th, led 3 out, rdn and edgd lft whn left clr last, all out.*........(6 to 4 fav tchd 13 to 8)   1

2403 RIMOUSKI [109] 6-10-0 Mr J Cambidge, *beh and pushed alng 6th, hdwy 8th, styd on frm 2 out, not rch wnr.*
..............................(33 to 1 tchd 50 to 1)   2

1845⁵ CAIRNCASTLE [109] 9-10-0 B Clifford, *slwly into strd, sn reco'red, hmpd 5th, lost pl 9th, hdwy appr 3 out, styd on r-in.*............(10 to 1 op 8 to 1 tchd 12 to 1)   3

2403 EVERALDO (Fr) [137] 10-12-0 M A FitzGerald, *beh, effrt tenth, styd on one pace frm 3 out.*
..............................(12 to 1 op 8 to 1 tchd 14 to 1)   4

2298² FLYER'S NAP [109] 8-10-0 S Earle, *chsd ldrs till wknd aftr 3 out*...........(6 to 1 tchd 5 to 1 and 8 to 1)   5

2009⁴ ULURU (Ire) [110] 6-10-1 C Llewellyn, *led to 3 out, sn btn.*
..............................(13 to 2 op 6 to 1 tchd 7 to 1)   6

2512³ METAL OISEAU (Ire) [112] (bl) 6-10-3 A Charlton, *lost tch frm 7th.*..............................(5 to 1 op 9 to 1)   7

1644 LEGAL BEAGLE [109] 7-10-0 M Perrett, *in tch till f 5th.*
..............................(20 to 1 op 16 to 1)   f

2109² MIZYAN (Ire) [120] 6-10-11 A Maguire, *in tch, ran on frm 3 out, crrd lft and ev ch whn f last....(7 to 1 op 6 to 1)*   f

Dist: 3½l, ½l, 12l, 6l, 2l, 30l. 6m 29.30s. a 40.30s (9 Ran).
(C A R Halliday), Mrs M Reveley

2598 Harwell Handicap Chase (5-y-o and up) £4,387 2½m................(3:45)

2174* KENTISH PIPER [127] 9-10-0 C Llewellyn, *made virtually all, quickened 2 out, ran on wl.*
..............................(5 to 2 op 9 to 4 tchd 11 to 4)   1

2145² ELFAST [132] 11-10-5² G McCourt, *chlgd 4th, mstk 8th, chald 11th, outpcd aftr 2 out, styd on r-in.*
..............................(2 to 1 tchd 5 to 2)   2

2266* UNCLE ELI [132] 11-10-5 S Earle, *in tch, chlgd 4 out, outpcd aftr 2 out, blun last, ran on.*
..............................(7 to 4 fav op 11 to 8 tchd 15 to 8)   3

1875³ ANOTHER CORAL [155] 11-12-0 A Maguire, *jmpd slwly 6th, al beh, lost tch 4 out, tld off whn pld up bef last.*
..............................(5 to 1 op 6 to 1 tchd 7 to 1)   pu

Dist: 2½l, sht-hd. 5m 27.40s. a 37.40s (4 Ran).
(Mrs Gordon Pepper), N A Gaselee

2599 The Year Of The Dog Novices' Hurdle (4-y-o and up) £3,116 2m 110yds (4:15)

2381⁶ CALIANDAK (Ire) 4-10-7 G McCourt, *in tch, chlgd frm 3 out, led aftr 2 out, drvn out*.........(5 to 1 op 5 to 2)   1

1174⁴ KNOCKAVERRY (Ire) 6-10-6 (7*) P Ward, *mid-div, hdwy to chase ldrs 5th, ev ch frm 3 out, not fluent last and one pace.*..............................(10 to 1 op 6 to 1)   2

2302² WITH IMPUNITY 5-11-9 C Llewellyn, *led till sn aftr 2 out, styd on one pace......(13 to 2 op 5 to 1 tchd 7 to 1)*   3

2147⁴ BRAVE HIGHLANDER (Ire) 6-11-4 D Murphy, *pld hrd, prmnt, str chal whn mstk 2 out, wknd appr last.*
..............................(5 to 2 op 3 to 1)   4

2366² KEEP ME IN MIND (Ire) 5-11-4 D Skyrme, *hld up, hdwy appr 5th, wknd 2 out.*
..............................(2 to 1 fav op 3 to 1 tchd 7 to 2)   5

2244⁵ LE BARON PERCHE (Fr) 5-11-4 M A FitzGerald, *prmnt, rdn 3 out, sn wknd*..............(33 to 1 op 20 to 1)   6

1734⁶ FLAPPING FREDA (Ire) 6-10-13 N Williamson, *hdwy 5th, wknd aftr 3 out*............(33 to 1 op 20 to 1)   7

2374⁵ MONAZITE 4-10-7 R Bellamy, *prmnt, ev ch 3 out, sn wknd*............(16 to 1 op 14 to 1 tchd 20 to 1)   8

1601³ CASTLE ORCHARD 10-11-4 A Maguire, *chsd ldrs till wknd 5th*...............(20 to 1 op 12 to 1 tchd 25 to 1)   9

2263 NIGHT FANCY 6-10-13 (5*) J McCarthy, *al beh.*
..............................(66 to 1 op 33 to 1)   10

2439 ALL THE JOLLY 6-10-13 S Earle, *al mid-div.*
..............................(66 to 1 op 33 to 1)   11

2430⁸ MA BELLA LUNA 5-10-13 A Charlton, *nvr better than mid-div.*..............................(33 to 1 op 25 to 1)   12

2315⁸ BONE SETTER (Ire) 4-10-0 (7*) Chris Webb, *prmnt to 5th, wknd 3 out.*...............(20 to 1 op 50 to 1 tchd 33 to 1)   13

2250⁸ ANLACE 5-10-13 M Perrett, *al beh...* (33 to 1 op 20 to 1)   14

2210 FILTHY REESH 5-11-4 D Bridgwater, *not fluent and al beh, tld off whn pld up bef 2 out.*
..............................(14 to 1 op 10 to 1 tchd 20 to 1)   pu

Dist: 7l, 1½l, 7l, 2½l, 8l, 4l, sht-hd, 5l, 1½l, 20l. 4m 25.60s. a 36.60s (15 Ran).
(G H Leatham), N Tinkler

UTTOXETER (soft)
Saturday February 12th
Going Correction: PLUS 1.25 sec. per fur. (races 1,5,7), PLUS 1.30 (2,3,4,6)

2600 Gulf Air Handicap Hurdle (0-135 4-y-o and up) £3,501 2¾m 110yds.....(1:30)

2403 BICKERMAN [107] (bl) 11-10-3 (7*) Miss T Spearing, *pld hrd, sn led, shaken up appr last, drw clr nr finish.*
..............................(11 to 2 op 4 to 1)   1

2507⁵ HIGH GRADE [102] 6-10-0 (5*) T Eley, *settled 3rd beh, took clr order 4 out, sstnd chal appr last, rdn and no extr r-in.*..............................(7 to 1 op 5 to 1)   2

2172 ROCHESTOWN LASS [105] (v) 8-10-8 N Mann, *hld up in tch, effrt and ev ch 2 out, sn rdn, one pace.*
..............................(14 to 1 op 12 to 1)   3

2009⁶ HOLY JOE [121] 12-11-5 (5*) T Jenks, *patiently rdn, improved 7th, chsd wnr 4 out, wknd aftr nxt.*
..............................(10 to 1 op 8 to 1)   4

2172⁷ ANDERMATT [114] 7-11-3 R Dunwoody, *settled towards rear, smooth prog 8th, shaken up to chal 3 out, no response...........(7 to 4 fav op 6 to 4 tchd 15 to 8)*   5

1311 POLLERTON'S PRIDE [97] 7-10-0 Diane Clay, *hld up, effrt hfwy, rdn and outpcd aftr 4 out...(14 to 1 op 12 to 1)*   6

2502⁸ FURRY BABY [104] 7-10-7 R Marley, *prmnt, rdn alng whn pace lifted 4 out, sn lost tch...*(4 to 1 tchd 5 to 1)   7

1299 SHIKARI KID [101] 7-10-4⁴ Mr K Green, *led to second, rdn and lost pl aftr 6th, sn tld off, pld up 4 out....(50 to 1)*   pu

Dist: 2½l, 8l, 8l, ½l, 12l, 5l. 5m 46.40s. a 35.40s (8 Ran).
SR: 9/1/-/4/-/   (B Dowling), J L Spearing

2601 J & B Novices' Chase For The Animal Health Trust (6-y-o and up) £7,405 3¼m............................(2:00)

2417* HONEST WORD 9-11-8 R Dunwoody, *made most, clr whn stumbled 3 out, unchlgd......(5 to 4 on op 6 to 4 on)*   1

2479* ROUYAN 8-11-4 I Lawrence, *rcd keenly*, *hld up in last pl*,
hdwy to chase wnr 4 out, no imprsn.
..............................(13 to 8 op 11 to 8 tchd 7 to 4)   2
2336* TARAMOSS 7-11-8 J Railton, *pressed wnr, slight ld 14th*,
rdn alng aftr 4 out, sn lost tch.
..............................(7 to 1 op 5 to 1 tchd 8 to 1)   3
Dist: Dist, 3½l. 7m 17.70s. a 61.70s (3 Ran).

(Mrs H J Clarke), M C Pipe

2602 Singer & Friedlander Handicap Chase
(0-145 5-y-o and up) £6,872 2m 7f (2:30)

2396* SHEER ABILITY [118] 8-10-7 R Dunwoody, *jmpd wl, prmnt*
till drpd rear 7th, rallied to ld tenth, shaken up whn
chlgd last, ran on gmely......(6 to 4 fav tchd 13 to 8)   1
2396² KALANSKI [113] 8-10-2 J Railton, *wtd with in tch, jnd on*
bit 2 out, chlgd last, unbl to quicken r-in.
..............................(3 to 1 op 5 to 2)   2
2403⁵ WILLSFORD [122] (bl) 11-10-11 I Lawrence, *chsd ldr, led*
6th to 9th, rdn and lost pl 12th, nvr dngrs aftr.
..............................(4 to 1 tchd 9 to 2 and 7 to 2)   3
2377⁵ WIDE BOY [117] 12-10-1 (5*) Guy Lewis, *settled rear, jmpd*
slwly 11th, took clr order appr 4 out, rdn and wknd
nxt..............................(10 to 1 tchd 12 to 1)   4
1345³ KEEP TALKING [135] 9-11-10 S Smith Eccles, *led to 6th, led*
9th to nxt, wknd appr 4 out, tld off whn pld up 2 out.
..............................(7 to 1 op 5 to 1)   pu
Dist: ½l, 25l, 20l. 6m 12.20s. a 42.20s (5 Ran).

(Michael Devlin), C J Mann

2603 Marstons Pedigree Novices' Handicap Chase (5-y-o and up) £4,999 2m
..............................(3:00)

2304* NAKIR (Fr) [103] 6-11-10 R Dunwoody, *al wl plcd, jnd ldr*
whn lft clr 4 out, slight mstk nxt, unchlgd.
..............................(6 to 4 fav tchd 7 to 4 and 11 to 8)   1
2319³ MISTER ODDY [80] 8-9-11¹ (5*) T Jenks, *hit 1st, hld up*,
rdn to improve 4 out, sn chasing wnr, outpcd appr 2
out..............................(6 to 1 op 5 to 1 tchd 13 to 2)   2
2249² LOCAL MANOR [79] 7-10-0 M Richards, *pressed ldr, rdn*
alng 8th, sn btn..........(5 to 2 op 7 to 4 tchd 11 to 4)   3
2361⁵ ELITE LEO [79] 9-10-0 C Maude, *rear, mstk 4th, effrt appr*
four out, wknd nxt..............(14 to 1 op 10 to 1)   4
1949⁶ VERSATILE [79] 10-10-0 S McNeill, *al rear, mstk 6th, sn tld*
off..............................(50 to 1 op 33 to 1)   5
2319² PEACEMAN [103] 8-11-10 E Murphy, *set gd pace and sn*
clr, slight ld whn slpd badly and uns rdr 4 out.
..............................(5 to 1 op 4 to 1)   ur
Dist: 15l, 3½l, 15l, dist. 4m 14.20s. a 25.20s (6 Ran).
SR: 52/14/9/

(Jim Lewis), S Christian

2604 Houghton Vaughan 'National Hunt' Novices' Hurdle (5-y-o and up) £1,955 3m 110yds.
..............................(3:30)

2295² CORNER BOY 7-11-2 R Dunwoody, *settled rear, took clr*
order tenth, slight ld 3 out, made nxt, styd on to draw
clr r-in..........(5 to 4 fav tchd 11 to 10 and 11 to 8)   1
2459³ GRAY'S ELLERGY 8-11-0 J Railton, *led to 3rd, led 11th to 3*
out, rdn and ev ch last, ran on one pace.
..............................(6 to 4 op 5 to 4 tchd 7 to 4)   2
2426² DO BE HAVE (Ire) 6-10-12 I Lawrence, *hld up, mstk 8th, jnd*
issue 3 out, ev ch whn pckd nxt, no extr appr last.
..............................(4 to 1 op 3 to 1)   3
2404⁷ JURASSIC CLASSIC 7-10-7 T Eley, *took keen hold, led*
3rd, sn clr, wknd and hdd 11th, tld off.
..............................(20 to 1 op 33 to 1 tchd 14 to 1)   4
Dist: 4l, 1½l, dist. 6m 26.20s. a 47.20s (4 Ran).

(Mrs E W Wilson), D Nicholson

2605 Mount Argus Hunters' Chase (5-y-o and up) £1,945 2m 7f.
..............................(4:00)

CENTRE ATTRACTION 15-11-7 (7*) Miss Y Beckingham,
jmpd wl, hld up, improved 11th, slight ld last, sn clr,
wknd and veered badly lft cl hme, fnshd 1st, relegated
to 3rd..............................(25 to 1)   1D
MOUNT ARGUS 12-11-9 (5*) Mr S Brookshaw, *chsd ldrs*,
led 11th to last, sn hrd rdn, btn whn squeezed out nr
line, dead-heated for second, awarded dead-heat race.
..............................(4 to 1 op 3 to 1)   1+
2456* FIFTH AMENDMENT (bl) 9-12-0 (7*) Mr R Ponsonby, *sn wl*
beh, hdwy 12th, rdn and ran on appr last, hld whn
hmpd cl hme, dead-heated for second, awarded dead-
heat 1st..........(5 to 2 fav op 2 to 1 tchd 11 to 4)   1+
QUEEN'S CHAPLAIN 10-11-7 (7*) Mrs M Morris, *jmpd slwly*
1st, in rear till hdwy hfwy, styd on wl appr last, nvr
nrr..............................(8 to 1 op 7 to 1)   4
ARCTIC TEAL 10-11-11 (3*) Mr J Durkan, *pressed ldrs, ev*
ch appr 2 out, sn rdn and btn..........(7 to 1 op 6 to 1)   5
HARLEY 14-11-9 (7*) Mr D McCain, *jmpd wl, led to 3rd, cl*
up till wknd appr 2 out..........(14 to 1 op 10 to 1)   6
2456 SPORTING MARINER (bl) 10-11-7 Mr D Bloor, *prmnt to*
9th, wl beh whn pld up bef 13th..........(50 to 1)   pu
KONRAD WOLF (Fr) (bl) 10-11-7 (7*) Mr J R Barlow, *al beh*,
tld off and pld up bef 13th..........(12 to 1 op 10 to 1)   pu

ROYAL GREEK 12-11-7 (7*) Mr R Jones, *led 3rd to 6th*,
mstk and lost pl nxt, tld off whn pld up bef 12th.
..............................(25 to 1)   pu
AH JIM LAD 10-11-7 (7*) Mr A Mcpherson, *prmnt till wknd*
and pld up aftr 9th..............(50 to 1 op 33 to 1)   pu
THE ARTFUL RASCAL 10-11-7 (7*) Mr C J B Barlow, *trkd*
ldrs, wkng whn mstk 3 out, pld up bef nxt.
..............................(10 to 1 op 12 to 1)   pu
ASTRE RADIEUX (Fr) 9-11-7 (7*) Mr C Stockton, *chsd ldrs*,
led 6th to 11th, wknd appr 4 out, pld up bef nxt.
..............................(33 to 1 op 50 to 1)   pu
975⁴ PORTAVOGIE 10-11-9 (5*) Mr R H Brown, *prmnt to 8th, sn*
wknd, beh whn pld up 2 out......(14 to 1 op 16 to 1)   pu
Dist: ¾l, dd-ht, ¾l, 12l, 25l. 6m 26.10s. a 56.10s (13 Ran).
(Mrs H J Clarke & Rupert Ponsonby), S A Brookshaw & C J Clarke

2606 Levy Board Novices' Handicap Hurdle
(4-y-o and up) £1,913 2m...... (4:30)

1751² SAINT CIEL (USA) [80] 6-10-6 R Supple, *hld up in rear*,
smooth prog hfwy, led 2 out, sn clr, easily.
..............................(4 to 1 tchd 7 to 2 and 9 to 2)   1
2308⁵ SHARPSIDE [74] 7-10-0 C Maude, *led second to 7th, led 3*
out to nxt, sn rdn, one paced......(8 to 1 op 6 to 1)   2
1867⁸ MAHONG [74] (v) 6-10-0 V Slattery, *mstk 1st, cl up till lost*
pl 7th, styd on ag'n frm 2 out......(25 to 1 op 20 to 1)   3
2404 SMITH'S BAND (Ire) [98] 6-11-10 I Lawrence, *hld up and*
beh, rdn whn pace lifted 6th, sn lost tch.
..............................(7 to 1 op 6 to 1)   4
2445³ UPWARD SURGE (Ire) [80] 4-10-6 S McNeill, *led to second*,
led 7th to 3 out, rdn and btn......(3 to 1 op 5 to 1)   5
2485* RAFTERS [90] 5-11-2 R Dunwoody, *trkd ldrs, effrt and ev*
ch 3 out, sn rdn and wknd.
..............................(5 to 4 fav op 11 to 10 tchd 13 to 8)   6
Dist: 8l, 8l, 12l, 1½l, 7l. 4m 4.10s. a 25.10s (6 Ran).
SR: 17/13/5/17/-/-/

(Tam Racing), F Jordan

LEOPARDSTOWN (IRE) (heavy)
Sunday February 13th
Going Correction: PLUS 1.00 sec. per fur. (races 1,2,-
4,6,7), PLUS 1.25 (3,5)

2607 John Gibbons Maiden Hurdle (5-y-o and up) £5,520 2m. . . . . (1:40)

ANABATIC (Ire) (bl) 6-10-13 (5*) K L O'Brien, ... (10 to 1)   1
MAJOR RUMPUS 6-11-12 T J Taaffe, ...(10 to 1)   2
2314⁹ CAPTAINS BAR 7-11-9 H Rogers, ...(20 to 1)   3
THE TOASTER 7-10-11 (7*) B Bowens, ...(20 to 1)   4
2161⁷ THE REAL ARTICLE (Ire) 5-11-9 H Rogers, ... (10 to 1)   5
2389 BALLYBODEN 7-11-4 P Niven, ...(16 to 1)   6
2552² FINNEGANS WAKE 7-11-4 R Dunwoody, ...(6 to 1)   7
2123 SUMMING UP 7-11-4 P M Verling, ...(20 to 1)   8
2309 VISTAGE (Ire) 6-11-12 B Sheridan, ...(20 to 1)   9
1687 COMERAGH MOUNTAIN 7-11-4 A J O'Brien, . .(20 to 1) 10
WHITBY 6-11-4 T Horgan, ...(20 to 1) 11
2394⁹ BOB NELSON 7-11-4 M Duffy, ...(20 to 1) 12
21557 JIMMY O'GOBLIN 7-10-11 (7*) F Byrne, ...(20 to 1) 13
BUSTHAT 7-11-9 (3*) T P Treacy, ...(12 to 1) 14
2177⁵ RHABDOMANCY (Ire) 6-11-0 (7*) L A Hurley, ...(14 to 1) 15
2199⁵ GALE TOI (Ire) 5-11-9 A Maguire, ...(5 to 2 fav) 16
2128 GLEN SALGIUS (Ity) 5-11-1 S H O'Donovan, ...(16 to 1) 17
1814⁸ HOLY FOX (Ire) 6-11-4 N Williamson, ...(10 to 1) 18
NO FRONTIERS (Ire) 5-11-1 J F Titley, ...(20 to 1) 19
2056⁴ ARDSHUIL 6-10-10 (5*) D P Geoghegan, ...(16 to 1) 20
2278 KELLYMOUNT 8-11-12 K F O'Brien, ...(8 to 1) 21
1822 BRIGADIER SUPREME (Ire) 5-10-10 (5*) J P Broderick,
. . . .(20 to 1) 22
2199 ISLAND ROW (Ire) 5-11-1 G Bradley, ...(20 to 1) 23
FIRE KING 8-11-4 C F Swan, ...(12 to 1) 24
1815 LOOK NONCHALANT (Ire) 5-10-3 (7*) B Murtagh, . .(33 to 1) 25
SIMPLY PHRASED (Ire) 5-11-1 J Shortt, ...(20 to 1) 26
Dist: 6l, ½l, 10l, ¾l. 4m 8.70s. a 20.70s (26 Ran).
SR: 43/45/36/34/30/-/

(William J Phelan), M J P O'Brien

2608 National Irish Bank Hurdle (Listed) (4-y-o) £11,500 2m. . . . . (2:10)

2285² SHIRLEY'S DELIGHT (Ire) 10-12 P Carberry, *hld up, prog to*
track ldr 2 out, dsptd ld appr last, slightly hmpd, rdn to
lead ins fnl 100 yards..............(7 to 4 on)   1
968² TROPICAL LAKE (Ire) 10-9 K F O'Brien, *trkd ldr, prog 3 out*,
rdn aftr nxt, lft disputing ld after last, hdd and no extr
ins fnl 100 yards..............(9 to 2)   2
2156⁶ MAGIC FEELING (Ire) 10-9 C F Swan, *hld up, prog 3 out*,
trkd ldrs nxt, rdn, wknd appr last......(4 to 1)   3
2156² MAYASTA (Ire) 10-9 C O'Dwyer, *mid-div, rdn and no extr*
appr 2 out..............................(10 to 1)   4
2388⁵ SHEREGORI (Ire) 11-0 N Williamson, *hld up, rdn appr 2*
out, no extr and wknd r-in..........(16 to 1)   5
1846* GLOWING VALUE (Ire) (bl) 11-0 B Sheridan, *trkd ldr, rdn*
and lost pl appr 2 out, wknd..........(14 to 1)   6
1816² THE BERUKI (Ire) 10-9 T P Treacy, *led, clr hfwy, rdn aftr 2*
out, hmpd appr last, blun and f, dead..........(5 to 1)   f
Dist: 3l, 13l, 4l, 9l. 4m 12.10s. a 24.10s (7 Ran).
SR: 3/-/-/-/-/

(Liam Doherty), Noel Meade

2609 WinElectric Chase Series Final (Listed) (5-y-o and up) £11,500 2m 5f (2:40)

2179* MERRY GALE (Ire) 6-11-12 K F O'Brien, *led, mstk 6th, jnd nxt, lft clr aftr 2 out, rdn appr last, styd on.* (13 to 8 on) 1
2286³ BUCKS-CHOICE 7-11-6 A Maguire, *in 4th pl whn mstk 6th, lost tch wth ldrs appr four out, kpt on frm 2 out, eased when btn r-in.* .... (4 to 1) 2
2075³ CHRKKRAR 7-12-0 R Dunwoody, *trkd ldr, rdn and lost pl appr 4 out, wknd.* .... (10 to 1) 3
2079 SIMENON 8-11-2 J P Banahan, *al rear, lost tch aftr 6th, tld off 5 out.* .... (50 to 1) 4
2286² BELVEDERIAN 7-11-12 G Bradley, *trkd ldr, dsptd ld 7th till stumbled and f 2 out.* .... (5 to 2) f
Dist: 20l, dist, dist. 5m 49.30s. a 35.30s (5 Ran).
SR: 8/-/- *(Herb M Stanley), J T R Dreaper*

2610 Convital Performance Handicap Hurdle (4-y-o and up) £13,000 2m. . (3:10)

2124⁸ THE SHAUGHRAUN [-] 8-10-6 T Horgan, ... (20 to 1) 1
1894³ JUPITER JIMMY (-) 10-10-J Magee, ... (100 to 30) 2
2279³ DEEP INAGH [-] 8-11-7 D P Fagan, ... (14 to 1) 3
2201* THATCH AND GOLD (Ire) [-] 6-10-8 M Duffy, ... (9 to 1) 4
2392⁴ COCK COCKBURN [-] 8-11-6 R Dunwoody, . . (3 to 1 fav) 5
2054² GRAND TOUR (NZ) [-] (bl) 6-10-2 L P Cusack, . . . (16 to 1) 6
2079⁵ TIME FOR A RUN [-] 7-11-10 C F Swan, ... (15 to 2) 7
2079² ARCTIC WEATHER (Ire) [-] 5-11-3 N Williamson, ...(5 to 1) 8
1686* FAMILY WAY [-] 7-10-7 F Woods, ... (100 to 30) 9
1234 LOSHIAN (Ire) [-] 5-11-8 B Sheridan, ... (12 to 1) 10
21807 IF YOU SAY YES (Ire) [-] 6-10-0 A Maguire, ... (14 to 1) 11
584² PRACTICE RUN [-] [-] 6-10-10 M Dwyer, ... (20 to 1) 12
2026³ FINAL FAVOUR (Ire) [-] (bl) 5-11-7 M Flynn, ... (12 to 1) 13
Dist: Nk, 2½l, sht-hd, 8l. 4m 7.80s. a 19.80s (13 Ran).
SR: 40/43/51/38/42/-/ *(Mrs G T McKey), P Hughes*

2611 Hennessy Cognac Gold Cup (Listed) (5-y-o and up) £43,125 3m. . . . . . (3:45)

2259³ JODAMI 9-12-0 M Dwyer, *wl plcd, smooth prog to dispute ld 4 out, lft clr aftr 2 out, eased r-in.* . . . . (5 to 4 fav) 1
1895* DEEP BRAMBLE 7-12-0 P Niven, *in tch, prog 6 out, mstk nxt, sn rdn, kpt on wl frm 2 out, no ch wth wnr.* (5 to 1) 2
2288⁵ FORCE SEVEN 7-11-9 A Maguire, *hld up, prog 5 out, rdn aftr 3 out, kpt on one pace.* .... (12 to 1) 3
2173² CHATAM (USA) 10-12-0 R Dunwoody, *trkd ldr, led 5th, jnd 4 out, mstk and hdd nxt, wknd.* .... (5 to 2) 4
1895⁶ CAHERVILLAHOW 10-12-0 N Williamson, *led to 5th, mstk 9th, sn rdn, kpt on one pace frm 3 out.* .... (25 to 1) 5
2189 FLASHING STEEL 9-12-0 K F O'Brien, *hld up, prog 6 out, dsptd ld 3 out, mstk and f nxt.* .... (4 to 1) f
Dist: 7l, 6l, 2½l, ½l, 2l. 44m 43.30s. a 31.30s (6 Ran).
SR: 87/80/69/71/66/-/ *(J N Yeadon), P Beaumont*

2612 Deloitte And Touche Hurdle (5-y-o and up) £13,000 2¼m. . . . . (4:15)

2287² DANOLI (Ire) 6-11-10 C F Swan, ... (5 to 4 on) 1
1986* COQ HARDI AFFAIR (Ire) 6-11-10 P Carberry, ... (10 to 1) 2
1891* WHAT A QUESTION (Ire) 6-11-5 G Bradley, ... (14 to 1) 3
2178 IDIOTS VENTURE 7-11-12 B Sheridan, ... (9 to 2) 4
1429* YUKON GOLD (Ire) (bl) 5-11-7 C O'Dwyer, . . . (100 to 30) 5
2287⁶ PADASHPAN (USA) 5-11-9 A Maguire, ... (7 to 1) 6
2391² COURT MELODY (Ire) 6-11-10 J P Broderick, ... (20 to 1) 7
Dist: 10l, 2½l, ½l, 2l. 44m 40.80s. a 24.80s (7 Ran).
SR: 28/18/10/16/9/-/-/ *(D J O'Neill), Thomas Foley*

2613 Le Coq Hardi Flat Race (5-y-o and up) £5,520 2m. . . . . (4:45)

1904² DOONANDORAS (Ire) 6-12-4 Mr J E Kiely, ... (9 to 2) 1
2467⁵ DROICHEAD LAPEEN 7-11-11 (7*) Mr T J Beattie, (20 to 1) 2
1230 THE SUBBIE (Ire) 5-11-11 (7*) Mr T J Murphy, ... (11 to 4) 3
2128¹ DONBOLINO (Ire) 6-11-13 Mr A P O'Brien, . . (12 to 1) 4
MASAI (Ire) 5-11-5 (3*) Mr D Valentine, ... (9 to 2) 5
2470⁴ TREANAREE (Ire) 5-11-3 (5*) Mr H F Cleary, ... (50 to 1) 6
2314* POWER PACK (Ire) 6-11-13 (5*) Mr B R Hamilton, . . (6 to 1) 7
2289¹ BUCK THE TIDE (Ire) 5-12-4 Mr T Mullins, ... (11 to 8 fav) pu
Dist: 3l, 2½l, 8l, 8l. 4m 6.00s. (8 Ran).

(E P King), J E Kiely

CLONMEL (IRE) (soft)
Monday February 14th

2614 Redmonstown Maiden Hurdle (4-y-o) £2,760 2m. . . . . (2:00)

2099² DANCING VISION (Ire) 10-9 C F Swan, ... (5 to 4 on) 1
2099³ MAN OF ARRAN (Ire) 10-11 (3*) T J O'Sullivan, ... (5 to 1) 2
2349² KHARASAR (Ire) 10-7 (7*) R A Hennessy, ... (4 to 1) 3
NURSE MAID (Ire) 10-9 J Jones, ... (12 to 1) 4
2547 ONOMATOPOEIA (Ire) 10-9 M Duffy, ... (12 to 1) 5
2099³ PERSIAN GEM (Ire) 10-4 C O'Dwyer, ... (12 to 1) 6
2099⁹ TINNEY JOUR (Ire) 10-9 T Horgan, ... (12 to 1) 7
2547 TRES JOUR (Ire) 10-4 P M Verling, ... (20 to 1) 8
2388 ABEREDW (Ire) 10-4 A Powell, ... (20 to 1) 9

2388⁶ RISKY GALORE 10-4 (5*) K P Gaule, ... (8 to 1) 10
CRISSY (Ire) 10-4 J Shortt, ... (20 to 1) pu
Dist: 2½l, sht-hd, 9l, 4½l. 4m 12.20s. (11 Ran).
(Golden Vale Racing Syndicate), Augustine Leahy

2615 The Gerry Chawke Hurdle (5-y-o) £3,110 2m. . . . . (2:30)

FOR REG (Ire) 11-9 M Duffy, ... (9 to 4) 1
2024* BE MY HOPE (Ire) 11-4 P Carberry, ... (5 to 2 on) 2
2279⁶ FABULIST (Ire) 11-1 (3*) T P Treacy, ... (9 to 1) 3
2231 PORT PRINCESS (Ire) 10-12 Mr T Doyle, ... (25 to 1) 4
2041 SALTY SNACKS (Ire) 11-3 A Powell, ... (25 to 1) 5
Dist: 2l, 20l, 11l, dist. 4m 11.90s. (5 Ran).
(D H O'Reilly), Patrick Joseph Flynn

2616 Powerstown EBF Mares Mdn Hdle (Qualifier) (4-y-o and up) £3,105 2½m . . . . (3:00)

2123⁵ CREATIVE BLAZE (Ire) 5-11-6 C F Swan, ... (100 to 30) 1
2586 SIOBHAILIN DUBH (Ire) 5-10-7 (5*) K P Gaule, . . . (14 to 1) 2
2197 JOES MISTIMARE 7-10-8 (7*) D M Drewett, ... (20 to 1) 3
1174⁸ THE COBH GALE 7-11-1 H Rogers, ... (25 to 1) 4
2464⁸ MARBLE FONTAINE 7-10-12 (3*) Miss M Olivefalk, (20 to 1) 5
945* BADEN (Ire) 6-11-6 (3*) T P Treacy, ... (6 to 4 fav) 6
1822⁸ HAZY ROSE (Ire) 5-11-6 J F Titley, ... (10 to 1) 7
2231⁷ TWO HILLS FOLLY (Ire) 5-10-12 T Horgan, ... (16 to 1) 8
2197⁴ FURRY DUCK (Ire) 6-11-9 B Sheridan, ... (8 to 1) 9
1766⁸ WATERLOO BALL (Ire) 5-11-1 (5*) M J Holbrook, . . (7 to 1) 10
1898⁸ FAIR ADELINE 7-11-1 P M Verling, ... (33 to 1) 11
2311⁶ KIZZY ROSE 7-10-10 (5*) J P Broderick, ... (14 to 1) 12
1898⁶ BALLINGOWAN STAR 7-10-8 (7*) M S O'Donnell, (16 to 1) 13
WEEKLY SESSIONS 7-11-9 P Carberry, ... (20 to 1) 14
KILLOSKEHAN QUEEN 7-10-12 (3*) C O'Brien, . . (20 to 1) 15
2197⁷ PARKBOY LASS 7-11-2 (7*) J M Donnelly, ... (20 to 1) 16
1401 GALES JEWEL 8-10-10 (5*) M G Cleary, ... (33 to 1) 17
1608 SMOOTH COUP 8-10-8 (7*) Mr D K Budds, ... (33 to 1) 18
2311 SHIMMERETTO 8-10-10 (5*) T P Rudd, ... (33 to 1) 19
2353 CROSSABEG ROSE 6-10-12 (3*) D P Murphy, (25 to 1) 20
Dist: 3l, 1½l, 12l. 5m 15.80s. (20 Ran).
(W J Austin), W J Austin

2617 Ladbrokes Handicap Hurdle (0-123 4-y-o and up) £3,450 2½m. . . . . (3:30)

2098* RIYADH DANCER (Ire) [-] 4-10-1 (5*) J R Barry, (3 to 1 fav) 1
1899³ IM MELODY (Ire) [-] 6-10-9 (5*) J P Broderick, ... (5 to 1) 2
2590⁷ RATHCORE [-] 7-10-13 L P Cusack, ... (5 to 1) 3
2590³ SUPER TACTICS (Ire) [-] 6-10-7 (5*) P A Roche, . . . (4 to 1) 4
1913⁷ BRINDLEY HOUSE [-] 7-11-5 J Shortt, ... (10 to 1) 5
2351³ SO PINK (Ire) [-] (bl) 6-10-13 (3*) T P Treacy, ... (7 to 1) 6
2039⁵ TARA'S SERENADE (Ire) [-] 5-9-8¹ C F Swan, ... (14 to 1) 7
2180² DEGO DANCER [-] 7-10-1 (3*) T J Mitchell, ... (8 to 1) 8
2549² HAKI SAKI [-] 8-11-5 T Horgan, ... (14 to 1) ur
Dist: ½l, 3½l, 6l, 11l. 5m 11.40s. (9 Ran).
(Miss C M Coady), Patrick Joseph Flynn

2618 The White Sands Catering Steeplechase (5-y-o and up) £3,110 2½m . . . . (4:00)

2550³ COMMANCHE NELL 6-11-3 J F Titley, ... (5 to 2) 1
2124⁵ RICH TRADITION (Ire) 6-11-4 J Shortt, ... (6 to 1) 2
2233⁴ BEAU GRANGE (Ire) 6-11-4 L P Cusack, ... (12 to 1) 3
2550⁷ CHELSEA NATIVE 7-10-8 (5*) Susan A Finn, ... (8 to 1) 4
2553⁸ DAVE FLECK (Ire) 6-11-4 C O'Dwyer, ... (12 to 1) 5
1900 MAMMY'S FRIEND 10-10-9 (3*) D P Murphy, . . . (14 to 1) 6
2282 FARNEY GLEN 7-11-8 C F Swan, ... (2 to 1 fav) 7
2277⁴ CROGEEN LASS 7-10-13 H Rogers, ... (14 to 1) 8
2313⁶ FAYS FOLLY (Ire) 5-9-11 (7*) D J Kavanagh, ... (25 to 1) 9
2160⁶ LINVAR 11-11-4 A Powell, ... (12 to 1) 10
2280 BLAZING DAWN 7-11-11 S H O'Donovan, ... (14 to 1) 11
Dist: 8l, 3l, 5l, 9l. 5m 43.40s. (11 Ran).
(Lisselan Farms Ltd), Fergus Sutherland

2619 Ballyvaughan Q.R. Handicap Chase (0-109 5-y-o and up) £2,760 3m. . (4:30)

2350 RUSSIAN GALE [-] 6-10-4¹¹ (7*) Mr D P Daly, (12 to 1) 1
2233³ GOOLDS GOLD [-] 8-10-12¹ (5*) Mr W M O'Sullivan, ... (4 to 1 jt-fav) 2
2350² IFFEEE [-] 7-11-8 (5*,3ex) Mr H F Cleary, ... (4 to 1 jt-fav) 3
2393³ MERLYNS CHOICE [-] 10-10-4¹ (3*) Mr J A Nash, . . (5 to 1) 4
1402 CARRIGEEN GALA [-] 7-10-4 (3*) Miss M Olivefalk, (20 to 1) 5
2235⁸ ITS A SNIP [-] 9-9-7 (7*) Mr T J Murphy, ... (14 to 1) 6
1402 ROSSI NOVAE [-] (bl) 11-12-3 Mr P Fenton, ... (20 to 1) 7
2100⁵ KIL KIL CASTLE [-] 7-9-10 (7*) Mr A O'Shea, ... (16 to 1) 8
2312³ KITES HARDWICKE [-] 7-10-6 Mr J P Dempsey, . . (9 to 1) 9
2393² GALLEY GALE [-] 8-10-10 (7*) Mr K Whelan, ... (25 to 1) f
2312⁴ GOLDEN CARRUTH (Ire) [-] 6-10-11 (7*) Mr B Moran, ... (6 to 1) f
2235 LISNAVARAGH [-] 8-10-7⁴ (3*) Mr A R Coonan, . . . (25 to 1) pu
Dist: ½l, 12l, 8l, 8l. 6m 43.80s. (12 Ran).
(J J Canty), E McNamara

2620 Templemore Flat Race (5-y-o and up) £2,760 2m................... (5:00)

1858[5]	DAWN ADAMS (Ire) 6-11-4 (5") Mr H F Cleary, ...(7 to 1)	1
2182[3]	WEST BROGUE (Ire) 5-11-11 Mr J P Dempsey, (5 to 4 fav)	2
2128	CARRAIG-AN-OIR (Ire) 5-11-11 Mr M Phillips, ... (12 to 1)	3
	LANCASTRIANS DREAM (Ire) 5-11-6 Mr A P O'Brien,	
	....(4 to 1)	4
	STEVIE BE (Ire) 6-11-7 (7") Mr B Moran, ...(7 to 1)	5
2128[9]	DEEP WAVE 7-11-9 (5") Mr C T G Kinane, ... (12 to 1)	6
107	BENTLEY'S FLYER (Ire) 5-11-6 Mr D M O'Brien, ...(6 to 1)	7
2553	LIME LADY (Ire) 5-10-13 (7") Mr M J Bowe, ... (14 to 1)	8
2353[3]	MIGHTY HAGGIS 7-11-7 (7") Mr N C Kelleher, ... (8 to 1)	9
	SALMOOSKY (Ire) 5-10-13 (7") Mr B Lennon, ... (10 to 1)	10
	SLIABH BLOOM (Ire) 5-10-13 (7") Mr F Cowman, ..(10 to 1)	11
2553	SHUIL SHELL (Ire) 5-11-3 (3") Mrs J M Mullins, ...(14 to 1)	12

Dist: 8l, 1½l, 2l, 14l. 4m 15.40s. (12 Ran).

(Jerome Sheehan), F Flood

FOLKESTONE (soft (races 1,4,6), good to soft (2,3,5))
Wednesday February 16th
Going Correction: PLUS 1.30 sec. per fur. (races 1,4,6), PLUS 1.05 (2,3,5)

2621 North Foreland Novices' Hurdle (5-y-o and up) £1,543 2m 1f 110yds.... (1:40)

2494*	BALLET ROYAL (USA) 5-11-6 M Perrett, hld up, prog to track ldr 3 out, led appr last, sn clr, cmftbly.	
	.... (6 to 4 op 7 to 4 tchd 11 to 8)	1
	ISAIAH 5-11-0 T Kent, led aftr second till appr last, wknd r-in... ....(33 to 1 op 8 to 1)	2
2335[3]	RIO TRUSKY 5-11-0 J Railton, hld up, prog 4th, rdn aftr 2 out, kpt on one pace................ (20 to 1 op 6 to 1)	3
2291*	GOOGLY 5-11-1 A Maguire, hld up, prog to track ldrs 5th, rdn betw last 2, not quicken.	
	.....................(5 to 4 on op 11 to 10 tchd 5 to 4)	4
2430[7]	MOVE A MINUTE (USA) 5-11-3 (3") P Hide, prmnt till wknd rpdly 2 out...........(16 to 1 op 5 to 1 tchd 20 to 1)	5
1840	SYLVAN SABRE (Ire) 5-11-0 J Osborne, in tch till wknd 5th, sn tld off................ (20 to 1 op 8 to 1)	6
2430	KITSBEL 6-11-0 L Harvey, led aftr 1st till after nxt, wknd 5th, sn tld off............(66 to 1 op 20 to 1)	7
	AUTO CONNECTION 8-10-9 N Dawe, led and mstk 1st, sn hdd, beh 5th, tld off and pld up bef last.	
	.... (66 to 1 op 33 to 1)	pu
2494	LB'S GIRL 5-10-9 N Williamson, beh 4th, sn tld off, pld up bef last.........................(66 to 1 op 33 to 1)	pu

Dist: 10l, 3½l, nk, 30l, dist, 3½l. 4m 24.70s. a 27.70s (9 Ran).
SR: 43/27/23/-/-/

(Park Farm Thoroughbreds), G Harwood

2622 Canterbury Handicap Chase (0-120 5-y-o and up) £2,635 2m 5f..... (2:10)

2319[4]	MAJOR INQUIRY (USA) [86] 8-10-6 D Murphy, hld up gng easily, prog to join ldr 12th, led 2 out, rdn out.	
	....................................(6 to 1 op 9 to 2)	1
2223[3]	GALLANT EFFORT (Ire) [100] 6-11-6 A Maguire, pressed ldr frm 3rd, led 12th till hdd and mstk 2 out, hrd rdn, no extr.................... (6 to 4 fav op 7 to 4 tchd 15 to 8)	2
2457[3]	FAARIS [85] 13-10-5 J Railton, in tch to 11th, kpt on appr 2 out, no dngr.........(20 to 1 op 10 to 1 tchd 25 to 1)	3
2047	ZAMIL (USA) [106] 9-11-12 N Williamson, led second to 12th, wknd 3 out....(3 to 1 op 11 to 4 tchd 100 to 30)	4
2454[4]	SECRET RITE [94] 11-11-0 Peter Hobbs, led to second, pushed alng 5th, beh 11th...........(7 to 2 op 9 to 4)	5
2520	MOZE TIDY [88] 9-10-8 T Grantham, al rear, rdn and lost tch 9th, tld off whn pld up bef 11th.	
	....................(33 to 1 op 20 to 1 tchd 50 to 1)	pu

Dist: 2½l, 20l, 20l, 1½l. 5m 37.90s. a 27.90s (6 Ran).
SR: 20/31/-/

(Mrs T Brown), J T Gifford

2623 Kent Handicap Chase (0-130 5-y-o and up) £3,366 3¼m............... (2:40)

2431*	FIDDLERS THREE [101] (bl) 11-11-6 (3") R Farrant, prmnt, led 4 out, clr 2 out, wknd r-in, all out.	
	....................(13 to 8 fav op 5 to 4 tchd 2 to 1)	1
2518[3]	BETTY HAYES [100] 10-11-1 (7") P Carey, mstks 7th and 11th, lost tld till rdn and outpcd 4 out, rallied r-in, not rch wnr...............(11 to 2 op 3 to 1 tchd 6 to 1)	2
2305[3]	SMOOTH ESCORT [106] (v) 10-12-0 N Williamson, led to 4th, led 6th till rdn and hdd four out, not quicken aftr, btn whn mstk last.......(11 to 4 op 5 to 1 tchd 3 to 1)	3
2396[3]	ROCKMOUNT ROSE [85] 9-10-0 (7") L Dace, cl up till outpcd 5th, no prog aftr.	
	..........................(7 to 1 op 4 to 1 tchd 8 to 1)	4
2188[3]	RUNNING SANDS [88] 10-10-5 (5") C Burnett-Wells, keen hold, led 4th to 6th, in tch whn mstk 13th, stumbled and uns rdr nxt......................(8 to 1 op 4 to 1)	ur
2336[2]	CARRIGLAWN [78] 9-10-0[3] (3") P Hide, uns rdr second.	
	....................(16 to 1 op 12 to 1 tchd 20 to 1)	ur

Dist: 1½l, 2l, 30l. 7m 6.40s. a 54.40s (6 Ran).

(Simon Sainsbury), Capt T A Forster

2624 Valentine Gorton Juvenile Hurdle (4-y-o) £1,543 2m 1f 110yds....... (3:10)

2189[5]	MARIUS (Ire) 10-12 D Murphy, trkd ldrs, led on bit last, easily................(10 to 1 op 7 to 2)	1
2374[3]	NAWAR (Fr) 11-4 A Maguire, mstks, cl up, rdn and ev ch appr last, unbl to quicken.... (9 to 4 on op 2 to 1 on)	2
2422[3]	VISIMOTION (USA) 10-12 T Kent, trkd ldr, led 3 out, rdn and hdd and mstk last, wknd r-in. (50 to 1 op 10 to 1)	3
2300	FOOLS ERRAND (Ire) 11-4 S McNeill, led till rdn and hdd 3 out, wknd appr last....................(5 to 2 op 6 to 4)	4
	PALACE PARADE (USA) 10-12 N Dawe, mstk 4th, in tch till f 3 out......................(100 to 1 op 14 to 1)	f

Dist: 2l, 8l, 1½l. 4m 29.10s. a 32.10s (5 Ran).

(Mrs Leonard Simpson), J T Gifford

2625 Manston Novices' Handicap Chase (5-y-o and up) £2,135 2m......... (3:40)

2603[2]	MISTER ODDY [80] 8-11-5 (5") T Jenks, jmpd lft, made all, wl clr 3 out, unchlgd... (6 to 4 op 5 to 4 tchd 13 to 8)	1
	HARBINGER [77] 9-11-7 D Murphy, rear whn mstk 7th, sn beh, styd on to take second r-in.... (11 to 2 op 5 to 1)	2
2397[2]	HANDSOME NED [82] 8-11-12 J Railton, chsd wnr, no imprsn 3 out, wknd appr last.	
	...................(11 to 10 on op Evens tchd 6 to 5)	3
2399[3]	LETTS GREEN (Ire) [56] (bl) 6-10-0 D Morris, rear, blun 8th and 9th, tld off whn refused nxt.	
	.................(40 to 1 op 10 to 1 tchd 50 to 1)	ref

Dist: 25l, 3l. 4m 20.30s. a 25.30s (4 Ran).
SR: 11/

(Mrs R M Hill), J S King

2626 Goodwins Handicap Hurdle (0-120 4-y-o and up) £2,196 2m 1f 110yds ....(4:10)

2521*	RUN HIGH [102] 11-10-10 (7ex) Mr R Teal, set very slow pace, quickened clr 2 out, mstk last, rdn out.	
	.......(6 to 5 fav op 5 to 4 tchd 13 to 8)	1
2432	FAMOUS DANCER [92] 6-10-0 A Maguire, hld up last, mstk 3rd, outpcd 2 out, ran on one pace appr last.	
	.................(11 to 2 op 4 to 1 tchd 6 to 1)	2
2267[8]	TOP WAVE [117] 6-11-11 M A FitzGerald, trkd wnr till outpcd 2 out, ran on one pace appr last.	
	............(5 to 4 op 6 to 4 tchd 11 to 10)	3
2400[5]	NOVA SPIRIT [92] 6-10-0 D Murphy, hld up, effrt to chase wnr aftr 2 out, sn one pace.	
	................(12 to 1 op 6 to 1 tchd 14 to 1)	4

Dist: 4l, 1½l, 1l. 4m 58.80s. a 61.80s (4 Ran).

(Mrs Patricia Mitchell), P Mitchell

SOUTHWELL (A.W) (std)
Wednesday February 16th
Going Correction: PLUS 0.65 sec. per fur.

2627 Corn Exchange Amateur Riders' Handicap Hurdle (0-115 4-y-o and up) £1,715 2¼m................... (2:25)

2530*	BURN BRIDGE (USA) [91] (v) 8-11-4 (7",6ex) Mr D Parker, chsd clr ldr, effrt and hdwy to ld appr 3 out, lft wl clear....(2 to 1 fav op 2 to 1 tchd 9 to 4 and 7 to 4)	1
2530[4]	RAIN-N-SUN [68] 8-9-12[3] (7") Mr I McLelland, beh and pushed alng through out, styd on frm 3 out, no ch wth wnr.................................(9 to 1 op 8 to 1)	2
2421[2]	ALDINGTON CHAPPLE [70] 6-9-11 (7") Miss L Boswell, chsd ldrs, rdn aftr 4 out and sn btn, hit last.	
	...........................(6 to 1 op 5 to 1)	3
2423[3]	SANTA PONSA BAY [77] 7-10-4 (7") Mr B Pollock, chsd ldrs, rdn aftr 4 out, 3rd and wl hld whn badly hmpd 3 out.	
	...................(5 to 2 tchd 11 to 4)	4
2227[3]	SHAMSHOM AL ARAB (Ire) [80] 6-10-7 (7") Miss V Haigh, chsd ldrs till lost pl 5 out, sn btn....(8 to 1 op 6 to 1)	5
1738[2]	RUSTY ROC [90] 13-11-3 (7") Mr N Miles, led and sn clr, rdn and hdd appr 3 out, second and wknd whn f three out.....................(6 to 1 op 5 to 1 tchd 13 to 2)	f

Dist: 12l, 2l, 7l, 4l. 4m 31.40s. a 19.40s (6 Ran).
SR: 20/-/-/

(M J Pipe), T H Caldwell

2628 Prince Rupert Selling Hurdle (4-y-o and up) £1,675 2m............. (2:55)

2421[4]	CHAGHATAI (USA) (bl) 8-11-4 Mr B Leavy, chsd ldrs, rdn and outpcd appr 4 out, gd hdwy to ld 3 out, ridden and styd on wl..........(20 to 1 op 20 to 1 tchd 25 to 1)	1
2331[6]	SHARP DANCE 5-10-13 B Powell, pld hrd, hld up, hdwy appr 4 out, rdn nxt, styd on one pace.	
	.......................(10 to 1 op 16 to 1)	2
2395[2]	MAJOR'S LAW (Ire) 5-11-10 W McFarland, trkd ldrs, hdwy 4 out, effrt and led briefly appr nxt, sn hrd drvn and ev ch, wknd last. (5 to 4 on op 7 to 4 on tchd 6 to 5 on)	3
1927[9]	GREEN MILL 4-10-8 B Dalton, led till aftr 1st, led 3rd to 5th, led 6th till rdn, hdd and wknd appr 3 out. (33 to 1)	4

2118[5] BALADIYA 7-10-13 N Mann, *prmnt, rdn 4 out, wknd appr nxt*.................... (9 to 2 op 5 to 1 tchd 4 to 1) 5

3333[5] BUSTLING AROUND 7-10-13 M Bosley, *hld up, effrt and rdn 4 out, no hdwy*.................... (7 to 1 op 4 to 1) 6

2439[6] NEVER SO LOST 4-10-8 D Bridgwater, *prmnt, led aftr 1st to 3rd, led 5th till hdd and hit nxt, rdn and mstk 4 out, sn wknd and pld up bef next*.................... (33 to 1) pu

1384[4] CHILTERN HUNDREDS (USA) 4-10-1 (7") Mr C Bonner, *chsd ldrs, hit 5th and sn lost pl, beh whn pld up bef 3 out*.
.... (20 to 1) pu

2500 SHATRAVIV 6-10-13 B Storey, *al rear, beh whn pld up bef 3 out*.................... (12 to 1 op 10 to 1) pu

Dist: 2½l, hd, 12l, 8l, 2l. 4m 6.30s. a 20.30s (9 Ran).

(Mrs M Robertson), W Clay

2629 White Hart Novices' Hurdle (4-y-o and up) £1,484 2¼m............... (3:25)

2092* ALLEGATION (v) 4-11-4 R Dunwoody, *made all, sn clr, eased r-in, unchlgd*.
.... (13 to 8 on op 5 to 4 on tchd Evens) 1

BEDOUIN PRINCE (USA) 7-11-4 G McCourt, *slwly into strd and beh, hdwy hfwy, rdn bef 3 out, kpt on, no ch wth wnr*.................... (7 to 1 op 5 to 1 tchd 8 to 1) 2

2422[2] BOZO BAILEY 4-10-8 R Campbell, *chsd wnr, rdn appr 3 out, plugged on one pace*...... (6 to 1 op 4 to 1) 3

2303 MULLED ALE (Ire) 4-10-3 M Richards, *slwly into strd and beh, hdwy 8th, rdn nxt, plugged on one pace*.
.... (16 to 1 op 12 to 1) 4

2327[3] SCRABO VIEW 6-11-4 L O'Hara, *unruly strt, in tch, rdn and wknd 4 out*.................... (11 to 2 op 7 to 2) 5

2327[5] TANGO IN PARIS (Arg) (bl) 4-10-3 (5") S Curran, *chsd wnr to hfwy, sn wknd and wl beh*.
.... (25 to 1 op 33 to 1 tchd 20 to 1) 6

2530 IMPERIAL TOKAY (USA) (v) 4-10-3 (5") T Eley, *mid-div, hit 3rd, tld off hfwy, pld up bef 3 out*.
.... (33 to 1 tchd 40 to 1) pu

1374[7] BRESIL (USA) 5-11-4 D Bridgwater, *mid-div, hdwy to chase ldrs 5th, rdn and wknd quickly 5 out, tld off whn pld up bef 3 out*.................... (25 to 1) pu

Dist: 5l, 3½l, 1l, 8l, 15l. 4m 29.80s. a 17.80s (8 Ran).

SR: 29/24/10/4/11/

(Southern Depots), M C Pipe

2630 Viscountess Ossington's Novices' Handicap Hurdle (4-y-o and up) £1,484 3m........................... (3:55)

2225[8] MUTUAL BENEFIT [58] (bl) 7-10-2 R Dunwoody, *made all, rdn clr appr 3 out, styd on wl*.......(6 to 1 op 5 to 1) 1

2117[2] MEKSHARP [71] 7-10-10 (5") T Eley, *chsd ldrs, rdn and outpcd tenth, plugged on und pres frm 3 out*.
.... (9 to 2 op 4 to 1) 2

2531[2] ARCTIC LIFE (Ire) [84] 5-12-0 Mr P Graffin, *trkd ldrs, hdwy 9th, jnd wnr nxt, rdn and wknd appr 3 out, blun badly three out and next*. (11 to 4 fav op 5 to 2 tchd 3 to 1) 3

1595 LAFHEEN (Ire) [56] 6-10-0 W Humphreys, *prmnt, rdn and outpcd tenth, plugged on und pres frm 3 out*.
.... (10 to 1 op 7 to 1) 4

2424* RED COLUMBIA [70] 13-11-0 Mrs G Adkin, *prmnt till f 4th, dead*.................... (3 to 1 tchd 7 to 2) f

2417 STORM ISLAND [67] 9-10-11 W McFarland, *chsd ldrs, rdn aftr 9th, sn tld off, pld up after 4 out*. (5 to 1 op 4 to 1) pu

MOUNT AILEY [65] 8-10-9 J Corkell, *in tch till blun badly 3rd, pld up lme*.................... (25 to 1 tchd 33 to 1) pu

Dist: 15l, ¾l, 1½l. 6m 18.60s. a 41.60s (7 Ran).

(T Casey), T Casey

2631 Queens Sconce Claiming Hurdle (4-y-o and up) £1,719 2½m....... (4:25)

2424* KANNDABIL (bl) 7-11-13 G McCourt, *mid-div, pushed along and hdwy 7th, rdn to ld 3 out, jmpd rght last three, kpt on*.................... (5 to 2 op 9 to 4 tchd 11 to 4) 1

1860[4] ELDER PRINCE 8-11-5 G Harker, *prmnt, led 4th till rdn and hdd 3 out, kpt on one pace*.
.... (12 to 1 op 14 to 1 tchd 16 to 1) 2

1394[6] OBIE'S TRAIN (bl) 8-11-11 R Dunwoody, *al prmnt, rdn appr 4 out, sn btn*.................... (9 to 4 op 7 to 1) 3

2116[4] TESEKKUREDERIM 7-11-3 Diane Clay, *mid-div, effrt and rdn alng 7th, wknd nxt*.......(12 to 1 op 10 to 1) 4

2458 THE JET SET 7-11-3 V Slattery, *jmpd rght thrght, prmnt till lost pl and beh frm hfwy*.... (25 to 1 tchd 33 to 1) 5

2425[3] FOR HEAVEN'S SAKE (Fr) 9-11-7 Wall, *led, reminders 3rd, hdd and f nxt, dead*...... (7 to 4 fav tchd 15 to 8) f

VITAL SINGER 9-11-0 (5") T Eley, *al rear, tld off 7th, pld up bef 3 out*.................... (66 to 1 op 50 to 1) pu

Dist: 10l, 6l, 3½l, 7l. 5m 15.20s. a 34.20s (7 Ran).

(Neil McAndrews), N Tinkler

2632 Hercules Clay Handicap Hurdle (0-110 5-y-o and up) £1,748 2¾m...... (4:55)

DESERT FORCE (Ire) [87] 5-10-1 M Richards, *hld up and beh, steady hdwy 4 out, led aftr 3 out, blun badly nxt, kpt on gmely und pres r-in*........ (10 to 1 op 12 to 1) 1

2425[2] COURT CIRCULAR [114] (v) 5-12-0 Diane Clay, *dsptd ld, led 4 out, sn rdn, hdd appr nxt, ev ch till no extr nr finish*.
.... (3 to 1 op 7 to 2 tchd 9 to 2) 2

1521[8] TRUST DEED (USA) [93] (bl) 6-10-7 D Gallagher, *dsptd ld till 4 out, sn rdn and drvn frm nxt*. (16 to 1 op 20 to 1) 3

2418[3] CORLY SPECIAL [86] 7-10-0 R Marley, *chsd ldrs, rdn 4 out and one pace*.................... (20 to 1 op 10 to 1) 4

348[2] BAHRAIN QUEEN (Ire) [94] 6-10-8 M Ranger, *mid-div, effrt and rdn appr 4 out, sn btn*........ (20 to 1 op 14 to 1) 5

2487[7] ST VILLE [108] 8-11-3 (5") S Mason, *dsptd ld till rdn 4 out, sn wknd*.................... (5 to 1 op 7 to 2) 6

2425* COSMIC DANCER [114] (bl) 7-12-0 A Carroll, *hld up and beh, hdwy 9th, smooth hdwy to ld appr 3 out, blun badly three out, sn hdd, pld up aftr nxt*.
.... (11 to 10 on op Evens tchd 11 to 10) pu

Dist: ½l, 6l, 2l, 1l, 30l. 5m 46.60s. a 37.60s (7 Ran).

(T R Pearson), R J Weaver

LEICESTER (heavy (races 1,2,6), good to soft (3,4,5))
Thursday February 17th
Going Correction: PLUS 2.60 sec. per fur. (races 1,2,6), PLUS 2.10 (3,4,5)

2633 Oadby 'National Hunt' Novices' Hurdle (5-y-o and up) £2,021 2½m 110yds ....(2:10)

CELTIC TOWN 6-10-12 M Richards, *nvr far away, drvn ahead aftr 3 out, styd on strly to go clr last*... (10 to 1) 1

2147 THREE OF CLUBS (Ire) 5-10-12 A Maguire, *set modest pace, quickened up appr 4 out, hdd bef nxt, one pace frm betw last 2*.................... (9 to 2 op 7 to 2) 2

2361 BATHWICK BOBBIE (bl) 7-10-12 S McNeill, *al hndy, blun 5th, led appr 3 out, blunded and sn hdd, rdn and no extr*.................... (9 to 2 op 4 to 1) 3

2262[3] FLAPJACK LAD 5-10-12 C Llewellyn, *patiently rdn, improved to take clr order 4 out, ridden aftr nxt, one pace*.................... (15 to 8 fav op 6 to 4 tchd 2 to 1) 4

1503 BRADWALL 10-10-9 (3") A Thornton, *trkd ldrs, struggling and lost grnd aftr 4 out, lost tch and pld up bef last*.
.... (33 to 1) pu

CASTLE BANKS 10-10-12 I Lawrence, *in tch, chsd alng to keep up hfwy, tld off whn pld up bef 4 out*. (33 to 1) pu

2220[8] THE PIPE FITTER (Ire) 6-10-12 P Niven, *trkd ldg bunch, struggling bef 4 out, lost tch and pld up before 2 out*.
.... (7 to 2 op 4 to 1) pu

Dist: 15l, 3½l, nk. (Time not taken) (7 Ran).

(Lady Helen Smith), O Sherwood

2634 Vicarage Novices' Claiming Hurdle (4 & 5-y-o) £1,780 2m............. (2:40)

2207[3] BAND SARGEANT (Ire) 5-11-8 (5") N Leach, *patiently rdn, chalg whn hit 3 out, led betw last 2, drvn clr, kpt on*.
.... (9 to 2 op 5 to 2) 1

2401[6] ERLEMO (v) 5-11-9 Diane Clay, *nvr far away, nosed ahead 3 out, hdd betw last 2, one pace*...... (16 to 1) 2

2523[2] BITRAN 4-11-0 A S Smith, *al hndy, effrt and drvn alng 3 out, styd on same pace frm nxt*...... (7 to 2 op 3 to 1) 3

FILOU FLIGHT (Fr) 4-11-0 A Maguire, *wtd wth, improved to join issue 3 out, kpt on same pace frm betw last 2*.
.... (9 to 1 op 6 to 1 tchd 10 to 1) 4

2414 COUSIN WENDY 4-10-2 (3") A Thornton, *chsd ldrs, feeling pace and drvn alng aftr 4 out, no imprsn frm nxt*.
.... (50 to 1 op 33 to 1) 5

2271[4] PRIORY PIPER 5-11-0 (5") T Eley, *tried to make all, hdd and rdn 3 out, sn outpcd*...............(20 to 1) 6

2140 ANNE CARTER 5-11-0 M Ranger, *trkd ldrs, hrd rdn to stay in tch appr 4 out, tld off*.................. (33 to 1) 7

KOSVILLE (Fr) 4-11-7 M Richards, *tucked away beh ldg bunch, improved 4 out, wknd quickly nxt, lost tch and pld up bef last*.
.... (11 to 8 on op 7 to 4 on tchd 5 to 4 on) pu

Dist: 2l, 2l, 2l, 2½l, 3l, dist. 4m 41.80s. a 58.80s (8 Ran).

(E R Madden), G Richards

2635 Trial Handicap Chase (0-120 5-y-o and up) £4,503 3m................. (3:10)

2499[2] VIVA BELLA (Fr) [90] (bl) 7-9-9 (7") Mr D Parker, *nvr far away, scrubbed alng and looked btn 3 out, styd on grimly to ld r-in, forged clr*...... (2 to 1 op 7 to 4) 1

2325* MORGANS HARBOUR [98] 8-10-10 P Niven, *wtd wth, improved to join ldr ful circuit, led 3 out, rdn and jmpd lft last, sn hdd and no extr*.
.... (6 to 5 fav op 5 to 4 on tchd 11 to 8) 2

2370[3] RIFLE RANGE [115] 11-11-3 A Maguire, *tried to make all, jnd ful circuit, hdd 3 out, fnshd tired*.
.... (5 to 1 tchd 6 to 1) 3

2410[4] BARKIN [97] 11-10-9 M Moloney, *trkd ldrs, hrd drvn and lost grnd bef 5 out, tld off*.
.... (16 to 1 op 14 to 1) 4

2448 DEEP COLONIST [116] 12-12-0 R Garritty, *trkd ldrs, blun 7th, sn lost pl, pld up bef 11th*,..... (16 to 1 op 14 to 1) pu

Dist: 5l, dist, dist. 6m 48.10s. a 56.10s (5 Ran).
SR: 17/20/   (L H Froomes), Mrs S A Bramall

2636   Wren Handicap Chase (0-115 5-y-o and up) £2,836 2½m 110yds.....(3:40)

1866⁴ BOLL WEEVIL [98] 8-11-4 M Richards, *dsptd ld, drvn alng whn pace lifted 5 out, rallied to forge ahead aftr 3 out, styd on, eased considerably cl hme.*
....................................(9 to 2 op 5 to 1 tchd 6 to 1)   1
2507* SHANNON GLEN [104] (bl) 8-11-10 I Lawrence, *made most, quickened clr 5 out, almost f nxt, hdd aftr 3 out, blun next, kpt on same pace.....* (100 to 30 jt-fav op 3 to 1)   2
1733⁴ REJOINUS [108] 9-12-0 A Maguire, *settled off the pace, effrt hfwy, reminders 4 out, rallied nxt, one pace.*
....................................(7 to 2 op 3 to 1 tchd 4 to 1)   3
2486* SPOONHILL WOOD [84] (bl) 8-10-4 B Dalton, *nvr far away, ev ch whn blun badly 3 out and nxt, wknd quickly betw last 2.*...................(7 to 2 op 3 to 1)   4
2334* DUO DROM [99] (v) 9-11-5 E Murphy, *chsd ldg bunch, struggling to keep up whn f 5 out.*........(100 to 30 jt-fav op 3 to 1 tchd 7 to 2)   f
2293 SMILES AHEAD [80] 6-9-9 (5*) T Eley, *chsd ldg pair to hfwy, struggling 4 out, tld off whn pld up betw last 2.*
....................................(14 to 1 op 33 to 1)   pu
Dist: 2½l, 12l, 25l. 6m 3.30s. a 60.30s (6 Ran).
(John Bolsover), O Sherwood

2637   Thurnby Novices' Chase (5-y-o and up) £2,476 2m 1f............. (4:10)

2538⁴ DAN DE LYON 6-11-2 A Maguire, *patiently rdn, improved gng wl 4 out, led on bit last, easily.*
....................................(9 to 2 op 7 to 2 tchd 5 to 1)   1
2501² PRECIPICE RUN 9-11-8 N Doughty, *mstks, al hndy, lft in ld 5 out, blun and hdd last, sn btn.*
....................................(11 to 10 fav tchd 11 to 8)   2
1308 TURF RUN 7-11-2 S McNeill, *wth ldr, led 5th till f 5 out.*
....................................(6 to 1 op 8 to 1)   f
2002⁵ TAURIAN PRINCESS 5-10-2 W Humphreys, *tracking ldrs whn f 5th.*....................(25 to 1 tchd 33 to 1)   f
2497 THE PUB 8-11-2 J Corkell, *led to 5th, 3rd and struggling whn impeded by loose horse, refused, landed in ditch 4 out.*....................................(100 to 1)   f
ALMANZORA 10-11-2 I Lawrence, *in tch, broke dwn and pld up bef 7th.*...................(7 to 2 op 6 to 4)   pu
Dist: 10l. 5m 5.10s. a 56.10s (6 Ran).
(Michael Kerr-Dineen), D Nicholson

2638   Somerby Novices' Hurdle (4-y-o) £1,909 2m................ (4:40)

2471⁴ MARROS MILL 10-13 A Maguire, *al gng best, led on bit bef 3 out, clr whn hit last, easily.......* (11 to 4 op 7 to 1)   1
2275⁴ EVE'S TREASURE 10-2 (5*) S Lyons, *settled in tch, took clr order aftr 4 out, styd on, not rch wnr.*
....................................(20 to 1 op 33 to 1)   2
2135* NATIVE WORTH 11-5 (5*) P Williams, *al hndy, drvn alng whn hit 3 out, rallied, kpt on same pace r-in.*
....................................(5 to 1 op 4 to 1)   3
2471³ PAPER DAYS 10-12 E Murphy, *trkd ldrs, blun second, effrt and bustled alng aftr 4 out, one pace.*
....................................(9 to 4 fav tchd 5 to 2)   4
2564⁴ PRIMO FIGLIO (bl) 10-9 (3*) A Thornton, *settled to track ldrs, effrt and drvn alng 4 out, sn outpcd.....* (14 to 1)   5
2291⁸ VOLUNTEER POINT (Ire) 10-7 (5*) J Burke, *tried to make all, jnd 4 out, sn ld aftr, tld off.......*(20 to 1)   6
2387⁸ MASTER TOBY 10-12 C Llewellyn, *al struggling, tld off appr 4 out.*.......(16 to 1 op 10 to 1 tchd 20 to 1)   7
2478³ SHAMSHADAL (Ire) 10-12 L Wyer, *pressed ldrs, effrt and drvn alng 4 out, wknd rpdly and pld up bef nxt.*
....................................(6 to 1 op 5 to 1 tchd 7 to 1)   pu
Dist: 2½l, 1l, 10l, 20l, 3½l, 6l. 4m 34.10s. a 51.10s (8 Ran).
(Mrs Claire Smith), D Nicholson

LINGFIELD (heavy)
Thursday February 17th
Going Correction: NIL

2639   Pretty Girl Claiming Chase (5-y-o and up) £2,420 2½m 110yds........(2:50)

2318⁵ HOMME D'AFFAIRE 11-11-2 D O'Sullivan, *led till hdd 6th, rgned ld appr 11th, sn headed, rallied to lead 2 out, styd on wl.*...................(8 to 1 op 5 to 1)   1
SWITCH (bl) 8-12-0 D Gallagher, *nvr far away, led aftr 11th till hdd 2 out, unbl to quicken.*
....................................(9 to 1 op 4 to 1 tchd 10 to 1)   2
STAR'S DELIGHT 12-12-0 J Lower, *trkd ldrs till led 6th, hdd appr 11th, sn wknd.*
....................................(6 to 4 on op 6 to 4 tchd 13 to 8 on)   3
2396⁶ RADICAL REQUEST 11-10-13 (5*) D Fortt, *al beh, tld off.*
....................................(16 to 1 op 12 to 1 tchd 20 to 1)   4
2402⁵ SERDARLI 12-10-3 (7*) Mr J O'Shaughnessy, *in tch, 5th whn f 7th.*........................(50 to 1)   f

---

1923² JAMES MY BOY 14-11-2 M Brennan, *chsd ldg bunch till wknd frm 9th, tld off whn pld up bef 3 out...* (14 to 1)   pu
2020 CEDAR RUN 11-11-1 D Meade, *niggled alng 3rd, sn struggling in rear, tld of whn pld up bef 7th.*
....................................(50 to 1 op 33 to 1)   pu
2397* NATHIR (USA) 8-11-10 R Greene, *not fluent, al beh, tld off whn pld up bef 3 out.*.......(7 to 1 op 4 to 1)   pu
2429⁵ FALSE ECONOMY (bl) 9-11-8 Richard Guest, *chsd ldrs till wknd 7th, beh whn pld up aftr 9th.* (10 to 1 op 5 to 1)   pu
Dist: 4l, dist, 8l. (Time not taken) (9 Ran).
(Miss Nicola M Pfann), R J O'Sullivan

LINGFIELD (A.W) (std)
Thursday February 17th
Going Correction: MINUS 0.05 sec. per fur.

2640   Juliet Novices' Hurdle (4-y-o and up) £1,722 2¼m................. (1:50)

2440² BOBBY SOCKS 8-11-2 W McFarland, *al tracking ldrs, hit 6th, led appr 3 out, sn jnd, hld on amely r-in.*
....................................(5 to 4 fav op Evens)   1
2529* DULZURA 6-11-3 R Greene, *led to second, styd hndy and chlgd frm 3 out, still ev ch last, kpt on.*
....................................(9 to 4 tchd 5 to 2)   2
1316⁴ EARLY DRINKER 6-10-13 (3*) J McCarthy, *chsd ldrs, ran on to go 3rd appr 3 out, styd on one pace.*
....................................(3 to 1 op 4 to 1)   3
2440³ SWING LUCKY (bl) 8-11-2 R Campbell, *led second till hdd appr 3 out, wknd.*..................(14 to 1)   4
1710⁸ HERETICAL MISS (bl) 4-10-2 D Gallagher, *hld up in midfield till lost tch frm 9th, tld off.*.......(12 to 1)   5
1085⁶ LUCKNAM DREAMER 6-11-2 E Byrne, *in tch, awkward 5th, mstk 7th, sn wknd and tld off.* (20 to 1 op 33 to 1)   6
2430 GIVE ALL 8-10-9 (7*) M Appleby, *slwly away, al beh, tld off.*......................(33 to 1)   7
2455 APOLLO VENTURE 6-10-9 (7*) S Arnold, *jmpd slwly 1st, last and niggled alng 7th, sn tld off.*
....................................(33 to 1 op 25 to 1)   8
Dist: Nk, 8l, 15l, dist, 25l, 15l, 3l. 4m 8.98s. a 7.98s (8 Ran).
(Martin Stillwell), R Lee

2641   Valentine Selling Handicap Hurdle (4-y-o and up) £1,799 2m........ (2:20)

2343⁸ BARTON ROYAL (Ire) [75] (v) 4-10-6 Richard Guest, *al tracking ldr, led aftr 3 out, jnd last, rdn and ran on wl.*
....................................(11 to 1 op 8 to 1 tchd 12 to 1)   1
2343⁴ MILL BURN [75] 5-10-6 R Campbell, *patiently rdn, smooth hdwy frm 7th, sn chasing ldrs, chlgd last, no extr run-un..*....................(3 to 1 op 9 to 4)   2
2542⁴ RED INK [74] (bl) 5-9-12 (7*) W J Walsh, *al hndy, till rdn and one pace aftr 3 out, sn no imprsn.*
....................................(10 to 1 op 7 to 1)   3
2545 CYRILL HENRY (Ire) [75] 5-10-6 A Merrigan, *in tch till no hdwy frm 3 out.*.............(10 to 1 op 8 to 1)   4
2545⁴ CANDLE KING (Ire) [72] 6-10-2⁶ (7*) M Appleby, *hld up, pushed alng and hdwy 6th, wknd frm 8th.*
....................................(8 to 1 tchd 9 to 1)   5
2342² SAFETY (USA) [93] (bl) 7-11-10 D Skyrme, *led till hdd aftr 3 out, wknd whn mstk nxt, sn wl beh.*
....................................(6 to 4 fav tchd 13 to 8)   6
1719⁶ HATS HIGH [78] 9-10-9 M Crosse, *lost tch frm 8th.*
....................................(16 to 1 op 12 to 1)   7
2271⁷ CASHABLE [69] 4-10-0 D Gallagher, *trkd ldrs till lost pl 3rd, sn beh, tld off.*........(14 to 1 op 12 to 1)   8
Dist: 3l, 12l, ½l, 25l, 4l, dist. 3m 40.77s. a 7.77s (8 Ran).
(D Tye), P C Ritchens

2642   Romeo Mares' Only Novices' Hurdle (4-y-o and up) £1,737 2½m......(3:20)

2204⁹ GLENGARRA PRINCESS 7-10-13 (3*) J McCarthy, *led second, made nxt, drw clr frm 3 out, easily.*
....................................(5 to 4 fav op 13 to 8)   1
2543² LIZZIES LASS 9-10-9 (7*) G Crone, *led to second, remained hndy till outpcd 11th, ran on qu'n und pres frm 2 out to snatch second nr finish.*...........(10 to 1 op 8 to 1)   2
2343² HULLO MARY DOLL 5-10-9 (7*) Chris Webb, *trkd wnr, effrt appr 3 out, sn rdn and no imprsn, wknd lost second nr finish..*....................(5 to 1 op 9 to 2)   3
2428⁷ LA POSADA (v) 4-9-12 (7*) P Moore, *chase ldrs till no hdwy frm tenth..*.................(6 to 1 op 5 to 1)   4
2492 FREEBYJOVE 4-9-12 (7*) S Arnold, *chsd ldrs till lost tch frm tenth, tld off..*.............(33 to 1)   5
2599⁷ FLAPPING FREDA (Ire) 6-11-2 D Gallagher, *al beh, tld off..*.........................(5 to 4 op 9 to 2)   6
2167⁴ MERTON MISTRESS 7-11-2 A Merrigan, *beh, shrtlvd effrt tenth, sn wknd, tld off...* (33 to 1 op 20 to 1)   7
2426 HERES A RONDO 7-11-2 A Dobbin, *al wl beh, tld off..*.......................(33 to 1)   8
SAMJAMALIFRAN 5-11-2 J Lower, *not jump wl, sn well beh, tried to refuse 3rd, tld off whn pld up aftr 8th.*
....................................(5 to 1 op 9 to 2)   pu
Dist: 20l, nk, 30l, 10l, 10l, 6l, dist. 4m 43.75s. a 12.75s (9 Ran).
(T J Whitley), D R Gandolfo

366

2643 Red Rose Handicap Hurdle (0-120 4-y-o and up) £1,722 2½m........ (3:50)

2544² CONSTRUCTION [86] 9-10-0 D Gallagher, *trkd ldr gng wl, led appr 3 out, sn clr, eased r-in*... (12 to 1 op 10 to 1) 1

2440* TOO CLEVER BY HALF [92] 6-10-6 Mr G Johnson Houghton, *tucked in hndy, niggled alng 9th, hdwy 11th, mstk 2 out, ran on und pres, no ch wth wnr.* (8 to 1 op 5 to 1) 2

2330* ELEGANT KING (Ire) [108] 5-11-8 R Greene, *in tch, effrt 11th, ran on one pace frm 2 out*...... (7 to 2 op 5 to 2) 3

2131⁶ CARFAX [88] 9-10-2² M Hoad, *outpcd and wl beh till styd on frm 3 out, nrst finish.*

.... (16 to 1 op 12 to 1 tchd 20 to 1) 4

2346² WEST BAY [86] 8-9-12¹ (3*) A Dicken, *al hndy, led 11th till bef nxt, sn rdn and unbl to quicken.*

................................(7 to 1 op 4 to 1 tchd 8 to 1) 5

2441* TELE THON [98] (v) 7-10-12 W McFarland, *led till hdd 11th, sn rdn and wknd*............... (9 to 4 fav op 7 to 2) 6

2109³ LUSTY LAD [114] 9-11-7 (7*) Chris Webb, *trkd ldrs, niggled alng and lost pl 9th, beh whn f 2 out, broke shoulder, destroyed*.............. (3 to 1 op 9 to 4 tchd 11 to 4) f

Dist: 3l, nk, 5l, 3l, 5l. 4m 42.25s. a 11.25s (7 Ran).

(N R T Racing), R Ingram

2644 Casanova Conditional Jockeys' Handicap Hurdle (0-115 4-y-o and up) £1,614 2m..................... (4:20)

2544³ ROYAL CIRCUS [89] 5-10-13 S Wynne, *made all, rdn clr aftr 2 out, easily*.............. (5 to 4 op 11 to 8) 1

2317⁵ MY SENOR [81] (v) 5-10-1 (4*) J Clarke, *trkd ldr, niggled alng 6th, wknd 3 out, lft remote second appr last.*

.... (12 to 1 op 6 to 1 tchd 14 to 1) 2

1249⁹ PRESENT TIMES [83] 8-10-7 A Dicken, *hld up, mstk 4th, pushed alng 8th, sn lost tch, lft remote 3rd appr last.*

.... (40 to 1 op 25 to 1) 3

2443* DONOSTI [104] 10-12-0 D Fortt, *wtd wth, hdwy appr 3 out, no imprsn on wnr whn pld up approaching last, broke leg, destroyed.*

.... (6 to 5 on op 5 to 4 on tchd 11 to 10 on) pu

Dist: 15l, 15l. 3m 44.70s. a 11.70s (4 Ran).

(P W Hiatt), P W Hiatt

2645 Sweetheart Novices' Handicap Hurdle (0-100 4-y-o and up) £1,830 2m.. (4:55)

2057⁵ MAJAL (Ire) [87] 5-11-9 (5*) P Midgley, *took keen hold, mstk 4th and lost pl, sn reco'red, chlgd 2 out, rdn to ld r-in.*

................................(3 to 1 op 9 to 4) 1

864 DELIFFIN [65] 8-10-1 (5*) D Fortt, *trkd ldr till led 3rd, hdd and not quicken r-in*............ (14 to 1 op 10 to 1) 2

2441⁴ YAAFOOR (USA) [69] (v) 5-10-10 O O'Sullivan, *handily plcd, ev ch whn jmpd slwly 3 out, sn outpcd.*

.... (20 to 1 op 16 to 1) 3

2343* HIGHLAND FLAME [70] 5-10-11 D Gallagher, *led to 3rd, styd hndy till wknd 3 out*...... (7 to 4 fav tchd 2 to 1) 4

2494⁷ DUTY SERGEANT (Ire) [80] 5-11-4 (3*) J McCarthy, *in tch till wknd frm 8th*.......... (9 to 1 op 8 to 1 tchd 10 to 1) 5

1758 LUCKY AGAIN [76] 7-11-3 B Powell, *beh second, rdn 8th, no dngr*................................(7 to 1 op 12 to 1) 6

2530² LORD NASKRA (USA) [77] 5-11-4 R Campbell, *in tch till rdn 7th, sn struggling...* (6 to 1 op 3 to 1 tchd 8 to 1) 7

2088 CAOIMSEACH (Ire) [70] 6-10-11 S Mackey, *in tch, jmpd slwly 6th, rdn 8th, wknd*......... (10 to 1 op 6 to 1) 8

2647 RED LEADER (Ire) [60] 4-10-1 D Meade, *in tch, rdn appr 8th, sn wknd*................................ (33 to 1) 9

Dist: 1l, 20l, 6l, 1½l, 10l, 2l, 8l, 1½l. 3m 39.61s. a 6.61s (9 Ran).

SR: 26/3/-/-/-/-/ (Mrs P Wake), J S Wainwright

SANDOWN (soft (races 1,4,6), good to soft (2,3,5)) Thursday February 17th

Going Correction: PLUS 1.40 sec. per fur. (races 1,4,6), PLUS 1.10 (2,3,5)

2646 Village Novices' Hurdle (5-y-o and up) £2,905 2m 110yds............. (2:00)

2217² ASLAN (Ire) 6-11-4 M Dwyer, *trkd ldrs, chlgd and mstk 2 out, led appr last, rdn clr r-in, eased nr finish.*

.... (11 to 4 op 9 to 4) 1

1840* SHUJAN (USA) 5-11-8 G McCourt, *led to 5th, led nxt to 2 out, sn led ag'n, rdn and hdd appr last, one pace.*

.......................(11 to 4 on op 5 to 2 on tchd 9 to 4) 2

1908³ ATOURS (USA) (bl) 6-11-0 G Bradley, *pressed ldr, led 5th to nxt, lost and hit 2 out, sn hdd, kpt on one pace.*

.... (20 to 1 op 10 to 1) 3

1695⁵ FENGARI 5-11-0 N Williamson, *hld up beh, effrt aftr 3 out, kpt on beh nxt*......................(50 to 1 op 25 to 1) 4

JAMES IS SPECIAL (Ire) 6-11-0 V Smith, *al beh, tld off 3 out*..................... (33 to 1 op 25 to 1 tchd 40 to 1) 5

Dist: 2½l, 1l, 25l, 4l. 4m 16.30s. a 29.30s (5 Ran).

SR: 28/29/20/-/-/ (Raymond Anderson Green), J G FitzGerald

2647 Fairmile Novices' Handicap Chase (5-y-o and up) £3,876 3m 110yds... (2:35)

2378⁷ ONE MORE RUN [87] 7-10-4 B Powell, *hld up in tch, hdwy whn mstks 18th and nxt, prog appr 3 out, led and lft clr last, pushed out.....* (25 to 1 op 20 to 1 tchd 33 to 1) 1

2514³ SPIKEY (NZ) [100] 8-11-3 N Williamson, *led second to 5th, mstk nxt, led and mistake 12th, hdd and one pace appr last.*............ (11 to 4 jt-fav op 2 to 1 tchd 3 to 1) 2

2264 EMERALD STORM [90] 7-10-7 M A FitzGerald, *jnd ldrs 11th, rdn to ld betw last 2, hdd and blun last, not reco'r*......................(9 to 1 op 7 to 1 tchd 10 to 1) 3

2493⁵ YORKSHIRE GALE [103] 8-11-6 D Murphy, *led to second, cl up till rdn and wknd 3 out.*

.... (7 to 2 op 5 to 1 tchd 7 to 1) 4

2493* LUCKY LANE [103] (bl) 10-11-6 (4ex) C Maude, *chsd ldrs till wknd 4 out....*(13 to 2 op 5 to 1 tchd 7 to 1) 5

YOUNG ALFIE [83] (bl) 9-10-0 M Hourigan, *mstk and uns rdr 4th*...............(40 to 1 op 25 to 1 tchd 50 to 1) ur

2260³ MR FLANAGAN [101] 8-11-4 G Bradley, *prmnt till wknd 14th, last and no ch whn mstk and uns rdr 17th.*

.......................(10 to 1 op 7 to 1 tchd 11 to 1) ur

2559 DRAW LOTS [83] 10-10-0 I Shoemark, *beh 11th, tld off whn pld up bef 17th*..............(100 to 1 op 50 to 1) pu

2355² FAIR CROSSING [107] 8-11-10 J Osborne, *in tch, prog to track ldrs 11th, wknd rpdly 3 out, pld up bef last..........*(11 to 4 jt-fav op 5 to 2 tchd 100 to 30) pu

1205² HOWARYAFXD [97] 7-11-0 M Perrett, *led 5th to 12th, wknd rpdly nxt, pld up bef 16th.*

.......................(10 to 1 op 7 to 1 tchd 11 to 1) pu

Dist: 10l, 5l, 8l, 7l. 6m 40.90s. a 41.90s (10 Ran).

(Michael Jackson Bloodstock Ltd), G B Balding

2648 Londesborough Handicap Chase (5-y-o and up) £4,440 2½m 110yds (3:10)

2416⁷ JAILBREAKER [104] 7-10-2 M A FitzGerald, *hld up, blun 13th, prog 3 out, led appr last, drvn out.*

.......................(2 to 1 fav op 6 to 4 tchd 9 to 4) 1

2431² LOVE ANEW (USA) [102] 9-10-0 N Williamson, *hld up, prog tenth, wth wnr last, sn rdn and not quicken.*

................................(7 to 1 op 6 to 1 tchd 8 to 1) 2

2476³ BUCK WILLOW [119] 10-11-3 D Murphy, *prmnt, led 7th till rdn and hdd appr last, one pace....* (5 to 2 op 3 to 1) 3

2513 MIGHTY FALCON [115] (bl) 9-10-13 J Osborne, *rear whn reminders 5th and 7th, prog to chase ldr aftr 14th, sn wknd, no ch when blun last.....* (8 to 1 tchd 10 to 1) 4

2143⁹ CATCH THE CROSS [128] (bl) 8-11-12 M Foster, *hld up, mstks 7th and tenth, sn lost tch.*

.......................(9 to 2 op 5 to 1 tchd 6 to 1) 5

NORMAN CONQUEROR [121] (bl) 9-11-5 S Smith Eccles, *led 4th to 7th, lost pl 13th, no dngr aftr.*

.......................(10 to 1 op 7 to 1) 6

2462 BALDA BOY [120] 10-11-4 B Powell, *led to 4th, mstk 12th, rdn and wknd appr 3 out.*

.......................(20 to 1 op 16 to 1 tchd 25 to 1) 7

Dist: 3l, 6l, 12l, 2½l, 3l, 3l. 5m 26.80s. a 27.30s (7 Ran).

SR: 27/22/33/17/27/17/13/ (Jack-Del-Roy), B R Millman

2649 Wavendon Handicap Hurdle (0-145 4-y-o and up) £3,127 2m 110yds (3:45)

1799⁷ EDIMBOURG [122] 8-12-0 J Osborne, *made all, drw clr appr last, eased nr finish.*

.......................(13 to 8 fav op 6 to 4 tchd 7 to 4) 1

2379² NORTHERN SADDLER [113] 7-11-5 B Powell, *chsd wnr till mstk 3 sn rdn, kpt on one pace appr last.*

.......................(6 to 1 op 5 to 2) 2

2267 CLURICAN (Ire) [112] 5-11-4 G McCourt, *hld up, prog and brght wide in strt, rdn and not quicken 2 out.*

.......................(13 to 2 op 6 to 1 tchd 15 to 2) 3

2366⁴ MAESTRO PAUL [104] 8-10-10 D Murphy, *hld up, effrt appr last, nvr nr to chal...........* (9 to 2 tchd 11 to 2) 4

2400⁶ RED BEAN [94] 6-10-0 M Perrett, *al rear, no prog appr 2 out...........................* (40 to 1 op 33 to 1) 5

2463² MIAMI SPLASH [116] 7-11-8 M Hourigan, *hld up in tch, prog to track wnr 3 out, rdn and wkng whn blun nxt,*

.......................(4 to 1 tchd 7 to 2 and 9 to 2) 6

1834³ GALAXY HIGH [100] 6-11-7 M J A Fitzgerald, *rear, effrt appr 2 out, sn no prog*............(12 to 1 op 10 to 1) 7

Dist: 3l, hd, 1l, 15l, 2½l, ¾l. 4m 14.60s. a 27.60s (7 Ran).

SR: 55/43/42/33/8/27/30/ (Mrs Iva Winton), Miss H C Knight

2650 Wilfred Johnstone Hunters' Chase (6-y-o and up) £1,702 2½m 110yds (4:15)

2301* DOUBLE SILK 10-11-13 (5*) Mr R Treloggen, *made all, drw clr frm 3 out, easily.*

.......................(15 to 8 on op 2 to 1 on tchd 7 to 4 on) 1

LOR MOSS 14-11-3 (7*) Mr G Hogan, *hld up, prog to chase wnr 4 out, ev ch nxt, sn btn.*

.......................(66 to 1 op 50 to 1 tchd 100 to 1) 2

2301 MY MELLOW MAN 11-11-5 (5*) Miss P Curling, *hmpd second, chsd ldrs, lft second 12th, wknd 4 out.*

.......................(10 to 1 op 16 to 1 tchd 25 to 1) 3

CROCK-NA-NEE 13-11-8 (7*) Mr C Vigors, *chsd wnr, cl up whn f 12th...........*(25 to 1 op 20 to 1 tchd 33 to 1) f

RADICAL VIEWS 9-11-11 (7*) Mr E Bailey, *wth wnr till f second*.......................... (9 to 4 tchd 5 to 2) f
CERTAIN LIGHT 16-11-8 (7*) Mr T Hills, *hld up, refused 6th*.
.... (14 to 1 op 12 to 1 tchd 16 to 1) ref
DECRETO 13-10-13 (7*) Mr E James, *prmnt to 6th, tld off whn pld up bef 12th*.
.... (100 to 1 op 66 to 1 tchd 150 to 1) pu
Dist: 25l, 12l. 5m 38.00s. a 38.50s (7 Ran).

(R C Wilkins), R C Wilkins

2651 Spring Novices' Handicap Hurdle (4-y-o and up) £3,208 2¾m....... (4:50)

2419² DIVINE CHANCE (Ire) [90] 6-11-4 J Osborne, *led till rdn and hdd appr 2 out, lft in ld aftr last, jst hld on*.
.... (7 to 4 fav op 9 to 4) 1
2380² EMPIRE BLUE [96] 11-11-10 M Bosley, *trkd ldrs, led appr 2 out, 3 ls clr whn blun last, sn hdd, rallied, jst fld*.
.... (7 to 2 tchd 4 to 1) 2
2435* THE BUD CLUB (Ire) [95] 6-11-9 N Williamson, *mstks, hld up, trkd ldrs 3 out, wknd bef nxt*... (2 to 1 tchd 9 to 4) 3
2428² UNEXIS [72] 9-10-0 M Perrett, *wth wnr to 8th, wknd 2 out*.
.... (7 to 1 tchd 10 to 1) 4
2361⁶ ROCK DIAMOND [79] 8-10-7 E Leonard, *drpd last and pushed alng 5th, no prog*.......... (12 to 1 op 7 to 1) 5
Dist: Hd, 25l, 8l, 20l. 5m 46.10s. a 40.10s (5 Ran).
SR: -/3/

(R E Morris-Adams), N A Gaselee

TAUNTON (good to soft)
Thursday February 17th
Going Correction: PLUS 1.75 sec. per fur.

2652 Blackdown Juvenile Novices' Hurdle (4-y-o) £1,780 2m 1f........... (2:05)

MALAIA (Ire) 10-9 T Grantham, *hld up and al gng wl, steady hdwy frm 3 out, quickened clr r-in*.
.... (8 to 1 op 6 to 1) 1
1517³ YOUNG TESS 10-4 (5*) D Matthews, *hmpd aftr second, hdwy 5th, 3rd whn hit last, styd on*.
.... (14 to 1 tchd 12 to 1) 2
2398* HABASHA (Ire) 11-5 R Farrant, *prmt rnk, lft in ld 4th, sn hdd, hrd rdn to lead 2 out, headed last, wknd r-in*.
.... (11 to 10 fav op 6 to 4 tchd Evens) 3
2398⁴ SILVER STANDARD 11-3 (3*) R Farrant, *al prmnt, rdn 2 out, sn btn*.................... (7 to 2 op 3 to 1 tchd 4 to 1) 4
2430⁶ AUSTRAL JANE 10-9 D Bridgwater, *trkd ldrs, hit 5th, rdn to ld bef nxt, hdd 2 out, wkng whn blun last*.
.... (16 to 1 op 20 to 1 tchd 33 to 1) 5
2207⁴ PLAIN SAILING 11-0 W Marston, *trkd ldrs, led aftr 4th, wkng whn nstk 3 out*............ (50 to 1 op 20 to 1) 6
890 ABU DANCER (Ire) 11-0 A Charlton, *mid-div, hdwy 5th, wknd 3 out, tld off*.............. (66 to 1 op 33 to 1) 7
2478 ZAYAN (USA) 11-0 P Holley, *slwly away, al beh, tld off*.
.... (33 to 1 op 20 to 1) 8
2245⁷ PRINCESS TATEUM (Ire) 10-9 Lorna Vincent, *led, clr second, blun badly sn uns rdr 9th*.
.... (9 to 2 op 7 to 2 tchd 11 to 2) ur
WALID'S PRINCESS (Ire) 10-9 J Frost, *al beh, tld off 5th, pld up bef 2 out*.................... (66 to 1 op 33 to 1) pu
890 IMAGERY 10-9 L Harvey, *prmnt to 4th, sn beh, tld off whn pld up bef 2 out*................... (66 to 1 op 33 to 1) pu
Dist: 5l, 2½l, 15l, 20l, 15l, 15l, 8l. 4m 22.30s. a 35.30s (11 Ran).
SR: 26/21/28/14/-/-/

(Count K Goess-Saurau), J A B Old

2653 Porlock Conditional Jockeys' Selling Handicap Hurdle (4-y-o and up) £1,780 2m 1f........................(2:35)

1788⁵ CHANDIGARH [77] 6-11-6 P McLoughlin, *hld up in rear, making hdwy whn mstk 5th, led 2 out, sn rdn, all out*.
.... (8 to 1 op 5 to 1 tchd 9 to 1) 1
SOVEREIGN NICHE (Ire) [65] (v) 6-10-8 L Reynolds, *led second to 6th, rdn and outpcd, rallied und pres to go second last*.................... (6 to 4 fav op 2 to 1) 2
CHARCOAL BURNER [79] 9-11-8 R Davis, *prmnt, wnt second aftr 4th, led 6th, sn clr, wkng whn hdd 2 out*.
.... (9 to 1 op 7 to 1) 3
1927⁶ GROGFRYN [67] 4-10-10 P Hide, *hld up, styd on past btn horses frm 3 out*................. (10 to 1 op 14 to 1) 4
1519⁷ SLICK CHERRY [68] 7-10-11 A Procter, *beh, hdwy frm 3 out, nvr nr to chal*................. (16 to 1 op 14 to 1) 5
460³ STAR MOVER [73] 5-11-2 R Darke, *in tch till outpcd 5th, nvr drgns aftr*.................... (9 to 1 op 7 to 1) 6
2361⁵ CHICKABIDDY [81] 6-11-10 D Salter, *beh, rdn 5th, outpcd*.
.... (11 to 2 op 7 to 2 tchd 6 to 1) 7
2082⁵ GARDA'S GOLD [80] 11-11-9 D Meredith, *al beh*.
.... (9 to 1 op 14 to 1) 8
1592 ITS ALL OVER NOW [70] 10-10-13 R Farrant, *prmnt to 4th, beh frm nxt, tld off*.............. (11 to 1 op 8 to 1) 9
2343⁶ VERRO (USA) [57] 7-10-0 S Curran, *beh whn mstk 4th, tld off frm nxt*.................... (33 to 1) 10
2146⁸ PALM SWIFT [75] 8-11-4 T Jenks, *led to second, wknd quickly appr 5th, tld off whn pld up bef nxt*.
.... (20 to 1 op 16 to 1) pu
Dist: 3l, 8l, 6l, 3½l, 4l, 4l, nk, 15l. 4m 24.40s. a 37.40s (11 Ran).

SR: 16/1/7/-/-/-/

(Michael Broke), R Lee

2654 Bet With The Tote Novices' Chase Qualifier (6-y-o and up) £2,944 3m 3f ....(3:05)

1704² FLORIDA SKY 7-10-10 R Supple, *led second, made rst, clr frm 4 out, hit last, unchlgd*....(7 to 2 jt-fav op 5 to 2) 1
2206⁴ MARTELL BOY (NZ) 7-10-10 J Frost, *blun 4th, al prmnt, wnt second four out, no ch wth wnr*. ....(7 to 2 jt-fav op 9 to 2) 2
2017 MELDON 7-10-7 (3*) R Davis, *trkd wnr frm 5th, rdn and wknd from 4 out*................. (16 to 1 op 14 to 1) 3
2206⁹ STAUNCH RIVAL (USA) 7-11-3 D Bridgwater, *hld up, gd hdwy frm 13th, rdn 5 out, sn btn*.
.... (5 to 1 op 4 to 1 tchd 11 to 2) 4
2493⁴ MISS MUIRE 8-10-5 D Morris, *hmpd 3rd, al beh, tld off*.
.... (25 to 1 op 20 to 1) 5
2378 SHOREHAM LADY 9-10-5 Lorna Vincent, *al beh, tld off frm 5 out*..................... (33 to 1 op 25 to 1) 6
2403 BRAVO STAR (USA) 9-10-10 W Marston, *trkd ldrs, jmpd slwly 8th, sn beh, tld off*......... (20 to 1 op 14 to 1) 7
2417² DOLLY OATS 8-10-5 R Dunwoody, *led to second, f nxt*.
.... (7 to 1 op 6 to 1) f
2362² KIWI VELOCITY (NZ) 7-10-5 Peter Hobbs, *hmpd and uns rdr 3rd*.......................... (9 to 2 op 7 to 2) ur
FRENCH PLEASURE 8-10-5 P Holley, *hld up, hdwy 7th, 3rd whn blun and uns rdr 11th*..... (12 to 1 op 8 to 1) ur
1700 JUDYS LINE 10-10-0 (5*) D Salter, *al beh, tld off whn pld up bef tenth*.......................... (50 to 1 op 25 to 1) pu
2295 PHILIPPONNAT (USA) 8-10-10 B Clifford, *sn tld off, pld up bef 9th*.......................... (50 to 1 op 33 to 1) pu
1273 HILL TRIX 8-10-10 A Tory, *in tch till wknd quickly 14th, tld off whn pld up bef 4 out*.
.... (16 to 1 op 10 to 1 tchd 20 to 1) pu
Dist: 20l, 15l, 15l, 12l, 30l, 20l. 7m 38.90s. a 63.90s (13 Ran).

(Andrew L Cohen), John R Upson

2655 Taunton Members Handicap Hurdle (0-125 4-y-o and up) £2,801 2m 3f 110yds........................(3:35)

1869⁷ HANDY LASS [94] 5-9-12³ (5*) D Matthews, *al in tch, led appr 2 out, hdd last, rallied and led ag'n cl hme*.
.... (20 to 1 op 14 to 1) 1
2554* AAL EL AAL [94] 7-9-7 (7*) N Parker, *nvr far away, wnt second 3 out, led on bit last, rdn and hdd nr finish*.
.... (13 to 8 fav op 5 to 4) 2
2554⁸ MARICLINO [94] 7-10-0 W Marston, *hld up, hdwy last, styd on, nvr nrr*................... (10 to 1 op 33 to 1) 3
2496⁷ PRIZE MATCH [94] 5-10-0 R Supple, *hld up in tch, rdn 3 out, one pace*.................... (20 to 1 op 16 to 1) 4
2379³ ELEMENTARY [119] 11-11-11 R Marley, *hld up in rear, hdwy 6th, ev ch appr 2 out, rdn and wknd bef last*.
.... (11 to 1 op 8 to 1) 5
2457³ RAMBLE (USA) [94] 7-10-0 T Grantham, *wl beh 5th, kpt on one pace frm 2 out*....(9 to 1 op 8 to 1 tchd 10 to 1) 6
2366⁶ SMILING CHIEF (Ire) [94] 6-9-11² (5*) T Jenks, *beh, effrt 3 out, wknd nxt*..................... (25 to 1 op 20 to 1) 7
2379⁴ LYNCH LAW (Ire) [110] (bl) 6-11-2 R Dunwoody, *prmnt, led 7th, hdd sn aftr nxt, wknd*...... (2 to 1 op 3 to 1) 8
2019² BROUGHTON'S TANGO (Ire) [98] 5-10-4 S Keightley, *al beh, lost tch 7th*..................... (11 to 1 op 8 to 1) 9
2496³ SURCOAT [98] 7-10-4 L Harvey, *hld up in rear, outpcd frm 7th*.................... (14 to 1 op 12 to 1) 10
2432⁴ KELLING [94] (bl) 7-9-9 (5*) Guy Lewis, *prmnt, led appr 6th, hdd nxt, wknd quickly, tld off*.... (16 to 1 op 14 to 1) 11
2366 ANTI MATTER [102] 9-11-7 (7*) Mr J Culloty, *led till hdd appr 6th, wknd rpdly, tld off*.
.... (50 to 1 op 33 to 1 tchd 66 to 1) 12
Dist: 1l, 10l, 2l, 1½l, ½l, 10l, 1¼l, nk, 25l. 5m 0.60s. a 39.60s (12 Ran).
SR: 17/16/6/-/22/-/

(G W Hackling), Mrs A Knight

2656 South West Racing Club Handicap Chase (0-125 5-y-o and up) £2,840 3m ....(4:05)

2318³ SUNLEY BAY [101] 8-10-3 (5*) Guy Lewis, *wtd wth, hdwy tenth, led sn aftr 4 out, ran on wl*.
.... (13 to 2 op 5 to 1 tchd 7 to 1) 1
2429* GHOFAR [115] (bl) 11-11-8 P Holley, *trkd ldrs, rdn to go second aftr 3 out, ridden and ran on*.
.... (7 to 2 op 3 to 1) 2
2416² SARAVILLE [117] 7-11-10 R Dunwoody, *led to 3rd, led 6th till sn aftr 4 out, rdn and one pace frm nxt*.
.... (13 to 8 fav op 9 to 4 tchd 6 to 4) 3
2246³ AUCTION LAW [94] [119] 10-11-12 J Frost, *nvr far away, wnt 3rd 4 out, wknd 2 out*........ (5 to 1 op 7 to 2) 4
2557⁵ LA CERISE [93] (bl) 11-9-7 (7*) M Moran, *tld off frm 8th, refused and uns rdr 4 out*......... (66 to 1 op 33 to 1) ref
2363⁵ NOUGAT RUSSE [100] 13-10-7 D Bridgwater, *sn beh, tld off whn pld up bef 9th*................... (66 to 1 op 33 to 1) pu
1698 HOLY FOLEY [101] 8-12-10 Peter Hobbs, *mstk 3rd, al beh, tld off whn pld up bef 9th*....... (25 to 1 op 4 to 1) pu
2047 POWDER BOY [93] 9-9-11² (5*) T Jenks, *chsd ldrs till wknd quickly 12th, tld off whn pld up run in*.
.... (20 to 1 op 14 to 1) pu

368

2363^{7} CHANNELS GATE [115] 10-11-8 J Railton, *trkd ldr, led 3rd to 6th, wknd quickly aftr 12th, tld off whn pld up bef 5 out*..................................(8 to 1 op 6 to 1) pu
Dist: 2l, 10l, 3l. 6m 40.60s. a 53.60s (9 Ran).
(Mrs Marianne G Barber), P F Nicholls

2657 Cranmore Novices' Handicap Hurdle (0-100 4-y-o and up) £1,822 3m 110yds ....(4:35)

2483* LANSDOWNE [89] 6-11-3 (7*) R Darke, *al gng wl, led 2 out, drvn clr r-in*..........................(4 to 1 op 5 to 2) 1
2483^{2} WARFIELD [84] 7-11-0 (5*) Guy Lewis, *wtd wth in tch, hdwy appr 8th, rdn alng frm 3 out, wnt second r-in.* ....(7 to 2 fav op 5 to 2) 2
2362 MAHATMACOAT [70] 7-9-12 (7*) Mr J Culloty, *led to 4th, led 7th, rdn and hdd 2 out, no extr r-in.* ....(20 to 1 tchd 16 to 1) 3
2208^{4} MOBILE MESSENGER (NZ) [87] 6-11-1 (7*) Mr G Shenkin, *hld up, hdwy 7th, no imprsn frm 3 out.* .... (10 to 1 op 6 to 1) 4
2034^{5} LAUGHING GAS (Ire) [75] 5-10-10 R Supple, *beh, hdwy 8th, rdn 3 out, wknd bef nxt*........... (20 to 1 op 14 to 1) 5
2428^{4} UP ALL NIGHT [65] 5-10-0 D Morris, *al in rear*....(12 to 1) 6
2141 CADOLIVE [65] 6-9-11 (3*) D Meredith, *prmnt till rdn and wknd 8th, tld off*..................(33 to 1 op 25 to 1) 7
1457 FREDS MELODY [84] 9-11-5 G Upton, *prmnt till wknd appr 6th, tld off whn pld up bef 9th.* ....(16 to 1 op 12 to 1 tchd 20 to 1) pu
2524 HEAR A NIGHTINGALE [77] 7-10-5 (7*) Miss J Brackenbury, *al beh, tld off frm 8th, pld up bef 2 out.* .... (33 to 1 op 20 to 1) pu
2483^{5} FIRST LESSON (NZ) [81] 8-11-2 Peter Hobbs, *prmnt till wknd quickly 9th, tld off whn pld up bef 2 out.* ....(9 to 1 op 7 to 1) pu
2302^{4} NAVAL BATTLE [65] 7-9-11^{2} (5*) T Jenks, *prmnt, led 4th to 7th, rdn and wknd nxt, tld off whn pld up bef 2 out.* ....(14 to 1 tchd 12 to 1) pu
2208^{5} HENRY VILL (Ire) [86] 6-11-7 D Bridgwater, *prmnt to 8th, tld off whn pld up bef 2 out*..........(10 to 1 op 7 to 1) pu
2428 VERY LITTLE (Ire) [85] (bl) 6-11-6 S Earle, *beh till hdwy 8th, rdn and sn wknd, tld off whn pld up bef 2 out.* ....(9 to 1 op 6 to 1) pu
2300^{3} LOVE YOU MADLY (Ire) [86] 4-11-7 R Dunwoody, *mid-div, rdn 8th, sn wknd, pld up bef 2 out.* .... (11 to 2 op 6 to 1 tchd 5 to 1) pu
Dist: 5l, 1½l, 5l, 20l, 25l, dist. 6m 26.90s. a 52.40s (14 Ran).
SR: 1/-/-/-/-/-/ (R F Denmead), G A Ham

THURLES (IRE) (soft)
Thursday February 17th

2658 Horse And Jockey Hurdle (5 & 6-y-o) £2,243 2m..................... (2:00)

2348* COMMON POLICY (Ire) 5-11-0 (3*) T J O'Sullivan, (11 to 4) 1
2281^{3} MISTER DRUM (Ire) 5-10-10 (7*) Mr J T McNamara, (7 to 2) 2
2281* SEEK THE FAITH (USA) 5-11-6 B Sheridan, ..(11 to 10 fav) 3
2123 COURSING GLEN (Ire) 6-11-2 M Duffy, ... (20 to 1) 4
2586 ISN'T THAT NICE (Ire) 6-11-2 J Shortt, ... (14 to 1) 5
2236^{7} LADY BUDD (Ire) 6-10-11 A J O'Brien, ... (16 to 1) 6
PALLAS CHAMPION (Ire) 5-10-13 F Woods, ... (33 to 1) 7
1978 DEEP DOVE (Ire) 6-10-11 (5*) J P Broderick, ... (25 to 1) 8
2465^{5} BLACK DOG (Ire) 6-10-11 (5*) D T Evans, ...(12 to 1) pu
Dist: ½l, 5l, dist, 2½l. 4m 7.20s. (9 Ran).
(Patrick O'Leary), Patrick O'Leary

2659 E.B.F. Novice Chase (5-y-o and up) £3,550 2¾m 110yds............ (2:30)

2282^{3} BART OWEN 9-11-8 C F Swan, ... (11 to 10 fav) 1
2550* GYPSY LASS 7-11-6 T Horgan, ... (6 to 4) 2
2235^{2} MAKE ME AN ISLAND 9-10-12 (5*) J P Broderick, .. (5 to 1) f
806 BIG JAMES 12-11-1 (3*) T J Mitchell, ... (16 to 1) ur
Dist: 6l. 6m 13.90s. (4 Ran).
(Mrs Sandra McCarthy), P Mullins

2660 Devils Bit Handicap Hurdle (0-130 4-y-o and up) £2,243 3m............(3:00)

2617^{5} BRINDLEY HOUSE [-] 7-11-9 J Shortt, ...(10 to 1) 1
2468^{2} CALMOS [-] 7-10-4 C F Swan, ... (7 to 4 fav) 2
2468^{4} BALLYMOE BOY (Ire) [-] 6-10-0 (5*) K P Gaule, ...(10 to 1) 3
2468^{5} MISGIVINGS (Ire) [-] 6-9-8 (7*) J M Donnelly, ... (8 to 1) 4
2392^{9} LUMINOUS LIGHT [-] 7-10-11 Mr M Phillips, ...(7 to 1) 5
2468 RED THUNDER [-] 7-10-0 D P Fagan, ...(8 to 1) 6
2160^{3} BARRONSTOWN BOY [-] 10-10-2 F Woods, ...(8 to 1) 7
2587^{5} PARSON'S RUN [-] 7-10-7 (5*) P A Roche, ...(8 to 1) 8
2040^{5} SHANNON KNOCK [-] 9-10-6 P M Verling, ... (16 to 1) 9
2311^{2} POOR MOTHER (Ire) [-] 6-9-10 F J Flood, ... (10 to 1) 10
131 GOLDEN RAPPER [-] (bl) 9-10-0 (5*) J P Broderick, (20 to 1) 11
1826 CAPINCUR EILE [-] 8-12-0 J F Titley, ... (20 to 1) 12
2278 SARAKIN (Ire) [-] 6-9-0^{4} (7*) D O'Driscoll, ...(33 to 1) 13
Dist: 1l, 12l, 2½l, ½l. 5m 58.90s. (13 Ran).
(Brindley Advertising Ltd), J E Mulhern

2661 Seskin Novice Chase (5-y-o and up) £2,243 3m.................... (3:30)

2550^{2} CARRIGEEN KERRIA (Ire) 6-11-9 Mr P J Healy, (13 to 8 fav) 1
2157 MOONCAPER 8-11-9 T Horgan, ...(7 to 1) 2
116 TAKE THE TOWN 9-11-9 J F Titley, ...(7 to 1) 3
2234^{2} BALADINE 7-11-4 S H O'Donovan, ...(10 to 1) 4
MALTELINA 8-11-1 (3*) C O'Brien, ...(16 to 1) 5
2588^{8} DHARKOUM 7-11-9 J A White, ... (14 to 1) 6
1823 PEGUS PRINCE (Ire) 5-10-4 (7*) Mr D P Daly, ... (16 to 1) 7
2390^{5} THE MAD MONK 9-12-0 M Flynn, ...(14 to 1) 8
2550^{5} MONKS AIR 7-11-4 A J O'Brien, ...(12 to 1) 9
2588 LISNABOY PRINCE 7-11-4 (5*) K P Gaule, ... (20 to 1) 10
2282^{5} CARRON HILL 7-12-0 F Woods, ... (7 to 1) 11
2550 ARDCARN GIRL 7-11-4 J Shortt, ...(20 to 1) 12
177 GIVE IT A MISS 8-11-6 (3*) D P Murphy, ...(14 to 1) 13
1451^{6} TAWNEY FLAME 8-12-0 J Magee, ...(4 to 1) ur
2550 COOL CARLING 7-11-4 L P Cusack, ... (20 to 1) pu
2390^{4} LE BRAVE 8-11-9 K F O'Brien, ...(10 to 1) pu
Dist: 11l, 20l, 7l, 5½l. 6m 37.10s. (16 Ran).
(Mrs R H Lalor), R H Lalor

2662 Holy Cross Handicap Chase (0-116 4-y-o and up) £2,243 3m........ (4:00)

2549^{3} LADY BAR [-] 7-11-7 P M Verling, ...(9 to 4 fav) 1
2235^{6} DEL MONTE BOY [-] 9-9-7 (7*) M D Murphy, ...(6 to 1) 2
2619 GOLDEN CARRUTH (Ire) [-] 6-9-13 (5*) J P Broderick, ...(8 to 1) 3
2100^{6} DUSKY LADY [-] 8-10-6 J F Titley, ...(7 to 1) 4
2619^{5} CARRIGEEN GALA [-] 7-9-2 (5*) M G Cleary, ...(10 to 1) 5
2550^{9} DELIGHTFUL CHOICE (Ire) [-] 6-9-10^{2} F Woods, .. (16 to 1) 6
2619^{7} ROSSI NOVAE [-] (bl) 11-11-3 A J O'Brien, ... (16 to 1) 7
1381 KNOCKNACARRA LAD [-] 9-11-0 J Shortt, ... (10 to 1) 8
2589^{5} MR MYAGI [-] 10-9-11 (3*) D Bromley, ...(8 to 1) 9
2183^{5} MACAMORE GALE [-] 8-11-3 (3*) C O'Brien, ...(10 to 1) 10
1901^{7} PROPUNT [-] 9-11-8 T Horgan, ...(8 to 1) pu
Dist: 2½l, 8l, 3l, 9l. 6m 41.90s. (11 Ran).
(Mrs T M Cleary), Michael Croke

2663 Tipperary INH Flat Race (4-y-o) £2,243 2m.......................... (4:30)

GAMBOLLING DOC (Ire) 11-2 (3*) Mrs S McCarthy, (5 to 1) 1
2592^{3} GRAPHIC IMAGE (Ire) 11-5 Mr A P O'Brien, ...(2 to 1 fav) 2
OAKLER (Ire) 10-12 (7*) Miss F Crowley, ...(8 to 1) 3
KERRYHEAD GIRL (Ire) 10-7 (7*) Mr E Norris, ... (8 to 1) 4
KILCARBERY (Ire) 10-11 (3*) Mrs J M Mullins, ...(8 to 1) 5
PERSIAN VIEW (Ire) 11-2 (3*) Mr J A Nash, ... (9 to 2) 6
2290^{9} CASTLEGRACE BOY (Ire) 10-12 (7*) Mr M P Dunne, ...(20 to 1) 7
KUDA CHANTIK (Ire) 10-9 (5*) Mr H F Cleary, ... (8 to 1) 8
KERKY (Ire) 10-12 (7*) Miss C O'Neill, ...(14 to 1) 9
WHITECHURCH LADY (Ire) 10-7 (7*) Mr B Hallihan, (12 to 1) 10
2547^{6} ROYAL RANK (USA) 11-2 (3*) Miss M Olivefalk, ... (10 to 1) 11
TEN BUCKS (Ire) 10-12 (7*) Mr D K Budds, ... (8 to 1) 12
2547 EMERALD BREFFNI (Ire) 10-12 (7*) Mr M McLoughney, ...(20 to 1) 13
CAPTAIN KIZZY (Ire) 10-12^{1} (3*) Mr P Fanning, ...(20 to 1) 14
GREENORE GLEN (Ire) 11-5 Mr P Fenton, ...(8 to 1) 15
Dist: 2l, 2½l, 2½l, 14l. 4m 2.20s. (15 Ran).
(Mrs M O'Leary), P Mullins

2664 Clonoulty INH Flat Race (6-y-o and up) £2,243 2m.................... (5:00)

2203^{2} RING THE ALARM (Ire) 6-11-4 (5*) Mr G J Harford, (8 to 1) 1
2394^{3} TOTAL CONFUSION 7-11-2 (7*) Mr T J Beattie, ... (8 to 1) 2
2289^{5} DUEONE (Ire) 6-11-4 (5*) Mr H F Cleary, ...(12 to 1) 3
2128^{3} SOFT WINTER (Ire) 6-11-6 (3*) Mrs M Mullins, .. (5 to 2 fav) 4
NEPI LAD (Ire) 6-11-9 Ms Rosemary Rooney, ... (8 to 1) 5
2586^{5} IFALLELSEFAILS 6-11-9 Mr A J Martin, ... (11 to 2) 6
QUIET ONE 9-10-11 (7*) Miss U Corcoran, ... (33 to 1) 7
2038^{9} MOONSHEE (Ire) 6-11-1 (3*) Miss M Olivefalk, ... (20 to 1) 8
2353^{6} VENT VERT (Ire) 6-10-11 (7*) Mr E Norris, ...(14 to 1) 9
1760 GOLDEN NUGGET 7-11-2 (7*) Mr P O'Keeffe, ... (12 to 1) 10
1501 CABBERY ROSE (Ire) 6-11-4 Mr J A Flynn, ... (20 to 1) 11
MERCHANTS ROAD 7-11-6 (3*) Mr J A Nash, ... (10 to 1) 12
YOU KNOW WHO (Ire) 6-11-6 (3*) Mrs J M Mullins, (7 to 2) 13
2278 CLONE (Ire) 6-11-6 (3*) Mr D Marnane, ...(33 to 1) 14
2394 BORRISMORE FLASH (Ire) 6-11-2 (7*) Mr P J Kelly, (20 to 1) 15
1401 AUSSIE BREEZE (Ire) 6-11-1 (3*) Mr T Lombard, .. (33 to 1) 16
2128 PURRIT THERE 8-11-9 Mr T Doyle, ...(20 to 1) 17
SHEEP WALK (Ire) 6-10-11 (7*) Mr D P Daly, ... (20 to 1) 18
BE KIND TO ME 8-11-0^{3} (7*) Mr J P Moloney, ...(20 to 1) 19
942^{7} SWEET PETEL 7-11-0^{3} (7*) Mr N Henley, ...(33 to 1) 20
OUR BLOSSOM (Ire) 6-10-11 (7*) Mr E Henley, ...(25 to 1) 21
NIGHT SERVICE (Ire) 6-10-11 (7*) Mr J Connolly, .. (25 to 1) 22
Dist: 2l, 2½l, 3½l, 7l. 4m 0.90s. (22 Ran).
(Miss Bernadette Curran), Martin Michael Lynch

FAKENHAM (good)
Friday February 18th
Going Correction: PLUS 0.75 sec. per fur.

2665 Sheringham Selling Handicap Hurdle (4-y-o and up) £2,983 2m 110yds (2:10)

2581² PINECONE PETER [86] (v) 7-11-6 M Brennan, *in tch, led appr 2 out, clr last, rdn out.*
......................(100 to 30 op 3 to 1 tchd 7 to 2 and 4 to 1) 1
2540⁴ NAGOBELIA [90] 6-11-10 A Maguire, *hld up in mid-div, rdn and styd on one pace frm 2 out.*
....(2 to 1 fav op 5 to 2) 2
2405⁴ MORIARITY [75] 7-10-6 (3*) J McCarthy, *led til hdd 3rd, led ag'n 6th, headed and not quicken appr 2 out.*
...............................(5 to 1 op 4 to 1 tchd 11 to 2) 3
1627² WEEKDAY CROSS (Ire) [86] 6-11-10 J Railton, *hld up in rear, ran on frm 3 out, one pace betw last 2 flights.*
......................(9 to 2 op 5 to 1 tchd 6 to 1) 4
1810⁸ ELEGANT FRIEND [88] 6-11-8 M Richards, *beh, moderate effrt 3 out, no imprsn on ldrs.*
...............................(9 to 1 op 6 to 1 tchd 10 to 1) 5
666⁵ SALISONG [94] 5-11-7 (7*) Mr M Gingell, *pressed ldrs til wknd aftr 2 out.*..................(12 to 1 op 10 to 1) 6
SWAN WALK (Ire) [88] 6-11-8 N Williamson, *rear most of way, tld off.*........................(14 to 1 op 10 to 1) 7
2405 LADY KHADIJA [66] 8-9-11 (3*) R Farrant, *led 3rd, hdd 6th, sn wknd, tld off.*....................(50 to 1 op 33 to 1) 8
1620 CUPID'S COURAGE (Ire) [66] 5-9-7 (7*) Honey Pearce, *chsd ldrs til lost pl 6th, tld off.*..........(50 to 1 op 33 to 1) 9
Dist: 8l, 2½l, 1l, 1½l, 6l, 20l, dist, dist. 4m 10.20s. a 20.20s (9 Ran).
SR: 14/10/-/6/2/2/ (Mrs B A Burgass), O Brennan

2666 Prince Carlton Handicap Chase (0-120 5-y-o and up) £4,143 3m........ (2:40)

2363² NEW HALEN [93] 13-10-1 R Bellamy, *wth ldrs, jmpd slwly at 3rd, led tenth, made rst, styd on strly frm 2 out.*
....(11 to 2 op 9 to 2) 1
1512³ SANDYBRAES [120] 9-12-0 A Maguire, *hdwy 8th, chsd wnr frm 14th, one pace frm 2 out, fnshd very tired.*
......................(7 to 2 op 4 to 1 tchd 9 to 2) 2
2294 NOTARY-NOWELL [92] (bl) 8-10-0 Gee Armytage, *jmpd rght at 1st, sn wth ldrs, lost pl 12th, tld off frm nxt.* (33 to 1) 3
2434* MR TITTLE TATTLE [102] (bl) 8-10-10 N Williamson, *led 3rd, hdd tenth, mstk and wknd 15th, tld off.*
..............................(3 to 1 op 5 to 2 tchd 7 to 2) 4
ROYAL FLAMINGO [101] 8-10-9 R J Beggan, *hld up in rear, shrtlvd effrt 11th, sn wknd, poor 3rd whn blun 2 out, refused last.*........................(7 to 1 tchd 8 to 1) ref
PRINCE NEPAL [92] 10-10-0 M Hourigan, *al beh, tld off whn pld up bef 15th.*..........(40 to 1 op 33 to 1) pu
2363⁷ TOCHENNA [109] 10-11-3 D Bridgwater, *led to 3rd, wknd tenth, lost tch and pld up bef 14th.*
.........................(7 to 1 op 4 fav op 4 to 1 tchd 7 to 1) pu
Dist: 25l, 6l. 6m 16.10s. a 24.10s (7 Ran).
SR: 12/14/-/-/ (Mrs Sally Siviter), A P James

2667 EBF 'National Hunt' Novices' Hurdle Qualifier (5,6,7-y-o) £2,794 2m 5f (3:10)

2404 COILED SPRING 7-11-0 A Maguire, *ldg grp, hit 7th and nxt, led and quickened clr aftr 2 out, eased nr line.*
..............................(13 to 8 op 7 to 4 tchd 2 to 1) 1
2419* CHIEF RAGER 5-11-10 D Bridgwater, *chsd ldr, led 6th, hdd aftr 2 out, outpcd and hit last.*
(11 to 8 on 6 to 4 on tchd 5 to 4 on and 11 to 10 on) 2
634³ FLAMEWOOD 5-10-9 W Marston, *led to 6th, rnwd effrt appr 2 out, sn rdn and no extr......*(10 to 1 op 8 to 1) 3
1930 MANDYS LAD 5-11-0 W Humphreys, *pld hrd, effrt frm 7th, wknd 2 out.*..........................(33 to 1 op 25 to 1) 4
2419 FINKLE STREET (Ire) 6-11-0 N Williamson, *mid-div, jmpd slwly 5th, outpcd frm 8th.*........(33 to 1 op 50 to 1) 5
2333 FAR VIEW (Ire) 5-11-0 D Skyrme, *trkd ldrs til wknd 8th, tld off.*....................................(66 to 1 op 50 to 1) 6
2140⁹ MERRY PANTO (Ire) 5-11-0 R Supple, *al beh, rdn alng 7th, sn tld off.*......................(16 to 1 tchd 20 to 1) 7
2339 CLOWN AROUND 6-10-9 Mr L Lay, *al beh, tld off whn pld up bef 8th.*..........(66 to 1 op 50 to 1 tchd 100 to 1) pu
Dist: 15l, 5l, 10l, 15l, dist, 20l. 5m 14.90s. a 21.90s (8 Ran).
SR: 25/20/-/-/-/ (Mrs James West), D Nicholson

2668 Bet With The Tote Novices' Chase Qualifier (6-y-o and up) £2,892 3m
.... (3:40)

2206² MASTER JOLSON 6-11-3 A Maguire, *wl plcd, mstk 9th, blun nxt, led aftr 2 out, jmpd lft last, drvn clr.*
..............................(7 to 4 fav op 2 to 1 tchd 5 to 2) 1
2479⁴ SALLY'S GEM 9-10-10 W McFarland, *led to second, led 5th to 6th, wth 9th till aftr 2 out, kpt on same pace.*
.....................(2 to 1 op 11 to 4 tchd 3 to 1) 2
2479⁵ BRABAZON (USA) 9-10-10 M Richards, *settled rear, reminders 8th, hdwy 12th, ran on one pace frm 3 out.*
....(20 to 1 op 14 to 1) 3
2402³ VITAL WITNESS (Can) 7-10-10 A S Smith, *hld up, hdwy aftr 13th, rdn and one pace 3 out.*............(8 to 1) 4
1043³ PARDON ME MUM (bl) 9-11-3 N Williamson, *hld up rear, improved 12th, no hdwy frm 15th....*(8 to 1 op 7 to 1) 5

2536 DONT TELL THE WIFE 8-11-3 D Bridgwater, *rear and not fluent early, mstk 14th, no prog aftr.*
....(6 to 1 tchd 7 to 1) 6
TRUE SHADE 8-10-10 M Hourigan, *led second to 5th, led 6th to 9th, wknd 3 out.*..........(10 to 1 tchd 12 to 1) 7
1934 SILENT CHANT (v) 10-10-3 (7*) Mr G Hogan, *trkd ldrs, drpd rear 8th, tld off.*....................(25 to 1 op 16 to 1) 8
2264 CRAIGSTOWN (Ire) 6-10-10 J Railton, *improved frm rear 15th, 4th whn f 2 out.*......................(33 to 1) f
2565⁵ EMERALD GEM (v) 8-10-10 M Brennan, *chsd ldrs till lost tch frm 13th, pld up bef 15th......*(25 to 1 op 16 to 1) pu
LE BUCHERON 8-10-10 J Ryan, *in tch till beh 11th, pld up bef 15th.*...............(25 to 1 op 16 to 1) pu
2417 KEV'S LASS (Ire) 6-9-12 (7*) P Murphy, *mid-div till wknd and pld up bef 14th...*(16 to 1 op 14 to 1) pu
Dist: 2½l, nk, 30l, dist, ½l, 7l, 25l. 6m 23.60s. a 31.60s (12 Ran).
(Mrs E Roberts), D Nicholson

2669 Walter Wales Memorial Cup Hunters' Chase (5-y-o and up) £2,635 2m 5f 110yds....................... (4:10)

KILFINNY CROSS (Ire) 6-11-10 Mr J Greenall, *hit 3rd, in tch, led tenth, clr appr last, pushed out.*
....(9 to 4 fav op 6 to 2) 1
MAN O'MAGIC 13-11-3 (7*) Mrs T Bailey, *improved frm rear 12th, styd on from 3 out, fnshd wl....* (6 to 1 op 5 to 1) 2
HOUGHTON 8-11-3 (7*) Major M Watson, *mid-div, not fluent 9th, hdwy nxt, styd on one pace 3 out.*
....(6 to 1 op 7 to 1) 3
SKINNHILL (bl) 10-11-3 (7*) Mr G Hogan, *cld on ldrs 8th, blun 2 out, btn appr last........*(14 to 1 op 10 to 1) 4
BOLD KING'S HUSSAR 11-11-3 (7*) Miss A Plunkett, *mstk second, hdwy tenth, no extr frm 3 out.*
....(16 to 1 op 12 to 1) 5
RAGLAN ROAD 10-11-3 (7*) Miss A Embiricos, *mid-div, effrt 6th, no imprsn on ldrs frm 14th.*
....(6 to 1 tchd 7 to 1) 6
HILARION (Fr) 10-11-3 (7*) Mr D Bloor, *strtd slwly, cld tenth, wknd 14th.*.........................(50 to 1) 7
2570³ ROYAL PAVILION 11-11-3 (7*) Mr C Gordon, *ldg grp, wth ldr tenth, wknd 3 out.*......................(10 to 1) 8
2482⁴ PORTER'S SONG 13-11-3 (7*) Mr L Lay, *ldg grp till beh 6th.*
....(14 to 1) 9
2456⁴ LE CHAT NOIR 11-11-74 (7*) Mr C Newport, *mstks, sn rear, tld off hfwy.*..............(3 to 1 op 9 to 2) 10
EXPRESS FRED 6-11-7 (3*) Mr Simon Andrews, *chasing ldrs whn mstk 8th, blun and uns rdr nxt.*
...............................(8 to 1 op 10 to 1 tchd 6 to 1) ur
ARPAL BREEZE 9-11-5 (5*) Mr P Harding-Jones, *sn rear, pld up bef 13th....*.................(12 to 1 op 9 to 1) pu
RALLYE STRIPE 10-11-3 (7*) Mr C Ward, *led to tenth, sn lost pl, pld up bef 12th..........*(50 to 1 op 33 to 1) pu
Dist: 2l, 12l, 3/4l, 6l, nk, 15l, 6l, 12l, 5l. 5m 41.30s. a 29.30s (13 Ran).
(J E Greenall), Miss C Saunders

2670 Cromer Handicap Hurdle (0-125 4-y-o and up) £3,501 2m 110yds...... (4:40)

2296⁴ ZEALOUS KITTEN (USA) [98] 6-10-4 (3*) J McCarthy, *ldg grp, sstnd chal frm 2 out, lft in ld last, ran on strly.*
...............................(7 to 1 op 6 to 1 tchd 8 to 1) 1
2403 CHILD OF THE MIST [119] 8-12-0 A Maguire, *hld up in tch, ev ch 2 out, not quicken betw last two, lft second fnl flight.*..........(3 to 1 jt-fav tchd 100 to 30 and 7 to 2) 2
1559 EDEN'S CLOSE [119] 5-12-0 M Richards, *hld up, effrt aftr 5th, rdn and one pace frm 2 out......*(7 to 1 op 6 to 1) 3
2401⁴ TYNRON DOON [91] (bl) 5-10-0 N Williamson, *rear til effrt 3 out, wknd appr nxt........*(100 to 30 op 11 to 2) 4
2471 ABJAR [100] 4-10-4 (5*) A Bates, *trkd ldrs, hit 5th, btn appr 2 out.......*(100 to 30 op 14 to 1 tchd 7 to 2) 5
2580* RATIFY [103] 7-10-12 (5ex) A S Smith, *led 4th til f last.*
...............................(3 to 1 jt-fav op 4 to 1) f
2306⁶ OLD EROS [102] 10-10-11 P Niven, *led to 4th, wknd quickly nxt, tld off whn pld up bef 2 out.*
..............................(4 to 1 op 5 to 1) pu
Dist: 7l, 1l, 2½l, 6l. 4m 7.50s. a 17.50s (7 Ran).
SR: 28/42/41/10/13/-/-/ (M F Oseman), R J Price

SANDOWN (good to soft)
Friday February 18th
Going Correction: PLUS 1.25 sec. per fur. (races 1,4,-6,7), PLUS 1.20 (2,3,5)

2671 EBF 'National Hunt' Novices' Hurdle Qualifier (5,6,7-y-o) £3,046 2m 110yds
.... (1:40)

2315² HAWAIIAN YOUTH (Ire) 6-11-5 G McCourt, *nvr far away, rdn to ld 2 out, all out.....................*(5 to 4 op 6 to 4) 1
2333³ SLIPMATIC 5-10-9 R Dunwoody, *al prmnt, rdn to press wnr frm 2 out, no extr cl hme.*
......................(10 to 1 op 14 to 1 tchd 16 to 1) 2

2194³ DUTCH MONARCH 7-10-11 (3") A Dicken, *prmnt till out-pcd 3 out, styd on frm nxt.*
.... (20 to 1 op 14 to 1 tchd 25 to 1) 3
1840⁷ VITAL WONDER 6-11-0 P Holley, *led aftr second, mstks nxt 2, hdd two out, wknd.*
.... (11 to 2 op 9 to 2 tchd 6 to 1) 4
AVENA 7-10-9 G Upton, *al prmnt, dsptd ld 3 out, wknd nxt.*....................(6 to 1 tchd 7 to 1) 5
2176⁶ MRS MONEYPENNY 5-10-2 (7") P Ward, *hld up, hdwy 3 out, rdn and one pace.*
.... (66 to 1 op 20 to 1 tchd 100 to 1) 6
2477* ROSE KING 7-11-10 D Murphy, *mid-div, hdwy 4th, rdn and btn whn hmpd 2 out.*
.... (7 to 8 fav op 6 to 4 tchd 5 to 1) 7
CHARGED 5-11-0 Peter Hobbs, *mid-div, rdn 3 out, sn btn, tld off.*..........(100 to 1 op 50 to 1 tchd 100 to 1) 8
1536⁷ GILPA VALU 5-11-0 I Lawrence, *al rear, tld off.*
.... (20 to 1 op 14 to 1) 9
1536⁹ RAGTIME BOY 6-11-0 B Clifford, *al beh, tld off.*
.... (66 to 1 op 50 to 1) 10
COSMICECHOEXPRESS 7-10-9 S Earle, *al beh, tld off.*
.... (100 to 1 op 50 to 1) 11
2380⁴ TOPPING TOM (Ire) 5-11-10 C Llewellyn, *hld up rear, hdwy 3 out, rdn and btn in 5th whn slpd and f nxt.*
.... (7 to 1 op 9 to 2) f
IDIOM 7-10-0 M A FitzGerald, *led till aftr second, wkng whn mstk 3 out, pld up bef nxt...* (100 to 1 op 50 to 1) pu
343 STANDAROUND (Ire) 5-10-9 A McCabe, *al beh, tld off whn pld up bef 2 out...*............(100 to 1 op 33 to 1) pu
2141 SARACEN'S BOY (Ire) 6-10-7 (7") Mr B Pollock, *tld off 4th, pld up bef 2 out...*..................(100 to 1 op 50 to 1) pu
BREYFAX 5-10-7 (7") G Crone, *sn beh, tld off whn pld up bef 4th...*..................(100 to 1 op 50 to 1) pu
Dist: Nk, 12l, 2½l, 10l, 8l, 4l, 12l, 8l, ½l, 10l. 4m 13.00s. a 26.00s (16 Ran).
SR: 37/26/19/-/1/-/4/-/-/ (G Redford), R Rowe

2672 Squirrel Handicap Chase (5-y-o and up) £4,760 2m..........(2:10)

2488² UNCLE ERNIE [145] 9-11-6 M Dwyer, *wtd wth in tch, wnt second 8th, led sn aftr 2 out, ran on wl.*
.... (11 to 10 fav op Evens tchd 6 to 5) 1
2383² YOUNG SNUGFIT [149] 10-11-10 J Osborne, *led till untidy and hdd 3rd, led nxt, hit 2 out, sn headed, one pace r-in...*..................(5 to 4 op 11 to 10 tchd 6 to 5) 2
2481² SETTER COUNTRY [125] 10-10-0 R Dunwoody, *led 3rd to 4th, jmpd wl till mstk 5 out, cl third whn f nxt, rmntd to finish...*..................(6 to 1 tchd 13 to 2) 3
Dist: 3l, dist. 4m 10.50s. a 22.00s (3 Ran).
SR: 64/65/-/ (J G FitzGerald), J G FitzGerald

2673 Stag Handicap Chase (5-y-o and up) £4,543 3m 110yds.............(2:40)

2513³ THE WIDGET MAN [120] 8-10-6 (3") P Hide, *not al fluent, hld up, trkd ldr frm 13th, led 2 out, jmpd lft last, ran on.*
.... (11 to 10 on tchd Evens) 1
2460 INDIAN TONIC [124] 8-10-13 C Maude, *led to 2 out, ev ch till one pace r-in...*..................(9 to 4 op 6 to 4) 2
2536 THE LEGGETT [115] (bl) 11-10-4 M A FitzGerald, *trkd ldr to 13th, hit nxt, wkng whn blun 16th, sn tld off, eased r-in...*..................(33 to 1 tchd 50 to 1) 3
2258⁵ CELTIC SHOT [135] 12-11-10 G Bradley, *hld up in tch, jmpd slwly 15th, lost pl, effrt 17th, held in 3rd whn pld up lme bef 2 out...*.....(7 to 2 op 4 to 1 tchd 3 to 1) pu
Dist: 10l, dist. 6m 44.90s. a 45.90s (4 Ran).
(A Ilsley), J T Gifford

2674 Philip Barnard Memorial Conditional Jockeys' Handicap Hurdle (0-125 4-y-o and up) £2,862 2¾m...........(3:15)

2019 MISS PURBECK [95] 7-9-12³ (5") S Fox, *rcd keenly, trkd ldr, led 7th, styd on wl frm 2 out.*
.... (20 to 1 op 25 to 1 tchd 33 to 1) 1
2403 CARIBOO GOLD (USA) [119] 5-11-10 A Thornton, *hld up, hdwy 3 out, rdn nxt, styd on one pace to go second r-in.*
.... (4 to 1 op 3 to 1 tchd 9 to 2) 2
2515* SUNSET AND VINE [118] 7-11-9 A Dicken, *hld up mid-div, cld 3 out, ev ch nxt, wknd r-in.*
.... (2 to 1 fav op 7 to 4 tchd 15 to 8) 3
2515² CRABBY BILL [101] (v) 7-10-6 A Procter, *in tch, rdn appr 2 out, one pace...........*(9 to 1 op 10 to 1) 4
2496 BRIGHTLING BOY [97] (bl) 9-10-2 D Fortt, *rear, effrt 3 out, nvr dngrs.*..................(14 to 1 op 10 to 1) 5
2515⁷ SEA BUCK [114] 8-11-5 R Davis, *al beh, rdn 6th, nvr on terms.*.....(16 to 1 op 12 to 1 tchd 20 to 1) 6
2496 ACCESS SUN [95] 7-10-0 T Jenks, *led to 7th, rdn and wkng whn hmpd 2 out, nvr recv'r, tld off.*
.... (20 to 1 op 14 to 1 tchd 25 to 1) 7
2528⁷ WICKET [95] 9-9-8¹ (7") P Ward, *hld up, mstk 6th, rdn 3 out, btn whn f nxt...*(6 to 1 tchd 16 to 1) f
2507² LEAVENWORTH [100] 10-9-12 (7") Pat Thompson, *prmnt whn blun and uns rdr 4th...*......(6 to 1 tchd 13 to 2) ur
2044⁶ WINABUCK [95] 11-10-0 D Meredith, *chsd ldrs, rdn 3 out, wkng whn brght dwn nxt.*
.... (25 to 1 op 20 to 1 tchd 33 to 1) bd

Dist: 6l, 5l, 2½l, 6l, 1½l, 30l. 5m 40.10s. a 34.10s (10 Ran).
SR: 6/24/18/-/-/3/ (Martin Hill), Mrs J G Retter

2675 Badger Novices' Chase (5-y-o and up) £4,072 2½m 110yds............(3:45)

2458* COONAWARA 8-11-9 B Powell, *made all, jmpd wl, quickened 5 out, sn clr, imprsv......*(3 to 1 on op 4 to 1 on) 1
2402² LOS BUCCANEROS 11-11-2 G Upton, *chsd wnr, outpcd whn mstk 4 out, no imprsn aftr.*
.... (10 to 1 op 8 to 1 tchd 12 to 1) 2
1637 COULDNT BE BETTER 7-11-2 G Bradley, *al last, blun 6th, hdwy 8th, dsptd second 4 out till wknd 2 out.*
.... (7 to 2 op 3 to 1 tchd 4 to 1) 3
Dist: 20l, 2l. 5m 27.80s. a 28.30s (3 Ran).
SR: 58/31/29/ (Simon Sainsbury), Capt T A Forster

2676 Cat & Mouse Novices' Hurdle (4-y-o) £2,851 2m 110yds.............(4:20)

1692⁶ BAGALINO (USA) 11-7 M Perrett, *nvr far away, hdwy appr 2 out, led last, all out...*(6 to 1 tchd 13 to 2) 1
EDITHMEAD (Ire) 10-9 M A FitzGerald, *dsptd ld early, hld up in tch aftr second, hdwy to chal appr last, pressed wnr to line...........*(5 to 1 op 4 to 1 tchd 11 to 2) 2
2471² ERCKULE 11-0 C Llewellyn, *trkd ldr aftr second, made most frm 4th till wknd and hdd last.*
.... (2 to 1 fav tchd 5 to 2) 3
COLLIER BAY 11-0 T Grantham, *jmpd big in rear, styd on aftr 3 out, nvr nrr.........*(5 to 2 op 2 to 1) 4
2374⁶ KARAR (Ire) 11-0 R Dunwoody, *rcd keenly, frnt rnk till wknd appr 2 out.....*(6 to 1 op 8 to 1 tchd 10 to 1) 5
2503³ LODESTONE LAD (Ire) 10-11 (3") D Meredith, *led to 4th, dsptd ld till rdn aftr 3 out, sn btn.*
.... (50 to 1 op 20 to 1 tchd 66 to 1) 6
2398⁶ WOLLBOLL 11-4 Richard Guest, *hmpd 1st, outpcd aftr second, effrt 4th, nvr dngrs.*
.... (50 to 1 op 20 to 1 tchd 66 to 1) 7
2320⁶ PHROSE 11-0 Peter Hobbs, *blun 1st, outpcd 4th, tld off.*
.... (50 to 1 op 20 to 1 tchd 50 to 1) 8
2522³ MANILA BAY (USA) 11-0 J R Kavanagh, *hld up, hdwy 3rd, mstk 3 out, wknd quickly, tld off.*
.... (14 to 1 op 16 to 1 tchd 50 to 1) 9
Dist: Nk, 1½l, 7l, 10l, 2l, 10l, dist, 1l. 4m 15.70s. a 28.70s (9 Ran).
SR: 12/-/2/-/-/-/ (Sir Eric Parker), G Harwood

2677 Sandown Open National Hunt Flat Race (4,5,6-y-o) £1,926 2m 110yds ....(4:55)

GO BALLISTIC 5-10-10 (7") R Massey, *trkd ldrs gng wl, led o'r 3 fs out, pushed out fnl furlong.*
.... (25 to 1 op 20 to 1 tchd 33 to 1) 1
NAHLA 4-9-11 (5") S Curran, *hld up rear, hdwy 6 fs out, dsptd ld 2 out, edgd rght und pres, no extr cl hme.*
.... (33 to 1 tchd 50 to 1) 2
2339² KILLONE ABBOT (Ire) 5-11-3 T Grantham, *hld up rear, hdwy 5 fs out, chsd ldg pair frm 2 out.*
.... (6 to 4 fav op 5 to 4 tchd 7 to 4) 3
CASTLE CHIEF 5-11-3 D Murphy, *hld up mid-div, cld o'r 3 fs out, styd on one pace.*
.... (12 to 1 op 10 to 1 tchd 14 to 1) 4
JIBBER THE KIBBER (Ire) 5-10-10 (7") D Bohan, *nvr far away, ev ch 3 fs out, sn outpcd.*
.... (12 to 1 op 10 to 1 tchd 14 to 1) 5
HUGE MISTAKE 5-11-3 C Llewellyn, *rear, sn rdn alng, styd on one pace fnl 3 fs.*
.... (10 to 1 op 8 to 1 tchd 12 to 1) 6
MASTER HOPE (Ire) 5-11-3 Mr R Bevan, *in tch till outpcd fnl 3 fs...........*(8 to 1 tchd 10 to 1) 7
1996² LEAD VOCALIST (Ire) 5-11-5 (5") C Burnett-Wells, *hld up in tch, no hdwy fnl 3 fs...* (9 to 2 op 6 to 1 tchd 7 to 1) 8
QUADRAPOL 5-10-5 (7") P Melia, *in tch, rdn 4 fs out, no hdwy.*....................(33 to 1 op 20 to 1) 9
BLUE DOCTOR 4-10-7 R Dunwoody, *prmnt, led 6 fs out, rdn and rcd o'r 3 out, wknd.....*(20 to 1 op 16 to 1) 10
JOLLY SENSIBLE 5-10-5 (7") J Brown, *al mid-div.*
.... (25 to 1 op 16 to 1) 11
2210² LIGHTENING LAD 6-10-10 (7") Mr E James, *prmnt, dsptd ld o'r 3 fs out, rdn and wknd quickly.*
.... (10 to 1 op 8 to 1 tchd 12 to 1) 12
EMMA'S WAY (Ire) 5-10-5 (7") M Keighley, *in tch till wknd 4 fs out.............*(7 to 1 op 10 to 1 tchd 8 to 1) 13
PURBECK CAVALIER 5-10-10 (7") Mr J Culloty, *al rear.*
.... (20 to 1) 14
2210⁴ SO HOPEFUL (NZ) 5-11-0 (3") R Davis, *prmnt till wknd 5 fs out.*.........(20 to 1 op 10 to 1 tchd 25 to 1) 15
2176 STRAY HARMONY 4-9-11 (5") T Jenks, *beh, some hdwy hfwy, wknd o'r 4 fs out, tld off.....*(33 to 1 op 20 to 1) 16
MISS PANDY 6-10-12 M Perrett, *al beh, tld off.*
.... (50 to 1 op 33 to 1) 17
FINAL SEASON 5-11-3 B Powell, *led to 6 fs out, wknd o'r 3 out, tld off.....*..................(50 to 1) 18
1126 FIVEPERCENT 6-11-3 B Clifford, *prmnt early, beh hfwy, tld off.*.....(50 to 1 op 25 to 1) 19
DEPTFORD BELLE 4-9-9 (7") G Crone, *prmnt on outsd, wknd rpdly 4 fs out.*..................(50 to 1 op 25 to 1) 20

2269 JAY EM ESS (NZ) 5-11-3 J Frost, *al beh, tld off.*
....(25 to 1 op 20 to 1)   21
2269 LEENEY 5-11-3 M Bosley, *al beh, tld off.*
....(50 to 1 op 33 to 1)   22
Dist: ¾l, 5l, 10l, nk, ¾l, 3l, 6l, 1l, ¾l, nk. 4m 9.80s. (22 Ran).
(Mrs B J Lockhart), D Nicholson

GOWRAN PARK (IRE) (heavy)
Saturday February 19th

2678
Red Mills Premier Maiden Hurdle (4-y-o) £3,105 2m................ (2:00)

2547⁸ GENTLE REEF (Ire) 10-4 C N Bowens, ...(20 to 1)   1
2547² WICKLOW WAY (Ire) 10-9 K F O'Brien, ...(Evens fav)   2
2614⁵ ONOMATOPOEIA (Ire) 10-9 M Duffy, ...(10 to 1)   3
2285⁶ TEXAS FRIDAY (Ire) 10-9 C F Swan, ...(8 to 1)   4
2024 BERESFORD LADY (Ire) 10-4 C O'Dwyer, ...(8 to 1)   5
BORN TO WIN (Ire) 10-4 P M Verling, ...(14 to 1)   6
SPECIAL OFFER (Ire) 9-11 (7⁵) F Byrne, ...(12 to 1)   7
2122 LIBRAN ROCK (Ire) 10-9 J Shortt, ...(12 to 1)   8
2663 EMERALD BREFFNI (Ire) 10-9 H Rogers, ...(33 to 1)   9
2614⁸ TRES JOUR (Ire) 9-11 (7⁵) P Morris, ...(20 to 1)   f
SOUL EMPEROR 10-7 (7⁵) T Martin, ...(12 to 1)   ur
2608⁵ SHEREGORI (Ire) 10-4 (5⁵) K L O'Brien, ...(5 to 2)   bd
Dist: 2l, 14l, nk, hd. 4m 22.30s. (12 Ran).
(B T Moore), W T Bourke

2679
Red Mills Quality Feed Maiden Hurdle (5-y-o) £3,105 2m.............. (2:30)

2389³ BUTCHES BOY (Ire) 11-11 S H O'Donovan, ...(11 to 10 fav)   1
2607 GLEN SALGIUS (Ity) 11-0 (3⁵) T P Treacy, ...(16 to 1)   2
2553* NINE O THREE (Ire) 11-6 (5⁵) J P Broderick, ...(5 to 1)   3
2155⁵ INAUGURATION 11-3 B Sheridan, ...(8 to 1)   4
2389⁹ JOHNSTONS BUCK (Ire) 10-10 (7⁵) D Finnegan, ...(8 to 1)   5
2348⁵ WEJEM (Ire) 11-3 P M Verling, ...(7 to 1)   6
2348⁴ TURALITY (Ire) 11-3 M Duffy, ...(8 to 1)   7
2348 ABAVARD (Ire) 11-6 (5⁵) M J Holbrook, ...(12 to 1)   8
2464⁹ RADICAL NURSE (Ire) 10-5 (7⁵) P J Mulligan, ...(25 to 1)   9
2465 SILVERFORT LAD (Ire) 10-12 (5⁵) T P Rudd, ...(20 to 1)   10
2465 SMALL TALK (Ire) 10-12 H Rogers, ...(25 to 1)   11
1822 STRUGGLING LASS (Ire) 10-12 C F Swan, ...(12 to 1)   12
DRINDOD (Ire) 10-10 (7⁵) D A McLoughlin, ...(12 to 1)   13
27⁹ TODDY MARK (Ire) 11-3 P L Malone, ...(33 to 1)   14
WHITE OAK BRIDGE (Ire) 10-5 (7⁵) P P Curran, ...(20 to 1)   15
2155 ANOTHER STAR (Ire) 10-12 M Moran, ...(25 to 1)   16
Dist: 5½l, 2½l, 5l, 2l. 4m 19.70s. (16 Ran).
(Mrs Bridget Kennedy), P A Fahy

2680
Red Mills Trial Hurdle (5-y-o and up) £6,900 2m................. (3:00)

2610⁸ ARCTIC WEATHER (Ire) (bl) 5-10-12 (5⁵) K L O'Brien, (9 to 4)   1
2467³ NOVELLO ALLEGRO (USA) 6-11-12 P Carberry, (7 to 4 fav)   2
2392 SHANKORAK 7-11-5 (7⁵) D J Kavanagh, ...(10 to 1)   3
AUTUMN GORSE (Ire) 5-11-3 C F Swan, ...(8 to 1)   4
Dist: 2½l, 8l, 12l. 4m 28.60s. (4 Ran).
(Richard Bomze), M J P O'Brien

2681
Red Mills Trial Chase (5-y-o and up) £3,450 2½m................. (3:30)

2609² BUCKS-CHOICE 7-11-9 J F Titley, ...(11 to 10 fav)   1
2282 THREE BROWNIES 7-11-9 C O'Dwyer, ...(7 to 1)   2
1497⁴ BORN DEEP 8-11-7 T Horgan, ...(4 to 1)   3
2351* MACAMORE STAR 8-11-4 (3⁵) C O'Brien, ...(10 to 1)   4
2282² SCRIBBLER 8-11-9 L P Cusack, ...(4 to 1)   f
2390² TITIAN BLONDE (Ire) 6-11-4 C F Swan, ...(20 to 1)   pu
Dist: Nk, 20l, dist. 5m 37.30s. (6 Ran).
(Hudson Valley Equine Inc), P Mullins

2682
Red Mills Hi-Pro Handicap Hurdle (0-130 4-y-o and up) £3,450 2½m (4:00)

2617² IM MELODY (Ire) [-] 6-10-0 (5⁵) J P Broderick, (4 to 1 jt-fav)   1
2468* DOWHATYOULIKE (Ire) [-] 5-10-0 (6ex) P Carberry, (9 to 2)   2
2548² IAMWHATIAM [-] 8-10-0 S H O'Donovan, ...(4 to 1 jt-fav)   3
2550 PANDA (Ire) [-] 6-10-7 K F O'Brien, ...(12 to 1)   4
2392 MICK O'DWYER [-] 7-10-5 F J Flood, ...(10 to 1)   5
2468 TERZIA [-] 7-11-4 T Horgan, ...(8 to 1)   6
2389 TRIMMER WONDER (Ire) [-] 6-9-4 (3⁵) C O'Brien, ...(14 to 1)   7
1984³ BEGLAWELLA [-] 7-10-4 T P Treacy, ...(6 to 1)   8
KELLY'S PEARL [-] 7-12-0 C F Swan, ...(6 to 1)   9
BROOKVILLE STAR (Ire) [-] 7-9-0 (7⁵) T Martin, ...(33 to 1)   10
Dist: 2½l, 4l, 8l, 3l. 5m 32.50s. (10 Ran).
(The Brouge Syndicate), Michael Hourigan

2683
Red Mills Stable Feed Novice Chase (5-y-o and up) £3,450 2¼m...... (4:30)

2588³ BLUE RING 10-11-9 F Woods, ...(5 to 1)   1
WALLYS RUN 7-11-9 (5⁵) D T Evans, ...(11 to 2)   2
2282⁶ THE WEST'S ASLEEP (bl) 9-11-11 (3⁵) J Magee, ...(10 to 1)   3
2588 SUPER MIDGE 7-12-0 T Horgan, ...(4 to 1)   4
2351 BARRAFONA (Ire) 6-11-9 (5⁵) J P Broderick, ...(12 to 1)   5
2233⁶ NO BETTER BUACHAIL (Ire) 6-12-0 F J Flood, ...(7 to 1)   6

2353⁴ TUL NA GCARN 9-12-0 J Shortt, ...(14 to 1)   7
2053⁴ CARTON 7-12-0 K F O'Brien, ...(10 to 1)   f
1893 FEATHERED GALE 7-12-0 T J Taaffe, ...(7 to 4 fav)   ur
2661 GIVE IT A MISS 8-11-11 (3⁵) D P Murphy, ...(20 to 1)   pu
2588 CRACKLING FROST (Ire) 6-11-9 (5⁵) T P Rudd, ...(20 to 1)   pu
Dist: 1½l, dist, 6l, 2½l. 5m 3.90s. (11 Ran).
(Mrs L Mangan), James Joseph Mangan

2684
Red Mills Vital I.N.H. Flat Race (5-y-o and up) £3,105 2m 1f.......... (5:00)

2470³ RUN BAVARD (Ire) 6-11-7 (7⁵) Mr P English, ...(10 to 1)   1
2586 CORYMANDEL (Ire) 5-11-4 (7⁵) Mr D P Carey, ...(12 to 1)   2
2553³ KEEPHERGOING (Ire) 5-10-13 (7⁵) Mr R P Burns, ...(8 to 1)   3
EMMA HAAN (Ire) 5-11-6 Mr T Mullins, ...(7 to 4 fav)   4
2620² WEST BROGUE (Ire) 5-11-11 Mr J P Dempsey, ...(10 to 1)   5
OH RIVER (Ire) 5-11-1 (5⁵) Mr J P Berry, ...(33 to 1)   6
2128⁴ SKY VISION (Ire) 5-10-13 (7⁵) Mr K F O'Donnell, ...(16 to 1)   7
2470² BALLYHIRE LAD (Ire) 5-11-11 Mr A P O'Brien, ...(3 to 1)   8
2177² WHALE OF A KNIGHT (Ire) 5-11-6 (5⁵) Mr T P Hyde, (6 to 1)   9
PERCUSIONIST 7-12-0 Mr A J Martin, ...(20 to 1)   10
NELLOES PET (Ire) 5-10-13 (7⁵) Mr F McGirr, ...(14 to 1)   11
2464² ANNIE FOX 7-11-9 Mr P Fenton, ...(7 to 1)   12
2394 DRUMCILL LASS (Ire) 6-11-2 (7⁵) Mr K Whelan, ...(33 to 1)   13
2620⁸ LIME LADY (Ire) 5-10-13 (7⁵) Mr M J Bowe, ...(20 to 1)   14
709⁹ FOUR MOONS (Ire) 5-10-13 (7⁵) Mr D L Bolger, ...(14 to 1)   15
2394 QUEENLIER (Ire) 5-10-13 (7⁵) Miss F M Crowley, ...(16 to 1)   16
YOUCAT (Ire) 5-11-4 (7⁵) Mr M G Holden, ...(12 to 1)   17
CANUIG (Ire) 5-11-11 Mr M McNulty, ...(10 to 1)   18
2464 LOVELY AFFAIR (Ire) 5-11-1 (5⁵) Mr H F Cleary, ...(12 to 1)   19
2553⁵ NAKURU (Ire) 5-11-1 (5⁵) Mrs A M O'Brien, ...(12 to 1)   20
Dist: 1l, 7l, 2½l, 7l. 4m 33.90s. (20 Ran).
(J R Kidd), Thomas Foley

NOTTINGHAM (good to soft)
Saturday February 19th
Going Correction: PLUS 0.90 sec. per fur.

2685
St Anns Juvenile Novices' Hurdle (4-y-o) £2,015 2m................. (1:35)

DARK DEN (USA) 10-10 T Kent, *jmpd wl, led second, clr 4th, stumbled 2 out, eased r-in, unchlgd.*
....(9 to 4 fav op 2 to 1)   1
2503² PRIME OF LIFE (Ire) 10-10 S McNeill, *hld up in tch, hdwy hfwy, chsd wnr appr 4 out, rdn and hit nxt, no ch with winner*....................................(7 to 1 op 5 to 1)   2
2371³ THE PREMIER EXPRES 11-4 A Maguire, *led to second, rdn alng 4th, sn one pace, poor 3rd whn blun last.*
....(7 to 1 op 8 to 1)   3
2381 ACANTHUS (Ire) 10-5 (5⁵) T Eley, *chsd ldrs, rdn 5th, styd on same pace frm 3 out.*...............(50 to 1 op 33 to 1)   4
2494 MIGAVON 10-5 D Gallagher, *hld up beh, effrt and rdn 3 out, nvr a factor.*...................(66 to 1 op 50 to 1)   5
2398² MILLMOUNT (Ire) (v) 10-5 W McFarland, *prmnt, rdn alng 5th, beh 4 out.*............(15 to 2 op 8 to 1 tchd 9 to 1)   6
2002⁴ HYDE'S HAPPY HOUR 11-4 G McCourt, *hld up, hdwy 4th, rdn appr four out, sn btn, blun last.* (9 to 2 op 7 to 2)   7
2381⁷ DYAB (USA) 10-10 S Keightley, *al rear, tld off hfwy.*
...............................(12 to 1 op 14 to 1 tchd 16 to 1)   8
2503 RUMPUS (Ire) 10-5 W Marston, *prmnt, hit 3rd, sn beh, tld off hfwy.*................(13 to 2 op 4 to 1 tchd 7 to 1)   9
Dist: 10l, 15l, 5l, ¾l, 1½l, hd, 25l, dist. 3m 40s. a 19.40s (9 Ran).
SR: 32/22/15/2/-/-/7/-/-/
(George L Ohrstrom), Mrs J Cecil

2686
Colwick Park Novices' Handicap Hurdle (0-100 4-y-o and up) £2,061 2m 5f 110yds. .... (2:05)

2404⁶ TRAVELLING LIGHT [92] 8-11-10 Mr S Swiers, *in tch, hdwy to ld 3 out, quickened clr appr last, easily.*
....(8 to 1 op 6 to 1)   1
2575* VERY EVIDENT (Ire) [89] 5-11-7 J Callaghan, *hld up, hdwy appr 3 out, chlgd nxt, sn rdn, one pace approaching last.*..............................(12 to 1 op 10 to 1)   2
2358⁴ LACURVA (Ire) [76] 6-10-1 (7⁵) P Ward, *mid-div, effrt and hdwy 3 out, rdn nxt, one pace appr last.*
....(11 to 2 op 7 to 1)   3
2498⁷ MAC RAMBLER [68] 7-10-5 S Turner, *reluctant strt and beh, hdwy 3 out, styd on one pace und pres appr last.*
....(25 to 1 op 16 to 1)   4
1442 DUNDEE PRINCE (NZ) [85] 6-11-3 N Williamson, *hld up, hdwy appr 3 out, sn rdn, one pace.* (10 to 1 op 7 to 1)   5
2308³ LEINTHALL PRINCESS [68] 8-10-0 A Maguire, *prmnt till outpcd 4 out, styd on one pace frm 2 out.*
....(14 to 1 tchd 12 to 1)   6
3617 MUZO (USA) [69] 7-10-1 W Humphreys, *slwly into strd, nvr rch ldrs.*............................(33 to 1)   7
1239* FATHER FORTUNE [85] (bl) 6-11-3 (7⁵) J McCarthy, *prmnt, led 3rd, sn clr, rdn and hdd 3 out, soon wknd.*
....(6 to 1 op 5 to 1)   8
2239⁷ ARTIC MISSILE [68] 7-10-0 Ann Stokell, *mid-div, hdwy appr 3 out, sn rdn and btn.*...............(50 to 1)   9
1386⁴ GREEN WALK [68] 7-10-0 B Powell, *prmnt till rdn appr 3 out, sn wknd.*..........(20 to 1 op 16 to 1)   10

2483 PETRADARE [68] 7-9-7 (7*) P McLoughlin, *prmnt, hit second, rdn and wknd hfwy, sn beh*............ (100 to 1) 11
EASTERN PLEASURE [82] 7-11-0 Diane Clay, *beh hfwy.*
.... (20 to 1 op 16 to 1) 12
1930 SALINGER [70] 6-10-2 V Smith, *pld hrd, hld up till hdwy
appr 4 out, rdn nxt, sn wknd*......(25 to 1 op 20 to 1) 13
2141⁷ COLETTE'S CHOICE (Ire) [88] 5-11-1 (5*) D Fortt, *prmnt, lost
pl and beh 6th*.................... (14 to 1 op 12 to 1) 14
2578* SCARF (Ire) [90] (bl) 6-11-8 M Dwyer, *hmpd strt, hdwy to
track ldrs 4th, effrt and ev ch whn f 3 out.*
.... (7 to 4 fav tchd 2 to 1) f
2141 PENLEA LADY [68] 7-10-0 D Gallagher, *led to 3rd, prmnt
till rdn and wkng whn hmpd 3 out, pld up.*
.................................(50 to 1 tchd 100 to 1) pu
Dist: 8l, ½l, 15l, nk, ¾l, 2l, 12l, ½l, 2l, 25l. 5m 39.60s. a 37.60s (16 Ran).
(Mrs J R Ramsden, Mrs J R Ramsden

2687 BBC Radio Nottingham Novices' Hunters' Chase (5-y-o and up) £1,164 2m 5f 110yds................. (2:35)

2484² MINERS MELODY (Ire) 6-12-0 Mr J Greenall, *al prmnt, hit
5th, led appr 5 out, sn clr, unchlgd.*
.............(13 to 8 on op 2 to 1 on tchd 6 to 4 on) 1
SPARTAN RANGER 9-11-7 (7*) Mr C Bonner, *led till appr 5
out, sn rdn, styd on one pace, lft remote second 2 out.*
.............................(7 to 1 op 5 to 1) 2
UP THE LADDER 10-11-7 (7*) Miss C Thomas, *hld up, effrt
and some hdwy hfwy, sn wknd, lft remote 3rd 2 out.*
............................(14 to 1 op 10 to 1) 3
2555 SAGARO SUN 8-11-7 (7*) Mr C Campbell, *in tch, hit 6th, sn
rdn alng, lost pl and tld off 12th.* (33 to 1 tchd 50 to 1) 4
TIRLEY MISSILE 8-11-7 (7*) Mr M Rimell, *not jump wl, al
prmnt, chsd wnr 4 out, poor second whn f 2 out.*
............................(11 to 2 op 5 to 1) f
BEN HEAD 12-11-7 (7*) Mr R Bevis, *beh, some hdwy 12th,
poor 4th whn brght dwn 2 out*.... (10 to 1 op 8 to 1) bd
ABADARE (USA) 10-11-7 (7*) Mr G Hogan, *al rear, tld off
12th, pld up bef 4 out.*..............(66 to 1 op 50 to 1) pu
AUTUMN SPORT 13-11-9 (5*) Mr R Hale, *jmpd slwly, beh,
tld off whn pld up bef 5 out.*........................(20 to 1) pu
AINTREE OATS 7-11-3¹ (7*) Mr J Holt, *chsd ldrs, hit 3rd,
lost pl 12th, sn beh, tld off whn pld up bef 4 out.*
.................................(50 to 1) pu
Dist: Dist, 3½l, dist. 5m 48.60s. a 35.60s (9 Ran).
(J E Greenall, P Cheesbrough

2688 Michael Seely Nottinghamshire Novices' Chase Grade 2 (5-y-o and up) £9,560 2m..................... (3:10)

1919³ COUNTRY LAD (Ire) 6-11-5 S McNeill, *chsd ldrs, rdn 3 out,
blun nxt, hit last, styd on to ld last 100 yards.*
............................(14 to 1 op 8 to 1) 1
2304² FRONT LINE 7-11-5 N Williamson, *in tch, hdwy 5 out, effrt
2 out, rdn to ld briefly r-in, hdd and no extr last 100
yards*.............................(33 to 1 op 20 to 1) 2
2268* CURRENT EXPRESS 7-11-5 M A FitzGerald, *trkd ldrs,
hdwy 5th, led 5 out, blun 2 out, rdn and blunded last,
hdd and no extr r-in.*
........(6 to 5 fav op 11 to 10 tchd Evens and 5 to 4) 3
2399* HOPS AND POPS 7-11-0 S Earle, *led, jmpd rght and
mstks, hdd 5 out, sn rdn alng, ev ch till no extr frm last.*
............................(7 to 1 op 5 to 1 tchd 8 to 1) 4
2584² SEON 8-11-5 L Wyer, *hld up, hit 5th, sn rdn alng and
outpcd.*.............................(33 to 1 op 20 to 1) 5
1919* NATIVE MISSION 7-11-12 M Dwyer, *blun 1st 2, rdn alng to
track ldrs 6th, effrt and ev ch 4 out, sn ridden, wknd
quickly.*.............................(7 to 1 tchd 5 to 1) 6
2584³ CALDECOTT 8-11-5 Gary Lyons, *prmnt, lost pl 5th, sn
beh, tld off whn pld up bef 4 out.* (100 to 1 op 50 to 1) pu
Dist: 1l, 3½l, nk, 3l, dist. 4m 9.70s. a 18.70s (7 Ran).
SR: 48/47/43/37/39/-/-/ (S A Douch, Mrs S D Williams

2689 Roseland Group City Trial Hurdle (Limited Handicap) (4-y-o and up) £4,727 2m..................... (3:45)

2046 HIGHBROOK (USA) [134] 6-10-7 A Maguire, *trkd ldrs,
hdwy to chal 3 out, sn led, quickened clr, unchlgd.*
...............(15 to 8 op 13 to 8 tchd 2 to 1) 1
2385³ STRATH ROYAL [134] 8-10-7 M Brennan, *trkd ldr, wide
strt, rdn appr 2 out, sn one pace.* (3 to 1 tchd 11 to 4) 2
2402 COULTON [155] 7-12-0 M Dwyer, *led, quickened 4 out, jnd
nxt, sn hdd and btn.* (11 to 8 fav op 5 to 4 on Evens tchd 6 to 4) 3
PHILS PRIDE [134] 10-10-7 P Niven, *pld hrd, in tch till lost
pl 5th, sn beh.*.....................(14 to 1 op 10 to 1) 4
Dist: 7l, 15l, 20l. 4m 3.60s. a 19.60s (4 Ran).
SR: 27/20/26/-/ (Nick Cook, M H Tompkins

2690 Letheby & Christopher Handicap Chase (0-110 5-y-o and up) £3,080 3m 110yds..................... (4:15)

1742* ASTINGS (Fr) [90] 6-11-0 M Dwyer, *cl up gng wl, rdn 3 out,
styd on und hrd driving frm last to ld on line.*
.............................(11 to 8 fav tchd 6 to 4) 1

2305² YOUNG MINER [95] 8-11-5 G Upton, *led to 6th, led tenth,
rdn 3 out, hit nxt, hrd drvn r-in, ct on line.*
.............................(9 to 2 op 4 to 1) 2
2493² IRISH BAY [100] (bl) 8-11-10 J Railton, *hld up, hdwy 11th,
effrt 2 out, ev ch last, wnt rght r-in, no extr nr finish.*
.............................(6 to 1 op 5 to 1) 3
2429² LITTLE GENERAL [89] 11-10-13 A Maguire, *prmnt, blun
tenth, hit 5 out, sn wknd.*.........(4 to 1 op 5 to 1) 4
2363⁴ UNDER OFFER [79] (bl) 13-9-7 M C Hancock, *chsd
ldrs, hit 8th, rdn alng tenth, sn lost pl.*
.............................(12 to 1 op 14 to 1) 5
ROYAL SUNSHINE [90] 9-11-0 L Harvey, *al rear, tld off
whn pld up bef 5 out.*...............(20 to 1 op 16 to 1) pu
2294 WOODY WILL [99] 8-11-6 (3*) J McCarthy, *cl up, led 6th to
tenth, rdn and wknd 5 out, pld up bef 3 out.*
.............................(12 to 1 op 8 to 1) pu
Dist: Hd, 7l, 15l. 6m 32.90s. a 37.90s (7 Ran).

2691 Nottingham Open National Hunt Flat Race (4,5,6-y-o) £1,570 2m.......(4:45)

CAVINA 4-10-2 L Wyer, *in tch, hdwy o'r 4 fs out, led appr
last, sn rdn, ran on...* (6 to 1 op 12 to 1 tchd 14 to 1) 1
2373² WHO IS EQUINAME (Ire) 4-10-7 A Maguire, *led 3 fs, cl up till
led o'r 4 out, hdd appr last, kpt on...*(3 to 1 op 5 to 2) 2
2509² PETE THE PARSON (Ire) 5-11-3 T Grantham, *in tch, hdwy 5
fs out, rdn and kpt on one pace frm 3 out.*
.............................(9 to 4 fav op 2 to 1 tchd 5 to 2) 3
GOTT TO APPROACH 6-10-10 (7*) M Keighley, *in tch, drvn
alng o'r 4 fs out, kpt on one pace.* (16 to 1 op 12 to 1) 4
BARTON SANTA (Ire) 5-11-3 N Williamson, *pld hrd, hdwy
hfwy, chsd ldrs 4 out, rdn and outpcd fnl 2 fs.*
.............................(5 to 1 op 3 to 1) 5
NOW YOUNG MAN (Ire) 5-11-3 J Railton, *al prmnt, effrt 4
fs out, sn rdn and one pace.*...........(25 to 1) 6
1660* DUNNOHALM 5-11-5 Mr S Swiers, *unruly strt, slwly into
strd and beh, headwy o'r 4 fs out, not rch ldrs.*
.............................(8 to 1 op 5 to 1) 7
2176⁹ CHIEF LADY NICOLA 4-9-9 (7*) E Tolhurst, *nvr rch ldrs.*
.............................(33 to 1) 8
SHAMELESS LADY 4-10-2 S Mackey, *prmnt till wknd o'r 3
fs out.*.............................(33 to 1) 9
2490⁶ BANOFFI (Ire) 5-11-3 M Dwyer, *chsed ldrs till rdn and
wknd o'r 3 fs out.*.................(16 to 1 op 14 to 1) 10
ELANDS CASTLE (Ire) 6-10-5 (7*) P Ward, *al mid-div.*
.............................(25 to 1 op 20 to 1) 11
MARY KNOLL (Ire) 6-10-5 (7*) Mr P Hanly, *nvr a factor.*
.............................(50 to 1) 12
OPERA TALENT (Ire) 5-10-10 (7*) G Tormey, *pld hrd, led
aftr 3 fs, rcd wide, hdd and wknd o'r 4 out.*
.............................(10 to 1 op 16 to 1) 13
2387 MY LISA TOO 5-10-12 R Garritty, *al beh.*........(33 to 1) 14
DABALARK 5-11-3 A O'Hagan, *al beh, tld off hfwy.*
.............................(50 to 1) 15
901⁸ CRADLERS 6-11-3 B Powell, *trkd lea ders till puled up
lme approching fnl fs.*.............(25 to 1 op 20 to 1) pu
LOVELARK 5-10-12 V Smith, *beh, ran wide strt, pld up 4
fs out.*.............................(50 to 1) pu
TIR NA NOG 5-10-10 (7*) Mr J O'Shaughnessy, *tld off hfwy,
pld up 3 fs out.*.....................(50 to 1) pu
Dist: 5l, 10l, sht-hd, 4l, 3l, 12l, 4l, 1l, ¾l, nk. 4m 7.70s. (18 Ran).
(Paul G Jacobs, N A Graham

WINDSOR (soft)
Saturday February 19th
Going Correction: PLUS 1.15 sec. per fur. (races 1,3,6), PLUS 1.08 (2,4,5)

2692 EBF King John 'National Hunt' Novices' Hurdle Qualifier (5,6,7-y-o) £2,267 2m..................... (1:50)

2558³ SPREAD YOUR WINGS (Ire) 6-10-9 J Osborne, *made virtually all, rdn clr frm 2 out.*..........(3 to 1 op 2 to 1) 1
2426* NO PAIN NO GAIN (Ire) 6-11-10 E Murphy, *wth ldrs, chsd
wnr frm 5th, rdn and not quicken from 2 out.*
.............(11 to 8 on op 5 to 4 tchd 6 to 4) 2
2048⁷ FORTUNES COURSE (Ire) 5-10-9 J R Kavanagh, *ran on frm
rear 4th, rdn and one pace appr 2 out.*
.............................(33 to 1 op 20 to 1) 3
1646⁷ SO AUDACIOUS 6-11-0 R Supple, *chsd ldrs, no extr appr
2 out...*.............................(9 to 1 op 33 to 1) 4
2556 SPIRIT IN THE NITE (Ire) 5-11-5 D Murphy, *trkd wnr to 5th,
sn rdn and btn.*........(4 to 1 op 5 to 2 tchd 9 to 2) 5
2176 ARCHIE'S SISTER 5-10-6 (3*) D Meredith, *lost tch frm 4th.*
.............................(66 to 1 op 33 to 1) 6
2048 CELTIC LAIRD 6-11-0 I Lawrence, *in tch til rdn and lost
pos aftr 5th.*.............(16 to 1 op 14 to 1 tchd 20 to 1) 7
2176 DO LETS 5-10-9 R Dunwoody, *al beh, lost tch frm 4th.*
.............................(33 to 1 op 20 to 1) 8
ARAGON MIST 5-10-9 M Bosley, *wl plcd to 4th, sn wknd,
pld up bef 3 out.*.................(66 to 1 op 50 to 1) pu

373

FINALLY FANTAZIA 5-10-9 R J Beggan, *rear whn mstks 3rd and 4th, sn lost tch, pld up bef 3 out.*
................(20 to 1 op 12 to 1 tchd 25 to 1) pu
Dist: 12l, 4l, 4l, 10l, 15l, 2l, 2l. 4m 9.00s. a 24.00s (10 Ran).
SR: 25/28/9/10/5/-/ (T J Whitley), D R Gandolfo

2693 Magna Carta Novices' Chase (5-y-o and up) £2,721 2m 5f.......... (2:25)

2427² NEW GHOST 9-10-10 (7*) Mr S Mulcaire, *mstk second, hdwy to ld 6th, not fluent nxt, lft wl clr 2 out.*
................(6 to 1 tchd 8 to 1) 1
2400³ MR MATT (Ire) 6-11-3 Peter Hobbs, *al wl-plcd, jmpd rght tenth, rdn 12th, lft moderate second 2 out, no imprsn.*
................(6 to 4 fav op 9 to 4 tchd 5 to 2) 2
2260 TIMUR'S KING 7-11-3 M Perrett, *jmpd slwly 4th, rdn alng and kpt on one pace frm 12th.*
................(20 to 1 op 10 to 1 tchd 33 to 1) 3
2208⁷ THE PORTSOY LOON 7-11-3 D Bridgwater, *not fluent 4th, staying on whn hmpd 3 out, nvr nrr.*
................(50 to 1 op 16 to 1 tchd 66 to 1) 4
2378⁵ POPPETS PET 7-11-5 (5*) S Curran, *led to 6th, rdn 11th, wknd nxt.*................(9 to 1 op 3 to 1 tchd 10 to 1) 5
2458³ KETTI (v) 9-10-12 R Dunwoody, *not fluent second, chsd ldrs til wknd 9th, tld off.*
................(8 to 1 op 6 to 1 tchd 10 to 1) 6
DISCO DUKE 9-10-10 (7*) J Clarke, *in tch til drpd rear tenth, tld off.*................(50 to 1 op 16 to 1) 7
2527* JOHNNY WILL 9-11-10 J Osborne, *blun 4th, jmpd slwly 8th, pushed alng 11th, disputing 3rd pl whn f 3 out.*
................(3 to 1 op 9 to 4 tchd 10 to 1) f
2504³ BUCKELIGHT (Ire) 6-11-0 (3*) R Farrant, *prog 7th, chsd wnr 11th, cl second whn f 2 out.*
................(15 to 1 op 9 to 2 tchd 8 to 1) f
2459 PENIARTH 8-10-12 V Slattery, *not fluent 1st, lost tch and jmpd rght tenth, pld up bef 4 out.* (66 to 1 op 33 to 1) pu
2176 PINE VALE 6-10-5 (7*) S Fox, *sn beh, blun 8th, tld off whn pld up bef nxt.*................(33 to 1 op 16 to 1) pu
Dist: 10l, 4l, 4l, 5l, 20l, 4l. 5m 40.50s. a 29.50s (11 Ran).
SR: 21/11/7/3/5/-/ (G W Giddings), G W Giddings

2694 Hatch Bridge Hurdle (4-y-o) £5,173 2m .... (2:55)

2374² MY BALLYBOY 11-2 S Smith Eccles, *led til aftr 4th, wl-plcd, swtchd rght and ran on frm last, led last strd.*
................(2 to 1 op 11 to 8) 1
2503* HOSTILE WITNESS (Ire) (v) 10-12 M Richards, *hdwy frm rear to ld aftr 4th, hdd und pres last strd.*
................(11 to 10 op 6 to 4) 2
1885⁴ RICH LIFE (Ire) 11-2 Peter Hobbs, *pld hrd, pressed ldrs frm 4th, ev ch 2 out, btn appr last.*
................(7 to 1 op 5 to 1 tchd 8 to 1) 3
2169⁸ SHARED GOLD 10-12 M Bosley, *drpd rear appr 5th, nvr nr to chal aftrwards.* (16 to 1 op 10 to 1 tchd 20 to 1) 4
2430² FOREVER SHINEING 10-7 M Perrett, *hld up, hdwy 5th, wknd appr 2 out.*......(13 to 2 op 7 to 1) 5
2150 BAJAN AFFAIR 10-7 A Thornton, *hld second, dsptd ld nxt, wknd 5th, tld off.*......(20 to 1 op 12 to 1) 6
2245⁹ CLEAR LOOK 10-7 J Osborne, *chsd ldrs til wknd 3 out, tld off.*................(33 to 1 op 20 to 1) 7
Dist: Sht-hd, 15l, 3l, 2l, 20l, 20l. 4m 12.20s. a 27.20s (7 Ran).
(A Bailey), A Bailey

2695 Fairlawne Chase (5-y-o and up) £8,052 3m................................ (3:25)

1843 BLACK HUMOUR 10-11-8 G Bradley, *jmpd wl, made all, clr 2 out, cmftbly.*................(2 to 1 op 11 to 8) 1
2474² ZETA'S LAD 11-11-12 R Supple, *pckd at 3rd, ev ch 15th, hit 3 out, rdn and outpcd frm nxt.*
................(2 to 1 op op 13 to 8 on tchd 6 to 4 on) 2
1895⁸ GOLD OPTIONS (bl) 12-11-12 J Osborne, *hld up wl in tch, mstk and lost grnd 12th, rallied and hit 15th, wknd 3 out.*................(8 to 1 op 5 to 1 tchd 12 to 1) 3
Dist: dist, dist. 6m 22.30s. a 27.30s (3 Ran).
SR: 80/-/-/ (Lady Lloyd Webber), C P E Brooks

2696 Staines Handicap Chase (0-125 5-y-o and up) £2,882 2m............... (3:55)

2481* SAILORS LUCK [112] 9-11-5 E Murphy, *led 6th, mstk and hdd nxt, not fluent 8th, led 4 out, drw clr frm 2 out.*
................(Evens fav op 5 to 4 on tchd 5 to 4) 1
NOS NA GAOITHE [117] 11-11-10 R Marley, *hld up, jmpd slwly 4th, wth wnr four out, rdn and no extr frm 2 out.*
................(5 to 1 op 3 to 1 tchd 11 to 2) 2
1363² THATS THE LIFE [117] 9-11-7 (3*) T Jenks, *pld hrd, led to 6th, led 7th, hdd 4 out, one pace whn mstk nxt.*
................(3 to 1 op 5 to 2 tchd 100 to 30) 3
1623⁴ COTAPAXI [93] 9-10-0 R Dunwoody, *chsd ldrs til mstk 4 out, sn lost tch, tld off.*...(4 to 1 op 3 to 1 tchd 9 to 2) 4
Dist: 7l, 1½l, 25l. 4m 19.30s. a 23.30s (4 Ran).
SR: 31/29/27/-/ (Geoffrey C Greenwood), P G Murphy

2697 Runnymede Handicap Hurdle (0-120 4-y-o and up) £2,495 2m....... (4:25)

2507³ ISLAND JEWEL [99] 6-11-0 M Bosley, *ldg grp, rdn alng frm 3 out, led und pres aftr last, styd on gmely.*
................(5 to 1 op 4 to 1 tchd 13 to 2) 1
2002* EASTHORPE [110] 6-11-11 J Osborne, *led, rdn frm 2 out, hdd and no extr aftr last.*
................(11 to 8 fav op 5 to 4 tchd 13 to 8) 2
FUNAMBULIEN (USA) [95] 7-10-10 R Marley, *in tch, cld on ldrs frm 5th, ev ch 2 out, wknd last.*
................(10 to 1 tchd 7 to 1) 3
2457² SOLEIL DANCER (Ire) [94] 6-10-9 Peter Hobbs, *mid-div, rdn and no imprsn on ldrs frm 3 out.* (3 to 1 op 9 to 2) 4
1945³ SURE PRIDE (USA) [98] 6-10-6 (7*) J Clarke, *wl-plcd, rdn 5th, blun nxt, wknd and pckd 2 out.*
................(9 to 1 op 7 to 1 tchd 10 to 1) 5
J BRAND [95] 7-10-10 A Tory, *al beh.*
................(20 to 1 op 12 to 1 tchd 25 to 1) 6
ROCK LEGEND [90] 6-10-5 R Supple, *al in rear, tld off.*
................(20 to 1 op 16 to 1 tchd 33 to 1) 7
STATE OF AFFAIRS [98] 7-10-13 R J Beggan, *mid-div til wknd 5th, tld off.*....(12 to 1 op 7 to 1 tchd 14 to 1) 8
Dist: 7l, 5l, 10l, 12l, 3½l, 10l, 6l. 4m 8.60s. a 23.60s (8 Ran).
SR: 34/38/18/7/-/ (M F Cartwright), J R Bosley

PUNCHESTOWN (IRE) (soft)
Sunday February 20th

2698 Red House Inn Handicap Chase (0-137 5-y-o and up) £4,830 2m........ (2:15)

1450 MERAPI [-] 8-10-12 B Sheridan, ...(16 to 1) 1
2590⁸ LADY OLEIN (Ire) [-] 6-10-5 J P Banahan, ...(7 to 1) 2
2466⁶ LASATA [-] 9-11-11 N Williamson, ...(8 to 1) 3
1459⁸ KINGSTON WAY [-] 8-9-13 A Maguire, ...(12 to 1) 4
2591⁵ WHO'S TO SAY [-] 8-9-3 G Bradley, ...(10 to 1) 5
2280⁵ THIRD QUARTER [-] 9-10-6 (7*) D J Kavanagh, ...(6 to 1) 6
2549 SARAEMMA [-] 8-11-9 J Shortt, ...(10 to 1) 7
2466* BALLAD SONG [-] 11-10-0 (6ex) C F Swan, ...(5 to 2 fav) 8
2466⁵ MAD TOM [-] 9-11-4 (5*) J P Broderick, ...(8 to 1) 9
2179² SORRY ABOUT THAT [-] 8-10-1 P Carberry, ...(8 to 1) 10
2590⁶ PARLIAMENT HALL [-] 8-11-0 K F O'Brien, ...(7 to 1) ur
Dist: 1l, 1½l, 6l, 10l. 4m 27.00s. (11 Ran).
(Miss Marian P Hanlon), R Coonan

2699 Murphys Irish Stout Hurdle (4-y-o) £10,400 2m....................... (2:45)

2608² TROPICAL LAKE (Ire) 10-9 K F O'Brien, ...(2 to 1) 1
2608³ MAGIC FEELING (Ire) 10-9 B Sheridan, ...(8 to 1) 2
2388* ANDANTE (Ire) 10-9 C F Swan, ...(6 to 4 fav) 3
391² MICKS DELIGHT (Ire) 11-0 P Carberry, ...(12 to 1) 4
2547* NANNAKA (USA) 10-9 G Bradley, ...(100 to 30) 5
2608⁴ MAYASTA (Ire) 10-9 C O'Dwyer, ...(14 to 1) 6
Dist: 4½l, 4l, 3l. 4m 32.10s. (6 Ran).
(G A Hoggard), Michael Hourigan

2700 Frank Ward & Co Solicitors Chase (Listed - Grade 3) (5-y-o and up) £8,280 2¼m... (3:15)

2126 DOORSLAMMER 9-10-9 F Woods, *made all, dist clr 4th, reduced advantage four out, four ls ld 2 out, rdn and kpt on wl.*................(20 to 1) 1
2286* ATONE 7-11-7 K F O'Brien, *mid-div, prog to ld chasing grp aftr 5th, stdly cld on ldr till pckd on landing 2 out, sn rdn, no extr after last.*..........(7 to 2 on) 2
ULTRA FLUTTER 7-10-9 (5*) J P Broderick, *hld up, kpt on one pace frm 4 out, nrst finish.*..........(8 to 1) 3
2588 MONKEY AGO 7-11-0 C O'Dwyer, *mid-div, mstk 4th, rdn and no extr aftr four out.*................(20 to 1) 4
2469 TALK TO YOU LATER 8-11-7 H Rogers, *led chasing grp, mstks 5th and 6th, sn lost pl, no imprsn aftr 4 out.*
................(20 to 1) 5
1914* CASTLE KNIGHT 8-11-4 W T Slattery Jnr, *mid-div, rdn and wknd aftr 4 out.*................(9 to 1) 6
2157⁶ ENQELAAB (USA) 6-11-0 J P Banahan, *al rear, tld off aftr 6th.*................(12 to 1) 7
Dist: 2l, 15l, 20l, 4½l. 5m 1.30s. (7 Ran).
(Mrs B M Browne), Mrs B M Browne

2701 Gain National Trial (Listed - Grade 3) (5-y-o and up) £8,280 3¼m 110yds .... (3:45)

2125² CALLMECHA [-] (bl) 9-9-13 A Maguire, *hld up, prog 5 out, trkd ldr nxt, led aftr 2 out, kpt on.*................(10 to 1) 1
2125* NUAFFE [-] 9-9-12 S H O'Donovan, *led, mstk 11th, hdd aftr 2 out and kpt on.*................(5 to 1) 2
2288³ SON OF WAR [-] 7-11-2 F Woods, *wl plcd, mstk 4 out, rdn, no extr appr 2 out.*................(9 to 2) 3
2589⁶ ANOTHER RUSTLE [-] 11-9-7 W T Slattery Jnr, *trkd ldr, rdn 4 out, no extr aftr last.*................(33 to 1) 4
2611⁵ CAHERVILLAHOW [-] 12-10-2 N Williamson, *mid-div, rdn 4 out, kpt on one pace, not threaten ldrs.*........(8 to 1) 5
1850⁹ LAURA'S BEAU [-] (bl) 10-10-5 C O'Dwyer, *mid-div, rdn and lost pl aftr 5 out, wknd.*................(14 to 1) 6

2312⁵ GREEN TIMES [-] 9-9-7 C F Swan, mid-div, rdn aftr 5 out,
no extr and wknd after 3 out.................(14 to 1)   7
2125⁷ OPRYLAND [-] 9-9-2 (5") J P Broderick, wl plcd, rdn and
lost pl aftr 5 out, wknd.....................(14 to 1)   8
2591⁴ CAPTAIN BRANDY [-] 9-10-6 K F O'Brien, mid-div, rdn and
lost pl 6 out, wknd, pld up bef 3 out...........(8 to 1)   pu
2126³ SPEAKING TOUR (USA) [-] 6-9-4 (3") C O'Brien, mid-div
whn dp on landing 6th, sn rear, rdn aftr 5 out, pld up
bef 2 out....................................(14 to 1)   pu
2393* BERMUDA BUCK [-] 8-9-7 P Carberry, mid-div, rdn aftr
11th, lost pl quickly, tld off and pld up bef 6 out.
....(5 to 2 fav)   pu
2619³ IFFEEE [-] 7-9-5³ (5") P A Roche, al rear, tld off aftr 6 out,
pld up bef 2 out.............................(14 to 1)   pu
Dist: 2l, 6l, 9l, sht-hd. 7m 30.80s. (12 Ran).

(T P O'Sullivan), Augustine Leahy

2702 Irish National Hunt Novice Hurdle Series Final (Listed - (5-y-o and up) £6,900 2¼m 110yds........... (4:15)

2587* DORANS PRIDE (Ire) 5-11-4 (5") J P Broderick, trkd ldr, led
briefly appr last, rallied gmely und pres to ld cl hme.
....(9 to 4 fav)   1
2612⁴ IDIOTS VENTURE 7-12-0 B Sheridan, wl plcd, prog to
lead cl out, rdn to ld appr last, hdd and no extr cl
hme...(5 to 2)   2
2612⁶ PADASHPAN (USA) 5-11-9 A Maguire, mid-div, rdn appr 2
out, no extr and wknd entering strt.............(9 to 1)   3
2389² DARU (USA) (bl) 5-10-13 C F Swan, stmd slwly, rdn 4 out,
sn lost aftr nxt.............................(8 to 1)   4
2236 TIP THE CAN (Ire) 6-11-2 A Powell, al rear, lost tch 4 out.
....(100 to 1)   5
2076* HEIST (bl) 5-11-7 P Carberry, f 1st...............(6 to 1)   f
2052¹ HARCON (Ire) 6-11-8 K F O'Brien, led till appr last, f.
....(8 to 1)   f
Dist: ½l, 15l, dist, 15l. 4m 59.10s. (7 Ran).

(T J Doran), Michael Hourigan

2703 Long-Stone Handicap Hurdle (0-109 4-y-o and up) £3,105 2m....... (4:45)

2232⁴ JO JO BOY (Ire) [-] 5-11-9 F J Flood,............(13 to 2)   1
2310 FIDDLERS BOW VI (Ire) [-] 6-10-8 P Carberry,......(8 to 1)   2
1851¹ STEEL DAWN [-] 7-11-8 B Sheridan,................(8 to 1)   3
2552* UNCLE BABY (Ire) [-] 6-11-2 (5",6ex) K P Gaule,....(8 to 1)   4
2392³ FERRYCARRIG HOTEL (Ire) [-] 5-11-13 D H O'Connor,
....(7 to 4 fav)   5
2310⁴ BELLE O' THE BAY (Ire) [-] 5-9-9 (3") D Bromley,.. (20 to 1)   6
2230⁴ KYLE HOUSE VI (Ire) [-] 5-10-6 C F Swan,.........(10 to 1)   7
2617⁸ DEGO DANCER [-] 7-10-11 (5") J P Broderick,......(12 to 1)   8
2027⁸ MARINA (Ire) [-] 5-10-7 P Mooney,................(33 to 1)   9
392² MILLENIUM LASS (Ire) [-] 6-10-6 (7") F Byrne,......(20 to 1)   10
2586 TOP RUN (Ire) [-] 6-10-2 H Rogers,...............(33 to 1)   11
2614⁷ TENCA (Ire) [-] (bl) 4-10-7 J Shortt,..............(16 to 1)   12
2552⁹ SHIRWAN (Ire) [-] 5-10-12 (7") D J Kavanagh,.....(12 to 1)   13
2281⁷ TAGANINI (Ire) [-] 6-10-7 F Woods,...............(20 to 1)   14
2552⁶ LAWYER'S BRIEF (Fr) [-] 7-11-5 L P Cusack,.......(10 to 1)   f
2391⁶ REASILVIA (Ire) [-] 4-11-2 N Williamson,.........(14 to 1)   pu
Dist: 7l, 5½l, 2½l, 6l. 4m 17.60s. (16 Ran).

(Raymond McConn), F Flood

2704 Irish National Bookmakers Flat Race Final (4-y-o and up) £4,830 2m.. (5:15)

2283⁴ THATS A SECRET 6-11-11 (7") Mr P English,..... (13 to 2)   1
1858³ MARYJO (Ire) 5-11-0 (3") Mr A E Lacy,...........(5 to 1)   2
1916⁵ BELGARRO (Ire) 5-11-8 (7") Mr E Norris,.....(2 to 1 jt-fav)   3
2236* NOPADDLE 10-12-1 (3") Mrs J M Mullins,..........(7 to 1)   4
2283⁵ PRODIGAL PRINCE 6-12-4 Mr A J Martin,.....(2 to 1 jt-fav)   5
2389 DORAN'S DELIGHT 7-11-11 (7") Mr B Lennon,....(14 to 1)   6
Dist: 1l, 7l, dist, 6l. 4m 17.20s. (6 Ran).

(T Power), Thomas Foley

FOLKESTONE (heavy (races 1,4,6), soft (2,3,5))
Wednesday February 23rd
Going Correction: PLUS 2.35 sec. per fur. (races 1,4,6), PLUS 1.45 (2,3,5)

2705 EBF 'National Hunt' Novices' Hurdle Qualifier (5,6,7-y-o) £2,709 2m 1f 110yds...................... (1:55)

2048* SQUIRE SILK 5-11-5 S McNeill, hld up, prog to track ldr
6th, led 2 out, clr appr last, rdn out. (7 to 2 op 5 to 2)   1
2505³ SPUFFINGTON 6-11-0 D Murphy, prmnt, led 3rd to 2 out,
rdn and no imprsn appr last.
....(25 to 1 op 8 to 1)   2
1040² GLENCARRIG GALE (Ire) 6-11-0 Peter Hobbs, mstks, chsd
ldrs, outpcd 3 out, kpt on to take 3rd nr finish.
....(12 to 1 op 5 to 1 tchd 14 to 1)   3
2494⁸ DENVER BAY 7-11-0 E Murphy, chsd ldg pair till rdn and
wknd aftr 2 out........(20 to 1 op 7 to 1 tchd 25 to 1)   4

1539 GOOD INSIGHT (Ire) 6-11-0 G Bradley, lost pl 5th, sn struggling......................................(3 to 1 op 5 to 2)   5
2505 HENRY'S SISTER 7-10-2 (7") P Ward, al beh, staying on
but no ch whn blun last..............(33 to 1 op 12 to 1)   6
2361 MAKING TIME 7-10-9 B Powell, led to 3rd, wknd 6th, sn
tld off............................(25 to 1 op 14 to 1)   7
HARRISTOWN (Ire) 6-11-0 N Williamson, hld up in tch,
mstk 5th, wknd rpdly, tld off whn pld up bef 2 out.
....(10 to 1 op 6 to 1)   pu
Dist: 6l, 15l, hd, 12l, ½l, dist. 4m 43.00s. a 46.00s (8 Ran).
SR: 42/31/16/16/4/   (Robert Ogden), Andrew Turnell

2706 EBF Novices' Chase (5-y-o and up) £2,535 2m 5f.................. (2:25)

2517* YELLOW SPRING 9-12-0 Peter Hobbs, made all, mstk
tenth, rdn clr 2 out, styd on wl.
....(3 to 1 on op 9 to 4 on)   1
2455 NICKSLINE 8-11-4 D Murphy, trkd wnr, ev ch appr 2 out,
not quicken...............................(8 to 1 op 5 to 1)   2
2338 LOBRIC (bl) 9-11-4 A Maguire, chsd ldg pair, mstk tenth,
outpcd nxt, no ch aftr....................(4 to 1 op 5 to 2)   3
2647 YOUNG ALFIE (bl) 9-11-4 Miss S Belcher, blun second, sn
lost tch, tld off 7th...............(33 to 1 op 14 to 1)   4
Dist: 15l, 5l, dist. 5m 50.50s. a 40.50s (4 Ran).

(Mrs R Howell), D M Grissell

2707 'Gay Record' Challenge Trophy Handicap Chase (0-125 5-y-o and up) £3,427 2m.................... (2:55)

1659* AROUND THE HORN [111] 7-11-0 S McNeill, trkd ldr 5th,
led 9th, clr appr last, rdn out.
.......(6 to 4 fav op 5 to 4 tchd 11 to 10 and 7 to 4)   1
2337³ DEXTRA DOVE [102] 7-10-5 S Earle, in tch, chsd wnr aftr 3
out, rdn and ev ch appr nxt, no extr.
....(7 to 2 tchd 4 to 1)   2
2397³ FRED SPLENDID [98] 11-10-1¹ R Dunwoody, hld up, prog
to track ldg pair appr 2 out, sn rdn and no imprsn.
...............................(10 to 1 op 8 to 1 tchd 12 to 1)   3
2539* ATLAAL [125] (v) 9-12-0 S Smith Eccles, hld up, prog 5th,
mstks nxt 2, wknd rpdly two out.....(7 to 1 op 9 to 1)   4
2307 GREENHEART [125] 11-12-0 Mr P Bull, mstks, led to 9th,
wknd rpdly aftr 3 out, tld off whn pld up bef last.
..............................(50 to 1 op 25 to 1)   pu
2143 FILE CONCORD [115] (bl) 10-11-4 D Murphy, lost pl and
rdn aftr 5th, sn tld off, pld up bef 3 out.
...............................(11 to 4 op 3 to 1 tchd 4 to 1)   pu
Dist: 5l, 1½l, dist. 4m 22.10s. a 27.10s (6 Ran).
SR: 47/33/27/   (Pell-Mell Partners), J T Gifford

2708 Hythe Novices' Handicap Hurdle (0-100 4-y-o and up) £1,553 2m 1f 110yds...................... (3:25)

2452³ AUGUST TWELFTH [60] 6-10-0 Mr Raymond White, beh,
rapid prog frm 3 out, rdn to ld last, wndrd und pres,
hld on....................................(50 to 1)   1
2335 SCOTTISH BALL [72] 5-10-12 M Crosse, rear whn hmpd
5th, rapid prog aftr nxt, led last 2, hdd last, hrd
rdn and styd on.......(13 to 2 op 5 to 1 tchd 7 to 1)   2
2483 FERRUFINO (Ire) [62] 6-10-2 P McDermott, hld up gng
easily, prog to ld 3 out, hdd then last 2, hrd rdn, not
quicken.......................(16 to 1 op 33 to 1 tchd 50 to 1)   3
3204⁴ BOLD STREET BLUES [80] 7-11-6 J Railton, led second to
5th, sn lost pl and beh, ran on appr last, fnshd wl.
....(7 to 1 op 5 to 1)   4
2315 GRAND COLONIST [60] 7-9-11 (3") A Procter, beh, rdn 5th,
styd on und pres frm 2 out, not rch ldrs.......(50 to 1)   5
2606* SAINT CIEL (USA) [84] 6-11-10 R Supple, hld up in tch,
prog 3 out, ev ch betw last 2, sn wknd.
....(13 to 8 fav op 2 to 1 tchd 9 to 4)   6
2015 GIVEITAGO [88] (bl) 8-11-9 (5") D Fortt, prmnt till wknd 3
out...(16 to 1 op 10 to 1)   7
2361 EMALLEN (Ire) [60] (v) 6-10-0 J R Kavanagh, mid-div, wknd
3 out.......................................(50 to 1 op 33 to 1)   8
2599⁹ CASTLE ORCHARD [64] 10-10-4 A Maguire, in tch till
wknd aftr 3 out.......(10 to 1 op 7 to 1 tchd 12 to 1)   9
2625 LETTS GREEN (Ire) [62] 6-10-2 D Morris, led to second, led
5th to 3 out, wknd rpdly, tld off whn pld up bef last.
....(20 to 1 op 12 to 1)   pu
2320² THE WHIP [85] 7-11-11 Peter Hobbs, hld up in tch, mstk
6th, wknd rpdly, tld off whn pld up bef last.
....(9 to 2 op 5 to 1)   pu
2492¹ WITCHWAY NORTH [76] (v) 4-11-2 V Smith, prmnt, wth ldr
5th to 3 out, wknd rpdly nxt, tld off whn pld up bef last.
...........................(12 to 1 op 6 to 1 tchd 14 to 1)   pu
Dist: Nk, 15l, ¾l, nk, 3½l, 2½l, 3l, 5l. 4m 49.00s. a 52.00s (12 Ran).

(D C O'Brien), D C O'Brien

2709 Tenterden Maiden Hunters' Chase (5-y-o and up) £1,521 2m 5f....... (3:55)

NO FIZZ 8-11-9 (7") Mr P Bull, hld up, prog 6th, led 9th,
drw clr appr 2 out, easily.........(7 to 4 tchd 2 to 1)   1
REGGIE (v) 12-12-0 (7") Mr A Hickman, led aftr 1st to 4th,
rdn 9th, chsd wnr 11th, no imprsn. (14 to 1 op 20 to 1)   2

TRUNDLE (bl) 8-12-0 (7*) Mr G Maundrell, *prmnt till wknd frm 11th*................ (12 to 1 op 8 to 1 tchd 14 to 1) 3
TOUSHTARI (USA) 8-12-4 (3*) Mr P Hacking, *led till aftr 1st, led 4th to 6th, jnd wnr 9th, f nxt.*
.... (11 to 10 fav op 5 to 4 on) f
KNOWAFENCE (bl) 8-11-11 (5*) Mr P Macewan, *prmnt to 8th, wkng whn hmpd tenth, f nxt.* (40 to 1 op 20 to 1) f
1023[9] BLACK ARROW 7-12-0 (7*) Mr Raymond White, *mstk second, 6th whn blun and uns rdr sixth.*
.... (50 to 1 op 33 to 1) ur
CASPIAN FLYER (bl) 11-12-6[6] (7*) Mr P Hickman, *strted slwly, sn tld off, pld up bef 7th....* (40 to 1 op 25 to 1) pu
978 MISSILE RUN 10-12-0 (7*) Mr M P Jones, *mstk 4th, tld off 7th, pld up bef 9th*................ (33 to 1 op 20 to 1) pu
2570[4] SONNENDEW 11-12-0 (7*) Mrs N Ledger, *beh 7th, tld off whn pld up bef tenth*...............(33 to 1 op 16 to 1) pu
JAYSMITH 8-12-0 (7*) Mr C Gordon, *prmnt, led 6th till hdd and mstk 9th, sn wknd, blun 12th, pld up bef nxt.*
.... (7 to 1 tchd 8 to 1) pu
Dist: 15l, 20l. 6m 2.50s. a 52.50s (10 Ran).

(Mrs A Bailey), Mrs D M Grissell

2710 Folkestone Handicap Hurdle (0-115 4-y-o and up) £2,427 2¾m 110yds
.... (4:25)

KOVALEVSKIA [84] 9-10-2 A Maguire, *al prmnt, led appr last, rdn and quickened clr.*
.... (9 to 2 op 3 to 1 tchd 5 to 1) 1
2535[3] THE PAPPARAZI [94] 14-10-12 D Murphy, *rcd wide, hld up last, prog 8th, ev ch appr last, not quicken.*
.... (4 to 1 op 3 to 1 tchd 6 to 1) 2
2082[7] PUNCHBAG (USA) [85] 8-10-3 B Powell, *prog 8th, rdn and outpcd aftr 2 out, styd on r-in.*
.... (8 to 1 op 10 to 1 tchd 12 to 1 and 14 to 1) 3
1120[4] DERRING VALLEY [100] 9-11-8 S McNeill, *led second till appr last, one pace.*............... (14 to 1 op 8 to 1) 4
2655[7] SMILING CHIEF (Ire) [87] (bl) 6-10-5 R Dunwoody, *hld up, prog 8th, ev ch betw last 2, rdn and no extr.*
.... (15 to 2 op 7 to 1 tchd 8 to 1 and 9 to 1) 5
2496[5] VILLA PARK [82] 12-10-0 N Williamson, *prmnt, rdn 2 out, wknd appr last, fnshd tired.*
.... (16 to 1 op 14 to 1 tchd 8 to 1) 6
2361[3] STYLE AND CLASS [95] 5-10-8 (5*) C Burnett-Wells, *hld up, prog 7th, ev ch 2 out, hrd ridn and wknd rpdly.*
.... (11 to 4 fav op 5 to 2 tchd 7 to 2) 7
ATTIKI [83] 12-10-1 Gee Armytage, *pld hrd, prmnt till wknd 8th, pulled up bef nxt*........ (33 to 1 op 16 to 1) pu
2597 LEGAL BEAGLE [105] (h) 7-11-9 M Perrett, *hld up, rdn and lost tch aftr 6th, tld off whn pld up bef last.*
.... (14 to 1 tchd 12 to 1 and 14 to 1) pu
1567[5] FOREST FEATHER (Ire) [97] 6-11-1 Peter Hobbs, *set slow pace to second, prmnt till wknd 2 out, pld up bef last.*
.... (13 to 2 op 6 to 1 tchd 7 to 1 and 8 to 1) pu
Dist: 10l, ¾l, sht-hd, 3l, 10l. dist. 6m 26.60s. a 72.60s (10 Ran).

(D A Wilson), D A Wilson

LINGFIELD (A.W) (Std)
Thursday February 24th
Going Correction: PLUS 0.05 sec. per fur.

2711 Nicholas Nickleby Conditional Jockeys' Claiming Handicap Hurdle (4-y-o and up) £1,722 2¾m..... (1:50)

CHEAP METAL [69] (bl) 9-10-10 A Thornton, *hld up in rear, rdn 5 out, cld o'r 3 out, chsd ldr aftr nxt, looking reluctant whn lft clr last.*
.... (12 to 1 op 10 to 1 tchd 14 to 1) 1
2346[4] GREENWINE (USA) [83] 8-11-5 (5*) D Meade, *jmpd slwly second and drpd rear, tld off 9th, styd on frm 3 out, snatched second cl hme.*.............(5 to 2 op 2 to 1) 2
2131 BRIGHT SAPPHIRE [59] 8-9-11 (3*) Guy Lewis, *made most til hdd 5 out, one pace frm 2 out, lost second whn rdr drpd hands cl hme.*............... (33 to 1 op 25 to 1) 3
2346[6] QUALITAIR MEMORY (Ire) [80] 5-11-7 J McCarthy, *cl up, hit 9th and sn pushed alng, outpcd.* (7 to 4 fav op 5 to 4) 4
2341[3] OMIDJOY (Ire) [66] 4-10-0 (7*) W J Walsh, *trkd ldrs till lost pl 5th, no dngr aftr.*................(10 to 1 op 8 to 1) 5
2642[4] LA PUSHKIN [61] (v) 4-10-4 A Procter, *wth ldr, wkng whn mstk 4 out.*.................... (14 to 1 op 12 to 1) 6
2064[6] WAR BEAT [70] 6-10-6 (5*) P McLoughlin, *al hndy, mstk tenth, led 5 out, sn clr, f last, dead.*
.... (5 to 1 op 6 to 1 tchd 7 to 1) f
2440[6] TAKE A FLYER (Ire) [68] 4-10-9 T Jenks, *in tch, rdn to cl 9th, sn outpcd, tld off whn pld up bef last.*
.... (9 to 1 op 8 to 1 tchd 10 to 1) pu
Dist: 7l, ½l, 15l, 15l, dist. 5m 13.50s. a 14.50s (8 Ran).

(H G Norman), R Ingram

2712 Hard Times Juvenile Novices' Hurdle (4-y-o) £1,676 2m............... (2:20)

2652 PRINCESS TATEUM (Ire) 10-7 Lorna Vincent, *jmpd rght, made all, sn clr, unchlgd.*...................(11 to 8 jt-fav op 5 to 4 on tchd 6 to 4) 1
2541[3] ARAMON 10-12 D Gallagher, *chsd ldg pair, hdwy appr last, sn took second pl, no ch wth wnr.*
.... (7 to 2 tchd 3 to 1) 2
2398 CLASSY KAHYASI (Ire) 10-7 W McFarland, *chsd wnr, lost second pl whn awkward last, wknd r-in.*
.... (50 to 1 op 25 to 1) 3
2516[2] RISING WOLF 10-12 D O'Sullivan, *pld hrd early, hld up in rear, not jump wl, lost tch aftr 4 out, tld off.* (11 to 8 jt-fav op 6 to 4 tchd 13 to 8 and 5 to 4) 4
2541 SUNBEAM CHARLIE 10-12 M Richards, *hld up, mstk 3rd, al beh, tld off*................... (33 to 1 op 25 to 1) 5
Dist: 20l, 8l, 15l, 6l. 3m 44.80s. a 11.80s (5 Ran).

(J R Good), M R Channon

2713 David Copperfield Claiming Hurdle (4-y-o and up) £1,691 2m......... (2:50)

2641[2] MILL BURN 5-11-4 R Campbell, *hld up, hmpd by loose horse aftr 4th, cld on ldg pair nxt, pushed alng and led 3 out, clr appr last, rdn out.*
.... (11 to 2 op 3 to 1 tchd 6 to 1) 1
2441[2] SPARKLER GEBE 8-11-6 D O'Sullivan, *wth ldr, ev ch 3 out, one pace und pres frm nxt....* (13 to 8 on op 5 to 4 on) 2
2343[7] BLAKE'S TREASURE (bl) 7-11-4 S Smith Eccles, *led til hdd 3 out, hrd rdn and sn outpcd.*
.... (25 to 1 op 12 to 1 tchd 33 to 1) 3
2645[3] YAAFOOR (USA) (v) 5-11-4 M Richards, *al beh, lost tch frm 6th, tld off*.............. (20 to 1 op 10 to 1) 4
2542[3] MASROUG 7-10-9 (7*) J Clarke, *took keen hold early, cl 3rd whn blun and uns rdr 4th......* (4 to 1 op 3 to 1) ur
2062 SECRET CASTLE 6-11-8 T Wall, *pld hrd, mstks in rear, tld off whn pulled up bef last.*
.... (10 to 1 op 7 to 1 tchd 12 to 1) pu
2525[9] BELLE LOCK 6-10-6 (7*) J Neaves, *keen hold early, in cl tch till wknd 6th, pld up bef nxt...* (50 to 1 op 33 to 1) pu
Dist: 6l, 15l, 20l. 3m 42.70s. a 9.70s (7 Ran).
SR: 1/-/-/-/

(Ms S Miller), I Campbell

2714 Barnaby Rudge Maiden Hurdle (4-y-o and up) £1,676 2½m........... (3:20)

2645[2] DELIFFIN 8-11-2 (5*) D Fortt, *made all, slpd clr 3 out, ran on wl.*................. (9 to 4 op 7 to 4 tchd 5 to 2) 1
2440[4] PIE HATCH (Ire) (bl) 5-11-2 R J Beggan, *hld up beh ldrs, jmpd awkwardly and lost grnd 4 out, sn hrd rdn, hdwy to chase wnr frm 2 out, styd on.*
.... (5 to 4 fav tchd 11 to 8 and 6 to 4) 2
PIGALLE WONDER 6-11-7 D O'Sullivan, *hld up, cld 7th, wknd 2 out.*................. (13 to 2 op 7 to 2 tchd 7 to 1) 3
2454[5] MISS PARKES 5-10-9 (7*) T Dascombe, *al prmnt, pushed alng appr 3 out, sn wknd.*........... (50 to 1) 4
2542[2] RUMBELOW 5-11-7 M Richards, *al beh, tld off.*
.... (7 to 2 op 4 to 1 tchd 9 to 2 and 5 to 1) 5
2559 OURPALWENTY 7-11-7 R Marley, *trkd ldr till lost pl aftr 4 out, tld off.*................. (50 to 1 op 33 to 1) 6
2190[5] BRIGHTON BREEZY 4-10-10 R Rowell, *beh whn blun 4th, tld off 6th, pld up bef 3 out.*............(50 to 1) pu
Dist: 7l, 25l, 8l, 20l, hd. 4m 42.40s. a 11.40s (7 Ran).

(Mrs G M Temmerman), R M Flower

2715 Great Expectations Handicap Hurdle (0-125 4-y-o and up) £1,660 2¼m (3:50)

2644* ROYAL CIRCUS [89] 5-11-13 D Bridgwater, *made all, hrd drvn frm 2 out, hld on gmely.*
.... (100 to 30 op 9 to 4 tchd 7 to 2) 1
LYPH (USA) [88] 8-11-10 M Richards, *hld up, rdn 4 out, sn cld on wnr, ev ch whn hng rght appr last, rallied r-in.*
.... (7 to 1 op 9 to 2) 2
2643* CONSTRUCTION [81] 9-11-5 (6ex) D Gallagher, *cl up, lost pl 4th, chased four out, rdn and outpcd frm nxt.*
.... (6 to 5 on op Evens tchd 11 to 10 and 11 to 8 on) 3
2442[2] SING THE BLUES [78] 10-11-2 D Morris, *cl up, pushed alng aftr 4 out, sn wknd.*.......... (4 to 1 tchd 5 to 1) 4
Dist: Hd, 12l, 10l. 4m 8.90s. a 7.90s (4 Ran).
SR: 29/26/9/-/

(P W Hiatt), P W Hiatt

2716 Bleak House National Hunt Flat Race (4,5,6-y-o) £1,576 2m....... (4:20)

2546* COLOSSUS OF ROADS 5-12-1 (3*) A Dicken, *hld up beh ldrs, cld 4 fs out, led appr last, all out.*
.... (6 to 4 fav op 5 to 4 tchd 13 to 8) 1
CHILDHAY MILLIE 5-10-8 (5*) Guy Lewis, *trkd ldrs, led 4 fs out till hdd appr last, rallied und pres.*
.... (14 to 1 op 12 to 1) 2
2546[5] LLAMA LADY 5-10-6 (7*) L Reynolds, *hld up, hrd rdn 3 fs out, one pace frm 2 out.*........ (50 to 1 op 25 to 1) 3
WINNOW 4-9-11 (7*) P McLoughlin, *keen hold early, cl up till short of room and snatched up 5 fs out, closed 3 out, wknd appr last.*................(7 to 4 op 11 to 4) 4
CUBAN AIR (Ire) 5-10-6 (7*) G Bazin, *cl up, led 5 fs out to 4 out, wknd o'r 2 out.*................(10 to 1 op 3 to 1) 5
IRENE'S ROLFE 5-10-6 (7*) J Neaves, *hld up in rear, nvr on terms.*....................... (33 to 1 op 20 to 1) 6

LADY AEDEAN 4-10-1 (3*) T Jenks, *led, drvn alng hfwy, hdd 5 fs out, sn lost pl*............(25 to 1 op 14 to 1) 7

NANOOK 5-10-11 (7*) Mr E Williams, *took keen hold early, cl up till drpd rear aftr 4 fs, sn tld off.*
......................(16 to 1 op 8 to 1 tchd 20 to 1) 8

Dist: Hd, 6l, 12l, 2½l, 12l, 12l, 20l. 3m 38.40s. (8 Ran).

(David F Wilson), T Thomson Jones

WINCANTON (good to soft)
Thursday February 24th
Going Correction: PLUS 1.10 sec. per fur. (races 1,3,6), PLUS 1.25 (2,4,5)

2717
K. J. Pike & Sons Claiming Hurdle (4-y-o and up) £2,910 2m.........(2:05)

2631* KANNDABIL (bl) 7-11-7 G McCourt, *chsd ldrs, slight ld 2 out, drvn out*....(100 to 30 fav op 3 to 1 tchd 7 to 2) 1

2418 SCHWEPPES TONIC 8-11-0 D J Burchell, *al prmnt, led 3 out to nxt, ev ch 2 out, wth wnr whn mstk last, not quicken*..........................(12 to 1 op 8 to 1) 2

1800 PRINCE RUBEN 7-11-7 (3*) R Farrant, *al prmnt, lft in ld 5th, hdd nxt, rdn and styd on one pace.*
......................................(33 to 1 op 25 to 1) 3

23667 MISS EQUILIA (USA) 8-10-12 R Dunwoody, *beh, rdn alng aftr 3 out, styd on frm nxt, nxt nrr.*
.................(4 to 1 tchd 9 to 2 and 7 to 2) 4

1717 GENERALLY JUST (bl) 9-11-2 Mr S Stickland, *prmnt, cl up whn pckd 4th, outpcd aftr 3 out, hrd rdn and styd on one pace.*..................(100 to 1 op 50 to 1) 5

1946 EAGLES LAIR 8-11-4 D Gallagher, *beh 3rd, styd on aftr 3 out, not rch ldrs.*................(100 to 1 op 50 to 1) 6

24966 MILDRED SOPHIA 7-10-6 (7*) Miss S Mitchell, *chsd ldrs, no imprsn frm 3 out.*..................(25 to 1 op 14 to 1) 7

2432 CLOGHRAN LAD 7-11-0 W Marston, *beh, hdwy aftr 4th, one pace 3 out*....... (25 to 1 op 20 to 1 tchd 33 to 1) 8

CASTLE SECRET 8-11-9 Mr S Blackwell, *hld up, mstk 3rd, rdn alng and some hdwy aftr 5th, no imprsn.*
....(9 to 2 op 3 to 1) 9

GREYFRIARS BOBBY 8-11-6 M A FitzGerald, *chsd ldrs, wknd appr 2 out*.......(6 to 1 op 7 to 1 tchd 9 to 1) 10

2461 TURKISH STAR 9-10-9 S Mackey, *prmnt, in tch and rdn alng aftr 5th, wknd 3 out.*
......................(50 to 1 op 33 to 1 tchd 100 to 1) 11

2430 ROBENKO (USA) (bl) 5-11-5 N Williamson, *nvr rch ldrs.*
........................(33 to 1 op 25 to 1) 12

25387 FIRST COMMAND (NZ) 7-11-7 B Powell, *nvr rch ldrs.*
......................................(50 to 1 op 25 to 1) 13

TUMBLED BRIDE 8-11-0 C Maude, *led, mstk and hdd 5th, wknd quickly.*......................(50 to 1 op 25 to 1) 14

LYCIAN MOON 5-10-12 E Byrne, *hmpd 1st, al beh.*
......................................(100 to 1 op 50 to 1) 15

24184 OAK PARK (Ire) 6-10-13 (5*) T Eley, *prmnt till wknd quickly aftr 4th.*....(25 to 1 op 16 to 1 tchd 33 to 1) 16

21123 MUSICAL PHONE 4-10-7 A Maguire, *chsd ldrs till wknd quickly aftr 4th.*......(100 to 1 op 20 to 1) 17

2398 BORDER DREAM 4-10-3 (7*) R Darke, *chsd ldrs, wknd quickly aftr 5th.*................(100 to 1 op 50 to 1) 18

2361 ENTERPRISE PRINCE 8-11-1 E Murphy, *slwly away, sn reco'red, chsd ldrs till wknd quickly aftr 4th.*
......................................(100 to 1 op 50 to 1) 19

16964 KATIEM'LU 8-10-4 (7*) Mr B Pollock, *al beh.*
..............(66 to 1 op 33 to 1 tchd 100 to 1) 20

2269 NORDEN (Ire) 5-11-5 A Tory, *beh 3rd.* (66 to 1 op 33 to 1) 21

23068 TITUS GOLD 9-11-5 Diane Clay, *f 1st.* f

2558 FORT RANK 7-10-13 J Frost, *beh whn brght dwn 3rd, dead.*...........................(16 to 1 op 14 to 1) bd

2621 AUTO CONNECTION 8-10-10 N Dawe, *slpd up aftr 3rd, broke leg, destroyed.*..............(100 to 1 op 33 to 1) su

ist: 2½l, 3½l, 5l, 2½l, 2l, ½l, ½l, 1½l, 3l, 5l. 4m 1.90s. a 24.90s (24 Ran).

R: 20/10/16/-/-/-/-/5/1/ (Neil McAndrews), N Tinkler

2718
Stewart Tory Memorial Trophy Handicap Chase For Amateur Riders (0-130 5-y-o and up) £4,276 2m 5f......(2:35)

18892 DUBLIN FLYER [125] 8-11-7 (7*) Mr Richard White, *led 5th, drw clr aftr 3 out, easily.*
......................(11 to 8 fav op 6 to 4 tchd 13 to 8) 1

16562 DRAGONS DEN [107] 8-10-92 (3*) Mr J Durkan, *prmnt to 4th, steadied, hdwy aftr 9th, chsd ldg trio, 3rd whn mstk four out, no imprsn after.*..................(5 to 1) 2

CALABRESE [125] (bl) 9-11-7 (7*) Major M Watson, *beh and outpcd aftr 7th, lft moderate 3rd 3 out.*
.............(8 to 1 op 7 to 1 tchd 9 to 1) 3

24296 FIGHT TO WIN (USA) [108] 6-10-0 (7*) Mr B Pollock, *pckd 8th, chsd ldrs, 4th whn mstks 5 out and nxt, btn whn blun last.*....................(20 to 1 op 14 to 1) 4

21846 VAVASIR [98] 8-9-8 (7*) Mr D Parker, *lost pl and pushed alng aftr 6th, al struggling.*........(7 to 1 op 6 to 1) 5

2416 ICARUS (USA) [122] (bl) 8-11-4 (7*) Mr A Rebori, *led to 5th, pressed ldr till wknd 4 out, 3rd and btn whn f nxt.*
......................................(14 to 1 op 12 to 1) f

1883 WHATEVER YOU LIKE [114] 10-10-12 (5*) Miss P Curling, *blun and uns rdr second.*.........(14 to 1 op 12 to 1) ur

2361 BLAKEINGTON [97] (bl) 8-9-7 (7*) Miss S Mitchell, *sn tld off, blun and ran out 9th.*............(100 to 1 op 66 to 1) ro

2437 SAMSUN [97] (bl) 12-9-7 (7*) Miss S White, *beh 4th, tld off whn pld up aftr 9th.*..............(100 to 1 op 66 to 1) pu

2605* FIFTH AMENDMENT [121] (bl) 9-11-52 (7*) Mr R Ponsonby, *chsd ldrs, lost pl aftr 8th, jmpd slwly nxt, beh whn jumped slowly and pld up after 6 out.*
......................................(13 to 1 op 5 to 1) pu

Dist: 20l, 12l, 8l, 8l. 5m 39.70s. a 33.70s (10 Ran).

SR: 25/-/-/-/-/ (J B Sumner), Capt T A Forster

2719
Kingwell Hurdle Grade 2 (4-y-o and up) £12,320 2m.................(3:05)

24752 VALFINET (Fr) 7-11-7 R Dunwoody, *led, drw clr 3 out, hdd nxt, wnt lft aftr last, drvn out r-in.*
..........................(7 to 4 on op 13 to 8 on) 1

2079 ROYAL DERBI (bl) 9-11-10 A Maguire, *chsd ldr, mstk second, blun 5th, sn outpcd, rdn and rallied aftr 2 out, styd on r-in, not quicken.*..........(4 to 1 op 3 to 1) 2

2595 HIGH BARON 7-11-2 M Hourigan, *chsd ldg pair to 3rd, sn beh, rdn and rallied aftr 3 out, styd on frm nxt.*
..................................(7 to 1 op 3 to 1) 3

26553 MARIOLINO 7-11-2 W Marston, *sn beh, styd on aftr 3 out, nvr dngrs.*.........................(100 to 1) 4

23668 ASHFIELD BOY 10-11-2 M A FitzGerald, *wnt moderate 3rd aftr third, mstk nxt, sn lost tch, tld off after 3 out.*
..................(66 to 1 op 50 to 1 tchd 100 to 1) 5

Dist: 2½l, 6l, 10l, dist. 3m 59.60s. a 22.60s (5 Ran).

SR: 43/43/29/19/-/ (Frank A Farrant), M C Pipe

2720
Jim Ford Challenge Cup Chase (5-y-o and up) £10,188 3m 1f 110yds...(3:35)

1841* SEE MORE INDIANS 7-11-7 G Bradley, *pckd 3rd, wnt second 8th, mstk tenth, cl up and ev ch 6 out, mistake last, sn led, drvn out.*..............(2 to 1 tchd 7 to 4) 1

2598 ANOTHER CORAL 11-11-2 W Marston, *led second, blun 3 out, tired and wnt lft aftr nxt, mstk last, hdd r-in, rallied nr finish*.....(20 to 1 op 16 to 1 tchd 25 to 1) 2

2474* SECOND SCHEDUAL 9-11-12 A Maguire, *hld up last, cl up whn lft 3rd 5 out, wknd quickly 3 out, virtually pld up r-in, broke blood vessel*....(5 to 4 on op 11 to 10 on) 3

2011 TOPSHAM BAY 11-11-2 J Frost, *led to second, chsd ldr, cl 3rd whn stumbled and uns rdr aftr 5 out.*
................(9 to 2 op 4 to 1 tchd 5 to 1) ur

Dist: 2l, dist. 7m 2.50s. a 46.50s (4 Ran).

(Paul K Barber), P F Nicholls

2721
Georgie Newall Novices' Chase (5-y-o and up) £3,704 2m.................(4:05)

25954 THUMBS UP 8-11-8 R Dunwoody, *trkd ldr till led 3 out, drvn out.*...................(6 to 4 fav op 2 to 1) 1

2299 SHAAB TURBO 8-11-2 S Burrough, *chsd ldrs, slightly outpcd aftr 4 out, styd on after nxt, took second pl r-in, kpt on nr finish*.....(16 to 1 op 10 to 1 tchd 20 to 1) 2

2511 WHAT'S IN ORBIT 9-11-8 G Bradley, *led, blun second, hdd 3 out, rdn and not quicken*......(13 to 2 op 4 to 1) 3

8078 COQ HARDI SMOKEY (Ire) 6-11-2 N Williamson, *chsd ldrs, effrt 4 out, no imprsn.*
..................(14 to 1 op 10 to 1 tchd 50 to 1) 4

BEACH BUM 8-11-2 G Upton, *lost tch aftr 7th, tld off.*
......................................(50 to 1 op 33 to 1) 5

21447 SIMON JOSEPH 7-11-2 B Powell, *hmpd second and 6th, sn lost tch*..................(25 to 1 op 14 to 1) 6

2637* DAN DE LYON 6-11-8 A Maguire, *hld up, hdwy 5th, 4th whn f nxt*..................(6 to 1 tchd 5 to 1) f

2402 SECOND CALL 5-9-13 (3*) R Farrant, *f second*
..................................(2 to 1 tchd 5 to 2) f

Dist: 2½l, 4l, 8l, 12l, 10l. 4m 16.20s. a 25.20s (8 Ran).

SR: 42/33/35/21/9/ (Michael Buckley), N J Henderson

2722
Mere Maiden Hurdle (4-y-o) £2,390 2m ....(4:35)

16472 GROUND NUT (Ire) 11-0 J Osborne, *al prmnt, led 5th, styd on til whn chlgd appr last, drvn out r-in.*
..........................(7 to 4 op 9 to 4) 1

25222 FORMAL AFFAIR 10-9 A Maguire, *hld up, hdwy 3 out, rdn to chal r-in, not quicken nr finish.*
.............(9 to 2 op 8 to 1 tchd 9 to 1) 2

GENERAL MOUKTAR 11-0 R Dunwoody, *trkd ldrs aftr 4th, cl up 3 out, chlgd and gng wl appr last, not quicken r-in.*........................(9 to 2 op Evens tchd 13 to 8) 3

22452 JUST YOU DARE (Ire) 11-0 J Lower, *hld up, hdwy aftr 5th, ev ch appr 2 out, wknd. (7 to 1 op 8 to 1 tchd 14 to 1) 4

12616 DOCTOOR (USA) 11-0 G McCourt, *prmnt, mstk 4th, ev ch appr 2 out, wknd betw last two....(16 to 1 op 14 to 1) 5

2624 PALACE PARADE (USA) 11-0 N Dawe, *chsaed ldrs, mstk 4th, rdn alng nxt, in tch till wknd aftr 2 out.*
......................................(100 to 1 op 50 to 1) 6

SCORESHEET (Ire) 11-0 D Murphy, *hld up, hdwy to track ldrs aftr 5th, ev ch appr 2 out, sn wknd, prmsg.*
......................................(16 to 1 op 7 to 1) 7

2478 FORMAESTRE (Ire) 10-9 B Powell, *beh second, pushed*
alng aftr 4th, nvr rch ldrs........(100 to 1 op 66 to 1) 8
2541⁶ NUTTY BROWN 11-0 Peter Hobbs, *led to 5th, wknd*
quickly aftr 3 out, tld off........(33 to 1 op 16 to 1) 9
253⁴ ROOTSMAN (Ire) 11-0 M A FitzGerald, *mstk 1st, beh aftr*
3rd, tld off 3 out.... (50 to 1 op 25 to 1 tchd 66 to 1) 10
2503⁶ NOBLE RISK 11-0 S McNeill, *pld hrd early, lost tch aftr*
4th, tld off 3 out.... (50 to 1 op 20 to 1 tchd 66 to 1) 11
2461⁹ WEST END 11-11 Mr S Swiers, *beh whn pld up bef 3rd*.
..................................(100 to 1 op 66 to 1) pu
1710 ORCHESTON 10-9 Richard Guest, *lost tch aftr 4th, tld off*
whn pld up bef 2 out.............(100 to 1 op 33 to 1) pu
2471 HARROW WAY (Ire) 11-0 E Murphy, *lost tch aftr 4th, tld off*
whn pld up bef 2 out. (50 to 1 op 20 to 1 tchd 66 to 1) pu
Dist: ¾l, ½l, 4l, 12l, 5l, 4l, 12l, 30l, 3½l, dist. 3m 59.60s. a 22.60s (14 Ran).
SR: 36/30/34/30/18/13/9/-/-/   (V McCalla), Miss H C Knight

KEMPTON (Soft)
Friday February 25th
Going Correction: PLUS 1.70 sec. per fur. (races 1,5,6), PLUS 1.45 (2,3,4)

2723 Bedfont Novices' Hurdle (5-y-o and up) £2,763 2m 5f.............. (2:25)

2263² TOP SPIN 5-11-5 A Maguire, *hld up, cld 6th, led appr 2*
out, quickened clr last, eased nr finish.
...............(11 to 4 op 3 to 1 tchd 5 to 2) 1
2430³ EALING COURT 5-10-10 V Slattery, *prmnt, pushed alng*
7th, outpcd appr nxt, rdn and styd on wl r-in.
....................(33 to 1 op 14 to 1) 2
2572* FRIENDLY FELLOW 5-11-5 P Holley, *hld up rear, hdwy*
6th, led briefly 3 out, one pace nxt.
....................(10 to 1 op 8 to 1 tchd 12 to 1) 3
1193³ NADJATI (USA) 5-10-10 R Dunwoody, *mid-div, cld appr 3*
out, ch approaching nxt, wknd r-in.
....................(10 to 1 op 8 to 1 tchd 12 to 1) 4
2021⁴ ORSWELL LAD 5-10-10 Peter Hobbs, *chsd ldrs, rdn aftr 3*
out, wknd......................(100 to 1 op 20 to 1) 5
2477³ RAINBOW CASTLE 7-10-10 E Murphy, *hld up, cld 7th png*
wl, wknd aftr nxt.... (33 to 1 op 20 to 1 tchd 50 to 1) 6
361² ACROBATE (USA) 5-10-10 C Llewellyn, *cl up till lost pl 6th,*
awkward nxt, no dngr aftr.
....................(33 to 1 op 14 to 1 tchd 50 to 1) 7
597⁸ GRANGE CHIEF (Ire) 6-10-10 M Richards, *prmnt, led*
briefly aftr 3 out, btn whn f nxt.
....................(66 to 1 op 16 to 1 tchd 100 to 1) f
2649* EDIMBOURG 8-11-5 J Osborne, *led to 3 out, wknd*
quickly, pld up bef nxt........ (Evens fav tchd 11 to 8) pu
2599 NIGHT FANCY 6-10-7 (3*) J McCarthy, *al beh, tld off whn*
pld up bef nxt.....(100 to 1 op 66 to 1 tchd 200 to 1) pu
2419⁴ SWEET MANATTE 7-10-5 C Maude, *not fluent, al beh, tld*
off whn pld up bef 7th.
....................(100 to 1 op 66 to 1 tchd 200 to 1) pu
2404² OVER THE POLE 7-10-10 D Murphy, *chsd ldg grp, lost pl*
whn pld up bef 3 out....(7 to 1 tchd 8 to 1) pu
Dist: 1l, 4l, 3l, 10l, 10l, 6l. 5m 33.50s. a 40.50s (12 Ran).
SR: 43/33/38/26/16/6/   (J M Long), J R Jenkins

2724 Corinthian Hunters' Chase (5-y-o and up) £2,388 3m............... (2:55)

2484* TEAPLANTER 11-12-2 (5*) Mr R Russell, *made all, mstk*
13th, ran on wl frm 3 out.
.................(11 to 8 on op 5 to 4 on tchd 11 to 10 on) 1
2482* MR MURDOCK 9-12-4 (3*) Mr R Alner, *cld 9th, chsd wnr*
frm 4 out, not fluent last 3, kpt on.
....................(11 to 4 op 2 to 1 tchd 3 to 1) 2
THE MALAKARMA 8-12-1 (3*) Mr I McKie, *hld up last, cld*
14th, one pace appr 3 out.
....................(6 to 1 op 4 to 1 tchd 8 to 1) 3
2526³ KNOCKUMSHIN 11-12-2 (5*) Mr T Byrne, *cld 9th, outpcd*
appr 3 out, tld off.... (9 to 1 op 7 to 1 tchd 14 to 1) 4
2605 SPORTING MARINER (bl) 12-12-0 (7*) Mr D Bloor, *trkd wnr,*
reminders 12th, wknd 14th, tld off.
....................(100 to 1 op 66 to 1) 5
Dist: 5l, 25l, 30l, 10l. 6m 34.50s. a 45.50s (5 Ran).
(R G Russell), Miss C Saunders

2725 Manor Novices' Chase (5-y-o and up) £3,752 3m................... (3:25)

2601* HONEST WORD 9-11-10 R Dunwoody, *made all, pckd 3*
out, ran on strly, not extended.
....................(11 to 4 on op 5 to 2 on tchd 9 to 4 on and 3 to 1 on) 1
2378 FANTUS 7-11-10 G Bradley, *hld up last, cld 9th, rdn to*
chal wnr 3 out, sn outpcd........(4 to 1 op 11 to 4) 2
2427³ WILLOW GALE 7-10-13 M A FitzGerald, *cl up, outpcd 13th,*
styd on wl frm 3 out...............(20 to 1 op 14 to 1) 3
2623 RUNNING SANDS 10-11-4 G McCourt, *in cl tch, mstks 7th*
and 4 out, wknd nxt.
....................(66 to 1 op 20 to 1 tchd 100 to 1) 4
1805⁶ REAL PROGRESS (Ire) 6-11-4 Peter Hobbs, *in cl tch, blun*
tenth and lost touch, reminders 12th, tld off.
....................(50 to 1 op 16 to 1) 5

2597⁵ FLYER'S NAP 8-11-4 S Earle, *f 3rd.*
....................(16 to 1 op 14 to 1 tchd 20 to 1) f
Dist: 3l, 7l, 25l, dist. 6m 29.30s. a 40.30s (6 Ran).
SR: 41/38/20/   (Mrs H J Clarke), M C Pipe

2726 Portlane Handicap Chase (0-135 5-y-o and up) £3,590 2½m 110yds.....(3:55)

2266³ BIBENDUM [128] 8-11-10 M A FitzGerald, *hld up, hdwy to*
cl aftr 4 out, led 2 out, easily.
....................(100 to 30 op 7 to 2 tchd 4 to 1 and 3 to 1) 1
2462* LAKE TEEREEN [123] 9-11-5 C Maude, *made most, pushed*
alng 3 out, hdd nxt, no extr und pres.
....................(15 to 8 fav op 7 to 4) 2
2248 AMBASSADOR [122] (bl) 11-11-4 R Dunwoody, *wth ldr till*
wknd appr 3 out....(11 to 2 op 7 to 2 tchd 4 to 1) 3
2569⁴ RODEO STAR (USA) [120] 8-11-2 G McCourt, *hld up, cld*
12th, pushed alng 4 out, wknd nxt, tired whn f heavily
2 out....................(2 to 1 op 6 to 4 tchd 5 to 2) f
Dist: 15l, 30l. 5m 38.40s. a 45.40s (4 Ran).
(Robert Waley-Cohen), R Waley-Cohen

2727 Littleton Handicap Hurdle (0-135 5-y-o and up) £3,392 2m 5f.......... (4:25)

2459⁵ ELAINE TULLY (Ire) [106] 6-10-2 Peter Hobbs, *chsd ldrs, led*
appr 2 out, shaken up and ran on wl. (9 to 1 op 7 to 1) 1
2649⁴ MAESTRO PAUL [105] 8-10-11 D Murphy, *hld up, hdwy*
frm 7th, ev ch appr 2 out, one pace approaching last.
....................(4 to 1 fav tchd 5 to 1) 2
2247 PARLEZVOUSFRANCAIS [104] 10-10-0 M Foster, *trkd ldrs,*
one pace appr 2 out....(33 to 1 tchd 40 to 1) 3
2172⁸ KADI (Ger) [132] 5-12-0 A Maguire, *hld up, cld 4 out, one*
pace 2 out....................(10 to 1 tchd 11 to 1) 4
2507⁴ VICTOR BRAVO (NZ) [104] 7-10-0 C Llewellyn, *beh, plenty*
to do 4 out, rdn and hdwy appr 2 out, styd on, nrst
finish.................(14 to 1 op 12 to 1 tchd 16 to 1) 5
2512⁵ PRIME DISPLAY (USA) [122] (bl) 8-11-4 M Richards, *led 3rd*
till appr 2 out, wknd.....................(20 to 1) 6
2571* MANEREE [115] 7-10-11 R Campbell, *hld up, niggled alng*
5th, in tch till wknd aftr 3 out.
....................(9 to 2 op 5 to 1 tchd 11 to 2) 7
646² JIMBALOU [106] 11-10-2 W Humphreys, *blun 5th, al beh.*
....................(16 to 1) 8
2571³ ROBINGO (Ire) [126] (bl) 5-11-8 D Gallagher, *chsd ldrs, drvn*
and outpcd aftr 3 out, rallied briefly, wknd 2 out.
....................(8 to 1 op 7 to 1) 9
2515⁴ FAIR BROTHER [105] 8-10-0² (3*) R Davis, *hld up, cld aftr 4*
out, wknd und pres appr 2 out.
....................(10 to 1 op 8 to 1 tchd 11 to 1) 10
2403⁴ MISTER MAJOR [113] 6-10-9 Richard Guest, *al beh, tld off.*
....................(8 to 1) 11
1650⁶ PROPAGANDA [112] 6-10-8 M A FitzGerald, *trkd ldrs till*
rdn and wknd aftr 3 out, tld off.. (20 to 1 op 14 to 1) 12
2256 TAP DANCING [104] 8-9-7 (7*) Mr N Bradley, *al beh, tld off*
whn pld up bef 7th.
....................(100 to 1 op 66 to 1 tchd 200 to 1) pu
2423* BENTLEY MANOR [104] 5-10-0 C Maude, *led to 3rd, wknd*
aftr 3 out, pld up bef nxt........ (33 to 1 tchd 40 to 1) pu
2175 ARCHIE BROWN [120] 7-11-2 J Osborne, *hld up mid-div,*
cld 4th, mstk 7th, wknd quickly, pld up bef 2 out.
....................(9 to 1 op 10 to 1 tchd 8 to 1) pu
Dist: 7l, 7l, 2l, 1l, 10l, 10l, 1l, ¾l, 3½l, dist. 5m 34.30s. a 41.30s (15 Ran).
SR: 18/10/2/28/-/7/   (Mrs P G Wilkins), P J Hobbs

2728 EBF 'National Hunt' Novices' Hurdle Qualifier (5,6,7-y-o) £2,574 2m.. (4:55)

1082³ CLOGHANS BAY (Ire) 5-11-10 R Dunwoody, *made all, jmpd*
lft 2 out, kpt on und pres.
....................(11 to 8 fav op 5 to 4 tchd 13 to 8) 1
1768² QUARRY HOUSE (Ire) 6-11-0 J Railton, *hld up in tch, cld 3*
out, awkward nxt, kpt on wl und pres frm last.
....................(6 to 1 op 5 to 1) 2
2556* GOSPEL (Ire) 5-11-5 C Llewellyn, *mid-div, pushed alng 4*
out, hrd rdn appr 2 out, one pace. (100 to 30 op 9 to 4) 3
2315 CREDON 6-11-0 A Maguire, *nvr far away, cld on wnr aftr*
3 out, hrd rdn appr last, one pace.
....................(14 to 1 op 10 to 1 tchd 16 to 1) 4
BEAUREPAIRE (Ire) 6-11-0 D Murphy, *chsd ldrs, outpcd*
aftr 3 out, btn whn mstk nxt.
....................(10 to 1 op 8 to 1) 5
2269 SHINING LIGHT (Ire) 5-10-7 (7*) G Hogan, *prmnt in chasing*
grp, hrd rdn 3 out, sn btn.
....................(50 to 1 op 25 to 1 tchd 66 to 1) 6
2426 POLICEMANS PRIDE (Fr) 5-11-0 G McCourt, *beh, hrd rdn 3*
out, no response.....(50 to 1 tchd 66 to 1) 7
2426⁵ KINDLE'S DELIGHT 6-11-0 J Osborne, *trkd wnr till wknd*
quickly aftr 3 out.............(6 to 1 op 7 to 1) 8
NONAME 5-11-0 Peter Hobbs, *sn beh, tld off whn pld up*
bef 2 out....................(10 to 1 tchd 14 to 1) pu
Dist: 2l, 4l, hd, 15l, 10l, 4l, 6l. 4m 15.10s. a 35.10s (9 Ran).
SR: 17/5/6/1/-/-/   (Sid Williams), M C Pipe

TOWCESTER (heavy)
Friday February 25th

Going Correction: PLUS 1.73 sec. per fur.

2729 Oak Selling Handicap Hurdle (4-y-o and up) £2,101 2m 5f. . . . . (2:15)

2674 LEAVENWORTH [102] 10-11-7 (7") S Fox, *hld up in tch, cld up aftr 6th, rdn to ld 2 out, drw clr r-in, styd on wl.*
. . . . (7 to 1 op 7 to 2) 1
2185 ONE MORE POUND [74] (v) 4-10-0 N Williamson, *led til hdd and hit 2 out, one pace.* . . . . (14 to 1 op 12 to 1) 2
2530³ IT'S NOT MY FAULT [74] [77] 6-10-3 P McDermott, *chsd ldrs frm 5th, ev ch 2 out, not quicken.* . . . .(12 to 1 op 7 to 1) 3
2292³ JOKERS PATCH [74] 7-10-0 L Harvey, *beh, hdwy aftr 4 out, styd on one pace.*
. . . . (10 to 1 tchd 12 to 1 and 9 to 1) 4
2308⁹ ARMASHOCKER [74] 6-10-0 V Smith, *hld up and beh, rdn and gd hdwy aftr 4 out, ev ch appr nxt, wknd approaching 2 out.* . . . .(10 to 1) 5
2338⁶ GROTIUS [75] (bl) 10-9-10 (5") D Fortt, *hld up, hdwy aftr 6th, chsd ldrs 4 out, no headway frm nxt.*
. . . . (14 to 1 tchd 16 to 1) 6
2215⁷ THANKSFORTHEOFFER [74] 6-10-0 W Marston, *chsd ldg grp, wnt 3rd 6th, styd prmnt til wknd 3 out.*
. . . . (33 to 1 op 20 to 1) 7
2524 MOUNTSHANNON [83] 8-10-9 B Powell, *beh, styd on one pace frm 4 out.* . . . .(25 to 1 op 20 to 1) 8
1711⁶ AL SAHIL (USA) [89] (bl) 9-10-8 (7") P McLoughlin, *hld up, hdwy aftr 7th, chsd ldrs after nxt, wknd after 3 out.*
. . . . (13 to 2 fav op 5 to 1 tchd 7 to 1) 9
GAELGOIR [74] 10-10-0 M Hourigan, *beh 4th, hdwy aftr 6th, wknd 3 out.* . . . . .(16 to 1 tchd 20 to 1 and 25 to 1) 10
2535⁴ ENBORNE LAD [80] (bl) 10-10-6 M Perrett, *al beh.*
. . . .(9 to 1 op 7 to 1) 11
2292⁴ BAYBEEJAY [74] 7-10-0 D Bridgwater, *al beh.*
. . . . (16 to 1 op 10 to 1) 12
2479 VITAL SCORE [74] (bl) 8-10-0 J R Kavanagh, *pressed ldrs to 5 out, wknd quickly, tld off whn refused 2 out.*
. . . . (33 to 1 op 20 to 1) ref
2153 NESSFIELD [92] 8-11-4 A S Smith, *hld up, hdwy 6th, chsd ldrs til wknd quickly aftr 3 out, beh whn pld up r-in.*
. . . .(25 to 1 op 16 to 1) pu
2528 DUCKHAVEN [85] (bl) 11-10-11 W Irvine, *prmnt til wknd quickly aftr 4 out, tld off whn pld up bef 2 out.*(20 to 1) pu
2639 CEDAR RUN [74] 11-9-11 (3") D Meredith, *trkd ldrs frm second, wnt second 5th, mstk 4 out, wknd quickly, tld off whn pld up bef 2 out.* . . . .(33 to 1 op 20 to 1) pu
2530⁶ FEARSOME [84] 8-10-5 (5") Guy Lewis, *beh and rdn alng aftr 4th, tld off whn pld up bef 2 out.*
. . . . (33 to 1 op 20 to 1) pu
2019⁶ BOOTSCRAPER [100] 7-11-12 M Brennan, *prmnt early, lost pl aftr 4th, tld off whn pld up bef 2 out.*
. . . . (8 to 1 op 14 to 1) pu
2600 SHIKARI KID [74] 7-10-0 Mr K Green, *beh, rdn alng aftr 4th, tld off whn pld up bef 2 out.* . . .(33 to 1 op 20 to 1) pu
2461³ NORTHERN OPTIMIST [87] 6-10-6 (7") Mr J L Llewellyn, *al beh, tld off whn pld up bef 3 out.*. .(16 to 1 op 14 to 1) pu
2544² ALICE'S MIRROR [78] (v) 5-10-4 W McFarland, *pressed ldr and ev ch til wknd quickly aftr 4 out, tld off whn pld up r-in.* . . . .(10 to 1 op 7 to 1) pu
Dist: 7l, 12l, 4l, 4l, 2½l, 2½l, 1½l, 2½l, 3l, 7l. 5m 43.00s. a 44.00s (21 Ran).
SR: 23/-/-/-/-/-/

(A Gardiner-Hill), Mrs J G Retter

2730 Ash Novices' Chase (5-y-o and up) £2,537 2m 110yds. . . . . (2:45)

2030 COUNTRY MISTRESS 7-10-11 T Grantham, *hld up in last pl, hdwy aftr 4 out, led 2 out, drvn out.*
. . . .(7 to 4 fav op 11 to 10 tchd 2 to 1) 1
2170 CRUISING ON 7-10-11 W Marston, *led second, hdd briefly 4 out, sn led ag'n, headed 2 out, soon one paced.*
. . . . (5 to 2 op 2 to 1 tchd 11 to 4) 2
STORMY FASHION 7-11-2 I Lawrence, *led to second, led and slpd on landing 4 out, wknd.*
. . . .(11 to 2 op 6 to 1 tchd 8 to 1) 3
2331 SINGING GOLD 8-10-11 (5") S Curran, *chsd ldg pair till mstk 4th, sn beh, tld off 5 out.* . . . .(10 to 1 op 6 to 1) 4
HELLO LADY 7-10-4 (7") Mr J O'Shaughnessy, *mstk 1st, lost tch aftr 4th, tld off whn pld up bef 2 out.*
. . . .(11 to 2 op 6 to 1 tchd 8 to 1) pu
Dist: 3l, 20l, 30l. 4m 38.90s. a 36.90s (5 Ran).

(Count K Goess-Saurau), J A B Old

2731 EBF 'National Hunt' Novices' Hurdle Qualifier (5,6,7-y-o) £2,164 2m. . (3:15)

OVERLORD 5-11-0 M Perrett, *trkd ldrs, led briefly aftr 4 out, jmpd slwly and lost pl nxt, rallied appr 2 out, led approaching last, styd on wl.* . . . . . .(10 to 1 op 5 to 1) 1
2405³ MARINER'S AIR 7-10-9 N Williamson, *hld up, trkd ldrs frm 5th, ev ch 2 out, not quicken appr last.*
. . . . (12 to 1 op 8 to 1) 2
2505⁴ MR PICKPOCKET (Ire) 6-11-5 L Harvey, *al prmnt, led 5th, hdd briefly, led ag'n 3 out til hdd appr last, one pace.* . . . . (7 to 4 fav op 5 to 4 tchd 6 to 4) 3
1716² GLENFINN PRINCESS 6-11-0 T Wall, *hld up and beh, hdwy to chase ldg grp aftr 4 out, kpt on one pace frm 2 out.* . . . .(11 to 2 op 5 to 1 tchd 7 to 1) 4

2606⁴ SMITH'S BAND (Ire) 6-11-0 I Lawrence, *trkd ldg grp frm 4th, cl up and ev ch appr 2 out, sn no imprsn.*
. . . .(4 to 1 op 5 to 1 tchd 6 to 1) 5
2633³ BATHWICK BOBBIE (bl) 7-10-9 (5") D Fortt, *trkd ldr, ev ch aftr 3 out, wknd appr nxt.*
. . . . (16 to 1 op 10 to 1 tchd 20 to 1) 6
2558 SLIEVE LEAGUE (Ire) 5-10-9 R Bellamy, *led till hdd 5th, wknd aftr nxt.* . . . . (20 to 1 op 14 to 1) 7
1386⁶ COUNTRY FLING 6-10-9 B Powell, *prmnt til drpd rear aftr 4th, sn last, styd on past btn horses after 2 out.*
. . . . (14 to 1 op 10 to 1) 8
2509⁸ BEATSON (Ire) 5-11-0 D Bridgwater, *hld up, hdwy to chase ldg grp aftr 4th, cl up and ev ch appr 2 out, wknd quickly.* . . . . .(11 to 2 op 5 to 1 tchd 6 to 1 and 7 to 1) 9
TEX MEX (Ire) 6-11-0 S McNeill, *hld up, hdwy to track ldrs aftr 4th, cl up and ev ch til wknd quickly appr 2 out.*
. . . . (10 to 1 op 12 to 1) 10
TRUE STORM 5-10-9 W Marston, *hld up and beh, nvr rch ldrs, lost tch aftr 4 out.* . . . .(20 to 1 op 14 to 1) 11
2525 RARE PADDY 5-10-9 R Supple, *hld up and beh, nvr rch ldrs, lost tch aftr 4 out.* . . . .(20 to 1 op 12 to 1) 12
Dist: 3l, 2½l, ½l, 2l, 10l, 15l, 5l, 1l, 8l, 3½l. 4m 17.50s. a 34.50s (12 Ran).
SR: 18/10/17/11/9/-/

(D J Deer), W R Muir

2732 Beech Novices' Handicap Chase (5-y-o and up) £2,713 2¾m. . . . . (3:45)

2601³ TARAMOSS [99] 7-11-10 N Williamson, *led to second, dsptd ld til led ag'n aftr 4 out, mstk lft 2 out, all out.*
. . . . (13 to 8 fav op 6 to 4 tchd 7 to 4 and 2 to 1) 1
2559⁴ TRIMAGE (Ire) [75] 6-10-0 B Powell, *led second to 4th, dsptd ld til four out, wknd frm nxt, rallied to take second pl appr last, not rch wnr.* . .(15 to 2 op 10 to 1) 2
1621⁵ LEESWOOD [80] 6-10-5 L Harvey, *blun second, chsd ldr frm 7th, wnt second aftr 3 out, rdn and no imprsn.*
. . . . (8 to 1 op 10 to 1 tchd 12 to 1) 3
2295³ JUST A SECOND [76] (v) 9-10-1 S McNeill, *wnt second 7th, led nxt til hdd and pckd 4 out, sn wknd, btn whn jmpd slwly 2 out.* . . . .(6 to 1 op 4 to 1 tchd 13 to 2) 4
2453 WHAT A NOBLE [76] 8-10-1⁴ (3") A Thornton, *hld up, hdwy 8th, cl up whn mstk nxt, wknd quickly 4 out, tld off.*
. . . . (15 to 2 op 5 to 1 tchd 8 to 1) 5
2596⁶ VICAR OF BRAY [75] 7-10-0 E Leonard, *blun second, blundered and uns rdr nxt.* . .(12 to 1 op 8 to 1 tchd 14 to 1) ur
2666³ NOTARY-NOWELL [78] (bl) 8-10-3 Gee Armytage, *rcd reluctantly, reminders appr 5th, mstk nxt, rdn to join ldrs 8th, lost pl aftr next, beh whn refused last.*
. . . . (16 to 1 op 8 to 1) ref
2406⁵ UNDERWYCHWOOD (Ire) [76] 6-10-1 I Lawrence, *jmpd very slwly 1st, sn reco'red, chsd ldrs aftr 3rd, beh whn pld up aftr 5th.* . . . .(13 to 2 op 3 to 1 tchd 7 to 1) pu
2362⁴ BRORA ROSE (Ire) [75] 6-10-0 I Shoemark, *jmpd slwly 3rd and 6th, sn beh, tld off last whn pld up aftr nxt.*
. . . . (25 to 1 op 20 to 1) pu
Dist: 6l, 2½l, 12l, 30l. 6m 19.20s. a 53.20s (9 Ran).

(Howard Parker), J A C Edwards

2733 Elm Handicap Chase (0-115 5-y-o and up) £3,670 3m 1f. . . . . (4:15)

2635* VIVA BELLA (Fr) [98] (bl) 7-10-8 (5",6ex) J Burke, *trkd ldrs, cl up 5 out, led aftr nxt, drw clr aftr 3 out, unchlgd.*
. . . . (9 to 2 fav op 4 to 1 tchd 6 to 1 and 13 to 2) 1
2536⁴ POSTMAN'S PATH [102] 8-11-3 B Powell, *wnt second aftr tenth, chlgd ldr nxt, outpcd after 3 out, no imprsn.* . . . . (9 to 1 op 8 to 1) 2
2623³ SMOOTH ESCORT [106] 10-11-7 D Bridgwater, *drpd rear, pushed alng aftr 8th, styd on after 3 out, nvr nrr.* . . . . (10 to 1 op 8 to 1) 3
2363 SUNBEAM TALBOT [100] 13-11-1 S McNeill, *drpd rear, pushed alng aftr 8th, sn beh, styd on past btn horses 3 out, nvr nrr.* . . . . (16 to 1 op 14 to 1) 4
2453⁵ LEAGAUNE [85] (bl) 12-10-0 E Byrne, *mstk 1st, beh frm 6th, sn lost tch, tld off.* . .(16 to 1 op 10 to 1 tchd 20 to 1) 5
2247 MWEENISH [107] 12-11-8 R Bellamy, *led til hdd 4 out, sn wknd, btn whn mstk 2 out, tld off.* (12 to 1 op 8 to 1) 6
2499³ ISLAND GALE [98] 9-10-10 (3") A Thornton, *pressed ldrs till lost pl aftr 9th, sn beh, tld off after 4 out.*
. . . . (6 to 1 op 4 to 1) 7
2429³ BERESFORDS GIRL [100] 9-11-1 R Supple, *hld up, mstk 6th, beh and pushed alng aftr 8th, sn lost tch, behind whn f 2 out.* . . . .(7 to 1 tchd 9 to 1) f
2623² BARTY HAYES [98] 10-10-6 (7") P Carey, *pressed ldr, wnt second aftr 6th, cl up whn blun and uns rdr 9th.*
. . . . (10 to 1 op 7 to 1) ur
2363 SAM SHORROCK [89] (bl) 12-10-4 Mr G Johnson Houghton, *blun and uns rdr 3rd.* . . . .(16 to 1 op 14 to 1) ur
2596³ HILLWALK [104] 8-11-5 D Morris, *hld up, hdwy 6th, cl up whn mstk tenth, ev ch whn hmpd and uns rdr 4 out.*
. . . . (13 to 2 op 4 to 1 tchd 7 to 1) ur
2453 TRUSTY FRIEND [88] 12-10-3 S Burrough, *hld up, beh and pushed alng aftr 8th, tld off whn pld up bef last.*
2506⁴ PAMBER PRIORY [113] 11-12-0 G Rowe, *jmpd slwly 3rd and 4th, blun nxt, sn beh, tld off aftr 6 out, pld up bef last.* . . . .(14 to 1 op 12 to 1) pu

NATIONAL HUNT RESULTS 1993-94

2668 KEV'S LASS (Ire) [85] 6-10-0 N Williamson, *hld up, wnt 3rd 6th, cl up whn blun 4 out, wknd quickly aftr nxt, beh when pld up bef last.* (16 to 1 op 14 to 1 tchd 20 to 1) pu
Dist: 25l, sht-hd. 7m 10.60s. a 55.60s (14 Ran).

(L H Froomes), Mrs S A Bramall

2734 Chestnut Handicap Hurdle (0-120 4-y-o and up) £1,982 2m...........(4:45)

1956 JALINGO [104] 7-11-3 B Clifford, *hld up, cld on ldrs aftr 3 out, led nxt, clr last, cmftbly......* (10 to 1 op 8 to 1) 1
1991⁵ IVEAGH HOUSE [115] 8-11-9 (5*) D Fortt, *hld up, hdwy to track ldrs aftr 3 out, sn ev ch, rdn and not quicken betw last 2.........................* (7 to 1 op 5 to 1) 2
2697² ISLAND JEWEL [105] 6-11-4 (6ex) M Bosley, *hld up, hdwy to track ldg grp aftr 5th, cl up and ev ch appr 2 out, rdn and not quicken betw last two.*
.............................(7 to 4 fav tchd 2 to 1 and 13 to 8) 3
2515⁸ RED RING [96] 7-10-9 W Marston, *led to 3rd, pressed ldr, rdn alng aftr 5th, kpt on one pace frm 2 out.*
....(5 to 1 op 6 to 1) 4
2627⁵ SHAMSHOM AL ARAB (Ire) [87] 6-9-7 (7*) Miss V Haigh, *hld up and beh, hdwy to track ldg grp aftr 3 out, cl up and ev ch appr nxt, sn outpcd.* (20 to 1 op 14 to 1) 5
2655⁴ PRIZE MATCH [87] 5-10-0 R Supple, *led 3rd to 5th, rallied appr 2 out and ev ch, sn rdn and wknd.*
..........................(5 to 1 op 9 to 2 tchd 11 to 2) 6
2477² JYMJAM JOHNNY (Ire) [94] 5-10-7 L Harvey, *cl up, wnt second 4th, led nxt til hdd appr 2 out, sn rdn and wknd.*
....(7 to 1 op 4 to 1) 7
2483 OAKLANDS WORD [87] (bl) 5-9-7 (7*) P McLoughlin, *mstks, drpd rear 3rd, sn beh, kpt on one pace frm 3 out.*
....(33 to 1 op 14 to 1) 8
2296 MRS MAYHEW (Ire) [94] (bl) 6-10-7 D Bridgwater, *hld up, pushed alng aftr 5th, wknd quickly.* (9 to 1 op 4 to 1) 9
1215⁷ SALLY SOHAM (Ire) [87] 6-9-7 (7*) P Murphy, *lost pl aftr 3rd, sn tld off.......................* (20 to 1 op 14 to 1) 10
Dist: 4l, 1½l, 2½l, 10l, 6l, 2l, 12l, ½l, dist. 4m 20.10s. a 37.10s (10 Ran).
SR: -/2/-/-/-/-/   (Mrs Amanda Shelton), P J Makin

EDINBURGH (Good)
Saturday February 26th
Going Correction: PLUS 0.30 sec. per fur.

2735 Port Seton Maiden Hurdle (Div I) (4-y-o and up) £1,966 2m..........(1:15)

2315³ THE CHANGELING (Ire) 5-11-7 R J Beggan, *al prmnt, led appr last, rdn clr r-in.*
.............................(11 to 10 fav op 5 to 4 tchd 11 to 8) 1
2573⁴ KNOW-NO-NO (Ire) 5-11-4 (3*) D Bentley, *chsd ldrs, rdn 2 out, styd on one pace.* (12 to 1 op 8 to 1 tchd 10 to 1) 2
2445 JUSTICE IS DONE (Ire) 4-10-12 Peter Hobbs, *hld up in tch, hit 4th, hdwy 2 out, effrt and ch appr last, sn rdn, not quicken r-in.....................* (33 to 1 op 25 to 1) 3
2573³ DAYADAN (Ire) 4-10-12 T Reed, *hld up beh, hdwy appr 3 out, effrt nxt, sn rdn, styd on one pace und pres.*
....(3 to 1 op 5 to 2) 4
2148³ MONTRAVE 5-11-7 B Storey, *prmnt, led 3rd, hit 2 out, hdd appr last, wknd r-in...........* (7 to 1 op 6 to 1) 5
2485 SCARABEN 6-11-4 (3*) N Bentley, *hld up beh, hdwy appr 2 out, kpt on, nvr dngrs.*
........................(40 to 1 op 33 to 1 tchd 50 to 1) 6
2573⁷ FALLEGIO 5-11-7 A Dobbin, *mid-div, hdwy 4th, effrt and hit 2 out, sn rdn and wknd...........* (20 to 1 op 14 to 1) 7
MARINER'S WALK 7-11-4 (3*) R Farrant, *nvr rch ldrs.*
.......................(25 to 1 op 20 to 1 tchd 33 to 1) 8
2581 MR WESTCLIFF (bl) 6-11-2 (5*) P Waggott, *mid-div, hdwy to chase ldrs 4th, rdn 3 out, sn wknd.*
.....................................(50 to 1 op 33 to 1) 9
547 WEE WARRIOR (v) 6-11-0 (7*) P Kennedy, *led till hdd and hit 3rd, sn wknd...................*(100 to 1) 10
2140 HAZEL CREST 7-11-0 (7*) F Leahy, *chsd ldrs, rdn alng 4 out, wknd nxt........* (14 to 1 op 10 to 1 tchd 25 to 1) 11
ROCK OPERA (Ire) 6-11-7 A Merrigan, *al rear.*
....................................(50 to 1 op 33 to 1) 12
429 MIDDLEHAM CASTLE 5-11-2 (5*) F Perratt, *cl up till rdn and wknd 2 out........................*(100 to 1 op 50 to 1) 13
1408 TODDEN 4-10-9 (3*) D J Moffatt, *mid-div, lost pl 4th, sn beh...............................* (50 to 1 op 50 to 1) 14
Dist: 4l, ½l, 3½l, sht-hd, 3l, 6l, 10l, 2l, 5l, 10l. 3m 51.00s. a 13.00s (14 Ran).
SR: 11/7/-/-/2/-/   (D B Clark), G C Bravery

2736 Edinburgh University Turf Club 'B.A. Mug Punter' Novices' Handicap Chase (5-y-o and up) £2,502 3m (1:45)

OPAL'S TENSPOT [77] 7-10-12 (3*) R Farrant, *chsed ldrs, hdwy to chal 4 out, led 2 out, sn rdn, ran on wl r-in.*
.... 1
2528² COSMIC FORCE (NZ) [81] 10-11-5 Jacqui Oliver, *al prmnt, lft in ld 11th, jnd 4 out, jmpd rght nxt, rdn and hdd 2 out, hit last, kpt on......* (3 to 1 tchd 11 to 4) 2
2579³ RAIN MAN (NZ) [80] 9-10-11 (7*) Mr C Bonner, *chsd ldrs, hit 7th, wknd appr 4 out.* (16 to 1 op 10 to 1) 3

ROSEHIP [79] 9-11-3 K Johnson, *mid-div, hit second, effrt 12th, rdn appr 4 out, sn one pace.*
..............................(14 to 1 op 12 to 1 tchd 16 to 1) 4
2355 HEATHVIEW [83] 7-11-0 (7*) F Leahy, *not jump wl, in tch till rdn and wknd 5 out......................*(5 to 1 op 4 to 1) 5
2071³ JUNIORS CHOICE [71] 11-10-9 A Merrigan, *prmnt, led 3rd till slpd and f 11th................*(9 to 1 op 7 to 1) f
2071* DONEGAL STYLE (Ire) [74] 6-10-12 A Dobbin, *hld up, hdwy 13th, ev ch whn f 4 out, broke leg, destroyed.*
............................(11 to 4 fav op 5 to 2 tchd 7 to 2) f
2565⁸ EBRO [86] 8-11-5 (5*) F Perratt, *prmnt till lost pl tenth, sn beh, tld off whn pld up bef 3 out...*(16 to 1 op 14 to 1) pu
2497 MOW CREEK [70] 10-10-3 (5*) P Williams, *al beh, tld off 5th, pld up bef 3 out...........*(20 to 1 op 16 to 1) pu
POTATO MAN [68] 8-10-3 (3*) D Bentley, *led to 3rd, prmnt till blun 13th, sn wknd, tld off whn pld up bef 3 out.*
....(20 to 1) pu
Dist: ½l, 15l, 3½l, 25l. 6m 11.40s. a 21.40s (10 Ran).
(Miss Joy Mailes), J M Bradley

2737 Longniddry Claiming Hurdle (5-y-o and up) £1,987 3m..............(2:15)

2575⁷ HOTDIGGITY 6-10-5 (3*) T Jenks, *beh, hdwy 8th, sn pushed alng, led aftr 2 out, drvn out r-in.*
.............................(100 to 1 op 66 to 1) 1
2152* FIRM PRICE 13-11-3 (7*) G Lee, *in tch, hit 7th and 8th, hdwy 3 out, effrt appr last, sn rdn, not quicken.*
.................................(6 to 4 on op 5 to 4 on tchd Evens) 2
2535 MISTIC GLEN (Ire) 5-10-13 A Dobbin, *mid-div, hdwy hfwy, effrt 2 out, sn rdn, styd on appr last.*
....(9 to 2 tchd 5 to 1) 3
2435² HOT PUNCH 5-11-1 (5*) P Waggott, *prmnt, rdn and ev ch 2 out, wknd appr last...................* (16 to 1) 4
82 LUCAS COURT 8-10-9 (3*) D J Moffatt, *hdwy hfwy, rdn 2 out, kpt on one pace...........* (66 to 1 op 50 to 1) 5
2330³ GYMCRAB DAWN 9-11-0 P Harley, *prmnt, led 9th till hdd and wknd aftr 2 out..............* (50 to 1 op 33 to 1) 6
2578⁴ CLASSIC MINSTREL 10-10-11 (5*) P Williams, *mid-div, hit 6th, effrt and hdwy appr 3 out, sn rdn, one pace nxt.*
......................................(20 to 1 op 16 to 1) 7
2321 YACHT CLUB 12-10-12 O Pears, *prmnt, rdn and wknd appr 2 out..............................*(100 to 1) 8
2575⁵ VALIANT DASH 8-10-13 (5*) F Perratt, *led to 6th, chsd ldrs till rdn and wknd appr 3 out.........* (8 to 1 op 5 to 1) 9
2425⁵ CLASSIC STATEMENT 8-10-11 (3*) A Larnach, *beh hfwy.*
....(50 to 1 op 25 to 1) 10
2575⁸ GOLDEN REVERIE (USA) 6-10-12 A Merrigan, *chsd ldrs till rdn and wknd hfwy.*
.............................(66 to 1 op 50 to 1 tchd 100 to 1) 11
2437⁶ LAPIAFFE 10-10-9 (7*) S Taylor, *prmnt, rdn and wknd 4 out..........................*(14 to 1 op 12 to 1 tchd 16 to 1) 12
2502⁴ MR FENWICK 10-11-2 A Mulholland, *prmnt, led 6th to 9th, wknd 4 out, tld off.......*(50 to 1 op 33 to 1) 13
PICKTHEMONEYUPALF 7-11-7 K Johnson, *al rear, tld off hfwy...*(100 to 1) 14
2579 MISTER CUMBERS 7-10-12 A S Smith, *in tch to 5th, sn lost pl and tld off, pld up bef 2 out.*
..........................(100 to 1 op 66 to 1) ur
Dist: 3l, 1l, 11l, 7l, ½l, 3l, 7l, 6l, 5l, nk. 5m 59.70s. a 19.70s (15 Ran).
(Lt-Col W L Monteith), P Monteith

2738 Edinburgh University Turf Club 'Hole In The Wall' Handicap Chase (0-125 5-y-o and up) £2,697 2m.......(2:45)

2563² KIND'A SMART [100] 9-10-3 A S Smith, *hld up in tch, hdwy on ins to ld 4 out, quickened clr appr 2 out, easily.................................*(6 to 4 fav tchd 13 to 8) 1
2450* SONSIE MO [115] 9-11-13 (5*) P Williams, *cl up, led 3rd to 7th, rdn and kpt on one pace......* (9 to 4 op 7 to 4) 2
2436³ GOLDEN ISLE [97] 10-10-0 B Storey, *led to 3rd, led 7th till hdd and rdn 4 out, one pace nxt.*
.........................(9 to 2 op 5 to 1 tchd 11 to 2) 3
2412⁴ ONE FOR THE POT [108] 9-10-8 (3*) T Jenks, *hld up, hdwy and ev ch 4 out, rdn nxt, sn wknd...* (9 to 2 op 7 to 1) 4
2251 STRONG SILVER (USA) [97] (bl) 9-10-0 K Johnson, *al rear, tld off appr 4 out....................*(66 to 1 op 50 to 1) 5
Dist: 3l, 3l, 2½l, dist. 3m 58.60s. a 8.60s (5 Ran).
SR: 37/44/23/31/-/   (B Parker), K A Morgan

2739 Haddington Maiden Chase (5-y-o and up) £2,242 2½m...............(3:20)

2186³ RUSSINSKY 7-11-2 R J Beggan, *hld up in tch, hdwy appr 4 out, outpcd nxt, rdn and headway whn lft second 2 out, sn led and clr................* (2 to 1 fav op 5 to 4) 1
2411⁵ MAYOR OF LISCARROL 9-11-7 G Harker, *led, jnd 4 out, hdd nxt, cl up whn blun 2 out, lft in ld, sn headed and no extr.....................*(66 to 1 op 33 to 1) 2
2104 KIRKCALDY (Ire) 10-11-2 T Reed, *al rear, hmpd 8th, blun 11th, styd on one pace frm 4 out...*(50 to 1 op 33 to 1) 3
2563⁶ BALLYBELL 9-11-7 B Storey, *prmnt, rdn appr 4 out, sn wknd................*(20 to 1 op 16 to 1 tchd 25 to 1) 4
2575⁴ FLING IN SPRING (v) 8-11-2 (5*) P Williams, *in tch, blun 9th, sn lost pl.....................*(7 to 1 op 6 to 1) 5

380

2489 COZZI (Fr) 6-11-4 (3*) R Farrant, *prmnt till rdn and wknd 11th, sn beh*....................(12 to 1 tchd 14 to 1) 6
2584⁴ KRISSOS (bl) 7-11-2 (5*) P Waggott, *not jump wl, al rear, beh hfwy*..........................(33 to 1 tchd 50 to 1) 7
1182⁶ NORTHERN VISION 7-11-0 (7*) M A Manners, *in tch, wknd 11th, sn beh, tld off 4 out*..........(20 to 1 op 16 to 1) 8
2501³ ZARBANO 8-11-7 A Merrigan, *mid-div, hdwy to chase ldrs 5 out, rdn nxt, sn wknd, virtually pld up r-in*.
...........................(7 to 1 op 5 to 1 tchd 8 to 1) 9
2486³ OVER THE ISLAND (Ire) 6-11-2 A Dobbin, *prmnt, chlgd 4 out, slight ld 3 out till f nxt*.
...........................(9 to 4 op 2 to 1 tchd 5 to 2) f
1223 CORNISH BAY 6-10-9 (7*) P Kennedy, *rear whn blun and uns rdr 8th*..................(100 to 1 op 50 to 1) ur
MISS JEDD 7-10-13 (3*) T Jenks, *steadied strt, beh whn refused and uns rdr 3rd*............(50 to 1 op 33 to 1) ref
2497⁸ GRAAL LEGEND 9-11-2 (5*) F Perratt, *mstks, blun 8th and pld up*......................(100 to 1 op 50 to 1) pu
Dist: 6l, 15l, 2½l, 1½l, 5l, 25l, 3½l, dist. 5m 10.40s. a 20.40s (13 Ran).
(Mrs E A Clark), G C Bravery

2740 Scottish Racing Club Handicap Hurdle (0-120 4-y-o and up) £2,346 2½m (3:50)

2405⁶ FORTUNE'S GIRL [90] 6-9-11 (3*) D Bentley, *hld up in tch, hdwy 3 out, chlgd nxt, rdn and sn led, clr appr last*.
.......................(5 to 1 op 7 to 2 tchd 11 to 2) 1
2566⁴ THE GREEN FOOL [108] 7-11-4 B Storey, *chsd ldrs, led 3 out, jnd nxt, sn hdd, one pace and dres*.
.......................(11 to 2 op 6 to 1) 2
1322⁸ TROODOS I[11] 8-11-7 T Reed, *prmnt, rdn appr 2 out, kpt on one pace*..............(20 to 1 op 14 to 1) 3
2108⁵ ELGIN [90] 5-10-0 A Dobbin, *beh, styd on frm 2 out, nrst finish*..........................(20 to 1 op 16 to 1) 4
2580² J P MORGAN [92] (v) 6-9-13 (3*) T Jenks, *prmnt, rdn 3 out, wknd nxt*..............(11 to 2 op 9 to 2 tchd 6 to 1) 5
1793 RAPID MOVER [92] (bl) 7-10-2⁷ (5*) P Williams, *prmnt, led 3rd to 5th, rdn and wkng whn hit 2 out*.
.......................(40 to 1 op 25 to 1) 6
2367³ MAJOR BELL [98] 6-10-8 M Moloney, *cl up, led aftr 7th to 3 out, rdn and wknd nxt*..........(9 to 2 op 7 to 2) 7
2566⁷ ONLY A ROSE [101] 5-10-11 D Wilkinson, *in tch, rdn and outpcd appr 3 out, beh whn blun last*.
.......................(100 to 30 fav op 3 to 1 tchd 7 to 2) 8
1481⁸ MIDLAND EXPRESS [90] 11-9-12³ (5*) P Waggott, *prmnt till rdn and wknd aftr 4 out*..........(50 to 1 op 33 to 1) 9
2449⁶ KIR (Ire) [95] (bl) 6-10-0 (5*) F Perratt, *in tch till rdn and wknd*..................(50 to 1 op 33 to 1) 10
2150⁸ RED TEMPEST (Ire) [90] 6-10-0 O Pears, *al beh*.......(40 to 1 op 33 to 1 tchd 50 to 1) 11
2153⁷ REXY BOY [94] 7-10-4⁴ G Harker, *chsd ldrs, led 5th till aftr 7th, rdn wn, wknd*.
.......................(40 to 1 op 33 to 1 tchd 50 to 1) 12
2385 NODFORM WONDER [118] 7-11-11 (3*) D J Moffatt, *led to 3rd, sn lost pl, pld up aftr 6th*....(10 to 1 tchd 14 to 1) pu
Dist: 6l, 5l, 6l, 1l, 1½l, 2l, 10l, 3l, 1½l, 4l. 4m 51.90s. a 13.90s (13 Ran).
SR: -/5/3/-/-/-/ (Million In Mind Partnership (3)), M D Hammond

2741 Port Seton Maiden Hurdle (Div II) (4-y-o and up) £1,955 2m..........(4:20)

2430⁵ KING ATHELSTAN (USA) 6-11-7 A S Smith, *made all, clr 2 out, rdn appr last, hld on wl r-in*.
.......................(5 to 2 fav op 13 to 8) 1
2485⁷ COMBELLINO 4-10-5 (7*) Mr C Bonner, *chsd ldrs, hdwy 3 out, chased wnr nxt, led last, styd on wl r-in*.
.......................(11 to 2 op 7 to 2 tchd 6 to 1) 2
2573⁶ TEMPLERAINEY (Ire) 6-11-2 (5*) P Williams, *hld up, hdwy 4 out, rdn appr 2 out, styd on....*..........(33 to 1) 3
2072⁸ COMMANCHE CREEK 4-10-9 (3*) A Larnach, *beh, styd on frm 2 out, nvr a factor*...............(33 to 1) 4
1103⁷ HOLD YOUR HAT ON 5-11-7 D Wilkinson, *in tch, hdwy to chase ldrs aftr 3 out, sn rdn and one pace*.
.......................(6 to 1 op 4 to 1) 5
1800⁸ SUPER SHARP (NZ) 6-11-7 J Jacqui Oliver, *prmnt, rdn 3 out, wknd bef nxt*..................(10 to 1 op 5 to 2) 6
2409 BUZZ-B-BABE 4-10-12 T Reed, *prmnt till rdn and wknd 3 out*..................(40 to 1 op 33 to 1 tchd 50 to 1) 7
GLORIOUS HEIGHTS 6-10-11 (5*) F Perratt, *sn beh, tld off 4th*......................(20 to 1) 8
2401⁸ LANCASTER PILOT 4-10-12 A Mulholland, *al rear, tld off 4 out*..................(33 to 1 op 25 to 1) 9
2382 BRAVE AND TENDER (Ire) 5-11-7 A Dobbin, *chsd wnr till rdn and wknd quickly aftr 3 out, sn tld off*.
.......................(3 to 1 op 7 to 4 tchd 8 to 1) 10
2404 TOMASHENKO 5-11-7 M Moloney, *al rear, tld off whn pld up bef 2 out*......................(66 to 1) pu
1125⁷ LITTLE FREDDIE (bl) 5-11-7 B Storey, *chsd ldrs to 5th, sn lost pl, tld off whn pld up bef 2 out*.........(100 to 1) pu
Dist: Nk, 4l, dist, 6l, dist, 3l, 8l, 1l, nk. 3m 49.70s. a 11.70s (12 Ran).
SR: 24/14/19/-/-/-/ (Ian Guise), K A Morgan

KEMPTON (soft)
Saturday February 26th
Going Correction: PLUS 1.55 sec. per fur. (races 1,2,-4,8), PLUS 1.35 (3,5,6,7)

2742 Rendlesham Hurdle Grade 2 (4-y-o and up) £9,240 3m 110yds......(1:25)

1756⁴ BALASANI (Fr) 8-11-5 R Dunwoody, *hld up, hdwy to track ldrs 9th, chlgd last, sn led, quickened clr*.
.......................(5 to 2 op 9 to 4) 1
2487² CAB ON TARGET 8-11-5 P Niven, *chsd ldr, nudged alng frm 9th, led 2 out, not fluent last, sn hdd and outpcd*.
.......................(9 to 4 op Evens tchd 5 to 4) 2
TRUTH BE TOLD 10-11-5 D Murphy, *hld up, hdwy to track ldrs 9th, ev ch appr 2 out, wknd approaching last*.
.......................(12 to 1 op 16 to 1 tchd 20 to 1) 3
2257⁴ BURGOYNE 8-11-5 A Maguire, *led, sn clr, hdd 2 out, wknd rpdly, tld off*.............(7 to 2 op 3 to 1) 4
2595⁷ WELSHMAN 8-11-5 D Gallagher, *in tch till wknd 9th, tld off whn pld up bef 2 out*.
.......................(25 to 1 op 16 to 1 tchd 33 to 1) pu
Dist: 5l, 8l, dist. 6m 34.80s. a 47.80s (5 Ran).
(M D Smith), M C Pipe

2743 Dovecote Novices' Hurdle Grade 2 (4-y-o and up) £6,520 2m.........(1:55)

1509* JAZILAH (Fr) 6-11-3 G McCourt, *mid-div, hdwy to track ldrs 3 out, chlgd nxt, sn led, drvn out*.
.......................(5 to 2 op 15 to 8) 1
2014³ BARNA BOY (Ire) 6-11-3 M A FitzGerald, *hld up, hdwy to track ldrs appr 2 out, chlgd last, styd on, not pace of wnr*..................(11 to 1 op 12 to 1 tchd 10 to 1) 2
2356⁴ ARCTIC KINSMAN 6-11-3 C Llewellyn, *chsd ldr, led aftr 3 out, hdd after 2 out, wknd quickly appr last*.
.......................(13 to 2 op 6 to 1 tchd 7 to 1) 3
2250² SUPER COIN 6-11-10 A Maguire, *hdwy 5th, styd on same pace frm 2 out*..............(14 to 1 op 10 to 1 tchd 16 to 1) 4
2452* PARADISE NAVY 5-11-3 R Dunwoody, *led till hdd aftr 3 out, wknd 2 out*..............(9 to 1 op 8 to 1 tchd 10 to 1) 5
2356* CUMBRIAN CHALLENGE (Ire) 5-11-10 L Wyer, *in tch, rdn 2 out, sn wknd*..............(9 to 4 fav tchd 2 to 1 and 5 to 2) 6
2621* BALLET ROYAL (USA) 5-11-3 M Perrett, *chsd ldrs, rdn 3 out*..........................(5 to 1 tchd 6 to 1) 7
2599⁸ MONAZITE 4-10-7 R Bellamy, *beh frm 4th, tld off*...........(100 to 1 op 50 to 1) 8
2439 NOTED STRAIN (Ire) 6-11-3 S Arnold, *beh frm 4th, tld off*...........(100 to 1 tchd 200 to 1) 9
2665⁶ SALISONG 5-11-3 N Williamson, *mstks, al beh, tld off whn pld up bef 2 out*...................(100 to 1) pu
Dist: 2½l, 15l, 2l, 5l, 10l, 10l, dist. 4m 7.90s. a 27.90s (10 Ran).
SR: 58/55/40/45/33/30/13/-/-/ (S Aitken), R Akehurst

2744 Emblem Chase (5-y-o and up) £6,775 2m.......................(2:25)

REMITTANCE MAN 10-12-0 R Dunwoody, *chlgd 5th to 7th, trkd ldr 3 out, chald 2 out, led sn aftr last, ran on wl*.
.......................(5 to 2 op 9 to 4 tchd 11 to 4) 1
2594⁴ DEEP SENSATION 9-12-0 D Murphy, *made most till definite advantage 8th, hdd sn aftr last, kpt on same pace*.
.......................(3 to 1 op 11 to 4 tchd 100 to 30) 2
2594² WONDER MAN (Fr) 9-11-7 A Maguire, *with ldrs 5th till hit 9th, rallied 3 out, sn beh*.
.......................(6 to 5 fav op 11 to 10 tchd 11 to 8) 3
1666³ SPACE FAIR 11-12-0 P Niven, *al in 4th, lost tch frm four out*..................(14 to 1 op 10 to 1 tchd 16 to 1) 4
Dist: 3½l, 15l, 30l. 4m 9.70s. a 22.70s (4 Ran).
SR: 89/85/63/40/ (J E H Collins), N J Henderson

2745 Adonis Hurdle Grade 2 (4-y-o) £10,183 2m...........................(3:00)

2568* MYSILV 11-1 A Maguire, *made all, not fluent 3 out, steadied, quickened clr ag'n 2 out, hit last easily*.
.......................(5 to 1 on op 4 to 1 on tchd 6 to 1 on) 1
2381* WINTER FOREST (USA) 11-2 J Osborne, *dsptd second till chsd wnr frm 5th, effrt aftr 3 out, sn lft toiling*.
.......................(11 to 2 op 5 to 1 tchd 6 to 1) 2
611² LEGAL ARTIST (Ire) 10-12 D Murphy, *dsptd second till aftr 4th, lost tch frm 3 out*.
.......................(20 to 1 op 12 to 1 tchd 25 to 1) 3
Dist: 30l, 15l. 4m 10.70s. a 30.70s (3 Ran).
SR: 28/-/-/ (Million In Mind Partnership (3)), D Nicholson

2746 Pendil Novices' Chase Grade 2 (5-y-o and up) £9,570 2½m 110yds.....(3:35)

2378* MONSIEUR LE CURE 8-11-3 N Williamson, *led second to 3rd, chlgd nxt, led 11th, hdd 13th, led 3 out, in command whn lft clr 2 out, pushd tired*.
.......................(9 to 4 tchd 2 to 1 and 11 to 4) 1
2458² IN THE NAVY 8-11-3 J Lower, *wnt 3rd frm 8th but nvr in contention, lft dist second 2 out*...(20 to 1 op 8 to 1) 2
2455* LORD RELIC (NZ) 8-11-3 R Dunwoody, *led to second, led 3rd to 11th, led 13th, hdd 3 out, tiring and hld whn f 2 out*..................(9 to 4 on op 11 to 10 tchd 5 to 4 on) f
2208⁹ DARINGLY 5-10-7 R Bellamy, *beh, pld up bef 12th*.......(200 to 1 op 66 to 1) pu
Dist: Dist. 5m 41.00s. a 48.00s (4 Ran).
(Hector H Brown), J A C Edwards

NATIONAL HUNT RESULTS 1993-94

2747 Racing Post Handicap Chase Grade 3
(5-y-o and up) £29,700 3m...... (4:10)

2259⁴	ANTONIN (Fr) [142] 6-10-4 (5*) J Burke, trkd ldrs, hit 5th, led and hit 15th, hdd 4 out and outpcd, rdn to ld last, ran on wl..(7 to 1) 1
1843⁷	DOCKLANDS EXPRESS [155] 12-11-8 N Williamson, in tch 9th, hdwy 13th, chlgd 3 out, led nxt, hdd last, styd on one pace..........................(20 to 1 op 16 to 1) 2
1843³	THE FELLOW (Fr) [160] (bl) 9-11-13 A Kondrat, mid-div, hdwy to track ldrs 13th, hmpd bend appr 3 out, one pace frm 2 out...................(9 to 2 fav op 8 to 1) 3
2598²	ELFAST [138] 11-10-5⁵ G McCourt, pressed ldrs, led 4 out, hdd 2 out, not quicken.....(50 to 1 op 33 to 1 tchd 66 to 1) 4
2557²	RYDE AGAIN [143] 11-10-10 G Bradley, hdwy tenth, rdn 4 out, no ch wth ldrs whn hmpd last. ....(7 to 1 tchd 8 to 1 and 13 to 2) 5
1889*	FIGHTING WORDS [135] 8-10-2¹ D Murphy, led second, sn hdd, lost pl 12th, hdwy nxt, wknd 4 out. ....(7 to 1 op 8 to 1 tchd 9 to 1) 6
2377⁶	ROMANY KING [143] 10-10-10 Richard Guest, mid-div whn hit 14th, nvr dngrs aftr...........(20 to 1 tchd 25 to 1) 7
2384*	CARBISDALE [143] 8-10-10 P Niven, nvr jumping wl, al beh...(10 to 1 op 8 to 1) 8
2448⁴	SPARKLING FLAME [135] 10-10-2 M A FitzGerald, chsd ldrs to 15th, sn wknd.....(50 to 1 op 25 to 1 tchd 66 to 1) 9
1439*	COGENT [152] 10-11-0 (5*) D Fortt, led aftr second, hdd 9th, hdd 15th, sn wknd.................(10 to 1 tchd 12 to 1) 10
2513²	ROUGH QUEST [133] 8-10-0 R Dunwoody, in tch, trkd ldrs 15th, chlgd 3 out to nxt, disputing 4th whn f last. ....(5 to 1 tchd 11 to 2) f
2259⁵	GAMBLING ROYAL [142] 11-10-9 A Maguire, al beh, hit 7th, tld off whn pld up bef 3 out. ....(25 to 1 op 20 to 1 tchd 33 to 1) pu
1340*	SOLIDASAROCK [133] 12-10-0 M Perrett, led 1st, sn hdd, rear 7th, tld off whn pld up bef 14th. ....(50 to 1 op 25 to 1 tchd 66 to 1) pu
2656²	GHOFAR [133] (bl) 11-10-0 P Holley, al beh, tld off whn pld up bef 2 out........(66 to 1 op 50 to 1 tchd 100 to 1) pu
2377	TOBY TOBIAS [135] 12-10-2 I Lawrence, mstks, rear and rdn 9th, tld off whn pld up bef 3 out. ....(50 to 1 op 25 to 1 tchd 66 to 1) pu
1757²	LATENT TALENT [144] (bl) 10-10-11 J Osborne, mid-div till wknd and pld up aftr 13th.........(16 to 1 op 20 to 1) pu

Dist: 6l, 1l, hd, 8l, 25l, 15l, 15l, ¾l, hd. 6m 28.20s. a 39.20s (16 Ran).
SR: 13/20/24/2/-/-/ (M Stanners), Mrs S A Bramall

2748 Greenalls Gold Cup Handicap Chase
(5-y-o and up) £22,159 3½m 110yds ....(4:40)

2318*	MASTER OATS [135] 8-10-2 N Williamson, hdwy to track ldrs 9th, hit 11th, led 18th, came clr frm 4 out easily. ....(11 to 4 jt-fav op 3 to 1 tchd 7 to 2) 1
2173*	MOORCROFT BOY [136] 9-10-3 A Maguire, beh, reminder 15th, hdwy 17th, styd on frm 3 out, no ch wth wnr. ....(11 to 4 jt-fav op 3 to 1 tchd 7 to 2) 2
2448⁵	MERRY MASTER [133] 10-10-0 Gee Armytage, pressed ldrs till led 13th, hdd 18th, one pace frm 4 out. ....(33 to 1 op 25 to 1 tchd 50 to 1) 3
2576²	GENERAL PERSHING [143] 8-10-10 N Doughty, in tch, chsd ldrs 16th, wknd 3 out. ....(10 to 1 op 12 to 1 tchd 14 to 1) 4
2460³	FIDDLERS PIKE [133] 13-10-0 Mrs R Henderson, sn led, hdd 13th, styd on same pace frm 4 out...........(50 to 1) 5
2384²	AVONBURN (NZ) [133] 10-10-0 M Richards, mid-div, hdwy 14th, wknd 4 out.....(25 to 1 op 20 to 1 tchd 33 to 1) 6
2377³	SOUTHERN MINSTREL [133] 11-10-0 B Powell, prmnt, chlgd 16th to 17th, wknd 4 out.
2474³	YOUNG HUSTLER [154] 7-11-7 C Llewellyn, in tch, rdn alng 16th, 5th and no ch whn f 2 out. (8 to 1 op 7 to 1) f
2506²	GLENBROOK D'OR [133] 10-10-0 B Clifford, prmnt early, sn beh, f 17th.......................(25 to 1 tchd 33 to 1) f
1652⁴	LIGHT VENEER [133] 9-10-0 D Gallagher, nvr nr ldrs, tld off whn pld up bef 3 out. (5 to 1 to 7 tchd 9 to 2) pu
2557*	GARRISON SAVANNAH [145] 11-10-12 G Bradley, nvr gng wl, al beh, tld off whn pld up bef 17th. ....(9 to 1 op 8 to 1 tchd 10 to 1) pu
2318⁶	DIAMOND FORT [133] 9-10-0 S McNeill, beh frm 13th, tld off whn pld up bef 17th...........(100 to 1 op 150 to 1) pu

Dist: 15l, 2l, 7l, 12l, 20l, 8l. 7m 52.70s. (12 Ran).
(P A Matthews), K C Bailey

2749 Kempton National Hunt Flat Race
(4,5,6-y-o) £2,763 2m.......... (5:10)

	PUNTERS OVERHEAD (Ire) 6-11-3 (7*) L Reynolds, prmnt, led 3 out, ran on wl fnl 2 fs. ....(16 to 1 op 10 to 1 tchd 20 to 1) 1
	SEXTON GREY (Ire) 5-11-3 (7*) N Parker, took str hold, prmnt, ran on fnl 2 fs, not pace of wnr. ....(20 to 1 op 14 to 1) 2
	SMART ROOKIE (Ire) 4-10-7 (7*) R Massey, chsd ldrs, styd on one pace fnl 2 fs...........(9 to 4 fav op 5 to 1) 3

692* CALLISOE BAY (Ire) 5-12-3 Mr J Durkan, rcd freely, chsd ldrs, led 5 fs out, hdd 3 furlongs out, outpcd fnl 2 furlongs.........................(10 to 1 op 7 to 1) 4

2269⁶ ACE PLAYER (NZ) 6-11-3 (7*) S Fox, led till hdd 5 fs out, outpcd fnl 3 furlongs.........(12 to 1 tchd 14 to 1) 5

GOING AROUND 6-11-7 (3*) A Thornton, in tch hfwy, chsd ldrs 5 fs out, rdn and no imprsn frm o'r 3 furlongs out. ....(12 to 1 op 8 to 1) 6

2560³ BOYFRIEND 4-10-7 (7*) N Willmington, some hdwy 5 fs out, not rch ldrs..............................(8 to 1 op 6 to 1) 7

WHAT'S YOUR STORY (Ire) 5-11-3 (7*) Mr G Hogan, beh, some prog fnl 3 fs.... (25 to 1 op 16 to 1 tchd 33 to 1) 8

2490⁸ SECOND SLIP 5-11-5 (5*) E Husband, hdwy hfwy, wknd o'r 3 fs out.................................(20 to 1 op 14 to 1) 9

BUCKWHEAT BERTHA (Ire) 5-10-12 (7*) Mr G Haine, chsd ldrs 11 fs..............................(50 to 1 op 33 to 1) 10

NORSE RAIDER 4-10-9 (5*) D Matthews, chsd ldrs hfwy, wknd 4 fs out.......(33 to 1 op 25 to 1 tchd 50 to 1) 11

CRACKING IDEA (Ire) 6-11-7 (3*) R Davis, effrt to chase ldrs 6 fs out, wknd o'r 3 fs out. ....(10 to 1 op 12 to 1 tchd 8 to 1) 12

PRE-EMPTIVE STRIKE 4-10-7 (7*) M D Parker, in tch hfwy, rdn and wknd o'r 3 fs out. ....(3 to 1 op 6 to 4 tchd 7 to 2) 13

2387⁷ KING LUCIFER (Ire) 5-11-3 (7*) M Keighley, prmnt ten fs. ....(25 to 1 op 16 to 1 tchd 33 to 1) 14

2509 GLENSKI 5-11-3 (7*) N Collum, al beh. ....(33 to 1 op 25 to 1 tchd 50 to 1) 15

WARNER FOR SPORT 5-11-3 (7*) Mr Richard White, prmnt ten fs..............(25 to 1 op 14 to 1 tchd 33 to 1) 16

1626⁹ BECKFORD 5-11-3 (7*) Mr R Griffiths, beh frm hfwy. ....(50 to 1 op 33 to 1) 17

HIGHLY REPUTABLE (Ire) 4-10-7 (7*) T Dascombe, al beh. ....(6 to 1 op 5 to 1 tchd 13 to 2) 18

MERRY BENVILLE 6-11-3 (7*) T Thompson, effrt hfwy, sn btn.................................(50 to 1 op 33 to 1) 19

NEARLY PERFECT 6-11-2 (3*) A Dicken, al beh. ....(50 to 1 op 33 to 1) 20

Dist: 3l, 6l, 2l, 2½l, 3l, 2½l, sht-hd, nk, 12l, nk. 4m 11.40s. (20 Ran).
(J N Hutchinson), M C Pipe

NAAS (IRE) (heavy)
Saturday February 26th

2750 Saggart Maiden Hurdle (4-y-o) £3,105
2m.......................(2:00)

2678	SHEREGORI (Ire) (bl) 10-11 (5*) K L O'Brien, .. (2 to 1 fav) 1
2678³	ONOMATOPOEIA (Ire) 11-2 M Duffy,..............(7 to 2) 2
2678⁵	BERESFORD LADY (Ire) 10-11 C O'Dwyer,.......(5 to 1) 3
	SPRUNG RHYTHM (Ire) 10-11 (5*) Mr D Walsh, .. (20 to 1) 4
2122⁶	TOUCHING MOMENT (Ire) 11-2 (5*) T P Rudd,....(7 to 1) 5
2590⁹	PRINTOUT (Ire) 10-11 H Rogers,.................(10 to 1) 6
1853⁶	BOBADIL (Ire) 10-9 (7*) P J Smullen,..............(7 to 1) 7
2290⁸	CONCLAVE (Ire) 11-2 R Hughes,.................(12 to 1) 8
	TASSET (Can) 11-0 (7*) T Martin, ...(14 to 1) 9
2349⁹	LADYS BID (Ire) 10-4 (7*) J M Donnelly,........(25 to 1) 10
2663	ROYAL RANK (USA) 11-2 C F Swan,..............(6 to 1) 11
1432	LIMAHEIGHTS (Ire) 10-11 H P Cusack, ...(16 to 1) 12
2614⁹	ABEREDW (Ire) 10-11 A Powell,..................(14 to 1) 13
2537⁷	MONTEJUSTICE (Ire) 10-11 (5*) D P Geoghegan,...(33 to 1) 14
	FOOLISH LAW (Ire) 10-11 S H O'Donovan,......(10 to 1) 15
2349	BOSSY PATRICIA (Ire) 10-4 (7*) D M Bean, ...(33 to 1) 16

Dist: 6l, 4l, nk, ¾l. 4m 4.50s. (16 Ran).
(D P Sharkey), M J P O'Brien

2751 Kilcullen Handicap Hurdle (0-130 5-y-o and up) £3,105 3m............(2:30)

2403	GIMME FIVE [-] (bl) 7-11-2 C F Swan, ... (3 to 1 fav) 1
2660²	CALMOS [-] 7-9-3 (5*) K R Donoghue,...........(7 to 2) 2
2619²	GOOLDS GOLD [-] 8-9-7 (5*) J P Broderick,.....(7 to 1) 3
2468	LOAVES AND FISHES [-] 6-9-7 (7*) B D Murtagh, ..(20 to 1) 4
2468³	FRIGID COUNTESS [-] 7-9-6 (7*) L A Hurley, ...(5 to 1) 5
2467²	TEMPLERAN PRINCE [-] 7-11-1 C N Bowens, (100 to 1) 6
2682⁶	TERZIA [-] 7-11-4 T Horgan,.....................(8 to 1) 7
2617⁷	TARA'S SERENADE (Ire) [-] 5-9-4 (3*) C O'Brien, ..(25 to 1) 8
2389⁷	MAN OF IRON [-] 7-9-8⁶ (5*) D Walsh,...........(20 to 1) 9
2390	SPUR OF THE MOMENT [-] 7-9-13 J P Banahan, (12 to 1) 10

Dist: 1½l, 1l, nk, 2l. 6m 16.20s. (10 Ran).
(J P McManus), E J O'Grady

2752 Foran Equine Products Novice Chase
(5-y-o and up) £3,795 3m...... (3:00)

2661²	MOONCAPER 8-12-0 T Horgan,................(11 to 10 fav) 1
2588	CHOSEN SON 6-11-9 (5*) D P Geoghegan,......(6 to 1) 2
	DELGANY DEER 8-11-9 (5*) M G J Harford,.....(10 to 1) 3
2618⁸	CROGEEN LASS 7-11-9 H Rogers,...............(14 to 1) 4
2588	DEER TRIX 9-11-9 J Shortt,......................(5 to 1) f
2661	CARRON HILL 7-12-0 F Woods,..................(5 to 1) f
11⁵	DUNBOY CASTLE (Ire) 6-11-9 (5*) K P Gaule, ...(10 to 1) f

Dist: 20l, 2½l, dist. 7m 17.60s. (7 Ran).
(John J Nallen), A P O'Brien

2753

EBF Johnstown Hurdle (Listed - Grade 3) (5-y-o and up) £5,520 2m . . . . . (3:30)

2587² SOUND MAN (Ire) 6-11-4 C F Swan, *trkd ldrs, prog to ld appr 3 out, rdn aftr last, eased cl hme.* . . . . .(10 to 9 on)	
2079 AIYBAK (Ire) (bl) 6-11-7 B Sheridan, *mid-div, prog 2 out, rdn appr last, kpt on, not trble wnr.* . . . . (12 to 1)	1
2702² IDIOTS VENTURE 7-11-5 (5*) K P Gaule, *hld up, prog entering strt, trkd ldr appr last, sn rdn, no extr and wknd r-in.* . . . . (5 to 1)	2
2612⁷ COURT MELODY (Ire) 6-11-2 (5*) J P Broderick, *hld up, prog appr 3 out, ev ch nxt, rdn, no extr and wknd r-in.*	3
	4
2613³ THE SUBBIE (Ire) 5-10-11 J Shortt, *led or dsptd ld till appr 3 out, rdn bef nxt, kpt on one pace.* . . . .(14 to 1)	5
2612⁵ YUKON GOLD (Ire) (bl) 5-11-4 C O'Dwyer, *mid-div, prog 3 out, rdn bef nxt, wknd appr last.* . . . . (9 to 2)	6
2702 HEIST (bl) 5-11-4 P Carberry, *al rear, rdn whn mstk 3 out, wknd aftr nxt.* . . . . (8 to 1)	7
2587⁹ DUNFERNE CLASSIC (Ire) 5-10-11 T Horgan, *dsptd ld till appr 3 out, rdn and wknd bef nxt.* . . . .(33 to 1)	8

Dist: 1l, ¾l, 4l, nk. 4m 8.70s. (8 Ran).

(David Lloyd), E J O'Grady

2754

Robertstown Handicap Hurdle (4-y-o and up) £6,900 2m. . . . .(4:00)

2610³ DEEP INAGH [-] 8-11-13 D P Fagan, ...(8 to 1)	1
2615* FOR REG (Ire) [-] 5-11-0 (5*,4ex) J R Barry, ... (6 to 1)	2
2610⁴ THATCH AND GOLD (Ire) [-] 6-11-1 M Duffy, ... (10 to 1)	3
2610* THE SHAUGHRAUN [-] 8-11-4 (5ex) T Horgan, ... (9 to 2)	4
2610 IF YOU SAY YES (Ire) [-] 6-10-7 K F O'Brien, ... (25 to 1)	5
2610² JUPITER JIMMY [-] 5-11-3 C F Swan, ...(7 to 4 fav)	6
2680* ARCTIC WEATHER (Ire) [-] 5-11-4 (5*) K L O'Brien, . .(6 to 1)	7
2391⁷ FINAWAY BOY [-] 6-10-6 J P Banahan, ...(33 to 1)	8
2699⁵ NANNAKA (USA) [-] 4-10-7 (3*,4ex) T P Treacy, ...(14 to 1)	9
2231⁶ KAWA-KAWA [-] 7-9-4 (3*) T J O'Sullivan, ... (33 to 1)	10
2690⁴ PARLIAMENT HALL [-] 8-11-5 (5*) J P Broderick, . .(14 to 1)	11
2680⁴ AUTUMN GORSE (Ire) [-] 5-11-9 (5*) K P Gaule, ...(14 to 1)	12

Dist: 5l, 12l, 1½l, 8l. 4m 0.30s. (12 Ran).

(Noel McMullan), J R H Fowler

2755

Newlands Handicap Chase (0-130 5-y-o and up) £3,450 2m 3f. . . . .(4:30)

JASSU [-] 8-11-6 C F Swan, ... (6 to 1)	1
2159³ BOB DEVANI [-] 8-10-13 P Carberry, ...(9 to 2)	2
2469* ROYAL MOUNTBROWNE [-] 6-11-11 J F Titley, (7 to 4 fav)	3
2466⁴ TORANFIELD [-] 10-11-6 (5*) J P Broderick, ... (5 to 1)	4
2662* LADY BAR [-] 7-11-2 (6ex) P M Verling, ... (6 to 1)	5
2591³ THE REAL UNYOKE [-] (bl) 9-10-9 (3*) D P Murphy, (14 to 1)	6
1231⁹ TENNESSEE PASS [-] 14-9-12 (7*) J Butler, ... (20 to 1)	7
2280 LIFE OF A LORD [-] 8-11-8 S H O'Donovan, ... (12 to 1)	8
2591⁷ GOOD TEAM [-] 9-11-6 T J Taaffe, ...(10 to 1)	pu

Dist: 2l, 7l, nk, 14l. 5m 35.30s. (9 Ran).

(Bruno Buser), J E Kiely

2756

Rathcoole INH Flat Race (5-y-o and up) £3,105 2m 3f. . . . . (5:00)

2470* MARINGO (Ire) 5-11-12 (3*) Mrs J M Mullins, . . . (5 to 2 fav)	1
2684* RUN BAVARD (Ire) 6-11-11 (7*) Mr P English, ... (8 to 1)	2
2470⁶ DUN CARRAIG (Ire) 6-11-8 (3*) Mr A R Coonan, . . .(14 to 1)	3
2632³ DROICHEAD LAPEEN 7-11-11 (7*) Mr T J Beattie, . .(7 to 2)	4
2682³ IAMWHATIAM 8-11-11 (7*) Mr E Norris, ... (5 to 1)	5
2613⁶ TREANAREE (Ire) 5-11-3 (5*) Mr H F Cleary, ...(16 to 1)	6
2618⁵ DAVE FLECK (Ire) 6-11-8 (3*) Mr D Marnane, ...(25 to 1)	7
2684⁸ BALLYHIRE LAD (Ire) 5-11-8 Mr A P O'Brien, ...(9 to 1)	8
2616⁷ HALEY SEA (Ire) 5-11-3 (7*) Mr D G Murphy, ...(12 to 1)	9
2684* EMMA HAAN (Ire) 5-11-3 Mr T Mullins, ... (6 to 1)	10
2027 DIAMOND BUCK (Ire) 6-11-4 (7*) Mr D A Harney, .(100 to 1)	11

Dist: 9l, 3l, sht-hd, 12l. 4m 52.30s. (11 Ran).

(Alexander McCarthy), W P Mullins

PLUMPTON (good to soft)
Monday February 28th

Going Correction: PLUS 1.70 sec. per fur. (races 1,3,-4,6), PLUS 1.25 (2,5)

2757

New Cross Novices' Hurdle (4-y-o and up) £1,543 2½m. . . . . (2:20)

136² STRONG CASE 6-11-2 R Dunwoody, *hld up in tch, led on bit appr 2 out, tired and reminder approaching last, rdn out.* . . . . . . (7 to 4 on op 6 to 4 on tchd 11 to 8 on)	1
2494² OUROWNFELLOW (Ire) 5-11-2 D Morris, *hld up in tch, hdwy 8th, led appr 3 out till bef nxt, rdn and ducked lft aftr last, kpt on one pace.* . . . . (10 to 1 op 8 to 1 tchd 12 to 1)	2
2320⁵ ESPRIT DE FEMME (Fr) 8-10-11 A Maguire, *led till appr 3 out, sn outpcd.* . . . .(12 to 1 op 7 to 1)	3
2599⁴ BRAVE HIGHLANDER (Ire) 6-11-2 D Murphy, *mid-div, hdwy 8th, wkng whn mstk 2 out.* . . . .(9 to 1 op 7 to 1)	4

1707⁹ HOT 'N ROSIE 5-10-11 P Holley, *rear till hdwy 4th, outpcd four out, collapsed aftr race, dead.* . . . . (50 to 1 op 20 to 1 tchd 100 to 1)	5
2426⁴ OLDHILL WOOD (Ire) 4-10-7 S Earle, *chsd ldr frm 3rd, rdn 4 out, wknd nxt.* . . . .(7 to 1 op 5 to 1 tchd 15 to 2)	6
2244⁴ FLY GUARD (NZ) 7-11-2 J Frost, *frnt rnk till rdn and wknd appr 4 out, tld off.* . . . .(25 to 1 op 14 to 1)	7
2671 COSMICECHOEXPRESS 7-10-11 N Williamson, *beh 4th, tld off.* . . . . (66 to 1 op 50 to 1 tchd 100 to 1)	8
2708⁵ GRAND COLONIST 7-10-13 (3*) A Procter, *hld up, lost tch 8th, tld off.* . . . .(66 to 1 op 33 to 1 tchd 100 to 1)	9
VENN BOY 5-10-9 (7*) T Murphy, *beh 3rd, jmpd rght 3rd, rdn to stay in tch, wknd 7th, tld off.*	
. . . . (66 to 1 op 50 to 1 tchd 100 to 1)	10

Dist: 1½l, 12l, 8l, 3l, 6l, 30l, 12l, 12l, dist. 5m 16.80s. a 39.80s (10 Ran).
SR: 30/28/11/8/-/-/

(Mrs L M Sewell), M C Pipe

2758

Wally Coomes Handicap Chase (0-115 5-y-o and up) £2,544 3m 1f 110yds . . . . (2:50)

2495² ROSITARY (Fr) [91] (bl) 11-10-4 J Osborne, *jmpd wl, al prmnt, wnt second aftr mstk 13th, led appr 5 out, clr nxt, eased r-in.* . . . . (8 to 1 op 7 to 1 tchd 9 to 1)	1
2518* SILVERINO [101] (bl) 8-11-0 M Richards, *sn beh and outpcd, rdn 4 out, styd on and pres to go second r-in.* . . . . (11 to 4 fav op 3 to 1)	2
2453* SHASTON [100] (bl) 9-10-13 P Holley, *led, clr whn jmpd slwly 8th, hit 13th, hdd appr 5 out, wkng when hit last, lost second r-in.* . . . . . (3 to 1 op 11 to 4 tchd 100 to 30)	3
1625⁴ SIDE OF HILL [114] 9-11-13 R Dunwoody, *slwly away, sn in tch, chsd ldr 4th till hit 13th, wknd nxt, tld off.* . . . . (9 to 2 op 4 to 1 tchd 5 to 1)	4
2125⁹ BROMPTON ROAD [108] 11-11-7 A Maguire, *f second.* . . . .(4 to 1 op 7 to 2)	f
2690⁵ UNDER OFFER [87] (bl) 13-10-0 J R Kavanagh, *chsd ldr to 4th, poor fourth whn blun and uns rdr tenth.* . . . . (33 to 1 op 25 to 1 tchd 50 to 1)	ur
2453⁶ CAMDEN BELLE [87] 12-9-12³ (5*) C Burnett-Wells, *al beh, tld off whn pld up bef 8th.* . . . . (50 to 1 op 33 to 1)	pu
2011⁶ BIT OF A CLOWN [115] 11-12-0 L Harvey, *lost tch 4th, tld off whn pld up bef 14th.* . . . .(16 to 1 op 12 to 1)	pu

Dist: 12l, 3l, 30l. 7m 7.30s. a 55.30s (8 Ran).

(P Winkworth), P Winkworth

2759

Coomes Handicap Hurdle (0-125 4-y-o and up) £2,924 2½m. . . . .(3:20)

2636² SHANNON GLEN [120] (bl) 8-11-5 (7*) D Bohan, *made all, rallied gmely whn chlgd appr 2 out, drw clr bef last.* . . . .(4 to 1 op 9 to 2 tchd 5 to 1)	1
2400* DAMIER BLANC (Fr) [103] (bl) 5-10-9 R Dunwoody, *chsd wnr most of way to 7th, rdn and outpcd 3 out, staying on one pace whn hit last, wnt second r-in.* . . . .(7 to 4 fav op 6 to 4 tchd 15 to 8)	2
2496 THE MRS [95] 8-10-11 S Earle, *hld up, hdwy frm 7th, wnt second appr 3 out, chlgd bef nxt, wknd approaching last.* . . . .(33 to 1 op 25 to 1)	3
2674⁴ CRABBY BILL [102] (v) 7-10-8 A Dicken, *hld up in rear, styd on frm 3 out, nvr nrr.* . . . .(4 to 1 op 9 to 2 tchd 9 to 2)	4
2400 MANHATTAN BOY [100] 12-10-6 A Maguire, *chsd ldrs till wknd appr 4 out.* . . . . .(12 to 1 op 10 to 1 tchd 14 to 1)	5
2247⁹ LESBET [97] 9-10-3 D Morris, *al rear, kpt on frm 3 out, nvr dngrs.* . . . . (12 to 1 op 10 to 1)	6
1465⁴ VAGADOR (Can) [122] 11-12-0 M Perrett, *in tch till wknd 8th, tld off.* . . . .(10 to 1 op 7 to 1 tchd 11 to 1)	7
2504 FANTASY WORLD [99] 8-10-5 D Murphy, *prmnt, wnt second appr 4 out, wknd quickly bef nxt, tld off.* . . . . (10 to 1 op 8 to 1)	8

Dist: 10l, 1l, 6l, 1¾l, 1½l, 15l, 1l. 5m 16.70s. a 39.70s (8 Ran).
SR: 41/14/5/6/-/-/3/-/

(Mrs Elizabeth Hitchins), Mrs J Pitman

2760

Coomes Selling Handicap Hurdle (4,5,6-y-o) £1,814 2m 1f. . . . .(3:50)

2454³ BAYLORD PRINCE (Ire) [73] (bl) 6-10-3³ M Hoad, *hld up, hdwy 3 out, rdn to ld last, sn clr.* (33 to 1 tchd 50 to 1)	1
DAYS OF THUNDER [94] 6-11-10 A Maguire, *hld up, rear, hdwy 4 out, wnt second appr 2 out, ev ch till one pace one r-in.* . . . .(9 to 2 op 3 to 1 tchd 5 to 1)	2
2247 DERISBAY (Ire) [84] (bl) 6-11-0 D O'Sullivan, *al prmnt, led 6th, rdn and hdd last, wknd r-in, fnshd lme.* . . . .(9 to 4 fav op 3 to 1)	3
2640⁵ HERETICAL MISS [72] 4-10-2³ (3*) A Thornton, *in tch, chlgd 3 out, wknd quickly bef nxt.* . . . . (12 to 1 op 8 to 1)	4
2523⁸ BOOGIE BOPPER (Ire) [73] (v) 5-10-3 R Dunwoody, *chsd ldr till wknd quickly aftr 4th, tld off.* . . . .(8 to 1 op 6 to 1 tchd 9 to 1)	5
1942⁴ SKIMMER HAWK [77] 5-10-7 V Smith, *hld up, hdwy 4th, chsd ldr 6th, wknd rpdly aftr 3 out, tld off.*	6
MAGGIES LAD [89] 6-11-5 M A FitzGerald, *led to 6th, wknd, tld off whn pld up bef last.* . . . .(9 to 1 op 7 to 1)	pu
2414 LEGAL WIN (USA) [75] 6-10-4⁶ (7*) Mr G Shenkin, *refused to race.* . . . .(9 to 1 op 7 to 1 tchd 10 to 1)	l

Dist: 10l, ½l, 20l, 25l, 3l. 4m 35.80s. a 43.80s (8 Ran).

(Miss J A Ewer), R P C Hoad

2761 Coomes Senior Citizens Novices' Chase (5-y-o and up) £2,225 2m (4:20)

2132[4] PHILIP'S WOODY 6-11-3 J R Kavanagh, *trkd ldr, chalg whn hit 3 out, led nxt, rdn out.*
.... (10 to 1 op 7 to 1 tchd 11 to 1) 1
1844[4] HANGOVER 8-11-3 A Maguire, *mid-div, hdwy into 3rd 7th, styd on und pres to go second r-in.*
.... (11 to 4 op 5 to 2 tchd 3 to 1) 2
2625* MISTER ODDY 8-11-7 (3*) T Jenks, *led to 2 out, one pace aftr.* .... (5 to 1 op 9 to 2 tchd 11 to 2) 3
1493[3] WAYWARD WIND 10-11-3 W McFarland, *al beh, tld off 4 out.* .... (33 to 1 op 14 to 1) 4
2268[5] PRIVATE JET (Ire) 5-10-6 (3*) A Thornton, *al beh, tld off 7th.*
.... (33 to 1 op 16 to 1) 5
2436* SLIEVENAMON MIST 8-11-10 N Williamson, *trkd ldrs till hit 7th, sn rdn, btn 5 out, tld off whn pld up bef 2 out.*
.... (Evens fav tchd 5 to 4 on and 11 to 10) pu
BLARNEY CASTLE 7-11-3 R Rowell, *al beh, tld off 6th, pld up bef 8th.* .... (66 to 1 op 50 to 1 tchd 100 to 1) pu
Dist: 2½l, 4l, dist, 12l. 4m 15.70s. a 25.70s (7 Ran).
SR: 32/29/32/-/ (B R Wilsdon), N J Henderson

2762 Catford Maiden Hurdle (4-y-o and up) £1,543 2m 1f................ (4:50)

2621[2] ISAIAH 5-11-7 T Kent, *trkd ldr, led 3rd, rdn and hit last, ran on wl.* ..... (2 to 1 op 9 to 4 tchd 7 to 4) 1
WHITECHAPEL (USA) 6-11-7 R Dunwoody, *led to 3rd, mstk 5th, rdn to chal appr 2 out, ev ch till no extr r-in.*
.... (13 to 8 on op 2 to 1 on tchd 6 to 4 on) 2
1490 WEE WINDY (Ire) 5-11-7 D Murphy, *rear till hdwy 6th, wnt 3rd appr last, no ch wth 1st 2.*
.... (25 to 1 op 20 to 1) 3
2544[4] KINGSFOLD PET 5-11-7 C Llewellyn, *al 1st 4, wnt 3rd four out, wknd appr last.*
.... (40 to 1 op 33 to 1 tchd 25 to 1 and 50 to 1) 4
KILLTUBBER HOUSE 8-11-7 A Maguire, *mid-div, nvr on terms.* .... (33 to 1 op 20 to 1 tchd 40 to 1) 5
1994 ROYAL GAIT (NZ) 6-11-7 J Frost, *al beh, tld off.*
.... (66 to 1 op 50 to 1) 6
1601[4] BLUE GLEN (Ire) (bl) 6-11-7 Richard Guest, *chsd 1st 2, hit 6th, wknd quickly 4 out, tld off..* (20 to 1 op 12 to 1) 7
2692 FINALLY FANTAZIA 5-11-2 R J Beggan, *al beh, tld off.*
.... (25 to 1 op 14 to 1) 8
1710 JULY BRIDE 4-10-8 B Powell, *al beh, tld off whn pld up bef 2 out.* .... (66 to 1 op 50 to 1 tchd 100 to 1) pu
2333 MAC'S LEAP 6-11-7 L Harvey, *al beh, tld off whn pld up bef 2 out.* .... (66 to 1 op 50 to 1) pu
NATIONAL FLAG (Fr) 4-10-13 M A FitzGerald, *al beh, tld off whn pld up bef 2 out.* .... (66 to 1 op 20 to 1) pu
Dist: 3½l, 7l, 15l, 8l, 10l, 2l, 15l. 4m 34.60s. a 42.60s (11 Ran).
(Mrs D MacRae), Mrs J Cecil

NOTTINGHAM (heavy (race 1), good to soft (2,3,5), soft (4,6)) Tuesday March 1st
Going Correction: PLUS 1.20 sec. per fur.

2763 Junior Selling Hurdle (4-y-o) £1,845 2m............... (2:20)

2292[2] RAGGERTY (Ire) 11-4 R Dunwoody, *nvr far away, led and edgd lft 3 out, veered badly left bef nxt, left clr, blun last, styd on, disqualified.* .... (5 to 1 op 7 to 2) 1D
2135[7] HO-JOE (Ire) 10-12 N Smith, *settled midfield, effrt whn hit 4th and nxt, rallied to chal 3 out, hmpd nxt, no ch wth wnr, awarded race.* (4 to 1 op 5 to 1 tchd 9 to 2) 1
2492[4] MANON LESCAUT 10-7 W McFarland, *nvr far away, drvn alng whn pace quickened 3 out, one pace frm nxt, fnshd 3rd, plcd second.* .... (20 to 1 op 14 to 1) 2
2652[6] PLAIN SAILING (Fr) (bl) 10-12 W Marston, *settled midfield, imprvg whn blun 4 out, drvn alng frm nxt, sn btn, fnshd fourth, plcd 3rd.*
.... (12 to 1 op 16 to 1 tchd 33 to 1) 3
2522[9] TEJANO GOLD (USA) 10-12 W Humphreys, *led till 3 out, 4th and btn whn f 2 out.* .... (33 to 1) f
2224[6] WATER DIVINER 10-12 J Ryan, *co'red up in midfield, effrt appr 3 out, 6th and rdn whn blun and uns rdr nxt.*
.... (50 to 1 op 33 to 1) ur
2634[5] COUSIN WENDY 10-4 (3*) A Thornton, *blun and uns rdr 1st.*...................... (25 to 1 op 16 to 1) ur
BETTY KENWOOD (bl) 10-4 (3*) R Farrant, *patiently rdn, improved alng wl appr 3 out, cl second whn blun and uns rdr 2 out.* .... (33 to 1) ur
2364* MR GENEALOGY (USA) (bl) 11-4 A Maguire, *patiently rdn, improved und pres 3 out, ev ch whn crrd out nxt.*
.... (5 to 4 on op 11 to 8 on tchd Evens) co
2530[5] HOT OFF THE PRESS 10-12 R J Beggan, *beh, effrt and reminders 5th, no ch whn pld up bef 2 out.*
.... (12 to 1 op 5 to 1 tchd 14 to 1) pu
2083 NORTHERN JUDY (Ire) 10-4 (3*) S Wynne, *reluctant to leave paddock, co'red up in midfield, outpcd aftr 4 out, no ch whn pld up bef 2 out.*..... (25 to 1 op 20 to 1) pu

HARLOSH 10-7 (5*) P Midgley, *nvr gng wl, tld off whn pld up bef 3 out.*.......................... (33 to 1) pu
2530 BASKERVILLE BALLAD 10-7 T Wall, *beh till pld up bef 4th.*
.... (50 to 1 op 33 to 1) pu
Dist: 15l, 10l, 20l. 4m 14.00s. a 30.00s (13 Ran).
(S Ho), J M Carr

2764 Long Eaton Handicap Chase (0-100 5-y-o and up) £3,012 3m 3f 110yds .... (2:50)

2495[3] DOROBO (NZ) [81] (bl) 6-10-6 (3*) R Farrant, *nvr far away, nosed ahead 4 out, hrd drvn betw last 2, styd on.*
.... (11 to 4 fav op 7 to 4) 1
2294[9] SHEEPHAVEN [94] 10-11-8 M Richards, *al wl plcd, drw level 4 out, rdn betw last 2, one pace.*
.... (11 to 1 op 14 to 1) 2
2294[7] TRIBAL RULER [95] 9-11-9 G McCourt, *al wth, improved fnl circuit, led briefly 7 out, rdn 4 out, no extr.*
.... (5 to 1 op 4 to 1) 3
2733 TRUSTY FRIEND [88] 12-11-2 M A FitzGerald, *trkd ldg grp, struggling fnl circuit, lost tch frm 5 out.*
.... (11 to 1 op 10 to 1 tchd 12 to 1) 4
2406 INCONCLUSIVE [87] 7-10-10 (5*) J Burke, *not fluent, took clr order fnl circuit, 5th and btn whn f 2 out.*
.... (14 to 1 tchd 16 to 1 and 20 to 1) f
2325[4] KILDOWNEY HILL [92] 8-11-6 A Maguire, *al hndy, led 8th till hdd briefly 7 out, headed 4 out, fourth and btn whn blun and uns rdr nxt.* .... (3 to 1 op 7 to 2) ur
2495 PHAROAH'S LAEN [98] 13-11-12 S Earle, *in tch one circuit, lost touch quickly and pld up bef 14th..* (25 to 1) pu
2656 LA CERISE [72] (bl) 11-10-0 W Marston, *chsd ldg grp, blun 7th, lost tch fnl circuit, pld up bef seven out...* (25 to 1) pu
2576[4] CAROUSEL CALYPSO [94] 8-11-8 P Niven, *tucked away, no ch whn pld up bef 3 out.* .... (13 to 2 op 5 to 1) pu
367[3] KNOX'S CORNER [90] 9-10-11 (7*) G Crone, *chsd ldg grp one ciruit, lost tch quickly and pld up bef 14th.*
.... (33 to 1 op 20 to 1) pu
Dist: 3½l, 20l, 2½l. 7m 37.80s. a 49.80s (10 Ran).
(Lady Lewinton), Capt T A Forster

2765 Times Rising Stars Hunters' Chase (Qualifier) (6,7,8-y-o) £2,005 3m 110yds.......................... (3:20)

2555* SUNNY MOUNT 8-12-5 Mr J Greenall, *al wl plcd, mstk 3rd, led 11th till mistake 13th, pckd nxt, disputing ld whn lft clr last........* (11 to 8 on op 6 to 4 on tchd 5 to 4 on) 1
2508 JOLLY ROGER 7-11-12 (7*) Mr Michael J Jones, *sn wth ldr, led briefly 13th, lost pl nxt, lft second last, styd on.*
.... (14 to 1 op 16 to 1) 2
2301[3] RUSTY BRIDGE 7-11-5 (7*) Mr R Johnson, *led till mstk tenth, lost pl appr 4 out, styd on r-in.*
.... (12 to 1 op 10 to 1) 3
MICK'S TYCOON (Ire) 6-12-5 Mr S Swiers, *mstks, led briefly tenth, lost pl appr 4 out, kpt on same pace frm last..* .... (6 to 1 op 5 to 1) 4
KINGS GUNNER 7-11-5 (7*) Miss S Vickery, *no hdwy frm 14th.* .... (14 to 1 op 12 to 1) 5
HARVEST SPLENDOUR (USA) 7-11-0 (7*) Mr M Worthington, *hld up in rear, mstks 12th and 4 out, sn lost tch, tld off.*
.... (50 to 1) 6
JOHNNY'S CHOICE 8-12-5 (3*) Mr A Hill, *settled in rear, prog and mstk tenth, led appr 14th, disputing ld whn f last....* .... (7 to 2 op 3 to 1) f
2482 DOUBTING DONNA 8-11-7 (7*) Mr V Hughes, *hld up, beh whn blun and uns rdr 8th...........* (33 to 1) ur
Dist: 3½l, nk, 4l, 4l, 20l. 6m 56.80s. a 61.80s (8 Ran).
(J E Greenall), Miss C Saunders

2766 Soar Handicap Hurdle (0-120 4-y-o and up) £2,910 3m 110yds...... (3:50)

2256[2] RUSTINO [90] 8-10-7 P Niven, *settled midfield, steady prog hfwy, led aftr 3 out, rdn and ran on wl r-in.*
.... (10 to 1 op 8 to 1) 1
2519[2] TALBOT [101] 8-11-4 J Osborne, *al frnt rnk, led 6th till aftr 3 out, edgd rght r-in, one pace.*
.... (7 to 1 op 6 to 1 tchd 8 to 1) 2
2597[2] RIMAOSKI [100] 6-11-3 Mr J Cambidge, *rear till prog 9th, hit last, no extr...........* (8 to 1 op 7 to 1) 3
2502* MISS CAPULET [85] (bl) 7-9-11 (5*) T Eley, *pressed ldrs till rdn and lost pl 8th, styd on ag'n frm 2 out.*
.... (9 to 1 op 7 to 1 tchd 10 to 1) 4
2400[4] GEORGE BUCKINGHAM [93] 9-10-10 M A FitzGerald, *wtd wth, hdwy 8th, no further prog frm 3 out.*
.... (25 to 1 op 20 to 1) 5
2512[4] SIR CRUSTY [94] 12-10-4 (7*) P Maddock, *hld up in rear, mstk 6th, styd on frm 2 out, not rch ldrs.*
.... (25 to 1 op 20 to 1) 6
2561[3] FARMER'S CROSS [90] 10-10-7 Mrs A Farrell, *some prog whn mstk 8th, lost pl appr 3 out, no dngr aftr.*
.... (25 to 1 op 20 to 1) 7
2507 SPARTAN TIMES [103] 10-11-6 B Powell, *jnd ldrs 3rd, rdn and lost pl hfwy, no dngr aftr.*
.... (12 to 1 op 10 to 1 tchd 16 to 1) 8

2502 SKIRCOAT GREEN [88] 9-10-5 R Dunwoody, *led till 6th, mstks 8th and 9th, sn btn*............(7 to 2 fav op 9 to 2) 9
2528⁵ DECIDED (Can) [94] 11-10-6 (5*) Miss P Jones, *chsd ldrs till wknd appr 3 out*............................(20 to 1) 10
2338² GORT [109] 6-11-12 A Maguire, *mid-div till drpd rear 4th, wl beh frm 7th*......................(12 to 1 op 10 to 1) 11
2500² IVY HOUSE (Ire) [105] 6-11-8 M Dwyer, *shrtlvd effrt 9th.* ....(6 to 1 op 5 to 1) 12
2502³ BADASTAN (Ire) [83] 5-10-0 N Williamson, *chsd ldg grp, rdn hfwy, struggling whn mstk 8th*....(12 to 1 op 10 to 1) 13
2536³ CAMBO (USA) [91] 8-10-8 D Skyrme, *pressed ldrs till wknd appr 3 out*....................(20 to 1 op 16 to 1) 14
2600³ ROCHESTOWN LASS [104] (v) 8-11-7 N Mann, *wl plcd to hfwy, tld off whn pld up bef 3 out.* (16 to 1 op 14 to 1) pu
2428⁵ MOUNTAIN MASTER [83] 8-9-11 (3*) J McCarthy, *wl plcd till mstk 7th, tld off whn pld up bef 2 out.* ....(25 to 1 op 20 to 1) pu
2600⁶ POLLERTON'S PRIDE [90] 7-10-7 Diane Clay, *in rear, rdn 6th, sn tld off, pld up bef 2 out*..............(25 to 1) pu
Dist: 3½l, 1½l, 15l, ½l, 2½l, 12l, 2l, nk, 8l, ½l. 6m 22.40s. a 34.40s (17 Ran).
SR: 29/36/33/3/10/8/-/3/-/   (Mrs E A Kettlewell), Mrs M Reveley

2767 Derwent Novices' Chase (5-y-o and up) £2,596 2m 5f 110yds....... (4:20)

2524⁶ MELEAGRIS 10-11-2 A Maguire, *hld up in rear, prog hfwy, led last, edgd lft, rdn out.* ....(9 to 2 op 5 to 1 tchd 6 to 1) 1
2406³ COMEDY SPY 10-11-2 M A FitzGerald, *cl up, hit 5th, led 14th to last, rdn and ran on*...........(6 to 1 op 9 to 2) 2
2355 HUDSON BAY TRADER (USA) 7-11-2 Mrs A Farrell, *wl beh 9th, kpt on past btn horses r-in*....(14 to 1 op 12 to 1) 3
2427* RAKAIA RIVER (NZ) 7-11-8 B Powell, *wl plcd, hit 6th, dsptd ld 11th till blun 13th, mstk nxt, wknd 2 out.* ....(5 to 1 op 7 to 2) 4
2273 HOW DOUDO 7-10-11 R Bellamy, *prmnt, hit 6th, sn lost pl and wl beh, hdwy 13th, wknd 4 out.*........(20 to 1) 5
1754 WANDERWEG (Fr) 6-11-2 J Osborne, *led second till 14th, wknd 3 out*.......................(7 to 2 op 5 to 2) 6
2577² JUPITER MOON 5-10-7 J Railton, *led till hdd and f second*......................................(12 to 1 op 20 to 1) f
2493³ YOUR WELL 8-11-8 B Clifford, *hmpd and uns rdr second.* .....(11 to 4 fav op 2 to 1 tchd 3 to 1 and 100 to 30) ur
2637 TAURIAN PRINCESS 5-10-2 D Bridgwater, *blun and uns rdr second*....................(25 to 1 tchd 33 to 1) ur
Dist: 1½l, 20l, 1l, 5l, 12l. 5m 52.10s. a 39.10s (9 Ran).
(D J Jackson), D Nicholson

2768 Woodborough Novices' Handicap Hurdle (0-100 4-y-o and up) £1,553 2m 5f 110yds.................... (4:50)

1137 PATROCLUS [66] 9-9-9 (5*) T Eley, *led briefly aftr 3rd, led 8th, edgd lft r-in, ran on wl und pres*............(33 to 1) 1
2144⁹ SOLO GENT [66] 5-10-0 S McNeill, *settled in rear, improved 8th, chlgd last, kpt on same pace*....(14 to 1) 2
2583² ALI'S ALIBI [90] 7-11-10 P Niven, *hld up and beh, hdwy frm hfwy, wknd quickly last.*..(9 to 4 fav tchd 3 to 1) 3
2483³ RACE TO THE RHYTHM [78] 7-10-12 C Llewellyn, *in rear, lost tch hfwy, styd on past btn horses r-in.* ....(9 to 2 op 4 to 1 tchd 5 to 1) 4
2428* ANILAFFED [78] (v) 4-10-12 D Gallagher, *prmnt, lost pl 6th, rnwd effrt 8th, wknd appr 3 out.* ....(5 to 1 op 7 to 2 tchd 11 to 2) 5
2686³ LACURVA (Ire) [77] 6-10-4 (7*) P Ward, *prog 7th, wknd appr 3 out*...........................(9 to 2 tchd 6 to 1) 6
2483⁶ THE OVERTRUMPER [66] 7-10-0 R Dunwoody, *led 4th to 8th, mstk 9th, lost pl quickly appr 3 out.* ....(10 to 1 op 8 to 1 tchd 12 to 1) 7
2686 EASTERN PLEASURE [81] 7-11-1 Diane Clay, *effrt 5th, wknd 7th, tld off*.................(25 to 1 op 20 to 1) 8
2686 PENLEA LADY [66] 7-10-0 A Maguire, *wl plcd to hfwy, tld off whn pld up bef 3 out.* ....(9 to 1 op 8 to 1 tchd 10 to 1) pu
2361 SNICKERSNEE [66] 6-10-0 W Marston, *led till aftr 3rd, hit 5th, lost pl quickly 8th, pld up aftr nxt*.......(10 to 1) pu
2275 STREPHON (Ire) [80] 4-11-0 M Dwyer, *shrtlvd effrt 7th, tld off whn pld up bef 3 out*............(12 to 1) pu
2409 JUST WOODY [71] 6-9-12 (7*) G Tormey, *wth ldrs whn pld up lme aftr 9th, destroyed*..............(14 to 1) pu
Dist: 2½l, 30l, ¾l, 8l, ½l, ½l. Dist: dsm 5m 39.00s. a 37.00s (12 Ran).
(Applied Signals Limited), J Mackie

BORDEAUX LE BOUCAT (FR) (very soft)
Wednesday March 2nd

2769 Grande Course de Haies du Bouscat (Hurdle) (5-y-o and up) £8,581 2m 1f 110yds.................... (1:00)

1840⁴ MAN TO MAN (NZ) 7-10-4 A Kondrat, *made all*........... 1
MARCUS MATHEUS (Fr) 6-10-12 H Serveau, ... 2
LINE SAJ (Fr) 5-10-10 C Pieux, ... 3
Dist: Nk, 8l, 1½l. (Time not taken) (10 Ran).
(Stanley Clarke), F Doumen

DOWNPATRICK (IRE) (heavy)

Wednesday March 2nd

2770 Erdelistan Opportunity Maiden Hurdle (6-y-o and up) £1,380 2m 1f 172yds ....(2:30)

2236 TREACYS CROSS 8-11-4 (2*) P A Roche, ...(8 to 1) 1
2586 SISTER NORA (Ire) 6-10-13 (2*) M M Mackin, ...(6 to 1) 2
2351 BOY BLUE 7-11-6 T J O'Sullivan, ...(8 to 1) 3
SLANEY BACON 7-11-2 (4*) D J Kavanagh, ...(5 to 1) 4
2464 BLACK AVENUE (Ire) 6-11-1 T J Mitchell, ...(7 to 2 fav) 5
2464 PILS INVADER (Ire) 6-10-13 (2*) D T Evans, ...(25 to 1) 6
2311 SERIOUS NOTE (Ire) 6-10-13 (2*) K P Gaule, ...(10 to 1) 7
YANKEE TRADER 7-11-5 (4*) D Fisher, ...(14 to 1) 8
SHEPHERDS KATE (Ire) 6-10-13 (2*) D Walsh, ...(10 to 1) 9
FRED 'N'GINGER (Ire) 6-11-2 (4*) J P Broderick, ...(22 to 1) 10
1379 MIRASEL 7-11-5 (4*) M Kelly, ...(5 to 1) 11
BREACADH AN LAE (Ire) 6-10-11 (4*) P Stafford, ..(10 to 1) 12
BASTILLE DAY 7-11-10 (4*) T Martin, ...(14 to 1) 13
2311 BRISCE HILL (Ire) 6-11-1 K B Walsh, ...(20 to 1) 14
1832 FOYLE BOREEN 7-10-11 (4*) D O'Driscoll, ...(25 to 1) 15
Dist: 2l, 1l, 2l, 3½l. (Time not taken) (15 Ran).
(Richard St John), H de Bromhead

2771 Rea's Hotel & Restaurant Maiden Hurdle (4 & 5-y-o) £1,380 2m 1f 172yds ....(3:00)

2465⁷ OVER THE MALLARD (Ire) 5-11-1 (3*) D Bromley, (3 to 1 jt-fav) 1
2349⁷ DUCHESS AFFAIR (Ire) 4-10-1 (7*) C McCormack, (16 to 1) 2
2314⁷ JULEIT JONES (Ire) 5-10-13 F J Flood, ...(9 to 2) 3
2679⁹ RADICAL NURSE (Ire) 5-10-6 (7*) P Mulligan, ...(20 to 1) 4
2703⁹ NATINA (Ire) 5-10-13 P Mooney, ...(10 to 1) 5
2056⁵ RAHAN BRIDGE (Ire) 5-10-13 M A Martin, ...(6 to 1) 6
MAJA GRADDNOS 4-10-10 (3*) K B Walsh, ...(20 to 1) 7
2586 MY HALL DOOR 5-10-13 (5*) D T Evans, ...(20 to 1) 8
2679 SILVERFORT LAD (Ire) 5-10-13 (5*) T P Rudd, ...(8 to 1) 9
2750⁶ PRINTOUT (Ire) 4-10-8 H Rogers, ...(3 to 1 jt-fav) 10
2314⁸ THE THIRD MAN (Ire) 5-10-13 (5*) J P Broderick, ..(14 to 1) 11
2678⁷ SPECIAL OFFER (Ire) 4-10-8 B Sheridan, ...(12 to 1) 12
253 TANDRAGEE LADY (Ire) 4-10-1 (7*) R J Gordan, ..(33 to 1) 13
2464 SIMONE STAR (Ire) 5-10-13 A Powell, ...(16 to 1) 14
2586 LIFFEYSIDE LADY (Ire) (bl) 5-10-6 (7*) D M Bean, ..(25 to 1) 15
Dist: ¾l, 7l, 1½l, ½l. (Time not taken) (15 Ran).
(Mallard Racing Syndicate), Peter Casey

2772 Harp Lager National EBF Handicap Chase (0-116 5-y-o and up) £4,140 3 ½m........................(3:30)

2619⁴ MERLYNS CHOICE [-] 10-9-7 T Horgan, ...(7 to 1) 1
2312* IL TROVATORE (USA) [-] 8-11-0 P Carberry, ...(4 to 1) 2
2701⁷ GREEN TIMES [-] 9-11-5 C F Swan, ...(8 to 1) 3
2053² LA-GREINE [-] 7-10-3 (3*) Mr P McMahon, ...(8 to 1) 4
2590* SADDLESTOWN GLEN [-] 9-10-3 H Rogers, ...(10 to 1) 5
2393⁴ WRECKLESS MAN [-] 7-10-12 (5*) P A Roche, ...(8 to 1) 6
2662⁸ KNOCKNACARRA LAD [-] 9-11-1 J Shortt, ...(16 to 1) 7
2025* WYLDE HIDE [-] 7-9-12 F Woods, ...(7 to 2 fav) 8
2662⁴ DUSKY LADY [-] 8-10-7 J F Titley, ...(10 to 1) 9
2125 LACKEN BEAU [-] 10-11-9 (5*) J P Broderick, ...(25 to 1) 10
2393 CASTLE BRANDON [-] 8-11-5 F J Flood, ...(7 to 1) ur
Dist: ¾l, nk, 1½l, 13l. (Time not taken) (11 Ran).
(J A Keogh), A P O'Brien

2773 Fuel Services (NI) Hunters' Chase (5-y-o and up) £1,380 3m......... (4:00)

2551³ TASSE DU THE 7-10-13 Mr A J Martin, ...(6 to 4 on) 1
NEDA CHARMER 8-10-11 (7*) Mr L J Gracey, ...(4 to 1) 2
LUCY'S CYGNET 11-10-11 (7*) Mr W Ewing, ...(14 to 1) 3
GLENSPORT VI 8-10-6³ (7*) Mr J A Quinn, ...(12 to 1) 4
ITSUPTOME VI 7-10-11 (7*) Mr J Bright, ...(20 to 1) 5
WHITESIDES FORT 11-10-11 (7*) Mr D M Christie, (33 to 1) f
SWORDBENDER (Ire) 5-10-5 (5*) Mr B R Hamilton, (8 to 1) f
1013 MASTER MILLER 8-10-11³ (7*) Mr R J Patton, ...(12 to 1) ur
COCO DANCER 12-10-11⁴ (7*) Mr C A McBratney, (9 to 1) pu
FITIZIT 7-10-6 (7*) Mr B Morgan, ...(33 to 1) pu
Dist: 7l, 1½l, ½l. Dist. (Time not taken) (10 Ran).
(Mrs M E Foster), Capt D C Foster

2774 P J McCartan Bookmaker Novice Chase (5-y-o and up) £1,380 2¼m ....(4:30)

1894⁹ FOGELBERG (USA) 6-12-0 C O'Dwyer, ...(5 to 1) 1D
2181³ JIMS CHOICE 7-11-2 (7*) Mr R J Patton, ...(25 to 1) 1
2313⁷ REDELVA 7-11-4 F Woods, ...(7 to 2) 3
2661⁸ THE MAD MONK 9-12-0 M Flynn, ...(12 to 1) 3
2313³ SPARKLING BLAKE 8-11-2¹ (7*) Mr I Buchanan, ..(8 to 1) 4
2618 LINVAR 11-12-0 J Jones, ...(12 to 1) 5
1576 SHANDONAGH BRIDGE 7-11-9 F J Flood, ...(8 to 1) 6
22 TRASSEY BRIDGE 7-11-9 A Powell, ...(12 to 1) 7
JIMMYS DOUBLE 8-11-2 (7*) Mr J J Canavan, ...(33 to 1) 8
1832 FIDSPRIT 7-11-1 (3*) K B Walsh, ...(20 to 1) 9
2309 GALZIG 6-11-9 H Rogers, ...(16 to 1) f

2703 MILLENIUM LASS (Ire) 6-11-4 C F Swan, ... (3 to 1 fav) f
LUCKY LANCER (Ire) 6-11-9 J F Titley, ... (12 to 1) pu
Dist: 3½l, 12l, 3½l, 3l. (Time not taken) (13 Ran).
(Mrs M E Hagan), William Patton

2775 Rhyme 'N' Reason Flat Race (4 & 5-y-o) £1,380 2m 1f 172yds......... (5:00)

2465^{9} KEY WEST (Ire) 5-11-13 Mr A J Martin, ... (10 to 1) 1
2177^{8} CUTTER'S WHARF (Ire) 5-11-8 (5*) Mr B R Hamilton, ... (11 to 4) 2
2616^{2} SIOBHAILIN DUBH (Ire) (bl) 5-11-8 Mr A P O'Brien, ... (Evens fav) 3
GRANDOLLY (Ire) 5-11-5 (3*) Mr D Marnane, ... (10 to 1) 4
BONDIR (Ire) 5-11-10 (3*) Mr P McMahon, ... (20 to 1) 5
EASY WONDER (Ire) 4-11-2 (3*) Mr A R Coonan, .. (10 to 1) 6
COTHU NA SLAINE (Ire) 4-10-7 (7*) Mr B Morgan, (20 to 1) 7
BARNISH DAWN (Ire) 4-10-7 (7*) Mr S Kerr, ... (25 to 1) 8
DRUMRUSK (Ire) 4-10-7^{1} (7*) Mr L J Gracey, ... (12 to 1) 9
MICHAEL'S PET (Ire) 4-10-7 (7*) Mr C Andrews, ... (33 to 1) 10
2470 SECRET COURSE (Ire) 5-11-1 (7*) Mr J McGuinness, ... (20 to 1) su
Dist: Sht-hd, 5½l, 10l, sht-hd. (Time not taken) (11 Ran).
(Mrs David Sherlock), Patrick Mooney

FONTWELL (good to soft)
Wednesday March 2nd
Going Correction: PLUS 1.50 sec. per fur.

2776 Littlehampton Gazette Novices' Claiming Hurdle (4-y-o and up) £1,922 2¼m.......................... (2:10)

2433* ERICOLIN (Ire) 4-11-5 G McCourt, *patiently rdn in tch, smooth hdwy appr 3 out, sn chalg, led last, drvn out.* .... (7 to 4 on tchd 6 to 4 on) 1
1456 TALLAND STREAM 7-11-10 (3*) R Farrant, *al prmnt, led appr 2 out till hdd last, hrd rdn and one pace.* .... (12 to 1 op 8 to 1 tchd 14 to 1) 2
LEAVE IT OUT 12-11-3 J Frost, *wl beh till styd on frm 2 out, nrst finish*..............(66 to 1 op 33 to 1) 3
2652^{7} ABU DANCER (Ire) 4-11-1 A Charlton, *wl beh till some hdwy frm 2 out, nvr a dngr.* .... (50 to 1 op 25 to 1 tchd 66 to 1) 4
2033 COUNTRYWIDE LAD 5-11-9 Peter Hobbs, *hld up in midfield, hdwy aftr 5th and sn chasing ldrs, wknd appr 2 out*.............................. (20 to 1 op 16 to 1) 5
2708 LETTS GREEN (Ire) 6-11-1 D Morris, *hld up and beh, moderate hdwy frm 2 out, nvr able to chal.* .... (50 to 1 op 25 to 1) 6
1589^{7} TEA-LADY (Ire) 6-11-4 S McNeill, *handily plcd, ev ch 3 out, sn wknd*....... (16 to 1 op 12 to 1 tchd 20 to 1) 7
486 MINT FRESH (bl) 7-10-12 (7*) Mr E James, *prmnt till wknd frm 6th*.......................... (66 to 1 op 33 to 1) 8
2454^{4} BORRETO 10-10-8 (7*) Katherine Davis, *al beh.* .... (14 to 1 op 10 to 1) 9
2147^{7} BIDDLESTONE BOY (NZ) 7-11-2 (7*) Mr G Shenkin, *al prmnt, led 3 out, sn hdd and wknd quickly.* .... (8 to 1 op 6 to 1 tchd 10 to 1) 10
2708 WITCHWAY NORTH (v) 4-11-0 V Smith, *led till hdd 3 out, sn rgned ld till wknd quickly appr nxt.* .... (14 to 1 op 10 to 1) 11
1632^{6} NORTHERN TRIAL (USA) 6-11-11 A Carroll, *prmnt till niggled alng and lost pl hfwy, beh whn pld up bef 2 out.* ....(7 to 1 op 4 to 1 tchd 11 to 1 and 12 to 1) pu
2560 PINBER 6-10-9 (7*) Mr S Mulcaire, *midfield, niggled alng hfwy, sn wknd, tld off whn pld up bef 2 out.* .... (66 to 1 op 33 to 1) pu
Dist: 1½l, 12l, 6l, 8l, 2l, 20l, 2l, ½l, 1½l, ½l. 4m 48.60s. a 38.60s (13 Ran).
(Gormley Marble Ltd), N Tinkler

2777 Monaveen Handicap Chase (0-110 5-y-o and up) £2,484 2m 3f...... (2:40)

WYLAM [84] 7-10-4 D Murphy, *cl up gng wl, led 12th, clr 3 out, cmftbly*............(9 to 2 op 4 to 1 tchd 5 to 1) 1
2491* SARTORIUS [108] 8-12-0 B Powell, *wl plcd, led 9th, hdd 12th, sn pushed alng and not pace of wnr.* ....(11 to 8 fav op 5 to 4 tchd 6 to 4) 2
2491^{3} GENERAL MERCHANT [90] (bl) 14-10-10 R Dunwoody, *trkd ldrs, rdn aftr 3 out, sn unbl to quicken.* ....(5 to 1 op 4 to 1) 3
2120^{7} AIR COMMANDER [101] 9-11-0 (7*) Mr S Joynes, *led to 9th, wknd frm 4 out, tld off*............ (33 to 1 op 16 to 1) 4
2622^{4} ZAMIL (USA) [105] (bl) 9-11-11 N Williamson, *trkd ldr till hit 7th, sn lost pl and not look keen, tld off.* ....(8 to 1 op 6 to 1 tchd 9 to 1) 5
2520^{5} ON YOUR WAY [80] (v) 12-10-0 A Maguire, *not jump wl, al beh, tld off whn pld up bef 12th*... (20 to 1 op 16 to 1) pu
2142^{8} CHIAROSCURO [80] 8-10-0 M Hourigan, *sn beh, tried to refuse 7th, pld up bef nxt*.......... (6 to 1 tchd 7 to 1) pu
Dist: 10l, 3l, dist, dist. 5m 9.00s. a 34.00s (7 Ran).
SR: 21/35/14/-/ (Mrs J S Wootton), J T Gifford

2778 Portobello Trader Novices' Chase (5-y-o and up) £2,185 2¼m........ (3:10)

1644^{5} ALL FOR LUCK 9-11-4 R Dunwoody, *lft in ld 4th, hdd 7th, led 9th, clr whn jmpd rght last 3, easily.* ....(9 to 2 op 4 to 1) 1
1594^{3} URBAN COWBOY 7-11-4 S McNeill, *hld up and beh, styd on frm 4 out, wnt second nxt, no ch wth wnr.* ....(16 to 1 tchd 20 to 1) 2
2528^{4} JACKSON FLINT 6-11-4 S Smith Eccles, *cl up, ev ch whn mstk 4 out (water), second and no imprsn when blun nxt, sn btn*........................ (3 to 1 tchd 4 to 1) 3
2458 WHYFOR 6-10-13 (5*) D Salter, *pld hrd, trkd ldrs, ev ch appr 4 out, wknd bef nxt*........ (100 to 1 op 50 to 1) 4
2625^{2} HARBINGER 9-11-1 (3*) P Hide, *lft second 4th, led 7th till hdd 9th, sn lost pl*....(16 to 1 op 14 to 1 tchd 20 to 1) 5
2527 ESSEN AITCH 5-10-5 V Slattery, *lost tch frm 9th, tld off.* .... (100 to 1 op 50 to 1) 6
1124 AMTRAK EXPRESS 7-11-10 M A FitzGerald, *led till o'r-jmpd and f 4th*............(Evens fav op 6 to 4 on) f
Dist: 25l, 4l, 12l, 1½l, dist. 4m 56.10s. a 36.10s (7 Ran).
(B J Craig), M C Pipe

2779 Tuscan 'National Hunt' Novices' Hurdle (5-y-o and up) £2,138 2¾m.. (3:40)

2459* SEE ENOUGH 6-11-7 A Tory, *al prmnt, led 2 out, rdn out.* ....(9 to 4 op 2 to 1 tchd 5 to 2) 1
2604^{3} DO BE HAVE (Ire) 6-11-0 J Osborne, *led aftr 3rd, hng lft and hdd 2 out, ran on one pace.* ....(4 to 1 op 9 to 2 tchd 5 to 1) 2
2459^{2} BOOK OF MUSIC (Ire) 6-11-7 D Murphy, *patiently rdn, steady hdwy 5th, ev ch 3 out, ridden appr nxt, unbl to quicken*............ (11 to 8 fav op 5 to 4 tchd 6 to 4) 3
1715 BALLYGRIFFIN LAD (Ire) 5-11-0 W McFarland, *chsd ldg grp, no hdwy frm 8th*.......................... (100 to 1) 4
2426 GOLDEN DROPS (NZ) 6-11-0 C Maude, *beh and rdn alng 5th, sn no imprsn*................. (16 to 1 op 14 to 1) 5
TULLYKYNE BELLS 5-11-0 D Gallagher, *chsd ldg grp till wknd 8th*..................... (100 to 1 op 50 to 1) 6
2494^{6} GREEN'S GAME 6-11-0 G Upton, *led to 3rd, mstk nxt and sn lost pl*.................................. (100 to 1) 7
1548^{5} A FORTIORI (Ire) (bl) 6-11-0 R Dunwoody, *took keen hold, wth ldr, ev ch 8th, wknd appr nxt.* .... (14 to 1 op 10 to 1 tchd 16 to 1) 8
2519 ALTESSE ROXANNE 5-10-2 (7*) Mr B Pollock, *al beh, tld off*.. (100 to 1) 9
2042 BISHOPS TRUTH 8-11-0 D Morris, *al beh, no ch whn f 3 out*..(100 to 1) f
2558 LADY CAROTINO 10-10-9 L Harvey, *al beh, tld off whn pld up aftr 7th*.............................. (100 to 1) pu
2671 SARACEN'S BOY (Ire) 6-10-9 (5*) D Salter, *chsd ldrs till lost pl and rdn alng 7th, beh whn pld up bef nxt.* (100 to 1) pu
1595^{6} TIME ENOUGH (Ire) 5-11-0 R Supple, *trkd ldrs, mstk 4th, rdn 7th, sn wknd, tld off whn pld up bef 2 out.* .... (50 to 1 op 20 to 1) pu
Dist: 2½l, 8l, 25l, 6l, sht-hd, 3½l, 4l, dist. 5m 47.70s. a 38.70s (13 Ran).
SR: 36/26/25/-/-/-/ (J A G Meaden), R H Buckler

2780 Silver Shadow Novices' Handicap Chase (5-y-o and up) £2,306 3¼m 110yds...................... (4:10)

2518 PUNCH'S HOTEL [90] 9-11-5 (5*) C Burnett-Wells, *beh till hdwy tenth, led 3 out, drvn out.* .... (7 to 1 op 5 to 1 tchd 15 to 2) 1
2524^{5} HERE COMES CHARTER [77] 9-10-11 R Dunwoody, *sn led, mstk 17th, hdd nxt, led 4 out to next, hrd rdn and kpt on*................................ (9 to 2 op 7 to 2) 2
962^{2} CASTLE BLUE [84] 7-11-4 J Osborne, *trkd ldr, led 18th to nxt, styd on one pace.* ....(2 to 1 fav op 9 to 4 tchd 5 to 2) 3
2654^{3} MELDON [77] 7-10-11 S Burrough, *trkd ldrs till drpd last 15th, tld off*........... (9 to 4 op 2 to 1 tchd 5 to 2) 4
1463 MAJOR ELSTON [66] 9-9-13^{2} (3*) P Hide, *in tch till wknd 16th, tld off*.........(50 to 1 op 33 to 1 tchd 66 to 1) 5
2543 PAPER STAR [69] 7-10-3 M Ahern, *in tch, wkng whn blun 17th, tld off*.................... (10 to 1 tchd 12 to 1) 6
2706^{4} YOUNG ALFIE [80] 9-11-0 Miss S Belcher, *not fluent, al beh, tld off whn pld up bef 13th*... (33 to 1 op 20 to 1) pu
2654^{5} MISS MUIRE [72] 8-10-6 D Morris, *not fluent, lost tch frm 16th, beh whn pld up bef 3 out.* .... (14 to 1 op 12 to 1 tchd 16 to 1) pu
2717 KATIEM'LU [66] 8-9-9 (5*) D Salter, *trkd ldrs till wknd 15th, beh whn pld up bef 4 out*........... (50 to 1 op 33 to 1) pu
Dist: 3l, 1½l, dist, 2½l, dist. 7m 28.10s. a 58.10s (9 Ran).
(Mrs A E Dawes), R Rowe

2781 Comedy Of Errors Handicap Hurdle (4-y-o and up) £2,267 2¼m...... (4:40)

2710* KOVALEVSKIA [90] 9-11-7 (6ex) A Maguire, *hld up in tch, hdwy 6th, led nxt, pushed clr r-in.* ....(2 to 1 fav op 5 to 2) 1
2142^{3} ALOSAILI [89] 7-11-6 M Stevens, *hld up, hdwy aftr 3 out, wnt second nxt, styd on one pace r-in.* ....(8 to 1 op 7 to 1 tchd 9 to 1) 2
2653^{3} CHARCOAL BURNER [79] 9-10-10 S Burrough, *keen hold, prmnt, ev ch appr 2 out, sn no extr.* ....(7 to 2 op 3 to 1 tchd 4 to 1) 3

24784 STAR MARKET [77] 4-10-8 T Wall, *trkd ldrs, led 6th to nxt, wknd appr 2 out*...... (10 to 1 op 7 to 1 tchd 11 to 1) 4
27177 MILDRED SOPHIA [73] 7-9-11 (7") Miss S Mitchell, *hld up, hdwy appr 6th, ev ch bef 2 out, sn btn.*
.... (6 to 1 tchd 7 to 1) 5
26414 CYRILL HENRY (Ire) [73] 5-10-4 C Maude, *patiently rdn, took clr order appr 3 out, shaken up aftr nxt, sn wknd.*
.... (12 to 1 op 10 to 1) 6
26976 J BRAND [93] 7-11-10 A Tory, *led on 6th, wknd 3 out.*
.... (12 to 1 op 10 to 1) 7
24009 LUCKY OAK [75] 8-10-6 R Dunwoody, *wth ldr till wknd quickly appr 3 out, sn last, tld off.*
.... (10 to 1 op 12 to 1 tchd 14 to 1) 8
Dist: 7l, 15l, 1½l, 1l, 20l, 2l, dist. 4m 43.40s. a 33.40s (8 Ran).
SR: 29/21/-/-/-/-/ (D A Wilson), D A Wilson

WETHERBY (soft)
Wednesday March 2nd
Going Correction: PLUS 1.70 sec. per fur.

2782 Bramham Hunters' Chase (6-y-o and up) £1,660 2½m 110yds........(1:55)

26054 QUEEN'S CHAPLAIN 10-11-10 (7") Mrs M Morris, *in tch, hdwy to dispute ld aftr 6th, mstk 2 out, styd on wl r-in.*
...... (15 to 8 fav op 7 to 4 tchd 13 to 8 and 2 to 1) 1
GOGGINS HILL 7-11-7 Mr J Greenall, *hld up beh, hdwy aftr 6th, led or dsptd ld frm nxt, rdn aftr 3 out, no extr r-in*.............................. (9 to 4 op 3 to 1) 2
BACK IN BUSINESS 11-11-0 (7") Miss H McCaul, *in tch, dsptd ld tenth, ev ch 4 out, sn rdn, mstk 2 out, kpt on same pace*....................... (5 to 1 op 4 to 1) 3
CONVINCING 10-11-0 (7") Mr P Cornforth, *cl up, led 5th till aftr nxt, wknd after 11th, beh whn pld up bef 2 out.*
.... (33 to 1) pu
IVEAGH LAD 8-11-2 (5") Mr N Tutty, *led to 5th, prmnt till wknd aftr 11th, beh whn pld up bef 4 out.*
.... (3 to 1 op 2 to 1) pu
Dist: 2l, 4l. 5m 50.70s. a 54.20s (5 Ran).
(E F Astley-Arlington), Mrs M Morris

2783 Harewood Novices' Hurdle (4-y-o) £2,354 2m.................. (2:25)

2573* BEND SABLE (Ire) 11-3 B Storey, *mstk 1st, hld up in tch, rdn appr 2 out, ran on wl.*
.... (8 to 1 tchd 10 to 1) 1
25642 CALL MY GUEST (Ire) 10-3 (7") F Leahy, *trkd ldrs, led 3 out to nxt, kpt on, no ch wth wnr.*
.... (11 to 10 fav op 6 to 4 tchd Evens) 2
24853 WEAVER GEORGE (Ire) 10-5 (5") J Supple, *in tch, styd on wl und pres frm 2 out.*................ (6 to 1 op 5 to 1) 3
26386 VOLUNTEER POINT (Ire) 10-5 (5") J Burke, *led to 3 out, sn rdn, kpt on same pace*............. (25 to 1 op 20 to 1) 4
I'M A DREAMER (Ire) 10-10 R Garritty, *beh, hdwy aftr 5th, kpt on same pace 3 out*............. (16 to 1 op 14 to 1) 5
25649 ZAAHEYAH (USA) 10-0 (5") S Lyons, *beh, hdwy aftr 6th, nvr rch ldrs*................................. (33 to 1) 6
14837 QUEEN OF THE QUORN 10-5 J Callaghan, *cl up, dsptd ld 6th till wknd aftr 3 out*............. (16 to 1 op 14 to 1) 7
23693 REBEL KING 10-10 A Dobbin, *chsd ldrs till wknd appr 3 out*.. (16 to 1) 8
25645 FREF (USA) 11-0 (3") N Bentley, *prmnt till wknd appr 3 out*........................... (11 to 1 op 8 to 1) 9
22755 GYMCRAK TIGER (Ire) 10-10 R Marley, *in tch till wknd appr 6th*.. (20 to 1) 10
SUDDEN SPIN 10-10 O Pears, *in tch till wknd appr 6th, tld off*.......................... (8 to 1 op 7 to 1) 11
CIRCUS COLOURS 10-10 Richard Guest, *in tch till wknd appr 6th, tld off*.......................... (8 to 1 op 7 to 1) 12
25646 CIVIL LAW (Ire) 10-10 C Hawkins, *al beh, lost tch and pld up bef 6th*.......................... (11 to 1 op 8 to 1) pu
24337 THATCHED (Ire) 10-10 N Smith, *prmnt till wknd appr 6th, beh whn pld up bef last*....................... (50 to 1) pu
2564 LINGCOOL 10-5 L Wyer, *in tch till wknd quickly appr 6th whn pld up bef 3 out*.......... (33 to 1 op 25 to 1) pu
Dist: 4l, 2l, 7l, 1½l, 1½l, 3½l, nk, 8l, 10l, 4l. 4m 15.00s. a 34.00s (15 Ran).
SR: 21/10/8/1/-/-/ (F S Storey), F S Storey

2784 Sicklinghall Novices' Chase (6-y-o and up) £3,817 3m 110yds...... (2:55)

26683 BRABAZON (USA) 9-11-0 M Richards, *blun 1st, sn pushed alng, outpcd hfwy, rallied appr 4 out, led nxt, hit 2 out, styd on und pres*.............. (5 to 1 op 6 to 1 tchd 7 to 1) 1
11845 UNGUIDED MISSILE (Ire) 6-11-0 N Doughty, *led to 3 out, sn same pace*................... (20 to 1 op 12 to 1) 2
2497* LO STREGONE 8-11-9 M Dwyer, *mstk second, trkd ldr, rdn approaching 4 out, wknd aftr nxt.*
.... (11 to 10 fav tchd Evens and 6 to 5) 3
24975 IRISH GENT 8-11-0 K Johnson, *not jump wl, sn beh and pushed alng, lost tch hfwy, tld off.* (33 to 1 op 20 to 1) 4
2137 BRACKENFIELD 8-11-9 P Niven, *trkd ldrs till f 11th.*
.... (7 to 4 op 5 to 4 tchd 15 to 8) f
Dist: 10l, dist, dist. 7m 12.90s. a 66.90s (5 Ran).
(P H Betts (Holdings) Ltd), M H Tompkins

2785 Hoechst Panacur EBF Mares 'National Hunt' Novices' Hurdle Qualifier (5-y-o and up) £2,427 2½m 110yds..... (3:25)

24473 CARNETTO 7-11-0 (7") F Leahy, *trkd ldrs, pushed alng appr 3 out, led approaching last, styd on wl.*
.... (11 to 2 op 4 to 1) 1
2573 SCRABBLE 5-10-7 Richard Guest, *sn prmnt, slight ld 3 out, hdd appr last, no extr*........ (14 to 1 op 10 to 1) 2
23562 MEGA BLUE 9-11-7 J Callaghan, *cl up, led 7t to 3 out, one pace*.................. (5 to 1 op 4 to 1 tchd 11 to 2) 3
23262 MANETTIA (Ire) 5-10-7 P Niven, *hld up in tch, hdwy hfwy, ev ch 7th, wknd appr 3 out.*
.... (100 to 30 op 3 to 1 tchd 7 to 2) 4
2500 CROSS REFERENCE 6-10-7 T Reed, *pld hrd early, in tch till wknd aftr 7th*........... (50 to 1 op 33 to 1) 5
23267 CATCH THE PIGEON 5-10-7 N Smith, *in tch till wknd aftr 7th*................... (50 to 1 op 33 to 1) 6
17516 BIN LID (Ire) 5-10-0 (7") B Harding, *in tch till wknd aftr 7th.*........................... (33 to 1 op 20 to 1) 7
MIDNIGHT FLOTILLA 8-10-7 C Hawkins, *led to 7th, sn wknd.*................................. (50 to 1) 8
2500 COMPANY SECRETARY 6-10-11 (7") A Linton, *in tch, rdn aftr 7th, sn wknd*........................ (50 to 1) 9
22202 LOCH SCAVAIG (Ire) 5-10-11 (3") D J Moffatt, *mid-div whn f 4th*..................... (2 to 1 fav op 5 to 2) f
26714 MRS MONEYPENNY 5-10-7 (7") P Ward, *cl up whn f 4th.*.................................... (7 to 1 op 10 to 1) f
2407 CACAHWETE 5-10-0 (7") Mr D Parker, *in tch whn bright dwn 4th*.............................. (33 to 1) bd
2409 MIDORI 6-10-4 (3") A Thornton, *tld off whn pld up bef 7th.*.............................. (50 to 1) pu
23262 CHORUS LINE (Ire) 5-10-7 M Dwyer, *beh whn pld up bef 3 out*..................... (25 to 1 tchd 33 to 1) pu
Dist: 4l, 8l, 20l, 15l, 4l, 20l, 8l, 15l. 5m 33.20s. a 46.20s (14 Ran).
(Mrs R Brewis), R Brewis

2786 East Keswick Handicap Chase (0-140 5-y-o and up) £4,077 2½m 110yds
.... (3:55)

24893 PRINCE YAZA [107] 7-10-1 L O'Hara, *in tch, jnd ldrs 8th, drvn alng aftr 11th, slight ld after 4 out, kpt on wl und pres r-in*...................... (33 to 1 op 20 to 1) 1
24885 DAWSON CITY [135] 7-12-0 L Wyer, *cl up, dsptd ld 8th till no extr und pres r-in.*
.... (6 to 5 on op 11 to 10 on tchd 5 to 4 on) 2
21395 CANDY TUFF [118] 8-10-3 P Niven, *not fluent, in tch, effrt aftr tenth, no imprsn till styd on wl frm 2 out.*
.... (9 to 4 op 2 to 1 tchd 5 to 2) 3
22466 REPEAT THE DOSE [130] 9-11-9 M Richards, *led or dsptd ld, mstk 3rd, hdd aftr 4 out, sn btn.*
.... (5 to 1 tchd 11 to 2) 4
STRONG SOUND [107] 7-10-0 K Johnson, *in tch, blun tenth, sn wknd, beh whn pld up bef 2 out.*
.... (20 to 1 op 14 to 1) pu
Dist: 1½l, 7l, 4l. 5m 44.90s. a 48.40s (5 Ran).
(Mrs M E Curtis), J W Curtis

2787 Diamond Seal Windows Lady Riders' Handicap Chase (0-125 5-y-o and up) £2,742 2½m 110yds............. (4:25)

2536* BALTIC BROWN [115] 9-12-0 Gee Armytage, *made all, cmftbly*...... (5 to 4 fav tchd 11 to 10 and 11 to 8) 1
2563* MILITARY HONOUR [100] (bl) 9-10-6 (7") Miss R Clark, *blun 3rd, al chasing wnr, rdn aftr 2 out, no imprsn.*
.... (11 to 8 op 11 to 10) 2
2242 HICKELTON LAD [89] 10-9-9 (7") Miss S Higgins, *pld hrd early, al beh*...................... (10 to 1 op 12 to 1) 3
2042 MOSS BEE [87] 7-10-0 Mrs A Farrell, *chsd ldrs, lost tch aftr 6th*........................... (9 to 1 op 12 to 1) 4
Dist: 7l, dist, dist. 5m 50.20s. a 53.70s (4 Ran).
(Mrs S Smith), Mrs S J Smith

2788 Micklethwaite Handicap Hurdle (0-135 4-y-o and up) £3,288 2½m 110yds
.... (4:55)

24874 PEANUTS PET [126] 9-11-10 R Garritty, *hld up, hdwy aftr 6th, effrt appr 3 out, styd on wl to ld nr finish.*
.... (7 to 1 op 5 to 1) 1
26493 CLURICAN (Ire) [112] 5-10-5 (5") E Husband, *mid-div, effrt aftr 7th, led after 3 out, edgd lft last, hdd and no extr nr finish*......................... (10 to 1 op 8 to 1) 2
24875 VIARDOT (Ire) [126] 5-11-10 P Niven, *hld up, hdwy effrt appr 3 out, ev ch last, kpt on same pace*..... (9 to 1 op 7 to 2) 3
22222 AMBLESIDE HARVEST [111] 7-10-4 (3") A Roche, *hld up, hdwy aftr 7th, ch 3 out, sn rdn and btn.*
.... (9 to 1 op 12 to 1) 4
2403 DUHALLOW LODGE [108] 7-10-6 Richard Guest, *sn tracking ldrs, dsptd ld 7th till wknd aftr 3 out.*
.... (25 to 1 op 20 to 1) 5
20083 MASTER BOSTON (Ire) [102] 6-10-0 A Dobbin, *in tch, ch 3 out, sn rdn and wknd*........... (20 to 1 op 16 to 1) 6

2515⁵ ABBOT OF FURNESS [124] 10-11-8 N Doughty, *trkd ldrs,
led or dsptd ld frm 5th till wknd aftr 3 out.*
...................(11 to 1 op 10 to 1 tchd 12 to 1)   7
2222⁷ BELLTON [124] 6-11-8 M Dwyer, *mid-div, ev ch 3 out,
wknd quickly, tld off*................(14 to 1 op 8 to 1)   8
2528* CHIEF RAIDER (Ire) [115] 6-10-13 K Jones, *prmnt till wknd
aftr 7th, tld off*........................(11 to 1 op 10 to 1)   9
GRIS ET VIOLET (Fr) [113] 7-10-4 (7*) G Tormey, *al beh, tld
off whn pld up bef 3 out*...................(20 to 1 op 14 to 1)   pu
2256* NODDLE (USA) [114] 6-10-12 T Reed, *led till pld up lme bef
3rd*...................(7 to 4 fav op 5 to 2 tchd 11 to 4)   pu
2385 TEMPLE GARTH [105] 5-10-3 C Hawkins, *mstks, lft in ld
bef 3rd, hdd 5th, dsptd lead 7th till wknd quickly and
pld up beofre 3 out*...................(25 to 1 op 20 to 1)   pu
Dist: Nk, 2l, 10l, 3l, 7l, 4l, 25l, 15l. 5m 26.20s. a 39.20s (12 Ran).
SR: 52/37/49/24/18/5/23/-/-/   (The Ivy Syndicate), T P Tate

LUDLOW (good)
Thursday March 3rd
Going Correction: PLUS 0.80 sec. per fur. (races 1,2,-
4,7), PLUS 0.90 (3,5,6)

2789 Corvedale Novices' Hurdle (4-y-o and up) £1,550 2m.................(2:00)

2525² MONTY ROYALE (Ire) 5-11-0 (3*) A Thornton, *nvr far away,
second 2 out, rdn and quickened to ld r-in, ran on wl.*
...................(6 to 1 op 4 to 1)   1
2522* SQUIRE YORK 4-11-1 D Gallagher, *led, rdn appr last, hdd
r-in, rallied and kpt on.*
...................(13 to 8 fav op 9 to 4 tchd 5 to 2 and 6 to 4)   2
2291⁴ BENTICO 5-11-3 C Llewellyn, *al prmnt, ev ch appr 2 out,
rdn and wknd approaching last....(7 to 1 op 10 to 1)   3
2525* FED ON OATS 6-11-9 A Maguire, *al prmnt, second aftr 3
out, one pace frm nxt.*
...................(3 to 1 op 11 to 4 tchd 100 to 30)   4
2525⁶ BIG PAT 5-11-3 V Slattery, *chsd ldr till wknd appr 2 out.*
...................(6 to 1 op 5 to 1)   5
NEWHALL PRINCE 6-10-12 (5*) T Eley, *mid-div, mstk 3 out,
nvr dngrs*...................(50 to 1)   6
2599 ANLACE 5-10-12 M Perrett, *al towards rear.*
...................(50 to 1 op 33 to 1)   7
2426⁹ PRECIOUS JUNO (Ire) 5-10-5 (7*) L O'Hare, *hld up, hdwy
5th, wknd appr 2 out, tld off*......(16 to 1 op 14 to 1)   8
2045 FRANK RICH (bl) 7-11-9 J Osborne, *slwly away, al rear,
tld off*...................(50 to 1 op 40 to 1)   9
JUST FOR A LAUGH 7-10-5 (7*) R Massey, *hld up in tch,
hdwy 4th, wknd stdly appr 2 out, tld off....(100 to 1)   10
SANDY'S SONG 8-10-10 (7*) R Walker, *reluctant to race,
blun second, uns rdr nxt.*.........(100 to 1 op 50 to 1)   ur
FICHU (USA) 6-11-3 R J Beggan, *al beh, tld off whn pld
up bef 2 out.*...................(50 to 1)   pu
LLES LE BUCFLOW 6-11-3 M Hourigan, *al beh, tld off whn
pld up bef 2 out.*...................(100 to 1 op 50 to 1)   pu
BAR THREE (Ire) 5-10-12 (5*) Guy Lewis, *prmnt to 5th, tld
off whn pld up bef 2 out.*........(100 to 1 op 66 to 1)   pu
705 HOW HUMBLE (Ire) 5-10-12 T Wall, *prmnt till wknd 5th,
tld off whn pld up bef 2 out.*..................(100 to 1)   pu
2599 FILTHY REESH (bl) 5-11-3 W Humphreys, *rcd on outsd in
tch till wknd quickly aftr 3 out, pld up bef nxt.*(33 to 1)   pu
2573 SEABURN 4-10-4 (5*) J Supple, *in tch till wknd 5th, tld
off whn pld up bef 2 out.*...................(50 to 1)   pu
Dist: ½l, 12l, 2½l, 20l, 10l, dist. 3m 55.40s. a 18.40s (17 Ran).
SR: 33/30/20/23/13/12/4/-/-/   (M Worcester), K C Bailey

2790 Border Conditional Jockeys' Selling Hurdle (4-y-o and up) £1,791 2m (2:30)

2554⁴ STYLUS 5-11-6 (5*) R Massey, *nvr far away, second 5th,
led on bit appr 2 out, rdn approaching last, all out.*
...................(5 to 4 fav op 5 to 4 on)   1
2717⁴ MISS EQUILIA (USA) 8-11-4 (5*) L Reynolds, *beh till hdwy 3
out, second nxt, ev ch till not quicken cl hme.*
...................(7 to 2 op 4 to 1 tchd 9 to 2)   2
887 NOBLE INSIGHT 7-11-9 (5*) M Berry, *hld up in rear, hdwy
3 out, styd on, nvr nrr...................(7 to 1 op 4 to 1)   3
2523³ ANDRATH (Ire) 6-11-4 D Meade, *led till appr 2 out, ev ch
till rdn approaching last, one pace.*
...................(10 to 1 op 25 to 1)   4
994³ ALWAYS READY 8-11-4 (7*) J Bond, *mid-div, hdwy aftr
5th, kpt on one pace frm 2 out...* (12 to 1 tchd 14 to 1)   5
2729⁷ THANKSFORTHEOFFER 6-11-1 (3*) Pat Thompson,
towards rear till hdwy appr 2 out, nvr dngrs. (50 to 1)   6
251⁹ TANAISTE (USA) 5-10-13 (5*) Leanne Eldredge, *hit 1st, rear
...................(33 to 1)   7
2535⁶ THE HIDDEN CITY 8-11-11 A Thornton, *al beh...... (20 to 1)   8
2543⁴ COLONIAL OFFICE (USA) (bl) 8-10-13 (5*) N Juckes, *al beh,
tld off...................(33 to 1)   9
748 SULTAN'S SON 8-11-4 (7*) M Griffiths, *prmnt to 4th, sn
beh, tld off...................(16 to 1 op 14 to 1)   10
FARM STREET 7-10-13 (5*) N Collum, *chsd ldr to 5th,
wknd stdly, tld off...................(33 to 1)   11
2333 SEATWIST 5-11-4 T Eley, *beh whn hmpd 3rd, tld off.*
...................(25 to 1 op 20 to 1)   12
2302 HIGHLAND BRAVE 7-10-11 (7*) S Arnold, *prmnt to 4th, sn
beh, tld off...................(50 to 1)   13

1768 ROCKY TYRONE (bl) 7-10-11 (7*) D Webb, *prmnt to 4th, sn
beh, tld off...................(50 to 1)   14
2581 SOLO CORNET 9-11-4 S Wynne, *slwly away, beh whn f
3rd...................(33 to 1)   f
SPORTING IDOL 9-11-7 (7*) R Walker, *chsd ldrs till drpd
out quickly 3 out, sn pld up.......(20 to 1 op 16 to 1)   pu
Dist: ½l, 3½l, 2l, 2½l, 2½l, ½l, dist, 1½l, 25l. 3m 58.80s. a 21.80s (16
Ran).
SR: 7/4/5/-/-/-/   (Capt J Macdonald-Buchanan), D Nicholson

2791 Forbra Gold Challenge Cup Handicap Chase (0-135 5-y-o and up) £4,713 3m ....(3:00)

2666* NEW HALEN [106] 13-9-9 (5*) Miss P Jones, *mostly jmpd
wl, led appr 3rd, made rst, ran on well r-in.*
...................(6 to 1 tchd 7 to 1)   1
2656* SUNLEY BAY [106] 8-9-9 (5*) Guy Lewis, *ran in snatches
and not fluent, hdwy whn jmpd slwly 12th, rallying
when hit 2 out, kpt on.........(4 to 1 co-fav op 5 to 2)   2
1220³ ROSS VENTURE [120] 9-11-0 T Reed, *led till appr 3rd,
chsd wnr till wknd approaching last..(4 to 1 co-
fav op 3 to 1)   3
2656⁴ AUCTION LAW (NZ) [116] 10-10-10 A Maguire, *chsd ldrs till
hit 7th, hdwy 4 out, rdn whn hit 2 out, sn btn.*
...................(4 to 1 co-fav op 7 to 2)   4
1757 FLASHTHECASH [93] 8-11-10 M Perrett, *hit 1st, hld up,
hdwy 7th, cld 4 out, rdn and wkng whn mstk 2 out.*
...................(11 to 2 op 13 to 2 tchd 5 to 1)   5
ACE OF SPIES [106] 13-10-0 C Llewellyn, *hld up in tch,
wknd 13th.....(14 to 1 op 10 to 1 tchd 16 to 1)   6
2143⁸ WARNER FOR WINNERS [106] 8-10-0 J Osborne, *mstk
3rd, al struggling in rear, tld off whn pld up bef 4 out.*
...................(5 to 1 tchd 9 to 2)   pu
Dist: 4l, 7l, 1l, 20l, 7l. 6m 15.80s. a 26.80s (7 Ran).
SR: 20/16/23/18/12/-/-/   (Mrs Sally Siviter), A P James

2792 Henley Hall Gold Challenge Cup Handicap Hurdle (0-110 4-y-o and up) £2,836 2m 5f 110yds...........(3:30)

2209³ SMITH TOO (Ire) [105] 6-11-4 (7*) D Bohan, *patiently rdn,
3rd 3 out, led sn aftr last, ran on wl.*
...................(17 to 2 op 7 to 1 tchd 9 to 1)   1
1964⁷ CAPTAIN WY CHEEK (Ire) [85] 6-10-5 C Llewellyn, *hld up
in rear, hdwy frm 3 out, jnd wnr last, rdn and outpcd
fnl 50 yards...................(20 to 1 op 14 to 1)   2
2528³ SUPER SPELL [101] 8-11-7 A Maguire, *prmnt, hit 4th and
6th, led appr 2 out, hit last, sn hdd, no extr.*
...................(6 to 1 op 5 to 1)   3
2222 LOGICAL FUN [93] 6-10-8 (5*) A Roche, *prmnt till lost pl
appr 5th, hdwy approaching 2 out, ev ch last, wknd.*
...................(25 to 1 op 20 to 1)   4
2528⁶ LITTLE BIG [86] 7-9-13 (7*) N Collum, *hld up in rear, hdwy
appr 2 out, ran on, nvr nrr...........(8 to 1 op 6 to 1)   5
2685⁴ ACANTHUS (Ire) [80] 4-9-9 (5*) T Eley, *pld hrd, prmnt, rdn
and ev ch appr 2 out, wknd bef last.*(8 to 1 op 12 to 1)   6
1753⁵ SILLIAN [102] 12-11-5 (3*) S Wynne, *in rear whn mstk 5th,
hdwy nxt, wknd appr last......(20 to 1 op 16 to 1)   7
2528⁸ LING (USA) [93] 9-10-13 R J Beggan, *hld up in rear, hdwy
7th, wknd appr 2 out, tld off.......(8 to 1 op 7 to 1)   8
2719⁴ MARIOLINO [85] 7-10-5 M Hourigan, *in tch to 6th, tld off.*
...................(3 to 1 fav op 7 to 2)   9
2256 SWILLY EXPRESS [92] 8-10-12 M Perrett, *rcd wide, prmnt
till wknd 5th, tld off.............(14 to 1 op 10 to 1)   10
2487 NEGATORY (USA) [98] 7-11-4 W Worthington, *beh whn
mstk 7th, sn tld off................(33 to 1)   11
4247 SUEZ CANAL (Ire) [95] 5-10-12 (3*) A Thornton, *led to 5th,
wknd quickly, tld off whn pld up bef last, lme.*
...................(25 to 1 op 20 to 1)   pu
2209 FACTOR TEN (Ire) [100] 6-11-6 J Osborne, *hld up, hdwy
3rd, cld 5th till wknd aftr 3 out, tld up bef nxt.*
...................(9 to 2 op 4 to 1 tchd 11 to 2)   pu
Dist: 3l, 4l, 1½l, 2l, 1½l, 4l, 25l, 3l, 4l, 5l. 5m 26.40s. a 29.40s (13 Ran).
(Smith Mansfield Meat Co Ltd), Mrs J Pitman

2793 Ludlow Hunters' Chase for the Ludlow Gold Cup (6-y-o and up) £1,679 3m ....(4:00)

BONANZA BOY 13-11-13 (7*) Mr D Pipe, *al prmnt, rdn
appr 12th, styd on to ld last, ran on. (8 to 1 op 4 to 1)   1
2451² ONCE STUNG 8-12-6 Mr J Greenall, *trckd ldrs, rdn 8th, led
12th, wndrd in frnt and hdd last, ridden and no extr.*
...................(11 to 10 on op 5 to 4 tchd 5 to 4 on)   2
2456³ MANDRAKI SHUFFLE (bl) 12-11-13 (7*) Mr A Harvey, *led
appr 3rd till 12th, styd prmnt, one pace frm 2 out.*
...................(8 to 1 op 5 to 1)   3
SANDBROOK 10-11-7 (7*) Mr K Cousins, *al prmnt, dsptd
ld 7th to 4 out, ev ch till wknd appr last.*
...................(50 to 1 op 33 to 1)   4
2526⁷ DOWNSVIEW LADY 10-11-2 (7*) Mr M Sheppard, *nvr on
terms.*...................(50 to 1)   5
VERY CHEERING 11-11-7 (7*) Mr B Crawford, *mstks in
rear, nvr on terms.*...................(50 to 1)   6
ADAMARE 10-11-12³ (5*) Mr C Bealby, *led till appr 3rd,
wknd 4 out.*...................(8 to 1 tchd 12 to 1)   7

388

RADIO CUE 11-11-13 (7*) Mr J A Llewellyn, *chsd ldrs, hit 13th, wknd appr 3 out, tld off*...... (14 to 1 op 8 to 1) 8

2526⁵ MY NOMINEE 6-11-7 (7*) Mr C Stockton, *mstk 1st, al beh, tld off*........................(25 to 1 op 20 to 1) 9

CELTIC FLEET (v) 13-11-13 (7*) Miss T Spearing, *mid-div whn f 9th*........................(20 to 1 op 14 to 1) f

MIG 9-11-8 (7*) Miss Y Beckingham, *mstk second, rear whn hmpd and uns rdr 9th*......(50 to 1 op 33 to 1) ur

JUDGMENT DAY 12-11-13 (7*) Mr Michael J Jones, *chsd ldrs to 6th, tld off whn pld up bef 12th*.

....(25 to 1 op 16 to 1) pu

2482 CLONONY CASTLE (bl) 8-11-7 (7*) Mr P Hanly, *al beh, tld off whn pld up bef 2 out*......................(50 to 1) pu

SPRINGMOUNT 10-11-7 (7*) Miss K Swindells, *outpcd, tld off whn pld up bef 3 out*........(50 to 1 op 33 to 1) pu

2526⁴ NGERU 8-11-7 (7*) Mr A Edwards, *mstk 1st, prmnt early, beh whn blun 12th, tld off when pld up bef 3 out*

....(20 to 1 op 16 to 1) pu

2526 LOCHINGALL 9-11-7 (7*) Mr D Duggan, *mstks in rear, tld off whn pld up bef 4 out*..........(12 to 1 op 8 to 1) pu

STORMY WAGER 9-11-7 (7*) Mr E Andrewes, *prmnt early, tld off 12th, tld off whn pld up bef 3 out*......... (50 to 1) pu

Dist: 5l, 5l, 2½l, 20l, sht-hd, 5l, 10l, 8l. 6m 26.00s. a 37.00s (17 Ran).

(Mrs Angie Malde), M C Pipe

2794
Bromfield Novices' Chase (5-y-o and up) £2,898 2½m .... (4:30)

2527² VAZON BAY (bl) 10-11-4 I Lawrence, *trkd ldr frm 4th, led appr tenth, rdn and tired last, edgd lft und pres, all out, fnshd 1st, plcd second*.

.........................(9 to 2 op 3 to 1 tchd 5 to 1) 1D

1805⁴ BALLY PARSON 8-11-1 (3*) A Thornton, *chsd ldrs, second whn hit 3 out, chlgd and crrd lft r-in, ran on, jst fld, fnshd second, awarded race*.......(20 to 1 op 14 to 1) 1

2293 RAMSTAR 6-11-9 A Maguire, *trkd ldrs, 3rd whn blun 11th, tried to cl when mstk 3 out, one pace*.

....(5 to 2 fav op 3 to 1) 3

2721³ WHAT'S IN ORBIT 9-11-4 (5*) Guy Lewis, *nvr far away, ev ch whn blun 3 out, sn btn*.

.........................(3 to 1 op 5 to 2 tchd 100 to 30) 4

2524⁴ PETTY BRIDGE 10-11-9 R Bellamy, *mid-div, not fluent, wknd 4 out, tld off*.............(12 to 1 op 8 to 1) 5

2580⁷ MASTER'S CROWN (USA) 6-11-4 W Worthington, *al beh, wknd 4 out*..................(20 to 1 op 16 to 1) 6

2714⁶ OURPALWENTY 7-11-4 R Marley, *led 4th till appr tenth, wknd quickly, pld up bef four out*...........(50 to 1) pu

2527 HAPPY DEAL 8-11-4 T Wall, *jmpd badly in rear, tld off wh18 mstk 9th*............................(66 to 1 op 33 to 1) pu

2361⁹ ROYAL REFRAIN 9-11-4 C Llewellyn, *tn tch to 9th, tld off whn pld up bef 4 out*...............(10 to 1 op 8 to 1) pu

STUBS GUEST 8-11-4 J Osborne, *pld last, tld to 4th, sn beh, tld off whn pulled up aftr 9th.* (14 to 1 op 12 to 1) pu

2209⁵ PERCY SMOLLETT 6-11-4 M Hourigan, *al beh, tld off whn pld up bef 11th*......................(20 to 1 op 33 to 1) pu

Dist: Nk, 20l, ¾l, 25l, 25l. 5m 15.20s. a 24.20s (11 Ran).

SR: 28/27/12/11/-/-/

(G Hutsby), J Chugg

2795
Clee Hill Novices' Hurdle (4-y-o and up) £1,896 2m 5f 110yds .... (5:00)

1994⁵ GOLDEN SPINNER 7-11-4 J R Kavanagh, *took second appr 3rd, led 7th, drw clr approaching 2 out, mstk last, pushed out*............(11 to 2 op 6 to 1 tchd 5 to 1) 1

2404* CYBORGO (Fr) 4-11-1 R Dunwoody, *led to 7th, hrd rdn appr 2 out, hit last, kpt on to take second r-in*.

.........................(11 to 8 on op 2 to 1 on tchd 5 to 4 on) 2

2667* COILED SPRING 7-11-10 A Maguire, *hld up in rear, hdwy to take 3rd 6th, second appr 2 out, wknd r-in.*

.........................(9 to 2 tchd 7 to 2 tchd 9 to 4) 3

1974⁵ GOD SPEED YOU (Ire) 5-11-4 C Llewellyn, *mid-div, rdn 3rd, lost tch frm 5th, tld off*......(66 to 1 op 50 to 1) 4

2525⁷ CARLSAN 8-11-4 Mr M Jackson, *mstks, in tch to 4th, tld off*...(100 to 1) 5

2428⁹ EMPERORS WARRIOR 8-11-4 Jacqui Oliver, *in tch whn mstk 5th, sn wknd, tld off*..(50 to 1 op 100 to 1) 6

2210 FUN SPORT (Ire) 5-11-4 R Bellamy, *rear, tld off whn pld up bef 5th*...................................(100 to 1) pu

2339 ABSOLUTELYMUSTARD (Ire) 5-11-4 J Osborne, *trkd ldr till appr 3rd, wknd aftr nxt, tld off whn pld up bef 2 out.* pu

Dist: 10l, 4l, dist, 15l, 15l. 5m 27.60s. a 30.60s (8 Ran).

(Sir Peter Miller), N J Henderson

TAUNTON (good to soft)
Thursday March 3rd
Going Correction: PLUS 1.30 sec. per fur. (races 1,2,- 4,6), PLUS 1.40 (3,5)

2796
EBF 'National Hunt' Novices' Hurdle Qualifier (5,6,7-y-o) £2,347 2m 3f 110yds .... (2:10)

1327⁵ MARSHALL SPARKS 7-11-0 J Lower, *trkd ldg pair, led 4 out, sn drw clr, unchlgd*..........(9 to 4 op 11 to 8) 1

1871² STORMY SUNSET 7-10-2 (7*) Mr N Moore, *hdwy 3rd, rdn alng 4 out, btn third whn mstk last, styd on r-in, not trble wnr*......................(10 to 1 op 6 to 1) 2

2042⁴ TOO SHARP 6-10-6 (3*) J McCarthy, *led til hdd 4 out, rdn and rallied aftr nxt, sn btn.*

.........................(7 to 4 fav op 6 to 4 tchd 15 to 8) 3

2426⁸ BRIDEPARK ROSE (Ire) 6-10-9 M Ahern, *not fluent, trkd ldr, mstk 6th, wknd aftr 3 out..* (4 to 1 op 8 to 1) 4

2505 BARON RUSH 6-11-0 Tracy Turner, *rdn and wknd aftr 5th, tld off after 4 out*............(6 to 1 op 33 to 1) 5

2757 VENN BOY 5-10-7 (7*) T Murphy, *drpd rear and reminders aftr 5th, tld off frm nxt*..............(66 to 1 op 33 to 1) 6

2558⁵ GLADYS EMMANUEL 7-10-9 S Burrough, *chsd ldg grp til wknd quickly appr 5th, sn tld off, pld up bef 2 out.*

....(20 to 1 op 16 to 1) pu

HOLD IM TIGHT 6-11-0 J Frost, *hld up, drpd rear aftr 4th, tld off whn pld up after 6th*.......(66 to 1 op 33 to 1) pu

AMBER REALM 6-10-9 B Powell, *hdwy appr 4th, pushed alng and lost pl aftr nxt, sn tld off, pld up bef 2 out.*

....(33 to 1 op 20 to 1) pu

Dist: 15l, 1l, 15l, dist, nk. 4m 57.70s. a 36.70s (9 Ran).

(D M Beresford), M C Pipe

2797
Crocombe Novices' Selling Hurdle (4 & 5-y-o) £1,770 2m 1f .... (2:40)

2653⁶ STAR MOVER 5-10-2 (7*) R Darke, *wnt 3rd 4th, trkd ldr till led 2 out, drvn out r-in*.........(5 to 1 tchd 11 to 2) 1

2118⁷ FORGETFUL 5-10-9 D J Burchell, *led to 2 out, rdn and wknd aftr last*..................(7 to 2 fav op 4 to 1) 2

KNYAZ 4-10-0 (7*) Mr L Jefford, *hld up, prmnt 4th, drvn alng aftr four out, no imprsn appr 2 out.*

....(16 to 1 op 12 to 1) 3

1546⁵ DANCING DANCER 5-10-9 J Frost, *hld up, beh 4th, hdwy aftr 3 out, styd on one pace.*

.........................(20 to 1 op 12 to 1 tchd 25 to 1) 4

2634² ERLEMO (v) 5-10-11 (3*) R Davis, *pressed ldr, drvn alng aftr 4 out, 3rd and btn whn blun last.*

....(6 to 1 tchd 7 to 1) 5

2717 NORDEN (Ire) 5-11-0 W Irvine, *mid-div, pushed along aftr 5th, no hdwy 4 out*..............(25 to 1 op 20 to 1) 6

2653⁴ GROGFRYN (bl) 4-10-9 C Maude, *trkd ldr, 4th and rdn alng aftr four out, wknd quickly.* (12 to 1 op 10 to 1) 7

2215 BALTIC EXCHANGE (Can) 5-11-0 J Lower, *beh 4th, lost tch aftr nxt, tld off whn pld up bef 2 out.*

.........................(13 to 2 op 9 to 2 tchd 7 to 1) pu

1717 LIZZIE DRIPPIN (Can) 5-10-9 B Powell, *hld up, pushed alng and sn beh aftr 4th, tld off whn pld up bef 3 out.*

....(25 to 1 op 10 to 1) pu

2430 PATONG BEACH 4-10-2 M Ahern, *hld up, hdwy 5th, chsd ldrs, wknd quickly aftr 5th, beh whn pld up and dismounted bef last*............(16 to 1 op 14 to 1) pu

2461⁸ MINI FETE (Fr) 5-10-9 S Earle, *mid-div, pushed alng aftr 4th, sn lost tch, tld off whn pld up bef 2 out.*

.........................(9 to 1 op 6 to 1 tchd 10 to 1) pu

1749 SCOTTISH TEMPTRESS 4-10-1⁴ (5*) D Matthews, *wknd quickly aftr 4th, sn beh, tld off whn pld up bef four out.*

....(6 to 1 op 33 to 1) pu

PARIS BY NIGHT (Ire) 4-9-11² (7*) T Thompson, *chsd ldrs 4th, rdn alng and wknd aftr nxt, tld off whn pld up bef 2 out*........................(14 to 1 op 12 to 1) pu

DOUBLE DEALING (Ire) 4-10-7 S McNeill, *mid-div whn mstk 5th, sn lost tch, tld off when pld up bef 2 out.*

....(33 to 1 op 16 to 1) pu

Dist: 12l, 12l, 10l, 6l, 1½l. 4m 15.20s. a 28.20s (14 Ran).

SR: 20/8/-/-/-/-/

(O J Stokes), W G M Turner

2798
Orchard FM Handicap Chase (0-130 5-y-o and up) £2,723 2m 110yds (3:10)

2476⁴ L'UOMO PIU [99] 10-10-3 S Earle, *chsd ldrs, mstks 4th and four out, rdn and rallied aftr nxt, led last, drvn out.*

....(5 to 1 op 4 to 1) 1

1798* GALAGAMES (USA) [96] 7-10-0 B Powell, *led to 3rd, mstk 6th, led ag'n 7th to nxt, led again aftr 4 out, wknd and hdd appr last, not quicken*....................(9 to 2 op 4 to 1) 2

2248⁴ BROUGHTON MANOR [120] 9-11-7 (3*) R Davis, *led 3rd to 7th, ev ch 5 out, styd on frm 3 out, not quicken.*

.........................(11 to 2 op 6 to 1 tchd 7 to 1) 3

2672³ SETTER COUNTRY [113] 10-11-3 W Irvine, *pushed alng aftr 5th, wnt second 7th, led nxt til aftr 4 out, sn btn.*

.........................(7 to 2 jt-fav tchd 4 to 1) 4

2696* SAILORS LUCK [119] 9-11-9 E Murphy, *hld up, pushed alng aftr 7th, no ch frm 5 out*..........(7 to 2 jt-fav op 11 to 4 tchd 4 to 1) 5

2397 RATHER SHARP [96] 8-10-0 S McNeill, *rear whn blun and uns rdr 6th*............(14 to 1 tchd 16 to 1) ur

2718 WHATEVER YOU LIKE [114] 10-11-4 C Maude, *hld up, lost tch aftr 6th, beh whn blun badly 8th, pld up bef nxt.*

....(14 to 1 op 12 to 1) pu

2425⁴ SWEET GEORGE [101] 7-10-5⁵ D J Burchell, *mstk 5th, sn beh, tld off whn pld up bef 4 out.*

.........................(28 to 1 op 20 to 1 tchd 33 to 1) pu

Dist: 2½l, 6l, 6l, 12l. 4m 25.00s. a 27.00s (8 Ran).

SR: 36/30/48/35/29/

(C J Spencer), A Barrow

2799 Blackdown Hills Novices' Handicap Hurdle (0-100 4-y-o and up) £1,945 3m 110yds. .... (3:40)

2454* DERRYMOSS [96] (v) 8-11-12 J Lower, *led aftr 3rd, clr 8th, styd on wl frm 2 out, easily* ....(8 to 1 op 6 to 1)   1
2651⁵ ROCK DIAMOND [70] 8-10-0 E Leonard, *hld up, beh 7th, hdwy aftr 3 out, mstks last 2, no imprsn on wnr.*
 ....(12 to 1 op 9 to 1)   2
2657⁴ MOBILE MESSENGER (NZ) [84] 6-10-7 (7*) Mr G Shenkin, *hld up, hdwy to chase ldr aftr 6th, styd on frm 3 out, btn whn mstk last.*................(6 to 1 tchd 7 to 1)   3
2424² DEVIOSITY (USA) [70] 7-10-0 I Shoemark, *beh 7th, rdn and hdwy aftr nxt, one pace frm 3 out.* (20 to 1 op 12 to 1)   4
2459 CHERYLS PET (Ire) [83] 6-10-13 B Powell, *beh and pushed alng aftr 7th, styd on frm 4 out, one pace.* ...(9 to 2 jt-fav op 5 to 1 tchd 4 to 1)   5
2558⁸ SOLO GIRL (Ire) [70] 6-10-0 S McNeill, *rdn and hdwy aftr 7th, no imprsn frm 3 out.*
 ....(14 to 1 op 10 to 1 tchd 16 to 1)   6
2558 KEMMY DARLING [70] 7-10-0 M Ahern, *hld up, steady hdwy aftr 4 out, in tch appr 2 out, wknd quickly.*
 ....(50 to 1 op 33 to 1)   7
1867³ SPIRIT LEVEL [70] 6-9-7 (7*) Miss S Mitchell, *beh frm 7th, tld off aftr 4 out.*..............(16 to 1 op 14 to 1)   8
1837⁴ SUASANAN SIOSANA [74] (v) 9-9-11 (7*) J James, *pressed ldr til rdn alng aftr 8th, wknd quickly, tld off aftr 3 out.*
 ....(13 to 2 op 5 to 1)   9
 FRENCHLANDS WAY [72] 10-10-2² S Mackey, *prmnt till wknd quickly aftr 8th, tld off whn pld up after 3 out.*
 ....(20 to 1 op 16 to 1)   f
2657³ MAHATMACOAT [71] 7-9-9¹ (7*) Mr J Culloty, *pressed ldr in second pl til wknd quickly aftr 8th, beh whn f nxt.*
 ....(9 to 2 jt-fav op 3 to 1)   f
2558⁹ ALICE SPRINGS [70] 5-10-0 C Maude, *hld up, pressed ldr aftr 5th, ev ch 4 out, fifth and btn whn f 2 out.*
 ....(33 to 1 op 25 to 1)   f
 LOWLANDS [81] 8-10-8 (3*) R Davis, *beh frm 7th, sn lost tch, tld off bef pld up before last...*(25 to 1 op 16 to 1)   pu
2686⁶ FATHER FORTUNE [85] (bl) 6-10-12 (3*) J McCarthy, *led til aftr 3rd, chsd ldr until wknd quickly, pld up bef nxt.*................................(7 to 1 op 5 to 1)   pu
Dist: 12l, 5l, 6l, ¾l, 3½l, 2½l, dist, ¾l. 6m 14.50s. a 40.00s (14 Ran).
SR: 17/-/-/-/-/-/   (Mrs J K L Watts), M C Pipe

2800 Taunton Hunters' Chase (6-y-o and up) £1,716 3m.................(4:10)

 NEARLY SPLENDID 9-11-5 (7*) Mr T Greed, *hld up on last pl, steady hdwy to track ldrs aftr 12th, lft second 6 out, led 3 out, drvn out r-in, styd on wl.*
 ....(13 to 8 fav op 11 to 8 tchd 7 to 4)   1
 PARSONS PLEASURE 11-11-12 (7*) Mr C Morlock, *hld up, mstk 1st, hdwy tenth, led 6 out, hdd and mistake 3 out, rdn and rallied r-in, not quicken nr finish.*
 ....(9 to 2 op 4 to 1 tchd 5 to 1)   2
 WALK IN THE WOODS 7-11-0 (7*) Mrs S Palmer, *jmpd lft, led aftr 3rd til jumped slwly and hdd 6th, led ag'n 9th to six out, wknd quickly after 4 out, tld off.*
 ....(20 to 1 op 14 to 1)   3
 EAGLE TRACE 11-11-5 (7*) Miss W Southcombe, *mstks 1st and second, hdwy 9th, mistake 12th (water), lost tch aftr nxt, tld off 5 out.*...........(40 to 1 op 25 to 1)   4
 ANOTHER LUCAS 10-11-5 (7*) Mr S Slade, *hdwy aftr 12th, chsd ldrs till wknd 5 out, tld off..* (40 to 1 op 33 to 1)   5
 COLCOMBE CASTLE 11-11-12 (7*) Mr I Dowrick, *mstk 3rd, f nxt (water).*......................(66 to 1 op 50 to 1)   f
 JUST SILVER 9-11-5 (7*) Mr J Culloty, *prmnt whn f 6th.*
 ....(150 to 1 op 66 to 1 tchd 200 to 1)   f
 ROVING REPORT 7-12-2 (3*) Mr R Alner, *hld up, in tch whn f tenth.*...........(85 to 40 op 5 to 4 tchd 5 to 2)   f
2696² NOS NA GAOITHE (v) 11-12-8 (7*) Mr Richard White, *hld up, wnt 3rd 9th, cl second whn blun and uns rdr 6 out.*
 ....(15 to 2 op 10 to 1 tchd 12 to 1)   ur
 LATE SESSION (bl) 10-12-0 (5*) Mr A Farrant, *led 7th to 9th, styd in tch til wknd quickly aftr 11th, beh whn pld up after nxt.*.........(150 to 1 op 66 to 1 tchd 200 to 1)   pu
 FLOOD MARK 10-11-12 (7*) Mr S Mulcaire, *hld up, hdwy aftr 11th, wknd 13th, beh whn pld up after 5 out.*
 ....(40 to 1 op 25 to 1)   pu
 CADEAU D'ARAGON 7-11-0 (7*) Mr N Harris, *hld up, hdwy 12th, chsd ldrs till wknd quickly aftr 5 out, tld off whn pld up bef 2 out.*............(50 to 1 op 33 to 1)   pu
 HIGHLAND ECHO 11-11-12 (7*) Miss A Turner, *prmnt till lost pl and wknd quickly aftr tenth, tld off whn pld up after 5 out.*....................(16 to 1 op 12 to 1)   pu
Dist: 1l, dist, 4l, 2l. 6m 41.00s. a 54.00s (13 Ran).
                            (S R Stevens), S R Stevens

2801 Pitminster Handicap Hurdle (0-120 5-y-o and up) £1,913 2m 3f 110yds ....(4:40)

2727 FAIR BROTHER [101] 8-10-10 J Frost, *hld up, hdwy to ld aftr 5th, made rst, drvn out r-in.*
 ....(2 to 1 op 7 to 4 tchd 9 to 4)   1

THE MINDER (Fr) [91] 7-9-9 (5*) D Salter, *hld up, wnt 3rd 6th, wth wnr 2 out, ev ch last, rdn and not quicken nr finish.*......................(11 to 1 op 9 to 1)   2
882³ SUKAAB [119] 9-11-7 (7*) T Dascombe, *pressed ldrs til lost pl and pushed alng aftr 6th, rallied 2 out, rdn and styd on nr finish.*...............(100 to 1 op 8 to 1)   3
2655* HANDY LASS [103] 5-10-7 (5*) D Matthews, *led 4th to nxt, pressed ldr frm next, ev ch appr 2 out, not quicken betw last two.*...........(13 to 8 fav op 6 to 4 tchd 7 to 4)   4
2528 LAND OF THE FREE [91] 5-10-0 L Harvey, *pressed ldrs frm 3rd, pushed alng aftr 6th, wknd 2 out.*
 ....(10 to 1 op 14 to 1)   5
2461² TENDRESSE (Ire) [91] 6-10-0 W Irvine, *hld up in last pl, lost tch aftr 5th, beh frm nxt.*..........(7 to 1 tchd 8 to 1)   6
2302⁶ PRINCE VALMY (Fr) [91] 9-10-0 B Powell, *led to 4th, led nxt, sn hdd, lost pl 6th, soon beh.* (100 to 1 op 50 to 1)   7
Dist: ½l, ½l, 1½l, 6l, 20l, 7l. 5m 2.50s. a 41.50s (7 Ran).
                            (Mrs S Watts), G B Balding

WARWICK (good to soft)
Thursday March 3rd
Going Correction: PLUS 1.10 sec. per fur. (races 1,3,-5,7), PLUS 1.25 (2,4,6)

2802 Watergall Maiden Hurdle (4-y-o and up) £2,241 2½m 110yds........(1:50)

2505⁵ A N C EXPRESS 6-11-7 J R Kavanagh, *sn in tch, led 8th, drvn clr aftr 2 out.*..........................(10 to 1)   1
2335⁴ DEDUCE 5-11-7 N Williamson, *hdwy 6th, chsd wnr appr 2 out, no imprsn.*...............(3 to 1 op 4 to 1)   2
934³ SHEARMAC STEEL 7-11-7 Peter Hobbs, *sn prmnt, chlgd 7th, rdn and one pace appr 2 out.*
 ....(11 to 1 op 7 to 1 tchd 12 to 1)   3
2505 TAKE CHANCES 6-11-7 P Holley, *hdwy 6th, wknd aftr 3 out.*..............................(33 to 1 op 25 to 1)   4
2599² KNOCKAVERRY (Ire) 6-11-2 R Supple, *in tch 5th, chsd ldrs 8th, rdn and wknd aftr 3 out.*....(10 to 1 op 8 to 1)   5
2646³ ATOURS (USA) (bl) 6-11-7 G Bradley, *in tch, chlgd 6th, slight ld 7th to nxt, wknd quickly appr 2 out.*
 ....(6 to 4 fav op 11 to 8 tchd 9 to 4)   6
2638² EVE'S TREASURE 4-10-2 (5*) S Lyons, *made most to 7th, wknd 3 out.*.....................(14 to 1)   7
2629³ BOZO BAILEY 4-10-12 R Campbell, *in tch, wkng whn mstk 8th.*......................(20 to 1 op 16 to 1)   8
993* FOULKSCOURT DUKE (Ire) 6-11-7 W Marston, *in tch, chsd ldrs aftr 6th, hit nxt, sn wknd.*......(11 to 1 op 7 to 1)   9
2459 TONGADIN 8-11-7 R Dunwoody, *effrt 7th, sn wknd.*
 ....(14 to 1 op 10 to 1)   10
2633 CASTLE BANKS 10-11-7 G McCourt, *beh 5th, tld off whn pld up bef 7th.*.................(100 to 1 op 66 to 1)   pu
1717 VALIANTHE (USA) (bl) 6-11-7 M Foster, *mstks, al beh, tld off whn pld up bef 7th.*........(33 to 1 op 25 to 1)   pu
 CHEQUE BOOK 6-11-7 Mr D Verco, *prmnt to 6th, tld off whn pld up bef 4 out.*..........(100 to 1 op 66 to 1)   pu
2477 RIFFLE 7-11-7 D Murphy, *sn beh, tld off whn pld up bef 4 out.*........................(20 to 1 op 16 to 1)   pu
 DALEHOUSE LANE 6-11-7 Gary Lyons, *beh 5th, tld off whn pld up bef 4 out.*..........(100 to 1 op 66 to 1)   pu
2327⁶ TIME WON'T WAIT (Ire) 5-11-7 J Railton, *beh 5th, tld off whn pld up bef 2 out.*..........(33 to 1 op 25 to 1)   pu
2269 PARAMOUNT (v) 5-11-7 S Smith Eccles, *sn beh, tld off whn pld up bef 4 out.*...............(50 to 1)   pu
Dist: 8l, 12l, nk, 12l, hd, 7l, 20l, hd, hd. 5m 20.80s. a 33.30s (17 Ran).
                     (ANC Owners Group), J S King

2803 Eastgate Novices' Chase (5-y-o and up) £3,571 2m.................(2:20)

2416³ CASTLE DIAMOND 7-12-0 R Dunwoody, *led till appr 6th, styd chasing ldr, outpcd aftr 3 out, stayed on frm nxt, drvn to ld r-in, all out.*...........(7 to 4 op 2 to 1)   1
 LADY GHISLAINE (Fr) 7-10-11 W McFarland, *chlgd 4th, led appr 6th, clr aftr 3 out, rdn and held last, wknd and hdd r-in.*..............(8 to 1 op 7 to 1 tchd 9 to 1)   2
2523* BEAUFAN 7-11-2 Gary Lyons, *beh, hit 3rd, hdwy appr 6th, in tch whn blun 4 out, sn btn.*
 ....(10 to 1 tchd 11 to 1)   3
1593² HIDDEN PLEASURE 8-11-2 G Upton, *hld up, hdwy to track ldrs aftr 5th, rdn 4 out, sn btn.*
 ....(11 to 8 fav op 5 to 4)   4
2653 PALM SWIFT 8-10-11 A Tory, *prmnt, chlgd 4th to 5th, wknd 7th.*..........(25 to 1 op 20 to 1)   5
2399² DEEP IN GREEK 8-10-9 (7*) Mr G Hogan, *al beh.*
 ....(10 to 1 op 16 to 1)   6
2538⁶ WINGED WHISPER (USA) 5-10-8 N Williamson, *al beh.*
 ....(10 to 1 op 16 to 1)   7
Dist: 1l, 25l, 8l, 15l, 1½l, 2½l. 4m 18.50s. a 26.50s (7 Ran).
SR: 35/17/-/-/   (Mrs S Kavanagh), H M Kavanagh

2804 Emscott Claiming Handicap Hurdle (4 - 7-y-o) £2,374 2m............(2:50)

2653² SOVEREIGN NICHE (Ire) [67] (v) 6-10-9 R Dunwoody, *led to 3rd, led ag'n appr 4th, styd on wl frm 2 out.*
 ....(7 to 4 fav op 9 to 4)   1

2665³ MORIARTY [71] 7-10-13 L Wyer, *mid-div, hdwy aftr 3rd, chsd wnr frm 5th, no imprsn frm 2 out.*
.................(5 to 2 op 3 to 1 tchd 9 to 4) 2
2523⁴ COBB GATE [80] (bl) 6-11-8 M Stevens, *chsd ldrs, one pace frm 3 out.*..........................(9 to 1 op 7 to 1) 3
2717⁸ CLOGHRAN LAD [80] 7-11-8 W Marston, *beh, pushed alng 5th, ran on frm last, not a dngr.....*(11 to 2 op 7 to 2) 4
2653* CHANDIGARH [81] 6-11-2 (7*) P McLoughlin, *slwly into strd, effrt 4th, sn wknd........*(11 to 2 op 4 to 1) 5
355 NOW BOARDING [58] 7-10-0* (7*) Mr G Hogan, *al beh, tld off.................*(50 to 1 op 33 to 1) 6
2329² GLOSSY [82] 7-11-3 (7*) G Robertson, *mstk 1st, led 3rd, hdd appr 4th and mistake, wkng whn mistake nxt, tld off....................*(12 to 1 op 8 to 1) 7
Dist: 8l, 6l, 25l, nk, dist, sht-hd. 4m 3.70s. a 23.70s (7 Ran).
SR: 20/16/19/-/ (Avalon Surfacing Ltd), M C Pipe

2805 Crudwell Cup Handicap Chase (0-145 5-y-o and up) £4,922 3m 5f..... (3:20)

CAPTAIN FRISK [118] 11-10-7 N Williamson, *jmpd wl, chsd ldrs, led 5th, sn hdd, led ag'n nxt, soon clr, pushed out, eased cl hme.......*(9 to 1 op 7 to 1) 1
2748 GLENBROOK D'OR [116] 10-10-5 B Clifford, *hdwy 5th, chsd wnr frm 17th, no imprsn.................*(7 to 2 jt-fav tchd 4 to 1) 2
2462² CYTHERE [112] 10-9-12 (3*) P Hide, *in tch, hdwy to chase ldrs 16th, one pace 4 out.............*(7 to 2 jt-fav) 3
2506³ ROC DE PRINCE (Fr) [132] 11-11-7 R Dunwoody, *led aftr 5th to nxt, led tenth to 11th, led after 15th to next, wknd and hit 16th..................*(7 to 1 op 6 to 1) 4
2602³ WILLSFORD [115] (bl) 11-10-4 D Murphy, *led till aftr 5th, led 6th to tenth, led 11th till hdd and hit 15th, wknd nxt, tld off........................*(13 to 2 op 10 to 1) 5
1471⁵ ASKINFARNEY [111] 7-10-0 R Supple, *hit 3rd, beh 6th, no ch whn blun 3 out, tld off........*(12 to 1 op 8 to 1) 6
2173⁵ ALL JEFF (Fr) [130] 10-11-5 G Bradley, *sn tld off, pld up bef 2 out......................*(4 to 1 op 7 to 2 tchd 9 to 2) pu
2506 DUNTREE [130] (bl) 9-11-5 W Marston, *lost tch 5th, ridden to stay in tch 12th, wknd 14th, tld off whn pld up bef 16th....................*(16 to 1 op 10 to 1) pu
Dist: 4l, 6l, 25l, dist, dist. 7m 48.90s. a 39.90s (8 Ran).
SR: 43/37/27/22/-/ (Mrs H J Clarke), K C Bailey

2806 Blackdown Handicap Hurdle (0-140 4-y-o and up) £3,525 2½m 110yds
.................................(3:50)

1880⁵ SPRING MARATHON (USA) [110] 4-10-0 P Holley, *chsd ldrs 4th, led appr 2 out, drvn out.........*(8 to 1 op 6 to 1) 1
2403² CASTIGLIERO (Fr) [120] (bl) 6-10-10 G Bradley, *chsd ldr, lft in ld briefly 3rd, sn steadied, styd chasing leader, rdn 3 out, stayed on and bumped 2 out, not quicken.
.....................(2 to 1 op 9 to 4 tchd 5 to 2) 2
2473⁶ JEASSU [134] 11-11-7 (3*) T Jenks, *hld up, hdwy 8th, led 3 out, sn rdn, hdd nxt, soon outpcd.
..............................(7 to 1 op 8 to 1) 3
2595 WINNIE THE WITCH [119] 10-10-9 D Bridgwater, *lft in ld aftr 3rd, hdd 3 out, sn wknd, tld off.
.....................(7 to 1 op 8 to 1 tchd 10 to 1) 4
2540² SO PROUD [110] 9-10-0 M Foster, *led till mstk and uns rdr 3rd......................*(7 to 4 fav tchd 2 to 1) ur
Dist: 2l, 8l, dist. 5m 21.50s. a 34.00s (5 Ran).
(Mrs Nerys Dutfield), Mrs P N Dutfield

2807 Town Of Warwick Foxhunters' Trophy Chase (5-y-o and up) £1,674 3¼m
.................................(4:20)

2650* DOUBLE SILK 10-12-4 (5*) Mr R Treloggen, *jmpd wl, made virtually all, clr appr 14th, unchlgd.
.....................(5 to 1 on op 4 to 1 on) 1
2605* MOUNT ARGUS 12-12-4 (5*) Mr S Brookshaw, *hdwy tenth, chsd wnr frm 3 out, no ch..........*(11 to 2 op 7 to 2) 2
2605⁵ ARCTIC TEAL 10-11-13 (3*) Mr J Durkan, *dsptd ld to 3rd, chsd wnr, chlgd 11th, ct for second 3 out, one pace.
.......................(20 to 1 op 10 to 1) 3
SHIPMATE 12-11-9 (7*) Miss H Irving, *mstks, beh 11th.
.......................(50 to 1 op 25 to 1) 4
ASHPIT 13-11-9 (7*) Mr T Garton, *effrt tenth, sn wknd.
.......................(40 to 1 op 25 to 1) 5
ROYLE SPEEDMASTER 10-11-13 (7*) Mr Julian Taylor, *beh till mstk and uns rdr 15th.........*(25 to 1 op 12 to 1) ur
Dist: 30l, 6l, 25l, 10l. 7m 2.10s. a 48.10s (6 Ran).
(R C Wilkins), R C Wilkins

2808 Edstone Mares Only Novices' Hurdle (4-y-o and up) £2,255 2m....... (4:50)

2731² MARINER'S AIR 7-11-0 N Williamson, *trkd ldrs, led aftr 3 out, rdn out......................*(7 to 1 tchd 8 to 1) 1
2692* SPREAD YOUR WINGS (Ire) 6-11-7 J Railton, *prmnt, chsd ldr aftr 3rd to 3 out, dsptd ld till hit last and one pace.
.......................(8 to 8 fav op 6 to 4 tchd 2 to 1) 2
2657 LOVE YOU MADLY (Ire) (bl) 4-10-13 M Foster, *wl beh till hdwy frm 4th, no imprsn appr 2 out.
.......................(10 to 1 op 8 to 1) 3

2712* PRINCESS TATEUM (Ire) 4-10-13 Lorna Vincent, *led aftr second, clr after nxt, hdd aftr 3 out, sn wknd.
.....................(5 to 1 op 4 to 1) 4
2428⁶ THE QUAKER 8-11-0 D Bridgwater, *led briefly second, lost pl 5th, styd on frm 2 out.
.......................(20 to 1 op 33 to 1 tchd 50 to 1) 5
2300 VELVET HEART (Ire) 4-10-13 S Burrough, *chsd ldrs, wknd 3 out.......................*(9 to 1 op 8 to 1) 6
2642 SAMJAMALIFRAN 5-10-7 (7*) L Reynolds, *nvr rch ldrs.
.......................(33 to 1) 7
MARCONDA (Ire) 5-10-G Upton, *nvr rch ldrs.
.......................(50 to 1 op 33 to 1) 8
1215² SAIL BY THE STARS 5-10-11 (3*) R Farrant, *in tch whn hit 4th, sn wknd.......................*(20 to 4 op 4 to 1) 9
5657 ANNABEL'S BABY (Ire) 5-11-0 P McDermott, *al beh.
.......................(50 to 1 op 33 to 1) 10
2335⁵ TENAYESTELIGN 6-11-0 Peter Hobbs, *hdwy to chase ldrs aftr 4th, wkng whn blun last, eased r-in.....*(10 to 1) 11
2535⁷ BROUGHTON'S GOLD (Ire) 6-11-0 N Mann, *al beh.
.......................(50 to 1 op 33 to 1) 12
RUNNING KISS 9-11-0 W McFarland, *hmpd 1st, al beh.
.......................(25 to 1 op 20 to 1) 13
1797 ARLEY GALE 6-11-0 G McCourt, *al beh.
.......................(50 to 1 op 33 to 1) 14
2405 UPTON LASS (Ire) (bl) 5-10-9 (5*) D Fortt, *chsd ldrs to 5th, sn wknd.......................*(25 to 1 op 20 to 1 tchd 33 to 1) 15
1779⁸ CELTIC EMERALD 6-11-0 D Gallagher, *al beh.
.......................(50 to 1 op 33 to 1) 16
2401⁴ FOXY LASS 5-11-0 Mr J Cambidge, *al beh.
.......................(66 to 1 op 50 to 1) 17
2691 ELANDS CASTLE (Ire) 6-11-0 R Supple, *beh till f 4th.
.......................(50 to 1 op 33 to 1) f
OPALKINO 9-11-0 W Marston, *uns rdr 1st.
.......................(66 to 1 op 50 to 1) ur
2717 LYCIAN MOON 5-11-0 E Byrne, *al beh, tld off whn pld up bef 3 out.......................*(66 to 1 op 50 to 1) pu
Dist: 3l, 20l, 4l, 8l, 15l, 3l, 1½l, 1½l, 1½l, 20l. 4m 4.50s. a 24.50s (20 Ran).
SR: 17/21/-/-/-/-/ (Mrs Peter Badger), J L Spearing

KELSO (soft)
Friday March 4th
Going Correction: PLUS 1.95 sec. per fur. (races 1,3,-5,6), PLUS 1.15 (2,4,7)

2809 Cyril Alexander Memorial Novices' Chase (Div I) (6-y-o and up) £2,835 2¾m 110yds.............................(1:20)

2577* GALLATEEN 6-11-6 N Doughty, *jmpd wl, cl up, led 12th, pushed out frm last.
.......................(3 to 1 on op 7 to 2 on tchd 11 to 4 on) 1
2565* EQUINOCTIAL 9-11-6 K Jones, *in tch, trkd wnr frm 12th, kpt on from 2 out, no imprsn.
.......................(7 to 1 op 6 to 1 tchd 8 to 1) 2
2411⁶ BIG MAC 7-11-0 L Wyer, *led till 12th, remained prmnt, kpt on same pace frm 2 out......*(12 to 1 op 8 to 1) 3
2170 PLAYFUL JULIET (Can) (v) 6-11-1 Pat Caldwell, *beh, hdwy aftr 4 out, kpt on same pace frm 2 out.
.......................(25 to 1 op 14 to 1) 4
2103⁴ KILCOLGAN 7-11-0 B Storey, *in tch, mstk 9th, grad wknd aftr 3 out.....................*(14 to 1 op 10 to 1) 5
2446² HERE COMES TIBBY 7-10-9 T Reed, *in tch, wknd aftr 3 out.......................*(33 to 1 op 25 to 1 tchd 40 to 1) 6
2736 MOW CREEK 10-10-9 (5*) P Williams, *cl up till wknd aftr 4 out.......................*(150 to 1 op 100 to 1) 7
RUPERT STANLEY 10-11-0 Richard Guest, *al beh, lost tch aftr 12th, tld off whn pld up bef 2 out.
.......................(33 to 1 op 25 to 1) pu
Dist: 5l, 2½l, 1l, 5l, 20l, 5l. 6m 21.90s. a 54.90s (8 Ran).
(E R Madden), G Richards

2810 Harcros Scottish Juvenile Championship Qualifier Novices' Hurdle (4-y-o) £2,495 2m 110yds.............. (1:50)

2541* RUSTY REEL 11-8 R Campbell, *al prmnt, led 2 out, ran on wl.................*(7 to 4 fav tchd 2 to 1 and 9 to 4) 1
2445² CALLERNOY (Ire) 10-5 (7*) Mr A Manners, *made most, hdd 2 out, no extr..........*(5 to 2 op 7 to 2 tchd 4 to 1) 2
2072* GENSERIC (Fr) 11-4 R Garritty, *jmpd slwly 1st, in tch, hdwy aftr 3 out, kpt on und pres frm last.
.......................(2 to 1 op 6 to 4) 3
2409⁶ ON GOLDEN POND (Ire) 10-13 J Callaghan, *chsd ldrs, pushed alng appr 3 out, kpt on same pace.
.......................(14 to 1 op 8 to 1) 4
1584⁶ SHARP AT SIX (Ire) 10-5 (7*) A Linton, *prmnt, ev ch appr 2 out, one pace.......................*(25 to 1 op 14 to 1) 5
2564 FRIENDLY KNIGHT 10-12 A Dobbin, *beh, hdwy appr 3 out, wknd approaching nxt............*(50 to 1 op 33 to 1) 6
2564 PREMIER STAR 10-12 T Reed, *in tch, effrt aftr 3 out, sn btn.......................*(25 to 1 op 14 to 1) 7
1920 ADMISSION (Ire) 10-12 A Merrigan, *al beh, lost tch aftr 3 out, tld off.................*(100 to 1 op 50 to 1) 8

MOSS PAGEANT 10-8 B Storey, *pld hrd, led aftr 3rd till hdd 4th, wknd after nxt, tld off whn pulled up bef 2 out*............................(100 to 1 op 50 to 1)   pu
SEVERE STORM 10-3 (5") F Perratt, *refused to race, took no part*......................(200 to 1 op 50 to 1)   l
Dist: 6l, 1l, 5l, 2l, 15l, 12l, 25l. 4m 13.30s. a 30.30s (10 Ran).
(S M Perry), I Campbell

2811 Times 'Rising Stars' Hunters' Chase Qualifier (6,7,8-y-o) £1,900 3m 1f (2:20)

2451* DAVY BLAKE 7-12-10 (5") Mr J M Dun, *made all, quickened aftr 2 out, drvn out r-in.*
............(11 to 10 on op 5 to 4 on tchd Evens)   1
DAMNIFICATION 8-11-5 (7") Mr A Parker, *al tracking ldrs, ev ch last, kpt on und pres*..........(9 to 2 op 4 to 1)   2
GREEN SHEEN (Ire) 6-11-5 (7") Mr Chris Wilson, *trkd ldrs, ev ch 2 out, sn btn*....................(6 to 1 op 5 to 1)   3
TRICKSOME 7-11-7 (5") Mr N Wilson, *dsptd ld to 15th, styd prmnt till grad wknd frm 2 out.*
..............................(7 to 2 op 4 to 1 tchd 9 to 2)   4
GO SILLY 8-11-5 (7") Miss P Robson, *sn beh, lost tch aftr 15th, tld off.*......................(66 to 1 op 50 to 1)   5
Dist: 2l, 12l, 4l, dist. 6m 58.70s. a 56.70s (5 Ran).
SR: 35/16/4/-/-/   (T N Dalgetty), T N Dalgetty

2812 Hennessy Cognac Special Novices' Hurdle (4-y-o and up) £11,186 2¼m
............................(2:50)

2356⁷ MORCELI (Ire) 6-11-7 D J Moffatt, *jmpd wl, made all, clr 2 out, styd on well*................(7 to 1 tchd 10 to 1)   1
2585* FIVE TO SEVEN (USA) 5-11-3 D Wilkinson, *al chasing wnr, mstk 6th, kpt on wl frm 2 out, no ch with winner.*
..............................(7 to 2 op 5 to 2)   2
2382⁴ MARCHWOOD 7-11-3 K Johnson, *al chasing ldrs, styd on wl frm 2 out.*............(15 to 2 op 7 to 1 tchd 9 to 1)   3
2568² BURNT IMP (USA) 4-11-2 J Callaghan, *chsd ldrs, no extr frm 2 out.*..............(9 to 2 op 7 to 2 tchd 5 to 1)   4
2740⁷ MAJOR BELL 6-11-3 M Moloney, *in tch, kpt on wl frm 2 out, not trble ldrs.*................(16 to 1 op 12 to 1)   5
2510⁵ VASILIEV (v) 6-11-3 L Wyer, *in tch, outpcd appr 3 out, no dngr aftr.*........................(16 to 1 op 12 to 1)   6
2646* ASLAN (Ire) 6-11-3 M Dwyer, *chsd ldrs, wknd aftr 3 out.*
..................(11 to 8 fav op 7 to 4 tchd 2 to 1)   7
2498² FLASH OF REALM (f) 8-11-3 A Dobbin, *nvr dngrs.*
..............................(25 to 1 tchd 33 to 1)   8
258¹ BANNTOWN BILL (Ire) 5-11-3 T Reed, *al beh.*
..............................(25 to 1 tchd 50 to 1)   9
2561² COQUI LANE 7-11-3 B Storey, *slwly into strd, al beh.*
..............................(25 to 1 op 20 to 1)   10
2220 STRONG DEEL 6-11-3 N Doughty, *sn wl beh.*
..............................(150 to 1 op 200 to 1)   11
2445⁴ EMERALD SEA (USA) 7-11-3 S Turner, *in tch till wknd aftr 6th.*................................(150 to 1)   12
2500⁶ D'ARBLAY STREET (Ire) 5-11-3 S McDougall, *in tch till wknd aftr 6th.*........................(150 to 1)   13
Dist: 12l, 2l, 8l, 11l, ½l, 8l, 20l, hd, 7l. 4m 31.30s. a 24.30s (13 Ran).
SR: 57/41/39/30/19/11/10/2/-/   (Mrs J M Corbett), J H Johnson

2813 Hamilton Memorial Chase Handicap For Amateur Riders (5-y-o and up) £4,270 3½m................ (3:20)

2264⁵ VELEDA II (Fr) [100] 7-9-11 (3") Mrs A Farrell, *jmpd wl, led 4th, drw clr frm 3 out, easily.*............(11 to 10 fav)   1
1063³ BLUFF KNOLL [124] 11-11-3 (7") Mr A Robson, *sn chasing wnr, pushed alng frm 12th, outpcd appr 3 out...* (5 to 4)   2
2718 SAMSUN [100] (bl) 12-9-7 (7") Miss S White, *led to 4th, sn lost tch, wl tld off.*................(25 to 1 op 33 to 1)   3
2324⁴ GATHERING TIME [100] 8-9-9² (7") Miss V Haigh, *blun and uns rdr 4th.*............(11 to 2 op 5 to 1 tchd 6 to 1)   ur
Dist: Dist, dist. 8m 2.10s. a 72.10s (4 Ran).
(L H Froomes), Mrs S A Bramall

2814 Cyril Alexander Memorial Novices' Chase (Div II) (6-y-o and up) £2,835 2¾m 110yds.................. (3:50)

2514 CLYDE RANGER 7-11-6 L Wyer, *made all, clr last, cmft-bly.*................................(2 to 1 on)   1
2238 GREENFIELD MANOR 7-11-0 A Merrigan, *chsd wnr frm 5th, drvn alng appr 2 out, no imprsn, sddl slpd.*
..............................(50 to 1 op 33 to 1)   2
2497⁶ POLLY MORRISSEY 7-11-0 A Dobbin, *in tch, effrt aftr 4 out, sn on same pace.*............(25 to 1 op 33 to 1)   3
2105 CEILIDH BOY 8-11-6 B Storey, *prmnt till wknd aftr 3 out.*
..............................(9 to 4 op 4 to 1)   4
2218⁸ CELTIC SONG 7-11-7 T Reed, *beh, some hdwy frm 4 out, nvr dngrs.*........................(7 to 1 op 5 to 1)   5
1587⁶ COUNT SURVEYOR 7-11-0 K Johnson, *al beh.*
..............................(12 to 1 op 9 to 1 tchd 16 to 1)   6
2446³ STAGSHAW BELLE 10-10-9 Mr J Bradburne, *lost tch frm 11th, tld off whn pld up lme r-in*............(50 to 1)   pu
SNOOK POINT 7-11-0 Richard Guest, *in tch, hdwy to track ldrs 9th, mstk 12th, sn wknd, wl beh whn pld up bef 3 out.*................................(200 to 1)   pu

Dist: 15l, ¾l, 1½l, sht-hd, 10l. 6m 25.00s. a 58.00s (8 Ran).
(I Bray), M D Hammond

2815 Harrow Hotel Dalkeith Handicap Hurdle (0-120 4-y-o and up) £2,827 2¼m
............................(4:20)

2540* BRAMBLEBERRY [104] 5-10-12 Richard Guest, *made all, quickened appr 6th, kpt on wl frm last.*
..............................(9 to 4 fav op 3 to 1)   1
2371* ARAGON AYR [105] 6-10-13 A Dobbin, *hld up in tch, hdwy hfwy, chsd wnr frm 7th, no imprsn.* (4 to 1 op 3 to 1)   2
2222 IT'S THE PITS [103] 7-10-11 T Reed, *hld up in tch, effrt appr 7th, kpt on same pace frm 2 out.*
..............................(5 to 2 tchd 11 to 4)   3
2437⁴ SWEET CITY [107] 9-11-1 Mr R Hale, *chsd wnr till outpcd aftr 7th.*..............(12 to 1 op 8 to 1 tchd 14 to 1)   4
2580³ PERSONAL HAZARD [92] (bl) 5-10-0 L Wyer, *chsd ldrs, wknd appr 3 out.*..........(11 to 2 op 5 to 1 tchd 6 to 1)   5
2575⁶ KAMBALDA RAMBLER [92] 10-10-0 B Storey, *chsd ldrs till wknd appr 3 out.*............(40 to 1 op 33 to 1 tchd 50 to 1)   6
2740⁹ MIDLAND EXPRESS [92] 11-9-13⁴ (5") P Waggott, *beh frm 7th.*..........................(50 to 1 op 33 to 1)   7
1922⁵ BAY TERN (USA) [107] 8-10-8 (7") A Linton, *chsd ldrs till 7th.*................................(10 to 1 op 8 to 1)   8
2581⁴ COOL DUDE [92] 8-9-12¹ (3") D J Moffatt, *beh frm 7th.*
..............................(11 to 1 op 8 to 1)   9
Dist: 7l, 4l, 20l, 4l, 5l, 15l, 12l, 2l. 4m 38.90s. a 31.90s (9 Ran).
(Mrs S Smith), Mrs S J Smith

LINGFIELD (heavy)
Friday March 4th
Going Correction: PLUS 1.10 sec. per fur.

2816 Keep Novices' Chase (5-y-o and up) £2,575 2½m 110yds........... (2:15)

2340² GINGER TRISTAN 8-11-5 Peter Hobbs, *led till aftr second, led 5th, drw clr frm 2 out, eased r-in.*
..............(11 to 4 op 7 to 4 tchd 3 to 1)   1
2517² NICKLUP 7-11-6 B Powell, *in tch, hdwy to track wnr frm 6th, rdn appr 3 out, tired and jmpd lft nxt, no headway.*..........................(11 to 4 op 2 to 1)   2
2639² SWITCH (bl) 8-11-5 G Bradley, *in tch till mstk and lost pl 7th, rdn to cl on ldr appr 3 out, sn btn.*
..............(4 to 1 fav tchd 2 to 1 and 6 to 4)   3
2461* ONE TO NOTE 10-11-5 M Ahern, *hld up, struggling in rear frm 5th, blun 7th and 9th, tld off whn pld up bef nxt, continued.*..............(16 to 1 op 10 to 1)   4
PURPLE SPRAY 9-11-5 M Hoad, *in tch whn mstk 5th, wknd bef nxt, tld off when pld up before tenth.*
..............................(33 to 1 op 16 to 1)   pu
2730³ STORMY FASHION 7-11-5 R Dunwoody, *led aftr second to 5th, wknd bef 8th, pld up bef nxt.* (14 to 1 op 7 to 1)   pu
Dist: 5l, 2l, dist. 5m 42.70s. a 41.70s (6 Ran).
(Mrs Christine Notley), D M Grissell

2817 EBF Rampart 'National Hunt' Novices' Hurdle Qualifier (5,6,7-y-o) £1,646 2m 110yds......................... (2:45)

1779* THERMAL WARRIOR 6-11-0 T Grantham, *trkd ldrs, hdwy 3 out, led appr nxt, rdn clr.* (11 to 10 on op 5 to 4 on)   1
2250⁵ CAWARRA BOY 6-10-7 (7") Mr E James, *rcd in 4th pl, rdn 5th, edgd lft and wnt second last, no ch whn wnr.*
..............(100 to 30 op 5 to 2 tchd 7 to 2)   2
1354⁸ YOUNG BUDRIC 7-11-0 J Lawrence, *led to second, led 3 out, rdn and hdd bef nxt, wkng whn bumped on landing last.*....................(12 to 1 tchd 10 to 1)   3
2057⁷ IN FOR A POUND (Ire) 5-11-0 R Dunwoody, *al beh, in tch till wknd appr 5th, tld off.*
..............(9 to 1 op 8 to 1 tchd 10 to 1)   4
1536 FERAL BAY (Ire) 5-11-0 G Bradley, *led second till hdd 3 out, wkng in 4th pl whn pld up bef nxt.*
..............................(6 to 1 op 5 to 1)   pu
Dist: 10l, 5l, 25l. 4m 26.30s. a 35.30s (5 Ran).
(C J Oakley), J A B Old

2818 Fort Handicap Chase (0-110 5-y-o and up) £3,392 2m..................(3:15)

2761³ MISTER ODDY [85] 8-10-4 (3") T Jenks, *trkd ldr, cld 7th, led bef nxt, wnt clr appr 3 out, unchlgd.*
..............................(5 to 2 tchd 3 to 1)   1
2463³ RAFIKI [106] 9-12-0 S Burrough, *chsd ldrs, outpcd 8th, blun 3 out, hit nxt, styd on to go second cl hme.*
..............................(5 to 1 op 7 to 2)   2
2603 PEACEMAN [103] 8-11-11 D Murphy, *set pd pace, mstk 7th, sn hdd, outpcd appr 3 out, clr second till wknd r-in.*
..............(7 to 4 fav op 6 to 4 tchd 15 to 8)   3
2707³ FRED SPLENDID [92] 11-11-0 R Dunwoody, *al beh, lost tch frm 7th, tld off.*........(13 to 2 op 5 to 1 tchd 7 to 1)   4
2639 NATHIR (USA) [100] 8-11-8 N Williamson, *al last, outpcd frm 4th, tld off.*..........(8 to 1 op 5 to 1 tchd 9 to 1)   5
Dist: 8l, 1½l, 30l, 30l. 4m 25.10s. a 31.10s (5 Ran).
(Mrs R M Hill), J S King

2819 Portcullis Handicap Hurdle (0-120 4-y-o and up) £2,745 2m 110yds.....(3:45)

2494[4] FONTANAYS (Ire) [95] 6-10-3 (5") E Husband, *hld up in tch, hdwy to ld sn aftr 2 out, clr whn hit last, cmftbly.*
...............................(7 to 2 op 11 to 4) 1
2697[3] FUNAMBULIEN (USA) [95] 7-10-8 R Dunwoody, *trkd ldrs, rdn 2 out, kpt on to go second r-in.............2 to 1 jt-*
fav tchd 5 to 2) 2
2649[2] NORTHERN SADDLER [114] 7-11-13 G McCourt, *led, mstk 3 out, hrd rdn and hdd sn aftr nxt, wknd r-in.*
.................(2 to 1 jt-fav op 11 to 8 tchd 9 to 4) 3
2626[4] NOVA SPIRIT [88] 6-10-1 B Powell, *trkd ldr till outpcd 3 out, rallied briefly, wknd appr 2 out.*
...............(5 to 1 op 9 to 2 tchd 6 to 1) 4
2521[4] AVERON [87] 14-10-0 Lorna Vincent, *al last, tld off frm 4th.*..............................(33 to 1 op 25 to 1) 5
Dist: 2½l, 7l, 8l, 6l. 4m 18.60s. a 27.60s (5 Ran).

(Pegasus Racing Partnership), Mrs M McCourt

2820 Dave Freeman Memorial Handicap Chase (0-125 5-y-o and up) £2,736 3m ....(4:15)

2602* SHEER ABILITY [122] 8-12-0 R Dunwoody, *led, jmpd slwly 5th, hdd 7th, led 9th to 13th, led ag'n nxt, drw clr frm 2 out.*......................(11 to 4 on tchd 6 to 4 on) 1
2462[2] CITY KID [120] 9-11-5 (7") J J Brown, *dsptd ld 5th, led 7th to 9th, led 13th to nxt, ev ch till wknd 2 out.*
...........................(11 to 4 op 5 to 2 tchd 3 to 1) 2
FIRE AT WILL [102] 11-10-8 B Powell, *mstk 8th, blun tenth, sn lost tch, tld off.*
........(14 to 1 op 10 to 1 tchd 16 to 1 and 20 to 1) 3
BUDDINGTON [112] 9-11-1 (3") R Farrant, *in tch to hfwy, outpcd whn jmpd slwly 11th, pld up aftr 13th.*
..........................(6 to 1 op 4 to 1) pu
Dist: 6l, 15l. 6m 53.20s. a 60.20s (4 Ran).

(Michael Devlin), C J Mann

2821 Moat Maiden Hurdle (4-y-o) £1,695 2m 110yds........................(4:45)

2676[4] COLLIER BAY 11-0 T Grantham, *made most, drw clr frm 2 out, very easily.*
........(11 to 8 op 11 to 10 tchd 6 to 4 and 13 to 8) 1
2722[3] GENERAL MOUKTAR 11-0 R Dunwoody, *hld up, wnt second 3 out, rdn appr nxt, sn btn.*
............(11 to 8 on op 5 to 4 on tchd 13 to 8 on) 2
2624[3] VISIMOTION (USA) 11-0 T Kent, *pld hrd, dsptd ld second and 3rd, trkd wnr till wknd quickly 3 out, tld off.*
..........................(10 to 1 op 8 to 1 tchd 12 to 1) 3
2760[4] HERETICAL MISS 10-6 (3") A Thornton, *beh and not fluent, wknd appr 4th, sn tld off.*.........(66 to 1 op 33 to 1) 4
Dist: 20l, dist, dist. 4m 14.10s. a 23.10s (4 Ran).
SR: 37/17/-/-/

(W E Sturt), J A B Old

NEWBURY (good)
Friday March 4th

Going Correction: PLUS 1.10 sec. per fur. (races 1,3,-4,5), PLUS 0.85 (2,6)

2822 Ardington Novices' Chase (5-y-o and up) £3,557 2m 1f..............(2:00)

2721[5] BEACH BUM 8-11-8 C Maude, *hit 5th, hdwy 7th, chsd ldrs 4 out, drvn to ld last, all out.* (20 to 1 tchd 33 to 1) 1
2675[2] LOS BUCCANEROS 11-11-8 G Upton, *in tch, hit 8th, pressed ldrs 9th, led 3 out to last, hrd rdn, no extr.*
..................(5 to 4 fav op 11 to 10 tchd 11 to 8) 2
1405 PICKETSTONE 7-11-8 R Bellamy, *l/ft in ld 8th, hdd 3 out, btn whn blun nxt.*.................(12 to 1 op 10 to 1) 3
2538[5] QUENTIN DURWOOD 8-11-8 S McNeill, *prmnt, pressed ldr 8th to 9th, wknd rpdly aftr 4 out...(4 to 1 tchd 7 to 2) 4
2532 ALWAYS REMEMBER 7-11-8 B Clifford, *led till mstk and uns rdr 4th..................(11 to 2 op 4 to 1) ur
2455[4] HERMES HARVEST 6-11-1 (7") Mr G Hogan, *uns rdr 3rd.*
............................(14 to 1) ur
2304[4] EMERALD RULER 7-11-8 R J Beggan, *al beh, tld off whn pld up bef 3 out......(11 to 1 op 10 to 1 tchd 12 to 1) pu
741[4] ON THE TEAR 8-11-8 D Gallagher, *al beh, tld off whn pld up bef 4 out.*........(12 to 1 tchd 25 to 1 and 16 to 1) pu
1866 PARSON'S WAY 7-11-8 W McFarland, *mstks, al beh, tld off whn pld up bef 4 out.*........................ pu
Dist: 3l, 25l, 25l. 4m 32.10s. a 31.10s (9 Ran).

(Mrs Judy Young), Mrs J A Young

2823 Radcot Handicap Hurdle (0-145 5-y-o and up) £3,730 3m 110yds......(2:30)

2597 BRAVE BUCCANEER [118] 7-11-9 P Niven, *in tch 6th, chlgd 3 out, led nxt, drvn out.*
...........................(10 to 30 op 5 to 2 tchd 7 to 2) 1
2763[3] RIMOUSKI [100] 6-10-5 Mr J Cambidge, *hdwy 3 out, sn hrd rdn, rallied last, styd on, not rch wnr.*
...........................(9 to 1 op 7 to 1) 2

2824 Hampshire Handicap Chase (0-140 5-y-o and up) £3,668 3m........ (3:00)

1512[2] TIPP MARINER [106] 9-10-0 J Osborne, *trkd ldr, hit second, lost pl 12th, rallied frm 4 out, chlgd 2 out, sn led, pushed out..........*(13 to 2 op 8 to 1 tchd 10 to 1) 1
2359[3] MANDER'S WAY [109] 9-10-3[3] G Upton, *in tch, chsd ldr 12th, led 4 out till aftr 2 out, sn rdn, found little.*
...........................(9 to 2 op 4 to 1 tchd 5 to 1) 2
2536[2] LOCH BLUE [108] 12-10-2 A Dicken, *lost pos 14th, styd on frm 4 out, kpt on r-in...(11 to 2 op 5 to 1 tchd 6 to 1) 3
2474 KING'S CURATE [130] 10-11-10 M Perrett, *led to 4 out, wkng whn hit nxt.*
...........................(11 to 8 fav op 11 to 10 on tchd 6 to 4) 4
2648[4] MIGHTY FALCON [110] (bl) 9-10-4 P Holley, *al beh, jmpd slwly 9th, lost tch 12th, tld off whn pld up bef last.*
...........................(5 to 1 tchd 6 to 1) pu
Dist: 3½l, 2l, 25l. 6m 28.80s. a 40.80s (5 Ran).

(Mrs Jean R Bishop), S E Sherwood

2825 Geoffrey Gilbey Handicap Chase (5-y-o and up) £4,172 2m 1f........(3:30)

2337[2] SPREE CROSS [123] 8-10-0 A Maguire, *made all, pckd 7th, wnt clr 3 out, unchlgd.*............(9 to 4 op 2 to 1) 1
2383* FOR A LAUGH [123] 10-9-7 (7") Mr D Parker, *chsd ldrs, blun 4 out, styd on same pace..*(9 to 4 op 2 to 1) 2
2672* YOUNG SNUGFIT [147] 10-11-10 J Osborne, *wth wnr to 4th, rdn 3 out, sn one pace.*
...........................(1 to 1 fav op 7 to 4 tchd 9 to 4) 3
615[6] PALM READER [125] 10-10-2 J R Kavanagh, *hld up, not fluent, hit 4 out, sn wknd..........*(8 to 1 tchd 9 to 1) 4
2645[6] LUCKY AGAIN [123] 7-10-0 S McNeill, *strt hold, in tch, 5th and fdg whn f 3 out................*(33 to 1 op 50 to 1) f
Dist: 15l, 5l, nk. 4m 22.10s. a 21.10s (5 Ran).
SR: 48/33/52/29/-/

(P L Mason), Mrs D Haine

2826 Peter Hamer Memorial Hunters' Chase (6-y-o and up) £2,276 3m (4:00)

ANDROS PRINCE 9-11-2 (7") Mr M Felton, *prmnt, led tenth, wnt clr frm 4 out.*..........(11 to 8 op 5 to 4) 1
SWINHOE CROFT 12-11-8 (7") Mr C Stockton, *led second to tenth, chlgd 13th, lost tch frm 4 out.*
...........................(5 to 4 fav op Evens tchd 11 to 8) 2
2482[3] MATSIX 13-11-4 (5") Miss P Jones, *prmnt till wknd 12th, disputing poor second whn f last, rmntd to finish 3rd.*
...........................(11 to 2 op 5 to 1 tchd 6 to 1) 3
DOMINICS CROSS 10-11-2 (7") Mr B Pollock, *in tch, rdn appr 14th, sn wknd, tld off whn pld up bef 4 out.*
...........................(8 to 1 op 12 to 1 tchd 14 to 1) pu
Dist: Dist, dist. 6m 33.30s. a 45.30s (4 Ran).

(Miss C Gordon), Miss C Gordon

2827 Whatcombe Novices' Handicap Hurdle (5-y-o and up) £3,213 2m 5f.. (4:30)

2403[3] GLENTOWER (Ire) [100] 6-10-3 A Maguire, *in tch, chlgd 3 out, led last, drvn out.*...........(5 to 1 op 8 to 1) 1
1953* CASTLE COURT (Ire) [104] 6-10-7 J Osborne, *trkd ldrs, chlgd 3 out, sn led gng wl, hdd last, shaken up and one pace r-in..........*(5 to 1 op 7 to 1 tchd 8 to 1) 2
2556[4] CONEY ROAD [98] 5-10-1 P Holley, *hdwy and pushed alng 4 out, styd on same pace 2 out.....*(11 to 4 jt-fav op 3 to 1 tchd 100 to 30 and 5 to 2) 3
2599[3] WITH IMPUNITY [97] 5-10-0 C Llewellyn, *led aftr 1st till after 3 out, wknd rpdly.*
...........................(10 to 1 tchd 8 to 1 and 12 to 1) 4
2505* CUNNINGHAMS FORD (Ire) [121] 6-11-3 (7") Mr A Harvey, *chsd ldrs 4th, chlgd four out, rdn and wknd rpdly appr nxt.................*(11 to 4 jt-fav op 9 to 4 tchd 3 to 1) 5
2556[2] BOND JNR (Ire) [104] 5-10-2 (5") Guy Lewis, *mid-div, chsd ldrs 7th, wknd appr 3 out.*
...........................(15 to 2 op 8 to 1 tchd 9 to 1) 6
2452[2] MAMES BOY [97] 7-9-11 (3") P Hide, *prmnt, rdn whn ran out 7th.*............................(8 to 1 op 5 to 1) ro
1542[9] PECTORUS (Ire) [97] 6-10-0 M Foster, *al beh, tld off whn pld up bef 4 out......*(16 to 1 op 14 to 1 tchd 20 to 1) pu

1167* WORLD WITHOUT END (USA) [114] 5-11-3 Diane Clay, *led till aftr 1st, wknd quickly 6th, tld off whn pld up bef 3 out*.....................(16 to 1 op 12 to 1 tchd 20 to 1) pu
Dist: 7l, 12l, 20l, 12l, 25l. 5m 15.30s. a 22.30s (9 Ran).
SR: 30/27/9/-/-/-/ (Lord Swaythling), N J Henderson

DONCASTER (good)
Saturday March 5th
Going Correction: PLUS 0.30 sec. per fur.

2828 Boughton And District Social Club Novices' Hurdle (4-y-o and up) £2,547 2½m.........................(1:55)

2068* OUTSET (Ire) 4-10-8 (7") Mr C Bonner, *made all, clr 2 out, ran on wl, cmftbly....* (6 to 1 op 11 to 2 tchd 13 to 2) 1
23612 ACT OF PARLIAMENT (Ire) 6-11-10 N Williamson, *trkd ldrs, rdn appr 3 out, kpt on, no ch wth wnr.*
............................(7 to 2 op 3 to 1) 2
25858 TUSKY 6-11-1 (3") N Bentley, *chsd ldrs, slightly outpcd appr 3 out, kpt on und pres approaching last.* (33 to 1) 3
1773* LYPHANTASTIC (USA) 5-11-4 M Dwyer, *trkd ldr, rdn aftr 3 out, wknd after nxt.*.............(5 to 1 op 7 to 2) 4
26385 PRIMO FIGLIO 4-10-4 (5") P Williams, *in tch, outpcd aftr 5th, styd on wl frm 2 out, nvr dngrs.*
............................(20 to 1 op 16 to 1) 5
25004 STOP THE WALLER (Ire) 5-11-4 A Dobbin, *in tch, hdwy to track ldrs 7th, sn pushed alng, wknd appr 3 out.*
............................(20 to 1) 6
21157 DOC SPOT 4-10-9 D Byrne, *nvr nr ldrs*.........(50 to 1) 7
27234 NADJATI (USA) 5-11-4 M Richards, *hld up, effrt appr 3 out, sn btn*.........(7 to 4 fav op 2 to 1 tchd 9 to 4) 8
1490 SCEPTICAL 6-11-4 T Reed, *nvr nr to chal.*
............................(50 to 1 op 33 to 1) 9
25738 TROY BOY 4-10-9 J Callaghan, *al beh*.............(25 to 1) 10
26465 JAMES IS SPECIAL (Ire) 6-11-4 V Smith, *in tch, effrt appr 7th, sn btn*.............(16 to 1 op 12 to 1) 11
25348 LEGATA (Ire) 5-10-8 (5") P Midgley, *in tch to hfwy.*
............................(100 to 1 op 50 to 1) 12
24098 HERBALIST 5-11-1 (3") A Larnach, *al beh*.........(33 to 1) 13
2204 CLOSE OF PLAY 5-10-13 (5") D Fortt, *in tch, hdwy to chase ldrs 6th, wknd quickly appr 3 out.*
............................(66 to 1 op 50 to 1) 14
HEDDON HAUGH (Ire) 6-11-4 K Johnson, *al beh, tld off whn pld up bef 3 out*.............(66 to 1 op 50 to 1) pu
Dist: 10l, 2l, 8l, 5l, hd, nk, 10l, 15l, 4l. 4m 49.10s. a 11.10s (15 Ran).
SR: 36/35/27/19/5/9/-/8/-/ (Mark Kilner), M D Hammond

2829 Midday Interiors Novices' Chase (5-y-o and up) £3,133 2m 110yds...(2:25)

24365 FULL O'PRAISE (NZ) 7-11-2 T Reed, *pld hrd early, hld up, hdwy appr 4 out, staying on whn lft in ld 2 out, sn clr.*
............................(5 to 1 op 4 to 1) 1
11282 SHREWD JOHN 8-11-8 R Garritty, *hld up, hdwy appr 4 out, styd on wl frm 2 out*.............(7 to 1) 2
9096 THE COUNTRY TRADER 8-11-2 N Doughty, *al chasing clr ldrs, kpt on wl frm 2 out*.........(25 to 1 op 20 to 1) 3
25382 NEWLANDS-GENERAL 8-11-2 M Dwyer, *chsd ldr, blun badly 4 out, lft cl second 2 out, sn btn.*
............................(5 to 4 fav op 7 to 4 tchd 6 to 4) 4
26687 TRUE SHADE 8-11-2 B Dalton, *chsd clr ldrs till wknd aftr 4 out.*.............(8 to 1 op 7 to 1 tchd 9 to 1) 5
4384 APRIL CITY 5-10-3 M Ranger, *al beh*.............(25 to 1) 6
BULAMONTEE 6-11-2 N Williamson, *hit 4th and 6th, al beh.*.............(6 to 1 op 5 to 1) 7
8416 SAFFAAH (USA) 7-11-2 M Richards, *led second, hit nxt, hit 6th, clr whn f 2 out.*.............(8 to 1 tchd 9 to 1) f
2584 FAVOURED VICTOR (USA) 5-11-2 A S Smith, *led to second, prmnt till wknd quickly aftr 6th, tld off whn pld up bef 3 out*.............(14 to 1 tchd 16 to 1) pu
Dist: 4l, 2l, 12l, 20l, 3l, 8l. 4m 5.60s. a 10.60s (9 Ran).
SR: 32/34/26/14/-/-/ (Lord Zetland), P Calver

2830 Light Infantry Plate Handicap Hurdle (0-140 4-y-o and up) £3,042 3m 110yds
............................(3:00)

26742 CARIBOO GOLD (USA) [120] 5-11-9 N Williamson, *hld up, steady hdwy to ld aftr 3 out, edgd rght appr last, jst held on, fnshd 1st, plcd second.* (9 to 4 fav tchd 5 to 2) 1D
2403 ATTADALE [121] 6-11-10 T Reed, *hld up, hdwy aftr 7th, rdn to chal 3 out, swtchd appr last,styd on wl und pres,fnshd second plcd 1st*
............................(9 to 1 op 8 to 1 tchd 10 to 1) 1
2403 POLISHING [116] 7-11-10 (5") S Lyons, *beh and rdn aftr 6th, rallied frm 3 out, fnshd wl*.....(12 to 1 tchd 14 to 1) 3
24038 ACROW LINE [118] 9-11-7 D J Burchell, *trkd ldrs, rdn to ld 3 out, sn hdd, no extr...*(13 to 2 op 7 to 1 tchd 8 to 1) 4
26433 ELEGANT KING (Ire) [121] 6-11-10 R Greene, *prmnt, rdn appr 3 out, kpt on same pace.......*(12 to 1 op 8 to 1) 5
25723 WELSH LUSTRE (Ire) [120] 5-11-9 W Marston, *in tch, out-pcd aftr 3 out, no dngr after.......*(13 to 2 op 11 to 2) 6
2597 MIZYAN (Ire) [120] 6-11-9 S Keightley, *hld up, hdwy aftr 7th, rdn appr 3 out, sn btn.*.........(5 to 1 op 4 to 1) 7

24876 SPROWSTON BOY [114] 11-11-3 W Worthington, *led till hdd 4th, prmnt till wknd aftr 8th.* (25 to 1 op 16 to 1) 8
2153* IF YOU SAY SO [97] 8-10-0 A Mulholland, *wth ldr, led 4th, mstk 7th, hdd 3 out, wkng whn mistake nxt.*
............................(12 to 1 tchd 14 to 1) 9
1119* NORTHUMBRIAN KING [107] 8-10-10 J Callaghan, *chsd ldrs till wknd aftr 8th.*.............(25 to 1 op 16 to 1) 10
16574 I'M TOBY [107] 7-10-10 M Dwyer, *beh and rdn aftr 7th, tld off...*.............(14 to 1 op 12 to 1) 11
Dist: Hd, 2½l, 3l, 4l, 3l, nk, 7l, 5l, 8l. 6m 1.10s. a 21.10s (11 Ran).
(C H McGhie), L Lungo

2831 Velka Pardubicka Grimthorpe Handicap Chase (0-140 5-y-o and up) £7,181 3½m.........................(3:35)

24482 SHRADEN LEADER [117] 9-10-6 N Williamson, *prmnt, led tenth, rdn appr 2 out, styd on wl.*
............................(3 to 1 fav tchd 100 to 30 and 7 to 2) 1
2105* WHAAT FETTLE [124] 9-10-13 M Moloney, *al prmnt, ev ch 3 out, kpt on wl, no imprsn on wnr.*
............................(9 to 1 op 8 to 1 tchd 10 to 1) 2
2246 HIGH PADRE [113] 8-10-2 M Dwyer, *in tch till lost pl and beh hfwy, rdn aftr 12th, rallied appr 4 out, fnshd wl.*
............................(12 to 1) 3
24566 TEAM CHALLENGE [112] 12-10-0 M Richards, *led till hdd tenth, remained prmnt, ev ch 4 out, kpt on same pace.*
............................(50 to 1 op 33 to 1) 4
20113 MISTER ED [129] 11-11-4 D Morris, *in tch, rdn alng and outpcd aftr 13th, kpt on frm 3 out....*(8 to 1 op 7 to 1) 5
25763 HE WHO DARES WINS [117] 11-10-6 K Johnson, *in tch, pushed alng frm hfwy, outpcd aftr 15th, no dngr after.*
............................(10 to 1) 6
23704 SHOON WIND [117] 11-10-6 L Wyer, *in tch till wknd aftr 15th, tld off.*.............(9 to 1 op 10 to 1) 7
1875² MR BOSTON [135] 9-11-10 P Niven, *al beh, lost tch aftr 16th, tld off...........*(7 to 2 op 4 to 1 tchd 100 to 30) 8
25823 NO MORE TRIX [112] 8-10-1¹ R Garritty, *trkd ldrs till mstk and uns rdr 13th.............*(11 to 2 op 6 to 1) ur
2384 MUSTHAVEASWIG [120] 8-10-9 W Marston, *chsd ldrs till pld up bef 16th, broke blood vessel.*
............................(10 to 1 tchd 11 to 1) pu
Dist: 3½l, 4l, 2l, nk, 1½l, 25l, 2½l. 7m 4.80s. (10 Ran).
(W R J Everall), K C Bailey

2832 Mitsubishi Shogun Handicap Chase (0-135 5-y-o and up) £5,800 2m 3f 110yds.........................(4:05)

2738* KIND'A SMART [107] 9-10-0 A S Smith, *hld up, gd hdwy aftr tenth, led aftr 3 out, ran on strly.*
............................(17 to 2 op 8 to 1) 1
23594 SNITTON LANE [110] 8-10-3 M Richards, *sn tracking ldrs, hmpd 9th, led 4 out, hdd aftr nxt, kpt on, no ch wth wnr.*.............(12 to 1 op 10 to 1) 2
23833 JUST FRANKIE [117] 10-10-10 M Dwyer, *hld up in tch, steady hdwy to chal 4 out, one pace frm nxt.*
............................(10 to 1 tchd 10 to 1) 3
15852 BOARDING SCHOOL [107] 7-10-0 B Storey, *beh hfwy, styd on wl frm 3 out, nrst finish....................*(33 to 1) 4
15632 FARDROSS [108] 8-10-1 N Williamson, *prmnt, mstk 3rd, lft in ld 9th, hdd 11th, grad wknd frm 4 out.*
............................(8 to 1 op 7 to 1) 5
2488 ARMAGRET [135] 9-12-0 L Wyer, *beh hfwy till styd on wl frm 3 out, nrst finish.*.............(20 to 1 op 16 to 1) 6
24122 MAUDLINS CROSS [115] 9-10-8 P Niven, *al beh.*
............................(9 to 1 op 10 to 1 tchd 8 to 1) 7
22182 POLITICAL TOWER [109] 7-10-2 A Dobbin, *prmnt, hmpd 9th, led 11th, mstk and hdd 4 out, sn btn.*
............................(5 to 1 op 11 to 2 tchd 6 to 1) 8
22483 TRIMLOUGH [128] 9-11-7 W Marston, *chsd ldrs till wknd aftr 4 out.*.............(20 to 1 op 16 to 1) 9
2151² BISHOPDALE [108] 13-10-1¹ A Merrigan, *nvr better than mid-div.*.............(20 to 1) 10
19334 DRIVING FORCE [115] 8-10-5 (3") T Jenks, *beh frm tenth.*
............................(16 to 1 op 14 to 1) 11
2718 ICARUS (USA) [122] (bl) 8-11-1 Mr A Rebori, *chsd ldrs, hmpd 9th, wknd quickly appr 4 out, tld off....*(50 to 1) 12
2227* CORRARDER [114] 10-10-7³ Mr J Smyth-Osbourne, *mstks, in tch whn f 8th........*(9 to 1 op 8 to 1 tchd 10 to 1) f
2437* SIR PETER LELY [120] (bl) 7-10-6 (7") Mr C Bonner, *led till f 9th.............*(100 to 30 fav op 6 to 1) f
26363 REJOINUS [109] 9-10-2¹ R Garritty, *al beh, hmpd 9th, tld off whn pld up bef 4 out.....................*(16 to 1) pu
Dist: 8l, 6l, nk, sht-hd, nk, 2l, nk, 2l. 4m 54.50s. a 8.50s (15 Ran).
SR: 46/41/42/31/32/59/27/13/30/ (B Parker), K A Morgan

2833 Danka/Nec Handicap Hurdle (0-145 4-y-o and up) £3,179 2m 110yds (4:40)

2670 RATIFY [109] 7-10-0 A S Smith, *cl up, led 5th, ran on wl frm last.........................*(12 to 1 op 10 to 1) 1
1278* BOTTLES (USA) [121] 7-10-12 S Keightley, *nvr far away, chsd wnr appr last, no imprsn.*
............................(9 to 1 op 5 to 1 tchd 11 to 2) 2
22584 PONTYNYSWEN [127] (v) 6-11-4 D J Burchell, *prmnt, chlgd 3 out, sn rdn, kpt on same pace...*(10 to 1 op 8 to 1) 3

2566[3] GYMCRAK SOVEREIGN [109] 6-10-0 R Marley, *led till hdd 5th, remained prmnt, kpt on same pace frm 3 out.* ....(14 to 1) 4

1571[2] ARCOT [127] 6-11-4 T Reed, *pld hrd early, hld up, hdwy appr 3 out, rdn aftr nxt, no imprsn.* ....(11 to 4 fav op 3 to 1 tchd 100 to 30) 5

2689[2] STRATH ROYAL [120] 8-10-11 M Brennan, *mid-div, rdn and outpcd aftr 5th, styd on wl frm last.* ....(11 to 2 op 6 to 1 tchd 5 to 1) 6

2360* HOME COUNTIES (Ire) [128] (v) 5-11-2 (3*) D J Moffatt, *trkd ldrs, effrt aftr 3 out, sn btn.*..........(8 to 1 op 7 to 1) 7

2385* BO KNOWS BEST (Ire) [131] 5-11-8 Mr S Swiers, *chsd ldrs till outpcd hfwy, no dngr aftr.*......(9 to 1 op 8 to 1) 8

1559[5] TAROUDANT [133] 7-11-10 P Niven, *hld up in tch, effrt appr 3 out, sn btn.*.....(15 to 2 op 7 to 1 tchd 8 to 1) 9

2580[5] DUAL IMAGE [109] 7-9-7 (7*) F Leahy, *chsd ldrs till wknd appr 3 out.*..........(16 to 1 op 20 to 1) 10

2307 VAIN PRINCE [117] (bl) 7-10-3 (5*) E Husband, *beh most of way, tld off.*..........(50 to 1) 11

GOLDEN GUNNER (Ire) [109] 6-9-11 (3*) T Jenks, *beh most of way, tld off.*..........(33 to 1) 12

1735[3] RED INDIAN [115] 8-10-6 D Byrne, *hld up, effrt appr 3 out, no ch whn f nxt.*..........(14 to 1 op 16 to 1) f

Dist: 4l, 2½l, 1½l, 1½l, ½l, 7l, hd, ½l, 5l. 3m 58.30s. a 7.80s (13 Ran).

SR: 44/52/55/35/51/43/44/47/48/ (J C Fretwell), K A Morgan

2834 'St Ninian' Open National Hunt Flat Race (4,5,6-y-o) £1,940 2m 110yds ....(5:10)

2749 HIGHLY REPUTABLE (Ire) 4-10-9 J Lower, *hld up in tch, steady hdwy 5 out, led 2 out, ran on wl.* ....(7 to 2 fav op 5 to 2 tchd 9 to 2) 1

2677* GO BALLISTIC 5-11-3 (7*) R Massey, *cl up, led o'r 3 out, hdd 2 out, kpt on, no ch wth wnr.*....(9 to 2 op 3 to 1) 2

MR BUSKER (Ire) 5-11-3 Mr J Durkan, *in tch, outpcd 4 out, kpt on wl fnl 2 fs.*..........(16 to 1 tchd 20 to 1) 3

2387[6] CAPENWRAY (Ire) 5-11-10 B Storey, *hld up, smooth hdwy 4 out, rdn 2 fs out, kpt on same pace.* ....(20 to 1 op 14 to 1) 4

2387[3] DISSINGTON DENE 5-10-12 (5*) P Midgley, *wth ldr, led hfwy, hdd o'r 3 fs out, kpt on same pace.* ....(8 to 1 tchd 9 to 1 and 10 to 1) 5

2407[2] VALERIOS KING (Ire) 5-11-3 V Slattery, *led to hfwy, remained cl up, rdn o'r 4 fs out, grad wknd.* ....(5 to 1 tchd 6 to 1) 6

LOCHNAGRAIN (Ire) 6-11-3 P Niven, *in tch, no hdwy fnl 4 fs.*..........(10 to 1 tchd 12 to 1) 7

2677[7] MASTER HOPE (Ire) 5-11-3 Mr R Bevan, *chsd ldrs till wknd o'r 3 fs out.*..........(14 to 1 op 10 to 1) 8

2339[7] MACKABEE (Ire) 5-11-3 N Doughty, *trkd ldrs, effrt 4 fs out, sn wknd.*..........(9 to 1 op 10 to 1 tchd 8 to 1) 9

STORMY PETREL (Ire) 5-10-12 Mr P Macewan, *chsd ldrs till wknd 4 fs out.*..........(12 to 1 op 8 to 1) 10

2339[3] ARDENT LOVE (Ire) 5-10-5 (7*) R Moore, *nvr dngrs.* ....(12 to 1 op 8 to 1) 11

2387[5] GREY SMOKE 4-10-2 (7*) J Driscoll, *chsd ldrs till wknd 4 fs out.*..........(20 to 1) 12

2373[6] VAN DER GRASS 5-11-3 A Dobbin, *nvr better than mid-div.*..........(33 to 1 op 25 to 1) 13

2387 SPY DESSA 6-11-3 R Hodge, *ran wide aftr 3 fs, al beh.* ....(50 to 1) 14

SPONTANEOUS PRIDE 6-11-3 N Williamson, *pld very hrd, in tch to hfwy, sn beh.*..........(14 to 1 op 6 to 1) 15

HIGH MOOD 4-10-6 (3*) T Jenks, *al beh.* ....(14 to 1 op 16 to 1 tchd 20 to 1) 16

SKELTON LASS (Ire) 5-10-5 (7*) C Woodall, *loose bef strt, al beh.*..........(20 to 1 tchd 25 to 1 and 33 to 1) 17

2691 OPERA TALENT (Ire) 5-11-3 M Dwyer, *dwlt, in tch till wknd quickly 5 fs out, tld off.*.....(20 to 1 op 16 to 1) 18

Dist: 3½l, hd, ½l, 4l, 7l, 3l, 2l, 4l, ¾l, sht-hd. 3m 53.70s. (18 Ran).

(W J Gredley), M C Pipe

HEREFORD (soft)
Saturday March 5th

Going Correction: PLUS 1.25 sec. per fur. (races 1,3,-5,7), PLUS 0.90 (2,4,6)

2835 Teme Novices' Hurdle (4-y-o and up) £1,864 2m 1f..........(1:55)

DREAMS END 6-11-3 M Hourigan, *jmpd wl, trkd ldr, led 4 out, drw clr aftr 2 out, easily* ....(5 to 4 on op 6 to 4 on tchd 6 to 4) 1

1658[6] GOTTA BE JOKING 6-11-7 (3*) J McCarthy, *led second til hdd 4 out, chsd ldr, rdn and no imprsn frm 2 out.* ....(6 to 1 op 4 to 1) 2

2652[2] YOUNG TESS 4-10-4 S Burrough, *mstks, hld up, pushed alng 4th, styd on frm 3 out, nvr nrr.* (7 to 2 op 3 to 1) 3

FOIL THE FOX 6-10-9 (3*) A Thornton, *chsd ldr frm 5th, wnt 3rd 3 out, sn rdn and one pace* (12 to 1 op 16 to 1) 4

2494[9] TEMPLE KNIGHT 5-11-3 S Earle, *led to second, chsd ldr til wknd aftr 4 out.*..........(33 to 1) 5

2525[8] ADMIRAL BYNG (Fr) 7-11-0 (3*) D Meredith, *prmnt to 6th, wknd quickly, tld off whn pld up aftr 2 out.* ....(8 to 1 op 12 to 1) pu

2335[9] MERRYHILL MADAM 5-10-12 W Humphreys, *chsd ldr, mstk 5th, sn wknd, tld off whn pld up aftr 2 out.* ....(33 to 1) pu

1277[6] CHILDSWAY 6-11-3 G Upton, *drpd rear aftr 3rd, not fluent, sn tld off, jmpd slwly and pld up after 3 out.* ....(10 to 1 op 8 to 1) pu

Dist: 15l, hd, 8l, 4l. 4m 12.20s. a 26.20s (8 Ran).

SR: 40/32/12/12/13/ (T G Price), P J Hobbs

2836 Newent Handicap Chase (0-105 5-y-o and up) £2,827 2m 3f..........(2:25)

2707[2] DEXTRA DOVE [102] 7-11-11 S Earle, *led 3rd, hdd 8th, led nxt, styd on wl frm 2 out, rdn out* (9 to 4 fav op 2 to 1) 1

2406[6] OLD ROAD (USA) [77] (bl) 8-10-0 P McDermott, *led to 3rd, pressed ldr til led ag'n 8th, hdd nxt, rdn and no imprsn frm 2 out.*..........(10 to 1 tchd 11 to 1) 2

2527 DUNKERY BEACON [77] 8-9-7 (7*) P McLoughlin, *hld up, wnt 3rd 9th, chsd ldg pair, kpt on frm 3 out, not quicken.*..........(33 to 1 op 20 to 1) 3

2205[2] PITHY [100] 12-11-2 (7*) Mr G Hogan, *hld up, effrt and rdn 5 out, styd on frm 3 out, nvr nrr.* (100 to 30 op 5 to 2) 4

1933[2] CHAIN SHOT [105] 9-12-0 R Bellamy, *hld up, rdn alng 5 out, no imprsn aftr nxt.*..........(12 to 1 op 8 to 1) 5

2639 JAMES MY BOY [90] 14-10-10 (3*) R Davis, *hld up, drpd rear 11th, btn whn mstk 2 out.* ....(16 to 1 op 12 to 1 tchd 20 to 1) 6

2406 MO ICHI DO [86] (bl) 8-10-6 (3*) T Eley, *mstk 5th, rdn nxt, wknd 8th, btn whn mistake 2 out.* (11 to 1 op 10 to 1) 7

2504[4] BARELY BLACK [87] 6-10-10 W Humphreys, *in tch, blun 5th, not fluent aftr, beh after 5 out.* (5 to 2 tchd 3 to 1) 8

Dist: 6l, 2l, 4l, 10l, 12l, 4l, 10l. 5m 1.60s. a 31.60s (8 Ran).

(Dextra Lighting Systems), R H Alner

2837 March Novices' Selling Hurdle (4-y-o and up) £1,550 2m 3f 110yds....(2:55)

2631[5] THE JET SET 7-11-2 (3*) R Davis, *hld up, hdwy to track ldrs aftr 5 out, led 2 out, drvn out*..(11 to 2 op 5 to 1) 1

2430[9] BEE BEAT 6-11-5 M Bosley, *hld up and beh, hdwy aftr 6th, led after 4 out til hdd 2 out, not quicken.* ....(8 to 1 tchd 10 to 1) 2

1354[9] MOON MONKEY (Ire) 6-11-5 M Hourigan, *hld up, hdwy 5 out, chsd ldg pair, sn no imprsn, btn whn mstk last.* ....(6 to 1) 3

2558 ORCHESTRATED CHAOS (Ire) 5-11-0 Mr J Mead, *hld up, hdwy 5th, led 5 out til aftr nxt, wknd 3 out, tld off.* ....(25 to 1 op 16 to 1) 4

2341[6] JUMPING JUDGE 7-11-5 S Earle, *chsd ldr to 6th, wknd 3 out, tld off.*..........(11 to 2 op 5 to 1) 5

2776 NORTHERN TRIAL (USA) 6-10-12 (7*) N Juckes, *f 1st.* ....(9 to 4 fav op 7 to 4) f

2291[7] NORTH HOLLOW 9-11-0 (5*) Mr D McCain, *brght dwn 1st.* ....(14 to 1 op 12 to 1) bd

2291 WHAT A MOUNT 11-11-5 R Bellamy, *prmnt til wknd quickly aftr 6th, tld off whn pld up bef 4 out.* ....(20 to 1 op 16 to 1) pu

2730 HELLO LADY 7-10-7 (7*) Mr J O'Shaughnessy, *led to 5 out, wknd aftr nxt, tld off whn pld up bef 2 out.* ....(20 to 1 op 12 to 1) pu

2789 SONNY'S SONG 8-11-2 (3*) A Thornton, *beh 6th, tld off whn pld up bef 4 out.*..........(25 to 1 op 16 to 1) pu

2291[5] MISTRESS MINX 5-11-0 R J Beggan, *drpd rear 5th, sn beh, tld off whn pld up bef 3 out.*....(8 to 1 op 7 to 1) pu

2144 CUMREWS NEPHEW 6-11-5 T Wall, *presesed ldr to 5 out, wknd quickly, tld off whn pld up bef 2 out.* ....(20 to 1 op 12 to 1) pu

2762 NATIONAL FLAG (Fr) 4-10-10 B Clifford, *drpd rear 5th, sn beh, tld off whn pld up bef 3 out.*. (25 to 1 op 10 to 1) pu

WOLF'S HABITAT (v) 4-10-5 J R Kavanagh, *al beh, lost tch aftr 6th, tld off whn pld up bef 3 out* ....(20 to 1 op 12 to 1) pu

Dist: 5l, 10l, 30l, 3l. 5m 13.10s. a 52.10s (14 Ran).

(T J Parrott), Mrs H Parrott

2838 Charlie Knipe Hunters' Chase (6-y-o and up) £1,511 3m 1f 110yds....(3:25)

2526[2] CAPE COTTAGE 10-11-7 (7*) Mr A Phillips, *hld up, pckd 3rd, mstk 10th, cld up 5 out, led aftr 3 out, styd on wl.* (11 to 8 on op 5 to 4 on tchd 6 to 5 on and 6 to 4 on) 1

CARRICKMINES 9-11-11 (7*) Mr G Hogan, *led to 9th, led ag'n 6 out till aftr 3 out, rdn and no imprsn.* ....(4 to 1 op 5 to 2) 2

2765 DOUBTING DONNA 8-11-6 (7*) Mr V Hughes, *hld up in last pl, not fluent, hdwy 10th, wnt moderate 3rd appr 3 out, no imprsn, tld off.*.... (14 to 1 op 8 to 1 tchd 16 to 1) 3

2482[5] CURAHEEN BOY 14-12-0 (7*) Miss J Butler, *chsd ldg pair til wknd 9th, sn tld off, plodded around.* ....(12 to 1 op 6 to 1 tchd 14 to 1) 4

2605 THE ARTFUL RASCAL 10-11-7 (7*) Mr C J B Barlow, *trkd ldr, led 9th till mstk and hdd 6 out, mistake nxt, sn beh, pld up bef 3 out.*..........(4 to 1 op 3 to 1) pu

NORMANDY BILL 7-11-9 (5*) Mr D McCain, *blun second, beh whn mstk 9th, tld off when pld up bef 12th.* ....(33 to 1 op 20 to 1) pu

Dist: 5l, 30l, 12l. 6m 52.90s. a 40.90s (6 Ran).

(D J Caro), D J Caro

2839 Bosbury Handicap Hurdle (0-115 4-y-o and up) £2,326 2m 1f........... (3:55)

1799[3] GOLDINGO [88] 7-10-3 (3*) R Davis, *hld up, mstk 5th, cld up 3 out, mistake nxt, sn led, rdn out r-in, styd on wl.* ....(7 to 2 op 3 to 1) 1
2532[2] BALLERINA ROSE [82] 7-9-11 (3*) A Procter, *trkd ldrs, cl up and ev ch 3 out, rdn and not quicken aftr nxt.* ....(7 to 1 op 6 to 1 tchd 8 to 1) 2
262* ON THE SAUCE [110] (bl) 7-11-7 (7*) T Dascombe, *led till hdd aftr 3 out, styd on one pace.* ....(3 to 1 fav op 5 to 1 tchd 7 to 2) 3
1890[5] TILT TECH FLYER [105] 9-11-2 (7*) N Collum, *hld up, trkd ldrs frm 5th til wknd aftr 3 out.*......(7 to 1 op 5 to 1) 4
JUST (Fr) [86] (v) 8-10-4 M Foster, *in tch, cl up and ev ch 4 out, led aftr nxt, mstk and hdd 2 out, wknd appr last.* ....(6 to 1 op 5 to 1 tchd 7 to 1) 5
2717[2] SCHWEPPES TONIC [97] 8-10-10 (5*) D Matthews, *pressed ldr in second pl till wknd quickly aftr 3 out.* ....(100 to 30 op 5 to 2) 6
2717 TITUS GOLD [100] (v) 9-11-4 D Bridgwater, *drpd rear aftr 5th, sn beh*........................(20 to 1 op 14 to 1) 7
25[9] BANKONIT (Ire) [104] 6-11-1 (7*) Mr J O'Shaughnessy, *hld up, drpd rear and rdn alng aftr 5th, sn no imprsn.* ....(14 to 1 op 12 to 1 tchd 16 to 1) 8
VISCOUNT TULLY [100] 9-11-4 W Humphreys, *hld up in last pl, lost tch aftr 5th*............(25 to 1 op 12 to 1) 9

Dist: 8l, 1l, 1l, 6l, 10l, 8l, 6l, ½l. 4m 15.70s. a 29.70s (9 Ran).
SR: -/-/7/1/-/-/ (G M Price), G M Price

2840 Malvern Novices' Chase (5-y-o and up) £2,522 2m.................(4:25)

2803* CASTLE DIAMOND 7-11-12 (3ex) M Bosley, *wnt second 5th, pressed ldr, rdn 3 out, led nxt, mstk last, drvn out.* ....(11 to 10 on op 5 to 4 on) 1
2458[4] HIGHLAND POACHER 7-11-2 J Railton, *led to 6th, led ag'n 3 out to nxt, ev ch whn mstk last, not quicken r-in.* ....(7 to 2 op 4 to 1) 2
2822 ALWAYS REMEMBER 7-11-2 B Clifford, *cl up, led 6th, jmpd slwly 4 out, hdd nxt, ev ch whn mstk last, not quicken r-in*.........................(5 to 2 op 7 to 4) 3
MICRONOVA 8-11-2 R Bellamy, *mstks, lost tch 7th, tld off whn refused last*...............(14 to 1 tchd 16 to 1) ref
2542[5] ALL ELECTRIC (bl) 9-10-13 (3*) R Farrant, *mstks, reminders aftr 4th, tld off whn mistake and pld up after 3 out.* .... (33 to 1 op 20 to 1) pu

Dist: 5l, ¾l. 4m 9.20s. a 20.20s (5 Ran).
SR: 40/25/24/-/-/ (Mrs S Kavanagh), H M Kavanagh

2841 Levy Board Novices' Handicap Hurdle (0-100 4-y-o and up) £1,906 2m 3f 110yds........................ (4:55)

2142[5] LUCKY BLUE [66] 7-10-0 S Earle, *led to second, chsd ldr aftr 6th, led 3 out, hdd nxt, rdn to ld ag'n last, jst hld on*..(20 to 1) 1
2692[3] FORTUNES COURSE (Ire) [75] 5-10-9 J R Kavanagh, *chsd ldr frm 6th, pushed alng 4 out, rallied aftr 2 out, 3rd whn mstk last, styd on nr finish, jst fld.* .... (11 to 2 op 5 to 1) 2
2414[2] RASTA MAN [80] 6-11-0 N Mann, *hld up, hdwy 6th, led 2 out, sn hdd, swtchd appr last not quicken r-in.* ....(5 to 1 op 3 to 1) 3
2708[4] BOLD STREET BLUES [78] 7-10-12 C Llewellyn, *beh, rdn and hdwy aftr 7th, styd on frm nxt, no imprsn after 2 out*...............................(5 to 1 tchd 11 to 2) 4
2763 RAGGERTY (Ire) [83] 4-11-0 (3*) N Bentley, *lost pl 6th, beh til styd on frm 3 out, nvr nrr*........(8 to 1 op 7 to 1) 5
2523[7] MUCH [72] 7-10-6[5] Mr M Jackson, *hld up, hdwy 6th, chsd ldrs 4 out, wknd 2 out*....................... (33 to 1) 6
2606[2] SHARPSIDE [67] 7-9-13[1] (3*) R Davis, *chsd ldr, wnt second 5th, mstk 3 out, sn wknd.* ....(7 to 2 fav op 3 to 1 tchd 4 to 1) 7
2694[4] SHARED GOLD [87] 4-11-7 M Bosley, *sn wl beh, styd on aftr 4 out, not rch ldrs*..........(10 to 1 tchd 11 to 1) 8
SARAH'S WROATH [66] 9-10-0 R Bellamy, *chsd clr ldr to 6th, sn beh*.....................(20 to 1 tchd 25 to 1) 9
BRENDA HUNT (Ire) [66] 5-10-0 M Ahern, *hld up, hdwy to chase clr ldr aftr 5th til wknd 4 out*........... (33 to 1) 10
2421[7] JANET SCIBS [66] 8-9-9 (5*) Guy Lewis, *mid-div til wknd aftr 7th, sn beh*.............................(33 to 1) 11
2606[6] RAFTERS [90] 5-11-7 (3*) R Farrant, *hit 5th, wknd aftr nxt, tld off whn pld up bef 3 out*.........(9 to 1 op 7 to 1) pu
1448[2] MR POPPLETON [70] 5-10-4 D Bridgwater, *led second, wl clr aftr nxt, hdd 3 out, wknd quickly, beh whn pld up bef last*.................(6 to 1 op 5 to 1 tchd 7 to 1) pu
1994[7] LOYAL GAIT (NZ) [66] 6-10-0 B Clifford, *lost tch aftr 5th, tld off whn pld up bef 3 out*...........(10 to 1 tchd 12 to 1) pu

Dist: Nk, 1½l, 8l, 1½l, 1½l, 6l, 1½l, nk, 10l, 15l. 5m 3.30s. a 42.30s (14 Ran).
(Mrs S M Palmer), N B Thomson

NAVAN (IRE) (heavy)
Saturday March 5th

2842 Castletown Handicap Hurdle (0-123 4-y-o and up) £3,105 2m........ (1:30)

2703[2] FIDDLERS BOW VI (Ire) [-] 6-9-13 P Carberry,.. (3 to 1 fav) 1
2284[5] OPERA HAT (Ire) [-] 6-11-4 A Powell,.............(11 to 2) 2
2180* STEEL MIRROR [-] 5-11-9 J Shortt,...............(5 to 1) 3
2552[7] MISS LIME [-] 7-11-1 (7*) R A Hennessy,.........(10 to 1) 4
2754[8] FINAWAY BOY (Ire) [-] 6-11-2 J P Banahan,.......(12 to 1) 5
2590 MONTE FIGO [-] 7-10-13 F Woods,..............(25 to 1) 6
2464[3] MINIGIRLS NIECE (Ire) [-] 6-10-5 D P Fagan,......(12 to 1) 7
2054[3] CELTIC SAILS (Ire) [-] 6-11-4 B Sheridan,..........(9 to 1) 8
2590 STAR ROSE [-] 12-10-12 (7*) J Butler,............(20 to 1) 9
2703[8] DEGO DANCER [-] 7-10-2 (5*) J P Broderick,...... (8 to 1) 10
2586 BARNAGEERA BOY (Ire) [-] 5-9-13 H Rogers,.....(12 to 1) 11
2309* DAMODAR [-] 5-10-9 F J Flood,..................(6 to 1) 12
466[7] NORTHERN BREGA [-] 7-9-7 P L Malone,.........(50 to 1) 13
2552[8] FAIRY STRIKE (Ire) [-] 5-10-5 K F O'Brien,........ (25 to 1) pu

Dist: 1½l, ¾l, 6l, 10l. 4m 14.60s. (14 Ran).
(Mrs A T B Kearney), Noel Meade

2843 E.B.F. Novice Chase Series Final (Listed) (5-y-o and up) £7,000 2¾m..(2:00)

2609* MERRY GALE (Ire) 6-12-0 K F O'Brien, *made all, jmpd wl, easily*.................................... (7 to 2 on) 1
2588* BELMONT KING (Ire) 6-11-8 L P Cusack, *trkd wnr till rdn and wknd 2 out, mstk last*.................... (7 to 1) 2
2681* BUCKS-CHOICE (bl) 7-11-11 J F Titley, *mstks, niggled alng appr 8th, rdn and btn 3 out, injured tendons, dead.* ....(7 to 2) 3
2659 BIG JAMES 12-11-1 (3*) T J Mitchell, *lost tch frm 6th, pld up aftr 8th*.................................. (33 to 1) pu

Dist: 25l, dist. 6m 23.50s. (4 Ran).
(Herb M Stanley), J T R Dreaper

2844 INH Stallion Owners EBF Novice Hurdle Series Final (Listed) (6-y-o and up) £8,280 2¾m.................. (2:30)

2753[4] COURT MELODY (Ire) 6-11-6 (5*) J P Broderick, *prog frm mid-div into second 4 out, rdn to ld appr last, ran on r-in*..................................... (Evens fav) 1
2389* CHANCE COFFEY 9-11-9 G M O'Neill, *wtd wth, prog to track ldrs appr 3 out, second and ev ch last, not quicken r-in*...................................(9 to 2) 2
2468[6] WILD VENTURE (Ire) 6-11-6 A Powell, *led 1st, sn clr, reduced advantage 4 out, rdn and hdd appr last.* ....(7 to 1) 3
2548* PRECARIUM (Ire) 6-11-9 C O'Dwyer, *led chasing grp, mstk 5th, rdn 4 out, wknd and btn 2 out*............(3 to 1) 4
2548[6] HI-WAY'S GALE 7-11-1 C F Swan, *wl plcd till rdn and wknd aftr 4 out*...............................(33 to 1) 5
1330 CALLERBANN 7-11-1 K F O'Brien, *al rear, wknd 4 out, pld up bef 2 out*................................ (16 to 1) pu

Dist: ½l, 9l, 20l, 12l. 5m 57.50s. (6 Ran).
(P P Johnson), Michael Hourigan

2845 Baltinglass Novice Chase (5-y-o and up) £3,105 2m...................(3:00)

2588[2] GLENCLOUD (Ire) 6-11-10 P Carberry,...... (2 to 1 jt-fav) 1
2698[2] LADY OLEIN (Ire) 6-11-5 J P Banahan,...... (2 to 1 jt-fav) 2
2051[6] PRINCESS CASILIA 9-11-5 B Sheridan,...........(6 to 1) 3
2617[6] SO PINK (Ire) 6-11-5 K F O'Brien,.................(7 to 1) 4
2588[7] WINTERBOURNE ABBAS (Ire) 5-11-2 T Horgan,.. (14 to 1) 5
2157 OXFORD QUILL 7-11-5 T J Taaffe,................(7 to 1) 6
2177[7] PROFESSOR STRONG (Ire) 6-11-5 L P Cusack,.. (25 to 1) 7
2469[5] BALLYCANN 7-11-7 (3*) T J Mitchell,............ (14 to 1) 8
2683[5] BARRAFONA (Ire) 6-11-0 (5*) J P Broderick,...... (14 to 1) 9
1685 PRIDE OF ERIN 10-11-10 H Rogers,.............(20 to 1) ref
2313[2] AUTUMN RIDE (Ire) 6-11-5 F Woods,............ (10 to 1) ref

Dist: 2½l, 20l, 3l, 15l. 4m 48.80s. (11 Ran).
(D Tierney), Noel Meade

2846 Long Distance Handicap Hurdle (4-y-o and up) £6,900 3m..............(3:30)

2659* BART OWEN [-] 9-10-12 C F Swan,...............(4 to 1) 1
2751[2] CALMOS [-] 7-9-2 (5*) K P Gaule,..........(100 to 30 fav) 2
2682[2] DOWHATYOULIKE (Ire) [-] 5-9-11 P Carberry,......(4 to 1) 3
2180[4] SOCIETY BAY (USA) [-] 8-10-10 (7*) R A Hennessy, (10 to 1) 4
2772[7] KNOCKNACARRA LAD [-] 9-10-6 (3*) T J Mitchell, (16 to 1) 5
2751[6] TEMPLEROAN PRINCE [-] 7-11-0 C N Bowens,....(6 to 1) 6
2682[7] TRIMMER WONDER (Ire) [-] 6-9-7 P L Malone,....(25 to 1) 7
SONOFBOA [-] 8-9-4 (3*) C O'Brien,.............(25 to 1) 8
2660[6] RED THUNDER [-] 7-9-2 (5*) J P Broderick,.......(14 to 1) 9
2751[7] TERZIA [-] (bl) 7-11-3 P P Curran,............... (12 to 1) 10
IRISH PEACE (Ire) [-] 6-12-0 K F O'Brien,.........(10 to 1) f
2590[5] ROSIN THE BOW (Ire) [-] 5-9-4 (3*) T J O'Sullivan, (16 to 1) pu

Dist: 1½l, 3½l, dist, 1½l. 6m 29.60s. (12 Ran).
(Mrs Sandra McCarthy), P Mullins

2847 Trim Handicap Chase (0-109 4-y-o and up) £3,105 3m..................(4:00)

2661[3] TAKE THE TOWN [-] 9-11-13 J F Titley,.......... (10 to 1) 1

2661* CARRIGEEN KERRIA (Ire) [-] 6-11-9 (4ex) Mr P J Healy, ...(5 to 2) 2
2235[5] KINGS HILL [-] 12-9-11 (7*) J Butler, ...(10 to 1) 3
2025 ALL A QUIVER [-] 7-10-12 C N Bowens, ...(12 to 1) 4
2681[2] THREE BROWNIES [-] 7-11-8 C O'Dwyer, ... (7 to 4 fav) 5
2053 SET YOUR SIGHTS [-] 11-11-5 D P Geoghegan, .. (12 to 1) 6
2662[9] MR MYAGI [-] (bl) 10-10-7 (3*) D Bromley, ... (12 to 1) 7
2662[5] CARRIGEEN GALA [-] 7-10-4 A Powell, ... (16 to 1) f
2591 WINNING CHARLIE [-] 8-12-0 K F O'Brien, ... (8 to 1) pu
2313* BUMBO HALL VI (Ire) [-] 6-11-7 F J Flood, ...(7 to 1) pu
2282 MONEY MADE [-] (bl) 7-9-7 W T Slattery Jnr, ... (33 to 1) pu
Dist: 5l, 4½l, 7l, 20l. 7m 3.50s. (11 Ran).
(Western Syndicate), Patrick G Kelly

2848 Ballivor INH Flat Race (4-y-o) £3,105 2m............................(4:30)

BRANDANTE (Ire) 11-3 (7*) Mr A F Doherty, ...(11 to 4) 1
CHIEF RANI (Ire) 11-10 Mr T Mullins, ...(4 to 1) 2
BOLD CHEVALIER (Ire) 11-3 (7*) Mr R P Cody, ... (8 to 1) 3
MORE DASH THANCASH (Ire) 11-3 (7*) Mr B Lennon, ...(12 to 1) 4
SHANNON DEE (Ire) 11-2 (3*) Mr J A Nash, ...(10 to 1) 5
2663[3] OAKLER (Ire) 11-10 Mr A P O'Brien, ...(7 to 4 fav) 6
PRINCESS LU (Ire) 11-3 (7*) Mr T Farrell, ...(10 to 1) 7
GREAT THYNE (Ire) 11-7 (3*) Mr A R Coonan, ...(10 to 1) 8
BEN-GURIAN (Ire) 11-7 (3*) Mr M F Barrett, ...(5 to 1) 9
Dist: 15l, 4l, ½l, 4½l. 4m 31.10s. (9 Ran).
(M D McGrath), J R H Fowler

2849 Bective INH Flat Race (5-y-o and up) £3,105 2m.....................(5:00)

2664[2] TOTAL CONFUSION 7-11-8 (3*) Mr J A Nash, ...(8 to 1) 1
2607[2] MAJOR RUMPUS 6-11-11 (7*) Mr H Murphy, (11 to 10 fav) 2
2664[5] NEPI LAD (Ire) 6-11-11 Mr M McNulty, ... (10 to 1) 3
1848[2] BELLS LIFE (Ire) 5-12-2 Mr J E Kiely, ...(7 to 2) 4
2756[3] DUN CARRAIG (Ire) 6-11-4 (7*) Mr M O'Connor, ...(12 to 1) 5
RUEMARO THYNE (Ire) 5-11-2 (7*) Mr B M Cash, (20 to 1) 6
2613[4] DONBOLINO (Ire) 6-11-13 Mr A P O'Brien, ... (10 to 1) 7
14557 BOOKLEUP (Ire) 5-11-6 (3*) Mr D Marnane, / GANTELLER 5-11-2 (7*) Mr T J Corcoran Jnr, ...(40 to 1) / (25 to 1) 8
2664* RING THE ALARM (Ire) 6-11-13 (5*) Mr G J Harford, (7 to 1) 9
THE REAL JOKER (Ire) 5-11-6 (3*) Mr A R Coonan, (12 to 1) 10
FARRELL'S CROSS 8-11-11 (7*) Mr D J Donegan, (25 to 1) 11
2664[7] QUIET ONE 9-10-13 (7*) Miss U Corcoran, ... (20 to 1) 12
13
Dist: Nk, 2l, 1½l, 5l. 4m 33.70s. (13 Ran).
(John Weafer), Norman Cassidy

NEWBURY (good)
Saturday March 5th
Going Correction: PLUS 1.20 sec. per fur. (races 1,2,-4,7), PLUS 1.45 (3,5,6)

2850 Eastleigh Handicap Hurdle (4-y-o and up) £5,952 2m 110yds......... (12:30)

2379* DANCING PADDY [136] 6-11-2 D O'Sullivan, *made all, sn clr cmftbly*.............(9 to 2 tchd 4 to 1 and 5 to 1) 1
2670[2] CHILD OF THE MIST [120] 8-10-0 J R Kavanagh, *chsd wnr most of way, no imprsn frm 2 out.* ....(9 to 1 op 7 to 1 tchd 10 to 1) 2
1571* MAJED (Ire) [144] 6-11-10 P Niven, *prmnt till jmpd slwly second, hdwy 5th, rdn and one pace appr last.* .... (6 to 4 fav op 13 to 8 tchd 7 to 4 and 11 to 8) 2
2463* HIGHLAND SPIRIT [122] 6-10-2 R Dunwoody, *hld up, hdwy 5th, rdn and no imprsn frm 2 out*...(9 to 2 tchd 4 to 1) 4
2655[5] ELEMENTARY [120] 11-10-0 R Marley, *jmpd slwly second and beh, no ch whn blun 3 out*.... (14 to 1 op 12 to 1) 5
2079 NAHAR [130] 9-10-10 A Dicken, *prmnt till drpd out 5th.* ....(7 to 1 op 5 to 1) 6
CADENCY [122] 6-10-2[2] D Murphy, *took str hold in rear, quickened to chase wnr briefly 3rd, rear 5th, tld off whn pld up bef last.* (14 to 1 op 12 to 1 tchd 16 to 1) pu
Dist: 2½l, dd-ht, 12l, 5l, ½l. 4m 10.80s. a 21.80s (7 Ran).
SR: 68/49/73/39/32/41/-/ (Bychance Racing), K O Cunningham-Brown

2851 Berkshire Hurdle Grade 2 (4-y-o and up) £9,380 2m 5f............... (1:00)

2595[3] FLAKEY DOVE 8-11-7 R Dunwoody, *trkd ldr, chlgd aftr 3 out, led sn after 2 out, easily.* ....(2 to 1 on op 7 to 4 on tchd 9 to 4 on) 1
1992[5] IVOR'S FLUTTER (bl) 5-11-5 P Holley, *dsptd 3rd, rdn alng frm 5th, styd on to take second appr last, no ch wth wnr*................. (25 to 1 op 14 to 1 tchd 50 to 1) 2
2646[2] SHUJAN (USA) 5-11-9 G McCourt, *led, sn clr, hdd aftr 2 out, wknd appr last.* (100 to 30 op 5 to 2 tchd 7 to 2) 3
2172 GLAISDALE (Ire) 5-11-5 D Murphy, *dsptd 3rd till wknd 7th, tld off*..................(7 to 1 op 6 to 1 tchd 15 to 2) 4
2693[6] KETTI 9-11-0 Miss S Higgins, *al beh, lost tch frm 5th, tld off*.................(66 to 1 op 50 to 1 tchd 100 to 1) 5
Dist: 20l, 8l, dist, 2½l. 5m 20.80s. a 27.80s (5 Ran).
SR: 67/45/41/-/-/ (J T Price), R J Price

2852 North Sydmonton Handicap Chase (5-y-o and up) £5,640 2½m........ (1:30)

MIINNEHOMA [150] 11-12-0 R Dunwoody, *chsd ldr to 8th, reminder appr 4 out, led 3 out, narrowly hdd last, rallied gmely to ld fnl 150 yards.* ....(11 to 2 op 5 to 1 tchd 6 to 1) 1
866[4] FOREST SUN [132] 9-10-10 G Bradley, *beh, hdwy frm 3 out, chlgd betw horses aftr 2 out, slight ld last, hdd fnl 150 yards, no extr*.................. (9 to 1 op 8 to 1) 2
2266 GUIBURN'S NEPHEW [130] 12-10-8 C Maude, *led to 3 out, still ev ch 2 out, outpcd appr last.* ....(13 to 8 fav op 5 to 4 tchd 7 to 4) 3
2557[4] SMARTIE EXPRESS [124] 12-10-2 B Powell, *pressed ldr 8th to 11th, chlgd ag'n 4 out, ev ch 2 out, sn wknd.* ....(7 to 2 op 4 to 1 tchd 9 to 2) 4
1706[4] MR ENTERTAINER [122] 11-10-0 C Llewellyn, *al in rear, lost tch frm 4 out, tld off*..........(7 to 2 tchd 4 to 1) 5
Dist: 2l, 12l, 6l, dist. 5m 21.20s. a 31.20s (5 Ran).
SR: 78/58/44/32/-/ (Freddie Starr), M C Pipe

2853 Highclere Novices' Hurdle (4-y-o) £3,132 2m 110yds............... (2:00)

2685* DARK DEN (USA) 11-4 T Kent, *made all, wl clr 3rd, kpt on well r-in*........ (5 to 4 fav tchd 11 to 10 and 11 to 8) 1
2599* CALIANDAK (Ire) 11-8 G McCourt, *chsd ldrs, rdn frm 2 out, took second r-in, not rch wnr.* .... (5 to 1 op 4 to 1 tchd 11 to 2) 2
2245[4] SUPREME MASTER 11-0 G Bradley, *hdwy to chase wnr 5th, rdn 2 out, sn one pace.* ....(6 to 1 op 7 to 1 tchd 8 to 1) 3
2624* MARIUS (Ire) 11-0 D Murphy, *hdwy aftr 4th, hit nxt, sn wknd*.................. (8 to 1 op 6 to 1 tchd 10 to 1) 4
2638 SHAMSHADAL (Ire) 11-0 S Smith Eccles, *prmnt, chsd wnr briefly aftr 4th, wknd 3 out, no ch whn blun nxt.* .... (33 to 1 op 20 to 1 tchd 50 to 1) 5
2694[7] CLEAR LOOK 10-9 J Osborne, *al beh, tld off whn f last.* .... (50 to 1 op 33 to 1 tchd 66 to 1) f
HORSERADISH 11-0 Richard Guest, *hit 3rd, effrt nxt, wkng whn f 5th*................ (50 to 1 tchd 66 to 1) f
2478* PREROGATIVE (v) 11-4 R Dunwoody, *chsd wnr to 4th, wknd nxt, tld off whn pld up bef 2 out.* ....(4 to 1 op 7 to 2) pu
LA SPEZIA 10-9 C Llewellyn, *sn beh, tld off whn pld up bef 2 out*.............. (50 to 1 op 33 to 1) pu
Dist: 1½l, 2½l, 25l, 2l. 4m 14.20s. a 25.20s (9 Ran).
SR: 36/38/27/2/-/-/ (George L Ohrstrom), Mrs J Cecil

2854 Wickham Novices' Chase (5-y-o and up) £3,522 3m..................(2:30)

2654 HILL TRIX 8-11-4 A Tory, *hdwy to chase ldrs 14th, led aftr 2 out, ran on wl*.....(50 to 1 op 33 to 1 tchd 66 to 1) 1
2732* TARAMOSS 7-12-0 J Osborne, *led aftr second, hdd 9th, styd on frm 3 out, no extr r-in.* ....(7 to 2 op 3 to 1 tchd 4 to 1) 2
2725[3] WILLOW GALE 7-10-13 G McCourt, *prmnt, led 9th, rdn frm 4 out, hdd aftr 2 out, wknd r-in.* .... (5 to 1 tchd 6 to 1 and 9 to 2) 3
2479[2] BOLLINGER 8-11-9 D Murphy, *in tch till lost pos 12th, rallied 14th, wknd frm 4 out*....(9 to 4 jt-fav op 5 to 2) 4
2647* ONE MORE RUN 7-11-9 G Bradley, *not fluent and beh, effrt appr 4 out, sn btn.* ....(9 to 4 jt-fav op 7 to 4 tchd 5 to 2) 5
2455[3] ELMORE 7-11-4 R Dunwoody, *led till aftr second, in tch till pld up after 8th*................ (8 to 1 tchd 9 to 1) pu
Dist: 3l, 8l, 4l, 1l. 6m 33.80s. a 45.80s (6 Ran).
(Mrs E K Ellis), K Bishop

2855 Jack O'Newbury Novices' Chase (5-y-o and up) £3,496 2½m........ (3:05)

2778* ALL FOR LUCK 9-11-4 R Dunwoody, *trkd ldr frm 7th, chlgd from 4 out, led sn aftr 2 out, pushed out.* ....(5 to 4 fav tchd 13 to 8) 1
2084[4] MUNKA (bl) 8-11-4 Peter Hobbs, *led till hdd aftr 2 out, sn outpcd*..................(4 to 1 op 7 to 2 tchd 9 to 2) 2
2012 CARDINAL RED 7-11-4 J Osborne, *sn beh, jmpd slwly 8th, hit 11th, took remote 3rd aftr 2 out, tld off.* .... (8 to 1 op 7 to 1 tchd 10 to 1) 3
2533* CREWS CASTLE 7-11-4 S Smith Eccles, *chsd ldrs till wknd aftr 6th, tld off*............ (14 to 1 op 10 to 1) 4
GOOD OLD CHIPS 7-11-4 L Harvey, *prmnt to 7th, lost tch frm 9th, tld off*........ (7 to 1 op 10 to 1 tchd 6 to 1) 5
2504[5] WINGS OF FREEDOM (Ire) (v) 6-11-4 G Bradley, *hdwy to go poor 3rd 12th, blun 3 out, tld off whn mstk nxt.* .... (12 to 1 op 8 to 1) 6
2706[2] NICKSLINE 8-11-4 D Murphy, *beh frm 7th, poor 4th whn f 12th*...............................(7 to 1 op 5 to 1) f
Dist: 10l, dist, 15l, 12l. 5m 27.30s. a 37.30s (7 Ran).
SR: 7/-/-/-/ (B J Craig), M C Pipe

2856 Levy Board Handicap Hurdle (0-135 4-y-o and up) £3,512 2m 5f...... (3:35)

2674* MISS PURBECK [103] 7-9-13 (5*) S Fox, *led to 4th, led aftr 5th, hdd 2 out, sn led ag'n, ran on gmely.
.................................(7 to 4 fav tchd 9 to 4) 1
2655⁸ LYNCH LAW (Ire) [110] (bl) 6-10-11 H Dunwoody, *hld up, hdwy to track ldrs 8th, chlgd frm 3 out till rdn and found no extr r-in*......(6 to 1 op 5 to 1 tchd 13 to 2) 2
2571² MYHAMET [105] 7-10-6 Peter Hobbs, *hdwy to track ldrs 8th, led 2 out, hdd, outpcd appr last.*
..............(11 to 4 op 5 to 2 tchd 9 to 4 and 3 to 1) 3
2517⁴ COKENNY BOY [123] 9-11-3 (7*) D Bohan, *took str hold, chsd ldrs, ev ch 3 out, sn outpcd.*
..........................(9 to 1 op 8 to 1 tchd 10 to 1) 4
2727 MISTER MAJOR [112] 6-10-13 Richard Guest, *hdwy to track ldrs 8th, fdd frm 3 out.*
..........................(9 to 1 op 8 to 1 tchd 10 to 1) 5
2571⁵ KAYTAK (Fr) [107] (v) 7-10-8 D Murphy, *sn beh, hit 6th, wknd frm 8th*..........(7 to 1 op 6 to 1 tchd 8 to 1) 6
2507⁷ BALLYSTATE [102] 6-10-3 L Harvey, *led 4th, hit 5th, sn hdd, beh frm 7th*....(16 to 1 op 20 to 1 tchd 25 to 1) 7
Dist: 1l, 10l, 7l, 10l, 15l, ¾l. 5m 24.80s. a 31.80s (7 Ran).
SR: 10/16/11/12/   (Martin Hill), Mrs J G Retter

STRATFORD (Good to soft)
Saturday March 5th
Going Correction: PLUS 1.63 sec. per fur. (races 1,4,6), PLUS 1.80 (2,3,5)

2857 Luddington Four Year Old Novices' Hurdle £1,912 2m 110yds...... (2:20)

2652* MALAIA (Ire) 11-0 T Grantham, *hld up, cld aftr 5th, ld appr last, rdn out*......................(5 to 2 op 9 to 4) 1
2694⁵ FOREVER SHINEING 10-7 M Perrett, *beh, hdwy 5th, styd on wl to take second r-in*.....................(8 to 1 op 5 to 1) 2
2722² FORMAL AFFAIR 10-7 A Maguire, *al prmnt, led appr 2 out, hdd whn hit last, wknd r-in.* (7 to 4 on op 5 to 4 on) 3
2398⁵ DON TOCINO 10-12 W McFarland, *trkd ldrs, wknd 2 out, tld off*.....................(20 to 1 op 10 to 1) 4
KEDGE 10-12 G Lyons, *led 1st, cl up till lost pl appr 3rd, tld off*.........................(33 to 1 op 14 to 1) 5
FLAMING MIRACLE (Ire) (bl) 10-12 D Gallagher, *took keen hold, led aftr 1st till hdd appr 2 out, wknd quickly, tld off*.........................(50 to 1 op 20 to 1) 6
2335 BARNIEMEBOY (v) 10-12 W Elderfield, *al beh, reminders 4th, tld off*.................(100 to 1 op 50 to 1) 7
KILLY'S FILLY 10-4 (3*) R Farrant, *in tch, wknd 5th, tld off whn pld up bef 2 out*..............(50 to 1 op 25 to 1) pu
2335 KING'S GOLD 10-7 (5*) C Burnett-Wells, *al beh, tld off whn pld up bef last*.................(66 to 1 op 33 to 1) pu
Dist: 8l, 4l, dist, 15l, 10l, dist. 4m 21.20s. a 32.20s (9 Ran).
SR: 33/18/14/-/-/-/   (Count K Goess-Saurau), J A B Old

2858 Marathon Novices' Chase (5-y-o and up) £3,668 3½m............... (2:50)

2524³ LASTOFTHEVIKINGS 9-11-3 D Gallagher, *jmpd soundly, in tch, styd on frm 4 out, jnd ldr last, sn led, stayed on wl.*
...........................(12 to 1 op 8 to 1) 1
2654* FLORIDA SKY 7-11-5 (3*) Mr D Costello, *hld up, hdwy tenth, led 16th, jnd last and sn hdd, one pace.*
..........(11 to 8 on op 6 to 4 on tchd 13 to 8 on) 2
2654 FRENCH PLEASURE 8-10-12 P Holley, *al prmnt, ev ch 4 out, mstk nxt and wknd*...............(7 to 1 op 4 to 1) 3
2630* MUTUAL BENEFIT (bl) 7-11-3 A Maguire, *led till hdd 16th, sn wknd, tld off*............(12 to 1 tchd 14 to 1) 4
2411⁸ JENNY'S GLEN 7-11-3 R Supple, *in tch, wknd 15th, tld off*..............(50 to 1 op 33 to 1 tchd 66 to 1) 5
2654 PHILIPPONNAT (USA) (bl) 8-11-3 N Mann, *wth ldr till wknd second*...............(50 to 1 op 33 to 1) 6
2427⁴ FREDDY OWEN 8-11-3 W McFarland, *blun and uns rdr*...............(9 to 1 op 10 to 1 tchd 16 to 1) ur
2525 BROADWOOD LAD 8-11-3 I Lawrence, *al towards rear, mstks, tld off whn pld up bef 16th.* (66 to 1 op 33 to 1) pu
MARNWORTH 8-10-12 Mr J Durkan, *in tch, mstk 14th, wknd nxt, tld off whn pld up bef 17th.*
...........................(8 to 1 op 7 to 1 tchd 6 to 1) pu
Dist: 8l, dist, dist, 5l, dist. 7m 55.30s. a 70.30s (9 Ran).
                                           (J L Needham), J L Needham

2859 Richardsons Oldbury Novices' Handicap Chase (5-y-o and up) £4,240 2½m .... (3:20)

2538³ CRYSTAL BEAR (NZ) [100] (bl) 9-11-10 B Powell, *jmpd slwly early and sn bustled alng to keep up, dashed into ld 12th, soon clr, easily....* (3 to 1 op 5 to 2 tchd 7 to 2) 1
2479³ NICKLE JOE [104] 8-12-0 D Gallagher, *led till hdd 7th, led and mstk 11th, headed nxt, outpcd.*
...........................(9 to 4 op 2 to 1 tchd 5 to 2) 2
2690* ASTINGS (Fr) [91] 6-11-1 A Maguire, *cl up, led 7th till hdd 11th, sn rdn and wknd quickly, tld off.*
.................(11 to 10 on op 5 to 4 on tchd Evens) 3
Dist: Dist, dist. 5m 23.40s. a 41.40s (3 Ran).
SR: 42/-/-/   (Lady Knutsford), Capt T A Forster

2860 Cherington 'National Hunt' Novices' Hurdle (4-y-o and up) £2,024 2m 110yds...................... (3:50)

2671⁵ AVENA 7-10-12 G Upton, *pld hrd, led 1st, led ag'n 4th till hdd last, kpt on und pres to ld again r-in.*
.................(2 to 1 tchd 7 to 4 and 9 to 4) 1
2083³ ABSOLUTELY AVERAGE (Ire) 4-10-9 R Supple, *al cl up, outpcd and pushed alng 2 out, rallied to ld last, hdd and no extr r-in.*
..............(7 to 4 fav op 2 to 1 tchd 11 to 4 and 3 to 1) 2
1646 DEVIL'S CORNER 6-10-10 (7*) L Reynolds, *beh, hdwy frm 3 out, styd on from last.*
..........................(66 to 1 op 50 to 1 tchd 100 to 1) 3
2269 MAGELLAN BAY (Ire) 6-11-3 I Lawrence, *cld on ldrs second, ev ch 2 out, rdn and wknd appr last.*
.................................(4 to 1 op 7 to 2) 4
1688⁶ METROPOLIS 7-11-3 J Frost, *beh, hdwy appr 3 out, nvr nr to chal*..............(8 to 1 tchd 7 to 1 and 9 to 1) 5
SOUTHERN DEALER 6-11-3 W McFarland, *mstk 1st, sn chsd ldrs, wknd 2 out*.............(33 to 1 op 20 to 1) 6
2505 CORNS LITTLE FELLA 6-10-12 (5*) J Supple, *chsd ldrs, pushed alng 5th, sn lost pl, tld off.*
..........................(66 to 1 op 50 to 1 tchd 100 to 1) 7
2599 BONE SETTER (Ire) 4-10-9 M Perrett, *beh, hdwy aftr 5th, sn wknd, tld off*...............(20 to 1 tchd 25 to 1) 8
1747 GRECIAN SAILOR 9-10-10 (7*) R Darke, *chsd ldr till wknd aftr 5th, tld off*....(66 to 1 op 50 to 1 tchd 100 to 1) 9
2692⁸ DO LETS 5-10-12 T Grantham, *in tch to 5th, sn tld off.*
.................................(66 to 1 op 33 to 1) 10
DIANE'S PRIDE (Ire) 5-10-12 G Lyons, *al beh, tld off.*
..............(50 to 1 op 20 to 1 tchd 66 to 1) 11
1223⁸ HECTOR MARIO 6-11-3 D Gallagher, *blun and uns rdr second*.................(20 to 1 tchd 25 to 1) ur
QUEEN OF THE CELTS 5-10-13* B Wright, *mid-div whn blun and uns rdr 4th.*
.................(33 to 1 op 20 to 1 tchd 40 to 1) ur
2333 BLURRED VISION (Ire) 5-11-3 B Powell, *led second till hdd 4th, sn lost pl, tld off whn pld up bef 2 out.*
.............................(9 to 1 op 50 to 1) pu
Dist: 2l, 1l, 7l, 20l, 6l, 12l, 6l, 10l, 1½l, dist. 4m 24.20s. a 35.20s (14 Ran).
SR: 1/-/3/-/-/-/   (Mrs Z S Clark), S Christian

2861 Bidford Handicap Chase (0-135 5-y-o and up) £4,201 2m 5f 110yds.... (4:20)

2450³ SIMPLE PLEASURE [110] 9-11-0 A Maguire, *in cl tch, out-pcd 12th, chsd ldr frm 3 out, led and jmpd lft last, hrd rdn, all out*..................(9 to 4 op 5 to 2) 1
980² BOLD CHOICE [96] 8-10-0 D Skyrme, *in cl tch, led aftr 3 out till hdd last, kpt on one pace.*
..............................(5 to 1 op 7 to 2 tchd 6 to 1) 2
2648* JAILBREAKER [109] 7-10-13 D Gallagher, *hld up in last pl, mstk tenth and outpcd, styd on appr 2 out.*
..................................(Evens fav op 2 to 1 on) 3
2648⁷ BALDA BOY [110] 10-11-0 B Powell, *led till hdd aftr 3 out, sn wknd, virtually pld up r-in*......(7 to 1 op 10 to 1) 4
Dist: 2l, 8l, 30l. 5m 50.20s. a 47.20s (4 Ran).
SR: 1/   (Mrs M Stirk), Mrs M Stirk

2862 Swan Handicap Hurdle (0-130 4-y-o and up) £3,057 2¾m 110yds..... (4:50)

FAST THOUGHTS [99] 7-11-0 P Holley, *wth ldr, led 5th, made rst, ran on wl frm 2 out....* (6 to 1 tchd 7 to 1) 1
2496* HAPPY HORSE (NZ) [107] 7-11-8 A Tory, *al prmnt, chsd wnr frm 3 out, no imprsn from nxt.*
................(9 to 4 fav op 7 to 4 tchd 5 to 2) 2
2766⁵ GEORGE BUCKINGHAM [93] (bl) 9-10-8 B Powell, *trkd ldrs to 5th, sn wknd, styd on r-in.*
..........................(9 to 1 op 10 to 1 tchd 12 to 1) 3
2676⁸ KARAR (Ire) [97] 4-10-12 M Perrett, *hld up in tch, rdn 6th, sn wknd, tld off.*...............(6 to 1 op 4 to 1) 4
2544⁶ JARRWAH [98] 6-10-13 A Maguire, *led till hdd 5th, wknd 3 out, tld off.*.............(6 to 1 op 5 to 1 tchd 8 to 1) 5
1777³ LASTING MEMORY [96] 8-10-11 J Frost, *al beh, tld off.*
..........................(10 to 1 op 8 to 1) 6
2480³ ALBERTITO (Fr) [102] 7-11-0 (3*) S Wynne, *chsd ldrs to 4th, sn wknd, tld off*..................(7 to 1 op 5 to 1) 7
2540⁶ KNIGHTS (NZ) [108] 8-11-9 Jacqui Oliver, *beh, shrtlvd effrt 7th, tld off whn pld up bef 3 out.*
.................(20 to 1 op 10 to 1 tchd 25 to 1) pu
VAL D'AUTHIE (Fr) [103] 6-11-4 D Skyrme, *mid-div, beh 5th, tld off whn pld up bef 3 out.*...........(33 to 1) pu
1206 LANDED GENTRY (USA) [109] 5-11-10 I Lawrence, *beh, shrtlvd effrt 4th, tld off whn pld up bef 2 out.*
..........................(10 to 1 op 8 to 1) pu
Dist: 12l, dist, 20l, 1½l, 25l, 4l. 5m 53.10s. a 41.10s (10 Ran).
SR: 42/38/-/-/-/-/   (W H Dore), D R Gandolfo

LEOPARDSTOWN (IRE) (heavy)
Sunday March 6th
Going Correction: PLUS 1.40 sec. per fur. (races 1,2,- 4,6,7), PLUS 1.80 (3,5)

2863 Cabinteely Maiden Hurdle (5-y-o and up) £3,105 2½m. . . . . (2:30)

2024[2] SIR MOSS 7-11-6 J F Titley, ... (5 to 1) 1
2389[6] TWIN RAINBOW 7-12-0 L P Cusack, ... (10 to 1) 2
1897[2] ARCHER (Ire) 6-11-6 K F O'Brien, ... (5 to 1) 3
2080[3] PIMBERLEY PLACE (Ire) 6-12-0 C F Swan, . . . (11 to 8 fav) 4
2607 BOB NELSON 7-11-6 M Duffy, ... (25 to 1) 5
2465 GARBONI (USA) 5-12-0 B Sheridan, ... (10 to 1) 6
1781[3] EMPEROR GLEN (Ire) 6-12-0 T Horgan, ... (16 to 1) 7
2586 BOBSVILLE (Ire) 6-11-6 C N Bowens, ... (25 to 1) 8
2607 WHITBY 6-11-1 (5*) J P Broderick, ... (16 to 1) 9
VITAL TRIX 7-11-1 P Carberry, ... (20 to 1) 10
2586[9] MIDNIGHT HOUR (Ire) 5-11-1 (5*) M G Cleary, ... (20 to 1) 11
2553 SERGEANT DAN (Ire) 6-11-1 (5*) D T Evans, ... (66 to 1) 12
2586 THE PERISHER (Ire) 5-11-6 J Shortt, ... (14 to 1) 13
2076[4] ANGAREB (Ire) 5-12-0 R Dunwoody, ... (8 to 1) 14
2024 CONQUEST OF LIGHT (Ire) 5-11-6 R Hughes, ... (33 to 1) 15
2664 BORRISMORE FLASH (Ire) 6-11-6 J P Banahan, . . (33 to 1) 16
2123 RATHFARDON (Ire) 6-11-6 A Powell, ... (66 to 1) 17
2607 RHABDOMANCY (Ire) 6-11-2 (7*) L A Hurley, ... (20 to 1) 18
2586 YOU'VE DONE WHAT (Ire) (bl) 6-11-1 (5*) K L O'Brien, ... (8 to 1) ur
2770 BASTILLE DAY 7-11-7 (7*) T Martin, ... (66 to 1) pu
2177[3] PUNTER'S SYMPHONY (Ire) 6-12-0 H Rogers, ... (14 to 1) pu
1236 SAFRANE 6-11-1 (5*) D P Geoghegan, ... (66 to 1) pu
1581 DOCS DILEMMA (Ire) 5-11-6 F Woods, ... (33 to 1) pu
QUICK LEARNER (Ire) 5-11-6 C O'Dwyer, ... (16 to 1) pu

Dist: 1½l, 4l, 7l, 10l. 5m 33.90s. a 48.90s (24 Ran).
(K J Martin), S A Kirk

2864 Hillcrest Hurdle (4-y-o) £3,105 2m . . . . (3:00)

2614[3] KHARASAR (Ire) 10-7 (7*) R A Hennessy, ... (7 to 1) 1
2750* SHEREGORI (Ire) (bl) 11-7 R Dunwoody, ... (7 to 2) 2
2699[4] MICKS DELIGHT (Ire) 11-7 P Carberry, ... (5 to 2) 3
2699[3] ANDANTE (Ire) (bl) 11-2 C F Swan, ... (2 to 1 fav) 4
1767 ANUSHA 10-4 (5*) J P Broderick, ... (20 to 1) 5
2678[2] WICKLOW WAY (Ire) 10-9 K F O'Brien, ... (10 to 1) 6
2614[2] MAN OF ARRAN (Ire) 10-11 (3*) T J O'Sullivan, ... (10 to 1) 7
2285[4] THE SALTY FROG (Ire) 11-2 (5*) M G Cleary, ... (12 to 1) 8
2614 CRISSY (Ire) 10-9 J Shortt, ... (66 to 1) 9
2678 SOUL EMPEROR 11-0 A Powell, ... (33 to 1) 10
2750[9] TASSET (Can) 10-7 (7*) T Martin, ... (33 to 1) 11
MY SPECIAL GUEST (Ire) 10-9 H Rogers, ... (25 to 1) pu
1111[8] LOUGHMOGUE (Ire) 10-9 F J Flood, ... (14 to 1) pu

Dist: 2½l, 6l, 4l, nk. 4m 15.30s. a 27.30s (13 Ran).
SR: 37/41/35/26/18/-/ (W Hennessy), Anthony Mullins

2865 Stepaside Chase (5-y-o and up) £4,140 2m 5f. . . . . (3:30)

2469[2] ALL THE ACES 7-11-11 T J Taaffe, ... (9 to 4 fav) 1
2681 SCRIBBLER 8-11-11 L P Cusack, ... (9 to 2) 2
2681[3] BORN DEEP 8-11-11 R Dunwoody, ... (6 to 1) 3
2681 TITIAN BLONDE (Ire) 6-11-6 F Woods, ... (8 to 1) 4
2282* BEAU BABILLARD 7-11-11 C F Swan, ... (7 to 2) 5
2618[7] FARNEY GLEN 7-11-11 T Horgan, ... (12 to 1) 6
2681[4] MACAMORE STAR 8-11-8 (3*) C O'Brien, ... (14 to 1) 7
2618* COMMANCHE NELL (Ire) 6-11-9 G M O'Neill, ... (8 to 1) 8
1851[9] PRINCIPLE MUSIC (USA) 6-11-4 (3*) Mr J A Nash, (16 to 1) f
2202[5] BACK DOOR JOHNNY 8-11-11 J Shortt, ... (12 to 1) ur
2700[7] ENQELAAB (USA) 6-11-7 J P Banahan, ... (25 to 1) pu

Dist: 2½l, 4l, 2l, 5l. 5m 58.10s. a 44.10s (11 Ran).
SR: 34/31/27/20/20/-/ (John P McManus), A L T Moore

2866 Brannockstown Handicap Hurdle (0-144 4-y-o and up) £4,140 2m. . (4:00)

2610[7] TIME FOR A RUN [-] 7-12-0 C F Swan, ... (4 to 1 fav) 1
2703[5] FERRYCARRIG HOTEL (Ire) [-] 5-10-6 D H O'Connor, ... (5 to 1) 2
2590[2] MR BOAL (Ire) [-] 5-10-12 (5*) J P Broderick, ... (7 to 1) 3
2754[4] THE SHAUGHRAUN [-] 8-11-1 T Horgan, ... (6 to 1) 4
2610[5] COCK COCKBURN [-] 8-11-11 R Dunwoody, ... (9 to 2) 5
2754[5] IF YOU SAY YES (Ire) [-] 6-10-2 K F O'Brien, ... (14 to 1) 6
2075[4] OH SO GRUMPY [-] 6-10-4 (3*) T J Mitchell, ... (14 to 1) 7
2023[3] LEGAL PROFESSION (Ire) [-] 6-10-4 (5*) A Maguire, (11 to 2) 8
PERSIAN POWER (Ire) [-] 6-11-11 P Carberry, ... (16 to 1) 9
2703 LAWYER'S BRIEF (Fr) [-] 7-9-11 F Woods, ... (14 to 1) 10
1450[9] JUST ONE CANALETTO [-] 6-9-7 P L Malone, ... (25 to 1) 11
2610 PRACTICE RUN (Ire) [-] 6-10-9 (5*) M G Cleary, . . . (20 to 1) 12
2467[4] SHARP INVITE [-] 7-11-11 B Sheridan, ... (12 to 1) 13

Dist: ½l, 2½l, hd, ¾l. 4m 28.10s. a 40.10s (13 Ran).
(John P McManus), E J O'Grady

2867 Kilteran Handicap Chase (5-y-o and up) £6,900 2m 5f. . . . . (4:30)

1985 FOURTH OF JULY [-] 10-10-0 J P Banahan, ... (12 to 1) 1
2698* MERAPI [-] 8-10-0 (3ex) A Powell, ... (7 to 1) 2
2755[6] THE REAL UNYOKE [-] 9-9-11 (3*) D P Murphy, ... (14 to 1) 3
2591* BUCKBOARD BOUNCE [-] 8-11-4 R Dunwoody, (2 to 1 fav) 4
2591[2] COMMERCIAL ARTIST [-] 8-10-13 A Maguire, ... (9 to 4) 5
2077[4] GARAMYCIN [-] 12-11-7 M Flynn, ... (16 to 1) 6
2695[3] GOLD OPTIONS [-] (bl) 12-11-6 P Carberry, ... (10 to 1) 7
2609[3] CHIRKPAR [-] 7-10-0 C F Swan, ... (6 to 1) f
2288[8] RIVER TARQUIN [-] 10-10-13 K F O'Brien, ... (12 to 1) pu
2288[7] GENERAL IDEA [-] 9-12-0 B Sheridan, ... (10 to 1) pu

Dist: 10l, hd, ½l, 9l. 5m 55.50s. a 41.50s (10 Ran).
SR: 35/25/25/42/28/-/ (Mrs J Keeling), M A O'Toole

2868 Firmount INH Flat Race (4-y-o) £3,105 2m. . . . . (5:00)

INVITATION CUP (Ire) 11-2 (3*) Mr J A Nash, ... (9 to 4 on) 1
2314[3] FEATHER SONG 10-11 (3*) Mr R Neylon, ... (8 to 1) 2
2290[4] MOSES PREY (Ire) 11-0 (5*) Mr H F Cleary, ... (8 to 1) 3
2663[2] GRAPHIC IMAGE (Ire) 11-5 Mr A P O'Brien, ... (5 to 1) 4
2290[7] SHINOUMA 11-2 (3*) Mrs J M Mullins, ... (14 to 1) 5
2663[9] KERKY (Ire) 10-12 (7*) Mr B Lennon, ... (33 to 1) 6
WHERE ARE THE KEYS (Ire) 10-7 (7*) Mr J Connolly, (7 to 1) 7
MON CHER AMI (Ire) 11-0 Mr J P Durkan, ... (25 to 1) 8
SELL EVERYTHING (Ire) 11-2 (3*) Mr D Valentine, (12 to 1) 9

Dist: 2l, 3l, 5½l, 6l. 4m 20.00s. (9 Ran).
(D K Weld), D K Weld

2869 Rockbrook INH Flat Race (5-y-o and up) £3,105 2m. . . . . (5:30)

2182[2] VENTANA CANYON (Ire) 5-11-12 Mr P Fenton, (7 to 4 fav) 1
2236[8] LITTLE BUCK (Ire) 6-11-7 (7*) Mr J S Cullen, ... (50 to 1) 2
DARAVIC (Ire) 5-11-5 (7*) Mr A V Murray, ... (25 to 1) 3
2076[5] MANHATTAN CASTLE (Ire) 5-11-5 (7*) Mr H Murphy, (7 to 1) 4
2620[5] STEVIE BE (Ire) 6-11-11 (3*) Mr A R Coonan, ... (14 to 1) 5
BALLINEVA (Ire) 5-11-9 (3*) Mrs J M Mullins, ... (8 to 1) 6
2389[5] JOHNNY SETASIDE (Ire) 5-11-9 (3*) Mr D Marnane, (10 to 1) 7
2592[4] HERO STATUS (Ire) 5-11-5 (7*) Mr T J Beattie, ... (33 to 1) 8
YOUR CALL (Ire) 5-11-9 (3*) Mr J A Nash, ... (10 to 1) 9
1337 SPANKERS HILL (Ire) 5-11-12 Mr J P Durkan, ... (25 to 1) 10
2080[6] JOHNY BELINDA (Ire) 6-11-9 Mr J P Dempsey, . . . (33 to 1) 11
2684 PERCUSIONIST 7-11-11 (3*) Miss C Hutchinson, . . (33 to 1) 12
2553[7] DOUBLE SYMPHONY (Ire) 6-11-2 (7*) Mr J P Dwan, ... (20 to 1) 13
RUDDS HILL (Ire) 6-11-7 (7*) Mr M McGrath, ... (33 to 1) 14
CLONROSH SLAVE 7-12-0 Mr T Mullins, ... (16 to 1) 15
1383[2] CAFE PRINCE (Ire) 5-11-9 (3*) Mr D Valentine, ... (5 to 2) 16
1039[7] UNSINKABLE BOXER (Ire) 5-11-5 (7*) Mr D K Budds, ... (50 to 1) 17
J J JACKSON (Ire) 5-11-5 (7*) Mr P J McGarry, ... (33 to 1) 18
2592[5] CLOVER MOR LASS (Ire) 5-11-0 (7*) Mr R F Coonan, ... (33 to 1) 19
2684 YOUCAT (Ire) 5-11-5 (7*) Mr M G Holden, ... (33 to 1) 20
2056[6] LAURA GALE (Ire) 5-11-0 (7*) Mr J P Walsh, ... (50 to 1) 21
ALAMILLO (Ire) 5-11-0 (7*) Mr P J McMahon, ... (16 to 1) 22
EIRE (Ire) 5-11-9 (3*) Mr R Neylon, ... (33 to 1) 23
TORY LAD (Ire) 5-11-5 (7*) Miss F M Crowley, ... (12 to 1) 24
THE COILTE 9-11-7 (7*) Mr J P Kilfeather, ... (50 to 1) pu
ARDMORE LEADER (Ire) 5-11-0 (7*) Mr E M Kelly, (16 to 1) pu
THE CAKE MAN (Ire) 5-11-5 (7*) Mr J Connolly, . . . (16 to 1) pu

Dist: 15l, 5l, 4½l, 10l. 4m 8.70s. (27 Ran).
(Philip F Myerscough), E J O'Grady

DONCASTER (good to firm) Monday March 7th

Going Correction: MINUS 0.20 sec. per fur. (races 1,2,5,7,8), NIL (3,4,6)

2870 Sprotbrough Claiming Hurdle (4-y-o and up) £2,302 2½m. . . . . (2:10)

2535* SO DISCREET (USA) 6-12-0 A Maguire, *hld up in tch, took clr order aftr 7th, rdn to ld last, ran on wl.* . . . . . (11 to 8 fav op 7 to 4) 1
2424[4] GENERAL SHOT 9-11-8 D Bridgwater, *in tch, pushed alng aftr 7th, hdwy appr 3 out, kpt on wl frm nxt, no imprsn on wnr r-in.* . . . . . (25 to 1 op 16 to 1) 2
2717* KANNDABIL (bl) 7-12-0 G McCourt, *wth ldr, led 5th, hdd last, no extr und pres.* . . . . . (9 to 2 op 4 to 1) 3
IRISH FLASHER 7-11-3 (5*) P Williams, *led to 5th, remained prmnt till grad wknd appr 2 out.* . . . . (33 to 1) 4
2686[7] MUZO (USA) 7-11-2 W Humphreys, *chsd ldrs 5th till outpcd appr 3 out, no dngr aftr.* . . . . . (25 to 1 op 20 to 1) 5
2689[4] PHILS PRIDE 10-11-10 M Dwyer, *hld up in tch, ev ch 3 out, sn rdn and btn.* . . . . (4 to 1 op 7 to 2 tchd 9 to 2) 6
2631[2] ELDER PRINCE (v) 8-11-6 G Harker, *chsd ldrs, hrd rdn aproaching 3 out, sn wknd.* . . . . . (14 to 1 op 12 to 1) 7
LATOSKY 6-11-4 P Harley, *in tch, pushed alng aftr 7th sn beh.* . . . . . (40 to 1 op 33 to 1 tchd 50 to 1) 8
2627* BURN BRIDGE (USA) (v) 8-11-8 Peter Caldwell, *prmnt till wknd quickly aftr 7th, tld off.* . . . . . (11 to 2 op 4 to 1 tchd 6 to 1) 9

Dist: 2½l, 3½l, 5l, 7l, 3l, 4l, 3½l, 15l. 4m 52.50s. a 14.50s (9 Ran).
(Ms M Horan), J White

2871 EBF 'National Hunt' Novices' Hurdle Qualifier (5,6,7-y-o) £2,755 2½m (2:40)

2556[3] THE FROG PRINCE (Ire) 6-11-0 C Llewellyn, *hld up, steady hdwy to ld appr 3 out, kpt on wl und pres frm last.* . . . . . (4 to 1 op 7 to 2) 1

2485² BANCHORY 5-11-0 M Dwyer, *al prmnt, chlgd 3 out, ev ch last, no extr und pres*..............(7 to 1 op 6 to 1) 2

2150 STAGGERING (Ire) 5-10-6 (3*) T Jenks, *hld up, steady hdwy aftr 6th, ev ch betw last 2, no extr und pres frm last*....................(40 to 1 op 33 to 1 tchd 50 to 1) 3

1872⁵ KENMORE-SPEED 7-11-5 Richard Guest, *trkd ldrs, led 4th, ran wide, hdd and lost pl appr 3 out, pushed alng aftr nxt, no hdwy.* (9 to 4 fav op 5 to 2 tchd 11 to 4) 4

2291³ GAYLOIRE (Ire) 5-10-7 (7*) Mr A Harvey, *cl up, led 3rd, hdd nxt, prmnt till wknd aftr 3 out.* ....(11 to 4 op 5 to 2 tchd 3 to 1 and 100 to 30) 5

1929 EMBLEY BUOY 6-10-9 (5*) S Curran, *hld up in tch, effrt appr 3 out, sn btn*..............(100 to 1 op 50 to 1) 6

2176 ALLERTON BARGE (Ire) (bl) 6-10-9 Gary Lyons, *prmnt till wknd appr 3 out*...(66 to 1 op 50 to 1 tchd 100 to 1) 7

HURRICANE LINDA 7-10-9 A Maguire, *nvr nr ldrs.* ....(12 to 1 tchd 14 to 1) 8

1804² CARAGH BRIDGE 7-11-0 R Supple, *in tch, hdwy to track ldrs hfwy, wknd appr 3 out*.................(12 to 1) 9

1490 HERESY (Ire) 5-10-9 S Smith Eccles, *al beh.* ....(66 to 1 op 50 to 1 tchd 100 to 1) 10

1957 FINWAG 7-10-11 (3*) T Eley, *chsd ldrs, pushed alng hfwy, wknd aftr 7th.*.................(100 to 1 op 50 to 1) 11

502⁴ THE MAN FROM CLARE (Ire) 6-11-0 R Greene, *in tch, pushed alng aftr 6th, sn beh*........(25 to 1 op 20 to 1) 12

STONE WARRIOR 7-11-0 M Robinson, *pld very hrd early, jmpd slwly 1st, led till hdd 3rd, wknd quickly aftr 5th, tld off whn pulled up bef last*....(66 to 1 op 50 to 1) pu

2604⁴ JURASSIC CLASSIC 7-11-0 D Bridgwater, *sn beh, tld off whn pld up bef 2 out*...........(16 to 1 tchd 20 to 1) pu

Dist: ¾l, 3l, 10l, 2l, 5l, 3½l, 7l, 3½l, 2l, 8l. 4m 49.30s. a 11.30s (14 Ran).
(Robert Cooper), N A Gaselee

2872 Pardubice Novices' Handicap Chase (5-y-o and up) £3,224 2m 3f 110yds ....(3:10)

1621 COCK SPARROW [78] 10-10-0 W Marston, *cl up, led aftr 8th, clr whn blun 3 out styd on wl.* ....(33 to 1 tchd 50 to 1) 1

1644 BUMPTIOUS BOY [78] 10-10-0 D Bridgwater, *hld up, hdwy appr 4 out, chsd wnr frm 2 out, no imprsn.* ....(7 to 1 op 6 to 1) 2

2330⁴ HOWGILL [79] 8-9-12 (3*) S Wynne, *prmnt, lft second 4 out, kpt on same pace.*.............(10 to 1 op 8 to 1) 3

SOUSON (Ire) [81] 6-10-3² R Garritty, *nvr on terms.* ....(12 to 1 tchd 14 to 1) 4

2636⁴ SPOONHILL WOOD [84] (bl) 8-10-6 B Dalton, *trkd ldrs, cl up whn blun badly tenth, nvt reco'r.* ....(5 to 1 tchd 9 to 2) 5

2636 SMILES AHEAD [78] 6-9-11 (3*) T Eley, *dsptd ld early, in tch till wknd aftr 11th.*....................(9 to 2) 6

2721⁴ COQ HARDI SMOKEY (Ire) [102] 6-11-7 (3*) A Thornton, *in tch whn f 9th, dead.*............(5 to 1 op 4 to 1) f

2603³ LOCAL MANOR [79] 7-10-1 J Osborne, *hld up, hdwy hfwy, chasing clr ldr whn f 4 out.* ....(11 to 10 fav op 7 to 4 tchd 15 to 8) f

2688 CALDECOTT [81] 8-10-3² Gary Lyons, *made most till hdd aftr 8th, wkng whn hmpd 4 out, sn pld up.* ....(20 to 1 op 14 to 1) pu

Dist: 8l, 3l, 15l, 12l, 2½l. 4m 53.00s. a 7.00s (9 Ran).
SR: 2/-/-/-/-/-/ (J F Broderick), J Mackie

2873 Dostihovy Spolek Novices' Chase (5-y-o and up) £3,224 3m..........(3:40)

2767* MELEAGRIS 10-11-10 A Maguire, *in tch gng wl, led on bit out, rdn betw last 2, ran on well.* ....(6 to 5 fav op 6 to 4 tchd 11 to 10) 1

2411² SILVER STICK 7-11-4 R Garritty, *in tch, effrt appr 4 out, rdn to chal 2 out, ev ch last, no extr.* ....(2 to 1 op 7 to 4 tchd 9 to 4) 2

2479⁶ BUCKS SURPRISE 6-11-4 W Marston, *mstks, prmnt, ev ch 2 out, grad wknd.*................(25 to 1 op 20 to 1) 3

2417³ SAYYURE (USA) (bl) 8-11-4 S Smith Eccles, *led to 7th, dsptd ld 13th, led appr 4 out, hdd nxt, sn btn.* ....(11 to 2 op 5 to 1) 4

2502⁹ GYMCRAK GAMBLE 6-11-4 Richard Guest, *in tch, led 7th, jnd 13th, grad wknd frm 4 out.*.....(11 to 1 op 8 to 1) 5

1527 HUNTING DIARY 8-10-13 (5*) S Curran, *beh most of way.* ....(33 to 1 op 25 to 1) 6

1694⁷ NUT TREE 9-10-13 D Bridgwater, *beh most of way.* ....(16 to 1 op 12 to 1) 7

1405⁴ OUTFIELD 8-10-13 G McCourt, *beh most of way.* ....(12 to 1 tchd 14 to 1) 8

Dist: 1½l, 12l, 20l, 15l, 5l, 11½l, ½l. 6m 11.00s. a 7.00s (8 Ran).
(D J Jackson), D Nicholson

2874 South Yorkshire Novices' Handicap Hurdle (4-y-o and up) £2,635 2m 110yds........................(4:40)

2217 CHIEF MINISTER (Ire) [98] 5-11-10 A Maguire, *al prmnt, chlgd 3 out, led betw last 2, ran on wl.* ....(9 to 1 op 8 to 1 tchd 11 to 1) 1

2585⁶ FLOATING LINE [85] 6-10-11 R Garritty, *nvr far away, led 2 out, sn hdd, kpt on same pace...* (14 to 1 tchd 16 to 1) 2

2135⁸ IJAB (Can) [74] 4-10-0 A Dobbin, *nvr far away, ev ch 2 out, kpt on same pace.*....................(33 to 1) 3

2356⁹ HIGH MIND (Fr) [88] 5-10-11 (3*) A Thornton, *cl up, led appr 3 out, hdd nxt, one pace.* ....(10 to 1 op 9 to 1 tchd 11 to 1) 4

1557³ ROSS GRAHAM [86] 6-10-12 P Holley, *in tch, styd on wl frm 3 out, not rch ldrs*.........(14 to 1 tchd 16 to 1) 5

2140 BLAYNEYS PRIVILEGE [74] 7-10-0 L Wyer, *mid-div, kpt on same pace frm 3 out*..........(20 to 1 op 14 to 1) 6

2485 SOUNDS GOLDEN [74] 6-10-0 R Marley, *beh, hdwy appr 3 out, staying on same pace whn badly hmpd last.* ....(33 to 1) 7

2405* SCARBA [74] 6-9-12⁶ (7*) K Davies, *chsd ldrs till wknd aftr 3 out*....................(10 to 1) 8

21507 TAHITIAN [77] 5-9-12 (5*) E Husband, *nvr dngrs.* ....(16 to 1 op 14 to 1) 9

2640² DULZURA [90] 6-11-2 R Greene, *led till hdd appr 3 out, sn btn*....................(14 to 1 op 10 to 1) 10

2381 ATHERTON GREEN (Ire) [87] 4-10-13 T Reed, *beh, rdn appr 3 out, no hdwy*....................(16 to 1 op 14 to 1) 11

2432⁷ ERZADJAN (Ire) [88] (bl) 4-11-0 G McCourt, *al beh, tld off appr 3 out, some late hdwy*.......(11 to 1 op 10 to 1) 12

2572⁶ PHIL'S DREAM [80] (bl) 6-10-6 I Lawrence, *beh most of way, no ch whn badly hmpd 2 out.* (16 to 1 op 14 to 1) 13

2217⁵ LEGION OF HONOUR [95] 6-11-4 (3*) T Jenks, *hld up in tch, effrt appr 3 out, btn whn badly hmpd nxt.* ....(9 to 1 op 10 to 1) 14

OTTER BUSH [80] 5-10-6 Richard Guest, *beh most of way.* ....(25 to 1) 15

1166 PYRRHIC DANCE [80] 4-10-6 R Bellamy, *prmnt, rdn aftr 5th, sn wknd.*................(16 to 1 op 14 to 1) 16

2741* KING ATHELSTAN (USA) [87] 6-10-13 A S Smith, *mid-div, mstk 5th, ch 3 out, sn rdn, fifth and btn whn f last.* ....(2 to 1 fav op 9 to 4 tchd 11 to 4) f

2640³ EARLY DRINKER [83] 6-10-6 (3*) J McCarthy, *trkd ldrs, wkng whn f 2 out*................(14 to 1 op 12 to 1) f

Dist: 6l, ½l, 3l, 5l, 2l, 11, nk, 8l, ¾l. 3m 52.70s. a 2.20s (18 Ran).
SR: 41/22/10/21/14/-/ (G Shiel), T Dyer

2875 Hambleton Hills Hunters' Chase (5-y-o and up) £1,607 2m 3f 110yds.... (4:40)

LINGHAM MAGIC 9-11-13 Mr S Swiers, *hld up, steady hdwy hfwy, chlgd 3 out, no extr frm last, held whn snatched up cl hme, fnshd second awarded race.* ....(6 to 1 tchd 11 to 2) 1

DALTON DANDY 12-11-7 (7*) Mr P Jenkins, *cl up, led 7th, kpt on wl frm last, edgd lft close hme, fnshd 1st, plcd* ....(33 to 1) 2

2669⁷ HILARION (Fr) 10-11-7 (7*) Mr D Bloor, *beh, hdwy appr 4 out, styd on wl frm 2 out, nrst finish.*........(50 to 1) 3

SPEAKERS CORNER 11-12-1 (7*) Mr M Sowersby, *in tch, kpt on same pace frm 4 out.* ....(9 to 2 op 4 to 1 tchd 7 to 2) 4

NISHKINA 6-11-7 (7*) Mr S Brisby, *al prmnt, ev ch appr 3 out, one pace.*....................(25 to 1) 5

HOBNOBBER 7-11-7 (7*) Mr A Sansome, *mid-div, effrt appr 4 out, kpt on same pace.*..............(33 to 1) 6

2838⁴ CURAHEEN BOY 14-11-10 (7*) Miss J Butler, *nvr dngrs.* ....(20 to 1 op 14 to 1) 7

911 FOUR TRIX 13-12-3 (5*) Mr R Hale, *nvr better than mid-div.*....................(33 to 1) 8

JOHN CORBET 11-11-11 (7*) Mr D Parker, *led to 3rd, cl up till grad wknd frm 4 out.*....................(9 to 1) 9

FRISKNEY DALE LAD 9-11-13 (5*) Mr M Buckley, *nvr dngrs.* ....(14 to 1 op 10 to 1) 10

2669³ HOUGHTON 8-12-1 (7*) Major M Watson, *chsd ldrs, ev ch 4 out, sn wknd.*...(11 to 1 op 10 to 1 tchd 12 to 1) 11

LACIDAR 14-12-5 (3*) Mrs A Farrell, *nvr better than mid-div, collapsed and died aftr race.* (12 to 1 op 10 to 1) 12

ANTINOUS 10-11-7 (7*) Mr N F Smith, *beh, blun 6th, f nxt, dead.*....................(33 to 1) f

2570* DUNCAN 9-12-1 (7*) Mr B Pollock, *nvr far away, chlgd 3 out, disputing ld whn blun and uns rdr nxt.* ....(7 to 2 op 4 to 1) ur

AFRICAN SAFARI (bl) 10-11-7 (7*) Mr P Murray, *prmnt till wknd aftr 8th, wl beh whn pld up bef tenth.* ....(66 to 1 op 50 to 1) pu

MAN O'MAGIC (bl) 11-11-7 (7*) Mrs T Bailey, *in tch whn blun and lost pl 9th, pld up bef nxt, dead.* ....(11 to 2 op 9 to 2) pu

BROWN SAUCE (NZ) 8-11-7 (7*) Mr A Price, *led 3rd, hit nxt, hdd 6th, lost pl quickly and pld up bef 9th.* ....(25 to 1 op 33 to 1 tchd 50 to 1) pu

Dist: 1½l, 12l, 2½l, ¾l, nd, 8l, 7l, 3½l, 2½l, 6l. 4m 56.00s. a 10.00s (17 Ran).
(J E Swiers), J E Swiers

2876 EBF Stakes National Hunt Flat Race (Div I) (4,5,6-y-o) £1,828 2m 110yds ....(5:10)

DON'T GEORGE 5-11-5 (5*) S Lyons, *beh, pushed alng and hdwy 4 out, ran on wl to ld o'r one out, sn clr.* ....(11 to 2 op 5 to 1 tchd 6 to 1) 1

WIZZO 4-10-9 (7*) D Rees, *in tch, effrt 4 out, ran on wl fnl furlong, nrst finish.*.............(20 to 1 op 16 to 1) 2

COXWELL QUICK STEP 5-11-5 Mr J M Pritchard, *trkd ldrs, chlgd o'r 2 out, ev ch till no extr fnl furlong.*
..........................(7 to 1 op 6 to 1 tchd 8 to 1) 3
RENT DAY 5-11-0 (5*) S Curran, *trkd ldrs, slight ld o'r 4 out till hdd over one out, sn btn...* (33 to 1 op 20 to 1) 4
REAL GLEE (Ire) 5-11-10 Mr J Durkan, *beh, styd on fnl 4 fs, nrst finish*..........(3 to 1 fav op 5 to 2 tchd 7 to 2) 5
HOT ADVICE (Ire) 5-11-7 (3*) A Thornton, *prmnt, one pace fnl 4 fs*..........................(25 to 1 op 20 to 1) 6
MISTRIC 5-10-12 (7*) D Bohan, *led till hdd o'r 4 out, grad wknd.*..................................... (7 to 1 op 9 to 1) 7
BUYERS DREAM (Ire) 4-10-13 (3*) A Larnach, *chsd ldrs till wknd o'r 4 out.*................................(20 to 1) 8
TIGH-NA-MARA 6-11-0 (5*) E Husband, *mid-div, effrt 5 out, no hdwy.*......(9 to 1 op 8 to 1 tchd 10 to 1) 9
HORTON TOWN 5-11-3 (7*) R Massey, *cl up till wknd o'r 3 out.*................................(33 to 1 op 25 to 1) 10
CHUKATEN 5-11-7 (3*) T Eley, *chsd ldrs till wknd 4 out.*
..........................(14 to 1 op 12 to 1) 11
2210 DREAM START 4-10-9 (7*) R Wilkinson, *chsd ldrs till wknd o'r 4 out.*............................(20 to 1) 12
FAIRY GARDEN (Ire) 6-11-3 (7*) R Moore, *nvr better than mid-div*........... (6 to 1 op 8 to 1 tchd 9 to 1) 13
RICASWORD 5-11-10 Mr Simon Andrews, *prmnt till wknd o'r 4 out.*........................(25 to 1 op 20 to 1) 14
MR DRUMMOND (Ire) 5-11-3 (7*) G McGrath, *prmnt till wknd o'r 5 out.*......................(8 to 1 op 7 to 1) 15
TORTULA 5-10-12 (7*) K Davies, *prmnt till wknd o'r 4 out.*
..........................(20 to 1) 16
BRIGG FOLLY 4-10-4 (7*) Annette Billany, *sn beh, tld off.*
..........................(33 to 1 op 20 to 1) 17
Dist: 4l, hd, 2½l, 2l, hd, 4l, 1½l, 2l, ¾l, 7l. 4m 2.10s. (17 Ran).
(Mrs J M L Milligan), M D Hammond

# 2877 EBF Stakes National Hunt Flat Race (Div II) (4,5,6-y-o) £1,814 2m 110yds
..........................(5:35)

THE BOUNDER 4-10-13 (3*) J McCarthy, *beh, hdwy 7 fs out, led o'r 2 out, ran on wl.*.....(9 to 4 fav op 3 to 1) 1
2509³ COURTOWN BOY 4-11-2 (7*) Mr G Hogan, *mid-div, smooth hdwy to chal o'r 2 fs out, sn rdn, kpt on, no ch wth wnr*.............(100 to 30 op 3 to 1) 2
LE MEILLE (Ire) 5-11-3 (7*) G McGrath, *in tch, gd hdwy 6 fs out, slight ld o'r 4 out, hdd 2 out, kpt on same pace.*..........................(8 to 1 op 10 to 1 tchd 7 to 1) 3
2210³ THE PADRE (Ire) 5-11-10 Mr J M Pritchard, *beh, styd on fnl 4 fs, nrst finish.*......................(4 to 1 op 3 to 1) 4
MIGHTY PROFILE (Ire) 5-11-3 (7*) K Davies, *hld up in tch, hdwy 6 out, kpt on same pace fnl 3 fs.*......... (20 to 1) 5
STORMY SESSION 4-10-9 (7*) G Tormey, *prmnt till grad wknd frm 4 fs out*......(15 to 2 op 5 to 1 tchd 10 to 1) 6
SHUIL POIPIN (Ire) 5-10-12 (7*) D Bohan, *cl up, slight aftr 6 fs, hdd o'r 4 out, grad wknd.*...........(8 to 1 op 6 to 1) 7
DIVINE COMEDY (Ire) 5-11-2 (3*) S Wynne, *hld up in tch, effrt 4 out, sn rdn, no hdwy.*......(16 to 1 op 20 to 1) 8
SAN GIORGIO 5-11-10 Mr T Stephenson, *prmnt, reminders 6 fs out, chlgd o'r 4 out, sn rdn and wknd.*
..........................(16 to 1) 9
1806 FORBURIES (Ire) 5-11-2 (3*) D Meredith, *mid-div till wknd 5 fs out, tld off*...................(20 to 1 op 16 to 1) 10
FORTRIA ROSIE DAWN 4-10-11 Mr R Heathfield, *badly hmpd and almost uns rdr aftr 6 fs, in tch till wknd 5 out, tld off.*......................(16 to 1 tchd 20 to 1) 11
CONNAUGHT'S SECRET 6-11-3 (7*) C Huggan, *chsd ldrs till wknd 5 fs out, tld off.*...................(20 to 1) 12
1957 MARINERS DANCE 6-10-12 (7*) R Massey, *dsptd ld aftr 6 fs till wknd six out, tld off*......................(20 to 1) 13
LOWGATE LAD (Ire) 5-11-5 (5*) P Midgley, *led 6 fs, cl up till wknd six out, tld off.*......................(20 to 1) 14
Dist: 5l, 2l, ¾l, 4l, 2l, 2½l, 3½l, 2l, 20l, 4l. 3m 57.40s. (14 Ran).
(T Stewart-Brown), O Sherwood

WINDSOR (soft)
Monday March 7th
Going Correction: PLUS 0.80 sec. per fur.

# 2878 Final Selling Hurdle (4 & 5-y-o) £1,707 2m.
..........................(2:20)

2763³ PLAIN SAILING (Fr) 4-10-7 N Williamson, *wth ldr to 3rd, chlgd 5th, outpcd appr 2 out, rallied to take slight ld last, all out.*..........(7 to 2 op 4 to 1 tchd 9 to 2) 1
2713⁴ YAAFOOR (USA) (bl) 5-11-0 M Richards, *led, gng best appr 2 out, narrowly hdd last, hrd rdn, swshd tail, not run on.*..........(6 to 1 op 7 to 1 tchd 5 to 1) 2
2776⁵ COUNTRYWIDE LAD 5-11-0 Peter Hobbs, *pld hrd in rear, hdwy to chase ldrs 4th, styd on same pace frm 3 out.*
..........................(5 to 1 op 4 to 1 tchd 11 to 2) 3
2454 OLIVIPET 5-10-9 M Crosse, *chsd ldrs till lost tch appr 3 out.*.......................(33 to 1 tchd 50 to 1) 4
2546⁶ HIZAL 5-10-7 (7*) M Appleby, *not fluent, al beh, lost tch 5th.*.......................(33 to 1 op 20 to 1) 5
2414⁴ JOKERS THREE (Ire) (bl) 5-11-0 M Perrett, *beh, drvn and effrt aftr 5th, sn wknd.* (11 to 2 op 4 to 1 tchd 6 to 1) 6

2492 CELTIC LILLEY 4-10-3¹ M Hoad, *al beh, lost tch 5th.*
..........................(33 to 1 op 20 to 1) 7
2428 MORAN BRIG (v) 4-10-7 E Leonard, *tracking ldrs whn stumbled and uns rdr 3rd.*
..........................(9 to 4 fav op 5 to 4 tchd 5 to 2) ur
1323⁹ EXCELLED (Ire) 5-10-9 R Dunwoody, *prmnt early, beh 5th, tld off whn pld up bef 3 out*......(12 to 1 tchd 16 to 1) pu
Dist: ½l, 7l, 15l, 12l, ¾l, 10l. 4m 12.80s. a 27.80s (9 Ran).
(Martyn Meade), Martyn Meade

# 2879 EBF Novices' Chase (5-y-o and up) £2,347 2m 5f.
..........................(2:50)

2390* ANOTHER EXCUSE (Ire) 6-11-12 Mr W O'Sullivan, *in tch, reminders appr 4 out, led 3 out, hit last, readily.*
..........................(Evens fav op 6 to 4 on) 1
992⁸ CHARDEN 8-11-2 S Earle, *chsd ldrs early, beh 11th, steady hdwy appr 4 out, chlgd 3 out, still ev ch nxt, outpcd whn hit last.*.......................(33 to 1) 2
2668 LE BUCHERON 8-11-2 J Ryan, *beh, blun 8th, hdwy 9th, styd on frm 3 out*......(25 to 1 op 20 to 1) 3
GYPSY KING (Ire) 6-11-2 S McNeill, *al pressing ldrs, ev ch 4 out, wknd frm 3 out*......(13 to 2 op 9 to 2) 4
2044³ SPECIAL ACCOUNT 8-11-2 N Mann, *in tch, rdn aftr 11th, sn wknd.*.......................(10 to 1 op 8 to 1) 5
2494⁵ RING CORBITTS 6-11-2 Peter Hobbs, *prmnt till wknd 11th*.......(16 to 1 op 14 to 1 tchd 20 to 1) 6
2247⁷ FAR TOO LOUD 7-10-13 (3*) P Davis, *chsd ldrs, hit 6th and lost pos, hdwy 11th, wknd aftr 4 out.*
..........................(12 to 1 tchd 14 to 1) 7
2223 STAR ACTOR 8-11-2 R Dunwoody, *led till hdd appr 3 out, sn wknd.*......................(8 to 1 tchd 10 to 1) 8
2733 KEV'S LASS (Ire) 6-10-11 N Williamson, *wnt prmnt 6th, chlgd aftr 11th, wknd frm 4 out...* (25 to 1 op 20 to 1) 9
2693 BUCKELIGHT (Ire) 6-10-13 (3*) R Farrant, *al beh.*
..........................(4 to 1 op 7 to 2 tchd 9 to 2) 10
BILLION DOLLARBILL 6-11-2 T Grantham, *beh whn mstk and uns rdr 3rd*......................(50 to 1) ur
2431 RICH NEPHEW 9-11-2 B Powell, *prmnt till drpd rear tenth, tld off whn pld up bef 3 out*............ (12 to 1) pu
Dist: 7l, 5l, 1½l, 7l, 1½l, 1½l, 30l, 5m 33.30s. a 23.30s (12 Ran).
SR: 33/16/11/9/2/-/ (Kilshannig Racing Syndicate), Eugene M O'Sullivan

2880 Pavilion Handicap Chase (0-130 5-y-o and up) £2,747 3½m 110yds...(3:20)

2791 WARNER FOR WINNERS [104] 8-10-7 Peter Hobbs, *hit second, chlgd 4th till led 4th, hit nxt, pckd tenth, led 14th, hit 2 out and last, hng lft r-in, ct to dead head on line.*..........(6 to 1 op 5 to 1 tchd 13 to 2) 1
2805* CAPTAIN FRISK [124] 11-11-13 (6ex) N Williamson, *chlgd 9th, chsd 15th till led 17th, hit 2 out, hng lft and hdd r-in, rallied to dead-heat on line.*
..........................(9 to 4 on op 5 to 2 on tchd 7 to 4 on) 2
2536⁵ SCOLE [108] 9-10-11 J R Kavanagh, *beh, lost tch 16th.*
..........................(7 to 1 op 9 to 2) 3
2690⁴ LITTLE GENERAL [97] 11-10-0 B Powell, *hit 6th, led ag'n 7th, hdd 14th, sn wknd.*
..........................(11 to 2 op 9 to 2 tchd 6 to 1) 4
Dist: Dd-ht, dist, 30l. 7m 38.00s. a 36.00s (4 Ran).
(Terry Warner Sports), P J Hobbs

2881 Thames Novices' Hurdle (4-y-o and up) £1,968 2m.....................(3:50)

2430* FIRST AVENUE 10-11-7 J Railton, *hld up, hdwy appr 3 out, led approaching last, ran on wl.*
..........................(5 to 1 op 4 to 1 tchd 11 to 2) 1
2676² EDITHMEAD (Ire) 4-10-2 R Dunwoody, *trkd ldrs, chlgd 3 out, led appr 2 out, hdd approaching last, sn one pace.*
(11 to 4 on op 5 to 2 on tchd 9 to 4 on and 3 to 1 on) 2
INTENTION (USA) 4-10-7 R Campbell, *chlgd 4th, led 5th, hdd appr 2 out, sn one pace.*
..........................(20 to 1 op 16 to 1 tchd 25 to 1) 3
2723 NIGHT FANCY 6-10-7 (7*) P McLoughlin, *beh, hdwy appr 3 out, sn one pace.*
..........................(66 to 1 op 50 to 1 tchd 100 to 1) 4
2335⁶ RAGAMUFFIN ROMEO 5-11-0 N Williamson, *in tch, pressed ldrs 5th, rdn 3 out, wknd appr 2 out.*
..........................(10 to 1 op 8 to 1 tchd 12 to 1) 5
2599 MA BELLA LUNA 5-10-9 A Charlton, *nvr rch ldrs.*
..........................(33 to 1 op 25 to 1 tchd 50 to 1) 6
2685⁵ MIGAVON 4-10-2 D Gallagher, *led to 5th, wknd appr 3 out.*......(50 to 1 op 20 to 1 tchd 66 to 1) 7
2708² SCOTTISH BALL 5-10-9 M Crosse, *in tch, jmpd slwly 3rd, hdwy 5th, wknd aftr 3 out.*
..........................(16 to 1 op 12 to 1 tchd 20 to 1) 8
FINNIGAN FREE 4-10-7 J R Kavanagh, *beh most of way.*
..........................(50 to 1 op 33 to 1 tchd 66 to 1) 9
NEOLOGIST 8-11-0 A Dicken, *al beh.*
..........................(66 to 1 op 50 to 1 tchd 100 to 1) 10
522⁸ WAAZA (USA) 5-10-9 M Bosley, *prmnt, chlgd 3rd to 4th, wknd quickly aftr 5th, tld off whn pld up bef 2 out.*
..........................(66 to 1 op 33 to 1) pu
2857⁷ BARNIEMEBOY (bl) 4-11-1⁸ W Elderfield, *chsd ldrs frm 3rd till wknd quickly appr 5th, tld off whn pld up bef 3 out.*
..........................(100 to 1 op 50 to 1 tchd 200 to 1) pu

Dist: 5l, 3l, 4l, 5l, 12l, 7l, 20l, 10l, 5l. 4m 6.60s. a 21.60s (12 Ran).
SR: 5/-/-/-/-/-/   (C J Drewe), C J Drewe

2882   Thames Valley Hunters' Chase (5-y-o and up) £1,646 3m . . . . (4:20)

BRIEF ENCOUNTER (NZ) 10-11-9 (5") Miss P Curling, chlgd
6th, led 9th, came clr frm 13th, unchald.
. . . .(6 to 5 fav op 5 to 4 tchd 11 to 8)   1
ZORRO'S MARK 7-11-7 (7") Mr J Dufosee, beh, lost tch 9th,
ran on frm 14th, chsd wnr aftr 4 out but no ch.
. . . .(5 to 1 tchd 11 to 2)   2
2669⁴ SKINNHILL (bl) 10-11-7 (7") Mr C Newport, led to 9th, wknd
4 out, tld off. . . . .(5 to 1 op 4 to 1)   3
GATTERSTOWN 11-11-7 (7") Mr S Mulcaire, blun 8th, chsd
ldr 11th till aftr 4 out, sn wknd, tld off.
. . . . (33 to 1 op 25 to 1)   4
PAMPERING 13-11-7 (7") Mr M Rimell, prmnt early, beh
frm 9th, tld off. . . . .(14 to 1)   5
SEE YOU THERE 12-11-7 (7") Mr M Portman, lost tch 11th,
tld off whn pld up bef 3 out. . . . .(6 to 1 op 5 to 1)   pu
TANGLE JIM 9-11-7 (7") Mr H Rowsell, pckd second, lost
tch 9th, tld off whn pld up bef 4 out. (11 to 2 op 5 to 1)   pu
Dist: Dist, 3l, dist, 30l. 6m 24.50s. a 29.50s (7 Ran).
. . . . (Mrs Bridget Nicholls), Richard Barber

2883   March Handicap Hurdle (0-120 4-y-o and up) £1,267 2m . . . .(4:50)

2432* MOVING OUT [100] 6-10-13 M Perrett, led to 3 out, outpcd
appr nxt, rallied r-in to ld ag'n cl hme. . . . . .(15 to 8 jt-
fav op 2 to 1 tchd 5 to 2 and 7 to 4)   1
2432² CARIBBEAN PRINCE [87] 6-10-0 R Dunwoody, chsd wnr
till led 3 out, rdn appr last, hdd and no extr cl hme.
. . . . (5 to 2 tchd 100 to 30 and 7 to 2)   2
1249⁶ WILL JAMES [90] (bl) 8-10-3³ J Railton, nvr rch ldrs.
. . . . (7 to 1 op 12 to 1)   3
2400⁸ MORE OF IT [110] 9-11-9 Peter Hobbs, beh, distant 3rd
whn blun last. . . . .(20 to 1 op 14 to 1 tchd 25 to 1)   4
DRAMATIC EVENT [96] 9-10-9 E Murphy, al beh.
. . . . (12 to 1 op 5 to 1 tchd 14 to 1)   5
2734² IVEAGH HOUSE [115] 8-11-9 (5") D Fortt, chsd ldrs till
wknd 3 out. . . . . . .(15 to 8 jt-fav op 9 to 4 tchd 5 to 2)   6
Dist: ½l, dist, 2½l, dist, 8l. 4m 19s. a 16.90s (6 Ran).
SR: 44/30/-/   (Mrs Shirley Brasher), Miss H C Knight

LEICESTER (good to soft)
Tuesday March 8th
Going Correction: PLUS 1.30 sec. per fur.

2884   Ian Langrish Maiden Hunters' Chase (6-y-o and up) £1,709 3m . . . . . . (2:00)

CLARE MAN (Ire) 6-12-7 Mr J Greenall, al prmnt, chlgd
appr last, hrd rdn to ld nr finish.
. . . .(11 to 4 fav op 7 to 2)   1
ST LAYCAR 9-12-2 (5") Mr G Tarry, wl beh and pushed
alng, virtually tld off 14th, rapid prog 3 out, led appr
last, hrd rdn and hdd nr finish. . . . . .(7 to 1 op 14 to 1)   2
2555² MR GOLIGHTLY 7-12-0 (7") Miss J Cobden, hld up, mstk
3rd, prog whn mistake 9th, led 4 out till appr last, unbl
to quicken. . . . .(7 to 2 tchd 11 to 4)   3
2782³ BACK IN BUSINESS 11-12-0 (7") Mr G Hogan, hld up,
reminder 7th, prog to chase ldrs tenth, rdn 2 out, one
pace. . . . . (8 to 1 op 14 to 1)   4
UBU VAL (Fr) 8-12-0 (7") Mr W Bethell, hld up, lost tch 14th,
styd on frm 2 out, nvr nrr.
. . . . (14 to 1 op 12 to 1 tchd 25 to 1)   5
HASTY SALVO 10-11-9 (7") Major G Wheeler, led 7th till 4
out, wknd 2 out. . . . .(16 to 1 op 10 to 1)   6
CARLY'S CASTLE 7-11-9 (7") Mr P Hanly, mstks, prmnt till
wknd 4 out, no ch whn hmpd last. (14 to 1 op 12 to 1)   7
DARTON RI 11-12-0 (7") Mr J Maxse, led till 7th, wknd 4
out. . . . .(66 to 1 op 50 to 1)   8
CHOCOLAT BLANC 13-12-0 (7") Mr N R Mitchell, chsd ldg
grp, lost tch 14th, no dngr aftr.
. . . . (16 to 1 op 14 to 1 tchd 20 to 1)   9
CAWKWELL DEAN 8-12-4 (3") Mr Simon Andrews, hld up
effrt to chase ldrs 11th, wknd 4 out. . . . .(16 to 1)   10
EASTER FROLIC 12-12-0 (7") Mr A Phillips, prmnt to 7th, sn
beh, tld off 14th. . . . .(50 to 1 op 33 to 1)   11
COUTURE TIGHTS 10-12-0 (7") Miss J Priest, al prmnt, ev ch
2 out, 4th and btn whn f last. . . . . (8 to 1 op 5 to 1)   f
SPACE MAN 11-12-0 (7") Mr P Howse, hld up rear, prog to
track ldrs whn f 11th. . . . .(16 to 1 op 10 to 1)   f
KELLY'S COURT 8-11-11 (5") Mr P Harding-Jones, chsd
ldrs, blun 8th, f tenth. . . . .(50 to 1)   f
2687 ABADARE (USA) 10-12-0 (7") Mr Michael J Jones, chsd ldrs
till wknd tenth, tld off and pld up bef 4 out.
. . . .(200 to 1 op 100 to 1)   pu
Dist: Hd, 7l, 5l, 7l, 8l, 20l, ¾l, nk, 6l, 12l. 6m 43.00s. a 51.00s (15 Ran).
. . . . (J E Greenall), Miss C Saunders

2885   City Merchants Investment Management 'Peter Jones' Hunters' Chase (6-

y-o and up) £1,520 2m 1f . . . .(2:30)

2669* KILFINNY CROSS (Ire) 6-12-4 Mr J Greenall, chsd ldr till led
5th, clr 4 out, shaken up aftr 2 out, mstk last, rdn out.
. . . .(5 to 2 on op 2 to 1 on tchd 7 to 4 on)   1
DENBERDAR 11-11-7 (7") Mr B Pollock, prog frm rear 5th,
mstk 7th, chsd wnr appr 2 out, ev ch aftr last, not
quicken. . . . .(20 to 1 op 16 to 1 tchd 25 to 1)   2
TRUST THE GYPSY 12-12-1 (7") Mr M Felton, in tch, chsd
wnr 8th, rdn and btn appr 2 out, eased.
. . . .(5 to 2 tchd 2 to 1)   3
PAID ELATION 9-11-2 (7") Mr J Wingfield Digby, prmnt till
4th and btn four out, sn tld off.
. . . .(40 to 1 op 33 to 1 tchd 50 to 1)   4
GRANNY'S BAY 11-11-9 (5") Mr D McCain, al beh, tld off
frm 4 out. . . . .(33 to 1 op 25 to 1)   5
DOUBLE LIGHT 12-11-7 (7") Mr James Young, al beh, tld
off . . . . (33 to 1 op 20 to 1)   6
2650 DECRETO 13-11-7 (7") Mr E James, prmnt till wknd rpdly
8th, tld off 3 out. . . . . (100 to 1 op 66 to 1)   7
2508 BOLD REPUBLIC (bl) 8-11-7 (7") Mr C Wadland, sn beh and
rdn alng, last whn blun and uns rdr 4th.
. . . . (100 to 1 op 66 to 1)   ur
PARADISE BEACH 9-11-7 (7") Mr M G Miller, led to 5th,
wknd rpdly, tld off and pld up 4 out.
. . . . (20 to 1 op 16 to 1)   pu
Dist: 4l, dist, 25l, 30l, dist, dist. 4m 44.40s. a 35.40s (9 Ran).
. . . .(J E Greenall), Miss C Saunders

2886   Leicestershire And Derbyshire Yeomanry Handicap Chase Amateur Riders' (0-105 5-y-o and up) £2,761 2 ½m 110yds. . . . . (3:00)

2437² DEADLINE [85] (bl) 11-10-7⁴ (7") Miss J Thurlow, rcd wide,
led second till appr 3 out, led ag'n and lft clr 2 out, styd
on wl. . . . . (7 to 2 op 3 to 1)   1
2297⁴ CHIASSO FORTE (Ity) [94] 11-10-12 (7") Mr S Mulcaire,
prmnt, led appr 3 out, hdd and hit 2 out, not quicken.
. . . . (3 to 1 fav tchd 7 to 2)   2
2639 SERDARLI [78] 12-9-10 (7") Mr J O'Shaughnessy, rear but
in tch, hmpd and lft 3rd 4 out, rdn and wknd nxt.
. . . .(20 to 1)   3
SEBEL HOUSE [85] (bl) 11-10-5 Mr D McCain, trkd ldrs,
prog 8th, wknd 4 out. . . . .(5 to 1 op 9 to 1)   4
1503⁷ OVERHEREOVERTHERE [99] 11-11-5 (7") Mr T Byrne, led to
second, 4th and ev ch whn f four out.
. . . .(13 to 2 op 6 to 1 tchd 7 to 1)   f
2328⁸ FLUTTER MONEY [83] 10-10-8¹⁵ (7") Mr R Griffiths, uns rdr
second. . . . .(50 to 1 op 33 to 1)   ur
1997² IMPECCABLE TIMING [77] 11-9-13⁴ (7") Mr A Mitchell, rear
but in tch till mstk and uns rdr 11th.
. . . .(7 to 2 tchd 4 to 1)   ur
2518 HOWARYADOON [103] 8-11-11 (3") Mr G Johnson
Houghton, trkd ldrs, lost pl 8th, rallied tenth, 3rd and ev
ch whn blun and uns rdr 4 out.
. . . .(6 to 1 op 5 to 1 tchd 13 to 2)   ur
Dist: 6l, dist, 5l. 5m 47.50s. a 44.50s (8 Ran).
. . . . (S Chadwick), S G Chadwick

2887   Walkers' Pies 'Roland Sheppard' Hunters' Chase (6-y-o and up) £3,002 3m. . . . .(3:30)

MY MELLOW MAN 11-11-5 (5") Miss P Curling, led 7th to
8th and frm nxt, clr 2 out, shaken up aftr last, ran on
strly. . . . .(12 to 1 op 8 to 1)   1
2526* BROWN WINDSOR 12-11-8 (7") Mr B Pollock, slwly into
strd, sn prmnt, chsd wnr 4 out, rdn and hld whn mstk 2
out, ran on one pace... (7 to 4 op 6 to 4 tchd 15 to 8)   2
2724³ THE MALAKARMA 8-11-12 (3") Mr I McKie, not fluent, hld
up, prog 9th, hrd rdn appr 2 out, unbl to quicken.
. . . .(11 to 10 fav op 5 to 4)   3
2724⁵ SPORTING MARINER 12-11-3 (7") Mr D Bloor, led 5th to
7th, reminders aftr nxt, rdn and btn whn mstk 2 out,
kpt on. . . . .(80 to 1 op 50 to 1 tchd 100 to 1)   4
ARTFUL ARTHUR 8-11-3 (7") Mr J Grassick, led to 5th, rdn
9th, beh whn mstk 4 out, tld off. . . . .(50 to 1)   5
WALTINGO 11-11-3 (7") Miss R Clark, hld up, mstk 9th, in
tch whn mistake and uns rdr 14th.
. . . .(14 to 1 op 10 to 1 tchd 16 to 1)   ur
2793 MIG 9-10-12 (7") Miss Y Beckingham, in tch, prog to join
wnr whn blun and uns rdr 14th.
. . . .(40 to 1 op 25 to 1 tchd 50 to 1)   ur
2765⁴ MICK'S TYCOON (Ire) (bl) 6-11-10 Mr S Swiers, in tch, led
and hit 8th, hdd nxt, wkng whn mstk 11th, tld off and
pld up bef last. . . . .(12 to 1 op 8 to 1)   pu
Dist: 6l, 5l, 5l, dist. 6m 44.50s. a 52.50s (8 Ran).
. . . . (W G Gooden), W G Gooden

2888   Robert Fleming 'Anthony Adams' Hunters' Chase (6-y-o and up) £1,744 2 ½m 110yds. . . . . (4:00)

2508* EASTERN DESTINY 16-11-9 (7*) Mr A Griffith, *blun 1st and 5th, prog 7th, 4th and no imprsn whn stumbled 3 out, rallied strly nxt, led aftr last, ran on wl.* .... (11 to 8 fav op 11 to 10 tchd 6 to 4) 1
2570 BEE GARDEN (bl) 13-11-11 (5*) Miss P Curling, *led till aftr last, not quicken*....... (13 to 2 op 5 to 1 tchd 7 to 1) 2
ROXALL CLUMP 10-11-3 (7*) Mr E Bailey, *trkd ldg pair, rdn 2 out, styd on one pace*...... (8 to 1 tchd 10 to 1) 3
2782* QUEEN'S CHAPLAIN 10-11-13 (7*) Mrs M Morris, *rear and nvr gng wl, styd on frm 2 out, nrst finish.* ....(4 to 1 tchd 7 to 2) 4
CROCK-NA-NEE 13-11-3 (7*) Mr C Vigors, *al pressing ldr, chlgd and ev ch 3 out, rdn nxt, wknd appr last.* .... (10 to 1 op 5 to 1) 5
948 CRAFTY CHAPLAIN 8-11-11 (5*) Mr D McCain, *mstks, hld up, prog 7th, wknd aftr 4 out.* .... (16 to 1 op 4 to 1 tchd 20 to 1) 6
2526 GANOON (USA) 11-11-3 (7*) Mr P Hanly, *in tch till 5th, mstk 7th, sn tld off*............... (66 to 1 op 33 to 1) 7
FOXTREE 11-11-3 (7*) Mr D Esden, *in tch till 6th, tld off and pld up bef 4 out*..............(50 to 1 op 25 to 1) pu
2508⁵ KAMEO STYLE 11-11-3 (7*) Mr B Pollock, *beh frm 5th, tld off and pld up bef 4 out*........... (33 to 1 op 20 to 1) pu
BARTINAS STAR 14-11-4¹ (7*) Mr C Stockton, *sn beh, last and tld off whn pld up bef 7th*..... (66 to 1 op 50 to 1) pu
Dist: 1l, 2½l, 3½l, 10l, dist, dist. 5m 47.20s. a 44.20s (10 Ran).
(E J W Griffith), Mrs J G Griffith

2889 Sidney Bailey Maiden Hunters' Chase (6-y-o and up) £1,631 2½m 110yds .... (4:30)

2482 KILLESHIN 8-12-0 (7*) Mr G Brown, *hld up beh, gd prog 8th, led 4 out, drw wl clr aftr nxt, imprsv.* .... (100 to 1 op 66 to 1) 1
FINE LACE 10-11-11 (5*) Mr G Tarry, *not jump wl, lost pl 5th, tld off 4 out, ran on strly aftr nxt, no ch wth wnr.* .... (11 to 10 fav op Evens tchd 5 to 4 on and 6 to 5) 2
PAMELA'S LAD 8-12-0 (7*) Mr G Hanmer, *hld up, prog 9th, chlgd and ev ch 3 out, wknd bef nxt.* (4 to 1 op 11 to 2) 3
TERRIFORN 9-12-4 (3*) Mr A Hill, *wtd wth, prog 8th, led tenth till nxt, 3rd whn mstk 4 out, btn when blun next.* .... (25 to 1 op 12 to 1) 4
FOURCEES 9-12-0 (7*) Mr P Howse, *trkd ldrs, prog to 3rd gng wl appr 3 out, sn wknd*....... (50 to 1 op 33 to 1) 5
HOOK HEAD 10-12-0 (7*) Mr C Vale, *prmnt, led 11th till nxt, wknd rpdly, tld off*.......... (20 to 1 op 14 to 1) 6
HYDROPIC 7-12-0 (7*) Mr J Beardsall, *prmnt till tenth, wl beh whn f 4 out*................. (33 to 1 op 25 to 1) f
ROSY PROSPECT 11-12-0 (7*) Mr Simon Robinson, *al beh, tld off whn pld up bef 7th*......... (33 to 1 op 20 to 1) pu
TEACHER'S DRAM 8-11-9 (7*) Mr R Hicks, *led to 3rd, sn drpd out, tld off whn pld up bef tenth*........(33 to 1) pu
MAJESTIC RIDE 10-12-2 (5*) Mr P Harding-Jones, *led 3rd till tenth, wknd rpdly, pld up bef 4 out*.......(50 to 1) pu
WAYSIDE BOY 9-12-0 (7*) Mr A Phillips, *prmnt till 6th, tld off whn pld up bef last*............ (50 to 1 op 33 to 1) pu
NATIONAL GYPSY 8-11-9 (7*) Mr M Felton, *al beh, tld off whn hmpd 4 out, pld up bef nxt*..............(33 to 1) pu
TENELORD 7-12-7 Mr J Greenall, *prmnt, blun 11th, rdn and btn whn mstks 3 out, wl beh when pld up bef last.* ....(5 to 1 op 3 to 1) pu
RACHELS ROCKER 7-11-9 (7*) Mr N R Mitchell, *hld up, lost tch 9th, tld off whn pld up bef 2 out.* (12 to 1 op 9 to 1) pu
Dist: 25l, 25l, 20l, 6l, dist. 5m 40.90s. a 37.90s (14 Ran).
(H J Manners), H J Manners

LINGFIELD (A.W) (std)
Tuesday March 8th
Going Correction: NIL

2890 Gettysburg National Hunt Flat Race (4,5,6-y-o) £1,478 2m........... (4:40)

2114* LINTON ROCKS 5-11-7 (5*) Mr M Buckley, *led 4 fs, led ag'n wl o'r four out, ran on strly frm 2 out.* .... (13 to 8 op 6 to 4 tchd 7 to 4) 1
2716² CHILDHAY MILLIE 5-10-9 (5*) Guy Lewis, *trkd ldrs, ev ch appr 2 fs out, sn rdn and kpt on wl.* ....(13 to 8 on op 6 to 4 on tchd 7 to 4 on) 2
LORD CAMBERLEY (Ire) 6-11-2 (3*) T Jenks, *wth ldr, led 12 fs out till wl o'r 4 out, outpcd.* .... (14 to 1 op 7 to 1 tchd 16 to 1) 3
ROCKFORD LADY 4-9-13 (7*) R Darke, *in cl tch till wknd o'r 5 fs out*....................... (33 to 1 op 20 to 1) 4
SNITTON STILE 6-11-0 Mr S Blackwell, *cl up till wknd wl o'r 4 fs out*.............................. (20 to 1 op 8 to 1) 5
Dist: 2l, 25l, 8l, 15l. 3m 33.90s. (5 Ran).
(Mrs C A Morrison), T Thomson Jones

SEDGEFIELD (good)
Tuesday March 8th
Going Correction: PLUS 0.60 sec. per fur. (races 1,4,6), PLUS 0.37 (2,3,5)

2891 John Wade Haulage Conditional Jockeys' Selling Handicap Hurdle (4-y-o and up) £1,830 2m 1f 110yds (2:20)

2090* REGAL ROMPER (Ire) [90] 6-11-8 (5*) D Towler, *mid-div, steady hdwy 5th, led 3 out, rdn last, ran on wl.* ....(8 to 1 tchd 10 to 1) 1
2408⁵ STATION EXPRESS (Ire) [63] 6-10-0 A Larnach, *beh, steady hdwy 3 out, effrt appr last, rdn and ran on r-in, jst fld.* ....(5 to 1 tchd 9 to 2) 2
2686⁴ MAC RAMBLER [66] 7-10-0 (3*) G Tormey, *in tch, hdwy 3 out, rdn nxt, styd on one pace*............ (14 to 1) 3
2581⁷ POINT TAKEN (USA) [70] 7-10-0 (7*) A Large, *chsd ldr, led 3rd, hdd 3 out, ev ch till rdn and wknd betw last 2.* ....(7 to 1) 4
2578⁷ STRATHBOGIE MIST (Ire) [63] 6-10-0 D J Moffatt, *beh, hdwy 3 out, hit nxt, sn rdn, one pace appr last.* ....(7 to 1 op 5 to 1) 5
2583 CARLA ADAMS [63] 8-10-0 J Supple, *sn led, hdd 3rd, prmnt till rdn 3 out, soon wknd.* .... (12 to 1 op 14 to 1 tchd 20 to 1) 6
2401² MASON DIXON [70] 5-10-2 (5*) K Davies, *al rear.* ....(9 to 2 fav op 3 to 1) 7
LOCAL DEALER [63] 6-9-11 (3*) F Leahy, *chsd ldrs, rdn 3 out, wknd bef nxt*....(12 to 1 op 14 to 1 tchd 20 to 1) 8
2581⁶ HYPNOTIST [85] 7-11-8 D Bentley, *prmnt till f 5th.* ....(12 to 1) f
CHADWICK'S GINGER [82] 6-11-5 A Thornton, *f 1st.* .... (25 to 1 op 14 to 1) f
2408⁶ ELVETT BRIDGE (Ire) [63] 6-10-0 F Perratt, *trkd ldrs till brght dwn 5th*.........(9 to 1 op 7 to 1 tchd 10 to 1) bd
2070 BEACH PATROL (Ire) [65] 6-9-11² (7*) S Melrose, *chsd ldrs, rdn 5th, sn wknd, tld off whn pld up bef 2 out.* (16 to 1) pu
2735 TODDEN [63] (bl) 4-9-11 (3*) D Ryan, *al rear, tld off 5th, pld up aftr 3 out*..................... (33 to 1 op 25 to 1) pu
Dist: Hd, 3l, 3½l, ¾l, 7l, 2l, dist. 4m 13.50s. a 18.50s (13 Ran).
SR: 20/-/-/-/-/-/ (Mrs S Smith), Mrs S J Smith

2892 Herbert's Grain Store Novices' Chase (5-y-o and up) £2,360 2m 1f..... (2:50)

2540³ DORADUS 6-10-10 (7*) F Leahy, *al prmnt, led 4 out, rdn last, edgd rght nr finish, kpt on*..... (7 to 2 op 3 to 1) 1
2688⁵ SEON 8-12-3 L Wyer, *beh, hdwy 4 out, effrt and rdn betw last 2, hrd drvn r-in, swtchd lft and hld nr finish.* ....(5 to 2 fav op 2 to 1 tchd 11 to 4) 2
2323⁶ DOWN THE ROAD 7-12-3 A Maguire, *hld up, steady hdwy hfwy, rdn 2 out, kpt on one pace appr last.* ....(7 to 2 op 3 to 1) 3
2565³ HIGHLANDMAN 8-11-3 A Dobbin, *cl up, led 4th till hdd and hit 7th, rdn 3 out, one pace frm nxt.* ....(12 to 1 tchd 14 to 1) 4
1100 MILO 8-11-3 T Reed, *beh, effrt and some hdwy 6th, sn one paced*.......................(66 to 1 op 50 to 1) 5
2739⁷ KRISSOS (bl) 7-10-12 (5*) P Waggott, *led to 4th, led 7th to four out, wknd nxt*..............(50 to 1 op 33 to 1) 6
1373² MAYWORK 7-10-12 P Niven, *al rear, tld off 8th.* .... (14 to 1 op 12 to 1) 7
2238 EBORNEEZER'S DREAM 11-11-3 D Telfer, *beh frm 6th, tld off*..............................(66 to 1 op 50 to 1) 8
2436⁴ ASHDREN 7-11-3 R Dunwoody, *in tch till lost pl and beh frm 8th*............... (13 to 2 op 6 to 1 tchd 7 to 1) 9
BALTIC BREEZE (Ire) 6-10-12 Gary Lyons, *sn beh, tld off frm 7th*.......................... (25 to 1 op 20 to 1) 10
2738⁵ STRONG SILVER (USA) 9-11-3 K Johnson, *in tch, rdn alng 7th and sn lost pl, beh whn f 4 out, dead.* .... (40 to 1 op 25 to 1) f
2565⁶ GRAZEMBER 7-11-3 R Garritty, *f 1st.* (16 to 1 op 12 to 1) f
Dist: 1l, 5l, hd, 15l, 2½l, dist, 6l, 2½l, 2½l. 4m 17.70s. a 12.70s (12 Ran).
SR: 25/38/33/19/4/1/ (Lady Halifax), J G FitzGerald

2893 McEwan's Durham National Handicap Chase (5-y-o and up) £4,207 3½m ....(3:20)

2561* PORTONIA [116] 10-11-10 P Niven, *led to 11th, cl up, led 6 out, rdn clr betw last 2, styd on wl*..........(5 to 2 jt-fav op 9 to 4) 1
2410² DUBIOUS JAKE [92] 11-10-0 N Williamson, *cl up, led 12th to 6 out, ev ch till hrd rdn and wknd appr last.* ....(5 to 1 op 9 to 2) 2
2813 GATHERING TIME [97] 8-10-5 R Dunwoody, *jmpd slwly and beh early, reminder 6th, hdwy and cl up 12th, hit 16th, effrt and rdn appr last, one pace.* ....(6 to 1 op 5 to 1) 3
2582² THE MALTKILN [101] (v) 11-10-9 L Wyer, *trkd ldrs, effrt and rdn 3 out, one pace aftr nxt*............(5 to 2 jt-fav op 2 to 1) 4
2499⁴ BOREEN OWEN [97] 10-10-0 (5*) A Roche, *cl up, hit 7th, led briefly 11th, rdn and hit 5 out, sn wknd.* ....(7 to 2 op 4 to 1) 5
Dist: 4l, ¾l, 3l, dist. 7m 11.30s. a 15.30s (5 Ran).
SR: 47/19/23/24/-/ (W H Strawson), Mrs M Reveley

2894 Gus Carter Handicap Hurdle (0-105 4-y-o and up) £2,490 3m 3f 110yds

.................................(3:50)

2578^{2} CARSON CITY [81] 7-10-4 P Niven, *trkd ldrs, hdwy hfwy, led 3 out, rdn clr appr nxt, drvn out r-in*...... (4 to 1) 1
2367^{4} PAR-BAR (Ire) [90] (v) 6-10-13 D Byrne, *beh, hdwy 8th, headway to chase wnr appr 2 out, rdn approaching last, styd on wl r-in*............ (10 to 1 tchd 12 to 1) 2
2371^{2} HUSO [91] 6-10-7 (7*) S Taylor, *hld up and beh, mstk second, hdwy 4 out, rdn 2 out, styd on one pace.* ....(9 to 2 op 5 to 1) 3
2740 REXY BOY [79] 7-10-2^{2} G Harker, *hld up, hdwy to track ldr 6th, reminders 5 out, hrd rdn and one pace aftr 3 out*..............................(25 to 1 tchd 33 to 1) 4
2322* JENDEE (Ire) [91] 6-10-11 (3*) A Larnach, *prmnt, rdn and one pace frm 3 out*............ (7 to 2 fav tchd 4 to 1) 5
2766^{9} SKIRCOAT GREEN [88] 9-10-11 R Dunwoody, *led, hdd 3 out, sn rdn and wknd appr nxt*.....(6 to 1 op 11 to 2) 6
2256^{9} LADY BE BRAVE [77] 11-9-10^{1} (5*) J Supple, *in tch, rdn alng 4 out, no hdwy*............................(50 to 1) 7
2434^{3} SCOTTISH GOLD [93] 10-11-2 A Maguire, *mid-div to 4th, sn lost pl and beh, tld off 5 out*..... (11 to 2 op 5 to 1) 8
2758 BROMPTON ROAD [105] 11-12-0 R Greene, *al rear, tld off 5 out*......................................(14 to 1) 9
1812 ITALIAN TOUR [77] 14-10-0 O Pears, *cl up, blun 7th, sn lost pl, tld off bef 3 out*........................(66 to 1) 10
2238 MERRYDALE FARM [77] 9-10-0 B Storey, *in tch, rdn alng 8th, sn lost pl, beh whn pld up bef 2 out*......(100 to 1) pu
2502^{6} MAKE ME PROUD (Ire) [80] (v) 5-10-3 L Wyer, *al rear, sn drvn alng, tld off off whn pld up aftr 4 out.* ....(9 to 1 op 8 to 1) pu

Dist: 1½l, 5l, 8l, 6l, 1l, 3l, dist, nk, 8l. 6m 54.40s. a 28.40s (12 Ran).
(Mrs M E Gray), Mrs M Reveley

2895 Robin And John Simpson Memorial Handicap Chase (0-120 5-y-o and up) £3,172 2m 5f.................... (4:20)

2205 COMEDY ROAD [95] 10-10-9 A Maguire, *trkd ldrs, smooth hdwy 4 out, led 2 out, clr appr last, cmftbly.* ....(7 to 2 op 3 to 1) 1
2574 BAD TRADE [96] 12-10-10 T Reed, *al prmnt, led 9th, rdn and hdd 2 out, sn one pace*.................. (16 to 1) 2
2403 BONANZA [114] 7-12-0 R Hodge, *in tch, reminders 8th, hit tenth and sn drvn alng, no imprsn aftr.* .... (7 to 2 op 11 to 4) 3
SANDY'S BEACON [97] 9-10-11 D Byrne, *hit 1st, mstk 5th, hdwy 9th, rdn 4 out, sn one pace*.... (6 to 1 op 4 to 1) 4
2243 COSMIC RAY [88] (bl) 9-10-2 N Williamson, *trkd ldrs, hdwy 9th, chsd lder nxt, rdn 4 out, wknd next.* .... (25 to 1 op 20 to 1) 5
2323^{2} MOUNTEBOR [89] 10-9-10 (7*) S Taylor, *cl up whn f 1st.* ...... (5 to 2 fav op 9 to 4 tchd 3 to 1 and 100 to 30) f
2274^{4} TRES AMIGOS [104] 7-11-1 (3*) A Larnach, *led till aftr 8th, sn lost pl and beh, tld off whn pld up lme bef last.* ....(7 to 2 op 7 to 1 tchd 8 to 1) pu
1486 BALLINROSTIG [102] 11-11-2 L Wyer, *cl up, rdn and lost pl tenth, sn beh, tld off whn pld up bef last*... (25 to 1) pu

Dist: 8l, 6l, 3l, 8l. 5m 24.00s. a 20.00s (8 Ran).
(Winsbury Livestock), R Lee

2896 Weatherbys 'Newcomers' Series Novices' Hurdle (4-y-o and up) £2,061 2m 5f 110yds..................... (4:50)

2788^{6} MASTER BOSTON (Ire) 6-11-8 R Garritty, *mid-div and pushed alng, steady hdwy appr 3 out, styd on to ld betw last 2, ran on strly und pres*.... (7 to 1 op 5 to 1) 1
1475* GREAT MAX (Ire) 5-11-1 (7*) Mr D Parker, *mid-div, hdwy hfwy, chlgd 3 out, led appr nxt, hdd betw last 2, kpt on und pres*.......................... (4 to 1 op 7 to 2) 2
2358^{8} SWEET NOBLE (Ire) 5-10-9 (7*) F Leahy, *in tch gng wl, chlgd 3 out, sn outpcd, styd on und pres appr last.* ....(8 to 1 op 7 to 1) 3
2212^{3} LAFANTA (Ire) 5-11-8 K Jones, *cl up, led second, rdn 3 out, hdd appr nxt, wknd bef last*....... (25 to 1 op 16 to 1) 4
1480^{5} FREE TRANSFER (Ire) 5-11-3 (5*) F Perratt, *hld up and beh, steady hdwy appr 3 out, rdn nxt, kpt on one pace.* .... (25 to 1 op 20 to 1) 5
2217 GERMAN LEGEND 4-10-7 A Merrigan, *chsd ldrs, rdn 3 out, kpt on same pace*................ (100 to 1 op 50 to 1) 6
2404^{4} ALJADEER (USA) 5-11-2 M Dwyer, *hld up and beh, smooth hdwy on outer 4 out, chlgd nxt, rdn appr next, sn btn.* ....(11 to 10 on tchd Evens and 5 to 4) 7
2564 BERING ISLAND (USA) 4-10-7 L Wyer, *chsd ldrs till rdn and wknd 3 out*.................. (33 to 1 op 25 to 1) 8
MISS CONSTRUE 7-10-11 P Niven, *beh, some hdwy hfwy, rdn 4 out and behind frm nxt*.......(25 to 1 op 20 to 1) 9
2578^{8} BASILICUS (Fr) 5-11-2 Richard Guest, *al rear.* .... (14 to 1 op 12 to 1) 10
2447^{5} FINNOW QUAY (Ire) 5-11-2 A Maguire, *prmnt, wknd whn hit 4 out, sn beh*......................(25 to 1 op 20 to 1) 11
2435^{7} CUMBERLAND BLUES (Ire) 5-10-11 (5*) S Lyons, *al rear.* ....(100 to 1 op 66 to 1) 12
2741^{4} COMMANCHE CREEK 4-10-4 (3*) A Larnach, *al rear, tld off 3 out*......................... (20 to 1 op 33 to 1) 13
COEDWGAN LUCIFER 7-11-2 N Williamson, *al beh, tld off 4 out*..............................(50 to 1 op 33 to 1) 14
1478 DESPERADO 6-11-0^{5} (7*) Mr S Pittendrigh, *al beh, tld off frm hfwy*........................ (100 to 1 op 66 to 1) 15
2583^{4} PESSOA 7-11-2 Gary Lyons, *led to second, cl up, lost pl 7th and sn beh. tld off whn pld up aftr 3 out.* (25 to 1) pu
2369^{6} NICHOLAS PLANT 5-11-2 T Reed, *cl up on outer till rdn and wknd 3 out, beh whn pld up bef last.* .... (20 to 1 op 33 to 1) pu

Dist: 4l, 4l, 8l, 3½l, 3½l, 3l, 3l, 1l, 20l, 4l. 5m 17.30s. a 26.30s (17 Ran).
(M K Oldham), R D E Woodhouse

BANGOR (soft)
Wednesday March 9th
Going Correction: PLUS 1.00 sec. per fur. (races 1,4,6), PLUS 1.40 (2,3,5)

2897 Chirk Novices' Hurdle (4-y-o and up) £2,295 2m 1f.................... (2:10)

1745 LE GINNO (Fr) 7-11-8 G Bradley, *early mstks, wth ldr, nosed ahead 2 out, clr last, ran on wl.* ....(3 to 1 op 2 to 1) 1
2339^{6} EVEN BLUE (Ire) 6-10-11 (5*) Mr D McCain, *jmpd wl, tried to make all, hdd 2 out, kpt on same pace.* .... (20 to 1 op 14 to 1) 2
2303^{5} TEST MATCH 7-11-2 Diane Clay, *nvr far away, ev ch appr 2 out, one pace frm betw last two.* .... (8 to 1 op 10 to 1 tchd 12 to 1) 3
2585^{2} STOPROVERITATE 5-10-11 A Maguire, *tucked away gng wl, ev ch 3 out, rdn alng bef nxt, one pace betw last 2.* ....(5 to 4 fav op 9 to 4) 4
1515 DIME BAG 5-10-11 J Railton, *al pressing ldrs, hrd at work appr 2 out, no extr*............... (12 to 1 op 7 to 1) 5
2564 DIWALI DANCER 4-11-0 N Mann, *chsd ldg bunch, niggled alng aftr 3rd, outpcd hfwy, tld off*.. (9 to 2 op 7 to 2) 6
1660^{9} CAPTIVA BAY 5-10-11 R Bellamy, *settled beh ldrs, feeling pace whn hit 5th, sn tld off*.......(66 to 1 op 33 to 1) 7
1494 MEGAMUNCH (Ire) 6-10-9 (7*) N Juckes, *beh whn blun and uns rdr 3rd*.................. (25 to 1 op 14 to 1) ur
2478 UNSUSPICIOUS (Ire) 4-10-8 P McDermott, *not fluent, al struggling, tld off whn pld up bef 2 out.* .... (66 to 1 op 33 to 1) pu
2204 COME ON CHARLIE 5-10-13 (3*) D Meredith, *settled mid-field, struggling hfwy, tld off whn pld up bef 2 out.* .... (100 to 1 op 33 to 1) pu

Dist: 6l, 1l, 1½l, ¾l, dist, 10l. 4m 13.30s. a 23.30s (10 Ran).
SR: 31/19/18/11/10/-/ (Irish World Partnership), C P E Brooks

2898 Times 'Rising Stars' Hunters' Chase Qualifier for the Hugh Peel Challenge Trophy (6,7,8-y-o) £2,221 3m 110yds ....(2:40)

KNIFEBOARD 8-12-0 (5*) Mr A Farrant, *pushed alng most of way, improved fnl circuit, jmpd slwly last 3, kpt on to ld last 50 yards*...... (11 to 4 op 5 to 2 tchd 3 to 1) 1
2765^{2} JOLLY ROGER 7-11-12 (7*) Mr Michael J Jones, *chsd clr ldg pair, improved fnl circuit, lft wl clear 3 out, wknd and ct last 50 yards*..............................(9 to 4 fav) 2
KINGS THYNE 8-11-5 (7*) Mr C J B Barlow, *chsd ldg trio, mstks and niggled alng fnl circuit, lost tch 6 out, tld off*.............................(14 to 1 op 8 to 1) 3
WORLESTON FARRIER 6-11-9^{4} (7*) Mr G Hanmer, *chsd ldrs for a circuit, tld off bef 6 out*...... (33 to 1 op 20 to 1) 4
2793 NGERU 8-11-5 (7*) Mr A Edwards, *not fluent, wth ldr, still hndy whn f tenth*..... (11 to 1 op 8 to 1 tchd 12 to 1) f
2555^{5} FLAME O'FRENSI 8-11-0 (7*) Miss J Cumings, *jmpd wl, tried to make all, 2 ls clr whn o'rjumped and f 3 out, unlucky*........................... (3 to 1 op 5 to 2) f
TIMURS LUCK 8-11-5 (7*) Mr O Warburton, *wtd wth, took clr order fnl circuit, ev ch whn f tenth.* .... (13 to 2 op 11 to 2) f

Dist: 1½l, dist, 10l. 6m 42.40s. a 52.40s (7 Ran).
(D G Williamson), Paul O J Hosgood

2899 Croxton Novices' Chase (5-y-o and up) £2,723 2½m 110yds............ (3:10)

2600^{5} ANDERMATT 7-11-5 W Marston, *settled gng wl, imprvg whn hit 3 out, led and jmpd lft last, sprinted clr.* .... (5 to 2 op 7 to 4 tchd 11 to 4) 1
2637^{2} PRECIPICE RUN 9-11-10 N Doughty, *made most, hdd briefly 3rd and nxt, jnd 3 out, headed and hit last, sn outpcd*..........................(Evens fav op 5 to 4) 2
2206 SQUIRES PRIVILEGE (Ire) 6-11-0 (5*) A Roche, *patiently rdn, steady hdwy whn mstk 8th (water), shaken up aftr 3 out, no imprsn*................ (5 to 1 op 4 to 1) 3
FOXY BLUE 9-11-5 G Bradley, *wth ldr, led briefly 3rd and nxt, blun 4 out, ev ch next, fdd.* .... (14 to 1 op 8 to 1 tchd 16 to 1) 4
2140 YOUNG PARSON 8-11-5 B Clifford, *not fluent, pressed ldrs, chsd alng aftr 6 out, sn lost tch.* .... (12 to 1 op 6 to 1) 5
ROSCOE'S GEMMA 10-10-11 (3*) D Meredith, *pressed ldrs to hfwy, sn lost tch, tld off whn pld up bef 2 out.* .... (50 to 1 op 25 to 1) pu

Dist: 7l, 10l, 4l, 10l. 5m 35.00s. a 44.00s (6 Ran).

(The Marston Sept), J Mackie

2900 Holywell Selling Hurdle (4-y-o and up) £1,955 2m 1f................... (3:40)

2575³ ALL GREEK TO ME (Ire) 6-11-3 (7*) F Leahy, *al hndy, drvn ahead bef 2 out, styd on und pres.*
.... (11 to 8 fav op 6 to 4 tchd 7 to 4 and 5 to 4) 1
2790⁵ ALWAYS READY (bl) 8-11-3 (7*) J Bond, *patiently rdn, improved 4 out, ev ch betw last 2, one pace.*
.... (8 to 1 op 7 to 1) 2
2729⁸ MOUNTSHANNON 8-11-10 Peter Caldwell, *settled beh ldg bunch, improved into midfield hfwy, effrt aftr 3 out, kpt on same pace.* .... (20 to 1 op 16 to 1) 3
ROYAL STANDARD 7-11-4 P McDermott, *al chasing ldrs, effrt and drvn alng aftr 3 out, one pace.*
.... (20 to 1 op 33 to 1 tchd 16 to 1) 4
2768⁸ EASTERN PLEASURE (v) 7-11-4 Diane Clay, *with ldr, led 4th, blun 3 out, hdd bef nxt, no extr.* (9 to 1 op 16 to 1) 5
2303 PERSIAN BUD (Ire) 6-11-4 M Bosley, *in tch, bustled alng whn pace lifted aftr 3 out, no imprsn.*
.... (14 to 1 tchd 20 to 1) 6
2645⁸ CAOIMSEACH (Ire) 6-11-4 A Maguire, *al tracking ldrs, hrd at work aftr 3 out, fdd.* (13 to 2 op 4 to 1 tchd 7 to 1) 7
AL SKEET (USA) 8-11-3 (7*) Mr G Hogan, *settled gng wl, smooth hdwy 4 out, pushed alng aftr nxt, no extr.*
.... (10 to 1 op 8 to 1) 8
2790⁷ TANAISTE (USA) 5-11-4 B Clifford, *settled rear, drvn alng aftr 4 out, nvr dngrs.* .... (10 to 1 op 8 to 1) 9
CHAPELSTREET BLUES 7-10-13 L Harvey, *in tch to hfwy, wknd quickly bef 3 out.* .... (66 to 1) 10
2789 BAR THREE (Ire) 5-10-13 (5*) Guy Lewis, *led to 4th, reminders nxt, drvn alng bef four out, sn lost tch, tld off.* .... (50 to 1 op 33 to 1) 11
2776⁷ TEA-LADY (Ire) 6-10-13 W Marston, *pressed ldrs to hfwy, tld off frm 4 out.* .... (14 to 1 tchd 20 to 1) 12
126² ALICANTE 7-11-10 J Railton, *tucked away in midfield, improved bef 3 out, wknd and pld up betw last 2.*
.... (16 to 1 tchd 20 to 1) pu
2329 PYRO PENNANT 9-11-4 D J Burchell, *settled gng wl, effrt hfwy, wknd quickly and pld up bef 2 out.*
.... (16 to 1 tchd 20 to 1) pu
2627³ ALDINGTON CHAPPLE 6-11-10 T Wall, *took keen hold, trkd ldrs to 3 out, wknd quickly and pld up bef nxt.*
.... (14 to 1 op 12 to 1) pu
Dist: 5l, 12l, 12l, 5l, 8l, 8l, dist. 4m 15.20s. a 25.20s (15 Ran).
SR: 14/12/9/-/-/-/ (Barry Hughes), J Parkes

2901 Llangollen Handicap Chase (0-135 5-y-o and up) £3,355 3m 110yds (4:10)

2593* BISHOPS ISLAND [129] 8-11-12 A Maguire, *chsd ldg pair, wnt second fnl circuit, led betw last 2, jmpd slwly last, drvn out.* .... (21 to 20 on op 6 to 4 on tchd Evens) 1
1932³ SIKERA SPY [125] 12-11-8 R Bellamy, *set str pace for o'r a circuit, jnd 2 out, sn hdd, rallied und pres.*
.... (3 to 1 tchd 7 to 2) 2
2733⁶ MWEENISH [103] 12-10-0 C Maude, *in tch, chsd alng to improve fnl circuit, rdn and one pace frm 5 out.*
.... (9 to 1 op 14 to 1) 3
2764³ TRIBAL RULER [105] 9-10-2² J Railton, *chsd clr ldr for a circuit, blun tenth, struggling aftr 5 out, one pace.*
.... (14 to 1 op 12 to 1) 4
2499 HOTPLATE [112] 11-10-9 N Doughty, *sn tld off last, pld up bef 6 out.* .... (11 to 1 op 8 to 1 tchd 12 to 1) pu
2298 STIRRUP CUP [131] 10-12-0 J Osborne, *chsd alng to keep up, effrt hfwy, sn struggling ag'n, tld off whn pld up bef 2 out.* .... (12 to 1 op 10 to 1 tchd 14 to 1) pu
Dist: 5l, 10l, hd. 6m 28.70s. a 38.70s (6 Ran).
SR: 54/45/13/15/-/-/ (Lord Vestey), D Nicholson

2902 Chorlton Novices' Handicap Hurdle (4-y-o and up) £2,379 2½m..... (4:40)

2768* PATROCLUS [63] 9-10-5 (3*,7ex) T Eley, *al hndy, hit 6th and 4 out, led aftr nxt, styd on wl.*
.... (13 to 8 fav op 6 to 4 tchd 15 to 8) 1
2523⁹ MARINE SOCIETY [70] (bl) 6-11-1 A Maguire, *tried to make all, clr hfwy, hdd bef 2 out, one pace.* (7 to 1 op 6 to 1) 2
2424 BLUE LYZANDER [56] 5-10-1 D Bridgwater, *nvr far away, hrd at work frm 3 out, no extr...* (16 to 1 tchd 25 to 1) 3
2405² PRINCETHORPE [69] 7-10-11 (3*) D Meredith, *trkd ldrs, drvn alng to keep up aftr 4 out, no imprsn frm betw last 2.* .... (7 to 1 op 3 to 1) 4
2381⁹ DON'T FORGET MARIE (Ire) [79] 4-11-10 S Smith Eccles, *patiently rdn, improved 4 out, ridden aftr nxt, sn struggling.* .... (7 to 2 op 5 to 1) 5
2478⁶ BOLD STAR [67] 4-10-12 J Osborne, *trkd ldrs, hrd at work bef 3 out, lost tch before nxt.*
.... (11 to 1 op 12 to 1 tchd 10 to 1) 6
SCARED STIFF [58] 6-10-3 D J Burchell, *in tch, struggling to keep up fnl circuit, tld off...* (25 to 1 op 14 to 1) 7
2145 RUSSELL ROVER [77] 9-11-8 C Maude, *blun and lost pl quickly 3rd, tld off whn pld up bef 6th.*
.... (33 to 1 op 16 to 1) pu
Dist: 10l, 4l, 2l, 8l, 15l, 15l. 5m 7.00s. a 31.00s (8 Ran).
(Applied Signs Limited), J Mackie

CATTERICK (good to soft) Wednesday March 9th
Going Correction: PLUS 0.35 sec. per fur. (races 1,3,- 5,7), PLUS 0.80 (2,4,6)

2903 Hornby Novices' Hurdle (4-y-o and up) £2,302 2m................... (2:00)

2445⁵ LITTLE BROMLEY 7-10-12 Mr R Hale, *led aftr 1st, made rst, hrd pressed frm 2 out, ran on wl.*
.... (16 to 1 op 20 to 1 tchd 14 to 1 and 33 to 1) 1
2783⁸ REBEL KING 4-10-9 A Dobbin, *sn chasing ldrs, ev ch frm 2 out till no extr aftr last.* .... (25 to 1) 2
2532* VANART 5-11-10 D Byrne, *in tch, hdwy hfwy, kpt on frm 2 out, no extr r-in.* .... (10 to 1 tchd 12 to 1) 3
2566⁵ SHAHGRAM (Ire) 6-11-3 M Dwyer, *hld up in tch, effrt aftr 2 out, hit last, sn btn.* .... (5 to 1 op 9 to 2) 4
2585⁷ IMPERIAL BID (Ire) 6-11-5 (5*) P Waggott, *al prmnt, ev ch whn mstk last, no extr...* (14 to 1 op 12 to 1) 5
2741² COMBELLINO 4-10-9 P Niven, *sn tracking ldrs, drvn alng appr 2 out, kpt on same pace.*
.... (7 to 2 fav op 4 to 1 tchd 9 to 2) 6
2485⁴ ZAJIRA (Ire) 4-10-4 R Hodge, *not fluent early, beh, steady hdwy frm 5th, nvr nr to chal...* (5 to 1 tchd 11 to 2) 7
2783 SUDDEN SPIN 4-10-9 O Pears, *in tch, hdwy to go prmnt 3 out frm appr nxt, grad wknd.* (100 to 1 op 50 to 1) 8
1920⁴ MHEMEANLES 4-10-9 L Wyer, *nvr dngrs.*
.... (10 to 1 op 8 to 1) 9
1082 MY ROSSINI 5-11-3 M Hourigan, *chsd ldrs till wknd appr 3 out.* .... (8 to 1 op 10 to 1 tchd 7 to 1) 10
BONNY HECTOR 10-10-12² (7*) Mr S Pittendrigh, *in tch, effrt aftr 3 out, sn btn.* .... (250 to 1 op 200 to 1) 11
2564³ STAR RAGE (Ire) 4-10-3¹ (7*) J Driscoll, *in tch, effrt appr 3 out, sn btn.* .... (11 to 2 op 7 to 1) 12
2369⁸ CALL THE SHOTS (Ire) 5-11-3 K Jones, *beh frm hfwy, tld off...* .... (150 to 1 op 100 to 1) 13
OTHER RANKS (Ire) 6-11-3 Mrs A Farrell, *beh most of way, tld off...* .... (50 to 1) 14
2585 HILLTOWN (Ire) 6-11-10 G McCourt, *al beh, tld off.*
.... (14 to 1 op 12 to 1) 15
2735³ JUSTICE IS DONE (Ire) 4-10-9 Richard Guest, *prmnt till wknd quickly aftr 3 out, tld off.* (10 to 1 tchd 12 to 1) 16
2237 ZIN ZAN (Ire) 6-11-3 G Upton, *beh, hdwy aftr 5th, wknd quickly appr 2 out, tld off...* (20 to 1 tchd 16 to 1) 17
2637 THE PUB 8-11-3 J Corkell, *led till badly aftr 1st, beh whn f 4th...* .... (100 to 1) f
AMY'S STAR 8-10-12 R Garritty, *al beh, tld off whn pld up bef 2 out...* .... (100 to 1) pu
Dist: 2¼l, sht-hd, 3l, nk, 7l, 1½l, ½l, 10l, 1½l, nk. 3m 53.30s. a 12.30s (19 Ran).
SR: 17/11/26/16/22/-/ (A Eubank), A Eubank

2904 Raby Novices' Hunters' Chase (5-y-o and up) £1,501 3m 1f 110yds.... (2:30)

2782² GOGGINS HILL 7-12-0 Mr J Greenall, *al prmnt, slight ld 12th, blun 14th, clr appr 3 out, easily.*
.... (13 to 8 on op 9 to 4 on tchd 6 to 4 on) 1
2782 CONVINCING 10-11-7 (7*) Mr P Cornforth, *in tch, outpcd aftr 12th, rallied appr 3 out, kpt on wl, no ch wth wnr.* .... (50 to 1) 2
727 REVILLER'S GLORY 10-11-11 (3*) Mrs A Farrell, *cl up, led aftr 5th, hdd 12th, chsd wnr after, no imprsn.*
.... (7 to 2 op 3 to 1) 3
PAPAS SURPRISE 9-11-7 (7*) Miss S Horner, *cl up, blun 9th, outpcd appr 3 out...* (16 to 1 op 14 to 1) 4
WENTBRIDGE 9-11-7 (7*) Mr M Sowersby, *in tch, wkng whn blun 4 out, mstk 2 out, tld off.* (20 to 1 op 16 to 1) 5
EASTLANDS MONKEY 12-11-2 (7*) Miss J Percy, *tld off frm hfwy...* .... (16 to 1) 6
2484 CELTIC HARRY 10-11-7 (7*) Mr J G Townson, *beh whn f 5th...* .... (25 to 1 op 20 to 1) f
STELZER 8-11-9 (5*) Mr M Buckley, *beh whn mstk and uns rdr 7th...* .... (7 to 1 op 6 to 1) ur
HELLCATMUDWRESTLER 13-11-7 (7*) Mr P Richmond, *blun badly 3rd, led till aftr 5th. lost tch frm hfwy, tld off whn pld up aftr 5th.* .... (10 to 1 op 16 to 1) pu
Dist: 7l, 12l, 2l, dist, 20l. 6m 52.20s. a 37.20s (9 Ran).
(J E Greenall), P Cheesbrough

2905 Weardale 'National Hunt' Novices' Hurdle (4-y-o and up) £2,197 2m 3f .... (3:00)

2785 LOCH SCAVAIG (Ire) 5-11-2 (3*) D J Moffatt, *hld up in tch, effrt aftr 3 out, hng lft and rdn to ld last, drvn out.*
.... (11 to 8 on tchd 5 to 4 on and 6 to 4 on) 1
2583* STRONG FLAME (Ire) 5-11-5 (5*) S Lyons, *led till aftr second, led ag'n 8th, hdd last, no extr.* (5 to 1 op 4 to 1) 2
SCOTTISH PERIL 7-11-3 B Storey, *in tch, hdwy aftr 6th, kpt on frm 2 out...* .... (25 to 1 op 20 to 1) 3
2629⁵ SCRABO VIEW (Ire) 5-11-3 L O'Hara, *chsd ldrs, ch appr 2 out, kpt on same pace...* .... (10 to 1) 4
2339 SUVLA BAY (Ire) 6-11-3 M Brennan, *beh, hdwy aftr 6th, nvr nr to chal...* .... (20 to 1) 5

GLEN DALUS (Ire) 5-11-3 A Dobbin, *hld up in midfield, chsd ldr frm 5th, rdn appr 2 out, sn btn.*
.............................(9 to 2 op 7 to 2 tchd 5 to 1) 6
1356⁵ DOLLY PRICES 9-10-7 (5*) P Waggott, *in tch till wknd appr 3 out.*..................................(33 to 1) 7
2239 ROSEBERRY TOPPING 5-11-3 P Niven, *nvr nr ldrs.*
.............................(12 to 1 op 10 to 1 tchd 14 to 1) 8
BALLINMUSIC 7-10-13³ (7*) Mr S Pittendrigh, *mid-div till wknd appr 3 out.*...........................(100 to 1) 9
2785 MIDORI 6-10-12 J Corkell, *lost tch frm 5th, tld off.*
.............................(200 to 1) 10
2413⁸ CARDINAL SINNER (Ire) 5-11-3 K Jones, *chsd ldrs till wknd quickly bef 5th, tld off.*.................(100 to 1) 11
2332 CANADIAN CRUISE 5-11-3 A Merrigan, *led aftr second till hdd 4th, wknd quickly bef nxt, wl tld off whn pld up before 2 out.*............................. (100 to 1) pu
THINK PINK 7-11-3 C Hawkins, *in tch, pushed alng aftr 4th, wknd after 6th, tld off whn pld up bef last.*
.............................(100 to 1) pu
Dist: 3l, 10l, 3½l, 7l, 5l, 12l, 10l, 12l, 15l, 20l. 4m 39.50s. (13 Ran).

(Mrs G A Turnbull), D Moffatt

2906
Peter Vaux Memorial Trophy Handicap Chase (0-110 5-y-o and up) £3,289 3m 1f 110yds. . . . . (3:30)

2690² YOUNG MINER [95] 8-11-2 G Upton, *al prmnt, slight ld 14th, hrd pressed and rdn frm 3 out, styd on wl, all out.*
.............................(7 to 2 op 3 to 1 tchd 4 to 1) 1
2562⁴ CHOICE CHALLANGE [93] 11-10-9 (5*) S Lyons, *al prmnt, drw clr wth wnr frm 4 out, ev ch last, no extr und pres.*
.............................(7 to 1 tchd 8 to 1) 2
2562* CHOCTAW [103] 10-11-10 C Hawkins, *led till hdd 14th, outpcd aftr 4 out, no dngr after.*
.............................(3 to 1 fav tchd 100 to 30) 3
2562² HEAVENLY CITIZEN (Ire) [90] 6-10-11 R Garritty, *in tch till outpcd aftr 13th, no dngr after.*.....(11 to 2 op 9 to 2) 4
2253³ MOULTON BULL [81] 8-10-2 L Wyer, *beh and pushed alng aftr tenth, some hdwy after 4 out, btn nxt.......*(7 to 1) 5
2582* TRUELY ROYAL [92] 10-10-13 B Storey, *in tch, pushed alng aftr 13th, sn outpcd, no dngr after.*
.............................(7 to 1 op 6 to 1) 6
2253⁴ HOUXTY LAD [83] 8-10-4¹ P Niven, *trkd ldrs, reminders aftr 11th, 4th and struggling whn f 15th.*
.............................(9 to 1 op 8 to 1 tchd 7 to 1 and 10 to 1) f
2787⁴ MOSS BEE [85] 7-10-6 T Reed, *al beh, lost tch aftr tenth, tld off whn pld up bef 14th.*.................(33 to 1) pu
Dist: 1l, 20l, 1l, 1l, 7l. 6m 41.00s. a 26.00s (8 Ran).

SR: 32/29/19/5/-/ (Mrs T J McInnes Skinner), Mrs T J McInnes Skinner

2907
Rudby Selling Hurdle (4-y-o) £2,005 2m. . . . . (4:00)

2763⁵ HO-JOE (Ire) 10-12 N Smith, *cl up, led 3 out, ran on wl, cmftbly.*....................(6 to 1 op 5 to 1 tchd 7 to 1) 1
1147⁶ GOLDMIRE 10-7 S Turner, *pld hrd early, trkd ldrs, chsd wnr 3 out, no imprsn, kpt on towards finish...*(10 to 1) 2
2783 THATCHED (Ire) (v) 10-9 (3*) D J Moffatt, *hld up, smooth hdwy appr 3 out, chsd wnr frm nxt, no imprsn.*(50 to 1) 3
2267⁷ GREAT EASEBY (Ire) 10-12 K Johnson, *chsd ldrs, pushed alng aftr 4th, outpcd appr 3 out, kpt on frm nxt.*
.............................(6 to 5 op 5 to 1) 4
2810⁴ ON GOLDEN POND (Ire) 10-13 J Callaghan, *prmnt till outpcd aftr 3 out, kpt on frm nxt...* (11 to 4 fav op 7 to 4) 5
2401 PAAJIB (Ire) 10-5 (7*) W Fry, *in tch till wknd aftr 3 out.*
.............................(33 to 1 op 25 to 1) 6
1655⁴ MR ABBOT 10-12 P Niven, *in tch, eff't aftr 3 out, no hdwy.*..........................(5 to 2 op 5 to 1 tchd 7 to 1) 7
2433 RYTHMIC RYMER 10-2 (5*) P Williams, *slight ld till hdd 4th, prmnt till wknd appr 2 out.* (25 to 1 tchd 33 to 1) 8
2433³ DIGNIFIED (Ire) 10-0 (7*) A Linton, *cl up, led 4th, hdd 3 out, grad wknd.*.............(5 to 1 op 9 to 2 tchd 11 to 2) 9
CIVIL ACTION (Ire) 10-12 C Hawkins, *pld hrd early, al beh.*
.............................(50 to 1) 10
2581⁹ UNNAB (bl) 10-2 (5*) P Waggott, *chsd ldrs, wknd appr 2 out.*...(20 to 1) 11
ONE FOR TONDY 10-7 T Reed, *chsd ldrs till wknd appr 3 out, tld off...*......................(100 to 1 op 50 to 1) 12
2490 HALF'N HALF 10-7 O Pears, *al beh, no ch whn brght dwn aftr 3 out.*..(50 to 1) bd
754 RED RONNIE 10-7 M Moloney, *chsd ldrs, wkng whn slpd up bend aftr 3 out.*.................(33 to 1 op 25 to 1) su
Dist: 8l, 1½l, 2½l, ¾l, 8l, 1½l, 2½l, 3l, 8l, 12l. 3m 57.60s. a 16.60s (14 Ran).

(S Ho), J M Carr

2908
Newby Novices' Handicap Chase (5-y-o and up) £2,672 3m 1f 110yds (4:30)

2579* DEVONGALE [87] 8-11-10 L Wyer, *in tch, hit 8th and lost pl, rallied aftr 13th, led and hit 4 out, lft wl clr 2 out, eased after last......*(7 to 2 fav op 3 to 1 tchd 4 to 1) 1
2579² DARK OAK [76] 8-10-13 L O'Hara, *led till hdd 4 out, sn outpcd.*..(9 to 2 op 4 to 1) 2
2434³ FOUR DEEP (Ire) [82] 6-11-5 A Dobbin, *cl up till outpcd aftr 4 out.*....................................(8 to 1 op 6 to 1) 3

2784⁴ IRISH GENT [84] (bl) 8-11-7 K Johnson, *prmnt, hit 13th, sn rdn and wknd, tld off.*
.............................(16 to 1 op 14 to 1 tchd 20 to 1) 4
2252⁵ BALISTEROS (Fr) [71] 5-10-8 R Garritty, *hld up, blun 6th and lost tch, some hdwy whn f 15th.*
.............................(14 to 1 op 12 to 1) f
2103⁵ FINCH'S GEM [84] (v) 6-11-7 S Turner, *trkd ldrs till f 13th.*
.............................(9 to 2 op 4 to 1) f
2325³ THE POD'S REVENGE [72] 9-10-9 R Hodge, *al prmnt, chsd wnr frm 4 out, second and btn whn blun and uns rdr 2 out.*..........................(4 to 1 op 5 to 1) ur
2497⁹ STRONG CHANCE [63] 8-10-0 B Storey, *not jump wl, sn beh, tld off whn pld up aftr 11th............*(33 to 1) pu
2736³ RAIN MAN (NZ) [74] (bl) 9-11-7 P Niven, *chsd ldrs till wknd quickly aftr 11th, tld off whn pld up bef 13th.*
.............................(8 to 1 tchd 9 to 1) pu
Dist: 30l, 5l, dist. 6m 43.10s. a 28.10s (9 Ran).

SR: 20/-/-/-/-/ (Victor Ogden), M H Easterby

2909
Grunwick Stakes National Hunt Flat Race (4,5,6-y-o) £1,318 2m. . . . . . (5:00)

VALLEY GARDEN 4-10-9 (7*) M Roberts, *in tch, hdwy 5 fs out, led one out, ran on wl.*
.............................(9 to 2 op 4 to 1 tchd 5 to 1) 1
CRANE HILL 4-10-13 (3*) S Wynne, *trkd ldrs, led 4 fs out, hdd one out, no extr...* (11 to 2 op 9 to 2 tchd 6 to 1) 2
2074² BENBEATH 4-10-11 (5*) S Lyons, *mid-div, hdwy 4 fs out, ch 2 out, no extr........................*(7 to 1 op 5 to 1) 3
LITTLE SERENA 4-10-6 (5*) E Husband, *mid-div, hdwy to chase ldrs 5 fs out, kpt on same pace fnl 3 furlongs.*
.............................(20 to 1 tchd 25 to 1) 4
1660² SKIDDAW SAMBA 5-10-12 (7*) M Herrington, *hld up in tch, chsd ldr frm 4 fs out, hit nxt, kpt on 7 to 1 op 7 to 2) 5
GENAWAY 5-11-10 Mr N Wilson, *sn beh, styd on frm 4 fs out, nvr dngrs...*......................................(33 to 1) 6
MY WARRIOR 6-11-7 (3*) R Davis, *chsd ldrs, eff'rt 4 fs out, no hdwy........................*(7 to 1 op 6 to 1) 7
OWES THE TILL 4-10-4 (7*) C Woodall, *nvr dngrs.* (20 to 1) 8
PERCY PIT 5-11-7 (3*) D J Moffatt, *chsd ldrs till hdd 4 fs out, wknd quickly....* (9 to 4 fav op 5 to 2 tchd 11 to 4) 9
ALLERBY 6-11-10 Mr R Ford, *beh frm hfwy......*(33 to 1) 10
ELI PECKANPAH (Ire) 4-10-9 (7*) Mr D Parker, *dwlt, nvr better than mid-div...*......................(16 to 1 op 20 to 1) 11
QUEEN BUZZARD 6-10-12 (7*) Mr J Weymes, *in tch till wknd 5 fs out...* (9 to 1 op 8 to 1 tchd 10 to 1) 12
TOP BANK 6-11-7 (3*) N Bentley, *prmnt, rdn o'r 6 fs out, sn wknd.*.....................................(20 to 1) 13
SALLY'S PRINCESS 4-10-11 Mr S Swiers, *al beh.*
.............................(20 to 1 tchd 33 to 1) 14
CEDAR LEAF (Ire) 4-10-5 (7*) P Waggott, *al beh...* (33 to 1) 15
BULLAFORD FAIR 6-11-5 (5*) J Supple, *prmnt till weakned 5 fs out....*...................................(33 to 1) 16
2490 WHATDIDYOUSAY 6-11-5 (5*) N Leach, *beh frm 5 fs out, vertually pld up fnl furlong.*
.............................(20 to 1 op 50 to 1 tchd 66 to 1) 17
GIDEONSCLEUCH 5-10-12 (7*) S Melrose, *al beh.*
.............................(33 to 1 tchd 50 to 1) 18
Dist: 1½l, 5l, 1l, 7l, 6l, 8l, 3l, 15l, hd, 2l. 3m 49.90s. (18 Ran).

(Guy Reed), C W Thornton

FOLKESTONE (good to soft (races 1,3,5), good (2,4,6,7))
Wednesday March 9th
Going Correction: PLUS 1.10 sec. per fur.

2910
Sandgate Maiden Hurdle (4-y-o and up) £1,553 2m 1f 110yds. . . . . (1:50)

2676³ ERCKULE 4-10-12 C Llewellyn, *trkd ldrs, prog to ld 6th, drw clr aftr 2 out, eased r-in.*
.............................(13 to 8 on op 6 to 4 on tchd 11 to 8 on) 1
RES IPSA LOQUITUR 7-11-6 D Gallagher, *beh till prog 6th, ran on frm 2 out, no ch wth wnr...* (50 to 1 op 33 to 1) 2
2705⁴ DENVER BAY 7-11-6 D Murphy, *prmnt, wth wnr frm 6th till aftr 2 out, hrd rdn and one pace.*
.............................(9 to 2 op 4 to 1 tchd 5 to 1) 3
2642⁶ FLAPPING FREDA 6-11-1 B Powell, *chsd ldrs, pushed alng 5th, one pace frm 3 out......*(33 to 1 op 14 to 1) 4
1974 SAIF AL ADIL (Ire) 5-11-6 V Smith, *chsd ldrs, disputing 3rd whn outpcd and mstk 3 out, sn btn.*
.............................(50 to 1 op 33 to 1) 5
2757⁹ GRAND COLONIST 7-11-3 (3*) A Procter, *al rear, no ch frm 3 out..*(50 to 1 op 33 to 1) 6
1622⁹ SARAZAR (USA) 5-10-13 (7*) S Ryan, *chsd ldrs, rdn 3 out, sn wknd.*................................(10 to 1 op 5 to 1) 7
2776⁴ ABU DANCER (Ire) 4-10-12 A Charlton, *hld up last, nvr nr ldrs.*..(50 to 1 op 16 to 1) 8
888 THE POWER OF ONE (v) 5-11-6 R Dunwoody, *wtd wth, eff'rt to chase ldrs 6th, sn btn, pld up bef last.*
.............................(8 to 1 op 7 to 1 tchd 9 to 1) pu
FELICE'S PET 4-10-4 (3*) A Thornton, *made most to 4th, wknd rapdly, tld off and pld up 3 out.*
.............................(9 to 1 op 8 to 1) pu
SARGANT (Ire) 5-11-6 R Supple, *al beh.*
.............................(50 to 1 op 33 to 1) pu

2667[6] FAR VIEW (Ire) (bl) 5-11-6 Mr Simon Andrews, *prmnt, led 4th till hdd and blun 6th, wknd rpdly, tld off and pld up bef last*...................(33 to 1 op 12 to 1) pu
ARRASAS LADY 4-10-7 Leesa Long, *prmnt till blun 5th, sn beh, tld off and pld up bef last.* (50 to 1 op 20 to 1) pu
2444[8] FAWLEY FLYER 5-11-6 M A FitzGerald, *jmpd badly, beh frm 5th, tld off and pld up bef 3 out.*
...................(50 to 1 op 14 to 1) pu
Dist: 4l, 6l, 15l, 4l, nk, 8l, 3l. 4m 37.10s. a 40.10s (13 Ran).
(The Saxon Partnership), N A Gaselee

2911 Fair Rosamund Handicap Chase (0-125 5-y-o and up) £3,395 3¼m (2:20)

2733 BETTY HAYES [98] 10-10-2 (7*) P Carey, *made all, rdn alng frm 15th, styd on wl from 2 out.*
...................(15 to 8 op 9 to 4 tchd 5 to 2) 1
2758* ROSITARY (Fr) [97] (bl) 11-10-8 (6ex) M Perrett, *trkd wnr, rdn appr 2 out, not quicken...* (Evens fav op 5 to 4 on) 2
2800 NOS NA GAOITHE [117] (v) 11-12-0 R Dunwoody, *trkd ldrs gng easily, rdn and not quicken appr 2 out, wknd last.*
...................(7 to 2 op 9 to 4) 3
2732 NOTARY-NOWELL [89] 8-10-0 Gee Armytage, *struggling frm 11th, sn wl beh...*(33 to 1 op 14 to 1 tchd 40 to 1) 4
Dist: 10l, 25l, hd. 6m 58.10s. a 46.10s (4 Ran).
(H S Butt), R H Alner

2912 Peasmarsh Conditional Jockeys' Selling Handicap Hurdle (4-y-o and up) £1,737 2m 1f 110yds.............(2:50)

2760* BAYLORD PRINCE (Ire) [64] 6-11-2 (6ex) D Fortt, *chsd ldrs, outpcd 5th, rdn and ran on frm 2 out, hmpd aftr last, sn led, styd on wl*.................(9 to 2 tchd 6 to 1) 1
2804* SOVEREIGN NICHE (Ire) [73] (v) 6-11-6 (5*,6ex) L Reynolds, *led, quickened 5th, wl clr 2 out, rdn and edgd lft aftr last, sn hdd and not quicken.*
...................(5 to 4 on tchd Evens and 11 to 8 on) 2
2797* STAR MOVER [78] 5-11-9 (7*,6ex) T Murphy, *chsd ldr aftr 4th, rdn and no imprsn 2 out, 3rd and btn whn hit last.*
...................(8 to 1 op 6 to 1 tchd 9 to 1) 3
2790[6] THANKSFORTHEOFFER [60] 6-10-12 T Jenks, *chsd ldr, rdn and lost pl aftr 4th, sn beh, no prog frm 2 out.*
...................(16 to 1 op 12 to 1 tchd 20 to 1) 4
2819[5] AVERON [68] 14-11-6 A Thornton, *hld up in tch, wnt 3rd and outpcd 5th, wknd 2 out, tld off.*
...................(14 to 1 op 10 to 1 tchd 16 to 1) 5
2653[5] SLICK CHERRY [64] 7-11-2 A Procter, *chsd ldrs, rdn aftr 4th, sn no ch, tld off*...............(10 to 1 op 5 to 1) 6
1627 BARCHAM [67] 7-11-5 A Dicken, *bolted bef strt, sn tld off, pld up aftr 4th*........(10 to 1 op 5 to 1 tchd 12 to 1) pu
2665[9] CUPID'S COURAGE (Ire) [48] 5-10-0 R Farrant, *rdn and lost tch aftr 4th, tld off and pld up bef nxt.*
...................(33 to 1 tchd 40 to 1) pu
(Miss J A Ewer), R P C Hoad

2913 Bet With The Tote Novices' Chase Qualifier (6-y-o and up) £3,525 3¼m ....(3:20)

CELTIC BARLE 10-10-10 S McNeill, *hld up in tch, trkd ldrs 7th, effrt aftr 3 out, led gng easily nxt, ran on wl.*
...................(10 to 1 op 6 to 1) 1
2340 SUFFOLK ROAD 7-10-10 R Dunwoody, *trkd ldg pair, mstk 15th, effrt aftr 3 out, sn ev ch, rdn and unbl to quicken.*
...................(2 to 1 tchd 9 to 4) 2
2559[3] YOUNG BRAVE 8-10-10 S Earle, *wth ldr, led tenth to 13th and sn nxt, hdd and hit 2 out, sn btn.*
...................(10 to 1 op 5 to 1) 3
2647[2] SPIKEY (NZ) 8-11-3 D Murphy, *led to tenth and frm 13th to nxt, rdn and wknd 4 out.*
...................(11 to 10 on op 11 to 8 on tchd Evens) 4
2496 PODRIDA 8-10-5 D O'Sullivan, *mstks, wl beh frm tenth, sn tld off*.........(33 to 1 op 20 to 1 tchd 50 to 1) 5
2361 TROPICAL ACE 7-10-5 A Tory, *blun 3rd, wl beh frm tenth, tld off and pld up bef 2 out*........(66 to 1 op 33 to 1) pu
1771[4] SANDY-BRANDY 9-10-10 J R Kavanagh, *wl beh frm tenth, tld off whn blun 4 out, pld up bef nxt.*
...................(50 to 1 op 20 to 1) pu
2761 BLARNEY CASTLE 7-10-10 R Rowell, *wl beh frm tenth, tld off and pld up bef 14th.*
...................(50 to 1 op 33 to 1 tchd 66 to 1) pu
Dist: 8l, 7l, dist, 20l. 7m 3.20s. a 51.20s (8 Ran).
(Mrs Irene Hodge), H B Hodge

2914 Somerfield Court Novices' Hurdle (4-y-o and up) £1,553 2m 1f 110yds (3:50)

2694[2] HOSTILE WITNESS (Ire) (v) 4-11-0 M Richards, *hld up in tch, trkd ldr 6th, led 2 out, sn clr, cmftbly.*
...................(11 to 8 on op 7 to 4 on tchd 5 to 4 on) 1
2757[3] ESPRIT DE FEMME (Fr) 8-10-11 M A FitzGerald, *led till hdd and mstk 2 out, sn rdn and one pace.* (7 to 1 op 8 to 1) 2
1284[3] LA VILLA ROSE (Fr) 4-10-3 D Murphy, *in tch till 3rd and no imprsn frm 2 out, wknd appr last...* (4 to 1 op 3 to 1) 3
2621[7] KITSBEL 6-11-2 W McFarland, *cl up, mstk 3 out, sn wknd, tld off*...............(20 to 1 op 10 to 1 tchd 25 to 1) 4

2522 MUSICAL HIGH (Fr) 4-10-3 R Dunwoody, *hld up, effrt 6th, sn wknd, tld off whn f last.*
...................(4 to 1 op 5 to 2 tchd 9 to 2) f
2599[6] LE BARON PERCHE (Fr) 5-11-2 S McNeill, *blun and uns rdr 1st*...................(12 to 1 tchd 14 to 1) ur
EWAR GOLD (Fr) 4-10-3 A Charlton, *lost tch and mstk 5th, sn tld off, pld up bef 3 out.*
...................(20 to 1 op 12 to 1 tchd 25 to 1) pu
Dist: 12l, 25l, 15l. 4m 36.30s. a 39.30s (7 Ran).
(The Pink Panthers), P R Hedger

2915 Cliftonville Handicap Chase (0-120 5-y-o and up) £2,422 2m........ (4:20)

2707* AROUND THE HORN [115] 7-12-0 S McNeill, *trkd ldr, led and mstk 7th, clr appr last, rdn out.*
...................(6 to 5 fav op 6 to 4 on tchd 5 to 4) 1
2539[3] PRIVATE AUDITION [114] 12-11-13 J R Kavanagh, *mstk second, al prmnt, chlgd appr 2 out, ran on one pace.*
...................(16 to 1 op 10 to 1 tchd 20 to 1) 2
2726[3] AMBASSADOR [115] (bl) 11-12-0 R Dunwoody, *led till 7th, wknd aftr 3 out...* (5 to 2 op 3 to 1 tchd 7 to 2) 3
2818[5] NATHIR (USA) [100] 8-10-13 M A FitzGerald, *mstk 1st, lost tch 8th, ran on aftr 3 out, 3rd and staying on whn f last*...................(12 to 1 op 6 to 1) f
2032* DARE SAY [105] 11-11-4 S Earle, *wth ldr whn blun and uns rdr 3rd*...........(5 to 2 op 2 to 1 tchd 11 to 4) ur
Dist: 1½l, 30l. 4m 18.60s. a 23.60s (5 Ran).
SR: 40/37/8/-/-/ (Pell-Mell Partners), J T Gifford

2916 Open National Hunt Flat Race (4,5,6-y-o) £1,308 2m 1f 110yds.............(4:50)

CROWN PROSECUTOR 4-10-9 M Richards, *trkd ldrs, led o'r 4 fs out, clr 2 out, rdn out...*...(6 to 4 fav op 2 to 1) 1
ENVOCAMANDA (Ire) 5-11-3 Peter Hobbs, *mid-div, prog 6 fs out, effrt to chase wnr 3 out, ran on one pace.*
...................(20 to 1 op 12 to 1 tchd 25 to 1) 2
2176[2] IDIOT'S LADY 5-10-5 (7*) D Bohan, *prmnt, led 8 fs out till o'r 4 out, styd on one pace aftr.*
...................(7 to 1 op 5 to 1) 3
2509[6] MOORE BONES 6-11-3 P Holley, *led for 3 fs, lost pl and hmpd bend 6 out, kpt on ag'n appr last.*
...................(16 to 1 op 8 to 1) 4
2560[7] RIVER LEVEN 5-11-0 (3*) J McCarthy, *prmnt till wknd o'r 3 fs out*...................(33 to 1 op 14 to 1) 5
2677[5] JIBBER THE KIBBER (Ire) 5-11-3 I Lawrence, *mid-div, prog to join ldrs 5 fs out, wknd wl o'r 3 out.*
...................(11 to 2 op 3 to 1 tchd 6 to 1) 6
POND HOUSE (Ire) 5-11-3 R Dunwoody, *trkd ldrs, smooth prog and ev ch 5 fs out, sn rdn and wknd.*
...................(11 to 4 op 3 to 1) 7
2269 WIN A HAND 4-10-4 C Llewellyn, *al beh, tld off.*
...................(33 to 1 op 20 to 1) 8
TINA SPARKLE (Ire) 5-10-12 D Murphy, *al rear, tld off.*
...................(20 to 1 op 12 to 1) 9
ANNS REQUEST 5-10-12 Mr J O'Brien, *chsd ldrs to hfwy, sn lost tch, tld off*...............(33 to 1 op 20 to 1) 10
MONKS SOHAM (Ire) 6-10-10 (7*) P Murphy, *al beh, tld off.*
...................(20 to 1 op 12 to 1 tchd 25 to 1) 11
VOLLEYBALL (Ire) 5-11-3 B Powell, *beh, effrt hfwy, wknd o'r 5 fs out, tld off*...............(33 to 1 op 20 to 1) 12
2509 KING'S COURTIER (Ire) 5-11-3 J Lower, *lost pl ten fs out, sn wl beh, tld off*..............(14 to 1 op 8 to 1) 13
TOP MISS 5-10-9 (3*) A Thornton, *al rear, tld off fnl 4 fs.*
...................(33 to 1 op 20 to 1) 14
2444[7] STEEL FAUCON (Ire) 5-11-3 Mr J Durkan, *led aftr 3 fs till 8 out, wknd rpdly, sn tld off.*...(33 to 1 op 20 to 1) 15
Dist: 3½l, 3½l, 20l, 3l, 10l, 5l, 15l, 1½l, 10l, 6l. 4m 34.30s. (15 Ran).
(D J Deer), W R Muir

TRALEE (IRE) (heavy)
Wednesday March 9th

2917 Castleisland Maiden Hurdle (4-y-o) £2,760 2m.....................(2:00)

2750[8] CONCLAVE (Ire) 10-13 R Hughes, ...(12 to 1) 1
2388[4] DARK SWAN (Ire) 10-13 (5*) C P Dunne, ...(7 to 2) 2
2547[4] DRESS DANCE (Ire) 10-13 A Powell, ...(4 to 1) 3
2864[7] MAN OF ARRAN (Ire) 11-1 (3*) T J O'Sullivan, ... (7 to 4 fav) 4
2547[7] TRIBAL MEMORIES (Ire) 10-5 (3*) C O'Brien, ...(25 to 1) 5
2547[5] BLAKE'S FABLE (Ire) 10-8 C F Swan, ...(8 to 1) 6
2771 SPECIAL OFFER (Ire) 10-8 B Sheridan, ...(25 to 1) 7
TISRARA LADY (Ire) 10-8 J F Titley, ...(25 to 1) 8
2750[7] BOBADIL (Ire) 10-6 (7*) P J Smullen, ...(8 to 1) 9
2750 ROYAL RANK (USA) 10-6 (7*) J M Donnelly, ...(12 to 1) 10
1377[9] RUNNING SLIPPER (Ire) 10-13 J P Cusack, ...(10 to 1) 11
2614 RISKY GALORE 10-8 (5*) K P Gaule, ...(14 to 1) 12
HEATHFIELD (USA) 10-11 (7*) R A Hennessy, ...(10 to 1) 13
COMMON BOND (Ire) 10-13? G M O'Neill, ...(8 to 1) 14
2547 BARLEY COURT (Ire) 10-8 (5*) P A Roche, ...(50 to 1) f
MISS PITTYPAT (Ire) 10-5 (3*) D P Murphy, ...(25 to 1) f
Dist: 2½l, 1½l, 2l, 3l. 4m 40.50s. (16 Ran).
(Mrs J R Mullion), D T Hughes

407

2918 Kingdom Maiden Hurdle (Div 1) (5-y-o and up) £2,760 2½m. . . . . (2:30)

2775³	SIOBHAILIN DUBH (Ire) 5-10-8 (5") K P Gaule, (7 to 2 jt-fav)	1
1379	DIRECT RUN 7-12-0 J F Titley, ...(5 to 1)	2
2353*	KING'S DECREE (Ire) 5-11-12 C F Swan, . . . (7 to 2 jt-fav)	3
2552	OZEYCAZEY (Ire) 5-11-4 F Woods, ...(8 to 1)	4
	GO GO GALLANT (Ire) 5-11-4 G M O'Neill, ... (9 to 2)	5
2348⁹	GODFREY TREVOR (Ire) 5-11-4 T Horgan, ...(25 to 1)	6
1902⁹	FIALADY 9-10-12 (3") T P Treacy, ...(25 to 1)	7
2616⁴	THE COBH GALE 7-11-1 H Rogers, ...(8 to 1)	8
2465	COOLGREEN (Ire) 6-11-6 P M Verling, ... (25 to 1)	9
2664	BE KIND TO ME 8-10-12 (3") C O'Brien, ...(12 to 1)	10
1859⁵	CORRIB HAVEN (Ire) 6-11-6 K F O'Brien, ...(12 to 1)	11
	CAILIN NAOFA 8-11-1 A Powell, ... (12 to 1)	pu
	KILLIMOR LAD 7-11-1 (5") J P Broderick, ... (14 to 1)	pu
	SHOT TO SAVE (Ire) (bl) 6-11-6 C O'Dwyer, ...(20 to 1)	pu
	BENSONS RETURN (Ire) 5-11-4 J P Banahan, ... (25 to 1)	pu
2586	SARVO (Ire) 6-11-3 (3") T J O'Sullivan, ... (14 to 1)	pu

Dist: 4l, 6l, 8l, 11l. 6m 10.40s. (16 Ran).

(Thomas O'Shea), A P O'Brien

2919 Kingdom Maiden Hurdle (Div 2) (5-y-o and up) £2,760 2½m. . . . .(3:00)

2465³	NO TAG (Ire) 6-11-6 J F Titley, ...(7 to 4 fav)	1
2620*	DAWN ADAMS (Ire) 6-11-9 F J Flood, ... (3 to 1)	2
2679³	NINE O THREE (Ire) 5-11-7 (5") J P Broderick, ... (4 to 1)	3
2664	CABBERY ROSE (Ire) 6-11-1 J Magee, ...(14 to 1)	4
2616	GALES JEWEL 8-10-8 (7") Mr F C Cahill, ...(20 to 1)	5
2616	FAIR ADELINE 7-11-1 P M Verling, ... (25 to 1)	6
2620⁶	DEEP WAVE 7-11-1 (5") Mr C T G Kinane, ...(12 to 1)	7
	POLLEROO (Ire) 6-11-9 J Jones, ...(12 to 1)	8
2702⁵	TIP THE CAN (Ire) 6-11-6 A Powell, ...(12 to 1)	9
1827	WINNIE WUMPKINS (Ire) 5-10-8 (5") M A Davey, . . (20 to 1)	10
2664	CLONE (Ire) 6-11-6 C F Swan, ...(14 to 1)	11
2096⁸	ORMOND BEACH (Ire) 5-11-4 T Horgan, ...(33 to 1)	12
	BAY VIEW PRINCE (Ire) 5-10-13 (5") C P Dunne, . . (14 to 1)	13
2658⁷	PALLAS CHAMPION (Ire) 5-11-4 F Woods, ... (25 to 1)	14
2620⁴	LANCASTRIANS DREAM (Ire) 5-10-8 (5") M J Holbrook,	
	. . . .(8 to 1)	pu
2592⁹	DESPERATE DAYS (Ire) 5-11-4 R Hughes, ... (10 to 1)	pu

Dist: 5½l, 5l, ¾l, 20l. 6m 16.90s. (16 Ran).

(Ms M Hynes), Patrick G Kelly

2920 Fenit Handicap Hurdle (4-y-o and up) £2,760 2m. . . . . (3:30)

2278⁸	BOHEMIAN CASTLE (Ire) [-] 5-10-13 C F Swan, . . . (6 to 1)	1
2703⁴	UNCLE BABY (Ire) [-] 6-10-13 (5") K P Gaule, ...(5 to 2 fav)	2
2703⁷	KYLE HOUSE VI (Ire) [-] 5-9-13 (7") J M Donnelly, . .(10 to 1)	3
2607⁶	BALLYBODEN [-] 7-10-13 K F O'Brien, ... (8 to 1)	4
2617⁴	SUPER TACTICS (Ire) [-] 6-11-4 (5") C P Dunne, . . (3 to 1)	5
2552⁵	SHANNON AMBER (Ire) [-] 5-11-6 (5") J P Broderick, (9 to 2)	6
2616	SHIMMERETTO [-] 8-9-5² (5") T P Rudd, ...(50 to 1)	7
1681	LEADING TIME (Fr) [-] 5-10-2 R Hughes, ...(12 to 1)	8
2658⁶	LADY BUDD (Ire) [-] 6-10-2 (3") C O'Brien, ...(14 to 1)	9

Dist: 3l, 3l, 9l, 13l. 4m 50.40s. (9 Ran).

(Mrs Orla Finucane), A J McNamara

2921 Spa Handicap Hurdle (4-y-o and up) £2,760 2¾m. . . . . (4:00)

2392⁶	PRINCE OLE (Ire) [-] 6-12-0 M Duffy, ... (7 to 4)	1
2160⁵	AEGEAN FANFARE (Ire) [-] (bl) 5-11-1 R Hughes, . . . (6 to 1)	2
2278	LEAVE IT TO JUDGE [-] 7-9-13 W T Slattery Jnr, . . (20 to 1)	3
2682*	IM MELODY (Ire) [-] 6-11-5 (5") J P Broderick, . . (6 to 4 fav)	4
2348³	CALL ME HENRY [-] 5-9-13 C F Swan, ...(6 to 1)	5
1823	HIGHLAND MINSTREL [-] 7-9-4 (5") M G Cleary, . . (14 to 1)	6
2616	BALLINGOWAN STAR [-] 7-9-4 (3") C O'Brien, ...(16 to 1)	7
2660	POOR MOTHER (Ire) [-] 6-9-11 F J Flood, ... (10 to 1)	8

Dist: 13l, 2l, ¾l, 2l. 6m 57.40s. (8 Ran).

(Mrs Patrick Flynn), Patrick Joseph Flynn

2922 Tralee Q.R. Handicap Chase (4-y-o and up) £2,760 2½m. . . . .(4:30)

2662²	DEL MONTE BOY [-] 9-11-6 (3") Mr T Lombard, ...(4 to 1)	1
2772⁹	DUSKY LADY [-] 8-11-7 (7") Mr N Goodwin, ...(10 to 1)	2
2393⁵	WHAT A MINSTREL [-] 8-10-1 (7") Mr J T McNamara,	
	. . . .(10 to 1)	3
2619⁶	ITS A SNIP [-] (bl) 9-9-7 (7") Mr T J Murphy, ...(12 to 1)	4
2662⁶	DELIGHTFUL CHOICE (Ire) [-] 6-10-7 (7") Mr K F O'Sullivan,	
	. . . .(16 to 1)	5
2619⁴	KILL KIL CASTLE [-] 7-10-0 (7") Mr A O'Shea, ...(16 to 1)	f
2661⁴	BALADINE [-] 7-11-4 Mr P Fenton, ... (4 to 1)	f
2619	GALLEY GALE [-] 8-11-5 (7") Mr R Walsh, ...(3 to 1 fav)	pu
2157⁵	THE MIGHTY BUCK [-] 11-11-9 (5") Mr W M O'Sullivan,	
	. . . .(14 to 1)	pu
2659	MAKE ME AN ISLAND [-] 9-11-3 (7") Mr R M Murphy, (9 to 2)	pu
2847	MONEY MADE [-] (bl) 7-9-9⁴ (7") Mr S P Hennessy, (66 to 1)	pu
2619*	RUSSIAN GALE [-] 6-10-5 (7") Mr D P Daly, ... (6 to 1)	pu

Dist: 10l, 6l, 11l, dist. 6m 19.80s. (12 Ran).

(Twenty First Racing Co Ltd), Augustine Leahy

2923 Lee Novice Chase (4-y-o and up) £2,760 2½m. . . . . (5:00)

2618⁶	MAMMY'S FRIEND 10-11-6 (3") D P Murphy, ... (12 to 1)	1
2661	TAWNEY FLAME 8-12-0 J Magee, ...(11 to 2)	2
2618⁴	CHELSEA NATIVE 7-11-4 (5") Susan A Finn, ... (6 to 1)	3
1683³	MUILEAR GRIDGE 7-12-0 J F Titley, ...(11 to 10 fav)	4
2588	TEL D'OR 9-11-7 (7") Mr P J Millington, ...(14 to 1)	5
2661⁵	MALTELINA 8-11-6 C O'Brien, ...(10 to 1)	6
1498⁸	JOHNNY SCATTERCASH 12-11-11 (3") T J Mitchell,	
	. . . .(10 to 1)	7
2752	DUNBOY CASTLE (Ire) 6-12-0 T Horgan, ...(12 to 1)	8
1857⁶	HIGHWAY LASS 8-11-9 S H O'Donovan, ...(16 to 1)	9
2618³	BEAU GRANDE (Ire) 6-12-0 L P Cusack, ...(6 to 1)	10
1497⁸	CLEAKILE 8-12-0 F Woods, ...(25 to 1)	pu
1822⁹	THE CRIOSRA (Ire) 5-11-1 (5") P A Roche, ...(25 to 1)	pu
2550	GODFREYS CROSS (Ire) 6-11-9 P M Verling, ... (25 to 1)	pu

Dist: ½l, 3l, 20l. 6m 25.50s. (13 Ran).

(Eric Mortell), John J Walsh

2924 Desmond Flat Race (4-y-o and up) £2,760 2m 1f. . . . . (5:30)

2664⁸	MOONSHEE (Ire) 6-11-6 (3") Miss M Olivefalk, ... (12 to 1)	1
2684⁵	WEST BROGUE (Ire) (bl) 5-11-12 Mr J P Dempsey,	
	. . . .(9 to 4 fav)	2
2869⁵	STEVIE BE (Ire) 6-11-7 (7") Mr T J Murphy, ...(5 to 2)	3
1982⁸	BACKTOWN JOHNNY (Ire) 5-11-5 (7") Mr S O'Donnell,	
	. . . .(16 to 1)	4
2553	THE LEFT FOOTER (Ire) 5-11-5 (7") Mr J T McNamara,	
	. . . .(10 to 1)	5
	RATH CAOLA 7-11-6 (3") Mr J A Nash, ...(6 to 1)	6
314⁸	UP FOR RANSOME (Ire) 5-11-12 Mr E Bolger, ... (10 to 1)	7
2849	QUIET ONE 9-11-2 (7") Miss U Corcoran, ... (20 to 1)	pu
1827	CAPTAIN CHARLES (Ire) 6-11-7 (7") Mr G Mulcaire, (33 to 1)	pu
990⁴	NOT MY LINE (Ire) 5-11-5 (7") Mr K Whelan, ... (7 to 1)	pu
2663⁸	KUDA CHANTIK (Ire) 4-10-6 (7") Mr E Norris, ... (7 to 1)	pu
2848⁹	BEN-GURIAN (Ire) 4-11-1 (3") Mr D Marnane, ... (8 to 1)	pu

Dist: 7l, 9l, 15l, 10l. 5m 5.70s. (12 Ran).

(Charles O M S Mansergh), Capt D G Swan

CARLISLE (heavy)
Thursday March 10th
Going Correction: PLUS 1.20 sec. per fur. (races 1,3,-5,7), PLUS 0.95 (2,4,6)

2925 Mackinnon Of Scotland 'National Hunt' Novices' Hurdle (4-y-o and up) £2,092 3m 110yds. . . . . (2:10)

2500³	WHITE DIAMOND 6-11-4 J Railton, trkd ldrs, shaken up to	
	ld 2 out, pushed out frm last.	
	. . . .(7 to 4 fav op 6 to 4 tchd 9 to 4)	1
2367⁹	NAWRIK (Ire) 5-11-4 T Reed, led to 1st, dsptd ld till	
	slightly outpcd aftr 2 out, kpt on wl und pres frm last.	
	. . . .(15 to 8 op 11 to 8 tchd 2 to 1)	2
2502⁷	BARNEY RUBBLE 9-11-4 M Moloney, led or dsptd ld frm	
	1st till hdd 2 out, sn btn. . . . . (8 to 1 tchd 9 to 1)	3
2578⁶	BELLS HILL LAD 7-11-13 A Dobbin, prmnt, pushed alng	
	aftr 7th, lost pl after nxt, kpt on frm 2 out.	
	. . . .(9 to 2 op 4 to 1 tchd 5 to 1)	4
2104	MOSSIMAN (Ire) 5-11-4 S Turner, in tch, outpcd appr 7th,	
	rallied aftr 9th, one pace frm 3 out. (33 to 1 op 25 to 1)	5
2785⁵	CROSS REFERENCE 6-10-13 B Storey, trkd ldrs, dsptd ld	
	appr 3 out, sn wknd. . . . .(50 to 1 op 33 to 1)	6
2436	ROYAL FIFE 8-10-8 (5") P Williams, reared strt, sn reco'red,	
	prmnt til wknd aftr 3 out. . . . .(50 to 1 op 33 to 1)	7
1181	THE WEATHERMAN 6-11-1 (3") N Bentley, in tch til outpcd	
	appr 7th, tld off. . . . .(16 to 1 op 14 to 1)	8
	NICKY'S BELLE 9-10-13 G Harker, beh, pushed alng and	
	lost tch hfwy, tld off whn pld up bef 8th. . . . . (200 to 1)	pu

Dist: 1l, 12l, 4l, 15l, 4l, 5l, 15l. 6m 32.80s. a 39.80s (9 Ran).

(M Allison), Mrs A Swinbank

2926 Jedburgh Kiltmakers Claiming Chase (5-y-o and up) £2,544 2m. . . . . . (2:40)

2815⁶	KAMBALDA RAMBLER 10-11-8 B Storey, jmpd wl, made	
	all, hld on well. . . . .(4 to 1 op 3 to 1 tchd 9 to 2)	1
2540⁷	YAHEEB (USA) 10-11-10 R Garritty, hld up, hdwy aftr 8th,	
	ev ch last, no extr. . . . .(5 to 2 jt-fav op 7 to 4)	2
2836⁶	JAMES MY BOY 14-11-0 P Niven, in tch, ev ch 3 out, sn	
	rdn, kpt on same pace. . . . .(9 to 2 op 11 to 2)	3
2736	EBRO 8-11-10 A Dobbin, prmnt, pushed alng frm 6th,	
	one pace from 3 out. . . . .(16 to 1 op 12 to 1)	4
1960⁷	REEF LARK 9-11-0 K Johnson, in tch, rdn and outpcd	
	3 out, no dngr after. (9 to 1 op 7 to 1 tchd 10 to 1)	5
1727⁴	PURA MONEY 12-12-0 N Doughty, hld up in tch, hdwy	
	aftr 7th, wknd wn mstk 3 out. (6 to 2 jt-fav op 3 to 1)	6
2255	SUPER SANDY 7-11-12³ Mr J Walton, cl up till grad wknd	
	frm 6th, tld off. . . . .(40 to 1 op 33 to 1)	7

Dist: 1½l, 6l, 1½l, 6l, 15l, 25l. 4m 22.80s. a 23.80s (7 Ran).

SR: 8/8/-/-/ (Mrs J G Dudgeon), C Parker

2927 **McEwans Lager Top Of North Novices' Hurdle Qualifier (4-y-o and up) £2,232 2½m 110yds. . . . . (3:10)**

2500* NORTHERN SQUIRE 6-11-5 (5*) P Williams, *not fluent, led aftr second, made rst, easily.* . . . . (3 to 1 on tchd 11 to 4 on) 1
1636⁴ FULL OF FIRE 7-11-2 N Doughty, *trkd ldrs till wknd appr 3 out, btn whn blun nxt.* (7 to 2 op 3 to 1 tchd 4 to 1) 2
2367 PRINCE ROSSINI (Ire) 6-11-2 T Reed, *led till hdd aftr second, wknd after 6th, sn wl beh.* (16 to 1 op 10 to 1) 3
2445⁷ PRECIOUS HENRY 5-11-2 J Railton, *prmnt, chsd wnr frm 7th, second and btn whn pld up aftr 3 out, lme.* . . . . (16 to 1 op 12 to 1) pu
2369 WEST AUCKLAND 5-11-2 A Merrigan, *pld up aftr 3rd, broke leg, dead.* . . . . (40 to 1 op 14 to 1) pu
2735 MIDDLEHAM CASTLE 5-11-2 A Dobbin, *in tch till wknd quickly aftr 7th, wl beh whn pld up after 3 out, lme.* . . . . (16 to 1 op 12 to 1) pu

Dist: Dist, 6l. 5m 23.60s. a 30.60s (6 Ran).
SR: 36/-/-/ (Mrs J M Davenport), J M Jefferson

2928 **Edinburgh Woollen Mill Novices' Chase (5-y-o and up) £5,702 2½m 110yds. . . . . (3:40)**

2323* BEACHY HEAD 6-11-7 M Dwyer, *jmpd wl, made all, cmftbly.* . . . . (5 to 4 on op 5 to 4 tchd 11 to 8) 1
2814* CLYDE RANGER 7-11-7 L Wyer, *al chasing wnr, rdn aftr 3 out, kpt on, no imprsn.* . . . . (2 to 1 op 7 to 4) 2
718* TARTAN TRADEWINDS 7-11-7 N Doughty, *chsd ldrs, outpcd aftr 4 out, no dngr after.* . . . . (14 to 1 op 8 to 1) 3
2892² SEON 8-11-7 P Niven, *chsd ldrs till wknd aftr 4 out.* . . . . (9 to 1 op 7 to 1 tchd 10 to 1) 4
2574 VAYRUA (Fr) 9-11-7 M Hourigan, *in tch, effrt aftr tenth, sn btn.* . . . . (10 to 1 op 8 to 1) 5
2411 SOUTH STACK 8-11-3 Gary Lyons, *sn beh, tld off whn pld up bef 12th.* . . . . (200 to 1 op 100 to 1) pu
2809⁶ HERE COMES TIBBY 7-10-12 T Reed, *lost tch frm tenth, tld off whn pld up bef 3 out.* . . . . (100 to 1 op 66 to 1) pu

Dist: 5l, dist, 3½l, 6l. 5m 26.70s. a 23.70s (7 Ran).
SR: 51/46/-/-/ (M Tabor), J J O'Neill

2929 **Clan Royal Conditional Jockeys' Handicap Hurdle (0-110 4-y-o and up) £2,511 2m 1f. . . . . (4:10)**

2371⁶ PALACEGATE KING [98] 5-11-0 (3*) B Harding, *made all, clr betw last 2, kpt on wl.* . . . (3 to 1 op 7 to 2 tchd 4 to 1) 1
2815² ARAGON AYR [105] 6-11-10 D J Moffatt, *hld up, effrt aftr 3 out, no hdwy till styd on wl appr last.* . . . . (6 to 4 fav op 11 to 10) 2
2686² VERY EVIDENT (Ire) [90] 5-10-9 N Bentley, *chsd ldrs, ev ch 3 out, kpt on same pace.* . . . . (9 to 4 op 2 to 1) 3
2634* BAND SARGEANT (Ire) [85] 5-10-4 N Leach, *chsd ldr, chlgd 3 out, sn rdn, wknd aftr nxt.* . . . . (7 to 1 op 6 to 1) 4
787⁶ KING OF NORMANDY (Ire) [81] 5-10-0 J Supple, *beh and pushed alng aftr 3rd, sn lost tch, tld off.* . . . . (100 to 1) 5

Dist: 2l, 2½l, 8l, dist. 4m 39.30s. a 32.30s (5 Ran).
(Chas N Whillans), A C Whillans

2930 **Pitlochry Knitwear Handicap Chase (0-130 5-y-o and up) £3,590 3¼m (4:40)**

2370* TARTAN TYRANT [125] 8-12-0 N Doughty, *hld up, steady hdwy to ld 2 out, mstk last, drvn out.* . . . . (6 to 5 fav op 5 to 4 on tchd 5 to 4) 1
2499* CAROUSEL ROCKET [97] 11-9-11 (3*) D Bentley, *chsd clr ldr, rdn to chal 2 out, kpt on und pres.* . . . . (5 to 2 op 9 to 4) 2
2576⁵ FORTH AND TAY [99] 12-10-2⁷ (5*) P Williams, *drpd rear hfwy, rallied aftr 3 out, kpt on und pres frm nxt.* . . . . (7 to 1 op 10 to 1) 3
2582 REGAL ESTATE [112] 10-11-1 R Garritty, *led and sn clr, hdd 2 out, wknd quickly, tld off.* . . . . (7 to 2 op 5 to 1) 4

Dist: 1½l, 1½l, dist. 7m 17.90s. a 47.90s (4 Ran).
(The Edinburgh Woollen Mill Ltd), G Richards

2931 **Heather Mills National Hunt Flat Race (4,5,6-y-o) £1,607 2m 1f. . . . . (5:10)**

2534⁴ ADIB (USA) 4-10-11 (3*) N Bentley, *chsd clr ldr, led o'r 2 out, drvn out.* . . . . (4 to 1 op 3 to 1 tchd 9 to 2) 1
MONY-SKIP (Ire) 5-11-5 (3*) D Bentley, *in tch, effrt o'r 3 out, kpt on fnl 2 fs, no imprsn on wnr.* . . . . (9 to 1 op 6 to 1 tchd 10 to 1) 2
BROADWATER BOY (Ire) 6-11-1 (7*) Mr C Bonner, *in tch, effrt 3 out, kpt on same pace fnl 2 fs.* (7 to 1 op 6 to 1) 3
2490⁵ MOREOF A GUNNER 4-10-9 (5*) P Williams, *hld up, pushed alng 5 out, kpt on fnl 3 fs, not dngrs.* . . . . (6 to 5 fav op 5 to 4 on tchd 5 to 4) 4
RADICAL CHOICE (Ire) 5-11-5 (3*) D J Moffatt, *mid-div, rdn o'r 3 out, no real hdwy.* . . . . (16 to 1) 5
ROLY PRIOR 5-11-3 (5*) S Lyons, *led, clr aftr 5 fs, wknd and hdd o'r 2 out, sn btn.* . . . . (25 to 1 op 20 to 1) 6
2074 BILLY BUOYANT 5-11-12⁴ Mr J Walton, *in tch till hng lft and wknd quickly o'r 3 out, tld off.* . . . . (50 to 1 op 33 to 1) 7
KINGS LANE 5-11-8 Mr J M Dun, *tld off frm hfwy.* . . . . (33 to 1 op 25 to 1) 8
SWISS ACCOUNT 5-10-10 (7*) Mr J Weymes, *in tch till wknd quickly o'r 4 out, tld off.* . . . . (13 to 2 op 8 to 1 tchd 6 to 1) 9
SUPERVISION 6-11-8 Mrs M Kendall, *sn beh, wl tld off.* . . . . (66 to 1 op 50 to 1) 10

Dist: 2l, 1½l, 5l, 3l, 3l, dist, 3l, dist, dist. 4m 34.80s. (10 Ran).
(N B Mason (Farms) Ltd), G M Moore

TOWCESTER (soft)
Thursday March 10th
Going Correction: PLUS 1.40 sec. per fur. (races 1,4,6), PLUS 1.05 (2,3,5)

2932 **Ginger Quill Novices' Chase (5-y-o and up) £2,401 2m 110yds. . . . . . (2:20)**

2730² CRUISING ON 7-10-11 W Marston, *led to 4th, cl up, led ag'n aftr 3 out, awkward nxt, styd on wl.* . . . . (13 to 8 op 6 to 4 tchd 11 to 8 and 7 to 4) 1
2730* COUNTRY MISTRESS 7-11-4 T Grantham, *beh 4th, jmpd slwly 6th and sn tld off, styd on appr last, fnshd wl.* . . . . (6 to 4 fav op 11 to 10 tchd 7 to 4) 2
2668 EMERALD GEM (v) 8-11-2 M Brennan, *al prmnt, pckd 5th, mstk 4 out, wknd.* . . . . (4 to 1 op 3 to 1 tchd 9 to 2) 3
461 BE PATIENT MY SON 13-11-2 S Earle, *beh 4th, jmpd slwly 7th, tld off.* . . . . (66 to 1 op 20 to 1) 4
2794 STUBS GUEST 8-10-13 (3*) A Procter, *pld hrd, hld up, led 4th, mstk four out, hdd aftr nxt, hard rdn and sn wknd, no ch whn f last.* . . . . (12 to 1 op 8 to 1 tchd 14 to 1) f

Dist: 20l, 25l, 15l. 4m 31.50s. a 29.50s (5 Ran).
SR: 19/6/ (Mrs J E Goodall), P T Dalton

2933 **Swan National Leasing Handicap Hurdle (0-130 4-y-o and up) £2,860 2m . . . .(2:50)**

2521² TAYLORS PRINCE [100] (v) 7-10-0 V Smith, *hld up, rapid hdwy to ld 3 out, rdn out.* . . . . (7 to 1 op 10 to 1) 1
2670* ZEALOUS KITTEN (USA) [103] 6-10-3 J Osborne, *trkd ldrs, lost pl 4 out, styd on wl to take second aftr last.* . . . . (3 to 1 jt-fav op 5 to 2 tchd 7 to 2) 2
2379⁷ SOOTHFAST (USA) [115] 5-11-1 T Grantham, *trkd ldrs, led aftr 4 out, hdd nxt, one pace frm 2 out.* . . . . (3 to 1 jt-fav tchd 7 to 2 and 11 to 4) 3
2566⁹ MARSH'S LAW [100] 7-10-0 M Brennan, *chsd ldrs, rdn aftr 3 out, styd on one pace.* . . . . (14 to 1 tchd 20 to 1) 4
1863⁷ NELTEGRITY [106] 5-10-6 Peter Caldwell, *hld up beh, mstk 5th, pushed alng 3 out, styd on, nvr on terms.* . . . . (11 to 1 op 8 to 1) 5
2734⁴ RED RING [100] 7-10-0 W Marston, *cl up, led briefly 4 out, sn btn.* . . . . (10 to 1 tchd 14 to 1) 6
2734* JALINGO [109] 7-10-9 Richard Guest, *hld up in tch, cld and ev ch 3 out, sn wknd.* . . . . (5 to 1 op 7 to 2) 7
961⁴ BRIGGS LAD (Ire) [104] (bl) 5-10-4⁴ M A FitzGerald, *led, ballooned 1st 2 sn clr, hdd 4 out, wknd, tld off.* . . . . (33 to 1 op 20 to 1) 8
2512² BUONARROTI [128] 7-11-7 (7*) Pat Thompson, *slpd up on flt aftr second.* . . . . (12 to 1 op 10 to 1 tchd 16 to 1) su

Dist: 2½l, 1l, 1½l, 5l, 3l, 30l, 12l. 4m 4.80s. a 21.80s (9 Ran).
SR: 22/22/33/16/17/8/ (H J Collingridge), H J Collingridge

2934 **Hoechst Panacur EBF Mares 'National Hunt' Novices' Hurdle Qualifier (5-y-o and up) £2,250 2m 5f. . . . . (3:20)**

2326⁴ ARTIC WINGS (Ire) 6-10-10 M Brennan, *al gng wl, mstk 4th, cld 7th, led on bit 2 out, easily.* . . . . (10 to 1 tchd 8 to 1) 1
2731⁴ GLENFINN PRINCESS 6-11-3 D Bridgwater, *hld up, cld aftr 6th, led 4 out till hdd 2 out, one pace.* . . . . (7 to 2 tchd 9 to 2) 2
2768⁴ RACE TO THE RHYTHM 7-10-10 C Llewellyn, *trkd ldrs, pushed alng appr 7th, one pace und pres frm nxt.* . . . . (5 to 1 tchd 7 to 1) 3
2667³ FLAMEWOOD 5-10-10 W Marston, *took keen hold, dsptd ld till led 5th, hdd 7th, wknd aftr nxt.* . . . . (8 to 1 op 5 to 1 tchd 10 to 1) 4
1935² LOVING AROUND (Ire) 6-10-10 M A FitzGerald, *trkd ldrs, pushed alng aftr 3 out, one pace.* . . . . (5 to 4 fav op 5 to 4 tchd 6 to 4) 5
2757⁸ COSMICECHOEXPRESS 7-10-10 S Earle, *dsptd ld till hdd 5th, wknd aftr nxt, tld off.* . . . . (66 to 1 op 33 to 1) 6
2686 GREEN WALK 7-10-5 (5*) C Burnett-Wells, *trkd ldrs, led 7th till hdd nxt, sn wknd, tld off.* (33 to 1 tchd 40 to 1) 7
2686⁶ LEINTHALL PRINCESS 8-10-10 Richard Guest, *hld up in tch till wknd 4 out, tld off.* . . . . (20 to 1 op 12 to 1) 8
2762⁸ FINALLY FANTAZIA 5-10-10 R J Beggan, *hit 1st, beh 5th, tld off whn pld up bef 2 out.* . . . . (40 to 1 op 20 to 1) pu

2785 CACAHWETE 5-10-3 (7*) Mr D Parker, *hld up in tch, drpd rear and tld off 6th, pld up bef last.

Dist: 8l, 5l, 2l, 1½l, 25l, 8l, hd. 5m 36.00s. a 37.00s (10 Ran). ....(50 to 1 op 20 to 1) pu

(Lady Anne Bentinck), O Brennan

2935 Swan National Leasing Handicap Chase (0-125 5-y-o and up) £3,574 3m 1f. ....(3:50)

2733⁴ SUNBEAM TALBOT [101] 13-10-4⁴ M FitzGerald, *trkd ldrs, pckd 11th, hrd rdn and styd on frm 4 out, lft second at last, sn led, ran on*...(14 to 1 op 10 to 1 tchd 16 to 1) 1
2733² POSTMAN'S PATH [102] 8-10-5 C Llewellyn, *hld up, hdwy 14th, outpcd appr 2 out, lft in ld last, sn hdd and no extr und pres*............(5 to 1 op 7 to 2 tchd 9 to 2) 2
2733³ SMOOTH ESCORT [103] 10-10-6 D Bridgwater, *led second till hdd 14th, sn hrd rdn and one pace.*
.................................(7 to 1 op 4 to 1) 3
2764² SHEEPHAVEN [97] 10-10-0 M Richards, *hld up in cl tch, led 5 out, clr whn f last.*............(10 to 1 op 8 to 1) f
2184 CLONROCHE GAZETTE [97] 14-10-0 Miss S Wallin, *in tch till drpd rear 9th, blun and uns rdr 13th.*
.................................(66 to 1 op 50 to 1) ur
2513⁴ THREEOUTOFFOUR [125] 9-12-0 M Brennan, *hld up in tch till wknd quickly and pld up aftr 13th.*
..............(11 to 4 op 7 to 4 tchd 3 to 1) pu
2733⁷ VIVA BELLA (Fr) [103] (bl) 7-10-1 (5*) J Burke, *led 1st, trkd ldrs, pushed alng 12th, sn lost pl, tld off whn pld up bef 2 out*..............(5 to 4 fav op 5 to 4) pu

Dist: 6l, 2l. 6m 57.10s. a 42.10s (7 Ran).
SR: 5/-/-/-/ (Mrs R Legouix), A P Jones

2936 Alfordshire Novices' Handicap Hurdle (4-y-o and up) £3,065 3m...... (4:20)

2428 MAKES ME GOOSEY (Ire) [85] 6-10-0 L Harvey, *took keen hold early, hld up in cl tch, jnd ldr whn awkward 3 out, led appr nxt, all out*............(7 to 1 op 14 to 1) 1
2515³ TEXAN BABY (Bel) [113] 5-12-0 C Llewellyn, *led til hdd appr 2 out, rdn and kpt on frm last.*
...................(3 to 1 op 5 to 2 tchd 7 to 2) 2
2505⁹ BLACK H'PENNY [88] 6-10-3 T Grantham, *hld up, hit 5th, er ch 4 out, outpcd frm nxt*......(3 to 4 fav op 7 to 2) 3
2766 GORT [109] 6-11-10 M A FitzGerald, *hld up, outpcd 8th, tld off*............(4 to 1 op 3 to 1 tchd 5 to 1) 4
2633* CELTIC TOWN [99] 6-11-0 J Osborne, *in cl tch whn f 8th.*
...................(5 to 1 op 4 to 1) f
2686 PETRADARE [85] (bl) 7-9-11 (3*) T Eley, *in tch, pushed alng 7th, sn wknd, tld off whn pld up bef 2 out.*
.................................(100 to 1 op 50 to 1) pu

Dist: 1½l, 6l, 15l. 6m 20.60s. a 34.60s (6 Ran).
SR: -/4/-/-/ (Alfordshire Ltd), Mrs I McKie

2937 John Wrathall Memorial Hunters' Chase (6-y-o and up) £1,604 3m 1f
.................................(4:50)

2807³ ARCTIC TEAL 10-12-3 (3*) Mr J Durkan, *hld up in cl tch, lft in clr ld 4 out, comf*...(9 to 1 op 7 to 1 tchd 10 to 1) 1
2807⁴ SHIPMATE 12-11-5 (7*) Miss H Irving, *made most till hdd 9th, sn drpd rear, styd on frm 3 out.*
.................................(33 to 1 op 20 to 1) 2
CLONEY GRANGE (Ire) 15-11-5 (7*) Mrs P Adams, *al hndy, led 9th till hdd and mstk 11th, sn wknd, tld off.*
.................................(40 to 1 op 25 to 1 tchd 50 to 1) 3
MISTER CHRISTIAN (NZ) (bl) 13-11-5 (7*) Mr E James, *trkd ldrs till wknd 13th, sn tld off, virtually pld up on r-in.*
...................(10 to 1 op 7 to 1 tchd 12 to 1) 4
2765* SUNNY MOUNT 8-12-6 Mr J Greenall, *in cl tch, led 11th till f 4 out*........(13 to 8 fav op 5 to 4 tchd 7 to 4) f
2800² PARSONS PLEASURE 11-11-13 (7*) Mr C Morlock, *hld up, 4th whn blun and uns rdr four out.*
.................................(4 to 1 op 7 to 2 tchd 9 to 2) ur
2765 JOHNNY'S CHOICE 8-11-12³ (3*) Mr A Hill, *hld up, cl second whn blun and hmpd 4 out, pld up bef 2 out.*
.................................(7 to 4 tchd 15 to 8) pu

Dist: 8l, 25l, 25l. 6m 59.60s. a 44.60s (7 Ran).
SR: 10/-/-/-/ (Mrs P Robeson), Mrs P Robeson

WEXFORD (IRE) (heavy)
Thursday March 10th

2938 Sports Wexford Ltd EBF Mares Maiden Hurdle (Qualifier) (4-y-o and up) £2,760 2m..................(2:30)

2587⁴ HAUNTING ANGLE (Ire) 5-11-5 (7*) T Martin, ...(9 to 4 fav) 1D
2616⁵ MARBLE FONTAINE 7-11-6 C F Swan,............(7 to 1) 1
1912⁸ ARABIAN SPRITE (Ire) 6-11-6 Mr P J Healy,.....(16 to 1) 2
2616⁹ FURRY DUCK (Ire) 6-12-0 B Sheridan, ...(6 to 1) 3
MY SUNNY GLEN 7-12-0 T Horgan, ...(13 to 2) 4
2770⁶ PILS INVADER (Ire) 6-11-1 (5*) D T Evans, ...(14 to 1) 5
FANCY STEP 8-11-11 (3*) T P Treacy, ...(11 to 2) 6
907⁵ SHUIL (Ire) 5-11-1 (3*) C O'Brien, ...(12 to 1) 7
2664⁹ VENT VERT (Ire) 6-11-6 M Duffy, ...(12 to 1) 8

DUST GALE (Ire) 5-11-4 P L Malone, ...(12 to 1) 9
2679 ANOTHER STAR (Ire) 5-11-4 M Moran, ...(20 to 1) 10
BLACK VALLEY (Ire) 5-11-1 (3*) D P Murphy, ...(20 to 1) 11
10 COOL COOPER 7-11-6 W T Slattery Jnr, ...(20 to 1) 12
1978⁸ NOBLE MADONNA (Ire) 6-11-6 K F O'Brien, ...(14 to 1) 13

Dist: 3l, 5l, 2½l, 4½l. (Time not taken) (14 Ran).
(W C Hodgins), D G Swan

2939 Pinnacle Handicap Hurdle (0-116 4-y-o and up) £2,760 2½m..........(3:00)

2658* COMMON POLICY (Ire) [-] 5-11-7 (3*) T J O'Sullivan, (6 to 1) 1
2234* BLAZING COMET [-] 8-10-2 F Woods, ...(10 to 1) 2
2284⁸ HORNER WATER (Ire) [-] 6-10-13 K F O'Brien, ..(8 to 1) 3
2617* RIYADH DANCER [-] 4-11-0 (5*) J R Barry, (9 to 4 fav) 4
2847 MYSTIC GALE (Ire) [-] 6-10-3 C F Swan, ...(10 to 1) 5
2310⁶ GRANADOS (USA) [-] 6-10-9 P Carberry, ...(12 to 1) 6
2755⁵ LADY BAR [-] 7-11-9 P M Verling, ...(8 to 1) 7
1335 TARA'S TRIBE [-] (bl) 7-10-4 M Duffy, ...(16 to 1) 8
1980⁸ GOODNIGHT IRENE (Ire) [-] 5-9-5³ (5*) M J Holbrook,
.................................(25 to 1) 9
2468⁸ ZVORNIK [-] 7-11-7 (3*) D P Murphy, ...(14 to 1) 10
2098⁵ MANTAS MELODY (Ire) [-] 6-10-4 (3*) C O'Brien, ..(12 to 1) 11
1892⁷ MOLLIE WOOTTON (Ire) [-] 6-9-12 W T Slattery Jnr, (25 to 1) 12
2586 TRAP ONE (Ire) [-] 6-9-7 (7*) D J Kavanagh, ...(25 to 1) 13
2552³ PUNTERS BAR [-] 7-10-10 C O'Dwyer, ...(8 to 1) 14
1976⁴ BETTYS THE BOSS (Ire) [-] 6-10-4 F J Flood, ...(14 to 1) 15

Dist: 2½l, ¾l, 2l, ¾l. 5m 30.00s. (15 Ran).
(Patrick O'Leary), Patrick O'Leary

2940 Garryrichard Novice Hurdle (6-y-o and up) £2,760 3m.............(3:30)

2846² CALMOS 7-11-4 C F Swan,..................(7 to 4 fav) 1
2548³ COUNTERBALANCE 7-10-13 B Sheridan, ...(10 to 1) 2
2055² DADDY LONG LEGGS 7-11-4 K F O'Brien, ...(5 to 2) 3
2618² RICH TRADITION (Ire) 6-12-0 C O'Dwyer, ...(5 to 1) 4
2616³ JOES NIGHTMARE 7-10-6 (7*) D M Drewett, ...(14 to 1) 5
636 JOHNNY THE FOX (Ire) 6-11-4 T Horgan, ...(8 to 1) 6
2863⁹ WHITBY 6-10-13 (5*) J P Broderick, ...(12 to 1) 7
2770³ BOY BLUE 7-11-4 G M O'Neill, ...(14 to 1) 8
2660³ BALLYMOE BOY (Ire) 6-10-13 (5*) K P Gaule, ...(12 to 1) 9
YOUR NEARLY THERE 8-10-13 M M Phillips, ...(20 to 1) 10
2616 WEEKLY SESSIONS (bl) 7-10-10 (3*) C O'Brien, ..(20 to 1) 11
2607 KELLYMOUNT 8-11-4 A J O'Brien, ...(12 to 1) pu
2234³ RATHNURE LADY (Ire) 6-10-6 (7*) D J Kavanagh, ..(16 to 1) pu
PADDYS TIPP (Ire) 6-11-1 (3*) T P Treacy, ...(20 to 1) pu

Dist: 5l, 15l, 11l, 3l. 6m 48.90s. (14 Ran).
(G A Murphy), A P O'Brien

2941 Bree Hunters Chase (5-y-o and up) £2,243 3m....................(4:00)

2551* ELEGANT LORD (Ire) 6-11-9 Mr E Bolger, ...(9 to 2 on) 1
GREENHALL 8-11-1¹ (3*) Mr D Valentine, ...(6 to 1) 2
SEATYRN 11-10-11 (7*) Mr B Moran, ...(16 to 1) 3
PHAIRY MIRACLES (Ire) 5-10-5¹ Mr P J Healy, ...(10 to 1) 4
CITIZEN MOSS 7-10-13 (5*) Mr W M O'Sullivan, ..(20 to 1) 5
2352² STYLISH STEPPER 9-10-11 (7*) Mr A K Wyse, ...(8 to 1) pu
15 BALLYDAY DAWN 7-10-6⁴ (7*) Mr J P Walsh, ...(25 to 1) pu
2352 BONZER BOB 8-10-11 (7*) Mr J T McNamara, ...(16 to 1) pu
SORE TOES 10-10-11 (7*) Mr W F Codd, ...(16 to 1) pu

Dist: 13l, 15l, 1½l, dist. 7m 1.00s. (9 Ran).
(John P McManus), E Bolger

2942 Red Mills Handicap Chase (0-102 5-y-o and up) £2,760 3m...........(4:30)

2101² NEW CO (Ire) [-] 5-11-7 C O'Dwyer, ...(9 to 4 fav) 1
2589⁷ ROYAL SEER [-] 8-11-5 L P Cusack, ...(7 to 1) 2
2589⁸ BOG LEAF VI [-] 11-9-4 (3*) C O'Brien, ...(10 to 1) 3
2772* MERLYNS CHOICE [-] 10-10-11 (4ex) T Horgan, ...(3 to 1) 4
906 MISCHIEF MOON [-] (bl) 9-11-3 (3*) D P Murphy, ..(16 to 1) 5
2589³ DEEP ISLE [-] 8-9-13 (5*) J P Broderick, ...(3 to 1) 6
THE QUIET MAN [-] 10-11-5 D H O'Connor, ...(7 to 1) pu
1612 WADI RUM [-] (bl) 8-10-10 J Shortt, ...(12 to 1) pu

Dist: 2l, ½l, 3l, 12l. 7m 10.30s. (8 Ran).
(Mrs L C Ronan), M F Morris

2943 Park House Stud Mares INH Flat Race (4-y-o and up) £2,760 2½m.....(5:00)

2028² THE BLUEBELL POLKA (Ire) 5-11-9 (5*) Mr H F Cleary,
.................................(4 to 1) 1
2394⁴ SISTER ALICE (Ire) 6-12-0 Mr P Fenton, ...(5 to 1) 2
FANDANGOLD 8-11-7 (7*) Mr E Norris, ...(25 to 1) 3
2155² LOTTOVER (Ire) 5-11-12 Mr J A Berry, ...(7 to 4 fav) 4
2464 MURPHY'S LADY (Ire) 5-11-5 (7*) Mr K Whelan, ..(20 to 1) 5
2660⁴ MISGIVINGS (Ire) 6-11-11 (3*) Miss M Olivefalk, ..(8 to 1) 6
BALLOUGH BUI (Ire) 5-11-12 Mr M J Holohan, ...(12 to 1) 7
2663⁵ KILCARBERY (Ire) 4-10-13 (3*) Mrs J M Mullins, ..(6 to 1) 8
THAT'S GOSPEL (Ire) 4-10-9 (7*) Mr J J Holohan, (12 to 1) 9
2203 BALLYHARRON 7-11-7 (7*) Mr J S Cullen, ...(25 to 1) 10
LOUGH NEAGH LADY 8-11-7 (7*) Mr D A Harney, ..(12 to 1) 11
2470 SLEMISH MIST 7-11-9 (5*) Mr G J Harford, ...(14 to 1) 12
2041³ CARRIG DANCER (Ire) 6-11-7 (7*) Mr M Budds, ...(14 to 1) 13
907⁴ TOURIG LE MOSS 7-11-7 (7*) Mr R J Foley, ...(14 to 1) 14

410

2553 RIGHT AND REASON (Ire) 5-11-5 (7*) Mr P M Cloke, ...(25 to 1) 15
Dist: 3½l, 2½l, 11l, 5l. 5m 36.80s. (15 Ran).
(Foster & Allen Syndicate), F Flood

2944 Bookmakers Pro/Am INH Flat Race (5-y-o) £2,760 2¼m.............. (5:30)

2869 SPANKERS HILL (Ire) 11-4 (7*) Mr P English, ...(20 to 1) 1
2465[4] TELLTALK (Ire) 11-4 (7*) Mr E Norris, ...(5 to 1) 2
2199 ROCK POOL 11-6 (5*) Mr H F Cleary, ...(7 to 4 fav) 3
2684[2] CORYMANDEL (Ire) 11-4 (7*) Mr D Carey, ...(7 to 2) 4
2470[7] SWEET CALLERNISH (Ire) 11-4 (7*) J M Donnelly, (14 to 1) 5
ANGEL'S BIT (Ire) 10-13 (7*) Mrs K Walsh, ...(25 to 1) 6
EVEN FLOW (Ire) 11-4 (7*) Mr M McCullagh, ...(10 to 1) 7
2684[6] OH RIVER (Ire) 11-1 (5*) Mr J P Berry, ...(14 to 1) 8
2620 SALMOOSKY (Ire) 10-13 (7*) Mr B Lennon, ...(20 to 1) 9
SIR JOHN (Ire) 11-4 (7*) J Butler, ... (16 to 1) 10
2039 LANCASTER COURT (Ire) 10-13 (7*) Mr J S Cullen, (25 to 1) 11
531[5] SLANEY GENT (Ire) 11-4 (7*) Miss L E A Doyle, ...(14 to 1) 12
BOLD TIPPERARY (Ire) 10-13 (7*) D O'Driscoll, ...(14 to 1) 13
ROSEL WALK (Ire) 11-6 (5*) Mr J P O'Brien, ...(16 to 1) pu
BLUE MONOPOLY (Ire) 11-4 (7*) C Eyre, ... (6 to 1) pu
Dist: 1l, 11l, 5l, 12l. 4m 43.10s. (15 Ran).
(Three Rock Syndicate), S J Treacy

WINCANTON (good)
Thursday March 10th

Going Correction: PLUS 0.50 sec. per fur. (races 1,3,6), PLUS 0.90 (2,4,5)

2945 Sparkford Novices' Claiming Hurdle (4-y-o) £1,882 2m..............(2:00)

2763 MR GENEAOLOGY (USA) (bl) 11-12 A Maguire, *al prmnt, trkd ldr frm 4th, led and lft clr 2 out, easily.*
.......(Evens fav op 11 to 10 tchd 11 to 8 and 6 to 4) 1
2000[7] SOUTHAMPTON 10-9 (5*) S Fox, *hld up in rear, blun 5th, rdn and hdwy 3 out, blunded last, rallied to go second cl hme.*..........(100 to 30 op 5 to 2 tchd 7 to 2) 2
2522[6] POCONO KNIGHT 10-12 G Upton, *hld up in tch, rdn to cl on ldrs 3 out, lft second and hit nxt, wknd r-in.*
.... (10 to 1 op 7 to 1) 3
2652 WALID'S PRINCESS (Ire) (bl) 10-6[1] J Frost, *trkd ldr to 4th, wknd nxt*.................(50 to 1 tchd 66 to 1) 4
2189 FATHER'S JOY 10-5 M Stevens, *f 1st.* (66 to 1 op 50 to 1) f
470[4] RED MICKS WIFE (Ire) 9-10 (7*) D Hobbs, *in rear, blun badly and uns rdr 3 out.*
......................(14 to 1 op 10 to 1 tchd 16 to 1) ur
2492[2] NANQUIDNO 10-2 (7*) T Dascombe, *led, rdn and jst hdd whn blun and uns rdr 2 out.*
.........................(9 to 2 op 3 to 1 tchd 5 to 1) ur
HARQUIN 11-10 N Mann, *prmnt, wkng whn mstk 3 out, sn tld off, pld up bef nxt*..........(20 to 1 op 12 to 1) pu
Dist: 30l, 2l, 8l. 4m 0.60s. a 23.60s (8 Ran).
(Mrs P A White), J White

2946 Forke Farm Mares Only Novices' Chase (5-y-o and up) £2,876 2m 5f ....(2:30)

2803[2] LADY GHISLAINE (Fr) 7-11-2 A Maguire, *led to tenth, cl second whn hit 5 out, steadied and ran on to ld 2 out, cmftbly.*
.... (13 to 8 fav op 7 to 4 tchd 2 to 1 and 6 to 4) 1
2146[2] PRUDENT PEGGY 7-11-8 J Frost, *jmpd wl, wth wnr, led tenth till hdd 2 out, kpt on one pace.* (6 to 1 op 5 to 1) 2
2299 PHYL'S LEGACY 9-11-2 G McCourt, *in rear till hdwy 8th, wkng whn f 11th*.................(50 to 1 op 33 to 1) f
2767[5] HOW DOUDO 7-11-2 R Bellamy, *mid-div till 7th, wl beh whn f 11th*........................(9 to 1 op 6 to 1) f
LITTLE CLARE 7-11-2 N Mann, *f second.*
.... (50 to 1 op 33 to 1) f
2759[8] FANTASY WORLD 8-11-2 D Murphy, *hld up, hdwy 6th, wknd tenth, remote and tired 3rd whn f last.*
.... (5 to 1 op 4 to 1 tchd 11 to 2) f
2693 PINE VALE 6-10-11 (5*) S Fox, *al towards rear, blun 8th, disputing 3rd but tld off whn f last.*
......................(25 to 1 op 12 to 1 tchd 33 to 1) f
2858[3] FRENCH PLEASURE 8-11-2 P Holley, *prmnt till blun and uns rdr 7th*..........................(7 to 2 op 3 to 1) ur
2527 COOMBESBURY LANE (bl) 8-11-2 W McFarland, *prmnt, wkng and btn 3rd whn jmpd slwly 4 out, tld off when refused last*.......................(16 to 1 op 10 to 1) ref
1805 STAPLEFORD LADY 6-11-2 B Powell, *prmnt, mstk 4th, wknd tenth, tld off whn pld up bef 3 out.*
.... (25 to 1 op 16 to 1) pu
2732 BRORA ROSE (Ire) 6-10-9 (7*) Miss S Cobden, *jmpd badly in rear, blun 9th, sn pld up*........(50 to 1 op 20 to 1) pu
CHASING GOLD 8-11-2 Peter Hobbs, *slwly away, blun 1st, tld off whn blunded 9th, sn pld up.*
.... (66 to 1 op 50 to 1) pu
Dist: 6l. 5m 37.50s. a 31.50s (12 Ran).
(Mrs P A White), J White

2947 Tommy Wallis Handicap Hurdle (0-135 4-y-o and up) £3,512 2m........ (3:00)

1842[4] ARABIAN BOLD (Ire) [128] 6-12-0 J R Kavanagh, *made all, rdn appr 2 out, sn drw clr.*
.... (15 to 8 op 5 to 4 tchd 2 to 1) 1
2655[2] AAL EL AAL [100] 7-10-0 Peter Hobbs, *chsd wnr thrght, hit 3 out, rdn and hld whn mstk nxt, no ch wth winner aftr.* (6 to 5 on op Evens tchd 11 to 10 and 5 to 4 on) 2
2455[2] SUN SURFER (Fr) [128] 6-12-0 B Powell, *in tch till rdn and outpcd frm 3 out*.................... (7 to 1 op 5 to 1) 3
2781[2] ALOSAILI [100] 7-10-0 A Maguire, *hld up, rdn and wnt 3rd briefly aftr 3 out, sn btn.*
.........(12 to 1 op 14 to 1 tchd 16 to 1 and 20 to 1) 4
1474 SOUTHOVER LAD (NZ) [106] 11-10-6[1] J Frost, *mstk 1st, blun and uns rdr second*.......... (33 to 1 op 16 to 1) ur
Dist: 8l, 12l, 6l. 3m 49.10s. a 12.10s (5 Ran).
SR: 59/23/39/5/-/ (Sheikh Amin Dahlawi), N J Henderson

2948 'Wincanton Ltd' Handicap Chase (0-140 5-y-o and up) £5,280 2m 5f (3:30)

2852[4] SMARTIE EXPRESS [124] 12-11-5 A Maguire, *hld up, hdwy tenth, led last, rdn out.* (5 to 1 op 4 to 1 tchd 11 to 2) 1
2747 ROUGH QUEST [130] 8-11-11 G McCourt, *hld up, gd hdwy 9th, led sn aftr 3 out, hdd last, hrd drvn and no extr fnl 50 yards*.........(11 to 10 fav op 5 to 4 tchd 11 to 8) 2
2747 GHOFAR [115] (bl) 11-10-10 P Holley, *al in tch, trkd ldr 9th to 5 out, ev ch till outpcd frm 2 out.*
.... (10 to 1 op 8 to 1 tchd 11 to 1) 3
ESHA NESS [133] 11-12-0 J White, *jmpd wl, trkd ldrs second to 9th, wnt second ag'n 5 out, ev ch whn slightly bumped 3 out, one pace, fnshd lme.*
.... (14 to 1 op 8 to 1 tchd 16 to 1) 4
1088* PANTO PRINCE [132] 13-11-13 B Powell, *led till hdd 5 out, pld up sn aftr, lme*................ (11 to 4 op 2 to 1) pu
SKETCHER (NZ) [105] 11-10-0 D Gallagher, *chsd ldr till hit second, wkng whn mstk tenth, hit 12th, tld off when pld up bef 4 out*......(33 to 1 op 16 to 1 tchd 50 to 1) pu
Dist: 1½l, 3½l, 5l. 5m 29.70s. a 23.70s (6 Ran).
SR: 43/47/28/41/-/-/ (S J Norman), R J Hodges

2949 Dick Woodhouse Hunters' Chase (5-y-o and up) £1,882 3m 1f 110yds (4:00)

SYNDERBOROUGH LAD 8-11-7 (7*) Mr M Felton, *pld hrd, rstrained in rear, steady hdwy 13th, led 4 out, all out whn lft clr last.*
............(6 to 1 op 9 to 2 tchd 13 to 2 and 7 to 1) 1
SONOFAGIPSY 10-12-0 (7*) Mr R Nuttall, *hld up, hdwy to track ldr 13th, wknd 4 out, lft poor second last.*
.... (16 to 1 op 8 to 1) 2
CONNATE (bl) 9-11-9 (5*) Miss P Curling, *nvr far away, chsd ldr 5th till mstk 13th, wknd appr 4 out.*
................................(4 to 1 op 3 to 1 tchd 9 to 2) 3
GLEN OAK 9-11-7 (7*) Mr J Pritchard, *beh whn mstk 4th, tld off 5 out, styd on frm 3 out*..... (50 to 1 op 33 to 1) 4
ABBOTSHAM 9-11-7 (7*) Mr D Pipe, *led till hdd 4 out, wknd quickly, tld off.* (11 to 1 op 8 to 1 tchd 12 to 1) 5
2724[2] MR MURDOCK 9-12-4 (3*) Mr R Alner, *not jump wl, trkd ldr till lost pl aftr jmpd slwly 5th, hdwy to chal 3 out, ev ch whn f last.*
(11 to 8 on op 5 to 4 on tchd 6 to 5 on and 6 to 4 on) f
2765[5] KINGS GUNNER 7-11-7 (7*) Miss S Vickery, *chsd ldrs till hit tenth, wkng whn f 12th*........(25 to 1 op 12 to 1) f
Dist: 30l, sht-hd, hd, dist. 6m 56.00s. a 40.00s (7 Ran).
(Stewart Pike), S Pike

2950 EBF 'National Hunt' Novices' Hurdle Qualifier (5,6,7-y-o) £2,197 2m.. (4:30)

2302[7] CHEMIN LE ROI 7-11-0 I Lawrence, *al prmnt, trkd ldr frm 4th, chlgd 2 out, hit last, led r-in, all out.*
....(7 to 1 op 5 to 1) 1
2642* GLENGARRA PRINCESS 7-10-11 (3*) J McCarthy, *led, rdn 2 out, hdd r-in*........ (2 to 1 fav op 7 to 4 tchd 9 to 2) 2+
2749 KING LUCIFER (Ire) 5-11-0 A Maguire, *beh till hdwy 2 out, ran on strly aftr nxt, nvr nrr*........ (4 to 1 op 6 to 1) 2+
2728[5] BEAUREPAIRE (Ire) 6-11-0 D Murphy, *hld up in mid-div, hdwy 3 out, ran on one pace frm nxt.*
.... (11 to 2 op 4 to 1 tchd 6 to 1) 4
FOX ON THE RUN 7-11-0 S McNeill, *al abt same pl, hdwy 3 out, kpt on one pace frm nxt*...... (14 to 1 op 10 to 1) 5
2147 FOUR HEARTS (Ire) 5-11-0 B Powell, *mid-div, nvr nr to chal*................. (12 to 1 op 10 to 1 tchd 16 to 1) 6
1542 FERNY BALL (Ire) 6-11-0 Peter Hobbs, *hld up, hdwy to go 3rd 3 out, wknd bef nxt*............(66 to 1 op 33 to 1) 7
1946[7] POLDEN PRIDE 6-10-11 (3*) R Davis, *al beh, effrt 3 out, nvr dngrs*.............................. (66 to 1 op 33 to 1) 8
2426 MAGGIE TEE 6-10-9 G Upton, *beh, hdwy whn hit 3 out, sn btn*.................................... (66 to 1 op 50 to 1) 9
2426 TITAN EMPRESS 5-10-9 M Perrett, *al in rear, tld off.*
.... (50 to 1 op 25 to 1) 10
2444* SEBASTOPOL 5-11-0 G Bradley, *chsd ldrs till wknd quickly 3 out, tld off*.................(5 to 1 op 9 to 2) 11
2315 EXE CRACKER 5-11-0 N Mann, *in rear whn f 3rd.*
.... (50 to 1 op 33 to 1 tchd 66 to 1) f

PAUL'S PRINCESS 7-10-4 (5") D Matthews, *al beh, tld off whn pld up bef 2 out*............. (66 to 1 op 50 to 1)   pu
AUGER BORE (Ire) 6-11-0 S Burnough, *al beh, tld off whn pld up bef 2 out*....................(66 to 1)   pu
2505 CELESTIAL STREAM 7-10-11 (3") R Farrant, *pld hrd, chsd ldr to 4th, wknd quickly, tld off whn pulled up bef 2 out*.................... (66 to 1 op 50 to 1)   pu
2332[7] HURRICANE SUE 5-10-9 R Greene, *beh whn hmpd 3rd, sn tld off, pld up bef 2 out*.................. (50 to 1)   pu
Dist: ¾l, dd-ht, 3l, nk, 25l, 1½l, 6l, 1½l, 15l, dist. 3m 57.00s. a 20.00s (16 Ran).

(Mrs Elizabeth Hitchins), Mrs J Pitman

AYR (soft (Races 1,4,6), good to soft (2,3,5)) Friday March 11th
Going Correction: PLUS 1.65 sec. per fur.

2951
Lagg Maiden Hurdle (4-y-o and up) £2,071 2m..................... (2:20)

2220[7] CAITHNESS CLOUD 6-11-7 B Storey, *made virtually all, hrd pressed frm 3 out, kpt on wl und pres nr finish.*
.... (100 to 30 op 7 to 2 tchd 4 to 1)   1
2573[2] CROMARTY 4-10-3 (5") A Roche, *hld up, hdwy hfwy, chlgd 3 out, slightly hmpd nxt, dsptd ld last, no extr nr finish*..............(11 to 10 fav tchd 5 to 4 and Evens)   2
2741[3] TEMPLERAINEY (Ire) 6-11-2 (5") P Williams, *trkd ldrs, chlgd 3 out, ev ch whn blun nxt, sn btn....* (8 to 1 op 5 to 1)   3
2373[7] OAT COUTURE 6-11-7 T Reed, *dsptd ld till outpcd appr 3 out, no dngr aftr*.................(20 to 1 op 12 to 1)   4
2106[8] EASBY JOKER 6-11-7 R Garritty, *hld up, hdwy hfwy, ev ch appr 3 out, sn rdn and wknd.*
.... (100 to 30 op 9 to 4 tchd 7 to 2)   5
PREAMBLE 5-11-2 A Merrigan, *in tch till wknd aftr 6th.*
.... (100 to 1 op 50 to 1)   6
2447[7] GOING PUBLIC 7-11-7 K Johnson, *nvr nr ldrs.*
.... (33 to 1 op 20 to 1)   7
723[3] KIRKTON GLEN 5-11-0 (7") Mr D Parker, *beh frm 6th.*
.... (66 to 1 op 33 to 1)   8
CANAAN VALLEY 6-11-7 Mr D Robertson, *dwlt, in tch till wknd aftr 5th, tld off whn pld up bef 2 out.*
.... (50 to 1 op 33 to 1)   pu
CORBY KNOWE 8-11-7 A Dobbin, *lost tch frm 5th, tld off whn pld up bef 2 out*................. (50 to 1 op 33 to 1)   pu
2373 AFRICAN GOLD 6-11-2 (5") F Perratt, *lost tch aftr 4th, tld off whn pld up bef 3 out*.........(100 to 1 op 50 to 1)   pu
2741[8] GLORIOUS HEIGHTS 6-11-2 P Niven, *mid-div till wknd aftr 6th, tld off whn pld up bef 2 out.*
.... (100 to 1 op 50 to 1)   pu
Dist: Sht-hd, 8l, 12l, 7l, 15l, 15l, 2l. 4m 10.00s. a 33.00s (12 Ran).
SR: 27/14/19/7/-/-/   (Raymond Anderson Green), C Parker

2952
Hollybush Novices' Chase (5-y-o and up) £2,606 3m 1f.............. (2:55)

2238[6] DUCHESS OF TUBBER (Ire) 6-10-9 (3") A Thornton, *in tch, rdn appr 3 out, styd on to ld aftr last, sn clr.*
.... (10 to 1 op 8 to 1 tchd 12 to 1)   1
2814[6] COUNT SURVEYOR 7-11-3 K Johnson, *al cl up, led appr last, sn hdd, no extr...* (9 to 1 op 7 to 1 tchd 10 to 1)   2
2784[2] UNGUIDED MISSILE (Ire) 6-11-3 N Doughty, *led, hit 9th, hdd appr last, sn btn.*........ (5 to 4 on op 5 to 4 on)   3
2739[3] KIRKCALDY (Ire) 5-10-2 (5") P Williams, *beh frm hfwy, some late hdwy, nvr dngrs.*........................(14 to 1)   4
2809[5] KILCOLGAN 7-11-3 A Dobbin, *in tch, reminders aftr 7th, pushed alng hfwy, outpcd appr 15th, no dngr after.*
.... (9 to 1 op 7 to 1 tchd 10 to 1)   5
2577[3] PIT PONY 10-11-3 T Reed, *cl up, disputing ld whn blun badly 2 out, not reco'r*............(20 to 1 op 12 to 1)   6
2894[8] SCOTTISH GOLD (v) 10-11-10 P Niven, *beh whn blun and uns rdr 4th.*.......................(12 to 1 op 7 to 1)   ur
2809[7] MOW CREEK 10-10-10 (7") A Watt, *al beh, no ch whn blun and uns rdr 2 out.*............. (100 to 1 op 33 to 1)   ur
2577[4] CAITHNESS PRINCE 8-11-3 B Storey, *in tch till pld up lme bef 6th*.......................... (8 to 1)   pu
2497[7] MY PARTNER (Ire) 6-11-3 K Jones, *chsd ldrs till wknd quickly aftr 11th, tld off whn pld up bef 13th.*
.... (33 to 1 op 25 to 1)   pu
Dist: 3l, 3½l, 5l, 3½l, 2l. 7m 3.90s. a 63.90s (10 Ran).
(Great Head House Estates Limited), R F Fisher

2953
Mad March Hare Handicap Chase (0-130 5-y-o and up) £3,062 2½m (3:30)

2574* RIVER PEARL [99] 9-10-13 T Reed, *hld up and beh, steady hdwy aftr 12th, led last, styd on wl.*
.... (5 to 2 op 9 to 4 tchd 11 to 4)   1
2786[3] CANDY TUFF [110] 8-11-10 P Niven, *led or dsptd ld till blun 9th, led 12th, hdd last, no extr.*
.... (7 to 4 fav op 9 to 4 tchd 5 to 2)   2
2574[3] DEEP DECISION [97] 8-10-11 K Johnson, *in tch, jnd ldr aftr 13th, ev ch 3 out, sn rdn and one pace.*
.... (9 to 1 op 7 to 2)   3
2832[4] BOARDING SCHOOL [101] 7-11-1 B Storey, *trkd ldrs, led 8th till hdd 12th, sn outpcd, no dngr aftr.*
.... (9 to 1 op 11 to 4)   4

2574 FUNNY OLD GAME [89] 7-10-0 (3") A Thornton, *in tch, jnd ldrs 12th, wknd aftr 4 out*...........(9 to 1 op 6 to 1)   5
2105 ZAM BEE [107] 8-11-7 C Grant, *dsptd ld to 6th, lost tch aftr 11th*........................(25 to 1 op 16 to 1)   6
Dist: 1½l, 10l, 8l, 12l, ½l. 5m 35.80s. a 48.80s (6 Ran).
(Mrs A G Martin), L Lungo

2954
Rosemount Handicap Hurdle (0-120 4-y-o and up) £2,242 3m 110yds (4:05)

2766* RUSTINO [94] 8-10-10 (4ex) P Niven, *mid-div, chsd ldr and reminders aftr 9th, led appr 3 out, sn clr.*
.... (11 to 8 on op 5 to 4 on tchd 6 to 4 on)   1
2766[4] MISS CAPULET [85] (bl) 7-9-12 (3") D Meredith, *cl up, led 8th, hdd appr 3 out, kpt on, no imprsn.*
.... (13 to 2 op 6 to 1 tchd 7 to 1)   2
2737[9] VALIANT DASH [100] 8-10-11 (5") F Perratt, *in tch, outpcd aftr 9th, kpt on frm 3 out, nvr dngrs.*......(66 to 1)   3
2153 ROSE TABLEAU [104] 11-11-1 (5") A Roche, *beh 7th, kpt on frm 3 out, nvr dngrs.*...........(20 to 1 op 16 to 1)   4
2822[5] CELTIC BREEZE [94] (v) 11-10-3 (7") Mr D Parker, *led till hdd 6th, sn drvn alng, wknd aftr 8th....*(10 to 1 op 8 to 1)   5
2740[2] THE GREEN FOOL [108] 7-11-10 A Dobbin, *hld up, hdwy hfwy, chsd clr ldrs aftr 9th, wknd after 3 out.*
.... (9 to 1 op 7 to 1)   6
2153[5] TRUMP [95] 5-10-11 B Storey, *hld up, hdwy hfwy, hrd rdn aftr 9th, wknd quickly*............(8 to 1 op 7 to 1)   7
2502[5] SANSOOL [96] 8-10-12 M Moloney, *blun second, sn beh, tld off whn pld up bef 8th.*
.... (10 to 1 op 8 to 1 tchd 11 to 1)   pu
THISTLEHOLM [112] 8-12-0 C Grant, *mid-div till wknd quickly aftr 8th, tld off whn pld up bef 3 out.*
.... (20 to 1 op 16 to 1 tchd 25 to 1)   pu
2737[7] CLASSIC MINSTREL [85] 10-10-1[6] (5") P Williams, *trkd ldrs, slight ld 6th till hdd 8th, wknd quickly aftr nxt, wl beh whn pld up bef last.*........................(50 to 1)   pu
Dist: 6l, 20l, 10l, 12l, 8l, 20l. 6m 37.00s. a 51.00s (10 Ran).
(Mrs E A Kettlewell), Mrs M Reveley

2955
Ayrshire Hunters' Challenge Cup Novices' Hunters' Chase (5-y-o and up) £1,450 2m 5f 110yds........ (4:35)

2687* MINERS MELODY (Ire) 6-12-2 Mr J Greenall, *sn cl up, led 12th, styd on wl frm 4 out.*
.... (4 to 1 on tchd 7 to 2 on and 9 to 2 on)   1
2793 CLONONY CASTLE (bl) 8-11-5 (5") Mr N Wilson, *trkd ldr frm 9th, reminders aftr 12th, chalg wnr whn mstk 4 out, mistakes last 2, no imprsn.*..........(66 to 1 op 12 to 1)   2
2687[2] SPARTAN RANGER 9-11-3 (7") Mr C Bonner, *led till hdd 12th, sn wknd...........* (4 to 1 op 3 to 1 tchd 9 to 2)   3
755 THE RAMBLING MAN 7-11-5 (5") Mr R Hale, *mstks, beh frm tenth, tld off whn pld up bef 14th...*(12 to 1 op 6 to 1)   pu
ST ELMO'S FIRE (NZ) 9-11-8[3] (5") Mr J M Dun, *tld off whn pld up bef 11th*........................(66 to 1 op 12 to 1)   pu
Dist: 3½l, dist. 6m 4.80s. a 59.80s (5 Ran).
(J E Greenall), P Cheesbrough

2956
Doon Handicap Hurdle (0-125 4-y-o and up) £2,221 2m..............(5:10)

2243[9] MASTER OF TROY [97] 6-9-8 (7") Mr D Parker, *hld up, hdwy appr 3 out, led aftr last, ran on wl.*
.... (9 to 4 op 3 to 1 tchd 2 to 1)   1
2449[2] DIZZY (USA) [120] 6-11-10 A Dobbin, *trkd ldrs, led 3 out, hdd aftr last, no extr.*
.... (11 to 8 fav op Evens tchd 6 to 4)   2
2498[5] HAMANAKA (USA) [98] 5-10-2[2] Mr S Love, *led till hdd 3 out, sn btn........*..................(66 to 1 op 25 to 1)   3
2360[7] NOTABLE EXCEPTION [101] 5-10-5 P Niven, *trkd ldr, effrt aftr 3 out, wknd aftr nxt...........*(2 to 1 op 9 to 4)   4
2005[8] RINGLAND (USA) [96] 6-9-7 (7") Carol Cuthbert, *reared strt, sn reco'red, in tch, mstk 5th, rdn appr 3 out, soon btn.*
.... (16 to 1 op 20 to 1 tchd 14 to 1)   5
Dist: ¾l, 10l, 3½l, ½l. 4m 20.40s. a 43.40s (5 Ran).
(Chilton Fawcett), C Parker

MARKET RASEN (good to soft) Friday March 11th
Going Correction: PLUS 0.55 sec. per fur. (races 1,4,-5,7), PLUS 1.45 (2,3,6)

2957
Cranwell Selling Hurdle (4 & 5-y-o) £1,861 2m 1f 110yds...........(2:10)

2634[3] BITRAN 4-10-8 A S Smith, *made all, clr frm 4 out, won easing dwn.*............(5 to 2 fav op 3 to 1 tchd 9 to 4)   1
2797[5] ERLEMO (v) 5-11-2 Diane Clay, *nvr far away, bustled alng whn ldg, quickened 4 out, styd on, no ch whn wnr.*
.... (13 to 1 op 5 to 1)   2
1655 MISSED THE BOAT (Ire) 4-10-8 Gary Lyons, *patiently rdn, improved to chase wnr hfwy, ridden and one pace frm 3 out.*........................(9 to 1 op 7 to 2)   3
2414[3] MARSHALL PINDARI 4-10-8 D Bridgwater, *in tch, improved into midfield hfwy, chsd alng frm 3 out, no extr.*........................(8 to 1 op 12 to 1)   4

2763 WATER DIVINER 4-10-8 J Ryan, *chsd ldg bunch, drvn alng frm hfwy, one pace from 3 out* .... (16 to 1) 5
26347 ANNE CARTER 5-10-11 M Ranger, *chsd alng in midfield, struggling 4 out, no extr* .... (33 to 1) 6
2485 WHATCOMESNATURALLY (USA) 5-10-4 (7*) R Moore, *bustled alng to go pace thrght, nvr able to rch ldrs*.
.... (12 to 1) 7
ARJIL 5-11-2 R Campbell, *trkd ldr, nrly f second, struggling abt aftr 4 out, fdd*.
.... (13 to 2 op 5 to 1 tchd 7 to 1) 8
2790 SEATWIST 5-10-13 (3*) T Eley, *shvd up wl wth chasing bunch till fdd aftr 4 out* .... (25 to 1 op 20 to 1) 9
2291 WOODYARD 5-11-2 V Slattery, *chsd ldg quartet, rdn hfwy, fdd* .... (33 to 1) 10
SULAAH ROSE 5-10-11 M Hourigan, *chsd ldg bunch to hfwy, sn tld off* .... (50 to 1) 11
2763 HARLOSH 4-10-6³ (5*) P Midgley, *settled wth chasing bunch, drvn alng appr 4 out, sn btn* ....(33 to 1) 12
18137 RELENTED 5-10-4 (7*) P McLoughlin, *chsd alng to go pace frm 4th, nvr a factor* .... (20 to 1 op 16 to 1) 13
1811 SALMON DANCER (Ire) 5-11-2 M Brennan, *al struggling, tld off frm hfwy* .... (50 to 1) 14
19984 ALBERSTAN (v) 4-10-8 S D Williams, *beh and struggling 4th, tld off whn pld up bef 3 out*.. (33 to 1 op 25 to 1) pu
MISS TYKE 4-10-3 W Worthington, *tld off till pld up appr 4th* .... (12 to 1 op 10 to 1) pu
Dist: 12l, 25l, 25l, 2l, 2l, ¾l, 12l, 12l, 20l, 6l. 4m 18.00s. a 16.00s (16 Ran).
SR: 16/12/-/-/-/-/   (W A Fouracres), K A Morgan

2958 Bet With The Tote Novices' Chase Qualifier (6-y-o and up) £3,249 3m 1f ....(2:45)

27673 HUDSON BAY TRADER (USA) 7-10-10 Mrs A Farrell, *nvr far away, scrubbed alng fnl circuit, 2 ls second whn lft clr last* .... (6 to 1 op 5 to 1) 1
URIZEN 9-10-10 C Hawkins, *mstks, al hndy, rdn and ev ch aftr 4 out, no extr frm betw last 2*.
.... (10 to 1 tchd 12 to 1) 2
2786* PRINCE YAZA 7-11-10 L O'Hara, *trkd ldrs, rdn whn pace lifted appr 4 out, plodded round* ..... (7 to 1 op 6 to 1) 3
2489* SUPPOSIN 6-11-3 Richard Guest, *dsptd early ld, ran on snatches, rdn frm 5 out, tld off* ...... (9 to 2 op 4 to 1) 4
22706 FIRST LORD 8-10-10 J Callaghan, *dsptd ld to 3rd, struggling hfwy, tld off* .... (33 to 1) 5
2767² COMEDY SPY 10-10-10 M Hourigan, *made most, quickened to go clr bef 4 out, 2 ls clear whn f last*.
.... (11 to 8 fav op 6 to 4) f
SUNCIA 10-10-5 Gee Armitage, *unruly strt, last and struggling whn blun and uns rdr 6th*.
.... (25 to 1 op 20 to 1) ur
Dist: 15l, 25l, 15l, 3l. 6m 44.90s. a 43.90s (7 Ran).
SR: 6/-/-/-/-/   (P C N Curtis), P Beaumont

2959 Beaumontcote Hunters' Chase (5-y-o and up) £1,856 3m 1f .... (3:15)

27936 VERY CHEERING 11-11-7 (7*) Mr B Crawford, *not jump wl, chsd alng to take clr order fnl circuit, styd on grimly to ld r-in* .... (14 to 1) 1
2456 ROYAL DAY 8-12-2 (5*) Mr R Russell, *dsptd ld, definite advantage 5th, hit 4 out, rdn and ct r-in*.
.... (3 to 1 op 5 to 2) 2
2838² CARRICKMINES 9-12-0 (5*) Mr T Jones, *slight ld to 5th, styd hndy and rdn alng 7 out, kpt on same pace last 3*.
.... (13 to 8 fav op 11 to 10) 3
2807⁵ ASHPIT 13-11-7 (7*) Mr T Garton, *nvr far away, feeling pace and drvn alng 5 out, outpcd aftr nxt, sn btn*.
.... (8 to 1 op 7 to 1) 4
DURIGHT 11-11-4 (5*) Mr N Tutty, *nvr far away, tracking ldr whn blun 6 out, rdn alng appr 3 out, fdd*.
.... (7 to 2 tchd 4 to 1) 5
ST ENTON 9-11-7 (7*) Mr K Green, *tracking ldrs whn blun and uns rdr second* .... (33 to 1 op 20 to 1) ur
JERRIGO 9-11-7 (7*) Mr M Sowersby, *rcd wide, pressed ldrs, ev ch fnl circuit, fdd 4 out, pld up before last*.
.... (14 to 1) pu
Dist: 3l, 8l, 20l, 6l. 6m 55.10s. a 54.10s (7 Ran).
                                                (Tim Brown), Miss M Rowland

2960 Scampton Maiden Claiming Hurdle (4,5,6-y-o) £2,530 2m 1f 110yds. . (3:50)

2763 BETTY KENWOOD (bl) 4-10-2 (3*) R Farrant, *settled midfield, chsd alng to improve 3 out, led bef last, forged clr*.
.... (9 to 4 fav op 5 to 2 tchd 11 to 4) 1
21644 BIRD WATCHER 5-11-3 (3*) D Bentley, *nvr far away, nosed ahead appr 2 out, hdd betw last two, not quicken r-in*.
.... (10 to 1) 2
2405 INNA (USA) 5-11-8 M Dwyer, *patiently rdn, steady hdwy frm 3 out, ev ch aftr nxt, found little r-in* ...(10 to 1) 3
2537³ CZAR NICHOLAS (v) 5-11-12 W Worthington, *made most till hdd appr 2 out, rdn and no extr betw last two*.
.... (10 to 1 op 8 to 1) 4
28028 BOZO BAILEY 4-10-12 R Campbell, *wtd wth, took clr order appr 3 out, ev ch aftr nxt, no extr*.
.... (13 to 2 op 5 to 1 tchd 7 to 1) 5

2573 WANG HOW 6-11-10 D Wilkinson, *settled off the pace, styd on frm 3 out, nrst finish* ...... (16 to 1 op 20 to 1) 6
16546 MUST BE MAGICAL (USA) 6-11-4 D Bridgwater, *wth ldrs, led briefly hfwy, hit 3 out, fdd frm nxt*.
.... (10 to 1 op 9 to 2) 7
2057 CRIMINAL RECORD (USA) (v) 4-11-2 Diane Clay, *pressed ldrs, rdn aftr 4 out, fdd* ....(14 to 1 op 12 to 1) 8
THEYDON PRIDE 5-10-11 (7*) P McLoughlin, *in tch, drvn alng to keep up appr 3 out, sn btn*. (33 to 1 op 25 to 1) 9
2275 KATIE'S BOY 4-10-12 A S Smith, *trkd ldrs, drvn alng to hold pl appr 4 out, sn btn* .... (14 to 1 op 10 to 1) 10
2763 COUSIN WENDY 4-10-2 (3*) T Eley, *wtd wth, improved into midfield hfwy, bustled alng aftr 4 out, sn btn*.
.... (33 to 1 op 20 to 1) 11
2802 CHEQUE BOOK 6-11-2 Mr D Verco, *unruly in paddock and at strt, pressed ldrs till appr 4 out, wknd quickly*.
.... (50 to 1 op 33 to 1) 12
1660 EMERALD QUEEN 5-11-4 M Brennan, *not fluent, beh whn nrly f 3rd, not reco'r* .... (14 to 1 op 10 to 1) 13
1860 ALIZARI (USA) (bl) 5-11-0 M Robinson, *scrubbed alng to keep up, nvr a factor* ....(50 to 1 op 33 to 1) 14
RUSTY PLUMBER (Ire) 6-11-2 (7*) P Midgley, *pressed ldrs to hfwy, wknd quickly, tld off* ....(25 to 1) 15
2581 INNOCENT GEORGE 5-11-4 W Marston, *patiently rdn, imprvg to go hndy whn f 4 out*. (33 to 1 op 25 to 1) f
Dist: 10l, 1½l, 8l, 1½l, 2½l, 6l, 5l, 12l, 2l, 2l. 4m 23.80s. a 21.80s (16 Ran).
                                                (M M Foulger), K G Wingrove

2961 Coningsby Handicap Hurdle (0-110 4-y-o and up) £3,048 2m 5f 110yds ....(4:20)

25667 CURTAIN FACTORY [80] 5-10-1 L Wyer, *hld up on ins, smooth hdwy to ld bef 2 out, drw clr*.
.... (13 to 2 op 7 to 1) 1
1772* COUTURE STOCKINGS [103] 10-11-7 (3*) T Eley, *hld up, improved frm midfield aftr 3 out, styd on one pace r-in*.
.... (9 to 2 op 4 to 1) 2
2766⁷ FARMER'S CROSS [90] 10-10-11 Mrs A Farrell, *led to second, styd upsides till led ag'n 5th, hdd bef 2 out, btn whn hit last* .... (10 to 1) 3
19646 MR TAYLOR [92] 9-10-13 V Smith, *reluctant to race, tld off hfwy, styd on frm 4 out, nvr nrr* .... (7 to 1 op 5 to 1) 4
25293 STRONG JOHN (Ire) [88] 6-10-9 D Bridgwater, *wth ldrs, ev ch and drvn alng 4 out, fdd aftr nxt*. (8 to 1 op 7 to 1) 5
SASKIA'S REPRIEVE [95] 10-11-2 D Byrne, *settled off the pace, prmsg effrt aftr 3 oput, rdn and no imprsn frm nxt* .... (12 to 1 op 10 to 1) 6
2729 NESSFIELD [87] 8-10-8 A S Smith, *led second to 5th, fdd und pres aftr 4 out* ....(16 to 1 op 14 to 1) 7
1740 MASTER OF THE ROCK [90] (v) 5-10-11 C Hawkins, *chsd ldg bunch to 4 out, wknd quickly frm nxt*.
.... (11 to 1 op 10 to 1 tchd 12 to 1) 8
2737³ MISTIC GLEN (Ire) [103] 5-11-3 (7*) F Leahy, *trkd ldg bunch, struggling whn f 4 out* ....(8 to 1 op 7 to 1) f
2710² THE PAPPARAZI [94] 14-11-1 E Murphy, *trkd ldrs, bustled alng appr 4 out, sn lost tch, pld up bef 2 out*.
.... (15 to 1 op 7 to 1 tchd 3 to 1) pu
Dist: 4l, 8l, 8l, 2l, 3l, 10l, dist. 5m 30.40s. a 26.40s (10 Ran).
                                                (Durham Drapes Ltd), M H Easterby

2962 Waddington Conditional Jockeys' Handicap Chase (0-120 5-y-o and up) £2,883 2m 1f 110yds ....(4:50)

2562 WHITWOOD [104] 9-11-3 D Fortt, *jmpd wl, made all, hit 4 out, styd on strly r-in* .... (5 to 1 op 6 to 1) 1
2272² RUPPLES [87] 7-10-0 P McLoughlin, *nvr far away, ev ch frm 4 out, rdn and not quicken r-in*.
.... (14 to 1 op 20 to 1) 2
2569³ ALAN BALL [106] 8-11-5 T Eley, *co'red up beh ldrs, idling whn blun and nrly uns rdr 6 out, drvn alng frm nxt, one pace* .... (3 to 1 fav) 3
1489 CAMPSEA-ASH [112] 10-11-8 (3*) P Murphy, *pressed ldrs, struggling to keep up 5 out, tld off frm nxt*.
.... (10 to 1 op 12 to 1 tchd 8 to 1) 4
2073 HAPPY BREED [87] 11-10-0 P Waggott, *beh and reminders hfwy, sn tld off*. .... (4 to 1 op 7 to 2) 5
2272* BOSTON ROVER [115] 9-11-9 (5*) R Moore, *hld up in rear whn blun and uns rdr 3rd*. .... (5 to 1 op 9 to 2) ur
2640* BOBBY SOCKS [110] 8-11-9 Guy Lewis, *tracking ldr whn blun and uns rdr second*. ....(4 to 1 op 7 to 2) ur
Dist: 6l, 4l, dist, dist. 4m 44.80s. a 30.80s (7 Ran).
SR: 35/12/27/-/   (J D Cable), Mrs V A Aconley

2963 Toft Newton National Hunt Flat Race (4,5,6-y-o) £1,953 1m 5f 110yds. . (5:20)

14946 BARNEY'S GIFT (Ire) 6-10-13 (7*) R Moore, *co'red up on ins, improved to ld over one furlong out, drifted lft, wnt badly left cl hme, ran off course aftr line*.
.... (7 to 2 op 9 to 2 tchd 5 to 1) 1
STIR FRY 4-10-7 (7*) Mark Roberts, *settled gng wl, led o'r 2 fs out till hdd and crowded over one furlong out, rallied and hmpd cl hme*.
.... (6 to 4 fav op 5 to 4 tchd 13 to 8) 2

413

2332² BORNE 4-10-9 (5") S Mason, *patiently rdn, steady hdwy to join issue last 2 fs, wndrd appr last, no extr.*
.... (11 to 4 op 2 to 1 tchd 3 to 1) 3
SABBAQ (USA) 4-10-9 (5") N Leach, *settled midfield, effrt appr strt, kpt on last 2 fs.* .... (9 to 1 op 8 to 1) 4
2332⁶ HOAGY POKEY 4-10-7 (7") J Driscoll, *settled midfield, effrt hdwy, rdn 2 fs out, no extr* .... (16 to 1 op 12 to 1) 5
1674 WHOCOMESNATURALLY 5-11-3 (3") T Eley, *trkd ldg bunch, effrt entering strt, rdn and wknd last 2 fs.*
.... (25 to 1) 6
CHUCKLES 4-11-0 Mr K Green, *nvr far away, rdn appr strt, wknd quickly.* .... (20 to 1 op 16 to 1) 7
MORE TO LIFE 5-10-10 (5") P Midgley, *al hndy, led appr strt till o'r 2 fs out, fdd.* .... (20 to 1 op 16 to 1) 8
1376 TWICE IN ONE NIGHT 5-11-1 (5") S Lyons, *wth ldrs, led aftr 3 fs till appr strt, fdd last 2 furlongs.....* (20 to 1) 9
CHEEKY CHIMP 4-10-4 (5") Mr M Buckley, *chsd ldrs to strt, wknd quickly 2 fs out.* .... (12 to 1 op 10 to 1) 10
2876 BRIGG FOLLY 4-10-2 (7") Annette Billany, *led for 3 fs, rdn and lost grnd appr strt, tld off.* .... (20 to 1) 11
Dist: 1l, 7l, 1l, 1½l, 12l, 6l, 2l, 5l, 20l. 3m 23.10s. (11 Ran).
(Richard J Marshall), O Brennan

SANDOWN (good to soft (races 1,4,6), good (2,3,5))
Friday March 11th
Going Correction: PLUS 0.83 sec. per fur. (races 1,4,6), PLUS 0.75 (2,3,5)

2964 Beech 'National Hunt' Novices' Hurdle (4-y-o and up) £2,996 2¾m.....(2:00)

2757² OUROWNFELLOW (Ire) 5-11-0 D Morris, *in tch, trkd ldrs 5th, led 3 out, clr aftr nxt, drvn out.*
.... (4 to 1 op 5 to 1 tchd 11 to 2) 1
2459⁶ ARCTIC COURSE (Ire) 6-11-4 A Maguire, *mid-div, hdwy 7th, rdn aftr 2 out, ran on und pres r-in, not rch wnr.*
.... (2 to 1 fav op 6 to 4) 2
1665⁷ CALL HOME (Ire) 6-11-4 D Murphy, *str hold, sn in tch, chsd wnr aftr 2 out, rdn and one pace r-in.*
.... (6 to 1 op 9 to 2) 3
2263⁹ ANTARCTIC CALL 7-11-0 J Osborne, *led till aftr 3rd, led 5th till appr nxt, ev ch 3 out, no hdwy frm next.*
.... (6 to 1 op 5 to 1 tchd 7 to 1) 4
2802³ SHEARMAC STEEL 7-11-0 Peter Hobbs, *sn in tch, chsd ldrs 3 out, wknd nxt.....* (8 to 1 tchd 9 to 1 and 7 to 1) 5
1804⁴ STORMY SWAN 8-11-0 S Smith Eccles, *chsd ldrs, led appr 6th to 3 out, wknd nxt.......* (66 to 1 op 33 to 1) 6
1935⁶ CATS RUN (Ire) 6-11-0 R Supple, *mid-div 5th, effrt nxt, wknd 2 out..................* (33 to 1 op 16 to 1) 7
2633² THREE OF CLUBS (Ire) 5-11-0 N Williamson, *sn beh, nvr rch ldrs.......................* (20 to 1 op 12 to 1) 8
1644 TRAIN ROBBER 9-11-0 W Irvine, *beh, rdn 5th, nvr dngrs.* .... (50 to 1 op 25 to 1 tchd 66 to 1) 9
2731⁹ BEATSON (Ire) 5-11-0 C Llewellyn, *prmnt whn pckd second, beh 5th...................* (33 to 1 op 14 to 1) 10
2361 MAYFIELD PARK 9-11-4 B Clifford, *chsd ldrs till wknd 7th.* .... (66 to 1 op 20 to 1) 11
2404 CAIPIRINHA (Ire) 6-10-9 G Upton, *hdwy and mstk 6th, sn wknd...........................* (66 to 1 op 33 to 1) 12
2734⁸ OAKLANDS WORD (bl) 5-10-7 (7") Mr E Williams, *led aftr 3rd to 5th, wknd 7th..........* (100 to 1 op 50 to 1) 13
BREECHES BUOY 8-11-0 D Gallagher, *al beh.*
.... (66 to 1 op 33 to 1) 14
2802 RIFFLE 7-10-11 (3") P Hide, *hdwy 7th, trkd ldrs 3 out till wknd rpdly nxt, tld off whn pld up bef last.*
.... (40 to 1 op 20 to 1 tchd 66 to 1) pu
Dist: 1½l, 7l, 3l, 2½l, ½l, 2l, 10l, 6l, 3l, 3l. 5m 36.00s. a 30.00s (15 Ran).
(Kings Of The Road Partnership), R Curtis

2965 Cray Systems Novices' Chase (5-y-o and up) £4,610 2½m 110yds.....(2:35)

2647⁴ YORKSHIRE GALE 8-11-10 D Murphy, *led 3rd to 13th, chlgd 4 out, sn led, pushed out.*
.... (Evens op 5 to 4 tchd 11 to 8) 1
2816* GINGER TRISTAN 8-11-7 Peter Hobbs, *led to 3rd, hit nxt, not fluent 7th, led 13th till aftr 4 out, effrt and stumbled 2 out, one pace.*
.... (6 to 5 on op 7 to 4 on tchd 11 to 10 on) 2
Won by 2l. 5m 21.10s. a 21.60s (2 Ran).
SR: 34/29/   *(Bill Naylor), J T Gifford*

2966 Horse And Hound Grand Military Gold Cup Chase For Amateur Riders (5-y-o and up) £4,758 3m 110yds.....(3:05)

QUICK RAPOR 9-11-7 Mr D Alers-Hankey, *led 8 to 12th, led 15th, sn clr, readily....* (9 to 1 op 8 to 1 tchd 10 to 1) 1
UNCLE RAGGY 11-11-7 Capt A Smith-Maxwell, *beh till hdwy 15th, styd on frm 3 out, not rch wnr.*
.... (25 to 1 op 16 to 1) 2
1889 TOUCHING STAR 9-12-7 Mr B Marquis, *beh till hdwy 15th, styd on frm 3 out, no imprsn on wnr.*
.... (16 to 1 op 10 to 1) 3

2484³ ON THE OTHER HAND 11-12-7 Capt A Ogden, *beh, hit 3rd, nvr nr ldrs..........* (7 to 2 fav op 3 to 1 tchd 4 to 1) 4
2623* FIDDLERS THREE (bl) 11-12-0 Mr C Ward Thomas, *chsd ldrs 9th, led 12th to 15th, hit 17th, sn wknd.*
.... (9 to 2 tchd 5 to 1) 5
2879² CHARDEN 8-11-7 Lt-Col R Webb-Bowen, *beh frm 8th.*
.... (14 to 1 op 16 to 1 tchd 12 to 1) 6
2718 FIFTH AMENDMENT (bl) 9-11-7 Mr R Ponsonby, *led to second, prmnt till wknd 12th.*
.... (11 to 1 op 10 to 1 tchd 12 to 1) 7
2764 KNOX'S CORNER 9-11-7 Mr J Wingfield Digby, *tld off 8th.*
.... (100 to 1) 8
2822³ PICKETSTONE 7-11-8¹ Mr J Fountain, *tld off 5th.*
.... (66 to 1 op 33 to 1) 9
CAPALL AOSTA 11-11-7 Mr C Farr, *sn tld off....* (100 to 1) 10
2718³ CALABRESE (bl) 9-12-0 Major M Watson, *chsd ldrs, chlgd 12th, 3rd and in tch whn f 4 out.*
.... (5 to 1 op 9 to 2 tchd 11 to 2) f
2504 FREE JUSTICE 10-11-7 Capt A Woodward, *f 1st, broke neck, dead...........* (40 to 1 op 20 to 1 tchd 50 to 1) f
2453² GENERAL BRANDY 8-12-0 Mr A Wood, *mid-div, 5th whn f 12th.....................* (25 to 1 op 14 to 1) f
GUNNER STREAM 10-12-7 Mr B Elliott, *mstk and uns rdr 3rd.......* (40 to 1 op 25 to 1 tchd 50 to 1) ur
2791⁶ ACE OF SPIES 13-12-7 Mr A Ayers, *mstk and uns rdr 1st.*
.... (33 to 1 op 25 to 1 tchd 40 to 1) ur
2602 KEEP TALKING 9-12-7 Major O Ellwood, *led second to 8th, 4th whn pitched and uns rdr 11th.*
.... (9 to 1 op 7 to 1 tchd 10 to 1) ur
2666 ROYAL FLAMINGO 8-11-9 Mr J Fuller, *mstk and uns rdr 4th........................* (14 to 1 op 16 to 1 tchd 12 to 1) ur
2555 OVER THE EDGE 8-11-7 Mr S Sporborg, *sn beh, tld off whn pld up bef 2 out.* .... pu
Dist: 20l, nk, 8l, 2l, 25l, dist, 8l. 6m 34.50s. a 35.50s (18 Ran).
(D G Alers-Hankey), Richard Barber

2967 Cognac Courvoisier Handicap Hurdle (4-y-o and up) £3,338 2¾m.....(3:40)

2788³ VIARDOT (Ire) [126] 5-11-7 R Hodge, *hdwy 7th, slight ld 2 out, wnt clr appr last............* (7 to 2 fav op 3 to 1) 1
2729* LEAVENWORTH [108] 10-10-0 (2") R Davis, *mid-div, hdwy 6th, rdn alng frm 3 out, styd on r-in, no imprsn on wnr.*
.... (5 to 1 op 7 to 2 tchd 11 to 2) 2
2781* KOVALEVSKIA [105] 9-10-0 (4ex) A Maguire, *beh, hdwy appr 2 out, rdn approaching last, styd on.*
.... (6 to 1 tchd 7 to 1) 3
2801³ SUKAAB [119] 9-10-7 (7") T Dascombe, *hdwy 6th, lost pl 3 out, rallied und pres frm nxt.....* (10 to 1 tchd 11 to 1) 4
2823 ULURU (Ire) [106] 6-10-1 J R Kavanagh, *chsd ldrs, chlgd 3 out, one pace nxt..........* (9 to 1 op 8 to 1 tchd 10 to 1) 5
2172 SUPER MALT (Ire) [109] 6-10-4 N Williamson, *beh 6th, rdn frm 3 out, one pace nxt..........* (10 to 1 tchd 11 to 1) 6
2759⁶ LESBET [105] 9-10-0 D Morris, *beh 6th, no dngr aftr.*
.... (25 to 1 op 20 to 1 tchd 33 to 1) 7
2473⁹ JOPANINI [133] (bl) 9-12-0 M A FitzGerald, *led, hit 5th, hdd 2 out, wknd quickly.....* (7 to 1 op 6 to 1 tchd 8 to 1) 8
2766³ SPARTAN TIMES [108] 10-10-0 B Powell, *beh hfwy.*
.... (33 to 1 op 20 to 1) 9
EARLY MAN [108] 7-10-3 Peter Hobbs, *beh, some prog 3 out, wknd nxt...............* (20 to 1 op 16 to 1) 10
2597³ CAIRNCASTLE [108] 9-10-3 N Mann, *chsd ldrs to 7th.*
.... (13 to 2 op 5 to 1 tchd 7 to 1) 11
QUIET DAWN [106] 8-10-1¹ G Rowe, *chsd ldrs to 6th.*
.... (100 to 1 op 66 to 1) 12
2657⁶ UP ALL NIGHT [105] 5-9-8¹ (7") G Crone, *mstk 3rd, al beh.*
.... (200 to 1 op 100 to 1) 13
2632 COSMIC DANCER [110] (bl) 7-10-2 (3") P Hide, *hdwy to chase ldrs 7th, rdn appr 2 out, wknd quickly, pld up bef last..............* (16 to 1 op 12 to 1) pu
Dist: 8l, 2½l, 1l, ¾l, 2½l, ¾l, sht-hd, 15l, 5l, 3l. 5m 28.00s. a 22.00s (14 Ran).
SR: 56/30/24/37/23/23/18/46/3/   (Exors Of The Late Mrs H North), Mrs M Reveley

2968 Duke Of Gloucester Memorial Hunters' Chase Past And Present (5-y-o and up) £2,034 3m 110yds...(4:10)

ELVERCONE 13-11-11 (7") Capt A Woodward, *led to 4th, prmnt, chlgd frm 3 out, slight ld last, hld on gmely.*
.... (5 to 1 op 5 to 1 tchd 13 to 2) 1
WILD ILLUSION 10-12-4 (7") Mr J Trice-Rolph, *sn in tch, hdwy to chase ldrs 11th, led 18th, narrowly hdd last, rallied gmely, jst fld..........* (11 to 8 op op 2 to 1 on) 2
BLUE DART 14-11-11 (7") Mr D Alers-Hankey, *chsd ldrs 11th, lost pos 14th, styd on frm 4 out, not rch ldrs.*
.... (7 to 1 tchd 8 to 1) 3
TUBBS 10-11-11 (7") Major O Ellwood, *hit 1st, chsd ldrs 9th, wknd 13th.............* (5 to 1 op 6 to 1 tchd 7 to 1) 4
NORSTOWN 12-11-11 (7") Capt R Inglesant, *al beh.*
.... (25 to 1 op 20 to 1 tchd 33 to 1) 5
ROARS OF APPLAUSE 12-11-11 (7") Mr S Sporborg, *chsd ldrs till wknd 11th, tld off whn pld up bef 2 out.* ..... pu
SECOND TIME ROUND 11-11-11 (7") Capt D R Parker, *mstks and beh, tld off whn pld up bef 12th.*
.... (16 to 1 op 12 to 1) pu

2793 STORMY WAGER 9-11-11 (7") Capt E Andrewes, *led 4th,*
hit 13th, hdd 18th, wknd rpdly, tld off whn pld up bef 3
out..................... (66 to 1 op 50 to 1) pu
Dist: Sht-hd, 20l, 1l, 15l. 6m 42.20s. a 43.20s (8 Ran).

(Mrs C M Scott), D Mills

2969 Lilac Novices' Handicap Hurdle (4-y-o) £3,208 2m 110yds........(4:40)

2722⁵ DOCTOOR (USA) [97] 11-9 D O'Sullivan, *al chasing ldrs,*
chlgd 2 out, slight ld last, hld on wl.
..............................(8 to 1 tchd 9 to 1) 1
2327² TEEN JAY [85] 10-11 J Osborne, *hld up, in tch 3 out, rdn*
and ran on frm last, no extr cl hme.
.... (6 to 1 op 5 to 1 tchd 13 to 2) 2
2694³ RICH LIFE (Ire) [98] 11-10 Peter Hobbs, *hdwy 5th, chlgd 2*
out, rdn and no extr cl hme.
.... (15 to 2 op 6 to 1 tchd 8 to 1) 3
2606⁵ UPWARD SURGE (Ire) [76] 10-2 N Williamson, *chsd ldrs 3rd,*
slight ld 2 out to last, one pace.
.... (100 to 30 fav op 5 to 2 tchd 7 to 2) 4
2776' ERICOLIN (Ire) [89] 11-1 (4ex) G McCourt, *beh, hdwy and*
ev ch 2 out, not quicken appr last.
..............................(9 to 2 op 4 to 1 tchd 7 to 2) 5
2685² PRIME OF LIFE (Ire) [96] 11-8 S McNeill, *prmnt, led briefly*
appr 2 out, ev ch last, wknd.
.... (5 to 1 op 4 to 1 tchd 11 to 2) 6
2638⁴ PAPER DAYS [90] 11-2 D Murphy, *made most till hdd*
wknd appr 2 out.................(10 to 1 tchd 12 to 1) 7
2685⁶ MILLMOUNT (Ire) [82] (v) 10-8 W McFarland, *prmnt, rdn 3*
out, wknd appr 2 out....(7 to 1 op 6 to 1 tchd 10 to 1) 8
2503⁵ AMILLIONMEMORIES [74] 10-0 P Holley, *al beh.*
..............................(33 to 1 tchd 50 to 1) 9
2275⁶ JACKSONS BAY [74] 9-9 (5") C Burnett-Wells, *beh hfwy.*
..............................(33 to 1 tchd 50 to 1) 10
Dist: Nk, sht-hd, 2l, ½l, 1l, 10l, 5l, 10l. 4m 11.00s. a 2±l.00s (10 Ran).

(I A Baker), R J O'Sullivan

AYR (soft)
Saturday March 12th
Going Correction: PLUS 1.10 sec. per fur.

2970 James Barclay Memorial Trophy Amateur Riders' Maiden Hurdle (4-y-o and up) £2,029 2¾m..........(1:40)

2447² KENILWORTH LAD 6-11-9 (5") Mr M Buckley, *hld up, hdwy*
hfwy, led 9th, sn clr, not extended.
.... (5 to 2 on op 3 to 1 on) 1
GLEN MIRAGE 9-11-7 (7") Miss S White, *dsptd ld till lost pl*
hfwy, rallied aftr 8th, styd on wl frm 3 out, no ch with
wnr....................(20 to 1 op 14 to 1) 2
2068⁷ DOUBLE STANDARDS (Ire) 6-11-7 (7") Mr D Parker, *hld up,*
hdwy hfwy, chsd wnr aftr 9th, sn rdn, no imprsn.
.... (15 to 2 op 6 to 1 tchd 8 to 1) 3
2896 NICHOLAS PLANT 5-11-7 (7") Mr C Bonner, *in tch, jnd ldrs*
hfwy, grad wknd frm 9th..........(25 to 1 op 20 to 1) 4
2785⁹ COMPANY SECRETARY 6-11-2 (7") Mr I McLelland, *in tch,*
wknd aftr 9th, tld off.......... (100 to 1 op bef 3 out) 5
SEA PET 5-11-2 (7") Mr S Johnson, *lost tch frm hfwy, tld*
off......................(50 to 1 op 33 to 1) 6
2739 MISS JEDD 7-11-6 (3") Mr J Bradburne, *led to 3rd, cl up till*
wknd hfwy, tld off.........(66 to 1 op 33 to 1) 7
TAUALERA 7-11-2 (7") Mr D Swindlehurst, *prmnt, led 6th,*
hdd 9th, sn wknd, tld off......(100 to 1 op 66 to 1) 8
2735 WEE WARRIOR (bl) 6-11-7 (7") Mr S de Burgh, *led 3rd till*
hdd 6th. sn wknd, tld off......(50 to 1 op 33 to 1) 9
2810⁵ SHARP AT SIX (Ire) 4-10-11 (7") Mr R Dyer, *chsd ldrs till*
wknd aftr 8th, tld off whn pld up bef 3 out.
..............................(10 to 1 op 8 to 1) pu
1707 SKI LADY 6-11-2 (7") Mr J Weymes, *beh frm 7th, wl tld off*
whn pld up bef 3 out...........(33 to 1 op 20 to 1) pu
Dist: 20l, 1l, 15l, dist, 12l, ¾l, 3½l, 25l. 6m 1.20s. a 51.20s (11 Ran).

(David Bell), Mrs M Reveley

2971 Marchburn Novices' Chase (5-y-o and up) £2,541 2m................(2:15)

2809' GALLATEEN 6-12-0 N Doughty, *cl up, slight ld frm 8th,*
drw clr aftr last, cmftbly.
..............................(9 to 2 on op 6 to 1 on tchd 4 to 1) 1
2565⁷ MACCONACHIE 7-11-4 T Reed, *slight ld aftr 3rd till hdd*
8th, ev ch 2 out, no imprsn on wnr. (33 to 1 op 20 to 1) 2
2739⁵ FLING IN SPRING (v) 8-10-13 (5") P Williams, *in tch, hdwy*
aftr 7th, ev ch 3 out, sn rdn and one pace.
..............................(16 to 1 tchd 20 to 1) 3
2007⁴ BULA NUDAY 9-11-4 K Johnson, *sn tracking ldrs, grad*
wknd aftr 4 out........ (15 to 2 op 6 to 1 tchd 8 to 1) 4
2739⁹ ZARBANO 8-11-4 A Merrigan, *prmnt till blun and lost pl*
6th, rdn to chase ldrs aftr nxt, wknd appr 4 out.
.... (16 to 1 op 14 to 1) 5
2739 CORNISH BAY 6-10-6 (7") P Kennedy, *f 1st......* (100 to 1) f
2218 BELLOFAGUS 9-10-13 (5") F Perratt, *slight ld till aftr 3rd,*
blun nxt, sn wl beh, tld off whn pld up bef 4 out.
..............................(100 to 1) pu
Dist: 5l, 1½l, 25l, 12l. 4m 12.30s. a 24.30s (7 Ran).

SR: 33/18/16/-/

(E R Madden), G Richards

2972 Harcros Scottish Juvenile Championship Qualifier Novices' Hurdle (4-y-o) £2,211 2m....................(2:50)

2135⁵ DEVILRY 11-4 J Callaghan, *hld up, hdwy aftr 5th, led 3*
out, ran on wl und pres...... (11 to 10 jt-fav op Evens) 1
2275³ BALLON 10-13 T Reed, *not fluent early, hld up and beh,*
hdwy aftr 5th, quickened to ld after nxt, hdd 3 out, kpt
on wl und pres.......(11 to 10 jt-fav op 11 to 10 on) 2
FUNNY ROSE 10-3 L O'Hara, *trkd ldrs, effrt aftr 6th,*
wknd after 3 out................. (66 to 1 op 50 to 1) 3
. 2369 AMERIGUE 10-7 M Moloney, *wth ldr, led 6th, sn hdd,*
wknd appr 3 out............(20 to 1 op 12 to 1) 4
2433⁸ FUNNY FEELINGS 10-9 (3") T Jenks, *slight ld till hdd 6th,*
wknd appr 3 out................. (25 to 1 op 12 to 1) 5
Dist: 2l, 12l, 8l, 1½l. 4m 17.50s. a 40.50s (5 Ran).

(Miss V Foster), G M Moore

2973 Elk Handicap Chase (0-120 5-y-o and up) £3,078 3m 1f..........(3:25)

JOHNNY'S SLIPPER [97] 9-10-10 J Callaghan, *made most,*
styd on wl frm 2 out...(11 to 2 op 5 to 1 tchd 13 to 2) 1
2906⁶ TRUELY ROYAL [92] 10-10-5 B Storey, *prmnt till outpcd*
appr 15th, rallied aftr 2 out, styd on wl r-in.
..............................(13 to 2 op 6 to 1 tchd 7 to 1) 2
2737 LAPIAFFE [90] 10-9-10 (7") Mr D Parker, *cl up, chlgd 4 out,*
ch 2 out, kpt on same pace........ (14 to 1 op 10 to 1) 3
2105² RUN PET RUN [107] 9-11-6 A Dobbin, *blun 1st, trkd ldrs,*
pushed alng aftr 15th, kpt on same pace.
..............................(5 to 2 fav op 9 to 4) 4
2325 LOTHIAN PILOT [98] 7-10-11 T Reed, *hld up and beh. blun*
tenth, effrt aftr 15th, staying on wl whn blunded last,
not recv'd........ (3 to 1 op 11 to 4 tchd 100 to 30) 5
2501⁴ ON THE HOOCH [96] 9-10-9 Mr J Bradburne, *trkd ldrs,*
pushed alng appr 11th, grad wknd, tld off whn pld up
bef last..................(5 to 1 op 7 to 2) pu
Dist: 1½l, 3½l, 1½l, 15l. 6m 55.40s. a 55.40s (6 Ran).

(N B Mason), N B Mason

2974 Ayrshire Yeomanry Cup Handicap Hurdle (0-110 4-y-o and up) £2,305 2 ½m.....................(4:00)

2815⁴ SWEET CITY [105] 9-12-0 N Doughty, *hld up in tch,*
pushed alng and slightly outpcd aftr 8th, hdwy to chal
3 out, led after last, held on wl...... (6 to 1 op 4 to 1) 1
2740 RED TEMPEST (Ire) [77] 6-9-9 (5") F Perratt, *chsd ldr, led*
6th, sn rdn and outpcd, kpt on wl und pres frm 2 out, ev
ch r-in, no extr cl hme.
.... (14 to 1 op 10 to 1 tchd 16 to 1) 2
2815³ IT'S THE PITS [103] 7-11-12 T Reed, *hld up, steady hdwy*
to ld 3 out, mstk nxt, sn hrd pressed, hdd and no extr
aftr last..... (Evens fav tchd 11 to 10 and 11 to 10 on) 3
2792⁴ LOGICAL FUN [93] 6-10-11 (5") A Roche, *mid-div, outpcd*
aftr 8th, kpt on frm 2 out.
..............................(3 to 1 op 9 to 4 tchd 100 to 30) 4
2815⁷ MIDLAND EXPRESS [85] 11-10-3 (5") P Waggott, *chsd ldrs,*
ev ch appr 3 out, grad wknd......(33 to 1 op 25 to 1) 5
2243 CAPTAIN TANCRED (Ire) [77] 6-10-0 E McKinley, *pld hrd, in*
tch, led 8th, hdd 3 out, sn btn....(25 to 1 tchd 33 to 1) 6
TALL MEASURE [95] 8-11-4 Mr D Swindlehurst, *led, clr aftr*
second, hdd 8th, sn wknd...... (20 to 1 op 14 to 1) 7
2575 BOLD MOOD [77] 5-9-8' (7") B Harding, *mid-div, rdn aftr*
7th, sn wknd............(20 to 1 op 16 to 1) 8
Dist: 1l, ½l, 5l, 8l, 6l, ½l. 5m 35.30s. a 56.30s (8 Ran).

(W J Peacock), G Richards

2975 Arthur Challenge Cup Handicap Chase (0-120 5-y-o and up) £3,387 2m ....(4:30)

2738⁴ ONE FOR THE POT [108] 9-11-2 (3") T Jenks, *hld up, chsd*
ldr frm 6th, led 4 out and quickened, 5 ls ahead whn lft
wl clr last.....................(11 to 4 op 9 to 4) 1
2788⁷ ABBOT OF FURNESS [115] 10-11-12 M Moloney, *mstk 3rd,*
chsd ldr to 6th, in tch till grad wknd frm 4 out, no ch
whn lft poor second and slightly hmpd last.
..............................(11 to 8 fav op 6 to 4) 2
2253³ PRESSURE GAME [89] 11-9-9 (5") F Perratt, *led till hdd 4*
out, sn wknd, tld off.......... (20 to 1 op 14 to 1) 3
2829² SHREWD JOHN [94] 8-10-5 R Garritty, *hld up, hdwy to*
chase wnr appr 3 out, no imprsn whn f last, rmntd.
..............................(9 to 4 op 15 to 8 tchd 13 to 8) 4
Dist: 12l, dist, dist. 4m 18.50s. a 30.50s (4 Ran).

(Philip Davies), M P Naughton

2976 Grunwick Stakes National Hunt Flat Race (4,5,6-y-o) £1,572 2m.....(5:00)

2834⁷ LOCHNAGRAIN (Ire) 6-11-1 (7") G Lee, *trkd ldrs, led 3 out,*
sn clr, pushed out fnl furlong.........(3 to 1 op 6 to 1) 1
BEN CRUACHAN (Ire) 4-10-9 (5") P Williams, *nvr far away,*
chsd wnr frm 2 out, kpt on, no imprsn.
.... (10 to 1 op 6 to 1) 2

BALLYALLIA CASTLE (Ire) 5-11-3 (5") J Burke, *prmnt, ev ch 3 out, kpt on same pace.*
............................(11 to 2 op 7 to 2 tchd 6 to 1)   3
BUITENVERWACHTING 5-10-12 (5") S Mason, *cl up, slightly hmpd aftr 4 fs, sn led, hdd 3 out, kpt on same pace.*...(33 to 1)   4
SIGMA RUN (Ire) 5-11-5 (3") T Jenks, *beh, hdwy 6 out, sn rdn and btn.*.........(7 to 4 fav op 2 to 1 tchd 9 to 1)   5
2373 CRAIGIE RAMBLER (Ire) 5-11-3 Mr D Robertson, *led, ran wide aftr 4 fs, sn hdd, outpcd 6 out, no dngr after.*
....(50 to 1)   6
DAY RETURN 5-10-12 (5") A Roche, *in tch till wknd 6 out.*
............................(9 to 1 op 7 to 1 tchd 10 to 1)   7
2373 OUR WILMA 5-10-10 (7") R McGrath, *in tch till wknd 6 out.*
....(66 to 1)   8
HENBRIG 4-10-4 (5") F Perratt, *in tch till wknd 6 out.*
............................(14 to 1 op 12 to 1)   9
2339 RUN ON FLO (Ire) 6-10-12 (5") P Waggott, *chsd ldrs till wknd 6 out, tld off.*...........................(66 to 1)   10
TROPICAL REEF (Ire) 4-10-7 (7") Mr D Parker, *lost tch frm 6 out, tld off.*.........................(8 to 1 op 6 to 1)   11
Dist: 2l, 12l, 4l, 12l, 10l, 3½l, 7l, 10l. 4m 11.00s. (11 Ran).
(Lightbody Of Hamilton Ltd), Mrs M Reveley

CHEPSTOW (Soft)
Saturday March 12th
Going Correction: PLUS 2.15 sec. per fur.

2977
Hywel Davies Retirement Hurdle (4-y-o) £4,810 2m 110yds.........(1:00)

2810* RUSTY REEL 11-0 R Campbell, *hld up, cld 4th, chalg whn lft in ld four out, clr 2 out, easily.*............(13 to 8 jt-fav op 5 to 4 on tchd 7 to 4)   1
2652³ HABASHA (Ire) 10-9 C Swan, *hld up, swshd tail, hdwy 4th, outpcd frm 3 out, tired whn hln last.*
....................(100 to 30 op 5 to 2 tchd 7 to 2)   2
2422 QUICK SILVER BOY 11-0 D J Burchell, *led till hdd and hmpd 4 out, btn whn hit nxt.*
....................(16 to 1 op 12 to 1 tchd 20 to 1)   3
2789² SQUIRE YORK 11-0 A Maguire, *trkd ldr, hit 3rd, led and f 4 out.*.........................(13 to 8 jt-fav op 3 to 1)   f
Dist: 30l, 10l. 4m 35.40s. a 49.40s (4 Ran).
(S M Perry), I Campbell

2978
Bishop Memorial Novices' Handicap Chase (5-y-o and up) £4,146 2m 3f 110yds......................(1:30)

2736* OPAL'S TENSPOT [82] 7-10-0 A Maguire, *led 7th to tenth, led appr 5 out, blun nxt, steadied, clr frm 2 out.*
............................(2 to 1 jt-fav tchd 9 to 4)   1
2418² AUVILLAR (USA) [86] 9½-10-0 D J Burchell, *led 4th, hdd appr 6th, rdn whn blun 5 out, wnt second approaching 2 out, fnshd tired.*........(11 to 2 op 9 to 2 tchd 5 to 1)   2
2693⁵ POPPETS PET [91] 7-10-4 (5") S Curran, *led to 4th, led appr 6th, hdd nxt, led tenth till approaching 5 out, second and hld whn blun 3 out.* (9 to 2 op 3 to 1 tchd 5 to 1)   3
2732 VICAR OF BRAY [82] 7-10-0 B Clifford, *al beh, tld off frm 8th.*.................................(14 to 1 op 10 to 1)   4
2859* CRYSTAL BEAR (NZ) [110] (bb) 9-12-0 B Powell, *reluctant to race, hdwy 5th, lost pl 8th, headway appr 5 out, 4th whn refused nxt.*...........(2 to 1 jt-fav op 7 to 4)   ref
Dist: 10l, 15l, dist. 5m 48.30s. a 61.30s (5 Ran).
(Miss Joy Mailes), J M Bradley

2979
Beaufort Hurdle (5-y-o) £11,815 2m 110yds......................(2:00)

2537² RELKEEL 11-5 A Maguire, *hld up, smooth hdwy to ld appr 4 out, clr frm nxt, hit last, not extended.*
....................................(Evens tchd 5 to 4)   1
2599⁵ KEEP ME IN MIND (Ire) 11-5 D Skyrme, *hld up, pushed alng frm 4 out, wnt second last, no ch wth wnr.*
............................(16 to 1 op 8 to 1)   2
2392⁸ DERRYMOYLE (Ire) 11-0 C Swan, *led till hdd appr 4 out, rdn and not resolute, wknd approaching last.*
............(11 to 8 op 11 to 8 tchd 11 to 10 and 6 to 4)   3
2671² SLIPMATIC 11-0 B Powell, *dsptd ld to 4th, rdn and wknd bef nxt, tld off.*........(13 to 2 op 6 to 1 tchd 9 to 1)   4
Dist: 10l, 5l, dist. 4m 30.60s. a 44.60s (4 Ran).
(Brig C B Harvey), D Nicholson

2980
Monmouthshire Novices' Chase (5-y-o and up) £2,665 3m.........(2:30)

2693⁴ THE PORTSOY LOON 7-11-3 D Bridgwater, *beh, hdwy frm 8th, styd on to go second 5 out, lft clr nxt, fnshd tired.*
............................(9 to 2 op 4 to 1 tchd 11 to 2)   1
2718 BLAKEINGTON (bl) 8-11-3 D Skyrme, *hld up 4th, second whn jmpd slwly 12th, one pace aftr, blun 3 out, fnshd tired.*........................(33 to 1 op 20 to 1)   2
1968 EBONY GALE 8-11-6 J R Kavanagh, *led to second, led briefly aftr 6, outpcd 12th, effrt appr 5 out, lft second nxt, fnshd very tired.*..............(2 to 1 op 6 to 4)   3

2739⁶ COZZI (Fr) 6-10-12 (5") Guy Lewis, *pld hrd, led 4th, blun nxt, hdd appr 8th, wkng whn blunded and uns rdr next.*.........................(14 to 1 op 10 to 1)   ur
2767⁴ RAKAIA RIVER (NZ) 7-11-6 B Powell, *hld up, hdwy to ld appr 8th, clr frm 12th, blun and uns rdr 4 out.*
............................(5 to 4 fav tchd 13 to 8)   ur
1794 OSCILANTE 6-11-3 M Foster, *led second, hit and hdd 8th, pld up bef 8th.*......(14 to 1 op 10 to 1 tchd 16 to 1)   pu
Dist: Dist, 12l. 7m 20.80s. a 90.80s (6 Ran).
(Mrs E J Crossman), J C Thorner

2981
Llangibby Handicap Chase (0-130 5-y-o and up) £2,833 2m 3f 110yds.. (3:00)

2818² RAFIKI [106] 9-10-12 S Burrough, *jmpd wl, led to 4th, led ag'n appr 6th, clr frm four out, unchlgd.*
............................(11 to 10 fav op 5 to 4 on)   1
1489⁶ LITTLE TOM [106] 9-10-12 J R Kavanagh, *not al fluent, hdwy to chase wnr frm 6th, cld 5 out, no imprsn from nxt, eased.*......(6 to 4 op 11 to 10 tchd 13 to 8)   2
1171 WINGSPAN (USA) [122] 10-12-0 D Bridgwater, *led 4th, wknd and hdd appr 6th, sn tld off.* (5 to 1 tchd 6 to 1)   3
Dist: Dist, dist. 5m 40.90s. a 53.90s (3 Ran).
(J P Carrington), Mrs J G Retter

2982
Curre Handicap Hurdle (0-135 4-y-o and up) £2,302 2½m 110yds....(3:35)

2806 SO PROUD [110] 9-11-10 C Swan, *hld up, wnt second 4 out, led on bit sn aftr 2 out, very easily.*
............................(5 to 4 fav op 6 to 4)   1
2823³ MAN FOR ALL SEASON (USA) [104] 8-11-4 M Hourigan, *trkd ldr, hit 3rd and 4th, outpcd four out, hld own whn rallied appr last, wnt second r-in.* (9 to 4 tchd 2 to 1)   2
2407 NICK THE DREAMER [110] 9-11-3 (7") R Darke, *trkd ldrs, led 5th, rdn appr 2 out, hdd sn aftr, wknd and lost second r-in.*...........(11 to 2 op 4 to 1 tchd 6 to 1)   3
2839³ VISCOUNT TULLY [98] 9-10-12 W Humphreys, *al beh, tld off.*..............................(16 to 1 op 14 to 1)   4
RAWHIDE [99] 10-10-13 J R Kavanagh, *led to 5th, wknd appr 4 out, sn tld off.* (12 to 1 op 7 to 1 tchd 14 to 1)   5
2816⁴ ONE TO NOTE [89] 10-10-3 M Ahern, *al in rear, tld off whn pld up bef 4 out.* (11 to 1 op 10 to 1 tchd 12 to 1)   pu
Dist: 1½l, 4l, dist, 25l. 5m 30.90s. a 49.90s (6 Ran).
SR: 38/30/32/   (Hon Mrs R Cobbold), M C Pipe

NAAS (IRE) (heavy)
Saturday March 12th

2983
Lakelands Maiden Hurdle (5-y-o and up) £3,105 2m.................(2:00)

2389⁸ YOUR THE MAN 8-12-0 J Shortt, ...(3 to 1 fav)   1
2607⁵ THE REAL ARTICLE (Ire) 5-11-12 H Rogers, ...(4 to 1)   2
1897⁹ ACKLE BACKLE 7-11-4 (5") J R Barry, ...(8 to 1)   3
2586⁸ BEST INTEREST (Ire) 6-11-11 (3") D Bromley, ...(6 to 1)   4
    GLENBALLYMA (Ire) 5-11-4 (3") T J Mitchell, ...(20 to 1)   5
2771⁸ MY HALL DOOR 5-11-7 (5") D T Evans, ...(33 to 1)   6
2770⁴ SLANEY BACON 7-11-7 (7") D J Kavanagh, ...(10 to 1)   7
2236 REPLACEMENT 7-12-0 G M O'Neill, ...(16 to 1)   8
2919 LANCASTRIANS DREAM (Ire) 5-11-2 (5") M J Holbrook,
....(20 to 1)   9
2658⁵ ISN'T THAT NICE (Ire) 6-12-0 K F O'Brien, ...(10 to 1)   10
2607⁸ ELUSIVE UP 7-12-0 P M Verling, ...(20 to 1)   11
    ILLUSIVE SOCIETY (Ire) 5-11-7 J A White, ...(20 to 1)   12
2679 SMALL TALK (Ire) 5-11-0 (7") J Butler, ...(50 to 1)   13
2231³ ELIADE (Ire) 5-11-7 C O'Dwyer, ...(7 to 2)   14
1332 NOBLE KNIGHT (Ire) 6-12-0 W T Slattery Jnr, ...(33 to 1)   15
1052⁸ METROLAMP (Ire) 6-11-9 (5") K P Gaule, ...(14 to 1)   16
2553 WHOTHATIS 8-11-9 D P Fagan, ...(33 to 1)   17
    MAZELLA (Ire) 5-11-7 M Duffy, ...(10 to 1)   18
2607 BUSTHAT 7-11-11 (3") T P Treacy, ...(8 to 1)   19
2679⁴ INAUGURATION (Ire) 5-11-12 B Sheridan, ...(8 to 1)   20
2050 SHINETHYME (Ire) 5-11-7 J P Banahan, ...(66 to 1)   21
2203⁹ BOWLING CHERRY (Ire) 6-12-0 P Kinane, ...(25 to 1)   22
    MAYFIELD PRINCE (Ire) 5-11-12 C Bowens, ...(8 to 1)   23
    DASHING GROOM (Ire) 6-11-7 (7") T Martin, ...(33 to 1)   24
2863 QUICK LEARNER (Ire) 5-11-12 A Powell, ...(50 to 1)   25
    GIFT ACCOUNT (Ire) 5-11-12 F J Flood, ...(20 to 1)   pu
Dist: 1½l, 5½l, 4l, 2l. 4m 13.00s. (26 Ran).
(Oliver Lehane), J H Scott

2984
Moat Handicap Chase (0-109 5-y-o and up) £3,105 3m.............(2:30)

2683* BLUE RING [-] 10-10-7 F Woods, ...(6 to 1)   1
2589² EDENAKILL LAD [-] 7-10-13 K F O'Brien, ...(9 to 4 fav)   2
2847* TAKE THE TOWN [-] 9-11-13 (4ex) J F Titley, ...(7 to 2)   3
2662⁷ ROSSI NOVAE [-] (bl) 11-11-2 (3") T P Treacy, ...(20 to 1)   4
1784⁸ MID-DAY GAMBLE [-] 10-10-13 L P Cusack, ...(12 to 1)   5
2701⁸ OPRYLAND [-] 9-11-1 (5") J P Broderick, ...(7 to 1)   6
2847⁴ ALL A QUIVER [-] 7-10-8 C N Bowens, ...(8 to 1)   7
2591⁹ AMERICAN EYRE [-] 9-11-4 (3") D P Murphy, ...(20 to 1)   8
2847⁶ SET YOUR SIGHTS [-] 11-10-10 (5") D P Geoghegan,
....(14 to 1)   9
2125 LANIGANS WINE [-] 12-11-7 T Horgan, ...(14 to 1)   10
2774⁵ LINVAR [-] 11-10-7 A Powell, ...(16 to 1)   11

CORBALLY HILL [-] 15-10-3 P L Malone, ... (12 to 1) f
2847^3 KINGS HILL [-] 12-9-7 (7*) J Butler, ... (7 to 1) ur
Dist: 4l, 2l, 2l, 2½l. 7m 19.10s. (13 Ran).
(Mrs L Mangan), James Joseph Mangan

2985 Fishery Hurdle (4-y-o and up) £3,105 3m............................(3:00)

2679* BUTCHES BOY (Ire) 5-11-7 (5*) K P Gaule, ... (4 to 1) 1
2679^5 JOHNSTONS BUCK (Ire) 5-11-5 (3*) Mr D Valentine, ... (10 to 1) 2
2587^6 LOVELY RUN 7-11-9 H Rogers, ... (11 to 2) 3
2863 YOU'VE DONE WHAT (Ire) 6-11-10 J F Titley, ... (8 to 1) 4
2863^3 ARCHER (Ire) 6-11-10 K F O'Brien, ...(7 to 4 fav) 5
1020^5 SIDCUP HILL (Ire) 5-11-3 T Horgan, ... (6 to 1) 6
WAYUPHILL 7-11-5 D P Fagan, ... (33 to 1) 7
2181^4 OLYMPIC D'OR (Ire) 6-12-0 C O'Dwyer, ... (10 to 1) 8
254 DAVY CROCKETT 7-11-7 (7*) Mr R Pugh, ... (14 to 1) 9
2547^3 CARHUE STAR (Ire) 4-10-10 (3*) T J O'Sullivan, ... (7 to 1) 10
2616 WATERLOO BALL (Ire) 5-10-12 (5*) M J Holbrook, (14 to 1) 11
2283^6 LOUGH CULTRA DRIVE (Ire) 6-11-10 G M O'Neill, (10 to 1) 12
2770^2 SISTER NORA (Ire) 6-11-0 (5*) M M Mackin, ... (12 to 1) pu
Dist: 2l, 12l, 2½l, sht-hd. 6m 36.80s. (13 Ran).
(Mrs Bridget Kennedy), P A Fahy

2986 Naas Handicap Hurdle (4-y-o and up) £6,900 2m 3f...................(3:30)

2866^5 COCK COCKBURN [-] 8-11-11 S R Murphy, ... (6 to 1) 1
2754^6 JUPITER JIMMY [-] 5-11-0 (3*) C O'Brien, ... (11 to 2) 2
2866^3 MR BOAL (Ire) [-] 5-10-12 (5*) J P Broderick, ... (7 to 1) 3
2231^2 MRS BARTON (Ire) [-] (bl) 6-9-2 (5*) J R Barry, ...(7 to 1) 4
2866^6 IF YOU SAY YES (Ire) [-] 6-10-2 K F O'Brien, ... (12 to 1) 5
2590^4 COIN MACHINE (Ire) [-] 5-9-11 T Horgan, ...(5 to 1) 6
2279^4 ASSERT STAR [-] 4-9-13 (5*) K P Gaule, ...(14 to 1) 7
2658^2 MISTER DRUM (Ire) [-] 5-10-0 (7*) Mr J T McNamara, ... (10 to 1) 8
2682^5 MICK O'DWYER [-] 7-10-3 F J Flood, ... (20 to 1) 9
2465* ROUBABAY (Ire) [-] 6-10-5 (3*) T P Treacy, ... (9 to 2 fav) 10
2682^9 KELLY'S PEARL [-] 7-11-13 S H O'Donovan, ...(16 to 1) 11
2680^2 NOVELLO ALLEGRO (USA) [-] 6-11-7 (7*) D J Kavanagh, ... (12 to 1) 12
2589* HAVE TO THINK [-] 6-9-7 F Woods, ... (10 to 1) 13
2754^3 THATCH AND GOLD (Ire) [-] 6-10-12 M Duffy, ... (8 to 1) 14
2351 ALTEREZZA (USA) [-] (bl) 7-11-10 B Sheridan, ... (12 to 1) 15
2772^5 SADDLESTOWN GLEN [-] 9-9-13 H Rogers, ... (14 to 1) 16
1987^3 PLUMBOB (Ire) [-] 5-9-8 (7*) P J Smullen, ... (25 to 1) f
Dist: Nk, 7l, ½l, sht-hd. 4m 58.20s. (17 Ran).
(D Kinsella), John Queally

2987 Nas Na Ri EBF Chase (Listed - Grade 3) (5-y-o and up) £5,520 2m 40yds ....(4:00)

2845* GLENCLOUD (Ire) 6-11-6 G M O'Neill, *dsptd ld 1st 2, trkd ldr nxt, rdn in 3rd two out, second at last, styd on und pres to lead 100 yards out*................. (5 to 4 fav) 1
2286^6 FABRICATOR 8-11-9 K F O'Brien, *dsptd ld 1st 2, led nxt till hdd and wknd last 100 yards*................ (15 to 8) 2
2125 ITS A CRACKER 10-11-6 (3*) D P Murphy, *settled in 3rd, prog to track ldr 6th, second 2 out, rdn and wknd appr last*...................................... (100 to 30) 3
2774^7 TRASSEY BRIDGE 7-10-11 A Powell, *lost tch 4th, sn tld off*.. (33 to 1) 4
2774^9 FIDSPRIT 7-10-8 (3*) K B Walsh, *beh whn f 4th*.. (33 to 1) f
2700^4 MONKEY AGO 7-11-2 C O'Dwyer, *uns rdr 1st*..... (8 to 1) ur
Dist: 1½l, 9l, dist. 4m 32.80s. (6 Ran).
(D Tierney), Noel Meade

2988 Johnstown Handicap Hurdle (0-116 4-y-o and up) £3,105 2m........ (4:30)

1175^5 GREEN GLEN (USA) [-] 5-11-10 B Sheridan, ... (12 to 1) 1
1904^6 DEEP THYNE (Ire) [-] 6-10-7 S H O'Donovan, ... (12 to 1) 2
2751^4 LOAVES AND FISHES [-] (bl) 6-10-4 (7*) B D Murtagh, ... (8 to 1) 3
2587^8 CABRA TOWERS [-] 7-10-4 (5*) M M Mackin, ... (14 to 1) 4
2347^4 FORTY ONE (Ire) [-] 6-10-5 (5*) J P Broderick, .. (9 to 2 fav) 5
2610^6 GRAND TOUR (NZ) [-] (bl) 6-11-4 L P Cusack, ... (5 to 1) 6
2842^9 STAR ROSE [-] 12-10-11 (7*) J Butler, ... (14 to 1) 7
1818 ROMAN FORUM (Ire) [-] 6-11-5 C Bowens, ... (8 to 1) 8
2842^8 CELTIC SAILS (Ire) [-] 6-11-3 K F O'Brien, ... (10 to 1) 9
1155^3 NORA ANN (Ire) [-] 5-9-8 (7*) D J Kavanagh, ... (12 to 1) 10
2845^8 BALLYCANN [-] 7-10-12 (7*) P J Mulligan, ... (16 to 1) 11
2309^5 PREMIER COUNTY [-] 8-10-4 T Horgan, ... (16 to 1) 12
2770 MIRASEL [-] 7-10-2 C O'Dwyer, ... (25 to 1) 13
2869^3 DARAVIC (Ire) [-] 5-10-7 J Shortt, ... (6 to 1) 14
1269^7 JIMMY THE JACKDAW [-] (bl) 7-10-1 H Rogers, ... (6 to 1) 15
Dist: 1½l, 1½l, 2l, ¾l. 4m 19.30s. (15 Ran).
(Neil S McGrath), Neil S McGrath

2989 Maudlins INH Flat Race (5-y-o) £3,105 2m............................(5:00)

FIFTH SYMPHONY (Ire) 11-12 Mr M Phillips, ... (8 to 1) 1
POPPEA (Ire) 11-0 (7*) Mr P Cashman, ... (10 to 1) 2
SCENIC ROUTE (Ire) 11-7 (5*) Mr T P Hyde, ... (6 to 4 on) 3
VERITATIS SPLENDOR (Ire) 11-9 (3*) Mr J A Nash, .. (7 to 1) 4
TIRCONNAIL (Ire) 11-9 (3*) Mr A R Coonan, ... (25 to 1) 5
2849^6 RUEMARO THYNE (Ire) 11-5 (7*) Mr B M Cash, ... (12 to 1) 6
BOBLONG (Ire) 11-12 Mr P Fenton, ... (7 to 1) 7
2869 UNSINKABLE BOXER (Ire) 11-5 (7*) Mr D K Budds, (33 to 1) 8
2849 CANTELIER 11-5 (7*) Mr T J Corcoran Jnr, ... (50 to 1) 9
1397^2 THE ODD TIME (Ire) 11-12 Mr J E Kiely, ... (9 to 2) 10
1337 LADY FONTAINE (Ire) 11-2 (5*) Mr G J Harford, ... (16 to 1) 11
COME ON BOBBY (Ire) 11-5 (7*) Mr M G Wiseman, (16 to 1) 12
114 THYNE OWN GIRL (Ire) 11-0 (7*) Mr J P Kilfeather, (33 to 1) 13
Dist: 2l, 6l, 6l, ½l. 4m 7.30s. (13 Ran).
(Gerard J O'Keeffe), James Joseph Mangan

SANDOWN (good (races 1,4,6), good to soft (2,3,5,7))
Saturday March 12th
Going Correction: PLUS 0.70 sec. per fur.

2990 Dick McCreery Cup Handicap Chase For Amateur Riders (0-135 5-y-o and up) £3,371 2½m 110yds.........(1:55)

1340 EASTSHAW [125] 12-11-7 (7*) Mr C Ward Thomas, *in cl tch, lost pl 4 out, rallied frm 2 out, led aftr last, styd on.* .... (25 to 1 op 16 to 1 tchd 33 to 1) 1
2305 HEY COTTAGE [110] 9-10-8 (5*) Mr D McCain, *hld up, cld 7th, ev ch last, no extr.* .... (12 to 1 op 14 to 1 tchd 20 to 1) 2
1507^7 THE MASTER GUNNER [110] 10-10-8^2 (7*) Mr D Alers-Hankey, *led to 4th, led 9th till aftr last, no extr.* .... (11 to 8 fav op 6 to 4 tchd 13 to 8 and 5 to 4) 3
2915^3 AMBASSADOR [115] (bl) 11-10-11 (7*) Mr J Wingfield Digby, *cl up, led 7th to 9th, jmpd slwly 11th, kpt on one pace frm last*........... (7 to 1 op 5 to 1 tchd 15 to 2) 4
2777^2 SARTORIUS [108] 8-10-7^3 (7*) Capt A Smith-Maxwell, *in cl tch, mstk 4th, hit 12th, ch 3 out, wknd appr last.* .... (9 to 4 op 2 to 1 tchd 5 to 2) 5
2476^5 AL HASHIMI [120] 10-11-2 (7*) Major G Wheeler, *cl up, led 4th to 7th, mstk tenth, blun 5 out, sn lost tch.* .... (6 to 1 op 5 to 1 tchd 7 to 1) 6
Dist: ¾l, ¾l, nk, 6l, 15l. 5m 26.40s. a 26.90s (6 Ran).
(Simon Sainsbury), Capt T A Forster

2991 High Speed Production 'National Hunt' Novices' Hurdle (4-y-o and up) £3,113 2m 110yds.............. (2:25)

2705* SQUIRE SILK 5-11-8 S McNeill, *mid-div, cld 4 out, led appr last, jst hld on*..... (9 to 2 op 3 to 1 tchd 5 to 1) 1
2102* REDEEMYOURSELF (Ire) 5-11-0 D Murphy, *hdwy 3rd, dsptd ld frm 2 out, ev ch r-in, ran on wl, jst fld.* .... (8 to 1 op 6 to 1 tchd 10 to 1) 2
2676^6 LODESTONE LAD (Ire) 4-10-4 (3*) D Meredith, *chsd ldrs, pushed alng aftr 5th, one pace frm 2 out.* .... (50 to 1 op 16 to 1) 3
1755^8 SOUND REVEILLE 6-11-0 G Bradley, *led, jnd 2 out, sn hdd, wknd appr last.* (20 to 1 op 16 to 1 tchd 25 to 1) 4
LOOKOUT MOUNTAIN (Ire) 6-10-9 (5*) D Fortt, *beh, styd on frm 2 out, nrst finish*............. (50 to 1 op 20 to 1) 5
2723^3 FRIENDLY FELLOW 5-11-8 P Holley, *hld up in mid-div, effrt aftr 3 out, not pace to chal.* .... (11 to 2 op 3 to 1 tchd 6 to 1) 6
2728^4 CREDON 6-11-0 G McCourt, *hld up, cld on ldrs 3 out, no hdwy frm nxt*........ (16 to 1 op 10 to 1 tchd 20 to 1) 7
2723^6 RAINBOW CASTLE 7-10-11 (3*) P Hide, *trkd ldrs, hit 4 out, wknd appr 2 out*..... (25 to 1 op 16 to 1 tchd 33 to 1) 8
2572^4 HOLD YOUR RANKS 7-11-4 J Frost, *nvr nr to chal.* .... (25 to 1 op 16 to 1) 9
TRIPLE TREAT (Ire) 5-11-0 R J Beggan, *wtd wth towards rear, effrt 5th, styd on in strt, improve.* .... (100 to 1 op 33 to 1) 10
2147^5 ILE DE SOO 8-11-0 M Perrett, *nvr dngrs.* .... (12 to 1 op 10 to 1 tchd 14 to 1) 11
2415 MISTER NOVA 5-11-4 M A FitzGerald, *hld up, hdwy appr 2 out, sn rdn and btn.* .... (11 to 4 fav op 3 to 1 tchd 7 to 2) 12
1126^5 DEAR DO 7-11-0 J Osborne, *nvr better than mid-div.* .... (25 to 1 op 14 to 1 tchd 33 to 1) 13
2509 GALES OF LAUGHTER 5-10-11 (3*) A Thornton, *nvr better than mid-div*...... (50 to 1 op 33 to 1 tchd 100 to 1) 14
2572^5 BALLYMGYR (Ire) 5-10-11 (3*) A Procter, *hld up in mid-div, wknd aftr 3 out*................. (100 to 1 op 33 to 1) 15
2779 BISHOPS TRUTH 8-11-0 D Morris, *al beh.* .... (200 to 1 op 50 to 1) 16
2692^7 CELTIC LAIRD 6-10-7 (7*) D Bohan, *trkd ldrs, rdn aftr 3 out, sn lost pl*........ (25 to 1 op 14 to 1 tchd 33 to 1) 17
2757^6 OLDHILL WOOD (Ire) 4-10-7 S Earle, *not fluent, al beh.* .... (20 to 1 op 10 to 1 tchd 25 to 1) 18
2477 PARLIAMENTARIAN (Ire) 5-11-0 M Dwyer, *al beh, tld off.* .... (66 to 1 op 33 to 1) 19
KIWI L'EGLISE (NZ) 8-10-11 (3*) R Davis, *chsd ldrs to 4th, sn wknd, tld off*.... (50 to 1 op 33 to 1 tchd 100 to 1) 20
AND WHY NOT 6-11-0 C Llewellyn, *cl up, wknd appr 2 out, no ch whn f last*.......................... (8 to 1) f

DEE EM AITCH 5-11-0 M Bosley, *trkd ldrs till wknd aftr 3rd, tld off whn pld up bef 2 out.* ....(50 to 1 op 33 to 1 tchd 66 to 1) pu
1950^{9} RHYMING PROSE 6-10-9 T Grantham, *al beh, tld off whn pld up bef 2 out.*................(33 to 1 tchd 50 to 1) pu
1277 MR WENDYL 6-11-0 V Slattery, *mid-div till drpd rear 3 out, pld up bef last.* (66 to 1 op 50 to 1 tchd 100 to 1) pu
2042 QUEEN'S AWARD (Ire) 5-11-0 L Wyer, *mid-div, sn beh, tld off whn pld up bef 2 out.*.........(100 to 1 op 33 to 1) pu
Dist: Sht-hd, 10l, nk, 12l, ½l, 3½l, 2½l, 1½l, ¾l, 4l. 4m 3.00s. a 16.00s (25 Ran).
SR: 50/42/25/31/19/26/14/11/13/ (Robert Ogden), Andrew Turnell

2992 Barclays Bank Handicap Hurdle For Amateur Riders (0-130 4-y-o and up) £4,138 2m 110yds............. (2:55)

2734^{5} SHAMSHOM AL ARAB (Ire) [94] 6-10-0 (7*) Miss V Haigh, *cld appr 3rd, led approaching 2 out, rdn out.* ....(50 to 1 op 33 to 1 tchd 66 to 1) 1
2862^{2} HAPPY HORSE (NZ) [107] 7-10-13 (7*) Mr J Wingfield Digby, *made most till appr 2 out, one pace.* (7 to 2 tchd 3 to 1) 2
2790^{3} NOBLE INSIGHT [94] 7-10-0 (7*) Mr S Righton, *hld up, outpcd 3 out, styd on one pace frm nxt.* ....(12 to 1 op 10 to 1 tchd 14 to 1) 3
2721 SECOND CALL [109] 5-11-1 (7*) Mr C Ward Thomas, *cl up, mstk 4th, wknd appr 2 out.*......(3 to 1 fav op 9 to 4) 4
2801* FAIR BROTHER [102] 8-10-10 (5*) Mr D McCain, *hld up, hrd rdn appr 2 out, no response.*.........(9 to 2 op 4 to 1) 5
2626^{3} TOP WAVE [115] 6-11-7 (7*) Mr D Alers-Hankey, *trkd ldrs till wknd aftr 2 out.*..............(6 to 1 tchd 13 to 2) 6
2192^{3} DJEBEL PRINCE [97] 7-10-8^{5} (7*) Major M Watson, *pckd second, lost pl nxt, wkng whn f 3 out.* ....(11 to 2 op 5 to 1 tchd 6 to 1) f
1338* CONVOY [94] (bl) 4-10-0 (7*) Mr J Beardsall, *hld up, tld off 3rd, pld up bef 2 out.*............(10 to 1 tchd 11 to 1) pu
Dist: 3l, 4l, 7l, 15l, sht-hd. 4m 6.80s. a 19.80s (8 Ran).
SR: -/6/-/-/-/ (Miss V Haigh), J R Jenkins

2993 Burnt Oak & Special Cargo Novices' Chase (5-y-o and up) £3,701 2m (3:30)

2567* CABOCHON 7-11-6 J Frost, *chsd ldr frm 4th, jmpd rght 8th, not fluent nxt 2, led aftr last, drvn out.* ....(11 to 4 op 9 to 4 tchd 100 to 30) 1
2268^{3} BIG BEAT (USA) 6-11-10 P Holley, *led, clr 3rd, awkward 7th, hdd aftr last, no extr.* ....(13 to 8 fav op 11 to 8 tchd 5 to 4) 2
1803 TUDOR FABLE (Ire) 6-11-6 M A FitzGerald, *in tch, hmpd 8th, outpcd 4 out, styd on frm 2 out.* ....(8 to 1 op 7 to 1 tchd 9 to 1) 3
2043 STRONG VIEWS 7-11-6 A Maguire, *hld up, hdwy 8th, ch 2 out, wknd appr last.*...(7 to 2 op 5 to 1 tchd 11 to 2) 4
DUKE OF APROLON 7-10-13 D Murphy, *awkward second, hld up, cld 3 out, btn nxt.* ....(10 to 1 op 8 to 1 tchd 12 to 1) 5
2366 COASTING 8-11-2 R Davis, *not fluent, al beh, tld off.* ....(33 to 1 op 25 to 1 tchd 40 to 1) 6
Dist: 1½l, 6l, 2l, 7l, dist. 4m 6.50s. a 18.00s (6 Ran).
SR: 24/26/16/14/-/-/ (Jack Joseph), R G Frost

2994 Sunderlands Imperial Cup Handicap Hurdle (4-y-o and up) £19,365 2m 110yds........................ (4:05)

1874 PRECIOUS BOY [138] 8-11-7 L Wyer, *al prmnt gng wl, led 2 out, sn drifted lft, hdd last, rallied und pres to ld r-in.* ....(33 to 1 tchd 40 to 1) 1
1561^{3} RIVA (NZ) [126] 7-10-9 C Llewellyn, *hld up, hdwy 5th, led last, hdd r-in, ran on.*...(8 to 1 op 7 to 1 tchd 9 to 1) 2
2046^{3} LEOTARD [141] 7-11-10 J Osborne, *hld up, swtchd rght to chal appr 2 out, one pace und pres approaching last.* ....(16 to 1 tchd 20 to 1) 3
1991^{2} HERE HE COMES [139] 8-11-1 (7*) S Ryan, *pld hrd early, hld up, hdwy appr 2 out, sn one pace.* ....(14 to 1 op 12 to 1) 4
2833^{7} HOME COUNTIES (Ire) [128] (v) 5-10-8 (3*) D J Moffatt, *hld up, cld appr 2 out, one pace approaching last.* ....(40 to 1 op 33 to 1 tchd 50 to 1) 5
2850^{6} NAHAR [130] 9-10-13 A Dicken, *hld up, pushed alng aftr 5th, kpt on, nvr on terms.* ....(40 to 1 op 33 to 1 tchd 50 to 1) 6
LEMON'S MILL (USA) [132] 5-11-1 D Murphy, *trkd ldrs gng wl, niggled alng aftr 3 out, sn btn, eased.* ....(6 to 1 op 7 to 1 tchd 8 to 1) 7
2473^{3} OLYMPIAN [136] (bl) 7-11-5 A Maguire, *led, hit 3 out, hdd nxt, wknd.*...............(9 to 4 fav tchd 5 to 2) 8
2788^{2} CLURICAN (Ire) [117] 5-9-9 (5*) E Husband, *chsd ldrs, f 5th.* ....(20 to 1 op 25 to 1 tchd 33 to 1) f
2723 EDIMBOURG [122] 8-10-5 M A FitzGerald, *cl up, mstks 1st 2, wknd aftr 3 out, pld up bef nxt.* ....(8 to 1 op 7 to 1 tchd 9 to 1) pu
2480^{2} KIVETON TYCOON (Ire) [123] (bl) 5-10-6 G Bradley, *mid-div, drpd rear 3rd, sn tld off, pld up bef last.* ....(16 to 1 op 14 to 1 tchd 20 to 1) pu
2595^{6} HER HONOUR [131] 5-11-0 J Lower, *hld up, shrtlvd effrt appr 2 out, pld up bef last.*.........(14 to 1 op 16 to 1) pu

2833^{5} ARCOT [127] (v) 6-10-10 G McCourt, *refused to race, took no part.*...............(11 to 2 op 5 to 1 tchd 6 to 1) l
Dist: ½l, 3l, 1l, nk, 3½l, 2½l, ¾l. 4m 1.10s. a 14.10s (13 Ran).
SR: 68/55/67/64/52/50/49/52/-/ (M R Johnson), M G Meagher

2995 H.M.S. Sandown Handicap Chase (0-14 5-y-o and up) £4,143 3m 110yds ....(4:40)

2648^{3} BUCK WILLOW [115] 10-10-1 D Murphy, *hld up, cld 13th, led 5 out, clr 2 out, easily.*..... (4 to 1 jt-fav op 7 to 2) 1
2506^{6} ANNIO CHILONE [115] 8-9-12 (3*) P Hide, *cl up, led 12th to 17th, outpcd 4 out, styd on to take second r-in.* (7 to 1) 2
2747 SOLIDASAROCK [125] 12-10-11 G McCourt, *trkd ldrs, lost pl 13th, rallied 16th, ev ch 3 out, outpcd.*.....(4 to 1 jt-fav op 7 to 2 tchd 9 to 2) 3
HENRY MANN [139] (bl) 11-11-11 J Osborne, *al beh, shrt-lvd effrt 13th, tld off.*....(9 to 2 op 4 to 1 tchd 5 to 1) 4
2747 GAMBLING ROYAL [142] 11-12-0 A Maguire, *nvr far away, led briefly 17th, second and ev ch whn f 3 out.* ....(7 to 1 op 6 to 1 tchd 8 to 1) f
2673^{3} THE LEGGETT [114] (bl) 11-10-0 R Bellamy, *led aftr 1st to 12th, mstk 15th and wknd, tld off whn pld up bef 2 out.* ....(12 to 1 op 50 to 1) pu
2786^{4} REPEAT THE DOSE [125] 9-10-11 M Dwyer, *hld up, reminder aftr 11th, sn wknd, pld up bef 13th.* ....(13 to 2 op 6 to 1 tchd 7 to 1) pu
2747^{9} SPARKLING FLAME [129] (bl) 10-11-1 M A FitzGerald, *led briefly 1st, cl up, wknd 15th, tld off whn pld up bef last.* ....(6 to 1 tchd 5 to 1 and 13 to 2) pu
Dist: 15l, 6l, dist. 6m 23.80s. a 24.80s (8 Ran).
(Mrs S N J Embiricos), J T Gifford

2996 'Au Revoir' National Hunt Flat Race (4,5,6-y-o) £1,954 2m 110yds.... (5:10)

FALMOUTH BAY (Ire) 5-11-8 Mr J Durkan, *led 5 fs, led five out, ran on wl.*......................(5 to 1 op 6 to 1) 1
2677^{4} CASTLE CHIEF (Ire) 5-11-5 (3*) P Hide, *al prmnt, ran green whn rdn 2 fs out, one pace.* ....(11 to 2 op 4 to 1 tchd 6 to 1) 2
FOXBOW (Ire) 4-10-7 (7*) R Massey, *chsd ldrs, hdwy 3 fs out, one pace ins last.* ....(10 to 1 op 12 to 1 tchd 14 to 1) 3
AIRTRAK (Ire) 5-11-1 (7*) Mr C Vigors, *mid-div, cld o'r 5 fs out, one pace 3 out.*...(10 to 1 op 5 to 1 tchd 12 to 1) 4
1126^{3} THE CAUMRUE (Ire) 6-11-5 (3*) R Davis, *beh, hdwy 4 fs out, hrd rdn 2 out, wknd fnl furlong.*.... (8 to 1 op 7 to 1) 5
2509^{5} COUNTRY CONCORDE 4-10-11 (3*) D Meredith, *trkd ldrs, rdn 5 fs out, styd on one pace frm 2 out.* ....(14 to 1 op 12 to 1) 6
WREKENGALE (Ire) 4-10-7 (7*) D Bohan, *hld up, outpcd 7 fs out, styd on wl frm o'r 2 out.*....(10 to 1 op 7 to 1) 7
TAMANDU 4-10-2 (7*) Katherine Davis, *beh, rdn and styd on fnl 2 fs, nrst finish.*............(50 to 1 op 33 to 1) 8
JAPACADA 4-10-9 (5*) D Fortt, *mid-div, cld 6 fs out, wknd o'r 2 out.*..........................(20 to 1 op 16 to 1) 9
ME FEIN (Ire) 6-11-1 (7*) Mr C Curley, *keen hold in mid-div, nvr nr to chal.*........(9 to 1 op 5 to 1 tchd 10 to 1) 10
EMBLEY QUAY 5-11-3 (5*) S Curran, *hld up, al beh.* ....(33 to 1) 11
2339^{9} NO MORE NICE GUY (Ire) 5-11-5 (3*) Miss A Harwood, *trkd ldrs, led aftr 5 fs to five out, wknd 3 out.* ....(14 to 1 op 12 to 1 tchd 16 to 1) 12
KATREE RUNNER 5-11-1 (7*) Pat Thompson, *beh, hdwy o'r 6 fs out, sn btn.*..................(10 to 1 op 5 to 1) 13
2509^{4} JUNGLE KING (NZ) 5-11-5 (3*) A Thornton, *trkd ldrs, pushed alng 5 fs out, btn 3 out.* ....(7 to 2 fav op 4 to 1 tchd 3 to 1) 14
ST MARTIN 6-11-8 Mr C Ward Thomas, *al beh.* ....(50 to 1 op 33 to 1) 15
2560 CHANCE DE LA VIE 5-11-1 (7*) M Keighley, *keen hold, trkd ldrs to hfwy.*....................(33 to 1 op 20 to 1) 16
2444 SURGICAL SPIRIT 4-10-2 (7*) P McLoughlin, *cl up, hrd rdn 5 fs out, wknd o'r 3 out.*..........(25 to 1 op 33 to 1) 17
2387 BLACK STAG (Ire) 5-11-1 (7*) Mr G Hogan, *al beh.* ....(33 to 1 op 25 to 1) 18
SCORPION BAY 6-11-8 A Dicken, *al beh.* ....(50 to 1 op 33 to 1) 19
SILENT SOVEREIGN 5-11-1 (7*) D Rees, *mid-div, beh hfwy.*...........................(50 to 1 op 33 to 1) 20
KEEP THE DREAM 4-10-2 (7*) L Reynolds, *al beh, sn tld off.*..(33 to 1) 21
DAYTIME BOMBER 4-10-7 (7*) N Juckes, *chsd ldrs, wknd aftr 6 fs, tld off whn pld up o'r 3 out.* ....(33 to 1 op 20 to 1) pu
Dist: 1½l, 2½l, 6l, 1½l, 4l, 1l, 2l, 2l, 3l, 1½l. 4m 3.30s. (22 Ran).
(James Morton), S E Sherwood

SOUTHWELL (good)
Saturday March 12th
Going Correction: PLUS 0.85 sec. per fur.

2997 Muskham Novices' Hurdle (5-y-o and up) £2,950 3m 110yds.......... (2:10)

2802⁵ KNOCKAVERRY (Ire) 6-10-7 R Supple, *al gng wl, nosed ahead on bit appr 2 out, readily.*
.................................(4 to 1 op 3 to 1 tchd 9 to 2) 1

2308 SON OF IRIS 6-10-12 P Niven, *patiently rdn, improved fnl circuit, led briefly aftr 3 out, no ch wth wnr.*
.................................(14 to 1 op 10 to 1) 2

2731⁵ SMITH'S BAND (Ire) (bl) 6-10-12 I Lawrence, *al hndy, ev ch 3 out, rdn bef nxt, one pace*.........(14 to 1 op 12 to 1) 3

1935 KONVEKTA CONTROL 7-10-12 M Richards, *tried to make all, hdd aftr 3 out, fnshd tired.*
.................................(5 to 4 fav tchd 11 to 10) 4

2419³ PENNANT COTTAGE (Ire) 6-10-7 J Railton, *wth ldr, hit 3rd, struggling 4 out, lost tch nxt, tld off.*
.................................(12 to 1 op 10 to 1) 5

2717 ROBENKO (USA) (bl) 5-10-12 N Williamson, *trkd ldg quartet hfwy, blun 4 out, sn lost pl. tld off.*
.................................(20 to 1 op 16 to 1) 6

2870⁸ LATOSKY 6-10-12 P Harley, *trkd ldg bunch, lost tch fnl circuit, pld up bef 3 out*..........(33 to 1 op 25 to 1) pu

2485 TRICYCLE (Ire) 5-10-12 Gary Lyons, *chsd ldrs to hfwy, tld off fnl circuit, pld up bef 5 out*...............(33 to 1) pu

2404 BUCKSHOT (Ire) 6-10-12 E Murphy, *in tch, struggling aftr one circuit, tld off whn pld up bef 5 out.*
.................................(9 to 1 op 8 to 1) pu

1620³ HINTON LADY 5-10-7 M Ranger, *al plcd whn hit 5th, sn lost tch, tld off when pld up bef 7th.*
.................................(13 to 1 op 25 to 1) pu

Dist: 10l, 12l, 30l, 20l, dist. 6m 18.50s. a 28.50s (10 Ran).
SR: 2/-/-/-/-/-/ (Mrs W Morrell), M J Wilkinson

2998 Fibreturf Claiming Hurdle (4-y-o and up) £4,269 2½m 110yds........(2:45)

2828³ TUSKY 6-11-3 N Bentley, *nvr far away, led 3 out, drvn alng last 2, kpt on gmely r-in*...... (4 to 1 tchd 7 to 2) 1

2895³ BONANZA 7-12-0 R Hodge, *al hndy, niggled alng to hold pl 5th, reminder 3 out, rallied, kpt on same pace r-in.*
.................................(11 to 8 on tchd 5 to 4 on and 6 to 4 on) 2

1721⁶ WINDWARD ARIOM (bl) 8-11-4 R Marley, *nvr far away, ev ch 3 out, feeling pace and rdn nxt, sn outpcd.*
.................................(16 to 1 op 12 to 1) 3

2033³ TRENTSIDE MIST 6-11-2 M Ranger, *wth ldr, led 6th to 3 out, fdd and pres*................(25 to 1 op 20 to 1) 4

2627² RAIN-N-SUN 8-11-2 T Wall, *wth ldrs, rdn bef 3 out, sn lost tch, tld off*..........(16 to 1 op 14 to 1 tchd 20 to 1) 5

2423³ TRISTAN'S COMET 7-11-4 D Gallagher, *chsd ldg bunch, struggling to keep up 4 out, tld off frm nxt.*
.................................(8 to 1 op 5 to 1) 6

BUD'S BET (Ire) 6-11-6 D Byrne, *in tch, struggling hfwy, sn lost touch, tld off.* (11 to 1 op 8 to 1 tchd 12 to 1) 7

2900⁹ TANAISTE (USA) (bl) 5-11-4 N Williamson, *slight ld to 6th, lost tch quickly 4 out, tld off*.......(33 to 1 op 20 to 1) 8

2792 NEGATORY (USA) 7-11-6 W Worthington, *reluctant to race, tld off thrght, nrly f 5 out, pld up bef 2 out.*
.................................(20 to 1 op 14 to 1) pu

Dist: ¾l, 20l, 8l, 15l, 10l, 12l, 25l, 20l. 5m 17.50s. a 24.00s (9 Ran).
SR: 23/33/3/-/-/-/ (Ms Sigrid Walter), G M Moore

2999 British Gas Novices' Chase (6-y-o and up) £5,668 3m 110yds.........(3:15)

1776⁵ UFANO (Fr) 8-11-4 Peter Hobbs, *led to second, styd hndy, led 8 out, jmpd wl to go clr, easily.* (20 to 1 op 16 to 1) 1

2706³ LOBRIC (bl) 9-11-4 J Railton, *led second to 8 out, outpcd and struggling 5 out, kpt on, no ch wth wnr.*
.................................(11 to 1 op 8 to 1 tchd 12 to 1) 2

2362* RUN UP THE FLAG 7-11-12 E Murphy, *trkd ldrs, struggling to keep up fnl circuit, lost tch 5 out, tld off.*
.................................(11 to 10 on op 5 to 4 on tchd Evens) 3

1952 CROFT MILL 8-11-8 N Williamson, *not jump wl, 4th and hndy whn f 11th*...................(7 to 1 op 6 to 1) f

2514⁴ LUSTY LIGHT 8-11-12 I Lawrence, *chsd ldg quartet till f 4th*........................(11 to 4 tchd 3 to 1) f

2896 PESSOA 7-11-4 Gary Lyons, *f 1st*.... (25 to 1 op 33 to 1) f

2809 RUPERT STANLEY 10-11-4 Richard Guest, *struggling to keep up aftr 4th, a fence beh whn pld up bef 7 out.*
.................................(50 to 1 op 33 to 1) pu

Dist: 30l, 15l. 6m 48.40s. a 50.40s (7 Ran).

(Nigel Harris), Capt T A Forster

3000 Rolleston Mill Novices' Handicap Chase (5-y-o and up) £6,961 2m (3:45)

2872³ HOWGILL [79] 8-10-6 (3*) S Wynne, *led till hdd 4 out, rallied, lft in ld nxt, styd on r-in*.. (10 to 1 op 7 to 1) 1

2665⁴ WEEKDAY CROSS (Ire) [75] 6-10-5 J Railton, *settled gng wl, smooth hdwy on bit appr 3 out, rdn betw last 2, found little*.........................(8 to 1 op 10 to 1) 2

2794⁶ MASTER'S CROWN (USA) [83] 6-10-13 W Worthington, *trkd ldrs, struggling to hold pl hfwy, tld off frm 6 out.*
.................................(33 to 1) 3

2794 VAZON BAY [92] (bl) 10-11-8 I Lawrence, *wth ldr, reminders hfwy, no response, tld off frm 6 out.*
.................................(3 to 1 fav tchd 7 to 2) 4

2584* GYMCRAK STARDOM [92] 8-11-8 R Marley, *chsd ldg bunch, rdn and struggling 6 out, poor 3rd whn f 3 out.*
.................................(7 to 2 tchd 4 to 1) f

1368² KEEP SHARP [94] 8-11-10 Richard Guest, *not fluent, disputing 4th and rdn alng whn f 6 out, broke shoulder destroyed*.......................(7 to 1 op 11 to 1 to 2) f

2304 FRONT STREET [95] 7-11-11 M Richards, *took keen hold, jmpd ahead 4 out, hrd pressed and rdn whn f nxt.*
.................................(4 to 1 op 7 to 2) f

1621 RIDDLEMEROO [70] (v) 9-9-11 (3*) T Eley, *struggling and lost tch hfwy, tld off whn pld up bef 3 out.*
.................................(50 to 1 op 33 to 1) pu

2402⁴ FROG HOLLOW (Ire) [76] 6-10-5 (3*) R Farrant, *chsd ldrs, struggling and lost grnd hfwy, tld off whn pld up bef 3 out*.......................(10 to 1 op 12 to 1) pu

Dist: 1l, dist, 20l. 4m 20.50s. a 21.50s (9 Ran).
SR: 2/-/-/-/-/ (Mrs Charles Lockhart), R Hollinshead

3001 Ossington Handicap Chase (0-145 5-y-o and up) £4,760 2½m 110yds...(4:20)

2787* BALTIC BROWN [120] 9-11-13 Richard Guest, *chsd clr ldg trio, relentless prog frm 4 out, ran on gmely to ld clr hme.*
.................................(11 to 4 op 5 to 2) 1

1932⁴ SIRRAH JAY [105] 14-10-12 N Williamson, *slight ld to 3rd, styd hndy till led ag'n bef 5 out, quickened clr, jst ct.*
.................................(20 to 1 tchd 25 to 1) 2

2785³ MEGA BLUE [112] 9-11-5 P Niven, *dsptd ld, led 3rd to 5th, struggling 4 out, tld off last 3.*
.................................(9 to 4 fav op 11 to 4 tchd 3 to 1) 3

2820² CITY KID [120] 9-11-6 (7*) J J Brown, *pressed ldg pair, led 5th till blun 5 out, tld off aftr nxt*... (4 to 1 op 3 to 1) 4

2707⁴ ATLAAL [121] (v) 9-12-0 S Smith Eccles, *struggling frm 6th, tld off whn pld up bef six out*.....(12 to 1 op 10 to 1) pu

2861* SIMPLE PLEASURE [113] 9-11-6 D Gallagher, *sn wl tld off, pld up bef 7 out*.......................(5 to 1) pu

Dist: ½l, dist, 30l. 5m 35.00s. a 32.00s (6 Ran).
(Mrs S Smith), Mrs S J Smith

3002 Egmanton Novices' Hurdle (4-y-o and up) £2,742 2¼m................(4:50)

2150⁴ WAMDHA (Ire) 4-10-9 A S Smith, *confidently rdn, smooth hdwy to draw level aftr 3 out, hrd ridden to ld post.*
.................................(3 to 1 op 2 to 1) 1

2405⁵ BIGWHEEL BILL (Ire) (bl) 5-11-2 S Smith Eccles, *al hndy, led 4 out, hrd pressed frm nxt, ran on, jst ct.*
.................................(5 to 2 fav op 3 to 1 tchd 7 to 2) 2

2812 D'ARBLAY STREET (Ire) 5-10-9 (7*) S McDougall, *dsptd ld, led hfwy to 4 out, rdn aftr nxt, fdd.*
.................................(7 to 1 op 6 to 1 tchd 8 to 1) 3

1509⁸ FITNESS FANATIC 6-11-8 E Murphy, *made most till hdd hfwy, rdn 4 out, sn wknd, virtually pld up r-in.*
.................................(5 to 1 op 3 to 1) 4

2245 KIMBERLEY BOY 4-10-8 N Williamson, *in tch to hfwy, tld off whn pld up bef 3 out*..............(7 to 1 op 10 to 1) pu

732³ BLUE RADIANCE 4-10-3 D Gallagher, *al beh, tld off whn pld up aftr 3 out*........(7 to 1 op 6 to 1 tchd 8 to 1) pu

2835 CHILDSWAY (bl) 6-11-2 G Upton, *dsptd ld, lang badly rght, tried to run out bend aftr 5th, pld up bef nxt.*
.................................(25 to 1 op 16 to 1) pu

Dist: Sht-hd, 30l, dist. 4m 53.50s. a 32.50s (7 Ran).
(T R Pryke), K A Morgan

HEREFORD (good)
Monday March 14th
Going Correction: PLUS 0.40 sec. per fur. (races 1,3,-6,7), PLUS 0.10 (2,4,5)

3003 Putley Selling Handicap Hurdle (4-y-o and up) £1,906 3¼m..........(2:10)

1592⁵ MISTRESS ROSS [73] 11-10-0 D Bridgwater, *hld up middiv, hdwy 4 out, chlgd 2 out, stly rdn to ld nr finish.*
.................................(11 to 1 op 10 to 1 tchd 12 to 1) 1

2729³ IT'S NOT MY FAULT (Ire) [77] 6-10-4 W Marston, *hld up rear, hdwy 6th, wnt second 9th, led aftr 3 out, hrd rdn and hdd nr finish*......(7 to 1 op 6 to 1 tchd 9 to 1) 2

2417 BARLEY MOW [76] 8-10-3 N Mann, *hld up, hdwy 7th, kpt on one pace frm 3 out*............(20 to 1 op 12 to 1) 3

2792⁵ LITTLE BIG [85] 7-10-5 (7*) N Collum, *prmnt, rdn 3 out, not pace to chal*......................(7 to 2 tchd 9 to 2) 4

2839³ ON THE SAUCE [108] (bl) 7-12-0 (7*) T Dascombe, *led till rdn and hdd aftr 3 out, wknd.*
.................................(7 to 4 fav op 6 to 4 tchd 15 to 8) 5

2711³ BRIGHT SAPPHIRE [73] 8-9-11 (3*) R Farrant, *prmnt, dsptd second 8th, wknd 4 out*..............(25 to 1) 6

2729 GAELGOIR [73] 10-10-0 W Humphreys, *al rear, tld off.*
.................................(12 to 1 op 8 to 1) 7

2729⁶ GROTIUS [73] (bl) 10-10-0 R Bellamy, *al rear, tld off.*
.................................(16 to 1 op 12 to 1) 8

2801⁷ PRINCE VALMY (Fr) [73] 9-10-0 B Powell, *rear whn hit 4th, tld off*....................................(50 to 1) 9

2535⁸ HELLO VANOS [76] 6-10-3⁶ (3*) A Thornton, *chsd ldr till wknd 7th, tld off*....................(50 to 1) 10

417⁴ MARLBOROUGH LADY [76] 8-10-3⁵ S Burrough, *al beh, tld off*..(33 to 1) 11

2776³ LEAVE IT OUT [80] 12-10-7⁷ J Frost, *prmnt second till wknd quickly 6th, pld up bef 8th.* (20 to 1 op 16 to 1) pu

2729 ENBORNE LAD [80] (bl) 10-10-7³ G McCourt, frnt rnk till
jmpd slvly and wknd 8th, tld off whn pld up bef last.
.... (16 to 1 op 12 to 1)   pu
2321 FILM LIGHTING GIRL [73] 8-10-0 R Supple, chsd ldrs till
pld up 8th, lme......................... (33 to 1)   pu
LEVY FREE [94] 9-11-0 (7") Mr N Bradley, loose bef strt, in
tch to 6th, tld off whn pld up before 8th.
.... (25 to 1 op 14 to 1)   pu
2760 LEGAL WIN (USA) [75] 6-10-0⁵ (7") Mr G Shenkin, refused to
race............................... (20 to 1)   pu
Dist: ½l, 12l, 2½l, nk, 15l, 30l, 8l, ½l, 2l, 3l. 6m 28.90s. a 28.90s (16 Ran).
(Dr Jane Van Tilborg), G Thorner

3004 Hagley Novices' Handicap Chase (5-y-o and up) £2,489 2m......... (2:40)

1557⁶ FRANKUS [72] 5-10-0 S Earle, made all, ran on gmely und
pres r-in, jst hld on....................(5 to 1 op 7 to 1)   1
2803³ BEAUFAN [72] 7-10-0 Gary Lyons, hld up, hdwy 8th, wnt
second 3 out, ran on strly und pres frm last, jst fld.
.... (11 to 2 op 5 to 1)   2
2794 PERCY SMOLLETT [78] 6-10-6 R Bellamy, prmnt, outpcd 3
out, rallied and not much room r-in.
.... (14 to 1 op 12 to 1)   3
2822 EMERALD RULER [80] 7-10-8 G McCourt, beh, hdwy 3rd,
rdn 7th, wknd 4 out..................... (7 to 1 op 5 to 1)   4
2761* PHILIP'S WOODY [96] 6-11-10 J R Kavanagh, not fluent,
chsd ldrs till lost pl 7th, tld off. (7 to 4 fav tchd 2 to 1)   5
2858 BROADWOOD LAD [72] 8-9-7 (7") P McLoughlin, rear, some
hdwy 8th, tld off........................ (50 to 1)   6
1615⁴ KING'S RARITY [74] 8-10-2 B Powell, prmnt to 4th, sn beh,
jmpd slvly four out, tld off................ (14 to 1)   7
1279 MARCH LANE [72] 7-10-0 D Bridgwater, al beh, tld off 6th.
.... (33 to 1)   8
2840³ ALWAYS REMEMBER [83] 7-10-11 B Clifford, prmnt, hit
second, ev ch 3 out, und pres in 4th whn f last.
.... (3 to 1 op 5 to 2)   f
Dist: Sht-hd, ¾l, 20l, 25l, 5l, 3l, dist. 3m 55.90s. a 6.90s (9 Ran).
SR: 19/19/24/6/-/-/   (Jack Woodward), S Mellor

3005 Hoechst Panacur EBF Mares 'National Hunt' Novices' Hurdle Qualifier (5-y-o and up) £2,228 2m 3f 110yds.... (3:10)

2841² FORTUNES COURSE (Ire) 5-10-12 J R Kavanagh, al prmnt,
rdn to ld sn aftr 2 out, pushed out.
.... (9 to 2 op 4 to 1 tchd 5 to 1)   1
2302³ GO MARY 8-11-5 W Marston, chsd ldrs, ev ch 2 out, not
pace of winr........................... (11 to 2 op 5 to 1 tchd 6 to 1)   2
2796³ TOO SHARP 6-10-9 (3") J McCarthy, led, hit 4 out, hrd rdn
and hld aftr 2 out, wknd......... (4 to 1 fav op 7 to 2)   3
1192 WONDERFULL POLLY 6-10-7 (5") Guy Lewis, hld up,
hdwy appr 7th, wknd approaching 2 out.
.... (7 to 1 op 5 to 1)   4
2789⁶ PRECIOUS JUNO (Ire) 5-10-12 I Lawrence, chsd ldrs, rdn 3
out, no hdwy............................ (7 to 1 op 5 to 1)   5
2796² STORMY SUNSET 7-10-5 (7") Mr N Moore, chsd ldr, hit
6th, prmnt till blun 3 out, sn btn..... (7 to 1 op 6 to 1)   6
1341³ ANNA VALLEY 8-11-5 Richard Guest, hld up in tch, wknd
4 out, eased, tld off................... (5 to 1 op 4 to 1)   7
2692⁶ ARCHIE'S SISTER 5-10-9 (3") D Meredith, al rear, tld off.
.... (33 to 1)   8
2558⁷ QUAGO 6-10-12 B Powell, prmnt to 6th, sn beh, tld off.
.... (20 to 1 op 14 to 1)   9
2808 ELANDS CASTLE (Ire) 6-10-12 R Supple, al beh, tld off.
.... (50 to 1)   10
1806 MISS PALEFACE 6-10-12 J Frost, al beh, tld off. (20 to 1)   11
2731 TRUE STORM 5-10-12 D Bridgwater, prmnt to 6th, sn beh,
tld off........................... (25 to 1 op 20 to 1)   12
BOOK OF RYMES 7-10-12 W Humphreys, hld up, tld off
7th................................... (40 to 1)   13
CRAZY DAISY 7-10-12 G Rowe, prmnt, hit 6th, wknd 4
out, tld off whn pld up bef last... (33 to 1 op 50 to 1)   pu
THE FOOLISH ONE 7-10-12 S Earle, mid-div to 5th, tld off
whn pld up bef 3 out............... (20 to 1 op 16 to 1)   pu
2808 ARLEY GALE 6-10-12 G McCourt, slwly away, lost tch
5th, tld off whn pld up bef 3 out............. (50 to 1)   pu
2860 DIANE'S PRIDE (Ire) 5-10-12 Mr B Leavy, al beh, tld off
whn hit 4 out, pld up bef nxt.................. (50 to 1)   pu
Dist: 2½l, 8l, 7l, 1½l, 2½l, 30l, 1l, 2½l, dist, ¾l. 4m 44.10s. a 23.10s (17 Ran).
(Mrs A J Garrett), J S King

3006 Trumpet Handicap Chase (0-110 5-y-o and up) £2,906 3m 1f 110yds.... (3:40)

2725 FLYER'S NAP [98] 8-11-10 S Earle, hld up rear, mstk 9th,
str hdwy frm 13th, led aftr 4 out, drw clr, easily.
.... (11 to 2 op 5 to 1 tchd 6 to 1)   1
2524* DEEPENDABLE [92] (bl) 7-11-4 J R Kavanagh, led to 3rd,
prmnt, no ch with winr frm 3 out.
.... (5 to 2 op 9 to 4 tchd 11 to 4)   2
2787³ HICKELTON LAD [79] 10-9-12 (7") Miss S Higgins, prmnt,
lost pl 7th, hit 12th, styd on frm 4 out.
.... (20 to 1 op 16 to 1)   3
1808 CASINO MAGIC [88] 10-11-0 W Marston, jmpd wl, led 3rd
till aftr 4 out, wknd.......................... (14 to 1)   4

1968³ SANDAIG [92] (bl) 8-11-1 (3") A Thornton, hld up, hdwy
appr 7th, wkng whn mstk 3 out.
.... (15 to 8 fav op 5 to 2 tchd 7 to 4)   5
2429⁴ THAMESDOWN TOOTSIE [87] 9-10-13 S McNeill, trkd ldrs
till wknd 14th, eased, tld off....... (5 to 1 op 4 to 1)   6
2733 SAM SHORROCK [89] (bl) 12-11-1 Mr G Johnson Houghton,
prmnt to 7th, tld off 13th, pld up bef 3 out.
.... (9 to 1 op 7 to 1)   pu
2499⁵ FAST CRUISE [86] 9-10-12 G McCourt, rear, tld off tenth,
pld up bef 3 out......................... (12 to 1)   pu
Dist: 12l, 1½l, 8l, 2½l, 25l. 6m 24.40s. a 12.40s (8 Ran).
(R J Tory), R H Alner

3007 Aylton Maiden Chase (5-y-o and up) £2,580 2m 3f.................. (4:10)

OH SO BOLD 7-11-2 (3") R Farrant, hld up in tch, hdwy 4
out, led aftr 2 out, ran on wl...... (14 to 1 op 12 to 1)   1
2378⁸ CANAVER 8-11-5 G McCourt, hld up, hdwy 4 out, ran on
wl to go second r-in...................... (12 to 1)   2
2417 RIDAKA 7-11-2 (3") T Eley, led 3rd, jmpd wl, clr tenth, rdn
and hld aftr 2 out, wknd r-in...... (14 to 1 op 12 to 1)   3
2778² URBAN COWBOY 7-11-5 S McNeill, hld up, hdwy 8th,
one pace 3 out.
.... (5 to 2 op 9 to 2 tchd 5 to 1 and 9 to 4)   4
2803⁶ DEEP IN GREEK 8-10-12 (7") Mr G Hogan, hld up, hdwy 4
out, nvr nr to chal........................ (20 to 1)   5
2504 EIGHTY EIGHT 9-11-5 W Marston, chsd ldrs, rdn 9th, sn
outpcd.................................. (50 to 1)   6
1684² COOLREE (Ire) 6-11-0 (5") Guy Lewis, prmnt till wknd
tenth, tld off.... (11 to 8 fav op 11 to 10 tchd 6 to 4)   7
2458 WILLIE McGARR (USA) 9-11-5 B Powell, led to 3rd, wknd
quickly 9th, tld off............... (6 to 1 op 5 to 1)   8
2822 PARSON'S WAY (bl) 7-11-5 L Harvey, al beh, tld off.
.... (50 to 1)   9
1994 MONKSANDER 8-11-5 Richard Guest, beh hfwy, tld off.
.... (33 to 1)   10
2795⁵ CARLSAN 8-11-5 Mr M Jackson, beh to 6th, some hdwy
whn f last............................. (6 to 1)   f
2829⁷ BULAMONTEE 6-11-2 (3") A Thornton, chsd ldrs 5th, wknd
4 out, f last.......................... (6 to 1 tchd 7 to 1)   f
2505 CELTIC ROMPER 7-11-5 R Bellamy, sn beh, pld up aftr
5th.................................. (20 to 1)   pu
2428⁹ RIVAGE BLEU 7-11-5 J R Kavanagh, chsd ldrs, blun 6th,
rallied 9th, wknd appr 3 out, pld up bef last...(14 to 1)   pu
2778⁶ ESSEN AITCH 5-10-5 D Bridgwater, al beh, tld off whn pld
up bef 3 out........................... (50 to 1)   pu
Dist: 4l, 3l, 8l, ½l, 7l, 8l, 15l, 5l, 30l. 4m 47.20s. a 17.20s (15 Ran).
(E A Hayward), J M Bradley

3008 Munsley Novices' Hurdle (Div I) (4-y-o and up) £1,553 2m 1f.......... (4:40)

1930⁶ GESNERA 6-10-13 G McCourt, hld up rear, hdwy 4 out,
led aftr 2 out, sn clr... (8 to 1 op 10 to 1 tchd 12 to 1)   1
2523⁵ BLAST FREEZE (Ire) 5-10-13 J R Kavanagh, hld up in tch,
hdwy to ld 2 out, sn hdd, outpcd.
.... (11 to 4 op 3 to 1 and 9 to 4)   2
2789* MONTY ROYALE (Ire) 5-11-8 (3") A Thornton, al prmnt, led
appr 3 out, hdd nxt, one pace. (5 to 4 fav tchd 13 to 8)   3
1716⁴ TIME FOR A FLUTTER 5-10-13 (7") Mr E James, al prmnt,
rdn appr 3 out, no imprsn aftr.
.... (9 to 2 op 3 to 1 tchd 5 to 1)   4
2147 COMEDIMAN 6-10-11 (7") Mr G Hogan, hld up in rear,
hdwy 6th, styd on one pace... (20 to 1 op 12 to 1)   5
2837² BEE BEAT 6-11-4 M Bosley, chsd ldrs, no hdwy frm 4 out.
.... (20 to 1 op 10 to 1)   6
2671⁸ CHARGED 5-11-4 M Hourigan, prmnt early, beh 5th, tld
off................................... (33 to 1 op 14 to 1)   7
2430 ROYAL GLINT 5-10-6 (7") Mr B Pollock, al in rear, tld off.
.... (50 to 1)   8
2762⁵ KILLTUBBER HOUSE 8-11-4 L Harvey, beh 5th, tld off.
.... (50 to 1)   9
1878 MARANO 6-11-4 I Lawrence, pld hrd, chsd ldr till wknd
5th, tld off........................... (100 to 1)   10
2789⁶ NEWHALL PRINCE 6-11-1 (3") T Eley, beh hfwy, tld off.
.... (100 to 1)   11
2789 LIES LE BUCFLOW 6-11-4 R Supple, sn wl beh, tld off
whn pld up bef 4th....................... (100 to 1)   pu
1108 SNOWSHILL SHAKER 5-11-4 D Bridgwater, led till ran
wide and hdd appr 3 out, sn btn, pld up bef last.
.... (25 to 1 op 16 to 1)   pu
Dist: 6l, 3½l, 1l, ½l, 8l, 12l, 3½l, 1l, 2½l, 20l. 3m 58.70s. a 12.70s (13 Ran).
SR: 26/20/28/22/19/11/   (Mrs V M Biggs), K White

3009 Munsley Novices' Hurdle (Div II) (4-y-o and up) £1,553 2m 1f.......... (5:10)

1390* CHAPEL OF BARRAS (Ire) 5-11-11 M Hourigan, hld up,
hdwy 5th, squeezed through to ld aftr 2 out, ran on wl.
.... (6 to 4 fav op 11 to 8 tchd 9 to 4)   1
2808* MARINER'S AIR 7-11-6 W Marston, al prmnt, ev ch 2 out,
rdn and one pace aftr.......... (2 to 1 tchd 7 to 4)   2
2808 TENAYESTELIGN 6-10-10 (3") J McCarthy, hld up, hdwy
6th, styd on, nvr threatened 1st 2.... (8 to 1 op 6 to 1)   3
2841⁶ MUCH 7-11-4 Mr M Jackson, chsd ldr, led 4th till hdd and
bumped aftr 2 out, wknd........ (50 to 1 op 33 to 1)   4

2790⁴ ANDRATH (Ire) 6-11-4 W Humphreys, *chsd ldrs till wknd 3 out*.................................. (10 to 1 op 16 to 1)   5
2878⁵ HIZAL 5-10-11 (7") M Appleby, *al rear*.
.... (66 to 1 op 50 to 1)   6
2834 STORMY PETREL 5-10-13 B Powell, *in tch till wknd appr 6th*.............................. (5 to 1 op 4 to 1)   7
TRIPLE SENSATION (NZ) 7-11-4 Jacqui Oliver, *beh, rdn 4th, nvr dngrs*.................................. (20 to 1 op 12 to 1)   8
2762⁶ ROYAL GAIT (NZ) 6-11-4 J Frost, *al beh*.........(50 to 1)   9
2088⁸ GIVE ME HOPE (Ire) 6-10-6 (7") Pat Thompson, *mid-div till lost tch 5th*....................... (50 to 1 op 33 to 1)   10
GANDERTON INT 7-11-4 S Earle, *in tch to 5th, sn beh, tld off*................................... (50 to 1 op 33 to 1)   11
1354⁷ KHAKI LIGHT 6-11-4 M Sharratt, *led to 4th, wknd quickly nxt, tld off*....................... (200 to 1 op 50 to 1)   12
2335 BEACHY GLEN 7-11-4 S Mackey, *al beh, tld off whn pld up bef 2 out*................................ (50 to 1)   pu
Dist: 2l, 4l, 5l, 20l, 2½l, 15l, sht-hd, 12l. 4m 2.60s. a 16.60s (13 Ran).

(Hawkridge Farmhouse Cheese Limited), P J Hobbs

PLUMPTON (Good)
Monday March 14th
Going Correction: PLUS 1.35 sec. per fur.

3010   Ardingly Novices' Hurdle (4-y-o and up) £1,543 2m 1f.............. (2:20)

2762³ WEE WINDY (Ire) 5-11-2 D Murphy, *wl in tch, led appr 2 out, shaken up and styd on strly frm last, eased nr line*.
.... (9 to 4 op 7 to 4 tchd 5 to 2)   1
1283⁹ SECRETARY OF STATE 8-11-2 J Railton, *hld up, cld on ldrs frm 7th, ev ch last, rdn and not quicken*.
.... (7 to 2 op 4 to 1 tchd 5 to 1 and 11 to 2)   2
1032⁴ SIR THOMAS BEECHAM 4-11-0 A Dicken, *hld up, improved 6th, ran on appr 2 out, one pace approaching last*.................. (9 to 4 op 2 to 1 op 5 to 4 fav op Evens)   3
2494 DOMITOR'S LASS 7-10-11 Mrs N Ledger, *led second, clr 4th, hdd and no extr appr 2 out*.
.... (50 to 1 op 20 to 1 tchd 66 to 1)   4
SHANAKEE 7-11-2 E Murphy, *effrt frm rear 6th, wknd appr 3 out*........................... (20 to 1 op 6 to 1)   5
2426 WORLDLY PROSPECT (USA) 6-10-11 A Maguire, *trkd ldrs til lost pos 7th, tld off*. (14 to 1 op 8 to 1 tchd 20 to 1)   6
RUN TO AU BON (Ire) 4-10-8 J Clarke, *led to second, wknd quickly 5th, tld off aftr nxt*.
.... (25 to 1 op 12 to 1 tchd 33 to 1)   7
KINON-PENNY 6-11-12 W McFarland, *beh most of way, lost tch 7th, tld off whn pld up bef last*
.... (100 to 1 op 20 to 1)   pu
Dist: 3½l, 5l, 10l, 12l, dist, 30l. 4m 30.10s. a 38.10s (8 Ran).

(W E Gale), J T Gifford

3011   Susan Payne 'Better Late Than Never' Valentines Novices' Chase (5-y-o and up) £2,350 2m 5f.............. (2:50)

2708 THE WHIP 7-11-4 J Railton, *pressed ldr, led 9th, reminders appr last, styd on wl*......(7 to 2 op 5 to 2)   1
2693⁷ DISCO DUKE 9-11-4 J Clarke, *l/ft in second pl frm tenth, ev ch 4 out, rdn and one pace appr last*.
.... (16 to 1 op 10 to 1)   2
IDLEIGH'S STAR 10-11-4 M Richards, *led to 9th, mstk nxt, sn wknd, blun 11th, tld off*......(14 to 1 op 5 to 1)   3
2761² HANGOVER 8-11-4 A Maguire, *with wnr whn f tenth*.
.... (11 to 4 on op 2 to 1)   f
Dist: 8l, dist. 5m 42.40s. a 37.40s (4 Ran).

(Mrs R Howell), D M Grissell

3012   Uckfield Selling Hurdle (4 & 5-y-o) £1,768 2m 1f.................. (3:20)

2878² YAAFOOR (USA) (bl) 5-11-3 M Richards, *made all, wl clr frm 7th, kpt on*.................. (9 to 4 tchd 5 to 1)   1
2781⁶ CYRILL HENRY (Ire) 5-11-8 (7") Mr G Cosgrove, *chsd ldrs til rdn alng and outpcd 6th, wnt second appr 3 out, no imprsn on wnr*........ (9 to 1 op 4 to 1 tchd 10 to 1)   2
2644² MY SENOR (v) 5-12-1 T Grantham, *chsd wnr frm 6th til sn wknd nxt, tld off*.......... (7 to 2 tchd 4 to 1)   3
1211 BARGIN BOY 5-11-3 Leesa Long, *in tch till blun 5th, mstk nxt, sn tld off*.......... (33 to 1 op 25 to 1)   4
2211⁴ QUIET CONFIDENCE (Ire) 4-9-13 (5") S Curran, *al beh, lost tch appr 6th, tld off*. (14 to 1 op 12 to 1 tchd 16 to 1)   5
2763² MANON LESCAUT 4-10-4 A Maguire, *trkd ldrs til pld up lme appr 6th*.................... (7 to 4 fav op 6 to 4)   pu
2797 PARIS BY NIGHT (Ire) 4-10-4 E Murphy, *tld off whn pld up aftr 6th*............. (25 to 1 op 20 to 1 tchd 33 to 1)   pu
Dist: 8l, 20l, 20l, sht-hd. 4m 33.00s. a 41.00s (7 Ran).

(P R Hedger), P R Hedger

3013   'Clapper' Challenge Cup Hunters' Chase (5-y-o and up) £1,548 3m 1f 110yds..................... (3:50)

2831⁴ TEAM CHALLENGE 12-11-7 (7") Mr J Rees, *led till hdd 3 out, led ag'n nxt, rdn out*..........(5 to 1 op 4 to 1)   1

BARON BOB 9-11-7 (7") Mr M G Miller, *hld up, hdwy hfwy, mstk 13th and 16th, led 3 out, pckd and hdd nxt, mistake last, kpt on nr finish*.
.... (5 to 4 on op Evens tchd 11 to 10)   2
2793³ MANDRAKI SHUFFLE (bl) 12-12-1 (7") Mr A Harvey, *not fluent, chsd wnr to 16th, sn btn*......(9 to 2 op 4 to 1)   3
TOPPING-THE-BILL 9-11-7 (7") Mr A Welsh, *mstks, chsd ldrs til rdn 15th, blun and wknd 17th*.
.... (16 to 1 op 8 to 1)   4
WREKIN HILL 12-11-7 (7") Mrs J Wilkinson, *jmpd slwly 4th, rear tenth, mstk 12th, lost tch 15th*. (12 to 1 op 8 to 1)   5
TRYUMPHANT LAD 10-11-12 (7") Mr S Deasley, *al racing towards rear, lost tch 15th, tld off*. (16 to 1 op 8 to 1)   6
BARON MANA 9-11-7 (7") Miss M Hill, *several poss, effrt 9th, wl beh frm 13th*............. (66 to 1 op 33 to 1)   7
Dist: ½l, 20l, 6l, 10l, 1½l, 15l. 7m 2.70s. a 50.70s (7 Ran).

(Mrs Elizabeth Hitchins), R Lee

3014   Don Butchers Challenge Trophy Handicap Hurdle (0-105 4-y-o and up) £2,162 2½m.................. (4:20)

2710⁵ SMILING CHIEF (Ire) [85] 6-11-0 S Smith Eccles, *chsd ldg grp, led 2 out, drvn out*. (5 to 1 op 6 to 1 tchd 7 to 1)   1
2711⁴ QUALITAIR MEMORY (Ire) [76] 5-9-12 (7") S Ryan, *wl in tch, led 3 out till nxt, ev ch last, kpt on und pres*.
.... (5 to 1 op 4 to 1)   2
2759⁵ MANHATTAN BOY [95] 12-11-10 A Maguire, *settled in mid-div, outpcd 7th, hdwy appr 2 out, nrst at finish*.
.... (8 to 1 op 7 to 1 tchd 9 to 1)   3
2759³ THE MRS [90] 8-11-0 (5") S Curran, *effrt frm rear 9th, rdn and one pace 3 out, wknd nxt*.
.... (3 to 1 fav op 7 to 2 tchd 4 to 1)   4
STRAIGHT LACED (USA) [93] (bl) 7-11-3 (5") D Fortt, *nvr nr to chal*............. (14 to 1 op 12 to 1 tchd 16 to 1)   5
2346 CAPSIZE [89] (v) 8-11-4 G Upton, *made most of rng till hdd 3 out, sn btn*................. (25 to 1 tchd 33 to 1)   6
2708⁹ CASTLE ORCHARD [71] 10-9-11 (3") A Procter, *chsd ldrs, rdn alng 7th, jmpd rght nxt, sn wknd*.
.... (40 to 1 op 33 to 1)   7
2715³ CONSTRUCTION [81] 9-10-10 D Gallagher, *wth ldr till wknd quickly appr 8th*............. (4 to 1 tchd 9 to 2)   8
2496⁹ WILTOSKI [71] 6-10-0 Mrs N Ledger, *beh frm 4th, sn lost tch*........................ (33 to 1 op 20 to 1)   9
2715² LYPH (USA) [90] 8-11-5 M Richards, *al beh, jmpd rght 8th, pld up bef nxt*..................... (9 to 2 op 7 to 2)   pu
Dist: ¾l, 15l, 6l, 3½l, hd, hd, 6l, 8l. 5m 12.20s. a 35.20s (10 Ran).
SR: 4/-/-/-/-/-/   (Mrs E A Tucker), R J Hodges

3015   Bolney Handicap Chase (0-105 5-y-o and up) £2,684 2m 5f.............. (4:50)

2656 POWDER BOY [90] 9-11-1 S Smith Eccles, *jnd ldrs at 4th, led 11th, hdd appr 3 out, slight advantage last, drvn out*........................ (20 to 1 op 16 to 1)   1
2623⁴ ROCKMOUNT ROSE [81] 9-10-1 (5") C Burnett-Wells, *led till 11th, jmpd slwly and lost pl 13th, rallied appr last*.
.... (5 to 1 tchd 11 to 2 and 6 to 1)   2
2622² GALLANT EFFORT (Ire) [100] 6-11-11 A Maguire, *cl up, mstk 8th, led appr 3 out, hdd last, wknd r-in*.
.... (11 to 8 fav op 7 to 4 tchd 5 to 4)   3
1491² GLENGRIFFIN [86] 9-10-11 D Murphy, *rear whn mstk 8th, hdwy 11th, styd on one pace frm 3 out*.
.... (5 to 1 op 3 to 1 tchd 11 to 2)   4
2495⁴ TAMMY'S FRIEND [103] (bl) 7-12-0 J Railton, *trkd ldrs till mstk 9th, wknd nxt*.................(7 to 1 op 5 to 1)   5
2495 BE SURPRISED [81] 8-10-6 G Upton, *in tch till rdn and lost touch tenth*.................... (16 to 1 tchd 7 to 1)   6
2836² OLD ROAD (USA) [77] (bl) 8-10-2 P McDermott, *beh frm 7th, pld up bef pld up bef last*......... (6 to 1 tchd 7 to 1)   pu
Dist: 2l, 3l, 3½l, 10l, 15l. 5m 40.20s. a 35.20s (7 Ran).
SR: 18/7/23/5/12/-/-/   (Don Hurford), R J Hodges

TAUNTON (good to soft)
Monday March 14th
Going Correction: PLUS 0.45 sec. per fur. (races 1,4,-5,7), PLUS 0.55 (2,3,6)

3016   March Juvenile Novices' Hurdle (4-y-o) £1,801 2m 1f.............. (2:00)

1243 FREE DANCER 10-4 (3") T Jenks, *dsptd ld till l/ft wth definite advantage 3rd, made rst, all out*.
.... (9 to 2 op 3 to 1 tchd 5 to 1)   1
2241 HEART OF SPAIN 10-12 T Wall, *chsd ldrs, chlgd 3 out to nxt, not quicken r-in*............. (11 to 2 op 3 to 1)   2
2634 KOSVILLE (Fr) 10-7 J Lower, *hdwy 3 out, stayin on whn hit 2 out, one pace*..(9 to 1 op 5 to 1 tchd 10 to 1)   3
2471⁶ FRONTIER FLIGHT (USA) 10-12 J Osborne, *chsd ldrs, shaken up appr 2 out, found little*.
.... (5 to 2 op 2 to 1 tchd 3 to 1)   4
PISTOL (Ire) 10-12 R J Beggan, *hld up in rear, hit 3rd, nvr dngrs*.................... (14 to 1 op 12 to 1)   5
2808⁴ PRINCESS TATEUM (Ire) 11-0 G Bradley, *wth wnr till f 3rd*......... (7 to 4 fav op 2 to 1 tchd 5 to 2 and 11 to 8)   f

2722[6] PALACE PARADE (USA) 10-12 N Dawe, *in tch whn hmpd and uns rdr 3rd*.......(7 to 1 tchd 11 to 2 and 8 to 1) ur
JEAN BRODIE 10-4 (3*) R Davis, *mstk 6th, sn wknd, tld off whn pld up bef 2 out*. (33 to 1 op 20 to 1 tchd 40 to 1) pu
Dist: 2½l, 5l, 5l, 20l. 4m 4.90s. a 17.90s (8 Ran).

(Mrs V E Hayward), R Brotherton

3017 Sheldon Claiming Chase (5-y-o and up) £2,287 2m 110yds.........(2:30)

2777[3] GENERAL MERCHANT 14-11-0 A Tory, *beh, hdwy to track ldrs 8th, styd on 3 out, slight ld 2 out, drvn out*.
.....................................(7 to 2 op 3 to 1) 1
2267 WELSH BARD 8-10-12-0 G Bradley, *trkd ldr till led 5th, made most till hdd 2 out, rallied r-in, jst fld*.
.................(100 to 30 jt-fav op 3 to 1 tchd 7 to 1) 2
2798 RATHER SHARP 8-11-8 A Dobbin, *took str hold, chlgd 8th to 4 out, still ev ch whn hit 3 out, sn wknd*.
.........................(13 to 2 op 5 to 1 tchd 7 to 1) 3
1944 MASTER SOUTH LAD 10-11-7 (7*) R Darke, *prmnt, lost pos 7th, drvn to chal ag'n nxt, wknd quickly 4 out*.
..............................(8 to 1 op 10 to 1 tchd 9 to 1) 4
2116[5] SAILOR'S DELIGHT 10-10-13 (7*) Mr S Joynes, *led, hit 4th, hdd 5th, wth ldr till 8th, wknd quickly frm four out*.
........................(12 to 1 op 10 to 1) 5
2316* DERRYMORE BOY 12-11-0 M A FitzGerald, *beh 5th, tld off whn pld up bef 4 out*.......(100 to 30 jt-fav op 3 to 1) pu
2803[6] PALM SWIFT 8-10-9 C Maude, *hit 8th and beh, tld off whn pld up bef 4 out*.........................(25 to 1) pu
Dist: Hd, 20l, 10l, 12l. 4m 14.20s. a 16.20s (7 Ran).
SR: 15/29/3/-/   (Mrs Susan Tate), R J Hodges

3018 Royal Bath And West Novices' Chase (5-y-o and up) £2,840 3m......(3:00)

2780[3] CASTLE BLUE 7-11-4 J Osborne, *trkd ldr, chlgd 14th, led 15th, in control whn lft clr last*.
.............................(6 to 4 fav op 13 to 8 tchd 7 to 4) 1
2654[4] STAUNCH RIVAL (USA) 7-11-10 C Llewellyn, *beh, hit 8th, hdwy 11th, chsd wnr appr 3 out, 3rd and one pace whn hmpd last, lft second r-in*.
.....................(11 to 4 op 5 to 2 tchd 3 to 1) 2
2718[6] VAVASIR (bl) 8-11-4 C Maude, *led till hdd 15th, wknd frm 4 out*........(4 to 1 op 3 to 1 tchd 9 to 2) 3
2647 DRAW LOTS 10-11-4 I Shoemark, *lost tch frm 8th, sn tld off and jmpd badly aftr*.
........................(50 to 1 op 33 to 1 tchd 66 to 1) 4
862[3] HOUSE OF ROSES (Ire) 6-11-4 G Bradley, *trkd ldrs, outpcd 4 out, rallied and ev ch 3 out, second and rdn whn f last*...........................(9 to 2 op 7 to 1) f
2559 ARCTICFLOW (USA) 9-11-4 A Tory, *tld off frm 9th, pld up bef 12th*.............(50 to 1 op 20 to 1 tchd 66 to 1) pu
2780 KATIEM'LU 8-10-8 (5*) D Salter, *lost tch frm 12th, tld off whn pld up bef 14th*.
.......................(66 to 1 op 50 to 1 tchd 100 to 1) pu
Dist: 3l, dist, dist. 6m 18.40s. a 31.40s (7 Ran).

(R J Parish), N J Henderson

3019 Bathpool Novices' Selling Hurdle (4 & 5-y-o) £1,812 2m 1f............(3:30)

SOPHISM (USA) 5-11-3 J Lower, *hld up, hdwy to ld 6th, rdn out*.......................(7 to 4 on op 11 to 10) 1
2878* PLAIN SAILING (Fr) 4-11-0 M A FitzGerald, *led to 6th, chlgd frm 3 out, rdn and styd on same pace from 2 out*.
.....................(4 to 1 op 7 to 2 tchd 5 to 1) 2
2717 MUSICAL PHONE 4-10-9 A Dobbin, *al prmnt, ev ch 3 out, one pace appr 2 out*......(7 to 2 op 3 to 1) 3
2945 RED MICKS WIFE (Ire) 4-10-1 (3*) R Davis, *chsd ldrs, hit 5th, outpcd 3 out, styd on ag'n frm nxt*.
...........................(14 to 1 op 10 to 1) 4
2808 LYCIAN MOON (bl) 5-10-12 E Byrne, *al beh*.
........................(33 to 1 op 16 to 1 tchd 40 to 1) 5
2716[6] IRENE'S ROLFE 5-10-5 (7*) J Neaves, *prmnt till hit 6th and wknd*........(66 to 1 op 25 to 1) 6
LOWRIANNA (Ire) 4-10-4 D J Burchell, *chsd ldrs to 6th, wknd 3 out, tld off whn pld up bef nxt*.
..............................(12 to 1 op 7 to 1) pu
2018[4] KRAKATOA (bl) 5-10-7 (5*) D Matthews, *beh, blun 3rd and 4th, sn pld up*.........(25 to 1 op 14 to 1) pu
2546[7] THE LATCHIKO (Ire) 4-10-9 M Perrett, *al beh, tld off whn pld up bef 2 out*.........(16 to 1 op 8 to 1) pu
Dist: 2l, 4l, 4l, 12l, 6l. 4m 10.40s. a 23.40s (9 Ran).

(M C Pipe), M C Pipe

3020 Haulwaste Handicap Hurdle (0-120 4-y-o and up) £2,918 2m 3f 110yds
....(4:00)

805[6] KHAZARI (USA) [108] 6-11-4 (3*) T Jenks, *hld up, drvn and hdwy appr 2 out, slight ld last, all out*.
........................(20 to 1 op 16 to 1 tchd 25 to 1) 1
2841* LUCKY BLUE [87] 7-9-7 (7*) T Thompson, *led to second, led ag'n 6th, hrd drvn frm 2 out, hdd last, rallied r-in, jst fld*.....................(25 to 1 op 20 to 1) 2

2801[2] THE MINDER (Fr) [90] 7-9-12 (5*) D Salter, *beh till gd hdwy frm 3 out, str chal last, styd on same pace*.
.......................(11 to 2 op 4 to 1) 3
2801[5] LAND OF THE FREE [87] 5-10-0 J Osborne, *in tch 5th, chlgd frm 3 out till one pace from 2 out*.
.............................(14 to 1 op 10 to 1) 4
2781[7] J BRAND [90] 7-10-3 A Tory, *chsd ldrs, outpcd frm 3 out, rallied and ev ch last, one pace*...(9 to 1 op 10 to 1) 5
2839* GOLDINGO [94] 7-10-4 (3*) R Davis, *mid-div, gd hdwy to chal 2 out, wknd last*.
.........................(100 to 30 fav op 11 to 4 tchd 7 to 2) 6
2792[9] MARIOLINO [87] 7-9-7 (7*) M Moran, *str hold, mid-div, effrt 7th, wknd appr 2 out*.........(7 to 1 op 10 to 1) 7
2528 CHEERFUL TIMES [93] 11-10-6 D O'Sullivan, *hdwy to track ldrs 3 out, rdn appr out, sn wknd*.
.............................(10 to 1 op 8 to 1 tchd 12 to 1) 8
2727 PROPAGANDA [111] 6-11-10 M A FitzGerald, *led second to 6th, styd wth ldrs, wknd 2 out*...(10 to 1 op 11 to 1) 9
2692[4] SO AUDACIOUS [87] 6-10-0 C Llewellyn, *chsd ldrs to 7th, sn wknd*.............(10 to 1 op 8 to 1 tchd 11 to 1) 10
2839[5] JUST (Fr) [87] (v) 8-9-7 (7*) L Reynolds, *hld up, nvr rch ldrs*.
............................(6 to 1 tchd 8 to 1) 11
2839[4] TILT TECH FLYER [103] 9-11-2 G Bradley, *chsd ldrs till rdn and wknd aftr 3 out*.....(8 to 1 op 7 to 1 tchd 9 to 1) 12
BOADICEA'S CHARIOT [87] 7-10-0 C Maude, *lost tch frm 6th*........................(66 to 1 op 50 to 1) 13
CHIROPODIST [87] 10-10-0 V Slattery, *al beh*.
.............................(66 to 1 op 50 to 1) 14
Dist: Hd, ¾l, nk, 1½l, ¾l, 3l, hd, 12l, 8l, 15l. 4m 51.30s. a 30.30s (14 Ran).

(Mrs Clair Morse), R Brotherton

3021 Mitford Slade Challenge Trophy Hunters' Chase (5-y-o and up) £1,032 3m............................(4:30)

STRONG GOLD (bl) 11-12-0 (7*) Mr T McCarthy, *led 3rd, made rst, clr 3 out, hld on wl*......(8 to 1 op 6 to 1) 1D
2826* ANDROS PRINCE 9-11-12 (7*) Mr M Felton, *beh, plenty to do frm 4 out but styd on, ev ch r-in till hng lft and no extr.* (9 to 4 fav op 3 to 1 tchd 100 to 30 and 7 to 2) 1
COOL RELATION 8-11-7 (7*) Mr A Phillips, *led second to 3rd, styd prmnt, hit tenth and 11th, outpcd frm 3 out*.
.........................(9 to 2 op 3 to 1 tchd 5 to 1) 2
2887[3] ARTFUL ARTHUR 8-11-7 (7*) Mr J Grassick, *beh 6th, hit 9th, nvr dngrs*...............(100 to 1 op 50 to 1) 3
2882[4] GATTERSTOWN (bl) 11-11-7 (7*) Mr S Mulcaire, *hdwy to chase ldrs 8th, wknd frm 4 out*.
..........................(9 to 1 op 33 to 1 tchd 66 to 1) 4
SEARCHER 9-11-7 (7*) Miss L Blackford, *hdwy 12th, wknd 14th*.......................(20 to 1 op 16 to 1) 5
TOO LATE 11-11-7 (7*) Mr R Nuttall, *al beh*.
.........................(25 to 1 op 20 to 1 tchd 33 to 1) 6
2838[3] DOUBTING DONNA 8-11-8 (7*) Mr V Hughes, *beh frm 11th*.............(50 to 1 op 25 to 1) 7
DISTILLATION (bl) 9-12-0 (7*) Mr Richard White, *tld off frm 9th*....................(66 to 1 op 50 to 1 tchd 100 to 1) 8
TERRA DI SIENA 12-11-7 (7*) Mr J Creighton, *in tch to 11th, wl beh whn blun and uns rdr last*.................(50 to 1) ur
2800 COLCOMBE CASTLE 11-11-9[2] (7*) Mr H Rowsell, *blun and uns rdr 4th (water)*. (40 to 1 op 25 to 1 tchd 50 to 1) ur
CITY ENTERTAINER 13-12-0 (7*) Mr S Shinton, *led to second, wknd and pld up bef 5th*.....(20 to 1 op 12 to 1) pu
MARTIN THOMAS 11-11-12 (7*) Mr A Price, *beh frm 6th, tld off whn pld up bef 3 out*............(100 to 1 op 66 to 1) pu
2724[4] KNOCKUMSHIN 11-12-2 (5*) Mr T Byrne, *al beh, tld off whn pld up bef 3 out*....(3 to 1 op 7 to 4 tchd 9 to 2) pu
SANDBROOK 10-11-7 (7*) Mr K Cousins, *prmnt, hit 11th, wknd nxt, tld off whn pld up bef 3 out*.
.............................(10 to 1 op 6 to 1) pu
Dist: 2l, 10l, 20l, 1l, sht-hd, 15l, 3l, 15l. 6m 20.10s. a 33.10s (15 Ran).

(Miss C Gordon), Miss C Gordon

3022 Widcombe 'National Hunt' Novices' Handicap Hurdle (0-100 5-y-o and up) £1,780 2m 1f.................(5:00)

2432[9] HEDGEHOPPER (Ire) [79] 6-11-4 J Osborne, *made all, clr whn hit 2 out, easily*.. (4 to 1 op 11 to 2 tchd 7 to 1) 1
2505[7] BROAD STEANE [82] 5-11-7 M Perrett, *prmnt, pressed wnr frm to 3 out, one pace whn blun 2 out*.
.............................(7 to 2 fav op 5 to 2) 2
2808[5] THE QUAKER [65] 8-10-4 Lorna Vincent, *hdwy 4th, outpcd 3 out, styd on ag'n appr last*.......(10 to 1 op 8 to 1) 3
2841[7] SHARPSIDE [65] (bl) 7-10-4 C Maude, *chsd ldrs to 3 out*.
.........................(11 to 2 op 5 to 1 tchd 6 to 1) 4
2667[4] MANDYS LAD [70] 5-10-9 C Llewellyn, *prmnt till hit 5th, sn wknd*................(13 to 2 op 11 to 2 tchd 7 to 1) 5
2048 FALCONBRIDGE BAY [85] 7-11-10 M A FitzGerald, *hdwy 6th, chsd ldrs appr 2 out, sn rdn, found nothing*.
.............................(9 to 1 op 11 to 2 tchd 10 to 1) 6
2735[8] MARINER'S WALK [68] 7-10-7 A Dobbin, *sn beh*.
.........................(12 to 1 op 14 to 1) 7
1708 ODYSSEUS [70] 8-10-3[1] (7*) Mr Richard White, *al beh*.
.............................(66 to 1 op 33 to 1) 8
2713 BELLE LOCK [65] 6-9-11 (7*) J Neaves, *al beh, tld off whn pld up bef 2 out*.................(66 to 1 op 33 to 1) pu
Dist: 5l, 5l, 1½l, 10l, ¾l, dist, 10l. 4m 1.00s. a 14.00s (9 Ran).

SR: 26/24/2/-/-/9/ (David Knox), C Weedon

CHELTENHAM (good to soft)
Tuesday March 15th
Going Correction: PLUS 0.57 sec. per fur.

3023 Citroen Supreme Novices' Hurdle Grade 1 (4-y-o and up) £35,908 2m 110yds.................... (2:15)

2743³ ARCTIC KINSMAN 6-11-8 C Llewellyn, *al hndy, quickened ahead bef 3 out, drvn clr betw last 2, readily.* (50 to 1) 1
2374* PRIDWELL 4-11-0 J Lower, *settled off the pace, improved to join ldrs 3 out, styd on, not pace of wnr.*
.... (14 to 1 tchd 16 to 1 and 12 to 1) 2
2835* DREAMS END 6-11-8 Peter Hobbs, *nvr far away, ev ch 3 out, rdn and one pace frm nxt.*
.... (12 to 1 op 10 to 1 tchd 14 to 1) 3
2743⁶ CUMBRIAN CHALLENGE (Ire) 5-11-8 L Wyer, *trkd ldg bunch, improved into midfield hfwy, ev ch 3 out, one pace betw last 2.*............... (14 to 1 op 10 to 1) 4
2743⁴ SUPER COIN 6-11-8 W McFarland, *chsd ldg bunch, feeling pace hfwy, styd on grimly frm 2 out, nrst finish.*
.... (28 to 1 op 16 to 1 tchd 33 to 1) 5
2743² BARNA BOY (Ire) 6-11-8 M A FitzGerald, *badly hmpd 1st, given time to reco'r, styd on frm 3 out, nvr nrr.*
.... (10 to 1 op 6 to 1) 6
2438* RELUCTANT SUITOR 5-11-8 C Grant, *nvr far away, ev ch appr 3 out, rdn and no extr frm nxt.*
.... (25 to 1 op 16 to 1) 7
1849¹ WINTER BELLE (USA) 6-11-8 J Shortt, *patiently rdn, improved gng wl to join issue 3 out, ridden nxt, no extr.*
.... (4 to 1 op 7 to 2 tchd 9 to 1) 8
2753² AIYBAK (Ire) (bl) 6-11-8 B Sheridan, *trkd ldg bunch, blun 4th, drvn alng bef 3 out, no imprsn.*
.... (12 to 1 op 10 to 1 tchd 14 to 1) 9
2743⁵ SOUND MAN (Ire) 6-11-8 C Swan, *settled midfield, improved appr 3 out, sn ev ch, rdn nxt, fdd.*
.... (7 to 2 fav op 4 to 1 tchd 9 to 2) 10
2743⁵ PARADISE VIEW 5-11-8 P Niven, *pressed ldrs, reminders aftr 4th, fdd frm four out.*...........(50 to 1 op 25 to 1) 11
2638¹ MARROS MILL (bl) 4-10-9 A Maguire, *in tch, drvn into midfield hfwy, fdd frm 3 out.*......(33 to 1 op 20 to 1) 12
2510⁴ SCOBIE BOY (Ire) 6-11-8 J Osborne, *led second till appr 3 out, fdd frm nxt.....*(12 to 1 op 10 to 1 tchd 14 to 1) 13
2267³ FATACK 5-11-8 S Curran, *led to second, styd hndy till fdd frm 4 out.*.................(20 to 1) 14
1946⁴ BOLD STROKE 5-11-8 M Perrett, *not fluent, struggling in rear whn blun 4 out, sn lost tch..* (50 to 1 op 33 to 1) 15
1840⁵ DUKE OF EUROLINK 5-11-8 G McCourt, *not jump wl, struggling hfwy, lost tch frm 4 out.* (33 to 1 op 20 to 1) 16
2333¹ GALES CAVALIER (Ire) 6-11-8 M Dwyer, *trkd ldrs, feeling pace 4 out, sn btn, pld up betw last 2, dismounted, broke blood vessel.*.................. (10 to 1) pu
2871⁴ KENMORE-SPEED 7-11-8 Richard Guest, *hmpd 1st, improved to race in tch hfwy, fdd 4 out, pld up betw last 2.*...................... (20 to 1) pu
Dist: 8l, 3¹/₂l, 4l, ¹/₄l, ¹/₂l, 2l, 1¹/₄l, 4l, ³/₄l, 2l. 4m 2.90s. a 11.90s (18 Ran).
SR: 69/53/57/53/52/51/49/47/43/ (Mrs R E Hambro), N A Twiston-Davies

3024 Guinness Arkle Challenge Trophy Chase Grade 1 (5-y-o and up) £43,290 2m.......................... (2:50)

2603* NAKIR (Fr) 6-11-8 J Osborne, *jmpd wl, handily plcd gng well, lft disputing ld 3 out, quickened betw last 2, imprsv.*.................(9 to 1 op 8 to 1 tchd 10 to 1) 1
2472* BAYDON STAR 7-11-8 A Maguire, *al hndy, lft disputing ld 3 out till rdn betw last 2, not pace of wnr.*
.... (5 to 2 fav tchd 3 to 1) 2
2538¹ SOUTHOLT (Ire) 6-11-8 D Bridgwater, *jmpd slwly 1st 2 and sn beh, gd hdwy 4 out and soon ev ch, outpcd appr two out, styd on wl r-in.*............... (33 to 1 op 25 to 1) 3
2700² ATONE 7-11-8 K O'Brien, *cl up on outsd, drw level appr 2 out, rdn and no extr.*............(5 to 1 op 3 to 1) 4
2286⁵ MUBADIR (USA) 6-11-8 P Carberry, *settled gng wl, effrt hfwy, feeling pace bef 4 out, sn btn.*
.... (20 to 1 op 16 to 1 tchd 25 to 1) 5
2688⁴ COUNTRY LAD (Ire) 6-11-8 S McNeill, *chsd ldrs, effrt hfwy, feeling pace 5 out, sn wknd.*
.... (12 to 1 op 10 to 1 tchd 14 to 1) 6
2675* COONAWARA 8-11-8 B Powell, *jmpd wl in ld frm 4th till f 3 out.*..................(7 to 2 op 3 to 1 tchd 4 to 1) f
2721* THUMBS UP 8-11-8 C Swan, *patiently rdn, took clr order frm hfwy, close 5th and poised to chal whn brght dwn on 3 out.*...................(6 to 1 op 5 to 1) bd
2511³ HEBRIDEAN 7-11-8 S Earle, *slight ld to 4th, wknd frm 7th, no ch whn hmpd 3 out, pld up bef nxt.*
.... (100 to 1 op 50 to 1) pu
1886 ONE MORE DREAM 7-11-8 G Bradley, *hld up, losing tch whn blun 7th, tld off when pld up bef 3 out.*
.... (16 to 1 op 14 to 1 tchd 20 to 1) pu
Dist: 8l, 1¹/₂l, 2¹/₂l, 15l, 1l. 4m 4.20s. a 11.20s (10 Ran).
SR: 73/65/63/60/45/44/ (Jim Lewis), S Christian

3025 Smurfit Champion Hurdle Challenge Trophy Grade 1 (4-y-o and up) £99,933 2m 110yds.................... (3:30)

2851* FLAKEY DOVE 8-11-9 M Dwyer, *settled gng wl, quickened up to ld betw last 2, styd on gmely r-in.*
.... (9 to 1 op 10 to 1) 1
2595² OH SO RISKY 7-12-0 P Holley, *patiently rdn, improved to chal betw last 2, ridden aftr last, no extr.*
.... (9 to 4 fav op 5 to 2 tchd 11 to 4) 2
2595¹ LARGE ACTION (Ire) 6-12-0 J Osborne, *tucked away in midfield, drvn up to led 2 out, sn hdd, kpt on same pace frm last.*...................(8 to 1 op 7 to 1 tchd 9 to 1) 3
2475³ MOLE BOARD 12-12-0 T Grantham, *tucked away beh ldrs, drvn alng to improve 3 out, styd on one pace frm last.*..................(40 to 1 op 33 to 1 tchd 50 to 1) 4
2376⁶ ABSALOM'S LADY 6-11-9 S McNeill, *wtd wth, improved to take clr order aftr 4 out, outpcd aftr nxt, no extr.*
.... (33 to 1) 5
2475* MUSE 7-12-0 M Richards, *sluggish strt, given time to reco'r, effrt and reminders 3 out, outpcd frm nxt.*
.... (13 to 2 op 6 to 1 tchd 5 to 1 and 7 to 1) 6
2287⁴ GRANVILLE AGAIN 8-12-0 J Frost, *patiently rdn, effrt whn stumbled badly appr 3 out, sn reco'red, not pace of ldrs frm nxt.*............ (10 to 1 tchd 11 to 1) 7
2287³ SHAWIYA (Ire) 5-11-9 C Swan, *chsd ldr to hfwy, feeling pace and losing grnd whn hmpd by faller 2 out, sn lost tch.*...................(16 to 1 op 20 to 1 tchd 14 to 1) 8
1888⁴ HALKOPOUS (v) 8-12-0 D Murphy, *nvr far away, chsd ldr hfwy, ev ch till fdd aftr 3 out......*(13 to 2 op 6 to 1) 9
2719* VALFINET (Fr) 7-12-0 J Lower, *tried to make all, clr hfwy, wknd and hdd 2 out, sn lost tch............*(33 to 1) 10
2719³ HIGH BARON 7-12-0 M Hourigan, *co'red up in midfield, lost pl quickly aftr 4 out, sn btn.*
.... (66 to 1 op 50 to 1 tchd 100 to 1) 11
2595⁵ LAND AFAR 7-12-0 W Marston, *settled midfield, disputing 3rd and gng wl whn f 2 out.......*(25 to 1 op 20 to 1) f
   MERCHANT HOUSE (Ire) 6-12-0 Richard Guest, *chasing ldrs whn f 1st.................*(250 to 1 op 100 to 1) f
1664⁷ MORLEY STREET 10-12-0 G Bradley, *badly hmpd 1st, nvr able to reco'r, tld off till pld up bef 3 out.*
.... (16 to 1 op 14 to 1 tchd 20 to 1) pu
2376 KING CREDO 9-12-0 A Maguire, *hmpd 1st, chsd ldrs to keep up hfwy, reminders appr 3 out, pld up aftr nxt.*
.... (16 to 1 op 14 to 1) pu
Dist: 1¹/₂l, ³/₄l, 3¹/₂l, 5l, nk, 3¹/₂l, 2¹/₂l, 4l, 25l, 7l. 4m 2.30s. a 11.30s (15 Ran).
SR: 76/79/78/74/64/68/64/56/57/ (J T Price), R J Price

3026 Ritz Club National Hunt Handicap Chase (5-y-o and up) £31,045 3m 1f .... (4:05)

2747* ANTONIN (Fr) [148] 6-11-5 (5*) J Burke, *hit 1st, blun 6th, hdwy 13th and sn tracking ldrs, led aftr 3 out, soon clr, easily.*................... (4 to 1 fav op 7 to 2 tchd 9 to 2) 1
2791⁵ FLASHTHECASH [130] 8-10-6 J Frost, *patiently rdn, improved gng wl frm hfwy, ev ch 4 out, styd on one pace frm nxt.*................... (14 to 1 tchd 20 to 1) 2
2593³ GRANGE BRAKE [124] (bl) 8-10-0 C Llewellyn, *midfield, niggled alng hfwy, effrt appr 3 out, kpt on r-in.*
.... (11 to 1 op 10 to 1 tchd 12 to 1) 3
2673² INDIAN TONIC [124] 8-10-0 C Maude, *tried to make all, jnd 3 out, sn hdd and wknd frm nxt.*
.... (11 to 1 op 10 to 1 tchd 12 to 1) 4
2805⁴ ROC DE PRINCE (Fr) [132] 11-10-8 G McCourt, *hld up in midfield, reminders 11th, hdwy 14th, 4th whn hit four out, sn btn.*...................(16 to 1 op 14 to 1) 5
2384 USHERS ISLAND [131] 8-10-7 G Bradley, *mstk second and sn last, jmpd slwly 14th, nvr a factor.*
.... (9 to 2 op 4 to 1 tchd 5 to 1) 6
2593⁷ STRONG BEAU [124] 9-10-0 A Maguire, *trkd ldrs, began to feel pace hfwy, sldly lost tch, tld off.* (5 to 1 op 4 to 1) 7
2593⁵ ROCKTOR (NZ) [127] 9-10-3 D Gallagher, *rear of ldg bunch whn blun and uns rdr 7th.........*(12 to 1 op 10 to 1) ur
2416 COMPLETE OPTIMIST [124] 10-10-9 (5*) Guy Lewis, *prmnt till lost pl and reminders hfwy, beh whn pld up bef 12th.*...................(100 to 1 op 66 to 1) pu
1224 SPRINGALEAK [140] (bl) 9-11-2 J Osborne, *trkd ldr frm 4th till rdn alng 12th, wkng whn jmpd slwly 5 out, pld up bef 3 out.*.........(11 to 1 op 10 to 1 tchd 14 to 1) pu
2831² WHAAT FETTLE [124] 9-10-0 M Moloney, *trkd ldr to 4th, styd hndy till wknd quickly frm 6 out, pld up bef nxt.*...................(7 to 1 op 6 to 1 tchd 8 to 1) pu
Dist: 10l, 1¹/₄l, 2l, 15l, 15l, 20l. 6m 26.10s. a 20.10s (11 Ran).
SR: 37/9/1/-/-/-/ (M Stanners), Mrs S A Bramall

3027 Fulke Walwyn Kim Muir Challenge Cup Handicap Chase Amateur Riders (5-y-o and up) £17,636 3m 1f.... (4:40)

2747⁶ FIGHTING WORDS [134] 8-10-0 (7*) Mr T McCarthy, *sn last and pushed alng, gd hdwy hfwy, led 3 out, jnd last, hld on grimly.*.........(9 to 2 fav op 5 to 1 tchd 6 to 1) 1
   THE COMMITTEE [133] 11-10-3 (3*) Mr P McMahon, *settled midfield, rdn to join issue 3 out, drw level last, edgd lft, jst hld.*............... (10 to 1 op 8 to 1 tchd 11 to 1) 2

423

1932* TRI FOLENE (Fr) [127] (bl) 8-9-7 (7*) Mr N Moore, al hndy, reminders 11th, ev ch 4 out, rdn and one pace frm nxt.
.................................(11 to 1 op 12 to 1) 3

2506 WINDY WAYS [127] 9-9-13⁶ (7*) Mr C Vigors, nvr far away, lft in ld 4 out, hdd nxt, rdn and one pace frm betw last 2.................................(14 to 1 op 10 to 1) 4

2648⁵ CATCH THE CROSS [128] (bl) 8-10-1⁷ (7*) Mr Richard White, trkd ldrs gng wl, chlgd 3 out, rdn and no extr frm nxt.
.................................(16 to 1 op 14 to 1) 5

2384⁶ STUNNING STUFF [127] (bh) 9-9-9² (7*) Mr J Rees, not fluent, pushed alng in midfield, feeling pace 4 out, sn struggling.............(11 to 1 op 10 to 1 tchd 12 to 1) 6

2748⁵ FIDDLERS PIKE [127] 13-10-0⁷ (7*) Mrs R Henderson, wl plcd to 4th, lost tch quickly hfwy, styd on ag'n aftr last.................................(33 to 1 op 25 to 1) 7

2791* NEW HALEN [127] 13-9-7 (7*,4ex) Miss C Thomas, trkd ldrs, led 8th to 13th, wknd quickly bef 4 out, tld off.
.................................(20 to 1 op 25 to 1) 8

2666 TOCHENKA [129] 10-10-2⁹ (7*) Mr M Rimell, made most to 8th, led ag'n 13th till f 4 out.....................(33 to 1) f

2720² ANOTHER CORAL [155] 11-11-7 (7*) Mr G Hogan, mstks, struggling frm 7th, pld up bef 11th.
.................................(10 to 1 tchd 10 to 1) pu

2593² RATHVINDEN HOUSE (USA) [127] 7-9-11 (3*) Mr M Buckley, patiently rdn, improved to join issue hfwy, ev ch appr 3 out, wknd and pld up bef last.
.................................(50 to 1 op 33 to 1) pu

2153 OFF THE BRU [131] (v) 9-10-4⁷ (3*) Mr J Bradburne, wth ldrs, led briefly 6th, wknd quickly 11th, pld up bef 4 out.................................(50 to 1 op 33 to 1) pu

2448* OVER THE DEEL [127] 8-9-9 (5*) Mr D Parker, trkd ldrs, lost pl quickly 9th, tld off whn pld up bef 12th.
.................................(8 to 1 op 7 to 1 tchd 9 to 1) pu

1365 FAR SENIOR [138] 8-10-11 Mr M Armytage, nvr gng pace, tld off whn pld up bef 4 out.
.................................(13 to 2 op 6 to 1 tchd 7 to 1) pu

2867⁵ COMMERCIAL ARTIST [136] 8-10-6 (3*) Mr J Durkan, not jump wl, sn struggling in rear, pld up bef 12th.
.................................(9 to 1 op 8 to 1 tchd 10 to 1) pu

Dist: Sht-hd, 20l, 5l, 1l, 15l, 2½l, dist. 6m 23.00s. a 17.00s (15 Ran).

SR: 51/50/24/19/19/3/ ....(Pell-Mell Partners), J T Gifford

3028 Hamlet Cigars Gold Card Handicap Hurdle Final (4-y-o and up) £23,052 3¼m..................................(5:15)

2487³ TINDARI (Fr) [121] 6-10-9 (3*) P Williams, handily plcd, prmsg effrt appr 3 out, led nxt, hdd r-in, rallied to ld nr finish.................................(20 to 1 op 16 to 1 tchd 25 to 1) 1

2473* DARK HONEY [137] 9-12-0 A Dicken, al hndy, drvn alng 4 out, rallied to chal frm 2 out, led r-in, hdd nr finish.
.................................(20 to 1 op 25 to 1) 2

2403⁶ KILGARIFF [111] 8-10-2 P Harley, wtd wth, improved fnl circuit, jnd issue appr 2 out, hng rght and styd on wl r-in.................................(20 to 1 tchd 25 to 1) 3

2823² RIMOUSKI [109] 6-10-0 Mr J Cambidge, last at hfwy, gd hdwy 9th, rdn and outpcd appr 3 out, styd on frm nxt.
.................................(25 to 1) 4

2806² CASTIGLIERO (Fr) [120] (bl) 6-10-11 G Bradley, nvr far away, ev ch appr 3 out, ran on one pace frm nxt.
.................................(14 to 1 tchd 12 to 1) 5

2298 CORACO [109] (v) 7-10-0 D Bridgwater, trkd ldg bunch, effrt 4 out, ev ch 2 out, sn no extr.............(50 to 1) 6

2473 PEATSWOOD [129] 6-11-6 Lorna Vincent, wl beh hfwy till hdwy appr 4 out, kpt on same pace frm nxt.. (25 to 1) 7

2487* NORTHANTS [124] 8-11-1 A Carroll, hld up and wl beh till some hdwy aftr 8th, nvr rchd ldrs. (12 to 1 op 14 to 1) 8

2512* NEWTON POINT [127] 5-11-1 (3*) T Jenks, led till hdd 9th, sn lost pl.................................(12 to 1 op 14 to 1) 9

2655⁹ BROUGHTON'S TANGO (Ire) [109] 5-10-0 S Keightley, rear div till some hdwy 9th, not rch ldrs.
.................................(66 to 1 op 50 to 1) 10

2674⁶ SEA ROCK [109] 8-9-13² (3*) R Davis, rear div, moderate hdwy 3 out, no dngr.....................(50 to 1) 11

2734³ ISLAND JEWEL [111] 6-10-2² M Bosley, midfield, feeling pace 9th, sn btn.....................(50 to 1) 12

2604² GRAY'S ELLERGY [110] 8-10-1 P Holley, wl beh hfwy, some hdwy fnl circuit, nvr able to chal.
.................................(25 to 1 tchd 33 to 1) 13

2512 CAPTAIN DOLFORD [119] 7-10-7 (3*) J McCarthy, sn struggling to go pace, nvr able to chal............(14 to 1) 14

2403⁹ JUDGES FANCY [125] (bh) 10-11-2 C Llewellyn, settled midfield, improved hfwy, wknd appr 3 out.
.................................(50 to 1 op 33 to 1) 15

2403² SENDAI [125] 8-11-2 D Murphy, al in mid-div.
.................................(33 to 1) 16

2823* BRAVE BUCCANEER [122] 7-10-13 (4ex) P Niven, hld up, struggling to keep up aftr a circuit, nvr on terms.
.................................(9 to 1 op 8 to 1 tchd 10 to 1) 17

2044 KABAYIL [115] 5-10-6 J Osborne, wl plcd, improved aftr 4 out, ev ch till blun 2 out, not reco'r...........(33 to 1) 18

2265² FOX CHAPEL [119] 7-10-3 (7*) N Juckes, in tch for o'r a circuit, stdly lost pl.....................(33 to 1) 19

2751* GIMME FIVE [127] (bh) 7-11-4 C Swan, trkd ldg grp till lost pl frm hfwy.........(4 to 1 fav op 8 to 1 tchd 9 to 1) 20+

2830³ POLISHING [116] 7-10-2 (5*) S Lyons, ran in snatches, hdwy 6th and sn hndy, wknd frm 8th.........(20 to 1) 20+

2257⁸ AAHSAYLAD [128] (bl) 8-11-5 A Maguire, tucked away in midfield, moved up frm hfwy, no hdwy whn hmpd 3 out, sn wknd, dismounted aftr finish.
.................................(9 to 1 op 12 to 1) 22

2865⁵ BEAU BABILLARD [128] (bl) 7-11-5 T Horgan, in tch for o'r a circuit, sn btn.................(20 to 1 op 16 to 1) 23

2856⁵ MISTER MAJOR [112] 6-10-3 Richard Guest, al towards rear.................................(50 to 1) 24

2298 LINKSIDE [117] 9-10-8 L Wyer, ldg grp till lost pl frm hfwy.................................(33 to 1) 25

2759² DAMIER BLANC (Fr) [109] (bl) 5-9-9 (5*) J P Broderick, mid-field whn hit 8th, sn wknd..................(33 to 1) 26

2766 ROCHESTOWN LASS [109] (v) 8-10-0 N Mann, wth ldr to 8th, wknd..................(66 to 1 op 50 to 1) f

2856* MISS PURBECK [109] 7-10-0 (4ex) J R Kavanagh, nvr far away, led 9th till f 3 out......(16 to 1 op 20 to 1) f

2703³ STEEL DAWN [110] 7-9-12 (3*) C O'Brien, settled gng wl, steady hdwy frm 8th, poised to chal whn brght dwn 3 out.....................(16 to 1 op 12 to 1 tchd 20 to 1) bd

2172 MONTAGNARD [119] 10-10-10 S McNeill, wth ldrs till wknd quickly frm 8th, tld off whn pld up bef 3 out.
.................................(33 to 1) pu

2597⁴ EMERALD (Fr) [133] (bl) 10-11-10 M A FitzGerald, wl plcd frm 5th till wknd from 4 out, pld up betw last 2, lme.
.................................(25 to 1) pu

2740³ TROODOS [110] 8-10-1 D Wilkinson, midfield, reminders hfwy, sn wknd, pld up bef 4 out..............(10 to 1) pu

Dist: Sht-hd, 1l, 15l, 5l, 3½l, 1½l, 4l, 1½l, 12l, nk. 6m 44.40s. a 25.40s (32 Ran).

(Yorkshire Racing Club Owners Group), J M Jefferson

SEDGEFIELD (good to firm)
Tuesday March 15th
Going Correction: MINUS 0.25 sec. per fur.

3029 Monkey Puzzle Selling Handicap Hurdle (4-y-o and up) £1,876 3m 3f 110yds
.................................(2:00)

2737 CLASSIC STATEMENT [72] (v) 8-10-10 (3*) A Larnach, al prmnt, led 8th, pushed clr appr 2 out, easily.
.................................(8 to 1 op 10 to 1) 1

2500⁷ OVER THE ODDS (Ire) [71] 5-10-5 (7*) D Ryan, trkd ldrs, hdwy 3 out, rdn and kpt on one pace frm nxt.
.................................(4 to 1 fav op 7 to 2) 2

2894⁷ LADY BE BRAVE [65] (v) 11-10-6 K Johnson, hld up, hdwy hfwy, effrt 3 out and sn rdn, styd on one pace. (12 to 1) 3

971 FRIENDLY SOCIETY [61] 8-10-2² A Merrigan, hld up, steady hdwy hfwy, chsd ldrs 3 out, staying on one pace whn hit last.................................(50 to 1) 4

2256⁵ GUTE NACHT [75] (bl) 11-10-11⁵ (7*) P Midgley, prmnt, led 3rd to 8th, rdn 3 out, grad wknd.....(9 to 2 op 7 to 2) 5

2870⁷ ELDER PRINCE [83] 8-11-10 G Harker, chsd ldrs to hfwy, sn outpcd and beh.................(8 to 1 op 7 to 1) 6

2165⁴ MILLIE (USA) [59] 6-10-0 M Robinson, beh frm hfwy.
.................................(33 to 1 op 20 to 1) 7

2686⁹ ARTIC MISSILE [59] 7-10-0 Ann Stokell, al rear, tld off 4 out.................................(33 to 1) 8

2408 SHAHMIRAJ [66] 6-10-7 K Jones, al rear, tld off 4 out.
.................................(12 to 1 op 10 to 1) 9

2929⁵ KING OF NORMANDY (Ire) [60] (bl) 5-10-1 Miss J Thurlow, rcd wide, chsd ldrs till wknd hfwy, sn tld off.
.................................(25 to 1 op 20 to 1) 10

PRINCE KLENK [78] 13-10-12 (7*) P McLoughlin, mid-div till f 5th, dead................................. f

2321⁹ SERPHIL [73] (bl) 6-10-9 (5*) F Perratt, led, hit second, hdd nxt, chsd ldrs till rdn alng and f 3 out.
.................................(9 to 2 op 3 to 1) f

Dist: 7l, 8l, sht-hd, 5l, 5l, sht-hd, 10l, 2l. 6m 46.00s. a 20.00s (12 Ran).

(John Sisterson), J A Hellens

3030 McEwans 80/- Special Top Of The North Novices' Hurdle Qualifier (4-y-o and up) £1,861 2m 5f 110yds.... (2:35)

2783* BEND SABLE (Ire) 4-11-3 B Storey, hld up and beh, smooth hdwy appr 4 out, chsd ldr 2 out, led approaching last, pushed out.
(6 to 5 on op 5 to 4 on tchd 11 to 8 on and 11 to 10 on)1

2785⁸ MIDNIGHT FLOTILLA 8-10-9 C Hawkins, led, rdn and hdd appr last, kpt on and prm r-in....(20 to 1 op 14 to 1) 2

2578³ RUSSIAN CASTLE (Ire) 5-11-0 K Jones, al prmnt, rdn aftr 3 out, sn one pace.....................(7 to 2) 3

2435³ SLAUGHT SON (Ire) 6-10-11 (3*) A Thornton, al prmnt, rdn 3 out, sn beh.........................(5 to 1 op 4 to 1) 4

971 MISS PIMPERNEL 4-10-2 L O'Hara, in tch, hit 4th, rdn and lost pl four out, sn beh.................(33 to 1) 5

2896⁹ MISS CONSTRUE 7-10-9 R Hodge, hld up in tch, effrt and hit 6th, sn lost pl.............(12 to 1 tchd 14 to 1) 6

2435⁶ PANTO LADY 8-10-2 (7*) Miss S Lamb, prmnt till lost pl hfwy, sn beh.................................(100 to 1) 7

2737 PICKTHEMONEYUPALF 7-11-0 K Johnson, pld hrd, chsd ldrs till lost pl hfwy, tld off 3 out, pulled up bef last.
.................................(50 to 1) pu

Dist: 2l, 10l, 5l, 4l, 3l, 8l. 5m 13.40s. a 22.40s (8 Ran).

(F S Storey), F S Storey

3031 Times 'Rising Stars' Hunters' Chase Qualifier (4 - 7-y-o) £1,847 3m 3f (3:10)

OAKSEY 7-11-12[5] (5*) Mr R Shiels, *cl up, mstk 12th and sn pushed alng, outpcd 5 out, lft second appr 2 out, chlgd and left in ld two out, hit last.* (6 to 5 fav op 5 to 4 on) 1
FROZEN FOREST 6-11-5 (7*) Miss C Metcalfe, *mstks, lost tch frm 16th, lft poor second 2 out.* ....(15 to 2 op 8 to 1 tchd 9 to 1 and 7 to 1) 2
ITS A DEAL 8-11-5 (7*) Mr S Pittendrigh, *al prmnt, mstk 6th, hit 9th, chsd ldr frm 5 out, lft in ld appr 2 out, f two out*.................. (8 to 1 op 7 to 1 tchd 9 to 1) f
STELZER 8-11-7 (5*) Mr N Wilson, *led, mstks 7th and 13th, blun 16th, pld up lme appr 2 out.* .... (13 to 8 op 6 to 4 tchd 7 to 4) pu
Dist: 20l. 7m 7.90s. a 28.90s (4 Ran).
(R Shiels), R Shiels

3032 Butterwick Handicap Chase (0-135 5-y-o and up) £2,794 2m 1f...... (3:45)

1409[6] CLARES OWN [92] 10-10-5 K Jones, *made all, quickened clr 7th, rdn appr last, styd on wl..* (10 to 1 op 8 to 1) 1
2787[2] MILITARY HONOUR [100] (bl) 9-10-13 Mr S Swiers, *chsd wnr, rdn 3 out, styd one one pace und pres.* ....(13 to 8 fav op 6 to 4 tchd 7 to 4) 2
2563[5] TERRIBLE GEL (Fr) [110] 9-11-9 N Smith, *hld up, hdwy 5 out, effrt 3 out, rdn appr last, kpt on one pace.* ....(9 to 2 op 4 to 1) 3
2107[4] POSITIVE ACTION [101] 8-11-0 A Dobbin, *cl up, rdn 7th, lost pl and beh appr 3 out.* ....(9 to 2 op 4 to 1 tchd 5 to 1) 4
2832[7] MAUDLINS CROSS [115] 9-11-7 (7*) G Lee, *in tch till f 5 out, dead*........................ (5 to 2 op 2 to 1) f
Dist: 6l, 3½l, 10l. 4m 6.00s. a 1.00s (5 Ran).
SR: 25/27/33/14/-/ (John Wade), J Wade

3033 Border Knight Novices' Chase (5-y-o and up) £2,490 2m 5f............ (4:20)

2739[2] MAYOR OF LISCARROL 9-11-4 G Harker, *led appr second, lft clr 5th, blun last, unchlgd*........ (7 to 2 op 4 to 1) 1
2892[5] MILO 8-11-4 J Callaghan, *mid-div, hdwy 9th and sn rdn alng, plugged on one pace frm 4 out.* (8 to 1 op 5 to 1) 2
2892[6] KRISSOS (bl) 7-10-13 (5*) P Waggott, *chsd ldrs, mstk 4th, lft second 9th, rdn four out, plugged on one pace.* ....(20 to 1) 3
2424[9] GOLDEN BANKER (Ire) (bl) 6-11-4 K Jones, *prmnt, lft second 5th, hit nxt, blun 9th and tenth, sn tld off, blunded badly 3 out*.................. (50 to 1 op 33 to 1) 4
2739[8] NORTHERN VISION 7-10-11 (7*) Mr A Manners, *mid-div, hit 8th and lost pl, blun 11th, sn tld off, blunded last.* ....(33 to 1) 5
2565[4] KEEP BIDDING 8-11-10 T Reed, *led till appr second, chsd wnr till f 5th*.................... (11 to 10 fav op Evens) f
1502 EDEN STREAM 7-11-4 A Dobbin, *prmnt, chsd wnr 7th, f 9th*....................................(9 to 1 op 7 to 1) f
2892[7] MAYWORK 7-10-13 N Smith, *hld up and beh, some hdwy, poor 4th whn hmpd and uns rdr four out.* .... (16 to 1 op 14 to 1) ur
819 LA MOLINILLA 11-10-6 (7*) Miss S Lamb, *chsd ldrs till brght dwn 5th*................................(66 to 1) bd
Dist: Dist, 3l, 25l, 1½l. 5m 19.30s. a 15.30s (9 Ran).
(Malcolm Smith), M Smith

3034 Spennymoor Novices' Handicap Hurdle (4-y-o and up) £1,907 2m 1f 110yds ....(4:50)

2874 OTTER BUSH [80] 5-10-10 (7*) D Towler, *mid-div, hdwy appr 3 out, effrt and rdn to chal betw last 2, led and jmpd rght last, ran on*............(16 to 1 op 12 to 1) 1
2874[7] SOUNDS GOLDEN [63] 6-10-0 R Marley, *al prmnt, effrt appr 2 out, rdn and ev ch approaching last, kpt on r-in.* ....(6 to 1 op 5 to 1) 2
2735 HAZEL CREST [77] 7-10-7 (7*) F Leahy, *chsd ldrs, hdwy to ld appr 2 out, sn rdn, hmpd last, no extr und pres nr finish*.. (14 to 1) 3
2445[8] THREE STRONG (Ire) [87] 5-11-7 (3*) D J Moffatt, *beh till styd on frm 3 out*... (8 to 1) 4
2903[4] SHAHGRAM (Ire) [87] (bl) 6-11-10 Mrs A Farrell, *pld hrd, cl up till led 3rd and sn clr, hdd and wknd quickly bef 2 out*.............................(4 to 1 tchd 9 to 2) 5
2445[6] SHARP CHALLENGE [63] 7-9-7 (7*) D Ryan, *led to 3rd, prmnt till rdn and wknd appr 3 out.* ....(12 to 1 tchd 14 to 1) 6
766 GLASTONDALE [70] 8-10-7 E McKinley, *nvr rchd ldrs.* ....(66 to 1) 7
2735[6] SCARABEN [84] 6-11-7 R Garritty, *hld up, hdwy hfwy, jnd ldrs 3 out, rdn and wknd quickly appr nxt.* ....(6 to 1 op 8 to 1) 8
2874[3] IJAB (Can) [70] 4-10-7 A Dobbin, *uns rdr 1st.* .... (7 to 2 fav tchd 4 to 1) ur
FEELING FRAYL [63] 7-10-0 B Storey, *al rear, tld off whn pld up bef 2 out*...............................(100 to 1) pu
1483[9] MOONSHINE DANCER [75] 4-10-5 (7*) J Lonergan, *al rear, tld off whn pld up bef 2 out*..........(5 to 1 op 4 to 1) pu
Dist: ½l, nk, 10l, hd, ¾l, dist, 1½l. 4m 6.80s. a 11.80s (11 Ran).
(Mrs S Smith), Mrs S J Smith

SOUTHWELL (A.W) (std)
Tuesday March 15th
Going Correction: NIL

3035 Munich National Hunt Flat Race (4,5,6-y-o) £1,450 2m................. (4:55)

2534[3] MALACHITE GREEN 4-10-4 (7*) L Aspell, *trkd ldg pair, niggled alng o'r 7 fs out, effrt and rdn entering strt, led over one out, ran on wl*.......................(5 to 2) 1
PRIMO CARNERA (Ire) 4-10-4 (7*) G Tormey, *trkd ldr, drvn alng leaving back strt, led o'r 2 fs out, hdd over one out, not quicken*...................(5 to 2 op 7 to 4) 2
2909[5] SKIDDAW SAMBA 5-10-7 (7*) M Herrington, *led, quickened leaving back strt, rdn and hdd o'r 2 fs out, wknd over one out*........(5 to 4 on op 6 to 4 on tchd 6 to 5 on) 3
2490 CITY RHYTHM 4-10-11 Mrs D McHale, *settled in last pl, improved hfwy, lost tch o'r 4 fs out, tld off.* .... (20 to 1 op 12 to 1) 4
Dist: 1½l, 10l, dist. 4m 1.10s. (4 Ran).
(Rykneld Thoroughbred Co Ltd), R Hollinshead

CHELTENHAM (good to soft)
Wednesday March 16th
Going Correction: PLUS 0.40 sec. per fur. (races 1,3,7), PLUS 0.27 (2,4,5,6)

3036 Sun Alliance Novices' Hurdle Grade 1 (4-y-o and up) £39,504 2m 5f.... (2:15)

2612* DANOLI (Ire) 6-11-7 C Swan, *handily plcd, led 4 out, hrd pressed betw last 2, hit last, ran on gmely.* ....(7 to 4 fav tchd 2 to 1 and 13 to 8) 1
2382[3] CORROUGE (USA) 5-11-7 C Llewellyn, *led till aftr second, styd hndy, ev ch betw last 2, ran on.* ....(10 to 1 op 12 to 1 tchd 14 to 1) 2
2558* BRIEF GALE 7-11-2 D Murphy, *nvr far away, hdwy gng wl 4 out, ev ch 2 out, sn rdn and not quicken.* ....(8 to 1 op 7 to 1 tchd 9 to 1) 3
2612[2] COQ HARDI AFFAIR (Ire) 6-11-7 P Carberry, *sn hndy, effrt and ev ch appr 2 out, one pace.* ....(16 to 1 op 14 to 1 tchd 20 to 1) 4
2806* SPRING MARATHON (USA) 4-10-12 P Holley, *beh and niggled alng early, hdwy appr 3 out, staying on whn hmpd nxt, nvr nrr*............................(50 to 1) 5
2612[3] WHAT A QUESTION (Ire) 6-11-2 C O'Dwyer, *patiently rdn, hdwy 4 out, sn wth ldrs, ev ch 2 out, no extr.* ....(25 to 1 op 20 to 1 tchd 33 to 1) 6
2651[2] EMPIRE BLUE 11-11-7 M Bosley, *beh, styd on frm 3 out, not rch ldrs*............................... (100 to 1) 7
2727* ELAINE TULLY (Ire) 6-11-2 Peter Hobbs, *in tch, effrt hfwy, no imprsn frm 3 out*................(33 to 1 op 25 to 1) 8
2262* PONDERING (v) 4-10-12 M A FitzGerald, *dsptd ld to second, lost pl hfwy, no further dngr.* (14 to 1 op 16 to 1) 9
2505[2] MAD THYME 7-11-7 J Frost, *beh, improved 6th, no imprsn frm nxt*.......................... (50 to 1 op 33 to 1) 10
2671* HAWAIIAN YOUTH (Ire) 6-11-7 G McCourt, *mid-div, pushed alng 5th, wknd aftr nxt.* (100 to 1 op 66 to 1) 11
2651* DIVINE CHANCE (Ire) 6-11-7 R Supple, *trkd ldrs, rdn 5th, lost pl nxt*.................... (200 to 1 op 100 to 1) 12
2250[4] FINE THYNE (Ire) 5-11-7 M Perrett, *rear div, effrt 6th, sn no hdwy*.................................. (100 to 1) 13
2779[3] BOOK OF MUSIC (Ire) 6-11-7 P Hide, *led aftr second till after 4th, hndy till wknd appr 3 out*..........(50 to 1) 14
2769* MAN TO MAN (NZ) 7-11-7 A Kondrat, *ldg grp till lost pl 4 out*..............................(16 to 1 tchd 20 to 1) 15
2757* STRONG CASE (Ire) 6-11-7 J Lower, *mid-div, feeling pace 4 out, sn btn*.....................(33 to 1 tchd 40 to 1) 16
2897* LE GINNO (Fr) 7-11-7 G Bradley, *al rear.* ....(40 to 1 op 33 to 1 tchd 50 to 1) 17
2415* RIVER LOSSIE (bl) 5-11-7 J Osborne, *keen hold, wth ldrs, mstk 4th, wknd four out*.........(33 to 1 op 20 to 1) 18
2459[4] TOTHEWOODS 6-11-7 D Bridgwater, *hld up beh, hdwy frm 4 out, staying on whn f 2 out.* (50 to 1 op 66 to 1) f
2702* DORANS PRIDE (Ire) 5-11-7 J P Broderick, *in tch, hdwy appr 3 out, ev ch nxt, cl 3rd and rdn whn f last.* ....(14 to 1 op 10 to 1) f
2812* MORCELI (Ire) 6-11-7 D J Moffatt, *improved to ld aftr 4th, hdd four out, sn wknd, no ch whn blun and uns rdr last*..............................(12 to 1 op 10 to 1) ur
2723* TOP SPIN 5-11-7 A Maguire, *al beh, tld off whn pld up bef 5th*...............................(16 to 1 tchd 20 to 1) pu
2194[2] BAY MISCHIEF (Ire) 5-11-7 M Dwyer, *trkd ldrs till lost tch 4 out, pld up bef 2 out*..............................(33 to 1) pu
Dist: 2l, 5l, 2½l, 2l, 4l, 12l, hd, 3l, 2½l, 1½l. 5m 10.50s. a 11.50s (23 Ran).
SR: 62/60/50/52/41/41/34/29/22/ (D J O'Neill), Thomas Foley

3037 Queen Mother Champion Chase Grade 1 (5-y-o and up) £74,381 2m

NATIONAL HUNT RESULTS 1993-94

. . . . **(2:50)**

2594* VIKING FLAGSHIP 7-12-0 A Maguire, *al hndy, dsptd ld betw last 2, rdn to lead r-in, ran on gmely.*
. . . . (4 to 1 tchd 7 to 2 and 9 to 2) 1

1843 TRAVADO 8-12-0 J Osborne, *settled gng wl, led 3 out, jnd betw last 2, hdd r-in, ran on.*
. . . . (100 to 30 op 5 to 2 tchd 7 to 2) 2

2744² DEEP SENSATION 9-12-0 D Murphy, *patiently rdn, improved on bit to draw level betw last 2, ridden and not quicken r-in.*. . . . . .(15 to 2 op 6 to 1 tchd 8 to 1) 3

2744³ WONDER MAN (Fr) 9-12-0 C Swan, *trkd ldrs, effrt 4 out, feeling pace and rdn nxt, sn outpcd.*
. . . .(16 to 1 op 20 to 1) 4

1666* KATABATIC 11-12-0 S McNeill, *tucked away on ins, blun 5 out, feeling pace nxt, rdn and fdd 3 out.*
. . . .(14 to 1 op 10 to 1) 5

2744⁴ SPACE FAIR 11-12-0 P Niven, *led, jnd 4 out, hdd nxt, wkng whn almost uns rdr 2 out, jmpd slvly last.*
. . . . (100 to 1 tchd 150 to 1) 6

2594³ SYBILLIN 8-12-0 M Dwyer, *rcd freely, hld up last, effrt 4 out, sn rdn and btn....* (15 to 2 op 7 to 1 tchd 8 to 1) 7

2744* REMITTANCE MAN 10-12-0 M A FitzGerald, *nvr far away, chalg whn f 3 out...*(11 to 4 fav op 9 to 4 tchd 5 to 2) f
Dist: Nk, 1l, 10l, 7l, 5l, 4l. 6m 0.80s. a 7.80s (8 Ran).
SR: 65/64/63/53/46/41/35/-/ (Roach Foods Limited), D Nicholson

3038 Coral Cup Handicap Hurdle (5-y-o and up) £37,924 2m 5f. . . . . (3:30)

2866* TIME FOR A RUN [137] 7-11-8 C Swan, *patiently rdn, hdwy 3 out, led aftr last, drvn out.*
. . . . (11 to 1 op 10 to 1 tchd 14 to 1) 1

2982* SO PROUD [115] 9-10-0 M Perrett, *wtd wth, hdwy to join ldrs aftr 3 out, led betw last 2, hdd r-in, hng lft, no extr.*
. . . . (12 to 1 tchd 14 to 1) 2

2844² CHANCE COFFEY [116] 9-10-6 K O'Brien, *patiently rdn, hdwy r-in, ev ch appr 2 out, one pace r-in.*
. . . . (33 to 1 op 25 to 1) 3

2967* VIARDOT (Ire) [126] 5-10-11 P Niven, *settled rear, hdwy appr 3 out, led bef nxt, sn hdd and not quicken.*
. . . . (5 to 1 fav op 8 to 1) 4

2727⁴ KADI (Ger) [133] 5-11-4 A Maguire, *rear div, hdwy 3 out, ran on appr last, not rch ldrs.*. . . . .(25 to 1) 5

2823⁶ ZAMIRAH (Ire) [119] 5-10-1 (3*) T Jenks, *beh, styd on frm 3 out, nvr nrr.*. . . . .(20 to 1) 6

1878² KYTTON CASTLE [118] 7-10-0 (3*) D Meredith, *hld up midfield, hdwy frm 6th to join ldrs, led briefly 2 out, wknd.*
. . . .(33 to 1) 7

2473² DOMINANT SERENADE [135] 5-11-3 (3*) D Bentley, *settled midfield, hdwy aftr 4 out, kpt on, nvr able to chal.*
. . . .(20 to 1) 8

2759* SHANNON GLEN [120] (bl) 8-10-5 G McCourt, *nvr far away, niggled alng aftr 4th, led after 6th till appr 2 out, sn wknd.*. . . . .(20 to 1) 9

2788* PEANUTS PET [126] 9-10-11 R Garritty, *in tch, rdn aftr 4 out, not trble ldrs.*. . . . .(16 to 1 tchd 20 to 1) 10

2851² IVOR'S FLUTTER [115] (bl) 5-10-0 P Holley, *midfield, shrt-lvd effrt 4 out, nvr able to chal...*(16 to 1 tchd 20 to 1) 11

2851⁴ GLAISDALE (Ire) [130] (v) 5-11-1 M Richards, *trkd ldrs, styd on frm 4 out, drvn out, ran on*
. . . .(33 to 1) 12

2632² COURT CIRCULAR [115] (v) 5-10-0 Diane Clay, *ldg grp, rdn alng bef 6th, wknd.* (66 to 1 op 33 to 1 tchd 100 to 1) 13

2806³ JEASSU [134] (v) 11-11-5 B Clifford, *mstk 3rd, sn beh.*
. . . . (20 to 1 op 16 to 1) 14

2257⁵ DANCE OF WORDS (Ire) [131] 5-10-13 (3*) D J Moffatt, *last early, nvr a dngr.*. . . . .(25 to 1) 15

1561² WICK POUND [126] (bl) 8-10-11 T Grantham, *in tch till no hdwy frm 6th.*. . . . . (25 to 1 op 33 to 1) 16

29947 LEMON'S MILL (USA) [132] 5-11-3 M A FitzGerald, *rdn alng aftr 4th, sn struggling.*. . . . .(16 to 1) 17

2994⁸ OLYMPIAN [136] (bl) 7-11-7 J Lower, *led aftr second, hdd and mstk 4th, wknd.* (16 to 1 op 14 to 1 tchd 20 to 1) 18

2833⁸ BO KNOWS BEST (Ire) [131] 5-11-2 W Marston, *beh, struggling hfwy, nvr dngrs.*
. . . . (12 to 1 op 10 to 1 tchd 14 to 1) 19

2830 CARIBOO GOLD (USA) [120] (bl) 5-10-5 G Bradley, *chsd ldg bunch till wknd frm 4 out.*
. . . . (14 to 1 op 12 to 1 tchd 16 to 1) 20

1671* PURITAN (Can) [118] 5-10-3 M Dwyer, *in tch till wknd appr 4 out.*. . . . . (20 to 1) 21

2846⁶ TEMPLEROAN PRINCE [123] 7-10-8 C Bowens, *led 4th till aftr 6th, wknd quickly appr 2 out.*
. . . . (33 to 1 tchd 40 to 1) 22

PACTOLUS (USA) [124] 11-10-9 A Mulholland, *beh hfwy.*
. . . . (66 to 1 op 50 to 1 tchd 100 to 1) 23

2449* GREY POWER [128] 7-10-13 R Hodge, *nvr gng wl, al rear.*
. . . . (14 to 1 tchd 16 to 1) 24

2674³ SUNSET AND VINE [119] 7-10-4 A Dicken, *midfield whn f 5th....*. . . . . (33 to 1 tchd 40 to 1) f

2680³ SHANKORAK [139] 7-11-3 (7*) D J Kavanagh, *led till aftr second, wknd quickly 4th, brght dwn nxt.*
. . . . (33 to 1 op 20 to 1 tchd 40 to 1) bd

2856² LYNCH LAW (Ire) [115] (v) 6-9-9 (5*) J P Broderick, *beh whn brght dwn 5th.*. . . . .(33 to 1) bd

2842³ STEEL MIRROR [120] 5-10-5 J Shortt, *midfield whn brght dwn 5th.*. . . . . (20 to 1 tchd 25 to 1) bd

2727² MAESTRO PAUL [116] 8-10-1¹ D Murphy, *nvr a dngr, beh whn pld up bef 3 out.*. . . . . (40 to 1 op 33 to 1) pu

2403 STORMHEAD [123] (bl) 6-10-8 J Osborne, *in tch to hfwy, beh whn pld up bef 4 out, dismounted.*
. . . .(33 to 1 tchd 40 to 1) pu
Dist: 1½l, 8l, 2½l, 1½l, 5l, ¾l, 1l, 12l, nk, 1l. 5m 9.20s. a 10.20s (30 Ran).
SR: 76/52/45/52/57/38/36/52/25/ (J P McManus), E J O'Grady

3039 Sun Alliance Chase Grade 1 (5-y-o and up) £49,017 3m 1f. . . . . (4:05)

2746* MONSIEUR LE CURE 8-11-4 P Niven, *sn wl plcd, lft in ld 12th, quickened 3 out, drvn betw last 2, styd on strly r-in...*. . . . .(15 to 2 op 6 to 1 tchd 8 to 1) 1

1691* MARTOMICK 7-10-13 D Gallagher, *al wl plcd, led 4th till pckd and hdd 12th, rallied frm 2 out, styd on well.*
. . . .(20 to 1) 2

2472² CRYSTAL SPIRIT 7-11-4 J Frost, *nvr far away, second and staying on whn blun last, not reco'r.*
. . . . (10 to 1 tchd 14 to 1) 3

2609 BELVEDERIAN 7-11-4 A Maguire, *settled off the pace, mstk 12th, styd on frm 3 out, nvr rch ldrs.*
. . . . (13 to 2 op 5 to 1 tchd 7 to 1) 4

2720* SEE MORE INDIANS 7-11-4 G Bradley, *settled off the pace, improved appr 3 out, kpt on, nvr nrr.*
. . . . (6 to 1 tchd 11 to 2 and 13 to 2) 5

2448³ ARTHUR'S MINSTREL 7-11-4 C Grant, *patiently rdn, improved fnl circuit, outpcd aftr 4 out, styd on finish.*
. . . . (100 to 1 op 50 to 1) 6

2514 EARTH SUMMIT (bl) 6-11-4 C Llewellyn, *wth ldrs early, lost grnd quickly aftr one circuit, no imprsn frm 4 out.*
. . . . (66 to 1 op 50 to 1) 7

2514 MUDAHIM 8-11-4 W Marston, *co'red up in midfield, drvn alng aftr one circuit, nvr a threat.*
. . . . (25 to 1 op 33 to 1) 8

2514* ONE MAN (Ire) 6-11-4 N Doughty, *wth ldrs, drw level whn blun 6 out, ev ch and rdn appr 3 out, 3rd and btn when blundered last, not reco'r.* (3 to 1 fav tchd 7 to 2) 9

2595⁵ GHIA GNEUIAGH 8-11-4 D Bridgwater, *sluggish strt, not jump wl, al beh.*. . . . .(100 to 1) 10

2601² ROUYAN 8-11-4 D Murphy, *chsd alng in midfield aftr one circuit, nvr a factor.*. . . . .(66 to 1 op 33 to 1) 11

2794⁵ PETTY BRIDGE 10-11-4 R Bellamy, *al struggling, tld off fnl circuit.*. . . . . (200 to 1 tchd 300 to 1) 12

2725* HONEST WORD 9-11-4 C Swan, *led to 4th, hndy till f tenth.*. . . . . (8 to 1 op 6 to 1 tchd 10 to 1) f

2576* KILLULA CHIEF 7-11-4 M Dwyer, *settled midfield, f 7th.*
. . . . (20 to 1 op 16 to 1 tchd 25 to 1) f

2879* ANOTHER EXCUSE (Ire) 6-11-4 Mr W O'Sullivan, *not jump wl, al struggling in rear, no imprsn whn f 6 out.*
. . . . (25 to 1 tchd 33 to 1) f

2784* BRABAZON (USA) 9-11-4 M Richards, *nvr gng wl, tld off whn pld up aftr 6 out.*. . . . . . . (66 to 1 op 50 to 1) pu

2514² MAOLIOM 8-11-4 J Osborne, *trkd ldg bunch, struggling fnl circuit, btn whn pld up bef 4 out.*
. . . . (14 to 1 tchd 16 to 1) pu

2596² THE GLOW (Ire) 6-11-4 P Holley, *chsd ldrs, hmpd tenth, losing tch whn hit 6 out, pld up bef 3 out.*
. . . . (25 to 1 op 20 to 1) pu
Dist: 3l, 8l, 7l, 12l, ½l, 3l, sht-hd, 15l, 2½l, 20l. 6m 18.30s. a 12.30s (18 Ran).
SR: 34/26/23/16/4/3/ (Hector H Brown), J A C Edwards

3040 124th Year Of The National Hunt Chase Challenge Cup Amateur Riders (5-y-o and up) £15,530 4m. . . . . . (4:40)

2406² CHRISTMAS GORSE 8-12-4 Mr M Armytage, *patiently rdn, hdwy frm 6 out, led betw last 2, pushed out r-in.*
. . . . (14 to 1 tchd 16 to 1) 1

2497³ EXTRA SPECIAL 9-12-0 Capt A Ogden, *beh, hdwy frm 3 out, str run to go second betw last 2, mstk last, one pace.*. . . . .(25 to 1) 2

2800* NEARLY SPLENDID 9-12-4 Mr T Greed, *beh, styd on wl frm 3 out, nvr nrr.*. . . . . (14 to 1 op 12 to 1) 3

2427 BINKLEY (Fr) 8-12-4 Mr M Rimell, *trkd ldrs, led 3 out till betw last 2, sn btn.*. . . . .(100 to 1) 4

2811² DAMNIFICATION 8-12-0 Mr A Parker, *beh, styd on frm 6 out, not rch ldrs.*. . . . .(20 to 1) 5

VALNAU (Fr) (bl) 7-12-0 Mr D Pipe, *chsd ldrs till moderate prog frm 3 out, nvr a dngr.*. . . . .(16 to 1 tchd 20 to 1) 6

2858² FLORIDA SKY 7-12-4 Mr D Costello, *hndy, led 5 out till 3 out, sn wknd.*. . . . .(10 to 1 tchd 12 to 1) 7

2858* LASTOFTHEVIKINGS 9-12-4 Mr W O'Sullivan, *beh whn mstk 14th, sn no hdwy.*. . . . . (14 to 1 op 16 to 1) 8

2700³ ULTRA FLUTTER 7-12-0 Mr G Hogan, *hld up, some hdwy whn blun and uns rdr 4 out.*
. . . . (11 to 2 op 4 to 1 tchd 6 to 1) ur

2654 DOLLY OATS 8-11-9 Mr D Duggan, *blun 6th, beh whn mstk and uns rdr 12th.*. . . . .(50 to 1) ur

2984³ TAKE THE TOWN 9-12-4 Mr W Mullins, *jmpd rght, led bef 4th till 17th, wkng whn blun and uns rdr four out.*
. . . . (12 to 1 tchd 14 to 1) ur

2446* DURHAM SUNSET 7-12-2 Mr D Parker, *sn hndy, wth ldrs whn blun and uns rdr 12th.....* (7 to 1 tchd 15 to 2) ur

2855⁴ CREWS CASTLE 7-12-4 Mr P Graffin, *trkd ldrs for o'r one circuit, wkng whn brght dwn 4 out.....* (100 to 1) ur

426

2527 GOLDEN FARE 9-12-4 Mr M Buckley, *not jump wl, sn struggling in rear, tld off whn pld up bef 6 out.* ....(33 to 1 op 25 to 1) pu
2780[2] HERE COMES CHARTER 9-12-0 Mr Anthony Martin, *trkd ldrs, lost tch fnl circuit, beh whn pld up bef 4 out.* ....(33 to 1 tchd 40 to 1) pu
962[4] KELLY OWENS 9-12-0 Mr N Bradley, *mid-div, lost tch fnl circuit, beh whn pld up bef 4 out*..........(100 to 1) pu
2559[2] RAMPOLDI (USA) (bl) 7-12-4 Mr P Hacking, *not fluent, hdwy 13th, sn prmnt, led 17th to 5 out, soon wknd, beh whn pld up bef 3 out*..........(12 to 1) pu
2688[2] FRONT LINE 7-12-0 Mr E Bolger, *patiently rdn, hdwy fnl circuit, no imprsn frm 4 out, pld up bef nxt, lme.* ....(11 to 4 fav op 5 to 2 tchd 7 to 2) pu
2773* TASSE DU THE 7-11-13 Mr J Durkan, *led till bef 4th, hmpd 8th, beh whn pld up before 17th*..........(33 to 1) pu
Dist: 3½l, 4l, 12l, 4l, 20l, 3½l, 15l. 8m 36.60s. a 31.60s (19 Ran).
(D R Stoddart), N A Gaselee

3041 44th Year Of The Mildmay Of Flete Challenge Cup Handicap Chase (5-y-o and up) £26,337 2½m 110yds....(5:15)

2747[4] ELFAST [137] 11-11-4 G McCourt, *patiently rdn, improved hfwy, led 2 out, jmpd rght last, drvn out.* ....(8 to 1 tchd 10 to 1) 1
2718* DUBLIN FLYER [132] 8-10-13 B Powell, *jmpd wl, led 3rd to 5th, ev ch frm 3 out, kpt on strly r-in.* ....(7 to 1 tchd 8 to 1) 2
2948* SMARTIE EXPRESS [127] 12-10-8 (3ex) A Maguire, *tucked away in midfield, improved aftr 4 out, styd on frm betw last 2*..........(14 to 1 op 12 to 1) 3
2867* FOURTH OF JULY [129] 10-10-10 (6ex) J P Banahan, *chsd ldg bunch, pushed alng to improve aftr 4 out, styd on, nvr nrr*..........(10 to 1 op 7 to 1) 4
1843[6] NEVADA GOLD [125] 8-10-6 D Gallagher, *patiently rdn, improved frm hfwy, styd on from 3 out, not rch ldrs.* ....(15 to 2 op 6 to 1 tchd 8 to 1) 5
2416 MAN OF MYSTERY [119] 8-10-0 D Bridgwater, *al hndy, led 7th to 2 out, wknd quickly*..........(33 to 1 tchd 40 to 1) 6
2726* BIBENDUM [133] 8-11-0 M A FitzGerald, *settled midfield, chsd alng appr 4 out, not pace to chal.* ....(10 to 1 op 8 to 1) 7
2488[4] RICHVILLE [132] 8-10-13 S McNeill, *wtd wth, effrt and bustled alng fnl circuit, nvr able to rch ldrs.* ....(16 to 1 op 14 to 1) 8
2598* KENTISH PIPER [132] 9-10-13 C Llewellyn, *outpcd and struggling hfwy, nvr a factor*....(14 to 1 tchd 12 to 1) 9
1895[7] BISHOPS HALL [143] 8-11-10 C Swan, *trkd ldrs, chsd alng appr 5 out, sn lost tch*..........(25 to 1 op 20 to 1) 10
2520* FRENCH CHARMER [121] 9-10-2[2] D Murphy, *tucked away beh ldrs, improved hfwy, staying on one pace whn f 2 out*..........(33 to 1 op 25 to 1) f
2384[3] GNOME'S TYCOON [127] 8-10-8 J Railton, *settled midfield, improved 4 out, staying on one pace whn f 2 out.* ....(6 to 1 fav op 7 to 1) f
2706* YELLOW SPRING [127] 9-10-8 Peter Hobbs, *trkd ldrs, in tch whn blun and uns rdr 4 out.* ....(14 to 1 op 12 to 1 tchd 16 to 1) ur
2911[3] NOS NA GAOITHE [121] (v) 11-10-2[2] M Dwyer, *al beh, tld off whn pld up bef 3 out*..........(66 to 1 op 50 to 1) pu
2513[7] LUMBERJACK (USA) [125] (bl) 10-10-6 J Osborne, *al struggling, tld off whn pld up bef 8th*...(50 to 1 op 33 to 1) pu
2852[2] FOREST SUN [132] 9-10-13 G Bradley, *struggling bef hfwy, tld off whn pld up before 3 out.* ....(8 to 1 op 10 to 1) pu
1520 LOCAL WHISPER [119] 10-10-0 P Holley, *led to 3rd, led 5th to 7th, lost tch and pld up bef 3 out.* ....(100 to 1 op 66 to 1) pu
1706[5] WELL WRAPPED [130] 10-10-11 M Perrett, *wth ldrs, blun and lost grnd quickly 6 out, tld off whn pld up bef 4 out*..........(33 to 1 op 25 to 1 tchd 40 to 1) pu
Dist: ¾l, 4l, 12l, 1½l, 3½l, 6l, 5l, 8l, 20l. 5m 7.60s. a 7.60s (18 Ran).
SR: 69/63/54/44/38/28/36/30/22/ (John Webber), J Webber

3042 Bromsgrove Industries Festival Bumper National Hunt Flat Race (4,5,6-y-o) £12,720 2m 110yds...(5:50)

1403* MUCKLEMEG (Ire) 6-11-5 C Swan, *hld up in tch gng wl, hdwy to ld on ins 3 fs out, rdn appr last, ran on well.* ....(7 to 2 fav op 5 to 2 tchd 2 to 1 and 4 to 1) 1
1903* ARIES GIRL 5-11-3 (5*) J R Barry, *nvr far away, led 4 fs out to 3 out, sn rdn, kpt on wl.* ....(5 to 1 op 6 to 1 tchd 9 to 2) 2
2834[2] GO BALLISTIC 5-11-3 (7*) R Massey, *patiently rdn, hdwy o'r 3 fs out, not quicken frm 2 out.* ....(16 to 1 op 20 to 1 tchd 25 to 1) 3
RHYTHM SECTION (Ire) 5-11-8 (5*) J P Broderick, *cl up, drvn alng 6 fs out, styd on one pace frm 3 out.* ....(9 to 1 op 7 to 1 tchd 10 to 1) 4
2677[3] KILLONE ABBOT (Ire) 5-11-6 T Grantham, *beh, hdwy fnl 3 fs, gng on finish, nvr nrr*..........(25 to 1 op 20 to 1) 5
2756* MARINGO (Ire) 5-11-13 Mrs J M Mullins, *led to 4 fs out, sn not quicken*..........(12 to 1 op 10 to 1 tchd 14 to 1) 6
2269* DOMINIE (Ire) 6-11-10 J Osborne, *patiently rdn, hdwy 4 fs out, no imprsn frm 2 out*..........(12 to 1 op 10 to 1) 7
2290* SOVEREIGN CHOICE (Ire) (v) 4-11-2 Pat Shanahan, *trkd ldg bunch, pushed alng to improve o'r 5 fs out, sn no extr.* ....(12 to 1) 8
2677[8] LEAD VOCALIST (Ire) 5-11-10 M Perrett, *chsd ldg bunch, rdn 4 fs out, sn one pace*..........(66 to 1 op 50 to 1) 9
2691[2] WHO IS EQUINAME (Ire) 4-10-12 M Dwyer, *slwly away, wl beh till styd on fnl 3 fs, nvr a dngr*..........(50 to 1) 10
2387* LIEN DE FAMILLE (Ire) 4-10-11 (5*) E Husband, *in tch, hdwy 4 fs out, wknd wl o'r 2 out.* ....(14 to 1 op 33 to 1 tchd 12 to 1) 11
2877[2] COURTOWN BOY 4-10-9 (7*) Mr G Hogan, *beh, some hdwy o'r 5 fs out, no imprsn frm 3 out*..........(50 to 1) 12
2407* ST MELLION FAIRWAY (Ire) 5-11-6 (7*) Pat Thompson, *midfield on outsd, no hdwy fnl 3 fs*..........(33 to 1) 13
2749* PUNTERS OVERHEAD (Ire) 6-11-10 G McCourt, *trkd ldrs on outsd, no hdwy fnl 6 fs*......(20 to 1 tchd 25 to 1) 14
2509* BEAR CLAW 5-11-13 A Maguire, *midfield, pushed alng o'r 6 fs out, no imprsn*..........(14 to 1 op 10 to 1) 15
2834* HIGHLY REPUTABLE (Ire) 4-11-2 J Lower, *trkd ldrs, pushed alng o'r 5 fs out, sn lost pl.* ....(16 to 1 op 14 to 1 tchd 20 to 1) 16
2081* RANAGAR (Ire) 4-10-11 (5*) Mr H F Cleary, *prmnt on ins, rdn wl o'r 5 fs out, wknd quickly*. (20 to 1 tchd 25 to 1) 17
2592* EDGE OF NIGHT 5-11-13 J P Banahan, *ldg grp, rdn and wknd 5 fs out*..........(9 to 1 op 8 to 1 tchd 10 to 1) 18
1779 RED PARADE (NZ) 6-11-7 (3*) R Davis, *in tch till rdn alng hfwy, sn wknd*..........(50 to 1 op 33 to 1) 19
2490[2] MAYBE O'GRADY (Ire) 5-11-5 (5*) S Mason, *al rear div.* ....(25 to 1 op 20 to 1) 20
2490* FEELS LIKE GOLD (Ire) 6-11-10 M A FitzGerald, *beh hfwy.* ....(33 to 1 tchd 40 to 1) 21
2663* GAMBOLLING DOC (Ire) 4-11-2 G Bradley, *hdwy o'r 6 fs out, sn chasing ldrs, wknd quickly wl over 3 out.* ....(25 to 1 op 20 to 1) 22
1806* AUTO PILOT (NZ) 6-11-10 C Llewellyn, *beh hfwy, tld off.* ....(50 to 1 op 33 to 1) 23
2560* SPARKLING CONE 5-11-10 M Foster, *wth ldr till rdn and wknd quickly o'r 5 fs out, tld off*. (20 to 1 tchd 25 to 1) 24
2890* LINTON ROCKS 5-11-10 (3*) Mr M Buckley, *rear div whn uns rdr 5 fs out*..........(66 to 1 op 50 to 1) ur
Dist: 3l, 15l, ¾l, hd, ½l, 4l, 1½l, 4l, ½l, hd. 3m 53.70s. (25 Ran).
(J P McManus), E J O'Grady

HUNTINGDON (good to soft)
Wednesday March 16th

Going Correction: PLUS 1.35 sec. per fur. (races 1,3,5), PLUS 1.10 (2,4,6)

3043 Island Hall Novices' Chase (5-y-o and up) £2,576 2½m 110yds.........(2:10)

1324* HEARTS ARE WILD 7-11-9 B Powell, *wl in tch, led 13th, drw clr appr 2 out, unchlgd.* ....(5 to 4 on op 6 to 4 on tchd 11 to 10 on) 1
2668[4] VITAL WITNESS (Can) 7-11-2 A S Smith, *effrt frm rear tenth, no hdwy 12th, lft poor second last fence.* ....(6 to 1 tchd 7 to 1) 2
2886 FLUTTER MONEY 10-11-2 G Upton, *chsd ldr to tenth, wkng whn blun 13th, no extr*......(33 to 1 op 20 to 1) 3
2829[5] TRUE SHADE 8-11-2 B Dalton, *led till hdd 13th, sn wknd, tld off whn mstk 2 out.* (9 to 1 op 6 to 1 tchd 10 to 1) 4
JUST MAX 10-10-11 (5*) J Supple, *mid-div whn f tenth.* ....(33 to 1 op 20 to 1) f
2440 GLEN PENNANT 7-11-2 N Mann, *f 4th.* ....(33 to 1 op 20 to 1) f
INTERPLAY 9-11-2 D O'Sullivan, *in 3rd pl whn blun and uns rdr 9th*..........(10 to 1 op 7 to 1) ur
2794* BALLY PARSON 8-11-6 (3*) A Thornton, *hld up, hdwy tenth, chsd wnr frm 13th, wkng whn mstk 2 out, second when blun and uns rdr last.* ....(7 to 2 op 5 to 2 tchd 4 to 1) ur
2958 SUNCIA 10-10-4 (7*) P Ward, *al beh, tld off whn pld up bef 3 out*..........(20 to 1 op 12 to 1) pu
983 JACK DIAMOND 6-11-2 V Smith, *not jump wl, beh whn hmpd 9th, tld off when pld up bef 3 out*...... (33 to 1) pu
Dist: 30l, 3l, dist. 5m 30.70s. a 35.70s (10 Ran).
SR: 15/-/-/-/-/ (T F F Nixon), Capt T A Forster

3044 Ellington Novices' Hurdle (4-y-o and up) £2,107 2m 110yds.......... (2:40)

2505 BATTY'S ISLAND 5-11-2 T Wall, *chsd ldr till lft in ld aftr 3rd, pushed clr frm 3 out, unchlgd*... (3 to 1 op 5 to 2) 1
PETTAUGH (Ire) 6-10-13 (3*) A Thornton, *chsd ldrs, rdn alng 5th, styd on one pace frm 3 out.* ....(12 to 1 op 10 to 1) 2
2808 OPALKINO 9-10-8 (3*) S Wynne, *not jump wl, hdwy frm rear 4th, rdn and wknd appr 2 out*..........(20 to 1) 3
COLONEL CLOETE 6-10-13 (3*) R Farrant, *in tch till rdn alng and outpcd frm 5th, tld off.* ....(6 to 1 tchd 13 to 2 and 7 to 1) 4
2335 CAP DIAMANT (USA) 6-10-9 (7*) W J Walsh, *chsd ldrs to 5th, poor 4th whn f 3 out.* ....(11 to 1 op 7 to 1 tchd 12 to 1) f

2828[4] LYPHANTASTIC (USA) 5-11-2 J R Kavanagh, *led till hdd and reluctant to race aftr 3rd, sn tld off, pld up bef 3 out*........................ (6 to 4 on tchd 11 to 8 on) pu
Dist: 30l, 10l, dist. 4m 16.00s. a 29.00s (6 Ran).
(Mrs Mary Price), B Preece

3045 Country Landowners Association Handicap Chase (0-130 5-y-o and up) £3,444 3m..................... (3:10)

2718[2] DRAGONS DEN [107] 8-10-4 (3*) A Thornton, *hit 1st and 3rd, jmpd slwly tenth, chsd ldr frm 14th, hrd rdn to ld r-in*.. (7 to 2 op 3 to 1) 1
2824[2] MANDER'S WAY [103] 9-10-3[1] G Upton, *jmpd slwly 4th and 7th, cl up till led 3 out, hdd und pres r-in*. ....(7 to 2 op 3 to 1) 2
2748[6] AVONBURN (NZ) [119] 10-11-5 D O'Sullivan, *hld up, hdwy 13th, rdn and one pace appr 2 out*. ....(7 to 4 fav op 5 to 4) 3
2513[5] CUDDY DALE [125] 11-11-11 J R Kavanagh, *led till hdd 3 out, wknd appr nxt*.................. (3 to 1 op 4 to 1) 4
EBONY SWELL [106] 13-10-6[9] (5*) P Midgley, *pressed ldr till lost pl frm 12th, wknd appr 2 out, blun last*. .... (25 to 1 op 20 to 1) 5
2832 ICARUS (USA) [115] (bl) 8-11-1 Mr A Rebori, *mstk second, beh and rdn 11th, lost tch 13th, pld up bef 3 out*. .... (12 to 1 op 10 to 1 tchd 14 to 1) pu
Dist: 1½l, 8l, 10l, 15l. 6m 30.80s. a 42.80s (6 Ran).
(Christopher Heath), S E Sherwood

3046 Great Paxton Novices' Hurdle (4-y-o and up) £1,891 2m 5f 110yds.... (3:50)

2382[2] NIRVANA PRINCE 5-11-12 T Wall, *hld up, hdwy 6th, led aftr nxt, clr appr 2 out, kpt on frm last*. ....(9 to 4 on op 5 to 2 on tchd 2 to 1 on) 1
GILLAN COVE (Ire) 5-11-2 S Earle, *wl plcd, chsd wnr aftr 7th, styd on well r-in*. .... (14 to 1 op 12 to 1 tchd 16 to 1) 2
2705[6] HENRY'S SISTER 7-10-4 (7*) P Ward, *trkd ldrs, effrt appr 3 out, one pace and btn whn blun last*. .... (20 to 1 op 14 to 1) 3
2320[3] NEFARIOUS 8-11-5 (7*) L Dace, *hld up in rear, effrt 6th, no imprsn on ldrs frm 2 out*.......... (5 to 1 op 4 to 1) 4
2881[4] NIGHT FANCY 6-10-9 (7*) P McLoughlin, *hld up in rear, effrt 6th, no extr aftr 3 out*........ (25 to 1 op 20 to 1) 5
2224 THE GREY TEXAN 5-11-2 Richard Guest, *ldg grp, led briefly aftr 6th, sn hdd, wknd frm 3 out*. .... (25 to 1 op 20 to 1) 6
1835[5] MAN O MINE (Ire) 5-11-2 J R Kavanagh, *beh frm 5th*. .... (10 to 1 op 7 to 1) 7
SPIRITUALIST 8-10-13 (3*) A Thornton, *led till hdd aftr 6th, wknd nxt, tld off*............ (25 to 1 op 20 to 1) 8
GENERAL EDDIE 10-10-11 (5*) S Curran, *chsd ldrs to 6th, tld off*.. (33 to 1) 9
2505 LADY OF ROME 7-10-6 (5*) J Supple, *beh whn mstk 6th, tld off when pld up bef 3 out*...... (20 to 1 op 16 to 1) pu
1021 WESTRAY (Fr) 4-10-7 A Carroll, *ldg grp till wknd 6th, tld off whn pld up bef 3 out*.................... (33 to 1) pu
2905[5] SUVLA BAY (Ire) 6-11-2 M Brennan, *wl plcd to 6th, well beh whn pld up bef 3 out*............. (8 to 1 tchd 10 to 1) pu
Dist: 3l, 8l, 30l, 3l, 8l, 7l, 15l, 15l. 5m 27.80s. a 32.80s (12 Ran).
SR: 7/-/-/-/-/-/ (D Portman), B Preece

3047 Hartford Novices' Chase (5-y-o and up) £2,401 2m 110yds.......... (4:25)

2337* MARTHA'S SON 7-11-5 (3*) R Farrant, *handily plcd, led appr 2 out, clr whn jmpd lft last, eased nr finish*. ....(6 to 4 on op 7 to 4 on tchd 11 to 8 on) 1
1559 JIMMY THE GILLIE 8-11-1 G Upton, *chsd ldr to 6th, outpcd 3 out, rallied appr 2 out, styd on one pace frm last*. ....(7 to 1 op 8 to 1) 2
2778 AMTRAK EXPRESS 7-11-8 J R Kavanagh, *jmpd very big early fences, led, quickened 3 out, hdd appr 2 out, wknd r-in*.. (7 to 4) 3
2331[7] PHARGOLD (Ire) 5-10-7 T Wall, *in tch in rear whn pckd on landing at 3rd, outpcd 3 out, shrtlvd appr nxt, sn btn*. .... (33 to 1) 4
Dist: 1½l, 6l, 2½l. 4m 25.60s. a 27.60s (4 Ran).
SR: 41/32/33/15/ (M Ward-Thomas), Capt T A Forster

3048 Buckden Palace Handicap Hurdle (0-105 4-y-o and up) £2,407 2m 110yds ....(4:55)

2933[4] MARSH'S LAW [92] 7-11-7 M Brennan, *hld up, improved frm 5th, led appr 2 out, sn wl clr, eased nr finish*. ....(4 to 1 op 3 to 1 tchd 9 to 2) 1
2992* SHAMSHOM AL ARAB (Ire) [82] 6-10-4 (7*,7ex) Miss V Haigh, *ldg grp, led 5th, hdd nxt, kpt on one pace frm 2 out*. ....(3 to 1 fav op 5 to 2 tchd 7 to 2) 2
2243 EXPLORATION (USA) [85] 7-11-0 A S Smith, *ldg grp, led 3 out, hdd and outpcd appr nxt*. ....(11 to 2 op 6 to 1 tchd 7 to 1 and 5 to 1) 3
APPLIANCEOFSCIENCE [95] 7-11-10 J Ryan, *settled towards rear, effrt and rdn 5th, styd on one pace frm 2 out*........(7 to 1 op 8 to 1 tchd 10 to 1 and 12 to 1) 4
SANTARAY [93] 8-11-5 (3*) T Eley, *blun 3rd, chsd ldrs till lost pl 3 out*........... (8 to 1 op 10 to 1 tchd 12 to 1) 5
2697[7] ROCK LEGEND [87] 6-10-11 (5*) J Supple, *cl up, led second to nxt, wknd 5th*.................. (16 to 1 op 14 to 1) 6
1741[4] COOL SOCIETY (USA) [71] 5-10-0 N Mann, *wl plcd, led 3rd till hdd 5th, sn btn*................ (14 to 1 op 10 to 1) 7
2883[3] WILL JAMES [84] (bl) 8-10-13 I Lawrence, *settled towards rear, rdn and btn aftr 5th*........... (9 to 1 op 6 to 1) 8
2439[4] THE CAN CAN MAN [72] 7-10-1 M Robinson, *led to second, wknd quickly aftr 4th*.............. (8 to 1 op 6 to 1) 9
1040[5] MASNUN (USA) [93] 9-11-8 D O'Sullivan, *not jump wl, al beh, tld off whn pld up bef 2 out*. .... (13 to 2 op 4 to 1 tchd 7 to 1) pu
Dist: 15l, 12l, 3½l, 12l, 2l, sht-hd, 5l, 3l. 4m 11.10s. a 24.10s (10 Ran).
SR: 34/9/-/6/-/-/ (Mrs Violet J Hannigan), O Brennan

NEWTON ABBOT (good to soft)
Wednesday March 16th
Going Correction: PLUS 1.20 sec. per fur.

3049 Little Town Restricted Novices' Hunters' Chase (5-y-o and up) £1,064 2m 5f..........................(2:00)

WINTER'S LANE 10-11-7 (7*) Mr M Felton, *hld up rear, hdwy 11th, chalg whn jmpd slwly 3 out, rallied and led nxt, ran on wl*. (11 to 10 on op 11 to 8 on tchd Evens) 1
2800[3] WALK IN THE WOODS 7-11-2 (7*) Mrs S Palmer, *jmpd lft 1st, slow nxt 2, made most till hdd and mstk two out, one pace*.......... (9 to 4 op 2 to 1 tchd 5 to 2) 2
2889 NATIONAL GYPSY 8-11-2 (7*) Mr R Nuttall, *wtd wth, hdwy 11th, cl second whn blun 4 out, rdn and one pace nxt*. .... (12 to 1 op 20 to 1) 3
BANG ON TARGET 6-11-7 (7*) Mr J Culloty, *hld up, making hdwy whn hit tenth, rdn and btn when blun last*. ....(5 to 1 op 6 to 1) 4
OH BE JOYFUL 6-11-2 (7*) Mrs J Mills, *led briefly 1st, in tch till outpcd 4 out*............... (33 to 1 op 25 to 1) 5
TAPSTER LAD 10-11-7 (7*) Mr R Mills, *prmnt, dsptd ld 3rd, 4th and tenth, wknd appr 3 out*. .... (25 to 1 op 20 to 1 tchd 33 to 1) 6
KINGSLEY SINGER 6-11-7 (7*) Mr J Creighton, *not jump wl, in tch whn blun and uns rdr 9th*.......... (50 to 1) ur
2800 JUST SILVER 9-11-7 (7*) Mr B Pollock, *hld up, hdwy 8th, hit tenth and wknd, pld up bef 2 out*. ....(20 to 1 tchd 25 to 1) pu
Dist: 5l, 1½l, 3l, 3½l, 1½l. 5m 44.50s. a 44.50s (8 Ran).
(Stewart Pike), S Pike

3050 Tetley Bitter Novices' Chase (5-y-o and up) £2,497 2m 110yds...... (2:30)

2439[3] NEEDS MUST 7-10-11 (7*) R Darke, *led, hit 1st and hdd, settled in beh ldrs, wnt second 4 out, led appr 2 out, mstk last, ran on*....... (4 to 1 tchd 5 to 1 and 7 to 2) 1
2146 BARONESS ORKZY 8-10-13 (5*) Guy Lewis, *led 1st, hdd appr 2 out, hrd rdn and rallied last, no imprsn r-in*. .... (11 to 10 fav op 7 to 4 on) 2
2328[3] ALDAHE 9-11-4 S Burrough, *sn trkd ldr, rdn and wknd 4 out*.......(7 to 2 op 4 to 1 tchd 5 to 1 and 100 to 30) 3
2778[4] WHYFOR 6-10-13 (5*) D Salter, *beh early, hit 5th, hdwy whn hit 8th, wkng when blun 4 out*. (8 to 1 op 16 to 1) 4
2749 MERRY BENVILLE 6-11-4 A Tory, *al beh, lost tch 7th, tld off whn f 4 out*..................... (12 to 1 op 8 to 1) f
Dist: 2½l, 15l, 20l. 4m 23.50s. a 26.50s (5 Ran).
SR: 23/20/5/-/-/ (Miss J Du Plessis), R G Frost

3051 Carlsberg Pilsner 'National Hunt' Novices' Hurdle (4-y-o and up) £1,931 2 ¾m.......................... (3:00)

2655 KELLING 7-10-12 (5*) Guy Lewis, *wtd wth, hdwy 6th, rdn to ld sn aftr 3 out, unchlgd*......... (14 to 1 op 7 to 1) 1
1800[3] TAKE THE BUCKSKIN 7-11-3 S Smith Eccles, *hld up, chsd ldr 6th, led briefly 3 out, sn outpcd*. .... (15 to 8 op 2 to 1 tchd 6 to 4) 2
2841 JANET SCIBS 8-10-7 (5*) D Matthews, *hld up in rear, hdwy 6th, rdn 4 out, one pace*............... (50 to 1) 3
952[8] ABSENT MINDS 8-10-12 Miss S Young, *chsd ldr 3rd to 6th, rdn and wknd 3 out*............... (66 to 1 op 50 to 1) 4
1406[3] LIE DETECTOR 6-11-0 (3*) J McCarthy, *beh, hdwy frm 6th, rdn and wknd 3 out*. (7 to 4 on op 6 to 4 tchd 7 to 4) 5
2795[4] GOD SPEED YOU (Ire) (bl) 5-11-3 R Marley, *led second, hdd 3 out, wknd quickly*. ....(8 to 1 op 16 to 1 tchd 20 to 1 and 6 to 1) 6
2779[6] TULLYKYNE BELLS 5-11-3 M Hourigan, *nvr on terms*. .... (16 to 1 op 33 to 1) 7
2717[5] GENERALLY JUST (bl) 9-11-3 Mr S Stickland, *nvr on terms*. .... (25 to 1 op 16 to 1) 8
2657[7] CADOLIVE 6-10-12 S Mackey, *led to second, lost pl 4th, sn beh*.............................. (50 to 1 op 33 to 1) 9

RED MATCH 9-11-3 A Tory, *hld up, hdwy to chase ldrs 6th, sn rdn, wkng whn hit 3 out, pld up bef nxt.*
..................................(50 to 1 op 33 to 1) pu
2799 ALICE SPRINGS 5-10-12 C Maude, *beh, some hdwy 6th, wl btn whn pld up bef 2 out, lme*............(33 to 1) pu
2095⁴ CREAG DHUBH 5-11-3 M Foster, *prmnt till outpcd frm 6th, tld off whn pld up bef 3 out*....(12 to 1 op 8 to 1) pu
2779 SARACEN'S BOY (Ire) 6-10-10 (7") Mr B Pollock, *prmnt early, tld off whn pld up bef 7th.* (100 to 1 op 66 to 1) pu
Dist: 10l, 12l, 3l, 12l, 5l, 4l, 3½l, 6l. 5m 37.50s. a 38.50s (13 Ran).

(Colin Lewis), P F Nicholls

3052 Carlsberg-Tetley Handicap Chase (0-135 5-y-o and up) £3,322 3¼m 110yds.................... (3:40)

2085² RUFUS [109] (bl) 8-11-5 L Harvey, *trkd ldr, reminder appr 14th, cld nxt, hrd rdn to ld 2 out, all out.*
.........................(9 to 4 op 3 to 1 tchd 9 to 2) 1
2656³ SARAVILLE [114] 7-11-10 S Smith Eccles, *led, quickened pace 7th, mstk 13th, jmpd rght and hit nxt, rdn and hdd 2 out, fnshd tired.*
.............(6 to 5 fav op 11 to 10 tchd Evens and 5 to 4) 2
2764⁴ TRUSTY FRIEND [90] 12-10-0 C Maude, *trkd ldrs, reminder 7th, lost tch frm tenth...* (20 to 1 op 14 to 1) 3
2791² SUNLEY BAY [103] 8-10-8 (5") Guy Lewis, *al last, rdn aftr jmpd slwly 4th, nvr gng wl.*
..................................(9 to 4 op 5 to 4 tchd 5 to 2) 4
Dist: 10l, 20l, 2½l. 6m 58.50s. a 38.50s (4 Ran).
SR: 24/19/-/-/ (Mrs Dianne J Coleman), B Smart

3053 Carlsberg Export Handicap Hurdle (0-120 4-y-o and up) £2,380 2¾m (4:15)

2657² WARFIELD [86] 7-10-9 (5") Guy Lewis, *trkd ldrs, led appr 2 out, hrd rdn, jst hld on*........ (5 to 2 fav op 11 to 4) 1
2655 SURCOAT [94] 7-11-8 L Harvey, *hld up, rapid hdwy to ld sn aftr 3 out, hdd bef nxt, rallied to chal last, pressed wnr to lme.*...........................(7 to 2) 2
2654² MARTELL BOY (NZ) [96] 7-11-10 A Tory, *trkd ldrs to 3rd, nvr far away, lft in ld 3 out, sn hdd and wknd...* (4 to 1) 3
2710³ PUNCHBAG (USA) [84] 8-10-12 C Maude, *led to 5th, wknd appr 3 out, tld off, fnshd lme.*...............(7 to 2) 4
3003 LEGAL WIN (USA) [75] (bl) 6-9-12² (7") Mr G Shenkin, *chsd ldr frm 3rd, led 5th, slight advantage whn f 3 out.*
..................................(33 to 1) f
2653⁷ CHICKABIDDY [76] 6-9-13 (5") D Salter, *mid-div whn hit and uns rdr 3rd.*...........................(7 to 1) ur
2346 BLASKET HERO [93] (bl) 6-11-7 S Smith Eccles, *hld up, rdn appr 4 out, in tch whn badly hmpd nxt, sn pld up.*
..................................(7 to 2 op 5 to 1) pu
Dist: Sht-hd, 20l, dist. 5m 34.60s. a 35.60s (7 Ran).
SR: -/2/-/-/ (Colin Lewis), P F Nicholls

3054 Carlsberg Elephant Beer Handicap Chase (0-120 5-y-o and up) £2,864 2m 5f.................... (4:50)

2639* HOMME D'AFFAIRE [93] 11-10-5 M Hourigan, *made all, rdn appr 2 out, drvn clr bef last*..................... 1
1890³ CHANGE THE ACT [116] 9-11-11 (3") J McCarthy, *jmpd slwly 3rd and 5th, chsd wnr frm 7th, tried to cl 3 out, no imprsn nxt, eased.*..........(Evens fav op 5 to 4 on) 2
2596⁴ VILLA RECOS [92] 9-10-4 S Burrough, *trkd wnr till mstk 7th, rdn appr 9th, lost tch nxt.*
..................................(9 to 2 op 5 to 1 tchd 11 to 2) 3
Dist: 15l, 4l. 5m 30.90s. a 30.90s (3 Ran).
SR: 20/28/-/ (Miss Nicola M Pfann), R J O'Sullivan

3055 Swan Light Novices' Handicap Hurdle (4-y-o and up) £2,230 2m 1f..... (5:25)

2835⁵ TEMPLE KNIGHT [68] 5-10-2 L Harvey, *trkd ldr 3rd to 5th, came wide into strt, led 2 out, forged clr.*
..................................(5 to 2 op 5 to 2) 1
2817² CAWARRA BOY [90] 6-11-3 (7") Mr E James, *hld up, hdwy to go second 5th, led 3 out, hrd rdn and hdd nxt, outpcd.*...............(11 to 10 on op Evens tchd 15 to 8) 2
2717 TUMBLED BRIDE [73] 8-10-7 C Maude, *hld up 3rd, hdd 3 out, one pace aftr...*......(5 to 1 op 9 to 1 tchd 12 to 1) 3
COURTING NEWMARKET [69] 6-10-3³ S Burrough, *hld up in rear, gd hdwy 5th, wnt second briefly appr 2 out, wknd.*..........................(10 to 1 op 6 to 1) 4
1517⁷ ACROSS THE BOW (USA) [70] 4-10-4 M Hourigan, *prmnt till rdn and wknd 3 out.*
..................................(9 to 1 op 6 to 1) 5
2799⁸ SPIRIT LEVEL [66] 6-9-7 (7") Miss S Mitchell, *al beh, outpcd frm 5th*..........................(10 to 1 op 7 to 1) 6
2722 WEST END [78] 4-10-12¹² Mr S Stickland, *al beh, lost tch appr 5th, tld off*..............................(33 to 1) 7
Dist: 12l, 1l, 3l, ½l, 5l, dist. 4m 20.50s. a 30.50s (7 Ran).
(T A Johnsey), Miss C Johnsey

SEDGEFIELD (good to firm)
Wednesday March 16th
Going Correction: PLUS 0.30 sec. per fur.

3056 Sedgefield Cricket Club Maiden Hurdle (4-y-o) £1,905 2m 1f 110yds. .(2:25)

2241⁶ SHARKASHKA (Ire) 10-9 L Wyer, *al wl plcd, improved to ld bef 4th, shaken up aftr 2 out, ran on well frm last.*
..................................(2 to 1 jt-fav op 7 to 4) 1
2914³ LA VILLA ROSE (Fr) 10-9 A Dobbin, *tucked away on ins, took clr order 4 out, effrt 2 out, ev ch whn blun last, not reco'r.*............(2 to 1 jt-fav op 5 to 4 tchd 7 to 4) 2
2896 COMMANCHE CREEK 10-11 (3") A Larnach, *led til hdd bef 4th, styd hndy, drvn alng aftr 3 out, grad wknd.*
..................................(12 to 1 op 20 to 1) 3
2483⁹ SOLOMAN SPRINGS (USA) 11-0 B Storey, *settled on ins, feeling pace and pushed alng 3 out, fdd.*
..................................(11 to 2 op 6 to 1 tchd 5 to 1) 4
2828⁷ DOC SPOT 11-0 D Byrne, *hld up in last pl, steady hdwy aftr 3 out, shaken up aftr nxt, nvr nr to chal.* (8 to 1) 5
2891 TODDEN 10-7 (7") D Ryan, *nvr far away, drvn alng hfwy, sn struggling, virtually pld up betw last 2.*
..................................(100 to 1 op 66 to 1) 6
2810 SEVERE STORM 10-9 (5") F Perratt, *not fluent, pressed ldrs on outer, hit second, struggling to keep up aftr 4 out, btn whn f nxt.*...............(66 to 1 op 50 to 1) f
2907 ONE FOR TONDY (bl) 10-9 S Turner, *chsd ldg 3, lost pl aftr 3rd, struggling after nxt, tld off whn refused last.*
..................................(33 to 1 op 25 to 1) ref
Dist: 5l, 10l, 3l, 12l, dist. 4m 7.60s. a 12.60s (8 Ran).
SR: 8/3/-/-/-/ (C H Stevens), M H Easterby

3057 Dun Cow Handicap Hurdle (0-115 4-y-o and up) £2,180 2m 5f 110yds. . (2:55)

2894³ HUSO [91] 6-10-4 J Callaghan, *patiently rdn, improved to chal 3 out, led bef nxt, ran on strly.*
..................................(5 to 4 fav op 6 to 4) 1
2740 KIR (Ire) [89] (bl) 6-10-2 A Dobbin, *trkd ldg pair, effrt and drvn alng aftr 3 out, kpt on und prss frm last, not rch wnr.*...........................(14 to 1) 2
2788⁹ CHIEF RAIDER (Ire) [112] 6-11-11 K Jones, *led til rdn and hdd bef 2 out, kpt on same pace.*...........(5 to 2) 3
477² RED JAM JAR [87] 9-10-0 K Johnson, *rcd freely, settled on ins, shaken up 2 out, no imprsn whn hit last.*
..................................(9 to 2 op 4 to 1) 4
2737 FEN WICK [87] 10-10-0 B Storey, *pressed ldr, outpcd and lost grnd 3 out, no dngr aftr.* (12 to 1 op 10 to 1) 5
TV PITCH (Fr) [87] 6-10-0 W Dwan, *settled rear, struggling to keep up 3 out, sn btn.*......................(14 to 1) 6
2581⁸ SOME DO NOT [88] 10-10-1 A Merrigan, *hld up, blun 3rd, struggling appr 3 out, tld off.*
..................................(16 to 1 op 14 to 1 tchd 25 to 1) 7
Dist: 2l, 5l, 2½l, 4l, 6l, 6l, 25l. 5m 11.40s. a 20.40s (7 Ran).
(G Cole), P C Haslam

3058 Golden Lion Handicap Chase (0-125 5-y-o and up) £2,768 2m 5f...... (3:25)

RARE FIRE [91] 10-10-4 N Smith, *trkd ldg 3, improved 4 out, ev ch aftr nxt, led last, rdn out.* (3 to 1 op 5 to 2) 1
2895² BAD TRADE [96] 12-10-9 B Storey, *cl up, led second, quickened fnl circuit, hrd pressed aftr 3 out, hdd last, one pace.*...................(5 to 2 tchd 9 to 4) 2
2831 NO MORE TRIX [111] 8-11-10 L Wyer, *led til hdd second, styd prmnt, effrt and rdn bef 2 out, not quicken appr last.*...........................(5 to 4 fav op Evens) 3
2895⁵ COSMIC RAY [88] (bl) 9-10-1 W McFarland, *nvr far away, rdn and lost pl 4 out, mstk nxt, sn btn.*
..................................(11 to 1 op 10 to 1) 4
Dist: 2½l, 3½l, 25l. 5m 22.60s. a 18.60s (4 Ran).
(Mrs J N Askew), Mrs M Reveley

3059 Social Club Novices' Chase (5-y-o and up) £2,444 3m 3f............. (3:55)

2635² MORGANS HARBOUR 8-11-8 L Wyer, *slwly into strd, sn tracking ldrs, jnd issue 12th, led 5 out, lft wl clr 2 out.*
..................................(9 to 4 on op 5 to 2 on) 1
2908⁴ IRISH GENT (bl) 8-11-2 K Johnson, *chsd ldrs, mstk 6th, sn struggling, drvn hfwy, lft remote second 2 out.* (5 to 1) 2
1941⁵ MOYODE REGENT 10-10-9 (7") Mr A Manners, *chsd ldg 3, cl up and gng wl whn badly hmpd 16th, sn btn, tld off.*
..................................(9 to 2 tchd 5 to 1) 3
2497 SHELTON ABBEY 8-11-2 K Jones, *led or dsptd ld, wnt on 15th, hdd 5 out, five ls second and hld whn f 2 out.*
..................................(16 to 1) f
2355 LADY BLAKENEY 8-11-3 A Dobbin, *led or dsptd ld, hdd 15th, cl up whn blun badly and uns rdr nxt...* (7 to 1) ur
2434 RUSHING BURN 8-10-11 B Storey, *slwly into strd, beh and al detached, struggling fnl circuit, tld off whn pld up 3 out.*..................................(25 to 1) pu
Dist: Dist, dist. 7m 0.30s. a 21.30s (6 Ran).
(P C W Owen), Mrs M Reveley

3060 Ceddesfeld Hall Handicap Chase (0-100 5-y-o and up) £2,807 2m 1f (4:30)

2563³ TRESIDDER [100] 12-12-0 Mr S Swiers, *patiently rdn, improved fnl circuit, led last, pushed out.*
....(7 to 4 fav op 6 to 4 tchd 2 to 1) 1

1604⁵ HEIR OF EXCITEMENT [78] (v) 9-10-3 (3") A Larnach, *led second, hrd pressed frm 3 out, rdn nxt, hdd last, one pace*..(8 to 1) 2

1463³ ACHILTIBUIE [79] 10-10-7 W McFarland, *handily plcd, effrt and rdn aftr 3 out, outpcd nxt, styd on und pres r-in*..(8 to 1) 3

1923 SILVER HAZE [88] 10-10-13 (3") P Williams, *nvr far away, ev ch 3 out, one pace aftr nxt, wknd r-in.*
....(5 to 1 op 4 to 1) 4

2739⁴ BALLYBELL [72] 9-10-0 B Storey, *led to second, styd upsides, blun 5th, ev ch 3 out, wknd bef nxt.*
....(20 to 1 op 16 to 1) 5

1069 ORCHIPEDZO [84] 9-10-5 (7") Judy Davies, *keen hold, trkd ldrs, struggling to keep up 4 out, tld off.*
....(14 to 1 op 12 to 1) 6

2962⁵ HAPPY BREED [87] 11-11-1 L Wyer, *beh, mstk 7th, struggling 6 out, tld off whn pld up bef last.*
....(11 to 2 op 5 to 1) pu

Dist: 4l, 3l, 1l, 12l, 30l. 4m 16.10s. a 11.10s (7 Ran).
SR: 40/14/12/20/   (S H J Brewer), M W Easterby

3061   Crosshill Hotel Novices' Handicap Hurdle (0-100 4-y-o and up) £1,821 2m 5f 110yds...................(5:00)

1804 DOCTOR DUNKLIN (USA) [59] 5-10-0 B Storey, *al hndy, outpcd and drvn alng 3 out, lft cl second bef last, rallied to ld towards finish*........(33 to 1 op 25 to 1) 1

2435⁴ WHY NOT EQUINAME [73] 6-11-0 A Dobbin, *al hndy, effrt bef 2 out, lft in ld before last, rdn and ct nr finish.*
....(7 to 1 op 6 to 1) 2

2891⁶ CARLA ADAMS [59] 8-10-0 K Johnson, *led til hdd bef 6th, styd hndy, outpcd 3 out, sn struggling.*
....(14 to 1 op 12 to 1) 3

2583⁵ KINDA GROOVY [75] 5-11-2 N Smith, *hld up, struggling bef 4 out, nvr a factor*..............(13 to 2 op 5 to 1) 4

2483⁷ MANWELL [68] 7-10-9 L Wyer, *trkd ldrs, lost grnd aftr 4th, struggling after nxt, tld off*...(6 to 1 op 5 to 1) 5

2737⁶ GYMCRAK DAWN [83] (bl) 9-11-10 P Harley, *chsd ldg bunch, lost grnd fnl circuit, tld off..*(8 to 1 op 7 to 1) 6

2583³ HIGH PENHOWE [74] 6-11-1 D Byrne, *beh, struggling to keep up aftr one circuit, tld off.*
....(5 to 1 op 4 to 1 tchd 11 to 2) 7

2896⁴ LAFANTA (Ire) [70] 5-10-11 A Merrigan, *nvr far away, led bef 6th, clr before 2 out, broke leg and f before last, destroyed*...........................(7 to 2 fav) f

2409⁵ DUNREIDY BAY (Ire) [76] 6-11-0 (3") P Williams, *chasing ldrs whn blun and uns rdr 6th.*...........(7 to 1 op 6 to 1) ur

Dist: Nk, 30l, hd, 3½l. 5m 16.00s. a 25.00s (9 Ran).
        (Mrs V C Ward), Mrs V C Ward

CHELTENHAM (Good)
Thursday March 17th
Going Correction: PLUS 0.12 sec. per fur. (races 1,2,7), PLUS 0.23 (3,4,5,6)

3062   Daily Express Triumph Hurdle Grade 1 (4-y-o) £36,372 2m 1f.........(2:15)

2745* MYSILV 10-9 A Maguire, *slight ld to 3rd, styd hndy, led 3 out, stayed on strly frm last.*
....(2 to 1 fav op 5 to 2 tchd 11 to 4 and 7 to 4) 1

2516* MOORISH 11-0 D Murphy, *tucked away in midfield, hdwy on outsd aftr 3 out, kpt on wl r-in.*
....(12 to 1 op 16 to 1) 2

2608* SHIRLEY'S DELIGHT (Ire) 10-9 P Carberry, *patiently rdn, improved to go hndy aftr 3 out, styd on r-in.*
....(10 to 1 op 8 to 1) 3

2564⁸ BLUE GROTTO (Ire) 11-0 R Campbell, *settled off the pace, hdwy 3 out, outpcd betw last 2, rallied r-in.*
....(50 to 1 tchd 66 to 1) 4

2169* KADASTROF (Fr) 11-0 D Meredith, *pld hrd, wth ldrs, ev ch 3 out, rdn and one pace frm betw last 2.*
....(16 to 1 tchd 20 to 1) 5

1575* GLENSTAL FLAGSHIP (Ire) 11-0 C Swan, *nvr far away, drw level betw last 2, one pace r-in.*
....(11 to 1 op 10 to 1 tchd 12 to 1) 6

3023² PRIDWELL 11-0 J Lower, *tucked away in midfield, improved aftr 4 out, ev ch after 2 out, sprawled last, one pace r-in.*...............(12 to 1 op 8 to 1 tchd 14 to 1) 7

2169⁵ DUVEEN (Ire) 11-0 C Llewellyn, *chsd ldrs, effrt and drvn alng aftr 3 out, kpt on, nvr able to chal.*
....(50 to 1 op 33 to 1) 8

2629* ALLEGATION (v) 11-0 M Foster, *bustled alng in midfield hfwy, styd on frm 2 out, nrst finish.*
....(50 to 1 op 33 to 1) 9

2969* DOCTOOR (USA) 11-0 D O'Sullivan, *wth ldrs, feeling pace and rdn 3 out, fdd nxt.*
....(10 to 1 tchd 66 to 1) 10

2745² WINTER FOREST (USA) 11-0 W Marston, *niggled alng to go pace aftr 3rd, styd on frm 3 out, no imprsn.*
....(33 to 1 op 25 to 1) 11

2471* DEVILS DEN (Ire) 11-0 G Bradley, *patiently rdn, improved on ins aftr 4 out, ridden and no imprsn betw last 2.*
....(11 to 1 op 10 to 1 tchd 12 to 1) 12

851⁶ CONTRACT ELITE (Ire) 11-0 D Wilkinson, *blun second, sn lost tch, nvr able to rch ldrs...*(100 to 1 op 66 to 1) 13

2564* DARING PAST 11-0 P Niven, *tucked away in midfield, hdwy to join ldrs 3 out, rdn and btn aftr nxt.*
....(25 to 1 tchd 33 to 1) 14

2503⁴ STRICTLY PERSONAL (USA) 11-0 L Harvey, *settled beh ldrs, drvn alng to improve 3 out, btn aftr nxt.*
....(100 to 1 op 66 to 1) 15

2969⁷ PAPER DAYS (bl) 11-0 E Murphy, *sn beh, some hdwy frm 2 out, nvr dngrs*...........................(100 to 1) 16

2624² NAWAR (Fr) (bl) 11-0 J Railton, *wth ldr, led 3rd, jnd 4 out, hdd nxt, fdd*..............(33 to 1 tchd 40 to 1) 17

2781⁴ STAR MARKET 11-0 T Wall, *wth ldrs to hfwy, struggling aftr 4 out, sn lost tch*..(200 to 1 op 150 to 1) 18

2522⁷ GUNNER SUE 10-9 S McNeill, *settled midfield, effrt 3 out, rdn and btn nxt*..............(200 to 1 op 100 to 1) 19

2821² GENERAL MOUKTAR 11-0 G McCourt, *last early, some hdwy appr 3 out, wknd nxt.*
....(16 to 1 op 12 to 1 tchd 20 to 1) 20

2862⁴ KARAR (Ire) 11-0 B Powell, *behihnd, drvn alng hfwy, nvr a dngr*...........................(100 to 1 op 66 to 1) 21

2874 ATHERTON GREEN (Ire) 11-0 Richard Guest, *al struggling, nvr a factor*.....................(200 to 1 op 100 to 1) 22

2743⁸ MONAZITE 11-0 M Richards, *al beh, tld off 4 out.*
....(200 to 1 op 150 to 1) 23

2676⁹ MANILA BAY (USA) 11-0 J R Kavanagh, *in tch to hfwy, sn struggling, tld off*...............(200 to 1 op 100 to 1) 24

2694* MY BALLYBOY 11-0 S Smith Eccles, *wtd wth, improved appr 3 out, fdg whn f nxt.*......(33 to 1 tchd 40 to 1) f

2735⁴ DAYADAN (Ire) 11-0 M A FitzGerald, *chsd ldrs to hfwy, beh whn f 2 out*........................(200 to 1 op 100 to 1) f

2676* BAGALINO (USA) 11-0 M Perrett, *trkd ldrs, struggling hfwy, lost tch and pld up betw last 2.*
....(16 to 1 tchd 18 to 1) pu

2722* GROUND NUT (Ire) 11-0 J Osborne, *trkd ldrs till aftr 4 out, lost tch and pld up betw last 2.*...(16 to 1 op 14 to 1) pu

Dist: 3½l, 1½l, 3½l, 1½l, 1½l, 1½l, 1½l, 8l, sht-hd, 2¼l, 3l. 3m 59.50s. a 5.00s (28 Ran).
SR: 51/52/45/46/44/42/40/32/32/   (Million In Mind Partnership (3)), D Nicholson

3063   Bonusprint Stayers' Hurdle Grade 1 (4-y-o and up) £46,625 3m 110yds.....(2:50)

2257² AVRO ANSON 6-11-10 M Dwyer, *hld up, reminders and hdwy appr 7th, sn chasing ldrs, led last, veered lft r-in, all out, fnshd 1st, plcd second.....*(8 to 1 tchd 9 to 1) 1D

2742* BALASANI (Fr) 8-11-10 M Perrett, *patiently rdn gng wl, hdwy appr 2 out, chalg whn hmpd and swtchd rght r-in, fnshd second, plcd 1st....*(9 to 2 jt-fav op 3 to 1) 1

2467* MINELLA LAD 8-11-10 T Horgan, *wth ldrs, led 2 out till hdd last, crrd lft r-in, no extr last 100 yards.*
....(7 to 1 op 6 to 1 tchd 8 to 1) 3

2257* SIMPSON 9-11-10 T Grantham, *hld up in midfield, rdn alng and hdwy aftr 3 out wth ldrs, ev ch whn blun and hmpd 2 out, styd on wl.........*(9 to 1 op 8 to 1) 4

2473⁴ SWEET DUKE (Fr) 7-11-10 C Llewellyn, *nvr far away, led briefly appr 2 out, rdn and not quicken betw last two.*
....(11 to 2 op 5 to 1 tchd 6 to 1) 5

2376⁵ SWEET GLOW (Fr) 7-11-10 J Lower, *hld up and beh till styd on frm 2 out, nvr able to chal* (9 to 1 op 20 to 1) 6

2855³ CARDINAL RED (Fr) 11-10 S McNeill, *trkd ldrs, rdn alng and ev ch 3 out, wknd betw last 2.*
....(50 to 1 op 33 to 1 tchd 40 to 1) 7

2494⁴ DEB'S BALL 8-11-5 D J Moffatt, *hld up, reminders hfwy, nvr a dngr*......................(33 to 1 tchd 40 to 1) 8

2846³ BART OWEN 9-11-10 G Bradley, *trkd ldrs, led 5th till appr 2 out, sn wknd.*..................(33 to 1) 9

2742⁴ BURGOYNE 8-11-10 P Niven, *beh whn rdn aftr 6th, no response.*..........................(33 to 1) 10

2537² SEEKIN CASH (USA) 5-11-10 J Osborne, *trkd ldrs, mstk 6th, feeling pace whn pckd 3 out, sn wknd...*(9 to 2 jt-fav op 5 to 1 tchd 11 to 2) 11

2632² DESERT FORCE (Ire) 11-10 A Carroll, *al last, tld off.*
....(200 to 1 tchd 500 to 1) 12

2376⁴ TRIPLE WITCHING 8-11-10 A Maguire, *handily plcd, rdn in 6th and clsg whn f 2 out.....*(6 to 1 tchd 11 to 2) f

PRAGADA (bl) 11-11-10 C Swan, *led, jmpd slwly 3rd and 4th, hdd nxt, wknd 7th, tld off whn pld up betw last 2.*
....(11 to 1 op 8 to 1) pu

Dist: Sht-hd, 2½l, 1½l, hd, ¾l, ¾l, 20l, 10l, 20l, 20l. 5m 48.40s. a 8.40s (14 Ran).
SR: 43/43/40/38/38/37/36/11/6/   (M D Smith), M C Pipe

3064   Tote Cheltenham Gold Cup Chase Grade 1 (5-y-o and up) £118,770 3¼m 110yds......................(3:30)

2747³ THE FELLOW (Fr) (bl) 9-12-0 A Kondrat, *jmpd wl, nvr far away, led appr last, styd on strly r-in.*
....(7 to 1 op 5 to 1 tchd 8 to 1) 1

2611* JODAMI 9-12-0 M Dwyer, *settled midfield, jnd ldrs gng wl 4 out, chalg whn awkward last, ran on well r-in.*
.... (5 to 4 tchd 13 to 8)

2748 YOUNG HUSTLER 7-12-0 C Llewellyn, *slight ld to 3rd, led 16th till appr last, rdn and not quicken r-in.*
.... (20 to 1 tchd 25 to 1) 2

2611 FLASHING STEEL 9-12-0 J Osborne, *mstks, patiently rdn, hdwy to join ldrs 4 out, outpcd nxt, plld on strly frm last.* .... (10 to 1 tchd 12 to 1) 3

24744 BRADBURY STAR 9-12-0 D Murphy, *tucked away gng wl, hdwy 4 out, effrt and niggled alng 2 out, rdn and no extr.* .... (5 to 1 tchd 6 to 1) 4

24742 DOCKLANDS EXPRESS 12-12-0 D Gallagher, *co'red up gng wl, effrt whn outpcd 3 out, rallied betw last 2, no imprsn.* .... (14 to 1 op 12 to 1 tchd 16 to 1) 5

2852* MIINNEHOMA 11-12-0 A Maguire, *al hndy, reminders 13th, rallied 4 out, btn aftr nxt.*
.... (11 to 1 op 10 to 1 tchd 12 to 1) 6

2611² DEEP BRAMBLE 7-12-0 P Niven, *settled midfield, hdwy on outsd whn blun 4 out, no extr aftr nxt.*
.... (20 to 1 op 16 to 1 tchd 25 to 1) 7

2375³ RUN FOR FREE 10-12-0 M Perrett, *led 3rd to 16th, styd hndy, rdn aftr 3 out, blun nxt, fdd.*
.... (11 to 1 op 10 to 1 tchd 12 to 1) 8

2720 TOPSHAM BAY 11-12-0 J Frost, *nvr far away, feeling pace appr 4 out, fdd nxt.*
.... (100 to 1 op 50 to 1 tchd 150 to 1) 9

2611 CHATAM (USA) 10-12-0 G McCourt, *settled off the pace, hit 9th, improved 4 out, fdd aftr nxt.*
.... (33 to 1 op 25 to 1) 10

2288⁴ EBONY JANE 9-11-9 C Swan, *chasing ldrs whn blun and uns rdr 6 out.* .... (100 to 1 op 50 to 1) ur

2748 GARRISON SAVANNAH 11-12-0 B Gradley, *not fluent, nvr gng wl, tld off whn pld up bef 3 out.* .... (50 to 1) pu

2488* BLAZING WALKER 10-12-0 C Grant, *nvr gng wl, reminders hfwy, tld off whn pld up bef 4 out.*
.... (20 to 1 op 16 to 1 tchd 25 to 1) pu

1757 CAPABILITY BROWN 7-12-0 M A FitzGerald, *al beh, tld off whn pld up bef 5 out.* .... (200 to 1 op 100 to 1) pu
Dist: 1½l, 4l, ¾l, 5l, 1½l, 6l, sht-hd, 4l, 2½l, 1l. 6m 40.70s. a 7.70s (15 Ran).
SR: 84/82/78/77/72/70/64/64/60/ (Marquesa de Moratalla), F Doumen

3065 Christies Foxhunter Chase Challenge Cup (5-y-o and up) £13,580 3¼m 110yds. .... (4:05)

2807* DOUBLE SILK 10-12-0 Mr R Treloggen, *jmpd wl, made all, clr fnl circuit, shaken up r-in, styd on well.*
.... (5 to 2 op 3 to 1 on tchd 9 to 4) 1

2724* TEAPLANTER 11-12-0 Mr R Russell, *chsd wnr thrght, cld betw last 2, kpt on, unbl to chal.* .... (7 to 2 op 3 to 1) 2

2793² ONCE STUNG (bl) 8-12-0 Mr J Greenall, *trkd ldg pair, reminders 9th, blun 13th, btn whn mstk 5 out, no imprsn.* .... (7 to 1 op 5 to 1) 3

2875* SPEAKERS CORNER 11-12-0 Mr M Sowersby, *struggling whn mstk 12th, nvr a dngr, tld off.*
.... (40 to 1 op 20 to 1 tchd 50 to 1) 4

ARDESEE 14-12-0 Mr J Wintle, *lost tch frm hfwy, tld off.*
.... (66 to 1 op 100 to 1) 5
Dist: 5l, dist, 3l, 20l. 6m 44.50s. a 11.50s (5 Ran).
SR: 46/41/ (R C Wilkins), R C Wilkins

3066 122nd Year Of The Cheltenham Grand Annual Chase Challenge Cup Hand-icap (5-y-o and up) £24,309 2m 110yds .... (4:40)

2832² SNITTON LANE [122] 8-10-0 D Bridgwater, *settled gng wl, hdwy to ld appr 2 out, drvn out.*
.... (33 to 1 op 20 to 1 tchd 50 to 1) 1

2672* UNCLE ERNIE [145] 9-11-9 M Dwyer, *patiently rdn, hdwy appr 3 out, chlgd 2 out, sn ridden and unbl to quicken.*
.... (8 to 1 tchd 9 to 1) 2

2476² STORM ALERT [150] 8-12-0 S McNeill, *settled midfield, hdwy appr 4 out, styd on same pace frm 2 out.*
.... (7 to 1 op 6 to 1 tchd 8 to 1) 3

2611³ FORCE SEVEN [142] 7-11-6 A Maguire, *midfield, rdn 3 out, styd on frm nxt, nvr nrr.*
.... (13 to 2 op 6 to 1 tchd 15 to 2) 4

2171³ BILLY BATHGATE [140] 8-11-4 M A FitzGerald, *wl beh till styd on frm 3 out, nvr nr to chal.*
.... (9 to 1 op 8 to 1 tchd 10 to 1) 5

2798¹ L'UOMO PIU [122] 10-10-0 B Powell, *beh till styd on frm 2 out, nvr a threat.* .... (100 to 1) 6

2798⁴ SETTER COUNTRY [122] 10-10-0 W Irvine, *beh, shrtlvd effrt 6 out, no dngr.* .... (40 to 1 op 33 to 1) 7

2450² CLAY COUNTY [137] 9-11-1 B Storey, *wtd wth, hdwy to chal 3 out, btn bef nxt.* .... (20 to 1 op 16 to 1) 8

2248* NORTHERN JINKS [122] (bl) 11-9-11 (3*) D Meredith, *set fst pace till hdd appr 2 out, wknd quickly.*
.... (33 to 1 op 20 to 1) 9

2511² SAN LORENZO (USA) [124] 6-10-2 D Gallagher, *ldg grp till wknd appr 3 out.* .... (14 to 1 op 10 to 1) 10

2825² GOOD FOR A LAUGH [122] 10-9-9 (5*) Mr D Parker, *sn beh, mstk 4th, nvr gng pace.* .... (14 to 1 tchd 16 to 1) 11

2569* DIS TRAIN [135] 10-10-13 M Richards, *struggling frm hfwy, no dngr.* ...... (16 to 1 op 14 to 1 tchd 20 to 1) 12

2511* LACKENDARA [124] 7-10-2 J Osborne, *chsd ldrs till pckd 3 out, sn wknd.* ...... (5 to 1 fav op 6 to 1 tchd 7 to 1) 13

1560⁷ CYPHRATE (USA) [146] 8-11-10 C Swan, *hld up and beh, pushed alng aftr hfwy, nvr a factor.*
.... (16 to 1 op 14 to 1 tchd 20 to 1) 14

2594⁵ EGYPT MILL PRINCE [142] (bl) 8-11-6 G Bradley, *chsd ldr till 7th.* .... (13 to 2 op 7 to 1 tchd 8 to 1) f

2832⁹ TRIMLOUGH [128] 9-10-6 W Marston, *chsd ldg bunch till hmpd and uns rdr 7th.* .... (33 to 1 op 25 to 1) ur

2798⁵ SAILORS LUCK [122] 9-10-0 E Murphy, *nvr gng pace, tld off whn pld up bef 6 out.* ...... (40 to 1 op 33 to 1) pu
Dist: 6l, 2½l, 3½l, 12l, 1½l, 1l, sht-hd, sht-hd, 7l, 3½l. 4m 1.30s. a 5.30s (17 Ran).
SR: 57/74/76/64/50/30/29/44/29/ (H D White), W Clay

3067 Cathcart Challenge Cup Chase (6-y-o and up) £29,240 2m 5f. .... (5:15)

2504* RAYMYLETTE 7-11-0 M A FitzGerald, *jmpd wl, made all, jnd appr last, hng rght r-in, all out.*
.... (7 to 4 op 11 to 8 tchd 15 to 8) 1

2867⁴ BUCKBOARD BOUNCE 8-11-3 C Swan, *al tracking wnr, chalg whn last, ran on.*
.... (3 to 1 op 7 to 2 tchd 4 to 1) 2

3027 COMMERCIAL ARTIST 8-11-3 C Bowens, *al hndy, reminder 9th, rdn appr 3 out, kpt on wl frm nxt.*
.... (1 to 1 op 7 to 1 tchd 8 to 1) 3

2488⁵ HAWTHORN BLAZE 8-11-0 A Maguire, *settled last, jmpd slwly tenth, no imprsn whn mstk 3 out, tld off.*
.... (13 to 8 fav op 5 to 4 tchd 7 to 4) 4
Dist: ¾l, ½l, dist. 5m 17.60s. a 13.60s (4 Ran).
(Lady Lloyd Webber), N J Henderson

3068 75th Year Of The County Handicap Hurdle Grade 3 (5-y-o and up) £22,250 2m 1f. .... (5:50)

2956² DIZZY (USA) [120] 6-10-0 A Dobbin, *al hndy, feeling pace and drvn alng betw last 2, ran on strly to ld last strds.*
.... (12 to 1 op 16 to 1 tchd 20 to 1) 1

2587³ DIPLOMATIC [121] 5-10-1 J P Banahan, *patiently rdn, improved 3 out, led r-in, ct last strds.*
.... (16 to 1 op 14 to 1 tchd 20 to 1) 2

3028 STEEL DAWN [120] 7-9-11 (3*) C O'Brien, *wl beh, a lot to do 3 out, styd on strly betw last 2, fnshd fst.*
.... (16 to 1 op 12 to 1 tchd 20 to 1) 3

2994⁴ NAHAR [130] 9-10-10 D Bridgwater, *made most till betw last 2, rallied r-in, no extr cl hme.* (25 to 1 op 20 to 1) 4

2994 HER HONOUR [130] 5-10-10 C Swan, *last hfwy, styd on frm 3 out, str run frm last, fdd.*
.... (25 to 1 tchd 33 to 1) 5

2994 ARCOT [127] (v) 6-10-7 G McCourt, *wtd wth, hdwy to ld betw last 2, hdd and no extr r-in.*
.... (12 to 1 op 10 to 1 tchd 14 to 1) 6

2670³ EDEN'S CLOSE [120] 5-10-0 M Richards, *settled beh ldrs, improved aftr 3 out, styd on one pace betw last 2.*
.... (16 to 1 op 12 to 1 tchd 20 to 1) 7

2595⁸ NIJMEGEN [127] 6-10-7 M Dwyer, *settled midfield, ev ch appr 2 out, no extr frm last.* ...... (14 to 1 op 10 to 1) 8

2812² FIVE TO SEVEN (USA) [120] 5-10-0 D Wilkinson, *nvr far away, ev ch 2 out, no extr betw last.* (14 to 1 op 10 to 1) 9

2994* PRECIOUS BOY [145] 8-11-11 (7ex) L Wyer, *al hndy, ev ch and drvn alng 2 out, fdd appr last.*
.... (16 to 1 op 12 to 1 tchd 20 to 1) 10

2947* ARABIAN BOLD (Ire) [128] 6-10-8 M A FitzGerald, *al hndy, jnd ldr hfwy, fdd betw last 2.*
.... (12 to 1 op 10 to 1 tchd 14 to 1) 11

2994² RIVA (NZ) [126] 7-10-6 C Llewellyn, *wtd wth, improved 3 out, effrt betw last 2, no extr.*
.... (12 to 1 op 10 to 1 tchd 14 to 1) 12

2175⁵ STATAJACK (Ire) [120] (bl) 6-10-0 P Holley, *co'red up in midfield, feeling pace and rdn hfwy, nvr dngrs.*
.... (33 to 1) 13

2933⁶ RED RING [120] 7-10-0 W Marston, *trkd ldrs to hfwy, fdd frm 3 out.* .... (100 to 1) 14

2994⁴ HERE HE COMES [138] 8-10-11 (7*) S Ryan, *trkd ldrs gng wl, ev ch 2 out, fdd bef last.* ...... (14 to 1 tchd 16 to 1) 15

2079³ JUDICIAL FIELD (Ire) [133] (bl) 5-10-13 A Maguire, *patiently rdn, hdwy aftr 3 out, sn ev ch, wknd betw last 2.*
.... (9 to 2 fav op 7 to 2 tchd 5 to 1) 16

2819³ NORTHERN SADDLER [120] 7-9-9 (5*) D Fortt, *in tch, struggling to keep up 4 out, fdd.* .... (33 to 1) 17

2833⁹ TAROUDANT [133] 7-10-13 P Niven, *in tch, rdn alng to go pace hfwy, nvr a threat.*
.... (14 to 1 op 10 to 1 tchd 16 to 1) 18

1116* BATABANOO [144] 5-11-10 B Storey, *al struggling in rear, nvr a factor.* ...... (10 to 1 op 12 to 1) 19

2850* DANCING PADDY [143] 6-11-9 (7ex) D O'Sullivan, *pressed ldrs, feeling pace 3 out, fdd.*
.... (12 to 1 op 10 to 1 tchd 16 to 1) 20

2697² EASTHORPE [120] 6-10-0 J Osborne, *chsd ldrs to hfwy, sn tld off.* .... (33 to 1) 21

1991⁴ HOLY WANDERER (USA) [122] 5-10-2 G Upton, *settled gng wl, hdwy to chal aftr 2 out, 4th and btn whn f last.*
.... (25 to 1 op 16 to 1) f

2850⁵ ELEMENTARY [122] 11-10-2² D Murphy, *beh and chsd alng hfwy, tld off whn pld up betw last 2.* .... (50 to 1) pu

894² PONTOON BRIDGE [120] 7-10-0 M Perrett, *al beh, tld off
whn pld up betw last 2* . . . .(50 to 1 op 33 to 1)   pu
Dist: Nk, ¾, nk, hd, 1½l, ¾l, 3½l, 2½l, ¾l, hd. 3m 58.00s. a 3.50s (24 Ran).
SR: 57/57/55/64/64/59/51/54/44/   (Mrs E M Hislop), W G Reed
                                         (Lt-Col W L Monteith), P Monteith

DOWN ROYAL (IRE) (soft)
Thursday March 17th

3069 Paddy Maiden Hurdle (Div 1) (4-y-o) £1,208 2m. . . . .(2:10)

2547⁹ CHALLENGER ROW (Ire) 10-9 (7*) Mr J Quinn, ...(8 to 1)   1
2917⁹ BOBADIL (Ire) 10-9 (7*) P J Smullen, ...(8 to 1)   2
2388⁷ HUNCHEON CHANCE 10-9 (7*) Mr L J Gracey, ...(5 to 2)   3
2775⁷ COTHU NA SLAINE (Ire) 10-4 (7*) Mr B Morgan, . . .(14 to 1)   4
2917³ DRESS DANCE (Ire) 11-2 A Powell, ... (5 to 4 fav)   5
       BAJAN QUEEN (Ire) 10-4 (7*) T Martin, ...(4 to 1)   6
2122⁷ MANGANS HILL (Ire) 10-9 (7*) D M Bean, ...(10 to 1)   7
2717¹ MAJA GODDNOS 10-13 (3*) K B Walsh, ...(12 to 1)   8
2775 MICHAEL'S PET (Ire) 10-4 (7*) Mr C Andrews, ...(16 to 1)   f
Dist: 3l, ¾l, 3½l, 1l. (Time not taken) (9 Ran).
                                         (Victor Semple), W Rock

3070 Paddy Maiden Hurdle (Div 2) (4-y-o) £1,208 2m. . . . .(2:40)

2232 ANNADOT (Ire) 10-11 F J Flood, ...(11 to 4)   1
2917 RUNNING SLIPPER (Ire) 10-9 (7*) P J Smullen, . . .(9 to 2)   2
       STATION HOUSE (Ire) 11-2 Mr J P Dempsey, . . .(6 to 4 fav)   3
2771 TANDRAGEE LADY (Ire) 10-4 (7*) R J Gordon, ...(14 to 1)   4
2464 COMMANCHE LYN (Ire) 10-6 (5*) Mr D Walsh, ...(5 to 1)   5
       LITTLE TOWN (Ire) 10-11 P L Malone, ...(12 to 1)   6
2775⁸ BARNISH DAWN (Ire) 10-4 (7*) Mr S Kerr, ...(14 to 1)   7
Dist: 4½l, 4l, 13l, dist. (Time not taken) (7 Ran).
                                         (Leonard Kelly), F Flood

3071 I'm Yer Man INH Flat Race (Div 1) (5-y-o and up) £1,208 2m. . . . .(4:15)

       GLENALLA STAR (Ire) 5-11-5 (7*) Mr J Quinn, ...(5 to 1)   1
1581⁵ CABLE BEACH (Ire) 5-11-7 (5*) Mr G J Harford, (5 to 4 on)   2
       BOTTLE BLACK 7-11-7 (7*) Miss S Gladders, ...(14 to 1)   3
       LEGIBLE 6-11-7 (7*) Mr L J Gracey, ...(10 to 1)   4
2775⁴ GRANDOLLY (Ire) 5-11-4 (3*) Mr A R Coonan, ...(8 to 1)   5
       FAIRVIEW LASS (Ire) 5-11-0 (7*) Mr S Kerr, ...(20 to 1)   6
   23 GLAsha BRIDGE (Ire) 6-11-7 (7*) Mr M Ewing, ...(20 to 1)   7
2182²¹ MILLHAVEN PRINCESS 8-11-2 (7*) Mr J Gault, . . .(25 to 1)   8
2775⁵ BONDIFI (Ire) 5-11-9 (3*) Mr P McMahon, ...(7 to 1)   9
2770⁹ SHEPHERDS KATE (Ire) 6-11-2 (7*) Mr A Tate, ...(6 to 1)   10
       TOAD THE WETSPROCKET (Ire) 5-11-5 (7*) Mr F C O'Keeffe,
       . . . .(10 to 1)   11
       AGHALEE LADY (Ire) 5-11-0 (7*) Miss M Wyatt, ...(8 to 1)   12
       LUCY TWO SHOES (Ire) 5-11-0³ (7*) Mr C McCarren,
       . . . .(20 to 1)   13
Dist: 1½l, 20l, sht-hd, 1½l. (Time not taken) (13 Ran).
                                         (Samuel Hegarty), W Rock

3072 I'm Yer Man INH Flat Race (Div 2) (5-y-o and up) £1,208 2m. . . . .(4:50)

2775² CUTTER'S WHARF (Ire) 5-11-5 (7*) Mr R J Patton,
       . . . .(5 to 4 on)   1
       GRAMSCI (Ire) 6-11-7 (7*) Mr C J Stafford, ...(11 to 2)   2
2464⁵ AMME ENAEK (Ire) 5-11-0 (7*) Mr G Keane, ...(7 to 1)   3
2771 THE THIRD MAN (Ire) 5-11-9 (3*) Mr P McMahon, (16 to 1)   4
       HEN'S DAY (Ire) 6-11-6 (3*) Mr A R Coonan, ...(12 to 1)   5
2311 PRINCESS DILLY (Ire) 5-11-0 (7*) Mr J Bright, ...(14 to 1)   6
2587 KINROSS 7-11-2 (7*) Mr L J Gracey, ...(10 to 1)   7
2771 SIMONE STAR (Ire) 5-11-0 (7*) Mr A Tate, ...(10 to 1)   8
2658⁴ COURSING GLEN (Ire) 6-12-0 Mr A J Martin, ...(6 to 1)   9
2128 NOT AN INCH (Ire) 5-11-7 (5*) Mr G J Harford, ...(10 to 1)   10
2278 RHINESTALL 7-11-2 (7*) Mr S M Cox, ...(9 to 1)   11
       WAREZ (Ire) 5-11-0 (7*) Mr P Henley, ...(14 to 1)   12
2770 FRED 'N'GINGER (Ire) 6-11-7¹ (7*) Mr R I Arthur, . .(16 to 1)   13
Dist: 4½l, nk, 2½l, 3½l. (Time not taken) (13 Ran).
                                         (Brian Scullion), J F C Maxwell

HEXHAM (heavy)
Thursday March 17th
Going Correction: PLUS 2.25 sec. per fur.

3073 Allerwash Novices' Chase (5-y-o and up) £2,369 2m 110yds. . . . .(2:00)

2928 HERE COMES TIBBY 7-10-12 Miss R Robson, *led second,
       made rst, jnd betw last 2, lft wl clr last.*
       . . . .(9 to 2 tchd 5 to 1)   1
2372 BITOFANATTER 6-11-3 K Johnson, *not fluent, hld up in
       tch, lost touch strting fnl circuit, sn tld off.*
       . . . .(20 to 1 tchd 16 to 1)   2
2928⁴ SEON 8-12-3 R Garritty, *led til hdd second, cl second whn
       f 7th.* . . . .(13 to 8 on op 2 to 1 on tchd 6 to 4 on)   f
2815⁹ COOL DUDE 8-11-3 J Callaghan, *nvr far away, lft second
       7th, drw level betw last 2, sn rdn, ev ch whn f last.*
       . . . .(3 to 1)   f
Dist: Dist. 4m 51.10s. a 53.10s (4 Ran).

3074 Coastley Novices' Hurdle (4-y-o and up) £1,907 2m. . . . .(2:35)

2874⁸ SCARBA 6-11-2 (7*) K Davies, *nvr far away, improved to
       draw level bef last, mstk last, ran on gmely to lead
       towards finish.* . . . .(7 to 2 tchd 4 to 1)   1
2783⁴ VOLUNTEER POINT (Ire) 4-10-3 (5*) J Burke, *led, hrd
       pressed frm last, drvn alng, hdd towards finish.*
       . . . .(3 to 1 fav tchd 7 to 2)   2
1959⁴ COL BUCKMORE (Ire) 6-11-9 N Doughty, *patiently rdn,
       effrt 2 out, kpt on same pace appr nxt.*
       . . . .(100 to 30 op 7 to 4 tchd 7 to 2)   3
2960² BIRD WATCHER 5-10-13 (3*) D Bentley, *trkd ldrs, effrt and
       pushed alng aftr 2 out, sn one pace.* (6 to 1 op 5 to 1)   4
2925⁶ CROSS REFERENCE 6-10-11 R Hodge, *trkd ldr, lost ground
       2 out, sn btn, tld off.* . . .(6 to 1 op 16 to 1 tchd 7 to 1)   5
       CAMPTOSAURUS 5-11-2 J Callaghan, *strted slwly,
       beh, struggling to keep up 3 up, sn btn, tld off.*
       . . . .(12 to 1 op 5 to 1)   6
2106 PRINCE BALTASAR 5-11-2 R Garritty, *al beh, lost tch 3 out,
       tld off whn pld up bef last.* . . . .(33 to 1)   pu
       SHORE LANE 5-11-2 Mr Robert Robinson, *not jump wl,
       trkd ldrs, struggling hfwy, tld off whn pld up aftr 3
       out.* . . . .(33 to 1 op 25 to 1)   pu
Dist: Nk, 5l, 6l, dist, 7l. 4m 33.10s. a 43.10s (8 Ran).
SR: 24/8/18/5/-/   (Bryan Gordon), D T Garraton

3075 Barrier Fire Protection Novices' Handicap Chase (5-y-o and up) £2,583 3m 1f. . . . .(3:15)

2952* DUCHESS OF TUBBER (Ire) [82] 6-10-6 (3*,8ex) A Thornton,
       *chsd ldg bunch, hit 13th, moved up to chal betw last 2,
       led r-in, ran on wl.* . . . .(8 to 1 op 7 to 1)   1
2908 THE POD'S REVENGE [73] 9-9-11 (3*) A Procter, *al hndy,
       blun 14th, reco'red and led aftr nxt, hdd r-in, no extr
       und pres.* . . . .(6 to 1 tchd 13 to 2)   2
2925⁴ NAWRIK (Ire) [73] 5-9-9 (5*) F Perratt, *led to second, styd
       prmnt, lost pl 5 out, sn drvn alng, rallied frm last.*
       . . . .(8 to 1 op 7 to 1)   3
2355* ROAD BY THE RIVER (Ire) [101] 6-12-0 K Johnson, *nvr far
       away, effrt and drvn alng bef 2 out, sn one pace.*
       . . . .(6 to 1 tchd 5 to 1)   4
2978* OPAL'S TENSPOT [90] 7-11-0 (3*,8ex) R Farrant, *tucked
       away beh ldrs, improved 12th, effrt gng wl 2 out, sn rdn
       and btn.* . . . .(4 to 1 fav op 7 to 2)   5
2908 FINCH'S GEM [84] 6-10-11 N Doughty, *cl up, dsptd ld 9th,
       struggling to keep up aftr 3 out, fdd.* (8 to 1 op 6 to 1)   6
2736 POTATO MAN [73] 8-9-11 (3*) D Bentley, *led or dsptd ld,
       hdd aftr 5 out, styd prmnt, drvn 2 out, fdd.* . . .(33 to 1)   7
2908³ FOUR DEEP (Ire) [82] 6-10-9 J Callaghan, *pressed ldg
       bunch, f 5 out.* . . . .(10 to 1)   f
2908 BALISTEROS (Fr) [77] 5-10-4⁴ R Garritty, *sn beh, blun and
       uns rdr 3rd.* . . . .(14 to 1 op 10 to 1)   ur
2952⁸ PIT PONY [73] 10-10-0 R Hodge, *beh, blun 7th and sn pld
       up.* . . . .(33 to 1)   pu
2809³ BIG MAC [83] 7-10-3 (7*) Mr C Bonner, *dsptd ld 1st circuit,
       hit 11th, lost pl aftr nxt, hit 13th, hmpd and pld up
       after 15th.* . . . .(9 to 1 op 10 to 1 tchd 12 to 1)   pu
2497 BUCKWHEAT LAD (Ire) [80] 6-10-6⁴ (5*) T Byrne, *al beh,
       struggling whn pld up bef 14th.* . . .(25 to 1 op 20 to 1)   pu
Dist: 4l, 20l, 1½l, 5l, 1l, ¾l. 7m 18.10s. a 73.10s (12 Ran).
                                         (Great Head House Estates Limited), R F Fisher

3076 Riding Mill Novices' Hurdle (5-y-o and up) £1,768 3m. . . . .(3:50)

1994⁴ SUNY BAY 5-10-12 R Supple, *nvr far away, led 8th,
       hit nxt, drw clr betw last 2.* . . . .(7 to 2 op 3 to 1)   1
1295² BRIGADIER DAVIS (Fr) 7-10-12 R Garritty, *trkd ldrs, jnd
       issue 8th, ev ch 3 out, outpcd aftr nxt.*
       . . . .(3 to 1 op 9 to 4)   2
2893* PORTONIA 10-11-2 (5*) S Mason, *led til hdd 8th, lost tch
       nxt, tld off.* . . . . . .(7 to 4 fav op 6 to 4 tchd 9 to 4)   3
2812⁹ BANNTOWN BILL (Ire) 5-10-7 (5*) F Perratt, *tracking ldr
       whn stumbled and f aftr 7th.* . . . .(3 to 1 op 4 to 1)   f
   875 FOX TOWER 8-10-12 Miss P Robson, *settled towards rear,
       struggling to keep up aftr 6th, tld off whn pld up jst
       after 8th.* . . . .(33 to 1 op 20 to 1)   pu
2925⁷ ROYAL FIFE 8-10-4 (3*) P Williams, *patiently rdn, took clr
       order fnl circuit, ev ch 3 out, wknd aftr nxt, pld up bef
       last.* . . . .(33 to 1 op 20 to 1)   pu
Dist: Dist, dist. 6m 57.50s. a 70.50s (6 Ran).
                                         (Andrew L Cohen), John R Upson

3077 Win With The Tote Handicap Chase (0-120 5-y-o and up) £3,622 4m. . .(4:25)

2935 VIVA BELLA (Fr) [103] (bh) 7-10-10 (5*) J Burke, *al with ldrs,
       led 3 out, hdd bef last, rallied to rgn ld r-in, edgd lft
       towards finish, all out.* (5 to 1 op 4 to 1 tchd 11 to 2)   1
2930³ FORTH AND TAY [81] 12-10-11 (3*) P Williams, *hld up,
       steady hdwy fnl circuit, led bef last, rdn and hdd r-in,
       slightly hmpd nr finish.*
       . . . .(11 to 2 op 5 to 1 tchd 6 to 1)   2

432

2893[2] DUBIOUS JAKE [92] 11-9-13[2] (7*) C Woodall, *led or dsptd ld 3 out, sn drvn alng, outpcd bef last.* (5 to 1 tchd 9 to 2) 3
2748 DIAMOND FORT [109] 9-11-7 R Bellamy, *wth ldrs, hit 5th, led 15th to nxt, blun 6 out, ev ch 2 out, sn btn.* ....(7 to 1 op 5 to 1) 4
2930[2] CAROUSEL ROCKET [94] 11-10-3 (3*) D Bentley, *chsd ldg grp, blun and lost grnd 13th, blunded 18th, sn rdn and btn.*..................(5 to 1 op 4 to 1) 5
2942[4] MERLYNS CHOICE [88] 10-10-0 R Supple, *trkd ldrs, mstk 11th, drvn alng 18th, mistake nxt, sn struggling, wl beh whn blun and uns rdr 4 out.* ....(11 to 2 op 7 to 2 tchd 6 to 1) ur
2894[9] BROMPTON ROAD [108] 11-11-6 R Greene, *nvr far away, hit 9th, mstk and drvn alng 17th, lost tch 4 out, tld off whn pld up bef last.* (4 to 1 fav op 6 to 1 tchd 7 to 1) pu
Dist: 1½l, 20l, 4l, dist. 9m 41.20s. a 99.99s (7 Ran).

(L H Froomes), Mrs S A Bramall

3078 Fallowfield Conditional Jockeys' Handicap Hurdle (0-110 5-y-o and up) £1,676 2m.................. (5:00)

2929* PALACEGATE KING [104] 5-11-9 (7*,6ex) B Harding, *led to second, styd upside, rgned ld aftr 4th, hit nxt, drvn to go clr betw last 2, eased r-in*...(2 to 1 on op 9 to 4 on) 1
2891 HYPNOTIST [85] 7-10-11 N Bentley, *cl up, led second, hdd aftr 4th, styd prmnt, drvn alng bef 2 out, btn betw last two*.................. (7 to 4 tchd 2 to 1) 2
912 SWANK GILBERT [74] 8-9-7 (7*) Carol Cuthbert, *trkd ldrs, mstk 4th, sn lost tch, tld off*...... (20 to 1 op 16 to 1) 3
Dist: 20l, dist. 4m 37.20s. a 47.20s (3 Ran).

(Chas N Whillans), A C Whillans

3079 Levy Board National Hunt Flat Race (4,5,6-y-o) £2,015 2m........... (5:35)

2931* ADIB (USA) 4-11-4 (3*) N Bentley, *patiently rdn, improved to ld o'r 3 fs out, jnd entering strt, ran on wl.* ....(7 to 4 fav op 6 to 4 tchd 2 to 1) 1
LORD DORCET (Ire) 4-10-9 (5*) J Burke, *chsd ldg grp, improved to chal entering strt, no extr ins fnl furlong.* .... (12 to 1 op 10 to 1) 2
2909[8] OWES THE TILL 4-10-2 (7*) C Woodall, *nvr far away, drvn alng o'r 3 fs out, sn outpcd.* ....(10 to 1 op 7 to 1 tchd 12 to 1) 3
2931[6] ROLY PRIOR 5-11-1 (7*) Mark Roberts, *hld up, improved to track ldrs hfwy, drvn alng 4 fs out, fdd.* .... (8 to 1 op 16 to 1) 4
2909 QUEEN BUZZARD 6-10-10 (7*) Mr J Weymes, *patiently rdn, improved to ld o'r 4 fs out, hdd over 3 out, sn btn.* .... (12 to 1 op 10 to 1) 5
TALL FELLOW (Ire) 4-10-7 (7*) Mr W Burnell, *tucked away beh ldrs, drvn alng o'r 4 fs out, fdd.* ....(14 to 1 op 10 to 1 tchd 16 to 1) 6
2490 SKI PATH 5-10-10 (7*) G Tormey, *sn led, hdd o'r 4 fs out, soon btn, tld off*.................. (20 to 1 tchd 25 to 1) 7
2387 WARREN HOUSE 6-11-3 (5*) S Lyons, *mid-div, wknd 7 fs out, tld off*.................. (8 to 1 op 6 to 1) 8
JASON'S BOY 4-10-11 (3*) R Farrant, *chsd ldrs on ins, pushed alng 7 fs out, btn 5 out*.....(10 to 1 op 7 to 1) 9
PARSON'S LODGE (Ire) 6-10-12 (5*) F Perratt, *chsd ldrs, struggling to keep up o'r 4 fs out, tld off.* ....(7 to 1 op 8 to 1 tchd 6 to 1) 10
CORPORAL KIRKWOOD (Ire) 4-10-11 (3*) A Thornton, *settled on ins, rdn alng 7 fs out, sn btn, tld off.* ....(7 to 1 op 5 to 1) 11
2909 BULLAFORD FAIR 6-11-3 (5*) J Supple, *nvr on terms, tld off*..................(33 to 1 op 20 to 1) 12
MATACHON 4-11-0 Mr S Brisby, *chsd ldrs on ins, pushed alng o'r 7 fs out, grad lost pl, tld off.* ....(16 to 1 tchd 20 to 1) 13
PRIESTS MEADOW (Ire) 5-11-1 (7*) Carol Cuthbert, *settled towards rear, hmpd hfwy, sn lost tch, tld off.* ....(20 to 1 tchd 25 to 1) 14
WAR LADY 5-10-12 (5*) P Waggott, *beh and sn drvn alng, tld off frm hfwy*..................(25 to 1 op 20 to 1) 15
HARRY'S MIDGET 4-10-9 Miss P Robson, *mid-div, lost tch hfwy, tld off*..................(33 to 1 op 25 to 1) 16
2931 SUPERVISION (bl) 6-11-8 Mrs M Kendall, *chsd ldrs to hfwy, sn struggling, tld off whn pld up entering strt.* .... (33 to 1 op 25 to 1) pu
CHALET PIERRE 4-10-7 (7*) W Fry, *trkd ldrs, wknd 7 fs out, tld off whn pld up ins last, dismounted.* ....(9 to 1 op 6 to 1) pu
SKYVAL 4-10-9 Mr Robert Robinson, *settled on outer, lost tch 7 fs out, tld off whn pld up entering strt.* .... (33 to 1 op 25 to 1) pu
Dist: 6l, 30l, 3½l, 3½l, 20l, 20l, sht-hd, 6l, 3l, 2l. 4m 26.30s. (19 Ran).
(N B Mason (Farms) Ltd), G M Moore

LEOPARDSTOWN (IRE) (soft)
Thursday March 17th
Going Correction: PLUS 0.95 sec. per fur.

3080 Castrol GTX Hurdle (4-y-o and up) £4,140 2½m.................. (3:50)

2392[2] IMPERIAL CALL (Ire) 5-11-13 G M O'Neill,..........(7 to 2) 1
2753[3] IDIOTS VENTURE 7-12-1 B Sheridan,..........(9 to 4 fav) 2
2753[7] HEIST 5-11-7 (3*) Mr D Marnane,..................(10 to 1) 3
2863* SIR MOSS 7-11-9 F Woods,..................(8 to 1) 4
2753[5] THE SUBBIE (Ire) 5-11-1 J Shortt,..................(8 to 1) 5
2096[4] MALIHABAD (Ire) 5-11-4 (3*) T J Mitchell,..........(12 to 1) 6
2124 APPELLATE COURT 6-11-9 D H O'Connor,........(20 to 1) 7
1817[2] BROCKLEY COURT 7-11-12 (3*) Mr J A Nash,......(9 to 2) 8
2678* GENTLE REEF (Ire) 4-10-3 (3*) D Bromley,.........(16 to 1) 9
2468[9] ROCHE MELODY (Ire) 6-10-13 (5*) T P Rudd,......(25 to 1) 10
2607* ANABATIC (Ire) (bl) 6-11-4 (5*) K L O'Brien,.........(8 to 1) f
2027[3] RISZARD (USA) 5-10-8 (7*) A P McCoy,..........(7 to 1) bd
2614* DANCING VISION (Ire) 4-10-11 C O'Dwyer,........(10 to 1) pu
Dist: 15l, 5l, ¾l, 8l. 5m 27.20s. a 42.20s (13 Ran).
(Lisselan Farms Ltd), Fergus Sutherland

3081 Castrol R X Super Plus Handicap Chase (0-123 4-y-o and up) £4,140 3m .... (4:20)

1579[3] WILL PHONE [-] 8-11-3 (3*) Mr D Valentine,.... (2 to 1 fav) 1
2939[7] LADY BAR [-] 7-11-4 P M Verling,..................(6 to 1) 2
2701 CAPTAIN BRANDY [-] 9-11-13 C O'Dwyer,..........(9 to 1) 3
2922 GALLEY GALE [-] 8-9-7 (5*) M G Cleary,............(8 to 1) 4
1979[4] JOE WHITE [-] 8-11-6 G M O'Neill,..................(9 to 1) 5
2591[8] NEW MILL HOUSE [-] 11-11-6 F Woods,..........(16 to 1) 6
2867[3] THE REAL UNYOKE [-] 9-10-12 (3*) D P Murphy,... (5 to 1) 7
WELCOME PIN [-] 13-11-6 J Shortt,..............(16 to 1) 8
2025 KINDLY KING [-] 10-10-13 S R Murphy,...........(16 to 1) pu
943[6] GLEN OG LANE [-] 11-9-4 (7*) D Fisher,...........(20 to 1) pu
Dist: 5l, 3½l, 12l, ½l. 6m 39.00s. a 27.00s (10 Ran).
SR: 50/43/48/7/28/-/ (Miss G Maher), M J P O'Brien

3082 Burmah Castrol INH Flat Race (4-y-o and up) £3,450 2m..............(5:20)

2849[3] NEPI LAD (Ire) 6-11-11 Mr M McNulty,.......(4 to 1 co-fav) 1
FIRE DUSTER (Ire) 4-11-1 Mr A P O'Brien,.. (4 to 1 co-fav) 2
SUPREME WONDER (Ire) 4-10-7 (3*) Mrs M Mullins, ... (4 to 1 co-fav) 3
NOBULL (Ire) 4-10-3 (7*) Mr D Groome,...........(20 to 1) 4
2289[7] SPEAK OF THE DEVIL 7-11-11 (7*) Mr D McDonnell, ...(14 to 1) 5
GALAVOTTI (Ire) 5-11-2 (7*) Mr P O'Donovan,......(6 to 1) 6
2849[9] RING THE ALARM (Ire) 6-11-11 (7*) Mr P J McGarry, (7 to 1) 7
2869 RUDDS HILL (Ire) 6-11-4 (7*) Mr M McGrath,......(12 to 1) 8
923[6] BUCKLESFORDBERRY 5-11-2 (7*) Mr S P McCarthy, ...(7 to 1) 9
107 FERRYCARRIGCRYSTAL (Ire) 6-11-8 (3*) Mr D Valentine, ...(10 to 1) 10
DR FAUST (Ire) 4-10-12 (3*) Mr D Marnane,.......(10 to 1) 11
2592[6] PREMIUM BRAND (Ire) 5-11-6 (3*) Mr R Neylon,.. (14 to 1) 12
2464[7] SOLMUS (Ire) 6-11-3 (3*) Mr J A Nash,...........(10 to 1) 13
DELGANY SUNSET 7-11-4 (7*) Mr G Lawless,.... (33 to 1) pu
2943[4] LOTTOVER (Ire) 5-11-4 Mr J A Berry,..............(6 to 1) pu
Dist: 1½l, 7l, 7l, 1l. 4m 8.20s. (15 Ran).
(Stephen Boyes), J T R Dreaper

LIMERICK (IRE) (heavy)
Thursday March 17th

3083 Hugh McMahon Insurance Brokers Hurdle (5-y-o and up) £3,450 2m (2:20)

2754[2] FOR REG (Ire) 5-11-9 M Duffy,............. (11 to 10 fav) 1
2985* BUTCHES BOY (Ire) 5-11-4 (5*) K P Gaule,........ (5 to 1) 2
2986[8] MISTER DRUM (Ire) 5-10-13 (7*) Mr J T McNamara, (8 to 1) 3
2552[4] SAM VAUGHAN (Ire) 5-11-4 (5*) Mr W M O'Sullivan, (5 to 1) 4
2279 EAGLE ROCK (USA) 6-11-8 (3*) T J O'Sullivan,.....(8 to 1) 5
2616* CREATIVE BLAZE (Ire) 5-10-8 (7*) J M Donnelly,....(7 to 1) 6
2919[3] NINE O THREE (Ire) 5-10-9 (5*) J P Broderick,......(8 to 1) 7
NATIVE CHAMPION (Ire) 5-11-0 Mr P Fenton,.....(20 to 1) 8
2683[4] SUPER MIDGE 7-11-1 (7*) Mr D A Harney,....... (10 to 1) pu
Dist: Nk, 4l, nk, 3½l. 4m 5.20s. (9 Ran).
(D H O'Reilly), Patrick Joseph Flynn

3084 Limerick E.B.F. Mares Hurdle (Qualifier) (Div 1) (4-y-o and up) £3,105 2m ....(2:50)

2464* STRONG DESIRE (Ire) 5-11-7 (5*) Mr B R Hamilton, ...(7 to 4 on) 1
2127[5] PRINCESS BAVARD 9-11-10 A J O'Brien,.........(10 to 1) 2
KATE FISHER (Ire) 5-11-8 J Magee,..............(12 to 1) 3
2918* SIOBHAILIN DUBH (Ire) 5-11-7 (5*) K P Gaule,..... (3 to 1) 4
2771[4] RADICAL NURSE (Ire) 5-11-1 (7*) P J Mulligan,....(10 to 1) 5
2938[9] VENT VERT (Ire) 6-11-10 M Duffy,..............(9 to 1) 6
V'SOSKE GALE (Ire) 4-11-0 J F Titley,..........(12 to 1) 7
PRINCESS LENA (Ire) 4-10-7[5] (7*) Mr T J Nagle Jnr, (20 to 1) 8
2942[3] BOG LEAF VI 11-11-10 L P Cusack,.............(10 to 1) 9
2943[7] BALLOUGH BUI (Ire) 5-11-3 (5*) M J Holbrook,... (12 to 1) 10
1332 ERADA (Ire) 6-11-10 H Rogers,.................(16 to 1) 11

Dist: Hd, 2l, 3½l, sht-hd. 4m 28.40s. (11 Ran).

(H Morrison), J F C Maxwell

3085 J J O'Toole (Packaging) Handicap Hurdle (0-123 4-y-o and up) £3,450 2m
....(3:20)

1899⁵	TUG OF PEACE [-] 7-11-13 M Flynn, ...(7 to 1)	1
1899⁷	MARIAN WAKE [-] 8-10-11 J Collins, ...(12 to 1)	2
2842⁴	MISS LIME [-] 7-10-13 (7*) R A Hennessy, ...(5 to 1)	3
2617³	RATHCORE [-] 7-11-0 L P Cusack, ...(6 to 1)	4
56⁷	SIR SOOJE (Ire) [-] 5-10-3 J Magee, ...(8 to 1)	5
2920²	UNCLE BABY (Ire) [-]-6-10-2 (5*) K P Gaule, ...(100 to 30)	6
2468	GOLDEN OPAL [-] 9-10-13 (5*) J P Broderick, ...(9 to 1)	7
575⁵	PEARL'S CHOICE (Ire) [-] 6-9-7 M Duffy, ...(12 to 1)	8
2921³	LEAVE IT TO JUDGE [-] 7-9-9 W T Slattery Jnr, ...(10 to 1)	9
2660	GOLDEN RAPPER [-] 9-10-1 Mr S H O'Donovan, ..(14 to 1)	10
2618	BLAZING DAWN [-] 7-10-7 H Rogers,..........(14 to 1)	11
2920⁷	BOHEMIAN CASTLE (Ire) [-] 5-10-8 (6ex) J F Titley,	
	................................(9 to 4 fav)	12

Dist: 5l, 2½l, 8l, 2½l. 4m 12.90s. (12 Ran).

(W J Austin), W J Austin

3086 Limerick EBF Mares Hurdle (Qualifier) (Div 2) (4-y-o and up) £3,105 2m
....(3:55)

2938⁵	MY SUNNY GLEN 7-11-5 (5*) K P Gaule, ...(6 to 4 fav)	1
2938⁴	FURRY DUCK (Ire) (bl) 6-11-10 M Flynn, ...(100 to 30)	2
	RUN FOR FUN (Ire) 6-11-5 (5*) D T Evans, ...(4 to 1)	3
2039⁴	VON CARTY 5-11-5 (3*) T J O'Sullivan, ...(6 to 1)	4
	ALL-TOGETHER 7-11-5 (5*) M F Cleary, ...(14 to 1)	5
1265	CARRIGKEM (Ire) 6-11-5 (5*) A J Slattery, ...(14 to 1)	6
2684	DRUMCILL LASS (Ire) 6-11-10 J Collins, ...(9 to 1)	7
2663	WHITECHURCH LADY (Ire) 4-11-0 J Magee, ...(12 to 1)	8
	LA KESTREL (Ire) 5-11-8 A J O'Brien, ...(8 to 1)	9
2917⁸	TISRARA LADY (Ire) 4-11-0 J F Titley, ...(10 to 1)	pu

Dist: 3l, dist, 4½l, 1½l. 4m 17.00s. (10 Ran).

(E Flavin), A P O'Brien

3087 Rathkeale INH Flat Race (Div 1) (5-y-o and up) £2,760 2m...........(4:25)

2756²	RUN BAVARD (Ire) 6-11-11 (7*) Mr P English, ...(7 to 4 fav)	1
2944²	TELLTALK (Ire) 5-11-2 (7*) Mr E Norris, ...(9 to 4)	2
2849⁷	DONBOLINO (Ire) 6-11-8 (5*) Mr H F Cleary, ...(5 to 1)	3
2924³	STEVIE BE (Ire) 6-11-4 (7*) Mr T J Murphy, ...(8 to 1)	4
2924⁶	RATH CAOLA 7-10-13 (7*) Mr D C O'Connor, ...(8 to 1)	5
1501	DOONEAL HERO (Ire) 6-11-11 Mr P Fenton, ...(20 to 1)	6
2944⁶	ANGEL'S BIT (Ire) 5-10-11 (7*) Mrs K Walsh, ...(20 to 1)	7
2924⁴	BACKTOWN JOHNNY (Ire) 5-11-2 (7*) Mr S O'Donnell,	
	................................(8 to 1)	8
1786	MILENKEH (Ire) 5-11-2 (7*) Miss H E McNamara, ..(20 to 1)	pu

Dist: 5½l, 11l, 4l, 9l. 4m 7.30s. (9 Ran).

(J R Kidd), Thomas Foley

3088 Rathkeale INH Flat Race (Div 2) (5-y-o and up) £2,760 2m.............(4:55)

671³	BACK TO BLACK (Ire) 5-10-11 (7*) Mr T J Murphy, ..(6 to 1)	1
	KNOCKAVILLA 7-11-4 (7*) Mr K Whelan, ...(9 to 2)	2
2943²	SISTER ALICE (Ire) 6-11-6 Mr P Fenton, ...(11 to 4)	3
	FLAWLESS FINISH (Ire) 5-10-11 (7*) Mr J P Dwan, (10 to 1)	4
	SAVUTI (Ire) 5-11-9 Mr J E Kiely, ...(5 to 4 fav)	5
2924⁵	THE LEFT FOOTER (Ire) 5-11-2 (7*) Mr J T McNamara,	
	................................(10 to 1)	6
2863⁵	BOB NELSON 7-11-6 (5*) Mr H F Cleary, ...(10 to 1)	7
2684	NELLOES PET (Ire) 5-10-11 (7*) Mr F McGirr, ...(16 to 1)	8
	KING TYRANT (Ire) 5-11-6 (3*) Mr M F Barrett, ...(16 to 1)	pu

Dist: 2½l, 10l, 1½l, 20l. 4m 6.40s. (9 Ran).

(S McHugh), Michael Hourigan

FAKENHAM (good to soft (races 1,2,3), soft (4,5,6))
Friday March 18th
Going Correction: PLUS 0.85 sec. per fur. (races 1,2), PLUS 1.20 (3,4,5,6)

3089 Mount Pleasant Contracts Halstead Selling Handicap Hurdle (4-y-o and up) £3,046 2m 110yds.........(2:20)

2665⁶	PINECONE PETER [88] (v) 7-11-10 M Brennan, chsd ldr, led aftr 3 out, lft clr last.............(11 to 4 op 5 to 2)	1
2790	SULTAN'S SON [74] 8-10-10 D Bridgwater, hld up rear, hdwy 3 out, lft moderate second at last, no imprsn on wnr.....................(14 to 1 tchd 16 to 1)	2
2665⁷	SWAN WALK (Ire) [81] 6-11-0 (3*) S Wynne, in tch, rdn and one pace 3 out......................(33 to 1 op 20 to 1)	3
2841³	RASTA MAN [83] 6-11-5 S Smith Eccles, rear, effrt 7th, not rch ldrs frm 2 out.................(9 to 4 fav op 7 to 2)	4
2212	JOLI'S GREAT [87] (bl) 6-11-9 J Ryan, hld up, jnd ldr 3 out, wknd quickly nxt.......(11 to 1 op 6 to 1 tchd 14 to 1)	5
2420³	RUTH'S GAMBLE [78] 6-10-11 (3*) R Davis, wl plcd, wnt second appr 2 out, f last.......(5 to 1 op 4 to 1)	f

---

2891⁴	POINT TAKEN (USA) [70] 7-10-6 A S Smith, led till aftr 3 out, wknd quickly, pld up bef last.	
	......................(8 to 1 op 6 to 1 tchd 9 to 1)	pu

Dist: 5l, 10l, 3½l, 15l. 4m 11.60s. a 21.60s (7 Ran).

SR: 20/1/-/-/

(Mrs B A Burgass), O Brennan

3090 Topclean Novices' Chase (5-y-o and up) £2,795 3m.................(2:50)

2668	CRAIGSTOWN (Ire) 6-11-2 (3*) R Davis, hld up, led 15th, pushed clr r-in.....(15 to 8 op 6 to 4 tchd 2 to 1)	1
	SPARTAN RAFT 13-10-12 (7*) Mr M Gingell, mstks, led to 5th, lft in ld 12th, hdd 15th, rallied last, one pace.	
2840	MICRONOVA (bl) 8-11-5 D Bridgwater, hld up rear, chsd ldr 3 out till rdn and no extr appr last.	
	....................(6 to 1 op 7 to 1 tchd 10 to 1)	3
2879³	LE BUCHERON 8-11-5 J Ryan, led 5th, clr whn blun and uns rdr 12th.............(6 to 4 on op 2 to 1 on)	ur

Dist: 6l, 6m 47.90s. a 55.90s (4 Ran).

(Mrs A Emanuel), Mrs L C Jewell

3091 Jewson Handicap Chase (0-125 5-y-o and up) £4,182 2m 5f 110yds.... (3:20)

1954³	ARDCRONEY CHIEF [103] 8-11-1 P Holley, led to 5th, led 13th, wnt clr appr last...(6 to 1 op 7 to 1 tchd 5 to 1)	1
2648²	LOVE ANEW (USA) [99] 9-10-11 D Murphy, hld up, cld on ldr 13th, ev ch 2 out, no extr appr last.	
	....................(3 to 1 op 4 to 1)	2
2962	BOSTON ROVER [115] 9-11-13 M Brennan, not fluent, settled rear, rdn and kpt on one pace frm 4 out.	
	....................(6 to 1 op 4 to 1)	3
2915²	PRIVATE AUDITION [114] 12-11-9 (3*) A Thornton, wth ldr, led 5th to 13th, sn wknd...........(10 to 1 op 8 to 1)	4
2636	DUO DROM [99] (v) 9-10-5 D Bridgwater, trkd ldrs, rdn and no hdwy frm 3 out.........(6 to 5 op 5 to 1)	5
2832⁶	KIND'A SMART [114] 9-11-12 A S Smith, in tch till blun and uns rdr 9th.....(13 to 8 fav op Evens tchd 7 to 4)	ur
2966	ROYAL FLAMINGO [97] 8-10-9 R J Beggan, not fluent, beh 6th, blun nxt, lost tch 8th, refused last.	
	....................(10 to 1 tchd 14 to 1)	ref

Dist: 15l, 3½l, 4l, ½l. 5m 42.70s. a 30.70s (7 Ran).

SR: 38/19/31/26/10/-/-/

(W H Dore), D R Gandolfo

3092 Middleton Aggregates Handicap Hurdle (0-115 4-y-o and up) £3,688 2m 110yds........................ (3:50)

2833⁶	RATIFY [114] 7-11-7 (7*) Mr C Bonner, led to second, led aftr 5th, quickened clr 3 out, rdn out.	
	....................(7 to 4 op 6 to 4 tchd 2 to 1)	1
2933²	ZEALOUS KITTEN (USA) [103] 6-11-0 (3*) J McCarthy, hit 4th and lost pl, effrt and outpcd appr 3 out, ran on strly approaching last, fnshd wl.	
	....................(11 to 8 fav op 5 to 4 tchd 6 to 4)	2
	BROWNSIDE BRIG [89] 9-10-3¹ D Murphy, pld hrd, chsd wnr frm 6th, blun and eased appr last. (6 to 1 op 4 to 1)	3
2408²	SPANISH WHISPER [86] 7-10-0 N Mann, chsd ldrs till lost tch appr 3 out..................(7 to 1 tchd 8 to 1)	4
2496⁴	MASAI MARA (USA) [107] (bl) 6-11-7 M Hourigan, led second till aftr 5th, wknd appr 3 out....(6 to 1 tchd 7 to 1)	5

Dist: 1½l, 20l, 5l, 4l. 4m 15.20s. a 25.20s (5 Ran).

SR: 46/33/-/-/8/

(J C Fretwell), K A Morgan

3093 West Norfolk Novices' Hunters' Chase (5-y-o and up) £2,514 2m 5f 110yds
....(4:20)

	KINGS VICTORY 10-11-4 (3*) Mrs L Gibbon, in tch, lft in ld 11th, drw clr 13th, unchlgd........(25 to 1 op 20 to 1)	1
	HERON'S ROCK 10-11-0 (7*) Mr M Portman, settled in 3rd pl, mstks 4th and 5th, chsd wnr frm 11th, outpcd 13th.	
	....................(6 to 4 on tchd Evens and 11 to 8 on)	2
	SPANDULAY (USA) 13-10-9 (7*) Miss S Baxter, chsd frnt rnk, mstk 11th, blun and no imprsn frm 3 out.	
	....................(15 to 2 op 6 to 1 tchd 8 to 1)	3
	RURAL CUSTOM 10-10-9 (7*) Mr J G Townson, al rear, mstk 8th, tld off 11th.................(7 to 1 tchd 8 to 1)	4
	SPECULATION 12-11-0 (7*) Mr C Ward, led to second, chsd ldrs till wknd 11th, mstk 13th, tld off:	
	....................(10 to 1 op 7 to 1)	5
2482	R N COMMANDER 8-11-0 (7*) Mr J R Cornwall, rear till blun and uns rdr 7th.........(25 to 1 op 12 to 1)	ur

PRINCE ENGELBERT 9-11-0 (7*) Mr N King, *mstk 4th, sn beh, tld off whn pld up bef 12th...* (33 to 1 op 20 to 1) pu
2669 ARPAL BREEZE 9-11-2 (5*) Mr P Harding-Jones, *not jump wl, al rear, blunds 8th, 9th and 11th, pld up bef 12th.* ....(4 to 1 op 7 to 2 tchd 9 to 2) pu
2885^{4} PAID ELATION 9-10-10^{1} (7*) Mr J Wingfield Digby, *led second, clr whn took wrong course appr 11th, pld up.* .... (25 to 1 op 20 to 1) pu
Dist: 20l, dist, 1½l, ½l. 5m 59.90s. a 47.90s (9 Ran).
(Derek Ginbey), Mrs Julie Read

3094 Swaffham Greyhounds Novices' Handicap Hurdle Conditional Jockeys (4-y-o and up) £2,827 2m 110yds (4:50)

1316^{2} WORDY'S WONDER [77] 6-10-12 R Farrant, *in tch in mid-div, chsd ldr appr 6th, led 2 out, clr whn pckd last, hld on nr finish.*........................(8 to 1 op 6 to 1) 1
2804^{2} MORIARTY [71] 7-10-6 J McCarthy, *beh till ran on frm 6th, rdn and quickened appr last, fnshd wl.* ....(100 to 30 op 4 to 1) 2
2629^{4} MULLED ALE (Ire) [72] 4-10-7 R Davis, *prog frm rear 6th, rdn and one pace 2 out*.............(7 to 1 op 5 to 1) 3
2670^{4} TYNRON DOON [76] (bl) 5-10-11 S Wynne, *led to 2 out, sn btn*..................(11 to 4 fav op 3 to 1 tchd 7 to 2) 4
1708^{3} SWIFT ROMANCE (Ire) [81] 6-11-2 A Procter, *effrt frm rear aftr 5th, outpcd nxt, tld off*..........(6 to 1 op 5 to 1) 5
1457 MARTRAJAN [89] 7-11-10 L O'Hare, *chsd ldr till rdn and wknd aftr 5th, tld off*................(8 to 1 op 7 to 1) 6
2969^{4} UPWARD SURGE (Ire) [76] (bl) 4-10-11 A Thornton, *wl plcd till wknd appr 3 out, tld off*..........(9 to 2 op 3 to 1) 7
2912 CUPID'S COURAGE (Ire) [65] 5-9-10 (4*) Honey Pearce, *mid-div, drpd rear 5th, sn tld off*.......(66 to 1 op 50 to 1) 8
POLISH RIDER (USA) [80] 6-11-1 C Huggan, *in tch till hmpd on bend aftr 5th, sn drpd rear, tld off whn pld up bef 2 out*..........................(16 to 1 op 12 to 1) pu
Dist: 1½l, 6l, 7l, 20l, 20l, 25l, dist. 4m 16.80s. a 26.80s (9 Ran).
SR: 14/6/1/-/-/-/ (L Wordingham), L Wordingham

LINGFIELD (good to soft)
Friday March 18th

Going Correction: PLUS 0.75 sec. per fur. (races 1,4,6), PLUS 1.20 (2,3,5)

3095 Newleaf Maiden Hurdle (4-y-o) £1,984 2m 110yds.....................(2:00)

WARM SPELL 11-0 N Williamson, *hld up, trkd ldr appr 3 out, led aftr last, drvn out.* .... (9 to 4 op 2 to 1 tchd 11 to 4) 1
1885^{3} CHIEF'S SONG 11-0 M A FitzGerald, *trkd ldrs, led 5th till hdd aftr last, ran on und pres.* .... (Evens fav op 5 to 4 on tchd 5 to 4) 2
2083^{5} ANY MINUTE NOW (Ire) 10-7 (7*) S Ryan, *trkd ldrs, styd on frm 4 out, one pace appr 2 out.* .... (25 to 1 op 14 to 1 tchd 33 to 1) 3
2881^{3} INTENTION (USA) 11-0 R Campbell, *took keen hold, led til hdd 5th, wknd aftr nxt.* (4 to 1 op 7 to 2 tchd 9 to 2) 4
2712^{3} CLASSY KAHYASI (Ire) 10-9 W McFarland, *trkd ldrs till wknd appr 5th*.......(50 to 1 op 25 to 1 tchd 66 to 1) 5
2712^{4} RISING WOLF 11-0 D O'Sullivan, *wth ldr till lost pl appr 5th*.................. (12 to 1 op 7 to 1 tchd 14 to 1) 6
2478^{6} PRAIRIE GROVE 11-0 J R Kavanagh, *al beh, tld off.* ....(33 to 1 op 20 to 1 tchd 50 to 1) 7
3010^{7} RUN TO AU BON (Ire) (v) 11-0 D Gallagher, *in cl tch, pushed alng aftr 4th, sn lost pl, tld off.* ....(50 to 1 op 33 to 1 tchd 100 to 1) 8
SUSSEX MAESTRO 11-0 M Crosse, *hld up in rear, lost tch aftr 4th, tld off*..... (50 to 1 op 33 to 1 tchd 100 to 1) 9
Dist: 1½l, 25l, 15l, 1l, 10l, 10l, 30l, dist. 4m 8.90s. a 17.90s (9 Ran).
SR: 31/29/4/-/-/-/ (K Higson), G L Moore

3096 Times 'Rising Stars' Hunters' Chase Qualifier (6,7,8-y-o) £1,865 3m.. (2:30)

AVOSTAR 7-11-7 (5*) Mr R Russell, *led aftr 1st, made rst at slow pace, ran on*.................. (7 to 2 op 2 to 1) 1
2949* SYNDERBOROUGH LAD 8-11-12 (7*) Mr M Felton, *hld up, cld 12th, one pace whn hit last.* ....(7 to 4 fav op 5 to 4 tchd 2 to 1) 2
FIRST HARVEST 7-11-5 (7*) Mr M Jackson, *led 1st, trkd wnr till wknd appr last.* ....(16 to 1 op 14 to 1 tchd 20 to 1) 3
2875^{6} HOBNOBBER 7-11-5 (7*) Mr B Pollock, *not fluent, hld up, cld and hit 12th, wknd appr 15th, tld off.* ....(25 to 1 op 20 to 1 tchd 33 to 1) 4
2800 ROVING REPORT 7-12-0 (5*) Mr T Mitchell, *al beh, lost tch 14th, tld off*............ (4 to 1 op 7 to 2 tchd 9 to 2) 5
2709* NO FIZZ 8-11-7 (7*) Mr P Bull, *hld up, 3rd whn f 11th.* ....(4 to 1 tchd 9 to 2) f
Dist: 10l, 8l, 15l, 15l. 6m 52.80s. a 59.80s (6 Ran).
(R G Russell), Miss C Saunders

3097 Paice Group Maiden Chase (5-y-o and up) £2,794 3m..................(3:00)

2822 HERMES HARVEST 6-11-8 M A FitzGerald, *al hndy, led briefly aftr 4 out to nxt, led ag'n last, drvn out.* .... (16 to 1 op 14 to 1) 1
2879^{6} RING CORBITTS 6-11-8 Mr P Hacking, *mid-div, hdwy to ld tenth, hdd briefly aftr 4 out, led ag'n 3 out to last, no extr*.................................(5 to 1 op 4 to 1) 2
2223^{4} FROZEN DROP 7-11-8 Richard Guest, *in tch, beh tenth, rdn 13th, outpcd frm 4 out*..........(8 to 1 op 5 to 1) 3
2913^{3} YOUNG BRAVE 8-11-8 S Earle, *hld up in rear, effrt and not fluent 14th, nvr on terms*.....(3 to 1 fav op 2 to 1) 4
2732^{2} TRIMAGE (Ire) 6-11-8 B Powell, *cl up, led 5th to 7th, lost pl 9th, rapid hdwy 14th, wknd nxt.* ....(7 to 2 op 3 to 1 tchd 11 to 4 and 4 to 1) 5
2427 SHOCK TACTICS 7-11-8 S McNeill, *chsd ldrs, pushed alng 12th, wkng whn blun 14th, tld off.* ....(14 to 1 op 12 to 1 tchd 16 to 1) 6
2816 PURPLE SPRAY 9-11-8 N Williamson, *hld up, hdwy to ld 7th, hdd whn f tenth*........... (14 to 1 tchd 16 to 1) f
2732^{4} JUST A SECOND (v) 9-11-3 J Railton, *reminders in rear aftr 3rd, beh whn blun and uns rdr 11th.* ....(7 to 1 op 6 to 1 tchd 8 to 1) ur
INDIAN JEWEL 10-11-8 D O'Sullivan, *led to 5th, dsptd ld 13th, wknd aftr nxt, tld off whn pld up bef 2 out.* .... (20 to 1 op 16 to 1) pu
2732 UNDERWYCHWOOD (Ire) (bl) 6-11-8 I Lawrence, *chsd ldrs, led tenth to 12th, sn rdn and lost pl, pld up bef 2 out.* ....(8 to 1 op 8 to 1) pu
2879 BILLION DOLLARBILL 6-11-8 T Grantham, *al beh, pld up bef 11th*.. (50 to 1) pu
Dist: 4l, dist, 5l, 2l, dist. 6m 45.20s. a 52.20s (11 Ran).
(Miss B W Palmer), D L Williams

3098 Lambert & Foster Selling Handicap Hurdle (4-y-o and up) £2,092 2m 110yds........................(3:30)

1597^{6} ROGER'S PAL [81] 7-11-5 D Gallagher, *hld up, led 3 out, ran on gmely*..(12 to 1) 1
2440^{7} MILZIG (USA) [90] 5-12-0 D O'Sullivan, *hld up beh, hdwy appr 2 out, ran on wl frm last*.....(10 to 1 tchd 8 to 1) 2
2789 FICHU (USA) [73] 6-10-11 B Powell, *hdwy 5th, ev ch last, one pace*.. (33 to 1) 3
2801^{6} TENDRESSE (Ire) [80] 6-11-4 G McCourt, *hld up beh ldg grp, cld 4 out, drvn and hdwy appr 2 out, ev ch last, one pace*......................(3 to 1 fav tchd 11 to 4) 4
2781^{3} CHARCOAL BURNER [77] 9-11-1 M A FitzGerald, *al prmnt, one pace appr last*................(6 to 1 tchd 5 to 1) 5
ST ROBERT [66] 7-10-4 W McFarland, *al prmnt, niggled alng appr 3 out, one pace frm nxt.* (13 to 2 tchd 7 to 1) 6
2804^{5} CHANDIGARH [81] 6-10-12 (7*) P McLoughlin, *hld up in rear, hdwy aftr 3 out, btn after nxt.* ....(12 to 1 tchd 14 to 1) 7
2912* BAYLORD PRINCE (Ire) [74] 6-10-12 M Hoad, *prmnt till hmpd and lost pl aftr 5th, no dngr after.* ....(9 to 2 tchd 5 to 1) 8
2641^{7} HATS HIGH [71] 9-10-9 M Crosse, *nvr better than mid-div, no ch whn mstk 2 out.* .... (11 to 1 op 10 to 1 tchd 12 to 1) 9
2912^{5} AVERON [68] 14-10-6 Lorna Vincent, *hdwy 4th, led nxt till hdd 3 out, wknd*.............................(25 to 1) 10
1795^{7} KNIGHT IN SIDE [78] 8-11-2 C Maude, *hld up, nvr dngrs.* ....(10 to 1 tchd 11 to 1) 11
2653^{8} GARDA'S GOLD [74] 11-10-9 (3*) D Meredith, *beh, shrtlvd effrt aftr 3 out*..................................(14 to 1) 12
748 OTHET [83] 10-11-7 J Railton, *beh frm 4th*....... (20 to 1) 13
2521^{5} LLOYDS DREAM [77] 5-11-1 R Supple, *settled in mid-div, drvn 3 out, sn btn*.......... (10 to 1 tchd 11 to 1) 14
PARISIAN [62] 9-9-10^{3} (7*) A Lucas, *mid-div, wkng whn mstk 2 out, eased*.............................. (20 to 1) 15
2912 BARCHAM [67] 7-10-5 J R Kavanagh, *prmnt till rdn and wknd aftr 3 out*...............................(16 to 1) 16
ACROSS THE CARD [69] 6-10-7 J Clarke, *made most to 5th, wknd quickly, tld off*....... (20 to 1 tchd 25 to 1) 17
2316 COLNE VALLEY KID [62] (bl) 9-10-0 I Lawrence, *al beh, tld off*..(33 to 1) 18
961 FIVE CASTLES [62] 6-10-0 M Perrett, *hit 1st and uns rdr.* ....(20 to 1 tchd 25 to 1) ur
2837 HELLO LADY [62] 7-9-7 (7*) Mr J O'Shaughnessy, *led 1st, cl up till wknd quickly aftr 4th, pld up bef 3 out.* (33 to 1) pu
Dist: ½l, ½l, 1l, 3l, 2l, 5l, 3½l, ½l, ¾l, nk. 4m 15.20s. a 24.20s (20 Ran).
(K Higson), A Moore

3099 Set Aside Novices' Handicap Chase (5-y-o and up) £2,649 2m....... (4:00)

2697^{4} SOLEIL DANCER (Ire) [84] 6-11-1 J Railton, *wtd wth, cld 4 out, led r-in, ran on wl*............. (9 to 2 op 3 to 1) 1
2244 MEDINAS SWAN SONG [73] 6-10-4 A Tory, *pckd 1st, led to r-in, ran on*........................(7 to 1 op 10 to 1) 2
2674^{7} ACCESS SUN [81] 7-10-12 J R Kavanagh, *trkd ldrs, ev ch appr 3 out, sn btn*....(12 to 1 op 10 to 1 tchd 14 to 1) 3
2043^{2} CROOKED COUNSEL [97] 8-12-0 N Williamson, *wth ldr till wknd aftr 4 out*..................(5 to 2 fav op 7 to 4) 4
2118^{6} RUSTIC GENT (Ire) [84] 6-10-8 (7*) Mr B Pollock, *trkd ldrs, mstk 4 out, wkng whn blun nxt 2.* (33 to 1 op 20 to 1) 5
2431^{3} BUSH HILL [70] 9-10-11^{1} S McNeill, *sn beh, tld off.* ....(12 to 1 tchd 14 to 1) 6

2491[2] VICTORY GATE (USA) [77] 9-10-8 D Gallagher, *sn beh, tld off*..................(11 to 2 op 5 to 1 tchd 6 to 1) 7
2766 MOUNTAIN MASTER [80] 8-10-11 Mr J M Pritchard, *beh whn blun and uns rdr 4th*.........(16 to 1 op 14 to 1) ur
2732[3] LEESWOOD [80] 6-10-11 L Harvey, *chsd ldrs, blun 4th, sn drpd rear, pld up bef 8th.* ....(7 to 2 op 3 to 1 tchd 4 to 1) pu

Dist: 2l, 10l, 12l, 10l, 15l, 1½l. 4m 19.40s. a 25.40s (9 Ran).
SR: 25/12/10/14/-/-/ (Mrs John Grist), D M Grissell

3100 Gummer Handicap Hurdle (0-125 4-y-o and up) £2,375 2m 110yds...... (4:30)

1412* MISS MARIGOLD [104] (bl) 5-11-5 A Tory, *hld up in tch, led 2 out, pushed out.* (7 to 2 jt-fav op 4 to 1 tchd 3 to 1) 1
2545[3] WHIPPERS DELIGHT (Ire) [103] 6-11-1 (3*) D Meredith, *led til hdd 2 out, one pace*...........(7 to 2 jt-fav op 9 to 4) 2
2432[5] TIP TOP LAD [96] 7-10-11 J Railton, *cl up, pushed alng and wknd aftr 4th, styd on frm last to take modest 3rd.* ....(9 to 2 op 3 to 1) 3
2933[7] JALINGO [109] 7-11-10 Richard Guest, *wtd wth in last pl, cl appr 5th, sn outpcd*... (6 to 1 op 5 to 1 tchd 7 to 1) 4
2432 FRONT PAGE [90] 7-10-5 D Gallagher, *trkd ldr, pushed alng aftr 3 out, sn wknd, tld off*..... (9 to 2 op 7 to 1) 5
2839[8] BANKONIT (Ire) [99] 6-10-7 (7*) Mr J O'Shaughnessy, *pushed alng aftr second, mstk nxt, sn beh, tld off.* ....(20 to 1 op 10 to 1 tchd 25 to 1) 6
DARK DESIRE [109] 8-11-10 S McNeill, *prmnt till wknd 4th, tld off*.........................(7 to 1 op 6 to 1) 7

Dist: 3½l, 20l, 2½l, 12l, 4l, 1l. 4m 14.90s. a 23.90s (7 Ran).
(Mrs Angela Fayers), R J Hodges

LINGFIELD (A.W) (std)
Friday March 18th
Going Correction: NIL

3101 EBF Stakes National Hunt Flat Race (4,5,6-y-o) £1,450 2m............ (5:00)

KALISKO (Fr) 4-11-0 Mr J Durkan, *hld up beh ldg pair, led appr 2 fs out, sn clr, easily.* ....(5 to 4 on op 6 to 4 on tchd Evens) 1
2996 SURGICAL SPIRIT 4-10-4 (5*) S Curran, *trkd ldr, led wl o'r 4 fs out till hdd appr 2 out, outpcd.* (14 to 1 op 10 to 1) 2
PETILLE 4-10-2 (7*) W J Walsh, *strted slwly, rcd in last pl, cld o'r 4 fs out, outpcd frm 3 out*... (6 to 1 tchd 7 to 1) 3
2444[3] KEEL ROW 4-10-9 D Meade, *led, reminders and hdd wl o'r 4 fs out, sn wknd, tld off*..........(Evens op 5 to 4) 4

Dist: 10l, 3½l, 25l. 3m 37.10s. (4 Ran).
(Colin J Clarke), O Sherwood

SOUTHWELL (good to soft (races 1,2,3), soft (4,5,6))
Friday March 18th
Going Correction: PLUS 0.20 sec. per fur.

3102 Mansfield Bitter Maiden Hurdle (4-y-o and up) £1,861 3m 110yds...... (2:10)

2870[2] GENERAL SHOT 9-11-10 Diane Clay, *nvr far away, led aftr 4 out, clr after nxt, mstk last, unchlgd.* ....(5 to 1 op 4 to 1) 1
2897 MEGAMUNCH (Ire) 6-11-10 W Marston, *nvr far away, outpcd and struggling aftr 4 out, styd on to chase wnr r-in, no imprsn*...... (16 to 1 op 12 to 1 tchd 20 to 1) 2
2409[3] MILLION IN MIND (Ire) (bl) 5-11-10 A Maguire, *not fluent early, led til hdd aftr 4 out, drvn alng nxt, sn outpcd.* .... (7 to 4 on op 2 to 1 on tchd 11 to 8 on and 5 to 4 on) 3
2960[6] WANG HOW 6-11-10 D Wilkinson, *settled rear, struggling to keep in tch bef 4 out, tld off*.....(14 to 1 op 12 to 1) 4
2960[4] CZAR NICHOLAS (v) 5-11-10 W Worthington, *not fluent, pressed ldg grp, drvn alng 9th, outpcd aftr nxt, tld off.* ....(9 to 1 op 7 to 1) 5
2871[8] HURRICANE LINDA 7-11-0 (5*) J Burke, *settled on ins, improved 5 out, outpcd aftr nxt, sn btn, no ch whn f last*...................(10 to 1 op 8 to 1 tchd 12 to 1) f
2404 RED BRANCH (Ire) 5-11-10 P Niven, *handily plcd, drvn alng aftr 9th, outpcd after nxt, blun 3 out, no ch whn blunded and uns rdr next*...........................(25 to 1) ur
2790[9] COLONIAL OFFICE (USA) (bl) 8-11-3 (7*) N Juckes, *hld up, struggling to keep up 5 out, blun 3out, tld off whn pld up bef nxt*........... (16 to 1 op 25 to 1 tchd 33 to 1) pu
2411 BEN THE BOMBER 9-11-3 (7*) Judy Davies, *settled midfield, feeling pace and rdn alng bef 8th, sn drpd rear, pld up before nxt*.....................................(33 to 1) pu
2524 MARIDADI 8-11-10 C Llewellyn, *trkd ldrs, reminders bef 9th, outpcd frm nxt, tld off whn pld up before 2 out.* .... (16 to 1 op 10 to 1) pu

Dist: 15l, 2½l, 30l, 6l. 6m 23.70s. a 33.70s (10 Ran).
(H D White), W Clay

3103 Fisher Hargreaves Proctor Selling Hurdle (4-y-o and up) £1,845 2m (2:40)

2628[2] SHARP DANCE 5-10-11 M Richards, *confidently rdn in rear, smooth hdwy bef 3 out, led on bit aftr last, shaken up and ran on strly*................ (7 to 1 op 10 to 1) 1
2900[5] EASTERN PLEASURE (v) 7-11-2 Diane Clay, *chsd clr ldr, led bef 5th, hit fifth and nxt, hrd pressed whn hit last, sn hdd and no extr*..... (11 to 2 op 5 to 1 tchd 7 to 1) 2
2900[4] ROYAL STANDARD 7-11-2 P McDermott, *prmnt in chasing grp, took clr order hfwy, outpcd and drvn alng 3 out, styd on und pres frm last*............ (5 to 1 op 9 to 2) 3
2408[4] AT PEACE 8-12-0 A Maguire, *nvr far away in chasing grp, improved to chal bef 2 out, hit two out and sn rdn, one pace whn wkng and hit last.* .... (3 to 1 tchd 7 to 2 and 4 to 1) 4
QUIET MISTRESS 4-10-3 B Storey, *patiently rdn, pushed alng to improve 3 out, no imprsn frm nxt*..... (33 to 1) 5
2271[8] MILTON ROOMS (Ire) 5-10-11 (5*) E Husband, *cl up in chasing grp, rdn and ev ch aftr 3 out, btn nxt.* (10 to 1) 6
1253 ALIF (Ire) 5-11-2 Mr B Leavy, *in tch chasing grp, drpd rear hfwy, tld off last 3*.............................. (33 to 1) 7
2523[5] LOXLEY RANGE (Ire) (h,v) 6-11-1 (7*) N Juckes, *prmnt in chasing grp, mstk and drvn alng 4 out, sn btn, tld off.* .... (10 to 1 op 8 to 1) 8
2783[7] QUEEN OF THE QUORN 4-10-3 J Callaghan, *settled in chasing grp, drvn alng bef 5th, struggling frm nxt, tld off whn pld up before 2 out.* ....(11 to 4 fav op 2 to 1 tchd 3 to 1) pu
1731 CAPTAIN TANDY (Ire) 5-11-2 T Wall, *keen hold, led and sn clr, hit 3rd, rdn and hdd bef 5th, soon struggling, tld off whn pld up before 3 out*........................ (25 to 1) pu

Dist: 2½l, 10l, 10l, ½l, ½l, 15l, 15l. 4m 2.00s. a 10.00s (10 Ran).
SR: 15/17/7/9/-/-/ (The Big Eaters Partnership), B Smart

3104 Russell Scanlan Novices' Chase (5-y-o and up) £2,298 3m 110yds... (3:10)

2668[2] SALLY'S GEM 9-11-2 A Maguire, *jmpd rght, made all, lft wl clr 6 out, unchlgd.* ....(5 to 2 on op 9 to 4 on tchd 2 to 1 on) 1
2886[3] SERDARLI 12-10-11 C Llewellyn, *settled in last pl, wnt remote second 4 out, nvr dngrs*.... (10 to 1 op 20 to 1) 2
2355[5] THE LIGHTER SIDE 8-10-9 (7*) Judy Davies, *trkd ldrs, niggled alng virtually thrght, mstk 3rd, struggling whn lft poor second 6 out, tld off*... (11 to 2 op 4 to 1) 3
2839[7] TITUS GOLD (v) 9-10-13 (3*) T Eley, *trkd wnr, hmpd second, cl second whn blun and uns rdr 6 out.* ....(8 to 1 op 6 to 1) ur
2946 HOW DOUDO 7-10-11 R Bellamy, *rcd keenly, cl 3rd whn blun and uns rdr 11th*..............(14 to 1 op 12 to 1) ur

Dist: 25l, 15l. 6m 59.40s. a 61.40s (5 Ran).
(Brian Gatensbury), J White

3105 National Westminster Bank Plc Handicap Chase (0-115 5-y-o and up) £2,648 2½m 110yds.................. (3:40)

2794[3] RAMSTAR [92] 6-11-1 A Maguire, *patiently rdn, imprvg whn blun tenth, led bef 3 out, hdd nxt, rallied and rgned ld towards finish.* ....(100 to 30 op 3 to 1 tchd 7 to 2) 1
2574[2] CENTENARY STAR [99] 9-11-8 P Niven, *wth ldr, lost pl aftr 9th, ran on to ld nxt, mstk 4 out, hdd bef next, led ag'n 2 out, headed towards finish*...... (3 to 1 fav op 9 to 4) 2
3001[2] SIRRAH JAY [105] 14-12-0 L Wyer, *chsd ldg pair, outpcd 11th, effrt aftr 4 out, shaken up and hng lft frm nxt, one pace*................ (11 to 2 op 5 to 1 tchd 6 to 1) 3
2872* COCK SPARROW [82] 10-10-5 (6ex) W Marston, *hld up, f second*................................ (7 to 2 op 5 to 2) f
ENCHANTED MAN [91] 10-11-0 R Greene, *not fluent, in tch, improved strting fnl circuit, hit 11th, sn struggling, btn whn f 4 out*............. (11 to 2 op 12 to 1) f
2690 WOODY WILL [94] 8-11-3 M Richards, *made most til hdd tenth, outpcd 12th, sn btn, tld off whn pld up bef 3 out.* .... (9 to 1 op 12 to 1 tchd 8 to 1) pu

Dist: ½l, 5l. 5m 41.20s. a 38.20s (6 Ran).
(U K Home Computers), D Nicholson

3106 Pannell Kerr Forster Handicap Chase (0-120 5-y-o and up) £2,694 2m.. (4:10)

2832[3] JUST FRANKIE [117] 10-11-11 P Niven, *pressed ldr, led 6th, drw clr bef 3 out, very easily.* ....(2 to 1 on op 5 to 2 on tchd 15 to 8 on) 1
1975[6] TILDARG [115] 10-11-9 M Richards, *trkd ldg pair, jnd issue 7th, outpcd bef 3 out, sn btn and eased.* ....(2 to 1 op 7 to 4) 2
2707 GREENHEART [120] 11-12-0 C Grant, *keen hold, led til hdd 6th, blun badly and lost grnd nxt, pld up aftr 8th.* ....(10 to 1) pu

Dist: 25l. 4m 22.50s. a 23.50s (3 Ran).
(Lady Susan Watson), Mrs M Reveley

3107 Southwell 2000 Appeal Handicap Hurdle (0-115 4-y-o and up) £1,961 2½m 110yds.......................... (4:40)

2306[5] IN TRUTH [81] 6-10-13 C Grant, *al hndy, mstk 4th, led 7th, rdn clr betw last 2*....... (7 to 1 op 6 to 1 tchd 9 to 1) 1

2961* CURTAIN FACTORY [86] 5-11-4 (6ex) L Wyer, *trkd ldrs on ins, jnd issue 7th, ev ch bef 2 out, outpcd betw last two.*
..................(11 to 8 fav op Evens tchd 7 to 4) 2

2727 BENTLEY MANOR [85] 5-11-3 A Maguire, *settled rear, took clr order hfwy, drvn alng aftr 3 out, btn appr nxt.*
..................(3 to 1 op 7 to 2 tchd 5 to 2) 3

1742* WE'RE IN THE MONEY [68] (bl) 10-10-0 B Dalton, *led til mstk and hdd 7th, sn upsides, rdn and outpcd frm 3 out.* ....(11 to 1 op 10 to 1 tchd 12 to 1) 4

2894* REXY BOY [73] 7-10-5 G Harker, *wth ldr, struggling to keep up bef 7th, tld off.*...........(5 to 1 op 4 to 1) 5

1812 BROOK COTTAGE (Ire) [92] 6-11-10 T Wall, *hld up, drvn alng fnl circuit, sn btn, tld off whn pld up bef 3 out.*
..................(16 to 1 op 14 to 1) pu

Dist: 12l, ¾l, 2½l, 20l. 5m 29.60s. a 36.10s (6 Ran).
(Mrs E Houlton), M D Hammond

CHEPSTOW (soft)
Saturday March 19th
Going Correction: PLUS 1.80 sec. per fur. (races 1,2,- 4,6,7), PLUS 2.30 (3,5)

3108 Beagles Novices' Hurdle (4-y-o and up) £2,136 2m 110yds......... (2:20)

2762² WHITECHAPEL (USA) 6-11-2 M A FitzGerald, *made all, clr appr last, easily.*
..................(2 to 1 on op 4 to on tchd 15 to 8 on) 1

2339⁵ BILLYGOAT GRUFF 5-11-2 W Marston, *trkd ldrs, chsd wnr frm 3 out, no imprsn nxt.*..........(5 to 1 op 4 to 1) 2

2776 BIDDLESTONE BOY (NZ) 7-10-13 (3*) R Davis, *hld up, hdwy frm 4th, ev ch four out, btn whn hit 2 out.*
..................(25 to 1 op 16 to 1) 3

2015 MISS SOUTER 5-10-4 (7*) R Darke, *mid-div, reminders aftr 4th, lost pl, some late hdwy...* (50 to 1 op 25 to 1) 4

2522⁴ HONEY GUIDE 4-10-2 (7*) Mr G Hogan, *cl up till wknd appr 4 out.*..............(12 to 1 op 10 to 1) 5

1935 ESSDOUBLEYOU (NZ) 6-10-13 (3*) A Thornton, *cl up till rdn and wknd appr 4 out*.........(12 to 1 op 10 to 1) 6

2808⁷ SAMJAMALIFRAN 5-10-11 J Lower, *al beh, tld off aftr 4th.*
..................(16 to 1 op 10 to 1) 7

POLY VISION (Ire) 4-10-2 (7*) P McLoughlin, *al beh, tld off aftr 4th...*........(10 to 1 op 25 to 1) 8

BOUGHT THE ACES (Ire) 6-11-2 S Mackey, *prmnt, pushed alng aftr second, beh 4th, tld off.* (50 to 1 op 25 to 1) 9

17974 SAMS QUEEN 5-10-11 R Supple, *al beh, shrtlvd effrt aftr 3 out...*...............(20 to 1 op 16 to 1) 10

Dist: 8l, 25l, 10l, 12l, 12l, dist. 4m 20.40s. a 34.40s (10 Ran).
SR: 41/33/8/-/-/-/ (Queen Elizabeth), N J Henderson

3109 Bristol University Turf Club Novices' Handicap Hurdle (4-y-o and up) £2,192 3m......................... (2:50)

2779* SEE ENOUGH [117] 6-11-7 (7*) Mr G Hogan, *led briefly 1st, cl up, led 4 out, rdn out frm last.*
..................(7 to 4 op 3 to 1 jt-fav op 7 to 4 tchd 5 to 1) 1

2799³ MOBILE MESSENGER (NZ) [86] 6-10-0 T Wall, *hld up rear, hdwy 5 out, ev ch appr last, no extr.*
..................(14 to 1 op 12 to 1 tchd 16 to 1) 2

2799² DERRYMOSS [105] (v) 8-11-2 J Lower, *jmpd rght, led aftr 1st to 4 out, btn whn hit last, eased.*........(9 to 4 jt-fav op 3 to 1) 3

2657* LANSDOWNE [97] 6-10-8 M A FitzGerald, *hld up, shrtlvd effrt 4 out, nvr on terms, tld off.*
..................(5 to 1 op 9 to 2 tchd 11 to 2) 4

2768² SOLO GENT [90] 5-10-1¹ S McNeill, *chsd ldrs, lost pl aftr 5 out...*............(16 to 1 op 10 to 1) 5

2795² CYBORGO (Fr) [106] 4-11-3 M Foster, *pld hrd, in tch and ev ch whn 1 2 out.*......(11 to 2 op 4 to 1) f

2946 PHYL'S LEGACY [89] 9-10-0 R Supple, *hld up, lost tch 7th, tld off whn pld up bef 4 out.*......(100 to 1 op 66 to 1) pu

2841¹⁰ SARAH'S WROATH [89] 9-9-11 (3*) D Meredith, *mid-div, lost tch 8th, pld up bef nxt.*.......(50 to 1 op 33 to 1) pu

2459 CRANK SHAFT [100] (v) 7-10-11 M Hourigan, *trkd ldrs till wknd 5 out, pld up bef nxt...*.......(10 to 1 op 12 to 1) pu

Dist: 1½l, 20l, dist, 3½l. 6m 30.00s. a 52.00s (9 Ran).
SR: 12/-/-/-/-/ (J A G Meaden), R H Buckler

3110 Steel Plate And Sections Young Chasers Qualifier Novices (5 - 8-y-o) £2,607 2m 3f 110yds........... (3:20)

2859² NICKLE JOE 8-11-6 W Marston, *made all, mstk 9th, clr 5 out, eased r-in...*.............(7 to 4 fav op 2 to 1) 1

2879⁷ FAR TOO LOUD 7-10-13 (3*) R Davis, *reminders aftr second, in tch, outpcd 11th, wnt moderate second 4 out, no extr whn...*..........(5 to 1 op 9 to 2) 2

2816³ SWITCH (bl) 8-11-2 S McNeill, *tracking wnr whn blun tenth, sn outpcd, lost second pl 4 out.*
..................(11 to 4 op 3 to 1) 3

2946 BRORA ROSE (Ire) (bl) 6-10-4 (7*) Miss S Cobden, *al beh, tld off aftr 5th.*..........(66 to 1 op 50 to 1) 4

2840* CASTLE DIAMOND 7-11-10 M Bosley, *mstk 1st, reminders aftr nxt, in tch till mistake 11th, sn wknd, tld off.*
..................(5 to 2 tchd 11 to 4) 5

2404 KETFORD BRIDGE 7-10-13 (3*) D Meredith, *f 1st.*
..................(66 to 1 op 50 to 1) f

Dist: 15l, 20l, 10l. 5m 38.40s. a 51.40s (6 Ran).
SR: 26/7/-/ (Mrs E Tate), M Tate

3111 Future Chasers Conditional Jockeys' Selling Handicap Hurdle (4 - 7-y-o) £1,940 2½m 110yds........... (3:50)

1280 CRAZY HORSE DANCER (USA) [73] 6-10-0 R Farrant, *hld up, cld 5th, jmpd lft 2 out, ran on und pres to ld nr finish...*.............(14 to 1 op 20 to 1 tchd 33 to 1) 1

2902² MARINE SOCIETY [73] (bl) 6-9-6 (8*) J Bond, *led to 5th, led and hit 4 out, hit last, hdd nr finish. (7 to 2 op 3 to 1) 2

2912⁴ THANKSFORTHEOFFER [73] (v) 6-9-10 (4*) Pat Thompson, *chsd ldrs, cld and ev ch appr 4 out, styd on one pace.*
..................(8 to 1 op 12 to 1 tchd 20 to 1) 3

2760⁵ BOOGIE BOPPER (Ire) [73] (v) 5-9-6 (8*) O Burrows, *hld up rear, moderate late hdwy, nvr on terms...*.....(10 to 1) 4

2729 SHIKARI KID [76] 7-10-3¹ A Larnach, *hld up, cld 5th, wknd aftr 5 out, no ch whn mstk nxt...*........(33 to 1) 5

2420⁵ DAMCADA (Ire) [73] 6-10-0 R Davis, *al beh, tld off 5th.*
..................(7 to 1 op 9 to 2 tchd 8 to 1) 6

2729 NORTHERN OPTIMIST [82] 6-10-9 Guy Lewis, *trkd ldrs till wknd 6th, tld off...*............(12 to 1) 7

2902³ BLUE LYZANDER [73] 5-10-0 T Jenks, *cld ldrs, led 5th to 4 out, sn wknd, virtually pld up r-in...*

3003¹⁰ ON THE SAUCE [108] (bl) 7-12-3 (4*) L Reynolds, *trkd ldrs, jmpd slwly 5th, lost pl 7th, tld off.*
..................(3 to 1 fav tchd 7 to 2) 9

2729⁴ JOKERS PATCH [73] 7-10-0 A Thornton, *hld up rear, shrt-lvd effrt aftr 7th, tld off...*....(9 to 2 tchd 5 to 1) 10

ON THE LEDGE (USA) [99] 4-11-8 (4*) M Appleby, *trkd ldrs to 4th, drpd out quickly and pld up aftr nxt.*
..................(25 to 1 op 33 to 1) pu

Dist: 1l, 8l, 8l, 3l, dist. 5m 23.80s. a 42.80s (11 Ran).
SR: 13/12/4/-/-/-/ (Mrs Jean Haslam), F Jordan

3112 Ostler Handicap Chase (0-130 5-y-o and up) £3,738 2m 3f 110yds.... (4:20)

2981* RAFIKI [109] 9-11-10 M A FitzGerald, *made all, clr 8th, unchlgd...*......(7 to 2 op 4 to 1 on tchd 3 to 1) 1

2861⁴ BALDA BOY [108] (bl) 10-11-6 (3*) R Farrant, *trkd wnr, reminders 7th, lost tch nxt, mstk 9th. (3 to 1 op 5 to 2) 2

Won by Dist. 5m 41.80s. a 54.80s (2 Ran).
SR: -/-/ (J P Carrington), Mrs J G Retter

3113 Open National Hunt Flat Race (Div I) (4,5,6-y-o) £1,276 2m 1f......... (4:50)

AIR SHOT 4-10-2 (7*) M Keighley, *hld up gng wl, hdwy hfwy, led on tch sit, sn clr, easily...*......(4 to 1) 1

2407³ NORMAN'S CONVINCED (Ire) 4-10-2 (7*) L Reynolds, *trkd ldr aftr 4 fs, led 7 out to four out, one pace und pres.*
..................(4 to 1 jt-fav op 7 to 2) 2

LUV-U-FRANK (Ire) 5-11-3 J Lower, *strted slwly, beh, hdwy frm o'r 4 fs out, styd on, prmsg.*
..................(11 to 2 op 5 to 3 tchd 6 to 1) 3

2560⁶ BOURNEL 6-10-5 (7*) Mr G Hogan, *beh, hdwy o'r 5 fs out, wknd 2 out...*..........(20 to 1 op 14 to 1) 4

2407⁵ DOVETTO 5-10-10 (7*) P McLoughlin, *beh, cld on ldrs o'r 5 fs out, rdn and no imprsn 3 out.*
..................(15 to 2 op 5 to 1 tchd 8 to 1) 5

2444⁵ DUNLIR 4-10-2 (7*) T Thompson, *beh, styd on fnl 4 fs, nrst finish...*............(33 to 1 op 14 to 1) 6

2210⁵ PONGO WARING (Ire) 5-11-0 (3*) J McCarthy, *chsd ldrs till wknd o'r 4 fs out...*.....(6 to 1 op 4 to 1 tchd 13 to 2) 7

2834 HIGH MOOD 4-10-6 (3*) T Jenks, *pld hrd in rear, hdwy 5 fs out, no imprsn 3 out...*.......(7 to 1 op 5 to 1) 8

2691⁹ SHAMELESS LADY 4-10-4 S Mackey, *rcd freely, led ten fs, wknd o'r 4 out...*...........(33 to 1 op 20 to 1) 9

BORIS BAGLEY 4-10-9 (7*) N Willmington, *trkd ldrs to hfwy...*..................(33 to 1 op 9 to 1) 10

1957 BREAD OF HEAVEN 5-10-9 (3*) D Meredith, *trkd ldrs to hfwy...*.............(33 to 1 op 8 to 1) 11

MAC'S BOY 5-10-10 (7*) D Rees, *mid-div, cld on ldrs hfwy, wknd o'r 3 fs out.*
..................(7 to 1 op 14 to 1 tchd 10 to 1) 12

DERRYS PREROGATIVE 4-10-6 (3*) A Thornton, *mid-div till drpd rear hfwy...*.............(33 to 1 op 20 to 1) 13

2909⁷ MY WARRIOR 6-11-3 M A FitzGerald, *trkd ldr 4 fs, cl up till lost pl hfwy...*...........(10 to 1 op 6 to 1) 14

ORCADIAN ROSE 4-10-4 R Supple, *al beh, sn tld off.*
..................(33 to 1 op 20 to 1) 15

Dist: 5l, 20l, 20l, 5l, 3½l, 1½l, 5l, 1½l, 12l, 1½l. 4m 18.30s. (15 Ran).
(Mrs Peter Prowting), D Nicholson

3114 Open National Hunt Flat Race (Div II) (4,5,6-y-o) £1,276 2m 1f........ (5:20)

NATIVE ALLIANCE (Ire) 5-11-3 J Lower, *hld up, hdwy 7 fs
out, led on bit one out, imprsv.....* (4 to 1 tchd 6 to 1)   1
2677² NAHLA 4-9-13 (5*) S Curran, *hld up, hdwy 6 fs out, led 4
out till rdn and hdd one out, not pace of wnr.*
...............(15 to 8 fav op 6 to 4 tchd 9 to 4)   2
FAR EAST (NZ) 5-11-0 (3*) R Davis, *cld on ldrs aftr 4 fs, ev
ch 3 out, sn outpcd.*.................(20 to 1 op 8 to 1)   3
KEYU 5-10-12 M Hourigan, *pld hrd, in tch, led 5 fs out to
4 out, sn wknd.*....................(50 to 1 op 20 to 1)   4
JOBINGO 6-10-12 (5*) Guy Lewis, *pushed alng hfwy,
hdwy o'r 5 fs out, outpcd over 3 out.*
...............................(20 to 1 tchd 25 to 1)   5
2509 HAILE DERRING 4-10-6 (3*) D Meredith, *rcd wide, in tch
till wknd 4 fs out.*.................(50 to 1 op 20 to 1)   6
2916⁵ RIVER LEVEN 5-11-3 W Marston, *al beh, tld off.*
.................................(14 to 1 op 10 to 1)   7
2916⁴ CROWN PROSECUTOR 4-11-2 S McNeill, *prmnt till wknd
4 fs out, virtually pld up ins last.*
...............................(11 to 4 op 2 to 1 tchd 4 to 1)   8
TYDFIL LASS 5-10-12 D J Burchell, *trkd ldrs for o'r ten fs,
sn wknd, tld off....* (66 to 1 op 10 to 1 tchd 100 to 1)   9
KINGS GAMBLE 4-10-9 Ann Stokell, *trkd ldrs 9 fs, sn
wknd, tld off.....* (33 to 1 op 20 to 1 tchd 50 to 1) 10
TRY AGAIN JANE 4-10-4 M A FitzGerald, *led to 5 fs out, lost
pl quickly, tld off.....* (10 to 1 op 4 to 1 tchd 12 to 1) 11
SCBOO 5-11-3 V Slattery, *al beh, tld off whn pld up 4 fs
out.*.............................(50 to 1 op 20 to 1) pu
WELSH ORCHID 4-9-11 (7*) N Juckes, *unruly strt, refused
to race.*.........................(100 to 1 op 20 to 1)   I
Dist: 3½l, 25l, 3l, 4l, 3½l, 15l, 1½l. 4m 22.40s. (13 Ran).
(Mrs L M Sewell), M C Pipe

LINGFIELD (soft)
Saturday March 19th
Going Correction: PLUS 1.55 sec. per fur.

3115
Overtons Restaurants Novices' Hurdle (4-y-o and up) £2,061 2m 3f 110yds
.... (1:55)

1946³ SESAME SEED (Ire) 6-11-4 J R Kavanagh, *wl in tch till led
4th, clr appr last, easily.*...................(3 to 1 jt-
fav op 7 to 2 tchd 4 to 1)   1
2705² SPUFFINGTON 6-11-4 D Murphy, *hld up, hdwy 7th, chsd
wnr aftr 3 out, one pace betw last 2.*........(3 to 1 jt-
fav tchd 7 to 2)   2
2857² FOREVER SHINEING 4-10-4 M Perrett, *led up, ran on frm
3 out, one pace from nxt.*.........(7 to 1 op 5 to 1)   3
2802⁴ TAKE CHANCES 6-11-4 N Dawe, *lost pos aftr 4th, styd on
ag'n appr 2 out, not rch wnr.*.....(20 to 1 op 14 to 1)   4
2621³ RIO TRUSKY 5-11-4 J Railton, *ldg grp, chsd wnr frm 6th
till aftr 3 out, wknd nxt.* (12 to 1 op 8 to 1 tchd 14 to 1)   5
1840⁶ NATIVE CHIEFTAN 5-11-10 W McFarland, *hdwy 4th, blun
6th, effrt 3 out, wknd nxt.*
............................(6 to 1 op 5 to 1 tchd 7 to 1)   6
2910⁷ SARAZAR (USA) 5-10-11 (7*) S Ryan, *jnd ldrs 4th, wknd 3
out.*...............................(33 to 1 op 20 to 1)   7
2048⁵ MARROB 7-11-4 G McCourt, *hld up, shrtlvd effrt appr 3
out, sn btn, tld off....*(11 to 2 op 3 to 1 tchd 6 to 1)   8
LE DENSTAN 7-11-4 M Richards, *hdwy 6th, wknd 3 out,
tld off.*..........................(100 to 1 op 33 to 1)   9
2505 DREAMLINE 5-10-13 M Ahern, *led to 4th, wknd aftr 6th,
tld off.*..........................(100 to 1 op 33 to 1) 10
1490 MR GREY FELLOW (Ire) 6-10-11 (7*) T Dascombe, *beh frm
4th, tld off from 7th, drpd dead aftr race.*
.................................(100 to 1 op 50 to 1) 11
2269 I'M IN CLOVER (Ire) 5-11-4 D Meade, *wth ldrs till blun 5th,
sn drpd out, tld off.*................(100 to 1 op 50 to 1) 12
95 THE FUN OF IT 9-11-4 G Upton, *al beh, tld off.*
.................................(100 to 1 op 33 to 1) 13
MR ELECTRAMECH 7-11-4 S Earle, *jmpd very slwly and
uns rdr 1st.*.....................(100 to 1 op 50 to 1) ur
2910² RES IPSA LOQUITUR 7-11-4 D Gallagher, *wl plcd till hmpd
and mstk 7th, rnwd effrt 3 out, wknd and pld up bef
last.*.........................(8 to 1 op 11 to 2 tchd 10 to 1) pu
2546 JOALTO 4-10-9 S Smith Eccles, *pld hrd, prmnt to 4th,
blun 6th, tld off whn pulled up bef nxt.*
.................................(100 to 1 op 33 to 1) pu
Dist: 10l, 15l, 4l, 3½l, 2l, 10l, 25l, 1½l, dist, 1l. 5m 15.70s. a 41.70s (16 Ran).
(Raymond Tooth), N J Henderson

3116
Charlie Chester Club Handicap Chase (0-105 5-y-o and up) £2,807 2m . . (2:25)

2872⁵ SPOONHILL WOOD [84] (bl) 8-10-7 B Dalton, *hld up, quick
hdwy to ld 3 out, clr nxt.....*(3 to 1 jt-fav tchd 11 to 4)   1
2915 DARE SAY [105] 11-12-0 S Earle, *hld up, led 8th, hdd and
jmpd rght 3 out, wknd nxt.*...(3 to 1 jt-fav tchd 7 to 2)   2
2520⁴ SQUEEZE PLAY [80] (bl) 9-10-3 J Railton, *led to 6th,
pushed alng and lost pl 4 out, styd on through btn
horses frm last.*.......(4 to 1 op 7 to 2 tchd 9 to 2)   3
2825 LUCKY AGAIN [91] 7-11-0 M Richards, *blun 3rd, hdwy frm
rear 9th, stumbled on landing 3 out, no extr.*
.................................(5 to 1 op 4 to 1 tchd 11 to 2)   4

2696⁴ COTAPAXI [92] 9-11-1 G McCourt, *led 6th to 8th, very ch
whn badly bumped 3 out, sn wknd.*
............................(6 to 1 op 9 to 2 tchd 13 to 2)   5
2491 FIGHTING DAYS (USA) [94] (v) 8-11-3 D Gallagher, *wth ldr,
reminder 5th, beh 8th, tld off....* (8 to 1 op 6 to 1)   6
Dist: 25l, ½l, ¾l, 1½l, dist. 4m 27.90s. a 33.90s (6 Ran).
(R M Micklethwait), J Wharton

3117
Maxims Lingfield Gold Cup Handicap Hurdle (0-135 4-y-o and up) £7,253 2m 3f 110yds.......................... (2:55)

1840⁸ BILLY BORU [105] 6-10-8 D Gallagher, *not fluent 4th and
5th, jnd ldrs nxt, led appr 2 out, sn clr.*
............................(6 to 1 op 6 to 1 tchd 13 to 2)   1
2759⁷ VAGADOR (Can) [113] 11-11-2 M Perrett, *led to 6th, lost pl
appr 3 out, styd on ag'n frm last....*(10 to 1 op 8 to 1)   2
SORBIERE [110] 7-10-13 J R Kavanagh, *hld up, effrt appr
2 out, one pace betw last two flights.*
...............................(3 to 1 op 4 to 1 tchd 9 to 2)   3
2856⁴ COKENNY BOY [121] 9-11-3 (7*) D Bohan, *chsd ldrs, rdn
and no extr frm 4 out...*(9 to 1 op 8 to 1 tchd 10 to 1)   4
2649⁵ RED BEAN [97] 6-10-0 S Earle, *handily plcd, rdn alng in
3rd pl frm 3 out, no hdwy nxt.....*(50 to 1 op 33 to 1)   5
1890 BELLEZZA [117] 7-11-6 M Richards, *beh frm 5th.*
...............................(11 to 4 fav op 5 to 2)   6
2697⁵ SURE PRIDE (USA) [100] 6-10-3³ G Upton, *chsd ldrs to 6th,
sn btn.*.................(12 to 1 op 8 to 1 tchd 14 to 1)   7
2626* RUN HIGH [105] 11-10-8 Mr R Teal, *hdwy to ld 6th, hdd
appr 2 out, btn in second pl whn hit last, wknd rpdly.*
...........................(7 to 2 op 5 to 2 tchd 4 to 1)   8
2883⁴ MORE OF IT [102] 9-10-5 J Railton, *ldg grp till lost pl
quickly 6th, pld up bef 2 out......*(14 to 1 op 20 to 1) pu
Dist: 6l, nk, 4l, 3½l, nk, 5l, 5l. 5m 16.00s. a 42.00s (9 Ran).
(Ron Butler), Mrs M E Long

3118
Northern Trust Opal Novices' Chase Grade 2 (5-y-o and up) £9,880 2½m 110yds........................ (3:25)

3041 YELLOW SPRING 9-11-3 J Railton, *not fluent 1st, hld up,
led 3 out, clr frm nxt, eased r-in.*
.......................(13 to 8 on op 6 to 4 on tchd 11 to 8 on)   1
2675³ COULDNT BE BETTER 7-11-3 M Perrett, *rdn alng 9th,
prog 11th, chsd wnr frm 2 out, styd on one pace.*
...............................(6 to 1 op 5 to 1 tchd 13 to 2)   2
1662⁵ FESTIVAL DREAMS 9-11-3 N Dawe, *jnd ldrs 3rd, led 8th,
mstk and hdd 3 out, sn btn.*
.................................(20 to 1 op 12 to 1 tchd 25 to 1)   3
2739ᴵ RUSSINSKY 7-10-12 R J Beggan, *al beh.*
...............................(9 to 1 op 6 to 1 tchd 10 to 1)   4
2567² BLACK CHURCH 8-11-3 G McCourt, *led, mstk 7th, hdd
nxt, lost tch 11th, tld off.*...............(10 to 1)   5
2651⁴ UNEXIS 9-11-3 S Earle, *rcd in rear frm 3rd, mstk 7th, tld
off whn pld up bef tenth.*
...............................(66 to 1 op 25 to 1 tchd 100 to 1) pu
2966 GENERAL BRANDY 8-11-3 D Murphy, *mstk second, chsd
ldrs to 9th, wknd quickly, pld up bef 3 out.*
...........................(14 to 1 op 12 to 1 tchd 16 to 1) pu
Dist: 3l, 8l, 20l, 20l. 5m 37.30s. a 36.30s (7 Ran).
SR: 44/41/33/8/   (Mrs R Howell), D M Grissell

3119
Victoria Trading Novices' Handicap Hurdle (4-y-o and up) £2,530 2m 110yds........................ (3:55)

2762⁴ KINGSFOLD PET [75] 5-10-0 D Skyrme, *led 3rd, clr appr 2
out, easily.*.................(12 to 1 tchd 14 to 1)   1
2914 LE BARON PERCHE (Fr) [80] 5-10-5 J R Kavanagh, *prog 5th,
styd on one pace and pres appr 2 out, not rch wnr.*
...............................(7 to 1 tchd 8 to 1)   2
3062 MONAZITE [80] (bl) 4-9-12 (7*) E Tolhurst, *led to 3rd,
pressed wnr till rdn and outpcd aftr 3 out, hit nxt, no
extr.*..........................(25 to 1 op 20 to 1)   3
2819* FONTANAYS (Ire) [99] 6-11-3 (7*) W J Walshe, *hld up, prog 3
out, 4th and btn whn mstk last.* (2 to 1 fav tchd 5 to 2)   4
1557 GAMEFULL GOLD [88] 5-10-13 W McFarland, *mid-div,
improved 5th, lost pl nxt, kpt on ag'n frm 2 out.*
............................(16 to 1 op 12 to 1 tchd 20 to 1)   5
2827 MAMES BOY [93] 7-11-4 D Murphy, *hld up in mid-div,
reminder at the 4th, effrt 6th, no prog 2 out.*
.................................(4 to 1 op 3 to 1)   6
2762⁷ GOLD GLEN (Ire) [85] (bl) 6-10-10 S Earle, *chsd 1st 2, rdn
and outpcd aftr 3 out............*(12 to 1 tchd 14 to 1)   7
2910⁶ GRAND COLONIST [75] 7-10-0 T Kent, *wl plcd till wknd
quickly 3 out.*.....................(50 to 1)   8
2789⁷ ANLACE [75] 5-10-0 M Perrett, *beh most of way.*
.................................(10 to 1 op 6 to 1)   9
2747 JYMJAM JOHNNY (Ire) [94] 5-11-5 D Gallagher, *pld hrd
early stages, al in rear............*(8 to 1 op 6 to 1) 10
2841 BRENDA HUNT (Ire) [75] 5-10-0 M Ahern, *al beh.*
.................................(50 to 1 op 33 to 1) 11
2776⁶ LETTS GREEN (Ire) [75] 6-10-0 M Richards, *pld hrd early
stages, in tch till wknd appr 3 out, pulled up bef 2 out.*
.................................(50 to 1) pu
2731³ MR PICKPOCKET (Ire) [99] 6-11-3 (7*) S Ryan, *sddl slpd and
pld up appr second......*(7 to 1 op 6 to 1 tchd 15 to 2) pu

438

Dist: 15l, 1½l, 2½l, nk, 2l, ½l, 4l, 4l, 12l, 6l. 4m 20.90s. a 29.90s (13 Ran).
SR: 29/19/17/33/21/24/15/1/-/ (G E Nye), M J Haynes

3120 Golden Horseshoe Handicap Chase (0-110 5-y-o and up) £3,184 3m. . (4:25)

2518[4] THE TARTAN SPARTAN [97] 10-10-11 (7*) P Ward, *mstks second and 4th, led 8th, not fluent 14th, clr appr 3 out, mistake last*............(5 to 1 op 7 to 2 tchd 11 to 2) 1
2758 CAMDEN BELLE [82] 12-10-3 M Perrett, *led 5th to 8th, lost pl tenth, rallied appr 3 out, no imprsn frm nxt.* ....(20 to 1 op 16 to 1 tchd 12 to 1 and 25 to 1) 2
2758[2] SILVERINO [101] (bl) 8-11-8 M Richards, *led to 5th, sn pushed alng, reminders 9th, one pace frm 3 out.* ....(15 to 8 op 7 to 4 tchd 2 to 1) 3
2647[3] EMERALD STORM [90] 7-10-11 J R Kavanagh, *hld up, chsd wnr 14th till appr 3 out, shaken up and sn btn.* ....(11 to 8 on op 5 to 4 on) 4
Dist: 10l, 15l, 15l. 6m 58.90s. a 65.90s (4 Ran).
(Mrs Delyth Batchelor), M J Wilkinson

NAVAN (IRE) ((races 1,3,4), soft to heavy (2))
Saturday March 19th

3121 Simonstown Handicap Chase (5-y-o and up) £3,105 2¾m............(3:30)

2867 RIVER TARQUIN [-] (bl) 10-11-6 K F O'Brien,.......(12 to 1) 1
2701 BERMUDA BUCK [-] 8-10-0 F Woods,............. (7 to 2) 2
2617 HAKI SAKI [-] 8-11-4 G M O'Neill,.................. (4 to 1) 3
2755[7] TENNESSEE PASS [-] 14-9-7 (7*) J Butler,......... (25 to 1) 4
2037 RUST NEVER SLEEPS [-] 10-11-6 P Carberry,..... (12 to 1) 5
2867[6] GARAMYCIN [-] 12-12-0 B Sheridan,............. (14 to 1) 6
2755[8] LIFE OF A LORD [-] 8-10-6 S H O'Donovan,....... (10 to 1) 7
FANE BANKS [-] (bl) 12-10-0 H Rogers,............ (25 to 1) pu
2846[8] SONOFBOA [-] (bl) 8-9-7 (7*) D A McLoughlin,..... (25 to 1) pu
1382[2] GALE AGAIN [-] 7-11-7 (5*) C P Dunne,........(9 to 4 fav) pu
Dist: ½l, 5l, 15l, 5l. 6m 23.80s. (10 Ran).
(Robinstown Racing Syndicate), J T R Dreaper

3122 Dolans Maiden Hurdle (5-y-o and up) £3,105 2m..................... (4:00)

2983[2] THE REAL ARTICLE (Ire) 5-11-12 H Rogers,........ (4 to 1) 1
1449[2] MONALEE RIVER (Ire) 6-12-0 K F O'Brien,..... (10 to 9 on) 2
POKONO TRAIL (Ire) 5-11-4 G M O'Neill,...........(20 to 1) 3
2289[4] CLOGRECON BOY (Ire) 6-10-13 (7*) J P Broderick, (10 to 1) 4
2586[4] JESSIE'S BOY (Ire) 5-10-11 (7*) T Martin, ...(10 to 1) 5
2679[8] ABAVARD (Ire) 5-11-12 S H O'Donovan,............(12 to 1) 6
2586 STRONG HICKS (Ire) 6-11-6 F J Flood,........... (16 to 1) 7
1429[4] ALOHA (Ire) 5-10-13 M Duffy,....................(10 to 1) 8
1496 MRS HEGARTY 8-11-1 D P Fagan,...............(33 to 1) 9
2309 IF YOU BELIEVE (Ire) 5-10-11 (7*) Mr R Byrne,..... (25 to 1) 10
2394[6] COOMACHEO (Ire) 5-11-4 D H O'Connor,.......... (16 to 1) 11
2988 PREMIER COUNTY 8-11-6 T Horgan,.............(20 to 1) 12
2863 BORRISMORE FLASH (Ire) 6-11-6 J P Banahan,.. (50 to 1) 13
2943[3] FANDANGOLD 8-10-12 (3*) T J Mitchell,.......... (14 to 1) 14
2679 WHITE OAK BRIDGE (Ire) 5-10-6 (7*) P P Curran,..(50 to 1) 15
2703 TOP RUN (Ire) 6-10-13 (7*) C O'Neill,............ (50 to 1) 16
2314 COLLIERS HILL (Ire) 6-11-6 L P Cusack,.......... (20 to 1) 17
2849 FARRELL'S CROSS 8-12-0 A Powell,............. (20 to 1) 18
2470 THE ROCKING CHAIR (Ire) 6-11-6 P Kavanagh,...(20 to 1) 19
2849[5] DUN CARRAIG (Ire) 6-11-6 P Mooney,............ (12 to 1) 20
CRANNON BOY 7-11-1 (5*) K P Gaule,............ (25 to 1) 21
2983 METROLAMP (Ire) 6-10-13 (7*) N T Egan,......... (20 to 1) 22
2983[9] LANCASTRIANS DREAM (Ire) 5-10-8 (5*) M J Holbrook, ...(25 to 1) 23
2586 MAY GALE (Ire) 6-11-1 F Woods,................ (14 to 1) 24
27[6] CLON CAW (Ire) 6-11-3 (3*) C O'Brien,............ (33 to 1) 25
2770 FOYLE BOREEN 7-10-8 (7*) D O'Driscoll,......... (50 to 1) 26
MUSICAL SMOKE (Ire) 5-10-6 (7*) D J Kavanagh, (25 to 1) f
Dist: 1½l, 2½l, 6l, hd. 4m 11.90s. (27 Ran).
(William J Brennan), Gerard Stack

3123 Proudstown Park Handicap Chase (5-y-o and up) £6,900 2m.......... (4:30)

2698[5] WHO'S TO SAY [-] 8-9-9 T Horgan,................(8 to 1) 1
2549 DORAN'S TOWN LAD [-] 7-9-2 (5*) J P Broderick,.. (6 to 1) 2
1850 MASS APPEAL [-] 9-10-1 B Sheridan,.............(14 to 1) 3
2755[2] BOB DEVANI [-] 8-9-9 P Carberry,........... (5 to 2 jt-fav) 4
2845[2] LADY OLEIN (Ire) [-] 6-9-9 S R Murphy,....... (5 to 2 jt-fav) 5
2698[9] MAD TOM [-] 9-10-9 J P Banahan,................ (10 to 1) 6
2867 CHIRKPAR [-] 7-10-4 J F Titley,................... (5 to 1) 7
1327 THE RIDGE BOREEN [-] 10-10-8 F Woods,........ (25 to 1) pu
Dist: 5½l, 9l, sht-hd, 2l. 4m 40.70s. (8 Ran).
(Mrs P Mullins), P Mullins

3124 Royal Tara INH Flat Race (4-y-o and up) £3,105 2m...................(5:00)

ROSTARR (Ire) 5-11-7 Mr A P O'Brien,............ (7 to 2) 1
2756[6] TREANAREE (Ire) 5-11-5 (7*) Mr D K Budds,...... (14 to 1) 2
KILLINEY GAYLE (Ire) 5-11-4 (3*) Mrs J M Mullins,.. (5 to 1) 3
2290[6] KIMANICKY (Ire) 4-10-11 (7*) K D Maher,.......... (5 to 1) 4
THE GOPHER (Ire) 5-11-7 (5*) T F Lacy Jnr,........(14 to 1) 5
2470 PARADISE ROAD 5-11-12 Mr A J Martin,.......... (10 to 1) 6
1113[5] TRICKLE LAD (Ire) 5-11-5 (7*) Miss F M Crowley,.. (10 to 1) 7
2944[3] ROCK POOL 5-11-7 (5*) Mr H F Cleary,........(5 to 2 fav) 8
COLLON DIAMONDS (Ire) 6-11-2 (7*) Mr M Callaghan, ...(33 to 1) 9
CEBU GALE (Ire) 5-11-7 (5*) Mr P J Casey,........ (12 to 1) 10
2199 FINAWAY EXPRESS (Ire) 5-11-5 (7*) P J Mulligan, (14 to 1) 11
BOALINE (Ire) 6-11-6 (3*) Mr D Marnane,......... (10 to 1) 12
513[2] HAUGHTON LAD (Ire) 5-11-5 (7*) Mr D Groome,.. (10 to 1) 13
SUIRFONTAINE (Ire) 6-11-11 (3*) Mr D Valentine,.. (14 to 1) 14
2944[8] OH RIVER (Ire) 5-11-2 (5*) Mr J P Berry,........... (14 to 1) 15
2869 EIRE (Ire) 5-11-9 (3*) Mr R Neylon,.............. (20 to 1) 16
AUNTIE HONNIE (Ire) 6-11-2 (7*) Mr T N Cloke,.... (25 to 1) 17
2944 BOLD TIPPERARY (Ire) 5-11-0 (7*) J Butler,........ (50 to 1) 18
2353 SILKEN MOSS (Ire) 6-11-2 (7*) D M Bean,......... (33 to 1) 19
3072 WAREZ (Ire) 6-12-0 Mr J P Dempsey,............. (66 to 1) 20
RADICAL DUAL (Ire) 5-11-5 (7*) Mr R Burke,....... (20 to 1) 21
ANOTHER RHUMBA 8-11-6 (3*) T J Mitchell,...... (25 to 1) 22
Dist: 5½l, 1l, 4½l, sht-hd. 4m 6.90s. (22 Ran).
(T A Shirley), A P O'Brien

NEWCASTLE (good)
Saturday March 19th
Going Correction: PLUS 0.40 sec. per fur. (races 1,2,-4,6), PLUS 0.20 (3,5)

3125 Belford Novices' Claiming Hurdle (4-y-o and up) £2,050 2m 110yds... (2:15)

2812[8] FLASH OF REALM (Fr) 8-11-4 A Dobbin, *handily plcd, improved to ld betw last 2, drvn out frm last.* ....(2 to 1 op 7 to 4 tchd 9 to 4) 1
2969[5] ERICOLIN (Ire) 4-10-11 (5*) E Husband, *patiently rdn, improved to chal betw last 2, ridden and no extr last 100 yards*............... (6 to 4 fav op 7 to 4 tchd 2 to 1) 2
1959 INGLETONIAN 5-11-4 L Wyer, *settled on ins, improved 3 out, drvn alng betw last 2, edgd lft and no extr r-in.* ....(25 to 1 op 20 to 1) 3
2498[4] NIGHT OF MADNESS 7-10-9 (7*) B Harding, *settled mid-field, pushed alng to improve bef 3 out, not quicken before last*.................... (16 to 1 op 10 to 1) 4
PIMSBOY (v) 7-11-3 (5*) P Midgley, *patiently rdn, drvn alng to improve 3 out, not quicken betw last 2.* (50 to 1) 5
732[4] KISS IN THE DARK 4-10-4 (5*) S Mason, *in tch chasing grp, cld aftr 3 out, rdn and btn appr nxt.* ....(8 to 1 op 10 to 1) 6
2891[8] LOCAL DEALER 6-10-13 D Byrne, *chsd clr ldr, ev ch whn blun 2 out, grad wknd*............................(33 to 1) 7
2530[8] CHOIR'S IMAGE 7-10-11 A Mulholland, *led 1st and sn clr, hit 2 out, soon hdd and btn*..................(33 to 1) 8
2447 WOLF'S DEN 5-11-1 (5*) F Perratt, *hld up, pushed alng aftr 4 out, nvr able to chal*...... (300 to 1 op 200 to 1) 9
2907[7] MR ABBOT 4-10-10 P Niven, *settled rear, nvr nr to chal.* .... (12 to 1 op 10 to 1 tchd 14 to 1) 10
2960 INNOCENT GEORGE 5-11-2 J Callaghan, *settled on outer, drvn alng to improve bef 3 out, wknd appr nxt.* ....(20 to 1 op 16 to 1) 11
DARK MIDNIGHT (Ire) 5-10-11 (7*) Mr A Manners, *beh, struggling to keep up hfwy, tld off.* ....(150 to 1 op 100 to 1) 12
2972[4] AMERIGUE 4-10-2 (3*) P Williams, *in tch chasing grp to hfwy, sn lost touch, tld off*........(16 to 1 op 20 to 1) 13
WHAT A CARD 6-10-9 K Johnson, *beh, struggling to keep in tch hfwy, tld off*............. (150 to 1 op 100 to 1) 14
2999 RUPERT STANLEY 10-10-6 (7*) S McDougall, *not fluent, led to 1st, lost pl 3rd, sn struggling, tld off.* ....(150 to 1 op 100 to 1) 15
2905[9] BALLINMUSIC 7-11-3 (7*) Mr C Bonner, *prmnt in chasing grp, struggling to keep up bef 3 out, btn whn pld up before last*.......................(150 to 1 op 100 to 1) pu
Dist: 2½l, 6l, 3l, 5l, nk, 5l, 2½l, 4l, 2l, 3l. 4m 5.70s. a 12.70s (16 Ran).

SR: 29/24/20/15/16/2/1/-/1/ (Allan W Melville), P Monteith

3126 Matts Bank Novices' Hurdle (4-y-o and up) £1,966 3m.................(2:45)

2970* KENILWORTH LAD 6-11-10 P Niven, *rcd keenly, nvr far away, improved to chal last, sn rdn and hng lft, led r-in, all out*..................(9 to 4 on op 7 to 4 on) 1
2104[3] MAJORITY MAJOR (Ire) 5-11-4 K Johnson, *cl up, dsptd ld frm 4th, wnt on bef 2 out, jnd last and sn rdn, hdd r-in, rallied*............................. (5 to 2 op 7 to 4) 2
3002[3] D'ARBLAY STREET (Ire) 5-10-11 (7*) S McDougall, *settled in last pl, improved to track ldrs 4 out, rdn 2 out, sn outpcd*..........................(50 to 1 op 20 to 1) 3
2387 GRAND PASHA (Ire) 6-11-4 R Garritty, *hld up in tch, effrt and shaken up bef 2 out, wknd betw last two.* ....(50 to 1 op 16 to 1) 4
2500 CLARET AND GOLD 7-11-4 B Storey, *slight ld aftr 1st, jnd 4th, hdd bef 2 out, rdn and grad wknd.* ....(100 to 1 op 33 to 1) 5

29074 GREAT EASEBY (Ire) 4-10-8 A Merrigan, *not fluent, led to 1st, chsd ldrs, reminders and drpd rear aftr 7th, hit 9th, sn lost tch, tld off.* ....(17 to 2 op 8 to 1 tchd 7 to 1 and 9 to 1) 6
Dist: Nk, 20l, 3½l, 5l, dist. 6m 16.50s. a 34.50s (6 Ran).
(David Bell), Mrs M Reveley

3127 Arthur Stephenson Memorial Handicap Chase (5-y-o and up) £7,067 3m ....(3:15)

2747 COGENT [152] 10-11-9 (5*) D Fortt, *made all, wl clr frm 5th, pressed 3 out, ran on strly from last, readily.* ....(9 to 4 op 7 to 4 tchd 5 to 2) 1
28326 ARMAGRET [130] 9-10-6 L Wyer, *chsd clr ldr, took clr order 6 out, ev ch frm 3 out, rdn aftr nxt, outpcd r-in.* ....(6 to 4 fav tchd 13 to 8) 2
28316 HE WHO DARES WINS [124] 11-10-0 C Grant, *sn beh, drvn alng and lost tch strting fnl circuit, styd on frm 3 out, nvr dngrs.*.............................(9 to 4 op 5 to 2) 3
2906 HOUXTY LAD [124] 8-10-0 B Storey, *not fluent, struggling to keep up fnl circuit, tld off*...... (50 to 1 op 33 to 1) 4
2832 BISHOPDALE [124] 13-10-0 A Dobbin, *hld up, took clr order fnl circuit, rdn alng bef 5 out, lost tch aftr nxt, tld off*..................................(20 to 1 op 33 to 1) 5
Dist: 6l, 25l, 20l, dist. 5m 59.40s. a 9.40s (5 Ran).
SR: 54/26/ (Pell-Mell Partners), J A Glover

3128 Northern Champion Juvenile Handicap Hurdle (4-y-o) £6,937 2m 110yds ....(3:45)

29722 BALLON [85] 10-8 B Storey, *patiently rdn, relentless prog frm 2 out, ridden to ld last 50 yards, styd on wl.* (7 to 1) 1
27833 WEAVER GEORGE (Ire) [83] 10-6 P Niven, *settled on ins, effrt and drvn alng aftr 3 out, led betw last 2, hng lft frm last, hdd last 50 yards.* ....(9 to 1 op 8 to 1 tchd 10 to 1) 2
2828* OUTSET (Ire) [98] 11-0 (7*) Mr C Bonner, *led, hit 5th, hdd 2 out, rallied and ev ch last, kpt on same pace.* ....(11 to 4 fav op 3 to 1 tchd 5 to 2) 3
29036 COMBELLINO [81] 10-1 (3*) D Bentley, *tucked away beh ldrs, outpcd and drvn alng 4 out, styd on betw last 2, fnshd wl*............(12 to 1 op 10 to 1 tchd 14 to 1) 4
28103 GENSERIC (Fr) [90] 10-13 R Garritty, *chsd ldr, improved to ld 2 out, sn hdd, unbl to quicken frm last.* ....(7 to 1 op 6 to 1) 5
29693 RICH LIFE (Ire) [101] 11-5 (5*) D Fortt, *in tch on ins, drvn alng aftr 3 out, outpcd bef nxt*.......(6 to 1 op 7 to 1) 6
3034 IJAB (Can) [77] 10-0 A Dobbin, *chsd ldg grp, drpd rear 3rd, nvr dngrs aftr*......................(11 to 1 op 10 to 1) 7
2972* DEVILRY [91] 11-0 J Callaghan, *chsd ldg bunch, drvn alng bef 2 out, sn btn*...................(6 to 1 op 5 to 1) 8
26946 BAJAN AFFAIR [80] 10-0 (3*) P Williams, *hld up, hit 1st, struggling to keep up aftr 4 out, tld off.* ....(16 to 1 op 14 to 1) 9
27453 LEGAL ARTIST (Ire) [92] 11-1 L Wyer, *nvr far away, drvn alng bef 2 out, wknd quickly.* ....(13 to 2 op 8 to 1 tchd 6 to 1) 10
Dist: 1½l, 1½l, ½l, 2½l, 5l, 3½l, 1½l, 6l, 25l. 4m 4.40s. a 11.40s (10 Ran).
SR: 31/27/40/22/28/34/6/18/1/ (Whitworth Racing), M Dods

3129 Bellingham Novices' Chase (5-y-o and up) £2,723 2m 110yds.......... (4:15)

2829* FULL O'PRAISE (NZ) 7-11-8 L Wyer, *settled on ins, mstk 1st, improved to join issue 7th, led 9th, ran on wl fnl 3.* ....(13 to 8 jt-fav op 11 to 8) 1
27383 GOLDEN ISLE 10-11-2 B Storey, *led, jnd 7th, hdd 9th, rallied and ev ch last 3, one pace last 100 yards.* ....(13 to 8 jt-fav op 7 to 4 tchd 6 to 4) 2
28924 HIGHLANDMAN 8-11-2 A Dobbin, *handily plcd, blun tenth and sn drvn alng and outpcd, styd on frm last.* ....(5 to 1 op 4 to 1) 3
VICARIDGE 7-11-2 G Harker, *hld up, blun badly 4th, struggling 8th, styd on wl frm 2 out, nvr dngrs.* ....(16 to 1 op 14 to 1) 4
29267 SUPER SANDY 7-10-11 K Johnson, *trkd ldr, lost pl aftr 3rd, struggling to keep up bef 4 out, no imprsn.* ....(66 to 1 op 33 to 1) 5
22185 BE AMBITIOUS (Ire) 6-11-2 A Merrigan, *nvr far away, effrt aftr 4 out, wknd frm nxt*..........(33 to 1 op 25 to 1) 6
2892 GRAZEMBER 7-11-2 R Garritty, *cl up till outpcd bef 4 out, sn struggling, tld off*..............(16 to 1 op 12 to 1) 7
Dist: 2½l, 3½l, ¾l, 25l, 2½l, 15l. 4m 10.10s. a 9.10s (7 Ran).
SR: 36/27/23/22/ (Lord Zetland), P Calver

3130 Ulgham Handicap Hurdle (4-y-o and up) £2,827 2½m................(4:45)

2830 NORTHUMBRIAN KING [102] 8-10-4 J Callaghan, *nvr far away, jnd issue bef 3 out, led before nxt, ran on gmely whn hrd-pressed r-in*...(11 to 2 op 5 to 1 tchd 6 to 1) 1
29564 NOTABLE EXCEPTION [100] 5-9-11 (5*) S Mason, *patiently rdn, swtchd ins entering strt, sn ridden and outpcd, styd on wl last 100 yards*.......(7 to 2 fav tchd 4 to 1) 2
2502 FORWARD GLEN [98] 7-10-0 K Johnson, *nvr far away, improved to chase wnr bef 2 out, chlgd two out, drvn alng and kpt on frm last*..........(16 to 1 op 20 to 1) 3
29982 BONANZA [123] 7-11-11 R Hodge, *ran in snatches, drvn alng frm 4th, improved und pres bef last, one pace r-in.* ....(11 to 2 op 9 to 2 tchd 6 to 1) 4
23222 LEADING PROSPECT [110] 7-10-12 B Storey, *trkd ldrs on ins, effrt and rdn betw last 2, no extr r-in.* ....(4 to 1 tchd 9 to 2) 5
820 HURDY [115] 7-10-12 (5*) Mr D Parker, *co'red up beh ldrs, took clr order bef 3 out, sn pushed alng, hng lft and btn before last 2*..............................(5 to 1 op 4 to 1) 6
2788 TEMPLE GARTH [99] 5-10-1 C Hawkins, *made most till hdd bef 2 out, sn btn*........(9 to 1 op 8 to 1 tchd 10 to 1) 7
17289 MANGROVE MIST (Ire) [98] 6-10-0 A Dobbin, *settled rear, improved bef 3 out, sn rdn alng, btn whn blun nxt, tld off*..................................(12 to 1 op 10 to 1) 8
1487 SUNSET REINS FREE [98] 9-10-0 L Wyer, *wth ldr, drpd rear 5th, pld up bef 7th*............(14 to 1 op 12 to 1) pu
Dist: Nk, ½l, 2½l, 2½l, 30l, 1½l, dist. 5m 0.20s. a 17.20s (9 Ran).
(Mrs K Walton), Mrs K Walton

UTTOXETER (soft)
Saturday March 19th

Going Correction: PLUS 1.25 sec. per fur. (races 1,6,7), PLUS 1.55 (2,3,4,5)

3131 Centurion Commercials Claiming Hurdle (4-y-o and up) £2,320 2m (2:00)

2790* STYLUS 5-10-11 (7*) F Leahy, *hld up, hdwy appr 3 out, rdn to ld r-in, quickened clr.* ....(8 to 1 op 5 to 1 tchd 9 to 1) 1
2418* ROSGILL 8-11-0 A Maguire, *hld up in tch, chalg whn hit last, one pace r-in*..............(7 to 2 fav op 3 to 1) 2
28703 KANNDABIL (bl) 7-11-1 C Llewellyn, *made most frm second, und pres last, hdd and no extr r-in.* ....(5 to 1 tchd 11 to 2) 3
29025 DON'T FORGET MARIE (Ire) 4-9-12 (3*) A Procter, *hld up, hdwy 3 out, styd on, nvr nrr.* ....(14 to 1 tchd 16 to 1 and 12 to 1) 4
27179 CASTLE SECRET 8-11-1 (5*) Mr D McCain, *hld up in rear, hdwy 3 out, styd on, nvr nrr.* ....(9 to 1 op 10 to 1 tchd 12 to 1) 5
29335 NELTEGRITY 5-11-6 Peter Caldwell, *hld up, hdwy 4th, jnd ldrs 3 out, ev ch whn blun last, not reco'r.* ....(7 to 1 op 5 to 1) 6
2214 SMART DEBUTANTE (Ire) 5-10-7 (3*) T Eley, *mid-div, rdn appr 5th, no hdwy frm 3 out*........................(33 to 1) 7
2992 DJEBEL PRINCE 7-11-3 J Osborne, *chsd ldrs till wknd appr 3 out*......................(7 to 1 tchd 15 to 2) 8
29338 BRIGGS LAD (Ire) (bl) 5-11-7 N Mann, *mid-div, lost tch 4 out*..............................(50 to 1 op 33 to 1) 9
28396 SCHWEPPES TONIC 8-10-13 D J Burchell, *trkd ldrs, wnt second appr 3 out, wknd quickly bef nxt*...... (12 to 1) 10
29294 BAND SARGEANT (Ire) 5-11-0 N Doughty, *in tch till wknd 4 out, tld off*..................................(14 to 1) 11
21675 MISTY GREY 5-10-6 (7*) S Lycett, *al beh, tld off.* (100 to 1) 12
2802 DALEHOUSE LANE 6-10-13 Gary Lyons, *al beh, tld off.* ....(100 to 1) 13
2790 SPORTING IDOL 9-10-6 (7*) R Walker, *prmnt to 4th, sn rdn, wknd aftr nxt, tld off whn pld up bef 2 out.* ....(50 to 1) pu
28047 GLOSSY 7-10-6 (7*) G Robertson, *led to second, disputing ld whn jmpd rght 5th, sn wknd, tld off when pld up bef 2 out*..............................(25 to 1 op 20 to 1) pu
Dist: 5l, 1l, nk, 3½l, 4l, 12l, 4l, 2l, 4l, 10l. 4m 8.90s. a 29.90s (15 Ran).
(Mattie O'Toole), M C Chapman

3132 St Modwen Handicap Chase (0-145 5-y-o and up) £5,312 2m 5f......(2:30)

3041 LUMBERJACK (USA) [125] (bl) 10-10-10 J Osborne, *trkd ldr to 3rd, hit 9th, led on bit 3 out, clr whn hit nxt, readily.* ....(14 to 1 op 10 to 1) 1
27484 GENERAL PERSHING [143] 8-12-0 N Doughty, *led, pushed alng appr 4 out, hdd nxt, one pace.* ....(6 to 4 fav op 5 to 4) 2
27262 LAKE TEEREEN [123] 9-10-8 T Grantham, *trkd ldr frm 3rd, rdn 4 out, one pace from nxt*.......(15 to 8 op 7 to 4) 3
27477 ROMANY KING [138] 10-11-9 Richard Guest, *al last, rcd wide, in tch till rdn and wknd appr 3 out.* ....(100 to 30 op 3 to 1 tchd 7 to 2) 4
Dist: 8l, 1½l, 20l. 5m 41.30s. a 41.30s (4 Ran).
SR: -/5/-/-/ (Elite Racing Club), C R Egerton

3133 Bet With The Tote Novices' Chase Final Handicap (6-y-o and up) £14,395 3¼m.......................... (3:00)

28542 TARAMOSS [106] 7-11-8 J Osborne, *jmpd wl, made virtually all, rdn and styd on well frm 2 out.* ....(9 to 2 fav op 5 to 1) 1

2913² SUFFOLK ROAD [102] 7-11-4 N Doughty, *prmnt, second whn hit 13th, sn in tch ag'n, outpcd 4 out, rallied and wnt second 2 out, no imprsn r-in*.............(14 to 1) 2

2668⁶ DONT TELL THE WIFE [92] 8-10-8 D Bridgwater, *hld up rear, hdwy 15th, chsd wnr 4 out till wknd 2 out.*
....(12 to 1) 3

2854* HILL TRIX [100] 8-11-2 A Tory, *nvr far away, mstk 13th, ev ch 4 out, one pace nxt.* (9 to 1 op 8 to 1 tchd 10 to 1) 4

2832⁵ FARDROSS [108] 8-11-10 N Williamson, *wtd wth in tch, hdwy appr 4 out, rdn nxt, sn btn...* (15 to 2 op 5 to 1) 5

2767 YOUR WELL [107] 8-11-9 B Clifford, *in tch, hit 15th, hit 5 out, wknd appr 2 out*.....................(10 to 1) 6

2958* HUDSON BAY TRADER (USA) [99] 7-11-1 Mrs A Farrell, *in tch till wknd 14th, tld off*...............(14 to 1 op 12 to 1) 7

2647⁵ LUCKY LANE [103] (bl) 10-11-5 C Maude, *frnt rnk till wknd 14th, tld off whn pld up bef 2 out.*
....(14 to 1 op 12 to 1) pu

2958 COMEDY SPY [100] 10-11-2 M Dwyer, *rcd wide, wknd 12th, pld up bef nxt......* (6 to 1 op 7 to 1 tchd 8 to 1) pu

2355⁶ JOLLY JAUNT [84] 9-10-0 C Llewellyn, *mid-div to 9th, sn beh, tld off whn pld up bef 4 out.*
....(7 to 1 op 8 to 1 tchd 9 to 1) pu

2958⁴ SUPPOSIN [93] 6-10-9 Richard Guest, *blun 4th, mstk 13th, sn rear, tld off whn pld up bef 2 out.*
....(25 to 1 op 20 to 1) pu

2854⁵ ONE MORE RUN [71] 7-10-13 B Powell, *al beh, tld off whn pld up bef 2 out.*...............(10 to 1 op 7 to 1) pu
Dist: 4l, 10l, 1½l, 15l, 1l, dist. 7m 19.50s. a 63.50s (12 Ran).
(Howard Parker), J A C Edwards

3134

Tetley Bitter Midlands National Handicap Chase Grade 3 (6-y-o and up) £32,810 4¼m.................(3:35)

2805² GLENBROOK D'OR [118] 10-10-0 B Clifford, *hld up rear, hdwy 18th, mstk 3 out, styd on strly to ld appr last, drw clr r-in*..............................(10 to 1 op 8 to 1) 1

2987³ ITS A CRACKER [120] 10-10-2 C O'Dwyer, *hld up, hdwy 18th, led sn aftr 3 out, rdn and hdd appr last, kpt on one pace*.........................(20 to 1 tchd 25 to 1) 2

2701* CALLMECHA [128] (bl) 9-10-10 M Dwyer, *hld up, hdwy frm 16th, ev ch whn awkward 2 out, hit last, no extr.*
..................................(10 to 1 tchd 12 to 1) 3

2805³ CYTHERE [118] 10-9-12¹ (3*) P Hide, *led second to 4th, led 18th to 5 out, ev ch whn mstk 3 out, one pace.*
..................................(20 to 1 op 16 to 1) 4

2831* SHRADEN LEADER [122] 9-10-4 N Williamson, *hld up in tch, hdwy 17th, led 5 out, mstk and hdd sn aftr 3 out, wknd.*............(4 to 1 fav op 7 to 2 tchd 3 to 1) 5

2495* GOLD CAP (Fr) [120] 9-10-2 C Maude, *in tch to 14th, one pace frm 3 out.*..............................(20 to 1) 6

2460* JUST SO [120] (bl) 11-10-2² S Burrough, *al beh, tld off 5 out.*...........................(10 to 1 op 8 to 1) 7

2772³ GREEN TIMES [118] 9-10-0 C Swan, *al beh, mstk 13th, tld off*...........................(20 to 1 op 16 to 1) 8

2831⁵ MISTER ED [129] 11-10-11 D Morris, *mid-div, rdn appr 17th, btn 5 out, tld off whn pld up bef 2 out.*
....(8 to 1 op 7 to 1) pu

2460 RIVERSIDE BOY [142] 11-11-10 C Llewellyn, *prmnt, led 4th to 18th, rdn and wknd appr 5 out, tld off whn pld up bef 3 out.*...............(11 to 1 op 10 to 1 tchd 12 to 1) pu

2460 INTO THE RED [129] 10-10-11 A Maguire, *trkd ldrs, rdn and wknd quickly appr 3 out, pld up bef 2 out.*
....(13 to 2 op 7 to 1) pu

2748³ MERRY MASTER [125] 10-10-7 Gee Armytage, *trkd ldr frm 5th, led briefly 16th, wknd 5 out, pld up bef nxt.*
....(12 to 1 tchd 14 to 1) pu

2506* SUPERIOR FINISH [130] 8-10-12 J Osborne, *prmnt, rdn 16th, wknd 5 out, tld off whn pld up bef 2 out.*
....(7 to 1 op 13 to 2 tchd 8 to 1) pu

2813* VELEDA II (Fr) [118] 7-9-12³ (5*) J Burke, *led to second, styd prmnt, wkng whn blun 4 out, tld off when pld up bef 2 out.*..(11 to 1) pu

2893³ GATHERING TIME [118] 8-9-8¹ (7*) Miss V Haigh, *mstks in rear, rdn 11th, tld off whn pld up bef 4 out...*(100 to 1) pu
Dist: 5l, nk, 5l, 25l, 7l, 4l, 15l. 9m 23.40s. a 55.40s (15 Ran).
SR: 45/42/49/34/13/4/ (Tim Leadbeater), A J Wilson

3135

Tattersalls Mares Only Novices' Chase Final Limited Handicap (6-y-o and up) £7,067 2m 5f...........(4:10)

2067⁸ NORSTOCK [98] 7-11-5 A Maguire, *led second to 8th, led 5 out, styd on strly*.......(7 to 1 op 8 to 1 tchd 13 to 2) 1

2654 KIWI VELOCITY (NZ) [95] 7-11-2 L Harvey, *led to second, led 8th to 5 out, rdn aftr nxt, kpt one pace.* (10 to 1) 2

2953* RIVER PEARL [103] 9-11-10 N Williamson, *hld up rear, hdwy frm 8th, chlgd 3 out, rdn and wknd nxt, fnshd tired.*...........................(3 to 1 fav tchd 100 to 30) 3

2946² PRUDENT PEGGY [87] 7-10-8 J Frost, *al prmnt, dsptd ld 5 out, one pace nxt.*...........................(11 to 2) 4

2814⁵ CELTIC SONG [44] 7-11-1 Mrs A Farrell, *beh till hdwy tenth, wknd 4 out, tld off*......................(12 to 1) 5

2739 OVER THE ISLAND (Ire) [86] 6-10-7 C Llewellyn, *blun and uns rdr 1st.*..............................(10 to 1 op 8 to 1) ur

2851⁵ KETTI [86] (bl) 9-10-7 C Swan, *in tch till wknd 5 out, tld off whn pld up bef 3 out.*..........(16 to 1 op 10 to 1) pu

2293 CHICHELL'S HURST [91] 8-10-12 A Carroll, *mstks in rear, blun 9th, tld off whn pld up bef 11th.*
....(17 to 2 op 6 to 1 tchd 9 to 1) pu

2809⁴ PLAYFUL JULIET (Can) [86] 6-10-7 Pat Caldwell, *al beh, tld off whn blun 3 out, pld up bef nxt.*(16 to 1 op 14 to 1) pu

2816² NICKLUP [97] 7-11-4 B Powell, *beh whn rdn 8th, blun nxt, sn tld off, pld up bef 4 out......*(7 to 1 op 5 to 1) pu

2932* CRUISING ON [84] 7-10-7 M Dwyer, *prmnt, blun 9th, sn beh, tld off whn pld up bef 5 out...*(14 to 1 op 12 to 1) pu
Dist: 12l, 3½l, 1l, 30l. 5m 51.00s. a 51.00s (11 Ran).
(Nick Quesnel), J White

3136

Ladbroke Handicap Hurdle (0-135 5-y-o and up) £7,782 2¾m 110yds...(4:40)

2830⁷ ATTADALE [126] 6-11-8 A Maguire, *hld up gng wl, hdwy 6th, led 3 out, drw clr frm nxt, easily.*
....(6 to 1 op 5 to 1 tchd 13 to 2) 1

2862⁷ FAST THOUGHTS [109] 7-10-5 P Holley, *al prmnt, led appr 6th to 3 out, kpt on one pace.*
....(9 to 2 op 4 to 1 tchd 5 to 1) 2

2528 ISABEAU [104] 7-10-0 A S Smith, *prmnt, led 3rd till appr 6th, ev ch 3 out, one pace.*......(14 to 1 op 12 to 1) 3

2961² COUTURE STOCKINGS [104] 10-10-0 N Williamson, *in tch, ev ch whn mstk 3 out, rdn and wknd.*
....(8 to 1 tchd 9 to 1) 4

2830⁸ SPROWSTON BOY [110] 11-10-6 W Worthington, *led to 1st, rdn 4th, sn beh, styd on one pace frm 3 out...* (33 to 1) 5

2172 POWLEYVALE [107] 7-10-3 M Dwyer, *al beh.*
....(20 to 1 op 16 to 1) 6

3038² SO PROUD [119] 9-11-1 C Swan, *hld up, some hdwy aftr 6th, rdn 4 out, sn btn, tld off.*
....(15 to 8 fav op 7 to 4 tchd 2 to 1) 7

2486⁴ BEAUCHAMP GRACE [132] 5-11-9 (5*) J Burke, *mstk second, al beh, tld off.*...........(16 to 1 op 10 to 1) 8

3028 ROCHESTOWN LASS [104] (v) 8-10-0 N Mann, *led 1st to 3rd, frnt rnk till rdn and wknd aftr 6th, tld off.*
....(33 to 1 op 25 to 1) 9

2600⁴ HOLY JOE [116] 12-10-12 B Clifford, *al beh, tld off 5th, pld up bef 3 out.*...........(20 to 1 op 14 to 1) pu

2385 DOOLAR (USA) [106] 7-10-2 D Bridgwater, *mid-div, beh 6th, tld off whn pld up bef 2 out...*(33 to 1 op 25 to 1) pu

2496 THE GOLFING CURATE [104] 9-9-12¹ (3*) P Hide, *al rear, rdn 4 out, tld off whn pld up bef 2 out.*
....(16 to 1 op 14 to 1 tchd 20 to 1) pu

2792* SMITH TOO (Ire) [111] 6-10-7 J Osborne, *in tch till wknd 4 out, tld off whn pld up bef 2 out.*
....(10 to 1 op 8 to 1 tchd 11 to 1) pu
Dist: 10l, 2l, 7l, 15l, 4l, 30l, nk, dist. 5m 42.10s. a 31.10s (13 Ran).
SR: 64/37/30/23/14/7/-/1/-/ (C H McGhie), L Lungo

3137

Elite Racing Club 'National Hunt' Novices' Hurdle (4-y-o and up) £2,407 2½m 110yds....................(5:10)

2823⁴ CORNER BOY 7-11-9 A Maguire, *hld up rear, rdn and hdwy appr 3 out, led sn aftr last, edgd lft, all out.*
....(6 to 5 fav op 5 to 4 tchd 11 to 10) 1

2897² EVEN BLUE (Ire) 6-10-11 (5*) Mr D McCain, *sn trkd ldr, ev ch last, short of room and swtchd rght r-in, ran on.*
....(9 to 1 op 12 to 1) 2

2871* THE FROG PRINCE (Ire) 6-11-9 C Llewellyn, *al prmnt, led 6th till sn aftr last, no extr.*
....(4 to 1 op 3 to 1 tchd 9 to 2) 3

1769 JIMMY O'DEA 7-11-2 N Williamson, *led to 6th, wknd 3 out.*.............................(33 to 1) 4

2817³ YOUNG BALDRIC 7-11-2 I Lawrence, *pld hrd, hdwy 5th, rdn and wknd appr 3 out.*........(14 to 1 op 12 to 1 tchd 16 to 1) 5

2796* MAN OF THE GRANGE 8-11-2 Diane Clay, *chsd ldr to 1st, beh h'wy, tld off.*............(100 to 1 op 33 to 1) 6

2796* MARSHALL SPARKS 7-11-9 M Foster, *pld hrd, in tch whn f 4 out.*........................(3 to 1 op 9 to 4) f

JUNIOR ROGERS 6-11-2 R Marley, *rear whn hit second, rdn appr 6th, sn tld off, pld up bef 3 out.*
....(10 to 1 op 33 to 1) pu
Dist: ¾l, ¾l, 20l, dist, 6l. 5m 28.80s. a 45.80s (8 Ran).
(Mrs E W Wilson), D Nicholson

LINGFIELD (A.W) (std)
Monday March 21st
Going Correction: NIL

3138

Thyme National Hunt Flat Race (4,5,6-y-o) £1,436 2m.................(4:40)

2546² QUEENFORD BELLE 4-10-3 (3*) T Jenks, *hld up, led 7 fs out, drw wl clr frm 4 out, eased nr finish.*
....(6 to 4 on tchd 5 to 4 on and Evens) 1

DRUMMOND WARRIOR (Ire) 5-11-5 D Meade, *hld up in last pl, chsd wnr o'r 6 fs out, rdn sn outpcd.*
....(7 to 4 op Evens tchd 9 to 4) 2

ROSIE-B 4-10-1 (5*) J Burke, *led aftr one furlong, hdd 7 out, lost tch 5 out.*.............(33 to 1 op 20 to 1) 3

2716⁴ WINNOW 4-9-13 (7") P McLoughlin, *pld hrd, led for one furlong, prmnt till lost tch 5 out, tld off.*
....(5 to 1 op 7 to 2) 4
Dist: 15l, 15l, dist. 3m 36.20s. (4 Ran).

(R A B Whittle), P J Hobbs

NEWCASTLE (good to firm)
Monday March 21st
Going Correction: MINUS 0.05 sec. per fur. (races 1,2,4,6), NIL (3,5)

3139
Sandy Lane Conditional Jockeys' Claiming Handicap Hurdle (4-y-o and up) £2,284 2m 110yds......... (2:20)

2891² STATION EXPRESS (Ire) [65] 6-10-3 A Larnach, *settled midfield, hdwy appr 3 out, hng lft and rdn to ld fnl 100 yards, styd on......(7 to 2 fav tchd 4 to 1 and 3 to 1)* 1
2254⁹ CHARLYCIA [75] (v) 6-10-6 (7") M Clarke, *sn chasing clr ldr, led 2 out, hit last, hdd fnl 100 yards, no extr.*
....(10 to 1 op 7 to 1) 2
2891 CHADWICK'S GINGER [82] 6-11-6 A Thornton, *chsd ldrs, hdwy aftr 2 out, ch nr 2 out, no extr nr finish.*
................................(40 to 1 op 33 to 1 tchd 50 to 1) 3
2321 HIGHFIELD PRINCE [72] 8-10-5 (5") K Davies, *settled midfield, hdwy aftr 3 out, kpt on same pace nxt.*
....(14 to 1 op 16 to 1) 4
2870⁴ IRISH FLASHER [83] 7-11-7 P Williams, *settled midfield, effrt aftr 3 out, kpt on same pace....(7 to 1 op 9 to 2)* 5
2422⁴ BARSAL (Ire) [65] 4-10-0 (3") F Leahy, *beh, hdwy aftr 3 out, not rch ldrs...................(16 to 1 op 12 to 1)* 6
2970⁴ NICHOLAS PLANT [74] 5-10-12 S Lyons, *beh, styd on frm 3 out, nvr dngrs....................(12 to 1 op 8 to 1)* 7
2907⁵ ON GOLDEN POND (Ire) [75] 4-10-13 N Bentley, *early reminders, sn beh, kpt on frm 2 out, nvr dngrs.*
....(6 to 1 op 4 to 1) 8
2907³ THATCHED (Ire) [75] (v) 4-10-13 D J Moffatt, *hld up, effrt aftr 3 out, no hdwy.....(11 to 1 op 9 to 1 tchd 14 to 1)* 9
2891 BEACH PATROL (Ire) [62] 6-9-10³ (7") S Melrose, *in tch, hdwy hfwy, chsd ldrs aftr 3 out, wknd after nxt.*
....(33 to 1) 10
TOURAQUE (Fr) [62] 9-9-7 (7") I Jardine, *prmnt till wknd aftr 3 out......................(100 to 1)* 11
3061³ CARLA ADAMS [62] 8-10-0 J Supple, *pld hrd, hmpd and mstk 3rd, sn beh........................(20 to 1 op 14 to 1)* 12
1148⁶ TOP VILLAIN [90] 8-12-0 P Midgley, *led, clr 3rd, hdd 2 out, sn rdn and btn.........(25 to 1 op 20 to 1 tchd 33 to 1)* 13
2905⁷ DOLLY PRICES [62] 9-10-0 P Waggott, *chsd ldrs, wknd appr 3 out....................(20 to 1 op 25 to 1)* 14
2970⁶ SEA PET [62] 5-10-0 D Bentley, *chsd ldrs till wknd appr 3 out..........................(50 to 1 op 33 to 1)* 15
3030⁵ MISS PIMPERNEL [82] 4-11-6 B Harding, *chsd ldrs, reminders hfwy, wknd appr 3 out.*
................................(25 to 1 op 33 to 1 tchd 20 to 1) 16
2903 STAR RAGE (Ire) [83] (bl) 4-11-4 (3") J Driscoll, *mid-div till wknd aftr 3 out.................(8 to 1 op 5 to 1)* 17
Dist: 1½l, nk, 4l, 2l, nk, 1½l, nk, 4l, 3½l. 3m 58.50s. a 5.50s (17 Ran).

SR: 12/20/26/12/21/2/5/4/3/

(Mrs Gwen Smith), B Ellison

3140
EBF 'National Hunt' Novices' Hurdle Qualifier (5,6,7-y-o) £2,337 2½m (2:50)

2834⁴ CAPENWRAY (Ire) 5-11-0 P Niven, *hld up, hdwy whn hmpd 3 out, led on bit appr last, blun, drvn clr.*
....(7 to 1 op 8 to 1) 1
2812⁵ MAJOR BELL 6-11-10 M Moloney, *slight ld till aftr 5th, led 3 out, hrd pressed nxt, hdd appr last, kpt on, no ch wth wnr..............(8 to 1 op 6 to 1 tchd 9 to 1)* 2
2785* CARNETTO 7-10-12 (7") F Leahy, *nvr far away, trkd ldrs 3 out, sn pushed alng, kpt on same pace.*
....(3 to 1 op 5 to 2) 3
2068 ASTRALEON (Ire) 6-11-0 B Storey, *hld up, hdwy to join ldrs 3 out, dsptd ld nxt, wknd appr last.*
....(14 to 1 op 12 to 1) 4
2459 SCOTTON BANKS (Ire) 5-11-0 L Wyer, *dsptd ld, pushed alng aftr 3 out, wknd.*
................................(11 to 8 fav op Evens tchd 6 to 4) 5
2220⁹ MANOR COURT (Ire) 6-11-0 A Merrigan, *trkd ldrs, effrt appr 3 out, kpt on same pace.............(200 to 1)* 6
2485* TICO GOLD 6-11-0 K Johnson, *in tch, kpt on frm 3 out, nvr dngrs....................................(50 to 1)* 7
2785⁶ CATCH THE PIGEON 5-10-6 (3") D J Moffatt, *chsd ldrs, wknd appr 3 out, tld off....................(100 to 1)* 8
2485⁶ HICKSONS CHOICE (Ire) 6-10-11 (3") A Thornton, *chsd ldrs, drvn alng appr 3 out, sn wknd, tld off.*
................................(33 to 1 op 50 to 1) 9
1097 JUMPING CACTUS 5-11-0 Mr C Mulhall, *al beh, tld off..........................(100 to 1)* 10
2741 BRAVE AND TENDER (Ire) 5-11-0 A Dobbin, *al beh, tld off..............(20 to 1 op 12 to 1)* 11
2951⁴ OAT COUTURE 6-11-0 C Grant, *sn beh, tld off...........(14 to 1 op 12 to 1)* 12
1722⁶ RHYMING THOMAS 6-11-0 R Garritty, *trkd ldrs, led aftr 5th, hdd and f 3 out...........(50 to 1 op 100 to 1)* f

2106 SAMS-THE-MAN 6-11-0 C Hawkins, *sn beh, tld off whn pld up bef 2 out................(100 to 1 op 200 to 1)* pu
2252 ANOTHER SHOON 7-10-9 (5") J Supple, *sn beh, tld off whn pld up bef 2 out........(300 to 1 op 200 to 1)* pu
Dist: 7l, 5l, 7l, 7l, 2½l, 5l, 30l, 5l, 12l, 5l. 4m 53.20s. a 10.20s (15 Ran).

(Mrs Linda Woodward), R F Fisher

3141
Hazlerigg Handicap Chase (0-125 5-y-o and up) £2,736 2½m...... (3:20)

2832 SIR PETER LELY [120] (bl) 7-11-7 (7") Mr C Bonner, *led to 2 out, second and hld whn lft in ld last, drvn out.*
................................(13 to 8 fav op 6 to 4 tchd 7 to 4) 1
2437⁵ ABSAILOR [93] (v) 10-10-14 (3") P Williams, *cl up, dsptd ld 8th till wknd appr 2 out, lft second at last.*
....(11 to 1 op 8 to 1) 2
2222⁸ KUSHBALOO [115] 9-11-9 B Storey, *in tch till outpcd aftr 4 out, no dngr after...................(9 to 2 op 3 to 1)* 3
2151⁹ STEPFASTER [103] 9-10-8 (3") A Thornton, *in tch till outpcd aftr 4 out, no dngr after.....(14 to 1 op 12 to 1)* 4
2953⁶ ZAM BEE [100] 8-10-8 C Grant, *chsd ldrs, pushed alng hfwy, wknd appr 4 out...........(10 to 1 op 8 to 1)* 5
1921⁴ NIGHT GUEST [99] 12-10-7 A Dobbin, *hld up, pushed alng hfwy, wknd appr 4 out..(9 to 1 op 8 to 1 tchd 10 to 1)* 6
2786 STRONG SOUND [100] 7-10-8 K Johnson, *sn tracking ldrs, 2nd, 4 ls clr whn f last...(20 to 1 op 14 to 1)* f
2886* DEADLINE [92] (bl) 11-10-0 Miss J Thurlow, *hit second, sn beh, tld off whn pld up bef 2 out..(9 to 1 op 7 to 1)* pu
Dist: 3½l, 15l, 6l, 10l, 6l. 4m 56.90s. a 5.90s (8 Ran).
SR: 41/10/17/-/-/

(John Doyle Construction Limited), M D Hammond

3142
Melton Handicap Hurdle (0-135 4-y-o and up) £2,788 3m............(3:50)

3028 POLISHING [117] (v) 7-11-0 (5") S Lyons, *made most to 2 out, rallied to ld aftr last, pushed out.*
....(9 to 2 op 3 to 1) 1
3057* HUSO [98] 6-10-0 (4ex) J Callaghan, *hld up, hdwy to ld 2 out, sn rdn, hdd aftr last, no extr.*
....(2 to 1 fav op 7 to 4) 2
3130⁵ LEADING PROSPECT [110] 7-10-12 B Storey, *nvr far away, ev ch 2 out, kpt on same pace.*
....(9 to 2 op 7 to 1 tchd 5 to 1) 3
2954³ VALIANT DASH [98] 8-9-9 (5") Mr D Parker, *cl up, dsptd ld 9th till wknd appr 2 out...........(8 to 1 op 6 to 1)* 4
1585 JESTERS PROSPECT [108] 10-10-7 (3") P Williams, *prmnt till wknd appr 2 out..............(14 to 1 tchd 16 to 1)* 5
3028 TROODOS [110] 8-10-12 D Wilkinson, *in tch, effrt whn mstk 3 out, wknd appr nxt.*
....(17 to 2 op 7 to 1 tchd 10 to 1) 6
914⁷ SEXY MOVER [98] 7-10-0 K Johnson, *in tch till wknd aftr 9th......................(11 to 1 op 7 to 1 tchd 10 to 1)* 7
2954 THISTLEHOLM [107] 8-10-6 (3") D Bentley, *trkd ldrs, wknd appr 2 out.................(20 to 1 op 14 to 1)* 8
PALANQUIN [102] (bl) 12-10-4 Miss P Robson, *sn beh, tld off whn pld up bef 3 out, lme.......(12 to 1 op 8 to 1)* pu
Dist: 4l, 4l, 6l, sht-hd, 20l, 15l, 20l. 5m 45.20s. a 3.20s (9 Ran).
SR: 47/24/32/14/24/6/

(J D Gordon), M D Hammond

3143
Brunton Novices' Chase (5-y-o and up) £2,509 2½m............... (4:20)

2873² SILVER STICK 7-11-3 R Garritty, *trkd ldrs, effrt appr 2 out, styd on wl und pres to ld last strds.*
................................(5 to 4 on op 7 to 4 on) 1
2814² GREENFIELD MANOR 7-11-3 A Merrigan, *cl up, led 2 out, rdn aftr last, ct last strds.........(7 to 1 tchd 8 to 1)* 2
2577⁵ SHEILAS HILLCREST 8-11-10 (5") J Supple, *made most to 2 out, wknd.........(13 to 2 op 6 to 1 tchd 7 to 1)* 3
2270⁵ EDEN SUNSET 8-11-3 P Niven, *trkd ldrs, hit 12th, ch whn hit 2 out, sn rdn and btn.*
....(7 to 2 op 5 to 2 tchd 4 to 1) 4
2814 SNOOK POINT 7-11-3 B Storey, *hld up beh, effrt aftr 3 out, no hdwy.......................(25 to 1 op 20 to 1)* 5
KINROYAL 9-10-12 (5") A Roche, *in tch whn f 7th.*
................................(66 to 1 op 50 to 1 tchd 100 to 1) f
Dist: ½l, 10l, 3½l, 4l. 5m 15.40s. a 24.40s (6 Ran).

(Lord Manton), M W Easterby

3144
Newcastle Brown Ale Top Of The North Racing Novices' Handicap Hurdle Qualifier (4-y-o and up) £2,123 2½m....................... (4:50)

1726 SHAWWELL [87] 7-11-2 B Storey, *settled midfield, steady hdwy to ld 2 out, sn clr, cmftbly.....(8 to 1 op 6 to 1)* 1
2812 STRONG DEEL (Ire) [80] 6-10-9 L Wyer, *led to 5th, remained prmnt, styd on wl frm last, no ch wth wnr.*
................................(12 to 1 tchd 14 to 1) 2
2896⁵ FREE TRANSFER (Ire) [90] 5-11-5 A Dobbin, *nvr far away, ev ch 2 out, no extr und pres............(16 to 1)* 3
2974² RED TEMPEST (Ire) [77] 6-10-1 (5") Mr D Parker, *in tch, effrt aftr 3 out, btn whn hmpd last....(12 to 1 op 10 to 1)* 4
2874 ERZADJAN (Ire) [85] (bl) 4-11-0 G McCourt, *dsptd ld led 5th to 2 out, no extr.................(12 to 1 tchd 14 to 1)* 5

2740* FORTUNE'S GIRL [95] 6-11-3 (7*) Mr C Bonner, *hld up, effrt aftr 3 out, styd on frm nxt, nrst finish.*
.................................(9 to 4 fav op 7 to 4 tchd 5 to 2)   6
2735⁵ MONTRAVE [86] 5-11-1 N Doughty, *hld up, hdwy frm 3 out, nvr nr to chal*......................................(16 to 1)   7
2896⁶ GERMAN LEGEND [76] 4-10-5 A Merrigan, *trkd ldrs, ev ch 3 out, wknd*..(25 to 1)   8
2606³ MAHONG [71] 6-10-0 V Slattery, *sn pushed alng and beh, nvr dngrs*...........................(9 to 1 op 8 to 1 tchd 10 to 1)   9
2907² GOLDMIRE [75] 4-10-4 S Turner, *prmnt, dsptd ld 7th till aftr 3 out*.......................................(14 to 1 tchd 12 to 1) 10
3030⁷ PANTO LADY [71] 8-9-7 (7*) Miss S Lamb, *in tch till wknd aftr 7th, tld off*..................................(500 to 1) 11
2810⁸ ADMISSION (Ire) [72] 4-10-1¹ C Grant, *al beh, tld off.*
....(200 to 1) 12
2633 THE PIPE FITTER (Ire) [75] (bl) 6-9-13 (5*) A Roche, *in tch till wknd appr 2 out, tld off*..............(25 to 1 tchd 33 to 1) 13
      CA-KNOWE (Ire) [72] 5-10-1¹ M Moloney, *mstk 1st, al beh, tld off*..........................(100 to 1 op 66 to 1) 14
2874⁴ HIGH MIND (Fr) [88] 5-11-0 (3*) A Thornton, *trkd ldrs, hmpd and hit rail appr second, effrt aftr 3 out, kpt on, disputing second and hld whn f last.*
...................................(9 to 1 op 8 to 1 tchd 10 to 1)   f
2276 JUKE BOX BILLY (Ire) [77] 6-10-3 (3*) A Larnach, *trkd ldrs till ran out 6th*...............(5 to 1 op 6 to 1 tchd 7 to 1) ro
3034⁷ GLASTONDALE [71] 8-10-0 E McKinley, *sn beh, tld off whn pld up bef 7th*...(50 to 1) pu
Dist: 6l, 3½l, 1½l, ½l, ¾l, 3½l, 4l, 4l, 1½l, 25l. 4m 59.10s. a 16.10s (17 Ran).
                                      (Mr J J Straker), J I A Charlton

PLUMPTON (heavy)
Monday March 21st
Going Correction: PLUS 1.90 sec. per fur. (races 1,3,6), PLUS 1.50 (2,4,5)

3145 **Pease Pottage Novices' Hurdle (4-y-o and up) £1,543 2m 1f........... (2:30)**

2621⁴ GOOGLY 5-11-3 A Maguire, *hld up in rear, hdwy whn blun 4 out, hit 2 out, led appr last, easily.*
....(7 to 4 on op 5 to 4 on)   1
3010⁵ SHANAKEE 7-11-2 E Murphy, *cl up, led 4 out till hdd appr last, no ch wth wnr*....(8 to 1 op 12 to 1 tchd 6 to 1)   2
2494 YELLOW CORN 5-10-11 Peter Hobbs, *mstk 3rd, reminders in rear aftr 5th, styd on frm 2 out*..(12 to 1 op 6 to 1)   3
2535 PULMICORT 4-10-8 D Gallagher, *trkd ldrs till wknd aftr 4 out*..............(16 to 1 op 14 to 1 tchd 20 to 1)   4
2717⁶ EAGLES LAIR 8-11-2 S McNeill, *chsd ldrs till wknd 4 out, fnshd tired, tld off*....................(12 to 1 op 5 to 1)   5
      FERENS HALL 7-11-2 N Williamson, *led, sn clr, hdd 4 out, soon wknd, tld off*...................(33 to 1 op 20 to 1)   6
3012⁴ BARGIN BOY 5-11-2 Leesa Long, *hit 5th and reminders aftr, al beh, tld off*......(50 to 1 op 25 to 1 tchd 66 to 1)   7
1549⁸ WANOVOWERS (Ire) 6-11-2 S Smith Eccles, *al prmnt, 3rd and hld whn f 2 out*..................(12 to 1 op 10 to 1)   f
2621 LB'S GIRL 5-10-11 J R Kavanagh, *jmpd badly rght and ran out aftr 1st*............................(100 to 1 op 50 to 1) ro
2619 KING'S GOLD 4-10-8 B Powell, *mid-div, wknd 6th, tld off whn pld up bef 2 out*..............(100 to 1 op 50 to 1) pu
      STARSHADOW 5-10-9 (7*) J Neaves, *mstk 3rd, al beh, tld off whn pld up bef 7th.*
.................................(50 to 1 op 33 to 1 tchd 66 to 1) pu
Dist: 12l, 20l, 10l, dist, 6l. 4m 29.10s. a 37.10s (11 Ran).
SR: 41/28/3/-/-/-/   (Ms M Horan), J White

3146 **Hemsley Orrell Partnership Handicap Chase (0-105 5-y-o and up) £2,831 3m 1f 110yds.................... (3:00)**

2911* BETTY HAYES [103] 10-11-5 (7*) P Carey, *in cl tch, led 8th till hdd 11th, led ag'n 4 out, styd on wl.*
.................................(5 to 2 op 13 to 8 tchd 11 to 4)   1
2758³ SHASTON [100] (bl) 9-11-9 P Holley, *in cl tch, lft in ld aftr 5th, hdd 8th, led 11th till mstk and headed 4 out, one pace*.................................(9 to 2 tchd 5 to 1)   2
2305⁴ MISS FERN [91] 9-10-11 (3*) D Meredith, *hld up in cl tch gng nicely, pushed alng appr 4 out, sn no imprsn.*
....(7 to 2 tchd 4 to 1)   3
2995 THE LEGGETT [105] (bl) 11-12-0 R Bellamy, *led till ran out aftr 5th*.. ro
2911² ROSITARY (Fr) [96] (bl) 11-11-5 J Osborne, *in cl tch, mstk 9th (water), wknd quickly 11th, pld up aftr nxt.*
.................................(7 to 4 fav op 5 to 2) pu
Dist: 10l, 3l. 6m 56.70s. a 44.70s (5 Ran).
SR: 33/20/8/-/-/   (H S Butt), R H Alner

3147 **March Selling Handicap Hurdle (4,5,6-y-o) £1,876 2m 1f.............. (3:30)**

3098⁸ BAYLORD PRINCE (Ire) [75] 6-10-5 M Hoad, *in tch, pushed alng aftr 5th, cld 3 out, rdn and styd on wl to ld nr finish.*....................(5 to 2 co-fav op 2 to 1 tchd 11 to 4)   1
2067 KALAMOSS [70] 5-9-7 (7*) Miss S Mitchell, *made most till hdd nr finish*....................................(8 to 1 op 9 to 1)   2

3098 ACROSS THE CARD [70] 6-10-0 D Gallagher, *led briefly 1st, trkd ldrs, outpcd and rdn alng 6th, styd on appr last.*
....(10 to 1 tchd 12 to 1)   3
2804³ COBB GATE [77] (bl) 6-10-7 M Stevens, *trkd ldrs, hrd rdn appr 2 out, one pace*........(5 to 2 co-fav op 3 to 1)   4
2760² DAYS OF THUNDER [94] 6-11-10 A Maguire, *hld up, cld 3 out, wknd quickly appr last.*................(5 to 2 co-fav op 7 to 1 tchd 11 to 4)   5
3022 BELLE LOCK [70] 9-10-0 J Neaves, *trkd ldrs, pushed alng and ch 3 out, sn wknd.*
.................................(10 to 1 op 5 tchd 66 to 1)   6
2779⁹ ALTESSE ROXANNE [70] 5-10-0⁷ (7*) Mr B Pollock, *jmpd rght, trkd ldrs till wknd 3rd, tld off 7th.*
....(50 to 1 op 33 to 1)   7
3098 FIVE CASTLES [70] 6-10-0 M Perrett, *hld up in rear, hit 3rd and uns rdr*......(25 to 1 op 20 to 1 tchd 33 to 1) ur
Dist: Hd, 12l, 1l, 5l, 20l, dist. 4m 32.70s. a 40.70s (8 Ran).
                                      (Miss J A Ewer), R P C Hoad

3148 **Offham Novices' Chase (5-y-o and up) £2,276 2m................... (4:00)**

2946* LADY GHISLAINE (Fr) 7-11-5 A Maguire, *made all, clr appr last, not extended.*
.................................(11 to 8 on tchd 5 to 4 on and 6 to 4 on)   1
2625³ HANDSOME NED 8-11-4 J Railton, *cl up, reminders aftr 6th, ev ch 3 out, hit nxt, one pace.*
.................................(2 to 1 op 7 to 4 tchd 9 to 4)   2
954   QUEENS CURATE 7-10-13 B Powell, *mstk second, beh, hdwy appr 7th, one pace frm nxt.*
.................................(66 to 1 op 50 to 1 tchd 100 to 1)   3
2432 EXACT ANALYSIS (USA) 8-11-4 G Upton, *cl up, mstk 7th and sn wknd, no ch whn blun last.*
.................................(16 to 1 op 10 to 1 tchd 20 to 1)   4
2934⁷ GREEN WALK 7-10-13 T Grantham, *mstk 1st, in tch till wknd quickly appr 7th*........(8 to 1 tchd 10 to 1)   5
2644³ PRESENT TIMES 8-11-4 B Clifford, *in cl tch whn blun and uns rdr 6th*..........(33 to 1 op 25 to 1 tchd 40 to 1) ur
Dist: 5l, 10l, 7l, 5l. 4m 19.80s. a 29.80s (6 Ran).
SR: 33/27/12/10/-/-/   (Mrs P A White), J White

3149 **Fox Hill Novices' Handicap Chase (5-y-o and up) £2,464 3m 1f 110yds (4:30)**

1704⁴ ROYAL SQUARE (Can) [85] 8-11-2 M Perrett, *led to 5th, led 7th to 9th and briefly 11th, led 13th to appr 3 out, led approaching last, rdn out*........(2 to 1 fav op 9 to 4)   1
2858 FREDDY OWEN [74] 8-10-5 A Maguire, *wtd wth, hdwy to ld briefly 12th, rallied to lead ag'n appr 3 out till hdd approaching last, no extr*........(9 to 4 tchd 5 to 2)   2
2780* PUNCH'S HOTEL [93] 9-11-10 T Grantham, *cl up, led 9th to 11th, one pace appr 3 out.*
.................................(9 to 4 op 7 to 4 tchd 5 to 2)   3
2980² BLAKEINGTON [81] (bl) 8-10-12 D Skyrme, *cl up, reminders aftr 6th, lost tch 12th, tld off.*
.................................(9 to 1 op 20 to 1 tchd 25 to 1)   4
2453⁸ GINGER DIP [70] 12-10-1 B Powell, *blun and uns rdr second.*...........(14 to 1 op 10 to 1 tchd 16 to 1) ur
1712 SALVAGER [72] 10-10-3³ R Rowell, *not fluent, led 4th to 7th, lost tch 9th, tld off.*........(33 to 1 op 50 to 1) pu
Dist: 1½l, 2½l, dist. 6m 59.80s. a 47.80s (6 Ran).
                              (Park Farm Thoroughbreds), G Harwood

3150 **Lewes Amateur Riders' Handicap Hurdle (4-y-o and up) £2,045 2½m............................. (5:00)**

2708* AUGUST TWELFTH [73] 6-9-10³ (7*) Mr Raymond White, *trkd ldrs, led 3 out, clr appr last, ran on.*
.................................(7 to 1 op 6 to 1 tchd 14 to 1)   1
2710⁶ VILLA PARK [78] 12-9-12 (7*) Mr J Rees, *trkd ldrs, lost pl 8th, styd on frm 2 out, fnshd wl.*
.................................(12 to 1 op 10 to 1 tchd 14 to 1)   2
2781⁵ MILDRED SOPHIA [73] 7-9-7 (7*) Miss S Mitchell, *beh, hdwy 4 out, one pace appr last*.........(10 to 1 tchd 8 to 1)   3
2734⁶ PRIZE MATCH [81] 5-10-8 Mr M Armytage, *hld up beh ldrs, one pace appr last*...(5 to 2 fav op 3 to 1 tchd 7 to 2)   4
      CONNABEE [73] 10-9-12⁵ (7*) Mr F Telford, *led 3rd till hdd 4 out, sn one paced*......................(66 to 1 op 50 to 1)   5
2330⁶ DONNA'S TOKEN [78] 9-9-12 (7*) Mr R Johnson, *led to 3rd, led ag'n 4 out till mstk and hdd nxt, sn wknd.*
.................................(11 to 1 op 10 to 1 tchd 12 to 1)   6
3014³ MANHATTAN BOY [95] 12-11-1 (7*) Mr G Hogan, *trkd ldrs, hmpd and lost pl 7th, not reco'r.....*(7 to 1 op 4 to 1)   7
3014³ THE MRS [90] 8-10-10 (7*) Mr S Righton, *trkd ldrs till lost pl 8th*.................(9 to 1 op 7 to 2 tchd 8 to 1)   8
      RIBOVINO [88] 11-10-8 (7*) Mr L Baker, *chsd ldrs, wknd frm 7th, tld off*..(20 to 1)   9
      ANDY BOY [77] 10-9-11 (7*) Miss C Copper, *sn beh, tld off frm 5th*......................(33 to 1 op 50 to 1 tchd 50 to 1) 10
2915 NATHIR (USA) [97] 8-11-7 (3*) Mr J Durkan, *al beh, tld off.*
....(14 to 1 op 10 to 1) 11
2185² MILLY BLACK (Ire) [79] (v) 6-9-13 (7*) Mrs J Gault, *prmnt whn hit 6th and uns rdr.*
.................................(14 to 1 op 10 to 1 tchd 16 to 1) ur
2970² GLEN MIRAGE [86] 9-10-6 (7*) Miss S White, *tld off 4th, pld up bef four out.*.....................................(7 to 1) pu

Dist: 1½l, 4l, ½l, 1l, 3½l, 15l, 8l, dist, dist, dist. 5m 23.00s. a 46.00s (13 Ran).
(D C O'Brien), D C O'Brien

FONTWELL (good)
Tuesday March 22nd
Going Correction: PLUS 1.40 sec. per fur. (races 1,3,6), PLUS 1.60 (2,4,5)

3151 Walberton 'National Hunt' Novices' Hurdle (4-y-o and up) £1,543 2¼m ....(2:00)

2692^{2} NO PAIN NO GAIN (Ire) 6-11-8 D Murphy, *al hndy, dsptd ld 5th, wnt on nxt, clr 2 out, pushed out, cmftbly.* ....(5 to 2 fav op 11 to 4 tchd 100 to 30) 1
2133^{3} POLLY MINOR 7-10-11 M Perrett, *mstk 1st and sn beh, hdwy appr 3 out, styd on wl frm nxt, nrst finish.* ....(50 to 1 op 33 to 1) 2
2333^{2} RAMALLAH 5-11-8 W McFarland, *in tch, rdn appr 2 out, one pace.*............(3 to 1 op 2 to 1 tchd 100 to 30) 3
2776^{2} TALLAND STREAM 7-10-13 (3*) R Farrant, *nvr far away, rdn appr 2 out, styd on same pace.* ....(7 to 1 op 5 to 1 tchd 8 to 1) 4
2728^{7} POLICEMANS PRIDE (Fr) 5-11-2 T Grantham, *led till hdd 6th, wknd frm 2 out.*..............(50 to 1 op 33 to 1) 5
2494^{3} ZULU PEARL 6-10-11 E Murphy, *hld up, mstk 4th, niggled alng and some hdwy aftr nxt, lost pl frm 3 out.* ....(9 to 2 op 3 to 1 tchd 5 to 1) 6
2705^{3} GLENCARRIG GALE (Ire) 6-11-2 Peter Hobbs, *trkd ldrs till wknd appr 3 out*......(10 to 1 op 7 to 1 tchd 12 to 1) 7
1929^{2} SMART IN SABLE 7-10-11 M Richards, *hld up, shrtlvd effrt aftr 6th, nvr a dngr.* ....(7 to 1 op 5 to 1 tchd 8 to 1) 8
2950^{9} MAGGIE TEE 6-10-11 D Skyrme, *pld hrd, wth ldr till wknd aftr 5th, tld off whn pulled up bef 2 out.* ....(33 to 1 op 25 to 1 tchd 50 to 1) pu

Dist: 5l, 7l, 1½l, 1½l, 12l, 3½l, 4l. 4m 41.30s. a 31.30s (9 Ran).
SR: 33/17/21/13/11/-/ (Mrs B J Curley), B J Curley

3152 'Certain Justice' Challenge Cup Handicap Chase (0-115 5-y-o and up) £2,531 2¼m..........................(2:30)

2861^{2} BOLD CHOICE [95] 8-10-9 J Frost, *hld up in tch, hit 9th, hdwy aftr 11th and sn ev ch, rdn to ld r-in, all out.* ....(3 to 1 op 7 to 2 tchd 4 to 1) 1
2517^{3} CONGREGATION [101] 8-11-1 J Railton, *trkd ldrs till jmpd ahead 3 out, hdd r-in, jst hld.*...............(5 to 2 jt-fav op 3 to 1 tchd 7 to 2) 2
2990^{5} SARTORIUS [106] 8-11-6 D Meade, *nvr far away, led aftr 5th till hdd 3 out, no extr last.*............(5 to 2 jt-fav op 7 to 4 tchd 11 to 4) 3
3017* GENERAL MERCHANT [93] (bl) 14-10-7 (6ex) A Tory, *trkd ldrs till outpcd and lost pl 11th, kpt on one pace frm 3 out.*..................................(6 to 1 op 9 to 2) 4
PEACE OFFICER [114] 8-12-0 M Richards, *wtd wth, gd hdwy tenth, wknd frm 12th.* ....(7 to 1 op 8 to 1 tchd 6 to 1) 5
2316 MASTER COMEDY [88] (bl) 10-10-2^{2} M Stevens, *led till aftr 5th, lost pl frm 9th.*..........................(33 to 1 op 20 to 1) 6
2491^{4} UNIQUE NEW YORK [86] 11-10-0 D Gallagher, *nvr gng wl, sn in rear, tld off whn pld up bef 3 out.* ....(25 to 1 op 20 to 1) pu

Dist: Hd, 2½l, 8l, 5l, 1½l. 4m 54.70s. a 34.70s (7 Ran).
SR: 22/28/30/9/25/-/-/ (Jack Joseph), R G Frost

3153 Mundham Selling Handicap Hurdle (4-y-o) £1,722 2¼m...............(3:00)

2492^{3} ROWLANDSONS GOLD (Ire) [77] 11-1 Lorna Vincent, *led till appr second, rgned ld aftr 3 out, jnd nxt, shaken up betw last 2, cmftbly.* ....(2 to 1 fav op 5 to 2 tchd 11 to 4) 1
2992 CONVOY [90] (bl) 12-0 G McCourt, *hld up in tch, gd hdwy aftr 3 out, chlgd nxt, one pace appr last.* ....(4 to 1 op 9 to 4) 2
2910^{8} ABU DANCER (Ire) [65] 10-3 A Charlton, *patiently rdn, smooth hdwy 6th and sn ev ch, ridden appr 2 out, unbl to quicken.*......................(13 to 2 op 5 to 1) 3
2957^{5} WATER DIVINER [62] 10-0 J Ryan, *hld up, hrd rdn appr 3 out, styd on frm nxt.* (20 to 1 op 16 to 1 tchd 25 to 1) 4
2722^{8} FORMAESTRE (Ire) [65] 10-3 D Murphy, *hld up in tch, gd hdwy to join ldrs aftr 3 out, wknd nxt.* ....(8 to 1 op 10 to 1 tchd 12 to 1 and 7 to 1) 5
1702^{7} MY SISTER LUCY [73] 10-11 S Burrough, *in tch, led 6th till aftr nxt, wknd.*......................(12 to 1 op 8 to 1) 6
2711^{5} OMIDJOY (Ire) [62] 10-0 D Gallagher, *hld up in tch, niggled alng hfwy, wknd appr 3 out.* ....(6 to 1 op 5 to 1 tchd 13 to 2) 7
2395^{5} DO BE WARE [62] 10-0^{3} (3*) A Thornton, *prmnt early, lost pl frm hfwy*...........(9 to 1 op 6 to 1 tchd 11 to 1) 8
2945 FATHER'S JOY [64] 10-2^{2} M Stevens, *pld hrd, led appr second, clr nxt, ran wide bend aftr 5th and hdd next, sn wknd, tld off whn pulled up bef 2 out.*........(50 to 1) pu

Dist: 3½l, 5l, 12l, 5l, 2l, 1½l, ½l. 4m 48.70s. a 38.70s (9 Ran).
(Rowlandsons Ltd (Jewellers)), M R Channon

3154 Geoffrey Osbourne R.N.L.I. Novices' Chase (5-y-o and up) £2,607 3¼m 110yds.......................(3:30)

1845^{7} HURRICANE BLAKE (bl) 6-11-8 Peter Hobbs, *jmpd carefully, sn led, hdd 7th, led ag'n tenth, lft clr 17th, unchlgd.*..........(Evens fav op 11 to 10 tchd 6 to 5) 1
2999^{2} LOBRIC (bl) 9-11-8 J Railton, *not fluent, trkd ldrs, niggled alng 15th, lft remote second 17th, no imprsn.* ....(7 to 4 op 5 to 4) 2
2567^{3} GROOMSMAN 8-11-8 W Humphreys, *patiently rdn in tch, hit 13th, second and gng wl whn f 17th.* ....(5 to 1 op 6 to 1 tchd 7 to 1) f
1324^{6} VISION OF WONDER 10-11-8 J R Kavanagh, *led 7th till hdd tenth, stdly lost pl, lft remote 3rd 17th, blun and pld up aftr 2 out*..... (20 to 1 op 16 to 1 tchd 25 to 1) pu
2640^{8} APOLLO VENTURE 6-11-8 E Byrne, *sn beh, tld off whn pld up aftr 15th, continued till pulled up bef 2 out.* ....(50 to 1 op 33 to 1) pu

Dist: 25l. 7m 40.90s. a 70.90s (5 Ran).
(Exors Of The Late Mr P D Rylands), D M Grissell

3155 Horse And Hound Charlton Hunt Challenge Cup Hunters' Chase (5-y-o and up) £1,618 2m 3f...............(4:00)

2889* KILLESHIN 8-11-13 (7*) Mr G Brown, *hld up and wl beh early, smooth hdwy fnl circuit, chlgd appr last, quickened to ld r-in, sn clr*...........(7 to 4 fav op 6 to 4) 1
MIC-MAC EXPRESS 11-11-7 (7*) Mr N R Mitchell, *trkd ldg grp, led 8th, clr 3 out, hdd and outpcd r-in.* ....(12 to 1 op 6 to 1 tchd 14 to 1) 2
ALL GOLD BOY 9-11-7 (7*) Mr C Ward Thomas, *hld up in tch, mstk tenth, styd on frm 3 out, no dngr*....(50 to 1) 3
MAGICAL MORRIS 12-11-11 (3*) Mr P Hacking, *led till aftr second, styd in tch till rdn and wknd frm 12th.* ....(10 to 1 op 6 to 1 tchd 11 to 1) 4
REMPSTONE 8-11-2 (7*) Mr R Nuttall, *trkd ldrs, hit 9th, wnt second aftr 4 out, ran wide bend appr nxt, sn wknd*..............................(50 to 1 op 33 to 1) 5
2885^{3} TRUST THE GYPSY 12-12-2 (7*) Mr M Felton, *led 3rd to 7th, styd hndy till wknd aftr 4 out*.....(3 to 1 op 11 to 4) 6
763^{7} AS GOOD AS GOLD 8-11-7 (7*) Mr D Birkmyre, *trkd ldrs till mstk 4 out (water), wkng whn f nxt*..........(50 to 1) f
POWERSURGE 7-11-7 (7*) Mr C Gordon, *beh till f 7th.* ....(25 to 1 op 14 to 1) f
2889^{4} TERRIFORN 9-11-12^{1} (3*) Mr A Hill, *hld up and beh till f 11th*..................(20 to 1 op 10 to 1) f
WELSHMAN'S GULLY 10-11-13 (7*) Mr C Newport, *al beh, no ch whn uns rdr 3 out.* (9 to 2 op 5 to 2 tchd 5 to 1) ur
2709 SONNENDEW 11-11-7 (7*) Mrs N Ledger, *led aftr second till 3rd, niggled alng hfwy, sn lost pl, tld off whn pld up bef 3 out*.........................(50 to 1 op 33 to 1) pu
3093 PAID ELATION 9-11-2 (7*) Mr J Wingfield Digby, *mstks, in tch, led 7th to 8th, lost pl frm hfwy, tld off whn pld up bef 3 out*.......................(20 to 1 tchd 33 to 1) pu

Dist: 6l, 15l, 5l, 15l, 1l. 5m 17.90s. a 42.90s (12 Ran).
(H J Manners), H J Manners

3156 Midhurst Handicap Hurdle (0-120 4-y-o and up) £2,194 2¼m..........(4:30)

2743^{7} BALLET ROYAL (USA) [113] 5-11-11 M Perrett, *hld up in tch, took clr order frm hfwy, led aftr 3 out, shaken up r-in, styd on*................(6 to 4 on tchd 5 to 4 on) 1
2496^{8} CARRIKINS [89] (bl) 7-10-1^{1} Peter Hobbs, *nvr far away, rdn and ev ch 3 out, rallied appr last, ran on one pace.* ....(15 to 2 op 5 to 1 tchd 8 to 1) 2
2265 PAPERWORK BOY [93] 9-10-2 (3*) R Farrant, *beh till hdwy frm 5th, rdn to chal appr 2 out, unbl to quicken.* ....(20 to 1 op 14 to 1) 3
2883^{5} DRAMATIC EVENT [88] 9-10-0 E Murphy, *rcd wide, pld hrd and prmnt, led appr 6th till hdd aftr nxt, sn wknd.* ....(10 to 1 op 7 to 1 tchd 12 to 1) 4
2480^{7} SHARRIBA [107] 5-11-5 D Murphy, *hld up, some hdwy appr 3 out, wknd nxt*..............(6 to 1 op 5 to 1) 5
1599 PERSIAN LUCK [95] 8-10-0 (7*) P McLoughlin, *trkd ldrs, rdn aftr 3 out, sn wknd.* ....(13 to 2 op 7 to 1 tchd 10 to 1) 6
3012^{3} MY SENOR [88] (v) 5-10-0 T Grantham, *led till hdd appr 6th, wknd quickly*... (12 to 1 op 10 to 1 tchd 16 to 1) 7
2781^{8} LUCKY OAK [88] 8-9-7 (7*) L Dace, *al beh, tld off.* ....(33 to 1 op 25 to 1 tchd 50 to 1) 8
2862 VAL D'AUTHIE (Fr) [97] 6-10-9 D Skyrme, *in tch, mstk 5th, wknd appr nxt, tld off*..........(20 to 1 op 12 to 1) 9
2132^{7} YUVRAJ [88] 10-10-0 V Smith, *sn beh, rdn hfwy, tld off whn pld up bef 2 out.* (25 to 1 op 20 to 1 tchd 33 to 1) pu

Dist: 3l, 4l, 15l, 7l, 12l, 8l, 12l, 3l. 4m 43.80s. a 33.80s (10 Ran).
SR: 11/-/-/-/-/-/ (Park Farm Thoroughbreds), G Harwood

NEWCASTLE (good to firm)
Tuesday March 22nd
Going Correction: MINUS 0.30 sec. per fur.

3157 Universal Forwarding Novices' Hunters' Chase (5-y-o and up) £960 2½m.............................. (2:40)

POPESHALL 7-12-2 (5") Mr R H Brown, *prmnt, led aftr 11th till aftr 4 out, rdn and styd on to ld r-in.*
................................(9 to 1 op 6 to 1) 1
2904* GOGGINS HILL 7-13-0 Mr J Greenall, *trkd ldrs, prog to ld 3 out, rdn appr last, wknd and hdd r-in, broke blood vessel*...........................(2 to 1 on op 6 to 4) 2
JOG-ALONG 5-11-7 (5") Mr R Hale, *prmnt, led briefly aftr 4 out, blun nxt, wknd*...............(33 to 1 op 20 to 1) 3
MILL KNOCK 12-12-0 (7") Miss P Robson, *hmpd second, al beh, tld off 8th, moderate late prog.*
....................................(40 to 1 op 25 to 1) 4
2898³ KINGS THYNE 8-12-0 (7") Mr C J B Barlow, *led, blun 11th, sn hdd and wknd*..................(33 to 1 op 20 to 1) 5
AH JIM LAD 10-12-0 (7") Mr A McPherson, *mstks, beh 8th, tld off*..................................(25 to 1 op 66 to 1) 6
SPOTTED HEUGH 10-12-0 (7") Mr T Scott, *prmnt to 4th, wkng whn f 7th*..........................(100 to 1) f
LITTLE WENLOCK 10-12-0 (7") Miss J Percy, *f 1st.*
....................................(25 to 1 tchd 33 to 1) f
PRIDEAUX PRINCE (bl) 8-12-0 (7") Mr P Atkinson, *f second.*
....................................(50 to 1 op 33 to 1) f
2955² CLONONY CASTLE (bl) 8-12-0 (7") Mr C Mulhall, *last whn hmpd and uns rdr 1st*................(8 to 1 op 5 to 1) ur
PARSON'S QUEST 8-12-0 (7") Miss Y Beckingham, *chsd ldrs, 5th and struggling whn blun and uns rdr tenth.*
....................................(12 to 1 op 8 to 1) ur
LINN FALLS 9-11-9 (7") Mrs V Jackson, *al beh, tld off whn pld up bef 3 out*.....................(33 to 1 op 25 to 1) pu
Dist: 3½l, 30l, 15l, 4l, 10l. 5m 11.00s. a 20.00s (12 Ran).
(T Williamson), Miss Sally Williamson

3158 Grouse And Claret Intermediate Hunters' Chase (6-y-o and up) £1,725 3m................................. (3:10)

2955* MINERS MELODY (Ire) 6-12-6 Mr J Greenall, *led to 3rd, wth ldr aftr, led 3 out, clr aftr nxt, rdn out.*
................................(11 to 4 on op 5 to 2 on tchd 9 to 4) 1
CONVINCING 10-11-0 (7") Mr P Cornforth, *blun 1st, chsd ldrs, chsd and outpcd 14th, ran on und pres frm last.*
....................................(40 to 1 op 33 to 1) 2
2955³ SPARTAN RANGER 11-11-0 (7") Mr D Bonner, *led 3rd to 8th, chsd ldrs aftr, outpcd aftr 4 out, kpt on frm last.*
....................................(14 to 1 op 8 to 1) 3
SHARP OPINION 11-11-0 (7") Miss P Robson, *sn rdn alng, al chasing ldrs, nvr able to chal*...(5 to 1 tchd 9 to 2) 4
DOXFORD HUT 10-11-2 (5") Mr R Hale, *prmnt, led 8th to 3 out, wknd whn hit nxt, eased r-in*........(200 to 1) 5
THE CHAP 11-11-0 (7") Mr W Burnell, *tld off 6th.*
....................................(33 to 1 op 25 to 1) 6
KAFFIR ALMANAC 7-11-3 (7") Miss K Barnett, *in tch till f 11th*.................................(50 to 1 op 25 to 1) f
LITTLE GLEN 6-11-0 (7") Mr D Scott, *in tch till f tenth.*
....................................(14 to 1 tchd 12 to 1) f
SICILIAN MELODY 10-11-3¹ (5") Mr P Johnson, *blun and uns rdr 4th*.............................(100 to 1) ur
1014⁸ HAWAIIAN GODDESS (USA) 7-11-12 Mr S Swiers, *in tch whn hmpd 11th, not reco'r, pld up bef 15th.*
....................................(16 to 1 op 12 to 1) pu
Dist: 7l, 2½l, 2½l, 3l, dist. 6m 2.60s. a 12.60s (10 Ran).
(J E Greenall), P Cheesbrough

3159 Northumberland Hussars Hunters' Chase (6-y-o and up) £3,870 3m (3:40)

2875² DALTON DANDY 12-11-10 Mr P Jenkins, *trkd ldrs, led 14th, rdn 2 out, kpt on gmely nr finish.*
................................(7 to 1 op 5 to 1 tchd 8 to 1) 1
2811* DAVY BLAKE 7-11-13 Mr J M Dun, *led to second, led tenth to 14th, chsd wnr aftr, unbl to quicken appr last.*
............(4 to 1 on op 9 to 2 on tchd 7 to 2 on) 2
FINAL CHANT 13-11-13 Mr R H Brown, *led second to tenth, wknd 4 out*.....(12 to 1 op 8 to 1 tchd 14 to 1) 3
NO PANIC 10-11-10 Mr S Whitaker, *trkd ldrs gng easily till wknd appr 3 out*..........................(33 to 1) 4
FAST STUDY 9-12-2 Mr Simon Robinson, *nrly uns rdr 3rd, beh aftr, no ch whn pld up and dismounted appr last, rmntd to finish*.................(25 to 1 op 16 to 1) 5
2959⁵ DURIGHT 11-11-5 Mr N Tutty, *trkd ldrs, outpcd 15th, 4th and no ch whn f 3 out.*
................................(14 to 1 op 12 to 1 tchd 16 to 1) f
STRING PLAYER 12-11-10 Mr D Barlow, *in tch, wkng whn mstk 13th, tld off when pld up bef 3 out.*
CLASSIC BART 10-11-10 Mr T Scott, *hld up, lost tch 13th, tld off whn pld up bef 2 out, dismounted.*
....................................(100 to 1 op 66 to 1) pu
Dist: ½l, 20l, 1½l, dist. 6m 1.00s. a 11.00s (8 Ran).
(Keith Middleton), Mrs Sarah L Dent

3160 Michael Jobling Wines Ladies' Hunters' Chase (6-y-o and up) £1,725

3m.......................................(4:10)
STEELE JUSTICE 10-11-7 (7") Miss P Robson, *prmnt, led 14th, drw clr frm 3 out, easily.*
................(13 to 8 on op 6 to 4 on tchd 7 to 4 on) 1
POSEIDONIA 8-10-9 (7") Miss J Percy, *led to 14th, rdn 3 out, no ch whn aftr*.............(33 to 1 op 20 to 1) 2
SECOND ATTEMPT 10-10-13 (3") Mrs A Farrell, *chsd ldrs, wknd 13th, tld off r-in*......(33 to 1 op 150 to 1) 3
2875 FRISKNEY DALE LAD 9-11-0 (7") Miss S Hunter, *f 3rd.*
....................................(8 to 1 op 6 to 1) f
2887 MIG 9-10-9 (7") Mrs V Jackson, *trkd ldrs, cl up whn f 13th.*
................(11 to 4 op 5 to 2 tchd 3 to 1) f
ROBINS CHOICE 10-10-13 (7") Mrs F Needham, *mstk 1st, hld up, lost tch 7th, tld off whn pld up bef 12th.*
....................................(25 to 1 tchd 33 to 1) pu
Dist: 12l, dist. 6m 6.90s. a 16.90s (6 Ran).
(W Manners), W Manners

3161 Town And Country Hunters' National Open £3,220 4m 1f............... (4:40)

2875⁸ FOUR TRIX 13-11-12 (5") Mr R Hale, *trkd ldrs, led aftr 4 out, ran on wl*..........(3 to 1 op 5 to 2 tchd 7 to 2) 1
MAN'S BEST FRIEND 7-11-7 (7") Mr R Ford, *led to 19th, chsd wnr 3 out, unbl to quicken*..........(6 to 4 on) 2
BELLWAY 13-11-4 (7") Mr C Bonner, *in tch whn mstk 13th, beh 17th, tld off*...............(20 to 1 op 16 to 1) 3
ISOBAR 8-11-7 (7") Mr D Barlow, *in tch, wkng whn mstk 15th, tld off 18th*...............(25 to 1 tchd 33 to 1) 4
GENERAL HARMONY (bl) 11-11-4 (7") Mr S Brisby, *prmnt, led 19th till aftr 4 out, wknd rpdly.*
................(13 to 2 op 6 to 1 tchd 7 to 1) pu
Dist: 4l, dist, 12l, 10l. 8m 48.10s. a 37.10s (5 Ran).
(Mrs Stewart Catherwood), G Richards

3162 Meldon Village Storage And Drying Hunters' Chase (6-y-o and up) £1,035 2m 110yds.................... (5:10)

2508² DARK DAWN 10-12-3 Mr J Greenall, *sn prmnt, trkd ldr 5th, led dppr 3 out, soon clr, imprsv.*
................(7 to 4 fav op 6 to 4 tchd 2 to 1) 1
2875* LINGHAM MAGIC 9-11-9 Mr S Swiers, *cl up, trkd ldg pair frm 8th, pushed alng 3 out, styd on, no ch wth wnr.*
................(5 to 2 op 9 to 4 tchd 11 to 4) 2
2888⁶ CRAFTY CHAPLAIN 8-11-2 (5") Mr D McCain, *rear and pushed alng, lost tch 6th, ran on frm 9th, fnshd wl, took 3rd cl hme.*...........................(33 to 1) 3
ASTRE RADIEUX (Fr) 9-11-10 (7") Mr C Stockton, *set fst pace till appr 3 out, chsd wnr aftr till wknd last.*
................(11 to 2 op 25 to 1 tchd 5 to 1) 4
WAY OF LIFE (Fr) 9-11-10 (7") Mr C Bonner, *mid-div, effrt 9th, styd on, nvr able to chal*......(7 to 1 op 5 to 1) 5
2875⁹ JOHN CORBET 11-11-9 (5") Mr R H Brown, *prmnt till wknd 4 out*..............................(14 to 1 op 10 to 1) 6
2875 HOUGHTON (bl) 8-11-10 (7") Major M Watson, *chsd ldrs, rdn 3 out, no ch whn mstks last 2*...........(10 to 1) 7
SUPER TRUCKER 11-11-10 (7") Miss P Robson, *al beh, tld off 8th*.............................(16 to 1 op 20 to 1) 9
SILENT RING (USA) (v) 8-11-10 (7") Mr C Mulhall, *prmnt, mstk 4th, wknd 8th, sn tld off*.................(50 to 1) 9
LOVE ON THE ROCKS (bl) 9-11-5 (7") Mr S Hope, *rear and rdn 7th, sn tld off*...........................(100 to 1) 10
395² TROOPER THORN 10-11-0 (7") Mr S Pittendrigh, *f 1st.*
....................................(33 to 1 op 25 to 1) f
AFRICAN SAFARI (bl) 11-11-10 (7") Mr P Murray, *prmnt to 4th, tld off whn pld up bef 3 out.*....(50 to 1 op 33 to 1) pu
RIVER CEIRIOG 13-11-10 (7") Mr D Barlow, *mstks, prmnt to 7th, tld off whn pld up bef last....* (50 to 1 op 33 to 1) pu
LOUGHLINSTOWN BOY 9-11-10 Mr S Bell, *sn beh, tld off whn pld up bef 8th.*........................(25 to 1) pu
Dist: 15l, 1½l, hd, 3½l, 5l, 1½l, 15l, 8l, ¾l. 4m 4.30s. a 3.30s (14 Ran).
SR: 21/-/4/4/-/-/   (J E Greenall), P Cheesbrough

NOTTINGHAM (soft)
Tuesday March 22nd
Going Correction: PLUS 1.50 sec. per fur.

3163 Welland Novices' Chase (5-y-o and up) £2,380 2m 5f 110yds........ (1:50)

2899¹ ANDERMATT 7-11-10 N Williamson, *patiently rdn, improved to join issue fnl circuit, jmpd ahead 3 out, kpt on strly r-in*............(9 to 4 op 2 to 1 tchd 5 to 2) 1
2504² RIVER MANDATE 7-11-10 B Powell, *wth ldr, lft in ld 8 out, jnd 4 out, hdd nxt, rallied r-in.*
................(11 to 8 fav op 11 to 10 tchd 6 to 4) 2
2829⁶ APRIL CITY 5-10-4 M Ranger, *settled off the pace, improved aftr one circuit, rdn and outpcd 6 out, no imprsn*...........................(50 to 1 op 33 to 1) 3
MR INVADER 7-11-4 C Llewellyn, *led or dsptd ld for a circuit, feeling pace and lost grnd 6 out, tld off.*
....................................(14 to 1 op 8 to 1) 4
2799 FATHER FORTUNE 6-11-3 (3") J McCarthy, *tracking ldrs whn f 7th*.............................(12 to 1 op 8 to 1) f

2879[4] GYPSY KING (Ire) 6-11-4 S McNeill, *led or dsptd ld, definite advantage 8th, slight lead whn f 8 out.* .... (9 to 2 op 5 to 1 tchd 11 to 2) f
1624 KING TASMAN (NZ) 7-11-4 C Maude, *jmpd sluggishly, struggling frm 5th, tld off whn pld up bef 8 out.* .... (50 to 1 op 25 to 1) pu

Dist: 1l, dist, dist. 5m 51.10s. a 38.10s (7 Ran).
SR: 37/36/-/-/ (The Marston Sept), J Mackie

3164 EBF 'National Hunt' Novices' Hurdle Qualifier (5,6,7-y-o) £1,952 2m.. (2:20)

2303[9] ANNIE KELLY 6-10-9 B Dalton, *nvr far away, nosed ahead bef 2 out, hdd and rdn whn lft clr last.* ....(20 to 1 op 16 to 1 tchd 33 to 1 and 25 to 1) 1
GARRISON COMMANDER (Ire) 5-11-0 S McNeill, *tucked away in midfield, outpcd whn ldrs quickened appr 3 out, rallied betw last 2, nrst finish.* (14 to 1 op 10 to 1) 2
1626[5] THE BARGEMAN (NZ) 6-11-0 C Llewellyn, *set steady pace, quickened up appr 3 out, hdd nxt, sn rdn and outpcd.* .... (6 to 1 op 5 to 1 tchd 13 to 2) 3
2860[3] DEVIL'S CORNER 6-11-0 M Bosley, *trkd ldg bunch, effrt and pushed alng appr 3 out, fdd frm nxt.* ....(6 to 1 op 4 to 1) 4
2860 HECTOR MARIO 6-11-0 N Williamson, *took keen hold, improved to take clr order aftr 4 out, hit 2 out, sn rdn and btn.* .... (14 to 1) 5
2303 MOZEMO 7-11-10 S Smith Eccles, *nvr far away, led briefly 3 out, sprawled on landing nxt, sn btn.* .... (12 to 1 op 10 to 1) 6
ALEX THUSCOMBE 6-11-0 D Telfer, *wth ldrs to hfwy, sn struggling, no imprsn frm 3 out*....(50 to 1 op 33 to 1) 7
2860[4] MAGELLAN BAY (Ire) 6-11-0 I Lawrence, *al hndy, 4th and rdn whn f 3 out*.......... (7 to 2 tchd 4 to 1 and 3 to 1) f
2789[4] FED ON OATS 6-11-5 A Maguire, *patiently rdn, improved to join ldrs 3 out, slight ld whn f last, unlucky.* .... (6 to 4 fav tchd 2 to 1) f

Dist: 10l, 5l, 6l, 10l, 2½l, 5l. 4m 21.40s. a 37.40s (9 Ran).
(Mrs R Hoare), J Wharton

3165 17th/21st Lancers Challenge Cup A Hunters' Chase (5-y-o and up) £1,192 3m 110yds.....................(2:50)

2887[2] BROWN WINDSOR (bl) 12-11-12 (7*) Mr B Pollock, *al wl plcd, led tenth, hrd pressed frm 4 out, gd jump to go clr ag'n last, ran on*.................... (2 to 1 op 7 to 4) 1
2807[2] MOUNT ARGUS 12-12-2 (5*) Mr S Brookshaw, *patiently rdn, improved appr 4 out, ev ch and ridden last 3, kpt on same pace*.................. (6 to 4 fav op 5 to 4) 2
2888[4] QUEEN'S CHAPLAIN 10-12-3 (7*) Mrs M Morris, *jmpd stickily 1st circuit, improved hfwy, outpcd 6 out, styd on ag'n betw last 2*.................. (7 to 1 op 6 to 1) 3
2887[4] SPORTING MARINER 12-11-7 (7*) Mr D Bloor, *al hndy, led 7th to tenth, feeling pace whn hit 6 out, sn lost pl, no imprsn*...........................(25 to 1 op 20 to 1) 4
PARSON'S CROSS 10-11-7 (7*) Mr A Sansome, *chsd ldrs, niggled to keep up aftr one circuit, wl beh frm 6 out.* ....(25 to 1) 5
PADRIGAL 11-11-9 (5*) Mr C Bealby, *trkd ldg bunch for a circuit, tld off frm 6 out.* .... (12 to 1 op 8 to 1 tchd 14 to 1) 6
SHILGROVE PLACE 12-11-9 (5*) Mr D Parker, *co'red up beh ldrs, blun and uns rdr second*..... (25 to 1 op 20 to 1) ur
2889[6] HOOK HEAD 10-11-7 (7*) Mr C Vale, *led to 7th, styd hndy till fdd fnl circuit, tld off whn pld up bef 4 out.* .... (25 to 1 op 20 to 1) pu

Dist: 4l, 20l, hd, 3l, dist. 6m 44.00s. a 49.00s (8 Ran).
(W Shand Kydd), Miss C Saunders

3166 Sherwood Rangers Yeomanry Handicap Hurdle (0-120 4-y-o and up) £2,505 3½m.................. (3:20)

1533 RIDWAN [93] 7-10-10 A S Smith, *settled off the pace, took clr order 3 out, led betw last 2, drvn out.* .... (14 to 1 op 10 to 1 tchd 16 to 1) 1
2894* CARSON CITY [87] 7-10-4 P Niven, *patiently rdn, improved frm midfield to join issue 3 out, ridden and one pace from betw last 2.* ....(5 to 2 fav op 7 to 2 tchd 9 to 2) 2
3028[4] RIMOUSKI [106] 6-11-9 Mr J Cambidge, *settled in rear, steady hdwy fnl circuit, styd on frm 2 out, nvr nrr.* ....(13 to 2 op 4 to 1 tchd 7 to 1) 3
2428[3] PRINCE OF SALERNO [85] 7-10-2 R Supple, *patiently rdn, improved hfwy, led 4 out till betw last 2, one pace.* .... (14 to 1 op 10 to 1) 4
2600[7] FURRY BABY [99] 7-11-2 R Garritty, *settled gng wl, improved to chal 3 out, rdn aftr nxt, no extr.* .... (10 to 1 op 6 to 1) 5
2936[4] GORT [105] 6-11-8 M A FitzGerald, *al hndy, ev ch and drvn alng appr 3 out, no extr frm nxt.* ....(14 to 1 op 10 to 1 tchd 16 to 1) 6
2967[9] SPARTAN TIMES [97] 10-11-0 B Powell, *al wl plcd, led aftr 9th to 4 out, styd hndy till fdd after nxt.* .... (20 to 1 op 16 to 1 tchd 25 to 1) 7
2896[3] SWEET NOBLE (Ire) [94] 5-10-4 (7*) F Leahy, *trkd ldg bunch, improved appr 3 out, hit nxt, sn btn.* .... (12 to 1 op 8 to 1) 8
1928 STORM DRUM [101] 5-11-4 N Williamson, *chsd ldg bunch, hrd drvn aftr 4 out, sn btn*........ (14 to 1 op 12 to 1) 9
2967[7] LESBET [92] 9-10-9 D Morris, *led till hdd aftr 9th, fdd und pres bef 3 out*...........(7 to 1 op 6 to 1 tchd 8 to 1) 10
2862[3] GEORGE BUCKINGHAM [92] (bl) 9-10-9 A Maguire, *al chasing ldrs, feeling pace frm 4 out, fdd.* (10 to 1 op 7 to 1) 11
2766[6] SIR CRUSTY [94] 12-10-4 (7*) P Maddock, *strted very slwly, tld off till hdwy hfwy, lost tch ag'n bef 3 out.* .... (20 to 1 op 14 to 1) 12
2733 BERESFORDS GIRL [107] 9-11-5 (5*) D Matthews, *settled midfield, wnt hndy 4th, drvn alng bef 3 out, sn btn.* ....(10 to 1 op 20 to 1 tchd 25 to 1) 13
1227[4] ARR EFF BEE [99] (bl) 7-10-13 (3*) T Eley, *in tch, stumbled bend appr 7th, rdn and blun tenth, sn lost touch.* .... (33 to 1 op 20 to 1) 14
2727 TAP DANCING [83] 8-9-7 (7*) Mr N Bradley, *wth ldrs for o'r a circuit, tld off whn pld up bef 4 out.* .... (50 to 1 op 25 to 1) pu

Dist: 2½l, 1½l, 2½l, 12l, 4l, 2l, ¾l, ¾l, 3l, 3l. 7m 28.30s. a 48.30s (15 Ran).
SR: 19/10/27/3/5/7/ (Tom Barr), K A Morgan

3167 Bendigo Mares Novices' Handicap Hurdle (4-y-o and up) £1,950 2m 5f 110yds........................ (3:50)

2997* KNOCKAVERRY (Ire) [91] 6-11-10 R Supple, *settled gng wl, imprvg whn badly hmpd by faller 4 out, reco'red to ld on bit bef last, readily*............ (5 to 2 tchd 11 to 4) 1
2802[7] EVE'S TREASURE [83] 4-11-2 A Maguire, *dsptd ld, lft in lead briefly 4 out, nosed ahead 2 out, sn hdd, not pace of wnr*..................................(10 to 1) 2
2934[3] RACE TO THE RHYTHM [77] 7-10-10 C Llewellyn, *al hndy, led aftr 4 to 2 out, rdn last, one pace.* ....(4 to 1 tchd 7 to 2) 3
2950 TITAN EMPRESS [67] 5-10-0 S Earle, *nvr far away, effrt and scrubbed alng appr 3 out, outpcd frm nxt.* (20 to 1) 4
2088[5] BOWLAND GIRL (Ire) [67] 5-9-11 (3*) S Wynne, *al wl plcd, hrd drvn 3 out, sn rdn and btn*..... (12 to 1 op 8 to 1) 5
2934* ARTIC WINGS (Ire) [85] 6-11-4 M Brennan, *patiently rdn, steady hdwy appr 3 out, ridden nxt, no response.* ....(7 to 4 fav op 6 to 4 tchd 2 to 1) 6
2808 BROUGHTON'S GOLD (Ire) [73] 6-10-6 N Mann, *tucked away beh ldrs, effrt aftr 4 out, no imprsn frm nxt.* ....(33 to 1) 7
2326 GAY'S GAMBIT [67] 5-9-9 (5*) Mr D Parker, *trkd ldg bunch, improved to go hndy appr 3 out, fdd frm nxt, tld off.* .... (25 to 1 op 33 to 1) 8
3007 ESSEN AITCH [67] 5-10-0 V Slattery, *tried to make all, drvn alng whn f 4 out*.......................... (100 to 1) f
2964 CAIPIRINHA (Ire) [70] 6-10-3[2] G Upton, *al wl plcd, 3rd and ev ch whn brght dwn 4 out*...................(33 to 1) bd
2136 CAROUSEL CROSSETT [67] 13-9-11[4] (7*) Mr S Walker, *in tch, struggling aftr one circuit, tld off whn pld up bef 3 out*.......................... (50 to 1 op 40 to 1) pu
LOST IN SPACE [67] 7-10-0 A S Smith, *pushed alng to hold pl hfwy, tld off whn pld up bef 3 out.* ....(14 to 1 op 33 to 1) pu
2799[6] SOLO GIRL (Ire) [68] 6-10-1[1] S McNeill, *in tch, struggling to keep up hfwy, tld off whn pld up bef 3 out.* .... (14 to 1 op 20 to 1) pu

Dist: 3½l, ½l, 15l, 3l, 15l, 4l, dist. 5m 45.90s. a 43.90s (13 Ran).
(Mrs W Morrell), M J Wilkinson

3168 Trent Handicap Chase (0-120 5-y-o and up) £3,088 3m 3f 110yds.... (4:20)

1577 BIANCONI [90] 8-10-1 C Llewellyn, *settled gng wl, improved to ld 6 out, jmpd clr 2 out, styd on well.* ....(7 to 1 op 5 to 1) 1
2906* YOUNG MINER [96] 8-10-7 G Upton, *al disputing ld, led briefly aftr 4th, ev ch and bustled alng frm four out, one pace from betw last 2.* ....(13 to 8 fav op 5 to 4 tchd 7 to 4) 2
2935* SUNBEAM TALBOT [96] 13-10-7 M A FitzGerald, *tucked away beh ldrs, improved fnl circuit, hrd drvn 6 out, outpcd last 3*..........(13 to 2 op 5 to 1 tchd 7 to 1) 3
2906[3] CHOCTAW [103] 10-11-0 C Hawkins, *led aftr 4th till hdd 6 out, hit nxt, btn bef four out*........(7 to 1 op 5 to 1) 4
2666 PRINCE NEPAL [89] 10-10-0 B Powell, *tracking ldg bunch whn blun and uns rdr 9th*.........(66 to 1 op 33 to 1) ur
1459 SOONER STILL [101] (bl) 10-10-5 (7*) Judy Davies, *made most till aftr 4th, styd hndy till wknd fnl circuit, tld off whn pld up bef four out*......... (20 to 1 tchd 33 to 1) pu
2935 CLONROCHE GAZETTE [89] 14-10-0 Miss S Wallin, *struggling to keep up hfwy, tld off whn pld up bef 3 out.* .... (66 to 1 op 40 to 1) pu
1720[7] RED AMBER [91] (bl) 8-10-2 J Osborne, *lost pl quickly aftr 5th, hit 8th, tld off whn pld up bef 14th.* ....(9 to 1 op 7 to 1) pu
2831[3] HIGH PADRE [113] 8-11-10 M Dwyer, *sn trailing in rear, nvr gng wl, tld off whn pld up bef 7 out.* ....(4 to 1 tchd 7 to 2) pu

Dist: 5l, 30l, 15l. 7m 35.80s. a 47.80s (9 Ran).
SR: 8/9/-/-/-/-/ (Saguaro Stables), N A Gaselee

3169 Levy Board National Hunt Flat Race (4,5,6-y-o) £2,076 2m. . . . . (4:50)

2749[8] WHAT'S YOUR STORY (Ire) 5-11-1 (7*) Mr G Hogan, *led early, styd prmnt, shaken up and stayed on to ld nr finish*. . . . . . (4 to 1 op 7 to 2) 1
2996 ME FEIN (Ire) 6-11-1 (7*) Mr C Curley, *wtd wth, gd hdwy entering strt, hrd rdn to ld blw dist, hdd cl hme*. . . . . . (8 to 1 op 7 to 1) 2
NATIVE MONY (Ire) 5-11-1 (7*) R Wilkinson, *took clr order hfwy, ev ch 2 fs out, styd on same pace*. . . . . . (33 to 1) 3
ERMINE STREET 6-11-1 (7*) R Moore, *patiently rdn, hdwy entering strt, effrt and not much room 2 fs out, one pace*. . . . . . (20 to 1) 4
WINDSWEPT LADY (Ire) 5-10-10 (7*) M Herrington, *hld up, hdwy o'r 4 fs out, not pace to chal*. (10 to 1 op 4 to 1) 5
1376* SOUNDS FYNE (Ire) 5-11-8 (7*) G Tormey, *hld up in tch, hdwy o'r 4 fs out, wknd fnl 2 furlongs*. . . . . . (7 to 1 op 2 to 1) 6
BOOLAVOGUE (Ire) 4-10-2 (7*) P Maddock, *settled mid-field, effrt 4 fs out, not trble ldrs*. . . (50 to 1 op 33 to 1) 7
FIXTURESSECRETARY (Ire) 5-11-1 (7*) R Massey, *prmnt, led o'r 5 fs out to blw dist, sn wknd*. . . . . . (7 to 4 fav op 7 to 2) 8
HOLY STING (Ire) 5-11-5 (3*) T Jenks, *pressed ldrs, rdn alng entering strt, grad wknd*. . . . . (14 to 1 op 10 to 1) 9
RHINE RIVER (USA) 4-11-0 Mr N Wilson, *al in rear, tld off*. . . . . . (33 to 1) 10
STONEGREY (Ire) 6-11-1 (7*) J Driscoll, *nvr a factor, tld off*. . . . . . (16 to 1) 11
2963[7] CHUCKLES 4-11-0 Mr K Green, *al beh, tld off*. . . . . . (50 to 1 op 33 to 1) 12
2176[8] ONLY JESTING 4-10-2 (7*) Lorna Brand, *led aftr 2 fs till ten out, sn led ag'n, hdd 6 out, grad wknd, tld off*. (33 to 1) 13
GREET THE GREEK 5-11-3 (5*) J Burke, *al in rear, tld off*. . . . . . (20 to 1 op 16 to 1 tchd 25 to 1) 14
2876 TORTULA 5-10-10 (7*) K Davies, *prmnt for 11 fs, sn rdn and wknd, tld off*. . . . . . (33 to 1) 15
2963[4] SABBAQ (USA) 4-10-9 (5*) N Leach, *in rear whn pld up 8 fs out, lme*. . . . . . (8 to 1 op 6 to 1) pu
LUCKY HOLLY 4-10-2 (7*) C Woodall, *iron broke early, led briefly ten fs out to 8 out, wknd and pld up o'r 4 out*. . . . . . (50 to 1 op 33 to 1) pu

Dist: 1½l, 8l, 1l, 2l, 3½l, 2l, ½l, 4l, 15l, 20l. 4m 12.80s. (17 Ran).

(Jerry Wright), D Nicholson

EXETER (good to soft)
Wednesday March 23rd
Going Correction: PLUS 0.90 sec. per fur. (races 1,4,-5,7), PLUS 1.05 (2,3,6)

3170 EBF 'National Hunt' Novices' Hurdle Qualifier (5,6,7-y-o) £2,411 2¼m (2:00)

2426[3] BASS ROCK 6-11-0 J Frost, *trkd ldr, led 4th, pushed clr frm 2 out, cmftbly*. . . . . . (5 to 4 fav tchd 13 to 8) 1
2459 NAZZARO 5-10-12 (7*) R Darke, *al prmnt, no imprsn frm 2 out*. . . . . . (4 to 1 op 3 to 1) 2
1161[4] BELL ONE (USA) 5-11-0 Peter Hobbs, *nvr far away, rdn and kpt on one pace frm 2 out*. . . . . . (8 to 1 op 5 to 1) 3
2657 NAVAL BATTLE 7-11-0 J R Kavanagh, *in rear, hdwy appr 2 out, styd on, nvr nrr*. . . . . . (16 to 1 op 12 to 1) 4
3053 CHICKABIDDY 6-10-9 (5*) D Salter, *hld up, hdwy frm 3 out, kpt on, nvr nrr*. . . . . . (14 to 1 op 10 to 1) 5
2021[7] SHIMBA HILLS 6-11-0 M A FitzGerald, *towards rear, styd on frm 2 out, nvr dngrs*. (6 to 1 op 5 to 1 tchd 8 to 1) 6
2021[8] IVE CALLED TIME 6-10-9 (5*) Guy Lewis, *mid-div, wkng whn hit 2 out*. . . . . . (25 to 1 op 16 to 1) 7
2964 OAKLANDS WORD (bl) 5-10-7 (7*) P McLoughlin, *in tch, rdn 2 out, sn btn*. . . . . . (66 to 1 op 50 to 1) 8
2789[9] FRANK RICH 7-11-10 G Upton, *chsd ldrs till wknd appr 2 out*. . . . . . (12 to 1 op 7 to 1) 9
2333 RECTORY GARDEN (Ire) 5-10-11 (3*) R Farrant, *chsd ldrs till wknd 5th*. . . . . . (20 to 1 op 10 to 1) 10
2950 AUGER BORE (Ire) 6-11-0 S Burrough, *sn beh, tld off whn f 4th*. . . . . . (66 to 1 op 50 to 1) f
2950 PAUL'S PRINCESS 7-10-6 (3*) A Thornton, *beh frm second, tld off whn pld up bef 2 out*. . . . . . (66 to 1 op 50 to 1) pu
1867[5] PIRATE OF PENZANCE 6-11-0 Mrs C Wonnacott, *chsd ldrs till wknd 3 out, tld off whn pld up bef last*. . . . . . (33 to 1 op 25 to 1) pu
2950 EXE CRACKER 5-11-0 W McFarland, *al beh, tld off whn pld up bef last*. . . . . . (66 to 1 op 25 to 1) pu
2426 DEVIL'S STING (Ire) 5-11-0 D Bridgwater, *led to 4th, sn rdn, tld off whn pld up bef last*. . . . . . (14 to 1 op 7 to 1) pu

Dist: 5l, 1½l, 2½l, ½l, 2½l, ½l, 2l, 12l, ½l. 4m 21.90s. a 21.90s (15 Ran).
SR: 29/29/22/19/18/15/14/12/10/ (Queen Elizabeth), I A Balding

3171 Robert Webb Travel Hunters' Chase (5-y-o and up) £1,297 3¼m. . . . . (2:30)

SAMS HERITAGE 10-11-10 (7*) Mr J M Pritchard, *nvr far away, wnt second 6 out, led 4 out, drw clr*. . . . . . (10 to 1 op 8 to 1) 1
2882* BRIEF ENCOUNTER (NZ) 10-12-5 (5*) Miss P Curling, *al prmnt, dsptd ld 9th, led 12th till hdd 4 out, one pace*. . . . . . (9 to 4 op 5 to 2 tchd 2 to 1) 2
2838* CAPE COTTAGE 10-12-3 (7*) Mr J Trice-Rolph, *nvr far away, no imprsn appr 4 out*. . . . . . (9 to 2 op 4 to 1) 3
2793* BONANZA BOY 13-12-3 (7*) Mr D Pipe, *trkd ldrs, no hdwy frm 5 out*. . . . . . (2 to 1 fav op 6 to 4 tchd 9 to 4) 4
3013[3] MANDRAKI SHUFFLE 12-12-3 (7*) Mr A Harvey, *mid-div, nvr nr to chal*. . . . . . (12 to 1 op 10 to 1) 5
3021[9] DISTILLATION 9-11-10 (7*) Mr Richard White, *beh, some late hdwy, nvr dngrs*. . . . . . (66 to 1 op 50 to 1) 6
2937* ARCTIC TEAL 10-12-7 (3*) Mr J Durkan, *made most till twelfth, wknd stdly*. (11 to 1 op 10 to 1 tchd 12 to 1) 7
3013[5] WREKIN HILL 12-12-3 (7*) Mrs J Wilkinson, *towards rear, some hdwy 11th, tld off*. . . . . . (33 to 1 op 25 to 1) 8
MONTGOMERY (bl) 13-11-10 (7*) Mr S Mulcaire, *al beh, tld off*. . . . . . (100 to 1) 9
ANOTHER LUCAS 10-11-10 (7*) Mr S Slade, *al beh, tld off*. . . . . . (100 to 1 op 50 to 1) 10
YARRON KING 8-11-10 (7*) Mr B Dixon, *al beh, tld off*. . . . . . (66 to 1 op 50 to 1) 11
3021 COLCOMBE CASTLE 11-11-10 (7*) Mr J Culloty, *in tch till wknd rpdly appr 4 out, tld off*. . . . . . (66 to 1) 12
SANCREED 9-11-10 (7*) Mr I Hambly, *al beh, tld off frm 11th*. . . . . . (33 to 1) 13
WATERSMEET DOWN 11-11-10 (7*) Miss C Wright, *prmnt till blun and uns rdr 5th*. . . . . . (50 to 1) ur
3021 TERRA DI SIENA 12-11-10 (7*) Mr J Creighton, *al beh, tld off whn pld up bef 2 out, broke leg, destroyed*. . . . . . (66 to 1 op 50 to 1) pu
SKERRY MEADOW 10-11-10 (7*) Mr I Widdicombe, *al beh, tld off whn pld up bef 2 out*. . . . . . (20 to 1 op 16 to 1) pu
BINCOMBE TOP 10-11-10 (7*) Mr L Jefford, *al beh, tld off whn pld up bef 4 out*. . . . . . (100 to 1 op 66 to 1) pu

Dist: 10l, 15l, 7l, 5l, 2l, 2½l, 25l, ¾l, 10l, 2½l. 6m 51.50s. (17 Ran).

(C G Smedley), P G Warner

3172 Heavitree Brewery Challenge Cup Handicap Chase (0-140 5-y-o and up) £5,684 2¼m. . . . . (3:00)

2798[3] BROUGHTON MANOR [120] 9-11-5 M A FitzGerald, *made all, rdn appr 4 out, ran on gmely und pres r-in, all out*. . . . . . (2 to 1 fav op 3 to 1) 1
3066[6] L'UOMO PIU [106] 10-10-5 S Earle, *trkd wnr to 6th, rdn and lost pl appr 4 out, rallied aftr 2 out, kpt on und pres r-in*. . . . . . (4 to 1 op 11 to 4) 2
2205[3] ITS NEARLY TIME [125] 11-11-5 (5*) Guy Lewis, *hld up, hdwy appr 4 out, rdn and one pace frm 2 out*. . . . . . (12 to 1 op 8 to 1 tchd 14 to 1) 3
1947 MINE'S AN ACE (NZ) [109] 7-10-8 J Frost, *hld up in rear, gd hdwy 5 out, ev ch nxt, wknd 2 out*. . . (9 to 1 op 5 to 1) 4
2429 HOLTERMANN (USA) [114] 10-10-13 D Bridgwater, *blun 3rd, beh but in tch 5 out, weaekened nxt*. . . . . . (14 to 1 op 10 to 1) 5
2990[4] AMBASSADOR [113] (bl) 11-10-12 J Lower, *hdwy appr 5th, wkng und pres whn f 4 out*. . . . . . (7 to 1 op 5 to 1 tchd 8 to 1) f
2861[3] JAILBREAKER [109] 7-10-8 J Osborne, *al prmnt, trkd wnr 6th, gng wl whn blun and uns rdr 4 out*. . . . . . (7 to 2 tchd 9 to 2) ur

Dist: ¾l, 3l, 2l, 25l. 4m 34.70s. a 23.70s (7 Ran).
SR: 43/28/44/26/6/-/-/ (W R Cook), Mrs J G Retter

3173 Robert Webb Travel Novices' Selling Hurdle (4 & 5-y-o) £1,891 2¼m. . (3:30)

2797[3] KNYAZ 4-10-4 (7*) Mr L Jefford, *hld up in tch, cld 3 out, led sn aftr nxt, hdd last, rallied to ld post*. . . . . . (7 to 2 op 3 to 1 tchd 4 to 1) 1
3019* SOPHISM (USA) 5-11-11 J Lower, *hld up in rear, smooth hdwy 3 out, led briefly nxt, steadied and led on bit last, rdn and found nil, hdd post*. . . . . . (Evens fav op 5 to 4 on tchd 11 to 10) 2
3019[2] PLAIN SAILING (Fr) 4-11-3 M A FitzGerald, *trkd ldr, led 5th to 2 out, rdn and sn btn*. . . . . . (3 to 1 tchd 7 to 2) 3
2797[6] NORDEN (Ire) 5-11-5 W Irvine, *hld up, effrt 3 out, sn outpcd*. . . . . . (25 to 1 op 20 to 1) 4
2215 NYMPH ERRANT 4-9-13 (7*) Mr N Moore, *prmnt till wknd quickly 2 out*. . . . . . (20 to 1 tchd 33 to 1) 5
2021 FRIENDLY VIKING 4-10-11 Miss A Turner, *blun second, al beh, tld off*. . . . . . (50 to 1 op 20 to 1) 6
2525 ON THE BOOK 5-11-0 S McNeill, *in tch, cld 4th whn f 5th*. . . . . . (10 to 1 op 12 to 1 tchd 16 to 1) f
3012[5] QUIET CONFIDENCE (Ire) 4-10-1 (5*) S Curran, *led, hit 3rd and 4th, hdd nxt, rdn whn blun and uns rdr 3 out*. . . . . . (25 to 1 op 20 to 1) ur
2914 EWAR GOLD (Fr) (bl) 4-10-6 D Bridgwater, *hld up in tch, hmpd 5th, rdn and sn btn, tld off whn pld up bef last*. . . . . . (25 to 1 op 8 to 1 tchd 33 to 1) pu

Dist: Hd, 12l, ½l, 30l, dist. 4m 32.00s. a 32.00s (9 Ran).

(Terence M Molossi), L G Cottrell

3174 Robert Webb Travel Handicap Hurdle (0-125 4-y-o and up) £2,490 2¼m (4:00)

1162 GREEN ISLAND (USA) [97] 8-11-7 Peter Hobbs, *hld up, gd hdwy 3rd, second whn mstk 2 out, led and jmpd rght last, hng lft r-in, all out.*
.......................(5 to 1 op 4 to 1 tchd 11 to 2) 1

3119 MR PICKPOCKET (Ire) [99] 6-11-9 L Harvey, *hld up, hdwy 3rd, pld ldrs 2 out, hrd rdn and ev ch whn short of room r-in, ran on.........*(100 to 30 op 2 to 1 tchd 7 to 2) 2

2719⁵ ASHFIELD BOY [90] 10-11-0 M A FitzGerald, *sn trkd ldr, led appr 3rd till hdd and wknd approaching last.*
.....................(13 to 2 op 11 to 2 tchd 7 to 1) 3

2856⁷ BALLYSTATE [97] 6-11-7 G Upton, *led till hdd appr 3rd, wknd approaching 2 out.*
.....................(12 to 1 op 8 to 1 tchd 14 to 1) 4

3020⁴ LAND OF THE FREE [86] 5-10-10 J Osborne, *prmnt till lost pl second, effrt 5th, rdn and sn btn.*
.....................(11 to 4 fav op 5 to 2 tchd 4 to 1) 5

2964⁹ TRAIN ROBBER [76] 9-10-0 W Irvine, *prmnt early, beh frm 3rd.............*(25 to 1 op 20 to 1 tchd 33 to 1) 6

2819⁴ NOVA SPIRIT [84] 6-10-8 W McFarland, *prmnt till wknd appr 2 out...........*(11 to 2 op 6 to 1 tchd 5 to 1) 7

2947 SOUTHOVER LAD (NZ) [100] 11-11-7 (3*) R Davis, *hld up, effrt 3rd, rdn and wknd 5th, tld off whn pld up bef 2 out.............*(12 to 1) pu

Dist: Nk, 7l, 10l, 1½l, 5l, 6l. 4m 23.30s. a 23.30s (8 Ran).
SR: 22/23/7/4/-/   (J E Moloney), A J K Dunn

3175 Diamond Edge Challenge Trophy Novices' Handicap Chase (5-y-o and up) £4,068 2m 7f 110yds............ (4:30)

3135² KIWI VELOCITY (NZ) [95] 7-11-7 L Harvey, *al prmnt, led 8th, wnt clr 5 out, unchlgd.........*(7 to 1 op 4 to 1) 1

1467³ OLD BRIG [96] (bl) 8-11-8 J Lower, *prmnt, led to 8th, lost tch wth wnr frm 5 out...........*(7 to 1 op 9 to 2) 2

3054³ VILLA RECOS [92] (v) 9-11-4 M A FitzGerald, *hld up, hdwy 5 out, wnt second briefly appr last, jmpd slwly, no extr.*
.....................(20 to 1 op 16 to 1 tchd 25 to 1) 3

2999* UFANO (Fr) [85] 8-10-11 Peter Hobbs, *chsd ldrs till wknd quickly 5 out..................*(3 to 1 tchd 100 to 30) 4

2993⁶ COASTING [78] 8-10-1 (3*) R Davis, *chsd ldrs, rdn and wnt second briefly tenth, wknd 5 out.*(20 to 1 op 12 to 1) 5

2948 SKETCHER (NZ) [91] 11-11-3 J Frost, *led till 8th, wknd tenth, tld off...................*(8 to 1 op 10 to 1) 6

2879 BUCKLIGHT (Ire) [87] (bl) 6-10-10 (3*) R Farrant, *wtd wth, hdwy tenth, disputing 3rd whn blun and uns rdr 5 out.*
.....................(7 to 1 op 5 to 1 tchd 15 to 2) ur

3007⁸ WILLIE McGARR (USA) [89] 9-11-1 W McFarland, *al beh, tld off whn pld up bef twelfth.....*(33 to 1 op 20 to 1) pu

2946 CHASING GOLD [74] (bl) 8-10-0 M Hourigan, *slwly away, sn tld off, pld up bef 8th...........*(50 to 1 op 25 to 1) pu

3006* FLYER'S NAP [103] 8-12-1 (Sex) S Earle, *mstks, hit 6th, dsptd ld 9th, rdn 5 out, sn btn, tld off whn pld up bef 2 out...............*(2 to 1 fav tchd 9 to 4) pu

Dist: 30l, 4l, 5l, 10l, 4l. 6m 11.40s. a 36.40s (10 Ran).
(A D Stoddart), P J Hobbs

3176 H.M.S. Exeter Mares Only National Hunt Flat Race (4,5,6-y-o) £2,015 2¼m
.... (5:00)

SISTER STEPHANIE (Ire) 5-11-4 (3*) J McCarthy, *al prmnt, led wl o'r 2 fs out, ran on gmely und pres, all out.*
.....................(5 to 2 fav tchd 3 to 1) 1

GARRYLOUGH (Ire) 5-11-4 (3*) A Thornton, *hld up in rear, gd hdwy o'r 5 fs out, chlgd 2 out, pressed wnr to line.*
.....................(10 to 1 op 4 to 1) 2

SWEET REVELATION 5-11-0 (7*) T Dascombe, *wtd wth in tch, hdwy 4 fs out, chlgd 2 out, no extr cl hme.*
.....................(5 to 1 op 5 to 2) 3

DOUJAS 4-10-6 (7*) Miss S Cobden, *hld up in rear, gd hdwy 4 fs out, ev ch o'r 2 furlongs out, wknd appr last.*
.....................(33 to 1) 4

URBAN LILY 4-10-6 (7*) T Thompson, *in rear till hdwy 4 fs out, wknd 2 out......*(16 to 1 op 14 to 1 tchd 20 to 1) 5

WREN WARBLER 4-10-13 Mr J Durkan, *hld up, hdwy hfwy, wnt second 6 fs out, wknd quickly 3 out.*
.....................(5 to 1 op 3 to 1) 6

NOVA NITA 4-10-6 (7*) P McLoughlin, *prmnt till wknd 3 fs out..............*(16 to 1 op 20 to 1 tchd 12 to 1) 7

UP THE TEMPO (Ire) 5-11-0 (7*) M Moran, *nvr on terms.*
.....................(25 to 1 op 20 to 1) 8

FREE HANDOUT 4-10-6 (7*) Mr Richard White, *mid-div.*
.....................(33 to 1 op 20 to 1) 9

MARTHA'S DAUGHTER 5-11-4 (3*) R Farrant, *prmnt, led 6 fs out, hdd and wknd quickly wl o'r 2 furlongs out.*
.....................(8 to 1 op 4 to 1) 10

KIWI CRYSTAL (NZ) 5-11-4 (3*) R Davis, *beh, hdwy aftr 6 fs, wknd o'r 4 out.............*(10 to 1 op 6 to 1) 11

2444⁴ FURIOUS OATS (Ire) 6-11-0 (7*) Mr L Jefford, *led till hdd 6 fs out, wknd quickly, tld off.*
.....................(5 to 1 op 10 to 1 tchd 11 to 2) 12

2021 BESSIE BOSSY BOOTS 4-10-8 (5*) D Salter, *prmnt till wknd 6 fs out, tld off...........*(20 to 1 op 16 to 1) 13

2996 KEEP THE DREAM 4-10-6 (7*) R Darke, *pld hrd, chsd ldrs till wknd sn aftr hfwy, tld off...........*(20 to 1) 14

MADAM MARGEAUX (Ire) 5-11-0 (7*) Mr J Culloty, *al beh, tld off...................*(10 to 1 op 20 to 1 tchd 8 to 1) 15

ROALY 5-11-7 D Meade, *prmnt till wknd quickly 5 fs out, tld off..........................*(20 to 1 tchd 25 to 1) 16

NEARLY A BROOK 4-10-8 (5*) Guy Lewis, *al beh, tld off.*
.....................(20 to 1 op 8 to 1) 17

Dist: Nk, ½l, 12l, 25l, hd, 6l, 1l, 3½l, nk, 3l. 4m 24.70s. (17 Ran).
(The Antwick Partnership), Mrs M McCourt

KELSO (soft)
Wednesday March 23rd
Going Correction: PLUS 2.00 sec. per fur. (races 1,3,6), PLUS 1.65 (2,4,5)

3177 Dolphin Hotel & Fleet Inn 'National Hunt' Novices' Hurdle (5-y-o and up) £2,425 2¾m 110yds............ (2:10)

2278* JOHNNY KELLY 7-11-7 M Dwyer, *cl up gng wl, led 2 out, shaken up aftr last, styd on well.*
......(13 to 8 on op 6 to 4 on tchd 11 to 8 on and 5 to 4 on) 1

2812 COQUI LANE 7-11-7 Mr J M Dun, *led or dsptd ld till hdd 2 out, no extr.....................*(7 to 2 op 3 to 1) 2

2358 ARIADLER (Ire) 6-11-7 K Johnson, *trkd ldrs, pushed alng hfwy, outpcd appr 3 out, kpt on wl frm nxt.*
.....................(16 to 1 op 10 to 1) 3

PARLEBIZ 5-10-4 (5*) J Burke, *mid-div, hdwy to join ldrs 7th, rdn appr 2 out, grad wknd....*(66 to 1 op 33 to 1) 4

3034⁶ SHARP CHALLENGE 7-11-0 A Merrigan, *hld up in tch, kpt on frm 3 out, not trble ldrs........*(66 to 1 op 50 to 1) 5

3076 BANNTOWN BILL (Ire) 5-11-0 C Grant, *cl up, outpcd aftr 7th, no dngr after.....*(13 to 2 op 5 to 1 tchd 7 to 1) 6

2737* HOTDIGGITY 6-11-7 A Dobbin, *nvr on terms.*
.....................(20 to 1 op 14 to 1) 7

3061 DUNREIDY BAY (Ire) 6-10-11 (3*) P Williams, *prmnt till wknd appr 3 out....................*(33 to 1 op 20 to 1) 8

2905³ SCOTTISH PERIL 7-11-0 B Storey, *beh, some hdwy aftr 7th, sn wknd....................*(25 to 1 op 20 to 1) 9

2583 KERRY TO CLARE 8-10-2 (7*) Mark Roberts, *pushed alng hfwy, sn beh, tld off whn pld up bef 8th.*
.....................(200 to 1 op 100 to 1) pu

1787 BOWLANDS HIMSELF (Ire) 6-10-9 (5*) Mr D Parker, *in tch, blun 6th, sn beh, tld off whn pld up bef 3 out.*
.....................(100 to 1 op 50 to 1) pu

MR MCAFF (Ire) 5-10-7 (7*) P Carr, *beh frm hfwy, tld off whn pld up bef 8th...................*(200 to 1) pu

Dist: 5l, 2½l, 2l, 2½l, 3½l, 5l, 8l, 12l. 6m 4.60s. a 53.60s (12 Ran).
SR: 7/2/-/-/-/-/   (Mrs M Dickinson), J J O'Neill

3178 Potterton Myson Novices' Chase (5-y-o and up) £2,721 2m 1f........ (2:40)

2896 BASILICUS (Fr) 5-10-8 Gary Lyons, *cl up, chlgd appr 3 out, led aftr nxt, sn clr, easily............*(8 to 1 op 6 to 1) 1

2121⁸ ABLE PLAYER (USA) (bl) 7-11-3 (5*) J Burke, *in tch, blun 6th, mstk 9th, kpt on frm 2 out, no ch wth wnr.*
.....................(6 to 1 op 9 to 2 tchd 7 to 1) 2

3129² GRAZEMBER 7-11-2 R Garritty, *hld up, effrt whn mstk 3 out, sn pushed alng, nvr on terms.*(25 to 1 op 16 to 1) 3

2829³ THE COUNTRY TRADER 8-11-2 N Doughty, *hit 1st, in tch till wknd appr 3 out.*
.....................(5 to 8 fav op 6 to 4 tchd 20 to 1) 4

3129³ HIGHLANDMAN 8-11-2 A Dobbin, *chsd ldrs, mstk 8th, wknd appr 3 out.............*(4 to 1 op 7 to 2) 5

2971² MACCONACHIE 7-11-2 A Merrigan, *led, hrd pressed appr 3 out, hdd aftr nxt, wkng whn blun last.*
.....................(4 to 1 op 9 to 2 tchd 5 to 1) 6

MASTER MATHEW 7-11-2 Miss P Robson, *in tch, pushed alng whn f 8th....................*(33 to 1 op 20 to 1) f

Dist: 15l, 25l, hd, 10l, 15l. 4m 39.30s. a 33.30s (7 Ran).
SR: 27/26/-/-/   (Trevor Hemmings), Mrs S J Smith

3179 Lothian Plumbing Supplies Novices' Hurdle (4-y-o and up) £2,425 2¼m
.... (3:10)

2810² CALLERNOY (Ire) 4-10-1 (7*) Mr A Manners, *slightly hmpd 1st, chsd clr ldr, slight ld 3 out, shaken up and styd on aftr last.............*(100 to 30 op 5 to 2 tchd 7 to 2) 1

2951² CROMARTY 4-10-3 M Dwyer, *hld up, hdwy aftr 6th, ch last, kpt on same pace.*
.....................(7 to 4 fav op 2 to 1 tchd 9 to 4) 2

2737⁵ RALLEGIO 5-10-11 (5*) J Burke, *hld up, gd hdwy aftr 6th, chalg whn mstk 2 out, ev ch when mistake last, no extr.*
.....................(20 to 1 op 16 to 1) 3

2812 EMERALD SEA (USA) 7-11-2 S Turner, *prmnt, led 7th, hdd 3 out, one pace frm nxt.............*(16 to 1 op 14 to 1) 4

1787 LONDON HILL 6-11-2 C Dennis, *chsd ldrs till outpcd aftr 6th, no dngr after...............*(33 to 1 op 25 to 1) 5

3034* OTTER BUSH 5-11-1 (7*) D Towler, *in tch, ev ch 2 out, hit last, swtchd r-in and not run on.* (16 to 1 op 12 to 1) 6

2154 THALEROS 4-10-8 J Callaghan, *hld up, some hdwy aftr 6th, wknd 3 out.............*(16 to 1 op 10 to 1) 7

2903 CALL THE SHOTS (Ire) 5-10-13 (3*) P Williams, *al beh.*
.....................(100 to 1 op 100 to 1) 8

2903* LITTLE BROMLEY 7-11-3 Mr R Hale, *led, clr till 6th, hdd nxt, wknd appr 2 out...............*(5 to 1 op 4 to 1) 9

1918⁸ BACK BEFORE DAWN 7-11-2 L O'Hara, *hld up, hdwy aftr 6th, wknd appr 2 out*............ (25 to 1 tchd 33 to 1) 10
1607 DOUGAL'S BIRTHDAY 8-11-2 A Merrigan, *sn wl beh, tld off*................. (200 to 1 op 100 to 1) 11
2407 TUESDAYNIGHTMARE 5-10-4 (7*) I Jardine, *f 1st.* (50 to 1) f
    KAVLAD 7-11-2 A Dobbin, *wl beh whn slpd up bend appr 2 out*............................ (66 to 1 op 50 to 1) su
2367 KIRKTON GREY 7-10-11 (5*) Mr D Parker, *slightly hmpd 1st, mid-div till wknd aftr 6th, tld off whn pld up bef 2 out*........................ (12 to 1 op 14 to 1 tchd 16 to 1) pu
2951⁷ GOING PUBLIC 7-11-2 K Johnson, *chsd ldrs till wknd aftr 7th, wl beh whn pld up after last.* (50 to 1 op 33 to 1) pu
2810 MOSS PAGEANT 4-10-8 R Hodge, *pld hrd, prmnt to hfwy, tld off whn pulled up bef 2 out.*
    .... (50 to 1 op 33 to 1) pu
2828 HEDDON HAUGH (Ire) 6-11-2 C Grant, *sn wl beh, tld off whn pld up bef 3 out*............ (50 to 1 op 33 to 1) pu
    HIGH BURNSHOT 7-11-2 B Storey, *beh frm hfwy, tld off whn pld up bef 3 out*............... (66 to 1 op 33 to 1) pu
    TANGO COUNTRY 5-10-11 P Niven, *beh frm 6th, tld off whn pld up bef 2 out*........... (33 to 1 op 50 to 1) pu
Dist: 3½l, 1½l, 10l, 5l, 5l, ½l, 3l, 4l, 7l, dist. 4m 52.00s. a 45.00s (19 Ran).
(R R Lamb), R R Lamb

3180 King's Own Scottish Borderers Challenge Cup Handicap Chase (0-135 5-y-o and up) £4,123 3m 1f.........(3:40)

1725⁴ PINK GIN [102] 7-10-9 C Grant, *chsd ldrs, rdn alng aftr 4 out, led appr last, drvn clr.*
    .... (7 to 1 op 6 to 1 tchd 8 to 1) 1
2813² BLUFF KNOLL [121] 11-12-0 G Harker, *in tch, reminders hfwy, outpcd aftr 13th, rallied after 4 out, kpt on und pres r-in*......................... (5 to 1 op 9 to 2) 2
2635³ RIFLE RANGE [110] 11-11-3 P Niven, *made most till hdd 13th, chsd ldr aftr, chlgd last, kpt on same pace.*
    .... (14 to 1 op 12 to 1) 3
2930⁴ REGAL ESTATE [109] 10-11-2 R Garritty, *hld up in tch, effrt aftr 15th, no hdwy*............ (10 to 1 op 12 to 1) 4
2973² TRUELY ROYAL [93] 10-10-0 B Storey, *in tch til outpcd aftr 12th, no dngr after*...........(11 to 2 op 5 to 1) 5
2973⁴ RUN PET RUN [105] 9-10-12 A Dobbin, *cl up, led 13th, hdd appr last, sn btn.*... (7 to 2 fav op 4 to 1) 6
    FISH QUAY [93] 11-9-7 (7*) Miss S Lamb, *in tch, outpcd aftr 13th, sn beh*........... (33 to 1 op 25 to 1) 7
2764 INCONCLUSIVE [93] 7-9-9 (5*) Mr D Parker, *in tch whn f 6th*................. (20 to 1 tchd 25 to 1 and 33 to 1) f
2973⁵ LOTHIAN PILOT [94] 7-10-1 L Wyer, *lost tch, pld up and dismounted aftr 13th*............... (4 to 1 op 7 to 2) pu
Dist: 8l, 4l, 2l, 4l, 10l. 7m 0.90s. a 58.90s (9 Ran).
(B Kennedy), M D Hammond

3181 Sport Of Kings Classic Racewear Hunters' Chase (5-y-o and up) £2,320 3m 1f.........................(4:10)

    ROYAL JESTER 10-10-11 (7*) Mr C Storey, *led to 3rd, chsd ldr, led 15th, pushed clr frm last.* (5 to 4 on op Evens) 1
2605 CENTRE ATTRACTION 15-11-5 (5*) Mr N Wilson, *hld up, hdwy to chase wnr 2 out, rdn aftr last, no imprsn.*
    ....(11 to 10 op Evens tchd 5 to 4) 2
    KINNESTON 10-11-5 (5*) Mr D Parker, *led 3rd till hdd 15th, wknd aftr 2 out, tld off*......... (12 to 1 op 10 to 1) 3
    JACK OF CLUBS 14-11-3 (7*) Mrs E Wright, *lost tch hfwy, wl tld off*..................(66 to 1 op 50 to 1) 4
Dist: 10l, dist, 30l. 7m 19.00s. a 77.00s (4 Ran).
(Mrs A D Wauchope), Mrs Jane Storey

3182 A. & J. Scott Handicap Hurdle (0-125 4-y-o and up) £2,635 2¼m...... (4:40)

1940³ WEE WIZARD (Ire) [98] 5-10-5 A Dobbin, *in tch, reminder aftr 4th, hit 3 out, kpt on wl und pres to ld towards finish*.................... (7 to 1 op 8 to 1 tchd 9 to 1) 1
3078⁴ PALACEGATE KING [102] 5-10-2 (7*) B Harding, *trkd ldrs, rdn appr 2 out, cl second whn lft poor last, wknd and hdd towards finish*................ (4 to 1 tchd 9 to 2) 2
2815⁵ PERSONAL HAZARD [98] 5-10-0 L Wyer, *chsd ldr till outpcd appr 2 out, no dngr aftr.*
    ....(14 to 1 op 12 to 1 tchd 16 to 1) 3
2788⁸ BELLTON [121] 6-11-7 (7*) F Leahy, *in tch till outpcd aftr 6th, tld off*............. (10 to 1 op 8 to 1) 4
2815* BRAMBLEBERRY [111] 5-11-4 Gary Lyons, *led, jst in frnt and gng best whn f last*......... (2 to 1 fav op 6 to 4) f
2961⁸ MASTER OF THE ROCK [93] 5-10-0 C Hawkins, *lost tch frm 6th, tld off whn pld up bef 2 out.* (16 to 1 tchd 20 to 1) pu
Dist: 2½l, 8l, dist. 4m 47.60s. a 40.60s (6 Ran).
SR: 31/32/15/ (Armstrong/Greenwell), M A Barnes

SOUTHWELL (A.W) (std)
Wednesday March 23rd
Going Correction: NIL

3183 Salsa National Hunt Flat Race (4,5,6-y-o) £1,604 2m................(4:45)

2534² HULLBANK 4-10-8 (3*) D J Moffatt, *hld up, smooth hdwy o'r 4 fs out, led 2 furlongs out, pushed clr fnl furlong.*
    ....(6 to 4 on op 7 to 4 on tchd 5 to 4 on) 1
    OUR MAIN MAN 4-10-8 (3*) A Procter, *hld up, hdwy on outer 4 fs out, effrt 2 furlongs out, sn rdn and styd on.*
    .... (12 to 1 op 10 to 1) 2
    MIDVALE GRADUATE (Ire) 5-11-0 (5*) D Fortt, *hld up, steady hdwy hfwy, effrt to chal 2 out, led briefly, ev ch till rdn and one pace appr fnl furlong.*
    .... (10 to 1 op 7 to 1) 3
976⁹ RAYLEO (Ire) 5-10-12 (7*) S Spence, *cl up, led aftr 5 fs, rdn 3 furlongs out, sn hdd and wknd.*
    ....(16 to 1 op 20 to 1) 4
3035* MALACHITE GREEN 4-10-11 (7*) L Aspell, *hld up, hdwy 6 fs out, rdn 3 furlongs out and sn one pace.*
    ....(9 to 2 op 5 to 2) 5
2074⁹ SEAHAWK RETRIEVER 5-10-12 (7*) G Tormey, *trkd ldrs, hdwy hfwy, effrt to chase lder 4 fs out, rdn 3 furlongs out, wknd 2 furlongs out.*
    ....(7 to 1 op 5 to 1 tchd 8 to 1) 6
    PRESTHOPE 6-11-0 (5*) E Husband, *chsd ldrs, rdn alng 6 fs out, wknd o'r 4 furlongs out.*.... (6 to 1 op 20 to 1) 7
    MISSISSIPPISTEAMER (Ire) 5-11-0 (5*) Mr D McCain, *pld hrd, set steady pace, hdd aftr 5 fs, cl up till wknd fine furlongs out and sn beh*............(14 to 1 op 10 to 1) 8
2877⁹ SAN GIORGIO 5-10-12 (7*) P Ward, *trkd ldrs, pushed alng 5 fs out and sn lost pl*..............(10 to 1 op 7 to 1) 9
Dist: 1¾l, ½l, 6l, ¾l, 7l, 25l, sht-hd, 15l. 4m 5.10s. (9 Ran).
(D Gibbon), W W Haigh

WORCESTER (good)
Wednesday March 23rd
Going Correction: PLUS 0.65 sec. per fur. (races 1,3,-6,7), PLUS 0.55 (2,4,5)

3184 Pitchcroft Novices' Hurdle (4-y-o and up) £2,184 2m 5f 110yds........ (2:20)

2374⁷ DEMILUNE (USA) 4-10-7 C Llewellyn, *al wl plcd, led 3 out, sn clr, eased nr finish.* (5 to 1 op 3 to 1 tchd 11 to 2) 1
3005 CRAZY DAISY 7-10-5¹ (7*) T Murphy, *al prmnt, shaken up appr 2 out, one pace*........ (66 to 1 op 33 to 1) 2
2874⁵ ROSS GRAHAM 6-11-2 P Holley, *settled mdifield, hdwy 6th, one pace 3 out*...... (15 to 2 op 8 to 1 tchd 7 to 1) 3
2802² DEDUCE 5-11-2 A Maguire, *led, sn clr, hdd 3 out, soon outpcd*.................... (11 to 10 on op 5 to 4 on) 4
1837³ OCEAN LEADER 7-11-8 D Murphy, *wtd with in rear, cld 7th, btn whn hit 2 out*........... (4 to 1 tchd 7 to 2) 5
1878 OUR ARNOLD 7-10-9 (7*) P Maddock, *al beh, rdn 4th, no imprsn, tld off*................. (33 to 1 op 20 to 1) 6
    PERTEMPS JOBSHOP 8-11-2 N Williamson, *hld up, hdwy 7th, wknd appr 2 out*............(33 to 1 op 20 to 1) 7
2910⁵ SAIF AL ADIL (Ire) 5-11-2 V Smith, *lost tch 6th, tld off.*
    ....(66 to 1 op 33 to 1) 8
2897⁷ CAPTIVA BAY 5-10-11 R Bellamy, *mid-div, wknd 6th, tld off*.................... (66 to 1 op 33 to 1) 9
    CELTIC TOKEN 5-11-2 W Marston, *al beh, tld off 5th, f 3 out*................. (33 to 1 op 20 to 1) f
2525 HIGH BACCARAT 5-11-2 A Tory, *chsd ldrs to hfwy, sn wknd, tld off whn pld up bef 3 out.*
    .... (100 to 1 op 50 to 1) pu
3005 BOOK OF RYMES (bl) 7-10-11 W Humphreys, *chsd ldrs to hfwy, wknd quickly, tld off whn pld up bef 3 out.*
    .... (100 to 1 op 50 to 1) pu
    WATERJO 7-11-2 V Slattery, *al rear, tld off hfwy, pld up 3 out*.....................(100 to 1 op 50 to 1) pu
Dist: 5l, 1½l, 3½l, 15l, 15l, 7l, 10l, 1l. 5m 18.00s. a 24.00s (13 Ran).
(Mrs S Tainton), N A Twiston-Davies

3185 Stourport Handicap Chase (0-120 5-y-o and up) £3,659 2m...........(2:50)

    STARLAP [96] 10-10-12 A Maguire, *hld up beh, hdwy to chal 3 out, sn led, quickened clr last, easily.*
    .... (9 to 4 tchd 5 to 2) 1
2798² GALAGAMES (USA) [99] 7-11-1 B Powell, *led till appr 6th, led aftr 8th, hdd and hit 2 out, sn btn.*
    ....(5 to 4 on op 11 to 10 on tchd 5 to 4 on Evens) 2
3017³ RATHER SHARP [88] 8-10-4 C Maude, *pld hrd, chsd ldrs, led appr 6th till aftr 8th, rdn and btn whn mstk 2 out.*
    ....(100 to 30 op 9 to 4 tchd 7 to 2) 3
Dist: 15l, nk. 4m 6.20s. a 17.20s (3 Ran).
SR: -/-/8/ (Mrs D A La Trobe), R J Hodges

3186 Weatherbys 'Newcomers' Series Handicap Hurdle (0-115 4-y-o and up) £2,700 2m 5f 110yds.........(3:20)

2792² CAPTAIN MY CAPTAIN (Ire) [88] 6-10-4 C Llewellyn, *hld up, hdwy und pres appr 3 out, styd on to ld nr finish.*
    ....(12 to 1 op 8 to 1) 1
    MAYFAIR MINX [114] 5-11-11 (3*) T Jenks, *led till aftr 1st, led 7th, hit last, hrd rdn and ct nr finish.*
    ....(14 to 1 op 10 to 1) 2

2967^{5} ULURU (Ire) [103] 6-11-5 A Maguire, *al wl plcd, ev ch whn hit 2 out, rallied und pres r-in.* .... (11 to 2 op 5 to 1 tchd 6 to 1) 3
2766 CAMBO (USA) [89] 8-10-5 D Skyrme, *led aftr 1st till after 4th, rdn 2 out, kpt on*................(12 to 1 op 8 to 1) 4
2502^{2} INTEGRITY BOY [90] (bl) 7-10-6^{1} D Murphy, *trkd ldrs, rdn 3 out, styd on frm last*................ (6 to 1 tchd 7 to 1) 5
2982^{4} VISCOUNT TULLY [93] 9-10-9 W Humphreys, *prmnt, rdn appr 2 out, one pace*.............. (25 to 1 op 20 to 1) 6
2830^{5} ELEGANT KING (Ire) [106] 5-11-8 N Williamson, *prmnt till rdn and wknd appr 2 out.* .... (10 to 1 op 8 to 1 tchd 12 to 1) 7
2153^{6} PIMS GUNNER (Ire) [87] 6-10-0 (3*) D Bentley, *nvr plcd to chal*.............................. (16 to 1 op 12 to 1) 8
2515^{6} SYLVIA BEACH [97] 8-10-8 (5*) D Matthews, *chsd ldrs, rdn and wknd appr 2 out*................(12 to 1 op 8 to 1) 9
2528 BOREEN JEAN [93] 10-10-9 R Supple, *al rear.* .... (33 to 1 op 20 to 1) 10
GARSTON LA GAFFE [96] 9-10-12 P Holley, *in tch, shrtlvd effrt 7th, wknd 3 out.* (16 to 1 op 12 to 1 tchd 20 to 1) 11
2496 CAPPUCCINO GIRL [94] 7-10-10 M Crosse, *hld up in tch, rdn and wknd appr 2 out, tld off.* (20 to 1 op 16 to 1) 12
2961^{4} MR TAYLOR [89] 9-10-5 V Smith, *al beh, rdn 5th, no response, tld off*..... (9 to 2 fav op 6 to 1 tchd 7 to 1) 13
2788^{5} DUHALLOW LODGE [106] 7-11-8 Richard Guest, *pld hrd, led aftr 4th to 7th, wknd 3 out, tld off.* .... (12 to 1 op 8 to 1) 14
850 HIRAM B BIRDBATH [98] (bl) 8-10-7 (7*) Mr T McCarthy, *al beh, tld off hfwy*................. (20 to 1 op 16 to 1) 15
3020 BOADICEA'S CHARIOT [84] 7-10-0 C Maude, *al beh, tld off*................................(100 to 1 op 50 to 1) 16
1190^{2} LORD'S FINAL [87] 7-10-3 N Mann, *al beh, tld off.* .... (16 to 1 op 12 to 1) 17
3003 LEVY FREE [94] 9-10-3 (7*) Mr N Bradley, *al beh, tld off 7th, pld up bef last*.................... (66 to 1 op 50 to 1) pu
Dist: 1l, 1½l, 1½l, nk, 1½l, 2l, 1½l, ½l, 10l, 2l. 5m 21.60s. a 27.60s (18 Ran).
(Mrs A Burton), R Brotherton

3187 Brewery Traders Handicap Chase (0-135 5-y-o and up) £4,914 2m 7f (3:50)

2820* SHEER ABILITY [129] 8-12-0 A Maguire, *al cl up gng wl, dsptd ld 11th, led 14th, clr 2 out, pushed out.* ....(6 to 5 on op 11 to 8 on tchd 11 to 10) 1
1326^{5} TOMPET [101] 8-10-0 C Llewellyn, *al prmnt, led aftr 9th to 14th, ev ch 3 out, sn rdn and btn.* ....(9 to 4 op 5 to 2 tchd 2 to 1) 2
2305 MATT REID [110] 10-10-9 Mr W Morgan, *sn beh, some hdwy frm 3 out, nvr nrr*...... (9 to 1 op 7 to 1 tchd 10 to 1) 3
2674 WINABUCK [116] 11-10-12 (3*) D Meredith, *led 6th till aftr 9th, wknd 12th, tld off.* (9 to 1 op 8 to 1 tchd 10 to 1) 4
1458 BEL COURSE [101] 12-10-0 W Marston, *led to 6th, sn lost pl, rdn whn mstk 11th, tld off when blun 4 out.* .... (14 to 1 op 10 to 1) 5
Dist: 4l, 8l, 5l, dist. 6m 1.10s. a 17.10s (5 Ran).
SR: 54/22/23/24/-/ (Michael Devlin), C J Mann

3188 EBF St Barnabas Novices' Chase (5-y-o and up) £2,999 2½m 110yds (4:20)

2964^{5} SHEARMAC STEEL 7-11-3 G McCourt, *hld up, chlgd 4 out, led appr nxt, drvn out.* ....(6 to 5 fav op 5 to 4 tchd 11 to 8) 1
2721^{6} SIMON JOSEPH 7-11-3 B Powell, *pld hrd, hld up rear, mstk 6th, blun 11th, styd on frm 3 out, no ch wth wnr.* .... (2 to 1 op 11 to 8 tchd 9 to 4) 2
2999 PESSOA 7-11-3 Richard Guest, *led till appr 3 out, sn rdn, btn whn hit last*..................(20 to 1 op 14 to 1) 3
2767 TAURIAN PRINCESS 5-10-3 D J Burchell, *jmpd slwly 1st and 7th, pressed ldrs till wknd appr 2 out.* ....(16 to 1 tchd 20 to 1) 4
MERRY MUSE 8-10-12 C Llewellyn, *prmnt till blun and uns rdr 8th*......... (12 to 1 op 10 to 1 tchd 14 to 1) ur
OPENING OVERTURE (USA) 8-10-12 A Maguire, *hld up rear, lost tch appr 2 out, pld up bef last.* .... (8 to 1 op 7 to 1 tchd 10 to 1) pu
Dist: 6l, 1½l, 5l. 5m 30.00s. a 27.00s (6 Ran).
(Shearmac Steel Services Ltd), P J Hobbs

3189 Pershore Novices' Hurdle (4-y-o and up) £2,061 2m..................(4:50)

2802^{6} ATOURS (USA) (bl) 6-11-2 A Maguire, *made most to 5th, led 2 out, rdn clr r-in*...... (5 to 2 op 7 to 4 tchd 11 to 4) 1
2881^{5} RAGAMUFFIN ROMEO 5-11-2 G McCourt, *hld up, hdwy hfwy, shaken up appr 3 out, kpt on und pres, no ch wth wnr*............. (6 to 1 tchd 8 to 1 and 11 to 2) 2
3009^{2} MARINER'S AIR 7-11-3 N Williamson, *prmnt, led 5th to 2 out, rdn and hit last, sn btn.* ....(9 to 4 fav tchd 2 to 1 and 5 to 2) 3
LOBILIO (USA) (v) 5-11-2 D J Burchell, *hld up in tch, jmpd slwly 3rd, hdwy and rdn 3 out, not pace to chal.* .... (4 to 1 op 6 to 1 tchd 13 to 2) 4
EIGHTANDAHALF (Ire) 5-10-11 (5*) P Midgley, *prmnt, ev ch 2 out, rdn and wknd appr last.* ....(7 to 1 op 8 to 1 tchd 9 to 1) 5
2328 DAUPHIN BLEU (Fr) 8-11-2 Dr P Pritchard, *al rear, tld off.* .... (66 to 1 op 50 to 1) 6
3022^{3} THE QUAKER 8-10-11 Lorna Vincent, *dsptd ld to 5th, wkng whn blun 3 out, tld off*..... (20 to 1 op 16 to 1) 7
2857^{6} FLAMING MIRACLE (Ire) 4-10-8 D Gallagher, *lost tch hfwy, tld off*...(50 to 1) 8
SCORPOTINA 5-11-2^{5} Mr G Hanmer, *al rear, tld off.* .... (66 to 1 op 50 to 1) 9
LELLAJES 5-10-11 V Smith, *al beh, tld off.* .... (50 to 1 op 20 to 1) 10
1951^{6} PEACE FORMULA (Ire) 5-11-2 W Marston, *al rear, tld off 3 out*.............................. (50 to 1 op 33 to 1) 11
ROISTER DOISTER 4-10-2^{4} (5*) D Matthews, *prmnt to hfwy, wknd quickly and pld up bef 3 out.* .... (33 to 1 op 20 to 1) pu
Dist: 6l, 5l, ½l, 1½l, 15l, hd, 12l, 15l, 12l, 1l. 3m 57.50s. a 16.50s (12 Ran).
SR: 27/21/17/15/13/-/ (Saeed Manana), C P E Brooks

3190 Open National Hunt Flat Race (4,5,6-y-o) £1,528 2m.................(5:20)

2749^{3} SMART ROOKIE (Ire) 4-10-9 A Maguire, *hld up in tch, shaken up to ld o'r one furlong out, edgd lft and rdn clr fnl furlong*.........(11 to 10 fav op 6 to 4 tchd Evens) 1
HENRY CONE 5-11-3 G McCourt, *al wl plcd, chsd wnr appr fnl furlong, no imprsn.* ....(14 to 1 op 8 to 1 tchd 16 to 1) 2
2996^{6} COUNTRY CONCORDE 4-10-6 (3*) D Meredith, *pld hrd, chsd ldrs, rdn and one pace fnl 2 fs.* ....(12 to 1 op 14 to 1 tchd 6 to 1) 3
2877^{3} LE MEILLE (Ire) 5-11-3 N Williamson, *hld up rear, hdwy 6 fs out, not rch ldrs.* ....(7 to 2 op 5 to 1 tchd 6 to 1 and 3 to 1) 4
2890^{3} LORD CAMBERLEY (Ire) 6-10-10 (7*) Mr G Hogan, *led 12 fs, rdn and styd on one pace*.......... (33 to 1 op 20 to 1) 5
MR PRESIDENT (Ire) 5-10-10 (7*) M Berry, *hld up, cld 9 fs out, led o'r 3 out till over one out, one pace.* ....(12 to 1 op 7 to 1 tchd 16 to 1) 6
NOVA RUN 5-11-3 R Marley, *wtd wth, hdwy o'r 5 fs out, nvr nrr*.............................. (14 to 1 op 10 to 1) 7
WELSH'S GAMBLE 5-11-3 T Grantham, *patiently rdn, hdwy o'r 5 fs out, wknd over one out.* .... (9 to 1 op 7 to 1 tchd 10 to 1) 8
2332 VOLCANIC ROC 4-10-9 Richard Guest, *hld up, cld 6 fs out, rdn and wknd o'r 2 out*.................................(50 to 1) 9
2749 BUCKWHEAT BERTHA (Ire) 5-10-5 (7*) Mr G Haine, *pressed ldr, slight ld 4 fs out, sn hdd and wknd.* .... (33 to 1 op 20 to 1) 10
CALL HER A STAR (Ire) 4-10-4 Miss M Maher, *hld up, effrt entering strt, nvr nr to chal*....... (50 to 1 op 33 to 1) 11
SHANNON RUN (Ire) 5-10-10 (7*) R Moore, *hld up beh, wnt prmnt 5 fs out, wknd o'r 3 out*.................(50 to 1) 12
2444^{6} SOBER ISLAND 5-11-3 C Llewellyn, *hdwy hfwy, jnd ldrs 4 fs out, sn rdn and wknd.* ....(12 to 1 op 8 to 1 tchd 14 to 1) 13
2677 FIVEPERCENT 6-11-3 B Clifford, *prmnt for o'r 9 fs, sn lost tch*.............................. (50 to 1 op 33 to 1) 14
2877 FORBURIES (Ire) 5-10-12 R Bellamy, *al rear.* .... (50 to 1 op 33 to 1) 15
WOODYOU 4-10-9 R Supple, *prmnt ten fs*....... (33 to 1) 16
MY BOY BARNEY 4-10-9 B Powell, *nvr a factor.* .... (50 to 1 op 33 to 1) 17
2996 BLACK STAG (Ire) 5-11-3 D Murphy, *al beh.* .... (50 to 1 op 33 to 1) 18
2407^{8} SHERWOOD GRANGE (Ire) 6-11-3 M Brennan, *pld hrd, hld up, al rear, tld off*.................(33 to 1 op 20 to 1) 19
RUSTIC BRIDGE 5-11-0 (3*) S Wynne, *beh hfwy, tld off.* ....(25 to 1 op 20 to 1 tchd 33 to 1) 20
MISTER JAY DAY 4-10-9 D J Burchell, *al beh, tld off.* .... (33 to 1 op 16 to 1) 21
PLEASURE CRUISE 4-10-9 W Marston, *al rear, tld off fnl 6 fs*.................................(50 to 1 op 33 to 1) 22
Dist: 5l, 10l, 6l, ½l, 1l, ½l, 1½l, ½l, ½l, 2l. 3m 55.30s. (22 Ran).
(Mrs Shirley Robins), D Nicholson

STRATFORD (good to soft)
Thursday March 24th

Going Correction: PLUS 0.95 sec. per fur. (races 1,3,6), PLUS 1.25 (2,4,5)

3191 EBF 'National Hunt' Novices' Hurdle Qualifier (5,6,7-y-o) £2,070 2m 110yds ....(2:30)

2356 NATIVE FIELD (Ire) 5-11-0 M Dwyer, *pressed ldrs, chlgd 4th, led nxt, hit 3 out and hdd, led ag'n aftr 2 out, drvn clr whn wnt badly rght last, all out.* .... (9 to 2 op 11 to 4 tchd 5 to 1) 1
2874^{6} BLAYNEYS PRIVILEGE 7-11-0 R Garritty, *prmnt, led aftr 3 out, hdd after 2, rdn and styd on same pace r-in.* ....(14 to 1 tchd 16 to 1 and 20 to 1) 2
1557^{7} MUSKORA (Ire) 5-11-5 G McCourt, *beh, steady hdwy 4th, hit 5th, outpcd appr last, rallied r-in.* .... (85 to 40 fav op 2 to 1 tchd 7 to 4 and 9 to 4) 3

2692[5] SPIRIT IN THE NITE (Ire) 5-11-5 D Murphy, *prmnt, chlgd 4th, styd chasing ldrs till outpcd appr last, rallied r-in.* ....(11 to 4 op 3 to 1) 4
SAILOR'S ROSE 6-10-9 J Lower, *hld up, steady hdwy 5th, chsd ldrs 2 out, wknd quickly r-in.* (16 to 1 op 12 to 1) 5
BOLLINGTON (Fr) 5-11-0 S McNeill, *beh, hdwy 5th, wknd frm 3 out*..........................(50 to 1 op 25 to 1) 6
2996 JUNGLE KING (NZ) 5-11-0 C Maude, *nvr better than mid-div*......................(8 to 1 op 5 to 1 tchd 9 to 1) 7
2860[6] SOUTHERN DEALER 6-11-0 W McFarland, *beh most of way*.................................(16 to 1 op 10 to 1) 8
2950 HURRICANE SUE 5-10-9 N Williamson, *chsd ldrs till appr 5th, tld off*...................................(50 to 1) 9
2991 DEE EM AITCH 5-11-0 M Bosley, *al beh, tld off.* ....(100 to 1 op 50 to 1) 10
3009 KHAKI LIGHT 6-11-0 M Sharratt, *led to 5th, wknd quickly, tld off*..............................(100 to 1 op 50 to 1) 11
2950 CELESTIAL STREAM 7-11-0 B Powell, *prmnt to 4th, beh whn f last*........................(100 to 1 op 50 to 1) f
2332 GOOD FEELING 5-11-0 D Bridgwater, *mstk and beh, tld off whn ran out 2 out*..........................(50 to 1) ro
Dist: 5l, ¾l, ½l, hd, 4l, 15l, sht-hd, dist, 20l. 4m 12.70s. a 23.70s (13 Ran).
SR: 6/1/5/4/-/-/ (R L White), J G FitzGerald

3192 Newbold Novices' Chase (5-y-o and up) £3,057 3m....................(3:00)

2733 HILLWALK 8-11-8 D Morris, *made most till mstk 2 out and sn hdd, rallied und pres r-in to ld cl hme.* ....(3 to 1 op 5 to 2 tchd 7 to 2) 1
1631[2] UNHOLY ALLIANCE 7-11-8 N Williamson, *hld up, steady hdwy frm tenth, chsd wnr from 4 out, mstk 2 out, sn ld, rdn r-in, found little and ct cl hme.* ....(7 to 4 fav op 2 to 1) 2
2879[5] SPECIAL ACCOUNT 8-11-2 N Mann, *wth wnr till lost tch frm 4 out*...............................(8 to 1 op 7 to 1) 3
2766 POLLERTON'S PRIDE 7-10-11 D Bridgwater, *beh, styd on frm 3 out to take 4th pl r-in*......(14 to 1 tchd 16 to 1) 4
2855[5] GOOD OLD CHIPS 7-11-2 S McNeill, *in tch, not fluent, rdn 12th, sn wknd*........................(12 to 1 op 8 to 1) 5
3099 MOUNTAIN MASTER 8-11-2 Mr J M Pritchard, *hld up, hdwy 12th, sn wknd*.............. (33 to 1 op 20 to 1) 6
3007[6] EIGHTY EIGHT 9-11-2 W Marston, *prmnt to 12th.* ....(66 to 1 op 50 to 1) 7
2630[2] MEKSHARP 7-10-13 (3*) T Eley, *hit 1st, in tch, wkng whn hit tenth and 11th, no ch when blun badly 4 out.* ....(33 to 1) 8
LEINTHALL DOE 8-10-11 J Kavanagh, *beh till f tenth.* ....(33 to 1) f
2960 CHEQUE BOOK 6-11-2 Mr D Verco, *not fluent and beh till blun and uns rdr 13th*............(100 to 1 op 50 to 1) ur
3043 JUST MAX 10-10-11 (5*) J Supple, *prmnt early, beh frm 11th, tld off whn pld up bef 4 out*............. (50 to 1) pu
2980 RAKAIA RIVER (NZ) 7-11-8 G McCourt, *prmnt, hit 8th, wknd 12th, tld off whn pld up bef 4 out.* ....(4 to 1 op 3 to 1) pu
Dist: 1½l, dist, 8l, ½l, 7l, 6l, 2½l. 6m 23.00s. a 36.00s (12 Ran).
SR: 34/32/-/-/-/-/ (M L Shone), R Curtis

3193 Studley Handicap Hurdle (0-125 4-y-o and up) £2,810 2m 110yds...... (3:30)

3020[6] GOLDINGO [94] 7-10-0 (3*) R Davis, *trkd ldrs, chlgd 2 out, led appr last, shaken up and styd on wl r-in.* ....(8 to 1 op 6 to 1) 1
2883* MOVING OUT [105] 6-11-0 M Perrett, *led to 3rd, led ag'n 5th, not fluent 3 out or 2 out, hdd appr last, styd on und pres*..........................(5 to 1 op 4 to 1) 2
2461[4] CELTIC BOB [91] 14-10-0 V Slattery, *prmnt, rdn alng frm 5th, styd on same pace from 2 out.* ....(40 to 1 op 33 to 1 tchd 50 to 1) 3
3048* MARSH'S LAW [101] 7-10-10 (7ex) M Brennan, *beh till hdwy 5th, rdn frm 3 out, styd on r-in.* ....(7 to 4 fav op 6 to 4 tchd 2 to 1) 4
2792[7] SILLIAN [100] 12-10-9 N Williamson, *beh, effrt 3 out, wknd 2 out*.............................(14 to 1 op 12 to 1) 5
1437 MIDDLE MARKER (Ire) [119] 5-12-0 Diane Clay, *beh frm 3rd.* ....(14 to 1 op 12 to 1 tchd 16 to 1) 6
2833 GOLDEN GUNNER (Ire) [107] 6-11-2 G McCourt, *mid-div till hdwy 5th, rdn 3 out, sn wknd.* ....(15 to 2 op 8 to 1 tchd 6 to 1) 7
2379 NO SIR ROM [103] 8-10-9 (3*) D Meredith, *chsd ldr till led 3rd, hdd 5th, wknd quickly, pld up bef last*....(33 to 1) pu
2788 GRIS ET VIOLET (Fr) [110] 7-11-5 M Dwyer, *mid-div till drpd rear 4th, sn rdn, tld off whn pld up bef 2 out.* ....(14 to 1 op 8 to 1) pu
2480[4] SEAGULL HOLLOW (Ire) [96] 5-10-5 L Wyer, *beh, effrt 5th, sn wknd, tld off whn pld up bef last.* (4 to 1 op 3 to 1) pu
Dist: 1½l, 11l, nk, 11l, 9l, 1½l. 4m 8.80s. a 19.80s (10 Ran).
SR: 34/43/18/27/15/25/11/-/-/ (G M Price), G M Price

3194 Bishopton Handicap Chase (0-125 5-y-o and up) £3,434 2½m.......... (4:00)

1206[8] MIDFIELDER [107] 8-10-13 G McCourt, *hld up, hdwy to track ldrs 7th, led tenth, sn clr, rdn frm 2 out, ran on wl*..................................(3 to 1 tchd 7 to 2) 1
3105* RAMSTAR [99] 6-10-5 (7ex) W Marston, *hdwy to track ldrs 5th, chlgd 2 out, one pace appr last.* ....(15 to 8 fav op 6 to 4 tchd 2 to 1) 2
3024 KIBREET [109] 7-10-8 (7*) P Carey, *chsd ldr till blun second, chased lder ag'n frm 5th, chlgd eigith, wknd from 4 out*..................................(5 to 2 op 7 to 4) 3
2718[4] FIGHT TO WIN (USA) [104] (bl) 6-10-10 R Supple, *hit 3rd, al beh, lost tch 9th, tld off.* ....(8 to 1 op 10 to 1 tchd 11 to 1 and 12 to 1) 4
1190 JOYFUL NOISE [122] 11-12-0 Miss S Barraclough, *chsd ldr second to 5th, chlgd 8th, wknd and hit 11th, tld off.* ....(16 to 1 op 10 to 1) 5
2777[4] AIR COMMANDER [98] 9-10-4 T Wall, *led to tenth, sn wknd, tld off whn pld up bef 4 out.* (12 to 1 op 10 to 1) pu
Dist: 7l, dist, 7l, dist. 5m 13.00s. a 31.00s (6 Ran).
SR: 25/10/-/ (Bournstream '6'), P J Hobbs

3195 John And Nigel Thorne Memorial Cup A Hunters' Chase (5-y-o and up) £2,052 3m.................... (4:30)

2966 CALABRESE (bl) 9-11-7 (7*) Major M Watson, *led aftr second, made rst, in command whn lft clr last.* ....(2 to 1 fav tchd 9 to 4) 1
2889[2] FINE LACE 10-11-4 (5*) Mr G Tarry, *beh, hit 9th, hdwy 12th, staying on one pace in 3rd whn lft second at last.* ....(7 to 2 tchd 4 to 1) 2
GOOD WORD (bl) 12-11-7 (7*) Mr C Vigors, *chsd wnr 4th to 6th, rdn 14th, sn btn, tld off*...... (20 to 1 op 14 to 1) 3
2888* EASTERN DESTINY 16-12-3 (7*) Mr E Griffith, *beh and mstks, hdwy 12th, wknd 4 out, tld off.* .... (6 to 1 op 4 to 1 tchd 13 to 2) 4
2937 SUNNY MOUNT 8-12-10 Mr J Greenall, *prmnt, chsd wnr frm 6th, chlgd 7th to 8th, hit 14th, second and hld whn f last*..................................(3 to 1 tchd 100 to 30) f
PROPLUS 12-12-3 (7*) Mr T Edwards, *led till aftr second, blun 7th, tld off tenth, pld up bef 4 out.* ....(8 to 1 op 6 to 1 tchd 9 to 1) pu
HEADIN' ON 14-11-7 (7*) Mr S Joynes, *beh, reminders 5th, tld off whn pld up bef 12th*........(66 to 1 op 33 to 1) pu
HOLY MACKEREL 7-11-7 (7*) Mr N Sutton, *al beh, tld off tenth, pld up bef 3 out*............(66 to 1 op 50 to 1) pu
Dist: 5l, dist, 1½l. 6m 25.90s. a 38.90s (8 Ran).
SR: 11/1/-/-/-/ (Major M Watson), N J Henderson

3196 Idlicote 'National Hunt' Novices' Handicap Hurdle (4-y-o and up) £2,070 2¾m 110yds.................... (5:00)

2667[2] CHIEF RAGER [92] 5-11-6 D Bridgwater, *chsd ldrs 5th, drvn alng 8th, led aftr 3 out, driven out*......(5 to 2 jt-fav op 2 to 1) 1
2768[5] ANILAFFED [77] (v) 4-10-5 W Marston, *al chasing ldrs, led appr 3 out, hdd approaching 2 out, rallying whn mstk last, jst fld*.............................(10 to 1 op 7 to 1) 2
2757[4] BRAVE HIGHLANDER (Ire) [88] 6-11-2 D Murphy, *beh, steady hdwy frm 3 out, chsd ldrs from nxt, no imprsn.* .... (6 to 1 op 9 to 2 tchd 13 to 2) 3
2686[5] DUNDEE PRINCE (NZ) [83] 6-10-11 N Williamson, *ran in snatches, hdwy 6th, hit 3 out, styd on same pace.* ....(7 to 1 tchd 8 to 1) 4
2686 SCARF (Ire) [91] (bl) 6-11-5 M Dwyer, *chsd ldrs till outpcd frm 3 out*.......... (5 to 2 jt-fav op 2 to 1 tchd 3 to 1) 5
3020 SO AUDACIOUS [74] 6-10-2 R Supple, *mid-div 3rd, hdwy 6th, wknd 8th*............................(14 to 1 op 10 to 1) 6
1421[3] BROWNHALL [95] 6-11-2 (7*) Mr B Pollock, *led, clr 3rd, hdd and weakneed appr 3 out*......... (16 to 1 op 10 to 1) 7
2934[8] LEINTHALL PRINCESS [72] 8-10-0 J R Kavanagh, *chsd ldrs to 7th*..........................(25 to 1 op 20 to 1) 8
2779[4] BALLYGRIFFIN LAD (Ire) [72] 5-9-7 (7*) W J Walsh, *prmnt early, beh frm 4th*................(25 to 1 op 20 to 1) 9
GRATUITY [83] 9-10-11 N Mann, *al beh.* ....(50 to 1 op 25 to 1) 10
2860[7] CORNS LITTLE FELLA [72] 6-9-9 (5*) J Supple, *chsd ldrs to 7th, sn wknd*.....................(66 to 1 op 33 to 1) 11
2871[6] EMBLEY BUOY [72] 6-9-9 (5*) S Curran, *beh 4th, hdwy to press ldrs 8th, wknd frm 3 out*................(50 to 1) 12
2358 OTTOMAN EMPIRE [100] 7-12-0 M Brennan, *beh and hmpd second, mstk 6th, nvr dngrs.* .... (14 to 1 op 10 to 1 tchd 16 to 1) 13
Dist: ½l, 7l, 15l, 5l, nk, 6l, nk, ¾l, 1½l, 20l. 5m 44.70s. a 32.70s (13 Ran).
(James Cheetham), N A Twiston-Davies

THURLES (IRE) (heavy)
Thursday March 24th

3197 Ballyduff Maiden Hurdle (5-y-o) £2,243 2m............................(2:30)

3088* BACK TO BLACK (Ire) 11-9 K F O'Brien, ...(9 to 4 fav) 1
292 THE WICKED CHICKEN (Ire) 11-1 C F Swan, ... (6 to 1) 2
3122[6] ABAVARD (Ire) 12-0 S H O'Donovan, ...(10 to 1) 3
2924 NOT MY LINE (Ire) 11-3 (3*) C O'Brien, ...(14 to 1) 4
3124 FINAWAY EXPRESS (Ire) 11-3 (3*) T J Mitchell, ...(16 to 1) 5
2918[3] KING'S DECREE (Ire) 12-0 J P Banahan, ...(7 to 1) 6
3085[5] SIR SOOJE (Ire) 11-6 J Magee, ...(7 to 1) 7

2983 MAZELLA (Ire) 10-10 (5*) J R Barry, ...(12 to 1) 8
3122 LANCASTRIANS DREAM (Ire) 10-10 (5*) M J Holbrook, ...(20 to 1) 9
2983 ELUSIVE SOCIETY (Ire) 11-1 J A White, ...(12 to 1) 10
2983 ELIADE (Ire) 11-9 C O'Dwyer, ...(9 to 1) 11
2607 BRIGADIER SUPREME (Ire) 11-1 (5*) J P Broderick, (20 to 1) 12
2919 BAY VIEW PRINCE (Ire) 11-1 (5*) C P Dunne, ... (25 to 1) 13
ON THE BRIDLE (Ire) 10-12 (3*) T J O'Sullivan, ... (16 to 1) 14
3122 WHITE OAK BRIDGE (Ire) 10-8 (7*) P P Curran, ...(20 to 1) 15
2592[8] AUNT ROSE (Ire) 11-1 L P Cusack, ... (33 to 1) 16
PARABELLUM (Ire) 11-1 F J Flood, ...(12 to 1) 17
NO DIPLOMACY (Ire) 11-1 M Duffy, ...(14 to 1) 18
2553 MISS BERTAINE (Ire) 10-12 (3*) D P Murphy, ...(16 to 1) f
2470[8] BEDFORD RAMBLER (Ire) 11-6 T Horgan, ...(12 to 1) bd
MANOFI (Ire) 11-6 J Shortt, ...(20 to 1) pu

Dist: 7l, hd, hd, 3l. 4m 8.90s. (21 Ran).

(S McHugh), Michael Hourigan

3198 Ballyduag Novice Chase (5-y-o and up) £2,243 2¾m 110yds.........(3:00)

2987 MONKEY AGO 7-12-0 P Carberry, ...(6 to 1) 1
2282[4] PARSONS BRIG 8-11-9 (5*) J P Broderick, ... (4 to 1) 2
557 PORT TIME 7-12-0 M Duffy, ... (10 to 1) 3
2683[3] THE WEST'S ASLEEP 9-12-0 J Magee, ... (10 to 1) 4
2923[8] DUNBOY CASTLE (Ire) 6-12-0 T Horgan, ... (16 to 1) 5
2923[9] HIGHWAY LASS 8-11-9 S H O'Donovan, ... (20 to 1) 6
2988 BALLYCANN 7-11-11 (3*) T J Mitchell, ... (20 to 1) 7
1891[3] FINAL ISSUE 7-12-0 A Powell, ... (7 to 1) 8
2097[4] BUCK'S DELIGHT (Ire) 6-12-0 C O'Dwyer, ... (8 to 1) f
2923 CLEAKILE 8-12-0 F Woods, ... (20 to 1) f
2940[4] RICH TRADITION (Ire) 6-12-0 J Shortt, ... (5 to 2 fav) ur
2922 THE MIGHTY BUCK 11-12-0 J F Titley, ... (14 to 1) pu
2055 MR BARNEY 7-12-0 J K Kinane, ... (33 to 1) pu
50 BAR LASS 7-11-9 D H O'Connor, ... (33 to 1) pu
LOST COIN 7-11-6 (3*) D P Murphy, ... (33 to 1) pu
340[2] SILVER LIGHT (Ire) 6-12-0 K F O'Brien, ... (14 to 1) pu

Dist: 4l, 3l, 1l, 7l. 6m 37.10s. (16 Ran).

(Mrs Audrey Healy), P Mullins

3199 W.T. O'Grady Memorial Hurdle (5-y-o and up) £2,243 2¼m............(3:30)

3083* FOR REG (Ire) 5-11-12 M Duffy, ... (3 to 1) 1
3085[3] MISS LIME 7-10-10 (7*) R A Hennessy, ...(6 to 1) 2
2939* COMMON POLICY (Ire) 5-11-9 (3*) T J O'Sullivan, (5 to 2 jt-fav) 3
1850 FINAL TUB 11-11-4 G M O'Neill, ... (14 to 1) 4
2988[7] STAR ROSE 12-10-10 (7*) J Butler, ... (10 to 1) 5
2232 PERCY BRENNAN (bl) 7-11-1 (7*) J M Donnelly, ...(16 to 1) 6
2986 KELLY'S PEARL 7-11-9 C F Swan, ...(5 to 2 jt-fav) 7
2939[9] GOODNIGHT IRENE (Ire) 5-10-6 (5*) M J Holbrook, (66 to 1) 8
3084[9] BOG LEAF VI 11-10-10 (3*) C O'Brien, ... (33 to 1) 9

Dist: 1l, 2½l, 20l, 2½l. 4m 45.80s. (9 Ran).

(D H O'Reilly), Patrick Joseph Flynn

3200 Bansha Handicap Chase (0-109 5-y-o and up) £2,243 2¼m............(4:30)

3063[9] BART OWEN [-] 9-12-0 C F Swan, ... (7 to 4 fav) 1
2550 HIGHBABS [-] 8-9-7 T Horgan, ...(7 to 1) 2
2393 CITIZEN LEVEE [-] 8-11-1 (5*) Mr W M O'Sullivan, (12 to 1) 3
2350[4] BALLYHEIGUE [-] 8-10-3 (3*) D P Murphy, ... (6 to 1) 4
2772[6] WRECKLESS MAN [-] 7-11-7 J Shortt, ... (8 to 1) 5
2922 KIL KIL CASTLE [-] 7-9-0 (7*) Mr A O'Shea, ... (14 to 1) 6
2589[9] PINEWOOD LAD [-] 7-10-7 (5*) C P Dunne, ... (10 to 1) 7
2036 SQUIRRELLSDAUGHTER [-] (bl) 7-9-8 J Jones, ... (25 to 1) 8
2200[5] BENS DILEMMA [-] 9-9-7 (5*) J P Broderick, ... (12 to 1) 9
1499 FAIRY PARK [-] 9-11-1 F Woods, ... (7 to 1) 10
2922 MONEY MADE [-] (bl) 7-9-2 (5*) M G Cleary, ... (50 to 1) 11
2700[6] CASTLE KNIGHT [-] 8-11-6 W T Slattery, ... (8 to 1) f

Dist: 5l, 1½l, 4l, 3l. 5m 5.70s. (12 Ran).

(Mrs Sandra McCarthy), P Mullins

3201 Ballygermane I N H Flat Race (5-y-o and up) £2,243 2m..............(5:30)

3122 DUN CARRAIG (Ire) 6-11-11 (3*) Mr A R Coonan, ... (8 to 1) 1
THE OSTRICH BLAKE (Ire) 5-11-0 (7*) Mrs C Doyle, (10 to 1) 2
2684[3] KEEPHERGOING (Ire) 5-11-0 (7*) Mr T J Murphy, ... (7 to 2) 3
1500 TORONTO TELEGRAM 8-11-4 (5*) Mr J P Berry, ... (8 to 1) 4
2586[2] TAITS CLOCK (Ire) 5-11-7 (5*) Mr H F Cleary, ... (2 to 1 fav) 5
1989[8] MISS POLLERTON (Ire) 6-11-2 (7*) Mr M J Bowe, (12 to 1) 6
LADY OF TARA 8-11-6 (3*) Mrs J M Mullins, ... (8 to 1) 7
2236[6] RAHEEN FLOWER (Ire) 6-11-9 Mr D M O'Brien, ... (12 to 1) 8
RIVER OF PEACE (Ire) 6-11-2 (7*) Mr T Power, ... (12 to 1) 9
2869 CLONROSH SLAVE 7-11-9 (5*) Mr P M Kelly, ... (14 to 1) 10
2924 QUIET ONE 9-11-2 (7*) Miss U Corcoran, ... (20 to 1) 11
3124 OH RIVER (Ire) 5-11-0 (7*) Mr T N Cloke, ... (12 to 1) 12
2983 NOBLE KNIGHT (Ire) 6-12-0 Mr P Fenton, ... (14 to 1) 13
DANGEROUS LADY (Ire) 5-11-4 (3*) Mr D Marnane, (12 to 1) 14
CLEAR ROUND 7-11-9 Mr M Phillips, ... (8 to 1) 15
HOLLOW SOUND (Ire) 5-11-7 Mr A J Martin, ... (10 to 1) 16
1832[9] START SINGING (Ire) 5-11-4 (3*) Mrs S McCarthy, .. (8 to 1) 17
XIMUN (Fr) 8-11-9 (5*) Mr G J Harford, ... (16 to 1) 18
SWALLOW REEF (Ire) 6-11-9 Mr T S Costello, ... (14 to 1) 19
2869 DOUBLE SYMPHONY (Ire) 6-11-2 (7*) Mr J P Dwan, ...(10 to 1) su

Dist: 1l, 4l, ¾l, 4½l. 4m 7.50s. (20 Ran).

(Mrs C P Smith), Patrick Mooney

WINCANTON (good to soft) Thursday March 24th

Going Correction: PLUS 0.60 sec. per fur. (races 1,3,-5,7), PLUS 0.95 (2,4,6)

3202 Somerton Novices' Hurdle (4-y-o and up) £2,337 2m..................(2:15)

2979[2] KEEP ME IN MIND (Ire) 5-11-2 D Skyrme, *hld up in tch, hdwy 4th, led aftr 3 out, sn clr, unchlgd.* ....(7 to 4 fav op 2 to 1 tchd 6 to 4) 1
DARZEE 4-10-8 M Richards, *hld up, steady hdwy frm 4th, kpt on to go second r-in.* ....(10 to 1 op 5 to 1 tchd 12 to 1) 2
2789[3] BENTICO 5-11-2 C Llewellyn, *wth ldr and ev ch 3 out, sn rdn, chsd wnr till wknd r-in.* ....(9 to 4 op 11 to 4 tchd 100 to 30) 3
1642[9] SHIRLEY'S TRAIN (USA) (bl) 5-11-2 Peter Hobbs, *al prmnt, ev ch 3 out, rdn and sn outpcd*......(10 to 1 op 7 to 1) 4
CASPIAN BELUGA 6-11-2 S Burrough, *made most till hdd sn aftr 3 out, wknd*..................(8 to 1 op 5 to 1) 5
3016 PALACE PARADE (USA) 4-10-8 N Dawe, *mid-div, lost tch 3 out, tld off*.......................(16 to 1 op 10 to 1) 6
3051[8] GENERALLY JUST (bl) 9-11-2 Mr S Stickland, *prmnt to 4th, sn beh, tld off*...................(100 to 1 op 33 to 1) 7
BUCKLEY'S COURT 5-11-2 L Harvey, *al beh, tld off.* ....(14 to 1 op 10 to 1) 8
2653 VERRO (USA) 7-11-2 I Shoemark, *al beh, tld off.* ....(100 to 1 op 50 to 1) 9
HEAD OF DEFENCE 9-11-2 Mr S Shinton, *in tch, wkng whn blun 5th, tld off*.............(200 to 1 op 66 to 1) 10
INCHINA 8-10-11 Ann Stokell, *mid-div whn mstk 3rd, tld off when f 2 out*..........(200 to 1 op 66 to 1) f
3051 RED MATCH 9-11-2 A Tory, *in tch whn hit 4th, sn beh, tld off when pld up bef last*..........(66 to 1 op 50 to 1) pu
2804[6] NOW BOARDING 7-10-4 (7*) Mr Richard White, *mstk 1st, prmnt to 4th, tld off whn pld up bef 2 out.* ....(200 to 1 op 66 to 1) pu
2525 AMYS DELIGHT 6-10-11 R Dunwoody, *al beh, tld off whn pld up bef 2 out*.................(100 to 1 op 66 to 1) pu

Dist: 20l, 2½l, 1l, 5l, 30l, 12l, 25l, 12l, dist. 3m 52.30s. a 15.30s (14 Ran).

SR: 31/3/8/7/2/-/ (P C Tory), N R Mitchell

3203 West Country Veterans' Chase £3,574 2m 5f.............................(2:45)

2598[3] UNCLE ELI 11-11-2 S Earle, *trkd ldr frm 5th, led appr 3 out, drvn out*...........(5 to 2 op 9 to 4 tchd 2 to 1) 1
2747[5] RYDE AGAIN 11-11-2 J Osborne, *al prmnt, rdn and chalg whn hit 2 out, mstk last, no imprsn r-in.* ....(7 to 4 on op 6 to 4 on tchd 5 to 4 on) 2
2020[5] CHANCERY BUCK 11-10-12 J Frost, *al beh, lost tch 12th, tld off whn lft 3rd 2 out*........... (66 to 1 op 50 to 1) 3
3018[4] DRAW LOTS 10-10-12 I Shoemark, *jmpd slwly in rear early, hdwy 4th, wknd appr 9th, tld off.* ....(200 to 1 op 100 to 1) 4
SATIN NOIR (Fr) 10-10-12 A Maguire, *led till hdd appr 3 out, btn 3rd whn f nxt.* (7 to 1 op 10 to 1 tchd 6 to 1) f
3041 NOS NA GAOITHE (v) 11-10-12 R Dunwoody, *hld up in rear, hdwy to cl on ldrs tenth, rdn and ev ch whn blun and uns rdr 3 out*...............(16 to 1 tchd 20 to 1) ur

Dist: 2l, dist, 8l. 5m 41.60s. a 35.60s (6 Ran).

(James Burley), R H Alner

3204 Motcombe Mares Only Novices' Hurdle (4-y-o and up) £2,057 2¾m.. (3:15)

2796 AMBER REALM 6-10-13 (3*) R Farrant, *hld up, hdwy 5th, led 2 out, ran on gmely und pres*...(50 to 1 op 33 to 1) 1
3008[4] TIME FOR A FLUTTER 5-11-1 (7*) Mr E James, *nvr far away, mstk 3 out, led briefly appr nxt, rdn and ev ch whn mistake last, kpt on und pres.* ....(7 to 4 fav op 2 to 1 tchd 9 to 4) 2
2808[8] MARCONDA (Ire) 5-11-2 G Upton, *pld hrd, prmnt till blun 6th, rallied 8th, wknd quickly appr 2 out, tld off.* ....(14 to 1 op 16 to 1 tchd 20 to 1) 3
2642[2] LIZZIES LASS 9-11-2 M Crosse, *led to 6th, led 4 out to nxt, wknd quickly, tld off*.............(20 to 1 op 16 to 1) 4
2946 LITTLE CLARE 7-11-2 B Clifford, *sn beh, tld off.* ....(50 to 1 op 33 to 1) 5
2016[8] BORROWED AND BLUE 4-10-7 Peter Hobbs, *hld up, hdwy 6th, cl second whn mstk and uns rdr 2 out.* ....(20 to 1 tchd 25 to 1) ur
2871 HERESY (Ire) 5-11-2 M Hourigan, *sn trkd ldr, wknd 6th, tld off whn pld up bef last*.........(50 to 1 op 33 to 1) pu
STRATTON FLYER 4-10-2 (5*) Guy Lewis, *mstk 1st, tld off whn pld up bef 7th*................(66 to 1 op 33 to 1) pu
2731[8] COUNTRY FLING 6-11-2 C Llewellyn, *al beh, tld off 7th, pld up bef 2 out*......(14 to 1 op 16 to 1 tchd 12 to 1) pu
1660[5] LEXY LADY (Ire) 6-11-2 R Dunwoody, *prmnt, led 6th to 4 out, led ag'n nxt, sn hdd and wknd quickly, pld up bef last*.................(100 to 30 op 5 to 2 tchd 4 to 1) pu

2835⁴ FOIL THE FOX 6-10-13 (3*) A Thornton, *pld hrd, prmnt whn mstk 4th, wknd aftr nxt, tld off when blun 8th, pulled up bef nxt*.......................(9 to 4 op 11 to 4) pu
2934⁶ COSMICECHOEXPRESS 7-11-2 S Earle, *in rear whn jmpd rght 5th, tld off when pld up bef last*.
..............................(66 to 1 op 50 to 1) pu
Dist: 1l, dist, 30l, 20l. 5m 42.20s. a 36.20s (12 Ran).

(Mrs C J Dunn), R H Buckler

3205 Wincanton Golf Course Handicap Chase (0-130 5-y-o and up) £4,435 3m 1f 110yds.....................(3:50)

2791⁴ AUCTION LAW (NZ) [113] 10-11-10 J Frost, *hld up, hdwy 14th, chlgd 2 out, led last, all out*......(4 to 1 op 6 to 1) 1
2824* TIPP MARINER [102] 9-10-13 J Osborne, *hld up early, cld on ldrs 6th, 3rd whn mstk 15th, led appr 3 out, hrd rdn and hdd last, ran on*..........(9 to 4 jt-fav op 11 to 4) 2
2995² ANNIO CHILONE [113] 8-11-7 (3*) P Hide, *hld up, hdwy 14th, ev ch 4 out, one pace frm nxt*.
..............................(11 to 2 op 5 to 1 tchd 5 to 1) 3
3027 TOCHENKA [109] 10-11-6 C Llewellyn, *led second till mstk 4th, led 9th to nxt, led 12th till mistake and hdd four out, one pace aftr*..............(9 to 4 jt-fav op 6 to 4) 4
2294 JIMSTRO [101] 9-10-12 J Railton, *led to second, led tenth to 12th, mstk 16th, led briefly 4 out, wknd*.
..............................(20 to 1 op 14 to 1) 5
1720 HONEYBEER MEAD [100] (bl) 12-10-11 R Dunwoody, *hld to 9th, wknd quickly, tld off whn pld up bef 12th*.
..............................(33 to 1 op 25 to 1) pu
TROUT ANGLER [100] 13-10-11 A Tory, *beh till hdwy aftr 13th, wknd quickly 5 out, tld off whn pld up bef 3 out*.
..............................(50 to 1 op 25 to 1) pu
Dist: Nk, 12l, sht-hd, 13l. 6m 54.30s. a 38.30s (7 Ran).

(Mrs Brenda Gittins), D H Barons

3206 Quantock Handicap Hurdle (0-125 4-y-o and up) £2,882 2m...........(4:20)

3000 FRONT STREET [98] 7-10-10 J Osborne, *hld up, hdwy 4th, led appr 2 out, hdd sn aftr last, rallied und pres to ld ag'n on line*........(6 to 4 fav op 9 to 4 tchd 5 to 2) 1
3020⁸ CHEERFUL TIMES [93] 11-10-5 R Dunwoody, *hld up in rear, rapid hdwy to go second 2 out, led sn aftr last, hrd rdn and ct on line*......(7 to 1 op 6 to 1 tchd 8 to 1) 2
2992³ NOBLE INSIGHT [92] 7-10-4 C Llewellyn, *in rear, outpcd 4th, hdwy 3 out, rdn and wknd nxt*. (6 to 1 op 5 to 1) 3
MIDDLEWICK [100] 9-10-7 (5*) D Leahy, *trkd ldrs, ev ch 3 out, outpcd bef nxt*.......(10 to 1 op 8 to 1) 4
621 ICE STRIKE (USA) [106] 5-11-4 J Railton, *dsptd ld, led 3rd to 5th, rdn and wknd appr 2 out*.
..............................(7 to 1 op 6 to 1 tchd 15 to 2) 5
2649⁷ GALAXY HIGH [112] 7-11-10 M A FitzGerald, *led till mstk 3rd, led 5th, hdd and wknd quickly appr 2 out, clambered o'r last, tld off*........(8 to 1 op 6 to 1) 6
Dist: Sht-hd, 12l, 5l, 1¼l, 30l. 3m 56.00s. a 19.00s (6 Ran).

(Mrs Jean R Bishop), S E Sherwood

3207 EBF Corton Denham Novices' Chase (5-y-o and up) £3,038 2m 5f.... (4:50)

2473 BOSCEAN CHIEFTAIN 10-11-3 R Dunwoody, *led to second, led 8th, hdd nxt, led appr 3 out, clr whn mstks last 2*.
..............................(2 to 1 op 9 to 4 tchd 5 to 2) 1
2993² BIG BEAT (USA) 6-11-10 P Holley, *led second to 8th, led ag'n nxt, hdd appr 3 out, btn whn blun 2 out*.
..............................(15 to 8 fav op 6 to 4 tchd 2 to 1) 2
WISE CUSTOMER 10-11-3 Mr J Rees, *in tch to 9th, tld off*.
..............................(10 to 1 op 8 to 1) 3
2993⁵ DUKE OF APROLON 7-11-0 (3*) P Hide, *mid-div till lost tch tenth, tld off*..........(6 to 1 op 4 to 1 tchd 5 to 1) 4
2045⁴ PRINCE'S COURT (bl) 11-11-5 (5*) D Fortt, *mid-div, wl beh whn mstk tenth, tld off*.......(10 to 1 op 8 to 1) 5
2361⁸ TEARFUL PRINCE 10-11-3 J Railton, *in rear whn blun 5th, blunded and uns rdr 7th*..........(33 to 1) ur
2799 FRENCHLANDS WAY 10-11-3 L Harvey, *al beh off whn pld up bef tenth*..............(66 to 1 op 33 to 1) pu
1534² RYTON GUARD 9-11-3 G Upton, *prmnt to 5th, tld off whn pld up bef 12th*.............(14 to 1 op 14 to 1) pu
1805³ IT'S AFTER TIME 9-10-12 (5*) Guy Lewis, *trkd ldrs till wknd tenth, tld off whn pld up bef 3 out*.
..............................(25 to 1 op 16 to 1) pu
MASTER KIWI (NZ) 7-11-3 A Tory, *in rear, tld off whn pld up bef 4 out*..............(50 to 1 op 10 to 1) pu
1593⁷ JHAL FREZI 6-11-3 M A FitzGerald, *chsd ldrs, mstk 6th, wknd quickly 9th, tld off whn pld up bef 4 out*.
..............................(50 to 1 op 33 to 1) pu
Dist: 20l, 30l, 8l, 30l. 5m 29.50s. a 23.50s (11 Ran).
SR: 54/41/4/-/-/-/

(Miss Christine Olds), Mrs J G Retter

3208 Levy Board National Hunt Flat Race (4,5,6-y-o) £2,230 2m...........(5:20)

BERUDE NOT TO (Ire) 5-11-8 Mr J Durkan, *hld up in tch, rdn o'r 3 fs out, ran on to ld cl hme*. (6 to 1 op 5 to 1) 1

BUNGEE JUMPER 4-10-11 (3*) R Farrant, *al prmnt, rdn to ld ins fnl furlong, edgd rght, hdd cl hme*.
..............................(16 to 1 tchd 12 to 1) 2
2387⁴ EXCLUSIVE EDITION (Ire) 4-10-6 (3*) A Thornton, *trkd ldrs, led 3 fs out, hdd ins last, kpt on one pace*.
..............................(12 to 1 op 14 to 1) 3
SEVSO 5-10-10 (7*) R Massey, *hld up, hdwy o'r 2 fs out, ran on, nvr nrr*.......(6 to 1 op 5 to 1 tchd 7 to 1) 4
2749⁷ BOXFRIEND 4-10-7 (7*) N Willmington, *al prmnt, one pace fnl 2 fs*.........(3 to 1 fav op 7 to 2 tchd 9 to 4) 5
2677⁹ QUADRAPOL 5-10-10 (7*) P Melia, *prmnt, led 5 fs out, ran wide and hdd 3 out, kpt on till wknd wl o'r one out*.
..............................(7 to 1 op 9 to 1) 6
QUAKER WALTZ 4-10-9 D Meade, *beh till hdwy 5 fs out, wknd o'r 2 out*..............(50 to 1 op 25 to 1) 7
1494 GAY MUSE 5-10-10 (7*) C Quinlan, *in tch till wknd wl o'r 2 fs out*..............(20 to 1 op 25 to 1) 8
HAZEL GALE (Ire) 5-10-12 (5*) D Leahy, *in tch till outpcd 3 fs out*..............(7 to 2 op 3 to 1 tchd 9 to 2) 9
GAME DOMINO 4-10-6 (3*) A Procter, *al mid-div*.
..............................(50 to 1 op 20 to 1) 10
WHAT A MOPPET (Ire) 5-11-0 (3*) J McCarthy, *sl'wly away, nvr on terms*..............(20 to 1 op 12 to 1) 11
HIGHWAY LAD 5-11-1 (7*) T Thompson, *al beh*.
..............................(33 to 1 op 25 to 1) 12
JACK A HOY 4-10-11 (3*) T Jenks, *hld up, hdwy o'r 4 fs out, wknd wl over 2 out*........(33 to 1 op 25 to 1) 13
INKY 5-10-10 (7*) Mr S Mulcaire, *in tch till wknd 5 fs out*.
..............................(50 to 1 op 33 to 1) 14
LYRICAL SEAL 4-10-4 (5*) D Fortt, *al beh*.
..............................(50 to 1 op 25 to 1) 15
WHISKEY CASTLE (Ire) 5-11-3 (5*) Guy Lewis, *al beh*.
..............................(16 to 1 op 12 to 1) 16
2534⁵ TELEPHONE 5-11-1 (7*) Pat Thompson, *pld hrd, led for 2 fs, wknd quickly o'r 3 out*.
..............................(14 to 1 op 12 to 1 tchd 16 to 1) 17
MARYLAND BOY 6-11-1 (7*) R Darke, *pld hrd, led aftr 2 fs, hdd 5 out, wknd quickly*.........(50 to 1 op 25 to 1) 18
Dist: Sht-hd, 1½l, 2½l, hd, 8l, 6l, hd, nk, 8l, 5l. 4m 1.80s. (18 Ran).

(G Addiscott), O Sherwood

LUDLOW (good to firm)
Friday March 25th
Going Correction: NIL (races 1,3,6), PLUS 0.30 (2,4,5)

3209 Aston Munslow Novices' Hurdle (4-y-o and up) £1,822 2m.............(2:15)

964⁵ LABURNUM 6-11-9 R Dunwoody, *chsd ldrs, shaken up appr last, ran on to ld nr finish*.......(8 to 1 op 6 to 1) 1
3008* GESNERA 6-11-4 G McCourt, *wtd wth, steady hdwy frm 3 out, slight ld last, hrd rdn and hdd cl hme*.
..............................(13 to 8 fav op 5 to 4 tchd 7 to 4 and 2 to 1) 2
BROWNED OFF 5-11-2 D Bridgwater, *patiently rdn, took clr order hfwy, slight ld 2 out, hdd last, ridden and unbl to quicken*..............(25 to 1 op 20 to 1) 3
1840 ROCA MURADA (Ire) 5-11-2 W Marston, *hld up in rear, hmpd paddock bend, hdwy appr 2 out, ran on one pace*..............(25 to 1 op 14 to 1) 4
2244⁶ ROXY RIVER 5-11-4 M Hourigan, *pressed ldrs, ev ch appr 2 out, sn rdn and wknd*. (9 to 1 op 6 to 1 tchd 10 to 1) 5
1809 ALIAS SILVER 7-10-9 (7*) Mr N Bradley, *in tch, effrt und pres appr 2 out, not rch ldrs*......(100 to 1 op 50 to 1) 6
2119⁷ KELLY'S DARLING 8-11-4 (5*) S Curran, *prmnt, rdn appr 2 out, sn btn*..............(20 to 1 tchd 33 to 1) 7
2525⁴ WILKINS 5-11-2 R Marley, *pressed ldrs, rdn and ev ch 2 out, sn wknd*......(11 to 2 op 4 to 1 tchd 6 to 1) 8
2871⁹ CARAGH BRIDGE 7-11-2 R Supple, *led, quickened clr 5th, wknd and hdd 2 out*........(25 to 1 op 20 to 1) 9
870⁴ EUPHONIC 4-11-2 B Powell, *in tch to hfwy, sn lost pl, nvr dngrs*..............(25 to 1 op 16 to 1) 10
2302⁹ STERLING BUCK (USA) 7-10-11 (5*) D Leahy, *al beh, tld off*..............(33 to 1 op 20 to 1) 11
1990 DEE RAFT (USA) 4-10-9 M Richards, *pld hrd, prmnt till wknd appr 2 out, tld off*.
..............................(11 to 2 op 8 to 1 tchd 14 to 1) 12
3044³ OPALKINO 9-10-11 I Lawrence, *al beh, tld off*. (100 to 1) 13
547⁴ TOTAL UP (Ire) 5-10-11 (5*) Mr D McCain, *mstks, al beh, sn tld off, pld up bef 2 out*........(100 to 1 op 50 to 1) pu
2691 DABALARK 5-11-2 A O'Hagan, *in rear, effrt 3 out, wknd and pld up bef nxt*..............(10 to 1 op 8 to 1) pu
Dist: ¾l, hd, 6l, 7l, 3l, ¾l, 2½l, nk, 2½l, 10l. 3m 47.20s. a 10.20s (15 Ran).

(The Icy Fire Partnership), C J Mann

3210 Aston Handicap Chase (0-135 5-y-o and up) £3,022 2m.............(2:45)

1659³ WICKFIELD LAD [97] 11-10-0 D Bridgwater, *hld up in rear, gd hdwy appr 3 out, led nxt, rdn out flt*.
3066⁹ NORTHERN JINKS [119] 11-11-5 (3*) D Meredith, *cl up, rdn and lost pl 6th, rallied 9th, ev ch 2 out, one pace*.
..............................(7 to 2 op 5 to 2 tchd 4 to 1) 2
2990⁶ AL HASHIMI [118] 10-11-7 A Tory, *led 5th to 7th, led 9th to 2 out, hrd rdn and one pace flt*.
..............................(8 to 1 op 10 to 1 and 11 to 1) 3

2696[3] THATS THE LIFE [117] 9-11-3 (3*) T Jenks, *led to 5th, wknd 9th, sn beh*.............(5 to 1 op 4 to 1 tchd 11 to 2) 4
3017[2] WELSH BARD [121] 10-11-10 M Richards, *chsd ldrs, effrt and hrd rdn appr 2 out, wknd last*...(9 to 1 op 6 to 1) 5
2962[3] ALAN BALL [106] 8-10-9 G McCourt, *pld hrd, cl up till led 7th, hdd 9th, ev ch 2 out, sn rdn and wknd, broke blood vessel*...........................(13 to 2 op 5 to 1) 6
2825[4] PALM READER [125] 10-12-0 R Dunwoody, *settled rear, effrt and mstk 7th, lost tch appr 3 out, tld off*.
.............................(7 to 1 op 6 to 1) 7
2365[3] SHU FLY (NZ) [125] 10-12-0 Jacqui Oliver, *hld up in rear, pld up bef 8th, broke blood vessel*.
....................(11 to 4 fav op 5 to 2 tchd 3 to 1) pu
Dist: 3l, 6l, 7l, sht-hd, 5l, 15l. 4m 2.20s. a 10.20s (8 Ran).

SR: 18/37/30/22/26/6/10/-/   (A M Tombs), N M Babbage

3211 Seifton Novices' Selling Hurdle (4,5,6-y-o) £1,555 2m................(3:15)

3098[3] FICHU (USA) 6-11-4 B Powell, *patiently rdn, smooth hdwy 3 out, led appr last, drvn out*.
...........................(11 to 2 op 7 to 1 tchd 5 to 1) 1
2957[3] MISSED THE BOAT (Ire) 4-10-10 G McCourt, *hld up midfield, shaken up to improve 5th, styd on und pres flt*.
.......................(9 to 1 op 8 to 1 tchd 10 to 1) 2
2912[3] STAR MOVER 5-10-13 (7*) R Darke, *trkd ldr, slight ld 2 out, wknd, one pace flt*............(6 to 1 op 4 to 1) 3
2960[8] CRIMINAL RECORD (USA) (v) 4-10-10 Diane Clay, *chsd ldrs, rdn appr 2 out, one pace*........(20 to 1 op 14 to 1) 4
2945 NANQUIDNO (v) 4-10-5 R Dunwoody, *led to 2 out, eased whn btn appr last*.
.............(7 to 4 fav op 6 to 4 tchd 2 to 1 and 9 to 4) 5
1506[5] SWISS MOUNTAIN 4-10-2 (3*) T Eley, *settled midfield, hdwy 3 out, rdn and edgd lft appr last, sn btn*.
.......................(14 to 1 tchd 16 to 1) 6
3103 CAPTAIN TANDY (Ire) 5-11-4 D Bridgwater, *steadied strt, in rear whn mstk 4th, effrt appr 2 out, not rch ldrs*.
...........................(66 to 1 op 50 to 1) 7
3131 DALEHOUSE LANE 6-11-1 (3*) D Meredith, *nvr nr to chal*...........................(50 to 1) 8
BECKY BOO 4-10-5 R Supple, *prmnt whn mstk second, sn lost pl*......................(66 to 1 op 50 to 1) 9
3005 ARLEY GALE 4-10-8 (5*) Mr D McCain, *chsd ldg pair, rdn appr 2 out, sn btn*...........(66 to 1 op 50 to 1) 10
2331 PIPERS REEL 4-10-5 Richard Guest, *trkd ldrs to 3 out, sn lost tch, tld off*............(40 to 1 op 33 to 1) 11
2797 DOUBLE DEALING (Ire) 4-10-10 S McNeill, *in tch, hit 3rd, sn lost pl, tld off*.............(66 to 1 op 50 to 1) 12
2837 CUMREWS NEPHEW 6-11-1 (3*) T Jenks, *chsd ldrs to 3 out, sn wknd, tld off*............(50 to 1 op 33 to 1) 13
2957[9] SEATWIST 5-11-4 V Slattery, *mstk 3rd, sn beh, tld off*.
.......................(25 to 1 op 20 to 1) 14
MAC TOMB 4-10-10 M Hourigan, *cl up whn mstk 4th, sn lost pl, tld off*........(5 to 1 op 16 to 1 tchd 33 to 1) 15
2421[3] DOUBLE THE STAKES (USA) 5-11-11 D J Burchell, *wtd wth, smooth hdwy 5th, jnd ldrs 2 out, ev ch whn f last*.
.......................(8 to 1 op 5 to 1) f
Dist: 1¼l, 6l, 3l, nk, 1¾l, 5l, 2½l, 6l, 4l, 15l. 3m 49.60s. a 12.60s (16 Ran).

(Graham Thorner), G Thorner

3212 Aldon Hunters' Chase (6-y-o and up) £1,584 3m....................(3:50)

2968[2] WILD ILLUSION 10-11-12 (7*) Mr J Trice-Rolph, *hld up gng wl, prog 14th, led last, ran on well*.
.......................(5 to 1 op 6 to 4 tchd 13 to 8) 1
GLEN OAK 9-11-7 (7*) Mr D Duggan, *chsd ldrs, rdn entering strt, hit 2 out, kpt on flt*.......(20 to 1 op 16 to 1) 2
2949[2] SONOFAGIPSY 10-11-12 (7*) Mr R Nuttall, *chsd ldr, led 13th to last, rdn and one pace*.
.......................(11 to 1 op 12 to 1 tchd 8 to 1) 3
2889[3] PAMELA'S LAD 8-11-7 (7*) Mr S Hanmer, *hld up, mstk 9th, hdwy 11th, one pace frm 3 out*....(20 to 1 op 16 to 1) 4
2887* MY MELLOW MAN 11-12-0 (5*) Miss P Curling, *prmnt till wknd 11th, sn tld off*............(20 to 1 op 16 to 1) 5
WARLEGGAN 13-12-0 (5*) Mr S Brookshaw, *settled middiv, effrt 12th, wknd 14th, tld off*..(20 to 1 op 16 to 1) 6
2650[2] LOR MOSS 14-11-12 (7*) Mr G Hogan, *al in rear, tld off frm 13th*...........................(14 to 1 tchd 16 to 1) 7
COMBO (Cze) 10-11-12 (7*) Mr Paul Morris, *al wl beh, tld off, pld up bef last*............(20 to 1 tchd 25 to 1) pu
2508 NO ESCORT 10-12-0 (5*) Mr R Russell, *jmpd wl, pld hrd, led to 13th, wknd quickly nxt, beh whn pulled up bef 3 out*.....................(5 to 2 op 7 to 4 tchd 11 to 2) pu
2884[4] BACK IN BUSINESS 11-11-7 (7*) Mr A Dalton, *prmnt till mstk 12th, sn lost tch, tld off whn pld up bef last*.
.......................(20 to 1 op 14 to 1) pu
Dist: 3½l, 4l, ½l, 20l, 12l, hd. 6m 12.30s. a 23.30s (10 Ran).

(Col A Clerke-Brown), Miss Jennifer Pidgeon

3213 Bitterly Novices' Chase (5-y-o and up) £2,788 2½m..................(4:20)

2524[2] RABA RIBA 9-11-9 V Slattery, *led aftr 1st, clr 11th, jmpd rght and mstk 3 out, unchlgd*....(5 to 2 tchd 11 to 4) 1

3043* HEARTS ARE WILD 7-11-9 B Powell, *outpcd, wnt poor 3rd 7th, chsd wnr frm 3 out, no imprsn*.
.......................(15 to 8 on op 2 to 1 on tchd 7 to 4 on) 2
2803[4] HIDDEN PLEASURE 8-11-3 G Upton, *led till aftr 1st, wth wnr till wknd tenth, sn btn*.
.........(10 to 1 op 8 to 1 tchd 11 to 1 and 12 to 1) 3
3005[9] QUAGO 6-10-9 (3*) R Farrant, *outpcd, al beh*.
.......................(50 to 1 op 33 to 1) 4
2693 PENIARTH 8-10-12 I Lawrence, *al outpcd and beh*.
.......................(100 to 1 op 50 to 1) 5
2208 ROSEN THE BEAU (Ire) 6-11-3 R Supple, *chsd ldg pair to 7th, rdn and lost tch 9th*.........(25 to 1 op 16 to 1) 6
1704 WAYWARD SAILOR 8-11-3 W Marston, *mstk 3rd, rdn 9th, al outpcd, tld off*..........(50 to 1 op 25 to 1) 7
3007 CARLSAN 8-11-3 Mr M Jackson, *mstks, al wl beh, tld off*.
.......................(100 to 1 op 50 to 1) 8
3004[6] BROADWOOD LAD 8-10-10 (7*) P McLoughlin, *jmpd badly, al in rear, tld off*...(66 to 1 op 50 to 1 tchd 100 to 1) 9
2208 CARLINGFORD BELLE 8-10-12 Richard Guest, *nvr nr ldrs, tld off whn pld up bef 3 out*.....(100 to 1 op 50 to 1) pu
Dist: 8l, 25l, 10l, 1½l, ¾l, dist, 6l, dist. 5m 2.50s. a 11.50s (10 Ran).

SR: 40/32/1/-/-/-/   (Jeff McCarthy), J L Spearing

3214 Downton Handicap Hurdle (0-135 4-y-o and up) £2,612 2m 5f 110yds.. (4:50)

3038 LYNCH LAW (Ire) [114] (v) 6-11-5 R Dunwoody, *wtd wth in rear, steady hdwy appr 2 out, chlgd and hit last, sn led, cmftbly*......(9 to 4 fav tchd 5 to 2 and 11 to 4) 1
2982[3] NICK THE DREAMER [110] 9-10-8 (7*) R Darke, *al cl up, dsptd ld frm 2 out, unbl to quicken flt*.
.......................(100 to 30 op 5 to 2) 2
2346[3] SHIMMERING SCARLET (Ire) [98] 6-10-3 B Powell, *led till aftr second, led appr 2 out to flt, rdn and no extr*.
.......................(7 to 2 tchd 4 to 1 and 9 to 2) 3
3028 FOX CHAPEL [119] 7-11-3 (7*) N Juckes, *trkd ldrs, effrt appr 2 out, sn outpcd*........(12 to 1 op 8 to 1) 4
3020[9] PROPAGANDA [111] 6-11-2 G McCourt, *hld up and beh, effrt 3 out, hrd rdn nxt, sn btn*....(10 to 1 op 8 to 1) 5
3009[4] MUCH [95] 7-10-0 Mr M Jackson, *led aftr second till appr 2 out, sn rdn and wknd*............(50 to 1) 6
2330[7] KAHER (USA) [100] 7-10-5 D Bridgwater, *hld up in tch, wknd appr 3 out, tld off whn pld up bef nxt*.
.............(3 to 1 op 4 to 1 tchd 9 to 2 and 5 to 1) pu
Dist: 3l, nk, 12l, 12l, nk. 5m 2.60s. a 5.60s (7 Ran).

SR: 35/28/15/24/4/-/-/   (Frank A Farrant), M C Pipe

NEWBURY (good)
Friday March 25th
Going Correction: PLUS 0.75 sec. per fur.

3215 Alvescot Maiden Hurdle (4-y-o and up) £3,142 2m 5f..................(1:55)

2710 FOREST FEATHER (Ire) 6-11-9 Peter Hobbs, *trkd ldrs, cld 2 out, led appr last, rdn out*........(33 to 1 op 20 to 1) 1
3036 MAD THYME 7-11-9 J Frost, *cld on ldrs 6th, ev ch appr last, one pace and pres*........(5 to 2 fav op 7 to 2) 2
2295[6] KILLURA (Ire) 6-11-9 N Williamson, *al prmnt, dsptd ld 2 out, one pace appr last*. (15 to 2 op 6 to 1 tchd 8 to 1) 3
2723 OVER THE POLE 7-11-6 (3*) P Hide, *beh whn badly hmpd 7th, styd on wl frm appr 2 out, nrst finish*.
.......................(8 to 1 op 7 to 1 tchd 10 to 1) 4
2315[6] DESERT RUN (Ire) 6-11-9 A Maguire, *trkd ldrs, dsptd ld 2 out, wknd appr last*....(8 to 1 op 7 to 1 tchd 9 to 1) 5
2910[3] DENVER BAY 7-11-9 D Murphy, *hld up in rear, cld 7th, one pace frm 3 out*.....(12 to 1 op 10 to 1 tchd 14 to 1) 6
1974[4] HIT THE FAN 5-11-9 C Llewellyn, *mstk 1st, wth ldr, led 5th till hdd 2 out, wknd*. (14 to 1 op 12 to 1 tchd 16 to 1) 7
2250[9] TREGURTHA 8-11-6 (3*) R Davis, *hld up in mid-div, effrt 3 out, outpcd appr nxt*...........(33 to 1 op 33 to 1) 8
2991 DEAR DO 7-11-9 M A FitzGerald, *chsd ldrs, pushed alng appr 3 out, sn outpcd*...........(16 to 1 op 12 to 1) 9
2828[5] PRIMO FIGLIO (bl) 4-10-11 (3*) A Thornton, *drvn appr 3 out, wknd quickly nxt*....(33 to 1 op 25 to 1) 10
2577 FLY GUARD (NZ) 7-11-9 J R Kavanagh, *beh whn badly hmpd 7th, not reco'r*.............(33 to 1 op 20 to 1) 11
2112[4] NO DEBT 6-11-4 P Niven, *cl up till wknd 6th*.
.......................(50 to 1 op 33 to 1) 12
2144 ACHIEVED AMBITION (Ire) 6-11-9 W McFarland, *chsd ldrs to 6th*...........................(50 to 1 op 33 to 1) 13
2505[6] HECTOR'S RETURN 6-11-9 S Earle, *nvr dngrs*.
.......................(20 to 1 op 14 to 1) 14
SEATTLE BRAVE 7-11-9 M Perrett, *chsd ldrs till wknd aftr 4 out*.............(20 to 1 op 12 to 1 tchd 33 to 1) 15
3008[7] CHARGED 5-11-9 B Clifford, *mid-div, reminders aftr 4th, beh whn slightly hmpd 7th*........(13 to 1 op 25 to 1) 16
2964[4] ANTARCTIC CALL 7-11-9 J Osborne, *in cl tch whn f 7th*.
.............(13 to 2 op 5 to 1 tchd whn f 7th) f
2404 GRUNGE (Ire) 6-11-9 D Gallagher, *mid-div whn f 7th*.
.......................(33 to 1 op 20 to 1) f
2991 KIWI L'EGLISE (NZ) 8-11-2 (7*) Mr G Shenkin, *al beh, tld off whn pld up bef last*............(50 to 1) pu
PROSPECTING 6-11-9 J Railton, *mid-div to 6th, beh whn pld up bef 8th, dead*. (25 to 1 op 20 to 1 tchd 33 to 1) pu

2048 PRETTY BOY GEORGE 5-11-9 M Ahern, *led till hdd 5th, sn
lost pl, pld up bef 3 out*.................... (50 to 1)   pu
2779⁵ GOLDEN DROPS (NZ) 6-11-9 C Maude, *sn pushed alng in
rear, tld off whn pld up bef 2 out*. (33 to 1 op 20 to 1)   pu
STORMTRACKER (Ire) 5-11-9 D O'Sullivan, *jmpd badly in
rear, tld off whn pld up bef 4 out*.
.... (33 to 1 op 14 to 1 tchd 50 to 1)   pu
Dist: 3l, 1½l, 11l, 4l, 4l, 2½l, 1l, 3½l, 2l, 6l. 5m 19.90s. a 26.90s (23 Ran).

(David Knox), C Weedon

3216 Times 'Rising Stars' Hunters' Chase Final (6,7,8-y-o) £7,100 3m...... (2:25)

3096² SYNDERBOROUGH LAD 8-12-0 Mr M Felton, *hld up beh
ldrs, jnd lder 4 out, led appr last, ran on wl.*
.... (6 to 1 op 5 to 1 tchd 7 to 1)   1
SOME-TOY 8-11-7 Miss L Blackford, *trkd ldrs, styd on wl
und pres to take second r-in*...... (20 to 1 op 14 to 1)   2
3021³ COOL RELATION 8-11-7 Mr A Phillips, *made most, jnd 4
out, hdd appr last, one pace*....... (12 to 1 tchd 14 to 1)   3
2884³ MR GOLIGHTLY 7-11-7 Miss J Cobden, *beh, styd on wl
appr last, nxt finish*............ (10 to 1 tchd 12 to 1)   4
3096 NO FIZZ 8-11-9 Mr P Bull, *al beh, blun 11th, tld off*.
.... (9 to 1 op 6 to 1 tchd 10 to 1)   5
2765⁶ HARVEST SPLENDOUR (USA) 7-11-2 Mr M Worthington,
mid-div whn mstk and uns rdr tenth.......... (33 to 1)   ur
2898* KNIFEBOARD (bl) 8-12-0 Mr T Jones, *al beh, pld up bef 4
out*.................... (9 to 1 op 7 to 1 tchd 10 to 1)   pu
2898 NGERU 8-11-7 Mr A Edwards, *wth ldrs, mstk 4th, wknd
appr 9th, pld up bef 13th*.................... (33 to 1)   pu
TRUNDLE (bl) 8-11-9² Mr J Dufosee, *al beh, pld up bef
13th*.................... (33 to 1 op 20 to 1)   pu
2898 FLAME O'FRENSI 8-11-2 Miss J Cumings, *trkd ldrs till
wknd, pld up bef 2 out*......... (9 to 1 op 10 to 1)   pu
THURS LUCK 8-11-7 Mr O Warburton, *beh whn blun 5
out, pld up bef 3 out*.................... (33 to 1)   pu
3096³ FIRST HARVEST 7-11-7 Mr P Harding-Jones, *chsd ldrs to
13th, beh whn pld up bef 3 out*...(14 to 1 op 25 to 1)   pu
2937 JOHNNY'S CHOICE 8-11-10³ Mr A Hill, *al beh, pld up bef
14th*.................... (11 to 1 op 10 to 1 tchd 12 to 1)   pu
GREEN SHEEN (Ire) 6-11-7 Mr Chris Wilson, *mid-div, pld
up bef 14th*.................... (14 to 1 tchd 16 to 1)   pu
2885* KILFINNY CROSS (Ire) 6-12-7 Mr J Greenall, *chsd ldrs,
pushed alng and hmpd frm 3 out, wknd quickly and
pld up bef last*.................... (3 to 1 fav tchd 100 to 30)   pu
Dist: 1½l, 5l, 2½l, dist. 6m 21.30s. a 33.30s (15 Ran).

(Stewart Pike), S Pike

3217 Betterton Handicap Chase (0-140 5-y-o and up) £3,626 3¼m 110yds.. (2:55)

2948³ GHOFAR [115] (bl) 11-10-8 P Holley, *made virtually all,
ran on gmely frm last*.................... (8 to 1 op 7 to 1)   1
2901* BISHOPS ISLAND [130] 8-11-9 A Maguire, *wtd wth, cld 4
out, shaken up aftr 2 out, hng lft and pres r-in, not
quicken*.......... (Evens fav op 11 to 10 tchd 5 to 4)   2
2831⁸ MR BOSTON [135] 9-12-0 P Niven, *cl up, jnd wnr 15th, ev
ch last, wknd r-in*.................... (6 to 1 op 5 to 1)   3
2805 ALL JEFF (Fr) [130] (bl) 10-11-9 J Osborne, *mstk second,
drpd rear 5th, cld tenth, pushed alng 14th, tld off frm 4
out*.................... (14 to 1 op 12 to 1)   4
3027⁶ STUNNING STUFF [122] (bl) 9-11-1 N Williamson, *in cl tch,
ev ch 16th, pckd nxt and sn pushed alng, blun whn btn
3 out and next*.......... (8 to 1 op 10 to 1 tchd 12 to 1)   5
2966 ACE OF SPIES [107] 13-10-0 C Llewellyn, *in cl tch, wkng
whn f 13th*.......... (20 to 1 op 25 to 1 tchd 14 to 1)   f
3026 ROCKTOR (NZ) [127] 9-11-6 J Frost, *hld up, cld 5th, blun
and uns rdr 8th*.................... (10 to 1 op 8 to 1)   ur
Dist: 1½l, 5l, 25l, 8l. 7m 3.90s. a 35.90s (7 Ran).

(Sir Hugh Dundas), D R C Elsworth

3218 Sabin Du Loir Handicap Chase (0-145 5-y-o and up) £3,362 2½m... (3:25)

1706² MENEBUCK [115] 8-10-8 E Murphy, *in cl tch, slight mstk
9th, jnd ldr 3 out, led appr nxt, ran on wl frm last.*
.... (3 to 1 op 4 to 1)   1
2852³ GUIBURN'S NEPHEW [122] 12-11-4 C Maude, *led, slight
mstk 9th, jnd 3 out, hdd appr nxt, jmpd lft last, no extr.*
.... (7 to 2 op 4 to 1)   2
3026² FLASHTHECASH [87] 8-11-6 A Maguire, *in cl tch till mstk
5 out, rdn appr nxt, sn btn, tld off*.
.... (7 to 4 fav op 6 to 4 tchd 15 to 8)   3
3066 DIS TRAIN [135] 10-12-0 J Osborne, *al hndy, 3rd whn f 3
out, dead*.................... (7 to 1 op 9 to 2)   f
Dist: 7l, dist. 5m 21.90s. a 31.90s (4 Ran).

(Lady Sarah Clutton), Lady Herries

3219 Railway Conditional Jockeys' Handicap Hurdle (0-140 4-y-o and up) £2,784 2m 110yds............. (4:00)

812⁵ NOCATCHIM [122] 11-10-2 J McCarthy, *trkd ldr frm 3rd,
led 3 out, ran on wl*.................... (4 to 1 tchd 9 to 2)   1
3100² WHIPPERS DELIGHT (Ire) [103] 6-10-9 D Meade, *led til hdd
3 out, kpt on gmely*.................... (4 to 1 op 7 to 2)   2

2862² ALBERTITO (Fr) [97] 7-10-3 S Wynne, *beh 4th, styd on one
pace frm 3 out*.................... (5 to 1 op 7 to 1)   3
2043⁷ DURRINGTON [94] 8-10-0 P Hide, *cld second, outpcd frm
4 out*.................... (33 to 1 op 20 to 1 tchd 40 to 1)   4
2994 CLURICAN (Ire) [117] 5-11-9 E Husband, *in cl tch till wknd
frm 4 out, tld off*...(7 to 2 jt-fav op 3 to 1 tchd 4 to 1)   5
1521⁵ FAUX PAVILLON [94] 10-10-0 S Fox, *in tch, outpcd frm 4
out, tld off*.......... (7 to 2 jt-fav op 3 to 1 tchd 4 to 1)   6
RIYADH LIGHTS [102] 9-10-1 (7*) G Carroll, *wth ldr, wkng
whn hit 3rd, tld off*. (16 to 1 op 20 to 1 tchd 14 to 1)   7
Dist: 2l, 7l, 15l, 20l, nk, 25l. 4m 6.40s. a 17.40s (7 Ran).
SR: 50/29/16/-/1/-1/-/   (Miss N Carroll), S E Sherwood

3220 Wantage Novices' Hurdle (4-y-o and up) £2,932 3m 110yds......... (4:30)

2779² DO BE HAVE (Ire) 6-11-4 J Osborne, *wth ldr, led 3rd, jnd 3
out, hdd nxt, led ag'n appr last, edgd rght, ran on wl.*
.... (7 to 2 jt-fav op 11 to 2)   1
2964* OUROWNFELLOW (Ire) 5-11-12 D Morris, *al hndy, jnd ldr
3 out, led nxt till hdd appr last, no extr.*
.... (8 to 1 op 7 to 1)   2
2404⁵ FUN MONEY 7-11-4 A Maguire, *hld up, effrt frm 3 out,
styd on one pace.*
.... (9 to 1 op 10 to 1 tchd 12 to 1 and 8 to 1)   3
2723⁷ ACROBATE (USA) 5-11-4 C Llewellyn, *led to 3rd, trkd ldrs,
rdn appr 3 out, sn btn*.................... (33 to 1 op 20 to 1)   4
3036⁷ EMPIRE BLUE 11-11-8 M Bosley, *chsd ldrs, blun badly 4
out, rdn and no dngr aftr.*
.... (9 to 2 op 3 to 1 tchd 5 to 1)   5
2795* GOLDEN SPINNER 7-11-8 J R Kavanagh, *hit 4th, trkd
ldrs, effrt appr 3 out, sn wknd.*
.... (9 to 2 op 3 to 1 tchd 5 to 1)   6
2332⁹ ERINS BAR (Ire) 5-11-4 N Williamson, *al beh, tld off.*
.... (20 to 1 op 12 to 1)   7
2367* SEVEN TOWERS (Ire) 5-11-12 P Niven, *hld up in rear, nvr
gng wl, lost tch 7th, pld up bef 3 out*........(7 to 2 jt-
fav op 9 to 2)   pu
1871⁶ BROWN ROBBER 6-11-4 Mr W Henderson, *trkd ldrs till
drpd rear 6th, tld off whn pld up bef 2 out*.
.... (50 to 1 op 33 to 1)   pu
3046² GILLAN COVE (Ire) 5-11-4 S Earle, *mid-div till drpd rear
aftr 7th, pld up bef 3 out*.......... (8 to 1 tchd 10 to 1)   pu
Dist: 3l, 7l, 15l, 9l, 20l, 20l. 6m 22.40s. a 33.40s (10 Ran).

(David P Walker), Mrs J Pitman

BANGOR (good to soft)
Saturday March 26th
Going Correction: PLUS 0.80 sec. per fur.

3221 Penley Novices' Hurdle (4-y-o and up) £2,316 2m 1f.................. (2:10)

3044⁶ BATTY'S ISLAND 5-11-5 (7*) Mr S Joynes, *chsd ldr, led 4th,
quickened clr appr 2 out, unchlgd.*
.... (6 to 5 on op 6 to 4 on tchd 11 to 10 on)   1
2841⁵ RAGGERTY (Ire) 4-11-9 (7*) P McLoughlin, *sn pushed alng,
cld 3 out, styd on r-in, no ch wth wnr.*
.... (9 to 2 op 4 to 1 tchd 5 to 1)   2
1751⁴ KADARI (v) 5-11-1 Mr B Leavy, *led to 4th, prmnt till outpcd appr 2 out*.................... (15 to 2 op 5 to 1)   3
2857⁵ KEDGE 4-10-12 Diane Clay, *trkd ldrs to 6th, sn rdn and
outpcd*.................... (20 to 1 op 16 to 1)   4
610⁷ ATHASSEL ABBEY 8-11-6 W McFarland, *prmnt to hfwy,
tld off*.................... (33 to 1 op 25 to 1)   5
2837 NORTH HOLLOW 9-11-1 (5*) Mr D McCain, *rear, reminders
aftr 3rd, sn tld off*.................... (33 to 1 op 25 to 1)   6
2244 HURRICANE RYAN (Ire) 6-11-6 P Holley, *steadied strt, hld
up rear, cld 5th, wknd appr 3 out, pld up bef last, lme.*
.... (4 to 1)   pu
Dist: 10l, 1½l, 10l, dist., 25l. 4m 13.80s. a 23.80s (7 Ran).

(Mrs Mary Price), B Preece

3222 Cross Lanes Conditional Jockeys' Selling Handicap Hurdle (4-y-o and up) £2,155 2m 1f.............. (2:40)

2900* ALL GREEK TO ME (Ire) [99] 6-11-9 (5*) F Leahy, *al wl plcd,
quickened to ld appr last, sn clr*... (8 to 1 op 6 to 1)   1
3009⁵ ANDRATH (Ire) [71] 6-9-11 (3*) D Meade, *sn chasing ldrs,
led aftr 4th till appr last, one pace*... (8 to 1 op 7 to 1)   2
3089² SULTAN'S SON [72] 8-10-1 D Leahy, *sn tld off, hdwy
entering strt, styd on, too much to do.*
.... (13 to 2 op 7 to 1 tchd 9 to 1)   3
2717 OAK PARK (Ire) [82] 6-10-11 T Eley, *al wl plcd, reminders 2
out, sn btn*.................... (20 to 1 op 16 to 1)   4
2900⁸ AL SKEET (USA) [75] 8-10-4 J McCarthy, *wtd wth, prog frm
hfwy, wknd 3 out*.......... (7 to 1 op 6 to 1 tchd 8 to 1)   5
2900³ MOUNTSHANNON [84] 8-10-13 R Farrant, *rear, rdn alng
5th, styd on frm 2 out, nvr nrr*......(11 to 1 op 8 to 1)   6
2900² ALWAYS READY [91] (bl) 8-10-13 (7*) J Bond, *beh, virtually
tld off hfwy, some hdwy frm 2 out, not rch ldrs.*
.... (8 to 1 op 11 to 1)   7
1948 NORDROSS [72] 6-10-11 A Thornton, *keen hold, chsd ldrs
to 3 out, sn rdn and wknd*........(50 to 1 op 25 to 1)   8

455

2119² EASTERN MAGIC [88] 6-10-10 (7*) L Arnold, *in tch, effrt 5th, wknd aftr nxt*.................. (9 to 1 op 7 to 1) 9
748 MOST INTERESTING [83] 9-10-12 R Davis, *cl up till weakeend quickly appr 2 out, tld off*....(20 to 1 op 16 to 1) 10
2713 SECRET CASTLE [80] 6-10-6 (3*) P McLoughlin, *pressed ldrs to 5th, sn rdn and wknd, tld off*.......... (33 to 1) 11
3131 SPORTING IDOL [73] 9-9-9 (7*) R Walker, *prmnt, rdn alng whn mstk 3 out, wknd quickly, tld off*. ....(50 to 1 tchd 33 to 1) 12
3125⁷ LOCAL DEALER [71] 6-9-11 (3*) E Husband, *led till aftr 4th, wkng whn mstk 6th, tld off*.................. (20 to 1) 13
2794 HAPPY DEAL [71] 8-10-0 A Roche, *lost pl hfwy, tld off whn pld up bef 2 out*..............................(50 to 1) pu

Dist: 4l, 6l, nk, 6l, 3l, 1½l, 1½l, 4l, 15l, ½l. 4m 11.10s. a 21.10s (14 Ran).
SR: 25/-/-/-/-/ (Barry Hughes), J Parkes

3223 Althrey Woodhouse Handicap Chase (0-130 5-y-o and up) £4,346 2½m 110yds........................ (3:10)

3006 FAST CRUISE [88] 9-10-2⁵ (3*) A Thornton, *pressed ldr, led 4th to 6th, led 11th to nxt, led 3 out, rdn out*. .... (12 to 1 op 8 to 1) 1
3032⁴ POSITIVE ACTION [98] 8-10-12 A Dobbin, *wtd wth in rear, cld 11th, hrd rdn appr last, not rch wnr*. .... (7 to 2 op 11 to 4 tchd 4 to 1) 2
2826² SWINHOE CROFT [100] 12-11-0 S McNeill, *led to 4th, led 6th to 11th, led 12th to 3 out, ev ch nxt, sn rdn and outpcd*............................ (4 to 1 op 7 to 2) 3
2895* COMEDY ROAD [102] 10-10-11 (5*) D Fortt, *chsd ldg pair, effrt and ev ch 11th, wknd quickly nxt, tld off*. .... (5 to 4 fav op Evens) 4
3060⁶ ORCHIPEDZO [86] 9-9-9² (7*) Judy Davies, *al beh, tld off 9th*................................ (20 to 1 op 14 to 1) 5
2926⁶ PURA MONEY [90] 12-9-11 (7*) B Harding, *hld up, hdwy 6th, wknd 12th, eased whn btn 2 out, virtually pld up r-in*.............................. (13 to 2 op 6 to 1) 6
2926³ JAMES MY BOY [86] 14-9-13² (3*) R Davis, *not jump wl, in tch till wknd 9th, tld off whn pld up bef 2 out*. .... (8 to 1 tchd 9 to 1) pu

Dist: 3½l, 4l, dist, dist. 5m 19.10s. a 28.10s (7 Ran).
(Chiman Patel), E H Owen Jun

3224 Miles Macadam Novices' Handicap Chase (5-y-o and up) £3,712 3m 110yds........................ (3:45)

3075³ NAWRIK (Ire) [73] 5-9-12 (3*) R Farrant, *al wl plcd, lft in ld 3 out, hrd rdn, hld on well*....... (14 to 1 tchd 12 to 1) 1
2928³ TARTAN TRADEWINDS [92] 7-11-6 N Doughty, *al cl up, ev ch whn hmpd 3 out, rallied to join wnr nxt, hrd rdn and no extr r-in*............ (4 to 1 jt-fav tchd 9 to 2) 2
2899³ SQUIRES PRIVILEGE (Ire) [81] 6-10-4 (5*) A Roche, *settled midfield, mstk tenth, effrt 13th, rdn appr last, one pace*.............................. (13 to 2 op 6 to 1) 3
3104 TITUS GOLD [85] (v) 9-10-10 (3*) T Eley, *cl up, blun 8th, outpcd 14th, sn beh*.............. (25 to 1 op 20 to 1) 4
2693³ TIMUR'S KING [77] 7-10-5 S Earle, *trkd ldrs, rdn 3 out, ran on one pace*................................ (7 to 1) 5
3075* DUCHESS OF TUBBER (Ire) [89] 6-11-0 (3*) A Thornton, *chsd ldrs, mstk and lost pl 12th, no dngr aftr*. ....(5 to 1 op 4 to 1) 6
2149² TRAVEL BOUND [75] 9-10-3 A Dobbin, *wtd wth in rear, hdwy 7th, wknd aftr 15th*......... (16 to 1 op 20 to 1) 7
3135 PLAYFUL JULIET (Can) [83] (v) 6-10-11 Pat Caldwell, *strted slwly, al beh, tld off*.............(25 to 1 op 16 to 1) 8
3104³ THE LIGHTER SIDE [84] 8-10-5 (7*) Judy Davies, *f 4th*. .... (25 to 1 op 20 to 1) f
3040⁷ FLORIDA SKY [96] 7-11-10 R Supple, *led till f 3 out*. ....(4 to 1 jt-fav op 3 to 1) f
2899⁵ YOUNG PARSON [74] 8-10-2 B Clifford, *beh, effrt 8th, blun and uns rdr nxt*.................. (25 to 1 op 20 to 1) ur
3090* CRAIGSTOWN (Ire) [79] 6-10-4 (3*) R Davis, *hld up, cld hfwy, close 3rd whn brght dwn 3 out*. .... (11 to 1 op 8 to 1) bd
2137 BOWLANDS WAY [72] 10-10-0 M Hourigan, *al beh, tld off whn pld up bef 13th*.............................. (33 to 1) pu
2425 KING OF SHADOWS [75] 7-10-3 D Skyrme, *al rear, tld off whn pld up bef 13th*..............(50 to 1 op 33 to 1) pu

Dist: ½l, 5l, 15l, ½l, 2½l, 2¼l, 25l. 6m 26.80s. a 36.80s (14 Ran).
(Mrs J K Peutherer), L Lungo

3225 Lightwood Green Novices' Handicap Hurdle (5-y-o and up) £2,368 3m (4:20)

2902* PATROCLUS [75] 9-9-11 (3*) T Eley, *made most, quickened clr appr 2 out, cmftbly*. (11 to 4 op 3 to 1 tchd 7 to 2) 1
2998* TUSKY [93] 6-11-4 N Bentley, *settled off the pace, edgd clr hfwy, chsd wnr frm 3 out, no imprsn*. .... (11 to 2 op 4 to 1) 2
SEARCY [75] 6-9-9 (5*) D Leahy, *wtd wth, hdwy 7th, kpt on same pace frm 3 out*............ (20 to 1 op 14 to 1) 3
2925* WHITE DIAMOND [87] 6-10-12 J Railton, *sn tracking ldrs, effrt and rdn 8th, soon lost tch*. .... (5 to 2 fav tchd 11 to 4) 4
2531³ VAZON EXPRESS [75] 8-9-8¹ (7*) D Winter, *wth wnr to 6th, sn rdn, wknd 3 out*............... (20 to 1 op 16 to 1) 5
2936 CELTIC TOWN [99] 6-11-7 (3*) J McCarthy, *pressed ldrs till wknd appr 3 out*.......................... (11 to 2 op 4 to 1) 6
2575² BUSMAN (Ire) [90] 5-11-1 M Hourigan, *hld up rear, cld 7th, wknd nxt, tld off*....... (9 to 1 op 8 to 1 tchd 10 to 1) 7
2828⁶ STOP THE WALLER (Ire) [82] 5-10-7 A Dobbin, *keen hold, trkd ldrs to 8th, wknd quickly, tld off*. .... (8 to 1 op 10 to 1) 8
2900 BAR THREE (Ire) [75] 5-10-0 V Smith, *al rear, lost tch 7th, tld off whn pld up bef 2 out*................... (100 to 1) pu
2731⁷ SLIEVE LEAGUE (Ire) [75] 5-10-0 R Bellamy, *dsptd ld till aftr 1st, rdn and wknd 6th, tld off whn pld up bef 2 out*. .... (50 to 1 op 33 to 1) pu

Dist: 5l, 1½l, 10l, 6l, 1¾l, 15l, 7l. 6m 1.80s. (10 Ran).
(Applied Signs Limited), J Mackie

3226 Maelor Novices' Chase (5-y-o and up) £2,788 2m 1f 110yds............ (4:55)

2971* GALLATEEN 6-11-12 N Doughty, *jmpd wl, led 3rd to nxt, led 6th, clr appr last, eased nr finish*. ....(7 to 2 on op 4 to 1 on tchd 11 to 4 on) 1
3007³ RIDAKA 7-11-1 (3*) T Eley, *blun second, sn chasing ldrs, ev ch 2 out, soon rdn and outpcd*... (12 to 1 op 8 to 1) 2
3004² BEAUFAN 7-11-4 R Supple, *wtd wth, hdwy 7th, staying on whn blun last*.................(9 to 1 op 6 to 1) 3
2822 ON THE TEAR 8-11-4 S McNeill, *led 4th to 6th, cl up till wknd 3 out, tld off*................ (33 to 1 op 20 to 1) 4
2840² HIGHLAND POACHER 7-11-4 J Railton, *led to 3rd, sn lost tch, tld off whn pld up bef 3 out*. ....(8 to 1 op 5 to 1 tchd 9 to 1) pu

Dist: 8l, 2½l, dist. 4m 32.30s. a 26.30s (5 Ran).
(E R Madden), G Richards

3227 Grunwick Stakes National Hunt Flat Race (4,5,6-y-o) £1,924 2m 1f....(5:25)

3113* AIR SHOT 4-11-2 (7*) M Keighley, *al gng wl, led o'r 2 fs out, sn clr*........ (2 to 1 on op 13 to 8 on tchd 6 to 4 on) 1
2976³ BALLYALLIA CASTLE (Ire) 5-11-7 (3*) A Thornton, *al wl plcd, rdn and ev ch 2 fs out, sn outpcd*... (10 to 1 op 5 to 1) 2
CURRAHEEN VIEW (Ire) 5-11-2 (3*) J McCarthy, *settled midfield, prog hfwy, slight ld 3 fs out, sn hdd, one pace*. .... (14 to 1 op 10 to 1) 3
HENNERWOOD OAK 4-10-4 (7*) P McLoughlin, *hld up rear, styd on fnl 2 fs, too much to do*. ....(9 to 1 op 10 to 1 tchd 20 to 1 and 8 to 1) 4
2996⁹ JAPACADA 4-10-11 (5*) D Fortt, *pressed ldrs, led o'r 4 fs out to 3 out, sn rdn and btn*........ (11 to 1 op 7 to 1) 5
KNUCKLEBUSTER (Ire) 4-10-9 (7*) F Leahy, *nvr nr ldrs*. .... (50 to 1 op 20 to 1) 6
EARLYMORNING LIGHT (Ire) 5-11-3 (7*) B Harding, *wtd wth, cld hfwy, ev ch o'r 3 fs out, wknd*. .... (16 to 1 op 8 to 1) 7
SIERRA MADRONA (USA) 4-10-11 Mr Chris Wilson, *in tch for o'r 12 fs, sn wknd*.............(33 to 1 op 20 to 1) 8
3079 CHALET PIERRE 4-10-9 (7*) W Fry, *al rear, tld off*. .... (50 to 1 op 25 to 1) 9
GAYMOOR GALE 4-10-11 Mr B Leavy, *cl up 12 fs, sn rdn and wknd, tld off*................ (33 to 1 op 20 to 1) 10
BEN DARWI 5-11-3 (7*) S Arnold, *sluggish strt, cld 7 fs out, sn ev ch, rdn and wknd 4 out, tld off*..........(50 to 1) 11
2876 CHUKATEN 5-11-7 (3*) T Eley, *mid-div till wknd o'r 4 fs out, tld off*........................(33 to 1 op 16 to 1) 12
SHARP TOUCH 4-10-11 (5*) Mr D McCain, *strted slwly, al beh, tld off*.............................(50 to 1 op 20 to 1) 13
1494 WHATAPICKLE (Ire) 5-11-7 (3*) R Davis, *led for o'r 12 fs, sn lost tch, tld off*......................(33 to 1 op 20 to 1) 14
BOWLANDS GEM 4-10-11 (5*) S Lyons, *prmnt to hfwy, sn wknd, tld off*.........................(50 to 1 op 33 to 1) 15

Dist: 11l, 2l, 3½l, 1¼l, 15l, 6l, ¾l, 8l, ½l. 4m 10.40s. (15 Ran).
(Mrs Peter Prowting), D Nicholson

NEWBURY (good)
Saturday March 26th
Going Correction: PLUS 0.65 sec. per fur.

3228 Lambourn Handicap Hurdle (4-y-o) £5,630 2m 110yds.............. (1:30)

3062 DARING PAST [96] 10-9 R Dunwoody, *sn prmnt, chlgd and hit 4th, dsptd ld frm 2 out, slight lead aftr last, drvn out*..................(100 to 30 op 11 to 4 tchd 7 to 2) 1
3095* WARM SPELL [106] 11-5 N Williamson, *chlgd second, led 3rd, rdn 2 out, hdd sn aftr last, not quicken*. ....(5 to 2 fav op 11 to 4 tchd 3 to 1) 2
2914* HOSTILE WITNESS (Ire) [106] 11-5 M Richards, *prmnt 3rd, chlgd 5th, rdn appr 3 out, styd on one pace*. .... (15 to 2 op 6 to 1) 3
2910* ERCKULE [104] 11-3 C Llewellyn, *beh, jmpd slwly second, hdwy to chase ldrs frm 5th, one pace from 3 out*. ....(7 to 1 op 8 to 1) 4
2568³ GRAND APPLAUSE (Ire) [111] 11-10 D Gallagher, *hdwy to chase ldrs 5th, fdg whn hmpd 3 out*. (10 to 1 op 8 to 1) 5
2853⁴ MARIUS (Ire) [99] 10-12 D Murphy, *beh, effrt and hit 5th, wkng whn hmpd 3 out*. .... (14 to 1 op 10 to 1 tchd 16 to 1) 6

2991³ LODESTONE LAD (Ire) [87] 9-11 (3*) D Meredith, *led to 3rd, rdn to stay prmnt appr 5th, wknd frm 3 out.*
..................(7 to 1 op 8 to 1 tchd 9 to 1) 7
1244² CHIAPPUCCI (Ire) [96] (bl) 10-9 A Maguire, *prmnt 3rd, chlgd frm 4th, mdn and f 3 out.* ....(7 to 1 op 10 to 1) f
Dist: 1l, 11l, ¾l, 15l, 1½l, 1½l. 4m 4.60s. a 15.60s (8 Ran).
SR: 32/41/30/27/19/5/-/-/ (John A Petty), M D Hammond

3229 Brown Chamberlin Handicap Chase (6-y-o and up) £5,608 3m...... (2:00)

3041⁵ NEVADA GOLD [118] 8-10-0 D Murphy, *hld up, steady hdwy 14th, chlgd and hit 2 out, slight ld last, readily.*
..................(15 to 8 fav op 7 to 4 tchd 9 to 4) 1
2995³ SOLIDASAROCK [125] 12-10-0 D Bridgwater, *chsd ldrs till led 6th, narrowly hdd last, ran on same pace.*
..................(9 to 2 op 1 to 1 tchd 11 to 2) 2
3041 FOREST SUN [132] 9-10-7 R Dunwoody, *trkd ldrs 14th, rdn 2 out, no imprsn...* (13 to 2 op 7 to 1 tchd 6 to 1) 3
BAPTISMAL FIRE [128] 10-10-3 J Ryan, *beh, hit 11th, lost tch frm 14th, tld off.*..................(33 to 1) 4
3026³ GRANGE BRAKE [125] (bl) 8-10-0 C Llewellyn, *beh but in tch whn f 5th.*..........(5 to 1 op 4 to 1 tchd 11 to 2) f
3052* RUFUS [125] (bl) 8-10-0 L Harvey, *chsd ldrs, 4th and hld whn uns rdr four out.*......................(12 to 1) ur
ARCTIC CALL [153] (bl) 11-12-0 J Osborne, *led and blun 1st, hit 4th, hdd 6th, hit 7th and 12th, tld off whn pld up bef 14th.*............(7 to 2 op 3 to 1 tchd 4 to 1) pu
Dist: 5l, ½l, dist. 6m 14.30s. a 26.30s (7 Ran).
(Maltsword Ltd), F J Yardley

3230 Hoechst Panacur EBF Mares 'National Hunt' Novices' Hurdle Final Handicap (5-y-o and up) £9,014 2m 5f..... (2:30)

3005² GO MARY [105] 8-10-0 W Marston, *chsd ldrs, led 2 out, edgd rght, ran on wl r-in.*
..................(20 to 1 op 16 to 1 tchd 25 to 1) 1
2728³ GOSPEL (Ire) [105] 5-10-0 C Llewellyn, *hdwy 8th, chasing wnr whn slightly hmpd aftr 2 out, not quicken r-in.*
..................(7 to 1 op 6 to 1 tchd 8 to 1) 2
2905¹ LOCH SCAVAIG (Ire) [105] 5-9-13² (3*) D J Moffatt, *prmnt, chlgd 6th to 7th, rdn 8th, styd on same pace...*(12 to 1) 3
2830⁶ WELSH LUSTRE (Ire) [109] 5-10-4 M A FitzGerald, *mid-div, hdwy 6th, rdn and not quicken frm 3 out.*
..................(7 to 1 op 5 to 1 tchd 8 to 1) 4
3036³ BRIEF GALE [133] 7-12-0 D Murphy, *hdwy 6th, pressed ldrs 3 out, sn one pace.*.........(2 to 1 fav op 11 to 4) 5
3005* FORTUNES COURSE (Ire) [105] 5-10-0 J R Kavanagh, *prmnt, chlgd 6th, led 7th, hdd 2 out, sn outpcd.*
..................(14 to 1 op 12 to 1 tchd 16 to 1) 6
3038⁷ KYTTON CASTLE [118] 7-10-10 (3*) D Meredith, *beh, effrt 8th, rdn and no imprsn.*............(5 to 1 op 7 to 2) 7
3005⁷ ANNA VALLEY [105] 8-9-7 (7*) R Massey, *beh 4th, nvr rchd ldrs.*....................(33 to 1 op 25 to 1 tchd 50 to 1) 8
2459 CARLINGFORD LAKES [105] 6-10-0 J Osborne, *led to 7th, chlgd 8th, wknd aftr 3 out...* (16 to 1 op 12 to 1) 9+
2934² GLENFINN PRINCESS [105] 6-10-0 D Bridgwater, *beh till hdwy 8th, chlgd 3 out, sn wknd.*
..................(16 to 1 op 20 to 1 tchd 25 to 1) 9+
2796 GLADYS EMMANUEL [108] (bl) 7-10-3³ S Burrough, *prmnt, chlgd 8th, sn wknd.*..................(10 to 1) 11
2979⁴ SLIPMATIC [107] 5-10-2² R Dunwoody, *in tch, hdwy 6th, wknd aftr 7th.*.........(15 to 2 op 7 to 1 tchd 9 to 1) 12
3046³ HENRY'S SISTER [105] 7-10-0 N Williamson, *al beh, f 3 out.*
..................(66 to 1 op 50 to 1) f
3040 DOLLY OATS [105] 8-10-0 D Gallagher, *mid-div to 5th, tld off whn pld up bef 3 out.*............(50 to 1 op 33 to 1) pu
Dist: 1½l, 10l, nk, ½l, sht-hd, 1½l, 5l, 25l, sht-hd, 7l. 5m 9.90s. a 16.90s (14 Ran).
SR: 40/38/28/31/54/26/37/19/-/ (Miss C Phillips), Miss C Phillips

3231 Final Novices' Hurdle (Div I) (4-y-o and up) £2,840 2m 110yds.......... (3:05)

1305² DESTINY CALLS 4-11-0 R Dunwoody, *prmnt, chlgd on bit frm 3 out, led last, sn clr, eased nr finish.*
..................(4 to 1 tchd 9 to 2 and 7 to 2) 1
2630³ ARCTIC LIFE 5-11-7 B Powell, *led to 3rd, led aftr 5th, kpt narrow ld til hdd last, styd on, no ch wth wnr.*
..................(14 to 1 tchd 16 to 1) 2
2991⁷ CREDON 6-11-7 M Richards, *chsd ldrs, ev ch frm 3 out, outpcd appr last.*........(8 to 1 op 6 to 1 tchd 9 to 1) 3
869 SOLAR KESTREL (Ire) 6-11-7 M A FitzGerald, *gd hdwy 3 out, chsd ldrs frm nxt, no imprsn.* (20 to 1 op 14 to 1) 4
3008 SNOWSHILL SHAKER 5-11-7 D Bridgwater, *gd hdwy 5th, ev ch frm 3 out, rdn and outpcd appr last.*
..................(14 to 1 op 33 to 1) 5
FIGHTING BRAVE 7-11-7 N Williamson, *gd hdwy 5th, chsd ldrs frm 3 out, one pace appr last...* (9 to 1 op 16 to 1) 6
2646⁴ FENGARI 5-11-7 D Morris, *gd hdwy 3 out, dsptd ld 2 out, wknd last.*..................(14 to 1 op 12 to 1) 7
2381 LIVONIAN 4-11-0 J Osborne, *in tch, dsptd ld frm 3 out, wknd quickly aftr 2 out...*....(8 to 1 op 6 to 1) 8
AMBER FOLLY 5-11-2 Peter Hobbs, *al beh, tld off.*
..................(25 to 1 op 16 to 1) 9

BODKIN 4-10-9 A S Smith, *prmnt early, beh frm hfwy, tld off...*..................(16 to 1 op 20 to 1 tchd 14 to 1) 10
WELSH MILL (Ire) 5-11-7 G McCourt, *not fluent, hdwy to track ldrs 5th, sn wknd, tld off.*
..................(9 to 4 fav op 2 to 1 tchd 5 to 2) 11
ELEGANT STYLE 4-10-9 B Wright, *al beh, tld off.* (33 to 1) 12
2727⁷ SCORESHEET (Ire) 4-11-0 D Murphy, *in tch, ev ch frm 3 out, wknd from 2 out, no chance whn f last.*
..................(8 to 1 op 7 to 1) f
GARRY'S CHOICE 5-11-7 G Rowe, *led 3rd, hdd and wknd quickly aftr 5th, tld off whn pld up bef last...* (33 to 1) pu
Dist: 6l, 3½l, nk, 1¼l, 1¾l, 5l, 1l, dist, 30l, 3l. 4m 9.00s. a 20.00s (14 Ran).
(Simon Harrap), N A Gaselee

3232 March Novices' Handicap Chase (5-y-o and up) £3,622 2½m....... (3:35)

2855* ALL FOR LUCK [109] 9-11-10 R Dunwoody, *prmnt, chlgd tenth, mstk 12th, sn reco'red to press ldrs, led last, easily.*..................(7 to 4 tchd 9 to 4 and 7 to 4) 1
2854³ WILLOW GALE [86] 7-10-11 M A FitzGerald, *in tch, chlgd 4 out, led 3 out, hdd and hit last, sn outpcd.*
..................(4 to 1 op 7 to 2 tchd 9 to 2) 2
3011 HANGOVER [95] 8-10-10 C Llewellyn, *beh, hdwy to chase ldrs appr 12th, chlgd 3 out to 2 out, outpcd approach-ing last.*..................(6 to 1 op 7 to 1 tchd 8 to 1) 3
2780⁶ PAPER STAR [85] 7-10-0 B Powell, *beh, rdn and hdwy 12th, wknd 3 out...*......(50 to 1 op 33 to 1 tchd 66 to 1) 4
3040 CREWS CASTLE [85] 7-10-0 N Williamson, *led second to 5th, chlgd tenth to 11th, wknd 3 out.*
..................(33 to 1 op 25 to 1 tchd 50 to 1) 5
1712* CANOSCAN [108] 9-11-9 E Murphy, *led to second, led 5th to 3 out, sn wknd...* (3 to 1 op 11 to 4 tchd 100 to 30) 6
2822* BEACH BUM [93] 8-10-8 G Upton, *chsd ldrs, hit second and tenth, lost tch frm 12th...*..........(6 to 1 op 7 to 1) 7
Dist: 5l, 10l, 6l, 9l, ½l, 1¼l. 5m 22.80s. a 22.80s (7 Ran).
(B J Craig), M C Pipe

3233 Final Novices' Hurdle (Div II) (4-y-o and up) £2,840 2m 110yds...... (4:05)

1878 SENIOR STEWARD 6-11-7 R Dunwoody, *beh, rdn 3 out, plenty to do frm 2 out, styd appr last, drvn to ld r-in, all out.*..................(10 to 1 op 7 to 1) 1
TICKERTY'S GIFT 4-11-0 M Richards, *prmnt, chsd ldrs 5th, led and f 2 out, wnt lft last, hdd and no extr r-in.*
..................(8 to 1 op 10 to 1) 2
2380³ MR JERVIS (Ire) 5-11-7 D Murphy, *mstk second, in tch, led 4th, hdd 5th, lft in ld 3 out, headed aftr 2 out, slightly hmpd last, one pace...* (5 to 1 op 9 to 2 tchd 11 to 2) 3
2991 AND WHY NOT 6-11-7 C Llewellyn, *chsd ldrs to 4th, rdn and outpcd 3 out, styd on ag'n appr last.*
..................(7 to 1 op 6 to 1) 4
PERSIANSKY (Ire) 4-11-0 G McCourt, *nvr rchd ldrs.*
..................(7 to 1 op 14 to 1 tchd 15 to 2) 5
SMART CASANOVA 5-11-7 N Williamson, *mstk second, al beh...*..................(25 to 1 op 14 to 1) 6
3027 GENERALLY JUST (bl) 9-11-7 Mr S Stickland, *pressed ldrs 3rd to 4th, wknd nxt.*
..................(66 to 1 op 50 to 1 tchd 100 to 1) 7
GENERAL SIKORSKI 6-11-7 Richard Guest, *hdwy 3rd, dsptd ld 3 out, rdn 2 out, 5th and wkng whn f last.*
..................(7 to 1 op 6 to 1 tchd 10 to 1) f
2881² EDITHMEAD (Ire) 4-10-9 M A FitzGerald, *trkd ldrs, led 5th, gng wl whn f 3 out.*
..................(7 to 1 op 9 to 4 tchd 5 to 2 and 7 to 4) f
TOUCHEE BOUCHEE 4-10-6⁴ (7*) G Bazin, *led to 4th, wknd rpdly, f nxt.*..................(66 to 1 op 50 to 1) f
ESTELLE MARIE 5-11-2 Peter Hobbs, *mstks and al beh, tld off whn pld up bef 5th.*
..................(20 to 1 op 12 to 1 tchd 25 to 1) pu
Dist: 3½l, 3½l, ¾l, 20l, 12l, 2l. 4m 8.00s. a 19.00s (11 Ran).
SR: 10/-/2/1/-/-/ (R J Lavelle), G B Balding

3234 Spring National Hunt Flat Race (4,5,6-y-o) £2,024 2m 110yds.... (4:35)

KNIGHTSBRIDGE STAR (Ire) 5-11-0 (7*) Mr G Hogan, *hdwy hfwy, led o'r 2 fs out, clr ins last.*
..................(12 to 1 op 8 to 1 tchd 16 to 1) 1
LIVELY KNIGHT (Ire) 5-11-4 (3*) P Hide, *steady hdwy frm 6 fs out, chsd wnr fnl 2 furlongs, no imprsn.*
..................(8 to 1 op 10 to 1) 2
2749 NORSE RAIDER 4-10-9 (5*) D Matthews, *chsd ldrs, led 4 fs out, hdd o'r 2 out, wknd...*(33 to 1 op 20 to 1) 3
SCARLET RAMBLER 5-11-4 (3*) T Jenks, *chsd ldrs, ev ch 4 fs out, kpt on one pace.*
..................(12 to 1 op 8 to 1 tchd 16 to 1) 4
MERLINS DREAM (Ire) 5-11-7 Mr J Durkan, *took str hold, hdwy 7 fs out, styd on one pace frm 3 out.*
..................(11 to 4 fav op 4 to 1 tchd 5 to 2) 5
UNCLE ALGY 5-11-4 (3*) D Meredith, *hdwy 5 fs out, styd on fnl 2 furlongs.*..................(20 to 1) 6
LISAHANE VILLE 5-11-7 Mr Raymond White, *hdwy 5 fs out, no imprsn fnl 2 furlongs.*......(20 to 1 tchd 25 to 1) 7
2677 PURBECK CAVALIER 5-11-2 (5*) S Fox, *styd on fnl 3 fs, nrst finish.*..................(33 to 1 op 20 to 1) 8

2996[4] AIRTRAK (Ire) 5-11-0 (7") Mr C Vigors, *chsd ldrs, ev ch 4 fs out, wknd 3 out*.....................(5 to 1 op 7 to 2)   9
MY MAN IN DUNDALK (Ire) 5-11-0 (7") Mr C Curley, *hld up, nvr plcd to chal*........(9 to 2 op 5 to 1 tchd 10 to 1)   10
2996[5] THE CAUMRUE (Ire) 6-11-2 (5") D Salter, *hdwy hfwy, chsd ldrs 4 fs out, sn wknd*.
.....................(14 to 1 op 10 to 1 tchd 16 to 1)   11
GOLF WORLD (Ire) 5-10-9 (7") M Berry, *trkd ldrs, ev ch 4 fs out, wknd 3 out*.
.........(16 to 1 op 14 to 1 tchd 12 to 1 and 20 to 1)   12
2916[3] IDIOT'S DELIGHT 4-10-9 (7") D Bohan, *made most till hdd 4 fs out, sn wknd*.....................(5 to 1 op 6 to 1)   13
2996[7] WREKENGALE (Ire) 4-10-7 (7") L O'Hare, *wth ldr, ev ch 4 fs out, wknd quickly*....(12 to 1 op 6 to 1 tchd 20 to 1)   14
CHEER'S BABY 4-10-11 (3") D J Moffatt, *nvr better than mid-div*..............(16 to 1 op 20 to 1 tchd 33 to 1)   15
SPIN ECHO (Ire) 5-11-7 Mr M Armytage, *wth ldr, wknd 4 fs out*.................(16 to 1 op 20 to 1 tchd 20 to 1)   16
FLORLESS GUY (Ire) 6-11-2 (5") C Burnett-Wells, *al beh*.
.....................(33 to 1 op 20 to 1)   17
FLEMINGS DELIGHT 4-10-2 (7") R Massey, *prmnt 6 fs*.
.....................(33 to 1 op 20 to 1)   18
2876 MR DRUMMOND (Ire) 5-11-0 (7") G McGrath, *al beh*.
.....................(20 to 1 op 14 to 1)   19
BE HOPEFULL 4-10-9 Mr J O'Brien, *pld hrd, prmnt 6 fs*.
.....................(33 to 1 op 20 to 1)   20
1494 DESTINY ANGEL 5-10-9 (7") Mr G Cosgrove, *al beh, virtually pld up, tld off*.............(33 to 1 op 25 to 1)   21
Dist: 7l, nk, ¾l, 11l, 3½l, 2½l, 4l, 5l, nk, hd. 3m 58.90s. (21 Ran).
(Knightsbridge BC), D Nicholson

SEDGEFIELD (good to firm)
Saturday March 26th
Going Correction: MINUS 0.20 sec. per fur.

3235 Pensher Security Doors Novices' Selling Hurdle (4-y-o and up) £1,779 3m 3f 110yds...........................(1:55)

3029[3] LADY BE BRAVE (v) 11-11-4 K Johnson, *al cl up, led appr tenth, rdn clr 2 out, styd on*.
.....................(11 to 4 op 3 to 1 tchd 7 to 2)   1
2424[6] HIGHLAND FRIEND (bl) 6-11-4 (5") J Supple, *trkd ldrs, effrt and hdwy 3 out, rdn nxt, styd on und pres*.
.....................(7 to 1 op 5 to 1)   2
2891 ELVETT BRIDGE (Ire) 6-11-9 B Storey, *hld up, hdwy tenth, chsd wnr 2 out, sn rdn, hng lft and one pace r-in*.
.....................(7 to 1 tchd 8 to 1)   3
2828 LEGATA (Ire) 5-10-13 (5") P Midgley, *hld up and beh, hdwy and hit tenth, effrt nxt, rdn 2 out, one pace*.
.....................(16 to 1 op 12 to 1)   4
2957[7] WHATCOMESNATURALLY (USA) 4-11-4 W Worthington, *al rear*...................(8 to 1 op 7 to 1 tchd 9 to 1)   5
CELTIC PEACE 7-11-4 C Hawkins, *cl up, ev ch 3 out, rdn and wknd quickly appr 2 out*.
.....................(16 to 1 op 12 to 1 tchd 20 to 1)   6
3150 GLEN MIRAGE 9-11-9 Miss S White, *trkd ldrs till lost pl 9th, sn beh, tld off frm 3 out*....(5 to 2 fav op 7 to 4)   7
3167 CAROUSEL CROSSETT (bl) 13-10-11 (7") K Davies, *led till aftr 9th, blun tenth, pld up lme after*.
.....................(33 to 1 op 20 to 1)   pu
2957 RELENTED 5-11-4 L O'Hara, *not fluent, mid-div, some hdwy 4 out, rdn and wknd nxt, tld off whn pld up bef 2 out*.................(25 to 1 op 16 to 1)   pu
Dist: 4l, 1l, 6l, 6l, 7l. 7m 9.70s. a 43.70s (9 Ran).

(J F Roberts), W Storey

3236 Grant Thornton Business Advisers Maiden Hurdle (4-y-o and up) £2,110 2m 5f 110yds.................(2:25)

3061[4] KINDA GROOVY (bl) 5-11-7 N Smith, *al prmnt, led 3 out, hdd briefly nxt, sn led ag'n, clr last*.
.....................(14 to 1 op 12 to 1)   1
3030[3] RUSSIAN CASTLE (Ire) 5-11-7 A Merrigan, *trkd ldrs, hdwy appr 3 out, effrt and led briefly nxt, sn rdn and one pace*.........................(5 to 1 tchd 11 to 2)   2
3056[5] DOC SPOT 4-11-0 D Byrne, *hdwy appr 3 out, sn rdn, styd on one pace betw last 2*.(8 to 1 op 7 to 1 tchd 10 to 1)   3
2737[4] HOT POTATO 4-11-0 (5") P Waggott, *hld up, smooth hdwy and sn ev ch, rdn 3 out, wknd aftr nxt*.
.....................(7 to 1 op 4 to 1 tchd 4 to 1)   4
3075 BALISTEROS (Fr) 5-11-7 R Garritty, *al prmnt, rdn and hit 3 out, sn one pace*...................(20 to 1 op 16 to 1)   5
3056[4] SOLOMAN SPRINGS (USA) 4-11-0 J Callaghan, *chsd ldrs, outpcd appr 4 out, sn btn*.
.....................(8 to 1 op 6 to 1 tchd 9 to 1)   6
2573 FINDOGLEN 8-11-4 (3") A Larnach, *nvr rch ldrs*.
.....................(100 to 1 op 50 to 1)   7
3030[6] MISS CONSTRUE 7-11-2 R Hodge, *al rear*.
.....................(11 to 1 op 8 to 1)   8
3030[2] MIDNIGHT FLOTILLA 8-11-2 C Hawkins, *led, hit 4th, mstk four out, hdd nxt, sn wknd*.
.....................(2 to 1 fav op 11 to 4 tchd 9 to 4)   9

2311 ALLOON BAWN 8-11-2 Mr C Mulhall, *prmnt, rdn and wknd quickly appr 4 out*.........(50 to 1 op 33 to 1)   10
TRIENNIUM (USA) 5-11-7 B Storey, *al rear*.
.....................(16 to 1 op 10 to 1)   11
2789 SEABURN 4-10-9 (5") J Supple, *mstks, al rear*...(33 to 1)   12
LET'S BE ON 6-10-9 (7") B Grattan, *al rear, tld off whn pld up bef 3 out*............(16 to 1 op 10 to 1)   pu
Dist: 8l, 3½l, ¾l, 7l, 20l, 4l, 4l, 1¼l. 5m 9.70s. a 18.70s (13 Ran).
(Ian Park), I Park

3237 Darlington Building Society Handicap Chase (0-120 5-y-o and up) £2,733 3m 3f...........................(2:55)

2908* DEVONGALE [94] 8-11-8 L Wyer, *wtd wth, hdwy 11th, led 3 out, clr appr last*............(6 to 4 on op 2 to 1 on)   1
2973[3] LAPIAFFE [89] 10-11-3 B Storey, *al prmnt, ev ch 4 out, sn rdn and styd on one pace frm nxt*....(5 to 1 op 4 to 1)   2
2954 CLASSIC MINSTREL [89] 10-11-0 (3") P Williams, *pld hrd and not jump wl, hld up, hdwy and blun 14th, effrt and blunded 3 out, rdn alng 3 out, kpt on, hit last*.
.....................(14 to 1 op 12 to 1 tchd 16 to 1)   3
2764 CAROUSEL CALYPSO [90] 8-11-1 (3") D Bentley, *in tch, blun 14th sn rdn alng, hit 5 out and soon beh*.
.....................(8 to 1 op 9 to 1)   4
1679 WHEELIES NEWMEMBER [89] 11-11-3 K Johnson, *dsptd ld, lost pl and outpcd 12th, hdwy 14th, rdn and wknd 5 out, sn beh*............(40 to 1 op 25 to 1)   5
2448 RED UNDER THE BED [96] 7-11-5 (5") Mr D Parker, *led, rdn 4 out, hdd nxt, 3rd and btn whn uns rdr 2 out*.
.....................(9 to 1 tchd 12 to 1)   ur
Dist: 6l, 1½l, 20l, 6l. 6m 53.30s. a 14.30s (6 Ran).
(Victor Ogden), M H Easterby

3238 Provident Mutual Novices' Chase (5-y-o and up) £2,634 3m 3f.........(3:30)

3059[3] MOYODE REGENT 10-10-9 (7") Mr A Manners, *in tch, hmpd 6th, hdwy 14th, led 4 out, styd on*.
.....................(9 to 4 op 2 to 1)   1
2858[5] JENNY'S GLEN 7-11-2 B Storey, *made most till hdd 12th and sn outpcd, hit 15th and 16th, styd on frm 4 out till chlgd and hit 2 out, kpt on und pres*.........(33 to 1)   2
3033[3] KRISSOS (bl) 7-10-11 (5") P Waggott, *cl up, led 12th till hdd 4 out, rdn and hit nxt, wl btn 3rd whn f 2 out*.
.....................(9 to 1 op 12 to 1 tchd 11 to 1)   f
KINGS LAW 8-11-2 Mr D Scott, *prmnt, hit 3rd, f 6th*.
.....................(9 to 1 tchd 8 to 1 and 10 to 1)   f
2103[6] TALLYWAGGER 7-11-2 L Wyer, *trkd ldrs, cl up whn pld up lme aftr 13th...*(6 to 5 on op 5 to 4 on tchd Evens)   pu
Dist: 3l. 6m 58.90s. a 19.90s (5 Ran).
(J K Britton), R R Lamb

3239 Tote Handicap Chase (0-115 5-y-o and up) £3,496 2m 1f...............(4:00)

3032* CLARES OWN [98] 10-11-2 (3") P Williams, *chsd ldg pair, hdwy appr 4 out, effrt 2 out, led last, rdn and ran on wl r-in*............(11 to 4 op 2 to 1 tchd 3 to 1)   1
2975[4] SHREWD JOHN [94] 8-11-1 R Garritty, *hld up, steady hdwy 5 out, effrt to chal last, rdn and ev ch r-in, no extr nr finish*......(5 to 2 fav op 11 to 4 tchd 3 to 1)   2
3032[3] TERRIBLE GEL (Fr) [107] 9-12-0 N Smith, *prmnt, blun badly and lost pl 7th, styd on frm 2 out*.
.....................(7 to 2 op 9 to 2 tchd 5 to 1)   3
2975[3] PRESSURE GAME [79] 11-9-9 (5") F Perratt, *led, hdd last, rdn and wknd r-in*............(14 to 1 tchd 16 to 1)   4
2892[3] DOWN THE ROAD [98] 7-11-0 (5") Mr D Parker, *hit 1st, in tch till blun 8th, sn beh*.
.....................(11 to 4 op 3 to 1 tchd 9 to 1)   5
WAIT YOU THERE (USA) [97] 9-10-13 (5") P Waggott, *not fluent, al rear*...................(16 to 1 tchd 20 to 1)   6
Dist: 5½l, 2½l, ¾l, 8l, nk. 4m 7.10s. a 2.10s (6 Ran).
SR: 36/28/38/9/20/18/
(John Wade), J Wade

3240 Bet With The Tote Handicap Hurdle (0-125 4-y-o and up) £2,929 2m 1f 110yds.................(4:30)

140* WHO'S TEF (Ire) [108] 6-11-10 L Wyer, *al prmnt, led to chal 2 out, led appr last, drvn clr r-in*.
.....................(4 to 1 op 3 to 1 tchd 9 to 2)   1
1487[9] ANY DREAM WOULD DO [85] 5-10-1 C Hawkins, *hld up in tch, hdwy hfwy, led 3 out, rdn nxt, hdd appr last, no extr und pres*.........(10 to 1 op 7 to 1 tchd 11 to 1)   2
3130[2] NOTABLE EXCEPTION [101] 5-10-12 (5") S Mason, *in tch, hdwy 3 out, sn rdn and one pace frm nxt*.
.....................(2 to 1 fav op 3 to 1 tchd 7 to 4)   3
2360[5] SAYMORE [100] 8-10-13 (3") S Wynne, *in tch, rdn appr 3 out, one pace*.............(11 to 2 op 9 to 2)   4
2833[4] GYMCRAK SOVEREIGN [108] 6-11-10 R Marley, *led, hdd 3 out, sn rdn and wknd nxt*..........(9 to 2 op 7 to 2)   5
HEY JOE [84] 7-10-0 A Merrigan, *al beh, blun 5th, sn tld off*.....................(33 to 1)   6
3057[2] KIR (Ire) [90] (bl) 6-10-6 B Storey, *chsd ldrs, hdwy till dsptd ld and uns rdr 3 out*....(13 to 2 op 8 to 1 tchd 6 to 1)   ur
Dist: 6l, 2l, 9l, 2½l. dist. 4m 5.10s. a 10.10s (7 Ran).

458

(T E F Freight (Scarborough) Ltd), M H Easterby

TIPPERARY (IRE) (heavy)
Saturday March 26th

3241 Camas Park Handicap Chase (0-109 4-y-o and up) £3,450 2m. (3:00)

2036	BLACKPOOL BRIDGE [-] 9-9-11 (5*) D T Evans,	(8 to 1)	1
3081^{4}	GALLEY GALE [-] 8-10-11 C F Swan,	(4 to 1)	2
2865^{7}	MACAMORE STAR [-] 8-11-0 (3*) C O'Brien,	(7 to 2 fav)	3
2923*	MAMMY'S FRIEND [-] 10-10-5 (3*,6ex) D P Murphy,	(4 to 1)	4
928^{9}	WAKE UP LUV [-] 9-11-11 S H O'Donovan,	(10 to 1)	5
1179^{2}	VINEYARD SPECIAL [-] 8-11-2 K F O'Brien,	(9 to 2)	f
1856^{2}	QUIET CITY [-] 7-10-13 (7*) Mr J T McNamara,	(5 to 1)	f
2588^{9}	BALLYFIN BOY [-] 8-10-0 (5*) J P Broderick,	(25 to 1)	ur

Dist: 12l, 7l, ¾l, dist. 4m 22.40s. (8 Ran).

(Mrs Teresa O'Flynn), Timothy O'Callaghan

3242 Pierse Motors Handicap Hurdle (0-123 4-y-o and up) £3,450 2½m. (3:30)

3085^{2}	MARIAN YEAR [-] 8-10-11 J Collins,	(12 to 1)	1
2660^{9}	SHANNON KNOCK [-] 9-10-1 P M Verling,	(25 to 1)	2
2939	PUNTERS BAR [-] 7-10-4 C O'Dwyer,	(14 to 1)	3
2921^{5}	CALL ME HENRY [-] 5-9-6 (3*) C O'Brien,	(14 to 1)	4
2939^{2}	BLAZING COMET [-] 8-9-10 F Woods,	(10 to 1)	5
2983^{8}	REPLACEMENT [-] 7-10-1 (3*) T J O'Sullivan,	(33 to 1)	6
1913^{6}	TOT EM UP [-] 7-9-2 (7*) M D Murphy,	(14 to 1)	7
3085^{4}	RATHCORE [-] 7-11-0 L P Cusack,	(8 to 1)	8
2771*	OVER THE MALLARD (Ire) [-] 5-10-0 (3*) D Bromley,	(12 to 1)	9
2921^{4}	IM MELODY (Ire) [-] 6-11-6 J F Titley,	(7 to 1)	10
2943	LOUGH NEAGH LADY [-] 8-9-10 R Hughes,	(25 to 1)	11
2986^{6}	COIN MACHINE (Ire) [-] 5-10-8 T Horgan,	(8 to 1)	12
2660*	BRINDLEY HOUSE [-] 7-11-10 J Shortt,	(9 to 1)	13
2660^{7}	BARRONSTOWN BOY [-] 10-9-12 F J Flood,	(14 to 1)	14
2986	SADDLESTOWN GLEN [-] 9-10-10 P Carberry,	(16 to 1)	15
3085^{9}	LEAVE IT TO JUDGE [-] 7-9-9 W J Slattery Jnr,	(25 to 1)	16
3085^{7}	GOLDEN OPAL [-] 9-11-4 K F O'Brien,	(12 to 1)	17
2986	ROUBABAY (Ire) [-] 6-11-5 C F Swan,	(5 to 2 fav)	f
519	ANNFIELD LADY (Ire) [-] 6-9-5^{1} (3*) T J Mitchell,	(25 to 1)	pu

Dist: 4l, 3l, 4l, 8l. 5m 33.30s. (19 Ran).

(Thomas Walker), Thomas Walker

3243 Ormond Maiden Hurdle (Div 1) (6-y-o and up) £2,760 2m. (4:00)

	BARNA MOSS (Ire) 6-10-12 (3*) C O'Brien,	(33 to 1)	1
2465^{8}	OLD ABBEY (Ire) 6-11-6 T Horgan,	(4 to 1)	2
3122	FARRELL'S CROSS 8-12-0 A Powell,	(16 to 1)	3
2919^{2}	DAWN ADAMS (Ire) 6-11-9 F J Flood,	(5 to 4 fav)	4
3122	FANDANGOLD (bl) 8-10-12 (3*) T J Mitchell,	(10 to 1)	5
2704*	THATS A SECRET 6-11-11 (3*) T P Treacy,	(5 to 1)	6
2918	CORRIB HAVEN (Ire) 6-11-6 G M O'Neill,	(20 to 1)	7
1833^{8}	SAME DIFFERENCE (Ire) 6-11-6 P P Kinane,	(12 to 1)	8
2918	KILLIMOR LAD 7-11-6 K F O'Brien,	(33 to 1)	9
1764^{8}	LADY HA HA 7-10-8 (7*) J Butler,	(16 to 1)	10
2919^{7}	DEEP WAVE 7-11-1 (5*) Mr C T G Kinane,	(20 to 1)	11
	SINGHANA (Ire) 6-11-9 J Magee,	(20 to 1)	12
2943	SLEMISH MIST 7-11-1 P L Malone,	(14 to 1)	13
2940	YOUR NEARLY THERE 8-11-1 Mr M Phillips,	(33 to 1)	14
	SALMON TRAIL (bl) 7-10-13 (7*) Mr F McGirr,	(33 to 1)	15
	TWO HILLS 7-11-3 (3*) T J O'Sullivan,	(33 to 1)	ur
3122	BORRISMORE FLASH (Ire) 6-11-6 J P Banahan,	(20 to 1)	ur

Dist: 5l, 3l, 5½l, 4l. 4m 48.70s. (17 Ran).

(D O'Brien), D O'Brien

3244 Ormond Maiden Hurdle (Div 2) (6-y-o and up) £2,760 2m. (4:30)

3040	ULTRA FLUTTER 7-11-6 K F O'Brien,	(5 to 1)	1
3122^{2}	MONALEE RIVER (Ire) 6-12-0 C F Swan,	(5 to 4 on)	2
2392^{7}	GROUND WAR 7-12-0 F Woods,	(13 to 2)	3
2983	SUMMING UP 7-11-6 P M Verling,	(20 to 1)	4
2983^{3}	ACKLE BACKLE 7-11-6 (3*) Mr J A Nash,	(8 to 1)	5
2940^{6}	JOHNNY THE FOX (Ire) 6-11-6 T Horgan,	(14 to 1)	6
2236^{5}	ANOTHER ROLLO (Ire) 6-11-3 (3*) T P Treacy,	(20 to 1)	7
2863	VITAL TRIX 7-11-1 P Carberry,	(14 to 1)	8
3122	METROLAMP (Ire) 6-11-1 (5*) K P Gaule,	(20 to 1)	9
2919	CLONE (Ire) (bl) 6-10-13 (7*) J M Donnelly,	(33 to 1)	10
3122	THE ROCKING CHAIR (Ire) 6-11-6 J Shortt,	(25 to 1)	11
2869	PERCUSIONIST 7-11-6 L P Cusack,	(20 to 1)	12
2918^{7}	FIALADY 9-11-1 A J O'Brien,	(50 to 1)	13
3086^{3}	RUN FOR FUN (Ire) 6-10-10 (5*) D T Evans,	(12 to 1)	14
	BENAUGHLIN (Ire) 6-11-1 F J Flood,	(14 to 1)	15
2919^{4}	CABBERY ROSE (Ire) 6-11-1 J Magee,	(10 to 1)	f

Dist: 20l, nk, 8l, 1l. 4m 30.20s. (16 Ran).

(Donal Higgins), Michael Hourigan

3245 Scarteen INH Flat Race (4-y-o) £2,760 2m. (5:00)

3082^{3}	SUPREME WONDER (Ire) 11-0 Mrs M Mullins,	(3 to 1 fav)	1
	ROCKFIELD NATIVE (Ire) 11-5 Mr A P O'Brien,	(100 to 30)	2
2848^{4}	MORE DASH THANCASH (Ire) 11-2 (3*) D P Murphy,	(10 to 1)	3
	LENEY MOSS (Ire) 10-7 (7*) Mr E Norris,	(14 to 1)	4
2848^{3}	BOLD CHEVALIER (Ire) 10-12 (7*) Mr R P Cody,	(8 to 1)	5
2868^{5}	SHINOUMA 11-5 Mr W P Mullins,	(9 to 1)	6
2943^{8}	KILCARBERY (Ire) 10-11 (3*) Mrs J M Mullins,	(4 to 1)	7
	KILBRICKEN MAID (Ire) 10-7 (7*) Mr P English,	(20 to 1)	8
2943^{9}	THAT'S GOSPEL (Ire) 10-11 (3*) Mr J A Nash,	(8 to 1)	9
	ASHPARK ROSE (Ire) 10-7 (7*) Mrs K Walsh,	(20 to 1)	10
	TIME TO SMILE (Ire) 10-7 (7*) Mr S O'Donnell,	(20 to 1)	11
	KILBRICKEN DANCER (Ire) 10-7 (7*) G T Hourigan,	(14 to 1)	12
3084^{8}	PRINCESS LENA (Ire) 10-7 (7*) Mr T J Murphy,	(20 to 1)	13
	PENNINE VENTURE (Ire) 10-7 (7*) Mr P M Cloke,	(20 to 1)	14
2663	GREENORE GLEN (Ire) 10-12 (7*) Miss S J Leahy,	(14 to 1)	15
	CLIFFORD HALL (Ire) 11-5 Mr T Mullins,	(14 to 1)	16
	CALL BOB (Ire) 10-12 (7*) Mr T J Nagle Jnr,	(50 to 1)	17
	HERONIMUS BOSCH (Ire) 10-7 (7*) M D Murphy,	(12 to 1)	18

Dist: 2½l, 6l, 4l, 15l. 4m 28.20s. (18 Ran).

(Mrs G P Gaffney), Anthony Mullins

NAAS (IRE) (heavy)
Sunday March 27th

3246 Naas Hurdle (4-y-o) £3,105 2m. (3:00)

2750^{2}	ONOMATOPOEIA (Ire) 11-7 M Duffy,	(6 to 1)	1
2864*	KHARASAR (Ire) 11-6 (7*) R A Hennessy,	(6 to 4 fav)	2
	PUSH THE BUTTON (Ire) 11-2 C F Swan,	(10 to 1)	3
2917*	CONCLAVE (Ire) 11-13 R Hughes,	(8 to 1)	4
2864	SOUL EMPEROR 11-7 A Powell,	(25 to 1)	5
2750^{5}	TOUCHING MOMENT (Ire) 11-2 (5*) T P Rudd,	(12 to 1)	6
	EUROPE (USA) 11-0 (7*) A P McCoy,	(14 to 1)	7
2281^{5}	BOTHSIDESNOW (Ire) 11-7 P Carberry,	(12 to 1)	8
3069^{3}	HUNCHEON CHANCE 11-4 (3*) T J Mitchell,	(10 to 1)	9
2663	TEN BUCKS (Ire) 11-7 M Flynn,	(66 to 1)	10
2750^{3}	BERESFORD LADY (Ire) 11-2 C O'Dwyer,	(8 to 1)	11
	BRAVE RAIDER (Ire) 11-7 B Sheridan,	(10 to 1)	12
2864	TASSET (Can) 11-0 (7*) T Martin,	(50 to 1)	13
2848^{7}	PRINCESS LU (Ire) 11-0 (7*) Mr P J Kelly,	(25 to 1)	14
1432	SPORTSTYLE (Ire) 11-7 J Shortt,	(14 to 1)	15
2917	HEATHFIELD (USA) 11-7 S H O'Donovan,	(33 to 1)	16
	PUB TALK (Ire) 11-2 (5*) D Walsh,	(33 to 1)	17
3070^{4}	TANDRAGEE LADY (Ire) 10-9 (7*) R J Gordon,	(100 to 1)	18
	JANZOE (Ire) 11-2 M Moran,	(20 to 1)	19
2864^{5}	ANUSHA 10-11 (5*) J P Broderick,	(5 to 2)	f
	COTTAGE GUEST (Ire) 10-9 (7*) J A Power,	(33 to 1)	f
	NOVARO EXPRESS (Ire) 11-2 C N Bowens,	(20 to 1)	pu

Dist: Sht-hd, 15l, 1l, hd. 4m 15.50s. (22 Ran).

(David O'Reilly), Patrick Joseph Flynn

3247 Brophy Farrell Handicap Hurdle (0-137 4-y-o and up) £3,795 2m. (3:30)

2986^{4}	MRS BARTON (Ire) [-] (bl) 6-9-4 (5*) J R Barry,	(9 to 2)	1
2842^{2}	OPERA HAT (Ire) [-] 6-10-8 A Powell,	(7 to 2 jt-fav)	2
2988^{5}	FORTY ONE (Ire) [-] 6-9-9 (5*) J P Broderick,	(8 to 1)	3
2842	DAMODAR [-] 5-9-12 F J Flood,	(16 to 1)	4
2986	PLUMBOB (Ire) [-] 5-9-10 (7*) P J Smullen,	(8 to 1)	5
2986^{7}	ASSERT STAR [-] 4-10-1 (5*) K P Gaule,	(16 to 1)	6
2699^{6}	MAYASTA (Ire) [-] 4-10-0 C O'Dwyer,	(5 to 1)	7
2027^{7}	BEAT THE SECOND (Ire) [-] 6-9-7 T Horgan,	(16 to 1)	8
2988^{9}	CELTIC SAILS (Ire) [-] 6-9-13 (7*) P O Casey,	(12 to 1)	9
1907^{3}	PERSIAN HALO (Ire) [-] 6-11-3 D H O'Connor,	(8 to 1)	10
2866^{8}	LEGAL PROFESSION (Ire) [-] 6-10-11 C F Swan,	(7 to 2 jt-fav)	11
1232	ROWAN REX [-] 9-10-2 B Sheridan,	(20 to 1)	12
2866	PRACTICE RUN (Ire) [-] 6-10-10 (5*) M G Cleary,	(20 to 1)	13

Dist: 7l, 2l, 8l, 2l. 4m 12.70s. (13 Ran).

(Mrs Patrick Flynn), Patrick Joseph Flynn

3248 Fairgreen Hurdle (5-y-o and up) £6,900 2m 3f. (4:00)

2986*	COCK COCKBURN 8-11-8 S R Murphy,	(Evens fav)	1
2866^{9}	PERSIAN POWER (Ire) 6-11-4 P Carberry,	(4 to 1)	2
3083^{5}	EAGLE ROCK (USA) 6-11-8 (3*) C O'Brien,	(10 to 1)	3
3083^{6}	CREATIVE BLAZE (Ire) 5-11-1 C F Swan,	(10 to 1)	4
	ROCKET DANCER 8-11-4 H Rogers,	(20 to 1)	5
3038	SHANKORAK 7-11-1 (7*) D J Kavanagh,	(6 to 1)	6
2658^{3}	SEEK THE FAITH (USA) 5-11-6 B Sheridan,	(6 to 1)	7
1334	HAPPY PERCY 9-11-8 C O'Dwyer,	(16 to 1)	8

Dist: 2½l, 8l, 3½l, 25l. 5m 11.10s. (8 Ran).

(D Kinsella), John Queally

3249 Abbey Bridge Handicap Chase (0-123 5-y-o and up) £3,105 3m. (4:30)

2772^{2}	IL TROVATORE (USA) [-] 8-10-11 P Carberry,	(6 to 1)	1
2662^{3}	GOLDEN CARRUTH (Ire) [-] 6-9-9 (5*) J P Broderick,	(12 to 1)	2
2752*	MOONCAPER [-] 8-10-12 T Horgan,	(5 to 1)	3
2772	CASTLE BRANDON [-] 8-11-1 F J Flood,	(9 to 1)	4
2589^{4}	ANOTHER GROUSE [-] 7-10-1 (3*) C O'Brien,	(10 to 1)	5
	STRAMORE [-] 7-10-8 K F O'Brien,	(12 to 1)	6
2984^{4}	ROSSI NOVAE [-] 11-10-6 (3*) T P Treacy,	(10 to 1)	7
2701^{6}	LAURA'S BEAU [-] 10-12-0 C O'Dwyer,	(14 to 1)	8
2847	BUMBO HALL VI (Ire) [-] 6-10-4 (3*) T J Mitchell,	(16 to 1)	9

1826 WATERLOO KING [-] 7-10-8 (3") D P Murphy, ... (25 to 1) 10
2701 IFFEEE [-] 7-10-11 S H O'Donavan, ...(10 to 1) 11
2984 LANIGANS WINE [-] 12-10-11 G M O'Neill, ... (25 to 1) 12
2847 CARRIGEEN GALA [-] (bl) 7-9-2 (5") M G Cleary, .. (25 to 1) f
2847 MR MYAGI [-] (bl) 10-9-5¹ (3") D Bromley, ...(16 to 1) f
2312⁶ MARKET MOVER [-] 8-11-5 S R Murphy, ...(20 to 1) pu
2984⁵ MID-DAY GAMBLE [-] 10-10-3 L P Cusack, ...(12 to 1) pu
3121² BERMUDA BUCK [-] 8-11-3 F Woods, ...(4 to 1 fav) pu
Dist: 2½l, ½l, 15l, 1½l. 7m 7.40s. (17 Ran).

(J Hunt), Noel Meade

3250 Tandy Bridge INH Flat Race (4 & 5-y-o) £3,105 2m.....................(5:30)

1916² CONQUERING LEADER (Ire) 5-11-8 Mr A P O'Brien, (8 to 1) 1
2663⁴ KERRYHEAD GIRL (Ire) 4-10-7 (7") Mr E Norris, ... (9 to 2) 2
3124³ KILLINEY GAYLE (Ire) 5-11-5 (3") Mrs J M Mullins, (7 to 2 jt-fav) 3
       NEAR GALE (Ire) 4-10-11 (3") Mrs S McCarthy, ...(8 to 1) 4
2868⁹ SELL EVERYTHING (Ire) 4-11-2 (3") Mr D Valentine, (14 to 1) 5
2989⁴ VERITATIS SPLENDOR (Ire) 5-11-10 (3") Mr J A Nash,
       ....(7 to 2 jt-fav) 6
3088⁴ FLAWLESS FINISH (Ire) 5-11-1 (7") Mr R P Cody, ..(12 to 1) 7
       REGAL FELLOW (Ire) 5-11-10 (3") Mr R Neylon, ...(25 to 1) 8
3082 LOTTOVER (Ire) 5-11-8 Mr J P Berry, ...(10 to 1) 9
       SIGMA WIRELESS (Ire) 5-11-10 (3") Mr D Marnane, (8 to 1) 10
       CAILIN GLAS (Ire) 5-11-1 (7") Mr M Dunne, ...(20 to 1) 11
2989⁸ UNSINKABLE BOXER (Ire) 5-11-6 (7") Mr D A Harney,
       ....(25 to 1) 12
2869 ALAMILLO (Ire) 5-11-1 (7") Mr P J McMahon, ...(20 to 1) 13
2989⁹ CANTELIER 5-11-6 (7") Mr T J Corcoran Jnr, ...(50 to 1) 14
       FOREST FORT (Ire) 5-11-13 Mr T Mullins, ...(20 to 1) 15
Dist: 12l, 1½l, 3½l, 11l. 4m 14.00s. (15 Ran).

(M C Casey), A P O'Brien

NEWTON ABBOT (soft)
Monday March 28th
Going Correction: PLUS 1.35 sec. per fur. (races 1,5), PLUS 1.88 (2,3,4,6,7)

3251 West Country Novices' Chase (5-y-o and up) £2,412 2m 5f...........(2:10)

1804 CROSULA 6-11-3 R Dunwoody, made all, jmpd tidily, clr frm 4 out, not extended.
       ....(14 to 1 op 12 to 1 tchd 16 to 1) 1
2855² MUNKA (bl) 8-11-3 Peter Hobbs, chsd wnr, awkward second and 9th, mstk 11th, rdn and no imprsn aftr.
       ....(11 to 10 fav op Evens tchd 11 to 10 on) 2
3135⁴ PRUDENT PEGGY 7-11-3 J Frost, trkd ldrs, lost tch frm tenth....................(7 to 2 op 3 to 1 tchd 4 to 1) 3
2841⁴ BOLD STREET BLUES 7-11-3 C Llewellyn, blun second and 5th, wl beh till hdwy aftr 8th, wknd tenth, tld off.
       ....(14 to 1 op 12 to 1 tchd 20 to 1) 4
3097 PURPLE SPRAY 9-11-3 S McNeill, hld up, hdwy to chase ldrs 8th, und pres and wkng whn f tenth.
       ....(20 to 1 op 10 to 1 tchd 25 to 1) f
3110² FAR TOO LOUD 7-11-3 M A FitzGerald, al beh, tld off frm 8th, refused 4 out.................(9 to 2 op 7 to 2) ref
2836³ DUNKERY BEACON 8-11-3 B Powell, blun 3rd and struggling in rear aftr, tld off whn pld up bef 4 out.
       ....(12 to 1 op 12 to 1) pu
Dist: 13l, 20l, dist. 5m 34.80s. 5m 34.80s (7 Ran).
SR: 25/12/-/-/   (Bisgrove Partnership), M C Pipe

3252 South West Of England Novices' Hurdle (4-y-o and up) £1,909 2m 1f..(2:40)

3023³ DREAMS END 6-11-8 C Llewellyn, trkd ldrs, led sn aftr 3 out, clr whn untidy nxt, eased r-in.
       ....(5 to 1 on op 4 to 1) 1
3056² LA VILLA ROSE (Fr) 4-10-4 A Maguire, trkd ldr, led appr 5th, hdd sn aftr 3 out, one pace after.
       ....(11 to 2 op 8 to 1) 2
2440⁸ EL GRANDO 4-10-9 A Charlton, hld up, hdwy frm 5th, nvr nrr...........................(100 to 1 op 50 to 1) 3
2746 DARINGLY 5-11-8 Mr G Brown, beh and nvr on terms.
       ....(66 to 1 op 16 to 1) 4
2802 VALIANTHE (USA) (bl) 6-11-2 J Lower, reluctant to race, blun 1st, some hdwy aftr 4th.
       ....(40 to 1 op 15 to 1 tchd 50 to 1) 5
3016³ KOSVILLE (Fr) 4-10-4 R Dunwoody, led till hdd appr 5th, wknd stdly.................(11 to 1 op 10 to 1 tchd 12 to 1) 6
2333 MYRTILLA 5-10-11 L Harvey, mid-div, cld on ldrs 5th, rdn and sn btn, tld off.....(16 to 1 op 12 to 1 tchd 20 to 1) 7
1271 SET-EM-ALIGHT 4-10-9 J Frost, in tch to 4th, tld off.
       ....(100 to 1 op 66 to 1) 8
3016 JEAN BRODIE 4-10-2¹ (3") R Davis, beh whn f 4th.
       ....(100 to 1 op 50 to 1) f
       ROYAL HONEY BEE 6-10-4 (7") N Jefford, beh whn uns rdr 5th...............(100 to 1 op 66 to 1 tchd 500 to 1) ur
3008⁶ BEE BEAT 6-10-10¹ (7") M Appleby, beh, effrt hfwy, remote 4th whn ran out last........(66 to 1 op 25 to 1) ro
1516 MR ZIEGFELD (USA) (bl) 5-11-2 W McFarland, tld off frm 4th, pld up bef 2 out...........(66 to 1 op 50 to 1) pu
Dist: 5l, 2½l, 25l, 5l, nk, 15l, 12l. 4m 30.20s. a 40.20s (12 Ran).

SR: 12/-/-/-/-/-/   (T G Price), P J Hobbs

3253 Haytor Mares Only Novices' Hurdle (4-y-o and up) £2,621 2¾m.....(3:10)

3036⁸ ELAINE TULLY (Ire) 6-11-10 (7") Mr S Mulcaire, led till aftr second, styd prmnt, led appr 2 out, rdn out.
       ....(6 to 5 op Evens tchd 5 to 4) 1
3167* KNOCKAVERRY (Ire) 6-11-12 R Supple, hld up in rear, steady hdwy 4 out, unt second appr 2 out, rdn and no imprsn...................(11 to 10 fav op 7 to 4) 2
3005⁶ STORMY SUNSET 7-10-9 (7") Mr N Moore, led aftr second, hdd after 3 out, 3rd whn blun nxt.
       ....(12 to 1 tchd 14 to 1) 3
3055⁶ SPIRIT LEVEL 6-10-11² (7") Mr R Payne, prmnt early, beh 6th, plugged on one pace aftr....(100 to 1 op 50 to 1) 4
3051³ JANET SCIBS 8-10-11 (5") D Matthews, trkd ldrs, rdn 3 out, wknd quickly...(50 to 1 op 25 to 1 tchd 66 to 1) 5
2878⁷ CELTIC LILLEY 4-10-7 M Hoad, in tch till outpcd 4 out, tld off.................................(100 to 1) 6
2797⁴ DANCING DANCER 5-11-2 J Frost, prmnt till wknd aftr 8th, tld off.........................(66 to 1 op 50 to 1) 7
2427 HAND OUT 10-11-2 B Powell, prmnt, wkng whn hit 3 out, tld off...............(40 to 1 op 25 to 1) 8
       MATCH HANS 9-11-2 M A FitzGerald, beh frm strt, tld off whn pld up bef 4 out............(100 to 1 op 50 to 1) pu
Dist: 2l, 25l, nk, 7l, 20l, 2l, 5l. 5m 47.30s. a 48.30s (9 Ran).
SR: 34/27/-/-/-/-/   (Mrs P G Wilkins), P J Hobbs

3254 Old Saw Mill Handicap Hurdle (0-110 4-y-o and up) £2,633 2m 1f.....(3:40)

2089⁵ CELCIUS [97] (bl) 10-11-10 R Dunwoody, hld up in rear, jmpd slwly 5th, cld on ldrs appr 2 out, led on lst line, rdn out...................(9 to 2 op 5 to 1 tchd 7 to 1) 1
1884⁶ SAILOR BLUE [93] 7-11-6 L Harvey, trkd ldr, rdn and led sn aftr 2 out, hdd last, one pace...........(7 to 1) 2
3020³ THE MINDER (Fr) [91] 7-10-13 (7") D Salter, led chasing grp till rdn appr 2 out, rallied to keep on and go 3rd ag'n r-in..................(6 to 1 op 5 to 1 tchd 13 to 2) 3
2883² CARIBBEAN PRINCE [90] 6-11-3 M A FitzGerald, hld rdn and hdd sn aftr 2 out, wknd...............(11 to 4 jt-fav op 5 to 2 tchd 2 to 1 and 3 to 1) 4
3150³ MILDRED SOPHIA [73] 7-9-7 (7") Miss S Mitchell, in tch, rdn appr 2 out, one pace. (8 to 1 op 10 to 1 tchd 12 to 1) 5
435² HEAD TURNER [83] 6-10-10 A Maguire, hld up in rear, tried to cl appr 2 out, wknd bef last.........(11 to 4 jt-fav op 5 to 2 tchd 100 to 30) 6
2998³ WINDWARD ARIOM [80] 8-10-7 R Marley, in tch till wknd 3 out...................(16 to 1 op 12 to 1) 7
Dist: 1½l, 5l, ¾l, nk, 6l, 7l. 4m 28.20s. a 38.20s (7 Ran).
SR: 34/28/21/19/1/5/-/   (Martin Pipe Racing Club), M C Pipe

3255 Gunners Handicap Chase (0-110 5-y-o and up) £3,134 2m 5f.........(4:10)

3049* WINTER'S LANE [81] 10-11-10 A Maguire, hld up, hdwy to track ldr frm 9th, led 3 out, pushed clr nxt.
       ....(2 to 1 fav op 3 to 1 tchd 100 to 30) 1
1834² SOCIAL CLIMBER [95] 10-11-10 S McNeill, trkd ldrs, led appr 9th, hdd 3 out, rdn and one pace.
       ....(100 to 30 op 5 to 2 tchd 7 to 2) 2
3050* NEEDS MUST [84] 7-10-13 J Frost, settled in rear, outpcd 11th, nvr dngrs aftr...(9 to 1 op 5 to 1 tchd 10 to 1) 3
3015* POWDER BOY [94] 9-11-9 R Dunwoody, hld up in tch, hld tenth, rdn and wknd appr 3 out, tired whn f last, lme.
       ....(3 to 1 op 5 to 2 tchd 100 to 30) f
2879⁸ STAR ACTOR [91] 8-11-6 M A FitzGerald, trkd ldr, hit 4th, led nxt, hdd appr 9th, wknd four out, pld up bef 2 out..................................pu
2902 RUSSELL ROVER [95] 9-11-10 C Maude, pld hrd, led to 5th, wknd quickly aftr nxt, tld off whn pulled up bef 9th.................(25 to 1 op 16 to 1 tchd 33 to 1) pu
Dist: 12l, 6l. 5m 40.70s. a 40.70s (6 Ran).
(Stewart Pike), S Pike

3256 Red Devils Open National Hunt Flat Race (Div I) (4,5,6-y-o) £1,864 2m 1f
..............................(4:40)

3114⁷ RIVER LEVEN (bl) 5-10-11 (3") J McCarthy, hld up, outpcd 7 fs out, rallied 4 out, hrd rdn to ld wl ins last.
       ....(20 to 1 op 16 to 1 tchd 25 to 1) 1
2749⁶ GOING AROUND 6-11-0 N Williamson, al prmnt, led 6 fs out, hrd rdn 2 out, edgd lft, hdd wl ins last.
       ....(Evens fav op 5 to 4 on tchd 11 to 10) 2
       PRINCE NASHA (Ire) 4-10-7 A Charlton, rdn hfwy, cld on ldrs 7 fs out, ev ch 2 out, no extr ins.
       ....(9 to 1 op 8 to 1 tchd 16 to 1) 3
       MUTLEY 4-10-7 Peter Hobbs, hld up in rear, hdwy 7 fs out, ev ch 2 out, one pace.
       ....(7 to 2 tchd 4 to 1 and 3 to 1) 4
       MANOR COTTAGE (Ire) 5-10-7 (7") N Collum, in tch, led hfwy to 6 fs out, wknd 4 out, tld off
       ....(14 to 1 op 12 to 1 tchd 20 to 1) 5
       PADDITATE (Ire) 5-11-0 R Dunwoody, trkd ldrs till wknd 6 fs out, tld off.................(10 to 1 op 5 to 1) 6

3176 MADAM MARGEAUX (Ire) 5-10-9 M A FitzGerald, *made most for 7 fs, rdn and sn wknd, tld off.*
.... (14 to 1 op 20 to 1 tchd 33 to 1) 7
SPIKEIE ROSE 4-10-2 A Maguire, *in tch, led briefly aftr 7 fs, sn rdn and lost pl, tld off whn virtually pld up 4 furlongs out.........* (12 to 1 op 10 to 1 tchd 8 to 1) 8
Dist: 1¼l, 1¾l, 2½l, 30l, 30l, 2½l. 4m 24.90s. (8 Ran).

(D R Gandolfo) D R Gandolfo

3257 Red Devils Open National Hunt Flat Race (Div II) (4,5,6-y-o) £1,864 2m 1f
.... (5:10)

2677 BLUE DOCTOR 4-10-7 R Dunwoody, *made virtually all, drw clr o'r 2 fs out.*............... (7 to 2 op Evens) 1
2677 EMMA'S WAY (Ire) 5-10-9 A Maguire, *wtd wth, gd hdwy sn aftr hfwy, wnt second 5 fs out, rdn and no imprsn fnl 2.*
.... (15 to 8 op 5 to 4 tchd 2 to 1) 2
PRIVILEGEDTOSERVE 5-10-2 (7*) M Moran, *in tch till outpcd 7 fs out, one pace aftr.*
.... (6 to 1 op 8 to 1 tchd 10 to 1) 3
QUICKRETREAT 5-11-0 B Powell, *nvr on terms, tld off.*
.... (10 to 1 tchd 16 to 1) 4
KING OF THE MICKS 4-10-0 (7*) Mr N Moore, *prmnt, led briefly 7 fs out, rdn and wknd o'r 3 out, tld off.*
.... (25 to 1 op 20 to 1) 5
3113⁹ SHAMELESS LADY 4-10-2 S Mackey, *al beh, tld off.*
.... (16 to 1 op 10 to 1) 6
NEARLY AT SEA 5-10-2 (7*) Mr L Jefford, *al beh, tld off.*
.... (25 to 1 op 10 to 1) 7
3113 BORIS BAGLEY 6-10-7 (7*) N Willmington, *trkd wnr till wknd rpdly hfwy, tld off.*
.... (12 to 1 op 20 to 1 tchd 25 to 1) 8
Dist: 7l, 30l, 20l, 2½l, 1½l, nk. tld off. 4m 21.60s. (8 Ran).

(Mrs E A Eagles) R J Hodges

SANDOWN (good)
Tuesday March 29th
Going Correction: PLUS 0.20 sec. per fur.

3258 Gunner Heritage Campaign Chase Handicap (5-y-o and up) £4,370 2½m 110yds. .... (2:20)

3121 GALE AGAIN [144] 7-11-11 D Murphy, *jmpd wl, hld up gng nicely, cld 9th, led last, ran on well, not extended.*
.... (13 to 8 fav op 6 to 4 tchd 7 to 4) 1
2990² EASTSHAW [125] 12-10-6 B Powell, *trkd ldr, mstk 12th, led appr 2 out to last, rdn and one pace.*
.... (5 to 2 op 9 to 4 tchd 11 to 4) 2
3091² LOVE ANEW (USA) [119] 9-10-0 N Williamson, *jmpd slwly early, hld up in tch, ch 3 out, kpt on wl frm last.*
.... (8 to 1 op 7 to 1 tchd 9 to 1) 3
YOUNG POKEY [147] 9-12-0 J Osborne, *led till hdd appr 2 out, wknd r-in.........* (11 to 2 op 4 to 1 tchd 6 to 1) 4
3132⁴ ROMANY KING [131] 10-10-12 Richard Guest, *hld up, in tch whn hmpd and uns rdr 4 out...* (6 to 1 tchd 7 to 1) ur
2780 YOUNG ALFIE [116] (bl) 9-9-11⁴ (7*) S Arnold, *trkd ldrs, in cl tch whn blun and uns rdr 4 out.*
.... (150 to 1 op 100 to 1) ur
Dist: 2½l, 4l, 8l. 5m 21.90s. a 22.40s (6 Ran).

(P Piller) T Stack

3259 British Aerospace Rapier Novices' Chase (5-y-o and up) £4,134 2½m 110yds. .... (2:55)

3047* MARTHA'S SON 7-11-8 R Dunwoody, *hld up gng wl, quickened to ld appr last, pushed clr, easily.*
.... (15 to 8 on op 7 to 4 on tchd 2 to 1 on) 1
2965* YORKSHIRE GALE 8-11-4 D Murphy, *cl up, led 7th, mstk 4 out, hdd appr last, no extr.*.................... (7 to 2) 2
2965² GINGER TRISTAN 8-11-0 Peter Hobbs, *led, hdd 7th, mstk 9th, ev ch 3 out, sn outpcd.*
.... (6 to 1 op 5 to 1 tchd 13 to 2) 3
3043 BALLY PARSON 8-11-0 N Williamson, *in cl tch whn f 7th.*
.... (20 to 1 op 10 to 1) f
Dist: 14l, 13l. 5m 15.80s. a 16.30s (4 Ran).

(M Ward-Thomas), Capt T A Forster

3260 Royal Artillery Gold Cup Chase (5-y-o and up) £3,712 3m 110yds...... (3:25)

2363⁸ WELKNOWN CHARACTER 12-12-7 Mr D Alers-Hankey, *led 7th, clr 17th, easily.*................ (6 to 1 op 5 to 1) 1
2966⁷ FIFTH AMENDMENT (bl) 9-12-7 Mr C Ward Thomas, *led briefly 1st, trkd ldrs, chsd wnr frm 13th, no imprsn.*
.... (10 to 1 op 12 to 1) 2
2901⁴ TRIBAL RULER 9-12-3 Mr D McCain, *chsd ldrs, blun 17th, styd on one pace.*...... (14 to 1 op 4 to 1 tchd 16 to 1) 3
2966³ TOUCHING STAR 9-12-7 Mr B Marquis, *mid-div, plugged on one pace frm 2 out.*...... (9 to 2 jt-fav tchd 5 to 1) 4
1302 KILLBANON 12-11-8³ Mr C Trietline, *nvr jump wl, trkd ldrs till outpcd 15th.*.................. (33 to 1 op 1 to 1) 5

2935³ SMOOTH ESCORT (v) 10-12-0 Mr D Line, *mstk 3rd, mid-div, outpcd frm hfwy.* (10 to 1 op 8 to 1 tchd 12 to 1) 6
SCRUMPY COUNTRY 9-11-3 Maj C Marriott, *nvr on terms.*
.... (16 to 1 op 20 to 1) 7
EAGLE TRACE 11-11-3 Miss W Southcombe, *al beh.*
.... (50 to 1 op 33 to 1) 8
2780⁵ MAJOR ELSTON 9-11-3 Mr D Warren, *chsd ldrs to hfwy, no ch whn blun 16th (water)......* (66 to 1 op 50 to 1) 9
2968⁵ NORSTOWN 12-11-3 Capt R Inglesant, *al beh....* (50 to 1) 10
3168 PRINCE NEPAL 10-11-7 Mr C Farr, *al beh.*
.... (50 to 1 op 33 to 1 tchd 66 to 1) 11
2966⁸ KNOX'S CORNER 9-12-0 Mr Simon Robinson, *al beh, tld off.*........................ (50 to 1) 12
2824³ LOCH BLUE 12-12-3 Mr A Wood, *chasing ldrs whn f 6th.*
.... (5 to 1 op 9 to 2) f
2966 GUNNER STREAM 10-12-7 Mr B Elliott, *led second to 7th, beh whn blun and uns rdr 12th.*............ (50 to 1) ur
1966⁴ WARNER'S END (bl) 13-11-7 Mr J Fountain, *chsd ldrs, blun and uns rdr 12th.....* (50 to 1 op 33 to 1 tchd 66 to 1) ur
878⁹ NEVER BE GREAT 12-12-7 Miss J Southcombe, *trkd ldrs, mstk 13th, blun and uns rdr 16th (water).*
.... (20 to 1 tchd 25 to 1) ur
2990³ THE MASTER GUNNER 10-12-7 Mr J Trice-Rolph, *hld up, cld whn blun 11th and lost pl, hdwy 14th, wknd 4 out.*
.... (9 to 2 jt-fav op 7 to 2) pu
Dist: 30l, 8l, 1l, 15l, 2½l, hd, sht-hd, 4l, 1¾l, 5l. 6m 21.10s. a 22.10s (17 Ran).

(R W Humphreys), P F Nicholls

3261 Alanbrooke Memorial Chase Handicap (5-y-o and up) £5,181 3m 110yds
.... (3:55)

2995* BUCK WILLOW [126] 10-10-1¹ D Murphy, *in cl tch, led 17th, ran on wl.* (11 to 10 on op 11 to 10 tchd 6 to 5) 1
1447 BONSAI BUD [125] 11-10-0 D Gallagher, *in tch, drpd rear 12th, cld 14th, ev ch 3 out, kpt on one pace.*
.... (5 to 1 op 11 to 2 tchd 9 to 2) 2
2824 MIGHTY FALCON [125] (bl) 9-10-0 P Holley, *mstk 7th, in tch, outpcd appr 3 out, styd on frm nxt.*
.... (50 to 1 op 33 to 1) 3
3041⁸ RICHVILLE [132] 8-10-7 N Williamson, *hld up, cld appr 3 out, sn rdn, one pace whn mstk last.*
.... (4 to 1 tchd 9 to 2) 4
2995⁴ HENRY MANN [135] (bl) 11-10-10 N Dunwoody, *hld up, cld 14th, outpcd aftr 4 out...........* (8 to 1 tchd 9 to 1) 5
3229 ARCTIC CALL [153] (bl) 11-12-0 J Osborne, *not fluent, led til hdd 17th, wknd appr 3 out......* (8 to 1 op 7 to 1) 6
3146 THE LEGGETT [125] (bl) 11-10-0 R Bellamy, *with ldr, drpd rear 16th, tld off...* (66 to 1 op 50 to 1 tchd 100 to 1) 7
Dist: 3½l, 2l, sht-hd, ¾l, 12l, dist. 6m 17.00s. a 18.00s (7 Ran).

(Mrs S N J Embiricos), J T Gifford

3262 Royal Ordnance Chase Handicap (5-y-o and up) £4,751 2m.......... (4:25)

2825* SPREE CROSS [127] 8-11-0 A Maguire, *made virtually all, pckd 8th, rdn appr last, jst hld on.*
.... (6 to 5 fav op 11 to 8) 1
2205² MULBANK [125] 8-10-12 C Maude, *with ldr, led briefly aftr 2 out, ev ch r-in, jst fld.*
.... (4 to 1 op 11 to 8 tchd 13 to 8) 2
1440³ BOUTZDAROFF [137] 12-11-10 M Dwyer, *wtd wth beh ldg pair, outpcd frm 4 out, eased whn btn.*
.... (100 to 30 op 3 to 1 tchd 4 to 1) 3
Dist: Sht-hd, dist. 3m 54.90s. a 6.40s (3 Ran).
SR: 54/52/-/
(P L Mason), Mrs D Haine

3263 'Ubique' Hunters' Chase (5-y-o and up) £2,052 2½m 110yds........ (4:55)

761³ AMARI KING 11-11-3 (7*) Mr C Ward Thomas, *hld up, cld on ldrs 9th, led 4 out, styd on wl...* (13 to 2 op 9 to 2) 1
TREYFORD 14-11-5 (7*) Mr A Steel, *cl up, led 9th till hdd 4 out, ev ch nxt, one pace.*.......... (20 to 1 op 16 to 1) 2
2885² DENBERDAR 11-11-7 (5*) Mr D Parker, *chsd ldrs, styd on one pace frm 3 out.*............ (8 to 1 op 6 to 1) 3
MINSTREL MAN 10-11-7 (7*) Mr T McCarthy, *hld up, cld and ev ch 4 out, one pace frm nxt.*
.... (8 to 1 tchd 25 to 1) 4
2875³ HILARION (Fr) 10-11-5 (7*) Mr D Bloor, *not jump wl in rear, ran on well frm last, nrst finish.*
.... (20 to 1 op 12 to 1 tchd 25 to 1) 5
2888³ ROXALL CLUMP 10-11-9 (7*) Mr M Felton, *not jump wl, trkd ldrs till rdn and wknd 3 out...* (11 to 2 op 9 to 2) 6
3162³ CRAFTY CHAPLAIN 8-11-11 (5*) Mr D McCain, *blun second, al beh.*.... (25 to 1 op 20 to 1 tchd 33 to 1) 7
DROMIN LEADER 9-11-7 (5*) Mr P Harding-Jones, *trkd ldrs till wknd aftr 4 out.*.... (20 to 1 op 8 to 1) 8
2875⁷ CURAHEEN BOY 14-11-9 (7*) Miss J Butler, *blun 3rd, sn pushed alng in rear, tld off...........* (20 to 1) 9
2888² BEE GARDEN (bl) 13-11-11 (5*) Miss P Curling, *made most till hdd 9th, wknd appr 4 out, pld up bef last.*
.... (7 to 1 op 6 to 1) pu
3021⁵ GATTERSTOWN (bl) 11-11-5 (7*) Mr S Mulcaire, *al beh, pld up bef 4 out...* (50 to 1 op 33 to 1 tchd 66 to 1) pu

2966* QUICK RAPOR 9-11-13 (7*) Mr D Alers-Hankey, *mstk 1st, led briefly 6th, wknd 11th, pld up bef 3 out.* ....(5 to 4 fav op 7 to 4) pu

Dist: 3l, 3½l, 10l, 1¾l, 3l, 3l, 12l, 20l. 5m 15.00s. a 15.50s (12 Ran).

(M Ward-Thomas), J Wall

ASCOT (good)
Wednesday March 30th

Going Correction: PLUS 0.10 sec. per fur. (races 1,4,-6,7), PLUS 0.35 (2,3,5)

3264 EBF 'National Hunt' Novices' Hurdle Qualifier (5,6,7-y-o) £2,879 2½m (1:20)

2356[5] BUTLER'S TWITCH 7-11-7 J Osborne, *trkd ldr, lft in ld 4 out, jnd aftr nxt, styd on strly r-in.* ....(7 to 2 op 4 to 1 tchd 9 to 2) 1

2964[3] CALL HOME (Ire) 6-11-5 D Murphy, *trkd ldrs, lft 3rd 4 out, left second 2 out, kpt on same pace.* ....(9 to 1 op 7 to 1 tchd 10 to 1) 2

2950[2] KING LUCIFER (Ire) 5-11-0 W Marston, *patiently rdn, steady hdwy appr 4 out, styd on wl frm last, nvr nrr.* ....(14 to 1 op 10 to 1) 3

3169[2] ME FEIN (Ire) 6-11-0 E Murphy, *beh aftr second till styd on stdly frm 3 out, nvr nr to chal.* ....(12 to 1 op 7 to 1 tchd 14 to 1) 4

1648[6] JULIOS GENIUS 7-11-7 M Dwyer, *trkd ldrs till no hdwy frm 4 out*....................(14 to 1 op 10 to 1 tchd 16 to 1) 5

2147 JOURNEYS FRIEND (Ire) 6-11-0 R Dunwoody, *hld up, steady hdwy aftr 6th, no imprsn frm 3 out.* ....(33 to 1 op 25 to 1) 6

2991 TRIPLE TREAT (Ire) 5-11-0 R J Beggan, *nvr able to chal.* ....(33 to 1 op 25 to 1) 7

2916 MONKS SOHAM (Ire) 6-11-0 J R Kavanagh, *beh frm hfwy.* ....(33 to 1 op 20 to 1 tchd 50 to 1) 8

2643[2] TOO CLEVER BY HALF 6-11-5 Mr G Johnson Houghton, *prmnt to hfwy, sn lost pl*....................(33 to 1 op 20 to 1) 9

3009[6] HIZAL 5-10-7 (7*) M Appleby, *mstk second, al beh.* ....(100 to 1) 10

1804 REFERRAL FEE 7-11-0 S Earle, *prmnt to hfwy, wknd quickly*....................(66 to 1 op 25 to 1) 11

3036 TOTHEWOODS 6-11-7 C Llewellyn, *hld up in midfield, clsg whn hmpd 4 out, trying to reco'r when f nxt.* ....(7 to 4 fav tchd 2 to 1) f

2795[3] COILED SPRING 7-11-7 A Maguire, *made most till f 4 out, broke neck, dead*......(8 to 1 op 7 to 1 tchd 10 to 1) f

2896* MASTER BOSTON (Ire) 6-11-7 R Garritty, *nvr far away, lft second 4 out, rdn whn mstk and uns rdr 2 out.* ....(14 to 1 op 10 to 1 tchd 16 to 1) ur

3115 MR ELECTRAMECH 7-11-0 A Tory, *not jump wl, sn struggling, tld off whn pld up bef 2 out.* ....(100 to 1 op 66 to 1) pu

Dist: 4l, 2½l, 12l, hd, 3½l, 1½l, 5l, 8l, 10l, 4l. 4m 58.10s. a 17.10s (15 Ran).

(Christopher Heath), O Sherwood

3265 'Merlin' Novices' Hunters' Chase (5-y-o and up) £3,566 3m 110yds...(1:55)

RICHARD HUNT 10-11-7 (7*) Miss L Rowe, *hld up in midfield, took mclr order frm hfwy, led 5 out, styd on wl from 2 out*....................(7 to 1 op 5 to 1 tchd 8 to 1) 1

2884[2] ST LAYCAR 9-11-9 (5*) Mr G Tarry, *hld up and beh, gd hdwy to chase ldrs frm 12th, ev ch 2 out, unbl to quicken*....................(7 to 1 op 6 to 1) 2

3040[3] NEARLY SPLENDID 9-12-0 (7*) Mr T Greed, *beh till took clr order frm hfwy, ev ch 3 out, kpt on one pace from nxt.* ....(4 to 1 tchd 9 to 2) 3

3171[3] CAPE COTTAGE 10-12-0 (7*) Mr A Phillips, *hdwy 12th, ev ch 3 out, one pace*....(12 to 1 op 10 to 1 tchd 14 to 1) 4

DERRING BUD 10-11-7 (7*) Mr M Jackson, *beh till gd hdwy 15th, sn chasing ldrs, wknd appr 4 out.* ....(16 to 1 op 14 to 1 tchd 20 to 1) 5

JIMMY CONE 11-11-7 (7*) Mr B Pollock, *drpd last 11th, mstk nxt, unbl to chal*............(33 to 1 op 16 to 1) 6

3021[2] ANDROS PRINCE 9-12-0 (7*) Mr M Felton, *handily plcd, led 8th to 5 out, wknd 2 out.* ....(11 to 2 op 5 to 1 tchd 6 to 1) 7

QUICK REACTION 11-11-11 (3*) Mrs L Gibbon, *beh, shrtlvd effrt aftr 14th, sn wknd*..........(25 to 1 op 16 to 1) 8

SCALISCRO 13-11-7 (7*) Mr C Wadland, *trkd ldrs till wknd appr 11th, tld off whn f 4 out.* ....(50 to 1 op 33 to 1 tchd 66 to 1) f

2884 EASTER FROLIC 12-11-7 (7*) Mr G Brown, *f second.* ....(50 to 1 op 25 to 1) f

TAMAR LASS 9-11-2 (7*) Mr D E Stephens, *beh till hdwy 11th, cl up whn blun and uns rdr 13th.* ....(40 to 1 op 25 to 1) ur

3096* AVOSTAR 7-12-2 (5*) Mr R Russell, *led second till blun and uns rdr 6th*......(100 to 30 fav op 3 to 1 tchd 7 to 2) ur

CHERRYHILL BEAUTY 10-11-7 (7*) Mr M Gingell, *led to second, lft in ld 6th till hdd 8th, wknd 4 out, tld off whn pld up bef last*....................(14 to 1 op 12 to 1) pu

Dist: 3½l, 5l, 2½l, 8l, 5l, 10l, 3l. 6m 19.40s. a 15.90s (13 Ran).

SR: 26/22/24/21/6/1/ (Mrs P Rowe), V H Rowe

3266 Golden Eagle Novices' Chase (5-y-o and up) £8,169 2m 3f 110yds.... (2:30)

2688[4] HOPS AND POPS 7-10-13 S Earle, *made all, clr frm 7th, unchlgd*...........(100 to 30 op 3 to 1 tchd 7 to 2) 1

2993* CABOCHON 7-11-4 J Frost, *hld up, hdwy to chase wnr frm aftr tenth, effrt 4 out, no imprsn.* ....(7 to 4 op 7 to 4 tchd 2 to 1) 2

3097* HERMES HARVEST 6-11-4 R Dunwoody, *in tch till rdn and wknd frm 4 out*....................(25 to 1 op 33 to 1) 3

2472[3] BAS DE LAINE (Fr) 8-11-8 J Osborne, *chsd wnr till aftr tenth, wknd appr 3 out.* ....(11 to 8 fav op 11 to 8 tchd 6 to 4) 4

1102[2] BUSTINELLO (Ire) 6-11-4 C Swan, *hld up, hdwy 11th, hit nxt, wknd appr 4 out, tld off, fnshd tired*.....(12 to 1) 5

3148[4] EXACT ANALYSIS (USA) 8-11-4 P Niven, *not fluent, al beh, tld off whn pld up bef 12th*......(66 to 1 op 100 to 1) pu

Dist: 9l, 3½l, 2l, dist. 4m 54.30s. a 12.80s (6 Ran).

SR: 25/21/17/19/-/-/ (B Dennett), R H Alner

3267 Letheby & Christopher Long Distance Hurdle Grade 2 (4-y-o and up) £13,100 3m...........................(3:00)

3063[6] SWEET GLOW (Fr) 7-11-7 R Dunwoody, *hld up and beh, steady hdwy frm 8th, chlgd last, rdn to ld last 50 yards.* ....(9 to 2 op 6 to 1) 1

3063 AVRO ANSON 6-11-3 M Dwyer, *hld up in midfield, hdwy 7th, ev ch 2 out, led last, hdd last 50 yards.* ....(3 to 1 op 9 to 4 tchd 100 to 30) 2

3038* TIME FOR A RUN 7-11-3 C Swan, *patiently rdn, steady hdwy frm 7th, hmpd bend appr 2 out, ran on one pace from nxt*..........(11 to 4 fav op 7 to 2 tchd 4 to 1) 3

3063[5] SWEET DUKE (Fr) 7-11-10 W Humphreys, *led 4th till aftr nxt, led 6th till hdd last, no extr.* ....(9 to 1 op 8 to 1 tchd 10 to 1) 4

3028[2] DARK HONEY 9-11-3 A Dicken, *ever far away, drvn alng appr 3 out, no imprsn bef nxt.* ....(9 to 1 op 7 to 1 tchd 10 to 1) 5

3063 BURGOYNE 8-11-7 P Niven, *beh and drvn alng 6th, hdwy 8th, hrd rdn and no imprsn frm nxt.* ....(33 to 1 tchd 40 to 1) 6

3063 TRIPLE WITCHING 8-11-7 W Marston, *al prmnt, rdn and ev ch 3 out, wknd nxt*... (7 to 1 op 6 to 1 tchd 8 to 1) 7

2830[4] ACROW LINE 9-11-3 D J Burchell, *niggled alng 6th, sn no imprsn*....................(66 to 1) 8

3063 PRAGADA (bl) 11-11-10 M Perrett, *led to 4th, reminders to ld aftr nxt till hdd 6th, wknd frm 8th.* ....(25 to 1 op 20 to 1 tchd 33 to 1) 9

DARA DOONE 8-11-3 E Murphy, *trkd ldrs till wknd 8th.* ....(50 to 1 op 33 to 1) 10

2873[4] SAYYURE (USA) 8-11-7 J Osborne, *prmnt to 3rd, sn struggling, tld off whn pld up bef 2 out.* (66 to 1 op 50 to 1) pu

2473 LORNA-GAIL 8-10-12 S Earle, *trkd ldrs to 7th, losing pl whn pld up bef nxt*...............(50 to 1 op 40 to 1) pu

Dist: Hd, 8l, 2l, 2½l, 2l, 1½l, 20l, 7l, 4l. 5m 40.40s. a 7.40s (12 Ran).

SR: 43/39/31/36/26/28/26/2/2/ (L B Hyman), M C Pipe

3268 Peregrine Handicap Chase (5-y-o and up) £8,286 2m 3f 110yds........ (3:35)

2981[2] LITTLE TOM [120] 9-10-0 J R Kavanagh, *jmpd wl, trkd ldr till led 8th, hng lft r-in, all out.* ....(20 to 1 op 16 to 1 tchd 25 to 1) 1

3041[3] SMARTIE EXPRESS [127] 12-10-7 R Dunwoody, *al hndy, niggled alng and slightly outpcd 12th, chlgd 3 out, rallied r-in*................(7 to 4 on tchd 13 to 8 on) 2

2962[4] CAMPSEA-ASH [121] 10-10-1[1] D Murphy, *hld up, effrt 12th and sn ev ch, wknd appr 2 out.* ....(20 to 1 op 16 to 1 tchd 25 to 1) 3

3172[3] ITS NEARLY TIME [125] 11-10-5 J Osborne, *hld up, hdwy 11th, one pace frm nxt.* ....(3 to 1 op 5 to 2 tchd 100 to 30) 4

2539[2] EMSEE-H [120] 9-10-0 C Swan, *led till jmpd slwly and hdd 8th, rdn aftr 11th, sn wknd, eased whn btn.* ....(10 to 1 tchd 12 to 1) 5

Dist: ½l, 12l, 12l, 20l. 4m 56.50s. a 15.00s (5 Ran).

(Mark O'Connor), J S King

3269 Kestrel Hurdle Limited Handicap (4-y-o and up) £4,833 2m 110yds...(4:15)

3025 HIGH BARON [142] 7-11-8 R Dunwoody, *trkd ldrs, led appr 2 out, clr nxt, readily*.........(4 to 1 tchd 9 to 2) 1

2833[3] PONTYNYSWEN [127] (v) 6-10-7 D J Burchell, *took keen hold, led 4th till hdd appr 2 out, not pace of wnr.* ....(4 to 1 op 5 to 2 tchd 9 to 2) 2

2079 KILCASH (Ire) [144] (bl) 6-11-10 M Richards, *hld up, effrt 5th, rdn aftr nxt, one pace*..........(5 to 1 op 7 to 2) 3

2994[3] LEOTARD [141] 7-11-7 J Osborne, *led to 3rd, styd hndy till rdn and wknd appr 2 out.* ....(13 to 8 fav op 2 to 1 tchd 9 to 4) 4

INDIAN QUEST [133] 5-10-13 D Murphy, *wth ldr, led 3rd to nxt, wknd appr 3 out*................(8 to 1 op 6 to 1) 5

1714 GANDOUGE GLEN [127] 7-10-4 (3*) P Hide, *hld up, lost tch frm 5th*.............(20 to 1 op 16 to 1 tchd 25 to 1) 6

Dist: 6l, 5l, 3l, 10l, 10l. 3m 49.50s. a 3.50s (6 Ran).
SR: 75/54/66/60/42/26/   (Miss C A James), R H Alner

3270   Sparrow Hawk Novices' Handicap Hurdle (4-y-o and up) £3,696 2m 110yds . . . . (4:45)

3151[5] NO PAIN NO GAIN (Ire) [99] 6-11-5 (4ex) E Murphy, *hld up in tch, took clr order aftr 4th, led r-in, drvn out.* . . . . (3 to 1 fav tchd 7 to 2)	1
3022* HEDGEHOPPER (Ire) [88] 6-10-8 M Richards, *led till hdd r-in, not quicken.* . . . . (5 to 1 tchd 6 to 1)	2
3115 RES IPSA LOQUITUR [90] 7-10-10 D Gallagher, *hld up, hdwy 4 out, ran on strly aftr last, nvr nrr.* . . . . (25 to 1)	3
2440[5] KING'S TREASURE (USA) [104] 5-11-10 W Irvine, *nvr far away, second and ev ch whn pckd 3 out, kpt on frm last.* . . . . (16 to 1 op 12 to 1 tchd 20 to 1)	4
3115[3] FOREVER SHINEING [84] 4-10-4 M Perrett, *hld up, hdwy 4 out, styd on same pace fnl 2.* . . . . (16 to 1 tchd 20 to 1)	5
2969[2] TEEN JAY [88] 4-10-8 J Osborne, *midfield, effrt appr 3 out, one pace frm nxt.* . . . . (8 to 1 op 6 to 1)	6
3062 DOCTOOR (USA) [103] 4-11-9 D O'Sullivan, *trkd ldrs till lost pl aftr 4th, 5th and rallying whn blun 2 out, not reco'r.* . . . . (13 to 2 op 9 to 2 tchd 7 to 1)	7
3119[3] MONAZITE [80] (bl) 4-9-7 (7*) E Tolhurst, *trkd ldrs, ev ch 3 out, wknd bef nxt.* . . . . (33 to 1)	8
2835[2] GOTTA BE JOKING [90] 6-10-10 D Murphy, *wth ldr till rdn and appr 3 out.* . . . . (10 to 1)	9
3044[2] PETTAUGH (Ire) [80] 6-10-0 J R Kavanagh, *al beh.* (33 to 1)	10
3022[6] FALCONBRIDGE BAY [82] 7-10-2 R Dunwoody, *tucked away in midfield till wknd appr 3 out, beh whn pld up bef 2 out.* . . . . (20 to 1)	pu
1464[5] BENGALI (Ire) [94] 4-11-0 J Railton, *drpd last frm 4th, beh whn pld up bef 2 out.* . . . . (25 to 1)	pu
3009* CHAPEL OF BARRAS (Ire) [103] 5-11-9 Peter Hobbs, *pld hrd, hld up in rear till no hdwy frm 4 out, beh whn pulled up bef 2 out.* . . . . . (4 to 1 op 9 to 2 tchd 5 to 1)	pu

Dist: ½l, nk, 3l, 5l, 2l, 3l, 8l, 10l, 4l. 3m 52.90s. a 6.90s (13 Ran).
SR: 38/26/27/38/13/15/27/-/-/   (Mrs B J Curley), B J Curley

DOWNPATRICK (IRE) (heavy)
Wednesday March 30th

3271   Ballee E.B.F. Mares Hurdle (Qualifier) (4-y-o and up) £1,380 2m 1f 172yds . . . . (2:30)

3084[5] RADICAL NURSE (Ire) 5-11-1 (7*) P J Mulligan, ... (4 to 1)	1
2938[6] PILS INVADER (Ire) 6-11-5 (5*) D T Evans, ... (4 to 1)	2
2771[6] RAHAN BRIDGE (Ire) 5-11-8 Mr A J Martin, ... (9 to 1)	3
3071[5] GRANDOLLY (Ire) 5-11-3 (5*) Mr B R Hamilton, ... (6 to 1)	4
2985[7] WAYUPHILL 7-11-10 D P Fagan, ... (6 to 1)	5
2983 SHINETHYME (Ire) 5-11-8 S R Murphy, ... (50 to 1)	6
2842[7] MINIGIRLS NIECE (Ire) 6-11-10 A Powell, ... (6 to 4 fav)	7
2985 SISTER NORA (Ire) 4-11-5 (5*) M M Mackin, ... (6 to 1)	8
2770[7] SERIOUS NOTE (Ire) 6-11-8 D Sheridan, ... (20 to 1)	9
1760 JEMMA'S GOLD (Ire) 6-11-10 J P Banahan, ... (25 to 1)	10
3072[6] PRINCESS DILLY (Ire) 5-11-1 (7*) Mr J Bright, ... (20 to 1)	11
2988 MIRASEL 7-11-10 C O'Dwyer, ... (14 to 1)	12
3070[7] BARNISH DAWN (Ire) 4-10-7 (7*) Mr S Kerr, ... (50 to 1)	13
WADABLAST (Ire) 4-10-11 (3*) C O'Brien, ... (33 to 1)	14
3122 MUSICAL SMOKE (Ire) 5-11-1 (7*) D J Kavanagh, . (20 to 1)	pu

Dist: 1½l, 6l, 1l, 1½l. (Time not taken) (15 Ran).

(B Maguire), B Maguire

3272   Down Claiming Hurdle (5-y-o and up) £1,207 2m 1f 172yds . . . . (3:00)

2771[5] NATINA (Ire) 5-10-1 P Mooney, ... (9 to 4)	1
503[3] TOP GENERATION 5-10-4 (3*) T J Mitchell, ... (7 to 2)	2
2987 FIDSPRIT 7-10-3 A Powell, ... (20 to 1)	3
2922[4] ITS A SNIP (Ire) 9-10-12 B Sheridan, ... (7 to 1)	4
39 THE PARSONS ROSE (Ire) 6-10-0 (3*) Mr P McMahon, ... (10 to 1)	5
3122 TOP RUN (Ire) 6-11-8 H Rogers, ... (12 to 1)	6
2351[2] CHARMING EXCUSE 10-10-9 (5*) Mr C T G Kinane, ... (2 to 1 fav)	7
GARVHILL (Ire) 5-10-8 (7*) R K Gordon, ... (14 to 1)	8

Dist: ½l, 4l, 4½l, dist. (Time not taken) (8 Ran).

(G G Racing Syndicate), Patrick Mooney

3273   Thoroughbred Insur. Services Handicap Hurdle (0-116 4-y-o and up) £1,380 2½m . . . . (3:30)

3242 BRINDLEY HOUSE [-] 7-12-0 J Shortt, ... (6 to 1)	1
2846[9] RED THUNDER [-] 7-9-13 D P Fagan, ... (8 to 1)	2
2468[7] RUNAWAY GOLD [-] 7-10-0 F Woods, ... (10 to 1)	3
2939[6] GRANADOS (USA) [-] 6-10-6 P Carberry, ... (6 to 1)	4
3198[7] BALLYCANN [-] 7-10-13 (7*) P J Mulligan, ... (14 to 1)	5
2703[6] BELLE O' THE BAY (Ire) [-] 5-9-4 (3*) D Bromley, . . (14 to 1)	6
3084[4] SIOBHAILIN DUBH (Ire) [-] 5-9-9 (5*) K P Gaule, (7 to 2 fav)	7
3128[8] ALOHA (Ire) [-] 5-10-9 M Duffy, ... (10 to 1)	8
2127[9] IM OK (Ire) [-] 6-9-0 (7*) T Martin, ... (50 to 1)	9
2770 BRISCE HILL (Ire) [-] 6-9-0 (7*) D A McLoughlin, . (50 to 1)	10
2940[5] JOES NIGHTMARE [-] 7-9-2 (7*) D Fisher, ... (20 to 1)	11

3122 PREMIER COUNTY [-] 8-10-2 (3*) T J Mitchell, ... (20 to 1)	pu
2988[4] CABRA TOWERS [-] 7-10-7 (5*) M M Mackin, ... (6 to 1)	pu
2310[8] FATHER GREGORY (Ire) [-] 5-9-0[1] (7*) C McCormack, ... (20 to 1)	pu
2846 ROSIN THE BOW (Ire) [-] 5-10-1 C O'Dwyer, ... (12 to 1)	pu

Dist: 12l, nk, 20l, 3½l. (Time not taken) (15 Ran).

(Brindley Advertising Ltd), J E Mulhern

3274   Downpatrick Handicap Chase (0-109 4-y-o and up) £2,070 3m . . . . (4:00)

3134[8] GREEN TIMES [-] 9-11-9 (5*) Mr G J Harford, . . . (9 to 4 fav)	1
2774* JIMS CHOICE [-] 7-10-9 (5*) Mr R J Patton, ... (5 to 2)	2
2774[3] THE MAD MONK [-] 9-10-1 (5*) D T Evans, ... (8 to 1)	3
2774[2] REDELVA [-] 7-9-12 F Woods, ... (9 to 2)	4
2619[3] KITES HARDWICKE [-] (bl) 7-9-11 F J Flood, ... (6 to 1)	5
2751 SPUR OF THE MOMENT [-] 7-11-10 J P Banahan, (9 to 2)	6
2984 LINVAR [-] 11-10-7 A Powell, ... (10 to 1)	7
2774[8] JIMMYS DOUBLE [-] 8-9-4[4] (7*) Mr J J Canavan, . (33 to 1)	8

Dist: 2l, 10l, 15l, ½l. (Time not taken) (8 Ran).

(Noel McGrady), Michael Cunningham

3275   Frank Magee Memorial Novice Chase (5-y-o and up) £1,207 2½m . . . . . . (4:30)

3071[3] BOTTLE BLACK 7-11-9 J P Banahan, ... (12 to 1)	1
2683[6] NO BETTER BUACHAIL (Ire) 6-11-9 F J Flood, ... (6 to 1)	2
3198 RICH TRADITION (Ire) 6-12-0 J Shortt, ... (11 to 8 fav)	3
2774 FOGELBERG (USA) 6-12-0 C O'Dwyer, ... (5 to 2)	4
2774[4] SPARKLING BLAKE 8-11-2 (7*) Mr I Buchanan, . . (10 to 1)	5
2232[9] RATHBRIDES JOY 7-12-0 T Horgan, ... (6 to 1)	f
2983[7] SLANEY BACON 7-11-2 (7*) D J Kavanagh, ... (10 to 1)	ur
1076 RUBDAN (USA) 7-11-9 A J O'Brien, ... (20 to 1)	pu
2752[3] DELGANY DEER 8-11-4 (5*) Mr G J Harford, ... (12 to 1)	pu

Dist: 2l, 1½l, 15l, dist. (Time not taken) (9 Ran).

(Mrs M H Davies), John Davies

3276   Sean P. Graham Memorial I.N.H. Flat Race (4-y-o and up) £3,450 2m 1f 172yds . . . . (5:00)

2586[6] I AM 6-11-13 (5*) Mr P J Casey, ... (8 to 1)	1
2465 NO DOZING (Ire) 5-11-4 (5*) Mr B R Hamilton, . . . (14 to 1)	2
2283 TOURIST ATTRACTION (Ire) 6-11-8 (3*) Mrs J M Mullins, ... (6 to 1)	3
3071[2] CABLE BEACH 5-11-4 (5*) Mr G J Harford, ... (9 to 1)	4
3124* ROSTARR (Ire) 5-11-11 Mr A P O'Brien, ... (9 to 1)	5
2775* KEY WEST (Ire) 5-12-2 Mr A J Martin, ... (10 to 1)	6
3201 DANGEROUS LADY (Ire) 5-11-1 (3*) Mr D Marnane, (25 to 1)	7
3072[4] THE THIRD MAN (Ire) 5-11-6 (3*) Mr P McMahon, (25 to 1)	8
3069 MICHAEL'S PET (Ire) 4-10-3 (7*) Mr C Andrews, . . (10 to 1)	9
3082 DELGANY SUNSET 7-11-4 (7*) Mr G Lawless, ... (20 to 1)	10
2314 LITTLE BALLYWOODEN (Ire) 6-10-13 (7*) Mr E Magee, ... (33 to 1)	pu
3071[7] GLASHA BRIDGE (Ire) 6-11-4 (7*) Mr R Sylvia, . . (33 to 1)	pu
2203* MISS MUPPET (Ire) 5-11-8 (3*) Mrs M Mullins, . . (6 to 4 fav)	pu
3070[5] COMMANCHE LYN (Ire) 4-10-3 (7*) Miss M A Burroughs, ... (33 to 1)	pu

Dist: 1l, 2½l, 14l, 1½l. (Time not taken) (14 Ran).

(Liam McAteer), Liam McAteer

WORCESTER (good)
Wednesday March 30th
Going Correction: PLUS 0.05 sec. per fur. (races 1,3,-5,7), PLUS 0.17 (2,4,6)

3277   Newland Novices' Hurdle (4-y-o and up) £2,153 2m 5f 110yds . . . . (2:10)

2438[3] TITIAN GIRL (bl) 5-10-8 (3*) A Thornton, *al wl plcd, wnt second 5th, hit 2 out, led and hit last, all out.* . . . . (7 to 1 op 10 to 1)	1
1800 THE SHAW TRADER 5-11-2 D Bridgwater, *led till appr 3 out, sn hrd rdn, styd on r-in.* . . . . (12 to 1 op 8 to 1 tchd 14 to 1)	2
2263 SKEOUGH (Ire) 6-11-8 R Bellamy, *chsd ldrs appr 5th, rdn approaching 3 out, sn btn.* . . . . (10 to 1 op 6 to 1)	3
TONY MURPHYS LADY 8-10-11 R Supple, *jmpd slwly 1st, tld off frm 5th.* . . . . (12 to 1)	4
3113[6] DUNLIR 4-10-1 (7*) T Thompson, *in rear whn mstk 3rd, tld off frm 5th.* . . . . (33 to 1 op 20 to 1)	5
3184[7] PERTEMPS JOBSHOP 8-11-2 N Williamson, *hld up and sn wl beh, some prog 6th, wknd aftr nxt, tld off.* . . . . (16 to 1 op 14 to 1 tchd 20 to 1)	6
MISTER MOSS MAN (Ire) 5-11-2 R Marley, *in rear, tld off frm 5th.* . . . . (25 to 1 op 12 to 1)	7
2430[4] KALAKATE 9-11-2 B Powell, *prog 5th, hit 7th, led appr 3 out, hit nxt, hdd and f last.* . . . . (5 to 2 op 4 to 1 tchd 9 to 2 and 9 to 4)	f
SURE SHOT NORMAN 5-10-9 (7*) P McLoughlin, *in tch till wknd 5th, tld off whn pld up aftr 7th.* . . . . (50 to 1 op 25 to 1)	pu
1090* SOUND CARRIER (USA) 6-11-5 (3*) J McCarthy, *pressed ldr to 5th, rdn and wknd 6th, pld up aftr nxt, lme.* . . . . (Evens fav op 6 to 4 on)	pu

2341 BALUSTRADE 7-11-2 W McFarland, *strted slwly, tld off whn trying to refuse 5th, sn pld up.* .... (50 to 1 op 25 to 1) pu
Dist: ¾l, 20l, dist, 6l, 10l, 6l. 5m 6.40s. a 12.40s (11 Ran).
(R J Wilkinson), Miss L C Siddall

3278 EBF Mares' Novices' Handicap Chase (5-y-o and up) £2,999 2m 7f..... (2:40)

868^{2} GILSTON LASS [90] 7-11-7 (3*) T Jenks, *made all, lft clr 2 out, unchlgd.*...........................(5 to 1 jt-fav) 1
2899 ROSCOE'S GEMMA [66] 10-9-11 (3*) D Meredith, *improved hfwy, styd on frm 2 out, no ch wth wnr.*...... (33 to 1) 2
SEASAMACAMILE [84] 7-11-4 B Powell, *hld up, prog 8th, bad mstk and lost pl 13th, styd on ag'n frm 2 out.* .... (14 to 1 op 12 to 1) 3
2520^{2} RINANNA BAY [74] 7-10-1 (7*) P Carey, *hld up, hdwy 11th, rdn and btn whn mstk 3 out.* ....(5 to 1 jt-fav op 4 to 1 tchd 11 to 2) 4
3104 HOW DOUDO [69] 7-10-3 R Bellamy, *wl beh whn mstk 14th, some hdwy frm 3 out.* .... (11 to 1 op 10 to 1 tchd 12 to 1) 5
3192^{4} POLLERTON'S PRIDE [82] 7-11-2 D Bridgwater, *chsd ldrs, btn whn lft second 2 out, wknd quickly.* .... (11 to 2 op 5 to 1 tchd 6 to 1) 6
3110^{4} BRORA ROSE (Ire) [67] (v) 6-9-8 (7*) Miss S Cobden, *al in rear, tld off frm 14th*............. (25 to 1 op 20 to 1) 7
2873^{8} OUTFIELD [74] 8-10-8 G McCourt, *al in rear, tld off frm 12th*.........................(10 to 1 tchd 12 to 1) 8
3051^{9} CADOLIVE [70] 6-10-4^{4} G Upton, *al in rear, tld off frm 11th*.............................. (33 to 1 op 25 to 1) 9
1803^{2} APRIL'S MODEL LADY [69] 8-10-3 N Williamson, *wtd wth, prog 11th, btn whn f 4 out*........... (8 to 1 op 9 to 2) f
1805 NEW PROBLEM [70] 7-10-4 C Maude, *al chasing wnr, clr second but rdn whn f 2 out*.................. (25 to 1) f
3104^{2} SERDARLI [71] 12-10-5 J Ryan, *blun and uns rdr second.* .... (16 to 1 op 12 to 1) ur
3224^{8} PLAYFUL JULIET (Can) [83] (v) 6-11-3 Pat Caldwell, *wl plcd to hfwy, no ch whn hmpd and refused last.* .... (20 to 1 op 14 to 1) ref
2946 STAPLEFORD LADY [70] 6-10-4 W McFarland, *blun 1st and second, rdr lost irons, pld up bef 3rd*.......... (25 to 1) pu
3097 JUST A SECOND [76] (v) 9-10-10 S McNeill, *in rear whn blun 8th, sn tld off, pld up bef last*...(8 to 1 op 6 to 1) pu
Dist: 10l, 4l, 2l, nk, 5l, 7l, dist, 20l. 5m 57.20s. a 13.20s (15 Ran).
SR: 3/-/-/-/-/-/ (Marlborough Racing Partnership), J S King

3279 Borchester Novices' Hurdle (4-y-o and up) £1,999 3m..................(3:10)

1401 WOLF WINTER 9-11-2 T Grantham, *made all, rdn out r-in.* ....(5 to 1 op 6 to 1) 1
3102* GENERAL SHOT 9-11-8 Diane Clay, *al prmnt, rdn and tried to chal last, no imprsn r-in.* ....(5 to 1 op 9 to 2 tchd 6 to 1) 2
2479 CALLEROSE 7-11-2 B Powell, *hld up in rear, gd hdwy appr 7th, kpt on one pace frm 3 out.* (11 to 2 op 9 to 2) 3
2633^{4} FLAPJACK LAD 5-11-2 D Bridgwater, *beh, not fluent, hdwy aftr mstk 8th, wknd 3 out*..... (5 to 1 op 5 to 1) 4
2796^{6} VENN BOY 5-10-9 (7*) T Murphy, *chsd ldrs till wknd 8th, tld off*.............................(66 to 1 op 50 to 1) 5
2015 RUFFINSWICK 8-11-2 C Maude, *rcd wide, prmnt to 3rd, tld off frm hfwy*............................ (100 to 1) 6
2964^{6} STORMY SWAN 8-11-2 S Smith Eccles, *prmnt till wknd quickly appr 3 out, tld off*..................... (10 to 1) 7
2996 ST MARTIN 6-11-2 Mr J Wingfield Digby, *in tch whn mstk 7th, sn beh, tld off*..........................(100 to 1) 8
3005^{8} ARCHIE'S SISTER 5-10-8 (3*) D Meredith, *prmnt to hfwy, sn beh, tld off*.............................. (33 to 1) 9
2900 CHAPELSTREET BLUES 7-10-11 L Harvey, *al beh, tld off.* .... (100 to 1 op 50 to 1) 10
2828^{2} ACT OF PARLIAMENT (Ire) 6-11-8 N Williamson, *hld up in tch, in frnt rnk whn pckd and uns rdr 8th.* ....(7 to 4 fav op 11 to 8 tchd 2 to 1) ur
3170 AUGER BORE (Ire) 6-11-2 S Burrough, *pld hrd, hdwy 3rd, wknd 6th, tld off whn pulled up bef 3 out.* .... (66 to 1 op 50 to 1) pu
3131 MISTY GREY 5-10-9 (7*) S Lycett, *chsd wnr till wknd 6th, tld off whn pld up bef 2 out*................(100 to 1) pu
Dist: 4l, 1l, 8l, dist, ½l, 10l, 15l, 4l, nk. 5m 49.50s. a 13.50s (13 Ran).
(Victor Dartnall), J A B Old

3280 Sonny Somers Handicap Chase (0-145 5-y-o and up) £4,146 2m 7f...... (3:40)

3041^{6} MAN OF MYSTERY [114] 8-10-0 D Bridgwater, *made all, blun tenth, rdn frm 3 out, ran on gmely.* .... (15 to 8 fav op 2 to 1 tchd 7 to 4 and 9 to 4) 1
3187^{4} WINABUCK [116] 11-9-13 (3*) D Meredith, *trkd wnr, blun 13th, steadied and lost pl aftr nxt, rallied to go second ag'n 3 out, hrd rdn, no imprsn r-in.* (10 to 1 op 7 to 1) 2
2995 SPARKLING FLAME [124] 10-10-10 M A FitzGerald, *hld up in tch, outpcd 11th, hdwy and ev ch 4 out, sn rdn, kpt on r-in*..........................(11 to 2 op 4 to 1) 3
3064 CAPABILITY BROWN [142] 7-12-0 G McCourt, *hld up in tch, hdwy to go second aftr 5 out, rdn 3 out, one pace after*....................(5 to 2 op 9 to 4 tchd 11 to 4) 4

2462 GAY RUFFIAN [133] 8-11-5 Richard Guest, *nvr gng wl, hit 4th and 8th, tld off aftr 9th, pld up bef 11th.* ....(7 to 2 op 2 to 1) pu
Dist: 5l, ¾l, ½l. 5m 51.60s. a 7.60s (5 Ran).
SR: 35/32/39/56/-/ (PCJF Bloodstock), N A Twiston-Davies

3281 Levy Board Novices' Handicap Hurdle (0-100 4-y-o and up) £2,421 2m.. (4:10)

3055* TEMPLE KNIGHT [78] 5-11-2 L Harvey, *al in tch, rdn 3 out, chalg whn pckd last, sn led, drvn out.* ....(7 to 1 op 5 to 1 tchd 8 to 1) 1
2405^{7} ALMAMZAR (USA) [77] 4-11-1 G McCourt, *hld up, hdwy frm 5th, led appr 2 out, blun last, sn hdd, no extr.* .... (13 to 2 op 4 to 1 tchd 7 to 1) 2
3222^{2} ANDRATH (Ire) [69] 6-10-7 D Meade, *mid-div, hdwy 4th, ev ch 2 out, one pace*................(11 to 1 op 12 to 1) 3
2014^{9} GEORGE LANE [65] 6-10-3 J Lodder, *al prmnt, rdn and ev ch 2 out, wknd appr last.* ....(20 to 1 op 12 to 1 tchd 10 to 1) 4
3094^{2} MORIARTY [75] 7-10-10 (3*) J McCarthy, *hld up in rear, hdwy appr 3 out, nvr dngrs*..........(8 to 1 op 7 to 1) 5
3005^{4} WONDERFULL POLLY (Ire) [78] 6-10-11 (5*) Guy Lewis, *wl beh till hdwy appr 3 out, styd on frm nxt, nvr nrr.* .... (10 to 1 op 6 to 1) 6
3014^{7} CASTLE ORCHARD [62] 10-9-11 (3*) A Procter, *wl in rear till some late hdwy*.............................. (33 to 1) 7
2531^{4} KOA [73] 4-10-11 D Bridgwater, *al mid-div, no hdwy frm 5th*.................. (11 to 1 op 7 to 1 tchd 12 to 1) 8
2874 KING ATHELSTAN (USA) [86] 6-11-10 A S Smith, *prmnt till rdn and wknd quickly 2 out.* ....(15 to 2 op 5 to 1 tchd 8 to 1) 9
3202^{6} PALACE PARADE (USA) [74] (bl) 4-10-12 N Dawe, *al beh.* ....(25 to 1) 10
3055^{5} ACROSS THE BOW (USA) [66] 4-10-4 M Hourigan, *al beh.* ....(33 to 1) 11
2708^{3} FERRUFINO (Ire) [62] 6-10-0 P McDermott, *in rear till gd hdwy to ld 3rd, wknd and hdd appr 2 out*..... (25 to 1) 12
ARJUNA [81] 9-10-12 (7*) Mr Richard White, *al in rear.* ....(33 to 1) 13
1601^{6} JOHNS JOY [76] 9-11-0 C Maude, *prmnt to 4th, sn beh.* ....(25 to 1) 14
2685^{8} DYAB (USA) [72] 4-10-10 S Keightley, *chsd ldrs, ev ch 5th, rdn and sn wknd*................(3 to 1 fav op 9 to 2) 15
2641* BARTON ROYAL (Ire) [84] (v) 4-11-8 Richard Guest, *led to 3rd, wknd aftr 5th, tld off*........(12 to 1 op 10 to 1) 16
3094^{5} SWIFT ROMANCE (Ire) [79] 6-10-10 (7*) Mr G Hogan, *pld hrd, prmnt to 4th, wkng whn f nxt.* .... (20 to 1 op 25 to 1) f
3062 STAR MARKET [75] 4-10-13 T Wall, *f 4th.* .... (20 to 1 op 25 to 1) f
Dist: 2½l, 6l, 5l, 2l, 1¾l, hd, 2l, 1l, 3l, 4l. 3m 47.70s. a 6.70s (18 Ran).
SR: 29/25/11/2/10/11/-/4/16/ (T A Johnsey), Miss C Johnsey

3282 Western Counties Handicap Chase (0-125 5-y-o and up) £3,579 2½m 110yds........................ (4:40)

3152^{5} PEACE OFFICER [114] 8-11-9 D Bridgwater, *al in tch, led 5th, hit 4 out, pushed out, cmftbly.* (4 to 1 tchd 9 to 2) 1
2246 GLOVE PUPPET [103] 9-10-12 M A FitzGerald, *led to 5th, styd in tch, rdn and kpt on one pace frm 2 out.* .... (9 to 1 op 7 to 1 tchd 10 to 1) 2
3045* DRAGONS DEN [107] 8-11-2 G Upton, *hld up, jmpd poorly in rear, hdwy to hold ev ch 4 out, no extr frm nxt.* ....(6 to 4 fav op 5 to 4 on) 3
3141^{4} STEPFASTER [103] 9-10-9 (3*) A Thornton, *in cl tch till wknd 3 out*.........................(11 to 2 op 8 to 1) 4
GREEK FLUTTER [119] 9-11-7 (7*) F Leahy, *hld up, hdwy 8th, mstk 4 out, wkng whn blun nxt, sn pld up.* ....(100 to 30 op 5 to 2 tchd 7 to 2) pu
Dist: 2½l, 10l, 6l. 5m 11.80s. a 8.80s (5 Ran).
SR: 42/28/22/12/-/ (J J Whelan), A Barrow

3283 Grandstand Handicap Hurdle (0-135 4-y-o and up) £2,458 3m........ (5:10)

2992^{2} HAPPY HORSE (NZ) [107] 7-10-7 A Tory, *al gng wl beh ldrs, led appr last, slight mstk, pushed out.* .... (11 to 2 op 4 to 1) 1
3053^{3} MARTELL BOY (NZ) [100] 7-9-13^{2} (3*) R Davis, *trkd ldr, led appr 3 out, rdn and hdd bef last, no extr.* ....(10 to 1 op 12 to 1 tchd 14 to 1) 2
2727^{5} VICTOR BRAVO (NZ) [104] 7-10-4 R Supple, *hld up in rear, mstk 3rd, rdn 7th, hdwy 4 out, styd on one pace.* ....(9 to 2 op 7 to 2) 3
2528 WELSH SIREN [100] 8-9-7 (7*) F Leahy, *towards rear till hdwy appr 3 out, one pace aftr*....(16 to 1 op 14 to 1) 4
3186^{3} ULURU (Ire) [102] 6-10-2 R Marley, *in tch, rdn 8th, wknd 3 out*.....................(4 to 1 jt-fav tchd 9 to 2) 5
3166 SIR CRUSTY [100] 12-9-7 (7*) P Maddock, *slwly away, al in rear, rdn 4 out, tld off whn blun 2 out.* ....(16 to 1 op 14 to 1 tchd 20 to 1) 6
2727^{3} PARLEZVOUSFRANCAIS [104] 10-10-4 J Lower, *led to second, jmpd slwly 7th, sn beh, tld off.* (8 to 1 op 6 to 1) 7

2727⁶ PRIME DISPLAY (USA) [122] (bl) 8-11-5 (3*) J McCarthy, *hld up in mid-div, lost tch 4 out, tld off*.
....(12 to 1 tchd 14 to 1) 8
3038 COURT CIRCULAR [109] (v) 5-10-9 Diane Clay, *sn struggling in rear, tld off frm hfwy*.....(14 to 1 op 10 to 1) 9
2999 CROFT MILL [104] 8-10-4⁴ M A FitzGerald, *al beh, tld off*.
....(20 to 1 op 14 to 1) 10
2982² MAN FOR ALL SEASON (USA) [105] (bl) 8-10-5 M Hourigan, *led second till rdn and hdd appr 3 out, wknd rpdly, tld off*................(4 to 1 jt-fav op 7 to 2 tchd 5 to 1) 11
1081 VOLCANIC DANCER (USA) [102] 8-10-2⁵ (3*) A Thornton, *refused to race*....................................(33 to 1) f
Dist: 3l, sht-hd, 12l, ¾l, 20l, nk, 11l, 20l, 2½l, 3½l. 5m 43.80s. a 7.80s (12 Ran).
SR: 13/3/7/-/-/-/   (Major Ian Manning), Mrs J Renfree-Barons

CARLISLE (soft (races 1,2,4,6), heavy (3,5))
Saturday April 2nd
Going Correction: PLUS 0.95 sec. per fur. (races 1,2,-4,6), PLUS 1.05 (3,5)

3284
Warwick Bridge 'National Hunt' Novices' Hurdle (4-y-o and up) £2,149 2½m 110yds.................. (2:05)

3023 KENMORE-SPEED 7-11-8 Richard Guest, *jmpd wl, led, hdd 5th, rgned ld bef nxt, styd on strly fnl 2*.
..........................(11 to 4 op 5 to 2 tchd 3 to 1) 1
2976* LOCHNAGRAIN (Ire) 6-11-2 P Niven, *keen hold in midfield, improved and ev ch bef 2 out, rdn and outpcd appr last*......................(6 to 4 fav tchd 2 to 1) 2
3177⁴ PARLEBIZ 5-10-11 B Storey, *nvr far away, outpcd and drvn alng aftr 3 out, styd on frm last, no ch wth 1st 2*.
.............................(9 to 2 op 5 to 1 tchd 6 to 1) 3
1287⁶ TIGHTER BUDGET (USA) 7-11-8 M Moloney, *wth wnr, led 5th, hdd bef nxt, effrt before 2 out, wkng whn blun last*.
....(33 to 1) 4
2891⁵ STRATHBOGIE MIST (Ire) 6-10-13 (3*) D J Moffatt, *al hndy, struggling to keep up 4 out, sn one pace*.
.............................(33 to 1 op 50 to 1) 5
2220 GILMANSCLEUCH (Ire) 6-10-6 (5*) F Perratt, *in tch, feeling pace and drvn alng aftr 3 out, btn bef nxt*....(100 to 1) 6
2785⁴ MANETTIA (Ire) 5-10-11 R Hodge, *mstks, settled on outer, outpcd aftr 3 out, btn frm nxt*.........(9 to 1 op 7 to 1) 7
3126³ D'ARBLAY STREET (Ire) 5-10-9 (7*) S McDougall, *patiently rdn, improved into midfield hfwy, pushed alng 3 out, no imprsn*...........................(50 to 1 op 33 to 1) 8
2903 BONNY HECTOR 10-10-9 (7*) Mr A Manners, *settled rear, drvn alng to improve aftr 4 out, not pace to chal*.
....(100 to 1) 9
3074⁵ CROSS REFERENCE 6-10-11 T Reed, *in tch on outer, drpd rear hfwy, nvr dngrs aftr*.............(25 to 1) 10
KIBBY BANK 5-11-2 A Dobbin, *settled rear, outpcd aftr 4 out, struggling frm nxt*........(12 to 1 op 8 to 1) 11
1736 EMERALD CHARM (Ire) 6-10-6 (5*) J Burke, *settled midfield, hit 5th, struggling to keep up aftr 4 out, sn btn*.
.............................(25 to 1 op 20 to 1) 12
3125⁹ WOLF'S DEN 5-11-2 K Johnson, *hld up in rear, struggling to keep up bef 7th, tld off last 3*........(50 to 1) 13
2154 BROWN BOMBER 5-11-2 R Garritty, *cl up, drpd rear hfwy, tld off whn pld up bef 3 out*.........(100 to 1) pu
2960 RUSTY PLUMBER (Ire) 6-10-11 (5*) P Midgley, *chsd ldg bunch, drpd rear aftr 5th, sn lost tch, tld off whn pld up bef 4 out*.................................(100 to 1) pu
Dist: 7l, 7l, ¾l, 3½l, 1½l, 1l, 5l, 15l, 9l. 8l. 5m 23.60s. a 30.60s (15 Ran).
                                          (K M Dacker), Mrs S J Smith

3285
Cummersdale Conditional Jockeys' Selling Handicap Hurdle (4-y-o and up) £1,744 2m 1f............... (2:35)

3139⁶ BARSAL (Ire) [66] 4-9-11 (3*) F Leahy, *settled midfield, took clr order hfwy, led 2 out, clr whn blun last, styd on*.
....(4 to 1 op 7 to 2) 1
2907⁸ RYTHMIC RYMER [66] 4-9-11 (3*) G Tormey, *al wl plcd, improved to ld bef 3 out, hdd nxt, not quicken*.
.........................(8 to 1 op 6 to 1 tchd 9 to 1) 2
2960³ INAN (USA) [82] 5-10-11 (5*) K Davies, *patiently rdn, improved to chase ldrs aftr 4 out, ridden aftr nxt, one pace betw last 2*. (100 to 30 fav op 3 to 1 tchd 7 to 2) 3
2498⁸ EMPEROR ALEXANDER (Ire) [66] 6-10-0 A Roche, *nvr far away, blun 4th, sn reco'red, effrt and rdn aftr 3 out, grad wknd*....................(14 to 1 op 12 to 1) 4
3139 TOURAQUE (Fr) [66] 9-9-7 (7*) I Jardine, *handily plcd, outpcd and lost grnd bef 3 out, styd on und pres frm last*..........................(25 to 1 op 20 to 1) 5
2970⁷ MISS JEDD [67] 7-10-1¹ J Burke, *led til hdd bef 3 out, fdd, tld off*......................(33 to 1 op 25 to 1) 6
3125 AMERIGUE [66] 4-10-8 A Harding, *settled rear, rdn to improve bef 3 out, sn struggling, tld off*.
.............................(14 to 1 op 10 to 1) 7

3139⁷ NICHOLAS PLANT [72] (bl) 5-10-6 F Perratt, *hld up on outsd, drvn alng hfwy, struggling aftr 4 out, wl btn whn blun last*.......................(5 to 1 op 4 to 1) 8
3125 RUPERT STANLEY [90] (bl) 10-10-0⁵ (5*) S McDougall, *wth ldr, drpd rear aftr 4th, sn wl beh, tld off*.....(100 to 1) 9
3057⁷ SOME DO NOT [74] 10-10-8 J Supple, *hld up, struggling 4 out, tld off*.........................(6 to 1 op 7 to 1) 10
2903 HILLTOWN (Ire) [90] 6-11-3 (7*) D Waters, *settled on outer, struggled to keep up bef 4 out, tld off*. (8 to 1 op 6 to 1) 11
2149 NOBBY [66] (bl) 8-10-0 A Larnach, *settled towards rear, improved aftr 4th, struggling bef 3 out, tld off whn pld up before last*.................(14 to 1 op 12 to 1) pu
Dist: 8l, ¾l, 20l, 7l, 1½l, 1¼l, 15l, 15l, 1½l, 25l. 4m 39.10s. a 31.10s (12 Ran).
                                          (W A Sellers), J Parkes

3286
Border Garden Centre Novices' Chase (5-y-o and up) £2,466 2½m 110yds......................... (3:05)

2899² PRECIPICE RUN 9-11-8 N Doughty, *nvr far away, led 4th to nxt, cl up whn blun 3 out, reco'red and led nxt, hrd pressed last, ran on*..........(3 to 1 op 11 to 4) 1
3135³ RIVER PEARL 9-11-9 T Reed, *confidently rdn in rear, relentless prog to chase ldrs 4 out, ch rn-in, kpt on*.
.............................(7 to 4 fav tchd 2 to 1) 2
3133⁷ HUDSON BAY TRADER (USA) 7-11-8 Mrs A Farrell, *handily plcd, outpcd 5 out, styd on and ev ch aftr last, no extr towards finish*................(7 to 1 op 6 to 1) 3
2446 HOWCLEUCH 7-10-11 B Storey, *settled rear, improved fnl circuit, effrt and rdn 3 out, kpt on same pace frm nxt*................................(25 to 1 op 20 to 1) 4
2925³ BARNEY RUBBLE 9-11-2 M Moloney, *hmpd 1st, beh till styd on fnl 3, nvr dngrs*.............(12 to 1 op 10 to 1) 5
2814³ PADDY MORRISSEY 7-11-2 A Dobbin, *handily plcd, feeling pace 5 out, btn bef nxt*...........(14 to 1 op 20 to 1) 6
3143⁴ EDEN SUNSET 8-11-2 P Niven, *nvr far away, struggling to keep up aftr 4 out, fdd*..........(14 to 1 op 20 to 1) 7
3033* MAYOR OF LISCARROL 9-11-8 G Harker, *chsd ldrs, outpcd bef 6 out, sn struggling, tld off*............(10 to 1) 8
3073* HERE COMES TIBBY 7-10-12 (5*) P Waggott, *prmnt, led 6th, hdd 2 out, fdd, tld off*..........(15 to 1 op 14 to 1) 9
2896 DESPERADO 6-10-9 (7*) Mr A Manners, *blun and uns rdr 1st*....................................(200 to 1) ur
2928 SOUTH STACK 8-11-2 Richard Guest, *led till hdd 4th, styd hndy, effrt aftr four out, btn aftr 2 out, pld up r-in*.
.............................(66 to 1 op 50 to 1) pu
2971 ROYLE BURCHLIN 8-10-13 (3*) D J Moffatt, *jmpd badly in rear, struggling fnl circuit, tld off whn blun 3 out, pld up bef last*...........................(50 to 1) pu
2971 BELLOFAGUS 9-10-11 (5*) F Perratt, *hld up, improved into midfield fnl circuit, struggling aftr 5 out, tld off whn pld up bef last*.......................(20 to 1) pu
FARMER'S HAND 7-10-11 (5*) J Burke, *settled on outer, struggling bef 6 out, tld off whn pld up before 3 out*.
.............................(33 to 1 op 25 to 1) pu
3073² BITOFANATTER 6-11-2 K Johnson, *beh, struggling fnl circuit, tld off whn pld up bef 3 out*.........(100 to 1) pu
2896 COEDWGAN LUCIFER 7-11-2 A Merrigan, *hld up, blun tenth, sn struggling, tld off whn pld up bef 4 out*.
....(100 to 1) pu
Dist: Nk, ¾l, 9l, 5l, 8l, 5l, 20l, 11l. 5m 35.80s. a 32.80s (16 Ran).
                                          (Cumbrian Racing Club), G Richards

3287
Quilter Goodison Handicap Hurdle (0-105 4-y-o and up) £2,302 3m 110yds ....(3:35)

2954 SANSOOL [91] (v) 8-11-0 M Moloney, *in tch, effrt aftr 4 out, styd on to ld r-in, rdn out*. (20 to 1 op 16 to 1) 1
2954⁵ CELTIC BREEZE [92] (v) 11-10-10 (5*) J Burke, *wth ldr, led 5 out, clr aftr nxt, hdd r-in, one pace*. (16 to 1 op 12 to 1) 2
2974⁴ LOGICAL FUN [91] 6-11-0 M Dwyer, *handily plcd, effrt gng wl bef 2 out, rdn and kpt on same pace frm last*.
.............................(9 to 1 op 8 to 1) 3
2487⁸ LION OF VIENNA [100] 7-11-9 B Storey, *settled on ins, improved hfwy, outpcd bef 3 out, styd on und pres frm last*.........................(12 to 1 op 10 to 1) 4
2894⁵ JENDEE (Ire) [91] 6-10-11 (3*) A Larnach, *al prmnt, rdn alng 4 out, one pace betw last 2*. (15 to 2 op 7 to 1 tchd 8 to 1) 5
2954² MISS CAPULET [87] (bl) 7-10-7 (3*) T Eley, *nvr far away, hit 4 out, effrt bef 2 out, one pace appr last*.
.............................(5 to 1 op 9 to 2) 6
3177² HOTDIGGITY [89] 6-10-12 A Dobbin, *hld up, improved 5 out, rdn aftr 3 out, btn bef last*.....(16 to 1 op 12 to 1) 7
3142⁴ VALIANT DASH [95] 8-10-13 (5*) F Perratt, *sn wl beh, styd on fnl 3, nvr nr to chal*..........(25 to 1 op 20 to 1) 8
3166² CARSON CITY [91] 7-11-0 P Niven, *wl plcd, effrt and wnr 3 out, btn betw last 2, virtually pld up r-in*.
.............................(12 to 1 op 10 to 1) 9
3029²⁵ GUTE NACHT [77] (bl) 11-10-0⁵ (5*) S Lyons, *sn beh, struggling frm 7th, nvr a factor*...............(33 to 1) 10
3029 SERPHIL [78] (bl) 6-10-11 C Grant, *mid-div, struggling hfwy, nvr on terms*.....................(20 to 1) 11
2632⁶ ST VILLE [99] 8-11-3 (5*) S Mason, *beh, struggling to keep up frm 7th, tld off*........(25 to 1 op 20 to 1) 12

3061⁶ GYMCRAK DAWN [77] 9-10-0⁷ (7") G Tormey, *handily plcd, struggling bef 4 out, fdd, tld off..* (25 to 1 op 20 to 1) 13
2954⁴ ROSE TABLEAU [101] 11-11-3 (7") Miss Sue Nichol, *beh, blun and lost tch 3rd, al struggling, tld off.*
.... (33 to 1 op 25 to 1) 14
3235⁷ LADY BE BRAVE [77] (v) 11-9-9 (5") J Supple, *settled mid-field, drpd rear hfwy, tld off....* (25 to 1 op 20 to 1) 15
2957 SULAAH ROSE [77] 5-9-7 (7") S Taylor, *al beh, struggling aftr one circuit, tld off.........................*(200 to 1) 16
2974⁵ MIDLAND EXPRESS [80] 11-9-12 (5") P Waggott, *beh, feel-ing pace hfwy, tld off....* (33 to 1 op 25 to 1) 17
3142⁷ SEXY MOVER [92] 7-11-1 K Johnson, *chsd ldg bunch, struggling to keep up aftr 7th, tld off whn pld up bef 3 out.*.......................... (20 to 1 op 16 to 1) pu
914 ROYAL QUARRY [77] 8-10-0 C Dennis, *beh, struggling hfwy, tld off whn pld up bef 3 out.*
.... (100 to 1 op 66 to 1) pu
2322⁵ DIG DEEPER [105] 7-11-9 (5") A Roche, *led til hdd 5 out, btn nxt, pld up bef 3 out.*........(16 to 1 op 14 to 1) pu
2925⁵ MOSSIMAN (Ire) [77] 6-10-0 S Turner, *reluctant to race and al wl beh, tld off whn pld up bef 4 out.........*(33 to 1) pu
Dist: ¾l, 3l, ½l, 1¼l, ¾l, 1¼l, 25l, 9l, 4l, 5l. 6m 22.80s. a 29.80s (21 Ran).
SR: 21/21/17/25/14/9/9/-/-/ (A C Whillans) A C Whillans

3288 Brackenridge Handicap Chase (0-120 5-y-o and up) £2,880 2m....... (4:05)

2926* KAMBALDA RAMBLER [94] 10-10-4 B Storey, *made vir-tually all, hdd briefly r-in, styd on gmely.*
.... (7 to 1 op 6 to 1) 1
3032² MILITARY HONOUR [100] (bl) 9-10-10 Mr S Swiers, *settled towards rear, improved 5 out, effrt and hit nxt, led briefly r-in, kpt on same pace towards finish.*
.... (4 to 1 chd 9 to 2 and 5 to 1) 2
2953⁵ FUNNY OLD GAME [90] 7-10-0 K Johnson, *nvr far away, pushed alng 5 out, outpcd aftr nxt.*
.... (16 to 1 op 14 to 1 tchd 20 to 1) 3
3162⁵ WAY OF LIFE (Fr) [97] 9-10-7 C Grant, *al prmnt, pushed alng 5 out, ev ch 4 out, btn 3 out....*(9 to 1 op 8 to 1) 4
2261 STRONG APPROACH [118] 9-11-9 (5") J Burke, *trkd ldrs, improved and ev ch 4 out, fdd............*(14 to 1) 5
2926² YAHEEB (USA) [94] 10-10-4 R Garritty, *settled in last pl, mstk 4th, hmpd and f 7th.*
.... (11 to 2 op 6 to 1 tchd 5 to 1) f
2975² ABBOT OF FURNESS [109] 10-11-5 M Moloney, *cl up, chalg whn f 6 out...............* (11 to 2 op 5 to 1) f
3223² POSITIVE ACTION [98] 8-10-8 A Dobbin, *trkd ldg pair, outpcd whn f 6th.................* (3 to 1 fav op 5 to 1) f
3135⁵ CELTIC SONG [91] 7-10-1 Mrs A Farrell, *towards rear, hit 5th, brght dwn 6th................*(16 to 1 op 14 to 1) bd
Dist: 1¾l, 20l, 7l, ¾l. 4m 20.10s. a 21.10s (9 Ran).
SR: 33/37/7/7/27/-/ (Mrs J G Dudgeon), C Parker

3289 Carlisle Club Members Novices' Hurdle (4-y-o and up) £2,134 2m 1f.. (4:35)

2828 TROY BOY 4-10-10 J Callaghan, *hld up in tch, led 2 out, ran on strly frm last..................*(20 to 1 op 14 to 1) 1
2951* CAITHNESS CLOUD 6-11-8 B Storey, *nvr far away, led aftr 3 out to nxt, one pace whn blun last.*
.... (11 to 8 fav op 5 evens tchd 6 to 4) 2
3074² VOLUNTEER POINT (Ire) 4-10-5 (5") J Burke, *trkd ldr, out-pcd and drvn alng bef 3 out, no extr nxt.*
.... (9 to 4 op 2 to 1 tchd 5 to 2) 3
3034⁵ SHAHGRAM (Ire) 6-11-2 M Dwyer, *patiently rdn, hdwy bef 3 out, ridden betw last 2, fdd.*
.... (7 to 2 op 9 to 2 tchd 5 to 1) 4
2905⁶ GLEN DALUS (Ire) 5-11-2 A Dobbin, *beh, struggling hfwy, tld off....................*(12 to 1 op 10 to 1) 5
3125 WHAT A CARD 6-10-11 K Johnson, *hld up, struggling bef 3 out, nvr on terms, tld off.................*(100 to 1) 6
3144⁴ RED TEMPEST (Ire) 6-10-11 (5") F Perratt, *al hndy, outpcd and nvr bef 4th, styd on to track ldrs before 3 out, wknd quickly nxt, tld off.........*(12 to 1 op 10 to 1) 7
2970⁸ TAUVALERA (bl) 7-10-11 Mr D Swindlehurst, *led till aftr 3 out, wknd, tld off..................*(100 to 1) 8
3177 MR MCAFF (Ire) 5-10-9 (7") P Carr, *sn beh, lost tch 5th, tld off whn pld up bef last.................*(200 to 1) pu
Dist: 6l, 3½l, 1¾l, 25l, 20l, 4l, 9l. 4m 32.90s. a 25.90s (9 Ran).
(J D Gordon), G M Moore

MALLOW (IRE) (heavy)
Saturday April 2nd

3290 Bantry Maiden Hurdle (5-y-o) £2,243 2m...............................(2:00)

3197² THE WICKED CHICKEN (Ire) 6-11-0 C F Swan, (5 to 2 jt-fav) 1
3084³ KATE FISHER (Ire) 10-11 (3") C O'Brien, ...(5 to 2 jt-fav) 2
DEARBORN TEC (Ire) 11-5 J F Titley, ... (14 to 1) 3
2348⁸ MY SUNNY WAY (Ire) 10-12 (7") Mr D K Budds, ... (12 to 1) 4
3250⁷ FLAWLESS FINISH (Ire) 10-9 (5") K P Gaule, ... (12 to 1) 5
2679⁷ TURALITY (Ire) 11-5 S H O'Donovan, ... (8 to 1) 6
2756⁹ HAIRY ROSE (Ire) 11-5 (5") D T Evans, ... (10 to 1) 7
3197⁸ MAZELLA (Ire) 11-0 M Duffy, ... (12 to 1) 8
2944* SPANKERS HILL (Ire) 11-10 (3") T P Treacy, ...(13 to 1) 9

3197 BRIGADIER SUPREME (Ire) 11-0 (5") J P Broderick, (20 to 1) 10
BUTLER JOHN (Ire) 11-5 K F O'Brien, ... (14 to 1) 11
2684 LOVELY AFFAIR (Ire) 10-7 (7") L Fleming, ...(50 to 1) 12
2353⁹ RAMBLE ALONG (Ire) 11-7 (7") M D Murphy, ...(16 to 1) 13
2465 ARISTOLOMAN 11-0 (5") D P Geoghegan, ... (25 to 1) 14
1858 DUN OENGUS (Ire) 11-0 J Magee, ... (12 to 1) 15
BROOK QUEEN (Ire) 10-7 (7") J M Willis, ... (16 to 1) 16
3197 PARABELLUM (Ire) 11-0 F J Flood, ... (14 to 1) 17
CROSS ANGORLADY (Ire) 10-11 (3") T J O'Sullivan,
.... (33 to 1) 18
2944 SIR JOHN (Ire) 10-12 (7") J Butler, ... (14 to 1) 19
IDEAL PARTNER (Ire) 11-5 F Woods, ...(12 to 1) 20
SHELLY'S DELIGHT (Ire) 10-11 (3") T J Mitchell, ..(20 to 1) 21
2679 STRUGGLING LASS (Ire) 11-0 T Horgan, ...(20 to 1) 22
2918 BENSONS RETURN (Ire) 11-5 J P Banahan, ...(50 to 1) 23
3086⁹ LA KESTREL (Ire) 11-0 A J O'Brien, ...(50 to 1) 24
3197 MISS BERTAINE (Ire) 10-11 (3") D P Murphy, ...(20 to 1) ur
Dist: 4l, ½l, 4½l, sht-hd. 4m 10.30s. (25 Ran).
(Mrs Sandra McCarthy), P Mullins

3291 Cobh Maiden Hurdle (6-y-o and up) £2,243 2m.................... (2:30)

2943* THE BLUEBELL POLKA (Ire) 5-11-9 F J Flood, (3 to 1 fav) 1
3087⁴ STEVIE BE (Ire) 6-11-6 K F O'Brien, ...(10 to 1) 2
2938³ ARABIAN SPRITE (Ire) 6-11-1 Mr P J Healy, ...(10 to 1) 3
3086⁶ CARRIGEEN (Ire) 6-11-1 A J Slattery, ...(33 to 1) 4
3244⁴ SUMMING UP 7-11-6 P M Verling, ...(10 to 1) 5
3243⁶ THATS A SECRET 6-11-11 (3") T P Treacy, ...(8 to 1) 6
3243² OLD ABBEY (Ire) 6-11-6 F Woods, ...(4 to 1) 7
3244⁹ METROLAMP (Ire) 6-10-13 (7") Mr J O'Neill, ...(14 to 1) 8
3087⁵ RATH CAOLA 7-11-1 J Jones, ...(14 to 1) 9
2943 CARRIG DANCER (Ire) 6-10-8 (7") Mr K Whelan, ..(20 to 1) 10
3243 TWO HILLS 7-11-3 (3") T J O'Sullivan, ...(25 to 1) 11
3201 DOUBLE SYMPHONY (Ire) 6-10-10 (5") M J Holbrook,
.... (10 to 1) 12
2985 LOUGH CULTRA DRIVE 6-12-0 C O'Dwyer, ...(10 to 1) 13
ALICES RUN 7-11-9 T Horgan, ... (6 to 1) 14
2943⁹ MARBLE FONTAINE 7-11-1 C F Swan, ...(8 to 1) 15
3243⁹ KILLIMOR LAD 7-11-1 (5") J P Broderick, ...(25 to 1) 16
3244 CLONE (Ire) 6-11-6 A Powell, ...(25 to 1) 17
36 GOLDEN ARRANGEMENT 9-11-3 (3") T J O'Sullivan, (25 to 1) 18
CASTLEMAHON CHICK (Ire) 6-10-8 (7") Mr D C O'Connor,
.... (25 to 1) 19
3243 YOUR NEARLY THERE 8-11-1 Mr M Phillips, ...(16 to 1) 20
2102 FEARSOME LORD (Ire) 6-11-6 S H O'Donovan, ..(33 to 1) 21
2664 OUR BLOSSOM (Ire) 6-10-8 (7") M D Murphy, ...(33 to 1) pu
3122 CLON CAW (Ire) 6-11-6 L P Cusack, ...(25 to 1) pu
Dist: 2½l, sht-hd, 5½l, 4l. 4m 10.60s. (23 Ran).
(Foster & Allen Syndicate), F Flood

3292 Greenvale Hurdle (5-y-o and up) £2,243 2m 5f.................. (3:00)

3244* ULTRA FLUTTER 7-12-0 K F O'Brien, ...(11 to 8 on) 1
3086² FURRY DUCK (Ire) 6-11-4 M Flynn, ...(14 to 1) 2
3084² PRINCESS BAVARD 9-11-4 A J O'Brien, ... (8 to 1) 3
2548⁵ CORRIBLOUGH (Ire) 6-11-9 C O'Dwyer, ...(16 to 1) 4
EXTRA DAYS 7-11-9 Mr E Bolger, ... (8 to 1) 5
2940² COUNTERBALANCE 7-11-4 B Sheridan, ...(10 to 1) 6
3067 DRUMCILL LASS (Ire) 6-11-4 P M Verling, ...(33 to 1) 7
2919* NO TAG (Ire) 6-12-0 J F Titley, ...(9 to 2) 8
3242² TOT EM UP 7-11-10 (7") M D Murphy, ...(16 to 1) 9
3244 CABBERY ROSE (Ire) 6-11-4 J Magee, ...(14 to 1) 10
3243⁵ FARRELL'S CROSS 8-11-9 A Powell, ...(14 to 1) 11
2684⁷ SKY VISION (Ire) 5-11-3 S H O'Donovan, ...(33 to 1) 12
CORSTON DANCER (Ire) 6-11-3 (3") D P Murphy, (20 to 1) 13
2863 SERGEANT DAN (Ire) 6-11-4 (5") D T Evans, ...(50 to 1) pu
Dist: 13l, 1½l, 5l, 6l. 6m 7.80s. (14 Ran).
(Donal Higgins), Michael Hourigan

3293 Lee Novice Chase (5-y-o and up) £2,243 2m.......................(3:30)

2157 BROGUESTOWN 9-12-0 F J Flood, ...(12 to 1) 1
2923⁴ MUILEAR OIRGE 7-12-0 J F Titley, ...(3 to 1 fav) 2
2923⁶ MALTELINA 8-11-4 S R Murphy, ...(14 to 1) 3
2683 FEATHERED GALE 7-11-11 (3") C O'Brien, ...(6 to 1) 4
2756⁷ DAVE FLECK (Ire) 6-11-9 L P Cusack, ...(16 to 1) 5
2923³ CHELSEA NATIVE 7-11-4 (5") Susan A Finn, ...(5 to 1) 6
2661⁹ MONKS AIR 7-10-13 (5") Mr W M O'Sullivan, ...(33 to 1) 7
2845⁴ SO PINK (Ire) 6-11-9 K F O'Brien, ...(8 to 1) 8
3198⁵ DUNBOY CASTLE (Ire) 6-12-0 T Horgan, ...(20 to 1) 9
3198⁶ HIGHWAY LASS 8-11-4 S H O'Donovan, ...(20 to 1) 10
2923⁵ TEE D'OR 9-11-2 (7") Mr P J Millington, ...(20 to 1) 11
2923² TAWNEY FLAME 8-12-0 J Magee, ... (5 to 1) 12
1857 MELDRUM MISS (Ire) 6-11-4 P M Verling, ...(33 to 1) 13
1332 CHERISHED PRINCESS (Ire) 6-11-4 F Woods, ...(33 to 1) 14
BRIDGIE TERRIE (Ire) 6-11-4 C F Swan, ...(6 to 1) 0
2940⁸ BOY BLUE 7-11-9 J Shortt, ...(14 to 1) pu
Dist: 2l, 9l, ¾l, 15l. 6m 49.70s. (16 Ran).
(Michael Dalton), F Flood

3294 Banteer Handicap Hurdle (0-123 4-y-o and up) £2,243 2m.............(4:00)

3247* MRS BARTON (Ire) [-] (bl) 6-10-4 (5") J R Barry, (6 to 4 fav) 1

3083^{4} SAM VAUGHAN (Ire) [-] 5-11-2 (5*) Mr W M O'Sullivan, ... (6 to 1) 2
3199^{6} PERCY BRENNAN [-] 7-9-4 (7*) J M Donnelly, ... (12 to 1) 3
3083^{7} NINE O THREE (Ire) [-] 5-9-9 (5*) J P Broderick, ... (10 to 1) 4
3242* MARIAN YEAR [-] 8-11-3 J Collins, ... (7 to 1) 5
2588 COOL CHARACTER (Ire) [-] 6-11-3 J F Titley, ... (10 to 1) 6
3242^{6} REPLACEMENT [-] 7-10-0 (3*) T J O'Sullivan, ... (16 to 1) 7
3242 ANNFIELD LADY (Ire) [-] 6-9-7 F Woods, ... (25 to 1) 8
1018^{2} MERRY PEOPLE (Ire) [-] 6-11-3 T Horgan, ... (10 to 1) 9
800^{6} MACK A DAY [-] 7-11-1 A J O'Brien, ... (12 to 1) 10
2920^{9} LADY BUDD (Ire) [-] 6-9-1 (7*) D J Kavanagh, ... (20 to 1) 11
3247^{4} DAMODAR [-] 5-10-7 F J Flood, ... (12 to 1) 12
1912^{4} MINSTREL FIRE (Ire) [-] 6-9-11 J Magee, ... (14 to 1) 13
2770* TREACYS CROSS [-] 8-9-10 (5*) P A Roche, ... (10 to 1) 14
807^{9} SUNSHINE SEAL [-] 7-9-11 (3*) T J Mitchell, ... (20 to 1) 15
Dist: 3l, 4l, 2½l, 1l. 4m 10.80s. (15 Ran).
(Mrs Patrick Flynn), Patrick Joseph Flynn

3295 Rathbarry Stud Maiden Hunters Chase (4-y-o and up) £5,520 3m (4:30)

504^{5} OUT THE DOOR (Ire) 5-11-0 (7*) Mr K Whelan, ... (12 to 1) 1
RED EXPRESS VI 9-11-7 (7*) Mr S O'Brien, ... (20 to 1) 2
2551^{2} MATTY TYNAN 7-12-0 Mr P Fenton, ... (7 to 4 fav) 3
THE VICARETTE (Ire) 6-11-2 (7*) Mr P Cashman, .. (25 to 1) 4
WHAT THING (bl) 7-11-2 (7*) Mr T J Murphy, ... (12 to 1) 5
2551^{7} GARRYLUCAS 8-12-0 Mr T Lombard, ... (8 to 1) 6
GLYNN CROSS (Ire) 6-11-4 (5*) Mr W M O'Sullivan, (25 to 1) 7
2941^{4} PHAIRY MIRACLES (Ire) 5-11-2 Mr P J Healy, ... (12 to 1) 8
NATIVE VENTURE (Ire) 6-11-9 (5*) Mr G J Harford, (10 to 1) 9
NORTHERN MOSS 7-12-0 Mr D M O'Brien, ... (25 to 1) 10
ELWILL WAY 9-11-6 (3*) Mr J A Nash, ... (25 to 1) 11
TAMMYIRIS 8-11-9 Mr M Phillips, ... (16 to 1) 12
853^{5} THE SILVER ROLLS 6-11-11 (3*) Mr D P Costello, (10 to 1) f
2941^{2} GREENHALL 8-11-7 (7*) Mr A D Evans, ... (5 to 1) f
OKDO 7-11-7 (7*) Mr D P Murphy, ... (14 to 1) f
FAIRY MIST (Ire) 6-11-7 (7*) Mr D A Harney, ... (25 to 1) f
MOSS CASTLE 9-11-7 (7*) Mr D G Murphy, ... (10 to 1) f
DARA'S COURSE (Ire) 5-11-2 Mr R Hurley, ... (12 to 1) f
LAURA'S PURSUIT (Ire) 5-10-9 (7*) Mr G F Ryan, .. (16 to 1) f
2941^{3} SEATYRN 11-11-7 (7*) Mr R P Burns, ... (8 to 1) pu
2941^{5} CITIZEN MOSS 7-11-7 (7*) Mr K Taylor, ... (33 to 1) pu
HOWLIN' WOLF 7-11-7 (7*) Mr S O'Callaghan, ... (33 to 1) pu
FUNNY BUSINESS 7-11-7 (7*) Mr J Lombard, ... (25 to 1) pu
Dist: 9l, hd, 7l, 1l. 6m 51.60s. (23 Ran).
(William Gleeson), John F Gleeson

3296 Kinsale Flat Race (6-y-o and up) £2,243 2m 5f. ... (5:00)

INDESTRUCTIBLE (Ire) 6-12-0 Mr P J Healy, ... (10 to 1) 1
3201^{7} LADY OF TARA 8-11-6 (3*) Mrs J M Mullins, ... (12 to 1) 2
2394^{5} LACKEN CROSS (Ire) 6-12-0 Mr A P O'Brien, ... (4 to 1) 3
3201^{6} MISS POLLERTON (Ire) 6-11-2 (7*) Mr M J Bowe, (10 to 1) 4
3201^{4} TORONTO TELEGRAM 8-11-4 (5*) Mr J P Berry, ... (6 to 1) 5
FOXED (Ire) 6-11-9 Mr D M O'Brien, ... (14 to 1) 6
2553^{6} PEGUS GOLD 7-11-4 (5*) Mr G J Harford, ... (8 to 1) 7
3244 RUN FOR FUN (Ire) 6-11-6 (3*) Mr J A Nash, ... (10 to 1) 8
3201^{9} RIVER OF PEACE (Ire) 6-11-2 (7*) Mr T J Power, ... (20 to 1) 9
BLUE GAYLE 9-11-7 (7*) Mr P O'Keeffe, ... (14 to 1) 10
3088^{2} KNOCKAVILLA 7-11-7 (7*) Mr K Whelan, ... (2 to 1 fav) 11
2924 CAPTAIN CHARLES (Ire) 6-11-7 (7*) Mr G Mulcaire, (25 to 1) 12
3201 CLEAR ROUND 7-11-9 Mr M Phillips, ... (12 to 1) 13
990 ALL A STRUGGLE (Ire) (bl) 6-11-9 Mr J A Flynn, ... (20 to 1) 14
DISTRICT JUSTICE 7-11-7 (7*) Mr E Norris, ... (10 to 1) 15
3087^{6} DOONEAL HERO (Ire) 6-12-0 Mr P Fenton, ... (16 to 1) 16
CULM BARON 6-11-7 (7*) Mr C Sadik, ... (14 to 1) pu
CREDO'S CAMPAIGN (Ire) 6-11-2 (7*) Mr J T McNamara, ... (20 to 1) pu
ALLESIO 7-11-9 (5*) Mr H F Cleary, ... (10 to 1) pu
CLODAS PET (Ire) 6-11-2 (7*) Mr S P Hennessy, ... (14 to 1) pu
Dist: ½l, ½l, 4l, 4l. 5m 57.20s. (20 Ran).
(John Quane), Augustine Leahy

NEWTON ABBOT (heavy)
Saturday April 2nd
Going Correction: PLUS 1.55 sec. per fur.

3297 Easter Bunny Novices' Chase (5-y-o and up) £2,670 2m 110yds. ... (2:15)

3050^{3} ALDAHE 9-11-2 S Burrough, *in cl tch, led aftr 8th, mstk 2 out, idled r-in, found extr nr finish.* ... (5 to 1 tchd 4 to 1) 1
3050^{4} WHYFOR 6-11-2 C Maude, *hld up, ran on appr 2 out, ev ch r-in, no extr nr finish.* ... (10 to 1 op 8 to 1) 2
1321* ROXTON HILL 9-11-8 R Dunwoody, *led til stumbled badly on landing aftr 8th, sn hdd, short lived effrt 3 out, soon btn.* ... (3 to 1 on op 4 to 1 on tchd 5 to 2 on) 3
2860^{9} GRECIAN SAILOR 9-11-2 J Frost, *in cl tch til drpd rear 9th.* ... (9 to 1 op 14 to 1 tchd 16 to 1 and 8 to 1) 4
Dist: ½l, 10l, 7l. 4m 35.80s. a 38.80s (4 Ran).
(B R Millman), B R Millman

3298 Dartmoor Selling Handicap Hurdle (4-y-o and up) £2,073 2¾m. ... (2:45)

3111^{4} BOOGIE BOPPER (Ire) [68] (v) 5-10-2^{2} R Dunwoody, *hld up in rear, steady hdwy frm 4 out, rdn to cl appr 2 out, led last, drvn out.* ... (5 to 1 op 6 to 1 tchd 9 to 2) 1
2799^{9} SUASANAN SIOSANA [68] 9-9-9 (7*) J James, *wth ldr, led appr 2 out till hdd last, no extr.* ... (13 to 2 op 9 to 2 tchd 7 to 1) 2
3186 BOREEN JEAN [90] (v) 10-11-7 (3*) T Jenks, *hld up, cld 4 out gng wl, ev ch 2 out, one pace*... (13 to 2 op 4 to 1) 3
3003^{6} BRIGHT SAPPHIRE [66] 8-9-9 (5*) Guy Lewis, *made most til hdd appr 2 out, wknd approaching last.* ... (16 to 1 op 10 to 1) 4
3111^{3} THANKSFORTHEOFFER [66] (v) 6-9-7 (7*) Pat Thompson, *sn trkd ldg pair, outpcd appr 2 out.* ... (15 to 2 op 5 to 1 tchd 8 to 1) 5
3053^{4} PUNCHBAG (USA) [80] 8-11-0 C Maude, *chsd ldrs till rdn and wknd aftr 4 out.* ... (4 to 1 fav tchd 5 to 1) 6
3170^{5} CHICKABIDDY [70] 6-9-13 (5*) D Salter, *beh, hdwy 6th, sn btn, tld off.* ... (9 to 2 op 4 to 1) 7
2982 ONE TO NOTE [82] 10-11-2 M Ahern, *al beh, tld off.* ... (12 to 1 op 8 to 1) 8
3003 LEAVE IT OUT [71] 12-10-5^{5} J Frost, *cld to track ldrs 3rd, wknd 4 out, tld off.* ... (14 to 1 op 12 to 1) 9
3053 LEGAL WIN (USA) [70] (bl) 6-10-0^{5} (7*) Mr G Shenkin, *refused to race, took no part.* ... (20 to 1 op 12 to 1) ref
3020 CHIROPODIST [70] (v) 10-9-13 (5*) D Leahy, *chsd ldrs, reminders aftr 4 out, btn appr nxt, pld up bef 2 out.* ... (10 to 1 op 7 to 1) pu
3003 MARLBOROUGH LADY [69] (bl) 8-10-3^{3} S Burrough, *trkd ldrs till wknd 6th, tld off whn pld up bef 2 out.* ... (25 to 1 op 16 to 1) pu
3003^{9} PRINCE VALMY (Fr) [66] 9-9-12^{3} (5*) D Matthews, *al beh, tld off whn pld up bef 2 out.* ... (25 to 1 op 20 to 1) pu
Dist: 3l, 6l, 20l, ¾l, hd, 25l, dist. 5m 53.90s. a 54.90s (13 Ran).
(M C Pipe), M C Pipe

3299 'Touch Of Spring' Handicap Chase (0-135 5-y-o and up) £3,143 3¼m 110yds. ... (3:15)

3027^{5} CATCH THE CROSS [128] (bl) 8-12-0 R Dunwoody, *hld up, al gng wl, quickened to ld betw last 2, pushed clr.* ... (5 to 2 op 7 to 4) 1
3229 RUFUS [115] (bl) 8-11-1 L Harvey, *made most, rdn alng 15th, hdd betw last 2, sn outpcd.* ... (5 to 2 op 3 to 1 tchd 7 to 2) 2
3052^{3} TRUSTY FRIEND [100] 12-10-0 C Maude, *wth ldr, pushed alng whn pace quickened 15th, one pace frm 4 out.* ... (33 to 1 op 16 to 1) 3
2316^{2} PLAYPEN [105] 10-10-5^{5} J Frost, *al beh, lost tch 16th, tld off.* ... (8 to 1 op 5 to 1) 4
3146* BETTY HAYES [108] 10-10-1 (7*) P Carey, *not jump wl, blun badly 15th, no ch aftr, tld off.* ... (6 to 4 fav tchd 7 to 4) 5
Dist: 5l, 15l, 20l, 25l. 7m 21.40s. a 61.40s (5 Ran).
(D A Beswick), M C Pipe

3300 Mile End Maiden Hurdle (5-y-o and up) £2,192 2m 1f. ... (3:45)

3055^{3} TUMBLED BRIDE 8-11-2 C Maude, *made virtually all, clr appr last, ran on wl.* ... (7 to 1 op 5 to 1) 1
3253^{4} SPIRIT LEVEL 6-10-9 (7*) Mr R Payne, *beh, tld off aftr 4th, styd on frm 2 out, fnshd wl.* ... (14 to 1 op 8 to 1 tchd 16 to 1) 2
2950^{7} FERNY BALL (Ire) 6-11-7 M Hourigan, *in tch, hdwy aftr 3 out, sn ev ch, wknd quickly appr nxt.* ... (14 to 1 op 8 to 1) 3
2315^{7} MR WILBUR 8-11-7 J Frost, *trkd ldrs gng wl, ch appr 2 out, found little.* ... (5 to 2 tchd 7 to 4 and 11 to 4) 4
PUKKA SAHIB 7-11-4 (3*) R Davis, *hld up in cl tch, f 5th.* ... (8 to 1 op 4 to 1) f
POLAR HAT 6-11-7 R Dunwoody, *wth ldr till wknd quickly aftr 3 out, pld up bef last.* ... (5 to 4 fav op 7 to 4 tchd 2 to 1) pu
3208 MARYLAND BOY 6-11-0 (7*) R Darke, *al beh, tld off whn pld up bef 2 out.* ... (33 to 1 op 14 to 1) pu
Dist: 8l, 3½l, 2½l. 4m 29.90s. a 39.90s (7 Ran).
(V G Greenway), V G Greenway

3301 Haccombe Handicap Chase (0-120 5-y-o and up) £3,245 2m 110yds (4:15)

3210^{3} AL HASHIMI [115] 10-11-10 R Dunwoody, *made all, drvn out.* ... (3 to 1 op 9 to 4 tchd 100 to 30) 1
3152* BOLD CHOICE [96] 8-10-5 J Frost, *hld up in tch, ev ch last, hng lft und pres r-in, ran on.* ... (7 to 4 fav op 5 to 4 tchd 15 to 8) 2
3066^{7} SETTER COUNTRY [113] 10-11-8 W Irvine, *in tch, ev ch appr 2 out, wknd quickly.* ... (2 to 1 op 5 to 2) 3
3116^{4} LUCKY AGAIN [91] 7-10-0 C Maude, *strted slwly, sn reco'red, in tch whn blun 7th, soon tld off, pld up bef last.* ... (8 to 1 op 10 to 1) pu
Dist: ¾l, 20l. 4m 27.80s. a 30.80s (4 Ran).
SR: 45/25/22/-/ (Major A W C Pearn), R J Hodges

3302 South West Racing Club Challenge Trophy Handicap Hurdle (0-130 4-y-o

and up) £2,633 2m 1f.......... (4:45)

3098⁵ CHARCOAL BURNER [87] 9-9-11² (5°) S Fox, *wth ldr, led last, drvn out.*........................ (7 to 1 op 6 to 1) 1

3254⁴ CARIBBEAN PRINCE [90] 6-10-3 R Dunwoody, *led til hdd last, ran on und pres.*........(6 to 4 fav tchd 7 to 4) 2

3206² CHEERFUL TIMES [96] 11-10-9 J Frost, *hld up, rdn appr 2 out, one pace.*.................... (11 to 4 op 9 to 4) 3

1868⁵ ATHAR [bbr] [111] 5-11-10 L Harvey, *in cl tch, wknd appr 2 out, no ch whn f last (dead).*
.... (11 to 4 op 2 to 1 tchd 3 to 1) f

Dist: ¾l, 10l. 4m 28.00s. a 38.00s (4 Ran).

(T M Schwalm), Mrs J G Retter

PLUMPTON (heavy)
Saturday April 2nd
Going Correction: PLUS 2.10 sec. per fur. (races 1,3,5), PLUS 2.00 (2,4,6)

3303 St Peter-St James Hospice Handicap Chase (0-115 5-y-o and up) £2,758 2 ¼m.......................... (2:30)

3148* LADY GHISLAINE (Fr) [91] 7-10-6 W McFarland, *in tch, led aftr 6th, drw clr appr 2 out, styd on wl.*
......(5 to 4 fav op 11 to 8 tchd 6 to 4 and 11 to 10) 1

3150 NATHIR (USA) [98] 8-10-13 N Williamson, *hld up and beh, hdwy aftr 5 out, styd on after 3 out, no ch wth wnr.*
.... (12 to 1 op 8 to 1) 2

3152² CONGREGATION [101] 8-11-2 J Railton, *chsd ldr, rdn 4 out, no imprsn appr 2 out.*
............................(2 to 1 op 9 to 4 tchd 5 to 2) 3

3099⁵ RUSTIC GENT (Ire) [85] 6-10-0 J R Kavanagh, *pressed ldr, cl up and ev ch 4 out, no imprsn aftr 3 out.*
.............................(50 to 1 op 33 to 1 tchd 66 to 1) 4

3194³ KIBREET [109] 7-11-10 S Earle, *chsd ldr, rdn 4 out, wknd appr 2 out.*............. (11 to 2 op 7 to 2 tchd 6 to 1) 5

2818⁴ FRED SPLENDID [90] 11-10-5 D Murphy, *hld up and beh, mstk 4 out, behind whn pld up bef last.*
.... (10 to 1 op 8 to 1 tchd 12 to 1) pu

3011³ IDLEIGH'S STAR [85] 10-10-0 D Gallagher, *led till hdd aftr 6th, wknd quickly after 5 out, tld off whn pld up bef 2 out.*...................(40 to 1 op 20 to 1 tchd 50 to 1) pu

Dist: 15l, 1¼l, 1½l, 5l. 5m 1.20s. a 42.20s (7 Ran).
SR: 34/26/27/9/28/-/-/

(Mrs P A White), J White

3304 Hallands Selling Handicap Hurdle (4,5,6-y-o) £1,861 2m 1f........ (3:00)

3147² KALAMOSS [73] 5-10-3 (7°) Miss S Mitchell, *in tch, led aftr 4th, made rst, drw clr after 2 out, styd on wl.*
...........................(7 to 4 op 2 to 1) 1

2395⁴ AL FORUM (Ire) [87] 4-11-10 D O'Sullivan, *hld up in tch, chsd wnr aftr 4 out, rdn and no imprsn after 2 out.*
..............................(11 to 8 fav tchd 6 to 4) 2

3153⁸ DO BE WARE [63] 4-10-0 J R Kavanagh, *chsd ldr, hit 6th, hrd rdn aftr 4 out, sn wknd.*
........................(16 to 1 op 12 to 1 tchd 20 to 1) 3

3012* YAAFOOR (USA) [80] (bl) 5-11-3 M Richards, *led second, chsd ldr, pushed alng aftr 5th, wknd after 4 out, tld off.*
.... (7 to 2 op 11 to 4 tchd 4 to 1) 4

3145⁷ BARGIN BOY [63] (bl) 5-10-0 Leesa Long, *hld up, hdwy aftr 5th, in tch after 6th, rdn and wknd quickly after 3 out, tld off.*...........(10 to 1 op 33 to 1 tchd 50 to 1) 5

3147 FIVE CASTLES [63] 6-10-0 M Perrett, *hld up, drpd rear aftr 5th, sn beh, tld off whn pld up bef 2 out.*
.............................(25 to 1 op 16 to 1) pu

Dist: 10l, 15l, dist, 5l. 4m 36.30s. a 44.30s (6 Ran).

(N R Mitchell), N R Mitchell

3305 Drones Restaurant Novices' Chase (5-y-o and up) £2,422 2m 5f....... (3:30)

2693² MR MATT (Ire) 6-11-2 Peter Hobbs, *led second, made rst, drw clr aftr 4 out, unchlgd.*.....(11 to 10 on op 6 to 4) 1

3015³ GALLANT EFFORT (Ire) 6-11-8 W McFarland, *chsd ldr, jmpd slwly 8th, no imprsn frm 3 out.*
...........................(3 to 1 op 5 to 2 tchd 100 to 30) 2

2886 HOWARYADOON 8-11-8 J Railton, *chsd ldr frm 3rd till wknd aftr 5 out.*........ (9 to 1 op 5 to 1 tchd 10 to 1) 3

2622* MAJOR INQUIRY (USA) 8-11-8 D Murphy, *hld up, effrt aftr tenth, sn wknd, tld off.*........ (3 to 1 tchd 100 to 30) 4

3011² DISCO DUKE 9-11-2 D Gallagher, *chsd ldrs to 9th, wknd quickly aftr nxt, tld off.*.......... (33 to 1 op 20 to 1) 5

Dist: 30l, 5l, 1l, dist. 5m 56.60s. a 51.60s (5 Ran).
SR: 13/-/

(Mrs Eric Boucher), D M Grissell

3306 Hailsham Novices' Hurdle (4-y-o and up) £1,543 2m 1f.............. (4:00)

2991² REDEEMYOURSELF (Ire) 5-11-0 D Murphy, *trkd ldr in second pl till led 6th, sn drw clr, unchlgd.*
.... (5 to 4 on op 6 to 4 on tchd 11 to 10 on) 1

2914² ESPRIT DE FEMME (Fr) 8-10-9 Peter Hobbs, *led to 6th, rdn alng aftr nxt, styd on to take moderate second appr 2 out, no imprsn.*........ (9 to 1 op 12 to 1 tchd 14 to 1) 2

3145* GOOGLY 5-11-9 N Williamson, *hld up, rdn and some hdwy aftr 6th, chsd ldr, wknd after 3 out, tld off.*
..................................(5 to 4 op 6 to 4) 3

3277 BALUSTRADE (bl) 7-11-0 W McFarland, *whipped round strt, beh and rdn alng aftr 4th, behind whn pld up after 6th.*..................(100 to 1 op 66 to 1) pu

3010 KINON-PENNY 6-11-0 M Stevens, *jmpd slwly second, beh and pushed alng aftr 4th, pld up after 6th.*
...................(100 to 1 op 66 to 1 tchd 200 to 1) pu

Dist: 30l, dist. 4m 33.40s. a 41.40s (5 Ran).
SR: 12/-/

(Mrs T Brown), J T Gifford

3307 Abergavenny Challenge Cup Handicap Chase (0-110 5-y-o and up) £2,807 3m 1f 110yds................ (4:30)

3006⁶ THAMESDOWN TOOTSIE [85] 9-10-7 D Murphy, *led to 5th, led 6th to 9th, led ag'n six out, styd on wl.*
...........................(11 to 2 op 5 to 1 tchd 6 to 1) 1

3259³ GINGER TRISTAN [97] 8-11-5 Peter Hobbs, *led 5th to 6th, led 9th to six out, mstk 4 out, rdn and no imprsn 2 out.*
.........................(11 to 8 fav op 13 to 8) 2

2622³ FAARIS [81] 13-10-3³ J Railton, *led to second, chsd ldrs, ev ch 4 out, styd on one pace appr 2 out.*
...........................(33 to 1 op 20 to 1 tchd 40 to 1) 3

3120* THE TARTAN SPARTAN [102] 10-11-3 (7°) P Ward, *hld up, mstk 7th, pushed alng aftr 9th, wknd 12th, styd on one pace frm 4 out.*...................(9 to 4 tchd 5 to 2) 4

3118 GENERAL BRANDY [87] 8-10-6 (3°) P Hide, *led second to nxt, chsd ldrs till wknd quickly aftr 11th, sn beh.*
........................(10 to 1 op 8 to 1 tchd 12 to 1) 5

3120² CAMDEN BELLE [82] 12-10-4 M Perrett, *tld off 8th, pld up bef tenth.*...............(12 to 1 op 8 to 1 tchd 16 to 1) pu

Dist: 3½l, 7l, 8l, 15l. 7m 13.80s. a 61.80s (6 Ran).
SR: -/5/-/

(J F O'Donovan), A P Jones

3308 Hurstpierpoint Handicap Hurdle (0-110 4-y-o and up) £2,162 2½m (5:00)

3091 ROYAL FLAMINGO [94] 8-11-10 R J Beggan, *hld up, hdwy 5th, led 8th, styd last, rdn and kpt on wl nr finish, all out.*..................................(20 to 1 tchd 25 to 1) 1

3150* AUGUST TWELFTH [80] 6-10-10 Mr Raymond White, *hld up in tch, cld up aftr 4 out, rdn to chal after 2 out, wth wnr last, ridden and not quicken nr finish.*
.............................(10 to 1 op 14 to 1 tchd 11 to 2) 2

3119⁵ GAMEFULL GOLD [87] 5-11-3 A Dicken, *hld up, beh 3rd, hdwy aftr 7th, chsd ldrs, no imprsn appr 2 out.*
.............................(4 to 1 fav tchd 9 to 2) 3

3147* BAYLORD PRINCE (Ire) [80] 6-10-10 M Hoad, *hld up, hdwy 4 out, rdn and styd on one pace.*
........................(13 to 2 op 5 to 1 tchd 7 to 1) 4

3119⁸ GRAND COLONIST [70] 7-9-11 (3°) A Procter, *hld up, beh 4th, effrt aftr 8th, wknd after 3 out.*
..........................(33 to 1 tchd 50 to 1) 5

3014* SMILING CHIEF (Ire) [90] (bl) 6-11-6 S Smith Eccles, *chsd ldrs to 8th, wknd 4 out.* (11 to 2 op 5 to 1 tchd 6 to 1) 6

3014² QUALITAIR MEMORY (Ire) [79] (v) 5-10-2 (7°) S Ryan, *sn prmnt, led aftr 6th, hdd 8th, wknd quickly, beh frm 4 out.*..................(9 to 2 op 4 to 1 tchd 5 to 1) 7

2881⁸ SCOTTISH BALL [82] (v) 5-10-12 M Crosse, *chsd ldrs to 6th, wknd aftr 8th, beh whn f 3 out.*
........................(10 to 1 op 7 to 1 tchd 12 to 1) f

2545 EDDIE WALSHE [84] 9-11-0 Leesa Long, *led to 7th, wknd rpdly, beh whn pld up aftr nxt.*
........................(25 to 1 op 20 to 1 tchd 33 to 1) f

3156² CARRIKINS [88] 7-11-4 Peter Hobbs, *hld up, rear and drvn alng aftr 6th, sn beh, pld up bef 3 out.*
.........................(7 to 1 op 6 to 1 tchd 8 to 1) pu

Dist: Hd, 10l, 12l, 2l, 15l, dist. 5m 23.00s. a 46.00s (10 Ran).
SR: 36/22/19/-/-/-/

(9th/12th Royal Lancers), G C Bravery

TOWCESTER (soft)
Saturday April 2nd
Going Correction: PLUS 1.30 sec. per fur. (races 1,2,-4,5), PLUS 1.20 (3,6)

3309 Turf Club Novices' Chase (5-y-o and up) £3,018 2¾m............... (2:20)

3163² RIVER MANDATE 7-11-10 B Powell, *in tch, rdn alng frm 12th, styd on to ld 2 out, all out.*
.......................(5 to 4 fav op 6 to 4 tchd 13 to 8) 1

3007² CANAVER 8-11-4 G McCourt, *wnt prmnt 6th, led 12th, hdd and wknd 2 out.*..(11 to 2 op 7 to 1 tchd 8 to 1) 2

3192* HILLWALK 8-12-0 D Morris, *led and pckd tenth, hit 11th, hdd 12th, rallied appr 2 out and mstk, sn btn.*
..................(2 to 1 op 5 to 4 tchd 9 to 4) 3

LUCKY LANDERS 9-11-4 D Bridgwater, *wth ldr to 4th, fdg whn f 9th.*.........................(20 to 1 op 10 to 1) f

3192³ SPECIAL ACCOUNT (v) 8-11-4 N Mann, *f 1st.*
...................(11 to 1 op 10 to 1 tchd 12 to 1) f

3043 INTERPLAY 9-11-4 E Murphy, *sn tld off, jmpd slwly second, pld up bef 4th.*.................(16 to 1 op 12 to 1) pu

2227[6] STYLISH GENT (bl) 7-11-4 I Lawrence, *prmnt till drpd rear 8th, tld off whn pld up bef 11th*....(33 to 1 op 10 to 1) pu
3007[9] PARSON'S WAY (bl) 7-11-4 P Holley, *hit 6th and 7th, rdn whn hmpd 9th, tld off when pld up bef 12th*.
.... (33 to 1 op 8 to 1) pu
Dist: 13l, 1¼l. 6m 4.50s. a 38.50s (8 Ran).
(Anne Duchess Of Westminster), Capt T A Forster

3310
29th Year Of The Schilizzi 1906 Commemorative Challenge Cup Handicap Chase (0-130 5-y-o and up) £3,671 2 ¾m.......................... (2:50)

2406 INVASION [101] (v) 10-11-10 M Brennan, *beh, rdn 7th, led aftr 3 out, all out*........(3 to 1 op 7 to 2) 1
2935[2] POSTMAN'S PATH [97] 8-11-6 B Powell, *beh, hdwy tenth, rdn and no imprsn frm 3 out*.
.... (13 to 8 fav op 5 to 4 tchd 7 to 4) 2
2901[3] MWEENISH [95] 12-11-4 G McCourt, *chsd ldrs, hit 8th, uns rdr 9th*..............(5 to 2 op 3 to 1 tchd 9 to 4) ur
2639 FALSE ECONOMY [98] (bl) 9-11-7 D Bridgwater, *bit but jmpd hesitantly, clr 5th, jumped very slwly 3 out, sn hdd, 3rd and no ch whn refused last*.
.... (8 to 1 op 6 to 1 tchd 10 to 1) ref
2823[5] DERRING VALLEY [100] (bl) 9-11-9 M A FitzGerald, *prmnt till wknd 9th, tld off tenth, jmpd slwly 11th and pld up*.
.... (8 to 1 op 6 to 1 tchd 10 to 1) pu
Dist: 15l. 6m 9.70s. a 43.70s (5 Ran).
(Lady Anne Bentinck), O Brennan

3311
National Letterbox Marketing Handicap Hurdle (0-120 4-y-o and up) £2,722 2m.................... (3:20)

2833[6] STRATH ROYAL [119] 8-12-0 M Brennan, *in tch, hdwy to chase ldr 4th, led 3 out, clr nxt*............(3 to 1 jt-fav tchd 7 to 2) 1
3100* MISS MARIGOLD [109] (bl) 5-11-4 A Tory, *reluctant to line up and slwly into strd, hdwy to chase ldr 3rd to 4th, styd on one pace frm 2 out*.................(3 to 1 jt-fav op 9 to 4 tchd 7 to 2) 2
2933* TAYLORS PRINCE [103] (v) 7-10-12 V Smith, *hdwy 3 out, chsd wnr appr 2 out, sn wknd*....... (7 to 1 op 33 to 1) 3
3100[6] BANKONIT (Ire) [93] 6-10-2 I Lawrence, *drpd rear 4th, styd on ag'n undr pres frm 2 out*....... (50 to 1 op 33 to 1) 4
3193[3] CELTIC BOB [91] 14-10-0 V Slattery, *in tch, rdn 3 out, sn wknd*...................(20 to 1 op 10 to 1) 5
3020 TILT TECH FLYER [96] (v) 9-10-5 W Marston, *led, clr 3rd, hdd 3 out, sn btn*.................(9 to 1 op 14 to 1) 6
3156[4] DRAMATIC EVENT [91] 9-10-0 E Murphy, *chsd ldrs 4th, wknd 3 out*.............(12 to 1 tchd 14 to 1) 7
2992[6] TOP WAVE [114] 6-11-9 M A FitzGerald, *al beh*.
.......................(4 to 1 tchd 5 to 1) 8
Dist: 25l, 6l, 2½l, 1½l, 2½l, 12l. dist. 4m 6.60s. a 23.60s (8 Ran).
SR: 56/21/9/-/-/ (Lady Anne Bentinck), O Brennan

3312
33rd Year Of The Schilizzi Challenge Bowl Handicap Chase (0-125 5-y-o and up) £3,442 2m 110yds..... (3:50)

3152[3] SARTORIUS [106] 8-11-2 G McCourt, *wth ldr, led 6th to 7th, led ag'n 4 out, hdd briefly frm 2 out, narrow ld again last, all out*. (11 to 4 fav op 5 to 2 tchd 3 to 1) 1
3091[3] BOSTON ROVER [115] 9-11-11 M Brennan, *hdwy 6th, led appr 2 out, hdd approaching last, styd on one pace*.
........................(4 to 1 op 7 to 2) 2
3152[4] GENERAL MERCHANT [92] bl) 14-10-2 A Tory, *al prmnt, rdn and styd on same pace frm 2 out*.
.... (9 to 1 op 6 to 1 tchd 10 to 1) 3
2307[3] DR ROCKET [113] 9-11-6 (3*) D Meredith, *hdwy 4 out, no imprsn frm 3 out*..... (100 to 30 op 5 to 1 tchd 13 to 2) 4
3066 SAILORS LUCK [114] 9-11-10 E Murphy, *led to 6th, wknd 3 out*......................(11 to 2 op 5 to 1 tchd 7 to 1) 5
3185[3] RATHER SHARP [90] 8-10-0 P Holley, *prmnt, led 7th, hdd 4 out, sn wknd*......... (10 to 1 op 7 to 1 tchd 11 to 1) 6
1566 BLUE BUCCANEER [91] 11-10-4 M A FitzGerald, *al beh, tld off whn pld up bef last*.
.... (14 to 1 op 8 to 1 tchd 16 to 1) pu
Dist: ½l, 7l, 9l, 20l, 2½l. dist. 4m 28.80s. a 26.80s (7 Ran).
SR: 34/42/12/24/5/-/-/ (M Popham), T Thomson Jones

3313
Empress Elizabeth Of Austria Hunters' Chase (5-y-o and up) £2,469 3m 1f......................... (4:20)

3065[2] TEAPLANTER 11-12-5 (5*) Mr R Russell, *lft in ld 1st, hdd tenth, led 12th, clr appr 2 out*.
.... (11 to 4 on tchd 5 to 2 on) 1
BLAKES ORPHAN 8-11-7 (7*) Mr T Illsley, *hit 1st, chsd ldrs, hit 11th, no imprsn on wnr frm 3 out*.
.... (8 to 1 tchd 9 to 2 and 7 to 2) 2
NICK THE BRIEF 12-11-9 (5*) Mr T Byrne, *chlgd 6th, led tenth, hdd 12th, wknd appr 2 out*.
.... (4 to 1 tchd 9 to 2 and 7 to 2) 3
2937 PARSONS PLEASURE 11-11-7 (7*) Mr C Morlock, *beh, hit 12th, effrt appr 3 out, 4th and no ch whn f last*.
.... (8 to 1 tchd 10 to 1) f

PARSON'S CROSS 10-11-11 (3*) Mr G Johnson Houghton, *f 1st*.................................(33 to 1 op 14 to 1) f
3165[3] QUEEN'S CHAPLAIN 10-12-3 (7*) Mrs M Morris, *hmpd 1st, hit 5th and 12th, tld off 14th, pld up bef 4 out*.
.... (14 to 1 op 8 to 1 tchd 16 to 1) pu
Dist: 30l, 15l. 7m 0.00s. a 45.00s (6 Ran).
(R G Russell), Miss C Saunders

3314
Grace Novices' Hurdle (4-y-o) £1,830 2m........................... (4:50)

1880 GIORDANO (Ire) 11-4 Gary Lyons, *in tch, led second to 3rd, led ag'n last, pushed out*............(5 to 2 op 7 to 2) 1
3228[4] ERCKULE 11-4 R Supple, *sn in tch, slight ld 2 out, hdd last, one pace*.................(6 to 4 fav op 11 to 10 on) 2
606[4] ROMALITO 10-12 M A FitzGerald, *in tch, hdwy to chal and mstk last, not quicken*... (14 to 1 tchd 16 to 1) 3
DOC COTTRILL 10-12 D Bridgwater, *led aftr 3rd till 4th, styd pressing ldrs till wknd aftr 2 out*.
.... (2 to 1 op 7 to 4 tchd 9 to 4) 4
DARING KING 10-12 V Smith, *led to second, led ag'n 3rd, sn hdd, led 4th, still in narrow ld whn mstk and uns rdr 3 out*.....................(14 to 1 op 10 to 1) ur
SEATTLE AFFAIR (Ire) 10-4 (3*) D Meredith, *jmpd slwly 4th, al beh, tld off whn pld up bef 3 out*. (33 to 1 op 16 to 1) pu
SPIKE 10-12 M Bosley, *al beh, tld off whn pld up bef last*.
.... (25 to 1 op 12 to 1) pu
Dist: 3l, sht-hd, 3l. 4m 19.60s. a 36.60s (7 Ran).
(John Pugh), P D Evans

UTTOXETER (heavy)
Saturday April 2nd
Going Correction: PLUS 1.85 sec. per fur.

3315
Invest In East Staffordshire Maiden Hurdle (4-y-o and up) £3,012 2m (2:25)

2897[3] TEST MATCH 7-11-6 Diane Clay, *hld up in tch, cld on ldrs 3 out, led nxt, hit last, rdn out*.
.... (8 to 1 op 7 to 1 tchd 10 to 1) 1
3042[3] GO BALLISTIC 5-11-6 A Maguire, *in tch, led appr 3 out, hdd nxt, one pace aftr*.
.... (2 to 1 on tchd 13 to 8 on and 6 to 4 on) 2
3108[2] BILLYGOAT GRUFF 5-11-6 J Osborne, *al prmnt, dsptd ld 2 out, sn one pace*.............(4 to 1 op 3 to 1) 3
2900 PYRO PENNANT 9-11-6 D J Burchell, *rcd wide, chsd ldr till lost pl 6th, rallied 3 out, no imprsn frm nxt*.
.... (2 to 1 op 3 to 1 tchd 4 to 1) 4
2276[9] MRS NORMAN 5-10-10 (5*) E Husband, *rcd wide, in tch to 3 out*...........(25 to 1 op 20 to 1 tchd 33 to 1) 5
3008[9] KILLTUBBER HOUSE 8-10-13 (7*) P McLoughlin, *mid-div, some hdwy appr 6th, wknd 3 out, tld off*.
.... (33 to 1 op 25 to 1) 6
RULLY 5-11-6 W Worthington, *al towards rear, tld off*.
.... (66 to 1 op 25 to 1) 7
2691 TIR NA NOG (bl) 5-11-6 J Ryan, *al beh, tld off*.
.... (66 to 1 op 3 to 1) 8
1297[2] SOUND AND FURY 10-11-6 T Grantham, *led till wknd and hdd aftr 4 out, blun and uns rdr nxt*.
.... (14 to 1 op 10 to 1 tchd 20 to 1) ur
SEEMENOMORE 5-11-1 T Wall, *al beh, tld off whn pld up bef last*...................(66 to 1 op 25 to 1) pu
2905 THINK PINK 7-11-6 C Hawkins, *prmnt till hrd rdn and wknd appr 6th, tld off whn pld up bef 3 out*.
.... (66 to 1 op 50 to 1) pu
3074[6] CAMPTOSAURUS (Ire) 5-11-6 A S Smith, *lost tch 4th, tld off whn pld up bef 2 out*..........(33 to 1 op 20 to 1) pu
Dist: 5l, 2l, 10l, 6l, 30l, 4l, 30l. 4m 15.00s. a 36.00s (12 Ran).
SR: 28/23/21/11/-/-/ (T A Theaker), W Clay

3316
Festival Park Novices' Chase (5-y-o and up) £3,558 3¼m........... (2:55)

3039 BRABAZON (USA) 9-11-9 A Maguire, *patiently rdn, briefly outpcd 12th, steady hdwy to join ldr 3 out, shaken up to ld sn aftr last*...........(2 to 1 op 6 to 4) 1
2913* CELTIC BARLE 10-11-9 S McNeill, *trkd ldr for most of way till led 5 out, pushed along frm nxt, hdd sn aftr last, no extr*....................(5 to 4 fav op 11 to 10 tchd 11 to 8) 2
2958[2] URIZEN 9-11-3 C Hawkins, *mstk second, in frnt rnk and ev ch 3 out, one pace frm nxt*......(4 to 1 tchd 9 to 2) 3
3278 SERDARLI 12-10-12 J Ryan, *hld up, btn whn f 4 out*.
.... (25 to 1 op 16 to 1) f
3213[5] REPRINTH 8-10-9 (3*) A Thornton, *led, blun 7th, hdd 5 out, remote 4th and exhausted whn f 2 out*.
.... (33 to 1 op 20 to 1) f
3043 SUNCIA 10-10-9 (3*) R Farrant, *rcd wide, hit 5th, struggling frm tenth, tld off whn pld up bef 12th*.
.... (25 to 1 op 16 to 1) pu
Dist: 5l, 5l. 7m 36.90s. a 80.90s (6 Ran).
(P H Betts (Holdings) Ltd), M H Tompkins

3317
Octagon Centre Selling Handicap Hurdle (4-y-o and up) £2,001 2½m 110yds .... (3:25)

3103² EASTERN PLEASURE [80] (bl) 7-11-7 Diane Clay, *al hndy,
led 3 out, hit nxt, hrd rdn and ran on wl.*
.... (13 to 2 op 6 to 1) 1
3215 PRIMO FIGLIO [84] 4-11-2 (3") A Thornton, *hld up, hdwy
6th, drvn to chal last, no imprsn r-in.*(7 to 1 op 6 to 1) 2
2328 RUSTY MUSIC [62] 8-9-10 (7") Mr J L Llewellyn, *al prmnt,
rdn to ld appr 6th, mstk and hdd 3 out, one pace frm
nxt.*.................................. (33 to 1 op 20 to 1) 3
3131⁷ SMART DEBUTANTE (Ire) [69] (bl) 5-10-3 (7") P McLoughlin,
*hld up in tch, hdwy frm hfwy, not rch ldrs from 3 out,
sddl slpd.*........................(14 to 1 op 16 to 1) 4
3103³ ROYAL STANDARD [78] 7-11-5 P McDermott, *led to second,
rdn and ev ch 3 out, wknd*...........(9 to 1 op 8 to 1) 5
3111² MARINE SOCIETY [75] (bl) 6-11-2 A Maguire, *prmnt till
wknd appr 3 out.*(100 to 30 fav op 5 to 2 tchd 7 to 2) 6
3222⁶ MOUNTSHANNON [82] 8-11-9 Peter Caldwell, *hld up in
rear, hdwy 5th, rdn 3 out, sn btn.*
.... (13 to 2 op 6 to 1 tchd 7 to 1) 7
3167⁵ BOWLAND GIRL (Ire) [61] 5-9-13 (3") S Wynne, *al beh.*
.... (8 to 1 tchd 10 to 1 and 12 to 1) 8
2998 NEGATORY (USA) [64] 7-10-5 W Worthington, *al beh, tld off
frm 6th.*.................................. (25 to 1 op 20 to 1) 9
2461⁵ PREENKA GIRL (Fr) [83] 5-11-10 J Lower, *prmnt till wknd
rpdly appr 3 out, tld off.*............(7 to 1 op 6 to 1) 10
2737⁸ YACHT CLUB [64] 12-10-5 O Pears, *beh, hdwy to ld 3rd,
hdd appr 6th, wknd quickly, tld off whn pld up bef 3
out.*.................................. (33 to 1 op 25 to 1) pu
3111⁷ CRAZY HORSE DANCER (USA) [76] 6-11-0 (3") R Farrant,
*mid-div, rdn aftr 6th, sn btn, tld off whn pld up bef 3
out.*.................................. (11 to 2 op 5 to 1 tchd 6 to 1) pu
2997 LATOSKY [59] (bl) 6-9-9² (7") W Fry, *beh, tld off whn pld up
bef 6th.*.................................. (33 to 1) pu
Dist: 2½l, 2½l, 12l, 4l, 2l, sht-hd, 6l, 30l. 5m 28.70s. a 45.70s (13 Ran).
SR: 15/10/-/-/-/-/ (T Wood), W Clay

3318 St Modwen Handicap Chase (0-135
5-y-o and up) £4,095 2m 5f..... (3:55)

3132⁴ LUMBERJACK (USA) [132] (bl) 10-12-0 J Osborne, *trkd
ldrs, led 5th, hdd appr 8th, led on bit and lft clr 2 out,
unchal.*.................................. (7 to 4 op 11 to 8 tchd 15 to 8) 1
3223⁷ FAST CRUISE [106] 9-10-2⁵ (3") A Thornton, *trkd ldr, led
4th to 5th, wknd appr 3 out, lft poor second nxt.*
.... (7 to 1 op 6 to 1 tchd 8 to 1) 2
2639⁴ RADICAL REQUEST [104] (bl) 11-10-0 A Maguire, *hld up in
rear, clsg whn mstk 8th, gd hdwy 5 out, wknd appr 3
out, tld off.*.................................. (8 to 1 op 7 to 1 tchd 9 to 1) 3
3052² SARAVILLE [114] 7-10-10 J Lower, *led to 4th, led appr 8th,
rdn, hdd and f 2 out.*
.... (11 to 10 fav op 5 to 4 tchd 11 to 8) f
Dist: 10l, 25l. 5m 51.90s. a 51.90s (4 Ran). (Elite Racing Club), C R Egerton

3319 Raynesway Park Novices' Handicap
Hurdle (4-y-o and up) £3,084 2m (4:25)

3281⁵ MORIARTY [78] 7-9-11 (3") J McCarthy, *al prmnt, rdn appr
2 out, rallied and ran on wl to ld sn aftr last.*
.... (6 to 1 tchd 7 to 1) 1
3023 MARROS MILL [104] 4-11-12 A Maguire, *hld up, hdwy to
go second appr 5th, led 2 out, strly rdn and hdd sn aftr
last, no extr.*.................................. (5 to 8 fav op 5 to 4 tchd 6 to 4) 2
3062⁹ ALLEGATION [106] (v) 4-12-0 J Lower, *al prmnt, led 4th,
rdn and hdd 2 out, ridden and wknd r-in.*
.... (9 to 4 op 7 to 4) 3
2797² FORGETFUL [78] 5-10-0 D J Burchell, *led to 4th, rdn and
wknd 3 out.*........... (13 to 2 op 8 to 1 tchd 10 to 1) 4
1303 GOLDEN MADJAMBO [88] 8-10-2² J Lodder, *pushed alng
frm 4th, lost tch 6th, tld off.*
.... (25 to 1 op 20 to 1 tchd 33 to 1) 5
2896 FINNOW QUAY (Ire) [78] 5-10-0 A S Smith, *hld up in rear,
effrt aftr 5th, wknd nxt, tld off whn pld up bef 3 out.*
.... (33 to 1 op 20 to 1) pu
2583⁶ MY ADVENTURE (Ire) [78] 4-10-0 L Wyer, *in tch till rdn and
lost pl 5th, tld off whn pld up bef 3 out.*
.... (8 to 1 op 6 to 1) pu
Dist: 2½l, 1l, 15l, 20l. 4m 14.50s. a 35.50s (7 Ran).
SR: 13/36/37/-/ (Mrs K Oseman), R J Price

3320 Orbital Centre Handicap Hurdle (0-140
4-y-o and up) £3,081 2m....... (4:55)

2947³ SUN SURFER (Fr) [120] 6-11-2 B Powell, *wtd wth, mstk
5th, hdwy 6th, in ld whn sprawled on landing nxt, clr
frm 2 out.*.................................. 1
2933³ SOOTHFAST (USA) [115] 5-10-11 T Grantham, *hld up, outpcd appr 3 out, styd on to go second bef nxt, no ch wth
wnr.*.................................. (7 to 4 jt-fav op 5 to 2) 2
3219² WHIPPERS DELIGHT (Ire) [104] 6-10-8 D Meade, *trkd ldr
till one pace frm 3 out.*....(7 to 4 jt-fav op 5 to 4) 3
2449⁶ BORO SMACKEROO [128] 9-11-10 A S Smith, *led till hdd
and wknd appr 3 out, sn btn.*
.... (7 to 1 op 6 to 1 tchd 8 to 1) 4
Dist: 11l, 15l, 20l. 4m 16.90s. a 37.90s (4 Ran).
SR: 5/ (Simon Sainsbury), Capt T A Forster

FAIRYHOUSE (IRE) (soft)

Monday April 4th

3321 Galtee Traditional Gold Hurdle (4-y-o)
£4,140 2m..................... (2:05)

2864³ MICKS DELIGHT (Ire) 11-7 P Carberry, ... (3 to 1 fav) 1
3246³ PUSH THE BUTTON (Ire) 10-9 C F Swan, ...(4 to 1) 2
2547 BISSTAMI (Ire) 11-7 G M O'Neill, ...(9 to 2) 3
MOUSSAHIM (USA) 11-0 L P Cusack, ...(14 to 1) 4
2864⁶ WICKLOW WAY (Ire) 10-9 K F O'Brien, ...(10 to 1) 5
2678⁶ BORN TO WIN (Ire) 10-9 S R Murphy, ...(20 to 1) 6
2868⁴ GRAPHIC IMAGE (Ire) 10-9 (5") K P Gaule, ...(12 to 1) 7
3080⁹ GENTLE REEF (Ire) 11-2 C N Bowens, ...(20 to 1) 8
THE OUTBACK WAY (Ire) 11-0 D H O'Connor, ...(33 to 1) 9
2122⁸ FRIENDLY FLYER (Ire) 10-9 C O'Dwyer, ...(12 to 1) 10
3246 SPORTSTYLE (Ire) 11-0 J F Titley, ...(25 to 1) 11
3069⁵ DRESS DANCE (Ire) 11-0 J P Banahan, ...(20 to 1) 12
OWENDUFF (USA) 11-0 F Woods, ...(20 to 1) 13
PETOFI 11-0 A Powell, ...(33 to 1) 14
MINUS ONE (USA) 11-0 B Sheridan, ...(33 to 1) 15
DANCEALOT (Ire) 11-0 J Shortt, ...(33 to 1) 16
2771² DUCHESS AFFAIR (Ire) 10-2 (7") C McCormack, ..(20 to 1) 17
2750 FOOLISH LAW (Ire) 10-9 H O'Donovan, ...(50 to 1) 18
3246 PUB TALK 10-9 (5") D Walsh, ...(50 to 1) 19
3246 HEATHFIELD (USA) 10-7 (7") R A Hennessy, ...(50 to 1) 20
MARY'S CASE (Ire) 10-7 (7") Mr M O'Connor, ...(33 to 1) 21
Dist: 2l, ¾l, 3l, 9l. 4m 8.20s. (21 Ran).

(M J McCarthy), Noel Meade

3322 Leinster Petroleum/Shell Handicap
Hurdle (Listed - Grade 3) (4-y-o and
up) £6,900 2¾m................... (2:40)

3086⁴ MY SUNNY GLEN [-] 7-9-9 (5") K P Gaule, *wl plcd, prog 3
out, quickened to ld appr last, styd on strly...*(10 to 1) 1
2939³ HORNER WATER (Ire) [-] 6-10-4 K F O'Brien, *mid-div, prog 4
out, ev ch 2 out, no extr appr last, ran on wl ag'n cl
hme.*.................................. (14 to 1) 2
2986⁹ MICK O'DWYER [-] 7-10-9 F J Flood, *mid-div, steady prog
to ld appr 3 out, rdn aftr nxt, hdd approaching last,
kpt on.*.................................. (16 to 1) 3
2940⁷ CALMOS [-] 7-10-4 J Osborne, *wl plcd, rdn 3 out, no extr
appr last, kpt on.*.................................. (16 to 1) 4
3242³ PUNTERS BAR [-] 7-9-10 (5") P A Roche, *mid-div, prog 5th,
rdn, no extr appr last, kpt on.*...........(11 to 1) 5
2846³ DOWHATYOULIKE (Ire) [-] 5-10-7 P Carberry, *mid-div, prog
3 out, one pace.*.................................. (8 to 1) 6
1851⁴ LOVE AND PORTER (Ire) [-] 6-11-5 D H O'Connor, *hld up,
prog 5 out, rdn 3 out, kpt on one pace.*.......(12 to 1) 7
3273³ RUNAWAY GOLD [-] (bl) 7-9-4 (3") C O'Brien, *mid-div, rdn 3
out, kpt on wthout threatening ldrs.*.......(25 to 1) 8
3038 TEMPLEROAN PRINCE [-] 7-11-0 (7") B Bowens, *rear, prog
4 out, kpt on one pace.*.................................. (14 to 1) 9
2939⁵ MYSTIC GALE (Ire) [-] 6-9-9 S R Murphy, *rear, prog 4 out,
kpt on one pace.*.................................. (25 to 1) 10
2921² AEGEAN FANFARE (Ire) [-] (bl) 5-10-7 R Hughes, *mid-div,
rdn 2 out, no extr aftr nxt.*.................................. (16 to 1) 11
2284⁶ CASH CHASE (Ire) [-] 6-10-2 L P Cusack, *mid-div, prog 4
out, trkd ldr nxt, no extr appr 2 out, wknd....*(25 to 1) 12
3242 COIN MACHINE (Ire) [-] 5-10-4 T Horgan, *wl plcd, rdn 4 out,
wknd aftr nxt.*.................................. (10 to 1) 13
3083² BUTCHES BOY (Ire) [-] 5-11-5 M Dwyer, *trkd ldr, rdn 4 out,
wknd aftr nxt.*.................................. (6 to 1) 14
2985³ LOVELY RUN [-] 7-10-10 H Rogers, *mid-div, some prog 4
out, rdn and wknd aftr nxt.*.................................. (14 to 1) 15
3085⁴ TUG OF PEACE [-] 7-11-13 M Flynn, *mid-div, prog 5 out,
rdn 3 out, sn wknd.*.................................. (8 to 1) 16
3242 GOLDEN OPAL [-] 9-10-9 (5") J P Broderick, *al rear.*
.... (25 to 1) 17
2844³ WILD VENTURE (Ire) [-] 6-10-2 A Powell, *mid-div, rdn 4 out,
wknd aftr nxt.*.................................. (12 to 1) 18
2844⁴ PRECARIUM (Ire) [-] 6-10-10 C O'Dwyer, *mid-div, rdn and
wknd quickly aftr 3 out.*.................................. (12 to 1) 19
3200⁷ BART OWEN [-] 9-11-13 C F Swan, *led aftr second, rdn
and hdd after 4 out, wknd quickly......*(9 to 2 fav) 20
3248⁸ HAPPY PERCY [-] 9-11-0 B Sheridan, *al rear.....*(20 to 1) 21
2846⁴ REGALING (Ire) [-] 6-10-10 F Woods, *mid-div, mstk and f 3
out.*.................................. (16 to 1) f
2078⁹ YOUNG GALE [-] 10-11-2 J Shortt, *mid-div, wknd 6 out,
pld up bef 4 out.*.................................. (25 to 1) pu
2587⁷ LAW BRIDGE [-] 7-11-8 J F Titley, *rear, rdn 6 out, wknd
and pld up bef 4 out.*.................................. (10 to 1) pu
2284 CONSTANT 'N CONTROL [-] 5-10-0 (3") T J Mitchell, *mid-
div, rdn and wknd appr 3 out, pld up bef last.*(20 to 1) pu
Dist: 2½l, sht-hd, 2l, hd. 5m 54.60s. (26 Ran).

(E Flavin), A P O'Brien

3323 Jameson Gold Cup Hurdle (Listed -
Grade 2) (5-y-o and up) £11,500 2m
.... (3:15)

2391⁴ KLAIRON DAVIS (Fr) 5-11-13 T Horgan, *pld hrd, prog 3 out,
trkd ldr nxt, led appr last, styd on strly.* (2 to 1 jt-fav)

3023 SOUND MAN (Ire) 6-11-11 C F Swan, *trkd ldr, prog 3 out, ev ch nxt, rdn appr last, kpt on without threatening wnr*.....................................(2 to 1 jt-fav) 2
3080² IDIOTS VENTURE 7-12-0 J Osborne, *led, clr aftr second, reduced advantage 3 out, hdd appr last, wknd*. (6 to 1) 3
3080³ HEIST 5-11-10 P Carberry, *wl plcd, rdn 3 out, no extr and wknd appr nxt*............................ (12 to 1) 4
2287⁷ PADRE MIO (Ire) 6-12-0 K F O'Brien, *hld up, rdn 3 out, no extr and wknd bef nxt*........................(5 to 1) 5
3023⁹ AIYBAK (Ire) (bl) 6-11-11 B Sheridan, *mid-div, rdn and lost tch aftr 4 out*..................................(6 to 1) 6
2281² NIGHTMAN 5-11-7 C O'Dwyer, *hld up, mstk 4 out, sn rdn, btn whn mistake at nxt*.......................(14 to 1) 7
Dist: 1½l, 5l, 14l, 1½l. 4m 8.50s. (7 Ran).
(C Jones), A L T Moore

3324 Jameson Irish Grand National Handicap Chase (Listed-Grade 1) (4-y-o and up) £58,200 3m 5f.......... (3:55)

2701³ SON OF WAR [-] 7-10-10 F Woods, *wl plcd, prog 4 out, mstk nxt, rdn, effrt appr last, styd on strly to ld r-in*. ....(12 to 1) 1
2701² NUAFFE [-] 9-10-0 S H O'Donovan, *led, mstks, quickened 6 ls clr aftr 4 out, rdn, hdd after last, no extr*....(16 to 1) 2
3064 EBONY JANE [-] 9-11-1 L P Cusack, *wl plcd, rdn 3 out, no extr aftr nxt, kpt on*.......................... (10 to 1) 3
3081³ CAPTAIN BRANDY [-] 9-10-0 F J Flood, *mid-div, prog 5 out, trkd ldrs aftr nxt, rdn and no extr appr 2 out, kpt on*..(25 to 1) 4
3067³ COMMERCIAL ARTIST [-] 8-10-12 C N Bowens, *mid-div, prog 5 out, trkd ldrs 3 out, rdn and wknd appr nxt*. ....(20 to 1) 5
3001* BALTIC BROWN [-] 9-10-0¹ (4ex) Richard Guest, *mid-div, prog 13th, trkd ldrs 4 out, rdn and wknd aftr nxt*. ....(25 to 1) 6
3134³ CALLMECHA [-] (bl) 9-10-0 T Horgan, *mid-div, rdn 6 out, wknd aftr nxt, tld off*.........................(12 to 1) 7
2755* JASSU [-] 8-10-0 C O'Brien, *mid-div, prog aftr half-way, rdn after 6 out, wknd, tld off*.................. (10 to 1) 8
3123³ MASS APPEAL [-] 9-10-0 B Sheridan, *mid-div, mstk 15th, rdn 6 out, sn wknd, tld off*..................(50 to 1) 9
3039⁴ BELVEDERIAN [-] 7-10-8 J Osborne, *wl plcd, tracking ldr whn f 6 out*..(6 to 1) f
3121⁵ RUST NEVER SLEEPS [-] 10-10-12 P Carberry, *rear, some prog hfwy, rdn 6 out, wknd, pld up bef 3 out*. (20 to 1) pu
3121* RIVER TARQUIN [-] (bl) 10-10-8 (1ex) K F O'Brien, *wl plcd, lost pos aftr hfwy, wknd, pld up bef 6 out*.....(20 to 1) pu
2288* HIGH PEAK [-] 10-10-7 C F Swan, *mid-div, mstks 3rd and 4th, rdn hfwy, wknd and pld up bef four out*. .... (9 to 4 fav) pu
2867² MERAPI [-] 8-10-0 A Powell, *al rear, pld up bef last*. ....(50 to 1) pu
3067² BUCKBOARD BOUNCE [-] 8-11-3 J Shortt, *mid-div whn blun 12th, rdn and lost tch 6 out, pld up bef 4 out*. ....(20 to 1) pu
3134* GLENBROOK D'OR [-] 10-10-0 (2ex) B M Clifford, *al rear, pld up bef 5 out*...................................(12 to 1) pu
2865* ALL THE ACES [-] 7-10-0 C O'Dwyer, *al rear, tld off whn refused last*.......................................(14 to 1) pu
3064⁸ DEEP BRAMBLE [-] 7-11-13 M Dwyer, *mid-div, wknd quickly and pld up 16th*............................. (8 to 1) pu
Dist: 4½l, 9l, 3l, hd, 6l, dist. 8m 10.30s. (18 Ran).
(Mrs V O'Brien), Peter McCreery

3325 Osmonds Teat Seal Novice Chase (5-y-o and up) £6,900 2¼m........ (4:35)

2845³ PRINCESS CASILIA 9-11-9 B Sheridan,...........(3 to 1) 1
2845⁵ WINTERBOURNE ABBAS (Ire) 5-11-7 J Shortt, ... (14 to 1) 2
3198³ PORT TIME 7-11-9 (5*) D Walsh,.................. (5 to 1) 3
2987⁴ TRASSEY BRIDGE 7-11-9 F Woods, ...(33 to 1) 4
3198⁸ FINAL ISSUE 7-12-0 A Powell,.....................(16 to 1) 5
3275 SLANEY BACON 7-11-9 C O'Dwyer, ...(20 to 1) 6
2588⁴ PROGRAMMED TO WIN 7-12-0 T Horgan, ... (5 to 1) f
2683² WALLYS RUN 7-11-9 (5*) D T Evans, ...(5 to 2 fav) f
2588⁵ HEMISPHERE (Ire) 5-10-13 S R Murphy, ... (10 to 1) f
2845⁷ PROFESSOR STRONG (Ire) 6-11-9 L P Cusack, .. (16 to 1) f
3293⁵ DAVE FLECK (Ire) 6-11-4 (5*) J P Broderick, ... (25 to 1) bd
2028⁴ JIMMY GORDON 7-11-9 K F O'Brien, ... (25 to 1) pu
173* MICHAEL'S STAR (Ire) 6-11-11 (3*) T J Mitchell, ... (16 to 1) pu
Dist: 7l, 5½l, 2½l, dist. 5m 9.90s. (13 Ran).
(Michael O'Dowd), W P Mullins

3326 Nuzum Ltd Handicap Chase (0-109 5-y-o and up) £4,140 2½m...... (5:05)

1909⁶ MINISTER FOR FUN (Ire) [-] 6-11-7 C F Swan, ..(5 to 4 fav) 1
3241² GALLEY GALE [-] 8-10-12 K F O'Brien, ... (13 to 2) 2
3249² GOLDEN CARRUTH (Ire) [-] (bl) 6-10-7 (5*) J P Broderick, ...(3 to 1) 3
2942 THE QUIET MAN [-] 10-10-11 D H O'Connor, ... (12 to 1) 4
3274⁶ SPUR OF THE MOMENT [-] (bl) 7-11-9 J P Banahan, ...(10 to 1) 5
2772⁴ LA-GREINE [-] 7-10-11 (3*) Mr P McMahon, ... (6 to 1) f
2313⁵ RAMBLING LORD (Ire) [-] 6-10-9 P Carberry, ... (20 to 1) f
2845 AUTUMN RIDE (Ire) [-] 6-10-9 F Woods, ...(16 to 1) f
3274⁴ REDELVA [-] 7-9-8 (3*) T J Mitchell, ...(10 to 1) f
2922⁵ DELIGHTFUL CHOICE (Ire) [-] (bl) 6-9-10 T Horgan, (20 to 1) f
1830⁷ HO FRETTA [-] 8-10-4 (3*) C O'Brien, ... (14 to 1) pu
Dist: 15l, 25l, 15l, 8l. 5m 41.90s. (11 Ran).
(John P McManus), E J O'Grady

3327 Texacloth Wool Merchants I N H Flat Race (5 & 6-y-o) £4,140 2m..... (5:35)

2470⁹ COLLEEN'S BELLE (Ire) 6-11-6 (3*) Mr D Valentine, (14 to 1) 1
ROYAL ALBERT (Ire) 5-11-13 Mr T Mullins, ...(3 to 1 fav) 2
2869⁴ MANHATTAN CASTLE (Ire) 5-11-6 (7*) Mr H Murphy, (4 to 1) 3
2869² LITTLE BUCK (Ire) 6-11-7 (7*) Mr J S Cullen, ... (8 to 1) 4
ROUNDWOOD (Ire) 5-11-6 (7*) Miss J Lewis, ... (14 to 1) 5
3124⁹ COLLON DIAMONDS (Ire) 6-11-2 (7*) Mr M Callaghan, ...(14 to 1) 6
2465⁶ SPECTACULAR STAR (Ire) 5-11-13 Mr A J Martin, (16 to 1) 7
PHARSILK (Ire) 5-11-13 Mr M McNulty, ... (7 to 1) 8
3071⁴ LEGIBLE 6-11-7 (7*) Mr L J Gracey, ...(14 to 1) 9
2869⁶ BALLINEVA (Ire) 5-11-10 (3*) Mrs J M Mullins, ...(8 to 1) 10
CLERICAL COUSIN (Ire) 5-11-8 (5*) Mr C T G Kinane, ...(20 to 1) 11
EUROBUCK (Ire) 6-11-2 (7*) Miss A M O'Brien, ...(8 to 1) 12
3124 CEBU GALE (Ire) 5-11-10 (3*) Mr P J Casey, ... (25 to 1) 13
1403 DOCTOR SHODDY (Ire) 6-12-0 Mr J P Dempsey, ..(14 to 1) 14
2869 JOHNY BELINDA (Ire) 6-11-9 Mr P Fenton, ... (16 to 1) 15
2203 MEDIEVAL BEAUTY (Ire) 6-11-2 (7*) Mr P E I Newell, ...(33 to 1) 16
3124⁸ ROCK POOL 5-11-8 (5*) Mr H F Cleary, ... (10 to 1) 17
3082⁹ BUCKLESFORDBERRY 5-11-6 (7*) Mr S McCarthy, ...(14 to 1) 18
2684 FOUR MOONS (Ire) 5-11-1 (7*) Mr D L Bolger, ... (33 to 1) 19
2278⁹ LEVEL VIBES 5-11-10 (3*) Mr J A Nash, ...(100 to 30) 20
2470 BALLY UPPER (Ire) 6-11-7 (7*) Mr S O'Brien, ...(25 to 1) 21
3072 NOT AN INCH (Ire) 5-11-6 (7*) Mr K Whelan, ... (33 to 1) 22
2203⁵ CHAINMAIL (Ire) 6-12-0 Mr A R Coonan, ... (10 to 1) 23
ZINZAN BANK (Ire) 5-11-8 (5*) Mr P M Kelly, ... (20 to 1) 24
WOODHAVEN LAD 6-11-7 (7*) Mr J A Smith, ... (25 to 1) 25
REDZ LAST STAND (Ire) 5-11-1 (7*) Mr F Fagan, .. (33 to 1) 26
PADDY RED (Ire) 5-11-8 (5*) Mr G J Harford, ...(25 to 1) 27
Dist: ¾l, 1l, hd, 6l. 4m 7.70s. (27 Ran).
(Stonewall Racing Syndicate), M J P O'Brien

FAKENHAM (soft)
Monday April 4th
Going Correction: PLUS 1.35 sec. per fur.

3328 Raynham Selling Handicap Hurdle (4-y-o and up) £3,111 2m 110yds... (2:30)

3089* PINECONE PETER [91] (v) 7-11-8 M Brennan, *cl up, led aftr 3 out, clr nxt, rdn out*...........(2 to 1 fav op 5 to 2) 1
3089 RUTH'S GAMBLE [78] 6-10-9 J Callaghan, *hld up, effrt to chase wnr appr 2 out, drvn and no imprsn*. ....(9 to 2 op 4 to 1 tchd 5 to 1) 2
3153² CONVOY [90] (bl) 4-11-7 S Smith Eccles, *chsd ldrs, effrt 3 out, sn rdn, little response*..........(9 to 2 op 3 to 1) 3
3092⁴ SPANISH WHISPER [80] 7-10-4 (7*) W J Walsh, *prmnt till rdn and swshd tail 3 out, not run on aftr*. .... (10 to 1 op 8 to 1 tchd 12 to 1) 4
3048⁴ APPLIANCEOFSCIENCE [93] 7-11-3 (7*) Pat Thompson, *settled rear, effrt appr 3 out, sn rdn and btn*. ....(12 to 1 op 10 to 1 tchd 16 to 1) 5
2960⁵ BOZO BAILEY [74] (v) 4-10-5 R J Beggan, *prmnt to 4th, not run on frm nxt*..........................(8 to 1 op 5 to 1) 6
3153 FATHER'S JOY [72] 4-10-3³ M Stevens, *pulling and hld up in rear, lost tch 3 out, tld off*..... (33 to 1 op 20 to 1) 7
1214⁵ SEA BREAKER (Ire) [92] (bl) 6-11-2 (7*) P Murphy, *hld up, wnt prmnt 4th, lost pl appr nxt, not keen, tld off and pld up last*.............................(14 to 1 op 8 to 1) pu
3048³ EXPLORATION (USA) [83] 7-11-0 A S Smith, *led till aftr 3 out, wknd rpdly, tld off and pld up last*. .... (6 to 1 op 5 to 1 tchd 13 to 2) pu
Dist: 7l, 5l, 3l, ¾l, 20l, 2l. 4m 20.30s. a 30.30s (9 Ran).
SR: 14/-/1/-/-/-/
(Mrs B A Burgass), O Brennan

3329 Queen's Cup, An Eastern Counties Hunters' Chase (5-y-o and up) £2,595 3m.............................(3:05)

3195* CALABRESE (bl) 9-11-5 (7*) Major M Watson, *led second, clr 3 out, easily*............. (7 to 4 on tchd 6 to 4 on) 1
AS YOU WERE (bl) 12-11-5 (7*) Miss Z Turner, *trkd ldrs, wnt second 4 out, drvn and no imprsn frm 2 out*. ....(8 to 1 tchd 10 to 1) 2
CHERRY CHAP 9-11-5 (7*) Miss L Hollis, *hld up and beh, last pl till styd on frm 3 out, rdn to go 3rd nr finish*. .... (33 to 1 op 16 to 1) 3
TARA BOY 9-11-5 (7*) Mr J Ferguson, *mstks, beh frm 6th, no ch from 13th*.................. (20 to 1 op 16 to 1) 4
3093⁵ SPECULATION 12-11-1 (7*) Mr C Ward, *dsptd second pl till wknd 3 out*........................ (33 to 1 op 25 to 1) 5
FLASHY BUCK 10-11-6¹ (7*) Mr S Stearn, *hld up in rear, 7th whn f tenth*.................... (8 to 1 op 12 to 1) f

LAD LANE 10-11-5 (7") Mr M Gingell, *led to second, dsptd second pl till 4 out, sn btn, very tired whn f last.*
.... (50 to 1 op 33 to 1) f
SKYGRANGE 13-11-7 (5") Mr P Harding-Jones, *in trch till rdn and wknd 12th, tailing off whn jmpd very slwly nxt, sn pld up*..........(4 to 1 op 7 to 2 tchd 9 to 2) pu
SAINT BENE'T (Ire) 6-11-5 (7") Mr M Jennings, *struggling frm hfwy, tld off and pld up 15th.*
.... (25 to 1 op 16 to 1 tchd 33 to 1) pu
Dist: 8l, 20l, 1l, 2l. 6m 44.50s. a 52.50s (9 Ran).

(Major M Watson), N J Henderson

3330 Event Caterers Handicap Hurdle (0-100 4-y-o and up) £3,647 2m 5f (3:40)

3142² HUSO [96] 6-11-11 J Callaghan, *midfield and gng wl, chlgd 3 out, dsptd ld aftr, finishing very slwly but ran on und pres flt...* (5 to 2 jt-fav op 11 to 4 tchd 3 to 1) 1
3147⁴ COBB GATE [75] (bl) 6-10-4 M Stevens, *hld up, gd hdwy to join ldr 3 out, dsptd ld aftr till very tired and btn fnl strd....................* (7 to 1 op 5 to 1) 2
2766 BADASTAN (Ire) [80] 5-10-9 M Brennan, *reminders 3rd, chsd ldrs till drpd to rear 3 out, rallied appr last, fnshd wl, too much to do...................*(7 to 1 op 5 to 1) 3
2957* BITRAN [76] 4-10-5 A S Smith, *led till 3 out, sn lost pl und pres...........................*(5 to 2 jt-fav tchd 9 to 4) 4
3014⁵ STRAIGHT LACED (USA) [93] (bl) 7-11-8 Leesa Long, *chsd ldrs to 3 out, sn outpcd.....................* (12 to 1) 5
2708⁸ EMALLEN (Ire) [71] 6-9-7 (7") Pat Thompson, *drvn alng 4 out, sn tld off.....................* (33 to 1 op 20 to 1) 6
2711* CHEAP METAL [74] (bl) 9-10-3³ R J Beggan, *al rear, tld off 3 out, pld up last..................*(7 to 1 op 12 to 1) pu
1772⁵ COXANN [77] 8-9-13 (7") E Tolhurst, *al rear, rdn and no response hfwy, tld off and pld up last.*
.... (16 to 1 op 10 to 1) pu
AQIQ [71] 7-9-7 (7") W J Walsh, *wth ldrs till wknd rpdly appr 3 out, sn tld off, pld up last.* (33 to 1 op 20 to 1) pu
2874 PYRRHIC DANCE [78] 4-10-7² S SMITH ECCLES, *wth ldr till wknd rpdly appr 3 out, not keen aftr, tld off and pld up last.....................*(16 to 1 op 20 to 1) pu
Dist: Sht-hd, 7l, 7l, 15l, 6l. 5m 32.00s. a 39.00s (10 Ran).

(G Cole), P C Haslam

3331 Robert Hoare Memorial Hunters' Chase (5-y-o and up) £2,507 2m 110yds.................. (4:15)

3155⁶ TRUST THE GYPSY 12-11-10 (7") Mr M Felton, *jmpd wl, hld up and cl up, led 3 out, hdd appr last, sn led ag'n r-in, drvn alng and fnshd tired.*
.... (5 to 4 fav op 5 to 4 on tchd 11 to 8) 1
3263⁸ DROMIN LEADER 9-11-6 (5") Mr P Harding-Jones, *trkd ldrs, led 7th till 3 out, led and jmpd slwly last, sn hdd and not quicken und pres.*
.... (2 to 1 op 9 to 4 tchd 5 to 2) 2
EXPRESS FRED 6-11-4 (7") Mr M Gingell, *jmpd slwly in last pl, al wl beh, wnt remote 3rd at last.*
.... (3 to 1 op 6 to 1) 3
3093 PRINCE ENGELBERT 9-11-4 (7") Mr C Ward, *made most to 7th, wknd nxt, jmpd slwly 4 out, tld off......* (50 to 1) 4
BERKANA RUN 9-11-4 (7") Mr S Sporborg, *cl up till lost tch 8th, distant 3rd whn blun and uns rdr last.*
.... (9 to 1 op 6 to 1 tchd 10 to 1) ur
Dist: 2½l, 20l, 15l. 4m 27.60s. a 30.60s (5 Ran).
SR: 20/11/

(Mrs B Whettam), J W Dufosee

3332 Betty And Herbert Cassell Memorial Handicap Chase (0-100 5-y-o and up) £4,201 2m 5f 110yds........... (4:50)

3118⁴ RUSSINSKY [82] 7-10-11 R J Beggan, *hld up and beh, hmpd 9th, steady prog 3 out, led aftr nxt, clr whn hit last........................*(7 to 2) 1
2668⁸ SILENT CHANT [71] (v) 10-10-0 Gee Armytage, *gd hdwy to join ldrs 8th, led 3 out, hdd aftr nxt, rdn and btn whn mstk and rdr lost irons last........*(33 to 1 op 25 to 1) 2
3045⁵ EBONY SWELL [97] 13-11-7 (5") P Midgley, *prmnt, und pres 5 out, ev ch nxt, sn wknd.*
.... (16 to 1 op 10 to 1 tchd 20 to 1) 3
2895 MOUNTEBOR [89] 10-11-4 J Callaghan, *made most til hdd and jmpd slwly 3 out, wknd rpdly...*(7 to 2 op 4 to 1) 4
3152⁶ MASTER COMEDY [79] (bl) 10-10-8 M Stevens, *mstks, sn beh, lost tch 8th.......*(14 to 1 op 10 to 1 tchd 20 to 1) 5
2777 ON YOUR WAY [71] 12-10-0 P Harley, *midfield til blun badly and uns rdr 9th......................*(25 to 1) ur
3090² SPARTAN RAFT [73] 13-9-10¹ (7") P Murphy, *hit second, dsptd ld to 5th, lost tch 8th, tld off and pld up 4 out.
.... (16 to 1 op 14 to 1) pu
2437 BARKISLAND [94] 10-11-9 M Brennan, *jmpd hesitantly in last pl, brief effrt 4 out, no ch whn blun badly 2 out, sn pulled up..................* (4 to 1 op 7 to 2) pu
3194² RAMSTAR [95] 6-11-10 S Smith Eccles, *drpd to rear and reminders 11th, tld off and pld up 4 out.*
.... (7 to 4 fav op 6 to 4 tchd 2 to 1) pu
Dist: 10l, 2½l, 10l, 3l. 5m 52.50s. a 40.50s (9 Ran).

(Mrs E A Clark), G C Bravery

3333 St John Ambulance Novices' Handicap Hurdle (4-y-o and up) £2,570 2m 110yds...................... (5:25)

3094* WORDY'S WONDER [84] 6-11-1 (3") R Farrant, *trkd ldrs, rdn 4th, led 3 out, clr hwr, ran on gmely......*(5 to 2 jt-fav tchd 3 to 1) 1
2735* THE CHANGELING (Ire) [94] 5-12-0 R J Beggan, *not fluent, hld up, prog 3 out, chsd wnr und pres frm nxt, btn whn mstk last.............*(11 to 4 op 3 to 1 tchd 7 to 2) 2
3002² BIGWHEEL BILL (Ire) [75] (bl) 5-10-9 S Smith Eccles, *prmnt, rdn alng aftr 4th, one pace and btn 2 out....*(5 to 2 jt-fav op 7 to 2) 3
2763 TEJANO GOLD (USA) [67] 4-10-11 J Callaghan, *chsd ldrs, wnt second 3 out, wknd and pres nxt.*
.... (33 to 1 op 20 to 1) 4
2714⁴ MISS PARKES [66] 5-10-0 Leesa Long, *led till hdd and wknd rpdly 3 out..................*(33 to 1 op 25 to 1) 5
3002* WAMDHA (Ire) [82] 4-11-2 A S Smith, *hld up, mstk 4th, nvr on terms aftr.....................*(5 to 1 op 4 to 1) 6
3125⁵ PIMSBOY [82] (v) 7-11-0 (5") P Midgley, *hld up, effrt 4th, rdn and btn appr 2 out, pld up last.* (14 to 1 op 8 to 1) pu
2645⁴ HIGHLAND FLAME [69] 5-10-3 Gee Armytage, *prmnt, wknd quickly 3 out, tld off and pld up last.*
.... (9 to 1 op 7 to 1 tchd 10 to 1) pu
Dist: 8l, 6l, 1½l, 12l, 20l. 4m 19.40s. a 29.40s (8 Ran).
SR: 19/21/-/-/-/

(L Wordingham), L Wordingham

HEREFORD (soft)
Monday April 4th
Going Correction: PLUS 0.45 sec. per fur.

3334 Ross-on-Wye Novices' Hurdle (Div I) (4-y-o and up) £1,896 2m 1f..... (2:30)

3209³ BROWNED OFF 5-11-2 D Bridgwater, *wtd wth, prog frm hfwy, rdn to ld 2 out, ran on wl und pres.*
.... (13 to 8 fav op 6 to 4 tchd 7 to 4) 1
3005³ TOO SHARP 6-10-11 R Marley, *second till led 6th, hdd 2 out, sn rdn, kpt on same pace.........*(7 to 2 op 3 to 1) 2
2525⁵ MERLINS WISH (USA) 5-11-8 J Lower, *hld up, hdwy 6th, no further prog frm 3 out..........* (3 to 1 tchd 7 to 2) 3
3209⁷ KELLY'S DARLING 8-11-1 (7") P McLoughlin, *took str hold, mid-div, no prog frm 6th......*(10 to 1 tchd 12 to 1) 4
1053⁶ FOURTH IN LINE (Ire) 6-11-2 C Maude, *beh frm hfwy, no ch whn hit 3 out...................* (10 to 1 op 5 to 1) 5
FIVE STARS (v) 7-10-11 N Mann, *led to 6th, sn lost pl, tld off............................*(20 to 1 op 14 to 1) 6
FOND KISS 9-10-6 (7") J Bond, *chsd ldrs till lost pl quickly appr 6th, tld off.........*(16 to 1 op 12 to 1) 7
PINK SUNSET (Ire) 6-11-2 J R Kavanagh, *al in rear, tld off.*
.... (50 to 1 op 33 to 1) 8
WETANDRY 6-11-2 M Bosley, *chsd ldrs to hfwy, tld off.*
.... (50 to 1 op 33 to 1) 9
GIRTON BELLE 4-10-5 N Williamson, *in rear, bad blund 5th, sn tld off......................*(50 to 1 op 25 to 1) 10
3209 DABALARK 5-11-2 A O'Hagan, *in rear, tld off frm 4th, pld up bef 3 out...................*(50 to 1 op 33 to 1) pu
Dist: 4l, 12l, 8l, 3l, dist. 3m 59.10s. a 13.10s (11 Ran).
SR: 34/25/24/16/7/-/

(Mrs Lorna Berryman), N A Twiston-Davies

3335 James Daly Hunters' Chase (5-y-o and up) £1,966 2m 3f.............. (3:05)

RAMPALLION 11-12-0 (7") Mr S Blackwell, *made all, drw clr frm 11th, mstk last, unchlgd......*(5 to 1 op 4 to 1) 1
HENRYK 10-11-3 (7") Mr R Johnson, *chsd wnr frm 5th, no imprsn whn mstk 2 out.*
.... (4 to 1 fav op 7 to 2 tchd 9 to 2) 2
CONNEMARA DAWN 10-11-7 (7") Dr P Pritchard, *pressed ldrs, hit 7th, outpcd appr 3 out, styd on frm nxt.*
.... (6 to 1 op 7 to 2) 3
BUSTED ROCK 9-11-3 (7") Mr S Shinton, *wl plcd till wknd aftr 11th........*(14 to 1 op 12 to 1 tchd 16 to 1) 4
SHARINSKI 7-11-7 (7") Mr J Rudge, *al beh, tld off.*
.... (13 to 2 op 6 to 1 tchd 8 to 1) 5
CWM GWAUN 10-11-7 (7") Mr M Jackson, *al in rear, tld off...........................*(25 to 1 op 20 to 1) 6
3263⁹ CURAHEEN BOY (bl) 14-12-3 (7") Miss J Butler, *sluggish strt, beh whn blun and uns rdr 3rd.*
.... (25 to 1 op 20 to 1) ur
2885 PARADISE BEACH 9-11-9 (5") Mr P Macewan, *beh frm hfwy, tld off whn pld up bef 3 out............*(33 to 1) pu
KISSANE 13-11-8¹ (7") Mr J Wintle, *chsd wnr till hit 5th, reminders 8th, sn struggling, tld off whn pld up bef last..........................*(13 to 2 op 5 to 1) pu
ABBEYDORE 12-11-7 (7") S Joynes, *al in rear, tld off whn pld up bef 9th......................*(33 to 1) pu
3212⁷ LOR MOSS 14-11-7 (7") Mr C Hancock, *beh frm hfwy, tld off whn pld up bef 2 out........*(5 to 1 op 8 to 1) pu
CORRIANNE 7-10-12 (7") Mrs D Smith, *chsd ldrs to hfwy, tld off whn pld up bef 3 out.....*(25 to 1 op 20 to 1) pu
KERRY HILL 8-11-3 (7") Mr M Wilding, *in rear whn mstk 6th, tld off whn pld up bef 9th....*(33 to 1 op 20 to 1) pu

IN THE WATER 7-11-3 (7*) Mr G Brown, *not jump wl, sn tld off, pld up bef 7th*................(25 to 1 op 20 to 1) pu
Dist: 15l, 4l, 15l, 15l, 3½l. 4m 48.50s. a 18.50s (14 Ran).
SR: 8/-/-/-/-/-/ (A P Gent), P G Warner

3336 Newton Williams Handicap Chase (0-100 5-y-o and up) £3,048 3m 1f 110yds........................ (3:40)

2305 NEARCO BAY (NZ) [100] 10-12-0 J R Kavanagh, *trkd ldrs, improved tenth, led 3 out, drvn out.* (10 to 1 op 7 to 1) 1
3146[3] MISS FERN [91] 9-10-12 (7*) P Carey, *sn pressing ldr, led 11th to 3 out, kpt on same pace frm nxt.* ....(2 to 1 fav op 7 to 2) 2
3006[5] SANDAIG [91] (bl) 8-11-5 N Williamson, *wtd wth, prog 13th, rdn appr 3 out, ev ch nxt, sn btn.*....(7 to 2 op 4 to 1) 3
2886 IMPECCABLE TIMING [77] 11-10-5 V Slattery, *improved frm rear hfwy, rdn and outpcd 15th.* ....(8 to 1 op 12 to 1) 4
3205 TROUT ANGLER [95] 13-11-9 G Upton, *wl plcd till wknd aftr 16th*.........................(20 to 1 op 16 to 1) 5
1838[6] JIMSTER [91] 12-10-12 (7*) Mr C Hancock, *hld up, mstk second, prog hfwy, wkng whn mistake 14th.* ....(9 to 2 op 4 to 1) 6
2656 NOUGAT RUSSE [97] 13-11-11 D Bridgwater, *led aftr 1st, hdd 11th, sn drvn alng, wkng whn mstk 14th, tld off.* ....(8 to 1 op 7 to 1) 7
2978[4] VICAR OF BRAY [72] 7-10-0 N Mann, *al in rear, tld off frm 12th*................(16 to 1 op 20 to 1 tchd 33 to 1) 8
2733[5] LEAGAUNE [80] 12-10-8 R Marley, *prmnt till rdn and drpd rear 11th, sn tld off*.................(8 to 1 op 7 to 1) 9
2088 MINT-MASTER [75] 9-9-10 (7*) P McLoughlin, *led till aftr 1st, sn toiling, tld off frm 12th*....(33 to 1 op 20 to 1) 10
3175[6] SKETCHER (NZ) [84] 11-10-5 (7*) Mr G Shenkin, *hld up in rear, improved stdly frm 6th, wknd appr 3 out, 4th and no ch whn blun and uns rdr last.* (12 to 1 op 10 to 1) ur
Dist: 2½l, 5l, 13l, 1½l, 15l. 6m 29.60s. a 17.60s (11 Ran).
SR: 39/27/22/-/11/-/ (Queen Elizabeth), N J Henderson

3337 Holiday Selling Hurdle (4 - 7-y-o) £1,500 3¼m................... (4:15)

3111[9] ON THE SAUCE (bl) 7-11-12 J Lower, *made most, reminders appr 6th, drw clr betw last 2, idled r-in, all out*...............................(6 to 4 fav op 5 to 4) 1
3166[6] GORT 6-11-12 J R Kavanagh, *hld up, prog appr 5th, reminders aftr nxt, dsptd ld till outpcd betw last 2, rallied r-in*............(13 to 8 op 6 to 4 tchd 7 to 4) 2
2799[7] KEMMY DARLING 7-10-11 M Ahern, *al chasing ldrs, styd on same pace frm 3 out*...........(33 to 1 op 16 to 1) 3
3103[8] LOXLEY RANGE (Ire) 6-11-5 (7*) P McLoughlin, *beh, mstk second, hdwy appr 9th, wknd aftr 3 out.* ....(20 to 1 op 16 to 1) 4
3003[4] LITTLE BIG (bl) 7-11-1 (7*) N Collum, *dsptd ld to 8th, sn wknd, tld off whn pld up bef 3 out.* ....(9 to 2 op 3 to 1 tchd 5 to 1) pu
2768 SNICKERSNEE (bl) 6-11-2 S Burrough, *al beh, lost tch 8th, tld off whn pld up bef nxt*........(20 to 1 op 10 to 1) pu
2016[9] SECRET FORMULA 4-10-8 W Humphreys, *al in rear, tld off whn pld up bef 2 out.* ....(20 to 1 op 16 to 1 tchd 33 to 1) pu
1301 SIXTH IN LINE (Ire) 6-11-2 C Maude, *pld hrd early, lost tch hfwy, tld off whn pulled up bef 9th.* ....(50 to 1 op 20 to 1) pu
Dist: 1¼l, 5l, 12l. 6m 35.00s. a 35.00s (8 Ran).
(Goldsmith, Langham & Thompson Partners), M C Pipe

3338 Marlbrook Novices' Chase (5-y-o and up) £2,770 2m...................(4:50)

1508* MACEDONAS 6-10-10 (7*) M Berry, *mstk second, chsd ldr 4th, led appr 3 out, jst hld on.* (7 to 4 fav op 11 to 10) 1
3150[6] DONNA'S TOKEN 9-10-5 (7*) P McLoughlin, *prmnt till slpd badly and lost pl 3rd, hdwy 8th, rdn to go second aftr 3 out, str brst r-in, jst fld*..............(14 to 1 op 8 to 1) 2
2319 SPINNING STEEL 7-11-3 S Burrough, *trkd ldrs till wknd appr 3 out*..........(16 to 1 op 12 to 1 tchd 20 to 1) 3
3174[5] LAND OF THE FREE 5-10-5 V Slattery, *in rear, reminders bef 5th, no ch frm 8th*...............(10 to 1 op 7 to 1) 4
2822[4] QUENTIN DURWOOD (bl) 8-11-3 G Upton, *chsd ldr to 4th, wknd 3 out*..........................(7 to 1 op 7 to 2) 5
3004* FRANKUS 5-11-3 N Mann, *led, blun 3rd, hdd appr 3 out, third and btn whn f last.* (9 to 4 op 7 to 4 tchd 5 to 2) f
TOKANDA 10-11-3 J R Kavanagh, *al in rear, lost tch 8th, tld off whn pld up bef 3 out*......(20 to 1 op 10 to 1) pu
3175[3] VILLA RECOS 9-11-3 D Bridgwater, *beh, drvn alng aftr 3rd, lost tch 8th, tld off whn pld up bef 3 out.* ....(11 to 2 op 8 to 1 tchd 5 to 1) pu
Dist: Sht-hd, 30l, 2½l, 1l. 4m 3.50s. a 14.50s (8 Ran).
SR: 16/11/-/-/-/ (Jim McCarthy), C P E Brooks

3339 Ross-on-Wye Novices' Hurdle (Div II) (4-y-o and up) £1,896 2m 1f..... (5:25)

3008[2] BLAST FREEZE (Ire) 5-10-11 J R Kavanagh, *al gng easily, led 6th, drw clr frm 3 out, mstk last, imprsv.* ....(5 to 4 on tchd Evens) 1
3145[4] PULMICORT 4-10-10 D Gallagher, *al chasing ldr, chlgd 6th, styd on same pace frm 3 out*...(20 to 1 op 14 to 1) 2
3209[8] WILKINS (bl) 5-11-2 R Marley, *led to 6th, hrd drvn and styd on same pace frm 3 out.* ....(11 to 4 op 5 to 2 tchd 3 to 1) 3
1794[5] ICE MAGIC 7-10-9 (7*) P McLoughlin, *hld up, improved 4th, wknd appr 3 out*...........(14 to 1 tchd 16 to 1) 4
TRUE MARCH 6-10-9 (7*) S Drake, *pld hrd, jmpd slwly and mstk second, sn prmnt, lost pl hfwy, tld off.* ....(33 to 1 op 16 to 1) 5
3055[4] COURTING NEWMARKET 6-11-2 S Burrough, *shrtlvd effrt 5th, tld off*..........................(10 to 1 op 8 to 1) 6
3202 HEAD OF DEFENCE 9-11-2 Mr S Shinton, *struggling frm hfwy, tld off*...............(100 to 1 op 20 to 1) 7
POETS COVE 6-11-2 D Bridgwater, *toiling frm 5th, tld off.* ....(8 to 1 op 5 to 1 tchd 10 to 1) 8
MENEFORT 6-11-2 Mr M Jackson, *in rear whn f 3rd.* ....(100 to 1 op 20 to 1) f
1023 NORDIC FLIGHT 6-11-2 V Slattery, *al in rear, tld off whn pld up bef 2 out*..................(50 to 1 op 20 to 1) pu
Dist: 15l, 2½l, 9l, dist, 14l. 4m 3.40s. a 17.40s (10 Ran).
(Pioneer Heat-Treatment), N J Henderson

3340 Peterstow Novices' Handicap Hurdle (0-100 4-y-o and up) £2,386 2m 3f 110yds........................ (5:55)

2796[4] BRIDEPARK ROSE (Ire) [75] 6-10-3 M Ahern, *settled mid-div, smooth prog to ld 8th, sn clr, easily.* ....(10 to 1 op 14 to 1) 1
3020[2] LUCKY BLUE [87] 7-11-1 C Maude, *al handily plcd, rdn to go second 3 out, no ch wth wnr*......(4 to 1 op 5 to 1) 2
MARINERS LOVE [76] 8-10-4[4] M Bosley, *hdwy frm rear 8th, no further prog from 3 out*....(33 to 1 op 25 to 1) 3
2088[7] PROJECT'S MATE [82] 7-10-3 (7*) P McLoughlin, *al chasing ldrs, reminders aftr 6th, mstk 8th, sn btn.* ....(11 to 2 op 4 to 1 tchd 6 to 1) 4
2522[5] DANGER BABY [73] 4-9-8 (7*) P Carey, *led till appr 3rd, btn 3 out*..............................(10 to 1 op 6 to 1) 5
3230 GLADYS EMMANUEL [78] (bl) 7-10-6 S Burrough, *chsd ldg grp till wknd 3 out*...............(25 to 1 op 16 to 1) 6
2768[7] THE OVERTRUMPER [72] 7-10-0 Lorna Vincent, *al in rear.* ....(12 to 1 op 8 to 1) 7
3215[3] KILLURA (Ire) [107] 6-12-7 N Williamson, *wl plcd, wnt second 5th till wknd 3 out, eased whn btn frm nxt.* ....(5 to 1 op 4 to 1) 8
2432 CHARLAFRIVOLA [74] 6-10-2[2] M Sharratt, *al trailing, tld off*.................................(33 to 1 op 16 to 1) 9
2671 RAGTIME BOY [78] 6-10-6 J R Kavanagh, *al in rear, tld off frm 7th*...........................(25 to 1 op 16 to 1) 10
3144[9] MAHONG [72] 6-10-0 V Slattery, *trkd ldrs, reminders aftr 6th, sn struggling, tld off whn pld bef 2 out.* ....(20 to 1 op 16 to 1) pu
3202[3] BENTICO [90] 5-11-4 D Bridgwater, *not jump wl, led appr 3rd till 8th, lost pl quickly, tld off whn pld up bef last.* ....(9 to 4 fav op 3 to 1) pu
3108[5] HONEY GUIDE [77] 4-10-5[2] G Upton, *al beh, tld off whn pld up bef 3 out*...................(14 to 1 op 8 to 1) pu
Dist: 8l, 8l, 6l, 1l, 6l, 6l, 1l, 15l. 4m 46.40s. a 25.40s (13 Ran).
(Tom Segrue), M P Muggeridge

MARKET RASEN (soft)
Monday April 4th
Going Correction: PLUS 1.60 sec. per fur. (races 1,3,6), PLUS 0.95 (2,4,5,7)

3341 Ancomb Novices' Chase (5-y-o and up) £2,860 2½m................(2:15)

2784 BRACKENFIELD 8-12-7 P Niven, *jmpd wl, dsptd ld till led appr 3 out, ran on well.* ....(6 to 5 on op 13 to 8 on tchd 5 to 4 on) 1
HIGHLAND RALLY (USA) 7-11-7 L Wyer, *dsptd ld till hdd 3 out, one pace fnl 2*..........................(25 to 1) 2
3090 LE BUCHERON 8-11-7 J Ryan, *hld up, hdwy frm 12th, not rch ldrs*..........................(7 to 2 op 4 to 1) 3
3178[3] GRAZEMBER 7-11-7 C Hawkins, *chsd ldrs frm 9th, one pace from 3 out*.....................(7 to 1 op 6 to 1) 4
3000[3] MASTER'S CROWN (USA) 6-11-7 W Worthington, *led to second, prmnt till wknd hfwy, sn tld off.* ....(10 to 1 op 14 to 1) 5
2998[4] TRENTSIDE MIST 6-11-7 M Ranger, *al prmnt, 3rd and btn whn f last*..............................(20 to 1) f
3033[4] GOLDEN BANKER (Ire) 6-11-0 (7*) D Ryan, *in tch, mstks, beh whn blun and uns rdr 9th*.....(33 to 1 op 50 to 1) ur
Dist: 12l, 10l, 13l, dist. 5m 30.40s. a 38.40s (7 Ran).
SR: 43/17/7/-/ (Guy Faber), Mrs M Reveley

3342 Rase Selling Handicap Hurdle (4,5,6-y-o) £1,938 2m 1f 110yds........(2:45)

3139[2] CHARLYCIA [78] (v) 6-10-13 (7*) M Clarke, *led 1st, led ag'n appr 4th, clr whn hit 2 out, unchlgd*..........(4 to 1) 1

2957² ERLEMO [73] (v) 5-11-1 Diane Clay, *chsd ldrs, wth wnr 3 out, sn rdn and unbl to quicken.*
.................................(7 to 2 fav tchd 4 to 1) 2

3089³ JOLI'S GREAT [81] (bl) 6-11-9 J Ryan, *hld up, ran on frm 2 out, not rch ldrs.*....................(13 to 2) 3

3285³ INAN (USA) [82] 5-11-3 (7*) F Leahy, *hld up, hdwy frm 3 out, ran on one pace from nxt.*........(5 to 1 op 4 to 1) 4

3094 POLISH RIDER (USA) [78] 6-10-13 (7*) C Huggan, *prmnt till wknd appr 2 out.*....................(12 to 1 op 10 to 1) 5

2797 MINI FETE (Fr) [68] 5-10-10 P Niven, *beh frm 4th.*
.................................(9 to 1 op 8 to 1 tchd 10 to 1) 6

3029⁷ MILLIE (USA) [58] (bl) 6-10-0 M Robinson, *led 1st, hdd appr 4th, wknd rpdly.*....................(33 to 1 op 25 to 1) 7+

2059⁴ NEGD (USA) [65] (bl) 4-10-7 L Wyer, *wth ldrs to 4th, wknd quickly.*....................(5 to 1 op 4 to 1) 7+

2957⁶ ANNE CARTER [60] 5-10-2 M Ranger, *wth ldrs till wknd quickly 5th, tld off whn pld up bef 2 out.*
.................................(40 to 1 op 25 to 1 tchd 50 to 1) pu

Dist: 14l, 4l, 1l, 15l, 4l, ½l, dd-ht. 4m 25.20s. a 23.20s (9 Ran).
SR: 26/7/11/11/-/-/ (Mrs V Chilton), T J Carr

3343 West Lindsey Easter Cup Novices' Handicap Chase (5-y-o and up) £3,562 3m 1f.........................(3:20)

3224* NAWRIK (Ire) [76] 5-9-9 (5*) F Perratt, *led to 3rd, led 5th to 7th, led tlk clr 15th, drvn out.*..............(7 to 2) 1

3224⁷ TRAVEL BOUND [76] 9-9-7 (7*) F Leahy, *prmnt, lft poor second 14th, ev ch 2 out, wknd last.*
.................................(14 to 1 op 16 to 1) 2

3033² MILO [76] 8-10-0 C Hawkins, *hld up, mstk and lost pl 14th, nvr dngrs aftrwards.*..............(33 to 1) 3

3075⁵ OPAL'S TENSPOT [89] 7-10-13 P Niven, *chsd ldrs, pckd 13th, disputing ld whn f 15th.*....(6 to 1 tchd 13 to 2) f

3237* DEVONGALE [100] 8-11-10 L Wyer, *blun 6th, sn wl beh, hdwy 14th, cl 3rd whn f 15th.*
.................................(85 to 40 fav op 13 to 8 tchd 9 to 4) f

2952² COUNT SURVEYOR [84] 7-10-8 K Johnson, *led 7th to 9th, cl up whn f 14th.*..............(9 to 2 op 4 to 1) f

3238² JENNY'S GLEN [76] 7-9-11 (3*) D Meredith, *prmnt whn f tenth.*..............(20 to 1 op 33 to 1 tchd 50 to 1) f

2908² DARK OAK [76] 8-10-0 L O'Hara, *led 3rd, hdd whn blun and uns rdr 5th.*......(9 to 1 op 10 to 1 tchd 8 to 1) ur

2579⁴ CANTGETOUT [76] 8-10-0 Mr A Pickering, *al in rear, bright dwn 14th.*....................(25 to 1) bd

3059 SHELTON ABBEY [81] 8-10-0 (5*) J Supple, *blun badly second, sn pld up.*....................(14 to 1) pu

Dist: 15l, dist. 7m 2.60s. a 61.60s (10 Ran).
(Mrs J K Peutherer), L Lungo

3344 Roseland Group Handicap Hurdle (0-110 4-y-o and up) £3,252 2m 3f 110yds.........................(3:55)

2566² WAKE UP [93] 7-10-8 (7*) F Leahy, *hld up, hdwy frm 6th, effrt 2 out, quickened to ld flt.*
.................................(11 to 2 op 5 to 1 tchd 6 to 1) 1

1639² MY SWAN SONG [92] 9-10-11 (3*) S Wynne, *hdwy frm 6th, led 2 out, hit last, not reco'r.*
.................................(11 to 1 op 12 to 1 tchd 12 to 1) 2

3186⁵ INTEGRITY BOY [90] (bl) 7-10-12 O Pears, *wth ldr till wknd appr 3 out.*..............(13 to 2 op 6 to 1) 3

3107* IN TRUTH [88] 6-10-7 (3*) D Meredith, *hdwy frm 3 out, nvr trbld ldrs.*....................(5 to 1 op 4 to 1) 4

2256 FLASS VALE [85] (v) 6-10-7 C Hawkins, *led till hdd appr 2 out, sn btn.*..............(20 to 1 tchd 25 to 1) 5

3136⁵ SPROWSTON BOY [105] 11-11-13 W Worthington, *beh till some hdwy appr 3 out, nvr nr to chal.*.....(16 to 1) 6

2632⁵ BAHRAIN QUEEN (Ire) [85] 6-10-7 M Ranger, *some hdwy frm hfwy, nvr nr to chal.*........(12 to 1 op 14 to 1) 7

3186⁷ ELEGANT KING (Ire) [106] 5-12-0 T Jarvis, *chsd ldrs to hfwy, grad lost pl.*..............(12 to 1 op 10 to 1) 8

3206³ SCRABO VIEW (Ire) [78] (bl) 6-10-0 L O'Hara, *nvr dngrs.*
.................................(10 to 1) 9

3048⁹ THE CAN CAN MAN [78] 7-10-0 M Robinson, *beh whn pld up bef 8th.*....................(25 to 1) pu

MARA ASKARI [90] 6-10-12 B Dalton, *prmnt to 7th, sn lost pl, tld off whn pld up bef 2 out.*............(33 to 1) pu

23067 MYTHICAL STORM [91] 7-10-13 P Niven, *beh most of way, tld off whn pld up bef 3 out.*...........(10 to 1) pu

3107² CURTAIN FACTORY [86] 5-10-8 L Wyer, *nvr trbld ldrs, tld off whn pld up bef 2 out.*...(3 to 1 fav op 11 to 10) pu

Dist: 1l, 20l, 2½l, 3½l, 11l, hd, 10l, 20l. 4m 58.50s. a 25.50s (13 Ran).
SR: 17/15/-/-/-/-/ (Steve Hammond), R O'Leary

3345 Pro-Lec Electrical EBF 'National Hunt' Novices' Hurdle Qualifier (5,6,7-y-o) £2,617 2m 3f 110yds...........(4:30)

3230⁷ KYTTON CASTLE 7-11-2 (3*) D Meredith, *al prmnt, led 2 out, clr last, jst hld on.*.........(11 to 8 fav op 7 to 4) 1

2768³ ALI'S ALIBI 7-11-5 P Niven, *hld up, hdwy to chase ldrs 3rd, outpcd aftr 3 out, str run appr last, jst fld.* (5 to 1) 2

3191* NATIVE FIELD (Ire) 5-11-3 (7*) F Leahy, *trkd ldr, slight ld 6th till hdd and mstk 2 out, hit last, one paced.*
.................................(100 to 30 op 7 to 4 tchd 7 to 2) 3

2871² BANCHORY 5-11-0 L Wyer, *al prmnt, dsptd ld 2 out, wkng whn hit last.*....................(5 to 1) 4

3140⁹ HICKSONS CHOICE (Ire) 6-10-7 (7*) L O'Hara, *nvr dngrs.*
.................................(33 to 1 op 25 to 1) 5

3183⁴ RAYLEO (Ire) 5-10-11 (3*) S Wynne, *prmnt to 3rd, sn beh, tld off.*............(20 to 1 op 25 to 1) 6

2960⁹ THEYDON PRIDE 5-11-0 P Naughton, *prmnt frm 4th, wknd aftr 6th, tld off.*....................(50 to 1) 7

KAMADORA 7-11-0 C Hawkins, *sn beh, tld off whn pld up bef 7th.*....................(50 to 1) pu

2327 MANDY LOUISE 6-10-9 T Jarvis, *led to 6th, wknd quickly, tld off whn pld up bef 2 out.*...........(50 to 1) pu

Dist: Sht-hd, 14l, 8l, 5l. 5m 0.30s. a 27.30s (9 Ran).
SR: 3/3/-/-/-/-/ (Joint Partnership), R Allan

3346 'Easter Bunny' Handicap Chase (0-120 5-y-o and up) £3,484 2m 1f 110yds ....(5:00)

3116* SPOONHILL WOOD [90] (bl) 8-10-1 B Dalton, *trkd ldr, led 3 out, lft clr last.*..............(3 to 1 op 7 to 2) 1

2953³ DEEP DECISION [94] 8-10-5 K Johnson, *hld up, some hdwy frm 3 out, rdn out flt.*.........(7 to 2 op 4 to 1) 2

3312⁴ DR ROCKET [113] 9-11-7 (3*) D Meredith, *al in rear.*
.................................(7 to 1 op 6 to 1) 3

3239³ TERRIBLE GEL (Fr) [105] 9-11-2 P Niven, *led 3 to three out, rnwd chal and ev ch whn f last.*......(4 to 1 op 7 to 2) f

3060⁴ SILVER HAZE [89] 10-10-4 L O'Hara, *prmnt to hfwy, beh whn pld up bef 2 out.*....................(14 to 1) pu

2962* WHITWOOD [110] 9-11-7 C Hawkins, *led to 3rd, wknd quickly, pld up bef 8th.*.........(9 to 4 fav op 7 to 4) pu

Dist: 3½l, dist. 4m 51.60s. a 37.60s (6 Ran).
(R M Micklethwait), J Wharton

3347 EBF Stakes National Hunt Flat Race (4,5,6-y-o) £1,800 1m 5f 110yds. . (5:30)

3183² OUR MAIN MAN 4-10-7 (3*) S Wynne, *al prmnt, led 3 fs out, rdn out.*..............(4 to 1 op 5 to 1) 1

3603² STIR FRY 4-10-3 (7*) S Taylor, *al prmnt, ev ch 2 fs out, kpt on wl cl hme.*............(5 to 4 fav tchd 6 to 4) 2

ROBINS PRIDE (Ire) 4-10-3 (7*) F Leahy, *gd hdwy entering strt, ran on one pace fnl 2 fs.......*(6 to 1 op 5 to 1) 3

976 UNCLE BENJI (Ire) 5-10-9 (7*) Miss V Haigh, *hdwy fnl 4 fs, ran on one pace.*............(33 to 1 op 20 to 1) 4

2490⁹ TERRINGTON 4-10-3 (7*) J Driscoll, *hld up, hdwy 4 fs out, ran on one pace.*.........(10 to 1 op 8 to 1) 5

2332⁸ HIGHLAND HEIGHTS (Ire) 6-10-8 (3*) D Meredith, *prmnt o'r 8 fs, no hdwy fnl 2.*..............(14 to 1 op 7 to 1) 6

3079 PARSON'S LODGE (Ire) 6-10-6 (5*) F Perratt, *led aftr 3 fs, hdd a nr pace fnl three furlongs.*
.................................(16 to 1 op 14 to 1) 7

ASK FOR BARNEY (Ire) 5-10-11 (5*) J Supple, *nvr better than middle div.*....................(20 to 1) 8

HOLIDAY HOME 6-10-9 (7*) B Grattan, *prmnt whn wnt wide aftr 3 fs, wknd 4 furlongs out.* (20 to 1 op 16 to 1) 9

KILNAMARTYRA GIRL 4-10-0 (5*) E Husband, *hld up, hdwy 5 fs out, in tch 3 out, wknd quickly o'r one out.*
.................................(12 to 1 tchd 14 to 1) 10

3169 SABBAQ (USA) 4-10-10 Mr B Crawford, *nvr trbld ldrs.*
.................................(10 to 1 tchd 12 to 1) 11

2877 CONNAUGHT'S SECRET 6-10-9 (7*) C Huggan, *mid-div till wknd o'r 4 fs out.*....................(20 to 1) 12

3079⁷ SKI PATH 5-10-4 (7*) P Naughton, *led aftr 7 fs, hdd and wknd 3 furlongs out.*....................(25 to 1) 13

2963 CHEEKY CHIMP 4-10-5 Mr A Pickering, *slight ld lead 3 fs, sn wknd, beh frm hfwy.*..........(33 to 1 op 25 to 1) 14

2963 BRIGG FOLLY 4-9-12 (7*) Annette Billany, *al in rear, tld off.*....................(33 to 1) 15

OYSTER SNATCHER (Ire) 5-10-9 (7*) K Davies, *al in rear, tld off.*..............(16 to 1 op 14 to 1) 16

Dist: Nk, 8l, 9l, nk, 2½l, ¾l, nk, 4l, hd, 10l. 3m 25.30s. (16 Ran).
(R M Whitaker), R M Whitaker

NEWTON ABBOT (heavy)
Monday April 4th
Going Correction: PLUS 2.25 sec. per fur. (races 1,3,-5,6), PLUS 2.00 (2,4)

3348 Independent Cellars Selling Handicap Hurdle (4 - 7-y-o) £1,937 2m 1f. . (2:15)

2912² SOVEREIGN NICHE (Ire) [83] (v) 6-10-12 R Dunwoody, *made all, clr 3 out, eased r-in.*
.................................(6 to 4 fav op 2 to 1 tchd 5 to 2) 1

TAKE TWO [95] 6-11-10 A Maguire, *al prmnt, chsd wnr frm 5th, no imprsn from 2 out.*
.................................(9 to 4 tchd 5 to 2 and 2 to 1) 2

3131⁸ DJEBEL PRINCE [95] 7-11-10 J Railton, *hld up in rear, effrt to cl appr 3 out, sn no imprsn...*(6 to 1 op 9 to 1) 3

3254⁵ MILDRED SOPHIA [71] 7-9-7 (7*) Miss S Mitchell, *hld up, cld aftr 4th, no imprsn frm nxt...*(6 to 1 op 4 to 1) 4

2018⁶ ROCKY BAY [73] 5-9-9 (7*) Mr J L Llewellyn, *cl up, mstk 5th, sn pushed alng and wknd, pld up bef last.*
.................................(10 to 1 op 6 to 1 tchd 12 to 1) pu

2523 SANDRO [78] (bl) 5-10-2 (5*) D Salter, *trkd ldrs whn blun badly 4th, wknd nxt, tld off when pld up bef 2 out.*
.... (10 to 1 op 5 to 1)   pu
1468[6] PIONEER PETE [77] 7-10-6[6] J Frost, *prmnt till lost pl aftr 4th, tld off whn pld up bef 2 out...* (25 to 1 op 16 to 1)   pu
Dist: 15l, 12l, 10l. 4m 35.80s. a 45.80s (7 Ran).
SR: 9/6/-/-/   (Avalon Surfacing Ltd), M C Pipe

3349 Happy Shopper Handicap Chase
(0-130 5-y-o and up) £3,081 2m 5f (2:50)

2602[2] KALANSKI [115] 8-11-10 J Railton, *sn trkd ldr, pushed alng 3 out, chlgd nxt, led appr last, all out.*
.... (10 to 10 op 11 to 8 on tchd 6 to 5)   1
3172 JAILBREAKER [109] 7-11-4 R Dunwoody, *led, mstks 3rd and 4th, hdd appr last, rallied und pres.*
.... (5 to 4 on tchd Evens)   2
3203[3] CHANCERY BUCK [97] 11-10-6[6] J Frost, *in tch till outpcd frm 9th, tld off.........* (9 to 1 op 7 to 1 tchd 12 to 1)   3
Dist: Nk, dist. 5m 47.80s. a 47.80s (3 Ran).
SR: 38/31/-/   (I Kerman), C R Egerton

3350 Courage Handicap Hurdle (0-135 4-y-o
and up) £2,608 2¾m............ (3:25)

1890[4] BALLY CLOVER [121] 7-11-0 M A FitzGerald, *trkd ldr, led aftr 6th, hdd nxt, led ag'n after 3 out, hrd rdn, all out.*
.... (100 to 30 op 5 to 2)   1
3038 OLYMPIAN [135] (bl) 7-12-0 R Dunwoody, *led till hdd and reminders aftr 6th, ev ch whn hit 2 out, hrd rdn and every chance r-in, no extr nr finish.*
.... (5 to 4 on op 6 to 4 on tchd 11 to 10 on)   2
3214[4] FOX CHAPEL [113] 7-9-13 (7*) N Juckes, *in cl tch frm 4th, led 7th till aftr 3 out, wknd appr nxt.*
.... (3 to 1 tchd 7 to 2)   3
2862[6] LASTING MEMORY [113] 8-10-6[6] J Frost, *al last, tld off frm 7th................* (16 to 1 op 14 to 1 tchd 20 to 1)   4
Dist: ¾l, 25l, dist. 6m 0.90s. a 61.90s (4 Ran).
                                              (Mrs E Roberts), N J Henderson

3351 Taunton Cider Novices' Chase (5-y-o
and up) £2,670 3¼m 110yds.... (4:00)

3104* SALLY'S GEM 9-11-9 A Maguire, *led 1st, wth ldr, reminders aftr 13th, led 16th, sn clr, mstk 2 out, ran on.*
.... (6 to 5 op Evens tchd 5 to 4)   1
3175* KIWI VELOCITY (NZ) 7-11-4 R Dunwoody, *led second, mstk 8th, jmpd slwly and hdd 16th, no ch whn pckd last, virtually pld up r-in.*
.... (Evens fav op 5 to 4 tchd 11 to 10)   2
1273 SENEGALAIS (Fr) 10-11-3 J Frost, *al beh, lost tch frm 13th, tld off................................* (14 to 1 op 10 to 1)   3
1080[4] HALF A MO 9-10-12 J Railton, *chsd ldg pair to tenth, tld off whn pld up bef 15th............* (14 to 1 op 10 to 1)   pu
Dist: 25l, dist. 7m 35.10s. a 75.10s (4 Ran).
                                                    (Brian Gatensbury), J White

3352 Lyons Tetley Conditional Jockeys'
Novices' Handicap Hurdle (0-100 4-y-o
and up) £1,909 2¾m............ (4:35)

3184[2] CRAZY DAISY [66] 7-9-9 (7*) T Murphy, *al hndy, led aftr 6th, clr appr 2 out, styd on wl.*
.... (7 to 4 op 5 to 4 tchd 2 to 1)   1
3109[2] MOBILE MESSENGER (NZ) [91] 6-11-8 (5*) N Juckes, *in cl tch, reminders aftr 6th, ev ch 3 out, sn hrd rdn, btn appr nxt............* (13 to 8 fav op Evens tchd 7 to 4)   2
3108[4] MISS SOUTER [70] 5-10-6 S Fox, *beh 4th, tld off frm 6th.*
.... (4 to 1 op 7 to 1 tchd 8 to 1)   3
MISHY'S STAR [64] (bl) 12-10-0 D Salter, *led second till hdd aftr 6th, sn wknd, poor 3rd whn refused last.*
.... (20 to 1 tchd 33 to 1)   ref
2902[7] SCARED STIFF [64] (bl) 6-10-0 C Burnett-Wells, *led 1st, drpd rear 4th, tld off frm 6th, pld up bef 2 out.*
.... (12 to 1 op 10 to 1)   pu
Dist: 25l, dist. 6m 3.60s. a 64.60s (5 Ran).
                                              (Mrs Philomena Reich), W G M Turner

3353 Thurlestone Hotel Four Yrs Old Nov-
ices' Hurdle £1,891 2m 1f...... (5:10)

2821* COLLIER BAY 11-5 T Grantham, *jmpd wl, made all, clr frm 5th, unchlgd..................* (3 to 1 op 5 to 1 on)   1
3153[6] MY SISTER LUCY 11-0 M A FitzGerald, *hld up, chsd clr wnr frm 5th, sn no imprsn.*
.... (3 to 1 op 5 to 1 tchd 7 to 1)   2
STRIKE-A-POSE 10-0 (7*) Mr J L Llewellyn, *in cl tch till outpcd 5th, tld off.................* (10 to 1 op 7 to 1)   3
PRIMO PRINCE 10-12 J Frost, *took keen hold, in cl tch till wknd quickly aftr 4th, pld up bef nxt.*
.... (6 to 1 tchd 10 to 1 tchd 16 to 1)   pu
3176[3] FREE HANDOUT 10-7 J Railton, *in tch till wknd 5th, tld off whn pld up bef 2 out.*
.... (20 to 1 op 12 to 1 tchd 25 to 1)   pu
Dist: Dist, 15l. 4m 32.90s. a 42.90s (5 Ran).
                                                   (W E Sturt), J A B Old

---

WETHERBY (good)
Monday April 4th
Going Correction: PLUS 0.55 sec. per fur. (races 1,4,6), PLUS 0.90 (2,3,5)

3354 Wilstrop Novices' Hurdle Amateur
Riders (5-y-o and up) £2,320 2½m
110yds......................... (2:20)

3177[3] ARIADLER (Ire) 6-11-6 Mr J Greenall, *al prmnt, reminders 7th, moderate second whn lft in ld 2 out, kpt on.*
.... (9 to 4 op 7 to 4)   1
3133 SUPPOSIN 6-10-7 (7*) Mr W Halliday, *trkd ldrs till wknd appr 3 out...........................* (7 to 1 op 6 to 1)   2
3046[8] SPIRITUALIST 8-10-7 (7*) Mr L Donnelly, *rcd wide, pressed ldr frm 4th to 6th, reminders 7th, wknd appr 3 out.*
.... (20 to 1 op 14 to 1)   3
3140[4] ASTRALEON (Ire) 6-10-7 (7*) B Storey, *prmnt, rdn 3 out, btn 3rd whn f 2 out..............* (11 to 4 tchd 3 to 1)   f
3076[2] BRIGADIER DAVIS (Fr) 7-10-7 (7*) Mr C Bonner, *led, clr 3 out, blun and uns rdr 2 out....* (2 to 1 fav tchd 9 to 4)   ur
VILLA TARANTO 9-11-1[3] (7*) Mr R Brunt, *reluctant to jump off, tld off whn pld up bef second.*
.... (100 to 1 op 33 to 1)   pu
Dist: 14l, 4l. 5m 8.30s. a 21.30s (6 Ran).
                                              (J A Stephenson), P Cheesbrough

3355 Huddersfield Novices' Chase (5-y-o
and up) £3,418 2½m 110yds..... (2:50)

3143* SILVER STICK 7-11-8 R Garritty, *al prmnt, dsptd ld frm 8th, led 5 out, drw clr from 3 out, pushed out.*
.... (5 to 2 op 9 to 4 tchd 11 to 4)   1
3178* BASILICUS (Fr) 5-11-1 Gary Lyons, *led to second, remained cl up, reminders aftr 5 out, dsptd ld nxt, one pace frm 3 out.............* (9 to 4 fav tchd 5 to 2)   2
2928[3] VAYRUA (Fr) 9-11-11 (3*) A Larnach, *hld up in tch, trkd ldrs into strt, no imprsn frm 3 out.* (11 to 2 op 4 to 1)   3
2368[2] CONCERT PAPER (v) 10-11-8 (7*) K Davies, *led second, mstk 3rd, hdd 5 out, grad wknd.....* (7 to 1 op 6 to 1)   4
3178* THE COUNTRY TRADER 8-11-2 N Doughty, *prmnt, reminders tenth, wknd aftr 5 out.....* (7 to 1 op 5 to 1)   5
3178[2] ABLE PLAYER (USA) (bl) 7-11-3 (5*) J Burke, *prmnt till wknd 5 out.....................* (7 to 1 op 5 to 1)   6
Dist: 7l, 6l, 9l, 3l, 1¾l. 5m 25.00s. a 28.50s (6 Ran).
                                              (Lord Manton), M W Easterby

3356 Leeds Intermediate Handicap Chase
(0-120 5-y-o and up) £3,452 2m.. (3:20)

2975* ONE FOR THE POT [110] 9-11-11 (3*) T Jenks, *al prmnt, hit 4th, prog to ld 3 out, kpt on gmely und pres frm nxt.*
.... (5 to 1 op 7 to 2)   1
2584 ISSYIN [99] 7-11-3 R Garritty, *hld up rear, prog to track ldrs 3 out, str chal r-in, jst fld.*
.... (11 to 2 op 6 to 1 tchd 13 to 2)   2
3186[8] PIMS GUNNER (Ire) [96] 6-11-0 G Grant, *al prmnt, ev ch 2 out, kpt on one pace............* (14 to 1 op 10 to 1)   3
2242[2] HIGHLY DECORATED [84] 9-10-2[2] Gary Lyons, *prmnt till outpcd 5 out, prog and ch 2 out, sn rdn and wknd.*
.... (10 to 1 op 8 to 1)   4
3060[2] HEIR OF EXCITEMENT [82] (v) 9-10-0 S Turner, *led till 3 out, sn wknd.......................* (20 to 1 op 16 to 1)   5
722[4] ALGARI [103] 7-11-0 (7*) B Harding, *in tch till wknd quickly appr 4 out............* (8 to 1 op 7 to 1)   6
3073 SEON [103] 8-11-7 N Bentley, *prmnt whn blun and uns rdr 5th......* (5 to 1 op 4 to 1 tchd 11 to 2)   ur
3129* FULL O'PRAISE (NZ) [100] 7-11-4 T Reed, *hld up in tch, prog to track ldrs whn ran out 4 out.*
.... (3 to 1 fav op 5 to 2)   ro
3129[2] GOLDEN ISLE [93] 10-10-6 (5*) B Storey, *prmnt, chsd ldr into strt, wknd 3 out, pld up bef last.* (8 to 1 op 6 to 1)   pu
Dist: Nk, 2½l, 8l, 13l, 20l. 4m 12.10s. a 20.10s (9 Ran).
SR: 43/31/25/5/-/-/   (Philip Davies), M P Naughton

3357 Wharfedale Selling Handicap Hurdle
(4-y-o and up) £2,110 2m...... (3:50)

2891* REGAL ROMPER (Ire) [96] 6-11-7 (7*) D Towler, *al prmnt, cld and gng wl to track ldr 3 out, dsptd ld nxt, sn led and clr, rdn out....* (3 to 1 jt-fav op 5 to 2 tchd 100 to 30)   1
3078[2] HYPNOTIST [74] 8-10-8 N Bentley, *trkd ldrs, led aftr 4 out, rdn appr nxt, hdd after 2 out, fdd. ....* (3 to 1 jt-fav op 7 to 2)   2
3139[4] HIGHFIELD PRINCE [72] 8-10-4 R Garritty, *mid-div, prog to track ldrs entering strt, kpt on one pace.*
.... (9 to 1 op 7 to 1)   3
AUSTHORPE SUNSET [93] 10-11-11 Mr R Armson, *led til 4 out, sn rdn, wknd frm nxt.......* (14 to 1 op 10 to 1)   4
3139 TOP VILLAIN [84] 8-11-2 Mr S Bell, *trkd ldrs till wknd appr 3 out..................* (12 to 1 op 8 to 1)   5
3139[3] CHADWICK'S GINGER [84] 6-11-2 S Turner, *rear, some prog whn blun 4 out, no dngr aftr.* (5 to 1 tchd 6 to 1)   6
2240[6] SINGING SAM [68] (bl) 9-10-0 N Smith, *rear, some prog hfwy, no imprsn frm 4 out.................* (33 to 1)   7

SEE THE LIGHT [68] 7-9-9 (5*) H Bastiman, *rear, no dngr frm 4 out*..........................(66 to 1 op 33 to 1) 8

2785[7] BIN LID (Ire) [68] 5-9-8[1] (7*) B Harding, *al rear.* ....(10 to 1 op 8 to 1 tchd 11 to 1) 9

912 OLD MORTALITY [80] 8-10-5 (7*) S Melrose, *mid-div, wknd 4 out*............................(10 to 1 op 12 to 1) 10

2665[6] LADY KHADIJA [68] 8-10-0 W Dwan, *trkd ldr, led 4 out, sn hdd and wknd*.....................(100 to 1 op 50 to 1) 11

1746 MY LINDIANNE [84] 7-11-2 C Dennis, *beh and pushed alng aftr second, tld off frm 4th, pld up 3 out.* ....(8 to 1 op 5 to 1) pu

2408 SUMMERS DREAM [70] (bl) 4-10-2 D Byrne, *lost tch frm 4th, tld off whn pld up 3 out*.......(14 to 1 op 10 to 1) pu

Dist: 7l, nk, 8l, 12l, 6l, 10l, 3l, 6l, 4l, 9l. 3m 57.10s. a 16.10s (13 Ran).

SR: 27/-/-/8/-/-/ (Mrs S Smith), Mrs S J Smith

3358 Wetherby Handicap Chase (0-140 5-y-o and up) £7,156 3m 110yds.....(4:20)

3127[2] ARMAGRET [130] 9-11-4 D Byrne, *trkd ldr, mstk 11th, second whn blun 4 out, kpt on und pres to ld r-in.* ....(11 to 2 op 4 to 1) 1

2953[2] CANDY TUFF [112] 8-10-0 N Smith, *mid-div, prog and gng wl to ld appr 4 out, clr 3 out, wknd and hdd r-in.* ....(9 to 2 tchd 5 to 1) 2

2784[3] LO STREGONE [115] 8-10-3[3] R Garritty, *rear till prog to track ldr hfwy, effrt frm 4 out, blun last, ran on flt.* ....(7 to 1 op 13 to 2) 3

3180[2] BLUFF KNOLL [120] 11-10-8 G Harker, *beh and outpcd frm hfwy, styd on from 2 out, nrst finish.* ....(14 to 1 op 10 to 1) 4

2006 IDA'S DELIGHT [120] 15-10-8 T Reed, *trkd ldr till wknd 11th.*............................(25 to 1 op 20 to 1) 5

2901[2] SIKERA SPY [121] 12-10-9 R Bellamy, *led and clr to hfwy, hdd appr 4 out, sn wknd.* ....(6 to 1 op 5 to 1 tchd 7 to 1) 6

2831[7] SHOON WIND [117] 11-10-5[5] C Grant, *beh frm hfwy.* ....(12 to 1 op 10 to 1 tchd 14 to 1) 7

3134 VELEDA II (Fr) [112] 7-9-9 (5*) J Burke, *in tch to 6th, beh and pld up aftr 9th*.............(16 to 1 op 14 to 1) pu

1616 WHISPERING STEEL [140] 8-12-0 N Doughty, *rear, prog to track ldrs 5 out, sn nudged alng, wknd bef nxt, pld up 3 out*............................(2 to 1 fav op 7 to 4) pu

Dist: 1½l, nk, 15l, 7l, 1l, 25l. 6m 34.20s. a 28.20s (9 Ran).

SR: 29/9/11/1/-/-/ (Mrs R M Wilkinson), B E Wilkinson

3359 Arkendale Novices' Handicap Hurdle (4-y-o and up) £2,477 3m 1f.....(4:50)

2905[2] STRONG FLAME (Ire) [88] 5-10-1 (5*) S Lyons, *made all, drw clr frm 2 out, eased cl hme*......(7 to 2 op 6 to 4) 1

3126* KENILWORTH LAD [106] 6-11-7 (3*) Mr M Buckley, *trkd ldrs, mstk 3 out, rdn aftr nxt, no imprsn.* ....(5 to 2 fav op 9 to 4 tchd 11 to 4) 2

3126[2] MAJORITY MAJOR (Ire) [97] 5-11-1 C Grant, *trkd ldr, ev ch 3 out, no imprsn frm nxt.* (3 to 1 op 5 to 2 tchd 7 to 2) 3

3144[2] STRONG DEEL (Ire) [88] 6-10-6[8] T Reed, *trkd ldr till rdn 4 out, sn wknd.*........................(7 to 1 op 5 to 1) 4

2905 MIDORI [85] 6-11-0 J Corkell, *lost tch quickly aftr 3rd, sn wl tld off.*...................(100 to 1 op 50 to 1) 5

1371[4] SQUIRES TALE (Ire) [82] 6-10-0 B Storey, *lost tch 7th, tld off whn pld up bef 3 out.* ....(9 to 1 op 7 to 1 tchd 10 to 1) pu

Dist: 3½l, 1¼l, 15l, dist. 6m 21.50s. a 26.50s (6 Ran).

(Trevor Hemmings), M D Hammond

WINCANTON (soft)
Monday April 4th
Going Correction: PLUS 1.25 sec. per fur.

3360 Pay And Play 'National Hunt' Novices' Hurdle (4-y-o and up) £2,372 2¾m ....(2:00)

3196[3] BRAVE HIGHLANDER (Ire) 6-11-0 D Murphy, *hld up, hdwy 4th, led 3 out, drw clr frm nxt.* ....(7 to 2 fav op 3 to 1 tchd 4 to 1) 1

3170[2] NAZZARO 5-11-0 (7*) R Darke, *trkd ldr, led appr 7th, hdd 3 out, no imprsn frm nxt.*.........(6 to 1 op 5 to 1) 2

2723[5] ORSWELL LAD 5-11-0 M Hourigan, *mstk second, chsd ldrs, wkng whn lft poor 3rd 2 out...*(10 to 1 op 8 to 1) 3

3151[3] RAMALLAH 5-11-7 W McFarland, *al beh, blun 7th, tld off.* ....(9 to 2 op 3 to 1) 4

3115[4] TAKE CHANCES 6-11-0 P Holley, *chsd ldrs, mstk 5th, wknd 3 out, no ch whn f nxt.* ....(9 to 1 op 8 to 1) f

2558[4] FOREST PRIDE (Ire) 5-10-6[3] A Thornton, *hld up in rear, hdwy appr 7th, 3rd and ev ch whn blun and uns rdr 2 out.*........................(5 to 1 op 4 to 1) ur

3233[7] GENERALLY JUST (bl) 9-11-0 Mr S Stickland, *led till hdd appr 7th, wknd rpdly, pld up bef nxt.* ....(100 to 1 op 50 to 1) pu

3051* KELLING 7-11-2 (5*) Guy Lewis, *hit second, rdn appr 4th, lost tch 6th, tld off whn pld up bef 8th.* ....(5 to 1 op 4 to 1 tchd 11 to 2) pu

1248 POLYNOGAN 8-11-0 B Powell, *al beh, tld off whn pld up bef 2 out.*............................(66 to 1) pu

Dist: 9l, 7l, dist. 5m 56.30s. a 56.30s (9 Ran).

(S N J Embiricos), J T Gifford

3361 Gardens Night Club Novices' Chase (5-y-o and up) £3,174 2m 5f.....(2:30)

3207[3] WISE CUSTOMER 10-11-0 Mr J Rees, *jmpd wl, trkd ldr to 11th, lft second nxt, led 5 out, left clr 3 out, easily.* ....(9 to 2 op 3 to 1 tchd 4 to 1) 1

2794[4] WHAT'S IN ORBIT 9-11-2 (5*) Guy Lewis, *mid-div, hdwy 5 out, lft second 3 out, no ch wth wnr.* (6 to 1 op 4 to 1) 2

3007 MONKSANDER 8-11-0 A Tory, *mid-div, nvr on terms.* ....(66 to 1 op 25 to 1) 3

3203[4] DRAW LOTS 10-11-0 I Shoemark, *al beh and not jump wl, blun badly 4 out, tld off last of four whn uns rdr 2 out.* ....(100 to 1 op 50 to 1) ur

3133[9] YOUR WELL 8-11-7 W McFarland, *prmnt till blun and lost pl 3rd, hdwy 8th, lft in ld 12th, hdd nxt, hld whn blunded and uns rdr 3 out.*..........(4 to 1 op 3 to 1) ur

3207[2] BIG BEAT (USA) 6-11-7 P Holley, *led, hit 3rd, clr whn hit 7th, blun and ran rdr 12th.* ....(11 to 1 op fav op Evens tchd 11 to 8) ur

KERRYS EYE 10-10-7 (7*) T Thompson, *beh, tld off 5th, pld up bef tenth.*..............(66 to 1 op 50 to 1) pu

1711[5] CHEEKY FOX 8-11-0 I Lawrence, *in tch till wknd tenth, tld off whn pld up bef 5 out.*..(33 to 1 op 25 to 1) pu

3219[4] DURRINGTON 8-11-0 S Earle, *al beh, tld off whn pld up bef 11th.*........................(33 to 1 op 16 to 1) pu

2858[4] MUTUAL BENEFIT 7-11-0 A Jones, *in rear whn blun 5th, blunded 9th, pld up bef nxt.* ....(28 to 1 op 20 to 1 tchd 33 to 1) pu

3004[7] KING'S RARITY 8-11-0 B Powell, *chsd ldrs till wknd 11th, tld off whn pld up bef 5 out.*.......(66 to 1 op 25 to 1) pu

Dist: 8l, 20l. 5m 55.30s. a 49.30s (11 Ran).

(Miss T A White), S E Sherwood

3362 Green Eagle Claiming Hurdle (4,5,6-y-o) £2,232 2m...............(3:00)

LASSIE (Fr) 5-11-11 (3*) R Davis, *trkd ldrs, led appr 2 out, sn clr...*............(11 to 1 to 2 op 7 to 2) 1

1509 TOOMUCH TOOSOON (Ire) 6-10-6 (5*) S Curran, *hld up in rear, hdwy 5th, chsd wnr frm 2 out.* ....(12 to 1 tchd 11 to 1) 2

2439 OUR NIKKI 4-10-1 I Shoemark, *led, blun 1st, sn clr, hdd appr 2 out, wknd...*..........(33 to 1 op 16 to 1) 3

3019[4] RED MICKS WIFE (Ire) 4-9-10[1] (5*) Guy Lewis, *mstk second, trkd ldr, ev ch appr 2 out, rdn and sn wknd.* ....(4 to 1 tchd 9 to 2) 4

3173[2] SOPHISM (USA) 5-11-9 D Murphy, *hld up in rear, in tch whn rdn aftr 3 out, no response, tld off.* ....(5 to 4 on op 7 to 4 on tchd 11 to 10 on) 5

LADY MAVIS 4-9-12 (7*) M Moran, *beh till hdwy 3rd, ev ch whn hit 3 out, sn btn, tld off...*....(20 to 1 op 8 to 1) 6

2834 SPONTANEOUS PRIDE 6-11-5 (3*) A Thornton, *refused to race...................*(6 to 1 op 4 to 1 tchd 13 to 2) ref

3055[7] WEST END 4-9-12 (7*) J Neaves, *in tch till ran out appr 4th....................*(50 to 1 op 25 to 1) ro

Dist: 7l, 14l, 8l, 25l, 12l. 4m 11.10s. a 34.10s (8 Ran).

(A J Richards), K O Cunningham-Brown

3363 Gardens Night Club Handicap Hurdle (0-115 4-y-o and up) £3,233 2¾m (3:30)

3038 MAESTRO PAUL [107] 8-11-6 D Murphy, *hld up, steady hdwy 6th, led and mstk last, pushed out.* ....(100 to 30 op 4 to 1 tchd 3 to 1) 1

2044 SALMON PRINCE [87] 8-9-9 (5*) S Curran, *trkd ldr, led 8th, rdn appr 2 out, ran on gmely, hdd last, no extr.* ....(33 to 1 op 20 to 1) 2

3053* WARFIELD [91] 7-9-13 (5*) Guy Lewis, *hld up in tch, gd hdwy 7th, ev ch appr 2 out, rdn and wknd bef last.* ....(11 to 4 fav op 3 to 1) 3

2790[2] MISS EQUILIA (USA) [92] 8-9-12 (7*) L Reynolds, *hld up in rear, gd hdwy 6th, rdn appr 2 out, found little, sn btn.* ....(6 to 1 op 5 to 1) 4

3150[3] RIBOVINO [87] 11-9-9 (5*) D Leahy, *in tch till rdn and wknd 3 out, tld off*..........(33 to 1 op 14 to 1) 5

BEE DEE BOY [87] 6-10-01 Lawrence, *chsd ldrs till outpcd 8th, wknd, tld off...* (16 to 1 op 20 to 1 tchd 14 to 1) 6

3214[2] NICK THE DREAMER (Ire) [99] 9-11-1 (7*) R Darke, *led, hit 7th, hdd nxt, wknd quickly appr 2 out, tld off.* ....(4 to 1 op 9 to 2) 7

2967[4] SUKAAB [115] 9-11-7 (7*) T Dascombe, *al in rear, lost tch 6th, tld off whn pld up bef 2 out...*(7 to 1 tchd 6 to 1) pu

3186 GARSTON LA GAFFE [96] 9-10-9 M P FitzGerald, *chsd ldrs till ran wide one bend appr 4th, lost tch nxt, tld off whn pld up bef 2 out.*.......(9 to 1 op 7 to 1 tchd 10 to 1) pu

Dist: 1½l, 9l, 20l, 15l, hd, nk. 5m 50.40s. a 44.40s (9 Ran).

(H T Pelham), J T Gifford

3364 Improve Your Handicap Chase (0-125 5-y-o and up) £3,808 3m 1f 110yds ....(4:00)

3052⁴ SUNLEY BAY [103] 8-10-5 (5*) Guy Lewis, *led 3rd to tenth,
led 12th to 15th, led last, ran on wl.* (6 to 1 op 5 to 1) 1
2518² COOL AND EASY [100] 8-10-7 D Murphy, *trkd ldrs, jmpd
slwly 7th, led tenth to 12th, jumped slowly 14th, led
nxt, rdn 3 out, hdd last, no extr.*
.................................(100 to 30 op 4 to 1 tchd 3 to 1) 2
1140² DOONLOUGHAN [98] 9-10-2 (3*) R Davis, *lft in ld 1st, hdd
3rd, stumbled and lost pl 13th, sn in tch ag'n, wknd 5
out.*...................................(16 to 1 op 10 to 1) 3
1720³ PURBECK DOVE [94] 9-10-1 S Earle, *not fluent, hld up in
rear, hdwy 12th, wknd 5 out.*
.................................(6 to 1 op 1 to 1 tchd 7 to 1) 4
3146² SHASTON [100] (bl) 9-10-0 (7*) R Darke, *led till f 1st.*
....(6 to 1 op 9 to 2) f
3217* GHOFAR [117] (bl) 11-11-10 P Holley, *prmnt till outpcd
16th, sn beh, tld off whn refused last.*
..................................(9 to 4 fav op 2 to 1 tchd 11 to 4) ref
3133⁴ HILL TRIX [100] 8-10-7 A Tory, *al beh, rdn and lost tch
appr 13th, blun 6 out, pld up bef nxt.*
.................................(13 to 2 op 5 to 1 tchd 7 to 2) pu
Dist: 2l, 25l, 2l. 7m 9.20s. a 53.20s (7 Ran).

(Mrs Marianne G Barber), P F Nicholls

3365 Nine Hole Novices' Hurdle (4-y-o and up) £2,495 2m..................(4:30)

3202² KEEP ME IN MIND (Ire) 5-11-7 D Skyrme, *al gng wl, led aftr
3 out, ran on strly.*......................(2 to 1 op 6 to 4) 1
3023 FATACK 5-11-2 (5*) S Curran, *made most to 5th, led ag'n
bef nxt, hdd aftr 3 out, rdn and no imprsn.*
....(Evens fav op 6 to 4) 2
2950* CHEMIN LE ROI 7-11-7 I Lawrence, *hld up in tch, hdwy
4th, wknd appr 2 out.*...(11 to 2 op 9 to 2 tchd 6 to 1) 3
SPRING SAINT 5-11-0 A Tory, *beh, effrt 5th, one pace frm
nxt.*..(100 to 1 op 33 to 1) 4
3215⁵ DESERT RUN (Ire) 6-10-9 (5*) Guy Lewis, *wth ldrs till wknd
3 out.*......................................(7 to 1 op 6 to 1) 5
DOMINOS RING (Ire) 5-11-0 B Powell, *al beh, lost tch 3
out.*...............................(16 to 1 op 25 to 1 tchd 14 to 1) 6
ALACUE 4-10-3 S Earle, *beh but in tch till wknd 5th.*
....(66 to 1 op 33 to 1) 7
3151⁵ POLICEMANS PRIDE (Fr) 5-11-0 D Murphy, *chsd ldrs, led
5th, sn hdd, uns rdr nxt.*...........(33 to 1 op 14 to 1) ur
ALFA VITA 8-10-9 I Shoemark, *beh whn crrd out bend
appr 3rd.*.................................(100 to 1 op 33 to 1) co
GYPSY CRYSTAL (USA) 4-9-10 (7*) Miss S Cobden, *pld md,
prmnt till ran out 3rd.*..............(100 to 1 op 33 to 1) ro
1313³ WILL BONNY (NZ) 7-10-7 (7*) J Neaves, *al beh, tld off whn
pld up bef 2 out.*.........................(50 to 1 op 20 to 1) pu
Dist: 10l, 20l, 5l, 12l, 2½l, ¾l. 4m 1.90s. a 24.90s (11 Ran).
SR: 44/34/14/2/-/-/ (P C Tory), N R Mitchell

FAIRYHOUSE (IRE) (soft to heavy)
Tuesday April 5th

3366 Autozero Maiden Hurdle (5-y-o and up) £4,830 2¾m..............(2:10)

2863² TWIN RAINBOW 7-12-0 L P Cusack, ...(11 to 2) 1
2278⁶ UNA'S CHOICE (Ire) 6-12-0 F J Flood, ...(6 to 1) 2
3247⁸ BEAT THE SECOND (Ire) 6-11-6 G M O'Neill, ...(16 to 1) 3
1434³ FINE TUNING (Ire) 6-11-6 F Woods, ...(10 to 1) 4
3087³ DONBOLINO (Ire) 6-11-9 T Horgan, ...(14 to 1) 5
3122⁴ CLOGRECON BOY (Ire) 6-11-1 (5*) J P Broderick, (12 to 1) 6
2940³ DADDY LONG LEGGS 7-11-6 K F O'Brien, ...(8 to 1) 7
2076² STRALDI (Ire) 6-11-7 (7*) E G Callaghan, ...(5 to 1) 8
2985² JOHNSTONS BUCK (Ire) 5-11-2 (3*) Mr D Valentine,
....(9 to 4 fav) 9
2863 TWIN RAINBOW (Ire) 6-11-3 (3*) C O'Brien, ...(66 to 1) 10
3292 SERGEANT DAN (Ire) 6-11-1 (5*) T Evans, ...(66 to 1) 11
3243 BORROSHANE FLASH (Ire) 6-11-6 J P Banahan, ...(50 to 1) 12
3248⁸ VITAL TRIX 7-11-1 P Carberry, ...(20 to 1) 13
RAMPANT ROSIE (Ire) 6-11-1 C F Swan, ...(14 to 1) 14
3291⁹ RATH CAOLA 7-11-1 J Jones, ...(20 to 1) 15
1683⁷ THE PARISH PUMP (Ire) 6-11-6 J Osborne, ...(16 to 1) 16
1848 STORMPROOF (Ire) 5-11-0 (5*) M G Cleary, ...(14 to 1) 17
1434⁴ BOB MONEY (Ire) 6-11-6 D H O'Connor, ...(20 to 1) 18
2586 DENNETT VALLEY (Ire) 5-11-2 J Shortt, ...(20 to 1) 19
2863⁸ BOBSVILLE (Ire) 6-11-6 C N Bowens, ...(25 to 1) 20
CALLEROGAN 7-11-6 M Moran, ...(50 to 1) 21
2919 DESPERATE DAYS (Ire) 5-11-5 S R Murphy, ...(33 to 1) 22
2607 FIRE KING 8-11-6 R Hughes, ...(20 to 1) 23
3290 SIR JOHN (Ire) 5-10-12 (7*) J Butler, ...(25 to 1) 24
3071 TOADTHEWETSPROCKET (Ire) 5-10-12 (7*) P Stafford,
....(50 to 1) 25
BLACKSTONE 7-11-1 H Rogers, ...(33 to 1) f
MIDNIGHT SERVICE (Ire) 5-11-5 C O'Dwyer, ...(20 to 1) pu
Dist: 9l, 2l, hd, 2l. 6m 4.20s. (27 Ran).

(Raymond E Moore), P D Osborne

3367 R.F.L. Steel Hurdle (5-y-o and up) £5,520 2m..................(2:40)

3244² MONALEE RIVER (Ire) 4-11-4 K F O'Brien, ...(6 to 1) 1
3068² DIPLOMATIC 5-11-10 J P Banahan, ...(3 to 1) 2
3122* THE REAL ARTICLE (Ire) 5-11-10 H Rogers, ...(8 to 1) 3

2124⁶ STARK CONTRAST (USA) 5-11-0 (7*) C McCormack,
....(20 to 1) 4
2988* GREEN GLEN (USA) 5-11-13 B Sheridan, ...(8 to 1) 5
3248³ EAGLE ROCK (USA) 6-11-11 (3*) C O'Brien, ...(10 to 1) 6
3199² MISS LIME 7-10-10 (7*) R A Hennessy, ...(6 to 1) 7
2615² BE MY HOPE (Ire) 5-11-5 P Carberry, ...(2 to 1 fav) 8
2938* HAUNTING ANGLE (Ire) 5-10-9 (7*) T Martin, ...(14 to 1) 9
2552 HURRICANE EDEN 7-10-12 (5*) M A Davey, ...(16 to 1) 10
3080⁴ SIR MOSS 7-11-11 C F Swan, ...(7 to 1) 11
2842⁵ FINAWAY BOY (Ire) 6-11-8 (3*) T J Mitchell, ...(33 to 1) 12
Dist: 2l, sht-hd, 2½l, nk. 4m 16.10s. (12 Ran).

(Donal O'Connor), W P Mullins

3368 Power Gold Cup (Chase) (Listed Race - Grade 1) (5-y-o and up) £18,200 2½m..............................(3:15)

2843* MERRY GALE 6-11-7 K F O'Brien, *made all, clr 2 out,
easily.*...................................(15 to 8 on) 1
2987* GLENCLOUD (Ire) 6-11-7 P Carberry, *trkd ldr, niggled
alng 4 out, rdn nxt, grad wknd.*...............(15 to 2) 2
3024⁴ ATONE 7-11-7 C F Swan, *f 1st.*................(2 to 1) f
Dist: Dist. 5m 30.20s. (3 Ran).

(Herb M Stanley), J T R Dreaper

3369 Bisquit Cognac Handicap Hurdle (Listed Race - Grade II) (4-y-o and up) £11,500 2m..............(3:50)

2986² JUPITER JIMMY [-] 5-10-11 C O'Brien, *mid-div, prog to
chal betw last 2, 3rd last, quickened r-in to ld cl hme.*
....(7 to 1) 1
2610⁹ FAMILY WAY [-] 7-10-5 F Woods, *prog frm mid-div to track
ldrs 3 out, led shrtly aftr 2 out till hdd cl hme.* (10 to 1) 2
20/99 COCKNEY LAD (Ire) [-] 5-10-6 C F Swan, *prog frm mid-div
to track ldrs 2 out, ev ch last, wknd cl hme.*....(7 to 1) 3
3199* FOR REG (Ire) [-] 5-11-0 (2ex) M Duffy, *wl plcd in chasing
grp, rdn to dispute ld appr 2 out, sn hdd and no extr
und pres betw last two.*.....................(10 to 1) 4
2703* JO JO BOY [-] 5-10-7 F J Flood, *wl plcd, mstk 3 out,
rdn and wknd betw last 2.*...................(10 to 1) 5
2754* DEEP INAGH [-] 8-11-9 D P Fagan, *led 1st till jnd appr 2
out, wknd betw last 2.*.......................(14 to 1) 6
2986⁵ IF YOU SAY YES (Ire) [-] 6-9-9 S R Murphy, *rear, kpt on frm
3 out without rchng ldrs.*....................(16 to 1) 7
3062⁶ GLENSTAL FLAGSHIP (Ire) [-] 4-10-11 J Osborne, *wd plcd,
mstk 6th, rdn and btn whn mistake 2 out.*......(7 to 1) 8
3248² PERSIAN POWER (Ire) [-] 6-11-5 P Carberry, *rear, nvr rch
ldrs.*..(10 to 1) 9
2610 FINAL FAVOUR (Ire) [-] 5-11-3 K F O'Brien, *trkd ldrs till rdn
and wknd 3 out.*.............................(10 to 1) 10
2754⁷ ARCTIC WEATHER (Ire) [-] 5-11-1 J F Titley, *mid-div, effrt 3
out, btn nxt.*................................(16 to 1) 11
2866² FERRYCARRIG HOTEL (Ire) [-] 5-10-1 D H O'Connor, *mid-
div, rdn 3 out, sn wknd.*......................(6 to 1) 12
2866 SHARP INVITE [-] (bl) 7-11-3 B Sheridan, *al rear.*..(16 to 1) 13
2866⁴ THE SHAUGHRAUN [-] 8-10-9 T Horgan, *mid-div till rdn
and wknd 3 out.*.............................(14 to 1) 14
3325* PRINCESS CASILIA [-] 9-11-6 Mr W P Mullins, *al rear, pld
up aftr 3 out.*...............................(16 to 1) pu
Dist: ½l, 1½l, 7l, 3l. 4m 9.20s. (15 Ran).

(James F Murphy), J E Kiely

3370 Lark Developments Joseph R.O'Reilly Memorial Cup (Hunter Chase) (5-y-o and up) £4,830 3m 1f..........(4:25)

2941* ELEGANT LORD (Ire) 6-12-3 Mr E Bolger, ...(5 to 2 on) 1
LINEKER 7-10-10 (5*) Mr G J Harford, ...(12 to 1) 2
TALE OF ENDURANCE (Ire) 6-11-1 Mr P Fenton, ..(9 to 2) 3
3295⁵ WHAT THING (bl) 7-10-13 (7*) Mr T J Murphy, ...(12 to 1) 4
SERLA EXPRESS 8-10-12⁴ (7*) Mr R Donohue, ...(66 to 1) pu
3295 DARA'S COURSE (Ire) 5-10-4¹ Mr A Coonan, ...(12 to 1) pu
COUNTESS MARK 7-10-7 (3*) Mr J A Nash, ...(25 to 1) pu
Dist: 10l, 12l, dist. 7m 14.00s. (7 Ran).

(J P McManus), E Bolger

3371 Anglo Irish Refrigeration Handicap Chase (0-116 5-y-o and up) £4,140 2¾m 110yds..............(5:00)

2986 HAVE TO THINK [-] 6-11-4 (5*) T P Rudd, ...(9 to 4 fav) 1
2984⁸ AMERICAN EYRE [-] 9-10-8 (5*) J P Broderick, ...(14 to 1) 2
3200³ CITIZEN LEVEE [-] 8-10-9 (5*) Mr W M O'Sullivan, ..(6 to 1) 3
1825 WINDS OF WAR [-] 9-12-0 C O'Dwyer, ...(6 to 1) 4
2662 PROPUNT [-] 9-11-7 J F Titley, ...(12 to 1) 5
3121 FANE BANKS [-] (bl) 12-11-1 P Carberry, ...(14 to 1) 6
2922 RUSSIAN GALE [-] 6-9-8¹ J Jones, ...(12 to 1) 7
3081⁸ WELCOME PIN [-] 13-11-8 J Shortt, ...(20 to 1) 8
3249 WATERLOO KING [-] 7-10-12 (3*) D P Murphy, ...(10 to 1) 9
GAELIC RAMBLER [-] 12-9-4³ (7*) D M Bean, ...(20 to 1) 10
3081² LADY BAR [-] 7-11-11 P M Verling, ...(12 to 1) f
2984⁷ ALL A QUIVER [-] 7-10-0 C N Bowens, ...(10 to 1) pu
Dist: ½l, 1l, 9l, 15l. 6m 27.40s. (12 Ran).

(Peter M Law), A L T Moore

3372 Hamilton Osborne King INH Flat Race (4-y-o) £4,140 2m..............(5:30)

CHEF COMEDIEN (Ire) 10-10 (7*) Miss S Kauntze,..(7 to 1) 1
3082[2] FIRE DUSTER (Ire) 11-3 Mr A P O'Brien,..........(5 to 2) 2
3245* SUPREME WONDER (Ire) 11-2 (3*) Mrs M Mullins, (10 to 1) 3
MAGIC MOONBEAM (Ire) 10-5 (7*) Mr P Carey,... (33 to 1) 4
2848* BRANDANTE (Ire) 11-3 (7*) Mr A F Doherty,.... (6 to 4 fav) 5
3042 GAMBOLLING DOC (Ire) 11-7 (3*) Mrs S McCarthy, (10 to 1) 6
2290[3] SHANES HERO (Ire) 11-3 Mr P F Graffin,..........(6 to 1) 7
3042 RANAGAR (Ire) 11-5 (5*) Mr H F Cleary,..........(12 to 1) 8
3124[4] KIMANICKY (Ire) 10-10 (7*) Mr P English,.........(14 to 1) 9
FONTAINE FABLES (Ire) 11-0 (3*) Mr D Marnane,..(12 to 1) 10
3245[7] KILCARBERY (Ire) 10-9 (3*) Mrs J M Mullins,......(25 to 1) 11
CONAGHER BOY (Ire) 10-12 (5*) Mr D McGoona, (20 to 1) 12
BEAGAN ROSE (Ire) 10-5 (7*) Mr M O'Connor,.... (25 to 1) 13
ARCTICTALDI (Ire) 10-10 (7*) Mr T J Murphy,......(25 to 1) 14

Dist: 11l, 2½l, ¾l, 3l. 4m 13.60s. (14 Ran).

(Mrs Michael Kauntze), Michael Kauntze

WETHERBY (good)
Tuesday April 5th

Going Correction: PLUS 0.40 sec. per fur. (races 1,2,-4,6,7), PLUS 0.90 (3,5)

3373 Yorkshire Museum Novices' Hurdle (4-y-o) £2,337 2m..............(2:05)

2857[3] FORMAL AFFAIR 10-5 A Maguire, *nvr far away, drvn ahead bef 2 out, hit last, styd on*.....(4 to 1 op 7 to 2) 1
2853[2] CALIANDAK (Ire) 11-2 G McCourt, *patiently rdn, improved frm midfield aftr 3 out, drvn alng from nxt, styd on r-in.*
(5 to 4 on op 11 to 10 on tchd Evens and 11 to 8 on) 2
2000[8] MISTROY 10-2 (3*) D Bentley, *settled beh ldg bunch, improved bef 3 out, sn pushed alng, styd on wl r-in.*
.... (25 to 1 op 20 to 1) 3
3128[5] GENSERIC (Fr) 11-2 R Garritty, *al tracking ldrs, effrt and drvn alng 3 out, styd on one pace frm nxt*..... (12 to 1) 4
3062 STRICTLY PERSONAL (USA) (v) 10-3 (7*) P Ward, *trkd ldrs, improved to nose ahead whn hit 3 out, rdn and one pace*.................. (13 to 2 op 7 to 1 tchd 11 to 2) 5
CESAR DU MANOIR (Fr) 10-5 (5*) J Burke, *sn hndy, dsptd ld appr 3 out, rdn and fdd bef nxt.* (25 to 1 op 16 to 1) 6
3016[2] HEART OF SPAIN 10-10 T Wall, *nvr far away, led aftr 4th to 3 out, fdd*...................... (16 to 1 op 14 to 1) 7
971[8] WANZA 11-2 C Grant, *made most to 4th, feeling pace and drvn alng appr 3 out, fdd*......... (16 to 1 op 12 to 1) 8
2903[2] REBEL KING 10-10 A Dobbin, *pressed ldg bunch till wknd und pres appr 3 out*................ (16 to 1 op 14 to 1) 9
WILD EXPRESSION 10-10 A S Smith, *dsptd ld, led briefly 4th, wknd frm 3 out*............... (50 to 1 op 25 to 1) 10
2628 CHILTERN HUNDREDS (USA) 10-5 (5*) P Midgley, *struggling frm hfwy, tld off*.............. (50 to 1 op 25 to 1) 11
2903[8] SUDDEN SPIN 10-10 J Callaghan, *struggling hfwy, tld off whn pld up bef 3 out*.............. (50 to 1 op 33 to 1) pu
872[6] GRINNELL 10-10 K Johnson, *struggling frm 3rd, tld off whn pld up bef 3 out*.............. (50 to 1 op 33 to 1) pu

Dist: 2½l, 1½l, hd, 1½l, 15l, 3l, 10l, 1l, ½l, 8l. 3m 56.00s. a 15.00s (13 Ran).

(The Plough Partnership), D Nicholson

3374 Yorkshire Racing Club Handicap Hurdle (0-130 4-y-o and up) £2,929 3m 1f ....(2:35)

3130* NORTHUMBRIAN KING [105] 8-10-4 J Callaghan, *tucked away gng wl improved to nose ahead bef 2 out, hrd pressed r-in, ran on*..........................(8 to 1) 1
3166[5] FURRY BABY [101] 7-10-0 A Maguire, *settled midfield, improved aftr 3 out, str chal r-in, jst hld.*
.... (13 to 2 op 6 to 1) 2
3142[3] LEADING PROSPECT [108] 7-10-7 B Storey, *wth ldrs, made most frm aftr 6th till nrly f 3 out, sn hdd, kpt on und pres from last*............................(10 to 1) 3
3038[4] VIARDOT (Ire) [129] 5-12-0 P Niven, *settled beh ldrs, took clr order 3 out, rdn and one pace frm betw last 2.*
.... (7 to 4 fav tchd 15 to 8) 4
2927* NORTHERN SQUIRE [101] 6-10-0 A Dobbin, *wth ldrs gng wl, dsptd ld fnl circuit, rdn bef 3 out, fdd aftr nxt.*
.... (6 to 1 op 11 to 2) 5
2737[2] FIRM PRICE [117] 13-10-9 (7*) G Lee, *wtd wth, steady hdwy fnl circuit, rdn bef 3 out, sn lost pl.*
.... (11 to 1 op 10 to 1) 6
3130[3] FORWARD GLEN [101] 7-10-0 K Johnson, *tucked away on ins, effrt aftr one circuit, fdd bef 3 out, tld off.*
.... (12 to 1 op 10 to 1) 7
3043[2] VITAL WITNESS (Can) [112] 7-10-11 A S Smith, *last and hld up, effrt fnl circuit, lost tch and pld up bef 3 out.*
..................................(12 to 1) pu
3058[3] NO MORE TRIX [108] 8-10-7 R Garritty, *slight ld till aftr 6th, reminders and lost grnd 4 out, pld up bef nxt.*
.... (12 to 1 op 10 to 1) pu
2961 MISTIC GLEN (Ire) [101] 5-9-7 (7*) F Leahy, *chsd ldg bunch, struggling frm 4 out, wknd quickly and pld up bef 2 out*.............................. (25 to 1 op 20 to 1) pu

Dist: ½l, 3½l, 1½l, 12l, 5l, dist. 6m 16.30s. a 21.30s (10 Ran).

(Mrs K Walton), Mrs K Walton

3375 Yorkshire Car Collection Handicap Chase (0-135 5-y-o and up) £3,687 2 ½m 110yds..................(3:05)

3141 STRONG SOUND [100] 7-10-0 K Johnson, *patiently rdn, smooth hdwy to join issue 4 out, jmpd ahead last, drvn out*.................(5 to 2 fav op 2 to 1 tchd 11 to 4) 1
2906[2] CHOICE CHALLANGE [100] 11-9-13[4] (5*) S Lyons, *nvr far away, nosed ahead 2 out, hdd last, kpt on same pace.*
.....................................(7 to 1 op 8 to 1) 2
3162[7] HOUGHTON [100] (bl) 8-10-0 W Marston, *made most, hit 8th and 6 out, hdd 2 out, styd on same pace*... (12 to 1) 3
3239[6] WAIT YOU THERE (USA) [100] 9-9-13[4] (5*) P Waggott, *co'red up beh ldrs, improved bef 3 out, ev ch frm nxt, one pace r-in*..................(33 to 1 op 25 to 1) 4
3239* CLARES OWN [102] 10-10-2 A Maguire, *nvr far away, drvn up on ins 4 out, reminders bef last, kpt on same pace*..................................(7 to 2 tchd 4 to 1) 5
3045[2] MANDER'S WAY [103] 9-10-3[1] G Upton, *in tch, jmpd slwly 7th, drvn alng frm 6 out, nvr able to chal.*
.... (11 to 2 op 5 to 1) 6
1793 CHARMING GALE [100] 7-10-0 A Dobbin, *settled wth chasing grp, feeling pace bef 4 out, no imprsn*......(20 to 1) 7
2958[3] PRINCE YAZA [109] 7-10-9 L O'Hara, *trkd ldg bunch, chsd alng whn ldrs quickened appr 4 out, no imprsn.*
.... (12 to 1 op 10 to 1) 8
3026 WHAAT FETTLE [124] 9-11-10 M Moloney, *dsptd ld, ev ch and drvn alng appr 4 out, fdd aftr nxt.*
..................................(9 to 1 op 7 to 1) 9

Dist: 2½l, 1¼l, 1l, ¾l, 7l, 1½l, 5l, nk. 5m 19.40s. a 22.90s (9 Ran).
SR: 28/25/23/22/23/17/12/16/30/ (Mrs H Scotto), P Cheesbrough

3376 Tetley's Brewery Wharf Handicap Hurdle (0-140 4-y-o and up) £4,532 2 ½m 110yds..................(3:35)

3057[3] CHIEF RAIDER (Ire) [112] 6-10-8 A Maguire, *al wl plcd, led bef 4 out, styd on strly to go clr betw last 2.*
..................................(7 to 1 tchd 13 to 2) 1
3142[8] THISTLEHOLM [104] 8-9-11 (3*) D Bentley, *patiently rdn, improved gng wl aftr 4 out, ridden betw last 2, one pace*.............................. (16 to 1 op 10 to 1) 2
2812[6] VASILIEV [104] (v) 6-10-0 C Grant, *settled midfield, drvn up to draw level 3 out, sn rdn, kpt on same pace frm last*................................ (12 to 1 op 14 to 1) 3
3136[3] ISABEAU [104] 7-10-0 A S Smith, *dictated pace till appr 4 out, rdn alng bef nxt, sn btn.*
..................(5 to 2 fav tchd 11 to 4 and 9 to 4) 4
1863[9] LOCH GARANNE [114] 6-10-10 D Byrne, *nvr far away, ev ch 4 out, rdn and wknd bef nxt.*
.... (5 to 1 op 4 to 1 tchd 11 to 2) 5
3038 GREY POWER [128] 7-11-10 P Niven, *nvr gng wl, struggling hfwy, tld off*...................(3 to 1 op 5 to 2) 6
3130[4] BONANZA [122] 7-11-4 R Hodge, *niggled alng to go pace thrght, tld off bef 3 out.* (8 to 1 op 7 to 1 tchd 9 to 1) 7
3130[6] HURDY [115] 7-10-6 (5*) J Burke, *settled midfield, wknd quickly 4 out, pld up bef nxt*.......(12 to 1 op 10 to 1) pu

Dist: 11l, ½l, 8l, 20l, 4l, 10l. 4m 59.00s. a 12.00s (8 Ran).
SR: 41/22/21/13/3/13/-/-/ (John Wade), J Wade

3377 Scarborough Millennium Novices' Hunters' Chase (5-y-o and up) £1,811 3m 110yds.....................(4:05)

996[5] WHATAGALE 7-11-10 (3*) Mr J Durkan, *patiently rdn, improved gng wl to ld 4 out, styd on strly frm last.*
.................................(9 to 4 fav op 2 to 1) 1
3158[3] SPARTAN RANGER 9-11-5 (7*) Mr C Bonner, *wth ldrs, made most frm hfwy till hdd 4 out, rallied from last.*
.....................................(9 to 1 op 8 to 1) 2
COT LANE 9-11-5 (7*) Mr R Walmsley, *in tch, struggling to keep up fnl circuit, styd on grimly frm 3 out, nrst finish*..........................(10 to 1 op 12 to 1) 3
3157* POPESHALL 7-11-7 (5*) Mr R H Brown, *nvr far away, dsptd ld fnl circuit, feeling pace aftr 4 out, fdd nxt.*
.....................................(3 to 1 op 7 to 2) 4
HELLCATMUDWRESTLER 13-11-5 (7*) Miss T Gray, *dictated pace, hit 4th, blun and uns rdr 9th*..... (50 to 1) ur
DALMORE 8-11-5 (7*) Mr P Atkinson, *chsd alng to keep up thrght, tld off whn pld up bef 2 out*.......... (50 to 1) pu
3158 HAWAIIAN GODDESS (USA) 7-11-7 Mr S Swiers, *reminders to keep up 5th, tld off whn pld up bef 4 out.*
.... (33 to 1 op 25 to 1) pu
CAWKWELL DEAN 8-11-9 (3*) Mr Simon Andrews, *chsd ldg bunch, bad mstk 9th, lost tch frm 6 out, pld up bef 2 out.*
.... (14 to 1 op 12 to 1) pu
LIFE OF A KING (Ire) 6-11-12 Mr J Greenall, *al frnt rnk, lft in ld 9th, hdd hfwy, styd hndy till wknd and pld up bef last*.............................. (5 to 2 op 9 to 4) pu

Dist: 1½l, 2l, 30l. 6m 44.90s. a 38.90s (9 Ran).

(C Coxen), O Sherwood

3378 Yorkshire And Humberside Tourist Board Novices' Hurdle (Div I) (5-y-o and up) £2,215 2m..............(4:35)

2951[3] TEMPLERAINEY (Ire) 6-10-5 (5*) J Burke, *al hndy, nosed ahead 2 out, hdd last, rallied to ld last 50 yards.* ....(9 to 2 jt-fav op 4 to 1 tchd 5 to 1) 1
3289[4] SHAHGRAM (Ire) 6-10-10 M Dwyer, *patiently rdn, steady hdwy on ins aftr 3 out, nosed ahead last, hdd and not run on last 50 yards*.............. (6 to 1 tchd 13 to 2) 2
3179 GOING PUBLIC 7-10-10 K Johnson, *nvr far away, drw level 3 out, sn rdn and outpcd, no imprsn.* ....(33 to 1 tchd 50 to 1) 3
3189[5] EIGHTANDAHALF (Ire) 5-10-6[1] (5*) P Midgley, *dictated pace till hdd 3 out, sn drvn alng, fdd*..............(9 to 2 jt-fav op 7 to 2 tchd 5 to 1) 4
2874 LEGION OF HONOUR 6-11-0 (3*) T Jenks, *wth ldrs, slight ld and mstk 3 out, hdd nxt, fdd*...... (5 to 1 op 4 to 1) 5
2308 TWIN STATES 5-10-10 (7*) W Fry, *patiently rdn, improved to go hndy appr 3 out, pushed alng and outpcd bef nxt, sn btn*........................... (16 to 1 op 14 to 1) 6
2409 MISCHIEVOUS GIRL 6-10-5 Mrs F Needham, *pressed ldg bunch, drvn alng aftr 4 out, sn btn*........... (50 to 1) 7
3074[4] BIRD WATCHER 5-10-7 (3*) D Bentley, *pressed ldg bunch till wknd und pres appr 3 out*..... (16 to 1 op 14 to 1) 8
2691[7] DUNNOHALM 5-10-5 Mr S Swiers, *very unruly at strt, settled off the pace, nvr nr to chal.* ....(5 to 1 tchd 13 to 2) 9
2154[6] VAL DE RAMA (Ire) 5-10-5 (5*) P Waggott, *chsd ldg bunch, feeling pace aftr 4 out, sn btn*..... (14 to 1 op 10 to 1) 10
2735 ROCK OPERA (Ire) 6-10-10 A Merrigan, *in tch, chsd alng to keep up 4 out, sn btn*....................... (66 to 1) 11
2074[7] ONE LAST CHANCE 5-10-5 B Storey, *chsd ldrs to hfwy, sn struggling, tld off*........................... (33 to 1) 12
MORE IMPORTANT 7-10-5 A Dobbin, *in tch to hfwy, wknd frm 4 out, tld off*.......................(66 to 1) 13
MODEST HOPE (USA) 7-10-10 A Maguire, *settled gng wl, ev ch till wknd and pld up bef 3 out.* ....(11 to 1 op 12 to 1 tchd 14 to 1 and 10 to 1) pu
3169 STONEGREY (Ire) 6-10-10 R Garritty, *struggling in mid-field and pld up bef 3 out*.................... (20 to 1) pu
GULER-A 6-10-3 (7*) R Moore, *al beh, tld off whn pld up bef 2 out*......................... (25 to 1 op 20 to 1) pu

Dist: ½l, 15l, 8l, nk, 1½l, 1¼l, 3l, 4l, 2½l, ½l. 3m 57.20s. a 16.20s (16 Ran).

(Lady Harris), Mrs S C Bradburne

3379 Yorkshire And Humberside Tourist Board Novices' Hurdle (Div II) (5-y-o and up) £2,197 2m..............(5:05)

2510[3] GORTEERA 8-11-3 M Brennan, *patiently rdn, led aftr 4 out, idled and ridden last, jst lasted.* .... (11 to 10 fav op 5 to 4 on) 1
2741[5] HOLD YOUR HAT ON 5-10-10 D Wilkinson, *tucked away beh ldrs, improved frm 3 out, styd on wl from last.* .... (20 to 1 op 16 to 1) 2
3125 INNOCENT GEORGE 5-10-7 (3*) A Thornton, *nvr far away, effrt and drvn alng frm 3 out, styd on one pace.* .... (50 to 1 op 33 to 1) 3
3034[2] SOUNDS GOLDEN 6-10-10 R Marley, *al hndy, led aftr 4th till after four out, rdn and not quicken nxt 3.* .... (16 to 1 op 12 to 1) 4
1668[4] JUNGLE RITES (Ire) 6-10-10 M Dwyer, *tucked away, improved to track ldr appr 3 out, wknd quickly frm nxt.* ....(5 to 1 tchd 6 to 1) 5
3209[4] ROCA MURADA (Ire) 5-10-10 A Maguire, *patiently rdn, shaken up 3 out, nvr plcd to chal.* ....(3 to 1 op 7 to 2 tchd 4 to 1) 6
2154[5] PHILDAN (Ire) 5-10-7 (3*) D J Moffatt, *pressed ldrs, hrd rdn aftr 4 out, fdd*....................(16 to 1 op 12 to 1) 7
2500 CROFTON LAKE 6-10-10 L O'Hara, *trkd ldrs, feeling pace aftr 4 out, sn btn*............................ (50 to 1) 8
2834 SKELTON LASS (Ire) 5-9-12 (7*) F Leahy, *sn struggling to keep up, nvr a factor*.............(50 to 1 op 33 to 1) 9
3179 HEDDON HAUGH (Ire) 6-10-10 K Johnson, *f 1st*... (50 to 1) f
BOURSIN (Ire) 5-10-10 T Reed, *al struggling, pld up bef 4 out*.................................. (16 to 1 op 14 to 1) pu
2835 MERRYHILL MADAM 5-10-5 Gary Lyons, *led till aftr 4th, styd hndy till lost tch and pld up bef 3 out*.... (50 to 1) pu
2785 CHORUS LINE (Ire) 5-10-5 C Hawkins, *pressed ldrs to hfwy, lost tch quickly and pld up bef 3 out*....(50 to 1) pu

Dist: ½l, 2l, 6l, sht-hd, 15l, 15l, 1¾l. 3m 58.80s. a 17.80s (13 Ran).

(Miss P Harding), O Brennan

ASCOT (soft (races 1,4,5,7,8), good to soft (2,3,6)) Wednesday April 6th

Going Correction: PLUS 0.85 sec. per fur. (races 1,4,-5,7,8), PLUS 0.60 (2,3,6)

3380 Lily Tree Novices' Hurdle (4-y-o and up) £3,087 2½m................(1:55)

3023[6] BARNA BOY (Ire) 6-11-7 M A FitzGerald, *hld up in tch, cld on ldrs aftr 6th, led and hit last, rdn out.* ......(11 to 8 fav op 6 to 4 tchd 7 to 4 and 11 to 10) 1
FEEL THE POWER (Ire) 6-11-7 D Gallagher, *al in tch, ev ch whn outpcd 2 out, rallied to go second r-in.* .... (33 to 1 op 25 to 1) 2
3191[4] SPIRIT IN THE NITE (Ire) 5-11-7 D Murphy, *al frnt rnk, led 4 out, hdd appr last, no extr r-in.* .... (20 to 1 op 14 to 1 tchd 25 to 1) 3
1501[3] COURT MASTER (Ire) 6-11-7 B Powell, *hld up in rear, gd hdwy frm 5th, ev ch 2 out, hit last, outpcd.* .... (25 to 1 op 20 to 1) 4
2572 WINNOWING (Ire) 6-11-2 J Osborne, *wtd wth, hdwy 3 out, styd on, nvr nrr*......... (5 to 1 op 6 to 1 tchd 7 to 1) 5
3036 STRONG CASE (Ire) 6-11-7 R Dunwoody, *rcd in tch, hdwy 5th, mstk 3 out, wknd bef nxt.* .... (10 to 1 op 8 to 1 tchd 11 to 1) 6
3036 BOOK OF MUSIC (Ire) 6-11-4 (3*) P Hide, *hld up in rear, some hdwy 6th, wknd nxt.* .... (12 to 1 op 8 to 1 tchd 14 to 1) 7
3196* CHIEF RAGER 5-11-7 D Bridgwater, *prmnt till wknd appr 3 out*..............(11 to 1 op 8 to 1 tchd 16 to 1) 8
3173* KNYAZ 4-10-7 (7*) Mr L Jefford, *prmnt to 5th, wknd, beh whn hit 4 out*........ (50 to 1 op 33 to 1 tchd 66 to 1) 9
3036 HAWAIIAN YOUTH (Ire) 6-11-7 M Perrett, *led till hdd 4 out, rdn and wknd quickly.* .... (10 to 1 op 8 to 1 tchd 12 to 1) 10
2728[2] QUARRY HOUSE (Ire) 6-11-7 J Railton, *al beh, tld off.* .... (20 to 1 op 12 to 1 tchd 25 to 1) 11
GREY EARL 6-11-7 Mr Raymond White, *slwly away, not jump wl, tld off frm 5th, pld up bef 4 out.* .... (50 to 1 op 33 to 1 tchd 66 to 1) pu
3264[4] ME FEIN (Ire) 6-11-7 E Murphy, *mid-div, lost tch 6th, tld off whn pld up bef 2 out.* .... (10 to 1 op 4 to 1 tchd 12 to 1) pu

Dist: 2l, 1¼l, 2½l, 3l, 1½l, 5l, 13l, 1¼l, hd, 9l. 5m 4.90s. a 23.90s (13 Ran).

SR: 24/22/20/17/9/12/7/-/-/ (Lynn Wilson), N J Henderson

3381 Fairview New Homes Novices' Chase (5-y-o and up) £10,996 3m 110yds ....(2:30)

3118[2] COULDNT BE BETTER 7-11-8 R Dunwoody, *made most to 5th, led tenth to 11th, led 4 out, wnt clr appr last, rdn out*.................(5 to 2 fav op 9 to 4 tchd 11 to 4) 1
3117[4] COKENNY BOY 9-11-8 J Osborne, *hld up in mid-div, hit 9th, outpcd 6 out, styd on to go second appr last, ran on*........................ (8 to 1 op 6 to 1 tchd 9 to 1) 2
3040 RAMPOLDI (USA) (bl) 7-11-8 M A FitzGerald, *in frnt rnk till lost pl hfwy, styd on aftr 3 out.* ....(7 to 1 op 6 to 1 tchd 8 to 1) 3
2822[2] LOS BUCCANEROS 11-11-8 G Upton, *mid-div, rdn 3 out, kpt on one pace*.........(9 to 1 op 6 to 1 tchd 10 to 1) 4
3133[2] SUFFOLK ROAD 7-11-8 J Railton, *led 5th to tenth, led nxt to 4 out, pressed wnr till wknd rpdly appr last.* ....(100 to 30 op 3 to 1 tchd 7 to 2 and 11 to 4) 5
2855 NICKSLINE 8-11-8 D Murphy, *in tch, 3rd whn blun and lost pl 11th, rallied 5 out, mstk nxt, sn btn, tld off.* .... (12 to 1 op 10 to 1 tchd 14 to 1) 6
1346[4] THEO'S FELLA 10-11-8 J Frost, *al beh, tld off whn pld up bef 13th*......................... (20 to 1 tchd 25 to 1) pu
2778[5] HARBINGER 9-11-8 P Hide, *prmnt, dsptd ld 7th, wknd quickly 11th, pld up bef 13th*....... (33 to 1 op 20 to 1) pu
2732[5] WHAT A NOBLE (bl) 8-11-8 Mr G Hogan, *jmpd badly in rear, tld off whn pld up bef 14th*.............. (33 to 1) pu
3040 KELLY OWENS 9-11-8 Mr N Bradley, *in tch whn hit 11th, sn lost pl, tld off when pld up bef 4 out*.......(100 to 1) pu
2780[4] MELDON 7-11-8 R Davis, *in tch to 11th, rallied appr 6 out, wknd and pld up bef 2 out.* (20 to 1 tchd 25 to 1) pu
3097[3] FROZEN DROP (v) 7-11-8 Richard Guest, *beh frm 6th, lost tch 11th, tld off whn pld up bef 15th.* ....(33 to 1 tchd 50 to 1) pu

Dist: 1¼l, 9l, 5l, 1½l, dist. 6m 29.40s. a 25.90s (12 Ran).

(R A B Whittle), C P E Brooks

3382 Daily Telegraph Novices' Chase Handicap (5-y-o and up) £14,005 2m 3f 110yds........................ (3:05)

2378[2] WELL BRIEFED [102] 7-10-3 B Powell, *tucked in beh ldrs, chlgd 4 out, led nxt, styd on wl*. ....(4 to 1 jt-fav tchd 5 to 1) 1
3207* BOSCEAN CHIEFTAIN [126] 10-11-13 R Dunwoody, *al prmnt, lft second 8th, led tenth to 3 out, one pace frm nxt*..............(4 to 1 jt-fav op 9 to 2 tchd 5 to 1) 2
3039 GHIA GNEUIAGH [116] 8-11-3 D Bridgwater, *hld up, hdwy 9th, rdn 4 out, one pace frm nxt.* .... (11 to 1 op 10 to 1 tchd 12 to 1) 3
2721[2] SHAAB TURBO [106] 8-10-7 S Burrough, *chsd ldrs, hit and lost pl 7th, rallied 5 out, wknd aftr nxt.* ....(6 to 1 tchd 13 to 2) 4
2596[2] JUMBEAU [110] 9-10-8 (3*) P Hide, *hld up, hdwy 9th, outpcd and wknd 4 out.* .... (6 to 1 op 5 to 1 tchd 13 to 2) 5
3118* YELLOW SPRING [127] 9-12-0 Peter Hobbs, *prmnt, second whn f 8th*...................... (10 to 1 tchd 12 to 1) f

3118⁵ BLACK CHURCH [99] 8-10-0 M Perrett, *beh till brght dwn*
8th..............................(66 to 1 tchd 100 to 1) bd
3361 BIG BEAT (USA) [123] 6-11-10 P Holley, *led, blun 7th, hit*
9th, hdd tenth, wknd quickly and pld up bef nxt.
........................(10 to 1 op 8 to 1 tchd 12 to 1) pu
3024⁶ COUNTRY LAD (Ire) [118] 6-11-5 D Murphy, *hld up in rear,*
blun 6th, not reco'r, pld up.
.............................(11 to 2 op 5 to 1 tchd 6 to 1) pu
3133⁵ FARDROSS [108] 8-10-9 J Osborne, *hld up in tch, wknd*
quickly 6 out, tld off whn pld up bef 3 out.
..............................(12 to 1 tchd 14 to 1) pu
Dist: 3½l, 20l, 15l, 1½l. 4m 57.30s. a 15.80s (10 Ran).
SR: 34/54/24/-/1/-/   (J R Barr), R H Buckler

3383 Trillium Handicap Hurdle (4-y-o and up) £5,073 2m 110yds......... (3:35)

3269² PONTYNYSWEN [127] (v) 6-11-1 D J Burchell, *rcd keenly,*
trkd ldr, cld appr 5th, led sn aftr, very easily.
.............................(13 to 8 op 6 to 4 tchd 7 to 4) 1
3174³ ASHFIELD BOY [112] 10-10-0 R Dunwoody, *led, clr 3rd,*
hdd sn aftr 5th, no imprsn aftr.
..............................(10 to 1 op 12 to 1 tchd 16 to 1) 2
3270³ RES IPSA LOQUITUR [112] 7-10-0 D Gallagher, *al last, wl*
beh 3rd, nvr on terms..(5 to 1 op 6 to 1 tchd 13 to 2) 3
Dist: 7l, 5l. 4m 5.00s. a 19.00s (3 Ran).
SR: 37/15/10/   (J L Thomas), D Burchell

3384 Alpine Meadow Handicap Hurdle (4-y-o and up) £5,015 3m......... (4:10)

3136* ATTADALE [130] 6-10-5 T Reed, *hld up, hit 6th and lost pl,*
gd hdwy appr 4 out, led approaching 2 out, rdn out.
..............................(15 to 8 fav op 2 to 1 tchd 5 to 4) 1
3028⁵ CASTIGLIERO (Fr) [126] (bl) 6-10-1¹ R Dunwoody, *hld up in*
tch, hdwy 7th, styd on to go second appr last, ran on.
.............................(13 to 2 op 6 to 1 tchd 7 to 1) 2
2978 CRYSTAL BEAR (NZ) [131] 9-10-6 B Powell, *hld up in rear,*
cld on ldrs 7th, led briefly aftr 3 out, wknd appr last.
..............................(25 to 1 tchd 33 to 1) 3
2933 BUONARROTI [128] 7-10-3 T Grantham, *al prmnt, ev ch 3*
out, one pace aftr..................(8 to 1 op 10 to 1) 4
3038⁸ DOMINANT SERENADE [135] 5-10-7 (3*) D Bentley, *in tch,*
rdn 3 out, wknd nxt.......................(7 to 1 op 6 to 1) 5
3267⁴ SWEET DUKE (Fr) [153] 7-11-7 (7*) Mr S Joynes, *led till hdd*
3 out, hrd rdn and sn wknd.
..............................(6 to 1 op 5 to 1 tchd 13 to 2) 6
3117⁶ BILLY BORU [125] 6-10-0 D Gallagher, *al prmnt, led briefly*
3 out, rdn and wknd quickly.....(20 to 1 op 33 to 1) 7
3028 SEA BUCK [125] 8-10-0³ (3*) R Davis, *al in rear, lost tch 4*
out, tld off..............(50 to 1 op 33 to 1 tchd 66 to 1) 8
3267⁸ ACROW LINE [125] 9-10-0 D J Burchell, *mid-div till wknd*
appr 4 out, tld off....(12 to 1 op 10 to 1 tchd 14 to 1) 9
2517⁵ SUPER SENSE [139] 9-11-0 C Maude, *al beh, tld off.*
..............................(20 to 1 tchd 25 to 1) 10
3267 DARA DOONE [143] 8-11-4 D Bridgwater, *al beh, tld off.*
..............................(10 to 1 tchd 12 to 1) 11
3028 SENDAI [127] 8-10-2² D Murphy, *trkd ldr till wknd 4 out,*
pld up bef 2 out........(7 to 1 op 8 to 1 tchd 13 to 2) pu
Dist: 1l, 15l, 3l, 12l, nk, 5l, 13l, 15l, 9l, 19l, 15l. 5m 55.20s. a 22.20s (12 Ran).
SR: 59/54/44/38/33/50/17/2/-/   (C H McGhie), L Lungo

3385 Mahonia Hunters' Chase (5-y-o and up) £3,387 2m 3f 110yds......... (4:45)

SHEER JEST 9-12-5 (3*) Mr A Hill, *wtd wth, cld on ldrs 8th,*
led 4 out, drw clr frm 2 out.
..............................(6 to 5 on op 5 to 4 on tchd Evens) 1
3263⁵ HILARION (Fr) 10-11-7 (7*) Mr D Bloor, *mstk 4th, outpcd*
tenth, styd on to go second appr last, no ch wth wnr.
..............................(25 to 1 op 20 to 1 tchd 33 to 1) 2
3263³ DENBERDAR 11-11-9 (5*) Mr D Parker, *trkd ldrs, led appr 6*
out, hdd 4 out, wknd quickly frm 2 out.
..............................(6 to 1 op 5 to 1 tchd 13 to 2) 3
2875 DUNCAN 9-12-1 (7*) Mr B Pollock, *hld up, hdwy frm 7th,*
wknd 5 out..................(11 to 4 op 2 to 1 tchd 3 to 1) 4
LUPO NERO 12-11-7 (7*) Mr S Hope, *led aftr 4th, hdd appr*
6 out, btn 3rd whn hit 3 out.
..............................(5 to 1 op 9 to 2 tchd 6 to 1) 5
3263 BEE GARDEN (bl) 13-12-3 (5*) Miss P Curling, *led till hdd*
aftr 4th, wknd appr 6 out, tld off whn pld up bef 2 out.
..............................(12 to 1 op 12 to 1 tchd 20 to 1) pu
BEE-KAY-ESS 11-11-7 (7*) Miss L Blackford, *in tch to 6th,*
tld off whn pld up bef six out.....(100 to 1 op 66 to 1) pu
2669⁸ ROYAL PAVILION 11-11-7 (7*) Mr T Hills, *blun 3rd, pld up*
5th..............................(33 to 1 tchd 50 to 1) pu
Dist: 15l, 15l, 13l, 12l. 5m 6.40s. a 24.90s (8 Ran).
                                            (Mrs Judy Wilson), W J Warner

3386 EBF Wild Boar Stakes National Hunt Flat Race (Div I) (4,5,6-y-o) £2,389 2m 110yds......... (5:20)

3113³ LUV-U-FRANK (Ire) 5-10-13 (7*) L Reynolds, *trkd ldrs, led*
o'r 3 fs out, clr ins fnl 2.
..............................(7 to 2 fav op 4 to 1 tchd 3 to 1) 1

3042 LIEN DE FAMILLE (Ire) 4-11-0 (7*) G Tormey, *al prmnt, ev ch*
2 fs out, rdn and one pace.
..............................(5 to 1 op 4 to 1 tchd 13 to 2) 2
3176* SISTER STEPHANIE (Ire) 5-11-5 (3*) J McCarthy, *al prmnt,*
one pace ins fnl 3 fs.... (5 to 1 op 10 to 1 tchd 9 to 2) 3
BIETSCHHORN BARD 4-10-9 (5*) D Leahy, *hld up in rear,*
hdwy 6 fs out, nvr nrr............(50 to 1 op 20 to 1) 4
ICE HOUSE STREET (NZ) 6-10-13 (7*) R Darke, *mid-div,*
one pace fnl 4 fs.....(16 to 1 op 10 to 1 tchd 12 to 1) 5
2916² ENVOCAMANDA (Ire) 5-11-1 (5*) D Fort, *prmnt till wknd 3*
fs out..............................(14 to 1 op 6 to 1) 6
2509⁸ COUNTRY PARSON (Ire) 5-11-1 (5*) S Curran, *pld hrd*
early, in tch till no hdwy fnl 4 fs. (50 to 1 op 25 to 1) 7
3169⁸ FIXTURESSECRETARY (Ire) 5-10-13 (7*) Mr G Hogan, *hld*
up, hdwy aftr 7 fs, ev ch 4 out, sn rdn and wknd.
..............................(5 to 1 op 9 to 1 tchd 9 to 2) 8
THE REVEREND BERT (Ire) 4-11-3 (3*) R Davis, *hld up,*
hdwy hfwy, no ch fnl 4 fs........(33 to 1 op 16 to 1) 9
STARLIGHT FOOL 5-11-6 Mr M Armytage, *beh, effrt 5 fs*
out, sn btn......................(16 to 1 op 12 to 1) 10
1548⁸ SPRINTFAYRE 6-11-6 (7*) M Keighley, *led till hdd o'r 3 fs*
out, wknd quickly... (25 to 1 op 20 to 1 tchd 33 to 1) 11
I'LL CHANCE IT (Ire) 5-10-13 (7*) Pat Thompson, *hld up,*
hdwy aftr 6 fs, wknd 5 out.
..............................(10 to 1 op 8 to 1 tchd 12 to 1) 12
TENBIT (Ire) 4-10-7 (7*) Mr S Joynes, *loose bef strt, beh till*
effrt hfwy, sn btn.....(16 to 1 tchd 20 to 1) 13
2749 CRACKING IDEA (Ire) 6-11-3 (3*) P Hide, *mid-div, rdn 4 fs*
out, sn btn..................(16 to 1 op 10 to 1 tchd 20 to 1) 14
HAN LINE 6-10-13 (7*) N Willmington, *mid-div, rdn 5 fs out,*
wknd.........................(33 to 1 op 20 to 1 tchd 50 to 1) 15
3176⁴ DOUJAS 4-10-2 (7*) Miss S Cobden, *al beh.*
..............................(50 to 1 op 20 to 1) 16
2876⁵ REAL GLEE (Ire) 5-11-6 Mr J Durkan, *trkd ldr, rdn 6 fs out,*
sn wknd.......................(12 to 1 op 4 to 1 tchd 14 to 1) 17
2749 NEARLY PERFECT 6-11-1 A Dicken, *al beh, tld off.*
..............................(50 to 1 op 20 to 1) 18
VEXFORD MODEL 4-10-4² (7*) Mr Richard White, *al beh, tld*
off......................(50 to 1 op 20 to 1) 19
Dist: 5l, 13l, sht-hd, 1l, 1¾l, 3½l, 4l, 3½l, 2½l, sht-hd. 3m 59.80s. (19 Ran).
                                            (Frank A Farrant), M C Pipe

3387 EBF Wild Boar Stakes National Hunt Flat Race (Div II) (4,5,6-y-o) £2,379 2m 110yds......... (5:55)

2834⁵ DISSINGTON DENE 5-10-13 (7*) W Fry, *mid-div, hdwy 5 fs*
out, drvn to ld wl ins last, all out.
..............................(12 to 1 op 10 to 1 tchd 14 to 1) 1
MANDALAY 5-10-13 (7*) Pat Thompson, *hld up in rear, rcd*
wide, rapid hdwy 5 fs out, ev ch entering last, ran on.
..............................(4 to 1 op 6 to 1) 2
BUCKHOUSE BOY 4-10-7 (7*) Mr S Joynes, *trkd ldr, led o'r*
6 fs out, hrd rdn and hdd wl ins last, no extr.
..............................(7 to 1 op 4 to 1 tchd 8 to 1) 3
2976⁵ SIGMA RUN (Ire) 5-11-3 (3*) R Davis, *hld up in tch, hdwy*
and ev ch o'r 3 fs out, wknd 2 out.
..............................(13 to 2 op 5 to 1 tchd 7 to 1) 4
HOW SUIR (Ire) 6-10-13 (7*) J J Brown, *mid-div, outpcd*
hfwy, kpt on fnl 2 fs. (33 to 1 op 25 to 1 tchd 50 to 1) 5
2332* CANTEEN ANGLE 5-11-6 (7*) Mr S Mulcaire, *trkd ldrs, out-*
pcd fnl 3 fs...............(7 to 2 op 4 to 1 tchd 11 to 2) 6
3234⁸ PURBECK CAVALIER 5-11-1 (5*) S Fox, *chsd ldrs till wknd*
4 fs out.....................(20 to 1 op 14 to 1 tchd 25 to 1) 7
UNIVERSAL MAGIC (Ire) 5-11-6 M P FitzGerald, *in tch on*
outsd, rdn to chal 4 fs out, wknd 3 out.
..............................(9 to 4 fav op 3 to 1) 8
HARLEY STREET 6-11-1 (5*) S Curran, *beh, hdwy 5 fs out,*
eased whn btn 3 out...(8 to 1 op 7 to 1 tchd 10 to 1) 9
ALONGWAYDOWN (Ire) 5-10-13 (7*) L O'Hare, *in tch till*
wknd 4 fs out, tld off. (25 to 1 op 16 to 1 tchd 50 to 1) 10
FENCING MASTER 5-11-6 Miss K Holmes, *pld hrd, hdwy*
aftr 5 fs, dsptd ld 7 out, wknd 4 out, tld off.
..............................(20 to 1 tchd 33 to 1) 11
3190⁵ LORD CAMBERLEY (Ire) 6-10-13 (7*) Mr G Hogan, *led, clr*
aftr 2 fs, hdd o'r 6 out, rdn and wknd 4 out, tld off.
..............................(20 to 1 op 12 to 1) 12
AWARLI 5-11-3 (3*) P Hide, *al beh, tld off.*
..............................(33 to 1 op 25 to 1) 13
LULA RIDGE 4-10-7 (7*) R Darke, *al beh, tld off.* (33 to 1) 14
Dist: ½l, 2l, 15l, 1l, ½l, 2½l, 1l, ½l, ½l, 25l, 3l. 4m 2.30s. (14 Ran).
                                            (D A & W Wyllie), J Norton

FAIRYHOUSE (IRE) (soft)
Wednesday April 6th

3388 Tattersalls (Ire) Maiden Hurdle (5-y-o and up) £4,140 2m............. (2:15)

2863⁴ PIMBERLEY PLACE (Ire) 6-12-0 C F Swan, ...(10 to 9 on) 1
2985⁴ YOU'VE DONE WHAT (Ire) 6-11-6 J F Titley, ...(8 to 1) 2
THAT'S POLITICS (Ire) 5-11-5 S H O'Donovan, ...(20 to 1) 3
3197⁵ FINAWAY EXPRESS (Ire) 5-10-12 (7*) P J Mulligan, (16 to 1) 4
3201⁵ TAITS CLOCK (Ire) 5-11-5 P Carberry, ...(8 to 1) 5
2607⁴ CAPTAINS BAR 7-11-11 (3*) Mr P McMahon, ...(11 to 4) 6
150² SIR HENRY KNYVET (Ire) 5-11-5 S R Murphy, ...(12 to 1) 7

2983 INAUGURATION (Ire) 5-11-5 A Powell, ... (20 to 1) 8
2983⁶ MY HALL DOOR 5-11-0 (5*) D T Evans, ... (25 to 1) 9
2289 SWANING AROUND (Ire) 5-11-5 C O'Dwyer, ... (33 to 1) 10
3197 BEDFORD RAMBLER (Ire) 5-11-0 (5*) J P Broderick,
. . . . (20 to 1) 11
2309 EARLY RISER (Ire) 6-11-1 J P Banahan, ... (66 to 1) 12
2197 MAID OF GLENDURAGH (Ire) 6-11-9 B Sheridan, . . (9 to 1) 13
709 NIGHT SERVICE (Ire) 6-10-10 (5*) D P Geoghegan, (50 to 1) 14
2664 NIGHT SERVICE (Ire) 6-10-10 (5*) D P Geoghegan, (50 to 1) 15
       SUCCESS EXPRESS 5-11-0 (5*) D Walsh, ... (20 to 1) 16
Dist: ½l, 4l, nk, 8l. 4m 2.60s. (16 Ran).

(William Alan Jones), P Mullins

3389 Oliver Freaney & Co. Dan Moore H'cap Chase (Listed) (4-y-o and up) £6,900 2m. . . . . (2:45)

2466² KINGS ENGLISH [-] 8-11-1 F Woods, trkd ldr, led appr 3
       out, lft clr last, rdn out. . . . . (11 to 2) 1
2549⁶ DESERT LORD [-] 8-10-13 C F Swan, hld up, prog to track
       ldrs whn mstk 3 out, rdn aftr nxt, styd on wthout
       threatening wnr. . . . . (8 to 1) 2
2987² FABRICATOR [-] 8-10-10 K F O'Brien, led, hdd appr 3 out,
       sn rdn, btn aftr nxt. . . . . (5 to 2 fav) 3
3123* WHO'S TO SAY [-] 8-10-12 (3*) T J Mitchell, mid-div, mstk
       4th, rdn to track ldrs 3 out, bad mistake nxt, wknd.
       . . . . (3 to 1) 4
2466⁷ VALRODIAN (NZ) [-] 11-10-6 J A White, al rear, rdn and
       lost tch appr 4 out. . . . . (20 to 1) 5
3123⁵ LADY OLEIN (Ire) [-] 6-10-8 J P Banahan, hld up, smooth
       prog to track ldrs 3 out, rdn aftr nxt, ev ch whn f last.
       . . . . (6 to 1) f
3123² DORAN'S TOWN LAD [-] 7-10-6 J P Broderick, mid-div,
       mstk and lost pl 4th, lost tch aftr nxt, rear whn f last.
       . . . . f
Dist: 3½l, 12l, 14l, 4½l. 4m 19.40s. (7 Ran).

(Mrs J N Anthony), A L T Moore

3390 Brown Thomas Festival Novice Hurdle (Listed) (5-y-o and up) £6,900 2½m . . . . (3:15)

2844⁶ COURT MELODY 6-11-9 (5*) J P Broderick, hld up,
       trkd ldr 3 out, smooth hdwy to dispute ld appr last, rdn
       to lead r-in. . . . . (5 to 2) 1
3322⁷ LOVE AND PORTER (Ire) 6-11-6 D H O'Connor, trkd ldr,
       dsptd ld appr last, rdn, hdd and no extr r-in. (10 to 1) 2
3036⁴ COQ HARDI AFFAIR (Ire) 6-11-11 P Carberry, led, 6 ls clr
       aftr 1st, reduced advantage 7th, rdn entering strt, jnd
       appr last, hdd, wknd r-in. 3
3038³ CHANCE COFFEY 9-11-8 G M O'Neill, al rear, rdn aftr 3
       out, sn wknd. . . . . (5 to 1) 4
2756⁴ DROICHEAD LAPEEN 7-10-11 (7*) Mr T J Beattie, rear, prog
       3 out, rdn and wknd appr nxt. . . . . (20 to 1) 5
Dist: 3l, 1½l, 15l, 2l. 5m 2.80s. (5 Ran).

(P P Johnson), Michael Hourigan

3391 Aer Rianta Dublin Airport Drivers for Romania H'cap Chase (5-y-o and up) £9,750 2½m. . . . . (3:45)

3199⁴ FINAL TUB [-] 11-10-12 C O'Dwyer, ... (10 to 1) 1
2286⁴ VISIBLE DIFFERENCE [-] 8-10-9 C F Swan, ... (4 to 1) 2
3121³ HAKI SAKI [-] 8-11-9 G M O'Neill, ... (4 to 1) 3
3081⁵ JOE WHITE [-] 8-10-2 S R Murphy, ... (11 to 1) 4
3123⁴ BOB DEVANI [-] 8-10-2 P Carberry, ... (9 to 2) 5
2755 GOOD TEAM [-] 9-10-7 F Woods, ... (14 to 1) 6
2865² SCRIBBLER [-] 8-10-5 L P Cusack, ... (10 to 4 fav) f
2280⁶ STIGON [-] 8-10-7 C O'Brien, ... (20 to 1) pu
Dist: 3l, 4l, 4½l, 25l. 5m 32.60s. (8 Ran).

(Sean O'Brien), V T O'Brien

3392 County Club (Dunshaughlin) Handicap Chase (4-y-o and up) £5,520 3m 1f . . . . (4:15)

2772⁸ WYLDE HIDE [-] 7-9-10 F Woods, ... (7 to 1) 1
2865⁴ TITIAN BLONDE (Ire) [-] 6-11-7 C F Swan, ... (7 to 2 fav) 2
3249⁴ CASTLE BRANDON [-] 8-11-3 F J Flood, ... (10 to 1) 3
2288 DYSART LASS [-] 9-11-6 (5*) M G Cleary, ... (20 to 1) 4
3040 TASSE DU THE [-] 7-9-11 A Powell, ... (14 to 1) 5
3249* IL TROVATORE (USA) [-] 8-11-5 (6ex) P Carberry, . (5 to 1) 6
3249 MR MYAGI [-] (bl) 10-9-4 (3*) D Bromley, ... (25 to 1) 7
2591⁶ PROVERB PRINCE [-] 10-11-0 J P Banahan, ... (14 to 1) f
3249⁶ ANOTHER GROUSE [-] 7-10-3 (3*) C O'Brien, ... (10 to 1) f
3274² JIMS CHOICE [-] 7-10-3 C O'Dwyer, ... (7 to 1) f
3249 IFFEEE [-] (bl) 7-10-10 (3*) D P Murphy, ... (16 to 1) ur
2200⁴ WALLS COURT [-] 7-9-11 P L Malone, ... (14 to 1) ur
3249³ MOONCAPER [-] 8-11-0 K F O'Brien, ... (6 to 1) pu
Dist: 2½l, dist, 9l, 1l. 6m 59.60s. (13 Ran).

(Mrs A L T Moore), A L T Moore

3393 Jet Oil Dunshaughlin Champion Flat Race (4-y-o and up) £4,140 2m. . (4:45)

2849² MAJOR RUMPUS 6-12-4 Mr A J Martin, ... (7 to 4 fav) 1

3276³ TOURIST ATTRACTION (Ire) 6-11-12 Mr W P Mullins,
       . . . . (10 to 1) 2
       MAID FOR DANCING (Ire) 5-11-5 Mr A R Coonan, (20 to 1) 3
2592² GLEN TEN (Ire) 5-11-12 Mr T Mullins, ... (14 to 1) 4
3042⁶ MARINGO (Ire) 5-12-3 (3*) Mrs J M Mullins, ... (2 to 1) 5
3042⁴ RHYTHM SECTION (Ire) 5-11-13 (7*) Mr M Brennan, (9 to 2) 6
2849* TOTAL CONFUSION 7-12-1 (3*) Mr J A Nash, ... (10 to 1) 7
2613⁷ POWER PACK (Ire) 6-11-13 (5*) Mr B R Hamilton, (16 to 1) 8
2988 DARAVIC (Ire) 5-11-10 Mr J P Dempsey, ... (16 to 1) 9
Dist: Hd, 3½l, 1½l, ½l. 3m 55.40s. (9 Ran).

(Frank Conroy), A L T Moore

3394 Seamus Maguire & Co. Flat Race (4-y-o and up) £4,140 2m. . . . . . . (5:15)

3250⁵ SELL EVERYTHING (Ire) (bl) 4-11-3 (3*) Mr D Valentine,
       . . . . (13 to 2) 1
2394 DERBY HAVEN 7-12-0 Mr A R Coonan, ... (25 to 1) 2
       THREE PHILOSOPHERS (Ire) 5-11-10 (3*) Mrs J M Mullins,
       . . . . (4 to 1) 3
       JAFFAPPEAL (Ire) 6-11-11 (3*) Miss C Hutchinson, (10 to 1) 4
2289² GLINT OF EAGLES (Ire) 5-11-6 (7*) Mr S P McCarthy, (5 to 1) 5
3244⁷ ANOTHER ROLLO (Ire) 6-11-7 (7*) Mr N Stokes, . . (20 to 1) 6
2983⁴ BEST INTEREST (Ire) 6-12-0 Mr A J Martin, ... (9 to 4 fav) 7
       AGITATO (Ire) 6-11-3 (3*) Mr R Neylon, ... (12 to 1) 8
2664 GOLDEN NUGGET 7-11-7 (7*) Mr M Budds, ... (14 to 1) 9
       PRACTICIAN (Ire) 4-11-3 (3*) Mr J A Nash, ... (20 to 1) 10
       ANTIGUA'S TREASURE (Ire) 5-11-6 (7*) Mr B M Cash,
       . . . . (14 to 1) 11
       IOLARA (Ire) 5-11-7 (7*) Mr M J Gilhooly, ... (33 to 1) 12
2848² CHIEF RANI (Ire) 4-11-6 Mr T Mullins, ... (7 to 1) 13
2024⁹ DRUMREAGH LAD (Ire) 6-11-11 (3*) Mr P McMahon, (7 to 1) 14
Dist: 1l, 2l, hd, 1l. 4m 12.60s. (14 Ran).

(T J Moore), M J P O'Brien

LUDLOW (good to soft)
Wednesday April 6th

Going Correction: PLUS 0.75 sec. per fur. (races 1,2,-4,7), PLUS 1.00 (3,5,6)

3395 Caynham Novices' Selling Hurdle (4-y-o and up) £1,553 2m 5f 110yds (2:15)

3137⁶ MAN OF THE GRANGE 8-11-4 Diane Clay, wl beh still
       steady hdwy frm 7th, str run to ld last, pushed clr,
       fnshd distressed. (33 to 1 op 25 to 1) 1
3108⁷ SAMJAMALIFRAN 5-10-13 J Lower, trkd ldr, led appr 3
       out, clr whn dived rght and almost uns rdr nxt, hdd
       last, not quicken, fnshd lme.
       . . . . (14 to 1 op 10 to 1 tchd 16 to 1) 2
3022⁴ SHARPSIDE (bl) 7-11-4 A Maguire, led till hdd aftr 3 out,
       sn rdn and not quicken. . . . . (4 to 1 fav op 5 to 1) 3
3281⁸ KOA 4-11-2 (3*) T Jenks, trkd ldr, led briefly aftr 3 out, sn
       rdn, hdd and no extr. . (11 to 2 op 5 to 1 tchd 6 to 1) 4
3157² RULLY 5-11-4 W Worthington, chsd ldrs till mstk 5th, nvr
       7th, sn one pace. . . . . (33 to 1) 5
2998⁸ TANAISTE (USA) (v) 5-11-4 Gary Lyons, wl beh till mode-
       rate hdwy frm 2 out, nvr nrr. . . . . . (16 to 1 op 25 to 1) 6
3236³ DOC SPOT 4-10-12 D Byrne, in tch, rdn alng 6th, wkng
       whn mstk 3 out. . . . . (11 to 2 op 4 to 1) 7
1640⁵ IS SHE QUICK 4-10-7 N Dawe, in tch till lost pl frm 7th,
       btn whn blun 2 out. . . . . (14 to 1 op 16 to 1) 8
2837³ MOON MONKEY (Ire) 6-11-4 S McNeill, midfield,
       reminders aftr 4th, nvr a dngr. . . . . (14 to 1 op 12 to 1) 9
1142 SARANNPOUR (Ire) (bl) 5-11-4 G McCourt, chsd ldrs till
       rdn and wknd quickly aftr 3 out. . . . . (6 to 1 op 9 to 2) 10
       SOLUNIOUS 7-11-4 W Marston, mstk 1st, beh and rdn
       alng aftr 4th, tld off. . . . . (40 to 1 op 33 to 1) 11
3317⁸ BOWLAND GIRL (Ire) 5-10-10 (3*) S Wynne, midfield, rdn
       aftr 4th, blun and uns rdr 7th. . . . . . (12 to 1 op 10 to 1) ur
1304⁸ JORURI 9-10-11 (7*) P McLoughlin, midfield, rdn alng
       whn mstk 7th, sn wknd, tld off when pld up bef 2 out.
       . . . . (50 to 1 op 33 to 1) pu
       WHITEHOUSE GEM 11-10-13 V Slattery, al beh, tld off
       whn pld up bef 2 out. . . . . (33 to 1 op 20 to 1) pu
3019⁵ LYCIAN MOON (bl) 5-10-13 E Byrne, mstk 3rd, sn in rear,
       tld off whn pld up bef 2 out. . . . . . . (33 to 1 op 25 to 1) pu
       BURFORDS DELIGHT 5-10-10 (3*) D Meredith, drpd last
       aftr 4th, wl beh whn pld up aftr nxt. . . . . . . (20 to 1) pu
2808 FOXY LASS 5-10-13 Mr J Cambidge, al beh, tld off whn
       pld up bef 2 out. . . . . (25 to 1) pu
3191⁹ HURRICANE SUE 5-10-13 R Supple, in tch till mstk 4th
       and sn lost pl, beh whn pld up bef 7th.
       . . . . (33 to 1 op 16 to 1) pu
Dist: 8l, 5l, 2l, 4l, 13l, 12l, ¾l, 15l, 6l, dist. 5m 34.30s. a 37.30s (18 Ran).

(Richard J Marshall), W Clay

3396 EBF 'National Hunt' Novices' Hurdle Qualifier (5,6,7-y-o) £2,267 2m. . (2:45)

2991* SQUIRE SILK 5-11-10 S McNeill, hld up in midfield,
       smooth hdwy appr 3 out, rdn bef nxt, styd on wl frm
       last to ld nr finish. . . . . . (11 to 4 op 3 to 1 tchd 7 to 2) 1
2525³ CAPTAIN KHEDIVE 6-11-0 G McCourt, in tch, effrt aftr 3
       out, quickened to ld bef nxt, clr last, ct nr finish.
       . . . . (7 to 1 op 5 to 1) 2

481

3023⁵ SUPER COIN 6-11-10 A Maguire, *hld up in midfield, hdwy to join issue 3 out, rdn nxt, wknd r-in.*
.................................(2 to 1 fav op 6 to 4 tchd 9 to 4) 3
3264 TOTHEWOODS 6-11-7 (3*) T Jenks, *sn led, hit second, hdd appr 2 out, wknd bef last*...........(9 to 2 op 4 to 1) 4
3113⁶ DOVETTO 5-10-7 (7*) P McLoughlin, *not fluent, beh till gd hdwy to join ldrs appr 3 out, rdn and no extr frm nxt.*
..............................(25 to 1 op 50 to 1 tchd 66 to 1) 5
3009⁸ TRIPLE SENSATION (NZ) 7-11-0 Jacqui Oliver, *in tch to 3 out, wkng whn hit nxt, no extr*...........(100 to 1) 6
3108 SAMS QUEEN 5-10-9 R Supple, *beh, rdn and some hdwy aftr 3 out, sn no imprsn*.........(100 to 1 op 66 to 1) 7
3221* BATTY'S ISLAND 5-11-3 (7*) D Bohan, *took keen hold, chsd ldr to 5th, rdn and wknd appr 2 out.*
...............................(12 to 1 tchd 14 to 1) 8
1642 TRUSTINO 6-10-9 J R Kavanagh, *in tch, ev ch 3 out, wknd appr nxt*....................................(100 to 1) 9
LA SUSIANE 7-10-6 (3*) R Farrant, *beh till shrtlvd effrt 5th, sn wknd*.................(100 to 1 op 66 to 1) 10
3189⁹ SCORPOTINA 5-10-9 Gary Lyons, *al beh*........(100 to 1) 11
3170⁹ FRANK RICH 7-11-10 M Richards, *trkd ldrs on tns till rdn and wknd aftr 3 out*..............(25 to 1 op 20 to 1) 12
2560 DIAMOND FLIER (Ire) 5-11-0 R Marley, *prmnt till wknd quickly frm 3 out, tld off*........(100 to 1 op 66 to 1) 13
2667 CLOWN AROUND 6-10-9 Mr A Charles-Jones, *al beh, tld off*...(100 to 1) 14
2534⁷ MOPHEAD KELLY 5-11-0 Mr B Leavy, *trkd ldrs till mstk 4th, sn wknd, tld off*.......................(100 to 1) 15
3191 DEE EM AITCH 5-11-0 M Bosley, *whipped round and uns rdr strt*...(100 to 1) ur
2250 CAPTAIN BERT 5-11-0 I Lawrence, *midfield whn slpd up aftr 3 out*..(100 to 1) su
2558 G'IME A BUZZ 6-10-9 M Foster, *prmnt to 3rd, sn lost pl, tld off whn pld up bef last*........(14 to 1 op 10 to 1) pu
Dist: ½l, 10l, 2½l, 15l, ½l, ½l, 2½l, 4l, 4l, 3l. 3m 53.20s. a. 16.20s (18 Ran).
SR: 54/43/43/40/15/14/8/20/1/   (Robert Ogden), Andrew Turnell

3397 Attwood Memorial Trophy Handicap Chase (0-135 5-y-o and up) £3,875 2½m.....................(3:20)

3310 FALSE ECONOMY [104] 9-9-11 (3*) T Jenks, *prmnt, pckd tenth, effrt aftr 4 out, ev ch whn mstk 2 out, styd on wl to ld r-in*......................................(25 to 1 op 16 to 1) 1
3268* LITTLE TOM [111] 9-10-7 (7ex) J R Kavanagh, *jmpd wl, nvr far away, led 5 out, hdd and unbl to quicken r-in.*
....(3 to 1 op 2 to 1) 2
2747 TOBY TOBIAS [132] 12-12-0 I Lawrence, *made most till hdd 5 out, sn rdn alng, styd on wl frm last.*
....(6 to 1 op 5 to 1) 3
3091* ARDCRONEY CHIEF [110] 8-10-6 S McNeill, *al prmnt, mstk 11th, rdn to chal appr 3 out, blun 2 out, one pace.*
.................................(5 to 2 fav op 9 to 4 tchd 3 to 1) 4
3172⁵ HOLTERMANN (USA) [111] 10-10-7 D Byrne, *hld up, nvr plcd to chal*..............................(11 to 1 op 10 to 1) 5
1138* DRUMSTICK [127] 8-11-6 (3*) A Thornton, *hld up and beh, no imprsn whn blun 4 out, sn btn.*
.................................(9 to 2 op 4 to 1 tchd 5 to 1) 6
1566⁵ JIM VALENTINE [104] 8-10-0 W Marston, *hld up in tch till no hdwy frm 5 out, btn whn f 3 out.*
....(12 to 1 tchd 16 to 1) f
Dist: 4l, 6l, 2l, 20l, 20l. 5m 17.90s. a. 26.90s (7 Ran).
SR: 3/6/21/-/   (J A C Edwards), J A C Edwards

3398 Sara Hamilton-Russell Memorial Trophy Handicap Hurdle (0-120 4-y-o and up) £3,022 2m 5f 110yds.......(3:50)

3186⁶ VISCOUNT TULLY [93] 9-10-6 W Humphreys, *patiently rdn, smooth hdwy frm 6th, chlgd 2 out, led last, ran on wl*.......................................(9 to 1 op 10 to 1) 1
TOUCH OF WINTER [102] (bl) 8-11-1 S McNeill, *trkd ldr, led 7th to nxt, rgned ld appr 2 out, hdd last, no extr.*
.................................(12 to 1 op 12 to 1 tchd 16 to 1) 2
3136 SMITH TOO (Ire) [111] 6-11-3 (7*) D Bohan, *trkd ldrs to 3rd, styd on ag'n appr 2 out, unbl to chal.*
......................................(10 to 1 op 7 to 1) 3
3020* KHAZARI (USA) [111] 6-11-10 A Maguire, *hld up and beh, steady hdwy aftr 3 out, one pace frm nxt.*
...................................(11 to 1 op 7 to 1 tchd 12 to 1) 4
2967 QUIET DAWN [87] 8-10-0 J R Kavanagh, *trkd ldrs, rdn 5th, jmpd rght last 2, kpt on same pace*...........(25 to 1) 5
3166³ RIMOUSKI [109] 6-11-8 Mr J Cambidge, *hld up and beh, moderate hdwy und pres frm 2 out, nvr able to chal.*
....(8 to 1 op 7 to 1 tchd 9 to 1) 6
3020⁷ MARIOLINO [87] 7-9-7 (7*) M Moran, *trkd ldrs till rdn and wknd appr 2 out*..................(14 to 1 op 11 to 1) 7
3028 DAMIER BLANC (Fr) [99] (bl) 5-10-12 J Lower, *hld up till hdwy 4th and sn tracking ldrs, mstk 6th, soon btn.*
....(5 to 1 op 4 to 1) 8
3186⁴ CAMBO (USA) [89] 8-10-2 D Skyrme, *in tch, rdn 5th, no imprsn*.......................(10 to 1 op 8 to 1) 9
3283 VOLCANIC DANCER (USA) [98] 8-10-6 (5*) E Husband, *al rear div*..................................(50 to 1) 10
3174⁴ BALLYSTATE [93] 6-10-3⁴ (7*) Mr E James, *led till hdd 7th, sn rdn and wknd*..........(33 to 1 op 20 to 1) 11

3184* DEMILUNE (USA) [87] 4-9-11 (3*) T Jenks, *al prmnt, led 3 out, sn rdn and hdd, wknd bef nxt.*
.................................(9 to 4 fav op 7 to 4 tchd 5 to 2) 12
2528 BALAAT (USA) [87] 6-10-0 W Worthington, *in tch 5th, sn in rear*...(33 to 1 op 25 to 1) 13
3170⁸ OAKLANDS WORD [87] (bl) 5-9-7 (7*) P McLoughlin, *in tch to hfwy, tld off*...................(100 to 1 op 66 to 1) 14
BATTLEPLAN [87] 9-10-0 T Wall, *drpd last 3rd, tld off whn pld up bef 3 out*.....................(100 to 1 op 50 to 1) pu
Dist: 6l, 4l, 2l, 3½l, 12l, ¾l, 3l, 15l, 1½l, 4l. 5m 23.60s. a. 26.60s (15 Ran).
(D Craddock), C F C Jackson

3399 Chase Meredith Memorial Trophy Hunters' Chase (6-y-o and up) £1,840 3m...........................(4:20)

3212* WILD ILLUSION 10-11-12 (7*) Mr J Trice-Rolph, *patiently rdn, took clr order 12th and wnt second frm 14th, led 2 out, quickened r-in.*
.................(11 to 8 on op 6 to 4 on tchd 5 to 4 on and 11 to 10 on) 1
3195 SUNNY MOUNT 8-12-5 Mr J Greenall, *al hndy, pckd 3rd, led 14th, hdd 2 out, not pace of wnr r-in.*
....(11 to 4 op 2 to 1 tchd 3 to 1) 2
3265 TAMAR LASS 9-11-2 (7*) Mr I Widdicombe, *nvr far away, bustled alng aftr 4 out, one pace...*(16 to 1 op 20 to 1) 3
3021 KNOCKUMSHIN 11-12-0 (5*) Mr T Byrne, *hld up, smooth hdwy 12th, mstk 14th, no imprsn frm nxt.*
....(5 to 1 op 4 to 1) 4
3335⁶ CWM GWAUN 10-11-7 (7*) Mr M Jackson, *prmnt, led 8th to 8th, wknd aftr 11th*.........................(50 to 1) 5
CAREFREE TIMES (v) 7-11-7 (7*) Miss C Burgess, *led to 5th, rgned ld 8th till hdd 14th, wknd*..........(50 to 1) 6
PADRIGAL 11-11-10⁵ (5*) Mr C Bealby, *trkd ldrs till lost pl and mstk 5th, reminders 9th, tld off*............(14 to 1) 7
3157⁵ KINGS THYNE 8-11-7 (7*) Mr C J B Barlow, *lost tch frm 12th, tld off whn pld up bef 2 out.* (40 to 1 op 33 to 1) pu
Dist: 5l, 15l, 2½l, 25l, 6l, dist. 6m 28.40s. a 39.40s (8 Ran).
(Col A Clerke-Brown), Miss Jennifer Pidgeon

3400 Buttercross Novices' Chase (5-y-o and up) £2,807 2m..................(4:55)

2818³ PEACEMAN 8-11-10 A Maguire, *jmpd wl, made all, sn clr, unchlgd*.........(11 to 10 fav tchd 11 to 8 and 7 to 5) 1
3004 ALWAYS REMEMBER 7-11-3 L Harvey, *al chasing wnr in vain, no imprsn frm 4 out*..........(14 to 1 op 12 to 1) 2
2308 WALLISTRANO (bl) 7-11-3 R Supple, *chsd ldr, no hdwy frm 4 out*..(25 to 1 op 14 to 1) 3
3050² BARONESS ORKZY 8-11-0 (5*) Guy Lewis, *in tch till wknd aftr 4 out*...........................(14 to 1 op 10 to 1) 4
3226³ BEAUFAN 7-11-3 Gary Lyons, *rear, moderate effrt 8th, nvr able to chal*......................(12 to 1 tchd 14 to 1) 5
2213⁵ CARLINGFORD LIGHTS (Ire) 6-11-3 V Slattery, *al rear div.*
....(50 to 1 op 33 to 1) 6
3259 BALLY PARSON 8-11-10 J R Kavanagh, *outpcd whn mstk 3rd, sn struggling*.....(12 to 1 op 14 to 1 tchd 16 to 1) 7
3107 BROOK COTTAGE (Ire) 6-11-3 T Wall, *mstk 3rd, reminders 5th, nvr a dngr*...........................(33 to 1 op 25 to 1) 8
1519⁹ TARMON (Ire) 6-11-3 W Humphreys, *jmpd lft, al struggling, tld off*............................(33 to 1 tchd 50 to 1) 9
3188 OPENING OVERTURE (USA) 8-10-9 (3*) R Farrant, *in tch till wknd 9th, tld off*...(16 to 1 op 25 to 1 tchd 40 to 1) 10
3099⁴ CROOKED COUNSEL 8-11-7 (3*) A Thornton, *f 1st.*
....(6 to 1 op 5 to 1) f
3099² MEDINAS SWAN SONG 6-11-3 A Tory, *f 1st.*
....(8 to 1 op 5 to 1) f
Dist: 20l, 2½l, 5l, 15l, 3½l, 2½l, 11l, 25l, 25l. 4m 13.00s. a 21.00s (12 Ran).
SR: 46/19/16/13/-/-/   (Sir Peter Gibbings), Mrs D Haine

3401 Mrs Muck Mares Only National Hunt Flat Race (4,5,6-y-o) £1,276 2m..(5:25)

CERTAINLY STRONG (Ire) 4-10-7 (7*) R Massey, *handily plcd gng wl, led o'r 3 fs out, pushed out, cmftbly.*
....(9 to 4 fav op 6 to 4) 1
3176² GARRYLOUGH (Ire) 5-11-3 (3*) A Thornton, *hld up in tch, chsd wnr fnl 3 fs, kpt on*..........(9 to 2 op 5 to 2) 2
3176³ SWEET REVELATION 5-10-13 (7*) T Dascombe, *trkd ldr led hfwy to o'r 3 fs out, sn rdn and unbl to quicken.*
....(3 to 1 tchd 5 to 1) 3
CORNBELT 5-11-3 (3*) D Meredith, *midfield, rdn alng hfwy, hdwy o'r 4 fs out, kpt on same pace.*
....(16 to 1 op 50 to 1) 4
MAGICAL MINSTER 4-10-7 (7*) G Robertson, *wth ldrs, rdn o'r 3 fs out, sn no extr*............(50 to 1 tchd 66 to 1) 5
FRA'S GIRL 6-11-6 Mr M Jackson, *nvr far away, ev ch 4 fs out, sn btn*.............................(5 to 1 op 3 to 1) 6
3176⁵ URBAN LILY 4-10-7 (7*) T Thompson, *beh, styd on fnl 4 fs, nvr able to chal*.......................(20 to 1 op 14 to 1) 7
BROOKSONG 4-10-11 (3*) T Jenks, *midfield, rdn alng hfwy, ran on o'r 4 fs out till no no hdwy fnl 3.*
....(66 to 1 op 33 to 1) 8
ARIOSO 6-10-13 (7*) N Collum, *in tch till wknd o'r 4 fs out*.........................(50 to 1 op 33 to 1) 9
MORNING BLUSH (Ire) 4-10-7 (7*) O Burrows, *chsd ldrs to hfwy, stdly lost pl*..........................(16 to 1 op 10 to 1) 10

GOLD OR BUST 4-11-0 Mr B Leavy, *nvr a dngr.* ....(25 to 1 op 33 to 1) 11
3227[4] HENNERWOOD OAK 4-10-7 (7*) P McLoughlin, *chsd ldg bunch till no hdwy fnl 4 fs*..........(9 to 1 op 5 to 1) 12
WINDERMERE TERRACE 4-11-0 N Bentley, *led to hfwy, sn btn*..................................(33 to 1 op 25 to 1) 13
ZANDALEE 5-10-13 (7*) S Arnold, *midfield till lost pl frm hfwy*..........................(100 to 1 op 50 to 1) 14
2996[8] TAMANDU 4-10-7 (7*) Katherine Davis, *slwly away, al beh.* ....(20 to 1 op 16 to 1) 15
CASTLE ROUGE 5-11-1 (5*) Mr D McCain, *chsd ldrs till rdn and wknd quickly o'r 5 fs out*.... (100 to 1 op 33 to 1) 16
SHEILA'S SUPRISE 5-11-3 (3*) T Eley, *wth ldrs till wknd quickly wl o'r 3 fs out*........................(25 to 1) 17
PALM SUNDAY 5-11-3 (3*) S Wynne, *chsd ldg bunch on ins till rdn and lost pl quickly 5 fs out, tld off.* ....(33 to 1 op 25 to 1) 18
Dist: 2½l, 20l, 2l, ¾l, sht-hd, 4l, 5l, 10l, 2½l, 1½l. 3m 49.70s. (18 Ran).
(Nick Skelton), D Nicholson

AINTREE (soft (races 1,2,3,5,6,7), good to soft (4))
Thursday April 7th
Going Correction: PLUS 1.40 sec. per fur. (races 1,5,7), PLUS 1.25 (2,3,4,6)

3402 Seagram Top Novices' Hurdle Grade 2 (4-y-o and up) £11,272 2m 110yds ....(2:00)

2743* JAZILAH (Fr) 6-11-6 G McCourt, *settled wth chasing grp, improved hfwy, led jst aftr last, hld on wl r-in.* ....(7 to 4 fav op 6 to 4 tchd 15 to 8) 1
3062 WINTER FOREST (USA) 4-11-0 A Maguire, *patiently rdn, mstk second, improved 3 out, ev ch whn struck by rival's whip r-in, hng lft, not go past.* ....(11 to 1 op 7 to 1 tchd 12 to 1) 2
3252* DREAMS END 6-11-2 Peter Hobbs, *tucked away gng wl, led 2 out, mstk last, sn hdd, one pace r-in.* ....(9 to 4 op 7 to 4 tchd 5 to 2) 3
3062 DEVILS DEN (Ire) 4-10-10 R Dunwoody, *nvr far away, led 3 out to nxt, wknd und pres betw last 2.* ....(6 to 1 tchd 7 to 1) 4
3023[4] CUMBRIAN CHALLENGE (Ire) 5-11-6 L Wyer, *trkd ldr, feeling pace and rdn 3 out, fdd und pres bef nxt.* ....(7 to 1 op 6 to 1 tchd 8 to 1) 5
2874[2] FLOATING LINE 6-11-2 R Garritty, *wtd wth, imprvg whn stumbled 4 out, effrt aftr nxt, fdd betw last 2.* ....(100 to 1 op 50 to 1) 6
3164[6] MOZEMO 7-11-2 S Smith Eccles, *led, jmpd rght 1st 2, rdn and hdd 3 out, wknd quickly.* ....(50 to 1 op 33 to 1 tchd 66 to 1) 7
2881* FIRST AVENUE 10-11-2 J Railton, *in tch, feeling pace and lost grnd 4 out, tld off whn f last.* ....(14 to 1 op 16 to 1 tchd 12 to 1) f
Dist: Nk, 8l, 11l, 7l, 20l, 1½l. 4m 15.60s. a 27.60s (8 Ran).
SR: 47/40/34/17/20/ (S Aitken), R Akehurst

3403 Martell Cup Chase Grade 2 (5-y-o and up) £28,820 3m 1f.............. (2:35)

3064[6] DOCKLANDS EXPRESS 12-11-5 R Dunwoody, *jmpd wl, led 4th, jnd 3 out, edgd lft r-in, kpt on gmely.* ....(5 to 2 op 2 to 1) 1
2695* BLACK HUMOUR 10-11-5 G Bradley, *not fluent, wtd wth, improved aftr 4 out, rallied and swtchd r-in, hld cl hme*..........(9 to 4 op 2 to 1 tchd 5 to 2) 2
2513* DUBACILLA 8-11-4 D Gallagher, *settled gng wl, drw level 3 out, rdn last, no extr.* ....(6 to 4 fav op 11 to 8 tchd 13 to 8) 3
3261[6] ARCTIC CALL (bl) 11-11-5 J Osborne, *not jump wl, led to 4th, blun and lost grnd 12th, not reco'r, tld off.* ....(12 to 1 op 16 to 1 tchd 20 to 1) 4
Dist: ½l, 8l, dist. 6m 54.00s. a 49.00s (4 Ran).
(R H Baines), K C Bailey

3404 Sandeman Maghull Novices' Chase Grade 2 (5-y-o and up) £15,481 2m ....(3:10)

3024* NAKIR (Fr) 6-11-10 J Osborne, *led to 5 out, dsptd ld till led betw last 2, ran on strly.* ....(6 to 5 fav op 5 to 4 tchd 11 to 8) 1
3047[2] JIMMY THE GILLIE 8-11-3 G Upton, *wth ldr, led 5 out till betw last 2, drifted lft r-in, no extr.* ....(12 to 1 tchd 14 to 1) 2
3024 THUMBS UP 8-11-3 R Dunwoody, *trkd ldg pair, blun 4th, blunded and lost grnd 5 out, struggling last 3.* ....(6 to 4 op 5 to 4) 3
3172[4] MINE'S AN ACE (NZ) 7-11-3 J Frost, *chsd clr ldg trio, struggling bef 4 out, no imprsn*.... (33 to 1 op 16 to 1) 4
2866[7] OH SO GRUMPY 6-11-3 M Dwyer, *settled off the pace, hit second, outpcd hfwy, nvr a threat.* ....(20 to 1 tchd 25 to 1) 5
2993[4] STRONG VIEWS 7-11-3 A Maguire, *settled off the pace, nvr able to rch chalg pos*..........(10 to 1 op 14 to 1) 6
Dist: 3½l, 11l, 3½l, 15l, 1l. 4m 12.60s. a 23.60s (6 Ran).
SR: 60/49/38/34/19/18/ (Jim Lewis), S Christian

3405 John Hughes Memorial Trophy Chase Handicap (0-145 5-y-o and up) £24,319 2¾m.......................... (3:45)

3026[4] INDIAN TONIC [120] 8-10-4 C Maude, *jmpd wl, made most, hrd pressed frm 4 out, kpt on gmely r-in.* ....(5 to 1 fav tchd 11 to 2) 1
3041[9] KENTISH PIPER [128] 9-10-12 J Osborne, *settled wth chasing grp, improved frm tenth (Becher's), ev ch appr 2 out, styd on wl r-in*.............. (7 to 1 tchd 8 to 1) 2
3105[3] SIRRAH JAY [116] 14-10-0 L Wyer, *wtd wth, improved aftr 13th (Valentine's), ev ch and rdn 2 out, no extr appr last*..................................(14 to 1 op 12 to 1) 3
2990[2] HEY COTTAGE [116] 9-10-0 D Gallagher, *settled off the pace, improved frm 13th (Valentine's), styd on from 2 out, nvr able to chal*..........................(20 to 1) 4
3141[3] KUSHBALOO [116] 9-10-0 B Storey, *wth ldr, niggled alng to hold pl appr 3 out, rdn and no extr betw last 2.* ....(10 to 1 op 12 to 1) 5
3027 OVER THE DEEL [117] 8-10-1 A Dobbin, *settled wth chasing grp, feeling pace and lost grnd bef tenth (Becher's), no imprsn frm 13th (Valentine's).* (14 to 1 op 12 to 1) 6
2847 WINNING CHARLIE [116] 8-10-0 K O'Brien, *sn struggling to go pace, lost tch hfwy, tld off 12th (Canal Turn).* ....(20 to 1) 7
2995 GAMBLING ROYAL [142] 11-11-12 A Maguire, *led briefly 1st, blun second, lost pl bef tenth (Becher's), no dngr aftr*..................................(10 to 1 op 7 to 1) 8
3027[3] TRI FOLENE (Fr) [122] (bl) 8-10-6 R Dunwoody, *blun and lost grnd second, struggling in rear aftr, tld off hfwy.* ....(8 to 1 tchd 9 to 1) 9
3027[8] NEW HALEN [116] 13-10-0 R Bellamy, *sn disputing ld, 3rd whn blun and lost grnd tenth (Becher's), rallied 12th (Canal Turn), fdd frm 5 out*....... (16 to 1 op 14 to 1) 10
2893[4] THE MALTKILN [116] (v) 11-10-0 C Grant, *f 1st.* ....(20 to 1 tchd 25 to 1) f
2984* BLUE RING [116] 10-10-0 F Woods, *patiently rdn, hdwy 12th (Canal Turn), effrt 4 out, 6th and no imprsn whn f 2 out*..................................(20 to 1 op 25 to 1) f
2948[2] ROUGH QUEST [130] 8-11-0 G McCourt, *patiently rdn, jnd ldrs 12th (Canal Turn), 3rd and ev ch whn f 4 out.* ....(6 to 1 op 5 to 1) f
3141[2] ABSAILOR [116] (v) 10-10-0[5] (5*) J Burke, *chasing ldg grp whn blun and uns rdr 7th*.........(20 to 1 op 33 to 1) ur
2294 GADBROOK [120] (v) 12-10-4[4] Mr M Armytage, *beh 3rd (Chair), jmpd slwly 5th, tld off whn pld up bef 9th.* ....(100 to 1) pu
3282[2] GLOVE PUPPET [118] 9-10-2[2] M A FitzGerald, *chsd ldrs, struggling to keep up whn blun 12th (Canal Turn), sn tld off, pld up bef 2 out*.......... (25 to 1 tchd 33 to 1) pu
Dist: Nk, 13l, 15l, ¾l, 14l, 2l, 4l, 8l, 5l. 5m 58.50s. a 30.50s (16 Ran).
SR: 46/53/28/13/12/-/-/18/-/ (Mrs Joanne Richards), N A Twiston-Davies

3406 Glenlivet Anniversary 4-y-o Hurdle Grade 2 £25,176 2m 110yds..... (4:20)

2699* TROPICAL LAKE (Ire) 10-9 K O'Brien, *settled midfield, improved gng wl 4 out, led appr last, ran on strly.* ....(10 to 1 op 7 to 1 tchd 11 to 1) 1
3062[5] KADASTROF (Fr) 11-0 D Meredith, *nvr far away, improved to ld briefly appr 3 out, rdn last, kpt on one pace.* ....(9 to 1 op 7 to 1 tchd 10 to 1) 2
3062* MYSILV 10-13 A Maguire, *sn led, hit 4th, hdd briefly appr 3 out, headed approaching last, one pace r-in.* ....(11 to 10 on op Evens tchd 11 to 10) 3
3062[3] SHIRLEY'S DELIGHT (Ire) (bl) 10-9 P Carberry, *settled to track ldrs, feeling pace aftr 4 out, lost tch after nxt.* ....(13 to 2 op 5 to 1) 4
2812[4] BURNT IMP (USA) 11-0 J Callaghan, *chsd alng to go pace aftr 4th, some hdwy frm four out, nvr nr to chal.* ....(25 to 1 tchd 33 to 1) 5
3062[7] PRIDWELL 11-0 R Dunwoody, *settled midfield, lost grnd hfwy, tld off*.......... (9 to 1 op 7 to 1 tchd 10 to 1) 6
2783[2] CALL MY GUEST (Ire) 11-0 M Dwyer, *struggling hfwy, tld off whn pld up aftr 4 out*.........(50 to 1 op 33 to 1) pu
2783 CIRCUS COLOURS 11-0 Richard Guest, *rdn alng aftr 3rd, sn lost tch, pld up after nxt*...... (100 to 1 op 66 to 1) pu
3062[8] DUVEEN (Ire) 11-0 D Bridgwater, *chsd ldrs to 4th, sn lost tch, tld off whn pld up bef 2 out*... (25 to 1 op 16 to 1) pu
2897[6] DIWALI DANCER (bl) 11-0 S Smith Eccles, *struggling hfwy, lost tch and pld up bef 6th.* (100 to 1 op 50 to 1) pu
1880 ADMIRAL'S WELL (Ire) 11-0 G McCourt, *chsd ldrs, feeling pace hfwy, lost tch and pld up aftr 4 out.* ....(25 to 1 op 20 to 1 tchd 33 to 1) pu
2853* DARK DEN (USA) 11-0 T Kent, *chsd ldg trio, hit 1st, lost pl hfwy, tld off whn pld up aftr 4 out.* ....(13 to 2 op 5 to 1 tchd 7 to 1) pu
Dist: 5l, ¾l, 30l, sht-hd, 15l. 4m 14.00s. a 26.00s (12 Ran).
SR: 52/52/50/16/21/6/ (G A Hoggard), M Hourigan

3407 Cuvee Napa Handicap Chase (5-y-o and up) £8,654 3m 1f........... (4:50)

3229 GRANGE BRAKE [130] 8-10-0 D Bridgwater, *wth ldr, led 8th, reminder to quicken fnl circuit, drw clr aftr 4 out, eased finish*..........(14 to 1 op 16 to 1 tchd 12 to 1)   1

3039[6] ARTHUR'S MINSTREL [130] 7-10-0 C Grant, *trkd ldrs, hit 9th and 6 out, styd on frm 2 out, not rch vnr.*
.... (11 to 1 op 14 to 1 tchd 10 to 1)   2

3218[3] FLASHTHECASH [130] 8-10-0 A Maguire, *co'red up, hit 4th, imprvg whn hit 11th, reminders bef nxt, drvn alng when blun 3 out, sn outpcd.*
...............(9 to 2 op 4 to 1 tchd 5 to 1)   3

3041[7] BIBENDUM [133] 8-10-3 M A FitzGerald, *settled midfield, struggling whn pace quickened fnl circuit, no imprsn when jmpd slwly 2 out.*...............(5 to 1 op 9 to 1)   4

3205* AUCTION LAW (NZ) [130] 10-10-0 C Maude, *chsd ldg grp, struggling 6 out, pld up bef 3 out.* (14 to 1 op 16 to 1)   pu

3261[2] BONSAI BUD [130] 11-10-0 D Gallagher, *chsd ldrs, outpcd and lost grnd 9th, tld off whn pld up bef 6 out.*
......................................(7 to 1 op 6 to 1)   pu

3280[4] CAPABILITY BROWN [142] 7-10-12 R Dunwoody, *led to 8th, lost tch fnl circuit, pld up bef 4 out.*
......................(7 to 1 op 6 to 1 tchd 8 to 1)   pu

3127* COGENT [155] 10-11-6 (5*) D Fortt, *trkd ldg pair, effrt fnl circuit, struggling 5 out, pld up bef 3 out.*
......................(9 to 4 fav op 7 to 4 tchd 5 to 2)   pu

Dist: 14l, 14l, dist. 6m 56.50s. a 51.50s (8 Ran).

(Mrs J Mould), N A Twiston-Davies

3408   Barton & Guestier Handicap Hurdle (5-y-o and up) £9,648 3m 110yds (5:20)

2473[8] MEDITATOR [128] 10-11-2 (5*) S Curran, *settled midfield, improved fnl circuit, styd on to ld aftr 3 out, drw clr.*
.... (20 to 1 op 16 to 1)   1

3028 LINKSIDE [113] 9-10-6 C Swan, *sn wl beh, prog fnl circuit, styd on frm 2 out, nvr nrr*.............(12 to 1 op 14 to 1)   2

1274 SAYFAR'S LAD [116] 10-10-9 D Bridgwater, *set gd pace, led till aftr 3 out, rdn and one pace.*
......................(14 to 1 op 10 to 1 tchd 16 to 1)   3

3136[2] FAST THOUGHTS [108] 7-10-1 P Holley, *al hndy, drvn alng 3 out, kpt on same pace....*(11 to 2 fav op 6 to 1)   4

3038 PEANUTS PET [126] 9-11-5 R Garritty, *beh and struggling aftr one circuit, tld off*............(10 to 1 tchd 12 to 1)   5

3038 LEMON'S MILL (USA) [131] 5-11-10 R Dunwoody, *wtd wth, effrt aftr one circuit, struggling 4 out, tld off.*
..................................(12 to 1 tchd 14 to 1)   6

3028[7] PEATSWOOD [129] 6-11-8 Lorna Vincent, *chsd ldrs one circuit, sn struggling, tld off.*....(12 to 1 tchd 14 to 1)   7

3253* ELAINE TULLY (Ire) [119] 6-10-12 (4ex) Peter Hobbs, *midfield whn brght drwn aftr 3rd....* (10 to 1 tchd 11 to 1)   bd

3028[3] TINDARI (Fr) [128] 6-11-7 A Dobbin, *settled midfield, slpd up aftr 3rd...........*(8 to 1 op 7 to 1 tchd 9 to 1)   su

2967[8] JOPANINI [131] (bl) 9-11-10 M A FitzGerald, *chsd ldrs, lost grnd quickly aftr one circuit, pld up aftr 7th.*
........................(16 to 1 op 14 to 1 tchd 20 to 1)   pu

2293 ASK THE GOVERNOR [113] 8-10-6 A Maguire, *nvr a factor, pld up aftr 7th.......*(16 to 1 op 14 to 1 tchd 20 to 1)   pu

2830[7] MIZYAN (Ire) [118] 6-10-11 G McCourt, *chsd ldrs one circuit, tld off whn pld up bef 2 out.* (20 to 1 op 16 to 1)   pu

3028[3] KILGARIFF [115] 8-10-8 P Niven, *sn wl beh, tld off whn pld up bef 3 out...................* (7 to 1 op 6 to 1)   pu

3206[3] NOBLE INSIGHT [107] 7-10-0 M Perrett, *tld off 13th, pld up aftr 7th.........*(66 to 1 op 50 to 1 tchd 100 to 1)   pu

3156[3] SHARRIBA [107] 5-10-0 B Powell, *sn beh, tld off whn pld up aftr 7th...................*(33 to 1 tchd 50 to 1)   pu

3038 DANCE OF WORDS (Ire) [130] 5-11-9 W Marston, *pressed ldrs, struggling aftr one circuit, tld off whn pld up bef 3 out....*........................(20 to 1 op 16 to 1)   pu

2999 LUSTY LIGHT [110] 8-10-3 J Osborne, *al beh, tld off whn pld up aftr 7th........*(20 to 1 op 16 to 1 tchd 25 to 1)   pu

3832[2] MARTELL BOY (NZ) [107] 7-9-13[2] (3*) R Davis, *chsd ldg pair one circuit, lost tch and pld up bef 3 out*
...........................(20 to 1 op 25 to 1)   pu

2172* TOOGOOD TO BE TRUE [130] 6-11-9 L Wyer, *settled midfield, improved gng wl hfwy, struggling fnl circuit, pld up bef 4 out...................*(6 to 1 tchd 7 to 1)   pu

3136[8] BEAUCHAMP GRACE [129] 5-11-3 (5*) J Burke, *trkd ldrs, struggling hfwy, lost tch and pld up aftr 7th.* (33 to 1)   pu

Dist: 10l, 3½l, hd, dist, 8l, 4l. 6m 34.90s. a 47.40s (20 Ran).

(Miss Jacqueline S Doyle), Miss Jacqueline S Doyle

AINTREE (heavy)
Friday April 8th
Going Correction: PLUS 2.25 sec. per fur. (races 1,5,6), PLUS 2.40 (2,3,4,7)

3409   Martell Mersey Novices' Hurdle Grade 2 (4-y-o and up) £11,318 2½m (2:00)

3109 CYBORGO (Fr) 4-10-8 R Dunwoody, *set steady pace, quickened hfwy, hdd 3 out, 4th r-in, rallied to ld last 50 yards..................*(8 to 1 op 7 to 1 tchd 10 to 1)   1

3367* MONALEE RIVER (Ire) 6-11-5 (4ex) K O'Brien, *settled gng wl, improved on bit to draw level last, sn led, wknd and ct last 50 yards.........*(8 to 1 op 10 to 1 tchd 7 to 1)   2

3025[3] LARGE ACTION (Ire) 6-11-9 J Osborne, *trkd ldr, led 3 out, mstk nxt, jnd last, sn hdd and one pace.*
...................(9 to 4 on op 5 to 2 on tchd 2 to 1 on)   3

2812[7] ASLAN (Ire) (bl) 6-11-1 M Dwyer, *pld hrd, co'red up beh ldrs, effrt on outsd aftr 3 out, rdn, no extr.*
........................(10 to 1 op 8 to 1)   4

2204 KONVEKTA KING (Ire) 6-11-1 A Maguire, *tucked away on ins, effrt and niggled alng appr 3 out, wknd rpdly nxt, tld off...................*(10 to 1 op 14 to 1)   5

2344* DEBACLE (USA) 5-11-1 D Murphy, *in tch, struggling to hold pl hfwy, lost touch bef 4 out, pld up before nxt.*
.......................(66 to 1 op 50 to 1 tchd 100 to 1)   pu

Dist: 1¼l, 1½l, 7l, dist. 5m 26.00s. a 48.00s (6 Ran).

SR: 50/59/61/46/-/-/   (County Stores (Somerset) Holdings Ltd), M C Pipe

3410   Mumm Melling Chase Grade 1 (5-y-o and up) £38,898 2½m (2:35)

3037[5] KATABATIC 11-11-10 S McNeill, *led to 3rd, styd hndy, led aftr tenth, quickened clr last 2, stayed on strly.*
...........................(14 to 1 op 10 to 1)   1

3037[2] TRAVADO 8-11-10 J Osborne, *patiently rdn, blun 9th and 4 out, effrt appr 3 out, styd on one pace r-in.*
........................(9 to 4 jt-fav op 7 to 4)   2

3037[3] DEEP SENSATION (bl) 9-11-10 D Murphy, *wtd wth, improved on outsd to chal aftr 4 out, rdn and no extr betw last 2...........*(3 to 1 op 2 to 1 tchd 100 to 30)   3

3037 REMITTANCE MAN 11-11-10 R Dunwoody, *trkd ldr, led 3rd, hit tenth, sn hdd, wknd quickly, jmpd slwly 3 out, tld off...................*(9 to 4 jt-fav op 2 to 1 tchd 5 to 2)   4

3066[4] FORCE SEVEN 7-11-5 T Horgan, *blun and uns rdr second.*
.......................(8 to 1 op 16 to 1 tchd 20 to 1)   ur

Dist: 15l, 8l, dist. 5m 43.80s. a 53.80s (5 Ran).

SR: 38/23/15/-/-/   (Pell-Mell Partners), J T Gifford

3411   Mumm Mildmay Novices' Chase Grade 2 (5-y-o and up) £20,652 3m 1f (3:10)

3039[4] MONSIEUR LE CURE 8-11-9 P Niven, *jmpd boldly, made most, quickened 6 out, imprsv.*
........................(7 to 4 fav op 2 to 1 tchd 6 to 4)   1

3039[3] CRYSTAL SPIRIT 7-11-6 J Frost, *al hndy, jnd wnr hfwy, drvn alng 6 out, no ch wth winner last 4.*
.....................................(9 to 2 op 3 to 1)   2

2873* MELEAGRIS 10-11-3 A Maguire, *wtd wth, improved hfwy, struggling whn pace quickened 6 out, sn outpcd.*
........................(10 to 1 tchd 12 to 1)   3

3024[3] SOUTHOLT (Ire) 6-11-3 D Bridgwater, *trkd ldrs, blun 13th, lost tch 6 out, tld off....*(10 to 1 op 9 to 1 tchd 12 to 1)   4

3226* GALLATEEN 6-11-3 N Doughty, *dsptd early ld, not fluent aftr 3rd, losing tch whn blun 12th, pld up bef 6 out.*
.....................................(9 to 2 op 6 to 1)   pu

3039[2] MARTOMICK 7-11-1 N Williamson, *not fluent, chsd alng and jmpd lft ith and 7th, losing tch whn blun 5 out, pld up bef nxt...........................*(4 to 1 op 9 to 2)   pu

Dist: 20l, 14l, dist. 7m 18.80s. a 73.80s (6 Ran).

(Hector Brown), J A C Edwards

3412   Martell Fox Hunters' Chase (6-y-o and up) £11,990 2¾m (3:45)

3155* KILLESHIN 8-12-0 Mr G Brown, *beh 3rd (Chair), improved into midfield tenth (Becher's), styd on wl to ld r-in, gmely...........................*(8 to 1 op 7 to 1)   1

3081* BROWN WINDSOR (bl) 12-12-0 Mr B Pollock, *al hndy, ev ch frm 3 out, led r-in, hdd and one pace last 50 yards.*
.......................(10 to 1 op 12 to 1)   2

539[5] ALLEZMOSS 8-12-0 Mr E Bolger, *trkd ldg grp, hmpd 12th (Canal Turn), reco'red to ld nxt (Valentine's), quickened 3 out, hdd r-in, kpt on same pace.*
.......................(11 to 2 op 4 to 1)   3

3162* DARK DAWN 10-12-0 Mr J Greenall, *rcd freely frnt rnk, stumbled tenth (Becher's), led nxt, hmpd 12th (Canal Turn), hdd next (Valentine's), btn 2 out.*
.......................(7 to 2 fav op 4 to 1)   4

3171[5] MANDRAKI SHUFFLE (bl) 12-12-0 Mr A Harvey, *chsd alng beh ldrs, feeling pace whn blun 11th, styd on frm 3 out, nvr nr to chal....................*(20 to 1)   5

NO REBASSE 12-12-0 Mr Simon Andrews, *sn beh, improved 12th (Canal Turn), drvn alng appr 4 out, not pace of ldrs...........*(33 to 1 op 25 to 1)   6

2966[4] ON THE OTHER HAND 11-12-0 Capt A Ogden, *wth ldrs, struggling to hold pl aftr 13th (Valentine's), fdd 3 out.*
.......................(12 to 1 op 14 to 1 tchd 16 to 1)   7

2888 KAMEO STYLE (bl) 11-12-0 Miss S Lea, *nvr gng pace, tld off tenth (Becher's).............*(150 to 1 op 200 to 1)   8

3284* WAY OF LIFE (Fr) 9-12-0 Mr C Bonner, *wth ldrs, led 4th to 11th, hndy till tld off 3 out.*
.......................(33 to 1 op 20 to 1 tchd 50 to 1)   9

3313[3] NICK THE BRIEF 12-11-10 Mr T Byrne, *led to 4th, hndy till f 7th..................*(25 to 1 op 33 to 1)   f

3260 GUNNER STREAM 10-12-0 Capt R Inglesant, *f 1st.*
.......................(150 to 1 op 200 to 1)   f

3171[8] WREKIN HILL 12-12-0 Mrs J Wilkinson, *tld off whn f 7th.*
...........................(100 to 1)   f

3161* FOUR TRIX 13-12-0 Mr R Hale, *settled midfield, chsd alng whn f 9th*..................................(25 to 1) f
2882³ SKINNHILL (bl) 10-12-0 Mr C Newport, *al beh, tld off whn f 2 out*.....................................(66 to 1) f
3159* DALTON DANDY 12-12-0 Mr P Jenkins, *settled midfield, hmpd and f 9th*.................(20 to 1 op 16 to 1) f
3021* STRONG GOLD (bl) 11-12-0 Mr T Hills, *hmpd 1st, f 8th*.
....(14 to 1 op 12 to 1) f
3162⁴ ASTRE RADIEUX (Fr) 9-12-0 Mr C Stockton, *settled midfield, pushed alng whn f tenth (Becher's)*.
...............................(66 to 1 op 50 to 1 tchd 100 to 1) f
3159⁴ NO PANIC 10-12-0 Mr N Bannister, *beh whn blun and uns rdr 8th*......................................(100 to 1) ur
3212³ SONOFAGIPSY 10-12-0 Mr M Felton, *chasing ldrs whn blun and uns rdr 7th*.......................(33 to 1) ur
RAGLAN ROAD 10-12-0 Miss A Embiricos, *brght dwn 1st*.
....(33 to 1) bd
2800 LATE SESSION 10-12-0 Miss L Blackford, *struggling whn refused 7th*..................(150 to 1 op 200 to 1) ref
2959³ CARRICKMINES 9-12-0 Mr T Jones, *al beh, hmpd and refused 13th (Valentine's)*............(66 to 1 op 50 to 1) ref
RAISABILLION 12-12-0 Mr P Murray, *wl beh whn pld up bef 13th (Valentine's)*..........(150 to 1 op 200 to 1) pu
3013* TEAM CHALLENGE 12-12-0 Mr J Rees, *hit 3rd (Valentine's), sn lost tch, hmpd and pld up bef 13th (Valentine's)*...................(12 to 1 op 8 to 1) pu
2888⁵ CROCK-NA-NEE 13-12-0 Mr C Vigors, *struggling to keep up whn baulked tenth (Becher's), tld off when pld up bef last*.............................(66 to 1 op 100 to 1) pu
SANDSTONE ARCH 11-12-0 Mr L Brennan, *wth ldrs to 7th, losing tch whn baulked and pld up 13th (Valentine's)*.
....(100 to 1) pu
3263⁴ MINSTREL MAN 10-12-0 Mr P Hacking, *hmpd 1st, tld off whn pld up bef last*................(50 to 1 op 33 to 1) pu
3168* BIANCONI 8-12-0 Mr M Armytage, *wl beh tenth (Becher's), tld off whn pld up bef 2 out*.
....(11 to 2 op 6 to 1) pu
Dist: 1¼l, 1l, 12l, 12l, 15l, dist, dist. 6m 26.40s. a 58.40s (28 Ran).
SR: 44/42/41/16/2/-/ (H J Manners), H J Manners

3413 Oddbins Handicap Hurdle (4-y-o and up) £13,177 2½m..............(4:20)

3038⁵ KADI (Ger) [133] 5-11-7 A Maguire, *patiently rdn, improved 4 out, strly ridden to ld r-in*.
.......................(7 to 1 op 6 to 1 tchd 8 to 1) 1
3038⁶ ZAMIRAH (Ire) [118] 5-10-6 D Bridgwater, *settled midfield, led aftr 4 out, sn clr, hdd r-in, no extr*.
.......................(6 to 1 op 8 to 1 tchd 10 to 1) 2
3214⁴ LYNCH LAW (Ire) [117] (v) 6-10-5 R Dunwoody, *wtd wth, improved 4 out, drvn alng and no imprsn frm 2 out*.
....(11 to 2 op 4 to 1) 3
2994 KIVETON TYCOON (Ire) [120] (bl) 5-10-8 G Bradley, *patiently rdn, wnt second 3 out, ev ch 3 out, ridden and one pace nxt*................(14 to 1 op 16 to 1) 4
1851 RISING WATERS (Ire) [128] 6-11-2 K O'Brien, *struggling to go pace hfwy, nvr a factor, tld off*.
....(16 to 1 op 14 to 1 tchd 20 to 1) 5
2727⁵ MANEREE [115] 7-10-3 J Osborne, *wth ldrs, feeling pace appr 5 out, sn fdd, tld off*...............(7 to 1 op 8 to 1) 6
3182 BRAMBLEBERRY [113] 5-10-11 Richard Guest, *led till appr 6th, led nxt till aftr 4 out, fdd, tld off*.
....(9 to 2 fav op 4 to 1 tchd 5 to 1) 7
2382⁶ WESTHOLME (USA) [119] 6-10-7 L Wyer, *al hndy, wth ldr aftr 5th, wknd nxt, pld up*. (9 to 1 op 7 to 1) pu
3038 SUNSET AND VINE [122] 7-10-10 A Dicken, *sn beh, tld off 5 out, pld up bef 3 out*...(9 to 1 op 8 to 1 tchd 10 to 1) pu
2986³ MR BOAL (Ire) [126] 5-11-0 C Swan, *al struggling, tld off whn pld up bef last*.................(5 to 1 tchd 11 to 2) pu
LEINTHALL FOX [112] 8-10-0 T Wall, *wth ldrs, led appr 6th to nxt, lost tch quickly, pld up bef 2 out*.
....(66 to 1 op 50 to 1 tchd 100 to 1) pu
Dist: 1l, 15l, 7l, 20l, dist, dist. 5m 40.60s. a 62.60s (11 Ran).
(J E Brown), D Nicholson

3414 Belle Epoque Sefton Novices' Hurdle Grade 2 (4-y-o and up) £8,032 3m 110yds......................(4:50)

3137* CORNER BOY 7-11-4 A Maguire, *settled gng wl, improved on bit to ld 3 out, styd on well r-in*. (10 to 1 op 7 to 1) 1
3036² CORROUGE (USA) 5-11-4 D Bridgwater, *nvr far away, led 4 out to nxt, rallied, kpt on r-in*.
.......................(15 to 8 fav op 6 to 4 tchd 11 to 8) 2
3036⁶ WHAT A QUESTION (Ire) 6-11-2 C O'Dwyer, *tucked away gng wl, hit 8th, ev ch frm 3 out, styd on one pace from last*.............................(7 to 1 op 6 to 1 tchd 9 to 1) 3
3177* JOHNNY KELLY 7-11-4 M Dwyer, *trkd ldg trio, improved on bit to join ldrs appr 2 out, rdn and one pace r-in*.
....(11 to 2 op 9 to 2 tchd 6 to 1) 4
3036 DIVINE CHANCE (Ire) 6-11-4 D Murphy, *made most to 4 out, fdd und pres aftr nxt*..............(33 to 1 op 20 to 1) 5
2812³ MARCHWOOD 7-11-4 K Johnson, *wth ldrs, ev ch aftr 4 out, fdd betw last 2*......(10 to 1 op 16 to 1 tchd 20 to 1) 6
3115⁴ SESAME SEED (Ire) 6-11-4 R Dunwoody, *pld hrd, pressed ldrs till und pres appr 3 out, tld off*.
....(13 to 2 op 5 to 1 tchd 7 to 1) 7

3220* DO BE HAVE (Ire) 6-11-4 J Osborne, *trkd ldr, led briefly appr 8th, lost tch and pld up bef 3 out*.
....(12 to 1 op 14 to 1 tchd 16 to 1) pu
3184* DEDUCE 5-11-4 N Williamson, *chsd alng whn hit 6th, lost tch aftr nxt, tld off when pld up bef 4 out*.
....(33 to 1 op 20 to 1) pu
3036⁵ SPRING MARATHON (USA) 4-10-13 P Holley, *wtd wth, improved hfwy, reminders aftr 4 out, lost tch and pld up bef last*..........................(8 to 1 op 7 to 1) pu
3046⁷ MAN O MINE (Ire) 5-11-4 C Swan, *struggling hfwy, tld off whn pld up bef 3 out*.........(10 to 1 op 25 to 1) pu
Dist: 2l, 2l, 5l, 20l, 2l, 25l. 7m 13.20s. a 85.70s (11 Ran).
(Mrs E W Wilson), D Nicholson

3415 Perrier Jouet Handicap Chase (5-y-o and up) £8,985 2½m...............(5:20)

3280* MAN OF MYSTERY [120] 8-10-0 (4ex) D Bridgwater, *pressed ldr, struggling to hold pl 9th, rallied to ld 5 out, sn drw clr, unchlgd*.........................(2 to 1 op 7 to 4) 1
3265⁵ BUSTINELLO (Ire) [120] 6-10-0 F Woods, *nvr far away, hmpd 6th, rallied, hampered and lft in ld tenth, hdd 5 out, wknd quickly, virtually pld up r-in*.
....(16 to 1 op 8 to 1 tchd 20 to 1) 2
2928* BEACHY HEAD [123] 6-10-3 M Dwyer, *led, blun 3rd, jnd aftr nxt, gng wl whn f tenth*.
....(6 to 4 on op 2 to 1 on tchd 11 to 8 on) f
1523⁵ GREENHILL RAFFLES [120] 8-10-0 Peter Hobbs, *tracking ldrs whn blun and uns rdr 6th*.
....(8 to 1 op 4 to 1 tchd 9 to 1) ur
Dist: Dist. 5m 57.80s. a 67.80s (4 Ran).
(PCJF Bloodstock), N A Twiston-Davies

HEREFORD (soft)
Saturday April 9th
Going Correction: PLUS 0.95 sec. per fur. (races 1,3,6), PLUS 0.75 (2,4,5)

3416 Bredwardine Novices' Selling Hurdle (4,5,6-y-o) £1,553 2m 1f........(2:10)

2118⁴ BAYRAK 4-10-8 J Railton, *al prmnt, wnt second aftr 4th, led appr 3 out, ran on strly*.
....(11 to 2 op 3 to 1 tchd 6 to 1) 1
3042² AL FORUM (Ire) 4-11-2 D O'Sullivan, *hld up in tch, gd hdwy frm 4th, wnt second appr 2 out, rdn and no imprsn r-in*............(6 to 4 fav tchd 11 to 8 on) 2
3319⁴ FORGETFUL 5-10-11 D J Burchell, *led till hdd appr 3 out, kpt on one pace aftr*..............(9 to 2 op 6 to 1) 3
3098⁷ CHANDIGARH 6-10-9 (7*) P McLoughlin, *hld up in rear, hdwy appr 5th, fdd 2 out*..........(8 to 1 op 6 to 1) 4
2957⁴ MARSHALL PINDARI 4-10-5 (3*) T Eley, *hld up, hdwy 5th, wknd quickly appr 2 out*............(14 to 1 op 8 to 1) 5
HAWAYMYSON (Ire) 4-10-8 C Maude, *chsd ldrs, mstk 5th, sn wknd, tld off*....(16 to 1 op 20 to 1 tchd 12 to 1) 6
2119⁵ BECKY BOO 4-10-0 (3*) A Procter, *al beh, tld off*.
....(16 to 1 op 14 to 1) 7
2837⁴ ORCHESTRATED CHAOS (Ire) 5-10-11 Mr J Mead, *al beh, lost tch 4th, tld off*........................(33 to 1 op 14 to 1) 8
2945 HARQUIN 4-10-8 J R Kavanagh, *al beh, tld off whn pld up bef 2 out*...(9 to 1 op 20 to 1 tchd 33 to 1 and 8 to 1) pu
2117 OHCUMGACHE 4-11-2 M Hourigan, *blun 1st, wnt second aftr nxt, hit 4th, wknd next, tld off whn pld up 2 out*.
....(14 to 1 op 12 to 1) pu
MR JAZZ DANCER (Ire) 4-10-8 P McDermott, *al beh, tld off frm 4th, pld up bef 3 out*..........(16 to 1 op 12 to 1) pu
2522 FULL COURT 4-10-8 R Bellamy, *al beh, tld off whn pld up bef 3 out*...........................(33 to 1) pu
Dist: 3l, 2¼l, 25l, 4l, 14l, 3l. 4m 8.30s. a 22.30s (12 Ran).
SR: 18/23/15/-/-/-/ (Elite Racing Club), C R Egerton

3417 Cusop Handicap Chase (0-120 5-y-o and up) £3,048 3m 1f 110yds....(2:40)

2880* WARNER FOR WINNERS [106] 8-11-6 Peter Hobbs, *al prmnt, mstk 11th, led 4 out till 2 out, rallied and led last, drvn out*.....................(5 to 1 op 7 to 2) 1
3336² MISS FERN [91] 9-10-2 (3*) D Meredith, *al prmnt, moved clr 13th, pressed wnr 4 out till led 2 out, hdd last, kpt on*.
....(7 to 2 jt-fav op 3 to 1) 2
3077⁴ DIAMOND FORT [106] 9-11-6 R Bellamy, *hld up, mstk 6th, hdwy 5 out, outpcd 3 out, rdn and styd on strly r-in*.
....(8 to 1 op 6 to 1) 3
2085³ RU VALENTINO [108] 10-11-8 Mr G Hanmer, *hld up, hdwy 5 out, wknd quickly appr 2 out*.
....(16 to 1 op 8 to 1 tchd 20 to 1) 4
1769 SADDLER'S CHOICE [99] 9-10-13 J Railton, *prmnt, hit 11th, wknd 5 out*.....(12 to 1 op 10 to 1 tchd 14 to 1) 5
2966⁵ FIDDLERS THREE [103] (bl) 11-11-3 W Powell, *sn prmnt, dsptd ld 9th, led 12th till 4 out, wknd quickly*. (7 to 2 jt-fav op 4 to 1) 6
3168 SOONER STILL [95] 10-10-9 C Maude, *prmnt early, beh frm 8th, tld off*..........(25 to 1 op 33 to 1 tchd 20 to 1) 7
2593⁶ CATCHAPENNY [109] (bl) 9-11-2 (7*) P Ward, *jmpd moderately in rear, lost tch 13th, tld off*. (5 to 1 op 7 to 2) 8

3217 ACE OF SPIES [103] 13-11-3 W Humphreys, *al beh, not jump wl, tld off whn clambered o'r 2 out, sn pld up.*
.... (16 to 1 op 10 to 1)   pu
3026 COMPLETE OPTIMIST [100] 10-10-9 (5*) Guy Lewis, *chsd ldrs till wknd 13th, tld off whn pld up bef 3 out.*
.... (25 to 1 op 20 to 1)   pu
3187³ MATT REID [110] 10-11-10 Mr W Morgan, *al beh, jmpd slwly 7th, tld off whn hit tenth, pld up bef nxt.*
.... (20 to 1 op 14 to 1)   pu
3015 OLD ROAD (USA) [87] (bl) 8-10-11 P McDermott, *made most till 12th, wknd quickly nxt, tld off whn pld up bef 3 out.*
.... (33 to 1)   pu
Dist: 2l, 2¹⁄₂l, 20l, 4l, 7l, 13l, 4l. 6m 36.60s. a 24.60s (12 Ran).
SR: 37/20/32/14/1/-/   (Terry Warner Sports), P J Hobbs

3418 Longtown Handicap Hurdle (0-125 4-y-o and up) £2,326 2m 1f........(3:10)

2554³ CABIN HILL [102] 8-11-1 (5*) D Leahy, *led 4th till hdd 3 out, rallied and led ag'n appr last, ran on wl.*
.... (3 to 1 co-fav op 2 to 1 tchd 100 to 30)   1
3131 SCHWEPPES TONIC [95] 8-10-13 D J Burchell, *al in tch, led 3 out, rdn and hdd appr last, one pace.*
.... (8 to 1 op 6 to 1 tchd 10 to 1)   2
3193* GOLDINGO [100] 7-11-1 (3*) R Davis, *hld up, hdwy 4th, ev ch 3 out, kpt on one pace frm nxt.*..........(3 to 1 co-fav op 5 to 2 tchd 100 to 30)   3
3099 LEESWOOD [91] 6-10-9 W McFarland, *trkd ldr, rdn and mstk 5th, kpt on one pace.*
.... (12 to 1 op 14 to 1 tchd 16 to 1)   4
3348³ DJEBEL PRINCE [95] 7-10-13 J Railton, *hld up in rear, gd hdwy 5th, rdn appr 2 out, no extr, eased.*
....(6 to 1 op 5 to 1)   5
3314* GIORDANO (Ire) [106] 4-11-10 Gary Lyons, *in tch whn mstk 5th, one pace frm nxt.*........(3 to 1 co-fav op 7 to 2)   6
2306 CARDINAL BIRD (USA) [93] (bl) 7-10-4 (7*) Chris Webb, *al beh, nvr on terms, tld off.*............(8 to 1 op 7 to 1)   7
420 ONENINEFIVE [82] 8-10-0 B Powell, *led to 4th, wknd quickly, tld off.*............................ (50 to 1)   8
Dist: 2l, 2l, 1¹⁄₄l, 1l, ¹⁄₂l, 25l, dist. 4m 9.70s. a 23.70s (8 Ran).
SR: 17/8/11/-/3/13/-/-/   (The Kinnersley Crew), S Christian

3419 Garway Novices' Hunters' Chase (5-y-o and up) £1,426 2m 3f.......(4:20)

3216³ COOL RELATION 8-11-9 (5*) Mr S Bush, *led to 3rd, led 4 out, gng wl whn lft well clr last.*
....(5 to 2 op 9 to 4 tchd 2 to 1)   1
WELSH LEGION 9-11-7 (7*) Miss C Burgess, *in tch till outpcd 5 out, lft poor second last....* (4 to 1 op 3 to 1)   2
MISS SHAW 8-11-2 (7*) Mr A Griffith, *prmnt till lost tch 5 out.*............... (12 to 1 op 16 to 1 tchd 10 to 1)   3
3157 CLONONY CASTLE (bl) 8-11-7 (7*) Mr J Rudge, *hld up, hdwy 6th, outpcd frm 9th.*........ (16 to 1 op 12 to 1)   4
HENRYANA 12-11-2 (7*) Miss S Lea, *sn wl beh, tld off frm 5th.*............................ (50 to 1 op 20 to 1)   5
2884* CLARE MAN (Ire) 6-12-7 Mr J Greenall, *made most frm 3rd to 4 out, rdn and still ev ch whn f last.*
....(6 to 5 fav op 11 to 10 tchd Evens and 11 to 8)   f
TAMERS GLEN 7-11-11 (7*) Mr E Griffith, *prmnt till wknd tenth, no ch whn blun 3rd out, pld up bef nxt.*
.... (40 to 1 op 33 to 1)   pu
Dist: 20l, 11l, 2¹⁄₂l, dist. 5m 1.80s. a 31.80s (7 Ran).
(D J Caro), D J Caro

3420 Pandy Novices' Chase (5-y-o and up) £2,568 2m 3f.................(4:50)

3004³ PERCY SMOLLETT 6-11-4 R Bellamy, *led to 4 out, hugged ins rail, hrd rdn and lft second last, sn led, ran on.*
....(3 to 1 tchd 4 to 1)   1
1999 STAGE PLAYER 8-11-1 (3*) T Eley, *trkd ldr, strly rdn frm 2 out, lft in ld last, sn hdd, kpt on....*(11 to 2 op 3 to 1)   2
3148³ QUEENS CURATE 7-10-13 B Powell, *hld up, jnd ldrs 9th, wknd 4 out, tld off....*(14 to 1 op 20 to 1 tchd 12 to 1)   3
3188⁴ TAURIAN PRINCESS 5-10-5 D J Burchell, *in tch but not jump wl, beh aftr blun 7th, tld off whn pld up bef last, continued.*............................(14 to 1 op 8 to 1)   4
3338* MACEDONAS 6-11-4 (7*) M Berry, *al in tch, mstk 6th, made most frm 4 out, hrd rdn whn f last.*
.... (5 to 4 on op 7 to 4 on tchd 11 to 10 on)   f
Dist: 1l, dist, dist. 5m 4.10s. a 34.10s (5 Ran).
(R G Murray), J C McConnochie

3421 Broad Oak Novices' Hurdle (4-y-o and up) £1,553 3¹⁄₄m.............(5:25)

2766² TALBOT 8-11-4 J Railton, *trkd ldr, al gng wl, led 4 out, clr nxt, unchlgd.*
.... (6 to 5 on op 11 to 10 on tchd 11 to 8 on)   1
3230⁴ WELSH LION 6-11-4 (7*) R Massey, *hld up in tch, hdwy appr 9th, wnt second bef 3 out, no ch whn wnr.*
.... (11 to 4 tchd 4 to 1 and 7 to 4)   2
3137⁴ JIMMY O'DEA 7-11-4 M Hourigan, *led till hdd 4 out, wknd quickly, tld off....*(33 to 1 op 25 to 1 tchd 40 to 1)   3
3351 HALF A MO 9-10-6 (7*) S Drake, *al beh, tld off frm 11th.*
.... (33 to 1 op 16 to 1)   4

3230⁸ ANNA VALLEY 8-11-2 (3*) R Davis, *chsd ldrs till wknd appr 9th, tld off whn pld up bef 3 out.*
.... (12 to 1 op 8 to 1)   pu
3339 NORDIC FLIGHT (bl) 6-10-11 (7*) P McLoughlin, *prmnt, 3rd whn mstk 7th, rdn and sn beh, tld off when pld up bef 4 out.*..(200 to 1 op 100 to 1)   pu
3170⁷ IVE CALLED TIME 6-10-13 (5*) Guy Lewis, *chsd ldrs till blun 9th, sn beh, tld off.*..........(50 to 1 op 25 to 1)   pu
1806 BIG BAD WOLF (Ire) 6-11-4 J R Kavanagh, *al beh, not jump wl, tld off 7th, pld up bef 3 out....*(33 to 1 op 16 to 1)   pu
3005 TRUE STORM 5-10-13 V Slattery, *al beh, tld off whn pld up aftr 8th....*..................(66 to 1 op 33 to 1)   pu
Dist: 20l, dist, 2¹⁄₂l. 6m 43.80s. a 43.80s (9 Ran).
(J F Dean), C R Egerton

AINTREE (heavy)
Saturday April 9th
Going Correction: PLUS 2.35 sec. per fur. (races 1,3,6), PLUS 2.00 (2,4,5)

3422 Cordon Bleu Handicap Hurdle (5-y-o and up) £18,342 2m 110yds..... (1:45)

3369⁴ FOR REG (Ire) [127] 5-10-1 A Maguire, *tucked away gng wl, improved on bit to chal whn blun last, rallied to ld last 100 yards....................*(4 to 1 op 6 to 1)   1
3025 LAND AFAR [144] 7-11-4 W Marston, *settled gng wl, hdwy to ld appr 2 out, jnd last, hdd and outpcd last 100 yards....................*(8 to 1 op 6 to 1)   2
2719² ROYAL DERBI [151] 9-11-11 M Perrett, *trkd ldrs, ev ch appr 3 out, rdn betw last 2, no extr.*
....(14 to 1 tchd 16 to 1)   3
3025⁵ ABSALOM'S LADY [151] 6-11-11 P Holley, *last and niggled alng hfwy, styd on und pres frm 3 out, nvr nr to chal.*
....(8 to 1 op 9 to 1)   4
3068⁵ HER HONOUR [132] 5-10-6 R Dunwoody, *trkd ldrs, effrt hfwy, feeling pace and reminders 3 out, sn btn.*
....(13 to 2 op 5 to 1)   5
2595⁹ NIKITAS [126] 9-10-0 S McNeill, *pressed ldrs, feeling pace and drvn alng 3 out, fdd nxt.*
....(16 to 1 op 12 to 1 tchd 20 to 1)   6
2702³ PADASHPAN (USA) [140] 5-11-0 C Swan, *nvr far away, ev ch appr 3 out, outpcd nxt, fdd.*
....(15 to 2 op 7 to 1 tchd 8 to 1)   7
3092* RATIFY [126] 7-10-0 A S Smith, *set steady pace, hit second, jmpd right nxt, quickened 5th, hdd and wknd quickly appr 2 out....*(15 to 2 op 7 to 1 tchd 8 to 1)   8
3068⁸ NIJMEGEN [127] 6-10-1¹ M Dwyer, *co'red up in midfield, effrt and drvn alng appr 3 out, sn btn, tld off.*
....(13 to 2 op 7 to 1 tchd 7 to 1)   9
3193⁶ MIDDLE MARKER (Ire) [126] 5-10-0 Diane Clay, *co'red up beh ldrs, effrt appr 3 out, disputing 3rd and rdn whn blun and uns rdr last.*..............(66 to 1 op 50 to 1)   ur
3269³ KILCASH (Ire) [144] (bl) 6-11-4 M Richards, *chsd ldrs, struggling 3 out, lost tch and pld up bef nxt.*
....(6 to 1 tchd 11 to 2 and 13 to 2)   pu
Dist: 3l, 8l, 1¾l, 8l, 15l, 8l, 15l, 15l. 4m 30.70s. a 42.70s (11 Ran).
SR: 34/48/47/45/18/7/15/-/-/   (D H O'Reilly), P J Flynn

3423 Martell Aintree Chase Limited Handicap Grade 2 (5-y-o and up) £26,110 2m.............................(2:20)

3066² UNCLE ERNIE [145] 9-10-8 M Dwyer, *al gng wl, cruised up on bit to dispute ld 3 out, led bef last, sn clr.*
....(3 to 1 op 5 to 2 tchd 100 to 30)   1
3037* VIKING FLAGSHIP [165] 7-12-0 A Maguire, *nvr far away, led 3 out till betw last 2, no ch with wnr.*
....(5 to 4 on tchd 100 to 30)   2
MY YOUNG MAN [150] 9-10-13 G Bradley, *led to 3 out, sn drvn alng, outpcd betw last 2....*(20 to 1 op 16 to 1)   3
3066* SNITTON LANE [144] 8-10-7 D Bridgwater, *mstks, co'red up beh ldrs, ev ch 3 out, fdd und pres betw last 2.*
....(12 to 1 tchd 14 to 1)   4
3066 TRIMLOUGH [144] 9-10-7 W Marston, *in tch, reminders 5th, sn lost grnd, tld off.*
....(40 to 1 op 25 to 1 tchd 50 to 1)   5
3066³ STORM ALERT [149] 8-10-12 S McNeill, *trkd ldg pair, hit 1st, reminders 6th, fdg whn f 5 out....*(3 to 1 op 2 to 1)   f
3066⁸ CLAY COUNTY [144] 9-10-7 R Dunwoody, *trkd ldr, hit 6th, level 5 out, wknd quickly, pld up bef last.*
....(10 to 1 op 12 to 1)   pu
2698³ LASATA [144] 9-10-7 C O'Dwyer, *mstks, nvr gng wl, no ch whn jmpd slwly 3 out, pld up bef nxt.*
....(10 to 1 op 12 to 1)   pu
Dist: 11l, 11l, 2¹⁄₂l, dist. 4m 21.30s. a 32.30s (8 Ran).
SR: 77/86/56/48/-/   (J G FitzGerald), J G FitzGerald

3424 Martell Aintree Hurdle Grade 1 (4-y-o and up) £30,585 2¹⁄₂m...........(2:55)

3036* DANOLI (Ire) 6-11-7 C Swan, *trkd clr ldr gng wl, drw level 4 out, sn led, clear last, easily.*
....(9 to 2 op 4 to 1 tchd 5 to 1)   1

3025⁴ MOLE BOARD 12-11-7 T Grantham, *patiently rdn, improved on outsd to chal aftr 3 out, ridden and one pace betw last 2*.......... (8 to 1 op 7 to 1 tchd 9 to 1) 2

2287* FORTUNE AND FAME 7-11-7 A Maguire, *setted wth chasing grp, improved aftr 4 out, rdn bef 2 out, no imprsn.*
.... (3 to 1 op 7 to 2 tchd 4 to 1) 3

3025⁶ MUSE 7-11-7 P Holley, *unruly strt, sn clr ld, jnd hfwy, hdd bef 3 out, soon btn.* (13 to 2 op 6 to 1 tchd 7 to 1) 4

3025* FLAKEY DOVE 8-11-2 R Dunwoody, *trkd ldg pair, ev ch appr 3 out, rdn and btn nxt.*
.... (9 to 4 fav op 7 to 4 tchd 5 to 2) 5

3025⁸ SHAWIYA (Ire) 5-11-2 J F Titley, *nvr far away, ev ch 4 out, rdn and btn nxt, tld off.*
.... (33 to 1 op 20 to 1 tchd 40 to 1) 6

3025⁹ HALKOPOUS 8-11-7 D Murphy, *sn beh, struggling hfwy, tld off whn pld up bef 3 out.*
.... (14 to 1 op 12 to 1 tchd 16 to 1) pu

2689³ COULTON 7-11-7 J Osborne, *al beh, tld off whn pld up bef 3 out*............ (33 to 1 op 20 to 1 tchd 50 to 1) pu

3025 VALFINET (Fr) 7-11-7 J Lower, *nvr gng wl, reminder 7th, tld off whn pld up bef 3 out*........ (33 to 1 op 50 to 1) pu

Dist: 8l, nk, 20l, 5l, dist. 5m 26.20s. a 48.20s (9 Ran).

SR: 81/73/72/52/42/-/ (D J O'Neill), Thomas Foley

3425 Martell Grand National Chase Handicap Grade 3 (115+) £115,606 4½m
.... (3:50)

30647 MIINNEHOMA [150] 11-10-8 R Dunwoody, *nvr far away, led 17th to 21st, stumbled nxt (Becher's), led 24th (Canal Turn) to next (Valentine's), steadied 3 out, led elbow, ran on gmely.* (16 to 1 op 14 to 1 tchd 20 to 1) 1

31347 JUST SO [145] 11-10-3³ S Burrough, *wl beh 1st circuit, gd hdwy 22nd (Becher's), led 25th (Valentine's) till bef 3 out, rallied r-in, no extr cl hme...* (20 to 1 op 25 to 1) 2

27482 MOORCROFT BOY [142] 9-10-0 A Maguire, *patiently rdn, smooth hdwy to go hndy hfwy, hit 5 out, led 2 out to elbow, one pace.*............ (9 to 2 fav op 7 to 1) 3

33243 EBONY JANE [143] 9-10-1 L Cusack, *wtd wth, improved aftr one circuit, led 21st to 24th (Canal Turn), led bef 3 out to nxt, fdd.*................ (25 to 1 op 28 to 1) 4

30277 FIDDLERS PIKE [142] 13-10-0 Mrs R Henderson, *sluggish strt, beh till gd hdwy fnl circuit, feeling pace 22nd (Becher's), kpt on frm 25th (Valentine's), no imprsn.*
.... (100 to 1) 5

30266 ROC DE PRINCE (Fr) [142] 11-10-0 J Lower, *not jump wl, al struggling in rear, tld off aftr one circuit....* (100 to 1) 6

3041* ELFAST [146] 11-10-4⁴ G McCourt, *midfield whn f 1st.*
.... (18 to 1 op 16 to 1 tchd 20 to 1) f

32615 HENRY MANN [142] (bl) 11-10-0 C Swan, *rear div whn f 1st.*..................... (50 to 1 op 33 to 1) f

3324 RUST NEVER SLEEPS [142] 10-10-0 P Carberry, *chsd ldg grp for o'r one circuit, outpcd 22nd (Becher's), tld off whn f 4 out.*.............. (66 to 1 op 100 to 1) f

3280 GAY RUFFIAN [142] 8-10-0 R Farrant, *rear div whn f 7th.*
.... (150 to 1 tchd 200 to 1) f

30816 NEW MILL HOUSE [142] 11-10-0 T Horgan, *struggling to keep up whn f 6th (Becher's).*............... (150 to 1) f

26952 ZETA'S LAD [155] 11-10-13 R Supple, *sn struggling to go pace, wl beh whn blun 22nd (Becher's), tld off whn f last.*.................. (16 to 1 tchd 18 to 1) f

3258 ROMANY KING [143] 10-10-1 Richard Guest, *chasing ldrs whn f 4th.*................... (22 to 1 op 20 to 1) f

32499 LAURA'S BEAU [142] (bl) 10-10-0 B Sheridan, *beh whn f 6th (Becher's).*................... (40 to 1 op 50 to 1) f

30414 FOURTH OF JULY [142] 10-10-0 J P Banahan, *rear div whn f 1st.*.......................... (50 to 1) f

32173 MR BOSTON [144] 9-10-2² P Niven, *chsd alng to keep in tch, baulked 11th, f 13th.*......... (16 to 1 tchd 20 to 1) f

34032 BLACK HUMOUR [154] 10-10-12 G Bradley, *settled midfield, 6th and staying on whn hesitated and f 15th (Chair).*................................ (33 to 1) f

3065* DOUBLE SILK [146] 10-10-4⁴ Mr R Treloggen, *led to 3rd, led ag'n 5th to 12th, third and ev ch whn f nxt.*
.... (6 to 1 op 7 to 1 tchd 8 to 1) f

3064* THE FELLOW (Fr) [160] (bl) 9-11-4 A Kondrat, *nvr far away, hit 1st, 22nd (Becher's) and nxt, 4th and ev ch whn f 24th (Canal Turn).*............. (9 to 1 tchd 10 to 1) f

31342 ITS A CRACKER [142] 10-10-0 C O'Dwyer, *chsd alng to keep in tch whn f 6th (Becher's).*
.... (33 to 1 op 50 to 1 tchd 66 to 1) f

27482 MASTER OATS [142] 8-10-0 N Williamson, *patiently rdn, imprvg whn hmpd and f 13th.*
.... (9 to 1 op 7 to 1 tchd 10 to 1) f

3134 MISTER ED [142] 11-10-0 D Morris, *struggling to go pace to hfwy, 8th and staying on whn baulked and uns rdr 24th (Canal Turn)....* (50 to 1 op 33 to 1) ur

3064 TOPSHAM BAY [153] 11-10-11 J Frost, *trkd ldrs, pushed alng whn hmpd and uns rdr 13th.*
.... (25 to 1 op 33 to 1 tchd 28 to 1) ur

3134 INTO THE RED [142] 10-10-0 J White, *chsd ldg bunch till rdn and outpcd 20th (Canal Turn), rallied 4 out, 5th and no imprsn whn blun and uns rdr last....* (25 to 1) ur

33244 CAPTAIN BRANDY [142] 9-10-0 K O'Brien, *beh whn blun and uns rdr 9th (Valentine's)....* (50 to 1 op 33 to 1) ur

30266 USHERS ISLAND [142] 8-10-0 A Dobbin, *midfield whn blun and uns rdr 3rd.*........................ (66 to 1) ur

QUIRINUS (Cze) [166] 12-11-10 J Brecka, *slwly away, tld off whn uns rdr 15th (Chair).*
.... (250 to 1 op 200 to 1) ur

32613 MIGHTY FALCON [142] (bl) 9-10-0 P Holley, *struggling in rear whn hmpd and brght dwn 13th.*
.... (250 to 1 op 200 to 1) bd

30643 YOUNG HUSTLER [154] 7-10-12 D Bridgwater, *al hndy, 4th whn brght dwn 11th.* (16 to 1 op 14 to 1 tchd 20 to 1) bd

3064 GARRISON SAVANNAH [145] (bl) 11-10-3 J Osborne, *wth ldrs on ins, led hfwy till hmpd and refused 17th.*
.... (25 to 1 tchd 28 to 1) ref

30649 RUN FOR FREE [163] 10-11-7 M Perrett, *wtd wth, improved into midfield 12th, pushed alng whn hmpd and refused 17th.*.............. (25 to 1) ref

3134 RIVERSIDE BOY [142] (bl) 11-10-0 M Richards, *al hndy, led 3rd to 5th, led aftr 12th to hfwy, tried to run out after 16th (water), wide whn refused 18th.*........ (33 to 1) ref

2656 CHANNELS GATE [142] 10-10-0 T Jenks, *in tch one circuit, wkng whn refused 18th.*................. (100 to 1) ref

27487 SOUTHERN MINSTREL [143] 11-10-11 M Dwyer, *chsd alng to keep in tch, pld up bef 11th....* (50 to 1 op 33 to 1) pu

2363 PACO'S BOY [142] (bl) 9-10-0 M Foster, *in tch one circuit, struggling whn pld up bef 17th.*............ (200 to 1) pu

31273 HE WHO DARES WINS [142] 11-10-0 C Grant, *al struggling, tld off whn pld up bef 17th.* (66 to 1 op 150 to 1) pu

Dist: 1¼l, 20l, 25l, 9l, dist. 10m 18.80s. a 80.80s (36 Ran).

(Freddie Starr), M C Pipe

3426 Chivas Regal Amateur Riders Novices' Handicap Chase (5-y-o and up) £7,595 2½m........ (4:40)

3232* ALL FOR LUCK [115] 9-11-4 (5°) Mr B R Hamilton, *nvr far away, led 2 out, clr whn jmpd rght last, easily.*
.... (9 to 4 fav op 7 to 4 tchd 5 to 2) 1

3135 KETTI [97] (bl) 9-10-0² (7°) Mr G Hogan, *led to 4th, styd hndy, led 5 out to 2 out, stayed on same pace.*
.... (25 to 1 op 16 to 1 tchd 33 to 1) 2

31183 FESTIVAL DREAMS [97] 9-10-0² (7°) Mr L Jefford, *patiently rdn, hit 5th, hmpd 9th, styd on, no imprsn.*
.... (10 to 1 op 8 to 1) 3

3080⁸ BROCKLEY COURT [120] 7-11-9 (5°) Mr J Nash, *chsd ldr, led aftr 4th, hit 9th, hdd after 5 out, one pace.*
.... (8 to 1 op 7 to 1) 4

3232³ HANGOVER [97] 8-10-13 (7°) Mr J Rees, *settled off the pace, hit second and 7th, nvr rch chalg pos.*
.... (10 to 1 op 7 to 1) 5

3355³ VAYRUA (Fr) [102] (v) 9-10-7² (5°) Mr N Wilson, *chsd ldg trio till f 9th.*.................... (10 to 1 tchd 12 to 1) f

3143² GREENFIELD MANOR [97] 7-10-5 Mr S Swiers, *settled midfield, pushed alng whn f 5th....* (33 to 1 op 14 to 1) f

3040⁴ BINKLEY (Fr) [97] 8-10-2⁴ (7°) Mr M Rimell, *trkd ldg grp, lost tch 5 out, tld off whn pld up bef last.*
.... (13 to 2 op 9 to 2 tchd 7 to 1) pu

29783 POPPETS PET [97] 7-10-1³ (7°) Mr C Vigors, *pressed ldrs to 4th, wknd hfwy, pld up bef 5 out.*
.... (14 to 1 op 12 to 1 tchd 16 to 1) pu

3135* NORSTOCK [108] 7-11-2 Mr J Durkan, *chsd ldg grp till lost tch 6 out, pld up bef 4 out.*
.... (3 to 1 op 7 to 2 tchd 4 to 1) pu

Dist: Dist, 7l, 12l, 25l. 5m 37.20s. a 47.20s (10 Ran).

SR: 23/-/-/-/-/-/ (B J Craig), M C Pipe

3427 Martell Champion National Hunt Flat Race (4,5,6-y-o) £7,448 2m 110yds .... (5:15)

3114² NAHLA 4-10-9 S Curran, *settled gng wl, improved to ld on bit 2 fs out, sn clr....* (8 to 1 op 6 to 1 tchd 9 to 1) 1

3190* SMART ROOKIE (Ire) 4-11-4 Mr G Hogan, *settled midfield, crrd wide paddock bend, reco'red to ld 3 fs out, hdd 2 out, one pace.* (100 to 30 fav op 7 to 2 tchd 4 to 1) 2

3042 RED PARADE (NZ) 6-11-10 R Darke, *al wl plcd, effrt and drvn alng 2 fs out, kpt on same pace.*
.... (25 to 1 op 20 to 1) 3

3079* ADIB (USA) 4-11-8 N Bentley, *chsd ldr, led 4 fs out to 3 out, sn drvn alng, outpcd 2 out.*
.... (13 to 2 op 8 to 1 tchd 9 to 1) 4

28343 MR BUSKER (Ire) 5-11-6 Mr J Durkan, *led 3 fs, hndy till rdn and wknd 2 out.*.............. (10 to 1 op 8 to 1) 5

2716* COLOSSUS OF ROADS 5-12-0 A Dicken, *chsd ldrs, hrd drvn 2 fs out, fdd.*........ (12 to 1 tchd 14 to 1) 6

3234 IDIOT'S LADY 5-11-1 D Bohan, *wtd wth, crrd wide paddock bend, sn lost tch, virtually pld up last 2 fs.*
.... (20 to 1 op 14 to 1) 7

3079² LORD DORCET (Ire) 4-11-3 J Burke, *wth ldrs, led aftr 3 fs to 4 out, wknd rpdly, virtually pld up last 2 furlongs.*
.... (9 to 1 op 8 to 1 tchd 10 to 1) 8

2041¹ FIONANS FLUTTER (Ire) 6-11-10 N Willmington, *pld hrd, wtd wth, effrt appr strt, sn lost tch, virtually pulled up last 2 fs.*...................... (4 to 1 tchd 5 to 1) 9

3042 HIGHLY REPUTABLE (Ire) 4-11-4 T Dascombe, *wtd wth, effrt and drvn alng 4 fs out, sn wknd, virtually pld up last 2 furlongs.*............ (12 to 1 op 8 to 1) 10

22902 SUBLIME FELLOW (Ire) 4-11-0 Mr C Vigors, *al beh, virtually pld up last 2 fs.*............. (11 to 2 op 4 to 1) 11

NATIONAL HUNT RESULTS 1993-94

3347 SABBAQ (USA) 4-11-0 N Leach, *al last, lost tch hfwy,*
      virtually pld up last 2 fs..........(66 to 1 op 33 to 1) 12
Dist: 9l, 12l, 1¼l, 6l, 20l. 4m 29.50s. (12 Ran).
                                    (The Safe Six), Miss Jacqueline S Doyle

KELSO (good to soft)
Monday April 11th
Going Correction: PLUS 0.80 sec. per fur. (races 1,3,-5,6), PLUS 0.95 (2,4,7)

3428 Glengoyne Highland Malt Tamerosia Series Qualifier Novices' Chase (5-y-o and up) £2,965 2¾m 110yds.....(2:00)

1200² BENNAN MARCH 7-11-6 A Dobbin, *mid-div, hdwy to track ldrs hfwy, led 2 out, hrd pressed aftr last, styd on wl und pres*....................(25 to 1 op 16 to 1) 1
3286² RIVER PEARL 9-11-5 T Reed, *hld up, hdwy aftr 11th, chlgd aftr last, ev ch till no extr und pres fnl 100 yards*
      ....(7 to 4 op 2 to 1 tchd 9 to 4) 2
2952⁴ KIRKCALDY (Ire) 5-10-8 A Maguire, *chsd ldrs, outpcd aftr 12th, styd on wl frm last*..........(20 to 1 op 14 to 1) 3
2971⁴ BULA NUDAY 9-11-2 B Storey, *hld up, hdwy hfwy, kpt on same pace frm 3 out*...........(10 to 1 tchd 12 to 1) 4
3286⁵ BARNEY RUBBLE 9-11-2 N Williamson, *mid-div, mstk 12th, lost pl, no dngr aftr*.
      ....(16 to 1 op 14 to 1 tchd 20 to 1) 5
3129⁵ SUPER SANDY 7-10-11 K Johnson, *prmnt, led 11th to 2 out, sn wknd*..................(66 to 1) 6
2736 JUNIORS CHOICE 11-11-2 Mr A Parker, *led to 11th, wknd, tld off*....................(33 to 1 op 16 to 1) 7
3029⁴ FRIENDLY SOCIETY 8-11-2 A Merrigan, *mstks, al beh, blun 3 out, tld off*..................(100 to 1) 8
      LINLITHGOW PALACE 12-10-11 (5°) P Waggott, *in tch, hit 5th, wknd aftr 12th, tld off*.......(200 to 1) 9
3341° BRACKENFIELD 8-12-0 P Niven, *cl up whn f 3rd*.
      ....(5 to 4 fav op Evens tchd 1 to 8) f
2497⁴ NORRISMOUNT 8-11-2 M Moloney, *in tch whn f 9th*.
      ....(10 to 1 op 16 to 1) f
3224 BOWLANDS WAY 10-11-2 C Grant, *sn tld off, pld up bef 8th*...................(50 to 1 op 33 to 1) pu
Dist: 1½l, 15l, 3½l, hd, 10l, 30l, 5l, 3½l. 5m 55.00s. a 28.00s (12 Ran).
                                                (Brian O'Kane), P Monteith

3429 E. Scarth & Son Builders Claiming Hurdle (4-y-o and up) £2,722 2¼m
          ....(2:30)

3222° ALL GREEK TO ME (Ire) 6-11-3 (7°) F Leahy, *in tch, effrt appr 3 out, styd on wl und pres to ld r-in, all out*.
      ....(3 to 1 jt-fav op 5 to 1) 1
3131³ KANNDABIL (bl) 7-11-10 G McCourt, *prmnt, led appr 2 out, clr last, hdd and no extr r-in*.
      ....(100 to 30 op 11 to 4 tchd 7 to 2) 2
3374⁶ FIRM PRICE 13-11-12 R Hodge, *beh, hdwy appr 3 out, styd on und pres nxt, nrst finish*.
      ....(5 to 1 op 4 to 1 tchd 11 to 2) 3
3179⁵ LONDON HILL 6-11-0 C Dennis, *sn tracking ldrs, rdn appr 2 out, kpt on same pace*......(25 to 1 op 20 to 1) 4
2974⁴⁶ CAPTAIN TANCRED (Ire) 6-11-6 A Merrigan, *sluly into strd, beh, hdwy aftr 7th, mstk 2 out, not rch ldrs*.. (33 to 1) 5
3320⁴ RORO SMACKEROO 9-11-6 A Dobbin, *led till appr 2 out, wknd*..........(3 to 1 jt-fav op 7 to 2 tchd 9 to 2) 6
3285⁶ MISS JEDD 7-10-4 (5°) J Burke, *prmnt till wknd aftr 3 out*.
      ....(100 to 1) 7
2436⁷ AYIA NAPA 7-11-2 A Dobbin, *in tch, effrt aftr 7th, no hdwy*..........................(66 to 1) 8
3179 TUESDAYNIGHTMARE 5-11-0 T Reed, *tld off hfwy, some late hdwy, nvr dngrs*............(33 to 1 op 10 to 1) 9
3357 OLD MORTALITY (v) 8-11-2 Miss P Robson, *chsd ldrs, wknd 3 out*........................(33 to 1) 10
2956³ HAMANAKA (USA) 5-10-13 Mr S Love, *nvr dngrs*.
      ....(20 to 1 tchd 25 to 1) 11
3144 GLASTONDALE 8-11-2 L O'Hara, *nvr dngrs*......(100 to 1) 12
3317 YACHT CLUB 12-11-0 O Pears, *nvr dngrs*..(100 to 1) 13
3346 SILVER HAZE 10-11-2 N Williamson, *prmnt till wknd aftr 3 out*..................(25 to 1 op 20 to 1) 14
3179 MOSS PAGEANT 4-11-3 K Johnson, *prmnt till wknd quickly aftr 5th*..................(200 to 1) 15
      ANGELS KISS 8-10-9 J Callaghan, *beh hfwy*....(100 to 1) 16
      NO BOUNDARIES 8-11-4 K Jones, *tld off hfwy*. (200 to 1) 17
282   TREASURE BEACH 5-10-5 (7°) A Linton, *beh 7th*. (200 to 1) 18
2970 SKI LADY 6-10-13 B Storey, *beh whn f 7th*......(100 to 1) f
1094 LUGER (Ire) 6-11-2 N Smith, *hmpd and uns rdr 1st*.
      ....(100 to 1) ur
3103⁵ QUIET MISTRESS 4-10-6 C Grant, *mstk 1st, sn beh, tld off whn hmpd and ran out aftr 4 out*............(50 to 1) ro
1668 TOLL BOOTH 5-10-11 Mrs J Speight, *in tch whn blun 5th, sn beh, pld up bef nxt*....................(100 to 1) pu
Dist: 2½l, 2½l, 2½l, 3½l, 2½l, 20l, hd, 8l, 10l, 1½l. 4m 32.70s. a 25.70s (22 Ran).
SR: 10/7/6/-/-/-/   (Barry Hughes), J Parkes

3430 'Horse And Hound' Buccleuch Cup Maiden Hunters' Chase (5-y-o and up)

£2,233 3m 1f...................(3:00)

      PRESS FOR ACTION 9-11-9 (5°) Mr D Mactaggart, *made all, lft clr 7th, blun 13th, hld on wl frm last*.
      ....(10 to 1 op 8 to 1 tchd 12 to 1) 1
      GALE STORM 10-11-2 (7°) Mr D Scott, *in tch, effrt aftr 3 out, styd on und pres frm last, no imprsn*.
      ....(50 to 1 op 33 to 1) 2
      WHINSTONE MILL 6-11-7 (7°) Mr A Robson, *in tch, chsd wnr frm 13th, no extr from last*.... (14 to 1 op 16 to 1) 3
      WIRE LASS 10-11-4 (5°) Miss J Thurlow, *blun 4th, sn tld off, styd on wl frm 3 out, not rch ldrs*.
      ....(100 to 1 op 50 to 1) 4
      GLEN LICKY 10-11-7 (7°) Miss C Metcalfe, *tld off 11th*.
      ....(100 to 1 op 50 to 1) 5
3158⁴ SHARP OPINION 11-11-7 (7°) Miss P Robson, *blun 3rd, beh whn f 8th*......................(2 to 1 op 7 to 4) f
      REDE REBEL 8-11-2 (7°) Mr T Scott, *wth wnr till f 7th*.
      ....(11 to 10 op 11 to 10 tchd 5 to 4) f
      MILL KNOCK 12-11-9 (5°) Mr J M Dun, *chsd wnr frm 7th till blun and uns rdr 13th*...........(16 to 1 op 20 to 1) ur
      EVE PET 10-11-9 Mr J Walton, *hmpd 8th, tld off whn pld up bef tenth*..........(50 to 1 op 33 to 1) pu
Dist: 3½l, nk, 6l, dist. 6m 47.50s. a 45.50s (9 Ran).
                            (S H Shirley-Beavan), S H Shirley-Beavan

3431 Queens Head 'National Hunt' Novices' Hurdle (4-y-o and up) £2,722 2¾m 110yds...................(3:30)

3177² COQUI LANE 7-11-8 Mr J M Dun, *led aftr 1st, made rst, styd on gmely frm last*..........(2 to 1 fav op 7 to 4) 1
2951⁵ EASBY JOKER 6-11-2 N Doughty, *trkd wnr frm 6th, rdn aftr 2 out, styd on wl, no imprsn*.
      ....(5 to 1 op 9 to 2 tchd 11 to 2) 2
3140⁶ MANOR COURT (Ire) 6-11-2 A Merrigan, *settled midfield, chsd ldrs aftr 7th, kpt on same pace frm 2 out*.
      ....(20 to 1 op 16 to 1) 3
3284³ PARLEBIZ 5-10-11 B Storey, *settled midfield, hdwy aftr 7th, kpt on same pace frm 3 out*.
      ....(5 to 1 op 9 to 2 tchd 11 to 2) 4
3225⁴ WHITE DIAMOND 6-11-8 J Railton, *trkd ldrs, lost pl aftr 6th, sn out of wl frm last*........(8 to 1 op 6 to 1) 5
3177⁶ BANNTOWN BILL (Ire) 5-11-2 T Reed, *led till aftr 1st, prmnt till outpcd after 7th, no dngr after*.
      ....(8 to 1 op 7 to 1 tchd 10 to 1) 6
1875⁵ STRONG MEASURE (Ire) 6-11-2 K Johnson, *hld up, hdwy to track ldrs 3 out, wknd aftr nxt*. (20 to 1 op 14 to 1) 7
2500⁵ LAST REFUGE (Ire) 5-11-2 N Williamson, *trkd ldrs till wknd aftr 3 out*..................(16 to 1 op 14 to 1) 8
      FULL OF CHAT (Ire) 5-10-11 A Dobbin, *beh, hdwy hfwy, wknd 3 out*..................(66 to 1 op 50 to 1) 9
3177⁵ SHARP CHALLENGE 7-11-2 A Maguire, *trkd ldrs till wknd aftr 3 out*..................(8 to 1 op 7 to 1) 10
3076 ROYAL FIFE 8-10-8 (3°) D J Moffatt, *prmnt till wknd aftr 8th*..................................(100 to 1) 11
      HIGHLAND RIVER 7-10-11 Carol Cuthbert, *al beh*.
      ....(100 to 1 op 50 to 1) 12
2497 LORD BERTRAM (Ire) 6-10-13 (3°) A Larnach, *blun and uns rdr second*.............(100 to 1 op 50 to 1) ur
2951 CORBY KNOWE 8-11-2 S Turner, *sn wl beh, tld off whn pld up bef 2 out*..................(100 to 1) pu
      MASCULINE 7-10-9 (7°) W Fry, *tld off whn pld up bef 7th*.
      ....(200 to 1) pu
3114 TRY AGAIN JANE 4-10-5 R Marley, *trkd ldrs till wknd quickly aftr 5th, tld off whn pld up bef 7th*.
      ....(20 to 1 tchd 25 to 1) pu
Dist: 1½l, 6l, 4l, 2½l, 1½l, 1¼l, 4l, 6l, 15l, 12l. 5m 46.30s. a 35.30s (16 Ran).
                                                (J M Dun), J R Dur

3432 Tim Doody Scottish Champion Hunters' Chase (5-y-o and up) £4,084 3m 1f...................(4:00)

3181° ROYAL JESTER 10-12-0 Mr C Storey, *cl up, rdn to ld last, styd on wl und pres*..........(11 to 4 tchd 3 to 1) 1
      LOUGHLINSTOWN BOY 9-12-4 Mr A Robson, *wth ldr, led tenth to last, no extr und pres*.....(25 to 1 op 20 to 1) 2
      AGATHIST (USA) 11-12-4 Mr K Anderson, *trkd ldrs, lost pl aftr 13th, rdn after last, no imprsn*.
      ....(11 to 10 fav tchd 5 to 4) 3
      GONE ASTRAY 9-11-9 Mr J Walton, *made most till jmpd sluly and lost pl tenth, beh whn jumped slowly 15th, no ch aftr*..................(25 to 1 op 20 to 1) 4
      STEELE JUSTICE 10-12-0 Miss P Robson, *prmnt till outpcd aftr 12th, sn tld off*......(9 to 4 op 7 to 4) 5
Dist: 2l, 11l, 10l, 6l. 6m 40.50s. a 38.50s (5 Ran).
                            (Mrs A D Wauchope), Mrs Jane Store

3433 Croall Bryson Handicap Chase for the Clyde Bridge Challenge Cup (0-130 5-y-o and up) £3,338 2m 1f.....(4:30)

3001 SIMPLE PLEASURE [113] 9-11-10 A Maguire, *in tch, outpcd appr 3 out, styd on wl und pres aftr last, led nr finish*....................(3 to 1 op 7 to 2 tchd 4 to 1)

3288* KAMBALDA RAMBLER [96] 10-10-7 B Storey, *jmpd wl, led, jnd 2 out, ev ch r-in till no extr nr finish.*
.........................(13 to 8 fav op 6 to 4 tchd 2 to 1) 2
3405 ABSAILOR [91] (v) 10-10-1⁴ (5*) J Burke, *in tch, pushed alng aftr 7th, hdwy after nxt, dsptd ld 2 out, slight lead r-in, hdd and wknd nr finish.*
.........................(11 to 4 op 3 to 1 tchd 100 to 30) 3
3141⁶ NIGHT GUEST [92] 12-10-3 A Dobbin, *chsd ldr, outpcd aftr 2 out, styd on wl nr finish.*......(6 to 1 op 4 to 1) 4
Dist: Hd, 3½l, sht-hd. 4m 25.30s. a 19.30s (4 Ran).

SR: 39/22/13/14/ (Mrs M Stirk), Mrs M Stirk

3434 Tennent Quaich Handicap Hurdle
(0-130 4-y-o and up) £2,652 2m 110yds
.........................(5:00)

3125* FLASH OF REALM (Fr) [100] 8-10-0 A Dobbin, *trkd ldrs, quickened to ld last, styd on wl und pres.*
.........................(7 to 2 op 4 to 1) 1
3182² PALACEGATE KING [104] 5-10-4 M Moloney, *led to last, kpt on wl und pres.*.........(9 to 4 tchd 5 to 2) 2
3000 GYMCRAK STARDOM [124] (bl) 8-11-10 R Marley, *hld, up in tch, chlgd on bit approching last, sn rdn, no extr.*
.........................(7 to 1 op 9 to 1) 3
3179⁴ EMERALD SEA (USA) [100] 7-10-0 S Turner, *cl up, chlgd last, sn rdn and one pace.*...................(33 to 1) 4
2956* MASTER OF TROY [101] 6-9-10 (5*) Mr D Parker, *f second.*
.........................(11 to 8 fav op 5 to 4 tchd 6 to 1) f
Dist: 1½l, 3½l, nk. 4m 3.30s. a 20.30s (5 Ran).

SR: 26/28/44/19/-/ (Allan W Melville), P Monteith

SEDGEFIELD (good)
Tuesday April 12th
Going Correction: PLUS 0.40 sec. per fur.

3435 John Wade Haulage Novices' Selling Hurdle (4-y-o and up) £1,984 2m 5f 110yds.........................(2:20)

3236⁴ HOT PUNCH 5-10-11 (5*) P Waggott, *trkd ldrs, chlgd appr 2 out, rdn to ld last, styd on und pres.*
.........................(5 to 2 op 6 to 4) 1
3285² RYTHMIC RYMER 4-9-11 (7*) G Tormey, *with ldrs, led and mstk 2 out, hdd last, kpt on wl und pres.*
.........................(7 to 1 op 8 to 1 tchd 10 to 1) 2
3236⁸ MISS CONSTRUE 7-10-4 (7*) G Lee, *wth ldrs, slight ld appr 2 out, sn hdd, ch last, kpt on und pres.*
.........................(14 to 1 op 10 to 1) 3
2961³ FARMER'S CROSS 10-11-8 Mrs A Farrell, *made most till hdd appr 2 out, kpt on same pace.*
.........................(2 to 1 fav op 7 to 4 tchd 9 to 4) 4
3079³ OWES THE TILL 4-9-13² (7*) C Woodall, *trkd ldrs, rdn appr 2 out, one pace.*...................(14 to 1 op 10 to 1) 5
2925⁸ THE WEATHERMAN 6-10-9 (7*) N Stocks, *prmnt, outpcd aftr 3 out, styd on frm nxt.*
.........................(16 to 1 op 14 to 1 tchd 20 to 1) 6
2951 GLORIOUS HEIGHTS 6-10-11 A Merrigan, *hld up, effrt aftr 3 out, no hdwy.*..........(66 to 1 op 50 to 1) 7
3341 FARAH 5-10-4 (7*) W Fry, *nvr dngrs.* (14 to 1 op 10 to 1) 8
3341 GOLDEN BANKER (Ire) 6-11-2 K Jones, *chsd ldrs, drvn alng hfwy, grad wknd.*............(50 to 1 op 33 to 1) 9
LODGING (v) 7-11-2 R Garritty, *hld up, steady hdwy to track ldrs aftr 3 out, wknd appr nxt.*.........(33 to 1) 10
1938 HOWARD'S POST 5-11-2 A Dobbin, *prmnt till wknd aftr 3 out.*..................(14 to 1 tchd 16 to 1) 11
3034 FEELING FRAYL 7-10-4 (7*) M Clarke, *prmnt till wknd aftr 3 out.*.........(50 to 1 op 50 to 1) 12
2485 ABLE MCCLEOD 4-10-9 J Callaghan, *sn beh.*
.........................(50 to 1 op 33 to 1) 13
3140 SAMS-THE-MAN (bl) 6-11-2 C Hawkins, *al beh.*
.........................(66 to 1 op 50 to 1) 14
3279 CHAPELSTREET BLUES 7-10-4 (7*) F Leahy, *in tch till aftr 3 out.*..........(50 to 1 op 33 to 1) 15
1097 TINSTONE 4-9-11 (7*) Mark Roberts, *pld hrd, beh most of way.*.........................(12 to 1 op 12 to 1) 16
3030 PICKTHEMONEYUPALF 7-11-2 K Johnson, *tld off early, some hdwy aftr 3 out, no ch whn f last.*
.........................(66 to 1 op 50 to 1) f
3284⁹ BONNY HECTOR 10-10-9 (7*) Mr A Manners, *chsd ldrs till pld up lme aftr 3 out.*.........................(50 to 1) pu
Dist: ¾l, 1¾l, 7l, 6l, sht-hd, 4l, 7l, 3½l, 1½l, 20l. 5m 25.60s. a 34.60s (18 Ran).

(Hamish Alexander), H Alexander

3436 John Joyce Handicap Hurdle (0-120 4-y-o and up) £2,490 2m 1f 110yds
.........................(2:50)

3240² ANY DREAM WOULD DO [88] 5-10-0 C Hawkins, *trkd ldrs, effrt appr 2 out, styd on wl und pres to ld towards finish.*..........(6 to 1 tchd 13 to 2) 1
3240* WHO'S TEF (Ire) [116] 6-12-0 L Wyer, *trkd ldrs, led appr 2 out, sn rdn, hdd and no extr towards finish.*
.........................(7 to 2 fav op 9 to 4 tchd 4 to 1) 2

3057⁴ RED JAM JAR [88] 9-10-0 K Johnson, *hld up and pld hrd, gd hdwy appr 2 out, styd on wl und pres, nrst finish.*
.........................(5 to 1 op 4 to 1) 3
3344⁵ FLASS VALE [88] (v) 6-9-11 (3*) D Bentley, *led till hdd appr 2 out, kpt on same pace.*.........(33 to 1) 4
2214 SASKIA'S HERO [90] 7-10-2 W Dwan, *prmnt, rdn appr 2 out, grad wknd.*...................(9 to 1 op 8 to 1) 5
FIERY SUN [112] 9-11-10 N Smith, *in tch, pushed alng aftr 3 out, no hdwy.*..........(20 to 1 op 16 to 1) 6
1474 MIAMI BEAR [99] 8-10-11 P Harley, *prmnt till wknd appr 2 out.*.........................(33 to 1 tchd 50 to 1) 7
3139* STATION EXPRESS (Ire) [88] 6-9-7 (7*) F Leahy, *hld up, effrt appr 2 out, no hdwy.*...................(16 to 1 op 14 to 1) 8
2436⁶ FLOWING RIVER (USA) [101] 8-10-13 B Storey, *hld up, pushed alng aftr 3 out, no hdwy.*.........................(9 to 2 op 4 to 1) 9
BUCKRA MELLISUGA [93] 10-10-5 C Grant, *trkd ldrs, chlgd appr 2 out, sn wknd.*......(20 to 1 tchd 25 to 1) 10
2573 DERWENT LAD [88] 5-10-0 A Dobbin, *beh most of way.*
.........................(100 to 1) 11
1213⁹ STAY AWAKE [113] 8-11-11 R Hodge, *in tch till wknd aftr 3 out.*.........................(11 to 1 op 10 to 1) 12
2498* DUTCH BLUES [88] 7-10-0 D Wilkinson, *sn chasing ldrs, lost tch aftr 3 out, wl beh whn pld up bef nxt.*
.........................(14 to 1 op 16 to 1) pu
Dist: ½l, 1½l, 7l, 6l, hd, 2l, ¾l, 2½l, ¾l, 15l. 4m 15.60s. a 20.60s (13 Ran).

(Mrs C M G Cawte), P Beaumont

3437 Reg Lamb Memorial Handicap Chase
(0-120 5-y-o and up) £3,042 3m 3f (3:20)

3059* MORGANS HARBOUR [103] 8-11-4 N Smith, *sn tracking ldrs, hit 14th, chlgd 4 out, led 2 out, pushed out r-in.*
.........................(13 to 8 fav op 7 to 4) 1
3237⁴ CAROUSEL CALYPSO [87] 8-10-2 A Dobbin, *prmnt, slight ld 4 out, hdd 2 out, kpt on und pres.*..........(20 to 1) 2
3168⁴ CHOCTAW [102] 10-11-3 C Hawkins, *led to 7th, cl up, led 14th to 4 out, no extr.*...............(8 to 1 tchd 9 to 1) 3
3134 GATHERING TIME [97] 8-10-5 (7*) Miss V Haigh, *beh, some late hdwy, nvr dngrs.*...................(16 to 1) 4
3194⁴ FIGHT TO WIN (USA) [99] (bl) 6-11-0 G Upton, *cl up, led tenth, dsptd ld 14th till wknd aftr 4 out.*
.........................(25 to 1 op 20 to 1) 5
3127⁵ BISHOPDALE [104] 13-11-5 A Merrigan, *chsd ldrs, hrd rdn aftr 13th, sn lost tch, tld off.*......(20 to 1 op 16 to 1) 6
2880⁴ LITTLE GENERAL [85] 11-10-0 M Perrett, *prmnt till lost tch aftr 14th, tld off.*..........(10 to 1 op 8 to 1) 7
3238* MOYODE REGENT [85] 10-9-12⁵ (7*) Mr A Manners, *sddl slpd, lost tch aftr 14th, tld off.*.........(8 to 1 op 7 to 1) 8
3077³ DUBIOUS JAKE [92] 11-10-7 M Dwyer, *chsd ldrs till blun and uns rdr 9th.*..........(8 to 1 tchd 9 to 1) ur
3286⁷ EDEN SUNSET [86] 8-10-1¹ J Callaghan, *blun and uns rdr 1st.*..........................(20 to 1 tchd 25 to 1) ur
3237² LAPIAFFE [89] 10-10-4 B Storey, *cl up, led 7th to tenth, wknd aftr 16th, wl beh whn pld up bef last.*
.........................(8 to 1 op 7 to 1) pu
2958⁵ FIRST LORD [85] (bl) 8-9-9 (5*) J Supple, *mstk 1st, sn beh and rdn alng, tld off whn pld up bef 3 out.*....(33 to 1) pu
2448 MAJIC RAIN [86] 9-10-1 C Grant, *sn tld off, pld up bef 14th.*.........................(10 to 1 op 66 to 1) pu
3059 LADY BLAKENEY [85] 8-10-0 L Wyer, *lost tch aftr 13th, wl beh whn pld up bef 4 out.*..........(33 to 1 op 20 to 1) pu
Dist: 1¾l, 25l, 8l, 3½l, 30l, ½l, 13l. 7m 4.10s. a 25.10s (14 Ran).

(P C W Owen), Mrs M Reveley

3438 Vaux Breweries Sedgefield Champion Novices' Chase (5-y-o and up) £4,274 2m 1f.........................(3:55)

2090² EXPLOSIVE SPEED (USA) 6-11-9 C Grant, *cl up, led aftr 7th, clr whn hit last, styd on.*......(6 to 1 op 5 to 1) 1
2892* DORADUS 6-11-9 F Leahy, *hld up in tch, ev ch 4 out, slightly outpcd aftr nxt, kpt on frm last.*
.........................(9 to 2 op 7 to 2) 2
3239² SHREWD JOHN 8-11-9 M Dwyer, *in tch, chsd wnr frm 3 out, no imprsn.*............(4 to 1 jt-fav tchd 5 to 1) 3
3356² ISSYIN 7-11-9 R Garritty, *hld up, hdwy aftr 8th, kpt on same pace frm 2 out.*..........(4 to 1 jt-fav op 7 to 2) 4
1571⁵ BEAUCADEAU 8-11-3 A Dobbin, *chsd ldrs till wknd aftr 3 out.*.........................(20 to 1 op 16 to 1) 5
3238 KINGS LAW 8-11-3 M D Scott, *sn beh, no ch whn blun and almost uns rdr 2 out.*...................(20 to 1) 6
2971⁵ ZARBANO 8-11-3 A Merrigan, *prmnt till wknd aftr 4 out.*.........................(33 to 1 op 20 to 1) 7
DOLITINO 10-12-12 R Trend, *beh frm hfwy.*
.........................(66 to 1 op 33 to 1) 8
3033 EDEN STREAM 7-11-3 G Upton, *mstks, al beh.*
.........................(20 to 1 op 16 to 1) 9
3286⁶ MAYOR OF LISCARROL 9-11-9 G Harker, *led till stumbled badly and lost pl aftr 7th, mstk nxt, no ch after.*
.........................(10 to 1) 10
2879 RICH NEPHEW 9-11-3 M Perrett, *sn beh.*
.........................(25 to 1 op 33 to 1) 11
3341⁴ GRAZEMBER 7-11-3 C Hawkins, *hld up in tch, hdwy aftr 8th, disputing 4th and staying on whn f 2 out.*
.........................(25 to 1 op 20 to 1) f
1287 SPLIT SECOND (bl) 5-10-10 P Harley, *blun and uns rdr 5th.*.........................(33 to 1 op 25 to 1) ur

3179 DOUGAL'S BIRTHDAY 8-11-3 K Jones, *sn wl beh, tld off whn pld up bef last*..........................(100 to 1)   pu
Dist: 6l, ½l, hd, 30l, 15l, 3½l, 1½l, 1½l, 3l, 2l. 4m 17.80s. a 12.80s (14 Ran).
SR: 35/29/28/-/-/   (Wetherby Racing Bureau Plc), M D Hammond

3439 Stanley Thompson Memorial Hunters' Chase (5-y-o and up) £1,702 3m 3f
.................................(4:30)

3157² GOGGINS HILL 7-11-12 Mr J Greenall, *trkd ldrs, led 4 out, drvn out aftr last.*
.... (6 to 5 on op 5 to 4 on tchd 11 to 10 on)   1
3165⁴ SPORTING MARINER 12-11-0 (7*) Mr D Bloor, *cl up, led 6th, hdd 4 out, kpt on wl frm last*.............. (6 to 1)   2
LINEBACKER 10-11-0 (7*) Mr N F Smith, *prmnt, dsptd ld 12th to 14th, ev ch till slightly outpcd aftr 4 out, kpt on frm 2 out*..........................(10 to 1 op 8 to 1)   3
BIRTLEY GIRL 10-10-9 (7*) Miss Sue Nichol, *beh, hdwy aftr 14th, wknd appr 3 out.*............(25 to 1 op 14 to 1)   4
2959* VERY CHEERING 11-11-5 (7*) Mr B Crawford, *jmpd badly rght, sn beh, tld off whn blun and uns rdr 16th.*
..........................(7 to 1 op 6 to 1)   ur
SECOND ATTEMPT (bl) 10-11-2 (5*) Mr D Parker, *led to 6th, wkng whn blun 14th, tld off when pld up bef 16th.*
..........................(33 to 1 op 25 to 1)   pu
3377 DALMORE 8-11-0 (7*) Mr P Atkinson, *in tch till wknd quickly appr 4 out, tld off whn pld up aftr nxt.*
..........................(50 to 1 op 33 to 1)   pu
RIVERBOAT QUEEN 11-10-9 (7*) Mr P Jenkins, *beh frm 7th, tld off whn hit 17th, pld up bef 4 out.*
..........................(10 to 1 op 8 to 1)   pu
LETHAL WEAPON 10-11-13¹³ (7*) Mr Simon Robinson, *sn tld off, pld up bef 6th.*............(66 to 1 op 50 to 1)   pu
Dist: 3½l, 2l, 30l. 7m 16.20s. a 37.20s (9 Ran).
(J E Greenall), P Cheesbrough

3440 Jump Into Spring Novices' Handicap Hurdle (4-y-o and up) £2,521 2m 110yds....................(5:00)

3378⁶ TWIN STATES [79] 5-9-10 (7*) W Fry, *trkd ldrs, led aftr 3 out, rdn and styd on wl r-in*...............(8 to 1)   1
2903 OTHER RANKS (Ire) [76] 6-10-0 C Dennis, *sn tracking ldrs, chsd wnr appr 2 out, kpt on und pres, no imprsn.*
..........................(33 to 1 op 20 to 1)   2
823 BRIAR'S DELIGHT [76] 6-10-0 B Storey, *sn tracking ldrs. effrt appr 2 out, kpt on same pace.* (25 to 1 op 20 to 1)   3
3277* TITIAN GIRL [84] (bl) 5-10-8 T Reed, *outpcd and lost pl hfwy, no dngr aftr*.................(6 to 1 op 5 to 1)   4
3144⁸ GERMAN LEGEND [77] 4-10-11 A Merrigan, *prmnt till wknd aftr 3 out*...(20 to 1 on 14 to 1 tchd 33 to 1)   5
3264⁹ TOO CLEVER BY HALF [92] 6-11-2 Mr G Johnson Houghton, *nvr dngrs*.....................(7 to 1 op 6 to 1)   6
3144 JUKE BOX BILLY (Ire) [77] 6-10-1 A Dobbin, *led aftr second till hdd aftr 3 out, wknd appr nxt...(7 to 1 op 6 to 1)   7
3139⁸ ON GOLDEN POND (Ire) [76] (bl) 4-9-11 (3*) D Bentley, *prmnt till wknd appr 2 out*...........(12 to 1 tchd 14 to 1)   8
OLLIVER DUCKETT [76] 5-10-0 C Hawkins, *mstk 1st, beh, hdwy hfwy, wknd appr 2 out*..............(20 to 1)   9
3136⁶ POWLEYVALE [102] 7-11-12 M Dwyer, *rcd wide, in tch till wknd aftr 5th*..............................10
3345² ALI'S ALIBI [90] 7-10-11 (3*) Mr M Buckley, *mstks, al beh.*
..........................(7 to 4 fav op 6 to 4 tchd 15 to 8)   11
3236⁹ MIDNIGHT FLOTILLA [76] (bl) 8-9-7 (7*) B Grattan, *led till aftr second, beh frm hfwy*..........(14 to 1 op 10 to 1)   12
3284⁴ TIGHTER BUDGET (USA) [76] 7-10-0 M Moloney, *wth ldrs till wknd aftr 3 out, tld off whn pld up bef nxt.*
..........................(5 to 1 op 7 to 1)   pu
Dist: 5l, 11l, 20l, 4l, 2½l, 10l, 4l, nk, 3½l, 9l. 5m 16.10s. a 25.10s (13 Ran).
(J R Turner), J R Turner

UTTOXETER (heavy)
Tuesday April 12th
Going Correction: PLUS 1.55 sec. per fur.

3441 Applied Signs Novices' Handicap Hurdle (0-100 4-y-o and up) £2,155 2¾m 110yds....................(2:10)

3317² PRIMO FIGLIO [80] (bl) 4-11-6 A Maguire, *al prmnt, led 6th, styd on wl frm 3 out*.........(14 to 1 op 8 to 1)   1
3340³ MARINERS LOVE [65] 8-10-5 R Dunwoody, *hld up in mid-div, hdwy hfwy, chsd wnr frm 3 out, no imprsn.*
..........................(12 to 1 tchd 14 to 1)   2
2902⁴ PRINCETHORPE [68] 7-10-5 (3*) D Meredith, *hld up, gd hdwy 4 out, no imprsn frm nxt.*
..........................(12 to 1 op 8 to 1 tchd 14 to 1)   3
3225* PATROCLUS [83] 9-11-6 (3*) T Eley, *led to 6th, styd in tch, rdn 3 out, no extr*......(5 to 2 fav op 7 to 2 tchd 11 to 2)   4
2964⁷ CATS RUN (Ire) [78] 6-11-4 R Supple, *trkd ldrs, wknd 3 out*...................(12 to 1 tchd 14 to 1)   5
3221³ KADARI [68] (v) 5-10-8 Diane Clay, *in tch till 4 out.*
..........................(16 to 1 op 14 to 1)   6
3196⁸ LEINTHALL PRINCESS [64] 8-10-4 T Wall, *prmnt frm 3rd, wknd 4 out*.........(33 to 1 op 20 to 1 tchd 50 to 1)   7

COTSWOLD CASTLE [73] 8-10-8 (5*) S Fox, *in tch till wknd appr 3 out*.............................(20 to 1)   8
3170⁴ NAVAL BATTLE [68] 7-10-8 J R Kavanagh, *in rear till hdwy 6th, wknd appr 3 out...(9 to 1 op 10 to 1 tchd 7 to 1)   9
3196 GRATUITY [80] 9-11-6 N Mann, *al beh, tld off.*
..........................(50 to 1 op 33 to 1)   10
3109 SARAH'S WROATH [60] 9-10-0 R Bellamy, *al beh, tld off frm 6th*........................(50 to 1 op 25 to 1)   11
3153* ROWLANDSONS GOLD (Ire) [84] 4-11-10 Lorna Vincent, *chsd ldrs till wknd 6th, tld off.....(16 to 1 op 10 to 1)   12
3287 GUTE NACHT [72] (bl) 11-10-7 (5*) P Midgley, *prmnt whn blun 5th, sn wknd, tld off.........(25 to 1 op 16 to 1)   13
2185* MOYNSHA HOUSE (Ire) [69] 6-10-3 D Murphy, *hld up, hdwy 6th, wknd quickly appr 2 out, tired 5th whn f last.*.......................(5 to 4 fav op 3 to 1)   f
KERRY MY HOME [60] 7-10-0 E Murphy, *tld off second, pld up appr 6th*..........(8 to 1 op 5 to 1 tchd 20 to 1)   pu
3196² ANILAFFED [84] (v) 4-11-10 D Gallagher, *trkd ldr till wknd hfwy, tld off whn pld up bef 3 out, lme.*
..........................(10 to 1 op 7 to 1)   pu
Dist: 8l, 2l, 13l, 15l, 2½l, 5l, 8l, sht-hd, 20l, 5l. 5m 52.80s. a 41.80s (16 Ran).
SR: 23/-/1/3/-/-/   (Townville C C Racing Club), Miss L C Siddall

3442 Phillips Florists Novices' Handicap Chase (5-y-o and up) £2,944 3¼m
.................................(2:40)

3316* BRABAZON (USA) [112] 9-11-13 A Maguire, *hld up, al gng wl, hdwy 12th, led on bit 2 out, very easily.*
..........................(3 to 1 fav op 7 to 2 tchd 4 to 1)   1
3309 SPECIAL ACCOUNT [85] (v) 8-10-0 N Mann, *hld up in mid-div, gd hdwy to go second 4 out, led and hit nxt, hdd 2 out, rdn and no imprsn.*
..........................(14 to 1 op 12 to 1 tchd 16 to 1)   2
3358 VELEDA II (Fr) [107] 7-11-3 (5*) J Burke, *make most till hdd 3 out, rdn and wknd nxt.*.........(10 to 1 op 7 to 1)   3
3188* SHEARMAC STEEL [85] 7-10-0 Peter Hobbs, *in tch, mstk 8th, ev ch 4 out, rdn and sn btn....(7 to 1 tchd 8 to 1)   4
3343² TRAVEL BOUND [85] 9-10-0 L Harvey, *frnt rnk till wknd 5 out*.........................(16 to 1 op 12 to 1)   5
2764* DOROBO (NZ) [86] (bl) 6-9-12 (3*) R Farrant, *prmnt, rdn 7th, wknd appr 4 out*.....................(7 to 2 op 3 to 1)   6
3224⁶ DUCHESS OF TUBBER (Ire) [89] 6-10-4 N Williamson, *pressed ldr till hit 5 out, wknd nxt, btn whn blun 2 out.*
..........................(12 to 1 op 10 to 1)   7
3077 MERLYNS CHOICE [87] 10-10-2² R Dunwoody, *prmnt till wknd 12th, tld off...(11 to 1 op 10 to 1 tchd 12 to 1)   8
1967⁶ BILLHEAD [85] 8-9-11 (3*) T Eley, *in rear, lost tch 12th, tld off whn pld up bef 5 out..........(50 to 1 op 20 to 1)   pu
3343 CANTGETOUT [86] 8-10-11 Mr A Pickering, *beh, tld off frm off 7th, pld up bef 12th*.......(33 to 1 op 20 to 1)   pu
3040⁸ LASTOFTHEVIKINGS [85] 9-10-0 D Gallagher, *mstk 3rd, tld off 7th, pld up bef 12th.(9 to 1 op 7 to 1 tchd 10 to 1)   pu
2980* THE PORTSOY LOON [92] 7-10-7 D Bridgwater, *mstks, al in rear, tld off whn pld up bef 4 out...(12 to 1 op 8 to 1)   pu
3224 CRAIGSTOWN (Ire) [85] 6-10-0 J R Kavanagh, *hld up, hdwy 11th, wknd rpdly appr 4 out, pld up bef 2 out.*
..........................(8 to 1 op 7 to 1)   pu
Dist: ¾l, 20l, 8l, 9l, 5l, nk, 30l. 7m 21.00s. a 65.00s (13 Ran).
(P H Betts (Holdings) Ltd), M H Tompkins

3443 Hawksworth Graphics & Print Handicap Chase (0-130 5-y-o and up) £3,461 2m 5f..........................(3:10)

3112* RAFIKI [109] 9-10-10 M A FitzGerald, *trkd ldr most of way, led 2 out, ran on wl*... (11 to 4 op 5 to 2 tchd 3 to 1)   1
3112² BALDA BOY [103] 10-10-4 B Powell, *led, jmpd lft 7th, wnt clr appr 4 out, rdn and hdd 2 out, no extr.*
..........................(16 to 1 op 14 to 1 tchd 20 to 1)   2
2836⁷ MO ICHI DO [99] 8-9-11 (3*) T Eley, *mid-div, pushed alng frm 8th, effrt appr 4 out, btn whn lft 3rd last.*
..........................(33 to 1 op 25 to 1)   3
3163* ANDERMATT [109] 7-10-10 N Williamson, *hld up in rear, gd hdwy appr 8th, outpcd 5 out, rdn frm nxt, btn 3rd whn f last.*.........................(9 to 2 op 4 to 1)   f
2995 REPEAT THE DOSE [120] 9-11-7 G McCourt, *nvr gng wl, tld off whn jmpd rght 9th and tenth, pld up bef 3 out.*
..........................(8 to 1 op 6 to 1 tchd 10 to 1)   pu
3180 INCONCLUSIVE [101] 7-10-2⁷ (5*) J Burke, *al beh, tld off whn pld up bef 3 out.*............(33 to 1 op 20 to 1)   pu
3041 GNOME'S TYCOON [127] 8-12-0 J Railton, *trkd ldrs, second whn hit 6th, rdn and wknd appr 4 out, pld up aftr nxt.*..........................(7 to 2 op 5 to 2)   pu
Dist: 3½l, 7l. 5m 46.60s. a 46.60s (7 Ran).
(J P Carrington), Mrs J G Retter

3444 Peter Davis Tractors Novices' Hurdle (4-y-o) £1,686 2m..............(3:45)

2853 PREROGATIVE (v) 12-0 R Dunwoody, *made all, hrd drvn frm 2 out, all out.*
..........................(11 to 10 on op 6 to 4 on tchd Evens)   1
3314³ ROMALITO 11-0 D Gallagher, *hld up, cld on ldrs 4 out, wnt second appr 2 out, jnd wnr last, no extr nr finish.*
..........................(2 to 1 op 7 to 4 tchd 6 to 4)   2

3289³ VOLUNTEER POINT (Ire) 10-9 (5*) J Burke, *al prmnt, wnt second appr 5th, rdn and wkng whn hit 2 out, eased.*
....(5 to 1 op 4 to 1) 3
3365 GYPSY CRYSTAL (USA) 10-9 M A FitzGerald, *pld hrd, trkd wnr till wknd appr 5th, sn tld off.*
.......................(25 to 1 op 50 to 1 tchd 20 to 1) 4
3211 MAC TOMB 10-11 (3*) J McCarthy, *in tch, wknd appr 5th, tld off whn blun nxt, sn pld up.*.............. (50 to 1) pu
Dist: 1½l, 20l, dist. 4m 15.30s. a 36.30s (5 Ran).

(D A Johnson), M C Pipe

3445 'Happy Birthday Viv' Novices' Chase (5-y-o and up) £2,612 2m 5f..... (4:20)

3133³ DONT TELL THE WIFE 8-11-10 D Bridgwater, *wtd wth, hdwy to track ldr frm 6th, led and hit 2 out, drvn out.*
.... (15 to 8 op 2 to 1 tchd 9 to 4 and 7 to 4) 1
3251* CROSULA 6-11-10 R Dunwoody, *led, clr whn mstk 3rd, mistake and hdd 2 out, hrd rdn and wknd r-in.*
....................................(5 to 4 fav op 6 to 4 on) 2
3224 KING OF SHADOWS 7-11-4 Gary Lyons, *in tch, lost pl 4th, cld on ldrs 8th, wknd four out, tld off.*
....(66 to 1 op 33 to 1) 3
2792⁶ LING (USA) 9-11-4 T Wall, *hld up, hdwy 5 out, wkng whn blun 3 out, tld off....* (14 to 1 op 10 to 1 tchd 16 to 1) 4
3102 BEN THE BOMBER 9-10-11 (7*) Judy Davies, *in tch, wknd 8th, tld off frm 5 out.*..................(50 to 1 op 33 to 1) 5
3224⁴ TITUS GOLD 9-11-1 (3*) T Eley, *in tch, wknd appr 5 out, tld off whn pld up bef nxt.*
..........................(13 to 2 op 14 to 1 tchd 6 to 1) pu
2899⁴ FOXY BLUE 9-11-4 S McNeill, *trkd ldr to 6th, wknd 8th, tld off whn pld up bef 3 out.*
.....................(16 to 1 op 14 to 1 tchd 20 to 1) pu
3278⁷ BRORA ROSE (Ire) (v) 6-10-6 (7*) Miss S Golden, *al beh, tld off 8th, pld up bef 3 out.*..........(50 to 1 op 33 to 1) pu
Dist: 6l, dist, ¾l, dist. 5m 46.60s. a 46.60s (8 Ran).

(H & K Commissions), Mrs D Haine

3446 Lycett Blinds & Awnings Handicap Hurdle (0-120 4-y-o and up) £2,583 2m ....(4:55)

2998⁵ RAIN-N-SUN [87] 8-10-0 T Wall, *trkd ldr, led 3 out, hdd nxt, rallied and led ag'n r-in.*
..........................(7 to 1 op 6 to 1 tchd 10 to 1) 1
2833 RED INDIAN [115] 8-12-0 D Byrne, *hld up in rear, gd hdwy frm 4 out, led on bit 2 out, sn rdn, hdd r-in.*
....................................(6 to 4 fav op Evens) 2
3136 DOOLAR (USA) [99] 7-10-12 N Mann, *led, hdd 3 out, wknd nxt.*........................(7 to 4 op 5 to 2 tchd 6 to 4) 3
3344 MARA ASKARI [90] (v) 6-10-3 R Dunwoody, *3rd till wknd appr 3 out, tld off.*..................(4 to 1 op 3 to 1) 4
Dist: 1¼l, 9l, dist. 4m 14.00s. a 35.00s (4 Ran).

(Mrs M Bostock), J L Harris

DOWN ROYAL (IRE) (soft)
Wednesday April 13th

3447 Dumfries Maiden Hurdle (Div 1) (4-y-o and up) £1,382 2m.............(2:30)

1978⁵ STRONG PLATINUM (Ire) 6-11-6 C O'Dwyer, (7 to 4 jt-fav) 1
3122⁷ STRONG HICKS (Ire) 6-11-6 F J Flood, ...(8 to 1) 2
529 RYE HILL QUEEN (Ire) 4-10-10 C F Swan, ...(12 to 1) 3
3388⁹ MY HALL DOOR 5-11-0 (5*) D T Evans, ...(16 to 1) 4
2863 DOCS DILEMMA (Ire) 5-11-0 (5*) J P Broderick, ...(20 to 1) 5
2470 PATS FAREWELL (Ire) 6-11-6 J Shortt, ...(16 to 1) 6
3388² YOU'VE DONE WHAT (Ire) 6-11-6 J F Titley, ...(7 to 4 jt-fav) 7
3227 GRAMSCI (Ire) 6-11-6 K F O'Brien, ...(7 to 1) 8
2309⁷ REMO GROVE (Ire) 6-11-1 (5*) M M Mackin, ...(20 to 1) 9
3122 COLLIERS HILL (Ire) 6-11-6 L F Cusack, ...(20 to 1) 10
3071⁶ MILLHAVEN PRINCESS 8-10-8 (7*) R J Gordon, ..(50 to 1) 11
3276⁸ THE THIRD MAN (Ire) 5-10-12 (7*) T Martin, ...(33 to 1) 12
GRANDEUR (Ire) 4-10-8 (7*) Mr S A Quilty, ...(10 to 1) 13
3072* CUTTER'S WHARF (Ire) 5-11-8 (5*) Mr B R Hamilton,
....(10 to 1) 14
JOHNSON'S HILL (Ire) 5-11-0 (5*) L Flynn, ...(33 to 1) 15
DANESFORT (Ire) 5-11-5 H Rogers, ...(20 to 1) 16
2938 DUST GALE (Ire) 5-11-0 P L Malone, ...(33 to 1) ref
TOP CAT (Ire) 4-10-8 (7*) D Fisher, ...(33 to 1) pu
Dist: 6l, hd, 6l, 1½l. (Time not taken) (18 Ran).

(Mrs Theresa McCoubrey), P Burke

3448 Dumfries Maiden Hurdle (Div 2) (4-y-o and up) £1,382 2m.............(3:00)

2607³ THE TOASTER 7-10-13 (7*) B Bowens, ...(5 to 4 fav) 1
2771³ JULEIT JONES (Ire) 5-11-0 F J Flood, ...(6 to 1) 2
3122 IF YOU BELIEVE (Ire) 5-11-5 J F Titley, ...(12 to 1) 3
3388 BEDFORD RAMBLER (Ire) 5-11-0 (5*) J P Broderick,
....(14 to 1) 4
3276⁶ KEY WEST (Ire) 5-11-10 (3*) T J Mitchell, ...(8 to 1) 5
3069⁸ MAJA GRADDNOS 4-10-12 (3*) K B Walsh, ...(25 to 1) 6
3069² BOBADIL (Ire) 4-10-8 (7*) P J Smullen, ...(9 to 1) 7
3271² PILS INVADER (Ire) 6-10-10 (5*) D T Evans, ...(7 to 1) 8
3244 PERCUSIONIST 7-11-6 L P Cusack, ...(20 to 1) 9

3072⁸ SIMONE STAR (Ire) 5-10-9 (5*) K P Gaule, ...(25 to 1) 10
HELLO DAWN (Ire) 6-11-6 J Shortt, ...(20 to 1) 11
SCENT JAR (Ire) 4-10-10 C O'Dwyer, ...(16 to 1) 12
3246⁷ EUROPE (USA) 4-10-13 (7*) A P McCoy, ...(7 to 1) 13
2983 WHOTHATIS 8-11-1 D P Fagan, ...(20 to 1) 14
2989⁶ RUEMARO THYNE (Ire) 5-11-5 H Rogers, ...(10 to 1) 15
3326 REDELVA 7-11-1 F Woods, ...(14 to 1) 16
ROCK SUPREME 7-10-13 (7*) Mr L J Gracey, ...(25 to 1) 17
Dist: Nk, 7l, 15l, ½l. (Time not taken) (17 Ran).

(Mrs K Owens), Victor Bowens

3449 Top Of The World Handicap Hurdle (0-116 5-y-o and up) £1,382 2½m (3:30)

2842* FIDDLERS BOW VI (Ire) [-] 6-10-10 P Carberry, (11 to 8 fav) 1
3273² RED THUNDER [-] 7-10-1 D P Fagan, ...(8 to 1) 2
3080 ROCHE MELODY (Ire) [-] 6-9-11 (3*) C O'Brien, ...(20 to 1) 3
3273⁷ SIOBHAILIN DUBH (Ire) [-] 5-10-2 C F Swan, ...(10 to 1) 4
3242⁹ OVER THE MALLARD (Ire) [-] 5-10-6 (3*) D Bromley, (14 to 1) 5
2026⁶ MR FIVE WOOD (Ire) [-] 6-10-7 (5*) Mr B R Hamilton, (6 to 1) 6
3272⁵ THE PARSONS ROSE (Ire) [-] 6-9-5¹ (5*) J P Broderick,
....(25 to 1) 7
2284⁹ SECRET SCEPTRE [-] 7-10-12 F Woods, ...(12 to 1) 8
3273⁶ BELLE O' THE BAY (Ire) [-] 5-9-5⁵ (7*) A P McCoy, (20 to 1) 9
3272* NATINA (Ire) [-] 5-9-10 (7*,6ex) T Martin, ...(10 to 1) 10
3276* I AM [-] 6-10-13 (3*) Mr P J Casey, ...(4 to 1) 11
2310³ MCCONNELL GOLD [-] 9-9-13 (5*) K P Gaule, ...(16 to 1) 12
2752 CARRON HILL [-] 7-10-10 K F O'Brien, ...(14 to 1) 13
SKI NUT [-] 7-11-0 H Rogers, ...(20 to 1) 14
3294 DAMODAR [-] 5-10-12 F J Flood, ...(10 to 1) 15
3272² TOP GENERATION [-] 5-10-1 (3*) T J Mitchell, ...(12 to 1) 16
LA CIENAGA [-] 10-11-5 (7*) S G Anderson, ...(20 to 1) pu
Dist: ½l, 2½l, ¾l, ¾l. (Time not taken) (17 Ran).

(Mrs A T B Kearney), Noel Meade

3450 Bradstock Insurance Brokers (Mares) INH Flat Race (4-y-o and up) £1,552 2m
..................................(5:00)

CAPITAL ROSE (Ire) 5-11-6 (7*) Mr P English, (3 to 1 jt-fav) 1
3291 DOUBLE SYMPHONY (Ire) 6-11-7 (7*) Mr G R Ryan, (4 to 1) 2
3271³ RAHAN BRIDGE (Ire) 5-11-13 Mr A J Martin, ...(12 to 1) 3
3271⁴ GRANDOLLY (Ire) 5-11-8 (5*) Mr B R Hamilton, ...(14 to 1) 4
3296² LADY OF TARA 8-11-11 (3*) Mrs J M Mullins, ...(4 to 1) 5
2983⁵ GLENBALLYMA (Ire) 5-11-8 (5*) Mr H F Cleary, (3 to 1 jt-fav) 6
BRAMBLESHINE (Ire) 4-11-3 (3*) Mrs M Mullins, ...(10 to 1) 7
LE MINTER (Ire) 5-11-13 Mr A R Coonan, ...(16 to 1) 8
BLENNERVILLE (Ire) 4-11-1 (5*) Mr G J Harford, ...(20 to 1) 9
3372 BEAGAN ROSE (Ire) 4-10-13 (7*) Mr M O'Connor, (33 to 1) 10
3072³ AMME ENAEK (Ire) 5-11-6 (7*) Mr G Rahane, ...(14 to 1) 11
3327 EUROBUCK (Ire) (bl) 6-11-7 (7*) Mr D Valentine, .(10 to 1) 12
3327⁶ COLLON DIAMONDS (Ire) 6-11-7 (7*) Mr M Callaghan,
....(6 to 1) 13
2848⁵ SHANNON DEE (Ire) 4-11-3 (3*) Mr A J Nash, ...(10 to 1) 14
MOUNTMEAD (Ire) 4-10-13 (7*) Mr A Harris, ...(33 to 1) 15
KINGS PEARL (Ire) 6-11-7 (7*) Mr B M Cash, ...(20 to 1) 16
SHANES BAY (Ire) 4-10-13 (7*) Mr J P Harvey, ...(20 to 1) 17
Dist: ¾l, 1l, 4l, ½l. (Time not taken) (17 Ran).

(M Phelan), M Phelan

WORCESTER (good to soft)
Wednesday April 13th
Going Correction: PLUS 0.70 sec. per fur. (races 1,3,- 5,7,8), PLUS 0.60 (2,4,6)

3451 Musket Novices' Hurdle (4-y-o and up) £2,323 2m..................... (2:25)

2303 BALLYHYLAND (Ire) 5-11-4 R Bellamy, *hdwy 5th, rdn 3 out, styd on to ld last hundred yards.*
..................................(12 to 1 op 12 to 1) 1
1642⁴ THE MILLWRIGHT 7-11-2 P Holley, *al prmnt, led appr 3 out, clr 2 out, hdd fnl hundred yards.*
..................................(10 to 1 op 12 to 1) 2
3115⁶ RIO TRUSKY 5-11-2 J Railton, *al prmnt, ran on one pace frm 3 out.*......................(16 to 1 tchd 14 to 1) 3
3098² MILZIG (USA) 5-11-9 D O'Sullivan, *gd hdwy 5th, one pace frm 2 out.*...................(14 to 1 op 20 to 1) 4
1509⁴ COLTRANE (v) 6-11-2 R Dunwoody, *led to 3rd, led 4th till appr 3 out, hrd rdn and wknd approaching 2 out.*
..................................(15 to 8 fav op 6 to 4 tchd 2 to 1) 5
RUSSIAN EMPIRE 4-10-10 J Osborne, *al prmnt, not quicken frm 2 out....* (12 to 1 op 7 to 1 tchd 14 to 1) 6
1610 WISE STATEMENT (Ire) 5-11-2 E Leonard, *led 3rd to 4th, wknd 3 out, mstk last....*......(66 to 1 op 50 to 1) 7
2834⁸ MASTER HOPE (Ire) 5-11-2 A Maguire, *hdwy 4th, no extr frm 3 out.*......................(12 to 1 op 8 to 1) 8
3164² GARRISON COMMANDER (Ire) 5-11-2 S McNeill, *prmnt to 5th.*...........................(12 to 1 op 10 to 1) 9
FREESHLOCH 5-10-11 (5*) D Fortt, *hdwy 3 out, staying on whn blun last, not reco'r.*....................(33 to 1) 10
2665² NAGOBELIA 6-11-2 J McLaughlin, *prmnt to 3 out, btn whn blun nxt.*........................(33 to 1) 11
3108⁸ POLY VISION (v) 4-10-3 (7*) P McLoughlin, *nvr nr to chal.*
..................................(66 to 1 op 50 to 1) 12

3004⁴ BLACK HEDGES 7-11-2 T Reed, *swrvd badly rght strt, wl beh till some late hdwy*............(33 to 1 op 25 to 1) 13

IZACOMIN (Ire) 5-10-11 R Supple, *swrvd badly rght strt, nvr nr ldrs*..............................(66 to 1) 14

2430 CASTILLO 7-10-9 (7*) Mr Richard White, *beh frm 3rd*.
....(66 to 1) 15

3010* WEE WINDY (Ire) 5-11-9 D Murphy, *prmnt till wknd 5th*.
....(9 to 2 op 5 to 1) 16

3044⁴ COLONEL CLOETE 6-11-2 B Powell, *al beh*.
....(50 to 1 op 33 to 1) 17

OLD COMRADES 7-11-2 G McCourt, *tld off frm 4th*.
....(66 to 1 op 50 to 1) 18

2691⁴ GOTT TO APPROACH 6-11-2 W Marston, *hdwy 5th, btn whn f 2 out*..................(16 to 1 op 12 to 1) f

TOO PLUSH 5-11-2 L Harvey, *mid-div whn blun and uns rdr 3 out*....................................(33 to 1) ur

METER MAN 4-10-10 M A FitzGerald, *tld off frm 4th, pld up bef 3 out*.................................(66 to 1) pu

Dist: 2l, 6l, 3l, 3½l, 6l, 2½l, nk, 4l, 1½l, 11l. 3m 58.70s. a 17.70s (21 Ran).

SR: 25/21/15/19/8/-/ (Mrs David Blackburn), J Webber

3452 Restoration Handicap Chase (0-125 5-y-o and up) £3,088 2½m 110yds
....(2:55)

ERRANT KNIGHT [116] 10-11-10 R Dunwoody, *hld up gng wl, hdwy 3 out, led last, drvn out*.
....(9 to 1 op 6 to 1 tchd 10 to 1) 1

2205 PERSIAN SWORD [98] 8-10-6 A Maguire, *nvr far away, effrt 2 out, wnt second aftr last, not quicken*.
....(5 to 1 tchd 11 to 2) 2

3054* HOMME D'AFFAIRE [88] 7-11-0 D O'Sullivan, *led second, led 7th to tenth, ev ch 3 out, sn lost pl, styd on frm last*.
....(5 to 1 op 11 to 2) 3

2832 DRIVING FORCE [115] (bl) 8-11-9 G McCourt, *chsd ldrs, led tenth to last, wknd quickly*.
....(9 to 1 op 7 to 1 tchd 10 to 1) 4

3213² HEARTS ARE WILD [104] 7-10-12 B Powell, *jmpd slwly and drpd rear 6th, mstks 7th and 8th, blun 9th, hdwy tenth, wknd 2 out*......................(7 to 4 fav tchd 9 to 5) 5

3172² L'UOMO PIU [106] 10-11-0 J Osborne, *led second to 7th, hrd rdn and drpd rear aftr tenth, no ch after*.
....(4 to 1 op 7 to 2) 6

2397 KISU KALI [93] 7-10-1 T Wall, *prmnt till wknd appr 3 out, tld off*..................................(33 to 1) 7

Dist: 2l, 14l, ¾l, 7l, ½l, 26l. 5m 20.10s. a 17.10s (7 Ran).

SR: 48/28/14/30/12/13/-/ (Mrs N J Bird), M C Pipe

3453 Levy Board Novices' Hurdle (4-y-o and up) £2,528 3m............(3:30)

2964² ARCTIC COURSE (Ire) 6-11-8 A Maguire, *hdwy 7th, led last, all out*.
....(5 to 2 fav op 11 to 4 tchd 3 to 1 and 9 to 4) 1

3279* WOLF WINTER 9-11-8 T Grantham, *led to last, ran on wl*.
....(7 to 1 op 11 to 2) 2

3279³ CALLEROSE 7-11-2 B Powell, *al prmnt, rdn 3 out, ran on frm last*..........................(8 to 1 tchd 10 to 1) 3

3225⁶ CELTIC TOWN 6-11-5 (3*) J McCarthy, *al prmnt, ran on one pace frm 3 out*.........................(20 to 1) 4

2505⁸ BETTER BYTHE GLASS (Ire) 5-11-2 D Bridgwater, *hdwy 8th, styd on one pace frm 3 out*.....(14 to 1 op 8 to 1) 5

3380² FEEL THE POWER (Ire) 6-11-2 N Williamson, *steady hdwy 8th, ev ch 3 out, btn whn mstk last*...(3 to 1 op 2 to 1) 6

3119⁶ MAMES BOY 7-11-8 D Murphy, *hdwy 7th, ev ch appr 3 out, one pace*....................(20 to 1 tchd 22 to 1) 7

2802* A N C EXPRESS 6-11-8 J R Kavanagh, *mstks 5th and 6th, in tch till wknd 9th, tld off*..........(6 to 1 op 9 to 2) 8

2141 ARDSCUD 7-11-2 P Holley, *hdwy 8th, hrd rdn and wknd appr 3 out, tld off*..................(66 to 1 op 50 to 1) 9

1715 MONKTON (Ire) 6-10-13 (3*) R Farrant, *rdn 6th, beh frm 8th, tld off*....................(33 to 1 op 25 to 1) 10

3163 GYPSY KING (Ire) 6-11-2 S McNeill, *beh frm 8th, tld off*.
....(33 to 1 op 20 to 1) 11

3184 CELTIC TOKEN 5-10-9 (7*) Mr G Hogan, *prmnt to 8th, tld off*..(40 to 1) 12

2338 CHRISTIAN SOLDIER 7-11-2 W Elderfield, *hrd rdn 6th, sn tld off, pld up bef 3 out*.......(100 to 1 op 66 to 1) pu

CALLYR 7-11-2 W Humphreys, *tld off whn pld up bef 3 out*.........................(33 to 1 op 100 to 1) pu

1626³ DUQUES 9-10-11 R Dunwoody, *tld off whn pld up bef 3 out*.........................(20 to 1 op 12 to 1 tchd 25 to 1) pu

3051⁷ TULLYKYNE BELLS (bl) 5-11-2 D Gallagher, *prmnt till wknd 6th, tld off whn pld up bef 3 out*.
....(66 to 1 op 33 to 1) pu

3137 JUNIOR ROGERS 6-11-2 R Marley, *tld off whn pld up bef 7th*..(100 to 1) pu

3395 SOLUNIOUS 7-10-13 (3*) T Jenks, *prmnt to 7th, tld off whn pld up bef 3 out*.....................(100 to 1) pu

TITCHWELL MILLY 5-10-11 M A FitzGerald, *tld off whn pld up bef 7th*...............................(100 to 1 op 33 to 1) pu

Dist: ½l, 3l, 1¼l, 1¼l, 1l, sht-hd, dist, ¾l, 15l, 30l. 6m 3.90s. a 27.90s (19 Ran).

(Mrs Shirley Robins), D Nicholson

3454 City Novices' Chase (5-y-o and up) £3,046 2½m 110yds............(4:00)

3004⁴ EMERALD RULER 7-11-4 G McCourt, *hdwy 9th, led appr last, ran on wl*..................(11 to 2 op 12 to 1) 1

2721 DAN DE LYON 6-11-9 A Maguire, *led 5th, mstk 9th, hdd appr last, not quicken*.
....(10 to 4 fav op 2 to 1 tchd 3 to 1) 2

2967 EARLY MAN 7-11-4 Peter Hobbs, *mstks, al prmnt, ev ch 3 out, one pace*............(4 to 1 op 7 to 2) 3

1621 THE YOKEL 8-11-1 (3*) T Eley, *led to 5th, ev ch 2 out, ran on one pace*....................(50 to 1 op 33 to 1) 4

3207⁴ DUKE OF APROLON 7-11-4 D Murphy, *mstks, blun 7th, prmnt till wknd 3 out*................(9 to 2 op 7 to 2) 5

3251 PURPLE SPRAY 9-11-4 R Dunwoody, *prmnt till wknd appr 3 out*...(50 to 1) 6

3192⁷ EIGHTY EIGHT 9-11-4 W Marston, *mstk 7th, tld off frm 8th*...................................(50 to 1 op 33 to 1) 7

2654⁷ BRAVO STAR (USA) 9-11-4 S Burrough, *tld off frm 8th*.
....(25 to 1) 8

FORCE 7-10-11 (7*) Mr S Joynes, *tld off frm 8th*.
....(33 to 1 tchd 50 to 1) 9

3316 PENIARTH 8-10-13 V Slattery, *al wl beh, tld off frm 8th, uns rdr last, rmntd*...(50 to 1 op 33 to 1 tchd 66 to 1) 10

3163 FATHER FORTUNE 6-11-1 (3*) J McCarthy, *f second*.
....(10 to 1 op 7 to 1) f

PECHE D'OR 10-11-4 Mr G Brown, *tld off whn pld up bef 3 out*......................................(33 to 1) pu

3309 STYLISH GENT (bl) 7-11-4 I Lawrence, *tld off whn pld up bef 3 out*........................(50 to 1 op 33 to 1) pu

3175⁵ COASTING 8-11-4 J Railton, *prmnt till wknd tenth, pld up bef 3 out*.............(20 to 1 op 14 to 1) pu

3317³ RUSTY MUSIC 8-10-11 (7*) Mr J A Llewellyn, *beh whn blun 7th, tld off whn pld up bef 9th*.........(25 to 1) pu

3188 MERRY MUSE 8-10-13 R Supple, *tld off frm 6th, pld up bef 3 out*......................(20 to 1 op 16 to 1) pu

Dist: 3½l, 8l, 3½l, 7l, dist, dist, 1¼l, 25l, dist. 5m 22.40s. a 19.40s (16 Ran).

SR: 19/20/7/3/-/-/ (Roger Nicholls), J Webber

3455 Commandery Handicap Hurdle (0-125 4-y-o and up) £2,197 2¼m......(4:35)

3038 CARIBOO GOLD (USA) [125] (bl) 5-12-0 N Williamson, *chsd ldr, hrd rdn 2 out, mstk last, ran on to ld fnl hundred yards*...............................(6 to 1 op 9 to 2) 1

3379* GORTEERA [106] 8-10-9 (7ex) M Brennan, *hdwy 5th, led 3 out, hdd last hundred yards*.
....(9 to 2 fav op 4 to 1 tchd 5 to 1) 2

2883⁶ NEAGH HOUSE [113] 8-11-2 A Maguire, *hdwy 5th, outpcd appr 3 out, styd on frm 2 out*.
....(13 to 2 op 11 to 2 tchd 7 to 1) 3

3206⁴ MIDDLEWICK [97] 9-9-9 (5*) D Leahy, *nrst finish*.
....(11 to 2 op 5 to 1) 4

3350³ FOX CHAPEL [113] (bl) 7-11-2 R Dunwoody, *led 3 out, hrd rdn and wknd nxt*..................(8 to 1 op 7 to 1) 5

3117² VAGADOR (Can) [113] 11-11-2 M Perrett, *badly hmpd 5th, no ch aftr*.........................(6 to 1 op 5 to 1) 6

3117 MORE OF IT [99] (bl) 9-10-2² Peter Hobbs, *prmnt till wknd appr 3 out*...............................(25 to 1) 7

3309 INTERPLAY [101] 9-10-4³ D O'Sullivan, *nvr nr to chal*.
....(50 to 1 op 33 to 1) 8

BAYPHIA [97] 6-10-0 D Skyrme, *prmnt till wknd appr 3 out*..(50 to 1) 9

2554⁷ ECOSSAIS DANSEUR (USA) [87] 8-10-0 R Supple, *al beh*.
....(33 to 1) 10

2336 MUSIC SCORE [97] 8-9-8¹ (7*) P Ward, *prmnt till wknd 6th*..(33 to 1) 11

BURSANA [97] 8-10-0 W Marston, *prmnt till wknd 6th*.
....(12 to 1 op 20 to 1) 12

202⁵ SUKEY TAWDRY [105] 8-10-8⁸ W Elderfield, *al wl beh*.
....(33 to 1) 13

3174² MR PICKPOCKET (Ire) [102] (v) 6-10-5 L Harvey, *prmnt till f 5th*....................(11 to 2 tchd 13 to 2) f

3125⁴ NIGHT OF MADNESS [97] 7-10-0 A S Smith, *beh whn pld up bef 3 out*..............................(33 to 1) pu

Dist: 2l, 2½l, 7l, ¾l, 15l, 9l, 12l, ¾l, sht-hd, 12l. 4m 27.00s. a 19.00s (15 Ran).

SR: 36/15/19/-/11/-/ (Sheikh Marwan Al Maktoum), K C Bailey

3456 Cromwell Conditional Jockeys' Handicap Chase (0-115 5-y-o and up) £2,652 2m........(5:10)

2818* MISTER ODDY [92] 8-11-10 T Jenks, *made all, ran on wl*.
....(Evens fav op 5 to 4 on tchd 11 to 10) 1

3312³ GENERAL MERCHANT [87] (bl) 14-11-5 R Farrant, *chsd wnr, hrd rdn appr last, not quicken*.
....(11 to 4 op 5 to 2 tchd 3 to 1 and 100 to 30) 2

3303⁴ RUSTIC GENT (Ire) [78] 6-10-10 R Davis, *chsd ldrs, one pace frm 3 out*.......................(9 to 1 op 10 to 1) 3

3148⁵ GREEN WALK [68] 7-10-0 C Burnett-Wells, *in rear till hdwy 7th, rdn appr 2 out, one pace*.
....(12 to 1 op 9 to 1 tchd 14 to 1) 4

3312⁶ RATHER SHARP [85] 8-11-3 J Burke, *prmnt to 6th, tld off whn f 3 out*............(13 to 2 op 7 to 1 tchd 6 to 1) f

Dist: 7l, 15l, sht-hd. 4m 8.80s. a 19.80s (5 Ran).

(Mrs R M Hill), J S King

3457 Open National Hunt Flat Race (Div I) (4,5,6-y-o) £1,444 2m......(5:35)

2677 LIGHTENING LAD 6-11-3 J R Kavanagh, *hdwy aftr 6 fs, chlgd 2 furlongs out, led ins fnl furlong, all out.*
.... (16 to 1 op 12 to 1) 1
3227⁴ AIR SHOT 4-10-13 (7*) M Keighley, *hdwy aftr 6 fs, led o'r one furlong out till ins fnl furlong, ran on wl nr finish.*
.... (5 to 2 fav op 6 to 4 tchd 3 to 1) 2
3042 WHO IS EQUINAME (Ire) 5-10-9 M A FitzGerald, *made most till hrd rdn and hdd o'r one furlong out, ran on.*
.... (5 to 1 op 4 to 1) 3
3190² HENRY CONE 5-11-3 G McCourt, *hdwy 6 fs out, ev ch 2 furlongs out, edgd lft, not quicken.*
.... (11 to 4 op 4 to 1 tchd 9 to 2) 4
INNER TEMPLE 4-10-9 B Powell, *hdwy fnl 2 fs, nvr nrr.*
.... (12 to 1 op 16 to 1) 5
3114⁶ HAILE DERRING 4-10-9 R Bellamy, *prmnt till wknd 2 fs out.*
.... (100 to 1 op 50 to 1) 6
3234⁴ SCARLET RAMBLER 5-11-0 (3*) T Jenks, *hdwy 6 fs out, one pace fnl 3 furlongs.* (8 to 1 op 6 to 1 tchd 10 to 1) 7
2909⁴ LITTLE SERENA 4-10-8 S Turner, *jnd ldr on ins 6 fs out, wknd 3 furlongs out.* .... (20 to 1 op 12 to 1) 8
STEEL BELLS (Ire) 5-10-10 (7*) M Berry, *prmnt till wknd 3 fs out.* .... (16 to 1 op 10 to 1) 9
2509 WOODLANDS POWER 6-11-0 (3*) R Davis, *nvr nr to chal.*
.... (100 to 1 op 50 to 1) 10
3169⁴ ERMINE STREET 6-11-3 M Brennan, *pld hrd, with ldrs till wknd 3 fs out.* .... (14 to 1 op 12 to 1) 11
3176 FURIOUS OATS (Ire) 6-10-9 (7*) Mr L Jefford, *in tch till wknd 4 fs out.* .... (50 to 1 op 25 to 1) 12
3347⁸ ASK FOR BARNEY (Ire) 5-10-12 (5*) J Supple, *nvr trbld ldrs.* .... (33 to 1 op 20 to 1) 13
3176⁷ NOVA NITA 4-9-11 (7*) P McLoughlin, *outpcd.*
.... (50 to 1 op 33 to 1) 14
3114⁵ JOBINGO 6-10-12 (5*) Guy Lewis, *beh fnl 5 fs...* (25 to 1) 15
3114 KINGS GAMBLE 4-10-9 Ann Stokell, *nvr on terms.*
.... (100 to 1 op 50 to 1) 16
RED DUST 5-10-12 A Maguire, *wth ldrs till wknd 5 fs out.*
.... (20 to 1 op 14 to 1) 17
3208 INKY 5-10-5 (7*) Mr S Mulcaire, *al beh.*
.... (100 to 1 op 50 to 1) 18
3401 ZANDALEE 5-10-5 (7*) S Arnold, *outpcd.*
.... (100 to 1 op 33 to 1) 19
3176 NEARLY A BROOK 4-10-4 A Tory, *prmnt till wknd 6 fs out.*
.... (66 to 1 op 33 to 1) 20
3113 ORCADIAN ROSE 4-10-4 R Supple, *tld off.*
.... (100 to 1 op 50 to 1) 21
Dist: Nk, 2½l, 2½l, 6l, 4l, 3l, 8l, 12l, 1¾l, 5l. 3m 54.70s. (21 Ran).

(Richard Peterson), J S King

3458 Open National Hunt Flat Race (Div II) (4,5,6-y-o) £1,434 2m .... (6:05)

NO NEAR MISS 4-10-4 A McCabe, *hld up in rear, gd hdwy 5 fs out, led o'r 3 furlongs out, sn clr, pushed out.*
.... (10 to 1 op 8 to 1) 1
SEACHANGE 5-10-10 (7*) P Ward, *hdwy 5 fs out, wnt second o'r 2 furlongs out, hng lft over one furlong out, no imprsn.* .... (33 to 1 op 20 to 1) 2
2834⁶ VALERIOS KING 5-11-3 G Upton, *al prmnt, rdn 3 fs out, ran one pace....* (7 to 2 op 3 to 1 tchd 9 to 2) 3
3256³ PRINCE NASHA (Ire) 4-10-9 A Maguire, *al prmnt, led o'r 4 fs till over 3 furlongs out, one pace.*
.... (12 to 1 op 10 to 1) 4
2909⁴ CRANE HILL 4-10-6 (3*) S Wynne, *al prmnt, ev ch 4 fs out, not quicken......* (3 to 1 fav op 4 to 1 tchd 5 to 1) 5
3234 CHEER'S BABY 4-10-6 (3*) D J Moffatt, *nvr nr to chal.*
.... (50 to 1 op 25 to 1) 6
3401⁶ FRA'S GIRL 6-10-5 (7*) P McLoughlin, *al mid-div, one pace fnl 2 fs......* .... (20 to 1) 7
3208² BUNGEE JUMPER 4-10-6 (3*) R Farrant, *hdwy aftr 5 fs, ev ch 3 furlongs out, rdn and one pace.* (4 to 1 op 5 to 1) 8
3208 GAME DOMINO 4-10-1 (3*) A Procter, *nvr nrr.* 9
3190³ COUNTRY CONCORDE 4-10-6 (3*) D Meredith, *prmnt till wknd 4 fs out.* .... (12 to 1 op 8 to 1) 10
FREDDIE MUCK 4-10-2 (7*) A Shakespeare, *led till o'r 4 fs out, wknd 3 furlongs out.* .... (14 to 1 op 10 to 1) 11
3138³ ROSIE-B 4-10-4 W McFarland, *nvr trbld ldrs....* (50 to 1) 12
3169⁷ BOOLAVOGUE (Ire) 4-9-11 (7*) P Maddock, *nvr on terms.* 13
1957⁷ THE MEXICANS GONE 6-11-3 Mr T Byrne, *prmnt till wknd 5 fs out.* .... (14 to 1 op 10 to 1) 14
2916⁸ WIN A HAND 4-9-13 (5*) Guy Lewis, *prmnt till wknd 6 fs out.* .... (50 to 1) 15
3079⁹ JASON'S BOY 4-10-9 N Williamson, *beh fnl 6 fs.* 16
3208⁸ GAY MUSE 5-10-5 (7*) C Quinlan, *prmnt till hrd rdn and wknd one m out.* .... (33 to 1 op 25 to 1) 17
3176⁸ UP THE TEMPO (Ire) 5-10-5 (7*) M Moran, *al beh.* 18
2916⁷ POND HOUSE (Ire) 5-11-3 R Dunwoody, *rdn 6 fs out, sn wl beh.* .... (8 to 1 op 6 to 1) 19
3234 GOLF WORLD (Ire) 5-10-5 (7*) M Berry, *wth ldr till wknd quickly o'r 3 fs out.* .... (12 to 1 op 14 to 1) 20
3257⁵ KING OF THE MICKS 4-10-9 M A FitzGerald, *outpcd.*
.... (50 to 1) 21

3208 WHAT A MOPPET (Ire) 5-10-9 (3*) J McCarthy, *hdwy aftr 6 fs, wth ldrs six furlongs out, wknd quickly.*
.... (33 to 1 op 20 to 1) 22
Dist: 7l, 6l, nk, 7l, 2½l, 3½l, 2½l, 1¼l, 4l, 3½l. 3m 51.60s. (22 Ran).

(The Radio Three), D R C Elsworth

AYR (good)
Thursday April 14th
Going Correction: PLUS 0.35 sec. per fur. (races 1,3,6), PLUS 0.55 (2,4,5)

3459 Gold Cup Hospitality 'National Hunt' Novices' Hurdle (4-y-o and up) £2,029 2m .... (2:20)

3074³ COL BUCKMORE (Ire) 6-11-2 (7*) B Harding, *trkd ldrs, mstk 4th, chlgd on bit 2 out, led last, quickened clr, easily.*
.... (11 to 4 op 7 to 2) 1
3140 RHYMING THOMAS 6-11-4 J Railton, *led till hdd last, kpt on, no ch wth wnr.* .... (7 to 1 op 5 to 1) 2
3347⁷ PARSON'S LODGE (Ire) 6-10-13 T Reed, *hld up, pld hrd early, hdwy aftr 3 out, mstk last, nrst finish.*
.... (16 to 1 op 20 to 1) 3
2373³ RHOSSILI BAY 6-11-4 P Niven, *prmnt, chlgd 3 out, hng lft and wknd betw last 2.*
.... (7 to 4 fav op 6 to 4 tchd 15 to 8) 4
3378⁹ DUNNOHALM 5-10-13 Mr S Swiers, *hld up, hdwy to track ldrs 3 out, fdd frm nxt.* (13 to 2 op 6 to 1 tchd 7 to 1) 5
2749⁹ SECOND SLIP 5-11-4 M Dwyer, *chsd ldrs till wknd aftr 3 out......* (8 to 1 op 7 to 1 tchd 10 to 1) 6
2573 KERNEL GRAIN (Ire) 5-11-1 (3*) D J Moffatt, *hld up, hdwy appr 3 out, rdn betw last 2, btn whn f last.*
.... (16 to 1 op 14 to 1) f
3284 EMERALD CHARM (Ire) 6-11-3 B Storey, *chsd ldrs till wknd frm 3 out, no ch whn brght dwn last.*
.... (33 to 1 op 20 to 1) bd
3284 BROWN BOMBER 5-11-4 C Grant, *lost tch frm 5th, tld off whn pld up bef 3 out......* (200 to 1 op 100 to 1) pu
Dist: 4l, 6l, 3½l, 7l, 4l. 3m 56.50s. a 19.50s (9 Ran).

(Brian Buckley), G Richards

3460 Ilph Copenhagen Memorial Novices' Chase (5-y-o and up) £3,387 2m (2:50)

3286* PRECIPICE RUN 9-12-0 N Doughty, *jmpd badly rght thrght, led till hdd second, mstk 4th, led appr four out, hld on wl r-in......* (7 to 4 op 11 to 8 tchd 15 to 8) 1
2435⁵ PAKENHAM 8-11-2 R Dunwoody, *hld up in tch, mstks second and 6th, shaken up to chase wnr betw last 2, ev ch r-in, nvr extr towards finish....* (14 to 1 op 12 to 1) 2
3429⁸ AYIA NAPA 7-11-2 A Merrigan, *trkd ldrs, ev ch 2 out, one pace....* .... (50 to 1 op 33 to 1) 3
1593⁵ FIDDLER'S DRUM 7-11-2 J Osborne, *led second, hdd appr 4 out, grad wknd......* (16 to 1 op 14 to 1) 4
3034⁸ SCARABEN 6-11-2 N Bentley, *mstk 1st, lost tch 4th, tld off whn blun and uns rdr 6th......* (33 to 1 op 50 to 1) ur
SOUND PROFIT 6-10-11 L O'Hara, *blun and uns rdr second......* .... (33 to 1 op 10 to 1) ur
3356 FULL O'PRAISE (NZ) 7-12-0 T Reed, *hld up in tch, chalg on bit whn badly hmpd and uns rdr 4 out.*
.... (11 to 8 on op Evens tchd 11 to 10) ur
Dist: Hd, 6l, 5l. 4m 3.40s. a 15.40s (7 Ran).
SR: 34/22/16/11/ (Cumbrian Racing Club), G Richards

3461 Friendly Hotels Handicap Hurdle (0-135 4-y-o and up) £2,827 3¼m 110yds. .... (3:20)

3287² CELTIC BREEZE [101] (v) 11-9-12¹ (3*) T Jenks, *made all, pushed alng appr 3 out, styd on wl.*
.... (11 to 2 op 6 to 1 tchd 5 to 1) 1
3028 AAHSAYLAD [125] (bl) 8-11-10 A Maguire, *in tch, rdn aftr 4 out, styd on to chase wnr appr last, no imprsn r-in.*
.... (7 to 4 fav op 6 to 4 tchd 15 to 8) 2
3374³ LEADING PROSPECT [108] 7-10-7 B Storey, *trkd ldrs, effrt appr 3 out, kpt on frm last.*
.... (5 to 1 op 6 to 1 tchd 9 to 2) 3
3142* POLISHING [120] (v) 7-11-0 (5*) S Lyons, *in tch, chlgd 3 out, ev ch till wknd appr last......* (9 to 2 op 4 to 1) 4
3343 SHELTON ABBEY [107] 8-10-6⁶ K Jones, *chsd wnr till wknd appr 3 out......* (25 to 1 op 20 to 1) 5
3166* RIDWAN [101] 7-10-0 A S Smith, *hld up, effrt appr 3 out, wknd appr last.* .... (9 to 2 op 4 to 1) 6
Dist: 3½l, 2l, 1l, 20l, 30l. 6m 37.70s. a 24.70s (6 Ran).

(Hugh Gething), M P Naughton

3462 Royal Scots Dragoon Guards Cup Hunters' Chase (6-y-o and up) £4,719 3m 3f 110yds. .... (3:50)

GENERALS BOY 12-12-0 Mr P Craggs, *hld up, mstk second, smooth hdwy aftr 16th, led 2 out, cmftbly.*
.... (5 to 4 on tchd 6 to 5 on) 1

JIMMY RIVER 11-12-0 Mr K Anderson, *in tch, trkd ldr frm 9th, led 16th, mstk and hdd 2 out, sn btn.*

3377² SPARTAN RANGER 9-12-0 Mr C Bonner, *led till hdd 16th, grad wknd frm nxt.*...........(11 to 1 op 10 to 1) 3

3160 MIG 9-11-9 Miss Y Beckingham, *in tch till wknd appr 4 out.*................................(25 to 1 op 20 to 1) 4

OCEANUS 13-12-0 Mr J Walton, *chsd ldr to 9th, lost tch aftr 12th, tld off.*..........................(50 to 1 op 33 to 1) 5

Dist: 5l, 8l, 5l, dist. 7m 12.10s. a 29.10s (5 Ran).

(P F Craggs), Mrs Nicki Craggs

3463 George Graham Memorial Handicap Chase (0-135 5-y-o and up) £3,668 3m 1f..(4:20)

3358* ARMAGRET [136] 9-12-4 (6ex) D Byrne, *sn chasing ldr, led last, styd on wl.*....................(5 to 1 op 4 to 1) 1

3205² TIPP MARINER [104] 9-10-0 J Osborne, *led till hdd last, no extr.*......................(9 to 4 jt-fav tchd 5 to 2) 2

3217⁴ ALL JEFF (Fr) [128] (bl) 10-11-10 A Maguire, *in tch, mstk 15th, rdn aftr 3 out, ch appr last, kpt on towards finish.*..................................(10 to 1 tchd 12 to 1) 3

2973 ON THE HOOCH [105] 9-10-11 R Dunwoody, *prmnt, rdn aftr 4 out, sn btn.*..................(10 to 1 op 8 to 1) 4

3127⁴ HOUXTY LAD [104] 8-10-0 B Storey, *in tch, effrt appr 4 out, no hdwy, btn whn blun 2 out.* (33 to 1 op 25 to 1) 5

2733⁷ ISLAND GALE [104] 9-10-0 K Johnson, *badly hmpd 5th, no dngr aftr.*....................(16 to 1 op 12 to 1) 6

2928² CLYDE RANGER [113] 7-10-9 C Grant, *prmnt whn blun and uns rdr 5th.*...................(9 to 4 jt-fav op 7 to 4) ur
CAMIONNAGE [107] 13-10-3³ A Merrigan, *lost tch and tried to run out aftr tenth, sn pld up.*
....(50 to 1 op 33 to 1) pu

Dist: 2l, nk, 13l, 8l, 5l. 6m 23.10s. a 23.10s (8 Ran).

SR: 11/-/-/-/-/-/ (Mrs R M Wilkinson), B E Wilkinson

3464 Royal Burgh Of Ayr Handicap Hurdle (0-135 4-y-o and up) £3,156 2m..(4:50)

2445⁵ SURREY DANCER [112] 6-10-7 P Niven, *hld up, hdwy aftr 5th, led after 3 out, clr whn mstk last, ran on wl.*
..........................(13 to 8 fav op 6 to 4 tchd 7 to 4) 1

2929² ARAGON AYR [106] 6-10-1 A Dobbin, *mid-div, effrt aftr 3 out, styd on wl frm nxt, not rch wnr.*
....(14 to 1 op 10 to 1) 2

2473⁷ HIGH ALTITUDE (Ire) [133] (bl) 6-12-0 A Maguire, *cl up, led aftr 6th till hdd after 3 out, kpt on same pace.*
....................................(9 to 1 op 6 to 1 tchd 10 to 1) 3

2994⁵ HOME COUNTIES (Ire) [127] (v) 5-11-8 M Dwyer, *hld up in midfield, hdwy appr 3 out, one pace frm nxt.*
....(11 to 2 op 4 to 1) 4

3288 ABBOT OF FURNESS [121] 10-10-9 (7*) B Harding, *made most till hdd aftr 6th, grad wknd.*
....(11 to 2 op 4 to 1) 4

3206* FRONT STREET [105] 7-10-0 J Osborne, *mid-div till out-pcd appr 3 out, no dngr aftr.*......(6 to 1 op 5 to 1) 5

1005⁵ CHANTRY BARTLE [108] 8-10-3 D Wilkinson, *prmnt, dsptd ld 4th till wknd aftr 3 out.*.........(12 to 1 op 10 to 1) 6

3311⁸ TOP WAVE [113] (bl) 6-10-8 M A FitzGerald, *trkd ldrs, effrt appr 3 out, sn btn.*..................(14 to 1) 7

3434 MASTER OF TROY [105] 6-9-9 (5*) Mr D Parker, *mstks, al beh.*....................(10 to 1 op 8 to 1) 9

Dist: 3½l, 2l, 4l, 6l, 3l, 2l, 8l, 1½l. 3m 46.00s. a 9.00s (9 Ran).

SR: 45/35/60/50/38/19/20/17/ (Laurel (Leisure) Limited), Mrs M Reveley

CLONMEL (IRE) (heavy)
Thursday April 14th

3465 County Chase (5-y-o and up) £2,243 3m..(3:30)

3039 ANOTHER EXCUSE (Ire) 6-11-8 (5*) Mr W M O'Sullivan,
....(5 to 2 fav) 1

2865⁸ COMMANCHE NELL (Ire) 6-11-5 G M O'Neill,.......(7 to 1) 2

3371⁴ WINDS OF WAR 9-11-7 C O'Dwyer,..............(20 to 1) 3

3040 TAKE THE TOWN 9-11-7 J F Titley,...............(10 to 1) 4

3198* MONKEY AGO 7-11-7 P Carberry,................(10 to 1) 5

2660 CAPINCUR EILE 8-11-3 J Jones,................(20 to 1) 6

3198² PARSONS BRIG 8-10-12 (5*) J P Broderick,......(10 to 1) 7

2939 ZVORNIK 7-11-0 (3*) C O'Brien,................(25 to 1) 8

2923 BEAU GRANDE (Ire) 6-11-3 L P Cusack,.........(14 to 1) 9

3275³ RICH TRADITION (Ire) 6-11-3 J Shortt,.........(10 to 1) 10

2550⁸ EXTRA MILE 7-10-12 S H O'Donovan,..........(25 to 1) 11

3322 HAPPY PERCY 9-11-3 K F O'Brien,.............(20 to 1) f

3028 BEAU BABILLARD 7-11-7 C F Swan,.............(6 to 1) pu

3326 DELIGHTFUL CHOICE (Ire) (bl) 6-10-12 T Horgan,.(8 to 1) pu

2940 RATHNURE LADY (Ire) 6-10-5 (7*) D J Kavanagh, .(25 to 1) pu

Dist: Hd, 10l, 3l, 3l. 6m 38.40s. (15 Ran).

(Kilshannig Racing Syndicate), Eugene M O'Sullivan

3466 Cashel Maiden Hurdle (4-y-o and up) £2,243 2m..(4:00)

2391⁵ CASH IT IN (Ire) 6-10-12 (3*) D P Murphy,..........(8 to 1) 1

3242⁴ CALL ME HENRY 5-11-5 F Woods,...............(8 to 1) 2

3321² PUSH THE BUTTON (Ire) 4-11-1 C F Swan, ...(Evens fav) 3

3290⁸ MAZELLA (Ire) 5-11-0 M Duffy,..................(8 to 1) 4

2231 HAVE A BRANDY (Ire) 5-11-5 Mr D M O'Brien,...(20 to 1) 5

2917⁶ BLAKE'S FABLE (Ire) 4-10-3 (7*) J M Donnelly,....(20 to 1) 6

2616 KILLOSKEHAN QUEEN 7-10-12 (3*) C O'Brien,...(20 to 1) 7

2938⁷ FANCY STEP 8-11-6 (3*) T P Treacy,..............(10 to 1) 8

2919⁸ POLLEROO (Ire) 6-11-9 J Jones,.................(20 to 1) 9

3243⁷ CORRIB HAVEN (Ire) 6-11-1 (5*) J P Broderick,.....(12 to 1) 10
PARTICULAR (Ire) 4-10-13 (7*) Mr S A Quilty,.....(10 to 1) 11

3291⁸ METROLAMP (Ire) 6-10-13 (7*) Mr J J O'Neill,.....(14 to 1) 12

3084⁷ V'SOSKE GALE (Ire) 4-10-10 J F Titley,...........(14 to 1) 13

2128 CASTLE CLUB (Ire) 5-10-11 (3*) Mr R O'Neill,......(25 to 1) 14

3243⁸ SAME DIFFERENCE (Ire) 6-11-6 P P Kinane,......(12 to 1) 15

671 MOOREFIELD GIRL (Ire) 5-11-8 M Moran,.......(10 to 1) 16

2123 ABBEY EMERALD 8-11-1 K F O'Brien,............(33 to 1) 17

2917 COMMON BOND 4-11-1 G M O'Neill,.............(14 to 1) 18

3321 FOOLISH LAW (Ire) 4-10-10 S H O'Donovan,.....(33 to 1) 19

3290 MISS BERTAINE (Ire) 5-11-0 A Powell,..........(25 to 1) ref

Dist: 3½l, sht-hd, 1l, 5l. 4m 38.70s. (20 Ran).

(J P Berry), J A Berry

3467 Roscrea Hurdle (5-y-o and up) £2,243 3m..(4:30)

3322⁴ CALMOS 7-12-0 C F Swan,...................(7 to 4 fav) 1

3292⁶ COUNTERBALANCE 7-11-4 B Sheridan,...........(7 to 1) 2

991⁹ POOR TIMES (Ire) 6-10-13 (5*) M A Davey,........(8 to 1) 3

3292 SKY VISION (Ire) 5-11-2 S H O'Donovan,.........(25 to 1) 4

2985 WATERLOO BALL (Ire) 5-10-11 (5*) M J Holbrook, .(20 to 1) 5

3366 RAMPANT ROSIE (Ire) 6-10-13 (5*) K P Gaule, ...(20 to 1) 6

3371³ CITIZEN LEVEE 8-10-13 (5*) Mr W M O'Sullivan, ..(8 to 1) 7

3366⁵ DOONDORRA (Ire) 6-11-4 T Horgan,.............(8 to 1) 8

3326³ GOLDEN CARRUTH (Ire) 6-11-4 (5*) J P Broderick, (14 to 1) 9

3296 CLEAR ROUND (Ire) 7-10-11 (7*) M D Murphy,...(25 to 1) 10

3122⁵ JESSIE'S BOY (Ire) 5-11-0 (7*) T Martin,..........(14 to 1) 11

3199⁹ BOG LEAF VI 11-11-1 (3*) C O'Brien,............(20 to 1) 12

3391³ HAKI SAKI 8-12-0 G M O'Neill,...................(7 to 2) ur

3296⁸ RUN FOR FUN (Ire) 6-11-1 (3*) T P Treacy,.......(10 to 1) pu

Dist: 3l, 14l, dist, 2l. 6m 27.70s. (14 Ran).

(G A Murphy), A P O'Brien

3468 Templemore Handicap Hurdle (0-116 5-y-o and up) £2,243 2m.......(5:00)

2347³ ANOTHER COURSE (Ire) [-] 6-10-12 C F Swan,.....(7 to 1) 1

3294² SAM VAUGHAN (Ire) [-] 5-11-9 (5*) Mr W M O'Sullivan,
....(7 to 2 jt-fav) 2

3294³ PERCY BRENNAN (-) 7-9-11 (7*) J M Donnelly,....(8 to 1) 3

3677 MISS LIME [-] 7-11-6 (7*) R A Hennessy,....(7 to 2 jt-fav) 4

2615³ FABULIST (Ire) [-] 5-11-4 (3*) T P Treacy,..........(8 to 1) 5

3367 HURRICANE EDEN [-] 7-10-7 (5*) M A Davey,......(7 to 1) 6

2754 KAWA-KAWA [-] 7-9-11 (3*) T J O'Sullivan,.......(12 to 1) 7

1450 KNOCNAGORE (Ire) [-] 5-10-1 A Powell,..........(25 to 1) 8

2846⁷ TRIMMER WONDER (Ire) [-] 6-10-6 K F O'Brien,..(14 to 1) 9
IRON MARINER (-) [-] 6-10-8 (7*) D M McCullagh, (14 to 1) 10

3294⁴ NINE O THREE (Ire) [-] 5-10-2 (5*) J P Broderick,..(20 to 1) 11

2098 NISHIKI (USA) [-] 5-10-2 C O'Dwyer,.............(20 to 1) 12
CAINSBRIDGE QUEEN [-] 9-10-3 (7*) M Kelly, ...(25 to 1) 13

607 ALTAR BOY [-] 10-11-10 S H O'Donovan,..........(25 to 1) 14

2348⁶ MAGNUM STAR (Ire) [-] 5-11-7 (3*) D O'Driscoll, ...(16 to 1) ur

Dist: 4½l, 1½l, sht-hd, nk. 4m 18.20s. (15 Ran).

(Patrick Heffernan), Patrick Heffernan

3469 Cahir I N H Flat Race (5-y-o and up) £2,243 2½m...................(5:30)

BUCK ROGERS (Ire) 5-11-6 (7*) Mr A G Costello,....(7 to 1) 1

3290⁵ FLAWLESS FINISH (Ire) 5-11-1 (7*) Mr G R Ryan, ..(8 to 1) 2

2924² WEST BROGUE (Ire) (bl) 5-11-13 Mr J P Dempsey, (8 to 1) 3

2232 MILLER'S CROSSING 7-11-9 Mr T Doyle,.........(16 to 1) 4

3296⁴ MISS POLLERTON (Ire) 6-11-2 (7*) Mr M J Bowe, (10 to 1) 5

2967 PEGUS GOLD 7-11-4 (5*) Mr G J Harford,.........(14 to 1) 6

3201³ KEEPHERGOING (Ire) 5-11-1 (7*) Mr T J Murphy,..(7 to 1) 7

3250³ KILLINEY GAYLE (Ire) 5-11-5 (3*) Mrs J M Mullins,
....(3 to 1 fav) 8
KERMESINA (Ire) 5-11-1 (7*) Mr J S Cullen,......(20 to 1) 9

3366⁹ JOHNSTONS BUCK (Ire) 5-11-10 (3*) Mr D Valentine,
....(4 to 1) 10
ASK ME LATER (Ire) 5-11-10 (3*) Mr T Lombard, ..(13 to 2) 11

2869 LAURA GALE (Ire) 5-11-3 (5*) Mr P M Kelly,......(20 to 1) 12

3201⁸ RAHEEN FLOWER (Ire) 6-11-9 Mr D M O'Brien,...(16 to 1) 13
FRENCH MYLE (Ire) 6-11-7 (7*) Mr K Whelan,.....(25 to 1) 14
SHOW ME THE LIGHT (Ire) 6-11-7 (7*) Mr J M Roche,
....(16 to 1) 15

3197⁴ NOT MY LINE (Ire) 5-11-13 Mr F Fenton,.........(12 to 1) 16

3200⁸ SQUIRRELLSDAUGHTER 7-11-2 (7*) Mr M Fehily, (50 to 1) 17
MR BORIS 5-11-13 Mr A J Martin,...............(20 to 1) 18

2353 JENAWAY (Ire) 5-11-5 (3*) Mr J A Nash,..........(33 to 1) 19
LOOPIN'S BOY 6-11-7 (7*) Mr R Eastwood, ...(33 to 1) pu

Dist: 1½l, ½l, 10l, 5½l. 5m 14.30s. (20 Ran).

(A G Costello), T Costello

AYR (good)
Friday April 15th
Going Correction: PLUS 0.05 sec. per fur. (races 1,3,6), MINUS 0.10 (2,4,5)

3470 Western House Restaurant Novices' Hurdle (4-y-o and up) £2,347 3m 110yds........................ (2:30)

3029[2] OVER THE ODDS (Ire) 5-11-0 K Johnson, *made all, clr 3 out, styd on wl*....................(6 to 4 op 13 to 8) 1
2741 LITTLE FREDDIE 5-11-0 L Wyer, *cl up, slightly outpcd aftr 8th, rdn to chase wnr appr 3 out, kpt on wl und pres, no imprsn*..........................(25 to 1 op 20 to 1) 2
2148 GOLDEN CAIRN (Ire) 5-11-0 T Reed, *in tch, mstk 6th, effrt aftr 8th, wknd appr 3 out*........ (25 to 1 op 20 to 1) 3
2014[8] THE BRUD 6-11-0 J Osborne, *trkd ldrs till drpd out quickly aftr 9th, tld off whn pld up bef 3 out, lme.* ....(6 to 4 on op 7 to 4 on) pu
Dist: 5l, 20l. 6m 16.00s. a 30.00s (4 Ran).
(Malcolm J Moss), D McCune

3471 Royal Highland Fusiliers Challenge Cup Handicap Chase (0-135 5-y-o and up) £3,395 2m..................(3:00)

2915* AROUND THE HORN [115] 7-11-9 S McNeill, *in tch gng wl, jnd ldrs 4 out, led appr 2 out, pushed clr aftr last, easily*.........................(5 to 4 fav op 11 to 10) 1
3106* JUST FRANKIE [120] 10-12-0 P Niven, *chsd ldr, slight ld aftr 4 out, hit nxt, hdd appr 2 out, kpt on, no ch wth wnr*...(2 to 1) 2
3054[2] CHANGE THE ACT [116] (bl) 9-11-10 J Osborne, *in tch, reminders aftr 7th, sn wknd*........(3 to 1 op 11 to 4) 3
3239[4] PRESSURE GAME [92] 11-9-9 (5*) F Perratt, *led till hdd aftr 4 out, wknd quickly*.............(20 to 1 tchd 25 to 1) 4
Dist: 8l, 20l, 13l. 3m 50.60s. a 2.60s (4 Ran).
SR: 53/50/26/-/ (Pell-Mell Partners), J T Gifford

3472 Ken Oliver Octogenarian Celebration 'National Hunt' Novices' Hurdle (4-y-o and up) £5,680 2½m............(3:30)

3140[2] MAJOR BELL 6-11-7 M Moloney, *made virtually all, styd on wl*..............(8 to 1 op 10 to 1 tchd 12 to 1) 1
3215[4] OVER THE POLE 7-11-2 P Hide, *in tch gng wl, tracking wnr whn mstk 3 out, shaken up aftr nxt, styd on well, not rch winner*... (11 to 4 jt-fav op 9 to 4 tchd 3 to 1) 2
2827[5] CUNNINGHAMS FORD (Ire) 6-11-7 Mr A Harvey, *prmnt, effrt appr 3 out, kpt on same pace*..........(11 to 4 jt-fav tchd 9 to 4 and 3 to 1) 3
3359[2] KENILWORTH LAD 6-11-7 P Niven, *hld up, effrt appr 3 out, kpt on same pace*... (5 to 1 op 7 to 1 tchd 8 to 1) 4
3264 MASTER BOSTON (Ire) 6-11-7 A Maguire, *in tch till wknd aftr 7th, tld off*...................(4 to 1 tchd 9 to 2) 5
3179* CALLERNOY (Ire) 4-11-0 Mr A Manners, *dsptd ld early, cl up till wknd aftr 7th, tld off*.......(12 to 1 op 10 to 1) 6
MR KNITWIT 7-11-2 N Doughty, *in tch till wknd quickly aftr 7th, tld off whn pld up bef 3 out.* ....(50 to 1 op 33 to 1) pu
Dist: 1¼l, 3l, 1¼l, dist, 2½l. 4m 46.40s. a 7.40s (7 Ran).
SR: 29/22/24/22/ (A C Whillans), A C Whillans

3473 Hillhouse Quarry Handicap Chase for the Hamilton Campbell Challenge Cup (0-130 5-y-o and up) £5,550 2½m (4:00)

2953[4] BOARDING SCHOOL [96] 7-10-0 B Storey, *in tch, effrt aftr 13th, led betw last 2, styd on und pres.* ....(5 to 1 op 9 to 2) 1
3105[2] CENTENARY STAR [99] 9-10-3 P Niven, *led 3rd to 8th, led 9th till hdd 4 out, led ag'n nxt, headed betw last 2, no extr*.................................(7 to 2 op 4 to 1) 2
3288[5] STRONG APPROACH [110] 9-11-0 A Maguire, *prmnt, led 4 out, hdd nxt, fdd*.....(15 to 2 op 10 to 1 tchd 7 to 1) 3
3397* FALSE ECONOMY [104] 9-10-5 (3*,6ex) T Jenks, *in tch, effrt aftr 13th, wknd frm 4 out*.......(8 to 1 op 6 to 1) 4
3091 KIND'A SMART [114] 9-11-4 A S Smith, *hld up, effrt aftr 13th, sn btn*......(100 to 30 fav op 5 to 2 tchd 7 to 2) 5
3141* SIR PETER LELY [120] (bl) 7-11-10 C Grant, *led to 3rd, led 8th to 9th, wknd aftr nxt*...........(4 to 1 op 7 to 2) 6
Dist: 1¾l, 11l, 7l, 8l, 9l. 5m 1.70s. a 14.70s (6 Ran).
(Raymond Anderson Green), C Parker

3474 Souters Of Stirling Novices' Handicap Chase for the Eglinton Cup (5-y-o and up) £3,533 2½m................(4:30)

3355[5] THE COUNTRY TRADER [90] 8-10-0 M Moloney, *in tch, hdwy to track ldrs 13th, sn pushed alng, styd on strly frm 2 out, rdn r-in, led post*........(16 to 1 op 12 to 1) 1
3426 GREENFIELD MANOR [90] 7-10-0 A Maguire, *prmnt, led and mstk 3 out, almost brght dwn and lft clr nxt, rdn aftr last, ct post*.......(13 to 2 op 8 to 1 tchd 6 to 1) 2
2219[5] SANDEDGE [90] 7-9-13[4] (5*) P Waggott, *chsd ldrs, outpcd aftr 11th, styd on frm 3 out*.................(100 to 1) 3
3075[7] POTATO MAN [90] 8-9-11 (3*) D Bentley, *mid-div, effrt aftr 12th, no hdwy*...............................(50 to 1) 4
3178[5] HIGHLANDMAN [90] 8-10-0 A Dobbin, *mid-div, effrt whn blun 12th, no dngr aftr*......................(10 to 1) 5
2755[3] ROYAL MOUNTBROWNE [125] 6-12-7 J F Titley, *chsd ldrs, grad wknd frm 13th*..... (7 to 2 op 3 to 1 tchd 4 to 1) 6
3075 PIT PONY [90] 10-9-12[1] (3*) T Jenks, *al beh*.......(66 to 1) 7
2238 THE LORRYMAN (Ire) [90] 6-10-0 T Reed, *led 3rd till hdd 7th, wknd aftr tenth*.............. (66 to 1 op 50 to 1) 8
3143 KINROYAL [90] 9-9-7 (7*) Miss Sue Nichol, *sn beh.* ....(100 to 1) 9
3286[3] HUDSON BAY TRADER (USA) [96] 7-10-6 Mrs A Farrell, *al beh*.......................................(7 to 2 op 3 to 1) 10
3000[4] VAZON BAY [92] (bl) 10-10-2 J Osborne, *led to 3rd, led 7th till hdd 3 out, cl up and rdn whn f nxt.* ....(5 to 2 fav tchd 11 to 4) f
3286[4] HOWCLEUCH [90] 7-10-0 B Storey, *sn beh, pld up bef 2 out*..................................(25 to 1 op 20 to 1) pu
Dist: Hd, 20l, 5l, 1¼l, 3½l, 11l, 2½l, ¾l, 1¼l. 5m 2.20s. a 15.20s (12 Ran).
(The Edinburgh Woollen Mill Ltd), G Richards

3475 Ayrshire Agricultural Association Handicap Hurdle (0-125 4-y-o and up) £3,350 2½m................... (5:00)

2788[4] AMBLESIDE HARVEST [111] 7-10-11 (5*) A Roche, *trkd ldrs, effrt appr 3 out, chlgd aftr last, kpt on und pres to ld post*...........................(16 to 1 op 14 to 1) 1
2638[3] NATIVE WORTH [104] 4-10-9 L Wyer, *cl up, led 3 out, hrd pressed and rdn frm last, ct post*.............(12 to 1) 2
3376* CHIEF RAIDER (Ire) [118] 6-11-9 (6ex) A Maguire, *cl up, led 6th, hdd 3 out, rallied to dispute ld last, no extr und pres*...............(11 to 4 fav op 3 to 1 tchd 7 to 2) 3
3289[2] CAITHNESS CLOUD [100] 6-10-5 B Storey, *hld up, hdwy to chase ldrs aftr 7th, kpt on same pace frm 2 out.* ....(20 to 1 op 16 to 1) 4
3464[6] FRONT STREET [102] 7-10-4 (3*) T Jenks, *hld up, hdwy to track ldrs 8th, wknd appr 3 out*....(14 to 1 op 12 to 1) 5
3142[5] JESTERS PROSPECT [103] 10-10-8 T Reed, *led till hdd 6th, outpcd aftr nxt, kpt on frm 3 out.* ....(14 to 1 op 12 to 1) 6
2929[3] VERY EVIDENT (Ire) [95] 5-10-0 J Callaghan, *beh, hmpd 4th, some late hdwy, nvr dngrs*...................(16 to 1) 7
2974* SWEET CITY [108] 9-10-13 N Doughty, *chsd ldrs till wknd aftr 8th*..........................(12 to 1 op 14 to 1) 8
3219[5] CLURICAN (Ire) [112] 5-11-3 M Dwyer, *mid-div, effrt aftr 8th, sn btn*.........................(9 to 1 op 10 to 1) 9
2136[3] CROSS CANNON [119] 8-11-10 C Grant, *al beh*...(33 to 1) 10
3376[2] THISTLEHOLM [101] 8-10-3 (3*) D Bentley, *prmnt till wknd quickly appr 3 out*..................(7 to 1 op 6 to 1) 11
3130[8] MANGROVE MIST (Ire) [95] 6-10-0 A Dobbin, *hld up, hmpd 4th, hdwy aftr 7th, wknd appr 3 out.* ....(20 to 1 op 14 to 1) 12
1940[7] GREY MERLIN [95] 7-10-0 N Bentley, *wl beh frm 6th.* ....(33 to 1 op 20 to 1 tchd 50 to 1) 13
3344* WAKE UP [99] 7-9-11 (7*,6ex) F Leahy, *beh most of way.* ....(7 to 1 op 8 to 1) 14
2737 GOLDEN REVERIE (USA) [95] 6-9-9 (5*) F Perratt, *wl beh frm 7th*..(100 to 1) 15
1066[4] HAZEL LEAF [102] 8-10-7[3] R Hodge, *f 4th.* ....(20 to 1 tchd 25 to 1) f
3240[3] NOTABLE EXCEPTION [101] 5-10-1 (5*) S Mason, *mid-div, effrt aftr 7th, sn rdn, btn whn f 3 out.* ....(13 to 2 op 6 to 1 tchd 7 to 1) f
Dist: Sht-hd, 2½l, 2½l, 11l, ½l, 3½l, 1½l, ¾l, 1¼l, hd. 4m 48.00s. a 9.00s (17 Ran).
SR: 8/1/12/-/-/-/ (G & P Barker Ltd/Globe Engineering), J J O'Neill

TAUNTON (good)
Friday April 15th
Going Correction: PLUS 0.10 sec. per fur.

3476 Orchard Restaurant 'National Hunt' Novices' Hurdle (4-y-o and up) £2,102 2m 1f.........................(5:25)

2731* OVERLORD 5-11-7 M Richards, *trkd ldrs gng wl, slight ld 2 out, hit last, drvn out.* ....(11 to 4 fav op 3 to 1 tchd 7 to 2) 1
3270[2] HEDGEHOPPER (Ire) 6-11-7 Peter Hobbs, *led to 2 out, hit last, no extr*...........(3 to 1 tchd 5 to 2 and 7 to 2) 2
3042 LINTON ROCKS 5-11-0 S Smith Eccles, *mstk second, mid-div whn mistake 5th, sn rdn alng, prog appr 2 out, styd on r-in*....................................(12 to 1 op 8 to 1) 3
3334[2] TOO SHARP 6-10-9 R Marley, *al cl up, ev ch 2 out, no extr frm last*................(11 to 2 op 4 to 1 tchd 6 to 1) 4
1247 SHERWOOD BOY 5-11-0 N Williamson, *chsd ldr, ev ch 2 out, fdd r-in*.......... (12 to 1 op 8 to 1 tchd 14 to 1) 5
SPARTS FAULT (Ire) 4-10-8 G Upton, *hld up in rear, steady prog appr 2 out, shaken up and ran on r-in, better for race*.................. (16 to 1 op 8 to 1 tchd 20 to 1) 6
2671[4] VITAL WONDER 6-11-0 P Holley, *trkd ldrs, mstk 3rd, ev ch 3 out, wknd nxt*........(11 to 2 op 7 to 2 tchd 6 to 1) 7
3211* FICHU (USA) 6-11-7 B Powell, *al in rear, tld off.* ....(33 to 1 op 20 to 1) 8
3347[6] HIGHLAND HEIGHTS (Ire) 6-10-9 R Ranger, *al in rear, tld off*...................(50 to 1 op 20 to 1 tchd 66 to 1) 9
2560 COUNTRY LORD 5-11-0 M A FitzGerald, *al beh, tld off.* ....(40 to 1 op 20 to 1 tchd 50 to 1) 10

PIRATE BOY 7-10-7 (7*) T Murphy, *hdwy 5th, wl in tch*
whn f 3 out.......... (50 to 1 op 33 to 1 tchd 66 to 1)   f
3138* QUEENFORD BELLE 4-10-3 M Hourigan, *slwly away,*
improved 4th, mid-div whn brght dwn 3 out.
.... (12 to 1 op 10 to 1)   bd
2021 INDERRING ROSE 4-10-8 Tracy Turner, *tld off 9th, pld up*
bef 6th...........................(100 to 1 op 50 to 1)   pu
Dist: 4l, 3½l, hd, 2l, nk, 6l, dist, 20l. 3m 54.80s. a 7.80s (13 Ran).
SR: 32/28/17/12/15/8/8/-/   (D J Deer), W R Muir

3477 Silver Street Motors Handicap Chase (0-125 5-y-o and up) £3,035 3m. (5:55)

3213* RABA RIBA [109] 9-11-5 V Slattery, *led, hit second, hdd*
3rd, led 5th, bad mstk 16th, styd on gmely und pres frm
last........................... (3 to 1 fav op 4 to 1)   1
3336³ SANDAIG [91] 8-10-1 N Williamson, *hld up in tch, rdn to*
chal last, not quicken r-in..........(10 to 1 op 8 to 1)   2
3018² STAUNCH RIVAL (USA) [90] 7-10-0 D Bridgwater, *chsd ldrs*
frm 8th, hrd drvn and styd on r-in.. (8 to 1 op 7 to 1)   3
3364 SHASTON [100] (bl) 9-10-10 R Dunwoody, *chsd ldrs till*
5th, hit 13th, mstk 2 out, hld whn hit last.
.... (8 to 1 tchd 9 to 1)   4
3364⁴ PURBECK DOVE [94] 9-10-4 W McFarland, *chsd ldg grp,*
no imprsn whn mstk 3 out...........(7 to 1 op 8 to 1)   5
3364² COOL AND EASY [100] 8-10-10 D Murphy, *lost tch frm*
hfwy, tld off......................(9 to 2 op 6 to 1)   6
1720 DELGANY RUN [101] 10-10-11 M A FitzGerald, *led 3rd to*
5th, struggling frm 15th, tld off.
.... (16 to 1 op 14 to 1 tchd 20 to 1)   7
3166 BERESFORDS GIRL [100] 9-10-10 E Murphy, *al wl beh, tld*
off hfwy.......................(20 to 1 op 14 to 1 tchd 25 to 1)   8
2294 TAGMOUN CHAUFOUR (Fr) [90] 9-10-0 B Powell, *improved*
5th, lost pl hfwy, sn tld off.................(66 to 1)   9
LOCKWOOD PRINCE [107] 11-11-3 J Frost, *al in*
arrears, tld off frm hfwy.......... (66 to 1 op 50 to 1)   10
1459 NAUGHTY NICKY [90] 10-10-0 R Greene, *al struggling, tld*
off frm hfwy......................(25 to 1 op 20 to 1)   11
3336 SKETCHER (NZ) [90] 11-10-0 D Gallagher, *mstk 6th, sn*
toiling, tld off frm 12th...........(16 to 1 op 20 to 1)   12
2131⁴ SUNSET AGAIN [92] 9-10-2² Richard Guest, *al in rear, tld*
off frm hfwy......................(66 to 1 op 50 to 1)   13
3364* SUNLEY BAY [110] 8-11-1 (5*,7ex) Guy Lewis, *nvr gng*
pace, tld off frm hfwy.............(9 to 1 op 7 to 1)   14
3260 NEVER BE GREAT [114] 12-11-10 W Marston, *toiling frm*
hfwy, blun and uns rdr 16th.................(33 to 1)   ur
3338 VILLA RECOS [90] (bl) 9-10-1 J Harvey, *chsd ldrs, mstk 9th,*
sn lost pl, tld off whn pld up bef 3 out.
.... (33 to 1 op 25 to 1)   pu
Dist: 2l, nk, 3l, 6l, dist, nk, 15l, 8l, dist, hd. 6m 3.60s. a 16.60s (16 Ran).
(Jeff McCarthy), J L Spearing

3478 Spring Conditional Jockeys Novices' Selling Handicap Hurdle (4-y-o and up) £1,833 3m 110yds.......... (6:25)

2799⁴ DEVIOSITY (USA) [65] 7-10-9 R Farrant, *with ldrs, led aftr 3*
out, hdd nxt, rnwd effrt to ld nr line.........(4 to 1 jt-
fav op 11 to 2)   1
2118⁶ KEMALS DELIGHT [64] 7-10-3 (5*) N Collum, *al cl up, led*
aftr 2 out, hdd nr line.............(10 to 1 op 7 to 1)   2
3340⁶ GLADYS EMMANUEL [78] 7-11-8 P McLoughlin, *wtd wth,*
prog 8th, ev ch 2 out, kpt on same pace.
.... (14 to 1 op 10 to 1 tchd 20 to 1)   3
3281 PALACE PARADE (USA) [71] 4-11-1 D Leahy, *trkd ldrs till*
lost pl 5th, kpt on ag'n frm 2 out...(14 to 1 op 7 to 1)   4
1801 NEW STATESMAN [61] 6-10-5 S Curran, *hld up, steady*
hdwy 9th, led briefly 2 out, sn btn.
.... (10 to 1 tchd 12 to 1)   5
3147³ ACROSS THE CARD [63] 6-10-7 Guy Lewis, *no prog frm 3*
out.............................. (6 to 1 tchd 7 to 1)   6
3340⁵ DANGER BABY [73] 4-11-3 D Meredith, *led till hdd aftr 3*
out, sn rdn and btn....... (9 to 2 op 5 to 1 tchd 6 to 1)   7
1950⁶ REALLY NEAT [60] 8-10-4 D Matthews, *mid-div, effrt 9th,*
btn appr 2 out....................(33 to 1 op 20 to 1)   8
3281 ARJUNA [80] 9-11-3 (7*) C Quinlan, *beh, no ch frm 8th.*
.... (4 to 1 jt-fav op 12 to 1)   9
3111⁶ DAMCADA (Ire) [57] 6-10-1 R Davis, *in rear, no ch frm 8th.*
.... (9 to 1 op 6 to 1 tchd 10 to 1)   10
3018 ARCTICFLOW (USA) [56] (bl) 9-10-0 P Carey, *wth ldr till 3*
out, sn lost pl, tld off...............(50 to 1 op 33 to 1)   11
3298⁵ THANKSFORTHEOFFER [62] (v) 6-10-3 (3*) Pat Thompson,
hld up, prog 8th, wknd aftr 3 out, f last.
.... (12 to 1 tchd 14 to 1)   f
3173⁴ NORDEN (Ire) [70] 5-10-11 (3*) T Thompson, *settled mid-*
field, rdn aftr 7th, mstk nxt, sn struggling, blun 3 out,
pld up bef 2 out...................(14 to 1 op 10 to 1)   pu
3173 ON THE BOOK [64] 5-10-8 R Darke, *in rear, lost tch frm*
8th, tld off whn pld up bef 2 out.........(12 to 1)   pu
Dist: Nk, 2l, ¾l, 9l, 2l, 2½l, 6l, sht-hd, 2½l, dist. 5m 56.80s. a 22.30s (14 Ran).
(Mrs S L Hooper), N G Ayliffe

3479 Peter And Sybil Blackburn Memorial Challenge Trophy Novices' Chase (5-y-o and up) £2,549 2m 110yds...(6:55)

2829 SAFFAAH (USA) 7-11-3 M Richards, *set gd pace frm 3rd, sn*
clr, pressed 8th, drw clear ag'n betw last 2, easily.
.... (100 to 30 op 5 to 2 tchd 7 to 2)   1
3066 SAN LORENZO (USA) 6-11-13 N Williamson, *mstks, al cl*
up, hld whn lft second last.
.... (11 to 8 fav op 6 to 4 tchd 13 to 8)   2
3400² ALWAYS REMEMBER 7-11-3 Peter Hobbs, *al frnt rnk, no*
imprsn whn swtchd lft betw last 2.
.... (11 to 10 op 10 to 1 tchd 12 to 1)   3
3338² DONNA'S TOKEN 9-10-5 (7*) P McLoughlin, *hdwy und pres*
whn mstk 7th, no further prog frm tenth.
.... (6 to 1 tchd 7 to 1)   4
2065⁸ FANATICAL (USA) (bl) 8-11-3 L Harvey, *wtd wth, improved*
7th, mstk 9th, sn btn. (16 to 1 op 12 to 1 tchd 20 to 1)   5
LEMHILL 12-11-3 R Dunwoody, *pressed ldg grp till wknd*
und pres frm tenth......(7 to 1 op 6 to 1 tchd 8 to 1)   6
3361 KING'S RARITY 8-11-3 B Powell, *pressed ldrs till wknd*
7th, tld off.......................(66 to 1 op 50 to 1)   7
1325 WESSEX MILORD 9-11-3 R Greene, *al in rear, tld off whn*
mstk 8th...........................(66 to 1 op 50 to 1)   8
3297* ALDAHE 9-11-10 S Burrough, *al in rear, tld off frm 7th.*
.... (20 to 1 op 16 to 1 tchd 25 to 1)   9
3338³ SPINNING STEEL 7-11-3 W Marston, *led to 3rd, chsd wnr,*
second and hld whn f last.........(33 to 1 op 25 to 1)   f
1718 CREDIT NOTE 8-11-3 S Earle, *beh till f 3 out.*
.... (66 to 1 op 33 to 1)   f
3297² WHYFOR 6-11-3 C Maude, *jmpd lft in rear, tld off 6th, f*
tenth............................ (25 to 1 op 20 to 1)   f
1547 NEVER EVER 9-11-0 (3*) R Davis, *jmpd lft in rear, tld off*
6th, pld up bef tenth....................(100 to 1)   pu
DOWN DALE 9-10-10 (7*) R Darke, *in rear whn blun 5th,*
sn tld off, pld up bef 3 out..............(100 to 1)   pu
Dist: 6l, 3½l, 8l, 9l, 7l, dist, 6l, 8l. 4m 5.30s. a 7.30s (14 Ran).
SR: 33/37/23/10/6/-/   (Mrs H Levy), W R Muir

3480 Somerset Hunters' Chase (5-y-o and up) £1,201 3m 3f.............. (7:25)

3412 CARRICKMINES 9-11-9 (5*) Mr T Jones, *led to second,*
remained cl up, led 18th to 3 out, slight ld nxt, edgd lft
r-in, all out........................(14 to 1 op 12 to 1)   1
3399⁴ KNOCKAMSHIN 11-12-2 (5*) Mr T Byrne, *patiently rdn,*
steady prog frm 13th, chlgd 2 out, styd on...(12 to 1)   2
2949 MR MURDOCK 9-11-12³ (5*) Mr T Mitchell, *settled in mid-*
field, hit 13th, prog nxt, ev ch 3 out, styd on same pace.
.... (7 to 4 fav op 2 to 1)   3
KHATTAF 10-11-7 (7*) Miss J Cumings, *chsd ldr, bad mstk*
18th, led 3 out to 2 out, no extr......(8 to 1 op 6 to 1)   4
3265⁴ CAPE COTTAGE (bl) 10-11-9 (5*) Mr S Bush, *styd on frm 3*
out, nvr rckd ldrs... (12 to 1 op 10 to 1 tchd 14 to 1)   5
3212⁵ MY MELLOW MAN 11-12-2 (5*) Miss P Curling, *mstk 8th,*
effrt 15th, no imprsn frm 18th.......(10 to 1 op 8 to 1)   6
RANDOM PLACE 12-11-7 (7*) Mr I Pocock, *improved 7th,*
mstk 16th, sn struggling................(33 to 1)   7
2765³ RUSTY BRIDGE 7-11-7 (7*) Mr R Johnson, *mstks in rear,*
tld off frm 17th...................(10 to 1 op 16 to 1)   8
3171 WATERSMEET DOWN 11-12-0 (7*) Miss C Wright, *not jump*
wl, well plcd to tenth, sn struggling.
.... (66 to 1 op 50 to 1)   pu
POPESWOOD 11-12-0 (7*) Mr J Maxse, *in rear whn mstk*
7th, sn lost tch, tld off when pld up bef 17th.
.... (12 to 1 op 12 to 1 tchd 14 to 1)   pu
AUTUMN ZULU 15-12-0 (7*) Mr G Baines, *led second to*
18th, sn wknd, beh whn pld up bef 7th....(100 to 1)   pu
CERTAIN STYLE 11-12-0 (7*) Mr M Batters, *reluctant to*
race, tld off till pld up bef 7th.... (50 to 1 op 33 to 1)   pu
3171 COLCOMBE CASTLE 11-11-7 (7*) Mr J Culloty, *chsd ldrs till*
wknd 17th, tld off whn pld up bef 3 out......(100 to 1)   pu
2671 STANDAROUND (Ire) 5-11-2 (7*) Mr B Pollock, *slwly away,*
in rear, tld off whn pld up bef 3 out...... (100 to 1)   pu
Dist: ¾l, 4l, ½l, 3l, 5l, ½l, 20l. 7m 6.20s. a 31.20s (14 Ran).
(Lee Bowles), Lee Bowles

3481 Aspen Catering Mares Only Handicap Hurdle (0-135 4-y-o and up) £2,179 2m 1f.............................. (7:55)

1599⁵ WOLVER GOLD [90] 7-10-5 C Maude, *hld up, smooth prog*
to ld 6th, easily...................(7 to 2 op 9 to 2)   1
3304* KALAMOSS [85] 5-9-7 (7*) Miss S Mitchell, *chsd ldr till lost*
pos 4th, rnwd effrt 6th, chlgd 2 out, no ch wth wnr.
.... (8 to 1 op 7 to 1 tchd 9 to 1)   2
2214³ SHIMMERING SCARLET (Ire) [96] 6-10-11 B Powell, *led till*
mstk and hdd 6th, rnwd effrt und pres 2 out, fdd r-in.
.... (3 to 1 op 5 to 2)   3
3363⁴ MISS EQUILIA (USA) [92] 8-10-7 R Dunwoody, *wtd wth,*
effrt 6th, rdn aftr 3 out, sn btn.
.... (15 to 8 fav op 9 to 4 tchd 11 to 4)   4
3117⁶ BELLEZZA [113] 7-12-0 D Gallagher, *hld up and beh,*
pushed alng and struggling appr 6th, sn tld off.
.... (4 to 1 op 7 to 2 tchd 9 to 2)   5
REELING [85] 8-10-0 W Marston, *drpd out strt, tld off hrd,*
hdwy to join ldr aftr 4th, wkng whn mstk 3 out.
.... (16 to 1 tchd 20 to 1)   6
Dist: 5l, 3l, 15l, 15l, 10l. 3m 58.50s. a 11.50s (6 Ran).
(A L Roberts), B Palling

AYR (good)
Saturday April 16th

Going Correction: MINUS 0.05 sec. per fur. (races 1,3,6,7,8), PLUS 0.10 (2,4,5)

3482 Harcros Scottish Juvenile Series Championship Final Novices' Handicap Hurdle (4-y-o) £6,937 2m. . . (2:25)

3179[2] CROMARTY [85] 10-5 M Dwyer, *hld up, hdwy aftr 2 out, led r-in, ran on wl*......(9 to 1 op 8 to 1 tchd 10 to 1) 1
3030* BEND SABLE (Ire) [98] 11-4 B Storey, *hld up, effrt aftr 3 out, ev ch last, kpt on wl*......... (6 to 1 tchd 13 to 2) 2
2977* RUSTY REEL [108] 12-0 R Campbell, *chsd ldrs, slight ld 3 out, hrd pressed frm last, hdd r-in, no extr.*
......................................(8 to 1 tchd 10 to 1) 3
3128[2] WEAVER GEORGE (Ire) [87] 10-7 R Dunwoody, *led, blun second, jnd 3 out, dsptd ld r-in, wknd nr finish.*
......................................(7 to 1 tchd 8 to 1) 4
3228* DARING PAST [105] 11-11 P Niven, *prmnt till wknd aftr 3 out.*.............(5 to 1 jt-fav tchd 9 to 2) 5
3128[8] DEVILRY [91] 10-11 J Callaghan, *in tch, effrt appr 3 out, no hdwy.*.......................(16 to 1 op 14 to 1) 6
3128* BALLON [91] 10-11 T Reed, *steadied strt, hld up beh, hdwy aftr 6th, rdn appr 3 out, one pace.*
......................................(6 to 1 tchd 7 to 1) 7
3333[6] WAMDHA (Ire) [80] 10-0 A S Smith, *trkd ldr aftr 3rd, ev ch 2 out, wknd appr last.*...........(33 to 1 op 25 to 1) 8
3228 CHIAPPUCCI (Ire) [100] (bl) 11-6 A Maguire, *hld up, rdn appr 3 out, sn btn.*...........(5 to 1 jt-fav tchd 11 to 2) 9
3062 CONTRACT ELITE (Ire) [98] 11-4 D Wilkinson, *in tch, chlgd 3 out, sn wknd, no ch whn blun last.*
......................................(13 to 2 op 6 to 1 tchd 7 to 1) 10
Dist: 1¾l, ¾l, nk, 9l, ¾l, hd, hd, sht-hd, nk. 3m 47.10s. a 10.10s (10 Ran).

(Les Femmes Fatales), J J O'Neill

3483 Edinburgh Woollen Mill's Future Champion Novices' Chase Grade 1 (5-y-o and up) £19,560 2½m...... (2:55)

3039[5] SEE MORE INDIANS 7-11-8 R Dunwoody, *made all, drw clr frm 4 out, easily.*....................(7 to 2 op 3 to 1) 1
3411 GALLATEEN 6-11-8 N Doughty, *cl up till wknd frm 4 out.*
......................................(6 to 1 op 5 to 1) 2
3039 ROUYAN 8-11-8 I Lawrence, *in tch, ev ch appr 4 out, sn rdn and wknd.*......... (25 to 1 op 16 to 1) 3
3382* WELL BRIEFED 7-11-8 B Powell, *lost tch frm 12th, tld off.*
......................................(11 to 2 op 6 to 1 tchd 5 to 1) 4
3024[2] BAYDON STAR 7-11-8 A Maguire, *in tch, reminders aftr 8th and after 11th, cl up whn f 13th, destroyed.*
......................................(11 to 8 on tchd 5 to 4 on) f
Dist: 9l, 8l, dist. 4m 56.30s. a 9.30s (5 Ran).
SR: 21/12/4/-/-/ (Paul K Barber), P F Nicholls

3484 Littlewoods Pools Scottish Champion Hurdle Grade 2 (4-y-o and up) £12,620 2m......................... (3:25)

3414[2] CORROUGE (USA) 5-11-2 D Bridgwater, *made all, lft clr 3 out, ran on strly, eased nr finish.*..(4 to 1 tchd 5 to 1) 1
3189* ATOURS (USA) (bl) 6-11-2 A Maguire, *trkd wnr till eclipsd aftr 6th, styd on frm 2 out, no imprsn.*
......................................(16 to 1 op 14 to 1 tchd 20 to 1) 2
3380[4] COURT MASTER (Ire) 6-11-2 B Powell, *hld up, effrt appr 3 out, kpt on same pace.*.......(66 to 1 op 50 to 1) 3
3269* HIGH BARON 7-11-2 R Dunwoody, *in tch, effrt aftr 6th, no ch whn hmpd 3 out, one pace after.*
......................................(11 to 8 fav op 6 to 4) 4
3025[7] GRANVILLE AGAIN 8-11-10 J Frost, *hld up, effrt aftr 6th, sn btn, tld off.*....................(3 to 1 op 2 to 1) 5
2956[5] RINGLAND (USA) 6-11-2 B Storey, *hld up, blun 5th, lost tch aftr last, tld off.*.........(500 to 1 op 200 to 1) 6
3068* DIZZY (USA) 6-10-11 A Dobbin, *prmnt, chsd wnr frm 6th, plng and wkng whn f 3 out, dead.*....(9 to 2 op 4 to 1) f
Dist: 7l, ¾l, 1l, 25l, 7l. 3m 39.40s. a 2.40s (7 Ran).
SR: 56/49/48/47/30/15/-/ (Michael Gates), N A Twiston-Davies

3485 Stakis Scottish Grand National Handicap Chase Grade 3 (5-y-o and up) £29,700 4m 1f................ (4:05)

3039[7] EARTH SUMMIT [121] (bl) 6-10-0 D Bridgwater, *trkd ldrs, led 23rd, sn clr, easily.*...................(16 to 1) 1
3217[2] BISHOPS ISLAND [130] 8-10-9 A Maguire, *mstks, trkd ldrs, ev ch whn blun and lost pl 21st, styd on to go second 2 out, no chance with wnr.*.... (7 to 1 co-fav op 8 to 1) 2
3134 SUPERIOR FINISH [130] (bl) 8-10-9 P Niven, *dsptd ld, slight lead 19th to 23rd, no extr.*.............(7 to 1 co-fav op 8 to 1) 3
3425 RIVERSIDE BOY [142] (v) 11-11-7 R Dunwoody, *made most to 19th, dsptd ld to 23rd, kpt on same pace.*
......................................(14 to 1 op 20 to 1) 4
3134 MERRY MASTER [125] 10-10-4 Gee Armytage, *chsd ldrs till outpcd 21st, no dngr after*.....(12 to 1 op 10 to 1) 5

3425 INTO THE RED [129] 10-10-8 J F Titley, *chsd ldrs till wknd aftr 23rd.*............(11 to 1 op 9 to 1 tchd 12 to 1) 6
3425 MISTER ED [129] 11-10-8 D Morris, *beh, styd on frm 4 out, nvr nrr.*......................(12 to 1 op 10 to 1) 7
3077[5] CAROUSEL ROCKET [121] 11-9-11 (3*) D Bentley, *nvr dngrs.*......................................(100 to 1) 8
2805[5] WILLSFORD [121] 11-10-0 I Lawrence, *chsd ldrs till wknd aftr 20th.*..............................(33 to 1) 9
3405[6] OVER THE DEEL [121] 8-10-0 A Dobbin, *mid-div till wknd aftr 19th.*.................................(20 to 1) 10
3375[3] WHAAT FETTLE [124] 9-10-3 M Moloney, *chsd ldrs till wknd a 22nd.*.......................(12 to 1) 11
3027 OFF THE BRU [124] (v) 9-10-3? Mr J Bradburne, *prmnt till wknd aftr 18th.*..........(10 to 1 op 33 to 1) 12
3299[2] RUFUS [121] (bl) 8-10-0 B Powell, *al beh, tld off.*
......................................(33 to 1 tchd 25 to 1) 13
3203[2] RYDE AGAIN [139] 11-11-4 D Murphy, *mid-div whn wknd aftr 19th, beh whn pld up aftr nxt.*
......................................(11 to 1 op 12 to 1) pu
2893[5] BOREEN OWEN [121] 10-9-10? (5*) A Roche, *sn beh, tld off whn pld up bef 15th.*......................(200 to 1) pu
3180[5] TRUELY ROYAL [121] 10-10-0 B Storey, *in tch till wknd aftr 19th, tld off whn pld up bef 4 out.*.......(200 to 1) pu
3141[5] ZAM BEE [127] 8-10-6? T Reed, *in tch till wknd aftr 19th, no hdwy.*.......................(100 to 1) pu
3134[5] SHRADEN LEADER [122] 9-10-1 N Williamson, *in tch till pld up aftr 13th, lme.*...(7 to 1 co-fav op 10 to 1) pu
2930* TARTAN TYRANT [125] 8-10-4 M Doughty, *blun 5th, nvr on terms, beh whn pld up bef 23rd.*...(10 to 1 op 12 to 1) pu
3417[3] DIAMOND FORT [121] 9-10-0 M Brennan, *al beh, tld off whn pld up bef 19th.*...................(50 to 1) pu
3168 HIGH PADRE [123] (bl) 8-10-2? M Dwyer, *mid-div till wknd aftr 19th, beh whn pld up bef 23rd.*..........(25 to 1) pu
3425 CHANNELS GATE [121] 10-10-0 L Wyer, *sn beh, tld off whn pld up bef 22nd.*....................(50 to 1) pu
Dist: 14l, 7l, 1½l, 3½l, ¾l, ½l, 15l, ½l, 3½l, 8l. 8m 20.80s. a 16.80s (22 Ran).
(R I Sims), N A Twiston-Davies

3486 Steel Plate And Sections Young Chasers' Qualifier Novices' Chase (5-8-y-o) £3,516 3m 1f............. (4:40)

3411 MARTOMICK 7-11-7 N Williamson, *jmpd wl, made all, clr aftr 15th, easily.*
......................................(Evens fav op 11 to 8 on tchd 11 to 10) 1
3040 DURHAM SUNSET 7-11-7 A Maguire, *chsd wnr frm hfwy, effrt aftr 15th, sn thn.*
......................................(100 to 30 op 4 to 1 tchd 9 to 2 and 3 to 1) 2
3259[2] YORKSHIRE GALE 8-11-12 D Murphy, *prmnt till wknd aftr 14th.*......................................(6 to 1) 3
3224[2] TARTAN TRADEWINDS 7-11-8 N Doughty, *in tch till outpcd aftr 13th.*...........................(10 to 1) 4
2514 GRANVILLE GUEST 8-11-8 R Dunwoody, *in tch till wknd aftr 14th.*......... (6 to 1 tchd 11 to 2) 5
SAGARO BELLE 8-10-13 A Merrigan, *sn tld off.*
......................................(400 to 1 op 200 to 1) 6
3178 MASTER MATHEW 7-11-4 T Reed, *sn tld off, pld up bef 14th.*......................................(200 to 1) pu
3143[5] SNOOK POINT 7-11-4 B Storey, *mstk 1st, sn tld off, pld up bef 15th.*......................................(200 to 1) pu
2952 MY PARTNER (Ire) 6-11-4 K Jones, *sn chasing wnr, wknd quickly aftr 7th, tld off whn pld up bef 12th.*
......................................(200 to 1) pu
Dist: 30l, 9l, 2½l, 15l, dist. 6m 5.90s. a 5.90s (9 Ran).
SR: 59/29/25/18/3/-/ (Richard Shaw), K C Bailey

3487 Albert Bartlett & Sons Novices' Handicap Hurdle (4-y-o and up) £3,615 2¾m
.... (5:10)

3128[3] OUTSET (Ire) [101] 4-11-3 (7*) Mr C Bonner, *made all, pushed clr frm 2 out.*............ (5 to 2 fav op 9 to 4) 1
3196[5] SCARF (Ire) [90] (bl) 6-10-13 M Dwyer, *hld up, effrt appr 3 out, styd on frm nxt, no ch wth wnr.*
......................................(13 to 2 op 6 to 1) 2
3360* BRAVE HIGHLANDER (Ire) [93] 6-11-2 D Murphy, *pld hrd, hld up, hdwy to track wnr aftr 9th, chlgd 3 out, shaken up, sn wknd.*......................................(3 to 1) 3
3144* SHAWWELL [96] 7-11-5 B Storey, *trkd ldrs, effrt appr 3 out, sn wknd.*...........(6 to 1 tchd 11 to 2) 4
3363[3] WARFIELD [88] 7-10-11 A Maguire, *chsd ldr till wknd appr 8th, tld off.*............ (5 to 1 op 9 to 2) 5
2970[3] DOUBLE STANDARDS (Ire) [83] 6-10-1 (5*) Mr D Parker, *in tch till drpd out quickly and pld up bef 8th.*
......................................(25 to 1 op 20 to 1) pu
Dist: 4l, 6l, 6l, dist. 5m 22.80s. a 12.80s (6 Ran).
(Mark Kilner), M D Hammond

3488 Gold Cup Hospitality Open National Hunt Flat Race (Div I) (4,5,6-y-o) £1,786 2m...................... (5:45)

2387[2] CALL EQUINAME 4-10-12 (5*) F Perratt, *made all, pushed clr fnl furlong, cmftbly.*
......................................(7 to 4 fav op 9 to 4 tchd 5 to 2) 1

SPARKY GAYLE (Ire) 4-10-10 B Storey, *sn tracking ldrs, ev ch 2 fs out, kpt on fnl furlong, no chance wth wnr.*
....(33 to 1 op 25 to 1) 2
3387* DISSINGTON DENE 5-11-2 (7") W Fry, *mid-div, hdwy to track ldrs 5 fs out, ev ch and rdn 2 out, one pace.*
....(5 op 4 to 1) 3
LUCIMAN (Ire) 4-10-10 P Niven, *hld up, hdwy to track ldrs 3 fs out, ev ch 2 out, no extr.*
...................................(15 to 2 op 7 to 1 tchd 8 to 1) 4
MISTER BUZIOS 6-10-11 (5") A Roche, *trkd ldrs, effrt o'r 2 fs out, kpt on same pace.*.............(14 to 1 op 25 to 1) 5
2931⁵ RADICAL CHOICE (Ire) 5-11-2 R Dunwoody, *trkd wnr, rdn 3 fs out, one pace.*........................(16 to 1 op 33 to 1) 6
TARA RAMBLER (Ire) 5-11-2 L Wyer, *mid-div, hdwy to track ldrs 5 fs out, kpt on same pace frm 3 out.*
....(14 to 1 op 10 to 1) 7
2407⁴ MINTY'S FOLLY (Ire) 4-10-10 A Maguire, *nvr dngrs.*
.... 8
2976⁷ DAY RETURN 5-10-11 C Dennis, *chsd ldrs till wknd o'r 2 fs out.*...(50 to 1) 9
LANSBOROUGH 4-10-3 (7") B Harding, *mid-div, effrt o'r 3 fs out, no hdwy.*......(12 to 1 op 10 to 1 tchd 14 to 1) 10
BE BRAVE 4-10-10 D Wilkinson, *mid-div, effrt o'r 3 fs out, no hdwy.*................(11 to 1 op 7 to 1 tchd 12 to 1) 11
2931⁸ KINGS LANE 5-11-2 T Reed, *beh last 4 fs.*.......(200 to 1) 12
KELBURNE LAD (Ire) 5-11-2 N Williamson, *nvr dngrs.*
....(9 to 1 op 6 to 1 tchd 10 to 1) 13
YOUANDI 4-10-5 A Dobbin, *al beh.* (20 to 1 tchd 25 to 1) 14
2909 CEDAR LEAF (Ire) 4-10-5 R Hodge, *beh last 6 fs.* (200 to 1) 15
2691⁶ NOW YOUNG MAN (Ire) 5-11-2 C Grant, *whipped round strt, al beh.*...................(12 to 1 tchd 14 to 1) 16
RAMBLING LANE 5-10-9 (7") S Melrose, *chsd ldrs, wknd o'r 4 fs out, tld off.*..........................(100 to 1) 17
TWICE WEEKLY 5-10-4 (7") Miss Sue Nichol, *lost tch 6 fs out, tld off.*...................................(200 to 1) 18
LUCKY DOMINO 4-11-15 Miss T Waggott, *beh hfwy, tld off.*..(200 to 1) 19
Dist: 6l, 3½l, ¾l, ½l, 3l, 2l, 5l, ¾l, 3½l, 1l. 3m 38.60s. (19 Ran).

(Mrs Karen McLintock), D Eddy

3489 Gold Cup Hospitality Open National Hunt Flat Race (Div II) (4,5,6-y-o) £1,786 2m...............................(6:15)

2373* NAUGHTY FUTURE 5-11-4 (5") A Roche, *trkd ldrs gng wl, led 3 fs out, pushed clr fnl furlong.*
..............................(6 to 4 fav tchd 5 to 4 and 13 to 8) 1
INTO THE WEST (Ire) 5-11-2 A Dobbin, *trkd ldrs frm hfwy, ev ch 2 fs out, kpt on und pres, no chance wth wnr.*
....(33 to 1) 2
DUKES MEADOW (Ire) 4-10-10 C Grant, *chsd ldrs, ev ch 2 fs out, kpt on und pres.*............(14 to 1 op 8 to 1) 3
2931⁴ MOREOF A GUNNER 4-10-10 A Maguire, *cl up, slight ld 4 fs out to 3 out, sn rdn and one pace.*
..............................(13 to 2 op 7 to 1 tchd 8 to 1 and 6 to 1) 4
STORMY CORAL (Ire) 5-10-4 (5") Mr D Parker, *mid-div, kpt on wl fnl 3 fs, not rch ldrs.*......(33 to 1 op 20 to 1) 5
3169⁵ WINDSWEPT LADY (Ire) 5-10-4 (7") G Lee, *hld up, styd on fnl 3 fs, nrst finish...* (10 to 1 op 8 to 1 tchd 14 to 1) 6
2976⁶ CRAIGIE RAMBLER (Ire) 5-10-11 Mr D Robertson, *mid-div, kpt on fnl 3 fs.*.......................(20 to 1) 7
BECK AND CALL (Ire) 5-11-2 N Williamson, *prmnt, rdn o'r 3 fs out, fdd.*.........................(12 to 1 op 8 to 1) 8
3347² STIR FRY 4-10-3 (7") S Taylor, *in tch, pushed alng hfwy, wknd 3 fs out.*.....................(9 to 4 op 7 to 2) 9
2876⁸ BUYERS DREAM (Ire) 4-10-10 P Niven, *mid-div, rdn o'r 3 fs out, no hdwy.*........................(14 to 1) 10
3169 LUCKY HOLLY 4-9-12 (7") C Woodall, *nvr dngrs.* (50 to 1) 11
REEFSIDE (Ire) 5-10-9 (7") B Harding, *nvr dngrs.*
....(20 to 1 op 16 to 1) 12
MY RACING DREAM 4-10-10 M Dwyer, *nvr dngrs.*
....(14 to 1 op 10 to 1) 13
MALENSKI (Ire) 4-10-3 (7") I Jardine, *al beh.*
....(33 to 1 op 25 to 1) 14
LISMORE LAD 5-11-2 R Dunwoody, *nvr dngrs...*(33 to 1) 15
2976⁸ OUR WILMA 5-10-4 (7") R McGrath, *al div till rdn and wknd o'r 3 fs out.*..(200 to 1 op 100 to 1) 16
LOGANI 4-10-5 S Turner, *made most to 4 fs out, wknd quickly.*..(50 to 1) 17
MEADOWLECK 5-10-6 (5") J Burke, *dsptd ld till wknd 5 fs out.*...................................(50 to 1 op 33 to 1) 18
2976⁹ HENBRIG 4-10-5 Mr C Ewart, *al beh.* (33 to 1 op 25 to 1) 19
3079 PRIESTS MEADOW 5-11-2 Carol Cuthbert, *trkd ldrs till wknd 5 fs out.*.. 20
Dist: 3½l, ½l, 4l, 2l, 3l, 1½l, 5l, sht-hd, 3l, 4l. 3m 42.30s. (20 Ran).

(A K Collins), J J O'Neill

BANGOR (good)
Saturday April 16th
Going Correction: PLUS 0.40 sec. per fur.

3490 Bunbury Novices' Chase (5-y-o and up) £2,879 2m 1f 110yds........(2:10)

3400* PEACEMAN 8-11-9 E Murphy, *set str pace, untidy 3rd, clr whn bad mstk 3 out, unchlgd.*
..............................(6 to 5 on op 5 to 4 tchd 5 to 4 on) 1
3047⁴ PHARGOLD (Ire) 5-10-12 G McCourt, *wtd wth in rear, hit 7th, steady prog frm 4 out, styd on wl appr last.*
..................................(11 to 1 op 10 to 1 tchd 12 to 1) 2
3382 COUNTRY LAD (Ire) 6-11-13 S McNeill, *al chasing ldrs, no imprsn frm 2 out.*...................(9 to 4 op 6 to 4) 3
2978² AUXILLAR (USA) (v) 6-11-5 D J Burchell, *hld up in mid-div, effrt 9th, nvr nr to chal.*..........(12 to 1 op 8 to 1) 4
3226⁴ ON THE TEAR 8-11-2 (3") S Wynne, *chsd wnr to 8th, sn rdn and wknd.*......................(66 to 1 op 33 to 1) 5
3356⁴ HIGHLY DECORATED 9-11-5 Gary Lyons, *chsd ldrs till wknd appr 2 out, eased whn btn.* (14 to 1 op 10 to 1) 6
3022⁸ ODYSSEUS 8-11-2 (3") R Davis, *hld up, al towards rear, tld off frm 4 out.*.......................(50 to 1 op 33 to 1) 7
1999 NO LIGHT 7-11-5 L Harvey, *al in rear, 4th and no ch whn f last.*..................................(33 to 1 op 20 to 1) f
3022⁷ MARINER'S WALK 7-11-2 (3") R Farrant, *al beh, tld off whn pld up bef 3 out.*.........(66 to 1 op 50 to 1) pu
3400⁸ BROOK COTTAGE (Ire) 6-11-5 T Wall, *in rear, tld off whn pld up bef 6th.*................(66 to 1 op 50 to 1) pu
Dist: 5l, 6l, 15l, 20l, 1¼l, 30l. 4m 20.10s. a 14.10s (10 Ran).
SR: 24/8/17/-/-/-/ (Sir Peter Gibbings), Mrs D Haine

3491 Tilstone Handicap Hurdle (0-130 4-y-o and up) £3,198 3m.............(2:40)

3374² FURRY BABY [103] 7-10-5 R Garritty, *nvr far away, led 3 out to 2 out, quickened to ld nr finish.*
..............................(15 to 2 op 5 to 1 tchd 8 to 1) 1
3136⁴ COUTURE STOCKINGS [101] 10-10-3 R Supple, *sn chasing ldrs, led 2 out, hrd rdn and ct cl hme.* (9 to 1 op 7 to 1) 2
3408² LINKSIDE [115] 9-10-12 (5") D Fortt, *hld up in rear, took clr order 8th, styd on appr last, nvr nrr.*
....(9 to 2 fav op 4 to 1) 3
3068 RED RING [102] 7-10-4⁴ G McCourt, *patiently rdn, hdwy hfwy, jnd ldrs 2 out, sn ridden, no extr.*
....(10 to 1 op 8 to 1) 4
3279² GENERAL SHOT [98] 9-10-0 Diane Clay, *trkd ldrs, rdn 8th, grad wknd.*...........(6 to 1 op 5 to 1 tchd 8 to 1) 5
3398² TOUCH OF WINTER [105] (bl) 8-10-7 S McNeill, *cl up, led 6th to 3 out, rdn and wknd appr last.* (6 to 1 op 9 to 2) 6
2729 BOOTSCRAPER [90] 6-10-0 C Maude, *al mid-div.*
....(20 to 1 op 16 to 1) 7
2837 PARLEZVOUSFRANCAIS [100] 10-10-2 J Lower, *pressed ldrs to 6th, grad wknd.*
..................................(11 to 1 op 10 to 1 tchd 12 to 1) 8
3028 JUDGES FANCY [123] (bl) 10-11-8 (3") T Jenks, *in tch, mstk and lost pl 9th, sn btn.* (11 to 1 op 8 to 1 tchd 14 to 1) 9
3166 ARR EFF BEE [98] (bl) 7-9-9 (5") D Leahy, *al in rear.*
....(33 to 1) 10
STATED CASE [113] 9-11-1 S Smith Eccles, *led second to 4th, rdn 7th, wknd and pld up bef 2 out.*
....(16 to 1 op 14 to 1) pu
3028 MONTAGNARD [113] 10-11-1 M Richards, *sn wl beh, tld off whn pld up bef 7th.*.............(14 to 1 op 10 to 1) pu
1481 MONTIFIORE AVENUE [100] 8-10-2⁷ (7") S Lycett, *led to second, led 4th to 6th, wknd nxt, pld up bef last.*
....(50 to 1) pu
3136⁹ ROCHESTOWN LASS [98] (v) 8-10-0 N Mann, *in tch to hfwy, beh whn pld up bef 3 out...*(20 to 1 op 16 to 1) pu
Dist: Nk, 2l, 2½l, 15l, ¾l, 8l, 1l, 1¼l, 1¼l. 5m 44.70s. (14 Ran).

(K Hanson), M Avison

3492 Marchweil Novices' Handicap Chase (5-y-o and up) £3,035 2½m 110yds
....(3:10)

2873³ BUCKS SURPRISE [90] 6-10-13 R Supple, *al frnt rnk, jnd ldrs appr 2 out, led last, ran on wl.* (12 to 1 op 10 to 1) 1
2336 THE CARROT MAN [79] 6-10-2² J Railton, *sluggish strt, took clr order hfwy, led 9th to nxt, led 12th to last, hrd rdn, no extr.*...........(12 to 1 op 10 to 1 tchd 16 to 1) 2
3309² CANAVER [81] 8-10-4¹ G McCourt, *hld up, took clr order hfwy, blun badly 12th, styd on und pres frm 2 out.*
.............................(5 to 2 fav op 9 to 2) 3
3007⁴ OH SO BOLD [84] 7-10-4 (3") R Farrant, *chsd ldrs, effrt appr 3 out, no imprsn.* (6 to 1 op 5 to 1 tchd 13 to 2) 4
3443³ MO ICHI DO [83] 8-10-3 (3") T Eley, *hdwy 9th, rdn 3 out, sn wknd.*.............................(16 to 1 op 14 to 1) 5
3355⁴ CONCERT PAPER [94] (v) 10-10-10 (7") K Davies, *al cl up, led tenth to 12th, wkng whn mstk 2 out.*
....(16 to 1 op 14 to 1) 6
3135 CRUISING ON [77] 7-9-7 (7") D Winter, *trkd ldrs to tenth, sn lost pl.*...................................(16 to 1 op 14 to 1) 7
3286 SOUTH STACK [78] 8-10-1¹ Gary Lyons, *nvr a factor.*
....(14 to 1 op 12 to 1) 8
3354² SUPPOSIN [93] 6-11-2 Richard Guest, *al in rear, tld off.*
....(14 to 1 op 12 to 1) 9
3426⁵ HANGOVER [85] 8-10-8 R Greene, *cl up, blun and rdr lost irons 12th, not reco'r...*............(10 to 1 tchd 7 to 1) 10
3105 COCK SPARROW [83] 10-10-6 N Mann, *al beh, tld off.*
....(11 to 1 op 10 to 1) 11
3099³ ACCESS SUN [81] 7-10-1 (3") T Jenks, *led to 9th, blun badly nxt, pld up.*......................(12 to 1 op 10 to 1) pu

3341[2] HIGHLAND RALLY (USA) [88] 7-10-11 R Garritty, *al beh, tld off whn pld up bef 12th*.......... (14 to 1 op 10 to 1) pu
2350[5] MCMAHON'S RIVER [88] 7-10-11 V Slattery, *in rear whn mstk 3rd, tld off and pld up bef 9th*.......... (33 to 1) pu
DROMIN MIST [101] 7-11-10 S McNeill, *al rear div, tld off whn pld up bef 3 out*............. (16 to 1 op 12 to 1) pu
Dist: 2½l, 4l, 5l, 3½l, 1l, 5l, 6l, dist, 7l. 5m 10.20s. a 19.20s (15 Ran).
(Mrs L E Morton), J Mackie

3493 Jane McAlpine Memorial Hunters' Chase (6-y-o and up) £2,008 3m 110yds...................... (3:45)

3399[2] SUNNY MOUNT 8-12-0 Mr J Greenall, *hld up in tch, chalg whn lft in ld 12th, clr frm 3 out, hit last*. .... (11 to 4 op 5 to 2 tchd 3 to 1) 1
3260[2] FIFTH AMENDMENT (bl) 9-12-0 Mr J Durkan, *led to 9th, lost tch appr 3 out, sn btn*. (5 to 1 op 9 to 2 tchd 11 to 2) 2
2887[3] THE MALAKARMA 8-11-9 (5*) Mr T Byrne, *wtd wth in rear, steady prog frm hfwy, clsg whn blun 15th, nvr dngrs aftrwards*......................... (6 to 1 op 4 to 1) 3
3329* CALABRESE (bl) 9-11-7 (7*) Major M Watson, *chsd ldr, led 9th, blun and hdd 12th, grad lost tch*. .... (11 to 8 fav op 5 to 4) 4
3195[4] EASTERN DESTINY 16-11-11[4] (7*) Mr E Griffith, *patiently rdn, clsg whn blun and uns rdr 11th*. .... (11 to 1 op 7 to 1 tchd 12 to 1) ur
3419[4] CLONONY CASTLE (bl) 8-11-7 (7*) Mr J Rudge, *cl up, mstk 9th, sn rdn and lost pl, beh whn blun and uns rdr 3 out*. .... (50 to 1 op 25 to 1 tchd 66 to 1) ur
3263 GATTERSTOWN (bl) 11-11-7 (7*) Mr S Mulcaire, *al in rear, tld off whn pld up bef 14th*........ (66 to 1 op 33 to 1) pu
Dist: 13l, nk, ¾l. 6m 16.40s. a 26.40s (7 Ran).
(J E Greenall), Miss C Saunders

3494 Crewe Novices' Hurdle (Div I) (4-y-o and up) £2,326 2½m............(4:15)

3225[2] TUSKY 6-11-9 N Bentley, *trkd ldrs, wnt second and mstk 8th, shaken up appr last, swtchd lft r-in, quickened to ld nr finish*......................... (7 to 2 op 5 to 2) 1
3051[2] TAKE THE BUCKSKIN 7-11-3 S Smith Eccles, *al cl up, mstk 4th, led 6th, hrd rdn and ct close hme*. .... (7 to 2 op 3 to 1) 2
2903[7] ZAJIRA (Ire) 4-10-5 R Garritty, *steadied strt, hld up in rear, jmpd rght thrght, effrt 3 out, nvr nr to chal*. .... (3 to 1 fav tchd 5 to 1) 3
3022[5] MANDYS LAD 5-11-0 (3*) T Jenks, *wtd wth, hdwy hfwy, wknd aftr 3 out*......................... (14 to 1 op 8 to 1) 4
3277[3] SKEOUGH (Ire) 6-11-9 R Bellamy, *pressed ldrs to 8th, sn wknd*............................ (8 to 1 tchd 10 to 1) 5
3008 NEWHALL PRINCE 6-10-12 (5*) D Leahy, *hdwy hfwy, rdn and wknd appr 8th*.............................. (33 to 1) 6
3421[3] JIMMY O'DEA 7-11-3 M Hourigan, *led to appr 6th, sn lost tch, tld off*...................... (25 to 1 op 16 to 1) 7
3211 CUMREWS NEPHEW 6-11-0 (3*) T Eley, *al in rear, wl beh whn blun and uns rdr 3 out, broke shoulder, destroyed*. .... (100 to 1 op 50 to 1) ur
SWEET LIBERTY 10-10-9 (3*) R Davis, *chsd ldrs to 7th, wknd nxt, beh whn pld up bef 2 out*. .... (100 to 1 op 50 to 1) pu
ROSINA MAE 5-10-12 D J Burchell, *sluggish strt, al in rear, tld off whn pld up bef 8th*..... (4 to 1 op 3 to 1) pu
1800 PEBBLE ROCK 6-11-0 (3*) R Farrant, *pressed ldrs to hfwy, sn wknd, tld off whn pld up bef 2 out*. .... (25 to 1 op 20 to 1) pu
Dist: ½l, 9l, 15l, 4l, 3l, 20l. 4m 49.40s. a 13.40s (11 Ran).
SR: 41/34/13/10/12/3/ (Ms Sigrid Walter), G M Moore

3495 Emral Handicap Chase (0-130 5-y-o and up) £3,663 3m 110yds...... (4:45)

2633 BRADWALL [100] 10-9-11 (3*) S Wynne, *patiently rdn, prog 12th, chlgd 2 out, sn led, ridden and hld on wl*. .... (50 to 1) 1
2966 KEEP TALKING [128] 9-12-0 S Smith Eccles, *jmpd wl, led to 3rd, led 7th to 12th, led 14th to 2 out, rallied und pres nr finish*............... (14 to 1 op 12 to 1 tchd 20 to 1) 2
3180[3] RIFLE RANGE [105] 11-10-5 C Maude, *led 3rd to 7th, ev ch 3 out, rdn and wknd appr nxt*. ....(9 to 1 op 10 to 1 tchd 12 to 1 and 8 to 1) 3
3001[4] CITY KID [120] 9-10-13 (7*) J J Brown, *wtd wth in rear, some hdwy frm 3 out, nvr nrr*........ (9 to 1 op 7 to 1) 4
3187[2] TOMPET [100] 8-9-11 (3*) T Jenks, *cl up, led 12th to 14th, wknd quickly appr 2 out*. ....(4 to 1 op 7 to 2 tchd 9 to 2) 5
3310 MWEENISH [104] 12-10-4[4] G McCourt, *hld up in rear, cld hfwy, wknd appr 3 out*.............(16 to 1 op 12 to 1) 6
3223[3] SWINHOE CROFT [100] 12-10-0 S McNeill, *frnt rnk, rdn alng 11th, wknd 13th*.............(16 to 1 op 14 to 1) 7
3077 BROMPTON ROAD [105] 11-10-5 R Greene, *hld up, al in rear*..(20 to 1 op 14 to 1) 8
3349* KALANSKI [116] 8-11-2 J Railton, *pressed ldrs, blun badly tenth, sn lost tch, wl beh whn mstk 15th*. ....(11 to 4 fav op 7 to 2 tchd 4 to 1) 9
3045[3] AVONBURN (NZ) [118] 10-11-4 M Richards, *hld up in rear, effrt 13th, no imprsn*... (7 to 1 op 5 to 1 tchd 15 to 2) 10

3417[5] SADDLER'S CHOICE [100] (bl) 9-10-0[3] (3*) R Davis, *cl up till wknd 15th, tld off*.................(20 to 1 op 14 to 1) 11
3318[2] FAST CRUISE [100] 9-10-0 M Hourigan, *al in rear, wl beh whn pld up bef 13th*..............(12 to 1 op 10 to 1) pu
3133 COMEDY SPY [100] 10-10-0 R Bellamy, *improved hfwy, wknd quickly 15th, pld up bef 2 out*. .... (14 to 1 op 12 to 1) pu
Dist: ¾l, 15l, 6l, 3l, 1½l, 1¾l, 5l, 1¾l, 1l, 9l. 6m 6.10s. a 16.10s (13 Ran).
SR: 9/36/-/7/-/-/ (G B Barlow), Mrs A R Hewitt

3496 Crewe Novices' Hurdle (Div II) (4-y-o and up) £2,326 2½m............(5:15)

3315* TEST MATCH 7-11-9 Diane Clay, *patiently rdn, prog frm 6th, led 2 out, quickened clr, cmftbly*. (3 to 1 op 9 to 4) 1
2950[5] FOX ON THE RUN 7-11-3 S McNeill, *chsd ldrs, shaken up appr 2 out, sn outpcd*. ....(6 to 4 fav op 2 to 1 tchd 9 to 4) 2
2871 JURASSIC CLASSIC 7-11-0 (3*) T Eley, *took str hold, led to 7th, rdn appr 2 out, kpt on*........ (33 to 1 op 20 to 1) 3
3184[3] ROSS GRAHAM 6-11-3 M Richards, *trkd ldr, led 7th to 2 out, ran on one pace*.... (5 to 1 op 7 to 2 tchd 6 to 1) 4
3225[3] SEARCY 6-10-12 (5*) D Leahy, *trkd ldrs, rdn appr 2 out, sn outpcd*............. (11 to 2 op 4 to 1 tchd 6 to 1) 5
3164[5] HECTOR MARIO 6-11-0 (3*) R Davis, *steadied strt, hld up and beh, smooth hdwy 8th, rdn and wknd 2 out*. .... (25 to 1 op 20 to 1) 6
3184[9] CAPTIVA BAY 5-10-9 (3*) S Wynne, *hld up in rear, effrt appr 7th, wknd nxt, tld off*........ (66 to 1 op 50 to 1) 7
1199[6] EMRAL MISS 6-10-12 G McCourt, *al beh, tld off*. .... (11 to 1 op 10 to 1 tchd 14 to 1) 8
PASSAMEZZO (Ire) 4-10-10 T Wall, *hld up in rear, lost tch appr 7th, tld off*.... (25 to 1 op 50 to 1 tchd 100 to 1) 9
883 KIRBY OPPORTUNITY 6-10-12 C Maude, *chsd ldg pair to 6th, sn rdn and wknd, tld off*.....(33 to 1 op 20 to 1) 10
Dist: 3½l, 1¾l, 1½l, 1¼l, 2l, 8l, 11l, 15l, nk. 4m 55.20s. a 19.20s (10 Ran).
(T A Theaker), W Clay

STRATFORD (good to soft)
Saturday April 16th

Going Correction: PLUS 0.70 sec. per fur. (races 1,3,-6,7), PLUS 0.95 (2,4,5)

3497 Stayers Novices' Hurdle (Div I) (4-y-o and up) £2,122 2¾m 110yds.....(2:25)

3421* TALBOT 8-11-4 J Osborne, *made all, rdn and styd on wl r-in*................ (7 to 4 fav op 6 to 4 tchd 5 to 4) 1
3215* FOREST FEATHER (Ire) 6-11-4 Peter Hobbs, *al prmnt, wnt second 3 out, chalg whn hit last, rdn and no imprsn r-in*................(100 to 30 op 5 to 2 tchd 9 to 2) 2
2141* TOP BRASS (Ire) 6-11-4 D Gallagher, *hld up in mid-div, moved clr 3 out, hrd rdn appr last, no hdwy*. .... (3 to 1 op 11 to 4 tchd 100 to 30) 3
2934[4] FLAMEWOOD 5-10-7 W Marston, *al prmnt, ev ch 2 out, rdn and no further hdwy*......... (20 to 1 op 14 to 1) 4
3204 BORROWED AND BLUE 4-10-0 M Perrett, *mstk second, prmnt till wknd appr 2 out*. .... (12 to 1 op 8 to 1 tchd 14 to 1) 5
3395[5] RULLY 5-10-12 W Worthington, *chsd wnr to 3 out, sn wknd, tld off*.....................(66 to 1 op 33 to 1) 6
YOUNG MOSS 8-10-7 (5*) S Curran, *hit second, prmnt till wknd 3 out, tld off*. ....(33 to 1 op 25 to 1 tchd 20 to 1 and 50 to 1) 7
2881[9] FINNIGAN FREE 4-10-5 J R Kavanagh, *al beh, tld off*. .... (100 to 1 op 50 to 1) 8
2728[6] SHINING LIGHT (Ire) 5-10-5 (7*) Mr G Hogan, *al towards rear, tld off*....................... (33 to 1 op 16 to 1) 9
3345[6] RAYLEO (Ire) 5-10-5 (7*) S Spence, *blun and uns rdr 1st*. .... (66 to 1 op 33 to 1) ur
1935 MARINERS MEMORY 6-10-12 W Humphreys, *refused to race*........................... (100 to 1 op 33 to 1) ref
MISS MAGIC 9-10-7 T Grantham, *al beh, tld off whn pld up bef last*...................... (50 to 1 op 25 to 1) pu
3204[5] LITTLE CLARE 7-10-7 B Clifford, *al beh, tld off 6th, pld up bef 8th*.......................... (66 to 1 op 50 to 1) pu
3396 CLOWN AROUND 6-10-0 (7*) R Massey, *prmnt till wknd 6th, tld off whn pld up bef last*... (100 to 1 op 50 to 1) pu
Dist: 7l, 2½l, 8l, 6l, dist, 1l, 20l, 20l. 5m 37.20s. a 25.20s (14 Ran).
(J F Dean), C R Egerton

3498 Long Marston Novices' Chase (6-y-o and up) £4,175 3m.............(2:55)

2047[4] GLENSHANE LAD 8-11-2 D Gallagher, *nvr far away, chalg whn hit 5 out, hrd rdn to ld appr 2 out, all out*. .... (10 to 1 op 8 to 1 tchd 12 to 1) 1
3305* MR MATT (Ire) 6-11-2 Peter Hobbs, *chsd ldr for most of way till led 5 out, hdd appr 2 out, no extr r-in*. .... (100 to 30 op 7 to 2) 2
2854[4] BOLLINGER 8-10-13 (3*) P Hide, *mid-div whn blun badly 4th, steadied towards rear, styd on frm four out, nvr nrr*.. (7 to 1) 3
3309[3] HILLWALK 8-11-2 M Perrett, *al frnt rnk, wkng whn hit last 2*............................ (6 to 1 op 11 to 2) 4

3133 JOLLY JAUNT 9-10-9 (7*) P Ward, *mid-div, in tch whn hit 12th, wknd 4 out*.................. (25 to 1 op 16 to 1)   5
1615³ CROWN EYEGLASS 8-10-12 M A FitzGerald, *hld up, lost tch frm 11th*.......................(50 to 1 op 33 to 1)   6
3361* WISE CUSTOMER 10-11-2 Mr J Rees, *al in rear*.
.... (8 to 1 op 7 to 1 tchd 10 to 1)   7
3278* GILSTON LASS 7-10-11 J R Kavanagh, *led till mstk and hdd 5 out, wknd rpdly, tld off*...... (11 to 2 op 6 to 1)   8
3192²⁶ MEKSHARP 7-10-12 W Marston, *in rear whn blun 8th, tld off frm hfwy*........................(50 to 1 op 33 to 1)   9
3192 CHEQUE BOOK 6-10-12 Mr D Verco, *sluly away, in rear whn blun and uns rdr 7th*........(100 to 1 op 66 to 1)   ur
3278² ROSCOE'S GEMMA 10-10-4 (3*) D Meredith, *sluly away, al beh, tld off whn pld up bef 2 out*. (66 to 1 op 50 to 1)   pu
3381 HARBINGER 9-10-9 (3*) J McCarthy, *al beh, tld off whn pld up bef 2 out*.................. (33 to 1 tchd 40 to 1)   pu
3381² COKENNY BOY 9-10-12 J Osborne, *hld up, gd hdwy 9th, wknd 12th, pld up bef 3 out*.
...................(3 to 1 fav tchd 7 to 2 and 11 to 4)   pu
3277⁶ PERTEMPS JOBSHOP 8-10-12 W Humphreys, *chsd ldrs till wknd quickly 12th, pld up bef 4 out*........(66 to 1)   pu
Dist: 3½l, 12l, 1½l, 10l, 5l, 8l, 25l, dist. 6m 15.00s. a 28.00s (14 Ran).
SR: 36/32/20/18/8/-/   (Mrs Harry J Duffey), K C Bailey

3499 Jenkinsons Handicap Hurdle (0-135 4-y-o and up) £3,018 2m 110yds (3:25)

ROYAL PRINT (Ire) [101] 5-9-11 (3*) J McCarthy, *hld up, rapid hdwy 3 out, led aftr nzt, sn clr*.
.... (10 to 1 op 8 to 1 tchd 12 to 1)   1
3365² FATACK [120] 5-11-0 (5*) S Curran, *prmnt till lost pl aftr 4th, rallied appr last to go second r-in*.
............................(4 to 1 op 7 to 2)   2
2762¹ ISAIAH [109] 5-10-8 T Kent, *led aftr second till hdd aftr 2 out, wknd*.................. (11 to 4 jt-fav tchd 3 to 1)   3
1799⁷ KING'S SHILLING (USA) [109] 7-10-8 Jacqui Oliver, *hld up in rear, hdwy 4th, one pace frm 2 out*.
..............................(8 to 1 op 7 to 1)   4
499* KING WILLIAM [108] 9-10-7 W Marston, *hld up in rear, hdwy 5th, wknd appr 2 out*........(10 to 1 op 8 to 1)   5
2717 GREYFRIARS BOBBY [101] 8-9-12⁹ (5*) S Fox, *hld up in tch, outpcd 3 out, tld off*...........(20 to 1 op 14 to 1)   6
BRILLIANT FUTURE [101] 9-10-0 W Humphreys, *led till aftr second, prmnt till wknd appr 2 out, tld off*.
.... (66 to 1 op 50 to 1)   7
3219* NOCATCHIM [125] (v) 5-11-10 J Osborne, *hld up, gd hdwy 4th, outpcd 2 out, wknd, virtually pld up r-in*.
...............(11 to 4 jt-fav op 3 to 1 tchd 5 to 2)   8
3193⁷ GOLDEN GUNNER (Ire) [102] 6-10-1 D Gallagher, *hld up in tch till wknd 3 out, tld off*........ (14 to 1 op 12 to 1)   9
1213⁸ PALACE WOLF (NZ) [110] 10-10-9 R Marley, *hld up in tch, outpcd 3 out, no ch whn f last*.....(20 to 1 op 16 to 1)   f
Dist: 15l, 2½l, 3l, 10l, 20l, 2l, 4l, 7l. 4m 4.10s. a 15.10s (10 Ran).
SR: 37/41/27/24/13/-/-/4/-/   (Delamere Partnership), W R Muir

3500 Welford Handicap Chase (0-135 5-y-o and up) £4,416 2½m. . . . . (3:55)

3194⁷ MIDFIELDER [110] 8-10-5 Peter Hobbs, *blun gdly second and sn in rear, steady hdwy 9th, led on bit 2 out, soon clr, hrd hld*...... (7 to 2 fav op 6 to 1 tchd 100 to 30)   1
3258³ LOVE ANEW (USA) [105] 9-9-9 (5*) Guy Lewis, *hld up in tch, styd on frm 3 out to go second appr last, no ch wth wnr*.........................(20 to 1 tchd 25 to 1)   2
3268² SMARTIE EXPRESS [127] 12-11-8 M A FitzGerald, *nvr far away, rdn appr 2 out, one pace*.
.... (13 to 2 op 6 to 1 tchd 7 to 1)   3
3210⁵ WELSH BARD [114] 10-10-9 D Gallagher, *jmpd wl, led to second, led 4th to 8th, frnt rnk till wknd appr last*.
.... (25 to 1 op 20 to 1)   4
3397² LITTLE TOM [111] 9-10-6 J R Kavanagh, *wtd wth, hdwy to ld briefly 5 out, wknd appr 2 out*.
.... (9 to 1 op 8 to 1 tchd 7 to 1)   5
3282* PEACE OFFICER [115] 8-10-10 S Burrough, *sluly away, beh till hdwy 8th, wknd 3 out*....(10 to 1 tchd 12 to 1)   6
3218* MENEBUCK [121] 8-10-12³ (7*) Mr Andrew Lillingston, *not jump wl, al in rear*......................(4 to 1 tchd 9 to 2)   7
3210² NORTHERN JINKS [119] (bl) 11-10-11 (3*) D Meredith, *sluly away, rapid hdwy to ld second, hdd 8th, made most frm 8th till wknd, headed and hit 2 out, sn btn*.
.... (14 to 1 op 10 to 1)   8
3258² EASTSHAW [120] 12-11-1 M Perrett, *mid-div whn jmpd sluly 5th, wl beh frm 7th*........ (14 to 1 op 10 to 1)   9
3318* LUMBERJACK (USA) [132] (bl) 10-11-13 J Osborne, *in tch till wknd quickly appr 5 out*.
.... (6 to 1 op 5 to 1 tchd 13 to 2)   10
3203* UNCLE ELI [133] 11-12-0 S Earle, *hld up in mid-div, hit 6th, pld up bef nzt, lme*. (6 to 1 op 5 to 1 tchd 7 to 1)   pu
Dist: 6l, 1½l, 1½l, 6l, 4l, 5l, 8l, 6l, 5l. 5m 8.70s. a 26.70s (11 Ran).
SR: -/-/9/-/-/-/   (Bournstream '6'), P J Hobbs

3501 Baulking Green Trophy Hunters' Chase (6-y-o and up) £2,388 2m 5f 110yds. (4:25)

3263* AMARI KING 10-12-3 (7*) Mr C Ward Thomas, *mid-div whn hmpd 7th, sn reco'red to track ldrs, led 4 out, ran on wl*.
.... (5 to 4 fav op 7 to 4 tchd 11 to 10)   1
3313 PARSON'S CROSS 10-11-7 (7*) Mr A Sansome, *chsd ldrs, rdn to go second appr 2 out, kpt on one pace*.
.... (33 to 1 op 20 to 1)   2
3171 SKERRY MEADOW 10-11-7 (7*) Mr G Hogan, *hld up in rear, gd hdwy frm 6th, outpcd 3 out, rdn and ran on frm nzt*......................(16 to 1 op 12 to 1 tchd 20 to 1)   3
3335 LOR MOSS 14-11-7 (7*) Mr J Jukes, *prmnt, lft second 7th, led nzt, mstk and hdd 4 out, one pace frm 2 out*.
.... (33 to 1 op 20 to 1)   4
ABBOTSHAM 9-11-7 (7*) Mr C Morlock, *hld up, gd hdwy 8th, hit tenth and 3 out, wknd appr 2 out*.
.... (14 to 1 op 10 to 1 tchd 16 to 1)   5
3263⁶ ROXALL CLUMP 10-12-0 Mr M Armytage, *beh, lost tch hfwy, tld off*................(5 to 1 op 10 to 1 tchd 9 to 2)   6
811⁴ GEMBRIDGE JUPITER 16-12-0⁷ (7*) Mr C Trietline, *al towards rear, tld off*.........(20 to 1 op 10 to 1 tchd 16 to 1)   7
3335* RAMPALLION 11-12-0 (7*) Mr S Blackwell, *led till f 7th*.
....................(9 to 4 op 5 to 2 tchd 2 to 1)   f
SOLDIER BANK 9-11-9 (5*) Mr S Bush, *in rear till blun and uns rdr 11th*........ (50 to 1 op 33 to 1 tchd 66 to 1)   ur
3335 KISSANE 13-11-10³ (7*) Mr J Wintle, *trkd ldr, lft in ld 7th, hdd nzt, wknd 5 out, tld off whn pld up bef last*.
.... (25 to 1 op 20 to 1 tchd 33 to 1)   pu
NORTHERN DAWN 12-11-7 (7*) R Telford, *in rear whn hit 5th, sn tld off, pld up bef 4 out*.
.... (50 to 1 tchd 66 to 1)   pu
2800 HIGHLAND ECHO 11-11-7 (7*) Mr J Rees, *in tch till wknd tenth, tld off whn pld up bef 5 out*. (33 to 1 op 20 to 1)   pu
TERRIFORN 9-11-11 (3*) Mr A Hill, *al in rear, tld off whn pld up bef tenth*......(25 to 1 op 20 to 1 tchd 50 to 1)   pu
Dist: 2½l, 2l, ¾l, 20l, dist, 2l. 5m 38.90s. a 35.90s (13 Ran).
                                                  (M Ward-Thomas), J Wall

3502 Ilmington Novices' Handicap Hurdle (0-100 4-y-o and up) £2,304 2m 110yds . . . .(4:55)

3270⁶ TEEN JAY [87] (v) 4-11-2 J Osborne, *al in tch and gng wl, led 2 out, clr whn heavily eased r-in, jst hld on*.
.......................(9 to 2 op 10 to 1 tchd 12 to 1)   1
3281² ALMAMZAR (USA) [83] 4-10-7 (5*) E Husband, *hld second, wl in rear till picked up bit appr last, fnshd fst, jst fld*.
....................(4 to 1 fav op 9 to 2 tchd 11 to 2)   2
2903⁹ MHEMEANLES [80] 4-10-9 Peter Hobbs, *hld up, hdwy 4th, rdn to go second appr last, one pace r-in*.
.... (10 to 1 op 10 to 1)   3
3074* SCARBA [80] 6-10-9 D Byrne, *hld up, rdn and hdwy 3 out, kept on whn hit last*.............(7 to 1 op 9 to 2)   4
3055² CAWARRA BOY [89] 6-10-11 (7*) Mr E James, *hld up in rear, hdwy 3 out, nvr nr to chal*....(10 to 1 op 7 to 1)   5
3365⁶ DOMINOS RING (Ire) [85] 5-11-0 W Marston, *trkd ldr, led 5th, rdn and hdd 2 out, sn btn*.
......................(20 to 1 op 14 to 1 tchd 25 to 1)   6
3009³ TENAYESTELIGN [84] 6-10-10 (3*) J McCarthy, *hld up in rear, gd hdwy 5th, rdn and wknd appr last*.
..................(12 to 1 op 10 to 1 tchd 14 to 1)   7
1642⁶ BRIMPTON BERTIE [85] 5-11-0 G Upton, *rcd wide, no hdwy frm 3 out*....................(25 to 1 op 20 to 1)   8
3137⁵ YOUNG BALDRIC [84] 7-10-13 W McFarland, *in tch till outpcd 3 out*........(14 to 1 op 10 to 1 tchd 16 to 1)   9
3339² PULMICORT [83] 4-10-12 D Gallagher, *al beh*.
.... (14 to 1 op 10 to 1 tchd 16 to 1)   10
3191² BLAYNEYS PRIVILEGE [80] 7-10-2 (7*) P McLoughlin, *hld up, hdwy to track ldrs 5th, wknd quickly aftr 2 out*.
.........................(14 to 1 op 10 to 1 tchd 16 to 1)   11
2652⁴ SILVER STANDARD [92] 4-11-7 J R Kavanagh, *al towards rear, lft beh 3 out*...............(14 to 1 op 10 to 1)   12
3300* TUMBLED BRIDE [80] 8-10-9 M Perrett, *led to 5th, wknd quickly, tld off whn pld up bef 2 out*.
.... (14 to 1 op 10 to 1)   pu
1442⁸ ORUJO (Ire) [96] 6-11-11 R Marley, *hld up in rear, tld off whn pld up bef 2 out*.. (16 to 1 op 10 to 1 tchd 20 to 1)   pu
2728⁸ KINDLE'S DELIGHT [85] 6-11-0 M A FitzGerald, *hld up, tld off whn pld up bef last*. (14 to 1 op 12 to 1)   pu
3119 JYMJAM JOHNNY (Ire) [89] 5-11-4 L Harvey, *al in rear, tld off whn pld up bef 2 out*.
..................(16 to 1 op 10 to 1 tchd 20 to 1)   pu
Dist: ½l, 3½l, 4½l, 2l, 2l, 6l, 6l, 1½l, 9l, 1l. 4m 7.00s. a 18.00s (16 Ran).
SR: 23/18/11/6/13/7/   (F J Bush), S E Sherwood

3503 Stayers Novices' Hurdle (Div II) (4-y-o and up) £2,122 2¾m 110yds. . . . . (5:25)

2318 MIDNIGHT CALLER 8-10-12 J Osborne, *made all, drw clr appr 2 out, hit last, unchlgd*.
.....................(9 to 1 op 5 to 1 tchd 10 to 1)   1
3230⁶ FORTUNES COURSE (Ire) 5-10-13 J R Kavanagh, *chsd wnr thrght, rdn appr 2 out, no ch aftr*....(7 to 1 op 5 to 1)   2
3220⁵ EMPIRE BLUE 11-11-4 M Bosley, *hld up in mid-div, steady hdwy 3 out, kpt on one pace*.
........................(100 to 30 op 5 to 1)   3
2934⁵ LOVING AROUND (Ire) 6-10-7 M A FitzGerald, *chsd ldrs, kpt on one pace frm 3 out*.
.... (5 to 1 op 5 to 1 tchd 13 to 2)   4

3360 FOREST PRIDE (Ire) 5-10-7 D Gallagher, *chsd ldrs, ev ch*
    whn rdn 3 out, wknd............(7 to 1 tchd 10 to 1)   5
32273 CURRAHEEN VIEW (Ire) 5-10-7 P Holley, *chsd ldrs, wkng*
    whn blun 3 out, tld off.
    ....(14 to 1 op 10 to 1 tchd 20 to 1)   6
2303 DISTINCTIVE (Ire) 5-10-5 (7*) P Ward, *hld up in tch, wknd*
    quickly 3 out, tld off.............(20 to 1 op 10 to 1)   7
18789 OUR WIZZER (Ire) 5-10-12 S Earle, *al beh, tld off.*
    ....(66 to 1 op 20 to 1)   8
3113 MAC'S BOY 5-10-12 Peter Hobbs, *hit second, in tch till*
    wknd 8th, beh whn f 2 out.....(66 to 1 op 20 to 1)   f
33397 HEAD OF DEFENCE 9-10-5 (7*) P McLoughlin, *al beh, tld*
    off whn pld up bef 2 out.........(66 to 1 op 33 to 1) pu
    DARK DEB 9-10-7 P McDermott, *rcd wide, lost tch 6th, tld*
    off whn pld up bef 3 out..........(50 to 1 op 33 to 1) pu
2572 PROFESSOR LONGHAIR 7-10-12 M Perrett, *rdn frm 4th,*
    sn beh, tld of whn pld up bef 2 out.(66 to 1 op 33 to 1) pu
33966 TRIPLE SENSATION (NZ) 7-10-12 Jacqui Oliver, *in rear*
    whn mstk 5th, sn tld off, pld up bef 7th.
    ....(10 to 1 op 5 to 1 tchd 33 to 1) pu
3046 WESTRAY (Fr) 4-10-5 A Carroll, *beh frm strt, tld off whn*
    pld up bef 3 out....................(20 to 1 op 33 to 1) pu
24076 SPA KELLY 6-10-12 V Slattery, *al beh, tld off whn pld up*
    bef 2 out........................(66 to 1 op 33 to 1) pu
3164 FED ON OATS 6-11-4 W Marston, *hld up, gd hdwy 6th,*
    tracking ldrs whn pld up lme appr 3 out, dismounted.
    ....(11 to 4 fav op 5 to 2 tchd 100 to 30) pu
Dist: 8l, 3½l, 8l, 1½l, dist, ¾l, 2½l. 5m 38.30s. a 26.30s (16 Ran).
                              (M Worcester), S E Sherwood

BALLINROBE (IRE) (yielding)
Monday April 18th

3504   Rathcarren Maiden Hurdle (6-y-o and up) £2,243 3m...................(2:30)

33668 STRALDI (Ire) 6-11-7 (7*) E G O'Callaghan,........(9 to 2)   1
29436 MISGIVINGS (Ire) 6-11-1 C F Swan,.................(6 to 1)   2
3296* INDESTRUCTIBLE (Ire) 6-12-0 Mr P J Healy,.........(8 to 1)   3
32925 EXTRA DAYS 7-12-0 Mr E Bolger,..........(4 to 1 fav)   4
    BROGUESTOWN PRIDE (Ire) 6-11-6 K F O'Brien, (14 to 1)   5
3449 I AM 6-11-5 (7*) J P Broderick,.....................(8 to 1)   6
33905 DROICHEAD LAPEEN 7-11-7 (7*) Mr T J Beattie,..(8 to 1)   7
3292⁴ CORRIBLOUGH (Ire) 6-12-0 C O'Dwyer,.........(9 to 2)   8
29218 POOR MOTHER (Ire) 6-11-1 F J Flood,...........(10 to 1)   9
3122⁹ MRS HEGARTY 8-11-1 D P Fagan,..............(14 to 1) 10
3200 MONEY MADE (bl) 7-11-1 (5*) M G Cleary,.......(50 to 1) 11
3243 LADY HA HA 7-10-8 (7*) J Butler,...............(20 to 1) 12
2616 PARKBOY LASS 7-11-2 (7*) J M Donnelly,.......(33 to 1) 13
    BELVIEW LADY 7-11-1 B Sheridan,..............(20 to 1) 14
29217 BALLINGOWAN STAR 7-11-1 L P Cusack,........(14 to 1) 15
472⁴ COSHLA EXPRESSO (Ire) 6-11-6 W T Slattery Jnr, (33 to 1) 16
3276 GLASHA BRIDGE (Ire) 6-11-6 F Woods,.........(50 to 1) 17
Dist: ½l, 11l, 11l, 4l. 6m 41.80s. (17 Ran).
                   (Christopher Cronin), A J Maxwell

3505   Corrib Maiden Hurdle (4 & 5-y-o) £2,243 2m....................(3:00)

34697 KEEPHERGOING (Ire) 5-11-0 K F O'Brien,........(5 to 1)   1
3086 TISRARA LADY (Ire) 4-10-10 J F Titley,.........(25 to 1)   2
3276⁴ CABLE BEACH (Ire) 5-11-5 C F Swan,.......(7 to 2 fav)   3
3321 SPORTSTYLE (Ire) 4-11-6 B Sheridan,...........(9 to 2)   4
2388⁸ SHANGANOIR (Ire) 4-10-10 P Carberry,..........(8 to 1)   5
968 GLOWING LINES (Ire) 4-10-5 (5*) P Gaule,......(5 to 1)   6
6173 BOB THE YANK (Ire) 4-11-1 A J O'Brien,.......(12 to 1)   7
939 RUSHEEN BAY (Ire) 5-11-0 (5*) P A Roche,.....(33 to 1)   8
2771 PRINTOUT (Ire) 4-10-10 H Rogers,............(10 to 1)   9
2750 MONTEJUSTICE (Ire) 4-10-5 (5*) D P Geoghegan, (33 to 1) 10
29179 TRIBAL MEMORIES (Ire) 4-10-7 (3*) C O'Brien, ..(12 to 1) 11
2124⁸ REMAINDER LASS (Ire) 5-11-8 S H O'Donovan,..(10 to 1) 12
3447 JOHNSON'S HILL (Ire) 5-11-0 (5*) L Flynn,......(50 to 1) 13
3197 AUNT ROSE (Ire) 5-11-0 L P Cusack,..........(33 to 1) 14
3290 CROSS ANGORLADY (Ire) 5-10-11 (3*) T J O'Sullivan,
    ....(33 to 1) 15
    FAIRY FANTASY (Ire) 4-10-10 A Powell,.........(20 to 1) 16
1036 LOVE FOR LYDIA (Ire) (bl) 5-11-0 G M O'Neill, ..(12 to 1) 17
2989 THYNE OWN GIRL (Ire) 5-10-11 (3*) G Kilfeather, ..(25 to 1) pu
Dist: 5½l, 4l, 4½l, 4l. 4m 20.50s. (18 Ran).
                   (G Walsh), Michael Hourigan

3506   Mayo Handicap Hurdle (0-109 4-y-o and up) £2,243 2m.............(3:30)

3294⁸ ANNFIELD LADY (Ire) [-] 6-10-1 F Woods,.......(25 to 1)   1
3292⁸ NO TAG (Ire) [-] 6-11-2 J F Titley,...........(7 to 2 fav)   2
3322 CASH CHASE (Ire) [-] 6-11-2 L P Cusack,.......(8 to 1)   3
2985⁸ DAVY CROCKETT [-] 7-10-13 (7*) Mr R Pugh,...(16 to 1)   4
3290⁶ TURALITY (Ire) [-] 5-10-2 S H O'Donovan,........(8 to 1)   5
29883 LOAVES AND FISHES [-] (bl) 6-11-0 (7*) B D Murtagh,
    ....(8 to 1)   6
2920⁶ SHANNON AMBER (Ire) [-] 5-10-6 (5*) J P Broderick, (20 to 1)   7
3294⁶ COOL CHARACTER (Ire) [-] 6-12-0 Mr E Bolger, ...(8 to 1)   8
2983 ISN'T THAT NICE (Ire) [-] 6-10-13 J Shortt,.....(14 to 1)   9
2232 PREMIER LEAP (Ire) [-] 5-10-10 G M O'Neill,.....(8 to 1) 10
376 ANA CRUSIS (Ire) [-] 6-10-0 (5*) D P Geoghegan, ..(20 to 1) 11

3367 FINAWAY BOY (Ire) [-] 6-11-8 J P Banahan,.......(14 to 1) 12
2024⁸ DICK'S CABIN [-] 7-10-7 K F O'Brien,............(6 to 1) 13
2988 NORA ANN (Ire) [-] 5-10-3 (7*) D J Kavanagh,....(9 to 2) 14
2988 JIMMY THE JACKDAW [-] (bl) 7-10-10 P Carberry, (10 to 1) 15
3273⁹ IM OK (Ire) [-] (bl) 6-9-2 (7*) T Martin,.........(50 to 1) 16
3291 CLONE (Ire) [-] (bl) 6-9-11 (7*) J M Donnelly,....(33 to 1) 17
2670⁹ VISTAGE (Ire) [-] 6-10-12 H Rogers,.............(11 to 1) 18
Dist: 1½l, 2½l, 1l, 9l. 4m 20.80s. (18 Ran).
                  (Patrick Delaney), W P Mullins

3507   Ballinrobe Water Towers Novice Chase (5-y-o and up) £2,243 2½m
    ....(4:30)

2920⁵ SUPER TACTICS (Ire) 6-11-9 (5*) P A Roche,.....(5 to 1)   1
3198⁴ THE WEST'S ASLEEP 9-11-9 J Magee,...........(9 to 1)   2
2865 PRINCIPLE MUSIC (USA) 6-11-11 (3*) Mr J A Nash,
    ....(7 to 2 fav)   3
3325 DAVE FLECK (Ire) 6-11-9 (5*) P Broderick,.....(12 to 1)   4
20267 RANDOM PRINCE 10-12-0 P Carberry,..........(5 to 1)   5
29237 JOHNNY SCATTERCASH 12-11-6 (3*) T J Mitchell, (12 to 1)   6
34659 BEAU GRANDE (Ire) 6-11-9 L P Cusack,.........(8 to 1)   7
3325⁴ TRASSEY BRIDGE 7-11-9 F Woods,.............(7 to 1)   8
2550⁶ PALMROCK DONNA 7-11-4 J F Titley,..........(10 to 1)   9
3275⁴ FOGELBERG (Ire) 6-12-0 C O'Dwyer,............(7 to 1) 10
2310⁹ NORA'S ERROR (Ire) 5-10-13 K F O'Brien,......(33 to 1) 11
2683 CRACKLING FROST (Ire) 6-11-9 J Shortt,........(20 to 1) 12
3241 BALLYFIN BOY 8-11-11 (3*) Miss M Olivefalk,....(16 to 1) ur
3242 SADDLESTOWN GLEN 9-12-0 T Horgan,..........(8 to 1) pu
3198 MR BARNEY 7-11-9 J K Kinane,................(50 to 1) pu
Dist: Hd, 9l, 8l, 1½l. 5m 42.10s. (15 Ran).
                   (F P Taaffe), C Kinane

3508   River Robe Flat Race (4 & 5-y-o) £2,243 2m..................(5:30)

2290⁵ BALLYQUIN BELLE (Ire) 4-10-8 (7*) Mr E Norris, ..(4 to 1)   1
3327 BALLINEVA (Ire) 5-11-10 (3*) Mrs J M Mullins, ...(6 to 1)   2
33217 GRAPHIC IMAGE (Ire) 4-11-6 Mr A P O'Brien, (7 to 2 jt-fav)   3
2199⁷ THE BOBTAIL FOX (Ire) 5-11-10 (3*) Mr D Marnane,
    ....(7 to 2 jt-fav)   4
    VERY ADAPTABLE (Ire) 5-11-6 (7*) Mr T J Murphy, ..(9 to 1)   5
    LESS HASSLE (Ire) 4-10-8 (7*) Mr J J Holohan,.....(33 to 1)   6
    SNIPE'S BRIDGE (Ire) 4-10-13 (7*) Mr D McCartan, (25 to 1)   7
    FREQUENT VISION (Ire) 4-10-13 (7*) Mr T Cooper, (20 to 1)   8
3124 BOLD TIPPERARY (Ire) 5-11-6 (7*) Mr K Whelan, ..(33 to 1)   9
    DONWOOD (Ire) 5-11-8 Mr D M O'Brien,..........(16 to 1) 10
1581 MAHANKHALI (Ire) 5-11-13 Mr A J Martin,.......(16 to 1) 11
    APPLEFORT (Ire) 4-11-1 (5*) Mr G J Harford,.......(8 to 1) 12
    SINERGIA (Ire) 4-10-13 (7*) Mr R Pugh,...........(25 to 1) 13
3245⁹ THAT'S GOSPEL (Ire) 4-10-13 (3*) Mr J A Nash, ...(33 to 1) 14
    BEYOND THE BAY 4-11-6 Mr T S Costello,.......(14 to 1) 15
    CARRIG HEATHER 4-10-13 (7*) Mr M D Jennings, ..(20 to 1) 16
249 KEASHILL (Ire) 5-11-1 (7*) Mr J P Kilfeather,.....(50 to 1) 17
Dist: ½l, 5½l, 3½l, 3½l. 4m 23.00s. (17 Ran).
           (Mrs S Crawford), Patrick Joseph Flynn

TOWCESTER (good)
Tuesday April 19th
Going Correction: PLUS 0.70 sec. per fur. (races 1,3,-6,7), PLUS 0.90 (2,4,5)

3509   Chestnut Novices' Hurdle (Div I) (4-y-o and up) £2,136 2m 5f..........(2:20)

3253² KNOCKAVERRY (Ire) 6-11-5 (7*) P Ward, *hdwy 7th, led 2*
    out, ran on wl.....(2 to 1 jt-fav op 6 to 4 tchd 9 to 4)   1
3380⁶ STRONG CASE (Ire) (bl) 6-11-11 R Dunwoody, *hdwy 5th, ev*
    ch 2 out, hrd rdn, not quicken...........(7 to 1 op 5 to 1
    *   fav* tchd 9 to 1 and 7 to 1)   2
2817* THERMAL WARRIOR 6-11-11 T Grantham, *hdwy 7th, rdn*
    appr 2 out, ran on frm last.........(3 to 1 op 2 to 1)   3
3196⁶ SO AUDACIOUS 6-11-5 R Supple, *wth ldr, led appr 2 out,*
    sn hdd, one pace...(20 to 1 tchd 25 to 1 and 33 to 1)   4
3221⁶ NORTH HOLLOW 9-11-0 (5*) Mr D McCain, *styd on frm 2*
    out, not trble ldrs...................(50 to 1 op 33 to 1)   5
3497 MARINERS MEMORY 6-11-5 W Humphreys, *nrst finish.*
    ....(50 to 1)   6
3497 LITTLE CLARE 7-11-0 B Clifford, *outpcd 8th, styd on frm 3*
    out..............................(50 to 1)   7
2795 ABSOLUTELYMUSTARD (Ire) 5-11-5 M Richards, *prmnt till*
    wknd 3 out.....................(33 to 1 op 50 to 1)   8
3211⁸ DALEHOUSE LANE 6-11-2 (3*) D Meredith, *beh frm 8th.*
    ....(50 to 1)   9
3252³ EL GRANDO 4-10-12 A Charlton, *led second to 6th, led 8th*
    till wknd quickly appr 2 out.......(33 to 1 op 50 to 1) 10
1718⁵ IVYCHURCH (USA) 8-10-12 (7*) Karen Cook, *jnd ldr sec-*
    ond, wknd quickly 5th.
    ....(20 to 1 op 50 to 1 tchd 16 to 1) 11
    LION ROCK (Ire) 6-11-5 J Osborne, *led to second, led 6th*
    to 8th, ev ch 3 out, wknd rpdly....(16 to 1 op 10 to 1) 12
Dist: 4l, nk, ½l, 20l, 4l, 4l, 13l, 1¼l, 5l, 8l. 5m 37.00s. a 38.00s (12 Ran).
                 (Mrs W Morrell), M J Wilkinson

3510 Elm Novices' Chase (5-y-o and up) £2,810 2¾m.................... (2:50)

3361³ MONKSANDER 8-11-2 Richard Guest, *hdwy 11th, hmpd aftr 2 out, hit last, ran on to ld cl hme.*
....(16 to 1 op 20 to 1) 1
1197 TITUS ANDRONICUS (bl) 7-11-8 R Supple, *strted slwly, hdwy 6th, led appr last till cl hme...* (8 to 1 op 7 to 1) 2
3116³ SQUEEZE PLAY (bl) 9-11-2 Peter Hobbs, *hdwy 11th, ev ch appr last, not quicken...*(9 to 2 op 7 to 2 tchd 5 to 1) 3
1563⁶ LOOSE WHEELS (v) 8-11-2 R Marley, *led to 3rd, led 4th till edgd lft and wknd appr last.*
..................................(9 to 1 op 10 to 1 tchd 12 to 1 and 8 to 1) 4
3097⁴ YOUNG BRAVE 8-11-2 S Earle, *hdwy tenth, prmnt whn mstk 4 out, wknd nxt...................*(7 to 1 op 5 to 1) 5
3343 DARK OAK 8-11-2 L O'Hara, *prmnt till wknd 4 out.*
.....................................(11 to 2 op 4 to 1 tchd 6 to 1) 6
3309 PARSON'S WAY (bl) 7-11-2 L Harvey, *prmnt till hrd rdn and wknd 12th...............................*(33 to 1) 7
3163² APRIL CITY 5-10-3 M Ranger, *prmnt to 9th......* (33 to 1) 8
3154 VISION OF WONDER 10-11-2 J R Kavanagh, *wl beh frm tenth..........................*(20 to 1 tchd 33 to 1) 9
3454 PECHE D'OR 10-11-2 Mr G Brown, *sn wl beh, hrd rdn 5th, tld off..*(33 to 1) 10
3445 FOXY BLUE 9-11-2 S McNeill, *wl beh frm tenth, tld off.*
....(14 to 1 op 10 to 1) 11
3207 FRENCHLANDS WAY 10-11-2 B Powell, *tld off whn pld up bef 8th...* pu
3097 INDIAN JEWEL 10-11-2 J Railton, *led 3rd to 4th, wknd 11th, tld off whn pld up bef 2 out...............*(33 to 1) pu
3454² EIGHTY EIGHT 9-11-2 W Marston, *mstks, tld off whn blun and pld up 8th............................*(33 to 1) pu
2872 LOCAL MANOR 7-11-2 J Osborne, *prmnt till wknd quickly 11th, pld up bef nxt.*
.....................(100 to 30 fav op 5 to 2 tchd 4 to 1) pu
Dist: Nk, 1l, 14l, 13l, 5l, 9l, 3½l, 11l, 20l, 13l. 5m 59.90s. a 33.90s (15 Ran).

(John Pearl), P C Ritchens

3511 Beech Selling Hurdle (4-y-o and up) £2,059 2m.................... (3:20)

3416* BAYRAK (USA) 4-11-1 J Osborne, *al prmnt, led on bit 2 out, ran on..........................*(4 to 1 jt-fav tchd 5 to 1) 1
HAWTHORNE GLEN 7-11-0 D Gallagher, *led second to 2 out.....................................*(20 to 1 op 14 to 1) 2
2233⁸ ASHBORO (Ire) 5-11-7 D Murphy, *al prmnt, ev ch appr 2 out, ran on one pace.......................*(14 to 1 op 7 to 1) 3
3317* EASTERN PLEASURE (bl) 7-11-7 Diane Clay, *hdwy 4th, ran on frm last, nvr nvr................*(8 to 1 op 5 to 1) 4
3317⁵ ROYAL STANDARD 7-11-7 P McDermott, *led to second, styd prmnt, one pace frm 2 out...*(25 to 1 op 33 to 1) 5
3622² TOOMUCH TOOSOON (Ire) 6-10-9 (5*) S Curran, *nrst finish.............................*(14 to 1 op 12 to 1) 6
3103* SHARP DANCE 5-11-2 B Powell, *hdwy 5th, nvr nr to chal.*
.....................................(4 to 1 jt-fav op 5 to 1 tchd 7 to 1) 7
2891⁷ MASON DIXON 5-11-0 M Dwyer, *hdwy 5th, not rch ldrs.*
....(14 to 1 op 12 to 1) 8
3003⁷ GAELGIOR 10-11-7 W Humphreys, *nvr trbld ldrs.* (33 to 1) 9
3298⁸ ONE TO NOTE (bl) 10-11-0 M Ahern, *no hdwy frm 3 out.*
....(20 to 1 op 16 to 1) 10
2729⁹ ARMASHOCKER 6-11-7 V Smith, *nvr on terms.*
.....................................(7 to 1 op 10 to 1 tchd 6 to 1) 11
1812 FUSSY LADY 7-11-2 L Harvey, *prmnt till wknd 3 out.*
.....................................(20 to 1 op 14 to 1) 12
3334⁷ FOND KISS 9-10-9 W McFarland, *outpcd.*
....(20 to 1 op 25 to 1) 13
2729 BAYBEEJAY 7-11-2 D Bridgwater, *prmnt to 4th.*
....(33 to 1 op 20 to 1) 14
1668⁸ DHARAMSHALA (Ire) 6-11-0 M Brennan, *tld off.*
.....................................(12 to 1 op 14 to 1) 15
2439 GILT DIMENSION 7-11-0 R Supple, *tld off.*
....(12 to 1 tchd 14 to 1) 16
3252 BEE BEAR 6-10-7 (7*) M Appleby, *very slwly away, tld off till tried to refuse and uns rdr 4th.* (16 to 1 op 10 to 1) ur
3098 PARISIAN 9-10-7 (7*) A Lucas, *tld off whn pld up bef 2 out.
....(33 to 1) pu
3330 COXANN 8-11-7 (7*) E Tolhurst, *tld off frm 3rd, pld up bef 2 out........................*(20 to 1 op 10 to 1) pu
3222⁴ OAK PARK (Ire) 6-11-7 (7*) R Massey, *pld up bef 5th, destroyed..................................*(14 to 1) pu
Dist: 2l, 5l, sht-hd, 4l, 2l, 4l, sht-hd, sht-hd, 9l, 3l. 4m 6.60s. a 17.60s (20 Ran).

SR: 23/20/22/22/11/9/7/5/1/2/   (Elite Racing Club), C R Egerton

3512 Maple Handicap Chase (0-120 5-y-o and up) £3,663 3m 1f.......... (3:50)

3077* VIVA BELLA (Fr) [108] (bl) 7-11-2 (5*) J Burke, *al prmnt, rdn 3 out, styd on to ld last 100 yards....* (9 to 2 op 3 to 1) 1
1326⁴ LAUDERDALE LAD [90] 12-10-3 J R Kavanagh, *led, clr 2 out, hdd fnl 100 yards.*
....(9 to 1 op 16 to 1 tchd 20 to 1) 2
3310* INVASION [104] (v) 10-11-3 M Brennan, *beh, rdn 9th, blun 4 out, gd hdwy frm 3 out, swrvd rght aftr last, ran on.*
....(9 to 2 op 4 to 1 tchd 5 to 1) 3

3168³ SUNBEAM TALBOT [96] 13-10-9 M A FitzGerald, *hdwy tenth, ev ch appr last, one pace.*
.....................................(12 to 1 op 10 to 1 tchd 14 to 1) 4
3443 INCONCLUSIVE [87] 7-9-9 (5*) Mr D Parker, *hdwy 12th, mstk 4 out, one pace frm nxt...................*(33 to 1) 5
3332³ EBONY SWELL [96] 13-10-7³ (5*) P Midgley, *hdwy 11th, ev ch 3 out, wknd appr last.............*(25 to 1 op 16 to 1) 6
2758⁴ SIDE OF HILL [112] 9-11-11 R Dunwoody, *wth ldr, reminders 7th, ev ch 3 out, wknd nxt.* (8 to 1 op 7 to 1) 7
2758 BIT OF A CLOWN [115] 11-12-0 L Harvey, *nvr gng wl, hrd rdn tenth, no further hdwy.......*(16 to 1 op 10 to 1) 8
2429⁷ DANDY MINSTREL [101] 10-11-0 D Bridgwater, *rdn most of way, several poss, beh frm 14th....*(8 to 1 op 10 to 1) 9
3168 CLONROCHE GAZETTE [87] 14-10-0 Miss S Wallin, *tld off frm tenth, pld up bef 4 out.*
.....................................(50 to 1 op 33 to 1 tchd 66 to 1) pu
2328⁴ ROSCOE HARVEY [100] 12-10-6 (7*) M Berry, *prmnt till badly bumped and lost pl tenth, beh whn pld up bef 4 out................................*(20 to 1 tchd 25 to 1) pu
3168 RED AMBER [91] (v) 8-10-4 J Osborne, *tld off whn pld up bef 4 out.........................*(14 to 1 op 10 to 1) pu
3224 FLORIDA SKY [96] 7-10-9 R Supple, *hdwy 8th, wknd 13th, beh whn pld up bef 2 out.......*(3 to 1 fav tchd 7 to 2) pu
Dist: ½l, hd, 1¾l, 6l, 1¼l, 2½l, 7l, 5l. 6m 53.80s. a 38.80s (13 Ran).

(L H Froomes), Mrs S A Bramall

3513 Ash Handicap Chase (0-120 5-y-o and up) £3,042 2m 110yds.......... (4:20)

3312* SARTORIUS [107] 8-11-5 G McCourt, *jnd ldr 5th, led 3 out, sn clr.........................*(5 to 2 fav op 9 to 4) 1
3303⁵ KIBREET [106] 7-11-4 S Earle, *al prmnt, hrd rdn 2 out, no imprsn............................*(9 to 1 op 8 to 1) 2
3301* AL HASHIMI [116] 10-12-0 R Dunwoody, *led to 3 out, ran on one pace..........................*(11 to 2 op 5 to 1) 3
3255² SOCIAL CLIMBER [95] 10-10-7 S McNeill, *prmnt till out-pcd 6th, no ch aftr......*(3 to 1 op 7 to 2 tchd 4 to 1) 4
3400 MEDINAS SWAN SONG [91] 6-10-3³ A Tory, *no hdwy frm 4 out..*(25 to 1 op 20 to 1) 5
3492⁷ CRUISING ON [88] 7-10-0 W Marston, *al beh.*
....(33 to 1 op 25 to 1) 6
3312² BOSTON ROVER [115] 9-11-13 M Brennan, *hld up, blun 5th, hdwy 7th, ev ch 3 out, 4th and wkng whn blunded 2 out..*(7 to 2 op 3 to 1) 7
3312 BLUE BUCCANEER [89] 11-10-1 L Harvey, *wl beh frm 8th, tld off whn pld up bef 2 out......* (16 to 1 op 14 to 1) pu
2729 CEDAR RUN [90] 11-10-2² Mr A Charles-Jones, *mstks, sn tld off, blun badly and pld up 2 out...........*(33 to 1) pu
Dist: 6l, 6l, 3½l, 2½l, 12l, 9l. 4m 21.50s. a 19.50s (9 Ran).

SR: 45/38/42/17/10/-/-/-/   (M Popham), T Thomson Jones

3514 Oak Handicap Hurdle (0-115 4-y-o and up) £2,897 2m 5f.......... (4:50)

3398⁹ CAMBO (USA) [85] 8-10-4 M Richards, *al prmnt, led appr 2 out, all out..........*(10 to 1 tchd 8 to 1 and 12 to 1) 1
3166⁴ PRINCE OF SALERNO [85] 7-10-4 R Supple, *hdwy 8th, ev ch appr last, ran on wl nr finish.* (10 to 1 op 12 to 1) 2
3254² BLUE FLAW [97] 7-11-2 S McNeill, *al prmnt, led 7th to 8th, ev ch appr 2 out, not quicken..........*(16 to 1) 3
1474 CAVO GRECO (USA) [85] 5-10-4 D Skyrme, *hdwy 5th, jnd wnr and mstk 2 out, btn whn mistake last.*
.....................................(33 to 1 op 25 to 1) 4
2777 CHIAROSCURO [84] 8-10-3 R Bellamy, *nrst finish.*
....(33 to 1 op 25 to 1) 5
3196 OTTOMAN EMPIRE [94] 7-10-13 M Brennan, *beh whn hmpd aftr 6th, rapid hdwy to ld 8th, hdd and wknd appr 2 out........*(11 to 1 op 8 to 1 tchd 12 to 1) 6
2674⁵ BRIGHTLING BOY [94] (bl) 9-10-13 Peter Hobbs, *prmnt till wknd appr 2 out.......................*(8 to 1 op 10 to 1) 7
3308² AUGUST TWELFTH [85] 6-10-4 Mr Raymond White, *hdwy 7th, ev ch 3 out, sn wknd........*(12 to 1 op 10 to 1) 8
3186 CAPPUCCINO GIRL [90] 7-10-9 M Crosse, *hdwy 8th, wknd appr 2 out.................*(33 to 1 op 20 to 1) 9
3097 UNDERWYCHWOOD (Ire) [87] 6-9-13 (7*) Mr J O'Shaughnessy, *nvr trbld ldrs.....................*(33 to 1) 10
3344³ INTEGRITY BOY [88] (bl) 7-10-7 M Dwyer, *prmnt till wknd 3 out........*(10 to 1 tchd 8 to 1 and 9 to 1) 11
3363⁶ BEE DEE BOY [81] 6-9-9 (5*) D Fortt, *beh whn 8th.* (33 to 1) 12
3418⁴ LEESWOOD [90] 6-10-9 W McFarland, *mstk 8th, al beh..*(16 to 1) 13
3362* LASSIE (Fr) [90] 5-10-6 (3*) R Davis, *wl beh frm 8th.*
.....................................(12 to 1 op 10 to 1) 14
2936* MAKES ME GOOSEY (Ire) [90] 6-10-9 L Harvey, *wl beh frm 7th...*(10 to 1 op 7 to 1) 15
3311⁴ BANKONIT (Ire) [89] (bl) 6-10-8 E Byrne, *led till wknd quickly 7th..............................*(20 to 1 op 25 to 1) 16
3330⁵ STRAIGHT LACED (USA) [88] (bl) 7-10-7 I Lawrence, *wl beh frm 7th...................*(25 to 1 op 20 to 1 tchd 33 to 1) 17
3186 MR TAYLOR [86] 9-10-5 V Smith, *wl beh frm 8th.*
.....................................(10 to 1 op 7 to 1 tchd 12 to 1) 18
3363² SALMON PRINCE [85] 8-9-13 (5*) S Curran, *prmnt till mstk and pld up 6th................*(7 to 2 fav op 4 to 1) pu
Dist: Hd, 6l, nk, 7l, 8l, 2½l, 4l, sht-hd, 4l, hd. 5m 29.60s. a 30.60s (19 Ran).

(M C Banks), M C Banks

3515 Chestnut Novices' Hurdle (Div II) (4-y-o and up) £2,136 2m 5f........(5:20)

3167[6] ARTIC WINGS (Ire) 6-11-6 M Brennan, *steady hdwy 7th, led 2 out, edgd rght appr last, drvn out.* ....(6 to 4 on op 7 to 4) 1
3278[8] OUTFIELD 8-11-6 G McCourt, *hld up, led appr 3 out, edgd lft and hdd 2 out, ran on frm last*...(8 to 1 op 10 to 1) 2
2768 PENLEA LADY 7-10-7 (7*) P McLoughlin, *al prmnt, ran on one pace frm 3 out*................ (25 to 1 op 33 to 1) 3
2558[6] LAY IT OFF (Ire) 5-11-0 N Williamson, *no hdwy frm 3 out.* ....(10 to 1 op 5 to 1) 4
3215 GRUNGE (Ire) 6-11-5 D Gallagher, *led 3rd to 4th, led 6th till appr 3 out, sn wknd*..............(12 to 1 op 6 to 1) 5
3046[5] NIGHT FANCY 6-11-2 (3*) J McCarthy, *ev ch 7th, wknd appr 3 out*....................... (20 to 1 op 16 to 1) 6
3277[5] DUNLIR 4-10-5 (7*) T Thompson, *beh frm 7th*.....(33 to 1) 7
2934 FINALLY FANTAZIA 5-11-0 L Harvey, *hdwy 6th, wknd 8th.* ....(33 to 1 op 20 to 1) 8
3497[7] YOUNG MOSS 8-11-0 (5*) S Curran, *led 4th to 6th, wknd 8th*..(33 to 1) 9
3380 ME FEIN (Ire) 6-11-5 E Murphy, *led to 3rd, lost pl quickly aftr 5th, tld off whn pld up bef 7th*...(4 to 1 op 5 to 4) pu
3451 COLONEL CLOETE 6-11-5 B Powell, *tld off frm 6th, pld up bef 2 out*......................... (20 to 1 op 10 to 1) pu
WELTON RAMBLER 7-11-0 R Supple, *tld off whn pld up bef 2 out*.......................................(33 to 1) pu

Dist: 1½l, 20l, 7l, 6l, 9l, 5l, 5l, 6l. 5m 35.70s. a 36.70s (12 Ran).
(Lady Anne Bentinck), O Brennan

CHELTENHAM (good to firm) Wednesday April 20th

Going Correction: NIL (races 1,3,5,7,8), PLUS 0.10 (2,4,6)

3516 Cheltenham Sponsorship Club Handicap Hurdle (0-140 4-y-o and up) £5,108 2m 1f...................(1:50)

3068[6] ARCOT [127] (v) 6-11-5 G McCourt, *steady hdwy 3 out, jnd ldr on bit appr last, led flt, drvn out.* ....(13 to 2 op 5 to 1) 1
3131[5] CASTLE SECRET [112] 8-10-4 D J Burchell, *hdwy 3 out, led appr last till flt, ran on.* ....(7 to 2 fav tchd 3 to 1 and 4 to 1) 2
3436[2] WHO'S TEF (Ire) [116] 6-10-8 L Wyer, *beh till hdwy appr 2 out, hrd rdn approaching last, one pace.* ....(5 to 1 tchd 6 to 1) 3
3311* STRATH ROYAL [127] 8-11-5 M Brennan, *hdwy 3 out, hrd rdn 2 out, one pace*...............(7 to 1 op 6 to 1) 4
3068[4] NAHAR [132] 9-11-10 A Dicken, *led 3rd, lft wl clr 5th, hdd and wknd appr last*................(9 to 1 op 7 to 1) 5
1803[3] STAR OF THE GLEN [120] 8-10-12 R Dunwoody, *al wl beh, tld off*..........................(20 to 1 tchd 25 to 1) 6
3365* KEEP ME IN MIND (Ire) [111] 5-10-3 D Skyrme, *hdwy 5th, wknd appr 2 out, tld off.* ....(11 to 2 op 5 to 1 tchd 4 to 1) 7
3455[3] IVEAGH HOUSE [113] 8-10-5 A Maguire, *hdwy 5th, ev ch aftr 2 out, 4th and btn whn f last.* (8 to 1 tchd 9 to 1) f
3068 ARABIAN BOLD (Ire) [130] 6-11-8 M A FitzGerald, *led to 3rd, cl second whn f 5th*..........................(10 to 1) f

Dist: 1½l, 6l, 5l, 4l, dist, 20l. 3m 57.30s. a 2.80s (9 Ran).
SR: 63/46/44/50/51/-/ (Pell-Mell Partners), J A Glover

3517 S. W. Shower Supplies Novices' Chase (5-y-o and up) £5,061 2m 5f ....(2:25)

3382[2] BOSCEAN CHIEFTAIN 10-11-7 R Dunwoody, *led to hit 8th, led 11th, hrd rdn appr 2 out, ran on wl.* ....(15 to 8 op 11 to 4) 1
3411[2] CRYSTAL SPIRIT 7-11-10 J Frost, *al prmnt, wnt second 4 out, mstk 3 out, ev ch last, hrd rdn, ran on.* ....(13 to 8 fav op 11 to 8 tchd 7 to 4) 2
3443 ANDERMATT 7-11-3 J Osborne, *hdwy 12th, styd on frm 3 out, one pace flt*..... (12 to 1 op 10 to 1 tchd 14 to 1) 3
1537[5] SQUIRE JIM 10-11-10 D Bridgwater, *prmnt till blun 11th, styd on frm 2 out*.....(16 to 1 op 14 to 1 tchd 20 to 1) 4
3232[4] PAPER STAR 7-10-12 B Powell, *beh frm 8th.* ....(100 to 1 op 25 to 1) 5
3110* NICKLE JOE 8-11-7 W Marston, *in tch to 12th.* ....(12 to 1 op 7 to 1 tchd 14 to 1) 6
3338[4] LAND OF THE FREE 5-10-5 V Slattery, *blun tenth, al beh.* ....(100 to 1 op 33 to 1) 7
3381* COULDNT BE BETTER 7-11-10 G Bradley, *led 8th to 11th, wknd 3 out, virtually pld up aftr last.* ....(10 to 1 op 7 to 1) 8
3411[3] MELEAGRIS 10-11-7 A Maguire, *reared up and swrvd rght strt, hdwy 7th, 4th whn blun and uns rdr 12th.* ....(9 to 1 op 7 to 1 tchd 11 to 1) ur

Dist: Sht-hd, 8l, 15l, 2½l, 1l, 15l. 5m 10.60s. a 6.60s (9 Ran).
SR: 48/51/36/28/13/21/ (Miss Christine Olds), Mrs J G Retter

3518 EBF 'National Hunt' Novices' Hurdle Final Handicap Grade 3 (5,6,7-y-o) £17,125 2½m.................. (3:00)

3230[2] GOSPEL (Ire) [110] 5-11-3 D Bridgwater, *al prmnt, led appr 2 out, sn wl clr, easily*.........(7 to 1 co-fav op 7 to 1) 1
3233* SENIOR STEWARD [95] 6-10-2 R Dunwoody, *hmpd appr second, hdwy 7th, styd on frm 2 out, no ch wth wnr.* ....(8 to 1 op 7 to 1) 2
3233[3] MR JERVIS (Ire) [93] 5-10-0[3] (3*) P Hide, *gd hdwy frm 2 out, nvr nrr*..(16 to 1) 3
3396[4] TOTHEWOODS [118] 6-11-8 (3*) T Jenks, *gd hdwy 7th, hrd rdn and styd on frm 2 out.* ....(11 to 1 op 10 to 1 tchd 12 to 1) 4
3164[4] DEVIL'S CORNER [93] 6-10-0 B Powell, *wl beh till gd late hdwy*.. (50 to 1) 5
3409[5] KONVEKTA KING (Ire) [108] 6-11-1 A Maguire, *hdwy 3 out, rdn and no extr frm 2 out*..... (7 to 1 co-fav op 8 to 1) 6
3333* WORDY'S WONDER [93] 6-9-11 (3*) R Farrant, *hdwy 6th, ev ch 3 out, wknd last*...................... (20 to 1) 7
3345* KYTTON CASTLE [113] 7-11-3 (3*) D Meredith, *prmnt to 3 out*..(10 to 1) 8
3023[7] RELUCTANT SUITOR [119] 5-11-9 (3*) D Bentley, *chsd ldrs, rdn and wknd 7th*.................(9 to 1 op 10 to 1) 9
3380[3] SPIRIT IN THE NITE (Ire) [111] 5-11-4 D Murphy, *lft in ld aftr 1st, hdd 3rd, led 6th till wknd appr 2 out*...... (14 to 1) 10
3215[2] MAD THYME [110] (bl) 7-11-3 J Frost, *pld hrd, led 3rd to 6th, sn wknd, tld off*............. (10 to 1 op 12 to 1) 11
3137[3] THE FROG PRINCE (Ire) [98] 6-10-5 M Perrett, *hdwy 7th, ev ch 3 out, wknd 2 out, tld off*...(7 to 1 co-fav op 6 to 1) 12
3380 QUARRY HOUSE (Ire) [107] 6-11-0 J Railton, *hmpd appr second, al beh, tld off frm 8th*.................(33 to 1) 13
3374[5] NORTHERN SQUIRE [99] 6-10-6 L Wyer, *prmnt to 7th, tld off*...........................(20 to 1 op 16 to 1) 14
3365[3] CHEMIN LE ROI [93] 7-10-0 I Lawrence, *hdwy 6th, ev ch appr 2 out, sn wknd, tld off*......(20 to 1 tchd 25 to 1) 15
3359* STRONG FLAME (Ire) [96] 5-9-13[1] (5*) S Lyons, *led till jinked rght and uns rdr bend aftr 1st.* ....(12 to 1 tchd 14 to 1) ur

Dist: 6l, 2½l, ½l, 1¾l, 2l, ½l, 2½l, 1¼l, nk, 15l. 4m 45.00s. (16 Ran).
(Mrs J K Powell), N A Twiston-Davies

3519 Golden Miller Handicap Chase (5-y-o and up) £8,559 3¼m 110yds.....(3:35)

3407* GRANGE BRAKE [127] 8-10-13 D Bridgwater, *al prmnt, rdn 18th, led 3 out, all out*............... (4 to 1 op 7 to 2) 1
3261* BUCK WILLOW [119] 10-10-5 D Murphy, *steady hdwy 13th, mstk and lost pl 3 out, rallied and ev ch last, not quicken*..........(5 to 2 fav op 100 to 30 tchd 7 to 2) 2
3027[4] WINDY WAYS [125] 9-10-11 M A FitzGerald, *hdwy 12th, mstk 17th, ev ch last, not quicken.* (7 to 1 tchd 15 to 2) 3
3358[6] SIKERA SPY [116] 12-10-2 R Bellamy, *led to 6th, led 11th to 3 out, ran on one pace.* (8 to 1 tchd 7 to 1 and 9 to 1) 4
3405[9] TRI FOLENE (Fr) [122] (bl) 8-10-8 R Dunwoody, *middle div whn blun and lost pl 15th, styd on frm 2 out.* ....(8 to 1 op 6 to 1) 5
3027 FAR SENIOR [138] 8-11-10 Mr M Armytage, *prmnt till wknd 3 out*........... (11 to 1 op 8 to 1 tchd 12 to 1) 6
3425 MIGHTY FALCON [115] (bl) 9-10-1[1] P Holley, *mstks, hdwy 15th, wknd 18th, tld off*........... (20 to 1 op 12 to 1) 7
1459 VIRIDIAN [114] (bl) 9-10-0 R Supple, *led 6th to 11th, mstk and wknd 15th, tld off.* ....(40 to 1 op 20 to 1 tchd 50 to 1) 8
1963 GALA'S IMAGE [116] 14-10-2[9] (7*) Mr M Rimell, *beh whn f 17th*............................ (50 to 1 op 20 to 1) f
3425 HENRY MANN [128] (bl) 11-11-0 J Osborne, *in rear whn jmpd slwly 3rd, pld up bef 4th.* ....(14 to 1 op 7 to 1 tchd 16 to 1) pu
3417[8] CATCHAPENNY [114] (bl) 9-10-0 S Earle, *mstks, prmnt to 8th, hrd rdn and beh tenth, tld off whn pld up bef 15th.* ....(20 to 1 op 12 to 1) pu

Dist: 2½l, 1¼l, 1¼l, 8l, 4l, 20l, dist. 6m 38.30s. a 5.30s (11 Ran).
SR: 59/48/52/41/39/51/8/-/-/ (Mrs J Mould), N A Twiston-Davies

3520 S. W. Shower Supplies Handicap Hurdle (5-y-o and up) £5,186 3m 110yds ....(4:10)

3283[3] VICTOR BRAVO (NZ) [108] 7-10-0 J Osborne, *al prmnt, led jst aftr last, ran on wl*............... (7 to 2 op 4 to 1) 1
3408[6] LEMON'S MILL (USA) [130] 5-11-8 R Dunwoody, *al prmnt, led 2 out till aftr last, ran on.* ....(7 to 2 op 5 to 2 tchd 4 to 1) 2
3384[8] SEA BUCK [109] 8-10-0[2] (3*) R Davis, *beh, rdn 6th, styd on frm 2 out*..............(10 to 1 op 6 to 1 tchd 12 to 1) 3
3251 FAR TOO LOUD [108] 7-9-11[2] (5*) S Fox, *lost pl 7th, styd on frm 2 out*.......................... (14 to 1 op 12 to 1) 4
3186[9] SYLVIA BEACH [108] 8-9-7 (7*) D Bohan, *hdwy 9th, ev ch 2 out, sn rdn and wknd.* ....(16 to 1 op 10 to 1 tchd 20 to 1) 5
2710 LEGAL BEAGLE [108] (h) 7-10-0 M Perrett, *mstk 5th, beh frm 9th, tld off*..................... (20 to 1 op 10 to 1) 6
3384 DARA DOONE [133] 8-11-8 (3*) T Jenks, *rdn 8th, mstk 3 out, sn wknd, tld off*... (9 to 1 op 6 to 1 tchd 10 to 1) 7

3283⁶ SIR CRUSTY [108] (bl) 12-10-0 N Mann, *hdwy 7th, wknd 9th, tld off*..............................(20 to 1 op 14 to 1)   8
3408³ SAYFAR'S LAD [117] 10-10-8 D Bridgwater, *led, mstk 5th, hdd 2 out, 3rd and btn whn pld up bef last.*
.................................(9 to 4 fav op 5 to 2 tchd 11 to 4)   pu
1845⁶ CASH IS KING [120] (bl) 10-10-12 J R Kavanagh, *tld off 4th, mstk 5th, pld up bef 6th.*............(14 to 1 op 8 to 1)   pu
Dist: 1¾l, 20l, 4l, 1l, 25l, 10l, 7l. 5m 43.00s. a 3.00s (10 Ran).
SR: 42/62/21/16/15/-/5/-/-/   (Mrs R W S Baker), N A Gaselee

3521 Cooper Clegg Anniversary Hunters' Chase (5-y-o and up) £2,866 3¼m (4:45)

3385* SHEER JEST 9-12-3 (3*) Mr A Hill, *pld hrd, steady hdwy 14th, led 2 out, cmftbly.*......(5 to 4 on op 11 to 8 on)   1
3216* SYNDERBOROUGH LAD 8-12-1 (5*) Mr M Felton, *hdwy 14th, mstk 15th, led 3 out to 2 out, no ch wth wnr.*
....(7 to 2 op 9 to 2)   2
3480* CARRICKMINES 9-12-1 (5*) Mr T Jones, *led 4th to 9th, ev ch 3 out, ran on frm last.*.........(20 to 1 op 14 to 1)   3
BLUE DANUBE (USA) 10-11-7 (7*) Mr Andrew Martin, *led to second, mstk 6th, mistake and lost pl 18th, hdwy and ev ch 3 out, wknd 2 out.*
....................................(25 to 1 op 20 to 1 tchd 33 to 1)   4
3265* RICHARD HUNT 10-11-13 (7*) Miss L Rowe, *mstks, hdwy 15th, ev ch 3 out, wknd 2 out.*
..........................(6 to 1 op 5 to 1 tchd 13 to 2)   5
CELTIC LEISURE 10-12-0⁵ (5*) Mr T Mitchell, *sn prmnt, jnd ldr 18th, ev ch whn mstk 3 out, soon wknd.*
...........(10 to 1 op 8 to 1 tchd 11 to 1 and 12 to 1)   6
MATSIX 13-11-7 (7*) Mr K Cousins, *led 9th to 3 out, wknd appr last.*..........................(50 to 1 op 25 to 1)   7
3021⁴ ARTFUL ARTHUR 8-11-7 (7*) Mr J Grassick, *beh frm 12th.*
....(100 to 1 op 8 to 1)   8
HIGHLAND SON 13-11-7 (7*) Mr T Cox, *led to 4th, wknd 13th, tld off.*..................(100 to 1 op 25 to 1)   9
2898² JOLLY ROGER 7-11-7 (7*) Mr Michael J Jones, *prmnt till wknd appr 3 out, pld up bef 2 out.*
..........................(33 to 1 op 16 to 1 tchd 50 to 1)   pu
Dist: 6l, nk, 6l, 3l, 12l, 8l, 3l, 30l. 6m 56.40s. a 23.40s (10 Ran).
                              (Mrs Judy Wilson), W J Warner

3522 Rowanside National Hunt Flat Race (Div I) (4,5,6-y-o) £2,153 2m 1f... (5:15)

VITAMAN (Ire) 5-10-13 (7*) L O'Hare, *hdwy 6 fs out, led 2 furlongs out, ran on wl.*
...........................(14 to 1 op 10 to 1 tchd 16 to 1)   1
LEGENDRA 4-10-4 (5*) D Matthews, *hdwy 3 fs out, hrd rdn o'r one out, ran on ins last.*
..................................(16 to 1 op 7 to 1 tchd 20 to 1)   2
DISTANT ECHO (Ire) 4-11-0 Mr M Armytage, *al prmnt, led 4 fs out till 2 out, ran on.*..........(14 to 1 op 12 to 1)   3
1626 CAPO CASTANUM 5-11-3 (3*) A Procter, *al prmnt, ran on one pace fnl 2 fs.*.....................(20 to 1 op 12 to 1)   4
WESTCOTE LAD 5-10-13 (7*) Mr S Joynes, *al prmnt, ev ch 3 fs out, one pace.*..(16 to 1 op 12 to 1 tchd 20 to 1)   5
B MY LOVELY 4-10-2 (7*) P Maddock, *nrst finish.*
....(33 to 1 op 16 to 1)   6
3387⁶ CERTAIN ANGLE 5-11-6 (7*) P Ward, *al prmnt, no hdwy fnl 2 fs.*.................(8 to 1 op 6 to 1 tchd 5 to 1)   7
SENOR EL BETRUTTI (Ire) 5-10-13 (7*) M Berry, *strtd slwly, wl beh till gd hdwy 3 fs out, wknd o'r one out.*
..................................(20 to 1 op 10 to 1)   8
RELATIVE CHANCE 5-10-13 (7*) Mr G Hogan, *hdwy 3 fs out, nvr nr to chal...* (16 to 1 op 14 to 1 tchd 33 to 1)   9
3387³ BUCKHOUSE BOY 4-10-11 (3*) T Jenks, *prmnt till wknd 2 out.*..............(7 to 2 op 3 to 1 tchd 4 to 1)   10
LIXWM 5-10-8 (7*) Pat Thompson, *chsd ldrs, grad wknd fnl 3 fs.*.........................(16 to 1 op 6 to 1)   11
NUPDOWN EXPRESS (Ire) 4-11-0 Mr J Durkan, *chsd ldrs till wknd 4 fs out.*........(7 to 1 op 10 to 1 tchd 12 to 1)   12
ZAMBEZI SPIRIT (Ire) 5-11-3 (3*) D Meredith, *nvr trbld ldrs.*
....(33 to 1 op 20 to 1)   13
3208 LYRICAL SEAL 4-10-4 (5*) D Fortt, *hdwy 6 fs out, ev ch 3 out, sn wknd...*......................(25 to 1 op 14 to 1)   14
OH SO VITAL 5-11-3 (3*) P Hide, *hdwy 6 fs out, wknd 3 out, tld off...*..................(33 to 1 op 14 to 1)   15
STEEL GOLD 4-10-7 (7*) Richard Edwards, *led aftr 4 fs till four out, sn wknd, tld off...*........(9 to 1 op 8 to 1)   16
ARKANSAS 4-10-7 (7*) P McLoughlin, *prmnt one m, tld off.*
..................................(33 to 1 op 16 to 1)   17
3190 MY BOY BARNEY 4-10-9 (5*) C Burnett-Wells, *prmnt ten fs, tld off...*.............(33 to 1 op 20 to 1 tchd 50 to 1)   18
2877* THE BOUNDER 4-11-4 (3*) J McCarthy, *prmnt till wknd quickly 3 fs out, tld off.*
....................(9 to 4 fav op 6 to 4 tchd 11 to 4)   19
PEN-ALISA 4-10-2 (7*) T Thompson, *sn tld off.*
..................................(14 to 1 op 10 to 1 tchd 16 to 1)   20
WISBOROUGH GREEN (Ire) 4-10-9 A Dicken, *led 4 fs, wknd quickly 6 out, tld off...*........(33 to 1 op 20 to 1)   21
AIN ZARA (Ire) 5-10-8 (7*) Mr G Haine, *beh till hmpd and uns rdr 6 fs out.*............(33 to 1 op 14 to 1)   ur
Dist: ½l, 1¼l, 7l, 1l, 1½l, ¾l, 14l, 2½l, 2½l, 1½l. 3m 51.01s. (22 Ran).
             (Larkhall Nat Hlth/Cantassium Vitamins), Mrs J Pitman

3523 Rowanside National Hunt Flat Race (Div II) (4,5,6-y-o) £2,138 2m 1f. (5:45)

THE REPROBATE (Ire) 5-11-3 (3*) A Procter, *strtd slwly, hdwy 4 fs out, ran on to ld nr finish.*
....(20 to 1 op 10 to 1)   1
2749² SEXTON GREY (Ire) 5-11-3 (3*) P Hide, *al prmnt, led 4 fs out, sn clr, hrd rdn and hdd cl hme.*
..................................(3 to 1 tchd 4 to 1 and 5 to 2)   2
3386 TENBIT (Ire) 4-10-11 (3*) T Jenks, *hdwy aftr 6 fs, ev ch o'r 2 out, ran one pace....*....(9 to 1 op 8 to 1 tchd 10 to 1)   3
CLEVER REMARK 5-10-13 (7*) P McLoughlin, *al prmnt, ran on one pace fnl 2 fs.*.............(14 to 1 op 33 to 1)   4
2996* FALMOUTH BAY (Ire) 5-11-13 Mr J Durkan, *led aftr 4 fs till four out, wknd ins last.* (4 to 1 op 7 to 2 tchd 7 to 1)   5
TIRLEY LEADER 5-10-13 (7*) M Keighley, *al prmnt, ev ch 2 fs out, wknd fnl furlong...*...........(33 to 1)   6
MR BOBBIT (Ire) 4-10-7 (7*) M Berry, *hdwy 6 fs out, one pace fnl 2 furlongs...*........(20 to 1 tchd 25 to 1)   7
MISS DISKIN (Ire) 5-10-8 (7*) R Massey, *prmnt till wknd o'r 2 fs out.*............................(33 to 1)   8
ALFION (Ire) 5-11-1 (5*) C Burnett-Wells, *nrst finish.*
..................................(20 to 1 op 33 to 1)   9
CARNIVAL KID 4-10-7 (7*) M Moran, *nvr nr to chal.*
....(33 to 1)   10
3169* WHAT'S YOUR STORY (Ire) 5-11-7 Mr G Hogan, *prmnt one m, rallied 4 fs out, wknd o'r 2 out.*
....................................(10 to 1 op 5 to 1)   11
KALOORE 5-11-1 (5*) S Fox, *nvr nr ldrs.*
..................................(14 to 1 op 8 to 1)   12
MITTENWALD (Ire) 5-11-6 Mrs T Bailey, *whipped round strt, nvr on terms...*.........(20 to 1 op 14 to 1)   13
3208⁷ QUAKER WALTZ 4-10-4 (5*) D Matthews, *in tch till wknd 6 fs out...*..................................(33 to 1)   14
RISKY BID 4-10-6 (3*) J McCarthy, *prmnt till wknd 3 fs out.*........................(14 to 1 op 8 to 1)   15
COUNTRYMASTER 5-10-13 (7*) Pat Thompson, *nvr better than middle div...*........(14 to 1 op 7 to 1)   16
2877⁷ SHUIL POIPIN (Ire) 5-10-8 (7*) D Bohan, *prmnt till wknd 4 fs out...*..................(14 to 1 op 14 to 1)   17
SGT CHILDCRAFT 4-10-7 (7*) R Darke, *tld off...*..........(33 to 1)   18
DIXTON HILL 6-11-3 (3*) D Meredith, *hdwy aftr 6 fs, wknd quickly 2 out, tld off...*..................(33 to 1)   19
2996 EMBLEY QUAY 5-11-1 (5*) S Curran, *strtd slwly, al beh, tld off...*......................................(33 to 1)   20
LADY LIR 5-11-1 Miss S Young, *led 4 fs, wknd one m out, tld off...*..................................(33 to 1)   21
3256⁶ PADDITATE (Ire) 5-10-13 (7*) T Thompson, *tld off.* (33 to 1)   22
MUTUAL MEMORIES 4-10-13 (7*) Mr J O'Shaughnessy, *prmnt ten fs, tld off...*(12 to 1 op 8 to 1 tchd 14 to 1)   23
SAFFRON MOSS 4-11-0 Mr P Williams, *tld off fnl m.*
....(33 to 1)   24
OAKLANDS POPEYE (e/s) 5-10-13 (7*) R Williamson, *strtd slwly, tld off fnl m, virtually pld up...*...........(20 to 1)   25
Dist: ¾l, 3½l, 1½l, ½l, 7l, 1¾l, 1l, ½l, sht-hd, 2l. 3m 56.80s. (25 Ran).
                              (C J Ells), C R Egerton

GOWRAN PARK (IRE) (heavy)
Wednesday April 20th

3524 Bagenalstown Handicap Chase (0-116 4-y-o and up) £2,760 3m. (3:00)

3392* WYLDE HIDE [-] 7-10-5 (4ex) F Woods,.........(7 to 2 fav)   1
2942* NEW CO (Ire) [-] 5-10-12 C O'Dwyer,..............(9 to 2)   2
2922* DEL MONTE BOY [-] 9-10-2 (7*) M D Murphy,.....(6 to 1)   3
3081⁷ THE REAL UNYOKE [-] (bl) 9-11-10 (3*) D P Murphy,
....(12 to 1)   4
3371⁶ FANE BANKS [-] (bl) 12-11-4 P Carberry,..........(20 to 1)   5
3200⁵ WRECKLESS MAN [-] 7-10-12 (5*) P A Roche,......(12 to 1)   6
3371 ALL A QUIVER [-] 7-10-3 C N Bowens,..............(20 to 1)   7
3465⁴ TAKE THE TOWN [-] 9-11-10 J F Titley,..............(8 to 1)   8
2497 ROSSI NOVAE [-] (bl) 11-10-10 (3*) T P Treacy,....(12 to 1)   9
3294 MACK A DAY [-] 7-11-9 A J O'Brien,................(14 to 1)   10
3249⁹ BUMBO HALL VI (Ire) [-] 6-10-9 (3*) T J Mitchell,..(20 to 1)   11
2923³ WHAT A MINSTREL [-] (bl) 8-9-7 T Horgan,........(20 to 1)   12
3392³ CASTLE BRANDON [-] 8-11-8 F J Flood,............(10 to 1)   13
3392 IFFEEE [-] 7-11-3 S H O'Donovan,..................(14 to 1)   14
3425 LAURA'S BEAU [-] (bl) 7-11-1 (7*) D J Kavanagh, (16 to 1)   15
2507 TIRRY'S FRIEND [-] 12-9-3 (5*) M A Davey,.........(12 to 1)   f
2984⁶ OPRYLAND [-] 9-10-9 (5*) J P Broderick,............(12 to 1)   pu
3200 FAIRY PARK [-] 9-10-12 J Shortt,......................(20 to 1)   pu
3371⁹ WATERLOO KING [-] (bl) 7-11-1 K F O'Brien,........(25 to 1)   pu
2942⁵ MISCHIEF MOON [-] (bl) 9-9-4 (3*) C O'Brien,.....(50 to 1)   pu
Dist: 6l, 8l, 5l, 3½l. 6m 34.40s. (20 Ran).
                              (Mrs A L T Moore), A L T Moore

3525 Thomastown Maiden Hurdle (4 & 5-y-o) £2,760 2½m. (3:30)

3080 RISZARD (USA) 5-11-6 (7*) A P McCoy,.........(6 to 4 fav)   1
3448² JULEIT JONES (Ire) 5-11-6 F J Flood,................(6 to 1)   2
2983 SMALL TALK (Ire) 5-11-0 H Rogers,..................(33 to 1)   3
3325 HEMISPHERE (Ire) (bl) 5-11-5 R Hughes,............(7 to 1)   4
3447 GRANDEUR (Ire) 4-10-6 (7*) S A Quilty,............(12 to 1)   5D

30878 BACKTOWN JOHNNY (Ire) 5-11-5 L P Cusack, ... (33 to 1) 5
34674 SKY VISION (Ire) 5-11-0 S H O'Donovan, ... (10 to 1) 7
2943 JOYFUL RUNNER (Ire) 4-10-8 G M O'Neill, ... (25 to 1) 8
       RING FOUR (Ire) 5-11-0 T Horgan, ... (16 to 1) 9
       COOLING CHIMES (Ire) 4-10-6 (7") Mr P A Dunphy, (33 to 1) 10
       TOOLITTLE TOOLATE (Ire) 5-11-5 J Collins, ... (16 to 1) 11
23487 OVER THE JORDAN (Ire) 5-11-5 C O'Dwyer, ... (8 to 1) 12
32909 SPANKERS HILL (Ire) 5-11-10 (3") T P Treacy, ... (7 to 1) 13
       RIFAYA (Ire) 4-10-3 (5") K P Gaule, ... (14 to 1) 14
2943 HARD AND REASON (Ire) 5-10-11 (3") D P Murphy, (25 to 1) 15
2863 THE PERISHER (Ire) 5-11-5 J Shortt, ... (12 to 1) 16
2394 GOOD BYE MONEY (Ire) 5-11-5 (7") L J Flemming, (20 to 1) 17
3201 OH RIVER (Ire) 5-10-9 (5") P A Roche, ... (16 to 1) 18
2620 SHUIL SHELL (Ire) 5-11-0 K F O'Brien, ... (20 to 1) pu
       HENRY G'S (Ire) 4-10-8 A Powell, ... (25 to 1) pu
Dist: 3l, dist, 3l, 5½l. 5m 31.20s. (20 Ran).

(Henryk de Kwiatkowski), J S Bolger

3526 Kilkenny Opportunity Handicap Hurdle (0-123 4-y-o and up) £3,105 2m 1f ....(4:00)

33225 PUNTERS BAR [-] 7-9-13 (2") P A Roche, ...(8 to 1) 1
3246* ONOMATOPOEIA (Ire) [-] (bl) 4-10-6 (2") J R Barry, .. (7 to 1) 2
3197 ELIADE (Ire) [-] 5-9-7 (2") M A Davey, ...(16 to 1) 3
3247 PERSIAN HALO (Ire) [-] 6-11-7 (2") T P Rudd, ... (10 to 1) 4
33229 TEMPLEROAN PRINCE [-] 7-11-3 (4") B Bowens, (10 to 1) 5
32477 MAYASTA (Ire) [-] 4-10-0 (4") D J Kavanagh, ...(10 to 1) 6
32476 ASSERT STAR [-] 4-10-8 (2") K P Gaule, ... (10 to 1) 7
3322 TUG OF PEACE [-] 7-12-0 T J Mitchell, ...(8 to 1) 8
       SHEER MIST [-] 7-10-7 (2") M J Holbrook, ...(33 to 1) 9
3322 COIN MACHINE (Ire) [-] 5-9-13 (4") P P Curran, ...(10 to 1) 10
2842 DEGO DANCER [-] 7-10-0 D P Murphy, ...(16 to 1) 11
33218 GENTLE REEF (Ire) [-] 4-10-3 T P Treacy, ...(20 to 1) 12
18187 HIS WAY (Ire) [-] 5-9-9 (4") J M Sullivan, ...(16 to 1) 13
22816 PELEUS (USA) [-] 9-10-3 (2") M G Cleary, ...(20 to 1) 14
5847 RUSTY COIN [-] 9-11-10 T J O'Sullivan, ...(20 to 1) 15
2703 SHIRWAN (Ire) [-] 5-10-2 C O'Brien, ...(16 to 1) 16
2774 MILLENIUM LASS (Ire) [-] 6-9-9 (4") F Byrne, ...(20 to 1) pu
       GLEN MONEY [-] 8-11-5 (4") L J Flemming, ...(14 to 1) pu
       ORANGE RAGUSA [-] 8-11-0 (2") D T Evans, ...(25 to 1) pu
3197* BACK TO BLACK (Ire) [-] 5-10-3 (2") J P Broderick, ... (9 to 4 fav) pu
Dist: 15l, 15l, nk, 1½l. 4m 37.80s. (20 Ran).

(Cedars Racing Syndicate), Patrick Day

3527 Tetratema Perpetual Cup (5-y-o and up) £2,760 3m.................(4:30)

32958 PHAIRY MIRACLES (Ire) 5-10-12 Mr P J Healy, ...(12 to 1) 1
32952 RED EXPRESS VI 9-11-3 (7") Mr S O'Brien, ...(13 to 2) 2
       SOUTH OFTHE BORDER (bl) 8-10-12 (7") Mr K O'Sullivan, ...(8 to 1) 3
32954 THE VICARETTE (Ire) 6-10-12 (7") Mr P Cashman, ..(8 to 1) 4
2941 BALLYDAY DAWN 7-10-12 (7") Mr J P Walsh, ...(33 to 1) f
32959 NATIVE VENTURE (Ire) 6-11-7 (3") Mr J A Nash, ...(10 to 1) f
3295 FUNNY BUSINESS 7-11-10 Mr D M O'Brien, ... (25 to 1) f
3295 MOSS CASTLE 9-11-7 (3") Mr D P Costello, ...(5 to 2 fav) f
       SUIL EILE 7-11-5 (5") Mr J P Berry, ...(12 to 1) ur
32956 GARRYLUCAS 8-11-3 (7") Mr P English, ...(10 to 1) ref
32953 MATTY TYNAN 7-11-10 Mr P Fenton, ...(3 to 1) pu
5837 IF SO 8-11-7 (3") Mr D P Daly, ...(12 to 1) pu
33704 WHAT THING (bl) 7-11-0 (5") Mr H F Cleary, ...(8 to 1) pu
Dist: 15l, 6l, 3l. 6m 59.10s. (13 Ran).

(C Healy), P J Healy

3528 Mount Leinster INH Flat Race (Div 1) (6-y-o and up) £2,760 2m 1f..... (5:00)

       MISTER BADSWORTH (Ire) 6-12-0 Mr J E Kiely, ...(9 to 2) 1
       DROMARA BREEZE (Ire) 6-11-7 (7") Mr C J McKee, (8 to 1) 2
26077 FINNEGANS WAKE 7-12-0 Mr A P O'Brien, ... (9 to 4 fav) 3
1827 LISCAHILL HIGHWAY 7-11-7 (7") Mr P Carey, ...(14 to 1) 4
2394 SECRET MISSILE 7-11-11 (3") Mrs J M Mullins, ...(8 to 1) 5
27519 MAN OF IRON 7-11-7 (7") M Cooney, ...(14 to 1) 6
33946 ANOTHER ROLLO (Ire) 6-11-7 (7") Mr N Stokes, ... (10 to 1) 7
       RAINYS RUN 7-11-2 (7") D J Kavanagh, ...(10 to 1) 8
30828 RUDDS HILL (Ire) 6-11-9 (5") T P Rudd, ...(25 to 1) 9
3291 MARBLE FONTAINE 7-11-6 (3") Miss M Olivefalk, .. (6 to 1) 10
3124 WAREZ (Ire) 6-11-7 (7") Miss L Doyle, ...(33 to 1) 11
3447 COLLIERS HILL (Ire) 6-11-7 (7") Mr J P Harvey, ... (12 to 1) 12
       STORM POINT (Ire) 6-11-7 (7") Mr J Murphy, ...(8 to 1) 13
3201 SWALLOW REEF (Ire) 6-11-82 (3") Mr D P Costello, (33 to 1) 14
       FARRANDERRY (Ire) 6-11-2 (7") Mr S O'Donnell, .. (14 to 1) 15
       KOWABANGA 7-11-7 (7") Mr P F O'Callaghan, ...(12 to 1) 16
3327 BALLY UPPER (Ire) 6-11-7 (7") Mr B Foster, ...(20 to 1) su
       COOLHARBOUR LASS (Ire) 6-11-2 (7") Mr D W Cullen, ...(14 to 1) pu
Dist: 12l, 1½l, 6l, ½l. 4m 43.50s. (18 Ran).

(Mrs A S O'Brien), J E Kiely

3529 Mount Leinster INH Flat Race (Div 2) (6-y-o and up) £2,760 2m 1f..... (5:30)

2586 PLEASURE SHARED (Ire) 6-12-0 Mr A P O'Brien, ...(7 to 2) 1
32965 TORONTO TELEGRAM 8-11-4 (5") Mr J P Berry, ... (9 to 1) 2

2664 YOU KNOW WHO (Ire) 6-11-11 (3") Mrs J M Mullins, ...(10 to 1) 3
       SHAKE UP 10-11-2 (7") Mr P English, ...(14 to 1) 4
26643 DUEONE (Ire) 6-11-9 (5") M A Davey, ...(8 to 1) 5
3201 CLONROSH SLAVE 7-12-0 Mr T Mullins, ...(20 to 1) 6
       LISSELAN PRINCE (Ire) 6-12-0 Mr P Fenton, ... (6 to 4 fav) 7
3504 COSHLA EXPRESSO (Ire) 6-11-11 (3") Mr D Marnane, ...(66 to 1) 8
32914 CARRIGKEM (Ire) 6-11-6 (3") Mr J A Nash, ... (12 to 1) 9
       NELPHA (Ire) 6-11-9 (5") Mr H F Cleary, ...(7 to 1) 10
1687 MASTER EYRE (Ire) 6-11-7 (7") Mr M J Bowe, ...(20 to 1) 11
       PALEFOOT (Ire) 6-11-6 (3") Mr R O'Neill, ...(50 to 1) 12
2236 DICKS DELIGHT (Ire) 6-11-7 (7") Mr E Sheehy, ...(33 to 1) 13
32435 FANDANGOLD 8-11-2 (7") Mr E Norris, ...(12 to 1) 14
945⁴ WOLVER LAD (Ire) 6-12-0 Mr T Doyle, ...(12 to 1) 15
       MOSSA NOVA (Ire) 6-12-0 Mr J P Dempsey, ...(16 to 1) 16
1910 JOHNNYS GIRL 7-11-2 (7") Mr J P Deegan, ...(50 to 1) 17
18525 MARTINS PARTY 9-11-2 (7") Miss S A Quinn, ...(66 to 1) 18
Dist: 20l, 7l, 7l, 20l. 4m 40.30s. (18 Ran).

(M G St Quinton), A P O'Brien

NEWTON ABBOT (good)
Wednesday April 20th
Going Correction: PLUS 0.37 sec. per fur.

3530 Liskeard 'National Hunt' Novices' Hurdle (4-y-o and up) £1,982 2m 1f. .(5:40)

31152 SPUFFINGTON 6-11-2 E Murphy, al gng wl, led 5th, drw clr frm 3 out, cmftbly.
       ....(100 to 30 op 5 to 2 tchd 4 to 1) 1
3352* CRAZY DAISY 7-10-4 (7") T Murphy, in tch till outpcd 5th, styd on frm 2 out to take second r-in. (8 to 1 op 6 to 1) 2
27416 SUPER SHARP (NZ) 6-11-2 Jacqui Oliver, mid-div, hdwy 4th, lft second 2 out, no extr r-in. (16 to 1 op 12 to 1) 3
       GOLDEN FRAME 7-11-2 D Gallagher, hld up towards rear, styd on frm 2 out, nvr nrr.
       ....(14 to 1 op 12 to 1 tchd 16 to 1) 4
2404 BOX OF DELIGHTS 6-11-2 B Powell, hld up in tch, rdn and wknd aftr 3 out..............................(50 to 1) 5
778 KINGFISHER BLUES (Ire) 6-11-2 B Clifford, al mid-div, no hdwy frm 5th..........................(50 to 1 op 33 to 1) 6
       PERSIAN WOLF 6-11-2 V Slattery, in tch, hdwy 5th, rdn and wknd 3 out..........................(50 to 1) 7
29914 SOUND REVEILLE 6-11-2 G Bradley, prmnt, led 4th to nxt, wknd quickly appr 2 out.
       ....(6 to 4 fav op 2 to 1 tchd 5 to 2) 8
27318 BATHWICK BOBBIE 7-10-9 (7") Miss S Higgins, slwly away, tld off frm 3rd..........................(50 to 1) 9
31918 BOLLINGTON (Fr) 5-11-2 S McNeill, pld hrd, led aftr 1st, hdd 4th, wknd nxt, tld off..............(10 to 1 op 6 to 1) 10
34765 SHERWOOD BOY 5-11-2 J Railton, led till aftr 1st, styd prmnt, hld whn blun and uns rdr 2 out.
       ....(6 to 1 op 3 to 1) ur
       HAPPY VALLEY 6-10-11 Mr I Hambly, not jump wl, al beh, tld off whn pld up bef 2 out.....(10 to 1 op 33 to 1) pu
616 DUNNICKS WELL 5-11-2 C Maude, al beh, sn tld off, pld up bef 3 out..........................(50 to 1) pu
3300 POLAR HAT 6-11-2 R Dunwoody, al towards rear, tld off whn pld up bef 2 out.......(10 to 1 op 5 to 1) pu
2996 DAYTIME BOMBER 4-10-10 M Richards, al beh, tld off whn pld up bef 3 out........................(50 to 1) pu
Dist: 3l, ½l, 30l, 1½l, 3½l, 8l, 2½l, 10l, 12l. 4m 6.70s. a 16.70s (15 Ran).

(Julian Clopet), J T Gifford

3531 St Austell Novices' Claiming Hurdle (4-y-o and up) £2,091 2m 1f.... (6:10)

28817 MIGAVON 4-10-9 D Gallagher, led till second, styd prmnt, led appr 3 out, clr nxt.
       ....(20 to 1 op 10 to 1 tchd 25 to 1) 1
31455 EAGLES LAIR 8-11-3 S McNeill, hld up in tch, hdwy 5th, ev ch 3 out, held whn blun last..... (14 to 1 op 8 to 1) 2
17058 BUGLET 4-11-3 R Dunwoody, al prmnt, ev ch 3 out, rdn and one pace aftr..........(13 to 8 fav tchd 2 to 1) 3
2945* MR GENEAOLOGY (USA) (bl) 4-11-2 A Maguire, hld up in tch, lost pl 3 out, one pace aftr......(7 to 4 op 5 to 4) 4
33953 SHARPSIDE (bl) 7-11-3 C Maude, led second, hit 5th, sn hdd, wknd appr 2 out..........................(8 to 1) 5
3362 WEST END 4-11-04 Mr S Stickland, mid-div, hdwy aftr 4th, wknd 2 out............(66 to 1 op 50 to 1) 6
3202 RED MATCH 9-10-13 A Tory, slwly away, beh till hdwy appr 3 out, wknd bef nxt........(50 to 1 op 33 to 1) 7
31514 TALLAND STREAM 7-11-6 (3") R Farrant, mid-div, lost tch 5th..........................(9 to 1 op 6 to 1) 8
27173 PRINCE RUBEN 7-11-9 B Powell, prmnt till wknd appr 5th, tld off..........(13 to 2 op 9 to 2) 9
945⁴ WALID'S PRINCESS (Ire) (bl) 4-10-8 J Frost, al beh, tld off......(66 to 1 op 33 to 1) 10
3009 BEACHY GLEN 7-11-3 L Harvey, al beh, tld off whn pld up bef 2 out..........................(50 to 1 op 25 to 1) pu
       FOUROFUS 5-11-3 S Earle, beh frm second, tld off whn pld up bef 5th..........................(66 to 1 op 50 to 1) pu
       THUNDER (Ire) 6-10-8 (5") Guy Lewis, al beh, tld off whn pld up bef 2 out.....(20 to 1 tchd 25 to 1 and 16 to 1) pu

505

3153⁵ FORMAESTRE (Ire) 4-10-6 M Richards, *al beh, tld off whn*
pld up bef 2 out.................. (20 to 1 tchd 33 to 1) pu
3252 JEAN BRODIE 4-10-8 G Upton, *jmpd poorly in rear, tld*
off whn pld up bef 2 out.......... (66 to 1 op 50 to 1) pu
Dist: 7l, 12l, 6l, 5l, 2l, 7l, ½l, 15l, 1l. 4m 4.90s. a 14.90s (15 Ran).
(Laurie Snook), L A Snook

3532 Westcountry Television Amateur Riders' Handicap Chase (0-110 5-y-o and up) £3,320 3¼m 110yds . . . (6:40)

3265³ NEARLY SPLENDID [96] 9-10-11² (7") Mr T Greed, *hld up,*
hdwy frm 13th, led sn aftr 5 out, styd on wl.
........................(3 to 1 fav op 5 to 2 tchd 7 to 2) 1
3501³ SKERRY MEADOW [87] 10-10-0 (7") Mr J Culloty, *hld up,*
hdwy 7th, rdn 4 out, no imprsn aftr.
.....................................(5 to 1 tchd 6 to 1) 2
3351² KIWI VELOCITY (NZ) [100] 7-10-13 (7") Mr S Mulcaire, *trkd*
ldrs, lft in ld 6 out, hdd aftr nxt, one pace frm 3 out.
...............................(4 to 1 op 5 to 2) 3
669⁴ BARRACILLA [83] 9-10-3² (7") Mr K Hickey, *beh, hdwy frm 6*
out, nvr nrr..........................(16 to 1 op 12 to 1) 4
3336⁴ IMPECCABLE TIMING [80] 11-9-8¹ (7") Mr A Mitchell, *slwly*
away, wl beh till some hdwy frm 7th, nvr nr to chal.
..............................(20 to 1 op 14 to 1) 5
3006³ HICKELTON LAD [80] 10-9-7 (7") Miss S Higgins, *led till*
13th, blnkd aftr....................(16 to 1 op 12 to 1) 6
2191⁸ GUILDWAY [90] 11-10-3 (7") Mr M Rimell, *not jump wl, beh*
frm 13th............... (11 to 2 op 5 to 1 tchd 6 to 1) 7
3417⁴ RU VALENTINO [108] 10-11-7 (7") Mr G Hanmer, *trkd ldrs,*
led briefly 13th, wknd quickly 4 out.
.................................(16 to 1 op 10 to 1) 8
3477 SKETCHER [92] 9-10-11 (7") Mr G Shenkin, *mstk sec-*
ond, al prmnt, led appr 14th, blun and uns rdr 6 out.
..............................(20 to 1 op 16 to 1) ur
3310 DERRING VALLEY [100] (bl) 9-11-1 (5") Mr S Bush, *mid-div*
whn blun 8th, in tch when blunded and uns rdr 14th.
.................................(16 to 1 op 14 to 1) ur
2993³ TRUSTY FRIEND [83] 12-10-0 (3") Mr R Treloggen, *trkd ldr*
till 9th, blun 11th, tld off whn pld up bef 6 out.
.................(12 to 1 tchd 14 to 1 and 20 to 1) pu
3253⁸ HAND OUT [80] 10-9-7 (7") Mr G Baines, *tld off frm 7th, pld*
up bef 4 out...........................(25 to 1 op 20 to 1) pu
Dist: 4l, 12l, ½l, 12l, 2½l, 12l, 5l. 6m 43.00s. a 23.00s (12 Ran).
(S R Stevens), S R Stevens

3533 Crown Windows Selling Handicap Hurdle (4-y-o and up) £2,082 3m 3f
.... (7:10)

3491⁸ PARLEZVOUSFRANCAIS [100] 10-12-0 R Dunwoody, *led*
second to 5th, led aftr 8th, hrd rdn frm 3 out, lft clr whn
mstk last............. (2 to 1 fav op 3 to 1 tchd 7 to 2) 1
3003* MISTRESS ROSS [76] 11-10-6 D Bridgwater, *hld up in mid-*
div, hdwy 7th, rdn and held whn lft second last.
...........................(11 to 2 op 7 to 1) 2
FRESH-MINT [90] 10-11-4 I Shoemark, *hld up in rear,*
hdwy appr 4 out, one pace frm nxt.
...................(25 to 1 op 33 to 1 tchd 20 to 1) 3
DOMINION TREASURE [82] 9-10-10 L Harvey, *sn pushed*
alng in rear, styd on frm 3 out, nvr nrr...........(20 to 1) 4
1526 BOXING MATCH [72] 7-9-11 (3") R Farrant, *nvr far away, ev*
ch 4 out, wknd appr 2 out............(25 to 1 op 20 to 1) 5
3298² SUASANAN SIOSANA [72] 9-10-0 R Supple, *al prmnt, rdn*
3 out, sn btn........................(50 to 1 op 33 to 1) 6
2165⁵ HARPLEY [72] 7-9-9² (7") N Juckes, *mid-div, one pace frm*
4 out..................................(50 to 1 op 33 to 1) 7
3166 TAP DANCING [72] 8-10-0 Ann Stokell, *in tch till wknd 4*
out................................(50 to 1 op 25 to 1) 8
3479⁷ KING'S RARITY [87] (bl) 8-11-1 M A FitzGerald, *trkd ldrs till*
wknd appr 3 out, eased, tld off...(10 to 1 op 12 to 1) 9
3219⁷ RIYADH LIGHTS [94] 9-11-8 B Powell, *sn trkd wnr, led 5th*
till aftr 8th, wknd quickly appr 3 out, tld off.
..............................(12 to 1 op 10 to 1) 10
383* QUIET RIOT [76] 12-10-4 A Maguire, *hld up in rear, rapid*
hdwy 4 out, took second nxt, hrd rdn and held whn f
last...................... (7 to 1 op 6 to 1 tchd 8 to 1) f
3298³ BOREEN JEAN [88] (v) 10-10-11 (5") D Leahy, *mid-div, btn*
whn f last................(13 to 2 op 5 to 1 tchd 8 to 1) f
SEA BARN [82] 11-10-10 B Clifford, *mid-div, tld off 8th,*
pld up bef nxt........................(50 to 1 op 33 to 1) pu
2764 LA CERISE [87] (bl) 11-11-1 Miss J Southcombe, *tld off 6th,*
pld up bef nxt........................(50 to 1 op 33 to 1) pu
1427 KILTONGA [72] 7-10-0 M Hourigan, *al beh, tld off whn pld*
up bef 4 out..........................(50 to 1 op 33 to 1) pu
3279⁶ RUFFINSWICK [72] 8-10-0 Richard Guest, *led till second,*
wknd hfwy, tld off whn pld up bef 4 out.
.................................(50 to 1 op 33 to 1) pu
3186 BOADICEA'S CHARIOT [76] 7-10-4 C Maude, *slwly away,*
al beh, tld off whn pld up bef 3 out. (50 to 1 op 33 to 1) pu
2799² ROCK DIAMOND [72] 8-10-0 E Leonard, *al beh, tld off whn*
pld up bef 2 out......................(11 to 2 op 7 to 1) pu
Dist: 6l, 6l, 7l, 2l, 2l, nk, 15l, 30l, 10l. 6m 47.20s. a 33.20s (18 Ran).
(L B Hyman), M C Pipe

3534 Fowey Novices' Handicap Chase (5-y-o and up) £3,139 2m 5f . . . . (7:40)

3041 FRENCH CHARMER [107] 9-11-11 D Murphy, *al gng wl in*
tch, led appr 8th, hdd 5 out, led 3 out, mstk and headed
last, rallied gmely to ld cl hme.
.....................(5 to 1 op 9 to 2 tchd 11 to 2) 1
3445² CROSULA [96] 6-11-0 R Dunwoody, *led to second, led ag'n*
5 out, hdd 3 out, led last, hrd rdn and headed cl hme.
.................................(7 to 4 fav op 3 to 1) 2
COMMANCHERO [85] 7-10-3 A Tory, *trkd ldrs, ev ch and*
mstk 5 out, one pace frm 3 out..............(20 to 1) 3
1139³ STRONG MEDICINE [96] 7-11-0 D Gallagher, *al prmnt, led*
7th, hdd bef nxt, one pace frm 5 out.
.....................(13 to 2 op 4 to 1 tchd 9 to 1) 4
3426³ FESTIVAL DREAMS [97] 9-11-1 P Holley, *chsd ldrs, pushed*
alng frm 8th, wknd 4 out....................(10 to 1) 5
3163⁴ MR INVADER [82] 7-10-0 R Supple, *mid-div whn blun 8th,*
nvr dngrs aftr................(25 to 1 op 20 to 1) 6
3361 DURRINGTON [82] 8-10-0 Richard Guest, *al in rear.*
....(33 to 1) 7
3175 BUCKELIGHT (Ire) [87] (bl) 6-10-2 (3") R Farrant, *al beh, tld*
off..................................(12 to 1 op 10 to 1) 8
3255³ NEEDS MUST [84] 7-10-2 J Frost, *sn beh, tld off.*
.................................(20 to 1 op 14 to 1) 9
2647 HOWARYAFXD [97] 7-11-1 M A FitzGerald, *in tch to 7th, sn*
beh., tld off........................(14 to 1 op 12 to 1) 10
3255* WINTER'S LANE [91] 10-10-9 A Maguire, *hld up in rear,*
hdwy 8th, in tch whn blun and uns rdr 4 out.
.................................(7 to 2 op 11 to 4) ur
3477 VILLA RECOS [88] 9-10-6 B Powell, *al beh, tld off whn pld*
up bef 4 out......................................(33 to 1) pu
3343 OPAL'S TENSPOT [89] 7-10-2 (5") Guy Lewis, *chsd ldrs to*
8th, rdn and sn beh, pld up bef 4 out.........(12 to 1) pu
3149⁴ BLAKEINGTON [82] 8-10-0 D Skyrme, *al beh, tld off*
whn pld up bef 4 out...............(50 to 1 op 33 to 1) pu
Dist: Hd, 10l, 15l, 1½l, 8l, sht-hd, 25l, 6l, 5l. 5m 13.30s. a 13.30s (14 Ran).
SR: 42/31/10/6/5/-/ (H T Pelham), J T Gifford

3535 St Blazey Handicap Hurdle (0-120 4-y-o and up) £2,847 2¾m . . . . (8:10)

3363* MAESTRO PAUL [109] 8-11-10 D Murphy, *hld up in tch, gd*
hdwy 6th, led on bit appr 2 out, pushed out.
..................................(6 to 1 op 4 to 1) 1
3053² SURCOAT [95] 7-10-10 L Harvey, *hld up, gd hdwy 3 out,*
rdn and no imprsn frm nxt...........(7 to 1 op 8 to 1) 2
3308⁶ SMILING CHIEF (Ire) [88] (bl) 6-10-3 A Tory, *trkd ldrs, ev ch 3*
out, rdn and kpt on one pace.......(16 to 1 op 12 to 1) 3
3281* TEMPLE KNIGHT [86] 5-10-1 S Earle, *nvr far away, dsptd*
ld aftr 3 out, wknd frm nxt.
..............................(13 to 2 op 4 to 1) 4
3174⁷ NOVA SPIRIT [85] 6-10-0 V Slattery, *in rear till styd on frm*
3 out, nvr nrr........................(25 to 1 op 20 to 1) 5
SYDNEY BARRY (NZ) [85] 9-10-0 B Powell, *hld up in rear,*
styd on frm 3 out...................(25 to 1 op 20 to 1) 6
3028⁸ CORACO [108] (v) 7-11-9 D Bridgwater, *hld up, gd hdwy to*
ld briefly aftr 3 out, sn btn..........(5 to 2 fav op 6 to 1) 7
3408⁴ FAST THOUGHTS [109] 7-11-5 (5") D Leahy, *led till hdd*
appr 3 out, sn btn, eased...........(6 to 1 op 4 to 1) 8
3441 ANILAFFED [85] (v) 4-10-0 D Gallagher, *hld up, hdwy 6th,*
led briefly 3 out, wkng whn slpd on bend bef nxt.
.................................(14 to 1 op 12 to 1) 9
3109⁴ LANSDOWNE [95] 6-10-10 M A FitzGerald, *al towards rear.*
.................................(13 to 2 op 6 to 1 tchd 10 to 1) 10
3512 INNOCENT PRINCESS (NZ) [85] 7-10-0³ (3") R Davis, *trkd*
ldrs till wknd quickly appr 3 out, tld off.
.................................(20 to 1 op 12 to 1) 11
3380⁹ KNYAZ [85] 4-9-9 (5") D Salter, *in tch to 6th, sn beh, tld off.*
.................................(25 to 1 op 20 to 1) 12
3360 KELLING [85] 7-9-9 (5") Guy Lewis, *mid-div, effrt 4 out,*
wknd nxt, tld off....................(20 to 1 op 14 to 1) 13
3398⁸ DAMIER BLANC (Fr) [98] (bl) 5-10-13 R Dunwoody, *prmnt*
till rdn 6th, stdly lost tch, tld off...(10 to 1 op 6 to 1) 14
3298⁴ BRIGHT SAPPHIRE [88] 8-9-11 (3") R Farrant, *in frnt rnk*
till wknd quickly appr 4 out, tld off.......(100 to 1) 15
3053 BLASKET HERO [87] (bl) 6-10-2 S McNeill, *hld up in rear,*
rapid hdwy 3 out, 3rd and held whn blun and uns rdr
last..................................(16 to 1 op 14 to 1) ur
1721 ODSTONE PEAR [89] 9-10-4 C Maude, *sn wl beh, tld off*
whn pld up aftr 6th.................(50 to 1 op 33 to 1) pu
Dist: 1¾l, 8l, sht-hd, ¾l, 6l, 3l, 3½l, nk, 2½l, 20l. 5m 27.10s. a 28.10s (17 Ran).
(H T Pelham), J T Gifford

PERTH (good to firm)
Wednesday April 20th
Going Correction: MINUS 0.35 sec. per fur. (races 1,3,4,6,7), MINUS 0.10 (2,5)

3536 Party Has Started Maiden Hurdle (Div I) (4-y-o and up) £2,458 2½m 110yds
.... (3:30)

2664⁶ IFALLELSEFAILS 6-11-7 T Reed, *trkd ldrs, led 2 out, sn*
clr, easily..........................(Evens, easily) 1
3354 BRIGADIER DAVIS (Fr) 7-11-7 R Garritty, *sn tracking ldr,*
mstk second, led and mistake 3 out, hdd nxt, no extr
und pres....... (Evens fav op 5 to 4 on tchd 11 to 10) 2

506

3354 ASTRALEON (Ire) 6-11-7 B Storey, *hld up, hdwy appr 3 out, ev ch nxt, kpt on same pace und pres.*
.................................(9 to 2 op 5 to 1 tchd 4 to 1) 3
THE PRIOR 8-11-7 S Turner, *in tch, ev ch 3 out, sn wknd.*
.................................(100 to 1 op 200 to 1) 4
29713 FLING IN SPRING 8-11-4 (3*) P Williams, *beh, some late hdwy, nvr dngrs.*...............(20 to 1 op 16 to 1) 5
30563 COMMANCHE CREEK (v) 4-10-11 (3*) A Larnach, *chsd ldrs till wknd quickly aftr 3 out.*
.................................(16 to 1 op 14 to 1 tchd 20 to 1) 6
29705 COMPANY SECRETARY 6-11-2 Peter Hobbs, *in tch till wknd aftr 6th.*....................(66 to 1 op 50 to 1) 7
25617 BISHOPS CASTLE (Ire) 6-11-7 A Dobbin, *in tch till wknd aftr 7th.*........................(16 to 1 op 14 to 1) 8
LARLOCH 10-11-7 N Doughty, *led till hdd 3 out, wknd quickly.*......................................(50 to 1) 9
2069 HIGHRYMER 10-11-2 A Merrigan, *mstks, al beh.* (50 to 1) 10
33795 JUNGLE RITES (Ire) 6-11-7 M Dwyer, *hld up, hdwy to track ldrs 6th, disputing 3rd and ev ch whn f 2 out.*
.................................(9 to 1 op 8 to 1) f
FLAXON WORRIOR 10-11-7 C Grant, *sn beh, tld off whn pld up bef 2 out.*.............................(200 to 1) pu
34443 VOLUNTEER POINT (Ire) 4-10-9 (5*) J Burke, *chsd ldrs till pld up lme aftr 5th....* (8 to 1 op 10 to 1 tchd 12 to 1) pu
Dist: 7l, 3½l, dist, 2½l, 10l, 15l, 12l, 5l, 7l. 4m 48.00s. a 3.00s (13 Ran).
(R Gilbert), L Lungo

3537 Shepherd & Wedderburn Private Client Handicap Chase (0-125 5-y-o and up) £4,318 3m.................(4:00)

3498* GLENSHANE LAD [108] 8-11-7 (6ex) N Williamson, *hld up, took clr order 11th, chlgd 4 out, rdn to ld 2 out, styd on wl und pres.*...................(15 to 8 fav op 5 to 2) 1
33752 CHOICE CHALLANGE [93] 11-10-6 C Grant, *with ldr, led 14th, jnd 4 out, hdd 2 out, kpt on und pres.*
.................................(4 to 1 op 7 to 2) 2
24373 CORNET [115] (v) 8-12-0 M Dwyer, *hld up in tch, chsd ldrs frm 4 out, no imprsn....*(7 to 1 op 6 to 1 tchd 8 to 1) 3
34634 ON THE HOOCH [97] 9-10-101 Mr J Bradburne, *led till hdd 14th, wknd aftr 4 out...........*(14 to 1 op 10 to 1) 4
31806 RUN PET RUN [100] 9-10-13 A Dobbin, *prmnt, mstk 7th, wknd aftr 13th, tld off..*(9 to 2 op 5 to 1 tchd 6 to 1) 5
31807 FISH QUAY [87] 11-9-7 (7*) Miss S Lamb, *al beh, lost tch aftr 11th, mstk 14th, tld off.*..................(50 to 1) 6
32824 STEPFASTER [98] 9-10-11 P Niven, *losing tch whn mstk 12th, tld off....*.................(9 to 1 op 6 to 1) 7
2105 RAWYARDS BRIG [87] 11-10-0 A Merrigan, *lost tch aftr 8th....*.............................(100 to 1) 8
3463 CAMONNAGE [96] 13-10-4 (5*) P Waggott, *mstks, lost tch aftr 11th, wl tld off....*.......................(100 to 1) 9
34635 HOUXTY LAD [87] 8-10-0 B Storey, *lost tch aftr 11th, tld off whn pld up bef 3 out...........*(16 to 1 op 14 to 1) pu
Dist: 2½l, 12l, 12l, 30l, 15l, 1½l, 1¼l, 20l. 5m 59.20s. a 2.20s (10 Ran).
SR: 47/29/39/9/-/-/ (Mrs Harry J Duffey), K C Bailey

3538 Kemback Car Centre Handicap Hurdle (0-125 4-y-o and up) £3,582 2m 110yds ....(4:30)

2874* CHIEF MINISTER (Ire) [106] 5-10-10 Peter Hobbs, *chsd ldrs, rdn to ld between last 2, hit last, drvn clr.*
.................................(13 to 8 fav op 7 to 4 tchd 6 to 4) 1
21389 FAMILY LINE [98] 6-10-2 N Williamson, *led to 3rd, cl up, led appr 2 out, hdd betw last two, no extr........*(14 to 1) 2
24382 GYMCRAK STARDOM [124] 8-12-0 R Marley, *hld up, effrt appr 2 out, kpt on wl frm last........*(10 to 1 op 8 to 1) 3
24382 LEGITIM [96] 5-9-7 (7*) G Tormey, *mid-div, effrt appr 2 out, kpt on same pace....*...........(10 to 1 tchd 11 to 1) 4
27406 RAPID MOVER [96] (bl) 7-9-9 (5*) A Roche, *trkd ldrs, ev ch 2 out, sn rdn and btn....*........(40 to 1 op 33 to 1) 5
3182* WEE WIZARD (Ire) [103] 5-10-7 A Dobbin, *early reminders and sn drvn alng, no hdwy frm 3 out.*
.................................(4 to 1 op 7 to 2 tchd 9 to 2) 6
3436* ANY DREAM WOULD DO [96] 5-10-0 (6ex) C Hawkins, *hld up in tch, effrt aftr 3 out, sn btn.*
.................................(8 to 1 op 7 to 1 tchd 9 to 1) 7
3423 CLAY COUNTY [105] 9-10-9 B Storey, *cl up, led 3rd till appr 2 out, wknd quickly............*(6 to 1 op 5 to 1) 8
1746 MAGIC BLOOM [96] 8-10-03 (3*) A Larnach, *tld off frm hfwy....*..........................(33 to 1 op 25 to 1) 9
Dist: 6l, nk, 4l, 2½l, 12l, 1¾l, 30l. 3m 41.80s. a 2.20s (9 Ran).
SR: 46/32/57/25/22/17/8/-/-/ (G Shiel), T Dyer

3539 'Loon Cartoons' Novices' Hurdle (5-y-o and up) £2,458 2m 110yds...(5:00)

15394 BERTONE (Ire) 5-12-0 N Williamson, *made all, clr 2 out, easily....*...................(5 to 4 on op Evens) 1
33782 SHAHGRAM (Ire) 6-11-10 M Dwyer, *hld up in tch, hdwy aftr 3 out, kpt on frm nxt, no imprsn on wnr.*
.................................(9 to 1 op 8 to 1) 2
34094 ASLAN (Ire) 6-11-9 (5*) Mr D Parker, *sn tracking wnr, pushed alng aftr 5th, outpcd appr 2 out, kpt on frm last....*...............(2 to 1 op 7 to 4 tchd 9 to 4) 3

3378* TEMPLERAINEY (Ire) 6-11-4 (3*) P Williams, *hld up in tch, hdwy to chase wnr aftr 3 out, wknd betw last 2.*
.................................(9 to 1 op 8 to 1 tchd 10 to 1) 4
24459 SALDA 5-11-0 T Reed, *mstk 5th, nvr dngrs.*
.................................(14 to 1 op 12 to 1) 5
33793 INNOCENT GEORGE 5-11-0 P Niven, *prmnt till wknd aftr 3 out.*................................(50 to 1) 6
3378 ROCK OPERA (Ire) 6-11-0 A Merrigan, *chsd ldrs till wknd aftr 3 out.*..............................(500 to 1) 7
3236 TRIENNIUM (USA) 5-11-0 B Storey, *al beh, tld off.*
.................................(100 to 1) 8
1613 THISTLE PRINCESS 5-10-9 N Doughty, *alway beh, pld up bef 2 out....*.................(25 to 1 op 16 to 1) pu
JARROW LAD 7-11-0 C Grant, *jmpd badly, sn tld off, pld up aftr second.*...........................(500 to 1) pu
Dist: 7l, sht-hd, 4l, 9l, 12l, 5l, 25l. 3m 48.00s. a 4.00s (10 Ran).
SR: 2/-/-/-/-/ (Mrs Harry J Duffey), K C Bailey

3540 Tote Credit Maiden Chase (5-y-o and up) £3,468 2m.................(5:35)

3438 GRAZEMBER 7-11-7 C Hawkins, *hld up in tch, hdwy to join ldr 8th, btn whn lft clr aftr 2 out, eased r-in.*
.................................(4 to 1 op 7 to 2 tchd 9 to 2) 1
2579 CASTLE CROSS 7-11-7 B Storey, *hld up and beh, hdwy aftr 4 out, styd on wl, not rch wnr...........*(33 to 1) 2
2208 HIGH BEACON 7-11-7 N Williamson, *mstk second, sn prmnt, slightly outpcd aftr 4 out, kpt on frm 2 out.*
.................................(4 to 1 op 7 to 2 tchd 9 to 2) 3
30605 BALLYBELL 9-11-7 T Reed, *led to 3rd, prmnt till wknd aftr 8th....*........................(10 to 1 op 14 to 1) 4
1959 STRONG TRACE 5-11-0 C Grant, *al beh, tld off.*
.................................(20 to 1 op 16 to 1) 5
34388 DOLITINO 10-11-2 Mr T Morrison, *prmnt till blun and lost pl 6th, wl beh whn f 2 out.*..................(33 to 1) f
34603 AYIA NAPA 7-11-7 A Merrigan, *chsd ldrs, wkng whn f 4 out...........................*(5 to 1 op 7 to 1) f
3460 SOUND PROFIT 6-10-11 (5*) J Burke, *losing tch whn mstk 8th, tld off whn pld up bef 3 out.* (33 to 1 op 25 to 1) pu
3135 OVER THE ISLAND (Ire) 6-11-2 A Dobbin, *led 3rd, 3 ls clr whn blun 2 out and pld up lme...*(2 to 1 fav op 6 to 4) pu
Dist: 3½l, nk, 20l, 30l. 4m 0.30s. a 9.30s (9 Ran).
(Mrs M Ashby), P Beaumont

3541 Ballathie House Hotel Amateur Riders' Handicap Hurdle (0-115 4-y-o and up) £3,009 3m 110yds......(6:05)

34758 SWEET CITY [108] 9-11-2 (5*) Mr R Hale, *hld up, hdwy aftr 3 out, led last, styd on wl......*(12 to 1 op 10 to 1) 1
33747 FORWARD GLEN [94] 7-10-0 (7*) Mr A Manners, *wth ldrs, led 2 out, hdd last, edgd lft, kpt on und pres, fnshd second, plcd 3rd...................*(10 to 1 op 8 to 1) 2D
31669 STORM DRUM [99] (bl) 5-10-5 (7*) Mr A Parker, *trkd ldrs, effrt aftr 2 out, sn rdn, staying on but hld whn not much room towards finish, fnshd 3rd, plcd second.*
.................................(5 to 1 op 4 to 1) 2
32834 WELSH SIREN [97] 8-10-5 (5*) Mr N Wilson, *wth ldrs, led 3 out, hdd nxt, ev ch till wknd appr last.*
.................................(11 to 4 fav op 4 to 1 tchd 5 to 2) 4
32803 SPARKLING FLAME [112] 10-11-4 (7*) Mr C Vigors, *made most till hdd 4 out, rdn and wknd aftr nxt.*
.................................(5 to 1 op 6 to 1) 5
34354 FARMER'S CROSS [88] 10-9-12 (3*) Mrs A Farrell, *chsd ldrs aftr 2 out....*.........................(12 to 1) 6
29747 TALL MEASURE [95] 8-10-1 (7*) Mr D Swindlehurst, *trkd ldrs till wknd aftr 3 out, tld off....*(6 to 1 tchd 7 to 1) 7
29547 TRUMP [93] 5-10-1 (5*) Mr P Parker, *hld up, pushed alng aftr 4 out, sn btn, tld off.*
.................................(5 to 1 op 9 to 2 tchd 11 to 2) 8
2436 LOVING OMEN [87] 7-9-7 (7*) Mr T Morrison, *al beh, lost tch frm 4 out, tld off....*...................(50 to 1) 9
Dist: 1¼l, ½l, 3½l, 6l, 3l, 20l, 5l, ¾l. 5m 56.30s. a 11.30s (9 Ran).
(W J Peacock), G Richards

3542 Party Has Started Maiden Hurdle (Div II) (4-y-o and up) £2,444 2½m 110yds ....(6:35)

34294 LONDON HILL 6-11-7 L O'Hara, *in tch, hdwy aftr 3 out, str run to ld r-in, styd on wl.......*(12 to 1 op 8 to 1) 1
30947 UPWARD SURGE (Ire) 4-11-0 N Williamson, *hld up in tch, hdwy to track ldrs 6th, chlgd 2 out, ev ch till no extr r-in....................*(8 to 1 op 7 to 1 tchd 6 to 1) 2
3277 KALAKATE 9-11-7 D O'Sullivan, *made most frm 3rd till hdd r-in, no extr.*........................(10 to 1 op 12 to 1) 3
34402 OTHER RANKS (Ire) 6-11-7 C Dennis, *chsd ldrs, led last, sn hdd, no extr.*..................(10 to 1 op 12 to 1) 4
3144 HIGH MIND (Fr) 5-11-7 P Niven, *prmnt, ev ch 2 out, wknd appr last.*...............(2 to 1 op 5 to 2) 5
31793 RALLEGIO 5-11-7 A Dobbin, *mid-div, effrt aftr 3 out, kpt on same pace..........*(3 to 1 fav op 5 to 2 tchd 9 to 4) 6
2970 SHARP AT SIX (Ire) 4-11-0 Peter Hobbs, *mid-div, effrt aftr 3 out, wknd aftr nxt....*(16 to 1 tchd 20 to 1) 7
34319 FULL OF CHAT (Ire) 5-11-2 M Dwyer, *in tch till outpcd aftr 7th, no dngr after....*(20 to 1 op 16 to 1 tchd 25 to 1) 8

3431 ROYAL FIFE 8-10-13 (3*) P Williams, *chsd ldrs till outpcd aftr 7th, no dngr after*..........(100 to 1) 9
3284[8] D'ARBLAY STREET (Ire) 5-11-0 (7*) S McDougall, *beh most of way*..........(50 to 1 op 33 to 1) 10
3236[5] BALISTEROS (Fr) 5-11-7 R Garritty, *led to 3rd, wth ldr till wknd aftr 7th*..........(20 to 1 op 16 to 1) 11
3284 CROSS REFERENCE 6-11-2 T Reed, *prmnt till outpcd hfwy, sn beh*..........(50 to 1 op 33 to 1) 12
3236[7] FINDOGLEN 8-11-7 C Grant, *in tch till wknd appr 3 out*..........(100 to 1) 13
3429 TREASURE BEACH 5-11-0 (7*) A Linton, *sn beh, tld off whn pld up aftr 7th*..........(200 to 1) pu
2433[9] HOD-MOD (Ire) 4-10-11 (3*) Mrs A Farrell, *al beh, tld off whn pld up bef 2 out*..........(200 to 1) pu

Dist: 2½l, hd, ¾l, 9l, ½l, 4l, 3½l, 4l, 3l, 4l. 4m 56.10s. a 11.10s (15 Ran).
(Peter J S Russell), Mrs D Thomson

FONTWELL (good to firm)
Thursday April 21st
Going Correction: PLUS 0.25 sec. per fur.

3543 Amberley Novices' Hurdle (Div I) (4-y-o and up) £1,543 2¼m.......(2:20)

3383[3] RES IPSA LOQUITUR 7-11-2 D Gallagher, *nvr far away, styd on to ld sn aftr last, rdn and ran on*..........(5 to 1 op 9 to 2) 1
JEHOL 8-11-2 W Humphreys, *led, clr 4 out, rdn appr last, hdd r-in, no extr*..........(14 to 1 op 50 to 1) 2
2315 BOOTH'S BOUQUET 6-11-2 M Richards, *al prmnt, wnt second appr 2 out, rdn and wknd r-in*..........(50 to 1 op 25 to 1) 3
3115[6] NATIVE CHIEFTAN 5-11-8 A Dicken, *wtd wth, hdwy 5th, no imprsn appr last*. (2 to 1 fav op 5 to 2 tchd 7 to 2) 4
3270[4] KING'S TREASURE (USA) 5-12-0 J Frost, *chsd ldr till wknd appr 2 out*...... (9 to 4 op 11 to 4 tchd 7 to 2) 5
1519[2] OH SO HANDY 6-11-2 D Morris, *in tch, one pace frm 3 out*..........(33 to 1 op 20 to 1) 6
3151[8] SMART IN SABLE 7-10-11 M A FitzGerald, *mid-div, lost tch 3 out*..........(20 to 1 op 10 to 1) 7
3334[8] PINK SUNSET (Ire) 6-11-2 J R Kavanagh, *chsd ldrs till wknd appr 2 out*..........(66 to 1 op 50 to 1) 8
2405[8] WYJUME (Ire) 5-10-11 B Powell, *al mid-div*..........(66 to 1 op 33 to 1) 9
3333 HIGHLAND FLAME 5-11-1 (7*) Mr G Hogan, *chsd ldrs till wknd quickly 3 out*..........(50 to 1 op 25 to 1) 10
3270 BENGALI (Ire) (bl) 4-11-2 Peter Hobbs, *in frnt rnk till wknd quickly appr 3 out*... (25 to 1 op 16 to 1 tchd 33 to 1) 11
LAST MATCH 6-10-13 (3*) R Davis, *al in rear*..........(66 to 1 op 33 to 1) 12
2881 BARNIEMEBOY (bl) 4-10-10 W Elderfield, *beh frm hfwy, tld off*..........(100 to 1 op 50 to 1) 13
3095[8] RUN TO AU BON (Ire) 4-10-10 G Upton, *in tch to 5th, tld off*..........(66 to 1 op 50 to 1) 14
PHAE TINGO (Ire) 4-10-10 L Harvey, *slwly away, tld off frm 4th*..........(66 to 1 op 50 to 1) 15
INTERROGATE 6-10-11 S Earle, *in tch to 5th, tld off whn pld up bef 2 out*..........(50 to 1 op 20 to 1) pu
3114[4] KEYLU 5-10-11 M Hourigan, *slwly away, al beh, tld off whn pld up bef 2 out*..........(66 to 1 op 50 to 1) pu
LEAP INTO SPRING (Ire) 5-11-2 A Maguire, *beh, tld off whn pld up bef 2 out*..........(9 to 2 op 9 to 4 tchd 2 to 1 and 5 to 1) pu
3145 LB'S GIRL 5-10-11 R Rowell, *tld off frm 5th, pld up bef 2 out*..........(100 to 1 op 50 to 1) pu

Dist: 8l, ½l, 4l, 1l, 20l, 2½l, hd, 5l, 1¾l, 9l. 4m 20.00s. a 10.00s (19 Ran).
SR: 33/25/24/26/31/-/ (Richard J Gray), J E Long

3544 John Rogerson Memorial Challenge Trophy Handicap Chase (0-120 5-y-o and up) £3,054 3¼m 110yds.....(2:50)

3332[5] MASTER COMEDY [74] (bl) 10-10-0 M Stevens, *al prmnt, led 9th to 14th, rallied und pres appr last, led sn aftr, styd on*..........(33 to 1 op 25 to 1) 1
3364[3] DOONLOUGHAN [98] 9-11-7 (3*) R Davis, *al frnt rnk, led 14th to 6 out, rdn 3 out, kpt on r-in*. (7 to 1 op 10 to 1) 2
3203 SATIN NOIR (Fr) [102] 10-12-0 M A FitzGerald, *beh, steady hdwy fnl circuit, styd on frm 3 out*..........(12 to 1 op 8 to 1 tchd 14 to 1) 3
3149[3] PUNCH'S HOTEL [93] 9-11-0 (5*) C Burnett-Wells, *hld up in tch, rdn and hdwy appr 3 out, ridden and kpt on r-in*..........(8 to 1 op 6 to 1 tchd 9 to 1) 4
1411[6] ISLAND FOREST (USA) [92] 8-11-4 R Dunwoody, *al prmnt, led 6 out, hrd rdn whn hit last, sn hdd, no extr*..........(3 to 1 fav op 7 to 2 tchd 4 to 1 and 11 to 4) 5
3154* HURRICANE BLAKE [91] (bl) 6-11-3 Peter Hobbs, *al towards rear, lost tch fnl circuit*..........(7 to 2 op 3 to 1 tchd 4 to 1) 6
3307* THAMESDOWN TOOTSIE [87] 9-10-13 D Murphy, *in tch till wknd 14th*..........(13 to 2 op 5 to 1 tchd 7 to 1) 7
3477[9] TAGMOUN CHAUFOUR (Fr) [77] 9-10-3 B Powell, *led to 9th, wknd 15th, sn wl beh*..........(50 to 1) 8
3149 GINGER DIP [74] 12-9-11 (3*) R Farrant, *al beh, tld off whn pld up aftr 15th*..........(50 to 1) pu
3260[6] SMOOTH ESCORT [96] (v) 10-11-8 D Bridgwater, *sn beh, tld off whn pld up bef 9th*..........(5 to 1 tchd 11 to 2) pu
LAD LANE [74] 10-10-0 J R Kavanagh, *al beh, tld off 11th, pld up bef 13th*..........(50 to 1) pu
3258 YOUNG ALFIE [75] (bl) 9-10-1 A Maguire, *chsd ldrs, chalg whn hit 6 out, wknd quickly appr 3 out, pld up bef nxt*..........(16 to 1 tchd 20 to 1) pu

Dist: 2½l, sht-hd, hd, nk, 20l, 15l, 3½l. 6m 56.00s. a 26.00s (12 Ran).
(Miss J Wilkinson), B Stevens

3545 Lidsey Conditional Jockeys' Selling Handicap Hurdle (4-y-o and up) £2,061 2¾m..........(3:20)

3398[5] QUIET DAWN [85] 8-11-5 P Ward, *led till hdd 3 out, rallied wl to ld ag'n r-in, jst hld on*.....(11 to 2 fav op 5 to 1) 1
2225[5] TEMPORALE [67] 8-9-10 (5*) G Crone, *nvr far away, outpcd appr 2 out, ran on strly r-in, jst fld*..........(16 to 1 op 14 to 1) 2
1592[3] PEAK DISTRICT [80] 8-11-0 P McLoughlin, *al prmnt, led last, rdn and hdd r-in, no extr nr finish*..........(11 to 1 op 10 to 1 tchd 12 to 1) 3
3308[7] QUALITAIR MEMORY (Ire) [76] 5-10-5 (5*) S Ryan, *al prmnt, led appr 2 out, hdd last, wknd r-in*..........(6 to 1 op 5 to 1 tchd 13 to 2) 4
2523[6] IRISH TAN [66] 7-9-10[1] (5*) S Arnold, *mid-div, steady hdwy frm 3 out, hld whn mstk last*..........(11 to 1 op 10 to 1 tchd 12 to 1) 5
3150[2] VILLA PARK [79] 12-10-13 P Hide, *hld up, hdwy 7th, one pace frm 3 out*..........(8 to 1 op 12 to 1) 6
3174 SOUTHOVER LAD (NZ) [82] 11-11-2 R Davis, *mid-div, hdwy 4th, led and blun 3 out, sn hdd, wknd appr last*..........(25 to 1) 7
3192[6] MOUNTAIN MASTER [79] 8-10-13 R Farrant, *prmnt whn hit 4th, lost tch 3 out*..........(14 to 1 tchd 16 to 1) 8
3363[5] RIBOVINO [79] 11-10-13 D Leahy, *al mid-div*..........(20 to 1 op 16 to 1) 9
3098* ROGER'S PAL [90] 7-11-10 Guy Lewis, *mid-div, wknd appr 3 out*..........(12 to 1 op 10 to 1) 10
JIM BOWIE [76] 11-10-5 (5*) M Keighley, *al towards rear*..........(25 to 1 tchd 33 to 1) 11
2711[2] GREENWINE (USA) [80] 8-11-0 J McCarthy, *al mid-div*..........(7 to 1 op 6 to 1 tchd 8 to 1) 12
2729 FEARSOME [77] 8-10-6 (5*) N Juckes, *chsd wnr till wknd appr 3 out*..........(25 to 1) 13
3337 LITTLE BIG [82] (bl) 7-11-2 R Massey, *prmnt till wknd 7th, tld off*..........(14 to 1 op 10 to 1) 14
2225[3] FROSTY RECEPTION [89] (bl) 9-11-9 S Curran, *prmnt till wknd appr 4 out, tld off*..........(12 to 1 op 2 to 1 tchd 14 to 1) 15
3003 ENBORNE LAD [74] 10-10-8 A Dicken, *al beh, tld off*..........(20 to 1 op 16 to 1) 16
3155 POWERSURGE [81] 7-11-1 L O'Hare, *mid-div, lost tch 7th, tld off*..........(25 to 1) 17
1411 LAVALIGHT [79] (bl) 7-10-13 P Carey, *prmnt to 6th, sn beh, tld off*..........(12 to 1 op 10 to 1) 18
3156[8] LUCKY OAK [70] (bl) 8-10-4 C Burnett-Wells, *al beh, tld off*..........(20 to 1 op 14 to 1) 19
2554[8] HOME COUNTY [75] 12-10-9 A Procter, *al beh, tld off whn pld up bef 2 out*..........(33 to 1 op 25 to 1) pu

Dist: Sht-hd, 2l, 8l, 5l, 3l, 1l, 4l, 7l, 1½l, 9l. 5m 26.70s. a 17.70s (20 Ran).
(Mrs P M King), J S King

3546 Trundle Novices' Chase (5-y-o and up) £2,427 3¼m 110yds............(3:50)

3454[3] EARLY MAN 7-11-2 Peter Hobbs, *al prmnt, hmpd appr 7 out, led nxt, drvn out*..........(100 to 30 op 3 to 1 tchd 7 to 2) 1
3006[2] DEEPENDABLE (bl) 7-11-8 M A FitzGerald, *al prmnt, hmpd appr 7 out, hit nxt, hrd rdn, no imprsn r-in*..........(11 to 8 fav tchd 6 to 4 and 5 to 4) 2
3154 GROOMSMAN 8-11-2 W Humphreys, *wtd wth, hdwy 7 out, kpt on one pace frm 2 out*.......(8 to 1 op 5 to 1) 3
3454 COASTING 8-11-2 J Railton, *al prmnt, led 4th to 15th, styd in tch, rdn and wknd appr last*..........(20 to 1 op 14 to 1) 4
3099[7] VICTORY GATE (USA) (v) 9-11-2 D Gallagher, *led, hit 11th, led 15th, tried to run out and hdd bef nxt, rallied appr 3 out, wknd next*..........(14 to 1 op 10 to 1) 5
3265[6] JIMMY CONE 11-11-2 J Frost, *beh, some late hdwy*..........(9 to 1 op 8 to 1 tchd 14 to 1) 6
2780 MISS MUIRE 8-10-11 D Morris, *mid-div, nvr nr to chal*..........(25 to 1 op 20 to 1) 7
3207 TEARFUL PRINCE 10-11-2 B Powell, *mid-div, 4th whn blun 3 out, not reco'r*..........(50 to 1 op 33 to 1) 8
3421[4] HALF A MO (bl) 9-10-11 J R Kavanagh, *beh, lost tch 15th, tld off*..........(20 to 1 op 14 to 1) 9
3307[5] GENERAL BRANDY 8-11-8 D Murphy, *trkd ldr, lft in ld appr 7 out, hdd nxt, wknd quickly, tld off*..........(12 to 1 op 8 to 1) 10
3332 SPARTAN RAFT 13-10-9 (7*) Mr G Pewter, *al in rear, tld off whn pld up bef 12th*..........(50 to 1 op 33 to 1) pu
3118 UNEXIS 9-11-2 S Earle, *sn in rear, lost tch 15th, pld up bef 5 out*..........(33 to 1 op 25 to 1) pu

Dist: 1½l, 2½l, 5l, 8l, 1l, 1¾l, 3l, 15l, dist. 7m 0.60s. a 30.60s (12 Ran).
(Mrs John Grist), D M Grissell

3547 Royal Veterinary College Challenge Trophy 'National Hunt' Novices' Hurdle (4-y-o and up) £1,543 2¾m. . (4:20)

```
2427  WOODLANDS BOY (Ire) 6-11-2 M Hoad, al prmnt, lost pl 3
      out, hrd rdn and rallied to ld r-in. (50 to 1 op 33 to 1)    1
2991  ILE DE SOO 8-11-2 R Dunwoody, hld up in tch, hdwy 7th,
      jnd ldr 2 out, drvn to ld last, hdd and no extr r-in.
      ...........................(6 to 1 op 7 to 1 tchd 9 to 1)     2
3151²  POLLY MINOR 7-10-11 A Maguire, hld up, hdwy 4 out, led
      2 out, hdd last, one pace.
      .......................(5 to 1 op 6 to 1 tchd 7 to 1)         3
3204*  AMBER REALM 6-11-3 B Powell, al prmnt, led 4 out to 2
      out, ev ch till mstk last, no extr.....(10 to 1 op 6 to 1)    4
26719  GILPA VALU 5-11-2 J Osborne, made most till 4 out, one
      pace frm 2 out........(16 to 1 op 6 to 1 tchd 20 to 1)        5
3365  POLICEMANS PRIDE (Fr) 5-11-2 T Grantham, in tch till
      wknd appr 3 out........................(50 to 1 op 33 to 1)   6
2991  BISHOPS TRUTH 8-11-2 D Morris, beh, effrt 4 out, sn btn.
      ..........................(50 to 1 op 33 to 1)               7
      JUDY LINE 5-10-11 W Marston, dsptd ld till wknd appr 4
      out................................(100 to 1 op 50 to 1)     8
3345  MANDY LOUISE 6-10-11 D Bridgwater, al beh, tld off.
      ..........................(100 to 1 op 50 to 1)              9
      ROONA 5-10-4 (7*) P McLoughlin, al beh, tld off.
      ..........................(50 to 1 op 20 to 1)              10
3264²  CALL HOME (Ire) 6-11-8 D Murphy, tucked in beh ldrs, 4th
      and gng wl whn f 3 out.
      ........................(13 to 16 on op 2 to 1 on tchd 6 to 4 on)  f
3306  NINON-PENNY 6-11-2 M Stevens, al beh, tld off 5th, pld
      up aftr nxt..............................(100 to 1)          pu
3264  MR ELECTRAMECH 7-11-2 A Dicken, beh frm 4th, tld off
      whn pld up bef four out....................(100 to 1)        pu
Dist: 1½l, 2½l, nk, 1½l, 14l, 4l, 1¾l, dist, 12l. 5m 36.60s. a 27.60s (13 Ran).
                                          (Stan Moore), R P C Hoad
```

3548 Robert Gore Memorial Challenge Cup Handicap Chase (0-115 5-y-o and up) £2,970 2¼m. . . . . (4:50)

```
2836*  DEXTRA DOVE [106] 7-11-6 S Earle, al prmnt, led appr 3
      out, drvn out...........(10 to 2 op 9 to 2 tchd 6 to 1)      1
3099*  SOLEIL DANCER (Ire) [91] 6-10-5 J Railton, hld up, hdwy
      frm 9th, pressed wnr last, short of room r-in, ran on.
      ..........................(6 to 1 op 4 to 1)                 2
3301²  BOLD CHOICE [96] 8-10-10 J Frost, hld up in rear, gd
      hdwy 4 out, ev ch last, kpt on.........(6 to 1 op 6 to 1)    3
3303³  CONGREGATION [101] 8-11-1 M Perrett, hld up, hdwy
      9th, rdn and ch last, hng lft and no extr nr finish.
      ..........................(10 to 1 op 8 to 1)                4
3456²  GENERAL MERCHANT [87] (bl) 14-10-1 R Dunwoody, al in
      tch, led aftr 8th, hdd appr 3 out, pressed wnr till edgd
      lft r-in, hld whn hmpd cl hme.
      ..........................                                   5
3420  MACEDONAS [99] 6-10-13 G Bradley, hld up in tch, hdwy
      9th, ev ch 2 out till wknd r-in.  (5 to 1 fav tchd 6 to 1)   6
3303²  NATHIR (USA) [98] 8-10-12 J R Kavanagh, wl in rear till
      hdwy 9th, wknd appr 2 out......(12 to 1 tchd 14 to 1)        7
2545²  VICTORY ANTHEM [86] 8-10-0 l Lawrence, not jump wl, in
      tch till hit 5 out, sn btn..............(50 to 1 op 33 to 1) 8
1512⁵  COURT RAPIER [96] 7-12 10-10 A Maguire, led second till
      hdd aftr 8th, rdn and sn beh......(10 to 1 tchd 12 to 1)     9
3305⁴  MAJOR INQUIRY (USA) [90] 8-10-4⁴ (3*) P Hide, al beh.
      ........................(9 to 1 op 10 to 1 tchd 11 to 1)    10
3203  NOS NA GAOITHE [110] 11-11-10 B Powell, prmnt, disput-
      ing ld whn mstk 6 out, wknd rpdly 4 out.
      ........................(20 to 1 op 14 to 1 tchd 33 to 1)   11
2707  FILE CONCORD [111] 10-11-4 (7*) L O'Hare, wl beh frm 8th,
      tld off whn pld up bef 3 out......(14 to 1 tchd 16 to 1)     pu
3210⁴  THATS THE LIFE [114] 9-12-0 M A FitzGerald, led to second,
      wknd quickly 8th, pld up bef nxt. (20 to 1 op 14 to 1)       pu
Dist: ½l, 1l, 1l, 1½l, 3½l, 9l, 15l, 4l, 7l, sht-hd. 4m 35.90s. a 15.90s (13 Ran).
                                       (Dextra Lighting Systems), R H Alner
```

3549 Amberley Novices' Hurdle (Div II) (4-y-o and up) £1,543 2¼m. . . . . . . (5:20)

```
3342⁵  POLISH RIDER (USA) 6-10-9 (7*) C Huggan, al prmnt, rdn
      to ld last, ran on wl......................(50 to 1 op 25 to 1)   1
1341  KHALIDI (Ire) 5-11-8 P Holley, led, clr appr 2 out, rdn and
      hdd last, no extr.......(11 to 4 op 3 to 1 tchd 5 to 2)     2
3215⁹  DEAR DO 7-11-2 M A FitzGerald, nvr far away, ev ch 3 out
      till rdn and wknd appr last.
      ........................(6 to 1 op 5 to 1 tchd 7 to 1)       3
3209*  LABURNUM 6-12-0 R Dunwoody, al in tch, rdn 3 out,
      wknd appr last......(6 to 4 fav op 2 to 1 tchd 5 to 2)       4
2426⁶  PRINCE TEETON 5-11-2 B Powell, hld up, hdwy 3 out,
      styd on, nvr nrr.....................(11 to 1 op 8 to 1)      5
592  PANDY 8-10-13 (3*) R Farrant, in frnt rnk till rdn and
      wknd 3 out.............(16 to 1 op 20 to 1)                 6+
3010⁶  WORLDLY PROSPECT (USA) 6-10-4 (7*) S Arnold, mid-div,
      nvr nr to chal........(25 to 1 op 14 to 1 tchd 20 to 1)     6+
3136  THE GOLFING CURATE 9-11-9 (5*) C Burnett-Wells, in tch
      till wknd appr 3 out....(10 to 1 op 6 to 1 tchd 12 to 1)     8
1595⁵  JUNIPER LODGE 6-11-2 S Earle, al towards rear.
      ........................(33 to 1 op 20 to 1)                 9
```

```
1994  GREAT ORME (NZ) 7-11-2 M Perrett, al beh.
      ..........................(33 to 1 op 20 to 1)             10
      HORIZON (Ire) (bl) 6-11-2 S Smith Eccles, prmnt till wknd
      quickly appr 3 out.......(8 to 1 op 4 to 1 tchd 9 to 1)    11
2950⁸  POLDEN PRIDE 6-11-2 J Railton, chsd ldrs till wknd
      quickly appr 4 out....................(50 to 1 op 25 to 1) 12
3339⁵  TRUE MARCH 6-11-2 J R Kavanagh, al beh, tld off.
      ..........................(33 to 1 op 20 to 1 tchd 50 to 1) 13
      GLEN PARISH 9-10-11 A Tory, al beh, tld off.................14
      SYMMETRICAL 5-11-2 D Morris, al beh, tld off whn pld
      up bef 4 out..........................(50 to 1)             pu
2881  NEOLOGIST 8-11-2 B Clifford, sn tld off, pld up bef 4th.
      ..........................(50 to 1)                         pu
Dist: 4l, 5l, ¾l, 2½l, 9l, dd-ht, 1¼l, 2l, 9l, 2l. 4m 24.00s. a 14.00s (16 Ran).
                                        (Mrs Diana Haine), Mrs D Haine
```

MALLOW (IRE) (soft)
Thursday April 21st

3550 Lee Maiden Hurdle (4-y-o and up) £2,243 2m. (2:30)

```
2616⁸  BADEN (Ire) 6-11-6 (3*) T P Treacy, ..........(5 to 4 fav)  1
2917²  DARK SWAN (Ire) 4-11-1 (5*) P C Dunne, ........(8 to 1)     2
3291³  ARABIAN SPRITE (Ire) 6-11-1 Mr P J Healy, ......(8 to 1)   3+
3466⁷  KILLOSKEHAN QUEEN 7-10-12 (3*) C O'Brien, ..(20 to 1)     3+
3473³  RYE HILL QUEEN (Ire) 4-10-10 C F Swan, ........(6 to 1)     5
3466⁵  HAVE A BRANDY (Ire) 5-11-5 Mr D M O'Brien, ..(12 to 1)     6
2614⁴  NURSE MAID (Ire) 4-11-2 J Collins, ............(12 to 1)   7
3290⁴  MY SUNNY WAY (Ire) 5-10-12 (7*) Mr D K Budds, (12 to 1)    8
3294⁷  REPLACEMENT 4-10-10 Mr O'Neill, ..............(16 to 1)    9
      BIMSEY (Ire) 4-10-10 (5*) Susan A Finn, .......(50 to 1)   10
313⁸  BUCKINGHAM BOY 8-11-7 (7*) Miss C A Harrison, (20 to 1)    11
      BUILDERS LINE (Ire) 6-10-10 (5*) M A Davey, ..(25 to 1)    12
3290  BROOK QUEEN (Ire) 5-10-9 (5*) Mr W M O'Sullivan,
      ..........................(33 to 1)                        13
3291  ALICES RUN 7-11-9 T Horgan, .................(8 to 1)      14
557⁷  MOUNTHENRY STAR (Ire) 6-12-0 C O'Dwyer, ...(12 to 1)       15
2943  TOURIG LE MOSS 7-10-8 (7*) Mr R Finlay, ......(20 to 1)    16
3291  CARRIG DANCER (Ire) 6-10-8 (7*) Mr K Whelan, (20 to 1)     17
3291  GOLDEN ARRANGEMENT 9-11-5 (3*) J O'Sullivan,
      ..........................(33 to 1)                        18
3466  MISS BERTAINE (Ire) 5-10-11 (3*) T J Mitchell, ..(33 to 1) 19
1265  ORDONNANT (Fr) 6-11-1 (5*) T P Rudd, .........(12 to 1)    20
2938  COOL COOPER 7-10-10 (5*) P A Roche, ..........(25 to 1)    21
2944  ROSEL WALK (Ire) 5-11-5 A J O'Brien, ..........(33 to 1)   22
3466⁹  POLLEROO (Ire) 6-11-9 J Jones, ...............(10 to 1)    23
2918⁸  THE COBH GALE 7-11-1 H Rogers, ..............(12 to 1)     24
292⁴  SPOUT HOUSE 5-11-0 F Woods, ................(10 to 1)      25
3290  BUTLER JOHN (Ire) 5-11-5 K F O'Brien, .........(20 to 1)   26
      BOLD ALFIE 4-11-1 J F Titley, .................(25 to 1)   27
      CAMDEN BANNER (Ire) 4-10-10 (5*) J P Broderick, (25 to 1)  28
Dist: 7l, ½l, dd-ht, hd. 4m 2.60s. (28 Ran).
                                             (Max Hauri), P Mullins
```

3551 Blackwater Novice Chase (5-y-o and up) £2,243 3m. . . . . (3:30)

```
2985⁸  OLYMPIC D'OR (Ire) 6-12-0 C O'Dwyer, ..........(6 to 1)    1
410³  SILVERWEIR 11-12-0 T Horgan, ................(10 to 1)      2
3457  PARSONS BRIG 8-12-0 K F O'Brien, ..........(7 to 2 fav)     3
3293⁹  DUNBOY CASTLE (Ire) 6-12-0 M Moran, ..........(12 to 1)     4
2922  BALADINE 7-11-4 S H O'Donovan, .............(8 to 1)        5
3293³  MATELINA 8-11-4 S R Murphy, ..................(6 to 1)      6
3293⁶  MONKS AIR 7-10-13 (5*) Mr W M O'Sullivan, ...(20 to 1)     7
2984  KINGS HILL 12-11-2 (7*) J Butler, .............(8 to 1)     8
635  HIGH-SPEC 8-11-11 (3*) C O'Brien, .............(12 to 1)     9
2752²  CHOSEN SON 6-11-4 (5*) D P Geoghegan, ........(20 to 1)    10
3293  MELDRUM MISS (Ire) 6-11-4 P M Verling, .......(14 to 1)    11
2128  MAJOR BERT (Ire) 6-11-9 F Woods, .............(20 to 1)    12
2919⁶  FAIR ADELINE (Ire) 7-11-4 H Rogers, ..........(20 to 1)    13
2923  GODFREYS CROSS (Ire) 6-11-4 J F Titley, .......(20 to 1)   14
3293⁸  SO PINK (Ire) 6-11-2 (7*) P Murphy, ............(8 to 1)    f
3197  ELUSIVE SOCIETY (Ire) 5-10-8 J A White, ......(20 to 1)    pu
Dist: 1l, 12l, 12l, 3l. 6m 39.70s. (16 Ran).
                                         (Mrs Dorine Reihill), M F Morris
```

3552 E.B.F. Mares Spring I N H Flat Race (4,5,6-y-o) £2,588 2m. . . . . (5:30)

```
3290²  KATE FISHER (Ire) 5-11-10 Mr J E Kiely, ........(7 to 2)    1
3393⁴  GLEN TEN (Ire) 5-12-0 (3*) Mrs M J Mullins, ...(5 to 2 fav) 2
2704²  MARYJO (Ire) 5-11-3 (7*) Mr P English, .........(8 to 1)    3
      THRESA-ANITA (Ire) 6-11-4 (7*) Mr B Hassett, ..(10 to 1)    4
3469⁵  MISS POLLERTON (Ire) 6-11-4 (7*) Mr M J Bowe, (12 to 1)     5
585  DON'T ASK JOHNNY (Ire) 5-11-3 (7*) Mr S O'Brien, (14 to 1)   6
2464⁴  BALLYMADUN LASS (Ire) 5-11-5 (5*) Mr H F Cleary, (7 to 1)   7
      ELWOOD (Ire) 4-10-10 (7*) Mr D Murphy, .........(14 to 1)    8
3245  KILBRICKEN DANCER (Ire) 4-11-3 Mr P Fenton, ..(14 to 1)     9
803⁷  SCEAL SIOG (Ire) 5-11-7 (3*) Mr J A Nash, .....(12 to 1)    10
      CARSEAHELEN (Ire) 6-11-4 (7*) Miss F O'Flynn, ..(20 to 1)   11
      VERUNA (Ire) 4-10-10 (7*) Mr M A Cahill, ........(25 to 1)  12
      TURTANE CHOICE (Ire) 6-11-4 (7*) Mr J Tracey, ..(12 to 1)   13
3447  DUST GALE (Ire) 5-11-7 (3*) Mr J F Sleator, ....(14 to 1)   14
      STEPHANIE'S JOY (Ire) 5-11-7 (3*) Mr T Lombard, (14 to 1)   15
```

3197 WHITE OAK BRIDGE (Ire) 5-11-3 (7*) Mr T R Hughes, ...(14 to 1) 16
636 BALLYRANEBOW (Ire) 6-11-4 (7*) Mr M Flood, ...(25 to 1) 17
AWAYTODAY (Ire) 4-10-10 (7*) Mr J F Robinson, .. (33 to 1) 18
BAILEY HOUSE (Ire) 4-10-13^{3} (7*) Mr A J Kennedy, (20 to 1) 19
3245 HERONIMUS BOSCH (Ire) 4-11-0 (3*) Mr D Marnane, ...(33 to 1) 20
3291 OUR BLOSSOM (Ire) 6-11-4 (7*) Mr E Henley, ...(33 to 1) 21
BALLYWILLIAM STAR (Ire) 4-10-10 (7*) Mr P O'Keeffe, ...(25 to 1) 22

Dist: 3l, 2½l, 9l, 11l. 3m 56.70s. (22 Ran).
(James P O'Keeffe), J E Kiely

PERTH (good to firm)
Thursday April 21st
Going Correction: MINUS 0.30 sec. per fur. (races 1,3,5), NIL (2,4,6)

3553 Sporting Lounge And Olympic Suite Claiming Hurdle (4-y-o and up) £2,570 2m 110yds....................(2:00)

2070^{9} JOHN NAMAN (Ire) 5-10-10 A Dobbin, *in tch, effrt aftr 3 out, led betw last 2, ran on wl*... (16 to 1 tchd 20 to 1) 1
3416^{2} AL FORUM (Ire) 4-10-9 D O'Sullivan, *al cl up, led 2 out, sn hdd, no extr*........................(9 to 2 op 7 to 2) 2
2907^{9} DIGNIFIED (Ire) 4-9-11^{4} (7*) A Linton, *hld up, hdwy aftr 3 out, kpt on wl frm last*........... (16 to 1 op 20 to 1) 3
3436 BUCKRA MELLISUGA (v) 10-10-11 (3*) A Larnach, *trkd ldrs, ev ch 2 out, kpt on same pace*.....(10 to 1 op 12 to 1) 4
3378^{8} BIRD WATCHER 5-10-11 (3*) D Bentley, *trkd ldrs, ev ch 2 out, kpt on same pace*....................... (33 to 1) 5
3429^{2} KANNDABIL (bl) 7-11-4 G McCourt, *chsd ldrs, ev ch 2 out, kpt on same pace*.... (3 to 1 fav op 4 to 1 tchd 9 to 2) 6
3436 STAY AWAKE 8-12-0 P Niven, *in tch, hdwy aftr 5th, ev ch appr 2 out, one pace*. (10 to 1 op 8 to 1 tchd 11 to 1) 7
3342* CHARLYCIA (v) 6-10-6 (7*) M Clarke, *prmnt, one pace frm 3 out*.................................(6 to 1 op 8 to 1) 8
1791^{6} CLEAR IDEA (Ire) 6-11-8 N Doughty, *cl up, led 5th, hdd 2 out, sn wknd*....................(16 to 1 op 14 to 1) 9
3436^{6} FIERY SUN 9-11-4 N Smith, *in tch, no hdwy frm 3 out*. .... (11 to 2 op 7 to 2) 10
3144 CA-KNOWE (Ire) (v) 5-10-12 M Moloney, *in tch till wknd aftr 3 out*...................................(100 to 1) 11
2433^{5} SUPREME SOVIET 4-10-2 (3*) D J Moffatt, *sn led, hdd 5th, wknd aftr nxt*...............................(50 to 1) 12
3435^{7} GLORIOUS HEIGHTS 6-10-9 A Merrigan, *al beh*. .... (50 to 1 op 33 to 1) 13
2254 HILLTOWN BLUES 5-10-12 L Wyer, *al beh*. .... (16 to 1 op 14 to 1) 14
1584^{5} ASTRAC TRIO (USA) 4-10-10 (5*) J Burke, *beh frm hfwy*. .... (16 to 1 op 14 to 1) 15
2909 SALLY'S PRINCESS 4-10-2 S Turner, *sn beh*.....(100 to 1) 16
3285^{5} TOURAQUE (Fr) 9-10-7 (7*) I Jardine, *al beh*..... (100 to 1) 17
2951 AFRICAN GOLD 6-11-1 T Reed, *beh whn blun and uns rdr 4th*....................................(100 to 1) ur

Dist: 3½l, 1½l, sht-hd, sht-hd, ¾l, 2½l, 3½l, 2½l, 3l, ¾l. 3m 49.10s. a 5.10s (18 Ran).
(G Breen), M A Barnes

3554 Glengoyne Highland Malt Tamerosia Series Final Novices' Chase (5-y-o and up) £5,472 3m..............(2:30)

2149^{6} CAPITAL PUNISHMENT 8-11-12 C Grant, *hld up in tch, trkd wnr frm 4 out, led 2 out, styd on wl*. ....(4 to 1 op 7 to 2 tchd 9 to 2) 1
3428^{5} BARNEY RUBBLE 9-11-5 N Williamson, *jmpd lft thrght, led till hdd 2 out, no extr*.......... (25 to 1 op 16 to 1) 2
3358^{3} LO STREGONE 8-11-12 R Garritty, *prmnt, pushed alng aftr 11th, outpcd after 14th, no dngr after*. .... (5 to 4 on op Evens tchd 11 to 8 on) 3
3075 BUCKWHEAT LAD (Ire) 6-11-5 K Johnson, *sn pushed alng, kpt on frm 3 out, nvr dngrs*........(66 to 1 op 33 to 1) 4
3428* BENNAN MARCH 7-11-12 A Dobbin, *in tch, blun 14th, btn whn hit 3 out*........ (100 to 30 op 5 to 2 tchd 7 to 2) 5
3486 SNOOK POINT 7-11-5 Mr A Manners, *wth ldrs, hmpd several fences, wknd appr 3 out*... (50 to 1 op 33 to 1) 6
3428^{9} LINLITHGOW PALACE 12-11-5 P Waggott, *sn beh and rdn, tld off whn pld up aftr 12th*..... (200 to 1 op 100 to 1) pu
3428^{3} KIRKCALDY (Ire) 5-10-10 P Williams, *al beh, lost tch and pld up bef 3 out*..... (14 to 1 op 12 to 1 tchd 16 to 1) pu

Dist: 4l, 8l, 2l, 4l, 1½l. 6m 9.90s. a 12.90s (8 Ran).
(J N Hinchliffe), M D Hammond

3555 W. Green Scottish Law Publisher Handicap Hurdle (0-125 4-y-o and up) £3,566 2½m 110yds............ (3:00)

3455* CARIBOO GOLD (USA) [128] (bl) 5-12-3 (3ex) N Williamson, *hld up in tch, hdwy to track ldr 3 out, rdn to ld nxt, clr whn hit last*.......(11 to 8 fav op 6 to 4 tchd 13 to 8) 1
2432^{6} SOMERSET DANCER (USA) [99] 7-10-2^{2} D O'Sullivan, *cl up, led 6th, hdd 2 out, kpt on und pres*. (14 to 1 op 20 to 1) 2
3166^{8} SWEET NOBLE (Ire) [97] 5-9-7 (7*) F Leahy, *prmnt, ev ch 3 out, grad wknd*...... (12 to 1 op 10 to 1 tchd 16 to 1) 3
2954^{6} THE GREEN FOOL [107] 7-10-10 B Storey, *hld up, effrt appr 3 out, no hdwy*............... (7 to 1 tchd 8 to 1) 4
3539^{2} SHAHGRAM (Ire) [97] 6-10-0 Mrs A Farrell, *hld up, effrt aftr 3 out, no hdwy*...................(14 to 1 op 10 to 1) 5
3475 HAZEL LEAF [99] 8-10-2 R Hodge, *nvr on terms*. .... (11 to 1 op 10 to 1 tchd 12 to 1) 6
2815^{8} BAY TERN (USA) [103] 8-10-6 L Wyer, *led till aftr 1st, cl up till wknd appr 3 out*.......................(7 to 2 op 9 to 4) 7
3475 MANGROVE MIST (Ire) [97] 6-10-0 A Dobbin, *al beh*. ....(20 to 1 tchd 16 to 1) 8
2740 NODFORM WONDER [116] 7-11-5 G McCourt, *led aftr 1st till hdd 6th, sn beh, tld off*..........(12 to 1 op 8 to 1) 9

Dist: 4l, 12l, 4l, hd, 12l, 4l, 7l, 25l. 4m 44.60s. b 0.40s (9 Ran).
SR: 46/13/-/5/-/-/ (Sheikh Marwan Al Maktoum), K C Bailey

3556 R M C Catherwood Ltd 'Little Bay' Handicap Chase (0-130 5-y-o and up) £5,446 2m.................... (3:30)

2449^{3} JINXY JACK [125] 10-11-12 N Doughty, *led 3rd, hdd 8th, led nxt, drw clr frm 2 out, cmftbly*. ....(9 to 2 op 7 to 2 tchd 5 to 1) 1
3346 TERRIBLE GEL (Fr) [105] 9-10-6 P Niven, *cl up, led 8th, hdd nxt, chsd wnr aftr, kpt on, no imprsn*. ....(7 to 2 tchd 4 to 1) 2
3356 GOLDEN ISLE [99] 10-10-0 B Storey, *hld up in tch, hdwy aftr 4 out, rdn after nxt, kpt on same pace*. .... (14 to 1 op 12 to 1) 3
3397^{6} DRUMSTICK [127] 8-12-0 N Williamson, *hld up in tch, mstk 5th (water), effrt aftr 4 out, one paced*. ....(11 to 10 fav op 6 to 4) 4
2574^{4} KAMART [99] 6-10-0 A Dobbin, *in tch, outpcd aftr 4 out, no dngr after*.................... (66 to 1 op 50 to 1) 5
3282 GREEK FLUTTER [119] 9-11-6 M Dwyer, *trkd ldrs till wknd aftr 4 out*...........................(9 to 1 op 6 to 1) 6
1591^{7} TINAS LAD [105] 11-10-3 (3*) T Jenks, *led to 3rd, trkd ldrs aftr, ev ch whn blun and uns rdr 4 out*. ....(7 to 1 op 5 to 1) ur

Dist: 3½l, 12l, 3½l, ½l, hd. 3m 55.70s. a 4.70s (7 Ran).
SR: 51/27/9/33/4/24/-/ (Mrs B M McKinney), G Richards

3557 Steedman Ramage Centenary Novices' Hurdle (4-y-o) £2,486 2m 110yds ....(4:00)

1710^{9} SMUGGLER'S POINT (USA) 10-12 D O'Sullivan, *made all, wl clr hfwy, unchlgd*.... (5 to 1 op 6 to 1 tchd 7 to 1) 1
1217^{2} PRINCIPAL PLAYER (USA) 11-4 A Dobbin, *hld up, hdwy hfwy, chsd wnr frm 3 out, no imprsn*. .... (9 to 4 tchd 5 to 2 and 2 to 1) 2
3482^{2} BEND SABLE (Ire) 11-7 B Storey, *hld up in tch, hdwy hfwy, wknd aftr 3 out*... (11 to 8 on tchd 11 to 10 on) 3
SABERAGE 10-0 (7*) B Harding, *in tch, hdwy hfwy, wknd appr 2 out*.......................... (16 to 1 op 25 to 1) 4
2220 GRAND AS OWT 10-12 A Merrigan, *beh frm hfwy*. (33 to 1) 5
STYLISH ROSE (Ire) 10-7 K Johnson, *nvr on terms*. ....(25 to 1) 6
2285^{7} HOME PARK (Ire) 10-9 (3*) P Williams, *chsd wnr frm 4th till wknd aftr nxt*........(20 to 1 op 25 to 1 tchd 16 to 1) 7
2972^{3} FUNNY ROSE 10-7 L O'Hara, *chsd wnr till f 4th*. .... (25 to 1 op 20 to 1) f
3373 GRINNELL 10-12 N Williamson, *al beh, tld off whn pld up bef 2 out*.......................... (20 to 1 op 16 to 1) pu
FIRST RESERVE 10-12 M Moloney, *sn beh, tld off whn pld up bef last*.......................................(50 to 1) pu
MAJOR JACK 10-7 (5*) J Burke, *chsd ldrs till pld up lme aftr 4th*.......................................(66 to 1) pu
MURDER MOSS (Ire) 10-12 L Wyer, *sn beh, tld off whn pld up bef 2 out*.................... (25 to 1 tchd 14 to 1) pu

Dist: 15l, 30l, 8l, 10l, 15l, hd. 3m 43.90s. b 0.10s (12 Ran).
SR: 35/26/-/-/-/-/ (Four Bars Racing Club), J J Bridger

3558 Perth Hunt Balnakeilly Challenge Cup Hunters' Chase (5-y-o and up) £2,221 3m..........................(4:30)

3065^{3} ONCE STUNG 8-12-8 Mr J Greenall, *prmnt, dsptd ld 14th, led 2 out, lft clr last, drvn out, fnshd tired*. ....(2 to 1 on op 7 to 4 on) 1
DURIGHT 11-11-4 (5*) Mr N Tutty, *chsd ldrs till outpcd aftr 14th, kpt on frm 3 out, no ch wth wnr*. .... (25 to 1 op 16 to 1) 2
SHILGROVE PLACE 12-11-9 (5*) Mr D Parker, *mstks, led till hdd 13th, grad wknd frm nxt*....... (5 to 1 op 9 to 2) 3
2955 THE RAMBLING MAN 7-11-9 (5*) Mr R Hale, *mstks, beh frm 14th*................................ (40 to 1 op 33 to 1) 4
3462^{4} MIG 9-11-2 (7*) Miss Y Beckingham, *al beh*. .... (10 to 1 op 8 to 1) 5
GUNMETAL BOY 10-11-12 (7*) Mr A Parker, *in tch, led 13th, jnd nxt, hdd 2 out, cl up and ev ch whn f last*. ....(8 to 1 op 7 to 1) f
SILENT RING (USA) (bl) 8-11-7 (7*) Mr S Pittendrigh, *tld off frm 12th, pld up bef 4 out*..........(33 to 1 op 25 to 1) pu

Dist: 20l, 20l, 8l, 12l. 6m 10.80s. a 13.80s (7 Ran).
(J E Greenall), P Cheesbrough

LUDLOW (good to firm)
Friday April 22nd
Going Correction: PLUS 0.05 sec. per fur.

3559 Aga-Rayburn Novices' Selling Hurdle (4,5,6-y-o) £1,725 2m........... (5:40)

3416^{3} FORGETFUL 5-10-13 D J Burchell, *made most, clr hfwy, unchlgd*............... (9 to 2 op 4 to 1 tchd 11 to 2) 1
3211^{2} MISSED THE BOAT (Ire) 4-10-9 (3*) T Eley, *cld hfwy, wnt second appr 2 out, sn hrd rdn, no imprsn*. ....(8 to 1 op 6 to 1) 2
3416^{5} MARSHALL PINDARI 4-10-12 J Railton, *hld up, hdwy 3 out, hrd rdn appr last, one pace*... (33 to 1 op 20 to 1) 3
3221^{4} KEDGE 4-10-12 Diane Clay, *in tch, effrt und pres appr 2 out out, no imprsn*................ (10 to 1 op 8 to 1) 4
3098^{4} TENDRESSE (Ire) 6-10-13 A Maguire, *trkd ldrs, mstk 5th, effrt nxt, no imprsn*. ....(15 to 8 fav op 7 to 4 tchd 9 to 4) 5
3328^{3} CONVOY (bl) 4-11-10 G McCourt, *prmnt, rdn aftr 3 out, sn btn*.................... (4 to 1 op 3 to 1 tchd 9 to 2) 6
3451 POLY VISION (Ire) 4-10-5 (7*) P McLoughlin, *al rear, tld off*. .... (25 to 1 op 20 to 1) 7
3334 GIRTON BELLE 4-10-7 B Clifford, *al beh, tld off*. .... (50 to 1 op 33 to 1) 8
1734 WHAT DO YOU THINK 6-10-13 M Bosley, *al rear, tld off*. .... (33 to 1 op 20 to 1) 9
1526 GILBERT (Ire) 6-11-10 Lorna Vincent, *wth wnr to 3rd, wknd 5th, tld off*.................. (20 to 1 op 16 to 1) 10
3315 SEEMENOMORE 5-10-13 T Wall, *al beh, tld off*. .... (25 to 1 op 33 to 1 tchd 50 to 1) 11
1939^{9} DUKE OF BUDWORTH 4-10-12 W Marston, *chsd ldrs to 5th, wknd quickly, tld off*......... (33 to 1 op 20 to 1) 12
1532 ROYAL EXECUTIVE (Ire) 4-10-12 D Bridgwater, *al wl beh, tld off whn f 5th*.................. (33 to 1 op 20 to 1) f
3395 BURFORDS DELIGHT 5-10-6 (7*) Miss S Duckett, *al rear, tld off whn f 2 out*........................... (33 to 1) f
TASSAGH BRIDGE (Ire) 4-10-7 M Hourigan, *trkd ldrs to 4th, sn wknd, tld off whn pld up bef 2 out*......... (50 to 1) pu
3451 METER MAN 4-10-9 (3*) R Farrant, *chsd ldrs to 5th, sn lost tch, tld off whn pld up bef 2 out*............. (50 to 1) pu

Dist: 11l, 4l, 6l, 2l, 6l, 11l, 6l, 1¼l, 3l, 4l. 3m 45.40s. a 8.40s (16 Ran).
SR: 9/-/-/-/-/-/ (The Equus Club), D Burchell

3560 Bromfield Sand And Gravel Handicap Chase for the Oakly Park Challenge Cup (0-120 5-y-o and up) £3,525 2½m ....(6:10)

3415 GREENHILL RAFFLES [111] 8-11-10 Peter Hobbs, *hld up in tch, mstk 4th, hdwy 3 out, led last, rdn clr*. ....(6 to 1 op 7 to 1) 1
609^{5} MISTER FEATHERS [90] 13-10-3 J R Kavanagh, *al cl up, led appr 3 out to nxt, kpt on one pace*. (16 to 1 op 14 to 1) 2
2962 BOBBY SOCKS [110] 8-11-2 (7*) P McLoughlin, *trkd ldrs, mstk 5th, rdn 3 out, styd on r-in*.... (10 to 1 op 6 to 1) 3
3454^{2} DAN DE LYON [90] 6-10-3 A Maguire, *al wl plcd, led 12th till appr 3 out, led 2 out till mstk and hdd last, no extr r-in*................ (3 to 1 fav op 2 to 1 tchd 7 to 2) 4
3194 AIR COMMANDER [93] 9-10-6 T Wall, *set str pace to 12th, sn lost tch*.................................... (33 to 1) 5
3437^{5} FIGHT TO WIN (USA) [99] (bl) 6-10-12 G Upton, *al rear*. .... (20 to 1 op 16 to 1) 6
1216^{6} BARTONDALE [87] 9-9-11 (3*) R Farrant, *chsd ldrs to hfwy, sn lost tch, tld off*............................(33 to 1) 7
2334 GLEN CHERRY [108] (bl) 8-11-7 G McCourt, *cld hfwy, mstk tenth, wknd appr 3 out, tld off*.... (14 to 1 op 10 to 1) 8
3260 THE MASTER GUNNER [109] 10-11-5 (3*) R Davis, *mstk 3rd, al beh, tld off*...................... (8 to 1 op 5 to 1) 9
ALDINGTON BELL [94] (bl) 11-10-7 R Bellamy, *in tch, lost pl 9th, pld up bef 11th, lme*..........(16 to 1 op 10 to 1) pu
3116^{2} DARE SAY [105] 11-11-4 W McFarland, *al rear, tld off whn pld up bef 2 out*........ (8 to 1 op 7 to 1 tchd 12 to 1) pu
3017^{4} MASTER SOUTH LAD [90] 10-10-0^{4} (7*) R Darke, *al beh, tld off whn pld up bef 13th*. ....(20 to 1 op 16 to 1 tchd 33 to 1) pu
3038^{9} SHANNON GLEN [104] (bl) 8-11-3 J Osborne, *chsd ldr till jmpd slwly and lost pl 4th, wl beh whn pld up bef tenth*. ....(9 to 2 op 6 to 1 tchd 4 to 1) pu

Dist: 13l, 1½l, 1¼l, 20l, 3½l, 2½l, 25l, 14l. 4m 57.70s. a 6.70s (13 Ran).
SR: 39/5/23/1/-/-/ (Miss Janet Stephens), P J Hobbs

3561 D. J. Profiles Handicap Hurdle (0-130 4-y-o and up) £2,722 2m 5f 110yds ....(6:40)

3317^{7} MOUNTSHANNON [97] 8-10-4^{4} Peter Caldwell, *settled rear, prog 7th, chlgd 2 out, sn led, ran on wl*. (33 to 1) 1
2967^{6} SUPER MALT (Ire) [105] 6-10-12 M Hourigan, *hld up rear, hdwy appr 2 out, rdn and styd on wl r-in*. ....(4 to 1 op 7 to 2) 2
3038 PACTOLUS (USA) [117] 11-11-10 G McCourt, *hld up beh, effrt und pres 3 out, nvr nrr*........ (10 to 1 op 8 to 1) 3
3398^{4} KHAZARI (USA) [111] 6-11-4 A Maguire, *al prmnt, ev ch appr 2 out, rdn and wknd approaching last*. ....(4 to 1 op 7 to 2) 4
2643^{6} TEL E THON [98] (v) 7-10-0 (5*) D Leahy, *led, clr hfwy, rdn appr 2 out, hdd approaching last, sn btn*. ....(9 to 1 op 8 to 1) 5
3398^{3} SMITH TOO (Ire) [111] 6-10-11 (7*) D Bohan, *prmnt, lost pl hfwy, rdn appr 2 out, no imprsn*..........(7 to 2 jt-fav) 6
3398 DEMILUNE (USA) [93] 4-10-0 D Bridgwater, *pressed ldrs, ev ch 3 out, rdn and wknd appr nxt, tld off*.....(7 to 2 jt-fav op 3 to 1) 7
3455 MUSIC SCORE [93] 8-9-7 (7*) P Ward, *prmnt till wknd aftr 3 out, tld off*..................................(33 to 1) 8
3317 CRAZY HORSE DANCER (USA) [93] 6-9-11 (3*) R Farrant, *chsd ldg pair, wknd appr 3 out, tld off*........ (25 to 1) 9
3398 BATTLEPLAN [96] 9-10-3^{3} Mr A Charles-Jones, *al beh, tld off 7th*......................... (50 to 1 tchd 100 to 1) 10

Dist: 1½l, 9l, 4l, 1¼l, 8l, 14l, 9l, 8l, 20l. 5m 8.90s. a 11.90s (10 Ran).
(N G King), C C Trietline

3562 Ricoh Novices' Handicap Chase (5-y-o and up) £3,850 3m..............(7:10)

2017^{4} VISAGA [92] 8-10-11 D Bridgwater, *made all, hrd rdn r-in, hld on gmely*..................... (4 to 1 tchd 7 to 2) 1
2425 DEBT OF HONOR [81] 6-10-0 A Maguire, *al wl plcd, ev ch frm 2 out, swtchd lft last, hrd rdn and ran on well*. ....(20 to 1) 2
3336^{8} VICAR OF BRAY [81] (v) 7-10-0 J R Kavanagh, *patiently rdn, prog frm hfwy, ridden 3 out, sn btn*...... (50 to 1) 3
3207^{5} PRINCE'S COURT [94] 11-10-8 (5*) D Fortt, *trkd ldrs, rdn whn hit 3 out, sn wknd*...................... (12 to 1) 4
3442^{4} SHEARMAC STEEL [85] 7-10-4 Peter Hobbs, *chsd ldrs, rdn appr 3 out, sn wknd*................(7 to 1 op 11 to 2) 5
3477^{2} SANDAIG [91] 8-10-10 D Gallagher, *cl up till blun 9th, wknd 14th*.........(7 to 2 fav op 3 to 1 tchd 4 to 1) 6
3278 NEW PROBLEM [81] 7-9-7 (7*) Pat Thompson, *al rear, no ch whn mstk 2 out*...............(33 to 1 tchd 50 to 1) 7
2946 COOMBESBURY LANE [81] (bl) 8-9-9 (5*) D Leahy, *al beh, tld off*..(50 to 1) 8
3408 LUSTY LIGHT [105] 8-11-10 I Lawrence, *hdwy 5th, rdn 14th, sn wknd, tld off*. ....(16 to 1 op 14 to 1 tchd 20 to 1) 9
3278^{6} POLLERTON'S PRIDE [81] 7-9-11 (3*) T Eley, *al beh, tld off*. ....(20 to 1 op 16 to 1) 10
2872^{2} BUMPTIOUS BOY [81] 10-10-0 B Clifford, *trkd ldrs till blun and uns rdr 8th*............ (10 to 1 tchd 12 to 1) ur
3454 PENIARTH [81] 8-10-0 W Marston, *blun and uns rdr 4th*. ....(50 to 1) ur
3090^{3} MICRONOVA [81] (bl) 8-10-0 R Bellamy, *chsd ldrs to 7th, sn lost tch, tld off whn pld up bef 12th*........... (20 to 1) pu
427^{4} HELMAR (NZ) [86] 8-10-5 T Wall, *lost tch 12th, tld off whn blun 3 out, pld up bef nxt*......... (20 to 1 op 16 to 1) pu
3377* WHATAGALE [97] 7-11-2 J Osborne, *al rear, wl beh whn pld up bef 14th*......... (9 to 2 op 4 to 1 tchd 5 to 1) pu
2980 COZZI (Fr) [81] (v) 6-9-11 (3*) R Farrant, *chsd ldrs to hfwy, wknd and pld up bef 12th*.....................(50 to 1) pu

Dist: Sht-hd, 15l, 6l, 12l, ¾l, 1½l, dist, 4l, 1½l. 5m 59.40s. a 10.40s (16 Ran).
(L Hellstenius), N A Twiston-Davies

3563 Ludlow Racecourse Bookmakers Hunters' Chase for the Magnus-Allcroft Memorial Trophy (5-y-o and up) £1,725 3m..................(7:40)

SAMS HERITAGE 10-11-12 (7*) Mr J M Pritchard, *mstk 4th, hld up rear, prog 13th, led appr 2 out, hrd rdn r-in, all out*...................... (9 to 4 op 2 to 1 tchd 5 to 2) 1
3399* WILD ILLUSION 10-11-12 (7*) Mr J Trice-Rolph, *wtd wth in rear, prog 12th, rdn and outpcd appr 2 out, ran on strly nr finish*........... (11 to 8 fav op 6 to 4 tchd 5 to 4) 2
SAFFRON LORD 12-11-12 Mr J Durkan, *trkd ldr, led 5th, blun 9th, sn hdd, led appr 3 out to nxt, ev ch last, ran on wl*.......................... (16 to 1 op 20 to 1) 3
3480^{3} MR MURDOCK 9-12-0 (5*) Mr T Mitchell, *prmnt, disputing ld whn mstk 15th, ev ch last, not quicken*. ....(6 to 1 op 4 to 1 tchd 13 to 2) 4
3480^{2} KNOCKUMSHIN 11-12-0 (5*) Mr T Byrne, *wtd wth, hdwy 14th, shaken up appr last, not pace to chal*. ....(7 to 1 tchd 8 to 1) 5
3480^{7} RANDOM PLACE 12-11-12 (7*) Mr I Pocock, *hdwy 7th, led tenth to 3 out, sn rdn and wknd*...(33 to 1 op 25 to 1) 6
PADDY'S POND 16-11-5 (7*) Mr M Jackson, *led to 5th, rdn and wknd appr 3 out, tld off*...... (50 to 1 op 25 to 1) 7
MENDON ROSE 13-11-0 (7*) Mr B Norris, *lost pl 6th, tld off whn pld up bef 15th*..................(50 to 1 op 33 to 1) pu
SPIN THE COIN 8-11-5 (7*) Mr W McLaughlin, *rcd wide, pressed ldrs to 13th, sn wknd, beh whn pld up bef 2 out*. ....(50 to 1) pu

Dist: 1l, 1l, ¾l, 4l, 13l, 13l. 6m 12.50s. a 23.50s (9 Ran).
(C G Smedley), P G Warner

3564 Ironbridge Gorge Museum 'National Hunt' Novices' Hurdle (4-y-o and up) £1,725 2m 5f 110yds............(8:10)

2997⁴ KONVEKTA CONTROL (bl) 7-11-2 J Osborne, *wtd wth gng wl, hdwy to chal last, sn led, quickened clr.*
.... (2 to 1 fav op 5 to 4 tchd 100 to 30) 1
3360² NAZZARO 5-11-2 (7*) R Darke, *al cl up, slight ld 2 out till hdd and no extr r-in*............... (3 to 1 op 11 to 4) 2
3167 CAIPIRINHA (Ire) 6-10-11 G Upton, *rcd wide, trkd ldrs, hit 2 out, kpt on und pres r-in.*
.... (15 to 2 op 10 to 1 tchd 7 to 1) 3
3209⁶ ALIAS SILVER 7-11-2 Gary Lyons, *wth ldrs, ev ch appr 2 out, sn rdn, one pace*...........(10 to 1 op 20 to 1) 4
3215 ACHIEVED AMBITION (Ire) 6-11-2 W McFarland, *led to 2 out, hrd rdn and kpt on one pace.* (33 to 1 op 20 to 1) 5
3257² EMMA'S WAY (Ire) 5-10-11 A Maguire, *wtd wth in rear, hdwy frm 3 out, wknd appr last*..... (3 to 1 op 4 to 1) 6
BLAKENEY BLUE 7-10-11 J Railton, *chsd ldrs to hfwy, wknd, tld off.*........................(33 to 1 op 20 to 1) 7
3214⁶ MUCH 7-11-2 Mr M Jackson, *hld up rear, cld 7th, wknd appr 2 out, tld off.*............. (25 to 1 tchd 33 to 1) 8
3008 LLES LE BUCFLOW 6-10-13 (3*) R Farrant, *pressed ldrs, wknd quickly appr 2 out, tld off.*.............. (50 to 1) 9
3278 APRIL'S MODEL LADY 8-10-11 B Clifford, *al rear, tld off.*
.... (20 to 1 op 16 to 1) 10
2424⁷ MASTER FRITH 6-11-2 W Humphreys, *prmnt early, lost pl 5th, tld off.*............................(50 to 1) 11
3005 THE FOOLISH ONE 7-10-11 S Earle, *chsd ldrs to 7th, wknd quickly nxt, tld off whn pld up bef 2 out.*
.... (50 to 1 op 33 to 1) pu
Dist: 6l, 1l, nk, hd, 2l, 10l, 6l, 14l, 6l, dist. 5m 16.40s. a 19.40s (12 Ran).
(Konvekta Ltd), O Sherwood

PERTH (good to soft)
Friday April 22nd
Going Correction: PLUS 1.00 sec. per fur.

3565 Moet & Chandon Novices' Hurdle (5-y-o and up) £2,584 3m 110yds...(2:20)

3279 ACT OF PARLIAMENT (Ire) (bl) 6-11-6 N Williamson, *trkd ldrs, led aftr 7th, quickened clr after 3 out, mstk last, very easily...* (6 to 1 on op 5 to 1 on tchd 9 to 2 on) 1
3470* OVER THE ODDS (Ire) 5-11-6 K Johnson, *led till hdd aftr 7th, cl up till outpcd after 3 out, kpt on, no ch wth wnr.*
..................(8 to 1 op 6 to 1) 2
3378 ONE LAST CHANCE 5-10-9 B Storey, *mstks, outpcd aftr 8th, sn wl beh.*..................(40 to 1 op 25 to 1) 3
3470² LITTLE FREDDIE 5-11-0 L Wyer, *cl up, pushed alng aftr 9th, outpcd after 3 out, sn btn.*......(10 to 1 op 7 to 1) 4
Dist: 30l, 12l, nk. 6m 25.80s. a 40.80s (4 Ran).
(J Perriss), K C Bailey

3566 Norsk Jockeyklub Handicap Chase Amateur Riders (0-115 5-y-o and up) £3,343 2½m 110yds.......... (2:55)

3332 BARKISLAND [94] 10-10-11 (3*) Mrs A Farrell, *mstk 3rd, made all, kpt on wl und pres r-in*............. (10 to 1) 1
3537⁴ ON THE HOOCH [96] 9-10-13 (3*) Mr J Bradburne, *in tch, effrt aftr tenth, mstk 3 out, kpt on same peace.*
.... (5 to 1 tchd 6 to 1) 2
3433³ ABSAILOR [91] (v) 10-10-9⁵ (7*) Mr M Bradburne, *in tch till lost pl aftr 11th, kpt on frm 2 out.*
.... (3 to 1 fav op 4 to 1 tchd 9 to 4) 3
THE YANK [102] 8-11-1 (7*) Mr C Bonner, *prmnt till wknd aftr 11th, tld off.*.................. (9 to 1 op 5 to 1) 4
3141 DEADLINE [92] (bl) 11-10-9² (5*) Mr N Wilson, *hld up, effrt aftr 11th, ev ch whn f 4 out.*
.... (9 to 2 op 6 to 1 tchd 4 to 1) f
3473⁴ FALSE ECONOMY [108] 9-12-0 Mr J Greenall, *trkd wnr, cl up and ev ch whn jmpd rght and uns rdr 2 out.*
.... (9 to 2 op 4 to 1) ur
3428⁷ JUNIORS CHOICE [80] 11-9-11⁴ (7*) Mrs J Dun, *mstk and uns rdr 1st.*..........(16 to 1 op 14 to 1 tchd 20 to 1) ur
3437⁶ BISHOPDALE [104] 13-11-5 (5*) Miss J Thurlow, *sn wl beh, tld off whn pld up bef 3 out.*
.... (8 to 1 op 7 to 1 tchd 10 to 1) pu
Dist: 3l, 5l, 25l. 5m 27.60s. a 29.60s (8 Ran).
(John Veitch), P Beaumont

3567 Clerical Medical Chase for the Kilmany Cup (5-y-o and up) £7,035 3m (3:25)

3425 MASTER OATS 8-12-0 N Williamson, *in tch, jnd ldr tenth, led 12th, clr aftr 14th, hit last, very easily.*
.... (9 to 4 on op 5 to 2 on tchd 2 to 1 on) 1
3486² DURHAM SUNSET 7-11-3 N Doughty, *led to 3rd, in tch, lost pl aftr 5th, hdwy to go second 4 out, no imprsn on wnr.*.................. (7 to 2 op 4 to 1 tchd 9 to 2) 2
3358⁵ IDA'S DELIGHT 15-11-5 B Storey, *chsd ldr, pushed alng aftr tenth, outpcd after 14th, no dngr after.*
.... (25 to 1 op 20 to 1) 3
3541⁵ SPARKLING FLAME (bl) 10-11-5 P Niven, *led 3rd, jmpd lft frm 7th, hld 12th, beh from 14th, tld off.*
.... (5 to 1 tchd 11 to 2) 4
3077² FORTH AND TAY 12-11-8 P Williams, *sn tld off, pld up aftr 12th.*.................. (25 to 1 op 20 to 1) pu

Dist: 10l, 1¼l, dist. 6m 29.70s. a 32.70s (5 Ran).
SR: 13/-/ (P A Matthews), K C Bailey

3568 Campbell, Boath Claiming Handicap Hurdle (4-y-o and up) £2,794 3m 110yds....................... (4:00)

3330³ BADASTAN (Ire) [80] 5-10-9 R Garritty, *in tch, trkd ldrs frm 7th, led 2 out, hld on wl und pres from last.*
.... (7 to 2 op 4 to 1) 1
3029* CLASSIC STATEMENT [81] (v) 8-10-7 (3*) A Larnach, *cl up, made most frm 7th till hdd 2 out, rallied appr last, no extr und pres.*......................(9 to 2 tchd 5 to 1) 2
3139⁵ IRISH FLASHER [83] 7-10-9 (3*) P Williams, *hld up in tch, hdwy aftr 9th, chlgd 2 out, ev ch last, no extr und pres.*
.... (9 to 2 op 4 to 1 tchd 5 to 1) 3
3287⁸ VALIANT DASH [89] 8-10-13 (5*) F Perratt, *cl up, lft in ld aftr 4th, hdd 7th, wknd appr 2 out.*
.... (10 to 1 tchd 12 to 1) 4
3287⁷ HOTDIGGITY [84] 6-10-13 A Dobbin, *beh, rdn alng aftr 8th, wknd appr 2 out.*...... (5 to 2 fav op 3 to 1) 5
2385 THE DEMON BARBER [106] 12-12-0 (7*) B Harding, *hld up, rdn aftr 8th, wknd aftr 2 out.*.....(10 to 1 op 8 to 1) 6
3235² HIGHLAND FRIEND [71] (bl) 6-9-9 (5*) J Supple, *cl up, dsptd ld 9th till 3 out, sn rdn, wknd quickly appr nxt, tld off.*
.... (25 to 1 op 20 to 1 tchd 33 to 1) 7
2153 HELLO GEORGIE [71] (bl) 11-10-0 N Williamson, *led till pld up lme aftr 4th.*..............(33 to 1 op 20 to 1) pu
Dist: ¾l, 1¾l, 15l, 5l, 7l, dist. 6m 15.80s. a 30.80s (8 Ran).
SR: 18/18/18/9/-/14/-/-/ (B T Stewart-Brown), T P Tate

3569 John Bradburn & Company Novices' Chase (5-y-o and up) £3,501 2½m 110yds....................... (4:30)

3192² UNHOLY ALLIANCE 7-11-8 N Williamson, *made all, drw wl clr frm 4 out, very easily.*
.... (5 to 2 on op 3 to 1 on tchd 9 to 4 on) 1
3474* THE COUNTRY TRADER 8-11-8 M Moloney, *in tch, drvn alng frm 9th, wl outpcd from 4 out, lft poor second last.*
.... (5 to 1 op 7 to 1 tchd 11 to 4) 2
3536⁵ FLING IN SPRING (v) 8-11-3 Mr J Bradburne, *trkd wnr, rdn aftr 11th, outpcd frm 4 out, remote second whn uns rdr last, rmntd.*......... (16 to 1 op 10 to 1 tchd 20 to 1) 3
Dist: Dist, dist. 5m 26.80s. a 28.80s (3 Ran).
SR: 11/-/-/ (Mrs S C York), K C Bailey

3570 Scott Oswald Auld Lang Syne 'National Hunt' Novices' Handicap Hurdle (4-y-o and up) £2,892 2m 110yds....................... (5:05)

3179 BACK BEFORE DAWN [70] 7-10-8 L O'Hara, *hld up, mstk 5th, gd hdwy appr 2 out, led betw last two, sn clr, cmftbly.*.................. (14 to 1 op 12 to 1) 1
3034⁴ THREE STRONG (Ire) [85] 5-11-9 A Dobbin, *led till hdd 2 out, rallied appr last, no ch wth wnr.*
.... (4 to 1 tchd 9 to 2) 2
2447⁶ ORD GALLERY (Ire) [78] 5-11-2 L Wyer, *cl up, led 2 out, sn hdd, no extr*..................(12 to 1 op 8 to 1) 3
3459* COL BUCKMORE (Ire) [96] 6-11-13 (7*,6ex) B Harding, *hld up, hdwy to track ldrs 3 out, hit nxt, sn rdn and one pace.*..................(9 to 4 on tchd 11 to 10 on) 4
1094⁶ FELL WARDEN [73] 6-10-8 (3*) A Larnach, *trkd ldrs till wknd aftr 3 out, tld off.*..............(5 to 1 tchd 10 to 1) 5
3284 WOLF'S DEN [63] 5-9-10 (5*) F Perratt, *al beh, tld off.*
.... (25 to 1 op 20 to 1) 6
3553 TOURAQUE (Fr) [62] 9-9-7 (7*) I Jardine, *chsd ldrs till wknd appr 3 out, tld off*...............(66 to 1 op 100 to 1) 7
3429 LUGER (Ire) [62] 6-10-0 N Smith, *in tch till wknd aftr 5th, tld off whn pld up bef 2 out.....* (25 to 1 op 50 to 1) pu
WINNINGTONRIG [70] 6-10-8 M Moloney, *prmnt till wknd quickly aftr 3 out, pld up bef nxt...*(10 to 1 op 8 to 1) pu
Dist: 6l, hd, sht-hd, 30l, 10l, 12l. 4m 10.00s. a 26.00s (9 Ran).
(John Pirie), P Monteith

TAUNTON (good to firm (races 1,2,3), firm (4,5,6))
Friday April 22nd
Going Correction: MINUS 0.30 sec. per fur.

3571 April Amateur Riders' Novices' Handicap Hurdle (0-100 5-y-o and up) £1,865 2m 3f 110yds........... (5:25)

2799⁵ CHERYLS PET (Ire) [81] 5-11-0 (7*) Mr G Baines, *cl up till lost pl aftr 3rd, rdn 6th, str brst frm last, led close hme.*.................. (8 to 1 op 7 to 1) 1
3319⁵ GOLDEN MADJAMBO [71] 8-9-13⁶ (7*) Mr G Shenkin, *took keen hold, prmnt, led aftr 5th, rdn appr 2 out, clr last, ct cl hme.*..................(33 to 1 op 20 to 1) 2
3530⁹ BATHWICK BOBBIE [81] 7-10-3 (7*) Miss S Higgins, *prog appr 2 out, hrd rdn and styd on r-in.*
.... (20 to 1 tchd 33 to 1) 3

512

3270 FALCONBRIDGE BAY [75] 7-10-3⁶ (7") Mr C Vigors, *hld up,*
prog 7th, styd on same pace frm 2 out.
.............................(12 to 1 op 10 to 1 tchd 14 to 1) 4
3340 RAGTIME BOY [72] (v) 6-10-1⁷ (7") Mr B Pollock, *beh, prog*
7th, no real imprsn frm 2 out....... (25 to 1 op 14 to 1) 5
2708⁷ GIVEITAGO [85] 8-10-7 (7") Mr J Rees, *in rear, styd on frm*
2 out, not rch ldrs.......(9 to 1 op 8 to 1 tchd 10 to 1) 6
2320 RACK RATE (Ire) [79] 6-10-1 (7") Miss L Horsey, *steadied*
strt, prog frm 6th, wknd appr 2 out. (14 to 1 op 8 to 1) 7
3264 REFERRAL FEE [73] 7-9-9 (7") Mr S Righton, *al in rear.*
.... 8
2705⁷ MAKING TIME [73] 7-10-2⁹ (7") Mr Richard White, *al beh.*
......................(33 to 1 op 14 to 1 tchd 50 to 1) 9
1323* DISTANT MEMORY [95] 5-11-3 (7") Mr J Creighton, *beh till*
steady prog 5th, last pl 7th.
.....................................(17 to 2 op 9 to 1) 10
3008⁸ ROYAL GLINT [75] 5-9-12¹ (7") Mr G Brown, *led till aftr 5th,*
rdn and wknd appr 2 out............(3 to 1 op 20 to 1) 11
3281⁶ WONDERFULL POLLY (Ire) [76] 6-9-12 (7") Mr J Culloty, *wtd*
wth, hit 5th, hdwy nxt, cl 3rd whn tried to run out and
uns rdr 3 out.......(3 to 1 fav op 7 to 2 tchd 11 to 4) ur
3186 LORD'S FINAL [71] 7-9-13⁶ (7") Mr G Hogan, *pld up bef*
second.....................(9 to 2 op 7 to 2 tchd 5 to 1) pu
2196 KOBYRUN [77] 8-9-13 (7") Miss S Mitchell, *pld hrd, wl plcd*
till wknd aftr 6th, tld off whn pulled up bef 2 out.
...........................(25 to 1 op 14 to 1 tchd 33 to 1) pu
Dist: ¾l, 2l, ½l, 2l, 12l, 2½l, ½l, 4l, 1¼l, 5l. 4m 33.50s. a 12.50s (14 Ran).

(Peter Partridge), R H Buckler

3572 Motorway Selling Handicap Hurdle (4 & 5-y-o) £1,731 2m 3f 110yds. . . . (5:55)

3253⁷ DANCING DANCER [61] (bl) 5-10-7³ J Frost, *improved 5th,*
led 3 out, readily.......................(20 to 1 tchd 25 to 1) 1
2711 TAKE A FLYER (Ire) [61] 4-10-7 A Tory, *wtd wth, smooth*
prog 7th, wnt second appr 2 out, no extr r-in.
.................................(20 to 1 op 16 to 1) 2
1931 IRISH DOMINION [54] 4-10-0 C Maude, *hld up, hdwy appr*
7th, kpt on same pace frm 2 out.................(25 to 1) 3
3481² KALAMOSS [78] 5-11-3 (7") Miss S Mitchell, *prog hfwy, rdn*
and no imprsn frm 3 out. (7 to 2 op 3 to 1 tchd 4 to 1) 4
3395⁸ IS SHE QUICK [60] 4-10-6 N Dawe, *settled in rear, jmpd*
slwly second, hdwy aftr 6th, no imprsn appr 2 out.
...........................(16 to 1 op 10 to 1 tchd 20 to 1) 5
1519⁴ POLK (Fr) [66] 5-10-12 R Dunwoody, *led to 3rd, led appr*
7th, hdd 3 out, sn rdn and btn. (3 to 1 fav tchd 9 to 2) 6
3252⁴ DARINGLY [71] 5-10-10 (7") M Appleby, *nvr nr ldrs.*
...........................(16 to 1 op 10 to 1 tchd 20 to 1) 7
2130 COOCHIE [67] (bl) 5-10-13 L Harvey, *cl up, lost pos 5th,*
rallied nxt, wknd aftr 3 out.........(16 to 1 op 8 to 1) 8
3348 SANDRO [69] (bl) 5-11-1 Richard Guest, *cl up, led 3rd till*
appr 7th, lost pl sn aftr 3 out........(10 to 1 op 8 to 1) 9
3304⁴ YAAFOOR (USA) [73] (bl) 5-11-5 M Richards, *wl plcd to 6th,*
tld off....(12 to 1 op 7 to 1) 10
3328⁷ FATHER'S JOY [55] 4-10-1 M Stevens, *al in rear, tld off.*
....(50 to 1 op 33 to 1) 11
2364⁵ BOHEMIAN QUEEN [68] (bl) 4-11-0 V Slattery, *al in rear, tld*
off.....................(12 to 1 op 8 to 1 tchd 14 to 1) 12
3173⁵ NYMPH ERRANT [59] 4-10-5⁴ M A FitzGerald, *chsd ldrs to*
5th, wl beh whn mstk 2 out, tld off. (33 to 1 op 20 to 1) 13
3337 SECRET FORMULA [69] 4-11-1 M Sharratt, *effrt 5th, lost pl*
7th, tld off.........................(33 to 1 op 20 to 1) 14
2881 WAAZA (USA) [70] 5-11-2 Mr G Brown, *wl plcd to 5th, beh*
whn pld up bef 7th...................(20 to 1 op 10 to 1) pu
3353² MY SISTER LUCY [70] 4-11-2 S Burrough, *in rear, rdn alng*
hfwy, sn tld off, pld up bef 3 out...(12 to 1 op 7 to 1) pu
Dist: 4l, 4l, 7l, 2½l, 3l, 8l, ¾l, 3½l, 10l, 6l. 4m 36.40s. a 9.60s (16 Ran).

(A E C Electric Fencing Ltd (Hotline)), R G Frost

3573 Husbands Challenge Cup Handicap Chase (0-120 5-y-o and up) £2,752 2m 110yds. . . . . (6:25)

3479⁵ FANATICAL (USA) [88] (bl) 8-10-0 L Harvey, *wtd wth, steady*
prog frm 9th, hrd drvn betw last 2, kpt on to ld r hme.
.........................(25 to 1 op 10 to 1 tchd 33 to 1) 1
2110³ MURPHY [99] 10-10-11 M Richards, *chsd ldr till led 3rd,*
hit tenth, jmpd lft frm 3 out, edgd left r-in, ct cl hme.
.................(4 to 1 co-fav op 6 to 1 tchd 7 to 2) 2
3301³ SETTER COUNTRY [108] 10-11-6 R Dunwoody, *chsd ldrs,*
styd on same pace frm 2 out. ....(4 to 1 co-
fav op 5 to 1 tchd 7 to 2) 3
2106 ALAN BALL [106] 8-11-4 M A FitzGerald, *chsd ldrs, hit 7th,*
wnt second 9th, btn appr last.
..................................(8 to 1 op 6 to 1 tchd 9 to 1) 4
3500⁴ WELSH BARD [114] 10-11-12 G Bradley, *cl up till wknd*
aftr tenth.................................(8 to 1 op 11 to 1) 5
3479³ ALWAYS REMEMBER [88] 7-10-0 C Maude, *prmnt till lost*
pos 5th, bad mstk tenth, sn struggling.
.................................(5 to 1 op 7 to 2 tchd 11 to 2) 6
3185² GALAGAMES (USA) [99] 7-10-11 B Powell, *led to 3rd, beh*
frm tenth.........(4 to 1 co-fav op 7 to 2 tchd 9 to 2) 7
3301 LUCKY AGAIN [91] 7-10-3 S McNeill, *wtd wth, improved*
7th, hit 9th, sn toiling.
...........................(12 to 1 op 10 to 1 tchd 16 to 1) 8

444 DEEP DARK DAWN [116] 9-12-0 R Supple, *beh, bad mstk*
9th, 7th and no ch whn f 3 out.
.........................(25 to 1 op 20 to 1 tchd 33 to 1) f
3361 DRAW LOTS [88] 10-10-0 I Shoemark, *jmpd badly lft, sn*
tld off, pld up bef tenth.
......................(66 to 1 op 25 to 1 tchd 100 to 1) pu
3336 MINT-MASTER [88] 9-10-0 V Slattery, *sn tld off, pld up bef*
8th.........................(66 to 1 op 25 to 1) pu
Dist: ½l, 30l, 4l, 7l, 10l, 6l, 5l. 4m 0.30s. a 2.30s (11 Ran).
SR: -/10/16/10/11/-/ (Duckhaven Stud), R J Baker

3574 Melody Man Challenge Cup Handicap Hurdle (0-115 4-y-o and up) £2,452 2m 1f. . . . . (7:00)

1642² ROUTING [86] 6-10-0 Richard Guest, *took keen hold in*
mid-div, prog to ld appr 5th, rdn out.
..................................(16 to 1 tchd 20 to 1) 1
3048⁸ WILL JAMES [86] (bl) 8-9-9 (5") S Curran, *nvr far away,*
took clr order 6th, chsd wnr frm 3 out, rdn and kpt on
same pace r-in.......................(33 to 1 op 25 to 1) 2
3418³ GOLDINGO [100] 7-10-9 (5") Guy Lewis, *cl up, rdn 3 out,*
3rd and btn whn bad mstk last..... (12 to 1 op 8 to 1) 3
3340² LUCKY BLUE [88] 7-9-9 (7") P Carey, *lost pl and rdn hfwy,*
btn whn lft 5th and slightly hmpd 2 out.
.................................(12 to 1 tchd 14 to 1) 4
3214⁵ PROPAGANDA [99] (bl) 6-10-13 M A FitzGerald, *wl plcd,*
toiling whn lft 4th and hmpd 2 out. (9 to 1 op 8 to 1) 5
3311⁵ CELTIC BOB [86] 14-10-0 V Slattery, *chsd ldrs till lost pos*
4th, no dngr aftrwards................(33 to 1 op 20 to 1) 6
3267 MISTER LAWSON [96] 8-10-10 I Shoemark, *in rear till some*
prog frm 2 out, nvr dngrs.
................................(14 to 1 op 10 to 1 tchd 16 to 1) 7
KNOCK KNOCK [110] 9-11-10 J Frost, *hld up, al beh.*
......................(4 to 1 fav tchd 9 to 2 and 7 to 2) 8
3408 SHARRIBA [100] (bl) 5-11-0 B Powell, *jnd ldrs aftr 4th, lost*
pl 6th..................................(20 to 1 op 12 to 1) 9
3254* CELCIUS [103] (bl) 10-11-3 R Dunwoody, *rdn and shrtlvd*
effrt appr 6th..........(5 to 1 op 11 to 2 tchd 6 to 1) 10
2554⁵ CORRIN HILL [102] (bl) 7-11-2 A Tory, *led till appr 5th, sn*
struggling, tld off....................(20 to 1 op 14 to 1) 11
3014 LYPH (USA) [86] (v) 8-9-10¹ (5") S Fox, *chsd ldrs till wknd*
rpdly und pres appr 6th, sn tld off. (16 to 1 op 12 to 1) 12
3455 ECOSSAIS DANSEUR (USA) [86] (bl) 8-10-0 R Supple,
handily plcd till wknd rpdly 5th, tld off frm 3 out.
..................................(33 to 1 tchd 50 to 1) 13
2947⁴ ALOSAILI [89] 7-10-3 M Stevens, *tld off frm hfwy.*
..................................(14 to 1 tchd 16 to 1) 14
3481¹ WOLVER GOLD [97] 7-10-11 (7ex) C Maude, *settled in rear,*
steady prog frm 5th, rdn aftr 3 out, 4th and btn whn f
nxt...................................(11 to 2 op 5 to 1) f
3398⁷ MARIOLINO [86] 7-9-7 (7") M Moran, *beh whn blun and*
uns rdr 3rd.........(20 to 1 op 16 to 1 tchd 25 to 1) ur
Dist: 1¾l, 12l, 9l, 11l, 1¾l, 2l, 9l, 2l, 2l, 15l. 3m 47.10s. a 0.10s (16 Ran).
SR: 20/18/20/-/-/-/ (N G Ayliffe), N G Ayliffe

3575 Hemyock Novices' Chase (5-y-o and up) £2,710 3m. . . . . (7:30)

1593³ JAY JAY'S VOYAGE 11-10-9 (7") Mr B Pollock, *al handily*
plcd, led 13th, hdd briefly betw last 2, all out.
...........................(25 to 1 tchd 33 to 1) 1
3018 HOUSE OF ROSES (Ire) 6-11-2 G Bradley, *al cl up, rdn to*
chase wnr frm 13th, slight ld briefly betw last 2, unbl to
quicken close hme........(3 to 1 jt-fav tchd 100 to 30) 2
3338⁵ QUENTIN DURWOOD (bl) 8-11-2 S McNeill, *wtd wth,*
steady prog frm 12th, no imprsn on ldg pair frm 3 out.
.................................(12 to 1 op 14 to 1 tchd 20 to 1) 3
3108* CASTLE BLUE 7-11-8 M A FitzGerald, *led to 3rd, remained*
cl up, rdn 14th, no prog frm 3 out............(3 to 1 jt-
fav op 11 to 4 tchd 100 to 30) 4
3175² OLD BRIG (bl) 8-12-0 R Dunwoody, *led 3rd to 13th, wknd*
16th...................................(7 to 2 op 3 to 1) 5
3040 GOLDEN FARE 9-11-8 R Greene, *nvr a factor.*
..................................(7 to 1 op 6 to 1) 6
3007⁵ DEEP IN GREEK 8-10-9 (7") Mr G Hogan, *wl plcd till lost*
pos 6th, rnwd effrt 12th, struggling 14th, tld off.
..................................(16 to 1 op 20 to 1) 7
3316 SERDARLI 12-10-11 L Harvey, *bad mstk 8th, tld off 11th,*
pld up bef 14th.....................(50 to 1 op 33 to 1) pu
3361 KERRYS EYE 10-10-9 (7") T Thompson, *not jump wl, tld*
off frm 5th, pld up bef 14th........(66 to 1 op 50 to 1) pu
3351³ SENEGALAIS (Fr) 10-11-2 J Frost, *in rear, mstk 8th, sn tld*
off, pld up bef 14th..............(14 to 1 tchd 16 to 1) pu
3381 MELDON 7-11-2 Richard Guest, *pressed ldrs, drvn alng*
tenth, drpd rear and jmpd slwly 14th, pld up bef nxt.
.................................(12 to 1 op 10 to 1) pu
3115⁹ LE DENSTAN 7-11-2 D O'Sullivan, *not jump wl in rear, tld*
off 9th, pld up bef 3 out.
..................................(33 to 1 op 20 to 1) pu
3213⁶ ROSEN THE BEAU (Ire) 6-11-2 R Supple, *prmnt, dsptd ld*
6th till wknd quickly 13th, tld off whn pld up and
dismounted bef 3 out...............(20 to 1 op 14 to 1) pu
Dist: Nk, 12l, 2½l, 12l, sht-hd, 25l. 6m 2.60s. a 15.60s (13 Ran).

(Mrs J Scrivens), Mrs J Scrivens

NATIONAL HUNT RESULTS 1993-94

3576 Martock Maiden Hurdle (4-y-o and up) £2,109 2m 1f.................(8:00)

3202² DARZEE 4-11-0 M Richards, *al wl plcd, led appr 2 out, hld on well r-in*.......(11 to 10 fav op Evens tchd 5 to 4) 1
FLINTLOCK (Ire) 4-11-0 R Dunwoody, *pld hrd, trkd ldrs, chalg whn squeezed out 2 out, rallied r-in, ran on wl, unlucky*..............(7 to 1 op 8 to 1 tchd 10 to 1) 2
3314⁶ DOC COTTRILL 4-10-11 (3*) T Jenks, *took keen hold, al frnt rnk, wth wnr whn swrvd rght 2 out, hrd drvn and kpt on r-in*........(7 to 4 op 6 to 4 tchd 2 to 1) 3
3207 JHAL FREZI 6-11-6 B Powell, *set moderate pace, hng lft aftr 5th, hdd appr 2 out, sn btn*...(100 to 1 op 50 to 1) 4
SPRING SUNRISE 4-10-9 S McNeill, *took str hold, mstk 5th, no hdwy frm 3 out.*
.............................(20 to 1 op 16 to 1 tchd 33 to 1) 5
3208 TELEPHONE 5-11-6 M A FitzGerald, *wl plcd till wknd frm 3 out.*.......................(25 to 1 op 12 to 1) 6
3362⁶ LADY MAVIS 4-10-2 (7*) M Moran, *no imprsn frm 3 out.*
..............................(66 to 1 op 50 to 1 tchd 100 to 1) 7
TRUE SERENADE 5-11-6 V Slattery, *smooth prog 5th, lost pl 3 out*.............(50 to 1 op 25 to 1 tchd 66 to 1) 8
3315⁸ TIR NA NOG (bl) 5-11-6 J Ryan, *cl up, mstk second, hrd drvn and btn 3 out*.............(100 to 1 op 50 to 1) 9
2546⁹ NORTHERN SINGER 4-11-0 A Tory, *al beh.*
..............................(100 to 1 op 50 to 1) 10
DONTDRESSFORDINNER 4-11-0 S Burrough, *al in rear.*
..............................(50 to 1 op 33 to 1 tchd 66 to 1) 11
3476 PIRATE BOY 7-10-13 (7*) T Murphy, *not fluent, pld hrd, wl plcd till drpd rear frm 6th*.......(12 to 1 tchd 11 to 1) 12
BLUE FLAG (USA) 5-11-6 J Frost, *rcd wide, pld hrd, pressed ldrs to 6th, tld off*.......(20 to 1 tchd 33 to 1) 13
3339 MENEFORT 6-11-6 Richard Guest, *tld off whn tried to refuse and wnt lft 3rd, pld up bef 5th.*
..............................(100 to 1 op 50 to 1) pu
Dist: Nk, hd, 15l, 3½l, 1¾l, ½l, 8l, 8l, hd, 4l. 3m 57.90s. a 10.90s (14 Ran).
(Tony Walsh), P R Hedger

HEXHAM (heavy)
Saturday April 23rd
Going Correction: PLUS 1.95 sec. per fur. (races 1,3,-5,6), PLUS 2.20 (2,4)

3577 Chesters Stud Mares Only Novices' Chase (5-y-o and up) £2,284 2m 110yds.......................(5:50)

3428² RIVER PEARL 9-12-0 T Reed, *hld up in tch, trkd ldr frm 8th, rdn betw last 2, led r-in, all out.*
..............................(6 to 4 on op 7 to 4 on) 1
3428⁶ SUPER SANDY 7-11-0 P Niven, *led, rdn betw last 2, hdd r-in, no extr und pres.* (13 to 2 op 6 to 1 tchd 7 to 1) 2
3486⁶ SAGARO BELLE 8-11-0 A Merrigan, *prmnt, wknd appr 2 out.*.....................(33 to 1 op 20 to 1) 3
1723 EASTER OATS 7-11-0 N Smith, *beh, styd on frm 2 out, nvr dngrs.*...................(14 to 1 op 10 to 1) 4
2892 BALTIC BREEZE (Ire) 6-11-0 Gary Lyons, *in tch, wknd aftr 7th, wl beh frm 3 out*.......(20 to 1 tchd 25 to 1) 5
3429 HAMANAKA (USA) 5-10-7 Mr S Love, *al beh, tld off.*
..............................(12 to 1 op 10 to 1) 6
3286⁹ HERE COMES TIBBY 7-11-2 (5*) P Waggott, *in tch, outpcd aftr 7th, wl beh frm 3 out, tld off.*
..............................(4 to 1 op 7 to 2 tchd 9 to 2) 7
3377 HAWAIIAN GODDESS (USA) (bl) 7-11-7 C Dennis, *sn beh, tld off whn mstk and uns rdr last, rmntd.*
..............................(16 to 1 op 14 to 1) 8
3540 SOUND PROFIT 6-11-0 A Dobbin, *f second.*
..............................(40 to 1 op 20 to 1) f
3033 LA MOLINILLA 11-10-7 (7*) Miss S Lamb, *hmpd second, blun 4th, tld off whn pld up aftr 6th*...........(33 to 1) pu
2951⁶ PREAMBLE 5-10-7 Miss J Thurlow, *prtominent to hfwy, sn wknd, pld up bef last.* (20 to 1 op 16 to 1) pu
Dist: ½l, dist, 20l, 8l, dist, 4l, dist. 4m 36.80s. a 38.80s (11 Ran).

SR: 34/19/-/-/-/-/ (Mrs A G Martin), L Lungo

3578 Northumberland County Association Of Boys Clubs Handicap Hurdle (0-110 4-y-o and up) £1,999 2½m 110yds ....(6:15)

2974³ IT'S THE PITS [103] 7-11-10 T Reed, *hld up, took clr order 7th, led betw last 2, lft clr last, drvn out*.......(3 to 1 jt-fav op 5 to 2) 1
3308* ROYAL FLAMINGO [100] 8-11-7 R J Beggan, *trkd ldrs, ev ch 2 out, sn rdn and one pace.*(3 to 1 jt-fav tchd 7 to 2) 2
3434² PALACEGATE KING [103] 5-11-10 M Moloney, *cl up, led 7th till hdd betw last 2, sn btn*.......(4 to 1 op 5 to 2) 3
3461⁵ SHELTON ABBEY [89] 8-10-10 K Jones, *not jump wl, made most till mstk and lost pl 5th, outpcd aftr nxt, no dngr after*...............(9 to 1 op 8 to 1 tchd 10 to 1) 4
3475 GREY MERLIN [80] 7-9-10 (5*) F Perratt, *cl up till wknd frm 3 out, tld off*.....................(25 to 1 op 16 to 1) 5

3429⁵ CAPTAIN TANCRED (Ire) [81] 6-10-2² A Merrigan, *hld up, hdwy to track ldrs, 8th, chalg whn stumbled and f last.*
..............................(12 to 1 op 10 to 1) f
3475 WAKE UP [97] 7-11-4 P Niven, *beh, lost tch aftr 7th, tld off whn pld up bef 2 out*...........(11 to 1 op 8 to 1) pu
3073 COOL DUDE [87] 8-10-8 S Turner, *beh, lost tch aftr 7th, tld off whn pld up bef 2 out*...........(11 to 1 op 8 to 1) pu
3287 ROYAL QUARRY [79] (bl) 8-10-0 C Dennis, *cl up, led 5th till hdd 7th, wknd quickly appr 2 out, wl beh whn pld up bef last.*...............(50 to 1 op 33 to 1) pu
Dist: 9l, 6l, 4l, dist. 5m 44.10s. a 51.10s (9 Ran).
SR: 36/24/21/3/-/-/ (Currie Group), L Lungo

3579 Britannia Office Equipment Novices' Chase (5-y-o and up) £2,363 2½m 110yds.......................(6:45)

3288 CELTIC SONG 7-11-11 T Reed, *prmnt, led 8th, hdd 4 out, outpcd aftr nxt, 15 ls beh but staying on whn lft alone last.*.........................(5 to 2 op 7 to 4) 1
3492⁸ SOUTH STACK 8-11-4 Gary Lyons, *cl up, slight ld aftr 4 out, blundd and uns rdr nxt, rmntd.*
..............................(14 to 1 op 10 to 1) 2
2240⁴ CAPTAIN CUTE 9-11-4 R Garritty, *tld off frm 8th, refused tenth.*...............(13 to 2 op 5 to 1) ref
3332* RUSSINSKY 7-11-11 R J Beggan, *in tch, led 4 out, sn hdd, lft in ld nxt, soon wl clr, tired betw last 2, refused last, broke blood vessel*...............(11 to 8 on op Evens) ref
JELLIQUE 12-11-4 C Hawkins, *made most till hdd 8th, blun badly and lost pl nxt, sn pld up.*
..............................(33 to 1 op 20 to 1) pu
3286 FARMER'S HAND 7-11-4 A Dobbin, *lost tch frm 11th, tld off whn pld up bef 2 out*...............(16 to 1 op 10 to 1 tchd 20 to 1) pu
Dist: Dist. 6m 11.60s. a 70.60s (6 Ran).
(Miss Rosemary Jeffreys), W G Reed

3580 McEwans Best Scotch Top Of The North Novices' Hurdle Qualifier (4-y-o and up) £2,565 2½m 110yds.....(7:15)

3126⁶ GREAT EASEBY (Ire) 4-10-8 K Johnson, *in tch, hdwy aftr 3 out, rdn to ld betw last 2, hit last, all out.*
..............................(20 to 1 op 16 to 1) 1
3440 TIGHTER BUDGET (USA) 7-11-4 M Moloney, *led till hdd betw last 2, rdn*(10 to 1 tchd 14 to 1 and 16 to 1) 2
3333² THE CHANGELING (Ire) 5-11-4 R J Beggan, *chsd ldrs, ev ch 3 out, wknd appr nxt*....(9 to 2 op 4 to 1 tchd 5 to 1) 3
3139 MISS PIMPERNEL 4-10-3 L O'Hara, *in tch, ev ch 3 out, wknd appr nxt*.....................(33 to 1) 4
3289* TROY BOY 4-11-2 J Callaghan, *in tch, ev ch 3 out, wknd appr nxt*....................(9 to 4 fav op 7 to 2) 5
3139 SEA PET 5-10-9 A Merrigan, *slwly away, al beh.* (50 to 1) 6
3179⁸ CALL THE SHOTS (Ire) 5-11-0 Gary Lyons, *al beh, tld off.*........................(50 to 1 op 33 to 1) 7
3413 WESTHOLME (USA) 6-11-12 R Garritty, *cl up, lost pl aftr 7th, tld off whn pld up aftr 2 out*... (5 to 2 op 5 to 1) pu
1967⁷ SERIOUS TIME 6-11-0 N Smith, *sn beh, tld off whn pld up bef 2 out*..................(9 to 1 op 8 to 1) pu
3440⁹ OLLIVER DUCKETT 5-11-0 C Hawkins, *al beh, tld off whn pld up bef 2 out.*............(50 to 1 op 33 to 1) pu
3373 WILD EXPRESSION 4-10-8 A Dobbin, *al beh, tld off whn pld up bef last.*..............(50 to 1 op 33 to 1) pu
3435 HOWARD'S POST 5-10-7 (7*) D Waters, *prmnt, wknd aftr 6th, tld off whn pld up aftr 2 out.* (50 to 1 op 25 to 1) pu
3440* TWIN STATES 5-11-1 (7*) W Fry, *in tch, wknd appr 3 out, tld off whn pld up bef last*..............(6 to 1 op 8 to 1) pu
2905 CARDINAL SINNER 5-11-0 K Jones, *sn beh, tld off whn pld up aftr 6th.*..............(50 to 1 op 33 to 1) pu
3435 PICKTHEMONEYUPALF 7-11-5⁵ Mr P Johnson, *slwly away, al beh, tld off whn pld up bef 2 out.*
..............................(50 to 1 op 33 to 1) pu
Dist: 6l, 30l, ¾l, hd, 11l, dist. 5m 47.20s. a 54.20s (15 Ran).
(D C Batey), W Storey

3581 Gilesgate Volvo Heart Of All England Hunt Cup Maiden Hunters' Chase (5-y-o and up) £2,152 3m 1f.......(7:45)

ELASTIC 8-11-4 (5*) Mr R Hale, *mstks, made all, sn wl clr, kpt on well*...............(11 to 2 op 5 to 1) 1
COT LANE 9-11-7 (7*) Mr R Walmsley, *in tch, hdwy aftr 13th, styd on frm 3 out, no ch wth wnr.*
..............................(15 to 2 op 9 to 2 tchd 8 to 1) 2
3439⁴ BIRTLEY GIRL 10-11-2 (7*) Miss Sue Nichol, *in tch, mstk 10th (water), chsd wnr frm 14th, no imprsn*...(33 to 1) 3
PRIDEAUX PRINCE 8-11-7 (7*) Mr P Atkinson, *nvr dngrs.*
..............................(12 to 1 op 8 to 1) 4
BROAD CHARE 7-11-7 (7*) Mr C Storey, *chsd ldrs, wknd aftr 14th.*.................(12 to 1 tchd 14 to 1) 5
3430 MILL KNOCK 12-11-7 (7*) Mr H Dickson, *in tch, wknd aftr 13th, tld off*.............(33 to 1 op 33 to 1) 6
LADY LOCH 8-11-10⁸ (7*) Mr B Stonehouse, *mstks, sn beh, tld off*.................(16 to 1 op 14 to 1) 7
SARONA SMITH 7-11-9 Mr J Walton, *chsd ldrs, wknd aftr 15th, tld off*.................(8 to 1 op 10 to 1) 8

514

CAPTAIN CAVEMAN 9-11-7 (7*) Mr M Haigh, *chsd ldrs, blun 10th (water), f 12th*.........................(66 to 1) f
FROZEN FOREST 6-11-7 (7*) Miss G Metcalfe, *beh, hld off frm hfwy, 13th*...........................(50 to 1 op 33 to 1) f
AUGHAFATEN WILLIE 8-11-7 (7*) Mr Chris Wilson, *beh whn f 13th*..........................(100 to 1 op 66 to 1) f
3430 REDE REBEL 8-11-2 (7*) Mr T Scott, *in tch whn f 9th*.
.........................(9 to 4 fav op 2 to 1 tchd 5 to 2) f
3430⁵ GLEN LICKY 10-11-7 (7*) Miss J Percy, *chsd ldrs, wkng whn badly hmpd 13th, tld off when slpd up appr 3 out*.
...............................(100 to 1) su
TRUE FAIR 11-11-7 (7*) Mr A Robson, *mstks, chsd wnr, wknd aftr 14th, tld off whn pld up bef last, lme*.
.........................(12 to 1 op 14 to 1 tchd 16 to 1) pu
3430⁴ WIRE LASS 10-11-4 (5*) Miss J Thurlow, *sn beh, tld off whn pld up bef last*.....................(33 to 1 op 25 to 1) pu
RAIKES RUSTLER 10-11-9 (5*) Mr R H Brown, *tld off whn pld up aftr 13th*..................(16 to 1 op 14 to 1) pu
3430² GALE STORM 10-11-2 (7*) Mr D Scott, *beh whn pld up lme aftr 13th*.....................(10 to 1 op 8 to 1) pu
HAZLE WAND 7-12-0 Mr S Swiers, *wl beh whn pld up bef 13th*.............................(20 to 1) pu
Dist: 14l, nk, dist, 1½l, dist, 6l, 3½l. 7m 24.20s. a 79.20s (18 Ran).
(Mrs D Cockburn), R G Cockburn

3582 Gilesgate Volvo Handicap Chase (0-100 5-y-o and up) £2,609 2½m 110yds.........................(8:15)

3474⁴ POTATO MAN [72] 8-9-9 (5*) F Perratt, *al prmnt, mstk tenth, effrt aftr 3 out, led betw last 2, drvn clr*.
.........................(33 to 1 op 25 to 1) 1
3412²⁹ WAY OF LIFE (Fr) [89] 9-11-3 P Niven, *led till hdd betw last 2, mstk last, no extr*.............(14 to 1 op 10 to 1) 2
3433² KAMBALDA RAMBLER [97] 10-11-11 B Storey, *hit 3rd, trkd ldrs, ev ch 3 out, wknd appr nxt*.
.........................(5 to 2 op 3 to 1 tchd 7 to 2) 3
3343* NAWRIK (Ire) [82] 5-10-10 T Reed, *outpcd aftr 6th, beh whn hmpd and brght down 11th*.
.........................(9 to 4 fav op 2 to 1 tchd 7 to 4 and 5 to 2) bd
2107² PINEMARTIN [94] 11-11-8 M Moloney, *hld up, mstk tenth, sn lost tch, wl beh whn pld up bef 4 out*.
.........................(9 to 1 op 10 to 1 tchd 8 to 1) pu
3288² MILITARY HONOUR [100] (bl) 9-12-0 Mr S Swiers, *in tch till wknd aftr 4 out, tld off whn pld up bef 2 out*.
.........................(8 to 1 op 5 to 1) pu
3058² BAD TRADE [96] 12-11-7 (3*) A Larnach, *in tch, hit tenth, wknd aftr 4 out, tld off whn pld up bef last*.
.........................(10 to 1 op 8 to 1) pu
2886² CHIASSO FORTE (Ity) [94] 11-11-8 L O'Hara, *blun 5th, rdn aftr 7th, lost tch and pld up bef 4 out*.
.........................(10 to 1 op 7 to 1) pu
3288 POSITIVE ACTION [98] 8-11-12 A Dobbin, *chsd ldrs, wknd appr 3 out, tld off whn pld up bef last*.
.........................(7 to 1 op 5 to 1 tchd 8 to 1) pu
Dist: 20l, 1¾l. 5m 57.40s. a 56.40s (9 Ran).
(Chris Foster), Mrs S Taylor

MARKET RASEN (good)
Saturday April 23rd
Going Correction: PLUS 0.50 sec. per fur. (races 1,2,- 5,7,8), PLUS 0.75 (3,4,6)

3583 Kings Head Mares Only Novices' Hurdle (4-y-o and up) £2,903 2m 3f 110yds ....(2:15)

3056* SHARKASHKA (Ire) 4-10-12 L Wyer, *wth ldr, led 5th, sn clr, mstks last 2, styd on wl*.
.........................(100 to 30 op 3 to 1 tchd 4 to 1) 1
3230³ LOCH SCAVAIG (Ire) 5-11-7 (3*) D J Moffatt, *nvr far away, lost pl 6th, ran on frm 2 out, not rch wnr*.
.........................(7 to 2 op 5 to 2) 2
3128⁹ BAJAN AFFAIR 4-10-12 A Maguire, *nvr far away, rdn 3 out, styd on one pace frm nxt*.
.........................(16 to 1 op 12 to 1 tchd 20 to 1) 3
3509* CHOCKAVERRY (Ire) 6-11-3 (7*) P Ward, *hld up, hdwy 6th, wnt second 3 out, sn rdn, no extr frm last*.
.........................(15 to 8 fav op 6 to 1 tchd 9 to 1) 4
1239² SAFARI PARK 5-11-5 M Dwyer, *led to 5th, wknd 2 out*.
.........................(14 to 1 tchd 16 to 1) 5
3440 POWLEYVALE 7-11-10 R Supple, *chsd ldg bunch, rdn 3 out, sn wknd*.....................(12 to 1 op 8 to 1) 6
3164* ANNIE KELLY 6-11-5 B Dalton, *nvr rch ldrs*.
.........................(10 to 1 tchd 12 to 1) 7
1707 MISS NOSEY OATS 6-11-0 M A FitzGerald, *in tch to 7th*.
.........................(40 to 1 op 25 to 1 tchd 50 to 1) 8
3396 LA SUSIANE 7-10-11 (3*) R Farrant, *prmnt, rdn 6th, sn lost tch*.........................(50 to 1 op 25 to 1) 9
3379 MERRYHILL MADAM 5-11-0 Gary Lyons, *al beh*.
.........................(66 to 1 op 50 to 1) 10
2490 HUTCEL BRIG 5-10-7 (7*) J Driscoll, *in tch to hfwy*.
.........................(66 to 1 op 25 to 1) 11
2117 POP FESTIVAL 5-10-7 (7*) D Winter, *sn beh*.
.........................(100 to 1 op 66 to 1) 12

3379⁹ SKELTON LASS (Ire) 5-10-7 (7*) F Leahy, *al wl beh*.
.........................(66 to 1 op 50 to 1) 13
DALBEATTIE 5-11-0 N Mann, *tld off frm hfwy*.
.........................(20 to 1 op 33 to 1 tchd 50 to 1) 14
1100 WE'RE IN 7-11-0 Richard Guest, *f 1st*.(66 to 1 op 50 to 1) f
2834 ARDENT LOVE (Ire) 5-11-0 M Brennan, *hld up, effrt whn f 7th*.........................(25 to 1 op 20 to 1 tchd 33 to 1) f
Dist: 3½l, 7l, hd, 1½l, 10l, 5l, 15l, 3½l, 8l, dist. 4m 48.80s. a 15.80s (16 Ran).
SR: 23/13/24/17/12/2/-/-/ (C H Stevens), M H Easterby

3584 White Swan Selling Hurdle (4,5,6-y-o) £2,061 2m 5f 110yds.........................(2:45)

3284⁵ STRATHBOGIE MIST (Ire) 6-11-0 (7*) F Leahy, *hdwy hfwy, led 3 out, rdn clr appr last*.........(7 to 1 tchd 8 to 1) 1
2152⁵ SAOIRSE (Ire) 6-11-11 (3*) D J Moffatt, *beh, ran on appr last, nrst finish*...............(10 to 1 op 7 to 1) 2
2907⁶ PAAJIB (Ire) 4-10-7 (7*) M Clay, *beh, hdwy hfwy, wnt second appr 2 out, wknd last*.........(25 to 1 op 20 to 1) 3
3342² ERLEMO (v) 5-11-7 Diane Clay, *beh and rdn alng, ran on appr last, nrst finish*.....(5 to 1 op 4 to 1 tchd 11 to 2) 4
3395 SARANNPOUR (Ire) (bl) 5-11-2 (5*) E Husband, *styd on frm 2 out, nvr nrr*.....................(12 to 1 op 10 to 1) 5
2419 SEPTEMBER SAND 6-11-2 J Railton, *in tch to 4 out*.
.........................(66 to 1) 6
3435⁵ OWES THE TILL 4-10-2 (7*) C Woodall, *prmnt to 7th*.
.........................(14 to 1 op 10 to 1) 7
2760 MAGGIES LAD (bl) 6-12-0 M A FitzGerald, *nvr far away, led 7th, hdd aftr 3 out, sn wknd*.
.........................(9 to 1 op 20 to 1 tchd 8 to 1) 8
3235⁴ LEGATA (Ire) 5-10-11 (5*) P Midgley, *wth ldrs, led 5th, hdd and mstk 7th, sn btn*.....................(20 to 1) 9
490* GREEK CHIME (Ire) 5-12-0 A Maguire, *nvr far away, rdn 7th, wknd 3 out, pld up bef nxt*.(7 to 4 fav op 2 to 1) pu
1142⁵ SUNTAN (Fr) 5-11-7 L Wyer, *al beh, tld off frm hfwy, pld up bef 2 out*...............(12 to 1 op 10 to 1) pu
3225 BAR THREE (Ire) (bl) 5-11-7 V Smith, *led til aftr 5th, sn wknd, tld off whn pld up bef 2 out*.............(50 to 1) pu
2902⁶ BOLD STAR (bl) 4-11-0 S McNeill, *in tch to hfwy, sn rdn, tld off whn pld up bef 2 out*.......(15 to 2 op 6 to 1) pu
1374 BOSSYMOSS (Ire) 5-11-7 Susan Kersey, *al beh, tld off whn pld up bef 2 out*..................(50 to 1) pu
3429 QUIET MISTRESS 4-10-9 M Dwyer, *al beh, tld off frm hfwy, pld up bef 2 out*.........(25 to 1 op 20 to 1) pu
Dist: 9l, 7l, 2½l, 3l, 4l, dist, 1½l, nk. 5m 29.30s. a 25.30s (15 Ran).
(W A Sellers), J Parkes

3585 Victor Lucas Memorial Novices' Handicap Chase (5-y-o and up) £3,314 2m 1f 110yds.........................(3:20)

2481⁴ ROC COLOR (Fr) [105] 5-11-10 G Bradley, *nvr far away, led 6th to tenth, second and btn whn lft in ld last, ran on wl*.............(10 to 1 op 8 to 1 tchd 11 to 1) 1
2486⁵ MAGGOTS GREEN [81] 7-9-11 (3*) R Farrant, *nvr far away, led tenth, hdd 2 out, 3rd and btn whn lft second and ev ch last, no extr nr finish*...........(33 to 1 op 20 to 1) 2
3490⁶ HIGHLY DECORATED [83] 9-10-2² Richard Guest, *prog hfwy, rdn 3 out, one pace frm nxt*.
.........................(12 to 1 op 10 to 1 tchd 14 to 1) 3
3400 CROOKED COUNSEL [91] 8-10-10 S McNeill, *in tch, rdn 7th, wknd 4 out*.........(8 to 1 op 7 to 1 tchd 9 to 1) 4
3341⁵ MASTER'S CROWN (USA) [82] 6-10-1 W Worthington, *led 3rd til 6th, wknd 4 out*..........(33 to 1 op 20 to 1) 5
3460* PRECIPICE RUN [96] 9-11-1 N Doughty, *led to 3rd, wknd 5 out*.........................(6 to 1 op 4 to 1) 6
1405⁵ BALLAD RULER [88] 8-10-4 (3*) R Davis, *al wl beh*.
.........................(33 to 1 op 20 to 1) 7
3346* SPOONHILL WOOD [93] (bl) 8-10-12 B Dalton, *hdwy hfwy, wknd 5 out*.........................(6 to 1 op 5 to 1) 8
2932³ EMERALD GEM [81] 8-10-0 M Brennan, *not fluent, blun 8th, tld off*....................(33 to 1 op 20 to 1) 9
3438² DORADUS [95] 6-10-7 (7*) F Leahy, *al cl up, slight ld whn f 3 out*...............(5 to 1 op 4 to 1 tchd 11 to 2) f
3490² PHARGOLD (Ire) [88] 5-10-7 R Supple, *sluggish strt, jmpd wl, hdwy 6th, led 2 out, sn clr, f last, unlucky*.
.........................(7 to 2 fav op 4 to 1 tchd 11 to 2) f
1078⁴ BALLYHAMAGE (Ire) [81] 6-10-0 A Maguire, *blun and uns rdr 3rd*........................(6 to 1 op 8 to 1) ur
DANCING SENSATION (USA) [81] 7-10-0 M Hourigan, *al tld off whn pld up bef 3 out*...(10 to 1 op 14 to 1) pu
Dist: 1½l, 5l, 8l, 9l, 2l, 1l, dist, 3l. 4m 34.40s. a 20.40s (13 Ran).
SR: 23/-/-/-/-/-/ (Mrs Susan McCarthy), C P E Brooks

3586 Red Lion Handicap Chase (0-110 5-y-o and up) £4,207 2½m.........................(3:55)

2859³ ASTINGS (Fr) [91] 6-10-9 M Dwyer, *chsd ldg grp, led 8th till 12th, rdn to ld last, ran on wl*..........(11 to 4 jt-fav op 5 to 2 tchd 3 to 1) 1
3375³ HOUGHTON [93] (bl) 8-10-11 L Wyer, *led to 8th, led 12th, jmpd lft 3 out and 2 out, hdd last, one pace r-in*.
.........................(5 to 1 op 11 to 2 tchd 10 to 1) 2
3342² DEEP DECISION [92] 8-10-10 K Johnson, *chsd ldg bunch, rdn 2 out, kpt on r-in*...........(5 to 1 tchd 11 to 1) 3

3357³ HIGHFIELD PRINCE [82] 8-9-11⁴ (7*) K Davies, *rstrained in rear, hdwy 6 out, hit 2 out, rdn and mstk last, no extr r-in*..............................(25 to 1 op 20 to 1 tchd 33 to 1) 4
3452² PERSIAN SWORD [98] 8-11-2 A Maguire, *chsd ldg bunch to 4 out*..............(11 to 4 jt-fav op 3 to 1 tchd 5 to 2) 5
3105 ENCHANTED MAN [91] 10-10-9 D Byrne, *hit 4th, effrt 9th, wknd four out*........(16 to 1 op 14 to 1 tchd 20 to 1) 6
3107⁴ WE'RE IN THE MONEY [82] (bl) 10-10-0 B Dalton, *in tch to 8th*.................................. (25 to 1 op 20 to 1) 7
1997⁴ NEWMARKET SAUSAGE [82] 13-10-0 M Hourigan, *in tch, wknd hfwy*.....................(100 to 1 op 66 to 1) 8
3318³ RADICAL REQUEST [88] (bl) 11-10-6 M A FitzGerald, *in rear, hit 7th, sn tld off*..............(20 to 1 tchd 25 to 1) 9
2501* DOLIKOS [106] 7-11-10 Peter Caldwell, *prmnt, mstk and uns rdr 8th*........................(5 to 1 tchd 6 to 1) ur
3261⁷ THE LEGGETT [105] (bl) 11-11-9 A S Smith, *in tch, jmpd slwly 3rd, wknd 5th, sn tld off, pld up bef 3 out*.
..............................(33 to 1 op 25 to 1) pu
Dist: 3½l, 1l, 1¼l, 10l, 4l, 15l, 20l, ½l. 5m 12.50s. a 20.50s (11 Ran).
SR: 26/24/22/10/16/5/ (W A A Farrell), J G FitzGerald

3587 Jack Green Farewell Juvenile Handicap Hurdle (4-y-o) £2,302 2m 1f 110yds........................(4:25)

3330⁴ BITRAN [74] 10-2 A S Smith, *led to 6th, sn lost pl, ran on appr last, led cl hme.* (11 to 2 op 6 to 1 tchd 13 to 2) 1
3131⁴ DON'T FORGET MARIE (Ire) [82] 10-7 (3*) A Procter, *hld up, prog 6th, led appr last, ct last strds.* (5 to 1 tchd 6 to 1) 2
3478⁷ DANGER BABY [72] 10-0 M Brennan, *prog hfwy, hmpd 2 out, ran on ul r-in...*(16 to 1 op 14 to 1 tchd 20 to 1) 3
2685⁷ HYDE'S HAPPY HOUR [94] 11-8 M A FitzGerald, *hdwy 4th, sn rdn, one pace frm 2 out*..........(9 to 1 op 7 to 1) 4
3502³ MHEMEANLES [80] (bl) 10-8 L Wyer, *chsd ldg bunch, lost pl appr 2 out, no dngr aftr*..........(4 to 1 op 7 to 2) 5
3285* BARSAL (Ire) [76] 9-11 (7*) F Leahy, *chsd ldg bunch, hit 4th, wknd appr 2 out.* (10 to 1 op 8 to 1 tchd 12 to 1) 6
2381 REGAL AURA (Ire) [100] 12-0 N Bentley, *hld up, effrt 3 out, sn lost tch.*.....(9 to 1 op 8 to 1 tchd 10 to 1) 7
3252² LA VILLA ROSE (Fr) [82] 10-10 A Maguire, *hit 1st, prmnt, led and hit 6th, sn hdd, not much room and wknd.*
.......................(3 to 1 fav op 9 to 2) 8
3334 TEJANO GOLD (USA) [72] 9-11 (3*) T Eley, *hdwy hfwy, led aftr 3 out, quickened clr, f 2 out.*
..............................(33 to 1 op 20 to 1 tchd 50 to 1) f
3373³ MISTROY [80] 10-5 (3*) D Bentley, *chsd ldg grp, rdn and outpcd aftr 3 out, lft in ld 2 out, sn hdd, cl second whn f last.*.......................(5 to 1 op 9 to 1) f
Dist: Nk, 1¼l, 10l, 12l, 2½l, hd, 20l. 4m 16.50s. a 14.50s (10 Ran).
SR: 17/24/12/24/-/-/15/-/-/ (W A Fouracres), K A Morgan

3588 Chase Novices' Chase (5-y-o and up) £3,470 3m 1f..................(4:55)

3341 TRENTSIDE MIST 6-11-4 M Ranger, *nvr far away, led 3 out, rdn appr last, ran on wl.*
..............................(9 to 1 op 8 to 1 tchd 14 to 1) 1
3495⁹ KALANSKI 8-12-0 J Railton, *hld up gng wl, cld on ldrs and mstk 16th, rdn r-in, ran on, too much to do.*
..............................(6 to 4 on op 5 to 4 on) 2
3445 TITUS GOLD (bl) 9-11-1 (3*) T Eley, *led second, hdd 3 out, no extr r-in.*............(7 to 1 op 6 to 1 tchd 8 to 1) 3
3213⁷ WAYWARD SAILOR 8-11-4 S McNeill, *hld up, hdwy fnl circuit, hit 14th, wknd 2 out.*....(20 to 1 op 12 to 1) 4
3437 FIRST LORD 8-11-4 W McFarland, *led to second, beh fnl circuit.*.........(16 to 1 op 20 to 1 tchd 14 to 1) 5
HORCUM 9-11-1 (3*) R Davis, *al in rear, hit tenth, f 13th.*
..............................(50 to 1 op 33 to 1) f
3343 JENNY'S GLEN 7-11-4 J R Kavanagh, *nvr far away, dsptd ld frm 14th, f 4 out.*............(7 to 1 op 5 to 1 tchd 13 to 2) f
3286 ROYLE BURCHUN 9-11-1 (3*) D J Moffatt, *blun and uns rdr second.*..............(16 to 1 tchd 20 to 1) ur
2871 STONE WARRIOR 7-11-4 M Robinson, *sluggish strt, effrt 7th, in tch whn blun and uns rdr 11th.*
..............................(50 to 1 op 33 to 1) ur
3043 GLEN PENNANT 7-11-4 Richard Guest, *chsd ldg bunch to hfwy, tld off whn pld up bef 13th.*
..............................(25 to 1 tchd 33 to 1) pu
Dist: 1l, 4l, 15l, 30l. 6m 54.30s. a 53.30s (10 Ran).
(J Payne), C Smith

3589 Aston Arms National Hunt Flat Race (Div I) (4,5,6-y-o) £2,045 1m 5f 110yds ....(5:25)

MASTER BRACKEN 5-11-0 (7*) G Lee, *chsd ldg bunch, rdn to ld 2 fs out, styd on wl.*
..............................(5 to 1 tchd 7 to 1 and 6 to 1) 1
3190⁷ NOVA RUN 5-11-2 (5*) P Midgley, *prog 5 fs out, chsd wnr fnl furlong, ran on wl.*...(4 to 1 fav op 7 to 1) 2
3256² GOING AROUND 6-11-7 Mr J Durkan, *al beh, hdd 2 fs out, styd on same pace und pres*........(5 to 1 op 5 to 2) 3
3347* OUR MAIN MAN 4-11-6 (3*) S Wynne, *nvr far away, rdn 2 fs out, no extr appr last.*
..............................(11 to 2 op 3 to 1 tchd 6 to 1) 4

3234⁷ LISAHANE VILLE 5-11-7 Mr Raymond White, *chsd ldg bunch, rdn entering strt, no imprsn appr fnl furlong.*
..............................(9 to 2 op 6 to 1 tchd 14 to 1) 5
2876⁹ TIGH-NA-MARA 6-10-11 (5*) E Husband, *al hndy, rdn and ev ch 2 fs out, wknd fnl furlong..* (20 to 1 op 16 to 1) 6
2677 JAY EM ESS (NZ) 5-11-4 (3*) R Davis, *styd on fnl 2 fs, nrst finish.*.......................(20 to 1 op 16 to 1) 7
HERBERT BUCHANAN (Ire) 4-10-13 (3*) J McCarthy, *in tch, one pace fnl 3 fs.*...........(12 to 1 op 8 to 1) 8
FAST EXIT 6-10-9 (7*) D Towler, *hld up, ran on appr fnl furlong, nvr nrr.*..............(25 to 1 op 12 to 1) 9
2877⁶ STORMY SESSION 4-10-9 (7*) G Tormey, *nvr trbld ldrs.*
..............................(20 to 1 op 12 to 1) 10
MORCAT 5-11-2 Mr C Ratcliffe, *al mid-div.*
..............................(25 to 1 op 20 to 1 tchd 33 to 1) 11
1813 SKIDDER 5-11-7 Mr K Green, *prmnt, wknd 3 fs out.*
..............................(33 to 1 op 16 to 1) 12
PRINCE IVANHOE 5-11-4 (3*) T Eley, *prmnt to hfwy.*
..............................(33 to 1 op 16 to 1) 13
3347³ ROBINS PRIDE (Ire) 4-10-9 (7*) F Leahy, *mid-div, effrt 5 fs out, sn btn.*....................(6 to 1 op 5 to 1) 14
2909⁹ PERCY PIT 5-11-4 (3*) D J Moffatt, *chsd ldrs till wknd o'r 3 fs out.*............(12 to 1 op 16 to 1 tchd 10 to 1) 15
2963⁵ HOAGY POKEY 4-10-9 (7*) J Driscoll, *in tch, rdn and wknd o'r 4 fs out.*...........(25 to 1 op 16 to 1) 16
BARDAROS 5-11-2 (7*) R Massey, *prmnt to hfwy.*
..............................(25 to 1 op 16 to 1) 17
2407 DARING CREST 4-10-8 (3*) R Farrant, *tld off frm hfwy.*
..............................(25 to 1 op 12 to 1) 18
STALBRIDGE LASS 5-10-11 (5*) Mr D McCain, *tld off frm hfwy.*...........................(16 to 1 op 12 to 1) 19
QUANTUM LEADER (Ire) 5-11-0 (7*) K Davies, *sluggish strt, al wl beh, tld off and pld up 3 fs out.*
..............................(33 to 1 op 16 to 1) pu
Dist: 2l, 3l, 1l, ¾l, 2l, 2½l, hd, ¾l, 8l, 4l. 3m 13.90s. (20 Ran).
(Express Marie Curie Racing Club), Mrs M Reveley

3590 Aston Arms National Hunt Flat Race (Div II) (4,5,6-y-o) £2,030 1m 5f 110yds ....(5:55)

NEBAAL (USA) 4-10-13 (3*) R Farrant, *hld up, prog 5 fs out, chsd ldrs entering strt, led o'r 2 out, styd on wl.*
..............................(16 to 1 tchd 20 to 1) 1
3079⁵ QUEEN BUZZARD 6-10-9 (7*) Mr J Weymes, *hdwy hfwy, wnt second appr fnl furlong, no extr cl hme.*
..............................(9 to 1 op 7 to 1) 2
MONYMOSS (Ire) 5-11-0 (7*) R Wilkinson, *hdwy 5 fs out, chsd ldg bunch entering strt, one pace fnl furlong.*
..............................(20 to 1 op 16 to 1 tchd 25 to 1) 3
IMPERIAL COSSACK 4-10-9 (7*) G Robertson, *al hndy, rdn o'r 2 fs out, wknd appr fnl furlong*...........(10 to 1) 4
3227⁸ SIERRA MADRONA (USA) 4-10-4 (7*) S Leahy, *hdwy hfwy, no imprsn fnl 2 fs.*.........................(20 to 1) 5
SWEET MARTINI 4-10-4 (7*) J Bond, *prmnt, rdn entering strt, no imprsn.*..............(12 to 1 op 10 to 1) 6
TAKE THE LAST 4-10-9 (7*) Mr C Bonner, *hdwy 4 fs out, wknd appr last...........*(10 to 1 op 8 to 1) 7
JUNO'S SPECIAL (Ire) 6-11-2 Mr I McLelland, *wth ldrs, rdn and wknd o'r 2 fs out.*...........(25 to 1 op 20 to 1) 8
3347⁹ HOLIDAY HOME 6-11-0 (7*) B Grattan, *chsd ldrs, led 6 fs out, hdd and wknd o'r 2 out.*
..............................(25 to 1 op 20 to 1 tchd 16 to 1) 9
PANDORA'S FIRE 6-10-9 (7*) K Davies, *al mid-div.* (33 to 1) 10
SCILLY CAY 5-10-9 (7*) B Harding, *nvr trbld ldrs.*
..............................(7 to 1 op 5 to 1 tchd 8 to 1) 11
NABURN LOCH 4-10-4 (7*) J Driscoll, *nvr nr to chal.*
..............................(20 to 1) 12
HICKLETON GIRL 4-10-4 (7*) P McLoughlin, *slwly into strd, nvr dngrs.*.........................(33 to 1) 13
STEPPING 4-10-6 (5*) Mr D Parker, *led, hdd 6 fs out, wknd o'r 3 out.*........................(20 to 1) 14
IMPERIAL SMILE (NZ) 6-11-4 (3*) R Davis, *al beh.*
..............................(11 to 2 op 4 to 1) 15
WURZLE GUMMIDGE 5-11-4 (3*) A Procter, *pressed ldrs till wknd 4 fs out.*........(3 to 1 fav op 2 to 1 tchd 4 to 1) 16
RAKATINO 4-10-8 (3*) D J Moffatt, *in tch fnl 7 fs.*
..............................(9 to 1 op 7 to 1) 17
GIRL NAMED SUE 5-10-13 (3*) J McCarthy, *al beh.*
..............................(7 to 1 op 5 to 1 tchd 8 to 1) 18
1674 AHBEJAYBUS (Ire) 5-11-0 (7*) M Harris, *lost tch aftr 3 fs, sn tld off*..............................(66 to 1 op 50 to 1) 19
Dist: 1½l, 3l, 10l, 5l, nk, nk, 8l, 1½l, 15l, ¾l. 3m 13.40s. (19 Ran).
(C Humphry), G Thorner

3591 38th Whitbread Gold Cup Handicap Chase Grade 3 (5-y-o and up) £58,415 3m 5f 110yds..................(4:05)

3425 USHERS ISLAND [140] 8-10-0 C Swan, *hld up beh, not fluent 19th, lost pl, hdwy appr 3 out, ran on approaching last, switchd rght and led r-in, styd on wl.*
.... (25 to 1 op 20 to 1 tchd 33 to 1) 1

3026* ANTONIN (Fr) [154] 6-10-9 (5") J Raven, *mstk 4th, prmnt, led 18th till mistake and hdd nxt, not fluent four out and next, ran on strly frm last.......*(4 to 1 op 3 to 1) 2

3403* DOCKLANDS EXPRESS [155] 12-11-1 N Williamson, *al prmnt, drvn aftr 3 out, led appr last till hdd and no extr r-in.....................* (5 to 1 tchd 9 to 2) 3

3027* FIGHTING WORDS [140] 8-9-11 (3") P Hide, *hld up, hdwy to track ldrs tenth, led 19th to 3 out, ev ch last, one pace.....................*(8 to 1 tchd 9 to 1) 4

3064⁴ FLASHING STEEL [161] 9-11-7 R Dunwoody, *hld up beh ldrs, mstk 14th, drvn 3 out, one pace.*
.....................(100 to 30 tay op 7 to 2) 5

3425 YOUNG HUSTLER [162] 7-11-8 D Bridgwater, *trkd ldrs, led 11th, mstk 17th, hdd nxt, led 3 out till appr last, wknd and eased r-in.....................* (9 to 1 tchd 5 to 1) 6

3425 TOPSHAM BAY [153] 11-10-13 J Frost, *led to second, trkd ldrs till lost pl 15th, no dngr aftr.*
.....................(8 to 1 op 7 to 1 tchd 9 to 1) 7

3134⁴ CYTHERE [140] 10-10-0 M Richards, *beh 4th, pushed alng aftr 13th, sn lost tch.....................*(66 to 1 op 50 to 1) 8

3205³ ANNIO CHILONE [140] 8-10-0 E Murphy, *hld up, reminders 14th, af beh.....................*(66 to 1) 9

3299* CATCH THE CROSS [140] (bl) 8-10-0 M Perrett, *hld up, al beh, tld off.....................*(20 to 1 tchd 25 to 1) 10

3501⁵ ABBOTSHAM [140] 9-9-9 (5") D Fortt, *mstks, al beh, tld off.*
.....................(250 to 1 op 200 to 1) 11

3485³ SUPERFINE FINISH [140] (bl) 8-10-0 J Osborne, *led second to 11th, lost pl 17th, pld up bef 3 out.*
.....................(16 to 1 tchd 20 to 1) pu

Dist: 2½l, ½l, sht-hd, hd, 3½l, 25l, 2½l, 6l, 15l, 1½l. 7m 36.10s. a 23.10s (12 Ran).

SR: 62/73/73/58/71/68/34/18/12/ (R W L Bowden), J H Johnson

WORCESTER (good)
Saturday April 23rd
Going Correction: PLUS 0.25 sec. per fur.

3592 Sporting Life Happy Returns Novices' Hurdle (4-y-o and up) £2,738 3m (5:30)

2572² GREENHILL TARE AWAY 6-11-3 Peter Hobbs, *took str hold, al ldg grp, mstk 9th, pushed alng appr 3 out, led last, styd on und pres.......* (5 to 2 op 9 to 4 tchd 11 to 4) 1

3453² WOLF WINTER 9-11-10 T Grantham, *led till last, rdn and no extr r-in........*(11 to 8 fav op 7 to 4 tchd 5 to 4) 2

1468² ARMATEUR (Fr) 6-11-3 R Bellamy, *cl up, ev ch 3 out, outpcd nxt............*(9 to 1 op 10 to 1 tchd 12 to 1) 3

3119⁷ GOLD GLEN (Ire) (bl) 6-11-3 B Clifford, *ldg grp till wknd 3 out.....................*(33 to 1) 4

3196⁴ DUNDEE PRINCE (NZ) 8-11-3 D Gallagher, *wtd with, smooth prog frm 7th, wknd quickly 3 out.*
.....................(9 to 1 op 7 to 1 tchd 10 to 1) 5

3352³ MISS SOUTER 5-10-5 (7") R Darke, *struggling frm 8th.*
.....................(50 to 1 op 33 to 1) 6

3441⁸ COTSWOLD CASTLE 8-10-12 (5") S Fox, *chsd ldrs, rdn and wknd 8th.....................*(25 to 1 op 20 to 1) 7

2768⁶ LACURVA (Ire) 6-11-3 S Earle, *chsd frnt rnk till wknd 9th.*
.....................(14 to 1 op 12 to 1 tchd 16 to 1) 8

3381 WHAT A NOBLE 8-10-10 (7") R Rourke, *jmpd rght in rear, tld off frm 4th.......*(25 to 1 op 20 to 1 tchd 33 to 1) 9

2841 LOYAL GAIT (NZ) 6-11-3 R Greene, *handily plcd, wknd sn aftr hfwy, no ch whn mstk 3 out, tld off......*(50 to 1) 10

2295 SENNA BLUE 9-11-3 V Slattery, *al in rear, tld off.*
.....................(66 to 1 op 50 to 1) 11

2717 ENTERPRISE PRINCE 8-11-3 B Powell, *slwly away, al in rear, tld off whn pld up bef 2 out.* (100 to 1 op 50 to 1) pu

3478⁹ ARJUNA 9-11-3 L Harvey, *al in rear, tld off whn pld up bef 3 out.....................*(33 to 1) pu

3503 DARK DEB 9-10-12 P McDermott, *hld up and pld hrd, improved 4th, lost pl hfwy, tld off whn pulled up bef 3 out.....................*(100 to 1 op 50 to 1) pu

ISAMBARD 7-11-3 Mr K Hollowell, *drpd out strt, took str hold, wnt prmnt 3rd, lost pl 7th, tld off whn pld up bef 3 out.....................*(100 to 1 op 50 to 1) pu

3453 CELTIC TOKEN 5-10-10 (7") Mr G Hogan, *wl plcd to hfwy, tld off whn pld up bef 3 out.....*(66 to 1 tchd 100 to 1) pu

3416⁸ ORCHESTRATED CHAOS (Ire) 5-10-12 Mr J Mead, *jmpd slwly 1st, al in rear, tld off whn pld up bef 3 out.*
.....................(100 to 1 op 50 to 1) pu

3459⁶ SECOND SLIP 5-11-13 G McCourt, *in rear, rdn 5th, pld up aftr nxt.....................*(14 to 1 op 12 to 1) pu

Dist: 5l, 15l, 20l, 10l, 3l, ½l, hd, 30l, 2½l, 12l. 5m 56.40s. a 20.40s (18 Ran).

(Mrs P Payne), P J Hobbs

3593 Saga Magazine Venerable Anniversary Handicap Chase (0-125) £3,745 2m 7f.....................(6:00)

3223⁴ COMEDY ROAD [102] 10-10-5 A Maguire, *wtd wth, hdwy hfwy, slight ld 4 out, drvn clr appr last, ran on wl.*
.....................(4 to 1 op 5 to 1) 1

3205⁴ TOCHENKA [109] 10-10-12 W Humphreys, *cl up, led 9th till appr 4 out, ev ch nxt, styd on same pace frm 2 out.*
.....................(3 to 1 fav op 2 to 1) 2

3405 GLOVE PUPPET [103] 9-10-6 M A FitzGerald, *lost pos 11th, styd on ag'n frm 2 out.....................* (7 to 1 tchd 8 to 1) 3

3280² WINABUCK [115] 11-11-1 (3") D Meredith, *wth ldrs, ev ch 4 out, sn beh.....................* (5 to 1 op 9 to 2) 4

2852⁵ MR ENTERTAINER [115] 11-11-4 B Powell, *jmpd rght, led to 9th, slightly outpcd 14th, sn rallied and ev ch 4 out, soon wknd.....................*(13 to 2 op 6 to 1) 5

3336⁷ NOUGAT RUSSE [97] 13-9-12¹ (3") T Jenks, *sn beh, mstks 8th and 12th, soon tld off.*
.....................(16 to 1 op 12 to 1 tchd 20 to 1) 6

3417 COMPLETE OPTIMIST [97] 10-9-9 (5") Guy Lewis, *hld up and beh, f 9th.....................*(33 to 1 op 25 to 1) f

3492 COCK SPARROW [97] 10-10-0 W Marston, *wl plcd, beh briefly appr 4 out, wknd 3 out, not fluent nxt, pld up bef last.....................*(25 to 1 op 20 to 1) pu

3375⁶ MANDER'S WAY [102] 9-10-5 G Upton, *beh, jmpd slwly 14th, sn hrd rdn, tld off whn pld up bef 2 out.*
.....................(13 to 2 op 6 to 1) pu

Dist: 5l, 7l, 15l, 10l, 1¾l. 5m 54.30s. a 10.30s (9 Ran).

SR: 31/33/20/17/7/-/ (Winsbury Livestock), R Lee

3594 Radio Times Congratulatory Handicap Hurdle (0-120 4-y-o and up) £3,127 2m.....................(6:30)

3446* RAIN-N-SUN [85] 8-10-2 T Wall, *al frnt rnk, led appr 3 out, drw clr nxt, ran on strly.....*(16 to 1 op 20 to 1) 1

1213 SALMAN (USA) [96] 8-10-13 N Williamson, *settled in rear, improved 4th, chsd wnr aftr 3 out, one pace...*(20 to 1) 2

2998⁶ TRISTAN'S COMET [83] 7-10-0 D Gallagher, *trkd ldrs, rdn and outpcd appr 3 out, hrd drvn betw last 2, styd on r-in.....................*(25 to 1) 3

3436³ RED JAM JAR [87] 9-10-4 R Dunwoody, *prog 3rd, third and hld whn bad mstk 2 out.........*(5 to 1 op 6 to 1) 4

3311⁶ TILT TECH FLYER [91] 9-10-8 D Bridgwater, *pressed ldrs till wknd 3 out.....................*(14 to 1 op 12 to 1) 5

3281³ ANDRATH (Ire) [83] 6-10-0 A Maguire, *wl plcd till wknd 3 out.....*(12 to 1 op 16 to 1 tchd 20 to 1 and 10 to 1) 6

3499⁴ KING'S SHILLING (USA) [106] 7-11-9 Jacqui Oliver, *nvr rch ldrs.....................*(9 to 2 op 6 to 1) 7

3192⁴ MOVING OUT [107] 6-11-10 M Perrett, *prmnt till struggling frm hfwy.....................*(6 to 1 op 9 to 2) 8

2655 ANTI MATTER [90] 9-10-2 (5") S Fox, *handily plcd to hfwy.*
.....................(20 to 1 op 16 to 1) 9

3319⁹ BRIGGS LAD (Ire) [92] (bl) 5-10-9 N Mann, *led till appr 3 out, sn wknd.....................*(10 to 1) 10

HARD TO GET [83] (bl) 7-10-0 Ann Stokell, *jnd frnt rnk 3rd, lost pl aftr nxt.....................*(100 to 1) 11

2790⁸ THE HIDDEN CITY [83] 8-10-0 B Clifford, *al in rear.*
.....................(50 to 1) 12

3455 BURSANA [86] 8-10-3 W Marston, *mstk 1st, tld off frm 3rd.*
.....................(16 to 1 op 12 to 1) 13

OCEAN LAD [84] 11-10-1¹ B Powell, *al in rear, tld off.*
.....................(25 to 1) 14

TASHONYA [83] 12-10-0 J W Dacosta, *al in rear, tld off frm hfwy.....................*(100 to 1 op 50 to 1) 15

3499⁹ GOLDEN GUNNER (Ire) [98] (bl) 6-11-1 G McCourt, *midfield whn f 5th......*(14 to 1 op 12 to 1 tchd 10 to 1) f

STEVEYVUL [98] 10-11-1 V Slattery, *tld off whn pld up bef 4th.....................*(20 to 1) pu

2977 SQUIRE YORK [94] 4-10-11 M A FitzGerald, *wtd wth, smooth prog 5th, handily plcd whn blun badly 3 out, sn bhd.....................*(14 to 1 op 12 to 1 tchd 16 to 1) pu

Dist: 6l, 7l, 1l, 3l, sht-hd, 5l, 5l, 2½l, ¾l, 5l. 3m 51.60s. a 10.60s (18 Ran).

SR: 8/13/-/-/-/-/7/3/-/ (Mrs M Bostock), J L Harris

3595 Ring & Brymer Birthday Cake Handicap Chase (0-135 5-y-o and up) £4,411 2m.....................(7:00)

2806⁴ WINNIE THE WITCH [115] 10-10-13 D Bridgwater, *settled in last pl, steady prog frm 6th, led 4 out, drvn and forged clr appr 2 out, ran on wl.....................*(8 to 1 op 7 to 1) 1

3404⁴ MINE'S AN ACE (NZ) [109] 7-10-7 J Frost, *patiently rdn, hdwy 8th, wnt second 2 out, kpt on same pace.*
.....................(7 to 2 op 4 to 1 tchd 3 to 1) 2

3452⁴ DRIVING FORCE [112] (bl) 8-10-10 G McCourt, *beh, effrt 7th, struggling appr 4 out, hrd drvn betw last 2, styd on ag'n r-in.....................*(11 to 2 op 6 to 1) 3

3210* WICKFIELD LAD [102] 11-10-0 S Earle, *in rear till styd on frm 2 out, nrst finish.....................*(12 to 1 op 10 to 1) 4

3312⁵ SAILORS LUCK [109] 9-10-7 E Murphy, *wl plcd, blun 5th, ev ch 4 out, btn nxt, mstk last...*(14 to 1 tchd 16 to 1) 5

3262³ BOUTZDAROFF [130] 12-12-0 M Dwyer, *patiently rdn, effrt and ev ch 4 out, sn ridden, found nil.*
.....................(3 to 1 op 5 to 2) 6

3210⁷ PALM READER [118] 10-11-2 R Dunwoody, *led to 3rd, lft in ld nxt, hdd 4 out, sn wknd......* (11 to 1 op 10 to 1) 7

596² TRY ME NOW [102] 8-10-0 R Supple, *hld up and pld hrd, struggling frm 8th, tld off.....................*(9 to 1 op 8 to 1) 8

3185⁴ STARLAP [103] 10-10-1 A Maguire, *trkd ldrs, effrt 7th, ev ch 4 out, wknd nxt, mstk last, virtually pld up r-in.*
.....................(11 to 4 fav op 3 to 1 tchd 2 to 1) 9

3423[5] TRIMLOUGH [128] 9-11-12 W Marston, *wth ldr, led 3rd, f nxt*.......................................(11 to 1) f
Dist: 4l, 4l, 4l, 1¼l, 1¾l, 3l, 30l, 15l. 4m 2.20s. a 13.20s (10 Ran).
(Paddocks Thoroughbred Racing Ltd), K S Bridgwater

3596 Three Score Years And Ten Times Novices' Hunters' Chase (5-y-o and up) £2,696 2m 7f............... (7:30)

HERON'S ROCK 10-11-7 (7*) Mr M Portman, *hld up in rear, steady prog frm 9th, led on bit 2 out, drw clr, easily.* .... (15 to 2 op 7 to 1 tchd 9 to 1) 1
3419* COOL RELATION 8-12-0 (7*) Mr A Phillips, *cl up, hit 11th, lost pos 14th, styd on ag'n frm 2 out, no ch wth wnr.* ....(3 to 1 op 9 to 4) 2
3419[2] WELSH LEGION 9-11-7 (7*) Miss C Burgess, *in tch, mstk 4th, jnd ldr 8th, led 13th to 2 out, no extr.* .... (16 to 1 op 12 to 1) 3
RYTON RUN 9-11-7 (7*) Miss A Plunkett, *wl plcd till outpcd 14th, styd on ag'n frm 2 out*..................(50 to 1) 4
3480[8] RUSTY BRIDGE 7-11-7 (7*) Miss C Thomas, *wl beh hfwy, ran on frm 3 out, nrst finish*.................. (33 to 1) 5
3419 CLARE MAN (Ire) 6-12-7 Mr J Greenall, *cl up, lost pl 14th, rnwd effrt appr 4 out, wknd nxt.* .... (7 to 4 fav tchd 2 to 1) 6
SPACE PRINCE 13-11-7 (7*) Mr C Campbell, *chsd frnt rnk till wknd 13th*......................(50 to 1 op 25 to 1) 7
BENJAMIN LANCASTER 10-11-7 (7*) Mrs C Wonnacott, *led to 13th, wknd 4 out*.................(9 to 1 op 5 to 1) 8
3493 CLONONY CASTLE (bl) 8-11-7 (7*) Mr J Rudge, *nvr a factor*..........................(33 to 1 op 25 to 1) 9
3155 AS GOOD AS GOLD 8-11-7 (7*) Mr D Birkmyre, *al in rear, tld off*..........................(50 to 1 op 33 to 1) 10
3155[3] ALL GOLD BOY 9-11-7 (7*) Mr J Wingfield Digby, *in rear hfwy, mstk 11th, tld off*........... (33 to 1 op 20 to 1) 11
3399[3] TAMAR LASS 9-11-2 (7*) Mr I Widdicombe, *al in rear, tld off*..................(11 to 1 op 12 to 1 tchd 14 to 1) 12
3385[3] DENBERDAR 11-11-7 (7*) Mr B Pollock, *beh till broke leg and refused 13th, destroyed.* .... (10 to 1 op 8 to 1 tchd 11 to 1) ref
COMHAMPTON 13-11-7 (7*) Mr N Bradley, *al in rear, tld off whn blun 4 out, pld up bef nxt.* (66 to 1 op 20 to 1) pu
DUKE OF IMPNEY 7-11-7 (7*) Mr D S Jones, *mstk 4th, struggling frm 11th, tld off whn blun four out, pld up bef nxt*..........................(50 to 1 op 33 to 1) pu
BANG ON TARGET 6-11-9 (5*) Mr T Byrne, *beh, mstk 3rd, hit tenth, tld off whn pld up bef 12th.* ....(33 to 1 op 50 to 1) pu
Dist: 12l, ½l, 1l, 1¼l, 2½l, ½l, 12l, 2l, 12l, 15l. 6m 4.00s. a 20.00s (16 Ran).
(M H B Portman), P R Chamings

3597 OBS Special Day Return Novices' Hurdle (4-y-o and up) £2,878 2m (8:00)

3234 THE CAUMRUE (Ire) 6-11-0 J Frost, *wtd wth, prog 5th, slight ld last, kpt on wl fnl 100 yards.* .... (20 to 1 op 14 to 1 tchd 25 to 1) 1
3373* FORMAL AFFAIR 4-10-10 A Maguire, *hld up, hdwy 5th, led aftr 3 out, hdd last, no extr fnl 100 yards.* ....(3 to 1 op 5 to 2) 2
ZANYMAN 8-11-0 M A FitzGerald, *prog to chase ldrs appr 3 out, styd on strly r-in.* .... (14 to 1 op 10 to 1 tchd 16 to 1) 3
3334* BROWNED OFF 5-11-7 D Bridgwater, *hdwy to ld appr 3 out, sn hdd, wkng whn mstk 2 out.* .... (2 to 1 fav op 5 to 2 tchd 11 to 4 and 7 to 4) 4
3231[6] FIGHTING BRAVE 7-11-0 N Williamson, *hld up, improved 5th, wknd 2 out*.......................... (6 to 1 op 7 to 1) 5
2722 ROOTSMAN (Ire) 4-10-8 D Gallagher, *wtd wth, effrt 5th, outpcd frm 3 out*.................. (50 to 1 op 33 to 1) 6
3386[7] COUNTRY PARSON (Ire) 5-11-0 R Bellamy, *nvr rch ldrs.* ....(33 to 1) 7
2835 ADMIRAL BYNG (Fr) 7-10-11 (3*) D Meredith, *took keen hold, chsd ldrs to 5th*.............(25 to 1 op 33 to 1) 8
3231[8] LIVONIAN 4-10-8 J Osborne, *nvr a factor, tld off.* ....(6 to 1 tchd 8 to 1) 9
AFFORDABLE 6-11-0 Diane Clay, *al beh, tld off.* (33 to 1) 10
3451 NAGOBELIA 6-11-0 G Bradley, *chsd ldrs to hfwy, tld off.* .... (16 to 1 op 12 to 1) 11
3334[6] FIVE STARS (v) 7-10-9 L Harvey, *chsd clr ldr, led 5th, hdd appr 3 out, sn lost pl, tld off*.......(50 to 1 op 33 to 1) 12
3204 FOIL THE FOX 6-10-9 R Dunwoody, *al beh, tld off.* .... (14 to 1 op 10 to 1) 13
MOONLIGHT SHIFT 8-11-0 Mr B Leavy, *bad mstk 1st, al in rear, tld off*..................................(100 to 1) 14
BIRTHPLACE (Ire) 4-10-8 R Supple, *handily plcd, mstk 3rd, toiling nxt, tld off whn hmpd 3 out.* .... (16 to 1 op 25 to 1 tchd 33 to 1) 15
3339[8] POETS COVE 6-11-0 M Perrett, *al in rear, tld off.* .... (50 to 1 op 25 to 1) 16
TENDER DANCER (Ire) 6-11-0 J W Dacosta, *chsd ldrs till f 3rd*..(200 to 1) f
1622 GLASGOW (bl) 5-10-7 (7*) S Arnold, *led, sn clr, hdd 5th, wknd quickly, wl beh whn f 3 out*............(66 to 1) f
2692 ARAGON MIST 5-10-9 M Bosley, *in rear, bad mstk second, blun and uns rdr nxt*.......................(100 to 1) ur
IRISH GROOM 7-10-9 (5*) D Leahy, *brght dwn 3rd.* .... (66 to 1 op 50 to 1) bd
OLD EAGLE 8-11-0 W Marston, *pld hrd, al beh, tld off whn hmpd 3 out, sn pulled up*.............. (100 to 1) pu
Dist: 3½l, nk, 20l, 1l, hd, 12l, 3l, 12l, 3l, 5l. 3m 55.60s. a 14.60s (21 Ran).
(Mrs G B Balding), G B Balding

HEXHAM (heavy)
Monday April 25th
Going Correction: PLUS 1.70 sec. per fur.

3598 Dickinson Dees Maiden Hurdle (5-y-o and up) £2,512 2m.............(5:45)

3460 SCARABEN 6-11-0 A Maguire, *trkd ldr, led 5th, drvn clr aftr last*..........................(4 to 1 op 3 to 1) 1
3436 DERWENT LAD 5-11-0 A Dobbin, *sn tracking ldrs, rdn appr 2 out, ev ch till no extr approaching last.* .... (14 to 1 op 16 to 1) 2
1480[8] FIVE FLAGS (Ire) 6-11-0 Richard Guest, *in tch, sn rdn alng, pushed along to chase ldrs appr 3 out, kpt on same pace frm nxt*.......................(11 to 4 fav op 7 to 4) 3
2217 STONEY BROOK 6-11-0 B Storey, *trkd ldrs, dsptd ld 5th till wknd betw last 2*............... (3 to 1 tchd 7 to 2) 4
3289[6] WHAT A CARD 6-10-9 K Johnson, *in tch, effrt aftr 2 out, sn rdn and wknd*................................ (33 to 1) 5
671 CALL THE KING (Ire) 5-11-0 M Ahern, *prmnt till wknd betw last 2*...................(4 to 1 op 5 to 1 tchd 6 to 1) 6
3536 FLAXON WORRIOR 10-11-0 O Pears, *led to 5th, sn wknd, tld off whn pld up bef last*.........(50 to 1 op 33 to 1) pu
BDOORE (Ire) 6-10-4 (5*) A Roche, *lost tch hfwy, tld off whn pld up bef 2 out*..........................(33 to 1) pu
925 SON OF TEMPO (Ire) 5-10-7 (7*) Miss S Lamb, *lost tch hfwy, tld off whn pld up bef 2 out.* (33 to 1 op 25 to 1) pu
3379[8] CROFTON LAKE 6-11-0 L O'Hara, *in tch till wknd aftr 5th, tld off whn pld up bef last.* .... (16 to 1 op 14 to 1 tchd 20 to 1) pu
1736 SOLAR NOVA 6-10-9 N Smith, *beh, lost tch aftr 3 out, tld off whn pld up bef last*..............(20 to 1 op 33 to 1) pu
RORY JOHN 6-11-0 Mr C Mulhall, *prmnt till wknd aftr 5th, tld off whn pld up bef last*................(33 to 1) pu
Dist: 9l, nk, 15l, 11l, 10l. 4m 30.80s. a 40.80s (12 Ran).
(J Tennant), S E Kettlewell

3599 Gibson & Company Novices' Chase (5-y-o and up) £2,618 3m 1f..... (6:15)

3474 HUDSON BAY TRADER (USA) 7-11-12 Mrs A Farrell, *cl up, led 6th, drvn clr aftr 2 out*........... (3 to 1 op 2 to 1) 1
3343 COUNT SURVEYOR 7-11-5 K Johnson, *dsptd ld till lost pl appr 14th, rallied und pres to chase wnr approaching last, no imprsn*... (2 to 1 fav op 3 to 1 tchd 100 to 30) 2
3498[6] CROWN EYEGLASS 8-11-5 M A FitzGerald, *made most to 6th, cl up, rdn aftr 15th, ev ch 3 out, one pace.* ....(4 to 1 tchd 9 to 2) 3
3316[3] URIZEN 9-11-5 C Hawkins, *in tch, wnt second 14th, rdn aftr nxt, wknd after 3 out*........... (3 to 1 op 9 to 4) 4
2952[5] KILCOLGAN 7-11-5 B Storey, *in tch, mstk 4th, outpcd aftr 11th, lost touch appr 3 out*..........(11 to 1 op 8 to 1) 5
Dist: 7l, 14l, 3l, 8l. 7m 17.40s. a 72.40s (5 Ran).
(P C N Curtis), P Beaumont

3600 Stublic Conditional Jockeys' Selling Handicap Hurdle (4-y-o and up) £1,953 2m.............................(6:45)

3357[2] HYPNOTIST [76] 7-10-5 N Bentley, *dsptd ld, led 5th, rdn betw last 2, clr last, styd on wl.* (5 to 4 fav tchd 6 to 4) 1
3429[7] MISS JEDD [73] (v) 7-10-2[2] J Burke, *made most to 5th, wth wnr, rdn betw last 2, one pace*... (16 to 1 tchd 20 to 1) 2
2581* GREENACRES LAD [95] 11-11-10 S Lyons, *in tch, outpcd aftr 3 out, no dngr after.* (4 to 1 op 3 to 1 tchd 9 to 2) 3
3357[6] CHADWICK'S GINGER [84] 6-10-13 D J Moffatt, *in tch, outpcd aftr 3 out, no dngr after*.... (11 to 2 op 4 to 1) 4
3235[3] ELVETT BRIDGE (Ire) [71] 6-10-0 F Perratt, *trkd ldrs till wknd appr 2 out*....... (17 to 2 op 7 to 1 tchd 9 to 1) 5
3357[8] SEE THE LIGHT [71] 7-10-0 H Bastiman, *trkd ldrs, wknd appr 2 out, tld off*................ (16 to 1 op 33 to 1) 6
3342[4] INAN (USA) [82] 5-10-6 (5*) K Davies, *hld up, effrt aftr 3 out, sn btn, wknd betw last 2, tld off.* ....(4 to 1 op 7 to 2 tchd 9 to 2) 7
Dist: 8l, 9l, 3½l, 1½l, dist, 6l. 4m 27.20s. a 37.20s (7 Ran).
(P Goodall), W Bentley

3601 Wilkinson Maughan Novices' Hurdle (4-y-o) £2,145 2m...............(7:15)

2783[9] FRET (USA) 11-5 N Bentley, *trkd ldrs, led 3 out, clr aftr nxt, easily*..................... (5 to 4 fav tchd 2 to 1) 1
3144 GOLDMIRE 10-7 S Turner, *cl up, dsptd ld 3 out, ev ch appr nxt, kpt on, no chance wth wnr.* ....(3 to 1 op 5 to 2 tchd 9 to 4) 2
1532[4] SALLY OF THE ALLEY 10-7 Gary Lyons, *in tch, effrt aftr 3 out, wknd after nxt*.... (13 to 2 op 6 to 1 tchd 7 to 1) 3

3557 FIRST RESERVE (v) 10-12 M Moloney, *hld up, hdwy to track ldrs hfwy, ev ch appr 2 out, sn wknd.* ....(25 to 1 op 20 to 1) 4
2876 DREAM START 10-12 Richard Guest, *in tch, hmpd 4th, wknd aftr 3 out, tld off*..........(8 to 1 tchd 10 to 1) 5
2728[8] RUSHALONG 10-12 D Byrne, *led to 3 out, wknd quickly, tld off*..............................(20 to 1) 6
TO BE THE BEST 10-12 A Merrigan, *beh, mstk 4th, sn lost tch, tld off whn pld up bef 2 out.* (14 to 1 tchd 16 to 1) pu
3431 TRY AGAIN JANE 10-7 M A FitzGerald, *prmnt till wknd aftr 5th, tld off whn pld up bef 2 out.* ....(5 to 1 tchd 6 to 1) pu
Dist: 15l, 13l, 2l, dist, 9l. 4m 30.00s. a 40.00s (8 Ran).
(N Honeyman), G M Moore

3602 Ian Straker Memorial Trophy Handicap Chase (0-115 5-y-o and up) £3,127 3m 1f.........................(7:45)

3180 LOTHIAN PILOT [94] 7-11-2 T Reed, *hld up in tch, hdwy to ld 2 out, hrd pressed frm last, styd on wl.* ....(6 to 1 op 5 to 1) 1
3442[5] TRAVEL BOUND [78] 9-10-0 A Maguire, *cl up, rdn betw last 2, dsptd ld aftr last, shaken up and hng rght, kpt on und pres nr finish*...(11 to 2 op 6 to 1 tchd 7 to 1) 2
3485 BOREEN OWEN [92] (bl) 10-10-9 (5*) A Roche, *led to 2 out, no extr*..................(7 to 1 op 6 to 1 tchd 8 to 1) 3
3567 FORTH AND TAY [95] 12-11-0 (3*) P Williams, *beh, outpcd aftr 4 out, kpt on frm 2 out, nvr dngrs.* ....(5 to 1 tchd 11 to 2) 4
3437[3] CHOCTAW [102] 10-11-10 C Hawkins, *hld up, blun 14th, sn struggling, nvr dngrs*............(6 to 1 op 4 to 1) 5
3437 DUBIOUS JAKE [92] 11-11-0 M Dwyer, *in tch, pushed alng aftr 15th, btn whn mstk 2 out*.... (9 to 4 fav op 7 to 2) 6
3485 ZAM BEE [95] 8-11-3 B Storey, *trkd ldrs, chlgd appr 2 out, sn wknd*............(12 to 1 op 10 to 1 tchd 14 to 1) 7
3512[5] INCONCLUSIVE [86] 7-10-3 (5*) J Burke, *drpd rear 13th, tld off whn pld up bef 4 out.* ....(7 to 1 op 8 to 1 tchd 10 to 1) pu
Dist: Hd, 13l, 2½l, 3½l, 7l, 2½l. 7m 18.40s. a 73.40s (8 Ran).
(Crawford, Wares & Hamilton), L Lungo

3603 Law Society Legal Handicap Hurdle (0-100 4-y-o and up) £2,335 3m..(8:15)

2894[6] SKIRCOAT GREEN [85] 9-11-0 R Dunwoody, *led, rdn betw last 2, hdd aftr last, styd on gmely to ld nr finish.* ....(6 to 1 op 5 to 1) 1
3287* SANSOOL [95] (v) 8-11-3 (7*) B Harding, *cl up, reminders aftr 8th, drw clr wth wnr frm 3 out, slight ld after last, hdd and no extr close hme*.................... (7 to 2) 2
3580* GREAT EASEBY (Ire) [83] 4-10-12 (6ex) K Johnson, *hld up, effrt aftr 9th, sn btn, tld off.* ....(15 to 2 op 5 to 1 tchd 8 to 1) 3
3436 DUTCH BLUES [81] 7-10-10 D Wilkinson, *in tch, chsd ldrs frm 9th, wknd 3 out, tld off*........(20 to 1 op 14 to 1) 4
3431[5] WHITE DIAMOND [87] 6-11-2 A Maguire, *prmnt whn f 5th.* ....(2 to 1 fav op 7 to 2 tchd 4 to 1) f
3541[6] FARMER'S CROSS [87] 10-11-2 Mrs A Farrell, *in tch, effrt aftr 9th, sn btn, tld off whn pld up bef last.* ....(16 to 1 op 14 to 1) pu
3428 BOWLANDS WAY [76] 10-10-5 O Pears, *prmnt till wknd aftr 9th, tld off whn pld up bef last*.......... (33 to 1) pu
3514 INTEGRITY BOY [88] (bl) 7-11-3 M Dwyer, *hld up, reminders aftr 7th, wknd after nxt, tld off whn pld up bef 3 out*..........................(7 to 1 tchd 8 to 1) pu
3240[6] HEY JOE [73] 7-10-2 A Merrigan, *beh, reminders aftr 3rd, mstk 8th, lost tch after nxt, tld off whn pld up bef last.* ....(33 to 1) pu
3287[6] MISS CAPULET [85] (bl) 7-10-11 (3*) T Eley, *prmnt to hfwy, wknd aftr 8th, tld off whn pld up bef 3 out.* ....(5 to 1 op 4 to 1) pu
Dist: ¾l, dist, ¾l. 6m 34.10s. a 47.10s (10 Ran).
SR: 23/32/-/-/-/-/ (Calder Racing), P Beaumont

ASCOT (good)
Tuesday April 26th
Going Correction: MINUS 0.10 sec. per fur.

3604 Hosta Novices' Hurdle (5-y-o and up) £3,087 2½m.................. (5:30)

3380* BARNA BOY (Ire) 6-11-5 R Dunwoody, *hld up, pushed alng and hdwy 4 out, led 2 out, ran on wl.* ....(6 to 4 fav op 5 to 4 on) 1
3386[9] THE REVEREND BERT (Ire) 6-11-0 E Leonard, *hld up, cld aftr 3 out, styd on wl appr last*... (100 to 1 op 50 to 1) 2
3220[6] GOLDEN SPINNER 7-11-0 J R Kavanagh, *led til mstk and hdd 6th, ev ch 2 out, one pace*.....(8 to 1 tchd 10 to 1) 3
3215[6] DENVER BAY 7-11-0 D Murphy, *hld up in tch, hdwy to ld 6th, hdd 2 out, one pace.* ....(33 to 1 op 20 to 1 tchd 50 to 1) 4
3230* GO MARY 8-11-0 W Marston, *chsd ldrs, drvn 3 out, btn appr last*........................(100 to 30 op 5 to 1) 5
2950[4] BEAUREPAIRE (Ire) 6-10-11 (3*) P Hide, *hld up, steady hdwy frm 2 out, nvr plcd to chal*..(25 to 1 op 16 to 1) 6
3496[4] ROSS GRAHAM 6-11-0 P Holley, *mid-div, cld up 6th, rdn alng aftr nxt, wknd appr 2 out*... (100 to 1 op 33 to 1) 7
3414 MAN O MINE (Ire) 5-11-0 M Hourigan, *trkd ldrs till wknd aftr 3 out*..........(100 to 1 op 33 to 1 tchd 200 to 1) 8
NOBLE FORESTER (Ire) 6-11-0 G Upton, *in tch till outpcd frm 6th*.......................(100 to 1 op 50 to 1) 9
1715 MUSCLETON 9-11-0 A McCabe, *hld up, al beh.* ....(100 to 1 op 33 to 1 tchd 200 to 1) 10
3233[4] AND WHY NOT 6-11-0 D Bridgwater, *wth ldr till wknd aftr 6th*.................(20 to 1 op 14 to 1 tchd 25 to 1) 11
3264* BUTLER'S TWITCH 7-11-0 J Osborne, *al prmnt, ev ch 3 out, btn whn mstk nxt*...(4 to 1 op 7 to 2 tchd 9 to 2) 12
3396 DIAMOND FLIER (Ire) 5-11-0 R Marley, *mid-div, pushed alng aftr 4th, tld off frm 6th.* ....(100 to 1 op 33 to 1 tchd 200 to 1) 13
3231[3] CREDON 6-11-0 A Maguire, *in tch, reminders aftr 6th, sn wknd, tld off, virtually pld up r-in.* ....(20 to 1 op 16 to 1 tchd 25 to 1) 14
Dist: 6l, 6l, ¾l, 1l, 6l, 5l, 13l, ½l, nk, 5l. 4m 44.80s. a 3.80s (14 Ran).
SR: 33/22/16/15/14/8/3/-/-/ (Lynn Wilson), N J Henderson

3605 Michael Page Group Novices' Chase (6-y-o and up) £4,104 2m 3f 110yds ....(6:00)

2725[5] REAL PROGRESS (Ire) 6-11-5 R Dunwoody, *made virtually all, mstk 8th, ran on strly.* ....(11 to 2 op 5 to 1 tchd 6 to 1) 1
3479 SPINNING STEEL 7-11-5 W Marston, *trkd ldrs, took keen hold, ev ch 3 out, one pace frm nxt.* ....(15 to 2 op 8 to 1 tchd 10 to 1) 2
2829[4] NEWLANDS-GENERAL 8-11-5 M Dwyer, *hld up in last pl, hit 9th, effrt and hdwy appr 2 out, sn one pace.* ....(15 to 8 fav op 6 to 4 tchd 2 to 1) 3
2725[4] RUNNING SANDS 10-11-5 G McCourt, *trkd wnr to 3 out, one pace*..........................(11 to 2 op 4 to 1) 4
3454[5] DUKE OF APROLON 7-11-5 D Murphy, *hld up in rear, not fluent 12th, sn outpcd*...(4 to 1 op 3 to 1 tchd 9 to 2) 5
3544 YOUNG ALFIE (bl) 9-11-5 A Maguire, *trkd ldrs till rdn and outpcd 4 out*............................(12 to 1 tchd 14 to 1) 6
3332[2] SILENT CHANT (v) 10-11-5 Gee Armytage, *not fluent, lost tch 11th, tld off*...... (25 to 1 op 16 to 1 tchd 33 to 1) 7
Dist: 8l, 3½l, ½l, 6l, 14l, 15l. 4m 53.50s. a 12.00s (7 Ran).
(A Stennett), P J Hobbs

3606 Reservoir Hurdle Handicap (4-y-o) £3,371 2m 110yds.............. (6:30)

3406 DARK DEN (USA) [114] 10-13 T Kent, *made all, not fluent 4th and 3 out, clr appr last, ran on wl.* ......(6 to 5 fav op 11 to 8 tchd 6 to 4 and 11 to 10) 1
3402[2] WINTER FOREST (USA) [129] 12-0 A Maguire, *hld up in tch, hit 1st, not fluent nxt, chlgd aftr 3 out, sn chsd wnr, no imprsn*..........(2 to 1 op 5 to 4 tchd 9 to 4) 2
3314[2] ERCKULE [101] 10-0 J Osborne, *in cl tch, outpcd and drvn aftr 5th, sn rallied, btn after 3 out.* ....(4 to 1 tchd 9 to 2) 3
3228[6] MARIUS (Ire) [101] 10-0 D Murphy, *in cl tch, ev ch 3 out, sn wknd*........................... (10 to 1 tchd 12 to 1) 4
Dist: 5l, 6l, 6l. 3m 48.30s. a 2.30s (4 Ran).
SR: 46/56/22/16/ (George L Ohrstrom), Mrs J Cecil

3607 Moonshine Chase Handicap (5-y-o and up) £7,392 2m..............(7:05)

3410[3] DEEP SENSATION [162] 9-12-0 D Murphy, *hld up in rear, outpcd aftr 3 out, hdwy appr last, quickened to ld r-in, cleverly*.................(3 to 1 op 5 to 2 tchd 7 to 2) 1
3262* SPREE CROSS [134] 8-10-0 A Maguire, *led to 3rd, led 5th till mstk and hdd 8th, led ag'n 3 out, blun and headed aftr nxt, ev ch r-in, ran on wl.* ....(7 to 2 op 4 to 1 tchd 9 to 2) 2
3423* UNCLE ERNIE [151] 9-11-3 M Dwyer, *hld up in rear, hdwy appr 2 out, ev ch r-in, ran on wl.* (7 to 4 fav op 5 to 4) 3
2825[3] YOUNG SNUGFIT [145] 10-10-11 J Osborne, *trkd ldg pair, led 8th till hdd 3 out, led ag'n aftr nxt, headed r-in, no extr*............................. (4 to 1 tchd 9 to 2) 4
3268[3] CAMPSEA-ASH [134] 10-10-0 J R Kavanagh, *hld up in cl tch, rdn 3 out, one pace.* ....(66 to 1 op 50 to 1 tchd 100 to 1) 5
3500[8] NORTHERN JINKS [134] (bl) 11-9-11 (3*) D Meredith, *led 3rd to 5th, in cl tch, pushed alng aftr 3 out, outpcd.* ....(33 to 1 op 20 to 1 tchd 40 to 1) 6
Dist: 1¼l, hd, 1½l, 7l, 5l. 3m 48.00s. a 0.50s (6 Ran).
SR: 79/49/66/58/40/35/ (R F Eliot), J T Gifford

3608 Royal Fern Novices' Handicap Chase (6-y-o and up) £5,129 3m 110yds (7:35)

3445* DONT TELL THE WIFE [99] 8-10-11 J Osborne, *hld up, al gng wl, cld 15th, led aftr 2 out, narrow advantage whn lft clr last*........................... (7 to 1 op 6 to 1) 1
2913[4] SPIKEY (NZ) [109] 8-11-7 B Powell, *trkd ldrs, outpcd 15th, hampererd appr 3 out, styd on, lft second last.* ....(8 to 1 op 7 to 1 tchd 9 to 1) 2
3075[2] THE POD'S REVENGE [88] 9-9-11 (3*) A Procter, *hld up in tch, outpcd frm 3 out*........... (33 to 1 tchd 50 to 1) 3

3316² CELTIC BARLE [109] 10-11-7 S McNeill, *f 4th (water)*.
....(6 to 1 op 5 to 1 tchd 9 to 2)　f
3586* ASTINGS (Fr) [95] 6-10-7 (4ex) M Dwyer, *mstk 1st, trkd ldrs, led 4 out till hdd aftr 2 out, cl second and rdn whn f last*.......................(5 to 2 fav op 3 to 1 tchd 7 to 2)　f
3454⁶ PURPLE SPRAY [88] 9-9-11² (5") C Burnett-Wells, *not jump wl, al beh, lost tch 11th, tld off whn blun and uns rdr 4 out*.........................(50 to 1 tchd 66 to 1)　ur
3382³ GHIA GNEUIAGH [116] 8-12-0 D Bridgwater, *blun 4th (water) and uns rdr*.....(7 to 1 op 6 to 1 tchd 9 to 1)　ur
3351* SALLY'S GEM [112] 9-11-10 A Maguire, *made most to 5th, reminders aftr 12th, led ag'n 14th till mstk and hdd 4 out, wknd nxt, pld up lme bef 2 out*. (5 to 1 op 3 to 1)　pu
3381³ RAMPOLDI (USA) [95] (bl) 7-10-7 R Dunwoody, *wth ldr, led 5th till hdd 14th, ev ch 4 out, wknd quickly, pld up lme aftr nxt*....................(5 to 1 tchd 6 to 1)　pu
Dist: 9l, 30l. 6m 8.50s. a 5.00s (9 Ran).
SR: 9/10/-/-/-/-/　　　　　(H & K Commissions), Mrs D Haine

3609 Primula Hurdle Handicap (4-y-o and up) £4,671 3m.................(8:10)

3283* HAPPY HORSE (NZ) [111] 7-10-8 A Tory, *took keen hold early, trkd ldrs, led 3 out, ran on strly*.
..............................(100 to 30 op 11 to 4 tchd 7 to 2)　1
3520³ SEA BUCK [106] 8-10-3 J R Kavanagh, *hld up, pushed alng aftr 7th, hdwy appr 2 out, sn ev ch, outpcd approaching last*.........(9 to 1 op 7 to 1 tchd 10 to 1)　2
3117³ SORBIERE [110] 7-10-7 R Dunwoody, *hld up in tch, hdwy to hold ev ch 2 out, one pace appr last*.
....................(7 to 4 fav op 13 to 8 tchd 15 to 8)　3
3408⁷ PEATSWOOD [127] 6-11-10 Lorna Vincent, *led til hdd 3 out, rallied and ev ch nxt, one pace*.
...............................(7 to 1 tchd 8 to 1)　4
3363 SUKAAB [108] 9-10-5 A Maguire, *hld up in rear, outpcd frm 3 out, styd on from last, nrst finish*.
..............................(5 to 1 tchd 11 to 2)　5
2946 FANTASY WORLD [103] 8-9-11 (3") P Hide, *hld up, cld 8th, outpcd appr 2 out*...(25 to 1 op 20 to 1 tchd 33 to 1)　6
3442² SPECIAL ACCOUNT [104] (v) 8-10-1 N Mann, *cl up till wknd appr 3 out, hrd rdn approaching nxt, no imprsn*.
..............................(7 to 1 op 8 to 1 tchd 6 to 1)　7
552 MANDALAY PRINCE [103] 10-10-0 W Marston, *hld up, losing tch whn refused 6th*......(100 to 1 tchd 150 to 1)　ref
Dist: 1¼l, 5l, 1½l, 1½l, nk, 4l. 5m 42.50s. a 9.50s (8 Ran).
(Major Ian Manning), Mrs J Renfree-Barons

PUNCHESTOWN (IRE) (heavy)
Tuesday April 26th

3610 Kildare Chilling Hunters' Chase (Bish-opscourt Cup) (4-y-o and up) £2,760 2½m.................(2:15)

3370² LINEKER 7-11-6 (5") Mr G J Harford, ...(9 to 4)　1
GLENARD LAD (Ire) 6-11-11 Mr P F Graffin, ...(10 to 1)　2
TAMER'S RUN 8-11-6 (5") Mr P M Kelly, ...(8 to 1)　3
CAMDEN COURT 7-12-2 Mr A J Martin, ...(6 to 4 fav)　4
DAVY BUSTIN 8-11-4 (7") Mr R Shaw, ...(12 to 1)　5
709 PUSH GENTLY (Ire) 5-10-8 (5") Mr W M O'Sullivan, (33 to 1)　6
MOYGLEN 7-11-1 (5") Mr J P Berry, ...(9 to 1)　f
FINAL BRIEF 7-11-4 (7") Mr J A Quinn, ...(33 to 1)　ur
DISNEYS HILL 7-11-4 (7") Mr A K Wyse, ...(33 to 1)　ref
CARASHEL 9-11-6 Mr J P Dempsey, ...(20 to 1)　pu
ENFANT TERRIBLE 8-11-4 (7") Mr E C Sexton, ...(33 to 1)　pu
MASTER JULIAN 8-11-4 (7") Mr J Robinson, ...(33 to 1)　pu
Dist: 7l, 2l, 15l, 10l. 5m 33.70s. (12 Ran).
(F Shaw), Neil S McGrath

3611 Brown Thomas Chase (Ladies Perpetual Cup) (4-y-o and up) £7,050 3m.................(2:45)

HANDYFELLOW 9-11-6 (7") Mr E Bolger, ...(6 to 1)　1
EEZ-AWAY (Ire) 5-11-3 (3") Mr J A Nash, ...(10 to 1)　2
SERGEANT MULLARKEY (Ire) 6-11-13 Mr P Fenton,
....................................(5 to 4 fav)　3
RAINBOW FOUNTAIN 7-11-1 (7") Mr P J Millington, (8 to 1)　4
LUCY SOMERS 8-11-3 (5") Mr P M Kelly, ...(25 to 1)　5
ROYAL FIREWORKS 7-11-13 Mr G Hogan, ...(8 to 1)　6
TLAQUEPAQUE 10-11-6 (7") Mr J F Gleeson, ...(20 to 1)　7
RISK OF THUNDER (Ire) 5-10-13 (7") Mr K Whelan, (8 to 1)　8
CASTLE UNION 7-11-6 (7") Mr R Keogh, ...(33 to 1)　9
GENERALANAESTHETIC 9-11-6 (7") Mr D J Donegan,
....................................(25 to 1)　f
NO MISTAKE (Ire) 11-11-6 (7") Mr J T McNamara, (25 to 1)　f
2773 WHITESIDES FORT 11-11-10 (3") Mr P McMahon, (33 to 1)　ur
CLOGHER LORD (Ire) 5-11-6 Mr R Hurley, ...(14 to 1)　bd
BLUE SERAPH 9-11-6 (7") Mr A K Wyse, ...(25 to 1)　pu
2773⁴ GLENSPORT VI 8-11-8 Mr A J Martin, ...(10 to 1)　pu
GOLDEN MAC 7-11-10 (3") Mr T Lombard, ...(25 to 1)　pu
Dist: 2l, 14l, 20l, 12l. 6m 58.60s. (16 Ran).
(A J McNamara), A J McNamara

3612 B M W Drogheda Handicap Chase (Listed - Grade 2) (4-y-o and up)

£22,000 2m.................(3:20)

2698⁷ SARAEMMA [-] 8-10-12 K F O'Brien, *wl plcd, led appr 4 out, slight mstk 2 out, styd on well aftr last*...(16 to 1)　1
2549⁴ HOW'S THE BOSS [-] 8-11-2 J Magee, *wtd wth at rear of chasing grp, prog into 3rd 3 out, kpt on without rching wnr*...(8 to 1)　2
3389* KINGS ENGLISH [-] 8-11-7 (3ex) F Woods, *wl plcd, rdn in second appr 2 out, wknd betw last two*.........(11 to 4)　3
3682² GLENCLOUD (Ire) [-] 6-10-7 P Carberry, *mid-div, mstk 3rd, prog into third 4 out, rdn nxt, fdd*...........(13 to 2)　4
3410 FORCE SEVEN [-] 7-11-10 C F Swan, *trkd ldrs, pushed alng 4 out, sn wknd*.....................(9 to 4 fav)　5
848⁵ TRY A BRANDY [-] 12-10-7 T Horgan, *al rear*...(33 to 1)　6
3324⁵ COMMERCIAL ARTIST [-] 8-11-5 C N Bowens, *al rear, tld off 6th*...................................(8 to 1)　7
3324 BUCKBOARD BOUNCE [-] 8-11-9 J Shortt, *refused to race*.
....(8 to 1)　ref
3423 LASATA [-] 9-11-2 C O'Dwyer, *led 1st, clr 3rd, rdn and hdd appr 4 out, wknd and pld up lme bef 2 out*.......(10 to 1)　pu
Dist: 7l, 9l, 25l, 12l. 4m 14.10s. (9 Ran).
(D Cox), J H Scott

3613 Country Pride Champion Novice Hurdle (Listed - Grade 1) (5-y-o and up) £16,350 2m.................(3:55)

3323* KLAIRON DAVIS (Fr) 5-11-13 T Horgan, *wl plcd, 3rd 2 out, slight advantage last, ran on well*.........(7 to 4 fav)　1
3525* RISZARD (USA) 5-11-13 C N Bowens, *wl plcd, rdn to ld betw last 2, hdd last, kpt on*...................(20 to 1)　2
3323⁴ HEIST 5-11-13 P Carberry, *prog frm mid-div to track ldrs 2 out, ev ch last, ran on*.........................(20 to 1)　3
3369* JUPITER JIMMY 5-11-13 C O'Brien, *prog frm rear to track ldrs 2 out, no extr und pres appr last*...........(10 to 1)　4
3409² MONALEE RIVER (Ire) 6-12-0 K F O'Brien, *led 1st, hdd bef 5th, led ag'n before nxt till headed and wknd betw last 2*.......................................(8 to 1)　5
3023⁸ WINTER BELLE (Ire) 6-12-0 J Shortt, *prog frm rear into mid-div 3 out, no extr und pres from nxt*.........(5 to 2)　6
3323² SOUND MAN (Ire) 6-12-0 C F Swan, *mid-div, rdn appr 2 out, not rch ldrs*.............................(5 to 1)　7
3390* COURT MELODY (Ire) 6-12-0 J P Broderick, *niggled alng in mid-div 5th, no imprsn, eased strt*............(10 to 1)　8
3322 BUTCHES BOY (Ire) 5-11-13 C O'Dwyer, *wl plcd, led 5th till hdd bef nxt, sn btn*...................(40 to 1)　9
3388* PIMBERLEY PLACE (Ire) 6-12-0 G Bradley, *al rear, pld up bef last*....................................(25 to 1)　pu
Dist: 1l, nk, 6l, hd, 4½l. 4m 10.20s. (10 Ran).
(C Jones), A L T Moore

3614 Bradstock Insurance Chase (Listed - Grade 3) (5-y-o and up) £8,625 2½m.................(4:30)

3324 BELVEDERIAN 7-12-0 G Bradley, *led 8th till hdd bef tenth, led ag'n nxt, rdn appr last, styd on strly*...(5 to 4 on)　1
2843² BELMONT KING (Ire) 6-11-10 L P Cusack, *wl plcd, bad mstks 6 and 4 out, styd on und pres aftr last*...(8 to 1)　2
3465⁵ MONKEY AGO 7-11-6 P Carberry, *wl plcd, ev ch whn not fluent 3 out, rdn in second last, wknd*.........(14 to 1)　3
3324 ALL THE ACES 7-11-10 T Horgan, *led 1st till hdd bef 8th, led ag'n tenth till headed before nxt, rdn and fdd*.
....(5 to 1)　4
3405 BLUE RING 10-11-5 F Woods, *rear, styd on frm 4 out without rching ldrs*........................(10 to 1)　5
3426² KETTI 9-10-11 C F Swan, *mid-div, rdn and btn bef 4 out*.
....(14 to 1)　6
3120⁴ EMERALD STORM 7-11-6 M A FitzGerald, *rear, nvr rchd ldrs*..(12 to 1)　7
FOILACLUG FURRY 9-11-2 M G Cleary, *mid-div, mstk second*...........................(40 to 1)　8
2983* YOUR THE MAN 8-11-2 J Shortt, *al rear*.......(14 to 1)　9
2055 COMICALITY 6-11-2 T P Rudd, *mid-div tld mstk and lost pl 7th*...(50 to 1)　10
3551 SO PINK (Ire) 6-10-11 J T Titley, *tracking ldrs whn f tenth*.
....(20 to 1)　f
3325 PROGRAMMED TO WIN 7-11-2 K F O'Brien, *al rear, pld up bef tenth*..................................(20 to 1)　pu
Dist: 2l, 1½l, 20l, 20l. 5m 24.30s. (12 Ran).
(A J O'Reilly), M F Morris

3615 Berkeley Court Handicap Hurdle (4 & 5-y-o) £9,750 2¼m.................(5:00)

3367⁸ BE MY HOPE [-] 5-11-3 P Carberry, ...(5 to 1)　1
3369³ COCKNEY LAD (Ire) [-] 5-11-5 C F Swan, ...(11 to 4 fav)　2
3247⁵ PLUMBOB (Ire) [-] 5-10-5 L P Cusack, ...(16 to 1)　3
3413 MR BOAL (Ire) [-] 5-11-8 J Shortt, ...(14 to 1)　4
3367³ THE REAL ARTICLE (Ire) [-] 5-11-2 H Rogers, ...(6 to 1)　5
3367² DIPLOMATIC [-] 5-11-6 J P Banahan, ...(5 to 1)　6
3369³ JO JO BOY (Ire) [-] 5-11-5 F J Flood, ...(7 to 1)　7
3469 NOT MY LINE (Ire) [-] 5-9-7 C O'Brien, ...(66 to 1)　8
3468⁵ FABULIST (Ire) [-] 5-10-9 T P Treacy, ...(16 to 1)　9
3068 JUDICIAL FIELD (Ire) [-] (bl) 5-12-0 B Sheridan, ...(10 to 1)　10
3388⁸ INAUGURATION (Ire) [-] 5-9-7 F Woods, ...(33 to 1)　11
3080 DANCING VISION (Ire) [-] 4-10-12 G M O'Neill, ...(14 to 1)　12

3322 AEGEAN FANFARE (Ire) [-] (bl) 5-10-4 C O'Dwyer, (20 to 1) 13
3526 BACK TO BLACK (Ire) [-] 5-10-5 K F O'Brien, ... (10 to 1) pu
Dist: 3l, 8l, 1½l, 4½l. 4m 36.90s. (14 Ran).

(Mrs John Magnier), Noel Meade

3616 Tom O'Leary Memorial I.N.H. Flat Race (4-y-o) £6,900 2m. . . . . (5:30)

3250² KERRYHEAD GIRL (Ire) 10-8 (7") Mr E Norris, ... (9 to 1) 1
    UNCLE KEENY (Ire) 11-6 Mr J A Berry, ... (12 to 1) 2
3377² SHANES HERO (Ire) 11-6 Mr P F Graffin, ... (14 to 1) 3
    THE CARRIG RUA (Ire) 11-6 Mr A J Martin, ... (12 to 1) 4
3245² ROCKFIELD NATIVE (Ire) 11-6 Mr A P O'Brien,
    . . . . (100 to 30 fav) 5
    PARSON FROM HEAVEN (Ire) 10-12 (3") Mrs J M Mullins,
    . . . . (12 to 1) 6
3321⁹ THE OUTBACK WAY (Ire) 10-13 (7") Mr J T Codd, (20 to 1) 7
    ISLANDOO (Ire) 11-1 Miss C Townsley, ... (12 to 1) 8
    FAIRIES CROSS (Ire) 11-6 Mr P Fenton, ... (10 to 1) 9
3372⁴ MAGIC MOONBEAM (Ire) 10-8 (7") Mr D Carey, . . (16 to 1) 10
    BLUSHING SAND (Ire) 10-13 (7") Mr T J Beattie, . . (33 to 1) 11
    RHETORIC HOUSE (Ire) 11-1 (5") Mr P M Kelly, . . (16 to 1) 12
    GOOD GLOW 10-13 (7") Mr A G Donnelly, ... (14 to 1) 13
    MR BUCKSKIN (Ire) 11-1 Mr T Mullins, ... (5 to 1) 14
    MULDER'S FRIEND (Ire) 10-13 (7") Mr D Murphy, . (16 to 1) 15
2750⁴ SPRUNG RHYTHM (Ire) 11-6 Mr J P Durkan, ... (7 to 2) 16
3508⁶ LESS HASSLE (Ire) 10-8 (7") Mr J J Holohan, ... (16 to 1) 17
3246 TEN BUCKS (Ire) 11-6 Mr E Bolger, ... (50 to 1) 18
    BUCK THE WEST (Ire) 10-13 (7") Mr A Dempsey, . . (14 to 1) 19
    FIONAILE (Ire) 10-8 (7") Mr G Finlay, ... (20 to 1) 20
    RAINBOW EILE (Ire) 11-3 (3") Mr D Valentine, ... (14 to 1) 21
    BEIGINIS (Ire) 11-6 Mr R Hurley, ... (14 to 1) 22
    RIVERBASIN (Ire) 10-8 (7") Mr A Daly, ... (33 to 1) 23
    BURSTOWS LAW (Ire) 10-13 (7") Mr K Whelan, . . . (33 to 1) 24
3372 ARCTICTALDI (Ire) 10-13 (7") Mr T J Murphy, ... (50 to 1) 25
    SITE DEVELOPMENT (Ire) 10-13 (7") Mr M O'Connor,
    . . . . (33 to 1) 26
3450 SHANES BAY (Ire) 10-8 (7") Mr J P Harvey, ... (33 to 1) pu
    STONEY PIPER (Ire) 10-13 (7") Mr C M Healy, ... (33 to 1) pu
Dist: 9l, 4l, 9l, 2l. 3m 52.00s. (28 Ran).

(James R Browne), Patrick Joseph Flynn

WETHERBY (good)
Tuesday April 26th
Going Correction: PLUS 0.80 sec. per fur.

3617 Castleford Novices' Hurdle (4-y-o and up) £2,337 2m. . . . . (2:20)

3482⁴ WEAVER GEORGE (Ire) 4-10-8 R Dunwoody, hit 1st, chsd
    clr ldr, led 5th, pressed 3 out, ran on strly betw last 2.
    . . . . (4 to 1 fav op 7 to 2) 1
3179⁶ OTTER BUSH 5-11-0 (7") D Towler, handily plcd, ev ch and
    rdn 3 out, outpcd aftr nxt, styd on und prss frm last.
    . . . . (6 to 1) 2
3373⁸ WANZA 4-11-1 N Williamson, al hndy, ev ch bef 3 out,
    mstk nxt, unbl to quicken. . . . . (14 to 1 op 12 to 1) 3
3373⁴ GENSERIC (Fr) 4-10-8 (7") W Fry, nvr far away, drvn alng
    aftr 4 out, ch nxt, no extr. . . . . (7 to 1 tchd 6 to 1) 4
3379² HOLD YOUR HAT ON 5-11-0 D Wilkinson, settled on outer,
    improved to go hndy hfwy, rdn and ch nxt, grad wknd.
    . . . . (7 to 1) 5
3542⁵ HIGH MIND (Fr) 5-11-0 A Maguire, settled in chasing
    bunch, effrt and drvn alng bef 3 out, no extr before nxt.
    . . . . (6 to 1 op 7 to 1) 6
1959³ AUBURN BOY 4-11-7 M Dwyer, prmnt in chasing bunch,
    drvn to improve aftr 4 out, fdd after nxt.
    . . . . (7 to 1 op 11 to 2) 7
3378³ GOING PUBLIC 7-11-0 K Johnson, nvr far away, ev ch bef
    3 out, fdd frm nxt. . . . . (20 to 1) 8
3539⁶ INNOCENT GEORGE 5-11-0 A Dobbin, settled on outer,
    drvn alng whn pace lifted aftr 4 out, btn frm nxt.
    . . . . (20 to 1 op 16 to 1) 9
1872 ZAFARRANCHO (Ire) 5-10-7 (7") F Leahy, settled on ins,
    drvn alng whn tempo increased aftr 4 out, sn btn.
    . . . . (25 to 1) 10
3413 LEINTHALL FOX 8-10-9 T Wall, settled midfield, improved
    to go hndy bef 4 out, sn drvn alng, btn before nxt.
    . . . . (33 to 1) 11
    CHARLIE MCCARTHY 6-11-0 Mr C Mulhall, beh, shrtlvd
    effrt hfwy, lost tch fnl 3. . . . . (50 to 1) 12
3459⁴ RHOSSILI BAY 6-11-0 P Niven, settled rear, hmpd 4 out,
    sn no ch. . . . . (10 to 1 op 8 to 1) 13
3125³ INGLETONIAN 5-11-0 L Wyer, in tch on ins, struggling to
    keep up aftr 4 out, tld off. . . . . (20 to 1 op 16 to 1) 14
3429 SILVER HAZE 10-11-0 K Jones, settled in midfield, drvn
    alng aftr 4 out, sn btn. (50 to 1) 15
1114⁶ BELIEVE IT 5-10-9 (7") J Supple, beh, struggling hfwy, tld
    off. . . . . (25 to 1) 16
2834 SPY DESSA 6-11-0 R Hodge, beh, struggling 4 out, tld
    off. . . . . (50 to 1) 17
3378 GULER-A 6-11-0 M Brennan, beh, struggling whn blun 4
    out, tld off. . . . . (50 to 1) 18
2903³ VANART 5-11-7 D Byrne, f 1st. . . . . (12 to 1) f
1199⁴ SPIDERS DELIGHT 6-11-0 A Merrigan, led and sn clr, blun
    second, hdd 5th, wkng whn f 4 out. . . . . (50 to 1) f

HALF A BILLION 6-10-7 (7") Mr S Walker, mid-div, blun 4th,
    sn struggling, pld up bef four out. . . . . (50 to 1) pu
429² DOCTOR FOSTER (Ire) 6-11-0 Richard Guest, patiently
    rdn, lost tch 4 out, sn btn and eased, pld up bef 2 out.
    . . . . (12 to 1) pu
3378 STONEGREY (Ire) 6-10-7 (7") J Driscoll, beh, struggling
    hfwy, tld off whn pld up bef 3 out. . . . . (33 to 1) pu
3167⁸ GAY'S GAMBIT 5-10-9 R Garritty, al beh, struggling hfwy,
    tld off whn pld up bef 2 out. . . . . (50 to 1) pu
Dist: 4l, 8l, 3½l, hd, 5l, 2½l, 1½l, 11l, 2l, 5l. 3m 59.40s. a 18.40s (24 Ran).

SR: 24/33/19/15/14/9/13/4/-/

(Mrs M Tindale), J A Hellens

3618 Bickerton Handicap Hurdle (0-130 4-y-o and up) £3,013 2½m 110yds. . . (2:50)

3491² COUTURE STOCKINGS [103] 10-10-4 N Williamson, chsd
    clr ldr, led on bit 3 out, pushed clear aftr nxt, eased
    towards finish. . . . . (9 to 1 op 7 to 1) 1
2833² BOTTLES (USA) [122] 7-11-9 R Dunwoody, co'red up beh
    ldrs, improved on bit and ev ch appr 3 out, rdn nxt, no
    imprsn on winr. . . . . (9 to 4 fav op 7 to 2 tchd 2 to 1) 2
3578 WAKE UP [100] 7-10-11 Richard Guest, prmnt in chasing
    grp, drvn alng bef 3 out, sn outpcd, styd on frm last, no
    imprsn. . . . . (16 to 1 op 14 to 1) 3
3429¹ ALL GREEK TO ME (Ire) [106] 6-10-0 (7") F Leahy, settled in
    chasing bunch, drvn 4th, sn reco'red, led briefly bef 3
    out, grad wknd frm nxt. . . . . (10 to 1 op 7 to 1) 4
3193⁴ MARSH'S LAW [100] 7-10-1 M Brennan, patiently rdn,
    shaken up to go hndy aftr 4 out, ridden and not
    quicken frm nxt. . . . . (10 to 1 op 7 to 1) 5
3376⁶ GREY POWER [124] 7-11-11 P Niven, settled rear, pushed
    alng to improved aftr 4 out, not rch ldrs.
    . . . . (8 to 1 op 7 to 1 tchd 9 to 1) 6
3475³ CHIEF RAIDER [119] 6-11-6 A Maguire, led and sn clr,
    hdd bef 3 out, grad wknd. . . . . (7 to 2 op 9 to 2) 7
3446³ DOOLAR (USA) [99] 7-10-0 N Mann, dsptd second pl, hit
    second, rdn alng bef 3 out, wknd before nxt.
    . . . . (20 to 1 op 25 to 1) 8
2740⁸ ONLY A ROSE [100] 5-10-1 D Wilkinson, settled on outer,
    struggling to keep up aftr 4 out, sn btn.
    . . . . (20 to 1) 9
2998⁷ BUD'S BET (Ire) [99] 6-9-8 (5") F Perratt, hld up, rdn alng
    whn hit 3 out, sn btn. . . . . (33 to 1) 10
3472⁵ MASTER BOSTON (Ire) [104] 6-10-5 R Garritty, settled in
    chasing grp, drvn into midfield appr 4 out, fdd bef nxt,
    tld off. . . . . (16 to 1 op 14 to 1) 11
3193 GRIS ET VIOLET (Fr) [105] 7-10-6 M Dwyer, settled on ins,
    struggling to keep up 4 out, tld off. . . . . (20 to 1) 12
3355⁶ ABLE PLAYER (USA) [117] (bl) 7-10-13 (5") J Burke, al beh,
    detached frm 4th, tld off bef 3 out. (20 to 1 op 12 to 1) 13
Dist: 2½l, 7l, 2l, 2½l, 2½l, 3½l, nk, 11l, 2l, 3½l. 5m 8.30s. a 20.30s (13 Ran).

SR: 27/43/14/18/9/30/21/-/-/

(Couture Marketing Ltd), J Mackie

3619 Appleton Roebuck Handicap Chase (0-125 5-y-o and up) £3,485 2½m 110yds. (3:20)

3473² CENTENARY STAR [100] 9-10-3¹ P Niven, cl up, outpcd
    aft 5 out, imprvg and lft close 3rd 2 out, led after last,
    ran on wl. . . . . (9 to 2 op 4 to 1 tchd 5 to 1) 1
3356³ PIMS GUNNER (Ire) [97] 6-10-0 A Dobbin, nvr far away,
    jnd issue fnl circuit, led appr last, hdd r-in, rdn and
    not quicken. . . . . (9 to 1 op 8 to 1 tchd 10 to 1) 2
    GONER HOUSE [102] 9-10-5⁵ Mr C Mulhall, chsd ldg 4,
    mstk 8th, drpd rear bef 6 out, tld off whn lft remote 3rd
    last. . . . . (66 to 1 op 33 to 1) 3
3475 CROSS CANNON [109] 8-10-12 B Storey, settled rear,
    improved fnl circuit, ev ch 4 out, sn rdn, chalg whn f 2
    out. . . . . f
3443 GNOME'S TYCOON [125] 8-12-0 J Railton, led, hrd pressed
    frm 4 out, jst hdd whn f heavily last.
    . . . . (11 to 2 op 5 to 1 tchd 6 to 1) f
3375⁴ STRONG SOUND [102] 7-10-5 K Johnson, patiently rdn,
    steady hdwy whn blun badly and uns rdr 7th.
    . . . . (7 to 2 op 11 to 4) ur
3586² HOUGHTON [97] (bl) 8-10-0 L Wyer, mstks, cl up, blun 7th,
    sn btn, tld off whn pld up bef 4 out. (13 to 2 op 6 to 1) pu
3186 HIRAM B BIRDBATH [101] (bl) 8-9-13 (5") D Fortt, settled on
    ins, struggling to keep up 6 out, tld off whn pld up bef 4
    out. . . . . (20 to 1 op 16 to 1) pu
3517³ ANDERMATT [109] 7-10-12 N Williamson, settled rear,
    improved to go hndy fnl circuit, rdn 6 out, btn aftr nxt,
    pld up bef 2 out. . . (5 to 2 fav tchd 11 to 4 and 9 to 4) pu
Dist: 3½l, dist. 5m 16.90s. a 20.40s (9 Ran).

SR: 35/28/-/-/-/-/

(C C Buckley), Mrs M Reveley

3620 Bradford Novices' Hurdle (4-y-o and up) £2,250 2½m 110yds. . . . . (3:50)

3497² FOREST FEATHER (Ire) 6-11-7 Peter Hobbs, tucked away
    beh ldrs, improved to ld bef last, drvn out r-in.
    . . . . (7 to 2 tchd 9 to 1) 1
3140⁴ CAPENWRAY (Ire) 5-11-7 P Niven, settled off the pace,
    improved to go hndy bef 3 out, chlgd nxt, no extr r-in.
    . . . . (6 to 4 fav tchd 11 to 8) 2

3536* IFALLELSEFAILS 6-11-7 T Reed, *al wl plcd, led 5th, jnd 3 out, hdd bef last, not quicken.*
....(5 to 1 op 6 to 1 tchd 7 to 1) 3
3376³ VASILIEV (bl) 6-11-7 N Williamson, *led till hdd aftr 1st, styd hdwy, chlgd 3 out, slightly outpcd and swtchd betw last 2, no extr...*(12 to 1 op 10 to 1 tchd 14 to 1) 4
3109 CRANK SHAFT 7-11-0 D Byrne, *settled on outer, lost grnd 4 out, kpt on stdly fnl 2, nrst finish.*
....(14 to 1 op 10 to 1) 5
1406² KENILWORTH (Ire) 6-10-7 (7*) G Tormey, *co'red up in mid-field, improved and ev ch 3 out, btn aftr nxt.*
....(8 to 1 op 6 to 1) 6
31407 TICO GOLD 6-11-0 A Dobbin, *hld up, pushed alng aftr 4 out, no imprsn fnl 2.*.............(50 to 1) 7
2303 DYNAMITE DAN (Ire) 6-11-0 L Wyer, *keen hold, settled on ins, steady to chase ldg bunch bef 3 out, shaken up nxt, sn no extr and eased.*............(25 to 1 op 20 to 1) 8
3345⁴ BANCHORY 11-11-0 R Garritty, *nvr far away, drvn alng bef 3 out, virtually wknd.*
....(11 to 1 op 8 to 1 tchd 12 to 1) 9
34317 STRONG MEASURE (Ire) 6-11-0 K Johnson, *tucked away beh ldrs, drvn alng 5 out, btn bef 3 out.*
....(20 to 1 tchd 25 to 1) 10
33787 MISCHIEVOUS GIRL 6-10-9 Mrs F Needham, *chsd ldg bunch, blun 6th, sn btn, tld off*.........(50 to 1) 11
1833 I IS 7-10-7 (7*) W Fry, *settled midfield, improved and hndy aftr 4 out, fdd frm nxt, tld off*..........(33 to 1) 12
3345⁵ HICKSONS CHOICE (Ire) 6-11-0 K Jones, *chsd ldrs, strug-gling to keep up 4 out, tld off*............(50 to 1) 13
2237 ARTHUR BEE 7-11-0 Richard Guest, *strted wide, sn reco'red into midfield, struggling frm 6th, tld off whn pld up bef 3 out.*......................(50 to 1) pu
3347⁵ TERRINGTON 4-10-2¹ (7*) J Driscoll, *jmpd badly, pld hrd, led aftr 1st, hdd 5th, wknd aftr nxt, pulled up bef 3 out.*...(33 to 1) pu
BENSBROOK 5-11-0 B Storey, *beh, struggling fnl circuit, tld off whn pld up bef 3 out*.............(50 to 1) pu
Dist: 5l, 1¼l, 1l, 3½l, 5l, 1½l, 8l, ¾l, sht-hd, 15l. 5m 12.90s. a 25.90s (16 Ran).
(David Knox), C Weedon

3621 Bramham Novices' Handicap Chase (5-y-o and up) £2,948 3m 110yds (4:20)

3355* SILVER STICK [102] 7-12-0 R Garritty, *wth ldrs, led briefly tenth, styd upsides, led ag'n 3 out, forged clr bef last, easily.*.............................(4 to 1 op 7 to 2 tchd 9 to 2) 1
3154² LOBRIC (bl) 9-10-9 J Railton, *led to 3rd, styd hndy, blun 9th, outpcd 6 out, stayed on wl fnl 2, not rch wnr.*...(12 to 1 op 10 to 1) 2
3428⁴ BULA NUDAY [79] 9-10-5 B Storey, *patiently rdn, steady hdwy to led bef 4 out, hdd nxt, ridden and not quicken aftr 2 out.*......................(4 to 1 op 7 to 2) 3
3486⁴ TARTAN TRADEWINDS [94] 7-11-6 N Doughty, *nvr far away, led 3rd, hdd briefly tenth, headed bef 4 out, btn 2 out.*.............................(5 to 2 fav op 7 to 2 tchd 4 to 1) 4
2908 RAIN MAN (NZ) [74] 9-10-0 N Williamson, *patiently rdn, effrt strting fnl circuit, lost tch 6 out, tld off.*
....(25 to 1 op 20 to 1) 5
3437 LADY BLAKENEY [76] 8-10-2 A Dobbin, *hld up, struggling fnl circuit, tld off whn almost f last.*
....(25 to 1 op 20 to 1) 6
3492⁶ CONCERT PAPER [92] (v) 10-10-11 (7*) K Davies, *chasing ldrs whn f 6th.*..........................(14 to 1) f
1574⁸ QUIXALL CROSSETT [74] 9-9-10³ (7*) Mr S Walker, *not jump wl, in rear whn f 7th.*........(66 to 1 op 50 to 1) f
3188³ PESSOA [76] 7-10-2² Richard Guest, *handily plcd on outer, f 7th.*.............................(16 to 1) f
2579 JUST MOLLY [74] 7-10-0 L Wyer, *trkd ldg grp, losing grnd whn f 11th.*...................(20 to 1 op 14 to 1) f
3582 NAWRIK (Ire) [82] 5-10-8 T Reed, *cl up, 4th and drvn alng whn f 5 out.*...................(10 to 1 op 8 to 1) f
3224⁵ TIMUR'S KING [75] (bl) 7-10-1¹ S Earle, *beh, hmpd by faller 7th, struggling frm tenth, tld off whn pld up bef 5 out.*
....(14 to 1 op 12 to 1) pu
3492 HIGHLAND RALLY (USA) [88] 7-11-0 J Callaghan, *hld up, improved to go hndy fnl circuit, struggling 5 out, blun 3 out, sn pld up.*.................(11 to 2 op 25 to 1) pu
3437 EDEN SUNSET [78] 8-10-4 P Niven, *settled rear, strug-gling aftr 5 out, pld up bef 2 out.*..........(16 to 1) pu
3442 LASTOFTHEVIKINGS [83] 9-10-9 D Gallagher, *towards rear, lost tch fnl circuit, tld off whn pld up bef 4 out.*
....(11 to 1 op 16 to 1) pu
Dist: 11l, 5l, 1¾l, 30l, 5l. 6m 40.00s. a 34.00s (15 Ran).
(Lord Manton), M W Easterby

3622 Halifax Handicap Hurdle (0-125 4-y-o and up) £2,965 3m 1f......... (4:50)

3541² STORM DRUM [99] (bl) 5-10-8 N Williamson, *settled on ins, improved to ld 3 out, sn hrd pressed, styd on wl frm last.*............................(4 to 1 fav op 9 to 2) 1
3287⁴ LION O'S VIENNA [99] 7-10-8 R Hodge, *nvr far away, led aftr 4 out, hdd nxt, rallied and rnwd chal last 2, not quicken r-in.*...............(9 to 1 op 7 to 1 tchd 10 to 1) 2
3408 KILGARIFF [115] 8-11-3 (7*) F Leahy, *patiently rdn, improved and ev ch 3 out, ridden and no extr appr last.*
....(13 to 2 op 7 to 1 tchd 8 to 1) 3

2273⁶ THIS NETTLE DANGER [96] 10-10-5 M Brennan, *patiently rdn, smooth hdwy and ev ch 3 out, ridden and found little aftr nxt.*........................(20 to 1 op 12 to 1) 4
3461* CELTIC BREEZE [103] (v) 11-10-9 (3*) T Jenks, *pressed ldr, led 6th, hdd aftr 4 out, grad wknd after nxt.*
....(9 to 1 op 7 to 1) 5
3374* NORTHUMBRIAN KING [111] 8-11-6 J Callaghan, *settled on outer, outpcd and drvn alng 5 out, no imprsn last 3.*
....(11 to 2 op 5 to 1) 6
3429³ FIRM PRICE [112] 13-11-7 P Niven, *wtd wth, improved to track ldg bunch aftr 4 out, rdn and btn frm nxt.*
....(11 to 1 op 10 to 1 tchd 12 to 1) 7
3461⁴ POLISHING [119] 7-11-9 (5*) S Lyons, *mid-div on outer, drpd rear bef 4th, rdn fnl circuit, nvr dngrs.*
....(14 to 1 op 10 to 1) 8
3344⁶ SPROWSTON BOY [97] 11-10-6 W Worthington, *led til hdd 6th, lost pl 8th, sn rdn, btn last 3.*...(20 to 1 op 14 to 1) 9
3475⁶ JESTERS PROSPECT [103] 10-10-9 (3*) P Williams, *handily plcd, hit 5 out, sn drvn alng, btn bef 3 out, tld off.*
....(25 to 1 op 16 to 1) 10
3541 FORWARD GLEN [94] 7-10-3 K Johnson, *settled midfield, improved to track ldrs strt fnl circuit, rdn and btn frm 4 out, tld off...*.......................(10 to 1 tchd 12 to 1) 11
3491* FURRY BABY [106] 7-11-1 R Garritty, *co'red up in mid-div, took clr order 5 out, wknd bef 3 out, tld off.*
....(11 to 2 op 4 to 1) 12
1936 JUSTICE LEA [91] 14-10-0 Carol Cuthbert, *chsd ldg bunch, lost tch fnl circuit, tld off...*.....(100 to 1 op 50 to 1) 13
3491 STATECO CASE [113] 9-11-8 L Wyer, *settled rear, lost tch bef 4 out, pld up before nxt.*........(16 to 1 op 14 to 1) pu
3374 VITAL WITNESS (Can) [103] 7-10-12 A S Smith, *settled rear, struggling to keep up frm 4 out, tld off whn pld up bef 2 out.*... pu
Dist: 4l, 1¼l, 10l, 8l, 6l, 2l, 1l, nk, 11l, 12l. 6m 24.60s. a 29.60s (15 Ran).
(Mrs Shelley Fergusson), K C Bailey

CHELTENHAM (good to firm)
Wednesday April 27th
Going Correction: PLUS 0.30 sec. per fur.

3623 Clark Whitehill Novices' Handicap Hurdle (4-y-o and up) £3,095 2m 5f 110yds...................... (5:25)

3441 GRATUITY [74] 9-10-0 N Mann, *prmnt, chsd ldr appr 3 out, reminder approaching nxt, styd on to take slight ld last, stayed on.*..................(50 to 1 op 20 to 1) 1
3339* BLAST FREEZE (Ire) [98] 5-11-10 J R Kavanagh, *beh, hdwy 6th, led aftr 3 out to last, sn rdn, not quicken.*
....(7 to 2 fav op 5 to 2) 2
3509⁴ SO AUDACIOUS [74] 6-10-0 R Supple, *prmnt, not fluent, lost pos 6th, styd on ag'n aftr 3 out.*
....(11 to 2 op 5 to 1 tchd 6 to 1) 3
3174⁶ TRAIN ROBBER [74] 9-10-0 W Irvine, *beh, pushed alng frm 4th, styd on one pace frm 2 out...*(33 to 1 op 20 to 1) 4
3360 TAKE CHANCES [90] 6-10-9 (7*) R Darke, *beh, hdwy and not fluent 5th, wknd appr 2 out...*(20 to 1 op 12 to 1) 5
3008⁵ COMEDIMAN [90] 6-11-2 A Maguire, *mid-div whn stumbled aftr 4th, hdwy appr 3 out, sn wknd.*
....(9 to 2 op 7 to 2 tchd 5 to 1) 6
3281⁷ CASTLE ORCHARD [74] 10-10-0 N Williamson, *al in rear.*
....(50 to 1 op 25 to 1) 7
3421 ANNA VALLEY [89] 8-10-12 (3*) R Davis, *in tch till wknd 3 out.*..............................(14 to 1 op 10 to 1) 8
3530³ SUPER SHARP (NZ) [75] 6-10-1 Jacqui Oliver, *chsd ldr till led 4th, hdd aftr 3 out, wknd quickly 2 out.*
....(4 to 1 tchd 5 to 1) 9
2997³ SMITH'S BAND (Ire) [87] (bl) 6-10-13 I Lawrence, *in tch 4th, wknd 3 out, no ch whn f nxt.*
....(8 to 1 op 6 to 1 tchd 9 to 1) f
1057⁹ KINGSLY ARGUS [92] 7-11-4 J Osborne, *led to 4th, mstk and wknd quickly 6th, tld off whn pld up bef last.*
....(7 to 1 op 6 to 1) pu
3340⁷ THE OVERTRUMPER [74] 7-9-11 (3*) T Jenks, *al beh, tld off whn pld up bef 3 out.*...........(33 to 1 op 16 to 1) pu
Dist: 6l, 5l, 2½l, 20l, nk, 11l, 12l, 4l. 5m 17.00s. a 15.50s (12 Ran).
(Mrs L Field), C R Barwell

3624 Ledbury Novices' Handicap Chase (5-y-o and up) £4,901 3m 1f 110yds (6:00)

3517⁴ SQUIRE JIM [99] 10-10-10 J Osborne, *led second, hdd 3rd, hit 5th, rdn alng aftr 11th, beaten ag'n 16th, wknd, rallied approaching 2 out, led last, all out.*
....(5 to 2 fav op 11 to 10 tchd 9 to 4) 1
3510² TITUS ANDRONICUS [89] (bl) 7-10-0 R Supple, *prmnt, hit 8 and 9th, lost pl 11th, hdwy and hit 4 out, staying on whn hmpd 2 out, no extr r-in.*......(7 to 1 op 9 to 2) 2
3426 BINKLEY (Fr) [92] 8-10-0 (3*) T Jenks, *chsd ldrs 8th, lft in ld 14th, slightly hmpd whn left in definite lead 2 out, wknd and hdd last.*...........(10 to 1 op 6 to 1) 3
3492⁴ OH SO BOLD [89] 7-9-11 (3*) R Farrant, *mid-div, hdwy 16th, wknd 3 out.*.....................(14 to 1 op 12 to 1) 4
3149² FREDDY OWEN [89] 8-10-0 W McFarland, *not fluent, beh and lost tch 13th.*.....(33 to 1 op 12 to 1 tchd 50 to 1) 5

NATIONAL HUNT RESULTS 1993-94

3039 PETTY BRIDGE [91] 10-10-2 R Bellamy, *led 3rd to 5th, str chal frm 4 out, ev ch whn f 2 out.*
..................(14 to 1 op 10 to 1 tchd 16 to 1) f
3407² ARTHUR'S MINSTREL [117] 7-12-0 N Williamson, *led to second, led 5th till blun and uns rdr 14th.*
..................(5 to 1 op 1 tchd 11 to 2) ur
3381 THEO'S FELLA [89] 10-10-0 J R Kavanagh, *in tch till wknd 12th, tld off whn pld up bef 2 out.* (25 to 1 op 14 to 1) pu
3517 MELEAGRIS [109] 10-11-6 A Maguire, *steady hdwy 12th, in tch whn blun 14th, not reco'r and pld up.*
..................(11 to 4 tchd 5 to 2 and 100 to 30) pu
3381 KELLY OWENS [89] 9-9-9² (7*) Mr N Bradley, *jmpd badly in rear, tld off whn pld up bef 15th.* (100 to 1 op 25 to 1) pu
Dist: 2½l, 9l, 13l, 25l. 6m 40.30s. a 24.30s (10 Ran).
(R P Hiorns), N A Twiston-Davies

3625 Cheltenham Racecourse Bookmakers Handicap Hurdle (5-y-o and up) £5,160 2m 5f 110yds................. (6:35)

1964* FIRED EARTH (Ire) [102] 6-10-6 A Maguire, *prmnt, pressed ldr 4th, led appr last, faltered r-in, ran on und pres.*
..................(7 to 2 op 3 to 1) 1
3413³ LYNCH LAW (Ire) [115] (v) 6-11-5 R Dunwoody, *hld up, hdwy and not fluent 3 out, chlgd appr last, ev ch fnl 150 yards till no extr cl hme.*
..................(100 to 30 fav op 3 to 1 tchd 7 to 2) 2
646⁴ CHUCKLESTONE [101] 11-10-5 J R Kavanagh, *drvn 1st 2, led nxt to two out, sn led ag'n, hdd last, one pace.*
..................(9 to 1 op 10 to 1) 3
3520⁴ FAR TOO LOUD [97] 7-10-1 J Osborne, *led to 3rd, pressed ldrs till one pace appr last.*...(11 to 1 op 10 to 1) 4
3413² ZAMIRAH (Ire) [120] 5-11-10 D Bridgwater, *chsd ldrs, rdn and outpcd aftr 3 out, drvn to ld nxt, sn hdd and one pace.*..................(5 to 1 tchd 11 to 2) 5
2967 COSMIC DANCER [106] (bl) 7-10-7 (3*) P Hide, *beh, effrt appr 2 out, sn fdd.*.............(20 to 1 op 14 to 1) 6
3491⁴ RED RING [104] 7-10-8⁴ G McCourt, *mid-div, hdwy to chase ldrs 2 out, sn wknd.*..............(13 to 2 op 5 to 1) 7
3408 ASK THE GOVERNOR [111] 8-11-1 J Railton, *trkd ldrs to 2 out, wknd appr last.*.............(16 to 1 tchd 20 to 1) 8
3068⁷ EDEN'S CLOSE [119] 5-11-9 D Murphy, *in tch, chsd ldrs 3 out till wknd aftr nxt.* (15 to 2 op 7 to 1 tchd 8 to 1) 9
Dist: Sht-hd, 4l, nk, 2½l, 3l, 1l, 9l. 5m 19.80s. a 18.30s (9 Ran).
(Mrs J Fanshawe), J R Fanshawe

3626 Cheltenham Silver Trophy Chase Grade 2 (5-y-o and up) £16,225 2m 5f .... (7:10)

3258* GALE AGAIN 7-11-4 D Murphy, *hld up, al gng wl, hdwy 12th, quickened to ld last, ran on well.*
..................(6 to 4 fav op 7 to 4) 1
3425 ELFAST 11-11-0 G McCourt, *hdwy to chase ldrs 11th, led aftr 3 out to last, hrd drvn and kpt on, not pace of view.*
..................(9 to 4 op 6 to 4 tchd 5 to 2) 2
3519⁶ FAR SENIOR 8-11-0 Mr M Armytage, *hdwy to chase ldrs 12th, outpcd 3 out.*.............(10 to 1 op 8 to 1) 3
661² WIND FORCE 9-11-0 N Doughty, *led and mstk 1st, blun tenth and 4 out, hdd and wknd aftr 3 out.*
..................(5 to 1 op 7 to 1) 4
3425 SOUTHERN MINSTREL 11-11-0 A Maguire, *chsd ldrs till wknd aftr 3 out.*..................(20 to 1 op 12 to 1) 5
3425 GARRISON SAVANNAH (bl) 11-11-0 R Dunwoody, *chsd ldr, hit 12th, wknd 13th...* (7 to 1 op 11 to 2 tchd 6 to 1) 6
Dist: 1¼l, 25l, 4l, 11½l, 1½l. 5m 12.80s. a 8.80s (6 Ran).
SR: 65/59/34/30/28/26/   (P Piller), T Stack

3627 Holman Cup Handicap Chase (5-y-o and up) £5,628 2m 110yds...... (7:45)

3556⁴ DRUMSTICK [127] 8-10-11 N Williamson, *hld up, hdwy to ld 3 out, rdn and ran on wl frm last.*
..................(8 to 1 op 6 to 1 tchd 9 to 1) 1
3423⁴ SNITTON LANE [128] 8-10-12 D Murphy, *hld up in tch, chlgd 2 out, shaken up last, no imprsn r-in.*
..................(11 to 4 fav op 5 to 2 tchd 100 to 30) 2
3037⁶ SPACE FAIR [140] 11-11-10 A Maguire, *led to second, hit nxt, led 9th to 3 out, one ch frm next till outpcd r-in.*
..................(7 to 2 op 11 to 4) 3
3415* MAN OF MYSTERY [119] 8-10-3 D Bridgwater, *led second to 4th, led 6th to 9th, sn one pace.*
..................(7 to 1 op 6 to 1 tchd 8 to 1) 4
3452⁶ L'UOMO PIU [116] 10-10-0 B Powell, *led 4th to 6th, hit 8th, wknd nxt.*.................(33 to 1 op 25 to 1) 5
3066⁵ BILLY BATHGATE [138] 8-11-8 R Dunwoody, *hdwy to chase ldrs 7th, chlgd 9th, hld whn blun 2 out, wknd rpdly, tld off.*..................(4 to 1 tchd 9 to 2 and 7 to 2) 6
3258⁴ YOUNG POKEY [140] 9-11-10 J Osborne, *blun 1st, nvr gng wl aftr, tld off whn pld up bef 7th.* (13 to 2 op 7 to 1) pu
Dist: 1¼l, 25l, 6l, 5l, 6l, dist. 4m 3.70s. a 7.70s (7 Ran).
SR: 56/55/61/35/26/-/-/   (Sarah Lady Allendale), K C Bailey

3628 Dents Originals Conditional Jockeys' Novices' Hurdle (5-y-o and up) £2,900 2m 1f................. (8:15)

3597⁴ BROWNED OFF 5-11-4 T Jenks, *hdwy 5th, chsd ldrs 3 out, rdn appr last, rallied gmely r-in.* (3 to 1 op 5 to 1) 1
3502⁷ TENAYESTELIGN 6-10-9 J McCarthy, *steady hdwy frm 5th, led last, rdn r-in, ct cl hme.*
..................(20 to 1 op 12 to 1 tchd 25 to 1) 2
3539* BERTONE (Ire) 5-11-8 F Leahy, *led second, not fluent, hdd last, rdn and one pace.*
..................(6 to 1 on op 2 to 1 on tchd 9 to 4 on) 3
3386⁵ ICE HOUSE STREET (NZ) 6-11-0 R Darke, *led aftr 1st to second, styd prmnt, one pace appr last.*
..................(12 to 1 op 6 to 1) 4
3515⁶ NIGHT FANCY 6-11-0 P McLoughlin, *hdwy and hit 3 out, wknd aftr 2 out.*......(40 to 1 op 33 to 1 tchd 50 to 1) 5
COOLGARDIE 7-10-11 (3*) M Keighley, *strted slwly, sn reco'red, fdd 3 out.*..................(10 to 1 op 6 to 1) 6
2404 MRS TWEED 8-10-2 (7*) D Carey, *al beh.*
..................(66 to 1 op 33 to 1 tchd 100 to 1) 7
3530⁵ BOX OF DELIGHTS 6-11-0 D Meredith, *led till aftr 1st, rdn 3 out, sn wknd, no ch whn blun and uns rdr last.*
..................(33 to 1) 8
Dist: 1¼l, 5l, 1¼l, 3l, 8l, 25l. 4m 21.30s. a 26.80s (8 Ran).
(Mrs Lorna Berryman), N A Twiston-Davies

EXETER (good to firm)
Wednesday April 27th
Going Correction: PLUS 0.40 sec. per fur.

3629 Ridgeway Financial Services Conditional Jockeys Novices' Handicap Hurdle (0-100 4-y-o and up) £1,938 2¼m........................ (2:20)

3191³ MUSKORA (Ire) [88] 5-11-7 (5*) C Quinlan, *hld up in mid-div, hdwy to track ldrs aftr 5th, ev ch 2 out, chlgd last, led r-in, rdn out.*....(2 to 1 fav op 7 to 2 tchd 9 to 2) 1
2874 EARLY DRINKER [79] 6-11-3 J McCarthy, *in tch, wnt second 5th, led nxt, hdd 2 out, rdn to ld ag'n last, headed r-in, not quicken......*(9 to 1 op 7 to 1 tchd 10 to 1) 2
3478* DEVIOSITY (USA) [69] 7-10-7 R Farrant, *pressed ldrs, rdn appr 2 out, styd on one pace.......*(11 to 1 op 10 to 1) 3
1953⁶ MARINERS COVE [65] 6-10-3 D Meredith, *hld up and beh, hdwy to chase ldg grp aftr 5th, ev ch betw last 2, chlgd last, wknd r-in......*(10 to 1 op 14 to 1 tchd 16 to 1) 4
3478⁴ PALACE PARADE (USA) [70] 4-10-8 D Salter, *trkd ldrs, ev ch 3 out, wknd betw last 2.*
..................(16 to 1 op 14 to 1 tchd 20 to 1) 5
3494* MANDYS LAD [70] 5-10-8 T Jenks, *hld up, hdwy to press ldrs aftr 5th, led 2 out, hdd appr last, sn wknd.*
..................(10 to 1 op 8 to 1) 6
3016* FREE DANCER [80] 4-11-4 T Dascombe, *prmnt, led 4th to 3 out, rdn and wknd.*.............(16 to 1 op 12 to 1) 7
3478³ GLADYS EMMANUEL [77] 7-11-1 P McLoughlin, *hld up and beh, hdwy aftr 5th, pressed ldrs nxt, ev ch til wknd after 2 out.*..........(20 to 1 op 14 to 1) 8
3571⁵ RAGTIME BOY [72] (v) 6-10-10 S Curran, *hld up and beh, no hdwy frm 4 out.*..................(14 to 1) 9
2483 DOWRY SQUARE (Ire) [74] 6-10-9 (3*) D Bohan, *led to 4th, styd prmnt til wknd 2 out..........*(12 to 1 op 14 to 1) 10
1871⁵ GAVASKAR (Ire) [73] 5-10-11 R Davis, *hld up, nvr rchd ldrs......*(12 to 1 op 10 to 1) 11
1504⁶ APACHEE FLOWER [76] 4-11-0 S Fox, *prmnt to 4th, sn beh......*(20 to 1 op 14 to 1 tchd 16 to 1) 12
3545 POWERSURGE [81] (bl) 7-11-2 (3*) K Brown, *hld up, some hdwy aftr 5th, sn wknd.*.............(33 to 1) 13
2088 ALTISHAR (Ire) [68] 6-10-6 D Fortt, *hld up and beh, rdn and hdwy aftr 5th, chsd ldrs frm nxt, wknd after 2 out, btn whn f last......*(11 to 1 op 10 to 1 tchd 12 to 1) f
3215⁸ TREGURTHA [75] 8-10-10 (3*) N Juckes, *hld up and beh, lost tch aftr 5th, tld off whn pld up bef 2 out.*
..................(12 to 1 op 7 to 1) pu
3094⁶ MARTRAJAN [83] 7-11-7 L O'Hare, *hld up and beh, lost tch aftr 5th, tld off whn pld up bef 2 out.*
..................(16 to 1 op 14 to 1) pu
2652⁵ AUSTRAL JANE [70] 4-10-8 D Matthews, *hld up and beh, lost tch aftr 3rd, tld off whn pld up bef 2 out.*
..................(20 to 1 op 14 to 1) pu
3108³ BIDDLESTONE BOY (NZ) [83] 7-11-7 R Darke, *chsd ldrs to 5th, wknd aftr 4 out, beh whn pld up and dismounted r-in......*(16 to 1 op 10 to 1) pu
Dist: 1½l, 8l, 3l, nk, hd, 1¼l, 1l, 3½l, 5l, 6l. 4m 18.60s. a 18.60s (18 Ran).
(N C Savery), P J Hobbs

3630 Ridgeway Financial Services Mares 'National Hunt' Novices' Hurdle (5,6,7-y-o) £1,791 2¼m.............. (2:50)

3527² MYRTILLA 5-10-12 L Harvey, *hld up, wnt second 4 out, led 2 out, drvn out.*......(10 to 1 op 7 to 1) 1
3530² CRAZY DAISY 7-10-5 (7*) T Murphy, *led in mid-div, chsd clr ldr frm 5th, ev ch 2 out, not quicken appr last.*
..................(9 to 4 tchd 5 to 2) 2
ROSEMOSS 7-10-12 J Lower, *hld up and beh, hdwy aftr 3 out, styd on to take 3rd pl nr finish.* (5 to 1 op 9 to 4) 3
2042 HALL END LADY (Ire) 6-10-12 A Maguire, *hld up and beh, hdwy to chase ldr aftr 5th, not quicken betw last 2.*
..................(9 to 1 op 7 to 1 tchd 10 to 1) 4

523

NATIONAL HUNT RESULTS 1993-94

3503⁵ FOREST PRIDE (Ire) 5-10-12 N Williamson, *led, clr aftr second, hdd 2 out, sn rdn and wknd.*
........................(2 to 1 fav op 9 to 4 tchd 5 to 2) 5

1494 CAST ADRIFT 7-10-12 D Gallagher, *hld up and beh, styd on aftr 3 out, not quicken betw last 2.*
.... (20 to 1 op 12 to 1) 6

3515³ PENLEA LADY 7-10-5 (7*) P McLoughlin, *hld up and beh, styd on one pace frm 3 out, nvr rchd ldrs.*
.... (20 to 1 op 12 to 1) 7

2642⁷ MERTON MISTRESS 7-10-12 J Osborne, *al rear, nvr rchd ldrs.*
.... (20 to 1 op 33 to 1) 8

3251³ PRUDENT PEGGY 7-10-12 J Frost, *chsd clr ldr to 4th, beh aftr four out.*
.... (10 to 1 op 8 to 1) 9

2558 CLOUD CUCKOO 6-10-6¹ (6*) Miss J Brackenbury, *chsd clr ldr till rdn and wknd quickly appr 2 out.*
.... (50 to 1 op 33 to 1) 10

3151 MAGGIE TEE 6-10-12 B Powell, *hld up, dd hdwy aftr 4th, chsd ldr til wknd quickly 2 out.* (33 to 1 tchd 50 to 1) 11

3547⁹ MANDY LOUISE 6-10-12 D Bridgwater, *beh aftr second, al rear.*
.... (33 to 1 tchd 50 to 1) 12

3457 INKY 5-10-5 (7*) Mr S Mulcaire, *beh aftr 4th, nvr rchd ldrs.*
.... (66 to 1 op 33 to 1) 13

MALYDAKI 6-10-12 R Greene, *tld off aftr 4th, pld up bef 2 out.*
.... (66 to 1 op 33 to 1) pu

3252 ROYAL HONEY BEE 6-10-9⁴ (7*) Mr R Payne, *chsd clr ldr til wknd quickly aftr 5th, tld off whn pld up bef 2 out.*
.... (100 to 1 op 50 to 1) pu

1642 TRADESPARK 6-10-12 W McFarland, *beh aftr 3rd, tld off whn pld up bef 2 out.* ....(100 to 1 op 50 to 1) pu
Dist: 3½l, 2l, 1¼l, 5l, 9l, 4l, 7l, 3l, 12l, 3l. 4m 19.30s. a 19.30s (16 Ran).
(Robert Long), Andrew Turnell

3631 City Of Exeter Challenge Cup Handicap Chase (0-125 5-y-o and up) £3,579 2m 7f 110yds.............. (3:20)

3364 GHOFAR [117] (bl) 11-11-11 P Holley, *trkd ldrs, wnt second aftr 5 out, rdn to ld last, drvn out r-in.*
.... (5 to 1 op 3 to 1 tchd 11 to 2) 1

3544² DOONLOUGHAN [98] 9-10-6 A Maguire, *led 3rd to 6th, led ag'n 12th, rdn 4 out, hdd last, not quicken.*
.... (9 to 4 fav op 7 to 2) 2

1467⁵ OCEAN LINK [92] 10-10-0 S Earle, *trkd ldrs til lost pl and drpd rear aftr 11th, rdn and styd on wl frm 3 out, kpt on r-in.* .... (5 to 1 op 7 to 1) 3

3477 NAUGHTY NICKY [92] 10-10-0 R Greene, *wl beh 9th, rear til styd on appr 4 out, mstk 2 out, kpt on r-in.*
.... (20 to 1 op 12 to 1) 4

3397⁴ ARDCRONEY CHIEF [110] 8-11-4 J Osborne, *in tch, reminder aftr 9th, led appr nxt, hdd 6 out, rdn and no imprsn frm 4 out.* ....(4 to 1 op 5 to 2) 5

4477⁴ SHASTON [100] (bl) 9-10-8 N Williamson, *led to 3rd, led ag'n 6th to tenth, cl up whn blun nxt, chsd ldrs til wknd 4 out.* ....(10 to 4 to 1 tchd 13 to 2) 6

3007⁴ URBAN COWBOY [93] 7-10-1¹ S McNeill, *sn wl beh, some hdwy aftr 6 out, styd on aftr 4 out, kpt on one pace.*
.... (12 to 1 op 10 to 1) 7

3207 IT'S AFTER TIME [92] 9-10-0 L Harvey, *pressed ldrs til wknd quickly aftr 5 out, tld off....*(33 to 1 op 20 to 1) 8

3477⁸ BERESFORDS GIRL [95] 9-10-3 E Byrne, *lost tch aftr 8th, sn tld off.*........................(12 to 1 op 10 to 1) 9
Dist: 4l, nk, 2½l, ¾l, 2½l, 4l, 30l, 4l. 5m 53.70s. a 18.70s (9 Ran).
SR: 4/-/-/-/-/-/ (Sir Hugh Dundas), D R C Elsworth

3632 Portman Estate Agents Novices' Selling Hurdle (4,5,6-y-o) £1,906 2¼m ....(3:50)

3362⁵ SOPHISM (USA) 5-11-9 J Lower, *hld up, stedy hdwy aftr 5th, trkd ldrs, led on bit 2 out, easily.*
........................(13 to 8 fav op 5 to 2) 1

3453 TULLYKYNE BELLS (bl) 5-11-2 D Gallagher, *in tch, cl up and ev ch 3 out, rdn and no imprsn appr last.*
........................(8 to 1 op 6 to 1) 2

3395⁴ KOA 4-11-2 D Bridgwater, *trkd ldrs, jmpd sluly 3rd, sn drvn alng, styd on appr 2 out, hng lft betw last two, not quicken.* ....(3 to 1 op 7 to 4) 3

ROCKET RUN (Ire) 6-11-2 W McFarland, *trkd ldr, led 3rd to 5th, lft in ld aftr 3 out, hdd nxt, wknd quickly.*
.... (14 to 1 op 10 to 1) 4

3421 IVE CALLED TIME 6-10-9 (7*) Miss J Brackenbury, *prmnt till lost pl aftr 4th, styd on ag'n frm 2 out, nvr nrr.*
.... (14 to 1 tchd 16 to 1) 5

3252 MR ZIEGFELD (USA) (bl) 5-11-2 L Harvey, *hld up, pressed ldr frm 5th, wnt second nxt, chsd lder til wknd 2 out.*
.... (20 to 1 op 14 to 1) 6

3572 MY SISTER LUCY 4-10-11 S Burrough, *prmnt to 4th, sn lost pl.*........................(20 to 1 op 14 to 1) 7

3264 HIZAL 5-10-9 (7*) M Appleby, *hld up and beh, no imprsn frm 4 out.*........................(20 to 1 op 25 to 1) 8

3278 STAPLEFORD LADY 6-10-8 (3*) R Farrant, *jmpd slwly 3rd, hld up, some hdwy aftr 3rd, wknd after 5th, sn beh.*
.... (25 to 1 tchd 33 to 1) 9

1602 REACH FOR GLORY 5-10-9 (7*) T Murphy, *chsd ldrs to 5th, wknd quickly.*........................(14 to 1 op 10 to 1) 10

2871 THE MAN FROM CLARE (Ire) 6-11-2 Richard Guest, *hld up, lost tch aftr 4th.*........(7 to 1 op 6 to 1 tchd 8 to 1) 11

3337 SNICKERSNEE 6-10-9 (7*) M Moran, *led to 3rd, led ag'n 5th til hit nez, sddl slpd and pld up.*
.... (50 to 1 op 25 to 1) pu

3184 HIGH BACCARAT (bl) 5-11-2 A Tory, *hld up and beh, lost tch aftr 4th, tld off whn pld up bef 2 out.*
.... (66 to 1 op 33 to 1) pu

1546⁶ LAW FACULTY (Ire) 5-11-2 B Powell, *mid-div, pushed alng aftr 4th, lost tch 3 out, pld up and dismounted bef last.*
........................(8 to 1 tchd 12 to 1) pu

3478 ON THE BOOK 5-10-11 S McNeill, *lost tch aftr 3rd, tld off whn pld up bef 2 out.*
........................(25 to 1 tchd 20 to 1 and 33 to 1) pu
Dist: 6l, sht-hd, 25l, 5l, 4l, 3l, 2½l, 1½l, 7l, 6l. 4m 20.20s. a 20.20s (15 Ran).
(A J Lomas), M C Pipe

3633 Portman Building Society Handicap Chase (0-135 5-y-o and up) £3,060 2¼m.......................(4:20)

3262² MULBANK [125] 8-11-12 Peter Hobbs, *trkd ldr til led 4 out, hrd pressed o'r fnl 2, drvn out r-in, styd on wl.*
.... (5 to 4 on op 5 to 4) 1

3349² JAILBREAKER [109] 7-10-10 G McCourt, *trkd ldr, with wnr and ev ch 4 out, rdn and not quicken r-in.*
.... (3 to 1 op 11 to 4 tchd 7 to 2) 2

3595⁹ STARLAP [103] 10-10-4 A Tory, *hld up in last pl, outpcd aftr 5 out, no ch frm 3 out.*..........(9 to 1 op 7 to 1) 3

3172* BROUGHTON MANOR [121] 9-11-8 B Powell, *led til hdd 4 out, sn wknd.*.......(3 to 1 op 2 to 1 tchd 100 to 30) 4
Dist: 3l, 15l, 12l. 4m 25.90s. a 14.90s (4 Ran).
SR: 21/2/-/-/ (I L Shaw), P J Hobbs

3634 Portman Building Society Handicap Hurdle (0-130 4-y-o and up) £2,444 2¼m.......................(4:50)

3398 BALLYSTATE [93] 6-10-12 G Upton, *led, hit 2 out, rdn and styd on wl whn chlgd betw last two.*
........................(5 to 1 op 5 to 1 tchd 13 to 2) 1

3219⁶ FAUX PAVILION [90] 10-10-4 (5*) S Fox, *trkd ldg pair, lft second 4 out, chsd ldr, ev ch betw last 2, not quicken appr last.*........(11 to 4 co-fav op 2 to 1 tchd 3 to 1) 2

3344⁸ ELEGANT KING (Ire) [100] 5-11-5 Richard Guest, *hld up, rdn alng appr 2 out, kpt on betw last two, styd on r-in, not quicken.*.....(11 to 4 co-fav op 3 to 1 tchd 7 to 2) 3

3340⁹ CHARLAFRIVOLA [81] (bl) 6-10-0 W Humphreys, *hld up in last pl, hdwy to track ldrs aftr 3 out, cl up and ev ch betw last 2, not quicken r-in.*
.... (5 to 1 op 20 to 1 tchd 33 to 1) 4

3499⁵ KING WILLIAM [105] 9-11-3 (7*) Mr B Pollock, *hld up, cld up appr 3rd, close upand ev ch til wknd quickly 2 out, tld off....*(11 to 4 co-fav op 6 to 4 tchd 3 to 1) 5

3545 FROSTY RECEPTION [89] (bl) 9-10-8 L Harvey, *trkd ldr, second and ev ch whn f 5th.*
........................(6 to 1 op 5 to 1 tchd 13 to 2) f
Dist: 1½l, ½l, 1l, dist. 4m 18.40s. a 18.40s (6 Ran).
(Mrs R Stevens), C James

HUNTINGDON (firm)
Wednesday April 27th
Going Correction: MINUS 0.30 sec. per fur.

3635 Huntingdon Newcomers Evening Conditional Jockeys' Selling Handicap Hurdle (4-y-o and up) £2,169 2m 110yds...............................(5:15)

3153⁴ WATER DIVINER [62] 4-9-9 (5*) Pat Thompson, *al wl plcd, led 4 out, drvn clr last, styd on....*(33 to 1 op 25 to 1) 1

3328⁶ BOZO BAILEY [69] 4-10-2 (5*) M Godsafe, *trkd ldrs, pushed alng aftr 3 out, styd on frm betw last 2, nrst finish.*........................(12 to 1 tchd 16 to 1) 2

3089³ SWAN WALK (Ire) [77] 6-10-12 (3*) E Husband, *al wl plcd, drw level 3 out, rdn and one pace frm betw last 2.*
........................(8 to 1 op 6 to 1 tchd 9 to 1) 3

3222³ SULTAN'S SON [72] 8-10-10 D Leahy, *al in tch, drvn alng whn pace quickened appr 3 out, styd on same pace frm nxt.*........................(6 to 1 fav tchd 8 to 1) 4

3408 NOBLE INSIGHT [90] (bl) 7-11-9 (5*) M Berry, *patiently rdn, improved to track ldg pair hfwy, ridden bef 3 out, kpt on same pace.*........................(13 to 2 op 8 to 1) 5

2532⁴ GREEN'S SEAGO (USA) [72] 6-10-10 D J Moffatt, *al with ldrs, pushed alng aftr 3 out, not quicken frm nxt.*
........................(12 to 1 op 6 to 1) 6

3089 POINT TAKEN (USA) [64] 7-9-9 (7*) A Large, *took keen hold, made most to 4 out, fdd aftr nxt...* (20 to 1 op 14 to 1) 7

2713* MILL BURN [80] 5-11-4 T Eley, *settled off the pace, improved frm 3 out, staying on finish.*
........................(12 to 1 op 8 to 1) 8

2580⁶ WHAT IF [86] 10-11-5 (5*) M Moore, *wtd with, pushed alng to go hndy aftr 3 out, rdn frm nxt, no imprsn.*
........................(9 to 1 op 8 to 1) 9

3597 NAGOBELIA [86] 6-11-10 A Dickin, *trkd ldg bunch, blun second, effrt 4 out, fdd frm nxt.*
........................(8 to 1 op 7 to 1 tchd 9 to 1) 10

524

3328² RUTH'S GAMBLE [78] 6-10-9 (7*) Honey Pearce, *nvr far away, struggling to hold pl bef 3 out, sn btn.*
..................................(12 to 1 op 8 to 1) 11

3435 LODGING [63] (v) 7-10-1 A Larnach, *chsd ldg bunch, struggling to go pace bef 3 out, no extr.* (11 to 1 op 10 to 1) 12

2627⁴ SANTA PONSA BAY [74] 7-10-12 A Procter, *struggling to keep up hfwy, nvr a threat.*................(10 to 1) 13

3345⁷ THEYDON PRIDE [62] 5-9-9 (5*) W J Walsh, *struggling frm 3rd, nvr able to rch chalg pos.*..........(33 to 1) 14

2665⁵ ELEGANT FRIEND [83] 6-11-2 (5*) C Huggan, *al chasing ldrs, hrd at work aftr 4 out, sn struggling.*
..................................(12 to 1 op 6 to 1) 15

1472 ROLY WALLACE [62] (v) 5-9-9 (5*) G Roberson, *sn struggling to keep up, not pace of ldrs.*............(33 to 1) 16

2541⁵ CONBRIO STAR [73] 4-10-11 S Wynne, *sn beh and drvn alng, nvr factor.*..................(50 to 1 op 20 to 1) 17

3373 CHILTERN HUNDREDS (USA) [62] 4-9-11² (5*) C Woodall, *sn struggling, lost frm 4th.*........(50 to 1 op 20 to 1) 18

Dist: 3½l, ¾l, 1½l, sht-hd, sht-hd, nk, ½l, 2½l, 5l, 2½l. 3m 53.50s. a 6.50s (18 Ran).

(M M Foulger), K G Wingrove

3636 Gidding Handicap Chase (0-115 5-y-o and up) £3,057 2½m 110yds.....(5:50)

3207 RYTON GUARD [87] (bl) 9-9-9 (5*) D Leahy, *jmpd wl, made all, styd on strly to go clr frm 3 out.* (6 to 1 op 8 to 1) 1

3560³ BOBBY SOCKS [110] 8-11-9 M FitzGerald, *trkd ldg bunch, improved to chase wnr frm 5th, rdn from 3 out, one pace from betw last 2.*..........(3 to 1 fav op 9 to 4) 2

3006⁴ CASINO MAGIC [88] 10-10-1 V Slattery, *wtd wth, improved hfwy, outpcd and rdn alng appr 3 out, no imprsn.*
..................................(6 to 1 op 5 to 1) 3

1275⁵ SECRET SUMMIT (USA) [94] (v) 8-10-4 (3*) T Eley, *sn beh and struggling, relentless prog frm 3 out, nvr nr to chal.*............(14 to 1 op 12 to 1 tchd 16 to 1) 4

3405³ SIRRAH JAY [105] 14-11-4 B Clifford, *wl plcd, hrd rdn to hold pl 4 out, sn lost tch.*............(7 to 2 op 9 to 4) 5

3513 BLUE BUCCANEER [89] 11-10-2 M Brennan, *al struggling, tld off frm hfwy.*................(16 to 1 op 14 to 1) 6

3397 JIM VALENTINE [99] 8-10-5 (7*) Mr G Hogan, *sn struggling to keep up, tld off frm hfwy.*..........(20 to 1 op 16 to 1) 7

3091⁴ PRIVATE AUDITION [112] 12-11-11 M Hourigan, *trkd ldg pair, bustled alng and lost grnd hfwy, sn tld off.*
..................................(11 to 2 op 4 to 1) 8

COMETTI STAR [97] 10-10-10 B Dalton, *in tch, improved hfwy, chasing ldg pair whn blun and uns rdr 4 out.*
..................................(16 to 1 op 12 to 1 tchd 20 to 1) ur

Dist: 12l, 15l, 3½l, 6l, 3½l, dist, 2½l. 4m 54.20s. b 0.80s (9 Ran).

SR: 19/30/-/-/-/-/-/ (Mrs Adrian Ireland), S Christian

3637 Touche Ross Maiden Hurdle (4-y-o and up) £2,792 2m 5f 110yds.... (6:25)

THE PRUSSIAN (USA) 8-11-7 J Ryan, *patiently rdn, improved quickly appr 4 out, led bef 2 out, drvn clr r-in.*
..................................(20 to 1 op 16 to 1 tchd 25 to 1) 1

3233 EDITHMEAD (Ire) 4-10-9 M A FitzGerald, *nvr far away, ev ch and swtchd betw last 2, rdn and not quicken r-in.*
..................................(5 to 4 op 6 to 4 on tchd Evens) 2

3315⁵ MRS NORMAN 5-10-13 (3*) S Wynne, *settled midfield, improved to join issue 3 out, rdn betw last 2, one pace.*
..................................(16 to 1 tchd 9 to 1) 3

2991 PARLIAMENTARIAN (Ire) 5-11-0 (7*) R Rourke, *nvr far away, led bef 3 out till aftr nxt, one pace frm betw last 2.*..................(25 to 1 op 16 to 1 tchd 33 to 1) 4

2910⁴ FLAPPING FREDA (Ire) 6-11-2 S Smith Eccles, *trkd ldg bunch, effrt and drvn alng appr 3 out, outpcd frm nxt.*
..................................(12 to 1 op 7 to 1) 5

2000⁶ COEUR BATTANT (Fr) 4-10-9 (5*) E Husband, *pushed alng to keep up hfwy, styd on frm 3 out, nvr able to chal.*
..................................(12 to 1 op 8 to 1) 6

3270 PETTAUGH (Ire) 6-11-7 M Hourigan, *chsd alng to go pace hfwy, styd on frm 3 out, no imprsn.*
..................................(16 to 1 op 12 to 1) 7

3451 IZACONIN (Ire) 5-10-11 (5*) J Supple, *nvr far away, hit 4th, feeling pace and rdn 3 out, fdd.*
..................................(33 to 1 op 25 to 1) 8

RIP THE CALICO (Ire) 6-10-9 (7*) Miss C Spearing, *al pressing ldrs, hrd drvn bef 3 out, sn btn.* (33 to 1 op 25 to 1) 9

3189² RAGAMUFFIN ROMEO 5-11-2 (5*) S Curran, *beh and pushed alng, lost further grnd appr 3 out, tld off.*
..................................(11 to 2 op 7 to 1 tchd 5 to 1) 10

3509⁸ ABSOLUTELYMUSTARD (Ire) 5-11-7 M Richards, *trkd ldg bunch, hrd drvn aftr 4 out, sn lost tch.*
..................................(16 to 1 op 10 to 1) 11

2731 RARE PADDY 5-10-9 (7*) J James, *in tch for one circuit, struggling bef 4 out, tld off.*............(33 to 1 op 20 to 1) 12

CLAYDONS MONTY 5-11-7 T Wall, *sn chsd alng to go pace, tld off fnl circuit.*...........(33 to 1 op 25 to 1) 13

VARELITO (Ire) 4-10-7 (7*) J Neaves, *struggling to go pace thrght, nvr a factor.*............(33 to 1 op 16 to 1) 14

3396 BEE EM AITCH 5-11-7 M Bosley, *made most till hdd appr 3 out, fdd, tld off.*..................(33 to 1 op 25 to 1) 15

FINE TUDOR 8-11-0 (7*) P Ward, *shod up in frnt rnk till wknd quickly appr 4 out, tld off..*(33 to 1 op 25 to 1) 16

3190 SHANNON RUN (Ire) 5-11-7 M Brennan, *chsd ldg bunch, hrd drvn bef hfwy, tld off frm 3 out.*
..................................(16 to 1 op 12 to 1) 17

1263⁵ THE MINE CAPTAIN 7-11-7 E Murphy, *chsd alng to keep up hfwy, ran out appr 3 out whr.* (16 to 1 op 8 to 1) ro

CRYMLYN SWING 10-11-2 W Worthington, *struggling most of way, tld off whn pld up lme r-in.*
..................................(33 to 1 op 25 to 1) pu

Dist: 5l, 2½l, 2l, 12l, 7l, 2½l, hd, ¾l, 10l, 6l. 5m 4.20s. a 9.20s (19 Ran).

(First In Racing Partnership), K G Wingrove

3638 Christie's Hunters' Chase (5-y-o and up) £1,716 3m.................(7:00)

3563² WILD ILLUSION 10-12-2 (7*) Mr J Trice-Rolph, *al gng wl, led 3 out, clr frm nxt, readily.* (9 to 4 on op 5 to 2 on) 1

3439 VERY CHEERING 11-11-12 (7*) Mr B Crawford, *made most to 3 out, sn drvn alng, styd on one pace frm betw last 2.*
..................................(20 to 1 op 12 to 1 tchd 25 to 1) 2

3412 SONOFAGIPSY 10-12-0 (5*) Mr M Felton, *jmpd slwly 4th, improved to join wnr 7th, chsd alng 3 out, one pace.*
..................................(9 to 2 op 7 to 2) 3

3501² PARSON'S CROSS 10-11-7 (7*) Mr A Sansome, *wth ldrs, struggling to hold pl 5 out, sn outpcd, fnshd lme.*
..................................(5 to 1 tchd 6 to 1) 4

3265 EASTER FROLIC 12-11-7 (7*) Mr N Bloom, *nvr far quartet, struggling aftr one circuit, tld off frm 6 out.*
..................................(33 to 1 op 20 to 1) 5

LAWLEY 12-11-7 (7*) Mr T Hills, *rdn alng to go pace bef hfwy, sn tld off, pld up before 6 out.*
..................................(33 to 1 op 25 to 1) pu

Dist: 7l, 6l, 20l, dist. 6m 4.60s. a 16.60s (6 Ran).

(Col A Clerke-Brown), Miss Jennifer Pidgeon

3639 Bob Arnold Forty Years Of Service Novices' Chase (5-y-o and up) £2,654 2m 110yds......................(7:30)

1072 PINISI 9-11-2 B Dalton, *nvr far away, jnd ldr appr 2 out, led r-in, drvn out.*
..................................(13 to 2 op 7 to 1 tchd 10 to 1 and 6 to 1) 1

2715⁴ SING THE BLUES 10-11-2 D Morris, *jmpd wl, tried to make all, jnd bef 2 out, hdd r-in, one pace.*
..................................(8 to 1 op 5 to 1 tchd 10 to 1) 2

MANABOUTTHEHOUSE 7-11-2 M Hourigan, *al tracking ldrs, effrt hfwy, drvn alng aftr 3 out, rallied frm last, ran on.*................(4 to 1 op 5 to 2 tchd 9 to 2) 3

3416⁴ CHANDIGARH 6-10-13 (3*) S Wynne, *al hndy, jnd ldr hfwy, drvn alng aftr nxt, sn outpcd* (7 to 1 op 3 to 1) 4

3415² BUSTINELLO (Ire) 6-11-8 M A FitzGerald, *chsd ldr to hfwy, feeling pace aftr 5 out, sn struggling.*
..................................(5 to 4 fav op Evens tchd 13 to 8) 5

3334⁹ WETANDRY 9-11-2 M Bosley, *struggling to go pace 5th, sn lost tch, tld off.*..........(40 to 1 op 25 to 1) 6

2900 TEA-LADY (Ire) 6-10-11 B Clifford, *hit second, lost tch quickly 5th, tld off..*(20 to 1 op 16 to 1 tchd 25 to 1) 7

2538 SIMWELL (Ire) 6-10-9 (7*) M G Hogan, *hit 1st, al struggling in rear, tld off..*........(12 to 1 op 6 to 1) 8

Dist: 3½l, 3l, 15l, 8l, dist, ½l, 2½l. 4m 2.00s. a 4.00s (8 Ran).

(R Pitman), J Wharton

3640 Chiltern Radio 'National Hunt' Novices' Hurdle (4-y-o and up) £1,907 3¼m..........................(8:00)

2961⁵ STRONG JOHN (Ire) 6-11-8 M Hourigan, *al hndy, led gng wl 2 out, drvn clr, easily.* (8 to 1 op 5 to 1 tchd 9 to 1) 1

2322⁵ CREWS CASTLE (bl) 7-11-8 S Smith Eccles, *nvr far away, drvn alng and outpcd aftr 3 out, styd on ag'n r-in.*
..................................(11 to 2 op 7 to 1) 2

3497⁴ FLAMEWOOD 5-10-11 M A FitzGerald, *made most frm second, outpcd 3 out, hdd nxt, one pace.*
..................................(5 to 4 fav op Evens tchd 11 to 8 and 6 to 4) 3

2997 BUCKSHOT (Ire) 6-11-2 E Murphy, *led to second, styd hndy and ev ch till outpcd 3 out, ran on ag'n r-in.*
..................................(11 to 2 op 6 to 1 tchd 9 to 1) 4

3196⁹ BALLYGRIFFIN LAD (Ire) 5-11-2 M Mann, *patiently rdn, improved aftr one circuit, effrt 4 out, outpcd nxt, sn btn.*..........(14 to 1 tchd 16 to 1 and 20 to 1) 5

3440⁶ TOO CLEVER BY HALF 6-11-8 Mr G Johnson Houghton, *wtd wth, improved aftr one circuit, rdn bef 4 out, fdd nxt.*........(8 to 1 op 7 to 1 tchd 9 to 1) 6

3235⁷ GLEN MIRAGE 9-11-2 Miss S White, *struggling most of way, nvr a factor..*(14 to 1 tchd 16 to 1 and 10 to 1) 7

3204 COSMICECHOEXPRESS 7-10-8 (3*) S Wynne, *chsd ldrs, hrd at work aftr one circuit, sn lost tch.*
..................................(33 to 1 op 20 to 1) 8

3147⁷ ALTESSE ROXANNE 5-10-11 B Clifford, *chsd ldg bunch for a circuit, tld off frm 4 out.*..........(33 to 1 op 20 to 1) 9

3497 RAYLEO (Ire) 5-11-2 M Brennan, *in tch, effrt hfwy, lost grnd aftr one circuit, tld off.*
..................................(25 to 1 op 20 to 1 tchd 33 to 1) 10

Dist: 8l, 1½l, hd, 10l, 7l, 5l, 15l, dist, 3l. 6m 13.50s (10 Ran).

(G A Hubbard), G A Hubbard

KELSO (good)

Wednesday April 27th
Going Correction: PLUS 0.40 sec. per fur.

3641 Z. Hinchliffe Novices' Handicap Hurdle (4-y-o and up) £2,867 2¾m 110yds ....(2:10)

2997^{2} SON OF IRIS [84] 6-10-12 P Niven, *hld up, hdwy hfwy, pushed alng and staying on whn slightly hmpd 2 out, rdn to ld r-in, all out*.............. (9 to 2 tchd 5 to 1) 1
3440^{3} BRIAR'S DELIGHT [72] 6-10-0 B Storey, *prmnt, chalg whn lft in ld 2 out, hdd r-in, no extr und pres.* .... (8 to 1 op 16 to 1) 2
3542* LONDON HILL [85] 6-10-13 (7ex) C Dennis, *outpcd and lost tch aftr 7th, styd on ag'n frm 2 out, nvr dngrs.* .... (13 to 2 op 6 to 1 tchd 7 to 1) 3
3431^{3} MANOR COURT (Ire) [86] 6-11-0 A Merrigan, *trkd ldrs, effrt appr 3 out, sn rdn, wknd aftr nxt.* .... (9 to 1 op 10 to 1 tchd 8 to 1) 4
3144^{3} FREE TRANSFER (Ire) [90] 5-11-4 A Dobbin, *in tch till wknd aftr 3 out*................... (14 to 1 op 10 to 1) 5
3236* KINDA GROOVY [76] (bl) 5-10-4 N Smith, *chsd ldr frm hfwy till wknd aftr 8th, tld off*........... (9 to 2 op 5 to 1) 6
3518 STRONG FLAME (Ire) [96] 5-11-5 (5*) S Lyons, *led, sn clr, jnd and pushed alng whn f 2 out.* (3 to 1 fav op 9 to 4) f
3144 PANTO LADY [72] 8-9-7 (7*) Miss S Lamb, *mstks, sn wl beh, tld off whn pld up bef 2 out*..... (200 to 1 op 100 to 1) pu
2252^{2} NINFA (Ire) [88] 6-10-9 (7*) B Harding, *in tch till wknd appr 3 out, tld off whn pld up bef last.* .... (11 to 1 op 8 to 1 tchd 12 to 1) pu
2500^{9} LOMOND SPRINGS (Ire) [72] 5-10-0 S Turner, *lost tch hfwy, tld off whn pld up bef 7th*...................(100 to 1) pu

Dist: 2½l, 15l, 2½l, 8l, dist. 5m 35.90s. a 24.90s (10 Ran).
(M H G Systems Ltd), Mrs M Reveley

3642 George Inter-Continental Edinburgh Trophy Novices' Chase (5-y-o and up) £3,415 2m 1f................... (2:40)

3438^{5} BEAUCADEAU 8-11-0 A Dobbin, *al prmnt, led last, sn clr, eased towards finish cmftbly.* .... (6 to 4 on tchd 5 to 4 on) 1
3540* GRAZEMBER 7-11-7 C Hawkins, *hld up in tch, hdwy aftr 5th, led bef 3 out, hdd last, kpt on, no ch wth wnr.* ....(2 to 1 tchd 9 to 4) 2
3429 OLD MORTALITY (v) 8-11-0 B Storey, *led till hdd bef 3 out, grad wknd*........................(25 to 1 op 20 to 1) 3
1723 MAN OF MOREEF 7-11-0 K Johnson, *outpcd aftr 5th, sn lost tch*........................... (25 to 1 op 20 to 1) 4
3033^{5} NORTHERN VISION 7-10-7 (7*) Mr A Manners, *not jump wl, prmnt till wknd quickly aftr 7th, tld off.* .... (25 to 1 op 20 to 1) 5
3540^{5} STRONG TRACE (Ire) 5-10-8 P Niven, *blun badly and uns rdr 4th*.......................... (12 to 1 tchd 16 to 1) ur

Dist: 1¾l, 15l, 13l, dist. 4m 19.40s. a 13.40s (6 Ran).
SR: 20/25/3/ (T A Barnes), M A Barnes

3643 Royal Bank Of Scotland Handicap Hurdle (0-135 4-y-o and up) £4,006 2m 110yds........................ (3:10)

3092^{3} BROWNSIDE BRIG [88] 9-10-4 P Niven, *hld up gng wl, hdwy to track ldrs 3 out, led last, rdn out.* ....(11 to 4 fav op 4 to 1) 1
3538^{6} WEE WIZARD (Ire) [103] 5-11-5 A Dobbin, *in tch, outpcd aftr 3 out, styd on wl und pres frm last, not rch wnr.* ....(8 to 1 op 7 to 1) 2
3538^{2} FAMILY LINE [98] 6-11-0 L O'Hara, *trkd ldrs, chlgd 2 out, ev ch last, no extr*.... (100 to 30 op 3 to 1 tchd 7 to 2) 3
3434* FLASH OF REALM (Fr) [101] 8-10-12 (5*) J Burke, *trkd ldr, slight ld bef 2 out, hdd last, sn wknd.* ....(100 to 30 op 11 to 4 tchd 7 to 2) 4
3429^{6} BORO SMACKEROO [106] 9-11-3 (5*) F Perratt, *led till hdd bef 2 out, sn btn*.................... (9 to 1 op 7 to 1) 5
3356 SEON [112] 8-12-0 N Bentley, *in tch, reminders hfwy, lost touch aftr 3 out*...................(8 to 1 tchd 9 to 1) 6
3484^{6} RINGLAND (USA) [84] 6-10-0 B Storey, *mstks, hld up, effrt aftr 3 out, sn btn, f nxt, dead*......(12 to 1 op 14 to 1) f

Dist: 3l, ½l, 6l, 1¼l, 12l. 3m 59.20s. a 16.20s (7 Ran).
(Mrs Lucy Gibbon), M H Tompkins

3644 Scottish Equitable Handicap Chase for the Haddington Jubilee Cup (0-135 5-y-o and up) £4,947 3m 1f...... (3:40)

3405^{5} KUSHBALOO [110] 9-10-3 B Storey, *jmpd wl, made all, styd on well*...........(9 to 2 op 5 to 1 tchd 11 to 2) 1
3358^{4} BLUFF KNOLL [116] 11-10-9 G Harker, *prmnt, pushed alng hfwy, rdn aftr 3 out, kpt on frm last.* ....(6 to 1 tchd 13 to 2) 2
3180* PINK GIN [107] 7-10-0 L Wyer, *hld up, reminders hfwy, hdwy aftr 15th, kpt on frm 2 out, nrst finish.* ....(100 to 30 jt-fav op 9 to 2 tchd 5 to 1) 3
3463* ARMAGRET [135] 9-12-0 D Byrne, *prmnt, chsd wnr aftr 2 out, no imprsn, wknd r-in*................(100 to 30 jt-fav op 3 to 1 tchd 7 to 2) 4
3537^{6} FISH QUAY [107] 11-9-7 (7*) Miss S Lamb, *badly hmpd 1st, sn tracking ldrs, kpt on same pace frm 2 out.* .... (100 to 1 op 66 to 1) 5
3425 HE WHO DARES WINS [115] 11-10-8 K Johnson, *in tch, pushed alng hfwy, sn lost pl, no dngr aftr.* ....(8 to 1 op 6 to 1) 6
JELUPE [109] 12-10-2 Mr R Sandys-Clarke, *beh frm 14th.* ....(25 to 1 tchd 33 to 1) 7
3433* SIMPLE PLEASURE [115] 9-10-8 Mr S Swiers, *in tch till wknd bef 3 out, tld off.* ....(14 to 1 op 12 to 1 tchd 16 to 1) 8
3537^{9} CAMIONNAGE [107] 13-9-13⁴ (5*) P Waggott, *prmnt till rdn and wknd aftr 13th, tld off*......(100 to 1 op 66 to 1) 9
3463^{6} ISLAND GALE [107] 9-9-9 (5*) F Perratt, *f 1st.* .... (25 to 1 op 16 to 1) f
3485^{8} CAROUSEL ROCKET [111] 11-10-4⁴ P Niven, *in tch, outpcd aftr 11th, staying on but plenty to do whn blun and uns rdr 2 out*...............(14 to 1 tchd 16 to 1) ur

Dist: 6l, 1l, nk, nk, 20l, nk, dist, ¾l. 6m 19.30s. a 17.30s (11 Ran).
SR: 2/2/-/19/-/-/ (Raymond Anderson Green), C Parker

3645 Charlie Brown Family United Border Hunt Chase (5-y-o and up) £2,360 3m 1f............................ (4:15)

3432* ROYAL JESTER 10-11-11 (7*) Mr C Storey, *trkd ldrs, led 15th, jnd last, styd on wl*........... (11 to 2 op 4 to 1) 1
3462* GENERALS BOY 12-12-4 Mr P Craggs, *hld up in tch, jnd ldrs 12th, chlgd last, sn rdn and no extr.* ....(7 to 4 on tchd 6 to 4 on) 2
3412 FOUR TRIX 13-11-13 (5*) Mr R Hale, *in tch, blun 12th, outpcd aftr 14th, styd on frm 2 out.* (8 to 1 tchd 9 to 1) 3
3558 GUNMETAL BOY (v) 10-11-11 (7*) Mr A Parker, *led, hdd 15th, ev ch whn mstk 2 out, sn rdn and btn.* .... (14 to 1 op 10 to 1 tchd 16 to 1) 4
3412 DALTON DANDY 12-11-11 (7*) Mr P Jenkins, *chsd ldrs till wknd aftr 16th, tld off, collapsed and died and after race*...............................(6 to 1 tchd 7 to 1) 5
SECOND ATTEMPT (bl) 10-11-7 (5*) Mr D Parker, *prmnt early, beh whn blun 11th, tld off when pld up bef 13th.* ....(66 to 1 op 100 to 1) pu
3439^{3} LINEBACKER 10-11-11 (7*) Mr N F Smith, *wl beh frm 13th, tld off whn pld up bef 2 out*....... (33 to 1 op 50 to 1) pu

Dist: 5l, 12l, 2½l, 25l. 6m 28.40s. a 26.40s (7 Ran).
(Mrs A D Wauchope), Mrs Jane Storey

3646 Cross Keys Hotel, Kelso Novices' Hurdle For Amateur Riders (4-y-o and up) £2,355 3m 3f............... (4:45)

3359^{3} MAJORITY MAJOR (Ire) 5-11-10 Mr J Greenall, *wth ldr, led bef 3 out, styd on wl und pres.* .... (11 to 4 op 3 to 1 tchd 5 to 2) 1
3431* COQUI LANE 7-12-0 (5*) Mr J M Dun, *made most till hdd bef 3 out, ev ch last, styd on und pres.* .... (11 to 4 op 5 to 2 tchd 3 to 1) 2
3076^{3} PORTONIA 10-11-11 (3*) Mr M Buckley, *cl up, outpcd aftr 9th, rallied appr last, kpt on, no imprsn.* ....(7 to 4 fav op 9 to 4) 3
2071^{6} MASTER MISCHIEF (bl) 7-11-10 Mr J Walton, *lost tch aftr 6th, tld off*...................................(33 to 1) 4
3431 HIGHLAND RIVER 7-10-12 (7*) Mrs H Johnston, *lost tch aftr 8th, tld off*...................................(66 to 1) 5
3554^{5} BENNAN MARCH 7-11-5 (5*) Mr D Parker, *chsd ldrs till outpcd aftr 9th, tld off whn pld up bef last.* .... (11 to 2 op 5 to 1) pu
3059 RUSHING BURN 8-10-12 (7*) Mr C Storey, *lost tch aftr 8th, tld off whn pld bef 2 out*..................... (50 to 1) pu

Dist: 2½l, 4l, dist, 5l. 6m 34.70s. a 20.70s (7 Ran).
SR: -/3/-/-/ (J A Stephenson), P Cheesbrough

PUNCHESTOWN (IRE) (yielding)
Wednesday April 27th

3647 Coolmore EBF Mares Hurdle Championship Final (4-y-o and up) £6,900 2½m.......................... (2:15)

3322* MY SUNNY GLEN 7-11-2 (5*) K P Gaule,..........(5 to 1) 1
3322 LOVELY RUN 7-11-5 H Rogers,...................(20 to 1) 2
3290^{7} HAZY ROSE (Ire) 5-10-10 (5*) D T Evans,.........(50 to 1) 3
3466* CASH IT IN (Ire) 6-11-2 (3*) D P Murphy,..........(16 to 1) 4
3550* BADEN (Ire) 6-11-2 (3*) T P Treacy,............(2 to 1 fav) 5
3248^{4} CREATIVE BLAZE (Ire) 5-10-13 (5*) J P Broderick, (16 to 1) 6
3244^{5} ACKLE BACKLE 7-10-11 (5*) J R Barry,..........(20 to 1) 7
3505* KEEPHERGOING (Ire) 5-11-4 K F O'Brien,........(12 to 1) 8
3504^{2} MISGIVINGS (Ire) 6-11-2 C F Swan,..............(14 to 1) 9
3550^{3} ARABIAN SPRITE (Ire) 6-11-2 Mr P J Healy,......(25 to 1) 10
2943^{5} MURPHY'S LADY (Ire) 5-10-12 (3*) C O'Brien,.....(50 to 1) 11
3449^{4} SIOBHAILIN DUBH (Ire) 5-10-11 (7*) Mr G F Ryan, (20 to 1) 12
3291* THE BLUEBELL POLKA (Ire) 5-11-5 F J Flood,.....(11 to 2) 13
3292^{3} PRINCESS BAVARD 9-11-2 T Horgan,.............(16 to 1) 14
3467^{2} COUNTERBALANCE 7-11-2 B Sheridan,..........(25 to 1) 15
3529^{9} CARRIGKEM (Ire) 6-10-11 (5*) A J Slattery,.......(33 to 1) 16
3466^{8} FANCY STEP 8-11-2 S H O'Donovan,............(33 to 1) 17

3388 MAID OF GLENDURAGH (Ire) (bl) 6-10-13 (3*) Mr B R Ham-
ilton, ... (14 to 1) 18
3450 AMME ENAEK (Ire) 5-10-12 (3*) K B Walsh, ... (50 to 1) 19
3271 JEMMA'S GOLD (Ire) 6-11-2 J P Banahan, ... (66 to 1) 20
3271⁶ SHINETHYME (Ire) 5-11-1 W Marston, ... (500 to 1) 21
3290 LOVELY AFFAIR (Ire) 5-11-1 C O'Dwyer, ... (50 to 1) 22
3290* THE WICKED CHICKEN (Ire) 5-11-4 R Dunwoody, (10 to 1) pu
Dist: 2½l, 5½l, 11l, 4½l. 5m 23.40s. (23 Ran).

(E Flavin), A P O'Brien

3648 Cappoquin Chickens Handicap Chase (4-y-o and up) £6,900 3m 1f. . . . . (2:45)

3524⁵ FANE BANKS [-] (bl) 12-11-2 P Carberry, ... (14 to 1) 1
3274* GREEN TIMES [-] 9-11-11 J P Banahan, ... (12 to 1) 2
3392 WALLS COURT [-] 7-10-3 T Horgan, ... (20 to 1) 3
2698⁴ KINGSTON WAY [-] 8-11-7 D M O'Brien, ... (12 to 1) 4
COLLIGAN RIVER [-] 11-11-9 J Magee, ... (25 to 1) 5
2589 JOHNEEN [-] 8-11-0 R Dunwoody, ... (12 to 1) 6
3293* BROGUESTOWN [-] 9-11-5 F J Flood, ... (14 to 1) 7
2661 LE BRAVE [-] 8-9-13 (3*) T J Mitchell, ... (33 to 1) 8
3326⁶ THE QUIET MAN [-] 10-10-5 D H O'Connor, ... (33 to 1) 9
3326² GALLEY GALE [-] 8-10-8 K F O'Brien, ... (12 to 1) 10
3524³ DEL MONTE BOY [-] 9-10-8 (7*) M D Murphy, ...(10 to 1) 11
2100⁹ SHUIL LE CHEILE [-] 7-9-4 (3*) C O'Brien, ... (25 to 1) 12
2934 FEATHERED GALE [-] 7-11-7 J Short, ... (12 to 1) 13
3524⁶ WRECKLESS MAN [-] 7-10-13 (5*) P A Roche, . . . (16 to 1) 14
3467⁹ GOLDEN CARRUTH (Ire) [-] 6-10-5 (5*) J P Broderick,
. . . . (14 to 1) 15
3371⁵ PROPUNT [-] 9-11-8 J F Titley, ... (20 to 1) 16
3371² AMERICAN EYRE [-] 9-11-5 R Murphy, ... (14 to 1) 17
NO DESERT [-] 10-11-9 L P Cusack, ... (33 to 1) f
3465² COMMANCHE NELL [-] 6-11-7 G M O'Neill, (9 to 2 fav) f
3524⁴ THE REAL UNYOKE [-] 9-11-11 (3*) D P Murphy, . .(14 to 1) ur
SILENT JET [-] 13-11-3 S H O'Donovan, ... (50 to 1) ref
2701⁴ ANOTHER RUSTLE [-] 11-10-3 W T Slattery Jnr, . . (14 to 1) pu
3392⁴ DYSART LASS [-] 9-11-13 C F Swan, ... (16 to 1) pu
3524 CASTLE BRANDON [-] 8-11-8 A Powell, ... (16 to 1) pu
3465 EXTRA MILE [-] 7-11-5 G Bradley, ... (33 to 1) pu
2149 QUIET MONEY [-] 7-10-3 F Woods, ... (33 to 1) pu
3524² NEW CO (Ire) [-] 5-10-13 C O'Dwyer, ...(5 to 1) pu
Dist: 2½l, 3l, 2l, ½l. 6m 56.30s. (27 Ran).

(Mrs M Cahill), Noel Meade

3649 Heineken Gold Cup (h'cap chase) (Listed) (4-y-o and up) £32,700 3m 1f (3:20)

3368* MERRY GALE (Ire) [-] 6-12-0 (2ex) K F O'Brien, wl plcd, led
at 6th, pressed frm 4 out, rdn and kpt on well from last.
. . . . (5 to 2) 1
3293 TAWNEY FLAME [-] 8-10-0 J Magee, hld up, mstk at 8th,
prog 5 out, ev ch appr last, rdn and no extr on r-in.
. . . . (40 to 1) 2
3039⁸ MUDAHIM [-] 8-10-13 W Marston, trkd ldr, ev ch 3 out, rdn
aftr nxt, no extr and wknd on r-in . . . . (14 to 1) 3
1905* FRIENDS OF GERALD [-] 8-10-12 C O'Brien, mid-div, ev ch
3 out, rdn aftr nxt, kpt on one pace. . . . . (10 to 1) 4
3415 BEACHY HEAD [-] 6-11-1 M Dwyer, wl plcd, rdn 3 out, no
extr and wknd appr last. . . . . (12 to 1) 5
3324² NUAFFE [-] 9-10-12 S H O'Donovan, led, hdd 6th, rdn 3
out, no extr and wknd appr last. . . . . (10 to 1) 6
3371* HAVE TO THINK [-] 6-10-6 (3ex) T P Rudd, mid-div, ev ch 3
out, rdn and wknd aftr nxt. . . . .(20 to 1) 7
3426* ALL FOR LUCK [-] 9-10-12 (7ex) R Dunwoody, mid-div,
mstk at 13th, slight mistake and lost pl 3 out, no extr
and wknd aftr nxt. . . . . (9 to 4 fav) 8
3391 SCRIBBLER [-] 8-10-8 G Bradley, mid-div, gd prog aftr 5
out, rdn 3 out, ran wide and lost grnd after nxt, wknd.
. . . . (20 to 1) 9
3392² TITIAN BLONDE (Ire) [-] 6-10-3 F Woods, mid-div, mstk at
11th, sn rdn and lost tch, tld off 4 out. . . . . (12 to 1) 10
3391⁵ BOB DEVANI [-] 8-10-5 P Carberry, al rear, rdn and lost
tch aftr 5 out, tld off nxt. . . . . (20 to 1) 11
3326* MINISTER FOR FUN (Ire) [-] 6-10-1 (8ex) C F Swan, mid-div
whn mstk and f 6 out. . . . . (8 to 1) f
3425 ITS A CRACKER [-] 10-10-6 C O'Dwyer, al rear, rdn and
lost tch aftr 6 out, pld up bef 2 out. . . . . (20 to 1) pu
2701 SPEAKING TOUR (USA) [-] 6-10-0 D H O'Connor, al rear,
lost tch 5 out, pld up bef 2 out. . . . .(40 to 1) pu
2865⁶ FARNEY GLEN [-] 7-10-0 T Horgan, mid-div, rdn and lost
tch 6 out, pld up bef 2 out. . . . . (33 to 1) pu
3249 BERMUDA BUCK [-] 8-10-1 J P Banahan, al rear, tld off 5
out, pld up bef 2 out. . . . . (33 to 1) pu
Dist: 3½l, 3l, 1l, 11l, nk. 6m 43.70s. (16 Ran).

(Herb M Stanley), J T R Dreaper

3650 Woodchester Credit Lyonnais Downshire Hurdle (Listed) (4-y-o and up) £21,800 2m. . . . . (3:55)

4243³ FORTUNE AND FAME 7-11-8 B Sheridan, mid-div, smooth
prog 3 out, trkd ldr aftr nxt, led appr last, easily.
. . . . (9 to 4 on) 1
3369⁶ DEEP INAGH 8-11-3 D P Fagan, trkd ldr, prog to ld 3 out,
rdn aftr nxt, hdd and no extr appr last. . . . . . . (20 to 1) 2

3068 DANCING PADDY 6-11-8 C F Swan, led, 5 ls clr at second,
reduced advantage 4 out, hdd nxt, wknd entering strt.
. . . . 3
3424⁶ SHAWIYA (Ire) (bl) 5-11-2 J F Titley, rcd in 3rd pl, rdn aftr 3
out, no extr and wknd after nxt. 4
4223³ ROYAL DERBI 9-11-8 M Perret, rear, some hdway frm 2 out,
nvr on terms. 5
3248* COCK COCKBURN 8-11-8 R Dunwoody, al rear, lost tch
aftr 4 out. . . . . (10 to 1) 6
3427³ PADASHPAN (USA) 5-11-7 K F O'Brien, mid-div, lost pl 4
out, rdn and no imprsn aftr nxt. . . . . (16 to 1) 7
3248⁵ ROCKET DANCER 8-11-8 P Carberry, al rear, lost tch aftr
4 out. . . . . (66 to 1) 8
Dist: 7l, 6l, 2l, 6l. 3m 59.20s. (8 Ran).

(Michael W J Smurfit), D K Weld

3651 Coleman Tunnelling Handicap Chase (Listed) (5-y-o and up) £8,625 2m 5f . . . . (4:30)

3391² VISIBLE DIFFERENCE [-] 8-10-8 K F O'Brien, hld up, prog 3
out, led aftr nxt, rdn and styd on strly frm last. (6 to 1) 1
3614⁴ ALL THE ACES [-] 7-10-4 P Carberry, trkd ldr, ev ch 2 out,
rdn appr last, kpt on wl. . . . . (10 to 1) 2
2698⁵ THIRD QUARTER [-] 9-10-3 C F Swan, hld up, prog 3 fs
out, chlgd appr last, rdn and no extr. . . . . (10 to 1) 3
2754 PARLIAMENT HALL [-] 8-10-6 T Horgan, wl plcd, led 4th till
aftr 2 out, rallied appr last, wknd r-in. . . . . . . (20 to 1) 4
3612⁶ TRY A BRANDY [-] 12-10-2 S H O'Donovan, mid-div, mstk
4th, kpt on one pace 3 out. . . . . (20 to 1) 5
5229³ FOREST SUN [-] 9-10-13 G Bradley, hld up, prog 6th, ev ch
3 out, rdn aftr nxt, no extr. . . . . (15 to 8 fav) 6
3371 LADY BAR [-] 7-10-0 P M Verling, mid-div, prog 5 out, rdn
and lost pl 3 out, kpt on one pace. . . . . (10 to 1) 7
3324 MERAPI [-] 8-10-9 F Woods, trkd ldrs, ev ch 2 out, rdn,
wknd appr last. . . . . (10 to 1) 8
539 GRATTAN PARK [-] 9-10-0 J Magee, mid-div, rdn 3 out,
wknd aftr nxt. . . . . (14 to 1) 9
3425 FOURTH OF JULY [-] 10-10-12 J P Banahan, mid-div, rdn 3
out, wknd aftr nxt. . . . . (7 to 1) 10
3121⁶ GARAMYCIN [-] 12-11-8 B Sheridan, mid-div, rdn 3 out, sn
wknd. . . . . (20 to 1) 11
3391¹ FINAL TUB [-] 11-11-0 C O'Dwyer, mstks, al rear. (10 to 1) 12
3389² DESERT LORD [-] 8-10-4 J F Titley, led to 4th, wl plcd till
rdn and wknd aftr 2 out, eased. . . . .(8 to 1) 13
Dist: 2l, sht-hd, 4½l, 5l. 5m 44.20s. (13 Ran).

(Patrick Heffernan), Patrick Heffernan

3652 Kilkea Castle Champion Hunters' Chase (5-y-o and up) £13,000 3m 1f . . . . (5:00)

3370* ELEGANT LORD (Ire) 6-11-11 Mr E Bolger, ... (2 to 1 on) 1
3313* TEAPLANTER 11-11-11 Mr R Russell, ...(9 to 4) 2
3527³ SOUTH OF THE BORDER (bl) 8-10-13 Mr K O'Sullivan,
. . . . (33 to 1) 3
3295 LAURA'S PURSUIT (Ire) 5-10-6 Mr G F Ryan, ... (33 to 1) 4
3610* LINEKER 7-11-8 (4ex) Mr G J Harford, ... (14 to 1) 5
3527 WHAT THING (bl) 7-10-13 Mr T J Murphy, ... (33 to 1) 6
EXEMPLAR (Ire) 6-11-4 Miss L Townsley, ... (20 to 1) f
3611* HANDYFELLOW 9-11-8 (4ex) Miss J Gayfer, ... (14 to 1) ur
3527 FUNNY BUSINESS 7-11-4 Mr D M O'Brien, ... (50 to 1) ur
BALD JOKER 9-11-8 Mr C A McBratney, ... (20 to 1) pu
3527⁴ THE VICARETTE (Ire) 6-10-13 Mr P Cashman, ... (33 to 1) pu
3370 DARA'S COURSE (Ire) 5-10-6 Mr A R Coonan, . . . (33 to 1) pu
GAELIC WARRIOR 7-11-4 Mr P J Millington, ... (40 to 1) pu
Dist: 4½l, 25l, 3½l, sht-hd. 7m 0.40s. (13 Ran).

(J P McManus), E Bolger

3653 Naas Traders I.N.H. Flat Race (5-y-o and up) £6,900 2m. . . . . (5:30)

3393² TOURIST ATTRACTION (Ire) 6-11-9 (3*) Mrs J M Mullins,
. . . . (6 to 1) 1
2869* VENTANA CANYON (Ire) 5-12-3 Mr P Fenton, . . (7 to 4 fav) 2
3394⁵ GLINT OF EAGLES (Ire) 5-11-3 (7*) Mr S McCarthy, (12 to 1) 3
3276⁵ ROSTARR (Ire) 5-11-12 Mr A P O'Brien, ... (8 to 1) 4
MAORI'S DELIGHT 5-10-12 (7*) Mr B Heffernan, . . (14 to 1) 5
3124² TREANAREE (Ire) 5-11-3 (7*) Mr D K Budds, ... (16 to 1) 6
9907 MR GLYNN (Ire) 5-11-3 (7*) Mr T J Murphy, ... (33 to 1) 7
2056² MOYGANNON COURT (Ire) 5-11-5 (5*) Mr H F Cleary,
. . . . (10 to 1) 8
3124⁶ PARADISE ROAD 5-11-10 P F Graffin, ... (14 to 1) 9
3250 CAILIN GLAS (Ire) 5-10-12 (7*) P Henley, ... (50 to 1) 10
3276⁷ DANGEROUS LADY (Ire) 5-11-3 (7*) Mr D Marnane, (50 to 1) 11
2989⁵ TIRCONNAIL (Ire) 5-11-3 (7*) Mr B M Cash, ... (20 to 1) 12
2989³ SCENIC ROUTE (Ire) 5-11-3 (7*) Miss C E Hyde, . . (4 to 1) 13
3525 SPANKERS HILL (Ire) 5-12-3 Mr J P J Durkan, ... (25 to 1) 14
1820⁴ DUDDON SANDS (Ire) 5-11-7 (3*) Mr J A Nash, . . (13 to 2) 16
SHORTSTAFF (Ire) 5-11-3 (7*) Mr A K Wyse, ... (20 to 1) 17
2620³ CARRAIG-AN-OIR (Ire) 5-11-5 (5*) Mr W M O'Sullivan,
. . . . (25 to 1) 18
2924⁷ UP FOR RANSOME (Ire) 5-11-3 (7*) Mr K Whelan, (50 to 1) 19
3508 MAHANKHALI (Ire) 5-11-3 (7*) Mr D W Cullen, . . . (33 to 1) 20
3394 IOLARA (Ire) 5-10-12 (7*) Mr M J Gilhooly, ... (50 to 1) 21
BEET STATEMENT (Ire) 5-11-2 (3*) D Valentine, . . (33 to 1) 22

3552 SCEAL SIOG (Ire) 5-10-12 (7*) Mr E Norris, ... (20 to 1) 23
1383 EXCUSE ME (Ire) 5-11-10 Mr A R Coonan, ... (25 to 1) 24
      MASTER HUNTER (Ire) 5-11-10 Mr A J Martin, ... (14 to 1) 25
      OFFICIAL PORTRAIT (Ire) 5-11-3 (7*) Mr D J Donegan,
      .... (33 to 1) 26
3327 ZINZAN BANK (Ire) 5-11-10 J P Dempsey, ... (50 to 1) 27
Dist: 2l, 7l, sht-hd, 2l. 4m 0.30s. (27 Ran).
                                    (North Kildare Racing Club), W P Mullins

PUNCHESTOWN (IRE) (good)
Thursday April 28th

3654 Sean Barrett Bloodstock Insurance
        Ltd Hurdle (0-127 4-y-o and up) £6,900
        2m... (2:00)

3526⁸ TUG OF PEACE [-] 7-11-6 (5*) J P Broderick, ... (25 to 1) 1
3083³ MISTER DRUM (Ire) [-] 5-10-7 (7*) Mr J T McNamara,
      .... (25 to 1) 2
3247² OPERA HAT (Ire) [-] 6-10-13 J Osborne, ... (10 to 1) 3
3504* STRALDI (Ire) [-] 6-10-11 D Murphy, ... (12 to 1) 4
3447* STRONG PLATINUM (Ire) [-] 6-10-10 (3ex) C O'Dwyer,
      .... (7 to 2) jt-fav) 5
3369 FERRYCARRIG HOTEL (Ire) [-] 5-11-0 D H O'Connor,
      .... (10 to 1) 6
3083 SUPER MIDGE [-] 7-11-0 R Dunwoody, ... (50 to 1) 7
1608* SEA GALE (Ire) [-] 6-10-7 C F Swan, ... (8 to 1) 8
3528³ FINNEGANS WAKE [-] 7-10-7 K P Gaule, ... (33 to 1) 9
2279⁶ KEPPOLS PRINCE [-] 7-10-4 A Powell, ... (50 to 1) 10
3294⁹ MERRY PEOPLE (Ire) [-] 6-10-12 M Dwyer, ... (20 to 1) 11
3369 THE SHAUGHRAUN [-] 8-11-6 T Horgan, ... (14 to 1) 12
2609⁴ SIMENON [-] 8-11-6 J P Banahan, ... (33 to 1) 13
3697 IF YOU SAY YES (Ire) [-] 6-10-7 A Maguire, ... (10 to 1) 14
2054⁵ DASHING ROSE [-] 6-10-9 P Carberry, ... (16 to 1) 15
      DONE INSTANTLY [-] 9-11-3 (3*) T P Treacy, ... (14 to 1) 16
3526 GLEN MONEY [-] 8-11-7 L P Cusack, ... (50 to 1) 17
3369² FAMILY WAY [-] 7-11-5 F Woods, ... (7 to 2 jt-fav) 18
2988² DEEP THYNE (Ire) [-] 6-10-7 S H O'Donovan, ... (33 to 1) 19
3367⁵ GREEN GLEN (USA) [-] 5-11-8 B Sheridan, ... (16 to 1) 20
3072² KINROSS [-] 7-10-4 (3*) T J Mitchell, ... (100 to 1) 21
3613⁶ MONALEE RIVER (Ire) [-] 6-11-8 K F O'Brien, ... (7 to 1) f
3468⁴ MISS LIME [-] 7-10-8 (7*) R A Hennessy, ... (14 to 1) pu
      FAY LIN [-] 7-11-3 G Bradley, ... (25 to 1) pu
3080⁶ MALIHABAD (Ire) [-] 5-10-11 F J Flood, ... (16 to 1) pu
Dist: 3l, 2½l, 2½l, 4l. 3m 54.00s. (25 Ran).
                                             (W J Austin), W J Austin

3655 Cox's Cash & Carry Chase (La Touche
        Cup) (5-y-o and up) £6,900 4m 1f (2:30)

2551⁶ LOVELY CITIZEN 11-11-1 (5*) Mr W M O'Sullivan, (16 to 1) 1
3425 NEW MILL HOUSE 11-11-6 T Horgan, ... (6 to 1) 2
635 BIRDIE'S PRINCE 9-11-6 C O'Dwyer, ... (33 to 1) 3
      MR MURRHILL (bl) 13-10-13 (7*) Mr W Ewing, ... (10 to 1) 4
1577⁴ HAVE A BARNEY 13-11-11 P Carberry, ... (9 to 1) 5
3295 FAIRY MIST (Ire) 6-10-13 (7*) Mr D A Harney, ... (25 to 1) 6
3336⁹ LEAGALINE 12-11-6 R Dunwoody, ... (16 to 1) 7
3272⁴ ITS A SNIP 9-11-4 (7*) Mr G Behan, ... (20 to 1) 8
3463³ ALL JEFF (Fr) (bl) 10-12-2 Mr E Bolger, ... (6 to 4 fav) 9
3611⁷ TLAQUEPAQUE (bl) 10-11-6 S R Murphy, ... (50 to 1) f
3504 MONEY MADE 7-10-13 (7*) Mr K Whelan, ... (33 to 1) f
      ADELAURE (Ire) 8-11-6 S McNeill, ... (66 to 1) ur
2922² DUSKY LADY 8-11-6 G M O'Neill, ... (9 to 1) ur
3611 GENERALANAESTHETIC 9-11-2³ (7*) Mr D J Donegan,
      .... (40 to 1) ur
2035⁹ PEJAWI 7-10-12 (3*) Mr A J Nash, ... (25 to 1) ur
3293 TEL D'OR 9-11-2³ (7*) Mr P J Millington, ... (14 to 1) ref
3524 OPRYLAND 9-12-7 Mr A R Coonan, ... (9 to 1) pu
      FEORES HILL 9-11-1 (5*) P A Roche, ... (33 to 1) pu
2619 LISNAVARAGH 8-11-1 (5*) J P Broderick, ... (33 to 1) pu
3392⁵ TASSE DU THE 7-11-6 Mr A J Martin, ... (12 to 1) pu
Dist: Sht-hd, 2l, 25l, 6l. 9m 40.10s. (20 Ran).
                                   (E J O'Sullivan), Eugene M O'Sullivan

3656 Murphys Irish Stout Champion Four
        Year Old Hurdle (Listed) £27,250 2m
        .... (3:05)

3369⁸ GLENSTAL FLAGSHIP (Ire) 11-0 C F Swan, trkd ldrs, rdn
      into second 2 out, led appr last, styd on strly... (6 to 1) 1
2699² MAGIC FEELING (Ire) 10-9 R Dunwoody, wl plcd, led 3 out,
      hdd appr last, kpt on und pres....................... (2 to 1) 2
3406* TROPICAL LAKE (Ire) 10-9 K F O'Brien, prog into 3rd 2 out,
      rdn and no extr appr last................... (9 to 4 fav) 3
3482³ RUSTY REEL 11-0 H Campbell, prog frm mid-div betw last
      2, kpt on r-in............................... (16 to 1) 4
3246² KHARASAR (Ire) 11-0 R A Hennessy, mid-div, travelling wl
      in 5th 2 out, rdn and no extr appr last......... (20 to 1) 5
3062² MOORISH 11-0 D Murphy, prog track ldrs 2 out, rdn and
      kpt on strt, fnshd lme........................ (5 to 2) 6
2864⁴ ANDANTE (Ire) 10-9 T J O'Sullivan, prmnt to hfwy, no
      imprsn 2 out................................ (20 to 1) 7
3321* MICKS DELIGHT (Ire) 11-0 A Maguire, rear, rdn 2 out, no
      rch ldrs................................... (10 to 1) 8

3406⁴ SHIRLEY'S DELIGHT (Ire) 10-9 P Carberry, mstk second,
      rear and rdn 6th, some prog appr 2 out, not rch ldrs.
      .... (6 to 1) 9
3321⁴ MOUSSAHIM (USA) 11-0 L P Cusack, nvr better than mid-
      div.. (33 to 1) 10
3246 ANUSHA 10-9 J P Broderick, trkd ldrs till rdn and wknd 3
      out.. (20 to 1) 11
3321³ BISSTAMI (Ire) 11-0 G M O'Neill, al rear.......... (25 to 1) 12
1111* LUSTRINO (USA) (bl) 11-0 Mr J A Nash, led till appr 3 out,
      wknd quickly................................ (14 to 1) 13
3466³ PUSH THE BUTTON (Ire) 10-9 F Woods, wl plcd till rdn
      and wknd bef 3 out.......................... (33 to 1) 14
Dist: 2½l, 3½l, ¾l, ½l, ½l. 3m 55.10s. (14 Ran).
                                             (Joseph Crowley), A P O'Brien

3657 Davenport Handicap Hurdle (Listed)
        (4-y-o and up) £8,625 3m....... (3:45)

3292* ULTRA FLUTTER [-] 7-10-6 K F O'Brien, prog to track ldrs
      tenth, led bef 3 out, rdn appr last, styd on strly. (7 to 2) 1
3267³ TIME FOR A RUN [-] 7-11-6 C F Swan, prog into 3rd 2 out,
      chlgd appr last, no extr...................... (5 to 2 fav) 2
3068³ STEEL DAWN [-] 7-10-0 A Maguire, prog into 5th 2 out, rdn
      and no extr betw last two.................... (7 to 2) 3
1851⁸ ALWAYS IN TROUBLE [-] 7-10-1² F Woods, prog frm mid-
      div to chase wnr 3 out, wknd nxt............ (12 to 1) 4
2846⁵ KNOCKNACARRA LAD [-] 9-10-0 T J Mitchell, rear till styd
      on frm 3 out, not rch ldrs.................... (33 to 1) 5
3390² LOVE AND PORTER (Ire) [-] 6-10-0 D H O'Connor, prog into
      3rd 3 out, rdn and wknd nxt................. (14 to 1) 6
3384² CASTIGLIERO (Fr) [-] 6-10-11 G Bradley, wl plcd, rdn and
      no imprsn 2 out............................. (12 to 1) 7
3413⁵ RISING WATERS (Ire) [-] 6-10-5 S McNeill, nvr better than
      mid-div.................................... (25 to 1) 8
3408 TINDARI (Fr) [-] 6-10-7 P Williams, mid-div, rdn appr 3 out,
      not rch ldrs................................ (14 to 1) 9
584⁵ CUILIN BUI (Ire) [-] 6-10-0 C O'Brien, wl plcd till rdn and
      wknd 4 out................................. (33 to 1) 10
2939⁴ RIYADH DANCER (Ire) [-] 6-11-4 M Duffy, al rear. (25 to 1) 11
2751⁵ FRIGID COUNTESS [-] 7-10-0 L A Hurley, led chasing grp,
      rdn and wknd 4 out.......................... (20 to 1) 12
3273* BRINDLEY HOUSE [-] 7-10-5 D Morris, led 1st, clr 4th, hdd
      and wknd bef 3 out.......................... (20 to 1) 13
3414³ WHAT A QUESTION (Ire) [-] 6-10-11 C O'Dwyer, mid-div,
      some prog tenth, sn btn..................... (12 to 1) 14
      BOTHAR NA SPEIRE [-] 9-10-0 R Dunwoody, wl plcd till
      rdn and wknd 4 out.......................... (33 to 1) 15
3273⁴ GRANADOS (USA) [-] 6-10-0 J P Banahan, al rear. (66 to 1) 16
787 FIXED ASSETS [-] 7-10-0 T Horgan, al rear....... (66 to 1) 17
2918² DIRECT RUN [-] 7-10-0 J P Broderick, al rear..... (33 to 1) 18
3241 VINEYARD SPECIAL [-] 8-10-0 P Carberry, prmnt till lost pl
      9th, tld off................................. (100 to 1) 19
3247 PRACTICE RUN (Ire) [-] 6-10-0 J Osborne, prmnt till rdn
      and lost pl 4 out, pld bef 2 out.............. (33 to 1) pu
3366* TWIN RAINBOW [-] 7-10-0 L P Cusack, al rear, pld up bef
      last....................................... (12 to 1) pu
Dist: 4½l, 1l, 13l, 4½l. 6m 6.70s. (21 Ran).
                                        (Donal Higgins), Michael Hourigan

3658 Bank Of Ireland (Colliers) Novice
        Chase (Listed) (5-y-o and up) £16,350
        2m... (4:15)

3404⁵ OH SO GRUMPY 6-11-8 J Osborne, prog track ldrs 8th,
      chlgd appr last, led and quickened r-in....... (20 to 1) 1
3404³ THUMBS UP 8-11-11 R Dunwoody, trkd ldrs, second 2
      out, dsptd lde appr last, kpt on............... (9 to 1) 2
3389 LADY OLEIN (Ire) 6-10-13 C F Swan, mid-div, mstk 3rd,
      styd on frm 4 out, nrst finish................. (8 to 1) 3
3465³ WINDS OF WAR 9-11-8 C O'Dwyer, wl plcd, led appr 8th
      till jnd approaching last, wknd.............. (20 to 1) 4
3612⁴ GLENCLOUD (Ire) 6-11-11 G M O'Neill, prmnt till lost pl
      8th, styd on ag'n strt....................... (14 to 1) 5
3024⁵ MUBADIR (USA) 6-11-8 P Carberry, mstk in mid-div 6th,
      rdn 3 out, not rch ldrs...................... (7 to 2) 6
3404² JIMMY THE GILLIE 8-11-4 G Upton, led till appr 8th,
      wknd....................................... (3 to 1) 7
3389³ FABRICATOR 8-11-11 K F O'Brien, al rear....... (16 to 1) 8
3426⁴ BROCKLEY COURT 7-11-8 J P Banahan, mid-div, rdn and
      btn 3 out.................................. (8 to 1) 9
3369 PRINCESS CASILIA 9-11-3 B Sheridan, mstk second, al
      rear....................................... (10 to 1) 10
Dist: 4½l, ¾l, sht-hd, 10l. 4m 51.10s. (10 Ran).
                                    (Mrs E Queally), Mrs John Harrington

3659 Castlemartin Stud Handicap Chase
        (Listed) (5-y-o and up) £11,500 3m 1f
        .... (4:45)

3612⁷ COMMERCIAL ARTIST [-] 8-11-5 C N Bowens, prog to
      track ldrs 9th, led bef 3 out, rdn nxt, styd on und pres
      r-in.. (10 to 1) 1
3324 HIGH PEAK [-] 10-10-13 C F Swan, wl plcd, led appr 8th
      till bef nxt, rdn 3 out, kpt on und pres frm next.
      .... (7 to 4 fav) 2
3041 BISHOPS HALL [-] 8-11-5 G Bradley, trkd ldrs, ev ch 3 out,
      rdn and no imprsn betw last 2................ (6 to 1) 3

3324* SON OF WAR [-] 7-11-11 F Woods, *led 1st till appr 5th, niggled alng in mid-div 8th, lost pl tenth, styd on frm 2 out*.......................................(5 to 1) 4
3425 CAPTAIN BRANDY [-] 9-10-4 A Maguire, *mid-div till ld appr 4 out, hdd and wknd bef nxt*.............(6 to 1) 5
2720³ SECOND SCHEDUAL [-] 9-12-0 R Dunwoody, *wtd wth, trkd ldrs 4 out, rdn nxt, no imprsn*.............(9 to 2) 6
3391⁴ JOE WHITE [-] 8-10-0 S R Murphy, *al rear*........(14 to 1) 7
3425 RUST NEVER SLEEPS [-] 10-10-12 P Carberry, *al rear*. ....(20 to 1) 8
3649 SPEAKING TOUR (USA) [-] 6-10-0 D H O'Connor, *led 5th till appr 8th, led 9th till bef 4 out, wknd quickly*. (20 to 1) 9
3324⁹ MASS APPEAL [-] 9-10-2 B Sheridan, *wl plcd till rdn and wknd 11th, tld off nxt*........................(20 to 1) 10
Dist: 4½l, 16l, 8l, 3l. 6m 42.10s. (10 Ran).
(Michael J O'Neill), Victor Bowens

3660 Jack White Memorial EBF Champion INH Flat Race (4-y-o and up) £9,750 2m ....(5:15)

3042² ARIES GIRL 5-12-1 Mr E Norris,...................(7 to 2) 1
3372* CHEF COMEDIEN (Ire) 4-11-7 Mr T P Hyde,.. (11 to 4 fav) 2
3372⁶ GAMBOLLING DOC (Ire) 4-11-7 Mr B R Hamilton, (20 to 1) 3
3042⁷ DOMINIE (Ire) 6-12-1 Mr D Marnane,............ (20 to 1) 4
3291⁶ THATS A SECRET 6-12-4 Mr P English,...........(33 to 1) 5
3042* MUCKLEMEG (Ire) 6-11-13 Mr P Fenton,...........(7 to 2) 6
1076² HOTEL MINELLA 7-12-4 Mr A P O'Brien,.........(10 to 1) 7
2613* DOONANDORAS (Ire) 6-12-4 Mr H F Cleary,........(8 to 1) 8
3080⁵ THE SUBBIE (Ire) 5-12-3 Mr J P Dempsey,....... (12 to 1) 9
2080⁴ GALLOWS HILL (Ire) 5-12-0 Mrs J M Mullins,......(10 to 1) 10
2394* GAILY RUNNING (Ire) 5-12-0 Mr T Mullins,.........(9 to 2) 11
2989* FIFTH SYMPHONY (Ire) 5-12-0 Mr J A Nash,..... (16 to 1) 12
Dist: 6l, 5½l, ¾l, 3l. 3m 56.40s. (12 Ran).
(W E Sturt), Patrick Joseph Flynn

BANGOR (good to firm)
Friday April 29th
Going Correction: NIL

3661 Colwyn Bay Selling Hurdle (4-y-o and up) £2,123 2m 1f............... (5:45)

790⁴ MADAM GYMCRAK 4-10-5 R Marley, *jnd ldrs 3rd, led 5th, drw clr appr 2 out, pushed out r-in*. (10 to 1 op 7 to 1) 1
3222 MOST INTERESTING 9-11-9 B Clifford, *wtd wth in rear, hdwy 3 out, ran on und pres r-in, not rch wnr*. (25 to 1) 2
1261³ VINEY (USA) 4-10-10 Peter Hobbs, *mstk 4th, prog appr 3 out, wnt second nxt, no extr frm last*. .....(100 to 30 fav op 4 to 1 tchd 11 to 2 and 5 to 1) 3
3594⁶ ANDRATH (Ire) 6-11-2 D Meade, *cl up till wknd 2 out*. .... (11 to 2 op 7 to 2) 4
3561 BATTLEPLAN 9-12-0 W Humphreys, *improved hfwy, hld whn hit 2 out*..................... (33 to 1 op 20 to 1) 5
1370⁶ RICHMOND (Ire) 6-11-8 D Wilkinson, *nvr rchd ldrs*. .... (16 to 1 op 14 to 1) 6
3501⁴ LOR MOSS 14-12-0 M A FitzGerald, *led to second, led 4th, blun and hdd nxt, wknd appr 2 out*. .... (16 to 1 op 14 to 1) 7
3214 KAHER (USA) 7-11-13 (7*) A Shakespeare, *led second to 4th, wknd appr 2 out*...(9 to 1 op 7 to 1 tchd 10 to 1) 8
2960⁷ MUST BE MAGICAL (USA) 6-10-13 (3*) T Eley, *cl up till wknd quickly 2 out*.....(6 to 1 op 5 to 1 tchd 13 to 2) 9
2900 ALICANTE 7-11-3 (5*) Mr D McCain, *nvr in the hunt*. .... (20 to 1 op 14 to 1) 10
3559 SEEMENOMORE 5-10-11 T Wall, *nvr a factor*. .... (33 to 1 op 25 to 1) 11
3491 MONTIFIORE AVENUE 8-11-1 (7*) S Lycett, *al beh*. .... (25 to 1 op 20 to 1) 12
2401 CAPITAL LAD 5-11-2 R Garritty, *mid-div whn mstk 3 out, sn struggling*.....................(33 to 1 op 25 to 1) 13
3395 FOXY LASS 5-10-11 Mr J Cambidge, *al in rear*. .... (33 to 1 op 25 to 1) 14
2628* CHAGHATAI (USA) (bl) 8-11-8 Mr B Leavy, *prmnt, blun 3rd, lost pl hfwy, tld off*.............(14 to 1 tchd 16 to 1) 15
3395 WHITEHOUSE GEM 11-10-8 (3*) D Meredith, *wl plcd till rdn and wknd aftr 5th, tld off*.....(33 to 1 op 25 to 1) 16
3017 PALM SWIFT 8-10-11 Mr G Brown, *mid-div whn bad mstk 4th, sn toiling, tld off*............ (33 to 1 op 25 to 1) 17
2130 KUTAN (Ire) (bl) 4-10-7 (3*) R Farrant, *wl plcd till wknd quickly aftr 6th, sn pld up, sddl slpd*. .... (14 to 1 op 12 to 1) pu
3211⁷ CAPTAIN TANDY (Ire) 5-11-2 D Bridgwater, *whipped round strt, al in rear, tld off whn pld up bef 2 out*. .... (7 to 1 op 14 to 1 tchd 16 to 1) pu
Dist: 1¼l, 4l, 9l, ½l, ½l, 1l, 1¾l, ¾l, 2½l, 6l. 3m 59.20s. a 9.20s (19 Ran).
SR: -/1/-/-/-/-/ (The Gymcrak Thoroughbred Racing Club), G Holmes

3662 Rhyl Conditional Jockeys' Handicap Chase (0-125 5-y-o and up) £3,517 2 ½m 110yds.................... (6:15)

3560⁹ THE MASTER GUNNER [109] 10-11-4 R Davis, *al gng wl, led appr 2 out, sn clr, easily*....... (10 to 1 op 8 to 1) 1
3495* BRADWALL [101] 10-10-10 S Wynne, *beh, pckd 1st, mstk 7th, styd on und pres appr 2 out, no ch wth wnr*. ....(7 to 2 op 3 to 1) 2
3443² BALDA BOY [103] 10-10-12 R Farrant, *led, mstk 8th (water), hdd nxt, led 11th till headed and no extr appr 2 out*..................(13 to 2 op 6 to 1 tchd 7 to 1) 3
3560² MISTER FEATHERS [91] 13-10-0 T Jenks, *trkd ldrs, mstk tenth, rdn aftr nxt, sn no imprsn*. ....(5 to 2 fav op 9 to 4 tchd 11 to 4) 4
1649³ PATS MINSTREL [106] (bl) 9-11-1 J Burke, *chsd ldr, led 9th to 11th, wknd aftr 3 out*........... (13 to 2 op 6 to 1) 5
3582 PINEMARTIN [94] 11-10-0 (3*) B Harding, *wtd wth, rdn and effrt tenth, hit 3 out, eased whn btn betw last 2*. .... (11 to 2 op 5 to 1 tchd 6 to 1) 6
3223⁵ ORCHIPEDZO [91] 9-9-11 (3*) Judy Davies, *took str hold, lost tch frm 11th, tld off whn pld up bef 2 out*. .... (50 to 1 op 33 to 1) pu
3490⁵ ON THE TEAR [91] 8-10-0 D Meredith, *slwly away, rdn alng tenth, struggling whn mstk 12th, tld off when pld up bef 2 out*................................. (33 to 1) pu
Dist: 6l, 1¾l, 6l, 12l, sht-hd. 5m 2.50s. a 11.50s (8 Ran).
(Major-Gen R L T Burges), K C Bailey

3663 Red Mills Irish Horse Feeds Novices' Handicap Hurdle (4-y-o and up) £2,873 2m 1f..........................(6:45)

3587² DON'T FORGET MARIE (Ire) [82] 4-11-7 (3*) A Procter, *wtd wth, prog 6th, lft in ld last, drvn out*. ....(4 to 1 fav op 3 to 1) 1
3511⁷ SHARP DANCE [76] 5-11-4 M Richards, *drpd out strt, improved frm rear 6th, lft second and impeded last, no extr*...................(13 to 2 op 8 to 1 tchd 6 to 1) 2
3496⁶ HECTOR MARIO [75] 6-11-0 (3*) R Davis, *slwly away, mstk 4th, hdwy frm 3 out, styd on same pace r-in*. .... (12 to 1 op 10 to 1) 3
3494⁶ NEWHALL PRINCE [68] 6-10-5 (5*) D Leahy, *prog hfwy, outpcd 2 out, btn whn hmpd by loose horse r-in*. .... (16 to 1 op 14 to 1 tchd 20 to 1) 4
3281 SWIFT ROMANCE (Ire) [74] 6-10-13 (3*) R Farrant, *hrd drvn and no prog appr 2 out*............(12 to 1 op 8 to 1) 5
3441² MARINERS LOVE [66] 8-10-5 (3*) T Jenks, *handily plcd, no imprsn frm 3 out*....................(7 to 1 op 4 to 1) 6
3334⁵ FOURTH IN LINE (Ire) [80] 6-11-8 M A FitzGerald, *toiling frm 5th, tld off*....................... (12 to 1 op 8 to 1) 7
1629⁴ CALL ME EARLY [82] 9-11-10 M Brennan, *shrtlvd effrt 6th, tld off*..................................(16 to 1 op 14 to 1) 8
1592 COME ON LUCY [59] 5-10-1 D Bridgwater, *effrt frm 3 out, in tch whn hng rght nxt, wknd quickly, tld off*. ....(20 to 1 op 25 to 1 tchd 16 to 1) 9
3046⁶ THE GREY TEXAN [74] 5-11-2 Richard Guest, *cl up, drvn alng 6th, sn lost pl, tld off*....... (14 to 1 tchd 16 to 1) 10
3281⁴ GEORGE LANE [65] 6-10-7 J Lodder, *wth ldrs gng wl, led 5th till f last*.......................(7 to 1 tchd 8 to 1) f
3441³ PRINCETHORPE [68] 7-10-7 (3*) D Meredith, *not fluent, drvn alng 4th, sn lost pl, beh whn pld up bef 6th*. ....(7 to 1 op 5 to 1) pu
3617 LEINTHALL FOX [79] (bl) 8-11-7 T Wall, *led, pushed alng and hdd 5th, sn struggling, tld off whn pld up bef last*. ....(12 to 1 tchd 10 to 1) pu
2057 QUINBERRY [58] 6-10-0 J R Kavanagh, *prmnt to hfwy, tld off whn pld up bef 2 out*...................... (33 to 1) pu
Dist: 2l, 5l, 3½l, 2l, 1½l, 20l, ¾l, 2l, dist. 3m 56.80s. a 6.80s (14 Ran).
SR: 28/20/14/3/7/-/ (Gordon Mytton), A Bailey

3664 J. Scott Furnishers Marchwiel Novices' Handicap Chase (5-y-o and up) £3,594 2m 1f 110yds............(7:15)

3400⁵ BEAUFAN [78] 7-10-4 Gary Lyons, *al wl plcd, slight ld last, rdn out*............................ (8 to 1 op 7 to 1) 1
HOT PURSUIT [74] 8-9-9 (5*) D Fortt, *patiently rdn, hdwy 9th, led 3 out till last, no extr*.... (20 to 1 tchd 25 to 1) 2
3000* HOWGILL [84] 8-10-7 (3*) S Wynne, *in rear till styd on appr 2 out, nrst finish*...(9 to 2 op 5 to 1 tchd 4 to 1) 3
3585² MAGGOTS GREEN [76] 7-9-13 (3*) R Farrant, *chsd ldr, led 8th, mstk and hdd 3 out, sn btn*. ....(9 to 4 fav op 5 to 2 tchd 11 to 4) 4
2683 CARTON [90] 7-11-2 G Upton, *settled in rear, lost tch frm 9th, tld off*........................ (12 to 1 tchd 14 to 1) 5
2736⁵ HEATHVIEW [77] 7-9-10 (7*) F Leahy, *trkd ldrs, mstk 4th, prog to chal whn hit 3 out, sn lost pl*. .... (15 to 2 op 7 to 1 tchd 8 to 1) 6
3456* MISTER ODDY [98] 8-11-7 (3*) T Jenks, *led, mstk 7th, hdd nxt, sn rdn and wknd, tld off*. .... (5 to 2 op 9 to 4 tchd 11 to 4) 7
Dist: 2l, 6l, 9l, 10l, 8l, 30l. 4m 12.00s. a 6.40s (7 Ran).
SR: 12/6/10/-/ (D Craddock), B R Cambidge

3665 Mold Novices' Hunters' Chase (5-y-o and up) £1,662 3m 110yds...... (7:45)

3493* SUNNY MOUNT 8-12-8 Mr J Greenall, *wl plcd, stumbled appr 8th, pckd 11th (water), slight ld 2 out, rdn and wndrd last, edgd lft r-in, all out*. ....(11 to 8 on op 7 to 4 on tchd 5 to 4 on) 1

SCALLY MUIRE 10-11-2 (7*) Mr A H Crow, *led to 3rd, led ag'n 11th to 2 out, rnwd effrt und pres r-in.*
...................................(4 to 1 op 7 to 2)   2

AH JIM LAD 10-11-7 (7*) Mr M S Williamson, *rcd wide, led 3rd to 11th, wknd 14th, lft poor third 2 out.*
...................................(20 to 1 op 16 to 1)   3

FOWLING PIECE 9-11-7 (7*) Mr M Harris, *wtd wth, mstk 8th, rdn and lost tch 14th, tld off.* (25 to 1 op 20 to 1)   4

MY NOMINEE 6-11-7 (7*) Mr A Griffith, *mstks 4th and 7th, lost tch 14th, tld off.*............... (16 to 1 op 14 to 1)   5

THE ARTFUL RASCAL 10-11-7 (7*) Mr C J B Barlow, *wl plcd, bumped 9th, 3rd and in tch whn f 3 out.*
...................................(11 to 2 op 5 to 1 tchd 6 to 1)   f

SNAPPIT 12-11-9 (5*) Mr D McCain, *in rear, mstk second, drvn alng hfwy, tld off whn pld up aftr 11th.*
...................................(33 to 1 op 25 to 1)   pu

3501 NORTHERN DAWN 12-11-7 (7*) Mr F Telford, *hld up, rdn sn aftr hfwy, mstk 13th, soon struggling, tld off whn pld up bef 3 out.*............... (100 to 1)   pu

Dist: ¾l, dist, 30l, 20l. 6m 13.00s. a 23.00s (8 Ran).

(J E Greenall), Miss C Saunders

3666 Prestatyn Novices' Hurdle (4-y-o and up) £2,389 3m ....(8:15)

3509² STRONG CASE (Ire) (bl) 6-11-9 R Dunwoody, *led to second, led 7th, wl clr 3 out, eased to a walk r-in, unchlgd.*
...................................(6 to 4 on op 2 to 1 on)   1

PERCY THROWER 7-11-3 D Bridgwater, *led second, mstk 3rd, awkward and hdd 7th, outpcd frm nxt.*
...................................(7 to 2 op 4 to 1 tchd 5 to 1)   2

3279⁸ ST MARTIN 6-11-0 (3*) T Jenks, *in rear, lft poor 3rd 8th, tld off.*......................(33 to 1 op 20 to 1)   3

3564 MASTER FRITH (bl) 6-11-3 W Humphreys, *pushed alng 5th, sn tld off.*...............(50 to 1 op 25 to 1)   4

3491⁵ GENERAL SHOT (v) 9-11-9 Diane Clay, *cl up, 3rd and gng wl whn pld up lme bef 8th.*.........(100 to 30 op 9 to 4)   pu

ALTHREY BLUE (Ire) 5-11-3 Gary Lyons, *not fluent, al in rear, tld off whn pld up aftr 7th.*
...................................(100 to 1 op 50 to 1 tchd 150 to 1)   pu

Dist: 20l, dist, dist. 5m 47.00s. (6 Ran).

(Mrs L M Sewell), M C Pipe

NEWTON ABBOT (good to firm)
Friday April 29th
Going Correction: MINUS 0.20 sec. per fur.

3667 Alliance And Leicester Building Society Amateur Riders Handicap Chase (0-125 5-y-o and up) £2,801 2m 110yds ....(2:25)

3116⁵ COTAPAXI [92] 9-9-11 (7*) Miss S Mitchell, *hld up, hdwy aftr 4 out, chsd ldr appr 2 out, led and blun last, drvn out r-in.*...............(11 to 2 op 9 to 2 tchd 7 to 1)   1

2981³ WINGSPAN (USA) [115] 10-11-6 (7*) Mr M Rimell, *led till hdd last, not quicken r-in.*
...................................(25 to 1 op 16 to 1 tchd 33 to 1)   2

3573⁷ GALAGAMES (USA) [99] 7-10-4 (7*) Mr G Baines, *chsd ldr, rdn 3 out, ev ch whn pckd 2 out, sn btn.*
...................................(11 to 1 op 6 to 1 tchd 12 to 1)   3

3573² MURPHY [99] 10-10-11 Mr J Durkan, *sent 3rd 4th, prmnt whn mstk 6th, lost pl aftr nxt, styd on one pace frm four out.*............(7 to 4 fav op 2 to 1 tchd 9 to 4)   4

3513³ AL HASHIMI [116] 10-11-7 (7*) Major G Wheeler, *mstks, beh frm 6th, styd on one pace from 3 out.* (6 to 1 op 4 to 1)   5

3106 GREENHEART [115] 11-11-6 (7*) Mr P Bull, *pressed ldr till rdn and wknd 5 out.*...............(100 to 1 op 25 to 1)   6

3556 TINAS LAD [105] 11-10-10 (7*) Mr G Hogan, *pressed ldr till lost pl aftr 7th, sn beh.*............(9 to 2 op 5 to 1)   7

3573* FANATICAL (USA) [88] (bl) 8-9-13⁶ (7*,7ex) Mr B Pollock, *hld up, 7th whn f 5 out, dead.*
...................................(9 to 2 op 7 to 2 tchd 11 to 2)   f

PANTECHNICON [88] 14-10-7 (7*) Mr D Puddy, *nvr wnt pace, lost tch 6th, tld off whn pld up bef 4 out.*
...................................(33 to 1 op 20 to 1)   pu

Dist: 4l, 8l, 10l, 7l, 20l, 1½l. 3m 59.00s. a 2.00s (9 Ran).

SR: 23/42/18/8/18/-/   (Mrs Barbara Lock), R J Hodges

3668 Boddingtons Bitter Conditional Jockeys' Selling Handicap Hurdle (4,5,6-y-o) £1,900 2m 1f ....(2:55)

3572* DANCING DANCER [65] (bl) 5-11-1 (7ex) R Darke, *hld up, cld on ldrs aftr 4th, led 2 out, drvn out.*
...................................(6 to 4 fav op 7 to 4 tchd 5 to 4)   1

3252⁵ VALIANTHE (USA) [65] (bl) 6-10-12 (3*) L Reynolds, *hld up, cld on ldrs aftr 5th, rdn and styd on wl betw last 2, kpt on r-in.*...............(6 to 1 op 5 to 2)   2

1597 ALMOST A PRINCESS [60] 6-10-10 P Carey, *led, jmpd slwly, hdd aftr 1st, led ag'n 3rd to 4th, styd cl up, ev ch appr 2 out, not quicken r-in.*
...................................(9 to 1 op 16 to 1 tchd 8 to 1)   3

3572⁸ COOCHIE [67] (bl) 5-11-3 D Matthews, *chsd ldg pair, cld up aftr 4th, close up and ev ch appr 2 out, sn wknd.*
...................................(8 to 1 tchd 10 to 1)   4

2652 IMAGERY [55] 4-10-2 (3*) Pat Thompson, *hld up in last pl, rdn and cld on ldrs aftr 5th, ev ch appr 2 out, sn wknd.*
...................................(16 to 1 op 12 to 1 tchd 20 to 1)   5

3012² CYRILL HENRY (Ire) [74] 5-11-10 C Burnett-Wells, *led aftr 1st, hdd 3rd, led nxt till 2 out, sn wknd.*
...................................(11 to 1 op 4 to 1)   6

3511⁶ TOOMUCH TOOSOON (Ire) [70] 6-11-6 S Curran, *hld up, cld on ldrs aftr 4th, pushed alng on ins aftr 3 out, sn btn.*.........(11 to 4 op 5 to 2 tchd 9 to 4 and 3 to 1)   7

Dist: 2l, 1¼l, 9l, 1l, 1¼l, 6l. 4m 5.70s. a 15.70s (7 Ran).

(A E C Electric Fencing Ltd (Hotline)), R G Frost

3669 Stella Artois Handicap Chase (0-140 5-y-o and up) £3,156 3¼m 110yds ....(3:30)

3532² SKERRY MEADOW [99] 10-11-4 (7*) Mr G Hogan, *hld up, struggling and outpcd aftr 6th, reminders aftr 13th, hmpd and lft in ld 5 out, hrd pressed after 3 out, all out.*
...................................(5 to 2 op 9 to 4)   1

3532 SKETCHER (NZ) [99] 11-10-0 R Greene, *mstks, sn last and struggling aftr 6th, lft moderate second 5 out, rallied after nxt, ev ch whn hng rght 2 out, not quicken.*
...................................(11 to 2 op 6 to 1 tchd 7 to 1)   2

3132³ LAKE TEEREEN [123] 9-11-10 T Grantham, *pressed ldr till led aftr 14th, f 5 out.*...............(11 to 4 op 6 to 4)   f

589* SKIPPING TIM [120] 15-11-7 R Dunwoody, *led till hdd aftr 14th, cl second whn blun and uns rdr 5 out.*
...................................(11 to 8 fav op Evens tchd 15 to 8)   ur

Dist: 2l. 6m 38.30s. a 18.30s (4 Ran).

(O J Carter), O J Carter

3670 Murphys Irish Stout Novices' Hurdle (4-y-o and up) £2,037 2m 1f .....(4:05)

3502* TEEN JAY (v) 4-11-9 J Osborne, *trkd ldrs, cl up and ev ch 3 out, rdn to ld last, ran on wl.*.......(2 to 1 op 6 to 4)   1

3334³ MERLINS WISH (USA) 5-11-7 R Dunwoody, *hld up in tch, wnt second aftr 3 out, led nxt, hdd last, rallied r-in, not quicken.*........(6 to 4 fav tchd 7 to 4 and 11 to 8)   2

3476⁷ VITAL WONDER 6-11-0 P Holley, *sn in tch, led aftr 4th, hdd 2 out, one pace.*...............(11 to 4 op 9 to 4)   3

3458 BOOLAVOGUE (Ire) 4-10-4 V Slattery, *hld up, beh 4th, hdwy aftr 5th, pushed alng after nxt, kpt on one pace.*
...................................(14 to 1 op 10 to 1 tchd 33 to 1)   4

MR SUNNYSIDE 8-11-0 J Frost, *prmnt till lost pl aftr 4th, ran on ag'n after 3 out, styd on one pace.*
...................................(33 to 1 op 20 to 1)   5

GATHERING 5-11-0 S McNeill, *slwly away, sn last, hdwy 5th, rdn and kpt on one pace aftr 3 out.*
...................................(20 to 1 op 10 to 1 tchd 25 to 1)   6

3339⁶ COURTING NEWMARKET 6-11-0 S Burrough, *hld up, effrt aftr 5th, chsd ldrs and in tch after 3 out, sn wknd.*
...................................(14 to 1 op 8 to 1)   7

3444² GYPSY CRYSTAL (USA) 4-10-4 W Irvine, *hld up, beh 4th, hdwy aftr 5th, kpt on one pace.*
...................................(25 to 1 op 33 to 1 tchd 40 to 1)   8

297⁸ GREEN'S STUBBS (bl) 7-11-0 B Powell, *led till aftr second, chsd ldrs till wknd after 5th.* (100 to 1 op 33 to 1)   9

3300 MARYLAND BOY (bl) 6-11-0 J Railton, *led aftr second, hdd after 4th, stdly wknd.*
...................................(150 to 1 op 50 to 1 tchd 200 to 1)   10

3365 ALFA VITA 8-10-9 I Shoemark, *mstk 1st, wl beh aftr 4th, sn tld off, pld up bef 2 out.*.......(66 to 1 op 33 to 1)   pu

3173⁶ FRIENDLY VIKING 4-10-9 Miss S Young, *wl beh aftr 3rd, tld off after nxt, pld up bef 2 out.* (100 to 1 op 33 to 1)   pu

Dist: 1½l, 8l, 20l, 7l, 1¼l, 3l, 2½l, 15l, 10l. 4m 0.80s. a 10.80s (12 Ran).

(F J Bush), S E Sherwood

3671 Newquay Steam Beer Novices' Chase (5-y-o and up) £2,983 2m 5f .....(4:40)

3534² CROSULA 6-11-9 R Dunwoody, *led, lft clr tenth, rdn 2 out, styd on wl.*
...................................(13 to 8 on op 9 to 4 on tchd 6 to 4 on)   1

3251⁸ BOLD STREET BLUES 7-11-4 L Harvey, *beh, mstk 1st, lft 3rd tenth, wnt second aftr nxt, chsd ldr, hrd rdn after 2 out, not quicken.*..............(14 to 1 op 8 to 1)   2

3363 GARSTON LA GAFFE 9-11-4 P Holley, *chsd ldr, lft second tenth, rdn and no imprsn frm 3 out.*
...................................(10 to 1 op 11 to 2)   3

3517⁷ LAND OF THE FREE 5-10-6 J Osborne, *beh, jmpd rght 7th, hmpd tenth, one pace frm 4 out.*
...................................(5 to 1 op 9 to 2 tchd 11 to 2)   4

3051⁴ ABSENT MINDS 8-10-13 Miss S Young, *pressed ldr till stdly wknd aftr tenth.*............(50 to 1 op 16 to 1)   5

1411 TIJUCA 15-10-11 (7*) Mr N Moore, *chsd ldr to 8th, lost tch tenth.*...............(33 to 1 op 16 to 1)   6

3297⁴ GRECIAN SAILOR 9-11-4 J Frost, *badly hmpd 1st, jmpd slwly second, lost tch aftr 9th.*.... (14 to 1 op 33 to 1)   7

3213⁴ QUAGO 6-10-13 B Powell, *chsd ldr to 7th, beh and struggling aftr nxt.*...............(33 to 1 op 16 to 1)   8

3400^{6} CARLINGFORD LIGHTS (Ire) 6-11-4 V Slattery, *wnt second 8th, ev ch whn f tenth.* ....(20 to 1 op 12 to 1 tchd 25 to 1) f
3097^{6} SHOCK TACTICS 7-11-4 S McNeill, *jmpd rght 1st, jumped very slwly, sn wl beh, last whn sddl slpd and uns rdr aftr 5th*..............(12 to 1 op 10 to 1 tchd 14 to 1) ur
3454^{9} FORCE 7-10-11 (7*) Mr S Joynes, *jmpd slwly, sn wl beh, tld off whn pld up and dismounted bef 4 out.* ....(100 to 1 op 33 to 1) pu
Dist: 1¾l, 25l, 5l, 3½l, 2½l, 4l, 1½l. 5m 11.30s. a 11.30s (11 Ran).
(Bisgrove Partnership), M C Pipe

3672 Heineken Draught Lager Handicap Hurdle (0-130 4-y-o and up) £2,242 2m 1f............................ (5:10)

3302* CHARCOAL BURNER [86] 9-9-13^{4} (5*) S Fox, *led till aftr 1st, trkd ldr till led ag'n after 3 out, drvn out r-in, styd on wl*..............(7 to 2 op 4 to 1 tchd 100 to 30) 1
3254^{6} HEAD TURNER [86] 6-10-0 P Holley, *hld up, hdwy to chase ldrs aftr 4th, wnt second appr 2 out, hit second last, rdn, not quicken r-in.* ....(13 to 8 fav op 7 to 4 tchd 6 to 4) 2
VISION OF FREEDOM (Ire) [86] 6-10-0 W McFarland, *chsd ldg pair, wnt second briefly aftr 4th, drvn alng 3 out, sn one pace*..........(11 to 1 op 6 to 1 tchd 12 to 1) 3
3574 CORRIN HILL [102] 7-11-2 A Tory, *hld up, pushed alng and not go pace aftr 5th, sn beh*....(11 to 1 op 8 to 1) 4
3444* PREROGATIVE [110] (v) 4-11-10 R Dunwoody, *led aftr 1st, mstk 3 out, hrd rdn, hdd appr nxt, sn wknd.* ....(7 to 4 op 5 to 4) 5
Dist: 1¼l, 1l, 2l, 15l. 3m 58.30s. a 8.30s (5 Ran).
(T M Schwalm), Mrs J G Retter

SEDGEFIELD (good to firm)
Friday April 29th
Going Correction: MINUS 0.10 sec. per fur.

3673 Campbells Selling Handicap Hurdle (4-y-o and up) £2,184 2m 5f 110yds .... (5:30)

3553^{4} BUCKRA MELLISUGA [90] 10-11-7 A Maguire, *nvr far away, led 4 out, clr bef 2 out, ran on wl.* ....(3 to 1 fav op 7 to 2 tchd 11 to 4) 1
1238^{2} HUNMANBY GAP [90] 9-11-7 C Hawkins, *settled on ins, improved bef 2 out, not quicken whn hit last.* ....(7 to 1 op 5 to 1) 2
3600^{5} ELVETT BRIDGE (Ire) [69] 6-10-0 B Storey, *tucked away on ins, rdn aftr 3 out, hit last, no imprsn.* .... (25 to 1 op 16 to 1) 3
3533^{8} TAP DANCING [69] 8-10-0 Ann Stokell, *trkd ldrs on ins, drvn alng bef 3 out, kpt on same pace betw last 2.* .... (50 to 1 op 33 to 1) 4
3475 GOLDEN REVERIE (USA) [78] 6-10-9 L Wyer, *settled on outsd, pushed alng bef 3 out, no extr.* .... (33 to 1 op 16 to 1) 5
2150 ERBIL (Ire) [83] 4-10-9 (5*) F Perratt, *settled off the pace, hdwy on bit bef 2 out, nvr plcd to chal.* .... (10 to 1 op 5 to 1) 6
3357^{7} SINGING SAM [69] (bl) 9-10-0 N Smith, *chsd ldrs, effrt 3 out, sn drvn alng, one pace betw last 2.* .... (66 to 1 op 33 to 1) 7
3435* HOT PUNCH [85] 5-10-11 (5*) P Waggott, *nvr far away, struggling 4 out, fdd nxt*............(5 to 1 op 4 to 1) 8
3542 FINDOGLEN [69] 8-10-0^{3} (3*) A Larnach, *settled midfield, drvn alng bef 3 out, wknd*........(50 to 1 op 33 to 1) 9
3429 YACHT CLUB [69] 12-10-0 O Pears, *beh, not jump wl, cld fnl circuit, wknd 3 out*........... (66 to 1 op 33 to 1) 10
3435^{2} RYTHMIC RYMER [70] 4-9-8 (7*) G Tormey, *settled midfield, cld fnl circuit, rdn 3 out, wknd, virtually pld up r-in*..................................(6 to 1 op 8 to 1) 11
3594 THE HIDDEN CITY [74] 8-10-5 Peter Caldwell, *settled midfield, feeling pace fnl circuit, btn 3 out.* .... (25 to 1 op 20 to 1) 12
2254 GYMCRAK CYRANO (Ire) [69] 5-10-0 N Bentley, *patiently rdn, improved fnl circuit, ridden aftr 4 out, btn nxt.* .... (50 to 1 op 33 to 1) 13
3535 BRIGHT SAPPHIRE [69] 8-10-0 W Marston, *wth ldr, led 3rd to 5th, led briefly aftr 6th, btn bef 2 out.* .... (33 to 1 op 20 to 1) 14
3533 BOREEN JEAN [88] (bl) 10-11-5 P Niven, *led to 3rd, wth ldr, led 5th till aftr nxt, wknd*..... (10 to 1 op 7 to 1) 15
3287 SULAAH ROSE [69] 5-10-0 D Morris, *trkd ldrs, struggling fnl circuit, tld off*................. (66 to 1 op 50 to 1) 16
3533^{5} BOXING MATCH [69] 7-10-0 N Williamson, *beh, struggling fnl circuit, tld off*..................... (12 to 1 op 8 to 1) 17
2408^{7} FIRE 'N' FURY [69] 8-10-0 K Johnson, *beh, blun 5th, tld off whn pld up bef 3 out*.............(20 to 1 op 16 to 1) pu
Dist: 12l, 1l, 3½l, ½l, 1¾l, 11l, sht-hd, nk, 6l, sht-hd. 5m 5.30s. a 14.30s (18 Ran).
(John Wade), J A Hellens

3674 Pepsi Max Conditional Jockeys' Novices' Hurdle (4-y-o and up) £1,968 2m 1f 110yds...................... (6:00)

3035^{3} SKIDDAW SAMBA 5-10-4 (5*) G Lee, *patiently rdn, hdwy aftr 4 out, led 2 out, ran on wl frm last.* ....(9 to 2 op 4 to 1 tchd 5 to 1) 1
3440^{8} ON GOLDEN POND (Ire) (bl) 4-10-10 N Bentley, *led to 1st, stasyed hndy, outpcd and drvn alng 6th, styd on wl frm last*...........................(10 to 1 op 11 to 1) 2
1735^{6} DE JORDAAN 7-11-0 W Fry, *patiently rdn, chlgd 2 out, kpt on same pace frm last*....................(50 to 1) 3
28^{2} MARIYDA (Ire) 5-10-9 S Lyons, *nvr far away, improved fnl circuit, ev ch bef 2 out, one pace betw last two.* .... (11 to 4 op 3 to 1 tchd 7 to 2) 4
3459 KERNEL GRAIN (Ire) 5-10-11 (3*) M Molloy, *keen hold early, settled beh ldrs, shaken up bef 2 out, btn before last.* ....(14 to 1) 5
ARITAM (Ire) 5-11-0 S Mason, *chsd ldg grp, rdn and wknd bef 3 out*..(33 to 1) 6
3164^{7} ALEX THUSCOMBE 6-10-9 (5*) R Moore, *rear, drvn alng bef 6th, nvr dngrs*................(50 to 1 op 33 to 1) 7
3553 AFRICAN GOLD 6-11-0 F Perratt, *beh, not fluent, struggling fnl circuit*..................................(50 to 1) 8
3315 CAMPTOSAURUS (Ire) 5-10-7 (7*) D Waters, *settled rear, shaken up aftr 3 out, sn btn*................. (33 to 1) 9
3079 HARRY'S MIDGET 4-10-3 J Supple, *mid-div, struggling to hold pl bef 3 out, sn btn*.........................(50 to 1) 10
3583 HUTCEL BRIG 5-10-6 (3*) J Driscoll, *jmpd poorly in rear, nvr on terms*....................................(33 to 1) 11
3435 FEELING FRAYL 7-10-4 (5*) M Clarke, *led 1st till bef 4th, wknd before nxt*................. (50 to 1 op 33 to 1) 12
3315 THINK PINK 7-10-7 (7*) B Grattan, *beh, struggling fnl circuit, tld off*.............................. (50 to 1) 13
3379 CHORUS LINE (Ire) (bl) 5-10-4 (5*) K Davies, *nvr far away, led bef 4th till aftr 3 out, fdd, tld off*..........(50 to 1) 14
3379^{7} PHILDAN (Ire) 5-11-0 D J Moffatt, *wth ldrs, ev ch bef 2 out, btn whn f last, destroyed*..........(10 to 1 op 8 to 1) f
2903^{5} IMPERIAL BID (Fr) 6-11-7 P Waggott, *nvr far away, led aftr 3 out, hdd whn stumbled and uns rdr after nxt.* ....(15 to 8 fav op 2 to 1 tchd 7 to 4) ur
Dist: 1¼l, 2½l, 6l, 10l, 6l, 2l, nk, 20l, 4l, ¾l. 4m 8.00s. a 13.00s (16 Ran).
(John Wills), Mrs M Reveley

3675 Guinness Novices' Chase (5-y-o and up) £2,275 3m 3f.............. (6:30)

3569* UNHOLY ALLIANCE 7-12-0 N Williamson, *patiently rdn, hit 9th, drw level 13th, lft in ld aftr nxt, sn clr, easily.* ....(4 to 1 on op 5 to 1 on tchd 7 to 2 on) 1
UPWELL 10-11-4 Mr P Johnson, *in tch, cld 7th, lft second bef 15th, no imprsn fnl 3*..........(20 to 1 op 16 to 1) 2
3486 MASTER MATHEW 7-11-4 B Storey, *led to 4th, styd hndy, outpcd last 5*................................. (12 to 1) 3
3287 LADY BE BRAVE (v) 11-10-13 K Johnson, *wth ldr, led 4th till slpd up bend aftr 14th*........................(7 to 1) su
3428^{8} FRIENDLY SOCIETY 8-11-4 A Merrigan, *not fluent early, trkd ldrs, cl second whn slpd up bend aftr 6th.* .... (25 to 1 op 20 to 1) su
3453 JUNIOR ROGERS 6-10-11 (7*) D Winter, *cl up, drpd rear 4th, struggling fnl circuit, tld off whn jmpd slwly four out, sn pld up*....................(50 to 1 op 33 to 1) pu
Dist: 6l, 6l. 6m 56.90s. a 17.90s (6 Ran).
(Mrs S C York), K C Bailey

3676 Castle Eden Ale Handicap Chase (0-125 5-y-o and up) £2,924 2m 5f (7:00)

3375^{4} WAIT YOU THERE (USA) [93] 9-10-3 L Wyer, *nvr far away, drw level 5 out, wth ldr whn lft clr 2 out, unchlgd.* .... (9 to 2 op 5 to 1 tchd 11 to 2) 1
3593* COMEDY ROAD [108] 10-11-4 (6ex) A Maguire, *settled rear, hit 3rd, improved bef 12th, outpcd aftr 4 out, lft second 2 out*...........................(15 to 8 fav op 5 to 2) 2
3376^{7} BONANZA [114] 7-11-10 R Hodge, *settled in tch, improved 8th, outpcd aftr 5 out, no imprsn fnl 2.* ....(7 to 1 op 6 to 1) 3
ANTHONY BELL [96] 8-10-6 B Storey, *patiently rdn, outpcd 4 out, styd on frm last, better for race.* .... (14 to 1 op 12 to 1) 4
1789^{7} SPEECH [92] 11-10-2^{2} A Merrigan, *not jump wl, chsd ldrs, drpd rear fnl circuit, tld off 3 out*............ (25 to 1) 5
3438* EXPLOSIVE SPEED (USA) [101] 6-10-11 P Niven, *led, jnd 5 out, f 2 out*........................(11 to 4 op 2 to 1) f
1792^{2} MARLINGFORD [99] 7-10-9 D Morris, *pressed ldr, rdn alng 11th, losing tch whn blun 3 out, pld up bef nxt.* .... (11 to 2 op 5 to 1) pu
Dist: 12l, 3l, ¾l, dist. 5m 6.70s. a 2.70s (7 Ran).
SR: 27/30/33/14/ (Hamish Alexander), H Alexander

3677 Woodpecker Cider Novices' Hurdle (4-y-o and up) £1,830 3m 3f 110yds (7:30)

3343 DEVONGALE 8-11-0 L Wyer, *led to 9th, led bef 2 out, hng rght, edgd lft frm last, all out*.. (13 to 8 fav op 2 to 1) 1
3144^{6} FORTUNE'S GIRL 6-11-2 A Maguire, *al hndy, led 9th till bef 2 out, ev ch whn not much room and swtchd before last, kpt on r-in*................. (7 to 4 op 5 to 4) 2
3236^{2} RUSSIAN CASTLE (Ire) 5-11-0 K Jones, *trkd ldrs, outpcd aftr 4 out*..(6 to 1) 3

3603 WHITE DIAMOND 6-11-7 Mr N Wilson, *keen hold, cl up,*
struggling 4 out, tld off .... (9 to 2 op 7 to 2) 4
CIRCLE BOY 7-11-0 A Merrigan, *cl up, struggling frm 4*
out, btn whn f last .... (33 to 1 op 20 to 1) f
Dist: ¾l, 20l, 25l. 6m 51.20s. a 25.20s (5 Ran).

(Victor Ogden), M H Easterby

3678 Whitbread Best Scotch Handicap Hurdle (0-110 4-y-o and up) £2,700 2m 5f 110yds........................ (8:00)

3436⁴ FLASS VALE [81] (v) 6-10-2 C Hawkins, *set str pace, made*
all, wnt clr appr 2 out, styd on wl. (10 to 1 op 14 to 1) 1
3561¹ MOUNTSHANNON [85] 8-10-6 (7ex) Peter Caldwell, *chsd*
ldg trio, effrt bef 3 out, kpt on und pres frm last, not rch
wnr .... (3 to 1 fav op 5 to 2) 2
3475 NOTABLE EXCEPTION [100] 5-11-2 (5*) S Mason, *settled*
rear, pushed alng 3 out, styd on wl frm last, nrst finish.
.... (4 to 1) 3
3107⁵ REXY BOY [83] 7-10-4⁴ G Harker, *al wl plcd, ev ch aftr 3*
out, hit last 2, not quicken. .... (20 to 1) 4
3107³ BENTLEY MANOR [84] 5-10-5 W Marston, *patiently rdn,*
improved and ev ch aftr 3 out, no extr nxt.
.... (8 to 1 op 7 to 1) 5
3578⁴ SHELTON ABBEY [89] 8-10-10 K Jones, *pressed wnr, out-*
pcd aftr 4 out, styd on und pres frm last, no imprsn.
.... (14 to 1 op 16 to 1) 6
3344 CURTAIN FACTORY [83] 5-10-4 L Wyer, *mid-div, outpcd*
and drvn alng aftr 4 out, btn nxt.... (4 to 1 op 9 to 2) 7
3374 MISTIC GLEN (Ire) [93] (bl) 5-11-0 A Maguire, *hld up in tch,*
effrt hfwy, wknd aftr 4 out .... (6 to 1 op 5 to 1) 8
3436⁷ MIAMI BEAR [95] 8-11-2 N Williamson, *mid-div, struggling*
to keep up aftr 4 out, sn btn, tld off .... (14 to 1) 9
3240 KIR (Ire) [90] (bl) 6-10-11 B Storey, *beh, struggling to go*
pace fnl circuit, tld off. .... (6 to 1 tchd 7 to 1) 10
3287 SEXY MOVER [84] 7-10-5 K Johnson, *in tch, drpd rear aftr*
4th, struggling fnl circuit, tld off. .... (16 to 1) 11
Dist: 6l, 1¾l, 1¼l, 1¼l, 7l, 6l, hd, 15l, ¾l, 6l. 4m 59.90s. a 8.90s (11 Ran).

(Goldspace T/a Sandal Business Services), C W Fairhurst

AUTEUIL (FR) (soft)
Saturday April 30th

3679 Prix Amadou (Hurdle) (4-y-o) £40,046 2 ¾m........................ (3:35)

TOPKAR (Fr) 9-13 C Gombeau, ... 1
PASQUINOBLE (Fr) 9-13 A Kondrat, ... 2
LAKE POWELL (Fr) 10-6 D Mescam, ... 3
3409* CYBORGO (Fr) 9-13 G Landau, *rear early, second aftr 3 fs,*
rdn 4 furlongs out, sn wknd. 4
Dist: 2½l, 4l, sht-nk, 10l, 1½l. 4m 47.00s. (6 Ran).

(H Try), J P Delaporte

HEREFORD (good to firm)
Saturday April 30th
Going Correction: MINUS 0.15 sec. per fur.

3680 Sun Valley Charities Novices' Hurdle (4-y-o and up) £1,725 2m 1f..... (2:20)

402 MUSICAL TREND (Ire) 6-11-2 J Osborne, *chsd ldrs, slight*
ld 3 out, pushed out. .... (7 to 1 op 5 to 1) 1
3209⁵ ROXY RIVER 5-11-3 W Marston, *led, narrowly hdd whn*
badly blun 3 out, tried to rally last, no extr.
.... (5 to 1 op 3 to 1 tchd 11 to 2) 2
3494⁵ SKEOUGH (Ire) 6-11-8 R Bellamy, *beh, drvn and styd on*
frm 6th, not pace to rch ldrs.
.... (8 to 1 op 6 to 1 tchd 9 to 1) 3
3476⁴ TOO SHARP 6-10-11 R Marley, *chsd ldrs, chlgd 6th, wknd*
aftr 3 out. .... (11 to 4 fav op 2 to 1 tchd 7 to 2) 4
FRENCH IVY (USA) 7-11-2 G Upton, *chsd ldrs till f dd appr*
3 out. .... (8 to 1 op 5 to 1 tchd 9 to 1) 5
3530 SHERWOOD BOY 5-11-2 S McNeill, *chsd ldrs, outpcd*
appr 5th, nvr dngrs aftr. .... (4 to 1 op 5 to 2) 6
3469⁹ PASSAMEZZO (Ire) 4-10-11 T Wall, *nvr rch ldrs.*
.... (33 to 1 op 20 to 1) 7
3113⁷ PONGO WARING (Ire) 5-10-13 (3*) R Farrant, *al beh, tld off.*
.... (16 to 1 op 12 to 1) 8
RING THE BANK 7-10-8 (3*) T Jenks, *sn beh, no ch whn f*
6th. .... (9 to 1 op 7 to 2 tchd 10 to 1) f
3597 TENDER DANCER (Ire) 6-11-2 J Da Costa, *al beh, tld off*
whn pld up bef 3 out. .... (100 to 1 op 50 to 1) pu
3494 SWEET LIBERTY 10-10-8 (3*) T Eley, *al beh, tld off whn*
pld up bef 3 out. .... (33 to 1 op 20 to 1) pu
3530⁷ PERSIAN WOLF 6-11-2 V Slattery, *sn beh and drvn alng,*
no ch whn hmpd 6th, tld off when pld up bef 2 out.
.... (50 to 1 op 25 to 1) pu
DIAMOND LIGHT 7-11-2 J R Kavanagh, *beh frm 4th, tld off*
whn pld up bef 2 out. .... (40 to 1 op 33 to 1) pu
3114⁹ TYDFIL LASS 5-10-11 D J Burchell, *sn beh, tld off whn pld*
up bef 3 out. .... (20 to 1 op 8 to 1) pu
Dist: 1¾l, 6l, 10l, 4l, 15l, nk, dist. 3m 53.40s. a 7.40s (14 Ran).

(P A Idris), O Sherwood

3681 Knight, Frank & Rutley Handicap Chase (0-120 5-y-o and up) £2,560 3m 1f 110yds..................... (2:50)

3336* NEARCO BAY (NZ) [105] 10-11-5 J R Kavanagh, *hld up,*
steady hdwy to chase ldrs 4 out, styd on wl 3 out, led
and hit last, drvn out. .... (6 to 4 fav tchd 7 to 4) 1
3498⁸ GILSTON LASS [95] 7-10-6 (3*) T Jenks, *led, clr 3 out, rdn,*
hdd and hit last, one pace.
.... (4 to 1 op 7 to 2 tchd 9 to 2) 2
548* HEIGHT OF FUN [93] (bl) 10-10-7 S Burrough, *chsd ldrs,*
rdn tenth, chlgd 11th, ridden ag'n 13th, outpcd frm 3
out. .... (7 to 1 op 5 to 1 tchd 8 to 1) 3
3495⁶ MWEENISH [95] 12-10-9 R Bellamy, *beh, hit 5th, nvr rchd*
ldrs. .... (9 to 1 op 4 to 1 tchd 10 to 1) 4
3562 BUMPTIOUS BOY [86] 10-10-0 W Marston, *in tch, hdwy to*
press ldrs tenth, wknd frm 4 out.... (10 to 1 op 7 to 1) 5
3307 CAMDEN BELLE [86] 12-10-0 A Tory, *al beh.*
.... (25 to 1 op 16 to 1) 6
2664⁴ MR TITTLE TATTLE [97] (bl) 8-10-11 S McNeill, *chsd ldrs,*
rdn 11th, wknd 15th.... .... (7 to 2 op 9 to 2) 7
3593 COMPLETE OPTIMIST [95] 10-10-9 L Harvey, *mstk 1st, tld*
off 7th, pld up bef tenth.... .... (33 to 1 op 16 to 1) pu
Dist: 3l, 20l, 8l, 5l, 12l, 20l. 6m 12.90s. a 0.90s (8 Ran).
SR: 44/31/9/3/-/

(Queen Elizabeth), N J Henderson

3682 Bonusprint Conditional Jockeys' Novices' Selling Handicap Hurdle (4-y-o and up) £1,553 2m 1f.......... (3:25)

3531⁵ SHARPSIDE [64] (bl) 7-11-2 (5*) C Quinlan, *hld up, chsd*
ldrs, chlgd 3 out, led last, held on wl. ....(7 to 2 jt-
fav op 5 to 2) 1
3145⁵ IRISH TAN [63] (bl) 7-10-13 (7*) S Arnold, *beh, rapid hdwy*
frm 4th, led aftr 5th, hdd last, not quicken... (7 to 2 jt-
fav op 3 to 1 tchd 4 to 1) 2
2900 ALDINGTON CHAPPLE [67] 6-11-10 T Jenks, *in tch, out-*
pcd 5th, hdwy 3 out, one paced frm 2 out.
.... (13 to 2 op 7 to 1 tchd 8 to 1) 3
3597 FIVE STARS [66] 7-11-9 J McCarthy, *chsd ldrs, led appr*
5th, hdd approaching nxt, sn one pace.
.... (13 to 2 op 4 to 1 tchd 7 to 1) 4
3395⁶ TANAISTE (USA) [54] (bl) 5-10-11 S Curran, *nvr rchd ldrs.*
.... (10 to 1 op 6 to 1) 5
3564³ LILES LE BUCFLOW [55] 6-10-12 R Farrant, *chsd ldrs to*
6th. .... (25 to 1 op 16 to 1) 6
3315⁴ PYRO PENNANT [60] 9-11-3 A Procter, *prmnt to 5th.*
.... (9 to 2 op 4 to 1 tchd 5 to 1) 7
3315⁶ KILLTUBBER HOUSE [65] 8-11-1 (7*) J Bond, *prmnt, mstk*
second, hit 5th and wknd.
.... (14 to 1 op 8 to 1 tchd 16 to 1) 8
567⁴ JUVENARA [61] (v) 8-11-4 T Eley, *al beh.*
.... (4 to 1 tchd 9 to 2) 9
3277 SURE SHOT NORMAN [60] (v) 5-11-3 P Carey, *sn beh, tld*
off whn pld up bef 2 out.... .... (33 to 1 op 20 to 1) pu
3147⁶ BELLE LOCK [55] 6-10-12 J Neaves, *al beh, tld off whn*
pld up bef last, dismounted.... ...(25 to 1 op 16 to 1) pu
3211 PIPERS REEL [55] 4-10-12 D Matthews, *led till appr 5th,*
wknd rpdly, tld off whn pld up bef 2 out.
.... (20 to 1 op 25 to 1) pu
Dist: 2½l, 5l, 20l, 5l, 10l, 1¾l, 10l, 1l. 3m 53.00s. a 7.00s (12 Ran).

(G J Green), P J Hobbs

3683 Sun Valley Only Best Will Doodle Do Novices' Chase (5-y-o and up) £3,210 2m 3f........................(3:55)

3479² SAN LORENZO (USA) 6-11-10 S McNeill, *trkd ldrs 7th,*
chlgd 9th, led tenth, hit last, readily.
.... (6 to 4 on op 5 to 4 on) 1
3454* EMERALD RULER 7-11-10 R Bellamy, *hld up, jmpd slwly*
7th, hdwy 4 out, blun nxt, styd on one pace.
.... (9 to 4 op 7 to 4) 2
3479⁴ DONNA'S TOKEN 9-10-12 W Marston, *jmpd slwly second,*
chsd ldrs, styd on und pessure frm 3 out.
.... (5 to 1 op 7 to 2 tchd 11 to 2) 3
3498 PERTEMPS JOBSHOP 81-3 W Humphreys, *led to tenth,*
rdn and wkng whn blun 2 out.... (40 to 1 op 33 to 1) 4
2043⁸ SEMINOLE PRINCESS (bl) 6-10-12 M Bosley, *chsd ldrs till*
wknd 9th. .... (50 to 1) 5
Dist: 5l, 5l, 15l, 1½l. 4m 49.30s. a 19.30s (5 Ran).

(James D Greig), K C Bailey

3684 Next Generation Hunters' Chase (5-y-o and up) £1,380 3m 1f 110yds (4:30)

3596⁵ RUSTY BRIDGE 7-11-7 (7*) Mr R Johnson, *led to second,*
led ag'n 4th, hdd 11th, led again 15th, rdn, hng lft and
jst hld on r-in. .... (25 to 1 op 20 to 1) 1
3493³ THE MALAKARMA 8-11-13 (5*) Mr T Byrne, *chsd ldrs, chlgd*
tenth, led 11th, hdd 15th, chald frm 3 out, styd on r-in,
jst hld. .... (4 to 1 op 3 to 1) 2
3563³ SAFFRON LORD 12-12-0 (7*) Mr G Hogan, *al prmnt, chsd*
ldrs frm 3 out, not quicken appr last.
.... (4 to 1 op 3 to 1 tchd 5 to 2 and 9 to 2) 3

NATIONAL HUNT RESULTS 1993-94

3480⁵ CAPE COTTAGE 10-11-11 (7") Mr A Phillips, *beh, steady hdwy to track ldrs 4 out, not clr run and snatched up bend appr last, one pace.*
.... (10 to 1 op 8 to 1 tchd 11 to 1) 4
MASTER MUCK 11-11-11 (7") Mr S Joynes, *prmnt, hit tenth, mstk and wknd 15th, tld off whn pld up bef 2 out.*.................... (20 to 1 op 14 to 1) pu
3412² BROWN WINDSOR (bl) 12-12-0 (7") Mr B Pollock, *beh, hit 6th, hdwy 8th, wknd 3 out, tld off whn pld up bef last.*
.... (12 to 1 op 2 to 1 tchd 9 to 4) pu
MENDON ROSE 13-11-2 (7") Mr B Norris, *al beh, tld off 5th, pld up bef 6th...* (50 to 1 op 25 to 1 tchd 66 to 1) pu
3412⁴ DARK DAWN 10-12-7 Mr J Greenall, *hdwy to track ldrs 9th, wknd appr 3 out, tld off whn pld up bef last.*
.... (9 to 4 op 6 to 4 tchd 5 to 2) pu
3412 SANDSTONE ARCH 11-12-0 (7") Mr L Brennan, *led second to 4th, beh 7th, hit 12th, tld off whn pld up bef 14th.*
.... (40 to 1 op 33 to 1) pu
Dist: Hd, 1½l, 1¼l. 6m 23.70s. a 11.70s (9 Ran).

(J I Johnson), J I Johnson

3685 Jail-break Novices' Handicap Hurdle (0-100 4-y-o and up) £1,725 2m 3f 110yds............... (5:00)

2543⁴ NEARLY HONEST [71] 6-10-9 A Tory, *hdwy 7th, led 4 out, ran on wl.*.............. (9 to 1 op 8 to 1 tchd 10 to 1) 1
3379⁶ ROCA MURADA (Ire) [85] 5-11-9 W Marston, *beh, hdwy 3 out, chsd wnr frm 2 out, no imprsn.* (5 to 1 tchd 6 to 1) 2
3502⁵ DOMINOS RING (Ire) [83] 5-11-2 (5") S Curran, *prmnt, pressed ldrs 4 out, kpt on same pace frm 2 out.*
.... (6 to 1 op 5 to 1 tchd 13 to 2) 3
2066⁵ ROAD TO AU BON (USA) [63] 6-9-12 (3") R Farrant, *beh, ran on frm 3 out, not a dngr.*.................... (20 to 1) 4
3574⁴ LUCKY BLUE [86] 7-11-3 (7") P Carey, *prmnt, led 7th, hdd 4 out, wknd frm 3 out....* (11 to 2 op 5 to 1 tchd 6 to 1) 5
2092² NO SHOW (Ire) [63] 4-10-1 W Humphreys, *al beh.* (20 to 1) 6
3535⁴ TEMPLE KNIGHT [86] 5-11-10 L Harvey, *al beh.*
.... (7 to 2 fav op 5 to 2 tchd 4 to 1) 7
3209 STERLING BUCK (USA) [67] 7-10-5 B Clifford, *beh frm 6th.*
.... (10 to 1 op 8 to 1 tchd 13 to 2) 8
3502⁸ BRIMPTON BERTIE [81] 5-11-5 G Upton, *in tch, drvn to chase ldrs 3 out, wknd quickly 2 out.*
.... (10 to 1 op 7 to 1) 9
1645³ IT'S DELICIOUS [77] 8-10-8 (7") Mr G Hogan, *prmnt, rdn 4 out, sn wknd.......* (10 to 1 op 8 to 1 tchd 14 to 1) 10
3571⁴ FALCONBRIDGE BAY [79] 7-11-3 J R Kavanagh, *beh, hdwy 7th, wknd 4 out.*.................... (8 to 1 op 7 to 1) 11
3571 KOBYRUN [73] 8-10-11 S Burrough, *prmnt to 5th, tld off whn pld up bef 2 out.*.................... (20 to 1 op 14 to 1) pu
3559 GILBERT (Ire) [74] 6-10-12 D J Burchell, *led to 7th, sn wknd, tld off whn pld up bef 2 out.* (20 to 1 op 16 to 1) pu
2405⁹ TWIST 'N' SCU [77] 6-10-12 (3") T Jenks, *prmnt, drvn alng frm 6th, sn wknd, tld off whn pld up bef last.*
.... (7 to 1 op 5 to 1) pu
3549⁹ JUNIPER LODGE [70] 6-10-8 N Mann, *sn beh, tld off whn pld up bef 7th.*.................... (20 to 1 op 14 to 1) pu
3515⁸ FINALLY FANTAZIA [65] 5-10-5 R Bellamy, *al beh, tld off whn pld up bef 3 out.*.............. (20 to 1 op 16 to 1) pu
Dist: 5l, 1¼l, 7l, ½l, 2½l, 1¼l, sht-hd, 4l, 12l, ½l. 4m 39.90s. a 18.90s (16 Ran).

(Jock Cullen), R J Hodges

3686 EBF National Hunt Flat Race (4,5,6-y-o) £1,380 2m 1f.............. (5:30)

2876² WIZZO 4-10-7 (7") L Aspell, *hld up beh ldrs, chsd lder fnl 2 fs, ran on strly to lead nr finish.*
.... (5 to 1 op 3 to 1 tchd 11 to 2) 1
3138² DRUMMOND WARRIOR (Ire) 5-10-13 (7") T Dascombe, *hld up in tch, led 4 fs out till hdd nr finish.*
.... (15 to 2 op 4 to 1 tchd 8 to 1) 2
3589⁸ HERBERT BUCHANAN (Ire) 4-10-9 (5") D Matthews, *al prmnt, ev ch wl o'r 2 fs out, one pace.*
.... (33 to 1 op 14 to 1) 3
BEGGARS LANE 5-10-8 (7") P Melia, *chsd ldrs, outpcd o'r 2 fs out, styd on wl fnl furlong, better for race.*
.... (16 to 1 op 8 to 1) 4
FROWN 4-10-9 (5") S Curran, *pld hrd, led till hdd aftr 6 fs, outpcd o'r 2 furlongs out...* (4 to 1 jt-fav tchd 5 to 1) 5
3169⁹ HOLY STING 5-11-3 (3") T Jenks, *strted slwly, rdn hfwy, styd on, nvr nrr...* (6 to 1 op 5 to 1 tchd 7 to 1) 6
HYDEMILLA 4-10-2 (7") K Brown, *hld up beh, styd on fnl 3 fs, nrst finish.*.......... (33 to 1 op 25 to 1) 7
CORRIB SONG 5-11-3 (3") R Farrant, *chsd ldrs, no hdwy fnl 3 fs.*............. (12 to 1 op 7 to 1 tchd 14 to 1) 8
3234⁶ UNCLE ALGY 5-10-13 (7") Mr G Hogan, *strted slwly, sn reco'red to track ldrs, wknd over 3 fs out.*
.... (7 to 1 op 5 to 1 tchd 6 to 1) 9
2716⁸ NANOOK 5-10-13 (7") Mr E Williams, *hld up, nvr better than mid-div.......* (14 to 1 op 20 to 1 tchd 16 to 1) 10
HARINGTON HUNDREDS 4-10-11 (7") J McCarthy, *chsd ldrs, ev ch 4 fs out, sn outpcd.* (4 to 1 jt-fav tchd 5 to 1) 11
DANCING SUPREME 4-11-0 Miss S Wallin, *nvr dngrs.*
.... (33 to 1 op 25 to 1) 12
ONEMOREANWEGO 6-10-8 (7") P Carey, *al towards rear.*
.... (33 to 1 op 16 to 1) 13

3488 KELBURNE LAD (Ire) 5-11-6 Mrs T Bailey, *prmnt till wknd 3 fs out.*.................... (14 to 1 op 8 to 1) 14
AREAL (Ire) 5-10-8 (7") D Rees, *led aftr 6 fs till hdd 4 furlongs out, wknd.*.................... (33 to 1 op 16 to 1) 15
CHRISSYTINO 6-10-8 (7") M Godsafe, *chsd ldrs till wknd o'r 6 fs out.*.......... (20 to 1 op 12 to 1 tchd 25 to 1) 16
3227 BEN DARWI 5-10-13 (7") S Arnold, *pld hrd, cl up till lost pl quickly hfwy, tld off.*.......... (10 to 1 op 8 to 1) 17
Dist: ½l, 7l, ¾l, 4l, 1½l, 2l, 8l, ½l, 1¾l, ¾l. 3m 49.50s. (17 Ran).
(Mrs M M Palling), B Palling

HEXHAM (good to firm)
Saturday April 30th
Going Correction: PLUS 0.25 sec. per fur.

3687 North Tyne Maiden Hurdle (4-y-o and up) £1,550 3m............... (5:50)

3428 NORRISMOUNT 8-11-7 M Moloney, *cl up, led hfwy, drw clr frm 2 out, cmftbly.*.............. (6 to 1 op 5 to 1) 1
3359⁴ STRONG DEEL (Ire) 6-11-7 L Wyer, *prmnt, chsd wnr aftr 3 out, kpt on, no imprsn.*........ (11 to 4 fav tchd 3 to 1) 2
3429⁹ TUESDAYNIGHTMARE 5-11-2 T Reed, *not fluent, hld up, outpcd aftr 3 out, styd on frm nxt.* (5 to 1 op 12 to 1) 3
3431⁸ LAST REFUGE (Ire) 5-11-7 B Storey, *hld up, outpcd aftr 3 out, no dngr after.*.............. (10 to 1 op 8 to 1) 4
3440⁵ GERMAN LEGEND 4-11-0 A Merrigan, *hld up, hdwy aftr 8th, ev ch 3 out, wknd after nxt, 5th and btn whn blun last.*.................... (25 to 1 op 20 to 1) 5
3284⁷ MANETTIA (Ire) 5-11-2 P Niven, *in tch wl behd aftr 3 out, tld off.*.................... (3 to 1 op 2 to 1) 6
UNLUCKY FOR SOME (Ire) 5-11-7 N Doughty, *prmnt till wknd appr 3 out, tld off.*.............. (8 to 1 op 7 to 1) 7
3235⁶ CELTIC PEACE 7-11-2 C Hawkins, *made most till hdd hfwy, wknd quickly, tld off whn pld up bef 9th.*
.... (33 to 1 op 20 to 1) pu
3102² MEGAMUNCH (Ire) 6-11-7 Richard Guest, *trkd ldrs, rdn aftr 3 out, sn wknd, tld off whn pld up bef last, lme.*
.... (5 to 1 op 4 to 1) pu
Dist: 6l, 15l, 8l, 20l, 15l, 6l. 6m 17.70s. a 30.70s (9 Ran).
(Mrs Stewart Catherwood), G Richards

3688 Rooster Computers Challenge Cup An Amateur Riders' Hurdle (4-y-o and up) £2,092 2½m 110yds........... (6:20)

3541⁷ TALL MEASURE 8-11-1 (7") Mr D Swindlehurst, *made most, hrd pressed appr last, styd on strly.* (11 to 2 op 9 to 1) 1
3287 ROSE TABLEAU 11-10-10 (7") Miss Sue Nichol, *in tch, reminders aftr 6th and 7th, outpcd aftr 3 out, styd on wl frm nxt, not rch wnr.*.......... (8 to 1 tchd 9 to 1) 2
3598³ FIVE FLAGS 6-11-1 (7") Mr W Halliday, *hld up in tch, outpcd aftr 3 out, rallied aftr nxt, styd on wl frm last.*
.... (9 to 2 op 4 to 1) 3
3210 SHU FLY (NZ) 10-11-7 (7") Mr R Braham, *hld up, blun second, steady hdwy to track wnr 3 out, chlgd on bit bef last, rdn, found nil, wknd towards finish.*
.... (6 to 5 on op 5 to 4 on tchd 5 to 4) 4
3598 BDOORE (Ire) 6-10-10 (7") Miss F Barnes, *cl up till grad wknd frm 3 out.*.................... (50 to 1 op 33 to 1) 5
3181² CENTRE ATTRACTION 15-11-1 (7") Miss Y Beckingham, *in tch, drpd rear hfwy, wknd last. styd on frm nxt.* (7 to 1 op 5 to 1) 6
3429 GLASTONDALE 8-11-1 (7") Mr S Johnson, *mid-div till wknd aftr 3 out.*.................... (33 to 1) 7
3286 DESPERADO (bl) 6-11-1 (7") Mr S Pittendrigh, *in tch, rdn aftr 7th, wknd quickly, tld off...* (50 to 1 op 33 to 1) 8
Dist: 7l, 1¾l, 1¾l, 12l, 10l, 8l, dist. 5m 15.60s. a 22.60s (8 Ran).
(D J Swindlehurst), D G Swindlehurst

3689 Alistair Turnbull 40th Birthday Novices' Chase (5-y-o and up) £2,540 2½m 110yds........................ (6:50)

3474⁸ THE LORRYMAN (Ire) 6-11-3 T Reed, *led aftr second till mstk and hdd 2 out, rallied after last, styd on wl to ld cl hme.*.................... (14 to 1 tchd 12 to 1) 1
3474 HOWCLEUCH 7-10-12 B Storey, *in tch, led 2 out till hdd and no extr cl hme.......* (10 to 1 op 8 to 1) 2
3577⁴ EASTER OATS 7-10-12 K Johnson, *in tch till outpcd aftr 12th, rallied after 2 out, ev ch last, hng rght and no extr.*.................... (14 to 1) 3
3355² BASILICUS (Fr) 5-11-3 Gary Lyons, *trkd ldrs, chlgd 2 out, sn rdn, kpt on same pace....* (Evens fav tchd 11 to 10) 4
3577⁷ HERE COMES TIBBY 7-11-5 Mrs A Farrell, *trkd ldrs, ev ch 2 out, one pace.*.................... (12 to 1 op 10 to 1) 5
3577³ SAGARO BELLE 8-10-12 A Merrigan, *in tch, ev ch whn mstk 3 out, kpt on same pace frm nxt.*
.... (20 to 1 op 16 to 1) 6
3438 MAYOR OF LISCARROL 9-11-10 G Harker, *led, hit second, sn hdd, prmnt till wknd aftr 12th.*........ (7 to 1) 7
3143³ SHEILAS HILLCREST 8-11-12 (5") J Supple, *al beh, lost tch aftr 11th, tld off.*.............. (4 to 1 op 7 to 2) 8
3642 STRONG TRACE (Ire) 6-10-10 P Niven, *not jump wl, beh, lost tch hfwy, well tld off.*............ (16 to 1) 9
Dist: Nk, 5l, nk, ½l, hd, 13l, dist, dist. 5m 20.80s. a 19.80s (9 Ran).

533

(J K Huddleston), W G Reed

3690 Devils Water Selling Hurdle (4-y-o and up) £1,953 2½m 110yds.........(7:20)

3177^{9} SCOTTISH PERIL 7-11-3 B Storey, *hld up, gd hdwy to track ldrs 6th, led r-in, all out*....... (5 to 1 op 9 to 2) 1
3435^{6} THE WEATHERMAN 6-10-10 (7*) N Stocks, *cl up, led 6th till hdd r-in, hld whn snatched up close hme.* ....(10 to 1 tchd 14 to 1) 2
3511^{3} ASHBORO (Ire) 5-11-9 P Niven, *trkd ldrs, ev ch 2 out, sn rdn, kpt on same pace*........... (7 to 4 fav op 5 to 2) 3
3580^{4} MISS PIMPERNEL 4-10-6 L O'Hara, *mid-div, effrt aftr 3 out, nvr dngrs*.................... (12 to 1 op 10 to 1) 4
3580^{6} SEA PET 5-10-12 A Merrigan, *slwly into strd, nvr nr to chal*...(20 to 1) 5
3533^{7} HARPLEY (v) 7-11-8 (7*) N Juckes, *led aftr second till hdd after 6th, grad wknd frm 3 out*................(20 to 1) 6
3395^{7} DOC SPOT 4-10-11 L Wyer, *chsd ldrs to hfwy, sn beh.* ....(8 to 1 op 7 to 1) 7
3553 GLORIOUS HEIGHTS 6-10-7 (5*) F Perratt, *al beh.* ....(20 to 1 tchd 25 to 1) 8
3584 SUNTAN (Fr) (bl) 5-10-10 (7*) K Davies, *chsd ldrs till wknd aftr 3 out*........................ (14 to 1 op 12 to 1) 9
3598 FLAXON WORRIOR 10-11-3 O Pears, *led till aftr second, prmnt to hfwy, sn beh, tld off*................(33 to 1) 10
3553 ASTRAC TRIO (USA) 4-11-3 A Dobbin, *in tch to hfwy, sn beh, tld off*.............(11 to 2 op 4 to 1 tchd 6 to 1) 11
3579^{2} SOUTH STACK 8-11-9 Richard Guest, *mid-div, rdn aftr 6th, wknd after nxt, tld off*........ (8 to 1 op 10 to 1) 12
3111^{5} SHIKARI KID (v) 7-11-10 (5*) P Midgley, *prmnt till wknd aftr 6th, tld off whn pld up bef last.* .... (6 to 1 op 20 to 1 tchd 25 to 1) pu
3603 HEY JOE 7-11-4 (5*) J Burke, *slwly into strd, sn wl beh, tld off whn pld up aftr 2 out*..... (25 to 1 tchd 33 to 1) pu
3511^{8} MASON DIXON 5-11-3 R Garritty, *mid-div till wknd aftr 3 out, tld off whn pld up bef last.* .... (10 to 1 op 8 to 1 tchd 12 to 1) pu

Dist: 2½l, 4l, 25l, 20l, 3½l, 3l, 7l, 2½l, dist. 5m 7.40s. a 14.40s (15 Ran).
(Mrs V Scott Watson), R Allan

3691 Tant Pis Handicap Chase (0-105 5-y-o and up) £2,862 2m 110yds...... (7:50)

2450^{4} BELDINE [94] 9-12-0 A Dobbin, *made all, clr aftr 2 out, hld on wl und pres frm last, all out*...... (5 to 2 op 9 to 4) 1
2906 MOSS BEE [80] 7-11-0 T Reed, *trkd wnr, outpcd aftr 2 out, rdn bef last, kpt on wl und pres r-in.* ....(9 to 2 tchd 5 to 1) 2
3582^{2} WAY OF LIFE (Fr) [89] 9-11-9 P Niven, *mstk 3rd, trkd ldrs, pushed alng aftr 3 out, sn wknd*. (6 to 4 fav op 7 to 4) 3
3585^{3} HIGHLY DECORATED [75] (bl) 9-10-9 Richard Guest, *beh, effrt aftr 9th, no hdwy whn blun 3 out, tld off.* .... (11 to 4 op 5 to 2 tchd 3 to 1) 4
EMMET STREET [73] 14-10-7 K Jones, *sn tld off*. (25 to 1) 5

Dist: ¾l, dist, dist, 2l. 4m 9.40s. a 11.40s (5 Ran).
SR: 27/12/ (Lt-Col W L Monteith), P Monteith

3692 Michael Henderson Handicap Hurdle (0-120 4-y-o and up) £2,427 2m.. (8:20)

3580^{2} TIGHTER BUDGET (USA) [85] 7-10-0 M Moloney, *led second, made rst, styd on wl und pres frm last.* ....(10 to 1 op 8 to 1) 1
3578 CAPTAIN TANCRED (Ire) [85] 6-10-0 A Merrigan, *hld up in tch, effrt aftr 2 out, ev ch last, rdn and no extr.* .... (11 to 1 op 8 to 1 tchd 12 to 1) 2
3643* BROWNSIDE BRIG [94] 9-10-9 (6ex) P Niven, *hld up, hdwy aftr 3 out, ev ch after last, no extr und pres.* ....(11 to 8 fav op 5 to 2) 3
3536^{3} ASTRALEON (Ire) [88] 6-10-3 B Storey, *hld up, hdwy aftr 3 out, pushed alng betw last 2, no imprsn.* .... (15 to 2 op 6 to 1 tchd 8 to 1) 4
3475^{7} VERY EVIDENT (Ire) [89] 5-10-4 J Callaghan, *hld up, outpcd bef 3 out, no dngr aftr*................(8 to 1 op 5 to 1) 5
3555^{4} THE GREEN FOOL [104] 7-11-5 A Dobbin, *led to second, prmnt till wknd aftr 2 out*.......... (10 to 1 op 7 to 1) 6
2575^{9} PREOBLAKENSKY [113] 7-11-9 (5*) J Supple, *prmnt till wknd bef 3 out*......................(5 to 1 tchd 4 to 1) 7
3643^{6} SEON [112] 8-11-13 N Bentley, *beh frm hfwy.* .... (12 to 1 op 7 to 1) 8
3413^{7} BRAMBLEBERRY [110] 5-11-11 Richard Guest, *prmnt till wknd bef 2 out, tld off*..................(5 to 1 op 3 to 1) 9

Dist: 1½l, 3l, 6l, 8l, 2½l, 9l, 15l, 25l. 3m 59.10s. a 9.10s (9 Ran).
SR: 21/19/25/13/6/18/18/2/-/ (A Slack), Mrs E Slack

NAAS (IRE) (good to yielding)
Saturday April 30th

3693 Osberstown Handicap Hurdle (0-137 4-y-o and up) £3,105 2m........ (3:00)

3526^{4} PERSIAN HALO (Ire) [-] 6-11-7 (5*) T P Rudd, ...(9 to 4 fav) 1
2842^{6} MONTE FIGO [-] 7-10-9 F Woods, ... (5 to 1) 2
3247^{9} CELTIC SAILS (Ire) [-] 6-10-10 (3*) Mr P J Casey, .. (11 to 2) 3
3199^{5} STAR ROSE [-] 12-10-8 (7*) J Butler, ... (7 to 1) 4D
3123^{6} MAD TOM [-] 9-11-13 K F O'Brien, ... (8 to 1) 4
2845 PRIDE OF ERIN [-] 10-11-0 J P Dempsey, ... (12 to 1) 5
3507 SADDLESTOWN GLEN [-] (bl) 9-10-8 P Carberry, ..(10 to 1) 6
ORBIS (USA) [-] 8-11-9 (5*) Mr E J Kearns Jnr, ... (16 to 1) 7
1038^{8} JAMES GIRL [-] 10-9-6^{4} (5*) J P Broderick, ... (25 to 1) 8
2279^{8} GREEN MACHINE [-] 7-9-12 (7*) D J Kavanagh, ...(14 to 1) 9
NOTUS [-] 9-9-11^{1} H Rogers, ... (20 to 1) 10

Dist: 1l, nk, 12l, 1½l. 3m 53.80s. (11 Ran).
(Tematron Racing Club), Michael Kauntze

3694 Blessington INH Flat Race (4-y-o and up) £3,105 2m 3f............... (5:30)

3327^{2} ROYAL ALBERT (Ire) 5-11-13 Mr T Mullins, ... (7 to 2) 1
3394^{3} THREE PHILOSOPHERS (Ire) 5-11-10 (3*) Mrs J M Mullins, ...(9 to 1) 2
3327^{4} LITTLE BUCK (Ire) 6-11-7 (7*) Mr J S Cullen, ...(10 to 1) 3
2944^{7} EVEN FLOW (Ire) 5-11-6 (7*) Mr M McCullagh, ... (20 to 1) 4
3393^{3} MAID FOR DANCING (Ire) 5-11-8 Mr A R Coonan, ..(9 to 2) 5
MINELLA EXPRESS (Ire) 5-11-13 Mr A P O'Brien, ... (3 to 1 fav) 6
2944^{4} CORYMANDEL (Ire) 5-11-6 (7*) Mr D Carey, ... (10 to 1) 7
3653 DANGEROUS LADY (Ire) 5-11-5 (3*) Mr D Marnane, (25 to 1) 8
RED RAYNE (Ire) 5-11-13 Mr P Fenton, ...(12 to 1) 9
LIAMS FLASH (Ire) 4-10-8 (7*) Mr J P Harvey, ... (25 to 1) 10
3245^{4} LENEY MOSS (Ire) 4-10-8 (7*) Mr E Norris, ... (10 to 1) 11
3528 WAREZ (Ire) 6-11-7 (7*) Mr C Murphy, ...(50 to 1) 12
3124^{5} THE GOPHER (Ire) 5-11-10 (3*) Mr A E Lacy, ...(12 to 1) 13
969 WOLF 10-11-11 (3*) Mr J R Banahan, ... (33 to 1) 14
3507 NORA'S ERROR (Ire) 5-11-6 (7*) Mr J Lighthalder, (25 to 1) 15
2588^{6} TOPICAL TIP (Ire) 5-11-6 (7*) S P McCarthy, ... (12 to 1) 16
3366 BLACKSTONE 7-11-2 (7*) Mr T J Murphy, ... (25 to 1) 17
2314 THE SHIRALEE (Ire) 6-11-7 (7*) Miss A Commey, .. (50 to 1) 18
3469^{3} WEST BROGUE (Ire) (bl) 5-11-13 Mr J P Dempsey, (10 to 1) 19
3529 MARTINS PARTY 9-11-6^{4} (7*) W T Murphy, ... (50 to 1) 20
ROWSERSTOWN (Ire) 6-11-9 (5*) H F Cleary, ... (20 to 1) 21
CLONAGAM (Ire) 5-11-10 (3*) Mr J A Nash, ...(10 to 1) 22
3124 ANOTHER RHUMBA 8-11-4 (5*) Mr G J Harford, .. (50 to 1) 23
YOUNG WOLF 6-11-7 (7*) Mr P J Kelly, ... (20 to 1) 24
3394 ANTIGUA'S TREASURE (Ire) 5-11-8 (5*) P M Kelly, (20 to 1) su
LUGHNASA'S DANCE (Ire) 5-11-1 (7*) Mr A Lee, .. (20 to 1) pu
FATHER MALONE (Ire) 5-11-6 (7*) Mr R J Nevin, .. (20 to 1) pu

Dist: 2½l, nk, 13l. 4m 34.60s. (27 Ran).
(R P Behan), P Mullins

PLUMPTON (good to firm)
Saturday April 30th
Going Correction: MINUS 0.25 sec. per fur.

3695 Newick Novices' Chase (5-y-o and up) £2,360 2m..................... (5:35)

3004^{5} PHILIP'S WOODY 6-11-6 M A FitzGerald, *made all, hrd rdn aftr 2 out, styd on wl*................(7 to 2 op 5 to 2) 1
1956 DAWN CHANCE 8-11-0 I Lawrence, *trkd ldr, jnd wnr 5 out, ev ch 2 out, sn rdn, untidy last, not quicken r-in.* .... (16 to 1 op 10 to 1) 2
308^{4} MIRAGE DANCER 11-11-0 M Perrett, *hld up, outpcd aftr 8th, styd on after 4 out, kpt on one pace.* .... (33 to 1 op 16 to 1) 3
3404^{6} STRONG VIEWS 7-11-12 D Murphy, *hld up, wnt 3rd 8th, chsd ldg pair, rdn aftr 3 out, sn wknd, eased whn btn r-in*.......................... (11 to 4 on op 2 to 1 on) 4
3585^{7} BALLAD RULER 8-10-11 (3*) R Davis, *hld up, niggled alng aftr 7th, beh whn mstk 4 out*........(11 to 1 op 7 to 1) 5
3479 CREDIT NOTE 8-11-0 S Earle, *chsd ldg pair til mstks 8th and 9th, sn beh*.................. (50 to 1 op 25 to 1) 6

Dist: 2½l, 10l, 15l, 4l, 6l. 3m 55.00s. a 5.00s (6 Ran).
SR: 2/-/-/ (B R Wilsdon), N J Henderson

3696 Concord Bar At Brighton Claiming Hurdle (4-y-o and up) £2,199 2½m ....(6:05)

3145^{2} SHANAKEE 7-11-0 R Dunwoody, *trkd ldrs frm 6th, cl up and ev ch 5 out, led aftr 3 out, hit last, drvn out, fnshd lme*.................................(5 to 1 tchd 6 to 1) 1
3542^{3} KALAKATE 9-11-4 D O'Sullivan, *al prmnt, led aftr 4 out till after 3 out, rdn and rallied betw last 2, not quicken.* ....(5 to 1 tchd 6 to 1) 2
3545 ROGER'S PAL 7-10-13 D Gallagher, *wl beh 7th, rdn and hdwy aftr nxt, wnt 4th after four out, styd on one pace.* .... (10 to 1 op 12 to 1 tchd 14 to 1) 3
3014^{9} WILTOSKI (bl) 6-11-4 Mrs N Ledger, *pushed alng in mid-div, mstk 4th, outpcd 9th, styd on frm 3 out.* .... (50 to 1 op 33 to 1) 4
3509 IVYCHURCH (USA) 8-10-13 (7*) Karen Cook, *beh, rdn and styd on frm 4 out, one pace*.......(50 to 1 op 33 to 1) 5
2454^{6} BITTER ALOE 5-12-0 M Perrett, *led till aftr 3rd, led ag'n after 5th til 5 out, wknd 3 out.* .... (25 to 1 op 16 to 1 tchd 33 to 1) 6
3511 ARMASHOCKER 6-11-1 V Smith, *beh, rdn and effrt aftr 7th, chsd ldrs, wknd after nxt.* .... (25 to 1 op 20 to 1 tchd 33 to 1) 7
2543^{3} WHATMORECANIASKFOR (Ire) (bl) 6-10-6 (3*) R Davis, *led aftr 3rd till after 5th, sn wknd*.....(50 to 1 op 33 to 1) 8

2729 ALICE'S MIRROR 5-10-9 W McFarland, *lost tch aftr 6th, sn beh*..................... (20 to 1 tchd 33 to 1) 9
3308[4] BAYLORD PRINCE (Ire) 6-11-6 M Hoad, *jmpd badly in rear, al beh*.......... (10 to 1 op 8 to 1 tchd 14 to 1) 10
2878[4] OLIVIPET 5-10-4 (7*) G Crone, *wl beh 7th, rdn and no hdwy*....................(50 to 1 op 33 to 1) 11
3330[2] COBB GATE (bl) 6-11-0 M Stevens, *beh, rdn and hdwy aftr 7th, wknd quickly after nxt.*
............................(14 to 1 op 10 to 1 tchd 16 to 1) 12
3304 FIVE CASTLES 6-11-2 J Railton, *al beh, rear grp frm 7th.*
.....................................(50 to 1 op 33 to 1) 13
RED OXON 12-11-2 Leesa Long, *pressed ldrs till wknd quickly aftr 7th, tld off*.......(50 to 1 op 33 to 1) 14
2870* SO DISCREET (USA) 6-12-0 A Maguire, *trkd ldrs frm 5th, led 8th, hdd and chsd lders till rdn aftr 4 out, fourth and btn whn f 2 out*................ (9 to 4 fav tchd 5 to 2) f
QUAI D'ORSAY 9-11-4 D Murphy, *hld up, lost tch frm 6th, tld off whn pld up aftr 3 out*...... (5 to 1 tchd 6 to 1) pu
ADANUS 10-11-5 M Crosse, *beh frm 5th, tld off whn pld up and dismounted aftr 3 out.*..... (50 to 1 op 33 to 1) pu
2713[2] SPARKLER GEBE (bl) 8-11-2 M A FitzGerald, *hld up, hdwy 5th, chsd ldrs till wknd 7th, sn beh, tld off whn pld up aftr 3 out*......................... pu
Dist: 2l, 3l, 15l, ¾l, 1¼l, 2½l, 7l, 12l, ¾l, hd. 4m 43.70s. a 6.70s (18 Ran).

(Darren Croft), J Ffitch-Heyes

3697 Southern FM Handicap Chase (0-105 4-y-o and up) £2,782 2m....... (6:35)

3456[4] GREEN WALK [70] 7-9-11[2] (5*) C Burnett-Wells, *trkd ldr, wnt second 5th, jnd lder 5 out, led nxt, mstk last, sn reco'red, styd on wl.* (30 to 1 op 20 to 1 tchd 25 to 1) 1
3560[5] AIR COMMANDER [88] 9-11-4 T Wall, *led till hdd 4 out, rdn and rallied betw last 2, not quicken r-in.*
.....................(9 to 2 op 4 to 1 tchd 5 to 1) 2
3303 FRED SPLENDID [90] 11-11-6 R Dunwoody, *chsd ldrs, pushed alng 5 out, rallied to go 3rd aftr 4 out, lft btn third at last*............(7 to 1 op 9 to 2 tchd 15 to 2) 3
3456[3] RUSTIC GENT (Ire) [78] 6-10-5 (3*) R Davis, *hld up, hdwy 6th, trkd ldrs 4th whn blun four out, sn wknd, lft poor fourth at last, tld off..* (7 to 1 op 5 to 1 tchd 8 to 1) 4
3573[8] LUCKY AGAIN [86] 7-11-2 S Earle, *chsd ldr till mstk 6th, mistake 8th, sn wknd, lft poor 5th at last, tld off.*
................................(8 to 1 op 5 to 1) 5
3548[9] COURT RAPIER [96] 12-11-12 A Maguire, *hld up and beh, hdwy aftr 5 out, styd on one pace after 3 out, beh whn f last*.................... (9 to 4 fav op 5 to 2) f
3148[2] HANDSOME NED [80] (bl) 8-10-10 J Railton, *blun and uns rdr second*.............. (5 to 2 tchd 100 to 30) ur
Dist: 2½l, 15l, dist, 1l. 3m 55.30s. a 5.30s (7 Ran).

(C Cornwell), R Rowe

3698 A. R. Dennis Handicap Hurdle (0-110 4-y-o and up) £2,805 2½m...... (7:05)

1945[7] DIRECTORS' CHOICE [80] 9-10-2 M Hourigan, *hld up, rapid hdwy aftr 3 out, chlgd after nxt, hit last, rdn to ld nr finish*.......... (16 to 1 op 10 to 1 tchd 20 to 1) 1
3306[2] ESPRIT DE FEMME (Fr) [84] 8-10-6 Peter Hobbs, *chsd ldg grp, cl up and ev ch 5 out, led appr 2 out, hit last, hdd nr finish*..............................(3 to 1 op 5 to 2 tchd 7 to 2) 2
3514[4] CAVO GRECO (USA) [85] 5-10-7 D Skyrme, *hld up and beh, hdwy aftr 7th, chsd ldrs, rdn 3 out, no imprsn.*
.......................(3 to 1 op 5 to 1 tchd 6 to 1) 3
3555[2] SOMERSET DANCER (USA) [96] 7-11-4 A Maguire, *pressed ldr till wknd aftr 4 out, styd on one pace.*
.................................(5 to 1 fav op 5 to 2) 4
3068 PONTOON BRIDGE [106] 7-12-0 M Perrett, *al prmnt, led 4 out, hdd appr 2 out, sn wknd.*
........................(7 to 1 op 4 to 1 tchd 10 to 1) 5
3545 LUCKY OAK [78] (bl) 8-9-11[2] (5*) C Burnett-Wells, *beh, pushed alng aftr 7th, styd on one pace frm 3 out.*
.... (33 to 1 op 25 to 1 tchd 50 to 1) 6
3308[3] GAMEFULL GOLD [87] 5-10-9 A Dicken, *beh frm 7th, nvr rch ldrs*...............(10 to 1 op 6 to 1 tchd 16 to 1) 7
2496 DOUALAGO (Fr) [83] (bl) 4-10-5 R Dunwoody, *led till hdd 4 out, sn wknd*...........(8 to 1 op 6 to 1 tchd 10 to 1) 8
2761[5] PRIVATE JET (Ire) [78] 5-10-0[3] (3*) R Davis, *al beh, rear grp frm 6th*.......... (25 to 1 op 20 to 1 tchd 33 to 1) 9
COURAGE-MON-BRAVE [80] 6-10-2[2] M Hoad, *al beh.*
.........................(16 to 1 op 12 to 1 tchd 20 to 1) 10
3330 CHEAP METAL [82] (bl) 9-10-4[4] M A FitzGerald, *beh.*
................................(25 to 1 op 14 to 1 tchd 33 to 1) 11
3409 DEBACLE (USA) [97] 5-11-5 D Murphy, *hld up in mid-div, wknd aftr 7th*............(5 to 1 op 4 to 1 tchd 11 to 2) 12
3150[5] CONNABEE [80] 10-10-2[2] R Rowell, *pressed ldrs till rdn and wknd quickly aftr 7th, sn beh, tld off whn pld up bef 4 out*...........(33 to 1 op 25 to 1 tchd 50 to 1) pu
3441 ROWLANDSONS GOLD (Ire) [83] 4-10-5 Lorna Vincent, *sn last, tld off 5th, pld up bef 4 out.*
................................(12 to 1 op 7 to 1 tchd 14 to 1) pu
Dist: Hd, 10l, 10l, 1l, 3l, 6l, 20l, sht-hd, 1¾l, 8l. 4m 37.60s. a 0.60s (14 Ran).
SR: 18/22/13/14/23/-/ (T G Mills), T G Mills

3699 Uckfield Handicap Chase (0-105 5-y-o and up) £3,027 3m 1f 110yds.... (7:35)

3532[4] BARRACILLA [83] 9-10-10 J Railton, *hld up, steady hdwy aftr 9th, trkd ldrs frm 15th, led 3 out, rdn clr r-in, styd on wl*....(13 to 2 op 12 to 1 tchd 14 to 1 and 6 to 1) 1
3477[5] PURBECK DOVE [92] 9-11-5 A Maguire, *led to second, trkd ldrs, cl up and ev ch 5 out, wth lder 3 out, every chance whn mstk last, not quicken*
.............................(6 to 1 op 8 to 1 tchd 11 to 2) 2
3546[5] VICTORY GATE (USA) [73] 9-10-0 D Gallagher, *beh, hdwy 15th, ev ch frm nxt, rdn and styd on one pace from 3 out*........................(25 to 1 op 20 to 1) 3
2506 WOODLANDS GENHIRE [77] (v) 9-11-1 (3*) R Davis, *led to 5th, led ag'n tenth to 12th, led 6 out to 3 out, styd on one pace*.............(12 to 1 op 8 to 1 tchd 14 to 1) 4
3417[2] MISS FERN [91] 9-11-1 (3*) D Meredith, *pressed ldg grp, ev ch 5 out, sn rdn and no imprsn...* (7 to 2 op 9 to 2) 5
3307[2] GINGER TRISTAN [97] 8-11-10 Peter Hobbs, *mid-div, chsd ldg grp frm 14th, ev ch 5 out, sn rdn and no imprsn from 3 out*................... (7 to 1 op 5 to 1) 6
3493[3] CHANCERY BUCK [83] (bl) 11-10-10 J Frost, *hld up, mstks 9th and 14th, hdwy nxt, cl up and ev ch 5 out, sn wknd.*
.................................(14 to 1 tchd 16 to 1) 7
3544[4] PUNCH'S HOTEL [93] 9-11-1 (5*) C Burnett-Wells, *beh frm 6th, one pace from six out*...........(10 to 1 op 7 to 1) 8
3332 ON YOUR WAY [73] 12-10-0 W McFarland, *mid-div, wkng whn mstk 15th, sn beh*...........(33 to 1 op 20 to 1) 9
3532 TRISKY FRIEND [83] 12-10-10 S Earle, *pushed alng aftr 6th, drpd rear 11th, sn beh*.............(20 to 1 op 14 to 1) 10
3512[4] SUNBEAM TALBOT [96] 13-11-9 M A FitzGerald, *al rear grp, lost tch frm 14th.* (12 to 1 op 7 to 1 tchd 14 to 1) 11
3040[6] VALNAU (Fr) [84] (bl) 7-10-11 R Dunwoody, *led second to 4th, led ag'n 5th to tenth, led 12th to 6 out, stdly wknd.*
.................(10 to 4 fav op 9 to 4 tchd 11 to 4) 12
CENTAUR SONG [77] 14-10-4 Mr Raymond White, *f 3rd.*
...............................(33 to 1 op 25 to 1) f
3510 INDIAN JEWEL [73] 10-9-7 (7*) W J Walsh, *beh frm 12th, tld off whn f 4 out*...........(20 to 1 op 14 to 1) f
3546[7] MISS MUIRE [73] 8-10-0 D Morris, *f 3rd.*
.................................(33 to 1 op 20 to 1) f
Dist: 5l, 4l, 3½l, ¾l, 11l, 12l, 15l, ½l, 2l, 2l. 6m 20.10s. a 8.10s (15 Ran).

(Mrs Margaret Geake), G B Balding

3700 Hove Four Yrs Old Novices' Hurdle £1,543 2m 1f.................. (8:05)

3208[5] BOYFRIEND 11-0 P Holley, *trkd ldrs, cl up and ev ch 3 out, rdn to ld last, ridden out...*(3 to 1 fav op 4 to 1) 1
3094[3] MULLED ALE (Ire) 10-9 M Richards, *trkd ldrs, led appr 2 out, hdd last, not quicken.*
..................(4 to 1 op 9 to 2 tchd 7 to 2) 2
2821[3] VISIMOTION (USA) 11-0 T Kent, *led to 3rd, pressed ldr till lost pl aftr 3 out, rdn and rallied after 2 out, kpt on one pace*................... (7 to 2 op 5 to 2) 3
2857[4] DON TOCINO 11-0 D Skyrme, *led 3rd till hdd appr 2 out, mstk two out, one pace.*
....................(25 to 1 op 20 to 1 tchd 33 to 1) 4
870 GENTLEMAN SID 10-11 (3*) D Meredith, *hld up, chsd ldrs frm 4 out, sn no imprsn.*
....................(20 to 1 op 12 to 1 tchd 16 to 1) 5
2364[8] FINDON ACADEMY (Ire) 11-0 H Jenkins, *hld up, styd on one pace frm 4 out*.........(20 to 1 tchd 33 to 1) 6
2516[3] DESERT CHALLENGER (Ire) 11-0 A Maguire, *hld up and beh 5th, lost tch 4 out*...............(4 to 1 op 5 to 1) 7
KEEP SAFE 10-9 M Ahern, *beh frm 5th, sn lost tch.*
.................................(33 to 1 op 14 to 1) 8
3095[5] CLASSY KAHYASI (Ire) 10-9 W McFarland, *led by second, lme.*...................(13 to 1 op 14 to 1 tchd 25 to 1) pu
3253[6] CELTIC LILLEY 10-9 M Hoad, *jmpd badly, sn last and tld off, pld up aftr 5th*.....(33 to 1 op 16 to 1) pu
2914 MUSICAL HIGH (Fr) 10-9 R Dunwoody, *hld up, steady hdwy aftr 6th, in tch whn mstk 3 out, broke leg, pld up appr nxt. Destroyed*................(10 to 1 op 7 to 1) pu
Dist: 2½l, 15l, nk, sht-hd, 2½l, 20l, 20l. 4m 1.80s. a 9.80s (11 Ran).

(Mrs T Brown), D R C Elsworth

UTTOXETER (good (races 1,2,3,4), good to firm (5,6,7,8))
Saturday April 30th
Going Correction: MINUS 0.05 sec. per fur.

3701 Calor Gas Novices' Hurdle (4-y-o) £1,987 2m.................... (2:40)

3231* DESTINY CALLS 11-5 R Dunwoody, *hld up in 3rd pl, wnt second appr 5th, led 2 out, rdn clr r-in.*
..............(13 to 8 on op 5 to 2 on tchd 6 to 4 on) 1
TRIPPIANO 10-12 T Kent, *led till hdd 2 out, ran on one pace und pres.*........(3 to 1 op 5 to 2 tchd 100 to 30) 2
3557[4] SABERAGE 10-0 (7*) B Harding, *hld up in rear, hdwy 4 out, ev ch 2 out, wknd aftr.*(12 to 1 op 6 to 1) 3
3601[5] DREAM START 10-5 (7*) R Wilkinson, *hld up in tch till wknd 4 out.*.........................(50 to 1) 4
3587 TEJANO GOLD (USA) 10-12 Gary Lyons, *pld hrd, chsd ldrs till sddl slpd and pulled up bef 5th...* (5 to 1 op 8 to 1) pu
Dist: 4l, 2l, 20l. 3m 53.30s. a 14.30s (5 Ran).

(Simon Harrap), N A Gaselee

3702 Addison Of Newport Selling Handicap Hurdle (4-y-o) £1,686 2m.......(3:15)

3587³ DANGER BABY [73] 11-2 B Powell, *sn chsd ldr, led appr 2 out, rdn clr.*
.........(11 to 4 fav op 4 to 1 tchd 9 to 2 and 5 to 2) 1
3559⁶ CONVOY [85] (bl) 12-0 R Dunwoody, *hld up, hdwy 4 out, chsd wnr frm 2 out, no imprsn.*................(5 to 1) 2
3601³ SALLY OF THE ALLEY [57] 9-7 (7") D Towler, *al prmnt, rdn and one pace frm 2 out.* (6 to 1 op 9 to 2 tchd 13 to 2) 3
3211⁴ CRIMINAL RECORD (USA) [65] (v) 10-8 Diane Clay, *hld up in tch, hdwy 3 out, kpt on one pace.*
.................(13 to 2 op 6 to 1 tchd 7 to 1) 4
3252⁶ KOSVILLE (Fr) [76] 11-5 J Lower, *towards rear till hdwy 3 out, nvr nr to chal.*................(6 to 1 tchd 8 to 1) 5
3572 SECRET FORMULA [63] 10-6 M Sharratt, *al towards rear.*
.................(20 to 1 op 25 to 1 tchd 33 to 1) 6
3587⁶ BARSAL (Ire) [73] 11-2 A Maguire, *slwly away, nvr on terms.*................(13 to 2 op 5 to 1 tchd 7 to 1) 7
2422 SMART DAISY [57] 10-0 N Williamson, *hld up, hdwy 4 out, wknd aftr nxt.*....................(33 to 1 op 25 to 1) 8
2628 NEVER SO LOST [60] (bl) 10-3 D Bridgwater, *took str hold and sn clr, wkng and hdd whn hit 2 out, eased.*
.................(20 to 1 op 16 to 1) 9
3559³ MARSHALL PINDARI [69] 10-5 (7") P McLoughlin, *al beh, lost tch appr 3 out, tld off.........*(8 to 1 tchd 10 to 1) 10
Dist: 5l, 3l, 3l, 5l, 2l, 6l, 6l, hd, 25l. 3m 52.60s. a 13.60s (10 Ran).
(Mouse Racing), R Dickin

3703 PRD Fasteners Handicap Chase (0-135 5-y-o and up) £3,275 3¼m (3:45)

3417* WARNER FOR WINNERS [109] 8-10-13 Peter Hobbs, *al prmnt, trkd ldr 15th to 4 out, pressed lder nxt, hrd rdn to lead cl hme.*....................(4 to 1 tchd 7 to 2) 1
3537* GLENSHANE LAD [112] 8-11-2 N Williamson, *hld up in tch and gng wl, hdwy 15th, wnt second 4 out, led nxt, hrd rdn and hdd cl hme.*............(9 to 4 fav op 2 to 1) 2
3519⁵ TRI FOLENE (Fr) [120] (bl) 8-11-10 R Dunwoody, *trkd ldr till rdn and outpcd 15th, rallied to go 3rd r-in.*
.................(3 to 1 op 5 to 2) 3
3443* RAFIKI [112] 9-11-2 A Maguire, *led till hdd 3 out, wknd quickly nxt.*........(3 to 1 op 11 to 4 tchd 7 to 2) 4
3495⁷ SWINHOE CROFT [97] 12-9-12 (3") S Wynne, *wl beh till hdwy tenth, outpcd 13th, tried to make headway appr 4 out, one pace.*.....................(20 to 1 op 16 to 1) 5
3171⁷ ARCTIC TEAL [105] (bl) 10-10-9 M Richards, *chsd ldrs till outpcd 13th, wl beh aftr.*.............(10 to 1) 6
Dist: Hd, 15l, 3l, 5l, 20l. 6m 33.90s. a 17.90s (6 Ran).
(Terry Warner Sports), P J Hobbs

3704 Ladbroke Staffordshire Hurdle Grade 2 (4-y-o and up) £9,600 2½m 110yds ....(4:20)

3484* CORROUGE (USA) 5-11-6 D Bridgwater, *led to second, led aftr 5th till mstk and hdd last, rallied und pres to ld cl hme.*.................(5 to 4 fav op Evens) 1
3555* CARIBOO GOLD (USA) (bl) 5-11-2 N Williamson, *al frnt rnk, pressed wnr 3 out, led last, hrd rdn and hdd nr finish.*
.................(100 to 30 op 3 to 1) 2
3384³ CRYSTAL BEAR (NZ) 9-11-2 B Powell, *pushed alng in rear, some hdwy 3 out, nvr on terms...* (25 to 1 op 14 to 1) 3
3413* KADI (Ger) 5-11-2 A Maguire, *hld up in tch till wknd appr 3 out....................*(5 to 2 op 2 to 1) 4
3383² ASHFIELD BOY 10-11-2 R Dunwoody, *pld hrd, led second till aftr 5th, lost tch appr 4 out, tld off.*
.................(12 to 1 op 20 to 1) 5
Dist: ½l, 15l, 1¼l, dist. 4m 45.10s. a 2.10s (5 Ran).
(Michael Gates), N A Twiston-Davies

3705 Stainless Threaded Fasteners Handicap Chase (0-135 5-y-o and up) £3,566 2m 5f....................(4:50)

3261⁴ RICHVILLE [132] 8-12-0 N Williamson, *trkd ldrs, wnt second 12th, led 3 out, mstk last, styd on strly.*
.................(5 to 1 op 7 to 2) 1
3500* MIDFIELDER [115] 8-10-11 Peter Hobbs, *hld up in rear, steady hdwy tenth, ev ch whn mstk 2 out, one pace aftr.*............................(5 to 4 fav tchd 6 to 4) 2
3593⁵ MR ENTERTAINER [107] 11-10-3 B Powell, *led, hit 9th, jmpd rght 11th, hdd 3 out, one pace.*
.................(13 to 2 op 5 to 1) 3
3500⁷ MENEBUCK [121] 8-11-3 E Murphy, *hld up in tch, blun 7th, nvr on terms aftr...*(9 to 2 op 4 to 1 tchd 5 to 1) 4
3473³ STRONG APPROACH [108] 9-10-4⁶ (3") P Williams, *beh, outpcd hfwy, effrt 5 out, one pace frm nxt.*
.................(10 to 1 op 8 to 1 tchd 12 to 1) 5
3500 LUMBERJACK (USA) [132] (bl) 10-12-0 J Osborne, *trkd ldr till hit 12th, sn btn, tld off.........*(7 to 1 tchd 6 to 1) 6
Dist: 3½l, 5l, 20l, sht-hd, 25l. 5m 9.70s. a 9.70s (6 Ran).
(Major-Gen R L T Burges), K C Bailey

3706 Eurofast Petrochemical Supplies Amateur Riders' Novices' Chase (5-

y-o and up) £2,234 2m.........(5:25)

3263⁷ CRAFTY CHAPLAIN 8-11-5 (5") Mr D McCain, *trkd ldrs, led 4 out, ran on wl....................*(14 to 1 op 12 to 1) 1
3548⁶ MACEDONAS 6-11-10 Mr J Durkan, *hld up, hdwy 5 out, ev ch whn pckd 2 out, strly rdn, no imprsn r-in.*
.................(3 to 1 op 5 to 2 tchd 7 to 2) 2
3585 PHARGOLD (Ire) 5-10-12 Mr M Armytage, *hld up in tch, hdwy to go second 4 out, wknd appr last.*
.................(6 to 4 fav tchd 7 to 4 and 15 to 8) 3
3111⁷ NORTHERN OPTIMIST 6-10-6 (7") Mr J L Llewellyn, *trkd ldr, made most frm 5th till hdd 4 out, hit nxt, sn btn.*
.................(20 to 1) 4
3532⁵ IMPECCABLE TIMING 11-10-11 (7") Mr A Mitchell, *not jump wl in rear, nvr on terms....................*(14 to 1) 5
3605* REAL PROGRESS (Ire) 6-11-3 (7",6ex) Mr S Mulcaire, *led to 5th, wknd rpdly appr 3 out....................*(3 to 1) 6
3478 ARCTICFLOW (USA) (bl) 9-10-11 (7") Mr S Davis, *al beh, lost tch 7th....................*(50 to 1) 7
2892⁹ ASHDREN 7-10-13 (5") Mr D Parker, *al rear, not ch aftr jmpd slwly 6th....................*(10 to 1) 8
Dist: 2l, 6l, 12l, 15l, 3½l, 2l, 4l. 3m 55.30s. a 6.30s (8 Ran).
(D A Malam), D McCain

3707 Levy Board National Hunt Flat Race (Div I) (4,5,6-y-o) £2,060 2m.... (5:55)

2332³ CROWTHER HOMES 4-10-0 (7") S Knott, *al prmnt, led wl o'r 3 fs out, pushed out, cmftbly.*
.................(12 to 1 op 10 to 1 tchd 14 to 1) 1
THE SHY PADRE (Ire) 5-10-13 (5") D Fortt, *al prmnt, rdn 3 fs out, kpt on....................*(12 to 1 op 8 to 1) 2
3488⁵ MISTER BUZIOS 6-10-13 (5") A Roche, *al prmnt, ev ch o'r 2 fs out, rdn and one paced entering last.*
.................(11 to 2 op 3 to 1) 3
1674 SPEARHEAD AGAIN (Ire) 5-10-13 (5") D Leahy, *hld up, gd hdwy o'r 4 fs out, rdn over 2 out, kpt on.*
.................(3 to 1 fav op 6 to 1 tchd 8 to 1) 4
MOUNT SERRATH (Ire) 6-11-1 (3") A Procter, *hld up in rear, hdwy sn aftr hfwy, ev ch o'r 2 fs out, wknd appr last.*
.................(11 to 2 op 5 to 1) 5
MULTIPOWER 5-10-11 (7") P McLoughlin, *mid-div, effrt o'r 5 fs out, wknd wl over 2 out....................*(8 to 1 op 5 to 1) 6
3489 MY RACING DREAM 4-10-7 (5") E Husband, *mid-div, one paced fnl 4 fs....................*(10 to 1 op 8 to 1) 7
DUKE OF LANCASTER (Ire) 5-10-11 (7") J James, *hld up in rear, hdwy 5 fs out, rdn and wknd o'r 3 out.*
.................(5 to 1 op 4 to 1) 8
3256⁵ MANOR COTTAGE (Ire) 5-10-11 (7") N Collum, *made most till hdd wl o'r 3 fs out, wknd quickly...........*(14 to 1) 9
815 RUKIA 5-10-13 Mr J Durkan, *in tch till wknd o'r 5 fs out.*
.................(16 to 1 op 12 to 1) 10
KINGS GAL 6-10-10 (3") S Wynne, *al towards rear.*
.................(16 to 1 op 14 to 1) 11
3590 SCILLY CAY 5-10-6 (7") B Harding, *al beh.*
.................(16 to 1 op 12 to 1) 12
3190 PLEASURE CRUISE 4-10-5 (7") Pat Thompson, *prmnt, dsptd ld hfwy, drpd out quickly o'r 3 fs out.*
.................(50 to 1 op 33 to 1) 13
Dist: 3l, ¾l, 2l, 6l, 10l, 5l, 4l, 2½l, 1½l, 9l. 3m 45.10s. (13 Ran).
(Mrs Stella Barclay), E J Alston

3708 Levy Board National Hunt Flat Race (Div II) (4,5,6-y-o) £2,060 2m.... (6:25)

3208* BERUDE NOT TO (Ire) 5-11-11 Mr J Durkan, *al prmnt and gng wl, led o'r 3 fs out, ran on strly.* (8 to 1 op 5 to 1) 1
3401* CERTAINLY STRONG (Ire) 4-10-7 (7") R Massey, *trkd ldrs, stumbled badly 6 fs out, sn reco'red, ev ch till outpcd fnl 2 furlongs.........*(6 to 4 fav op Evens tchd 7 to 4) 2
ELUSIVE STAR 4-10-0 (7") P McLoughlin, *nvr far away, dsptd ld 4 fs out, sn rdn, one pace fnl 2.*
.................(6 to 1 op 4 to 1 tchd 8 to 1) 3
GWEEBARRA BAY (Ire) 5-10-11 (7") R Darke, *hld up in mid-div, prmnt frm hfwy, rdn o'r 2 fs out, one pace.*
.................(33 to 1 op 20 to 1) 4
ALFIE THE GREAT (Ire) 5-10-11 (7") Mr S Mulcaire, *hld up in rear, hdwy o'r 4 fs out, one pace fnl 2.*
.................(10 to 1 op 7 to 1) 5
3489⁵ STORMY CORAL (Ire) 4-10-7 (5") Mr D Parker, *mid-div, lft beh fnl 4 fs....................*(12 to 1 op 7 to 1) 6
MULLINGAR (Ire) 5-11-1 (3") P Williams, *hld up in rear, styd on fnl 4 fs, nvr dngrs....................*(25 to 1) 7
3401 MORNING BLUSH (Ire) 4-10-0 (7") L Reynolds, *prmnt till wknd o'r 3 fs out....................*(12 to 1 op 10 to 1) 8
GOING GREY 4-10-5 (7") N Wilmington, *al beh.*
.................(33 to 1 op 20 to 1) 9
MISTER GOODGUY (Ire) 5-11-4 Mr A H Crow, *trkd ldr, led aftr 6 fs, hdd o'r 3 out, wknd quickly.*
.................(5 to 1 op 8 to 1 tchd 7 to 2) 10
LEINTHALL THISTLE (Ire) 5-10-6 (7") N Collum, *al beh, tld off....................*(33 to 1 op 20 to 1) 11
THISTLE LOCH 5-10-6 (7") D Towler, *prmnt to hfwy, sn beh, virtually pld up.*....(25 to 1 op 20 to 1) 12
GLEN FIDEL (Ire) 6-11-1 (3") T Eley, *al beh, virtually pld up 2 fs out, completed.*.............(33 to 1 op 10 to 1) 13

KAYAK POINT 5-10-11 (7") D Winter, *led for 6 fs, wknd
rpdly and virtually pld up, completed.*
.... (33 to 1 op 20 to 1) 14
Dist: 8l, 2½l, 7l, ½l, 6l, 8l, 6l, nk, 8l, dist. 3m 41.70s. (14 Ran).

(G Addiscott), O Sherwood

GOWRAN PARK (IRE) (soft)
Sunday May 1st

3709   Silver Birch Novice Chase (5-y-o and
up) £3,450 2¼m............... (4:30)

3507⁵	RANDOM PRINCE 10-12-0 P Carberry, ... (6 to 1)	1
3325²	SLANEY BACON 7-11-9 C F Swan, ... (10 to 1)	2
3325²	WINTERBOURNE ABBAS (Ire) 5-11-7 B Sheridan, ..(9 to 2)	3
	OATFIELD LAD 7-12-0 K F O'Brien, ...(12 to 1)	4
1035	COOLADERRA LADY 8-11-4 J P Banahan, ...(50 to 1)	5
3275	DELGANY DEER 8-11-4 (5") D T Evans, ...(16 to 1)	6
	PERSIAN ABBEY 7-11-4 (5") Mr H F Cleary, ...(16 to 1)	7
3528⁶	MAN OF IRON 7-11-4 (5") D Walsh, ...(14 to 1)	8
3551	MAJOR BERT (Ire) 6-11-9 F Woods, ...(50 to 1)	9
3507	BALLYROY BOY 8-11-11 (3") Miss M Olivefalk, ...(14 to 1)	10
3275²	NO BETTER BUACHAIL (Ire) 6-11-9 F J Flood, ...(10 to 1)	11
3366	CALLEROGAN 7-11-9 M Moran, ...(20 to 1)	12
2919	ORMOND BEACH (Ire) 5-10-13 W T Slattery Jnr, ..(50 to 1)	13
3273	PREMIER COUNTY 8-11-6 (3") T J Mitchell, ...(20 to 1)	14
3198	BUCK'S DELIGHT (Ire) 6-11-9 C O'Dwyer, ...(9 to 1)	pu
3293²	MUILEAR OIRGE 7-12-0 J F Titley, ...(6 to 4 fav)	pu
Dist: ¾l, 2½l, 14l, 1l. 4m 48.00s. (16 Ran).		

(N Coburn), Noel Meade

3710   Avonmore Handicap Hurdle (0-137
4-y-o and up) £4,485 2m........ (5:00)

3506³	CASH CHASE (Ire) [-] 6-9-7 S H O'Donovan, ...(9 to 2)	1
3526	HIS WAY (Ire) [-] 5-10-6 J Shortt, ...(12 to 1)	2
3615⁴	MR BOAL (Ire) [-] 5-10-12 (5") J P Broderick, ...(7 to 2)	3
3664	THE SHAUGHRAUN [-] 8-11-1 K F O'Brien, ...(7 to 1)	4
3529³	SHEER MIST [-] 7-9-11 (5") M J Halbrook, ...(16 to 1)	5
	SLANEY SPECIAL [-] 7-11-0 F J Flood, ...(12 to 1)	6
1454⁶	BIZANA (Ire) [-] 4-10-3 P Carberry, ...(6 to 1)	7
3468	IRON MARINER (Ire) [-] 6-9-5 (7") D M McCullagh, (14 to 1)	8
3449	LA CIENAGA [-] 10-10-3 (7") S G Anderson, ...(25 to 1)	9
3369	ARCTIC WEATHER (Ire) [-] (bl) 5-11-7 C F Swan, .(3 to 1 fav)	pu
Dist: 1l, ½l, ¾l, 8l. 4m 1.10s. (10 Ran).		

(S Ryan), A J Keane

3711   Great Oak Novice Handicap Hurdle
(0-123 4-y-o and up) £2,760 2½m (5:30)

3654⁵	STRONG PLATINUM (Ire) [-] 6-10-13 (7",6ex) Mr J Connolly,	
	.... (7 to 2)	1
3322	PRECARIUM (Ire) [-] 6-11-0 C O'Dwyer, ...(14 to 1)	2
2040⁴	PEPPERONI EXPRESS (Ire) [-] (bl) 5-10-5 J P Banahan,	
	.... (14 to 1)	3
3526⁴	PUNTERS BAR [-] 7-10-7 (5",6ex) P A Roche, ...(13 to 2)	4
2027	AERODROME FIELD (Ire) [-] 6-10-3 B Sheridan, ...(33 to 1)	5
3613⁵	HEIST [-] 5-12-0 P Carberry, ...(9 to 4 fav)	6
2425⁵	BLAZING COMET [-] 8-10-0 F Woods, ...(12 to 1)	7
3020	STEEL MIRROR [-] 5-11-9 C O'Brien, ...(14 to 1)	8
3394⁹	GOLDEN NUGGET [-] 7-10-6 D Walsh, ...(20 to 1)	9
2939	BETTYS THE BOSS (Ire) [-] 6-9-12 C F Swan, ...(12 to 1)	10
3449²	RED THUNDER [-] 7-9-11 D P Fagan, ...(10 to 1)	11
3294	TREACYS CROSS [-] 8-9-12 (3") T J Mitchell, ...(25 to 1)	12
3506⁹	ISN'T THAT NICE (Ire) [-] 6-10-4 J Shortt, ...(14 to 1)	13
11⁸	AISEIRI [-] 7-10-9 K F O'Brien, ...(16 to 1)	14
3529	FANDANGOLD [-] (bl) 8-9-8 S H O'Donovan, ...(20 to 1)	15
231*	THE EXAMINER [-] 8-10-8 J Magee, ...(20 to 1)	16
3366	BORRISMORE FLASH (Ire) [-] (bl) 6-9-5 (5") J P Broderick,	
	.... (50 to 1)	17
96⁸	ARI'S FASHION [-] 9-9-7 W T Slattery Jnr, ...(50 to 1)	18
3197⁷	SIR SOOJE (Ire) [-] 5-10-2 S R Murphy, ...(20 to 1)	f
1685	GARYS GIRL [-] 7-10-0 (7") J M McCormack, ...(25 to 1)	pu
ist: 3l, nd, 2½l, hd. 5m 8.30s. (20 Ran).		

(Mrs Theresa McCoubrey), P Burke

3712   Thomastown I.N.H. Flat Race (4-y-o
and up) £2,760 2m............. (6:00)

3372²	FIRE DUSTER 4-11-3 Mr A P O'Brien, ...(9 to 4 fav)	1
3244³	GROUND WAR 7-11-11 (7") Mr M Budds, ...(8 to 1)	2
3372⁸	RANAGAR (Ire) 4-11-5 (5") Mr H F Cleary, ...(6 to 1)	3
3694³	LITTLE BUCK (Ire) 6-11-4 (7") Mr J S Cullen, ...(10 to 1)	4
4327*	COLLEEN'S BELLE (Ire) 6-11-13 Mr D Valentine, ...(9 to 1)	5
2704⁴	NOPADDLE 10-12-4 Mr W P Mullins, ...(14 to 1)	6
3071	DROICHEAD LAPEEN 7-11-11 (7") Mr T J Beattie, (16 to 1)	7
2733	DUNFERNE CLASSIC (Ire) 5-12-3 Mr P Fenton, ...(5 to 2)	8
3552²	GLEN TEN (Ire) 5-11-9 (3") Mrs J M Mullins, ...(6 to 1)	9
3552⁶	DUEONE (Ire) 6-11-11 Mr J A Nash, ...(14 to 1)	10
3552⁶	DON'T ASK JOHNNY (Ire) 5-11-2 (7") Mr F O'Brien,	
	.... (20 to 1)	12
1687	PERSPEX GALE (Ire) 6-11-3 (3") Mr D Marnane, ..(50 to 1)	13
2096	SWIFT SAILER (Ire) 5-11-4 (7") Mr M Cahill, ...(16 to 1)	14
3552	WHITE OAK BRIDGE (Ire) 5-10-12 (7") Mr T R Hughes,	
	.... (20 to 1)	15
1039	KESS (Ire) 5-11-5 Mr J R Banahan, ...(25 to 1)	16

	ITS ONLY JUSTICE 8-12-4 Mr M Halford, ...(25 to 1)	17
2983	BUSTHAT 7-11-11 (7") Mr P English, ...(20 to 1)	0
3201²	THE OSTRICH BLAKE (Ire) 5-10-12 (7") Miss C Doyle,	
	.... (12 to 1)	18
	BRENMAR ROSE 11-11-6 (7") Mr B J Harney, ...(25 to 1)	pu
	BUFFALO HOUSE (Ire) 4-11-3 Mr J P Dempsey, ..(20 to 1)	pu
Dist: 1l, 9l, 8l, ¾l. 3m 50.50s. (20 Ran).		

(T O'Hanlon), A P O'Brien

EXETER (firm)
Monday May 2nd
Going Correction: NIL

3713   South West Racing Club Novices' Hurdle (4-y-o and up) £1,558 2m 3f 110yds
.... (2:00)

3543⁵	KING'S TREASURE (USA) 5-12-0 J Frost, *al frnt rnk, led
3rd to 6th, led ag'n appr 2 out, hng rght r-in, all out.*
.............................(Evens fav tchd 5 to 4)	1
3253⁵	JANET SCIBS 8-10-2 (7") Pat Thompson, *hld up in rear, gd
hdwy appr 4th, led 6th till hdd approaching 2 out, strly
rdn and ran on r-in...*(14 to 1 op 8 to 1 tchd 16 to 1)	2
3531³	BUGLET (bl) 4-10-11 J Lower, *in tch till lost pl 6th, hrd
rdn and ran on 2 out....*(2 to 1 op 6 to 4 tchd 9 to 4)	3
1869	SHERWOOD FOX 7-10-7 (7") Mr G Hogan, *al prmnt, led to
3rd, rdn 2 out, rallied r-in.*
.......................(40 to 1 op 20 to 1 tchd 50 to 1)	4
2969⁹	AMILLIONMEMORIES 4-10-4 (5") D Matthews, *in tch till
rdn and lost pl 4th, rallied and hdwy 2 out, wknd r-in.*
.......................(20 to 1 op 12 to 1 tchd 25 to 1)	5
3629	APACHEE FLOWER 4-9-13 (5") S Fox, *prmnt early, led
5th, styd on frm 2 out....*(10 to 1 op 8 to 1)	6
3535	KNYAZ 4-10-9 (7") Mr L Jefford, *al beh.*
.......................(11 to 1 op 6 to 1 tchd 12 to 1)	7
3543	LAST MARCH 6-11-0 R Greene, *prmnt till rdn and wknd
appr 2 out....*(20 to 1 op 12 to 1)	8
3479	DOWN DALE 9-11-0 I Shoemark, *al beh, tld off 4 out, pld
up bef 2 out....*(50 to 1 op 20 to 1)	pu
Dist: ½l, ½l, hd, 2½l, 1½l, 4l, 1½l. 4m 36.00s. a 14.00s (9 Ran).		

(Paul Mellon), I A Balding

3714   Bramble Novices' Claiming Chase (5-
y-o and up) £2,593 2¼m........ (2:30)

3479⁹	ALDAHE 9-11-4 S Burrough, *patiently rdn, mstk 6th,
hdwy 4 out, 3rd whn lft clr 2 out.*...(12 to 1 op 7 to 1)	1
2693	JOHNNY WILL 9-11-8 L Harvey, *nvr far away, hdwy to
chase ldr 5th, second whn hmpd 2 out, not reco'r.*
.......................(3 to 1 tav op 5 to 2 tchd 7 to 2)	2
3400	OPENING OVERTURE (USA) 8-10-6 (5") D Matthews, *beh,
hdwy appr 5th, no ch frm 4 out.*
.......................(4 to 1 op 12 to 1 tchd 14 to 1)	3
3400⁴	BARONESS ORKZY 8-10-11 (3") R Davis, *chsd ldrs till
wknd appr 4 out....*(9 to 1 op 7 to 1)	4
1411²	LUCAYAN GOLD 10-11-8 R Greene, *prmnt, jmpd slwly
5th, sn beh....*(12 to 1 op 8 to 1)	5
3020	JUST (Fr) (v) 8-11-4 J Lower, *jmpd poorly in rear, al beh.*
.......................(7 to 1 op 9 to 1)	6
3575	MELDON 7-11-1 (5") S Fox, *al beh, tld off.*
.......................(11 to 1 op 8 to 1)	7
2065	BONDAID 10-11-1 (7") P McLoughlin, *f 1st.*
.......................(9 to 2 op 3 to 1 tchd 5 to 1)	f
3540³	HIGH BEACON (bl) 7-12-0 M Richards, *beh whn f 4th.*
.......................(7 to 1 op 5 to 1)	f
3255	STAR ACTOR 8-11-7 (7") Mr C Vigors, *led 4th, hit 7th, clr
whn crrd out by loose horse 2 out.*
.......................(15 to 2 op 4 to 1 tchd 8 to 1)	co
3575	SENEGALAIS (Fr) 10-11-0 J Frost, *beh whn hmpd 4th, tld
off whn pld up bef 5 out....*(16 to 1 op 8 to 1)	pu
2340	BALLINAMOE 9-10-7 (7") Mr G Hogan, *led to 4th, sn beh,
tld off whn pld up bef 5 out.*
.......................(40 to 1 op 20 to 1 tchd 50 to 1)	pu
3018	KATIEM'LU 8-10-4 (5") D Salter, *al beh, tld off whn pld up
bef last....*(50 to 1 op 25 to 1)	pu
Dist: 20l, 8l, nk, 3½l, 7l, dist. 4m 27.40s. a 16.40s (13 Ran).		

(B R Millman), B R Millman

3715   South West Racing Club Novices'
Handicap Hurdle (0-100 4-y-o and up)
£1,544 2¼m................ (3:00)

3330	PYRRHIC DANCE [72] 4-10-8 M Richards, *led till aftr sec-
ond, settled in 3rd pl, led 2 out, drw clr r-in.*
.......................(6 to 1 op 9 to 2)	1
3300⁴	MR WILBUR [78] 8-11-0 J Frost, *chsd ldr frm 3rd, ev ch 2
out till wknd r-in....*(6 to 1 op 4 to 1)	2
3153³	ABU DANCER (Ire) 6-10-0 L Harvey, *hld up, hdwy frm
4th, styd on one pace from 2 out.*
.......................(100 to 30 op 4 to 1 tchd 3 to 1)	3
3629³	MUSKORA (Ire) [88] 5-11-3 (7") C Quinlan, *rcd freely, led
aftr second, sn clr, rdn and hdd 2 out, no extr.*
.......................(11 to 10 on op 7 to 4 on tchd Evens)	4
3352	MISHY'S STAR [64] 12-9-10³ (7") Mr M Burrows, *prmnt
early, beh 3rd, tld off............*(66 to 1 op 20 to 1)	5

3670⁹ GREEN'S STUBBS [64] (bl) 7-10-0 W Irvine, *chsd ldrs till*
wknd appr 5th, tld off................(25 to 1 op 14 to 1) 6
1717 FORGED PUNT [64] 7-9-7 (7*) M Moran, *unruly strt, pld*
hrd and dsptd ld to second, beh nxt, tld off whn pulled
up bef 2 out....................(40 to 1 op 14 to 1) pu
Dist: 4l, 5l, 2l, 20l, 3½l. 4m 13.50s. a 13.50s (7 Ran).

(T W King), C J Mann

3716 South West Racing Club Selling Hurdle (4,5,6-y-o) £1,201 2¼m...... (3:30)

702⁷ ITS UNBELIEVABLE 4-10-9 (7*) P McLoughlin, *sn trkd ldrs,*
led 3 out, clr nxt, unchlgd....(3 to 1 jt-fav tchd 4 to 1) 1
3211⁵ NANQUIDNO (v) 4-10-4 J Lower, *hld up towards rear,*
hdwy 3rd, ev ch 3 out, outpcd, rallied to go second r-in.
.....................(7 to 2 op 3 to 1 tchd 4 to 1) 2
3342⁶ MINI FETE (Fr) 5-10-9 R Greene, *led till hdd 3 out, sn rdn,*
kpt on one pace....................(16 to 1 op 12 to 1) 3
3702² CONVOY (bl) 4-11-9 M Richards, *hld up in rear, pushed*
alng and hdwy frm 3rd, hrd rdn appr 2 out, one pace.
.........................(4 to 1 op 3 to 1) 4
3362⁴ RED MICKS WIFE (Ire) 4-10-1 (3*) R Davis, *al beh, tld off*
frm 5th....................(12 to 1 op 9 to 1) 5
2743⁹ NOTED STRAIN (Ire) 6-10-7 (7*) M G Hogan, *al beh, tld off.*
.........................(50 to 1 op 20 to 1) 6
FREDDIE JACK 4-10-9 S Burrough, *chsd ldrs till wknd*
quickly appr 3 out, tld off........(20 to 1 op 12 to 1) 7
3340 MAHONG 6-10-7 (7*) N Collum, *hld up, rdn and some*
hdwy 3 out, btn whn mstk and uns rdr nxt.
.........................(16 to 1 op 12 to 1) ur
2900⁶ PERSIAN BUD (Ire) 6-11-0 M Bosley, *pressed ldr till wknd*
appr 3 out, weakened nxt......(3 to 1 jt-fav op 5 to 1) pu
Dist: 12l, hd, ½l, 30l, 15l, 3½l. 4m 9.80s. a 9.80s (9 Ran).

(Gerald Hopkins), J White

3717 West Of England Open Hunters' Chase (6-y-o and up) £1,187 2m 7f 110yds........................ (4:00)

3521³ CARRICKMINES 9-11-4 (7*) Miss S Mitchell, *hld up, hdwy*
to go second 7th, steadied aftr blund 9th, led 11th,
made rst, edgd lft under pres r-in, all out.
.....................(9 to 2 op 7 to 2 tchd 5 to 1) 1
3563⁴ MR MURDOCK 9-11-4 (7*) Mr M G Miller, *prmnt early, lost*
pl appr tenth, steady hdwy frm 5 out, hrd rdn to press
wnr r-in....................(100 to 30 op 5 to 2) 2
3216 KNIFEBOARD 8-11-4 (7*) Mr J Culloty, *al in tch, wnt second 5 out, pressed wnr frm nxt till no extr nr finish.*
.........................(12 to 1 op 8 to 1) 3
SPACIAL (USA) 10-10-13 (7*) Miss M Hill, *led, hdd aftr mstk*
second, styd in tch till wknd appr 4 out.
.........................(7 to 1 op 5 to 1) 4
3591 ABBOTSHAM 9-10-13 (7*) Mr G Hogan, *led aftr second,*
hdd 11th, rdn and sn wknd.
.....................(11 to 2 op 5 to 1 tchd 13 to 2) 5
3532* NEARLY SPLENDID 9-11-7 (7*) Mr T Greed, *hld up in rear, f*
9th..........................(7 to 4 op 5 to 2) f
Dist: Nk, ½l, 15l, 1¾l. 5m 52.90s. a 17.90s (6 Ran).

(Lee Bowles), Lee Bowles

3718 South West Racing Club Handicap Hurdle (0-120 4-y-o and up) £2,008 2¼m........................ (4:30)

2632³ TRUST DEED (USA) [88] (bl) 6-10-2² S Burrough, *trkd ldr,*
led appr 3rd, hdd nxt, outpcd 3 out, styd on frm next,
drvn out to ld on line.
.....................(100 to 30 op 4 to 1 tchd 3 to 1) 1
3533³ FRESH-MINT [86] 10-10-0 I Shoemark, *hld up in rear,*
mstk 5th, rdn to ld appr last, kpt on, hld on line.
.....................(5 to 1 op 6 to 1 tchd 13 to 2) 2
3068 EASTHORPE [110] 6-11-10 L Harvey, *led, hdd appr 3rd,*
led ag'n nxt, hdd and headed appr approaching last, wknd
r-in..........................(3 to 1 fav op 7 to 1) 3
3574 MARIOLINO [86] 7-9-7 (7*) M Moran, *al in tch, chsd ldr 5th*
till one pace appr 2 out. (7 to 1 op 9 to 1 tchd 12 to 1) 4
3206⁶ GALAXY HIGH [107] 7-11-7 J Frost, *al in rear, rdn and*
some hdwy appr 2 out, sn btn, eased, tld off.
.....................(9 to 2 op 4 to 1 tchd 11 to 2) 5
3499⁶ GREYFRIARS BOBBY [95] 8-10-4 (5*) S Fox, *trkd ldrs, cl*
3rd whn blun badly 3 out, not reco'r, tld off.
.........................(6 to 1 op 8 to 1 tchd 9 to 2) 6
Dist: Sht-hd, 6l, 30l, 8l. 4m 11.70s. a 11.70s (6 Ran).

(Malcolm Enticott), Mrs A Knight

DOWN ROYAL (IRE) (good to yielding)
Monday May 2nd

3719 Bangor Opportunity Handicap Hurdle (0-116 4-y-o and up) £1,553 2½m (2:20)

3449⁶ MR FIVE WOOD (Ire) [-] 6-10-7 (2*) P A Roache, (5 to 4 fav) 1
3448* THE TOASTER [-] 7-10-6 (4*) B Bowens, ... (9 to 2) 2
3449³ ROCHE MELODY (Ire) [-] 6-9-13 C Everard, ... (6 to 1) 3
3506⁶ LOAVES AND FISHES [-] (bl) 6-10-11 (4*) B D Murtagh,
.........................(12 to 1) 4

3504⁹ POOR MOTHER (Ire) [-] 6-9-6 (4*) L J Fleming, ...(10 to 1) 5
3447⁴ MY HALL DOOR [-] 5-9-12 (2*) D T Evans, ...(10 to 1) 6
JOE'S A BOY [-] 9-10-11 D Bromley, ...(16 to 1) 7
3449⁷ THE PARSONS ROSE (Ire) [-] 6-9-6³ (2*) D Walsh, (16 to 1) 8
2⁹ GONE BY (Ire) [-] 6-10-4 (2*) D P Geoghegan, ...(4 to 1) 9
3467 JESSIE'S BOY [-] 5-10-1 (4*) T Martin, ... (16 to 1) 10
3448⁶ MAJA GRADDNOS [-] 4-9-6 (4*) D McLoughlin, ...(25 to 1) 11
3448 SIMONE STAR (Ire) [-] 5-9-3 (4*) T Horgan, ...(33 to 1) 12
2078 MASTER CRUSADER [-] 8-10-11 T J Mitchell, ...(10 to 1) 13
Dist: 5l, 3½l, sht-hd, 1l. (Time not taken) (13 Ran).

(Mrs T Doherty), J F C Maxwell

3720 Gain Horsefeeds (QR) Maiden Hurdle (4-y-o and up) £1,553 2¾m...... (2:50)

2773 MASTER MILLER 8-11-1 (5*) Mr B R Hamilton, ...(8 to 1) 1
COULIN LOCH (Ire) 5-11-0 (5*) Mr P M Kelly, ...(25 to 1) 2
3467⁶ RAMPANT ROSIE (Ire) 6-10-8 (7*) Mr G F Ryan, ...(6 to 1) 3
80² TADILA (Ire) 5-11-1 (7*) Mr J A Quinn, ...(7 to 4 on) 4
HAWAIIAN DANCE 7-11-3 (3*) Mrs C H Barker, ...(8 to 1) 5
KALAVO (Ire) 6-10-8 (7*) Mr K Ross, ...(10 to 1) 6
SCORPIO'S STAR 10-10-13 (7*) Mr C J Stafford, ..(33 to 1) 7
492 RAGS RAGOUILLE 8-10-13 (7*) Mr J A Gault, ...(14 to 1) 8
TOSS UP (Ire) 5-10-12 (7*) Mr W Ewing, ...(10 to 1) 9
EXECUTIVE BILL 8-10-8 (7*) Mr M Callaghan, ...(33 to 1) 10
692 BALLYBRAZIL BOY 5-11-5 Mr J P Dempsey, (12 to 1) 11
808 MONKS DEAR VI 7-11-1 Mr A R Coonan, ...(20 to 1) 12
MISS MAGUIRE 11-11-1 Mr M McNulty, ...(25 to 1) 13
ABDULLAH BULBUL 6-10-13 (7*) Mr S Smyth, ...(50 to 1) 14
MAGS SUPER TOI (Ire) 5-11-2 (3*) Mr P J Casey, ...(9 to 1) f
BAVARDAGE (Ire) 6-10-13 (7*) Mr L V Gracey, ...(33 to 1) pu
Dist: 3½l, 7l, 15l. (Time not taken) (16 Ran).

(M Ryan), Thomas Millar

3721 Governor's Perpetual Cup (Handicap Chase) (0-116 4-y-o and up) £1,553 2½m.......................(4:20)

3326 LA-GREINE [-] 7-10-7 (3*) Mr P McMahon, ...(7 to 2) 1
3121 SONOFBOA [-] (bl) 8-9-3 (7*) D A McLoughlin, ...(10 to 1) 2
3448 REDELVA [-] 7-9-2 (5*) Mr B R Hamilton, ...(10 to 1) 3
3392 JIMS CHOICE [-] 7-10-5 (5*) Mr R J Patton, ...(9 to 4 fav) 4
NO MORE THE FOOL [-] 8-9-11 (5*) P A Roche, ...(14 to 1) 5
2772 LACKEN BEAU [-] 10-11-11 (3*) Mr J A Nash, ...(12 to 1) 6
2200⁶ MUST DO [-] 8-10-7 (3*) T J Mitchell, ...(7 to 1) 7
3524⁷ ALL A QUIVER [-] 7-10-0 C N Bowens, ...(8 to 1) 8
DERRYNAP [-] 11-10-4 (5*) D P Geoghegan, ...(8 to 1) 9
3326 AUTUMN RIDE (Ire) [-] 6-10-0 (5*) D T Evans, ...(10 to 1) 10
Dist: 4½l, 5l, 4½l, 2l. (Time not taken) (10 Ran).

(T Bushe), I A Duncan

3722 W E Rooney Memorial Hunters' Chase (5-y-o and up) £1,380 3m 1f..... (4:50)

3527² RED EXPRESS VI 9-10-13 (5*) Mr H F Cleary, ...(11 to 4) 1
3611 GLENSPORT VI 8-10-8 (5*) Mr B R Hamilton, ...(14 to 1) 2
2773 COCO DANCER 12-10-11 (7*) Mr C A McBratney, (12 to 1) 3
TWO COVERS 7-11-9 Mr T S Costello, ...(7 to 4 fav) 4
ANOTHER MACHINE 7-10-10 (3*) Mr P McMahon, (14 to 1) 5
989⁶ WINDOVER LODGE 7-11-4 Mr J P Dempsey, ...(11 to 4) 6
2773² NEDA CHARMER 8-11-1 (3*) Mr J A Nash, ...(9 to 4) 0
Dist: 20l, 3½l, dist, 6l. (Time not taken) (7 Ran).

(O J Roche), O J Roche

3723 New Stand (QR) Ladies Flat Race (4-y-o and up) £1,382 2m........(5:20)

3508⁴ THE BOBTAIL FOX (Ire) 5-11-6 (7*) Miss C Hyde, (5 to 2 jt-fav) 1
DELPHI LODGE (Ire) 4-11-3 (3*) Miss M Olivefalk, ..(9 to 2) 2
81⁵ MRS COOPS 7-11-2 (7*) Miss A Harvey, ...(7 to 1) 3
3447⁹ REMO GROVE (Ire) 6-11-7 (7*) Miss C Gordon, ...(12 to 1) 4
39 PROUD KITTEN (Ire) 5-11-1 (7*) Miss S McDonogh, (14 to 1) 5
TEMPLEWOOD EXPRESS (Ire) 5-11-6 (7*) Miss L Robinson,
.........................(8 to 1) 6
3447 THE THIRD MAN (Ire) 5-11-6 (7*) Miss M Savage, (12 to 1) 7
3447⁵ DOCS DILEMMA (Ire) 5-11-6 (7*) Miss D Blair, ...(6 to 1) 8
3449⁸ BELLE O' THE BAY (Ire) 5-11-1 (7*) Miss J Cox, ...(10 to 1) 9
3201 START SINGING (Ire) (bl) 5-11-5 (3*) Mrs S McCarthy,
.........................(9 to 1) 10
KAVANAGHS DREAM (Ire) 5-11-10 (3*) Mrs C H Barker,
.........................(5 to 2 jt-fav) 11
OWNERS RISK (Ire) 4-10-8 (7*) Miss J Lewis, ...(10 to 1) 12
NEXT ADVENTURE (Ire) 5-11-1 (7*) Miss M A Burroughs,
.........................(14 to 1) 13
LORNA'S BEAUTY (Ire) 4-10-8 (7*) Miss L Townsley,
.........................(14 to 1) 14
215 DAYLIGHT LADY 7-11-2 (7*) Miss A McDonnell, ...(25 to 1) 15
3272⁸ GARVHILL (Ire) 5-11-1 (7*) Miss E Hyndman, ...(25 to 1) pu
Dist: 2l, 20l, 1l, ¾l. (Time not taken) (16 Ran).

(Mrs John Magnier), Noel Meade

FONTWELL (firm)
Monday May 2nd
Going Correction: NIL

3724 Beaumont Challenge Cup Amateur Riders' Chase (6-y-o and up) £2,469 3¼m 110yds. . . . . (2:00)

3544³ SATIN NOIR (Fr) 10-11-10 Mr M Armytage, *led to 3rd then 14th to 17th, cl second whn lft clr 2 out.* . . . . (Evens fav op 6 to 4 tchd 11 to 10 on)	1
3015² ROCKMOUNT ROSE 9-11-8 (7") Mr J Luck, *led 4th to 14th, lost tch frm 16th, lft poor second 2 out.* . . . . (4 to 1 op 3 to 1 tchd 11 to 4)	2
3425 PACO'S BOY (v) 9-11-3 (7") Dr J Naylor, *in rear, styd on frm 2 out, nvr a dngr.* . . . . . . (7 to 1 op 6 to 1 tchd 15 to 2)	3
3548 MAJOR INQUIRY (USA) 8-12-1 Mr J Durkan, *rear early, effrt 15th, outpcd frm 17th.* . . . . (11 to 2 op 9 to 2 tchd 7 to 1)	4
3166 LESBET 9-10-12 (7") Mr G Brown, *not jump wl, al beh, hld off.* . . . . (50 to 1 op 25 to 1)	5
2709 KNOWAFENCE 8-10-5 (7") Mr S Howe, *chsd ldrs early, outpcd frm beh, f 11th.* . . . . (50 to 1 op 25 to 1)	f
2535⁹ KILMYSHALL 8-10-10 (7") Mr D Breen, *mstk 6th, led 17th, rdn and ev ch whn blun and uns rdr 2 out.* . . . . (20 to 1 op 16 to 1 tchd 25 to 1)	ur

Dist: Dist, 5l, hd, dist. 7m 7.00s. a 37.00s (7 Ran).

(Erich Krahenbuhl), S Woodman

3725 News Selling Hurdle (4 & 5-y-o) £1,768 2¼m. . . . . (2:30)

3098 LLOYDS DREAM 5-11-1 (3") P Hide, *hld up, hdwy 5th, led bef 7th, sn clr.* . . . . (4 to 1 tchd 5 to 1 and 7 to 2)	1
3572 WAAZA (USA) 5-10-11 (7") M Appleby, *not jump wl, chsd ldrs, lost pl 4th, ran on frm 7th, no dngr.* . . . . (11 to 1 op 10 to 1 tchd 12 to 1)	2
959² CORINTHIAN GOD (Ire) 5-11-10 G Bradley, *hdwy 6th, one pace frm 2 out.* . . . . . . (9 to 4 fav op 7 to 4 tchd 5 to 2)	3
3572 FATHER'S JOY 4-10-8 M Stevens, *mstks 1st and second, in rear, hdwy frm 3 out, nvr a dngr.* . . . . (25 to 1 op 20 to 1 tchd 33 to 1)	4
3333⁵ MISS PARKES 5-10-13 S Earle, *in tch, improved bef 7th, one pace aftr.* . . . . (6 to 1 op 5 to 1 tchd 13 to 2)	5
3531⁶ WEST END (bl) 4-10-13 Mr S Stickland, *chsd ldrs frm 5th, mstk 7th, wknd 2 out.* . . . . (14 to 1 op 25 to 1)	6
3531 FORMAESTRE (Ire) 4-10-8 B Powell, *mid-div thrght.* . . . . (14 to 1 op 12 to 1 tchd 10 to 1)	7
BAN RI (Ire) 4-10-8 G Rowe, *dwlt, nvr on terms.* . . . . (5 to 1 op 10 to 1)	8
3304⁵ BARGIN BOY 5-11-4 Leesa Long, *al in rear, mstk 5th.* . . . . (33 to 1 op 25 to 1)	9
3632 HIGH BACCARAT (v) 5-11-4 A Tory, *led to 7th, wknd quickly, pld up 2 out.* . . . . (25 to 1 op 20 to 1)	pu
3543 BARNIEMEBOY (bl) 4-10-13 W Elderfield, *chasing ldrs til beh frm 6th, pld up bef 7th.* . . . . (33 to 1 op 25 to 1)	pu
1515 TINAS LASS 5-10-13 D Morris, *chsd ldrs to 6th, sn wknd, pld up 2 out.* . . . . (7 to 1 op 6 to 1)	pu

Dist: 15l, 2½l, ½l, 3½l, 1l, 6l, 12l, 5l. 4m 25.50s. a 15.50s (12 Ran).

(Mrs Eileen Sheehan), J J Sheehan

3726 Chichester Observer Novices' Chase (5-y-o and up) £2,232 2m 3f. . . . . (3:00)

3498² MR MATT (Ire) 6-11-8 J Railton, *led till hdd 12th, ran on 2 out, led last, ran on.* . . . . (6 to 5 on op 11 to 10)	1
3697* GREEN WALK 7-10-12 (5") C Burnett-Wells, *al hndy, led 12th, hrd rdn 2 out, hdd last and wknd.* . . . . (3 to 1 op 9 to 4)	2
2761⁴ WAYWARD WIND 10-11-2 W McFarland, *in tch early, outpcd 9th, styd on, no dngr.* . . . . (12 to 1 op 9 to 1)	3
3572⁷ DARINGLY 5-10-9 Mr G Brown, *chsd ldr 5th to 11th, outpcd frm 12th.* . . . . . . (25 to 1 tchd 33 to 1 and 20 to 1)	4
3426 POPPETS PET 7-11-3 (5") S Curran, *lost pl 7th, tld off frm 12th.* . . . . (4 to 1 op 5 to 1 tchd 9 to 2)	5
3454 STYLISH GENT (bl) 7-11-2 B Powell, *al beh, tld off frm 9th, pld up 11th.* . . . . (20 to 1 op 16 to 1 tchd 25 to 1)	pu

Dist: 10l, 1¼l, 3l, dist. 4m 47.70s. a 12.70s (6 Ran).

(Mrs Eric Boucher), D M Grissell

3727 Diane Oughton Memorial Challenge Trophy Handicap Chase (0-115 5-y-o and up) £2,831 2m 3f. . . . . (3:30)

3548* DEXTRA DOVE [108] 7-11-12 S Earle, *chsd ldrs to 3rd, mstks 6th, led aftr 9th, rdn 3 out, blun 2 out, hrd ridn on flt.* . . . . (7 to 4 on op 6 to 4 tchd 9 to 4)	1
3011² THE WHIP [85] 7-10-3 J Railton, *chsd ldr to 3rd, effrt 2 out, rdn and chlgd last, not quicken.* . . . . (2 to 1 op 7 to 4 tchd 9 to 4)	2
2020 SOCKS DOWNE [82] 15-10-0 B Powell, *led til 9th, outpcd frm 3 out.* . . . . . . (7 to 1 op 5 to 1 tchd 8 to 1)	3

Dist: 1½l, 9l. 4m 46.30s. a 11.30s (3 Ran).

(Dextra Lighting Systems), R H Alner

3728 Bradley Electrical Handicap Hurdle (0-120 5-y-o and up) £2,145 2¾m (4:00)

3481³ SHIMMERING SCARLET (Ire) [91] 6-11-9 B Powell, *led 3rd to 5th, led ag'n 2 out, hrd rdn.* . . . . (3 to 1 fav op 7 to 2 tchd 11 to 4)	1
3520⁶ LEGAL BEAGLE [90] 7-11-8 M Perrett, *led till lost pl 3rd, mstk 4th, ran on frm 3 out, ev ch last, not quicken.* . . . . (14 to 1 op 10 to 1 tchd 16 to 1)	2
CHASMARELLA [83] 9-11-1 D Morris, *hld up, hdwy frm 2 out, rdn but no extr aftr last.* . . . . (13 to 2 op 10 to 1 tchd 6 to 1)	3
3545² TEMPORALE [70] 8-9-9 (7") G Crone, *chsd ldrs, ev ch appr 2 out, one pace.* . . . . (4 to 1 op 9 to 2 tchd 11 to 2 and 7 to 1)	4
3609⁶ FANTASY WORLD [92] 8-11-7 (3") P Hide, *led frm 5th to 2 out, wknd appr last.* . . . . (6 to 1 op 5 to 1)	5
3308 CARRIKINS [83] (bl) 7-11-1 J Railton, *in tch, rdn frm 8th, wknd bef 2 out.* . . . . (14 to 1 op 8 to 1)	6
3514 STRAIGHT LACED (USA) [82] (bl) 7-11-0 Leesa Long, *al mid-div.* . . . . (16 to 1 op 20 to 1 tchd 14 to 1)	7
3547² ILE DE SOO [92] 8-11-5 (5") C Burnett-Wells, *al beh.* . . . . (7 to 1 op 5 to 1 tchd 11 to 2)	8
3594 OCEAN LAD [75] 11-10-7 A Tory, *al beh, pld up aftr 7th.* . . . . (33 to 1 op 25 to 1)	pu
3455⁷ MORE OF IT [90] (bl) 9-11-8 G Rowe, *chsd ldrs to 6th, beh 7th, pld up 2 out.* . . . . (20 to 1 op 16 to 1)	pu
3117⁵ RED BEAN [87] 6-11-5 A Dicken, *mstk 7th, lost pl and pld up appr 2 out.* . . . . . . (12 to 1 tchd 10 to 1 and 14 to 1)	pu

Dist: 2l, 1½l, 1¼l, 2½l, 9l, 15l, 30l. 5m 21.80s. a 12.80s (11 Ran).

(Peter Jones), R H Buckler

3729 West Sussex Gazette Novices' Hurdle (4-y-o and up) £1,543 2¼m. . . . . . (4:30)

FISIO SANDS 5-10-6 (3") P Hide, *al prmnt, led 4th, ran on frm 2 out, easily.* . . . . . (6 to 1 op 5 to 1 tchd 7 to 2)	1
3002⁴ FITNESS FANATIC 6-10-13 (7") J J Brown, *hdwy 5th, chsd wnr frm 7th, not quicken aftr.* . . . . (8 to 1 op 6 to 1 tchd 7 to 1)	2
CHINAMAN 5-11-0 A Tory, *in tch early, one pace frm 6th.* . . . . (10 to 1 op 6 to 1 tchd 12 to 1)	3
1945⁸ JOVIAL MAN (Ire) 5-11-6 M Perrett, *chsd ldrs, improved appr 6th, btn aftr nxt.* . . . . (15 to 8 fav op 2 to 1 tchd 9 to 4 and 7 to 4)	4
3543⁶ OH SO HANDY 6-11-0 D Morris, *hdwy aftr 5th, sn wknd.* . . . . (7 to 2 op 7 to 1)	5
3281 JOHNS JOY 9-11-0 W McFarland, *hdwy 6th, one pace frm 7th.* . . . . (10 to 1 op 12 to 1)	6
3571⁹ MAKING TIME 7-10-9 B Powell, *nvr a dngr.* . . . . (16 to 1 op 20 to 1 tchd 50 to 1)	7
MAJESTIC QUEEN 7-10-9 J Railton, *nvr a factor.* . . . . (33 to 1 op 25 to 1)	8
3145⁶ FERENS HALL 7-10-9 (5") C Burnett-Wells, *led to 3rd, hdd 4th, wknd 6th, tld off.* . . . . (5 to 1 op 16 to 1 tchd 33 to 1)	9
3455 SUKEY TAWDRY 8-10-11² W Elderfield, *nvr a dngr.* . . . . (50 to 1 op 33 to 1)	10
2910 FELICE'S PET 4-10-6² G Rowe, *rear, mstk second, f 3rd.* . . . . (50 to 1 op 25 to 1 tchd 66 to 1)	f
2817 FERAL BAY (Ire) 5-11-0 G Bradley, *chsd ldr to 3rd, sn lost pl, pld up aftr 5th.* . . . . (12 to 1 op 6 to 1)	pu
3547 MR ELECTRAMECH 7-11-0 A Dicken, *played up strt, beh frm 3rd, pld up aftr 5th.* . . . . (50 to 1 op 33 to 1)	pu

Dist: 6l, 4l, 1¼l, 6l, 11l, nk, 1½l, 20l, 20l. 4m 19.10s. a 9.10s (13 Ran).

(Mrs S A Willis), J T Gifford

GOWRAN PARK (IRE) (soft)
Monday May 2nd

3730 Richard Power (Bookmaker) Maiden Hurdle (4 & 5-y-o) £3,450 2m 1f. . (3:45)

3550⁵ RYE HILL QUEEN (Ire) 4-10-5 (5") K P Gaule, ... (5 to 1)	1
1853⁹ AULD STOCK (Ire) 4-11-1 M Duffy, ... (6 to 1)	2
PRINCE PERICLES (Ire) 5-10-12 (7") J M Sullivan, . . (5 to 1)	3
NORDIC SENSATION (Ire) 5-10-12 (7") A P McCoy, . (7 to 1)	4
3466² CALL ME HENRY 5-10-12 (7") Mr J T McNamara, ... (9 to 2 fav)	5
3250⁶ VERITATIS SPLENDOR (Ire) 5-11-5 S H O'Donovan, (6 to 1)	6
3505 TRIBAL MEMORIES (Ire) 4-11-3 (7") M P Kelly, . . (14 to 1)	7
A LITTLE EARNER 5-11-5 R Hughes, ... (12 to 1)	8
GALLOPING HOGAN (Ire) 5-11-0 (5") M A Davey, . .(14 to 1)	9
DANGER FLYNN (Ire) 4-11-1 A J O'Brien, ... (10 to 1)	10
3550 ROSEL WALK (Ire) 5-11-5 D M O'Brien, ... (20 to 1)	11
3246 PRINCESS LU (Ire) 4-10-8 (7") D J Kavanagh, . . . (20 to 1)	12
1333⁹ ALBERTA ROSE (Ire) 5-11-5 (3") D P Murphy, . . . (16 to 1)	13
3466 MOOREFIELD GIRL (Ire) 5-11-8 M Moran, ... (12 to 1)	14
3088⁸ THE LEFT FOOTER (Ire) 5-11-2 (3") T J O'Sullivan, (16 to 1)	15
3550⁷ NURSE MAID (Ire) 4-11-1 J Jones, ... (8 to 1)	16
3525 COOLING CHIMES (Ire) 4-10-8 (7") M P Dunphy, (20 to 1)	17
GAIN CONTROL (Ire) 5-10-11 C P Dunne, ...(10 to 1)	18
292 D'S AND DO'S (Ire) 5-10-9 (5") C P Dunne, ... (16 to 1)	19
2924 BEN-GURIAN (Ire) 4-11-1 W T Slattery Jnr, ... (16 to 1)	20

Dist: Nk, 1l, 8l, 7l. 4m 28.70s. (20 Ran).

(D Stuart), A P O'Brien

3731 A & R Supplies Acorn Pipe Handicap Hurdle (0-116 4-y-o and up) £3,105 3m .... (4:15)

3657[3] STEEL DAWN [-] 7-11-2 (7*) Mr R J Curran, ... (6 to 4 fav) 1
3467* CALMOS [-] 7-10-11 (5*,4ex) K P Gaule, ... (4 to 1) 2
3657 RIYADH DANCER (Ire) [-] 4-11-2 (5*) J R Barry, ... (12 to 1) 3
3197[9] LANCASTRIANS DREAM (Ire) [-] 5-9-7 (5*) M J Holbrook, ... (20 to 1) 4
3467[3] POOR TIMES (Ire) [-] 6-9-7 (5*) M A Davy, ... (12 to 1) 5
3292[9] TOT EM UP [-] 7-9-6 (7*) M D Murphy, ... (20 to 1) 6
3647[2] LOVELY RUN [-] 7-11-4 H Rogers, ... (8 to 1) 7
3322[6] DOWHATYOULIKE (Ire) [-] 5-11-2 Mr K F O'Sullivan, (8 to 1) 8
3468[9] TRIMMER WONDER (Ire) [-] 6-10-5 P L Malone, ... (20 to 1) 9
3242 LEAVE IT TO JUDGE [-] 7-9-12 W T Slattery Jnr, .. (50 to 1) 10
3526 COIN MACHINE (Ire) [-] 5-10-7 (3*) C O'Brien, ... (16 to 1) 11
3551* OLYMPIC D'OR (Ire) [-] 6-10-12 A J O'Brien, ... (10 to 1) 12
3551[4] DUNBOY CASTLE (Ire) [-] 6-11-3 M Moran, ... (12 to 1) 13
3468 MAGNUM STAR (Ire) [-] 5-10-9 J Magee, ... (20 to 1) 14
3504 BALLINGOWAN STAR [-] 7-9-7 S H O'Donovan, .. (25 to 1) 15
Dist: 1½l, 2½l, 15l, 6l. 5m 59.60s. (15 Ran).
(Ronald Curran), Ronald Curran

3732 A&R Supplies Triton Showers Handicap Hurdle (0-109 4-y-o and up) £3,105 2m 1f.................... (4:45)

3656[5] KHARASAR (Ire) [-] 4-11-7 (7*) R A Hennessy, .. (6 to 4 fav) 1
3388[4] FINAWAY EXPRESS (Ire) [-] 5-10-9 (7*) P J Mulligan, (7 to 1) 2
3654[9] FINNEGANS WAKE [-] 7-11-2 (5*) K P Gaule, ... (7 to 1) 3
3466[4] MAZELLA (Ire) [-] 5-10-7 M Duffy, ... (4 to 1) 4
3550 BUCKINGHAM BOY [-] 8-10-7 (7*) Miss C A Harrison, ... (20 to 1) 5
3657 VINEYARD SPECIAL [-] 8-11-11 (3*) C O'Brien, ... (14 to 1) 6
3526 DEGO DANCER [-] 7-10-10 (5*) J P Broderick, ... (12 to 1) 7
3506 JIMMY THE JACKDAW [-] (bl) 7-10-11 H Rogers, (10 to 1) 8
CHIEF JOSEPH [-] 7-10-2 (7*) M D Murphy, ... (20 to 1) 9
3242 BARRONSTOWN BOY [-] 10-10-2 (7*) J M Donnelly, ... (12 to 1) 10
967 IVY GLEN [-] 8-10-8 P L Malone, ... (33 to 1) 11
990* EAST HOUSTON [-] 5-11-9 (3*) W T Slattery Jnr, .. (10 to 1) 12
3506[5] TURALITY (Ire) [-] 5-10-3 S H O'Donovan, ... (8 to 1) f
38 LET THE RIVER RUN [-] 8-9-13 (7*) D J Kavanagh, (16 to 1) pu
Dist: 4l, 2½l, 3½l, 8l. 4m 24.10s. (14 Ran).
(W Hennessy), Anthony Mullins

3733 Dunraven Arms Hotel Flat Race (6-y-o and up) £3,450 2½m............ (5:15)

3504[5] BROGUESTOWN PRIDE (Ire) 6-12-0 A P O'Brien, ... (3 to 1 fav) 1
3552 CARSEAHELEN (Ire) 6-11-2 (7*) Miss F O'Flynn, ... (16 to 1) 2
3296[3] LACKEN CROSS (Ire) 6-11-7 (7*) D Valentine, ... (6 to 1) 3
3529[4] SHAKE UP 10-11-2 (7*) Mr P English, ... (10 to 1) 4
3528[7] ANOTHER ROLLO (Ire) 6-11-7 (7*) Mr N Stokes, .. (10 to 1) 5
3450[5] LADY OF TARA 8-11-6 (3*) Mrs J M Mullins, ... (9 to 2) 6
STICK WITH HER 7-11-2 (7*) Mr M Hartrey, ... (14 to 1) 7
124 DUNDOCK WOOD 6-11-9 Mr P Fenton, ... (20 to 1) 8
3529[8] COSHLA EXPRESSO (Ire) 6-11-10[3] (7*) Mr J F Gleeson, ... (20 to 1) 9
2553 BAUNFAUN RUN (Ire) 6-11-4 (5*) Mr J P Berry, ... (20 to 1) 10
2100[7] THE PHOENO 8-11-7 (7*) Mr T R Hughes, ... (20 to 1) 11
2586 GROUP HAT (Ire) 6-11-7 (7*) M Brennan, ... (8 to 1) 12
3394[4] JAFFAPPEAL (Ire) 6-11-7 (7*) S P McCarthy, ... (7 to 2) 13
ROCKMOUNT (Ire) (bl) 6-11-9 Mr D M O'Brien, ... (10 to 1) 14
FAIR REVIVAL 7-11-7 (7*) Mr D Dorgan, ... (20 to 1) 15
3469 SHOW ME THE LIGHT (Ire) 6-11-7 (7*) Mr J M Roche, ... (16 to 1) 16
1827 ELTON'S SON 8-11-7 (7*) Mr P Brett, ... (20 to 1) 17
1988 ATH DARA (bl) 7-11-2 (7*) Mr J T McNamara, ... (20 to 1) 18
3291 CASTLEMAHON CHICK (Ire) 6-11-2 (7*) Mr D C O'Connor, ... (20 to 1) pu
Dist: 5l, sht-hd, 1½l, hd. 5m 14.40s. (19 Ran).
(Michael Dalton), A P O'Brien

HAYDOCK (good to firm)
Monday May 2nd
Going Correction: MINUS 0.25 sec. per fur.

3734 Hell Nook Four Years Old Handicap Hurdle £10,747 2m............ (12:50)

3406 ADMIRAL'S WELL (Ire) [102] 10-12 C Swan, *hld up, hdwy aftr 4 out, led appr last, rdn out.* .... (11 to 4 fav op 5 to 2 tchd 3 to 1) 1
3482* CROMARTY [91] 10-1[1] M Dwyer, *beh, hdwy aftr 3 out, ev ch last, kpt on same pace*............ (5 to 1 op 6 to 1) 2
3557* SMUGGLER'S POINT (USA) [105] 11-1 D O'Sullivan, *led and sn clr, jmpd slwly and lost action 3rd, hdd bef nxt, styd in tch, ev ch last, not quicken*....... (6 to 1 op 5 to 1) 3
3482[5] DARING PAST [104] 11-0 R Dunwoody, *beh, hdwy 3 out, in tch last, one pace*................ (10 to 1 op 8 to 1) 4
3418[6] GIORDANO (Ire) [103] 10-13 Gary Lyons, *chsd clr ldr, in tch till wknd appr last*................ (33 to 1 op 25 to 1) 5
3475[2] NATIVE WORTH [109] 11-2 (3*) P Williams, *hld up, no hdwy frm 2 out*.......................... (14 to 1 op 12 to 1) 6
3606* DARK DEN (USA) [114] 11-10 T Kent, *in tch, led aftr 3 fs till appr last, rdn and wknd.* .... (3 to 1 op 5 to 2 tchd 100 to 30) 7
1007* MOSHAAJIR (USA) [100] 10-10 M Ranger, *prmnt till wknd 3 out, tld off*...................... (10 to 1 op 8 to 1) 8
3444[2] ROMALITO [98] 10-8[3] D Murphy, *in tch, wknd quickly appr 3 out, tld off*................ (33 to 1 op 20 to 1) 9
Dist: 2½l, ½l, 2½l, ½l, 10l, nk, 20l, 2½l. 3m 41.40s. a 1.40s (9 Ran).
SR: 30/16/29/25/23/19/23/-/-/ (A D Spence), R Akehurst

3735 Petros Long Distance Hurdle (5-y-o and up) £10,383 2m 7f 110yds... (1:25)

3267[2] AVRO ANSON 6-11-0 M Dwyer, *set slow pace, quickened aftr 2 out, hld on wl*......... (11 to 10 fav tchd 5 to 4) 1
3267* SWEET GLOW (Fr) 7-11-4 R Dunwoody, *hld up in tch, taking clr order whn hmpd appr 2 out, ev ch last, ran on wl*.................. (11 to 8 op Evens tchd 6 to 4) 2
3609[4] PEATSWOOD 6-11-0 Lorna Vincent, *wtd wth, outpcd aftr 2 out, sn beh*...................... (20 to 1 op 16 to 1) 3
3063[8] DEB'S BALL 8-10-9 D J Moffatt, *patiently rdn, moving up to chal whn hng lft aftr 3 out, ev ch, blun nxt, rdr lost iron, sn btn, disqualified.* .... (7 to 1 tchd 13 to 2 and 8 to 1) 0
Dist: 1l, 15l, 3l. 6m 16.50s. a 45.50s (4 Ran).
(B P Skirton), M J Camacho

3736 Crowther Homes Swinton Handicap Hurdle Grade 3 (4-y-o and up) £23,555 2m........................... (2:00)

3402[3] DREAMS END [130] 6-11-4 M Hourigan, *led 1st, styd in tch, led 2 out, rdn and ran on wl*... (10 to 1 op 8 to 1) 1
3422* FOR REG (Ire) [138] 5-11-12 M Dwyer, *beh, hdwy 3 out, chsd wnr appr last, no imprsn.* .... (14 to 1 op 12 to 1 tchd 16 to 1) 2
3206[5] ICE STRIKE (USA) [112] 5-10-0 A Dobbin, *wtd wth, hdwy 5th, styd on, not pace to chal.* .... (33 to 1 op 25 to 1 tchd 40 to 1) 3
LONESOME TRAIN (USA) [114] 5-10-2 Peter Hobbs, *in rear, ran on wl frm 2 out, nvr nrr*.................. (20 to 1) 4
3422[9] NIJMEGEN [124] 6-10-5 (7*) F Leahy, *in tch, led 1st till aftr second, led appr 3 out to nxt, sn one pace.* .... (16 to 1 op 14 to 1) 5
3615[2] COCKNEY LAD (Ire) [126] 5-11-0 C Swan, *settled in rear, hdwy 3 out, fouth whn hmpd last, not reco'r.* .... (8 to 1 op 12 to 1) 6
3383* PONTYNYSWEN [127] (v) 6-11-1 D J Burchell, *prmnt, ev ch 2 out, rdn and sn wknd*.......... (12 to 1 op 10 to 1) 7
3499* ROYAL PRINT (Ire) [112] 5-9-11 (3*) J McCarthy, *al abt same pl*.................................. (9 to 1 op 8 to 1) 8
3422 MIDDLE MARKER (Ire) [113] 5-10-1 Diane Clay, *hld up, hdwy 3 out, nrst finish.* .... (10 to 1 op 8 to 1 tchd 12 to 1) 9
3516[3] WHO'S TEF (Ire) [117] 6-10-5 L Wyer, *chsd ldrs, rdn 2 out, btn whn hmpd last*................ (12 to 1 op 14 to 1) 10
3464[4] HOME COUNTIES (Ire) [125] (v) 5-10-10 (3*) D J Moffatt, *hld up, beh whn hmpd last*............ (25 to 1 op 20 to 1) 11
1442 TEXAN TYCOON [118] 6-10-6 R Dunwoody, *prmnt till wknd appr 3 out, sn beh*......... (6 to 1 tchd 13 to 2) 12
3422[8] RATIFY [118] 7-10-6 A S Smith, *al beh*........... (16 to 1) 13
3538[3] GYMCRAK STARDOM [120] 8-10-8 R Marley, *mid-div, bad mstk 3rd, sn tld off*................ (16 to 1 op 14 to 1) 14
3499[8] NOCATCHIM [122] (bl) 5-10-10 J Osborne, *led aftr second till appr 3 out, btn whn hmpd last, virtually pld up flt.* .... (14 to 1 op 12 to 1 tchd 16 to 1) 15
3422[6] NIKITAS [119] 9-10-2 (5*) D Fortt, *chsd ldrs till f 5th.* .... (20 to 1 op 16 to 1) f
3516* ARCOT [133] (v) 6-11-7 D Murphy, *mid-div, hdwy aftr 3 out, in 3rd pl and staying on whn f last, dead.* .... (11 to 2 fav op 7 to 1 tchd 8 to 1) f
3516 IVEAGH HOUSE [112] 8-10-0 A Maguire, *pld up aftr second*.................................. (14 to 1 op 12 to 1) pu
Dist: 3½l, 8l, 1¼l, ½l, 1¼l, 1½l, ¾l, sht-hd, 1¼l, 3½l. 3m 37.90s. b 2.10s (18 Ran).
SR: 71/75/41/41/50/50/49/33/34/ (T G Price), P J Hobbs

3737 New Florida Mares' Only Handicap Hurdle (0-140 4-y-o and up) £3,356 2 ½m........................... (2:30)

3583[2] LOCH SCAVAIG (Ire) [108] 5-10-2 (3*) D J Moffatt, *chsd ldr, led last, drvn out*............... (100 to 30 op 5 to 2) 1
3520[2] LEMON'S MILL (USA) [131] 5-12-0 R Dunwoody, *led, mstks, hdd last, no extr.* .... (11 to 8 on op 5 to 4 on tchd 6 to 5 on) 2
3618[6] GREY POWER [124] 7-11-7 P Niven, *prmnt till wknd 3 out, sn beh*................ (13 to 2 op 6 to 1 tchd 7 to 1) 3
3408 DANCE OF WORDS (Ire) [129] 5-11-12 A Maguire, *wtd wth, hdwy 7th, wknd nxt, tld off*......... (6 to 1 op 5 to 1) 4
3344 MYTHICAL STORM [103] 7-9-13[2] (3*) Mr M Buckley, *hld up, lost tch 7th, tld off whn pld up bef 2 out.* .... (16 to 1 tchd 20 to 1) pu
Dist: 2½l, 20l, 10l. 4m 45.00s. a 6.50s (5 Ran).
(Mrs G A Turnbull), D Moffatt

3738 Edge Green Claiming Hurdle (4-y-o and up) £3,824 2½m. . . . . (3:00)

3568⁶ THE DEMON BARBER 12-11-0 A Dobbin, *hld up, hdwy to go 3rd hfwy, led 3 out, ran on wl.*
. . . . (12 to 1 op 10 to 1 tchd 14 to 1) 1
3574 CELCIUS (bl) 10-10-13 R Dunwoody, *wtd wth, took clr order 3 out, ev ch last, sn wkd one pace.*
. . . . (3 to 1 tchd 11 to 4) 2
867⁴ GREAT MILL (bl) 7-11-3 J Osborne, *made most till 3 out, one pace frm nxt...* (9 to 4 fav op 5 to 2 tchd 11 to 4) 3
2507⁶ OUR SLIMBRIDGE 6-11-5 R Campbell, *hld up, rdn alng 2 out, no response.* . . . . (7 to 2 op 5 to 2) 4
3553⁶ KANNDABIL (bl) 7-11-0 M Dwyer, *in tch, jmpd slwly 5th, sn beh.* . . . . (11 to 2 op 5 to 1) 5
3317⁶ MARINE SOCIETY (bl) 6-10-11 A Maguire, *wth ldrs to 5th, tld off...* (11 to 1 op 10 to 1 tchd 12 to 1) 6
3568³ IRISH FLASHER 7-10-8 (3*) P Williams, *in rear whn f 3rd.*
. . . . (12 to 1 tchd 14 to 1) f
Dist: 2½l, 5l, 3l, 3½l, dist. 4m 41.50s. a 3.00s (7 Ran).
SR: 6/2/1/-/ (Slotamatics (Bolton) Ltd), G Richards

3739 Dock Lane Novices' Hurdle (4-y-o and up) £2,514 2m. . . . . (3:30)

3570⁴ COL BUCKMORE (Ire) 6-11-4 N Doughty, *al travelling wl beh ldrs, led appr last, cmftbly.* . . (3 to 1 tchd 4 to 1) 1
3396³ SUPER COIN 6-11-7 A Maguire, *trkd ldr till led 3 out, hdd appr last, rdn and no extr.*
. . . . (11 to 8 on op 5 to 4 on) 2
3701 TEJANO GOLD (USA) 4-10-9 Gary Lyons, *led till 3 out, rdn and wknd appr last.* . . . . (10 to 1 tchd 9 to 1) 3
3451² THE MILLWRIGHT 7-11-0 P Holley, *chsd ldrs, effrt 4 out, outpcd frm nxt.* . . . . (4 to 1 op 3 to 1) 4
2749 WARNER FOR SPORT 5-11-0 Peter Hobbs, *hld up in rear, blun 3 out, sn beh, tld off.*. . . . . . (16 to 1 op 12 to 1) 5
Dist: 2½l, 11l, 5l, 30l. 3m 43.00s. a 3.00s (5 Ran).
SR: 20/20/ (Brian Buckley), G Richards

LUDLOW (firm)
Monday May 2nd
Going Correction: MINUS 0.35 sec. per fur.

3740 Tote Placepot Selling Hurdle (4-y-o and up) £1,658 2m. . . . . (2:30)

3222⁵ ALWAYS READY (bl) 8-10-13 (7*) J Bond, *led to 3rd, led ag'n aftr 2 out, styd on wl, jnshd lme.*
. . . . (7 to 1 op 4 to 1) 1
2837 NORTHERN TRIAL (USA) 6-11-1 J R Kavanagh, *hdwy 5th, one pace frm 2 out.* . . . . (4 to 1 op 4 to 1) 2
1860⁹ IMMORTAL IRISH 9-11-6 T Wall, *led 3rd till hdd aftr 2 out, one pace.* . . . . (14 to 1 op 7 to 1) 3
297³ SALAR'S SPIRIT 8-11-3 (5*) R Darke, *chsd ldrs, one pace frm 6th.* . . . . (7 to 1 op 5 to 1) 4
3635⁴ SULTAN'S SON 8-11-6 D Bridgwater, *prmnt till wknd 6th.*
. . . . (3 to 1 op 4 to 1 tchd 5 to 1) 5
3511 FOND KISS 9-10-10 W Humphreys, *prmnt till lost pl 4th, rallied 6th, wknd 2 out.* . . . . (12 to 1) 6
3334⁴ KELLY'S DARLING 8-11-6 Richard Guest, *hdwy 6th, wknd appr 2 out.* . . . . (11 to 4 fav op 3 to 1 tchd 7 to 2) 7
3533 BOADICEA'S CHARIOT 7-10-12 (3*) R Farrant, *nvr rchd ldrs.* . . . . (50 to 1 op 33 to 1) 8
3098 OTHET 10-11-11 M Mann, *al struggling.*
. . . . (14 to 1 op 12 to 1) 9
3559⁸ GIRTON BELLE 4-10-5 B Clifford, *gd hdwy 5th, wknd quickly aftr nxt, pld up bef 2 out.* (50 to 1 op 33 to 1) pu
1519 VITAL TYCOON 6-10-3 (7*) J Neaves, *al beh, pld up bef 2 out.* . . . . (50 to 1 op 25 to 1) pu
Dist: 5l, 5l, nk, 4l, 8l. 3m 40.20s. a 3.20s (11 Ran).
SR: 4/-/-/-/-/ (The Always Ready Partnership), R Lee

3741 St Johns' Novices' Hurdle (4-y-o and up) £1,780 2m 5f 110yds. . . . . . . (3:05)

3592⁶ MISS SOUTER 5-10-6 (5*) R Darke, *al hndy, led 6th, rdn and ran on wl frm 2 out.*
. . . . (5 to 2 op 3 to 1 tchd 7 to 2 and 2 to 1) 1
3543⁸ PINK SUNSET (Ire) 6-11-2 J R Kavanagh, *hdwy 8th, chsd wnr appr 2 out, no imprsn.*
. . . . (5 to 1 op 6 to 1 tchd 8 to 1) 2
3564⁵ ACHIEVED AMBITION 6-10-9 (7*) Mr M Rimell, *led to 6th, mstk and rdn nxt, sn btn.*
. . . . (11 to 4 op 7 to 4 on tchd 5 to 4 on) 3
3562 COZZI (Fr) 6-10-13 (3*) R Farrant, *chsd ldr to 6th, sn reminders, wknd und pres frm 2 out.*
. . . . (10 to 1 op 9 to 1) 4
Dist: 4l, 20l, 6l. 5m 8.00s. a 11.00s (4 Ran).
(Q J Jones), H S Howe

3742 Ludlow Golf Club Handicap Chase (0-125 5-y-o and up) £2,814 3m. . (3:35)

3544⁵ ISLAND FOREST (USA) [92] 8-11-6 J R Kavanagh, *al hndy, led appr 3 out, sn clr.*. . . . . (11 to 10 fav tchd 11 to 8) 1

3512⁹ DANDY MINSTREL [96] (bl) 10-11-10 D Bridgwater, *rear till hdwy 12th, hit 14th, sn rdn alng, ran on frm 3 out, not rch wnr.* . . . . (3 to 1 op 5 to 2) 2
3560⁷ BARTONDALE [80] 9-10-5 (3*) R Farrant, *in tch, one pace frm 15th.* . . . . (9 to 1 op 6 to 1) 3
3532⁷ GUILDWAY [87] (bl) 11-10-8 (7*) Mr M Rimell, *led, rdn alng frm 12th, hdd appr 3 out, fdd...* (6 to 1 op 5 to 1) 4
3560⁶ FIGHT TO WIN (USA) [94] (bl) 6-11-8 B Clifford, *pressed ldrs till wknd aftr 4 out.* . . . . (8 to 1 op 9 to 1) 5
3573 MINT-MASTER [72] (bl) 9-10-0 N Mann, *tld off 6th, pld up aftr 11th.* . . . . (25 to 1 tchd 33 to 1) pu
Dist: 4l, 20l, sht-hd, nk. 5m 52.10s. a 3.10s (6 Ran).
(John C Blackwell), P F Nicholls

3743 Bet With The Tote Handicap Hurdle (0-125 4-y-o and up) £2,730 2m. . (4:05)

3254⁷ WINDWARD ARIOM [86] (bl) 8-10-0 J R Kavanagh, *pld hrd and rstrained, quickened to ld 4th, sn clr, styd on wl frm 2 out.* . . . . (8 to 1 tchd 10 to 1) 1
3594 SQUIRE YORK [94] 4-10-8 Richard Guest, *chsd ldr frm 4th, rdn aftr 2 out, rallied flt, not rch wnr.*
. . . . (11 to 10 op Evens) 2
3594* RAIN-N-SUN [91] 8-10-5 T Wall, *led, reluctant to race and reminders 3rd, lost pl and struggling frm nxt.*
. . . . (11 to 10 on op 11 to 8 on tchd Evens) 3
Dist: 1l, 16l. 3m 48.10s. a 11.10s (3 Ran).
(Kendall White & Co Ltd), K R Burke

3744 Tripleprint Novices' Handicap Chase (5-y-o and up) £3,074 3m. . . . . . (4:35)

3575* JAY JAY'S VOYAGE [86] 11-11-3 (7*) Mr B Pollock, *hdwy to ld aftr 15th, clr nxt, styd on wl und pres flt.*
. . . . (3 to 1 op 2 to 1) 1
3575² HOUSE OF ROSES (Ire) [85] (bl) 6-11-9 J R Kavanagh, *hit 1st, effrt 13th, rdn to chal appr last, no extr flt.*
. . . . (7 to 4 fav op 6 to 4 tchd 2 to 1) 2
3175⁴ UFANO (Fr) [85] 8-11-9 D Bridgwater, *led 4th to 8th, reminders 12th, led ag'n 14th, hdd aftr nxt, hrd rdn appr last, wknd flt.* . . . . . . (2 to 1 tchd 9 to 4) 3
2206 WILD FORTUNE [65] 12-10-3 Mr G Johnson Houghton, *led to 4th, led ag'n 6th till hdd and uns rdr 14th.*
. . . . (5 to 1 op 14 to 1) ur
3454 MERRY MUSE [64] 8-10-2 Richard Guest, *sn tld off, pld up bef tenth.* . . . . (25 to 1 op 12 to 1) pu
Dist: 4l, 7l. 6m 0.60s. a 11.60s (5 Ran).
(Mrs J Scrivens), Mrs J Scrivens

3745 Red Cross Novices' Hurdle (4-y-o and up) £1,906 2m. . . . . (5:05)

3680² ROXY RIVER 5-11-2 J R Kavanagh, *made all, given breather aftr 3 out, pld clr frm last...* (5 to 2 op 2 to 1) 1
3576³ DOC COTTRILL 4-10-10 D Bridgwater, *hld up, improved hfwy, rdn and one pace frm 2 out.* (5 to 4 fav op Evens) 2
402³ ASTERIX 6-10-12 (3*) R Farrant, *chsd ldrs frm 3rd, one pace frm 2 out.* . . . . (7 to 2 op 7 to 1) 3
3339⁴ ICE MAGIC 7-11-1 Richard Guest, *cld up aftr 6th, wknd betw last 2.* . . . . (12 to 1) 4
1301 MAJESTIC GOLD 6-11-1 J Lodder, *lost tch frm 6th.*
. . . . (33 to 1 op 25 to 1) 5
LAURA 5-10-10 N Mann, *al beh....* (33 to 1 op 20 to 1) 6
3145 STARSHADOW 5-10-8 (7*) J Neaves, *lost tch hfwy till uns rdr 5th.* . . . . (50 to 1) ur
448⁷ AWESTRUCK (bl) 4-10-10 T Wall, *rcd wide, lost tch frm 4th, pld up bef last.* . . . . (16 to 1 op 10 to 1) pu
Dist: 8l, 3½l, 14l, 8l, 14l. 3m 37.20s. a 0.20s (8 Ran).
SR: 30/16/17/3/-/ (Mrs Liz Brazier), J L Spearing

NAVAN (IRE) (good to yielding)
Monday May 2nd

3746 Waterfood Food Ingredients Handicap Chase (5-y-o and up) £6,900 2½m
. . . . (4:00)

3657 BOTHAR NA SPEIRE [-] 10-10-10 (5*) T P Rudd, . . (33 to 1) 1
3392 PROVERB PRINCE [-] 10-10-9 J P Banahan, ... (20 to 1) 2
3658⁴ WINDS OF WAR [-] 9-11-4 C O'Dwyer, ... (4 to 1 fav) 3
3649⁹ SCRIBBLER [-] 8-11-7 F Woods, ... (11 to 2) 4
3659⁷ JOE WHITE [-] 8-11-1 P Carberry, ... (16 to 1) 5
3648⁴ KINGSTON WAY [-] 8-10-10 K F O'Brien, ... (7 to 1) 6
1577 BLENHEIM PALACE (USA) [-] 7-9-2 (5*) M G Cleary, (33 to 1) 7
3526 RUSTY COIN [-] 9-11-9 L P Cusack, ... (16 to 1) 8
446 DESELBY'S CHOICE [-] 9-9-5 (3*) T P Treacy, ... (20 to 1) 9
3474⁶ ROYAL MOUNTBROWNE [-] 6-12-0 G M O'Neill, . .(12 to 1) 10
3123⁷ CHIRKPAR [-] 7-11-13 B Sheridan, ... (12 to 1) 11
3648⁶ JOHNEEN [-] 8-10-3 S R Murphy, ... (14 to 1) 12
3524⁸ TAKE THE TOWN [-] 9-11-0 J F Titley, ... (16 to 1) ur
3659⁵ CAPTAIN BRANDY [-] 9-11-12 F J Flood, ... (12 to 1) pu
3651⁴ PARLIAMENT HALL [-] 8-11-11 T Horgan, ... (7 to 1) pu
3586 DOLIKOS [-] 7-10-10 J Shortt, ... (10 to 1) pu
Dist: Hd, 5l, 1½l, 6l. (Time not taken) (16 Ran).
(John M Mannion), M J P O'Brien

3747 Bective Maiden Hurdle (6-y-o and up) £3,105 2m 5f.................... (4:30)

3366[4] FINE TUNING (Ire) 6-11-6 F Woods, ...(2 to 1 fav) 1
2027[4] RIVERLAND (Ire) 6-11-6 B Sheridan, ...(8 to 1) 2
3447[2] STRONG HICKS (Ire) 6-11-6 F J Flood, ...(6 to 1) 3
2704[6] DORAN'S DELIGHT 7-12-0 J F Titley, ...(14 to 1) 4
THE BOOLYA (Ire) 6-11-6 S R Murphy, ...(9 to 2) 5
3366 RATHFARDON (Ire) 6-11-6 A Powell, ...(25 to 1) 6
3271[5] WAYUPHILL 7-10-12 (3*) T P Treacy, ...(14 to 1) 7
3271[7] MINIGIRLS NIECE (Ire) 6-11-1 D P Fagan, ...(12 to 1) 8
1760 MAMBO KING 7-11-6 P Carberry, ...(12 to 1) 9
3292[7] DRUMCILL LASS (Ire) 6-11-1 P M Verling, ...(14 to 1) 10
3244[6] JOHNNY THE FOX (Ire) 6-11-1 (5*) Mr G J Harford, (8 to 1) 11
3447[7] YOU'VE DONE WHAT (Ire) 6-11-3 (3*) T P Rudd, ... (8 to 1) 12
3366[3] BEAT THE SECOND (Ire) 6-11-6 G M O'Neill, ... (5 to 1) 13
STRONG HURRICANE 7-12-0 T Horgan, ...(14 to 1) 14
2161[5] ROSDEMON (Ire) 6-11-6 K F O'Brien, ...(12 to 1) 15
1892[6] CUCHULLAINS GOLD (Ire) 6-11-6 Mr A J Martin, (12 to 1) 16
1833 MORNING IN MAY (Ire) 6-11-6 J Shortt, ...(14 to 1) 17
GREENBELLE 7-10-10 (5*) M G Cleary, ...(20 to 1) 18
2590 QUEEN PERSIAN 7-10-8 (7*) R Burke, ...(33 to 1) 19
3448 HELLO DAWN (Ire) 6-11-6 P P Kinane, ...(33 to 1) 20
2607 HOLY FOX (Ire) 6-11-6 C O'Dwyer, ...(14 to 1) 21
3448[9] PERCUSIONIST 7-11-6 L P Cusack, ...(20 to 1) 22
2863 BASTILLE DAY 7-12-0 J P Byrne, ... (50 to 1) pu
746 THEKINDWORD VI (bl) 9-11-6 J P Banahan, ...(50 to 1) pu
Dist: 2l, sht-hd, 1l, sht-hd. (Time not taken) (24 Ran).
(Spencer Wood), A L T Moore

3748 Navan Races Hurdle (4 & 5-y-o) £4,140 2m.......................... (5:00)

3505[3] CABLE BEACH (Ire) 5-11-8 J P Banahan, ...(8 to 1) 1
2586* CURRENCY BASKET (Ire) 5-12-0 K F O'Brien, .. (Evens fav) 2
3505[4] SPORTSTYLE (Ire) (bl) 4-11-1 B Sheridan, ...(10 to 1) 3
1180[8] BROWNRATH KING (Ire) 5-11-8 J Shortt, ...(20 to 1) 4
2842 BARNAGEERA BOY (Ire) 5-11-8 P Carberry, ... (8 to 1) 5
HAVIN' A BALL (Ire) 5-11-3 F Woods, ... (40 to 1) 6
2684 CANUIG (Ire) 5-11-8 L P Cusack, ...(25 to 1) 7
1848[9] ANDROS GALE (Ire) 5-11-8 C O'Dwyer, ...(16 to 1) 8
DESERT LAUGHTER (Ire) 4-10-8 (7*) Mr J Bright, ..(40 to 1) ur
3367[4] STARK CONTRAST (USA) 5-11-7 (7*) C McCormack, ...(2 to 1) pu
Dist: 6l, 15l, 7l, 1l. (Time not taken) (10 Ran).
(Herb M Stanley), Michael Cunningham

3749 Kentstown Flat Race (4 & 5-y-o) £3,105 2¼m......................... (5:30)

2607 ARDSHUIL 6-11-13 Mr A J Martin, ...(8 to 1) 1
3250 SIGMA WIRELESS (Ire) 5-11-10 (3*) Mr D Marnane, (12 to 1) 2
LUCKY SALUTE (Ire) 5-11-6 (7*) Mr R P Cody, ... (10 to 1) 3
3450[7] BRAMBLESHINE (Ire) 4-10-8 (7*) Mr T M Cloke, ...(12 to 1) 4
APPALACHEE BAY (Ire) 4-10-13 (7*) Mr J T Codd, (20 to 1) 5
3388[3] THAT'S POLITICS (Ire) 5-11-10 (3*) Mrs M Mullins, ... (6 to 4 fav) 6
COURTLY CIRCLE (Ire) 5-11-8 Mr A R Coonan, ... (6 to 1) 7
SPLEODRACH (Ire) 4-10-12 (3*) Mr R Neylon, ...(14 to 1) 8
GRAFTON GIRL (Ire) 4-10-12 (3*) Mr P Casey, ...(7 to 1) 9
3327[8] PHARSILK (Ire) 5-11-13 Mr M McNulty, ... (7 to 1) 10
ROCKY CASHEL (Ire) 5-11-1 (7*) Mr S Jurak, ... (66 to 1) 11
3653[6] TREANAREE (Ire) 5-11-6 (7*) Mr D K Budds, ... (8 to 1) 12
3466 V'SOSKE GALE (Ire) 4-10-8 (7*) Mr J G O'Connell, (14 to 1) 13
TOR 4-11-1 (5*) Mr T P Hide, ... (10 to 1) 14
2679 DRINDOD (Ire) 5-11-6 (7*) Mr S O'Callaghan, ... (25 to 1) 15
JR MY FRIEND (Ire) 4-11-6 Mr P J Kelly, ... (16 to 1) 16
3327 CLERICAL COUSIN (Ire) 5-11-8 (5*) Mr C T G Kinane, ...(25 to 1) 17
PADDY'S PET (Ire) 5-11-6 (7*) Mr A K Wyse, ... (20 to 1) 18
ATHABASCA (Ire) 4-11-1 (5*) Mr G J Harford, ... (66 to 1) 19
LEITRIMS SECRET (Ire) 5-11-6 (7*) Mr M G Wiseman, ...(25 to 1) 20
2290 DERRYSHERIDAN 4-11-6 Mr J A Berry, ...(16 to 1) 21
BELLEW BOY (Ire) 4-10-13 (7*) Mr D M Cartan, ... (20 to 1) 22
BRISAN HERO (Ire) 4-10-8 (7*) Mr A Daly, ... (20 to 1) 23
PRATE BOX (Ire) 4-10-13 (7*) Mr G A Kingston, ...(14 to 1) ur
3327 REDZ LAST STAND (Ire) 5-11-1 (7*) Mr M J Dunne, (66 to 1) pu
QUIET POLLYANNA (Ire) 5-11-1 (7*) Mr C Rae, ... (25 to 1) pu
Dist: 4½l, 3l, 2l, ½l. (Time not taken) (26 Ran).
(N A McCarthy), A L T Moore

SOUTHWELL (good to firm)
Monday May 2nd
Going Correction: MINUS 0.75 sec. per fur.

3750 Devon Novices' Chase (5-y-o and up) £3,757 3m 110yds.............. (2:30)

3534[4] STRONG MEDICINE 7-11-8 N Williamson, *settled gng wl, improved to ld aftr 6 out, going clr whn blun 2 out, drvn out r-in*..........(11 to 10 fav tchd Evens and 6 to 5) 1
3621[2] LOBRIC (bl) 9-11-4 S Smith Eccles, *al cl up, mstk 4th, led 6th, hdd aftr six out, effrt bef 2 out, styd on wl frm last.* ....(5 to 2 tchd 11 to 4) 2
3442 CRAIGSTOWN (Ire) 6-11-8 M Brennan, *settled rear, improved to go hndy aftr one circuit, blun 5 out, no extr after nxt*......................(7 to 1 op 11 to 2) 3
3575[3] QUENTIN DURWOOD (bl) 8-11-4 G Upton, *pressed ldrs, jnd issue 8th, hit and lost grnd 13th, wknd last 3, tld off*..............................(5 to 1 tchd 11 to 2) 4
3498[9] MEKSHARP 7-11-1 (3*) T Eley, *blun and uns rdr second.* ....(16 to 1) ur
1807 GOLDEN SHOON 10-11-4 R Garritty, *jmpd rght, led til hit and hdd 6th, sn struggling, tld off whn pld up aftr 12th*..........................(25 to 1 tchd 33 to 1) pu
3510[7] PARSON'S WAY (bl) 7-11-4 D Byrne, *in tch, struggling to keep up aftr 7th, tld off whn pld up after 13th.* .... (40 to 1 op 33 to 1) pu
Dist: ½l, 14l, dist. 6m 8.50s. a 10.50s (7 Ran).
(Dr D B A Silk), K C Bailey

3751 Exmoor Selling Hurdle (4-y-o and up) £2,574 2½m 110yds............ (3:00)

3395* MAN OF THE GRANGE 8-11-13 N Williamson, *patiently rdn, took clr order fnl circuit, nosed ahead bef 2 out, forged clr betw last two*............(5 to 1 op 4 to 1) 1
3637[9] RIP THE CALICO (Ire) 6-10-8 (7*) Miss C Spearing, *al wl plcd, led 5 out, hdd bef 2 out, rdn and no extr.* ....(20 to 1 tchd 25 to 1) 2
2634[6] PRIORY PIPER 5-11-3 (3*) T Eley, *led till mstk and hdd 1st, pressed ldrs, outpcd bef 6th, styd on frm 2 out, nrst finish*............................(16 to 1 op 12 to 1) 3
3673[6] ERBIL (Ire) 4-11-2 (5*) F Perratt, *patiently rdn, steady hdwy fnl circuit, effrt and ridden bef 2 out, btn whn hit last*.................. (Evens fav op 6 to 4 tchd 2 to 1) 4
3478[2] KEMALS DELIGHT 7-11-1 Jacqui Oliver, *trkd ldrs, struggling aftr 3 out, sn btn*............. (6 to 1 op 5 to 1) 5
3395[2] SAMJAMALIFRAN (bl) 5-11-1 M Foster, *in tch, effrt and rdn 3 out, btn frm nxt*..............(4 to 1 tchd 5 to 1) 6
3235[5] WHATCOMESNATURALLY (USA) 5-11-1 W Worthington, *beh, reminders aftr 5th, sn btn*.... (16 to 1 op 12 to 1) 7
1427[4] KEY DEAR (Fr) 7-10-13 (7*) N Juckes, *keen hold, trkd ldrs, lft in ld 5th, hdd 7th, grad lost pl aftr nxt.* .... (10 to 1 op 8 to 1) 8
2401 ANAR (Ire) 5-10-13 (7*) R Massey, *not fluent in rear, struggling fnl circuit, tld off*...........(14 to 1 op 10 to 1) 9
3440 MIDNIGHT FLOTILLA 8-11-1 C Hawkins, *led 1st till f 5th.* ....(7 to 1) f
Dist: 10l, 12l, 1¼l, 1l, 2½l, 2½l, 2½l, dist. 4m 47.90s. b 5.60s (10 Ran).
SR: 1/-/-/-/-/-/ (Richard J Marshall), W Clay

3752 Greet Handicap Hurdle (0-115 4-y-o and up) £5,021 3m 110yds...... (3:30)

1310[5] JAWANI (Ire) [104] 6-11-10 A Carroll, *trkd ldr, drvn alng and outpcd bef 2 out, styd on and ev ch last, led nr finish*..................(3 to 1 op 4 to 1 tchd 9 to 2) 1
3535 BLASKET HERO [86] (bl) 6-10-6 N Williamson, *chsd ldg 4, reminders strting fnl circuit, improved to ld 2 out, hdd nr finish, lme*........................(5 to 1 op 6 to 1) 2
2961[6] SASKIA'S REPRIEVE [92] 10-10-12 D Byrne, *rstrained in rear, drvn alng aftr 4 out, improved betw last 2, no extr last 50 yards*........................ (8 to 1 op 11 to 2) 3
3622[4] THIS NETTLE DANGER [96] 10-11-2 M Brennan, *hld up in last pl, improved aftr 4 out, ch after 2 out, hit last, no extr*............... (2 to 1 fav op 5 to 2 tchd 11 to 4) 4
3219[3] ALBERTITO (Fr) [93] 7-10-10 (3*) S Wynne, *chsd ldrs on ins, lost pl strting fnl circuit, no dngr frm 2 out.* .... (11 to 2 op 4 to 1 tchd 6 to 1) 5
3455[5] FOX CHAPEL [103] 7-11-2 (7*) N Juckes, *trkd ldrs, struggling to keep up aftr 3 out, grad wknd.* ....(5 to 1 op 9 to 2) 6
3678[7] CURTAIN FACTORY [83] (bl) 5-10-3 R Garritty, *led til hdd 2 out, fdd*............................(7 to 1 op 5 to 1) 7
Dist: Sht-hd, 4l, 2½l, 7l, 4l, hd. 6m 5.80s. a 15.80s (7 Ran).
(Mrs Susan Scargill), Dr J D Scargill

3753 Sam Derry Challenge Cup Handicap Chase (0-135 5-y-o and up) £4,603 2½m 110yds................... (4:00)

3627* DRUMSTICK [129] 8-12-4 (4ex) N Williamson, *trkd ldg pair, mstk 5 out, chlgd nxt, led on bit 3 out, quickened last, eased r-in*...(13 to 8 on op 7 to 4 on tchd 11 to 8 on) 1
3636[5] SIRRAH JAY [105] 14-10-8 R Garritty, *led second, jnd 4 out, rdn and hdd nxt, kpt on r-in*.....(100 to 30 op 5 to 2) 2
FOOLISH AFFAIR [97] (bl) 10-10-0 M Brennan, *led to second, pressed ldrs, mstks 7th and 9th, sn struggling, refused nxt*......... (100 to 30 op 3 to 1 tchd 5 to 2) ref
Dist: 1½l. 5m 18.50s. a 15.50s (3 Ran).
(Sarah Lady Allendale), K C Bailey

3754 Fleet Novices' Handicap Chase (5-y-o and up) £3,132 2m..............(4:30)

3664[3] HOWGILL [84] 8-10-3 (3*) S Wynne, *pressed ldr, led 7th to nxt, sn drvn alng, lft clr 5 out, hld on wl frm 2 out.* ....(7 to 2 op 3 to 1) 1

3000² WEEKDAY CROSS (Ire) [79] 6-10-1 C Swan, *patiently rdn, improved to chase wnr bef 3 out, ridden and no extr frm last.*....................................(2 to 1 fav op 11 to 4) 2
612³ FASTBIT [113] 7-12-7 N Williamson, *settled in tch, badly hmpd by faller 5 out, sn drvn alng, btn 3 out, tld off.*
....(5 to 2 op 7 to 4) 3
3442 BILLHEAD [78] (bl) 8-9-11 (3") T Eley, *made most til hdd 7th, wkng whn blun 4 out, tld off.* (25 to 1 op 20 to 1) 4
SHEEP STEALER [80] 6-10-2 R Dunwoody, *nvr far away, improved to ld 8th, f nxt.*...................(5 to 2 op 7 to 4) f
Dist: 1¾l, 30l, 15l. 3m 53.90s. b 5.10s (5 Ran).
SR: 9/2/6/-/-/ (Mrs Charles Lockhart), R Hollinshead

3755 Witham Claiming Hurdle (4-y-o and up) £3,517 2m.............(5:00)

3670² MERLINS WISH (USA) 5-11-8 R Dunwoody, *settled on ins, effrt and rdn aftr 3 out, ev ch last, styd on gmely to ld cl hme.*.....................................(5 to 4 on op 2 to 1) 1
2645* MAJAL (Ire) 5-11-5 (5") P Midgley, *hld up, improved to track ldrs bef 4 out, led nxt, hrd pressed frm 2 out, kpt cl hme.*...(6 to 1 tchd 7 to 1) 2
3240⁴ SAYMORE 8-11-1 (3") S Wynne, *hld up, shaken up to improve 3 out, styd on frm nxt, nvr dngrs.*
....(8 to 1 op 7 to 1) 3
3328⁵ APPLIANCEOFSCIENCE (bl) 7-10-10 J Ryan, *nvr far away, led aftr 4 out, hdd nxt, rdn and not quicken.*
....(12 to 1 op 8 to 1) 4
3016⁴ FRONTIER FLIGHT (USA) (bl) 4-10-12 (3") J McCarthy, *chsd ldg bunch, effrt and rdn aftr 3 out, not quicken appr nxt.*..(11 to 1 op 7 to 1) 5
3594⁷ KING'S SHILLING (USA) 7-11-6 A Maguire, *hld up, drvn to improve 3 out, no imprsn.*
....(9 to 1 op 3 to 1) 6
3281 DYAB (USA) (bl) 4-10-11 R Campbell, *handily plcd, struggling to keep up 4 out, sn btn, eased fnl 2.*
....(16 to 1 op 10 to 1) 7
3584⁸ MAGGIES LAD (bl) 6-11-0 R Garritty, *led til hdd aftr 4 out, fdd.*...(20 to 1) 8
CREPT OUT (Ire) 5-10-10 Mr A Walton, *pld hrd, pressed ldr til lost pl hfwy, tld off.*..........................(33 to 1) 9
3436⁵ SASKIA'S HERO 7-11-6 D Byrne, *settled on outer, struggling to keep up hfwy, tld off.*..........(10 to 1 op 8 to 1) 10
Dist: Hd, 13l, ½l, 4l, 3l, 5l, hd, 30l, dist. 3m 46.60s. b 5.40s (10 Ran).
SR: 28/30/11/2/3/5/ (Malcolm B Jones), M C Pipe

3756 Beck Novices' Hurdle (4-y-o and up) £3,522 2¼m.................(5:30)

3406⁶ PRIDWELL 4-11-7 R Dunwoody, *trkd ldrs on ins, effrt whn hit 2 out, reco'red and led last, pushed out.*
.........................(2 to 1 op 9 to 4 on tchd 6 to 4 on) 1
3333³ BIGWHEEL BILL (Ire) (bl) 5-11-3 S Smith Eccles, *led, rdn bef 2 out, edgd rght and hdd last, not quicken.*
....(9 to 1 op 6 to 1) 2
2093* YAAKUM 5-11-6 C Swan, *patiently rdn, took clr order 3 out, effrt and ridden nxt, sn one pace.*
....(100 to 30 op 11 to 4) 3
2731 TEX MEX (Ire) 6-11-2 A Maguire, *pressed ldr, ev ch 2 out, blun last, no extr*.....................(8 to 1 op 10 to 1) 4
2637 TURF RUN 7-11-2 N Williamson, *settled rear, improved to go hndy bef 2 out, sn drvn alng and kpt on same pace.*
....(20 to 1) 5
3580 OLLIVER DUCKETT 5-11-2 C Hawkins, *tucked away in midfield, effrt and rdn bef 2 out, grad wknd.*
....(33 to 1 op 25 to 1) 6
3046 SUVLA BAY (Ire) 6-11-2 R Garritty, *al wl plcd, rdn alng appr 2 out, fdd.*................(20 to 1 tchd 25 to 1) 7
2963⁶ WHOCOMESNATURALLY 5-11-2 W Worthington, *settled on outer, struggling to keep up 5 out, tld off.*......(33 to 1) 8
3549* POLISH RIDER (USA) 6-10-13 (7") C Huggan, *settled on outer, blun and uns rdr 4 out.*...........(8 to 1 op 5 to 1) ur
Dist: 4l, 5l, sht-hd, 3l, 7l, 1½l, dist. 4m 25.60s. a 4.60s (9 Ran).
(Pond House Racing), M C Pipe

TOWCESTER (firm)
Monday May 2nd
Going Correction: MINUS 0.15 sec. per fur.

3757 Meadow Brown Novices' Selling Hurdle (4-y-o and up) £1,953 2m....(2:20)

3511² HAWTHORNE GLEN 7-11-0 D Gallagher, *wtd with in chasing grp, cld aftr 4 out, led after nxt, ran on wl.*
....(7 to 4 fav op 9 to 4) 1
3635² BOZO BAILEY 4-10-9 R J Beggan, *wtd with, cld aftr 4 out, chsd wnr frm nxt, one pace und pres appr last.*
....(2 to 1 tchd 9 to 4) 2
HICKORY WIND 7-10-7 (7") J James, *prmnt in chasing grp, styd on und pres appr 2 out.*
....(9 to 1 op 8 to 1 tchd 16 to 1) 3
3617⁹ INNOCENT GEORGE 5-11-0 W Marston, *mid-div, styd on appr 2 out.*..........................(5 to 1 op 7 to 2) 4
417 SUNDAY JIM 10-11-0 S McNeill, *hld up, effrt 3 out, no imprsn.*...........................(20 to 1 op 12 to 1) 5

3511 DHARAMSHALA (Ire) 6-10-7 (7") R Moore, *chsd ldrs till rdn and wknd appr 2 out.*...............(14 to 1 op 8 to 1) 6
3632 THE MAN FROM CLARE (Ire) 6-11-0 M A FitzGerald, *mid-div till outpcd aftr 4 out.*...............(14 to 1 op 8 to 1) 7
3416 HARQUIN (bl) 4-10-2 (7") A Shakespeare, *rcd freely, led, sn wl clr, mstk 3 out and soon hdd, wknd.*
....(33 to 1 op 50 to 1) 8
BOB-CAM 10-10-11 (3") A Procter, *led chasing grp till wknd 5th, tld off.*...................(25 to 1 op 14 to 1) 9
3184⁸ SAIF AL ADIL (Ire) (bl) 5-10-11 (3") T Jenks, *cl up in chasing grp, wknd quickly 4 out, pld up bef 2 out.*
....(50 to 1 op 33 to 1) pu
3189 ROISTER DOISTER 4-10-4 E Murphy, *sn struggling, tld off whn pld up aftr 4th.*............(33 to 1 op 25 to 1) pu
Dist: 5l, 3½l, 3l, 10l, 10l, 20l, 4l, 8l. 3m 46.80s. a 3.80s (11 Ran).
SR: 24/14/15/12/2/-/ (Mrs Gail Davison), Mrs M E Long

3758 Red Admiral Novices' Chase (5-y-o and up) £2,929 2m 110yds......(2:50)

3548⁶ VICTORY ANTHEM 8-11-2 I Lawrence, *hld up, jmpd slwly 6th, cld 4 out, led 2 out, jst held on.*
....(12 to 1 op 10 to 1 tchd 14 to 1) 1
3585⁴ CROOKED COUNSEL 8-11-8 D Gallagher, *led till 3 out, rallied appr last, ran on wl und pres, jst fld.*
....(2 to 1 op 6 to 4 tchd 9 to 4) 2
3226 HIGHLAND POACHER 7-10-11 (5") Mr D McCain, *in cl tch, blun 3rd, led 3 out to nxt, swtchd rght appr last, one pace.*..(25 to 1 op 14 to 1) 3
3110 KETFORD BRIDGE 7-10-13 (3") D Meredith, *lost tch 8th, tld off.*..(25 to 1) 4
3004⁸ MARCH LANE 7-11-2 R Bellamy, *pld hrd, cl up, lost tch 9th, tld off.*.......................(20 to 1 op 16 to 1) 5
3513⁴ SOCIAL CLIMBER 10-11-8 S McNeill, *blun and uns rdr 3rd.*..............(11 to 10 on op Evens tchd 5 to 4) ur
3588 GLEN PENNANT 7-11-2 W Marston, *hld up, lost tch 8th, pld up bef last.*.................(25 to 1 tchd 33 to 1) pu
Dist: Sht-hd, 6l, 15l, dist. 4m 10.70s. a 8.70s (7 Ran).
(P Gray Limited), P C Clarke

3759 Fred Withington Memorial Handicap Chase (0-125 5-y-o and up) £3,434 2m 110yds....................(3:20)

3513* SARTORIUS [113] 8-12-0 M A FitzGerald, *made virtually all, hrd pressed nr finish, jst hld on.*
....(11 to 8 fav op 5 to 4 on) 1
3060³ ACHILTIBUIE [85] 10-10-0 D Gallagher, *in cl tch, chsd wnr frm 3 out, swtchd rght and ran on strly from last, jst fld.*..........................(3 to 1 op 7 to 2 tchd 4 to 1) 2
3346² DR ROCKET [108] 9-11-6 (3") D Meredith, *hld up in cl tch, pushed alng and outpcd 4 out, one pace frm 2 out.*
................................(7 to 4 tchd 15 to 8 and 2 to 1) 3
STRANGELY QUIET [85] 12-10-0 I Lawrence, *trkd wnr, led briefly 7th, ev ch 4 out, wknd aftr nxt.*
....(9 to 1 op 10 to 1 tchd 11 to 1) 4
3513 CEDAR RUN [85] 11-10-0 Mr A Charles-Jones, *reluctant to race, strted 3 fences beh and completed in own time.*
....(50 to 1 op 20 to 1) 5
Dist: Hd, 20l, 20l, dist. 4m 7.80s. a 5.80s (5 Ran).
SR: 17/-/ (M Popham), T Thomson Jones

3760 Ronnie Beggan Farewell Handicap Hurdle (0-120 4-y-o and up) £3,111 2m 5f.......................(3:50)

3541⁴ WELSH SIREN [97] 8-11-2 (5") J Burke, *hld up beh ldrs, led aftr 3 out, rdn out.*..........................(7 to 1) 1
3535⁵ NOVA SPIRIT [80] 6-10-1 (3") A Procter, *hld up in rear, hdwy 4 out, ev ch last, no extr.*......(16 to 1 op 14 to 1) 2
3545* QUIET DAWN [89] 8-10-10 (3") D Meredith, *al hndy, ev ch 3 out, one pace frm nxt.*..................(8 to 1 op 7 to 1) 3
3574⁶ CELTIC BOB [80] 14-10-4 V Slattery, *hld up in rear, hdwy 5 out, one pace appr 2 out.*..........(20 to 1 op 14 to 1) 4
2655⁶ RAMBLE (USA) [89] 7-10-13 T Grantham, *hld up in rear, hdwy 4 out, sn one pace.*........(8 to 1 tchd 10 to 1) 5
3634³ ELEGANT KING [100] 5-11-10 M A FitzGerald, *trkd ldrs till wknd appr 2 out.*...(8 to 1 op 7 to 1 tchd 10 to 1) 6
3625⁷ RED RING [100] 7-11-10 W Marston, *trkd ldrs till wknd appr 2 out.*.........................(8 to 1 op 9 to 1) 7
3520⁵ SYLVIA BEACH [97] 8-11-7 E Murphy, *nvr better than middiv.*.....................................(10 to 1 op 8 to 1) 8
3545⁸ RIBOVINO [76] (bl) 11-9-9 (5") D Leahy, *trkd ldrs till wknd 4 out.*.................................(33 to 1 op 14 to 1) 9
MISS SIMONE [92] 8-10-13 (3") T Jenks, *led till hdd 3 out, wknd quickly, tld off.*.........(3 to 1 fav op 6 to 1) 10
2823 EMERALD SUNSET [95] 9-11-5 D Gallagher, *al beh, lost tch 6th, pld up bef 4 out.*..........(9 to 1 op 14 to 1 tchd 20 to 1) pu
3514* CAMBO (USA) [89] 8-10-13 D Skyrme, *al beh. pld up bef 2 out.*..(8 to 1) pu
3578² ROYAL FLAMINGO [100] 8-11-10 R J Beggan, *hld up, cld 4 out, btn appr 2 out, pld up bef last, lme.*
....(6 to 1 op 3 to 1) pu
3514³ SAILOR BLUE [89] 7-11-7 S McNeill, *cl up, led 3 out whn broke leg, dead.*.....................(8 to 1 op 6 to 1) pu
Dist: 1l, 15l, nk, 6l, ¾l, 8l, 1¼l, 2½l, dist. 5m 6.10s. a 7.10s (14 Ran).
(Quicksilver Racing Partnership), K C Bailey

3761 Speckled Wood Novices' Hunters' Chase (5-y-o and up) £1,811 2¾m (4:20)

FINE LACE 10-11-4 (5*) Mr G Tarry, *in cl tch, led 3 out, clr appr last, easily.* (11 to 8 on op 7 to 4 on tchd 2 to 1 on and 5 to 4 on) 1
3596⁴ RYTON RUN 9-11-7 (7*) Mr J Trice-Rolph, *hld up, blun 5th, hdwy to ld 12th, hdd 3 out, ev ch nxt, btn appr last.* (4 to 1 op 10 to 1 tchd 12 to 1) 2
LUPO NERO 12-11-7 (7*) Mr S Hope, *led til hdd 7th, cl up, mstk tenth, outpcd frm 3 out.* (8 to 1 op 5 to 1 tchd 10 to 1) 3
DAMERS TREASURE 8-11-7 (7*) Mr A Sansome, *hld up in cl tch, led 7th till hdd 12th, wknd aftr 3 out, tld off.* (12 to 1 op 10 to 1 tchd 16 to 1) 4
2889 TENELORD 7-12-0 Mr J Greenall, *cl up, mstk tenth, sn wknd, pld up aftr 3 out.* (7 to 2 op 5 to 2 tchd 4 to 1) pu
Dist: 15l, 20l, dist. 5m 45.80s. a 19.80s (5 Ran).
(G B Tarry), G J Tarry

3762 BBC Radio Northampton Novices' Handicap Hurdle (4-y-o and up) £2,757 3m (4:50)

3515⁴ LAY IT OFF (Ire) [62] 5-9-11 (3*) A Procter, *led 3rd till hdd 7th, cl up, hrd rdn to ld ag'n nr finish.* (11 to 1 op 8 to 1) 1
3564⁴ ALIAS SILVER [70] 7-10-8 Ann Stokell, *al cl up, led 4 out till hdd last strds.* (9 to 1 op 5 to 1 tchd 10 to 1) 2
3061* DOCTOR DUNKLIN (USA) [62] 5-9-11 (3*) D Meredith, *middiv, rdn appr 4 out, sn cld, ev ch approaching last, one pace.* (8 to 1 op 9 to 2 tchd 10 to 1) 3
2428 SPANISH BLAZE (Ire) [66] 6-10-4 M A FitzGerald, *hld up, hdwy 4 out, ev ch appr last, one pace r-in.* (16 to 1 op 8 to 1) 4
3167³ RACE TO THE RHYTHM [80] 7-11-1 (3*) T Jenks, *led to 3rd, hit 6th, chsd ldrs, mstk 4 out, wknd nxt.* (9 to 2 op 3 to 1) 5
3330⁶ EMALLEN (Ire) [62] 6-10-0 I Lawrence, *hld up, reminders 7th, wknd appr 3 out.* (33 to 1 op 16 to 1) 6
3530⁴ GOLDEN FRAME [79] 7-11-3 D Gallagher, *hld up, hdwy 4 out, ev ch 2 out, wknd quickly appr last.* (5 to 1 op 7 to 2 tchd 11 to 2) 7
3565² OVER THE ODDS (Ire) [73] 5-10-11 K Johnson, *nvr dngrs.* (7 to 2 fav op 5 to 1) 8
3496⁵ SEARCY [74] 6-10-7 (5*) D Leahy, *chsd ldrs till wknd o'r 3 out, pld up bef 2 out.* (4 to 1 op 7 to 2 tchd 3 to 1) pu
3515² OUTFIELD [86] 8-11-10 R Bellamy, *prmnt till wknd 7th, pld up bef 2 out.* (11 to 2 op 4 to 1 tchd 6 to 1) pu
3592 LOYAL GAIT (NZ) [62] 6-9-7 (7*) K Brown, *mstk second, al beh, pld up bef 2 out.* (33 to 1 op 16 to 1) pu
Dist: Sht-hd, 1¾l, sht-hd, 15l, 3½l, ½l, 25l. 5m 54.80s. a 8.80s (11 Ran).
(J G O'Neill), J G O'Neill

LES LANDES (JER) (good)
Monday May 2nd

3763 Hampton's, Gothard & Trevor Handicap Hurdle (4-y-o and up) £600 2m 1f (2:30)

CLEAR HOME 8-12-0 S Macky, (6 to 4) 1
3572 BOHEMIAN QUEEN 4-10-1⁸ M Sharratt, (Evens fav) 2
OUR TOPSIE 7-9-7 V Smith, (3 to 1) 3
Dist: Hd, 1l. 4m 32.00s. (3 Ran).
(T J Bougourd), T J Bougourd

NEWTON ABBOT (firm)
Tuesday May 3rd
Going Correction: MINUS 0.05 sec. per fur.

3764 Passage House Hotel Novices' Chase (5-y-o and up) £2,840 2m 110yds (1:55)

3361² WHAT'S IN ORBIT 9-11-9 G Bradley, *made virtually all, ran on wl.* (2 to 1 op 5 to 2 tchd 11 to 4) 1
3595² MINE'S AN ACE (NZ) 7-11-9 J Frost, *al prmnt, ev ch 2 out, not quicken frm last.* (Evens fav op 11 to 8 on tchd 11 to 10) 2
3499 PALACE WOLF (NZ) 10-11-4 R Dunwoody, *al prmnt, ev ch 3 out, one pace.* (9 to 2 op 4 to 1 tchd 13 to 2) 3
3534⁹ NEEDS MUST 7-11-4 (5*) R Darke, *wth wnr till wknd 4 out.* (16 to 1 op 10 to 1 tchd 20 to 1) 4
1926⁸ ROMANY SPLIT 9-11-4 M A FitzGerald, *strted slwly, al tld off.* (40 to 1 op 25 to 1 tchd 50 to 1) 5
2223 REAL HARMONY 8-11-4 D O'Sullivan, *al tld off.* (50 to 1 op 20 to 1) 6
3454⁸ BRAVO STAR (USA) 9-11-4 W Marston, *sn tld off.* (20 to 1 tchd 33 to 1) 7
484³ DARING CLASS 8-10-13 I Shoemark, *5th whn pld up lme aftr 6th.* (33 to 1 op 12 to 1 tchd 40 to 1) pu
Dist: 4l, 10l, 3½l, dist, 3l, sht-hd. 4m 1.20s. a 4.20s (8 Ran).
SR: 45/41/26/27/-/ (Paul K Barber), P F Nicholls

3765 H. A. Fox Rolls Royce Novices' Selling Hurdle (4,5,6-y-o) £1,939 2m 1f. . (2:25)

3559⁵ TENDRESSE (Ire) 6-10-9 R Dunwoody, *al prmnt, led 2 out, drvn out.* (7 to 2 op 2 to 1 tchd 4 to 1) 1
3531 WALID'S PRINCESS (Ire) (bl) 4-10-0¹ (5*) R Darke, *al prmnt, led 3 out to 2 out, ev ch whn mstk last, not quicken.* (25 to 1 op 12 to 1) 2
3395 BOWLAND GIRL (Ire) (v) 5-10-9 A Maguire, *al prmnt, ev ch 3 out, one pace.* (12 to 1 op 10 to 1 tchd 8 to 1) 3
3496 KIRBY OPPORTUNITY 6-10-9 J Frost, *beh, hdwy 5th, nvr nr to chal.* (3 to 1 op 8 to 1 tchd 12 to 1) 4
3716⁵ RED MICKS WIFE (Ire) 4-10-1 (3*) R Davis, *al beh.* (33 to 1 op 10 to 1) 5
1716 ELEGANT TOUCH (bl) 5-10-2 (7*) O Burrows, *led 3rd to 3 out, wknd quickly.* (12 to 1 op 7 to 1 tchd 14 to 1) 6
2714³ PIGALLE WONDER (bl) 6-11-0 D O'Sullivan, *al beh, tld off.* (14 to 1 op 10 to 1 tchd 16 to 1) 7
3632⁹ STAPLEFORD LADY 6-10-6 (3*) R Farrant, *f 1st.* (33 to 1 op 20 to 1 tchd 50 to 1) f
3632 SNICKERSNEE 6-10-7 (7*) M Moran, *led to second, wknd 5th, beh whn pld up bef 2 out.* (12 to 1 op 12 to 1 tchd 33 to 1) pu
3716 PERSIAN BUD (Ire) 6-11-0 M Bosley, *hmpd 1st, sn wl beh, pld up bef 2 out.* (16 to 1 op 8 to 1) pu
MIDGET GEM 4-10-9 S Burrough, *pld hrd, led second to 3rd, wknd quickly, tld off whn pulled up bef 5th.* (33 to 1 op 16 to 1) pu
2057³ LEEWA (Ire) 4-10-9 M Richards, *nvr gng wl, prmnt to 4th, 6th and btn whn pld up bef 2 out.* (11 to 10 fav op 2 to 1 tchd Evens) pu
Dist: 4l, 9l, 10l, 8l, 7l, dist. 4m 3.50s. a 13.50s (12 Ran).
(P E Axon), R J Hodges

3766 Flynns Bistro Handicap Chase (0-125 5-y-o and up) £3,088 2m 5f. . . . . . (2:55)

3452* ERRANT KNIGHT [119] 10-11-10 R Dunwoody, *hld up, hdwy 9th, led 2 out, cmftbly...* (11 to 8 fav op 13 to 8) 1
3548 NOS NA GAOITHE [103] (v) 11-10-8 B Powell, *led to 3rd, led 9th to 2 out, no ch wth wnr.* (12 to 1 op 10 to 1 tchd 14 to 1) 2
3500⁶ PEACE OFFICER [115] 8-11-6 M A FitzGerald, *led 3rd to 9th, ev ch 3 out, one pace.* (11 to 2 op 5 to 1 tchd 6 to 1) 3
152² FLYING ZIAD (Can) [96] 11-10-1 D Morris, *hdwy 8th, ev ch 4 out, rdn and wknd nxt.* (14 to 1 op 12 to 1 tchd 16 to 1) 4
3534 WINTER'S LANE [95] 10-10-0 A Maguire, *wl beh, hdwy 8th, wknd 11th.* (5 to 2 op 9 to 4) 5
3573³ SETTER COUNTRY [108] 10-10-13 W Irvine, *prmnt to 9th.* (5 to 1 op 9 to 2 tchd 11 to 2) 6
2798 WHATEVER YOU LIKE [109] (bl) 10-11-0 G Bradley, *prmnt to 7th, beh frm 9th, pld up bef 11th...* (16 to 1 op 12 to 1) pu
Dist: 7l, 2½l, 15l, 12l, 5l. 5m 4.70s. a 4.70s (7 Ran).
SR: 39/16/25/-/ (Mrs N J Bird), M C Pipe

3767 Passage House Hotel Novices' Hurdle (4-y-o and up) £2,410 2m 1f. . . . . (3:25)

1639* MISSY-S (Ire) 5-10-4 (7*) Mr J L Llewellyn, *chsd ldr frm 5th, led 2 out, easily.* (8 to 1 op 7 to 1 tchd 9 to 1) 1
3202⁵ CASPIAN BELUGA 6-11-2 S Burrough, *led, sn wl clr, blun and hdd 2 out, no ch wth wnr.* (10 to 1 op 7 to 1) 2
3531* MIGAVON 4-10-12 D Gallagher, *4th whn mstk fourth, sn beh, gd hdwy frm 2 out.* (9 to 2 op 11 to 4) 3
3231⁷ FENGARI 5-11-2 A Maguire, *gd hdwy frm 2 out, nvr nrr.* (9 to 2 op 5 to 1 tchd 4 to 1) 4
3549² KHALIDI (Ire) 5-11-8 P Holley, *mstk 4th, chsd ldr to 5th, wknd appr last...* (11 to 10 fav op 5 to 2 tchd 11 to 4) 5
3209 DEE RAFT (USA) 4-10-11 M Richards, *wl beh, hdwy 5th, wknd 2 out.* (10 to 1 op 7 to 1) 6
3549⁵ PRINCE TEETON 5-11-2 B Powell, *al beh, tld off.* (12 to 1 op 10 to 1) 7
3670 FRIENDLY VIKING 4-10-11 Miss S Young, *al tld off.* (100 to 1 op 33 to 1) 8
THANKS A MILLION 8-10-11 S Earle, *sn wl beh, pld up bef 2 out.* (33 to 1 op 20 to 1) pu
1645⁴ APARECIDA (Fr) 8-10-11 S McNeill, *tld off, pld up bef 2 out.* (9 to 1 op 6 to 1 tchd 10 to 1) pu
Dist: 5l, 1¾l, 2l, 13l, 7l, 20l, dist. 4m 1.50s. a 11.50s (10 Ran).
(B J Llewellyn), B J Llewellyn

3768 Passage House Hotel Novices' Hunters' Chase (5-y-o and up) £1,831 2m 5f (3:55)

CONNEMARA DAWN 10-11-7 (7*) Mr S Shinton, *jmpd wl, made virtually all, ran on well.* (6 to 1 op 8 to 1 tchd 5 to 1) 1
3521² SYNDERBOROUGH LAD 8-12-5 (5*) Mr M Felton, *hld up and beh, hdwy 5th, chsd wnr frm tenth, ev ch appr 2 out, no imprsn.* (2 to 1 on tchd 6 to 4 on) 2
BLACKGUARD (USA) 8-11-7 (7*) Mr J Grassick, *hdwy 8th, styd on frm 3 out, not rch 1st 2.* (8 to 1 op 8 to 1) 3

EXPOUND (USA) 9-11-7 (7*) Mr N R Mitchell, *hdwy 9th, one pace frm 4 out*.....................(33 to 1 op 14 to 1)   4
SWEET ON WILLIE (USA) 8-11-2 (7*) Miss A Turner, *chsd wnr, blun tenth, no ch aftr*.........(8 to 1 op 6 to 1)   5
BOGAZKOY 12-11-7 (7*) Mr G Brown, *prmnt early, sn lost tch*.................................(50 to 1 op 20 to 1)   6
OVAC STAR 8-11-7 (7*) Mr R Lawther, *al beh.*
.......................(12 to 1 op 16 to 1 tchd 25 to 1)   7
COLD MARBLE (USA) 9-11-7 (7*) Mr A Oliver, *al tld off.*
.......................(33 to 1 op 14 to 1)   8
FREE EXPRESSION 9-11-2 (7*) Mr R Payne, *beh whn pld up bef 2 out*......................(50 to 1 op 20 to 1)   pu
HAMPER 11-11-7 (7*) Mr R Nuttall, *beh whn pld up bef 11th*..................................(50 to 1 op 20 to 1)   pu
RANDOM CHARGE 13-11-7 (7*) Mr Richard White, *chsd ldrs, 5th and no ch whn blun 4 out, beh when pld up bef 2 out*..........................(50 to 1 op 16 to 1)   pu
TUDOR BAY 12-11-7 (7*) Mr S Parfimowicz, *beh frm 9th, pld up bef 11th*......................(33 to 1 tchd 50 to 1)   pu
HOLCOMBE BILL 11-11-7 (7*) Mr I Widdicombe, *prmnt, jmpd slwly 3rd, beh whn pld up bef 11th.*
.......................(50 to 1 op 20 to 1)   pu
RANSOME JRAG 9-11-9² (7*) Mr R Mills, *beh whn pld up bef 11th*............................(50 to 1 op 20 to 1)   pu
Dist: 10l, 7l, 25l, 7l, 30l, 5l, dist. 5m 9.10s. a 9.10s (14 Ran).

(John Tuck), John Tuck

3769   Westomatic Handicap Hurdle (0-130 4-y-o and up) £2,682 2¾m...... (4:25)

3594⁹ ANTI MATTER [85] 9-10-9 (5*) S Fox, *al prmnt, led 2 out, ran on wl*.................................(8 to 1 op 7 to 1)   1
34917 BOOTSCRAPER [92] 7-11-7 A Maguire, *dsptd ld, led 7th, hdd 2 out, ran on*.......(11 to 2 op 5 to 1 tchd 6 to 1)   2
2964 MAYFIELD PARK [75] 9-9-11 (7*) Mr G Hogan, *al prmnt, ev ch 2 out, one pace*.............(4 to 1 op 9 to 4)   3
SPORT OF FOOLS (Ire) [95] 5-11-10 W McFarland, *hdwy 6th, wknd appr 2 out*..............(7 to 1 op 4 to 1)   4
3535 ODSTONE PEAR [77] 9-10-6 J Frost, *al beh.*
.......................(20 to 1 op 14 to 1 tchd 25 to 1)   5
3561⁵ TEL E THON [95] (v) 7-11-10 R Dunwoody, *dsptd ld to 7th, wknd 3 out*................(7 to 4 fav tchd 2 to 1)   6
3418⁸ ONENINEFIVE [71] 8-10-0 B Powell, *al beh.*
.......................(25 to 1 op 20 to 1 tchd 33 to 1)   7
3533 KILTONGA [71] 7-10-0 M Hourigan, *sn tld off, pld up bef 2 out*...........................(33 to 1 op 20 to 1)   pu
3545 LAVALIGHT [71] 7-10-0 I Lawrence, *pld up bef 3rd, sddl slpd*...................(13 to 2 op 11 to 2 tchd 7 to 1)   pu
Dist: 3½l, 5l, 20l, 20l, 5l, 6l. 5m 16.70s. a 17.70s (9 Ran).

(T M Few), Mrs J G Retter

UTTOXETER (Good to firm)
Wednesday May 4th
Going Correction: PLUS 0.10 sec. per fur.

3770   Highland Park Novices' Claiming Hurdle (4-y-o and up) £2,494 2m.... (5:45)

3632* SOPHISM (USA) 5-11-9 R Dunwoody, *hld up, hdwy 6th, chlgd frm 2 out, drvn to ld r-in, all out.*
.......................(11 to 10 op 5 to 4 tchd 5 to 4)   1
3542² UPWARD SURGE (Ire) 4-11-7 N Williamson, *led, not fluent, mstk 2 out, hrd drvn appr last, hdd r-in, one pace.*
.......................(100 to 30 op 9 to 4 tchd 7 to 2)   2
3531² EAGLES LAIR 8-11-12 S McNeill, *hdwy 5th, trkd ldrs 3 out, styd on one pace.* (6 to 1 op 5 to 1 tchd 13 to 2)   3
3661 CAPTAIN TANDY (Ire) 5-11-3 D Bridgwater, *not fluent early, hdwy 6th, rdn 3 out, wknd nxt.*
.......................(16 to 1 op 12 to 1)   4
2760⁶ SKIMMER HAWK 5-11-0 V Smith, *in tch 5th, chsd ldr frm 7th to aftr 3 out, sn rdn and wknd.* (16 to 1 op 12 to 1)   5
3559⁴ KEDGE (v) 4-11-4 Diane Clay, *chsd ldrs to 7th.*
.......................(11 to 1 op 8 to 1 tchd 12 to 1)   6
3167 ESSEN AITCH 5-10-7 (5*) D Fortt, *wth ldr, hit 6th, rdn and wknd frm nxt.*..................(50 to 1 op 33 to 1)   7
3348 PIONEER PETE 7-11-3 J Frost, *beh frm 7th, tld off.*
.......................(50 to 1 op 33 to 1)   8
2478⁷ WAKT 4-11-2 W McFarland, *chsd ldrs to 5th, wkng whn mstk and uns rdr 7th*...............(14 to 1 op 7 to 1)   ur
2790 SOLO CORNET 9-10-11 Gary Lyons, *sn beh, hrd rdn aftr 6th, tld off whn pld up bef 2 out*...(25 to 1 op 20 to 1)   pu
PROSPECT OF WHITBY 8-10-12 (3*) R Davis, *al beh, tld off whn pld up bef 3 out*......................(50 to 1)   pu
2525 OLD TICKLERTON 5-11-4 (5*) Mr D McCain, *beh 7th, no ch whn blun 7th, tld off when pld up bef 2 out.*
.......................(50 to 1)   pu
Dist: ½l, 4l, 9l, 3½l, 11l, sht-hd, dist. 3m 49.40s. a 10.40s (12 Ran).
SR: 7/4/5/-/-/-/   (A J Lomas), M C Pipe

3771   Bunnahabhain Handicap Hurdle (0-125 5-y-o and up) £3,468 3m 110yds
.............................(6:15)

3283⁹ COURT CIRCULAR [105] (bl) 5-11-8 Diane Clay, *made all, styd on wl whn chlgd frm 3 out, drvn clr from 2 out.*
.......................(8 to 1 tchd 9 to 1)   1

3622* STORM DRUM [105] (bl) 5-11-8 (6ex) N Williamson, *hld up, hdwy tenth, chlgd 3 out, sn rdn and found nothing.*
.......................(Evens fav tchd 5 to 4)   2
3491 ARR EFF BEE [92] (bl) 7-10-4 (5*) D Leahy, *al chasing ldrs, rdn and outpcd appr 3 out.*
.......................(10 to 1 op 7 to 1 tchd 11 to 1)   3
3609² SEA BUCK [107] 8-11-10 J R Kavanagh, *sn pushed alng, chlgd 9th, wknd 4 out.* (5 to 2 op 2 to 1 tchd 11 to 4)   4
3350⁴ LASTING MEMORY [91] 8-10-8 S Earle, *chsd wnr 3rd to 8th, rdn tenth, sn wknd*...........(7 to 1 op 8 to 1)   5
Dist: 12l, 3l, 30l, 15l. 5m 54.50s. a 15.50s (5 Ran).

(B A S Limited), W Clay

3772   Famous Grouse Handicap Chase For Fred Dixon Memorial Trophy (0-135 5-y-o and up) £4,858 3¼m...... (6:45)

3519⁴ SIKERA SPY [115] 12-10-8 R Bellamy, *jmpd wl, made all, clr 5th, ran on well frm 3 out.*
.......................(15 to 8 fav op 2 to 1 tchd 7 to 4)   1
3560* GREENHILL RAFFLES [118] 8-10-11 Peter Hobbs, *slpd 3rd and beh, hit 13th, hdwy to chase wnr whn hit 3 out, sn outpcd.*................(9 to 4 op 2 to 1)   2
3494⁷ JIMMY O'DEA [107] (bl) 7-10-0 N Williamson, *chsd wnr to 9th, chased winner ag'n 12th, hit 4 out, wknd nxt.*
.......................(33 to 1 tchd 50 to 1)   3
3626³ FAR SENIOR [135] 8-12-0 Mr M Armytage, *prmnt, chsd wnr 9th to 12th, wknd appr 4 out*......(5 to 1 op 4 to 1)   4
3512⁸ BIT OF A CLOWN [110] 11-10-3 L Harvey, *nvr gng wl, tld off 12th, moderate prog und pres frm 4 out.*
.......................(25 to 1 op 16 to 1 tchd 33 to 1)   5
3229² SOLIDASAROCK [123] 12-11-2 G McCourt, *in tch, rdn 15th, sn wknd*...............(7 to 2 tchd 4 to 1)   6
Dist: 20l, 6l, 15l, 5l, 3l. 6m 35.00s. a 19.00s (6 Ran).

(D W Heys), Mrs A R Hewitt

3773   Tamdhu Trophy Selling Handicap Hurdle (4-y-o and up) £2,064 2m.... (7:15)

3348* SOVEREIGN NICHE (Ire) [89] (v) 6-11-7 R Dunwoody, *made all, clr appr 3 out, eased r-in, unchlgd.*
.......................(6 to 4 fav op 7 to 4 tchd 9 to 4)   1
3103⁴ AT PEACE [85] 8-11-3 W McFarland, *prmnt, chsd wnr frm 3 out, no imprsn*..............(8 to 1 tchd 10 to 1)   2
1801 FRENDLY FELLOW [68] (bl) 10-10-0 J Lodder, *hdwy 7th, styd on frm 3 out, not a danger.*...(12 to 1 tchd 14 to 1)   3
3098 KNIGHT IN SIDE [74] 8-10-6¹ M A FitzGerald, *beh, styd on frm 3 out, nvr nrr.*..................(12 to 1 op 10 to 1)   4
324² JOHNSTED [95] 8-11-13 Diane Clay, *prmnt, rdn 7th, wkng whn f 7th*...................(5 to 1 op 4 to 1 tchd 6 to 1)   5
3511 FUSSY LADY [74] (bl) 7-10-6 L Harvey, *mid-div, hdwy 6th, rdn and no imprsn frm 3 out*.....(12 to 1 op 10 to 1)   6
810⁵ SLIPPERY MAX [86] 10-10-11 (7*) N Juckes, *hdwy to chase ldrs 6th, wknd 3 out*............(16 to 1 op 14 to 1)   7
3131 GLOSSY [76] 7-10-8 G McCourt, *chsd wnr, wknd quickly 3 out*...........................(14 to 1)   8
3716 MAHONG [68] 6-10-0³ (3*) R Davis, *al beh.*
.......................(20 to 1 op 25 to 1)   9
3594 TASHONYA [68] 12-10-0 J Da Costa, *al beh*......(33 to 1)   10
3661 ALICANTE [68] 7-10-0 D Gallagher, *sn beh.*
.......................(12 to 1 op 16 to 1)   11
3279 MISTY GREY [68] 5-10-0 N Williamson, *al beh.*
.......................(33 to 1 op 25 to 1)   12
3661 MONTIFIORE AVENUE [92] 8-11-10 B Powell, *al beh.*
.......................(33 to 1 op 25 to 1)   13
VALTAKI [81] 9-10-6 (7*) P McLoughlin, *beh frm 4th, no ch whn f 7th*......................(20 to 1 tchd 25 to 1)   f
3222⁵ AL SKEET (USA) [74] 8-10-3 (3*) J McCarthy, *in tch whn hmpd and brght dwn 5th.*
.......................(6 to 1 op 5 to 1 tchd 13 to 2)   bd
3222 SECRET CASTLE [75] 6-10-7 T Wall, *disputing second whn ran out 5th*.....(33 to 1 op 25 to 1 tchd 50 to 1)   ro
3594 HARD TO GET [68] (bl) 7-10-0 Ann Stokell, *pld up aftr 1st, lme*....................................(12 to 1)   pu
Dist: 4l, 9l, 3½l, 8l, nk, 2½l, 6l, 7l, 10l, 3l. 3m 47.50s. a 8.50s (17 Ran).
SR: 24/16/-/-/7/-/   (Avalon Surfacing Ltd), M C Pipe

3774   Highland Park Novices' Handicap Chase (5-y-o and up) £3,826 2m 5f
.............................(7:45)

3341³ LE BUCHERON [82] 8-10-9 M Richards, *hld up, hdwy 12th, led 3 out, stumbled and nrly uns rdr last, reco'red, ran on.*.............(3 to 1 tchd 100 to 30)   1
3454⁴ THE YOKEL [73] 8-9-11 (3*) T Eley, *led, hdd 3 out, styd on, no ch with wnr*...........(3 to 1 op 5 to 1 tchd 7 to 1)   2
3492* BUCKS SURPRISE [97] 6-11-10 W Marston, *chsd ldrs frm 6th, rdn 3 out, not quicken.*................(2 to 1 jt-fav op 7 to 4 tchd 9 to 4)   3
CHARTERHARDWARE [82] 8-10-9 N Williamson, *hld up, rdn 9th, hdwy and mstk tenth, hit 12th, trkd ldrs 4 out, sn ridden and no response*...........(2 to 1 jt-fav tchd 9 to 4)   4
3586⁷ WE'RE IN THE MONEY [73] (bl) 10-10-0 B Dalton, *chsd ldrs, mstk tenth, wknd 4 out*.........(10 to 1 tchd 12 to 1)   5

3445³ KING OF SHADOWS [75] 7-10-2² Gary Lyons, *wth ldr, hit 12th, ev ch whn blun 4 out, wknd and mstk nxt.* ....(25 to 1 op 20 to 1 tchd 33 to 1) 6
Dist: 5l, 8l, ¾l, 2l, 2l. 5m 14.00s. a 14.00s (6 Ran).
(Mrs W L Sole), M J Ryan

3775 Famous Grouse Novices' Hurdle (4-y-o and up) £2,886 2¾m 110yds (8:15)

3666* STRONG CASE (Ire) (bl) 6-12-0 R Dunwoody, *not fluent, made all, clr 3 out, unchlgd.* ....(11 to 8 on op 11 to 10 on) 1
3220² OUROWNFELLOW (Ire) 5-11-7 D Morris, *chsd wnr 6th, chlgd 8th, rdn and outpcd frm 3 out.* ....(11 to 8 op 11 to 10 tchd 6 to 4) 2
THE JEWELLER (v) 7-11-0 N Williamson, *chsd ldrs, reminder aftr second, rdn frm 8th, no imprsn.* ....(20 to 1 op 25 to 1 tchd 16 to 1) 3
3189⁸ FLAMING MIRACLE (Ire) 4-10-5 (3*) R Farrant, *mstk 3rd, effrt 7th, one pace frm 8th*.........(66 to 1 op 33 to 1) 4
CINDERCOMBE 5-10-9 S Earle, *in tch, hdwy 7th, wknd aftr 8th*..........................(20 to 1 op 10 to 1) 5
3005 ELANDS CASTLE (Ire) 6-10-2 (7*) P Ward, *al beh, tld off.* ....(66 to 1 op 33 to 1) 6
2997 TRICYCLE (Ire) 5-11-0 Gary Lyons, *in tch, hit 4th, f 5th.* ....(100 to 1 op 50 to 1) f
3564⁷ BLAKENEY BLUE 7-10-9 J Railton, *sn beh, tld off whn pld up aftr 8th*.......................(50 to 1 op 25 to 1) pu
3421 TRUE STORM 5-10-9 W Marston, *in tch, wknd aftr 6th, hit 7th, tld off whn pld up after 8th.* ....(100 to 1 op 50 to 1) pu
Dist: 6l, 12l, 8l, 12l, dist. 5m 23.70s. a 12.70s (9 Ran).
(Mrs L M Sewell), M C Pipe

WETHERBY (good to firm)
Wednesday May 4th
Going Correction: PLUS 0.35 sec. per fur.

3776 Durham Edition Conditional Jockeys' Handicap Chase (0-120 5-y-o and up) £2,820 2m..................... (6:00)

3356⁶ ALGARI [101] 7-10-12 B Harding, *hld up towards rear, gd hdwy to go second 4 out, led appr last, rdn out.* ....(9 to 4 fav tchd 5 to 2) 1
3556⁶ GREEK FLUTTER [114] 9-11-11 F Leahy, *sn trkd ldr, led 4 out, hdd appr last, one pace.* ....(11 to 1 op 8 to 1 tchd 12 to 1) 2
3595⁴ WICKFIELD LAD [95] 11-10-6 J Supple, *in tch on outsd, ev ch 4 out, wkng whn hit 2 out*........(4 to 1 op 3 to 1) 3
3060* TRESIDDER [107] 12-11-4 J Driscoll, *hld up in rear, rdn appr 3 out, no hdwy*... (11 to 4 op 3 to 1 tchd 9 to 4) 4
3691³ WAY OF LIFE (Fr) [89] 9-10-0 S Lyons, *led, mstk 3rd, hdd 4 out, sn btn, tld off*................(11 to 1 op 10 to 1) 5
3556³ GOLDEN ISLE [89] 10-10-0 F Perratt, *trkd ldrs, jmpd slwly 5th, wknd appr 4 out, tld off whn refused last.* ....(5 to 1 op 7 to 1) ref
Dist: 2½l, 7l, 5l, dist. 4m 3.50s. a 11.50s (6 Ran).
SR: 25/35/9/16/-/-/ (C J Allan), G Richards

3777 Blazing Walker Handicap Chase (0-125 5-y-o and up) £3,427 2½m 110yds........................ (6:30)

3619 STRONG SOUND [102] 7-10-8 K Johnson, *hld up, hdwy to go 3rd 8th, wnt second 3 out, led sn aftr last, all out.* ....(9 to 4 fav op 2 to 1 tchd 5 to 2) 1
3485⁵ MERRY MASTER [122] (bl) 10-12-0 Gee Armytage, *led, pld hrd and jmpd rght, hit 5 out, hdd sn aftr last, rallied gmely, jst fld*...........(7 to 2 op 3 to 1 tchd 4 to 1) 2
3537² CHOICE CHALLANGE [94] 11-9-12³ (5*) S Lyons, *trkd ldr to 5th, outpcd aftr 7th, rallied 4 out, kpt on one pace.* ....(3 to 1 tchd 7 to 2) 3
3619 CROSS CANNON [109] 8-11-1 A Maguire, *wtd wth, hdwy to go second 5th, rdn and wknd 3 out.* ....(3 to 1 tchd 100 to 30) 4
3433⁴ NIGHT GUEST [94] 12-10-0 A Dobbin, *trkd ldrs till wknd 7th, tld off whn pld up bef 4 out.* (10 to 1 tchd 11 to 1) pu
Dist: Hd, 5l, 7l. 5m 14.00s. a 17.50s (5 Ran).
(Mrs H Scotto), P Cheesbrough

3778 Totty Construction Group Novices' Hurdle (4-y-o and up) £2,337 2½m 110yds........................ (7:00)

3620⁴ VASILIEV (bl) 6-11-7 A Maguire, *rcd keenly, hld up, gd hdwy 4 out, jnd ldr 2 out, edgd lft and sn led, clr whn hit rail r-in*..........................(7 to 2 op 5 to 1) 1
3455² GORTEERA 8-12-0 M Brennan, *hld up in mid-div, hdwy hfwy, led sn aftr 3 out, hng rght, bumped and hdd appr last, no extr r-in*... (3 to 1 jt-fav op 5 to 2 tchd 7 to 2) 2
BRABINER LAD 10-11-0 S Turner, *hld up, hdwy 4 out, btn 3rd whn jmpd badly rght last*................(20 to 1) 3
3536² BRIGADIER DAVIS (Fr) 7-11-0 R Garritty, *al prmnt, led aftr 4 out, blun nxt, sn hdd and btn*......(9 to 2 op 7 to 1) 4
1671⁴ ROYAL VACATION 5-12-0 J Callaghan, *hld up, hdwy appr 5th, ev ch 3 out, wknd*..............(8 to 1 op 6 to 1) 5
3414⁶ MARCHWOOD 7-11-7 K Johnson, *trkd ldrs till hrd rdn and wknd appr 3 out*.......... (3 to 1 jt-fav op 6 to 4) 6
2872⁴ SOUSON (Ire) 6-11-0 K Jones, *hld up in tch, rdn and wknd 6th, tld off whn pld up bef 3 out.* ....(20 to 1 op 16 to 1) pu
2252⁹ PRICELESS HOLLY 6-10-7 (7*) C Woodall, *al beh, tld off whn pld up bef 3 out*.............(100 to 1 op 50 to 1) pu
3438 SPLIT SECOND 5-11-0 A Dobbin, *chsd ldrs to 5th, sn wknd, tld off whn pld up bef 3 out.* ....(25 to 1 tchd 33 to 1) pu
1469 BECK COTTAGE 6-11-0 P Niven, *led till hdd and wknd aftr 4 out, pld up bef 2 out*......................(33 to 1) pu
1938⁸ ISLAND RIVER (Ire) 6-11-0 C Dennis, *al beh, tld off whn pld up bef 3 out*.................................(50 to 1) pu
3617 CHARLIE McCARTHY 6-11-0 Mr C Mulhall, *hld up, hdwy 4th, wknd aftr 6th, tld off whn pld up bef 3 out.* ....(66 to 1 op 50 to 1) pu
3557 MURDER MOSS (Ire) 4-10-1 (7*) A Linton, *trkd ldrs till wknd quickly 7th, pld up nxt*.................(50 to 1) pu
Dist: 1¾l, 7l, 1¼l, 6l, 8l. 5m 2.90s. a 15.90s (13 Ran).
SR: 6/11/-/-/-/-/ (R L Houlton), M D Hammond

3779 Chris Grant Novices' Chase (5-y-o and up) £3,626 3m 110yds.......... (7:30)

3624 MELEAGRIS 10-12-0 A Maguire, *reluctant to line up, sn in frnt rnk, led 3 out, rdn out.* ....(11 to 10 fav op 6 to 5 on) 1
3621³ BULA NUDAY 9-11-2 B Storey, *hld up in rear, hdwy 11th, jnd wnr 2 out, ev ch whn slight mstk last, kpt on.* ....(9 to 2 op 7 to 1) 2
3546³ GROOMSMAN 8-11-2 W Humphreys, *nvr far away, 3rd whn hit 3 out, rallied frm nxt*.....(5 to 1 tchd 11 to 2) 3
3621⁶ LADY BLAKENEY 8-11-3 A Dobbin, *al prmnt, led 5th till hdd 3 out, kpt on one pace*........ (20 to 1 op 16 to 1) 4
3599³ CROWN EYEGLASS 8-11-2 R Garritty, *in frnt rnk till wknd appr 4 out*...................(11 to 1 op 12 to 1) 5
3554 LINLITHGOW PALACE 12-11-2 A Merrigan, *hld up in rear, hdwy 11th, btn whn blun 4 out, not reco'r.* ....(66 to 1 op 33 to 1 tchd 100 to 1) 6
3621 PESSOA 7-11-2 Richard Guest, *led to 1st, wkng whn blun tenth, tld off when f 4 out, broke neck, dead.* ....(20 to 1 op 16 to 1) f
2238 CALMATA 13-10-11 G Harker, *mstk second, tld off 11th, pld up bef 4 out*...................(25 to 1 op 20 to 1) pu
3621 CONCERT PAPER (v) 10-11-2 L Wyer, *led 1st, mstk 4th, hdd nxt, wknd quickly and pld up aftr tenth.* ....(13 to 2 op 11 to 2 tchd 7 to 1) pu
Dist: 2l, 2½l, 1l, 15l, 15l. 6m 38.60s. a 32.60s (9 Ran).
(D J Jackson), D Nicholson

3780 Dobroyd Mills Shop Handicap Hurdle (0-125 4-y-o and up) £3,028 2m..(8:00)

3538* CHIEF MINISTER (Ire) [112] 5-11-1 A Maguire, *al gng wl, hld up in tch, led 2 out, rdn out.* ....(6 to 5 on op Evens tchd 11 to 10 and 5 to 4) 1
3516⁴ STRATH ROYAL [125] 8-12-0 M Brennan, *nvr far away, led appr 3 out, hdd nxt, ran on und pres.* ....(100 to 30 op 5 to 2 tchd 7 to 2) 2
3617 VANART [97] 5-10-0 D Byrne, *beh till hdwy appr 4 out, outpcd nxt, rallied and kpt on*.... (16 to 1 op 12 to 1) 3
3600³ GREENACRES LAD [97] 11-10-0 A Mulholland, *beh till styd on frm 3 out, nvr nrr*..............(25 to 1 op 14 to 1) 4
2833 VAIN PRINCE [110] 7-10-13 M Dwyer, *hld up, hdwy on ins 4 out, outpcd nxt, wknd*..........(25 to 1 op 20 to 1) 5
3692⁹ BRAMBLEBERRY [110] 5-10-13 Richard Guest, *trkd ldr, led 4th, hdd appr 3 out, wknd*...... (11 to 1 op 8 to 1) 6
3311³ TAYLORS PRINCE [100] (v) 7-10-3 V Smith, *al struggling in rear, tld off whn pld up bef 3 out*...(8 to 1 tchd 9 to 1) pu
3643⁵ BORO SMACKEROO [106] (bl) 9-10-4 (5*) F Perratt, *led to 4th, struggling four out, pld up bef 2 out*......(16 to 1) pu
Dist: 1¼l, 3l, 2l, 7l, 6l. 3m 52.60s. a 11.60s (8 Ran).
SR: 27/38/7/5/11/5/-/-/ (G Shiel), T Dyer

3781 Washdale Novices' Hurdle (4-y-o) £2,075 2m.................... (8:30)

3617* WEAVER GEORGE (Ire) 11-3 M Dwyer, *made all, quickened frm 2 out, ran on wl*................(7 to 4 op 9 to 4) 1
3597² FORMAL AFFAIR 10-12 A Maguire, *trkd wnr, hit 3rd, rdn appr last, no imprsn.* ....(11 to 8 fav op 6 to 4 tchd 11 to 10) 2
3557⁵ GRAND AS OWT 10-10 K Johnson, *trkd ldrs, outpcd appr 3 out, lft 3rd last*.................(50 to 1 op 33 to 1) 3
3620 TERRINGTON 10-10 R Garritty, *hld up in rear, not jump wl, some hdwy 4 out, jmpd badly nxt, outpcd.* ....(25 to 1 op 20 to 1) 4
GOSPATRIC (Ire) 10-10 N Smith, *al rear, outpcd whn hmpd 3 out, tld off*...............(50 to 1 op 33 to 1) 5
3557² PRINCIPAL PLAYER (USA) 11-3 A Dobbin, *pld hrd, trkd ldrs frm 3rd, cl third but hld whn f last.* ....(5 to 2 op 9 to 4 tchd 11 to 4) f
Dist: 1¾l, 20l, 1½l, 20l. 3m 58.50s. a 17.50s (6 Ran).
(Mrs M Tindale), J A Hellens

SEDGEFIELD (firm)
Thursday May 5th
Going Correction: MINUS 0.20 sec. per fur.

3782 John Wade Group Of Companies Selling Handicap Hurdle Series Final (4-y-o and up) £3,687 2m 5f 110yds (6:00)

3673³ ELVETT BRIDGE (Ire) [62] 6-10-0 A Dobbin, *al prmnt, led 3 out, clr nxt, styd on wl* .... (7 to 1 op 6 to 1) 1
3436⁸ STATION EXPRESS (Ire) [77] 6-11-1 R Dunwoody, *hld up, hdwy aftr 7th, chsd wnr frm 2 out, no imprsn.* .... (2 to 1 fav op 5 to 2 tchd 11 to 4 and 3 to 1) 2
3061⁵ MANWELL [64] 7-10-2¹ M Dwyer, *led to 3rd, prmnt till outpcd and lost pl hfwy, styd on wl ag'n frm 3 out.* .... (10 to 1 op 8 to 1) 3
3435³ MISS CONSTRUE [72] 7-10-3 (7") G Lee, *led 3rd till hdd 3 out, grad wknd* .... (8 to 1 op 6 to 1 tchd 9 to 1) 4
3690⁹ SUNTAN (Fr) [63] (bl) 5-9-8 (7") K Davies, *in tch till rdn and wknd bef 3 out* .... (14 to 1 op 8 to 1) 5
3673² HUNMANBY GAP [90] 9-12-0 C Hawkins, *in tch till rdn and wknd bef 3 out.* (100 to 30 op 5 to 2 tchd 7 to 2) 6
2566 STAGS FELL [84] 9-11-1 (7") N Stocks, *prmnt till wknd aftr 7th, tld off whn pld up bef 2 out.* .... (8 to 1 op 7 to 1) pu
3568⁷ HIGHLAND FRIEND [62] (v) 6-9-9 (5") J Supple, *mstk second, sn wl beh, tld off whn pld up bef 7th.* .... (16 to 1 op 20 to 1) pu
Dist: 5l, ½l, 10l, 1¾l, 1l. 5m 11.60s. a 20.60s (8 Ran).
(A Crampton), V Thompson

3783 Solmere Handicap Hurdle (0-105 5-y-o and up) £2,684 3m 3f 110yds.... (6:30)

3603 BOWLANDS WAY [76] (bl) 10-10-10 O Pears, *cl up, led 8th, wnt lft aftr last, all out* .... (20 to 1 op 16 to 1) 1
3568⁴ BADASTAN (Ire) [82] 5-11-2 R Garritty, *trkd ldrs, drvn alng bef 3 out, kpt on und pres to chase wnr frm nxt, no imprsn.* ....(15 to 8 op 5 to 4 tchd 2 to 1) 2
3673⁴ TAP DANCING [66] 8-10-0 Ann Stokell, *cl up, led 5th till hdd 8th, rdn aftr 3 out, kpt on same pace.* .... (16 to 1 op 14 to 1) 3
3688² ROSE TABLEAU [93] 11-11-13 R Dunwoody, *hld up, reminders aftr 7th, hdwy bef 3 out, sn rdn, one pace frm nxt.* ....(7 to 1 op 5 to 1) 4
3622 JUSTICE LEA [66] 14-10-0 Carol Cuthbert, *sn pushed alng and wl bhd, tld off...* (25 to 1 op 20 to 1 tchd 33 to 1) 5
3221⁵ ATHASSEL ABBEY [66] (bl) 8-10-0 W McFarland, *drvn alng and lost tch aftr 6th, wl tld off whn pld up aftr 3 out.* .... (50 to 1 op 25 to 1) pu
3426 NORSTOCK [94] 7-12-0 A Maguire, *made most till hdd 5th, prmnt till wknd aftr 3 out, tld off whn pld up bef last.* .... (7 to 4 fav op 3 to 1) pu
3584⁹ LEGATA (Ire) [66] 5-10-0 M Hourigan, *sn beh, tld off whn pld up aftr 3 out.* .... (25 to 1 op 20 to 1) pu
Dist: 3l, 1¾l, 1½l, dist. 6m 48.50s. a 22.50s (8 Ran).
(Mrs Lynn Campion), J L Eyre

3784 George Carpenter Memorial Handicap Chase (0-120 5-y-o and up) £2,768 3m 3f. .... (7:00)

3602⁵ CHOCTAW [100] 10-10-9 C Hawkins, *led to 6th, dsptd ld aftr, blun 14th, led nxt, drvn alng bef 3 out, styd on gmely und pres frm last.* .... (3 to 1 tchd 100 to 30) 1
3437 LAPIAFFE [92] 10-10-11 R Dunwoody, *in tch, hdwy to track wnr 16th, chlgd gng wl betw last 2, sn rdn, no extr und pres frm last.* .... (4 to 1 tchd 5 to 1) 2
3646³ PORTONIA [119] 10-12-0 P Niven, *in tch till lost pl aftr 12th, sn beh, styd on frm 3 out, nvr dngrs.* .... (2 to 1 fav tchd 7 to 4) 3
3437⁴ GATHERING TIME [97] 8-9-13 (7") Miss V Haigh, *beh, some hdwy aftr 13th, sn rdn and btn.*...(12 to 1 op 10 to 1) 4
3237 RED UNDER THE BED [96] 7-10-11 (5") J Burke, *cl up, led or dsptd ld frm 6th till hdd 15th, hit nxt, sn wknd.* .... (10 to 1 op 7 to 1) 5
3602³ BOREEN OWEN [92] (bl) 10-10-9 (5") A Roche, *hit 8th, sn beh, tld off whn pld up bef 16th.*......(6 to 1 op 9 to 2) pu
Dist: ½l, 20l, 8l, 10l. 6m 43.20s. a 4.20s (6 Ran).
(J N Yeadon), P Beaumont

3785 Dudley Dukes Antique Fair Handicap Chase (0-120 5-y-o and up) £2,611 2m 5f. .... (7:30)

3375⁵ CLARES OWN [102] 10-11-10 A Maguire, *made most, pushed clr frm 2 out, cmftbly.* ....(15 to 8 fav op 2 to 1 tchd 9 to 4) 1
3586⁶ ENCHANTED MAN [90] 10-10-12 M A FitzGerald, *cl up, pld wnr 13th, rdn bef 2 out, grad wknd.* ....(10 to 1 op 7 to 1 tchd 12 to 1) 2
3556⁵ KAMART [78] 6-10-0 A Dobbin, *in tch, hdwy to track ldrs aftr tenth, rdn bef 3 out, kpt on same pace.* ....(7 to 1 op 8 to 1) 3

3676⁴ ANTHONY BELL [96] 8-11-4 B Storey, *trkd ldrs, mstk 9th, sn lost pl, no dngr aftr* .... (5 to 2 op 3 to 1) 4
3058* RARE FIRE [94] 10-11-2 N Smith, *in tch till wknd aftr 11th.* ....(5 to 2 op 2 to 1) 5
Dist: 8l, sht-hd, 30l, 20l. 5m 9.20s. a 5.20s (5 Ran).
SR: 2/-/
(John Wade), J Wade

3786 Primera Novices' Handicap Chase (5-y-o and up) £2,535 2m 1f. .... (8:00)

3642² GRAZEMBER [70] 7-10-9 C Hawkins, *hld up in tch, hdwy to track ldrs 8th, led gng wl 2 out, rdn aftr last, all out.* ....(3 to 1 op 7 to 2 tchd 4 to 1) 1
3664² HOT PURSUIT [73] 8-10-7 (5") D Fortt, *in tch, ev ch 3 out, sn pushed alng, styd on wl und pres frm last.* ....(5 to 1 op 4 to 1) 2
1817⁴ CHIC AND ELITE [78] 7-10-12 (5") A Roche, *led to 6th, led ag'n 3 out, hdd nxt, kpt on und pres frm last.* .... (5 to 4 on op 5 to 4 tchd 11 to 8) 3
1790² WILD ATLANTIC [85] 11-11-10 K Jones, *cl up, led 6th, hdd 3 out, sn rdn and btn.*...........(10 to 1 op 7 to 1) 4
3438⁹ EDEN STREAM [74] 7-10-13 G Upton, *sn wl beh, tld off.* .... (20 to 1) 5
DOCTOR BRIGGS (Ire) [61] 5-10-0 D Morris, *lost tch frm 6th, tld off whn pld up aftr 3 out.* (66 to 1 op 25 to 1) pu
3033 MAYWORK [61] 7-10-0 N Smith, *jmpd rght, sn wl beh, tld off whn pld up aftr 3 out.*.......... (16 to 1 op 14 to 1) pu
Dist: Nk, 1l, 12l, 30l. 4m 7.00s. a 2.00s (7 Ran).
SR: 27/29/33/28/
(Mrs M Ashby), P Beaumont

3787 Northeast Press Novices' Hurdle (4-y-o and up) £2,040 2m 5f 110yds (8:30)

DASHING DULA 8-10-9 P Niven, *hld up, hdwy hfwy, led bef 3 out, clr nxt, rdn aftr last, all out.* ....(9 to 2 op 4 to 1) 1
3126⁵ CLARET AND GOLD 7-11-0 B Storey, *prmnt till outpcd and lost pl aftr 6th, rallied after 3 out, styd on wl frm nxt, not rch wnr* ....(6 to 1 tchd 7 to 1) 2
3641⁶ KINDA GROOVY 5-11-7 N Smith, *reminders bef hfwy, hdwy to chase ldr 7th, ev ch 3 out, sn outpcd, kpt on wl und pres frm last.*................. (5 to 4 fav op 7 to 4) 3
3620 MISCHIEVOUS GIRL 6-10-9 Mrs F Needham, *chsd ldrs till grad wknd frm 3 out.*.................. (14 to 1) 4
3431 SHARP CHALLENGE 7-11-0 K Jones, *led till hdd bef 3 out, sn btn.*...........................(9 to 2 tchd 4 to 1) 5
3641 PANTO LADY 8-10-2 (7") Miss S Lamb, *in tch till wknd bef 3 out.*..................(150 to 1 op 66 to 1) 6
2411 UNCLES-LAD 6-11-0 N Bentley, *beh, some hdwy bef 3 out, sn wknd.*.......................(20 to 1) 7
3690⁹ GLORIOUS HEIGHTS 6-10-9 A Dobbin, *in tch till stumbled badly bef 7th, sn wl beh, tld off...*(16 to 1 op 14 to 1) 8
3620 ARTHUR BEE 7-11-0 Richard Guest, *lost tch frm hfwy, tld off whn pld up bef 3 out.*............(100 to 1 op 66 to 1) pu
Dist: 1½l, nk, 15l, hd, 1½l, 15l, dist. 5m 11.60s. a 20.60s (9 Ran).
(Mrs J N Askew), Mrs M Reveley

TRAMORE (IRE) (yielding)
Thursday May 5th

3788 Nore Maiden Hurdle (5-y-o and up) £2,245 2m. .... (5:30)

3550⁶ HAVE A BRANDY (Ire) 5-11-5 Mr D M O'Brien, ... (6 to 1) 1
3660⁵ THATS A SECRET 6-11-11 (3") T P Treacy, ... (10 to 9 on) 2
3550 BUILDERS LINE (Ire) 6-11-2 M A Davey, ...(20 to 1) 3
1397 SWIFT GLIDER (Ire) 5-10-11 (3") D P Murphy, ...(33 to 1) 4
MINOR MATTER (Ire) 5-11-0 H Rogers, ...(25 to 1) 5
3550 CARRIG DANCER (Ire) 6-10-10 (5") K P Gaule, ...(16 to 1) 6
3550 POLLEROO (Ire) 6-11-9 J Jones, ...(10 to 1) 7
3647 FANCY STEP 8-11-2 (7") Mr B Lennon, ...(11 to 1) 8
3711 SIR SOQUE (Ire) 5-11-5 A J O'Brien, ...(10 to 1) 9
2347⁵ SLANEY AGAIN (Ire) 6-10-13 (7") Miss L E A Doyle, .(12 to 1) 10
2586 VALTORUS (Ire) 5-11-5 K F O'Brien, ...(14 to 1) 11
3550 GOLDEN ARRANGEMENT 9-11-3 (3") T J O'Sullivan, ... (50 to 1) 12
3550 COOL COOPER 7-10-10 (5") P A Roche, ...(33 to 1) 13
3525 OVER THE JORDAN (Ire) 5-11-5 C O'Dwyer, ...(6 to 1) 14
3291 CLON CAW (Ire) 6-11-6 L P Cusack, ...(50 to 1) 15
Dist: ½l, ¾l, 13l, 6l. 4m 8.30s. (15 Ran).
(Paddock Racing Syndicate), Francis M O'Brien

3789 Dungarvan Chase (4-y-o and up) £2,245 2m. .... (6:00)

2233* ALBERT'S FANCY 8-12-0 F J Flood, ...(6 to 1) 1
2845⁹ BARRAFONA (Ire) 6-11-9 J Magee, ...(20 to 1) 2
2920⁴ BALLYBODEN 7-11-4 (5") J P Broderick, ...(14 to 1) 3
3614⁹ MONKEY AGO 7-12-0 K F O'Brien, ...(7 to 4 fav) 4
3465⁸ ZVORNIK 7-11-4 (5") P A Roche, ...(14 to 1) 5
3709⁶ DELGANY DEER 8-11-4 (5") D T Evans, ...(20 to 1) 6
3200 CASTLE KNIGHT 8-12-0 W T Slattery Jnr, ...(7 to 1) 7
BRIDGEOFALLEN (Ire) 6-10-13 (5") Mr W M O'Sullivan, ... (20 to 1) 8
2866 LAWYER'S BRIEF (Fr) 7-11-9 L P Cusack, ...(8 to 1) 9
3709⁹ MAJOR BERT (Ire) 6-11-9 F Woods, ...(50 to 1) 10

3241 QUIET CITY 7-11-6 (3") T J O'Sullivan, ... (8 to 1) 11
3291 KILLIMOR LAD 7-11-6 (3") C O'Brien, ...(33 to 1) 12
3325⁵ FINAL ISSUE 7-11-9 A Powell, ...(10 to 1) 13
2923 THE CRIOSRA (Ire) 5-11-2 S H O'Donovan, ...(33 to 1) 14
3709* RANDOM PRINCE 10-12-0 P Carberry, ... (5 to 1) f
Dist: 1½l, hd, hd, sht-hd. 4m 18.30s. (15 Ran).
(Slaney Cooked Meats), P J P Doyle

3790 Waterford Opportunity Handicap Chase (0-109 4-y-o and up) £2,659 2 ¾m. . . . . (6:30)

3551⁸ KINGS HILL [-] 12-9-11 (4") J Butler, ...(12 to 1) 1
3746 TAKE THE TOWN [-] 9-11-12 (2") M G Cleary, ...(8 to 1) 2
3551⁷ MONKS AIR [-] 7-10-0 (4") M D Murphy, ...(25 to 1) 3
3392 ANOTHER GROUSE [-] 7-11-1 C O'Brien, ... (8 to 1) 4
3524 MISCHIEF MOON [-] (bl) 9-9-3 (4") L A Hurley, . . . (33 to 1) 5
3648 NEW CO (Ire) [-] 5-11-0 (2") M A Davey, ...(6 to 1) 6
3465⁶ CAPINCUR EILE [-] 8-11-1 T P Rudd, ...(14 to 1) 7
3524 WHAT A MINSTREL [-] (bl) 8-9-7 T J O'Sullivan, . . . (16 to 1) 8
3648 WRECKLESS MAN [-] 7-11-7 T J Mitchell, ... (14 to 1) 9
3524 IFFEEE [-] 7-11-7 D P Murphy, ...(10 to 1) 10
3655 PEJAWI [-] 7-9-10 (4") T Martin, ...(25 to 1) 11
3648⁵ COLLIGAN RIVER [-] 11-11-10 (2") D T Evans, ...(9 to 2) pu
WATERCOURSE [-] 10-11-3 (5") P A Roche, ...(2 to 1 fav) pu
3200⁹ BENS DILEMMA [-] (bl) 9-9-10 (2") K P Gaule, ...(16 to 1) pu
3241⁵ WAKE UP LUV [-] 9-11-8 (4") T M O'Sullivan, ...(16 to 1) pu
Dist: 15l, 1½l, 3l, 3½l. 5m 49.20s. (16 Ran).
(Mrs M Butler), Michael Butler

3791 Dunmore East Hunters Chase (4-y-o and up) £2,590 2¾m. . . . .(7:00)

3527 NATIVE VENTURE (Ire) 6-11-10 Mr E Bolger, ...(7 to 1) 1
KILARA 7-11-7 (3") Mr T Lombard, ...(100 to 30 fav) 2
2352* FAHA GIG (Ire) 5-10-10 (7") Mr P R Crowley, ...(7 to 1) 3
797⁸ SCREEN PRINTER (Ire) 5-10-5 (7") Mr T J Murphy, . (10 to 1) 4
2551⁵ TROPICAL GABRIEL (Ire) 6-11-10 Mr P J Healy, ...(12 to 1) 5
3652³ SOUTH OFTHE BORDER (bl) 8-10-12 (7") Mr K O'Sullivan, ...(7 to 1) 6
KILLANNA LASS (Ire) 5-10-6¹ (7") Mr N D Fehily, . . (25 to 1) 7
3527 MOSS CASTLE 9-11-7 (3") Mr D P Costello, ... (5 to 1) 8
SONNY SULLIVAN 7-11-5² (7") Mr N C Kelleher, . . (25 to 1) 9
ANCHOR EXPRESS (bl) 8-11-3 (7") Mr D Keane, . . . (7 to 1) 10
LYNDON ROSE 7-11-0 (5") Mr W M O'Sullivan, ...(25 to 1) 11
3610² GLENARD LAD (Ire) 6-11-10 Mr A J Martin, ...(8 to 1) 12
3652 FUNNY BUSINESS 7-11-10 Mr D M O'Brien, ...(33 to 1) f
2941 STYLISH STEPPER 9-11-3 (7") Mr A K Wyse, ... (12 to 1) ur
Dist: 3½l, 5l, 5½l, 1½l. 5m 54.90s. (14 Ran).
(Mrs Nora Corcoran), Patrick G Kelly

3792 Barrow Flat Race (4 & 5-y-o) £2,245 2 ½m. . . . . (8:30)

3469² FLAWLESS FINISH (Ire) 5-11-8 Mr A P O'Brien, (2 to 1 fav) 1
114⁶ HIGHLAND SUPREME (Ire) 5-11-13 Mr E Bolger, ... (5 to 1) 2
3087² TELLTALK (Ire) 5-11-6 (7") Mr E Norris, ... (4 to 1) 3
3694 LENEY MOSS (Ire) 4-10-7 (7") Mr P English, ...(14 to 1) 4
VALIYIST (Ire) 5-11-1 (7") Mr C Cronin, ... (20 to 1) 5
3466 CASTLE CLUB (Ire) 5-11-5 (3") Mr R O'Neill, ...(33 to 1) 6
2756 EMMA HAAN (Ire) 5-11-5 (3") Mrs J M Mullins, ... (7 to 2) 7
STARLIGHT FOUNTAIN (Ire) 5-11-6 (7") Mr T J Murphy, ...(14 to 1) 8
MILL OTHE RAGS (Ire) 5-11-6 (7") Mr B Lennon, . . (14 to 1) 9
3525³ SMALL TALK (Ire) 5-11-1 (7") Mr J P Codd, ... (16 to 1) 10
3197 ON THE BRIDLE (Ire) 5-11-1 (7") Mr P J Nolan, ... (20 to 1) 11
2944 SLANEY GENT (Ire) 5-11-6 (7") Mr C Murphy, ...(20 to 1) 12
1039⁸ CUL RUA CREEK (Ire) 5-11-1 (7") Mr E Sheehy, . . . (20 to 1) 13
MONA CURRA GALE (Ire) 4-10-7 (7") Mr K O'Sullivan, ...(25 to 1) 14
GOLDWREN (Ire) 5-11-8 Mr A J Martin, ...(25 to 1) 15
Dist: 5½l, 4l, 10l, 2l. 4m 42.80s. (15 Ran).
(Bogey Syndicate), A P O'Brien

DOWNPATRICK (IRE) (good)
Friday May 6th

3793 Murphy Jewellers Downpatrick Maiden Hurdle (4-y-o and up) £1,553 2m 1f 172yds. . . . . (5:30)

3447 CUTTER'S WHARF (Ire) 5-11-8 (5") Mr B R Hamilton, ...(7 to 4 fav) 1
3448⁸ PILS INVADER (Ire) 6-10-10 (5") D T Evans, ... (12 to 1) 2
3448⁶ KEY WEST (Ire) 5-11-10 (3") T J Mitchell, ... (5 to 1) 3
3647 AMME ENAEK (Ire) 5-11-0 M Duffy, ...(14 to 1) 4
3723⁷ THE THIRD MAN (Ire) 5-11-5 C F Swan, ... (14 to 1) 5
2863 RHABDOMANCY (Ire) 4-10-12 (7") L A Hurley, ... (10 to 1) 6
3366 DENNETT VALLEY (Ire) 5-11-5 K F O'Brien, ... (12 to 1) 7
6176 SISTER CARMEL (Ire) 4-10-10 J Shortt, ...(10 to 1) 8
529⁷ WARREN STREET (Ire) 4-11-1 C O'Dwyer, ...(8 to 1) 9
3647 LOVELY AFFAIR (Ire) 5-10-7 (7") L J Fleming, ...(20 to 1) 10
KEPPOLS HARRIER (Ire) 4-10-8 (7") B D Murtagh, .(10 to 1) 11
1267⁷ JODONLEE (Ire) 5-10-7 (7") A Wall, ...(14 to 1) 12
638 LOCAL SILK (Ire) 5-11-0 F J Flood, ... (8 to 1) 13
3272³ FIDSPRIT 7-10-8 (7") Mr L J Gracey, ... (16 to 1) 14

3794 Frank Fitzsimons Memorial Hunters Chase (4-y-o and up) £1,553 3m (7:00)

3722 NEDA CHARMER 8-11-3 (7") Mr R I Arthur, ... (5 to 4 fav) 1
3652 BALD JOKER 9-11-13 (7") Mr C A McBratney, ... (7 to 2) 2
HAYES CORNER 8-11-7 (3") Mr P McMahon, ...(10 to 1) 3
3722⁶ WINDOVER LODGE 7-11-10 Mr J P Dempsey, ...(20 to 1) 4
378⁶ CARRIGANS LAD (Ire) 6-11-3 (7") Mr R Pugh, ...(20 to 1) 5
SHATTERED ILLUSION 8-11-5 (5") Mr B R Hamilton, ...(12 to 1) 6
807 FIND OUT MORE (Ire) 6-11-3 (7") Mr W Ewing, . . . (25 to 1) 7
364⁵ BALLYVERANE 8-11-3 (7") Mr C Rae, ... (14 to 1) 8
3723³ COCO DANCER 12-11-3 (7") Mr B Morgan, ...(16 to 1) 9
3722² GLENSPORT VI 8-10-12 (7") Mr J A Quinn, ...(12 to 1) 10
NEW DAY (Ire) 6-10-12 (7") Mr I Buchanan, ...(8 to 1) 11
3610⁶ PUSH GENTLY (Ire) 5-10-7 (5") Mr W M O'Sullivan, (25 to 1) 12
NAYCAB 8-11-2 (3") Mr J A Nash, ...(16 to 1) 13
3611 WHITESIDES FORT 11-11-3 (7") Mr D M Christie, (25 to 1) ur
Dist: 2½l, 4½l, 2½l, sht-hd. (Time not taken) (14 Ran).
(Neda Syndicate), I R Ferguson

3795 Parce Puer Stimulis Novice Chase (5-y-o and up) £1,553 2¼m. . . . . . . (7:30)

2986 ALTEREZZA (USA) 7-12-0 B Sheridan, ... (5 to 4 fav) 1
THE MAD MONK 9-12-0 K F O'Brien, ...(5 to 1) 2
3507⁸ TRASSEY BRIDGE (bl) 7-11-9 F Woods, ...(8 to 1) 3
3275⁵ SPARKLING BLAKE 8-11-2 (7") Mr I Buchanan, . . (10 to 1) 4
3721³ REDELVA 7-10-13 (5") Mr B R Hamilton, ...(8 to 1) 5
201⁹ OYSTER LANE 8-11-1 (3") G Kilfeather, ...(16 to 1) 6
3709 NO BETTER BUACHAIL (Ire) 6-11-9 F J Flood, ...(7 to 1) 7
2051⁵ BALLINDERRY GLEN 8-11-4 (5") M G Cleary, ... (12 to 1) 8
3271 MIRASEL 7-11-4 H Rogers, ...(33 to 1) 9
LISTEN MAN 7-11-2 (7") A Wall, ...(33 to 1) 10
2588 GONE LIKE THE WIND 7-11-4 (5") L Flynn, ...(20 to 1) f
3709 PREMIER COUNTY 8-11-6 (3") T J Mitchell, ...(20 to 1) f
3326 RAMBLING LORD (Ire) 6-11-9 P Carberry, ... (10 to 1) f
THEM AND US 8-11-4 (5") D Walsh, ...(25 to 1) pu
Dist: 1l, 2l, 6l, 7l. (Time not taken) (14 Ran).
(M G Hynes), D K Weld

3796 Caithness Flat Race (Div 1) (4-y-o and up) £1,553 2m 1f 172yds. . . . . . . (8:00)

DENRON (Ire) 5-11-8 (5") Mr B Hamilton, . . . (15 to 8 fav) 1
3653 EXCUSE ME (Ire) 5-11-6 (7") Mr P English, ...(10 to 1) 2
FIVE A SIDE (Ire) 7-12-0 Mr A J Martin, ...(5 to 1) 3
TACTIX 4-11-1 Mr P Fenton, ... (7 to 2) 4
2311 ARCTIC TREASURE (Ire) 5-11-1 (7") Mr W Ewing, (14 to 1) 5
3327 PADDY RED (Ire) 5-11-10 (3") Mr P J Casey, ... (6 to 1) 6
3276 LITTLE BALLYWOODEN (Ire) 5-11-6 (7") Mr E Magee, ...(20 to 1) 7
3327 MEDIEVAL BEAUTY (Ire) 6-11-2 (7") Mr P E I Newell, ...(33 to 1) 8
1455 HAWTHORN'S WAY (Ire) 6-11-6 (3") Mr R Neylon, (16 to 1) 9
3508 SINERGIA (Ire) 4-10-13 (7") Mr R Pugh, ...(10 to 1) 10
TWICE AS LUCKY (Ire) 5-11-1 (7") Mr J Bright, ...(8 to 1) 11
WAYSIDE SPIN (Ire) 4-10-13 (7") Mr J Wilson, ...(16 to 1) 12
EMMAS FRONTIER (Ire) 4-10-8 (7") Mr M Callaghan, ...(14 to 1) 13
Dist: 4½l, 1½l, 6l, 2½l. (Time not taken) (13 Ran).
(J F C Maxwell), J F C Maxwell

3797 Caithness Flat Race (Div 2) (4-y-o and up) £1,553 2m 1f 172yds. . . . . . . (8:30)

3488² SPARKY GAYLE (Ire) 4-11-6 Mr A Parker, ... (7 to 2) 1
3694⁸ DANGEROUS LADY (Ire) 5-11-5 (3") Mr D Hanlon, . .(7 to 1) 2
SHERS DELIGHT (Ire) 4-10-13 (7") Mr G F Ryan, (7 to 4 fav) 3
2394 PRETTY PRETENDER (Ire) 6-11-2 (7") Mr P E I Newell, ...(33 to 1) 4
3276² NO DOZING (Ire) 5-11-10 (3") Mr B R Hamilton, ...(3 to 1) 5
3450 SHANNON DEE (Ire) 4-10-12 (3") Mr J A Nash, ... (7 to 1) 6
TWABLADE (Ire) 6-11-6 (3") Mrs J M Mullins, ...(7 to 1) 7
3450 MOUNTMEAD (Ire) 4-10-8 (7") Mr A Harris, ...(33 to 1) 8
DAWN DIEU (Ire) 4-11-1 (5") Mr G J Hartford, ...(20 to 1) 9
DROPAHINT (Ire) 4-10-13 (7") Mr R Pugh, ...(20 to 1) 10
ARDMORE KELINKA (Ire) 4-10-8 (7") Mr J Bright, . .(20 to 1) 11
Dist: 8l, 5½l, ¾l, 3l. (Time not taken) (11 Ran).
(Raymond Anderson Green), C Parker

MARKET RASEN (firm)
Friday May 6th
Going Correction: NIL

3798 May Selling Handicap Hurdle (4 & 5-y-o) £1,891 2m 3f 110yds. . . . . . . (5:45)

2960 ALIZARI (USA) [49] (bl) 5-10-0 M Robinson, *reminders aftr second, led briefly after nxt, kidded alng to ld ag'n after 4 out, styd on r-in.*
. . . .(14 to 1 op 12 to 1 tchd 16 to 1) 1

3702⁷ BARSAL (Ire) [73] 4-11-3 (7*) F Leahy, *al hndy, led briefly 6th till aftr 4 out, edgd rght and ev ch last 2, one pace.*
....(5 to 2) 2

3673 GYMCRAK CYRANO (Ire) [59] 5-10-10 N Bentley, *patiently rdn, pushed up to track ldg pair aftr 3 out, btn whn blun last.*..........................(9 to 1 op 7 to 1) 3

3584⁵ SARANNPOUR (Ire) [69] (bl) 5-11-6 M Dwyer, *slight ld till hdd briefly aftr 3rd, headed after 4 out, blun nxt, sn struggling.*.......................(2 to 1 fav op 6 to 4) 4

3584³ PAAJIB (Ire) [63] 4-10-7 (7*) W Fry, *trkd ldrs, hrd at work and lost grnd bef 3 out, tld off.*....... (3 to 1 op 9 to 4) 5

Dist: 5l, 15l, 25l, 6l. 4m 46.20s. a 13.20s (5 Ran).

(Newbridge Stables), J Mooney

3799 Geostar Novices' Hunters' Chase (5-y-o and up) £1,892 3m 1f........(6:15)

IVEAGH LAD 8-11-7 (7*) Mr N F Smith, *made all, clr frm 5th, unchlgd.*......................(5 to 1 op 4 to 1) 1

3562 WHATAGALE 7-12-5 Mr J Durkan, *patiently rdn, improved to chase wnr fnl circuit, ridden and no imprsn frm 3 out.*..............................(5 to 4 on op 6 to 4 on) 2

GENERAL PICTON 8-11-9 (5*) Mr P Harding-Jones, *chsd ldg pair, pushed alng whn blun tenth, hrd at work frm 5 out, no imprsn.*.....................(9 to 1 op 6 to 1) 3

GILLANBONE 12-11-7 (7*) Mr A Sansome, *not fluent, chsd wnr to hfwy, struggling 6 out, tld off.*
....(50 to 1 op 33 to 1) 4

SMART PAL 9-12-0 Mrs A Farrell, *in tch, effrt whn not fluent 12th (water), struggling frm 6 out, sn lost touch.*
....(4 to 1 op 7 to 2) 5

3546 SPARTAN RAFT 13-11-7 (7*) Mr M Gingell, *not fluent, chsd ldrs for a circuit, tld off frm 12th.* (20 to 1 op 16 to 1) 6

Dist: 14l, 20l, 20l, 30l, dist. 6m 29.90s. a 28.90s (6 Ran).

(Peter Sawney), Miss J Sawney

3800 AEG Maiden Hurdle (4-y-o and up) £3,260 2m 1f 110yds..........(6:45)

3587⁵ MHEMEANLES 4-11-0 R Garritty, *settled midfield, drvn alng to take clr order aftr 4 out, led betw last 2, styd on to go clr r-in.*...................(4 to 1 op 5 to 2) 1

3378⁴ EIGHTANDAHALF (Ire) 5-11-0 (5*) P Midgley, *nvr far away, lft in ld 4 out, clr aftr nxt, hdd betw last 2, one pace.*
..............................(7 to 2 op 4 to 1 tchd 9 to 4) 2

3745⁴ ICE MAGIC 7-11-5 D Gallagher, *chsd clr ldg trio, bustled alng to improve appr 3 out, rdn and one pace frm nxt.*
....(14 to 1 op 10 to 1) 3

3617⁵ HOLD YOUR HAT ON 5-11-5 D Wilkinson, *scrubbed alng to keep in tch, improved und pres 4 out, one pace frm aftr nxt.*...........................(5 to 2 fav tchd 3 to 1) 4

3497⁶ RULLY 5-11-5 W Worthington, *wth ldg pair, hrd at work bef 3 out, sn outpcd.*...............(50 to 1 op 25 to 1) 5

3620 I IS 7-10-12 (7*) W Fry, *chsd ldg bunch, drvn up to fitter aftr 4 out, wknd after nxt.*....................(33 to 1) 6

3637³ MRS NORMAN 5-10-9 (5*) E Husband, *settled wth chasing bunch, drvn alng to improve aftr 4 out, outpcd frm after nxt.*...................................(7 to 1) 7

2254 GASCOIGNE WOOD 6-11-5 Mrs F Needham, *set of pace, stumbled and hdd 4 out, rallied, wknd and eased last 2.*
....(50 to 1 op 33 to 1) 8

3589 SKIDDER 5-11-5 Mr K Green, *chsd ldrs to hfwy, sn struggling, tld off.*.....................(50 to 1 op 33 to 1) 9

3598 RORY JOHN 6-11-5 Mr C Mulhall, *wth ldg pair, hrd at work 4 out, lost tch, tld off.*
................................(25 to 1 op 33 to 1 tchd 50 to 1) 10

2407 BEN CONNAN (Ire) 4-10-11 (3*) R Davis, *al struggling to keep in tch, nvr a factor, tld off.*...(33 to 1 op 33 to 1) 11

3231 BODKIN 4-10-9 A S Smith, *al struggling, tld off frm 3rd, virtually pld up r-in.* (12 to 1 op 8 to 1 tchd 14 to 1) 12

3620⁶ DYNAMITE DAN (Ire) 6-11-5 L Wyer, *hld up and beh whn blun and uns rdr second.*
................................(8 to 1 op 7 to 1 tchd 9 to 1) ur

3781⁴ TERRINGTON 4-11-0 W Marston, *sn struggling to keep in tch, tld off whn pld up bef 4 out...*(16 to 1 op 12 to 1) pu

Dist: 6l, 3½l, ½l, 3l, 9l, hd, ¾l, dist, dist, 20l. 4m 8.50s. a 6.50s (14 Ran).

SR: 21/20/16/15/12/3/-/2/-/ *(C H Stevens), M H Easterby*

3801 Grahame Liles Handicap Hurdle (0-110 4-y-o and up) £3,951 2m 3f 110yds....................(7:15)

3618⁵ MARSH'S LAW [100] (v) 7-12-0 M Brennan, *patiently rdn, smooth hdwy appr 3 out, led bef nxt, ran on strly r-in.*
....(9 to 1 op 10 to 1) 1

3678⁵ BENTLEY MANOR [84] (v) 5-10-12 W Humphreys, *settled off the pace, took clr order aftr 4 out, styd on frm betw last 2, nrst finish.*..(5 to 1 op 9 to 2 tchd 11 to 2) 2

3344² MY SWAN SONG [96] 9-11-5 (5*) D Leahy, *wtd wth, improved into midfield hfwy, hrd at work to improve frm betw last 2, nrst finish.*........(13 to 2 op 11 to 3) 3

3444⁴ IN TRUTH [86] 6-11-0 A Dobbin, *al wl plcd, ev ch 3 out, rdn frm nxt, one pace.*.................(8 to 1 op 6 to 1) 4

3678* FLASS VALE [88] (v) 6-11-2 Gee C Hawkins, *led frm second, hdd 3 out, hdd bef nxt, second and rdn whn nrly f last, not reco'r.*.................(7 to 1 op 11 to 2) 5

3545³ PEAK DISTRICT [81] 8-10-2 (7*) P McLoughlin, *settled to track ldg bunch, improved aftr 3 out, rdn and one pace frm nxt.*.........................(10 to 1 tchd 12 to 1) 6

3594³ TRISTAN'S COMET [80] 7-10-8 D Gallagher, *chsd ldg bunch, hrd at work frm 3 out, not quicken.*
....(12 to 1 op 14 to 1) 7

3619 HOUGHTON [95] (bl) 8-11-9 W Marston, *led to second, styd upsides till drvn alng aftr 3 out, fdd.*
..............................(10 to 1 op 12 to 1 tchd 14 to 1) 8

3357 MY LINDIANNE [80] 7-10-5² (5*) P Midgley, *bustled alng to keep up hfwy, nvr able to rch chalg position.*...(25 to 1) 9

3587* BITRAN [78] 4-10-6 A S Smith, *wth ldrs early, lost pl quickly hfwy, tld off.*.........(5 to 1 fav tchd 6 to 1) 10

3102⁴ WANG HOW [79] 6-10-7 D Wilkinson, *chsd ldg bunch, effrt hfwy, outpcd 3 out, tld off.*........(25 to 1 op 20 to 1) 11

3398 VOLCANIC DANCER (USA) [80] 8-10-3 (5*) E Husband, *refused to race, took no part.*......(40 to 1 op 25 to 1) ref

3446⁴ MARA ASKARI [78] (v) 6-10-6 T Wall, *struggling to keep in tch hfwy, tld off whn pld up bef 2 out.*........(50 to 1) pu

3583⁴ LEGITIM [91] 5-11-5 M Dwyer, *beh and struggling frm hfwy, tld off whn pld up 2 out, lme.........*(8 to 1 tchd 10 to 1) pu

Dist: 3½l, 1½l, ½l, ¾l, 5l, 2½l, 1l, 12l, 7l, 12l. 4m 39.60s. a 6.60s (14 Ran).

SR: 34/14/24/13/14/2/-/12/-/ *(Mrs Violet J Hannigan), O Brennan*

3802 East Coast Slag Products Novices' Chase (5-y-o and up) £3,366 2¾m 110yds......................(7:45)

3664⁶ HEATHVIEW 7-10-7 (7*) F Leahy, *not fluent, nvr far away, chlgd frm 3 out, led and wnt rght last, styd on strly.*
....(7 to 1 op 9 to 2) 1

3585⁵ MASTER'S CROWN (USA) 6-11-0 W Worthington, *al hndy, nosed ahead tenth, hdd and crowded last, kpt on same pace.*..................................(7 to 1 op 5 to 1) 2

3224 YOUNG PARSON 8-11-0 T Wall, *sn beh, relentless prog frm 4 out, styd on r-in, nrst finish.*
................................(7 to 1 op 6 to 1 tchd 10 to 1) 3

3510⁴ LOOSE WHEELS (v) 8-11-0 R Marley, *tried to make all, hdd tenth, rallied, rdn and outpcd frm 3 out.*
....(7 to 4 fav tchd 5 to 2) 4

3343³ MILO 8-11-0 W McFarland, *patiently rdn, improved frm midfield aftr 4 out, ridden alng after nxt, one pace.*
....(10 to 1 op 6 to 1) 5

2227 KHOJOHN 6-11-0 G Upton, *settled off the pace, steady hdwy gng wl aftr 4 out, can improve.*(6 to 1 op 7 to 2) 6

3544 LAD LANE 10-11-0 Mr M Gingell, *chsd ldg bunch, drvn alng to keep up hfwy, struggling frm 4 out...*(33 to 1) 7

3338 TOKANDA 10-11-0 D Gallagher, *trkd ldrs, effrt aftr 4 out, rdn and outpcd frm nxt..........*(16 to 1 op 14 to 1) 8

3630 WANDER LODGE 6-10-6 (3*) A Proctor, *trkd ldrs, blun 3rd and 5 out, sn lost tch.*.............(50 to 1 op 33 to 1) 9

3588 STONE WARRIOR 7-11-0 M Robinson, *sluggish strt, improved hfwy, effrt aftr 4 out, fourth and rdn whn blun and uns rdr last.*..........(50 to 1 op 33 to 1) ur

3579 JELLIQUE 12-11-0 C Hawkins, *reminders to keep up aftr 4th, struggling hfwy, tld off whn pld up bef four out.*
....(50 to 1 op 33 to 1) pu

2892⁸ EBORNEEZER'S DREAM 11-11-0 D Telfer, *sn struggling in rear, tld off whn pld up aftr 4 out.* (25 to 1 op 20 to 1) pu

CRUISE CRACKER 8-10-9 M Ranger, *settled midfield, feeling pace fnl circuit, wknd and pld up bef tenth.*
....(50 to 1 op 33 to 1) pu

Dist: 1½l, 13l, 2½l, sht-hd, 3½l, 15l, 12l, 20l. 5m 44.70s. a 16.70s (13 Ran).

(W Hancock), J G FitzGerald

3803 Theodore West Memorial Handicap Chase (0-125 5-y-o and up) £4,045 2m 1f 110yds......................(8:15)

3471² JUST FRANKIE [117] 10-11-10 P Niven, *led till hdd aftr 6th (water), rgned ld 4 out, hrd pressed whn lft clr nxt, blun 2 out, easily.*
.....(11 to 10 on op Evens tchd 11 to 10 and 6 to 5 on) 1

3566* BARKISLAND [94] 10-10-1 Mrs A Farrell, *pressed ldr, led aftr 6th (water), hdd 4 out, wknd bef nxt, no imprsn whn lft second 3 out...........*(3 to 1 op 5 to 2) 2

3513⁷ BOSTON ROVER [115] 9-11-8 M Brennan, *settled travelling wl, cruised up to dispute ld whn blun and uns rdr 3 out, rmntd......................*(5 to 2 op 2 to 1) 3

Dist: 9l, dist. 4m 27.90s. a 13.90s (3 Ran).

(Lady Susan Watson), Mrs M Reveley

WINCANTON (firm)
Friday May 6th
Going Correction: MINUS 0.85 sec. per fur.

3804 Jamboree Novices' Handicap Hurdle (0-100 4-y-o and up) £2,206 2¾m (6:00)

3497⁵ BORROWED AND BLUE [78] 4-10-13 Peter Hobbs, *beh, hdwy frm 7th, chlgd 2 out, led and wnt lft last, quickened wl nr finish...................*(9 to 2 op 3 to 1) 1

3623* GRATUITY [82] 9-11-3 (8ex) N Mann, *chsd ldrs, led 3rd to nxt, led aftr 3 out to last, rallied r-in, sn rdn and outpcd.................*(6 to 1 op 5 to 1 tchd 7 to 1) 2

3623⁴ TRAIN ROBBER [70] 9-10-5 W Irvine, *prmnt early, sn rear, drvn and hdwy 3 out, styd on appr last.*
.......................(14 to 1 op 12 to 1 tchd 16 to 1) 3
3572² TAKE A FLYER (Ire) [67] 4-10-2 A Tory, *chsd ldrs 6th, chlgd 2 out, rdn and one pace appr last...* (11 to 1 op 12 to 1) 4
3629⁵ PALACE PARADE (USA) [70] 4-10-5 P Holley, *chsd ldrs, rdn 7th, drvn and styd on frm 2 out.*
.......................(16 to 1 op 14 to 1 tchd 20 to 1) 5
3685¹ LUCKY BLUE [86] 7-11-7 S Earle, *beh, rdn 7th, styd on und pres appr 2 out, not a dngr...* (16 to 1 op 10 to 1) 6
3046⁴ NEFARIOUS [93] 8-12-0 A Maguire, *in tch, chsd ldrs 7th, chlgd 3 out, ev ch nxt, wknd and mstk last.*
.... 7
3560⁸ GLEN CHERRY [88] (bl) 8-11-2 (7*) Mr Richard White, *chsd ldrs to 7th...........................*(33 to 1 op 14 to 1) 8
3543⁹ WYJUME (Ire) [70] 5-10-5 B Powell, *al beh, rcd wide, nvr dngrs.............................*(50 to 1 op 25 to 1) 9
3623⁷ CASTLE ORCHARD [65] 10-10-0 J R Kavanagh, *not fluent, al beh..............................*(50 to 1 op 20 to 1) 10
2874 PHIL'S DREAM [75] 6-10-10 I Lawrence, *al beh.*
.......................(16 to 1 op 14 to 1) 11
3572 YAAFOOR (USA) [69] (bl) 5-10-4 M Richards, *led to 3rd, led nxt till hdd and wknd rpdly aftr 3 out, tld off.*
.......................(33 to 1 op 20 to 1) 12
3630² CRAZY DAISY [80] 7-11-1 R Dunwoody, *chsd ldrs, wkng whn blun 3 out, tld off when pld up bef 2 out.*
.......................(5 to 2 fav op 7 to 2 tchd 4 to 1) pu
Dist: 2½l, 5l, 1½l, 10l, 6l, 1l, 5l, 12l, ½l, 6l. 5m 2.60s. b 3.40s (13 Ran).

(Brian Cooper), P J Hobbs

3805 Fonthill Novices' Handicap Chase (5-y-o and up) £3,116 2m 5f.......(6:30)

3534⁵ FESTIVAL DREAMS [97] 9-12-0 P Holley, *chsd ldrs, led 6th, styd on und pres frm 2 out, gmely.*
.......................(8 to 1 op 7 to 1 tchd 9 to 1) 1
3546⁴ COASTING [71] 8-10-2 J Railton, *chsd ldrs, pressed wnr frm 9th, str chal und pres r-in, jst fld.*
.......................(11 to 2 op 5 to 1) 2
3562⁴ PRINCE'S COURT [89] 11-11-1 (5*) D Fortt, *hdwy to chase ldrs 8th, effrt 4 out, wkng whn hit 3 out.*
.......................(6 to 1 tchd 13 to 2) 3
3517⁵ PAPER STAR [69] 7-10-0 B Powell, *chsd ldrs till outpcd 9th, no dngr aftr...*(9 to 2 op 5 to 1 tchd 13 to 2) 4
3695³ MIRAGE DANCER [76] 11-10-7 M Perrett, *al beh, no ch whn hit 3 out.....*(16 to 1 op 14 to 1 tchd 20 to 1) 5
3532 HAND OUT [75] 10-9-13 (7*) Mr G Hogan, *mstks, al beh, tld off.............................*(33 to 1 op 20 to 1) 6
3278⁴ RINANNA BAY [74] 7-10-5 A Maguire, *beh 6th, tld off.*
.......................(13 to 2 op 6 to 1 tchd 7 to 1) 7
3546⁸ TEARFUL PRINCE [69] 10-10-0 D Bridgwater, *beh whn f second..............................*(33 to 1 op 20 to 1) f
3534³ COMMANCHERO [85] 7-11-2 R Dunwoody, *in tch, hit 11th, 4th and btn whn f four out.*
.......................(3 to 1 fav op 5 to 2 tchd 100 to 30) f
3510⁹ VISION OF WONDER [70] 10-10-1 J R Kavanagh, *hit off whn pld up bef 4 out.........*(50 to 1 op 33 to 1) pu
3562⁸ COOMBESBURY LANE [70] (v) 8-10-1 N Williamson, *led to 3rd, prmnt till mstk 13th, sn wknd, tld off whn pld up aftr 3 out.................*(50 to 1 op 33 to 1) pu
3714⁴ BARONESS ORKZY [83] 8-11-0 M A FitzGerald, *led 3rd to 6th, wknd tenth, tld off whn pld up bef 3 out.*
.......................(16 to 1 op 12 to 1) pu
Dist: Hd, 14l, 20l, 12l, dist, 4l. 5m 3.20s. b 2.80s (12 Ran).

(Mrs Nerys Dutfield), Mrs P N Dutfield

3806 American Express Foreign Exchange Handicap Hurdle (0-120 4-y-o and up) £3,629 2m...................(7:00)

1557⁵ MULCIBER [92] 6-10-10 M Perrett, *mid-div, hdwy 5th, drvn to chal last, quickened wl to ld r-in, driven out.*
.......................(6 to 1 tchd 7 to 1) 1
3574¹ ROUTING [88] 6-10-6 Richard Guest, *hdwy 5th, led gng wl appr 2 out, shaken up r-in, hdd and one pace.*
.......................(4 to 1 op 5 to 1 tchd 11 to 2) 2
3574² WILL JAMES [86] (bl) 8-9-13 (5*) S Curran, *chsd ldrs, drvn appr 2 out, styd on r-in.*
.......................(13 to 2 op 11 to 2 tchd 7 to 1) 3
2229¹ NOBLELY (USA) [104] 7-11-8 R Dunwoody, *led aftr 1st till appr 2 out, wknd.*
.......................(3 to 1 fav tchd 11 to 4 and 100 to 30) 4
3628² TENAYESTELIGN [82] 6-9-11 (3*) J McCarthy, *hdwy to chase ldrs 3 out, rdn appr nxt, one pace.*
.......................(7 to 1 op 6 to 1) 5
3574² KALAMOSS [82] 5-9-7 (7*) Miss S Mitchell, *beh, hit second, ran on frm 3 out, not rch ldrs.....*(20 to 1 op 16 to 1) 6
1672⁵ ADMIRALTY WAY [106] 8-11-7 (3*) T Jenks, *chsd ldrs, hrd rdn appr 2 out, wknd approaching last.*
.......................(20 to 1 op 14 to 1 tchd 25 to 1) 7
3156⁶ PERSIAN LUCK [92] 8-10-10 A Maguire, *led, hit 1st and hdd, wth ldr till wknd aftr 3 out, tld off.*
.......................(14 to 1 op 10 to 1 tchd 16 to 1) 8
3571 DISTANT MEMORY [93] (bl) 5-10-11 M Hourigan, *prmnt, wknd 4th, no ch whn hmpd 3 out, tld off.*
.......................(12 to 1 op 8 to 1) 9

3302³ CHEERFUL TIMES [93] 11-10-11 J Railton, *beh till f 3 out.*
.......................(11 to 1 op 8 to 1 tchd 12 to 1) f
Dist: 1½l, 10l, hd, 2½l, 8l, ¾l, dist, 20l. 3m 28.30s. b 8.70s (10 Ran).
SR: 33/27/15/33/8/-/23/-/-/ (Mrs Penny Treadwell), G Harwood

3807 R. K. Harrison Insurance Brokers Novices' Hunters' Chase (6-y-o and up) £1,868 2m 5f...............(7:30)

RYMING CUPLET 9-11-7 (7*) Mr Richard White, *not fluent, lost tch 6th, hdwy 9th, staying on whn hit 4 out, rallied nxt, chlgd 2 out till quickened to ld r-in.*
.......................(11 to 10 on op 11 to 8 on tchd Evens) 1
DUBIT 9-11-7 (7*) Miss S Vickery, *chsd ldr 9th, chlgd 11th, led 13th, hit 3 out, hdd r-in, hrd drvn, no extr cl hme.*
.......................(7 to 2 op 9 to 2) 2
SKIPPING GALE 9-11-7 (7*) Mr N R Mitchell, *led, blun 5th and hdd, led 8th to 13th, wknd 3 out.*
.......................(3 to 1 op 5 to 2 tchd 7 to 2) 3
NATIONAL GYPSY 8-11-2 (7*) Mr R Nuttall, *led 5th to 8th, in tch, 4th and rear whn f tenth.......*(10 to 1 op 8 to 1) f
Dist: Nk, 25l. 5m 8.80s. a 2.80s (4 Ran).

(Gerald Tanner), M J Trickey

3808 Chedington Handicap Chase (0-120 5-y-o and up) £3,756 3m 1f 110yds
....................................(8:00)

3593² TOCHENKA [107] 10-11-7 (3*) T Jenks, *jmpd wl, chsd ldrs, led 5th, clr 4 out...*(11 to 4 fav op 9 to 4 tchd 3 to 1) 1
3631² DOONLOUGHAN [99] 9-11-2 A Maguire, *prmnt, hit 9th, chsd wnr frm 16th, hit 4 out, styd on, no imprsn.*
.......................(4 to 1 op 3 to 1 tchd 9 to 2) 2
3437² LITTLE GENERAL [84] 11-10-1 M Perrett, *in tch, pushed alng 14th, chsd ldrs 17th, outpcd 4 out.*
.......................(10 to 1 op 7 to 1) 3
3544⁸ TAGMOUN CHAUFOUR (Fr) [83] 9-10-0 B Powell, *led to 5th, prmnt, hit 17th, no dngr aftr.*
.......................(50 to 1 op 33 to 1 tchd 66 to 1) 4
3260⁴ TOUCHING STAR [107] 9-11-10 M Hourigan, *beh 6th, hdwy 14th, pressed ldrs 16th, wknd 4 out.*
.......................(50 to 1 op 33 to 1) 5
3669* SKERRY MEADOW [93] 10-10-10 (6ex) R Dunwoody, *prmnt, drpd rear 13th, rallied 15th, rdn whn mstk and uns rdr 17th...........................*(7 to 1 op 9 to 1) ur
3631³ OCEAN LINK [91] 10-10-8 S Earle, *pressed ldrs, lost pl 9th, rallied to chal 11th to nxt, second whn mstk and uns rdr 15th..........*(100 to 30 op 4 to 1 tchd 9 to 1) ur
Dist: 10l, 6l, 2l, 14l. 6m 15.10s. b 0.90s (7 Ran).

(R K Minton-Price), N A Twiston-Davies

3809 Whitsbury 'National Hunt' Novices' Hurdle (4-y-o and up) £2,355 2m (8:30)

3630* MYRTILLA 5-11-1 L Harvey, *in tch, str hold, chlgd aftr 2 out, slight ld last, drvn out.*
.......................(6 to 4 fav op 7 to 4 tchd 9 to 4) 1
3543⁷ SMART IN SABLE 7-10-8 M Richards, *rear, mstk 3rd, hdwy to ld 2 out, wnt lft, hdd last, styd on same pace.*
.......................(5 to 1 op 4 to 1 tchd 11 to 2) 2
3115⁸ MARROB 7-10-13 G McCourt, *hld up mid-div, hdwy and jmpd slwly 5th, rdn appr 2 out, sn btn.*
.......................(13 to 8 op 7 to 4 tchd 11 to 8) 3
3396 CAPTAIN BERT 5-10-13 I Lawrence, *chsd ldrs, rdn and one pace appr 2 out.* (33 to 1 op 16 to 1 tchd 50 to 1) 4
3530 BOLLINGTON (Fr) 5-10-13 (3*) J McCarthy, *sluly away, str hold, sn reco'red to ld, hdd aftr 3 out, wknd quickly.*
.......................(14 to 1 op 10 to 1 tchd 20 to 1) 5
3576⁸ TRUE SERENADE 5-10-13 V Slattery, *al beh.*
.......................(16 to 1 op 20 to 1 tchd 14 to 1) 6
2860 DO LETS 5-10-8 R Dunwoody, *trkd ldrs, led aftr 3 out to nxt, ev ch whn f last............*(12 to 1 tchd 16 to 1) f
Dist: 1½l, 6l, 1½l, 12l, 20l. 3m 39.90s. a 2.90s (7 Ran).
(Robert Long), Andrew Turnell

DOWNPATRICK (IRE) (good)
Saturday May 7th

3810 Toal Bookmakers Maiden Hurdle (4-y-o and up) £1,553 2m 1f 172yds (2:20)

3468⁸ KNOCNAGORE (Ire) 5-11-13 A Powell,........(5 to 2 fav) 1
3448⁴ BEDFORD RAMBLER (Ire) 5-11-8 (5*) J P Broderick, (5 to 1) 2
2774 GALZIG 6-12-0 H Rogers,.....................(16 to 1) 3
3723⁴ REMO GROVE (Ire) 6-11-9 (5*) M M Mackin,.....(7 to 1) 4
1814 GOLDEN PLAN (Ire) 6-12-0 C N Bowens,.........(9 to 2) 5
3388 EARLY RISER (Ire) 6-11-2 (7*) Mr G T Morrow,.....(20 to 1) 6
3273 FATHER GREGORY (Ire) 5-11-10 (3*) T J Mitchell, (20 to 1) 7
2919 WINNIE WUMPKINS (Ire) (bl) 5-11-3 (5*) M A Davey,
.......................(25 to 1) 8
BEAU'S CHOICE (Ire) 5-11-13 J Shortt,..........(10 to 1) 9
3201 HOLLOW SOUND (Ire) 5-11-8 C O'Dwyer,.......(14 to 1) 10
BOLD NOT BEAT (Ire) 4-11-6 J Collins,..........(10 to 1) 11
3273 BRISCE HILL (Ire) 6-11-2 (7*) D A McLoughlin,....(25 to 1) 12
2203 QUICK RAISE (Fr) 5-11-10 (3*) D Bromley,.........(8 to 1) 13
PHARVIONE (Ire) 4-11-1 C F Swan,..............(8 to 1) 14

3730⁷ TRIBAL MEMORIES (Ire) 4-10-8 (7") M P Kelly, ... (7 to 1) pu
Dist: 3l, 2½l, 7l, 3½l. (Time not taken) (15 Ran).

(T J Hanafin), Michael Flynn

3811 Irish Field (QR) Maiden Hurdle (4-y-o and up) £1,553 2¾m. . . . . (2:50)

3550³ KILLOSKEHAN QUEEN 7-11-1 Mr P Fenton, . .(13 to 8 fav) 1
38 WILLCHRIS 7-11-7⁸ (7") Mr C A McBratney, ...(12 to 1) 2
3450⁴ GRANDOLLY (Ire) 5-11-10 (3") Mr B R Hamilton, . .(3 to 1) 3
3447⁸ PATS FAREWELL (Ire) 6-11-6 Mr J P Dempsey, ...(7 to 1) 4
3733 THE PHOENIX 8-10-13 (7") Mr T R Hughes, ...(12 to 1) 5
3720⁶ KILRAY (Ire) 6-10-8 (7") Mr K Ross, ...(12 to 1) 6
RIVER MAGNET (Ire) 5-11-2 (3") Mr P McMahon, . .(10 to 1) 7
3506 IM OK (Ire) (bl) 6-10-8 (7") Mr B M Cash, ...(25 to 1) 8
1833 MONARROW (Ire) 6-11-3 (3") Mr J A Nash, ...(20 to 1) 9
KUSHDALAY (Ire) 5-11-5 Mr A R Coonan, ...(6 to 1) 10
SHEER INDULGENCE 7-11-6 Mr A J Martin, ...(14 to 1) 11
3723 DAYLIGHT LADY 7-10-8 (7") Mr L J Gracey, ...(33 to 1) 12
Dist: 1l, hd, ¾l, 12l. (Time not taken) (12 Ran).

(Mrs S Hamilton), L Young

3812 Willie Polly Memorial Handicap Hurdle (0-109 4-y-o and up) £1,725 2m 1f 172yds. . . . . (3:20)

3719⁶ MY HALL DOOR [-] 5-10-2 (5") D T Evans, ...(5 to 1) 1
3504⁶ I AM [-] 6-11-3 (5") J P Broderick, ...(5 to 1) 2
3719² THE TOASTER [-] 7-10-10 (7") B Bowens, ...(9 to 4 fav) 3
3449 TOP GENERATION [-] 5-10-6 (3") T J Mitchell, ... (10 to 1) 4
3719⁸ THE PARSONS ROSE (Ire) [-] 6-9-10 (5") K P Gaule, (16 to 1) 5
3719⁴ LOAVES AND FISHES [-] (bl) 6-11-1 (7") B D Murtagh,
. . . .(7 to 1) 6
2122 FALCARRAGH (Ire) [-] 4-10-7 C O'Dwyer, ...(16 to 1) 7
3447⁸ GRAMSCI (Ire) [-] 6-11-1 K F O'Brien, ... (10 to 1) 8
3273 ROSIN THE BOW (Ire) [-] (bl) 5-10-0 (7") P Morris, (14 to 1) 9
2158⁴ MR SNAGGLE (Ire) [-] 5-11-4 (3") C O'Brien, ...(7 to 1) 10
3272⁶ TOP RUN (Ire) [-] 6-9-11 D J Kavanagh, ...(20 to 1) 11
3693⁸ JAMES GIRL [-] 10-10-4 C F Swan, ...(14 to 1) 12
2939 MOLLIE WOOTTON (Ire) [-] 6-10-2 W T Slattery Jnr, (20 to 1) 13
3325 JIMMY GORDON [-] 7-11-3 J Shortt, ...(16 to 1) 14
3711 GARYS GIRL [-] 7-10-10 (7") J M McCormack, ...(8 to 1) f
Dist: 1l, 1l, 3l, 1½l. (Time not taken) (15 Ran).

(T C McGeary), A D Evans

3813 Holestone Bloodhounds Flat Race (4-y-o and up) £1,553 2½m. . . . . . . (4:50)

3723 KAVANAGHS DREAM (Ire) 5-11-8 (5") Mr H F Cleary, (4 to 1) 1
SHANECRACKEN (Ire) 6-11-11 (3") Mr P McMahon, (7 to 1) 2
POPEYE THE GUY (Ire) 5-11-6 (7") Mr C A McBratney,
. . . .(10 to 1) 3
CLUEN CASTLE (Ire) 6-11-6 (3") Mr D Valentine, . .(12 to 1) 4
TOM SNOUT (Ire) 6-12-0 Mr A J Martin, ... (15 to 8 fav) 5
DUPREY (Ire) 6-11-7 (7") Mr G Martin, ...(6 to 1) 6
TELEMAR (Ire) 5-11-1 (7") Mr J G Bates, ... (25 to 1) 7
JACK DANDY 8-11-7 (7") Mr J Gault, ... (20 to 1) 8
LAST DECADE (Ire) 6-11-7 (7") Mr J J Lamb, ...(6 to 1) 9
3370 SERLA EXPRESS 8-11-7 (7") Mr A J Smith, ...(20 to 1) 10
DEEYEHFOLLYME (Ire) 6-11-2 (7") Mr C Gainey, . .(20 to 1) 11
ARCTIC MO (Ire) 5-11-5 (3") Mr B R Hamilton, ...(7 to 1) 12
MAIASAURA (Ire) 5-11-6 (7") Mr C Rae, ...(7 to 1) 13
58 HASSLE FREE 7-11-7 (7") Mr D M Christie, ... (25 to 1) 14
Dist: 2l, 7l, 7l, 1½l. (Time not taken) (14 Ran).

(D G McArdle), Cecil Mahon

NEWCASTLE (firm)
Saturday May 7th
Going Correction: MINUS 0.45 sec. per fur.

3814 C.I.U. Convalescent Homes Handicap Chase (0-115 5-y-o and up) £3,345 3m
. . . . (5:50)

3644 CAROUSEL ROCKET [94] 11-10-12 A Dobbin, nvr far
away, drvn alng fnl circuit, outpcd bef 3 out, styd on to
ld r-in, gmely. . . . . (100 to 30 fav op 3 to 1 tchd 7 to 2) 1
3566² ON THE HOOCH [92] 9-10-10 Mr J Bradburne, in tch,
improved to draw level 12th, led briefly 5 out, outpcd
aftr nxt, styd on to ld last, hdd r-in, no extr.
. . . .(4 to 1 op 7 to 2 tchd 9 to 2) 2
3602⁷ ZAM BEE [92] 8-10-10 T Reed, with ldr, led 9th, hdd
briefly 5 out, drw clr bef 3 out, headed last, no extr. . . 3
3644⁷ JELUPE [104] 12-11-8 Mr R Sandys-Clarke, al hndy, jnd
leader 12th, led 5 out, weakened bef 3 out, styd on
r-in, no imprsn. . . . .(10 to 1 op 8 to 1) 4
3485 TRUELY ROYAL [91] 10-10-9 B Storey, settled in tch, drvn
alng bef 5 out, outpcd aftr nxt. . . . .(7 to 1 op 6 to 1) 5
3237⁵ WHEELIES NEWMEMBER [86] 11-9-13 (5") J Supple, slight
ld till hdd 9th, styd hndy, drvn alng aftr 5 out, wknd
frm 3 out. . . . . (33 to 1) 6
3644⁶ HE WHO DARES WINS [110] (bl) 11-12-0 K Johnson, nvr far
away, not fluent 9th, cl 5th whn f nxt, broke hock,
destroyed. . . . .(9 to 2 op 7 to 1) f

3784⁴ GATHERING TIME [97] 8-10-8 (7") Miss V Haigh, beh and
not jump wl, blun 6th, in pld up. . .(25 to 1 op 20 to 1) pu
Dist: 2l, 2l, 12l, nk. 5m 53.40s. a 3.40s (8 Ran).

(A Saccomando), M D Hammond

3815 McEwans Lager Novices' Hurdle (4-y-o and up) £2,102 2m 110yds. . .(6:25)

3617⁸ GOING PUBLIC 7-11-3 K Johnson, nvr far away, ev ch 2
out, rdn to ld r-in, styd on wl. . . . . .(14 to 1 op 10 to 1) 1
3692⁴ ASTRALEON (Ire) 5-11-3 T Reed, tucked away on ins,
improved on bit to ld 2 out, hdd aftr last, shaken up
last 50 yards, not run on. . . . .(3 to 1 tchd 7 to 2) 2
3674³ DE JORDAAN 7-10-10 (7") W Fry, patiently rdn, improved
and ev ch 2 out, ridden and not quicken frm last.
. . . .(12 to 1 op 10 to 1) 3
3459 EMERALD CHARM (Ire) 6-10-12 B Storey, patiently rdn,
smooth hdway hfwy, ev ch betw last 2, no extr r-in.
. . . .(50 to 1) 4
3617² OTTER BUSH 5-11-3 (7") D Towler, chsd ldg bunch,
improved on outer 3 out, ev ch nxt, not quicken frm
last. . . . .(5 to 2 fav op 6 to 4) 5
3617 INGLETONIAN (bl) 5-11-3 C Hawkins, settled on outer,
improved 4 out, rdn alng nxt, fdd betw last 2.
. . . .(25 to 1 op 16 to 1) 6
3617 BELIEVE IT 5-11-3 Miss T Waggott, led 1st, hdd 4 out,
struggling to keep up aftr nxt, sn btn. . . . .(50 to 1) 7
3598 SON OF TEMPO (Ire) 5-10-10 (7") Miss S Lamb, hld up,
shaken up bef 2 out, not rch ldrs.
. . . .(150 to 1 op 100 to 1) 8
3125 DARK MIDNIGHT (Ire) 5-10-10 (7") Mr A Manners, pld very
hrd, sn tracking ldrs, ev ch aftr 3 out, fdd frm nxt.
. . . .(66 to 1) 9
ANOTHER MEADOW 6-11-3 L O'Hara, nvr far away, ev ch
2 out, rdn and sn btn. . . . .(200 to 1) 10
3688⁵ BDOORE (Ire) 6-10-7 (5") F Perratt, led to 1st, trkd ldrs till
rdn and wknd bef 3 out. . . . .(50 to 1) 11
3598² DERWENT LAD 5-11-3 A Dobbin, settled midfield, imprvg
whn hit 3 out, sn btn. . . . .(14 to 1 op 12 to 1) 12
3578 ROYAL QUARRY (bl) 8-11-3 C Dennis, trkd ldg pair, led 4
out, hdd 2 out, sn btn. . . . .
. . . .(66 to 1 op 50 to 1) 13
3584 BOSSYMOSS (Ire) 5-11-3 Susan Kersey, hld up and struggling bef 3 out, tld off. . . . .(100 to 1 op 200 to 1) 14
3598 SOLAR NOVA 6-10-12 N Smith, beh, struggling hfwy, tld
off. . . . .(33 to 1) 15
2326⁶ HECKLEY SPARK 6-11-2⁴ Mr J Walton, mid-div, pushed
alng hfwy, struggling bef 3 out, tld off.
. . . .(33 to 1 tchd 50 to 1) 16
3617 HALF A BILLION 6-11-3 Mr R Hale, beh and sn struggling,
tld off last. . . . .(100 to 1) 17
FALLOWFIELD GIRL 5-10-12 G Harker, pld hrd, sn in mid-
field, lost grnd hfwy, tld off whn pulled up bef last.
. . . .(50 to 1) pu
3459² RHYMING THOMAS 6-11-3 J Railton, pld and dismounted
bef 1st, lme. . . . .(4 to 1 op 7 to 2 tchd 9 to 2) pu
Dist: 1½l, 3l, 3l, 1¼l, 10l, ¾l, ½l, 3½l, 2l, sht-hd. 3m 54.40s. a 1.40s (19 Ran).
SR: 1/-/-/-/-/ (Alan Cairns), P Cheesbrough

3816 Newcastle Brown Ale Amateur Riders' Handicap Chase for the John J. Straker Challenge Trophy (0-115 5-y-o and up) £3,360 2½m. . . (6:55)

3676⁴ WAIT YOU THERE (USA) [97] 9-11-7 Mr S Swiers, nvr far
away, led aftr tenth, jnd 12th, lft wl clr 4 out, unchlgd.
. . . .(6 to 1 op 11 to 8 on and 5 to 4 on) 1
3705⁵ STRONG APPROACH [100] 9-11-5 (5") Mr D Parker, led till
hdd bef 9th, blun and lost grnd nxt, no imprsn fnl 3.
. . . .(11 to 4 op 9 to 4 tchd 9 to 2) 2
3586⁸ NEWMARKET SAUSAGE [76] 13-9-9² (7") Mr M Coglan, al
beh, tld off fnl circuit. . . . .(33 to 1 op 25 to 1) 3
3579⁷ CELTIC SONG [91] 7-11-1 Mrs A Farrell, not fluent, pressed
ldr, led bef 9th, hdd aftr nxt, chlg whn f 4 out.
. . . .(4 to 1 op 7 to 2 tchd 9 to 2) f
Dist: 8l, 30l. 5m 2.50s. a 11.50s (4 Ran).

(Hamish Alexander), H Alexander

3817 Newcastle Breweries Top Of The North Novices' Handicap Hurdle Final (4-y-o and up) £3,371 2½m. . . . . .(7:25)

3687² STRONG DEEL (Ire) [84] 6-10-6³ T Reed, trkd ldrs, rdn aftr
3 out, styd on to ld bef last, ran on wl.
. . . .(8 to 1 op 9 to 1 tchd 12 to 1) 1
3354⁴ ARIADLER (Ire) [101] 6-11-9 K Johnson, settled on ins,
outpcd and lost grnd 4th, styd on und pres betw last 2,
unt second last 50 yards. . . . .(12 to 1 op 10 to 1) 2
3580 TWIN STATES [88] 5-10-3 (7") W Fry, nvr far away, lft in ld
and hit 2 out, hdd bef last, one pace.
. . . .(12 to 1 op 10 to 1) 3
3379⁴ SOUNDS GOLDEN [78] 6-10-0 A Dobbin, chsd ldrs, outpcd
and rdn 6th, styd on to chal 2 out, one pace frm last.
. . . .(33 to 1 op 20 to 1) 4
3487⁴ SHAWWELL [94] 7-11-2 B Storey, nvr fluent in rear,
improved to chase ldrs hfwy, crrd lft 2 out, no imprsn.
. . . .(13 to 1 op 5 to 1 tchd 10 to 1) 5

3692* TIGHTER BUDGET (USA) [90] 7-10-12 M Moloney, *wth ldr,*
rdn aftr 3 out, cl up whn badly hmpd nxt, sn btn.
....(7 to 1 op 8 to 1) 6
3487* OUTSET (Ire) [106] 4-11-7 (7*) Mr C Bonner, *jmpd wl, led till*
f 4 out...(9 to 4 op 5 to 4) f
3494* TUSKY [95] 6-11-3 N Bentley, *chsd ldrs, improved 5th,*
stumbled and uns rdr aftr nxt........(7 to 2 op 5 to 1) ur
Dist: 5l, ¾l, nk, 10l, 10l. 4m 44.70s. a. 1.70s (8 Ran).

(J Stephenson), W G Reed

3818 Newcastle Exhibition Novices' Chase
(5-y-o and up) £2,780 2½m.....(8:00)

3689* THE LORRYMAN (Ire) 6-12-0 T Reed, *led, hdd 9th, styd*
hndy, rgned ld last, pushed out.
...............(11 to 4 op 3 to 1 tchd 5 to 2 and 7 to 2) 1
3706* CRAFTY CHAPLAIN 8-12-0 (5*) Mr D McCain, *nvr far*
away, led aftr 4 out, blun 2 out, blunded and hdd last,
no extr.........(5 to 4 fav op 11 to 8 on tchd 11 to 8) 2
3581 TRUE FAIR 11-11-7 B Storey, *pressed ldr, led 9th, mstk 4*
out, sn hdd, rallied and ev ch whn swtchd bef last, one
pace..(7 to 1 op 6 to 1) 3
3566 JUNIORS CHOICE 11-11-7 A Merrigan, *trkd ldrs, hit 4 out,*
rn rdn alng, outpcd aftr nxt, tld off. (10 to 1 op 7 to 1) 4
3621⁵ RAIN MAN (NZ) 9-11-0 (7*) Mr C Bonner, *chsd ldrs, strug-*
gling fnl circuit, tld off last 5 fs.....(11 to 1 op 8 to 1) 5
AYSCOUGHFEE DEER 8-11-7 A Dobbin, *not fluent in*
rear, sn struggling, tld off whn pld up bef 3 out.
...............(16 to 1 op 25 to 1 tchd 33 to 1) pu
Dist: 5l, 3l, 3l, 3l. 4m 59.60s. a 8.60s (6 Ran).

(J K Huddleston), W G Reed

3819 McEwans Best Scotch Handicap Hurdle (0-115 4-y-o and up) £2,337 2m 110yds....................... (8:40)

3600* HYPNOTIST [82] 7-10-9 D Wilkinson, *hit 1st, wth ldr, led*
4th, hdd bef 2 out, sn rdn alng, rallying whn hit last,
styd on to ld cl hme............................(6 to 1 op 9 to 2) 1
3538⁷ ANY DREAM WOULD DO [90] 5-11-3 C Hawkins, *nvr far*
away, ev ch 3 out, led bef nxt, rdn and hng lft r-in, hdd
cl hme..............................(13 to 2 op 5 to 1 tchd 7 to 1) 2
3048² SHAMSHOM AL ARAB (Ire) [90] 6-10-10 (7*) Miss V Haigh,
chsd ldg bunch, rdn alng 3 out, styd on frm last, nrst
finish..........................(6 to 1 op 5 to 1 tchd 13 to 2) 3
3643³ FAMILY LINE [97] 6-11-10 M Dwyer, *led, mstk and hdd 4th,*
styd upsides, ev ch 3 out, rdn and one pace betw last 2.
....(11 to 4 fav op 7 to 2) 4
3553¹ JOHN NAMAN (Ire) [90] 5-11-3 A Dobbin, *keen hold, trkd*
ldrs, ev ch 3 out, rdn nxt, grad wknd. (7 to 1 op 6 to 1) 5
3578 COOL DUDE [81] 8-10-3 (5*) F Perratt, *hld up, struggling*
bef 3 out, tld off...............................(14 to 1 op 12 to 1) 6
3538⁹ MAGIC BLOOM [85] 8-10-9 (3*) A Larnach, *keen hold, chsd*
ldg grp, struggling to keep up 3 out, tld off.
..............................(16 to 1 op 10 to 1) 7
3621 QUIXALL CROSSETT [73] 9-9-11⁴ (7*) Mr A Manners, *beh,*
struggling frm hfwy, tld off.....(200 to 1 op 50 to 1) 8
125² NOUVELLE CUISINE [88] 6-11-1 Mr S Swiers, *hld up in*
rear, f heavily second...(4 to 1 op 7 to 2 tchd 9 to 2) f
Dist: ½l, 3½l, sht-hd, 12l, 20l, 1¼l, 20l. 3m 51.20s. b 1.80s (9 Ran).
SR: 25/32/28/35/16/-/

(P Goodall), W Bentley

WARWICK (good to firm)
Saturday May 7th
Going Correction: MINUS 0.30 sec. per fur. (races
1,3,6), MINUS 0.05 (2,4,5)

3820 Wasperton Hill Handicap Hurdle
(0-130 4-y-o and up) £2,905 2½m 110yds.......................... (6:00)

3594⁸ MOVING OUT [105] 6-10-8 M Perrett, *led aftr second, hdd*
3 out, rallied last, led r-in............(9 to 1 op 6 to 1) 1
3736⁸ ROYAL PRINT (Ire) [107] 5-10-10 M Richards, *cld on ldr 7th,*
hit nxt, led 3 out, hdd and one pace r-in.
.........(9 to 4 fav op 5 to 2 tchd 7 to 2 and 2 to 1) 2
3625⁴ FAR TOO LOUD [99] 7-9-11 (5*) S Fox, *prmnt til lost pl 4th,*
effrt 7th, styd on ag'n frm 2 out, fnshd wl.
..............................(15 to 2 op 8 to 1 tchd 9 to 1) 3
3625⁸ ASK THE GOVERNOR [106] 8-10-9 A Maguire, *chsd ldrs,*
rdn 8th, no hdwy frm 3 out.
.............................(5 to 1 op 10 to 1 tchd 9 to 2) 4
3678² MOUNTSHANNON [100] 8-10-3³ Peter Caldwell, *wl in tch*
til rdn and wknd frm 3 out.........(10 to 1 op 6 to 1) 5
3535⁷ CORACO [105] (v) 7-10-1 (7*) Mr G Hogan, *in tch in mid-*
div, outpcd frm 8th....(15 to 2 op 5 to 1 tchd 8 to 1) 6
3560 SHANNON GLEN [122] (bl) 8-11-11 R Dunwoody, *led till*
aftr second, reminders and lost pl 8th, jmpd slwly 3 out,
tld off..........(7 to 1 op 5 to 1 tchd 8 to 1 and 9 to 1) 7
3413⁴ KIVETON TYCOON (Ire) [118] (bl) 5-11-7 G Bradley, *wl plcd*
to 6th, hit nxt, lost tch and mstk 8th, tld off whn pld up
bef 2 out...(7 to 1 op 5 to 1) pu
Dist: ½l, ¾l, 9l, 2l, 7l, 25l. 4m 50.60s. a 3.10s (8 Ran).

(Mrs Shirley Brasher), Miss H C Knight

3821 Veterans Chase £4,581 3¼m....(6:30)

3591³ DOCKLANDS EXPRESS 12-12-0 N Williamson, *hld up gng*
wl, pressed ldr frm 16th, led aftr last, cleverly.
..............(7 to 2 on tchd 11 to 4 on and 5 to 2 on) 1
3485⁶ INTO THE RED 10-11-6 Richard Guest, *hdwy 11th, led*
15th, hdd aftr last, rallied gmely und prs.
....(7 to 1 op 5 to 1) 2
1889 LE PICCOLAGE 10-11-6 R Dunwoody, *led 5th, hdd and*
not fluent 15th, wknd 4 out, sn lost tch.
...............................(4 to 1 op 3 to 1 tchd 9 to 2) 3
3187⁵ BELCOURSE 12-10-12 W Marston, *in tch til drpd rear frm*
9th, not fluent 12th, lost touch aftr nxt, tld off.
...............................(100 to 1 op 33 to 1) 4
NEWS REVIEW 11-10-12 A Maguire, *led to 5th, mstk 13th,*
lost tch nxt, tld off..............(33 to 1 op 20 to 1) 5
Dist: ½l, dist, 20l, 12l. 6m 28.80s. a 14.80s (5 Ran).

(R H Baines), K C Bailey

3822 Barford Conditional Jockeys' Selling Hurdle (4,5,6-y-o) £1,576 2m.... (7:00)

3725² WAAZA (USA) 5-11-0 (5*) M Appleby, *rcd in second pl, not*
fluent 3 out, jnd ldr nxt, slight advantage last, rdn clr.
............................(15 to 2 op 4 to 1 tchd 8 to 1) 1
3635 ELEGANT FRIEND 6-11-10 (5*) M Godsafe, *settled in 3rd*
pl, led and hit 2 out, hdd and no extr last.
...............................(7 to 2 op 5 to 2 tchd 4 to 1) 2
3702⁶ SECRET FORMULA 4-11-0 R Davis, *ran on frm rear appr 3*
out, no imprsn on ldrs aftr nxt.
...............................(9 to 1 op 14 to 1 tchd 16 to 1) 3
1965⁶ THE COUNTRY DANCER 4-10-9 P McLoughlin, *led, wl clr*
aftr 3rd, hdd and rcd wide appr 2 out, sn btn.
...............................(6 to 1 op 7 to 1 tchd 10 to 1) 4
2945² SOUTHAMPTON 4-11-3 (7*) S Arnold, *jmpd big second,*
settled in rear, not fluent 3rd, rdn and outpcd frm nxt.
...............(10 to 1 op 6 to 1 on tchd Evens and 11 to 10) 5
3632⁶ MR ZIEGFELD (USA) (bl) 5-11-5 Pat Thompson, *in tch in*
mid-div til outpcd aftr 3rd............(20 to 1 op 14 to 1) 6
Dist: 2½l, 4l, 5l, 10l, 11l. 3m 49.20s. a 9.20s (6 Ran).

(H J Manners), H J Manners

3823 Godiva Kingmaker Novices' Chase Grade 2 (5-y-o and up) £10,005 2½m 110yds....................... (7:30)

3517¹ BOSCEAN CHIEFTAIN 10-11-3 R Dunwoody, *trkd ldrs, led*
11th, made nxt, drvn out.............(5 to 4 op 11 to 10) 1
3486⁴ MARTOMICK 7-11-2 N Williamson, *led and mstk 1st, sn*
hdd, led 7th to 9th, mistake 12th, chsd wnr frm 14th, ev
ch aftr 2 out, not quicken nr line.
................(Evens fav op 11 to 10 on tchd 5 to 4 on) 2
3477⁴ RABA RIBA 9-11-3 V Slattery, *led second to 7th, led ag'n*
9th, hdd 11th, outpcd frm 14th, wl btn whn bad mstk 2
out.......................................(6 to 1 op 7 to 1) 3
3614⁶ KETTI (bl) 9-10-12 A Maguire, *al outpcd, sn tld off.*
...............................(33 to 1 op 20 to 1) 4
3445⁴ LING (USA) 9-11-3 T Wall, *sn wl outpcd and tld off, pld up*
bef 13th.....................................(100 to 1 op 33 to 1) pu
Dist: Nk, dist, dist. 4m 56.40s. a 1.40s (5 Ran).
SR: 64/62/

(Miss Christine Olds), Mrs J G Retter

3824 Willoughby de Broke Challenge Trophy Novices' Hunters' Chase (5-y-o and up) £1,592 2½m 110yds.....(8:00)

SAILOR JIM 7-11-7 (7*) Mr D Bloor, *wth ldrs, led 8th, drw*
clr frm last..(8 to 1) 1
MALVERNIAN (bl) 8-11-7 (7*) Mr M Rimell, *in tch, sstnd*
chal frm 2 out, outpcd from last....(4 to 1 op 5 to 1) 2
PRINCE ROCKAWAY (Ire) 6-11-7 (7*) Mr C Hancock, *led to*
3rd, pressed ldrs, ev ch 2 out to last, no extr r-in.
................(15 to 2 op 6 to 1 tchd 8 to 1) 3
BALLYMAC GIRL 6-11-2 (7*) Mr G Hogan, *cld on ldrs frm*
tenth, chsd 2 out, kpt on same pace.
................(7 to 2 fav op 5 to 1 tchd 4 to 1) 4
BIBLICAL 7-11-2 (7*) Mr T Fowler, *ran on frm rear aftr*
tenth, rdn and styd on one pace 2 out.
.....................................(14 to 1 op 10 to 1) 5
3501 SOLDIER BANK 9-11-9 (5*) Mr S Bush, *trkd ldg grp,*
pushed alng and one pace frm 3 out.
...............................(33 to 1 op 25 to 1) 6
IRIDOPHANES 8-11-7 (7*) Mr S Edmunds, *hdwy tenth, no*
prog frm 3 out...............................(20 to 1 op 16 to 1) 7
HAPPY PADDY 11-11-7 (7*) Mr A Sansome, *wl plcd till*
wknd 11th...............................(50 to 1 op 33 to 1) 8
ARCTIC LINE (bl) 6-11-8¹ (7*) Mr S R Green, *settled in mid-*
div, beh 11th, tld off........................(100 to 1) 9
3581⁴ PRIDEAUX PRINCE 8-11-7 (7*) Mr P Atkinson, *settled in*
mid-div, in 7th pl whn f 3 out...............(8 to 1) f
3761² RYTON RUN 9-11-7 (7*) Miss A Plunkett, *in tch, cl 3rd whn*
blun and uns rdr 12th...(9 to 2 op 4 to 1 tchd 5 to 1) ur
YORK VALER 11-11-2 (7*) Mr S Johnson, *tld off whn*
refused tenth....................................(100 to 1) ref

552

SNOWY RUN 13-11-7 (7") Mr R Armson, *led 3rd to 8th, wknd aftr 11th, pld up bef 2 out...* (16 to 1 op 12 to 1) pu
3563 SPIN THE COIN 8-11-7 (7") Mr W McLaughlin, *beh whn pld up bef 8th.......................*(33 to 1 op 25 to 1) pu
MISTER JOE 7-11-7 (7") Mr M Smith, *slwly into strd, not jump wl, sn tld off, pld up bef tenth.*
......................................(100 to 1 op 50 to 1) pu
MOYNE CROSS 7-11-7 (7") Miss S Higgins, *mstks, beh till pld up bef 4 out...................*(16 to 1 op 12 to 1) pu
Dist: 4l, ½l, ¾l, 3½l, 10l, 2l, 11l, dist. 5m 16.50s. a 21.50s (16 Ran).

(D R Bloor), D R Bloor

3825 Leamington Novices' Handicap Hurdle (0-100 4-y-o and up) £2,384 2m
................................(8:30)

3663² SHARP DANCE [80] 5-11-2 R Dunwoody, *gd prog 4th, led 2 out, quickened clr r-in..........*(3 to 1 fav op 5 to 1) 1
2783 GYMCRAK TIGER (Ire) [70] 4-10-6 R Marley, *hld up in rear, improved appr 2 out, not fluent last, fnshd strly.*
......................................(16 to 1) 2
3688⁷ TOOMUCH TOOSOON (Ire) [65] 6-9-10 (5") S Curran, *hld up, cld on ldrs frm 5th, ev ch betw last 2, outpcd r-in.*
......................................(12 to 1 op 8 to 1) 3
2112⁷ SOLO CHARTER [65] 4-10-1 B Powell, *ran on frm 5th, kpt on one pace frm 2 out.........*(50 to 1 op 33 to 1) 4
3571³ BATHWICK BOBBIE [81] 7-10-10 (7") Miss S Higgins, *pressed ldrs, dsptd ld aftr 3rd to nxt, ev ch 2 out, no extr appr last...................*(14 to 1 op 12 to 1) 5
3502 KINDLE'S DELIGHT [80] 6-11-2 J Osborne, *ldg grp, led 4th, hdd 2 out, eased whn btn aftr last.*
......................................(10 to 1 tchd 16 to 1) 6
3629⁴ MARINERS COVE [64] 6-9-11 (3") D Meredith, *handily plcd, rdn and one pace appr 2 out....*(7 to 1 op 6 to 1) 7
3661⁴ ANDRATH (Ire) [75] 6-10-11 W Marston, *pressed ldrs, led aftr 3rd to nxt, btn appr 2 out.*
......................................(16 to 1 op 14 to 1 tchd 20 to 1) 8
3663⁸ CALL ME EARLY [80] 9-11-2 M Brennan, *in tch, no hdwy ....*(16 to 1) 9
2762 MAC'S LEAP [64] 6-10-0 L Harvey, *rapid prog 4th, wth ldrs 3 out, btn appr nxt..............*(50 to 1 op 33 to 1) 10
3663⁹ COME ON LUCY [64] 5-10-0 J R Kavanagh, *led till aftr 3rd, no prog frm 5th..............*(50 to 1 op 33 to 1) 11
3005⁵ PRECIOUS JUNO (Ire) [78] 5-11-0 I Lawrence, *chsd frnt rnk to 3 out.....................*(12 to 1) 12
3634⁴ CHARLAFRIVOLA [68] (bl) 6-10-4 W Humphreys, *al beh. ....*(11 to 1 op 10 to 1 tchd 12 to 1) 13
2380⁶ WILL'S BOUNTY [73] 11-10-9 N Williamson, *wknd frm 5th. ....*(14 to 1) 14
2991 BALLYMGYR (Ire) [75] (bl) 5-10-11 M Perrett, *in tch to 5th. ....*(20 to 1 op 16 to 1) 15
3680³ SKEOUGH (Ire) [88] 6-11-10 R Bellamy, *mid-div, no hdwy aftr 4th.................*(8 to 1 op 7 to 1 tchd 10 to 1) 16
3628⁵ NIGHT FANCY [69] 6-10-2 (3") J McCarthy, *chsd ldrs to hfwy.......................................*(7 to 1) 17
3629 GAVASKAR (Ire) [72] 5-10-8 A Maguire, *al beh. ....*(9 to 1 op 8 to 1 tchd 10 to 1) 18
Dist: 3½l, hd, 3l, 1l, 3½l, 2l, 5l, 3l, hd, 6l. 3m 41.30s. a 1.30s (18 Ran).
SR: 27/13/8/5/20/15/-/3/5/ (The Big Eaters Partnership), B Smart

WORCESTER (good)
Saturday May 7th
Going Correction: PLUS 0.20 sec. per fur.

3826 Himbleton Novices' Selling Hurdle (4-y-o and up) £2,323 2m.........(1:45)

3740² NORTHERN TRIAL (USA) (v) 6-11-2 J R Kavanagh, *hld up, hdwy 4th, led sn aftr 3 out, ran on strly.*
......................................(7 to 1 op 8 to 1) 1
SIRKA (Fr) 4-10-10 R Dunwoody, *hld up, hdwy 5th, rdn to take second appr 2 out, one pace.*
......................................(3 to 1 fav op 11 to 4) 2
3729⁶ JOHNS JOY 9-11-2 D O'Sullivan, *prmnt, ev ch 2 out, rdn and one pace....................*(20 to 1 tchd 25 to 1) 3
3740⁷ KELLY'S DARLING 8-11-9 A Maguire, *hld up, hdwy appr 3 out, rdn and one pace frm nxt......*(7 to 1 op 6 to 1) 4
3682¹ SHARPSIDE (bl) 7-10-9 (7") C Quinlan, *hld up, hdwy 4th, rdn appr 3 out, no headway.*
......................................(11 to 1 op 6 to 1 tchd 5 to 1) 5
3451 CASTILLO 7-10-9 (7") Mr M Rimell, *chsd ldrs, no hdwy frm 3 out........................*(50 to 1 op 33 to 1) 6
3740⁴ SALAR'S SPIRIT 8-11-4 (5") R Darke, *prmnt, ev ch 3 out, sn wknd.............................*(8 to 1) 7
3682⁴ FIVE STARS (v) 7-10-11 N Williamson, *made most till sn aftr 3 out, wknd........*(20 to 1 op 16 to 1) 8
3590⁸ JUNO'S SPECIAL (Ire) 6-10-8 (3") T Eley, *rear till rdn and some hdwy 4th, nvr on terms.*(25 to 1 op 20 to 1) 9
3125⁶ KISS IN THE DARK 4-10-12 P Niven, *hld up, effrt 5th, wknd bef nxt.................*(13 to 2 op 6 to 1) 10
2478 PACIFIC SPIRIT 4-9-12 (7") P McLoughlin, *al beh. ....*(50 to 1 op 33 to 1) 11
3559 DUKE OF BUDWORTH 4-10-10 W Marston, *al beh, tld off. ....*(50 to 1 op 33 to 1) 12

3396 MOPHEAD KELLY 5-11-2 Mr B Leavy, *al rear, tld off 3 out. ....*(50 to 1) 13
3531⁷ RED MATCH 9-11-2 A Tory, *prmnt, wknd 5th, tld off. ....*(33 to 1 op 25 to 1) 14
3479 NEVER EVER 9-11-2 G Upton, *al beh, tld off.....*(50 to 1) 15
ANDREA'S GIRL 4-9-13¹ (7") M G Hogan, *al beh, tld off. ....*(33 to 1 op 25 to 1) 16
3685 GILBERT (Ire) 6-11-9 Lorna Vincent, *led betw second and 3rd, wknd quickly nxt, tld off whn pld up bef 3 out. ....*(25 to 1 op 20 to 1) pu
GREEN'S EXHIBIT (bl) 5-11-2 A Charlton, *al beh, tld off whn pld up bef 3 out.*(20 to 1 op 16 to 1 tchd 25 to 1) pu
3416 FULL COURT 4-10-10 R Bellamy, *prmnt to 3rd, sn wknd, tld off whn pld up bef 3 out.......*(50 to 1 op 33 to 1) pu
2728 NONAME 5-11-2 Peter Hobbs, *in tch to 4th, tld off whn pld up bef last...................*(12 to 1 op 10 to 1) pu
Dist: 4l, 2½l, 1½l, 15l, ½l, 3½l, 8l, 1½l, 4l, 1¼l. 3m 54.30s. a 13.30s (20 Ran).
(Mrs Elaine M Burke), K R Burke

3827 Rhydd Novices' Chase (5-y-o and up) £2,851 2½m 110yds............(2:15)

3110⁵ CASTLE DIAMOND 7-11-13 R Dunwoody, *al prmnt, trkd ldr 6th, led aftr tenth, mstk 4 out, hit last and hld, rallied to ld r-in, all out.*(7 to 2 op 4 to 1 tchd 9 to 2) 1
3671 CARLINGFORD LIGHTS (Ire) 6-11-3 V Slattery, *hld up in tch, hdwy 7th, outpcd 2 out, hrd rdn and ran on wl to take second of hme.................*(20 to 1 op 16 to 1) 2
3675* UNHOLY ALLIANCE 7-11-13 N Williamson, *wtd wth, hdwy 6th, lft second tenth, pressed wnr 4 out, led last, hrd rdn and hdd r-in..........*(5 to 4 fav tchd 7 to 4) 3
3492 HANGOVER 8-11-3 M A FitzGerald, *hld up, hdwy tenth, one pace 3 out...............*(7 to 1 op 6 to 1) 4
3575 LE DENSTAN 7-11-3 M Richards, *mid-div, hdwy 7th, no imprsn frm 5 out, btn whn blun last.*
......................................(66 to 1 op 50 to 1) 5
3758⁴ KETFORD BRIDGE 7-11-0 (3") D Meredith, *chsd ldrs till wknd appr 4 out.....................*(33 to 1) 6
3560⁴ DAN DE LYON 6-11-9 A Maguire, *trkd ldr, led 4th, hmpd by loose horse 7th, sn led ag'n, blun and hdd tenth, rallied, wknd four out...........*(11 to 2 op 9 to 2) 7
3639² SING THE BLUES 10-11-3 D Morris, *led to 4th, wknd 7th, tld off...........................*(11 to 10 op 11 to 10 tchd 12 to 1) 8
3706⁷ ARCTICFLOW (USA) 8-11-3 (7") P Carey, *al beh, tld off. ....*(66 to 1 op 50 to 1) 9
3671⁷ GRECIAN SAILOR 9-11-3 J Frost, *blun and uns rdr second.........................*(33 to 1) ur
3102 COLONIAL OFFICE (USA) 8-10-10 (7") Mr M Rimell, *al beh, tld off whn pld up bef 9th.........*(66 to 1 op 50 to 1) pu
3637 CRYMLYN SWING 10-10-12 Mr D Verco, *not jump wl, al rear, tld off whn pld up bef 4 out.*(66 to 1 op 50 to 1) pu
3510 FOXY BLUE 9-11-3 G Bradley, *al beh, tld off whn pld up bef tenth.....................*(25 to 1) pu
3420⁴ TAURIAN PRINCESS 5-10-5 D J Burchell, *al beh, tld off whn pld up bef tenth.............*(33 to 1) pu
Dist: Hd, ¾l, 12l, 12l, 15l, 8l, 25l, dist. 5m 17.20s. a 14.20s (14 Ran).
(Mrs S Kavanagh), H M Kavanagh

3828 Madresfield Handicap Chase (0-115 5-y-o and up) £3,306 2m 7f......(2:45)

2761 SLIEVENAMON MIST [103] 8-11-6 N Williamson, *hld up, hdwy tenth, hit 3 out, led appr last, cmftbly.*
......................................(8 to 1 op 7 to 1 tchd 9 to 1) 1
3495⁵ TOMPET [100] 8-11-0 (3") T Jenks, *led 3rd, rdn and hdd appr last, one pace..............*(8 to 1 op 7 to 1) 2
3149* ROYAL SQUARE (Can) [88] 8-10-5 M Perrett, *hld up, hdwy tenth, rdn 3 out, kpt on one pace 2 out.*(9 to 1) 3
3619* CENTENARY STAR [102] 9-11-5 P Niven, *al frnt rnk, jmpd lft 3 out, one pace.* (11 to 2 fav op 5 to 1 tchd 6 to 1) 4
3624 PETTY BRIDGE [91] 10-10-8 R Dunwoody, *hld up, hdwy 6th, rdn 5 out, wknd aftr nxt.....* (6 to 1 tchd 8 to 1) 5
3593⁴ WINABUCK [107] 11-11-7 (3") D Meredith, *in tch till wknd 5 out...........................*(12 to 1 op 10 to 1) 6
3586⁵ PERSIAN SWORD [97] 8-11-0 A Maguire, *al beh. ....*(9 to 1 op 7 to 1 tchd 10 to 1) 7
3662⁴ MISTER FEATHERS [90] 13-10-7 J R Kavanagh, *hld up, hdwy tenth, wknd 5 out, tld off...*(16 to 1 op 12 to 1) 8
3534 HOWARYAFXD [92] 7-10-9 M A FitzGerald, *led 1st to 3rd, wknd quickly appr 4 out, tld off...*(20 to 1 op 14 to 1) 9
3512³ INVASION [104] (v) 10-11-7 M Brennan, *al beh, tld off 6th.......................*(9 to 1 op 7 to 1) 10
3681⁴ MWEENISH [90] 12-10-7 G McCourt, *chsd ldrs till f 11th...................*(16 to 1 tchd 20 to 1) f
3681 COMPLETE OPTIMIST [90] 10-10-7 M Richards, *prmnt early, rear whn f 11th.............*(50 to 1 op 33 to 1) f
2316³ HOPE DIAMOND [83] (bl) 11-10-0 W McFarland, *al beh, tld off whn pld up bef 4 out.........*(50 to 1 op 33 to 1) pu
3412 GUNNER STREAM [100] 10-11-3 B Powell, *led to 1st, beh 5th, tld off whn pld up bef 12th...*(50 to 1 op 33 to 1) pu
3452³ HOMME D'AFFAIRE [96] (v) 11-10-13 D O'Sullivan, *prmnt, wknd 13th, tld off whn pld up bef 3 out.*
......................................(12 to 1 op 10 to 1) pu
3548³ BOLD CHOICE [96] 8-10-13 J Frost, *rear, hdwy hfwy, wkng whn hit 13th, tld off when pld up bef last.*
......................................(7 to 1 op 8 to 1 tchd 9 to 1) pu

3514 UNDERWYCHWOOD (Ire) [83] 6-10-0 I Lawrence, *al beh, tld*
    off whn pld up bef 3 out..................... (33 to 1)   pu
Dist: 4l, 3½l, 1l, ¾l, 7l, 7l, 25l, 7l, dist. 5m 54.80s. a 10.80s (17 Ran).
SR: 30/23/7/20/8/17/   (I M S Racing), K C Bailey

3829 Blakedown Amateur Riders' Novices' Handicap Hurdle (0-100 4-y-o and up) £2,542 2m 5f 110yds.......... (3:15)

3571⁸ REFERRAL FEE [70] 7-10-3 (7*) Mr S Righton, *hld up in tch,*
    rdn 3 out, ran on strly und pres to ld nr finish.
    .... (33 to 1 op 25 to 1)   1
3702* DANGER BABY [78] 4-10-11 (7*) Miss S Duckett, *al prmnt,*
    led on bit appr 2 out, hrd rdn r-in, ct cl hme. (6 to 1 fav)   2
3592⁵ DUNDEE PRINCE (NZ) [82] 6-11-8 Mr J Durkan, *hld up,*
    hdwy 4 out, ev ch till hrd rdn appr last, one pace.
    .... (13 to 2 op 5 to 1 tchd 7 to 1)   3
3623⁸ ANNA VALLEY [83] 8-11-2 (7*) Mr K Hickey, *hld up, wl in*
    rear, styd on frm 3 out, nvr nrr....... (9 to 1 op 7 to 1)   4
3635⁶ GREEN'S SEAGO (USA) [72] 6-10-5 (7*) Mr M Mannish, *al*
    prmnt, one pace frm 3 out......... (16 to 1 op 14 to 1)   5
3497 CLOWN AROUND [60] 6-9-12⁵ (7*) Mr R Johnson, *al abt*
    same pl, no hdwy frm 3 out........(100 to 1 op 66 to 1)   6
3640⁶ TOO CLEVER BY HALF [84] (bl) 6-11-7 (3*) Mr G Johnson
    Houghton, *al prmnt, led aftr 4 out, hdd and wknd appr 2*
    out, one pace............................   7
27797 GREEN'S GAME [61] 6-9-8 (7*) Miss S Mitchell, *al towards*
    rear, some late hdwy.
    .... (14 to 1 op 25 to 1 tchd 50 to 1)   8
3680 PERSIAN WOLF [60] (bl) 6-9-7 (7*) Mr A Mitchell, *wl in rear*
    till hdwy 4 out, nvr on terms.................(50 to 1)   9
3098⁶ ST ROBERT [66] 7-9-13 (7*) Mr G Hogan, *chsd ldrs till*
    wknd 6th................................. (33 to 1 op 20 to 1)   10
3592⁴ GOLD GLEN (Ire) [84] (bl) 6-11-3 (7*) Mr M Rimell, *slwly*
    away, beh till hdwy appr 5th, rdn approaching 3 out,
    wknd bef nxt.............................(12 to 1 op 10 to 1)   11
3503⁸ OUR WIZZER (Ire) [60] 5-9-7 (7*) Mr S de Burgh, *al beh.*
    .... (66 to 1 op 50 to 1)   12
2795⁶ EMPERORS WARRIOR [71] 8-10-4 (7*) Mr N Bradley, *mid-*
    div till wknd 6th, tld off................. (16 to 1)   13
3225⁵ VAZON EXPRESS [63] 8-9-12² (7*) Mr R Bevis, *prmnt, led*
    6th till aftr nxt, wknd quickly, tld off........(25 to 1)   14
3222⁸ NORDROSS [60] 6-9-9² (7*) Miss S Lea, *hld up, hdwy 4th,*
    wknd four out, tld off................. (50 to 1 op 33 to 1)   15
3571⁶ GIVEITAGO [80] (bl) 8-10-13 (7*) Mr J Rees, *led to 6th, wknd*
    quickly appr 3 out, tld off............. (7 to 1 op 6 to 1)   16
    MIDNIGHT JESTOR (Ire) [68] 6-10-8¹⁵ (7*) Mr R Thuillier, *al*
    rear, tld off........................(100 to 1 op 66 to 1)   17
    MASCALLS LADY [62] 9-10-2⁹ (7*) Mr S Davis, *sn beh, tld*
    off whn f 4 out................. (33 to 1 tchd 66 to 1)   f
3725⁵ MISS PARKES [64] 5-10-4¹¹ (7*) Mr P Clarke, *prmnt to 8th,*
    beh whn f 6th...................... (50 to 1 op 33 to 1)   f
3696 RED OXON [80] 12-10-13 (7*) Mr J O'Brien, *al beh, tld off*
    5th, pld up bef 3 out...............(66 to 1 op 50 to 1)   pu
3637 THE MINE CAPTAIN [78] 7-10-11 (7*) Mr O Evans, *rear, effrt*
    5th, sn btn, tld off whn pld up bef 4 out........(12 to 1)   pu
3543 HIGHLAND FLAME [65] 5-10-0² (7*) Miss J Davis, *al beh, tld*
    off whn pld up bef 8th.................. (16 to 1)   pu
Dist: Hd, 9l, ¾l, 2½l, 1¼l, hd, 1½l, 6l, 10l, nk. 5m 12.30s. a 18.30s (22 Ran).
                         (Seamus Mullins), J W Mullins

3830 Ramsden Handicap Chase (0-120 5-y-o and up) £3,013 2½m 110yds... (3:45)

3631* GHOFAR [120] (bl) 11-12-0 P Holley, *dsptd ld on outsd to 4*
    out, rallied to chal 2 out, rdn to lead r-in.
    ....(5 to 1 op 4 to 1)   1
3662* THE MASTER GUNNER [115] 10-11-6 (3*) R Davis, *trkd*
    ldrs, led on bit 4 out, rdn appr last, one pace and hdd
    r-in..................... (5 to 2 op 9 to 4 tchd 11 to 4)   2
3627⁵ L'UOMO PIU [106] 10-11-0 B Powell, *trkd ldrs till outpcd*
    7th, rallied appr 4 out, one pace 2 out.
    .... (10 to 1 op 8 to 1)   3
3595* WINNIE THE WITCH [120] 10-12-0 R Dunwoody, *hld up,*
    hdwy 7th, lost pl appr 4 out, no dngr aftr.
    ....(2 to 1 fav op 7 to 4)   4
3500⁵ LITTLE TOM [109] 9-11-3 J R Kavanagh, *made most to 4*
    out, sn btn, eased, tld off.
    .... (9 to 2 op 5 tchd 5 to 1)   5
3636⁶ BLUE BUCCANEER [92] 11-10-0 L Harvey, *rear whn hit*
    9th, sn tld off, tld off bef nxt.......(25 to 1 op 20 to 1)   pu
    JUVEN LIGHT (Fr) [110] 13-11-4 D O'Sullivan, *jmpd poorly*
    in rear, tld off 8th, pld up bef 4 out. (40 to 1 op 25 to 1)   pu
Dist: 2l, 2½l, 3l, dist. 5m 14.30s. a 11.30s (7 Ran).
SR: 28/21/9/20/   (Sir Hugh Dundas), D R C Elsworth

3831 Stonehall Handicap Hurdle (0-115 4-y-o and up) £2,318 2m.......... (4:15)

3635⁹ WHAT IF [84] 10-10-0 M Brennan, *hld up, hdwy 4th, led*
    appr 2 out, sn clr................... (16 to 1 op 14 to 1)   1
2856⁶ KAYTAK (Fr) [103] (v) 7-11-5 N Williamson, *hld up, hdwy 3*
    out, outpcd nxt................... (10 to 1 op 8 to 1)   2
3193⁵ SILLIAN [96] 12-10-9 (3*) S Wynne, *hld up, hdwy appr 3*
    out, kpt on one pace................. (16 to 1 op 14 to 1)   3
3451* BALLYHYLAND (Ire) [105] 5-11-7 R Bellamy, *trkd ldrs, no*
    hdwy aftr 3 out......... (7 to 1 op 6 to 1 tchd 8 to 1)   4

34187 CARDINAL BIRD (USA) [91] 7-10-0 (7*) Chris Webb, *wl beh*
    till hdwy 4 out, ran on strly aftr 2 out, nvr nrr.
    .... (20 to 1 op 14 to 1)   5
3594⁵ TILT TECH FLYER [88] (bl) 9-10-4 W Marston, *mid-div, effrt*
    3 out, nvr dngrs...................(14 to 1 op 12 to 1)   6
3514 LASSIE (Fr) [84] 5-10-0 D Gallagher, *beh, hdwy 5th, rdn*
    and wknd appr 2 out.................(20 to 1 op 16 to 1)   7
3311⁷ DRAMATIC EVENT [84] 9-10-0 E Murphy, *led, clr second,*
    rdn and hdd appr 2 out, wknd.
    .... (11 to 2 op 5 to 1 tchd 7 to 1)   8
3455⁴ MIDDLEWICK [96] 9-10-7 (5*) D Leahy, *prmnt, rdn appr 3*
    out, wknd bef nxt.
    .... (9 to 2 fav op 5 to 1 tchd 11 to 2 and 4 to 1)   9
3574 ECOSSAIS DANSEUR (USA) [85] 8-10-1¹ J Osborne, *frnt*
    rnk till wknd quickly 2 out........(40 to 1 op 33 to 1)   10
3594 GOLDEN GUNNER (Ire) [98] (bl) 6-11-0 G McCourt, *al rear,*
    tld off.................(12 to 1 op 14 to 1 tchd 16 to 1)   11
3736 IVEAGH HOUSE [112] 8-12-0 A Maguire, *chsd ldrs till*
    wknd quickly aftr 3 out, tld off.......(8 to 1 op 5 to 1)   12
3516⁶ STAR OF THE GLEN [112] 8-12-0 R Dunwoody, *al beh,*
    eased whn btn 3 out, tld off.
    .... (13 to 1 tchd 12 to 1)   13
3535⁶ SYDNEY BARRY (NZ) [84] 9-10-0 B Powell, *rear till hdwy*
    3rd, wknd appr 3 out, btn whn f nxt.
    .... (11 to 2 op 5 to 1)   f
    BIDDERS CLOWN [85] 9-10-11 Gary Lyons, *al beh, tld off*
    whn pld up bef 2 out.................(33 to 1 op 25 to 1)   pu
3514 BANKONIT (Ire) [84] 6-10-0 I Lawrence, *sn beh, tld off whn*
    pld up bef 3 out.....................(33 to 1 op 20 to 1)   pu
Dist: 7l, 5l, 5l, 2½l, ½l, 2½l, 2½l, 6l, 2½l, 30l. 3m 49.50s. a 8.50s (16 Ran).
SR: 19/31/19/23/6/2/   (Brian Culley), O Brennan

3832 Open National Hunt Flat Race (Div I) (4,5,6-y-o) £1,402 2m...... (4:45)

3208³ EXCLUSIVE EDITION (Ire) 4-10-4 J Osborne, *made all, rdn*
    3 fs out, ran on wl....(8 to 1 op 10 to 1 tchd 12 to 1)   1
    SIGN 5-11-0 A Maguire, *nvr far away, took second 6 fs*
    out, hrd rdn o'r 2 out, no imprsn.
    .... (11 to 2 op 4 to 1 tchd 6 to 1)   2
3457* LIGHTENING LAD 6-11-7 J R Kavanagh, *hld up rear, hdwy*
    hfwy, rdn o'r 3 fs out, one pace.......(10 to 1 op 7 to 1)   3
3208⁶ QUADRAPOL 5-10-4 (5*) D Leahy, *hld up rear, hdwy*
    hfwy, one pace fnl 3 fs................(14 to 1 op 12 to 1)   4
3234³ NORSE RAIDER 4-10-4 (5*) C Burnett-Wells, *hld up, hdwy 6 fs*
    out, rdn 4 out, sn btn.(11 to 1 op 12 to 1 tchd 8 to 1)   5
3458⁹ GAME DOMINO 4-9-13 (5*) C Maude, *towards rear,*
    styd on fnl 3 fs, nvr nrr...................(50 to 1)   6
3523² SEXTON GREY (Ire) 5-10-11 (3*) P Hide, *hld up, hdwy o'r 4*
    fs out, not pace to chal.
    .... (5 to 2 fav op 3 to 1 tchd 4 to 1)   7
    LIVING ON THE EDGE (Ire) 5-10-11 (3*) A Procter, *mid-div,*
    nvr nr to chal.....................(14 to 1 op 12 to 1)   8
    STAC-POLLAIDH 4-9-11 (7*) F Leahy, *al mid-div.*
    .... (20 to 1 op 16 to 1)   9
    LANDSKER MISSILE 5-10-9 R Dunwoody, *prmnt till wknd*
    o'r 4 fs out........................ (7 to 1 op 5 to 1)   10
3458⁶ CHEER'S BABY 4-10-6 (3*) D J Moffatt, *chsd ldrs till wknd*
    5 fs out...........................(33 to 1 op 25 to 1)   11
2876⁴ RENT DAY 5-10-4 (5*) S Curran, *chsd ldrs till wknd 5 fs*
    out............................... (20 to 1)   12
3523³ TENBIT (Ire) 4-10-6 (3*) T Jenks, *chsd ldrs, wknd quickly*
    o'r 4 fs out......... (10 to 1 op 7 to 1 tchd 12 to 1)   13
    FLAMING SANDS (Ire) 5-10-9 D Gallagher, *al beh, tld off.*
    .... (66 to 1 op 50 to 1)   14
3347 KILNAMARTYRA GIRL 4-9-13 (5*) E Husband, *al rear, tld*
    off............................... (50 to 1)   15
3401 GOLD OR BUST 4-10-4 Mr B Leavy, *prmnt early, beh*
    hfwy, tld off........................(66 to 1 op 50 to 1)   16
2916 ANNS REQUEST 5-10-9 Mr J O'Brien, *al beh, tld off.*
    .... (66 to 1 op 50 to 1)   17
    CRUISE FREE 5-11-0 G Upton, *prmnt early, beh hfwy, tld*
    off...............................(14 to 1 tchd 20 to 1)   18
3208 JACK A HOY 4-10-9 W Marston, *al beh, tld off.*
    .... (66 to 1 op 50 to 1)   19
    QUEEN MARIANA 4-10-4 Gee Armytage, *al wl beh, tld off*
    whn pld up and dismounted ins fnl furlong...(50 to 1)   pu
Dist: 6l, 8l, 7l, 15l, 2l, ½l, 3½l, 15l, hd, 1½l. 3m 44.40s. (20 Ran).
               (V McCalla), Miss H C Knight

3833 Open National Hunt Flat Race (Div II) (4,5,6-y-o) £1,392 2m.......... (5:15)

    SUPREME RAMBLER (Ire) 5-11-0 J Osborne, *hld up in tch,*
    hdwy o'r 5 fs out, led appr last, edgd lft, rdn out.
    .... (12 to 1 op 8 to 1 tchd 14 to 1)   1
3458* NO NEAR MISS 4-10-11 A McCabe, *hld up, hdwy o'r 3 fs*
    out, chlgd appr last, short of room, one pace.
    .... (5 to 2 fav)   2
3589* MASTER BRACKEN 5-11-0 (7*) G Lee, *hld up, hdwy hfwy,*
    led 3 out, sn hdd, one pace.
    ....(9 to 2 op 4 to 1 tchd 5 to 1)   3
3457⁴ HENRY CONE 5-11-0 G McCourt, *hld up mid-div, hdwy 6*
    fs out, one pace aftr 3 out.
    .... (11 to 4 op 1 tchd 6 to 1)   4
3522 BUCKHOUSE BOY 4-10-6 (3*) T Jenks, *led to 5 fs out, led*
    o'r 3 out to 2 out, no extr.......... (8 to 1 op 12 to 1)   5

ROYAL COUP 5-11-0 B Powell, *hld up, hdwy 6 fs out, no imprsn frm 3 out*................(14 to 1 tchd 16 to 1) 6
3590[6] SWEET MARTINI 4-9-11 (7*) J Bond, *hld up rear, hdwy hfwy, kpt on one pace fnl 3 fs*................(20 to 1) 7
3190 CALL HER A STAR (Ire) 4-9-11 (7*) Miss M Maher, *beh, some late hdwy, nvr dngrs*..............(66 to 1 op 33 to 1) 8
3387[9] HARLEY STREET 6-10-9 (5*) S Curran, *trkd ldr, led 5 fs out, rdn and hdd o'r 3 out, wknd.*
....................(14 to 1 op 10 to 1 tchd 16 to 1) 9
GREY FINCH 5-11-0 Mr J Durkan, *beh, hdwy 6 fs out, wknd 3 out*........................(14 to 1 op 8 to 1) 10
2407 KENNINGTON KUWAIT 4-10-2 (7*) N Juckes, *al beh.*
....................................(66 to 1 op 33 to 1) 11
3522[5] WESTCOTE LAD 5-10-7 (7*) Mr S Joynes, *trkd ldrs till wknd wl o'r 2 fs out*..............(10 to 1 op 8 to 1) 12
GARNISHEE (Ire) 5-10-7 (7*) L O'Hare, *prmnt early, wknd o'r 4 fs out, tld off*..................(14 to 1 op 8 to 1) 13
2677 DEPTFORD BELLE 4-9-11 (7*) G Crone, *prmnt till wknd 5 fs out, tld off*..................(66 to 1 op 50 to 1) 14
3227 CHUKATEN 5-11-0 M A FitzGerald, *prmnt early, beh hfwy, tld off*..................(66 to 1 op 50 to 1) 15
MADAM ROSE (Ire) 4-10-4 W McFarland, *chsd ldrs, wknd o'r 5 fs out, tld off*................(50 to 1 op 33 to 1) 16
HOW FRIENDLY 4-10-9 J R Kavanagh, *al rear, tld off.*
....................................(66 to 1 op 33 to 1) 17
3707[7] MY RACING DREAM 4-10-4 (5*) E Husband, *al rear, tld off.*
....................................(20 to 1 op 16 to 1) 18
3457 KINGS GAMBLE 4-10-9 Ann Stokell, *prmnt, wknd hfwy, tld off*..............................(66 to 1 op 50 to 1) 19
3523 OAKLANDS POPEYE (e/c) 5-11-0 M Ahern, *al beh, tld off hfwy*............................(66 to 1 op 50 to 1) 20
3114 SCBOO 5-11-0 V Slattery, *tld off hfwy, pld up and dismounted one furlong out*..........(66 to 1 op 50 to 1) pu
KELLY'S CEFFYL 5-10-9 Mr A Charles-Jones, *beh whn pld up hfwy, broke leg, destroyed*.....(66 to 1 op 50 to 1) pu
Dist: ¾l, 7l, 1¼l, 7l, 1l, 4l, 2½l, 1l, 7l, 7l. 3m 48.70s. (22 Ran).
(Mrs L M Dresher), Miss H C Knight

KILLARNEY (IRE) (soft)
Sunday May 8th

3834 Killarney Vintners Maiden Hurdle (5-y-o and up) £3,450 2m 1f........(2:30)

3732[3] FINNEGANS WAKE 7-11-6 C F Swan,..........(9 to 4 fav) 1
3615[8] NOT MY LINE (Ire) 5-11-2 (3*) C O'Brien,..........(12 to 1) 2
3450[6] GLENBALLYMA (Ire) 5-11-0 F J Flood,............(10 to 1) 3
3731 MAGNUM STAR (Ire) (bl) 5-11-5 T Horgan,........(20 to 1) 4
3468[7] KAWA-KAWA 7-10-8 (7*) Mr J Collier,............(10 to 1) 5
URBAN DANCING (USA) 5-11-5 F Woods,.........(6 to 1) 6
3508[5] VERY ADAPTABLE (Ire) 5-11-5 K F O'Brien,........(8 to 1) 7
3788 VALTORUS (Ire) 5-11-0 (5*) J P Broderick,........(20 to 1) 8
3747[4] DORAN'S DELIGHT 7-12-0 J F Titley,.............(5 to 2) 9
2158[3] PROFIT MOTIVE (Ire) 5-11-10 (3*) T J O'Sullivan,..(10 to 1) 10
3730 THE LEFT FOOTER (Ire) 5-11-5 J Shortt,..........(16 to 1) 11
2098[8] COOL MOSS 8-11-9 (5*) P A Roche,..............(20 to 1) 12
3467[5] WATERLOO BALL (Ire) 5-11-8 M J Hallbrook,......(12 to 1) 13
3730 ROSEL WALK (Ire) 5-11-5 A J O'Brien,............(25 to 1) 14
3733 CASTLEMAHON CHICK (Ire) 6-11-1 J Jones,......(33 to 1) 15
ARGIDEEN FLYER (Ire) 5-11-0 G M O'Neill,........(20 to 1) 16
2919 PALLAS CHAMPION (Ire) 5-10-12 (7*) T Martin,....(33 to 1) 17
3525[5] BACKTOWN JOHNNY (Ire) 5-11-5 L P Cusack,....(14 to 1) 0
Dist: 3l, 2l, 11l, 3½l. 4m 37.20s. (18 Ran).
(Bracken Syndicate), A P O'Brien

3835 Randles/Nissan Mares Novice Chase (5-y-o and up) £3,450 2¾m......(3:05)

3657 CUILIN BUI (Ire) 6-11-11 (3*) C O'Brien,............(4 to 1) 1
3551[5] BALADINE 7-11-9 S H O'Donovan,.................(10 to 1) 2
3551 MELDRUM MISS (Ire) 6-11-9 P M Verling,.........(25 to 1) 3
3295[7] GLYNN CROSS (Ire) 6-11-9 J P Banahan,.........(16 to 1) 4
3652 THE VICARETTE (Ire) 6-11-2 (7*) Mr P Cashman,..(20 to 1) 5
3791[4] SCREEN PRINTER (Ire) 5-10-8 (5*) J P Broderick,..(10 to 1) 6
3295 ELWILL WAY 9-11-6 (3*) Mr J A Nash,............(20 to 1) 7
3790[3] MONKS AIR 7-11-4 (5*) Mr W M O'Sullivan,.......(12 to 1) 0
3468 NISHIKI (USA) 5-11-7 G M O'Neill,................(14 to 1) pu
3614 SO PINK (Ire) 6-12-0 J F Titley,..................(5 to 2 fav) pu
3551[6] MALTELINA 8-11-9 K F O'Brien,....................(7 to 1) pu
3551 GODFREYS CROSS (Ire) 6-11-9 P P Kinane,.......(50 to 1) pu
3293 CHERISHED PRINCESS (Ire) 6-11-9 F Woods,.....(33 to 1) pu
3293 BRIDGIE TERRIE (Ire) 6-11-9 T Horgan,..........(6 to 1) pu
SEEANDBESEEN 7-11-9 C O'Dwyer,...............(12 to 1) pu
Dist: 1½l, 14l, 25l, ¾l. 6m 18.50s. (15 Ran).
(Miss E Kiely), David J McGrath

3836 Murphys Irish Stout Handicap Hurdle (4-y-o and up) £13,000 2m 1f.... (3:35)

3711* STRONG PLATINUM (Ire) [-] 6-10-5 (7ex) C O'Dwyer, (8 to 1) 1
3656[2] MAGIC FEELING (Ire) [-] 4-10-0 C F Swan,...(4 to 1 jt-fav) 2
3613[2] RISZARD (USA) [-] 5-10-5 C N Bowens,......(4 to 1 jt-fav) 3
3656[3] TROPICAL LAKE (Ire) [-] 4-11-2 K F O'Brien,........(8 to 1) 4
3650[6] COCK COCKBURN [-] 8-11-11 S R Murphy,.......(12 to 1) 5
3732* KHARASAR (Ire) [-] 4-10-4 (2ex) R A Hennessy,.....(8 to 1) 6
3647* MY SUNNY GLEN [-] 7-10-0 (7ex) T Horgan,........(9 to 1) 7
3710[4] THE SHAUGHRAUN [-] (bl) 8-10-8 M Dwyer,.......(20 to 1) 8
3612[2] HOW'S THE BOSS [-] 8-11-11 J Magee,..........(16 to 1) 9
3710[3] MR BOAL (Ire) [-] 5-10-10 J Shortt,...............(20 to 1) 10
3649[4] FRIENDS OF GERALD [-] 8-11-0 C O'Brien,.......(14 to 1) 11
2610 LOSHIAN (Ire) [-] 5-11-6 R Dunwoody,............(14 to 1) 12
3248[7] SEEK THE FAITH (USA) [-] 5-10-5 B Sheridan,.....(14 to 1) 14
3389[4] WHO'S TO SAY [-] 8-10-12 T P Treacy,............(25 to 1) 15+
3654* TUG OF PEACE [-] 7-11-4 (5ex) J P Broderick,.....(16 to 1) 15+
2132 FIRST SESSION (Ire) [-] 6-10-0 F Woods,..........(25 to 1) 16
Dist: 2l, 2½l, sht-hd, 2½l. 4m 31.00s. (16 Ran).
(Mrs Theresa McCoubrey), P Burke

3837 Kerry Petroleum Flat Race (6-y-o and up) £3,450 2m 1f................ (5:35)

3450[2] DOUBLE SYMPHONY (Ire) 6-11-9 Mr A P O'Brien,
....(5 to 4 fav) 1
CELTIC SUNRISE 6-11-7 (7*) Mr H Murphy,.......(10 to 1) 2
3529[3] YOU KNOW WHO (Ire) 6-11-11 (3*) Mrs J M Mullins, (6 to 1) 3
3552[5] MISS POLLERTON (Ire) 6-11-2 (7*) Mr M J Bowe, (12 to 1) 4
3291[2] STEVIE BE (Ire) 6-11-11 (3*) Mr J A Nash,..........(7 to 2) 5
3528 SWALLOW REEF (Ire) 6-11-2 (7*) Mr M J Lombard, (33 to 1) 6
SAILIN BISHOP 7-12-0 Mr P J Healy,..............(12 to 1) 7
3712 PERSPEX GALE (Ire) 6-11-6 (3*) Mr D Marnane,....(33 to 1) 8
2664 SWEET PETEL 7-11-2 (7*) Mr E Henley,............(33 to 1) 9
1858 BUNNINADDEN PHIL (Ire) 6-11-2 (7*) Mr B Walsh, (33 to 1) 10
2607 JIMMY O'GOBLIN 7-11-7 (7*) Mr B Heffernan,.....(10 to 1) 11
2620[9] MIGHTY HAGGIS 7-11-11 (3*) Mr J Lombard,......(12 to 1) 12
3469[4] MILLER'S CROSSING 7-11-2 (7*) Miss C Doyle,..(12 to 1) su
3529 WOLVER LAD (Ire) 6-12-0 Mr T Doyle,............(12 to 1) pu
3528 BALLY UPPER (Ire) 6-11-7 (7*) Mr B Foster,.......(20 to 1) pu
BOSTON RUN 8-11-11 (3*) Mr D Valentine,.........(33 to 1) pu
3733[7] STICK WITH HER 7-11-2 (7*) Mr M Hartrey,........(12 to 1) pu
Dist: 1l, ¾l, 15l, 4l. 4m 36.00s. (17 Ran).
(Jet Syndicate), A P O'Brien

ENGHIEN (FR) (very soft)
Monday May 9th

3838 Prix de Montpellier (Chase) (5-y-o and up) £10,297 2¼m................(4:25)

KOMBOLOYE (Fr) 5-11-1 P Larbodiere,.................. 1
MEZOS (Fr) 5-9-11 (4*) E Diard,.......................... 2
CARDEPAL (Fr) 5-10-1 S Juteau,........................ 3
3585* ROC COLOR (Fr) 5-10-5 G Bradley,...................... 7
Dist: Nk, 3l, 10l, 6l, 6l, ¾l, 3l, 5l, 8l. 4m 30.20s. (10 Ran).
(Mme C de La Soudiere-Niault), Mme C de La Soudiere-Niault

KILLARNEY (IRE) (yielding to soft)
Monday May 9th

3839 Buckler Maiden Hurdle (4-y-o) £3,452 2m 1f............................(5:25)

617[4] NORDIC THORN (Ire) 11-7 A Powell,..............(8 to 1) 1
3246[6] TOUCHING MOMENT (Ire) 11-4 (3*) T P Rudd,......(6 to 1) 2
2388[2] SOVIET CHOICE (Ire) 10-11 (5*) C P Dunne,....(2 to 1 fav) 3
3730[2] AULD STOCK (Ire) 11-2 M Duffy,..................(3 to 1) 4
3466 FOOLISH LAW (Ire) 10-11 S H O'Donovan,........(50 to 1) 5
3616 TEN BUCKS (Ire) 11-2 B Sheridan,..............(25 to 1) 6
KING'S FROLIC (Ire) 10-9 (7*) Mr J T McNamara,..(20 to 1) 7
3505[7] BOB THE YANK (Ire) 11-2 A J O'Brien,.............(12 to 1) 8
NEPHIN FAR (Ire) 10-8 (3*) C O'Brien,.............(25 to 1) 9
3525[8] JOYFUL RUNNER (Ire) 10-11 G M O'Neill,.........(10 to 1) 10
3730 BEN-GURIAN (Ire) 11-2 W T Slattery Jnr,.........(50 to 1) 11
KATES WELL (Ire) 10-4 (7*) J M Willis,.............(25 to 1) 12
3321 PUB TALK (Ire) 11-2 F Woods,...................(50 to 1) 13
3550 CAMDEN BANNER (Ire) 10-11 (5*) J P Broderick,..(25 to 1) 14
3550 BOLD ALFIE 11-2 K F O'Brien,....................(25 to 1) 15
3525 RIFAYA (Ire) 10-6 (5*) K P Gaule,................(14 to 1) 16
3508[3] GRAPHIC IMAGE (Ire) 11-2 C F Swan,.............(4 to 1) f
3394 CHIEF RANI (Ire) 10-9 (7*) P Murphy,..............(8 to 1) f
Dist: ½l, 8l, 4½l, 8l. 4m 30.10s. (18 Ran).
(Peter Malone), Martin Brassil

3840 Killarney Racegoers Club Handicap Hurdle (0-102 4-y-o and up) £3,452 2½m.......................... (5:55)

3731 COIN MACHINE (Ire) [-] 5-11-8 P Carberry,........(8 to 1) 1
3322[2] HORNER WATER (Ire) [-] 6-11-13 K F O'Brien,..(7 to 4 fav) 2
3647 SIOBHAILIN DUBH (Ire) [-] 5-10-13 C F Swan,......(8 to 1) 3
2231 AWBEG ROVER (Ire) [-] 6-10-13 (3*) C O'Brien,....(20 to 1) 4
3710[8] IRON MARINER (Ire) [-] 6-11-5 (7*) D M McCullagh, (12 to 1) 5
3730[5] CALL ME HENRY [-] 5-11-0 F Woods,...............(7 to 1) 6
3732[7] DEGO DANCER [-] 7-11-2 (5*) J P Broderick,......(10 to 1) 7
2679[6] WEJEM (Ire) [-] 5-11-5 S R Murphy,................(8 to 1) 8
1913[8] COOLAHEARAC [-] 8-11-4 P P Kinane,............(20 to 1) 9
1823 SILENTBROOK [-] 9-10-1 (7*) Mr A O'Shea,.......(33 to 1) 10
3526[6] MAYASTA (Ire) [-] 4-11-10 C O'Dwyer,..............(8 to 1) 11
3812 MOLLIE WOOTTON (Ire) [-] 6-10-8 W T Slattery Jnr, (33 to 1) 12
3550 MOUNTHENRY STAR (Ire) [-] 6-11-8 J Shortt,.....(12 to 1) 13
3834[4] MAGNUM STAR (Ire) [-] (bl) 5-11-7 T Horgan,......(16 to 1) 14
3242[2] SHANNON KNOCK [-] 9-11-6 P M Verling,........(13 to 2) 15

3504 LADY HA HA [-] (bl) 7-9-9 (7") J M Donnelly, ... (16 to 1) 16
3711 TREACYS CROSS [-] 8-10-12 (5") P A Roche, ...(20 to 1) 17
3694 NORA'S EXPORT (Ire) [-] 5-10-10 A J O'Brien, ... (25 to 1) 18
Dist: ¾l, 2l, 4l, 9l. 5m 10.00s. (18 Ran).

(P Hughes), P Hughes

3841 Heineken Chase (5-y-o and up) £4,142 2½m. . . . . (6:55)

3651³ THIRD QUARTER 9-11-10 C F Swan, ... (5 to 4 fav) 1
3651 DESERT LORD 8-11-10 K F O'Brien, ...(7 to 1) 2
3746⁶ KINGSTON WAY 8-11-7 Mr D M O'Brien, ...(7 to 1) 3
2469 NORDIC SUN (Ire) 6-11-10 T Horgan, ...(7 to 1) 4
3389⁵ VALRODIAN (NZ) 11-11-0 J A White, ... (16 to 1) 5
3241⁴ MAMMY'S FRIEND 10-10-13 (3") D P Murphy, ...(10 to 1) 6
3651⁵ TRY A BRANDY 12-11-10 S H O'Donovan, ...(6 to 1) f
Dist: 2l, 6l, 4l, dist. 5m 23.70s. (7 Ran).

(John P McManus), Francis Berry

3842 Gleneagle Hotel INH Flat Race (4-y-o) £3,452 2m 1f. . . . . (8:25)

3749 V'SOSKE GALE (Ire) 11-7 Mr E Bolger, ... (8 to 1) 1
3250⁴ NEAR GALE (Ire) 11-2 (3") Mrs J M Mullins, ... (6 to 4 fav) 2
3616⁵ ROCKFIELD NATIVE (Ire) 11-10 Mr A P O'Brien, ...(7 to 2) 3
3616⁸ ISLANDOO (Ire) 10-12 (7") Miss L Townsley, ...(10 to 1) 4
3550 BIMSEY (Ire) 11-3 (7") Mr D Keane, ... (8 to 1) 5
3508 THAT'S GOSPEL (Ire) 11-2 (3") Mr J A Nash, ... (15 to 1) 6
  LUCKY BUST (Ire) 11-3 (7") Mr D A Harney, ...(20 to 1) 7
3616 RHETORIC HOUSE (Ire) 11-5 (5") Mr P M Kelly, ...(12 to 1) 8
  GLOW TINA (Ire) 11-2 (3") Mr J J O'Gorman, ...(16 to 1) 9
  PHARLEYGIRL (Ire) 11-2 (3") Mr D Marnane, ...(12 to 1) 10
3552⁸ ELWOOD (Ire) 10-12 (7") Mr D Murphy, ...(14 to 1) 11
  GRANNY BOWLY (Ire) 10-12 (7") Mr T J Murphy, . .(12 to 1) 12
  WYLD Bay (Ire) 10-12 (7") Mr K P Egan, ...(12 to 1) 13
  KING FOWLER (Ire) 11-3 (7") Mr J T McNamara, . . (20 to 1) 14
  SIDI MEDIENNE (Ire) 11-3 (7") Mr E Norris, ...(10 to 1) 15
  MISS HENBIT (Ire) 10-12 (7") Mr D K Budds, ... (25 to 1) 16
  SUNDANCE MADERA (Ire) 10-12 (7") Mr M P Dunne,
  . . . .(12 to 1) 17
3552⁹ KILBRICKEN DANCER (Ire) (bl) 11-5 Mr P Fenton, . .(7 to 1) pu
Dist: ¾l, 2½l, nk, 1½l. 4m 30.10s. (18 Ran).

(Michael Dixon), Patrick G Kelly

TOWCESTER (good)
Monday May 9th
Going Correction: PLUS 0.30 sec. per fur.

3843 David Capel Benefit Year Selling Hurdle (4,5,6-y-o) £1,784 2m. . . . .(6:00)

3559* FORGETFUL 5-11-1 D J Burchell, led, rdn 2 out, blun last, sn reco'red, all out.
  . . . .(13 to 8 on op 2 to 1 on tchd 6 to 4 on) 1
3696⁴ WILTOSKI (bl) 6-11-10 Mrs N Ledger, al chasing wnr, rdn and styd on betw last 2, chlgd last, not quicken nr finish. . . . .(6 to 1 op 4 to 1) 2
3503 WESTRAY (Fr) 4-10-11 B Powell, chsd ldr, kpt on frm 3 out, 3rd and btn whn mstk nxt. . . . (50 to 1 op 33 to 1) 3
3281 BARTON ROYAL (b) (v) 4-11-1 Richard Guest, chsd ldr 4th till rdn and wknd appr 2 out.
  . . . .(9 to 2 op 3 to 1 tchd 5 to 1) 4
3702⁹ NEVER SO LOST (bl) 4-10-11 D Bridgwater, hld up, chsd wnr 4th till wknd quickly aftr 3 out, tld off.
  . . . .(20 to 1 op 16 to 1 tchd 25 to 1) 5
2960 EMERALD QUEEN 5-10-11 M Brennan, pld hrd early, mstk 3rd, tld off aftr 5th. . . . . .(5 to 1 op 8 to 1 tchd 9 to 1) 6
3632⁸ HIZAL 5-10-9 (7") M Appleby, swrvd lft and slwly away, lost tch aftr 4th, sn tld off.
  . . . .(25 to 1 op 20 to 1 tchd 33 to 1) 7
3111 ON THE LEDGE (USA) 4-10-11 Mr G Brown, slwly away, hdwy aftr second, chsd ldr till lost tch aftr 4th, tld off whn pld up bef 3 out. . . . .(50 to 1 op 25 to 1) pu
3637 VARELITO (Ire) 4-10-6 (5") S Curran, chsd ldr 3rd till wknd quickly aftr 5th, sn beh, tld off whn pld up bef 2 out.
  . . . .(50 to 1 op 25 to 1) pu
Dist: 1l, 14l, hd, 25l, 8l, 2½l. 3m 56.40s. a 13.40s (9 Ran).
SR: 1/9/-/-/-/-/ (The Equus Club), D Burchell

3844 Wilcon Homes Novices' Chase (5-y-o and up) £2,654 2¾m. . . . .(6:30)

3608 GHIA GNEUIAGH 8-11-7 D Bridgwater, led aftr 4th, drw clr aftr 3 out, unchlgd.
  . . . .(11 to 8 fav op 5 to 4 on tchd 5 to 4) 1
2535 TRY NEXT DOOR 7-11-0 M Brennan, hld up, in tch 7th till lost pl aftr 9th, rdn and styd on after 3 out, not trble wnr. . . . .(33 to 1 op 25 to 1) 2
3562³ VICAR OF BRAY (v) 7-11-0 J R Kavanagh, hld up, rdn and hdwy aftr 6 out, kpt on one pace frm 2 out.
  . . . .(12 to 1 op 10 to 1 tchd 14 to 1) 3
3562⁶ SANDAIG 8-11-7 N Williamson, hld up, wnt 3rd 8th, chsd wnr tenth till wknd aftr 3 out. . . . .(7 to 1) 4
3513⁶ CRUISING ON 7-10-13 (3") T Jenks, al prmnt, wnt 3rd tenth, wknd aftr 4 out.
  . . . .(33 to 1 op 25 to 1 tchd 50 to 1) 5

3671⁴ LAND OF THE FREE 5-10-2 J Osborne, hld up, hdwy 8th, chsd wnr till wknd 5 out, tld off. (16 to 1 tchd 25 to 1) 6
3683³ DONNA'S TOKEN 9-10-9 W Marston, pushed alng aftr 6th, blun and uns rdr 9th.
  . . . .(7 to 1 op 5 to 1 tchd 8 to 1) ur
3562 MICRONOVA (v) 8-11-0 R Bellamy, jmpd poorly, tld off aftr 4th, refused 7th. . . . .(40 to 1 op 33 to 1) ref
3605⁴ RUNNING SANDS 10-11-0 G McCourt, led till aftr 4th, chsd wnr till wknd after 6 out, tld off whn pld up bef 2 out. . . . .(15 to 2 op 7 to 1 tchd 10 to 1) pu
3714³ OPENING OVERTURE (USA) 8-10-9 A Maguire, beh whn jmpd slwly 9th, tld off whn pld up bef nxt.
  . . . .(8 to 1 op 16 to 1 tchd 7 to 1) pu
3510* MONKSANDER 8-11-7 Richard Guest, lost pl aftr 6th, sn beh, tld off whn pld up bef 2 out... (8 to 1 tchd 9 to 1) pu
Dist: 6l, 9l, 8l, 1l, dist. 5m 48.70s. a 22.70s (11 Ran).

(Mrs S A Scott), N A Twiston-Davies

3845 Woodview Light Transport Handicap Hurdle (0-120 4-y-o and up) £2,442 2m 5f. . . . . (7:00)

3698³ CAVO GRECO (USA) [85] 5-10-3 D Skyrme, hld up, hdwy to track ldr 4 out, led appr 2 out, hit last, drvn out.
  . . . .(4 to 1 op 3 to 1 tchd 9 to 2) 1
3533⁴ DOMINION TREASURE [82] 9-10-0 L Harvey, hmpd 4th, led nxt, hdd 7th, led 3 out, sn headed, mstk nxt, rallied r-in, not quicken. . . . .(10 to 1 op 6 to 1) 2
3740⁵ SULTAN'S SON [82] 8-10-0 D Bridgwater, hld up, hdwy to track ldrs aftr 4 out, pushed alng aftr nxt, sn wknd.
  . . . .(10 to 1 op 7 to 1) 3
3630⁸ MERTON MISTRESS [83] 7-10-1¹ A Merrigan, trkd ldrs, pushed alng 4 out, wknd aftr nxt.
  . . . .(66 to 1 op 50 to 1 tchd 100 to 1) 4
3533⁷ MISTRESS ROSS [82] 11-10-0 I Lawrence, trkd ldr, led 7th to 3 out, sn wknd. . . . .(10 to 1 op 7 to 1) 5
  HIGHLAND BOUNTY [95] 10-10-13 D Gallagher, hld up in last pl, styd on aftr 3 out, nvr nrr. (33 to 1 op 25 to 1) 6
3514⁶ OTTOMAN EMPIRE [91] 7-10-9 M Brennan, hld up, hdwy 4 out, chsd ldrs till rdn and wknd appr 2 out.
  . . . .(7 to 2 op 4 to 1 tchd 9 to 2) 7
3592⁹ WHAT A NOBLE [82] 8-9-7 (7") R Rourke, prmnt whn hmpd 4th, chsd ldrs till wknd quickly aftr four out.
  . . . .(33 to 1 op 40 to 1 tchd 50 to 1) 8
2980³ EBONY GALE [108] 8-11-12 R Dunwoody, hld up mid-div, wknd quickly aftr 4 out, tld off. . . . .(5 to 1 op 9 to 2) 9
3491¹⁶ TOUCH OF WINTER [103] (bl) 8-11-7 N Williamson, led till 4th. . . . .(3 to 1 fav op 5 to 2 tchd 4 to 1) f
Dist: 2l, 9l, 6l, 1¾l, ¾l, hd, 6l, 20l. 5m 25.40s. a 26.40s (10 Ran).

(Jack Joseph), J Joseph

3846 Land Rover Gentlemen's Championship Hunters' Chase (5-y-o and up) £4,182 3m 1f. . . . .(7:30)

AVOSTAR 7-12-4 Mr R Russell, mstks, led 3rd to nxt, led aftr 6th, lft clr 4 out, styd on wl.
  . . . .(5 to 2 op 7 to 2 tchd 4 to 1) 1
BLAKES ORPHAN 8-11-9 Mr T Illsley, hdwy 8th, chsd ldr till outpcd 6 out, ran on aftr 3 out, not rch wnr.
  . . . .(12 to 1 op 14 to 1 tchd 16 to 1) 2
3563* SAMS HERITAGE 10-12-4 Mr J M Pritchard, hld up, cl 5th whn blun 9th, hdwy aftr 12th, wnt second 3 out, sn rdn, wknd betw last 2.
  . . . .(Evens fav op 5 to 4 on tchd 11 to 10) 3
STRONG BOND 13-12-0 Mr N R Mitchell, led clr aftr 1st, lost pl and rdn alng after mstk 11th, styd on one pace frm 4 out. . . . .(7 to 1 op 3 to 1) 4
EVENING RUSH 8-11-9 Mr K Drewry, drpd rear 5th, tld off tenth. . . . .(33 to 1 op 20 to 1) 5
GOOD WATERS 14-12-4 Mr L Streeton, lost tch 6th, sn tld off. . . . .(20 to 1 tchd 16 to 1 and 25 to 1) 6
MAHANA 10-11-9 Mr D Coates, led aftr 1st to 3rd, led nxt till after 6th, chsd ldr, lft second 4 out, wknd quickly.
  . . . .(33 to 1 op 16 to 1) 7
REGAN (USA) 7-11-13 Mr C Mulhall, beh whn collided wth rng rail aftr 5th, sn tld off. . . . . .(33 to 1 op 20 to 1) 8
3563⁶ RANDOM PLACE 12-12-0 Mr I Pocock, pressed ldr 8th, cl second whn f 4 out. . . . .(33 to 1 op 14 to 1) f
Dist: 8l, 1¾l, 9l, dist, 8l, 10l, 7l. 6m 43.50s. a 28.50s (9 Ran).

(R G Russell), Miss C Saunders

3847 Barwell Handicap Chase (0-115 5-y-o and up) £2,883 2m 110yds. . . . . . (8:00)

3548⁵ GENERAL MERCHANT [87] 14-10-0 R Dunwoody, in tch, mstk 6th, chsd ldr nxt, switchd aftr 2 out, led and hit last, drvn out. . . . .(7 to 2 op 11 to 4) 1
I LIKE IT A LOT [87] 11-10-0 J R Kavanagh, led, clr 6 out, hdd betw last 2, rallied r-in, not quicken nr finish.
  . . . .(33 to 1 op 25 to 1) 2
3513² KIBREET [106] 7-11-5 S Earle, lft second 5th, chsd ldr frm 5 out, hmpd 2 out, rdn and not quicken.
  . . . .(3 to 1 fav op 5 to 2) 3
860¹ THEY ALL FORGOT ME [87] 7-10-0 D Bridgwater, sn beh, styd on aftr 4 out, nvr nrr. . . . .(12 to 1 op 7 to 1) 4

NATIONAL HUNT RESULTS 1993-94

3697² AIR COMMANDER [88] 9-10-1 T Wall, *hld up, chsd ldr 5th till wknd aftr 6 out.....*(11 to 2 op 9 to 2 tchd 6 to 1) 5
3595³ DRIVING FORCE [112] (bl) 8-11-11 G McCourt, *hld up, drvn alng aftr 7th, no imprsn............*(4 to 1 op 7 to 2) 6
3727³ SOCKS DOWNE [87] 15-10-0 B Powell, *prmnt, mstk second, lost tch aftr 5th, sn beh.*
.................................(16 to 1 op 10 to 1 tchd 20 to 1) 7
3664⁴ MAGGOTS GREEN [87] 7-10-0 A Maguire, *second whn blun and uns rdr 5th..................*(11 to 2 op 5 to 1) ur
3759⁴ STRANGELY QUIET [87] 12-10-0 I Lawrence, *hld up, mstk 5th, lost tch aftr nxt, tld off whn pld up bef 2 out.*
.................................(9 to 1 op 14 to 1 tchd 33 to 1) pu
Dist: 1¼l, 3l, 12l, 20l, 4l, 12l. 4m 12.40s. a 10.40s (9 Ran).
SR: 18/16/32/1/-/2/ (Mrs Susan Tate), R J Hodges

3848 Michael Jones Jeweller And Breitling Novices' Hurdle (4-y-o and up) £2,180 2m...........................(8:30)

3515* ARTIC WINGS (Ire) 6-11-9 M Brennan, *hld up, hdwy 5th, led 2 out, drvn out.*
.................................(7 to 4 fav op 13 to 8 tchd 11 to 8) 1
3756 POLISH RIDER (USA) 6-11-0 (7*) C Huggan, *hld up, hdwy aftr 5th, ev ch 2 out, not quicken.*
.................................(7 to 2 tchd 5 to 2 and 4 to 1) 2
3549³ DEAR DO 7-11-0 M A FitzGerald, *hdwy 3rd, ev ch appr 2 out, not quicken...........*(3 to 1 op 7 to 2 tchd 4 to 1) 3
STRONG TOI 7-10-9 J Osborne, *trkd ldr, ev ch appr 2 out, rdn and kpt on one pace..........*(20 to 1 op 12 to 1) 4
3597 POETS COVE 6-11-0 M Perrett, *hld up, sn beh, hdwy aftr 3 out, nvr nvr......................*(33 to 1 op 12 to 1) 5
MERIVEL 7-11-0 B Powell, *hld up, trkd ldrs 5th, ev ch appr 2 out, sn wknd............*(33 to 1 tchd 40 to 1) 6
3630⁶ CAST ADRIFT 7-10-9 D Gallagher, *prmnt, led 3 out to nxt, sn wknd..................*(6 to 1 tchd 8 to 1) 7
1568 STORMING RUN (Ire) 6-11-0 W Marston, *led to 3 out, rdn and rallied, wknd nxt.*
.................................(40 to 1 op 33 to 1 tchd 50 to 1) 8
1027 SUNGIA (Ire) 5-11-0 D Bridgwater, *mstk 1st, beh 3rd, sn lost tch..................................*(40 to 1 op 33 to 1) 9
TRIAL TIMES (USA) 5-10-9 (5*) S Curran, *losing tch whn pckd 5th, sn beh..................*(33 to 1 op 20 to 1) 10
Dist: 3½l, ½l, 6l, 1¾l, 2½l, 10l, 6l, 4l, 5l. 4m 5.70s. a 22.70s (10 Ran).
(Lady Anne Bentinck), O Brennan

CHEPSTOW (good to firm)
Tuesday May 10th
Going Correction: MINUS 0.15 sec. per fur.

3849 Status Novices' Hurdle (4-y-o and up) £2,332 2½m 110yds...........(2:15)

3756* PRIDWELL 4-11-1 R Dunwoody, *hld up, gd hdwy 7th, chlgd 3 out, led last, ran on...*(3 to 1 on op 1 to 1 on) 1
3340* BRIDEPARK ROSE (Ire) 6-10-13 M Ahern, *al prmnt, led appr 4 out, rdn 2 out, hdd and hit last, one pace.*
.................................(11 to 2 op 6 to 1) 2
3685⁴ ROAD TO AU BON (USA) 6-11-1 L Harvey, *hld up, hdwy 7th, rdn 3 out, sn outpcd.........*(13 to 1 op 20 to 1) 3
3628⁶ COOLGARDIE 7-11-1 A Maguire, *pld hrd, in tch to 6th, rdn appr 4 out, no hdwy.............*(7 to 1 op 6 to 1) 4
3632² TULLYKYNE BELLS (bl) 5-11-1 D Gallagher, *led to second, led appr 5th till approaching 4 out, rdn and sn beh.*
.................................(33 to 1 op 20 to 1) 5
CHARLES HENRY 10-11-1 R Bellamy, *pld hrd, led second till aftr 4th, ran out nxt.*
.................................(33 to 1 op 50 to 1 tchd 100 to 1) ro
Dist: 4l, 25l, 6l, ¾l. 4m 48.60s. a 7.60s (6 Ran).
(Pond House Racing), M C Pipe

3850 Goldmark Novices' Chase (5-y-o and up) £3,038 3m.................(2:45)

3624* SQUIRE JIM 10-12-3 D Bridgwater, *hld up in rear, gd hdwy frm 12th, wnt second 4 out, led 2 out, eased whn clr r-in...............*(2 to 1 fav op 7 to 4 tchd 9 to 4) 1
3510⁵ YOUNG BRAVE 8-11-5 S Earle, *hld up, gd hdwy to go second appr 8th, led 5 out, hdd whn mstk 2 out, held when hit last....................*(8 to 1 tchd 10 to 1) 2
3546² DEEPENDABLE (bl) 7-11-11 M A FitzGerald, *chsd ldrs, one pace frm 4 out.........*(3 to 1 op 11 to 4 tchd 9 to 4) 3
3699⁸ PUNCH'S HOTEL 9-11-6 (5*) C Burnett-Wells, *chsd ldrs, rdn appr 5 out, one pace aftr.*
.................................(12 to 1 tchd 16 to 1 and 10 to 1) 4
3477³ STAUNCH RIVAL (USA) 7-11-11 J Frost, *in rear till hdwy 13th, wknd appr 3 out...........*(11 to 2 op 6 to 1) 5
3744 WILD FORTUNE 12-11-5 P Holley, *led to second, led 6th till wknd and hdd 5 out, sn beh, tld off.*
.................................(28 to 1 op 12 to 1 tchd 33 to 1) 6
3635⁵ SEMINOLE PRINCESS (bl) 6-10-7 (7*) R Williamson, *hld up, hdwy appr 8th, wkng whn blun and uns rdr 11th.*
.................................(66 to 1 op 25 to 1) ur
TOM PENNY 12-11-5 J R Kavanagh, *prmnt to 7th, sn beh, tld off whn pld up bef 3 out........*(66 to 1 op 33 to 1) pu
NONE SO WISE (USA) 8-11-5 B Powell, *hld up, hit 4th, in rear whn pld up bef tenth........*(10 to 1 op 13 to 2) pu

---

3764⁵ ROMANY SPLIT 9-11-5 D Gallagher, *pld hrd, hit tenth, effrt 13th, wknd appr 5 out, pulled up bef 3 out.*
.................................(20 to 1 op 16 to 1 tchd 33 to 1) pu
1879 SAM PEPPER (bl) 8-11-5 S Mackey, *led second to 6th, mstks 12th and 13th, sn beh, pld up bef 2 out.*
.................................(66 to 1 op 25 to 1) pu
Dist: 1¾l, 7l, 3l, nk, 15l. 6m 0.70s. a 10.70s (11 Ran).
(R P Hiorns), N A Twiston-Davies

3851 Ernst & Young Handicap Hurdle (0-125 4-y-o and up) £3,761 2½m 110yds
.................................(3:15)

3136 HOLY JOE [108] 12-11-10 M A FitzGerald, *hld up in rear, gd hdwy frm 7th, rdn 3 out, led appr last, drvn out.*
.................................(9 to 1 op 12 to 1 tchd 16 to 1) 1
3535 DAMIER BLANC (Fr) [95] (v) 5-10-11 R Dunwoody, *hld up in tch, led 7th, rdn and hdd appr last, kpt on one pace.*
.................................(13 to 2 op 5 to 1 tchd 9 to 2) 2
3634² FAUX PAVILLON [90] 10-10-1 (5*) S Fox, *led to 7th, pushed alng frm 4 out, ev ch 2 out, one pace r-in.*
.................................(5 to 1 op 9 to 2) 3
3625³ CHUCKLESTONE [103] 11-11-5 J R Kavanagh, *prmnt early, sn rdn in rear, hdwy appr 4 out, struggling frm nxt...........*(7 to 2 fav op 3 to 1 tchd 4 to 1) 4
3634 FROSTY RECEPTION [84] 9-9-9 (5*) S Curran, *sn trkd ldr, wknd 7th...........*(16 to 1 op 14 to 1 tchd 12 to 1) 5
3574 WOLVER GOLD [92] 7-10-8 Peter Hobbs, *hld up, hdwy 5th, wknd 3 out............*(7 to 1 op 6 to 1 tchd 9 to 1) 6
3697 ONENINEFIVE [84] (v) 8-10-0 B Powell, *prmnt early, tld off frm 5th...........*(66 to 1 op 50 to 1) 7
3609⁵ SUKAAB [106] 9-11-8 A Maguire, *pld up aftr hmpd 1st.*
.................................(9 to 2 op 4 to 1 tchd 5 to 1) pu
3282³ DRAGONS DEN [100] 8-11-2 J Osborne, *jmpd slwly 1st and struck into frm beh, pld up....*(11 to 2 op 5 to 1) pu
Dist: 3l, 1¼l, 14l, 1½l, 20l, dist. 4m 45.00s. a 4.00s (9 Ran).
SR: 25/9/2/1/-/-/ (Mrs J E Brookes), A J Wilson

3852 Status Handicap Chase (0-125 5-y-o and up) £3,579 2m 3f 110yds.... (3:50)

3661⁷ LOR MOSS [85] 14-10-3 R Kavanagh, *hld up in tch, hdwy 6th, hit tenth, led nxt, pushed out.*
.................................(9 to 1 op 5 to 1 tchd 33 to 1) 1
3830³ L'UOMO PIU [106] 10-11-10 M A FitzGerald, *led to 4th, lost pl 7th, rallied appr 5 out, tld appr nxt, hit 3 out, one pace...............*(11 to 2 op 5 to 1 tchd 9 to 1) 2
3490⁴ AUVILLAR (USA) [83] (v) 6-10-1 D J Burchell, *beh, mstk 4th, styd on frm 3 out, nvr nrr.............*(7 to 1 op 6 to 1) 3
811⁶ COUNTERBID [103] (v) 7-11-7 J Osborne, *hld up, hdwy 8th, rdn 4 out, sn wknd.............*(8 to 1 op 7 to 1) 4
3671* CROSULA [99] 6-11-3 R Dunwoody, *hld up, wnt second appr 6th, led 9th to 11th, second and rdn whn blun 4 out, not reco'r..................*(6 to 4 fav tchd 7 to 4) 5
3753³ SIRRAH JAY [98] 14-11-2 A Maguire, *trkd ldr, led 4th to 5th, beh frm nxt, sn tld off........*(5 to 1 tchd 11 to 2) 6
3662³ BALDA BOY [102] 10-11-6 B Powell, *led 5th to 9th, wkng whn blun 5 out, pld up bef 2 out...*(7 to 1 op 5 to 1) pu
Dist: 6l, 9l, 11l, 12l, dist. 4m 50.20s. a 3.20s (7 Ran).
SR: 14/29/-/6/ (S G Griffiths), S G Griffiths

3853 Cremanaze Claiming Hurdle (4-y-o and up) £2,164 2m 110yds...... (4:20)

3492 ACCESS SUN [7] 4-11-9 J R Kavanagh, *made all, rdn 2 out, drvn out r-in.......................*(15 to 2 op 12 to 1) 1
3773⁴ KNIGHT IN SIDE 8-10-11 A Maguire, *hld up in mid-div, hdwy 4th, pressed wnr frm 2 out, rdn and no extr cl hme.......................*(7 to 1 op 5 to 1) 2
3714 SENEGALAIS (Fr) 10-10-10 J Frost, *al frnt rnk, rdn 3 out, no imprsn frm nxt...........*(20 to 1 op 16 to 1) 3
3348⁴ MILDRED SOPHIA 7-9-13 (7*) Miss S Mitchell, *wl in rear till hdwy 3 out, nvr nrr.....*(33 to 1 op 20 to 1) 4
997⁶ BOLTROSE 4-10-11 A Maguire, *nvr far away, rdn 3 out, one pace aftr...................*(5 to 1 op 4 to 1 tchd 9 to 1) 5
3684⁴ SHU FLY (NZ) 10-11-8 Jacqui Oliver, *hld up in rear, hdwy 4th, rdn four out, wknd bef nxt.*
.................................(7 to 4 fav op 5 to 4 tchd 2 to 1) 6
2912⁶ SLICK CHERRY 7-10-5 A Charlton, *in rear, effrt 4th, one pace frm nxt..................*(40 to 1 op 33 to 1) 7
3100⁷ DARK DESIRE 8-11-2 M Richards, *effrt 4th, nvr on terms.....................*(9 to 1 op 7 to 1) 8
3572⁹ SANDRO (bl) 5-10-11 L Harvey, *hld up in rear, hdwy 4th, wknd quickly 3 out...........*(40 to 1 op 33 to 1) 9
IT'S VARADAN 10-10-11 J Osborne, *chsd ldrs till wknd appr 4 out, tld off.........*(5 to 1 op 4 to 1) 10
3728 OCEAN LAD 11-10-10 B Powell, *al beh, tld off.*
.................................(9 to 1 op 10 to 1 tchd 50 to 1) 11
3668³ ALMOST A PRINCESS 6-10-7 D Gallagher, *prmnt till rdn and wknd appr 4 out, beh whn f nxt.*
.................................(20 to 1 tchd 25 to 1) f
3533 SEA BARN 11-10-10 B Clifford, *chsd ldrs till pld up lme bef 4 out..............*(33 to 1 op 25 to 1 tchd 50 to 1) pu
Dist: ½l, 4l, 6l, ¾l, 7l, 6l, 12l, ½l, 20l, 30l. 3m 51.20s. a 5.20s (13 Ran).
SR: 9/5/-/-/-/-/ (Dajam Ltd), J S King

557

3854 Marlborough Book Shop Novices' Hunters' Chase (5-y-o and up) £1,670 3m..........................(4:50)

3596³ WELSH LEGION 9-11-7 (7*) Miss C Burgess, *nvr far away, hld whn lft in ld 2 out, styd on*..... (11 to 2 op 9 to 2) 1
3521⁸ ARTFUL ARTHUR 8-11-7 (7*) Mr J Grassick, *al prmnt, led 5th to 9th, lft second whn mstk 2 out, hmpd by loose horse aftr, kpt on r-in*.............(33 to 1 op 25 to 1) 2
SANDBROOK 10-11-7 (7*) Mr E Williams, *trkd ldr, led 9th till hdd 4 out, one pace*.(7 to 1 op 8 to 1 tchd 10 to 1) 3
MILLIE BELLE (bl) 8-11-2 (7*) Mr S Blackwell, *hld up, hdwy 8th, no ch frm 5 out*...............(20 to 1 op 16 to 1) 4
CHANNEL PASTIME 10-11-7 (7*) Mr G Hogan, *wl in rear till effrt appr 5 out, nvr on terms.*
.... (25 to 1 op 20 to 1 tchd 33 to 1) 5
UNITYFARM OLTOWNER 10-11-7 (7*) Mr E Evans, *in tch till wknd appr 5 out, tld off*..........(50 to 1 op 20 to 1) 6
WINNIE LORRAINE 9-11-3¹ (7*) Mr M G Miller, *f 1st.*
.... (12 to 1 op 10 to 1) f
DURZI 9-11-7 (7*) Mr M Rimell, *beh till hdwy 4th, wkng whn blun and uns rdr 5 out*........ (12 to 1 op 8 to 1) ur
3596⁷ SPACE PRINCE 13-11-7 (7*) Mr C Campbell, *led second to 5th, prmnt till wknd appr 5 out, blun and uns rdr nxt.*
..................................(50 to 1 op 20 to 1) ur
3768² SYNDERBOROUGH LAD 8-12-0 (7*) Mr J M Pritchard, *hld up wl in rear, rapid hdwy 13th, chlgd whn slight mstk 5 out, led nxt, in command when blun and uns rdr 2 out.*
.... (5 to 4 on tchd 11 to 10 on and 6 to 4 on) ur
CAPTAIN MANNERING (USA) 9-11-7 (7*) Mr M Harris, *prmnt early, beh frm 11th, refused one out.*
.................................(100 to 1 op 50 to 1) ref
3385 BEE-KAY-ESS 11-11-7 (7*) Mr S Shinton, *in tch till mstk 13th, sn wknd, tld off whn pld up bef 2 out.*
..................................(100 to 1 op 50 to 1) pu
MINS QUEST 10-11-7 (7*) Mr R Payne, *led to second, in rear whn jmpd rght 8th, sn pld up.*
..................................(100 to 1 op 50 to 1) pu

Dist: 5l, 8l, 12l, 9l. dist. 6m 7.30s. a 17.30s (13 Ran).

(G W Lewis), G W Lewis

3855 Baltyboys Open National Hunt Flat Race (4,5,6-y-o) £1,612 2m 110yds ....(5:20)

3522³ DISTANT ECHO (Ire) 4-10-9 R Dunwoody, *al gng wl, hld up beh ldrs, pushed out to ld ins fnl furlong, very easily.*
.... (11 to 10 on op 6 to 4 tchd 7 to 4) 1
3686³ HERBERT BUCHANAN (Ire) 4-10-9 M Perrett, *led aftr one furlong, hrd rdn and hdd ins last, no imprsn.*
.................................(9 to 1 op 5 to 1) 2
TIME HE WENT 5-11-0 A Maguire, *al in tch, hdwy 6 fs out, rdn 3 out, one pace fnl 2*..........(5 to 1 op 7 to 1) 3
TREMBLE 5-11-0 M A FitzGerald, *wl in rear till hdwy 4 fs out, styd on fnl 2, nvr nrr*......... (7 to 1 op 5 to 1) 4
3686⁶ HOLY STING (Ire) 5-10-11 (3*) T Jenks, *trkd ldrs, rdn and one pace fnl 3 fs*.....................(9 to 1 op 7 to 1) 5
3522 LYRICAL SEAL 4-9-13 (5*) D Fortt, *nvr far away, one pace fnl 3 fs*....................(50 to 1 op 33 to 1) 6
WYE OATS 5-10-9 R Bellamy, *prmnt, chsd ldrs 7 fs out till wknd 3 out*................ (33 to 1 op 25 to 1 tchd 40 to 1) 7
3523⁷ MR BOBBIT (Ire) 4-10-4² (7*) M Berry, *mid-div, hdwy 4 fs out, wknd o'r 2 out*...........(10 to 1 op 7 to 1) 8
3523 LADY LIFE 5-10-9 Miss S Young, *prmnt to hfwy, beh fnl 4 fs, tld off*........................(50 to 1 op 33 to 1) 9
3523 MUTUAL MEMORIES 6-10-7 (7*) Pat Thompson, *wl in rear till hdwy o'r 4 fs out, wknd 3 out, tld off.*
................................(20 to 1 op 16 to 1) 10
NURSERY STORY 6-11-0 J R Kavanagh, *beh till hdwy 5 fs out, wknd o'r 3 out, tld off*........(100 to 1 op 50 to 1) 11
POLYGAR 4-10-9 B Powell, *chsd ldrs till wknd 7 fs out, tld off*..............................(33 to 1 op 20 to 1) 12
3589 PRINCE IVANHOE 5-11-0 J Railton, *prmnt till wknd quickly 4 fs out, tld off*..........(50 to 1 op 33 to 1) 13
3686 NANOOK 5-11-0 D Gallagher, *led for one furlong, wknd quickly sn aftr hfwy, tld off*........(33 to 1 op 20 to 1) 14
3523 SAFFRON MOSS 4-10-9 S Mackey, *in tch till wknd o'r 5 fs out, tld off*...................(50 to 1 op 33 to 1) 15

Dist: 1¼l, 7l, ¾l, hd, 4l, 2l, 4l, 15l, 1¼l, 13l. 3m 45.70s. (15 Ran).

(Mel Fordham), D W P Arbuthnot

FOLKESTONE (good to firm) Tuesday May 10th
Going Correction: MINUS 0.10 sec. per fur.

3856 NFU Nuptials Maiden Hunters' Challenge Cup Chase (5-y-o and up) £1,579 2m 5f..........................(5:45)

AFALTOUN 9-12-0 (7*) Mr T Lacey, *sn prmnt, led 7th till 4 out, trkd ldr till led aftr aftr nxt, drvn out r-in, styd on wl.*
..(6 to 4 on op 5 to 4 on tchd 11 to 10 on and Evens) 1

MAGICAL MORRIS 12-12-4 (3*) Mr P Hacking, *hld up beh, rdn and hdwy aftr tenth, second after 2 out, ridden and no imprsn r-in.*
..................(100 to 30 op 11 to 4 tchd 7 to 2) 2
3629 POWERSURGE (bl) 7-12-0 (7*) Mr C Gordon, *hld up, hdwy aftr 9th, 3rd whn blun 3 out, rdn and styd on one pace.*
..................................(50 to 1 op 20 to 1) 3
RAH WAN (USA) 8-12-0 (7*) Mr C Vigors, *beh, hdwy aftr 9th, led 12th to nxt, hdd appr 2 out, one pace.*
.................................(33 to 1 tchd 50 to 1) 4
BASHER BILL 11-12-0 (7*) Mr S Deasley, *wl beh 8th, tld off aftr tenth*......................(100 to 1 op 33 to 1) 5
MOUNT PATRICK 10-12-4 (3*) Mr Simon Andrews, *beh 8th, tld off 5 out*.....................(50 to 1 op 20 to 1) 6
RYDAL PRIDE 9-12-0 (7*) Mr P Atkins, *chsd ldrs, prmnt whn f tenth*............................(66 to 1 op 25 to 1) f
KINGS HATCH (bl) 8-12-0 (7*) Mr Matthew J Jones, *chsd ldrs, prmnt whn f 9th*............(50 to 1 op 20 to 1) f
ALZAMINA 8-11-9 (7*) Mr J Best, *mid-div whn hmpd and uns rdr tenth*........ (10 to 1 op 5 to 1 tchd 12 to 1) ur
STEDE QUARTER 7-12-0 (7*) Mr A Hickman, *mstks, beh till some hdwy whn hmpd and uns rdr tenth.*
.... (20 to 1 op 14 to 1 tchd 33 to 1) ur
NETHERTARA 7-11-9 (7*) Mr P Bull, *mstk 1st, beh whn brght dwn tenth*................. (25 to 1 op 10 to 1) bd
BRUCE BUCKLEY 6-12-0 (7*) Mr T Hills, *chsd ldrs, prmnt whn brght dwn 9th.* (66 to 1 op 33 to 1 tchd 100 to 1) bd
FLASHING SILKS 9-11-9 (7*) Mrs N Ledger, *mstks, beh, pld up bef tenth.*..................(100 to 1 op 33 to 1) pu
PEMBRIDGE DANCER 7-12-0 (7*) Mr S Sporborg, *led to 7th, 4th whn blun 11th, sn drpd out, beh when pld up bef 2 out.*.........(20 to 1 op 16 to 1 tchd 33 to 1) pu

Dist: 4l, 4l, 2½l, dist, 4l. 5m 21.40s. a 11.40s (14 Ran).

(Miss J Winch), J Porter

3857 Grunwick United Hunts Open Challenge Cup Hunters' Chase (5-y-o and up) £2,022 2m 5f..............(6:15)

3501* AMARI KING 10-12-7 (7*) Mr C Ward Thomas, *hld up, 8th, hdwy aftr tenth, ev ch 4 out, led after 2 out, all out.*
.....................(13 to 8 on op 5 to 4 on) 1
DROMIN LEADER 9-12-2 (5*) Mr P Harding-Jones, *second 6th, led 5 out, hdd aftr 2 out, ev ch last, hrd rdn, not quicken.*...........................(6 to 1 op 4 to 1) 2
WELSHMAN'S GULLY 10-12-4 (7*) Mr C Newport, *hld up, beh 8th, rdn and hdwy aftr 5 out, one pace frm 2 out.*
.................................(7 to 1 tchd 12 to 1) 3
JOHN O'DEE 11-12-1¹ (7*) Mr I Marsh, *al prmnt, cl up and ev ch 4 out, second nxt, wknd appr 2 out.*
.... (25 to 1 op 14 to 1) 4
3412 SKINNHILL (bl) 10-12-4 (7*) Mr T McCarthy, *ran in snatches, mstk 3rd, beh and pushed alng aftr 7th, hdwy nxt, wknd after 6 out*........ (25 to 1 op 14 to 1) 5
3331* TRUST THE GYPSY 12-12-9 (5*) Mr M Felton, *hld up and beh, rdn and effrt aftr 5 out, wknd appr 2 out.*
.... (5 to 2 op 3 to 1 tchd 11 to 2) 6
DAN MARINO 12-12-0 (7*) Miss A Stedman, *mstks, hdwy 7th, led 9th to 5 out, wknd quickly, no ch whn mistake 2 out.*.........................(100 to 1 op 33 to 1) 7
ASTROAR 13-12-0 (7*) Mr H Lawther, *led to second, led 3rd to 9th, wknd 5 out*.. (25 to 1 op 14 to 1 tchd 33 to 1) 8
TARA BOY (bl) 9-12-4 (7*) Mr J Ferguson, *jmpd lft, led to 3rd, mstk tenth, sn wknd, tld off whn pld up bef 2 out.*
..................................(50 to 1 op 20 to 1) pu

Dist: 1l, 11l, 8l, 7l, nk, sht-hd, 7l. 5m 17.30s. a 7.30s (9 Ran).

SR: 20/12/5/-/-/-/ (M Ward-Thomas), J Wall

3858 Shepherd Neame United Hunts Open Champion Hunters' Chase (5-y-o and up) £3,045 3¼m..............(6:45)

3638* WILD ILLUSION 10-12-0 (7*) Mr J Trice-Rolph, *led, jmpd lft 14th, quickened r-in, easily...* (7 to 1 on op 7 to 1 on) 1
AS YOU WERE (bl) 12-12-0 (7*) Miss Z Turner, *trkd ldr, pushed alng 4 out, ev ch 2 out, sn outpcd.*
.... (5 to 1 tchd 6 to 1) 2

Won by 2½l. 6m 40.00s. a 28.00s (2 Ran).

SR: -/-/ (Col A Clerke-Brown), Miss Jennifer Pidgeon

3859 Eurocharing Novices' Hunters' Chase For Guy Peate Memorial Challenge Trophy (5-y-o and up) £1,852 3¼m ....(7:15)

NO FIZZ 8-11-12 (7*) Mr C Newport, *hld up, hdwy 13th, led 4 out, clr 2 out, styd on strly.*
.... (5 to 2 op 2 to 1 tchd 11 to 4) 1
DARTON RI 11-12-0 (7*) Mr J Maxse, *led till aftr 3rd, led after 5th to 7th, pressed ldr till 4 out, ran on to take second r-in. not trble wnr.*
.................(7 to 1 op 5 to 1 tchd 10 to 1 and 12 to 1) 2
3521⁵ RICHARD HUNT 10-12-3 (7*) Miss L Rowe, *hld up, rcd wide, not fluent, pushed alng aftr 14th, wnt second 3 out, wknd after 2 out*...... (11 to 8 on op 11 to 8 on) 3

NATIONAL HUNT RESULTS 1993-94

RUSTY RAILS 12-12-0 (7*) Mrs N Ledger, *hld up, 3rd 12th, chsd ldrs till lost pl aftr 14th, styd on one pace frm 4 out*.................. (20 to 1 op 14 to 1 tchd 25 to 1) 4
WHAT A GIG 11-12-0 (7*) Mr J Best, *hld up, rear frm 14th, styd on one pace from 4 out*...... (25 to 1 op 12 to 1) 5
FORGET THE BLUES (bl) 9-12-0 (7*) Mr P Bull, *pressed ldrs till wknd aftr tenth, tld off 5 out.* (66 to 1 op 25 to 1) 6
FRIENDLY BANKER (Aus) (bl) 10-12-0 (7*) Mr A Hickman, *led aftr 3rd, led 7th till after 5 out, wknd quickly, no ch whn f last*.........................(25 to 1 op 10 to 1) f
DIAMOND WAY 8-12-0 (7*) Mr Matthew J Jones, *prmnt whn blun and uns rdr tenth*............(66 to 1 op 20 to 1) ur
3596 ALL GOLD BOY (bl) 9-12-0 (7*) Mr C Ward Thomas, *mstk 4th, beh frm 12th, blun 14th, tld off whn pld up and dismounted bef last*................ (25 to 1 op 12 to 1) pu
Dist: 13l, ¾l, 8l, 1¾l, 30l. 6m 41.00s. a 29.00s (9 Ran).

(Mrs A Bailey), Mrs D M Grissell

3860 Grant's Cherry Brandy South East Champion Novices' Hunter Chase Final (5-y-o and up) £1,852 2m 5f (7:45)

KILN COPSE 10-12-0 (7*) Mr M Portman, *chsd ldrs frm tenth, cl up and ev ch 4 out, rdn to ld r-in, drvn out.*
.... (9 to 1 op 4 to 1 tchd 10 to 1) 1
WISEBOW 9-12-0 (7*) Mrs C Elliott, *led, jmpd rght 7th, rdn and hdd aftr last, not quicken nr finish.*
.......................(25 to 1 op 12 to 1) 2
WELSHMAN'S CREEK 8-12-0 (7*) Mr C Newport, *hld up, hdwy aftr 9th, cl up and ev ch 4 out, rdn and styd on betw last 2, wknd appr last*....... (4 to 1 tchd 5 to 1) 3
BARN ELMS 7-12-4 (3*) Mr P Hacking, *hld up, hdwy aftr 9th, 4th nxt, cl up and ev ch four out, rdn and wknd betw last 2*.................... (4 to 1 op 7 to 1) 4
RYME AND RUN 8-11-9 (7*) Mr N King, *beh, hdwy aftr 5 out, cl up and ev ch appr 2 out, sn wknd.*
.... (10 to 1 op 6 to 1 tchd 12 to 1) 5
ROLLESTON BLADE 7-12-0 (7*) Mr P Bull, *mstks 1st and 6th, chsd ldrs frm tenth, mistake 3 out, sn wknd.*
.......................(11 to 2 op 4 to 1) 6
BRIGHT CRUSADER 8-12-0 (7*) Mr A Warr, *mstks 5th and 6th, tld off frm 8th*................. (33 to 1 op 20 to 1) 7
PRINCE RONAN (Ire) 6-12-4 (7*) Mr J Ayton, *beh frm 8th, lost tch tenth, tld off*............... (50 to 1 op 25 to 1) 8
LITTLE ISLAND 8-11-9 (7*) Miss V Hardman, *mstk 3rd, chsd ldrs, 4th and ev ch whn blun four out, not reco'r.*
.......................(25 to 1 op 14 to 1) 9
JOHN ROGER 8-12-0 (7*) Mr G Brown, *hld up and beh, hdwy 9th, 5th and staying on whn f nxt.*
.....................(5 to 2 fav tchd 7 to 2) f
SECOND TIME ROUND 11-12-0 (7*) Mr C Gordon, *mid-div, in tch whn uns rdr on bend aftr 6th.*
.......................(10 to 1 op 12 to 1) ur
TRUE ILLUSIAN 8-11-9 (7*) Mr G Pewter, *beh frm 8th, lost tch aftr tenth, tld off whn refused last.*
.......................(33 to 1 op 25 to 1) ref
Dist: 1¾l, 11l, 1½l, 2l, 9l, 20l, 10l, 1½l. 5m 25.50s. a 15.50s (12 Ran).

(G P P Stewart), P R Chamings

3861 Ross And Co. Solicitors Devil's Advocate Open Hunters' Chase for the Royal Judgement Challenge Trophy (5-y-o and up) £2,040 3¼m..... (8:15)

ANOTHER TROUP (bl) 12-12-0 (7*) Mr P Bull, *beh, jmpd slwly 3rd, hdwy 6th, chsd ldrs frm 13th, ev ch 3 out, rdn to ld last, drvn out.*.......... (7 to 2 op 5 to 1 tchd 6 to 1) 1
HURRICANE HUGO 8-11-7 (7*) Mr J Luck, *hld up and beh, mstk 7th, hdwy 9th, 3rd 5 out, led nxt, hdd and rdr lost irons last, not quicken.*
.......................(14 to 1 op 12 to 1 tchd 20 to 1) 2
3638⁸ SONOFAGIPSY 10-12-6 (5*) Mr M Felton, *hld up, hmpd bend aftr tenth, hdwy 5 out, ev ch appr 2 out, not quicken*................. (6 to 1 op 9 to 1 tchd 7 to 1) 3
BANTEL BUCCANEER 12-12-0 (7*) Mr C Vigors, *pressed ldr, mstk tenth, led 12th to 4 out, rdn and wknd 2 out.*
.... (20 to 1 op 12 to 1) 4
GILT BRONZE 10-11-7 (7*) Mr N Bloom, *beh, cld up 5th, reminders aftr 11th, wknd after 14th, tld off.*
.... (25 to 1 op 16 to 1) 5
DISCAIN BOY 14-11-7 (7*) Mr A Welsh, *pressed ldrs till lost pl 13th, sn beh, tld off.*
.......................(50 to 1 op 33 to 1 tchd 100 to 1) 6
GROVELANDS 12-12-0 (7*) Mr R Hubbard, *tld off aftr 8th.*
.......................(100 to 1 op 50 to 1) 7
STRONG GOLD (bl) 11-12-4 (7*) Mr T McCarthy, *led, blun 7th, hdd 12th, wknd rpdly aftr 14th, sn tld, pld up after 3 out*......(6 to 4 on tchd 7 to 4 on and 5 to 4 on) pu
Dist: 4l, 3½l, 9l, 25l, ¾l, dist. 6m 37.30s. a 25.30s (8 Ran).

(P A Bull), Miss A Newton-Smith

HEXHAM (good to firm)
Tuesday May 10th
Going Correction: MINUS 0.10 sec. per fur.

3862 Devilswater Novices' Hurdle (4-y-o and up) £2,030 2m 5f 110yds.... (2:05)

3620³ IFALLELSEFAILS 6-11-7 T Reed, *patiently rdn, improved 4 out, led and quickened bef 2 out, ran on strly.*
.... (9 to 4 op 2 to 1 tchd 7 to 4) 1
3620² CAPENWRAY (Ire) 5-11-7 P Niven, *settled off the pace, smooth hdwy to join issue aftr 4 out, pushed alng and hit last 2, not pace of wnr*....... (Evens fav tchd 6 to 4) 2
3690² THE WEATHERMAN 6-10-7 (7*) N Stocks, *sn clr, jnd aftr 4 out, hdd bef 2 out, one pace.....* (14 to 1 tchd 16 to 1) 3
3641² BRIAR'S DELIGHT 6-11-0 B Storey, *sn beh, improved to join ldrs aftr 4 out, feeling pace nxt, no imprsn.*
.......................(8 to 1 op 10 to 1 tchd 12 to 1) 4
3641⁴ MANOR COURT (Ire) 6-11-0 A Merrigan, *blun and nrly uns rdr 1st, improved to go hndy aftr 4 out, hrd at work nxt, fdd*........................(12 to 1) 5
3673⁹ FINDOGLEN 8-10-11 (3*) A Larnach, *chsd clr ldr frm 3rd to 4 out, tdd und pres aftr nxt*............. (50 to 1) 6
3683³ FIVE FLAGS (Ire) 6-11-0 Richard Guest, *settled with chasing bunch, reminders 4th, lost tch 6th, tld off.*
.... (10 to 1 op 8 to 1 tchd 11 to 1) 7
3435⁹ GOLDEN BANKER (Ire) 6-11-0 K Jones, *chsd ldr to 3rd, struggling 6th, sn tld off*.................. (50 to 1) 8
3379 HEDDON HAUGH (Ire) 6-11-0 K Johnson, *settled off the pace, outpcd bef 4 out, tld off.....* (50 to 1 op 33 to 1) 9
3674 HARRY'S MIDGET 4-9-12 (5*) J Supple, *in tch, hrd at work and lost grnd bef 4 out, tld off*............... (50 to 1) 10
2275 DIDACTE (Fr) 4-10-3 (5*) P Waggott, *settled with chasing bunch, struggling bef 4 out, tld off.*
.......................(50 to 1 op 33 to 1) 11
LAURAS TEEARA (Ire) 6-10-9 C Hawkins, *in tch to hfwy, lost touch bef 4 out, tld off*.................(50 to 1) 12
Dist: 12l, 8l, ¾l, 15l, ¾l, 25l, 1½l, ½l, 25l, dist. 5m 1.00s. (12 Ran).

(R J Gilbert), L Lungo

3863 Beaufront Novices' Chase (5-y-o and up) £2,284 3m 1f............... (2:30)

3599⁴ URIZEN 9-11-2 C Hawkins, *with ldg pair, led 9th, lft clr 4 out, styd on wl frm betw last 2...* (2 to 1 fav op 9 to 4) 1
3779⁵ CROWN EYEGLASS 8-11-2 R Garritty, *wtd with, improved fnl circuit, chsd wnr last 3, kpt on same pace.*
.... (50 to 1 op 25 to 1) 2
3675² UPWELL 10-11-2 K Johnson, *with ldg pair, rdn to hold pl fnl circuit, struggling 6 out, no imprsn aftr.*
.... (15 to 2 op 6 to 1 tchd 8 to 1) 3
3588 JENNY'S GLEN 7-11-2 B Storey, *bustled alng wth chasing grp, struggling fnl circuit, tld off whn hmpd and jmpd slwly 2 out*....................(8 to 1 op 7 to 1) 4
3675³ MASTER MATHEW 7-11-2 T Reed, *slight ld till aftr 6th, struggling to keep up appr six out, sn tld off.*
.......................(7 to 1 op 8 to 1 tchd 10 to 1) 5
3675 FRIENDLY SOCIETY 8-11-2 A Merrigan, *chsd ldrs for o'r a circuit, tld off frm 6 out.........* (25 to 1 op 20 to 1) 6
3438⁶ KINGS LAW 8-11-2 Mr D Scott, *not jump wl, blun and lost grnd 11th, f nxt*................ (14 to 1 op 12 to 1) f
3678⁶ SHELTON ABBEY 8-11-2 K Jones, *dsptd ld, led aftr 6th to 9th, nrly uns rdr 4 out, second whn tried to refuse 3 out, refused nxt*........................(5 to 1 op 7 to 2) ref
Dist: 7l, 30l, 30l, 6l, dist. 6m 30.70s. a 25.70s (8 Ran).

(Mrs P A H Hartley), P Beaumont

3864 Oakwood Selling Hurdle (4-y-o and up) £2,045 2m................(3:00)

3553⁸ CHARLYCIA 6-11-5 (7*) M Clarke, *patiently rdn, improved to track ldrs hfwy, led betw last 2, ran on.*
.......................(7 to 2 fav op 2 to 1) 1
3661⁶ RICHMOND (Ire) 6-11-10 D Wilkinson, *settled midfield, improved aftr 3 out, styd on und pres r-in.*
.....................(4 to 1 op 5 to 2) 2
3702³ SALLY OF THE ALLEY 4-10-7 Richard Guest, *nvr far away, ev ch frm 3 out, kpt on one pace r-in.*
.......................(6 to 1 op 5 to 1 tchd 7 to 1) 3
3536⁹ LARLOCH 10-11-3 N Doughty, *tried to make all. quickened clr aftr 2 out, wknd and hdd bef last.*
.... (14 to 1 op 12 to 1 tchd 16 to 1) 4
SWIFT CARRIAGE 8-10-12 A Dobbin, *al hndy, ev ch 2 out, one pace frm betw last two.*
.......................(7 to 1 op 10 to 1 tchd 8 to 1) 5
PERSPICACITY 7-10-12 J Callaghan, *trkd ldrs, effrt hfwy, kpt on same pace frm 2 out.*
.... (20 to 1 op 16 to 1 tchd 25 to 1) 6
3435 TINSTONE 4-10-7 R Garritty, *steadied strt, improved into midfield hfwy, effrt 3 out, one pace.*
.......................(7 to 1 op 8 to 1 tchd 6 to 1) 7
3690 FLAXON WORRIOR 10-11-3 O Pears, *pressed ldrs, drvn alng to hold pl bef 3 out, no extr...* (33 to 1 op 20 to 1) 8
3740³ IMMORTAL IRISH 9-11-10 T Wall, *nvr far away, ev ch whn hit 3 out, fdd frm nxt*............ (10 to 1 op 20 to 1) 9
3798³ GYMCRAK CYRANO (Ire) 5-10-7 (5*) S Lyons, *wth ldrs, hrd at work bef 3 out, sn btn.*
.... (11 to 1 op 12 to 1 tchd 10 to 1) 10
CBS RANDOLPH (Ire) 5-10-12 (5*) A Roche, *beh and drvn alng, tld off frm 4 out*............. (16 to 1 op 14 to 1) 11

559

3601 TRY AGAIN JANE 4-10-7 D Byrne, *in tch to hfwy, tld off frm 3 out*.............(15 to 2 op 7 to 1 tchd 10 to 1) 12
3236 LET'S BE ON 6-10-5 (7") B Grattan, *in tch, wnt wide bend aftr 4th, slpd up bend bef nxt*......(33 to 1 op 25 to 1) su
3570 LUGAR HOUSE 6-11-3 N Smith, *not fluent, chsd ldg bunch to 4 out, lost tch and pld up bef last.*
..............................(16 to 1 tchd 20 to 1) pu
Dist: 3½sl, 2l, 5l, 1½l, 4l, 1¼l, 7l, 1¾l, ½l, dist. 4m 1.00s. a 11.00s (14 Ran).
(Mrs V Chilton), T J Carr

3865 Tynedale Handicap Chase (0-115 5-y-o and up) £2,586 2m 110yds.....(3:30)

3691² MOSS BEE [82] 7-10-6² T Reed, *made most, ran on strly to go clr betw last 2, hld on wl finish*......(3 to 1 jt-fav) 1
1789⁶ CLEVER FOLLY [87] 14-10-11 N Doughty, *wth ldrs, led briefly hfwy, feeling pace aftr 4 out, rallied r-in, fnshd wl*..........................(11 to 2 op 5 to 1) 2
3785³ KAMART [78] 6-10-2 A Dobbin, *al hndy, ev ch frm 4 out, rdn and jdd betw last 2*........ (3 to 1 jt-fav op 4 to 1) 3
3584⁴ HIGHFIELD PRINCE [81] 8-10-5 M Dwyer, *chsd alng to keep in tch hfwy, nvr a factor, tld off.*
..........................(100 to 30 op 5 to 2) 4
911 BEN TIRRAN [84] (v) 10-10-8 D Telfer, *struggling to stay in tch hfwy, tld off*..............(12 to 1 tchd 14 to 1) 5
3582 MILITARY HONOUR [100] 9-11-10 Mr S Swiers, *tracking ldrs whn pld up lme aftr 6th.*
..........................(4 to 1 op 7 to 2 tchd 9 to 2) pu
Dist: ¾l, 25l, 25l, 6l. 4m 4.00s. a 6.00s (6 Ran).
SR: 2/6/-/

3866 Battle Hill Handicap Hurdle (0-110 4-y-o and up) £2,511 2½m 110yds...(4:00)

3690* SCOTTISH PERIL [86] 7-10-7 B Storey, *patiently rdn, jnd ldrs hfwy, led betw last 2, forged clr r-in*......(8 to 1) 1
3692² CAPTAIN TANCRED (Ire) [88] 6-10-9 A Merrigan, *settled midfield, improved to track ldrs 3 out, rdn and kpt on same pace frm betw last 2*..........(10 to 1 op 7 to 1) 2
3817⁶ TIGHTER BUDGET (USA) [90] 7-10-11 M Moloney, *made most, hdd briefly 4th to 6th, headed betw last 2, wknd pace.*..........(6 to 1 op 7 to 1 tchd 8 to 1) 3
3622⁵ CELTIC BREEZE [103] (v) 11-11-5 (5") J Burke, *nvr far away, feeling pace and drvn alng 3 out, kpt on same pace*................(11 to 1 op 7 to 1 tchd 12 to 1) 4
3643² WEE WIZARD (Ire) [102] 5-11-9 A Dobbin, *al hndy, drvn alng whn pace quickened 3 out, no extr betw last 2.*
..........................(4 to 1 jt-fav op 7 to 2) 5
3678³ NOTABLE EXCEPTION [100] 5-11-7 P Niven, *settled midfield, effrt aftr 4 out, outpcd after nxt. ......(4 to 1 jt-fav) 6
3357⁴ AUSTHORPE SUNSET [93] 10-11-0 Mr R Armson, *took keen hold, led briefly 4th to 6th, fdd bef 3 out.*
..........................(12 to 1 tchd 14 to 1) 7
3603⁴ DUTCH BLUES [79] 7-10-0 D Wilkinson, *chsd ldrs, reminders hfwy, sn lost tch, tld off.*
..........................(14 to 1 op 12 to 1) 8
3622 FORWARD GLEN [94] 7-11-1 K Johnson, *chsd ldrs to hfwy, lost tch frm 4 out, tld off*..............(6 to 1) 9
3692⁶ THE GREEN FOOL [101] 7-11-8 T Reed, *tracking ldrs whn blun badly 3rd, sn lost pl, rdn and no imprsn frm hfwy.*
..........................(10 to 1) 10
3577 LA MOLINILLA [79] 11-9-7 (7") Miss S Lamb, *took str hold, jnd ldrs 3rd, wknd quickly 6th, tld off*........(50 to 1) 11
Dist: 10l, 1¼l, 1¼l, 3l, 10l, 4l, 15l, 2½l, 1½l, dist. 4m 56.80s. a 3.80s (11 Ran).
SR: 21/13/13/24/20/8/
(Mrs V Scott Watson), R Allan

3867 Romfords Caterers Hunters' Chase (6-y-o and up) £1,632 2½m 110yds (4:30)

3412⁷ ON THE OTHER HAND 11-11-7 (7") Capt A Ogden, *al hndy, led 9th, hdd briefly 3 out, rallied to go clr betw last 2.*
..........................(5 to 1 tchd 6 to 1) 1
3645⁴ GUNMETAL BOY (v) 10-11-9 (5") Mr J M Dun, *made most to 9th, rallied und pres betw last 2, styd on.*
..........................(6 to 1 op 5 to 1) 2
GONE ASTRAY 9-11-9 Mr J Walton, *settled midfield, feeling pace fnl circuit, styd on frm 2 out, nrst finish.*
..........................(8 to 1 op 7 to 1 tchd 9 to 1) 3
3684 DARK DAWN 10-12-6 Mr J Greenall, *al hndy, led briefly 3 out, jdd und pres betw last 2.* (Evens fav tchd 11 to 10) 4
3558² DURIGHT 11-11-2 (7") Mr N F Smith, *settled wth chasing bunch, rapid hdwy aftr 4 out, no imprsn frm betw last 2*...........................(12 to 1) 5
JOHN CORBET 11-11-9 (5") Mr R H Brown, *nvr far away, feeling pace fnl circuit, outpcd frm 3 out.*
..........................(12 to 1 op 14 to 1) 6
JACK OF CLUBS 14-11-7 (7") Mr S Heslop, *chsd alng to go pace hfwy, tld off frm 5 out*...............(33 to 1) 7
ST ELMO'S FIRE (NZ) 9-11-7 (7") Mr M Nicholson, *struggling to go pace 3 out, tld off frm hfwy*........(33 to 1) 8
3558⁵ MIG 9-11-2 (7") Miss Y Beckingham, *blun and uns rdr 1st.*
..........................(25 to 1 op 20 to 1 tchd 33 to 1) ur
POSEIDONIA 8-11-7 (7") Miss J Percy, *wth ldrs for a circuit, tld off whn pld up bef last*...............(14 to 1) pu
MR POD 8-11-7 (7") Mr A Manners, *drvn wth chasing grp, reminders 5 out, pld up bef nxt*...............(33 to 1) pu

3581 GALE STORM 10-11-7⁵ (7") Mr D Scott, *drvn alng to keep up hfwy, tld off whn pld up bef 4 out.*
..........................(20 to 1 tchd 25 to 1) pu
3581 GLEN LICKY 10-11-9 (5") Miss J Thurlow, *struggling hfwy, tld off whn pld up bef 5 out*...............(50 to 1) pu
Dist: 2l, 8l, 5l, 12l, 30l, 25l, 1l. 5m 16.80s. a 15.80s (13 Ran).
(Robert Ogden), Miss C L Dennis

3868 Hencotes Open National Hunt Flat Race (4,5,6-y-o) £1,413 2m......(5:00)

3707* CROWTHER HOMES 4-10-4 (7") S Knott, *patiently rdn, hdwy o'r 3 fs out, led 2 out, quickened over one out, ran on wl*...........................(5 to 1 op 4 to 1) 1
3183* HULLBANK 4-11-2 D Byrne, *patiently rdn, hdwy 4 fs out, ridden o'r 2 out, ran on wl*...........(3 to 1 jt-fav op 5 to 2 tchd 100 to 30) 2
3488⁶ RADICAL CHOICE (Ire) 5-11-0 B Storey, *towards rear, steady hdwy o'r 3 fs out, styd on wl und pres fnl furlong*..........(9 to 1 op 8 to 1 tchd 10 to 1) 3
3590³ MONYMOSS (Ire) 5-10-7 (7") R Wilkinson, *al prmnt, led hfwy, hdd 2 fs out, unbl to quicken. (7 to 1 op 6 to 1) 4
3589² NOVA RUN 5-11-0 R Marley, *mid-div, effrt o'r 6 fs out, rdn 3 out, kpt on one pace....* (3 to 1 jt-fav tchd 100 to 30) 5
3488 KINGS LANE 5-10-9 (5") F Perratt, *chsd ldrs, ev ch o'r 3 fs out, rdn and wknd over 2 out......(8 to 1 op 10 to 1) 6
3590 NABURN LOCH 4-10-0³ (7") J Driscoll, *mid-div, no hdwy fnl 3 fs*............(50 to 1 op 33 to 1) 7
3589⁶ TIGH-NA-MARA 6-10-2 (7") K Davies, *towards rear, styd on fnl 3 fs, nvr trble ldrs*..............(16 to 1) 8
3590⁵ SIERRA MADRONA (USA) 4-9-13 (5") F Leahy, *towards rear, effrt hfwy, no imprsn fnl 4 fs*............(16 to 1) 9
3079⁴ ROLY PRIOR 5-10-7 (7") Mark Roberts, *prmnt, reminders aftr 6 fs, rdn and wknd o'r 3 out...*(16 to 1 op 14 to 1) 10
3590 STEPPING 4-9-11 (7") W Fry, *chsd ldrs, rdn and wknd o'r 2 fs out*..........(33 to 1 op 25 to 1) 11
3489 LOGANI 4-10-4 S Turner, *sn prmnt, dsptd ld aftr 4 fs to hfwy, grad wknd frm four out...........(33 to 1) 12
3589 MORCAT 5-10-9 Mr C Ratcliffe, *prmnt to hfwy, grad wknd.....*...........................(25 to 1) 13
2931⁷ BILLY BUOYANT 5-11-5⁵ Mr J Walton, *steadied strt, al beh*...........................(50 to 1) 14
3488 BE BRAVE 4-10-9 D Wilkinson, *in tch o'r 9 fs, wl beh frm over 2 out*...........................(14 to 1) 15
3589⁴ FAST EXIT 6-10-2 (7") D Towler, *cl up 7 fs, drpd rear o'r 3 out*............(10 to 1 op 14 to 1) 16
2976 RUN ON FLO (Ire) 6-10-4 (5") P Waggott, *lost tch 6 fs out, tld off.*...........................(50 to 1) 17
3488 LUCKY DOMINO 4-11-0⁵ Miss T Waggott, *sn in rear, tld off.*...........................(50 to 1) 18
3488 NOW YOUNG MAN (Ire) 5-11-0 Mr N Wilson, *mid-div 6 fs, sn struggling, wl beh frm 4 out.*............(20 to 1) 19
3590 GIRL NAMED SUE 5-10-9 A S Smith, *made most to hfwy, sn outpcd, tld off....*........ (20 to 1 op 16 to 1) 20
3489 LISMORE LAD 5-10-7 (7") S Melrose, *drpd rear hfwy, tld off*..........(25 to 1 tchd 33 to 1) 21
Dist: 3½l, 2l, 1½l, 4l, 5l, 10l, 5l, 2l, 1½l, 1¾l. 3m 54.00s. (21 Ran).
(Mrs Stella Barclay), E J Alston

KILLARNEY (IRE) (yielding to soft (race 1), (2,3,4,5)) Tuesday May 10th

3869 M.D. O'Shea (Mares) Maiden Hurdle (5-y-o and up) £3,452 2½m.....(5:25)

3792* FLAWLESS FINISH (Ire) 5-11-13 C F Swan, ...(13 to 8 fav) 1
3243⁴ DAWN ADAMS (Ire) 6-12-0 F J Flood, ...(4 to 1) 2
3528⁶ RAINYS RUN 7-12-0 B Sheridan, ...(8 to 1) 3
3647⁷ ACKLE BACKLE 7-11-9 (5") J R Barry, ...(9 to 2) 4
3731⁵ POOR TIMES (Ire) 6-11-9 (5") M A Davey, ...(8 to 1) 5
3290 PRINCESS BAVARD 9-12-0 Mr M Phillips, ...(8 to 1) 6
3550 THE COSH GALE 7-12-0 H Rogers, ...(16 to 1) 7
3290 DUN OENGUS (Ire) 5-11-13 J Magee, ...(16 to 1) 8
3552 DUST GALE (Ire) 5-11-13 T Horgan, ...(25 to 1) 9
3290 RAMBLE ALONG (Ire) 5-11-8 (5") J P Broderick, ..(25 to 1) 10
2919⁵ GALES JEWEL 8-11-7 (7") Mr F P Cahill, ...(14 to 1) 11
3732⁹ CHIEF JOSEPH 7-11-7 (7") M D Murphy, ...(33 to 1) 12
3450³ RAHAN BRIDGE (Ire) 5-11-13 Mr A J Martin, ...(10 to 1) 13
3084 ERADA (Ire) 6-12-0 A Powell, ...(33 to 1) 14
3243 SLEMISH MIST 7-12-0 P L Malone, ...(25 to 1) 15
3723 START SINGING (Ire) 5-11-6 (7") P Murphy, ...(16 to 1) pu
Dist: 1l, 20l, 5l, 12l. 5m 12.80s. (16 Ran).
(Bogey Syndicate), A P O'Brien

3870 White Sands Hotel Opportunity Hurdle (6-y-o and up) £3,797 2m 1f.....(5:55)

2125 FOR KEVIN 7-11-2 (2") J P Broderick, ...(9 to 2) 1
3292 FARRELL'S CROSS 8-11-2 (2") M G Cleary, ...(10 to 1) 2
3550⁹ REPLACEMENT 7-11-4 T J O'Sullivan, ...(12 to 1) 3
3393⁷ TOTAL CONFUSION 7-11-0 (4") B D Murtagh, (7 to 2 jt-fav) 4
234 GO DEAS 7-10-11 (2") K P Gaule, ...(12 to 1) 5
3789³ BALLYBODEN 7-11-0 (4") D J Kavanagh, ...(10 to 1) 6
3507⁶ JOHNNY SCATTERCASH 12-11-2 (2") D Walsh, ...(10 to 1) 7

3528 MARBLE FONTAINE 7-11-2 (4*) J M Donnelly, ... (12 to 1) 8
3657 DIRECT RUN 7-11-4 D P Murphy, ... (5 to 1) 9
3654 DEEP THYNE (Ire) 6-10-13 T P Treacy, ... (7 to 2 jt-fav) 10
3296 DISTRICT JUSTICE 7-11-2 (2*) A J Slattery, ... (10 to 1) 11
3291 LOUGH CULTRA DRIVE (Ire) 6-11-4 C O'Brien, ... (10 to 1) 12
3296 CAPTAIN CHARLES (Ire) 6-11-2 (2*) P A Roche, ... (50 to 1) 13
2278[7] SOUTH WESTERLY (Ire) 6-11-2 (2*) J R Barry, ... (8 to 1) 14
Dist: Hd, 11l, 1l, 1½l. 4m 57.30s. (14 Ran).
(Donal Sheahan), Michael Hourigan

3871 Killarney Racegoers Club Novice Hurdle (4-y-o and up) £3,452 2½m.. (6:25)

3834* FINNEGANS WAKE 7-11-6 C F Swan, ... (9 to 2) 1
3654[2] MISTER DRUM (Ire) 5-10-12 (7*) Mr J T McNamara,
.... (9 to 4 jt-fav) 2
3504[8] CORRIBLOUGH (Ire) 6-11-2 C O'Dwyer, ... (14 to 1) 3
3468[2] SAM VAUGHAN (Ire) 5-11-3 (5*) Mr W M O'Sullivan,
.... (9 to 4 jt-fav) 4
3647[8] KEEPHERGOING (Ire) 5-10-9 (5*) J P Broderick, ... (13 to 2) 5
3290[3] DEARBORN TEC (Ire) 5-11-1 G M O'Neill, ... (9 to 1) 6
QUEEN OF THE LAKES (Ire) 4-10-2 F Woods, ... (33 to 1) 7
3834[7] VERY ADAPTABLE (Ire) 5-11-1 K F O'Brien, ... (8 to 1) 8
3730 NURSE MAID (Ire) (bl) 4-10-2 J Jones, ... (16 to 1) 9
3788 OVER THE JORDAN (Ire) 5-10-8 (7*) Miss L Townsley,
.... (14 to 1) 10
Dist: 2l, sht-hd, ½l, 6l. 5m 26.50s. (10 Ran).
(Bracken Syndicate), A P O'Brien

3872 Great Southern Hotels Novice Chase (4-y-o and up) £3,452 2½m..... (6:55)

3551[2] SILVERWEIR 11-12-0 T Horgan, ... (9 to 4 fav) 1
3293[6] CHELSEA NATIVE (bl) 7-11-4 (5*) Susan A Finn, ... (6 to 1) 2
3507[3] PRINCIPLE MUSIC (USA) 6-11-11 (3*) Mr J A Nash, (4 to 1) 3
3789[4] BRIDGEOFALLEN (Ire) 6-11-4 (5*) Mr W M O'Sullivan,
.... (14 to 1) 4
3709 BALLYHIN BOY 8-12-0 J Shortt, ... (12 to 1) 5
1555 IRISH LIGHT (Ire) 6-12-0 G M O'Neill, ... (20 to 1) 6
2661[7] PEGUS PRINCE (Ire) 5-11-4 (3*) T J O'Sullivan, ... (20 to 1) 7
3789 MAJOR BERT (Ire) 6-11-7 (7*) Mr T J Murphy, ... (50 to 1) 8
3709 ORMOND BEACH (Ire) 5-11-7 W T Slattery Jnr, ... (50 to 1) 9
3731 DUNBOY CASTLE (Ire) 6-11-9 (5*) K P Gaule, ... (8 to 1) ur
GORTALOUGH 12-12-0 L P Cusack, ... (33 to 1) pu
2075[6] INCA CHIEF 10-12-0 F Woods, ... (9 to 2) pu
3789 KILLIMOR LAD (bl) 7-11-9 (5*) J P Broderick, ... (20 to 1) pu
1897 PRINCE THEO 7-11-9 (5*) P A Roche, ... (16 to 1) pu
3449 DANGOAR 5-11-7 F J Flood, ... (8 to 1) pu
Dist: 9l, 14l, 4l, 2l. 5m 38.50s. (15 Ran).
(W J Purcell), A P O'Brien

3873 Niall Brosnan & Co. Solicitors Handicap Chase (0-102 4-y-o and up) £3,452 2m........................(7:25)

2922 MAKE ME AN ISLAND [-] 9-11-5 J F Titley, ... (6 to 1) 1
3467 BOG LEAF VI [-] (bl) 11-9-4 (3*) T J O'Sullivan, ... (10 to 1) 2
3273[5] BALLYCANN [-] 7-10-12 (3*) T J Mitchell, ... (8 to 1) 3
PARSONS SON [-] 9-11-3 S H O'Donovan, ... (14 to 1) 4
3524 TIRRY'S FRIEND [-] 12-10-0 (5*) M A Davey, ... (20 to 1) 5
3200[2] HIGHBABS [-] 8-10-4 T Horgan, ... (4 to 1) 6
2942[6] DEEP ISLE [-] 8-9-10 (5*) J P Broderick, ... (8 to 1) 7
FURLANA WONDER [-] 12-11-10 P Carberry, ... (14 to 1) 8
RIVERSTOWN LAD [-] 7-11-1 J P Banahan, ... (10 to 1) 9
3200[4] BALLYHEIGUE [-] 8-10-12 (3*) D P Murphy, ... (5 to 1) 10
3241[7] BLACKPOOL BRIDGE [-] 9-11-0 (3*) D T Evans, (3 to 1 fav) ur
532 PORTLAND LAD [-] 9-10-4 (3*) Miss M Olivefalk, .. (33 to 1) pu
Dist: 10l, 3½l, 9l, 1½l. 4m 47.90s. (12 Ran).
(John A Mitchell), Patrick G Kelly

HEREFORD (good to firm)
Wednesday May 11th
Going Correction: MINUS 0.20 sec. per fur.

3874 Weobley Novices' Hurdle (4-y-o) £1,553 2m 3f 110yds............. (2:15)

3781[2] FORMAL AFFAIR 11-2 A Maguire, sn prmnt, chlgd 6th, led
nxt, drvn clr frm 3 out.............. (7 to 2 op 9 to 4) 1
3734[3] SMUGGLER'S POINT (USA) 11-7 D O'Sullivan, not fluent,
hld up, rcd wide, hit 3 out, styd on frm three out, not
rch wnr...... (13 to 8 on op 7 to 4 on tchd 6 to 4 on) 2
3770[2] UPWARD SURGE (Ire) 11-0 R Dunwoody, in tch 5th, led 6th
to nxt, styd on same pace frm 3 out. (5 to 1 op 4 to 1) 3
3713[6] APACHEE FLOWER 10-4 (5*) Guy Lewis, chsd ldrs till outpcd appr 3 out..................... (25 to 1 op 16 to 1) 4
2808[6] VELVET HEART (Ire) 11-2 S Burrough, led till aftr 1st, wknd
7th............................. (14 to 1 op 10 to 1) 5
3629 AUSTRAL JANE 10-9 B Powell, prmnt till wknd 7th.
.... (50 to 1 op 25 to 1) 6
3668[5] IMAGERY 10-9 L Harvey, sn beh, tld off whn pld up bef
last................................ (50 to 1 op 16 to 1) pu
3314 VAN DEN MAN 10-9 M Bosley, led second to 6th, tld off nxt, pld
up bef last....................... (100 to 1 op 50 to 1) pu
3353 FREE HANDOUT 10-9 S Earle, sn beh, tld off 6th, pld up
bef 7th.......................... (100 to 1 op 50 to 1) pu

Dist: 15l, 1¼l, 6l, 2½l, 4l. 4m 35.00s. a 14.00s (9 Ran).
(The Plough Partnership), D Nicholson

3875 Canon Pyon Handicap Chase (0-125 5-y-o and up) £2,840 3m 1f 110yds ....(2:45)

3681* NEARCO BAY (NZ) [112] 10-11-10 J R Kavanagh, in tch,
jmpd wl, led 12th to 14th, chlgd 3 out, rdn out.
.... (15 to 8 fav op 6 to 4 tchd 2 to 1) 1
3593[3] GLOVE PUPPET [100] 9-10-12 J Frost, hld up, pushed
alng 11th, chlgd 13th, led nxt, hdd aftr 3 out, rdn and
styd on one pace....... (15 to 2 op 6 to 1 tchd 8 to 1) 2
3636[2] BOBBY SOCKS [103] 8-11-1 A Maguire, chsd ldrs 8th, kpt
on one pace und pres frm 2 out.... (5 to 1 tchd 13 to 2) 3
3405 NEW HALEN [107] 13-10-12 (7*) Mr G Hogan, beh, hit 8th,
hdwy 14th, wknd 16th... (9 to 2 op 5 to 1 tchd 4 to 1) 4
3512[7] SIDE OF HILL [109] 9-11-7 R Dunwoody, prmnt, led second
to 5th, led 7th to 12th, sn wknd.
.... (5 to 1 op 4 to 1 tchd 11 to 2) 5
3631[4] NAUGHTY NICKY [89] 10-10-1 R Greene, al tld off.
.... (8 to 1 op 10 to 1) 6
3593[6] NOUGAT RUSSE [89] 13-10-1 D Bridgwater, led 5th to 7th,
styd chalg till blun 11th, sn beh, tld off whn pld up bef 3
out......................... (14 to 1 op 16 to 1 tchd 12 to 1) pu
3699[4] WOODLANDS GENHIRE [88] (v) 9-10-03 (3*) R Davis, led to
second, drpd rear tenth, sn tld off, pld up bef 2 out.
.... (25 to 1 op 20 to 1) pu
Dist: 3½l, 2l, 25l, hd, dist. 6m 11.40s. b 0.60s (8 Ran).
SR: 51/35/36/15/17/
(Queen Elizabeth), N J Henderson

3876 Holmer Selling Hurdle (4 & 5-y-o) £1,696 2m 3f 110yds...........(3:15)

3702[4] CRIMINAL RECORD (USA) (bl) 4-10-12 G McCourt, in tch,
rdn appr 7th, drvn to chal 3 out, bumped nxt, sn led,
driven out........................(5 to 1 op 7 to 1) 1
3632 REACH FOR GLORY 5-10-10 (7*) T Murphy, chsd ldrs, led 4
out, bumped 2 out, sn hdd, outpcd appr last.
.... (25 to 1 op 16 to 1) 2
3770* SOPHISM (USA) 5-11-10 R Dunwoody, hld up, shaken up
aftr 4 out, no response.
.... (5 to 4 on op 6 to 4 on tchd 11 to 10 on) 3
3716[7] FREDDIE JACK 4-10-12 S Burrough, chlgd, led aftr second
to 5th, led 7th to 4 out, wknd nxt, tld off.
.... (50 to 1 op 33 to 1) 4
3597 ARAGON MIST 5-10-12 M Bosley, beh 5th, blun nxt, tld
off whn pld up bef 3 out.......(100 to 1 op 33 to 1) pu
3552[2] AL FORAN (Ire) 4-11-5 D O'Sullivan, led till aftr second,
styd chalg till led 5th, hdd 7th, wkng in 3rd whn wnt
lme and pld up bef 2 out.
.... (13 to 8 op 5 to 4 tchd 7 to 4) pu
Dist: 5l, 4l, dist. 4m 40.60s. a 19.60s (6 Ran).
(Ed Weetman (Haulage & Storage) Ltd), W Clay

3877 Brockhampton Hunters' Chase (5-y-o and up) £1,341 3m 1f 110yds.... (3:45)

3563[5] KNOCKUMSHIN 11-12-2 (5*) Mr T Byrne, al in tch, mstk
12th, led nxt, lft clr 3 out, drvn out r-in.
.... (13 to 8 op 5 to 4 tchd 7 to 4) 1
3684* RUSTY BRIDGE 7-12-0 (7*) Mr R Johnson, led till aftr 11th,
outpcd 14th, staying on whn lft second 3 out, kpt on,
not rch wnr..................... (5 to 2 tchd 11 to 4) 2
3335 CURAHEEN BOY (bl) 14-12-0 (7*) Miss J Butler, prmnt, led
aftr 11th to 13th, mstk 15th, sn wknd, no ch whn mistake 4 out, tld off..................... (9 to 2 tchd 6 to 1) 3
3412 LATE SESSION (bl) 10-11-7 (7*) Miss L Blackford, blun 6th,
beh, blunded 11th, 4th and no ch whn tried to refuse
and uns rdr last, rmntd.
.... (50 to 1 op 33 to 1 tchd 66 to 1) 4
3717* CARRICKMINES 9-12-2 (5*) Mr T Jones, chlgd second to
4th, drpd rear 8th, in tch tenth, chasing wnr and staying on whn blun and uns rdr 3 out.
.... (6 to 4 fav op 5 to 4) ur
Dist: 3½l, dist, dist. 6m 22.80s. a 10.80s (5 Ran).
(Sidney J Smith), Sidney J Smith

3878 St Richards School Novices' Handicap Hurdle (0-100 4-y-o and up) £1,553 2m 1f...........................(4:15)

3829[2] DANGER BABY [78] 4-11-1 (3*) D Meredith, hdwy to track
ldrs 5th, styd on wl to chal last, drvn to ld cl hme.
.... (11 to 4 fav op 5 to 2 tchd 7 to 2) 1
3571 ROYAL GLINT [70] 5-10-7 (7*) R Davis, beh, rapid hdwy 4
out, led 2 out, rdn r-in, ct cl hme, lme.
.... (20 to 1 op 16 to 1) 2
3725* LLOYDS DREAM [78] 5-11-4 (7ex) G McCourt, hdwy 4th,
chsd ldrs 2 out, staying whn blun last, rallied and not
much room cl hme..............(11 to 1 op 7 to 1) 3
3476[8] FICHU (USA) [80] 6-11-6 B Powell, in tch, kpt on same
pace frm 2 out...................(14 to 1 op 10 to 1) 4
3623[9] SUPER SHARP (NZ) [70] 6-10-10 Jacqui Oliver, sn in tch,
led 5th to 2 out, soon rdn and btn.... (9 to 1 op 3 to 1) 5

3685⁹ BRIMPTON BERTIE [78] 5-11-4 G Upton, *hld up rear, some prog frm 2 out, not a dngr.*
.......................(14 to 1 op 12 to 1 tchd 16 to 1) 6
3511 PARISIAN [60] 9-9-11⁴ (7") A Lucas, *hdwy 5th, sn one pace.*
.......................(50 to 1 op 25 to 1) 7
3635 RUTH'S GAMBLE [76] (v) 6-10-9 (7") Mr B Pollock, *chsd ldrs to 5th.*.................(14 to 1 op 12 to 1 tchd 16 to 1) 8
3559² MISSED THE BOAT (Ire) [75] 4-11-1 Richard Guest, *nvr rch ldrs.*.................(10 to 1 op 8 to 1 tchd 14 to 1) 9
2545⁵ MAMALAMA [83] 6-11-9 D O'Sullivan, *chsd ldrs till wknd appr 3 out.*............................(12 to 1 op 7 to 1) 10
3685 KOBYRUN [70] 8-10-10 S Burrough, *effrt 4th, wknd nxt.*
.......................(20 to 1 tchd 33 to 1 and 12 to 1) 11
3008 MARANO [60] 6-10-0 I Lawrence, *led 4th to nxt, sn wknd.*
.......................(50 to 1 op 25 to 1) 12
3663 GEORGE LANE [70] 6-10-10 J Lodder, *prmnt till wknd 2 out, no ch whn f last.*...............(7 to 2 op 3 to 1) f
3685 IT'S DELICIOUS [72] 8-10-12 D Bridgwater, *led to 4th, sn wknd, tld off whn pld up bef 3 out.* (14 to 1 op 10 to 1) pu
Dist: Hd, ½l, 9l, 1¼l, 1l, 1¾l, 1½l, 2l, 2½l, 15l. 3m 51.50s. a 5.50s (14 Ran).

SR: 1/-/-/-/-/-/ (Mouse Racing), R Dickin

3879 Tillington Novices' Chase (5-y-o and up) £2,529 2m. ....(4:45)

3827³ UNHOLY ALLIANCE 7-11-12 J Osborne, *led second to 5th, outpcd 4 out, shaken up and hdwy to chase ldr 2 out, chlgd last, sn led, readily.*
.............(13 to 8 on op 7 to 4 on tchd 6 to 4 on) 1
3695² DAWN CHANCE 8-11-3 G McCourt, *led to second, led 5th, hrd drvn frm 3 out, hdd sn aftr last, one pace.*
.......................(9 to 2 op 7 to 2) 2
3758¹ VICTORY ANTHEM 8-11-9 I Lawrence, *chsd ldr 8th to 2 out, sn outpcd.*.....................(5 to 1 op 7 to 2) 3
1525⁵ PECCAVI 10-11-3 D Bridgwater, *beh 7th, moderate prog frm 3 out.*............................(10 to 1 op 7 to 1) 4
3706⁴ NORTHERN OPTIMIST 6-10-5 (7") Mr J L Llewellyn, *beh frm 3rd.*.......................(12 to 1 op 10 to 1) 5
LA BELLE DE SANTO (bl) 11-10-12 J Da Costa, *mstk 1st, sn beh, not fluent, tld off.*...........(66 to 1 op 25 to 1) 6
3490 BROOK COTTAGE (Ire) 6-11-3 T Wall, *jmpd poorly, sn tld off, pld up bef 6th.*.............(25 to 1 op 20 to 1) pu
Dist: 3½l, 8l, 20l, 3l, dist. 3m 52.00s. a 3.00s (7 Ran).

SR: 36/23/21/-/-/ (Mrs S C York), K C Bailey

3880 Grunwick Stakes National Hunt Flat Race (4,5,6-y-o) £1,570 2m 1f. ...(5:15)

SAGAMILL (USA) 6-11-5 Mr C Morlock, *hdwy 7 fs out, led 3 out, sn clr, easily.*.................(5 to 1 op 2 to 1) 1
3458 FREDDIE MUCK 4-10-7 (7") A Shakespeare, *pressed ldrs, led hfwy to 7 fs out, kpt on, no ch wth wnr frm 2 out.*
.............(7 to 2 op 6 to 1 tchd 7 to 1 and 3 to 1) 2
CLARE'S CHOICE 5-10-11 (3") A Procter, *sn in tch, chsd ldrs, no imprsn frm 3 fs out.*......(50 to 1 op 16 to 1) 3
3708⁴ GWEEBARRA BAY (Ire) 5-11-0 (5") R Darke, *prmnt, led 7 fs out to 3 out, sn one pace.* (9 to 2 op 7 to 2 tchd 5 to 1) 4
3101⁴ KALISKO (Fr) 4-11-7 Mr A Durkan, *hdwy to track ldrs 7 fs out, rdn 4 out, sn btn.*
.......................(7 to 4 fav tchd 6 to 4 and 9 to 4) 5
GENTLE JESTER 5-10-7 (7") Mr Richard White, *chsd ldrs till wknd 4 fs out.*...............(33 to 1 op 14 to 1) 6
PINXTON POPPY 4-10-9 Mr B Leavy, *in tch 11 fs.*
.......................(20 to 1 op 12 to 1) 7
3708⁹ GOING GREY 4-10-7 (7") N Willmington, *chsd ldrs 11 fs.*
.......................(50 to 1 op 16 to 1) 8
NICKY'S CHOICE 5-10-11 (3") T Jenks, *al beh.*
.......................(16 to 1 tchd 20 to 1) 9
SEE YOU FURST 4-10-7 (7") Mr G Hogan, *led aftr 4 fs, hdd hfwy, sn wknd.*.................(25 to 1 op 12 to 1) 10
GREENFIELD MAID (Ire) 5-11-0 Mrs S Bosley, *hmpd strt, al beh.*.......................(33 to 1 op 16 to 1) 11
GOLD NITE 6-10-7 (7") N Collum, *al beh.*
.......................(20 to 1 op 10 to 1) 12
SPANISH HERO 6-11-0 (5") S Fox, *slwly into strd, al beh.*
.......................(11 to 1 op 4 to 1 tchd 12 to 1) 13
3387 LULA RIDGE 4-10-6 (3") D Meredith, *led 4 fs, wknd hfwy.*
.......................(50 to 1 op 33 to 1) 14
Dist: 12l, 3½l, 1½l, 15l, 7l, 14l, hd, 6l, 6l, 8l. 3m 48.50s. (14 Ran).
(Raymond Tooth), N J Henderson

HUNTINGDON (good to firm)
Wednesday May 11th
Going Correction: MINUS 0.20 sec. per fur. (races 1,3,6), MINUS 0.35 (2,4,5)

3881 Ladies Evening Novices' Selling Handicap Hurdle (4,5,6-y-o) £1,891 2m 5f 110yds. ....(6:05)

3751² RIP THE CALICO (Ire) [58] 6-9-11 (7") Miss C Spearing, *al prmnt, led 7th, made rst, rdn out.*...........(3 to 1 jt-fav 5 to 2 tchd 7 to 2) 1

3697⁷ ARMASHOCKER [71] 6-11-3 V Smith, *hdwy hfwy, chsd wnr frm 2 out, no extr.*
.......................(13 to 2 op 7 to 1 tchd 8 to 1 and 6 to 1) 2
3089⁴ RASTA MAN [78] 6-11-10 G Bradley, *dwlt strt, hdwy appr 3 out, chlgd and rdr lost stick last, unbl to quicken.*
.......................(100 to 30 op 6 to 4 tchd 7 to 2) 3
LEGAL LEGACY [77] 6-11-9 Miss S White, *made most, hdd 7th, ran on one pace.* (14 to 1 op 6 to 1 tchd 16 to 1) 4
3153⁷ OMIDJOY (Ire) [58] 4-10-4 Gee Armytage, *al middle div, no hdwy.*.........(8 to 1 op 5 to 1 tchd 9 to 1) 5
3478 DAMCADA (Ire) [54] 6-10-0 W Marston, *chsd ldrs to 6th, grad lost pl.*........(3 to 1 jt-fav op 5 to 2 tchd 7 to 2) 6
3696⁸ WHATMORECANIASKFOR (Ire) [54] (bl) 6-9-9 (5") S Curran, *wth ldr to 4th, no ch frm 3 out.*
.......................(16 to 1 op 8 to 1 tchd 20 to 1) 7
3757 SAIF AL ADIL (Ire) [65] (bl) 5-10-11 O Pears, *beh frm 6th, tld off.*..................(33 to 1 op 20 to 1 tchd 50 to 1) 8
3342 ANNE CARTER [54] 7-10-0 M Ranger, *no ch whn mstk 6th, tld off when pld up bef last.*
.......................(50 to 1 op 33 to 1 tchd 50 to 1) pu
Dist: 5l, nk, 15l, 8l, 3½l, 10l, 6l. 5m 1.60s. a 6.60s (9 Ran).

(Alan Bucknall), J L Spearing

3882 Cambridge Evening News Novices' Handicap Chase (5-y-o and up) £2,591 2½m 110yds. ....(6:35)

3758² CROOKED COUNSEL [86] 8-11-6 N Williamson, *chsd ldrs, led 12th, drw clr appr 2 out, unchlgd.*
.......................(4 to 1 op 3 to 1 tchd 9 to 2 and 5 to 1) 1
3605⁷ SILENT CHANT [71] (v) 10-10-5 Gee Armytage, *some hdwy frm 12th, no ch wth wnr.*
.......................(14 to 1 op 8 to 1 tchd 16 to 1) 2
3757⁵ DEEP IN GREEK [66] (bl) 8-9-7 (7") Miss S Higgins, *chsd ldr to 11th, sn btn.*...............(33 to 1 op 20 to 1) 3
3847 MAGGOTS GREEN [76] 7-10-10 W Marston, *nvr trble ldrs, kpt on one pace.*...............(10 to 1 op 8 to 1) 4
3636¹ RYTON GUARD [87] (bl) 9-11-2 (5") D Leahy, *f 3rd.*
.......................(11 to 4 op 6 to 1) f
3639⁷ TEA-LADY (Ire) [67] 6-10-1¹ S McNeill, *beh whn f tenth.*
.......................(33 to 1) f
3754⁴ BILLHEAD [66] (bl) 8-9-11 (3") T Eley, *beh till pld up bef last.*...............(33 to 1 op 20 to 1) pu
3714 STAR ACTOR [90] 8-11-10 R Dunwoody, *prmnt to 7th, lost pl and pld up bef 12th.*..(9 to 2 op 3 to 1 tchd 5 to 1) pu
2063⁵ NO WORD [85] 7-11-5 A Maguire, *led to 12th, wknd 14th, btn whn pld up bef 2 out.*
.......................(5 to 2 fav op 8 to 1 tchd 3 to 1) pu
Dist: 12l, 6l, 12l. 4m 56.90s. a 1.90s (9 Ran).
SR: 1/-/-/-/-/-/ (I R Scott & D J MacFarlane), K C Bailey

3883 MacMillan Nurse Appeal Birthday Celebration Handicap Hurdle (0-125 4-y-o and up) £2,442 3¼m. .....(7:05)

3609¹ HAPPY HORSE (NZ) [116] 7-12-0 A Tory, *hld up, hdwy frm 8th, wth ldr whn lft in ld appr last, ran on.*
.......................(2 to 1 fav op 3 to 1 tchd 100 to 30 and 7 to 2) 1
3728² LEGAL BEAGLE [90] 7-10-2 M Perrett, *led to 3rd, settled dwn and hld up, ran on ag'n frm 3 out.*
.......................(7 to 2 op 4 to 1 tchd 9 to 2) 2
3640² CREWS CASTLE [88] (bl) 7-10-0 A Maguire, *led 3rd to 5th, ran on one pace frm 8.*............(8 to 1 op 6 to 1) 3
3728 MORE OF IT [90] (bl) 9-10-2 M A FitzGerald, *prmnt to hfwy, beh frm 9th, tld off.*..............(33 to 1) 4
3640¹ STRONG JOHN (Ire) [95] 6-10-7 M Hourigan, *led aftr 4th till hdd 9th, wknd quickly, tld off.*
.......................(9 to 2 op 4 to 1) 5
3760¹ WELSH SIREN [103] 8-11-1 (6ex) N Williamson, *hdwy frm 4th, led 9th, slight ld whn pld up bef last, lme.*
.......................(4 to 1 op 3 to 1) pu
3625⁶ COSMIC DANCER [103] (bl) 7-10-12 (3") P Hide, *al in rear, pld up lme bef 9th.*..............(8 to 1 op 6 to 1) pu
Dist: 10l, 30l, 15l, 12l. 6m 3.90s. a 2.90s (7 Ran).
SR: 19/-/-/-/ (Major Ian Manning), Mrs J Renfree-Barons

3884 Robert Lenton Memorial Hunters' Chase (5-y-o and up) £1,674 3m (7:35)

3558¹ ONCE STUNG 8-12-7 Mr J Greenall, *al chasing ldr, hrd rdn frm 2 out, led nr finish.*
.......................(11 to 10 fav op 6 to 5 tchd 5 to 4) 1
3521⁴ BLUE DANUBE (USA) 10-11-7 (7") Mr Andrew Martin, *chsd ldrs till led aftr 12th, made rst till hdd and no extr nr finish.*...............(4 to 1 op 7 to 2 tchd 9 to 2) 2
FINAL CHANT 13-11-9 (5") Mr R H Brown, *led till hdd aftr 12th, kpt on frm 2 out.*............(6 to 1 op 9 to 2) 3
ROYAL APPROVAL 11-11-7 (7") Miss D Stanhope, *al beh.*
.......................(9 to 2 op 4 to 1) 4
3501 RAMPALLION 11-12-0 (7") Mr S Blackwell, *hld up, hdwy frm 13th, 3rd and in tch whn f 3 out.* (5 to 2 op 7 to 2) f
Dist: ½l, 6l, 12l. 6m 5.10s. a 17.10s (5 Ran).

(J E Greenall), P Cheesbrough

3885 Brent Walker Leisure Services Handicap Chase (0-115 5-y-o and up) £3,626

2½m 110yds. . . . . (8:05)

3742⁴ GUILDWAY [87] (bl) 11-10-7 (7*) Mr M Rimell, *led appr 6th, made rst, ran on wl approaching 2 out.*
. . . . (9 to 1 op 5 to 1 tchd 10 to 1) 1

3532⁶ HICKELTON LAD [74] 10-10-1 R Dunwoody, *al prmnt, kpt on frm 2 out, no ch wth wnr.*
. . . .(3 to 1 op 5 to 2 tchd 7 to 2) 2

3636 COMETTI STAR [97] 10-11-10 B Dalton, *hld up, some hdwy frm 13th, not rch ldrs...*(8 to 1 op 10 to 1 tchd 7 to 1) 3

3742³ BARTONDALE [80] 9-10-7 N Williamson, *led till hdd appr 6th, chsd wnr till lost pl last.*
. . . . (12 to 1 op 10 to 1 tchd 14 to 1) 4

3695⁵ BALLAD RULER [80] 8-10-4 (3*) R Davis, *prmnt till wknd appr 2 out.* . . . . (20 to 1 op 12 to 1) 5

3784⁵ RED UNDER THE BED [96] 7-11-4 (5*) J Burke, *hld up, mstk and uns rdr 9th.*. . . . . . (10 to 1 op 8 to 1 tchd 12 to 1) ur

3742² DANDY MINSTREL [96] (bl) 10-11-9 D Bridgwater, *nvr gng wl, al beh, tld off whn pld up bef 2 out, broke blood vessel....*(7 to 4 fav op 6 to 4 tchd 2 to 1 and 9 to 4) pu

3537⁷ STEPFASTER [91] 9-11-4 A Maguire, *prmnt to 7th, sn lost pl, tld off whn pld up bef 2 out............*(8 to 1) pu

Dist: 20l, 9l, ½l, 30l. 4m 53.80s. b 1.20s (8 Ran).

SR: 26/-/7/-/-/ (Mark G Rimell), N A Twiston-Davies

3886 SPS Advertising Maiden Hurdle (4-y-o and up) £2,617 2m 110yds. . . . . . (8:35)

3630⁵ FOREST PRIDE (Ire) 5-10-9 N Williamson, *al prmnt, led 2 out, ran on wl.*
. . . .(8 to 1 op 5 to 1 tchd 9 to 1 and 10 to 1) 1

2749⁵ ACE PLAYER (NZ) 6-11-0 A Maguire, *al prmnt, led 3 out, hdd 2 out, unbl to quicken.*
. . . .(7 to 1 op 5 to 1 tchd 12 to 1 and 14 to 1) 2

3604⁸ MAN O MINE (Ire) 5-11-0 M Hourigan, *hdwy frm 4th, ran on wl from 2 out.*. . . . .(14 to 1 tchd 16 to 1) 3

3701² TRIPPIANO 4-10-9 T Kent, *al prmnt, in tch frm 3 out, ran on one pace.*. . . . . (4 to 1 fav op 7 to 4) 4

3629² EARLY DRINKER 6-10-11 (3*) J McCarthy, *al prmnt, no hdwy frm 3 out.* . . . .(10 to 1 op 5 to 1) 5

3745³ ASTERIX 6-11-0 R Dunwoody, *prmnt, unbl to quicken frm 2 out.* . . . . (6 to 1 op 8 to 1 tchd 10 to 1) 6

1460 NIGEL'S LUCKY GIRL 6-10-9 J McLaughlin, *chsd ldr till led aftr 5th, hdd one wl bhnd 3 out.* . . . . .(16 to 1 op 10 to 1) 7

3231² ARCTIC LIFE (Ire) 5-11-0 B Powell, *prmnt till wknd quickly appr last.*. . . . .(10 to 1 op 5 to 1) 8

3729⁸ MAJESTIC QUEEN 7-10-9 J Railton, *al abt mid-div.*
. . . .(33 to 1 op 16 to 1) 9

3696⁵ IVYCHURCH (USA) 8-10-7 (7*) Karen Cook, *prmnt till wknd appr 3 out.* . . . .(33 to 1 op 25 to 1) 10

3115 THE FUN OF IT 9-11-0 G Upton, *al in rear div, tld off.*
. . . .(33 to 1 op 20 to 1) 11

3729⁹ FERENS HALL 7-11-0 M A FitzGerald, *led till hdd aftr 5th, sn wknd, tld off.*. . . . .(33 to 1 op 20 to 1) 12

3700⁸ KEEP SAFE 4-10-4 M Ahern, *mid-div to hfwy, wknd, tld off.*. . . . .(33 to 1 op 25 to 1) 13

3314 DARING KING 4-10-9 V Smith, *nvr better than mid-div, tld off.*. . . . . (12 to 1 op 7 to 1 tchd 14 to 1) 14

1027 SUPERFORCE 7-10-9 (5*) S Curran, *refused to strt.*
. . . .(33 to 1 op 20 to 1) ref

3010⁴ DOMITOR'S LASS 7-10-9 Mrs N Ledger, *refused to strt.*
. . . .(33 to 1 op 20 to 1) ref

DRAWL (Ire) 6-10-11 (3*) D Meredith, *beh whn pld up bef 2 out.*. . . . . (33 to 1 op 20 to 1) pu

2262⁴ AXEL 7-11-0 M Richards, *prmnt to hfwy, beh whn pld up bef 3 out.*. . . . . (9 to 2 op 12 to 1) pu

MY TREASURE 4-9-11 (7*) L O'Hare, *slow to strt, al in rear, tld off whn pld up bef 5th...*(33 to 1 op 25 to 1) pu

MISTER RAINMAN 5-11-0 W McFarland, *beh till pld up bef 2 out.* . . . .(33 to 1 op 25 to 1) pu

Dist: 3l, ½l, 1l, sht-hd, 2½l, 11l, 4l, 6l, 1¾l, 10l. 3m 49.80s. a 2.80s (20 Ran).
SR: 20/22/21/15/20/17/1/2/-/ (I M S Racing), K C Bailey

KILLARNEY (IRE) ()
Wednesday May 11th

3887 Gabys Handicap Hurdle (0-116 4-y-o and up) £3,450 2¾m. . . . . (2:05)

3731² CALMOS [-] 7-11-2 C F Swan, ... (11 to 10 fav) 1
3840³ SIOBHAILIN DUBH (Ire) [-] 5-9-10 (5*) K P Gaule, . . .(8 to 1) 2
3840 SHANNON KNOCK [-] 9-10-8 P M Verling, ... (10 to 1) 3
3840⁶ CALL ME HENRY [-] 5-10-2 F Woods, ...(8 to 1) 4
3551³ PARSONS BRIG [-] (bl) 8-11-2 (5*) J P Broderick, . .(10 to 1) 5
3085 GOLDEN RAPPER [-] 9-10-5 J F Titley, ...(33 to 1) 6
3731 LEAVE IT TO JUDGE [-] 7-9-12 W T Slattery Jnr, . .(50 to 1) 7
3719 MASTER CRUSADER [-] 8-10-12 J Shortt, ...(20 to 1) 8
3506 PREMIER LEAP (Ire) [-] 5-9-9 (7*) B Fenton, ...(12 to 1) 9
3294⁵ MARIAN YEAR [-] 8-11-3 J Collins, ...(7 to 1) 10
3711⁴ PUNTERS BAR [-] 7-11-2 C O'Dwyer, ...(4 to 1) 11
3654⁷ SUPER MIDGE [-] 7-11-11 T Horgan, ...(10 to 1) 12
3526 ORANGE RAGUSA [-] 8-11-8 (3*) D T Evans, ...(33 to 1) 13

Dist: 2½l, 9l, 3l. 5m 48.20s. (13 Ran).

(G A Murphy), A P O'Brien

3888 Laurels Hunter Chase (5-y-o and up) £3,450 3m. . . . . (2:35)

3791* NATIVE VENTURE (Ire) 6-12-0 Mr E Bolger, ...(5 to 1) 1
3791² KILARA 7-11-1 (3*) Mr T Lombard, ...(9 to 2) 2
3791⁶ SOUTH OFTHE BORDER (bl) 8-10-6 (7*) Mr K O'Sullivan,
. . . .(10 to 1) 3
BUCKSFERN 7-11-4 Mr P Fenton, ...(15 to 8 fav) 4
3791⁵ TROPICAL GABRIEL (Ire) 6-11-4 Mr P J Healy, ...(14 to 1) 5
3791³ FAHA GIG (Ire) 5-10-9 (7*) Mr P R Crowley, ...(12 to 1) 6
YOUNG NIMROD 7-10-13 (5*) Mr J Berry, ...(12 to 1) 7
MENATURE (Ire) 5-10-4 (7*) Mr G F Ryan, ...(16 to 1) 8
3295 NORTHERN MOSS 7-11-4 Mr D M O'Brien, ...(40 to 1) 9
3652 HANDYFELLOW 9-11-7 (7*) Mr J T McNamara, ...(10 to 1) pu
BALLY MURPHY BOY 9-11-4 Mr A R Coonan, ...(50 to 1) pu
3527 GARRYLUCAS 8-10-11 (7*) Mr T J Murphy, ...(8 to 1) pu
3722* RED EXPRESS VI 9-11-9 (5*) Mr H F Cleary, ...(7 to 1) pu
5727 WALKERS LADY (Ire) 6-10-6 (7*) Mr D Keane, ...(33 to 1) pu
LIGHT ARGUMENT (Ire) (bl) 5-10-6 Mr M Phillips, (16 to 1) pu

Dist: 11l, 13l, 7l. 6m 48.30s. (15 Ran).

(Mrs Nora Corcoran), Patrick G Kelly

3889 Menvier Handicap Hurdle (0-109 4-y-o and up) £3,450 2m 1f. . . . . (3:05)

798 SOLBA (USA) [-] 5-11-7 G M O'Neill, ...(12 to 1) 1
3526² ONOMATOPOEIA (Ire) [-] 4-11-6 (5*) J R Barry, (5 to 2 fav) 2
3550² DARK SWAN (Ire) [-] 4-11-1 (5*) C P Dunne, ...(5 to 1) 3
3840⁷ DEGO DANCER [-] 7-11-0 P Carberry, ...(9 to 1) 4
3615 BACK TO BLACK (Ire) [-] 5-11-7 K F O'Brien, ...(4 to 1) 5
2917 RISKY GALORE [-] 4-10-0 (5*) M J Holbrook, ...(12 to 1) 6
3732² FINAWAY EXPRESS (Ire) [-] 5-10-8 (7*) P J Mulligan,
. . . .(11 to 2) 7
3647 THE WICKED CHICKEN (Ire) [-] 5-10-12 C F Swan, (4 to 1) pu
3290 STRUGGLING LASS (Ire) [-] 5-10-7 T Horgan, ...(25 to 1) pu

Dist: ½l, 7l, dist, 1½l. 4m 37.90s. (9 Ran).

(Three Counties Syndicate), Augustine Leahy

3890 Jefferson Smurfit Group Handicap Chase (0-116 4-y-o and up) £6,902 2¾m. . . . . (4:05)

3648 GALLEY GALE [-] 8-10-7 K F O'Brien, ...(12 to 1) 1
3649 MINISTER FOR FUN (Ire) [-] 6-11-10 C F Swan, (5 to 2 fav) 2
3649² TAWNEY FLAME [-] 8-11-2 J Magee, ...(7 to 2) 3
3790⁶ WHAT A MINSTREL [-] (bl) 8-9-4 (3*) T J O'Sullivan, (25 to 1) 4
3524 MACK A DAY [-] 7-11-1 P Carberry, ...(20 to 1) 5
3651⁷ LADY BAR [-] 7-12-0 P M Verling, ...(6 to 1) 6
3790⁴ ANOTHER GROUSE [-] 7-10-7 (3*) C O'Brien, ...(12 to 1) 7
3648 DEL MONTE BOY [-] 9-10-9 P Carberry, ...(10 to 1) 8
3873³ BALLYCANN [-] 7-9-13 (3*) T J Mitchell, ...(12 to 1) 9
3873 BLACKPOOL BRIDGE [-] 9-10-4 T Horgan, ...(12 to 1) 10
3648 GOLDEN CARRUTH (Ire) [-] 6-10-4 (5*) J P Broderick,
. . . .(14 to 1) ur
3648 THE REAL UNYOKE [-] 9-11-8 (3*) D P Murphy, ...(10 to 1) pu
3790⁵ WRECKLESS MAN [-] 7-11-0 J Shortt, ...(14 to 1) pu
3648 QUIET MONEY [-] 7-10-2 F Woods, ...(33 to 1) pu

Dist: 1½l, 15l, 10l. dist. 6m 13.30s. (14 Ran).

(J J Connolly), Daniel O'Connell

3891 Killarney Racegoers Club INH Flat Race (5-y-o) £3,450 2m 1f. . . . . . . (5:05)

CROSSFARNOGUE (Ire) 11-0 (7*) Mr T N Cloke, . . .(11 to 1) 1
CASTLE ARMS HOTEL (Ire) 11-0 (7*) Mr R P Cody, (12 to 1) 2
3653⁷ MR GLYNN (Ire) 11-7 (7*) Mr T J Murphy, ...(8 to 1) 3
3653 CAILIN GLAS (Ire) 10-9 (7*) Mr P M Dunne, ...(25 to 1) 4
GALBOOLA (Ire) 10-9 (7*) Mr K Whelan, ...(25 to 1) 5
THE NOBLE ROUGE (Ire) 11-7 Mr P Fenton, ...(10 to 1) 6
36 FIRST SET (USA) 10-13 (3*) Miss M Olivefalk, ...(10 to 1) 7
3508 DONWOOD (Ire) 11-2 Mr D M O'Brien, ...(16 to 1) 8
3653 MAHANKHALI (Ire) 11-7 Mr A J Martin, ...(20 to 1) 9
3550⁶ MY SUNNY WAY (Ire) 11-0 (7*) Mr D K Budds, ...(16 to 1) 10
3122³ POKONO TRAIL (Ire) 11-2 (5*) Mr H F Cleary, (2 to 1 jt-fav) 11
3792² HIGHLAND SUPREME (Ire) 11-7 Mr E Bolger, (2 to 1 jt-fav) pu
SUNKEN LADY (Ire) 10-9 (7*) Mr P English, ...(16 to 1) pu
3712 THE OSTRICH BLAKE (Ire) 11-2 Mr T Doyle, ...(11 to 1) pu
3469 MR BORIS (Ire) 11-0 (3*) Mr T Lombard, ...(20 to 1) pu
PREMIER WALK 11-0 (7*) Mr A Ryan, ...(20 to 1) pu

Dist: 12l, 9l, 4l. 4m 35.30s. (16 Ran).

(G Stafford), Patrick Day

PERTH (good to firm)
Wednesday May 11th
Going Correction: PLUS 0.10 sec. per fur.

3892 Tamdhu 10 Y.O. Single Malt Juvenile Maiden Hurdle (4-y-o) £1,882 2m 110yds. . . . . (6:35)

3553³ DIGNIFIED (Ire) 10-2 (7*) A Linton, *settled wth chasing grp, drw level aftr 3 out, sn led, styd on wl r-in.*
. . . .(5 to 2 op 4 to 1) 1

2564[7] MAMARA REEF (v) 10-4 (5*) P Waggott, *patiently rdn, trkd ldg 4 appr 3 out, kpt on r-in, not rch wnr.*
.... (13 to 2 op 5 to 1 tchd 7 to 1) 2
3536[6] COMMANCHE CREEK 10-11 (3*) A Larnach, *chsd ldg pair, effrt aftr 3 out, kpt on same pace frm nxt.*
.... (14 to 1 op 12 to 1) 3
3553 SUPREME SOVIET 11-0 A Dobbin, *chsd clr ldr, led bef 4 out, hdd and rdn aftr nxt, no extr.* (25 to 1 op 20 to 1) 4
3557[7] HOME PARK (Ire) 11-0 B Storey, *chsd ldg grp, effrt appr 3 out, rdn and one pace nxt.* .... (20 to 1 op 16 to 1) 5
2485 FANFOLD (Ire) 10-9 L O'Hara, *settled wth chasing grp, rdn 4 out, sn lost tch, tld off.* .... (100 to 1) 6
3429 MOSS PAGEANT 11-0 K Johnson, *sn clr ldr, drvn alng and hdd bef 4 out, fdd nxt, tld off.* .... (33 to 1) 7
3557 MAJOR JACK 11-0 T Reed, *chsd ldg grp, effrt and drvn alng appr 3 out, no imprsn whn bumped and f nxt.*
.... (33 to 1) f
3701[3] SABERAGE 10-2 (7*) B Harding, *not fluent, improved frm midfield appr 3 out, rdn and no imprsn whn hmpd and f nxt.*............... (2 to 1 fav op 6 to 4) f
3601 TO BE THE BEST 11-0 A Merrigan, *al beh, tld off whn pld up bef 2 out.*......................... (66 to 1) pu
578[2] GRANDERISE (Ire) 11-0 Mr D Swindlehurst, *sn struggling, tld off whn pld up bef 2 out.*....(9 to 1 op 12 to 1) pu
3601[4] FIRST RESERVE (v) 11-0 M Moloney, *in tch, rdn 4 out, tld off whn pld up bef 2 out.*........(20 to 1 op 33 to 1) pu
448[8] AMGANTY 10-9 K Jones, *al tld off, pld up bef 4 out.*
.... (66 to 1) pu
3778 MURDER MOSS (Ire) 11-0 Peter Hobbs, *struggling hfwy, tld off whn pld up bef 2 out.*...... (40 to 1 op 33 to 1) pu

Dist: 4l, 5l, 1¼l, 7l, dist, 15l. 3m 55.10s. a 11.10s (14 Ran).

(Mrs Linda Dyer), T Dyer

3893 Glengoyne 10 Y.O. Single Malt Maiden Chase (5-y-o and up) £2,721 2m............................(6:50)

3573[6] ALWAYS REMEMBER 7-11-6 Peter Hobbs, *chsd clr ldr, drw level aftr 5 out, led 2 out, ran on wl frm last.*
.... (4 to 1 op 3 to 1) 1
3786[3] CHIC AND ELITE 7-10-10 (5*) A Roche, *sn clr, blun 7th, reco'red wl, hdd 2 out, ran on same pace frm last.*
.... (6 to 4 fav op 2 to 1) 2
3577 SOUND PROFIT 6-11-1 T Reed, *chsd alng to go pace, improved frm off the pace 3 out, styd on wl, nrst finish.*
.... (50 to 1 op 33 to 1 tchd 66 to 1) 3
3708[6] ASHDREN 7-11-6 A Dobbin, *chsd ldg trio, effrt and drvn alng aftr 5 out, no imprsn nxt.*..... (14 to 1 op 12 to 1) 4
3758[3] HIGHLAND POACHER 7-11-1 (5*) Mr D McCain, *chsd ldg pair, hit 4th and nxt, struggling 5 out, tld off.*
.... (6 to 1 op 5 to 1 tchd 13 to 2) 5
3540[2] CASTLE CROSS 7-11-6 B Storey, *settled midfield, imprvg into 3rd whn f 5 out.*....................... (10 to 1) f
3540 DOLITINO 10-11-1 D Byrne, *al struggling, tld off whn pld up bef 3 out.*............................... (50 to 1) pu
3642[5] NORTHERN VISION 7-11-6 A Merrigan, *struggling in midfield 5th, tld off whn pld up bef 3 out.*
.... (33 to 1 op 25 to 1) pu
3460[2] PAKENHAM 8-11-6 N Doughty, *nvr gng pace, reminders 5th, tld off whn pld up bef 3 out...* (4 to 1 tchd 9 to 2) pu

Dist: 2l, 3½l, 20l, 20l. 4m 2.00s. a 11.00s (9 Ran).

(Mrs S C Cockshott), P J Hobbs

3894 Famous Grouse Handicap Chase (0-125 5-y-o and up) £3,189 2½m 110yds......................(7:20)

3577* RIVER PEARL 9-11-1 T Reed, *patiently rdn, hdwy frm off the pace 4 out, ridden to ld last 50 yards, kpt on.*
.... (7 to 1 op 8 to 1) 1
3239[5] DOWN THE ROAD [96] 7-10-8[2] N Doughty, *jmpd lft, led second, rdn and hdd last, kpt on one pace.*
.... (11 to 1 op 10 to 1 tchd 12 to 1) 2
3776* ALGARI [101] 7-10-6 (7*) B Harding, *settled gng wl, jnd ldrs aftr 4 out, slight ld last, hdd and no extr last 50 yards.*
.... (9 to 2 op 5 to 1 tchd 11 to 4) 3
3582 CHIASSO FORTE (Ity) [94] 11-10-6 L O'Hara, *settled off the pace, hdwy fnl circuit, effrt and rdn 4 out, kpt on same pace.*........................... (50 to 1) 4
3619[2] PIMS GUNNER (Ire) [96] 6-10-8 A Dobbin, *al hndy, ev ch 4 out, rdn nxt, no extr betw last 2...* (5 to 2 tchd 11 to 4) 5
3582* POTATO MAN [88] 8-9-9 (5*) F Perratt, *led to second, hndy till several mstks and fdd frm 4 out.*.......... (16 to 1) 6
3537[3] CORNET [112] (v) 8-11-10 M Dwyer, *chsd ldg trio, reminders 9th, mstks aftr, lost tch 4 out, tld off.*
.... (4 to 1 op 5 to 1) 7
3375[7] CHARMING GALE [92] 7-10-4 B Storey, *in tch, struggling whn pace quickened 6 out, tld off whn pld up bef 2 out.*................................... (9 to 1 op 8 to 1) pu

Dist: 1¼l, 1¼l, 3l, 2l, 7l, 30l. 5m 4.60s. a 6.60s (8 Ran).

SR: 42/33/36/26/26/11/5/-/ (Mrs A G Martin), L Lungo

3895 Bunnahabhain 12 Y.O. Single Malt Selling Handicap Hurdle (4-y-o and up) £2,316 3m 110yds.........(7:50)

3568[4] VALIANT DASH [84] 8-10-8 (5*) F Perratt, *dsptd ld, led 2 out, styd on strly r-in.*..............(7 to 1 tchd 8 to 1) 1
3738 IRISH FLASHER [81] 7-10-10 Peter Hobbs, *settled midfield, improved to join ldrs 4 out, disputing ld whn stumbled 2 out, rdn and one pace r-in.*
.... (6 to 1 op 5 to 1) 2
3568[2] CLASSIC STATEMENT [81] 8-10-7 (3*) A Larnach, *made most till hdd and rdn 2 out, kpt on same pace frm last.*
.... (3 to 1 fav tchd 7 to 2) 3
3786 MAYWORK [71] 7-9-7 (7*) G Lee, *patiently rdn, improved gng wl 4 out, effrt and ridden 2 out, one pace whn hit last.*.......................... (25 to 1 op 14 to 1) 4
3545 JIM BOWIE [71] 11-9-7 (7*) B Harding, *nvr far away, drvn alng 3 out, no extr betw last 2...* (25 to 1 op 33 to 1) 5
3568[5] HOTDIGGITY [78] 6-10-7 A Dobbin, *feeling pace and drvn alng appr 3 out, kpt on, nvr able to chal.*
.... (11 to 2 op 6 to 1 tchd 7 to 1) 6
3801 VOLCANIC DANCER (USA) [80] (v) 8-10-4 (5*) E Husband, *nvr far away, feeling pace and drvn alng 3 out, fdd.*
.... (33 to 1 op 25 to 1) 7
3584[2] SAOIRSE (Ire) [78] 6-10-0 (7*) M Molloy, *settled midfield, losing grnd whn mstk 8th, rdn and btn 4 out.*
.... (9 to 1 op 8 to 1 tchd 10 to 1) 8
3603 INTEGRITY BOY [80] (bl) 7-10-9 M Dwyer, *trkd ldrs, effrt hfwy, niggled alng appr 3 out, fdd.*
.... (8 to 1 op 7 to 1 tchd 9 to 1) 9
3690 HEY JOE [74] 7-10-3[3] K Jones, *chsd ldg grp, struggling whn pace quickened appr 3 out, sn btn.........* (66 to 1) 10
3673[5] GOLDEN REVERIE (USA) [75] 6-10-4 B Storey, *settled off the pace, effrt and pushed alng aftr one circuit, btn 4 out.*............................ (16 to 1 op 20 to 1) 11
2862 KNIGHTS (NZ) [99] 8-12-0 V Slattery, *wtd with, imprvg on ins whn not much room appr 6th, effrt nxt, feeling pace bef 3 out, sn btn.*........................(6 to 1 op 5 to 1) 12
3787[6] GLORIOUS HEIGHTS [72] 6-10-1[1] A Merrigan, *chsd ldg grp, effrt hfwy, lost tch 4 out, tld off.*............. (33 to 1) 13
GRANNY'S BAY [71] 11-9-9 (5*) A Roche, *chsd ldrs, wknd quickly hfwy, tld off whn pld up bef 4 out.*
.... (80 to 1 op 66 to 1) pu

Dist: 12l, hd, ¾l, 12l, 4l, 1½l, 1¾l, 8l, 5l, 2½l. 5m 55.80s. a 10.80s (14 Ran).

SR: 1/-/-/-/-/-/ (J S Goldie), J S Goldie

3896 Coopers & Lybrand Novices' Chase (5-y-o and up) £2,788 3m......(8:20)

3428 BRACKENFIELD 8-12-4 P Niven, *made all, jmpd wl, jnd fnl circuit, drw clr 2 out, easily.* (5 to 4 on ch Evens) 1
3532[3] KIWI VELOCITY (NZ) 7-11-3 Peter Hobbs, *not fluent, al hndy, jnd wnr fnl circuit, blun and no extr 2 out.*
.... (5 to 4 op 11 to 10 tchd 11 to 8) 2
3818[4] JUNIORS CHOICE 11-11-3 A Merrigan, *pressed wnr, mstk 7th, feeling pace 6 out, sn lost tch, tld off.*
.... (25 to 1 op 20 to 1 tchd 33 to 1) 3
3665 SNAPPIT (bl) 12-10-12 (5*) Mr D McCain, *al tld off.* (66 to 1) 4
3689[6] SAGARO BELLE 8-10-12 A Dobbin, *tld off till pld up bef 12th.*............................. (20 to 1 op 16 to 1) pu

Dist: 9l, dist, dist. 6m 14.60s. a 17.60s (5 Ran).

(Guy Faber), Mrs M Reveley

3897 Highland Park 12 Y.O. Single Malt Conditional Jockeys' Handicap Hurdle (0-110 4-y-o and up) £2,221 2m 110yds ....(8:50)

2371[5] ALL WELCOME [96] 7-11-10 (3*) G Lee, *nvr far away, lft in ld 4th, hrd pressed last 2, styd on wl r-in........* (5 to 1) 1
3801 LEGITIM [91] 5-11-5 (3*) G Tormey, *trkd ldrs, drw level and mstk 2 out, ran on und pres frm last.*
.... (13 to 2 op 6 to 1 tchd 7 to 1) 2
3617[3] WANZA [87] 4-11-4 S Lyons, *trkd ldr, hmpd 4th, rallied, struggling 3 out, btn betw last 2.*
.... (9 to 4 fav tchd 5 to 2) 3
3094[4] TYNRON DOON [74] (bl) 5-10-5 F Leahy, *chsd ldrs, chlgd 3 out, rdn and no extr aftr nxt........* (8 to 1 tchd 9 to 1) 4
3815[2] ASTRALEON (Ire) [86] 6-10-10 (7*) S Melrose, *patiently rdn, improved 3 out, ridden nxt, no response.*
.... (9 to 1 op 5 to 1) 5
3819[4] FAMILY LINE [97] 6-11-2 J Supple, *led till f 4th.*
.... (5 to 1 op 4 to 1 tchd 9 to 2) f
3570[5] FELL WARDEN [70] 6-10-1 A Larnach, *chasing ldrs whn f 3rd........................* (14 to 1 op 12 to 1) f
3584 GREEK CHIME (Ire) [75] 5-10-6 F Perratt, *refused to race, took no part........* (10 to 1 op 12 to 1 tchd 14 to 1) l

Dist: ½l, 9l, 1¾l, 12l. 3m 53.50s. a 9.50s (8 Ran).

SR: 21/15/2/-/-/ (Lionville Builders Ltd), Mrs M Reveley

SOUTHWELL (good to firm) Wednesday May 11th
Going Correction: MINUS 1.10 sec. per fur.

3898 Delaney Novices' Hurdle (4-y-o and up) £1,922 2m.................(2:25)

3499³ ISAIAH 5-11-9 T Kent, *made all, clr aftr 3 out, ran on wl whn pressed frm last.*
........................(6 to 5 on op 5 to 4 on tchd Evens) 1
1930 SHELLHOUSE (Ire) 6-11-2 N Williamson, *strted slwly, beh whn blun 3rd, steady hdwy frm 5th, ev ch when awkward last, ran on wl und pres....* (33 to 1 op 25 to 1) 2
3543² JEHOL 8-11-2 W Humphreys, *trkd unr, rdn aftr 2 out, one pace..................* (11 to 2 op 9 to 2) 3
3755² MAJAL (Ire) 5-11-11 (5*) P Midgley, *trkd ldrs, one pace frm 2 out.........* (1 to 2 op 9 to 2) 4
1675³ LADY DONOGHUE (USA) 5-11-4 P Niven, *trkd ldrs, blun 4 out, sn btn................* (7 to 2 tchd 4 to 1) 5
3755³ CREPT OUT (Ire) 5-11-2 Mr A Walton, *trkd ldrs, outpcd frm 3 out.......* (50 to 1 op 33 to 1) 6
3598⁶ CALL THE KING 5-11-2 M Ahern, *wtd wth in rear, no ch whn blun badly 3 out.........* (33 to 1 op 16 to 1) 7
GALLANT JACK 5-11-2 M A FitzGerald, *strted slwly, nvr on terms................* (25 to 1 op 20 to 1) 8
3756⁶ OLLIVER DUCKETT 5-11-2 C Hawkins, *hld up, hdwy 5th, btn aftr nxt, eased................* (33 to 1 op 20 to 1) 9
3095⁹ SUSSEX MAESTRO 4-10-11 M Crosse, *hld up, al beh, tld off...................* (50 to 1) 10

Dist: 1l, 12l, 5l, 20l, 2½l, 25l, hd, 5l. 3m 41.30s. 6 10.70s (10 Ran).

SR: 26/18/6/15/-/-/ (Mrs D MacRae), Mrs J Cecil

3899 Bassingham Selling Hurdle (4-y-o and up) £1,876 2¼m............(2:55)

3600⁴ CHADWICK'S GINGER 6-11-3 S Turner, *al prmnt, led aftr 3 out till hdd last, rallied und pres to ld ag'n cl hme.*
........................(11 to 2 op 9 to 2) 1
2065³ LAKE DOMINION 5-11-8 D Skyrme, *hld up in mid-div, cld 4 out, led last till hdd close hme, ran on wl.*
........................(11 to 10 fav op 5 to 4 tchd 6 to 1) 2
3864² RICHMOND (Ire) 6-11-8 D Wilkinson, *mid-div, pushed alng and hdwy 6th, styd on wl frm 3 out.* (6 to 1 op 7 to 2) 3
3584⁶ SEPTEMBER SAND 6-10-11 J Railton, *drpd to last pl 5th, styd on wl appr 2 out, nvr nrr finish..........* (50 to 1) 4
3661 CAPITAL LAD 5-11-2 R Garritty, *hld up, took keen hold, led aftr 5th till aftr 3 out, wknd.*
........................(13 to 2 op 25 to 1) 5
2061³ SILK DYNASTY 8-10-13 (3*) S Wynne, *hld up in rear, hdwy appr 3 out, wknd nxt.*
........................(12 to 1 op 8 to 1 tchd 14 to 1) 6
3635 THEYDON PRIDE 5-11-2 M Ahern, *led til hdd aftr 5th, wkng whn mstk 3 out.......................*(50 to 1) 7
3769 LAVALIGHT 7-12-0 A Tory, *wth ldr till wknd aftr 6th.*
........................(8 to 1 op 6 to 1 tchd 10 to 1) 8
3635⁷ POINT TAKEN (USA) 7-10-9 (7*) A Large, *drpd rear 5th, nvr on terms...............*(12 to 1 op 10 to 1) 9
3661 CHAGHATAI (USA) (bl) 8-11-5 (3*) T Eley, *hld up in tch, beh frm 6th...................*(8 to 1 op 7 to 1) 10
PAPER CRAFT 7-11-2 A S Smith, *hld up, cld 5th, wknd aftr nxt................*(8 to 1 op 14 to 1) 11
3509⁹ DALEHOUSE LANE 6-11-2 Gary Lyons, *prmnt, rdn alng and lost pl aftr 5th................*(33 to 1 op 25 to 1) 12

Dist: Sht-hd, 10l, 20l, 8l, 20l, sht-hd, 2½l, 10l, 6l, ¾l. 4m 20.70s. ɓ 0.30s (12 Ran).

(W H Tinning), W H Tinning

3900 Bilsthorpe Novices' Hunters' Chase (5-y-o and up) £1,423 3m 110yds (3:25)

3596⁶ CLARE MAN (Ire) 6-12-5 Mr J Greenall, *trkd ldrs, led 2 out, ran on wl...* (6 to 4 on op 5 to 4 on tchd 11 to 10 on) 1
KNOWE HEAD 10-11-7 (7*) Mr S Brisby, *trkd ldr, led 13th till hdd 2 out, btn whn hit last.*
........................(9 to 2 op 7 to 2 tchd 5 to 1) 2
RAGALOO (bl) 8-11-7 (7*) Mr L Lay, *hld up beh ldrs, blun 14th, sn outpcd, styd on to take modest 3rd r-in.*
........................(50 to 1 op 20 to 1) 3
HELLCATMUDWRESTLER 13-11-7 (7*) Miss T Gray, *led til hdd 13th, sn outpcd, tld off........*(12 to 1 op 6 to 1) 4+
LORD FAWSLEY 11-11-9 (5*) Mr G Tarry, *hld up in rear, tld off frm 14th.............*(4 to 1 op 3 to 1) 4+
IM PRIVILAGED (bl) 10-11-7 (7*) Mr D Bloor, *mstk 8th, tld off nxt, pld up aftr 12th.*
........................(12 to 1 op 14 to 1 tchd 33 to 1) pu
DUNSBROOK LAD 12-11-7 (7*) Mr B Crawford, *al beh, mstk 7th, tld off frm 4 out, pld up bef nxt.*
........................(25 to 1 op 16 to 1) pu

Dist: 8l, dist, 5l, dd-ht. 6m 13.00s. ɓ 15.00s (7 Ran).

(J E Greenall), Miss C Saunders

3901 Bathley Novices' Chase (5-y-o and up) £2,649 3m 110yds..............(3:55)

3750⁸ STRONG MEDICINE 7-12-2 N Williamson, *lft in ld 6th, clr appr 3 out, cmftbly................*(7 to 4 op 11 to 8) 1
3621 HIGHLAND RALLY (USA) 7-11-2 R Garritty, *chsd wnr frm 6th, no imprsn whn pckd 2 out....* (25 to 1 op 16 to 1) 2
3724⁵ LESBET 9-10-11 D Morris, *cl up til outpcd 9th, styd on appr 2 out......................*(14 to 1 op 8 to 1) 3
3750³ CRAIGSTOWN (Ire) 6-11-9 M Brennan, *trkd ldrs till wknd 4 out, styd on appr last.....................*(10 to 1) 4

3562 POLLERTON'S PRIDE (v) 7-10-11 M A FitzGerald, *in cl tch till lost pl 13th, rallied 16th, sn outpcd.*
........................(15 to 2 op 10 to 1 tchd 11 to 1) 5
DOVEDONS GRACE 8-11-2 H Taylor, *al beh.*
........................(20 to 1 op 16 to 1 tchd 25 to 1) 6
3278⁵ HOW DOUDO 7-10-11 R Bellamy, *cl up, awkward 4th, drpd rear tenth, tld off.*
........................(16 to 1 op 10 to 1 tchd 20 to 1) 7
3750² LOBRIC (bl) 9-11-2 S Smith Eccles, *led til f 6th, dead.*
........................(13 to 8 fav op 5 to 4) f

Dist: 8l, 2l, 2½l, 12l, 2½l, 25l. 6m 14.20s. ɓ 16.20s (8 Ran).

(Dr D B A Silk), K C Bailey

3902 Thorp Handicap Chase (0-115 5-y-o and up) £3,435 2m...............(4:25)

3553⁷ STAY AWAKE [102] 8-11-1 N Williamson, *hld up, mstk 5th, hdwy aftr 4 out, led appr last, ran on wl.*
........................(5 to 1 op 7 to 1) 1
3754* HOWGILL [90] 8-10-0 (3*,6ex) S Wynne, *trkd ldrs, lft in ld aftr 7th, hdd appr last, no extr.*
........................(100 to 30 fav op 3 to 1 tchd 4 to 1) 2
3607⁵ CAMPSEA-ASH [105] 10-11-4 M Hourigan, *hld up, trkd ldrs frm 6th, wknd quickly appr 3 out.*
........................(9 to 2 op 5 to 2 tchd 5 to 1) 3
3633³ STARLAP [98] 10-10-11 A Maguire, *mstk second, chsd ldrs, hmpd 7th, sn outpcd.............*(20 to 1 op 16 to 1) 4
3595⁸ TRY ME NOW [87] 8-9-8¹ (7*) P Ward, *chsd ldrs, mstk 5th, outpcd frm 7th.............*(20 to 1 op 16 to 1) 5
3667² WINGSPAN (USA) [115] 10-11-7 (7*) Mr M Rimell, *wth ldr, stumbled and uns rdr aftr 7th.*
........................(5 to 1 op 11 to 2 tchd 7 to 1) ur
3667⁴ MURPHY [90] 10-10-12 M Richards, *led til hdd aftr 7th, blun 9th, pld up bef nxt.*
........................(6 to 1 op 5 to 1 tchd 6 to 1) pu
3667⁶ GREENHEART [110] 11-11-9 Mr P Bull, *blun badly 3rd, beh whn pld up bef 9th................*(50 to 1 op 20 to 1) pu
3667* COTAPAXI [96] 9-10-9 A Tory, *beh 7th, tld off whn pld up bef 3 out................*(11 to 2 op 4 to 1 tchd 7 to 1) pu

Dist: 1¾l, 20l, 6l, 15l. 3m 51.30s. ɓ 7.70s (9 Ran).

(Austin Donnellon), Mrs M Reveley

3903 Moorhouse Novices' Hurdle (4-y-o and up) £1,953 2½m 110yds.....(4:55)

3756² BIGWHEEL BILL (Ire) 8-11-2 N Williamson, *made most to 3rd, led ag'n 5th, made rst, rdn and ran on wl whn pressed frm 2 out.......................* 1
3637* THE PRUSSIAN (USA) 8-11-9 J Ryan, *trkd ldrs, jnd wnr 2 out, one pace appr last.................*(6 to 5 op 5 to 4) 2
3580³ THE CHANGELING (Ire) 5-11-9 R J Beggan, *chsd ldrs, lost pl 7th, hdwy 3 out, no imprsn whn hit 2 out.*
........................(9 to 4 fav op 5 to 2 tchd 3 to 1) 3
3308 SCOTTISH BALL 5-10-11 M Crosse, *mid-div, mstk 4th, hdwy aftr 3 out, styd on wl................*(16 to 1) 4
3685² ROCA MURADA (Ire) 5-11-2 A Maguire, *hld up in rear, clsg whn mstk 3 out, sn no extr.*
........................(100 to 30 op 5 to 2 tchd 7 to 2) 5
3800⁴ HOLD YOUR HAT ON 5-11-2 D Wilkinson, *hld up in rear, effrt 4 out, sn no imprsn.*
........................(6 to 1 op 11 to 2 tchd 7 to 1) 6
3597⁷ COUNTRY PARSON (Ire) 5-11-2 R Bellamy, *mid-div till lost pl appr 7th............*(14 to 1 op 10 to 1 tchd 16 to 1) 7
3637⁵ FLAPPING FREDA (Ire) 6-10-11 R Dunwoody, *trkd ldrs, rdn aftr 3 out, btn quickly............*(12 to 1 op 8 to 1) 8
3454 FATHER FORTUNE 6-10-13 (3*) J McCarthy, *chsd ldrs till wknd appr 3 out...............*(12 to 1 op 8 to 1) 9
3800 RORY JOHN (bl) 6-11-2 Mr C Mulhall, *racd freely, led briefly aftr 1st and ag'n frm 3rd to 5th, drpd rear 7th, tld off.*
........................(50 to 1 op 33 to 1) 10
LOUGH KENT (Ire) 6-11-2 M A FitzGerald, *hld up in rear, no ch whn pld up bef 2 out........*(25 to 1 op 20 to 1) pu
3637 CLAYDONS MONTY 5-11-2 M Hourigan, *tld off 6th, pld up bef 8th...............*(33 to 1 op 25 to 1) pu

Dist: 8l, 2l, 6l, 8l, 5l, 7l, 2½l, 15l, dist. 4m 48.70s. ɓ 4.80s (12 Ran).

(H J W Steckmest), G A Pritchard-Gordon

3904 Kelham Handicap Hurdle (0-115 4-y-o and up) £2,057 2m..........(5:25)

3063 DESERT FORCE [86] (bl) 5-10-5 M Richards, *cl up, led 4 out, pushed alng appr 2 out, ran on wl frm last.*
........................(7 to 1 op 6 to 1 tchd 8 to 1) 1
3773 AL SKEET (USA) [81] 8-9-11 (3*) M McCarthy, *hld up in tch, hdwy frm 3 out, styd on wl frm last.*
........................(14 to 1 op 12 to 1) 2
3819² ANY DREAM WOULD DO [90] 5-10-9 C Hawkins, *trkd ldrs, rdn alng aftr 4th, staying on whn blun 2 out, one pace und pres..............*(13 to 2 op 7 to 1 tchd 7 to 1) 3
3594² SALMAN (USA) [96] 8-11-1 N Williamson, *hld up, cld 6th, gng wl 3 out, sn rdn, btn whn blun 2 out.*
........................(7 to 1 op 6 to 1 tchd 8 to 1) 4
3755³ SAYMORE [99] 8-11-1 (3*) S Wynne, *chsd ldrs, hrd rdn appr 2 out, wl outpcd...........*(7 to 1 op 8 to 1) 5
3773* SOVEREIGN NICHE (Ire) [95] (v) 6-11-0 (6ex) R Dunwoody, *led til hdd 6th, sn hrd rdn, eased whn btn.*
........................(Evens fav op 5 to 4 tchd 11 to 8) 6

3619 HIRAM B BIRDBATH [97] (bl) 8-10-9 (7*) T Becton, *in cl tch till wknd appr 4 out*..............(33 to 1 op 16 to 1) 7
3754² WEEKLY CROSS (Ire) [85] 6-10-4 A Maguire, *hld up, al beh*... 8
3311² MISS MARIGOLD [109] (bl) 5-12-0 A Tory, *refused to race.* ....(8 to 1 op 7 to 1 tchd 9 to 1) ref
3618 BUD'S BET (Ire) [89] 6-10-8 S Turner, *lost tch 5th, pld up bef nxt*.. pu
Dist: 5l, 1l, 12l, ½l, 15l, 2½l, 2l. 3m 38.50s. a 13.50s (10 Ran).
SR: 36/26/34/28/30/11/10/-/-/   (J Naughton), R J Weaver

PERTH (good to firm)
Thursday May 12th
Going Correction: PLUS 0.10 sec. per fur.

3905 Interpart Maiden Hurdle (4-y-o and up) £2,039 3m 110yds.............(1:50)

2326⁵ GLANDALANE LADY 5-10-7 (7*) R McGrath, *patiently rdn, improved frm 4 out, chlgd last, styd on grimly to ld last strd*...................(11 to 2 op 5 to 1 tchd 6 to 1) 1
3498⁸ EMRAL MISS 6-11-0 N Doughty, *chsd clr ldr, led bef 4 out, rdn and stumbled 2 out, jst ct*......(11 to 9 op 8 to 1) 2
3690⁴ MISS PIMPERNEL 4-10-7 L O'Hara, *wiated wth, improved frm midfield aftr 4 out, switchd to chal r-in, ran on und pres*..(20 to 1) 3
2008 STEPDAUGHTER 8-11-0 C Dennis, *settled midfield, improved to join issue 4 out, rdn last, kpt on one pace.* ....(33 to 1) 4
3687⁵ GERMAN LEGEND 4-10-12 A Merrigan, *settled gng wl, smooth hdwy to track ldrs aftr 4 out, rdn after nxt, no extr*....................(16 to 1 op 25 to 1 tchd 33 to 1) 5
3102 HURRICANE LINDA 7-11-0 J Callaghan, *settled to track ldrs, feeling pace appr 3 out, btn bef nxt*......(14 to 1) 6
3674⁴ MARIYDA (Ire) 5-11-0 A Maguire, *not fluent, tucked away in midfield, ev ch 4 out, rdn nxt, sn btn*. ....(7 to 2 fav op 3 to 1) 7
3598⁴ STONEY BROOK 6-11-5 B Storey, *in tch for o'r a circuit, struggling bef 3 out, tld off*.
.................................(4 to 1 op 9 to 2 tchd 5 to 1) 8
NORTHERN NIKKI 7-10-7 (7*) S McDougall, *al wl beh, tld off aftr one circuit*.....................(100 to 1) 9
BY THE BYE 7-11-0 M Moloney, *beh whn blun and uns rdr bef second*..................(200 to 1 op 100 to 1) ur
3815 BDOORE (Ire) 6-10-9 (5*) A Roche, *in tch for a circuit, tld off whn pld up bef 4 out*.....(33 to 1 op 25 to 1) pu
3600² MISS JEDD (bl) 7-10-9 (5*) J Burke, *mstks, midfield whn blun 8th, pld up bef nxt*..........(8 to 1 tchd 9 to 1) pu
3778 BECK COTTAGE (bl) 6-11-5 P Niven, *racd freely, clr ldr till hdd bef 4 out, wknd quickly and pld up appr nxt.* ....(9 to 1 op 8 to 1) pu
HULA 6-11-0 (5*) F Perratt, *slow strter, al wl tld off, pld up bef 2 out*.....................................(100 to 1) pu
3565⁴ LITTLE FREDDIE 5-11-5 R Dunwoody, *trkd ldrs, ev ch appr 4 out, wknd quickly nxt, pld up bef 2 out.* ....(9 to 1 op 8 to 1 tchd 10 to 1) pu
RUN HECTOR (Ire) 6-11-5 S Turner, *chsd ldrs for o'r a circuit, lost tch quickly and pld up bef 3 out.* ....(33 to 1 op 25 to 1) pu
DRYDERDALE 5-11-5 K Jones, *beh whn pld up bef 6th.* ....(100 to 1) pu
Dist: Sht-hd, hd, 1¼l, 12l, 20l, nk, 20l, dist. 5m 59.50s. a 14.50s (17 Ran).
                                   (Mrs M O'Neill), J J O'Neill

3906 Rhone-Poulenc Povral Novices' Chase (5-y-o and up) £3,087 2½m 110yds....................(2:20)

3642* BEAUCADEAU 8-11-10 A Dobbin, *al hndy, jmpd ahead 4 out, clr whn mstk last, eased finish.* ....(6 to 5 fav op 11 to 10 tchd 5 to 4) 1
2511⁴ GLEMOT (Ire) 6-12-1 A Maguire, *tried to make all, blun 4th, bad mstk and hdd four out, one pace frm 3 out.* ....(13 to 8 op 5 to 4 tchd 7 to 4) 2
3569² THE COUNTRY TRADER 8-11-10 N Doughty, *wth ldrs, hit 3rd, feeling pace and reminders 8th (water), rdn and one pace frm 3 out*.........(12 to 1 op 10 to 1) 3
3577² SUPER SANDY 7-11-0 P Niven, *dsptd ld to hfwy, hrd at work to hold pl 4 out, sn btn*.......(6 to 1 tchd 7 to 1) 4
3577⁶ HAMANAKA (USA) 6-11-0 Mr S Love, *not jump wl, struggling in last pl whn pld up aftr 7th.* ....(100 to 1 op 66 to 1) pu
Dist: 2½l, 9l, 10l. 5m 11.50s. a 13.50s (5 Ran).
                                   (T A Barnes), M A Barnes

3907 MacDonalds Solicitors Quick Ransom Novices' Hurdle (4-y-o and up) £2,246 2m 110yds....................(2:55)

3539 THISTLE PRINCESS 5-10-2 (7*) B Harding, *nvr far away, nosed ahead aftr 3 out, rdn out frm last.* ....(5 to 1 op 6 to 1 tchd 8 to 1 and 9 to 1) 1
3641⁵ FREE TRANSFER (Ire) 5-11-2 (5*) J Burke, *patiently rdn, improved frm midfield to join issue 3 out, kpt on same pace frm last*.........(8 to 1 op 6 to 1 tchd 9 to 1) 2

3815⁴ EMERALD CHARM (Ire) 6-10-9 R Dunwoody, *settled gng wl, improved to join ldrs 3 out, rdn and not quicken frm last*...................................(5 to 1 op 4 to 1) 3
NODFORMS INFERNO 5-11-0 Peter Hobbs, *wtd wth, improved frm midfield appr 3 out, effrt betw last 2, one pace*.................................(6 to 1 op 5 to 1) 4
1356⁸ SHAYNA MAIDEL 5-10-9 L O'Hara, *settled midfield, improved appr 3 out, rdn aftr nxt, one pace.* ....(50 to 1 op 33 to 1) 5
3674⁵ KERNEL GRAIN (Ire) 5-10-7 (7*) M Molloy, *patiently rdn, improved to track ldg bunch aftr 3 out, fdd betw last 2.* ....(20 to 1 op 12 to 1) 6
YOUNG GALA 5-10-9 K Jones, *chsd ldg bunch, struggling to hold pl 4 out, outpcd frm nxt*.......(200 to 1) 7
BROUGHPARK JASMIN 5-10-9 (5*) A Roche, *chsd ldrs, hrd at work bef 4 out, fdd*...........(25 to 1 op 20 to 1) 8
3688⁷ GLASTONDALE 8-11-0 A Merrigan, *chsd ldg pair to hfwy, lost tch frm 4 out, tld off*.......(66 to 1 op 50 to 1) 9
3570² THREE STRONG (Ire) 5-11-0 A Maguire, *tried to make all, hit 4 out, hdd aftr nxt, wknd quickly and f last, dead.* ....(11 to 10 fav op Evens) f
3179 HIGH BURNSHOT 7-11-0 B Storey, *wth ldr to hfwy, lost pl frm 4 out, tld off un pld up betw last 2.* ....(33 to 1 op 25 to 1 tchd 40 to 1) pu
3074 SHORE LANE 5-11-0 Mr Robert Robinson, *in tch, struggling to keep up hfwy, tld off whn pld up betw last 2.* ....(100 to 1) pu
SPECTRE BROWN 4-10-2 (7*) R McGrath, *struggling to go pace hfwy, tld off whn pld up betw last 2*....(200 to 1) pu
Dist: 1¼l, 1¾l, nk, 2½l, 12l, 20l, sht-hd, 3l. 3m 56.00s. a 12.00s (13 Ran).
                                   (Joseph A Gordon), G Richards

3908 Curzon Heating Components Handicap Chase (0-120 5-y-o and up) £3,217 3m....................(3:25)

3437* MORGANS HARBOUR [108] 8-11-10 P Niven, *patiently rdn, improved to draw level 4 out, led 2 out, easily.* ....(2 to 1 fav tchd 5 to 2) 1
3622 JESTERS PROSPECT [103] 10-11-5 B Storey, *al wl plcd, led aftr tenth (water), jnd 4 out, hdd 2 out, one pace.* ....(33 to 1) 2
3554* CAPITAL PUNISHMENT [95] 8-10-11 R Garritty, *trkd ldrs, effrt appr 4 out, rdn alng bef nxt, one pace*...(4 to 1) 3
3814³ ZAM BEE [96] 8-10-12⁴ N Doughty, *wth ldr, ev ch appr 4 out, rdn and not quicken frm nxt*...(7 to 1 op 6 to 1) 4
3814 GATHERING TIME [97] 8-10-13 A Maguire, *ran in snatches, lost pl hfwy, styd on ag'n frm 3 out*.
....(20 to 1 op 16 to 1) 5
3644⁵ FISH QUAY [84] 11-9-7 (7*) Miss S Lamb, *wth ldr, lft in ld appr 5th, hdd aftr tenth (water), outpcd frm 4 out.* ....(12 to 1 op 16 to 1) 6
3814* CAROUSEL ROCKET [100] 11-11-2 (6ex) A Dobbin, *niggled alng most of way, lost grnd aftr one circuit, rdn and no imprsn frm 3 out*...............(10 to 1 op 6 to 1) 7
3814² ON THE HOOCH [92] 9-10-8 Mr J Bradburne, *trkd ldrs, pushed alng fnl circuit, 6th and fdg whn blun and uns rdr 5th.*................................(6 to 1 op 5 to 1) ur
3784² LAPIAFFE [89] 10-10-5 R Dunwoody, *led till pld up appr 5th*..................................(6 to 1) pu
Dist: 8l, ½l, 3l, 1½l, 3l, 8l. 6m 12.30s. a 15.30s (9 Ran).
                                   (P C W Owen), Mrs M Reveley

3909 Linlithgow & Stirlingshire Hunt Novices' Hunters' Chase (5-y-o and up) £2,355 2½m 110yds............(3:55)

UNOR (Fr) 8-11-9 (5*) Mr J M Dun, *jmpd wl, chsd clr ldr, led aftr 8th (water), styd on strly frm 3 out, easily.* ....(13 to 8 fav op 7 to 4 tchd 6 to 4 and 2 to 1) 1
MARSHALSTONESWOOD 9-11-7 (7*) Miss A Bowie, *patiently rdn, improved to track wnr fnl circuit, blun and rdr lost reins 3 out, kpt on same pace frm nxt.* ....(6 to 1 op 7 to 1) 2
AMBER PAYNE 10-11-9 (5*) Mr R Hale, *outpcd and sn wl beh, no imprsn fnl circuit*......(20 to 1 op 16 to 1) 3
LINN FALLS 9-11-2 (7*) Mrs V Jackson, *al struggling in rear, tld off thrght*................(3 to 1 op 5 to 2) 4
JOHNNIE REGGIE 8-11-7 (7*) Miss J Percy, *chsd ldrs for a circuit, sn struggling, tld off*....(100 to 1 op 66 to 1) 5
DERRY PRINCESS 8-11-2 (7*) Mr Robert Robinson, *wtd wth, early mstks, improve to join ldr whn blun and uns rdr 9th*...............................(7 to 1 tchd 8 to 1) ur
STONE ROW (Ire) 6-11-7 (7*) Mr T Scott, *set fst pace for a circuit, hdd aftr 8th, blun and uns rdr nxt.* ....(4 to 1 tchd 9 to 2) ur
Dist: 7l, dist, 8l, 20l. 5m 9.00s. a 11.00s (7 Ran).
SR: 11/4/-/-/-/   (Miss H B Hamilton), P Wilson

3910 Spring Fling Handicap Hurdle (0-120 4-y-o and up) £2,676 2½m 110yds....................(4:25)

3555⁸ MANGROVE MIST (Ire) [83] 6-10-0 A Dobbin, *nvr far away, jnd ldr gng wl 3 out, led nxt, clr last.* ....(12 to 1 tchd 14 to 1) 1

3673* BUCKRA MELLISUGA [98] 10-11-1 A Maguire, *al hndy, led*
4 out, jnd nxt, hdd 2 out, one pace.
.... (5 to 2 op 2 to 1 tchd 11 to 4)   2
1680* MYSTIC MEMORY [107] 5-11-10 P Niven, *patiently rdn,*
improved hfwy, feeling pace bef 3 out, not pace to chal.
...... (11 to 10 on op Evens tchd 11 to 10 and 5 to 4)   3
3578⁵ GREY MERLIN [83] 7-9-9 (5*) F Perratt, *dictated pace till*
hdd 4 out, rdn alng frm nxt, fdd...(66 to 1 op 50 to 1)   4
3541⁸ TRUMP [86] 5-10-3 B Storey, *trkd ldrs, feeling pace and*
drvn alng aftr 6th, no imprsn after.
.... (9 to 1 op 6 to 1 tchd 10 to 1)   5
NATIVE CROWN (Ire) [93] 6-10-10 L O'Hara, *wth ldrs, rdn*
frm 3 out, sn lost tch... (8 to 1 op 5 to 1 tchd 10 to 1)   6
Dist: 6l, 6l, 8l, 2½l, 15l. 4m 55.40s. a 10.40s (6 Ran).
SR: -/-/-/-/   (Coupar Capital Racing), P Monteith

TIPPERARY (IRE) (heavy)
Thursday May 12th

3911 Chestnut Novice Chase (4-y-o and up) £2,762 2½m................. (7:00)

3366⁷ DADDY LONG LEGGS 7-11-10 K F O'Brien, ... (9 to 4 fav)   1
3789⁵ ZVORNIK 7-11-5 (5*) P A Roche, ...(7 to 1)   2
3836 LOSHIAN (Ire) 5-10-12 T Horgan, ...(7 to 1)   3
3551⁹ HIGH-SPEC 8-11-7 (3*) C O'Brien, ...(12 to 1)   4
BARAVARD (Ire) 6-11-10 C O'Dwyer, ...(14 to 1)   5
2918⁵ GO GO GALLANT (Ire) 5-11-3 G M O'Neill, ...(13 to 2)   6
3709³ WINTERBOURNE ABBAS (Ire) 5-11-3 B Sheridan, ..(7 to 2)   7
881⁶ RUFO'S COUP 7-11-5 (5*) D Walsh, ...(14 to 1)   f
3835 MONKS AIR 7-11-0 (5*) Mr W M O'Sullivan, ...(10 to 1)   f
3198 BAR LASS 7-11-2 (3*) D P Murphy, ...(25 to 1)   ur
234 RED FOUNTAIN (Ire) 5-11-3 D H O'Connor, ...(25 to 1)   pu
Dist: 5l, dist, 13l, dist. 5m 25.00s. (11 Ran).

(Miss D Keating), J T R Dreaper

3912 Gowla Breeders International Mares Series Final (4-y-o and up) £4,142 2½m.......................... (8:00)

ROYAL GREENWOOD (Ire) 5-11-6 (7*) Mr E Norris, (7 to 1)   1
RAISE AN ACE 7-12-0 Mr P J Healy, ...(20 to 1)   2
GRACEMARIE KATE (Ire) 5-11-10 (3*) Mr T Lombard,
....(5 to 1)   3
3720³ RAMPANT ROSIE (Ire) 6-11-7 (7*) Mr G F Ryan, ...(8 to 1)   4
BLACKBERRY ROAD (Ire) 4-10-12 (7*) Mr F McGirr,
....(9 to 4 fav)   5
3370 COUNTESS MARK 7-11-7 (7*) Mr M Brennan, ...(20 to 1)   6
MORE BUBBLES 8-11-7 (7*) Mr M Greaney, ...(20 to 1)   7
MRS HUSHABYE (Ire) 5-11-6 (7*) Miss L Townsley, (16 to 1)   8
535 ROSCEEN BUI (Ire) 5-11-6 (7*) Mr T J Murphy, ...(12 to 1)   9
CLODAGH RIVER (Ire) 5-11-10 (3*) Mr J A Nash, ..(16 to 1)   10
JOYNEY 7-11-9 (5*) Mr P M Kelly, ...(20 to 1)   11
STRONG MARY (Ire) 5-11-13 Mr P Fenton, ...(8 to 1)   12
71 TYARA 8-11-7 (7*) Mr D Murphy, ...(20 to 1)   13
3552⁴ THRESA-ANITA (Ire) 6-11-7 (7*) Mr B Hassett, ...(5 to 1)   14
343⁵ HAZEL PARK 6-11-7 (7*) Mr P Henley, ...(14 to 1)   15
71 MARIENS TREASURE (Ire) 5-11-10 (3*) Mr D Marnane,
....(25 to 1)   16
HILARY'S IMAGE (Ire) 5-11-13 Mr A J Martin, ...(10 to 1)   17
AUNTIE PRICKLE PIN (Ire) 6-12-0 Mr A R Coonan, (16 to 1)   18
SPEAK OF THE DEVIL (Ire) 7-11-7 (7*) Mr R P Cody, ..(14 to 1)   pu
Dist: Dist, 10l, 10l, 9l. 5m 39.80s. (19 Ran).

(John M Dunford), David J McGrath

3913 Beech INH Flat Race (5-y-o and up) £2,762 2m..................... (8:30)

3712² GROUND WAR 7-11-11 (7*) Mr P English, ... (5 to 4 fav)   1
ORIENTAL SUNSET (Ire) 5-11-3 (7*) Mr B Hassett, (14 to 1)   2
3712⁷ DROICHEAD LAPEEN 7-11-11 (7*) Mr T J Beattie, (10 to 1)   3
CROHANE QUAY (Ire) 5-11-7 (3*) Mr J A Nash, ...(12 to 1)   4
3712 BUSTHAT 7-11-11 (7*) Mr E Norris, ...(7 to 1)   5
709 PRIORITY GALE (Ire) 5-10-12 (7*) Mr J Connolly, ..(16 to 1)   6
3712⁵ COLLEEN'S BELLE (Ire) 6-11-10 (3*) Mr D Valentine, (8 to 1)   7
3712 DON'T ASK JOHNNY (Ire) 5-10-12 (7*) Mr Sean O'Brien,
....(14 to 1)   8
3528⁴ LISCAHILL HIGHWAY 7-11-4 (7*) Mr P Carey, ...(14 to 1)   9
708 TIME UP (Ire) 6-11-11 Mr A J Martin, ...(33 to 1)   10
GOODBOY JOE (Ire) 5-11-3 (7*) Miss M Tulett, ...(20 to 1)   11
CELTIC GALE 7-11-6 (7*) Mr D Delaney, ...(33 to 1)   12
3450* CAPITAL ROSE (Ire) 5-11-7 (5*) Mr H F Cleary, ...(5 to 1)   13
3730 MOOREFIELD GIRL (Ire) 5-11-5 (7*) Miss F M Crowley,
....(10 to 1)   14
3327 FOUR MOONS (Ire) 5-11-7 Mr D L Bolger, ...(16 to 1)   15
FORABBY (Ire) 5-11-3 (7*) Mr K Dempsey, ...(33 to 1)   16
3505⁸ RUSHEEN BAY (Ire) 5-11-3 (7*) Mr A Daly, ...(20 to 1)   17
3788 CLON CAW (Ire) 6-11-4 (7*) Mr M Brennan, ...(33 to 1)   18
3082⁵ SPEAK OF THE DEVIL 7-11-11 (7*) Mr D McDonnell,
....(16 to 1)   su
Dist: 7l, 3½l, 6l, nk. 4m 29.90s. (19 Ran).

(K Dwan), Kevin Dwan

NEWTON ABBOT (good to firm)

Friday May 13th
Going Correction: PLUS 0.30 sec. per fur.

3914 Aegon Financial Services Novices' Hurdle (5-y-o and up) £1,948 2m 1f
....(6:00)

2802 TIME WON'T WAIT (Ire) 5-11-0 J Railton, *wtd wth in tch,*
hdwy 5th, led 2 out, rdn and wnt lft r-in, jst hld on.
.... (25 to 1 op 14 to 1 tchd 33 to 1)   1
3767² CASPIAN BELUGA 6-11-0 S Burrough, *led, quickened*
appr 5th, rdn and hdd 2 out, rallied r-in.
.... (11 to 2 op 4 to 1 tchd 6 to 1)   2
3826³ JOHNS JOY 9-11-0 D O'Sullivan, *hld up in tch, wnt sec-*
ond briefly 5th, kpt on one pace 2 out.
.... (50 to 1 op 16 to 1)   3
3809² SMART IN SABLE (v) 7-10-9 M Richards, *hld up, hdwy 5th,*
one pace appr 2 out... (6 to 1 op 4 to 1 tchd 7 to 1)   4
3597¹ THE CAUMRUE (Ire) 6-11-7 J Frost, *hld up, hdwy to go*
second 3 out, rdn and wknd bef nxt.........(9 to 4 jt-
fav op 7 to 4 tchd 3 to 1)   5
3714⁵ LUCAYAN GOLD 10-11-0 R Greene, *not jump wl, al in*
rear......................(50 to 1 op 16 to 1)   6
3257⁷ NEARLY AT SEA 5-10-2 (7*) Mr L Jefford, *al beh, tld off frm*
5th........................(66 to 1 op 25 to 1)   7
3670³ VITAL WONDER 6-11-0 P Holley, *chsd ldr till wknd*
quickly 3 out.............(13 to 2 op 9 to 2 tchd 7 to 1)   8
3670⁵ MR SUNNYSIDE 8-10-9 (5*) R Darke, *al beh, tld off frm*
5th.........................(20 to 1 op 10 to 1)   9
3628* BROWNED OFF 5-11-7 D Bridgwater, *nvr gng wl, effrt 3*
out, sn btn, pld up bef nxt.................(9 to 4 jt-
fav op 3 to 1 tchd 7 to 2 and 2 to 1)   pu
Dist: Nk, 4l, nk, 6l, 13l, 9l, 2½l, 6l. 4m 1.10s. a 11.10s (10 Ran).
SR: 26/25/21/15/21/1/   (Old Berks Partnership), R T Phillips

3915 Netherton Novices' Selling Hurdle (4,5,6-y-o) £1,956 2m 1f........(6:25)

3451⁴ MILZIG (USA) 5-11-7 D O'Sullivan, *hld up, gd hdwy on*
outsd appr 2 out, rdn and ran on wl to ld r-in.
.................(3 to 1 jt-fav op 2 to 1 tchd 100 to 30)   1
3826¹ NORTHERN TRIAL (USA) (v) 6-11-7 M A FitzGerald, *chsd*
ldrs, rdn to ld 2 out, hdd und pres r-in.
..................................(5 to 1 op 7 to 2)   2
3668² VALIANTHE (USA) (bl) 6-11-0 R Dunwoody, *hld up towards*
rear, hdwy 3 out, ev ch and mstk nxt, one pace.
.................(3 to 1 jt-fav op 2 to 1 tchd 9 to 2)   3
3765¹ TENDRESSE (Ire) 5-10-2 G McCourt, *hld up in tch, hdwy*
appr 5th, one pace frm 2 out.........(11 to 2 op 4 to 1)   4
3632⁷ MY SISTER LUCY (bl) 4-10-10 S Burrough, *chsd ldr to 4th,*
rdn appr 3 out, wknd.
.... (16 to 1 op 10 to 1 tchd 20 to 1)   5
3684⁴ COOCHIE (bl) 5-11-2 L Harvey, *hld up in rear, rdn appr*
5th, nvr on terms.................(12 to 1 op 10 to 1)   6
FAIR ENCHANTRESS 6-10-9 R Greene, *al prmnt, chsd ldr*
frm 4th, hit nxt, wknd aftr 3 out...(20 to 1 op 16 to 1)   7
3572³ IRISH DOMINION 4-10-8 S Earle, *al beh, tld off frm 3 out.*
.... (7 to 1 op 10 to 1 tchd 8 to 1)   8
3765² WALID'S PRINCESS (Ire) (bl) 4-9-12 (5*) R Darke, *al beh, lost*
tch 3 out, tld off..........(7 to 1 op 6 to 1 tchd 9 to 1)   9
3576 DONTDRESSFORDINNER 4-10-8 S McNeill, *led till rdn,*
hdd and f 2 out....................(33 to 1 op 16 to 1)   f
Dist: ¾l, 4l, 4l, 3l, 3½l, 1¼l, 14l, 2l. 4m 8.60s. a 18.60s (10 Ran).
(Jack Joseph), R J O'Sullivan

3916 M & B Marquees Handicap Chase (5-y-o and up) £2,827 2m 5f.......(6:55)

3766* ERRANT KNIGHT [124] 10-11-3 (5ex) R Dunwoody, *rcd*
keenly, tucked in beh ldrs and al gng wl, quickened to
ld 2 out, sn clr, eased r-in..........(Evens fav op 6 to 5)   1
3830* GHOFAR [125] (bl) 11-11-4 (5ex) P Holley, *made most till*
hdd 2 out, kpt on one pace.........(5 to 2 op 9 to 4)   2
3772⁴ FAR SENIOR [135] 8-12-0 Mr M Armytage, *jmpd wl, dsptd*
ld most of way till outpcd appr 2 out.
.... (9 to 1 op 9 to 2 tchd 10 to 1)   3
3753* DRUMSTICK [134] 8-11-13 (5ex) J Railton, *hld up in rear,*
took clr order 6th, outpcd six out, rdn appr 3 out, one
pace...................(5 to 2 op 6 to 4 tchd 11 to 4)   4
3671⁶ TIJUCA [108] 15-10-11 W McFarland, *ran in snatches, not*
fluent, lost tch 6 out, tld off whn pld up bef 2 out, lme.
.... (66 to 1 op 33 to 1)   pu
Dist: 2½l, 2½l, 3l. 5m 11.60s. a 11.60s (5 Ran).
SR: 36/34/41/37/-/   (Mrs N J Bird), M C Pipe

3917 J C Milton Electrical Novices' Handicap Hurdle (4-y-o and up) £2,379 2¾m
....(7:25)

3629³ DEVIOSITY (USA) [69] 7-10-9 M A FitzGerald, *hld up in tch,*
rdn to ld sn aftr 3 out, drvn out.
.... (9 to 2 op 4 to 1 tchd 5 to 1)   1
3629⁸ GLADYS EMMANUEL [76] 7-10-9 (7*) P McLoughlin, *hld up,*
hdwy 3 out, rdn ran on to go second r-in.
.... (16 to 1 op 12 to 1)   2

3716[4] CONVOY [84] 4-11-10 G McCourt, *al prmnt, dsptd ld frm 3 out till wknd appr last, fnshd lme.* (16 to 1 op 10 to 1) 3
3716[2] NANQUIDNO [68] (v) 4-10-8 R Dunwoody, *al rear, gd hdwy 4 out, rdn appr 2 out, one pace.*
....(8 to 1 op 6 to 1) 4
3671[2] BOLD STREET BLUES [77] 7-11-3 L Harvey, *hld up, hdwy 4 out, rdn and wknd appr 2 out...* (10 to 1 tchd 11 to 1) 5
3804[4] TAKE A FLYER (Ire) [67] 4-10-7 A Tory, *al prmnt, led 4 out, hdd sn aftr nxt, wknd.* (9 to 1 op 7 to 1 tchd 10 to 1) 6
3713[5] AMILLIONMEMORIES [68] 4-10-4[1] (5") D Matthews, *al mid-div, outpcd frm 3 out...............* (10 to 1 op 8 to 1) 7
3632[3] KOA [69] 4-10-9 D Bridgwater, *al in rear, tld off.*
....(12 to 1 op 10 to 1) 8
3629 TREGURTHA [70] 8-10-10 R Greene, *in tch till wknd 4 out, tld off................................*(20 to 1 op 16 to 1) 9
3769[3] MAYFIELD PARK [75] 9-10-8 (7") Mr G Hogan, *mid-div, rdn appr 4 out, sn beh, tld off whn pld up bef 2 out.*
....(5 to 1 op 4 to 1) pu
3804 YAAFOOR (USA) [69] (v) 5-10-9 M Richards, *led, mstk, hit 5th, hdd 4 out, wknd quickly, pld up bef 2 out.*
....(25 to 1 op 20 to 1) pu
3337[3] KEMMY DARLING [63] (bl) 7-10-3 M Ahern, *chsd ldr to 4 out, sn wknd, pld up bef last, lme.*
....(14 to 1 op 7 to 1 tchd 16 to 1) pu
3715[2] MR WILBUR [78] 8-11-4 J Frost, *al beh, tld off whn pld up aftr 6th, broke blood vessel.........* (10 to 1 op 7 to 1) pu
3729[7] MAKING TIME [70] 7-10-10 I Lawrence, *al beh, tld off whn pld up sn aftr 3 out...............* (33 to 1 op 20 to 1) pu
Dist: 2½l, 3½l, 3½l, 5l, 2½l, 5l, 20l, 12l. 5m 18.30s. a 19.30s (14 Ran).

(Mrs S L Hooper), N G Ayliffe

3918 End Of Spring Hunters' Chase (5-y-o and up) £1,830 3¼m 110yds.....(7:55)

SPRING FUN 11-11-7 (7") Mr M G Miller, *hld up, outpcd 9th, hdwy to go second 6 out, led sn aftr 4 out, ran on.*
....(9 to 4 op 8 to 1 tchd 10 to 1) 1
3717[5] ABBOTSHAM 9-11-0 (7") Mr I Widdicombe, *hld up, hdwy aftr 6th, wnt second appr 3 out, rdn and kpt on one pace..* (9 to 4 op 2 to 1) 2
KHATTAF 10-11-0 (7") Miss J Cumings, *chsd ldr to 6 out, rdn 4 out, one pace.* (2 to 1 fav op 6 to 4 tchd 5 to 2) 3
BUSTEELE 10-11-0 (7") Mr Richard White, *in rear, styd on frm 5 out, nvr dngrs.*
....(100 to 30 op 3 to 1 tchd 11 to 4 and 7 to 2) 4
3854[5] CHANNEL PASTIME 10-11-0 (7") Mr G Hogan, *led, clr 11th, jmpd rght frequently aftr, blun 4 out, sn hdd and wknd...*(16 to 1 op 12 to 1) 5
3768[6] BOGAZKOY 12-11-0 (7") Miss J Southcombe, *chsd ldrs till wknd 5 out, tld off...............* (33 to 1 op 20 to 1) 6
DANNY'S LUCK (NZ) 12-11-2[2] (7") Mr R Payne, *in tch till wknd 5 out, tld off...* (14 to 1 op 20 to 1 tchd 25 to 1) 7
3768[3] COLD MARBLE (USA) 9-11-9[9] (7") Mr A Oliver, *in rear, f 13th...* (33 to 1 op 25 to 1) f
Dist: 3½l, 11l, 10l, 2½l, 1¼l, 20l. 6m 51.30s. a 31.30s (8 Ran).

(David Young), David Young

3919 Pleasure Prints Handicap Hurdle (0-125 4-y-o and up) £2,766 2¾m (8:25)

3804[2] GRATUITY [82] 9-10-3 N Mann, *led aftr second, hrd rdn and hdd briefly last, rallied gmely, all out.* (11 to 4 jt-fav op 5 to 1) 1
3535[2] SURCOAT [96] 7-11-3 L Harvey, *hld up in rear, drvn alng and hdwy 4 out, wnt second appr 2 out, led briefly last, no extr nr finish...........................*(11 to 4 jt-fav op 5 to 1 tchd 7 to 4 and 3 to 1) 2
3769[2] BOOTSCRAPER [92] 7-10-13 G McCourt, *trkd ldrs, wnt second appr 4 out, rdn and wknd approaching 2 out.
....*(8 to 1 op 6 to 1) 3
3769* ANTI MATTER [92] 9-10-13 (7ex) M A FitzGerald, *hld up in mid-div, outpcd 6th, kpt on one pace aftr 3 out.
....*(5 to 1 op 4 to 1 tchd 11 to 2) 4
3672[4] CORRIN HILL [92] 7-10-13 R Dunwoody, *al beh, lost tch 4 out..............................* (8 to 1 op 7 to 1 tchd 10 to 1) 5
3845 TOUCH OF WINTER [103] (bl) 8-11-10 S McNeill, *led till aftr second, prmnt till wknd quickly 4 out.
....*(7 to 1 op 4 to 1) 6
3760 MISS SIMONE [92] 8-10-13 D Bridgwater, *in tch, 3rd whn hit 4 out, wknd quickly.* (7 to 1 op 5 to 1 tchd 8 to 1) 7
3698[4] SOMERSET DANCER (USA) [96] 7-11-3 D O'Sullivan, *al beh, tld off................* (11 to 2 op 7 to 1 tchd 14 to 1) 8
3574 ALOSAILI [85] 7-10-6 M Stevens, *slwly away, al beh, tld off whn pld up bef 2 out.*
....(20 to 1 op 12 to 1 tchd 25 to 1) pu
Dist: ¾l, 14l, 4l, 15l, 12l, sht-hd, 13l. 5m 16.20s. a 17.20s (9 Ran).

(Mrs L Field), C R Barwell

STRATFORD (good)
Friday May 13th
Going Correction: MINUS 0.25 sec. per fur.

3920 Red Horse Vale Novices' Hunters' Chase (5-y-o and up) £1,904 3m (6:15)

3596* HERON'S ROCK 10-11-13 (7") Mr M Portman, *trkd ldr, led 5 out to 3 out, second and btn whn lft clr nxt.
....*(6 to 4 fav tchd 7 to 4 and 5 to 4) 1
JACK SOUND 8-11-7 (7") Mr J Jukes, *led to 5 out, wknd 3 out, lft poor second nxt.
....*(13 to 2 op 5 to 1 tchd 15 to 2) 2
RIVER GALAXY 11-11-7 (7") Mr R Lawther, *lost pl 11th, styd on one pace frm 5 out, lft remote 3rd 2 out.
....*(50 to 1 op 25 to 1) 3
FOURCEES 9-11-7 (7") Mr P Howse, *mstks, chsd ldrs to 11th, beh 5 out, lft poor 4th 2 out.*(50 to 1 tchd 25 to 1) 4
MAID TO MATCH 9-11-2 (7") Miss K Mobley, *cl up whn f 4th..........................*(5 to 2 tchd 3 to 1 and 9 to 4) f
CELTIC ABBEY 6-11-7 (7") Mr D S Jones, *trkd ldrs, led 3 out till f nxt.....................*(9 to 1 op 6 to 1) f
3824[4] BALLYMAC GIRL 6-11-2 (7") Mr R Johnson, *blun and uns rdr second.....................* (16 to 1 op 8 to 1) ur
INDIAN KNIGHT 9-12-0[5] (5") Mr T Mitchell, *hld up, pushed alng 5 out, sn beh, poor 3rd whn pld up and dis-mounted bef 2 out.................*(16 to 1 op 10 to 1) pu
Dist: 25l, 7l, 20l. 6m 10.20s. a 23.20s (8 Ran).

(M H B Portman), P R Chamings

3921 Sheldon Bosley Memorial Trophy Novices' Chase (6-y-o and up) £3,111 3m....................................(6:40)

3624 THEO'S FELLA 10-10-12 J R Kavanagh, *trkd ldr, led 12th to 5 out, led 2 out, hrd rdn, jst hld on, fnshd lme.
....*(9 to 1 op 16 to 1) 1
3624[3] BINKLEY (Fr) 8-10-13 (3") T Jenks, *hld up, chsd ldg pair frm 12th, rdn alng 4 out, chlgd r-in, not quicken nr finish...................................*(7 to 1 op 8 to 1 tchd 9 to 1) 2
3608 ASTINGS (Fr) 6-11-5 M Dwyer, *led to 12th, led 5 out to 2 out, rallied last, not quicken nr finish.
....*(5 to 2 tchd 3 to 1) 3
3575* OLD BRIG (bl) 8-11-5 J Lower, *trkd ldrs, outpcd aftr 6 out, lost tch nxt...........................* (8 to 1) 4
3750 MEKSHARP 7-10-7 (5") D Leahy, *lost pl 5th, sn pushed alng, beh 7 out.........................* (50 to 1) 5
3588[4] WAYWARD SAILOR 8-10-12 W Marston, *mstks, lost tch aftr 11th, tld off.................* (33 to 1 tchd 40 to 1) 6
3510 PECHE D'OR (bl) 10-10-5 (7") Mr M Rimell, *hld up, outpcd aftr 11th, tld off 5 out.........*(100 to 1 op 66 to 1) 7
3779* MELEAGRIS 10-11-5 A Maguire, *3rd whn f 5th.
....*(11 to 8 fav op 11 to 10 tchd 6 to 4) f
3744* JAY JAY'S VOYAGE 11-10-12 (7") Mr B Pollock, *mstks, lost tch 12th, tld off whn pld up bef 5 out.
....*(6 to 1 tchd 13 to 2) pu
3588 HORCUM 9-10-5 (7") K Davies, *mstks, reminders aftr 7th, tld off 13th, pld up bef 5 out................*(100 to 1) pu
Dist: Sht-hd, hd, 13l, 2½l, dist, 1¾l. 6m 3.20s. a 16.20s (10 Ran).

(Theo Waddington (UK) Ltd), G B Balding

3922 Pragnell Trophy Novices' Hurdle (4-y-o and up) £2,108 2¾m 110yds (7:10)

3620* FOREST FEATHER (Ire) 6-11-12 Peter Hobbs, *hld up, hdwy 4th, trkd ldrs, second whn mstk 2 out, sn led, styd on wl.......................*(14 to 1 op 5 to 2 tchd 3 to 1) 1
3555[3] SWEET NOBLE (Ire) 5-10-9 (5") F Leahy, *trkd ldrs, ev ch 2 out, rdn and not quicken appr last.
....*(14 to 1 op 10 to 1) 2
2651[3] THE BUD CLUB (Ire) 6-11-6 N Williamson, *prmnt, led 3 out till aftr nxt, btn whn mstk last.
....*(8 to 1 op 6 to 1 tchd 10 to 1) 3
3503[2] FORTUNES COURSE (Ire) 5-11-1 J R Kavanagh, *led to 3 out, rdn and styd on one pace.
....*(11 to 2 op 5 to 1 tchd 6 to 1) 4
3421[2] WELSH LUSTRE (Ire) 5-11-7 A Maguire, *chsd ldrs 5th, beh 3 out.............................* (4 to 1 op 3 to 1 tchd 9 to 2) 5
3778[2] GORTEERA 8-11-12 M Brennan, *hld up, hdwy and mstk 7th, 4th whn hit 3 out, sn wknd....*(6 to 1 op 3 to 1) 6
3666[2] PERCY THROWER 7-10-11 (3") T Jenks, *mid-div till wknd quickly aftr 7th, tld off.
....*(10 to 1 op 12 to 1 tchd 14 to 1) 7
SHE'S NO NUN 7-10-9 G Upton, *beh 6th, tld off 5 out.
....*(33 to 1 op 25 to 1) 8
3775 TRICYCLE (Ire) 5-11-0 W Humphreys, *lost tch aftr 6th, tld off whn pld up after nxt.....................*(100 to 1) pu
LITTLE MAHARANEE 7-10-9 B Powell, *mstks, al beh, tld off 6th, pld up aftr nxt...................* (100 to 1) pu
3680 DIAMOND LIGHT 7-11-0 R Bellamy, *lost tch 6th, tld off whn pld up aftr 4 out...................*(100 to 1) pu
3547[8] JUDY LINE 5-10-9 W Marston, *prmnt till lost pl aftr 5th, tld off nxt, pld up aftr 4 out.................*(66 to 1) pu
3458 GOLF WORLD (Ire) 5-10-9 G Bradley, *prmnt till wknd quickly aftr 6th, tld off whn pld up after 4 out.
....*(33 to 1 op 20 to 1) pu
Dist: 8l, 2l, 4l, 12l, 2l, dist, 25l. 5m 19.40s. a 7.40s (13 Ran).

(David Knox), C Weedon

3923 Roddy Baker Gold Cup Handicap Chase (0-145 5-y-o and up) £4,183 2m 5f 110yds.....................(7:40)

3705² MIDFIELDER [115] 8-11-3 Peter Hobbs, *trkd ldr, led aftr 8th to tenth, lft in ld nxt, drw clr after 3 out, unchlgd.*
.................................(7 to 4 fav tchd 6 to 4)   1
3683* SAN LORENZO (USA) [122] 6-11-10 N Williamson, *trkd ldrs, lft second 6 out, led nxt, wknd 4 out.* (3 to 1 op 9 to 4)   2
3483⁴ WELL BRIEFED [112] 7-11-0 B Powell, *led to 9th, led and ran out 6 out, continued, fnshd 3rd, disqualified.*
.................................(11 to 4 op 9 to 4)   3D
3500² LOVE ANEW (USA) [103] 9-10-5 A Maguire, *slwly away, reluctant to race, jmpd slowly 5th, blun 8th and pld up, destroyed.*............... (9 to 2 op 5 to 1 tchd 6 to 1)   pu
Dist: 20l. dist. 5m 24.60s. a 21.60s (4 Ran).

(Bournstream '6'), P J Hobbs

3924 Needham & James Handicap Hurdle (0-120 4-y-o and up) £2,472 2m 110yds
.................................(8:10)

3806³ WILL JAMES [90] (bl) 8-9-9 (5*) S Curran, *hld up, hdwy 5th, led 3 out to nxt, led appr last, rdn and held on nr finish.*.........................(10 to 1 op 12 to 1)   1
3743² SQUIRE YORK [96] 4-10-6 Richard Guest, *trkd ldrs, ev ch 3 out, rdn and rallied aftr last, styd on nr finish.*
.................................(13 to 2 op 6 to 1 tchd 7 to 1)   2
3670* TEEN JAY [103] (v) 4-10-13 J Osborne, *prmnt, led 2 out till appr nxt, rdn and wknd r-in, fnshd lme.*
.................................(3 to 1 fav op 7 to 2 tchd 4 to 1)   3
3806 CHEERFUL TIMES [93] 11-10-3 N Williamson, *hld up, pushed alng 3 out, styd on appr last, nrst finish.*
.................................(16 to 1 op 12 to 1 tchd 20 to 1)   4
3692³ BROWNSIDE BRIG [94] 9-10-4 A Maguire, *hld up, hdwy 5th, wnt 3rd aftr 2 out, sn wknd....* (11 to 2 op 5 to 1)   5
3736⁴ LONESOME TRAIN (USA) [114] 5-11-10 Peter Hobbs, *in tch, cl up and ev ch 3 out, sn rdn, wknd quickly.*
.................................(7 to 2 op 11 to 4)   6
3743* WINDWARD ARIOM [90] (bl) 8-10-0 (7ex) J R Kavanagh, *beh 4th, sn lost tch, no ch frm four out.*
.................................(9 to 1 tchd 10 to 1)   7
ZUCCHINI [90] 8-9-7 (7*) Mr J L Llewellyn, *pressed ldr, led 5th to nxt, rdn and wknd quickly aftr 2 out.*
.................................(16 to 1 op 33 to 1)   8
1143* HALLO MAM (Ire) [98] 5-10-8 M Brennan, *hld up, hdwy to chase ldrs aftr 5th, rdn and wknd quickly after 2 out.*
.................................(12 to 1 op 10 to 1)   9
1044 STRIDING EDGE [90] (v) 9-10-0 D Gallagher, *led to 5th, in tch till wknd quickly aftr 3 out.* (14 to 1 tchd 12 to 1) 10
Dist: 1l, 6l, sht-hd, nk, 25l, 15l, ½l, 2½l, 3l, 3l. 3.10s (10 Ran).
SR: /-/5/6/-/-/-/   (Mrs Jenny Melbourne), C J Drewe

3925 Oxhill Novices' Handicap Hurdle (0-100 4-y-o and up) £2,164 2m 110yds
.................................(8:40)

3476² HEDGEHOPPER (Ire) [94] 6-12-0 Peter Hobbs, *led chasing grp, blun 4th, led nxt, clr aftr 2 out, easily.*
.................................(9 to 2 fav op 6 to 1 tchd 13 to 2)   1
3700² MULLED ALE (Ire) [79] 4-10-13 J Osborne, *chsd ldrs, chased wnr and pres appr last, no imprsn.*
.................................(13 to 2 tchd 6 to 1 tchd 8 to 1)   2
3825³ TOOMUCH TOOSOON (Ire) [66] 6-9-9 (5*) S Curran, *chsd ldrs, cld and ev ch 3 out, wknd aftr nxt.*
.................................(13 to 10 tchd 8 to 1)   3
3597⁵ FIGHTING BRAVE [85] 7-11-5 N Williamson, *al hndy, outpcd aftr 3 out, no ch whn mstk last.* (13 to 2 op 5 to 1)   4
3800 DYNAMITE DAN [80] 6-11-0 R Garritty, *beh, hdwy 5th, wknd nxt.*.................(9 to 1 op 6 to 1 tchd 10 to 1)   5
3482⁶ WAMDHA (Ire) [78] 4-10-12 A S Smith, *chsd ldrs 3 out.*
.................................(10 to 1 op 12 to 1 tchd 8 to 1)   6
3700⁴ DON TICINO [75] 4-10-9 A Maguire, *led, sn clr, wknd and hdd 5th, soon lost pl.*.........(10 to 1 op 10 to 1)   7
3737⁷ HEART OF SPAIN [82] (v) 4-11-2 T Wall, *beh 4th.*
.................................(16 to 1 op 12 to 1 tchd 20 to 1)   8
2881⁶ MA BELLA LUNA [75] 5-10-9 A Charlton, *hmpd 4th, al beh.*
.................................(14 to 1 op 12 to 1 tchd 16 to 1)   9
WEST ORIENT [80] 9-11-0 V Slattery, *beh, cld on ldrs gng till 5th, f 3 out.*.........................(20 to 1 op 14 to 1)   f
1085⁴ SINGERS IMAGE [87] (v) 5-11-4 (3*) R Davis, *hld up rear, f 4th.*........... (12 to 1 op 7 to 1 tchd 14 to 1)   f
3034³ HAZEL CREST [80] 7-11-0 M Dwyer, *hld up mid-div, nig-gled alng appr 4th, sn lost pl, tld off whn pld up bef 2 out.*.........................(8 to 1 op 5 to 1)   pu
3663⁴ NEWHALL PRINCE [68] 6-9-11 (5*) D Leahy, *al beh, tld off whn pld up bef last.* (14 to 1 tchd 16 to 1 and 12 to 1)   pu
Dist: 6l, 15l, 4l, 25l, 2l, 5l, 11l, 4l. 3m 51.20s. a 2.20s (13 Ran).
SR: 37/16/-/3/-/-/   (David Knox), C Weedon

BANGOR (good to firm)
Saturday May 14th
Going Correction: MINUS 0.05 sec. per fur.

3926 Penycae Claiming Hurdle (4 - 7-y-o) £2,442 2½m.................(11:35)

3738³ GREAT MILL (bl) 7-11-13 N Williamson, *made all, clr betw last 2, unchlgd.*...............(3 to 1 tchd 4 to 1)   1

3337⁷ ON THE SAUCE (bl) 7-11-1 R Dunwoody, *al wl plcd, chsd wnr appr 2 out, no imprsn.......* (5 to 4 fav op 7 to 4)   2
3635 SANTA PONSA BAY 7-11-2 J Railton, *wtd wth, took clr order hfwy, styd on one pace frm 2 out.*
.................................(25 to 1 op 20 to 1)   3
2354⁷ SHARE A MOMENT (Can) 4-10-2 (3*) S Wynne, *settled mid-div, effrt appr 3 out, not pace to chal.*
.................................(33 to 1 op 20 to 1)   4
3819* HYPNOTIST 7-11-13 A Maguire, *al wl plcd, rdn whn hit 2 out, sn btn............*(11 to 2 tchd 6 to 1 and 5 to 1)   5
3342⁷ MILLIE (USA) 6-10-6 M Robinson, *trkd ldrs to 7th, wknd nxt.*........................(100 to 1 op 50 to 1)   6
2855⁶ WINGS OF FREEDOM (Ire) (v) 6-11-13 D Gallagher, *al in rear...........*(7 to 1 op 5 to 1 tchd 8 to 1)   7
3584⁴ CHEERFUL TIMES (USA) (bl) 5-11-5 Diane Clay, *sn chasing ldrs, rdn alng 4th, wknd 7th.......*(14 to 1 op 20 to 1 tchd 25 to 1)   8
3773 ALICANTE 7-10-12 (5*) Mr D McCain, *strted slwly, al wl beh, tld off............*(50 to 1 op 33 to 1)   9
1603 SPEEDY SIOUX (bl) 5-10-3 (5*) F Perratt, *outpcd, al beh, tld off.....................*(50 to 1 op 33 to 1) 10
3751⁸ KEY DEAR (Fr) (v) 7-10-13 J Osborne, *strted very slwly, rdn, no response, tld off.......*(50 to 1 op 25 to 1) 11
Dist: 15l, 3l, 4l, 12l, 2½l, ¾l, 5l. 4m 41.30s. a 5.30s (11 Ran).
SR: 36/9/5/-/2/-/   (Mrs Harry J Duffey), K C Bailey

3927 North Western Area Point-to-Point Championship Final Hunters' Chase for Wynnstay Hunt Challenge Cup (5-y-o and up) £2,840 3m 110yds. .(12:05)

SIR NODDY 11-11-10 (7*) Mr C Stockton, *jmpd wl, made all, sn clr, unchlgd.*.................(5 to 1 op 7 to 2)   1
WARLEGGAN 13-11-12 (5*) Mr S Brookshaw, *hld up, took clr order hfwy, hrd rdn 2 out, kpt on.*
.................................(7 to 1 tchd 8 to 1)   2
3665² SCALLY MUIRE 10-11-5 (7*) Mr A H Crow, *al cl up, mstk 12th, styd on one pace frm 3 out.*
.................................(7 to 4 fav tchd 6 to 4 and 2 to 1)   3
3665⁵ MY NOMINEE 6-11-10 (7*) Mr A Griffith, *trkd ldrs, rdn and outpcd 14th, btn whn pckd last....*(25 to 1 op 20 to 1)   4
SPY'S DELIGHT 8-11-10 (7*) Mr E Woolley, *pressed ldrs, hit 6th, rdn 3 out, sn wknd...........*(16 to 1 op 12 to 1)   5
SIMPLY PERFECT 8-11-10 (7*) Miss K Swindells, *prmnt, blun 6th, lost tch 14th, tld off.......*(14 to 1 op 10 to 1)   6
CAREFREE TIMES (v) 7-11-10 (7*) Miss C Burgess, *in rear, rdn alng 13th, no imprsn, tld off.....*(66 to 1 op 33 to 1)   7
3665 THE ARTFUL RASCAL 10-11-10 (7*) Mr C J B Barlow, *trkd ldrs, chsd wnr frm 15th, wknd 3 out, tld off.*
.................................(7 to 1 tchd 5 to 1)   8
JAUNTY GIG 8-11-10 (7*) Mr A Gribbin, *al wl beh, tld off.*.................................(66 to 1 op 33 to 1)   9
RENARD QUAY 11-11-10 (7*) Miss C Wilberforce, *prmnt till wknd hfwy, tld off...........*(12 to 1 op 7 to 1) 10
JOSSESTOWN (bl) 11-11-10 (7*) Mr G Hanmer, *slpd up and uns rdr bef strt, whipped round start, al wl beh, tld off.*
.................................(66 to 1 op 33 to 1) 11
REAL CLASS 11-11-10 (7*) Mr J Evans, *mstk 3rd, sn wl beh, tld off whn pld up bef 13th.*
.................................(13 to 2 op 7 to 1 tchd 6 to 1)   pu
Dist: 3l, 6l, 10l, 3l, 15l, 3l, 1½l, 25l, 20l. 6m 10.20s. a 20.20s (12 Ran).

(G W Briscoe), J Groucott

3928 Turner Ties The Knot Novices' Hurdle (4-y-o and up) £2,400 2m 1f. .. . (12:35)

3663⁹ HECTOR MARIO 6-11-3 N Williamson, *patiently rdn, steady prog frm hfwy, chlgd 2 out, sn led, ran on strly.*
.................................(7 to 2 op 4 to 1 tchd 9 to 2)   1
3576² FLINTLOCK (Ire) 4-10-12 R Dunwoody, *hld up, hdwy hfwy, led aftr 3 out, mstk and hdd nxt, one pace.*
.................................(13 to 8 on tchd 5 to 4 and 7 to 4 on)   2
1627⁸ BASSIO (Bel) (h) 5-11-3 A Maguire, *pld hrd, pressed ldrs, ev ch 3 out, ran on one pace frm nxt.*(10 to 1 op 8 to 1)   3
3344 THE CAN CAN MAN 7-11-3 M Robinson, *led till aftr 4th, hrd rdn 3 out, one pace............*(20 to 1 op 10 to 1)   4
3756⁷ SUVLA BAY (Ire) 6-11-3 M Brennan, *cl up, led aftr 6th till appr 2 out, sn wknd.............*(14 to 1 op 12 to 1)   5
3396 SCORPOTINA 5-10-12 T Wall, *styd on frm 3 out, nvr nrr.*
.................................(50 to 1)   6
RUBY VISION (Ire) 5-10-12 Mr M Wilding, *chsd ldrs, led 5th till nxt, sn lost tch, tld off...........*(100 to 1)   7
3745⁶ LAURA 5-10-12 D Bridgwater, *al wl beh, tld off.*
.................................(50 to 1 op 33 to 1)   8
7307⁷ QUEENS TOUR 9-11-3 G Upton, *al beh, tld off.....*(50 to 1)   9
3458 WHAT A MOPPET (Ire) 5-10-12 J Osborne, *chsd ldr, led aftr 4th, sn hdd, rallied 3 out, wknd quickly nxt, tld off.*
.................................(14 to 1 op 12 to 1) 10
3666 ALTHREY BLUE (Ire) 5-11-3 Gary Lyons, *prmnt to hfwy, sn rdn and lost tch, tld off............*(100 to 1) 11
3597 IRISH GROOM 7-10-12 (5*) D Leahy, *mstk second, sn beh, tld off frm hfwy.........................*(100 to 1) 12
3597 AFFORDABLE 6-11-3 Diane Clay, *f 3rd, broke leg, destroyed.*.................(16 to 1 tchd 20 to 1)   f
Dist: 2½l, 9l, 2l, 8l, 2l, 8l, 20l, 1½l. 4m 3.40s. a 13.40s (13 Ran).

(R J McAlpine), J A C Edwards

3929 North West Racing Club Selling Handicap Chase (5-y-o and up) £3,269 2½m 110yds.................... (1:05)

37723 JIMMY O'DEA [80] (bl) 7-10-4 N Williamson, *jmpd wl, made all, sn clr, easily*............(7 to 2 tchd 4 to 1)   1
38259 CALL ME EARLY [87] (v) 9-10-11 M Brennan, *blun 1st, sn prmnt, chsd wnr frm 9th, hrd rdn 2 out, styd on.*
.... (12 to 1 op 10 to 1)   2
38522 LOR MOSS [92] 14-11-2 (7ex) J R Kavanagh, *al cl up, rdn 3 out, wknd nxt*..........(4 to 1 op 9 to 2 tchd 7 to 2)   3
37852 ENCHANTED MAN [85] 10-10-9 A Maguire, *hld up in rear, reminders 6th, hdwy 8th, wknd quickly tenth.*
.... (5 to 2 fav tchd 3 to 1)   4
37664 FLYING ZIAD (Can) [92] 11-10-9 (7°) G Crone, *hld up and beh, took clr order 9th, fdd quickly 11th, tld off.*
.... (9 to 1 op 8 to 1 tchd 10 to 1)   5
3566 BISHOPDALE [104] 13-12-0 A Dobbin, *hdwy 5th, wknd 9th, tld off*....................... (20 to 1 op 14 to 1)   6
37737 SLIPPERY MAX [85] 10-10-9 J Osborne, *chsd ldrs to 9th, sn lost tch, tld off.*...........................(20 to 1)   7
36999 ON YOUR WAY [76] (bl) 12-10-0 W McFarland, *cl up to 9th, wknd quickly, tld off whn f 12th.* (50 to 1 op 33 to 1)   f
37742 THE YOKEL [76] 8-9-11 (3°) T Eley, *cl up whn blun and uns rdr 3rd.*.. ur
3779 CONCERT PAPER [92] (v) 10-10-9 (7°) K Davies, *sn wl beh, tld off whn pld up bef tenth*.......(14 to 1 op 12 to 1)   pu
Dist: 4l, 10l, 2l, 25l, 30l, 7l. 4m 59.30s. a 8.30s (10 Ran).

(J S Harlow), T T Bill

3930 Win With The Tote Handicap Hurdle (0-135 4-y-o and up) £4,460 2m 1f (1:35)

3755* MERLINS WISH (USA) [101] 5-10-0 R Dunwoody, *al cl up and gng wl, led appr 2 out, ran on well.*
.... (7 to 2 fav tchd 4 to 1)   1
38061 NOBLELY (USA) [104] 7-10-3 N Williamson, *led till appr 2 out, styd on und pres*.................(4 to 1 op 3 to 1)   2
37802 STRATH ROYAL [125] 8-11-10 M Brennan, *wtd wth, hdwy hfwy, outpcd 3 out, sn btn*............(6 to 1 op 5 to 1)   3
30922 ZEALOUS KITTEN (USA) [106] 6-10-2 (3°) J McCarthy, *al in rear, rdn 5th, no imprsn*........(10 to 1 op 8 to 1)   4
37805 VAIN PRINCE [104] (bl) 7-10-3 J Osborne, *cl up, wknd appr 3 out*...........(16 to 1 op 14 to 1 tchd 20 to 1)   5
37363 MIDDLE MARKER (Ire) [113] 5-10-12 A Maguire, *trkd ldrs, rdn and lost tch 3 out, tld off*......(4 to 1 op 5 to 1)   6
3736 WHO'S TEF (Ire) [117] 6-11-2 R Garritty, *prmnt to 5th, wknd quickly, wl beh whn f 3 out.*
.... (5 to 1 op 9 to 2 tchd 11 to 2)   f
629 LUSTREMAN [106] 7-10-5 T Wall, *hld up, hdwy appr 6th, wkng whn hmpd nxt, pld up bef 2 out, lme.*
.... (14 to 1 op 12 to 1)   pu
Dist: 4l, 6l, 6l, 5l, 10l. 3m 52.40s. a 2.40s (8 Ran).

SR: 40/39/54/29/22/21/-/-/   (Malcolm B Jones), M C Pipe

3931 Ruabon Novices' Chase (5-y-o and up) £2,775 2m 1f 110yds........... (2:10)

3585 DORADUS 6-11-5 (5°) F Leahy, *al prmnt, led 3 out, hrd rdn appr last, hld on gmely.*
.... (6 to 1 op 5 to 1 tchd 13 to 2)   1
36928 SEON 8-12-2 A Maguire, *patiently rdn, took clr order 4 out, chalg whn hit last, swtchd and str run flt, jst fld.*
.... (7 to 1 op 4 to 1)   2
3754 SHEEP STEALER 6-11-4 R Dunwoody, *prog hfwy, rdn 2 out, ev ch last, unbl to quicken.*
.... (9 to 4 fav op 5 to 2 tchd 3 to 1)   3
36393 MANABOUTTHEHOUSE 7-11-4 M Hourigan, *led appr 4th to 6th, hrd rdn 2 out, ev ch last, one pace.*
.... (14 to 1 op 10 to 1)   4
37063 PHARGOLD (Ire) 5-10-12 T Wall, *prmnt, led 6th to 3 out, wknd quickly nxt*................(5 to 1 op 4 to 1)   5
37643 PALACE WOLF (NZ) 10-11-4 J Osborne, *chsd ldrs to 8th, sn lost tch, tld off*....(13 to 2 op 6 to 1 tchd 7 to 1)   6
36834 PERTEMPS JOBSHOP 8-11-4 W Humphreys, *led till appr 4th, wknd four out, tld off*.......(40 to 1 op 20 to 1)   7
38182 CRAFTY CHAPLAIN 8-11-11 (5°) Mr D McCain, *hld up mid-field, f 6th.*...................(8 to 1 op 6 to 1)   f
3629 MARTRAJAN 7-11-4 I Lawrence, *al wl beh, tld off whn pld up bef 3 out.*................(25 to 1 op 14 to 1)   pu
3662 ON THE TEAR 8-11-4 G Bradley, *disputing ld whn blun badly 3rd, sn lost pl, tld off when pld up bef 7th.*
.... (50 to 1 op 33 to 1)   pu
3827 TAURIAN PRINCESS 5-10-7 D J Burchell, *al in rear, tld off whn pld up bef 4 out.*................(50 to 1 op 33 to 1)   pu
Dist: Nk, ½l, 1¼l, 15l, 25l, 1½l. 4m 13.00s. a 7.00s (11 Ran).

SR: 17/22/9/7/-/-/   (Lady Halifax), J G FitzGerald

3932 Gobowen Novices' Handicap Hurdle (4-y-o and up) £2,463 2½m..... (2:40)

3564* KONVEKTA CONTROL [85] (bl) 7-11-0 J Osborne, *wtd wth in tch, quickened to ld last, rdn out.*
.... (3 to 1 fav tchd 7 to 2)   1

3751* MAN OF THE GRANGE [77] 8-10-3 (3°) T Eley, *took clr order hfwy, led aftr 3 out to last, rallied und pres.*
.... (11 to 2 op 6 to 1 tchd 5 to 1)   2
3715* PYRRHIC DANCE [80] 4-10-9 R Dunwoody, *chsd ldr, led 8th till aftr 3 out, sn rdn and outpcd.* (6 to 1 op 5 to 1)   3
35835 SAFARI PARK [84] 5-10-13 B Storey, *led to 8th, wknd appr 2 out*......................... (10 to 1 op 12 to 1)   4
3583 MERRYHILL MADAM [71] 5-10-0 W Humphreys, *settled in rear, some hdwy frm 3 out, nvr nrr.*
.... (66 to 1 op 50 to 1)   5
3817 TUSKY [95] 6-11-10 N Bentley, *wtd wth, hdwy hfwy, chlgd 3 out, sn rdn and wknd.*..... (13 to 2 op 5 to 1)   6
38293 DUNDEE PRINCE (NZ) [82] 6-10-11 N Williamson, *mstk second, prog 7th, wknd appr 3 out......(7 to 1 op 5 to 1)   7
38258 ANDRATH (Ire) [72] 6-10-1 W Marston, *nvr a factor.*
.... (20 to 1 op 16 to 1)   8
32708 MONAZITE [78] (bl) 4-10-0 (7°) E Tolhurst, *prmnt to 7th, sn wknd 8th, tld off*.....................(20 to 1 op 16 to 1)   9
38174 SOUNDS GOLDEN [71] 6-10-0 A Maguire, *cl up, wknd 7th, tld off*...................(7 to 1 op 5 to 1)   10
13569 JUST EVE [71] 7-10-0 D Bridgwater, *al in rear, tld off.*
.... (33 to 1)   11
38296 CLOWN AROUND [71] 6-9-7 (7°) R Massey, *prmnt to hfwy, sn rdn and wknd, tld off.*.... (66 to 1 op 50 to 1)   12
38788 RUTH'S GAMBLE [76] (v) 6-10-5 J R Kavanagh, *trkd ldrs to 8th, sn wknd, tld off.*...... (16 to 1 op 14 to 1)   13
3798* ALIZARI (USA) [71] 5-10-0 M Robinson, *sn rdn and lost tch, tld off frm hfwy, pld up bef 3 out.* (25 to 1 op 16 to 1)   pu
38173 TWIN STATES [87] 5-10-9 (7°) W Fry, *nvr trble ldrs, tld off whn pld up bef 3 out.*...... (10 to 1 op 8 to 1)   pu
Dist: ½l, 5l, 8l, 7l, 3½l, 8l, 1½l, 7l, 20l, 1l. 4m 40.40s. a 4.40s (15 Ran).
SR: 32/23/21/17/-/17/   (Konvekta Ltd), O Sherwood

NAVAN (IRE) (good)
Saturday May 14th

3933 Garlow Cross Handicap Chase (0-137 4-y-o and up) £3,082 2½m...... (3:30)

32248 JASSU [-] 8-11-11 C F Swan, ... (9 to 4 jt-fav)   1
33265 SPUR OF THE MOMENT [-] 7-10-2 S R Murphy, ... (8 to 1)   2
37462 PROVERB PRINCE [-] 10-10-10 P Carberry, ... (4 to 1)   3
36589 BROCKLEY COURT [-] 7-11-5 J P Banahan, .(9 to 4 jt-fav)   4
3217 MUST DO [-] 8-9-5 (3°) C O'Brien, ... (14 to 1)   5
3197 JOE'S A BOY [-] 9-10-7 K F O'Brien, ... (12 to 1)   6
3123 THE RIDGE BOREEN [-] 10-12-0 F Woods, ... (14 to 1)   7
37216 LACKEN BEAU [-] (bl) 10-10-9 (3°) T J Mitchell, ... (10 to 1)   8
3085 BLAZING DAWN [-] 7-10-13 S H O'Donovan, ... (14 to 1)   9
Dist: 1l, 1½l, ¾l, 10l. 5m 14.00s. (9 Ran).

(Bruno Buser), J E Kiely

3934 Osberstown Maiden Hurdle (4-y-o and up) £3,082 2¼m............... (4:00)

37306 VERITATIS SPLENDOR (Ire) 5-11-5 M Dwyer, ... (10 to 1)   1
3656 PUSH THE BUTTON (Ire) 4-10-8 (7°) D J Finnegan, .(6 to 1)   2
37472 RIVERLAND (Ire) 6-11-6 B Sheridan, ... (4 to 1)   3
3834 BACKTOWN JOHNNY (Ire) 5-11-5 L P Cusack, .. (16 to 1)   4
32469 HUNCHEON CHANCE 4-10-12 (3°) T J Mitchell, .. (10 to 1)   5
34798 MAMBO KING 7-11-6 P Carberry, ...(7 to 2 fav)   6
34798 MINIGIRLS NIECE (Ire) 6-11-1 D P Fagan, ...(10 to 1)   7
AMBLE SPEEDY (Ire) 4-10-12 (3°) T P Rudd, ...(20 to 1)   8
37308 A LITTLE EARNER 5-11-5 C F Swan, ... (8 to 1)   9
3839 RIFAYA (Ire) 4-10-10 T Horgan, ... (8 to 1)   10
MC GUINNESS FLINT (Ire) 5-11-5 R Hughes, ... (16 to 1)   11
37483 SPORTSTYLE (Ire) (bl) 4-11-6 K F O'Brien, ... (8 to 1)   12
PARADISE FOUND 6-11-6 F Woods, ... (10 to 1)   13
3448 EUROPE (USA) 4-10-13 (7°) A P McCoy, ... (14 to 1)   14
DEESIDE DOINGS (Ire) 6-11-6 H Rogers, ...(25 to 1)   15
2231 TOMMY'S RUN 7-11-11 (3°) D T Evans, ... (14 to 1)   16
3124 BOALINE (Ire) 6-11-1 J P Banahan, ... (20 to 1)   17
20232 HACKETTS CROSS (Ire) 6-12-0 A Powell, ... (11 to 2)   18
3747 CUCHULLAINS GOLD (Ire) 6-11-6 C O'Dwyer, .. (12 to 1)   19
3528 COLLIERS HILL (Ire) 6-11-6 S R Murphy, ... (20 to 1)   20
709 WITHOUT TRACE (Ire) 5-11-5 J Short, ... (12 to 1)   21
1681 DERRAVARAGH GALE (Ire) 5-10-7 (7°) D J Kavanagh,
.... (33 to 1)   22
2682 BROOKVILLE STAR (Fr) 7-11-3 (3°) C O'Brien, ... (33 to 1)   23
3388 SWANING AROUND (Ire) 5-11-5 P L Malone, ... (20 to 1)   24
3505 JOHNSON'S HILL (Ire) (bl) 5-10-12 (7°) Mr B M Cash,
.... (33 to 1)   25
3505 THYNE OWN GIRL (Ire) 6-11-1 S H O'Donovan, ...(33 to 1)   26
469 RATHCARRICK LASS (Ire) 5-10-11 (3°) G Kilfeather, (33 to 1)   27
3540 DRESSED IN BLACK (Ire) 6-11-1 (5°) D Walsh, ... (33 to 1)   28
Dist: 2½l, ½l, 1½l, ½l. 4m 18.10s. (28 Ran).

(Mrs John Harrington), Mrs John Harrington

3935 Donoughmore Handicap Hurdle (5-y-o and up) £6,850 2m............ (4:30)

36548 SEA GALE (Ire) [-] 6-9-11 C F Swan, ... (8 to 1)   1
37102 HIS WAY (Ire) [-] 5-10-3 J Shortt, ...(9 to 4 fav)   2
3710* CASH CHASE (Ire) [-] 6-9-7 S H O'Donovan, ... (10 to 1)   3
3836 TUG OF PEACE [-] 7-11-1 (5°) J P Broderick, ... (12 to 1)   4
3658* OH SO GRUMPY [-] 6-10-2 M Dwyer, ... (6 to 1)   5
3654 DASHING ROSE [-] 6-9-11 P Carberry, ...(12 to 1)   6

3748* CABLE BEACH (Ire) [-] 5-10-3 J P Banahan, ... (10 to 1) 7
1828² BAVARD DIEU (Ire) [-] 6-9-10 (3*) T J Mitchell, ...(14 to 1) 8
1686 DUHARRA (Ire) [-] (bl) 6-11-7 (3*) Mr J A Nash, . . . (14 to 1) 9
3693² MONTE FIGO [-] 7-9-9 F Woods, ... (10 to 1) 10
DINNYS CORNER (Ire) 10-9-4 (7*) B Bowens, ... (50 to 1) 11
2550 DOS ADVENTICA (Ire) [-] 10-10-0 A Powell, ... (50 to 1) 12
3836³ COCK COCKBURN [-] 8-11-13 S R Murphy, ... (6 to 1) pu
3650² DEEP INAGH [-] 8-12-0 D P Fagan, ... (8 to 1) pu
Dist: 4l, 3l, 2½l, 4½l. 3m 46.80s. (14 Ran).

(Simon J H Davis), E J O'Grady

3936 Rathfeigh Flat Race (Div 1) (4-y-o and up) £3,082 2m. . . . . (5:00)

3749² SIGMA WIRELESS (Ire) 5-11-10 (3*) Mr D Marnane,
. . . . (7 to 4 fav) 1
3653⁸ MOYGANNON COURT (Ire) 5-11-8 (5*) Mr H F Cleary,
. . . . (7 to 1) 2
3749³ LUCKY SALUTE (Ire) 5-11-6 (7*) Mr R P Cody, ... (5 to 1) 3
3528⁵ SECRET MISSILE 7-11-11 (3*) Mrs J M Mullins, . . . (10 to 1) 4
365⁴ GOOD DEER (Ire) 6-12-0 Mr P Fenton, ... (14 to 1) 5
3712⁴ LITTLE BUCK (Ire) 6-11-7 (7*) Mr J S Cullen, ... (6 to 1) 6
MADISON COUNTY (Ire) 4-10-13 (7*) Mr K A Dempsey,
. . . . (10 to 1) 7
3394⁷ BEST INTEREST (Ire) 6-11-11 (3*) Mr J A Nash, ... (3 to 1) 8
1762 MANTEGNA (Ire) 5-11-8 (5*) Mr G J Harford, ... (12 to 1) 9
THOUGHT RAIDER (Ire) 4-11-6 Mr J P Dempsey, (16 to 1) 10
THE FINANCIER (Ire) 5-11-6 (7*) Mr J Connolly, . . . (20 to 1) 11
3250 FOREST FORT (Ire) (bl) 5-11-6 (7*) R Whelan, . . (33 to 1) 12
PRESTBURY KING (Ire) 5-11-6 (7*) Mrs D McDonagh,
. . . . (16 to 1) 13
3653 BEAKSTOWN (Ire) 5-11-13 Mr T Mullins, ... (14 to 1) 14
620 LORD MONTE (Ire) 5-11-10 (3*) Mr D Valentine, . . (14 to 1) 15
832 PRECEPTOR (Ire) 5-11-13 Mr A R Coonan, ... (16 to 1) 16
1766 THE KINGS SEAL (Ire) 6-12-2 (7*) Mr D McCartan, (33 to 1) 17
3508 KEASHILL (Ire) 5-11-1 (7*) Mr J P Kilfeather, ... (33 to 1) 18
3616 RAINBOW EILE (Ire) 4-11-3 (3*) Mr R Jennings, . . . (14 to 1) 19
CALLMECHARLIE (Ire) 5-11-6 (7*) Mr E Norris, . . . (14 to 1) 20
3528 KOWABUNGA 7-11-7 (7*) Mr P F O'Callaghan, . . .(14 to 1) 21
3124 RADICAL DUAL (Ire) 5-11-6 (7*) Mr A K Wyse, . . . (33 to 1) 22
Dist: Sht-hd, 3½l, 2½l, 10l. 3m 47.00s. (22 Ran).

(J A Boyle), Noel Meade

3937 Rathfeigh Flat Race (Div 2) (4-y-o and up) £3,082 2m. . . . . (5:30)

OTTOWA (Ire) 4-11-3 (3*) Mr D Marnane, ... (5 to 2 fav) 1
162⁴ OLD ARCHIVES (Ire) 5-11-6 (7*) Mr J Connolly, . . .(10 to 1) 2
3837³ YOU KNOW WHO (Ire) 6-11-11 (3*) Mrs J M Mullins, (6 to 1) 3
2586³ LINDEN'S LOTTO (Ire) 5-11-6 (7*) Mr E Norris, ... (6 to 1) 4
3394² DERBY HAVEN 7-12-0 Mr A R Coonan, ... (8 to 1) 5
ACT THE WAG (Ire) 5-11-13 Mr J A Berry, ... (12 to 1) 6
3653 DUDDON SANDS (Ire) 5-11-10 (3*) Mr J A Nash, . . . (8 to 1) 7
2613⁵ MASAI (Ire) 5-11-10 (3*) Mr D Valentine, ... (14 to 1) 8
KINGS VENTURE (Ire) 4-10-13 (7*) Miss F M Crowley,
. . . . (8 to 1) 9
MOORLOUGH BAY (Ire) 4-11-3 (3*) Mr R Neylon, . .(33 to 1) 10
3616 SHANES BAY (Ire) 4-10-12 (3*) Mr P J Casey, ... (33 to 1) 11
3723⁵ PROUD KITTEN (Ire) 5-11-1 (7*) Miss S McDonogh, (16 to 1) 12
COLLON LEADER (Ire) 5-11-1 (7*) Mr M Callaghan, (20 to 1) 13
THATS FAR ENOUGH (Ire) 4-11-1 (5*) Mr P M Kelly, (20 to 1) 14
3616 MR BUCKSKIN (Ire) 4-11-6 Mr T Mullins, ... (12 to 1) 15
3290 HANDMASTER (Ire) 5-11-3 (5*) Mr H F Cleary, . . . (14 to 1) 16
AUT EVEN (Ire) 4-11-6 Mr P Fenton, ... (14 to 1) 17
FANE'S TREASURE (Ire) 5-11-8 (5*) Mr G J Harford, (20 to 1) 18
3813 HASSLE FREE 7-11-7 (7*) Mr F McGirr, ... (16 to 1) 19
3749 REDZ LAST STAND (Ire) 5-11-1 (7*) Mr M J Dunne, (66 to 1) 20
3813 DEEYEHFOLLYME (Ire) 6-11-2 (7*) Mr C Gainey, . . (66 to 1) 21
Dist: 2l, sht-hd, 4l, ½l. 3m 50.70s. (21 Ran).

(Miss G O'Brien), Noel Meade

FONTWELL (good to firm)
Monday May 16th
Going Correction: PLUS 0.15 sec. per fur.

3938 Nyton Novices' Hurdle (4-y-o and up) £1,553 2¼m. . . . . (2:25)

3729³ CHINAMAN 5-11-5 A Tory, in tch, pushed alng and cld 4
out, led aftr last, ran on wl. . . . . (10 to 1 op 14 to 1) 1
3008* REDEEMYOURSELF (Ire) 5-11-8 (3*) P Hide, in tch, led 4
out till hdd aftr last, no extr und pres.
. . . . (2 to 1 op tchd 7 to 4 on) 2
3848² POLISH RIDER (USA) 6-11-4 (7*) C Huggan, hld up, cld 5th,
ev ch 2 out, one pace. . . . . (10 to 1 op 8 to 1) 3
3543³ BOOTH'S BOUQUET 6-11-5 M Richards, cl up, led 3rd till
blun and hdd 4 out, one pace appr last, no extr und
pres. . . . . (12 to 1 op 10 to 1) 4
EDELWEISS 7-11-0 R Dunwoody, hld up beh ldrs, outpcd
appr 4 out. . . . . (13 to 2 op 4 to 1) 5
3145³ YELLOW CORN 5-11-0 Peter Hobbs, led till hdd 3rd, in
tch till wknd 4 out. (20 to 1 tchd 25 to 1 and 16 to 1) 6
3886 DOMITOR'S LASS 7-11-0 Mrs N Ledger, hld up, cld 4th,
one pace whn ran out appr 2 out. (100 to 1 op 66 to 1) ro
TRICKY TIMES 7-11-0 B Powell, prmnt to 4th, lost tch aftr
nxt, tld off whn pld up bef 2 out. . . . (66 to 1 op 50 to 1) pu

3729 FELICE'S PET 4-10-9 N Williamson, hld up in rear, not
jump wl, tld off 5th, pld up bef 2 out.
. . . . (100 to 1 op 66 to 1) pu
3543 LB'S GIRL 5-11-0 R Rowell, prmnt, mstk 3rd and lost pl
quickly, tld off whn pld up bef 6th.
. . . . (100 to 1 op 66 to 1) pu
3809⁵ BOLLINGTON (Fr) 5-11-2 (3*) J McCarthy, sn struggling, tld
off and pld up bef 2 out. . . . . (25 to 1 op 16 to 1) pu
Dist: 1¼l, 4l, sht-hd, 25l, 4l. 4m 22.40s. a 12.40s (11 Ran).

(John Light), Mrs J Renfree-Barons

3939 Kybo Handicap Chase (0-110 5-y-o and up) £2,831 3¼m 110yds. . . . .(2:55)

3808 OCEAN LINK [91] 10-10-13 S Earle, led 4th, made rst,
pushed alng four out, rdn out. . . . . . (8 to 1 op 6 to 1) 1
3808² DOONLOUGHAN [98] 9-11-6 A Maguire, nvr far away, hrd
rdn and rallied appr last, kpt on und pres. . .(4 to 1 jt-
fav op 5 to 1) 2
3519⁷ MIGHTY FALCON [102] (bl) 9-11-10 P Holley, reminders
5th, cl up frm 9th, ev ch 4 out, hrd rdn and one pace
from 2 out. (5 to 1 op 7 to 2 tchd 11 to 2 and 6 to 1) 3
3808³ LITTLE GENERAL [78] 11-10-0 M Perrett, hld up, styd on
frm 3 out, nvr dngrs. . . . . (12 to 1 op 8 to 1) 4
3724* SATIN NOIR (Fr) [106] 10-12-0 R Dunwoody, hld up in tch,
reminders 15th, outpcd nxt, tld off.
. . . . (11 to 2 op 4 to 1 tchd 6 to 1) 5
3821⁵ NEWS REVIEW [92] 11-10-12⁵ (7*) Mr E Williams, al beh, tld
off frm 16th. . . . . (25 to 1 op 33 to 1 tchd 20 to 1) 6
3546* EARLY MAN [87] 7-10-9 Peter Hobbs, trkd ldrs, pushed
alng whn f 5 out. . . . . (4 to 1 jt-fav op 3 to 1) f
3885* GUILDWAY [93] (bl) 11-10-8 (7*,6ex) Mr M Rimell, led to 4th,
drpd rear 8th, sn rdn alng, tld off whn pld up bef 3 out.
. . . . (5 to 1 op 9 to 2) pu
Dist: ½l, 5l, 1¾l, 30l, dist. 6m 48.20s. a 18.20s (8 Ran).

(N H S New), R H Alner

3940 May Selling Hurdle (4-y-o and up) £1,938 2¼m. . . . . (3:25)

3738² CELCIUS (bl) 10-12-3 R Dunwoody, hld up in mid-div, cld
aftr 4 out, shaken up to ld after last, pushed out.
. . . . (5 to 4 on op 6 to 4 on tchd 11 to 10 on) 1
3714 BONDAID 10-12-3 A Maguire, chsd ldrs, led appr 2 out till
hdd aftr last, no extr. . . . . . . (9 to 1 op 7 to 1 tchd 9 to 1) 2
3770³ EAGLES LAIR 8-11-7 S McNeill, hld up and beh, rapid
hdwy 3 out, awkward last 2, kpt on.
. . . . (5 to 1 op 6 to 1 tchd 9 to 1) 3
3843⁴ BARTON ROYAL (Ire) 4-11-9 Richard Guest, cl up, rdn to ld
4 out, hdd appr 2 out, outpcd. . . . . . (20 to 1 op 14 to 1) 4
3740⁹ OTHET 10-12-3 Peter Hobbs, mid-div, pushed alng aftr
5th and outpcd, styd on ag'n frm last.
. . . . (25 to 1 op 16 to 1) 5
3696³ ROGER'S PAL 7-12-3 D Gallagher, prmnt till rdn and lost
pl aftr 4 out. . . . . (9 to 1 op 8 to 1 tchd 10 to 1) 6
3725⁸ BAN RI (Ire) 4-10-11 N Williamson, beh, hdwy aftr 3 out,
btn nxt. . . . . (50 to 1 op 33 to 1) 7
3698⁵ LUCKY OAK (bl) 8-11-12 (5*) C Burnett-Wells, cl up till
wknd 3 out. . . . . (50 to 1 op 33 to 1) 8
3696 FIVE CASTLES 6-12-0 J Railton, al beh. . . . . (50 to 1) 9
OFFSPRING 5-11-2 A Dicken, towards rear, lost tch 4 out,
tld off. . . . . (50 to 1 op 33 to 1) 10
3698 CONNABEE 10-11-0 (7*) Mr T McCarthy, rcd freely, led till
hdd 4 out, wknd quickly, pld up bef 2 out.
. . . . (50 to 1 op 33 to 1) pu
604 JUST JAMIE 4-11-2 M Richards, chsd ldrs till wknd
quickly 4 out, pld up bef 2 out.
. . . . (50 to 1 op 33 to 1) pu
Dist: 3½l, 4l, 12l, 3l, hd, 25l, 5l, 2l, dist. 4m 22.70s. a 12.70s (12 Ran).
SR: 3/-/-/-/-/-/

(Martin Pipe Racing Club), M C Pipe

3941 Steel Lock Handicap Chase (0-110 5-y-o and up) £2,544 2¼m. . . . . (3:55)

3847² I LIKE IT A LOT [87] 11-11-4 J R Kavanagh, made all, ran on
wl. . . . . (11 to 2 op 4 to 1) 1
3726² GREEN WALK [73] 7-9-13 (5*) C Burnett-Wells, in tch, chsd
wnr frm 11th, hrd rdn appr last, ran on.
. . . . (6 to 1 op 5 to 1 tchd 7 to 1) 2
3605⁶ YOUNG ALFIE [75] (bl) 9-10-6 A Maguire, trkd ldrs, outpcd
5 out, styd on frm 2 out.
. . . . (12 to 1 op 10 to 1 tchd 14 to 1) 3
3548² SOLEIL DANCER (Ire) [92] 6-11-9 J Railton, beh, styd on
frm 2 out, nrst finish.
. . . . (8 to 5 fav op 9 to 4 tchd 5 to 2) 4
3667³ GALAGAMES (USA) [94] 7-11-4 (7*) Mr G Hogan, chsd wnr
to 11th, wknd aftr 3 out. . . . . (5 to 1 op 7 to 1) 5
3847⁴ THEY ALL FORGOT ME [86] 7-11-3 G McCourt, nvr on
terms. . . . . (11 to 2 op 5 to 1 tchd 6 to 1) 6
3847⁵ AIR COMMANDER [88] 9-10-12 (7*) Mr S Joynes, trkd ldrs
till rdn and outpcd 4 out.
. . . . (16 to 1 op 12 to 1 tchd 20 to 1) 7
3697⁴ RUSTIC GENT (Ire) [73] (v) 6-10-4 W McFarland, hld up,
shrtlvd effrt 9th, sn btn. . . . . (20 to 1 op 16 to 1) 8
2184 HALF BROTHER [97] 12-11-7 (7*) Mr T McCarthy, mid-div
till drpd rear 9th, pld up bef 3 out.
. . . . (25 to 1 op 14 to 1 tchd 33 to 1) pu

3697³ FRED SPLENDID [87] 11-11-4 R Dunwoody, *outpcd, tld off and pld up bef 9th....* (12 to 1 op 8 to 1 tchd 16 to 1) pu
Dist: 1½sl, 5l, 20l, 11l, ¾l, 5l, 15l. 4m 31.50s. a 11.50s (10 Ran).
SR: 2/-/-/-/-/-/-/ (Brian J D Lewis), John R Upson

3942 Billingshurst Novices' Chase (5-y-o and up) £2,318 2m 3f.......... (4:25)

2432⁸ ILEWIN 7-11-13 M Ahern, *chsd ldg pair, mstk 3rd, dsptd ld 3 out till wnt on appr last, jst hld on.*
....................................(11 to 4 tchd 3 to 1) 1
3828³ ROYAL SQUARE (Can) 8-11-13 M Perrett, *chsd ldr to appr 3 out, rallied last, ran on wl, jst fld.*
.................................(11 to 10 on op Evens) 2
3699³ VICTORY GATE (USA) 9-11-6 D Gallagher, *lost tch 9th, cld 11th, dsptd ld 3 out till appr last, ran on.*
......................(7 to 1 op 5 to 1 tchd 15 to 2) 3
3697 HANDSOME NED (bl) 8-11-6 J Railton, *led till hld 3 out, sn wknd...........................* (11 to 2 op 4 to 1) 4
3758 GLEN PENNANT 7-11-6 W Marston, *mstk 3rd, tld off frm 9th................................* (50 to 1 op 25 to 1) 5
Dist: Sht-hd, ¾l, dist, dist. 4m 50.70s. a 15.70s (5 Ran).
(Middx Packaging Ltd), M P Muggeridge

3943 Ford Handicap Hurdle (0-115 4-y-o and up) £1,999 2¾m............... (4:55)

3728⁵ FANTASY WORLD [88] 8-10-0¹ (3*) P Hide, *hld up, hdwy 7th, led 4 out, rdn clr frm last...................* (7 to 1) 1
3698² ESPRIT DE FEMME (Fr) [90] 8-10-4 Peter Hobbs, *chsd ldrs, wnt second and drvn appr last, one pace.*
...................(15 to 2 op 6 to 1 tchd 8 to 1) 2
3728³ CHASMARELLA [86] 9-10-0 D Gallagher, *cl up, rdn appr 2 out, one pace...................* (10 to 1 op 8 to 1) 3
3455⁸ INTERPLAY [86] 9-10-0 A Maguire, *chsd ldrs, one pace frm 3 out.........................* (7 to 1 op 7 to 1) 4
3851² DAMIER BLANC (Fr) [95] (v) 5-10-9 R Dunwoody, *prmnt till lost pl 4 out..............* (7 to 1 op 9 to 2 tchd 8 to 1) 5
3547* WOODLANDS BOY (Ire) [90] 6-10-4 M Hoad, *beh. effrt 4 out, nrst finish..................* (14 to 1 op 12 to 1) 6
3771⁴ SEA BUCK [105] 8-11-2 (3*) R Davis, *al beh.*
.................................(12 to 1 op 8 to 1) 7
3771² STORM DRUM [103] (bl) 5-11-3 N Williamson, *sn pushed alng in mid-div, no ch frm 4 out.*
..................(3 to 1 fav op 7 to 2 tchd 4 to 1) 8
APOLLO KING [114] 8-12-0 Mr R Teal, *al beh.*
.................................(33 to 1 op 20 to 1) 9
3545⁶ VILLA PARK [86] 12-9-11² (5*) C Burnett-Wells, *cl up, mstk 4th, wknd nxt.......* (20 to 1 op 25 to 1 tchd 50 to 1) 10
3760³ QUIET DAWN [87] 8-10-1 J R Kavanagh, *trkd ldrs till wknd 6th.......................* (12 to 1 tchd 14 to 1) 11
1138² ST ARMINA [100] (bl) 9-11-0 D Morris, *strtd slwly, reco'red to ld second, hdd 4 out, rdn whn f nxt.*
.................(16 to 1 op 14 to 1 tchd 20 to 1) f
3698⁵ PONTOON BRIDGE [105] 7-11-5 M Perrett, *making hdwy in 6th pl whn brght dwn 3 out.....* (10 to 1 op 8 to 1) bd
Dist: 10l, 5l, 2l, 15l, nk, 2½l, 20l, 2½l, nk, ½l. 5m 16.50s. a 7.50s (13 Ran).
SR: 32/24/15/13/7/1/13/-/-/ (A Ilsley), J T Gifford

MALLOW (IRE) (soft)
Monday May 16th

3944 Blarney Handicap Hurdle (0-116 4-y-o and up) £2,228 2m 5f.......... (5:30)

3870* FOR KEVIN [-] 7-10-1 (5*,6ex) J P Broderick, ... (6 to 1) 1
3887* CALMOS [-] 7-11-7 (6ex) C F Swan, ...(5 to 2 fav) 2
3840⁴ AWBEG ROVER (Ire) [-] 6-9-12 (3*) P Kinane, ...(10 to 1) 3
3887² SIOBHAILIN DUBH (Ire) [-] 5-9-8 (5*) K P Gaule, ...(4 to 1) 4
3870⁹ DIRECT RUN [-] 7-11-2 J F Titley, ...(12 to 1) 5
1231 GUESSWORK [-] 8-11-1 (5*) M G Cleary, ...(16 to 1) 6
3836⁸ THE SHAUGHRAUN [-] 8-12-0 P Carberry, ...(5 to 1) 7
3887⁶ GOLDEN RAPPER [-] (bl) 9-10-2 B Sheridan, ...(14 to 1) 8
3811* KILLOSKEHAN QUEEN [-] 7-9-6 (7*) D J Kavanagh, ...(9 to 1) 9
3732⁵ BUCKINGHAM BOY [-] 8-9-12 (7*) Miss C A Harrison,
.................................(20 to 1) 10
3812 JAMES GIRL [-] 10-9-7 R Hughes, ...(33 to 1) 11
3747 GREENBELLE [-] 7-10-1 S R Murphy, ...(33 to 1) 12
3788 COOL COOPER [-] 7-9-7 S H O'Donovan, ...(33 to 1) 13
1335 WHISTLING MICK [-] 9-10-5 H Rogers, ...(20 to 1) 14
Dist: 7l, 5½l, 3l, 8l. 5m 32.40s. (14 Ran).
(Donal Sheahan), Michael Hourigan

3945 Sugar Factory Greenvale Handicap Chase (0-109 4-y-o and up) £2,742 2m
.................................(7:00)

3890* GALLEY GALE [-] 8-11-2 (6ex) K F O'Brien, ... (7 to 4 fav) 1
3648⁹ THE QUIET MAN [-] 10-10-5 D H O'Connor, ...(10 to 1) 2
3890⁴ WHAT A MINSTREL [-] (bl) 8-9-4 (3*) T J O'Sullivan, (10 to 1) 3
3873⁴ PARSONS SON [-] 7-10-3 D O'Connor, ...(8 to 1) 4
3507⁷ BEAU GRANDE (Ire) [-] 6-10-10 L P Cusack, ...(10 to 1) 5
3873⁶ HIGHBABS [-] 7-8-9-8 T Horgan, ...(11 to 2) 6
3890 THE REAL UNYOKE [-] (bl) 9-11-7 (7*) Mr T N Cloke,
.................................(12 to 1) 7
3873 BALLYHEIGUE [-] 8-10-2 (3*) D P Murphy, ...(8 to 1) 8

3873⁸ FURLANA WONDER [-] 12-11-0 J F Titley, ...(20 to 1) 9
3872⁵ BALLYFIN BOY [-] 8-10-4² J Shortt, ...(8 to 1) 10
3790 WAKE UP LUV [-] 9-11-1 (7*) T M O'Sullivan, ...(30 to 1) 11
Dist: 7l, hd, 4l, ½l. 4m 10.80s. (11 Ran).
(J J Connolly), Daniel O'Connell

3946 Sugar Factory Greenvale Flat Race (4-y-o and up) £2,570 2m.......... (8:30)

2756⁸ BALLYHIRE LAD (Ire) 5-11-13 Mr A P O'Brien, ..(6 to 4 fav) 1
SHEAN HILL (Ire) 4-10-10 (5*) Mr E J Kearnes, ...(10 to 1) 2
3792⁷ EMMA HAAN (Ire) 5-11-8 Mr T Mullins, ...(10 to 1) 3
FIFTH GENERATION (Ire) 4-11-6 Mr A J Martin, ...(9 to 1) 4
3792³ TELLTALK (Ire) 5-11-6 (7*) Mr E Norris, ...(5 to 1) 5
3837⁵ STEVIE BE (Ire) 6-11-7 (7*) Mr T J Murphy, ...(8 to 1) 6
3250 UNSINKABLE BOXER (Ire) 5-11-6 (7*) Mr D A Harney,
.................................(20 to 1) 7
3749 JR MY FRIEND (Ire) 4-10-13 (7*) Mr J T McNamara, (10 to 1) 8
3529² TORONTO TELEGRAM 8-11-6² (5*) Mr J P Berry, (10 to 1) 9
ROSES WISH (Ire) 4-10-9¹ (7*) Miss N Rhodes, .. (20 to 1) 10
SEVENTY SEVEN MILL (Ire) 5-11-6 (7*) Miss C Cashman,
.................................(8 to 1) 11
2869 YOUCAT (Ire) 5-11-13 Mr J P Dempsey, ...(25 to 1) 12
3842 PHARLEYGIRL (Ire) 4-10-12 (3*) Mr D Marnane, ...(14 to 1) 13
SOUTH COAST STAR (Ire) 4-11-1 (5*) Mr H F Cleary,
.................................(12 to 1) 14
BOREEN LASS (Ire) 4-10-8 (7*) Mr P Crowley, ...(25 to 1) 15
3733⁹ COSHLA EXPRESSO (Ire) 6-11-9 (5*) Mr G J Harford,
.................................(33 to 1) 16
3837⁹ SWEET PETEL 7-11-2 (7*) Mr E Henley, ...(25 to 1) 17
3550 MISS BERTAINE (Ire) 5-11-8 Mr M Phillips, ...(25 to 1) 18
3552 STEPHANIE'S JOY (Ire) 5-11-8 (7*) Mr T Lombard, (25 to 1) 19
3616 BEIGINIS (Ire) 4-10-13 (7*) Miss S J Leahy, ...(12 to 1) 20
HEY PAT (Ire) 6-11-7 (7*) Mr K O'Sullivan, ...(33 to 1) 21
YOUNG ANAGLOG (Ire) 4-10-8 (7*) Mr P Cloke, ...(25 to 1) 22
531 BOLD TED (Ire) 5-11-10 (3*) Mr J A Nash, ...(10 to 1) 23
3245 TIME TO SMILE (Ire) 4-10-8 (7*) Mr C M Healy, ...(25 to 1) 24
3082 PREMIUM BRAND (Ire) 5-11-10 (3*) Mr R Neylon, (20 to 1) 25
PERFIC PINK (Ire) 6-12-0 Mr P Fenton, ...(25 to 1) 26
KASHABI (Ire) 4-10-13 (7*) Mr L J Temple, ...(14 to 1) 27
ROOUAN GIRL (Ire) 4-11-2¹ Mr R Hurley, ...(25 to 1) 28
3936 KOWABUNGA (bl) 7-11-7 (7*) Mr P F O'Callaghan, (25 to 1) 29
Dist: 5½l, 1½l, 1l, 2l. 3m 54.10s. (29 Ran).
(Mrs Anna Foxe), A P O'Brien

CHELTENHAM (good to firm)
Tuesday May 17th
Going Correction: PLUS 0.40 sec. per fur.

3947 Sue Williamson Novices' Hunters' Diamond Chase (5-y-o and up) £1,980 2m 5f......................... (5:45)

FLAME O'FRENSI 8-11-2 (7*) Miss J Cumings, *led to 8th and ag'n nxt, drw clr appr last, cmftbly.*
...........(9 to 4 fav op 5 to 2 tchd 11 to 4 and 2 to 1) 1
WILDNITE 10-11-7 (7*) Mr T Jackson, *prmnt in chasing grp, gd prog 12th, chsd wnr aftr 4 out, no imprsn appr last....................* (25 to 1 op 16 to 1) 2
CAUSEWAY CRUISER 8-11-7 (7*) Mr R Lawther, *prog to join ldrs 7th, chsd wnr 12th till rdn aftr 4 out, kpt on one pace......* (10 to 1 op 7 to 1 tchd 12 to 1) 3
MR MAYFAIR 11-11-7 (7*) Mr M Portman, *mid-div in chasing grp, rdn aftr 7th, ran on frm 13th, no imprsn after 3 out................* (33 to 1 op 20 to 1 tchd 50 to 1) 4
3824 SNOWY RUN 13-11-7 (7*) Mr R Armson, *mid-div in chasing grp, effrt and prog 13th, kpt on und pres.*
.................................(50 to 1 op 33 to 1) 5
ROMAN WOOD 12-11-2 (7*) Mrs T Hill, *prmnt in chasing grp, effrt 13th, nvr rch ldrs.......* (16 to 1 op 10 to 1) 6
TRY IT ALONE 12-11-7 (7*) Miss L Blackford, *mstk 3rd, nvr threatened ldrs...............* (12 to 1 op 6 to 1) 7
3824 RYTON RUN 9-11-2 (7*) Mr J Trice-Rolph, *mid-div in chasing grp, effrt 13th, nvr rch ldrs, wknd r-in.*
...........(9 to 1 op 7 to 1 tchd 10 to 1) 8
KINGS GUNNER 7-11-7 (7*) Miss S Vickery, *al beh and nvr gng wl....................* (14 to 1 op 8 to 1) 9
3824⁵ BIBLICAL 7-11-2 (7*) Mr T Fowler, *prmnt till wknd rpdly frm 12th...................* (33 to 1 op 20 to 1) 10
3724 KNOWAFENCE 8-11-2 (7*) Mr S Howe, *sn tld off.*
.................................(100 to 1 op 50 to 1) 11
POLITICAL MAN 10-11-7 (7*) Mrs K Hills, *prmnt in chasing grp to 8th, sn wknd and beh.....* (16 to 1 op 33 to 1) 12
3761⁴ DAMERS TREASURE 8-11-7 (7*) Mr A Sansome, *al rear, no ch whn mstk and uns rdr 12th.*
...............(3 to 1 op 16 to 1 tchd 12 to 1) ur
HARKEN PREMIER 9-11-8¹ (7*) Mr V Hughes, *chsd ldrs to 7th, sn wknd, tld off whn pld up bef last.......* (50 to 1) pu
MAGNOLIA EXPRESS 10-11-7 (7*) Mr S Blackwell, *mstks, wl beh whn pld up bef 9th..........* (33 to 1 op 25 to 1) pu
VERY TOUCHING 9-11-7 (7*) Mr C Millington, *nvr gng wl, al beh, tld off whn pld up aftr last.*
.............(5 to 1 op 4 to 1 tchd 11 to 2) pu

572

DOXFORD HUT 10-11-9 (5") Mr R Hale, *pressed wnr, led 8th to 9th, rdn and wknd 11th, beh whn pld up bef last.*
.................................(14 to 1 op 10 to 1 tchd 16 to 1) pu
3920⁴ FOURCEES 9-11-7 (7") Mr P Howse, *al beh, tld off whn pld up 3 out......................*(25 to 1 op 16 to 1) pu
3824⁶ SOLDIER BANK 9-11-9 (5") Mr S Bush, *in chasing grp till pld up aftr 7th.....................*(33 to 1 op 20 to 1) pu
COLONEL FAIRFAX 6-11-7 (7") Miss S Duckett, *beh, mstk 6th, tld off and pld up bef tenth.* (100 to 1 op 50 to 1) pu
Dist: 6l, 4l, 3l, 6l, 15l, sht-hd, 1¼l, 8l, 2½l, 8l. 5m 28.00s. a 24.00s (20 Ran).

(P J Clarke), K Cumings

3948 Colin Nash Memorial United Hunts' Challenge Cup Hunters' Chase (6-y-o and up) £2,253 3m 1f 110yds.... (6:20)

3768³ BLACKGUARD (USA) 8-11-10 (7") Mr J Grassick, *hld up beh, steady prog frm 16th, shaken up 2 out, led last, ran on wl..............*(13 to 2 op 6 to 1 tchd 8 to 1) 1
MATSIX 13-11-10 (7") Mr K Cousins, *led, drw clr 16th, hdd last, ran on one pace.............*(12 to 1 op 8 to 1) 2
BRIGHT BURNS (bl) 9-11-10 (7") Mr R Sweeting, *wtd wth in tch, prog to chase ldr 16th, chlgd and pckd 2 out, not run on.............*(100 to 30 op 7 to 2 tchd 3 to 1) 3
HIGHLAND SON 13-11-10 (7") Mr T Cox, *cl up, rdn and outpcd frm 16th, no prog aftr.*
.................................(25 to 1 op 20 to 1 tchd 33 to 1) 4
JANUARY DON (bl) 9-11-10 (7") Mr A Dalton, *prmnt to 16th, grad fdd.................*(33 to 1 op 20 to 1) 5
JOBURN 11-11-8³ (7") Mr J Pritchard, *hld up in tch, blun 14th, not reco'r........*(7 to 1 op 5 to 1 tchd 15 to 2) 6
MY MELLOW MAN 11-11-10 (7") Miss S Vickery, *lost pl and rdn 11th, sn tld off.....* (5 to 1 op 3 to 1 tchd 11 to 2) 7
BEECH GROVE 13-11-12 (5") Mr M Felton, *mstk 8th, chsd ldrs till wknd 16th, sn beh, eased.*
.................................(16 to 1 op 14 to 1 tchd 20 to 1) 8
LOST FORTUNE 11-11-10 (7") Mr H Wheeler, *hld up, in tch whn f 8th...................*(3 to 1 fav op 7 to 2) f
3854³ SANDBROOK 10-11-10 (7") Mr E Williams, *pressed ldr till wknd rpdly 14th, tld off and pld up bef 2 out.*
.................................(16 to 1 op 14 to 1) pu
MARY BOROUGH 8-11-3 (7") Mr A Charles-Jones, *not jump wl al beh, tld off and pld up bef 14th.*
.................................(100 to 1 op 50 to 1) pu
Dist: 7l, 10l, 9l, 6l, 2½l, 20l, ½l. 6m 47.20s. a 31.20s (11 Ran).

(L P Grassick), L P Grassick

3949 Keyline Champion Hunters' Chase (5-y-o and up) £4,123 3¼m 110yds (6:55)

3652² TEAPLANTER 11-12-6 Mr R Russell, *led to 3rd and frm 5th, mstk and hdd 18th, sn rdn alng, styd on to last, soon clr.....* (2 to 1 on tchd 7 to 4 on and 9 to 4 on) 1
3877² RUSTY BRIDGE 7-12-3 Mr R Johnson, *led 3rd to 5th, last frm 12th, mstk and lost tch 16th, styd on 2 out, took second nr finish.....* (14 to 1 op 12 to 1 tchd 16 to 1) 2
3854 SYNDERBOROUGH LAD 8-12-6 Mr M Felton, *hld up in tch, dropped wnr 12th till led 18th, hrd rdn 2 out, hdd and mstk last, wknd rpdly.*
.................................(7 to 2 op 3 to 1 tchd 4 to 1) 3
3877 CARRICKMINES 9-12-6 Mr T Jones, *trkd leaers 3rd and outpcd blun and uns rdr 6 out.*
.................................(13 to 2 op 6 to 1 tchd 7 to 1) ur
Dist: 10l, 1½l. 7m 2.30s. a 29.30s (4 Ran).

(R G Russell), Miss C Saunders

3950 Equestralite Hunters' Chase (6-y-o and up) £2,905 4m 1f.......... (7:30)

3717 NEARLY SPLENDID 9-11-10 (7") Mr T Greed, *hld up in tch, prog 18th, led 5 out, sn clr, jnd 2 out, styd on strly r-in.*
.................................(9 to 4 fav op 3 to 1 tchd 2 to 1) 1
3684² THE MALAKARMA 8-11-9 (5") Mr T Byrne, *trkd ldrs, prog to join wnr 4 out, chlgd 2 out, sn rdn, edgd rght and unbl to quicken r-in.........*(9 to 2 op 7 to 2 tchd 5 to 1) 2
KILSHEELAN LAD 11-11-7 (7") Mr J Jukes, *cl up, rdn and ev ch 5 out, sn outpcd, kpt on....*(16 to 1 tchd 20 to 1) 3
PROPLUS 12-11-10 (7") Mr J M Pritchard, *led till 6 out, rdn and btn frm 4 out.........*(20 to 1 op 25 to 1) 4
3846 RANDOM PLACE 12-11-7 (7") Mr I Pocock, *prmnt, rdn 5 out, btn frm nxt...............*(16 to 1 op 10 to 1) 5
3665⁴ FOWLING PIECE 9-11-7 (7") Mr M Harris, *pressed ldr, led 6 out till nxt, sn rdn, btn bef 3 out...*(50 to 1 op 33 to 1) 6
3861* ANOTHER TROUP 12-11-7 (7") Mr P Bull, *drpd last and mstk 15th, lost tch 19th, sn tld off...*(10 to 1 op 6 to 1) 7
COT LANE 9-11-7 (7") Mr R Walmsley, *in tch to 18th, tld off frm 21st.....................*(14 to 1 op 12 to 1) 8
ROYLE GODSMASTER 10-11-8¹ (7") Mr Julian Taylor, *prmnt, rdn and wknd rpdly 6 out.* (16 to 1 op 14 to 1) 9
SCRUMPY COUNTRY 9-11-7 (7") Maj C Marriott, *al rear, pushed alng 17th, sn lost tch, tld off.*
.................................(14 to 1 op 12 to 1) 10
QUE BELLA 8-11-2 (7") Mr L Brown, *lost pl 11th, beh frm 19th, tld off...................*(25 to 1 op 20 to 1) 11
LADDIE BALLINGER 12-11-7 (7") Dr P Pritchard, *uns rdr strt............................*(66 to 1) ur

ANOTHER LUCAS 10-11-7 (7") Mr L Jefford, *in tch till rdn and wknd 17th, mstk nxt, pld up bef 20th.*
.................................(66 to 1 op 50 to 1) pu
3645³ FOUR TRIX 13-11-12 (5") Mr R Hale, *hld up rear, effrt whn mstk 18th, sn lost tch, pld up bef 4 out.*
.................................(4 to 1 op 9 to 2 tchd 5 to 1) pu
Dist: 1¼l, 25l, 2l, sht-hd, 4l, 3½l, nk, 15l, 12l, 6l. 8m 54.70s. a 37.70s (Flag start) (14 Ran).

(S R Stevens), S R Stevens

3951 Vale Of Evesham Hunters' Chase (5-y-o and up) £2,284 2m 5f.......(8:05)

3884² BLUE DANUBE (USA) 10-11-7 (7") Mr Andrew Martin, *al prmnt, chsd ldr 3 out, rdn to chal last, led r-in, ran on wl.........................*(4 to 1 co-fav op 7 to 2) 1
3216 KILFINNY CROSS (Ire) 6-12-3 Mr J Greenall, *al prmnt, led appr 3 out, hrd rdn nxt, edgd lft and hdd r-in, no extr.*
.................................(4 to 1 co-fav op 3 to 1) 2
WHATS YOUR PROBLEM 11-11-7 (7") Mr J M Pritchard, *hld up in mid-div, prog 12th, wnt 3rd appr 2 out, ran on, nvr nr to chal................*(7 to 1 tchd 9 to 1) 3
TREYFORD 14-11-7 (7") Mr A Steel, *prmnt till wknd appr 3 out......................*(10 to 1 op 8 to 1) 4
3493⁴ CALABRESE (bl) 9-11-10 (7") Major M Watson, *trkd ldrs, mstk tenth, wknd 12th........*(4 to 1 co-fav op 3 to 1) 5
GABISH 9-11-7 (7") Mrs R Hewitt, *al beh.*
.................................(100 to 1 op 50 to 1) 6
3501 KISSANE 13-11-10³ (7") Mr J Wintle, *chsd ldrs, ev ch 12th, rdn and wknd 4 out.............*(40 to 1 op 33 to 1) 7
KAMEO STYLE (bl) 11-11-7 (7") Mr L Brown, *chsd ldrs till rdn and wknd 7th, sn beh.......*(50 to 1 tchd 40 to 1) 8
THE BATCHLOR 11-11-7 (7") Mr W Pugh, *outpcd, tld off whn f 4 out.....................*(40 to 1 op 33 to 1) f
GREAT POKEY 9-11-7 (7") Mr M Wilson, *chsd ldr till blun and wknd 8th, tld off whn f 3 out.*(100 to 1 op 50 to 1) f
3877⁴ LATE SESSION 10-11-7 (7") Mr S Shinton, *outpcd, tld off whn blun and uns rdr 11th......*(66 to 1 op 100 to 1) ur
BEE GARDEN (bl) 13-11-7 (7") Miss S Vickery, *set fst pace, mstks 13th and 14th, hdd appr nxt, wknd, pld up bef last...................*(14 to 1 op 10 to 1) pu
KNOCKBRACK 14-11-9 (5") Mr M Felton, *outpcd, blun whn pld up bef 13th..........*(66 to 1 op 33 to 1) pu
3480 AUTUMN ZULU 15-11-7 (7") Mr G Baines, *outpcd, tld off whn pld up bef 13th........*(66 to 1 op 100 to 1) pu
DEER FENCER 12-11-7 (7") Mr D Duggan, *outpcd, blun 8th, tld off whn pld up bef 13th.*
.................................(11 to 2 op 6 to 1 tchd 7 to 1 and 5 to 1) pu
Dist: 3½l, 4l, 15l, 20l, 2l, 6l, 1¼l. 5m 24.50s. a 20.50s (Flag start) (15 Ran).

(S G Allen), S G Allen

3952 Overbury Hunters' Chase (5-y-o and up) £2,211 2m 110yds.......... (8:40)

3856⁴ RAH WAN (USA) 8-11-13 (7") Mr C Vigors, *prmnt, led aftr 9th, clr 2 out, blun last, jst hld on.* (9 to 2 op 12 to 1) 1
3857³ WELSHMAN'S GULLY 10-12-3 (7") Mr C Newport, *hld up, gd prog 8th, 3rd and outpcd 3 out, ran on frm nxt, fnshd strly, jst fld................*(5 to 2 op 6 to 1) 2
3857⁶ TRUST THE GYPSY 12-12-8 (5") Mr M Felton, *keen hold, hld up in tch, chsd wnr 11th, ev ch 3 out, not quicken nxt, styd on r-in...*(6 to 4 fav tchd 7 to 4 and 11 to 8) 3
3854⁶ UNITYFARM OLTOWNER 10-11-13 (7") Mr E Evans, *mid-div, lost tch 9th, no progr aftr.....*(12 to 1 tchd 14 to 1) 4
3856 BRUCE BUCKLEY 6-11-13 (7") Mr T Hills, *chsd ldrs till wknd rpdly frm 11th, tld off......*(50 to 1 op 100 to 1) 5
3824⁸ HAPPY PADDY 11-11-13 (7") Mr A Sansome, *prmnt, ev ch 9th, hrd rdn and wknd nxt, tld off.* (33 to 1 op 50 to 1) 6
3824⁹ ARCTIC LINE 6-11-13 (7") Mr S R Green, *al rear, tld off whn tried to run out 3 out...........*(100 to 1) 7
FREE EXPRESSION 9-11-8 (7") Mr R Payne, *al rear, tld off whn blun 11th........*(25 to 1 op 20 to 1 tchd 33 to 1) 8
3854 BEE-KAY-ESS 11-11-13 (7") Mr S Shinton, *prmnt, led 6th till aftr 9th, wkng whn blun nxt, sn tld off.*
.................................(20 to 1 op 16 to 1 tchd 25 to 1) 9
3856 PEMBRIDGE DANCER 7-11-13 (7") Mr S Sporborg, *mstk 3rd, last whn blun and uns rdr 5th.*
.................................(20 to 1 op 16 to 1) ur
MOAT LEGEND 9-11-13 (7") Dr P Pritchard, *jmpd rght and mstks, tell till 6th, wknd and pld up 9th.*
.................................(11 to 1 op 20 to 1 tchd 12 to 1) pu
Dist: Sht-hd, 2½l, 25l, 25l, 7l, 20l, 3l, 1¼l. 4m 15.30s. a 19.30s (11 Ran).

(Mrs J Hadden-Wight), P R Chamings

MALLOW (IRE) (yielding to soft)
Tuesday May 17th

3953 Macroom Maiden Hurdle (5-y-o) £2,228 2m............. (5:30)

3834³ GLENBALLYMA (Ire) 11-0 F J Flood, ...(9 to 4) 1
3834² NOT MY LINE (Ire) 11-2 (3") C O'Brien, ... (7 to 4 fav) 2
3793⁴ AMME ENAEK (Ire) 11-0 M Duffy, ...(8 to 1) 3
3834⁸ VALTORUS (Ire) 11-5 J F Titley, ...(10 to 1) 4
3366 SIR JOHN (Ire) 10-12 (7") J Butler, ...(33 to 1) 5
3505 CROSS ANGORLADY (Ire) 11-0 C F Swan, ...(12 to 1) 6

573

3834 THE LEFT FOOTER (Ire) 11-2 (3*) T J O'Sullivan, .. (16 to 1) 7
3871⁹ VERY ADAPTABLE (Ire) 10-12 (7*) T J Murphy, ... (10 to 1) 8
HERESTHEDEAL (Ire) 11-5 J Jones, ... (10 to 1) 9
3653 UP FOR RANSOME (Ire) 11-5 S H O'Donovan, ... (14 to 1) 10
2096⁷ DONNASOO (Ire) 11-8 B Sheridan, ... (16 to 1) 11
LEVANTER'S BREEZE (Ire) 11-0 (5*) J P Broderick, (14 to 1) 12
SUPREME ARCTIC (Ire) 11-0 P McGrath, ... (14 to 1) 13
3788⁴ SWIFT GLIDER (Ire) 10-11 (3*) D P Murphy, ... (10 to 1) 14
3793 LOCAL SILK (Ire) (bl) 11-0 A Powell, ... (14 to 1) 15
SIR GREGORY (Ire) 11-5 L P Cusack, ... (10 to 1) 16
3290 BENSONS RETURN (Ire) 11-5 J P Banahan, ... (25 to 1) 17
ANDANTE ALLEGRO (Ire) 11-0 A J O'Brien, ... (33 to 1) 18
3730 D'S AND DO'S (Ire) 11-0 T Horgan, ... (25 to 1) f
Dist: 8l, 7l, 6l, 8l. 3m 57.80s. (19 Ran).

(Mrs J J Byrne), F Flood

3954 Blackwater Maiden Hurdle (6-y-o and up) £2,228 2m 5f. .... (6:00)

2756⁵ IAMWHATIAM 8-12-0 S H O'Donovan, ... (11 to 2) 1
3747³ STRONG HICKS (Ire) 6-11-6 F J Flood, ... (3 to 1 fav) 2
3504⁴ EXTRA DAYS 7-12-0 J F Titley, ... (7 to 1) 3
3466 CORRIB HAVEN (Ire) 6-11-1 (5*) J P Broderick, .. (20 to 1) 4
3647⁹ MISGIVINGS (Ire) 6-11-1 C F Swan, ... (7 to 1) 5
3733* BROGUESTOWN PRIDE (Ire) 6-11-9 (5*) K P Gaule, (7 to 2) 6
FLOWERHILL DAISY (Ire) 6-10-12 (3*) C O'Brien, .. (33 to 1) 7
3647 CARRICKEM (Ire) 6-10-10 (5*) A J Slattery, ... (16 to 1) 8
3747 DRUMCILL LASS (Ire) 6-11-1 P M Verling, ... (10 to 1) 9
3647 CORRTBALANCE (bl) 7-11-1 B Sheridan, ... (10 to 1) 10
3747⁶ RATHFARDON (Ire) 6-11-6 A Powell, ... (10 to 1) 11
3747 STRONG HURRICANE 7-12-0 T Horgan, ... (12 to 1) 12
3869⁸ PRINCESS BAVARD 9-11-9 Mr M Phillips, ... (10 to 1) 13
3870 LOUGH CULTRA DRIVE (Ire) 6-12-0 C O'Dwyer, .. (20 to 1) 14
3655 MONEY MADE 7-11-1 (5*) M G Cleary, ... (50 to 1) 15
3291 TWO HILLS 7-11-3 (3*) T J O'Sullivan, ... (33 to 1) 16
3810⁵ GOLDEN PLAN (Ire) 6-11-6 C N Bowens, ... (16 to 1) pu
Dist: Hd, 1½l, 5l, 1l. 5m 39.60s. (17 Ran).

(Seamus O'Farrell), Seamus O'Farrell

3955 Sugar Factory Greenvale Novice Chase (5-y-o and up) £2,742 2m (7:00)

3870⁶ BALLYBODEN 7-11-4 (5*) J P Broderick, ... (11 to 2) 1
3835 SO PINK (Ire) 6-11-9 J F Titley, ... (5 to 1) 2
3275 RATHBRIDES JOY 7-12-0 T Horgan, ... (7 to 1) 3
3872² CHELSEA NATIVE (Ire) 7-11-4 (5*) Susan A Finn, (4 to 1 fav) 4
3789² LAWYER'S BRIEF (Fr) 7-12-0 L P Cusack, ... (12 to 1) 5
3792² BARRAFONA (Ire) 6-11-9 J Magee, ... (7 to 1) 6
3911⁴ HIGH-SPEC 8-11-11 (3*) C O'Brien, ... (8 to 1) 7
2350 STRONG CHERRY 8-10-12¹ (7*) Mr K Taylor, ... (14 to 1) 8
3795⁸ BALLINDERRY GLEN 8-11-4 (5*) M G Cleary, ... (12 to 1) 9
3872⁹ ORMOND BEACH (Ire) 5-10-13 W T Slattery Jnr, .. (33 to 1) 10
3655 GENERALANAESTHETIC 9-11-2 (7*) A Powell, ... (33 to 1) 11
133² BERT HOUSE 8-11-9 T Kinane Jnr, ... (12 to 1) 12
3835⁶ SCREEN PRINTER (Ire) 5-10-8 C O'Dwyer, ... (12 to 1) 13
71 FAHA STAR (Ire) 5-10-13 S H O'Donovan, ... (25 to 1) 14
MASTER RAG (bl) 7-11-4 (5*) P A Roche, ... (25 to 1) 15
133⁹ J-TEC BOY 8-12-0 P P Kinane, ... (20 to 1) 16
Dist: ¾l, 2½l, 1l, 2½l. 4m 8.80s. (16 Ran).

(Exors Of The Late O McCormack), Michael Hourigan

3956 Munster INH Flat Race (5-y-o and up) £2,228 2m 5f. .... (8:30)

LORD SINGAPORE (Ire) 6-12-0 Mr M Phillips, ... (8 to 1) 1
3891³ MR GLYNN (Ire) 5-11-6 (7*) Mr T J Murphy, ...(7 to 4 fav) 2
2869⁹ YOUR CALL (Ire) 5-11-10 (3*) Mr J A Nash, ... (8 to 1) 3
3912⁴ RAMPANT ROSIE (Ire) 6-11-9 Mr A P O'Brien, ... (8 to 1) 4
112 CARRABAWN 8-11-2 (7*) Mr Patrick O'Keeffe, ... (20 to 1) 5
BULLENS BAY (Ire) 5-11-6 (7*) Mr N C Kelleher, .. (14 to 1) 6
MARLFIELD (Ire) 6-11-7 (7*) Mr K Whelan, ... (20 to 1) 7
MILEY SWEENEY 7-11-9 (5*) Mr B F Murphy, ... (20 to 1) 8
QUAYSIDE COTTAGE (Ire) 6-11-11 (3*) Mr T Lombard,
.... (12 to 1) 9
ONE EYED GER VI (Ire) 5-11-6 (7*) Mr T J Foley, ..(10 to 1) 10
DISTANT LADY 8-11-9 Mr P Fenton, ... (7 to 1) 11
124 GRAND SCENERY (Ire) 6-11-7 (7*) Mr D Keane, .. (10 to 1) 12
925 AYDOANALL (Ire) 5-11-6 (7*) Mr J T McNamara, .. (20 to 1) 13
3791² KILLANNA LASS (Ire) 5-11-1 (7*) Mr N D Fehily, .. (20 to 1) 14
DESSIE'S GIRL (Ire) (bl) 6-11-2 (7*) Mr A Daly, ... (20 to 1) 15
MY GOONY (Ire) 5-11-1 (7*) Mr G R Kenny, ... (20 to 1) 16
NEVER CRY GRIEF (Ire) 6-11-2 (7*) Miss L Townsley,
.... (20 to 1) 17
REDCHAIR EXPRESS 8-11-2 (7*) Mr D Duggan, .. (33 to 1) 18
3912⁷ MORE RUBBLES 8-11-2 (7*) Mr G Mulcaire, ... (20 to 1) 19
3611 CLOGHER LORD (Ire) 5-11-6 (7*) Miss S J Leahy, (14 to 1) 20
71 CANDY IS DANDY (Ire) 5-11-4³ (7*) Mr R Stack, .. (25 to 1) 21
Dist: 4½l, 2½l, ½l, 11l. 5m 35.90s. (21 Ran).

(Mrs E Farrelly), John J Walsh

LEOPARDSTOWN (IRE) (good)
Wednesday May 18th

3957 Seafield (QR) Handicap Hurdle (0-130 4-y-o and up) £3,084 2m. .... (8:15)

3656 LUSTRINO (USA) [-] (bl) 4-11-8 (3*) Mr J A Nash, ... (7 to 2) 1
3935² HIS WAY (Ire) [-] 5-11-6 (3*) Mr D Marnane, ...(7 to 4 fav) 2
3657⁸ RISING WATERS (Ire) [-] 6-11-11 (7*) Mr M Wiseman,
.... (16 to 1) 3
3247 LEGAL PROFESSION (Ire) [-] 6-11-7 (3*) Mr D Valentine,
.... (7 to 1) 4
3693³ CELTIC SAILS (Ire) [-] 6-11-1 (3*) Mr P J Casey, .. (8 to 1) 5
3810* KNOCNAGORE (Ire) [-] 5-9-13 (5*) Mr H F Cleary, ..(10 to 1) 6
VLADIMIR'S WAY (Ire) [-] 5-10-10 (5*) Mr M Kelly, (25 to 1) 7
3913 CELTIC GALE [-] 7-10-4 (7*) Mr T J Beattie, ... (25 to 1) 8
2054⁶ HEADBANGER [-] (bl) 7-11-10 Mr J P Dempsey, .. (14 to 1) 9
3836 MR BOAL (Ire) [-] 5-11-11 (7*) Mr M Brennan, ... (7 to 1) 10
3732 EAST HOUSTON [-] 5-11-0 (5*) Mr G J Harford, ... (33 to 1) 11
3693⁷ ORBIS (USA) [-] 8-11-12 (5*) Mr E J Kearns Jnr, ... (14 to 1) 12
Dist: 1l, nk, 7l, ½l. 3m 48.00s. (12 Ran).
SR: 41/38/46/31/24/-/   *(Michael H Watt), D K Weld*

3958 Holly Park INH Flat Race (4 & 5-y-o) £3,084 2m. .... (8:45)

EXPEDIENT OPTION (Ire) 4-11-3 Mr P Fenton, ... (8 to 1) 1
3712³ BANAGAR (Ire) 4-11-5 (5*) Mr H F Cleary, ...(5 to 1) 2
3508* BALLYQUIN BELLE (Ire) 4-10-12 (7*) Mr E Norris, ..(5 to 1) 3
3660 GALLOWS HILL (Ire) 5-12-0 (3*) Mrs J M Mullins, ..(6 to 1) 4
3394* SELL EVERYTHING (Ire) (bl) 4-11-7 (3*) Mr D Valentine,
.... (5 to 1) 5
3653⁵ MAORI'S DELIGHT 5-10-12 (7*) Mr B Heffernan, .. (11 to 2) 6
3653⁴ ROSTARR (Ire) 5-11-12 Mr A P O'Brien, ... (3 to 1 fav) 7
CHATTERBUCK (Ire) 5-11-10 Mr M McNulty, ... (10 to 1) 8
3792⁵ VALIYIST (Ire) 5-10-12 (7*) Mr C Cronin, ... (14 to 1) 9
BUGGY (Ire) 5-11-3 (7*) Mr T N Cloke, ... (25 to 1) 10
3796⁶ PADDY RED (Ire) 5-11-7 (3*) Mr P J Casey, ... (25 to 1) 11
SCEAL EILE (Ire) 4-10-5 (7*) Mr A K Wyse, ... (33 to 1) 12
Dist: 2l, 4½l, 4½l, 1½l. 3m 48.00s. (12 Ran).

(J Halley), P M J Doyle

SEDGEFIELD (firm)
Wednesday May 18th
Going Correction: MINUS 0.50 sec. per fur.

3959 End Of Season Claiming Hurdle (4-y-o and up) £1,892 2m 1f 110yds.... (2:20)

3866⁶ NOTABLE EXCEPTION 5-11-9 (5*) S Mason, mid-div, hdwy
aftr 3 out, styd on wl to ld cl hme. ....(7 to 2 jt-
fav op 3 to 1 tchd 11 to 4) 1
3780⁴ GREENACRES LAD 11-11-2 A Mulholland, trkd ldrs, led
aftr 2 out, mstk last, ct cl hme. ....(7 to 2 jt-
fav op 3 to 1 tchd 4 to 1) 2
3899³ RICHMOND (Ire) 6-10-13 D Wilkinson, hld up, gd hdwy to
track ldrs 3 out, ev ch betw last 2, no extr.
.... (7 to 1 op 5 to 1) 3
3864⁰ PERSPICACITY 7-10-8 J Callaghan, hld up, hdwy hfwy,
dsptd ld 3 out, ev ch appr last, one pace.
.... (14 to 1 op 10 to 1) 4
CROXDALE GREY 7-10-0 (5*) Mr D Parker, trkd ldrs, slight
ld 3 out, hdd aftr 3 out, wknd. ....(20 to 1) 5
3778 SOUSON (Ire) (bl) 6-10-13 K Jones, chsd ldrs, one pace frm
3 out. .... (20 to 1 op 10 to 1) 6
3782² STATION EXPRESS (Ire) 6-11-5 A Maguire, hld up, hdwy
aftr 3 out, one pace frm nxt. ....(5 to 1 op 7 to 2) 7
2870⁹ BURN BRIDGE (USA) (v) 8-11-2 Peter Caldwell, slwly into
strd, nvr dngrs. .... (8 to 1 op 6 to 1) 8
810⁶ POLDER 8-11-1 (7*) Miss S Higgins, prmnt till wknd aftr 3
out. .... (16 to 1 op 10 to 1) 9
3864⁸ FLAXON WORRIOR 10-10-10 O Pears, made most till hdd
3 out, sn wknd. .... (12 to 1 op 6 to 1) 10
3357⁵ TOP VILLAIN 8-10-13 K Johnson, trkd ldrs, rdn aftr 3 out,
sn wknd. .... (12 to 1 op 6 to 1) 11
3864 GYMCRAK CYRANO (Ire) (bl) 5-10-3 (5*) S Lyons, dsptd ld,
wkng wtn blun 4th, tld off...........(33 to 1 op 20 to 1) 12
3435 SAMS-THE-MAN (bl) 6-10-7 C Hawkins, slwly into strd,
beh most of way, tld off.
.... (12 to 1 op 33 to 1 tchd 50 to 1) 13
3868 RUN ON FLO (Ire) (bl) 6-10-12 (5*) P Waggott, beh frm hfwy,
tld off.. (50 to 1 op 20 to 1) 14
3815 SOLAR NOVA 6-11-0 N Smith, wth ldrs to 5th, wknd
quickly, tld off.................................. (50 to 1 op 33 to 1) 15
3864 LET'S BE ON 6-10-4 (7*) B Grattan, sn beh, wl tld off whn
pld up bef 3 out. .... (33 to 1) pu
Dist: Hd, 3l, 4l, 3½l, 3l, 4l, 9l, hd, sht-hd, ½l. 4m 0.00s. a 5.00s (16 Ran).

(Andrews & Wilson), Mrs M Reveley

3960 Reg Boyle Bookmaker Handicap Hurdle (0-125 5-y-o and up) £2,238 2m 5f 110yds. .... (2:50)

3801⁵ FLASS VALE [88] (v) 6-10-2 C Hawkins, made all, clr aftr 3
out, easily.................................(2 to 1 fav op 7 to 4) 1
3464⁷ CHANTRY BARTLE [104] 8-11-4 D Wilkinson, hld up, hdwy
hfwy, rdn to chase wnr aftr 7th, no imprsn.
.... (7 to 2 op 3 to 1) 2
3783* BOWLANDS WAY [86] (bl) 10-10-0 O Pears, prmnt till outpcd aftr 7th, styd on ag'n frm last. (8 to 1 tchd 7 to 1) 3
3782* ELVETT BRIDGE (Ire) [86] 6-10-0 A Dobbin, prmnt till wknd
bef 3 out............................ (14 to 1 op 12 to 1) 4

3819 NOUVELLE CUISINE [88] 6-10-2 N Bentley, *beh and reminders aftr 3rd, some hdwy after 6th, wknd bef 3 out*..................................(4 to 1 op 9 to 2) 5
3823[4] KETTI [110] 9-11-10 A Maguire, *in tch, pushed alng hfwy, wknd aftr 7th*..................................... (6 to 1) 6
3866 LA MOLINILLA [86] 11-9-7 (7*) Miss S Lamb, *lost tch frm hfwy, tld off*......................(100 to 1 op 50 to 1) 7
Dist: 10l, 9l, 3½l, nk, 4l, 25l. 4m 58.00s. a 7.00s (7 Ran).
(Goldspace T/a Sandal Business Services), C W Fairhurst

3961 John N. Dunn Novices' Chase (5-y-o and up) £2,186 3m 3f........... (3:20)

3863[3] UPWELL 10-11-2 K Johnson, *al prmnt, rdn to ld bef 2 out, styd on wl und pres*...............(11 to 1 op 10 to 1) 1
3863[2] CROWN EYEGLASS 8-11-2 A Maguire, *al prmnt, drvn alng aftr 4 out, kpt on wl und pres frm 2 out*. ....(4 to 1 tchd 7 to 2) 2
3779[4] LADY BLAKENEY 8-11-3 A Dobbin, *led to 4th, wth ldr, drvn alng and slightly outpcd aftr four out, one pace after*..................(11 to 2 op 5 to 1 tchd 6 to 1) 3
3863[5] MASTER MATHEW 7-10-11 (5*) J Burke, *led 4th till hdd bef 2 out, sn rdn, fdd*................. (25 to 1 op 20 to 1) 4
3828[5] PETTY BRIDGE 10-11-8 R Bellamy, *mstks, sn beh, tld off*. ....(7 to 4 fav op 6 to 4 tchd 2 to 1) 5
3779[6] LINLITHGOW PALACE (bl) 12-10-11 (5*) P Waggott, *sn beh, tld off*............................(66 to 1 op 50 to 1) 6
3437[8] MOYODE REGENT 10-11-1 (7*) Mr A Manners, *sn beh, tld off whn pld up bef 4 out*............(7 to 1 op 6 to 1) pu
3895 HEY JOE 7-11-2 K Jones, *sn beh, tld off whn pld up bef 14th*............................. (66 to 1 op 50 to 1) pu
3863[4] JENNY'S GLEN 7-11-2 B Storey, *in tch, pushed alng and no imprsn whn mstk 15th, wl behend when pld up bef 4 out*.................................(12 to 1 op 10 to 1) pu
Dist: 2½l, 9l, 8l, 30l, 4l. 6m 43.10s. a 4.10s (9 Ran).
(Robert Johnson), R Johnson

3962 Guy Cunard Northern Point-to-point Championship Hunters' Chase (5-y-o and up) £1,935 2m 5f........... (3:50)

3900[2] KNOWE HEAD 10-12-0 (7*) Mr S Brisby, *made all, pushed out aftr last, eased towards finish*. ....(5 to 4 fav tchd 11 to 8) 1
WALTINGO 11-12-0 (7*) Miss R Clark, *beh, took clr order hfwy, chsd wnr frm 2 out, ch bef last, no extr r-in*. ....(7 to 2 op 3 to 1) 2
CAPTAIN LYNDSEY 13-12-0 (7*) Mr A Robson, *in tch, chsd wnr frm tenth, ev ch 3 out, one pace from nxt*. ....(25 to 1 op 20 to 1) 3
CONTACT KELVIN 12-12-0 (7*) Mr M Haigh, *cl up, outpcd whn mstk tenth, sn beh*........................(8 to 1) 4
3645 LINEBACKER 10-12-3 (7*) Mr N F Smith, *blun 4th, sn beh, mstk 9th, nvr dngrs*..................... (5 to 1 op 4 to 1) 5
HOME DOVE 7-11-9 (7*) Mr M Sowersby, *in tch, blun 11th, sn wknd*......................... (14 to 1 op 12 to 1) 6
CERTAIN BEAT 9-12-0 (7*) Mr N Kent, *prmnt early, losing tch whn f 4 out*....................(16 to 1 op 14 to 1) f
SUNDAYSPORT SCOOP (bl) 9-12-2 (5*) Mr N Wilson, *sn lost tch, wl tld off whn pld up bef 2 out*. (50 to 1 op 33 to 1) pu
Dist: 2l, 4l, 20l, 1½l, nk. 5m 8.00s. a 4.00s (8 Ran).
(J Hodgson), Miss C A Blakeborough

3963 A1 Handicap Chase (0-125 5-y-o and up) £2,768 2m 1f............... (4:20)

3902* STAY AWAKE [107] 8-10-10 (5ex) P Niven, *trkd ldr frm 3rd, led gng wl bef last, quickened clr r-in, easily*. ....(2 to 1 op 7 to 4) 1
3785* CLARES OWN [105] 10-10-8 A Maguire, *led till hdd bef last, sn btn*.................... (11 to 10 fav op Evens) 2
3816[3] NEWMARKET SAUSAGE [97] 13-10-0 M Hourigan, *sn lost tch, tld off*....................................(50 to 1) 3
3595[6] BOUTZDAROFF [125] 12-12-0 M Dwyer, *tracking ldr whn broke leg and f 3rd, destroyed*......(3 to 1 tchd 7 to 2) f
Dist: 5l, dist. 4m 0.40s. b 4.60s (4 Ran).
SR: 43/36/-/-/ (Austin Donnellon), Mrs M Reveley

3964 Sedgefield Champion Novices' Hurdle (4-y-o and up) £2,921 2m 5f 110yds ....(4:50)

3787[3] KINDA GROOVY (bl) 5-11-6 N Smith, *cl up, led bef 7th, rdn betw last 2, styd on wl*............(14 to 1 op 10 to 1) 1
3862* IFALLELSEFAILS 6-11-7 (5*) F Perratt, *in tch, slightly outpcd aftr 3 out, kpt on frm nxt, no imprsn on wnr*. .... (6 to 5 on op 11 to 8 on tchd 11 to 10 on) 2
3825[5] BATHWICK BOBBIE 7-10-7 (7*) Miss S Higgins, *al prmnt, ev ch 2 out, kpt on same pace*........ (16 to 1 op 14 to 1) 3
3897[5] ASTRALEON (Ire) 6-11-0 A Maguire, *hld up, hdwy bef 3 out, rdn betw last 2, sn btn*........ (7 to 1 tchd 8 to 1) 4
3787[2] CLARET AND GOLD 7-11-0 B Storey, *chsd ldrs till outpcd aftr 7th, no dngr after*.............(12 to 1 op 8 to 1) 5
3778[5] ROYAL VACATION 5-11-12 J Callaghan, *hld up, blun 3rd, hdwy whn mstk 3 out, wknd bef nxt*. (4 to 1 op 3 to 1) 6
3905* GLANDALANE LADY 5-10-8 (7*) R McGrath, *in tch till wknd bef 3 out*.....................(10 to 1 op 7 to 1) 7

ARCTIC BLOOM 8-10-9 Mr N Wilson, *strted slwly, sn tld off, pld up bef 6th*.................(66 to 1 op 33 to 1) pu
3673[7] SINGING SAM (bl) 9-10-7 (7*) W Fry, *led till hdd bef 7th, wknd quickly, tld off whn pld up before 2 out*. (66 to 1) pu
3677[3] RUSSIAN CASTLE (Ire) 5-11-0 K Jones, *lost tch frm hfwy, tld off whn pld up bef 3 out*....... (20 to 1 op 16 to 1) pu
3862 DIDACTE (Fr) 4-10-3 (5*) P Waggott, *lost tch frm hfwy, tld off whn pld up bef 2 out*...........(66 to 1 op 33 to 1) pu
Dist: 3½l, 2l, 5l, 8l, 4l, 5l. 4m 58.00s. a 7.00s (11 Ran).
(Ian Park), I Park

WORCESTER (good to firm) Wednesday May 18th

Going Correction: PLUS 0.05 sec. per fur.

3965 Earls Croome Novices' Selling Hurdle (4-y-o and up) £2,059 2m....... (2:30)

3211 DOUBLE THE STAKES (USA) 5-11-7 D J Burchell, *rcd keenly and al gng wl, led sn aftr 3 out, clr whn mstk last, unchlgd*.......... (9 to 2 op 5 to 1 tchd 11 to 2) 1
3716[3] MINI FETE (Fr) 5-10-9 R Greene, *chsd ldrs, kpt on one pace frm 3 out*..........................(14 to 1 op 10 to 1) 2
922[4] DESERT PEACE (Ire) 5-11-0 G McCourt, *al prmnt, led briefly 3 out, btn whn hit last*. ....(7 to 2 op 3 to 1 tchd 5 to 2) 3
3822[3] SECRET FORMULA 4-10-9 W Humphreys, *hld up, hdwy 4th, outpcd frm 3 out*..............(20 to 1 op 12 to 1) 4
2061 SOL ROUGE (Ire) 5-10-9 Mr K Green, *hld up, hdwy 5th, wknd aftr nxt*....................(33 to 1 op 25 to 1) 5
3765[3] BOWLAND GIRL (Ire) 5-10-6 (3*) S Wynne, *hld up, hdwy 5th, btn whn hit 2 out*.............(20 to 1 op 12 to 1) 6
3826[2] SIRKA (Fr) 4-10-9 R Dunwoody, *whipped round strt, sn chsd ldr, led aftr 5th, hdd 3 out, wkng whn hit nxt*. .... (6 to 4 fav tchd 7 to 4) 7
3826[4] KELLY'S DARLING 8-11-2 (5*) S Curran, *hld up, hdwy appr 3 out, wknd bef nxt*........... (9 to 1 op 8 to 1) 8
3829 NORDROSS (bl) 6-10-9 D Bridgwater, *hld up, hdwy 4th, wknd appr 3 out*.................. (33 to 1 op 16 to 1) 9
3715[6] GREEN'S STUBBS (v) 7-11-0 B Powell, *mid-div, not fluent, lost tch 5th*................... (50 to 1 op 33 to 1) 10
3848 TRIAL TIMES (USA) 5-11-0 S McNeill, *hld up, lost tch 5th, tld off*...............................(33 to 1 op 20 to 1) 11
3661 FOXY LASS 5-10-9 Mr J Cambidge, *al beh, tld off*. ....(100 to 1 op 50 to 1) 12
3357 LADY KHADIJA 8-10-9 L O'Hara, *led till hdd sn aftr 5th, wknd rpdly, tld off*...............(100 to 1 op 50 to 1) 13
3826 DUKE OF BUDWORTH 4-10-9 W Marston, *beh and jmpd rght, sn tld off*.................. (100 to 1 op 50 to 1) 14
3827 CRYMLYN SWING (bl) 10-10-9 Mr D Verco, *prmnt till blun 4th, sn tld*...................... (100 to 1 op 50 to 1) 15
HIT THE BOX 9-11-0 M A FitzGerald, *hmpd 1st, beh whn hit 3rd, tld off*......................(50 to 1 op 25 to 1) 16
SAMANTHAS JOY 4-9-11 (7*) P McLoughlin, *al beh, tld off frm 4th*........................ (100 to 1 op 50 to 1) 17
620 MARCHING SEASON (Ire) 6-10-9 M Brennan, *jmpd badly rght in rear, tld off whn pld up aftr 5th*. ....(33 to 1 op 20 to 1) pu
3670 MARYLAND BOY (bl) 6-11-0 J Railton, *in tch to 3rd, tld off whn pld up 3 out*.................(66 to 1 op 50 to 1) pu
1734 OZONE LASS (Ire) 6-10-9 Mr M Smith, *beh frm 3rd, tld off whn pld up aftr 5th*.............(100 to 1 op 50 to 1) pu
Dist: 8l, 6l, 7l, ¾l, 1l, 9l, 6l, 1l, 2½l, 8l. 3m 48.30s. a 7.30s (20 Ran).
SR: 28/8/7/-/-/-/ (T G Brooks), D Burchell

3966 Handley Castle Novices' Chase (5-y-o and up) £2,420 2½m 110yds.....(3:00)

3706[2] MACEDONAS 6-11-9 S McNeill, *hld up in rear, mstk 3rd, hit 8th, hdwy appr 4 out, mistake nxt, ran on wl to ld r-in*....................(15 to 8 op 7 to 4 tchd 2 to 1) 1
3827 COLONIAL OFFICE (USA) 8-10-10 (7*) Mr M Rimell, *hld up, hdwy 8th, lft in ld 3 out, rdn and hdd r-in*. ....(100 to 1 op 50 to 1) 2
2993[3] TUDOR FABLE (Ire) 6-11-9 R Dunwoody, *led till aftr second, led 5th to 9th, led 5 out to 3 out, one pace frm nxt*. ....(11 to 10 on op 11 to 8 on tchd Evens) 3
3929 THE YOKEL 8-11-0 (3*) T Eley, *led aftr second, hdd 5th, beh 9th, effrt appr 4 out, one pace*. ....(10 to 1 op 8 to 1 tchd 12 to 1) 4
3774[6] KING OF SHADOWS 7-11-3 Gary Lyons, *jmpd lft, prmnt till wknd quickly aftr 5 out*........(25 to 1 op 14 to 1) 5
2966[9] PICKETSTONE 7-11-3 G McCourt, *hld up, gd hdwy appr 4 out, led, blun and uns rdr nxt*.....(12 to 1 op 10 to 1) ur
TOLL BRIDGE 7-10-12 D Bridgwater, *hld up, hdwy and lft second 7th, led 9th to 11th, wknd quickly, pld up bef nxt*............................ (33 to 1 op 16 to 1) pu
3000 FROG HOLLOW (Ire) (bl) 6-11-3 B Powell, *pld hrd, trkd ldrs, second whn blun badly 7th, not reco'r, pulled up bef 11th*............................(12 to 1 op 9 to 1) pu
Dist: ¾l, 2½l, 6l, 8l. 5m 11.10s. a 8.10s (8 Ran).
SR: 24/17/20/8/-/ (Jim McCarthy), C P E Brooks

3967 Ryall Handicap Hurdle (0-120 4-y-o and up) £2,051 2m 5f 110yds.... (3:30)

3618* COUTURE STOCKINGS [108] 10-11-12 N Williamson, *al gng wl beh ldrs, led appr 2 out, sn clr, cmftbly.*
.... (5 to 1 fav op 7 to 2) 1
3904* DESERT FORCE (Ire) [92] (bl) 5-10-10 (6ex) J R Kavanagh, *hld up, steady hdwy frm 4th, ev ch 3 out, rdn and one pace from nxt.*........ (5 to 1 op 9 to 2 tchd 11 to 2) 2
3283⁵ ULURU (Ire) [103] 6-11-7 R Dunwoody, *trkd ldr, hit 3rd, led appr 5th, hdd aftr 2 out, one pace.* (11 to 2 op 5 to 1) 3
3845* CAVO GRECO (USA) [91] 5-10-9 (6ex) D Skyrme, *hld up in tch, lost pl 4th, hdwy 6th, ev ch till one pace frm 2 out.*
.... (8 to 1 op 7 to 1 tchd 9 to 1) 4
3831⁶ TILT TECH FLYER [85] 9-10-3 W Marston, *al in cl tch, rdn and wknd appr 2 out.*.............. (14 to 1 op 12 to 1) 5
3496* TEST MATCH [95] 7-10-13 M A FitzGerald, *al prmnt, rdn 3 out, sn btn.*........ (9 to 2 op 4 to 1 tchd 5 to 1) 6
3692⁷ PREOBLAKENSKY [107] 7-11-6 (5*) J Supple, *led till hdd appr 5th, wknd approaching 3 out, tld off.*
.... (16 to 1 op 20 to 1) 7
3831* WHAT IF [91] 10-10-9 M Brennan, *hld up, hdwy appr 5th, ev ch 3 out, wkng whn blun nxt, eased, tld off.*
.... (13 to 2 op 11 to 2) 8
3851 SUKAAB [106] 9-11-5 (5*) Guy Lewis, *al beh, tld off 4 out.*
.... (10 to 1) 9
1783⁵ GOLDEN SHINE [102] 8-11-6 T Wall, *al beh, tld off 4 out.*
.... (33 to 1) 10
Dist: 6l, 1½l, 1½l, 2l, 5l, 15l, 2½l, 2l, dist. 5m 6.00s. a 12.00s (10 Ran).

(Couture Marketing Ltd), J Mackie

3968 Upton On Severn Handicap Chase (0-120 5-y-o and up) £3,556 2½m 110yds........................ (4:00)

3808* TOCHENKA [112] 10-11-12 D Bridgwater, *al cl up, led 9th, drw clr appr 4 out, hrd hld.*
.... (6 to 5 fav op Evens tchd 5 to 4) 1
2563⁴ VULRORY'S CLOWN [86] 16-10-0 M Brennan, *jmpd wl, led till aftr 6th, outpcd, lft poor second last.*
.... (20 to 1 op 16 to 1) 2
3803² BARKISLAND [94] 10-10-8 R Dunwoody, *sn trkd ldr, led aftr 6th, jmpd slwly 8th, hdd nxt, poor second whn blun badly last.*...................... (2 to 1 op 5 to 2) 3
3766³ PEACE OFFICER [114] 8-12-0 M A FitzGerald, *nvr gng wl in rear, some hdwy 5th, no ch aftr blun 5 out, brook blood vessel.*..................... (11 to 4 op 5 to 2 tchd 3 to 1) 4
Dist: 8l, 2½l, 9l. 5m 11.20s. a 8.20s (4 Ran).

SR: 26/-/-/8/   (R K Minton-Price), N A Twiston-Davies

3969 Kinnersley Hunters' Chase (5-y-o and up) £1,657 2m 7f.............. (4:30)

3768* CONNEMARA DAWN 10-12-0 (7*) Miss P Gundry, *made most and jmpd wl till hit last, sn hdd, rallied gmely to ld on line, collapsed aftr, dead.* (7 to 2 fav tchd 3 to 1) 1
YAHOO 13-11-7 (7*) Mr M Rimell, *al in tch, rdn 4 out, chlgd and led sn aftr last, ct on line.*
.... (4 to 1 op 7 to 2) 2
3854* WELSH LEGION 9-12-0 (7*) Miss C Burgess, *hld up in tch, hit 11th, rdn 3 out, ev ch nxt, ran on wl r-in.*
.... (7 to 1 op 6 to 1) 3
3807² DUBIT 9-11-7 (7*) Miss S Vickery, *prmnt, making hdwy whn mstk 11th, sn reco'red, one pace frm 3 out.*
.... (8 to 1 op 7 to 1 tchd 9 to 1) 4
3884 RAMPALLION 11-12-0 (7*) Mr M Jackson, *dsptd ld for most of race till wknd quickly 3 out, pshd lme, tld off.*
.... (9 to 2 op 4 to 1) 5
LOVE ON THE ROCKS 9-11-3* (7*) Mr S Hope, *al beh, tld off.*......................... (33 to 1) 6
3684 MASTER MUCK 11-12-0 (7*) Mr S Joynes, *mstks, rdn tenth, wknd 5 out, tld off.*................. (16 to 1) 7
NEW GAME 12-11-2 (7*) Mr G Maundrell, *prmnt till wknd 12th, tld off.*................... (7 to 1 op 6 to 1) 8
3854 CAPTAIN MANNERING (USA) 9-11-7 (7*) Mr M Harris, *sn tld off.*.............................. (100 to 1) 9
3854 DURZI 9-11-7 (7*) Mr S Blackwell, *mstks, al beh, tld off whn pld up bef 2 out.*.................. (20 to 1) pu
YOU'LL DO 11-11-7 (7*) Mr N Moore, *al beh, tld off whn pld up bef 4 out.*........ (25 to 1 op 20 to 1) pu
MISTER TUFTIE 9-11-7 (7*) Mr D Barlow, *prmnt, wkng whn mstk tenth, tld off when pld up bef 4 out.*
.... (33 to 1 op 25 to 1) pu
HYMER 5-11-0 (7*) Mr P Hamer, *hit 1st, sn tld off, pld up bef 4 out.*........ (50 to 1 op 33 to 1 tchd 66 to 1) pu
Dist: Sht-hd, ½l, 3½l, dist, 2½l, 4l, 14l, dist. 5m 53.60s. a 9.60s (13 Ran).

SR: 23/16/22/11/-/-/   (John Tuck), John Tuck

3970 Ripple Novices' Handicap Hurdle (0-110 4-y-o and up) £2,374 2m 5f 110yds........................ (5:00)

3829* REFERRAL FEE [75] 7-10-3 S Earle, *hld up towards rear, hdwy 6th, hmpd nxt, rallied 3 out, hrd rdn to ld r-in.*
.... (13 to 2 op 5 to 1) 1
3829⁴ ANNA VALLEY [83] 8-10-11 J Railton, *hld up, gd hdwy frm 5th, rdn 2 out, ran on strly to go second r-in.*
.... (11 to 2 op 9 to 2) 2

3829 EMPERORS WARRIOR [72] 8-10-0 Jacqui Oliver, *al in tch, led 6th, clr whn hit 2 out, edgd lft and hdd r-in.*
.... (25 to 1 op 16 to 1) 3
3825⁷ MARINERS COVE [72] 6-9-11 (3*) D Meredith, *hld up, hdwy appr 3 out, kpt on one pace, nvr nrr.*
.... (12 to 1 op 16 to 1 tchd 20 to 1) 4
3903⁴ SCOTTISH BALL [78] 5-10-6 M Crosse, *led till jmpd slwly 1st, nvr far away, no imprsn frm 2 out.*
.... (14 to 1 op 10 to 1) 5
3886 IVYCHURCH (USA) [72] 8-9-7 (7*) Karen Cook, *wl in rear till hdwy 3 out, ran on well r-in, nvr nrr.*.......... (20 to 1) 6
3592⁸ LACURVA (Ire) [75] 6-9-10 (7*) P Ward, *al abt same pl, ev ch 3 out, wknd appr last.*.......... (14 to 1 op 12 to 1) 7
3502 SILVER STANDARD [89] 4-11-3 B Powell, *prmnt, rdn and ev ch whn mstk 3 out, sn btn.*...... (14 to 1 op 10 to 1) 8
3825 NIGHT FANCY [72] 6-9-12¹ (3*) J McCarthy, *al mid-div, lost tch appr 3 out.*.................(20 to 1 op 16 to 1) 9
3878³ LLOYDS DREAM [74] 5-10-0¹ (3*) P Hide, *wl beh till hdwy 6th, wknd quickly appr 3 out.*
.... (11 to 4 fav op 3 to 1 tchd 4 to 1) 10
TROPICAL GALE [72] (v) 9-10-0 T Wall, *chsd ldrs till wknd appr 3 out, tld off.*............... (66 to 1 op 33 to 1) 11
3829⁸ GREEN'S GAME [75] 6-10-3³ G Upton, *led aftr 1st, hdd 4th, wknd appr last, tld off.*......... (25 to 1 op 20 to 1) 12
3775 TRUE STORM [74] 5-10-2² M Sharratt, *in frnt rnk till jmpd slwly 6th, sn beh, tld off.*.........(66 to 1 op 33 to 1) 13
3671 SHOCK TACTICS [73] (bl) 7-10-1¹ S McNeill, *jmpd badly in rear, already tld off whn hmpd aftr 4 out.*
.... (33 to 1 op 20 to 1) 14
3564 APRIL'S MODEL LADY [73] 8-10-1 D Bridgwater, *slwly away, f 1st.*..........(20 to 1 op 16 to 1 tchd 25 to 1) f
3848* ARTIC WINGS (Ire) [95] 6-11-9 (7ex) M Brennan, *hld up, hdwy 5th, 3rd and gng wl whn f 4 out.*
.... (9 to 2 op 3 to 1 tchd 5 to 1) f
3509⁷ LITTLE CLARE [72] 7-10-0 B Clifford, *prmnt, led 4th to 6th, sn wknd, tld off whn pld up bef 3 out.*
.... (33 to 1 tchd 50 to 1) pu
Dist: 2l, ½l, 3½l, nk, nk, 1¼l, 3½l, 6l, ½l, 10l. 5m 11.00s. a 17.00s (17 Ran).
(Seamus Mullins), J W Mullins

CLONMEL (IRE) (soft)
Thursday May 19th

3971 Templemore Maiden Hurdle (4-y-o) £2,228 2m........................ (5:30)

3889³ DARK SWAN (Ire) 11-4 (5*) C P Dunne, ... (6 to 1) 1
3505⁵ SHANGANOIR (Ire) 10-13 P Carberry, ...(10 to 1) 2
3505² TISRARA LADY (Ire) 10-13 G M O'Neill, ...(12 to 1) 3
3842* V'SOSKE GALE (Ire) 11-4 J F Titley, ...(5 to 1) 4
3372 KILCARBERY (Ire) 10-6 (7*) M Kelly, ...(14 to 1) 5
3839 GRAPHIC IMAGE (Ire) 11-4 P Carberry, ...(7 to 2 fav) 6
3839⁸ BOB THE YANK (Ire) 11-4 Mr D M O'Brien, ...(12 to 1) 7
3656 ANUSHA 11-1 (3*) J P Broderick, ...(5 to 1) 8
3839⁴ AULD STOCK (Ire) 11-4 M Duffy, ...(5 to 1) 9
3934 RIFAYA (Ire) 10-13 T Horgan, ...(16 to 1) 10
TIBOULEN (Ire) 10-10 (3*) T P Rudd, ...(25 to 1) 11
375⁸ PERCY LANE (Ire) 11-4 A Powell, ...(25 to 1) 12
3525 GRANDEUR (Ire) 10-11 (7*) S A Quilty, ...(10 to 1) 13
706 RATES RELIEF (Ire) 11-1 (3*) C O'Brien, ...(50 to 1) 14
3730 DANGER FLYNN (Ire) 11-4 A J O'Brien, ...(20 to 1) 15
ISLAND SHADOW (Ire) 10-13 J A White, ...(33 to 1) 16
3730 COOLING CHIMES (Ire) 10-11 (7*) Mr P A Dunphy, (33 to 1) 17
3842 KING FOWLER (Ire) 11-4 F Woods, ...(25 to 1) 18
HILLTOWN LADY (Ire) 10-13 D H O'Connor, ...(25 to 1) 19
3839⁷ KING'S FROLIC (Ire) 10-11 (7*) Mr J T McNamara, (25 to 1) f
Dist: 1l, hd, 2½l, 2½l. 4m 10.40s. (20 Ran).

(T J O'Mara), T J O'Mara

3972 Holycross Novice Chase (5-y-o and up) £2,228 2½m............... (6:00)

3648 FEATHERED GALE 7-11-9 J Shortt, ...(2 to 1 fav) 1
3872 DUNBOY CASTLE (Ire) 6-11-9 T Horgan, ...(5 to 1) 2
3835² BALADINE 7-10-13 S H O'Donovan, ...(4 to 1) 3
3872⁶ IRISH LIGHT (Ire) 6-11-4 J F Titley, ...(16 to 1) 4
3872⁷ PEGUS PRINCE (Ire) 5-11-9 (5*) T J O'Sullivan, ...(20 to 1) 5
3911 MONKS AIR 7-10-8 (5*) Mr M W O'Sullivan, ...(12 to 1) 6
3835 NISHIKI (USA) 5-10-11 C O'Brien, ...(20 to 1) 7
3835 SEEANDBESEEN 7-10-13 Mr M Phillips, ...(14 to 1) 8
3551 ELUSIVE SOCIETY (Ire) 5-10-3 J A White, ...(20 to 1) 9
3872⁸ MAJOR BERT (Ire) 6-11-4 F Woods, ...(25 to 1) 10
3911⁶ GO GO GALLANT (Ire) 5-10-8 G M O'Neill, ...(8 to 1) 11
3835³ MELDRUM MISS (Ire) 6-10-13 P M Verling, ...(10 to 1) f
3840 NORA'S ERROR (Ire) 5-10-8 J P Banahan, ...(25 to 1) f
3835 BRIDGIE TERRIE (Ire) 6-10-13 A J O'Brien, ...(8 to 1) bd
Dist: Hd, 1l, 11l, 11l. 5m 34.30s. (14 Ran).

(E P King), A L T Moore

3973 Avonmore Foods Handicap Hurdle (0-130 4-y-o and up) £3,598 2m. . (6:30)

3836⁶ KHARASAR (Ire) [-] 4-10-10 (7*) R A Hennessy, (6 to 4 fav) 1
3122 MAY GALE (Ire) [-] 6-9-11 P Carberry, ...(20 to 1) 2
3871* FINNEGANS WAKE [-] 7-10-12 C F Swan, ...(5 to 1) 3
3840⁵ IRON MARINER (Ire) [-] 6-9-8 (7*) D M McCullagh, (14 to 1) 4

3870² FARRELL'S CROSS [-] 8-9-13 A Powell, ...(6 to 1) 5
3506° ANNFIELD LADY (Ire) [-] 6-9-7 F Woods, ...(10 to 1) 6
3647⁴ CASH IT IN (Ire) [-] 6-10-0 (3") D P Murphy, ...(8 to 1) 7
3369 FINAL FAVOUR (Ire) [-] 5-11-7 (7") D J Kavanagh, . .(13 to 2) 8
3870³ REPLACEMENT [-] 7-9-5 (3") T J O'Sullivan, ...(14 to 1) 9
991⁷ BALLYTIGUE LORD [-] 8-10-8 G M O'Neill, ...(16 to 1) 10
Dist: 5l, 2l, 5l, 3l. 4m 5.90s. (10 Ran).
(W Hennessy), Anthony Mullins

3974 Tipperary Mares INH Flat Race (4-y-o and up) £2,228 2½m. . . . .(8:30)

3837 MILLER'S CROSSING 7-12-0 Mr T Doyle, ...(16 to 1) 1
3869³ RAINYS RUN 7-11-7 (7") Mr E Norris, ...(10 to 1) 2
3946⁹ TORONTO TELEGRAM 8-11-9 (5") Mr J P Berry, . . (12 to 1) 3
3797² DANGEROUS LADY (Ire) 5-11-10 (3") Mr D Marnane, (8 to 1) 4
LEAD THE BRAVE (Ire) 5-11-10 (3") Mr T Lombard, (16 to 1) 5
3733⁶ LADY OF TARA 8-11-11 (3") Mrs J M Mullins, ...(10 to 1) 6
3788³ BUILDERS LINE (Ire) 6-11-4 Mr P Fenton, ...(12 to 1) 7
SISTER ROSZA (Ire) 6-12-0 Mr P J Healy, ...(16 to 1) 8
3792⁴ LENEY MOSS (Ire) 4-10-12 (7") Mr R M Walsh, ...(14 to 1) 9
3733² CARSEAHELEN (Ire) 6-11-9 (5") Mr P M Kelly, ...(8 to 1) 10
3529 PALEFOOT (Ire) 6-11-11 (3") Mr R O'Neill, ...(33 to 1) 11
3198 LOST COIN 7-11-7 (7") Mr T N Cloke, ...(50 to 1) 12
3733⁴ SHAKE UP 10-11-7 (7") Mr M Brennan, ...(14 to 1) 13
3552 BALLYWILLIAM STAR (Ire) 4-10-12 (7") Mr H O'Keith-Daly,
. . . .(50 to 1) 14
3525² JULEIT JONES (Ire) 5-11-8 (5") Mr H F Cleary, . .(7 to 4 fav) 15
WHY EMERALD (Ire) 4-10-12 (7") Miss M FitzGerald,
. . . .(25 to 1) 16
2939⁸ TARA'S TRIBE (bl) 7-11-7 (7") Mr P R Lenihan, . . . (14 to 1) 17
3835 CHERISHED PRINCESS (Ire) (bl) 6-11-7 (7") Mr K O'Sullivan,
. . . .(20 to 1) 18
3912⁵ BLACKBERRY ROAD (Ire) 4-11-5 Mr A P O'Brien, . .(3 to 1) su
Dist: Nk, sht-hd, 6l, 3½l. 5m 2.30s. (19 Ran).
(F X Doyle), F X Doyle

EXETER (good to firm)
Thursday May 19th
Going Correction: PLUS 0.20 sec. per fur.

3975 Lapford Novices' Hurdle (4-y-o and up) £1,773 2¼m. . . . .(2:50)

3597³ ZANYMAN 8-11-2 M A FitzGerald, wtd wth, gd hdwy to
track ldr frm 5th, led 2 out, sn clr, easily.
. . . .(2 to 1 op 7 to 4 tchd 9 to 4 and 5 to 2) 1
3914² CASPIAN BELUGA 6-11-2 S Burrough, led, clr second, rdn
and hdd 2 out, no imprsn aftr. . . . . . . (9 to 2 op 7 to 2) 2
3713⁸ LAST MATCH 6-11-2 R Greene, chsd ldrs, hrd rdn frm 2
out, kpt on und pres. . . . .(3 to 1 op 20 to 1) 3
3770⁸ PIONEER PETE 7-11-2 R Darke, hld up, hdwy 5th, hrd
rdn frm 2 out, one pace. . . . .(100 to 1 op 50 to 1) 4
3204 COUNTRY FLING 6-10-11 B Powell, hit second, al beh, tld
off. . . . .(33 to 1 op 16 to 1) 5
3914⁷ NEARLY AT SEA 5-10-4 (7") Mr L Jefford, al beh, tld off.
. . . .(50 to 1 op 33 to 1) 6
DARKTOWN STRUTTER (bl) 8-11-2 Tracy Turner, chsd ldr to
4th, sn wknd, tld off. . . . .(100 to 1 op 66 to 1) 7
1695 TITIAN MIST 8-10-11 L Harvey, beh, effrt appr 3rd, sn btn,
tld off. . . . .(100 to 1 op 50 to 1) 8
3170* BASS ROCK 6-11-8 J Frost, prmnt, outpcd 5th, rdn appr
2 out, 4th 8th whn f last.
. . . .(11 to 8 on op Evens tchd 11 to 10) f
OPEN SESAME 8-11-2 P Holley, prmnt till wknd 4th, tld
off whn pld up bef 2 out.
. . . .(25 to 1 op 12 to 1 tchd 33 to 1) pu
STOUR HILL LAD 5-11-2 S Earle, al beh, tld off whn pld
up bef 2 out. . . . .(100 to 1 op 50 to 1) pu
3523 EMBLEY QUAY 5-10-11 (5") S Curran, slwly away, tld off
3rd, pld up bef 3 out. (40 to 1 op 33 to 1 tchd 50 to 1) pu
Dist: 11l, 1¾l, 1½l, dist, 15l, 20l, 10l. 4m 13.20s. a 13.20s (12 Ran).
(Mrs P Shaw), N J Henderson

3976 Dawlish Novices' Chase (5-y-o and up) £2,429 2¼m. . . . .(3:20)

3764² MINE'S AN ACE (NZ) 7-11-10 R Dunwoody, trkd ldr, led
5th, rdn whn hit 2 out, rallied und pres r-in, all out.
. . . .(11 to 10 fav op 11 to 10 on tchd 6 to 5) 1
3879* UNHOLY ALLIANCE 7-12-0 N Williamson, hld up in tch, cld
on ldrs frm 5th, lft second 5 out, strly rdn and ev ch
from 3 out, no extr close hme.
. . . .(13 to 8 op 6 to 4 tchd 7 to 4) 2
3826 RED MATCH 9-11-4 A Tory, in rear whn hmpd 3rd, lost tch
5th, hampered 5 out, tld off. . . . . . .(66 to 1 op 33 to 1) 3
3893* ALWAYS REMEMBER 7-11-10 Peter Hobbs, led to 5th, rdn
and cl second whn f 5 out.
. . . .(4 to 1 op 7 to 2 tchd 9 to 2) f
3827 GRECIAN SAILOR 9-11-4 R Darke, prmnt till wknd appr
5th, tld off whn stumbled on landing and f 4 out.
. . . .(66 to 1 op 33 to 1) f
3805 VISION OF WONDER 10-11-4 J R Kavanagh, in rear whn
hmpd and uns rdr 3rd. . . . .(33 to 1 op 20 to 1) ur
3744 MERRY MUSE 8-10-13 B Powell, chaseed ldrs till blun
and uns rdr 3rd. . . . .(66 to 1 op 332 to 1) ur

3298⁹ LEAVE IT OUT 12-11-4 J Frost, jmpd badly in rear, tld off
whn pld up aftr 4th. . . . .(66 to 1 op 33 to 1) pu
Dist: 1¼l, dist. 4m 20.90s. a 9.90s (8 Ran).
SR: 33/35/-/-/-/ (Michael A Knight), D H Barons

3977 Chudleigh Novices' Claiming Hurdle (4-y-o and up) £1,789 2m 3f 110yds
. . . .(3:50)

3806⁹ DISTANT MEMORY (bl) 5-11-6 M Hourigan, hld up, hdwy
to chal 2 out, led last, quickened clr. (5 to 1 op 4 to 1) 1
2808³ LOVE YOU MADLY (Ire) v) 4-10-12 R Dunwoody, hld up,
hdwy 6th, rdn appr 2 out, rallied to take second r-in.
. . . .(7 to 2 jt-fav op 9 to 4 tchd 4 to 1) 2
3876* CRIMINAL RECORD (USA) (bl) 4-11-5 G McCourt, hld up in
rear, hdwy 5th, led appr 2 out, hdd and mstk last,
wknd. . . . .(6 to 1 op 4 to 1) 3
3530 POLAR HAT (bl) 6-11-4 M Foster, hld up, hdwy 3rd, ev ch 3
out, rdn and wknd appr last.
. . . .(12 to 1 tchd 16 to 1 and 20 to 1) 4
3765 SNICKERSNEE 6-11-4 W Marston, led aftr second, hdd
nxt, styd prmnt, wknd appr 2 out. (33 to 1 op 20 to 1) 5
3713⁴ SHERWOOD FOX 7-11-1 (7") Mr G Hogan, prmnt till rdn
and wknd sn aftr 3 out. . . . .(7 to 2 jt-
fav op 5 to 1 tchd 6 to 1) 6
3915⁵ MY SISTER LUCY (bl) 4-10-4 S Burrough, mid-div, mstks,
lost tch 6th, tld off. . .(16 to 1 op 12 to 1 tchd 20 to 1) 7
3573 DRAW LOTS 10-10-12 I Shoemark, al beh, tld off.
. . . .(66 to 1 op 50 to 1) 8
3914⁶ LUCAYAN GOLD (bl) 10-11-0 R Greene, prmnt, led and
wnt clr frm 3rd, wknd quickly appr 2 out, eased, tld off.
. . . .(16 to 1 op 10 to 1 tchd 20 to 1) 9
3800³ ICE MAGIC 7-11-4 D Gallagher, al towards rear, tld off.
. . . .(11 to 2 op 7 to 2) 10
3765 STAPLEFORD LADY 6-10-13 G Upton, al beh, tld off.
. . . .(50 to 1 op 33 to 1) 11
3757⁵ SUNDAY JIM 10-10-9 (7") L Reynolds, mstk 1st, al, beh, tld
off. . . . .(16 to 1 op 14 to 1 tchd 20 to 1) 12
3503 HEAD OF DEFENCE (bl) 9-11-0 Mr S Shinton, al beh, tld off
whn pld up bef 3 out. . . . .(66 to 1 op 50 to 1) pu
3673 BOXING MATCH 7-11-0 N Williamson, tld till aftr second,
wknd quickly 4th, tld off whn pld up bef 3 out.
. . . .(16 to 1 op 12 to 1) pu
3365 WILL BONNY (NZ) 7-11-5 (7") T Murphy, prmnt early, tld
off whn pld up bef 3 out. . . . .(33 to 1 op 20 to 1) pu
Dist: 9l, 1¼l, 12l, 5l, 7l, 10l, 8l, 15l, 1½l. 4m 38.20s. a 16.20s (15 Ran).
(Mrs Ann Weston), P J Hobbs

3978 Whiddon Down Claiming Chase (5-y-o and up) £2,589 2m 7f 110yds. . . .(4:20)

3875⁶ NAUGHTY NICKY 10-11-5 R Greene, wl in rear whn mstk
tenth, gd hdwy appr 4 out, led sn aftr 2 out, wnt clr,
unchlgd. . . . .(25 to 1 op 12 to 1) 1
3477 LOCKWOOD PRINCE 11-11-2 J Frost, hld up in rear,
pushed alng and styd on frm 4 out, wnt second r-in.
. . . .(33 to 1 op 14 to 1) 2
3808⁴ TAGMOUN CHAUFOUR (Fr) 9-11-2 B Powell, al prmnt,
outpcd 5 out, kpt on frm 3 out. . . . .(40 to 1 op 25 to 1) 3
3260* WELKNOWN CHARACTER 12-11-5 (5") Guy Lewis, led till
aftr second, led ag'n 8th, hrd rdn 4 out, hdd sn after 2
out, wknd, fnshd tired. . . . .(7 to 4 tchd 6 to 4) 4
3828⁸ MISTER FEATHERS 13-10-12 R Kavanagh, hld up in mid-
div, gd hdwy to go second 5 out, chalg whn hit nxt, one
pace aftr. . . . .(16 to 1 op 10 to 1) 5
3699 TRUSTY FRIEND 12-10-12 S Earle, mid-div, rdn appr
tenth, nvr on terms. . . . .(40 to 1 op 20 to 1) 6
3885⁴ BARTONDALE 9-10-7 N Williamson, al towards rear, nvr
nr to chal. . . . .(25 to 1 op 12 to 1) 7
3669 SKIPPING TIM 15-10-12 R Dunwoody, led aftr second, hdd
8th, outpcd 5 out, btn whn hit last, tld off.
. . . .(11 to 10 fav op 5 to 4 tchd 6 to 4) 8
3714* ALDAHE 9-11-6 S Burrough, in rear till hdwy 9th, wknd
rpdly appr 4 out, tld off.
. . . .(16 to 1 op 8 to 1 tchd 20 to 1) 9
MOLOJEC (Pol) 13-11-3 (7") Mr J Culloty, prmnt till wknd
tenth, tld off whn pld up bef 4 out. . . (8 to 1 op 5 to 1) pu
3445 BRORA ROSE (Ire) 6-10-9 M A FitzGerald, al beh, tld off
whn pld up bef 4 out. . . . .(50 to 1 op 33 to 1) pu
Dist: 20l, 1l, 2½l, 2½l, 3l, 7l, 20l, dist. 5m 54.20s. a 19.20s (11 Ran).
(K Bishop), K Bishop

3979 Topsham Handicap Chase (0-125 5-y-o and up) £2,976 2¼m. . . . .(4:55)

3805* FESTIVAL DREAMS [101] 9-10-8 P Holley, rcd keenly, led
6th, drw clr frm 3 out, very easily.
. . . .(11 to 10 fav op 5 to 4) 1
3847³ KIBREET [106] 7-10-13 S Earle, al prmnt, chsd wnr frm
7th, outpcd and no ch whn no chance whn blun badly
last. . . . .(3 to 1 op 5 to 2 tchd 7 to 2) 2
3573 DEEP DARK DAWN [115] 9-11-8 J R Kavanagh, hld up in
rear, gd hdwy 5 out, rdn and one pace frm nxt.
. . . .(20 to 1 op 10 to 1) 3
3759² ACHILTIBUIE [93] 10-10-0 D Gallagher, in tch till wknd
appr 4 out.
. . . .(9 to 1 op 7 to 1 tchd 10 to 1 and 12 to 1) 4

3902 WINGSPAN (USA) [115] 10-11-8 N Mann, *led to 6th, wknd appr 8th, tld off*....................(7 to 1 op 3 to 1) 5
3902 COTAPAXI [96] 9-10-3 R Dunwoody, *al struggling in rear, last whn mstk 8th, tld off.*
........................(5 to 1 op 4 to 1 tchd 11 to 2) 6
Dist: 12l, 5l, 1¼l, 14l, 20l. 4m 24.10s. a 13.10s (6 Ran).
(Mrs Nerys Dutfield), Mrs P N Dutfield

3980 William Hill Handicap Hurdle (0-120 4-y-o and up) £2,368 2m 3f 110yds ....(5:25)

3804[3] TRAIN ROBBER [81] 9-10-0 W Irvine, *mid-div, cld on ldrs aftr 3 out, short of room and swtchd rght appr last, edgd lft r-in, hrd rdn to join on line.*
...................................(33 to 1 op 16 to 1) 1+
3806[6] KALAMOSS [81] 5-9-7 (7*) Miss S Mitchell, *hld up, gd hdwy appr 4th, led 3 out, hrd rdn and edgd lft r-in, jnd on line*..............................(16 to 1 op 12 to 1) 1+
3760[2] NOVA SPIRIT [82] 6-10-1 V Slattery, *wl in rear till hdwy appr 2 out, hrd rdn approaching last edgd and crrd slightly lft r-in, no extr cl hme*.......(5 to 1 op 3 to 1) 3
3831[7] LASSIE (Fr) [81] 5-10-0 N Williamson, *hld up, gd hdwy to track ldrs 5th, ev ch 2 out, one pace appr last.*
...................................(16 to 1 op 8 to 1) 4
3851[3] FAUX PAVILLON [90] 10-10-9 M A FitzGerald, *al prmnt, led 4th to 3 out, rdn nxt, wknd.*
............(4 to 1 op 5 to 1 tchd 11 to 2 and 6 to 1) 5
3919[2] SURCOAT [96] 7-11-1 L Harvey, *hld up, hdwy 3 out, rdn and wknd bef nxt.*
........(11 to 4 fav op 3 to 1 tchd 7 to 2 and 5 to 2) 6
3715[4] MUSKORA (Ire) [96] 5-11-1 Peter Hobbs, *hld up in rear, hdwy 5th, wknd quickly frm 2 out.*
........................(9 to 1 op 7 to 1 tchd 10 to 1) 7
3853* ACCESS SUN [95] 7-11-0 (7ex) J R Kavanagh, *led to 4th, wknd appr 2 out, tld off*.............(8 to 1 op 4 to 1) 8
3698[8] DOUALAGO (Fr) [81] (bl) 4-10-0 R Dunwoody, *prmnt, wth ldr 3rd, wknd appr 3 out, tld off*....(10 to 1 op 8 to 1) 9
3481[6] REELING [81] 8-10-0 R Greene, *prmnt to 4th, sn beh, tld off*..............................(66 to 1 op 20 to 1) 10
3718[4] MARIOLINO [83] 7-10-2 W Marston, *al beh, tld off.*
..................................(10 to 1 tchd 12 to 1) 11
3150 MILLY BLACK (Ire) [81] (v) 6-10-0 D Gallagher, *prmnt early, beh frm 5th, tld off whn pld up bef 2 out.*
...................................(25 to 1 op 14 to 1) pu
3904 MISS MARIGOLD [109] (bl) 5-12-0 A Tory, *hld up in tch, beh frm 5th, tld off whn pld up bef 2 out.*
........................(8 to 1 op 10 to 1 tchd 20 to 1) pu
Dist: Dd-ht, 1l, 3½l, 12l, ½l, 4l, 15l, 7l, 1l, dist. 4m 34.60s. a 12.60s (13 Ran).
(W G McKenzie-Coles & N R Mitchell), W G McKenzie-Coles & N R Mitchell

PERTH (firm)
Thursday May 19th
Going Correction: MINUS 0.45 sec. per fur.

3981 T Dyer & Co Maiden Hurdle (4-y-o and up) £2,242 2½m 110yds.........(6:35)

3620[5] CRANK SHAFT 7-11-6 D Byrne, *al gng best, jnd ldr 4 out, definate advantage nxt, clr 2 out, easily.*
....(13 to 8 on op 6 to 4 on tchd 7 to 4 on) 1
3862[4] BRIAR'S DELIGHT 6-11-6 B Storey, *patiently rdn, improved gng wl 3 out, effrt and ridden nxt, no ch wth wnr*..............................(7 to 2 tchd 4 to 1) 2
3907[5] SHAYNA MAIDEL 5-11-1 L O'Hara, *nvr far away, effrt and bustled alng aftr 3 out, one pace.*
...................................(11 to 1 op 8 to 1) 3
3815[7] BELIEVE IT 5-11-6 Miss T Waggott, *wtd wth, improved to track wnr 4th, outpcd bef four out, sn btn.*
......................(11 to 1 op 6 to 1 tchd 12 to 1) 4
3905 MISS JEDD (v) 7-10-10 (5*) J Burke, *set modest pace, quickened and jnd 4 out, hdd nxt, sn btn, tld off.*
...................................(14 to 1 op 10 to 1) 5
3429 TOLL BOOTH 5-10-10 (5*) Mr D Parker, *tucked away on ins, sddl slpd and pld up bef 3rd*.............(100 to 1) pu
3907[8] BROUGHPARK JASMIN 5-11-1 (5*) A Roche, *trkd ldrs, struggling to hold pl hfwy, tld off whn pld up aftr 3 out*..............................(20 to 1 op 12 to 1) pu
Dist: 11l, 8l, 1¼l, 25l. 4m 51.40s. a 6.40s (7 Ran).
(Charles McNulty), J F Bottomley

3982 Marquee Claiming Hurdle (4-y-o and up) £2,232 3m 110yds.......... (7:05)

3905[3] MISS PIMPERNEL 4-10-13 L O'Hara, *settled midfield, improved to draw level whn hit 2 out, styd on grimly to ld last 100 yards*....................(9 to 1 op 10 to 1) 1
3895[6] HOTDIGGITY 6-10-11 (5*) J Burke, *sn beh, scrubbed alng to improve fnl circuit, nosed ahead betw last 2, hdd and one pace last 100 yards.*
......................(10 to 1 op 8 to 1 tchd 11 to 1) 2
3895[3] CLASSIC STATEMENT (bl) 8-11-3 (3*) A Larnach, *tried to make all, jnd and rdn 2 out, sn hdd, rallied und pres r-in*..(3 to 1) 3

3728[4] TEMPORALE 8-10-13 (7*) G Crone, *al hndy, rdn whn pace quickened 2 out, btn last.*
..........................(8 to 1 op 7 to 1 tchd 9 to 1) 4
3820[4] ASK THE GOVERNOR 8-12-0 A Maguire, *settled gng wl, jnd ldr fnl circuit, dsptd ld 2 out, sn rdn and no extr.*
..........(5 to 4 on tchd 6 to 5 on and 11 to 10 on) 5
3862[8] GOLDEN BANKER (Ire) 6-11-2 K Jones, *nvr gng wl, scrubbed alng to keep in tch aftr one circuit, tld off.*
...................................(100 to 1 op 50 to 1) 6
3926 SPEEDY SIOUX (bl) 5-10-6 (5*) F Perratt, *chsd ldr for a circuit, struggling frm 4 out, tld off.*
...................................(100 to 1 op 66 to 1) 7
3289 MR MCAFF (Ire) 5-10-9 (7*) P Carr, *chsd ldrs, struggling to keep up fnl circuit, tld off frm 3 out*..........(100 to 1) 8
Dist: ½l, 1l, 7l, ¾l, 30l, hd, dist. 5m 48.40s. a 4.40s (8 Ran).
(Don Hazzard), J J Birkett

3983 Goldman Sachs Euro Novices' Handicap Hurdle (4-y-o and up) £2,284 2m 110yds......................... (7:35)

3825 GAVASKAR (Ire) [75] 5-10-0 A Dobbin, *settled gng wl, smooth hdwy to ld bef 2 out, drvn clr r-in.*
....................................(9 to 1 op 8 to 1) 1
3587[7] REGAL AURA (Ire) [99] 4-11-10 J Callaghan, *chsd clr ldr, improved 3 out, rdn alng frm nxt, kpt on same pace r-in*.............. (2 to 1 jt-fav op 7 to 4 tchd 9 to 4) 2
3570* BACK BEFORE DAWN [76] 7-10-1 L O'Hara, *settled off the pace, steady hdwy appr 3 out, effrt last, rdn and one pace*................(100 to 30 op 9 to 4 tchd 7 to 2) 3
3892* DIGNIFIED (Ire) [85] 4-10-3 (7*,7ex) A Linton, *led, wl clr till jnd aftr 3 out, sn hdd, fdd betw last 2*........(2 to 1 jt-fav op 3 to 1) 4
3600[7] INAN (USA) [75] 5-10-0 A Maguire, *patiently rdn, some hdwy aftr 4 out, nvr rchd ldrs.*
.......................(9 to 1 op 8 to 1 tchd 10 to 1) 5
3815 ANOTHER MEADOW [75] 6-10-0 B Storey, *in tch, reminders to keep up 4 out, sn struggling.*
...................................(25 to 1 op 16 to 1) 6
3815[9] DARK MIDNIGHT (Ire) [75] 5-9-12[5] (7*) Mr A Manners, *settled wth chasing bunch, rdn appr 4 out, sn lost tch.*
...................................(25 to 1 op 20 to 1) 7
Dist: 3½l, nk, 7l, 5l, 10l, 7l. 3m 45.40s. a 1.40s (7 Ran).
SR: -/4/-/-/ (Highflyers), G B Balding

3984 Goldman Sachs European Novices' Handicap Chase (5-y-o and up) £3,055 2½m 110yds...................(8:05)

3893 CASTLE CROSS [79] 7-10-0 B Storey, *settled off the pace, improved to go hndy 5 out, led bef 2 out, easily.*
...................................(12 to 1 op 10 to 1) 1
3852[4] COUNTERBID [103] (v) 7-11-10 A Maguire, *tried to make all, jnd 4 out, hdd bef 2 out, rdn and one pace.*
....................................(5 to 2 op 2 to 1) 2
3818[3] TRUE FAIR [79] 11-9-9 (5*) P Waggott, *settled rear, drvn alng to go hndy hfwy, struggling aftr 6 out, tld off.*
......................(14 to 1 op 12 to 1 tchd 16 to 1) 3
3906* BEAUCADEAU [102] 8-11-9 (7ex) A Dobbin, *tracking ldr whn f 5th*..................(2 to 1 on tchd 7 to 4 on) f
Dist: 12l, 30l. 5m 0.00s. a 2.00s (4 Ran).
(Mrs P Boynton), J I A Charlton

3985 Hilltown Property Co. Ltd Selling Handicap Chase (5-y-o and up) £3,225 2m.............................(8:35)

3471[4] PRESSURE GAME [73] 11-9-10 (5*) F Perratt, *led aftr 1st, made rst, kpt on strly r-in*.....(6 to 5 on op 5 to 4 on) 1
3667[7] TINAS LAD [100] 11-12-0 A Maguire, *not fluent, led till aftr 1st, pushed up for rnwd chal 4 out, kpt on same pace r-in*..........................(Evens tchd 11 to 10) 2
Won by 2l. 3m 57.80s. a 6.80s (2 Ran).
SR: -/-/ (Allan Gilchrist), B Mactaggart

3986 Bollinger Amateur Riders' Handicap Hurdle (0-115 4-y-o and up) £2,232 2½m 110yds.....................(9:05)

3895* VALIANT DASH [90] 8-10-2 (5*,6ex) Mr D Parker, *set scorching pace, made all, hit last 2, unchlgd.*
.................................(7 to 4 op 6 to 4 tchd 2 to 1) 1
3910[3] MYSTIC MEMORY [107] 5-11-7 (3*) Mr M Buckley, *patiently rdn, improved frm 3 out, effrt betw last 2, no imprsn.*
................................(11 to 8 fav op 6 to 4) 2
2502 DANCING DOVE (Ire) [90] 6-10-2 (5*) Mr R Hale, *chsd wnr till aftr 3 out, fdd betw last 2*........ (3 to 1 op 5 to 2) 3
3566 DEADLINE [83] (bl) 11-9-9 (5*) Miss J Thurlow, *struggling to go pace frm 4th, tld off whn pld up bef 2 out.*
...................................(12 to 1 op 16 to 1) 4
Dist: 11l, 9l. 4m 41.20s. b 3.80s (4 Ran).
SR: 25/31/5/-/ (J S Goldie), J S Goldie

UTTOXETER (good to firm)
Thursday May 19th
Going Correction: PLUS 0.30 sec. per fur.

3987
Addison Of Newport Novices' Hunters' Chase (5-y-o and up) £1,868 3¼m. .... (6:20)

FOX POINTER 9-11-7 (7°) Mr J Jukes, *led 5th, made rst, gng wl whn lft clr 2 out*. (6 to 1 op 4 to 1 tchd 7 to 1) 1
NODFORMS DILEMMA (USA) 11-11-9 (5°) Mr S Brookshaw, *mstks in rear, prog 13th, lft second and blun 2 out, no ch wth wnr*........................ (5 to 1 op 4 to 1) 2
BUTTERLEY BOY 11-11-7 (7°) Mr M Harris, *mid-div, effrt 5 out, styd on one pace*..............(12 to 1 op 8 to 1) 3
CELTIC KING 10-11-7 (7°) Mr K Needham, *chsd ldg pair till 5 out, one pace aftr, no ch whn hmpd 2 out*.
.... (12 to 1 op 6 to 1) 4
ALBERT BLAKE 7-11-7 (7°) Mr G Hanmer, *hld up, rdn and prog to chase ldg pair 5 out, wknd 3 out*.
.... (20 to 1 op 14 to 1 tchd 25 to 1) 5
COUTURE TIGHTS 9-11-7 (7°) Miss J Priest, *prmnt in chasing grp, rdn and no imprsn frm 4 out*.
.... (13 to 1 op 5 to 1) 6
3854[4] MILLIE BELLE (bl) 8-11-2 (7°) Mr S Blackwell, *hld up, prog 13th, nvr rch ldrs, wkng whn blun 2 out*.
.... (11 to 1 op 8 to 1) 7
3846[5] EVENING RUSH 8-11-7 (7°) Mr K Drewry, *prmnt in chasing grp, wknd und pres 14th, sn tld off*.
.... (25 to 1 op 14 to 1) 8
ADAMARE 10-11-9 (5°) Mrs J Saunders, *led second to 5th, chsd wnr aftr clr of rst, rdn and ev ch whn f 2 out*.
.... (15 to 8 fav op 7 to 4 tchd 5 to 2) f
RUSSIAN LION 13-11-7 (7°) Miss T Gray, *lost pl 9th, tld off whn pld up bef 3 out*............(50 to 1 op 25 to 1) pu
ARM IN ARM 9-11-8[1] (7°) Mr C Stockton, *al rear, tld off 13th, pld up bef 4 out*............(50 to 1 op 20 to 1) pu
3947 DAMERS TREASURE 8-11-7 (7°) Mr A Sansome, *drpd last at tenth, sn struggling, tld off whn pld up bef 5 out*.
.... (20 to 1 op 10 to 1) pu
PROCTORS ROW 7-11-7 (7°) Mr C J B Barlow, *led to second, prmnt in chasing grp aftr till wknd 5 out, pld up bef nxt*........................ (10 to 1 op 4 to 1) pu
Dist: 11l, nk, 1¾l, 2l, sht-hd, 20l, dist. 6m 28.70s (13 Ran).
(Mrs L T J Evans), Mrs L T J Evans

3988
W. Boden & Co. Maiden Hunters' Chase for the Pat Wint Cup (5-y-o and up) £1,881 2m 5f. .... (6:50)

3920 CELTIC ABBEY 6-11-12 (7°) Mr D S Jones, *hld up, prog 9th, rdn to chal 2 out, led aftr last, drvn out*.
.... (13 to 8 fav op 5 to 4) 1
3854 WINNIE LORRAINE 9-11-7 (7°) Mr M G Miller, *in tch, prog 5 out, led gng wl 2 out, hdd aftr last, found nothing*.
.... (6 to 1) 2
RED SCORPION 10-11-12 (7°) Mr A Newey, *not jump wl, mid-div, lost tch 11th, kpt on und pres to take poor 3rd nr finish*........................ (50 to 1 op 20 to 1) 3
FREDDIE FOX 8-11-12 (7°) Mr T Garton, *mstk 7th, rear, lost tch 11th, kpt on one pace*........(25 to 1 op 20 to 1) 4
3860[2] WISEBOW 9-11-12 (7°) Mrs C Elliott, *pld hrd, led to 4th, prmnt aftr till wknd 5 out*.
.... (10 to 1 op 16 to 1 tchd 20 to 1) 5
DALAMETRE 7-11-12 (7°) Mr J Smyth-Osbourne, *prmnt, mstk tenth, wknd 5 out*...........(12 to 1 op 10 to 1) 6
3807 NATIONAL GYPSY 8-11-9 (5°) Mr M Felton, *badly hmpd 1st, beh till effrt 9th, sn wknd*...........(33 to 1 op 20 to 1) 7
BENTON'S PRIDE 6-11-7 (7°) Mr G Hanmer, *f 1st*.
.... (33 to 1 op 20 to 1) f
MR FUDGE 7-11-12 (7°) Mr M Sowersby, *led 4th, mstk 7th, hdd and f 2 out*................(5 to 2 op 2 to 1) f
3900 IM PRIVILAGED 10-11-12 (7°) Mr D Bloor, *al beh, tld off 7th, pld up bef 4 out*................(50 to 1) pu
HAPPY HIGGINS 10-11-12 (7°) Mr C J B Barlow, *mid-div till wknd aftr 11th, beh whn pld up bef 4 out*.
.... (14 to 1 tchd 16 to 1) pu
TRIMBUSH 10-12-0 (5°) Mr R H Brown, *al rear, tld off whn pld up bef 4 out*..................(33 to 1 op 16 to 1) pu
TERRIFORN 9-12-2 (3°) Mr A Hill, *hld up, rdn and no prog 9th, tld off whn pld up bef 3 out*...(33 to 1 op 25 to 1) pu
ABITMORFUN 8-12-0 (5°) Mr S Brookshaw, *prmnt to 8th, sn wknd, tld off whn pld up bef 4 out*..............pu
Dist: 3½l, dist, hd, 2½l, 1¾l, 12l. 5m 15.60s. a 15.60s (14 Ran).
SR: 12/3/-/-/-/-/ (G J Powell), Mrs Christine Hardinge

3989
Sir Geoffrey Congreve Cup Open Hunters' Chase (5-y-o and up) £2,006 2m 7f. .... (7:20)

DUNCAN 9-12-0 (7°) Mr B Pollock, *hld up in tch, prog 5 out, gng wl whn lft in ld 2 out, rdn out r-in*.
.... (6 to 1 op 7 to 2) 1

CELTIC LEISURE 10-11-7 (7°) Mr Richard White, *mstks in mid-div, rdn and prog 5 out, staying on whn mistake and hmpd 2 out, ran on frm last*.... (7 to 2 op 4 to 1) 2
LINGHAM MAGIC 9-12-2 Mr S Swiers, *prmnt, led 5 out to nxt, rdn and unbl to quicken*.
.... (9 to 4 fav op 7 to 4 tchd 5 to 2) 3
GREEN ARCHER 11-11-7 (7°) Mrs T Hill, *led to 3rd, lost pl and rdn alng 12th, styd on und pres frm 2 out*. (12 to 1) 4
3877° KNOCKUMSHIN 11-12-2 (5°) Mr T Byrne, *hld up in tch, prog 5 out, rdn and not quicken 2 out*.
.... (3 to 1 op 2 to 1) 5
3877³ CURAHEEN BOY (bl) 14-12-0 (7°) Miss J Butler, *rear, effrt to chase ldrs 9th, no prog frm 4 out*...(33 to 1 op 12 to 1) 6
RAISABILLION 12-11-7 (7°) Mr C Stockton, *wl beh frm 5th, tld off*........................ (50 to 1 op 25 to 1) 7
ISOBAR (bl) 8-11-7 (7°) Mr D Barlow, *wl beh frm 5th, tld off*.
.... (50 to 1 op 20 to 1) 8
3684 SANDSTONE ARCH 11-12-0 (7°) Mr L Brennan, *led 3rd to tenth, wknd rpdly, sn tld off*... (50 to 1 op 20 to 1) 9
3918² ABBOTSHAM 9-11-7 (7°) Mr I Widdicombe, *prmnt, led tenth till 5 out, led ag'n nxt, one l up whn f 2 out*.
.... (8 to 1 op 7 to 1) f
STORMGUARD (v) 11-11-7 (7°) Mr G Hanmer, *in tch till wknd 11th, tld off and pld up bef 2 out*.
.... (50 to 1 op 33 to 1) pu
MAJUBA ROAD 14-11-4 (5°) Mr N Wilson, *in tch till rdn and wknd tenth, tld off and pld up bef 2 out*.
.... (33 to 1 op 25 to 1) pu
Dist: 3l, 1½l, 1¼l, 2½l, 12l, dist, 3½l, sht-hd. 5m 46.60s. a 16.60s (12 Ran).
SR: 10/-/-/-/-/-/ (C R Saunders), Miss C Saunders

3990
Lady Lichfield Open Hunters' Chase For Uttoxeter Premier Trophy (5-y-o and up) £2,739 4¼m. .... (7:50)

3884° ONCE STUNG 8-12-7 Mr J Greenall, *prmnt, led 4 out, styd on wl und pres frm 2 out*.
.... (11 to 10 fav op 5 to 4 tchd Evens) 1
SPEAKERS CORNER 11-11-7 (7°) Mr M Sowersby, *prmnt, led 11th to 4 out, pressed wnr aftr, till no extr r-in*.
.... (7 to 1 op 8 to 1) 2
3684 BROWN WINDSOR 12-11-12 (7°) Mr B Pollock, *trkd ldrs, wnt 3rd 6 out, outpcd aftr nxt, rdn and not quicken 3 out*........................ (2 to 1 op 11 to 8 tchd 9 to 4) 3
3808 SKERRY MEADOW 10-11-7 (7°) Mr I Widdicombe, *hld up, effrt 18th, outpcd appr 4 out, no imprsn aftr*.
.... (8 to 1 op 7 to 1) 4
SHIPMATE 12-11-7 (7°) Miss H Irving, *not fluent, chsd ldrs, pushed alng 17th, sn lost tch, kpt on frm 2 out*.
.... (14 to 1 op 12 to 1 tchd 10 to 1) 5
BELLWAY 13-11-7 (7°) Mr C Storey, *al last pair, tld off 17th*........................ (33 to 1 op 20 to 1) 6
WORLESTON FARRIER 6-11-7 (7°) Mr G Hanmer, *led till 11th, wknd aftr 5 out, pld up bef 3 out*.
.... (20 to 1 op 10 to 1) pu
Dist: ½l, 4l, 9l, ½l, dist. 8m 50.20s. a 22.20s (7 Ran).
(J E Greenall), P Cheesbrough

3991
Bradshaw Bros. Hunters' Chase for the Ingestre Trophy (5-y-o and up) £2,608 3¼m. .... (8:20)

3807° RYMING CUPLET 9-11-12 (7°) Mr Richard White, *cl up, mstk 15th and rdn, prog to chal 3 out, hrd ridden and ran on wl to ld nr finish*.......... (3 to 1 tchd 7 to 2) 1
3861³ SONOFAGIPSY 10-12-0 (5°) Mr M Felton, *prmnt, led 8th, rdn and hdd 15th, rallied to ld appr 2 out, headed und pres nr finish*..............(11 to 1 op 8 to 1) 2
3439° GOGGINS HILL 7-12-7 Mr J Greenall, *prmnt, led 4 out till aftr nxt, sn rdn and one pace*..........(5 to 2 jt-fav op 3 to 1 tchd 9 to 4) 3
3867⁵ DURIGHT 11-11-2 (7°) Mr N F Smith, *hld up in tch, prog to ld 15th, hdd and wknd 4 out*......(25 to 1 op 20 to 1) 4
3884³ FINAL CHANT 13-12-0 (5°) Mr R H Brown, *led to 8th, mstk and lost pl 13th, no imprsn on ldrs frm 4 out*.
.... (4 to 1 op 7 to 2) 5
MOUNT ARGUS 12-12-2 (5°) Mr S Brookshaw, *drpd last and pushed alng 6th, still last whn f 11th*...(5 to 2 jt-fav op 6 to 4) f
Dist: ½l, 7l, ½l, 2½l. 6m 49.70s. a 33.70s (6 Ran).
(Gerald Tanner), M J Trickey

3992
Peter Smith Sports Cars Novices' Hunters' Chase (5-y-o and up) £1,823 2m 5f. .... (8:50)

LONGSHOREMAN 7-11-7 (7°) Mr S Joynes, *al prmnt, led aftr 5 out, clr whn mstk 2 out, pushed out*.
.... (7 to 2 op 9 to 2 tchd 6 to 1 and 3 to 1) 1
3799° IVEAGH LAD 8-12-0 (7°) Mr N F Smith, *settled rear aftr 3rd, prog and prmnt 9th, chsd wnr 4 out, wknd after nxt*.
.... (9 to 4 op 5 to 4 tchd 7 to 4) 2
SWORDED KNIGHT 8-11-7 (7°) Mr G Hanmer, *wl beh, no ch frm tenth, staying on whn lft poor 3rd 3 out*.
.... (9 to 1 op 7 to 1) 3
BIFOCAL 7-11-7 (7°) Mr A Griffith, *not jump wl, al rear, no ch frm 9th*........................ (12 to 1) 4

CANTANTIVVY 9-11-2 (7") Mr R Johnson, *mid-div, pushed alng and lost tch 9th, sn no ch........*(6 to 1 op 5 to 1) 5
DE PROFUNDIS 10-11-7 (7") Miss T Gray, *al beh, tld off frm tenth........................*(50 to 1 op 20 to 1) 6
TUROLDUS (7") Mr S Brookshaw, *prmnt, led 7th till aftr 5 out, cl 3rd but btn whn f 3 out.*
..............................(12 to 1 op 8 to 1 tchd 14 to 1) f
3824* SAILOR JIM 7-12-0 (7") Mr D Bloor, *led 3rd to 7th, wknd 11th, lft poor third and f 3 out.*
.........................(7 to 2 op 5 to 2 tchd 4 to 1) f
CLOSEBUTNOCIGAR (bl) 10-11-7 (7") Mr P Bennett, *mstks, chsd ldg grp, wknd 11th, tld off whn refused 2 out.*
.............................(50 to 1 op 25 to 1) ref
ANGLESEY RAMBLER 12-11-7 (7") Mrs R Hewitt, *led to 3rd, wknd 8th, tld off and pld up bef 2 out.*
.............................(50 to 1 op 20 to 1) pu
Dist: 25l, 11l, 12l, ½l, dist. 5m 21.90s (10 Ran).
(Mrs Althea Barclay), Mrs A Barclay

DUNDALK (IRE) (firm (races 1,2,3,4), good to firm (5)) Friday May 20th

3993 Ardee Hurdle (4-y-o) £2,228 2m 135yds
.................................(5:30)

2099 LAKE OF LOUGHREA (Ire) 11-0 J Shortt, ...(10 to 1) 1
3839² TOUCHING MOMENT (Ire) 10-11 (3") T P Rudd, ...(6 to 1) 2
3246⁸ BOTHSIDESNOW (Ire) 11-0 P Carberry, ...(3 to 1 jt-fav) 3
3934² PUSH THE BUTTON (Ire) 10-9 K F O'Brien, .. (3 to 1 jt-fav) 4
3839* NORDIC THORN (Ire) 11-7 A Powell, ...(7 to 1) 5
3839⁶ TEN BUCKS (Ire) 11-0 M Flynn, ...(16 to 1) 6
3934⁵ HUNCHEON CHANCE 10-11 (3") T J Mitchell, ... (8 to 1) 7
INNOCENT MAN 11-0 L P Cusack, ...(20 to 1) 8
LA CENHERENTOLA (Ire) 10-9 H Rogers, ...(16 to 1) 9
2081⁹ CNOC AN RIOG (Ire) 11-0 J F Titley, ...(20 to 1) 10
3730* RYE HILL QUEEN (Ire) 11-2 C F Swan, ...(6 to 1) 11
3321 DANCEALOT (Ire) 11-0 C O'Dwyer, ...(33 to 1) 12
2592⁷ RUN TO GLORY (Ire) 10-6 (3") J P Broderick, ...(33 to 1) 13
PRINCE SABI (Ire) 10-7 (7") A Wall, ...(20 to 1) 14
FINAWAY LADY (Ire) 10-9 P L Malone, ...(20 to 1) 15
COME ON ROSELLA (Ire) 10-9 B Sheridan, ...(16 to 1) 16
3793 KEPPOLS HARRIER (Ire) 10-11 (3") Mr D Marnane, (20 to 1) ur
3321 DRESS DANCE (Ire) 11-0 J P Banahan, ...(10 to 1) pu
Dist: Sht-hd, 1½l, ¾l, 1½l. 3m 51.20s. (18 Ran).
(Bezwall Fixings Ltd), Kevin Prendergast

3994 Tallanstown Hunters Chase (5-y-o and up) £2,228 3m.................(6:00)

3794² BALD JOKER 9-11-13 (7") Mr C A McBratney, ... (7 to 1) 1
3888⁶ FAHA GIG (Ire) 5-11-3 Mr P F Graffin, ...(13 to 2) 2
3652⁵ LINEKER 7-11-10 (5") Mr G J Harford, ...(7 to 4 fav) 3
3794³ HAYES CORNER 8-11-7 (3") Mr P McMahon, ...(7 to 1) 4
3791 GLENARD LAD (Ire) 6-11-10 Mr A J Martin, ...(8 to 1) 5
VOLDI 7-11-3 (7") Mr J S Vance, ...(25 to 1) 6
HYPERION SON 7-11-3 (7") Mr P Humphries, ...(10 to 1) 7
BUAILE BOS 7-11-3 (7") Mr M O'Connor, ...(33 to 1) 8
3888 RED EXPRESS VI 9-11-8 (7") Mr S O'Brien, ...(6 to 1) f
3652⁴ LAURA'S PURSUIT (Ire) 5-10-5 (7") Mr G F Ryan, .. (7 to 1) ur
17 BELLAGHY BRIDGE 7-10-12 (7") Mr J Bright, ...(50 to 1) pu
Dist: 3½l, 8l, 7l, 20l. 6m 11.20s. (11 Ran).
(Mrs David McBratney), David McBratney

3995 Carroll Trophy Handicap Hurdle (Listed) (4-y-o and up) £5,782 2½m 153yds
.................................(6:30)

3836* STRONG PLATINUM (Ire) [-] 6-11-1 C O'Dwyer, *led till aftr 5th, led 3 out, jnd 2 out, quickened ag'n to ld r-in.*
...............................(5 to 2 jt-fav) 1
3736⁶ COCKNEY LAD (Ire) [-] 5-10-13 C F Swan, *hld up, prog to track ldrs entering strt, dsptd ld 2 out, rdn and no extr r-in.......................*(5 to 2 jt-fav) 2
3836⁷ MY SUNNY GLEN [-] 7-9-13 (5") K F Gaule, *trkd ldrs, ev ch 2 out, sn rdn and no extr.......................*(7 to 1) 3
3719* MR FIVE WOOD (Ire) [-] 6-9-9 (3") A Roche, *hld up, rdn to track ldrs entering strt, no extr aftr 2 out, kpt on.*
..............................(6 to 1) 4
3654³ OPERA HAT (Ire) [-] 6-10-5 A Powell, *wl plcd, wknd aftr 3 out, no extr 2 out.......................*(5 to 1) 5
3248⁶ SHANKORAK [-] 7-11-7 (7") D J Kavanagh, *mid-div, prog 4 out, rdn aftr nxt, wknd 2 out.......................*(7 to 1) 6
3710⁹ LA CIENAGA [-] 10-9-12¹ (7") S G Anderson, *hld up, rapid prog to ld aftr 5th, hdd 3 out, rdn, no extr and wknd after nxt.......................*(7 to 1) 7
3711 AISEIRI [-] 7-10-0 F Woods, *trkd ldr, lost pl appr 6th, rdn and wknd after 3 out.......................*(25 to 1) 8
3615³ PLUMBOB (Ire) [-] 5-9-7 (7") P J Smullen, *al rear, rdn and wknd aftr 3 out.......................*(12 to 1) 9
3935⁸ BAVARD DIEU (Ire) [-] 6-9-12 (3") T J Mitchell, *wl plcd, rdn 4 out, no extr and wknd aftr 2 out.......................*(10 to 1) 10
3836 FIRST SESSION (Ire) [-] 6-10-4 K F O'Brien, *mid-div, rdn 3 out, sn wknd.......................*(16 to 1) 11

3654 GLEN MONEY [-] 8-10-11 F J Flood, *mid-div, rdn and lost pl 4 out, wknd.......................*(25 to 1) 12
Dist: 4½l, 3l, 2½l, 8l. 4m 43.60s. (12 Ran).
(Mrs Theresa McCoubrey), P Burke

3996 Mickey McArdle Handicap Chase (0-116 4-y-o and up) £2,228 3m.. (7:00)

3648* FANE BANKS [-] (bl) 12-11-7 P Carberry, ...(100 to 30) 1
3721⁴ JIMS CHOICE [-] 7-10-12 C O'Dwyer, ...(10 to 1) 2
3721* LA-GREINE [-] 7-11-2 C F Swan, ...(11 to 4 fav) 3
3795² THE MAD MONK [-] 9-10-2 K F O'Brien, ...(11 to 2) 4
3746⁷ BLENHEIM PALACE (USA) [-] 7-9-12 H Rogers, ...(14 to 1) 5
3648⁷ BROGUESTOWN [-] 9-11-4 F J Flood, ...(11 to 2) 6
3657⁵ KNOCKNACARRA LAD [-] 9-11-0 (3") T J Mitchell, (10 to 1) 7
3795 RAMBLING LORD (Ire) [-] 6-10-3 S R Murphy, ...(20 to 1) 8
3933⁶ MUST DO [-] 8-10-10 J Shortt, ...(8 to 1) 9
3790² TAKE THE TOWN [-] 9-11-12 J F Titley, ...(8 to 1) ur
3721 AUTUMN RIDE (Ire) [-] (bl) 6-9-12 (3") D T Evans, ..(25 to 1) ur
3795⁵ REDELVA [-] 7-9-8¹ F Woods, ...(16 to 1) ur
3274⁷ LINVAR [-] 11-9-4 (7") D J Kavanagh, ...(16 to 1) ur
Dist: Sht-hd, 4l, 7l, 2½l. 6m 4.70s. (13 Ran).
(Mrs M Cahill), Noel Meade

3997 Greenore I.N.H. Flat Race (4-y-o) £2,228 2m 135yds.............(8:30)

CHERYL'S LAD (Ire) 11-4 (5") Mr P M Kelly, ...(10 to 1) 1
3842⁶ THAT'S GOSPEL (Ire) 11-4 Mr P Fenton, ...(16 to 1) 2
NATIVE STATUS (Ire) 11-4 (5") Mr G J Harford, ..(3 to 1 fav) 3
LOUISES FANCY (Ire) 10-11 (7") Mr P Hutchinson, (20 to 1) 4
2663⁶ PERSIAN VIEW (Ire) 11-6 (3") Mr J A Nash, ...(7 to 2) 5
3508⁷ SNIPE'S BRIDGE (Ire) 11-2 (7") Mr D McCartan, ..(12 to 1) 6
3749⁸ SPLEODRACH (Ire) 11-1 (3") Mr R Neylon, ...(7 to 2) 7
3946⁸ JR MY FRIEND (Ire) 11-2 (7") Mr J T McNamara, ..(10 to 1) 8
3937 SHANES BAY (Ire) 11-1 (3") Mr P J Casey, ...(14 to 1) 9
NEW LEGISLATION (Ire) 11-4 Mr J P Dempsey, ..(10 to 1) 10
NATIVE BABY (Ire) 11-1 (3") Mrs J M Mullins, ...(8 to 1) 11
3616 LESS HASSLE (Ire) 10-13 (5") Mr J P Berry, ...(14 to 1) 12
3842 WYLD BAY (Ire) 10-11 (7") Mr K P Egan, ...(14 to 1) 13
3839 CHIEF RANI (Ire) 11-9 Mr T Mullins, ...(6 to 1) 14
THE REAL BAVARD (Ire) 11-8⁶ (7") Mr I Mulcahy, ..(16 to 1) 15
TOUREEN LODGE (Ire) 11-4 (5") Mr H F Cleary, ...(10 to 1) 16
SPECTACLE (Ire) 11-6 (3") Mr D Marnane, ...(10 to 1) 17
3797 ARDMORE KELINKA (Ire) 10-11 (7") Mr J Bright, ..(33 to 1) 18
3796 SINERGIA (Ire) 11-5³ (7") Mr R Pugh, ...(25 to 1) ur
Dist: 3½l, 4l, 3½l, ½l. 3m 46.10s. (19 Ran).
(Mrs Marie Carolan), Adrian Taylor

FAKENHAM (good) Friday May 20th
Going Correction: MINUS 0.15 sec. per fur.

3998 KLFM Radio Selling Handicap Hurdle Amateur Riders (4-y-o and up) £3,143 2m 110yds.....................(6:15)

3822² ELEGANT FRIEND [75] 6-10-1² (3") Mrs L Gibbon, *hld up, prog 5th, led appr last, quickened clr.*
..........................(9 to 2 fav op 4 to 1 tchd 5 to 1) 1
2829 FAVOURED VICTOR (USA) [93] 7-10-13 (7") Mr S Walker, *pressed ldr, led 2 out, hdd appr last, one pace.*
..............................(8 to 1 op 5 to 1) 2
3755⁸ MAGGIES LAD [73] (bl) 6-9-9 (5") Mr D Parker, *ldg grp, led 6th til hdd 2 out, lft btn 3rd last...* (12 to 1 op 7 to 1) 3
3328⁴ SPANISH WHISPER [77] 7-9-12¹ (7") Mr K Loads, *outpcd til styd on frm 2 out, fnshd wl.*
..............................(8 to 1 op 5 to 1 tchd 9 to 1) 4
3755⁴ APPLIANCEOFSCIENCE [89] (bl) 7-10-9 (7") Mr I McLelland, *outpcd in rear til improved 6th, no extr frm 2 out.*
..............................(12 to 1 op 8 to 1) 5
3635 NAGOBELIA [84] 6-10-11 Mr S Swiers, *mid-div, effrt aftr 5th, wknd after 3 out...................*(8 to 1 op 5 to 1) 6
3682 BELLE LOCK [73] 6-9-7 (7") Mr L Baker, *outpcd frm 4th, tld off........................*(50 to 1 op 33 to 1) 7
3947 KNOWAFENCE [73] 8-10-0⁷ (7") Mr S Howe, *mstk 1st, sn beh, tld off bef hfwy...............*(50 to 1 op 33 to 1) 8
181⁵ NORTHERN CONQUEROR (Ire) [78] 6-10-4² (3") Mr M Buckley, *hdwy frm rear 6th, ev ch appr 2 out, btn 3rd whn f last.......................*(7 to 1 op 6 to 1) f
3767 THANKS A MILLION [74] 8-10-1⁸ (7") Mr S Davis, *blun and uns rdr at second hurdle.......*(50 to 1 op 33 to 1) ur
183* NORDIC FLASH [101] 7-11-9 (7") Mr P Harding-Jones, *rear frm 3rd, tld off whn pld up bef last.* pu
3418⁵ DJEBEL PRINCE [88] (bl) 7-11-1 Mr J Durkan, *made most of rng till hdd 6th, sn lost tch, pld up bef last.*
.............................(11 to 2 op 9 to 2) pu
Dist: 6l, 6l, 3l, 1½l, 3l, 12l, dist, dist. 3m 53.70s. a 3.70s (12 Ran).
SR: 12/24/-/-/9/-/ (Mark Tompkins Racing), M H Tompkins

3999 Hood, Vores And Allwood Hunters' Chase For Essandem Trophy (5-y-o and up) £2,635 3m.............(6:40)

3857² DROMIN LEADER 9-11-7 (5*) Mr P Harding-Jones, *wl in tch, led 3 out, drvn out.*
.... (13 to 8 fav op 7 to 4 tchd 2 to 1 and 11 to 8) 1
3858² AS YOU WERE (bl) 12-11-5 (7*) Miss Z Turner, *hld up, pressed ldr 11th til 3 out, ev ch betw last 2 fences, not quicken.* ....(7 to 2 op 5 to 2 tchd 5 to 1) 2
3951⁵ CALABRESE (bl) 9-12-1 (7*) Major M Watson, *chsd ldr frm 3rd, led tenth til 3 out, hrd rdn appr last, ran on same pace.* ....(9 to 4 op 7 to 4 tchd 5 to 2) 3
MR GOSSIP 12-11-7 (5*) Mr W Wales, *rdn alng most of way, outpcd frm 13th, tld off.*
.... (12 to 1 op 8 to 1 tchd 14 to 1) 4
3857⁴ JOHN O'DEE 11-11-11⁶ (7*) Mr I Marsh, *pressed ldrs to 9th, sn wknd, tld off 14th.*..............(16 to 1 op 8 to 1) 5
FOREVER SHY (Ire) 6-11-1 (7*) Miss S Lamb, *hld up in rear, outpcd frm 12th, tld off nxt.*........(20 to 1 op 10 to 1) 6
3799³ GENERAL PICTON 8-11-1 (7*) Mr M Gingell, *prmnt til mstk 4th, beh whn uns rdr nxt.*
.... (20 to 1 op 14 to 1 tchd 25 to 1 and 33 to 1) ur
3799⁶ SPARTAN RAFT 13-11-5 (7*) Mr A Ward, *led to tenth, lost tch 12th, pld up bef 3 out.*.........(50 to 1 op 25 to 1) pu
Dist: 1½l, 1½l, 25l, sht-hd, 2l. 6m 5.10s. a 13.10s (8 Ran).
(J M Turner), J M Turner

4000 Harris Kafton Handicap Hurdle Amateur Riders (0-100 4-y-o and up) £3,338 2m 110yds...........(7:05)

3924⁵ BROWNSIDE BRIG [94] 9-11-8 (3*) Mrs L Gibbon, *mstk 1st, pld hrd in rear, prog aftr 3 out, led appr last, edgd rght and ran on.*..............(6 to 1 op 4 to 1 tchd 7 to 1) 1
3826⁶ CASTILLO [69] 7-10-0² (7*) Miss C Thorner, *prmnt till lost pl aftr 5th, ran on ag'n 2 out, kpt on strly frm last.*
.... (7 to 2 op 5 to 2 tchd 5 to 1) 2
3915² NORTHERN TRIAL (USA) [80] (v) 6-10-6 (5*) Mr D Parker, *hld up in rch, chlgd betw last 2 flights, rdn and not quicken.*..............(11 to 2 op 4 to 1 tchd 6 to 1) 3
3806⁸ PERSIAN LUCK [86] 8-11-10 (7*) Mr A Welsh, *trkd ldrs, rdn and one pace frm 2 out.*.......(33 to 1 op 20 to 1) 4
3789³ VICTORY ANTHEM [90] 8-11-0 (7*) Mr P Clarke, *led second flight, hdd appr last, sn btn.*........(14 to 1 op 8 to 1) 5
3904² AL SKEET (USA) [74] 8-9-12 (7*) Mr G Hogan, *wl plcd, ev ch appr 2 out, found no extr.*
.... (7 to 2 op 9 to 4 tchd 4 to 1) 6
3897¹ AL WELLCOME [96] 7-11-11 (7*) Mr M Buckley, *hld up, effrt 5th, wknd 2 out, eased whn btn, tld off.*
.... (2 to 1 fav op 7 to 4 tchd 5 to 2 and 3 to 1) 7
3831⁸ DRAMATIC EVENT [82] 9-10-13 Mr J Durkan, *led to second, rdn alng and wl in tch till wknd aftr 6th, tld off.*
.... (11 to 4 op 5 to 1 tchd 7 to 1) 8
Dist: 1½l, 1¾l, 2½l, ½l, 1½l, 25l, 30l. 3m 56.70s (8 Ran).
SR: 5/-/-/-/-/ (Mrs Lucy Gibbon), M H Tompkins

4001 Prince Of Wales Cup Chase Amateur Riders (5-y-o and up) £3,485 2m 5f 110yds.................... (7:35)

3916⁴ DRUMSTICK 8-12-0 (7*) Mr G Hogan, *took str hold and hld up, led on bridle aftr 2 out, very easily.*
.... (11 to 8 on op 11 to 10 on tchd Evens) 1
3908⁶ FISH QUAY 11-11-5 (7*) Miss S Lamb, *hld up in rear, improved frm 3 out, no imprsn on unr appr last.*
.... (33 to 1 tchd 50 to 1) 2
MASTER SALESMAN 11-11-8¹ (5*) Mr C Bealby, *hld up, led and not fluent 3 out, hdd and blun nxt, sn wknd.*
.... (33 to 1 tchd 50 to 1) 3
3705² LUMBERJACK (USA) (bl) 10-12-7 Mr J Durkan, *led, mstk 3rd, hdd nxt, ev ch whn blun 3 out, no extr.*
.... (7 to 2 op 5 to 2 tchd 4 to 1 and 9 to 2) 4
3026 SPRINGALEAK 9-11-9 (7*) Mr J M Pritchard, *led 4th till 6th, jmpd slwly and lost tch 11th.*........(5 to 1 op 4 to 1) 5
3724² ROCKMOUNT ROSE 9-11-6 (7*) Mr J Luck, *mstk 1st, hdwy to ld 6th, hdd 3 out, wkng 4th whn uns rdr last.*
.... (7 to 1 op 14 to 1 tchd 16 to 1) ur
Dist: 2½l, 10l, 7l, 12l. 5m 27.60s. a 15.60s (6 Ran).
(Sarah Lady Allendale), K C Bailey

4002 Tote Novices' Hunters' Chase (5-y-o and up) £2,423 2m 5f 110yds.... (8:05)

FAIRFIELD'S BREEZE 9-11-5 (7*) Dr P Pritchard, *wth ldrs, led 7th, made rst, quickened wl clr frm 2 out.*
.... (6 to 1 op 8 to 1) 1
HONEST FRED 8-11-12 (5*) Mr P Harding-Jones, *in tch, effrt 13th, rdn and one pace frm 2 out.*
.... (5 to 1 op 3 to 1 tchd 6 to 1) 2
MASTER TREASURE 12-12-0 (7*) Mrs L Gibbon, *led to 7th, mstk 11th, rnwd effrt 13th, no imprsn frm 2 out.*
.... (25 to 1 op 20 to 1 tchd 33 to 1) 3
ZENISKA (Ire) 6-11-10 (7*) Mr S Cowell, *al handily plcd, no extr frm 3 out.*....................(8 to 1 op 4 to 1) 4
3802⁷ LAD LANE 10-11-10 (7*) Mr M Gingell, *al in rear, lost tch frm 7th, tld off.*.....................(33 to 1 op 20 to 1) 5
PRINCE ENGELBERT 9-11-10 (7*) Mr A Harvey, *beh whn blun and uns rdr 3rd...* (9 to 1 op 7 to 1 tchd 10 to 1) ur

SOUND OF JURA 9-11-10 (7*) Miss Z Turner, *beh whn mstk and lost tch 6th, blun and uns rdr nxt.*
.... (6 to 4 on op Evens tchd 5 to 4) ur
Dist: 10l, 10l, 2½l, dist. 5m 28.00s. a 16.00s (7 Ran).
(Miss Sarah George), Miss Sarah George

4003 Event Caterers Novices' Hurdle Amateur Riders (4-y-o and up) £2,757 2m 110yds...................... (8:35)

3898⁵ LADY DONOGHUE (USA) 5-11-2 (3*) Mr M Buckley, *hld up gng wl, prog 6th, quickened and led 2 out, not extended....* (Evens fav tchd 11 to 10 on and 5 to 4) 1
3886⁵ EARLY DRINKER 6-11-3 Mr J Durkan, *pressed ldrs, led 3 out, hdd nxt, outpcd appr last....*(6 to 4 op 5 to 4) 2
3773⁹ MAHONG 6-10-12² (7*) Mr A Dowson, *outpcd wl in rear til ran on frm 3 out, nrst at finish....* (25 to 1 op 10 to 1) 3
3815⁸ SON OF TEMPO (Ire) 5-10-10 (7*) Miss S Lamb, *effrt frm rear 5th, one pace frm 3 out.*
.... (12 to 1 tchd 16 to 1 and 20 to 1) 4
3899 PAPER CRAFT (bl) 7-10-10 (7*) Mr A Pickering, *led to 4th, led ag'n and hit 5th, hdd 3 out, wknd frm nxt.*
.... (20 to 1 tchd 25 to 1 and 33 to 1) 5
3829 MASCALLS LADY 9-10-5 (7*) Mr S Davis, *hld up in mid-div, effrt 5th, wknd bef 2 out, tld off.*
.... (5 to 1 op 20 to 1) 6
3829 MISS PARKES 5-10-5 (7*) Mr P Clarke, *midfield til outpcd and tld off frm 6th...* (16 to 1 op 12 to 1 tchd 25 to 1) 7
3800 BEN CONNAN (Ire) 4-10-7² (7*) Mr M Gingell, *wl plcd, led 4th to 5th, wknd aftr 3 out, tld off.*
.... (33 to 1 op 20 to 1 tchd 40 to 1) 8
3745 STARSHADOW 5-10-10 (7*) Mr L Baker, *mid-div, unbl to go pace frm 5th, pld up bef 2 out.*
.... (33 to 1 op 20 to 1 tchd 40 to 1) pu
Dist: 2½l, 6l, 7l, 4l, 25l, 9l, 20l. 4m 0.40s. a 10.40s (9 Ran).
(C C Buckley), Mrs M Reveley

STRATFORD (good)
Friday May 20th
Going Correction: PLUS 0.25 sec. per fur.

4004 Radway Conditional Jockeys' Novices' Handicap Hurdle (0-100 4-y-o and up) £2,122 2¾m 110yds.....(6:25)

3478⁵ NEW STATESMAN [64] 6-10-0 S Curran, *al in tch, wnt second 3 out, led appr last, pushed clr, very easily.*
.... (12 to 1 tchd 14 to 1) 1
3917² GLADYS EMMANUEL [76] 7-10-12 R Davis, *hld up, hdwy appr 4 out, kpt on frm 2 out.*......(13 to 2 op 11 to 2) 2
1067 EXARCH (USA) [88] (bl) 5-11-10 F Leahy, *al prmnt, led 3 out, sn rdn, hdd appr last, one pace r-in.*
.... (20 to 1 op 12 to 1) 3
3829 ST ROBERT [66] 7-10-2 S Fox, *hit second, chsd ldrs, one pace frm 3 out.*...................(16 to 1 op 14 to 1) 4
3762¹ LAY IT OFF (Ire) [69] 5-10-5 R Procter, *prmnt, sn trkd ldr, led appr 4 out, hdd nxt, wknd soon aftr 2 out.*
.... (9 to 1 op 6 to 1 tchd 10 to 1) 5
3804⁵ BORROWED AND BLUE [85] 4-11-7 G Tormey, *hld up, hdwy 4 out, nvr nr to chal.....* (13 to 8 fav op 7 to 4) 6
3741⁵ MISS SOUTER [69] 5-10-5 R Darke, *in tch to 7th, sn beh, tld off....*..............(14 to 1 op 8 to 1) 7
3874⁴ APACHEE FLOWER [70] 4-10-6 Guy Lewis, *prmnt till wknd 3 out, tld off....*..........(16 to 1 op 12 to 1) 8
3828 UNDERWYCHWOOD (Ire) [82] (bl) 6-11-4 L O'Hare, *mstk 3rd, hdwy 5th, rdn and wknd appr 4 out, tld off.*
.... (20 to 1 tchd 33 to 1) 9
3845⁸ WHAT A NOBLE [68] 8-10-4 R Rourke, *al beh, hit 5th, tld off frm 4 out......* (25 to 1 op 20 to 1) 10
3917⁸ KOA [69] (bl) 4-10-5 T Jenks, *led, hit second, rdn and already hdd whn hit 4 out, wknd quickly, tld off.*
.... (16 to 1 tchd 20 to 1) 11
3895⁴ MAYWORK [64] 7-10-0 G Lee, *al beh, effrt 4 out, sn tld off......*.....(6 to 1 op 8 to 1 tchd 11 to 2) 12
3583 POP FESTIVAL [64] 5-10-0 D Winter, *hld up in rear, hdwy 4 out, rdn and held whn f 3 out....* (100 to 1 op 33 to 1) f
3559⁷ POLY VISION (Ire) [67] (bl) 4-10-3 R Massey, *al beh, tld off whn pld up bef last........*(33 to 1 op 25 to 1) pu
Dist: 14l, ¾l, 2½l, 7l, 2l, 14l, 5l, ½l, 7l, 30l. 5m 23.10s. a 11.10s (14 Ran).
SR: 17/15/26/1/-/11/ (Robin Barwell), C R Barwell

4005 Charles Lea Memorial Trophy Novices' Chase (5-y-o and up) £2,900 2m 5f 110yds.................... (6:50)

3901* STRONG MEDICINE 7-11-7 N Williamson, *al gng wl, wnt second 4th, led tenth, drw clr four out, eased r-in.*
.... (Evens jt-fav) 1
3850* SQUIRE JIM 10-11-11 D Bridgwater, *hld up, hdwy 9th, outpcd 11th, rallied to chase wnr nxt, no ch aftr hit 4 out....*(Evens jt-fav op 11 to 10 on tchd 11 to 10) 2
3879⁵ NORTHERN OPTIMIST 6-11-1 (7*) Mr J L Llewellyn, *beh, rdn hfwy, nvr got into race....*(20 to 1 op 16 to 1) 3
3921⁷ PECHE D'OR (bl) 10-10-6 (7*) Mr M Rimell, *led second, hit and hdd tenth, wknd and headed aftr nxt....* (66 to 1) 4

BAKER CONTRACT 9-10-13 M A FitzGerald, *led till hit second, wknd quickly and tld off 6th, pld up bef 9th.*
....(100 to 1 op 66 to 1) pu
Dist: 15l, 8l, ¾l. 5m 23.70s. a 20.70s (5 Ran).
(Dr D B A Silk), K C Bailey

4006 Copacabana Handicap Hurdle (0-125 4-y-o and up) £2,580 3m 3f...... (7:20)

3625[2] LYNCH LAW (Ire) [121] (v) 6-12-0 R Dunwoody, *wtd wth, hdwy frm 6th, cld on ldrs 3 out, rdn to ld nr finish.*
....(5 to 1 op 9 to 2 tchd 4 to 1) 1
3520[*] VICTOR BRAVO (NZ) [112] 7-11-5 J Osborne, *hld up in tch, led appr last, strly rdn and hdd cl hme.*
....(5 to 2 fav op 11 to 4 tchd 3 to 1) 2
3771[4] COURT CIRCULAR [109] (bl) 5-11-2 G McCourt, *chsd ldr, led appr 3 out, hdd approaching last, wknd and pres r-in.*.. 3
3609[7] SPECIAL ACCOUNT [100] (v) 8-10-7 A Maguire, *hld up in tch, hdwy 7th, ev ch 2 out, rdn and wknd.*
....(9 to 1 op 7 to 1) 4
3779[3] GROOMSMAN [95] 8-10-2 W Humphreys, *hld up, rdn and hdwy 4 out, no imprsn frm nxt...*(16 to 1 tchd 20 to 1) 5
3820[3] FAR TOO LOUD [99] 7-10-6 M A FitzGerald, *prmnt to 7th, rallied 4 out, wknd nxt...............*(10 to 1 op 7 to 1) 6
3943[7] SEA BUCK [105] 8-10-12 J R Kavanagh, *al beh, tld off.*
....(14 to 1 op 11 to 1) 7
3622[8] POLISHING [119] (v) 7-11-7 (5[*]) S Lyons, *al beh, tld off.*
....(14 to 1 op 9 to 1) 8
3883[2] LEGAL BEAGLE [93] 7-10-0 M Perrett, *led, hit 1st, hdd appr 3 out, wknd rpdly and tld off.*
....(10 to 1 op 9 to 1 tchd 11 to 1) 9
PERRY WELL [93] 10-10-0 N Williamson, *beh till hdwy 8th, wknd aftr 4 out, tld off.*
....(14 to 1 op 12 to 1 tchd 16 to 1) 10
3783[3] TAP DANCING [93] 8-10-0 Ann Stokell, *prmnt till wknd 6th, tld off whn pld up bef 2 out.* (100 to 1 op 66 to 1) pu
3511 COXANN [93] 8-9-7 (7[*]) E Tolhurst, *beh, struggling frm 6th, tld off whn pld up bef 3 out.......* (66 to 1 op 50 to 1) pu
1643 POP SONG [93] 10-10-0 O Gallagher, *beh, rdn appr 9th, tld off whn pld up bef 3 out, lme...*(66 to 1 op 25 to 1) pu
3728[*] SHIMMERING SCARLET (Ire) [94] 6-10-1 B Powell, *prmnt, wknd appr 5th, tld off whn pld up approaching 3 out.*
....(9 to 1 op 8 to 1) pu
Dist: Nk, 5l, 13l, 6l, ½l, 25l, 4l, 2½l, 2½l. 6m 30.80s. a 11.80s (14 Ran).
SR: 49/39/31/9/-/1/ (Frank A Farrant), M C Pipe

4007 Tom Pettifer Handicap Chase (0-125 5-y-o and up) £2,965 3m........ (7:50)

3662[2] BRADWALL [101] 10-10-9 (3[*]) S Wynne, *wtd wth in rear, hit 8th, rdn 11th, hdwy 4 out, led 2 out, drvn out.*
....(13 to 2 op 5 to 1 tchd 7 to 1) 1
3875[2] GLOVE PUPPET [100] 9-10-11 M A FitzGerald, *hld up, hdwy 4 out, strly rdn to go second r-in.*
....(8 to 1 op 7 to 1) 2
3699[5] MISS FERN [91] 9-9-13 (3[*]) D Meredith, *nvr far away, led appr 3 out, hdd nxt, kpt on one pace.........*(10 to 1) 3
3816[2] STRONG APPROACH [97] 9-10-8 A Maguire, *al in tch, cld on ldrs 5 out, second whn blun 3 out, one pace aftr.*
....(7 to 1) 4
3703[6] ARCTIC TEAL [100] (bl) 10-10-11 M Richards, *beh till styd on frm 2 out, nvr nrr...............*(20 to 1 op 16 to 1) 5
3875[4] NEW HALEN [107] 13-11-4 R Bellamy, *trkd ldr, jmpd slwly 9th, led aftr 13th, hdd appr 3 out, outpcd whn mstk nxt.................*(16 to 1 op 20 to 1 tchd 14 to 1) 6
3828[2] TOMPET [100] 8-10-11 D Bridgwater, *led, mstk second, hdd aftr 13th, hit nxt, sn btn.*
....(13 to 2 op 7 to 1 tchd 6 to 1) 7
3808[5] TOUCHING STAR [103] 9-11-0 M Hourigan, *al beh, rdn tenth, tld off.*..(100 to 1) 8
3821[3] LE PICCOLAGE [117] 10-12-0 R Dunwoody, *trkd ldrs till blun 4 out, sn btn.......*(13 to 2 op 7 to 1 tchd 8 to 1) 9
3358[2] CANDY TUFF [110] 8-11-7 P Niven, *mstk second, mid-div whn f 7th, destroyed.*
....(11 to 4 fav op 7 to 2 tchd 4 to 1) f
3821[4] BEL COURSE [94] 12-10-5 W Marston, *mstk second, beh aftr blun 5th, tld off whn pld up bef 9th....* (33 to 1 tchd 50 to 1) pu
Dist: 2½l, 3l, 1½l, 3l, 6l, 12l, 2½l, ½l. 6m 5.60s. a 18.60s (11 Ran).
(G B Barlow), Mrs A R Hewitt

4008 Gay Sheppard Memorial Challenge Trophy Hunters' Chase (6-y-o and up) £2,108 3m.................... (8:20)

SPORTING MARINER 12-12-0 Mr J Greenall, *made most to 4th, jmpd slwly 7th and 8th, lft to finish alone frm 9th.*
....(9 to 4 op 11 to 10) 1
NO ESCORT 10-12-2 (5[*]) Mr R Russell, *made most frm 4th till f 9th.........* (6 to 4 on op 7 to 4 on tchd 5 to 4 on) f
Won by 6m 37.70s. a 50.70s (2 Ran).
SR: -/-/ (D R Bloor), D R Bloor

4009 Nuffield Orthotics Appeal Novices' Hurdle (4-y-o and up) £2,080 2m 110yds.................... (8:50)

3825[*] SHARP DANCE 5-11-7 R Dunwoody, *hld up, gd hdwy 3 out, chlgd and led sn aftr last, quickened clr.*
....(3 to 1 op 9 to 4) 1
3886[*] FOREST PRIDE (Ire) 5-11-0 N Williamson, *hld up in tch, mstk 1st, hdwy appr 3 out, hit nxt, led approaching 3 out, rallied and kpt on frm nxt...........*(11 to 8 fav tchd 5 to 4 and 6 to 4) 2
3573[4] ALAN BALL 8-10-12 G McCourt, *led to 1st, styd in tch, led 3 out, hdd appr last, no extr.*
....(8 to 1 op 10 to 1 tchd 12 to 1) 3
3878[2] ROYAL GLINT 5-10-4 (3[*]) R Davis, *hld up in rear, gd hdwy frm 5th, wknd appr last............*(10 to 1 op 8 to 1) 4
3700[5] GENTLEMAN SID 4-10-4 (3[*]) D Meredith, *chsd ldrs till mstk 3 out, rallied and kpt on frm nxt...(25 to 1 op 14 to 1) 5
3583 DALBEATTIE 5-10-0 (7[*]) D Winter, *led 1st, hdd 3 out, wknd quickly appr last...............*(100 to 1 op 66 to 1) 6
3938 BOLLINGTON (Fr) 5-10-9 (3[*]) J McCarthy, *prmnt till rdn and wknd 3 out.................*(50 to 1 op 33 to 1) 7
3886[6] ASTERIX 6-10-12 A Maguire, *al towards rear.*
....(9 to 1 op 6 to 1 tchd 10 to 1) 8
3878[5] SUPER SHARP (NZ) 6-10-12 Jacqui Oliver, *pld hrd, mstk 1st, prmnt to h/uy...............*(20 to 1 op 8 to 1) 9
3809[6] TRUE SERENADE 5-10-7 (5[*]) D Leahy, *prmnt, second whn mstk 4th, wknd 3 out..............*(100 to 1 op 50 to 1) 10
3826 PACIFIC SPIRIT 4-9-9 (7[*]) M McLoughlin, *al beh.*
....(100 to 1 op 66 to 1) 11
3925 WEST ORIENT 9-10-12 V Slattery, *pld hrd in mid-div, mstk 3rd, beh frm 5th......*(10 to 1 op 12 to 1 tchd 7 to 1) 12
3189 PEACE FORMULA (Ire) (bl) 5-10-12 W Marston, *in tch till wknd 5th, tld off....................*(66 to 1 op 33 to 1) 13
THEMOREYOUKNOW 5-10-12 M Sharratt, *al beh, tld off.*
....(100 to 1) 14
3849 CHARLES HENRY 10-10-12 R Bellamy, *pld hrd, mid-div whn ran out aftr 4th.*
....(50 to 1 op 66 to 1 tchd 100 to 1) ro
3231[9] AMBER FOLLY 5-10-7 Peter Hobbs, *mid-div, in rear to 5th, tld off whn pld up bef last...* (25 to 1 op 12 to 1) pu
Dist: 6l, 1½l, 3l, 7l, ¾l, 6l, 4l, 8l, 4l, 5l. 4m 2.20s. a 13.20s (16 Ran).
SR: 2/-/-/-/-/-/ (The Big Eaters Partnership), B Smart

CURRAGH (IRE) (good to yielding)
Saturday May 21st

4010 Landrover I.N.H. Flat Race (4-y-o and up) £6,850 2m.................(4:30)

2391[4] WHAT IT IS (Ire) 5-11-9 (3[*]) Mr J A Nash, ...(14 to 1) 1
3660[3] GAMBOLLING DOC (Ire) 4-11-4 (3[*]) Mr B R Hamilton, ...(6 to 1) 2
2127[*] GREAT SVENGALI (Ire) 5-11-10 (7[*]) Mr E Norris, (5 to 2 fav) 3
3393[6] RHYTHM SECTION (Ire) 5-12-3 Mr A J Martin, ...(7 to 2) 4
3913[5] BUSTHAT 7-11-8 (7[*]) Mr T J Murphy, ...(14 to 1) 5
3653[*] TOURIST ATTRACTION (Ire) 6-11-9 (3[*]) Mrs J M Mullins, ...(4 to 1) 6
3250[8] REGAL FELLOW (Ire) 5-11-4 (3[*]) Mr R Neylon, ...(50 to 1) 7
3653 SHORTSTAFF (Ire) 5-11-4 (3[*]) Mr A K Wyse, ...(33 to 1) 8
2080[7] FAITHFULL FELLOW 7-11-1 (7[*]) Mr S McCarthy, ...(16 to 1) 9
3936[8] BEST INTEREST (Ire) 6-11-5 (3[*]) Mr D Marnane, ...(16 to 1) 10
2290 LORD BARNARD (Ire) 4-10-11 (3[*]) Mrs C Barker, ...(33 to 1) 11
3937[5] DERBY HAVEN 7-11-1 (7[*]) Mr A F Doherty, ...(16 to 1) 12
3712 ITS ONLY JUSTICE 8-11-8 (7[*]) Mr M Halford, ...(33 to 1) 13
1160[*] CONQUINN (Ire) 5-12-0 Mr P F Graffin, ...(12 to 1) 14
LA MANCHA BOY (Ire) 4-11-0 Mr M McNulty, ...(33 to 1) 15
Dist: 3l, 1l, 3l, 3½l. 3m 46.05s. (15 Ran).
(Mrs M Holleran), J H Scott

SOUTHWELL (good to soft (races 1,2), soft (3,4,5,6))
Saturday May 21st
Going Correction: MINUS 0.20 sec. per fur.

4011 Wally Street - Celebration Novices' Hurdle (4-y-o and up) £2,057 2m (6:05)

3767[*] MISSY-S (Ire) 5-10-9 (7[*]) Mr J L Llewellyn, *trkd ldrs, hdwy 4th, led aftr nxt, clr appr 2 out, unchlgd.*
....(2 to 1 on op 15 to 8 on tchd 9 to 4 on) 1
3925[5] DYNAMITE DAN (Ire) 6-11-0 R Garritty, *hld up and beh, took clr order appr 5th, chsd wnr frm nxt, rdn and wknd approaching 2 out..............*(4 to 1 tchd 9 to 2) 2
3826[9] JUNO'S SPECIAL (Ire) 6-10-2 (3[*]) T Eley, *hld up and beh, hit second, hdwy 5th, rdn nxt, sn one pace....*(20 to 1) 3
3915[9] WALID'S PRINCESS (Ire) 4-10-6[2] J Frost, *led till appr 5th, sn rdn and wknd quickly nxt....*(12 to 1 tchd 14 to 1) 4
3898[6] CREPT OUT (Ire) 5-11-0 Mr A Walton, *chsd ldr till lost pl quickly 5th sn beh...........*(25 to 1 op 20 to 1) 5
3898[9] OLLIVER DUCKETT (Ire) 5-11-0 C Hawkins, *chsd ldrs, hdwy to ld appr 5th, hit fifth, sn rdn and hdd, wknd quickly nxt and soon tld off...............*(16 to 1 op 12 to 1) 6
Dist: 25l, 4l, 15l, ½l. 3m 54.00s. a 2.00s (6 Ran).

SR: 36/9/-/ (B J Llewellyn), B J Llewellyn

4012 — Ductile Castings Selling Hurdle (4,5,6-y-o) £1,940 2½m 110yds........ (6:35)

3770⁶ KEDGE (bl) 4-10-10 R Garritty, *not jump wl, trkd ldrs, hdwy to chase ldr 7th, rdn 2 out, hrd drvn flt and styd on to lead nr finish*...................(7 to 1 op 6 to 1) 1

3757⁶ DHARAMSHALA (Ire) 6-11-2 M Brennan, *hld up, hdwy to join ldrs 7th, rdn 2 out, kpt on.*
................................(12 to 1 op 16 to 1 tchd 20 to 1) 2

3926⁴ SHARE A MOMENT (Can) 4-10-7 (3*) S Wynne, *trkd ldrs, hdwy to ld 3 out, rdn nxt, hdd and no extr flt.*
...................................(7 to 1 op 5 to 1) 3

3584* STRATHBOGIE MIST (Ire) 6-11-3 (5*) F Leahy, *in tch, gd hdwy 4 out, rdn 2 out and one pace appr last.* (3 to 1 jt-
...........................fav op 11 to 4 tchd 5 to 2) 4

3637⁶ COEUR BATTANT (Fr) 4-10-10 G McCourt, *hld up and beh, hdwy to join ldrs 4 out, rdn appr 2 out and sn btn.*
....................................(3 to 1 jt-fav tchd 7 to 2) 5

3899⁴ SEPTEMBER SAND 6-10-11 J Railton, *led to second, cl up till led 7th, rdn and hdd 3 out, grad wknd.*......(25 to 1) 6

3826 KISS IN THE DARK 4-10-11 P Niven, *hld up in rear, not jump wl, tld off 4 out, pld up bef 2 out.*
.....................................(5 to 1 op 7 to 2) pu

3843³ WESTRAY 4-10-10 S Earle, *led second till appr 7th, sn lost pl and tld off whn pld up bef 2 out.*
.....................................(14 to 1 op 8 to 1) pu

Dist: 4l, nk, 2l, 3l, 2l. 5m 12.70s. a 19.20s (8 Ran).

(S Hibbert, A K Lowe), W Clay

4013 — East Midlands Electricity Handicap Chase (0-105 5-y-o and up) £3,184 3m 110yds........................ (7:05)

3630⁹ PRUDENT PEGGY [87] 7-10-11 J Frost, *al prmnt, chsd ldr frm 12th, hrd drvn appr last, styd on to ld nr line.*
.....................................(4 to 1 op 5 to 1) 1

3929² CALL ME EARLY [87] (v) 9-10-11 M Brennan, *prmnt, hdwy to dispute ld 11th, led nxt, jmpd rght 3 out and next, sn hrd rdn, hdd nr finish...*(3 to 1 op 7 to 2 tchd 4 to 1) 2

3978⁶ TRUSTY FRIEND [77] 12-10-1 S Earle, *led to 9th, cl up till wknd appr 11th, sn lost touch.* (10 to 1 op 16 to 1) 3

3885 RED UNDER THE BED [92] 7-10-11 (5*) J Burke, *hld up in rear, hit 5th, blun 11th, sn tld off.* (12 to 1 op 10 to 1) 4

3564⁴ THE YANK [98] (bl) 8-11-8 P Niven, *trkd ldrs, hdwy 7th, led 9th, hit 12th, sn hrd rdn and one pace, poor 3rd whn uns rdr last.*.............................(6 to 1 op 5 to 1) ur

3816* WIN YOU THERE (USA) [102] 9-11-12 Mr S Swiers, *hld up in tch, blun 6th, hdwy to join ldrs 8th, mstk 5 out, sn lost pl, beh whn pld up bef 3 out.* (2 to 1 fav op 5 to 4) pu

Dist: Sht-hd, 30l, 2l. 6m 32.90s. a 34.90s (6 Ran).

(Mrs J McCormack), R G Frost

4014 — Maun Motors Maiden Chase (5-y-o and up) £2,251 3m 110yds...... (7:35)

3844² TRY NEXT DOOR 7-11-7 M Brennan, *hld up, hit 6th and 7th, hdwy 9th, led 11th, rdn 2 out, styd on wl flt.*
................(6 to 4 fav op 11 to 8 tchd 13 to 8) 1

3810 SEMINOLE PRINCESS (bl) 6-11-2 M Bosley, *al prmnt, jnd wnr 12th, ev ch till rdn and wknd last.*........ (25 to 1) 2

3762 SEARCY 6-11-7 G Upton, *led to 5th, led 9th, hdd 11th, rdn nxt, wknd 3 out.*..............(3 to 1 tchd 7 to 2) 3

3818⁵ RAIN MAN (NZ) 9-11-7 P Niven, *prmnt, rdn 12th, wknd nxt.*...........................(5 to 1 op 4 to 1) 4

3575 SERDARLI 12-11-2 L Harvey, *mstk 1st, in tch whn f 5th.*
.....................................(12 to 1 tchd 14 to 1) f

3802 JELLIQUE 12-11-7 C Hawkins, *cl up, led 5th till hdd and hit 9th, close up till blun 11th and lost pl, pld up bef 4 out.*....................(25 to 1 tchd 33 to 1) pu

3474⁹ KINROYAL 9-11-0 (7*) Miss Sue Nichol, *in tch till lost pl and beh 9th, staying on and 4th whn pld up bef 3 out.*
.....................................(25 to 1) pu

3682⁵ TANAISTE (USA) 5-10-12 J R Kavanagh, *in tch till mstk and wknd 11th, hit nxt, beh whn pld up aftr 4 out.*
................(12 to 1 op 10 to 1 tchd 14 to 1) pu

3802 STONE WARRIOR 7-11-7 M Robinson, *beh till pld up aftr 4th.*....................................(12 to 1) pu

Dist: 10l, 20l, dist. 6m 34.40s. a 36.40s (9 Ran).

(M S Griffiths), O Brennan

4015 — British Coal Novices' Handicap Chase (5-y-o and up) £2,604 2m....... (8:05)

3941⁸ RUSTIC GENT (Ire) [73] (v) 6-10-7 J Railton, *al prmnt, hdwy 3 out, effrt nxt, rdn to ld last, styd on wl.*
.....................................(10 to 1 op 8 to 1) 1

3786* GRAZEMBER [77] 7-10-11 C Hawkins, *hld up, hit 5th, hdwy to ld 7th, rdn 2 out, hdd last, no extr.*
.....................................(3 to 1 op 5 to 2) 2

3786² HOT PURSUIT [78] 8-10-12 M Brennan, *al prmnt, ev ch 3 out, sn rdn and wknd nxt.*......(5 to 2 fav tchd 3 to 1) 3

3764⁴ NEEDS MUST [84] 7-11-4 J Frost, *led till hdd 7th, rdn and wknd aftr 4 out.*...............(4 to 1 op 7 to 2) 4

3902² HOWGILL [90] 8-11-7 (3*) S Wynne, *hit 1st, in tch, rdn alng 5 out, ev ch appr 3 out, sn hrd drvn and btn.*
.....................................(11 to 4 op 5 to 2) 5

Dist: 2½l, 9l, 11l, 3l. 4m 11.00s. a 12.00s (5 Ran).

(Sadlers Estate Agents), Mrs L C Jewell

4016 — Smith & Partners Handicap Hurdle For Amateur Riders (0-115 4-y-o and up) £2,092 2½m 110yds........... (8:35)

3661⁵ BATTLEPLAN [74] 9-10-3⁵ (7*) Mr A Charles-Jones, *hld up, outpcd aftr 3 out, hdwy after nxt, styd on strly to ld flt.*
.....................................(6 to 1 tchd 7 to 1) 1

3831⁹ MIDDLEWICK [93] 9-11-3 (7*) Mr M Rimell, *chsd ldr, led 5 out, rdn 2 out, hdd and no extr r-in.* (4 to 1 op 5 to 2) 2

3752⁷ CURTAIN FACTORY [76] 5-10-2 (5*) Mr D Parker, *pld hrd, trkd ldrs, hdwy 5 out, chlgd 2 out and ev ch till rdn and not quicken last...*(5 to 2 fav op 11 to 4 tchd 3 to 1) 3

3829⁵ GREEN'S SEAGO (USA) [72] 6-11-0⁴ (7*) Mr M Mannish, *led till 5 out, rdn and wknd appr 2 out.*
....(9 to 1 op 12 to 1) 4

3819³ SHAMSHOM AL ARAB (Ire) [90] 6-11-0 (7*) Miss V Haigh, *hld upin tch, effrt and hdwy 3 out, rdn nxt and sn btn.*
.....................................(3 to 1 op 11 to 4) 5

SONALTO [76] 8-10-0 (7*) Miss S Judge, *red wide, hit 3rd,mstk 6th and 7th, sn lost pl and btn.*
................(20 to 1 op 25 to 1 tchd 16 to 1) 6

Dist: 2l, 4l, 1l, 7l, 20l. 5m 21.90s. a 28.40s (6 Ran).

(Glyn Hughes), K S Bridgwater

WARWICK (good (races 1,2,3,4), good to soft (5,6,7))
Saturday May 21st
Going Correction: NIL

4017 — Elisabeth Chef Hurdle (5-y-o and up) £2,532 2m.................... (5:55)

3302² CARIBBEAN PRINCE (bl) 6-10-13 (5*) S Fox, *chsd ldrs till led 3 out, rdn 2 out, hit last, ran on wl r-in.*
.....................................(7 to 1 op 11 to 2) 1

3038 WICK POUND (bl) 8-10-12 T Grantham, *chsd ldrs, led 5th, hdd 3 out, stood ev ch nxt, sn rdn and found little.*
.....................................(2 to 1 tchd 7 to 4) 2

2480⁶ BADRAKHANI (Fr) 8-11-4 R Dunwoody, *in tch, chsd ldrs 4th, rdn 3 out, sn one pace.*
.....................................(7 to 1 op 5 to 1 tchd 8 to 1) 3

3878⁷ PARISIAN 9-10-5 (7*) A Lucas, *in tch, effrt and hit 4th, wknd aftr nxt...*..............(100 to 1 op 66 to 1) 4

3607⁴ YOUNG SNUGFIT 10-10-12 J Osborne, *led till hdd 5th, wknd grad frm 3 out.*
.................(Evens fav tchd 5 to 4 and 5 to 4 on) 5

3635³ SWAN WALK (Ire) 6-10-12 N Williamson, *in tch whn hit 5th, sn wknd.*....................(33 to 1 op 20 to 1) 6

3815 BOSSYMOSS (Ire) 5-10-12 Susan Kersey, *jmpd poorly, tld off aftr 3rd, refused and uns rdr nxt.*
.....................................(500 to 1 op 200 to 1) ur

Dist: 7l, 1¼l, 15l, 25l, 14l. 3m 45.70s. a 5.70s (7 Ran).

SR: 33/20/24/3/ (Mrs B Taylor), Mrs J G Retter

4018 — Watch Security Handicap Chase (0-135 6-y-o and up) £3,785 2½m 110yds........................ (6:25)

3916* ERRANT KNIGHT [128] 10-11-8 R Dunwoody, *hld up, hit 3rd, smooth hdwy 11th, led 12th, hdd nxt, led ag'n aftr 2 out, readily.*
.........(5 to 4 on tchd 11 to 10 and 11 to 8 on) 1

3519⁸ VIRIDIAN [106] 9-10-0 N Williamson, *led, hit 1st and hdd, led 3rd till aftr 7th, led after tenth, headed 12th, led nxt, headed and one pace after 2 out.*
................(11 to 1 op 16 to 1 tchd 8 to 1) 2

3705³ MR ENTERTAINER [106] 11-10-0 J Osborne, *led 6th till aftr 7th, styd pressing ldrs, hit 12th, sn rdn, stayed on same pace frm 2 out.*........(11 to 2 op 5 to 1 tchd 6 to 1) 3

3627³ SPACE FAIR [134] 11-12-0 A Maguire, *hdwy to chase ldrs 11th, rdn 3 out, sn wknd.*
.................(5 to 2 op 2 to 1 tchd 11 to 4) 4

3766² NOS NA GAOITHE [106] (v) 11-10-0 B Powell, *led aftr 1st, wknd 12th, tld off.*..............(16 to 1 tchd 20 to 1) 5

Dist: 7l, 5l, 1¼l, dist. 5m 8.60s. a 13.60s (5 Ran).

(Mrs N J Bird), M C Pipe

4019 — Malcolm Hawkesford Handicap Hurdle (0-140 4-y-o and up) £2,880 2m ...... (6:55)

3618² BOTTLES (USA) [122] 7-11-6 R Dunwoody, *hld up, hdwy 5th, chlgd 2 out, rdn, edgd lft and led last, styd on wl.*
................(13 to 8 fav op 7 to 4 tchd 2 to 1) 1

3806² ROUTING [102] 6-10-0 B Powell, *gd hdwy to chase ldrs 5th, led 3 out, hdd last, not quicken.* (8 to 1 op 6 to 1) 2

3806⁷ ADMIRALTY WAY [103] 8-9-12 (3*) T Jenks, *gd hdwy 5th, pressed ldrs 3 out, outpcd appr nxt.* (8 to 1 op 5 to 1) 3

3625⁹ EDEN'S CLOSE [114] 5-10-12 A Maguire, *chsd ldr 3rd to 5th, sn wknd...*.........(7 to 2 op 4 to 1 tchd 9 to 2) 4

3516 ARABIAN BOLD (Ire) [130] 6-11-7 (7") Pat Thompson, *led, clr appr 4th, hdd 3 out, sn wknd*.......(7 to 1 op 4 to 1) 5
3320³ WHIPPERS DELIGHT (Ire) [102] 6-10-0 D Meade, *chsd ldr to 3rd, wknd nxt*....................(10 to 1 op 12 to 1) 6
3736⁷ PONTYNYSWEN [127] (v) 6-11-11 O J Burchell, *in tch to 5th*.........................(7 to 1 op 5 to 1) 7
3718⁶ GREYFRIARS BOBBY [102] 8-9-12³ (5") S Fox, *beh 3rd, f nxt*.............................(33 to 1) f

Dist: 1½l, 15l, 13l, 1l, 20l, 1½l. 3m 43.50s. a 3.50s (8 Ran).
SR: 57/35/21/19/34/-/9/-/ (R C Taylor), J E Banks

4020 Rose And William Sutton Novices' Handicap Chase (5-y-o and up) £3,080 2½m 110yds.................(7:25)

3942² ROYAL SQUARE (Can) [88] 8-10-12 M Perrett, *chsd ldrs, chlgd tenth till led 12th, forged clr appr 2 out*.
.........................(9 to 4 fav op 7 to 2) 1
3251 DUNKERY BEACON [76] 8-9-7 (7") P McLoughlin, *beh 8th, hdwy 11th, chlgd 3 out, rdn and sn outpcd*.
.........................(25 to 1 op 20 to 1) 2
3695* PHILIP'S WOODY [96] 6-11-6 R Dunwoody, *led to 3rd, led ag'n 6th, hdd 12th, outpcd frm 3 out*. (3 to 1 op 2 to 1) 3
3517⁶ NICKLE JOE [104] 8-12-0 W Marston, *chsd ldrs, outpcd frm 4 out*.......................(3 to 1 op 7 to 2) 4
3498 ROSCOE'S GEMMA [76] 10-9-11 (3") D Meredith, *beh frm 7th*........................(40 to 1 op 33 to 1) 5
3534⁶ MR INVADER [79] 7-10-3 J Osborne, *beh 7th, hdwy and hit 11th, sn btn*.........(15 to 2 op 6 to 1 tchd 8 to 1) 6
3882 BILLHEAD [76] 8-10-0 N Williamson, *hit 5th, wknd 11th*.
.........................(50 to 1) 7
3805³ PRINCE'S COURT [89] 11-10-8 (5") D Fortt, *chsd ldrs 7th, hit 11th, sn wknd*.......(8 to 1 op 7 to 1 tchd 9 to 1) 8
3966 FROG HOLLOW (Ire) [79] (bl) 6-10-3¹ M A FitzGerald, *slight ld 3rd till hdd 6th, wknd 9th, pld up bef nxt*.
.........................(20 to 1 op 14 to 1) pu

Dist: 12l, 1½l, 10l, 15l, 7l, nk, 15l. 5m 17.10s. a 22.10s (9 Ran).
(Park Farm Thoroughbreds), G Harwood

4021 Ozbox Novices' Hurdle (4-y-o and up) £2,199 2½m 110yds............(7:55)

3606³ ERCKULE 4-11-2 M A FitzGerald, *in tch, hdwy to chase ldrs 7th, chlgd frm 2 out till hrd drvn r-in, led cl hme*.
.........................(3 to 1 fav op 4 to 1 tchd 9 to 2) 1
3874* FORMAL AFFAIR 4-11-3 A Maguire, *mid-div, hdwy 6th, led 3 out, rdn r-in, ct cl hme*.
.........................(7 to 2 op 5 to 2 tchd 4 to 1) 2
3831⁴ BALLYHYLAND (Ire) 5-11-9 R Bellamy, *al prmnt, chsd ldrs 3 out, outpcd frm 2 out*......(11 to 2 tchd 13 to 2) 3
3767⁵ KHALIDI (Ire) 5-11-8 M Dwyer, *chsd ldrs till led appr 6th, hdd 3 out, sn btn*..............(10 to 1 op 8 to 1) 4
3809³ MARROB 7-10-9 (7") S Ryan, *chsd ldrs, rdn 8th, sn btn*.
.........................(10 to 1 op 12 to 1 tchd 14 to 1) 5
3932* KONVEKTA CONTROL (bl) 7-12-0 J Osborne, *chsd ldrs, rdn 8th, wknd quickly*................(9 to 2 op 3 to 1) 6
3970 WAKT 4-10-5 W McFarland, *beh, hit 6th, styd on frm 3 out, not rch ldrs*.....(50 to 1 op 33 to 1 tchd 66 to 1) 7
3881* RIP THE CALICO (Ire) 6-10-10 (7") Miss C Spearing, *hdwy to chase ldrs 6th, wknd aftr nxt*............(33 to 1) 8
3453 CHRISTIAN SOLDIER (bl) 7-11-2 W Elderfield, *al beh*.
.........................(200 to 1 op 100 to 1) 9
3848⁶ MERIVEL 7-11-2 B Powell, *al beh*....(50 to 1 op 25 to 1) 10
3222 HAPPY DEAL 8-11-2 T Wall, *al beh*.
.........................(66 to 1 op 33 to 1 tchd 100 to 1) 11
3849³ ROAD TO AU BON (USA) 6-10-11 (5") Guy Lewis, *al beh*.
.........................(33 to 1) 12
3848⁴ STRONG TOI 7-10-11 N Williamson, *al beh*.
.........................(12 to 1 op 10 to 1) 13
3826 ANDREA'S GIRL 4-9-12 (7") Mr G Hogan, *al beh*.
.........................(200 to 1 op 100 to 1) 14
3932⁵ MERRYHILL MADAM 5-10-11 W Humphreys, *sn beh*.
.........................(50 to 1) 15
3970 TRUE STORM (bl) 5-10-11 M Sharratt, *pressed ldr, blun 4th, sn wknd, beh whn f 6th*......(200 to 1 op 100 to 1) f
3756³ YAAKUM 5-11-8 R Dunwoody, *prmnt till wknd 7th, tld off whn pld up bef last*.............(7 to 1 op 8 to 1) pu
3932 JUST EVE 7-10-11 D Bridgwater, *led till hdd appr 6th, sn wknd, tld off whn pld up bef last*.
.........................(200 to 1 op 100 to 1) pu
1277 TUDOR BLUES 7-10-6 (5") D Leahy, *al beh, tld off whn pld up bef 7th*...............(200 to 1 op 100 to 1) pu
3590 AHBEJAYBUS (Ire) 5-11-2 Susan Kersey, *al beh, tld off whn pld up bef last*........(200 to 1 op 100 to 1) pu
3009 GANDERTON INT 7-10-9 (7") P Ward, *al beh, tld off whn pld up bef 7th*...............(100 to 1 op 66 to 1) pu

Dist: ½l, 11l, 12l, 25l, 8l, 4l, 2l, 5l, 14l, 2l. 5m 2.90s. a 14.40s (21 Ran).
(The Saxon Partnership), N A Gaselee

4022 Yarnolds Of Stratford Hunters' Chase (5-y-o and up) £1,716 3¼m....(8:25)

3927² WARLEGGAN 13-11-4⁴ (7") Mr C Stockton, *chsd ldrs, hit 15th, drvn to ld appr 2 out, hld on wl*. (5 to 2 op 2 to 1) 1
3717² MR MURDOCK 9-11-7 (7") Mr M G Miller, *hld up, hit 14th, hdwy to chal frm 3 out, shaken up r-in, no extr cl hme*.
.........................(13 to 8 on op 6 to 4 on tchd 7 to 4 on) 2

3857⁵ SKINNHILL (bl) 10-11-7 (7") Mr G Hogan, *led to 4th, clr 13th, sn reminders, hit 14th, hdd appr 2 out, soon outpcd*.........................(6 to 1 op 5 to 1) 3
3501 HIGHLAND ECHO 11-11-0 (7") Miss A Turner, *led to 4th, hit tenth, lost tch frm 14th*.........(14 to 1 op 10 to 1) 4

Dist: Nk, 11l, dist. 6m 56.10s. a 42.10s (4 Ran).
(D A Malam), S A Brookshaw

4023 Grunwick 'Bumper' National Hunt Flat Race (4,5,6-y-o) £1,842 2m.....(8:55)

ZAMORSTON 5-11-0 (7") W Fry, *gd hdwy 6 fs out, led 4 out, clr fnl 2*........................(10 to 1 op 25 to 1) 1
TELL THE BOYS (Ire) 6-11-0 (7") P Ward, *hdwy 6 fs out, chlgd 4 out, styd on but no ch wth wnr fnl quarter-m*.
.........................(14 to 1) 2
SANDRIFT 5-10-13 (3") A Procter, *hdwy hfwy, rdn 5 fs out, styd on und press fnl quarter-m*.........(4 to 1 jt-fav op 3 to 1 tchd 9 to 2) 3
3457⁷ SCARLET RAMBLER 5-11-4 (3") T Jenks, *slwly into strd, gd hdwy 7 fs out, kpt on fnl quarter-m*.
.........................(7 to 1 op 5 to 1 tchd 8 to 1) 4
3855³ TIME HE WENT 5-11-0 (7") M Godsafe, *mid-div, hdwy 7 fs out, outpcd fnl 3 furlongs*.............(4 to 1 jt-fav op 5 to 1 tchd 6 to 1) 5
OWENS QUEST (Ire) 4-10-4 (7") R Rourke, *hdwy 4 fs out, no imprsn frm 3 out*............(12 to 1 op 16 to 1) 6
GARJUN (Ire) 5-10-13 (3") R Davis, *kpt on fnl 4 fs, not rch ldrs*...........................(16 to 1 op 10 to 1) 7
3833⁸ CALL HER A STAR (Ire) 4-10-11 Miss M Maher, *some prog frm 3 fs out, not a dngr*..........(16 to 1 tchd 33 to 1) 8
STICKY MONEY 6-10-9 (7") L Reynolds, *prmnt, sddl slpd aftr 6 fs, not reco'r*..............(10 to 1 op 6 to 1) 9
BOBBIE MO 4-10-9 (7") Mr R M Murphy, *gd hdwy 6 fs out, wknd 3 out*.........(25 to 1 op 20 to 1) 10
BRIDGNORTH LASS 5-10-9 (7") O Burrows, *prmnt till wknd 4 fs out*................(14 to 1 tchd 16 to 1) 11
3707⁵ MOUNT SERRATH (Ire) 6-11-7 Mr J Durkan, *led one furlong, styd prmnt till wknd o'r 5 fs out*.
.........................(10 to 1 op 4 to 1 tchd 12 to 1) 12
3079⁶ TALL FELLOW (Ire) 4-10-9 (7") Mr W Burnell, *nvr rchd ldrs*.........................(25 to 1) 13+
3522 AIN ZARA (Ire) 5-10-13 (3") J McCarthy, *nvr rchd ldrs*.
.........................(25 to 1 tchd 33 to 1) 13+
MONKS JAY (Ire) 5-11-0 (7") S Drake, *led aftr one furlong, made rst till hdd 4 out, sn btn*.....(6 to 1 tchd 9 to 1) 15
3708³ ELUSIVE STAR 4-10-4 (7") P McLoughlin, *pld hrd, prmnt till wknd hfwy*...............(6 to 1 tchd 5 to 1) 16
3832 LANDSKER MISSILE 5-10-9 (7") T Dascombe, *chsd ldrs, rdn 6 fs out, sn wknd*.........(14 to 1 op 12 to 1) 17
ANOTHER VENTURE (Ire) 4-11-2 N Bentley, *beh frm hfwy*.
.........................(6 to 1 op 8 to 1) 18
3589 BARDAROS 5-11-0 (7") Mr N Bradley, *al beh*......(50 to 1) 19
BAY MAG 4-10-9 (7") A Shakespeare, *al beh*.
.........................(20 to 1 op 25 to 1) 20
3707 KINGS GAL 6-10-9 (7") L Aspell, *slwly into strd, al beh*.
.........................(50 to 1 op 33 to 1) 21
DELWORTHY DANCER 5-11-0 (7") M Keighley, *strted slwly, al beh*.........................(50 to 1 op 33 to 1) 22
YOUWONNA 4-10-9 (7") Mr S Joynes, *prmnt to hfwy*.
.........................(50 to 1 op 33 to 1) 23
BLUE JADE 5-11-2 Mr L Lay, *tld off, pld up frm hfwy*.
.........................(50 to 1 op 33 to 1) pu

Dist: 15l, ¾l, nk, hd, 3½l, 1½l, 2l, 9l, ½l, hd. 3m 45.80s. (24 Ran).
(L M Wild), S G Norton

MARKET RASEN (good)
Monday May 23rd
Going Correction: PLUS 0.20 sec. per fur. (races 1,2,-4,5,6), MINUS 0.20 (3)

4024 Garth West Novices' Chase (5-y-o and up) £2,726 2½m.............(2:20)

3896* BRACKENFIELD 8-11-13 P Niven, *made all and sn clr, pressed fnl 2, shaken up and wnt clear r-in*.
.........................(5 to 2 on op 11 to 4 on tchd 9 to 4 on) 1
3894² DOWN THE ROAD 7-11-13 A Maguire, *nvr far away, mstk 5 out, improved and ev ch 2 out, outpcd r-in*...(3 to 1) 2
3901² HIGHLAND RALLY (USA) 7-11-3 R Garritty, *prmnt, dropd rear 4th, improved to chase ldrs 6 out, outpcd bef 3 out, sn btn*.................(12 to 1 op 8 to 1 tchd 14 to 1) 3
3931 ON THE TEAR 8-11-3 S McNeill, *wtd wth, improved 6 out, struggling bef 3 out, sn tld off*.............(50 to 1) 4
3802 CRUISE CRACKER 8-10-12 M Ranger, *handily plcd, struggling to keep up aftr 5 out, tld off last 3*.
.........................(100 to 1 op 50 to 1) 5
3628⁷ MRS TWEED 8-10-12 B Dalton, *in tch, mstk and drpd rear second, chasing ldrs whn blun and uns rdr 4 out*.
.........................(50 to 1 op 33 to 1) ur

Dist: 9l, 8l, 13l, dist. 5m 7.10s. a 15.10s (6 Ran).
(Guy Faber), Mrs M Reveley

4025 Clugston Selling Hurdle (4 & 5-y-o) £1,780 2m 1f 110yds............(2:50)

3757⁴ INNOCENT GEORGE 5-11-0 W Marston, *pressed ldr, improved to ld aftr 2 out, edgd rght and ran on wl frm last*....................(4 to 1 op 7 to 2 tchd 9 to 1) 1
3635* WATER DIVINER 4-10-9 J Ryan, *led, hdd aftr 2 out, kpt on same pace und pres r-in*............ (9 to 2 op 5 to 2) 2
3864⁷ TINSTONE 4-10-4 R Garritty, *not fluent in rear, improved aftr 4 out, ev ch 2 out, rdn and not quicken.*
.... (11 to 1 op 10 to 1) 3
3965⁶ BOWLAND GIRL (Ire) (v) 5-10-9 R Dunwoody, *settled midfield, rdn alng aftr 3 out, btn frm nxt*...........(7 to 1) 4
3357 SUMMERS DREAM 4-10-4 S Turner, *in tch, struggling to go pace 4 out, some late hdwy, nvr dngrs.*
...................................(10 to 1 op 7 to 1 tchd 12 to 1) 5
3668⁶ CYRILL HENRY (Ire) 5-11-10 A Merrigan, *patiently rdn, improved into midfield 4 out, effrt bef 2 out, fdd.*
....(10 to 1) 6
3881⁵ OMIDJOY (Ire) 4-10-4 Gee Armytage, *handily plcd, struggling to keep up appr 2 out, fdd...*(11 to 1 op 10 to 1) 7
3800⁹ SKIDDER 5-11-0 Mr K Green, *co'red up in midfield, outpcd and rdn 4 out, sn struggling, tld off.*
................................(40 to 1 op 33 to 1) 8
3892⁶ FANFOLD (Ire) (bl) 4-10-4 L O'Hara, *keen hold, trkd ldrs, blun 3 out, sn struggling, tld off...*(33 to 1 op 25 to 1) 9
3928³ BASSIO (Bel) (h) 5-11-0 A Maguire, *pld hrd in midfield, improved on outer 4 out, struggling nxt, tld off and pulled up bef 2 out...*(2 to 1 fav op 9 to 4 tchd 3 to 1) pu
3922 TRICYCLE (Ire) (bl) 5-11-0 W Humphreys, *keen hold in rear, shrtlvd effrt 4 out, struggling nxt, tld off whn pld up bef last*....................... (50 to 1 op 33 to 1) pu
Dist: 3l, 8l, 7l, hd, sht-hd, 3½l, dist, 12l. 4m 12.60s. a 10.60s (11 Ran).
SR: 15/7/-/-/-/7/   (Edward C Wilkin), Miss L C Siddall

4026 A W Bacon & Son Novices' Handicap Chase (5-y-o and up) £2,804 3m 1f ....(3:25)

3575⁴ CASTLE BLUE [86] 7-11-4 R Dunwoody, *nvr far away, outpcd 4 out, improved aftr nxt, led r-in, gmely.*
...................................(2 to 1 fav op 5 to 2 tchd 15 to 8) 1
3774⁵ WE'RE IN THE MONEY [68] (bl) 10-10-8 D Dalton, *led, clr aftr 4 out, rdn alng nxt, hdd r-in, no extr clsg stages.*
...................................(15 to 2 op 7 to 1 tchd 8 to 1) 2
3805⁵ MIRAGE DANCER [70] 11-10-2 I Lawrence, *patiently rdn, improved and ev ch 4 out, outpcd frm nxt.*
...................................(12 to 1 op 10 to 1) 3
3961³ LADY BLAKENEY [76] 8-10-8 A Maguire, *trkd ldrs, hit 4 out, sn struggling, tld off*.........(9 to 2 tchd 5 to 1) 4
3554⁴ BUCKWHEAT LAD (Ire) [80] 6-10-12 K Johnson, *in tch, reminders 5th, mstk 9th, uns rdr nxt*.(9 to 1 op 6 to 1) ur
3863* URIZEN [92] 9-11-10 C Hawkins, *not fluent, in tch, hit 6th, lost touch fnl circuit, tld off whn pld up bef 4 out.*
...................................(9 to 4 op 7 to 4 tchd 5 to 2) pu
Dist: 1¼l, 20l, 25l. 6m 24.90s. a 23.90s (6 Ran).
                         (R J Parish), N J Henderson

4027 Martin And Rodgers Maiden Hurdle (4-y-o and up) £2,164 2m 3f 110yds ....(3:55)

3892² MAMARA REEF (v) 4-10-2 (5*) P Waggott, *patiently rdn, effrt bef 2 out, str run frm last, led towards finish.*
...................................(4 to 1 op 7 to 2) 1
3925² MULLED ALE (Ire) (v) 4-10-7 J Osborne, *pressed ldr, led 4 out, quickened clr appr 2 out, wknd and hdd towards finish*......................(9 to 4 op 13 to 8) 2
3620 HICKSONS CHOICE (Ire) 6-11-4 K Jones, *patiently rdn, improved and ev ch bef 2 out, ridden and not quicken.*
...................................(20 to 1 op 33 to 1) 3
3928² FLINTLOCK (Ire) 4-10-12 R Dunwoody, *tucked in hndy, effrt and drvn alng bef 2 out, grad wknd.*
...................................(7 to 4 fav op 2 to 1) 4
3190 SHERWOOD GRANGE (Ire) 6-11-4 M Brennan, *hld up, struggling frm hfwy, tld off*......(20 to 1 op 25 to 1) 5
3674 THINK PINK 7-10-11 (7*) B Grattan, *pressed ldrs, lost tch hfwy, tld off*......................(50 to 1 op 20 to 1) 6
3800⁸ GASCOIGNE WOOD 6-11-4 Mrs F Needham, *led, blun 4 out, hdd nxt, 5th and hld whn f 2 out.*
...................................(50 to 1 op 33 to 1) f
3061² WHY NOT EQUINAME 6-11-4 A Maguire, *uns rdr 1st.*
...................................(1 to 2 op 5 to 1 tchd 6 to 1) ur
2997 HINTON LADY 5-10-13 M Ranger, *settled beh ldrs, lost grnd fnl circuit, tld off whn pld up bef 3 out.*
...................................(25 to 1 op 20 to 1) pu
SHINGLE PATH 4-10-0 (7*) Mark Brown, *pld hrd on outsd, struggling frm 5th, tld off whn pld up bef 4 out.*
...................................(25 to 1 op 20 to 1) pu
Dist: 1l, 9l, 9l, 25l, dist. 4m 45.50s. a 12.50s (10 Ran).
                         (C J Pennick), Denys Smith

4028 Cray Valley Handicap Chase (0-115 5-y-o and up) £3,548 2¾m 110yds ....(4:25)

3875³ BOBBY SOCKS [103] 8-11-0 (7*) P McLoughlin, *nvr far away, led 9th, drw clr frm 2 out, easily.*
...................................(11 to 4 op 9 to 4 tchd 3 to 1) 1

3586³ DEEP DECISION [92] 8-10-10 K Johnson, *al wl plcd, chsd wnr fnl 5, no extr frm 2 out*.....(9 to 4 fav op 2 to 1) 2
3894⁴ CHIASSO FORTE (Ity) [94] 11-10-12 L O'Hara, *led till jmpd slwly and hdd 1st, sn beh and mstks, effrt und pres bef 4 out, no imprsn frm nxt*.........(6 to 1 tchd 13 to 2) 3
3852² L'UOMO PIU [106] 10-11-10 B Powell, *led second, hdd 9th, struggling bef 4 out, tld off*...................... 4
3636³ CASINO MAGIC [82] 10-10-0 W Marston, *pld hrd, led 1st to nxt, styd hndy, struggling to keep up last 4, tld off.*
...................................(9 to 2 op 4 to 1) 5
3586 THE LEGGETT [104] (bl) 11-11-8 R Bellamy, *in tch, struggling frm 9th, tld off*..................(20 to 1) 6
Dist: 20l, 1l, 15l, 15l, dist. 5m 43.50s. a 15.50s (6 Ran).
                         (Martin Stillwell), R Lee

4029 H L Foods Handicap Hurdle (0-115 4-y-o and up) £2,320 2m 3f 110yds.. (4:55)

3344⁷ BAHRAIN QUEEN (Ire) [80] 6-10-4 M Ranger, *patiently rdn, mstk 7th, improved on bit to ld aftr 3 out, shaken up and ran on wl frm nxt*.........(11 to 2 op 4 to 1) 1
3801* MARSH'S LAW [104] (v) 7-12-0 M Brennan, *hld up, drvn to improve 4 out, ev ch bef 2 out, kpt on same pace.*
...................................(6 to 4 fav op 5 to 4 tchd 7 to 4) 2
3825 CHARLAFRIVOLA [76] (bl) 6-10-0 W Humphreys, *hld up, improved to chase ldg bunch aftr 3 out, rdn nxt, no extr*...................................(20 to 1 op 16 to 1) 3
3932⁴ SAFARI PARK [84] 5-10-8 R Dunwoody, *wth ldr, led appr 3 out, sn hdd, grad wknd*.......(13 to 2 op 5 to 1) 4
3594 BURSANA [84] (bl) 8-10-8 W Marston, *nvr far away, effrt and bef 2 out, one pace whn blun last.*
...................................(16 to 1 op 14 to 1) 5
3678⁴ REXY BOY [80] (v) 7-10-4⁴ G Harker, *led til hdd appr 3 out, rdn and grad wknd.*..............(11 to 2 op 5 to 1) 6
4016³ CURTAIN FACTORY [76] 5-10-0 S Turner, *chasing ldrs whn f 7th.*..................(9 to 2 op 5 to 1 tchd 4 to 1) f
BARON TWO SHOES [85] 8-10-6² (5*) P Midgley, *chsd ldrs, drpd rear strtng fnl circuit, tld off and pld up bef 2 out.*
...................................(33 to 1 op 20 to 1) pu
3306 BALUSTRADE [76] 7-10-0 I Lawrence, *settled towards rear, wkng whn hmpd by faller 7th, tld off when pld up bef 2 out.*....................(66 to 1 op 50 to 1) pu
Dist: 7l, 2½l, 9l, 2½l, 9l. 4m 42.90s. a 9.90s (9 Ran).
SR: 16/33/2/1/-/-/   (David J Thompson), C Smith

ROSCOMMON (IRE) (good)
Monday May 23rd

4030 Elphin Opportunity Handicap Hurdle (0-116 4-y-o and up) £3,084 2m.. (5:30)

3788* HAVE A BRANDY (Ire) [-] 5-10-5 (2*) P A Roche, ..(5 to 2 fav) 1
3935 MONTE FIGO [-] 7-11-7 T P Rudd, ...(4 to 1) 2
3793⁶ RHABDOMANCY (Ire) [-] 6-10-3 (4*) A P McCoy, .. (10 to 1) 3
1145 PEACE TRIBUTE (Ire) [-] 5-10-1 (4*) K O Maher, ... (20 to 1) 4
3466 ABBEY EMERALD [-] 8-9-7 J P Broderick, ...(16 to 1) 5
3840 MAGNUM STAR (Ire) [-] 5-10-6 (4*) D O'Driscoll, ..(14 to 1) 6
3719 JESSIE'S BOY [-] 5-10-5 (4*) T Hagger, ...(14 to 1) 7
3812 JIMMY GORDON [-] 7-11-0 T J Mitchell, ...(20 to 1) 8
3291⁵ SUMMING UP [-] 7-10-7 (2*) K P Gaule, ...(8 to 1) 9
LABESTE (Ire) [-] 6-10-2 P Stafford, ...(16 to 1) 10
3647 JEMMA'S GOLD (Ire) [-] 6-10-0 C O'Brien, ...(33 to 1) 11
745* BRAE (Ire) [-] 6-9-12 (4*) D J Kavanagh, ...(10 to 1) 12
3711 BORRISMORE FLASH (Ire) [-] 6-9-13 (4*) L A Hurley,
...................................(25 to 1) 13
3711 ARI'S FASHION [-] 9-9-10 (4*) R Burke, ...(33 to 1) 14
1269 CLOGS [-] (bl) 10-10-7 C Everard, ...(20 to 1) f
3506 ANA CRUISIS (Ire) [-] 6-10-2 (2*) D P Geoghegan, ..(16 to 1) f
3889 THE WICKED CHICKEN (Ire) [-] 5-10-12 T P Treacy, (5 to 1) f
Dist: 1½l, 1½l, 5l, ¾l. 3m 57.50s. (17 Ran).
                 (Paddock Racing Syndicate), Francis M O'Brien

4031 Ballygar Hurdle (4-y-o and up) £2,742 2m...(6:00)

924³ NEMURO (USA) 6-11-1 (7*) J Connolly, ... (7 to 4 on) 1
3954⁷ FLOWERHILL DAISY (Ire) 6-11-0 (3*) J P Broderick, (25 to 1) 2
3711 ISN'T THAT NICE (Ire) 6-11-8 C F Swan, ...(20 to 1) 3
3946 COSHLA EXPRESSO (Ire) 6-11-8 W T Slattery Jnr, (33 to 1) 4
SHES A STAR (Ire) 4-10-9 J F Titley, ...(12 to 1) 5
3891 SUNKEN LADY (Ire) 5-10-9 (7*) J M Donnelly, .(20 to 1) 6
3810 HOLLOW SOUND (Ire) 5-11-2 P Carberry, ...(20 to 1) 7
3747 MORNING IN MAY (Ire) 6-11-8 C O'Dwyer, ...(20 to 1) 8
1397 FREEWAY HALO (Ire) 5-11-3 (3*) T J Mitchell, ..(20 to 1) 9
3934 DERRAVARAGH GALE (Ire) 5-10-9 (7*) D J Kavanagh,
...................................(33 to 1) 10
133⁶ AHEEMA COTTAGE 8-12-0 F J Flood, ...(8 to 1) 11
211¹⁹ ABBEY TRINITY (Ire) 5-11-2 D M Bean, ...(33 to 1) 12
3466 SAME DIFFERENCE (Ire) 6-11-8 J K Kinane, ...(20 to 1) 13
WOLLONGONG (Ire) 4-10-9 A J O'Brien, ...(25 to 1) 14
3121⁷ LIFE OF A LORD 8-11-8 G M O'Neill, ...(12 to 1) 15
LOS ANGELES (Ire) 5-11-2 H Rogers, ...(14 to 1) 16
BLAZING DANCER 8-10-10 (7*) R J Gordon, ...(50 to 1) f
JUST 'R JAKE (Ire) 5-11-2 (5*) D P Geoghegan, ... (33 to 1) ro
Dist: 3½l, ½l, 7l, 13l. 3m 58.10s. (18 Ran).
                         (John Muldoon), P Aspell

4032 Frank Hannon Memorial Chase (5-y-o and up) £3,427 2½m. . . . . (6:30)

3789⁴	MONKEY AGO 7-11-10 P Carberry, ...(7 to 2)	1
3872*	SILVERWEIR 11-11-10 T Horgan, ...(7 to 2)	2
2035⁸	FANCY DISH 8-10-12 (3*) D P Murphy, ...(25 to 1)	3
3933⁴	BROCKLEY COURT 7-11-10 J P Banahan, ... (6 to 4 fav)	4
3889⁴	DEGO DANCER 7-10-12 (3*) J P Broderick, ... (25 to 1)	5
538	GOLDEN CLAW 7-11-6 F J Flood, ...(16 to 1)	6
853	GALA VOTE 8-10-10 (5*) D P Geoghegan, ...(50 to 1)	7
3655	DUSKY LADY 8-11-5 G M O'Neill, ...(14 to 1)	8
3913	TIME UP (Ire) 6-11-6 J Shortt, ...(50 to 1)	9
3709⁴	OATFIELD LAD 7-11-6 A Powell, ... (8 to 1)	10
3657	GRANADOS (USA) 6-11-6 S R Murphy, ... (16 to 1)	f
1980⁷	QUAYSIDE BUOY 11-11-10 J F Titley, ... (14 to 1)	su

Dist: 2l, 1l, 1l, 1l. 5m 4.20s. (12 Ran).

(Mrs Audrey Healy), P Mullins

4033 Derrane Handicap Chase (0-119 4-y-o and up) £2,742 2½m. . . . . (7:00)

3841³	KINGSTON WAY [-] 8-11-10 Mr D M O'Brien, . . (5 to 2 fav)	1
3795³	TRASSEY BRIDGE [-] (bl) 7-10-4 F Woods, ... (12 to 1)	2
3945²	THE QUIET MAN [-] 10-10-7 D H O'Connor, ... (7 to 2)	3
3890	GOLDEN CARRUTH (Ire) [-] 6-10-9 (3*) J P Broderick,	
	. . . .(10 to 1)	4
3721⁸	ALL A QUIVER [-] 7-10-2 C N Bowens, ...(14 to 1)	5
3933⁹	BLAZING DAWN [-] 7-11-13 S H O'Donovan, ... (14 to 1)	6
3933⁶	JOE'S A BOY [-] 9-11-8 H Rogers, ... (10 to 1)	7
3790	BENS DILEMMA [-] 9-9-10 (3*) T J Mitchell, ...20 to 1)	8
532	GONZALO [-] 11-11-5 A Powell, ...(10 to 1)	9
3873	PORTLAND LAD [-] 9-10-0 F J Flood, ...(33 to 1)	10
2235	HURRICANE TOMMY [-] (bl) 7-11-3 C F Swan, ...(6 to 1)	11
3507⁹	PALMROCK DONNA [-] 7-9-10 (5*) P A Roche, ...(14 to 1)	12
2157	OLD MONEY [-] 8-11-2 P Carberry, ...(16 to 1)	13
2618⁹	FAYS FOLLY (Ire) [-] 5-9-3 (7*) D J Kavanagh, ...(20 to 1)	ur
3721⁹	DERRYNAP [-] 11-10-0 D P Geoghegan, ...(16 to 1)	pu

Dist: 4½l, 4½l, 15l, 2½l. 4m 56.30s. (15 Ran).

(L T Fitzpatrick), Francis M O'Brien

4034 Kepak I.N.H. Flat Race (5-y-o and up) £3,427 2m. . . . . (8:30)

3956⁷	MANDALAY LINE (Ire) 7-11-7 (7*) Mr K Whelan, ...(10 to 1)	1
3956²	MR GLYNN (Ire) 5-11-13 Mr E Bolger, ... (6 to 4 fav)	2
	BEE MOY DO (Ire) 6-12-0 Mr P F Graffin, ...(10 to 1)	3
805⁷	LOUGH ATALIA 7-11-7 (7*) Mr A Daly, ... (16 to 1)	4
3956⁴	RAMPANT ROSIE (Ire) 6-11-9 (7*) Mr A Brennan, ... (5 to 1)	5
3872	KILLIMOR LAD 7-11-11 (3*) Mr D Marnane, ...(20 to 1)	6
3912	THRESA-ANITA (Ire) 6-11-2 (7*) Mr M T Harrison, ...(8 to 1)	7
3974⁵	LEAD THE BRAVE (Ire) 5-11-5 (3*) Mr T Lombard, ... (6 to 1)	8
	LINGERING HOPE (Ire) 6-11-9 (5*) Mr H F Cleary, ...(20 to 1)	9
	THE BUACHAILL (Ire) 5-11-6 (7*) Mr A V Murray, ...(20 to 1)	10
	BOTH SIDES (Ire) 5-11-9 (3*) Mr J A Nash, ...(10 to 1)	11
3891⁸	DONWOOD (Ire) 5-11-8 Mr D M O'Brien, ... (12 to 1)	12
3813⁷	TELEMAR (Ire) 5-11-1 (7*) Mr J G Bates, ...(25 to 1)	13
969⁶	TRUE SON 9-11-7 (7*) Mr E Norris, ...(10 to 1)	14
3953⁶	CROSS ANGORLADY (Ire) 5-11-8 Mr P Fenton, ...(10 to 1)	15
	FIRST VIEW (Ire) 6-11-7 (7*) Mr P J McMahon, ...(10 to 1)	16
3788	GOLDEN ARRANGEMENT 9-11-7 (7*) Mr P Carey, . . . (33 to 1)	17
	TALL ORDER (Ire) 5-11-10 (3*) Mr A R Coonan, ...(20 to 1)	18
	CARNMORE CASTLE (Ire) 6-11-12⁸ (7*) Mr P M Higgins,	
	. . . .(33 to 1)	19

Dist: 1½l, 1½l, 4½l, 1l. 3m 52.80s. (19 Ran).

(W F Treacy), W F Treacy

SEDGEFIELD (good)
Tuesday May 24th
Going Correction: MINUS 0.05 sec. per fur.

4035 Bamburgh Claiming Hurdle (4-y-o and up) £1,784 2m 5f 110yds. . . . . . . (2:10)

3910²	BUCKRA MELLISUGA 10-11-1 A Maguire, nvr far away, led 4 out, clr 2 out, easily.	
	. . . .(4 to 1 op 3 to 1 tchd 9 to 2)	1
3926*	GREAT MILL (bl) 7-11-7 N Williamson, al wl plcd, led briefly appr 4 out, struggling aftr nxt, wnt second after last, no imprsn. . . . .(5 to 4 on op 6 to 4 on)	2
3940*	CELCIUS (bl) 10-11-5 R Dunwoody, patiently rdn, chsd wnr aftr 3 out, sn pushed alng, no ch frm nxt.	
	. . . .(9 to 4 tchd 5 to 2)	3
3964	ARCTIC BLOOM 8-10-2¹ (7*) J Driscoll, chsd ldg grp, feeling pace aftr 4 out, nvr able to chal.	
	. . . .(150 to 1 op 100 to 1)	4
3673	YACHT CLUB 12-10-13 A Mulholland, mstks, led till appr 4 out, struggling nxt, sn btn. . . . . . . (66 to 1 op 50 to 1)	5
3862	HARRY'S MIDGET 4-9-11 (5*) J Supple, mid-div, lost pl 3rd, tld off fnl circuit. . . . .(66 to 1 op 50 to 1)	6
3895	GLORIOUS HEIGHTS 6-10-10 A Dobbin, in tch, drpd rear 4 out, sn lost touch, tld off. . . . . (66 to 1 op 50 to 1)	7
3819⁸	QUIXALL CROSSETT 9-10-4 (7*) Mr A Manners, al beh, struggling and reminders 4th, tld off fnl circuit.	
	. . . .(100 to 1 op 66 to 1)	8

| 3959 | SOLAR NOVA 6-10-12 N Smith, pressed ldr, lost grnd 4 out, wknd quickly, tld off. . . . .(66 to 1 op 50 to 1) | 9 |
| | ALBERTS TREASURE 6-11-3 Mr C Mulhall, handily plcd, struggling to keep up fnl circuit, tld off whn broke dwn and pld up aftr last, destroyed. (300 to 1 op 200 to 1) | pu |

Dist: 25l, 6l, 30l, 4l, 1¼l, dist, 5l, 30l. 5m 11.40s. a 20.40s (10 Ran).

(John Wade), J A Hellens

4036 Whitley Bay Novices' Hurdle (4-y-o) £1,645 2m 1f 110yds. . . . . (2:40)

3482	CONTRACT ELITE (Ire) 11-7 D Wilkinson, made all, drw clr appr 3 out, unchlgd. . . . .(6 to 4 on op 5 to 4 on)	1
3674²	ON GOLDEN POND (Ire) (bl) 11-2 N Bentley, nvr far away, reminders bef 4 out, outpcd before nxt, wnt poor second 2 out, no ch with wnr. . . . .(7 to 2 op 11 to 4)	2
3965⁷	SIRKA (Fr) (v) 11-0 R Dunwoody, keen hold, hld up in tch, wnt second 4 out, sn pushed alng, outpcd nxt, tld off.	
	. . . .(7 to 2 op 3 to 1 tchd 4 to 1)	3
	REGAL JEST 10-2 (7*) G Tormey, pld hrd, hld up, improved 4 out, struggling aftr nxt, tld off.	
	. . . .(50 to 1 op 20 to 1)	4
3601⁶	RUSHALONG 11-0 A Maguire, pressed ldr, drpd rear aftr 3rd, struggling fnl circuit, tld off. (25 to 1 op 20 to 1)	5

Dist: 30l, 8l, 4l, dist. 4m 10.60s. a 15.60s (5 Ran).

(Brian Whitelaw), C W Thornton

4037 Seahouses Handicap Hurdle (0-110 4-y-o and up) £1,900 2m 5f 110yds . . . . (3:10)

3964⁷	KINDA GROOVY [82] (bl) 5-10-6 (6ex) N Smith, nvr far away, led bef 5th, pressed 2 out, ran on strly.	
	. . . .(15 to 8 fav op 2 to 1 tchd 7 to 4)	1
3926²	ON THE SAUCE [103] (bl) 7-11-13 R Dunwoody, al wl plcd, ev ch 2 out, kpt on same pace appr last.	
	. . . .(9 to 2 op 7 to 2 tchd 5 to 1)	2
3960³	BOWLANDS WAY [79] 10-10-3 O Pears, beh, not jump wl, styd on frm 2 out, nvr a factor... (10 to 1 tchd 12 to 1)	3
3959⁷	STATION EXPRESS (Ire) [78] 6-9-13 (3*) A Larnach, patiently rdn, pushed alng to improve fnl circuit, outpcd 3 out, tld off. . . . .(11 to 1 op 10 to 1)	4
3863	SHELTON ABBEY [85] 8-10-9 A Maguire, in tch, drvn to improve 4 out, struggling aftr nxt, tld off.	
	. . . .(14 to 1 op 12 to 1)	5
3960*	FLASS VALE [94] (v) 6-11-4 (6ex) C Hawkins, made most till bef 5th, lost tch fnl circuit, tld off....(9 to 4 op 7 to 4)	6

Dist: 4l, dist, ¾l, 2½l, dist. 5m 7.90s. a 16.90s (6 Ran).

(Ian Park), I Park

4038 Seaham Handicap Chase (0-115 5-y-o and up) £2,586 3m 3f. . . . . (3:40)

3318	SARAVILLE [114] 7-12-0 R Dunwoody, jmpd rght, made all, shaken up and ran on strly 2 out, eased nr finish.	
	. . . .(6 to 5 fav op 11 to 10 on)	1
3961²	CROWN EYEGLASS [86] 8-10-0 N Williamson, al hndy, improved to track ldr 13th, effrt and rdn aftr 3 out, no extr after nxt. . . . .(7 to 1 op 6 to 1 tchd 8 to 1)	2
3939²	DOONLOUGHAN [98] 9-10-12 A Maguire, in tch, trkd ldrs 13th, outpcd 6 out, sn no ch. . . . .(5 to 4 tchd 6 to 5)	3
3814⁶	WHEELIES NEWMEMBER [86] 11-9-9¹ (3*) J Supple, with ldr, lost pl 11th, struggling frm 6 out, tld off. .(20 to 1)	4
	TIBER MELODY [86] 11-10-0 B Storey, al beh, struggling fnl circuit, tld off. . . . .(66 to 1 op 50 to 1)	5

Dist: 3½l, 30l, 3l, 3½l. 6m 46.90s. a 7.90s (5 Ran).

SR: 8/-/

(R V Cliff), M C Pipe

4039 Holy Island Novices' Chase (5-y-o and up) £2,064 2m 1f. . . . . (4:10)

3893²	CHIC AND ELITE 7-11-3 N Williamson, made all, sn clr, ran on wl last 3, unchlgd. . . . .(5 to 1 on)	1
3959	FLAXON WORRIOR 11-7-0 O Pears, nvr far away, chsd wnr 6 out, rdn 3 out, kpt on frm nxt, no imprsn.	
	. . . .(12 to 1 op 8 to 1)	2
3778	SPLIT SECOND 5-10-12 A Maguire, in tch, chsd wnr 6th to 8th, outpcd 4 out, sn btn. . . . .(6 to 1 op 5 to 1)	3
	DE GREY 7-11-4 S Turner, keen hold, in tch, struggling frm 6 out, tld off. . . . .(50 to 1 op 33 to 1)	4

Dist: 5l, 13l, 15l. 4m 10.20s. a 5.20s (4 Ran).

SR: 24/24/5/-/

(J R Weston), J J O'Neill

4040 Seaburn Open National Hunt Flat Race (4,5,6-y-o) £1,576 2m 1f 110yds . . . . (4:40)

3832⁴	QUADRAPOL 5-10-4 (5*) D Leahy, wl plcd, led on bit o'r 3 fs out, wnt clr entering strt.	
	. . . .(13 to 8 on op 6 to 4 on tchd 7 to 4 on)	1
	BOWLANDS LAW 5-11-0 O Pears, led till o'r 3 fs out, not quicken entering strt. . . . .(8 to 1 op 6 to 1)	2
2490	TASHREEF 4-10-2 (7*) B Harding, patiently rdn, outpcd o'r 3 fs out, styd on fnl furlong, nvr rchd.	
	. . . .(40 to 1 op 33 to 1)	3

3868 LOGANI 4-10-4 S Turner, *pld hrd, pressed ldrs, feeling pace 4 fs out, kpt on same pace entering strt.*
.................................(25 to 1 op 20 to 1) 4
3868[7] NABURN LOCH 4-10-2[5] (7") J Driscoll, *settled beh ldrs, improved 6 fs out, ev ch appr strt, drvn alng and no extr.*......................(6 to 1 op 8 to 1) 5
BUSTALLEY 4-10-9 A Dobbin, *nvr far away, lost grnd hfwy, btn 4 fs out, tld off.*..........(20 to 1 op 16 to 1) 6
3868 LUCKY DOMINO 4-10-13[4] Miss T Waggott, *co'red up beh ldrs, outpcd over 3 fs out, sn struggling, tld off.*
.................................(100 to 1) 7
THORONDOR 4-10-9 D Telfer, *settled on outsd, struggling o'r 5 fs out, tld off.*.........(20 to 1 op 12 to 1) 8
3489 LUCKY HOLLY 4-10-4 A Maguire, *pressed ldr, lost grnd o'r 4 fs out, eased, tld off.*..........(10 to 1 tchd 12 to 1) 9
FORTUNATA 6-10-9 C Dennis, *slwly into strd, hld up, struggling o'r 6 fs out, tld off.*...(66 to 1 op 50 to 1) 10
3868 STEPPING 4-9-11 (7") W Fry, *pld hrd, hld up, sddl slpd aftr 6 fs, lost tch o'r six out, tld off whn pulled up over 3 out.*.......................(20 to 1) pu
Dist: 14l, 2½l, 1¼l, 2½l, 15l, 9l, 4l, 30l. 4m 10.40s. (11 Ran).
(C D Harrison), S Christian

TRAMORE (IRE) (good to yielding)
Tuesday May 24th

4041 Brownstown Novice Chase (5 & 6-y-o) £2,228 2m.................... (7:00)

3525[7] SKY VISION (Ire) 5-11-2 S H O'Donovan, ...(10 to 1) 1
3872[3] PRINCIPLE MUSIC (USA) 6-11-11 (3") Mr J A Nash,
.................................(7 to 4 fav) 2
3955[2] SO PINK (Ire) 6-11-9 J F Titley, ...(5 to 1) 3
3872[4] BRIDGEOFALLEN (Ire) 6-11-4 (5") Mr W M O'Sullivan,
.................................(10 to 1) 4
3972[7] NISHIKI (USA) 5-10-13 (3") C O'Brien, ...(14 to 1) 5
3525 RIGHT AND REASON (Ire) 5-10-13 (3") D P Murphy, (25 to 1) 6
967[9] HUGH DANIELS 6-11-11 T P Rudd, ...(9 to 1) 7
3911[5] BARAVARD (Ire) 6-12-0 C O'Dwyer, ...(14 to 1) 8
3955[6] BARRAFONA (Ire) 6-12-0 J Magee, ...(5 to 1) f
PALACE KING (Ire) 5-11-4 (3") J P Broderick, ...(33 to 1) pu
Dist: 10l, 2½l, 11l, 1l. 4m 6.30s. (10 Ran).
(Kevin O'Donnell), Kevin O'Donnell

4042 Portlaw Handicap Chase (0-102 4-y-o and up) £2,228 2½m........... (7:30)

3972[6] MONKS AIR [-] 7-10-5 (5") P A Roche, ...(12 to 1) 1
1179[7] HURRYUP [-] 7-11-5 (3") C O'Brien, ...(14 to 1) 2
3200[6] KIL KIL CASTLE [-] 7-9-7 (3") J P Broderick, ...(20 to 1) 3
3873[2] BOG LEAF VI [-] (bl) 11-9-4 (3") T J O'Sullivan, ..(9 to 1) 4
3945[3] WHAT A MINSTREL [-] (bl) 8-9-12 C F Swan, ...(6 to 1) 5
3790[4] KINGS HILL [-] 12-10-8 (7") J Butler, ...(7 to 1) 6
3790[5] MISCHIEF MOON [-] (bl) 9-9-5 (7") L A Hurley, ...(20 to 1) 7
STANACATE [-] 9-10-3[2] (7") Mr N D Fehily, ...(16 to 1) 8
3709[5] COOLADERRA LADY [-] 8-10-0 J P Banahan, ...(16 to 1) 9
3789[4] ALBERT'S FANCY [-] 8-12-0 F J Flood, ...(7 to 2 fav) 10
3811[5] THE PHOENO [-] 8-9-11[6] (7") Mr T R Hughes, ...(20 to 1) 11
800 GARRYDOOLIS [-] 8-11-4 C O'Dwyer, ...(16 to 1) 12
3524[9] ROSSI NOVAE [-] (bl) 11-11-4 (3") T P Treacy, ...(14 to 1) 13
411[7] MANOR RHYME [-] (bl) 7-10-7 J Horgan, ...(25 to 1) f
3873[7] MAKE ME AN ISLAND [-] 9-11-10 J F Titley, ...(9 to 2) pu
Dist: 5l, ½l, 4l, 2½l. 4m 52.00s. (15 Ran).
(M Madden), Eugene M O'Sullivan

4043 Lismore Handicap Hurdle (0-109 4-y-o and up) £2,228 2m........... (8:00)

3973[3] FINNEGANS WAKE [-] 7-11-9 (5") K P Gaule, ...(5 to 1) 1
3973[6] ANNFIELD LADY (Ire) [-] 6-10-8 F Woods, ...(8 to 1) 2
3657 FIXED ASSETS [-] 7-11-5 (3") C O'Brien, ...(25 to 1) 3
3955[*] BALLYBODEN [-] 7-10-2 (3") J P Broderick, ...(7 to 1) 4
467[3] WESBEST (Ire) [-] 5-10-6 (7") D M McCullagh, ...(14 to 4 fav) 5
2232[5] NORDIC RACE [-] 7-10-4 W T Slattery Jnr, ...(14 to 1) 6
3870[8] MARBLE FONTAINE [-] 7-10-7 C F Swan, ...(10 to 1) 7
3468[6] HURRICANE EDEN [-] 7-10-12 (5") M A Davey, ...(9 to 1) 8
3792 SMALL TALK (Ire) [-] 5-10-3 H Rogers, ...(16 to 1) 9
2920[7] SHIMMERETTO [-] 8-9-9[1] (3") T P Rudd, ...(50 to 1) 10
2236[2] SLANEY FAYRE (Ire) [-] 6-10-10 F J Flood, ...(8 to 1) 11
2750 LIMAHEIGHTS (Ire) [-] (bl) 4-10-6 A Powell, ...(14 to 1) 12
3552 BALLYRANEBOW (Ire) [-] 6-10-3 (3") D P Murphy, ..(33 to 1) 13
2099 BAEZA [-] (bl) 4-9-12[6] (7") Mr K Whelan, ...(33 to 1) 14
1781 STRONG SERENADE (Ire) [-] 5-11-7 (3") T P Treacy, (8 to 1) pu
Dist: 2½l, sht-hd, 3½l, ¾l. 4m 0.00s. (15 Ran).
(Bracken Syndicate), A P O'Brien

4044 Tramore I.N.H. Flat Race (6-y-o and up) £2,228 2m................. (8:30)

3647 ARABIAN SPRITE (Ire) 6-11-9 Mr P J Healy, ...(6 to 1) 1
ASTITCHINTIME 7-11-7 (7") Mr C A Murphy, ...(8 to 1) 2
3936[4] SECRET MISSILE 7-11-11 (3") Mrs J M Mullins,
.................................(15 to 8 fav) 3
3797[7] TWABLADE (Ire) 6-11-9 Mr W P Mullins, ...(10 to 1) 4
3735[5] ANOTHER ROLLO (Ire) 6-12-0 Mr P Fenton, ...(5 to 1) 5
3974 PALEFOOT (Ire) 6-11-6 (3") Mr R O'Neill, ...(20 to 1) 6

3788[6] CARRIG DANCER (Ire) 6-11-2 (7") Mr K Whelan, .. (14 to 1) 7
1270 CARRIG BELLE 8-11-2 (7") Mr B Foster, ...(14 to 1) 8
3733 SHOW ME THE LIGHT (Ire) 6-11-7 (7") Mr J M Roche,
.................................(20 to 1) 9
3711 FANDANGOLD 8-11-4 (5") Mr H F Cleary, ...(8 to 1) 10
495[7] SONIC EXPERIENCE (Ire) 6-11-2 (7") Mr R Lawler, .(20 to 1) 11
PLEASE NO TEARS 7-11-6 (3") Mrs C Barker, ...(10 to 1) 12
3946 SWEET PERIL 7-11-2 (7") Mr E Henley, ...(20 to 1) 13
508[3] POLLY PLUM (Ire) 6-11-2 (7") Mr J E Coonan, ...(8 to 1) 14
WOODSTOWN BOY (Ire) 6-12-0 Mr D M O'Brien, (12 to 1) 15
Dist: 5½l, 10l, 2½l, ¾l. 3m 57.20s. (15 Ran).
(P J Healy), P J Healy

CARTMEL (good to firm)
Wednesday May 25th
Going Correction: MINUS 0.35 sec. per fur.

4045 Carpets By Huglin Selling Hurdle (4-y-o and up) £2,038 2¾m....... (2:00)

3977[2] LOVE YOU MADLY (Ire) (v) 4-10-11 R Dunwoody, *hld up in tch, hdwy to track ldr 6th, cl up and hit 2 out, quick-ened to ld last 75 yards.*
.................................(11 to 8 fav op 11 to 10 tchd 6 to 4) 1
3751 MIDNIGHT FLOTILLA 8-10-11 C Hawkins, *led, clr hfwy, rdn alng appr last, hdd and not quicken last 75 yards.*
.................................(8 to 1 op 7 to 1) 2
3970 TROPICAL GALE (v) 9-10-11 Peter Caldwell, *al prmnt, rdn 2 out, kpt on one pace r-in.*...................(25 to 1) 3
3895[8] SAOIRSE (Ire) 6-11-6 (3") D J Moffatt, *hld up, pushed alng 3 out, styd on frm nxt, nvr dngrs.*...........(9 to 2) 4
3690[5] SEA PET 5-10-11 A Merrigan, *in tch, effrt and pushed alng 3 out, rdn nxt and sn one pace.*
.................................(16 to 1 tchd 20 to 1) 5
3977[3] CRIMINAL RECORD (USA) (bl) 4-11-2 G McCourt, *in tch, hit second, hit 6th and lost pl, hdwy 3 out, rdn and blun last, sn btn.*..................(2 to 1 op 5 to 2) 6
3345 KAMADORA 7-11-2 Mr K Green, *chsd ldr to 6th, lost pl and beh frm 3 out.*................(50 to 1 op 40 to 1) 7
Dist: 4l, 1½l, 3l, 3½l, 14l, hd. 5m 28.40s. a 23.40s (7 Ran).
(Mrs Alison C Farrant), M C Pipe

4046 Swan Hotel Newby Bridge Handicap Chase (0-125 5-y-o and up) £2,749 2m 1f 110yds..................... (2:30)

3865[2] CLEVER FOLLY [87] 14-10-0 B Storey, *cl up, led 3 out, rdn and ran on wl r-in.*..(3 to 1 op 5 to 2 tchd 100 to 30) 1
3984 BEAUCADEAU [105] 8-11-4 A Dobbin, *hld up, smooth hdwy hfwy, led 7th, hdd 3 out, rdn and hit 2 out, styd on gmely und pres r-in.*
.................................(6 to 4 fav op 7 to 4 tchd 11 to 8) 2
3776[2] GREEK FLUTTER [114] 9-11-8 (5") F Leahy, *hld up and beh, hdwy 4 out, rdn nxt, kpt on one pace.*
.................................(7 to 2 op 3 to 1) 3
3979[5] WINGSPAN (USA) [115] (bl) 10-12-0 N Mann, *led, hdd 7th, wknd 4 out.*.......................(10 to 1) 4
3968[3] BARKISLAND [94] 10-10-7 R Dunwoody, *chsd ldp pair, hit 5th, reminders and lost pl hfwy, tld off frm 4 out.*
.................................(9 to 2 op 4 to 1) 5
Dist: Nk, 14l, 8l, 30l. 4m 12.10s. b 0.90s (5 Ran).
SR: 20/37/32/25/-/
(N B Mason (Farms) Ltd), G Richards

4047 Ladbroke Racing Handicap Hurdle (0-125 4-y-o and up) £2,814 2m 1f 110yds..................... (3:00)

3924[7] WINDWARD ARIOM [96] 8-10-11 R Dunwoody, *in tch, hdwy on inner 3 out, led aftr nxt, quickened clr r-in.*
.................................(12 to 1 op 8 to 1) 1
3736 HOME COUNTIES (Ire) [123] (v) 5-11-11 (3") D J Moffatt, *cl up, not fluent, rdn alng 2 out, effrt and ev ch last, sn drvn and one pace.*................(2 to 1 op 6 to 4) 2
3739[*] COL BUCKMORE (Ire) [100] 6-9-12 (7") B Harding, *hld up in tch gng wl, smooth hdwy 3 out, ev ch last, sn rdn and one pace r-in.*...............(11 to 8 on op Evens) 3
3959[8] BURN BRIDGE (USA) [99] (v) 8-10-4[3] Peter Caldwell, *led till hdd and wknd aftr 2 out.*
.................................(8 to 1 op 10 to 1 tchd 12 to 1) 4
3078[3] SWANK GILBERT [95] 8-10-0 Carol Cuthbert, *prmnt, till rdn and wknd 3 out, sn beh.*......(50 to 1 op 40 to 1) 5
Dist: 5l, nk, 20l, 20l. 4m 2.10s. a 2.10s (5 Ran).
SR: -/13/
(Kendall White & Co Ltd), K R Burke

4048 Barclays Bank Novices' Hurdle (4-y-o and up) £2,038 2m 1f 110yds... (3:30)

3800[5] RULLY 5-11-3 W Worthington, *made all, rdn appr last, ran on strly.*...................(7 to 1 op 8 to 1) 1
3464[*] SURREY DANCER 6-12-1 P Niven, *hld up, smooth hdwy to chase ldr 4th, rdn alng 2 out, hrd drvn last, no extr flt.*...................(7 to 1 op 8 to 1 on) 2
SILVER PROSPECT 13-10-12 (5") A Roche, *beh frm 3rd, tld off hfwy.*............(14 to 1 op 12 to 1 tchd 16 to 1) 3

3815 FALLOWFIELD GIRL 5-10-7 (5*) S Lyons, *chsd ldr to 4th, sn
lost pl and tld off whn pld up bef 2 out.
.... (33 to 1 op 25 to 1) pu
Dist: 6l, dist. 4m 3.40s. a 3.40s (4 Ran).
.... (Astaire & Partners (Holdings) Ltd), M C Chapman

4049 Henry, Cooke, Makin, Novices' Chase (5-y-o and up) £2,424 2m 5f 110yds
.... (4:00)

3852³ AUVILLAR (USA) (v) 6-11-3 D J Burchell, *prmnt, hdwy on
inner to ld 9th, jmpd lft last 2, rdn clr aftr last, styd on
wl*.................... (7 to 1 op 6 to 1 tchd 15 to 2) 1
3894* RIVER PEARL 9-12-0 P Niven, *hld up, hit 6th, hdwy to
chase ldrs 4 out, chlgd nxt, rdn and hmpd aftr last, kpt
on*..................(Evens fav tchd 11 to 10 and 5 to 4) 2
3894⁶ POTATO MAN 8-11-7 R Dunwoody, *led till hdd 9th, rdn 3
out, wknd appr last*.................... (9 to 1 op 8 to 1) 3
3818* THE LORRYMAN (Ire) 6-11-11 B Storey, *hld up, hdwy to
chase ldrs 5 out, sn rdn and wknd 3 out.*
................................(7 to 2 op 4 to 1 tchd 9 to 2) 4
3802* HEATHVIEW 7-11-2 (5*) F Leahy, *in tch on outer till blun
and wns rdr 7th*..................... (7 to 1 op 5 to 1) ur
3961⁴ MASTER MATHEW 7-10-12 (5*) J Burke, *cl up till wknd 5
out, beh whn pld up bef 3 out*..... (25 to 1 op 16 to 1) pu
Dist: 5l, dist, 15l. 5m 13.20s. a 1.20s (6 Ran).
SR: 2/8/-/ .... (Mrs J M Snape), D Burchell

4050 North West Racing Club Amateur Riders Handicap Hurdle for the Horace D. Pain Memorial Trophy (4-y-o and up) £2,495 3¼m....... (4:30)

3964² IFALLELSEFAILS [109] 6-11-6 Mr S Swiers, *hld up, gd
hdwy 6th, dsptd ld 3 out till led last, edr clr flt.*
.... (9 to 4 fav op 3 to 1) 1
3646* MAJORITY MAJOR (Ire) [105] 5-10-9 (7*) Mr A Manners, *al
prmnt, led 4 out, jnd nxt, rdn and ev ch whn hit last, no
extr flt*............................ (7 to 2 op 9 to 1) 2
3603* SKIRCOAT GREEN [89] 9-10-0 Mrs A Farrell, *in tch, rdn 4
out and kpt on one pace frm nxt....(11 to 2 op 5 to 1) 3
3802² MASTER'S CROWN (USA) [90] 6-9-8 (7*) Mrs F Needham,
led to 7th, cl up and ev ch till rdn 3 and gradually
wknd*.................................(6 to 1 tchd 7 to 1) 4
3866⁴ CELTIC BREEZE [102] (v) 11-10-8 (5*) Mr D Parker, *in tch,
reminders and outpcd appr 6th, nvr dfangerous aftr.*
..................................(5 to 1 op 9 to 2) 5
3541* SWEET CITY [113] 9-11-5 (5*) Mr R Hale, *in tch, rdn 4 out
and sn btnb*..............................(9 to 1 tchd 11 to 2) 6
3646⁵ HIGHLAND RIVER [89] 7-9-7 (7*) Mrs H Johnston, *al rear,
tld off bef 4 out*...............................(33 to 1) 7
3177 KERRY TO CLARE [89] 8-9-7 (7*) M M Coglan, *cl up, led 7th
till hdd and hit 4 out, wkng whn hit nxt and sn beh.*
....(33 to 1) 8
3910⁴ GREY MERLIN [89] 7-9-7 (7*) Mr C Bonner, *prmnt to hfwy,
sn lost pl and beh, pld up bef 3 out*..............(33 to 1) pu
Dist: 5l, 7l, 7l, 3l, 20l, 20l, 3l. 6m 4.50s. a 6.50s (9 Ran).
.... (R J Gilbert), L Lungo

HEREFORD (good to soft)
Thursday May 26th
Going Correction: PLUS 0.65 sec. per fur.

4051 Ansells Novices' Hurdle (4-y-o and up) £1,945 2m 3f 110yds........... (2:00)

4021² FORMAL AFFAIR 4-11-5 A Maguire, *al gng wl in tch, chsd
ldr appr 6th, chlgd 3 out, sn led and clr, easily.*
.... (3 to 1 on tchd 4 to 1) 1
3970⁸ SILVER STANDARD 4-11-3 B Powell, *led till aftr second,
lft in ld ag'n 3rd, rdn 4 out, hdd sn after nxt, no ch wth
wnr*.......................... (3 to 1 tchd 7 to 2) 2
3685⁶ NO SHOW (Ire) 4-10-10 W Humphreys, *sn prmnt, rdn 4
out, styd on to take poor 3rd r-in.*
..................................(16 to 1 tchd 20 to 1) 3
3977⁷ MY SISTER LUCY 4-10-12 S Burrough, *beh, hdwy to chase
ldrs 7th, rdn 4 out, sn wknd.*
.... (20 to 1 op 14 to 1) 4
3680 TENDER DANCER (Ire) 6-11-2 J Da Costa, *sn beh, tld off
frm 5th*......................................(100 to 1) 5
4009 CHARLES HENRY 10-11-2 R Bellamy, *strted slwly, bolted
into ld aftr second, ran out and crashed through wing
nxt*.............................. (50 to 1 op 25 to 1) ro
3975⁸ TITIAN MIST 8-10-11 L Harvey, *al beh, tld off whn pld up
bef 3 out*.......................... (100 to 1 op 50 to 1) pu
THE HOLLERY MADAM 9-10-11 M Hourigan, *jmpd very
slwly in rear, rdn 4th and tld off, pld up bef 2 out.*
.... (20 to 1 op 16 to 1 tchd 25 to 1) pu
Dist: 9l, 25l, 1¾l, dist. 4m 52.30s. a 31.30s (8 Ran).
.... (The Plough Partnership), D Nicholson

4052 Castlemaine XXXX Selling Handicap Hurdle (4-y-o and up) £1,990 2m 1f
.... (2:30)

3770⁴ CAPTAIN TANDY (Ire) [71] 5-10-0 D Bridgwater, *hdwy 5th,
hrd rdn to ld aftr 3 out, all out....* (12 to 1 op 16 to 1) 1
3098⁹ HATS HIGH [71] 9-9-7 (7*) G Crone, *in tch till lost pos appr
4 out, hdwy 2 out, ran on wl r-in, jst fld.*
.... (14 to 1 op 20 to 1) 2
3853² KNIGHT IN SIDE [80] 8-10-9 M A FitzGerald, *hdwy 5th,
chlgd 3 out to 2 out, rdn and not quicken r-in.*
..........................(9 to 2 co-fav op 7 to 2 tchd 5 to 1) 3
3773⁸ JOHNSTED [94] 8-11-9 N Williamson, *chsd ldrs, hrd rdn
appr 3 out, one pace*..........(9 to 2 co-fav op 4 to 1) 4
3853⁹ SANDRO [71] (bl) 5-10-0 L Harvey, *led second to 3 out sn
btn*..(20 to 1) 5
3773⁸ GLOSSY [71] 7-10-0 D Gallagher, *took str hold and prmnt,
chlgd frm 5th till led 3 out, sn hdd, rdn and btn.*
.... (16 to 1 op 14 to 1) 6
3661² MOST INTERESTING [83] 9-10-12 B Clifford, *mid-div,
shaken up and no imprsn frm 3 out*. (7 to 1 op 6 to 1) 7
3853 SEA BARN [71] 7-9-11 (7*) Miss S Mitchell, *lost pl 4th,
hdwy 5th, sn wknd*.............. (20 to 1 op 33 to 1) 8
3899⁶ SILK DYNASTY [71] 8-9-11 (3*) S Wynne, *al beh*...(25 to 1) 9
4021 HAPPY DEAL [71] 8-10-0 T Wall, *led 1st, sn hdd, beh frm
3rd*...............................(66 to 1 op 50 to 1) 10
3998 DJEBEL PRINCE [88] 7-11-3 J Osborne, *in tch, rdn 3 out,
sn btn*.....................(9 to 2 co-fav op 4 to 1) 11
3740* ALWAYS READY [95] (bl) 8-11-10 A Maguire, *chsd ldrs,
chlgd 5th to 3 out, sn wknd*..........(7 to 1 op 4 to 1) 12
3773 TASHONYA [71] 12-10-0 J Da Costa, *al beh.*
................................(66 to 1 op 50 to 1) 13
381* HELLO SAM [78] 11-10-7 R Greene, *prmnt to 4th.*
..................................(25 to 1 op 14 to 1) 14
MUMMY'S SONG [71] 9-10-0 I Lawrence, *mstk second, al
beh*.................................(66 to 1 op 50 to 1) 15
4009 PEACE FORMULA (Ire) [102] (bl) 5-11-10 (7*) P McLoughlin,
refused to race...................(100 to 1 op 33 to 1) ref
4019 GREYFRIARS BOBBY [89] 8-11-4 R Dunwoody, *prmnt till
pld up aftr 4th, lme....* (9 to 1 op 8 to 1 tchd 10 to 1) pu
Dist: ½l, nk, 7l, 7l, 2l, 3l, 2l, 12l, 3l, 5l. 4m 3.00s. a 17.00s (17 Ran).
SR: 13/12/20/27/-/-/4/-/-/ .... (Mrs C Kelly), K S Bridgwater

4053 Vanguard Handicap Chase (0-130 5-y-o and up) £3,368 2m 3f.........(3:00)

3968* TOCHENKA [119] 10-11-4 (7ex) D Bridgwater, *made al, rdn
frm 3 out, styd on wl*.......................(Evens fav) 1
4001* DRUMSTICK [136] 8-12-0 (7*,7ex) Mr G Hogan, *hld up in
tch, not fluent 6th, chsd wnr 4 out, gng wl nxt, rdn 2
out, found no extr.*
.............(7 to 4 op 6 to 4 tchd 2 to 1 and 9 to 4) 2
3595 TRIMLOUGH [128] 9-11-13 W Marston, *chsd ldr, chlgd 7th
to 9th, wknd 4 out.*...................(7 to 2 op 4 to 1) 3
Dist: 3l, dist. 4m 50.30s. a 20.30s (3 Ran).
SR: 10/24/-/ .... (R K Minton-Price), N A Twiston-Davies

4054 Carlsberg Pilsner Conditional Jockeys' Handicap Hurdle (0-120 4-y-o and up) £2,684 2m 3f 110yds.... (3:30)

3755⁶ KING'S SHILLING (USA) [97] 7-10-11 R Davis, *hld up,
hdwy 7th, led 4 out, clr nxt, eased r-in.*
.... (8 to 1 op 10 to 1) 1
3831³ SILLIAN [94] 12-10-8 S Wynne, *hld up, steady hdwy appr
3 out, chsd wnr frm aftr nxt, no imprsn whn not fluent
last*.............................. (7 to 1 op 6 to 1) 2
3967* COUTURE STOCKINGS [113] 10-11-13 (5ex) J McCarthy, *al
tracking ldrs, rdn frm 3 out, styd on same pace und
pres*.................(9 to 4 fav op 2 to 1 tchd 11 to 4) 3
3831 SYDNEY BARRY (NZ) [86] 9-9-11 (3*) P McLoughlin, *in tch,
drvn to chase wnr 2 out, sn rdn and wknd.*
..................................(17 to 2 op 6 to 1 tchd 9 to 1) 4
3561⁴ KHAZARI (USA) [110] 6-11-10 T Jenks, *al in rear, nvr
dngrs*................................(12 to 1 tchd 14 to 1) 5
3919⁶ TOUCH OF WINTER [100] 8-10-11 (3*) F Leahy, *made most
to 4th, chlgd 7th till four out, wknd nxt.*
..................................(8 to 1 op 6 to 1 tchd 9 to 1) 6
3672* CHARCOAL BURNER [90] 9-10-1 (3*) S Fox, *took str hold,
wth ldr, led 4th, hdd four out, sn rdn and wknd.*
..................................(9 to 2 op 4 to 1 tchd 5 to 1) 7
3418² SCHWEPPES TONIC [97] 8-10-8 (3*) D Matthews, *in tch till
wknd aftr 4th, tld off whn pld up bef 2 out.* (5 to 1) pu
Dist: 7l, 1l, 1½l, 15l, 1½l, 3½l. 4m 49.80s. a 28.80s (8 Ran).
.... (Keith M Pinfield), C D Broad

4055 Tetley Bitter Novices' Chase (5-y-o and up) £2,749 3m 1f 110yds.... (4:00)

3844* GHIA GNEUIAGH 8-12-2 D Bridgwater, *led till aftr 1st, styd
wth ldr till led tenth, hdd 12th, led ag'n 13th, made rst,
stayed on wl frm 3 out......* (2 to 1 on tchd 7 to 4 on) 1
3961⁵ PETTY BRIDGE 10-11-10 A Maguire, *led aftr 1st to tenth,
led ag'n 12th, to 13th, styd chasing wnr but no ch frm 3
out*.....................(7 to 2 op 4 to 1 tchd 9 to 2) 2
3828⁹ HOWARYAFXD 7-11-10 M A FitzGerald, *chsd ldrs, lost tch
frm 12th*...............(11 to 1 op 6 to 1 tchd 12 to 1) 3
3805⁴ PAPER STAR (bl) 7-10-13 B Powell, *beh frm 7th, hit tenth
and 11th, sn tld off*..................(7 to 1 tchd 8 to 1) 4
3921 HORCUM (v) 9-10-11 (7*) K Davies, *beh, rdn 7th, hit tenth,
sn tld off*..............................(66 to 1 op 33 to 1) 5

3498 CHEQUE BOOK 6-11-4 Mr D Verco, *hdwy to chase ldrs*
 7th, wknd 9th, sn tld off..........(66 to 1 op 33 to 1)   6
Dist: 3l, 30l, 5l, dist, 3l. 6m 37.40s. a 25.40s (6 Ran).
SR: 14/5/-/   (Mrs S A Scott), N A Twiston-Davies

4056 Carlsberg Tetley Novices' Handicap Hurdle (0-100 4-y-o and up) £1,997 2m 1f..............................(4:30)

3629[7] FREE DANCER [79] 4-10-6 (3*) T Jenks, *chsd ldrs, led 5th, mstk and hdd nxt, led ag'n 3 out, sn drvn alng, styd on und pres r-in*..........(8 to 1 op 7 to 1 tchd 12 to 1)   1
3983* GAVASKAR (Ire) [74] 5-10-4 (7ex) A Dobbin, *in tch, hdwy to chase ldrs 5th, rdn and styd on appr last, no imprsn on unr r-in*.........................(9 to 4 fav op 6 to 4)   2
3685* NEARLY HONEST [78] 6-10-8 A Tory, *chsd ldrs, ev ch 3 out, styd on frm nxt*....................(5 to 2 op 7 to 4)   3
3685[8] STERLING BUCK (USA) [70] 7-10-0 J R Kavanagh, *wth ldrs, led 3rd to 4th, led ag'n four out, hdd and ev ch nxt, outpcd appr last*........................(14 to 1)   4
4017[4] PARISIAN [70] 9-9-7 (7*) A Lucas, *wth ldrs, chlgd 5th to 3 out, sn rdn and pace frm nxt*. (10 to 1 op 14 to 1)   5
 1192 EARLY STAR [70] 5-10-0 R Greene, *hdwy 5th, chalg whn not fluent 2 out, sn rdn and wknd appr last*.
 ....(16 to 1 op 33 to 1)   6
3848[5] POETS COVE [80] 6-10-10 M Perrett, *pld hrd in rear, al beh*........................(9 to 1 op 7 to 1)   7
3940[4] BARTON ROYAL (Ire) [75] 4-10-0 (5*) S Fox, *led to 3rd, led ag'n 4th to 5th, wknd 3 out*.......(14 to 1 op 8 to 1)   8
3829[9] PERSIAN WOLF [70] (bl) 6-10-0 V Slattery, *not fluent and al beh, tld off*.......................(12 to 1 op 16 to 1)   9
 SHARP PRINCE [75] 5-10-5 A Maguire, *hdwy to track ldrs appr 5th, still gng wl 3 out, wknd rpdly, tld off whn pld up bef last*....................(10 to 1 op 7 to 1)   pu
Dist: 3l, 2l, nk, 1½l, 3¼l, 4l, 5l, dist. 4m 8.30s. a 22.30s (10 Ran).
                            (Mrs V E Hayward), R Brotherton

4057 Grunwick Stakes National Hunt Flat Race (4,5,6-y-o) £1,507 2m 1f....(5:00)

CHARMER'S WELL (Ire) 6-11-0 (3*) R Davis, *beh, shaken up and rapid hdwy 3 fs out, led ins last, drvn out*.
 ....(11 to 2 op 5 to 2)   1
3522[2] LEGENDRA 4-10-0 (7*) D Bohan, *chsd ldrs, led o'r 2 fs out, hdd jst ins last, styd on same pace*.
 ....(11 to 4 op 6 to 4 tchd 3 to 1)   2
3522[6] B MY LOVELY 4-10-0 (7*) P Maddock, *beh, hdwy 7 fs out, headway 3 out, styd on fnl furlong*.
 ....(9 to 2 op 4 to 1 tchd 5 to 1)   3
 GRAY ROSETTE 5-10-12 Mr A Griffith, *al chasing ldrs, rdn and styd on frm 2 fs out*..........(25 to 1 op 16 to 1)   4
 ERNEST ARAGORN 5-10-12 (5*) S Curran, *chsd ldrs, led 5 fs out, hdd o'r 2 furlongs out, sn btn*.
 ....(16 to 1 op 10 to 1)   5
 MISS TRAPPER (Ire) 6-10-5 (7*) L O'Hare, *chsd ldrs, led briefly appr fnl 5 fs, wknd 3 out...*(9 to 1 tchd 12 to 1)   6
3832[9] STAC-POLLAIDH 4-10-2 (5*) F Leahy, *chsd ldrs till wknd o'r 3 furlongs out*...............(14 to 1 op 10 to 1)   7
 TROJAN RED 4-10-5 (7*) Mr C Curley, *effrt 7 fs out, wknd o'r 3 furlongs out*............(25 to 1 op 16 to 1)   8
 FRONTRUNNER 6-10-12 Mrs S Hobbs, *beh, nvr rch ldrs*.
 ....(6 to 1 op 7 to 2)   9
3880[6] GENTLE JESTER 5-10-5 (7*) Mr Richard White, *mid-div till wknd 4 fs out*....................(25 to 1 op 20 to 1)   10
 COUP DE VENT 4-10-5 (7*) S Taylor, *prmnt to hfwy*.
 ....(5 to 2 fav tchd 3 to 1)   11
3855 NURSERY STORY 6-10-10 (7*) Mr E Williams, *led till hdd o'r 5 fs out, sn wknd*.....................(25 to 1)   12
 DERRING BRIDGE 4-10-5 (7*) Mr R Johnson, *sn beh*.
 ....(20 to 1 op 14 to 1)   13
 GALLI-CURCI (Ire) 6-10-7 (5*) D Leahy, *nvr better than mid-div*.....................(14 to 1 op 7 to 1)   14
 LE QUARANTIEME 5-10-5 (7*) Miss C Burgess, *beh frm hfwy*........................(25 to 1 op 14 to 1)   15
3183[7] PRESTHOPE 6-11-0 (3*) T Jenks, *dwlt, al beh*.
 ....(20 to 1 op 14 to 1)   16
3590 PANDORA'S FIRE 6-10-5 (7*) K Davies, *sn beh*.
 ....(25 to 1 op 14 to 1)   17
Dist: 3l, 2½l, 5l, ¾l, 7l, 7l, 1l, nk, 10l, 3½l. 4m 0.50s. (17 Ran).
                            (Mrs G B Balding), G B Balding

TIPPERARY (IRE) (good to soft) Thursday May 26th

4058 Limerick Junction Handicap Hurdle (0-123 4-y-o and up) £2,742 2½m (8:00)

3506[2] NO TAG (Ire) [-] 6-10-10 J F Titley,..............(5 to 1)   1
3995[3] MY SUNNY GLEN [-] 7-11-7 C F Swan,........(6 to 4 fav)   2
3935[3] CASH CHASE (Ire) [-] 6-10-11 S H O'Donovan,.....(8 to 1)   3
2231[8] SLANEY LAMB (Ire) [-] 6-10-8 (7*) C A Murphy, (20 to 1)   4
3889* SOLBA (USA) [-] 5-11-5 G M O'Neill,............(10 to 1)   5
3887[7] LEAVE IT TO JUDGE [-] 7-9-7 W T Slattery Jnr, ...(66 to 1)   6
3812[6] LOAVES AND FISHES [-] (bl) 6-10-5 (7*) B D Murtagh,
 ....(20 to 1)   7
3995[9] PLUMBOB (Ire) [-] 5-11-0 L P Cusack,.........(14 to 1)   8

3693[5] PRIDE OF ERIN [-] 10-10-12 (3*) C Everard,......(20 to 1)   9
3322[3] MICK O'DWYER [-] 7-11-4 F J Flood,.............(7 to 1)   10
3944[3] AWBEG ROVER (Ire) [-] 6-9-12 (3*) C O'Brien,.....(20 to 1)   11
3732[6] VINEYARD SPECIAL [-] 8-11-5 K F O'Brien,......(25 to 1)   12
3840[8] WEJEM (Ire) [-] 5-10-3 S R Murphy,.............(25 to 1)   13
3887[4] CALL ME HENRY [-] 5-9-12 F Woods,...........(16 to 1)   14
3887 SUPER MIDGE [-] 5-10-3 (3*) D P Murphy,........(20 to 1)   15
3870 DEEP THYNE (Ire) [-] 6-10-11 P Carberry,........(16 to 1)   16
3657[6] LOVE AND PORTER (Ire) [-] 6-11-6 (7*) Mr J T Codd,
 ....(10 to 1)   f
Dist: 2½l, sht-hd, 3½l, 3l. 4m 56.80s. (17 Ran).
                            (Ms M Hynes), Patrick G Kelly

4059 Grange Stud Maiden Hurdle (4 & 5-y-o) £3,427 2m...................(8:30)

3730[4] NORDIC SENSATION (Ire) 5-10-12 (7*) A P McCoy, (6 to 1)   1
3889 FINAWAY EXPRESS (Ire) 5-10-12 (7*) P J Mulligan,
 ....(2 to 1 fav)   2
3946[7] UNSINKABLE BOXER (Ire) 5-10-12 (7*) D O'Driscoll,
 ....(20 to 1)   3
3934[4] BACKTOWN JOHNNY (Ire) 5-11-5 L P Cusack,...(7 to 2)   4
3525[9] RING FOUR (Ire) 5-10-11 (3*) K P Gaule,........(10 to 1)   5
3788[5] MINOR MATTER (Ire) 5-11-0 H Rogers,.........(20 to 1)   6
3552[7] BALLYMADUN LASS (Ire) 5-11-0 F J Flood,.......(6 to 1)   7
2678[4] TEXAS FRIDAY (Ire) 4-10-12 (3*) T J O'Sullivan, ..(12 to 1)   8
3934[9] A LITTLE EARNER 5-11-5 C F Swan,............(8 to 1)   9
3946 MISS BERTAINE (Ire) 5-10-11 (3*) T J Mitchell, ...(25 to 1)   10
3971 KING'S FROLIC (Ire) 4-10-8 (7*) Mr J T McNamara, (14 to 1)   11
 OUT THE NAV (Ire) 5-10-12 (7*) M Whelan,......(12 to 1)   12
2553 BLAIR HOUSE (Ire) 5-10-9 (5*) D P Geoghegan, ...(10 to 1)   13
 FIDDLE FUND (Ire) 5-11-5 A Powell,............(20 to 1)   14
 AD EXTRA (Ire) 4-10-3 (7*) Mr E J O'Rourke,.....(16 to 1)   15
 FAT BARNEY (Ire) 4-11-1 B Sheridan,.............(20 to 1)   16
3839[9] NEPHIN FAR (Ire) 4-10-7 (3*) C O'Brien,.........(14 to 1)   17
3842 ELWOOD (Ire) 4-10-10 K F O'Brien,.............(20 to 1)   18
3936 CALLMECHARLIE (Ire) 5-11-0 (5*) P A Roche,....(20 to 1)   19
2663 CAPTAIN KIZZY (Ire) 4-10-10 D H O'Connor, ...(20 to 1)   20
Dist: 2l, ¾l, 1l, hd. 4m 5.70s. (20 Ran).
                            (Thomas McDonogh), J S Bolger

4060 Nenagh I.N.H. Flat Race (4-y-o and up) £2,742 2m....................(9:00)

3723* THE BOBTAIL FOX (Ire) 7-11-0 (7*) Miss C E Hyde, (12 to 1)   1
3749[4] BRAMBLESHINE (Ire) 4-10-5 (7*) Mr T N Cloke, ...(12 to 1)   2
3616[4] THE CARRIG RUA (Ire) 4-11-3 Mr P Fenton, ...(2 to 1 fav)   3
3946* BALLYHIRE LAD (Ire) 5-12-3 Mr A P O'Brien,......(5 to 1)   4
3870[4] TOTAL CONFUSION 7-12-1 (3*) Mr J A Nash, ...(10 to 1)   5
3871[3] CORRIBLOUGH (Ire) 6-11-13 (5*) Mr G J Harford, (12 to 1)   6
3616[6] PARSON FROM HEAVEN (Ire) 4-10-9 (3*) Mrs J M Mullins,
 ....(10 to 1)   7
 REGIT (Ire) 4-10-10 (7*) Mr M J Leahy,..........(20 to 1)   8
3956[8] MILEY SWEENEY 7-11-6 (5*) Mr B F Murphy, ...(33 to 1)   9
3749[5] APPALACHEE BAY (Ire) 4-10-7 (7*) Mr J T Codd, (12 to 1)   10
3912* ROYAL GREENWOOD (Ire) 5-11-5 (7*) Mr E Norris, (9 to 2)   11
 ALICE FOX (Ire) 6-10-13 (7*) Mr D K Budds,......(20 to 1)   12
3749 PRATE BOX (Ire) 4-10-10 (7*) Mr G A Kingston, ...(10 to 1)   13
3946 YOUCAT (Ire) 5-11-3 (7*) Mr P Crowley,.........(14 to 1)   14
2868[2] FEATHER SONG 4-10-9 (3*) Mr R Neylon,........(6 to 1)   15
3653 CARRAIG-AN-OIR (Ire) 5-11-10 Mr M Phillips, ...(25 to 1)   16
 SIN SCEAL EILE (Ire) 6-11-1 (5*) Mr H F Cleary, ...(20 to 1)   17
 DEAR MONEY (Ire) 4-10-5 (7*) Mrs S Hennessy, ...(25 to 1)   18
3616 BURSTOWS LAW (Ire) 4-10-10 (7*) Mr K Whelan, ..(50 to 1)   19
 FONTAINE LODGE (Ire) 4-10-7[2] (7*) Mr W Codd, ..(25 to 1)   20
Dist: 3½l, 1½l, 1l, 10l. 3m 54.50s. (20 Ran).
                            (Mrs John Magnier), Noel Meade

DUNDALK (IRE) (firm) Friday May 27th

4061 Point Maiden Hurdle (4-y-o and up) £2,228 2½m 153yds............(5:30)

3525 TOOLITTLE TOOLATE (Ire) 5-11-5 J Jones,........(8 to 1)   1
3748[6] HAVIN' A BALL (Ire) 5-10-7 (7*) T Martin, ...(33 to 1)   2
3946[6] STEVIE BE (Ire) 6-11-6 K F O'Brien,............(5 to 1)   3
3934[3] RIVERLAND (Ire) 6-11-8 B Sheridan,..........(7 to 4 fav)   4
3611[2] EEZ-AWAY (Ire) 5-11-5 F Woods,.............(14 to 1)   5
3971 PERCY LANE (Ire) 4-11-0 A Powell,.............(20 to 1)   6
3934 DEESIDE DOINGS (Ire) 6-11-6 H Rogers,.........(20 to 1)   7
3934[7] MINIGIRLS NIECE (Ire) 6-11-3 D P Fagan,.......(10 to 1)   8
3837* DOUBLE SYMPHONY (Ire) 6-11-9 C F Swan,......(5 to 2)   9
3993 DRESS DANCE (Ire) 4-11-0 J P Banahan,.........(12 to 1)   10
3934 COLLIERS HILL (Ire) 6-11-6 L P Cusack,.........(33 to 1)   11
3812[5] THE PARSONS ROSE (Ire) 6-10-12 (3*) K P Gaule, (12 to 1)   12
 MOORETOWN LAD (Ire) 6-10-13 (7*) D Halford, ...(25 to 1)   pu
Dist: 12l, hd, ½l, 4l. 4m 41.20s. (13 Ran).
                            (J C Harley), J C Harley

4062 Ravensdale Handicap Chase (0-116 4-y-o and up) £2,228 2m 3f....(7:30)

2865 BACK DOOR JOHNNY [-] 8-11-10 J Shortt,.......(3 to 1)   1
3841[4] NORDIC SUN (Ire) [-] 6-11-9 (5*) Mr H F Cleary,.....(4 to 1)   2
3996[3] LA-GREINE [-] 7-11-1 C F Swan,.............(5 to 2 fav)   3

3789 RANDOM PRINCE [-] 10-11-6 P Carberry, ...(5 to 1) 4
4043⁴ BALLYBODEN [-] 7-10-11 (3*) J P Broderick, ...(4 to 1) 5
906* ROSSBEIGH CREEK [-] 7-11-6 F J Flood, ...(8 to 1) 6
Dist: 1½l, 6l, 5l, 3l. 4m 42.90s. (6 Ran).
(Mrs S Guerin), M Halford

4063 Claremount Pro/Am I.N.H. Flat Race (4-y-o and up) £2,228 2m 135yds (8:30)

3388 SWINGER (Ire) 5-11-6 (7*) D J Kavanagh, ...(9 to 4 fav) 1
3870⁷ JOHNNY SCATTERCASH 12-12-0 Mr E Norris, ... (16 to 1) 2
3327⁵ ROUNDWOOD (Ire) 5-11-6 (7*) A J Dempsey, ...(7 to 2) 3
2332⁴ TIFASI (Ire) 4-10-13 (7*) Mr B Cash, ...(8 to 1) 4
3124 HAUGHTON LAD (Ire) 5-11-6 (7*) Mr D Groome, ...(7 to 1) 5D
EBONY KING (Ire) 4-10-13 (7*) M P Cooney, ...(10 to 1) 5
3936 THE KINGS SEAL (Ire) 6-11-2 (7*) Mr D McCartan, (33 to 1) 6
3936 FOREST FORT (Ire) (bl) 5-11-6 (7*) J Butler, ...(25 to 1) 7
3321 MINUS ONE (USA) 4-11-1 (5*) Mr H F Cleary, ...(12 to 1) 8
1455 FLIP THE LID (Ire) 5-11-1 (7*) Miss H McCourt, ...(33 to 1) 9
3913⁶ PRIORITY GALE (Ire) 5-11-1 (7*) Mr J Connolly, ... (6 to 1) 10
3796² EXCUSE ME (Ire) 5-11-6 (7*) Mr R I Arthur, ...(9 to 1) 11
3388 NIGHT SERVICE (Ire) 6-11-2 (7*) Mr K A Dempsey, (20 to 1) 12
3796⁵ ARCTIC TREASURE (Ire) 5-11-8 Mr W Ewing, ...(12 to 1) 13
MINNY DOZER (Ire) 5-11-6 (7*) J P Deegan, ... (25 to 1) 14
510³ SLIM-N-LITE 8-11-2 (7*) Mr L J Gracey, ...(20 to 1) 15
2989 COME ON BOBBY (Ire) 5-11-6 (7*) Mr M G Wiseman, ...(25 to 1) 16
PAULA'S BOY (Ire) 4-10-13 (7*) Mr R J Patton, ... (33 to 1) 17
2849 THE REAL JOKER (Ire) 5-11-6 (7*) Mr A F Doherty, ..(6 to 1) 18
3810 PHARVIONE (Ire) 4-10-10 (5*) Mr G J Harford, ... (16 to 1) 19
Dist: ½l, 1l, 2l, 9l. 3m 42.90s. (20 Ran).
(Mrs Margaret Dowling), Noel Meade

TOWCESTER (good to soft)
Friday May 27th
Going Correction: PLUS 0.30 sec. per fur.

4064 Heygate Selling Handicap Hurdle (4-y-o and up) £2,153 2m 5f........(6:30)

3511⁴ EASTERN PLEASURE [89] (bl) 7-11-11 N Williamson, *wth ldrs, led 3 out, rdn clr appr last, styd on wl.* ....(5 to 1 fav op 9 to 2 tchd 11 to 2) 1
3967⁸ WHAT IF [91] 10-11-13 M Brennan, *prog 7th, rdn and not quicken appr 2 out*...............(12 to 1 op 10 to 1) 2
3845⁵ MISTRESS ROSS [75] 11-10-11 D Bridgwater, *handily plcd, rdn and not quicken appr 2 out, styd on nr finish.* .... (16 to 1 op 14 to 1) 3
3970⁶ IVYCHURCH (USA) [69] 8-9-12 (7*) Karen Cook, *mid-div, styd on one pace frm 2 out*........(14 to 1 op 20 to 1) 4
3895⁷ VOLCANIC DANCER (USA) [73] (v) 8-10-4 (5*) E Husband, *hdwy 6th, rdn and no extr appr 2 out.* .... (25 to 1 op 20 to 1) 5
3853⁸ DARK DESIRE [86] 8-11-8 M Richards, *prog 7th, mstk 3 out, one pace appr nxt*............ (8 to 1 op 20 to 1) 6
3881² ARMASHOCKER [71] 6-10-7 V Smith, *effrt frm rear 7th, no prog from 3 out*....................(12 to 1 op 8 to 1) 7
4025⁴ BOWLAND GIRL (Ire) [64] (bl) 5-9-11 (3*) S Wynne, *cld on ldrs appr 3 out, rdn and no extr nxt*..........(33 to 1) 8
3980⁹ DOUALAGO (Fr) [80] (bl) 4-11-2 R Dunwoody, *led to 4th, led appr 6th to 3 out, sn btn.* .... (8 to 1 op 5 to 1 tchd 10 to 1) 9
FRANK DALE [64] 11-10-0 B Clifford, *slwly into strd, nvr nr to chal*........................(33 to 1 op 20 to 1) 10
4021⁸ RIP THE CALICO (Ire) [67] 6-9-10 (7*) Miss C Spearing, *wl plcd frm 6th, hit 3 out, sn btn*.....(16 to 1 op 14 to 1) 11
3895 KNIGHTS (NZ) [92] (v) 8-12-0 Jacqui Oliver, *led 4th till appr 6th, sn wknd, tld off*................ (14 to 1 op 8 to 1) 12
3533 RIYADH LIGHTS [87] 9-11-9 B Powell, *lost tch 6th, tld off whn pld up bef 3 out*............. (25 to 1 op 20 to 1) pu
3943³ CHASMARELLA [80] 9-11-2 D Gallagher, *chsd ldrs to 7th, pld up bef 2 out*......... (7 to 1 op 6 to 1 tchd 5 to 1) pu
ROYAL SHEPHERD [64] 11-10-0 A McCabe, *al beh, pld up bef 2 out*........................ (16 to 1 op 12 to 1) pu
4006 COXANN [66] (bl) 8-9-9 (7*) E Tolhurst, *chsd ldrs to 6th, beh whn pld up bef 2 out*............. (33 to 1 op 20 to 1) pu
3682² IRISH TAN [64] 7-10-0 A Maguire, *ldg gorup, wknd 7th, pld up bef 3 out*...................... (10 to 1 op 7 to 1) pu
3805 COMMANCHERO [76] 7-10-12 A Tory, *mid-div, no hdwy 6th, pld up bef 2 out*....(6 to 1 op 5 to 1 tchd 13 to 2) pu
4004⁹ UNDERWYCHWOOD (Ire) [82] (v) 6-11-4 J R Kavanagh, *rear till pld up bef 2 out*...(16 to 1 op 20 to 1 tchd 25 to 1) pu
3853⁴ MILDRED SOPHIA [65] 7-9-8 (7*) Miss S Mitchell, *in tch to 7th, pld up bef 2 out*...............(12 to 1 op 10 to 1) pu
Dist: 5l, 5l, 1¾l, 7l, 1¾l, 3½l, 2½l, 5l, 4l, nk. 5m 20.80s. a 21.80s (20 Ran).
(T Wood), W Clay

4065 Connell Wilson Handicap Chase (0-125 5-y-o and up) £3,096 3m 1f (6:55)

3828 INVASION [101] (v) 10-10-4 M Brennan, *hld up, prog 13th, hit 15th, led last, rdn clr*.... (5 to 2 jt-fav tchd 11 to 4) 1
3828 MWEENISH [97] 12-10-0 R Bellamy, *led, hit 15th, hdd last, one pace*.........................(12 to 1 op 10 to 1) 2
3850⁵ STAUNCH RIVAL (USA) [97] 7-10-0 D Bridgwater, *beh, improved frm 9th, one pace 2 out*.... (7 to 1 op 8 to 1) 3
3519 CATCHAPENNY [109] (bl) 9-10-12 G McCourt, *drpd rear 8th, rdn and lost tch 11th, styd on frm 3 out.* ....(7 to 1 op 5 to 1 tchd 15 to 2) 4
4008* SPORTING MARINER [97] 12-10-0 (7ex) A Maguire, *wl plcd, rdn and no extr appr 2 out*......(10 to 1 tchd 11 to 1) 5
3519 HENRY MANN [125] (bl) 11-12-0 R Dunwoody, *rear most of way*....................(7 to 1 op 5 to 1 tchd 8 to 1) 6
3544⁷ THAMESDOWN TOOTSIE [102] 9-10-5⁵ M A FitzGerald, *ldg grp, hit 3 out, sn btn*.............. (12 to 1 op 8 to 1) 7
3990⁴ SKERRY MEADOW [97] 10-10-0 N Williamson, *f 1st.* ....(14 to 1 op 20 to 1) f
2935 SHEEPHAVEN [97] 10-10-0 M Richards, *trkd ldr till rdn and lost pl 11th, effrt 13th, hit 3 out, sn wknd, pld up bef last*...........(5 to 2 jt-fav op 2 to 1 tchd 3 to 1) pu
Dist: 6l, ¾l, 7l, ½l, 2½l, nk. 6m 40.80s. a 25.80s (9 Ran).
(Lady Anne Bentinck), O Brennan

4066 Shoosmiths And Harrison Handicap Hurdle (0-125 4-y-o and up) £1,940 2m ....(7:20)

3930³ STRATH ROYAL [124] 8-12-0 M Brennan, *settled in 3rd pl, chsd ldr frm 5th, led 3 out, wl clr whn hit nxt, unchlgd.* .... (11 to 8 fav op 11 to 10 tchd 6 to 4) 1
3942* ILEWIN [96] 7-10-0 M Ahern, *rear, effrt 5th, chsd wnr appr 2 out, no imprsn*.. (5 to 1 op 4 to 1 tchd 6 to 1) 2
4019³ ADMIRALTY WAY [103] 8-10-4 (3*) T Jenks, *beh, rdn and effrt appr 3 out, not trble ldr.* .... (9 to 2 tchd 5 to 1 and 4 to 1) 3
4019⁴ EDEN'S CLOSE [114] 5-11-4 A Maguire, *led to 3 out, sn wknd*.............................(9 to 2 op 3 to 1) 4
4000⁴ PERSIAN LUCK [96] 8-9-7 (7*) P McLoughlin, *in tch in mid-div till wknd 5th, pld up bef last*..(33 to 1 op 20 to 1) pu
3240⁵ GYMCRAK SOVEREIGN [106] 6-10-10 R Marley, *trkd ldr, wknd 5th, pld up bef last.* .... (5 to 1 op 9 to 2 tchd 11 to 2) pu
Dist: 25l, 6l, 7l. 3m 51.40s. a 8.40s (6 Ran).
SR: 64/11/12/16/-/-/ (Lady Anne Bentinck), O Brennan

4067 Broadway Stampings Handicap Chase (0-125 5-y-o and up) £3,533 2m 110yds.......................(7:50)

3941³ YOUNG ALFIE [87] (bl) 9-10-0 A Maguire, *led to 2 out, rallied und pres to ld r-in.* ....(15 to 2 op 7 to 1 tchd 6 to 1 and 8 to 1) 1
3847* GENERAL MERCHANT [88] (bl) 14-10-1 R Dunwoody, *pressed ldr, hit 9th, led 2 out, hit last, wknd and hdd nr finish*............(11 to 10 fav op 5 to 4 tchd 6 to 4) 2
3803³ BOSTON ROVER [115] 9-12-0 M Brennan, *hld up rear, blun and lost tch 5th, hdwy 8th, no extr frm 2 out.* ....(6 to 4 op 5 to 4) 3
3941⁶ THEY ALL FORGOT ME [87] 7-10-0 D Bridgwater, *hld up rear, in tch 5th, rdn alng and outpcd nxt, tld off.* ....(7 to 1 op 6 to 1 tchd 8 to 1) 4
4020⁷ BILLHEAD [87] 8-10-0 N Williamson, *chsd ldg pair till wknd appr 3 out, tld off*..........(66 to 1 op 33 to 1) 5
Dist: ¾l, 25l, 25l, 15l. 4m 15.90s. a 13.90s (5 Ran).
(J F Panvert), J F Panvert

4068 Wilson Connolly Hunters' Chase (5-y-o and up) £1,308 3m 1f........(8:20)

3846* AVOSTAR 7-12-0 (7*) Mr B Pollock, *wth ldrs, led 7th, hit 12th, quickened appr 2 out, styd on strly*....(7 to 4 jt-fav op 5 to 4 tchd 2 to 1) 1
4007⁵ ARCTIC TEAL 10-11-11 (7*) Mr S Edmunds, *wl plcd, mstk 15th, chsd wnr appr 2 out, no imprsn approaching last.* ....(12 to 1 op 8 to 1) 2
3950² THE MALAKARMA 8-11-13 (5*) Mr T Byrne, *ldg grp, ev ch aftr 3 out, btn nxt.* (7 to 4 jt-fav op 2 to 1 tchd 5 to 2) 3
3989 ABBOTSHAM 9-11-7 (7*) Mr Richard White, *mstks, chsd ldrs till outpcd 3 out*.................(8 to 1 op 5 to 1) 4
3949² RUSTY BRIDGE 7-11-11 (7*) Mr R Johnson, *led to 7th, wknd aftr 11th, mstk 14th*............(11 to 2 op 5 to 1) 5
SHILGROVE PLACE 12-11-7 (7*) Mr C Ward, *in tch tenth till wknd appr 3 out*............(12 to 1 tchd 16 to 1) 6
3950⁶ FOWLING PIECE 9-11-7 (7*) Mr J M Pritchard, *hdwy frm rear 7th, lost pl 14th, rallied appr 2 out, btn 4th whn blun and uns rdr last*............ (20 to 1 op 50 to 1) ur
RENT A BANDIT 10-11-8¹ (7*) Mr S R Green, *slwly into strd, sn wl beh, tld off whn pld up bef last*... (100 to 1) pu
3857⁷ DAN MARINO 12-11-7 (7*) Miss A Stedman, *not jump wl, beh 4th, lost tch 7th, pld up bef tenth*........ (50 to 1) pu
Dist: 12l, 8l, 6l, nk, 8l. 6m 47.10s. a 32.10s (9 Ran).
(R G Russell), Miss C Saunders

4069 Abbcott Novices' Hurdle (4-y-o and up) £2,015 2m..................(8:50)

3543* RES IPSA LOQUITUR 7-11-7 A Maguire, *hld up in mid-div, led 3 out, clr whn hit last, styd on, easily.* ....(6 to 4 fav tchd 7 to 4) 1
3914⁵ THE CAUMRUE (Ire) 6-11-7 J Frost, *hld up, hdwy 5th, one pace frm 2 out*..........(2 to 1 op 6 to 4 tchd 9 to 4) 2
3757* HAWTHORNE GLEN 7-11-7 D Gallagher, *trkd ldrs, led briefly appr 3 out, no extr nxt*.....(4 to 1 tchd 5 to 1) 3

3965[4] SECRET FORMULA 4-10-9 W Humphreys, *rear, improved frm 5th, not rch ldrs appr 2 out.* ....(25 to 1 op 20 to 1 tchd 33 to 1) 4
3800[7] MRS NORMAN 5-10-4 (5*) E Husband, *led second till hdd and wknd appr 3 out.* (14 to 1 op 8 to 1 tchd 16 to 1) 5
3970[9] NIGHT FANCY 6-10-11 (3*) J McCarthy, *led to second, wknd 3 out.*........ (20 to 1 op 14 to 1 tchd 25 to 1) 6
3583 ARDENT LOVE (Ire) 5-10-9 M Brennan, *strted slwly, beh most of way*...................... (6 to 1 tchd 8 to 1) 7
3848[8] STORMING RUN (Ire) 6-11-0 W Marston, *outpcd frm hfwy.* ....(50 to 1 op 33 to 1) 8
JUST BRUCE 5-11-0 Mr S Cowell, *trkd ldrs till wknd 5th, tld off*............................(50 to 1 op 33 to 1) 9
3543 PHAE TINGO (Ire) 4-10-9 L Harvey, *al rear, tld off.* ....(50 to 1 op 33 to 1) 10
Dist: 6l, 5l, 30l, 2½l, 3l, 2½l, 9l, 30l, 2½l. 3m 56.60s. a 13.60s (10 Ran).
SR: 5/-/-/-/-/- (Brian Arthur Pearce), B A Pearce

CARTMEL (firm)
Saturday May 28th
Going Correction: MINUS 0.30 sec. per fur. (races 1,3,6), MINUS 0.20 (2,4,5)

4070 Crowther Homes Selling Handicap Hurdle (4-y-o and up) £2,178 3¼m ....(2:00)

3561[9] CRAZY HORSE DANCER (USA) [72] 6-11-4 J Lodder, *hld up in mid-div, hdwy 8th, chsd ldr 2 out, rdn to ld r-in.* ....(10 to 1 op 10 to 1 tchd 12 to 1) 1
3982[4] TEMPORALE [67] 8-10-6 (7*) G Crone, *chsd ldrs, took clr order 4 out, led nxt, rdn appr last, hdd r-in.* ....(3 to 1 fav op 7 to 2) 2
3533 QUIET RIOT [76] 12-11-8 J F Titley, *hld up and beh, hdwy appr 3 out, rdn nxt, kpt on one pace.* ....(7 to 2 tchd 4 to 1) 3
3298* BOOGIE BOPPER (Ire) [71] (v) 5-11-3 R Dunwoody, *hld up and beh, hdwy 8th, rdn to chase ldrs 3 out, sn one pace.* ....(100 to 30 op 7 to 2) 4
3853[3] SENEGALAIS (Fr) [78] 10-11-10 J Frost, *al prmnt, rdn appr 3 out, sn one pace*................(14 to 1 op 12 to 1) 5
4006 TAP DANCING [62] 8-10-8 Ann Stokell, *hld up, hdwy hfwy, rdn 4 out, one pace frm nxt*............(14 to 1) 6
3926[6] MILLIE (USA) [54] 6-10-0 M Robinson, *chsd ldrs, rdn 4 out, sn one pace*..................................(33 to 1) 7
3769[5] ODSTONE PEAR [73] 9-11-5 P Niven, *hld up, hdwy to chase ldrs 4, effrt and ev ch 3 out, rdn nxt, sn wknd.* ....(7 to 1 op 12 to 1) 8
3982[6] GOLDEN BANKER (Ire) [58] 6-10-4[4] K Jones, *chsd ldrs, wknd 4th, tld off four out*........(50 to 1 op 33 to 1) 9
3982[7] SPEEDY SIOUX [54] (bl) 5-9-9 (5*) F Perratt, *al beh, tld off 4 out*...(33 to 1) 10
3906 HAMANAKA (USA) [77] 5-11-9 Mr S Love, *led, hdd appr 4 out, sn wknd*..................(50 to 1 op 33 to 1) 11
3844 MICRONOVA [65] 8-10-11 L Harvey, *beh frm 4th, tld off four out, pld up bef last*..................... (50 to 1) pu
4045[3] TROPICAL GALE [65] (v) 9-10-11 Peter Caldwell, *cl up, led appr 4 out, hdd nxt, sn rdn and wknd quickly, beh whn pld up r-in*.................................. (12 to 1) pu
Dist: 1¾l, 8l, 4l, ½l, 2½l, 2½l, 20l, 12l, 12l, 12l. 6m 6.00s. a 8.00s (13 Ran).
(Mrs Jean Haslam), F Jordan

4071 Marten Julian Handicap Chase (0-110 5-y-o and up) £2,801 2m 1f 110yds ....(2:35)

3963* STAY AWAKE [109] 8-12-0 P Niven, *trkd ldr, cl up hfwy, led briefly 5 out, hit 3 out, led nxt, rdn clr r-in, easily.* ....(5 to 4 on tchd Evens) 1
4001[3] MASTER SALESMAN [96] 11-11-1 D Gallagher, *chsd ldg pair, pushed alng and outpcd aftr 2 out, styd on wl r-in*...................(7 to 1 op 8 to 1 tchd 9 to 1) 2
3865* MOSS BEE [81] 7-10-0 R Dunwoody, *led, hdd briefly 5 out, rdn and headed 2 out, one pace frm last.* ....(7 to 4 tchd 6 to 4) 3
3865[4] HIGHFIELD PRINCE [81] 8-9-9 (5*) F Leahy, *hld up, hdwy 4 out, rdn and hit nxt, one pace frm last.* ....(12 to 1 op 8 to 1) 4
3699[7] CHANCERY BUCK [88] (bl) 11-10-7[7] J Frost, *in tch, hit 1st and 6th, rdn 4 out, wkng whn mstk 2 out, sn beh.* ....(25 to 1 op 20 to 1 tchd 33 to 1) 5
Dist: 4l, 1¾l, 1½l, 12l. 4m 15.00s. a 2.00s (5 Ran).
SR: 45/28/11/9/4/ (Austin Donnellon), Mrs M Reveley

4072 Bass Handicap Hurdle (0-125 4-y-o and up) £2,346 2¾m............(3:10)

3737* LOCH SCAVAIG (Ire) [112] 5-10-13 (3*) D J Moffatt, *made all, clr 4th, quickened 2 out, rdn and ran on wl r-in.* ....(9 to 4 op 6 to 4) 1
4006* LYNCH LAW (Ire) [124] (v) 6-12-0 R Dunwoody, *in tch, not fluent 4th and 5th, hdwy to press wnr 2 out, rdn last, not quicken r-in*.................(Evens fav op 6 to 4) 2
3986[3] DANCING DOVE (Ire) [96] 6-9-9[2] (7*) B Harding, *hld up, in tch, hdwy 3 out, effrt nxt, rdn appr last, kpt on.* ....(10 to 1 op 14 to 1) 3
4029* BAHRAIN QUEEN (Ire) [96] 6-10-0 (4ex) M Ranger, *chsd ldr, effrt and ev ch 3 out, rdn and hit nxt, sn btn.* ....(7 to 2 op 6 to 1) 4
2528[9] RECORD LOVER (Ire) [97] 4-10-1[1] W Worthington, *chsd ldg pair, ev ch 3 out, sn rdn and btn nxt.* ....(16 to 1 op 33 to 1) 5
3866[2] CAPTAIN TANCRED (Ire) [96] 6-10-0 A Merrigan, *hld up pulling hrd, in tch till rdn 3 out, sn wknd.* ....(12 to 1 op 8 to 1) 6
Dist: 3l, 3l, 2l, 8l, 5l. 5m 20.70s. a 15.70s (6 Ran).
(Mrs G A Turnbull), D Moffatt

4073 Bass Maiden Hunters' Chase for the Fraser Cup (5-y-o and up) £1,891 3¼m ....(3:45)

SOLAR GREEN 9-11-9 (5*) Mr S Brookshaw, *led to 3rd, cl up till led 9th, hmpd by loose horse and hdd 13th, led 3 out, clr nxt, easily*............ (5 to 2 fav tchd 3 to 1) 1
3984[3] TRUE FAIR 11-11-7 (7*) Mr A Robson, *hld up, hdwy 7th, lft in ld 13th, hdd and mstk 3 out, sn one pace*...(12 to 1) 2
JOLLY FELLOW 10-11-7 (7*) Mr C Stockton, *beh, steady hdwy 11th, chsd ldrs 4 out, mstk nxt and sn one pace.* ....(20 to 1 op 14 to 1) 3
STILLTODO 7-11-2 (7*) Mr Chris Wilson, *beh, hdwy 6 out, sn rdn and plugged on one pace*...(14 to 1 op 50 to 1) 4
MR TOBIN 12-11-9 (5*) Mr K Darby, *chsd ldrs, rdn hfwy and sn wknd*....................(33 to 1 op 25 to 1) 5
EASTLANDS MONKEY 12-11-2 (7*) Mr J Nicholl, *sn beh, tld off bef 8th*.................................(50 to 1) 6
MAHANA 10-11-7 (7*) Mr D Coates, *chsd ldrs, 4th and staying on und pres whn f four out.* (11 to 2 op 9 to 2) f
SWEETING (bl) 9-11-7 (7*) Mr R Lawther, *prmnt till f 4th.* ....(3 to 1 op 6 to 1 tchd 5 to 2) f
GO SILLY 8-11-9 (5*) Miss J Thurlow, *beh whn f 7th.* ....(20 to 1) f
DEDAY 7-11-7 (7*) Mr T Scott, *cl up, led 3rd to 9th, hit 11th, rdn and wkng whn uns rdr 3 out*....... (33 to 1) ur
3927 JOSSESTOWN 11-11-7 (7*) Mr G Hanmer, *prmnt whn brght dwn 4th*.................................(20 to 1) bd
3988[3] RED SCORPION 10-11-7 (7*) Mr A Newey, *chsd ldrs, brght dwn 4th*....................(10 to 1 op 25 to 1) bd
ADDABITON (bl) 8-11-8[1] (7*) Mr D Barlow, *mid-div whn brght dwn 4th*..................(40 to 1 op 33 to 1) bd
BIRTLEY GIRL 10-11-2 (7*) Miss Sue Nichol, *al beh, tld off whn pld up bef 11th*................(11 to 2 op 7 to 2) pu
3909 DERRY PRINCESS (v) 8-11-2 (7*) Mr Robert Robinson, *in tch, lost pl hfwy, beh whn pld up bef 5 out.* ....(10 to 1 op 8 to 1) pu
Dist: 6l, 25l, 20l, 3l, dist. 6m 31.00s. a 14.00s (15 Ran).
(Reach Recruitment Limited), S A Brookshaw

4074 British Rail Novices' Chase for the McAlpine Cup (5-y-o and up) £2,398 3¼m.......................... (4:20)

4026 URIZEN 9-11-6 C Hawkins, *al prmnt, chsd ldr frm 9th, lft wl clr 3 out*.............(7 to 2 op 3 to 1 tchd 4 to 1) 1
GLORIOLE 10-11-2 Mr A Robson, *chsd ldrs, rdn 13th, lft poor second 3 out, plugged on one pace.* ....(25 to 1 op 20 to 1) 2
3961* UPWELL 10-11-6 Mr P Johnson, *chsd ldrs, outpcd and beh hfwy, reminders and styd on frm 5 out, no hdwy from 2 out*.........................(7 to 2 op 4 to 1) 3
3927[9] JAUNTY GIG 8-11-2 A Merrigan, *in tch, hit second, mstk 6th, sn lost pl and beh*............(33 to 1 op 25 to 1) 4
4015[4] NEEDS MUST 7-11-6 J Frost, *made rng, 4 ls clr and gng wl whn f 3 out*.................... (8 to 1 op 10 to 1) f
3802[3] YOUNG PARSON 8-11-2 J F Titley, *hld up, hdwy to chsd ldrs whn f 12th*.................(7 to 2 op 4 to 1) f
3783 NORSTOCK 7-11-6 (7*) P McLoughlin, *chsd ldr, jmpd slwly 7th and 8th, sn lost pl, beh whn pld up bef 13th.* ....(7 to 4 fav tchd 2 to 1) pu
Dist: 15l, 8l, 15l. 6m 31.30s. a 14.30s (7 Ran).
(Mrs P A H Hartley), P Beaumont

4075 Coniston Hall Enterprises Novices' Hurdle (4-y-o and up) £2,542 2m 1f 110yds...................... (4:55)

4003* LADY DONOGHUE (USA) 5-11-6 P Niven, *prmnt, hdwy to chase ldr 3rd, led 3 out, rdn clr last, kpt on.* ....(6 to 4 on tchd 11 to 8 on) 1
3598 CROFTON LAKE 6-11-3 L O'Hara, *chsd ldrs, rdn 3 out, mstk nxt, kpt on one pace und pres.* ....(25 to 1 op 20 to 1) 2
3907[2] FREE TRANSFER (Ire) 5-11-7 R Dunwoody, *led and sn clr, rdn and hdd 3 out, hrd drvn and hit last, one pace.* ....(6 to 4 tchd 13 to 8) 3
3476[9] HIGHLAND HEIGHTS (Ire) 6-10-12 M Ranger, *hit second, in tch, rdn and hit 5th, sn outpcd*....(12 to 1 op 20 to 1) 4
3824 YORK VALER 11-10-12 A Merrigan, *al rear, tld off frm hfwy*.......................................(66 to 1) 5
Dist: 5l, ½l, dist, dist. 4m 1.00s. a 1.00s (5 Ran).

NATIONAL HUNT RESULTS 1993-94

SR: 30/22/25/-/-/ (C C Buckley), Mrs M Reveley

FAIRYHOUSE (IRE) (good)
Saturday May 28th

4076 Porterstown Hurdle (4-y-o and up)
£3,082 2m. . . . . (3:30)

	AVOID THE RUSH (Ire) 4-10-10 J Shortt, ... (33 to 1)	1
3935⁵	OH SO GRUMPY 6-12-0 C F Swan, ... (3 to 1)	2
3321⁵	WICKLOW WAY (Ire) 4-10-5 K F O'Brien, ... (9 to 2)	3
3934	HACKETTS CROSS (Ire) 6-11-4 A Powell, ... (5 to 1)	4
3973⁷	CASH IT IN (Ire) 6-11-1 (3*) D P Murphy, ... (7 to 1)	5
3647⁵	BADEN (Ire) 6-11-1 (3*) T P Treacy, ... (5 to 4 fav)	6
3837⁸	PERSPEX GALE (Ire) 6-10-13 J P Banahan, ... (33 to 1)	7
	MARAMOURESH (Ire) 6-11-4 L P Cusack, ... (25 to 1)	8
3993	PRINCE SABI (Ire) 4-10-10 J P Byrne, ... (33 to 1)	9
	HAPPY REUNION 9-11-1 (3*) J P Broderick, ... (33 to 1)	10

Dist: Hd, 1l, 1l, 2½l. 3m 56.30s. (10 Ran).

(John Muldoon), Patrick Prendergast

4077 Baltrasna Handicap Hurdle (0-130 4-y-o and up) £3,082 2½m. . . . . (4:00)

1450³	SUPER FLAME (Can) [-] 7-11-4 P Carberry, ... (5 to 1)	1+
4043*	FINNEGANS WAKE [-] 7-11-9 (6ex) C F Swan, ... (11 to 2)	1+
3957³	RISING WATERS (Ire) [-] 6-12-0 K F O'Brien, ... (6 to 1)	3
3995⁴	MR FIVE WOOD (Ire) [-] 6-10-7 (5*) P A Roche, (5 to 4 fav)	4
3242	ROUBABAY (Ire) [-] 6-11-2 (3*) T P Treacy, ... (6 to 1)	5
3954	RATHFARDON (Ire) [-] 6-9-8¹ F Woods, ... (14 to 1)	6
880⁵	MABES TOWN (Ire) [-] 6-10-1 (3*) J P Broderick, . . . (14 to 1)	7
3935	DINNYS CORNER [-] 10-10-11 L P Cusack, ... (50 to 1)	8
904⁵	PALACE GEM [-] 7-10-11 (3*) Mr P J Casey, ... (14 to 1)	9
3873⁹	RIVERSTOWN LAD [-] 7-9-9 (7*) B Bowens, ... (20 to 1)	10
3710⁵	SHEER MIST [-] 7-10-10 S H O'Donovan, ... (12 to 1)	11
3526⁷	ASSERT STAR [-] 4-10-11 (3*) K P Gaule, ... (40 to 1)	12

Dist: Dd-ht, 5l, sht-hd, 4½l. 4m 43.20s. (12 Ran).

(N Stassen & Bracken Syndicate), Joseph M Canty & A P O'Brien

4078 Macetown INH Flat Race (4-y-o and up) £3,082 2m. . . . . (5:30)

3327⁹	LEGIBLE 6-11-11 (3*) Mr D Marnane, ... (14 to 1)	1
3937⁸	MASAI (Ire) 5-11-6 (7*) Miss A W O'Brien, ... (10 to 1)	2
3946	SEVENTY SEVEN MILL (Ire) 5-11-6 (7*) Miss C Cashman,	
	. . . . (14 to 1)	3
3124⁷	TRICKLE LAD (Ire) 5-11-13 Mr A P O'Brien, ... (7 to 1)	4
4010⁸	SHORTSTAFF 5-11-6 (7*) Mr A K Wyse, ... (9 to 1)	5
3958⁶	MAORI'S DELIGHT 5-11-1 (7*) Mr B Heffernan, ... (8 to 1)	6
3937⁷	DUDDON SANDS (Ire) 5-11-10 (3*) Mr J A Nash, . . . (10 to 1)	7
3973⁷	YOU KNOW WHO (Ire) 6-11-11 (3*) Miss A Harvey, (6 to 1)	8
3936²	MOYGANNON COURT (Ire) 5-11-8 (5*) Mr H F Cleary,	
	. . . . (11 to 4 fav)	9
3749⁷	COURTLY CIRCLE (Ire) 5-11-8 Mr A R Coonan, ... (5 to 1)	10
3913⁹	LISCAHILL HIGHWAY 7-11-7 (7*) Mr P Cleary, ... (20 to 1)	11
3937	COLLON LEADER (Ire) 5-11-1 (7*) Mr M O'Callaghan,	
	. . . . (20 to 1)	12
	COOL ROCKET (Ire) 5-11-6 (7*) Miss L Townsley, . . (16 to 1)	13
3937	PROUD KITTEN (Ire) 5-11-1 (7*) Miss S McDonogh, (25 to 1)	14
4034⁹	LINGERING HOPE (Ire) 5-11-7 (7*) Mr J G O'Connell,	
	. . . . (20 to 1)	15
	TENDER RIVER (Ire) 4-11-2³ (7*) Miss T Collins, . . . (10 to 1)	16
4010⁹	FAITHFULL FELLOW 7-11-7 (7*) Mr S P McCarthy, (10 to 1)	17
	SKEHANAGH BRIDGE (Ire) 5-11-6 (7*) Mr T Gilmore,	
	. . . . (16 to 1)	18
4044³	SECRET MISSILE 7-12-0 Mr W P Mullins, ... (10 to 1)	19
2989	LADY FONTAINE (Ire) 5-11-3 (5*) Mr G J Harford, . . (50 to 1)	20
	OAK LEAF COUNTY (Ire) 6-12-0 Mr T Mullins, ... (12 to 1)	21
3936	PRECEPTOR (Ire) 5-11-13 Mr J A Berry, ... (20 to 1)	22
	LISNATIERNEY (Ire) 4-10-8 (7*) Mr J Bright, ... (25 to 1)	23
3936	PRESTBURY KING (Ire) 5-11-6 (7*) Mrs D McDonogh,	
	. . . . (20 to 1)	24
	ROSES RED (Ire) 4-10-10 (5*) Mr P J Casey, ... (25 to 1)	25
3937	THATS FAR ENOUGH (Ire) 4-11-1 (5*) Mr P M Kelly, (20 to 1)	26
2868⁶	KERKY (Ire) 4-10-13 (7*) Mr E Norris, ... (20 to 1)	27
3937	FANE'S TREASURE 5-11-10 (3*) Mr D Valentine,	
	. . . . (25 to 1)	28
	CELTIC KINSHIP (Ire) 6-11-7 (7*) Mr G R Ryan, ... (16 to 1)	29
	DISTILLERY HILL (Ire) 6-11-7 (7*) Mr J Connolly, . . (12 to 1)	30

Dist: 6l, nk, nk, 6l. 3m 31.60s. (30 Ran).

(S P Tindall), I R Ferguson

HEXHAM (firm)
Saturday May 28th
Going Correction: MINUS 0.50 sec. per fur.

4079 Riding Novices' Hurdle (4-y-o and up)
£1,035 2½m 110yds. . . . . (2:15)

3620	STRONG MEASURE (Ire) 6-11-2 K Johnson, patiently tkn, improved on bit to ld bef last, shaken up and ran on strly r-in. . . . . (11 to 8 on op 5 to 4 on)	1
	SWISS BEAUTY 6-10-6 (5*) Mr D Parker, nvr far away, led appr 2 out, sn pushed alng, hdd bef last not quicken r-in. . . . . (4 to 1 op 7 to 2)	2

3983⁶ ANOTHER MEADOW 6-11-2 L O'Hara, al cl up, led 3 out till appr nxt, fdd. . . . . . . (15 to 1 op 7 to 1 tchd 8 to 1) 3
3673 SULAAH ROSE 5-10-4 (7*) S Taylor, blun and uns rdr second. . . . . (66 to 1 op 50 to 1) ur
3076 FOX TOWER 8-11-2 A Dobbin, jmpd slwly, drpd rear second, struggling 4th, tld off whn pld up bef 7th.
. . . . (25 to 1 tchd 33 to 1) pu
ROUGH LEA 7-11-2 B Storey, led, jmpd badly lft 5th, hdd 3 out, sn struggling, tld off whn pld up bef last.
. . . . (11 to 1 op 10 to 1 tchd 12 to 1) pu
Dist: 5l, 20l. 4m 58.80s. a 5.80s (6 Ran).

(Leading Star Racing), P Cheesbrough

4080 Ernst & Young Handicap Hurdle (0-105 4-y-o and up) £1,234 2m. . . . . . (2:45)

3538⁵ RAPID MOVER [82] (bl) 7-10-8² N Doughty, settled beh ldrs, improved to join issue 3 out, led last, rdn out.
. . . . (9 to 2 op 4 to 1) 1
3959³ RICHMOND (Ire) [80] (bl) 6-10-6 D Wilkinson, made most, jnd 4th, hdd last, no extr towards finish.
. . . . (5 to 1 op 4 to 1) 2
1092 JIM'S WISH (Ire) [74] (bl) 6-10-0 Carol Cuthbert, al wl plcd, drw level 4th, slightly outpcd 2 out, rallied and ev ch last, not quicken last 100yards. . . . (20 to 1 op 14 to 1) 3
3864* CHARLYCIA [86] 6-10-5 (7*) M Clarke, nvr far away, pushed alng aftr 3 out, sn outpcd, no imprsn frm last.
. . . . (4 to 1) 4
3634⁵ KING WILLIAM [102] 9-12-0 A Maguire, settled in last pl, blun second, outpcd 3 out, no dngr aftr.
. . . . (5 to 2 fav op 4 to 1 tchd 3 to 1) 5
3980⁵ FAUX PAVILLON [90] 10-11-2 M A FitzGerald, cl up, strug-gling to go pace aftr 3 out, fdd.
. . . . (9 to 1 op 11 to 4 tchd 100 to 30) 6
Dist: 1¼l, ¾l, 3½l, 4l, 12l. 4m 3.60s. a 13.60s (6 Ran).

(Elite Business Partners Ltd), D A Nolan

4081 Eastgate Novices' Chase (5-y-o and up) £1,198 2m 110yds. . . . . (3:15)

3931² SEON 8-12-2 A Maguire, jmpd wl, nvr far away, led 3 out, forged clr frm last. . . . . (5 to 4 fav op 11 to 8) 1
4039* CHIC AND ELITE 7-11-5 (6ex) M Dwyer, led, hdd 3 out, sn pushed alng, outpcd frm last. . . . . . (13 to 8 op 11 to 8) 2
3893 DOLITINO 10-10-13 Mr T Morrison, nvr far away, outpcd and rdn aftr 4 out, struggling after nxt.
. . . . (66 to 1 op 50 to 1) 3
1289 WSOM (Ire) 6-11-4 N Smith, hit 1st, beh and sn outpcd, shtlvd effrt frm rear aftr 4 out, then nxt, tld off.
. . . . (33 to 1 tchd 40 to 1) 4
4049 MASTER MATHEW 7-10-13 (5*) J Burke, in tch, struggling to keep up fnl circuit, tld off. . . . . . . (16 to 1 op 14 to 1) 5
4039² FLAXON WORRIOR 10-11-4 O Pears, wth ldr, blun 5th, 4th and losing grnd whn f 9th. . . . . (16 to 1) f
3959⁵ CROXDALE GREY 7-10-8 (5*) J Supple, not fluent, beh and sn struggling, tld off whn pld up bef 9th.
. . . . (8 to 1 tchd 10 to 1) pu
Dist: 12l, 20l, 7l, dist. 4m 0.40s. a 2.40s (7 Ran).

(C F Hunter Ltd), W Bentley

4082 Shire Selling Handicap Hurdle (4-y-o and up) £1,423 2m. . . . . (3:45)

3635 LODGING [71] 7-10-5⁵ M A FitzGerald, al hndy, improved to ld bef last, rdn and ran on strly. (10 to 1 op 8 to 1) 1
3959² GREENACRES LAD [90] 11-11-10 A Maguire, nvr far away, effrt and ev ch aftr 2 out, kpt on frm last, no chance wth wnr. (5 to 4 on tchd 11 to 10 on and 11 to 8 on) 2
3866⁷ AUSTHORPE SUNSET [90] (v) 10-11-10 Mr R Armson, taken early to post, chsd ldr, ev ch aftr 2 out, not quicken frm last. . . . . (11 to 2 op 9 to 2 tchd 6 to 1) 3
3139 CARLA ADAMS [66] 8-10-0 K Johnson, led, clr to 4th, hdd bef last, grad wknd. . . . . (14 to 1 op 20 to 1) 4
3981 TOLL BOOTH [66] 5-9-9 (5*) Mr D Parker, beh, steady hdwy frm 2 out, nrst finish. . . . . (33 to 1) 5
4047⁵ SWANK GILBERT [66] 8-10-0 Carol Cuthbert, in tch, rdn and outpcd appr 2 out, sn btn. . . . (33 to 1 op 50 to 1) 6
3285⁹ RUPERT STANLEY [66] 7-10-0⁵ (7*) S McDougall, beh, struggling to go pace fnl circuit, nvr a threat.
. . . . (6 to 1 op 33 to 1) 7
3139 BEACH PATROL (Ire) [66] (v) 6-10-0 B Storey, settled on ins, outpcd appr 3 out, tld off.
. . . . (9 to 1 op 8 to 1 tchd 10 to 1) 8
4025⁵ SUMMERS DREAM [66] 4-10-0 S Turner, chsd ldrs, drpd rear fnl circuit, sn struggling, tld off. . . . . (9 to 1) 9
3674 FEELING FRAYL [66] 7-9-10³ (7*) M Clarke, hld up, improved into midfield hfwy, outpcd frm 3 out, tld off.
. . . . (33 to 1) 10
Dist: 4l, 1¼l, 4l, 6l, 3l, 25l, 1l, 1¼l, sht-hd. 3m 49.00s. b 1.00s (10 Ran).

SR: 7/22/20/-/-/-/ (Mrs Jean Stapleton), B Ellison

4083 Ernst & Young Handicap Chase (0-115 5-y-o and up) £1,520 3m 1f. . . . . (4:15)

3908⁴ ZAM BEE [92] 8-11-10 A Dobbin, chsd ldr, chalg whn lft clr 5 out, unchlgd. . . . (6 to 5 fav op Evens tchd 5 to 4)

592

3814⁵ TRUELY ROYAL [89] 10-11-7 B Storey, *hndy, rdn and outpcd strtng fnl circuit, lft second 5 out, no imprsn.*
.................................(5 to 1 op 5 to 2) 2

4013⁴ RED UNDER THE BED [85] 7-10-12 (5*) J Burke, *hld up, mstk 7th, outpcd and rdn tenth, lft poor 3rd 5 out, some hdwy frm last, nvr dngrs.*
.................................(5 to 2 op 7 to 2 tchd 4 to 1) 3

4038⁵ TIBER MELODY [85] (bl) 11-11-3 A Maguire, *led, pressed whn f 5 out.*...................(10 to 1 op 12 to 1) f

Dist: 20l, 6l. 6m 23.10s. a 18.10s (4 Ran).

(J N Anthony), W G Reed

4084 Flying Ace Hunters' Chase (5-y-o and up) £1,660 2½m 110yds........(4:45)

HELLCATMUDWRESTLER 13-11-7 (7*) Miss T Gray, *made all, clr 4 out, unchlgd.*....................(8 to 1 op 10 to 1) 1

3989³ LINGHAM MAGIC 9-12-2 Mr S Swiers, *patiently rdn, shaken up to improve fnl circuit, styd on wl to go second nr finish.*....(11 to 8 fav op Evens tchd 6 to 4) 2

3909* UNOR (Fr) 8-12-2 (5*) Mr J M Dun, *in tch, effrt fnl circuit, wnt second aftr 2 out, one pace r-in.*
....................................(7 to 4 op 2 to 1 tchd 9 to 4) 3

LITTLE WENLOCK 10-11-7 (7*) Miss J Percy, *hld up, chsd wnr frm tenth, outpcd bef 2 out, fdd.*
.................................(33 to 1 op 25 to 1) 4

3947⁵ SNOWY RUN 13-11-7 (7*) Mr R Armson, *beh, pushed alng fnl circuit, nvr a threat.*............(14 to 1 op 16 to 1) 5

HYDROPIC 7-11-7 (7*) Mr J Beardsall, *beh, pushed alng fnl circuit, nvr able to chal, tld off.* (25 to 1 op 20 to 1) 6

3909 STONE ROW (Ire) 6-11-7 (7*) Mr A Manners, *pressed ldr, outpcd tenth, tld off.*...................(12 to 1) 7

ANZARNA 9-11-2 (7*) Mrs J Dun, *not fluent, al struggling in rear, tld off fnl circuit.*....................(33 to 1) 8

WITERO 11-11-7 (7*) Mr T Morrison, *not jump wl, beh, badly hmpd bef 5th.*.........................(50 to 1) 9

RAP UP FAST (USA) 5-11-0 (7*) Mr C Mulhall, *beh, hmpd bend bef 5th, sn struggling, tld off.*..........(33 to 1) 10

CAPTAIN CAVEMAN 9-11-7 (7*) Mr M Haigh, *towards rear whn slpd up bend bef 5th.*..................(50 to 1) su

NENNIUS 9-11-2 (7*) Miss P Robson, *sn lost tch, tld off whn pld up bef last.*.................(14 to 1 op 12 to 1) pu

Dist: 6l, ¾l, 20l, 3½l, 15l, dist, dist, 3l. 5m 5.70s. a 4.70s (12 Ran).

(Henry Bell), Henry Bell

CARTMEL (firm)
Monday May 30th
Going Correction: MINUS 0.45 sec. per fur.

4085 Burlington Slate Juvenile Maiden Hurdle (4-y-o) £2,262 2m 1f 110yds..(2:00)

3892³ COMMANCHE CREEK (bl) 11-0 R Dunwoody, *made all, pushed out r-in.*....(5 to 4 fav op 6 to 4 tchd Evens) 1

3925⁷ DON TOCINO 11-0 J F Titley, *cl up, niggled alng 2 out, no imprsn r-in.*....................(3 to 1 tchd 7 to 2) 2

DANCES WITH GOLD 10-4 (5*) Mr D Parker, *prmnt till lost pl hfwy, styd on one pace frm 2 out.*
....................................(12 to 1 tchd 14 to 1) 3

4025⁹ FANFOLD (Ire) 10-6 (3*) D J Moffatt, *hld up, styd on frm 3 out, nvr nrr.*....................(25 to 1 op 50 to 1) 4

4025³ TINSTONE 10-9 N Doughty, *slwly away, rear, prog 4th, rdn and wknd appr last.*............(7 to 1 op 8 to 1) 5

3892⁴ SUPREME SOVIET 11-0 A Dobbin, *prmnt, slwly lost pl, prog to join ldr 5th, pckd nxt, wknd appr last.*
....................................(11 to 2 op 9 to 2) 6

4040³ TASHREEF 11-0 D Wilkinson, *slwly away, refused 1st.*
....................................(12 to 1 op 10 to 1) ref

Dist: 6l, 6l, 2½l, 15l, 20l. 4m 0.90s. a 0.90s (7 Ran).

(Up The Creek Partners), J A Hellens

4086 Michael C. L. Hodgson Selling Handicap Hurdle (4,5,6-y-o) £2,122 2m 1f 110yds........................(2:35)

3819⁵ JOHN NAMAN (Ire) [87] 5-11-6 A Dobbin, *prog to track ldrs 5th, led aftr 2 out, pushed out.*.....(6 to 1 op 5 to 1) 1

4054⁴ SAOIRSE (Ire) [74] (v) 6-10-4 (3*) D J Moffatt, *in tch, chsd ldrs frm 5th, ran on to take second pl cl hme.*
....................................(9 to 1 op 8 to 1) 2

3983⁵ INAN (USA) [70] 5-9-10 (7*) K Davies, *prmnt, led 5th till aftr 2 out, kpt on one pace.*............(8 to 1, tchd 10 to 1) 3

3398 BALAAT (USA) [80] 6-10-13 W Worthington, *cl up till lost pl hfwy, styd on one pace frm 3 out.*(7 to 1 tchd 8 to 1) 4

3897 FELL WARDEN [70] 6-10-0 (3*) A Larnach, *al prmnt, chsd alng frm 3 out, kpt on one pace.*...(16 to 1 op 14 to 1) 5

4012 KISS IN THE DARK [67] 4-9-7 (7*) G Lee, *rear div, styd on one pace frm 3 out.*............(12 to 1 op 10 to 1) 6

3998³ MAGGIES LAD [71] (bl) 6-9-13 (5*) Mr D Parker, *prmnt till wknd hfwy.*.....................(10 to 1 op 8 to 1) 7

3773 SECRET CASTLE [69] 6-10-0³ (5*) R Waggott, *gd jump to track leaers second, ev ch 3 out, rdn and wknd nxt.*
....................................(33 to 1 op 20 to 1) 8

4025 BASSIO (Bel) [78] (bl) 5-10-11 N Doughty, *al rear.*
....................................(16 to 1 op 14 to 1) 9

3668* DANCING DANCER [75] (bl) 5-10-8 J Frost, *al rear.*
....................................(3 to 1 op 4 to 1) 10

3904⁶ SOVEREIGN NICHE (Ire) [95] (v) 6-12-0 R Dunwoody, *led till appr 5th, wknd nxt.*..........(7 to 4 fav op 5 to 2) 11

3895 GOLDEN REVERIE (USA) [68] 6-9-10 (5*) F Perratt, *al beh.*
....................................(25 to 1) 12

3635 CHILTERN HUNDREDS (USA) [69] 4-10-2² N Smith, *al rear.*
....................................(33 to 1 op 25 to 1) 13

3932 ALIZARI (USA) [67] (bl) 5-10-0 M Robinson, *rear, tld off whn pld up 2 out.*.................(33 to 1 op 20 to 1) pu

Dist: 1½l, 1¾l, 5l, 1¾l, 4l, 4l, 2½l, 7l, 5l. 3m 59.50s. b 0.50s (14 Ran).
SR: 18/3/-/2/-/-/

(G Breen), M A Barnes

4087 Burlington Slate Handicap Chase Amateur Riders (0-135 5-y-o and up) £2,697 2m 5f 110yds...........(3:10)

2832 CORRARDER [111] 10-10-10⁷ (7*) Mr J Smyth-Osbourne, *trkd ldrs, cld up 7th, led 4 out, rdn out r-in.*
....................................(11 to 4 op 7 to 1) 1

4053² DRUMSTICK [129] 8-11-9 (5*) Mr D Parker, *wtd wth, in tch, cld up 9th, chlgd r-in, no extr fnl hundred yards.*
....................................(7 to 4 on op 6 to 4 on) 2

3706⁵ IMPECCABLE TIMING [101] 11-10-0⁷ (7*) Mr A Mitchell, *beh, cl up 9th, rdn 3 out, styd on one pace.*
....................................(5 to 1 op 20 to 1) 3

4046⁵ BARKISLAND [101] 10-10-0 Mrs A Farrell, *dsptd ld till blun 7th, sn lost pl, beh frm 9th.*..........(7 to 1 op 6 to 1) 4

3978 MOLOJEC (Pol) [101] 13-9-11⁴ (7*) Mr J Culloty, *led or dsptd ld till 4 out, rdn alng and wkng 3rd whn f nxt.*
....................................(14 to 1 tchd 12 to 1) f

Dist: 3½l, 12l, dist. 5m 6.50s. b 5.50s (5 Ran).
SR: 40/54/14/-/-/

(Mrs E T Smyth-Osbourne), J A B Old

4088 Stanley Leisure Handicap Hurdle (0-125 4-y-o and up) £2,724 3¼m (3:45)

3784³ PORTONIA [108] 10-11-3 (7*) G Lee, *led second, made rst, ran on strly.*..................(4 to 1 tchd 5 to 1) 1

3919⁴ ANTI MATTER [89] 9-10-0 (5*) S Fox, *al prmnt, pressed ldr frm 4 out, ev ch last, no extr r-in.*.....(5 to 1 op 4 to 1) 2

3986* VALIANT DASH [95] 8-10-6 (5*) F Perratt, *nvr gng wl, pushed alng frm hfwy, rdn appr last, no imprsn.*
....................................(Evens fav op 5 to 4 on) 3

4072⁵ RECORD LOVER (Ire) [86] 4-10-2² W Worthington, *rear, cld up hfwy, effrt 2 out, wknd appr last.*
....................................(12 to 1 op 10 to 1) 4

3982³ CLASSIC STATEMENT [84] (bl) 8-10-0³ (3*) A Larnach, *led to second, remained cl up till rdn and wknd appr last.*
....................................(4 to 1 tchd 11 to 2) 5

3785⁵ JUSTICE LEA [84] 14-10-0 Carol Cuthbert, *beh frm hfwy, tld off frm 4 out.*..............(50 to 1 op 25 to 1) 6

Dist: 3½l, 4l, 7l, 2½l, dist. 5m 58.00s. (6 Ran).

(W H Strawson), Mrs M Reveley

4089 Victoria Trading Fruit Importers Ltd Novices' Chase (5-y-o and up) £2,397 2m 1f 110yds.................(4:20)

4046² BEAUCADEAU 8-11-12 A Dobbin, *hld up beh ldrs, cld up 4 out, led and lft clr 2 out, easily.*
....................................(5 to 4 on op 6 to 5 on) 1

4050⁴ MASTER'S CROWN (USA) 6-11-2 W Worthington, *pressed ldr, outpcd 5 out, styd on one pace frm 2 out.*
....................................(4 to 1 op 5 to 1 tchd 6 to 1) 2

4015² GRAZEMBER 7-11-12 P Niven, *in tch in rear, cld up 8th, kpt on one pace frm 3 out.*
....................................(2 to 1 tchd 7 to 4 and 9 to 4) 3

3882 NO WORD 7-11-2 J F Titley, *mstks 1st and second, led till hdd and f 2 out.*..................(11 to 1 op 7 to 1) f

Dist: 12l, 1½l. 4m 12.70s. b 0.30s (4 Ran).
SR: 22/-/8/-/

(T A Barnes), M A Barnes

4090 Trainer, Lawyer And Friends Novices' Hurdle (4-y-o and up) £1,968 2¾m ....(4:55)

3472⁴ KENILWORTH LAD 6-12-0 P Niven, *hld up in 3rd, cld up 4 out, led aftr 2 out, easily.*
....................................(11 to 10 fav op Evens tchd 5 to 4) 1

4048* RULLY 5-11-9 (5ex) W Worthington, *hld up in last, pushed into ld 4 out, hdd aftr 2 out, sn btn.* (7 to 2 op 4 to 1) 2

4027* MAMARA REEF (v) 4-10-7 (5*) P Waggott, *trkd ldr, rdn and wknd aftr 2 out.*.................(6 to 4 op 2 to 1) 3

4027⁶ THINK PINK 7-10-11 (7*) B Grattan, *led till aftr 4 out, sn wknd.*.........(25 to 1 op 20 to 1 tchd 33 to 1) 4

Dist: 15l, 4l, dist. 5m 18.00s. a 13.00s (4 Ran).

(David Bell), Mrs M Reveley

DOWN ROYAL (IRE) (good to firm)
Monday May 30th

4091 Dunmurry Maiden Hurdle (4-y-o and up) £1,370 3m.................(5:45)

3711⁵ AERODROME FIELD (Ire) 6-11-6 B Sheridan, ...(5 to 2 fav) 1

3954⁵ MISGIVINGS (Ire) 6-11-1 C F Swan, ...(3 to 1) 2
3840 MOLLIE WOOTTON (Ire) 6-11-1 W T Slattery Jnr, . .(25 to 1) 3
3793⁹ WARREN STREET (Ire) 4-10-12 M Duffy, ... (10 to 1) 4
1823 BAMANYAR (Ire) 6-11-7 (7") Mr J J Murphy, ...(4 to 1) 5
3811² WILLCHRIS 7-11-6 H Rogers, ...(8 to 1) 6
3793⁵ THE THIRD MAN (Ire) 5-11-2 (3") T P Treacy, ...(16 to 1) 7
3811³ GRANDOLLY (Ire) 5-10-11 (3") Mr B R Hamilton, . .(10 to 1) 8
3711 BETTYS THE BOSS (Ire) 6-11-9 F J Flood, ...(7 to 1) 9
4063 SLIM-N-LITE 8-10-12 (3") Mr P McMahon, ...(7 to 1) 10
3447 HALKMAN PRINCESS 8-10-8 (7") R J Gordon, . . .(25 to 1) 11
3813 MAIASAURA (Ire) 5-11-5 C N Bowens, ...(14 to 1) 12
3767 APARECIDA (Fr) 8-11-1 R Hughes, ...(10 to 1) f
3811⁴ PATS FAREWELL (Ire) 6-11-6 J Shortt, ...(9 to 1) pu
OLD KILMAINE 10-10-12 (3") K P Gaule, ... (20 to 1) pu
Dist: ½l, 9l, 8l, 5l. (Time not taken) (15 Ran).

(G Delahunt), Peter McCreery

4092 Belfast Vintners Maiden Hurdle (4-y-o and up) £1,370 2m. . . . .(6:15)

3993⁷ HUNCHEON CHANCE 4-10-8 (7") A P McCoy, ...(7 to 1) 1
3730³ PRINCE PERICLES (Ire) 5-11-5 J Shortt, ...(5 to 4 fav) 2
3973² MAY GALE (Ire) 6-11-1 C F Swan, ... (9 to 4) 3
1075 BOLERO DANCER (Ire) 6-11-7 (7") D J Kavanagh, (16 to 1) 4
3993⁸ INNOCENT MAN 4-11-1 L P Cusack, ...(8 to 1) 5
3953⁴ AMME ENAEK (Ire) 5-11-0 M Duffy, ...(12 to 1) 6
3072⁹ COURSING GLEN (Ire) 6-11-6 B Sheridan, ...(8 to 1) 7
GLENMAVIS 7-11-6 F J Flood, ...(20 to 1) 8
3869 START SINGING (Ire) 5-10-11 (3") T P Treacy, ...(10 to 1) 9
MON SHIQUE 7-11-6 C N Bowens, ...(25 to 1) 10
3448 ROCK SUPREME 7-10-13 (7") Mr L J Gracey, ...(25 to 1) 11
3993 FINAWAY LADY (Ire) 4-10-3 (7") M R Hunt, ...(20 to 1) 12
3069⁴ COTHU NA SLAINE (Ire) 4-10-10 H Rogers, ...(12 to 1) 13
Dist: Nk, 1½l, nk, 8l. (Time not taken) (13 Ran).

(Anthony McAleese), I R Ferguson

4093 Co Antrim Handicap Hurdle (0-109 4-y-o and up) £1,370 2m. . . . .(6:45)

3973⁴ IRON MARINER (Ire) [-] 6-11-0 (7") D M McCullagh, (6 to 1) 1
4043⁷ MARBLE FONTAINE [-] 7-10-13 C F Swan, ...(8 to 1) 2
3957⁷ VLADIMIR'S WAY (Ire) [-] 5-11-9 (5") Mr P M Kelly, . .(6 to 1) 3
3720⁴ MASTER MILLER [-] 8-11-2 (3") Mr B R Hamilton, . .(8 to 1) 4
3615 INAUGURATION (Ire) [-] 5-10-10 B Sheridan, ...(12 to 1) 5
4043⁶ NORDIC RACE [-] 7-10-10 W T Slattery Jnr, ...(10 to 1) 6
2842 FAIRY STRIKE (Ire) [-] 5-10-12 (7") B Bowens, ...(10 to 1) 7
3747 QUEEN PERSIAN [-] 7-10-3 (7") R Burke, ...(20 to 1) 8
3812⁹ ROSIN THE BOW (Ire) [-] (bl) 5-10-4 (7") P Morris, . .(20 to 1) 9
4030 THE WICKED CHICKEN (Ire) [-] 5-11-2 (3") T P Treacy,
. . . . (5 to 2 fav) 10
1549 STAR FLYER (Ire) [-] 6-10-8 (3") D Bromley, ...(20 to 1) 11
3246 TARDAGEE LADY (Ire) [-] 4-9-12 (7") R J Gordon, (33 to 1) 12
3723³ MRS COOPS [-] 7-10-11 J Shortt, ...(8 to 1) 13
1015* COQUALLA [-] (bl) 9-10-8 (7") Mr J P Geoghegan, . .(8 to 1) 14
3954 STRONG HURRICANE [-] 7-11-3 L P Cusack, ...(7 to 1) pu
Dist: 1½l, 3l, 4½l, 7l. (Time not taken) (14 Ran).

(D M McDonald), Michael McCullagh

4094 Guinness INH Flat Race (4-y-o and up) £1,370 2m. . . . . (8:15)

3797³ SHERS DELIGHT (Ire) 4-10-10 (7") Mr G F Ryan, (Evens fav) 1
3528 STORM POINT (Ire) 6-11-4 (7") Mr M T Dunne, ...(7 to 1) 2
4010 CONQUINN (Ire) 5-12-3 Mr P F Graffin, ...(4 to 1) 3
4063 ARCTIC TREASURE (Ire) 5-11-2 (3") Mr B R Hamilton,
. . . .(10 to 1) 4
4031 JUST 'R JAKE (Ire) 5-11-3 (7") Mr K Ross, ...(10 to 1) 5
MOORECHURCH GLEN 8-11-8 (3") Mr P McMahon, (20 to 1) 6
4034 TELEMAR (Ire) 5-10-12 (7") Mr J G Bates, ...(20 to 1) 7
PRIESTHILL (Ire) 5-11-3 (7") Mr L J Gracey, ...(25 to 1) 8
MADDYDOO (Ire) 6-11-4 (7") Mr R Marrs, ...(20 to 1) 9
DENDIEU (Ire) 5-11-7 (3") Mr J A Nash, ...(6 to 1) 10
JUST SUSIE (Ire) 5-10-12 (7") Mr C Rae, ...(20 to 1) 11
3506 DICK'S CABIN 7-11-4 (7") Mr M Wiseman, ...(9 to 1) l
Dist: Hd, 1l, 1l, 20l. (Time not taken) (12 Ran).

(G Reddin), A P O'Brien

FONTWELL (good to firm)
Monday May 30th
Going Correction: MINUS 0.15 sec. per fur.

4095 Ambrose Harcourt Hunters' Chase (5-y-o and up) £1,744 3¼m 110yds (2:00)

3991² SONOFAGIPSY 10-11-9 (5") Mr M Felton, prmnt, led 4 out,
chlgd 2 out, styd on. . . . . (11 to 4 op 7 to 2) 1
3918* SPRING FUN 11-12-0 (7") Mr M G Miller, al prmnt, chsd ldr
frm 7th to 17th, chlgd 4 out, kpt on same pace.
. . . . (7 to 2 tchd 5 to 1) 2
3854² ARTFUL ARTHUR 8-11-0 (7") Mr J Grassick, al in tch, rdn
and not quicken frm 17th, styd on frm 2 out.
. . . .(12 to 1 op 10 to 1 tchd 14 to 1) 3
3989⁵ KNOCKUMSHIN 11-12-2 (5") Mr T Byrne, effrt 5 out, rdn
nxt, one pace frm 2 out.
. . . .(5 to 2 fav tchd 11 to 4 and 9 to 4) 4

PRINCE ZEUS 15-11-0 (7") Mrs K Hills, in rear, styd on frm
2 out, nrst finish. . . . . .(25 to 1 op 14 to 1 tchd 33 to 1) 5
3948⁴ HIGHLAND SON 13-11-7 (7") Mr T Cox, chsd ldrs, mstk
15th, outpcd aftr nxt. . . . .(10 to 1 op 20 to 1) 6
EXPOUND (USA) 9-11-0 (7") Miss S Mitchell, in rear, mstk
13th, nvr a dngr. . . . .(66 to 1 op 20 to 1) 7
4022³ SKINNHILL 10-11-0 (7") Mr C Gordon, led 3rd, rdn frm
15th, hdd 4 out, sn wknd.
. . . .(16 to 1 op 20 to 1 tchd 25 to 1) 8
THE HUMBLE TILLER 11-11-0 (7") Miss J Waites, led to 3rd,
chsd ldr to 7th, lost pl 13th, tld off whn pld up bef 2 out.
. . . . (66 to 1 op 25 to 1) pu
RINGBOY 9-11-0 (7") Mr A Riley, al beh, tld off whn pld
up aftr 15th. . . . .(33 to 1 op 16 to 1) pu
COCK-OF-THE-ROCK 13-11-3³ (7") Miss Lucy Smith, al
beh, tld off whn pld up aftr 12th. . .(50 to 1 op 20 to 1) pu
3947⁴ MR MAYFAIR 11-11-0 (7") Mr M Portman, al beh, tld off
whn pld up bef 15th. (25 to 1 op 16 to 1 tchd 33 to 1) pu
3856² MAGICAL MORRIS 12-11-4 (3") Mr P Hacking, mstk 1st, al
beh, tld off whn pld up bef 3 out.
. . . .(9 to 1 op 5 to 1 tchd 10 to 1) pu
MR MCGREADY 11-11-0 (7") Mr M Gingell, al beh, tld off
bef being pld up 2 out. . . . .(66 to 1 op 33 to 1) pu
Dist: 1l, 5l, 20l, 7l, 2½l, 12l, 12l. 6m 46.30s. a 16.30s (14 Ran).

(Mrs B Whettam), J W Dufosee

4096 Southern FM News Selling Handicap Hurdle (4-y-o and up) £2,199 2¼m . . . .(2:30)

3977⁹ LUCAYAN GOLD [61] 10-10-0 D Morris, al in tch, hdwy frm
6th, led 2 out, pushed out. . . . .(14 to 1) 1
4052² HATS HIGH [76] 9-10-9 M Crosse, al prmnt, led 7th, hdd 2
out, one pace frm last. (10 to 1 op 8 to 1 tchd 12 to 1) 2
3843² WILTOSKI [77] (bl) 6-11-2 Mrs N Ledger, in tch, chsd ldr to
6th, not quicken nxt, kpt on appr last.
. . . .(10 to 1 op 11 to 1) 3
3940⁹ FIVE CASTLES [61] 6-9-11 (3") D Leahy, hld up, effrt 3 out,
not quicken frm nxt. . . . . . .(5 to 1 op 16 to 1 tchd 33 to 1) 4
4052³ KNIGHT IN SIDE [80] 8-11-5 W Irvine, mid-div, effrt 3 out,
nvr able to chal. . . . . (4 to 1 fav op 7 to 2) 5
4025⁶ CYRILL HENRY (Ire) [71] 5-10-10 B Powell, mid-div, hdwy
frm 5th, effrt 3 out, one pace. . . . (14 to 1 op 12 to 1) 6
3696 COBB GATE [77] (bl) 6-11-2 M Stevens, nvr a dngr.
. . . .(20 to 1 op 16 to 1) 7
3696 BAYLORD PRINCE (Ire) [80] 6-11-5 M Hoad, mid-div, rdn
frm 5th, nvr on terms. . . . .(10 to 1 op 7 to 1) 8
3940⁵ OTHET [72] 10-10-11 Peter Hobbs, in tch to 6th, sn wknd.
. . . .(20 to 1 op 16 to 1) 9
3940⁸ LUCKY OAK [61] (bl) 8-9-9 (5") C Burnett-Wells, nvr a factor. . . . .(8 to 1 op 10 to 1 tchd 7 to 1) 10
3980⁸ ACCESS SION [84] 7-11-2 (7") P Ward, chsd ldrs, mstk
second, wknd 3 out. . . . .(9 to 2 op 4 to 1) 11
3980 MILLY BLACK (Ire) [76] (bl) 6-11-1 P Holley, nvr on terms.
. . . .(12 to 1 tchd 14 to 1) 12
3845⁶ HIGHLAND BOUNTY [85] 10-11-10 D Gallagher, al beh.
. . . . (10 to 1 op 7 to 1) 13
3308 EDDIE WALSHE [77] 9-11-2 Leesa Long, led, hdd 3 out,
wknd appr 2 out. . . . . (16 to 1 op 12 to 1) 14
3545 ENBORNE LAD [63] (bl) 10-10-2 M Perrett, sn beh, struggling aftr 6th. . . . . . (25 to 1 op 16 to 1 tchd 33 to 1) 15
SERIOZHA [71] 11-10-3 (7") G Crone, mid-div, beh aftr 6th.
. . . .(25 to 1 op 20 to 1 tchd 33 to 1) 16
4052 HELLO SAM [78] 11-11-3 A Tory, chsd ldrs, mstk 4th, beh
whn pld up bef 2 out.
. . . .(12 to 1 op 14 to 1 tchd 16 to 1 and 10 to 1) pu
Dist: 8l, 3½l, ¾l, 3½l, 2½l, 2½l, 2½l, 1¾l, 2l, 3l. 4m 12.80s. a 2.80s (17 Ran).
SR: 17/18/21/4/19/7/10/10/-/ (Mrs E K Ellis), K Bishop

4097 Richard Gwynn Novices' Chase (5-y-o and up) £2,037 3¼m 110yds. . . . .(3:00)

4020* ROYAL SQUARE (Ire) 8-12-0 M Perrett, hld up, not fluent
3rd, hdwy strt, chsd ldrs 15th, led flt gmely.
. . . .(6 to 4 fav op Evens tchd 13 to 8) 1
3895³ JIM BOWIE 11-11-2 D Gallagher, led, clr 13th to 15th,
quickened and sn rdn, hdd flt, one pace.
. . . . (25 to 1 op 20 to 1 tchd 33 to 1) 2
3744² HOUSE OF ROSES (Ire) 6-11-2 G Bradley, chsd ldrs to 15th,
ev ch 4 out, one pace aftr.
. . . .(11 to 4 op 7 to 2 tchd 4 to 1) 3
3724 KILMYSHALL 8-10-13 (3") P Hide, chsd ldrs, rdn 16th,
outpcd 4 out, mstk 3 out, tld off.
. . . .(4 to 1 op 8 to 1 tchd 9 to 1) 4
3921* THEO'S FELLA 10-11-8 Peter Hobbs, in tch til 8th, rdn
14th, beh nxt, tld off whn pld up bef 4 out.
. . . .(5 to 1 op 5 to 2 tchd 11 to 2) pu
3764⁶ REAL HARMONY 8-11-2 B Powell, in tch, mstk 12th, beh
frm 15th, tld off and pld up bef 3 out.
. . . .(50 to 1 op 33 to 1) pu
Dist: 1¼l, 8l, dist. 6m 42.10s. a 12.10s (6 Ran).

(Park Farm Thoroughbreds), G Harwood

4098 Ted Triggs Memorial Challenge Cup Handicap Hurdle (0-115 4-y-o and up) £2,180 2¼m. . . . .(3:30)

3943 PONTOON BRIDGE [102] 7-11-10 M Perrett, *made virtually all, hdd briefly 3 out, rgned ld, clr 2 out, styd on wl*..........................(7 to 4 fav op 5 to 2) 1
3980⁴ LASSIE (Fr) [80] 5-10-2 D Gallagher, *chsd wnr, ev ch 3 out, sn and one pace*.....(9 to 2 op 4 to 1 tchd 6 to 1) 2
4066 PERSIAN LUCK [84] 8-10-3 (7ª) D Leahy, *chsd ldrs, ev ch 3 out, sn outpcd*..............(11 to 2 op 4 to 1) 3
3970 LLOYDS DREAM [78] 5-9-8 (5ª) D Fortt, *hld up, led and blun badly 3 out, not reco'r*........(4 to 1 op 5 to 1) 4
3729⁵ OH SO HANDY [78] 6-10-0 D Morris, *hld up, hdwy 6th, ev ch 3 out, sn outpcd*..........(8 to 1 tchd 7 to 1) 5
3924 STRIDING EDGE [86] (v) 9-10-8 B Powell, *beh frm 6th*.
...................(5 to 1 op 3 to 1 tchd 11 to 2) 6
Dist: 5l, 4l, 9l, 1l, 11l. 4m 14.20s. a 4.20s (6 Ran).
SR: 27/-/-/ (Peter Wiegand), G Harwood

4099 Lavington Challenge Cup Handicap Chase (0-125 5-y-o and up) £2,611 2 ¼m.......................... (4:00)

4067² GENERAL MERCHANT [97] (bl) 14-9-7 (7ª) Miss S Mitchell, *strted slwly, tld off to 9th, hdwy frm nxt, wnt second 2 out, ran on to ld flt*...................(13 to 2 op 4 to 1) 1
3941² GREEN WALK [97] 7-9-9 (5ª) C Burnett-Wells, *chsd ldrs, mstk 7th, led 8th, clr tenth, blun 2 out hdd flt*.
....................(7 to 1 op 8 to 1 tchd 10 to 1) 2
3943 ST ATHANS LAD [125] (bl) 9-12-0 D Morris, *led to 3rd, led 4th to aftr 8th, chsd ldrs till 2 out, wknd*.
.......................(6 to 4 op 7 to 4) 3
3941* I LIKE IT A LOT [97] 11-9-9 (5ª) Guy Lewis, *led 3rd to 4th, chsd ldr to 8th, lost tch frm tenth, pld up bef 3 out.
...............(5 to 4 fav op 11 to 10 tchd 11 to 8) pu
Dist: 2l, 2l. 4m 27.30s. a 7.30s (4 Ran).
(Mrs Susan Tate), R J Hodges

4100 Chris And Nicky Breakfast Show Novices' Hurdle (4-y-o and up) £1,553 2 ¾m.......................... (4:30)

3943² ESPRIT DE FEMME (Fr) 8-10-9 Peter Hobbs, *made all, quickened clr 2 out, cmftbly*.....(5 to 4 fav op 2 to 1) 1
2845⁶ OXFORD QUILL 7-11-0 D Morris, *prmnt frm 3rd, chsd wnr from 4th to 6th, outpcd from 2 out.
....................(10 to 1 op 8 to 1 tchd 11 to 1) 2
3938* CHINAMAN 5-11-6 A Tory, *prmnt, chsd wnr to 6th, one pace frm 3 out*........(7 to 4 op 6 to 4 tchd 2 to 1) 3
3943⁶ WOODLANDS BOY (Ire) 6-11-6 M Hoad, *in tch, effrt 3 out, sn outpcd*...................(10 to 1 op 6 to 1) 4
4003⁷ MISS PARKES 5-10-4 (5ª) D Fortt, *chsd wnr second to 3rd, tld off frm out, tld off*........(100 to 1 op 33 to 1) 5
345 THE FRUIT 15-11-0 Mrs N Ledger, *prmnt to 6th, sn lost pl, tld off frm 8th*.................(100 to 1 op 33 to 1) 6
ANNIE'S ARTHUR (Ire) 5-11-0 B Powell, *al beh, tld off frm 8th*...........(100 to 1 op 66 to 1 tchd 125 to 1) 7
3716⁶ NOTED STRAIN (Ire) 6-10-7 (7ª) Miss S Mitchell, *reluctant to race, mid-div and effrt 8th, wknd 2 out, tld off.
.................(100 to 1 op 33 to 1) 8
3970⁵ SCOTTISH BALL 5-10-9 M Crosse, *chsd wnr to second, beh frm 3rd, tld off whn pld up aftr 7th.
.....................(10 to 1 op 8 to 1) pu
Dist: 7l, 1¼l, 3½l, 25l, 30l, 4l, ½l. 5m 18.50s. a 9.50s (9 Ran).
(Mrs L R Browning), D W Browning

HEREFORD (good to firm)
Monday May 30th
Going Correction: MINUS 0.20 sec. per fur.

4101 Madley Novices' Hurdle (4-y-o and up) £1,833 2m 1f................... (2:30)

3209² GESNERA 6-10-11 (7ª) P McLoughlin, *hld up, al gng wl, led appr 3 out, rdn approaching last, ran on well.
.......................(7 to 4 on tchd 13 to 8 on) 1
3806⁵ TENAYESTELIGN 6-10-9 (3ª) J McCarthy, *hld up in tch, gd hdwy to chal 2 out, hrd rdn and slight mstk last, no extr r-in*...................(15 to 8 op 6 to 4) 2
3876⁴ FREDDIE JACK (bl) 4-10-12 S Burrough, *trkd ldr to 3rd, outpcd appr 3 out, sn beh.
....................(12 to 1 op 16 to 1 tchd 10 to 1) 3
3928⁸ LAURA 5-10-9 (3ª) T Jenks, *trkd ldr frm 3rd, led briefly 5th till outpcd appr 3 out*........(25 to 1 tchd 33 to 1) 4
3874 SPIKE 4-10-12 M Bosley, *led, briefly hdd whn mstk 6th, headed and wkng when blun and uns rdr 3 out.
.......................(50 to 1 op 25 to 1) ur
4003 STARSHADOW 5-10-10 (7ª) Mr E James, *not jump wl, outpcd frm 6th, tld off whn blun and uns rdr last.
.......................(66 to 1 op 33 to 1) ur
Dist: 1½l, 25l, sht-hd. 4m 0.40s. a 14.40s (6 Ran).
(Mrs V M Biggs), K White

4102 Edwardian Handicap Chase (0-125 5-y-o and up) £2,723 2m 3f...... (3:00)

3929³ LOR MOSS [88] 14-10-6¹ M A FitzGerald, *led to second, led 4th till appr 6th, rdn to ld 2 out, ran on strly.
.......................(7 to 2 op 9 to 2) 1

M I BABE [110] 9-11-7 (7ª) Mr C Vigors, *al prmnt, led appr 6th, clr 8th, rdn and hdd 2 out, one pace.
.......................(4 to 1 op 3 to 1) 2
4018⁵ NOS NA GAOITHE [99] (v) 11-11-0 (3ª) J McCarthy, *al in tch, ev ch 3 out, one pace frm nxt*........(8 to 1 op 4 to 1) 3
4020² DUNKERY BEACON [82] 8-9-7 (7ª) P McLoughlin, *hld up, hdwy 7th, one pace frm 3 out.
.......................(15 to 2 op 7 to 1 tchd 8 to 1) 4
4028³ CHIASSO FORTE (Ity) [94] 11-10-12 A Merrigan, *not jump wl, al beh, tld off*.......(6 to 1 op 5 to 1 tchd 10 to 1) 5
1591⁵ MARKET LEADER [84] 14-10-2 R Greene, *in rear, outpcd frm 8th, tld off*......(10 to 1 op 12 to 1 tchd 11 to 1) 6
3492 MCMAHON'S RIVER [88] 7-10-6 V Slattery, *in tch to 5th, sn beh, tld off*.........................(33 to 1 op 14 to 1) 7
3847⁷ SOCKS DOWNE [83] 15-10-14 (3ª) R Davis, *led second to 4th, wknd 6th, tld off*.......(25 to 1 op 14 to 1) 8
3776³ WICKFIELD LAD [89] 11-10-7 S Earle, *al towards rear, outpcd frm 8th, tld off whn pld up bef last.
.......................(5 to 2 fav op 3 to 1) pu
Dist: 6l, 3l, ½l, 30l, nk, dist, 20l. 4m 32.20s. a 2.20s (9 Ran).
SR: 18/34/20/2/-/-/ (S G Griffiths), S G Griffiths

4103 Clive Maiden Hunters' Chase (5-y-o and up) £1,329 3m 1f 110yds.... (3:30)

3988² WINNIE LORRAINE 9-11-2 (7ª) Mr P Henley, *al prmnt, led 5 out, hld nxt, upsides whn outjmpd last, rallied gmely to ld on line*..........(100 to 30 op 5 to 2 tchd 7 to 2) 1
3969⁴ DUBIT 9-11-7 (7ª) Miss S Vickery, *hld up, hdwy 11th, led 4 out, hrd rdn and hdd on line*.......(7 to 2 tchd 3 to 1) 2
3987³ BUTTERLEY BOY 11-11-7 (7ª) Mr M Harris, *in rear till hdwy 13th, styd on, nvr nrr*..........(8 to 1 op 7 to 1) 3
3987 ADAMARE 10-11-7 (7ª) Mr B Pollock, *not fluent, al prmnt, led tenth to 5 out, wknd appr 3 out.
.......................(2 to 1 fav op 5 to 2 tchd 11 to 4) 4
3992⁵ CANTANTIVY 9-11-2 (7ª) Mr R Johnson, *chsd ldrs, one pace frm 4 out*.......................(20 to 1 op 12 to 1) 5
4068 FOWLING PIECE 9-11-7 (7ª) Mr A Sansome, *al towards rear, lost tch 14th, tld off*................(16 to 1 op 8 to 1) 6
3920 INDIAN KNIGHT 9-11-7 (7ª) Mr C Vigors, *mid-div till lost tch frm 13th, tld off*..........(14 to 1 op 8 to 1) 7
LAKENHEATHER (NZ) 8-11-7 (7ª) Mr C Morlock, *beh frm 12th, tld off whn f last*...........(50 to 1 op 33 to 1) f
3998⁸ KNOWAFENCE 8-11-2 (7ª) Mr S Howe, *sn tld off, blun and uns rdr tenth*..............(50 to 1 op 33 to 1) ur
3947⁶ ROMAN WOOD 11-11-2 (7ª) Mrs T Hill, *lost to 4th, wknd 11th, tld off whn pld up bef 3 out*. (16 to 1 op 10 to 1) pu
3950 LADDIE BALLINGER 12-11-7 (7ª) Dr P Pritchard, *prmnt to 13th, tld off whn pld up bef last*...(50 to 1 op 33 to 1) pu
3947⁸ RYTON RUN 9-11-7 (7ª) Mr R Lawther, *in tch till outpcd 9th, wknd 11th, tld off whn pld up bef 2 out.(14 to 1 op 10 to 1) pu
DANDY REASON 10-11-7 (7ª) Mr C Stockton, *led 4th to tenth, wknd quickly four out, pld up bef 2 out.
.......................(14 to 1 op 25 to 1 tchd 12 to 1) pu
BANTABA 8-11-2 (7ª) Miss S Baskerville, *beh, tld off whn pld up bef 12th*................(33 to 1 op 20 to 1) pu
HANDSOME HARVEY 8-11-7 (7ª) Mr J Jukes, *al beh, tld off whn pld up bef last*......(10 to 1 op 8 to 1) pu
MISTER JOE 7-11-7 (7ª) Mr M Smith, *al beh, tld off whn pld up bef 12th*.............(50 to 1 op 33 to 1) pu
Dist: Sht-hd, 12l, ¾l, 8l, 25l, 10l. 6m 19.20s. a 7.20s (16 Ran).
(Mrs S Fry), H Wellstead

4104 Stoke Edith Selling Hurdle (4-y-o and up) £1,763 2m 1f.............. (4:00)

3998 THANKS A MILLION 8-10-9 (3ª) R Davis, *hld up, gd hdwy to ld appr 2 out, ran on wl*......(33 to 1 op 20 to 1) 1
3965² MINI FETE (Fr) 5-10-12 R Greene, *al prmnt, outpcd appr 3 out, rallied and ev ch nxt, hrd rdn, one pace.
.......................(15 to 8 fav op 5 to 2 tchd 7 to 4) 2
4052⁷ MOST INTERESTING 9-11-5 (7ª) Mr R Johnson, *nvr far away, ev ch 3 out, wknd last*..(100 to 30 op 5 to 2) 3
4052 ALWAYS READY (bl) 8-11-10 (7ª) J Bond, *led second till hdd appr 2 out, wknd*..........(100 to 30 op 5 to 2) 4
3977⁵ SNICKERSNEE 6-11-3 M A FitzGerald, *chsd ldrs, one pace frm 3 out*....................(7 to 1 tchd 9 to 1) 5
4051⁴ MY SISTER LUCY (bl) 4-11-0 S Burrough, *al in chasing grp, no hdwy frm 6th*............(6 to 1 tchd 7 to 1) 6
4052 HAPPY DEAL (bl) 8-11-3 T Wall, *hld up in tch, wnt second briefly 6th, rdn and wknd 4 out*......(20 to 1 op 12 to 1) 7
3715 FORGED PUNT 7-11-3 R Bellamy, *chsd ldrs till wknd 5th, tld off*.........................(50 to 1 op 33 to 1) 8
3977 HEAD OF DEFENCE (bl) 9-10-10 (7ª) P McLoughlin, *al in rear, tld off*..................(20 to 1 op 25 to 1) 9
3975⁷ DARKTOWN STRUTTER (bl) 8-11-3 Tracy Turner, *wl beh frm 5th, tld off*........(33 to 1 op 25 to 1) 10
CATHOS (Fr) 9-10-10 (7ª) N Juckes, *slwly away, nvr got into race, tld off*...............(14 to 1 op 10 to 1) 11
3843 ON THE LEDGE (USA) 4-10-6¹ (7ª) M Appleby, *not jump wl, al beh, tld off*..............(50 to 1 op 25 to 1) 12
3879⁶ LA BELLE OF SANTO 11-11-5 J Da Costa, *chsd ldrs till wknd 5th, tld off*..............(50 to 1 op 25 to 1) 13
3878 MARANO (bl) 6-11-3 V Slattery, *led to second, wknd 5th, tld off whn pld up bef 2 out*.......(16 to 1 op 10 to 1) pu
3559 BURFORDS DELIGHT 5-10-5 (7ª) Miss S Duckett, *al beh, tld off whn pld up bef 2 out*..........(20 to 1 op 14 to 1) pu

Dist: 3½l, 8l, 1l, 9l, ¾l, 1½l, 15l, 7l, 6l, 12l. 3m 54.00s. a 8.00s (15 Ran).

(R N Short), N B Thomson

4105 Eaton Bishop Novices' Chase (5-y-o and up) £2,481 2m.............(4:35)

3931⁶ PALACE WOLF (NZ) 10-11-4 M A FitzGerald, *wtd wth in tch, chlgd 3 out, led appr last, ran on.*
....(6 to 1 op 5 to 1) 1
3879⁴ PECCAVI 10-11-4 R Bellamy, *led to 3rd, led 6th, already hdd whn rdn and mstk last, one pace.*
....(6 to 1 op 5 to 1) 2
3931 CRAFTY CHAPLAIN 8-11-11 (5*) Mr D McCain, *hld up, hdwy 7th, ev ch 3 out, rdn and sn btn.*.........(3 to 1) 3
3979² KIBREET 7-12-2 S Earle, *trkd ldrs, not fluent, lost tch aftr 4 out....*(6 to 4 on op 11 to 8 on tchd 5 to 4 on) 4
4005⁴ PECHE D'OR (bl) 10-11-1 (3*) T Jenks, *led 3rd to 6th, wknd quickly 4 out.........*(16 to 1 op 12 to 1 tchd 20 to 1) 5
3965 OZONE LASS (Ire) 6-10-13 Mr M Smith, *slwly away, sn tld off, blun and uns rdr 8th........*(100 to 1 op 50 to 1) ur
3639⁶ WETANDRY 9-11-4 V Slattery, *jmpd badly lft, tld off 5th, pld up bef 3 out.................*(100 to 1 op 50 to 1) pu
Dist: 4l, 12l, 12l, 20l. 3m 54.10s. a 5.10s (7 Ran).

SR: 7/3/3/-/ (Michael H Watt), Miss H C Knight

4106 Carey Handicap Hurdle (0-110 4-y-o and up) £2,421 2m 3f 110yds... (5:05)

4054⁴ SYDNEY BARRY (NZ) [80] 9-10-9 M A FitzGerald, *al gng wl, led 7th, clr 2 out, very easily....* (6 to 4 fav op 7 to 4) 1
4064⁶ DARK DESIRE [86] 8-10-12 (3*) J McCarthy, *led 1st to 7th, outpcd 3 out, rallied to go second last, no ch wth wnr.*
....(5 to 1 op 7 to 2) 2
3773³ FRENDLY FELLOW [71] (bl) 10-10-0 J Lodder, *in tch, wnt second appr 3 out, btn whn wknd last.*
....(4 to 1 tchd 9 to 2) 3
4004⁸ APACHEE FLOWER [71] 4-9-7 (7*) P McLoughlin, *mid-div, rdn appr 7th, no hdwy frm 4 out...*(14 to 1 op 10 to 1) 4
3820⁵ MOUNTSHANNON [95] 8-11-10 Peter Caldwell, *al beh, lost tch frm 6th...............................*(5 to 1 op 9 to 2) 5
3831 ECOSSAIS DANSEUR (USA) [78] 8-10-4 (3*) R Davis, *sn trkd ldr, wknd quickly appr 3 out....*(16 to 1 op 10 to 1) 6
4064 FRANK DALE [71] 11-9-7 (7*) Mr R Johnson, *chsd ldrs, wknd whn hit 7th...................*(25 to 1 op 14 to 1) 7
958⁴ BY FAR (USA) [80] 8-10-9 V Slattery, *al beh, tld off whn pld up bef last...............*(13 to 2 op 5 to 1) pld
3931 TAURIAN PRINCESS [72] 5-10-1 D J Burchell, *led till jmpd slwly 1st, hit 4th, sn in rear, tld off whn pld up bef 3 out...................*(25 to 1 op 14 to 1) pu
Dist: 8l, 3½l, 12l, 7l, 15l, 3l. 4m 32.70s. a 11.70s (9 Ran).

(Peter Jones), R H Buckler

HUNTINGDON (good to firm)
Monday May 30th
Going Correction: MINUS 0.35 sec. per fur.

4107 East Midlands Electricity Novices' Selling Handicap Hurdle (4-y-o and up) £1,984 2m 110yds.........(2:00)

3354³ SPIRITUALIST [70] 8-10-12 O Pears, *made all, sn clr, ran on wl frm 2 out, unchlgd.*
...............................(12 to 1 op 8 to 1 tchd 14 to 1) 1
3822⁵ SOUTHAMPTON [70] 4-10-12 A Maguire, *chsd ldrs, chased wnr frm 2 out, sn no imprsn....*(3 to 1 jt-fav op 5 to 2) 2
1253 DOCTOR-J (Ire) [58] 4-10-0 W McFarland, *al prmnt, one pace frm 2 out....................*(20 to 1 op 10 to 1) 3
3914³ JOHNS JOY [82] 9-11-10 D O'Sullivan, *al prmnt, styd on one pace frm 2 out..............*(9 to 1 op 5 to 1) 4
3770⁵ SKIMMER HAWK [65] 5-10-7 V Smith, *hld up, effrt 3 out, sn no imprsn...................*(20 to 1 op 10 to 1) 5
4003³ MAHONG [63] 6-10-5 L Harvey, *nvr on terms.*
.............................(11 to 2 op 6 to 1 tchd 5 to 1) 6
3965³ DESERT PEACE (Ire) [78] 5-11-6 G McCourt, *prmnt, outpcd aftr 4 out....................*(9 to 2 op 5 to 2) 7
4025² WATER DIVINER [69] 4-10-11 J Ryan, *cl up to 5th.*
...................(4 to 1 jt-fav op 7 to 2 tchd 9 to 2) 8
2424⁵ PEARLY WHITE [58] 5-9-7 (7*) Miss S Higgins, *al beh, tch frm 4th, tld off..................*(25 to 1 op 16 to 1) 9
3770 SOLO CORNET [58] 9-10-0 W Humphreys, *al beh, tld off frm 5th........................*(40 to 1 op 25 to 1) 10
3886 THE FUN OF IT [62] (bl) 9-10-4 G Upton, *beh, rapid hdwy aftr 3rd, sn wknd, tld off whn pld up bef 3 out.*
.........(16 to 1 op 25 to 1 tchd 33 to 1 and 10 to 1) pu
Dist: 14l, ¾l, nk, 14l, 20l, 3½l, 7l. 3m 51.00s. a 4.00s (11 Ran).

(Mrs G S Plowright), Mrs G S Plowright

4108 Willmott Dixon Novices' Handicap Chase (5-y-o and up) £2,363 3m (2:30)

3844³ VICAR OF BRAY [71] (v) 7-10-8 A Maguire, *cl up, gd jump to ld 15th, hld betw last 2, edgd lft and kpt on wl und pres aftr last..................*(7 to 4 op 6 to 4 tchd 2 to 1) 1

4026² WE'RE IN THE MONEY [65] (bl) 10-10-2 B Dalton, *wtd wth, jmpd slwly 4th, cld 8th, led betw last 2, ev ch whn edgd rght and not quicken r-in.*
...........................(13 to 8 fav op 7 to 4 tchd 15 to 8) 2
GILT BRONZE [63] (bl) 10-10-0 D Skyrme, *cl up, reminders 12th, sn outpcd, tld off....................*(7 to 1 op 4 to 1) 3
4055³ HOWARYAFXD [87] 7-11-10 J Osborne, *led, hdd 15th, sn wknd, tld off......................*(4 to 1 tchd 7 to 2) 4
4002⁵ LAD LANE [63] (bl) 10-10-0 W Macfarland, *nvr gng wl, tld off frm 11th........................*(33 to 1 op 20 to 1) 5
Dist: 1l, dist, 25l, 2½l. 5m 55.00s. a 7.00s (5 Ran).

(The Cleric Partnership), G B Balding

4109 East Midlands Electricity Handicap Chase (0-115 5-y-o and up) £2,883 2m 110yds.....................(3:05)

3847⁶ DRIVING FORCE [108] (bl) 8-11-13 G McCourt, *wtd wth, cld 3 out, outpcd appr nxt, rallied und pres and styd on to ld aftr last......................*(5 to 1 op 7 to 2) 1
3963² CLARES OWN [102] 10-11-7 A Maguire, *led, hdd 2 out, rallied aftr last, ran on.*
............................(5 to 4 on op Evens tchd 5 to 4) 2
4005⁵ VICTORY ANTHEM [81] 8-10-0 I Lawrence, *trkd ldg pair, wnt second 8th, pushed alng 3 out, led nxt, hdd aftr last, no extr.............*(9 to 2 op 4 to 1 tchd 5 to 1) 3
3979³ DEEP DARK DAWN [105] 9-11-10 R Supple, *hld up, cld 7th, ev ch last, one pace............*(5 to 1 op 4 to 1) 4
3959⁹ POLDER [81] 8-9-7 (7*) Miss S Higgins, *wth ldr to 8th, outpcd aftr 3 out..................*(50 to 1 op 25 to 1) 5
3847 STRANGELY QUIET [81] 12-10-0 L Harvey, *lost tch aftr 4th, tld off...........................*(20 to 1 tchd 25 to 1) 6
Dist: 2l, nk, 2l, 14l, 30l. 3m 58.00s. (6 Ran).

SR: 41/33/11/33/-/-/ (B J Reid), Mrs M McCourt

4110 Qualitair Success Handicap Hurdle (0-130 4-y-o and up) £2,337 2m 5f 110yds.....................(3:45)

3903² THE PRUSSIAN (USA) [96] 8-11-1 J Ryan, *hld up in tch, cld aftr 4 out, hdwy to ld 2 out. ran on wl.*
....(5 to 1 tchd 11 to 2) 1
3752* JAWANI (Ire) [105] 6-11-10 G McCourt, *trkd ldg pair, hdwy to ld aftr 4 out, hdd 2 out, one pace.*
..........................(11 to 4 fav op 3 to 1 tchd 4 to 1) 2
3831² KAYTAK (Fr) [103] (v) 7-11-8 A Maguire, *trkd ldrs, one pace appr 2 out...................*(4 to 1 op 3 to 1) 3
3938³ POLISH RIDER (USA) [62] 6-10-4 (7*) C Huggan, *hld up in rear, effrt appr 4 out, sn one pace.*
..............................(9 to 1 op 8 to 1 tchd 10 to 1) 4
3982⁵ ASK THE GOVERNOR [95] 8-11-0 J Osborne, *hld up, pushed alng 5th, sn outpcd, tld off.*
....(6 to 1 tchd 13 to 2) 5
3932³ PYRRHIC DANCE [83] 4-10-2 W McFarland, *not fluent, wth ldr, blun 7th and lost pl, tld off.*
....(8 to 1 tchd 10 to 1) 6
2216² ALREEF [95] (v) 8-11-0 S Smith Eccles, *led, not fluent 6th, hdd aftr 4 out, wknd quickly, 5th and no ch whn f last.*
....(11 to 2 op 6 to 1) f
3728⁷ STRAIGHT LACED (USA) [81] (bl) 7-10-0 I Lawrence, *hld up in tch, outpcd 4 out, pld up bef 2 out.*
....(50 to 1 op 33 to 1) pu
Dist: 2½l, 6l, 12l, dist, dist. 4m 55.00s. (8 Ran).

SR: 12/18/10/-/-/ (First In Racing Partnership), K G Wingrove

4111 East Midlands Electricity, Mencap Novices' Chase (6-y-o and up) £2,087 2½m 110yds.....................(4:15)

3882* CROOKED COUNSEL 8-12-3 A Maguire, *made all, lft clr 5 out, jmpd left last, easily....*(6 to 5 on op 7 to 4) 1
3755 SASKIA'S HERO 7-11-3 R Marley, *chsd wnr, drw level 9th, lft second 5 out, sn no imprsn....*(10 to 1 tchd 12 to 1) 2
3998⁵ APPLIANCEOFSCIENCE 7-11-3 J Ryan, *lost tch aftr 8th, lft modest 3rd 5 out...*(15 to 2 op 8 to 1 tchd 10 to 1) 3
3639* PINISI (bl) 9-11-10 B Dalton, *not fluent 5th, drw level 9th, cl second and ev ch whn f 5 out.......*(7 to 4 op 2 to 1) f
4055⁶ CHEQUE BOOK 6-11-3 Mr D Verco, *hld up, blun and uns rdr 8th.................*(25 to 1 op 33 to 1 tchd 50 to 1) ur
Dist: 15l, 1½l. 5m 0.00s. a 5.00s (5 Ran).

(I R Scott & D J MacFarlane), K C Bailey

4112 Qualitair Supreme Maiden Hurdle (4-y-o and up) £2,045 2m 110yds... (4:45)

4021⁵ MARROB 7-11-5 G McCourt, *mid-div, cld appr 4th, led 3 out, sn hrd rdn, jnd nxt, ran on wl und pres, fnshd lme.*
....(9 to 2 op 5 to 1) 1
3539⁵ SALDA 5-11-5 W Humphreys, *keen hold, trkd ldrs, jnd wnr 2 out, ev ch r-in, kpt on....*(16 to 1 op 14 to 1) 2
3878⁶ BRIMPTON BERTIE 5-11-5 G Upton, *al hndy, outpcd appr 3 out, styd on frm last.............*(14 to 1 op 10 to 1) 3
3964³ BATHWICK BOBBIE 7-11-5 A Maguire, *al cl up, led aftr 4 out to 3 out, sn hrd rdn and one pace.*
....(7 to 2 op 3 to 1 tchd 4 to 1) 4
3915⁷ FAIR ENCHANTRESS (bl) 6-11-0 L Harvey, *beh, rdn and cld 3 out, one pace nxt.................*(33 to 1 op 20 to 1) 5

3829 THE MINE CAPTAIN 7-11-5 E Murphy, *beh, effrt appr 5th,*
nvr on terms. . . . . (16 to 1 op 8 to 1) 6
3886⁷ NIGEL'S LUCKY GIRL 6-11-0 J McLaughlin, *led, hdd aftr 4*
out, sn wknd. . . . . (10 to 1 op 8 to 1) 7
2645⁷ LORD NASKRA (USA) 5-11-5 Mr I McLelland, *al beh, lost*
tch 5th, tld off. . . . . (10 to 1 op 8 to 1) 8
3231 ELEGANT STYLE 4-10-9 M Ahern, *mid-div, lost tch 5th,*
tld off. . . . . (33 to 1) 9
3965 CRYMLYN SWING (bl) 10-11-0 Mr D Verco, *al beh, lost tch*
5th, tld off. . . . . (50 to 1 op 33 to 1) 10
4011³ JUNO'S SPECIAL (Ire) 6-10-7 (7*) M Harris, *rear whn blun*
sn rdr 3rd. . . . . (1 to 1 op 25 to 1 tchd 40 to 1) ur
4003² EARLY DRINKER 6-11-5 J Osborne, *trkd ldrs, wknd*
quickly aftr 4 out, pld up bef 2 out.
. . . . (5 to 4 fav op 6 to 4 tchd 5 to 2) pu
4003⁸ BEN CONNAN (Ire) 4-11-0 W McFarland, *al beh, lost tch*
5th, tld off whn pld up bef 2 out. . . . . (33 to 1) pu
Dist: Hd, 6l, 3l, 4l, 15l, 1½l, 11l, 25l, 1l. 3m 50.00s. a 3.00s (13 Ran).
SR: 3/3/-/-/-/-/ (R N C Lynch), R Akehurst

KILBEGGAN (IRE) (good to firm)
Monday May 30th

4113 Brusna Claiming Maiden Hurdle (5-y-o and up) £2,228 2m 3f. . . . . . . (5:30)

3366 VITAL TRIX 7-10-13 A Powell, ... (12 to 1) 1
3719⁹ GONE BY (Ire) 6-11-0 C O'Dwyer, ... (5 to 4 fav) 2
3974* MILLER'S CROSSING 7-10-13 Mr T Doyle, ... (6 to 1) 3
4030⁴ PEACE TRIBUTE (Ire) 5-10-12 (3*) J P Broderick, . . (6 to 1) 4
BONNY'S GAME 6-11-4 (5*) D P Geoghegan, ... (33 to 1) 5
3469 FRENCH MYLE (Ire) 6-11-2 J P Banahan, ... (33 to 1) 6
4031⁷ HOLLOW SOUND (Ire) 5-10-8 K F O'Brien, ... (14 to 1) 8
3366 DESPERATE DAYS 5-11-1 S R Murphy, ... (16 to 1) 9
3911 BAR LASS 7-10-6 (3*) D P Murphy, ... (33 to 1) 10
3611⁹ CASTLE UNION 7-10-7 (3*) T P Rudd, ... (33 to 1) 11
SWINGING SARI (Ire) 5-10-8 S H O'Donovan, ... (25 to 1) 12
503⁸ WEDDING DREAM (Ire) 5-10-6 (3*) D T Evans, ... (33 to 1) 13
OPIUM LASS (Ire) 6-10-9 F Woods, ... (33 to 1) 14
3912 HILARY'S IMAGE (Ire) 5-10-8 P L Malone, ... (16 to 1) 15
3793 JODONLEE (Ire) 5-10-13 (3*) T J Mitchell, ... (10 to 1) 17
3794 PUSH GENTLY (Ire) (bl) 5-10-5 (7*) P A Roche, . . . (33 to 1) 17
INDIANA GOLD (Ire) 4-10-7 (7*) B D Murtagh, . . . (16 to 1) 18
Dist: Sht-hd, 11l, 2l, 6l. 4m 29.70s. (18 Ran).
(Thomas Matthews), Thomas Matthews

4114 Horse Leap Maiden Hurdle (5-y-o and up) £2,228 2m 3f. . . . . (6:00)

3957⁸ CELTIC GALE 7-11-2 (7*) Mr T J Beattie, ... (5 to 1) 1
3954⁴ CORRIB HAVEN (Ire) 6-11-3 (3*) J P Broderick, . (5 to 4 fav) 2
4030⁸ JIMMY GORDON 7-11-11 (3*) T J Mitchell, ... (16 to 1) 3
3913 MOOREFIELD GIRL (Ire) 5-11-8 M Moran, ... (8 to 1) 4
2939 MANTAS MELODY (Ire) 6-10-12 (3*) C O'Brien, . . (12 to 1) 5
3840 SILENTBROOK 9-10-8 (7*) Mr J A Collins, ... (16 to 1) 6
3366 BOB MONEY (Ire) 6-11-6 D H O'Connor, ... (10 to 1) 7
3788 SLANEY AGAIN (Ire) 6-10-13 (7*) Miss L E A Doyle, (14 to 1) 8
3834 COOL MOSS 8-11-9 (5*) P A Roche, ... (10 to 1) 9
3972⁵ PEGUS PRINCE (Ire) 5-11-2 (3*) T J O'Sullivan, . . (14 to 1) 10
3953⁴ VALTORUS (Ire) 5-11-5 K F O'Brien, ... (4 to 1) 11
3748⁸ ANDROS GALE (Ire) 5-11-5 C O'Dwyer, ... (10 to 1) 12
473⁵ MISS FLINTSTONE VI (Ire) 6-10-8 (7*) D O'Driscoll, (33 to 1) 13
3974 LOST COIN 7-10-12 (3*) D P Murphy, ... (25 to 1) pu
Dist: 3l, ½l, 2½l, 1l. 4m 31.10s. (14 Ran).
(Mrs R Ardiff), Norman Cassidy

4115 Keenan Bros. Handicap Hurdle (0-116 4-y-o and up) £2,742 2m 3f. . . . . . (6:30)

4030⁸ ABBEY EMERALD [-] 8-9-4 (3*) J P Broderick, . (100 to 10) 1
3957⁶ KNOCNAGORE (Ire) [-] 5-10-6 A Powell, ... (6 to 1) 2
3711³ PEPPERONI EXPRESS (Ire) [-] (bl) 5-11-1 J P Banahan,
. . . . (3 to 1 fav) 3
3995 BAVARD DIEU (Ire) [-] (bl) 6-11-3 (5*) Mr G J Harford, (6 to 1) 4
3793* CUTTER'S WHARF (Ire) [-] 5-10-13 (5*) P A Roche, (7 to 1) 5
4030⁶ MAGNUM STAR (Ire) [-] (bl) 7-11-7 (7*) D O'Driscoll, (14 to 1) 6
3869⁵ POOR TIMES (Ire) [-] 6-9-7 (5*) M A Davey, ... (10 to 1) 7
3812 GARYS GIRL [-] 7-11-1 C O'Dwyer, ... (10 to 1) 8
3944⁸ GOLDEN RAPPER [-] (bl) 9-10-6 K F O'Brien, . . . (12 to 1) 9
2682⁸ BEGLAWELLA [-] 7-11-11 (3*) C O'Brien, ... (10 to 1) 10
4030 BORRISMORE FLASH (Ire) [-] 6-9-6 (7*) L A Hurley, (33 to 1) 11
3322 YOUNG GALE [-] 10-11-9 (5*) D P Geoghegan, . . . (12 to 1) pu
Dist: 4½l, sht-hd, 11l, ¾l. 4m 23.90s. (12 Ran).
(Miss R Easom), Michael Hourigan

4116 Dawn Dairies Novice Chase (4-y-o and up) £2,913 2m 5f. . . . . (7:00)

3972² DUNBOY CASTLE (Ire) 6-11-9 (5*) P A Roche, ... (10 to 1) 1
4033² TRASSEY BRIDGE 7-11-9 F Woods, ... (6 to 1) 2
3887⁵ PARSONS BRIG 8-12-0 K F O'Brien, ... (5 to 2 fav) 3
3789 THE CRIOSRA (Ire) 5-11-4 (3*) C O'Brien, ... (33 to 1) 4
2551⁸ BERRINGS DASHER 7-12-0 S H O'Donovan, ... (33 to 1) 5
4032 OATFIELD LAD 7-12-0 A Powell, ... (12 to 1) 6
2865 ENQELAAB (USA) 6-12-0 J P Banahan, ... (10 to 1) 7

3955⁸ STRONG CHERRY 8-11-2 (7*) Mr K Taylor, ... (16 to 1) 8
3972⁴ IRISH LIGHT (Ire) 6-11-7 (7*) Mr W Ewing, ... (20 to 1) 9
4032⁶ GOLDEN CLAW 7-12-0 P L Malone, ... (12 to 1) 10
3325 MICHAEL'S STAR (Ire) 6-11-11 (3*) T J Mitchell, . . (14 to 1) 11
3747 HOLY FOX (Ire) 6-12-0 C O'Dwyer, ... (12 to 1) 12
3869 ERADA (Ire) (bl) 6-11-6 (3*) T P Rudd, ... (20 to 1) 13
3655 ADELAURE (Fr) 9-12-0 S R Murphy, ... (33 to 1) f
4032³ FANCY DISH 8-11-6 (3*) D P Murphy, ... (5 to 1) pu
Dist: ¾l, 1½l, dist, ¾l. 5m 13.70s. (15 Ran).
(S J O'Sullivan), A P O'Brien

4117 Usher Challenge Cup (Handicap Chase) (0-116 4-y-o and up) £2,228 3m 1f. . . . . (7:30)

3659⁵ SPEAKING TOUR (USA) [-] 6-11-10 D H O'Connor, (14 to 1) 1
3790⁶ NEW CO (Ire) [-] 5-11-3 C O'Dwyer, ... (6 to 1) 2
3996⁴ THE MAD MONK [-] 9-10-0 A Powell, ... (4 to 1) 3
3945 WAKE UP LUV [-] 9-11-6 S H O'Donovan, ... (20 to 1) 4
3996 TAKE THE TOWN [-] (bl) 9-10-13 (7*) M G Cleary, . . (7 to 1) 5
4033⁴ GOLDEN CARRUTH (Ire) [-] 6-10-6 (3*) J P Broderick,
. . . . (10 to 1) 6
4042 MANOR RHYME [-] (bl) 7-9-8 J Magee, ... (20 to 1) 7
4033 HURRICANE TOMMY [-] (bl) 7-10-13 J P Banahan, (10 to 1) f
3790 WATERCOURSE [-] 10-11-4 (3*) D P Murphy, ... (8 to 1) pu
3911* DADDY LONG LEGGS [-] 7-11-7 K F O'Brien, . . (7 to 4 fav) pu
3648 SHUIL LE CHEILE [-] 7-9-4 (3*) C O'Brien, ... (14 to 1) pu
Dist: 1½l, 14l, 15l, 6l. 6m 17.80s. (11 Ran).
(E O'Dwyer), James Joseph O'Connor

4118 Tullaghansleek Stud Hunters Chase (5-y-o and up) £2,570 3m 1f. . . . . (8:00)

3994² FAHA GIG (Ire) 5-10-6 (7*) Mr P R Crowley, ... (8 to 1) 1
MRS PEGASUS 7-10-8 (7*) Mr T J Murphy, ... (9 to 4) 2
3888⁸ MENATURE (Ire) 5-10-10 (3*) Mr D Valentine, . . . (25 to 1) 3
3994³ LINEKER (bl) 7-11-6 (5*) Mr G J Harford, ... (8 to 1) 4
3527 BALLYDAY DAWN 7-10-8 (7*) Mr J P Walsh, ... (50 to 1) 5
SIR L MUNNY 10-10-13 (7*) Mr K Whelan, ... (14 to 1) 6
DERBY O'GILL (Ire) 8-10-13 (7*) Mr J T Codd, . . . (16 to 1) 7
THATSTHEFASHION (Ire) 6-10-8 (7*) Mr T N Cloke, (20 to 1) 8
IDEMOSS (bl) 7-10-8 (7*) Mr K O'Sullivan, ... (25 to 1) 9
3794⁹ COCO DANCER 12-10-13 (7*) Mr C A McBratney, (20 to 1) 10
3956 ONE EYED GER VI (Ire) 5-10-6 (7*) Mr P P Curran, (14 to 1) su
3722⁴ TWO COVERS 7-11-11 Mr J A Berry, ... (8 to 1) pu
3888* NATIVE VENTURE (Ire) 6-12-2 Mr E Bolger, . . . (5 to 4 fav) pu
3610 DISNEYS HILL (bl) 7-11-2³ (7*) Mr S O'Brien, . . . (50 to 1) pu
3994 LAURA'S PURSUIT (Ire) 5-10-8 Mr A R Coonan, . (10 to 1) pu
3994⁵ GLENARD LAD (Ire) 6-11-1 (5*) Mr J P Berry, . . . (20 to 1) pu
Dist: 2½l, 8l, sht-hd, 6l. 6m 28.30s. (16 Ran).
(P O'Mahony), Gerard Cully

4119 Lughnagore INH Flat Race (5-y-o and up) £2,228 2½m. . . . . (8:30)

4044⁵ ANOTHER ROLLO (Ire) 4-11-7 (7*) Mr T R Hughes, (12 to 1) 1
3201 QUIET ONE 9-11-2 (7*) Mr J Connolly, ... (16 to 1) 2
3974⁴ DANGEROUS LADY 5-11-5 (3*) Mr D Marnane, . . (8 to 1) 3
3891² CASTLE ARMS HOTEL (Ire) 5-11-13 Mr A P O'Brien,
. . . . (5 to 4 fav) 4
BALLYHANNON (Ire) 5-11-6 (7*) Mr T J Murphy, . . (5 to 1) 5
GLENPATRICK PEACH (Ire) 5-11-1 (7*) Mr G Flanagan,
. . . . (12 to 1) 6
SLANEY PEACE (Ire) 5-11-6 (7*) Mr C A Murphy, . (14 to 1) 7
3748⁴ BROWNRATH KING (Ire) 5-11-13 Mr P Fenton, . . . (6 to 1) 8
4047 CARRIG DANCER (Ire) 6-11-2 (7*) Mr K Whelan, . (25 to 1) 9
3953 LEVANTER'S BREEZE (Ire) 5-11-6 (7*) Mr B Moran, (8 to 1) 10
3796⁵ FIVE A SIDE (USA) 7-11-7 (7*) Mr G Elliot, ... (14 to 1) 11
4034 CARNMORE CASTLE (Ire) 6-11-9 (5*) Mr G J Harford,
. . . . (33 to 1) 12
3953⁷ THE LEFT FOOTER (Ire) 5-11-13 Mr J T McNamara,
. . . . (25 to 1) 13
3504 BELVIEW LADY 7-11-2 (7*) Mr E Norris, ... (25 to 1) 14
3733 ELTON'S SON 8-11-7 (7*) Mr P Brett, ... (25 to 1) 15
Dist: 1½l, 6l, ¾l, sht-hd. 4m 39.80s. (16 Ran).
(P J Stokes), P J Stokes

UTTOXETER (good to firm)
Monday May 30th
Going Correction: MINUS 0.30 sec. per fur.

4120 Twyford Bathrooms Novices' Hurdle (4-y-o and up) £1,882 2m. . . . . (2:30)

4009² FOREST PRIDE (Ire) 5-11-2 N Williamson, *patiently rdn,*
cld up 6th, led appr 2 out, clr last, easily.
. . . . (6 to 4 fav tchd 7 to 4) 1
3103⁷ ALIF (Ire) 7-10-8 D Bridgwater, *nvr far away, rdn and kpt*
on same pace frm 2 out. . . . . (33 to 1 op 16 to 1) 2
3938⁵ EDELWEISS 7-10-9 L Reynolds, *hld up in tch, outpcd 6th,*
kpt on frm 2 out, nvr nrr. . . . . (4 to 1 op 3 to 1) 3
4069⁵ MRS NORMAN 5-10-6 (3*) S Wynne, *nvr far away, rdn*
and wknd frm 3 out. . . . . (14 to 1 op 12 to 1) 4

4009[6] DALBEATTIE 5-10-2 (7*) D Winter, *led till appr 2 out, sn*
rdn, ran on one pace.
.... (16 to 1 tchd 20 to 1 and 14 to 1) 5
GALLOP TO GLORY 4-10-6 (3*) T Eley, *sn struggling, drvn*
alng 6th, tld off........................ (33 to 1 op 20 to 1) 6
4011* MISSY-S (Ire) 5-11-4 (5*) Mr J L Llewellyn, *trkd ldr to 6th,*
rdn 3 out, disputing 3rd but hld whn f 2 out, dead.
.... (13 to 8 op 5 to 4 tchd 7 to 4) f
Dist: 10l, nk, 1½l, ½l, dist. 3m 45.00s. a 6.00s (7 Ran).
(I M S Racing), K C Bailey

4121 R. L. Harrison Construction Selling Handicap Hurdle (4-y-o and up) £1,889 ....(3:00)

3328 SEA BREAKER (Ire) [85] 6-11-1 S McNeill, *settled rear,*
hdwy 7th, trkd ldrs 2 out, ran on to ld last strd.
.....................(3 to 1 fav op 10 to 1) 1
4052[4] JOHNSTED [94] 8-11-10 N Williamson, *nvr far away, led 2*
out, sn clr, rdn r-in, hdd last strd. (7 to 1 tchd 8 to 1) 2
4064[5] VOLCANIC DANCER (USA) [73] (v) 8-10-3 J R Kavanagh, *cld*
appr 3 out, rdn and ran on one pace approaching last.
.... (16 to 1 op 20 to 1) 3
3915[3] VALIANTHE (USA) [73] (bl) 6-9-10 (7*) O Burrows, *beh, styd*
on frm 2 out, nrst finish................ (8 to 1 op 7 to 1) 4
3926[3] SANTA PONSA BAY [74] 7-10-4 J Railton, *led to second, cl*
up till rdn and wknd appr last...... (9 to 1 op 14 to 1) 5
3775[4] FLAMING MIRACLE (Ire) [70] (bl) 4-9-9 (5*) S Curran, *chsd ldr*
5th till appr 2 out, sn rdn and wknd. (8 to 1 op 7 to 1) 6
3801[6] PEAK DISTRICT [79] (bl) 8-10-6 (3*) D Meredith, *mid-div,*
effrt 7th, rdn and wknd appr 2 out.
.... (8 to 1 op 10 to 1 tchd 7 to 1) 7
4052 PEACE FORMULA (Ire) [70] (bl) 5-10-0 W Marston, *rear,*
moderate late hdwy, nvr nr ldrs... (50 to 1 op 33 to 1) 8
3125 MR ABBOT [70] 4-9-11 (3*) T Eley, *str hold, chsd ldrs till*
rdn and wknd appr 3 out.................... (16 to 1) 9
4012[3] SHARE A MOMENT (Can) [70] 4-9-11 (3*) S Wynne, *led*
second to 2 out, sn rdn and btn............ (10 to 1) 10
3899 CHAGHATAI (USA) [71] (v) 8-10-1 Mr B Leavy, *al beh.*
.... (20 to 1 op 14 to 1) 11
3965 FOXY LASS [70] 5-10-0 Mr J Cambidge, *al beh...* (66 to 1) 12
3917 MAYFIELD PARK [70] 9-10-0 N Mann, *mid-div, outpaced 3*
out.............................. (10 to 1) 13
CISTOLENA [70] (bl) 8-10-0 L O'Hara, *al beh, tld off.*
.... (33 to 1) 14
3460[4] FIDDLER'S DRUM [80] 7-10-3 (7*) W Fry, *ran out second.*
.... (14 to 1 op 12 to 1) ro
3545[4] QUALITAIR MEMORY (Ire) [75] 5-10-5 T Grantham, *beh,*
hdwy 6th, prmnt whn slpd up appr 3 out.
.... (7 to 1 op 5 to 1) su
4016* BATTLEPLAN [82] 9-10-12 D Bridgwater, *in tch to 5th,*
wknd quickly, tld off whn pld up bef 7th.
.... (13 to 2 op 6 to 1 tchd 7 to 1) pu
3742 MINT-MASTER [70] 9-9-7 (7*) P Maddock, *beh hfwy, tld off*
whn pld up bef 3 out................(50 to 1) pu
Dist: ¾l, 6l, 15l, sht-hd, ¾l, 5l, 1½l, 9l, 6l, 7l. 4m 46.80s. a 3.80s (18 Ran).
(Don Cantillon), D E Cantillon

4122 Neville Lumb Silver Jubilee Handicap Chase (5-y-o and up) £2,749 3¼m ....(3:30)

3875* NEARCO BAY (NZ) [117] 10-11-0 J R Kavanagh, *al cl up, led*
4 out, sn hdd, led appr 2 out, all out.
.... (13 to 8 fav op 6 to 4) 1
4007* BRADWALL [106] 10-10-0 (3*) S Wynne, *led to 4 out, sn led*
ag'n, hdd appr 2 out, soon rdn, kpt on one pace r-in.
.....................(5 to 2 op 2 to 1) 2
3916[3] FAR SENIOR [131] 8-12-0 N Williamson, *patiently rdn,*
mstk 5th, cl up 13th, in tch till ridden and wknd frm 3
out...................... (4 to 1 op 3 to 1 tchd 9 to 2) 3
3828[6] WINABUCK [104] 11-9-12 (3*) D Meredith, *prmnt, pushed*
alng 13th, wknd nxt, tld off..................(9 to 1) 4
1130[2] BUDDY HOLLY (NZ) [104] 9-10-1[?] T Grantham, *cl up, chsd*
ldr frm 8 to 13th, rdn and wknd 15th, tld off whn pld up
bef 3 out................ (9 to 2 op 5 to 1 tchd 11 to 2) pu
Dist: ¾l, 6l, 30l. 6m 40.00s. a 24.00s (5 Ran).
(Queen Elizabeth), N J Henderson

4123 Lisa & Richard Oldham Marriage Novices' Handicap Hurdle (0-100 4-y-o and up) £1,997 3m 110yds...... (4:00)

3919* GRATUITY [70] 9-11-10 N Mann, *al cl up, led appr 3 out,*
clr 2 out, eased r-in........... (7 to 4 fav tchd 15 to 8) 1
3878* DANGER BABY [83] 4-11-3 (3*) D Meredith, *in tch, took clr*
order appr 3 out, chsd wnr approaching nxt, sn out-
pcd........................ (3 to 1 op 5 to 2) 2
4004 WHAT A NOBLE [64] (v) 8-10-1 W Marston, *wth ldr, not*
fluent 5th, wknd aftr 7th, sn lost tch.
.... (14 to 1 op 10 to 1) 3
4029[4] SAFARI PARK [84] 5-11-7 R Dunwoody, *led till appr 3 out,*
3rd and btn whn f 2 out............(3 to 1 tchd 7 to 2) f
3982* MISS PIMPERNEL [75] 4-10-12 L O'Hara, *prmnt till rdn*
and outpcd frm 4 out, tld off and pld up bef 2 out.
.... (7 to 1 op 3 to 1 tchd 4 to 1) pu
Dist: 20l, 5l. 5m 42.30s. a 3.30s (5 Ran).

4124 Houghton Vaughan Novices' Chase (5-y-o and up) £2,540 2m 7f..... (4:30)

4020[4] NICKLE JOE 8-12-0 W Marston, *led to tenth, rdn to rgn ld*
4 out, hrd ridden and kpt on gmely r-in.
.....................(3 to 1 op 5 to 2) 1
4005[3] NORTHERN OPTIMIST 6-10-11 N Williamson, *wth ldr till*
hdd, hld 4 out, ev ch frm 3 out, hrd rdn flt, no extr
cl hme...................... (10 to 1 tchd 12 to 1) 2
4005[2] SQUIRE JIM 10-11-13 (7*) Mr M Rimell, *cl up till rdn 9th, sn*
drpd rear, mstk 11th, ran on appr 4 out, ridden and
wknd bef 2 out...................... (9 to 4 op 7 to 4) 3
3621 EDEN SUNSET 8-11-2 Mr Chris Wilson, *cl up, rdn and*
ridden and wknd appr 4 out........(25 to 1 tchd 33 to 1) 4
4024[4] ON THE TEAR 8-11-2 S McNeill, *patiently rdn, cld up 8th,*
ridden and wknd appr 4 out.......(33 to 1 op 25 to 1) 5
3992* LONGSHOREMAN 7-11-8 R Dunwoody, *chsd ldrs to tenth,*
rdn and wknd 11th, tld off frm 4 out.
.... (7 to 4 fav op 9 to 4 tchd 13 to 8) 6
3893[3] HIGHLAND POACHER 7-11-2 J Railton, *jmpd slwly 1st,*
pushed alng and effrt 8th, wknd 13th, tld off whn pld
up bef last...................... (14 to 1 op 8 to 1) pu
Dist: Nk, 25l, 1½l, 9l, 20l. 5m 41.90s. a 11.90s (7 Ran).
(Mrs E Tate), M Tate

4125 Round Meadows Racing Stables Handicap Hurdle For Raisdorf Trophy (0-135 4-y-o and up) £2,253 2m.. (5:00)

3930[2] NOBELY (USA) [106] 7-11-5 N Williamson, *al cl up, led*
appr 2 out, pushed out r-in.
.... (11 to 4 op 5 to 2 tchd 7 to 2) 1
1650* SAND-DOLLAR [115] 11-12-0 S McNeill, *patiently rdn,*
took clr order 3 out, ev ch 2 out, one pace r-in.
.... (5 to 2 op 2 to 1) 2
SIMONE'S SON (Ire) [104] (bl) 6-11-3 D Bridgwater, *chsd*
ldrs, ev ch appr 2 out, rdn and one pace approaching
last...................... (6 to 1 op 7 to 1 tchd 8 to 1) 3
NAIYSARI (Ire) [115] 6-12-0 W Marston, *chsd ldrs, led and*
hit 3 out, sn hdd and btn.
4017[3] BADRAKHANI (Fr) [100] 8-10-13 R Dunwoody, *trkd ldr, led*
aftr 3 out, sn hdd and wknd... (5 to 2 fav tchd 3 to 1) 5
3636[4] SECRET SUMMIT (USA) [91] (v) 8-10-1 (3*) T Eley, *led, clr*
5th, hdd appr 3 out, sn btn.
.... (10 to 1 op 8 to 1 tchd 12 to 1) 6
Dist: 3l, 5l, ¾l, 8l, ½l. 3m 39.70s. a 0.70s (6 Ran).
SR: 36/42/26/36/13/3/ (D H Cowgill), N J H Walker

WETHERBY (good)
Monday May 30th
Going Correction: NIL

4126 Holiday Novices' Hurdle (4-y-o and up) £2,267 2m................(2:05)

3815* GOING PUBLIC 7-11-7 K Johnson, *trkd ldrs, chlgd 3 out,*
rdn aftr nxt, styd on wl to ld cl hme.
.... (5 to 2 fav tchd 3 to 1) 1
3815[5] OTTER BUSH 5-11-0 (7*) D Towler, *cl up, led aftr 6th, rdn*
betw last 2, hdd and no extr close hme.
.....................(4 to 1 op 7 to 2) 2
3333 PIMSBOY (v) 7-10-9 (5*) P Midgley, *hld up, hdwy aftr 3*
out, ev ch betw last 2, styd on wl frm last.
.... (33 to 1 op 20 to 1) 3
3617[4] GENSERIC (Fr) 4-11-2 R Garritty, *trkd ldrs, pushed alng to*
chal 3 out, one paced frm nxt.
.... (5 to 1 op 9 to 2 tchd 6 to 1) 4
3907* THISTLE PRINCESS 5-10-9 (7*) B Harding, *trkd ldrs, effrt*
aftr 3 out, sn rdn, wknd betw last 2.
.... (6 to 1 tchd 13 to 2) 5
3800 TERRINGTON 4-10-9 J Callaghan, *hld up, hdwy aftr 6th,*
rdn aftr 3 out, sn wknd.
.... (25 to 1 op 20 to 1 tchd 33 to 1) 6
4025* INNOCENT GEORGE 5-11-2 (5*) J Burke, *slight ld till hdd*
aftr 6th, wknd bef 3 out............(12 to 1 op 10 to 1) 7
3981[4] BELIEVE IT 5-11-0 Mr C Mulhall, *prmnt till wknd aftr 6th.*
.... (33 to 1 op 20 to 1) 8
4003[4] SON OF TEMPO (Ire) 5-10-7 (7*) Miss S Lamb, *mid-div till*
wknd bef 3 out...................... (33 to 1) 9
3983[4] DIGNIFIED (Ire) 4-10-4 (7*) A Linton, *in tch, hdwy to track*
ldrs 6th, wknd bef 3 out... (7 to 1 op 6 to 1) 10
3868 FAST EXIT 6-10-9 Gary Lyons, *beh frm hfwy, tld off whn*
pld up bef 3 out...................... (33 to 1) pu
Dist: ½l, nk, 3½l, 7l, 8l, sht-hd, 1l, 4l, 8l. 3m 51.60s. a 10.60s (11 Ran).
(Alan Cairns), P Cheesbrough

4127 Catterton Claiming Hurdle (4-y-o and up) £2,425 2m................(2:40)

3959* NOTABLE EXCEPTION 5-10-12 (5*) S Mason, *trkd ldrs, led*
2 out, ran on wl...................... (9 to 2 op 4 to 1) 1

3899* CHADWICK'S GINGER 6-10-12 S Turner, *in tch, hdwy hfwy, ev ch 3 out, sn pushed alng, kpt on wl frm last.*
....(12 to 1) 2
40007 ALL WELCOME 7-11-1 R Hodge, *led till hdd 2 out, no extr.*...........................(7 to 2 op 3 to 1 tchd 4 to 1) 3
3924⁹ HALLO MAM (Ire) 5-10-7 (7*) C Davies, *hld up, hdwy aftr 6th, ev ch whn mstk 3 out, kpt on same pace frm nxt.*
....(11 to 2 op 6 to 1 tchd 5 to 1) 4
3618⁴ ALL GREEK TO ME (Ire) 6-10-10 (5*) F Leahy, *trkd ldrs, pushed alng bef 3 out, kpt on same pace frm nxt.*
....(5 to 2 fav op 9 to 4) 5
4011² DYNAMITE DAN (Ire) 6-11-1 R Garritty, *hld up, hdwy hfwy, swtchd bef 3 out, pushed alng and ch whn blun nxt, sn btn.*..............................(11 to 1 op 12 to 1) 6
3600⁶ SEE THE LIGHT 7-9-13 (5*) H Bastiman, *hld up, hdwy bef 6th, rdn before nxt, sn btn.*...................(33 to 1) 7
3584 BAR THREE (Ire) 5-10-11 J Callaghan, *in tch, rdn and outpcd bef 6th, no dngr aftr.*...........(50 to 1 op 33 to 1) 8
3798² BARSAL (Ire) 4-10-5 B Clifford, *prmnt till wknd bef 6th.*
.... 9
3801⁹ MY LINDIANNE 7-10-1 (7*) Mr S Walker, *chsd ldrs till wknd aftr 6th.*...(33 to 1) 10
3598⁵ WHAT A CARD 6-10-4 K Johnson, *beh most of way.*
....(33 to 1) 11
3553 HILLTOWN BLUES 5-10-4 (7*) A Linton, *prmnt till wknd quickly aftr 6th.*.........................(25 to 1 op 20 to 1) 12
3284 RUSTY PLUMBER (Ire) (bl) 6-10-10 (5*) P Midgley, *not fluent, sn lost tch, wl tld off whn pld up bef 3 out.* (50 to 1) pu
Dist: 2l, 2l, 1l, 4l, 5l, 6l, 5l, 7l, 8l, 2½l. 3m 4.60s. a 8.60s (13 Ran).
SR: 3/-/-/-/-/-/ (Andrews & Wilson), Mrs M Reveley

4128 Roddy Armytage Handicap Chase (0-130 5-y-o and up) £3,548 3m 110yds ....(3:15)

3777² MERRY MASTER [122] (bl) 10-11-11 Gee Armytage, *jmpd rght, led 3rd, clr twelfth, blun 4 out, styd on wl.*
.....................................(11 to 8 fav op 6 to 4) 1
4007² GLOVE PUPPET [100] 9-10-3 B Clifford, *in tch, chsd wnr frm tenth, rdn aftr 14th, ch aftr 4 out, kpt on, no imprsn.*...(5 to 2 op 4 to 1) 2
3908² JESTERS PROSPECT [99] 10-10-2 B Storey, *not fluent, nvr on terms.*.........................(5 to 1 op 4 to 1) 3
3485 HIGH PADRE [109] 8-10-12 M Dwyer, *led to 3rd, outpcd aftr twelfth, no dngr after.*...........(6 to 1 op 7 to 1) 4
4001² FISH QUAY [97] 11-9-7 (7*) Miss S Lamb, *al beh, mstk 13th, tld off.*.................(16 to 1 op 14 to 1 tchd 20 to 1) 5
3814⁴ JELUPE [102] 12-10-5 Mr R Sandys-Clarke, *in tch, hdwy aftr twelfth, 3rd and btn whn pld up lme bef 4 out.*
....(14 to 1 op 12 to 1) pu
Dist: 3½l, 25l, 3l, dist. 6m 22.60s. a 16.60s (6 Ran).
(G Lansbury), R C Armytage

4129 Headley Handicap Hurdle (0-125 4-y-o and up) £2,630 2m.............(3:45)

3780³ VANART [93] 5-11-2 D Byrne, *made all, quickened aftr 3 out, cmftbly.*................(9 to 4 jt-fav op 2 to 1) 1
HOSTILE ACT [98] 9-11-7 M Richards, *hld up, hdwy aftr 6th, rdn after 3 out, styd on, no ch whn wnr.*
.....................................(14 to 1 op 12 to 1) 2
3904³ ANY DREAM WOULD DO [92] 5-11-1 C Hawkins, *in tch, rdn aftr 3 out, one paced.*....(3 to 1 op 7 to 2 tchd 4 to 1) 3
3983² REGAL AURA (Ire) [100] 4-11-9 J Callaghan, *prmnt, rdn aftr 6th, one pace frm 3 out.*..(9 to 4 jt-fav tchd 5 to 2) 4
2005⁹ LIABILITY ORDER [97] 5-11-6 R Garritty, *hld up, rdn aftr 3 out, no hdwy.*.........................(5 to 1 op 9 to 2) 5
3930⁵ VAIN PRINCE [101] (bl) 7-11-10 M Dwyer, *trkd wnr, rdn 3 out, sn btn.*.............(10 to 1 op 8 to 1) 6
Dist: 6l, 1¾l, 1¾l, hd, hd. 3m 54.80s. a 13.80s (6 Ran).
(W W Haigh), W W Haigh

4130 Guy Cunard Hunters' Chase (5-y-o and up) £2,178 3m 110yds.......(4:20)

3990* ONCE STUNG 8-12-7 Mr J Greenall, *al prmnt, mstk 11th, drw clr wth ldr frm 4 out, slight ld last, styd on und pres.*..................................(5 to 4 on op Evens) 1
3990² SPEAKERS CORNER 11-11-7 (7*) Mr M Sowersby, *prmnt, lft in ld hfwy, rdn aftr 3 out, hdd last, no extr und pres.*
.....................................(3 to 1 op 2 to 1) 2
3962³ CAPTAIN LYNDSEY 13-11-7 (7*) Mr A Robson, *trkd ldrs, ev ch 4 out, sn outpcd.*...................(28 to 1) 3
4084 CAPTAIN CAVEMAN 9-11-2 (7*) Mr M Haigh, *prmnt to hfwy, sn outpcd, tld off.*........................(50 to 1) 4
RIVERBOAT QUEEN 11-11-6 (7*) Mr P Atkinson, *in tch, some hdwy hfwy, sn outpcd, tld off.*
.....................................(20 to 1 op 16 to 1) 5
SILENT RING (USA) 9-11-7 (7*) Mr C Mulhall, *beh frm hfwy, no ch whn hmpd 4 out, tld off.*.........(33 to 1) 6
3962 CERTAIN BEAT 9-11-2 (7*) Mr N Kent, *led to 3rd, prmnt to hfwy, wl beh whn badly hmpd 4 out and blun nxt, well tld off.*..................................(40 to 1) 7
FAST STUDY 9-11-11 (7*) Mr Simon Robinson, *not jump wl, sn lost tch, well tld off whn badly hmpd last.*
.....................................(28 to 1 op 20 to 1) 8

BURNSWARK 13-11-7 (7*) Mr W Ramsay, *sn lost tch, wl tld off.*....................(40 to 1 op 33 to 1) 9
PYJAMAS 13-11-7 (7*) Miss L Whitaker, *led 3rd till tried to run out bend hfwy, continued, wl tld off whn f last.*
.....................................(20 to 1) f
3989 MAJUBA ROAD 14-11-4 (5*) Mr N Wilson, *beh early, steady hdwy to chase ldrs 13th, 4th and ch whn f four out.*
.....................................(100 to 1) f
3992⁶ DE PROFUNDIS 10-11-2 (7*) Miss T Gray, *hmpd and uns rdr sn aftr strt.*.........................(50 to 1) ur
TAMMY MY GIRL 11-11-6 (7*) Miss A Armitage, *sn lost tch, wl tld off whn badly hmpd by loose horse and uns rdr bef 3 out.*.........................(16 to 1 op 14 to 1) ur
GLEN LOCHAN 14-12-0 Mr S Swiers, *wl beh whn pld up bef 11th.*.............(16 to 1 op 20 to 1 tchd 25 to 1) pu
DEEP ARTISTE 8-11-2 (7*) Mr N F Smith, *wl beh whn pld up bef 13th.*........................(10 to 1 op 16 to 1) pu
Dist: ½l, 20l, dist, ½l, hd, 30l. 6m 21.00s. a 15.00s (15 Ran).
(J E Greenall), P Cheesbrough

4131 Bilbrough Novices' Handicap Hurdle (4-y-o and up) £2,232 2½m 110yds ....(4:50)

3981* CRANK SHAFT [95] 7-11-9 D Byrne, *hld up gng wl, steady hdwy to ld bef 3 out, clr nxt, easily.*
.....................................(9 to 4 fav op 7 to 2 tchd 4 to 1) 1
3817* STRONG DEEL (Ire) [89] 6-11-3 B Storey, *in tch till outpcd and beh aftr 7th, styd on wl frm 3 out, no ch wth wnr.*
.....................................(7 to 2 op 11 to 4) 2
3687² NORRISMOUNT [96] 8-11-10 M Moloney, *led till hdd bef 3 out, kpt on same pace.*........(3 to 1 op 5 to 2) 3
3895² IRISH FLASHER [81] 7-10-2 (7*) G Tormey, *mid-div, effrt bef 7th, rdn before 3 out, sn btn.*
.....................................(11 to 2 op 5 to 1 tchd 6 to 1) 4
3778³ BRABINER LAD [90] 10-11-4 S Turner, *in tch, mstk 5th, effrt aftr nxt, no hdwy whn jmpd rght 3 out, sn btn.*
.....................................(8 to 1 op 7 to 1) 5
4012⁴ STRATHBOGIE MIST (Ire) [77] 6-10-0 (5*) F Leahy, *in tch, rdn aftr 7th, sn btn.*.............(12 to 1 op 10 to 1) 6
TRAP DANCER [75] 6-9-12 (5*) J Supple, *chsd ldr till wknd aftr 7th, tld off whn blun last.*.....................(16 to 1) 7
Dist: 12l, 1½l, 7l, 8l, 20l, dist. 4m 53.00s. a 6.00s (7 Ran).
SR: 35/17/22/-/1/-/ (Charles McNulty), J F Bottomley

AUTEUIL (FR) (good to soft)
Tuesday May 31st

4132 Prix Millionaire II (Chase) (5-y-o and up) £34,325 2¾m.............(3:50)

3425 THE FELLOW (Fr) (bl) 9-10-10 A Kondrat, *al prmnt, led 2 out, pushed out.*................................... 1
REBAH (Fr) 7-10-4 D Mescam, ... 2
ALT'ELA (Fr) 7-10-8 P Havas, ... 3
3425⁴ EBONY JANE 9-9-13 P Chevalier, *rear but in tch, mstk tenth, rdn and lost touch 5 out.*..................... 6
Dist: 3l, 2l, 3l, 10l, 20l. 5m 29.00s. (6 Ran).
(Marquesa de Moratalla), F Doumen

HEXHAM (hard)
Tuesday May 31st
Going Correction: MINUS 0.30 sec. per fur.

4133 Joe Parker Amateur Riders Maiden Hurdle (4-y-o and up) £2,005 3m (6:40)

3775³ THE JEWELLER (v) 7-11-9 (5*) Mr D Parker, *led or dsptd ld, wnt on string fnl circuit, hdd 3 out, rallied and rgned lead bef last, went clr.*.....................(6 to 4 tchd 13 to 8) 1
4027 WHY NOT EQUINAME 6-11-7 (7*) Miss V Haigh, *al wl plcd, led 3 out, clr aftr nxt, wknd and hdd bef next, no extr.*
.....................................(11 to 8 fav op Evens) 2
3775⁵ CINDERCOMBE 5-11-2 (7*) Miss J Cumings, *al hndy, out-pcd bef 2 out, no imprsn aftr.*........(9 to 2 op 6 to 1) 3
4050⁷ HIGHLAND RIVER 7-11-2 (7*) Mrs H Johnston, *settled but in tch, struggling to keep up bef 2 out, sn btn.*
.....................................(12 to 1 op 10 to 1 tchd 14 to 1) 4
4035⁸ QUIXALL CROSSETT 9-11-7 (7*) Mr A Manners, *not fluent, led or dsptd ld for one circuit, lost tch 4 out, tld off.*
.....................................(40 to 1 op 33 to 1 tchd 50 to 1) 5
Dist: 15l, ¾l, 6l, dist. 5m 59.60s. a 12.60s (5 Ran).
(Mrs V C Ward), Mrs V C Ward

4134 Federation Brewery LCL Pils Lager Novices' Chase (5-y-o and up) £2,604 2½m 110yds................(7:10)

4024² DOWN THE ROAD 7-12-2 A Maguire, *made all, wnt clr 3 out, easily.*
.....................(7 to 4 on op 5 to 4 tchd 13 to 8 on and 6 to 4 on) 1
4074² JAUNTY GIG (bl) 8-11-4 A Merrigan, *hld up, improved to track wnr aftr 9th, blun 11th, pushed alng bef 2 out, no imprsn.*............................(16 to 1 op 20 to 1) 2

NATIONAL HUNT RESULTS 1993-94

3816 CELTIC SONG 7-12-3 A Dobbin, *nvr far away, outpcd 5*
out, sn btn, tld off......(15 to 8 op 2 to 1 tchd 7 to 4) 3
4081³ DOLITINO 10-10-13 Mr T Morrison, *pressed ldr, lost tch*
strting fnl circuit, tld off......... (12 to 1 op 10 to 1) 4
4084⁹ WITERO 11-11-4 Miss J Percy, *al beh and not jump wl, tld*
off fnl circuit........ (40 to 1 op 20 to 1 tchd 50 to 1) 5
Dist: 6l, dist, 25l, dist. 5m 7.80s. a 6.80s (5 Ran).

(R J Crake), J H Johnson

4135 Federation Brewery Medallion Lager Selling Hurdle (4-y-o and up) £1,799 2½m 110yds.................... (7:40)

3982² HOTDIGGITY 6-11-3 (5*) J Burke, *beh in chasing bunch,*
improved hfwy, outpcd and drvn alng 2 out, rallied to
ld r-in, kpt on..... (9 to 4 fav op 5 to 2 tchd 11 to 4) 1
4064 RIP THE CALICO (Ire) 6-10-10 (7*) Miss C Spearing, *cl up in*
chasing bunch, drvn to ld bef last, sn hrd pressed, hdd
r-in, no extr.............(9 to 2 op 4 to 1 tchd 6 to 1) 2
4035⁴ ARCTIC BLOOM 8-10-4 (7*) J Driscoll, *nvr far away, ev ch*
and drvn alng betw last 2, not quicken appr last.
.............................(33 to 1 op 25 to 1) 3
4082⁴ CARLA ADAMS 8-10-11 K Johnson, *led and clr to 5th, rdn*
and hdd bef last, fdd............. (6 to 1 tchd 7 to 1) 4
3960⁴ ELVETT BRIDGE (Ire) 6-11-8 A Dobbin, *in tch chasing*
bunch, hit 3rd, struggling frm 6th, tld off whn refused 3
out..................................(7 to 2 op 5 to 2) ref
4082⁵ TOLL BOOTH 5-10-7¹ (5*) Mr D Parker, *patiently rdn, effrt*
and pushed alng bef 3 out, wknd nxt, pld up before
last............................. (6 to 1 tchd 7 to 1) pu
4079 SULAH ROSE 5-10-4 (7*) S Taylor, *cl up in chasing*
bunch, struggling frm hfwy, tld off whn pld up bef last.
.............................(50 to 1 op 33 to 1) pu
3763² BOHEMIAN QUEEN (bl) 4-10-5 A Maguire, *chsd clr ldr,*
struggling to keep up frm 2 out, pld up bef last.
.............................(6 to 1 op 5 to 1) pu
PETTICOAT RULE 6-10-11 B Storey, *settled in chasing*
grp, struggling to keep up hfwy, tld off whn pld up bef
3 out.............................(33 to 1 op 20 to 1) pu
Dist: 3½l, 9l, 6l. 4m 53.30s. a 0.30s (9 Ran).
SR: 30/21/6/-/-/-/ (Lt-Col W L Monteith), P Monteith

4136 Federation Brewery Special Ale Novices' Hurdle (4-y-o and up) £1,970 2m ....(8:10)

3959⁴ PERSPICACITY 7-10-10 J Callaghan, *patiently rdn,*
improved gng wl to ld last, pushed clr.
.............................(9 to 4 op 2 to 1) 1
2500 JOYFUL IMP 7-10-10 L O'Hara, *al wl plcd, hmpd 3rd,*
chlgd 3 out, led betw last 2, edgd lft, hdd last, not
quicken, fnshd second, pld third.
.............................(14 to 1 op 12 to 1 tchd 16 to 1) 2D
3815³ DE JORDAAN 7-10-8 (7*) W Fry, *nvr far away, led bef 2 out*
till appr last, sn hmpd, not reco'r, fnshd 3rd, plcd
second................... (5 to 4 fav tchd 11 to 10) 2
3983⁷ DARK MIDNIGHT (Ire) 5-10-8 (7*) Mr A Manners, *settled off*
the pace, styd on fnl 2, nrst finish. (25 to 1 op 20 to 1) 4
4081 CROXDALE GREY 7-10-10 A Maguire, *made most, jmpd lft*
and reminders 3rd, hdd bef 2 out, sn btn.
.............................(5 to 1 op 11 to 2 tchd 6 to 1 and 9 to 2) 5
4082⁸ SWANK GILBERT 8-11-1 Carol Cuthbert, *cl up, dsptd ld*
frm 3rd, rdn alng bef 2 out, sn btn. (20 to 1 op 16 to 1) 6
3289⁸ TAUVALERA (bl) 7-10-10 Mr D Swindlehurst, *strted slwly,*
reco'red to join issue second, struggling to keep up 4
out.............................(16 to 1 op 14 to 1) 7
Dist: 9l, 6l, 8l, 4l, 3½l, dist. 3m 53.20s. a 3.20s (7 Ran).
SR: 2/-/-/-/ (Mrs J Lynne Mason), Mrs J L Mason

4137 Federation Brewery 75th Anniversary Handicap Chase (0-105 5-y-o and up) £3,557 2½m 110yds............ (8:40)

4046* CLEVER FOLLY [93] 14-11-4 (6ex) R Dunwoody, *made all,*
hrd pressed frm 5 out, drw clr bef last, eased r-in,
dismounted aftr line.
.............................(85 to 40 fav op 3 to 1 tchd 2 to 1) 1
4007⁴ STRONG APPROACH [97] 9-11-8 A Dobbin, *al wl plcd, drw*
level 5 out, no extr bef last.
.............................(9 to 2 op 4 to 1 tchd 5 to 1) 2
4081* SEON [106] 8-12-3 (3ex) A Maguire, *cl up, hit 4th,*
reminders 5 out, struggling frm nxt, no imprsn fnl 2.
.............................(7 to 2 op 3 to 1 tchd 9 to 2) 3
4083* ZAM BEE [98] 8-11-9 (6ex) B Storey, *chsd ldrs, lost pl 7th,*
shrtlvd effrt 4 out, sn btn.............(7 to 2 op 3 to 1) 4
4013 WAIT YOU THERE (USA) [102] 9-11-13 Mr S Swiers, *settled*
in tch, improved and prmnt 6th, struggling bef 4 out, sn
btn.............................(9 to 2 op 4 to 1 tchd 5 to 1) 5
3979⁴ ACHILTIBUIE [81] 10-10-6 K Johnson, *hld up in tch,*
pushed alng to improve 4 out, struggling frm nxt tld
off.............................(11 to 10 fav op 6 to 4) 6
Dist: 4l, 6l, 12l, nk, dist. 5m 2.50s. a 1.50s (6 Ran).
SR: 14/14/17/ (N B Mason (Farms) Ltd), G Richards

4138 Co-operative Bank Club Plan Handicap Hurdle (0-100 4-y-o and up)

£2,733 2½m 110yds............ (9:10)

4037* KINDA GROOVY [96] (bl) 5-12-5 (6ex) R J Beggan, *led till*
hdd appr 3rd, styd prmnt, not much room and swtchd
bef last, led r-in, kpt on wl.
.............................(11 to 8 fav op Evens tchd 6 to 4) 1
4080³ JIM'S WISH (Ire) [68] (bl) 6-10-5 Carol Cuthbert, *keen hold,*
chsd ldg 3, rdn to ld bef last, hdd r-in, no extr.
.............................(5 to 2 op 2 to 1) 2
4037⁴ STATION EXPRESS (Ire) [78] 6-11-1 R Dunwoody, *pld hrd,*
chsd ldrs, effrt and rdn bef last, one pace r-in.
.............................(3 to 1 tchd 11 to 4) 3
1793 PANDESSA [84] 7-11-0 (7*) W Fry, *pressed ldr, led appr*
3rd, hit 3 out, hdd bef last, sn btn....(6 to 1 op 8 to 1) 4
Dist: 2l, 4l, 12l. 5m 2.80s. a 9.80s (4 Ran).
(Ian Park), I Park

WORCESTER (firm)
Tuesday May 31st
Going Correction: MINUS 0.50 sec. per fur.

4139 Holt Maiden Hurdle (4-y-o and up) £2,015 2m 5f 110yds............ (2:20)

3427 HIGHLY REPUTABLE (Ire) 4-10-8 R Dunwoody, *hld up*
towards rear, hdwy appr 5th, jnd ldr 3 out, hrd rdn to
ld r-in................... (11 to 8 jt-fav op 11 to 10 on) 1
4004² GLADYS EMMANUEL 7-10-9 A Maguire, *hld up in tch,*
hdwy to go second 6th, led 3 out, rdn and hdd r-in,
fnshd lme.................(11 to 8 jt-fav op 2 to 1) 2
3762⁶ EMALLEN (Ire) 4-11-0 J Railton, *prmnt till lost pl 4th,*
rallied four out, kpt on one pace frm nxt...... (33 to 1) 3
3977⁶ SHERWOOD FOX 7-10-7 (7*) Mr J Culloty, *al prmnt, led*
appr 5th, hdd 3 out, one pace aftr.
.............................(14 to 1 op 10 to 1 tchd 16 to 1) 4
4021 STRONG TOI 7-10-9 N Williamson, *prmnt, rdn appr 3 out,*
sn btn.............. (14 to 1 op 10 to 1 tchd 16 to 1) 5
4051³ NO SHOW (Ire) 4-10-8 W Humphreys, *towards rear till*
styd on one pace frm 3 out, nvr nrr.
.............................(16 to 1 tchd 20 to 1) 6
4021⁹ CHRISTIAN SOLDIER (bl) 7-11-0 W Elderfield, *chsd ldrs,*
wknd 4 out..........................(100 to 1) 7
3975⁶ NEARLY AT SEA 5-10-2 (7*) Mr L Jefford, *mstk 4th, in rear*
frm 6th..............................(50 to 1) 8
4009 PACIFIC SPIRIT 4-9-10 (7*) P McLoughlin, *in rear till hdwy*
4 out, wknd quickly nxt, tld off..............(100 to 1) 9
3457 WOODLANDS POWER 6-10-11 (3*) R Davis, *al beh, tld off.*
.............................(50 to 1) 10
CAPTAIN MANNERING (USA) 9-11-0 G Upton, *led till hdd*
appr 5th, rdn and wknd quickly aftr nxt, tld off.
.............................(100 to 1) 11
3975 EMBLEY QUAY 5-10-9 (5*) S Curran, *chsd ldrs, mstks 5th*
and 6th, sn beh, tld off..................(100 to 1) 12
4021 ANDREA'S GIRL 4-10-3 W Marston, *jmpd badly in rear, sn*
tld off, pld up bef 3 out................(100 to 1) pu
Dist: 2½l, 11l, 1¾l, 6l, 1¼l, 8l, 1¾l, 25l, 8l, ½l. 4m 58.10s. a 4.10s (13 Ran).
(W J Gredley), M C Pipe

4140 Green Street Novices' Chase (5-y-o and up) £2,479 2½m 110yds..... (2:50)

3976 ALWAYS REMEMBER 7-11-8 Peter Hobbs, *pld hrd, led to*
second, led appr 8th, drw clr frm 2 out.
.............................(13 to 8 op 7 to 4) 1
3966³ TUDOR EAGLE (Ire) (bl) 6-11-8 R Dunwoody, *hld up, trkd*
wnr frm 8th, hit 3 out, sn rdn and btn whn hit last.
.............................(5 to 4 on op 7 to 4 on) 2
3732⁸ JIMMY THE JACKDAW 7-11-2 A Maguire, *hld up in rear,*
rdn to cl 4 out, sn wknd, fnshd lme.
.............................(8 to 1 tchd 10 to 1) 3
3829 VAZON EXPRESS 8-10-9 (7*) D Winter, *al in rear, rdn and*
cld 6th, hit nxt, lost tch 5 out...(33 to 1 op 16 to 1) 4
3966 TOLL BRIDGE 7-10-11 D Bridgwater, *led second till hdd*
appr 8th, wknd rpdly, pld up bef 5 out.
.............................(33 to 1 op 25 to 1) pu
Dist: 7l, 20l, 5l. 4m 59.00s. b 4.00s (5 Ran).
SR: 32/25/ (Mrs S C Cockshott), P J Hobbs

4141 St Martins Handicap Hurdle (0-120 4-y-o and up) £2,057 2¼m.... (3:20)

3738⁴ OUR SLIMBRIDGE [109] 6-11-10 R Campbell, *al in tch,*
wnt second 4 out, led appr 2 out, hdd briefly last,
pushed out......... (10 to 1 op 9 to 1 tchd 14 to 1) 1
3980³ NOVA SPIRIT [85] 6-10-0 N Williamson, *hld up, jmpd slwly*
4th, hdwy appr 3 out, led nxt, sn hdd, no extr.
.............................(10 to 1 op 8 to 1) 2
4054* KING'S SHILLING (USA) [97] 7-10-12 A Maguire, *al in tch,*
ev ch frm 2 out, hrd rdn and ran on r-in, fnshd lme.
.............................(11 to 10 fav op 6 to 4) 3
4047* WINDWARD ARIOM [94] 8-10-9 (6ex) R Dunwoody, *prmnt,*
rdn appr 2 out, one pace aftr, fnshd lme.
.............................(5 to 5 op 2 tchd 11 to 2) 4
3831⁵ CARDINAL BIRD (USA) [88] 7-10-3 M Perrett, *led reluc-*
tantly, jmpd rght 1st 2, hdd nxt, styd in tch till one
pace frm 3 out.....................(33 to 1 op 14 to 1) 5

3831 GOLDEN GUNNER (Ire) [92] (bl) 6-10-7 D Gallagher, *led to
3rd till wknd and hdd appr 2 out*. (25 to 1 op 20 to 1) 6
3977* DISTANT MEMORY [89] (bl) 5-10-4 M Hourigan, *hld up in
rear, rdn frm 6th, nvr on terms*..... (5 to 1 tchd 6 to 1) 7
4066³ ADMIRALTY WAY [100] 8-10-12 (3*) T Jenks, *pld hrd, al in
rear, fnshd lme*..... (16 to 1 op 14 to 1 tchd 20 to 1) 8
3853 IT'S VARADAN [91] 10-10-6¹ M A FitzGerald, *in frnt rnk till
wknd aftr 6th, fnshd lme*.
.... (16 to 1 tchd 25 to 1 and 14 to 1) 9
Dist: ½l, nk, 12l, 4l, 1¼l, 2½l, 8l, 10l. 4m 18.10s. a 10.10s (9 Ran).
(A N Fiber), C N Williams

4142 Lowesmore Novices' Handicap Chase (5-y-o and up) £2,498 2m....... (3:50)

3976³ RED MATCH [60] 9-10-4⁴ A Tory, *hld up, making hdwy
whn hit 3 out, led last, drvn out*. (20 to 1 tchd 33 to 1) 1
3984* CASTLE CROSS [72] 7-11-2 R Dunwoody, *trkd ldrs, lft
second 4 out, led nxt, hdd last, edgd left r-in, kpt on*.
.....................(7 to 4 fav op 11 to 8 tchd 15 to 8) 2
3827⁸ SING THE BLUES [80] 10-11-10 D Morris, *trkd ldr, led 5th
to 7th, lft in ld 4 out, hdd nxt, ev ch till wknd appr last*.
.....................(6 to 1 op 5 to 1 tchd 13 to 2) 3
3966 PICKETSTONE [73] 7-11-3 G McCourt, *hld up, in tch whn
hmpd 4 out, not reco'r*..........(3 to 1 tchd 100 to 30) 4
4099² GREEN WALK [76] 7-11-1 (5*) C Burnett-Wells, *hld up, hit
4th, sn struggling in rear, last whn hmpd four out*.
.....................(5 to 1 op 9 to 4) 5
3802⁸ TOKANDA [60] 10-10-4 D Gallagher, *led to 5th, led 7th till f
4 out*..........................(20 to 1 op 16 to 1) f
Dist: 1¾l, 10l, 8l, 8l. 3m 55.00s. a 6.00s (6 Ran).
(R J Hodges), R J Hodges

4143 Abberley Handicap Chase (0-120 5-y-o and up) £2,951 2m 7f.......... (4:20)

4018² VIRIDIAN [100] 9-10-11 N Williamson, *made virtually all,
drw clr frm 3 out, hit last, wknd r-in*.
.....................(7 to 3 to 1 tchd 4 to 1) 1
4007⁷ TOMPET [100] 8-10-11 D Bridgwater, *chsd wnr till lost pl
8th, rdn to go second ag'n tenth, dsptd ld appr 4 out,
outpcd nxt, ran on strly r-in*..........(4 to 1 op 5 to 2) 2
3978⁵ MISTER FEATHERS [89] 10-11-0 J R Kavanagh, *hld up in
tch, lost pl hfwy, rallied 5 out, 3rd and held whn hit 3
out*........................(14 to 1 op 10 to 1) 3
FAITHFUL STAR [115] 9-11-12 R Dunwoody, *mstks, chsd
ldrs till rdn appr 3 out, wknd quickly, fnshd tired*.
.....................(9 to 4 fav op 3 to 1) 4
3699* BARRACILLA [89] 9-10-0 B Clifford, *hit 1st, tld off frm 4th*.
.....................(7 to 2 op 3 to 1 tchd 9 to 2) 5
4001 ROCKMOUNT ROSE [89] 9-9-11² (5*) C Burnett-Wells, *in
tch, rdn 12th, hit nxt, sn wknd, tld off*.
.....................(14 to 1 op 10 to 1) 6
3875 NOUGAT RUSSE [89] 13-10-0³ (3*) T Jenks, *hld up, hdwy
to dispute ld 8th, wknd whn f tenth*. (20 to 1 op 14 to 1) f
3939⁶ NEWS REVIEW [89] 11-9-7 (7*) P McLoughlin, *jmpd slwly
second, in tch till wknd quickly hfwy, tld off whn pld
up bef 5 out*..........(20 to 1 op 16 to 1 tchd 25 to 1) pu
Dist: Nk, 11l, 20l, 3½l, 6l. 5m 40.60s. b 3.40s (8 Ran).
SR: 2/1/-/-/-/ (P Moriarty), E T Buckley

4144 Astwood Novices' Handicap Hurdle (0-100 4-y-o and up) £1,922 2m 5f 110yds..................... (4:50)

3970* REFERRAL FEE [78] 7-11-3 S Earle, *hld up, hdwy to track
ldrs 5th, led appr 3 out, rdn and hng lft approaching
last, kpt on*..........(9 to 4 fav op 5 to 2 tchd 3 to 1) 1
3845⁴ MERTON MISTRESS [61] 7-10-0 D Bridgwater, *in rear whn
hmpd second, drvn alng frm 5th, hdwy 4 out, hrd
driven and edgd lft appr last, no imprsn r-in*.
.....................(10 to 1 op 8 to 1 tchd 12 to 1) 2
3932² MAN OF THE GRANGE [85] 8-11-10 N Williamson, *hld up in
rear, hdwy 5th, mstk nxt, rdn appr 3 out, no imprsn
aftr*.....................(11 to 4 op 5 to 2 tchd 7 to 2) 3
4004⁷ MISS SOUTER [67] 5-10-6 R Darke, *prmnt till outpcd appr
3 out, no hdwy aftr*..........(14 to 1 op 10 to 1) 4
JUST CHARI IE [61] 5-9-9 (5*) F Leahy, *dsptd ld till lft in
frnt 3rd, rdn and hdd appr 3 out, wknd quickly, tld off*.
.....................(4 to 1 op 7 to 2 tchd 9 to 2) 5
3970 LITTLE CLARE [61] 7-10-0 B Clifford, *made most till f 3rd*.
.....................(33 to 1 op 20 to 1) f
3970³ EMPERORS WARRIOR [70] 8-10-9 Jacqui Oliver, *trkd ldr
frm 3rd, mstk 7th, sn wknd, tld off whn pld up bef last*.
.....................(4 to 1 op 7 to 2 tchd 5 to 1) pu
3977⁴ POLAR HAT [70] (bl) 6-10-9 R Dunwoody, *hld up, jmpd
slwly 5th, sn beh, tld off whn pld up bef 3 out*.
.....................(7 to 1 op 9 to 2) pu
Dist: 2½l, 7l, 1½l, 25l. 5m 1.80s. a 7.80s (8 Ran).
(Seamus Mullins), J W Mullins

CURRAGH (IRE) (good) Wednesday June 1st

4145 McLoughlins Garage I.N.H. Flat Race (4-y-o and up) £2,399 2m....... (8:00)

4010² GAMBOLLING DOC (Ire) 4-11-7 (3*) Mr B R Hamilton,
.....................(5 to 2 fav) 1
3834 WATERLOO BALL (Ire) 5-11-12 Mr A P O'Brien, ... (8 to 1) 2
3997* CHERYL'S LAD (Ire) 4-11-5 (5*) Mr P M Kelly, ... (6 to 1) 3
3958² RANAGAR (Ire) 4-11-5 (5*) Mr H F Cleary, ...(5 to 1) 4
3936* SIGMA WIRELESS (Ire) 5-11-2 (3*) Mr D Marnane, .. (8 to 1) 5
3913 GOODBOY JOE (Ire) 5-11-3 (7*) Mr J Connolly, ... (12 to 1) 6
4034* MARLFIELD (Ire) 6-11-11 (7*) Mr K Whelan, ...(14 to 1) 7
4044 PLEASE NO TEARS 7-11-3 (3*) Mrs C Barker, ...(20 to 1) 8
3913 SPEAK OF THE DEVIL 7-11-11 (7*) Mr D McDonnell,
.....................(16 to 1) 9
4078⁸ SEVENTY SEVEN MILL (Ire) 5-11-10 Mr P Fenton, .. (16 to 1) 10
BALLYMORE THATCH (Ire) 5-11-7 (7*) Mr E Norris, (10 to 1) 11
95 KINGQUILLO (Ire) 5-11-3 (7*) Mr T J Murphy, ...(16 to 1) 12
COOL IT (Ire) 4-11-3 Mr A R Coonan, ...(10 to 1) 13
REACTED (Ire) 4-10-5 (7*) Mr A K Wyse, ...(12 to 1) 14
DELVIN SPIRIT (Ire) 5-11-3 (7*) Mr G Elliot, ...(20 to 1) 15
RALOO (Ire) 4-10-5 (7*) Mr M A Naughton, ...(12 to 1) 16
4010 ITS ONLY JUSTICE 8-11-4 Mr M Halford, ...(20 to 1) 17
4078 FAITHFULL FELLOW 7-11-4 (7*) Mr S P McCarthy, (16 to 1) 18
3937 DEEYEHFOLLYME (Ire) 6-11-3 (7*) Mr C Gainey, .. (33 to 1) 19
DEES DARLING (Ire) 4-10-9 (3*) Mr J A Nash, ...(20 to 1) 20
ALIFONTAINE (Ire) 5-10-12 (7*) Mr H Murphy, ...(16 to 1) 21
Dist: 1l, hd, 1½l, 4½l. 3m 37.50s. (21 Ran).
(Mrs M O'Leary), P Mullins

BALLINROBE (IRE) (good) Thursday June 2nd

4146 Lough Carra Maiden Hurdle (4-y-o and up) £2,228 2m............. (5:20)

3971⁷ BOB THE YANK (Ire) 4-11-1 A J O'Brien, ...(7 to 2) 1
3971 RATES RELIEF (Ire) 4-11-1 C O'Dwyer, ...(14 to 1) 2
4031² FLOWERHILL DAISY (Ire) 6-10-8 (7*) Mr R P Burns,
.....................(6 to 4 fav) 3
3934 THYNE OWN GIRL (Ire) 5-10-11 (3*) G Kilfeather, .. (16 to 1) 4
1397 SHARP CIRCUIT 5-10-12 (7*) E G O'Callaghan, ... (12 to 1) 5
2464 AMAKANE LADY (Ire) 5-11-8 H Hughes, ...(6 to 1) 6
3913 RUSHEEN BAY (Ire) 5-10-12 (7*) G J Harford, ... (14 to 1) 7
CLEW BAY ROCKET (Ire) 4-10-3 (7*) T J Murphy, .. (14 to 1) 8
2917 BARLEY COURT (Ire) 4-10-10 (5*) C P Dunne, ... (14 to 1) 9
OMESMACJOY (Ire) 4-11-1 B Sheridan, ...(7 to 1) 10+
PERUVIAN GALE (Ire) 5-11-0 (5*) M J Holbrook, .. (14 to 1) 10+
3839 KATES WELL (Ire) 4-10-3 (7*) Mr J Sheehan, ...(14 to 1) 11
3839 CAMDEN BANNER (Ire) 4-10-12 (3*) J P Broderick, (10 to 1) 12
3839 BEN-GURIAN (Ire) 4-11-1 W T Slattery Jnr, ...(12 to 1) 13
3508 CARRIG HEATHER 4-10-10 (5*) D P Geoghegan, ..(16 to 1) 14
Dist: ½l, 1l, 4½l, 3l. 4m 12.80s. (15 Ran).
(R Phelan), Francis M O'Brien

4147 Harp Lager Novice Chase (5-y-o and up) £3,427 2½m................. (6:50)

3945 BALLYFIN BOY 8-12-0 J Shortt, ...(7 to 1) 1
1914⁶ BALLINAVEEN BRIDGE 7-11-9 W T Slattery Jnr, .. (12 to 1) 2
3791⁹ SONNY SULLIVAN 7-11-9 L P Cusack, ...(14 to 1) 3
4041⁴ BRIDGEOFALLEN (Ire) 6-10-13 (5*) Mr W M O'Sullivan,
.....................(7 to 1) 4
3527 IF SO 8-11-6 (3*) T J Mitchell, ...(14 to 1) 5
3944⁵ DIRECT RUN 7-11-9 B Sheridan, ...(5 to 2 jt-fav) 6
3888 LIGHT ARGUMENT (Ire) (bl) 5-10-8 C O'Dwyer, .. (13 to 2) 7
4030 LABESTE (Ire) 6-11-6 (3*) G Kilfeather, ...(14 to 1) 8
528⁷ HAYMAKERS JIG (Ire) 6-11-6 (3*) J P Broderick, (5 to 2 jt-fav) 9
4032⁹ TIME UP (Ire) (bl) 6-11-2 (7*) Mr A Daly, ...(20 to 1) f
Dist: 1l, 6l, 12l, 4l. 5m 30.20s. (10 Ran).
(Mrs Kathleen Deane), W J Austin

4148 Partry I.N.H. Flat Race (4-y-o and up) £2,228 2m................. (8:20)

TRICKY TINA (Ire) 5-11-3 (5*) Mr H F Cleary, ...(7 to 1) 1
3946 ROSES WISH (Ire) 4-10-8 (7*) Mr T J Murphy, ... (10 to 1) 2
NATIVE FLECK (Ire) 4-11-3 (3*) Mr D Marnane, ...(7 to 1) 3
DEIREADH AN SCEAL (Ire) 4-10-13 (7*) Mr A Dempsey,
.....................(8 to 1) 4
2203³ DROMOD POINT (Ire) 5-11-6 (7*) Mr E Norris, .. (5 to 4 fav) 5
3997⁵ PERSIAN VIEW (Ire) 4-11-3 (3*) Mr J A Nash, ...(5 to 1) 6
MYBLACKTHORN (Ire) 4-10-8 (7*) Mr M Connor, .. (14 to 1) 7
3937⁹ KINGS VENTURE (Ire) 4-10-13 (7*) Mr R P Cody, .. (10 to 1) 8
4060 FEATHER SONG 4-10-12 (3*) Mr R Neylon, ...(9 to 2) 9
4031⁶ SUNKEN LADY (Ire) 5-11-8 Mr H Murphy, ...(14 to 1) 10
3997 SPECTACLE (Ire) 4-11-1 (5*) Mr W M O'Sullivan, .. (12 to 1) 11
2775 SECRET COURSE (Ire) 5-11-1 (7*) Mr J McGuinness,
.....................(20 to 1) 12
MELONS LADY (Ire) 4-10-8 (7*) Mr T K Budds, ...(20 to 1) 13
3839 PUB TALK (Ire) 4-10-13 (7*) Mr K O'Sullivan, ...(14 to 1) 14
GALLANT DREAM (Ire) 4-10-8 (7*) Mr A Daly, ...(20 to 1) 15
3946 KASHABI (Ire) 4-10-13 (7*) Mr L J Temple, ...(14 to 1) 16
1832 FRIENDLY BID (Ire) 6-11-2 (7*) Mr N Moran, ...(25 to 1) 17
Dist: 2½l, 2l, 2½l, hd. 4m 5.30s. (17 Ran).
(J J Lennon), Thomas Foley

CLONMEL (IRE) (good)

Thursday June 2nd

4149 Galtee Hurdle (5-y-o and up) £2,228 2½m. .... (5:30)

4077*	FINNEGANS WAKE 7-12-0 C F Swan, ... (11 to 10 fav)	1
3944*	FOR KEVIN 7-11-7 (7*) Mr B Moran, ...(100 to 30)	2
3869*	ACKLE BACKLE 7-10-8 (5*) J R Barry, ... (5 to 1)	3
3840	MOUNTHENRY STAR (Ire) 6-11-4 A Powell, ... (14 to 1)	4
4041*	SKY VISION (Ire) 5-10-12 S H O'Donovan, ... (8 to 1)	5
3201	NOBLE KNIGHT (Ire) 6-10-13 (3*) A J Slattery, ...(25 to 1)	6
5587	HURRICANE MILLIE (Ire) 6-10-13 S R Murphy, ...(16 to 1)	7
3296	ALL A STRUGGLE (Ire) 6-10-13 J P Banahan, ...(33 to 1)	8
3946	PREMIUM BRAND (Ire) 5-11-3 J Collins, ...(33 to 1)	9
3244	FIALADY 9-10-10 (3*) T P Treacy, ...(33 to 1)	10
1610	RED VERONA 5-10-12 J Jones, ...(33 to 1)	11
3944	BUCKINGHAM BOY 8-10-11 (7*) Miss C A Harrison,	
	....(20 to 1)	pu
4061³	STEVIE BE (Ire) 6-11-4 K F O'Brien, ...(8 to 1)	bd

Dist: 8l, 1½l, nk, ¾l. 4m 38.90s. (13 Ran).

(Bracken Syndicate), A P O'Brien

4150 Cashel Handicap Chase (0-109 5-y-o and up) £2,228 2½m. .... (6:00)

3945*	GALLEY GALE [-] 8-11-11 K F O'Brien, ...(9 to 4 fav)	1
4118*	FAHA GIG (Ire) [-] 5-10-9 (6ex) S H O'Donovan, ...(6 to 1)	2
3524	FAIRY PARK [-] (bl) 9-11-4 F Woods, ...(12 to 1)	3
3721⁵	NO MORE THE FOOL [-] 8-10-4 (5*) P A Roche, ...(20 to 1)	4
3945⁸	BALLYHEIGUE [-] 8-10-8 C F Swan, ...(7 to 1)	5
3996⁵	BLENHEIM PALACE (USA) [-] 7-10-1 H Rogers, ...(12 to 1)	6
4058	VINEYARD SPECIAL [-] 8-11-7 T Horgan, ...(10 to 1)	7
3945⁶	HIGHBABS [-] (bl) 8-9-8 (3*) C O'Brien, ...(8 to 1)	8
4042⁸	STANACATE [-] 9-9-11 (7*) J Jones, ...(14 to 1)	9
5094	JAMES PIGG [-] 7-11-0 (3*) T P Treacy, ...(10 to 1)	10
4033	FAYS FOLLY (Ire) [-] 5-9-5 (7*) D J Kavanagh, ...(20 to 1)	11
4042⁵	WHAT A MINSTREL [-] (bl) 8-9-4 (3*) T J O'Sullivan, (15 to 2)	12
	ANOTHER VISION [-] 9-11-6 S R Murphy, ...(14 to 1)	13
4042⁹	COOLADERNA LADY [-] (bl) 8-9-4 (3*) D Bromley, ...(25 to 1)	ref
3873⁵	TIRRY'S FRIEND [-] 12-9-12 M Duffy, ...(20 to 1)	pu

Dist: Sht-hd, 7l, 2l, 8l. 5m 1.60s. (15 Ran).

(J J Connolly), Daniel O'Connell

4151 Mountain Handicap Hurdle (0-109 4-y-o and up) £2,228 2½m. .... (6:30)

4043³	FIXED ASSETS [-] 7-11-2 (3*) C O'Brien, ...(4 to 1)	1
4058²	MY SUNNY GLEN [-] 7-11-13 C F Swan, ...(Evens fav)	2
3840⁹	COOLAHEARAC [-] 8-10-8 A Powell, ...(20 to 1)	3
3974	TARA'S TRIBE [-] 7-10-7 M Duffy, ...(25 to 1)	5
4114⁵	MANTAS MELODY (Ire) [-] 6-10-0 (7*) Mr E J O'Rourke,	
	....(20 to 1)	6
330²	LANTERN LUCK (Ire) [-] 6-10-6 (5*) P A Roche, ...(10 to 1)	7
4091	APARECIDA (Fr) [-] 8-9-10 F J Flood, ...(10 to 1)	8
689	DANCINGCINDERELLA [-] 10-10-6 (7*) Mr B Moran, (8 to 1)	9

Dist: 6l, 11l, 1½l, sht-hd. 4m 34.80s. (9 Ran).

(L Casey), D Casey

4152 Corinthian I.N.H. Flat Race (4-y-o and up) £2,228 2m. ....(8:30)

3842³	ROCKFIELD NATIVE (Ire) 4-11-6 Mr A P O'Brien, (2 to 1 fav)	1
692²	HILL OF TULLOW (Ire) 5-11-10 (3*) Mr M F Barrett, (6 to 1)	2
4044⁶	PALEFOOT (Ire) 6-11-6 (3*) Mr R O'Neill, ...(16 to 1)	3
3469⁸	KILLINEY GAYLE (Ire) 5-11-8 Mr W P Mullins, ...(6 to 1)	4
	HIGHWAYS DAUGHTER (Ire) 5-11-5 (3*) Mrs J M Mullins,	
	....(4 to 1)	5
43⁹	CILL CHUILLINN (Ire) 6-11-7 (7*) Mr M A Cahill, ...(20 to 1)	6
	TOMMY PAUD (Ire) 5-11-13 Mr P Fenton, ...(8 to 1)	7
3913⁸	DON'T ASK JOHNNY (Ire) 5-11-1 (7*) Mr S O'Brien, (10 to 1)	8
3694	CLONAGAM (Ire) 5-11-13 Mr T Mullins, ...(10 to 1)	9
3730	PRINCESS LU (Ire) 4-10-13 (7*) Mr P G Kelly, ...(20 to 1)	10
29	LE SEPT 7-11-2 (7*) Mr R J Foley, ...(33 to 1)	11
3912³	GRACEMARIE KATE (Ire) 5-11-5 (3*) Mr T Lombard,	
	....(10 to 1)	12
3974	WHY EMERALD (Ire) 4-10-8 (7*) Miss M FitzGerald, (33 to 1)	13
3913	FORABBY (Ire) 5-11-6 (7*) Mr K A Dempsey, ...(33 to 1)	14
	ARKINFIELD (Ire) 5-11-1 (7*) Mr B Moran, ...(12 to 1)	15
	PLEASING MELODY (Ire) 5-11-1 (7*) Mr A K Wyse, (20 to 1)	16
3971	COOLING CHIMES (Ire) 4-10-13 (7*) Mr P A Dunphy,	
	....(20 to 1)	17
3946	ROOUAN GIRL (Ire) (bl) 4-10-8 (7*) Mr K Whelan, ...(25 to 1)	18

Dist: 2l, 4½l, 1l, 2l. 3m 39.60s. (18 Ran).

(M F McKeon), A P O'Brien

UTTOXETER (good to firm)
Thursday June 2nd

Going Correction: MINUS 0.25 sec. per fur.

4153 Blythe Pictures Novices' Hurdle (4-y-o and up) £2,337 2½m 110yds.....(2:20)

3975*	ZANYMAN 8-11-7 M A FitzGerald, *settled in rear, hdwy to ld aftr 6th, hit last, hrd rdn, all out.*	
	......................................(2 to 1 tchd 9 to 4 on)	1

4021³	BALLYHYLAND (Ire) 5-11-9 R Bellamy, *not strd out, patiently rdn, hdwy to chal last, hrd ridden and ran on wl.* ....(9 to 4 op 2 to 1 tchd 5 to 2)	2
	FRESHMANS ESSAY (Ire) 6-11-0 G McCourt, *hld up in rear, took clr order appr 4 out, rdn and one pace approaching last.* ....(14 to 1 op 10 to 1)	3
	SELDOM IN 8-11-0 W Marston, *trkd ldrs, rdn appr last, sn btn.* ....(50 to 1 op 25 to 1)	4
4009	THEMOREYOUKNOW 5-11-0 M Sharratt, *pressed ldr, led 4th till aftr 6th, wknd quickly nxt, tld off.* .....(50 to 1)	5
3583⁹	LA SUSIANE (bl) 7-10-9 B Powell, *chsd ldrs, rdn alng hfwy, tld off frm 4 out.* ....(33 to 1 op 33 to 1)	6
2808	RUNNING KISS 9-10-9 W McFarland, *cl up, jmpd slwly 1st, rdn alng and hit 6th, sn lost tch, tld off.*	
	......................................(50 to 1 op 33 to 1)	7
4021	GANDERTON INT 7-11-0 S Earle, *led to 4th, wknd four out, tld off whn pld up bef nxt...* (100 to 1 op 66 to 1)	pu

Dist: Nk, 5l, 3½l, dist, dist, 25l. 4m 50.90s. a 7.90s (8 Ran).

(Mrs P Shaw), N J Henderson

4154 Exchange Bar Diner Novices' Chase (5-y-o and up) £3,087 3¼m....(2:50)

4055*	GHIA GNEUIAGH 8-12-6 R Dunwoody, *jmpd wl, made all, came clr appr 4 out, unchlgd.*	
	............................(9 to 2 on op 5 to 1 on tchd 4 to 1 on)	1
3921⁵	MEKSHARP 7-11-2 A Maguire, *chsd wnr frm 7th, jmpd slwly 13th, outpcd appr 4 out.*	
	..........................(12 to 1 op 10 to 1 tchd 14 to 1)	2
3961	MOYODE REGENT 10-11-1 (7*) Mr A Manners, *hld up, took clr order hfwy, rdn and lost tch appr 16th, tld off.*	
	......................................(10 to 1 op 6 to 1)	3
3562	PENIARTH 8-10-11 J Lawrence, *wtd with in rear, steady hdwy 12th, outpcd 15th, sn tld off.* (33 to 1 op 20 to 1)	4
4055⁵	HORCUM (v) 9-10-9 (7*) K Davies, *dsptd ld, hit 3rd, blun 8th, sn rdn, lost tch and tld off frm 14th.*	
	......................................(33 to 1 op 33 to 1)	5
3896⁴	SNAPPIT (bl) 12-10-11 (5*) Mr D McCain, *cl up till jmpd slwly and lost pl 6th, rdn alng hfwy, tld off whn pld up bef 14th...* ....(33 to 1 op 16 to 1)	pu
3901⁶	DOVEDONS GRACE 8-11-2 Hugh Taylor, *sn wl beh, hdwy tenth, rdn and wknd 15th, tld off whn blun 2 out, pld up...* ....(14 to 1 op 10 to 1)	pu

Dist: 12l, 20l, 30l, dist. 6m 51.40s. a 35.40s (7 Ran).

(Mrs S A Scott), N A Twiston-Davies

4155 Walter J. Wallington Handicap Hurdle for the Ken Boulton Cup (0-135 4-y-o and up) £2,892 3m 110yds....... (3:20)

4006⁴	SPECIAL ACCOUNT [103] (v) 8-10-0 A Maguire, *al cl up, shaken up appr 3 out, led r-in, all out.*	
	....(7 to 1 op 5 to 1)	1
3398⁶	RIMOUSKI [109] 6-10-6 Mr J Cambidge, *wtd with in rear, took clr order 8th, rdn 3 out, styd on and ev ch r-in, no extr close hme.* ....(5 to 1 op 7 to 2)	2
3775*	STRONG CASE (Ire) [115] (bl) 6-10-12 R Dunwoody, *dsptd ld, led aftr 8th, clr last, wknd rpdly and hdd r-in.*	
	......................................(11 to 10 on op 5 to 4 on)	3
4050⁵	CELTIC BREEZE [103] (v) 11-10-0 A Dobbin, *pressed ldrs till wknd 2 out.* ....(8 to 1 op 6 to 1 tchd 9 to 1)	4
4037³	BOWLANDS WAY [103] (bl) 10-10-0 O Pears, *with ldr till wknd aftr 8th, tld off.* ......(5 to 1 op 4 to 1 tchd 6 to 1)	5
3492⁵	MO ICHI DO [103] 8-9-11 (3*) T Eley, *chsd ldrs to 7th, sn rdn and lost pl, tld off...* ....(50 to 1 op 25 to 1)	6
3851⁴	CHUCKLESTONE [103] 11-10-0 J R Kavanagh, *al in rear, rdn alng 7th, sn tld off...* ....(10 to 1 op 3 to 1)	7
4052	TASHONYA [103] 12-10-0 J Da Costa, *al beh, tld off frm hfwy...* ....(100 to 1 op 50 to 1)	8

Dist: ¾l, 2l, 1½l, dist, dist, 3l, dist. 5m 37.90s. b 1.10s (8 Ran).

SR: 22/27/31/17/-/

(Tony Fiorillo), C R Barwell

4156 P & C Morris Handicap Chase (0-130 5-y-o and up) £4,065 2m 5f..... (3:55)

3676²	COMEDY ROAD [105] 10-10-7 A Maguire, *sn pressing ldrs, led 11th, rdn clr appr last.*	
	........................(3 to 1 op 5 to 2 tchd 100 to 30)	1
3923*	MIDFIELDER [122] 8-11-10 Peter Hobbs, *prmnt till jmpd slwly and lost pl 9th, rdn and rallied 3 out, no imprsn frm nxt...* ....(9 to 4 fav op 3 to 1)	2
3979*	FESTIVAL DREAMS [110] 9-10-12 P Holley, *prmnt, mstk 12th, sn rdn, styd on one pace frm nxt.*	
	..........................(7 to 2 op 11 to 4 tchd 4 to 1)	3
4143³	VIRIDIAN [107] 9-10-9 (7ex) N Williamson, *led to 6th, mstk nxt, led aftr 8th to 11th, lost tch 13th...*	
	....(11 to 2 op 9 to 2)	4
4053*	TOCHENKA [125] 10-11-13 (7ex) R Dunwoody, *cl up till led 6th, hdd aftr 8th, wknd appr 4 out, tld off.*	
	....(5 to 1 op 7 to 2)	5
3865⁵	BEN TIRRAN [98] 9-9-9 (5*) S Curran, *al beh, tld off frm nxt...* ....(9 to 2 op 7 to 2)	6

Dist: 5l, 20l, 2l, dist, 25l. 5m 10.40s. a 10.40s (6 Ran).

(Winsbury Livestock), R Lee

4157 Ed Weetman Haulage & Storage Novices' Handicap Hurdle (4-y-o and up,

£2,400 2m. . . . . (4:30)

4126² OTTER BUSH [90] 5-11-7 A Maguire, *with ldr, led on bit appr 2 out, sn clr, drvn out.*
. . . . (7 to 2 op 11 to 4 tchd 4 to 1)   1

3848³ DEAR DO [85] 7-11-2 M A FitzGerald, *led, mstk 3rd, hdd appr 2 out, kpt on same pace.* . . . . (7 to 1 op 5 to 1)   2

3925 NEWHALL PRINCE [69] (bl) 6-9-11 (3°) D Leahy, *chsd ldrs, rdn and hit 3 out, sn outpcd, styd on und pres r-in.*
. . . . (12 to 1 op 14 to 1 tchd 16 to 1)   3

4009³ SHARP DANCE [93] 5-11-10 R Dunwoody, *hld up in rear, steady hdwy whn mstk 3 out, sn rdn and btn, blun last.*
. . . . (11 to 8 fav op 11 to 10 tchd 6 to 4)   4

4029³ CHARLAFRIVOLA [69] (bl) 6-10-0 W Humphreys, *wtd wth in rear, hmpd 4 out, not reco'r.*
. . . . (10 to 1 tchd 12 to 1 and 8 to 1)   5

4052⁹ SILK DYNASTY [69] 8-9-11 (3°) S Wynne, *chsd ldrs till rdn and outpcd appr 3 out, tld off.*
. . . . (16 to 1 op 14 to 1 tchd 20 to 1)   6

3897² LEGITIM [93] 5-11-3 (7°) G Tormey, *hld up in tch, 5th whn f 4 out.* . . . . (4 to 1 op 9 to 2 tchd 5 to 1 and 7 to 1)   f

Dist: 3½sl, 1½l, 5l, 1½l, 30l. 3m 45.90s. a 6.90s (7 Ran).

(Mrs S Smith), Mrs S J Smith

4158   Houghton Vaughan Novices' Hunters' Chase for the Feilden Challenge Cup (5 - 8-y-o) £2,208 2m 5f. . . . . . . (5:00)

3949³ SYNDERBOROUGH LAD 8-12-5 (5°) Mr M Felton, *chsd ldrs, led aftr 3 out, sn clr, easily.*
. . . . (5 to 2 on op 7 to 2 on tchd 2 to 1 on)   1

3988⁶ DALAMETRE 7-11-7 (7°) Mr J Smyth-Osbourne, *pld hrd, led 6th, pckd 3 out, sn hdd, ran on one pace.*
. . . . (9 to 1 op 7 to 1)   2

BENTON'S PRIDE 6-11-4² (7°) Mr G Hanmer, *hdwy und pres hfwy, rdn appr 4 out, no imprsn.* . . . . (20 to 1)   3

MUIRFIELD 8-11-7 (7°) Mr N Hargreave, *chsd ldrs till wknd appr 3 out.* . . . . (12 to 1 tchd 14 to 1)   4

3988⁴ FREDDIE FOX 8-11-7 (7°) Mr T Garton, *in tch, rdn hfwy, mstk 4 out, sn btn.* . . . . (16 to 1)   5

3480 STANDAROUND (Ire) 5-10-9 (7°) Mr B Pollock, *in rear, hdwy 11th, no imprsn whn blun 4 out.* . . . . (100 to 1)   6

PELOTA 8-11-2 (7°) Mr N King, *chsd ldrs to 9th, sn lost tch, tld off.* . . . . (100 to 1 op 50 to 1)   7

3909⁵ JOHNNIE REGGIE 8-11-7 (7°) Mr J Nicholl, *al towards rear, tld off.* . . . . (66 to 1 op 100 to 1)   8

4103 KNOWAFENCE 8-11-2 (7°) Mr S Howe, *led 4th to 6th, prmnt whn f tenth.* . . . . (50 to 1 op 100 to 1)   f

4103 MISTER JOE (v) 7-11-11⁴ (7°) Mr Paul Morris, *sn wl beh, tld off whn ran out 7th.* . . . . (100 to 1)   ro

OVAC STAR 8-11-7 (7°) Mr R Lawther, *led to second, hit 9th, grad wknd, tld off whn pld up bef 2 out.* (12 to 1)   pu

THE DUBLINER (bl) 8-11-7 (7°) Mr C Mulhall, *pld hrd, rcd very wide, led second to 4th, wknd quickly and pulled up bef tenth.* . . . . (100 to 1)   pu

NEWSTARSKY 8-11-7 (7°) Miss J Cumings, *in tch whn blun second, lost pl hfwy, tld off whn pld up bef 3 out.*
. . . . (16 to 1 op 14 to 1)   pu

Dist: 20l, 20l, nk, 12l, 15l, 20l, 20l. 5m 18.00s. a 18.00s (13 Ran).

(Stewart Pike), S Pike

4159   Tetley Bitter Open National Hunt Flat Race (4,5,6-y-o) £1,339 2m. . . . . . (5:30)

4023⁵ TIME HE WENT 5-10-7 (7°) P Maher, *settled midfield, hdwy entering strt, styd on to ld ins fnl furlong, sn clr.*
. . . . (12 to 1 op 6 to 1)   1

3832* EXCLUSIVE EDITION (Ire) 4-10-11 J Osborne, *led, quick-ened clr ten fs out, hdd and no extr ins fnl furlong.*
. . . . (9 to 4 op 3 to 1 tchd 6 to 4)   2

3880² FREDDIE MUCK 4-10-9 R Dunwoody, *al cl up, wnt second 7 fs out, ev ch 2 out, sn rdn and one pace.*
. . . . (10 to 1 op 5 to 1)   3

3833³ MASTER BRACKEN 5-11-0 (7°) G Lee, *wtd wth in rear, steady hdwy frm 4 fs out, shaken up o'r 2 out, kpt on one pace.* . . . . (10 to 1 op 6 to 1)   4

3868³ RADICAL CHOICE (Ire) 5-11-0 A Dobbin, *trkd ldrs, rdn 4 fs out, sn btn.* . . . . (14 to 1 op 10 to 1 tchd 16 to 1)   5

3833⁷ SWEET MARTINI 4-10-4 A Maguire, *wtd wth, effrt 6 fs out, no imprsn last 3 furlongs.* . . . . (14 to 1 op 8 to 1)   6

3833 KINGS GAMBLE 4-10-9 Ann Stokell, *nvr nrr.*
. . . . (100 to 1 op 50 to 1)   7

3855 PRINCE IVANHOE 5-11-0 J Railton, *rdn alng in mid-div, no imprsn.* . . . . (100 to 1 op 50 to 1)   8

3707 RUKIA 5-10-9 M Richards, *nvr rch ldrs.*
. . . . (14 to 1 op 7 to 1)   9

4023 TALL FELLOW (Ire) 4-10-9 R Garritty, *prmnt for 11 fs, grad wknd, tld off.* . . . . (25 to 1 op 16 to 1)   10

4023 BRIDGNORTH LASS 5-10-2 (7°) L Reynolds, *trkd ldrs to hfwy, sn wknd, tld off.* . . . . . (25 to 1 op 16 to 1)   11

4023 YOUWONNA 4-10-9 T Wall, *al in rear, tld off.*
. . . . (100 to 1 op 50 to 1)   12

4040 STEPPING 4-10-4 W Marston, *al beh, tld off frm hfwy.*
. . . . (100 to 1 op 50 to 1)   13

4040² BOWLANDS LAW 5-11-0 O Pears, *prmnt for 9 fs, sn rdn and wknd, tld off.* . . . . (16 to 1 op 14 to 1 tchd 20 to 1)   14

4040⁸ THORONDOR 4-10-4 (5°) S Curran, *al wl beh, tld off frm hfwy.* . . . . (100 to 1 op 50 to 1)   15

4023* ZAMORSTON 5-11-0 (7°) W Fry, *chsd ldrs, jnd issue 4 fs out, ev ch whn broke dwn and pld up 3 furlongs out.*
. . . . (7 to 4 fav op 6 to 4 tchd 11 to 4)   pu

Dist: 3½l, 5l, 4l, 5l, 12l, 8l, 12l, 2½l, 2l, 2½l. 3m 34.60s. (16 Ran).

(Lady Nelson Of Stafford), M H Tompkins

STRATFORD (good to firm)
Friday June 3rd
Going Correction: NIL

4160   Dealers Selling Handicap Hurdle (4 & 5-y-o) £1,716 2m 110yds. . . . . (6:35)

4107² SOUTHAMPTON [70] (v) 4-10-9 A Maguire, *patiently rdn, improved gng wl to draw level bef 2 out, led appr last, drvn out.* . . . . (4 to 1 co-fav op 7 to 2)   1

3876² REACH FOR GLORY [61] 5-9-9 (5°) P McLoughlin, *al hndy, led 3 out, rdn and hdd betw last 2, one pace whn hit last.* . . . . (4 to 1 co-fav tchd 9 to 2)   2

3876³ SOPHISM (USA) [85] 5-11-10 R Dunwoody, *nvr far away, effrt and drvn alng aftr 3 out, outpcd frm betw last 2.*
. . . . (4 to 1 co-fav op 3 to 1)   3

4107⁹ PEARLY WHITE [67] (v) 5-10-6⁵ M A FitzGerald, *trkd ldrs, effrt aftr one circuit, rdn 3 out, sn struggling.*
. . . . (33 to 1 op 20 to 1 tchd 40 to 1)   4

4107³ DOCTOR-J (Ire) [61] 4-10-0 W McFarland, *pressed ldrs, rdn aftr 3 out, fdd.* . . . . (12 to 1 op 10 to 1)   5

4052* CAPTAIN TANDY (Ire) [72] 5-10-11 (7ex) D J Burchell, *chsd ldr aftr second, hit nxt, rallied hfwy, fdd frm 3 out.*
. . . . (15 to 2 op 4 to 1 tchd 8 to 1)   6

2797 BALTIC EXCHANGE (Can) [79] 5-10-11 (7°) L Reynolds, *tried to make al, hdd and reminders 3 out, wknd quickly, tld off.* . . . . (16 to 1 op 10 to 1)   7

3635⁸ MILL BURN [80] 5-11-2 (3°) T Eley, *al pressing ldrs, effrt frm 3 out, tld off.* . . . . (11 to 2 op 8 to 1)   8

4064⁸ BOWLAND GIRL (Ire) [62] (bl) 5-9-12 (3°) S Wynne, *chasing ldrs whn f 1st.* . . . . . . (16 to 1 op 12 to 1 tchd 20 to 1)   f

3822⁴ THE COUNTRY DANCER [84] 4-11-9 D Skyrme, *in tch till jmpd badly rght 4th, sn tld off, pld up bef last.*
. . . . (25 to 1 op 16 to 1 tchd 33 to 1)   pu

Dist: 8l, 14l, 8l, 8l, ¾l, 8l, 25l, 1¼l. 3m 58.20s. a 9.20s (10 Ran).

(Highflyers), G B Balding

4161   Hunt Supporters' Novices' Handicap Chase (5-y-o and up) £2,802 2m 5f 110yds. . . . . (7:00)

4026³ MIRAGE DANCER [70] 11-10-4 I Lawrence, *wtd wth, improved hfwy, outpcd and rdn 2 out, ran on und str pres to ld r-in.* . . . . (16 to 1 op 12 to 1)   1

4067* YOUNG ALFIE [82] (bl) 9-11-2 (7ex) A Maguire, *made most, jnd fnl circuit, blun badly 6 out, rdn frm 2 out, hdd and no extr r-in...* (11 to 4 jt-fav op 5 to 2 tchd 100 to 30)   2

3883³ CREWS CASTLE [81] 7-11-1 N Williamson, *settled off the pace, improved hfwy, outpcd 3 out, rallied to chal last, kpt on same pace.* . . . . (7 to 1 tchd 8 to 1)   3

4074 NEEDS MUST [79] 7-10-13 J Frost, *wth ldrs, feeling pace and rdn aftr 4 out, sn lost tch.* . . . . . . (9 to 2 op 4 to 1)   4

4105⁵ PECHE D'OR [70] (bl) 10-10-3⁶ (7°) Mr M Rimell, *chsd ldg pair, rdn whn pace quickened aftr 4 out, tld off.*
. . . . (33 to 1 op 20 to 1)   5

3774* LE BUCHERON [90] 8-11-10 M Richards, *patiently rdn, improved to join ld hfwy, ridden frm 3 out, cl 4th whn f last.* . . . . (11 to 4 jt-fav op 5 to 1 tchd 9 to 1)   f

4105² PECCAVI [71] 10-10-5 R Bellamy, *chasing ldrs whn blun and uns rdr 3rd.* . . . . . . (13 to 2 tchd 9 to 1)   ur

4014² SEMINOLE PRINCESS [68] (bl) 6-10-2² R Dunwoody, *wth ldrs early, struggling bef hfwy, tld off whn pld up before tenth.* . . . . (9 to 1 op 8 to 1 tchd 10 to 1)   pu

4111 CHEQUE BOOK [72] 6-10-6⁶ Mr D Verco, *wth ldrs for o'r a circuit, lost tch 6 out, pld up bef 3 out.*
. . . . (50 to 1 op 33 to 1 tchd 66 to 1)   pu

Dist: 2½l, 3l, 25l, 25l. 5m 17.50s. a 14.50s (9 Ran).

(Miss C J E Caroe), Miss C J E Caroe

4162   Tarmac Construction Handicap Hurdle (0-120 4-y-o and up) £3,272 2m 110yds. . . . . (7:30)

4069* RES IPSA LOQUITUR [103] 7-11-5 (7ex) A Maguire, *settled midfield, improved to nose ahead 3 out, gng clr whn hit last.* . . . . (4 to 1 tchd 7 to 2)   1

4054² SILLIAN [94] 12-10-7 (3°) J Railton, *settled off the pace, imprvg whn hit 4 out, rallied frm nxt, ran on.*
. . . . (11 to 1 op 7 to 1)   2

3924* WILL JAMES [92] (bl) 8-10-3 (5°) S Curran, *trkd ldg bunch, drvn alng to chal aftr 3 out, one pace frm betw last 2.*
. . . . (11 to 2 op 4 to 1)   3

3904⁴ SALMAN (USA) [92] 8-10-8 N Williamson, *patiently rdn, blun 3rd, effrt aftr 4 out, ridden and no imprsn frm betw last 2.* . . . . (9 to 1 op 8 to 1 tchd 11 to 1)   4

3924[2] SQUIRE YORK [97] 4-10-13 M A FitzGerald, *nvr far away,
rdn aftr 3 out, sn struggling.*
............(11 to 2 op 1 to 2 tchd 5 to 1 and 6 to 1) 5
3930* MERLINS WISH (USA) [108] 5-11-10 R Dunwoody, *tried to
make all, hesitated 4th, hdd and hit 3 out, eased whn
btn bef last*........(2 to 1 fav op 9 to 4 tchd 11 to 4) 6
4127[4] HALLO MAM (Ire) [98] 5-11-0 M Brennan, *patiently rdn,
improved hfwy, hit 3 out and nxt, nvr able to chal.*
............(12 to 1 op 10 to 1 tchd 14 to 1) 7
4029[5] BURSAM [84] (bl) 8-10-0 W Marston, *unruly at strt,
refused to race, took no part.*
............(40 to 1 op 20 to 1 tchd 50 to 1) ref
4106 BY FAR (USA) [84] (bl) 8-10-0 V Slattery, *chsd ldrs till lost pl
hfwy, tld off whn pld up bef 2 out.* (33 to 1 op 20 to 1) pu
Dist: 6l, 4l, 25l, 15l, 11l, 2l. 3m 53.60s. a 4.60s (9 Ran).

SR: 45/30/24/-/-/-/   (Richard J Gray), B A Pearce

4163 30th Year Of The John Corbet Cup Champion Novices' Hunters' Chase (5-y-o and up) £3,551 3½m.....(8:00)

3988* CELTIC ABBEY 6-11-7 (7*) Mr D S Jones, *patiently rdn,
steady hdwy fnl circuit, ridden to ld last, ran on wl.*
............(7 to 2 op 5 to 1) 1
3987* FOX POINTER 9-11-7 (7*) Mr J Jukes, *tried to make all,
blun badly 14th, jnd last 3, mstk and hdd last, one
pace*............(11 to 2 op 5 to 1) 2
3991* RYMING CUPLET 9-11-7 (7*) Mr Richard White, *tucked
away in midfield, improved to join issue 3 out, rdn bef
last, kpt on same pace.*............(4 to 1 tchd 3 to 1) 3
4068[5] RUSTY BRIDGE 7-11-7 (7*) Mr J Johnson, *nvr far away,
feeling pace and drvn alng aftr 4 out, one pace frm nxt.*
............(11 to 1 op 8 to 1) 4
3846[3] SAMS HERITAGE 10-11-7 (7*) Mr G Hanmer, *settled off the
pace, hmpd by faller 12th, improved fnl circuit, outpcd
frm 4 out.*............(2 to 1 fav op 6 to 4 tchd 9 to 4) 5
3969[3] WELSH LEGION 9-11-7 (7*) Miss C Burgess, *chsd ldr, blun
tenth, drvn alng whn f 12th.*............(10 to 1 op 12 to 1) f
3846[2] BLAKES ORPHAN 8-11-8[1] (7*) Mr T Illsley, *beh and pushed
alng whn f 12th.*.....(12 to 1 op 10 to 1 tchd 14 to 1) f
WILDNITE 10-11-7 (7*) Mr T Jackson, *in tch, struggling to
hold pl fnl circuit, tld off whn pld up betw last 2.*
............(33 to 1 op 25 to 1) pu
Dist: 4l, 5l, 6l, 9l. 7m 9.60s. a 24.60s (8 Ran).

(G J Powell), Mrs Christine Hardinge

4164 Saddlers Handicap Chase (0-120 5-y-o and up) £2,921 2m 1f 110yds.... (8:30)

4125[6] SECRET SUMMIT (USA) [87] (v) 8-11-3 (3*) T Eley, *reluctant
to race, not fluent, drvn alng most of way, 7th and
looked btn last, ran on to ld last strds.*
............(12 to 1 op 10 to 1) 1
4102* LOR MOSS [94] 14-10-7 (7ex) J R Kavanagh, *nvr far away,
drvn ahead bef 2 out, ran on und pres, jst ct.*
............(6 to 1 op 3 to 1) 2
4067[3] BOSTON ROVER [115] 9-12-0 M Brennan, *settled off the
pace, plenty to do frm 4 out, ran on from last, nvr nrr.*
............(7 to 1 op 6 to 1 tchd 15 to 2) 3
4015[5] HOWGILL [88] 8-10-1 R Dunwoody, *al hndy, ev ch and
drvn alng frm 4 out, styd on one pace.*
............(11 to 2 fav op 4 to 1 tchd 13 to 2) 4
4105* PALACE WOLF (NZ) [94] 10-10-7 (7ex) M A FitzGerald, *al wl
in tch, ev ch and drvn alng frm 4 out, no extr r-in.*
............(6 to 1 op 4 to 1) 5
4109[5] POLDER [87] 8-9-7 (7*) Miss S Higgins, *settled midfield,
drvn up to fitter appr 3 out, not quicken frm nxt.*
............(40 to 1 op 33 to 1) 6
4109[4] DEEP DARK DAWN [105] 9-11-4 R Supple, *nvr far away,
ev ch and drvn alng 3 out, one pace frm nxt.*
............(7 to 1 tchd 6 to 1) 7
3929[4] ENCHANTED MAN [87] 10-10-0 A Maguire, *chsd ldrs, blun
4th, reminders nxt, struggling four out, tld off.*
............(10 to 1 op 8 to 1) 8
3985[2] TINAS LAD [98] 11-10-11 N Williamson, *tried to make all,
hdd bef 2 out, wknd quickly.*
............(9 to 1 op 6 to 1 tchd 10 to 1) 9
4071[2] MASTER SALESMAN [96] 11-10-9 D Gallagher, *al chasing
ldrs, effrt and drvn alng aftr 4 out, btn aftr nxt.*
............(9 to 1 op 8 to 1 tchd 10 to 1) 10
3941[7] AIR COMMANDER [87] 9-10-0 T Wall, *chsd ldr, feeling
pace 5 out, lost tch and pld up bef 2 out.*
............(10 to 1 op 14 to 1 tchd 8 to 1) pu
Dist: Hd, 3l, ¾l, 6l, 1¼l, 2½l, 25l, ¾l, 2l. 4m 17.50s. a 13.50s (11 Ran).

(Beamhurst Racing), A L Forbes

4165 Young Entry Novices' Handicap Hurdle (0-100 4-y-o and up) £2,094 2m 110yds....................... (9:00)

3917[6] TAKE A FLYER (Ire) [66] 4-10-0 R Dunwoody, *patiently rdn,
improved hfwy, nosed ahead betw last 2, styd on wl.*
............(5 to 1 op 4 to 1) 1
3843* FORGETFUL [82] 5-11-2 D J Burchell, *tried to make all,
hdd and rdn betw last 2, ran on same pace.*
............(7 to 1 op 5 to 1) 2

4120* FOREST PRIDE (Ire) [95] 5-11-10 (5*,10ex) F Leahy, *settled
off the pace, improved to join issue 3 out, rdn and kpt
on same pace frm betw last 2.*
............(11 to 4 fav op 3 to 1 tchd 100 to 30) 3
3914* TIME WON'T WAIT (Ire) [90] 5-11-10 J Railton, *wtd wth,
improved hfwy, rdn and ev ch frm 3 out, one pace.*
............(10 to 1 op 8 to 1) 4
3878 GEORGE LANE [66] 6-10-0 J Lodder, *wtd wth, improved to
join issue aftr 3 out, rdn bef nxt, fdd.*
............(10 to 1 op 8 to 1) 5
3998 NORTHERN CONQUEROR (Ire) [77] 6-10-11 M A FitzGerald,
nvr far away, feeling pace and drvn alng 3 out, sn btn.
............(16 to 1 op 12 to 1 tchd 20 to 1) 6
4012[2] DHARAMSHALA (Ire) [70] 6-10-4 M Brennan, *in tch, rdn to
hold pl aftr 4 out, tld off frm nxt.* (14 to 1 op 10 to 1) 7
3829[7] TOO CLEVER BY HALF [84] (bl) 6-11-4 R Supple, *in tch,
chsd alng whn pace lifted bef 3 out, sn lost touch.*
............(20 to 1 op 10 to 1) 8
3822* WAAZA (USA) [73] 5-10-7 N Williamson, *chsd ldg bunch,
rdn aftr 4 out, sn lost tch, tld off...*(10 to 1 op 5 to 1) 9
4056[7] POETS COVE [80] 6-11-0 R Bellamy, *slow away, beh and
drvn alng hfwy, tld off*............(14 to 1 op 9 to 1) 10
3016 PRINCESS TATEUM (Ire) [82] 4-11-2 G McCourt, *pressed
ldrs, struggling bef 3 out, tld off.* (12 to 1 tchd 14 to 1) 11
4016[4] GREEN'S SEAGO (USA) [72] 6-10-6 D Gallagher, *in tch,
struggling frm hfwy, tld off whn pld up bef 2 out.*
............(20 to 1 op 12 to 1) pu
4056 SHARP PRINCE [75] 5-10-9 A Maguire, *pressed ldrs till
wknd quickly 4 out, tld off whn pld up aftr nxt.*
............(16 to 1 op 7 to 1 tchd 20 to 1) pu
4029 BALUSTRADE [66] 7-10-0 I Lawrence, *struggling to go
pace hfwy, tld off whn pld up aftr 3 out.*
............(100 to 1 op 50 to 1) pu
Dist: 3l, ½l, 9l, 13l, 6l, 20l, 6l, dist, 8l, 25l. 3m 59.00s. a 10.00s (14 Ran).

(Bull & Bear Racing), R J Hodge

WEXFORD (IRE) (good (races 1,2), sof (3,4,5,6)) Friday June 3rd

4166 Premier Molasses Maiden Hurdle (4 y-o and up) £2,742 2¼m 100yds (5:00

3246[5] SOUL EMPEROR 4-11-6 A Powell,............(14 to 1)
3937[4] LINDEN'S LOTTO (Ire) 5-11-13 C O'Dwyer,........(4 to 1)
3616[7] THE OUTBACK WAY (Ire) 4-11-6 D H O'Connor,....(5 to 1)
3793[2] PILS INVADER (Ire) 6-11-13 (7*) D T Evans,.......(12 to 1)
213[4] CHARLIES DELIGHT (Ire) 6-11-11 (3*) K P Gaule,..(12 to 1)
4061[2] HAVIN' A BALL (Ire) 5-11-1 (7*) T Martin,........(14 to 1)
4059 CALLMECHARLIE (Ire) 5-11-8 (5*) P A Roche,......(50 to 1)
ORLAS CASTLE (Ire) 5-11-1 (7*) N T Egan,........(33 to 1)
3086[5] ALL-TOGETHER 7-11-4 (5*) Mr H F Cleary,.......(14 to 1)
4059[6] MINOR MATTER (Ire) 5-11-8 H Rogers,............(20 to 1)
4031 ABBEY TRINITY (Ire) 5-11-1 (7*) D M Bean,......(20 to 1)
3953 D'S AND DO'S (Ire) 5-11-8 T Horgan,............(33 to 1)
3321 HEATHFIELD (USA) 4-10-13 (7*) R A Hennessy, ..(33 to 1)
3788[2] THATS A SECRET 6-12-0 C F Swan,.........(11 to 10 fav)
2940 PADDYS TIPP (Ire) (bl) 6-12-0 S H O'Donovan, ...(25 to 1)
Dist: 6l, ¾l, 2l, 4½l. 4m 14.00s. (15 Ran).

(Luke Comer), Luke Come

4167 Greenvale Animal Feeds Hurdle (4 y-o and up) £2,742 2½m....... (5:30

3615[9] FABULIST (Ire) 5-11-7 T Horgan,................(6 to 1)
3993[4] PUSH THE BUTTON (Ire) 4-10-7 C F Swan,........(2 to 1)
3654[6] FERRYCARRIG HOTEL (Ire) 5-11-12 D H O'Connor,
............(6 to 4 fav)
MR GREENFIELD 10-11-6 (7*) J M Donnelly,.......(10 to 1)
3995 FIRST SESSION (Ire) 6-11-1 (7*) M Kelly,.........(7 to 1)
4076 HAPPY REUNION 9-11-7 C O'Dwyer,.............(14 to 1)
LIGHT OF OTHERDAYS 7-11-0 (7*) Mr B Lennon,..(33 to 1)
4059 CAPTAIN KIZZY (Ire) 4-10-7 H Rogers,...........(33 to 1)
Dist: 4½l, 4½l, 1½l, 8l. 5m 1.10s. (8 Ran).

(Mrs C A Moore), P Mulli

4168 Gowla Classic Handicap Chase (4-y-o and up) £3,427 2½m............(7:00

4042 ALBERT'S FANCY [-] 8-10-1 F J Flood,............(7 to 1)
3933* JASSU [-] 8-12-0 C F Swan,.................(11 to 8 fav)
3890[6] LADY BAR [-] 7-10-13 P M Verling,.............(8 to 1)
4032[2] SILVERWARE [-] 11-10-10 T Horgan,............(8 to 1)
3944[6] GUESSWORK [-] 8-10-13 (5*) M G Cleary,........(12 to 1)
4062[4] RANDOM PRINCE [-] 10-10-2 S R Murphy,........(8 to 1)
4032 QUAYSIDE BUOY [-] 11-10-0 (3*) C O'Brien,......(10 to 1)
3081 GLEN OG LANE [-] 10-9-7 F Woods,............(25 to 1)
4033[7] JOE'S A BOY [-] 9-9-3 (7*) Mr M G Wiseman,....(14 to 1)
637[9] ENNEREILLY RIVER [-] 11-11-1 (3*) T J Mitchell, ..(8 to 1)
Dist: Dd-ht, 8l, ½l, 2l. 5m 0.10s. (10 Ran).

(Slaney Cooked Meats & Bruno Buser), P J P Doyle & J E Kie

4169 Wellington Bridge Mares I.N.H. Fl Race (Div 1) (4-y-o and up) £2,742

¼m 100yds. . . . . (7:30)

3974² RAINYS RUN 7-11-7 (7*) Mr E Norris, ... (7 to 2) 1
3792 CUL RUA CREEK (Ire) 5-11-6 (7*) Mr E Sheehy, . . . (25 to 1) 2
4059⁵ RING FOUR (Ire) 5-11-13 Mr A P O'Brien, ... (5 to 4 on) 3
3953 SWIFT GLIDER (Ire) 5-11-6 (7*) Mr R P O'Keeffe, . . (14 to 1) 4
MARIES GALE (Ire) 4-11-3 (3*) Mrs J M Mullins, ... (8 to 1) 5
2620⁷ BENTLEY'S FLYER (Ire) 5-11-13 Mr D M O'Brien, . . . (8 to 1) 6
SANDY SHACK (Ire) 5-11-8 (5*) Mr H F Cleary, ... (8 to 1) 7
3084 BALLOUGH BUI (Ire) 5-11-6 (7*) Mr G F Ryan, ... (20 to 1) 8
4060 DEAR MONEY (Ire) 4-10-13 (7*) Mrs F Hennessy, . . (25 to 1) 9
3958 SCEAL EILE (Ire) 4-10-13 (7*) Mr A K Wyse, ... (20 to 1) 10
4063 NIGHT SERVICE (Ire) (bl) 6-11-7 (7*) Mr J Connolly, (20 to 1) 11
ANOTHER WHISTLE (Ire) 5-11-6 (7*) Mr B Lennon, (12 to 1) 12
GERAY LADY (Ire) 4-11-6 Mr P Fenton, ... (16 to 1) 13
GRADH MO CROI (Ire) 6-11-9 (5*) Mr P English, . . . (10 to 1) 14
Dist: 2½l, 4l, 15l, sht-hd. 4m 18.60s. (14 Ran).

(W Mooney), P Kiely

4170 Wellington Bridge Mares I.N.H. Flat Race (Div 2) (4-y-o and up) £2,742 2 ¼m 100yds. . . . . (8:00)

3997² THAT'S GOSPEL (Ire) 4-11-6 Mr P Fenton, ... (2 to 1 fav) 1
258⁸ OX EYE DAISY (Ire) 6-11-11 (3*) Mrs M Mullins, ... (7 to 1) 2
BALLYMACODA LADY (Ire) 5-11-13 Mr J A Flynn, . . (5 to 1) 3
CHRISALI (Ire) 5-11-13 Mr A P O'Brien, ... (8 to 1) 4
3956⁵ CARRABAWN 8-11-7 (7*) Mr P O'Keeffe, ... (16 to 1) 5
ANOTHER KAV (Ire) 4-11-6 Mr D M O'Brien, ... (16 to 1) 6
1160³ COTTON CALL (Ire) 5-11-10 (3*) Mrs J M Mullins, . . . (8 to 1) 7
1581⁶ CLOWATER LADY (Ire) 5-11-8 (5*) Mr P English, ... (6 to 1) 8
3891⁵ GALBOOLA (Ire) 5-11-6 (7*) Mr K Whelan, ... (14 to 1) 9
PENSTAL LADY (Ire) 4-10-13 (7*) Mr C A Murphy, (16 to 1) 10
SWEET VALLEY HIGH (Ire) 5-11-6 (7*) Miss N FitzGerald, ... (25 to 1) 11
4060 FONTAINE LODGE (Ire) 4-10-13 (7*) Mr J T Codd, (33 to 1) 12
3467 RUN FOR FUN (Ire) 6-11-11 (3*) Mr J A Nash, ... (12 to 1) 13
1814 LADY MARILYN (Ire) 6-11-9 (5*) Mr J P Berry, ... (16 to 1) 14
Dist: 3½l, 12l, 1½l, 3l. 4m 19.30s. (14 Ran).

(D Delahunty), Thomas Bergin

4171 Gold Blend I.N.H. Flat Race (4 & 5-y-o) £2,742 2¼m 100yds. . . . . (8:30)

4060² BRAMBLESHINE (Ire) 4-10-8 (7*) Mr T N Cloke, (6 to 4 fav) 1
3723⁶ TEMPLEWOOD EXPRESS (Ire) 5-11-8 (5*) Mr P English, ... (9 to 1) 2
3956³ YOUR CALL (Ire) 5-11-10 (3*) Mr J A Nash, ... (6 to 1) 3
PAEANDISPLAY (Ire) 4-10-13 (7*) Mr K Kirwan, ... (14 to 1) 4
3842⁸ RHETORIC HOUSE (Ire) 4-11-1 (5*) Mr P M Kelly, (12 to 1) 5
3936 LORD MONTE (Ire) (bl) 5-11-6 (7*) Miss A M O'Brien, ... (16 to 1) 6
3891⁹ MAHANKHALI (Ire) 5-11-13 Mr P Fenton, ... (14 to 1) 7
NORTHERN REEF (Ire) 4-11-1 (5*) Mr H F Cleary, . . (14 to 1) 8
DARAA DARAA (Ire) 4-11-3 (3*) Mrs M Mullins, ... (5 to 2) 9
3792 SLANEY GENT (Ire) 5-11-6 (7*) Mr C A Murphy, . . . (16 to 1) 10
3946 YOUNG ANAGLOG (Ire) 4-10-8 (7*) Mr P Cloke, . . . (33 to 1) 11
2231 THE BRIDGE TAVERN (Ire) 5-11-6 (7*) Mr R P Cody, (8 to 1) 12
4031 WOLLONGONG (Ire) 4-10-9¹ (7*) Mr P Cody, ... (33 to 1) 13
OFF YOU SAIL (Ire) 4-10-8 (7*) Mr J Connolly, ... (16 to 1) 14
Dist: 9l, ½l, 2½l, 2l. 4m 23.10s. (14 Ran).

(Kevin O'Donnell), Kevin O'Donnell

CHEPSTOW (soft)
Saturday June 4th
Going Correction: NIL

4172 Grunwick Stakes National Hunt Flat Race (4,5,6-y-o) £1,381 2m 110yds . . . . (9:15)

2444² IVY EDITH 4-10-2 (7*) S Ryan, *trkd ldrs, led 6 fs out, came o'r to stands side strt, pushed out.* . . . . (13 to 2 op 4 to 1 tchd 7 to 1) 1
4057² LEGENDRA 4-10-2 (7*) D Bohan, *mid-div, took clr order frm hfwy, ev ch 3 fs out, one pace*. . . . . (4 to 1) 2
3833² NO NEAR MISS 4-10-9 (7*) N Willmington, *hld up, hdwy hfwy, one pace fnl 3 fs*. . . . . (11 to 8 fav op 2 to 1) 3
4057⁴ GRAY ROSETTE 5-10-7 (7*) Richard Edwards, *al frnt rnk, plugged on one pace fnl 4 fs*. . . . . . (14 to 1 op 12 to 1) 4
4057³ B MY LOVELY 4-10-2 (7*) P Maddock, *hld up, hdwy 7 fs out, kpt on one pace fnl 3 furlongs*. (8 to 1 op 10 to 1) 5
KINO'S CROSS 5-10-12 (7*) K Brown, *mid-div, hdwy 6 fs out, no headway fnl 3 furlongs*. . . . . (20 to 1) 6
SISTER ELLY 4-10-6 (3*) R Davis, *beh till hdwy o'r 5 fs out, wknd 3 out*. . . . . (25 to 1) 7
3832 ANNS REQUEST 5-11-0 Mr J O'Brien, *prmnt early, beh frm hfwy, tld off*. . . . . (20 to 1 op 16 to 1) 8
4023 BOBBIE MO 4-10-7 (7*) Mr R M Murphy, *prmnt to hfwy, tld off*. . . . . (14 to 1 op 10 to 1) 9
4023⁹ STICKY MONEY 6-10-7 (7*) L Reynolds, *pld hrd, led till hdd and wknd quickly 6 fs out, tld off.* . . . . (6 to 1 tchd 7 to 1) 10
3686 ONEMOREANWEGO 6-10-7 (7*) Mr R Johnson, *al beh, tld off*. . . . . (25 to 1) 11
2509 RELAXED LAD 5-11-2 (3*) D Meredith, *al beh, tld off.* . . . . (25 to 1) 12
4023² TELL THE BOYS (Ire) 6-10-12 (7*) P Ward, *prmnt till wknd 6 fs out, tld off*. . . . . (5 to 1 op 4 to 1) 13
4023 MONKS JAY (Ire) 5-11-2 (3*) J McCarthy, *al beh, tld off.* . . . . (33 to 1) 14
4057⁹ FRONTRUNNER 6-11-0 Mrs S Hobbs, *prmnt early, beh hfwy, tld off*. . . . . (12 to 1 op 10 to 1) 15
4023 DELWORTHY DANCER 5-10-12 (7*) M Keighley, *al beh, tld off frm hfwy*. . . . . (14 to 1) 16
3386 VEXFORD MODEL 4-10-2 (7*) T Dascombe, *prmnt till wknd o'r 6 fs out, tld off whn pld up and collapsed over one furlong out*. . . . . (33 to 1) pu
Dist: 4l, 5l, 2½l, 1l, 12l, 7l, 20l, 1¼l, 3½l, 2½l. 4m 17.50s. (17 Ran).

(Glen Antill), T G Mills

MARKET RASEN (good to firm)
Saturday June 4th
Going Correction: NIL

4173 Lincolnshire Echo Novices' Chase (5-y-o and up) £3,263 2m 1f 110yds (6:25)

3726³ WAYWARD WIND 10-11-1 A Maguire, *chsd ldrs, led 3 out, styd on strly*. . . . . (2 to 1 fav op 9 to 4) 1
4014³ SEARCY 6-11-1 G Upton, *al prmnt, led aftr 6th, hdd 3 out, cl up whn mstk nxt, sn rdn and btn.* . . . . (4 to 1 op 5 to 1) 2
4029 BARON TWO SHOES (v) 8-11-1 (5*) P Midgley, *led, hdd aftr second, sn led ag'n, headed after 6th, one pace frm 3 out*. . . . . (12 to 1 op 10 to 1 tchd 14 to 1) 3
4111³ APPLIANCEOFSCIENCE 7-11-6 J Ryan, *in tch, 5th and btn whn f 3 out*. (6 to 1 tchd 7 to 1) f
3893³ SOUND PROFIT 6-10-10 A Dobbin, *hld up, hdwy 6th, jnd ldrs 3 out, wknd nxt, 3rd whn f last.* . . . . (5 to 2 op 6 to 4 tchd 11 to 4) f
4121 FIDDLER'S DRUM 7-11-1 M Brennan, *led aftr second, ran out nxt*. . . . . (11 to 1 op 10 to 1) ro
4081⁴ WSOM (Ire) 6-11-1 N Smith, *mstk 1st, tld off frm hfwy, pld up bef 3 out*. . . . . (25 to 1 op 20 to 1) pu
Dist: 6l, 6l. 4m 26.30s. a 12.30s (7 Ran).

(Andy Dobson), J White

4174 Evening Telegraph Selling Hurdle (4-y-o) £1,968 2m 1f 110yds. . . . .(6:55)

3716* ITS UNBELIEVABLE 11-12 A Maguire, *al hndy, led appr 2 out, ran on wl*. . . . . (11 to 8 on op 5 to 4 on) 1
4012⁵ COEUR BATTANT (Fr) 11-0 G McCourt, *hdwy 5th, rdn 3 out, chsd wnr nxt, hit last, one pace r-in.* . . . . (5 to 1 tchd 11 to 2) 2
TIL FRIDAY 10-9 J Ryan, *wl beh, rdn hfwy, ran on frm last, nrst finish*. (14 to 1 op 10 to 1) 3
2401³ WORKINGFORPEANUTS (Ire) 10-6 (3*) D J Moffatt, *mstks, beh, ran on frm 2 out, nvr nrr.* . . . . (11 to 1 op 10 to 1 tchd 12 to 1) 4
4085³ DANCES WITH GOLD (v) 10-9 N Williamson, *led, hit 5th, hdd appr 2 out, sn rdn and wknd.* (6 to 1 tchd 13 to 2) 5
4121⁹ MR ABBOT 10-11 (3*) T Eley, *chsd ldr, effrt appr 2 out, sn btn*. . . . . (16 to 1 op 12 to 1) 6
3690 ASTRAC TRIO (USA) 11-7 A Dobbin, *prmnt, rdn hfwy, wknd appr 2 out*. . . . . . . (9 to 1 op 8 to 1 tchd 10 to 1) 7
4101³ FREDDIE JACK 11-0 S Burrough, *hld up, effrt 4th, sn rdn and wknd*. . . . . (16 to 1 op 14 to 1) 8
4112 BEN CONNAN (Ire) 11-0 M A FitzGerald, *beh frm hfwy, tld off whn pld up bef 2 out*. . . . . (50 to 1) pu
Dist: 3l, 8l, 5l, 1l, sht-hd, 3l, 30l. 4m 11.20s. a 9.20s (9 Ran).
SR: 6/-/-/-/-/- (Gerald Hopkins), J White

4175 Colin Booth Transport Handicap Chase (0-110 5-y-o and up) £4,370 2 ¾m 110yds. (7:30)

4013² CALL ME EARLY [87] 9-10-7 M Brennan, *chsd ldrs, led 12th, mstk 2 out, wndrd appr last, ran on wl.* . . . . (5 to 1 op 8 to 1 tchd 9 to 2) 1
4028* BOBBY SOCKS [108] 8-12-0 A Maguire, *hld up, hdwy 7th, effrt appr 3 out, swtchd lft approaching last, sn rdn and unbl to quicken*. . . . . (6 to 4 fav op 5 to 4) 2
4108² WE'RE IN THE MONEY [80] (bl) 10-10-0 B Dalton, *hld up, outpcd tenth, rdn appr 3 out, nvr able to chal.* . . . . (9 to 1 op 6 to 1 tchd 10 to 1) 3
3908 LAPIAFFE [89] 10-10-9 R Dunwoody, *led to 12th, wknd 3 out*. . . . . (6 to 1 op 9 to 2) 4
3512⁶ EBONY SWELL [94] 13-10-9 (5*) P Midgley, *nvr dngrs.* . . . . (20 to 1 op 16 to 1) 5
4067⁴ THEY ALL FORGOT ME [80] 7-10-0 N Williamson, *chsd ldrs, rdn and wknd 3 out*. . . . . (16 to 1 op 12 to 1) 6
4137² STRONG APPROACH [97] 9-11-3 A Dobbin, *prmnt, rdn 4 out, grad wknd*. . . . . (9 to 2 op 4 to 1 tchd 5 to 1) 7
4087⁴ BARKISLAND [94] 10-11-0 Mrs A Farrell, *in tch till mstk 8th, beh whn pld up bef tenth*. . . . . (20 to 1 op 14 to 1) pu
Dist: 2l, 3l, 15l, sht-hd, 15l, 20l. 5m 37.80s. a 9.80s (8 Ran).

(J S Lammiman), O Brennan

4176 Newark Storage Handicap Hurdle (0-100 4-y-o and up) £3,634 2m 3f 110yds...................... (8:00)

4121* SEA BREAKER (Ire) [87] 6-11-4 (6ex) G Bradley, *hld up, hdwy hfwy, led 2 out, ran on wl.*
.... (11 to 2 op 5 to 1 tchd 6 to 1) 1
3910² MANGROVE MIST (Ire) [93] 6-11-10 A Dobbin, *al prmnt, jnd wnr 2 out, no extr r-in.* (11 to 2 op 9 to 2 tchd 6 to 1) 2
4157⁵ CHARLAFRIVOLA [70] (bl) 6-10-1 W Humphreys, *hld up, hdwy and ev ch 2 out, rdn appr last, unbl to quicken r-in.* ....(12 to 1 op 10 to 1 tchd 14 to 1) 3
4086² SAOIRSE (Ire) [74] (v) 6-10-2 (3*) D J Moffatt, *sn wl beh, ran on frm 2 out, nrst finish.* .... (10 to 1) 4
4080⁴ CHARLYCIA [84] (v) 6-10-8 (7*) M Clarke, *prmnt, rdn 3 out, styd on same pace.*................(12 to 1 op 10 to 1) 5
3287³ LOGICAL FUN [91] (bl) 6-11-8 A Maguire, *hld up, no hdwy frm 2 out.* .... (6 to 1) 6
4080* RAPID MOVER [82] (bl) 7-10-13 R Dunwoody, *hld up, rdn appr 2 out, no imprsn.*
..................(4 to 1 fav op 5 to 1 tchd 11 to 2) 7
3998⁴ SPANISH WHISPER [76] 7-10-7 N Williamson, *prmnt, led aftr 3 out, hdd and wknd appr nxt.*
.... (14 to 1 op 12 to 1) 8
4029⁶ REXY BOY [72] (v) 7-10-3² G Harker, *led to 3rd, led ag'n 5th, hdd and wknd 3 out.*........... (10 to 1 op 8 to 1) 9
4089² MASTER'S CROWN (USA) [86] 6-11-3 W Worthington, *beh, rdn hfwy, grad lost tch.*............(14 to 1 op 12 to 1) 10
2331 KALKO [88] 5-11-6 G McCourt, *prmnt, rdn 3 out, wknd whn f nxt.* ....(12 to 1) f
4121¹³ VOLCANIC DANCER (USA) [70] (v) 8-10-1 B Dalton, *refused to race.*...................(16 to 1 op 12 to 1) ref
4081 FLAXON WORRIOR [69] 10-10-0 O Pears, *led 3rd, hdd 5th, sn tld off, pld up bef 2 out.*.......(50 to 1 op 33 to 1) pu
4082* LODGING [74] 7-10-5 M A FitzGerald, *prmnt till wknd rpdly and pld up bef 2 out.*
.... (9 to 1 op 10 to 1 tchd 8 to 1) pu
Dist: 2l, ¾l, 5l, 1l, 1¼l, 3l, 8l, 7l, 2l. 4m 39.10s. a 6.10s (14 Ran).
SR: 29/33/9/8/17/22/10/-/-/- (Don Cantillon), D E Cantillon

4177 Pleasure Prints Novices' Handicap Chase (5-y-o and up) £3,327 2½m ....(8:30)

4081² CHIC AND ELITE [83] 7-10-12 N Williamson, *hld up, hdwy tenth, ev ch whn lft in ld 3 out, styd on strly.*
..........................(3 to 1 op 7 to 2) 1
3940² BONDAID [86] 10-11-1 A Maguire, *hld up, hdwy und pres 12th, lft second 3 out, one pace appr last.*
..........................(5 to 1 op 3 to 1) 2
4024 MRS TWEED [71] 8-10-0 B Dalton, *hld up, hdwy 8th, wth ldrs whn blun and lost pl tenth, effrt appr 3 out, btn when not fluent last 2.*..................... (33 to 1) 3
3646 BENNAN MARCH [95] 7-11-10 A Dobbin, *led to 8th, wknd 3 out.*............... (11 to 1 op 8 to 1 tchd 9 to 1) 4
4142² CASTLE CROSS [72] 7-10-1 R Dunwoody, *prmnt, led 8th to 11th, rdn and wknd 3 out.*
.... (2 to 1 fav op 5 to 2 tchd 11 to 4 and 3 to 1) 5
4014* TRY NEXT DOOR [80] 7-10-9 M Brennan, *wl beh frm hfwy.*
.... (3 to 1 op 11 to 4 tchd 7 to 2) 6
4049 HEATHVIEW [79] 7-10-3 (5*) F Leahy, *chsd ldrs, led 11th till f 3 out.*..................(6 to 1 tchd 7 to 1) f
Dist: 8l, 10l, ¾l, 25l, dist. 5m 3.60s. a 11.60s (7 Ran).
(J R Weston), J J O'Neill

4178 'Seasons Over' Novices' Hurdle (4-y-o and up) £2,882 2m 5f 110yds.... (9:05)

3734⁷ DARK DEN (USA) 4-11-6 T Kent, *prmnt, led 4th, styd on strly.*..........................(3 to 1 op 4 to 1) 1
4072* LOCH SCAVAIG (Ire) 5-11-4 (3*) D J Moffatt, *led to 3rd, chsd wnr appr 2 out, styd on one pace approaching last.*
..................(9 to 2 op 4 to 1 tchd 5 to 1) 2
3739² SUPER COIN 6-11-12 A Maguire, *hld up, hdwy 6th, rdn appr 2 out, sn btn.*................. (7 to 1 op 4 to 1) 3
4088⁴ RECORD LOVER (Ire) 4-11-2 W Worthington, *beh till ran on frm 2 out.*...................(40 to 1 op 33 to 1) 4
3970 ARTIC WINGS (Ire) 6-11-7 M Brennan, *hld up, hdwy hfwy, wknd 2 out.*...................(10 to 1 op 7 to 1) 5
SWERVIN MERVIN 6-11-2 G Bradley, *hld up and beh, nvr nrr.*............................ (66 to 1 op 50 to 1) 6
3849* PRIDWELL 4-11-6 R Dunwoody, *hld up in tch, rdn appr 2 out, btn whn mstk last.*....... (Evens fav op 6 to 5 on) 7
3928⁴ THE CAN CAN MAN 7-11-2 M Robinson, *hld up, hdwy hfwy, wknd 3 out.*...............(50 to 1 op 33 to 1) 8
4079² SWISS BEAUTY 6-10-8 (3*) A Larnach, *led 3rd to 4th, wknd 7th.*..........................(50 to 1 op 25 to 1) 9
4021 AHBEJAYBUS (Ire) 5-11-2 Susan Kersey, *al in rear, tld off frm 6th.*..................(200 to 1 op 100 to 1) 10
4133² WHY NOT EQUINAME 6-10-9 (7*) D Waters, *in tch to 7th, sn beh.*..................(50 to 1 op 25 to 1) 11
4025⁸ SKIDDER 5-11-2 Mr K Green, *unruly strt, in tch to hfwy, sn wl beh, tld off whn pld up bef 2 out.*
..................(200 to 1 op 100 to 1) pu
Dist: 3l, 13l, 3l, 4l, 20l, nk, ¾l, 2l, dist, 6l. 5m 15.50s. a 11.50s (12 Ran).
(George L Ohrstrom), Mrs J Cecil

STRATFORD (good)
Saturday June 4th
Going Correction: PLUS 0.40 sec. per fur.

4179 Whyte Melville Conditional Jockeys' Claiming Hurdle (4 & 5-y-o) £2,178 2m 110yds...................... (2:50)

3899² LAKE DOMINION 5-11-8 P McLoughlin, *settled gng wl, smooth hdwy to ld 2 out, ran on strly to go clr last.*
..........................(7 to 4 fav tchd 2 to 1) 1
4052⁵ SANDRO (bl) 5-11-0 D Leahy, *chsd clr ldr frm 3rd, led nxt, jnd 3 out, hdd 2 out, one pace.*
..................(12 to 1 op 10 to 1 tchd 14 to 1) 2
MORJINSKI 4-10-2 A Procter, *patiently rdn, improved to join issue bef 3 out, fdd nxt, tld off.*
..................(150 to 1 op 50 to 1) 3
1705 HOHNE GARRISON 4-10-6 (7*) K Davies, *reminders to keep up 3rd, effrt aftr 4 out, fdd nxt, tld off.*
.... (33 to 1 op 20 to 1) 4
4160⁷ BALTIC EXCHANGE (Can) 5-10-12 L Reynolds, *struggling to go pace hfwy, tld off frm 4 out...* (16 to 1 op 8 to 1) 5
4160⁴ PEARLY WHITE 5-10-9 Guy Lewis, *chsd clr ldr to 3rd, fdd und pres bef 3 out, tld off.*........(25 to 1 op 14 to 1) 6
4141⁷ DISTANT MEMORY (bl) 5-10-12 (7*) C Quinlan, *chsd ldrs, pushed alng in midfield whn f 3 out.*
..........................(9 to 4 tchd 5 to 2) f
3853⁵ BOLTROSE 4-11-0 (7*) C Huggan, *trkd ldrs, improved hfwy, 4th and rdn whn mstk, slpd on landing and uns rdr 2 out.*.............. (10 to 1 tchd 5 to 1 and 7 to 2) ur
4009 TRUE SERENADE 5-10-5 (7*) P Maddock, *wtd wth, effrt whn hmpd by faller and brght dwn paddock bend aftr 4th.*.............. (25 to 1 op 20 to 1 tchd 33 to 1) bd
GOLDEN SPHINX (Ire) 4-10-2 R Davis, *wtd wth, steady hdwy whn slpd up paddock bend aftr 4th.*
..................(50 to 1 op 25 to 1 tchd 66 to 1) su
4104 ON THE LEDGE (USA) 4-10-7³ (7*) M Appleby, *rcd freely in clr ld, hdd 4th, wknd quickly and pld up bef nxt.*
..................(200 to 1 op 50 to 1) pu
Dist: 12l, dist, 20l, 11l, 1l. 4m 6.80s. a 17.80s (11 Ran).
(Mrs Betty Bate and Mark Goodall), J White

4180 Gambling Prince Chase (5-y-o and up) £3,512 2m 5f 110yds........... (3:20)

4018⁵ ERRANT KNIGHT 10-11-6 R Dunwoody, *confidently rdn, hit 7th, led 4 out, clr last 2...* (3 to 1 on op 9 to 4 on) 1
4102³ NOS NA GAOITHE (v) 11-10-12 B Powell, *wth ldr, nosed ahead 3rd to 4 out, not pace of wnr last 2.*
.... (14 to 1 op 10 to 1) 2
3978² LOCKWOOD PRINCE 11-10-12 J Frost, *chsd ldrs, hit 4th, struggling hfwy, tld off.*
..................(25 to 1 op 33 to 1 tchd 50 to 1) 3
4018⁴ SPACE FAIR 11-12-0 A Maguire, *led to 3rd, styd upsides till ran out 4 out, continued, tld off.*
..................(100 to 30 op 9 to 4 tchd 7 to 2) 4
Dist: 25l, dist, dist. 5m 31.40s. a 28.40s (4 Ran).
(Mrs N J Bird), M C Pipe

4181 Flagstone Handicap Hurdle (0-120 5-y-o and up) £2,705 3m 3f.........(3:50)

4050³ SKIRCOAT GREEN [86] 9-10-7 Mrs A Farrell, *enterprisingly rdn, made all, drvn clr frm 2 out, styd on.*
.... (7 to 1 op 5 to 1) 1
4123* GRATUITY [93] 9-11-0 (6ex) N Mann, *chsd wnr thrght, rdn last 2, styd on r-in...* (3 to 1 fav tchd 7 to 2) 2
3943⁴ INTERPLAY [83] 9-10-4 D O'Sullivan, *patiently rdn, improved to go hndy fnl circuit, ridden 3 out, ran on one pace.*.............. (14 to 1 op 12 to 1) 3
3919³ BOOTSCRAPER [90] (bl) 7-10-11 A Maguire, *settled wth chasing bunch, effrt gng wl fnl circuit, one pace frm 3 out.*.............. (13 to 2 op 8 to 1) 4
4070² TEMPORALE [79] 8-9-7 (7*) G Crone, *last and hld up, took clr order fnl circuit, rdn 3 out, fdd.* (16 to 1 op 12 to 1) 5
4088² ANTI MATTER [89] 9-10-5 (5*) S Fox, *wtd wth, effrt hfwy, rdn bef 3 out, sn btn...* (9 to 1 op 7 to 1 tchd 10 to 1) 6
4054⁶ TOUCH OF WINTER [95] 8-11-2 N Williamson, *settled off the pace, effrt hfwy, rdn bef 3 out, no imprsn.*
..................(11 to 1 op 8 to 1 tchd 12 to 1) 7
4064 KNIGHTS (NZ) [87] 8-10-8 Jacqui Oliver, *hld up, pushed alng whn pace lifted fnl circuit, sn tld off.*
..................(14 to 1 op 12 to 1 tchd 16 to 1) 8
4070* CRAZY HORSE DANCER (USA) [79] 6-10-0 J Lodder, *settled midfield, improved aftr one circuit, fdd 3 out, tld off.*
..........................(12 to 1) 9
3845² DOMINION TREASURE [80] 9-10-1 L Harvey, *wl plcd early, lost tch 5th, tld off whn pld up bef 3 out.*
..................(13 to 2 op 6 to 1) pu
3764⁷ BRAVO STAR (USA) [102] 9-11-9 W Marston, *chsd ldrs to hfwy, lost pl quickly and pld up bef 3 out.*
..................(25 to 1 op 20 to 1 tchd 33 to 1) pu
4035³ CELCIUS [103] (bl) 10-11-10 R Dunwoody, *patiently rdn, improved fnl circuit, wknd quickly 4 out, pld up bef last.*..................(10 to 1 op 6 to 1) pu

4106[7] FRANK DALE [79] 11-9-7 (7*) Mr R Johnson, *struggling most of way, tld off whn pld up bef last.* ....(100 to 1 op 50 to 1) pu
Dist: 3l, 1½l, 1l, 15l, 7l, ½l, 30l, 20l. 6m 52.40s. a 33.40s (13 Ran).
(Calder Racing), P Beaumont

4182 35th Year Of The Horse And Hound Cup Final Champion Hunters' Chase (5-y-o and up) £7,230 3½m......(4:25)

MIGHTY FROLIC 7-11-9 Mr T Hills, *made most, jnd fnl circuit, styd on to go clr betw last 2.* ....(10 to 1 tchd 12 to 1) 1
4022[2] MR MURDOCK 9-12-0 Mr P Henley, *in tch, niggled alng 6th, jnd wnr fnl circuit, no extr frm 2 out.* ....(9 to 1 op 7 to 1) 2
3948* BLACKGUARD (USA) 8-12-0 Mr J Grassick, *wtd wth, improved fnl circuit, feeling pace whn blun 4 out, not quicken*..........................(12 to 1 op 10 to 1) 3
4022* WARLEGGAN 13-12-0 Mr S Brookshaw, *last for o'r a circuit, styd on frm 6 out, nvr nrr*..... (12 to 1 op 6 to 1) 4
3949 CARRICKMINES 9-12-0 Mr T Jones, *led early, styd hndy till rdn fnl circuit, fdd 5 out, tld off.* (16 to 1 op 8 to 1) 5
CELTIC FLAME 13-12-0 Mr R Lawther, *in tch, chsd ldr hfwy, struggling 6 out, tld off*..... (33 to 1 op 20 to 1) 6
3858* WILD ILLUSION 10-12-0 Mr J Trice-Rolph, *nvr far away, blun and slpd on landing 12th, rallied, lost tch 6 out, tld off*............... (9 to 4 fav op 2 to 1 tchd 5 to 2) 7
GENERALS BOY 12-12-0 Mr P Craggs, *patiently rdn, improved gng wl to track wnr whn f 14th.* ....(3 to 1 op 7 to 2) f
4065 SKERRY MEADOW 10-12-0 Mr I Widdicombe, *in tch for a circuit, jmpd slwly 7 out, pld up bef nxt.* .... (33 to 1 op 25 to 1) pu
3951* BLUE DANUBE (USA) 10-12-0 Mr Andrew Martin, *in tch, jmpd slwly 8th, tld off whn pld up bef 2 out.* ....(9 to 1 op 8 to 1) pu
3717[3] KNIFEBOARD 8-12-0 Mr J Culloty, *chsd ldg bunch till pld up and dismounted aftr 11th*...... (20 to 1 op 14 to 1) pu
4095* SONOFAGIPSY 10-12-0 Mr M Felton, *struggling to keep up aftr one circuit, tld off whn pld up bef 4 out.* .... (16 to 1 op 10 to 1) pu
Dist: 15l, 8l, 2l, 13l, 25l, 6l. 7m 21.70s. a 36.70s (12 Ran).
(Maurice E Pinto), Miss S Edwards

4183 Farriers Hurdle (5-y-o and up) £2,901 2¾m 110yds..................... (4:55)

4072[2] LYNCH LAW (Ire) (v) 6-11-2 R Dunwoody, *al gng best, cruised up on bit 3 out, led aftr last, readily.* .... (11 to 8 fav tchd 6 to 4) 1
4017[2] WICK POUND (bl) 8-10-12 T Grantham, *wtd wth, improved to join ldr 3 out, sn led, hdd aftr last, no extr.* .... (13 to 8 op 6 to 4 tchd 15 to 8) 2
3384[9] ACROW LINE 9-10-12 D J Burchell, *wl plcd till rdn and ran in snatches fnl circuit, one pace frm 3 out.* ....(3 to 1 op 7 to 2 tchd 4 to 1) 3
4131[5] BRABINER LAD 10-10-12 S Turner, *patiently rdn, improved aftr one circuit, ridden 3 out, no extr.* .... (50 to 1 op 25 to 1) 4
2067 LAABAS 11-10-12 D Gallagher, *tried to make all, hdd bef 2 out, fdd*...(100 to 1) 5
4080[6] FAUX PAVILLON (bl) 10-10-7 (5*) S Fox, *trkd ldrs, feeling pace bef 3 out, wknd quickly, virtually pld up r-in.* .... (25 to 1 op 14 to 1) 6
4112[4] BATHWICK BOBBIE 7-10-12 J R Kavanagh, *trkd ldrs, struggling fnl circuit, tld off.* .... (40 to 1 op 25 to 1 tchd 50 to 1) 7
4139[7] CHRISTIAN SOLDIER (bl) 7-10-12 W Elderfield, *chsd ldrs, mstk and reminders 7th, tld off aftr*.........(100 to 1) 8
3848[7] CAST ADRIFT 7-10-7 G Bradley, *struggling frm hfwy, tld off whn pld up bef last*........... (50 to 1 op 25 to 1) pu
Dist: 8l, 1¼l, 9l, 15l, dist, nk, dist. 5m 41.50s. a 29.50s (9 Ran).
(Frank A Farrant), M C Pipe

4184 Foxford Handicap Chase (0-120 5-y-o and up) £2,999 3m..............(5:25)

4038* SARAVILLE [114] 7-11-11 R Dunwoody, *jmpd wl, made most, ran on strly frm 3 out.* .... (6 to 4 fav op 5 to 4 tchd 13 to 8) 1
4013* PRUDENT PEGGY [94] 7-10-5[5] J Frost, *patiently rdn, improved to go hndy 3 out, ridden and ev ch nxt, kpt on same pace*.................................(8 to 1 op 7 to 1) 2
4007[3] MISS FERN [91] 9-9-13 (3*) D Meredith, *nvr far away, ev ch 3 out, rdn and no extr betw last 2.* (4 to 1 tchd 5 to 1) 3
4007[8] TOUCHING STAR [102] 9-10-13 M Hourigan, *al chasing ldrs, effrt fnl circuit, rdn and one pace frm 3 out.* .... (14 to 1 op 8 to 1) 4
4065[2] MWEENISH [90] 12-10-1 R Bellamy, *chsd ldrs, struggling whn pace lifted 5 out, tld off.* .... (6 to 1 op 5 to 1 tchd 13 to 2) 5
4065[5] SPORTING MARINER [90] (bl) 12-10-0[2] (3*) R Davis, *wth ldr, feeling pace and drvn alng fnl circuit, lost tch 4 out, tld off*..................................(16 to 1 op 12 to 1) 6
4068[4] ABBOTSHAM [95] 9-10-6 J R Kavanagh, *in tch, drvn alng to keep up whn f 15th.* (13 to 2 op 7 to 1 tchd 10 to 1) f
4143 NEWS REVIEW [89] 11-10-0 D Gallagher, *beh, shrtlvd effrt fnl circuit, lost tch and pld up bef 3 out.* .... (40 to 1 op 25 to 1) pu
3978[3] TAGMOUN CHAUFOUR (Fr) [89] 9-10-0 B Powell, *reminders and drvn alng 4th, sn lost tch, pld up bef 12th.* (33 to 1) pu
4055[4] PAPER STAR [89] 7-10-0 M Perrett, *dsptd ld early, struggling 5 out, lost tch an pld up bef 3 out.* .... (50 to 1 op 33 to 1 tchd 66 to 1) pu
Dist: 7l, 5l, nk, 25l, 7l. 6m 14.20s. a 27.20s (10 Ran).
(R V Cliff), M C Pipe

4185 Puppy Walkers Novices' Handicap Hurdle (0-100 4-y-o and up) £2,094 2¾m 110yds..................... (5:55)

4004* NEW STATESMAN [75] 6-10-8 (5*) S Curran, *settled gng wl, improved to ld 3 out, ran on strly r-in.* .... (5 to 2 fav op 3 to 1 tchd 7 to 2) 1
4104* THANKS A MILLION [62] 8-10-0[3] (3*,8ex) R Davis, *settled off the pace, drvn alng and gd hdwy fnl circuit, styd on, not rch wnr*........................ (8 to 1 op 7 to 1) 2
4135[2] RIP THE CALICO (Ire) [63] 6-9-10[2] (7*) Miss C Spearing, *nvr far away, effrt and reminders hfwy, ev ch 3 out, no extr frm nxt*.......................... (12 to 1 op 14 to 1) 3
4021[7] WAKT [62] 4-10-0 D Skyrme, *sn wl beh, relentless prog fnl circuit, styd on, nvr nrr.* .... (12 to 1 op 7 to 1 tchd 14 to 1) 4
4100[3] CHINAMAN [90] (bl) 5-12-0 A Tory, *pressed ldrs, feeling pace and drvn alng fnl circuit, btn aftr 4 out.* .... (10 to 1 op 8 to 1) 5
4021 ROAD TO AU BON (USA) [62] 6-10-0 M Perrett, *outpcd and drvn alng hfwy, styd on und pres frm 3 out, nvr able to chal*..(16 to 1) 6
4004[3] EXARCH (USA) [90] (bl) 5-11-9 (5*) P McLoughlin, *chsd ldrs, ev ch hfwy, struggling frm 3 out, tld off.* ....(8 to 1 op 6 to 1) 7
4004[4] ST ROBERT [66] 7-10-4 W McFarland, *wth ldrs, led 4th, jnd hfwy, hdd 3 out, fdd*......................(14 to 1) 8
4064[7] ARMASHOCKER [66] 6-10-4 R Dunwoody, *wtd wth, improved to take clr order fnl circuit, rdn 3 out, fdd frm nxt*..................................(9 to 1 op 7 to 1) 9
4144 EMPERORS WARRIOR [70] 8-10-8 Jacqui Oliver, *trkd ldrs, drw level hfwy, rdn alng 3 out, sn lost tch.* .... (14 to 1 op 10 to 1) 10
4014 SERDARLI [62] 12-10-0 L Harvey, *dsptd ld, blun 6th, sn lost pl, tld off frm 4 out*......... (33 to 1 tchd 50 to 1) 11
3765[6] ELEGANT TOUCH [62] (bl) 5-9-7 (7*) O Burrows, *beh hfwy, drvn alng fnl circuit, tld off*...... (33 to 1 op 25 to 1) 12
3829 RED OXON [62] 12-10-0 Mr J O'Brien, *not fluent, rcd freely in ld till hdd 4th, wknd quickly hfwy, tld off whn pld up bef last*................ (50 to 1 op 33 to 1) pu
3970[4] MARINERS COVE [66] 6-10-1 (3*) D Meredith, *wtd wth, improved hfwy, drvn alng bef 4 out, lost tch and pld up before last*............ (15 to 2 op 7 to 1 tchd 8 to 1) pu
Dist: 9l, 1½l, 9l, 2l, 3½l, 1½l, 5l, hd, dist, 10l. 5m 48.50s. a 36.50s (14 Ran).
(Robin Barwell), C R Barwell

SLIGO (IRE) (good)
Sunday June 5th

4186 Yeats Maiden Hurdle (4-y-o and up) £2,226 2m..................... (2:15)

3971 TIBOULEN (Ire) 4-10-7 (3*) T P Rudd,............. (6 to 1) 1
4092[8] GLENMAVIS 7-11-6 T J Mitchell,................ (14 to 1) 2
HELLO MONKEY 7-11-11 (3*) T P Treacy,.......(6 to 4 fav) 3
4031[5] SHES A STAR (Ire) 4-10-10 C O'Dwyer,.......... (11 to 4) 4
3810[6] EARLY RISER (Ire) 6-10-8 (7*) Mr G T Morrow,..... (10 to 1) 5
MANDYSWAY (Ire) 5-11-0 S H O'Donovan,....... (16 to 1) 6
3071 LUCY TWO SHOES (Ire) 5-11-0 F Woods,........ (25 to 1) f
4146[4] THYNE OWN GIRL (Ire) 5-10-11 (3*) G Kilfeather, ..(16 to 1) pu
Dist: 4l, 4l, 4½l, 2½l. 4m 0.00s. (8 Ran).
(Gerald Cooney), F J Lacy

4187 N.C.F. Meats Handicap Hurdle (0-109 4-y-o and up) £2,740 2m........ (2:45)

4043[2] ANNFIELD LADY (Ire) [-] 6-10-10 F Woods,........ (3 to 1) 1
4030[3] RHABDOMANCY (Ire) [-] 6-10-1 (7*) A P McCoy,.... (4 to 1) 2
4093[5] INAUGURATION (Ire) [-] (bl) 5-10-4 B Sheridan,... (14 to 1) 3
4113[4] PEACE TRIBUTE (Ire) [-] 5-10-3 (3*) T J Mitchell,.. (12 to 1) 4
4093[4] MASTER MILLER [-] 8-10-13 Mr B R Hamilton,... (14 to 1) 5
4115* ABBEY EMERALD [-] 8-9-11 (3*,6ex) J P Broderick, ... (7 to 4 fav) 6
4030 BRAE (Ire) [-] 6-10-3 C O'Dwyer,.................(10 to 1) 7
4031[9] FREEWAY HALO (Ire) [-] (bl) 5-9-6 (7*) D J Kavanagh, ...(16 to 1) 8
4030 CLOGS [-] (bl) 10-10-8 S H O'Donovan,............(20 to 1) 9
3647 SHINETHYME (Ire) [-] 5-9-6 (5*) M G Cleary,...... (50 to 1) 10
3995[7] LA CIENAGA [-] 10-11-7 (7*) S G Anderson,...... (12 to 1) 11
Dist: 3½l, ½l, 4l, 12l. 3m 51.30s. (11 Ran).
(Patrick Delaney), W P Mullins

4188 Larkhill Novice Chase (5-y-o and up) £2,226 2½m.................. (4:15)

4116²	TRASSEY BRIDGE (bl) 7-11-9 F Woods, ... (9 to 4 fav)	1
1234	CEDAR COURT (Ire) 6-11-11 (3*) J P Broderick, ... (9 to 2)	2
	CURRACLOE STAR 8-10-11 (7*) Mr J T Codd, ... (20 to 1)	3
3972³	BALADINE 7-11-4 S H O'Donovan, ... (9 to 2)	4
4041⁸	BARAVARD (Ire) 6-11-9 C O'Dwyer, ... (33 to 1)	5
4116	MICHAEL'S STAR (Ire) 6-11-11 (3*) T J Mitchell, . . (16 to 1)	6
4061³	SO PINK (Ire) 6-11-9 J Jones, ... (100 to 30)	7
4147⁸	DIRECT RUN (bl) 7-11-9 B Sheridan, ...(8 to 1)	8
3529²	CLONROSH SLAVE 7-11-6 (3*) D P Murphy, ...(16 to 1)	9
4147	LABESTE (Ire) 6-11-6 (3*) G Kilfeather, ...(20 to 1)	10

Dist: 4l, 14l, 5½l, 1l. 5m 6.40s. (10 Ran).

(Castleford Syndicate), Raymund S Martin

4189 Sportsman Pro/Am I.N.H. Flat Race (4 & 5-y-o) £2,226 2m. . . . . (5:15)

3552³	MARYJO (Ire) 5-11-3 (5*) Mr P English, ... (7 to 4 fav)	1
	DIVALI (Ire) 5-11-6 (7*) Mr T J Murphy, ...(5 to 2)	2
	SLANEY STAR (Ire) 5-11-6 (7*) D J Kavanagh, ...(14 to 1)	3
4063	EXCUSE ME (Ire) 5-11-13 T Martin, ... (33 to 1)	4
2863	MIDNIGHT HOUR (Ire) 5-11-8 (5*) Mr H F Cleary, . . . (9 to 2)	5
	DROP THE ACT (Ire) 4-10-13 (7*) Mr R Pugh, ... (20 to 1)	6
3652	DARA'S COURSE (Ire) 5-11-1 (7*) Mrs S Bolger, . . . (14 to 1)	7
	HALF VOLLEY (Ire) 5-11-1 (7*) E G O'Callaghan, . . (11 to 2)	8
4148	GALLANT DREAM (Ire) 4-10-8 (7*) Mr A Daly, ... (33 to 1)	9
	HARLEY-D (Ire) 5-11-6 (7*) Mr J A Quinn, ... (12 to 1)	10
4094	JUST SUSIE (Ire) 5-11-1 (7*) Mr C A Rae, ...(16 to 1)	11
3749	BRISAN HERO (Ire) 4-10-8 (7*) Mr J Kilfeather, . . (33 to 1)	12

Dist: Nk, 3l, 15l, 2½l. 3m 53.60s. (12 Ran).

(Thomas Keane), D P Kelly

TRALEE (IRE) (soft (races 1,2,3), yielding to soft (4))
Sunday June 5th

4190 Kingdom Novice Chase (5-y-o and up) £2,740 2m. (3:05)

4032⁵	DEGO DANCER 7-11-4 (5*) P A Roche, ... (5 to 1)	1
3872	INCA CHIEF 10-12-0 J Shortt, ... (10 to 1)	2
3955⁷	HIGH-SPEC 8-11-11 (3*) C O'Brien, ... (12 to 1)	3
3614⁸	FOILACLUG FURRY 9-12-0 S R Murphy, ...(6 to 1)	4
3955³	RATHBRIDES JOY 7-12-0 T Horgan, ... (100 to 30 fav)	5
3955	FAHA STAR (Ire) 5-10-0 (7*) Mr P J Crowley, ... (25 to 1)	6
4031	AHEEMA COTTAGE 8-12-0 F J Flood, ...(6 to 1)	7
4041⁵	NISHIKI (USA) 5-11-2 A Powell, ... (14 to 1)	8
3955	BERT HOUSE 8-12-0 T Kinane Jnr, ... (14 to 1)	9
3955	J-TEC BOY 8-12-0 P P Kinane, ... (20 to 1)	f
3911	RUFO'S COUP 7-12-0 C F Swan, ... (6 to 1)	pu
	WAR FLOWER (Ire) 6-11-2 (7*) Mr B Moran, ... (25 to 1)	pu

Dist: 9l, 4l, nk, 8l. 4m 20.00s. (12 Ran).

(Mrs Ann McAllen), Patrick McAllen

4191 Ballybeggan Racegoers Club Handicap Hurdle (0-123 4-y-o and up) £4,110 2m. (3:35)

3887	MARIAN YEAR [-] 8-11-5 J Collins, ... (7 to 2)	1
4077	SHEER MIST [-] 7-10-10 K F O'Brien, ... (11 to 1)	2
3957	EAST HOUSTON [-] 5-11-3 W T Slattery Jnr, ... (14 to 1)	3
3871²	MISTER DRUM (Ire) [-] 5-11-4 (7*) Mr J T McNamara, (9 to 4)	4
4149*	FINNEGANS WAKE [-] 7-12-1 (1ex) C F Swan, . . (Evens fav)	5

Dist: 2l, 6l, sht-hd, 2l. 4m 12.10s. (5 Ran).

(Thomas Walker), Thomas Walker

4192 Ballybeggan Racegoers Club Maiden Hurdle (4-y-o and up) £3,425 2½m . . . . (4:05)

3869²	DAWN ADAMS (Ire) 6-11-9 F J Flood, ... (2 to 1 fav)	1
3242	LOUGH NEAGH LADY 8-11-9 S R Murphy, ... (16 to 1)	2
3954⁶	BROGUESTOWN PRIDE (Ire) 6-12-0 C F Swan, ... (7 to 2)	3
4149⁴	MOUNTHENRY STAR (Ire) 6-12-0 A Powell, ... (7 to 1)	4
4059	MISS BERTAINE (Ire) 5-11-8 W T Slattery Jnr, ...(20 to 1)	5
3956	GRAND SCENERY (Ire) 6-12-0 P M Verling, ... (12 to 1)	6
	IRISH FOUNTAIN (Ire) 6-12-0 M P Hourigan, ...(14 to 1)	7
3974⁸	SISTER ROSZA (Ire) 6-11-6 (3*) C O'Brien, ... (12 to 1)	8
3869⁸	DUN OENGUS (Ire) 5-11-8 L P Cusack, ... (14 to 1)	9
4114²	CORRIB HAVEN (Ire) 6-12-0 K F O'Brien, ...(7 to 1)	10
4043	SHIMMERETTO 8-11-2 (7*) J M Donnelly, ... (33 to 1)	11
	COOLEGALE 8-12-0 T Horgan, ... (14 to 1)	12
3837⁷	SAILIN BISHOP 7-12-0 J Magee, ... (20 to 1)	13
2940	KELLYMOUNT 8-11-7 (7*) M Kelly, ... (12 to 1)	14
3971⁶	GRAPHIC IMAGE (Ire) 4-11-3 (3*) K P Gaule, ...(10 to 1)	15
4078	LISCAHILL HIGHWAY 7-11-7 (7*) R McGrath, ... (14 to 1)	16
3953⁹	HERESTHEDEAL (Ire) 5-11-13 J Collins, ... (20 to 1)	17
4076⁷	PERSPEX GALE (Ire) 6-11-9 J Shortt, ... (25 to 1)	18
	SPANISH ARCH (Ire) 5-11-6 (7*) Mr B Moran, ... (20 to 1)	19
3870	CAPTAIN CHARLES (Ire) 6-11-9 (5*) P A Roche, . . .(33 to 1)	pu

Dist: 7l, 8l, 20l, 3l. 4m 21.60s. (20 Ran).

(Jerome Sheehan), F Flood

4193 Sportsmans I.N.H. Flat Race (6-y-o and up) £2,740 2m 1f. . . . . (5:35)

4063²	JOHNNY SCATTERCASH 12-11-7 (7*) Mr E Norris, (8 to 1)	1
3837²	CELTIC SUNRISE 6-11-7 (7*) Mr H Murphy, ... (6 to 4 fav)	2
4044²	ASTITCHINTIME 7-11-7 (7*) Mr C A Murphy, ... (9 to 2)	3
3956⁹	QUAYSIDE COTTAGE (Ire) 6-11-11 (3*) Mr T Lombard,	
	. . . . (20 to 1)	4
	NECTANEBO (Ire) 6-12-0 Mr J E Kiely, ... (3 to 1)	5
4031	SAME DIFFERENCE (bl) 6-11-7 (7*) Mr G A Kingston,	
	. . . . (12 to 1)	6
4034⁷	THRESA-ANITA (Ire) 6-11-2 (7*) Mr M T Hartrey, . . (10 to 1)	7
4060	ALICE FOX (Ire) 6-11-9 Mr P Fenton, ... (16 to 1)	8
	ALL IN THE GAME (Ire) 6-12-0 Mr J A Flynn, ...(12 to 1)	9
3652	GAELIC WARRIOR 7-11-7 (7*) Mr J Millington, . . (20 to 1)	10
4044⁸	CARRIG BELLE 8-11-2 (7*) Mr B Foster, ... (14 to 1)	pu

Dist: 9l, hd, 8l, 1½l. 4m 22.50s. (11 Ran).

(Michael Purcell), Michael Purcell

608

Index to National Hunt Results 1993-94

5 **A FEW GOOD MEN(IRE)**, ch g Yashgan - Victorian Pageant by Welsh Pageant (E Bolger) 48³ 109⁷ 201² 331⁶

6 **A FORTIORI(IRE)**, b g Denel (FR) - Sofa River (FR) by Riverton (FR) (M C Pipe) 1548⁵ 2779⁸

8 **A GENTLEMAN TWO**, b h All Systems Go - Solar Honey by Roi Soleil (J L Eyre) 757² 1143⁵ 1485 1680³ 1788⁸ 2152³ 2498⁶

13 **A LAD INSANE**, br g Al Sirat (USA) - Endora by Royal Palm (K C Bailey) 697² 865⁷

5 **A LITTLE EARNER**, ch g The Parson - Welgenco by Welsh Saint (E J O'Grady) 3730⁸ 3934⁹ 4059⁹

5 **A MONKEY FOR DICK(IRE)**, br g Monksfield - Maggie's Turn by Garda's Revenge (USA) (J K Magee) 1833⁴ 2289

6 **A N C EXPRESS**, gr g Pragmatic - Lost In Silence by Silent Spring (J S King) 1542⁵ 2505⁵ 2802¹ 3453⁸

5 **A WINDY CITIZEN(IRE)**, ch m Phardante (FR) - Candolcis by Candy Cane (Eugene M O'Sullivan) 531 907 939

5 **A WOMAN'S HEART(IRE)**, b m Supreme Leader - Mary Black by Ardoon (M F Morris) 1858

8 **AAHSAYLAD**, b h Ardross - Madam Slaney by Prince Tenderfoot (USA) (J White) 156¹ 895¹ 1653⁹ 2257⁸ 3028 3461²

7 **AAL EL AAL**, b h High Top - Last Card (USA) by Full Out (USA) (P J Hobbs) 1053⁴ 1414³ 2554¹ 2655² 2947²

10 **ABADARE(USA)**, b g Robellino (USA) - Latonia Thrush by Tudor Minstrel (D Lowe) 2687 2884

5 **ABAVARD(IRE)**, ch g Le Bavard (FR) - Heroanda by Tepukei (A M Forte) 832 1020⁶ 1833¹ 2127³ 2348 2679⁸ 3122⁶ 3197³

8 **ABBEY EMERALD**, ch m Baptism - Key Note by Kythnos (Michael Hourigan) 689 1331⁶ 1496 1823 2038 2123 3466 4030⁵ 4115¹ 4187⁶

7 **ABBEY JACK**, b g Furry Glen - Abbey Princess (Thomas Bergin) 4405 93⁸ 178⁸ 691⁷

5 **ABBEY TRINITY(IRE)**, ch m Tender King - Nordic Maid by Vent Du Nord (R Donoghue) 48 58 98⁸ 162 211⁹ 4031 4166

12 **ABBEYDORE**, b g Rouser - Cagaleena by Cagirama (Mrs Christine Hardinge) 3335

6 **ABBEYLANDS(IRE)**, gr g Cardinal Flower - Findabair by Sunny Way (J H Johnson) 1114² 1362⁵

10 **ABBOT OF FURNESS**, b g The Parson - Chestnut Fire by Deep Run (G Richards) 1005⁴ 1106 1753² 1874³ 2005⁵ 2273⁴ 2515⁵ 2788⁷ 2975² 3288 3464⁵

9 **ABBOTSHAM**, b g Ardross - Lucy Platter (FR) by Record Token (O J Carter) 2949⁵ 3501⁵ 3591 3717⁵ 3918² 3989 4068⁴ 4184

11 **ABBREVIATION**, b g Torus - Worldling by Linacre (John Williams) 143 196

7 **ABDUL EMIR**, b g Ovac (ITY) - Azul by Majority Blue (Toby Watson) 4406 36 53 215

5 **ABDULLAH BULBUL**, b g Tina's Pet - Shercol by Monseigneur (USA) (D H Clyde) 3720

5 **ABELONI**, ch g Absalom - Agreloui by Tower Walk (R Hollinshead) 1059 1416⁷ 1472³ 1589⁸ 1794 1931 2331³ 2420¹ 2531¹

9 **ABERCROMBY CHIEF**, br g Buckskin (FR) - Free For Ever by Little Buskins (J H Johnson) 789² 1319 1725

4 **ABEREDW(IRE)**, b f Caerwent - Secret Hideaway (USA) by Key To The Mint (USA) (Martin Brassil) 2388 2614⁹ 2750

8 **ABITMORFUN**, ch g Baron Blakeney - Mary Mile by Athenius (S A Brookshaw) 4321 3988

4 **ABJAR**, br g Dominion - Rye Tops by Ile de Bourbon (USA) (P A Kelleway) 851¹ 2275² 2471 2670⁵

4 **ABLE MCCLEOD**, bl g Bold Owl - Slap Bang by Pitskelly (Mrs K Walton) 2485 3435

7 **ABLE PLAYER(USA)**, b or br g Solford (USA) - Grecian Snow (CAN) by Snow Knight (Mrs S A Bramall) 318⁶ 480³ 498¹ 586 694⁴ 974⁷ 1058 1146² 1570⁷ 2049 2121⁸ 3178² 3355⁶ 3618

9 **ABNEGATION**, b g Abednego - Autumn Magic by Arctic Slave (J H Johnson) 1033 1288

10 **ABSAILOR**, b g Kambalda - Tarsilogue by Tarqogan (Mrs S C Bradburne) 4300⁷ 288² 366¹ 560³ 722¹ 1203³ 1363¹ 1659⁴ 2107³ 2437⁵ 3141² 3405 3433³ 3566³

6 **ABSALOM'S LADY**, gr m Absalom - High Point Lady (CAN) by Knightly Dawn (USA) (D R C Elsworth) 1521¹ 1755¹ 1888³ 2046¹ 2376⁶ 3025⁵ 3422⁴

8 **ABSENT MINDS**, b m Lir - Forgotten by Forlorn River (B R J Young) 952⁸ 3051⁴ 3671⁵

6 **ABSENT RELATIVE**, ch m Absalom - Relatively Smart by Great Nephew (Miss B Sanders) 384¹ 629³ 961¹

5 **ABSOLUTE DANCER**, b m Myjinski (USA) - Absolutely Blue by Absalom (W Bentley) 315⁵ 622 912

4 **ABSOLUTELY AVERAGE(IRE)**, b g Montelimar (USA) - Dr Shadad by Reform (John R Upson) 2083³ 2860²

6 **ABSOLUTELY RIGHT**, ch g Absalom - Sun Worshipper by Sun Prince (J White) 126⁴

5 **ABSOLUTELYMUSTARD(IRE)**, ch g Crash Course - Stradbally Beg by Little Buskins (S E Sherwood) 2339 2795 3509⁸ 3637

5 **ABSOLUTLEY FOXED**, gr m Absalom - May Fox by Healaugh Fox (B A McMahon) 137⁴ 1079² 1252 1404⁷ 1562⁵ 1731 2093 2271¹ 2401⁷

4 **ABU DANCER(IRE)**, b g Heraldiste (USA) - Ottavia Abu by Octavo (USA) (K O Cunningham-Brown) 890 2652⁷ 2776⁴ 2910⁸ 3153³ 3715³

10 **ABU MUSLAB**, b or br g Ile de Bourbon (USA) - Eastern Shore by Sun Prince (G F Edwards) 385⁵ 438⁶ 794¹ 884 984¹ 1189²

4 **ACANTHUS(IRE)**, b c Slip Anchor - Green Lucia by Green Dancer (USA) (Miss S J Wilton) 2204⁸ 2381 2685⁴ 2792⁶

7 **ACCESS SUN**, b g Pharly (FR) - Princesse Du Seine (FR) by Val de Loir (J S King) 861⁴ 1198⁸ 1508⁴ 1721³ 2247⁵ 2496 2674⁷ 3099³ 3492 3853¹ 3980⁸ 4096

13 **ACE OF SPIES**, b g He Loves Me - Belle Bergere by Faberge II (N A Twiston-Davies) 2791⁶ 2966 3217 3417

6 **ACE PLAYER(NZ)**, b g Full On Aces (AUS) - C'est La Vie (NZ) by Dubassoff (USA) (Mrs J Renfree-Barons) 1996³ 2269⁶ 2749⁵ 3886²

INDEX TO NATIONAL HUNT RESULTS 1993-94

5 **ARAGON MIST,** b m Aragon - Feathers Fly by Busted (Mrs N S Sharpe) 2692 3597 3876

5 **ARAGONA,** b m Aragon - Polly Worth by Wolver Hollow (P D Cundell) 839

4 **ARAMON,** b g Aragon - Princess Mona by Prince Regent (FR) (G Lewis) 2190⁴ 2541³ 2712²

4 **ARAN EXILE,** b f Ahonoora - Gallic Pride (USA) by Key To The Kingdom (USA) (Noel Meade) 494⁴

7 **ARANY,** b g Precocious - Bellagio by Busted (M H Tompkins) 1240² 1395⁸ 1632⁴

6 **ARAQUEEPA(IRE),** b g Bowling Pin - Saint Cyde by Welsh Saint (John Joseph Murphy) 4

8 **ARBEE TWENTY,** b g Sunyboy - Town Flirt by Charlottown (Mrs J Pitman) 1327⁷ 1527 1590⁸ 2341⁵

6 **ARCHER(IRE),** b g Roselier (FR) - Suir Valley by Orchardist (J T R Dreaper) 1555⁴ 1786³ 1897² 2863³ 2985⁵

7 **ARCHIE BROWN,** b g Deep Run - Fairgoi by Baragoi (S E Sherwood) 2175 2727

5 **ARCHIE'S SISTER,** gr m Pitpan - Lo-Incost by Impecunious (R Dickin) 2176 2692⁶ 3005⁸ 3279⁹

6 **ARCOT,** b g Formidable (USA) - Pagan Queen by Vaguely Noble (J A Glover) 1034² 1225 1571² 2833⁵ 2994 3068⁶ 3516¹ 3736

9 **ARCTIC BARON,** b g Baron Blakeney - Learctic by Lepanto (GER) (G Raymond) 4394⁵

8 **ARCTIC BLOOM,** gr m Scallywag - Constant Rose by Confusion (G P Kelly) 4329 3964 4035⁴ 4135³

11 **ARCTIC CALL,** b g Callernish - Polar Lady by Arctic Slave (O Sherwood) 3229 3261⁶ 3403⁴

6 **ARCTIC COURSE(IRE),** ch g Crash Course - Polar Vixen by Arctic Slave (D Nicholson) 753 869⁴ 1108² 1624¹ 1992⁴ 2459⁶ 2964² 3453¹

6 **ARCTIC KINSMAN,** gr g Relkino - Arctic Advert by Birdbrook (N A Twiston-Davies) 1418¹ 1539⁶ 2250¹ 2356⁴ 2743³ 3023¹

5 **ARCTIC LIFE(IRE),** b g Roselier (FR) - Miss Dollar by Lucifer (USA) (J R Jenkins) 136⁷ 597 695⁵ 863² 1263³ 1729 1969³ 2093² 2531² 2630³ 3231² 3886⁸

6 **ARCTIC LINE,** b g Green Ruby (USA) - Sally Ann III by Port Corsair (R D Green) 227⁸ 323⁷ 456 3824⁹ 3952⁷

5 **ARCTIC MO(IRE),** b or br m Mandalus - Polarville by Charlottesvilles Flyer (J F C Maxwell) 3813

9 **ARCTIC OATS,** ch m Oats - Arctic Festival by Arctic Slave (W W Haigh) 289⁵ 424⁵ 594⁸ 2060¹ 2166² 2533²

10 **ARCTIC ROSE,** b m Soldier Rose - Cool Gipsy by Romany Air (Mrs R C Matheson) 4321

10 **ARCTIC TEAL,** b g Town And Country - Arctic Warbler by Deep Run (Mrs P Robeson) 2605⁵ 2807³ 2937¹ 3171⁷ 3703⁶ 4007⁵ 4068²

5 **ARCTIC TREASURE(IRE),** br m Treasure Hunter - Windy Winter by Le Bavard (FR) (Mayne Kidd) 1016⁵ 1455 1681 1848 2311 3796⁵ 4063 4094⁴

5 **ARCTIC WEATHER(IRE),** b g Montelimar (USA) - Brigadiers Nurse by Brigadier Gerard (M J P O'Brien) 1075² 1267² 1431² 1686⁸ 2079² 2610⁸ 2680¹ 2754⁷ 3369 3710

9 **ARCTICFLOW(USA),** ch g Arctic Tern (USA) - Bold Flora (USA) by Bold Favorite (USA) (N B Thomson) 4384⁵ 350⁶ 2399⁴ 2559 3018 3478 3706⁷ 3827⁹

4 **ARCTICTALDI(IRE),** br g Cataldi - Arctic Sue (M Brew) 3372 3616

9 **ARD T'MATCH,** b g Ardross - Love Match (USA) by Affiliate (USA) (A L Forbes) 548² 726⁴ 986³ 1242¹ 1512⁴ 1769

11 **ARDBRIN,** ch g Bulldozer - Hazels Fancy by Prefairy (T P Tate) 919⁴ 1123¹ 1538² 1887 2266

7 **ARDCARN GIRL,** b m Ardross - Rhein Maiden by Rheingold (P M Barrett) 1902⁶ 2277 2550 2661

8 **ARDCRONEY CHIEF,** ch g Connaught - Duresme by Starry Halo (D R Gandolfo) 487³ 609¹ 700³ 935⁴ 1089³ 1407¹ 1954³ 3091¹ 3397⁴ 3631⁵

6 **ARDEE FLO JO(IRE),** ch m Horage - Floppy Disk by Patch (L W Doran) 20

5 **ARDENT LOVE(IRE),** b m Ardross - Love Match (USA) by Affiliate (USA) (O Brennan) 2339³ 2834 3583 4069⁷

14 **ARDESEE,** ch g Le Coq D'Or - Katie Little by Nulli Secundus (D J Wintle) 3065⁵

5 **ARDFALLON(IRE),** b m Supreme Leader - Vamble by Vulgan (Thomas Bergin) 23 1036⁶

5 **ARDLEA HOUSE(IRE),** ch g Precocious - Palatana by Nonoalco (USA) (Oliver Finnegan) 37 362 1038⁹ 1780

4 **ARDMORE KELINKA(IRE),** b f Oats - Nicolas Pet by Boreen (FR) (Ms Nicola FitzGerald) 3797 3997

5 **ARDMORE LEADER(IRE),** b m Supreme Leader - Ardmore Lady by Quayside (Declan Gillespie) 2869

7 **ARDNAMONA,** b m Torus - Monica's Pet by Sovereign Gleam (S A Kirk) 4305⁸ 2 57⁷ 340⁵

8 **ARDORAN,** ch g Little Wolf - Smoke Creek by Habitat (Miss S J Wilton) 1084⁹ 1239 1624 1967

7 **ARDSCUD,** b g Le Bavard (FR) - Tudor Lady by Green Shoon (M Bradstock) 1935⁹ 2141 3453⁹

6 **ARDSHUIL,** b g Pennine Walk - Ordina (FR) by Northfields (USA) (A L T Moore) 2056⁴ 2607 3749¹

7 **ARDUBH,** b g Black Minstrel - Ardglass Belle by Carnival Night (T M Walsh) 4340⁴ 4380⁶ 35³ 82³ 1819³ 2025⁵

4 **ARE YOU HAPPY(IRE),** b f Glenstal (USA) - Aingeal by Fordham (USA) (John R Upson) 272³ 349⁴ 497 2303

5 **AREAL(IRE),** br m Roselier (FR) - Stream Flyer by Paddy's Stream (B Palling) 3686

6 **ARFER MOLE(IRE),** b g Carlingford Castle - Sharpaway by Royal Highway (J A B Old) 1309⁴ 1536⁴ 2014¹ 2510⁴

5 **ARFEY(IRE),** b g Burslem - Last Gunboat by Dominion (T Thomson Jones) 1390² 1642³

5 **ARGIDEEN FLYER(IRE),** b m Over The River (FR) - Killegney by Reformed Character (Andrew Lee) 3834

9 **ARI'S FASHION,** br f Aristocracy - Ballyellen by Bally Joy (Michael F Kearney) 4358⁵ 37 50 80⁸ 96⁸ 3711 4030

6 **ARIADLER(IRE),** b g Mister Lord (USA) - Arianrhod by L'homme Arme (P Cheesbrough) 656⁸ 1060¹ 1722⁴ 2358 3177³ 3354¹ 3817²

5 **ARIES GIRL,** ch m Valiyar - Ravaro by Raga Navarro (ITY) (P J Flynn) 1180¹ 1500¹ 1903¹ 3042² 3660¹

6 **ARIOSO,** b m True Song - Most by Our Mirage (J L Needham) 3401⁹

5 **ARISE(IRE),** b g Rising - What's The Point by Major Point (Andrew Kennedy) 109⁴

5 **ARISTODEMUS,** b g Politico (USA) - Easter Jane by Palm Track (A L T Moore) 1848 2465 3290

5 **ARISTOLIGHT(IRE),** b m Aristocracy - Lightning Girl by African Sky (Basil King) 4360 94 208

5 **ARITAM(IRE),** b g Aristocracy - Tamu by Malinowski (USA) (T J Carr) 3674⁶

616

10 **BALDA BOY,** b g Kambalda - Lady Coleman by Master Owen (Capt T A Forster) 995 2462 2648⁷ 2861⁴ 3112² 3443² 3662³ 3852

5 **BALISTEROS(FR),** b g Bad Conduct (USA) - Oldburry (FR) by Fin Bon (T P Tate) 1003⁷ 1114⁷ 2252⁵ 2908 3075 3236⁵ 3542

4 **BALLACASCADE,** b g Ballacashtal (CAN) - Pasha's Dream by Tarboosh (USA) (P C Haslam) 578⁷

8 **BALLAD RULER,** ch g Ballad Rock - Jessamy Hall by Crowned Prince (USA) (P A Pritchard) 4345 4395 596¹ 703⁴ 931⁶ 1324⁵ 1405⁵ 3585⁷ 3695⁵ 3885⁵

11 **BALLAD SONG,** br g Ballad Rock - Apt by Ragusa (Michael Cunningham) 2230⁵ 2466¹ 2698⁸

7 **BALLAGH COUNTESS,** br m King's Ride - Countess Spray by Even Say (W J Burke) 19 112 989⁹ 1035⁴ 1177

7 **BALLERINA ROSE,** b m Dreams To Reality (USA) - Ragtime Rose by Ragstone (M P Bielby) 4377 1187 1508⁸ 1810³ 2120⁴ 2331² 2532² 2839²

5 **BALLET ROYAL(USA),** b or br h Nureyev (USA) - Crystal Queen by High Top (G Harwood) 1509² 1729⁴ 2244² 2494¹ 2621¹ 2743⁹ 3156¹

7 **BALLINABOOLA GROVE,** b g Trimmingham - Beagle Bay (John Queally) 1233 1763⁵ 1909⁵

9 **BALLINAMOE,** b g Rymer - Superdora by Super Slip (R H Buckler) 1947 2186 2340 3714

8 **BALLINASCREENA,** b or br g Kampala - Nordic Maid by Vent Du Nord (Michael Hourigan) 1854²

7 **BALLINAVEEN BRIDGE,** b g Whitehall Bridge - Tanival by Carnival Night (Thomas Heffernan) 97 116 411⁶ 475⁴ 583⁴ 941 1399 1826 1914⁶ 4147²

8 **BALLINDERRY GLEN,** br m Furry Glen - Cornamucla by Lucky Guy (T F Lacy) 4399⁷ 38¹ 66 100⁷ 118² 199⁴ 275⁵ 493⁷ 574⁹ 805⁵ 1038³ 1178⁶ 1495⁶ 1857 2051⁵ 3795⁸ 3955⁹

5 **BALLINEVA(IRE),** b g Mummy's Treasure - Make-Up by Bleep-Bleep (W P Mullins) 2869⁶ 3327 3508²

7 **BALLINGOWAN STAR,** ch m Le Moss - Cherry Lodge by Charlottesvilles Flyer (A J Keane) 4357 4406³ 15⁹ 536⁶ 638⁸ 857³ 1332 1898⁶ 2616 2921⁷ 3504 3731

7 **BALLINMUSIC,** ch g Southern Music - Ballindoon by Doon (S I Pittendrigh) 2905⁹ 3125

11 **BALLINROSTIG,** ch g General Ironside - Mavar's Choice by Virginia Boy (Denys Smith) 1222 1486 2895

7 **BALLISTIC BLAZE,** ch g Le Bavard (FR) - Hansel's Queen by Prince Hansel (Kevin McQuillan) 1160

4 **BALLON,** b f Persian Bold - La Vosgienne by Ashmore (FR) (M Dods) 1920⁵ 2154¹ 2275³ 2972² 3128¹ 3482⁷

9 **BALLOO HOUSE,** ch g Le Moss - Forgello by Bargello (Mrs P Sly) 1150¹

5 **BALLOUGH BUI(IRE),** br m Supreme Leader - Bucks Princess by Buckskin (FR) (A P O'Brien) 2943⁷ 3084 4169⁸

7 **BALLY CLOVER,** ch g Deep Run - Miss de Jager by Lord Gayle (USA) (N J Henderson) 900⁶ 1703³ 1890⁴ 3501

8 **BALLY FLAME,** b g Balliol - Flame by Firestreak (Mrs M A Kendall) 316⁸ 394 477

9 **BALLY MURPHY BOY,** b g Rare One - Royal Dress (Mrs Jonah Wragg) 3888

8 **BALLY O ROURKE,** br g Copper Gamble - Bionic Girl by Fine Blade (USA) (M Flannery) 22 33⁹ 176⁵ 255⁷ 332⁹ 377

8 **BALLY PARSON,** b g The Parson - Ballyadam Lass by Menelek (J Chugg) 1593⁴ 1805⁴ 2794¹ 3043 3259 3400⁷

6 **BALLY RIOT(IRE),** br g Riot Helmet - Ballybrack by Golden Love (J E Kiely) 798 1018⁸

6 **BALLY UPPER(IRE),** b g Bustineto - Judy Browne by Pry (M Phelan) 4371⁹ 2470 3327 3528 3837

5 **BALLYALLIA CASTLE(IRE),** ch g Carlingford Castle - Clonsilla by Clever Fella (R F Fisher) 2976³ 3227²

9 **BALLYANTO,** b g Lepanto (GER) - Ballyarctic by Arcticeelagh (C Parker) 289⁴ 580⁶ 680

9 **BALLYBELL,** ch g Prince Mab (FR) - Lydien by Sandford Lad (J L Gledson) 1096 1602⁷ 1723 2149 2240² 2436⁸ 2563⁶ 2739⁴ 3060⁵ 3540⁴

7 **BALLYBODEN,** ch g Over The River (FR) - Dadooronron by Deep Run (Michael Hourigan) 1827⁴ 2123⁷ 2289⁹ 2389 2607⁶ 2920⁴ 3789³ 3870⁶ 3955¹ 4043⁴ 4062⁵

5 **BALLYBRAZIL BOY(IRE),** ch g Orange Reef - Munsters Pride by Hardboy (J H Scott) 393³ 638 692 3720

7 **BALLYBRIKEN CASTLE,** br m Le Bavard (FR) - Giolla's Trip by Giolla Mear (Edward P Mitchell) 4369 21 332 468⁷ 989⁴ 1179

8 **BALLYBRIT BOY,** ch g Merrymount - Royal Kate by Royal Trip (P D Osborne) 6⁹

6 **BALLYBROWN FLASH(IRE),** b g Spanish Place (USA) - Coalauct by Crash Course (Edward P Mitchell) 363 472¹ 1823

7 **BALLYCANN,** b g Bamboo Saucer - Dolly Button by Jukebox (B Maguire) 4339¹ 63³ 118³ 123 1551⁶ 1780⁶ 2180⁶ 2469⁵ 2845⁸ 2988 3198⁷ 3273⁵ 3873³ 3890⁹

7 **BALLYDAVIN,** br g Creative Plan (USA) - Princess Baroda by Hardicanute (John C Shearman) 9

7 **BALLYDAY DAWN,** br m Seclude (USA) - Green Orchid (J P Walsh) 15 2941 3527 4118⁵

5 **BALLYDAY SNOW(IRE),** br m Seclude (USA) - Green Orchid by Green Shoon (Mrs C M Brown) 7

6 **BALLYDOUGAN(IRE),** ch g The Parson - Get My Pint by Menelek (R Mathew) 1669⁵ 2045

8 **BALLYFIN BOY,** br g Smooth Stepper - Tumble Heather by Tumble Wind (USA) (W J Austin) 2282 2588⁹ 3241 3507 3709 3872⁵ 3945 4147¹

10 **BALLYGIBLIN LADY,** b m General Ironside - Clonbur Lass by Bluerullah (M C Casey) 4368⁸ 4408⁴ 36⁵ 169³

7 **BALLYGRANT,** br g Cut Above - Felicity Lot by Malacate (USA) (John Houghton) 67 538

5 **BALLYGRIFFIN LAD(IRE),** ch g Carlingford Castle - Calfstown Night by Bargello (T P McGovern) 864⁹ 1169 1715 2779⁴ 3196⁹ 3640⁵

6 **BALLYHAMAGE(IRE),** br g Mandalus - Deep Slaney by Deep Run (D Nicholson) 809² 1078⁴ 3585

5 **BALLYHANNON(IRE),** b g Strong Gale - Chestnut Fire by Deep Run (Michael Hourigan) 4119⁵

7 **BALLYHARRON,** ch f Deep Run - Tarmar by Sayfar (J S Cullen) 2203 2943

5 **BALLYHAYS(IRE),** ch g Glow (USA) - Relanca by Relic (R Akehurst) 1515⁹

8 **BALLYHEIGUE,** b g King's Ride - Star Of Canty by Konigssee (A J McNamara) 4369⁵ 4397 6⁵ 42 251² 330⁴ 377⁴ 430 506⁵ 573 1179 1550⁷ 1915¹ 2036³ 2350⁴ 3200⁴ 3873 3945⁸ 4150⁵

5 **BALLYHIRE LAD(IRE),** b g Carlingford Castle - Blajina by Bold Lad (IRE) (A P O'Brien) 2470² 2684⁸ 2756⁸ 3946¹ 4060⁴

5 **BALLYHOOK(IRE),** b m Phardante (FR) - Racy Lady by Continuation (Francis Berry) 709

7 **BARCHAM,** b g Blakeney - La Pythie (FR) by Filiberto (USA) (D A Wilson) 4331 1355 1627 2912 3098

5 **BARDAROS,** b g Lighter - Suttons Hill by Le Bavard (FR) (Mrs A L M King) 3589 4023

8 **BARDESAN,** b g Kambalda - Early Start by Wrekin Rambler (J G O'Neill) 325⁵ 442¹ 549² 612⁷

7 **BARDOLPH(USA),** b g Golden Act (USA) - Love To Barbara (USA) by Stevward (P F I Cole) 1509⁵

6 **BARE FISTED,** ch g Nearly A Hand - Ba Ba Belle by Petit Instant (J S King) 889 1324

8 **BARE HIGHLANDER,** b g Kambalda - Banross by Allangrange (R J Hodges) 301⁹ 415³ 502⁹

6 **BARELY BLACK,** br g Lidhame - Louisa Anne by Mummy's Pet (N M Babbage) 695⁸ 1059³ 1621¹ 1866³ 2504⁴ 2836⁸

9 **BARGAIN AND SALE,** br g Torenaga - Miss Woodville by Master Buck (D J Minty) 4374 417³ 593⁶ 892

10 **BARGE BOY,** b g Jimsun - Barge Mistress by Bargello (J A B Old) 710 899

5 **BARGIN BOY,** ch g Undulate (USA) - Chaddy by St Chad (J E Long) 1126 1211 3012⁴ 3145⁷ 3304⁵ 3725⁹

11 **BARKIN,** b g Crash Course - Annie Augusta by Master Owen (G Richards) 4300¹ 1419⁵ 1864 2253 2410⁴ 2635⁴

10 **BARKISLAND,** b g Prince Regent (FR) - Satlan by Milan (P Beaumont) 479⁵ 913³ 1312¹ 1409³ 2242⁵ 2437 3332 3566¹ 3803² 3968³ 4046⁵ 4087⁴ 4175

4 **BARLEY COURT(IRE),** gr g Milk Of The Barley - Kissing Gate by Realm (C Kinane) 2547 2917 4146⁹

8 **BARLEY MOW,** b g Wolverlife - Ellette by Le Levanstell (Mrs Barbara Waring) 4314 526² 607 843⁵ 1194² 1411 2417 3003³

7 **BARN ELMS,** ch g Deep Run - Leara by Leander (J C Peate) 3860⁴

6 **BARNA BOY(IRE),** b g Torus - Barna Beauty by Gala Performance (USA) (N J Henderson) 1442⁶ 2014³ 2743² 3023⁶ 3380¹ 3604¹

6 **BARNA MOSS(IRE),** b f Le Moss - Barna Glen by Furry Glen (D O'Brien) 3243¹

5 **BARNAGEERA BOY(IRE),** b m Indian King (USA) - Saint Simbir (T G McCourt) 2024⁶ 2232⁶ 2586 2842 3748⁵

9 **BARNEY RUBBLE,** b or br g Politico (USA) - Peak Princess by Charlottown (D W Whillans) 1722³ 1938⁵ 2295⁵ 2502⁷ 2925³ 3286⁵ 3428⁵ 3554²

6 **BARNEY'S GIFT(IRE),** ch g Exhibitioner - Run-A-Line by Deep Run (O Brennan) 1103² 1494⁶ 2963¹

4 **BARNIEMEBOY,** ch g Donor - Form Up by Gold Form (P M McEntee) 1510 2169 2335 2857² 2881 3543 3725

4 **BARNISH DAWN(IRE),** ch f King Luthier - Daddy's Folly by Le Moss (Brian Kerr) 2775⁸ 3070⁷ 3271

5 **BARNISH ROSE(IRE),** b m Scorpio (FR) - Monmore by Lochnager (Brian Kerr) 1581 2311

9 **BARON BOB,** ch g Baron Blakeney - Treasury by Henry The Seventh (H Wellstead) 3013²

9 **BARON MANA,** b g Baron Blakeney - Manalane by Manacle (Mrs B Hill) 3013⁷

6 **BARON RUSH,** b g Baron Blakeney - Orvotus (W G Turner) 1277 2505 2796⁵

8 **BARON TWO SHOES,** gr g Baron Blakeney - Win Shoon Please by Sheshoon (R Thompson) 4029 4173³

8 **BARONESS BELLE,** gr m Baron Blakeney - My Belleburd by Twilight Alley (Mrs E L Stocker) 952

8 **BARONESS ORKZY,** ch m Baron Blakeney - General's Daughter by Spartan General (P F Nicholls) 682¹ 1276¹ 1696³ 2146 3050² 3400⁴ 3714⁴ 3805

6 **BARR NA CRANEY(IRE),** b g Monksfield - Lavarna Lady by Rheingold (Desmond McDonogh) 4410⁵ 27⁵ 56

9 **BARRACILLA,** ch g Kambalda - Lady Coleman by Master Owen (G B Balding) 93⁷ 170⁶ 386⁴ 458⁴ 669⁴ 3532⁴ 3699¹ 4143⁵

6 **BARRAFONA(IRE),** ch g Green Shoon - Bulabos by Proverb (K Riordan) 1760⁶ 2027⁹ 2351 2683⁵ 2845⁹ 3789² 3955⁶ 4041

6 **BARRINGTONS CASTLE(IRE),** ch g Carlingford Castle - Dawning Glory by Hitite Glory (A J McNamara) 4402 41 71 108⁴

10 **BARRONSTOWN BOY,** br g Smooth Stepper - Blaze Gold by Arizona Duke (W J Austin) 1380 1609³ 1823⁸ 1980² 2160³ 2660⁷ 3242 3732

7 **BARRYMORE BOY,** ch g Rontino - Lilly Of Killarney by Funny Way (D T Hughes) 59⁷ 510²

4 **BARSAL(IRE),** b g Absalom - La Bella Fontana by Lafontaine (USA) (J Parkes) 1284⁵ 1476⁹ 2422⁴ 3139⁶ 3285¹ 3587⁶ 3702⁷ 3798² 4127⁹

9 **BART OWEN,** br g Belfalas - Ten Again by Raise You Ten (P Mullins) 1399 1497¹ 2125 2282³ 2659¹ 2846¹ 3063⁹ 3200¹ 3322

14 **BARTINAS STAR,** b g Le Bavard (FR) - Bartina by Bargello (G W Briscoe) 2888

8 **BARTON BANK,** br g Kambalda - Lucifer's Daughter by Lucifer (USA) (D Nicholson) 1031¹ 1556¹ 1843¹

5 **BARTON PRIDE(IRE),** b g Phardante (FR) - Ginosa by Kalamoun (M D Hammond) 243⁵ 339⁴ 447³ 514⁶

4 **BARTON ROYAL(IRE),** b g Petorius - Royal Sensation by Prince Regent (FR) (P C Ritchens) 668⁷ 1021⁷ 1243 1410 2130³ 2224⁴ 2343⁸ 2641¹ 3281 3843⁴ 3940⁴ 4056⁸

5 **BARTON SANTA(IRE),** b g Cataldi - Galloping Santa by Santa Claus (K C Bailey) 2691⁵

9 **BARTONDALE,** br m Oats - Miss Boon by Road House II (J M Bradley) 4334⁴ 154⁴ 271³ 345³ 397² 525⁴ 810² 1216⁶ 3560⁷ 3742³ 3885⁴ 3978⁷

15 **BARTRES,** ch g Le Bavard (FR) - Gail Borden by Blue Chariot (D J G Murray Smith) 4311⁴

8 **BARTS CASTLE,** ch g Carlingford Castle - Tavojina by Octavo (USA) (W M Halley) 4343 30⁸

8 **BAS DE LAINE(FR),** b g Le Pontet (FR) - La Gaina (FR) by New Chapter (O Sherwood) 1006¹ 1120² 1349³ 1844¹ 2472³ 3266⁴

11 **BASHER BILL,** b g Maystreak - Rugby Princess by El Gallo (K D Giles) 3856⁵

6 **BASICALLY(IRE),** b m Strong Gale - Carney's Hill by Le Prince (John R O'Sullivan) 926

5 **BASIE NOBLE,** ch g Local Suitor (USA) - Prima Ballerina (FR) by Nonoalco (USA) (John J McLoughlin) 1269 1780 1976⁶

5 **BASILICUS(FR),** b h Pamponi (FR) - Katy Collonge (FR) by Trenel (Mrs S J Smith) 1003⁶ 1369² 1582⁹ 1877² 2088³ 2578⁸ 2896 3178¹ 3355² 3689⁴

4 **BASKERVILLE BALLAD,** ch f Seymour Hicks (FR) - Tiny Feet by Music Maestro (K S Bridgwater) 2530 2763

6 **BASS ROCK,** b g Bellypha - Dunfermline by Royal Palace (I A Balding) 1027³ 1957³ 2269³ 2426³ 3170¹ 3975

5 **BASSETJA(IRE),** b m Lashkari - Belle Doche (FR) by Riverman (USA) (J F C Maxwell) 59² 1014⁵

INDEX TO NATIONAL HUNT RESULTS 1993-94

5 **BASSIANESE(IRE),** b m Dance Of Life (USA) - Inesdela by Wolver Hollow (Michael Cunningham) 256 747

5 **BASSIO(BEL),** b g Efisio - Batalya (BEL) by Boulou (BEL) (S Coathup) 1068 1313² 1424³ 1627⁸ 3928³ 4025 4086⁹

7 **BASTILLE DAY,** ch g Persian Bold - Marie Antoinette by Habitat (Mark McCausland) 2770 2863 3747

5 **BATABANOO,** ch g Bairn (USA) - For Instance by Busted (Mrs M Reveley) 781¹ 873¹ 1116¹ 3068

7 **BATHWICK BOBBIE,** b g Netherkelly - Sunwise by Roi Soleil (D L Williams) 998 1248³ 1457⁴ 1836 2361 2633³ 2731⁶ 3530⁹ 3571³ 3825⁵ 3964³ 4112⁴ 4183⁷

5 **BATTERY FIRED,** ch g K-Battery - Party Cloak by New Member (N B Mason) 1100 1289⁶ 1480⁹

7 **BATTLE STANDARD(CAN),** b g Storm Bird (CAN) - Hoist Emy's Flag (USA) by Hoist The Flag (USA) (Mrs S A Bramall) 316¹ 428¹

9 **BATTLEPLAN,** b g Hard Fought - Zoly (USA) by Val de L'orne (FR) (K S Bridgwater) 3398 3561 3661⁵ 4016¹ 4121

5 **BATTUTA,** ch m Ballacashtal (CAN) - Valpolicella by Lorenzaccio (G R Oldroyd) 137¹ 244² 346¹

5 **BATTY'S ISLAND,** b g Town And Country - Just Something by Good Times (ITY) (B Preece) 815⁹ 1428¹ 1813¹ 2505 3044¹ 3221¹ 3396⁸

6 **BAUNFAUN RUN(IRE),** b m Roselier (FR) - Lady Waters by Deep Run (Miss Ursula Ryan) 1501 2553 3733

6 **BAVARD DIEU(IRE),** ch g Le Bavard (FR) - Graham Dieu by Three Dons (Michael Cunningham) 61² 124³ 179¹ 400² 505¹ 938² 1453² 1685⁵ 1828² 3935⁸ 3995 4115⁴

6 **BAVARDAGE(IRE),** ch g Le Bavard (FR) - Glenrula Queen by Royal Match (Patrick Mooney) 3720

5 **BAWNROCK(IRE),** gr g Roselier (FR) - Dame Sue by Mandamus (A P O'Brien) 4361³ 172² 333¹ 555⁴ 2389

5 **BAY COTTAGE(IRE),** b m Quayside - Polly's Cottage by Pollerton (A P O'Brien) 3912

4 **BAY MAG,** b g Buzzards Bay - Chrome Mag by Prince de Galles (K S Bridgwater) 4023

5 **BAY MISCHIEF(IRE),** b g Crash Course - Regal Guard by Realm (N A Twiston-Davies) 162² 365¹ 1236¹ 1878¹ 2194² 3036

8 **BAY TERN(USA),** b h Arctic Tern (USA) - Unbiased (USA) by Foolish Pleasure (USA) (T Dyer) 4385 270³ 598¹ 736⁵ 1219⁴ 1728⁵ 1922⁵ 2815⁸ 3555⁷

5 **BAY VIEW PRINCE(IRE),** ch g Kambalda - Zoom Zoom by Bargello (T J O'Mara) 2919 3197

7 **BAYBEEJAY,** b m Buzzards Bay - Peak Condition by Mountain Call (R Brotherton) 224⁴ 659⁸ 1562³ 1699³ 2142⁷ 2292⁴ 2729 3511

7 **BAYDON STAR,** br g Mandalus - Leuze by Vimy (D Nicholson) 1071¹ 1228¹ 1348¹ 1558¹ 1754² 2268² 2472¹ 3024² 3483

4 **BAYFAN(IRE),** b g Taufan (USA) - Laurel Express by Bay Express (J S Moore) 3497 379⁵

5 **BAYLINER,** b m Skyliner - Gambling Wren by Knave To Play (Mrs V A Aconley) 2490

6 **BAYLORD PRINCE(IRE),** b g Horage - Miss Moat by Dike (R P C Hoad) 1272⁹ 2064 2227⁷ 2454³ 2760¹ 2912¹ 3098⁸ 3147¹ 3308⁴ 3696 4096⁸

5 **BAYPHIA,** ch g Bay Express - Sophie Avenue by Guillaume Tell (USA) (R Akehurst) 3455⁹

4 **BAYRAK(USA),** b g Bering - Phydilla (FR) by Lyphard (USA) (H R A Cecil) 790⁵ 1261² 1532² 1927² 2118⁴ 3416¹ 3511¹

8 **BAYSHAM(USA),** b g Raise A Native - Sunny Bay (USA) by Northern Bay (USA) (B R Millman) 791⁴

6 **BDOORE(IRE),** b m Petoski - Princess Biddy by Sun Prince (F Jestin) 3598 3688⁵ 3815 3905

6 **BE AMBITIOUS(IRE),** ch g Arapahos (FR) - Hilarys Mark by On Your Mark (S G Payne) 731⁹ 1181 2007⁷ 2218⁵ 3129⁶

4 **BE BRAVE,** b g Never So Bold - Boo by Bustino (C W Thornton) 3488 3868

6 **BE CREATIVE(IRE),** b g Ela-Mana-Mou - Ce Soir by Northern Baby (CAN) (A Redmond) 212 274 433

7 **BE HOME SHARP,** b g Montekin - Sciure (USA) by Sea-Bird II (J T R Dreaper) 20 45

4 **BE HOPEFULL,** ch f Full Of Hope - Too Familiar by Oats (J E Long) 3234

8 **BE KIND TO ME,** gr m Kind Of Hush - Sawk by Sea Hawk II (Michael Ronayne) 2664 2918

5 **BE MY HABITAT,** ch g Be My Guest (USA) - Fur Hat by Habitat (Miss L C Siddall) 4388⁵

5 **BE MY HOPE(IRE),** b m Be My Native (USA) - Diamond Gig by Pitskelly (Noel Meade) 2024¹ 2615² 3367⁸ 3615¹

13 **BE PATIENT MY SON,** b g Stanford - Try My Patience by Balliol (Miss C J E Caroe) 461 2932⁴

8 **BE SURPRISED,** ch g Dubassoff (USA) - Buckenham Belle by Royben (A Moore) 897 1140 2495 3015⁶

6 **BE THE BEST,** b g Rousillon (USA) - Shadywood by Habitat (John Whyte) 693⁹ 846 920 1371

8 **BEACH BUM,** gr g Scallywag - St Lucian Breeze by Vivify (Mrs J A Young) 2721⁵ 2822¹ 3232⁷

6 **BEACH PATROL(IRE),** b g Thatching - Waveguide by Double Form (R Allan) 1092 1791³ 2070 2891 3139 4082⁸

6 **BEACHOLME BOY(IRE),** b g Dominion - Bronte (USA) by Bold Forbes (USA) (J J Bridger) 460 520 592

7 **BEACHY GLEN,** b g Glenstal (USA) - Ampersand (USA) by Stop The Music (USA) (R J Baker) 2144 2335 3009 3531

6 **BEACHY HEAD,** gr g Damister (USA) - No More Rosies by Warpath (J J O'Neill) 741¹ 1358¹ 2323¹ 2928¹ 3415 3649⁵

4 **BEAGAN ROSE(IRE),** gr f Roselier (FR) - Addies Lass (Patrick Woods) 3372 3450

5 **BEAKSTOWN(IRE),** b g Orchestra - Little Shoon by Green Shoon (P Mullins) 3653 3936

5 **BEAM ME UP SCOTTY(IRE),** br g Orchestra - Bright Path by He Loves Me (Mrs S D Williams) 434 705⁶ 775² 953 1188⁸ 1506⁶

6 **BEANLEY BROOK,** ch m Meadowbrook - The Bean-Goose by King Sitric (K C Bailey) 1276

5 **BEAR CLAW,** br g Rymer - Carmarthen Honey by Eborneezer (D Nicholson) 2339¹ 2509¹ 3042

4 **BEAT THE BAGMAN(IRE),** b g Bob Back (USA) - Dacani by Polyfoto (J Akehurst) 188¹ 296² 570² 890¹

8 **BEAT THE RAP,** b g Wolverlife - Juries Slip (J R Millington) 79 177⁷ 342³

6 **BEAT THE SECOND(IRE),** gr g The Parson - Granpa's River by Over The River (FR) (V T O'Brien) 926² 1265³ 1681⁵ 1898² 2027⁷ 3247⁸ 3366³ 3747

5 **BEATSON(IRE),** gr g Roselier (FR) - Toevarro by Raga Navarro (ITY) (N A Twiston-Davies) 1957¹ 2269² 2509⁸ 2731⁹ 2964

623

INDEX TO NATIONAL HUNT RESULTS 1993-94

6 **BILLY LOMOND(IRE),** b g Lomond (USA) - Relko's Belle (FR) by Relko (K R Burke) 4322⁵ 203¹ 381³

10 **BILLY STRAYHORN,** b g Northfields (USA) - Tanaka by Tapalque (J R H Fowler) 4339

5 **BILLYGOAT GRUFF,** b g Afzal - Autumn Ballet by Averof (D Nicholson) 2339⁵ 3108² 3315³

12 **BILOXI BLUES,** gr g Blue Refrain - Haunting by Lord Gayle (USA) (Andrew Turnell) 4315¹

4 **BIMSEY(IRE),** b c Horage - Cut It Out by Cut Above (Mrs Edwina Finn) 3550 3842⁵

5 **BIN LID(IRE),** b m Henbit (USA) - Our Ena by Tower Walk (G Richards) 1183⁸ 1588⁴ 1751⁶ 2785⁷ 3357⁹

10 **BINCOMBE TOP,** gr g Revlow - Flying Streak by Blue Streak (Mrs J Hayes) 3171

8 **BINKLEY(FR),** ch g Bikala - Jinkitis by Irish Love (N A Twiston-Davies) 1968¹ 2209⁴ 2427 3040⁴ 3426 3624³ 3921²

6 **BIRCHALL BOY,** br g Julio Mariner - Polarita by Arctic Kanda (J C McConnochie) 934 1078⁶ 1320 1535

14 **BIRD OF SPIRIT,** b g Hot Brandy - Bird Of Honour by Dark Heron (M Scudamore) 4346

5 **BIRD WATCHER,** b g Bluebird (USA) - Grayfoot by Grundy (M D Hammond) 1639³ 1865⁶ 2164⁴ 2960² 3074⁴ 3378⁸ 3553⁵

9 **BIRDIE'S PRINCE,** b g Prince Regent (FR) - Watch The Birdie by Polyfoto (P J P Doyle) 92³ 200 411 635 3655³

4 **BIRTHPLACE(IRE),** b or br c Top Ville - Birthday Party (FR) by Windwurf (GER) (G Fierro) 3597

10 **BIRTLEY GIRL,** b m Le Coq D'Or - Goldness Abbey by Blackness (Dennis Hutchinson) 3439⁴ 3581³ 4073

8 **BISHOP'S TIPPLE,** b g Monksfield - Fair Vic by Fair Turn (T J Carr) 2411

13 **BISHOPDALE,** ch g Proverb - Garryduff Lady by Deep Run (S G Chadwick) 544 740 1222⁹ 1486⁸ 2151¹ 2832 3127⁵ 3437⁶ 3566 3929⁶

6 **BISHOPS CASTLE(IRE),** ch g Carlingford Castle - Dancing Princess by Prince Regent (FR) (T J Carr) 2074⁸ 2239² 2561⁷ 3536⁸

8 **BISHOPS HALL,** br g Pimpernels Tune - Mariner's Dash by Master Buck (H de Bromhead) 4356⁸ 76⁵ 422³ 539⁴ 943¹ 1226 1895⁷ 3041 3659³

8 **BISHOPS ISLAND,** b g The Parson - Gilded Empress by Menelek (D Nicholson) 1069 1507³ 1706² 2593¹ 2901¹ 3217² 3485²

8 **BISHOPS TRUTH,** gr g Scallywag - Coumenole by Beau Chapeau (R Curtis) 862 10407 2042 2779 2991 3547⁷

4 **BISSTAMI(IRE),** b g Kahyasi - Blissful Evening by Blakeney (Andrew Lee) 1911¹ 2547 3321³ 3656

7 **BIT OF A CHARACTER,** b g Orchestra - Royal Character by Reformed Character (Patrick Heffernan) 969³ 1270⁶

11 **BIT OF A CLOWN,** b g Callernish - Gusserane Lark by Napoleon Bonaparte (Mrs I McKie) 1732⁵ 2011⁶ 2758 3512⁸ 3772⁵

7 **BIT OF A FUSS,** b g Torus - Siamsa by My Swallow (W P Mullins) 508⁴ 538

8 **BIT OF A TOUCH,** b or br g Touching Wood (USA) - Edelliette (FR) by Edellic (A Lillingston) 4340⁵ 37 77 122 291

7 **BIT OF LIGHT,** ch g Henbit (USA) - Welsh Daylight by Welsh Pageant (R R Lamb) 1114⁹ 2068

7 **BITACRACK,** ch g Le Bavard (FR) - Gothic Arch by Gail Star (I R Ferguson) 4304² 18¹

7 **BITOFABANTER,** ch g Celtic Cone - Little Ginger by Ron (A L T Moore) 1431

6 **BITOFANATTER,** ch g Palm Track - Little Ginger by Cawston's Clown (R H Goldie) 823 2372 3073² 3286

4 **BITRAN,** gr c Midyan (USA) - Bishah (USA) by Balzac (USA) (K A Morgan) 851 1408⁹ 1532³ 1741² 2271² 2401 2523² 2634³ 2957¹ 3330⁴ 3587¹ 3801

5 **BITTER ALOE,** b g Green Desert (USA) - Sometime Lucky by Levmoss (G Harwood) 1515⁴ 2263 3464⁵ 3696⁶

4 **BIZANA(IRE),** b g Kings Lake (USA) - Intrinsic by Troy (Noel Meade) 470¹ 617¹ 968⁴ 1111⁵ 1454⁶ 3710⁷

7 **BLACK ARROW,** br g Full Of Hope - Snow Damsel by Mandamus (D C O'Brien) 1023⁹ 2709

6 **BLACK AVENUE(IRE),** br m Strong Gale - Shallow Run by Deep Run (F Flood) 331⁴ 2102³ 2236 2464 2770⁵

8 **BLACK CHURCH,** ch g Torus - Chantry Blue by Majority Blue (R Rowe) 933 1385⁵ 1691 2567² 3118⁵ 3382

6 **BLACK DOG(IRE),** bl g Spin Of A Coin - Granny's Needles by Linacre (W J Lanigan) 1076 2465⁵ 2658

6 **BLACK H'PENNY,** b m Town And Country - Black Penny by West Partisan (J A B Old) 1707⁵ 2505⁹ 2936³

7 **BLACK HEDGES,** b g Black Minstrel - Articinna by Arctic Slave (J A Glover) 3451

10 **BLACK HORSE LAD,** ch g Orchestra - Little Peach by Ragapan (Mrs J G Retter) 4345⁷

10 **BLACK HUMOUR,** b g Buckskin (FR) - Artiste Gaye by Artist's Son (C P E Brooks) 828¹ 1439³ 1843 2695¹ 3403² 3425

11 **BLACK MALACHA VI,** br m Black Minstrel - Unknown by Arcticeelagh (Mrs Helen O'Keeffe Daly) 79 101⁹ 250

5 **BLACK OPAL(IRE),** br g Strong Gale - Fast Adventure by Deep Run (Mrs J Pitman) 1027² 1418⁴

4 **BLACK PIPER(IRE),** b f Mr Fluorocarbon - Percussive by High Tack (Peter McCreery) 1432 1853 2349

7 **BLACK SAPPHIRE,** ch g Lomond (USA) - Star Of India by General Assembly (USA) (Major D N Chappell) 1972 2403 2528

12 **BLACK SPUR,** br g Spur On - Ravenside by Marcus Superbus (J I A Charlton) 2501⁵

5 **BLACK STAG(IRE),** b or br g Phardante (FR) - Light Whisper by Idiot's Delight (M J Wilkinson) 2387 2996 3190

5 **BLACK VALLEY(IRE),** br m Good Thyne (USA) - Slaney Valley by Even Money (J L Rothwell) 4382 2938

4 **BLACKBERRY ROAD(IRE),** br f Callernish - Arctic Raheen by Over The River (FR) (J R Curran) 3912⁵ 3974

7 **BLACKDOWN,** b h Rainbow Quest (USA) - Cider Princess by Alcide (T Dyer) 282⁴ 1064⁷ 1788

8 **BLACKGUARD(USA),** ch g Irish River (FR) - Principle (USA) by Viceregal (CAN) (L P Grassick) 3768³ 3948³ 4182³

9 **BLACKPOOL BRIDGE,** ch g Black Minstrel - Miss Stoker by Proverb (Timothy O'Callaghan) 690 929 1914² 2036 3241¹ 3873 3890

7 **BLACKSTONE,** gr m Crash Course - Sarsa by Sassafras (Gerard Stack) 3366 3694

5 **BLAIR HOUSE(IRE),** b m Heraldiste (USA) - Mrs Baggins by English Prince (A L T Moore) 2203⁶ 2553 4059

4 **BLAKE'S FABLE(IRE),** br f Lafontaine (USA) - Quality Blake by Blakeney (Capt D G Swan) 2547⁵ 2917⁶ 3466⁶

627

7 **BLAKE'S TREASURE,** b g Mummy's Treasure - Andamooka by Rarity (T Thomson Jones) 794 1241 1597⁸ 2111⁴ 2343⁷ 2713³

8 **BLAKEINGTON,** b g Baron Blakeney - Camina by Don Carlos (N R Mitchell) 1563 1869⁵ 2263 2361 2718 2980² 3149⁴ 3534

7 **BLAKENEY BLUE,** b m Baron Blakeney - Oxford Lane by Clever Fella (R T Phillips) 3564⁷ 3775

4 **BLAKES BEAU,** br g Blakeney - Beaufort Star by Great Nephew (M H Easterby) 588⁸ 784

6 **BLAKES FOLLY(IRE),** gr g Sexton Blake - Welsh Folly by Welsh Saint (J E Kiely) 305⁶

8 **BLAKES ORPHAN,** gr g Baron Blakeney - Orphan Grey by Crash Course (A E Illsley) 3313² 3846² 4163

7 **BLARNEY CASTLE,** ch g Le Moss - Miss Phyllis by Tepukei (J E Long) 2761 2913

6 **BLASKET HERO,** gr g Kalaglow - Glory Isle by Hittite Glory (Mrs S D Williams) 845⁶ 955³ 1474 2131¹ 2346 3053 3535 3752²

5 **BLAST FREEZE(IRE),** b m Lafontaine (USA) - Lady Helga by Aristocracy (N J Henderson) 9³ 31¹ 67² 88⁶ 252³ 3008² 3339¹ 3623²

7 **BLAYNEYS PRIVILEGE,** b g Morston (FR) - Flying Sister by St Paddy (R D E Woodhouse) 1478 1768⁶ 2003⁶ 2140 2874⁶ 3191² 3502

8 **BLAZING ACE,** ch m Ovac (ITY) - Belle Fillette by Beau Chapeau (P Towell) 1551 1764 1907⁷

8 **BLAZING COMET,** b m Deroulede - Guided Missile by Harwell (Miss P M Maher) 4338³ 907⁷ 991⁴ 1496⁴ 2038² 2234¹ 2939² 3242⁵ 3711⁷

8 **BLAZING DANCER,** b m Blazing Saddles (AUS) - Take More (FR) (E Quinn) 4031

7 **BLAZING DAWN,** b g Deep Run - Men's Fun by Menelek (John J Costello) 1856³ 2101⁶ 2280 2618 3085 3933⁹ 4033⁶

6 **BLAZING TRAIL(IRE),** gr g Celio Rufo - Bally Sovereign by Supreme Sovereign (P A Fahy) 675³ 808³

10 **BLAZING WALKER,** ch g Imperial Fling (USA) - Princess Kofiyah by High Line (P Cheesbrough) 2488¹ 3064

5 **BLAZON OF TROY,** b g Trojan Fen - Mullet by Star Appeal (T Thomson Jones) 551¹ 705² 916¹ 1152² 1424²

7 **BLENHEIM PALACE(USA),** gr g Hero's Honor (USA) - Hat Tip (USA) (J P Byrne) 4340³ 4405⁵ 357 97¹ 134⁹ 178⁷ 878⁸ 1268⁵ 1577 3746⁷ 3996⁵ 4150⁶

4 **BLENNERVILLE(IRE),** ch f General View - Hail And Hearty by Daring March (T F Lacy) 3450⁹

11 **BLITZKREIG,** gr g General Ironside - Tyrone Typhoon by Typhoon (E J O'Grady) 940⁶ 1336³ 1578⁷ 1847⁴ 2280⁸

6 **BLOW IT(IRE),** b g Nearly A Nose (USA) - Peaceful Pleasure by Silent Whistle (J T R Dreaper) 277³ 495² 620

6 **BLUE AEROPLANE,** ch g Reach - Shelton Song by Song (P F Nicholls) 144⁸

11 **BLUE BUCCANEER,** b g Fine Blue - Port Dancer by Port Corsair (Capt T A Forster) 987⁵ 1195³ 1566 3312 3513 3636⁶ 3830

9 **BLUE BURTON LADY,** b m Broadsword (USA) - Maggie-Now by Hard Sauce (C E Ash) 649

10 **BLUE DANUBE(USA),** ch g Riverman (USA) - Wintergrace (USA) (S G Allen) 3521⁴ 3884² 3951¹ 4182

14 **BLUE DART,** ch g Cantab - Maisie Owen by Master Owen (Richard Barber) 2968³

9 **BLUE DISC,** br g Disc Jockey - Kaotesse by Djakao (FR) (A L Forbes) 4345 370⁵

4 **BLUE DOCTOR,** gr g Sharrood (USA) - Altana by Grundy (R J Hodges) 2677 3257¹

9 **BLUE ENSIGN,** b g Beldale Flutter (USA) - Blue Rag by Ragusa (M P Muggeridge) 182⁵

5 **BLUE FLAG(USA),** b g Dixieland Band (USA) - Stuttsman County (USA) by Damascus (USA) (G Thorner) 3576

9 **BLUE GAYLE,** ch g Lord Gayle (USA) - Bunch Of Blue by Martinmas (M N O'Riordan) 3296

4 **BLUE GROTTO(IRE),** ch g Bluebird (USA) - Ganna (ITY) by Molvedo (M H Tompkins) 2564⁸ 3062⁴

5 **BLUE JADE,** ch m Afzal - Sparkling Blue by Hot Spark (C H Jones) 4023

4 **BLUE LAWS(IRE),** b g Bluebird (USA) - Claretta (USA) by Roberto (USA) (J G FitzGerald) 784²

5 **BLUE LYZANDER,** b m Petrizzo - Ol' Blue Eyes by Bluerullah (R Brotherton) 524⁷ 704⁷ 1526⁸ 1716⁷ 1948² 2295⁷ 2424 2903³ 3111⁸

5 **BLUE MONOPOLY(IRE),** b g Flash Of Steel - Blue Lookout by Cure The Blues (USA) (Declan Gillespie) 2944

4 **BLUE RADIANCE,** b f Skyliner - Stellaris by Star Appeal (J A Harris) 732³ 3002

10 **BLUE RING,** b m Young Barnaby - Alta Moda (FR) by Snob II (James Joseph Mangan) 1550² 1785² 1905⁵ 2051³ 2588³ 2683¹ 2984¹ 3405 3614⁵

9 **BLUE SERAPH,** br g Rusticaro (FR) - Saranita by Thatch (USA) (F M O'Donnell) 3611

6 **BLUE TAIL,** gr m Petong - Glyn Rhosyn by Welsh Saint (P Butler) 1040 1247⁸

4 **BLUE TRUMPET,** b g Respect - Sans Blague by Above Suspicion (B Palling) 1237 2211

8 **BLUEBELL TRACK,** b or br m Saher - Douriya (V Thompson) 559⁵ 770⁷ 1096 2152 2321

8 **BLUECHIPENTERPRISE,** br m Blakeney - Hey Skip (USA) by Bold Skipper (USA) (R C Darke) 143⁴ 198⁴ 297⁷

6 **BLUEJACKET(IRE),** ch g Thatching - Gitane Blue by Cure The Blues (USA) (Mrs D Haine) 4339 4401⁷ 369⁴

11 **BLUFF KNOLL,** b g New Brig - Tacitina by Tacitus (R Brewis) 822⁴ 1063³ 2813² 3180² 3358⁴ 3644²

5 **BLURRED VISION(IRE),** b g Vision (USA) - Yvonne's Choice by Octavo (USA) (G A Ham) 2333 2860

8 **BLUSHING DORA,** b m Blushing Scribe (USA) - Grecian Gift by Cavo Doro (M W Eckley) 2525

5 **BLUSHING GOLD,** ch m Blushing Scribe (USA) - Nonpareil (FR) by Pharly (FR) (Mrs J Jordan) 4350⁴ 818 912

4 **BLUSHING SAND(IRE),** ch g Shy Groom (USA) - Sandford Star by Sandford Lad (P T Leonard) 3616

9 **BLUSHING TIMES,** b g Good Times (ITY) - Cavalier's Blush by King's Troop (Mrs A Peach) 4355⁸

9 **BLUSTERY FELLOW,** b g Strong Gale - Paulas Fancy by Lucky Guy (J Chugg) 700² 919²

5 **BO KNOWS BEST(IRE),** ch g Burslem - Bo We Know by Derrylin (Mrs J R Ramsden) 648² 1122⁴ 1874⁶ 2138⁶ 2385¹ 2833⁸ 3038

6 **BO MULLEN(IRE),** ch m Be My Native (USA) - Fair Emma (Cecil Mahon) 341 510⁷

7 **BOADICEA'S CHARIOT,** b m Commanche Run - Indignie (USA) by Raise A Native (R J Manning) 3020 3186 3533 3740⁸

6 **BOALINE(IRE),** b m Balboa - Waterline by High Line (Noel Meade) 3124 3934

7 **BOARDING SCHOOL,** b g Glenstal (USA) - Amenity (FR) by Luthier (C Parker) 4386 560² 735 1132⁴ 1585² 2832⁴ 2953⁴ 3473¹

8 **BOB DEVANI**, br g Mandalus - Russell's Touch by Deep Run (Noel Meade) 806 966³ 1179¹ 1550¹ 1761¹ 1847³ 2159³ 2755² 3123⁴ 3391⁵ 3649

6 **BOB MONEY(IRE)**, ch g Deep Run - Cailin Cainnteach by Le Bavard (FR) (James Joseph O'Connor) 638 1074⁵ 1434⁴ 3366 4114⁷

7 **BOB NELSON**, b g Le Moss - Caplight by Capistrano (M C Gunn) 1330⁸ 2394⁹ 2607 2863⁵ 3088⁷

4 **BOB THE YANK(IRE)**, b g Bar Dexter (USA) - Jambrel (USA) by Tropic King II (Francis M O'Brien) 617³ 3505⁷ 3839⁸ 3971⁷ 4146¹

5 **BOB'S GIRL(IRE)**, ch m Bob Back (USA) - Norme (FR) by Dark Tiger (P Hughes) 276²

10 **BOB-CAM**, ch g Scallywag - Stolen Girl by Mountain Call (M D I Usher) 3757⁹

4 **BOBADIL(IRE)**, br f Bob Back (USA) - Thyme Music by Tudor Music (T F Lacy) 1377 1853⁶ 2750⁷ 2917⁹ 3069² 3448⁷

6 **BOBBIE MAGEE(IRE)**, br m Buckskin (FR) - Tengello by Bargello (J R Bryce-Smith) 967 115 341⁷

4 **BOBBIE MO**, br g Jupiter Island - Johnkeina (FR) by Johnny O'Day (USA) (J White) 4023 4172⁹

8 **BOBBY SOCKS**, b or br g Blakeney Point - Countesswells by Behistoun (R Lee) 4332⁴ 1489 2440² 2640¹ 2962 3560³ 3636² 3875³ 4028¹ 4175²

5 **BOBLONG(IRE)**, b g The Parson - Big Jump by Double Jump (H de Bromhead) 2989⁷

4 **BOBROSS(IRE)**, b g Bob Back (USA) - Testarossa (FR) by Kenmare (FR) (Peter McCreery) 802

5 **BOBS LADY(IRE)**, ch m Bob Back (USA) - Lohunda Lady by Ballymore (P Cluskey) 2024 2311

6 **BOBSVILLE(IRE)**, br g Strong Gale - Pampered Run by Deep Run (Victor Bowens) 2389 2586 2863⁸ 3366

6 **BOCELLIE**, ch m Royal Vulcan - Elmco by Boco (USA) (P W Hiatt) 524

4 **BODKIN**, b f Reference Point - Prickle by Sharpen Up (K A Morgan) 3231 3800

11 **BOG LEAF VI**, b m Roselier (FR) - Bog Cottage by Teaspoon (Patrick Carey) 93 250 468⁸ 691⁴ 1179⁴ 1268 1402³ 1550³ 1826 2036² 2100 2350³ 2589⁸ 2942³ 3084⁹ 3199⁹ 3467 3873² 4042⁴

12 **BOGAZKOY**, b g Hittite Glory - Lady Captain by Never Say Die (S G Barnett) 3768⁶ 3918⁶

6 **BOGGLE HOLE(IRE)**, b g Mazaad - Gentalyn by Henbit (USA) (Miss Anne Collen) 3

5 **BOHEMIAN CASTLE(IRE)**, b g Carlingford Castle - Gay Signal by Lord Gayle (USA) (A J McNamara) 990⁶ 1333⁷ 1610⁵ 1821² 2278⁸ 2920¹ 3085

4 **BOHEMIAN QUEEN**, ch f Doulab (USA) - Tittlemouse by Castle Keep (J L Spearing) 128 642² 1049⁷ 2364⁵ 3572 3763² 4135

7 **BOHOLA EXPRESS**, b g Ovac (ITY) - Elenas Beauty by Tarqogan (M H Dare) 4340 6 30

8 **BOKARO(FR)**, b g Air Du Nord - Tzara by Night And Day (C P E Brooks) 192¹ 267¹ 440¹

5 **BOLANEY GIRL(IRE)**, b m Amazing Bust - French Note by Eton Rambler (J J O'Neill) 1133⁴ 1660

4 **BOLD ACRE**, ch g Never So Bold - Nicola Wynn by Nicholas Bill (D Burchell) 851⁷ 1243⁵

4 **BOLD ALFIE**, br g Sulaafah (USA) - Miss Boldly by Flandre II (Michael Hourigan) 3550 3839

7 **BOLD AMBITION**, b g Ela-Mana-Mou - Queen Of The Dance by Dancer's Image (USA) (T Kersey) 1320⁷ 1571 1998

8 **BOLD BARNEY(NZ)**, br g So Bold (NZ) - War Belle (NZ) by War Hawk (Michael Robinson) 969⁵ 1270

5 **BOLD BOSS**, b g Nomination - Mai Pussy by Realm (M C Pipe) 1437¹

6 **BOLD BOSTONIAN(FR)**, b h Never So Bold - Miss Boston (FR) by River River (FR) (P J Hobbs) 1053³ 1460⁷ 2529²

6 **BOLD BREW(IRE)**, b g Brewery Boy (AUS) - Bold Tavo (Francis M O'Brien) 4368⁵ 4399 10

5 **BOLD CAT(IRE)**, b h Bold Arrangement - Le Chat by Burglar (Joseph Sheahan) 692

4 **BOLD CHEVALIER(IRE)**, gr g Roselier (FR) - Worling Gold by Connaught (Redmond Cody) 2848³ 3245⁵

8 **BOLD CHOICE**, b g Auction Ring (USA) - Inner Pearl by Gulf Pearl (R G Frost) 980² 2861² 3152¹ 3301² 3548³ 3828

6 **BOLD CRYSTAL(IRE)**, b g Persian Bold - Wineglass by Wolver Hollow (Patrick Prendergast) 4403² 271¹

11 **BOLD FLYER**, b g Peacock (FR) - Bold And True by Sir Herbert (Miss Anne Collen) 59⁵ 75² 132 364³ 422⁵ 708 2202² 2591

11 **BOLD IN COMBAT**, b g Junius (USA) - Malmsey by Jukebox (T Casey) 4394⁷

11 **BOLD KING'S HUSSAR**, ch g Sunyboy - Oca by O'Grady (Mrs David Plunkett) 2669⁵

5 **BOLD MELODY**, b m Never So Bold - Broken Melody by Busted (P C Haslam) 642³

5 **BOLD MOOD**, br g Jalmood (USA) - Boldie by Bold Lad (IRE) (J J Birkett) 1738 2108⁷ 2254⁴ 2321⁵ 2575 2974⁸

4 **BOLD NOT BEAT(IRE)**, gr g Bold Arrangement - Disco Beat by No Mercy (J C Harley) 3810

8 **BOLD REPUBLIC**, gr g Nishapour (FR) - Gallant Believer (USA) by Gallant Romeo (USA) (John Boswell) 2508 2885

11 **BOLD SPARTAN**, b g Bold Owl - Spartan's Girl by Spartan General (J K M Oliver) 2105

4 **BOLD STAR**, b c Persian Bold - Star Arrangement by Star Appeal (M F Barraclough) 1350 1522⁵ 1702³ 1931² 2094² 2276 2478⁵ 2902⁶ 3584

4 **BOLD STREET(IRE)**, ch g Shy Groom (USA) - Ferry Lane by Dom Racine (FR) (A Bailey) 1290

7 **BOLD STREET BLUES**, b g Bold Owl - Basin Street by Tudor Melody (J A Bennett) 888⁴ 1010 1448⁴ 2320⁴ 2708⁴ 3451³ 3671² 3917⁵

5 **BOLD STROKE**, br g Persian Bold - Fariha by Mummy's Pet (M C Pipe) 1695¹ 1946⁴ 3023

5 **BOLD TED(IRE)**, gr g Taufan (USA) - Alfambra (USA) by Nashua (Mrs John Harrington) 323¹ 531 3946

5 **BOLD TIPPERARY(IRE)**, b m Orchestra - Princess Annabelle by English Prince (Michael Butler) 2944 3124 3508⁹

7 **BOLD'N**, ch g Ardross - Princess Dina by Huntercombe (N B Mason) 875⁶

6 **BOLEREE(IRE)**, b m Mandalus - Damberee by Deep Run (Anthony Mullins) 10 45 636⁴ 1495 1855⁹

6 **BOLERO DANCER(IRE)**, b g Shareef Dancer (USA) - Legend Of Arabia by Great Nephew (Thomas O'Neill) 636⁵ 967⁵ 1075 4092⁴

8 **BOLL WEEVIL**, b g Boreen (FR) - Lavenham Lady by Precipice Wood (O Sherwood) 741³ 1081¹ 1311² 1511⁷ 1866⁴ 2636¹

6 **BOLLIN MAGDALENE**, b m Teenoso (USA) - Klairlone by Klairon (M H Easterby) 1481³ 1619 2086¹ 2273¹ 2403¹

6 **BOLLIN WILLIAM**, b h Nicholas Bill - Bollin Charlotte by Immortality (M H Easterby) 1005² 1322² 1617¹ 1756⁵ 2012²

INDEX TO NATIONAL HUNT RESULTS 1993-94

8 **BOLLINGER,** ch g Balinger - Jolly Regal by Jolly Good (J T Gifford) 1385² 1631¹ 2193² 2479² 2854⁴ 3498³

5 **BOLLINGTON(FR),** ch g Lightning (FR) - Secret Hideaway (USA) by Key To The Mint (USA) (D Marks) 3191⁶ 3530 3809⁵ 3938 4009⁷

7 **BOLTON SARAH,** b m Saher - Paddy's Team by Ballymore (James Joseph Mangan) 71⁸ 108⁶ 169 295⁹

4 **BOLTROSE,** b c Electric - Garnette Rose by Floribunda (K White) 870³ 997⁶ 3853⁵ 4179

7 **BON VIVANT(FR),** b g Noblequest - Bay Area by Youth 374³

5 **BON VIVEUR,** b g Petoski - Venetian Joy by Windjammer (USA) (A L T Moore) 990 1230

7 **BONANZA,** ch g Glenstal (USA) - Forliana by Forli (ARG) (Mrs M Reveley) 867⁵ 1148¹ 1322¹ 1561 2323² 2403 2893⁵ 2998² 3130⁴ 3376² 3676³

13 **BONANZA BOY,** b g Sir Lark - Vulmid by Vulgan (M C Pipe) 2793¹ 3171⁴

4 **BONAR BRIDGE(USA),** b or br g Quadratic (USA) - Merririver (USA) by Taylor's Falls (USA) (K R Burke) 1965⁵ 2094

4 **BOND JNR(IRE),** ch g Phardante (FR) - Sea Scope by Deep Run (P F Nicholls) 1110³ 1542¹ 1695⁴ 2556² 2827⁶

10 **BONDAID,** b g Main Reef - Regency Gold by Prince Regent (FR) (J White) 141¹ 195³ 298¹ 522² 681¹ 1153³ 1586³ 2065 3714 3940² 4177²

5 **BONDIR(IRE),** b g Jamesmead - Saltatrix by Grange Melody (I A Duncan) 2775⁵ 3071⁹

5 **BONE IDOL(IRE),** gr g Sexton Blake - Clarence Fort by Prefairy (Thomas F Walshe) 431

4 **BONE SETTER(IRE),** b g Strong Gale - Princess Wager by Pollerton (S Mellor) 2042⁹ 2315⁸ 2599 2860⁸

4 **BONITA BEE,** b f King Of Spain - Lady Annie Laurie by Pitcairn (J C McConnochie) 406 742

6 **BONNY BEAU,** b m Kinglet - Starlight Beauty by Scallywag (L J Williams) 2509

10 **BONNY HECTOR,** ch g Bonne Noel - Miss Bustle by Majority Blue (S I Pittendrigh) 2903 3284⁹ 3435

4 **BONNY PRINCESS,** br f Petoski - True Queen (USA) by Silver Hawk (USA) (W Storey) 642⁹

6 **BONNY'S GAME,** b m Mummy's Game - Ribonny (FR) by Fast Hilarious (USA) (D Buckley) 4113⁵

11 **BONSAI BUD,** b g Tug Of War - Keep The Day by Master Buck (D J G Murray Smith) 661 886¹ 1082² 1447 3261² 3407

4 **BONUS POINT,** ch g Don't Forget Me - Blue Aria by Cure The Blues (USA) (C R Egerton) 278³ 406³ 561¹ 872³ 1062⁶

8 **BONZER BOB,** bl g Kemal (FR) - Timber Line by High Line (Lady Earle) 2352 2941

5 **BOOGIE BOPPER(IRE),** b or br g Taufan (USA) - Mey by Canisbay (M C Pipe) 1404⁹ 1546⁴ 1699⁵ 1719 1867⁶ 2317³ 2523⁸ 2760⁵ 3111⁴ 3298¹ 4070⁴

6 **BOOK OF MUSIC(IRE),** b g Orchestra - Good Loss by Ardoon (J T Gifford) 1442³ 1648¹ 1992 2459² 2779³ 3036 3380⁷

9 **BOOK OF RUNES,** b g Deep Run - Wychelm by Allangrange (N A Twiston-Davies) 542² 2293 2479

7 **BOOK OF RYMES,** br m Rymer - Dunoon Court by Dunoon Star (Miss R J Patman) 3005 3184

4 **BOOLAVOGUE(IRE),** b f Torus - Easter Beauty by Raise You Ten (O O'Neill) 3169⁷ 3458 3670⁴

9 **BOOM TIME,** br g Strong Gale - Karin Maria by Double Jump (Mrs John Harrington) 1783⁶ 1909

6 **BOOTH'S BOUQUET,** b g Ginger Boy - Lismore by Relkino (Miss B Sanders) 982⁷ 2315 3543³ 3938⁴

7 **BOOTSCRAPER,** ch g Doc Marten - Impish Ears by Import (P Leach) 1721 2019⁶ 2729 3491⁷ 3769² 3919³ 4181⁴

4 **BORDER DREAM,** b g Electric - Be Still by Derring-Do (W G M Turner) 2398 2717

9 **BOREEN BRIDGE,** gr g Boreen (FR) - Lady Peacock by Peacock (FR) (Peter McCreery) 372

10 **BOREEN JEAN,** ch m Boreen (FR) - Kitty Quin by Saucy Kit (K S Bridgwater) 2216⁵ 2528 3186 3298³ 3533 3673

4 **BOREEN LASS(IRE),** gr f Cardinal Flower - Tara's Lady by General Ironside (D Dorgan) 3946

10 **BOREEN OWEN,** b g Boreen (FR) - Marble Owen by Master Owen (J J O'Neill) 975 1130⁴ 1359² 1471 1635⁶ 1939 2410⁵ 2499⁴ 2893⁵ 3485 3602³ 3784

5 **BORING(USA),** ch g Foolish Pleasure (USA) - Arriya by Luthier (W Storey) 1092³ 1607 1791⁷ 2150

6 **BORIS BAGLEY,** ch g Rymer - Lady Christine by Don Carlos (Dr D Chesney) 3113 3257⁸

8 **BORN DEEP,** ch g Deep Run - Love-In-A-Mist by Paddy's Stream (A P O'Brien) 575 635¹ 856² 1112² 1266 1497⁴ 2681³ 2865³

4 **BORN TO WIN(IRE),** b f Torus - Mugs Away by Mugatpura (M J Byrne) 2678⁶ 3321⁶

4 **BORNE,** b g Bairn (USA) - Mummy's Glory by Mummy's Pet (M J Camacho) 2332² 2963³

10 **BORO DOLLAR,** b g Smartset - Boro Nickel by Nicolaus (A P O'Brien) 1330 1496 1814 1897

8 **BORO EIGHT,** b g Deep Run - Boro Nickel by Nicolaus (P Mullins) 1335² 1431⁹

9 **BORO SMACKEROO,** b g Deep Run - Boro Nickel by Nicolaus (J H Johnson) 769⁵ 1065 1285⁵ 1737 2360⁴ 2449⁵ 3320⁴ 3429⁶ 3643⁵ 3780

10 **BORRETO,** b or br g Treboro (USA) - Fiji Express by Exbury (C James) 1353⁵ 1456⁶ 1645⁷ 2033² 2454⁴ 2776⁹

6 **BORRISMORE FLASH(IRE),** ch g Le Moss - Deep Goddess by Deep Run (James M Kiernan) 4343 2394 2664 2863 3122 3243 3366 3711 4030 4115

4 **BORROWED AND BLUE,** b f Local Suitor (USA) - Abielle by Abwah (P J Hobbs) 2016⁸ 3204 3497⁵ 3804¹ 4004⁶

10 **BOSCEAN CHIEFTAIN,** b g Shaab - Indian Stick by Indian Ruler (Mrs J G Retter) 2473 3207¹ 3382² 3517¹ 3823¹

7 **BOSSBURG,** b m Celtic Cone - Born Bossy by Eborneezer (D McCain) 4323⁴ 834² 1312² 1591³ 1771³ 2032⁴

4 **BOSSY PATRICIA(IRE),** ch f Glenstal (USA) - Biddy Mulligan by Ballad Rock (Owen Weldon) 2349 2750

5 **BOSSYMOSS(IRE),** b g Le Moss - Annes Wedding by Buckskin (FR) (R W Emery) 1078 1374 3584 3815 4017

9 **BOSTON ROVER,** b g Ovac (ITY) - Vulgan Ten by Raise You Ten (O Brennan) 913¹ 1098² 1566² 1737³ 2087⁷ 2272¹ 2962 3091³ 3312² 3513⁷ 3803³ 4067³ 4164³

8 **BOSTON RUN,** b g Deep Run - Chillaway by Arctic Slave (D J Barry) 3837

4 **BOTANIC VERSES(IRE),** ch f King Persian - Rose A Village by River Beauty (George Gracey) 1377

5 **BOTH SIDES(IRE),** b g Mandalus - Abi's Dream by Paddy's Stream (J H Scott) 4034

7 **BOTHA BOCHT,** b m Pauper - Tudor Saint by Tudor Music (D J Flannery) 554

10 **BOTHAR NA SPEIRE,** gr g Ovac (ITY) - Lady Peacock by Peacock (FR) (M J P O'Brien) 3657 3746[1]

4 **BOTHSIDESNOW(IRE),** b g Exhibitioner - Caroline's Mark by On Your Mark (Noel Meade) 1983[9] 2122 2281[5] 3246[8] 3993[3]

7 **BOTTLE BLACK,** b g Kemal (FR) - Deep Sea Diver by Deep Diver (John Davies) 3071[3] 3275[1]

7 **BOTTLES(USA),** b g North Pole (CAN) - Fooling Around by Jaazeiro (USA) (J E Banks) 1278[1] 2833[2] 3618[2] 4019[1]

6 **BOUGHT THE ACES(IRE),** gr g Flash Of Steel - Soubrette by Habat (G A Ham) 3108[9]

6 **BOULEY BAY,** b g Lightning Dealer - Cathedine Flyer by Green Shoon (Mrs I McKie) 502

6 **BOUNTIFUL HOLLOW(IRE),** b m Cataldi - Devine Lady by The Parson (A P O'Brien) 103 171[9]

9 **BOURNE LANE,** ch g Pollerton - Cherry Princess by Prince Hansel (D M Grissell) 2194[4]

6 **BOURNEL,** ch m Sunley Builds - Golden Granite by Rugantino (C R Barwell) 1806 2021[3] 2560[6] 3113[4]

5 **BOURSIN(IRE),** b g Taufan (USA) - Cloven Dancer (USA) by Hurok (USA) (P Calver) 3379

12 **BOUTZDAROFF,** ch g Dubassoff (USA) - Love Seat by King's Bench (J G FitzGerald) 631[4] 1009 1285[3] 1440[3] 3262[3] 3595[6] 3963

8 **BOWL OF OATS,** ch g Oats - Bishop's Bow by Crozier (Andrew Turnell) 1171[6] 1471[2] 1732 1838[4] 2191[1]

7 **BOWLAND CONNECTION,** ch g Crash Course - Bonnemahon by Polyfoto (J L Eyre) 4303 1480

5 **BOWLAND GIRL(IRE),** b m Supreme Leader - El Marica by Buckskin (FR) (R Hollinshead) 1747[5] 1926[7] 2088[5] 3167[5] 3317[8] 3395 3765[3] 3965[6] 4025[4] 4064[8] 4160

4 **BOWLANDS GEM,** ch g Nicholas Bill - Early Doors by Ballad Rock (J L Eyre) 3227

6 **BOWLANDS HIMSELF(IRE),** b g The Parson - Yellow Canary by Miner's Lamp (C Parker) 1787 3177

5 **BOWLANDS LAW,** b g Pitpan - Kilbride Madam by Mandalus (J L Eyre) 4040[2] 4159

10 **BOWLANDS WAY,** b g Al Sirat (USA) - Kilbride Lady VI by Menelek (J L Eyre) 2004[4] 2137 3224 3428 3603 3783[1] 3960[3] 4037[3] 4155[5]

6 **BOWLING CHERRY(IRE),** b g Bowling Pin - Lady Cherry by Bargello (Thomas Kinane) 1852[4] 2203[9] 2983

6 **BOX OF DELIGHTS,** br g Idiot's Delight - Pretty Useful by Firestreak (R Dickin) 1542 1800 2404 3530[5] 3628

7 **BOXING MATCH,** b g Royal Boxer - Mutchkin by Espresso (J M Bradley) 264[3] 344[3] 592[9] 699[1] 889[6] 1211[2] 1526 3533[5] 3673 3977

6 **BOY BILLY(IRE),** b g Balboa - Tanfirian Star (F Warren) 4382[7]

7 **BOY BLUE,** ch g Fine Blade (USA) - Shady Blue by Bluerullah (Andrew Lee) 1854[4] 2233[9] 2351 2770[3] 2940[8] 3293

5 **BOY BUSTER,** b g Pitpan - Medway Melody by Romany Air (F Gray) 2339

4 **BOYFRIEND,** b c Rolfe (USA) - Lady Sweetapples by Super Song (D R C Elsworth) 2560[3] 2749[7] 3208[5] 3700[1]

4 **BOZO BAILEY,** gr g Hadeer - Perceive (USA) by Nureyev (USA) (M H Tompkins) 2422[2] 2629[3] 2802[8] 2960[5] 3328[6] 3635[2] 3757[2]

9 **BRABAZON(USA),** b g Cresta Rider (USA) - Brilliant Touch (USA) by Gleaming (USA) (M H Tompkins) 2012[5] 2257[6] 2479[5] 2668[3] 2784[1] 3039 3316[1] 3442[1]

10 **BRABINER LAD,** ch g Celtic Cone - Bit Of A Madam by Richboy (T Laxton) 4362[3] 3778[3] 4131[5] 4183[4]

5 **BRACE OF PHEASANTS,** ch m Vital Season - Singing Trooper by Air Trooper (N R Mitchell) 216

7 **BRACKENAIR,** b m Fairbairn - Ulster Belle by Porto Bello (W J Bryson) 343[9] 491[6]

8 **BRACKENFIELD,** ch g Le Moss - Stable Lass by Golden Love (Mrs M Reveley) 733[1] 874 1033[1] 1537[3] 2137 2784 3341[1] 3428 3896[1] 4024[1]

9 **BRADBURY STAR,** b g Torus - Ware Princess by Crash Course (J T Gifford) 866[1] 1226[1] 1843[2] 2474[4] 3064[5]

10 **BRADWALL,** br g Strong Gale - Sweet Season by Silly Season (Mrs A R Hewitt) 1359 1503 2633 3495[1] 3662[2] 4007[1] 4122[2]

6 **BRAE(IRE),** b m Runnett - Peak by High Top (Cecil Ross) 4381[6] 17 81[4] 99[4] 160 513[3] 745[1] 4030 4187[7]

8 **BRAIDA BOY,** b h Kampala - Braida (FR) by Tissot (M Bradstock) 4362[1]

6 **BRAMBLE RUN(IRE),** b g Carlingford Castle - Bramble Lane by Boreen (FR) (F Kavanagh) 1555

5 **BRAMBLEBERRY,** gr g Sharrood (USA) - Labista by Crowned Prince (USA) (Mrs S J Smith) 1481[7] 1746[3] 2243[5] 2540[1] 2815[1] 3182 3413[7] 3692[9] 3780[6]

4 **BRAMBLESHINE(IRE),** b f Phardante (FR) - Shining Run by Deep Run (Kevin O'Donnell) 3450[7] 3749[4] 4060[2] 4171[1]

4 **BRANCEPETH BELLE(IRE),** b f Supreme Leader - Head Of The Gang by Pollerton (N B Mason) 278[2]

4 **BRANDANTE(IRE),** b g Phardante (FR) - Branston Lady by Deep Run (J R H Fowler) 2848[1] 3372[5]

9 **BRANDESTON,** b g Northern Treat (USA) - Fussy Budget by Wolver Hollow (G A Hubbard) 749[4] 897 1226 1387[3] 1664

6 **BRANDON PRINCE(IRE),** b g Shernazar - Chanson de Paris (USA) by The Minstrel (CAN) (I A Balding) 1442[5] 1878[4]

4 **BRASS BUTTON(IRE),** ch f Fools Holme (USA) - Nolnocan by Colum (B J Ryan) 228

5 **BRAVE AND TENDER(IRE),** b g Strong Gale - Brave Intention by Brave Invader (USA) (J H Johnson) 2382 2741 3140

7 **BRAVE BUCCANEER,** ch g Buckskin (FR) - Not So Dear by Dhaudevi (FR) (Mrs M Reveley) 2172[9] 2597[1] 2823[1] 3028

6 **BRAVE HENRY,** br g Miner's Lamp - Miss Posey by Pitskelly (A J McNamara) 304[3] 433[4] 540

6 **BRAVE HIGHLANDER(IRE),** b g Sheer Grit - Deerpark Rose by Arapaho (J T Gifford) 1442[7] 2147[4] 2599[4] 2757[4] 3196[3] 3360[1] 3487[3]

4 **BRAVE RAIDER(IRE),** ch g Dixieland Band (USA) - Trusted Partner (USA) by Affirmed (USA) (D K Weld) 3246

10 **BRAVE SHARON,** b m Scorpio (FR) - Sleigh Song by Ridan (USA) (Mrs P Collier) 169 229[9] 689 797

8 **BRAVE STAR,** b g Glen Quaich - Accidental by Energist (Francis Berry) 3 4

6 **BRAVEFOOT,** b h Dancing Brave (USA) - Swiftfoot by Run The Gantlet (USA) (J H Scott) 4404[3] 10[5] 24[1] 40[1] 106[3] 113 123 230[4] 232[1] 313[6] 376[1] 471[2] 637[6] 673[1] 831[3] 880[7]

9 **BRAVO STAR(USA),** b g The Minstrel (CAN) - Stellarette (CAN) by Tentam (USA) (K Bishop) 2403 2654⁷ 3454⁸ 3764⁷ 4181

4 **BRAXTON BRAGG(IRE),** ch c Glenstal (USA) - Chanting Music by Taufan (USA) (M D Hammond) 272⁵ 481⁴

6 **BREACADH AN LAE(IRE),** b m Mandalus - Clare Dawn by Prince Hansel (I J Keeling) 2770

5 **BREAD OF HEAVEN,** b m Kaytu - Nimble Star by Space King (R Evans) 1660 1957 3113

7 **BRECKENBROUGH LAD,** b g Uncle Pokey - Fabulous Beauty by Royal Avenue (D T Turner) 226⁷ 369¹

8 **BREECHES BUOY,** ch g Buckskin (FR) - Sea Fog by Menelek (A R Aylett) 2964

5 **BREEZE AWAY,** b m Prince Sabo - Ballad Island by Ballad Rock (D Eddy) 1675 1961

6 **BREFFNI MELODY(IRE),** b g Euphemism - Coolenearl Lady by Crash Course (Michael Cunningham) 675 877

5 **BRENDA HUNT(IRE),** gr m Huntingdale - Brenda by Sovereign Path (M P Muggeridge) 2841 3119

11 **BRENMAR ROSE,** b m Roselier (FR) - Corrib Lass (S G Walsh) 3712

5 **BRESIL(USA),** b g Bering - Clever Bidder (USA) by Bold Bidder (A P Jarvis) 1374⁷ 2629

5 **BREYFAX,** b g Rabdan - Celtic Love by Irish Love (G Gilio) 2671

6 **BRIAR'S DELIGHT,** b g Idiot's Delight - Briar Park by Timolin (FR) (R Allan) 717⁹ 823 3440³ 3641² 3862⁴ 3981²

7 **BRIC LANE(USA),** br g Arctic Tern (USA) - Spring Is Sprung (USA) by Herbager (J E Long) 1729

6 **BRIDEPARK ROSE(IRE),** b m Kemal (FR) - Elite Lady by Prince Hansel (M P Muggeridge) 535⁶ 857⁴ 993⁹ 2426⁸ 2796⁴ 3340¹ 3892²

15 **BRIDESWELL DEW,** ch g Deep Run - Merry Valley by Festive (Seamus Neville) 4380

5 **BRIDGE PEARL(IRE),** b g Millfontaine - Gay Profusion by Green God (Patrick G Kelly) 692⁸ 1820

7 **BRIDGE PLAYER,** ch m The Noble Player (USA) - Auction Bridge by Auction Ring (USA) (D Moffatt) 222¹ 424² 1057⁷

5 **BRIDGE STREET BOY,** ch g Risk Me (FR) - Bridge Street Lady by Decoy Boy (J R Bosley) 1046 1187⁸ 1325

6 **BRIDGEOFALLEN(IRE),** ch m Torus - Overdressed by Le Tricolore (Eugene M O'Sullivan) 3789⁸ 3872⁴ 4041⁴ 4147⁴

6 **BRIDGIE TERRIE(IRE),** b f Cardinal Flower - Garden Pit by Pitpan (John Queally) 3293 3835 3972

5 **BRIDGNORTH LASS,** b m Say Primula - Muskcat Rambler by Pollerton (M C Pipe) 4023 4159

10 **BRIEF ENCOUNTER(NZ),** b g Foreign Affair - Euphemia (NZ) by Piccolo Player (USA) (Richard Barber) 2882¹ 3171²

7 **BRIEF GALE,** b m Strong Gale - Lucky Chestnut by Lucky Brief (J T Gifford) 1196¹ 1536² 2558¹ 3036³ 3230⁵

9 **BRIGADIER BILL,** ch g Nicholas Bill - Sailing Brig by Brigadier Gerard (J White) 4377

7 **BRIGADIER DAVIS(FR),** b g R B Chesne - Styrene (FR) by Trenel (T P Tate) 1295² 3076² 3354 3536² 3778⁴

5 **BRIGADIER SUPREME(IRE),** b or br g Supreme Leader - Star Whistler by Menelek (Michael Hourigan) 98 217⁷ 469 1822 2607 3197 3290

4 **BRIGENSER(IRE),** b g Digamist (USA) - Lady Anna Livia by Ahonoora (G Barnett) 706⁷ 802

4 **BRIGG FOLLY,** b or br f Oedipus Complex - Lombard Street by Naucetra (J G Thorpe) 2876 2963 3347

10 **BRIGGS BUILDERS,** b g Absalom - Quenlyn by Welsh Pageant (R Rowe) 1391⁴ 1596⁴ 2248²

5 **BRIGGS LAD(IRE),** ch g Be My Native (USA) - Zestino by Shack (USA) (P T Dalton) 4344⁴ 594⁷ 867⁷ 961⁴ 2933⁸ 3131⁹ 3594

9 **BRIGHT BURNS,** b g Celtic Cone - Chanter Mark by River Chanter (C J R Sweeting) 3948³

8 **BRIGHT CRUSADER,** b g Lepanto (GER) - Snowdra's Daughter by Down Cloud (Mrs N Simm) 3860⁷

8 **BRIGHT HARBOUR,** b m Energist - Mystical Marina (J P N Parker) 4339

5 **BRIGHT IDEA(IRE),** b g Delamain (USA) - Coolkereen by My Swanee (James Grace) 157 503

8 **BRIGHT SAPPHIRE,** b g Mummy's Pet - Bright Era by Artaius (USA) (J M Bradley) 951 1072 1190⁹ 1485 2131 2711³ 3003⁶ 3298⁴ 3535 3673

9 **BRIGHTLING BOY,** ch g Deep Run - Susan La Salle by Master Owen (D M Grissell) 1711³ 2044¹ 2247⁴ 2496 2674⁵ 3514⁷

4 **BRIGHTON BREEZY,** b g Skyliner - Tree Mist by Bruni (J C Poulton) 2190⁵ 2714

6 **BRIGTINA,** b g Tina's Pet - Bristle-Moss by Brigadier Gerard (J M Bradley) 401² 477³ 586² 607 813⁶

9 **BRILLIANT FUTURE,** b m Welsh Saint - Autumn Gift by Martinmas (K S Bridgwater) 3499⁷

6 **BRILLIANT VENTURE(IRE),** ch m Le Moss - Troilena by Troilus (Anthony Mullins) 572⁹

5 **BRIMPTON BERTIE,** ch g Music Boy - Lady Of Bath by Longleat (USA) (Major D N Chappell) 983 1642⁶ 3502⁸ 3685⁹ 3878⁶ 4112³

7 **BRINDLEY HOUSE,** b g Deep Run - Annick (FR) by Breton (R Curtis) 1453 1913⁷ 2617⁵ 2660¹ 3242 3273¹ 3657

4 **BRISAN HERO(IRE),** br f Henbit (USA) - Miss Shamrock by Saritamer (USA) (S F Maye) 3749 4189

6 **BRISCE HILL(IRE),** b m Roselier (FR) - Mur's Girl by Deep Run (M V Manning) 2311 2770 3273 3810

5 **BRISTOL SPIRIT(IRE),** b m Evros - Bristol Bomber by Red Alert (A J Kennedy) 531

7 **BROAD CHARE,** b g Bishop Of Orange - Faultys Call Vii (E A Elliott) 3581⁵

5 **BROAD STEANE,** b g Broadsword (USA) - Banbury Cake by Seaepic (USA) (S Mellor) 1428⁴ 1768 2263⁵ 2505⁷ 3022²

6 **BROADWATER BOY(IRE),** b g Miner's Lamp - Down By The River by Over The River (FR) (M D Hammond) 2931³

8 **BROADWOOD LAD,** b g Broadsword (USA) - Spartaca by Spartan General (R J Eckley) 2404 2525 2858 3004⁶ 3213⁹

7 **BROCKLEY COURT,** b g Boreen (FR) - Arctic Free by Master Buck (Mrs John Harrington) 991¹ 1269¹ 1431¹ 1684¹ 1817² 3080⁸ 3426⁴ 3658⁹ 3933⁴ 4032⁴

8 **BRODESSA,** gr g Scallywag - Jeanne Du Barry by Dubassoff (USA) (Mrs M Reveley) 821¹ 983³ 1366²

9 **BROGUESTOWN,** b g King's Ride - Happy View by Royal Buck (F Flood) 1498 1684⁴ 1905 2157 3293¹ 3648⁷ 3996⁶

6 **BROGUESTOWN PRIDE(IRE),** b g Kemal (FR) - Una's Pride by Raise You Ten (A P O'Brien) 3504⁵ 3733¹ 3954⁶ 4192³

11 **CAPALL AOSTA,** b g Spitsbergen - Musk Lemon by Philemon (C M P Farr) 843⁶ 2966

6 **CAPDOO LADY(IRE),** b m Pollerton - No Dear by No Argument (Mark McCausland) 4400 374⁴

10 **CAPE COTTAGE,** ch g Dubassoff (USA) - Cape Thriller by Thriller (D J Caro) 2526² 2838¹ 3171³ 3265⁴ 3480⁵ 3684⁴

8 **CAPE SPY,** b g Scorpio (FR) - Glaspistol by Tumblewind (USA) (J R H Fowler) 878⁶ 966⁴ 1231⁵ 1268⁴ 1433¹ 1761

5 **CAPENWRAY(IRE),** br g Supreme Leader - Godetia by Be Friendly (R F Fisher) 2387⁶ 2834⁴ 3140¹ 3620² 3862²

5 **CAPICHE(IRE),** b g Phardante (FR) - Sainthill by St Alphage (J Etherington) 4407¹

12 **CAPINCUR BOY,** ch g The Parson - In The Limelight by Prince Hansel (Donal Hassett) 21⁴ 101² 178 303 332 532

8 **CAPINCUR EILE,** b g The Parson - Kenodon by Menelek (Michael J McDonagh) 905⁸ 1402⁶ 1499⁹ 1826 2660 3465⁶ 3790⁷

5 **CAPITAIN,** b g Idiot's Delight - Crosa by Crozier (A P Jones) 1996 2519

5 **CAPITAL LAD,** ch g Dublin Lad - Wellington Bear by Dragonara Palace (USA) (M Avison) 2401 3661 3899⁵

5 **CAPITAL LETTER(IRE),** b g Tumble Gold - Willetta by Will Somers (J P Leigh) 2387

8 **CAPITAL PUNISHMENT,** ch g Capitano - Loophole by London Gazette (M D Hammond) 542¹ 911¹ 1145⁴ 2069³ 2149⁶ 3554¹ 3908³

5 **CAPITAL ROSE(IRE),** b m Roselier (FR) - Capital Katie by Distinctly (USA) (M Phelan) 3450¹ 3913

5 **CAPO CASTANUM,** ch g Sula Bula - Joscilla by Joshua (Miss H C Knight) 1626 3522⁴

7 **CAPPUCCINO GIRL,** ch m Broadsword (USA) - Coffee Bob by Espresso (F Gray) 1462⁶ 2172 2338⁹ 2496 3186 3514⁹

8 **CAPSIZE,** ch g Capitano - Fogged Light by Fury Royal (A Moore) 899 1136² 1467⁴ 2346 3014⁶

5 **CAPTAIN BERT,** b g Capitano - Cavity by True Song (B de Haan) 1536 2250 3396 3809⁴

9 **CAPTAIN BRANDY,** ch g Step Together (USA) - Manhattan Brandy by Frankincense (F Flood) 800 1231 1553 2125³ 2591⁴ 2701 3081³ 3324⁴ 3425 3659⁵ 3746

9 **CAPTAIN CAVEMAN,** gr g Scallywag - Canadian Pacific by Spartan General (M Sams) 3581 4084 4130⁴

6 **CAPTAIN CHARLES(IRE),** b g Cataldi - Axxon Choice by Tarqogan (E Lacey) 930⁹ 1827 2924 3296 3870 4192

9 **CAPTAIN CUTE,** ro g Absalom - Cute by Hardicanute (D T Garraton) 4328⁶ 641³ 974⁶ 1425³ 2058³ 2240⁴ 3579

7 **CAPTAIN DOLFORD,** ch g Le Moss - Niatpac by Royal Highway (D R Gandolfo) 1274 1759⁵ 1972¹ 2298¹ 2437 2512 3028

11 **CAPTAIN FRISK,** bl g Politico (USA) - Jenny Frisk by Sunacelli (K C Bailey) 2805¹ 2880²

7 **CAPTAIN GREG,** ch g Cardinal Flower - Pottlerath by Paddy's Stream (Austin Broderick) 36

6 **CAPTAIN KHEDIVE,** ch g Deep Run - Wing On by Quayside (P J Hobbs) 815¹ 1329¹ 1548³ 2525³ 3396²

4 **CAPTAIN KIZZY(IRE),** b f Niels - Gibson Girlee (USA) by Gidouee (CAN) (James Joseph O'Connor) 2663 4059 4167⁸

13 **CAPTAIN LYNDSEY,** b g Major Point - Rosas by Harwell (J P Dodds) 509⁵ 3962³ 4130³

9 **CAPTAIN MANNERING(USA),** b g Tina's Pet - Independentia by Home Guard (USA) (T J Price) 3854 3969⁹ 4139

5 **CAPTAIN MARMALADE,** ch g Myjinski (USA) - Lady Seville by Orange Bay (D T Thom) 916⁶

12 **CAPTAIN MOR,** b g Welsh Captain - Oona More by Straight Deal (J L Eyre) 871⁵

6 **CAPTAIN MY CAPTAIN(IRE),** ch g Flash Of Steel - Amanzi by African Sky (R Brotherton) 1072 1619⁷ 1964⁷ 2792² 3186¹

6 **CAPTAIN TANCRED(IRE),** b g The Parson - Tudor Lady by Green Shoon (J J Birkett) 824⁷ 972 1357⁷ 2108 2243 2974⁶ 3429⁵ 3578 3692² 3866² 4072⁶

5 **CAPTAIN TANDY(IRE),** ch g Boyne Valley - Its All A Dream by Le Moss (D Burchell) 1731 3103 3211⁷ 3661 3770⁴ 4052¹ 4160⁶

8 **CAPTAIN TEACH,** b g Relkino - Pirate's Cottage by Pirate King (P Monteith) 4328³

7 **CAPTAINS BAR,** b g Lochnager - Precious Petra by Bing II (Bernard Jones) 2607⁴ 3388⁶

5 **CAPTIVA BAY,** b m Scorpio (FR) - Leading Line by Leading Man (Mrs A R Hewitt) 815 1660⁹ 2897⁷ 3184⁹ 3496⁷

7 **CAPWELL LADY,** b m Roi Guillaume (FR) - Wilden by Will Somers (John O'Callaghan) 540⁷

8 **CARA DEILISH,** ch m On Your Mark - Kilteelagh by King's Leap (V T O'Brien) 413⁷ 1178 1269

7 **CARAGH BRIDGE,** ch g Kambalda - Halcyon Years by Royal Highway (E T Buckley) 1169⁶ 1406⁸ 1658³ 1804² 2871⁹ 3209⁹

6 **CARAIBE(FR),** b m Top Dancer - Faytoria by Fayriland (A Chayrigues) 373¹

9 **CARASHEL,** b m Safari - Alegeach by Master Buck (James O'Haire) 3610

8 **CARBISDALE,** ch g Dunbeath (USA) - Kind Thoughts by Kashmir II (Mrs M Reveley) 842³ 921¹ 1670¹ 1875 2384¹ 2747⁸

5 **CARBON FIVE(IRE),** ch m Mr Fluorocarbon - Five Swallows by Crash Course (Anthony Mullins) 102⁷ 234⁷ 409⁹ 555 1495

8 **CARDAN,** b g Mandalus - Roamaway by Gala Performance (USA) (Michael J O'Connor) 583⁸ 635 799 905

6 **CARDENDEN(IRE),** b g Bustomi - Nana by Forlorn River (J Barclay) 642⁵ 818 1182⁴ 1587⁴ 1676

5 **CARDEPAL(FR),** b g Carmont - Adepale by Olmeto 3838³

7 **CARDINAL BIRD(USA),** b g Storm Bird (CAN) - Shawnee Creek (USA) by Mr Prospector (USA) (S Mellor) 1355¹ 1632¹ 1949¹ 2142⁴ 2306 3418⁷ 3831⁵ 4141⁵

7 **CARDINAL RED,** b g The Parson - Rose Ravine by Deep Run (B de Haan) 1030 1227 1665² 2012 2855³ 3063⁷

5 **CARDINAL SINNER(IRE),** br g Cardinal Flower - Andonian by Road House II (J Wade) 2413⁸ 2905 3580

5 **CARDINALS LADY(IRE),** b m Cardinal Flower - Spicy Lady by Decent Fellow (James H Kelly) 4306 3

6 **CARDISTOWN ROSE(IRE),** ch m King Persian - Sandfordgold by Sandford Lad (Noel Meade) 4337

5 **CAREFORMENOW(USA),** gr h Caro - Mlle Liebe (USA) by Bupers (Patrick Joseph Flynn) 1581² 1820² 2102² 2394² 2470⁵

7 **CAREFREE TIMES,** b g Good Times (ITY) - Danaka (FR) by Val de Loir (R Burgess) 139⁴ 223⁵ 3399⁶ 3927⁷

4 **CARELESS FARMER,** b f Waajib - Careless Whisper (USA) by Broadway Forli (USA) (N A Twiston-Davies) 516³ 606⁸

8 **CARELESS LAD,** ch g Precocious - Mousquetade by Moulton (J Joseph) 145²

7 **CARES OF TOMORROW,** b g Montekin - Fauchee by Busted (J S Bolger) 11⁴ 78⁶ 135 291¹ 410⁹

9 **CARFAX,** ch g Tachypous - Montana Moss by Levmoss (R P C Hoad) 149³ 1274⁵ 1533 1711 2067⁵ 2131⁶ 2643⁴

4 **CARHUE STAR(IRE),** gr f Petong - Crohane by Cracksman (Patrick O'Leary) 228 253 802² 968⁸ 1853² 1983² 2122² 2349¹ 2547³ 2985

6 **CARIBBEAN PRINCE,** ch g Dara Monarch - My Ginny by Palestine (Mrs J G Retter) 2432² 2883² 3254⁴ 3302² 4017¹

5 **CARIBBEAN SURFER(USA),** b h Summing (USA) - Caribbean Surfing (USA) by Northjet (Miss L A Perratt) 1223⁹ 2074⁵ 2332⁵

6 **CARIBEAN ROSE(IRE),** ch m Regular Guy - Sue Bell by Random Shot (Daniel O'Connell) 1912⁷ 2050⁴ 2311⁷

5 **CARIBOO GOLD(USA),** b h Slew O' Gold (USA) - Selket's Treasure (USA) by Gleaming (USA) (K C Bailey) 1544 2403 2674² 2830 3038 3455¹ 3555¹ 3704²

8 **CARLA ADAMS,** ch m Billion (USA) - Jupiters Jill by Jupiter Pluvius (W Storey) 2583 2891⁶ 3061³ 3139 4082⁴ 4135⁴

8 **CARLINGFORD BELLE,** ch m Carlingford Castle - Swiftly Belle by Deep Run (J L Needham) 1528 2208 3213

8 **CARLINGFORD GEM,** b m Carlingford Castle - Pai-Collect by Paico (D Buckley) 4371⁸ 3⁸ 59

6 **CARLINGFORD LAKES(IRE),** ch m Carlingford Castle - Silver Heights by Even Money (T Thomson Jones) 1386¹ 2162² 2459 3230⁹

4 **CARLINGFORD LASS(IRE),** ch f Carlingford Castle - Clanwilla by Pauper (F Jordan) 2210

6 **CARLINGFORD LIGHTS(IRE),** ch g Carlingford Castle - Chinese Queen by Tarim (O O'Neill) 2059³ 2213⁵ 3400⁶ 3671 3827²

7 **CARLINGFORD RUN,** ch m Carlingford Castle - Mariamne by Deep Run (Thomas Carver) 4371⁶ 43¹ 172³ 265⁵ 295⁴ 538⁹

8 **CARLSAN,** ch g Carlingford Castle - Lovely Sanara by Proverb (Mrs A Price) 1421 2525⁷ 2795⁵ 3007 3213⁸

7 **CARLY'S CASTLE,** b m Carlingford Castle - Ann Advancer by Even Money (Miss P M Whittle) 2487

5 **CARMELS DELIGHT(IRE),** ch m Invited (USA) - Knock Candy by Candy Cane (F Flood) 2470

7 **CARNETTO,** b m Le Coq D'Or - Carney by New Brig (R Brewis) 1183¹ 1475² 1918³ 2106¹ 2447³ 2785¹ 3140³

4 **CARNIVAL KID,** b g Latest Model - Easter Carnival by Pardigras (K Bishop) 3523

6 **CARNMORE CASTLE(IRE),** ch g Carlingford Castle - Bassett Girl by Brigadier Gerard (Martin Higgins) 4034 4119

11 **CAROGROVE,** b g Rusticaro (FR) - Heather Grove by Hethersett (E T Buckley) 4391

6 **CAROMANDOO(IRE),** b g Simply Great (FR) - Tanimara by Sassafras (FR) (A Barrow) 632⁵ 887⁴ 1051

8 **CAROUSEL CALYPSO,** ch g Whistling Deer - Fairy Tree by Varano (P Monteith) 1130³ 1359⁴ 1486 1962⁶ 2219 2576⁴ 2764 3237⁴ 3437²

13 **CAROUSEL CROSSETT,** b m Blind Harbour - Grange Classic by Stype Grange (E M Caine) 1960⁶ 2136 3167 3235

4 **CAROUSEL MAGIC,** ch c Dunbeath (USA) - Tap The Honey by Tap On Wood (M D Hammond) 754⁹

11 **CAROUSEL ROCKET,** ch g Whistling Deer - Fairy Tree by Varano (M D Hammond) 1572 1635⁴ 2001⁶ 2370⁵ 2499¹ 2930² 3077⁵ 3485⁸ 3644 3814¹ 3908⁷

10 **CARPET CAPERS(USA),** b g Dance Bid (USA) - Cofimvaba (FR) by Verrieres (J Ffitch-Heyes) 4314⁶ 148² 156² 205⁴ 463⁴ 601⁵ 701²

8 **CARPET SLIPPERS,** br m Daring March - Mollified by Lombard (GER) (Mrs D Haine) 916³ 1734¹ 2335²

8 **CARRABAWN,** b m Buckskin (FR) - Ice Cream Girl by Laurence O (Mrs Helen O'Keeffe Daly) 4338⁴ 30³ 112 3956⁵ 4170⁵

5 **CARRAIG LIATH(IRE),** b m Roselier (FR) - Cailin Run by Deep Run (Anthony Mullins) 12

5 **CARRAIG-AN-OIR(IRE),** b g Down The Hatch - Dont Rock by Rugged Man (Michael O'Connor) 1827 2128 2620³ 3653 4060

4 **CARRICK PIKE(USA),** ch g Proud Truth (USA) - Spring Adieu (CAN) by Buckpasser (J S Bolger) 290⁴ 391⁶

9 **CARRICKMINES,** ch g Deep Run - Gallant Breeze (USA) by Mongo (Lee Bowles) 4374 2838² 2959³ 3412 3480¹ 3521³ 3717¹ 3877 3949 4182⁵

8 **CARRICKROVADDY,** ch g Deroulede - Ballybeg Maid by Prince Hansel (B Smart) 4363² 630⁴

8 **CARRIG BELLE,** b m Torus - Belle Seeker by Status Seeker (M Phelan) 4381 969⁸ 1270 4044⁸ 4193

6 **CARRIG DANCER(IRE),** br m Cardinal Flower - Kilcronat Tune by Green Shoon (P D FitzGerald) 801 993⁸ 1403 1496 2041³ 2943 3291 3550 3788⁶ 4044⁷ 4119⁹

4 **CARRIG HEATHER,** ch g Power Reigns - Regal Santa by Royal And Regal (USA) (F B McGrath) 3508 4146

6 **CARRIGANN HOTEL(IRE),** ch m Duky - Bean Giolla by Giolla Mear (P M Lynch) 266 365⁶ 535 853

6 **CARRIGANS LAD(IRE),** b or br g Seclude (USA) - Feathermore by Crash Course (Patrick L Kerins) 27⁴ 97⁹ 133 201³ 378⁵ 3794⁵

7 **CARRIGEEN GALA,** b m Strong Gale - Carrigeensharragh by Walshford (R H Lalor) 1035⁸ 1402 2619⁵ 2662⁵ 2847 3249

6 **CARRIGEEN KERRIA(IRE),** b m Kemal (FR) - Carrigeensharraga by Walshford (R H Lalor) 929⁷ 1112⁶ 2550² 2661¹ 2847²

6 **CARRIGKEM(IRE),** br m Kemal (FR) - Carrigello by Bargello (T A Busteed) 930⁷ 1265 3086⁶ 3291⁴ 3529⁹ 3647 3954⁸

9 **CARRIGLAWN,** ch g Buckskin (FR) - Sonlara by Deep Run (J T Gifford) 864⁶ 1108⁷ 1206 1392⁵ 2336² 2623

7 **CARRIKINS,** b m Buckskin (FR) - Carrigello by Bargello (D M Grissell) 2192⁴ 2338⁸ 2496⁸ 3156² 3308 3728⁶

6 **CARROLLS MARC(IRE),** b g Horage - Rare Find by Rarity (P C Haslam) 656⁹ 1096⁸

7 **CARRON HILL,** b g Pollerton - Due Consideration by Sir Herbert (J R H Fowler) 637³ 689² 1453 1685³ 1782³ 1913⁴ 2282⁵ 2661 2752 3449

6 **CARSEAHELEN(IRE),** b m Kemal (FR) - Doll's Delight by Tug Of War (P Kiely) 3552 3732³ 3974

7 **CARSON CITY,** b g Carlingford Castle - Even More by Even Money (Mrs M Reveley) 2008 2367⁶ 2578² 2894¹ 3166² 3287⁹

7 **CARTON,** b g Pollerton - Wild Deer by Royal Buck (E H Owen Jun) 1268⁶ 1819⁶ 2053⁴ 2683 3664⁵

10 **CARTOON TIME(FR),** b g Graphite (FR) - Skitty Kitty (K Woods) 512 806

7 **CARTRON HOUSE,** b g Floriferous - Clonmore by Prince Hansel (F B McGrath) 378⁷ 801 969

INDEX TO NATIONAL HUNT RESULTS 1993-94

5 **CLONAGAM(IRE),** b g Phardante (FR) - Elite Lady by Prince Hansel (R Galvin) 3694 4152[9]

5 **CLONALEENAN,** ch g Ballacashtal (CAN) - Extra La by Exbury (T M Walsh) 99[3] 503[2]

6 **CLONE(IRE),** b g Final Straw - Highland Girl (USA) by Sir Ivor (Michael J Carroll) 1912 2278 2664 2919 3244 3291 3506

10 **CLONEENVERB,** b m Proverb - Cloneen Lady by Master Owen (Terence O'Brien) 86[8] 229[2] 276[6] 327[4] 690[5] 905 1179

15 **CLONEY GRANGE,** br g Bargello - Pampas Wind by Copernicus (Mrs Pauline Adams) 2937[3]

8 **CLONONY CASTLE,** ch g Lord Gayle (USA) - Early Morn by Sassafras (FR) (Miss U McGuinness) 2482 2793 2955[2] 3157 3419[4] 3493 3596[9]

9 **CLONROCHE DRILLER,** b g Pauper - Lady Abednego Vii (Mrs S A Bramall) 1095[6] 1222[6] 1352[4] 1635[5] 2294[8]

14 **CLONROCHE GAZETTE,** ch g Pauper - Clonrochess by London Gazette (Miss D J Baker) 2184 2935 3168 3512

7 **CLONROSH SLAVE,** br g Tesoro Mio - Clonrosh Artic by Pauper (Andrew Murphy) 2869 3201 3529[6] 4188[9]

9 **CLOSE AT HAND,** br m Kemal (FR) - Coldwater Morning by Laurence O (James O'Haire) 4342[2] 213[7] 72[2] 93[1] 134 364[7]

5 **CLOSE OF PLAY,** b g Vital Season - Last Alliance by Honour Bound (J Chugg) 1806 2204 2828

10 **CLOSEBUTNOCIGAR,** b g Paddy's Stream - Churchtown Breeze by Tarqogan (P A Bennett) 3992

8 **CLOSUTTON EXPRESS,** ch g Golden Love - Royal Bonnet by Beau Chapeau (W P Mullins) 538 689 903[2] 1037[6] 1434[5] 1829[8] 1897[5] 2052[5]

6 **CLOUD CUCKOO,** b m Idiot's Delight - Lampstone by Ragstone (P F Nicholls) 2558 3630

13 **CLOUGHTANEY,** b or br g Quayside - Coadys Fancy by No Time (J F Tormey) 1780

5 **CLOVER MOR LASS(IRE),** gr m Mandalus - Right Cash by Right Tack (Noel T Chance) 2592[5] 2869

5 **CLOWATER LADY(IRE),** br m Orchestra - Chief Dilkie by Saulingo (Thomas Foley) 832[7] 1020[2] 1455[3] 1581[6] 4170[8]

6 **CLOWN AROUND,** ch m True Song - Spartan Clown by Spartan General (J Hutsby) 2339 2667 3396 3497 3829[6] 3932

6 **CLUEN CASTLE(IRE),** ch m Carlingford Castle - Samarcand by Final Problem (A D Evans) 3813[4]

5 **CLURICAN(IRE),** ch g Dara Monarch - Jane Bond by Good Bond (N Tinkler) 781[6] 1005[8] 1225 1571[8] 1672[4] 1746[2] 1842[3] 2267 2649[3] 2788[2] 2994 3219[5] 3475[9]

7 **CLWYD LODGE,** b g Blakeney - High Caraval by High Top (R T Juckes) 153[5] 185[7] 262[5] 373

9 **CLYDE PRINCE,** b g Prince Regent (FR) - Clyde Avenue by Peacock (FR) (M Munnelly) 15[5] 58 160[9] 208[3] 489[5]

7 **CLYDE RANGER,** b g Kemal (FR) - Clyde Avenue by Peacock (FR) (M D Hammond) 1723[1] 1873[2] 2137[1] 2514 2814[1] 2928[2] 3463

6 **CLYRO,** b m Kind Of Hush - Clear As Crystal by Whitstead (P G Murphy) 264[1] 355[3]

4 **CNOC AN RIOG(IRE),** ch g Tender King - Kayousha by Thatching (T A Regan) 2081[9] 3993

6 **COAL NOT DOLE(IRE),** br g Miner's Lamp - Swans Bog by Over The River (FR) (John R Upson) 843 1247[4]

8 **COASTING,** b g Skyliner - Shantung Lassie (FR) by Shantung (G B Balding) 2366 2993[6] 3175[5] 3454 3546[4] 3805[2]

6 **COBB GATE,** b h Creetown - Glazepta Final by Final Straw (B Stevens) 4331[6] 1488[4] 1597[7] 1942[3] 2207[1] 2523[4] 2804[3] 3147[4] 3330[2] 3696 4096[7]

8 **COBBLERS ROCK,** gr g Step Together (USA) - Ardmoney by Sir Herbert (P A Fahy) 60 92[7] 97 176

4 **COBBS CROSS,** ch g Bairn (USA) - Trapani by Ragusa (T H Caldwell) 578[6]

8 **COCK COCKBURN,** ch g Sheer Grit - Merry Mirth by Menelek (John Queally) 2079[7] 2392[4] 2610[5] 2866[5] 2986[1] 3248[1] 3650[6] 3836[5] 3935

10 **COCK SPARROW,** b g Niniski (USA) - Hors Serie (USA) by Vaguely Noble (J Mackie) 1372 1621 2872[1] 3105 3492 3593

13 **COCK-OF-THE-ROCK,** b g Cantab - Cherry Bounce (Mrs Sarah Clarke) 4095

5 **COCKNEY LAD(IRE),** ch g Camden Town - Big Bugs Bomb by Skymaster (W M Roper) 102[8] 257[2] 555[1] 924[1] 1849[5] 2079[9] 3369[3] 3615[2] 3736[6] 3995[2]

12 **COCO DANCER,** ch g Corawice - Lisnaree Lass by Cantab (David McBratney) 2773 3722[3] 3794[9] 4118

8 **COE,** b or br g Coquelin (USA) - Gully by Dike (USA) (R Akehurst) 4394[4] 1140[5]

7 **COEDWGAN LUCIFER,** br g Mandabo - Lucia Bella Margh by Festive (W T Kemp) 2896 3286

4 **COEUR BATTANT(FR),** ch c General Holme (USA) - Feerie Boreale by Irish River (FR) (N Tinkler) 652[4] 830[8] 1290[3] 1476[3] 2000[6] 3637[6] 4012[5] 4174[2]

10 **COGENT,** b g Le Bavard (FR) - Cottstown Breeze by Autumn Gold (J A Glover) 1162[2] 1439[1] 2747 3127[1] 3407

7 **COILED SPRING,** b g Miramar Reef - Kitty Come Home by Monsanto (FR) (D Nicholson) 1428[3] 1674[1] 2404 2667[1] 2795[3] 3264

7 **COIN MACHINE(IRE),** b g Seclude (USA) - Penny Levy by Levmoss (P Hughes) 1232[8] 1400[8] 1780 2590[4] 2986[6] 3242 3322 3526 3731 3840[1]

11 **COINAGE,** br g Owen Dudley - Grisbi by Grey Sovereign (R F Johnson Houghton) 241

9 **COKENNY BOY,** b g Abednego - Northern Push by Push On (Mrs J Pitman) 1971[4] 2086[7] 2427 2517[4] 2856[4] 3117[4] 3381[2] 3498

6 **COL BUCKMORE(IRE),** b g King's Ride - Mugra by Mugatpura (G Richards) 658[7] 717[1] 915 1053[2] 1418[3] 1736[2] 1959[4] 3074[3] 3459[1] 3570[4] 3739[1] 4047[3]

8 **COLCANON,** ch g Callernish - Rose Of Spring (Joseph G Murphy) 1827 2353

11 **COLCOMBE CASTLE,** gr g Persian Plan (AUS) - Vet's Bill by Hardraw Scar (B F W Rendell) 2800 3021 3171 3480

9 **COLD MARBLE(USA),** b g Told (USA) - Coney Dell by Ercolano (USA) (Andrew Oliver) 3768[8] 3918

5 **COLETTE'S CHOICE(IRE),** b m Alzao (USA) - Madrilon (FR) by Le Fabuleux (G A Ham) 1303[4] 1716 2141[7] 2686

7 **COLIN'S MAN,** b g Mandalus - Iseult by Songedor (K C Hitchmough) 801

6 **COLLEEN'S BELLE(IRE),** b m Remainder Man - Aileen's Belle by The Parson (M J P O'Brien) 2470[9] 3327[1] 3712[5] 3913[7]

4 **COLLIER BAY,** b g Green Desert (USA) - Cockatoo Island by High Top (J A B Old) 2676[4] 2821[1] 3353[1]

6 **COLLIERS HILL(IRE),** b g Furry Glen - Joy's Argument by No Argument (D Harvey) 1016[6] 1989[7] 2314 3122 3447 3528 3934 4061

9 **COWLEY,** gr g Kalaglow - Loralane by Habitat (O Brennan) 728⁷ 1000³

9 **COWORTH PARK,** gr g Wolver Hollow - Sparkling Time (USA) by Olden Times (P Mitchell) 1890

8 **COXANN,** b g Connaught - Miss Nelski by Most Secret (J C McConnochie) 819⁴ 955⁵ 1190 1458⁹ 1533⁶ 1772⁵ 3330 3511 4006 4064

5 **COXWELL QUICK STEP,** b m Balinger - Stepout by Sagaro (Miss H C Knight) 2876³

6 **COZZI(FR),** gr g Cozzene (USA) - Land Girl (USA) by Sir Ivor (J M Bradley) 4336⁷ 1301⁸ 1528⁵ 1768 2015⁷ 2117³ 2489 2739⁶ 2980 3562 3741⁴

7 **CRABBY BILL,** br g Blakeney - Dancing Kathleen by Green God (Miss B Sanders) 1972⁶ 2067⁶ 2225² 2317¹ 2457¹ 2515² 2674⁴ 2759⁴

6 **CRACKING IDEA(IRE),** b g The Parson - Game Sunset by Menelek (J A C Edwards) 2749 3386

6 **CRACKLE N POP(IRE),** b g Step Together (USA) - Kilmessan Lass by Frigid Aire (Victor Bowens) 45 150 231

7 **CRACKLING ANGELS,** b m Martinmas - Freeze Frame by Averof (R H Buckler) 715³ 883 982⁵ 1412³ 1557⁹ 2063

6 **CRACKLING FROST(IRE),** b g Green Shoon - Moppet's Last by Pitpan (A L T Moore) 1814 2233⁷ 2588 2683 3507

6 **CRADLERS,** ch g Sunley Builds - Countess Mariga by Amboise (R Rowe) 901⁸ 2691

8 **CRAFTY CHAPLAIN,** ch g The Parson - She's Clever by Clever Fella (D McCain) 4384 129 194⁵ 325² 451² 517² 741 833¹ 948 2888⁶ 3162³ 32637 3706¹ 3818³ 3931 4105³

6 **CRAGHAN CRAFTY(IRE),** ch m Over The River (FR) - Cathryn's Court by Ardoon (S F Maye) 4357 25

5 **CRAIGIE RAMBLER(IRE),** b m Amazing Bust - Rambling Moss by Le Moss (D Robertson) 2373 2976⁶ 3489⁷

6 **CRAIGSTOWN(IRE),** b g Green Shoon - Only Gorgeous by King's Equity (W S Cunningham) 1170³ 1563⁶ 2264 2668 3090¹ 3224 3442 3750³ 3901⁴

4 **CRANE HILL,** b g Dancing Brave (USA) - Consolation by Troy (P Calver) 2909² 3458⁵

7 **CRANK SHAFT,** b g Strong Gale - Tullow Performance by Gala Performance (USA) (J F Bottomley) 1067³ 1362² 1775² 2459 3109 3620⁵ 3981¹ 4131¹

7 **CRANNON BOY,** gr g Abednego - Crannon Girl by Polaroid (A P O'Brien) 3122

6 **CRASH BANG WALLOP(IRE),** b h Le Johnstan - Attendre Moi by Saulingo (P M McEntee) 2224

7 **CRAZY DAISY,** ch m Turn Back The Time (USA) - Nicaline by High Line (W G M Turner) 3005 3184² 3352¹ 3530² 3630² 3804

7 **CRAZY GAIL,** b m Lord Gayle (USA) - Cracked Advice by Cracksman (A P O'Brien) 123

6 **CRAZY HORSE DANCER(USA),** b g Barachois (CAN) - Why Pass (USA) by Pass (USA) (F Jordan) 125⁷ 194⁶ 525⁶ 996⁶ 1280 3111¹ 3317 3561⁹ 4070¹ 4181⁹

8 **CRAZY LADY,** b m Bulldozer - Purranna (Capt D G Swan) 23 967 1176⁹ 1400⁹ 1764

5 **CREAG DHUBH,** br g Petong - Hawthorne Vale by Richboy (M C Pipe) 1126⁴ 2095⁴ 3051

4 **CREAGMHOR,** gr g Cragador - Cawstons Prejudice by Cawston's Clown (B J Llewellyn) 453³ 711² 1253⁶ 1522⁴ 1749⁵ 1931⁸ 2116⁶

5 **CREATIVE BLAZE(IRE),** b m Creative Plan (USA) - Blaze Gold by Arizona Duke (W J Austin) 1180⁵ 1337 1982¹ 2123⁵ 2616¹ 3083⁶ 3248⁴ 3647⁶

6 **CREDIT CALL(IRE),** br g Rhoman Rule (USA) - Maiacourt by Malacate (USA) (R G Brazington) 1027 1187

12 **CREDIT CUT,** b g Fine Blade (USA) - Vul's Money by Even Money (P W Hiatt) 1299

8 **CREDIT NOTE,** b g National Trust - Swaynes Folly by Midsummer Night II (R H Alner) 1718 3479 3695⁶

6 **CREDIT TRANSFER(IRE),** b m Kemal (FR) - Speedy Lady by Carlburg (F Flood) 4337⁹

6 **CREDO'S CAMPAIGN(IRE),** ch m Le Moss - Paupers Spring by Pauper (J R Walsh) 3296

6 **CREDON,** b g Sunyboy - Credo's Daughter by Credo (S Woodman) 1536 2042⁶ 2315 2728⁴ 2991⁷ 3231³ 3604

12 **CREEAGER,** b g Creetown - Teenager by Never Say Die (J Wharton) 1389⁷ 1671²

8 **CREGGYCONNELL,** b g Cut Above - Tangaroa by Lord Gayle (USA) (J W Boyers) 4357⁴ 245

4 **CREHELP EXPRESS(IRE),** br f Strong Gale - Canute Villa by Hardicanute (Victor Bowens) 706⁴ 802 1816⁶ 1983⁶ 2349⁶

5 **CREPT OUT(IRE),** ch h On Your Mark - Valbona (FR) by Abdos (J A Harris) 3755⁹ 3898⁶ 4011⁵

7 **CRESELLY,** b m Superlative - Gwiffina by Welsh Saint (R Allan) 399⁵

4 **CREST,** b g Dominion - High And Bright by Shirley Heights (Mrs V A Aconley) 2095³

5 **CRESTWOOD LAD(USA),** ch g Palace Music (USA) - Sweet Ellen (USA) by Vitriolic (Mrs M Reveley) 4337⁷

7 **CREW HILL,** gr m General Ironside - Raheen Princess by Raise You Ten (Michael J Carroll) 4343

7 **CREWS CASTLE,** ch g Carlingford Castle - Crews Girl by Gala Performance (USA) (J R Jenkins) 29⁵ 66⁴ 69² 197² 2117¹ 2428 2533¹ 2855⁴ 3040 3232⁵ 3640² 3883³ 4161³

4 **CRIMINAL RECORD(USA),** b c Fighting Fit (USA) - Charlie's Angel (USA) by Halo (USA) (W Clay) 754³ 896³ 2057 2960⁸ 3211⁴ 3702⁴ 3876¹ 3977³ 4045⁶

5 **CRIMSON CONSORT(IRE),** b g Red Sunset - Purple Princess by Right Tack (C W Thornton) 724⁹

4 **CRISSY(IRE),** ch f Entitled - Antipol by Polyfoto (R J Cotter) 2614 2864⁹

7 **CROBALLY,** ch m Carlingford Castle - Tip Your Toes by Prince Tenderfoot (USA) (W H Dooly) 2236

13 **CROCK-NA-NEE,** b g Random Shot - Saucy Slave by Arctic Slave (Mrs Fiona Vigors) 4311⁶ 2650 2888⁵ 3412

6 **CROCKALAWN(IRE),** ch g Arapahos (FR) - Naomi Night Vii (Daniel Lordan) 45 411

8 **CROFT MILL,** b g Furry Glen - Aplomb by Ballymore (Miss H C Knight) 957¹ 1770 1952 2999 3283

6 **CROFTON LAKE,** ch g Alias Smith - Joyful Star by Rubor (J E Dixon) 1053⁹ 2003 2500 3379⁸ 3598 4075²

7 **CROGEEN LASS,** br m Strong Gale - Hucklebuck Queen by Tanfirion (P J Casserly) 2277⁴ 2618⁸ 2752⁴

5 **CROGHAN BRIDGE(IRE),** ch g Seclude (USA) - Ballyfad Seeker by Status Seeker (Patrick John Murphy) 4382 31⁹ 95⁶ 150

7 **CROGHAN DEW,** b m Step Together (USA) - Ballyfad Seeker (Patrick John Murphy) 4343⁵ 19⁶

6 **CROGHAN MIST(IRE),** b m Le Patron - Ballyfad Seeker by Status Seeker (Patrick John Murphy) 61 105 277 508 618

650

4 **DANCES WITH GOLD,** b f Glint Of Gold - Northern Ballerina by Dance In Time (CAN) (P D Evans) 4085³ 4174⁵

5 **DANCING BAREFOOT,** ch m Scallywag - High Venture by High Award (A M Forte) 2095⁵

5 **DANCING BOAT,** b g Shareef Dancer (USA) - Sauceboat by Connaught (J L Harris) 1097⁹

6 **DANCING COURSE(IRE),** b m Crash Course - Imagination (FR) by Dancer's Image (USA) (Martin Higgins) 4337² 4406¹ 10² 56 88⁵ 174¹ 413⁵ 574² 673² 854⁵ 937⁴ 1685⁹ 1823⁵ 2284

5 **DANCING DANCER,** b m Niniski (USA) - Verchinina by Star Appeal (R G Frost) 599⁷ 891³ 1079⁵ 1253⁹ 1546⁵ 2797⁴ 3253⁷ 3572¹ 3668¹ 4086

8 **DANCING DAYS,** ch g Glenstal (USA) - Royal Agnes by Royal Palace (J Parkes) 4328⁵ 4385⁸ 2060

6 **DANCING DOVE(IRE),** ch m Denel (FR) - Curragh Breeze by Furry Glen (G Richards) 429¹ 524⁶ 1114⁴ 1204² 1614⁸ 2502 3986³ 4072³

6 **DANCING PADDY,** b h Nordance (USA) - Ninotchka by Niniski (USA) (K O Cunningham-Brown) 2046⁵ 2379¹ 2850¹ 3068 3650³

7 **DANCING SENSATION(USA),** b m Faliraki - Sweet Satina (USA) by Crimson Satan (R Akehurst) 3585

6 **DANCING STREET,** ch m Scottish Reel - Florence Street by Final Straw (T Craig) 2005 2150⁹

4 **DANCING SUPREME,** ch g Nestor - Vulgan's Joy by Vulgan Slave (W G Mann) 3686

4 **DANCING VISION(IRE),** br g Vision (USA) - Dewan's Niece (USA) by Dewan (USA) (Augustine Leahy) 688² 1432 1853⁴ 2099² 2614¹ 3080 3615

10 **DANCINGCINDERELLA,** b m Oats - June's Slipper by No Argument (Michael Hourigan) 21¹ 76¹ 100¹ 116¹ 134⁴ 306⁹ 532³ 689 4151⁹

10 **DANDY MINSTREL,** br g Black Minstrel - Julanda by Tarboosh (USA) (N A Twiston-Davies) 886³ 1050⁵ 1388⁴ 1748 1838² 2001 2334³ 2429⁷ 3512⁹ 3742² 3885

10 **DANDY REASON,** br g Abednego - Drumrainey by Arctic Slave (Mrs Pat Mullen) 4103

6 **DANE ST LADY(IRE),** b f Erin's Hope - Ballydowd Lady by Reformed Character (Augustine Leahy) 234⁶ 295 534 585

5 **DANESFORT(IRE),** ch h Hatim (USA) - Merriment (USA) by Go Marching (USA) (Thomas O'Neill) 3447

4 **DANGER BABY,** ch g Bairn (USA) - Swordlestown Miss (USA) by Apalachee (USA) (R Dickin) 1021 1297⁴ 1504⁵ 2000² 2245⁶ 2522⁵ 3340⁵ 3478⁷ 3587³ 3702¹ 3829² 3878¹ 4123²

4 **DANGER FLYNN(IRE),** b g Boreen (FR) - Stramillian by Furry Glen (Michael Condon) 3730 3971

5 **DANGEROUS LADY(IRE),** ch m Roselier (FR) - Decent Dame by Decent Fellow (D Carroll) 3201 3276⁷ 3653 3694⁸ 3797² 3974⁴ 4119³

6 **DANGEROUS REEF(IRE),** b g Burslem - Tamara's Reef by Main Reef (B Lalor) 4408⁵ 34⁶ 110⁷ 275⁶ 473² 991⁵ 1232³ 2098⁹ 2310¹

8 **DANNIGALE,** b g Strong Gale - No Bella Lady by No Time (John J Harding) 583⁹ 856 941⁴ 1177⁸ 1612⁵ 1904⁴

12 **DANNY'S LUCK(NZ),** b g St Puckle - Kiss Girl (NZ) by Palm Beach (B Scriven) 144 154⁸ 218⁴ 350⁵ 435⁷ 3918⁷

6 **DANOLI(IRE),** b g The Parson - Blaze Gold by Arizona Duke (Thomas Foley) 1265¹ 1576¹ 1849³ 2287² 2612¹ 3036¹ 3424¹

11 **DANRIBO,** b g Riboboy (USA) - Sheridans Daughter by Majority Blue (John Whyte) 347⁵ 461⁵ 589³

7 **DANTE'S NEPHEW,** b g Le Moss - Candy Coated by Candy Cane (M McCormack) 1161² 1844

6 **DANZARIN(IRE),** b g Kings Lake (USA) - Sodium's Niece by Northfields (USA) (R Akehurst) 728 1023⁴

5 **DAPHNIS(USA),** b h Lead On Time (USA) - Dancing Vaguely (USA) by Vaguely Noble (T Craig) 268⁵

8 **DARA DOONE,** b g Dara Monarch - Lorna Doone (USA) by Tom Rolfe (N A Twiston-Davies) 3267 3384 3520⁷

5 **DARA KNIGHT(IRE),** br g Dara Monarch - Queen Of The Dance by Dancer's Image (USA) (R B Smyth) 81 233

5 **DARA'S COURSE(IRE),** b m Crash Course - Sliabh Dara by Prince Hansel (E Bolger) 3295 3370 3652 4189⁷

4 **DARAA DARAA(IRE),** br g Dara Monarch - Orchestration by Welsh Pageant (Anthony Mullins) 4171⁹

7 **DARAVIC(IRE),** ch g Dara Monarch - Muligatawny by Malacate (USA) (G M Lyons) 2869³ 2988 3393⁹

5 **DARCARI ROSE(IRE),** b m Try My Best (USA) - Shikari Rose by Kala Shikari (F W Pennicott) 8⁷ 24⁴ 232⁸ 341⁵ 392⁸ 490² 805¹ 1400³ 1450¹ 1551³ 1764⁴

10 **DARCY'S THATCHER,** b or br g Thatching - Lancette by Double Jump (W P Browne) 1176⁸

7 **DARDO(POL),** 598³

11 **DARE SAY,** b g Kris - Pampered Dancer by Pampered King (R H Alner) 1168 1514² 2032¹ 2915 3162⁵ 3560

6 **DARI SOUND(IRE),** b g Shardari - Bugle Sound by Bustino (J G FitzGerald) 1296

8 **DARING CLASS,** b m Class Distinction - Darymoss by Ballymoss (P R Rodford) 4314 194 298 385² 418³ 484³ 3764

4 **DARING CREST,** b f Reesh - Hodsock Venture by Major Portion (K A Morgan) 2407 3589

4 **DARING KING,** b g King Of Spain - Annacardo by Derrylin (G A Pritchard-Gordon) 3314 3886

4 **DARING PAST,** b g Daring March - Better Buy Baileys by Sharpo (M D Hammond) 2083⁶ 2478² 2564¹ 3062 3228¹ 3482⁵ 3734⁴

8 **DARING STAR,** b g Derring Rose - Alice Starr by Windjammer (USA) (Victor Bowens) 618⁶

5 **DARINGLY,** b h Daring March - Leylandia by Wolver Hollow (H J Manners) 597 716⁷ 885⁹ 1079¹ 1163⁵ 1502⁹ 1882³ 2142 2208⁹ 2746 3252⁴ 3572⁷ 3726⁴

10 **DARK DAWN,** b g Pollerton - Cacodor's Pet by Chinatown (P Cheesbrough) 4351 2508² 3162¹ 3412⁴ 3684 3867¹

9 **DARK DEB,** b m Black Minstrel - Prospective Lady by Kabale (D J Wintle) 3503 3592

7 **DARK DEEP DAWN,** ch m Deep Run - Swinging Sovereign by Swing Easy (USA) (John R Upson) 194⁴ 269⁴ 279⁴ 407⁶

4 **DARK DEN(USA),** b c Val de L'orne (FR) - Covert (USA) by Turn To Mars (USA) (Mrs J Cecil) 2685¹ 2853¹ 3406 3606¹ 3734⁷ 4178¹

8 **DARK DESIRE,** b g Alzao (USA) - Treble Cloud by Capistrano (C P E Brooks) 3100⁷ 3853⁸ 4064⁶ 4106²

7 **DARK FOUNTAIN,** br g Royal Fountain - Another Joyful by Rubor (J E Dixon) 4326³ 315¹

9 **DARK HONEY,** b g Marechal (FR) - Caillou by Owen Anthony (S Dow) 861⁶ 1257¹ 1561¹ 1653 2009⁵ 2247¹ 2473¹ 3028² 3267⁵

5 **DARK MIDNIGHT(IRE),** br g Petorius - Gaelic Jewel by Scottish Rifle (R R Lamb) 3125 3815⁹ 3983⁷ 4136⁴

8 **DARK OAK,** br g Kambalda - Dusky Jo by Dusky Boy (J W Curtis) 1372² 1563³ 1770⁴ 2170⁶ 2411 2579² 2908² 3343 3510⁶

4 **DARK SWAN(IRE),** br g Soughaan (USA) - Last Stop by Charlottown (T J O'Mara) 1853³ 2388⁴ 2917² 3550² 3889³ 3971¹

7 **DARKBROOK,** b g Green Shoon - Pitpan Lass by Pitpan (D R Gandolfo) 1167 2427

8 **DARKTOWN STRUTTER,** ch g Pas de Seul - Princess Henham by Record Token (R W Pincombe) 483 567 3975⁷ 4104

4 **DARSING,** b g Chief Singer - Alydear (USA) by Alydar (USA) (G A Pritchard-Gordon) 604⁴ 830

11 **DARTON RI,** b g Abednego - Boogie Woogie by No Argument (Mrs S Maxse) 2884⁸ 3859²

5 **DARU(USA),** gr g Caro - Frau Daruma (ARG) by Frari (ARG) (E J O'Grady) 2199² 2389² 2702⁴

4 **DARZEE,** b g Darshaan - Royal Lorna (USA) by Val de L'orne (FR) (P R Hedger) 3202² 3576¹

6 **DASDILEMMA(IRE),** b m Furry Glen - Baloney by Balidar (Francis Ennis) 1236 1403 1501

8 **DASHING DULA,** b m Oats - Swift Wood by Precipice Wood (Mrs M Reveley) 3787¹

6 **DASHING GROOM(IRE),** ch g Shy Groom (USA) - Aunt 'ski by Prince Regent (FR) (Luke Comer) 2983

6 **DASHING ROSE,** b m Mashhor Dancer (USA) - Speedy Rose by On Your Mark (Noel Meade) 1686⁹ 1976 2054⁵ 3654 3935⁶

7 **DASHMAR,** b g Rare One - Ballinattin Girl by Laurence O (Martyn Wane) 721⁴ 875³ 1475 1677⁴ 2008⁸

7 **DASTARDLY DALE,** b g Baron Blakeney - Rue Talma by Vigo (J R Adam) 1723 2219

6 **DAUNTLESS KNIGHT(USA),** ch g Sir Ivor - Colinear (USA) by Cohoes (W Smith) 2847 445⁵ 565⁴ 683

8 **DAUPHIN BLEU(FR),** b g Direct Flight - Shabby (FR) by Carmarthan (FR) (Dr P Pritchard) 551⁶ 618⁸ 844³ 1040 1810⁹ 1929⁶ 2225⁷ 2328 3189⁶

8 **DAVARA,** gr g Dawn Johnny (USA) - News Belle by London Gazette (S J Leadbetter) 1588

6 **DAVE FLECK(IRE),** b g Kemal (FR) - Brickey Gazette by Fine Blade (USA) (Michael Kiernan) 1827 2102⁷ 2553⁸ 2618⁵ 2756⁷ 3229⁵ 3325 3507⁴

8 **DAVES DELIGHT,** ch m Lighter - The Deer Hound by Cash And Carry (Miss S Waterman) 773 1642⁸ 1695⁶ 1869¹ 2015

4 **DAVY BLAKE,** b g Cool Guy (USA) - True Grit by Klairon (T N Dalgetty) 2451¹ 2811¹ 3159²

8 **DAVY BUSTIN,** br g Bustineto - Tourney's Girl by Yankee Gold (J R Shaw) 3610⁵

7 **DAVY CROCKETT,** b g Buckskin (FR) - Branstown Lady by Deep Run (Derek Pugh) 4358¹ 4404¹ 25⁴ 2985⁹ 3506⁴

8 **DAWAAM,** b h Young Generation - Alys by Blakeney (M Dods) 970² 1148² 1603 1740⁷

7 **DAWADAR(USA),** b g Exceller (USA) - Damana (FR) by Crystal Palace (FR) (J S Goldie) 562³ 736¹

6 **DAWN ADAMS(IRE),** b or br m Kemal (FR) - Light Of Day by Normandy (F Flood) 1858⁵ 2620¹ 2919² 3243⁴ 3869² 4192¹

7 **DAWN APPEAL,** ch m Deep Run - Garry Niat by Le Bavard (FR) (A L T Moore) 28⁵

7 **DAWN CALL,** b m Rymer - Herald The Dawn by Dubassoff (USA) (N A Smith) 1707⁷

8 **DAWN CHANCE,** gr g Lighter - Main Chance by Midsummer Night II (R J Hodges) 1598⁷ 1795² 1956 3695² 3879²

11 **DAWN COYOTE(USA),** ch g Grey Dawn II - Beanery (USA) by Cavan (Mrs S Taylor) 819

4 **DAWN DIEU(IRE),** b g Convinced - Dieu Course by Crash Course (J K Magee) 3797⁹

5 **DAWN FLIGHT,** b g Precocious - Sea Kestrel by Sea Hawk II (Lady Herries) 1515³

6 **DAWN POPPY,** b m Martinmas - Goldaw by Gala Performance (USA) (R J Hodges) 321 520

7 **DAWSON CITY,** ch g Glint Of Gold - Lola Sharp by Sharpen Up (M H Easterby) 1029² 2488³ 2768²

5 **DAY RETURN,** b m Electric - Fly For Home by Habitat (Mrs D Thomson) 2976⁷ 3488⁹

4 **DAYADAN(IRE),** b c Shernazar - Dayanata by Shirley Heights (J G FitzGerald) 1290⁴ 1504 2573³ 2735⁴ 3062

7 **DAYLIGHT LADY,** ch m Deep Run - First Gal by General Ironside (Mark McCausland) 4406 179 215 3723 3811

6 **DAYS OF THUNDER,** ch g Vaigly Great - Silent Prayer by Queen's Hussar (J White) 2760² 3147⁵

4 **DAYTIME BOMBER,** ch g Royal Vulcan - Rue-The-Day by Rubor (K R Burke) 2996 3530

5 **DAZZLING FIRE(IRE),** b m Bluebird (USA) - Fire Flash by Bustino (C C Elsey) 151 227³ 486⁴

7 **DE GREY,** gr g Grey Ghost - A Certain Lusty by Ascertain (USA) (J E Swiers) 4039⁴

7 **DE JORDAAN,** br g Callernish - Gorge by Mount Hagen (FR) (W S Cunningham) 785⁵ 1092⁹ 1484⁵ 1735⁶ 3674³ 3815³ 4136²

10 **DE PROFUNDIS,** ch g Deep Run - Men's Fun by Menelek (Mrs F M Gray) 3992⁶ 4130

4 **DEAD CALM,** gr g Another Realm - Truly Bold by Bold Lad (IRE) (C Tinkler) 1483

11 **DEADLINE,** br g Strong Gale - Countess Charmere by Chamier (S G Chadwick) 4300⁴ 2437² 2886¹ 3141 3566 3986⁴

8 **DEADLY CHARM(USA),** b or br m Bates Motel (USA) - Certain Something by Solinus (D Nicholson) 1084⁷ 1307⁴ 1538¹ 2174⁴ 2266

5 **DEAL WITH HONOR,** b m Idiot's Delight - Vulgan's Honor by Paddy's Birthday (K S Bridgwater) 4319

8 **DEAR BUCK,** b g Buckskin (FR) - Not So Dear by Dhaudevi (FR) (F Lennon) 1113⁹ 1270

7 **DEAR DO,** b g Swinging Rebel - Earlsgift by Dusky Boy (N J Henderson) 901⁴ 1126⁵ 2991 3215⁹ 3549³ 3848³ 4157²

4 **DEAR MONEY(IRE),** b f Buckskin (FR) - Maestra Gama by Master Buck (Robert J McCarthy) 4060 4169⁹

5 **DEARBORN TEC(IRE),** br g Sexton Blake - Wild Deer by Royal Buck (Andrew Lee) 3290³ 3871⁶

8 **DEB'S BALL,** b m Glenstal (USA) - De'b Old Fruit by Levmoss (D Moffatt) 4389¹ 736³ 1030¹ 1438⁴ 1617² 2449⁴ 3063⁸ 3735

5 **DEB'S TURN(IRE),** b g Orchestra - Another Deb by African Sky (D K Weld) 4396 99⁶

5 **DEBACLE(USA),** b g Raft (USA) - Kuala (USA) by Hawaii (B J McMath) 185¹ 441¹ 628² 795⁴ 2344¹ 3409 3698

8 **DEBBIGENE,** ch m Royal Vulcan - Wicken Folly by Babu (D P Geraghty) 1707

8 **DELPIOMBO,** br g Lochnager - Precious Petra by Bing II (J G FitzGerald) 729 1093⁴ 1493⁴

5 **DELVIN SPIRIT(IRE),** ch m Rhoman Rule (USA) - Solarina by Solinus (A J Martin) 4145

5 **DELWORTHY DANCER,** b g Natroun (FR) - Traditional Miss by Traditionalist (USA) (A G Newcombe) 4023 4172

4 **DEMILUNE(USA),** b c Nijinsky (CAN) - Media Luna by Star Appeal (N A Twiston-Davies) 561³ 742³ 1634⁶ 2245³ 2374⁷ 3184¹ 3398 3561⁷

6 **DEMOFONTE,** ch g Aragon - Dusty Bluebell by Sky Gipsy (A B Coogan) 836

9 **DEMOKOS(FR),** ch g Dom Racine (FR) - Eagletown (FR) by Dictus (FR) (W L Barker) 591

11 **DENBERDAR,** b g Julio Mariner - Penumbra by Wolver Hollow (M J Clarke) 2885² 3263³ 3385³ 3596

7 **DENBY HOUSE LAD(CAN),** br h Assert - Queens Club (USA) by Cyane (C Parker) 1204⁸

5 **DENDIEU(IRE),** ch g Denel (FR) - Three Dieu by Three Dons (I R Ferguson) 4094

5 **DENIM BLUE,** ch h Mandrake Major - Delphinium by Tin King (W G Reed) 577⁴ 1588⁷

5 **DENNETT VALLEY(IRE),** b g Phardante (FR) - Khalketta by Khalkis (Desmond McDonogh) 1383⁶ 1786⁵ 1820⁹ 2586 3366 3793⁷

6 **DENNINGTON(IRE),** ch g Deep Run - La Flamenca by Brave Invader (USA) (G A Hubbard) 499³ 730³

6 **DENNY'S GUESS(IRE),** b g Denel (FR) - Nicky's Guess by Three Dons (J R Bryce-Smith) 801 942⁶

5 **DENRON(IRE),** b g Denel (FR) - Sakyron by Copper Gamble (J F C Maxwell) 3796¹

6 **DENTICULATA,** ch g Domynsky - Melody Song by Saintly Song (P Spottiswood) 1094⁷ 1602⁴ 1936⁶

7 **DENVER BAY,** b g Julio Mariner - Night Action by Dusky Boy (J T Gifford) 2494⁸ 2705⁴ 2910³ 3215⁶ 3604⁴

4 **DEPTFORD BELLE,** b f Sula Bula - Gemini Stone by Le Bavard (FR) (R Curtis) 2677 3833

11 **DEPUTY TIM,** ch g Crofter (USA) - Kindle by Firestreak (R Bastiman) 2581

7 **DERBY HAVEN,** b g Buckskin (FR) - Marie Goold by Arapaho (Capt S H Walford) 2394 3394² 3937⁵ 4010

6 **DERBY O'GILL(IRE),** b g King's Ride - Longford Lady by Reformed Character (James Joseph O'Connor) 4118⁷

7 **DERECHEF,** ch m Derrylin - Songe D'Inde by Sheshoon (Mrs J G Retter) 4375

6 **DERISBAY(IRE),** b g Gorytus (USA) - Current Bay by Tyrant (USA) (J J Bridger) 1006 1395⁵ 1597¹ 1945² 2247 2760³

5 **DERRAVARAGH GALE(IRE),** br m Strong Gale - Fairly Deep by Deep Run (Cecil Ross) 1681 3934 4031

4 **DERRING BRIDGE,** b g Derring Rose - Bridge Ash by Normandy (Mrs S M Johnson) 4057

10 **DERRING BUD,** br g Derring Rose - Tarune by Tarqogan (Lady Susan Brooke) 3265⁵

7 **DERRING DREAM,** b g Derring Rose - Mischievous by Le Mesnil (Michael Sheahan) 41 79 108 277 393⁹ 433

9 **DERRING VALLEY,** b g Derrylin - Chalke Valley by Ragstone (A P Jones) 696 1004⁶ 1120⁴ 2710⁴ 2823⁵ 3310 3532

8 **DERRY PRINCESS,** b m Workboy - Derry Island by Varano (R Robinson) 4329 3909 4073

6 **DERRY'S DIAMOND(IRE),** b m Cardinal Flower - Hi Style by Tarkhun (K Riordan) 4337

12 **DERRYMORE BOY,** br g Bonne Noel - Sweet Melody by Alcide (P F Nicholls) 2316¹ 3017

8 **DERRYMOSS,** b g Le Moss - Derrynaflan by Karabas (M C Pipe) 889 1528² 1717¹ 1794¹ 2015¹ 2208⁶ 2454¹ 2799¹ 3109³

5 **DERRYMOYLE(IRE),** b g Callernish - Luminous Lady by Girandole (Michael Cunningham) 115² 162¹ 365³ 504¹ 938¹ 1234² 1580¹ 1765² 2079⁴ 2392⁸ 2979³

11 **DERRYNAP,** b g Derrylin - Knapping by Busted (R Donoghue) 3721⁹ 4033

4 **DERRYS PREROGATIVE,** b g Nearly A Hand - Derrycreha Lass by Precipice Wood (N M Babbage) 3113

4 **DERRYSHERIDAN,** ch g Relkino - Joedes Janet by Bahrain (J A Berry) 2290 3749

5 **DERWENT LAD,** br g Lidhame - Swifter Justice by King's Bench (M A Barnes) 1223 2003 2237 2573 3436 3598² 3815

8 **DERWENT MIST,** b m Majestic Streak - Minimist by Bilsborrow (Miss S Clarke) 482

9 **DESELBY'S CHOICE,** b f Crash Course - Scrahan by Wily Trout (Michael G Holden) 4369¹ 4380² 44⁶ 3746⁹

4 **DESERT CHALLENGER(IRE),** b g Sadler's Wells (USA) - Verily by Known Fact (USA) (J R Jenkins) 1990⁵ 2516³ 3700⁷

5 **DESERT FORCE(IRE),** b h Lomond (USA) - St Padina by St Paddy (R J Weaver) 2632¹ 3063 3904¹ 3967²

4 **DESERT LAUGHTER(IRE),** ch g Desert Of Wind (USA) - Tickled To Bits by Sweet Revenge (Mark McCausland) 3748

8 **DESERT LORD,** gr g Step Together (USA) - Star Mill by Milan (A J McNamara) 76³ 119⁹ 532¹ 855 992³ 1552² 1850⁴ 2077³ 2549⁶ 3389² 3651 3841²

5 **DESERT MIST,** gr m Sharrood (USA) - Misty Halo by High Top (Denys Smith) 4301⁵ 337⁴

7 **DESERT OASIS,** br m Farhaan - Karry's Sister by Super Slip (Capt D G Swan) 1017

9 **DESERT PALM,** b m Palm Track - Diascia by Dike (USA) (R J Hodges) 359² 955 1087⁴ 1190³

5 **DESERT PEACE(IRE),** b g Last Tycoon - Broken Wide by Busted (R Akehurst) 658⁵ 922⁴ 3965³ 4107⁷

6 **DESERT RUN(IRE),** ch g Deep Run - Another Dutchess by Master Buck (P F Nicholls) 1935⁵ 2147² 2315⁶ 3215⁵ 3365⁵

5 **DESERT WALTZ(IRE),** ch h Gorytus (USA) - Desert Pet by Petingo (M Halford) 530

6 **DESMOND GOLD(IRE),** b g Tumble Gold - Stylish Princess by Prince Tenderfoot (USA) (E McNamara) 540 675 853

6 **DESPERADO,** b h Esclavo (FR) - Diane by Priamos (S I Pittendrigh) 4340 4405⁹ 124 136 304⁹ 1478 2896 3286 3688⁸

6 **DESPERATE,** ch g Saxon Farm - Menel Arctic by Menelek (N A Twiston-Davies) 646¹ 750

5 **DESPERATE DAYS(IRE),** b g Meneval (USA) - Grageelagh Lady by Laurence O (D T Hughes) 2592⁹ 2919 3366 4113⁹

6 **DESSIE'S GIRL(IRE),** ch m Orchestra - Rosas by Harwell (P J Casserly) 3956

5 **DESTINY ANGEL,** b m Native Bazaar - Hot Tramp by Country Retreat (P Winkworth) 1494 3234

4 **DESTINY CALLS,** ch g Lord Avie (USA) - Miss Renege (USA) by Riva Ridge (USA) (N A Gaselee) 1021² 1305² 3231¹ 3701¹

8 **DESTRIERO,** br g Ile de Bourbon (USA) - Tipperary Tartan by Rarity (Noel Furlong) 1906⁴ 2287⁵

186³ 387³ 416¹ 608¹ 889³ 1188³ 1323¹ 3571 3806⁹ 3977¹ 4141⁷ 4179

6 DISTANT MILL(IRE), b g Millfontaine - Distant Breeze by London Bells (CAN) (R Dickin) 1460 1622

9 DISTILLATION, b g Celtic Cone - Cauldron by Kabale (G F Edwards) 986⁷ 3021⁹ 3171⁶

6 DISTILLERY HILL(IRE), ch g Orchestra - Ollie's Pet by Tiepolo II (D T Hughes) 4078

5 DISTINCTIVE(IRE), ch g Orchestra - Zimuletta by Distinctly (USA) (M J Wilkinson) 844 1003⁹ 1768³ 2303 3503⁷

7 DISTRICT JUSTICE, b g Nishapour (FR) - Strokestown Girl by Henry Higgins (Patrick Joseph Flynn) 3296 3870

5 DIVALI(IRE), ch c Aristocracy - Capricious (FR) by Snob II (Michael Hourigan) 4189²

6 DIVINE CHANCE(IRE), b g The Parson - Random What by Random Shot (N A Gaselee) 1568⁸ 1969² 2088⁴ 2308¹ 2419² 2651¹ 3036 3414⁵

5 DIVINE COMEDY(IRE), ch m Phardante (FR) - Mawbeg Holly by Golden Love (Mrs A R Hewitt) 2877⁸

5 DIVINITY RUN(IRE), b m Commanche Run - No Distractions by Tap On Wood (F J Lacy) 1397⁷ 1500³ 1766¹ 1908⁴

4 DIWALI DANCER, gr g Petong - Dawn Dance (USA) by Grey Dawn II (A Bailey) 742⁵ 1290¹ 1473⁷ 2241² 2381³ 2564 2897⁶ 3406

4 DIXIE DIAMOND, ch f Then Again - Miss Dicky by Lepanto (GER) (N R Mitchell) 1338⁶

4 DIXIE HIGHWAY, gr f Absalom - Kip's Sister by Cawston's Clown (Mrs E Slack) 1147 1483⁸ 2072⁶

6 DIXTON HILL, b g Pitpan - Miss Silly by Silly Season (R Dickin) 3523

6 DIZZY(USA), gr m Golden Act (USA) - Bergluft (GER) by Literat (P Monteith) 1571 1940⁶ 2360² 2449² 2956² 3068¹ 3484

7 DIZZY DEALER, b m Le Bavard (FR) - Dizzy Dot by Bargello (Mrs R E Barr) 286⁵ 366 480⁵

7 DJEBEL PRINCE, b g Ile de Bourbon (USA) - Noirmont Girl by Skymaster (C R Egerton) 1599⁴ 1799² 2082² 2192³ 2992 3131⁸ 3348³ 3418⁵ 3998 4052

9 DO BE BRIEF, ch g Le Moss - Right Performance by Gala Performance (USA) (Mrs J Pitman) 1171¹ 1388³ 1503¹ 1732¹ 1993⁵

6 DO BE HAVE(IRE), b g Le Bavard (FR) - Darjoy by Darantus (Mrs J Pitman) 2263⁷ 2426² 2604³ 2779² 3220¹ 3414

4 DO BE WARE, b g Tinoco - Kitty Royal by Kinglet (J Ffitch-Heyes) 668⁶ 760⁴ 1261⁷ 1464⁶ 2063³ 2113³ 2395⁵ 3153⁸ 3304³

5 DO LETS, b m Pragmatic - Acushla Macree by Mansingh (USA) (C J Drewe) 2176 2692⁸ 2860 3809

4 DOC COTTRILL, b g Absalom - Bridal Wave by Julio Mariner (N A Twiston-Davies) 3314⁴ 3576³ 3745²

8 DOC LODGE, b m Doc Marten - Cooling by Tycoon II (J White) 4331

4 DOC SPOT, b g Doc Marten - Detonate by Derring-Do (Capt J Wilson) 2115⁷ 2828⁷ 3056⁵ 3236³ 3357² 3690⁷

9 DOC'S COAT, b g Tower Walk - Gold Loch by Lochnager (C P Wildman) 776⁶

4 DOCK OF THE BAY(IRE), ch g Broken Hearted - Zestino by Shack (USA) (P J McBride) 2335⁸ 2492⁵

12 DOCKLANDS EXPRESS, b g Roscoe Blake - Southern Moss by Sea Moss (K C Bailey) 4310¹ 1670³ 1843⁷ 2747² 3064⁶ 3403¹ 3591³ 3821¹

5 DOCS DILEMMA(IRE), br g Decent Fellow - Talkative Princess by Prince Regent (FR)

(I R Ferguson) 3⁵ 39⁵ 81⁸ 233³ 1016² 1581 2863 3447⁵ 3723⁸

7 DOCTER MAC, br m Strong Gale - Miss Lacemore (Robert Tyner) 6⁷ 97 293⁵ 507⁴ 929⁴ 989⁵

4 DOCTOOR(USA), ch g Cozzene (USA) - To The Top (USA) by Bold Hour (R J O'Sullivan) 1125² 1261⁶ 2722⁵ 2969¹ 3062 3270⁷

5 DOCTOR BRIGGS(IRE), ch g King Of Clubs - Great Meadow by Northfields (USA) (Mrs J Jordan) 3786

5 DOCTOR DUNKLIN(USA), b g Family Doctor (USA) - Mis Jenifer's Idea (USA) by Capital Idea (USA) (Mrs V C Ward) 227 310⁵ 441⁶ 814⁷ 1169 1287⁵ 1804 3061¹ 3763³

6 DOCTOR FOSTER(IRE), b g Rymer - Ash Copse by Golden Love (Mrs S J Smith) 429² 3617

6 DOCTOR SHODDY(IRE), b g Decent Fellow - Brave Wish by Brave Invader (USA) (G M Lyons) 1403 3327

8 DOCTOR'S REMEDY, br g Doc Marten - Champagne Party by Amber Rama (USA) (Mrs J Jordan) 280⁵ 316⁶ 477⁵ 818⁹ 2152⁸

4 DOCTOR-J(IRE), ch g Jareer (USA) - Velvet Breeze by Windjammer (USA) (J White) 193⁷ 321² 497⁵ 702³ 1253 4107³ 4160⁵

8 DOCTRINAIRE, b g Pragmatic - Doc's Dolly by Menelek (J P N Parker) 4343⁸ 15

7 DODGER DICKINS, gr g Godswalk (USA) - Sronica by Midsummer Night II (R Hollinshead) 1812

7 DOLIKOS, b g Camden Town - Wolveriana by Wolver Hollow (T H Caldwell) 722² 1132² 1489¹ 1733² 1966³ 2501¹ 3586 3746

10 DOLITINO, gr m Neltino - Sandoli by Sandford Lad (Miss Z A Green) 3438⁸ 3540 3893 4081³ 4134⁴

8 DOLLY OATS, ch m Oats - Royaldyne by No Argument (R J Eckley) 1210² 1707⁴ 1994⁶ 2417² 2654 3040 3230

9 DOLLY PRICES, b m Silly Prices - Miss Friendly by Status Seeker (W J Smith) 4355⁷ 1099⁹ 1183⁵ 1356⁵ 2905⁷ 3139

5 DOMINANT FORCE, b g Primo Dominie - Elan's Valley by Welsh Pageant (R Hannon) 1040¹ 1557² 1840⁹ 2228

5 DOMINANT SERENADE, b g Dominion - Sing Softly by Luthier (M D Hammond) 898⁶ 1116⁸ 1322³ 1922² 2473² 3038⁶ 3384⁵

10 DOMINICS CROSS, ch g Le Bavard (FR) - Killala Bay by Larkspur (N J Pomfret) 4342³ 2826

6 DOMINIE(IRE), b g Crash Course - Meneplete by Menelek (J A C Edwards) 1223² 1494⁵ 2269¹ 3042⁷ 3660⁴

9 DOMINION TREASURE, b or br g Dominion - Chrysicabana by Home Guard (USA) (R J Baker) 3533⁴ 3845² 4181

5 DOMINO'S RING(IRE), b h Auction Ring (USA) - Domino's Nurse by Dom Racine (FR) (Michael Kauntze) 314³ 555⁵ 803⁸

5 DOMINOS RING(IRE), b g Auction Ring (USA) - Domino's Nurse by Dom Racine (FR) (R H Buckler) 3365⁶ 3502⁶ 3685³

7 DOMITOR'S LASS, ch m Domitor (USA) - Spartan Flame by Owen Anthony (R R Ledger) 2244 2494 3010⁴ 3886 3938

9 DON LEONE, b g Don - Saintly Tune by Welsh Saint (Gerard Cully) 831

4 DON TOCINO, b c Dominion - Mrs Bacon by Balliol (J White) 2398⁵ 2857⁴ 3700⁴ 3925⁷ 4085⁵

9 DON VALENTINO, ch g Don - Hell's Mistress by Skymaster (Mrs J Pitman) 2170⁵

5 DON'T ASK JOHNNY(IRE), b m Crash Course - Sammy's Money Box by Le Bavard (FR) (J A Flynn) 585 3552⁶ 3712 3913⁸ 4152⁸

5 **DON'T DROP BOMBS(USA),** ch g Fighting Fit (USA) - Promised Star (USA) by Star de Naskra (USA) (P J Feilden) 1374[9] 1509[9]

4 **DON'T FORGET MARIE(IRE),** b f Don't Forget Me - My My Marie by Artaius (USA) (A Bailey) 1416[1] 1522[1] 2381[9] 2902[5] 3131[4] 3587[2] 3663[1]

5 **DON'T FORSAKE ME,** ch m Don't Forget Me - Pirate Lass (USA) by Cutlass (USA) (C R Egerton) 429[7] 524[3] 791 932[6] 1042

5 **DON'T GEORGE,** b g Fort Nayef - Merry Missus by Crash (D H Hammond) 2381

4 **DON'T JUMP(IRE),** ch f Entitled - Ruby River by Red God (M H Tompkins) 2381 2503[7]

8 **DON'T LIGHT UP,** b g Lighter - Hannah's Bar by Babu (P F Nicholls) 686[1] 1205 1273[2] 1503[3] 1700[1]

6 **DON'T TELL JUDY(IRE),** b g Strong Gale - Two In A Million by Rarity (J S Haldane) 1959[5] 2106[7] 2239[3]

6 **DONBOLINO(IRE),** b m Camden Town - Gobolino by Don (A P O'Brien) 1501[6] 1858[4] 2128[1] 2613[4] 2849[7] 3087[3] 3366[5] 3467[8]

9 **DONE INSTANTLY,** b g Day Is Done - Instanter by Morston (FR) (P Mullins) 3654

10 **DONEANEY GOLD,** b m Boreen (FR) - Misty Gold (W T Bourke) 4342

5 **DONEGAL PRINCESS(IRE),** b m Prince Bee - Sun Girl by Cassoum (FR) (R A Fahey) 2176

6 **DONEGAL STYLE(IRE),** b or br g Kemal (FR) - Donegal Lady by Indigenous (J H Johnson) 559[9] 771 910 2071[1] 2736

7 **DONERAILE PARK,** ch g Floriferous - Southfields by Northfields (USA) (John J Walsh) 571[6] 853[9]

5 **DONIA(USA),** ch m Graustark - Katrinka (USA) by Sovereign Dancer (USA) (J L Harris) 1313[1]

9 **DONNA'S TOKEN,** br m Record Token - Lyricist by Averof (R L Brown) 1799[5] 2060[3] 2330[6] 3150[6] 3338[2] 3479[4] 3683[3] 3844

5 **DONNASOO(IRE),** ch m Mansooj - Denowski by Malinowski (USA) (Seamus Spillane) 1821[6] 2096[7] 3953

10 **DONOSTI,** b g Rusticaro (FR) - Blue Flame (USA) by Crimson Satan (R Lee) 446[3] 1149[1] 2342[1] 2443[1] 2644

5 **DONT BE SHORT(IRE),** b m Long Pond - Candy Cross by Candy Cane (Mrs Edwina Finn) 4361 4400[8] 36[9]

8 **DONT GAMBLE,** gr g Spin Of A Coin - Dontlike by Amazon (Mrs P Townsley) 23[4] 53[6] 70[5] 112[6]

5 **DONT RISE ME(IRE),** b g Don't Forget Me - Raise A Plum (USA) by Raise A Cup (USA) (Michael Croke) 31

8 **DONT TELL THE WIFE,** br g Derring Rose - Dame Sue by Mandamus (Mrs D Haine) 750[6] 1711[8] 1999[2] 2170[3] 2340[1] 2536 2668[6] 3133[3] 3445[1] 3608[1]

4 **DONTDRESSFORDINNER,** b g Tina's Pet - Classic Times by Dominion (D R Tucker) 3576 3915

5 **DONWOOD(IRE),** b f King Persian - Birchwood by Fordham (USA) (Francis M O'Brien) 3508 3891[8] 4034

4 **DOOGAREY,** br c Lidhame - Good Time Girl by Good Times (ITY) (J White) 147[7] 180

7 **DOOLAR(USA),** b g Spend A Buck (USA) - Surera (ARG) by Sheet Anchor (P T Dalton) 2172 2385 3136 3446[3] 3618[8]

5 **DOONAGLERAGH(IRE),** b m King's Ride - Miss Leeway by Tarboosh (USA) (M J Carter) 469[3] 832[8] 1910[4]

6 **DOONANDORAS(IRE),** br g Cataldi - Welsh Beauty by Welsh Saint (J E Kiely) 990[2] 1555[1] 1904[2] 2613[1] 3660[8]

4 **DOONE BRAES(IRE),** b g The Noble Player (USA) - Bonnie Doon by Furry Glen (W A Murphy) 349

6 **DOONEAL HERO(IRE),** b g Remainder Man - Arcticality by Arctic Slave (John J Walsh) 1501 3087[6] 3296

6 **DOONEEN MIST(IRE),** b m Carlingford Castle - Hi-Way Dooradoyle by Wishing Star (N C Bell) 1687 1859

6 **DOONEGA(IRE),** b g Derring Rose - Monavalla by Kabale (David J McGrath) 293[8] 430[6] 557 854[8] 1178[2] 1380[3] 1609[5] 1900[3] 2101

9 **DOONLOUGHAN,** b g Callernish - Cora Swan by Tarqogan (G B Balding) 405[3] 436[4] 600[3] 714[5] 986[4] 1050 1140[2] 3364[3] 3544[2] 3631[2] 3808[2] 3939[2] 4038[3]

9 **DOORSLAMMER,** b m Avocat - Camdora by Cantab (Mrs B M Browne) 707[7] 929[8] 1857[4] 2051[4] 2126 2700[1]

6 **DORADUS,** br g Shirley Heights - Sextant by Star Appeal (J G FitzGerald) 1746[7] 2138[5] 2540[3] 2892[1] 3438[2] 3585 3931[1]

7 **DORAN'S DELIGHT,** ro g Energist - Astral Fairy by Prefairy (Anthony Mullins) 2283[8] 2389 2704[6] 3747[4] 3834[9]

7 **DORAN'S TOWN LAD,** b m Tumble Gold - Thomastown Girl by Tekoah (Anthony Mullins) 527[1] 556[5] 674[4] 1177[3] 1579[4] 1819 2549 3123[2] 3389

5 **DORANS PRIDE(IRE),** ch g Orchestra - Marians Pride by Pry (Michael Hourigan) 535[1] 798[2] 1862[9] 2178[2] 2392[1] 2587[1] 2702[1] 3036

13 **DORNVALLEY LAD,** ch g Anax - Lovely Diana by Supreme Sovereign (D T Garraton) 4328[7]

4 **DOROBO(NZ),** b g Ivory Hunter (USA) - Mountain Hi (NZ) by Rocky Mountain (FR) (Capt T A Forster) 650[2] 920[5] 1194 1511 1776[1] 1952[2] 2206[7] 2495[3] 2764[1] 3442[6]

10 **DOS ADVENTICA,** b or br m Welsh Pageant - Shallow Stream by Reliance II (Mrs E A McMahon) 2550 3935

5 **DOT'S JESTER,** b g Jester - Taylors Renovation by Frimley Park (E J Alston) 1094 1315

5 **DOTS DEE,** ch m Librate - Dejote by Bay Express (J M Bradley) 145[5]

6 **DOTTEREL(IRE),** b h Rhoman Rule (USA) - Miysam by Supreme Sovereign (R G Brazington) 4331 4372[7] 748 988 1079

4 **DOUALAGO(FR),** b g Rivelago (FR) - Lady Rock (FR) by Timmy Lad (USA) (M C Pipe) 1253[2] 1522[3] 1749[2] 1931[3] 2058 2094[1] 2212[1] 2496 3698[8] 3980[9] 4064[9]

4 **DOUBLE DEALING(IRE),** b g Double Schwartz - Mothers Blessing by Wolver Hollow (A P Jones) 2797 3211

12 **DOUBLE LIGHT,** b g Lighter - Salira by Double Jump (D J Wintle) 2885[7]

5 **DOUBLE SHERRY,** ch m Crofthall - Two's Up by Double Jump (D Eddy) 1096[2] 1475

10 **DOUBLE SILK,** b g Dubassoff (USA) - Yellow Silk by Counsel (R C Wilkins) 2301[1] 2650[1] 2807[1] 3065[1] 3425

6 **DOUBLE STANDARDS(IRE),** br g Entre Nous - Miss Minstrel VI by Beau Tudor (C Parker) 1202[4] 2068[7] 2970[3] 3487

6 **DOUBLE SYMPHONY(IRE),** ch m Orchestra - Darling's Double by Menelek (A P O'Brien) 2553[7] 2869 3201 3291 3450[2] 3837[1] 4061[9]

9 **DOUBLE THE BLACK,** ch f Black Minstrel - Oweena Jay by Doouble'U'jay (R G Frost) 155[5]

5 **DOUBLE THE STAKES(USA),** b g Raise A Man (USA) - Je'da Qua (USA) by Fleet Nasrullah (D Burchell) 932[1] 1460 1811[3] 2421[3] 3211 3965[1]

8 **DOUBTING DONNA,** gr m Tom Noddy - Dewy's Quince by Quorum (Mrs D Hughes) 2301 2482 2765 2838[3] 3021[8]

659

INDEX TO NATIONAL HUNT RESULTS 1993-94

8 **DOUCE ECLAIR,** b m Warpath - Sweet Clare by Suki Desu (Mrs Jean Brown) 577⁶ 770

8 **DOUGAL'S BIRTHDAY,** br g Glen Quaich - Ramla Bay by Rarity (G M R Coatsworth) 823 1607 3179 3438

5 **DOUGLAS PYNE(IRE),** b g Good Thyne (USA) - Princess Narva by Combine Harvester (Mrs B M Browne) 1827⁹ 2128

4 **DOUJAS,** b f Nearly A Hand - Doucement by Cheval (P R Rodford) 3176⁴ 3386

7 **DOUNHURST,** b m Saher - Wernlas by Prince Tenderfoot (USA) (R Rowe) 1390

8 **DOVEDONS GRACE,** b g Netherkelly - Grace Of Langley by Foggy Bell (G C Bravery) 3901⁶ 4154

6 **DOVEGROVE HOUSE(IRE),** b g Carlingford Castle - Susie Wuzie by Ardoon (A J McNamara) 73

8 **DOVEHILL,** gr g Pragmatic - Arconist by Welsh Pageant (R D Townsend) 1493 1712 2195⁵ 2340 2517

5 **DOVETTO,** ch g Riberetto - Shadey Dove by Deadly Nightshade (R J Price) 2407⁵ 3113⁵ 3396⁵

5 **DOWHATYOULIKE(IRE),** b m Remainder Man - Bell Walks Fancy by Entrechat (K Riordan) 1397⁴ 1608³ 1822¹ 2284³ 2468¹ 2682² 2846³ 3322⁶ 3731⁸

9 **DOWN DALE,** br g Hillandale - Indian Madness by Indian Ruler (D Bloomfield) 3479 3713

7 **DOWN THE BACK,** ch m Sandalay - Super Slaney by Brave Invader (USA) (James William Cullen) 708 945⁷ 1113⁸ 1902³ 2278⁴

5 **DOWN THE FELL,** b g Say Primula - Sweet Dough by Reindeer (J H Johnson) 976²

7 **DOWN THE ROAD,** br g Roi Guillaume (FR) - Killanny Bridge by Hallez (FR) (J H Johnson) 521⁵ 756² 974⁵ 1604¹ 1960² 2323⁶ 2892³ 3239⁵ 3894² 4024² 4134¹

9 **DOWN TOWN TO-NIGHT,** br m Kambalda - Dusky Smile by Dusky Boy (John Daly) 21⁷

6 **DOWNS DELIGHT(IRE),** b g Le Moss - Time Please by Welsh Saint (Francis Berry) 4382² 61

10 **DOWNSVIEW LADY,** ch m Sparkler - Lady Downsview by Prince Regent (FR) (J A Bullock) 2526⁷ 2793⁵

6 **DOWRY SQUARE(IRE),** b or br g Strong Gale - Bavette by Le Bavard (FR) (P G Murphy) 650⁷ 869⁷ 1392³ 1935⁸ 2361 2483 3629

10 **DOXFORD HUT,** b g Class Distinction - Tillside Brig by New Brig (W McKeown) 3158⁵ 3947

4 **DOYROY(IRE),** br f Doyoun - Royale Warning (USA) by Sir Ivor (J G Coogan) 706² 802

8 **DOZING STAR,** br g Bulldozer - Baltic Star by Ballyciptic (Michael Hourigan) 1498 2038⁷ 2123⁶ 2309⁶

4 **DR FAUST(IRE),** b g Bulldozer - Lucky Favour by Ballyciptic (Miss A M McMahon) 3082

7 **DR MACCARTER(USA),** gr g Dr Carter (USA) - Now Voyager (USA) by Naskra (USA) (A L Forbes) 2273

9 **DR ROCKET,** b g Ragapan - Lady Hansel by Prince Hansel (R Dickin) 4320² 931² 1105¹ 1649² 1798³ 2087² 2174⁵ 2307³ 3312⁴ 3346³ 3759³

8 **DRAGONS DEN,** b g Furry Glen - Ballygriffin by Deep Run (S E Sherwood) 677 842¹ 1050 1242 1656² 2718² 3045¹ 3282³ 3851

9 **DRAMATIC EVENT,** b g Kind Of Hush - Welsh Jane by Bold Lad (IRE) (J S Moore) 2883⁵ 3156⁴ 3311⁷ 3831⁸ 4000⁸

6 **DRAPERY SHOP(IRE),** ch g Le Moss - Kassina by Laurence O (G T Lynch) 620

10 **DRAW LOTS,** b g Ela-Mana-Mou - Raffmarie by Raffingora (P R Rodford) 592 1719 2195 2362³ 2559 2647 3018⁴ 3203⁴ 3361 3573 3977⁸

6 **DRAWL(IRE),** b g Alzao (USA) - Say Something by Reform (A B Coogan) 3886

4 **DREAM START,** b c Dreams To Reality (USA) - Bad Start (USA) by Bold Bidder (Mrs S J Smith) 2210 2876 3601⁵ 3701⁴

13 **DREAMCOAT(USA),** gr g Jig Time (USA) - Restless Polly (USA) by Restless Wind (R Lee) 154⁹ 261³ 382³ 700⁷

8 **DREAMERS DELIGHT,** b g Idiot's Delight - Just Jolly by Jolly Jet (D Nicholson) 899

5 **DREAMLINE,** ch m Capricorn Line - Hammerhill by Grisaille (M P Muggeridge) 901 1027 1957⁶ 2187⁴ 2505 3115

6 **DREAMS END,** ch h Rainbow Quest (USA) - Be Easy by Be Friendly (P J Hobbs) 2835¹ 3023³ 3252¹ 3402³ 3736¹

4 **DRESS DANCE(IRE),** b g Nordance (USA) - Pitaya by Princely Gift (Noel T Chance) 290 375⁴ 494³ 2547⁴ 2917³ 3069⁵ 3321 3993 4061

6 **DRESSED IN BLACK(IRE),** ch g Floriferous - Midi Skirt by Kabale (Peter McCreery) 255⁹ 414³ 540 3934

5 **DRINDOD(IRE),** b g Welsh Term - Clearing Mist by Double Jump (J T R Dreaper) 2679 3749

7 **DRINK UP DAN,** b g Down The Hatch - Avra Bay by Captain James (Patrick G Kelly) 538 708⁷ 801 939⁹ 1378⁵ 1496⁸ 1782

6 **DRIPSEY QUAY(IRE),** b m Quayside - Dirpsey Crystal by Mon Capitaine (Daniel Lordan) 4 32 73⁵

8 **DRIVING FORCE,** ch g Be My Native (USA) - Frederika (USA) by The Minstrel (CAN) (Mrs M McCourt) 698 936² 1072⁹ 1389⁴ 1514¹ 1630¹ 1933⁴ 2832 3452⁴ 3595³ 3847⁶ 4109¹

7 **DROICHEAD LAPEEN,** ch g Over The River (FR) - Merry Rambler by Wrekin Rambler (Norman Cassidy) 1236³ 2467⁵ 2613² 2756⁴ 3390⁵ 3504⁷ 3712⁷ 3913⁹

6 **DROMARA BREEZE(IRE),** b g Cataldi - Markup by Appiani II (H Kirk) 3528²

6 **DROMIN(IRE),** ch g Over The River (FR) - My Puttens by David Jack (Mrs A Swinbank) 563

9 **DROMIN LEADER,** b g Crash Course - Astral Fairy by Prefairy (J M Turner) 4311 3263⁸ 3331² 3857² 3999¹

7 **DROMIN MIST,** ch g Over The River (FR) - Ten-Cents by Taste Of Honey (J Mackie) 3492

13 **DROMINA STAR,** b or br g Pauper - Kitty The Hare by Hardicanute (Mrs S C Bradburne) 4302 396¹ 451⁴ 542 641⁶ 733² 768 2437⁷

5 **DROMOD POINT(IRE),** ch g Dromod Hill - Bright Point by Shackleton (Patrick Joseph Flynn) 114² 2203³ 4148⁵

4 **DROP THE ACT(IRE),** ch g Buckskin (FR) - Manna Rose by Bonne Noel (Derek Pugh) 4189⁶

5 **DROP THE HAMMER(IRE),** b g Good Thyne (USA) - Libby Jayne by Tumble Wind (USA) (Derek Pugh) 4360⁵ 4406 98⁴ 211² 1581 1786⁶

4 **DROPAHINT(IRE),** b g Torus - Dusky Joe by Dusky Boy (Derek Pugh) 3797

3 **DRU RI'S BRU RI,** b g Kafu - Bru Ri (FR) by Sir Gaylord (W J Smith) 2254⁵ 2321³ 2408⁹ 2581³

9 **DRUID'S DAWN,** b m Fine Blade (USA) - Curracloe by Push On (J A Berry) 4343 215⁸ 236

12 **DRUMALDA,** b or br g Kambalda - Drumgoole Star by Double-U-Jay (Kevin Dwan) 254

660

INDEX TO NATIONAL HUNT RESULTS 1993-94

ENBORNE LAD, gr g Celtic Cone - Blue Delphinium by Quorum (G P Enright) 4345 2535⁴ 2729 3003 3545 4096

ENCHANTED FLYER, b g Doulab (USA) - Enchanted by Song (T W Donnelly) 659 814⁵ 1070⁷ 1535⁸ 1751⁵

ENCHANTED MAN, b g Enchantment - Queen's Treasure by Queen's Hussar (R Lee) 3105 3586⁶ 3785² 3929⁴ 4164⁸

ENCHANTED QUEEN, b or br m Tender King - Magic Quiz by Quisling (Michael Hourigan) 573

END GAME(IRE), b g Glow (USA) - Tumbella by Tumble Wind (USA) (Noel Meade) 4402⁵ 647

ENERGANCE(IRE), ch m Salmon Leap (USA) - Rosemore by Ashmore (FR) (F Flood) 637 854 1987⁸ 2201⁵ 2347⁶

ENFANT DU PARADIS(IRE), b m Shernazar - Fille de L'orne (FR) by Jim French (USA) (P D Evans) 918⁷ 1068⁵

ENFANT TERRIBLE, b g Cheval - Lauregeen by Laurence O (Edward C Sexton) 3610

ENNEL VIEW(IRE), b m Le Bavard (FR) - Yankee View by Yankee Gold (F Flood) 990

ENNEREILLY RIVER, b g Mississippi - Burlington Miss by Burlington II (Daniel J Murphy) 4380 637⁹ 4168

ENNIS SEVEN FIFTY, b g Mljet - Polly Peril by Politico (USA) (Patrick J F Hassett) 178 363⁸ 466⁶ 673⁸

ENQELAAB(USA), b g Chief's Crown (USA) - Affirmatively (USA) by Affirmed (USA) (M A O'Toole) 489¹ 880² 1269⁶ 1450 1981³ 2157⁶ 2700⁷ 2865 4116⁷

ENSHARP(USA), b g Sharpen Up - Lulworth Cove by Averof (S Gollings) 1417 245

ENTERPRISE PRINCE, b g Lucky Wednesday - Avona by My Swallow (G P Murphy) 953 2361 2717 3592

ENTIRE, ch g Relkino - Tactless by Romulus (J D Hugill) 4335

ENVOCAMANDA(IRE), b g Supreme Leader - Cool Amanda by Prince Hansel (D M Grissell) 2916² 3386⁶

ENVOPAK TOKEN, ch g Proverb - Luck Token by Festive (G L Humphrey) 595 792

EPILENY, br g Random Shot - Charming Hostess by Khalkis (Miss P M Whittle) 4374

EQUATOR, ch g Nijinsky (CAN) - Sound Of Success (USA) by Successor (Mrs A E Lee) 4302⁴ 820⁵

EQUINOCTIAL, b g Skyliner - Night Rose by Sovereign Gleam (N Miller) 1477 2565¹ 2809²

ERADA(IRE), b m Spanish Place - Roamaway by Gala Performance (USA) (John J Walsh) 1332 3084 3869 4116

ERBIL(IRE), b c Shadari - Cretna by Golden Fleece (USA) (L Lungo) 1476 1584¹ 1791⁵ 2150 3673⁶ 3751⁴

ERCALL MILLER, b g Van Der Linden (FR) - Salica (ITY) by Hogarth (ITY) (K White) 2403

ERCKULE, b c Petoski - Mytinia by Bustino (N A Gaselee) 2245⁸ 2471² 2676³ 2910¹ 3228⁴ 3314² 3606³ 4021¹

ERIC'S TRAIN, b g Strong Gale - Star-Pit by Queen's Hussar (G B Balding) 1189 1339

ERICOLIN(IRE), ch g Ahonoora - Pixie Erin by Golden Fleece (USA) (N Tinkler) 1584³ 2303⁶ 2433¹ 2776¹ 2969⁵ 3125²

ERINS BAR(IRE), b g Erin's Hope - Vultellobar by Bargello (K C Bailey) 2332⁹ 3220⁷

ERLEMO, b h Mummy's Game - Empress Catherine by Welsh Pageant (W Clay) 2401⁶ 2634² 2797⁵ 2957² 3342² 3584⁴ 3926⁸

ERLKING(IRE), b g Fairy King (USA) - Cape Of Storms by Fordham (USA) (S Mellor) 462⁸ 611⁴ 870 2111² 2439¹ 2541²

ERMESHKA, b g Day Is Done - Orapa by Aureole (A P O'Brien) 4370⁸ 11 29⁸ 42

ERMINE STREET, ch g Relkino - Nearly Straight by Straight Lad (O Brennan) 3169⁴ 3457

ERNEST ARAGORN, b g Laxton - Passage To Freedom by Pals Passage (Mrs S Lamyman) 4057⁵

ERNEST MORSE(IRE), b g Boyne Valley - Sanvitalia by Right Tack (Robert O'Brien) 56 111 173⁸

ERRANT KNIGHT, ch g Deep Run - Dame Lucy by Prince Hansel (M C Pipe) 3452¹ 3766¹ 3916¹ 4018¹ 4180¹

ERSILLAS(FR), b g Labus (FR) - Misvaria (FR) by On My Way (USA) (M F Morris) 535²

ERZADJAN(IRE), b g Kahyasi - Ezana by Ela-Mana-Mou (N Tinkler) 872¹ 1032⁵ 1290² 1504³ 2003⁴ 2432⁷ 2874 3144⁵

ESHA NESS, b g Crash Course - Beeston by Our Babu (Mrs J Pitman) 2948⁴

ESPERER, b g Full Of Hope - Priory Maid by Malinowski (USA) (J O'Donoghue) 2134⁴ 2444⁹

ESPRIT D'ETOILE(USA), b g Spectacular Bid (USA) - Star Pastures by Northfields (USA) (Charles O'Brien) 421²

ESPRIT DE FEMME(FR), b m Esprit Du Nord (USA) - Bustelda (FR) by Busted (D W Browning) 1595³ 2320⁵ 2757³ 2914² 3306² 3698² 3943² 4100¹

ESPY, b g Pitpan - Minorette by Miralgo (C P E Brooks) 647¹ 1011⁶

ESSDOUBLEYOU(NZ), ch g Sambuk - Gardone by Petingo (Mrs J Renfree-Barons) 1490⁵ 1935 3108⁶

ESSEN AITCH, b m Lochnager - Eamon's Girl by Irish Star (M G Meagher) 1707 1869 2527 2778⁶ 3007 3167 3770⁷

ESTELLE MARIE, b m Royal Match - Trip To Heaven by Tower Walk (P J Hobbs) 3233

ESTHAL(IRE), b c Kalaglow - Chevrefeuille by Ile de Bourbon (USA) (R J Hodges) 1410⁹

EULOGY(FR), br h Esprit Du Nord (USA) - Louange (K R Burke) 1773⁷

EUPHONIC, br g Elegant Air - Monalda (FR) by Claude (I A Balding) 296¹ 870⁴ 3209

EURIDICE(IRE), ch m Woodman (USA) - Arctic Kite by North Stoke (W G M Turner) 715² 795 952⁹

EUROBUCK(IRE), b m Buckskin (FR) - Starcat by Avocat (M J P O'Brien) 3327 3450

EUROPA POINT, ch g Deep Run - Regal Dawn by Golden Love (Michael Robinson) 1827³

EUROPE(USA), b g Lear Fan (USA) - Clara Bow (USA) by Coastal (USA) (Gerard Stack) 3246⁷ 3448 3934

EUROTHATCH(IRE), gr g Thatching - Inch by English Prince (George Stewart) 746⁷

EUROTWIST, b g Viking (USA) - Orange Bowl by General Assembly (USA) (Mrs V A Aconley) 2243⁷ 2432 2580⁴

EVE PET, b m Politico (USA) - Gusty Lucy by White Speck (J W F Aynsley) 3430

EVE'S TREASURE, ch f Bustino - Before Long by Longleat (USA) (S W Campion) 1532 1655 1865² 2275⁴ 2638² 2802⁷ 3167²

EVEN BLUE(IRE), b g Gianchi - The Blue Pound by Even Money (Mrs C J Black) 1674⁴ 1806³ 2339⁶ 2897² 3137²

EVEN FLOW(IRE), b g Mandalus - Mariners Chain by Walshford (Michael McCullagh) 2944⁷ 3694⁴

665

INDEX TO NATIONAL HUNT RESULTS 1993-94

7 **FLAHERTYS BEST VI,** ch m Major Point - Corran View by Kambalda (L Young) 2352³ 2551

8 **FLAKEY DOVE,** b m Oats - Shadey Dove by Deadly Nightshade (R J Price) 1030⁴ 1347³ 1663⁴ 2046² 2258¹ 2376¹ 2595³ 2851¹ 3025¹ 3424⁵

8 **FLAME O'FRENSI,** b m Tudor Flame - Regal Rage by Fury Royal (K Cumings) 2555⁵ 2898 3216 3947¹

5 **FLAMEWOOD,** b m Touching Wood (USA) - Alan's Girl by Prince Hansel (Mrs D Haine) 634³ 2667³ 2934⁴ 3497⁴ 3640³

4 **FLAMING MIRACLE(IRE),** b g Vision (USA) - Red Realm by Realm (G Barnett) 2857⁶ 3189⁸ 3775⁴ 4121⁶

5 **FLAMING SANDS(IRE),** ch m Sandalay - Shady Ahan by Mon Capitaine (F J O'Mahony) 3832

5 **FLAPJACK LAD,** b g Oats - Reperage (USA) by Key To Content (USA) (N A Twiston-Davies) 1806⁴ 1957² 2262³ 2633⁴ 3279⁴

6 **FLAPPING FREDA(IRE),** ch m Carlingford Castle - Just Darina by Three Dons (J R Jenkins) 1027⁶ 1386⁷ 1734⁶ 2599⁷ 2642⁶ 2910⁴ 3637⁵ 3903⁸

8 **FLASH OF REALM(FR),** b h Super Moment (USA) - Light Of Realm by Realm (P Monteith) 821 1114⁵ 1356¹ 1607¹ 2254² 2498² 2812⁸ 3125¹ 3434¹ 3643⁴

9 **FLASHING SILKS,** b m Kind Of Hush - Hit The Line by Saulingo (A G Russell) 3856

9 **FLASHING STEEL,** b g Broadsword (USA) - Kingsfold Flash by Warpath (J E Mulhern) 1398¹ 1652¹ 1895² 2611 3064⁴ 3591⁵

8 **FLASHTHECASH,** b g Torus - Easter Beauty by Raise You Ten (G B Balding) 1123 1208 1436⁷ 1652⁷ 1757 2791⁵ 3026² 3218³ 3407³

10 **FLASHY BUCK,** b g Buckskin (FR) - Flashy Money by Even Money (Simon J Stearn) 1177 3329

6 **FLASS VALE,** b g Final Straw - Emblazon by Wolver Hollow (C W Fairhurst) 733 974⁸ 1150² 1311 1676 1874⁵ 2256 3344⁵ 3436⁴ 3678¹ 3801⁵ 3960¹ 4037⁶

5 **FLAWLESS FINISH(IRE),** ch m Le Bavard (FR) - Kiltarquin by Deep Run (A P O'Brien) 3088⁴ 3250⁷ 3290⁵ 3469² 3792¹ 3869¹

10 **FLAXON WORRIOR,** ch g Roman Warrior - Domino Smith by White Speck (A J Le Blond) 3536 3598 3690 3864⁸ 3959 4039² 4081 4176

6 **FLEMCUR(IRE),** ch g Buckskin (FR) - Golden Vixen by Goldhill (D K Weld) 4403⁸ 55¹ 136⁹

4 **FLEMINGS DELIGHT,** b f Idiot's Delight - Meadow Maid by Deep Run (A E Jessop) 3234

7 **FLEMINGS FOOTMAN,** br h Warpath - Ashmo by Ashmore (FR) (Peadar Matthews) 991

12 **FLEURCONE,** ch g Celtic Cone - Little Fleur by Tudor Wood (K White) 936⁵

5 **FLIGHT LIEUTENANT(USA),** b g Marfa (USA) - Lt Golden Girl (USA) by Lt Stevens (R Hannon) 1442⁴ 1840

8 **FLING IN SPRING,** b g Last Fandango - Lovely Season by Silly Season (Mrs S C Bradburne) 282³ 559² 656² 734⁴ 1183² 1356³ 1587⁵ 2007⁶ 2149⁴ 2575⁴ 2739⁵ 2971³ 3536⁵ 3569³

7 **FLINTERS,** b g Deep Run - En Clair by Tarqogan (G Richards) 1636⁵ 2573

4 **FLINTLOCK(IRE),** ch c Kris - Foolish Lady (USA) by Foolish Pleasure (USA) (N J Henderson) 3576² 3928² 4027⁴

5 **FLIP THE LID(IRE),** b or br m Orchestra - Punters Gold by Yankee Gold (T G McCourt) 255 1155⁸ 1455 4063⁹

11 **FLOATER(USA),** b g Vaguely Noble - Need A Dime (USA) by Three Bagger (P Monteith) 2003⁹ 2217

6 **FLOATING LINE,** ch g Bairn (USA) - County Line by High Line (P Wigham) 1668⁷ 2485⁵ 2585⁶ 2874² 3402⁶

10 **FLOOD MARK,** ch g High Line - Crystal Fountain by Great Nephew (Ian Hutchins) 2800

4 **FLORA LADY,** b f Mandalus - Dame Flora by Celtic Cone (W T Kemp) 2787⁴ 453 652

4 **FLORA WOOD(IRE),** b f Bob Back (USA) - Crannog by Habitat (Kevin Prendergast) 1846⁵ 2099⁷

7 **FLORIDA SKY,** b g Florida Son - Eskylane by Cantab (John R Upson) 1205 1563⁴ 1704² 2654¹ 2858² 3040⁷ 3224 3512

6 **FLORLESS GUY(IRE),** b g Floriferous - Wine List by Frigid Aire (R Rowe) 3234

7 **FLOWER OF GRANGE,** ch m Arapahos (FR) - Dara's Bishop by Bishop Of Orange (James William Cullen) 53⁸

6 **FLOWERHILL DAISY(IRE),** b m Torus - Little Else by Abednego (G T Lynch) 3954⁷ 4031² 4146³

8 **FLOWING RIVER(USA),** b h Irish River (FR) - Honey's Flag (USA) by Hoist The Flag (USA) (R Allan) 4354 543⁵ 657³ 739² 873⁴ 1128⁴ 1792 2436⁶ 3436⁹

6 **FLUIDITY(USA),** b g Robellino (USA) - Maple River (USA) by Clandestine (E T Buckley) 4331⁴ 4375⁶ 703 1422³ 2065⁹ 2229⁷

8 **FLUSTERED(USA),** b g Blushing Groom (FR) - Miss Mazepam (USA) by Nijinsky (CAN) (R O'Leary) 4398⁵ 35⁸ 47⁵ 556 2403

10 **FLUTTER MONEY,** b g Beldale Flutter (USA) - Berthe Mazet by Crepello (J Kirby) 1072 1396 1712 1967⁵ 2328⁶ 2886 3043³

6 **FLY BY NORTH(USA),** b g Northern Horizon (USA) - Lazy E (CAN) by Meadow Court (D Nicholson) 713⁷ 796

7 **FLY GUARD(NZ),** gr g Imperial Guard - Fly (IRE) by Three Legs (N M Babbage) 773⁷ 869⁸ 2244⁴ 2757⁷ 3215

9 **FLYAWAY(FR),** ch g Touching Wood (USA) - Flying Sauce by Sauce Boat (USA) (R W Emery) 1928² 2060² 2120² 2216³

8 **FLYER'S NAP,** b g Rolfe (USA) - English Flyer by English Prince (R H Alner) 1653⁶ 2034² 2298² 2597⁵ 2725 3006¹ 3175

4 **FLYING AMY,** ch f Norwick (USA) - Starky's Pet by Mummy's Pet (W G M Turner) 193 356⁵

7 **FLYING COLUMN,** b g Miner's Lamp - Curracloe by Push On (Dr C J Maguire) 1814 2161⁴ 2289³ 2553⁴

6 **FLYING CONNECTION,** b g Never So Bold - Gunner's Belle by Gunner B (W Clay) 260

9 **FLYING FINISH,** gr g Junius (USA) - Blue Alicia by Wolver Hollow (G R Graham) 1393 1712

6 **FLYING SOUTH(IRE),** b g Kemal (FR) - Magic User by Deep Run (Thomas Carberry) 20⁹ 113³ 131⁶ 493

6 **FLYING SPEED(USA),** b g Far North (CAN) - Diatoma (FR) by Diatome (M C Pipe) 2418

8 **FLYING WILD,** b g Another Hoarwithy - Valrina Miy by Carnival Boy (W Clay) 813⁷ 998

11 **FLYING ZIAD(CAN),** ch g Ziad (USA) - Flying Souvenir (USA) by Flying Relic (R Curtis) 4335⁴ 152² 3766⁴ 3929⁵

6 **FOGELBERG(USA),** b g Caro - La Paqueline (FR) by Sassafras (FR) (B V Kelly) 1495⁹ 1894⁹ 2774 3275⁴ 3507

6 **FOIL THE FOX,** b m Broadsword (USA) - Huntless by Songedor (K C Bailey) 2835⁴ 3204 3597

9 **FOILACLUG FURRY,** br g Furry Glen - Con's Dual Fair by Dual (D T Hughes) 3614⁸ 4190⁴

671

5 **GENE OF THE GLEN(IRE),** b m Golden Act (USA) - Keep The Faith by Furry Glen (Ms E Cassidy) 95 255 343⁶ 469 709

8 **GENERAL BRANDY,** b g Cruise Missile - Brandy's Honour by Hot Brandy (J T Gifford) 1107 1393⁶ 2223¹ 2453³ 2966 3118 3307⁵ 3546

4 **GENERAL BROOKS(IRE),** b g Governor General - Choral Park by Music Boy (R T Juckes) 180⁶ 462

4 **GENERAL CHASE,** ch f Scottish Reel - Make A Signal by Royal Gunner (USA) (D Burchell) 606¹ 754¹

10 **GENERAL EDDIE,** b g Chambrais - Corncrop (D P Geraghty) 3046⁹

11 **GENERAL HARMONY,** ch g True Song - Spartando by Spartan General (Miss G Sarah Jennings) 3161⁵

9 **GENERAL IDEA,** ch g General Assembly (USA) - Idealist by Busted (D K Weld) 119¹ 1226 1578² 1895⁴ 2288⁷ 2867

11 **GENERAL JAMES,** ch g General Ironside - Royal Bonnet by Beau Chapeau (J T Gifford) 825² 1466⁴

14 **GENERAL MERCHANT,** br g Legal Tender - Elissa Cheng by Chinese Lacquer (R J Hodges) 2491³ 2777³ 3017¹ 3152⁴ 3312³ 3456² 3548⁵ 3847¹ 4067² 4099¹

4 **GENERAL MOUKTAR,** ch c Hadeer - Fly The Coop by Kris (M C Pipe) 2722³ 2821² 3062

5 **GENERAL MURAKA(IRE),** b g Assembly General - Muraka by Off Key (Patrick J Smyth) 4396

8 **GENERAL PERSHING,** br g Persian Bold - St Colette by So Blessed (G Richards) 1001² 1226³ 1573⁴ 1664⁶ 1875¹ 2384⁴ 2576² 2748⁴ 3132²

8 **GENERAL PICTON,** b g Cut Above - Bodnant by Welsh Pageant (P Venner) 3799³ 3999

9 **GENERAL SHOT,** b g General Ironside - Kova's Daughter by Brave Invader (USA) (W Clay) 1173 1456 1602⁶ 2215² 2424⁴ 2870² 3102¹ 3279² 3491⁵ 3666

6 **GENERAL SIKORSKI,** b g Petoski - Cristalga by High Top (P J Makin) 3233

7 **GENERAL TONIC,** b g Callernish - Jude Lacy by Laurence O (D R Gandolfo) 150⁴ 277² 540² 1283⁷ 1502²

5 **GENERAL WOLFE,** ch g Rolfe (USA) - Pillbox by Spartan General (Capt T A Forster) 1110⁴ 1564¹ 2141⁴ 2519¹

9 **GENERALANAESTHETIC,** b g General Ironside - Sedate by Green Shoon (Martin Brassil) 3611 3655 3955

9 **GENERALLY JUST,** b g Golden Love - Petite Star by Super Seer (G Stickland) 650 953⁸ 1717 2717⁵ 3051⁸ 3202⁷ 3233⁷ 3360

12 **GENERALS BOY,** b g General Ironside - Even More by Even Money (Mrs Nicki Craggs) 4392¹ 3462¹ 3645² 4182

10 **GENEROUS SCOT,** b g Rarity - Galloping Santa by Santa Claus (A P James) 649 751³ 957⁴ 1081⁵ 1324⁴ 1525²

9 **GENIE MACK(IRE),** ch g Le Bavard (FR) - Shannon Ville by Deep Run (Michael Condon) 4403⁹ 1610 1821 2039

9 **GENISTA,** b or br g Furry Glen - Rossaleigh by Menelek (Mrs K A Heywood) 79 1737⁷

4 **GENSERIC(FR),** br g Groom Dancer (USA) - Green Rosy (USA) by Green Dancer (USA) (T P Tate) 784⁶ 1569² 2072¹ 2810³ 3128⁵ 3373⁴ 3617⁴ 4126⁴

5 **GENTLE JESTER,** br m Reesh - Mirthful by Will Somers (P F Nicholls) 3880⁶ 4057

4 **GENTLE REEF(IRE),** b f Orange Reef - Monica Carr by Top Ville (W T Bourke) 2349⁸ 2547⁸ 2678¹ 3080⁹ 3321⁸ 3526

11 **GENTLEMAN ANGLER,** ch g Julio Mariner - San Salvador (GER) by Klairon (S E Sherwood) 4313³ 4394 947 1191

4 **GENTLEMAN SID,** b c Brotherly (USA) - Eugenes Chance by Flashback (R Dickin) 870 3700⁵ 4009⁵

8 **GEOELITA(FR),** b m Rolling Bowl - Goela by Amarko (A de Mieulle) 372¹

5 **GEOFFREY TREVOR(IRE),** ch g Invited (USA) - Aerial Orchid by Perspex (T J O'Mara) 2348⁹ 2918⁶

9 **GEORGE BUCKINGHAM,** b g Royal Palace - Flying Idol by Acrania (G A Ham) 2400⁴ 2766⁵ 2862³ 3166

6 **GEORGE LANE,** b g Librate - Queen Of The Kop by Queen's Hussar (F Jordan) 1078⁹ 2014⁹ 3281⁴ 3663 3878 4165⁵

4 **GEORGE ROPER,** b g Hotfoot - Helewise by Dance In Time (CAN) (G L Moore) 668⁵

4 **GERAY LADY(IRE),** b f Roselier (FR) - Toevairo by Raga Navarro (ITY) (Michael G Holden) 4169

4 **GERMAN LEGEND,** br g Faustus (USA) - Fairfields by Sharpen Up (R R Lamb) 1147⁹ 1920⁷ 2217 2896⁶ 3144⁸ 3440⁵ 3687⁵ 3905⁵

6 **GEROLAS(IRE),** gr g Godswalk (USA) - Beecom Silk by English Prince (Gerard Stack) 66 342⁶

8 **GERRYMANDER,** br g Croghan Hill - Normandy Lady by Normandy (Mrs Pauline Gavin) 92 112 363

10 **GERTIES PRIDE,** b m The Parson - Gertie Owen by Master Owen (P M Lynch) 101⁴ 119 1347 170⁷ 1402⁴ 1499⁴ 1826 1901³ 2037

6 **GESNERA,** br m Rusticaro (FR) - Joie D'Or (FR) by Kashmir II (K White) 983⁵ 1930⁶ 3008¹ 3209² 4101¹

8 **GET STEPPING,** ch g Posse (USA) - Thanks Edith by Gratitude (Miss M Bragg) 4366

5 **GETA LEGUP,** ch g True Song - Dundonnel by Roan Rocket (Peter McCreery) 55⁷ 107⁸

4 **GETYERKITON(IRE),** ch g Parliament - Frisky Matron by On Your Mark (M A Barnes) 516

8 **GHIA GNEUIAGH,** b or br g Monksfield - Kindly by Tarqogan (N A Twiston-Davies) 1008¹ 1228² 1348⁴ 1691⁴ 1844 2264² 2472 2596⁵ 3039 3382³ 3608 3844¹ 4055¹ 4154¹

11 **GHOFAR,** ch g Nicholas Bill - Royale Final by Henry The Seventh (D R C Elsworth) 1396 1520² 1713³ 2429¹ 2656² 2747 2948³ 3217¹ 3364 3631¹ 3830¹ 3916²

5 **GIDEONSCLEUCH,** b m Beverley Boy - Wintersgame by Game Warden (R Allan) 2909

5 **GIFT ACCOUNT(IRE),** b g Auction Ring (USA) - Lucky Realm by Realm (F Flood) 2983

4 **GIFT OF PEACE(IRE),** br f Vision (USA) - Peace In The Woods by Tap On Wood (A P O'Brien) 225⁸

7 **GIFTED FELLOW(IRE),** b g Decent Fellow - Grilse by Raga Navarro (ITY) (J T Gorman) 4396 159⁴ 304⁶

4 **GIG TIME(IRE),** b f Digamist (USA) - Hazel Gig by Captain's Gig (USA) (Daniel O'Connell) 228 529

6 **GILBERT(IRE),** br g Dalsaan - Pennyala by Skyliner (D N Carey) 4393 416³ 565⁶ 773⁶ 891¹ 1047² 1192⁶ 1526 3559 3685 3826

5 **GILLAN COVE(IRE),** b g The Parson - Shanban by Shackleton (R H Alner) 3046² 3220

12 **GILLANBONE,** ch g Baptism - Joplin by Sandford Lad (Graham Wheatley) 3799⁴

6 **GILMANSCLEUCH(IRE),** b m Mandalus - Wreck-Em-All by Wrekin Rambler (J K M Oliver) 2220 3284⁶

5 **GILPA VALU,** ch g Ovac (ITY) - More Cherry by Bargello (Mrs J Pitman) 1536⁷ 2671⁹ 3547⁵

1686⁶ 1818⁴ 2079 2588² 2845¹ 2987¹ 3368² 3612⁴ 3658⁵

13 **GLENCOMMON,** ch g Forties Field (FR) - Deep Pearl by Deep Run (R W Pincombe) 776

5 **GLENDUN(IRE),** b g Forties Field (FR) - Pony's Mount by Choral Society (I R Ferguson) 1020⁷

6 **GLENFINN PRINCESS,** ch m Ginger Boy - Lady Amazon by Spartan General (K S Bridgwater) 4407³ 616⁴ 753⁵ 1110⁵ 1215³ 1535¹ 1716² 2731⁴ 2934² 3230⁹

7 **GLENGARRA PRINCESS,** ch m Cardinal Flower - Glengarra Queen by Laurence O (D R Gandolfo) 554 801¹ 1076⁵ 2204⁹ 2642¹ 2950²

9 **GLENGRIFFIN,** b g Furry Glen - Ballygriffin by Deep Run (J T Gifford) 860 1171⁷ 1491² 3015⁴

7 **GLENMAVIS,** b g King's Ride - Pink Quay by Quayside (I R Ferguson) 4092⁸ 4186²

5 **GLENPATRICK PEACH(IRE),** b f Lafontaine (USA) - Seat Of Learning by Balliol (Mrs John Harrington) 4119⁶

8 **GLENSHANE LAD,** b g Fidel - Molly Dancer by Choral Society (K C Bailey) 521 595² 677¹ 694³ 954⁴ 1081² 1262² 1486³ 1932 2047⁴ 3498¹ 3537¹ 3703²

7 **GLENSHANE PASS,** b g Fidel - Molly Dancer by Choral Society (I R Ferguson) 745⁴ 808⁶ 1157⁵ 1764

5 **GLENSKI,** b g Tout Ensemble - Glen Wise by Fair Decision (G B Balding) 2509 2749

8 **GLENSPORT VI,** b m Abednego - Leafy by Grange Melody (W Rock) 2773⁴ 3611 3722² 3794

4 **GLENSTAL FLAGSHIP(IRE),** b g Glenstal (USA) - Fourth Degree by Oats (A P O'Brien) 1377¹ 1575¹ 3062⁶ 3369⁸ 3656¹

7 **GLENSTAL PRIORY,** b m Glenstal (USA) - Jumbolia by Wolver Hollow (S B Avery) 4345 1100⁸ 1238 1425⁴ 2215

6 **GLENTOWER(IRE),** b g Furry Glen - Helens Tower by Dual (N J Henderson) 1800⁵ 2144³ 2404³ 2827¹

4 **GLIDING ALONG(IRE),** b f Bob Back (USA) - Naujella by Malinowski (USA) (T F Lacy) 2388 2592

4 **GLINDIGO(IRE),** br g Glow (USA) - Indigo Rose by Petingo (P Monteith) 1064⁵ 1221⁶

4 **GLINT OF AYR,** b f Glint Of Gold - Iyamski (USA) by Baldski (USA) (R H Goldie) 278⁵ 754⁵

5 **GLINT OF EAGLES(IRE),** b g Treasure Hunter - Double Damask by Ardoon (D P Kelly) 2289² 3394⁵ 3653³

8 **GLITTER GREY,** bl m Nishapour (FR) - Saraday by Northfields (USA) (J H Scott) 21⁶ 52⁹ 101⁸ 170³ 806⁸

8 **GLITTERING PAN,** b f Pitpan - Ever Shining by Indigenous (John Crowley) 1401

4 **GLOBE HABIT,** ch h Sayyaf - Samkhya by Crocket (P J Healy) 293 430 583

10 **GLORIOLE,** b g Indian King (USA) - Escorial by Royal Palace (Miss J L Rae) 4074²

6 **GLORIOUS HEIGHTS,** ch m Wolver Heights - Glorious Jane by Hittite Glory (V Thompson) 2741⁸ 2951 3435⁷ 3553 3690⁸ 3787⁸ 3895 4035⁷

10 **GLORY BEE,** ch g Bold Owl - Sweet Minuet by Setay (G A Ham) 885⁵ 953

7 **GLOSSY,** ch g Derrylin - Floor Show by Galivanter (Mrs M McCourt) 1068 1313⁵ 1749³ 2061¹ 2329² 2804⁷ 3131 3773⁸ 4052⁶

9 **GLOVE PUPPET,** ch g Nearly A Hand - April Belle by Grisaille (G B Balding) 1471⁸ 1720 2246 3282² 3405 3593³ 3875² 4007² 4128²

4 **GLOW TINA(IRE),** b f Glow (USA) - Bustina (FR) by Busted (A P O'Brien) 3842⁹

4 **GLOWING LINES(IRE),** br f Glow (USA) - Eyeliner (USA) by Raise A Native (A P O'Brien) 688³ 968 3505⁶

4 **GLOWING PATH,** b g Kalaglow - Top Tina by High Top (R J Hodges) 352¹ 1021 1271 1510⁸ 1949⁵

4 **GLOWING VALUE(IRE),** b g Glow (USA) - Party Piece by Thatch (USA) (Thomas J Taaffe) 968³ 1377⁴ 1454⁹ 1846¹ 2608⁶

6 **GLYNN CROSS(IRE),** b m Mister Lord (USA) - Arctic Survivor by Hard Run (Eugene M O'Sullivan) 3295⁷ 3835⁴

6 **GLYNN RIVER(IRE),** ch g Over The River (FR) - Golden Ash by Skymaster (William Patton) 4359⁵ 22⁵

8 **GNOME'S TYCOON,** br g Strong Gale - Fairgoi by Baragoi (R T Phillips) 1656¹ 1995¹ 2384³ 3041 3443 3619

5 **GO BALLISTIC,** br g Celtic Cone - National Clover by National Trust (D Nicholson) 2677¹ 2834² 3042³ 3315²

7 **GO DEAS,** ch g King Persian - St Louisan by St Chad (A P O'Brien) 234 3870⁵

5 **GO GO GALLANT(IRE),** b g Over The River (FR) - Joyful Anna by Blurullah (Fergus Sutherland) 2918⁵ 3911⁶ 3972

8 **GO MARY,** b m Raga Navarro (ITY) - Go Perrys by High Hat (Miss C Phillips) 2302¹ 3005² 3230¹ 3604⁵

6 **GO SILLY,** b g Silly Prices - Allez Stanwick by Goldhill (Miss L C Plater) 2811⁵ 4073

6 **GO UNIVERSAL(IRE),** br g Teofane - Lady Dorcet by Condorcet (FR) (M Bradstock) 1768

5 **GOD SPEED YOU(IRE),** gr g Roselier (FR) - Pitmark by Pitpan (C T Nash) 1406⁵ 1974⁵ 2795⁴ 3051⁶

6 **GODFREYS CROSS(IRE),** ch m Fine Blade (USA) - Serpentine Artiste by Buckskin (FR) (James Murphy) 929 989 1857 2550 2923 3551 3835

7 **GOGGINS HILL,** b g Slippered - Rathcreevagh by Harwell (P Cheesbrough) 2782² 2904¹ 3157² 3439¹ 3991³

6 **GOING AROUND,** b g Baron Blakeney - Elect by New Member (K C Bailey) 2749⁶ 3256² 3589³

9 **GOING DOWN,** b m Sayyaf - Neshoma by Realm (T F Archdeacon) 212

4 **GOING GREY,** gr g Little Wolf - Lion And Lamb by Royal And Regal (USA) (Miss S J Wilton) 3708⁹ 3880⁸

7 **GOING PUBLIC,** b g Strong Gale - Cairita by Pitcairn (P Cheesbrough) 2447⁷ 2951⁷ 3179 3378³ 3617⁸ 3815¹ 4126¹

7 **GOLA LADY,** b m Pollerton - Bregoge Bridge by Crash Course (Victor Bowens) 4359⁴ 1017⁶ 1159³ 1402 1830³ 1909² 2277

9 **GOLD CAP(FR),** ch g Noir Et Or - Alkmaar (USA) by Verbatim (USA) (P J Hobbs) 765³ 986 1365 1540 2495¹ 3134⁶

6 **GOLD GLEN(IRE),** ch g Red Sunset - Park Lady by Tap On Wood (P J Makin) 1601⁴ 2762⁷ 3119⁷ 3592⁴ 3829

10 **GOLD HAVEN,** ch g Pollerton - Coolbawn Lady by Laurence O (Andrew Turnell) 850¹ 1098 1459

6 **GOLD NITE,** b m Nesselrode (USA) - Melinite by Milesian (C D Broad) 3880

12 **GOLD OPTIONS,** ch g Billion (USA) - Foggy Park by Foggy Bell (Peter McCreery) 1231⁷ 1433² 1578 1895⁸ 2695³ 2867⁷

4 **GOLD OR BUST,** b f Amazing Bust - Going After Gold by King's Ride (W Clay) 3401 3832

11 **GOLD SHAFT,** b g Kambalda - Golden Goose by Prince Hansel (N W Padfield) 4317³ 761⁴ 860

8 **GOLD SHOT,** ch g Hard Fought - Cartridge (FR) by Jim French (USA) (P Bowen) 4374

8 **GOLDEN AMBITION,** b f Torus - Lasting Impression by Proverb (Ronald Curran) 1495 2201⁷

9 **GOLDEN ARRANGEMENT,** br g Kemal (FR) - Tober Moth by Rugged Man (Patrick Carey) 23 36 3291 3550 3788 4034

6 **GOLDEN BANKER(IRE),** ch g Sandalay - Stylistic by Bargello (J Wade) 782⁴ 909⁶ 974 2215⁶ 2424⁹ 3033⁴ 3341 3435⁹ 3862⁸ 3982⁶ 4070⁹

5 **GOLDEN CAIRN(IRE),** ch h Dromod Hill - Gilt Course by Crash Course (W G Reed) 2148 3470³

6 **GOLDEN CARRUTH(IRE),** br g Euphemism - Connie's Girl by Condorcet (FR) (Michael Hourigan) 1499 1826³ 1915⁴ 2183² 2312⁴ 2619 2662³ 3249² 3326³ 3467⁹ 3648 3890 4033⁴ 4117⁶

10 **GOLDEN CELTIC,** b g Rare One - Cooleen by Tarqogan (Miss H C Knight) 1507 2507

7 **GOLDEN CLAW,** br g Strong Gale - Dark Gold by Raise You Ten (F Flood) 495¹ 538 4032⁶ 4116

11 **GOLDEN CROFT,** ch g Crofter (USA) - Rossian by Silent Spring (T H Jackson) 4322⁷

6 **GOLDEN DROPS(NZ),** b g Dorchester (FR) - Super Maric (NZ) by Super Gray (USA) (Mrs J Renfree-Barons) 2426 2779⁵ 3215

9 **GOLDEN FARE,** ch g Scallywag - Katie Fare by Ritudyr (R Lee) 649⁴ 813² 1189¹ 1841⁴ 2527 3040 3575⁶

6 **GOLDEN FELLOW(IRE),** ch g Buckskin (FR) - Miss Argument by No Argument (Martyn Meade) 2014 2147

7 **GOLDEN FRAME,** ch h White Christmas - Can Bowl by Bowling Pin (D J G Murray Smith) 3530⁴ 3762⁷

12 **GOLDEN FREEZE,** b g Golden Love - Freezeaway by Vulgan (R Lee) 1363 2087 2463

6 **GOLDEN GUNNER(IRE),** ch g Mazaad - Sun Gift by Guillaume Tell (USA) (Mrs M McCourt) 2833 3193⁷ 3499⁹ 3594 3831 4141⁶

10 **GOLDEN ISLE,** b h Golden Fleece (USA) - Dunette (FR) by Hard To Beat (J I A Charlton) 4354² 543⁵ 1221⁷ 1735⁴ 1958² 2212³ 2436³ 2738³ 3129² 3356 3556³ 3776

7 **GOLDEN MAC,** ch g Court Macsherry - Prett Damsel by Prince Hansel (C Hennessy) 3611

8 **GOLDEN MADJAMBO,** ch h Northern Tempest (USA) - Shercol by Monseigneur (USA) (F Jordan) 316² 484⁴ 814³ 1070 1303 3319⁵ 3571²

9 **GOLDEN MOSS,** ch g Le Moss - Call Bird by Le Johnstan (J Ffitch-Heyes) 1274³ 1561⁶

7 **GOLDEN NUGGET,** b g Furry Glen - Ivy Rambler by Wrekin Rambler (Michael Purcell) 572 801² 1270³ 1760 2664 3394⁹ 3711⁹

9 **GOLDEN OPAL,** ch g Golden Love - Coquita by Go Match (Michael Hourigan) 1380⁵ 1609⁴ 2078¹ 2160¹ 2313⁸ 2468 3085⁷ 3242 3322

6 **GOLDEN PLAN(IRE),** b m Creative Plan (USA) - Miss Aglojo by Aglojo (Victor Bowens) 1401 1549 1760 1814 3810⁵ 3954

9 **GOLDEN RAPPER,** ch g General Ironside - Our Star by Laurence O (Patrick G Kelly) 1⁴ 69⁴ 122 131 2660 3085 3887⁶ 3944⁸ 4115⁹

6 **GOLDEN RECORD,** ch g Nicholas Bill - Halmsgiving by Free State (J W Curtis) 1376 1674 2237 2413⁷

6 **GOLDEN REVERIE(USA),** b g Golden Act (USA) - Our Reverie (USA) by J O Tobin (USA) (B Mactaggart) 1586 1940⁵ 2108⁴ 2222⁶ 2575⁸ 2737 3475 3673⁵ 3895 4086

4 **GOLDEN SAVANNAH,** b g Presidium - Golden Pampas by Golden Fleece (USA) (M W Easterby) 971⁶ 1147 1284¹ 1569⁵ 2405 2564

10 **GOLDEN SEE,** b g Crozier - Toison D'Or by Tanavar (P Rooney) 44 1785⁵ 364⁶

8 **GOLDEN SHINE,** b g Golden Love - Segiolla by Giolla Mear (J L Harris) 1685 1783⁵ 3967

10 **GOLDEN SHOON,** ch g Green Shoon - Marigold by High Perch (K R Burke) 1807 3750

5 **GOLDEN SICKLE(USA),** b g Amazing Prospect (USA) - Marisickle (USA) by Maris (A B Coogan) 916 1042 1404

6 **GOLDEN SLEIGH(IRE),** ch m Le Moss - Sno-Sleigh by Bargello (A J Kennedy) 73 109 169

4 **GOLDEN SPHINX(IRE),** ch f Carmelite House (USA) - Golden Carrier by Homing (K Bishop) 4179

7 **GOLDEN SPINNER,** ch g Noalto - Madame Russe by Bally Russe (N J Henderson) 1110² 1344² 1648⁴ 1994⁵ 2795¹ 3220⁶ 3604³

8 **GOLDEN SUPREME,** ch g Deep Run - Good Calx by Khalkis (J W Curtis) 1374 1607

10 **GOLDEN SWORD,** b g Golden Fleece (USA) - Bandit Queen (FR) by Jim French (USA) (Anthony Dunphy) 4399

4 **GOLDEN TARGET(USA),** b f Gold Crest (USA) - Freshet (USA) by Believe It (USA) (Miss L Shally) 406 497 702⁶

7 **GOLDEN TORQUE,** br g Taufan (USA) - Brightelmstone by Prince Regent (FR) (R Bastiman) 1872⁶ 2303² 2585⁵

11 **GOLDFINGER,** ch g Billion (USA) - Old Hand by Master Owen (J Pilkington) 1457

7 **GOLDINGO,** ch g Rustingo - Ruths Image by Grey Love (G M Price) 1799³ 2839¹ 3020⁶ 3193¹ 3418³ 3574³

4 **GOLDMIRE,** b f Norwick (USA) - Orange Parade by Dara Monarch (W H Tinning) 622² 1147⁶ 2907² 3144 3601²

6 **GOLDSMITH,** b g Sonnen Gold - Star Alliance by Big Morton (Mrs S J Smith) 138 238⁶

5 **GOLDWREN(IRE),** gr m Tumble Gold - Wren's Princess by Wrens Hill (D J Barry) 3792

5 **GOLF WORLD(IRE),** b m Mandalus - Early Start by Wrekin Rambler (C P E Brooks) 3234 3458 3922

9 **GONE ASTRAY,** ch m The Parson - Merry Missus by Bargello (F T Walton) 4325 3424⁴ 3867³

6 **GONE BY(IRE),** ch g Whistling Deer - French Strata (USA) by Permian (USA) (P Burke) 2⁹ 3719⁹ 4113²

7 **GONE LIKE THE WIND,** ch h Tumble Wind (USA) - Friendly Polly (P J Molloy) 341⁸ 746 804⁸ 1233⁸ 1981 2157 2588 3795

9 **GONER HOUSE,** ch g General Ironside - Slavesville by Charlottesville Flyer (J Mulhall) 4351⁵ 3619³

11 **GONZALO,** b g Strong Gale - Dereen by Boreen (FR) (F J Lacy) 97³ 121³ 200² 303¹ 474⁴ 532 4033⁹

6 **GOOD BLOW(IRE),** br g Strong Gale - Gerise by Nishapour (FR) (A J Wilson) 2209

5 **GOOD BYE MONEY(IRE),** b m Treasure Hunter - Clonaslee Baby by Konigssee (F Flood) 2394 3525

6 **GOOD DEER(IRE),** ch g Whistling Deer - Tina O'Flynn by Martinmas (C P Donoghue) 365⁴ 3936⁵

8 **GOOD EGG,** ch m Tachypous - Get Involved by Shiny Tenth (R Hollinshead) 4384⁶ 102

5 **GOOD FEELING,** gr g Belfort (FR) - Angela Edelson by Owen Dudley (A P Jarvis) 1027 1376 2332 3191

10 **GOOD FOR A LAUGH,** b g Idiot's Delight - Mekhala by Menelek (Mrs S A Bramall) 4379 76 132⁶ 336³ 479³ 590 913⁴ 1056¹ 1294¹ 1638³ 1975² 2261¹ 2383¹ 2825² 3066

11 **GREENACRES LAD,** ch g Billion (USA) - Moon Lady by Cash And Courage (J L Eyre) 1485[5] 1738[1] 1860[7] 2254[3] 2581[1] 3600[3] 3780[4] 3959[2] 4082[2]

7 **GREENBELLE,** b m Green Shoon - Bell Walks Fancy by Entrechat (Joseph G Murphy) 3747 3944

5 **GREENFIELD LODGE(IRE),** b g Lancastrian - Cambridge Lodge by Tower Walk (James Joseph O'Connor) 31[8] 102[9]

5 **GREENFIELD MAID(IRE),** ch m Red Johnnie - Cuan Maid by Whistling Top (Mrs N S Sharpe) 3880

7 **GREENFIELD MANOR,** ch g Move Off - Kerosa by Keren (N Chamberlain) 1218[4] 1637[3] 1790 2238 2814[2] 3143[2] 3426 3474[2]

8 **GREENHALL,** b g Creative Plan (USA) - South by Mount Hagen (FR) (A D Evans) 2941[2] 3295

5 **GREENHAM COMMON,** b g Cruise Missile - Willmon by Willipeg (J H Peacock) 1957

11 **GREENHEART,** br g Green Shoon - Giollaretta by Giolla Mear (R Dean) 2307 2707 3106 3667[6] 3902

6 **GREENHIL TARE AWAY,** b g Oats - Burlington Belle by Galivanter (P J Hobbs) 2147 2327[7] 2572[2] 3592[1]

9 **GREENHILL GO ON,** b or br m Oats - Ballylaneen by Master Buck (Mrs M E Long) 1386 1563 1715

8 **GREENHILL RAFFLES,** ch g Scallywag - Burlington Belle by Galivanter (P J Hobbs) 1343 1523[5] 3415 3560[1] 3772[2]

4 **GREENHILL WONDER,** ch f Nearly A Hand - Blue Wonder by Idiot's Delight (A J Chamberlain) 1990

4 **GREENORE GLEN(IRE),** br g Wolverlife - Cribasque by Gay Fandango (USA) (Augustine Leahy) 2663 3245

8 **GREENWINE(USA),** br h Green Dancer (USA) - Princesse Margo by Targowice (USA) (Mrs L Richards) 4316 610[4] 796[6] 1198[9] 1597[4] 2065 2113[1] 2346[4] 2711[2] 3545

5 **GREET THE GREEK,** b g Formidable (USA) - Yelney by Blakeney (Mrs S A Bramall) 3169

9 **GREGORY PECK,** br g Henbit (USA) - Indigo Rose by Petingo (L W Doran) 745[8]

13 **GRENAGH,** ch g Rouser - All Blarney by Blarney Stone (V R Bishop) 1544[3] 1884[2] 2298[5]

9 **GREY ADMIRAL,** gr g Alias Smith (USA) - Beech Tree by Fighting Ship (G Stickland) 1339[3] 1547

6 **GREY COMMANDER,** gr h Grey Desire - Melowen by Owen Dudley (M Brittain) 622[7] 970

6 **GREY EARL,** gr g Today And Tomorrow - Runager by Lochnager (D C O'Brien) 3380

5 **GREY FINCH,** gr g Nishapour (FR) - Swiftsand by Sharpen Up (O Sherwood) 3833

7 **GREY MERLIN,** gr g Derrylin - Sea Kestrel by Sea Hawk II (Mrs S Taylor) 4330[4] 1940[7] 3475 3578[5] 3910[4] 4050

10 **GREY MINSTREL,** gr g Black Minstrel - Sam's Can by Cantab (Denys Smith) 1203 1606[4] 2242[6] 2370[2] 2562[5]

7 **GREY POWER,** gr m Wolf Power (SAF) - Periquito (USA) by Olden Times (Mrs M Reveley) 2138[1] 2222[1] 2449[1] 3038 3376[6] 3618[6] 3737[3]

6 **GREY REALM,** ch m Grey Desire - Miss Realm by Realm (R E Barr) 622 755[9]

5 **GREY SEASON,** gr g Belfort (FR) - Cherry Season by Silly Season (T W Donnelly) 2485

4 **GREY SMOKE,** ch g Alias Smith (USA) - Salira by Double Jump (M W Easterby) 2387[5] 2834

6 **GREY TRIX(IRE),** gr g Le Moss - Moll Of Kintire by Politico (USA) (T P Tate) 1320[6] 1736[4]

8 **GREYFRIARS BOBBY,** ch g Hard Fought - Victorian Pageant by Welsh Pageant (Mrs J G Retter) 2717 3499[6] 3718[6] 4019 4052

6 **GRIFFINS BAR,** b g Idiot's Delight - Milly Kelly by Murrayfield (Mrs P Sly) 1251[3] 1654 1969[4] 2291[6]

10 **GRILLADIN(FR),** b h Bellypha - Gentop (FR) by High Top (M Munnelly) 254 496[5]

4 **GRINNELL,** ch g Gypsy Castle - Rosinka by Raga Navarro (ITY) (D McCune) 872[6] 3373 3557

7 **GRIS ET VIOLET(FR),** ch g Iron Duke (FR) - Darkeuse (FR) by Dark Tiger (J G FitzGerald) 2788 3193 3618

5 **GROG(IRE),** b g Auction Ring (USA) - Any Price by Gunner B (S E Sherwood) 716[6] 934[8] 1642[5] 2064[3] 2129[2]

6 **GROGAN CREST(IRE),** b m Farhaan - Sweetham by Tudenham (Thomas Bergin) 36

4 **GROGFRYN,** ch f Nicholas Bill - Connaughts' Trump by Connaught (C L Popham) 296[9] 379 608[3] 890[5] 1097[1] 1271[7] 1404[5] 1702[5] 1927[6] 2653[4] 2797[7]

8 **GROOMSMAN,** ch g Shy Groom (USA) - Octet by Octavo (USA) (N M Babbage) 2567[3] 3154 3546[3] 3779[3] 4006[5]

10 **GROTIUS,** ch g Ardross - Tudor Whisper by Henry The Seventh (G A Ham) 994[7] 1299[5] 1643[6] 1884 2142[6] 2338[6] 2729[6] 3003[8]

4 **GROUND CONTROL(IRE),** b c Digamist (USA) - Space Of Time (USA) by Timless Moment (USA) (J A Berry) 688 802 968

4 **GROUND NUT(IRE),** ch g Fools Holme (USA) - Corn Seed by Nicholas Bill (Miss H C Knight) 1510[4] 1647[2] 2722[1] 3062

7 **GROUND WAR,** b g Tug Of War - Shannon Lek by Menelek (Kevin Dwan) 2284[2] 2392[7] 3244[3] 3712[2] 3913[1]

6 **GROUP HAT(IRE),** b g Mister Lord (USA) - Arctic Sue by Arctic Slave (Mrs John Harrington) 1555 1786[7] 1910[3] 2128[7] 2586 3733

5 **GROUSE-N-HEATHER,** gr m Grey Desire - Heldigvis by Hot Grove (Miss J L Rae) 656[7] 821[5] 910

8 **GROVE WALK,** b or br m Croghan Hill - Supple by Poynton (Joseph G Murphy) 169

12 **GROVELANDS,** ch g Balinger - Oca by O'Grady (Mrs D Schilling) 3861[7]

5 **GRUBBY,** b m Green Ruby (USA) - Via Vitae by Palm Track (R Hollinshead) 323[9] 680[4] 950[4] 1153[2] 2118[9]

4 **GRUMPY'S GRAIN(IRE),** b g Horage - Godwyn by Yellow God (Miss L A Perratt) 272[7]

6 **GRUNGE(IRE),** b or br g Crash Course - Hills Of Fashion by Tarqogan (D J G Murray Smith) 2404 3215 3515[5]

8 **GUESSWORK,** b g Strong Gale - Martiness by Martinmas (R H Lalor) 291 306[5] 422[7] 943[5] 1231 3944[6] 4168[5]

12 **GUIBURN'S NEPHEW,** ch g National Trust - Arran Sunset by Miracle (P J Hobbs) 897[1] 1226 1436[2] 1698[3] 2266 2852[3] 3218[2]

11 **GUILDWAY,** b g Bulldozer - Lucky Favour by Ballyciptic (N A Twiston-Davies) 865[5] 1565[8] 1925[2] 2191[8] 3532[7] 3742[4] 3885[1] 3939

5 **GUITING GIRL,** b m Primo Dominie - Emily Kent by Royal Palace (N A Twiston-Davies) 605 1564

6 **GULER-A,** b g King Of Spain - Wayleave by Blakeney (R Craggs) 3378 3617

10 **GUNMETAL BOY,** b g Warpath - Geranium by Ragusa (Miss Lucinda V Russell) 3558 3645[4] 3867[2]

4 **GUNNER BE GOOD,** b f Gunner B - Immodest Miss by Daring Display (USA) (J K Cresswell) 406[8]

INDEX TO NATIONAL HUNT RESULTS 1993-94

10 **GUNNER STREAM,** ch g Gunner B - Golfers Dream by Carnoustie (P G Murphy) 2966 3260 3412 3828

4 **GUNNER SUE,** b f Gunner B - Sujono by Grey Mirage (M Scudamore) 742⁹ 997⁴ 1297³ 1767 2016⁵ 2164³ 2522⁷ 3062

10 **GUNNER'S FLIGHT,** ch m Celtic Cone - Lady Lucy by Hardraw Scar (Mrs A C Wakeham) 2484

4 **GUNS OF GOLD,** ch g Gunner B - Yellow Stag by Arapaho (J G M O'Shea) 2509

7 **GUSHKA,** b g Le Moss - Saucy Serene by Tarqogan (Mrs M McCourt) 1779 2141 2505

11 **GUTE NACHT,** ch g Laurence O - Cherry Branch (S W Campion) 1351 1533 1745⁴ 1862 2256⁵ 3029⁵ 3287 3441

5 **GWEEBARRA BAY(IRE),** b g Colonel Godfrey (USA) - Palhiri by Pall Mall (G A Ham) 3708⁴ 3880⁴

5 **GYMCRAK CYRANO(IRE),** b m Cyrano de Bergerac - Sun Gift by Guillaume Tell (USA) (N Chamberlain) 1060 1791 1961 2152 2254 3673 3798³ 3864 3959

9 **GYMCRAK DAWN,** b g Rymer - Edwina's Dawn by Space King (J Hetherton) 1877³ 2162¹ 2330³ 2737⁶ 3061⁶ 3297

6 **GYMCRAK GAMBLE,** b g Beldale Flutter (USA) - Baridi by Ribero (T Dyer) 4301³ 2502⁹ 2873⁵

6 **GYMCRAK SOVEREIGN,** b g Ballacashtal (CAN) - Get Involved by Shiny Tenth (G Holmes) 1487⁶ 1746¹ 1863⁴ 2119⁵ 2566³ 2833⁴ 3240⁵ 4066

8 **GYMCRAK STARDOM,** b g Comedy Star (USA) - Chemin de Guerre by Warpath (G Holmes) 1034⁷ 1218⁶ 1743³ 1953⁸ 2584¹ 3000 3434³ 3538³ 3736

4 **GYMCRAK TIGER(IRE),** b g Colmore Row - Gossip by Sharp Edge (G Holmes) 1767⁸ 2275⁵ 2783 3825²

4 **GYPSY CRYSTAL(USA),** gr f Flying Saucer - U R Grounded (USA) by Grounded (P R Rodford) 3365 3444⁴ 3670⁸

6 **GYPSY KING(IRE),** b g Deep Run - Express Film by Ashmore (FR) (Andrew Turnell) 2879³ 3163 3453

7 **GYPSY LASS,** br m King's Ride - Vagrant Lass by Peter Jones (W Harney) 1785¹ 1893³ 2286 2550¹ 2659²

4 **GYPSY LEGEND,** b f Legend Of France (USA) - Gipsy Scott by Sky Gipsy (W G M Turner) 1965 2130

4 **HABASHA(IRE),** b f Lashkari - Haughty Manner by High Top (M C Pipe) 1166³ 1297¹ 2398¹ 2652³ 2977²

8 **HABTON WHIN,** b g Le Bavard (FR) - Bob's Hansel by Prince Hansel (M H Easterby) 975¹

6 **HACKETTS CROSS(IRE),** b g Rusticaro (FR) - Anglesea Market by Sea Hawk II (Noel T Chance) 804⁴ 1449³ 2023² 3934 4076⁴

7 **HADLEIGHS CHOICE,** b g Fairy King (USA) - Jillette by Fine Blade (USA) (J Mooney) 517 586 729 950⁸ 1627 1860

5 **HAGAR,** ch g Viking (USA) - Blue Mistral (USA) by Monteverdi (J I A Charlton) 2565²

4 **HAILE DERRING,** br g Derring Rose - Haile Lady by Menelek (M Scudamore) 2509 3114⁶ 3457⁶

8 **HAIRY MAC,** b g Carlingford Castle - Mandy Pop by Mandalus (J White) 694 882

7 **HAITHAM,** b h Wassl - Balqis (USA) by Advocator (R H Buckler) 4316¹

8 **HAKI SAKI,** ch g Tug Of War - Shannon Lek by Menelek (Augustine Leahy) 938⁷ 1231⁴ 1578³ 1611² 1856 2288⁶ 2549² 2617 3121³ 3391³ 3467

6 **HALF A BILLION,** b g Nicholas Bill - Half Asleep by Quiet Fling (USA) (E M Caine) 3617 3815

9 **HALF A MO,** b m Sunyboy - Motif by St Elmo (C T Nash) 962⁵ 1080⁴ 3351 3421⁴ 3546⁹

12 **HALF BROTHER,** br g Faraway Times (USA) - Sinzinbra by Royal Palace (S Dow) 4310³ 2184 3941

5 **HALF VOLLEY(IRE),** b f Cataldi - Good Court by Takeawalk (A J Maxwell) 4189⁸

4 **HALF'N HALF,** br f Skyliner - Wharton Manor by Galivanter (Mrs V A Aconley) 2490 2907

4 **HALHAM TARN(IRE),** b g Pennine Walk - Nouniya by Vayrann (D R C Elsworth) 2245¹ 2374⁴ 2471⁵

8 **HALKOPOUS,** b g Beldale Flutter (USA) - Salamina by Welsh Pageant (M H Tompkins) 1663² 1888⁴ 3025⁹ 3424

6 **HALL END LADY(IRE),** b m Tumble Wind (USA) - Avise La Fin by Scottish Rifle (J White) 1309⁶ 1688⁵ 2042 3630⁴

5 **HALLO MAM(IRE),** br m Tender King - Fruit Of Passion by High Top (O Brennan) 4364¹ 499⁸ 591 849¹ 972² 1143¹ 3924⁹ 4127⁴ 4167⁷

9 **HALLOW FAIR,** b h Wolver Hollow - Fingers by Lord Gayle (USA) (C A Horgan) 601⁷

5 **HAMANAKA(USA),** b m Conquistador Cielo (USA) - Tastefully (USA) by Hail To Reason (J Love) 519⁸ 644⁵ 1680⁵ 1788⁷ 1936⁷ 2498⁵ 2956³ 3429 3577⁶ 3906 4070

11 **HAMPER,** ch g Final Straw - Great Care by Home Guard (USA) (J W Dufosee) 4314⁹ 3768

6 **HAN LINE,** ch g Capricorn Line - Nine Hans by Prince Hansel (M J Coombe) 3386

10 **HAND OUT,** b m Spare A Dime - Stolen Ember by Burglar (R H Buckler) 954² 1411³ 1644⁶ 1696² 1879 2146⁶ 2427 3253⁸ 3532 3805⁶

4 **HANDMAIDEN,** gr f Shardari - Flyaway Bride (USA) by Blushing Groom (FR) (S G Norton) 2095¹ 2534¹

8 **HANDSOME HARVEY,** b g Push On - April Airs by Grey Mirage (H W Lavis) 4103

8 **HANDSOME NED,** br g Netherkelly - Beau Wonder by Veiled Wonder (USA) (D M Grissell) 861 1042³ 1599² 2192⁶ 2397² 2625³ 3148² 3697 3942⁴

5 **HANDY LASS,** b m Nicholas Bill - Mandrian by Mandamus (Mrs A Knight) 889² 1047¹ 1303¹ 1516² 1716¹ 1869⁷ 2655¹ 2801⁴

9 **HANDYFELLOW,** br g Strong Gale - Alsipola (FR) by Sigebert (A J McNamara) 3611¹ 3652 3888

7 **HANG A RIGHT,** b g Enchantment - Martina's Magic by Martinmas (P Mullins) 12⁹ 877⁶ 1174 1379⁴

8 **HANGOVER,** b or br g Over The River (FR) - Falcade by Falcon (R Lee) 1469³ 1844⁴ 2761² 3011 3232³ 3426⁵ 3492 3827⁴

11 **HAPPY BREED,** b g Bustino - Lucky Realm by Realm (M H Easterby) 1737² 2073 2962⁵ 3060

4 **HAPPY DAYS BLANCHE,** b g Never So Bold - Veronica Ann by Henbit (USA) (K A Morgan) 1290

8 **HAPPY DEAL,** b h Mon Cheval - Straight Look by Don't Look (B Preece) 2527 2794 3222 4021 4052 4104⁷

11 **HAPPY ELIZA,** b m Laurence O - Whipper Snapper by Menelek (James Joseph O'Connor) 22⁶ 72⁶ 116 134

10 **HAPPY HIGGINS,** b g Strong Gale - Quayville by Quayside (R K Aston) 3988

7 **HAPPY HORSE(NZ),** ch g Gaiter (NZ) - Silver Valley (NZ) by Retained (Mrs J Renfree-Barons) 1396⁹ 1711¹ 2034⁴ 2400² 2496¹ 2862² 2992² 3283¹ 3609¹ 3883¹

5 **HIGH BACCARAT,** ch g Formidable (USA) - By Surprise by Young Generation (A J Chamberlain) 2525 3184 3632 3725

7 **HIGH BARON,** gr g Baron Blakeney - High Finesse by High Line (R H Alner) 894¹ 1106 1347⁵ 1559³ 1888² 2267² 2595 2719³ 3025 3269¹ 3484⁴

7 **HIGH BEACON,** ch g High Line - Flaming Peace by Queen's Hussar (K C Bailey) 2208 3540³ 3714

7 **HIGH BURNSHOT,** br g Cardinal Flower - Andonian by Road House II (C Parker) 3179 3907

7 **HIGH CASTE,** ch g Carwhite - Brazen by Cash And Courage (Capt J Wilson) 339³

6 **HIGH GRADE,** b g High Top - Bright Sun by Mill Reef (USA) (Miss S J Wilton) 1072⁵ 1280³ 1462 1633¹ 2265⁴ 2507⁵ 2600²

8 **HIGH HAGBERG,** b g Cree Song - Persian Breakfast by Deep Diver (J R Jenkins) 1714 2064

8 **HIGH IDEALS,** b g Swan's Rock - British Queen by King's Leap (J S Cullen) 15

14 **HIGH IMP,** ch g Import - High Walk by Tower Walk (P Leach) 1275 2020

5 **HIGH MIND(FR),** br g Highest Honor (FR) - Gondolina (FR) by Vaguely Noble (Miss L C Siddall) 910⁴ 1010³ 1414² 2154³ 2356⁹ 2874¹ 3144 3542⁵ 3617⁶

4 **HIGH MOOD,** b g Jalmood (USA) - Copt Hall Princess by Crowned Prince (USA) (T R George) 2834 3113⁸

8 **HIGH PADRE,** b g The Parson - High Energy by Dalesa (J G FitzGerald) 921⁷ 1145¹ 1375⁴ 2246 2831³ 3168 3485 4128⁴

10 **HIGH PEAK,** ch g Prominer - Ardmayle by Raise You Ten (E J O'Grady) 1784⁵ 2125 2288¹ 3324 3659²

6 **HIGH PENHOWE,** ch m Ardross - Spritely by Charlottown (Mrs V A Aconley) 482⁶ 626² 717⁵ 2237² 2583³ 3061⁷

7 **HIGH STREET BLUES,** b g White Prince (USA) - Crendle Hill by French Beige (A B Coogan) 346 425 837⁵

5 **HIGH TONE(IRE),** ch g Orchestra - High Reign by Bahrain (J R Cox) 1681 1815² 2289

7 **HIGH WATER,** ch g High Line - Sextant by Star Appeal (A J Le Blond) 369

8 **HIGH-SPEC,** b g Strong Gale - Shine Your Light by Kemal (FR) (J E Kiely) 135 291⁹ 410 557⁸ 635 3551⁹ 3911⁴ 3955⁷ 4190³

8 **HIGHBABS,** b m Baptism - High Fi by High Hat (John J Walsh) 4397⁴ 21² 44⁴ 72⁴ 82² 134 250⁴ 327² 554² 1857⁹ 2036⁸ 2550 3200² 3873⁶ 3945⁶ 4150⁸

6 **HIGHBROOK(USA),** b m Alphabatim (USA) - Tellspot (USA) by Tell (USA) (M H Tompkins) 1559² 1755⁴ 2046 2689¹

6 **HIGHCLIFF HOTEL(IRE),** b f Asir - Erskine Melody by Melody Rock (F W Pennicott) 239⁹ 400⁹

5 **HIGHCLIFFE JESTER,** b g Jester - Canty Day by Canadel II (P Beaumont) 640 912 1097⁷

8 **HIGHFIELD PRINCE,** b g Prince Tenderfoot (USA) - Parler Mink by Party Mink (R O'Leary) 1143⁹ 1357⁹ 2321 3139⁴ 3357³ 3586⁴ 3865⁴ 4071⁴

10 **HIGHLAND BOUNTY,** b g High Line - Segos by Runnymede (Mrs M E Long) 3845⁶ 4096

7 **HIGHLAND BRAVE,** b g Crofter (USA) - Calling Bird by Warpath (J Colston) 2302 2790

5 **HIGHLAND BREEZE,** b g Green Ruby (USA) - Highland Rossie by Pablond (Ms Nicola FitzGerald) 338³

6 **HIGHLAND BRIDGE(IRE),** ch g Sallust - Break Of Day by On The Mark (R F Dalton) 1685

9 **HIGHLAND BUD,** b h Northern Dancer - Fleur D'Or by Exclusive Native (J Sheppard) 817²

11 **HIGHLAND ECHO,** b g Impecunious - Scotchemup by Raisin (Mrs John C Edwards) 2800 3501 4022⁴

5 **HIGHLAND FLAME,** ch g Dunbeath (USA) - Blakesware Saint by Welsh Saint (A G Blackmore) 551⁷ 1384² 1509⁶ 1930⁷ 2227⁵ 2343¹ 2645⁴ 3333 3543 3829

6 **HIGHLAND FRIEND,** ch g Highlands - Friendly Wonder by Be Friendly (F Watson) 1588 2117⁴ 2424⁶ 3235² 3568⁷ 3782

6 **HIGHLAND HEIGHTS(IRE),** b m Lomond (USA) - Climb The Heights (USA) by Majestic Light (USA) (C Smith) 2332⁸ 3347⁶ 3476⁹ 4075⁴

7 **HIGHLAND MINSTREL,** b f Black Minstrel - Quefort by Quayside (T F Lacy) 466⁸ 1330⁷ 1495 1764 1823 2921⁶

7 **HIGHLAND POACHER,** ch g Netherkelly - Spartiquick by Spartan General (D McCain) 848³ 1505⁶ 1774³ 2030³ 2458⁴ 2840² 3226 3758³ 3893⁵ 4124

7 **HIGHLAND RALLY(USA),** b g Highland Blade (USA) - Fast Trek (FR) by Trepan (FR) (M Avison) 3341² 3492 3621 3901² 4024³

7 **HIGHLAND RIVER,** b m Salmon Leap (USA) - Sigtrudis by Sigebert (T A K Cuthbert) 3431 3646⁵ 4050⁷ 4133⁴

13 **HIGHLAND SON,** b g Sunyboy - Highland Path by Jock Scot (Richard J Smith) 4315⁵ 3521⁹ 3948⁴ 4095⁶

6 **HIGHLAND SPIRIT,** ch m Scottish Reel - Salacious by Sallust (M C Pipe) 4388² 1051³ 2463¹ 2850⁴

4 **HIGHLAND SUNBEAM,** b g Barley Hill - Oaklands Sunbeam by Grand Roi (D Moffatt) 578⁸ 790⁷

5 **HIGHLAND SUPREME(IRE),** b g Supreme Leader - Right Love by Golden Love (Patrick G Kelly) 4406² 58⁹ 114⁶ 3792³ 3891

5 **HIGHLANDER(IRE),** b g Shernazar - Bonny Brae by Cure The Blues (USA) (P Aspell) 48² 95² 172¹

8 **HIGHLANDMAN,** b h Florida Son - Larne by Giolla Mear (J S Haldane) 1724 2007⁵ 2251 2565³ 2892⁴ 3129³ 3178⁵ 3474⁵

9 **HIGHLY DECORATED,** b g Sharpo - New Ribbons by Ribero (Mrs S J Smith) 1743⁴ 1861² 2242² 3356⁴ 3490⁶ 3585³ 3691⁴

4 **HIGHLY REPUTABLE(IRE),** ch g Persian Heights - Reputation by Tower Walk (M C Pipe) 2749 2834¹ 3042 3427 4139¹

7 **HIGHLY SUSPICIOUS,** b g Never Got A Chance - Annagh Delight by Saint Denys (Donal Hassett) 540⁵ 930¹

10 **HIGHRYMER,** gr m Rymer - On My Way by Town Crier (J Threadgall) 820 1060 1677⁵ 2069 3536

5 **HIGHWAY LAD,** b g Nearly A Hand - Hilda's Way by Royal Highway (R J Hodges) 3208

8 **HIGHWAY LASS,** br m Candy Cane - Highway Spark by Royal Highway (Gerard Cully) 1332 1496 1608⁸ 1857⁶ 2923⁹ 3198⁶ 3293

5 **HIGHWAYS DAUGHTER(IRE),** b m Phardante (FR) - Highway Mistress by Royal Highway (P Hughes) 4152⁵

10 **HILARION(FR),** br g Gay Mecene (USA) - Helvetie II by Klairon (D R Bloor) 2669⁷ 2875³ 3263⁵ 3385²

5 **HILARY'S IMAGE(IRE),** ch m Phardante (FR) - Hilarys Pet by Bon Noel (A J Martin) 3912 4113

5 **HILL OF TULLOW(IRE),** b or br g Roselier (FR) - Clonmeen Mist by Mugatpura (A J Kennedy) 331⁵ 530⁶ 692² 4152²

7 **HILL RANGER,** b m Love Tale - Corbally Supreme by Pitpan (W T Murphy) 65⁵ 103

INDEX TO NATIONAL HUNT RESULTS 1993-94

8 **HILL TRIX,** b g Le Moss - Up To Trix by Over The River (FR) (K Bishop) 1273 2654 2854¹ 3133⁴ 3364

6 **HILLHEAD PRINCE(IRE),** b g Young Grillo - West Park Hall by Garland Knight (James Nicholl) 491 675 808

4 **HILLSDOWN BOY(IRE),** ch g Dominion Royale - Lady Mary by Sallust (S Dow) 462²

5 **HILLTOP BAVARD(IRE),** b g Le Bavard (FR) - Chantecler by Sayyaf (John Joseph Murphy) 4399

6 **HILLTOWN(IRE),** b g Camden Town - Chaconia by Record Run (J H Johnson) 1959¹ 2585 2903 3285

5 **HILLTOWN BLUES,** gr g Le Solaret (FR) - Herminda by King Of Spain (T Dyer) 4299⁷ 2254 3553 4127

4 **HILLTOWN LADY(IRE),** ch f Be My Native (USA) - Another Tune by Red God (James Joseph O'Connor) 3971

8 **HILLWALK,** b g Croghan Hill - Bell Walks Fancy by Entrechat (R Curtis) 1248¹ 1393 1691³ 2596³ 2733 3192¹ 3309³ 3498⁴

7 **HINTERLAND,** ch g The Noble Player (USA) - Sevens Wild by Malinowski (USA) (Noel Meade) 24

5 **HINTON LADY,** b m Ilium - Lavender Rose by Beau Lavender (C Smith) 1215⁶ 1472⁵ 1620³ 2997 4027

5 **HIP HOP(IRE),** gr g Phardante (FR) - Iron Mermaid by General Ironside (Mrs S A Bramall) 1478⁶ 1787⁸ 2354⁶

8 **HIRAM B BIRDBATH,** b g Ragapan - At The King's Side (USA) by Kauai King (J A Glover) 371¹ 426¹ 523⁴ 679² 850 3186 3619 3904⁷

5 **HIS WAY(IRE),** br g His Turn - Bay Foulard by Shantung (Kevin Prendergast) 4357¹ 2⁴ 46⁵ 62¹ 118¹ 362² 392 432⁵ 471 1269 1400⁶ 1782 1818⁷ 3526 3710² 3935² 3957²

8 **HISTORY GRADUATE,** ch g Carlingford Castle - Muriel's Pet by Goldhill (A J McNamara) 4398¹ 6³

9 **HIT THE BOX,** ch g Quayside - Three Dieu by Three Dons (C R Beever) 3965

5 **HIT THE FAN,** b or br g Lear Fan (USA) - Embroglio (USA) by Empery (USA) (N A Twiston-Davies) 1747⁷ 1974⁴ 3215⁷

7 **HITCHIN A RIDE,** b g Dublin Taxi - Farmers Daughter by Red Slipper (M P Muggeridge) 1526⁷

5 **HIZAL,** b g Afzal - Hi Darlin' by Prince de Galles (H J Manners) 2546⁶ 2878⁵ 3009⁶ 3264 3632⁸ 3843⁷

8 **HO FRETTA,** b or br m Mandalus - Lefkara by Steeple Aston (Cecil Mahon) 364⁸ 512⁴ 806¹ 966⁶ 1158¹ 1268 1550⁸ 1830⁷ 3326

4 **HO-JOE(IRE),** b g Burslem - Walkyria by Lord Gayle (USA) (J M Carr) 1569⁸ 1920 2083⁹ 2135⁷ 2763¹ 2907¹

4 **HOAGY POKEY,** b g Uncle Pokey - L'ancressaan by Dalsaan (C Tinkler) 2332⁶ 2963⁵ 3589

4 **HOBBS(IRE),** b g Phardante (FR) - Merry Watt by Last Fandango (G A Pritchard-Gordon) 1244 1541⁴

9 **HOBBYS GIRL,** b m Straight Knight - Owen's Hobby by Owen Anthony (Mrs S C Bradburne) 4325

7 **HOBNOBBER,** br g True Song - Speakalone by Articulate (Mrs J H Docker) 2875⁶ 3096⁴

4 **HOD-MOD(IRE),** b g Digamist (USA) - Sallymiss by Tanfirion (Miss Z A Green) 2433⁹ 3542

7 **HODGESTOWN,** b f Cut Above - David's Pleasure by Welsh Saint (Neil S McGrath) 17⁹ 91 122

4 **HOHNE GARRISON,** b g Cragador - Chanita by Averof (J White) 1410⁸ 1705 4179⁴

11 **HOLCOMBE BILL,** b g Sovereign Bill - Holcombe Lady by Hardraw Scar (Miss J Du Plessis) 3768

6 **HOLD IM TIGHT,** b g Teamwork - Holdmetight by New Brig (R G Frost) 2796

5 **HOLD YOUR HAT ON,** ch g Celestial Storm (USA) - Thatched Grove by Thatching (C W Thornton) 1103⁷ 2741⁵ 3379² 3617⁵ 3800⁴ 3903⁶

7 **HOLD YOUR RANKS,** b g Ranksborough - Holdmetight by New Brig (R G Frost) 1542⁴ 1871¹ 2572⁴ 2991⁹

6 **HOLIDAY HOME,** ch g Monsanto (FR) - Holiday Hymn by Saintly Song (P Beaumont) 3347⁹ 3590⁹

5 **HOLIDAY ISLAND,** ch g Good Times (ITY) - Green Island by St Paddy (R Akehurst) 885⁶

5 **HOLLOW SOUND(IRE),** ch m Orchestra - Bells Hollow by Rarity (B V Kelly) 3201 3810 4031⁷ 4113⁸

6 **HOLLOW VISION(IRE),** b g Cataldi - Clonderlaw by Kalamoun (Michael Hourigan) 853

5 **HOLME LATER(IRE),** br m Fools Holme (USA) - Latin Guest by Be My Guest (USA) (Lady Sarah Barry) 174

10 **HOLTERMANN(USA),** b g Mr Prospector (USA) - Royal Graustark (USA) by Graustark (J G M O'Shea) 761¹ 1195¹ 1391² 2429 3172⁵ 3397⁵

9 **HOLY AWL,** b g Buckskin (FR) - Saint Audrey by Cracksman (G C Evans) 2526

12 **HOLY FOLEY,** b g The Parson - En Clair by Tarqogan (Miss S Pitman) 1275⁴ 1698 2656

6 **HOLY FOX(IRE),** ch g The Parson - Lucifer's Dream by Lucifer (USA) (M F Morris) 1496 1814⁸ 2607 3747 4116

12 **HOLY JOE,** b g The Parson - Doonasleen by Deep Run (A J Wilson) 1274 1438⁷ 1561 2009⁶ 2600⁴ 3136 3851¹

7 **HOLY MACKEREL,** ch g The Parson - Shallow Run by Deep Run (J Porter) 3195

5 **HOLY STING(IRE),** b g The Parson - Little Credit by Little Buskins (N A Twiston-Davies) 3169⁹ 3686⁶ 3855⁵

7 **HOLY WANDERER(USA),** b g Vaguely Noble - Bronzed Goddess (USA) by Raise A Native (D W P Arbuthnot) 1991⁴ 3068

5 **HOME COUNTIES(IRE),** ch g Ela Mana Mou - Safe Home by Home Guard (USA) (D Moffatt) 1034⁴ 1221² 1874² 2138² 2360¹ 2833⁷ 2994⁵ 3464⁴ 3736 4047²

12 **HOME COUNTY,** ch g Homing - Hants by Exbury (M P McNeill) 2554⁸ 3545

7 **HOME DOVE,** ch m Homeboy - Onaea by Prince de Galles (M E Sowersby) 3962⁶

4 **HOME PARK(IRE),** ch g Shernazar - Home Address by Habitat (Mrs S C Bradburne) 2122⁹ 2285⁷ 3557⁷ 3892⁵

4 **HOMEMAKER,** b f Homeboy - Ganadora by Good Times (ITY) (P G Murphy) 570⁴ 702¹

6 **HOMILE,** b g Homing - Rocas by Ile de Bourbon (USA) (G Fierro) 307⁹ 520² 592 748¹ 916

11 **HOMME D'AFFAIRE,** br g Lord Gayle (USA) - French Cracker by Klairon (R J O'Sullivan) 1041⁴ 1262 2318⁵ 2639¹ 3054¹ 3452³ 3828

8 **HONEST FRED,** br g Mandalus - Quayside Fairy by Quayside (J M Turner) 4002²

9 **HONEST WORD,** ch g Touching Wood (USA) - Amerella by Welsh Pageant (M C Pipe) 1842⁶ 2084¹ 2417¹ 2601¹ 2725¹ 3039

4 **HONEY GUIDE,** b c Hadeer - Diana's Bow by Great Nephew (R J Baker) 2016⁷ 2364³ 2522⁴ 3108⁵ 3340

7 **HONEY'S FORTUNE,** gr g Magic Mirror - Close To You by Nebbiolo (D R Tucker) 567⁹ 685

689

INDEX TO NATIONAL HUNT RESULTS 1993-94

9 **INCH LADY,** b m Bulldozer - Gayfield by Light Thrust (W J Burke) 539 928³

8 **INCH MAID,** b m Le Moss - Annie Augusta by Master Owen (W J Burke) 4405 22² 72¹ 116 509³ 583² 691² 906⁶

8 **INCHINA,** ch m Grey Ghost - Chinese Falcon by Skymaster (M F Barraclough) 3202

7 **INCONCLUSIVE,** b g Roselier (FR) - Kilbride Madam by Mandalus (Mrs S A Bramall) 2406 2764 3180 3443 3512⁵ 3602

4 **INDERRING ROSE,** br g Derring Rose - Whisky Lima by Midsummer Night II (W G Turner) 2021 3476

6 **INDESTRUCTIBLE(IRE),** ch g Duky - Chatty Actress by Le Bavard (FR) (Augustine Leahy) 3296¹ 3504³

10 **INDIAN JEWEL,** b g Arapaho - Daughterly by Tyrant (USA) (J R Jenkins) 3097 3510 3699

9 **INDIAN KNIGHT,** b g Kinglet - Indian Whistle by Rugantino (C A Green) 4374 3920 4103⁷

8 **INDIAN MAESTRO,** b g Music Maestro - Indian Wells by Reliance II (G F Edwards) 715⁶ 773 988 1187

7 **INDIAN ORCHID,** b m Warpath - Flower Child by Brother (Mrs M Reveley) 976⁵ 1215 2140

5 **INDIAN QUEST,** b g Rainbow Quest (USA) - Hymettus by Blakeney (N A Gaselee) 3269⁵

6 **INDIAN RIVER(IRE),** b g Indian King (USA) - Chaldea by Tamerlane (J G FitzGerald) 1582⁷ 1865⁷ 2413³

5 **INDIAN RUN(IRE),** b g Commanche Run - Excitingly (USA) by Val de L'orne (FR) (R J Hodges) 829 1012⁴

4 **INDIAN SECRET(IRE),** ch g Indian Forest (USA) - Pendle's Secret by Le Johnstan (Mrs V A Aconley) 1483 1584⁸

14 **INDIAN SHOT,** ch g Ete Indien (USA) - Tonophos by Bowsprit (J H Peacock) 1325

8 **INDIAN TONIC,** br g Ovac (ITY) - Green Hedge by Goldhill (N A Twiston-Davies) 956 1208² 1365¹ 1652⁶ 1881 2011⁵ 2460 2673² 3026⁴ 3405¹

6 **INDIANA GOLD(IRE),** b m Commanche Run - Golden Carrier by Homing (Norman Cassidy) 4113

4 **INFANTRY GLEN,** gr g Infantry - Rage Glen by Grey Mirage (G R Oldroyd) 2275 2381

6 **INFERRING,** b g Alleging (USA) - Be My Darling by Windjammer (USA) (J S Wainwright) 4385⁵ 582¹

5 **INGLETONIAN,** b g Doc Marten - Dreamy Desire by Palm Track (B E Wilkinson) 1494 1736⁵ 1959 3125³ 3617 3815⁶

6 **INK BY THE DRUM(USA),** ch h Salutely (USA) - Sharp Pencil (USA) by Olden Times (E J O'Grady) 293⁶ 377¹

5 **INKY,** b or br m Impecunious - Latanett by Dairialatan (G W Giddings) 3208 3457 3630

4 **INNER TEMPLE,** b g Shirley Heights - Round Tower by High Top (Capt T A Forster) 3457⁵

5 **INNOCENT GEORGE,** b g Hallgate - Are You Guilty by Runnett (Miss L C Siddall) 2581 2960 3125 3379³ 3539⁶ 3617⁹ 3757⁴ 4025¹ 4126⁷

4 **INNOCENT MAN(IRE),** gr g Neltino - Cry Of Truth by Town Crier (B V Kelly) 290⁸ 529⁸

4 **INNOCENT MAN,** gr g Neltino - Cry Of Truth by Town Crier (G A Cusack) 3993⁸ 4092⁵

7 **INNOCENT PRINCESS(NZ),** ch m Full Of Aces (NZ) - Kia Court (NZ) by Barcas (USA) (D H Barons) 219⁵ 3512² 3535

7 **INSPIRED GUESS(USA),** b g Robellino (USA) - Inspire (USA) by Tell (USA) (D A Nolan) 818

8 **INTEC(NZ),** b g· Sir Avon (NZ) - Ride The Storm (NZ) by Crest Of The Wave (W W Dennis) 4374

7 **INTEGRITY BOY,** b g Touching Wood (USA) - Powderhall by Murrayfield (R O'Leary) 767¹ 1057 1361⁴ 2256³ 2502² 3186⁵ 3344³ 3514 3603 3895⁹

4 **INTENTION(USA),** b c Shahrastani (USA) - Mimi Baker (USA) by What Luck (USA) (I Campbell) 2881³ 3095⁴

11 **INTERIM LIB,** b g Lighter - Ballinew by New Brig (Mrs S C Bradburne) 822⁶ 876⁴

9 **INTERPLAY,** ch g Be My Guest (USA) - Intermission by Stage Door Johnny (R J O'Sullivan) 3043 3309 3455⁸ 3943⁴ 4181³

6 **INTERROGATE,** b m In Fijar (USA) - Artipiar by Tyrant (USA) (R H Alner) 3543

7 **INTO THE FUTURE,** b g Mummy's Game - Valley Farm by Red God (A P Stringer) 4299³

10 **INTO THE RED,** ch g Over The River (FR) - Legal Fortune by Cash And Courage (J White) 2173³ 2460 3134 3425 3485⁶ 3821²

10 **INTO THE TREES,** b g Over The River (FR) - Diana's Flyer by Charlottesvilles Flyer (Michael D Abrahams) 4387⁶

5 **INTO THE WEST(IRE),** b or br g Roselier (FR) - Caherelly Cross by Royal Buck (T J Carr) 3489²

5 **INTREPID FORT,** gr g Belfort (FR) - Dauntless Flight by Golden Mallard (B W Murray) 1961⁶

7 **INTUITIVE JOE,** b g Petorius - Super Girl by Super Sam (R H Buckler) 216 260 416⁴

10 **INVASION,** b g Kings Lake (USA) - St Padina by St Paddy (O Brennan) 1144¹ 1375² 1565¹ 1732³ 2323⁵ 2406 3310¹ 3512³ 3828 4065¹

9 **INVERINATE,** b g Lomond (USA) - Major Concession by Major Portion (L Lungo) 759⁵ 819⁸ 909⁸ 974⁴ 1091³ 1184¹ 1477⁵ 1676¹ 1962

10 **INVERTIEL,** b g Sparkling Boy - Phyl's Pet by Aberdeen (P Monteith) 824⁹ 1127⁷ 1586

5 **INVISIBLE ARMOUR,** gr g Precocious - Haunting by Lord Gayle (USA) (P C Haslam) 339⁵ 622¹

2 **INVITATION CUP(IRE),** ch c Persian Heights - Often by Ballymore (D K Weld) 2868¹

12 **INVITE D'HONNEUR(NZ),** ch g Guest Of Honour (NZ) - Jillion's Joy (NZ) by Khan Sahib (C D Broad) 4345⁴ 659 970⁵ 1299⁹

5 **IOLARA(IRE),** br m Good Thyne (USA) - Le Idol by Le Bavard (FR) (M J Gilhooly) 3394 3653

7 **IPANEMA,** b m Auction Ring (USA) - Alta (FR) by Luthier (W Fennin) 1398 1981 2160⁸

6 **IRELANDS GALE(IRE),** b or br g Strong Gale - Killyhevlin by Green God (F Flood) 4382⁶ 4⁹ 49

5 **IRENE'S ROLFE,** b m Rolfe (USA) - Porto Irene by Porto Bello (D C Tucker) 2716⁶ 3019⁶

8 **IRIDOPHANES,** ch g Import - Grouse by March Past (Mrs P Robeson) 3824⁷

8 **IRISH BAY,** b g Derrylin - Sea Kestrel by Sea Hawk II (C R Egerton) 1544⁵ 1861 2223 2493² 2690³

7 **IRISH DITTY(USA),** ch g Irish River (FR) - Devon Ditty by Song (K A Morgan) 2360 2581

4 **IRISH DOMINION,** b g Dominion - Irish Cookie by Try My Best (USA) (P Leach) 147⁶ 352 4867 793⁷ 1517⁵ 1640⁷ 1931 3572³ 3915⁸

7 **IRISH FLASHER,** b g Exhibitioner - Miss Portal by St Paddy (J M Jefferson) 2870⁴ 3139⁵ 3568³ 3738 3895² 4131⁴

6 **IRISH FOUNTAIN(IRE),** b g Royal Fountain - Four In A Row by Cracksman (Michael J McDonagh) 4192⁷

8 **IRISH GENT,** br g Andretti - Seana Sheo by Seana Sgeal (P Cheesbrough) 756⁴ 1091⁵ 1862 2497⁵ 2784⁴ 2908⁴ 3059²

693

8 **IRISH GOSSIP,** br g Express Foto - Little Enda by Little Buskins (Miss Suzy Barkley) 4359 145

7 **IRISH GROOM,** b g Shy Groom (USA) - Romany Pageant by Welsh Pageant (J P Smith) 3597 3928

6 **IRISH LIGHT(IRE),** ch g Orchestra - Lets Cruise by Deep Run (Michael J McDonagh) 1555 3872⁶ 3972⁴ 4116⁹

6 **IRISH PEACE(IRE),** ch g Hold Your Peace (USA) - Tajniak (USA) by Irish River (FR) (Liam Browne) 2846

7 **IRISH PERRY,** b f Le Moss - Lady Bluebird by Arapaho (Martin Comber) 7⁶ 73⁴ 109 124

6 **IRISH ROVER(IRE),** ch g Chair Lift - Animalean by Beau Chapeau (Timothy O'Callaghan) 71⁶

5 **IRISH STAMP(IRE),** b g Niniski (USA) - Bayazida by Bustino (J Pearce) 1371² 1677³

7 **IRISH TAN,** br h Tanfirion - Anglesea Market by Sea Hawk II (A R Aylett) 1303 2196⁵ 2361 2523⁶ 3545⁵ 3682² 4064

8 **IRISH VELVET,** b g Ballacashtal (CAN) - Normandy Velvet by Normandy (R G Frost) 4373 152

5 **IRON BARON(IRE),** b g Sure Blade (USA) - Riverine (FR) by Riverman (USA) (Mrs V A Aconley) 597³ 771² 915¹

6 **IRON MARINER(IRE),** b or br m Mandalus - Mariners Chain by Walshford (Michael McCullagh) 3468 3710⁸ 3840⁵ 3973⁴ 4093¹

4 **IS SHE QUICK,** ch f Norwick (USA) - Get Involved by Shiny Tenth (Mrs P N Dutfield) 570⁷ 1125⁶ 1338³ 1410⁴ 1640⁵ 3395⁸ 3572⁵

7 **ISABEAU,** b m Law Society (USA) - Elodie (USA) by Shecky Greene (USA) (K A Morgan) 1462⁹ 1863¹ 2273³ 2528 3136³ 3376⁴

5 **ISAIAH,** gr g Bellypha - Judeah by Great Nephew (Mrs J Cecil) 2621² 2762¹ 3499³ 3898¹

7 **ISAMBARD,** b g Star Appeal - Mertola by Tribal Chief (John R Upson) 3592

6 **ISHRAAQ(USA),** ch g Alydar (USA) - Water Lilly (FR) by Riverman (USA) (R Akehurst) 4331²

7 **ISIPINGO,** b g Pitskelly - Nemoralis by Great White Way (USA) (Mrs L C Jewell) 1621

5 **ISLAND BLADE(IRE),** b g Sure Blade (USA) - Queen's Eyot by Grundy (R Akehurst) 1729⁹

8 **ISLAND FOREST(USA),** ch h Green Forest (USA) - Bonnie Isle by Pitcairn (P F Nicholls) 311¹ 404² 464² 712⁵ 962¹ 1140³ 1411⁶ 3544⁵ 3742¹

9 **ISLAND GALE,** br g Strong Gale - Island Varra by Deep Run (D McCune) 1669³ 1941² 2105¹ 2355³ 2499³ 2733⁷ 3463⁶ 3644

8 **ISLAND JETSETTER,** ch g Tolomeo - Baridi by Ribero (Mrs S J Smith) 4332⁵ 676⁴ 946⁴ 1132¹ 1285⁴ 1409² 1583

6 **ISLAND JEWEL,** ch g Jupiter Island - Diamond Talk by Counsel (J R Bosley) 1443⁴ 1521² 1721² 2044⁴ 2306² 2507³ 2697¹ 2734³ 3028

6 **ISLAND RIVER(IRE),** ch g Over The River (FR) - Diana's Flyer by Charlottesvilles Flyer (J L Goulding) 1736⁶ 1938⁸ 3778

5 **ISLAND ROW(IRE),** br g Buckskin (FR) - Sharon's Pet by Raise You Ten (Michael Hourigan) 1821⁹ 2199 2607

4 **ISLAND SHADOW(IRE),** ch f Nearly A Nose (USA) - Book Choice by North Summit (John A White) 3971

4 **ISLAND VISION(IRE),** b c Vision (USA) - Verandah by Jaazeiro (USA) (Kevin Prendergast) 1377⁶ 1432⁸ 1846⁸

4 **ISLANDOO(IRE),** ch f Convinced - Ascot Princess by Prince Hansel (Ms Rosemary Rooney) 3616⁸ 3842⁴

6 **ISN'T THAT NICE(IRE),** b g Delamain (USA) - Rescue Run by Laurence O (J H Scott) 801⁶ 908² 993 1760⁴ 1833 2278 2586 2658⁵ 2983 3506⁹ 3711 4031³

8 **ISOBAR,** b g Another Realm - Lady Eton by Le Dieu D'Or (Michael Mullineaux) 3161⁴ 3989⁸

7 **ISSYIN,** ch g Oats - Spiders Web by Big Deal (M W Easterby) 1358⁵ 1735² 1960¹ 2357² 2489² 2584 3356² 3438⁴

13 **IT'S A PRY,** b g Pry - Clogga Girl by Levanter (Mrs E Moscrop) 478³ 564⁵ 759⁷ 2451

9 **IT'S AFTER TIME,** b g Newski (USA) - Lavenanne by Tacitus (Mrs R Brackenbury) 1547 1805³ 3207 3631⁸

7 **IT'S CONFIDENTIAL(NZ),** ch g State Of Kings (USA) - Kind Thought (NZ) by Greek God (D H Barons) 1622 1871⁴ 2144

8 **IT'S DELICIOUS,** b m Idiot's Delight - Bellardita by Derring-Do (Mrs T D Pilkington) 1414⁵ 1645³ 3685 3878

6 **IT'S NOT MY FAULT(IRE),** b g Red Sunset - Glas Y Dorlan by Sexton Blake (D J Wintle) 859⁸ 1299³ 1603 1719² 1801² 2058¹ 2530³ 2729³ 3003²

7 **IT'S THE PITS,** b g Tender King - Pithead by High Top (L Lungo) 1614¹ 1728³ 2222 2815³ 2974³ 3578¹

10 **IT'S VARADAN,** ch h Rabdan - Miss Casanova by Galivanter (Miss H C Knight) 3853 4141⁹

14 **ITALIAN TOUR,** ch g Coliseum - Follow Me by Guide (Mrs G S Plowright) 1238⁶ 1485 1812 2894

10 **ITS A CRACKER,** b g Over The River (FR) - Bob's Hansel by Prince Hansel (J A Berry) 1233¹ 1381⁵ 1553² 1763² 1895⁶ 2125 2987³ 3134² 3425 3649

8 **ITS A DEAL,** b g Lochnager - J J Caroline by Track Spare (S I Pittendrigh) 3031

9 **ITS A SNIP,** ch g Monksfield - Snipkin by Straight Lad (T M Walsh) 2036⁹ 2235⁸ 2619⁶ 2924⁴ 3272⁴ 3655⁸

10 **ITS ALL OVER NOW,** b g Martinmas - Devon Lark by Take A Reef (Mrs A L M King) 4377⁷ 297¹ 344¹ 418² 1127⁵ 1592 2653⁹

5 **ITS GRAND,** b g Sula Bula - Light Of Zion by Pieces Of Eight (R J Manning) 901 1169 1542

11 **ITS NEARLY TIME,** br g Newski (USA) - Lavenanne by Tacitus (Mrs R Brackenbury) 1752³ 1933¹ 2205³ 3172³ 3268⁴

8 **ITS ONLY JUSTICE,** b g Hays - Tolaytala by Be My Guest (USA) (M Halford) 3712 4010 4145

4 **ITS UNBELIEVABLE,** ch g Kalaglow - Avon Royale by Remainder (J White) 247¹ 296⁴ 570⁵ 702⁷ 3716¹ 4174¹

5 **ITS YOUR CHOICE(IRE),** b m Cataldi - Ramblers Choice by Run The Gantlet (USA) (P Beirne) 363⁹

7 **ITSUPTOME VI,** b g Not To Worry - Gay Cantella Vii by Cantab (L W Doran) 2773⁵

8 **ITYFUL,** gr g Bellypha - Tants by Vitiges (FR) (B E Wilkinson) 911⁶

6 **IVE CALLED TIME,** b g Sergeant Drummer (USA) - Alice Rairthorn by Romany Air (Mrs R Brackenbury) 2021⁸ 3170⁷ 3421 3632⁶

8 **IVEAGH HOUSE,** b g Be My Guest (USA) - Waffles by Wollow (D Nicholson) 1991⁵ 2734² 2883⁶ 3455³ 3516 3736 3831

8 **IVEAGH LAD,** br g Irish Star - Lady McQuaid by Mick McQuaid (Miss J Sawney) 2782 3799¹ 3992²

5 **IVOR'S FLUTTER,** b g Beldale Flutter (USA) - Rich Line by High Line (D R C Elsworth) 1010⁸ 1442⁹ 1643⁸ 1992⁵ 2851² 3038

7 **IVORLINE,** ch g Pollerton - Lady In Red by Royal Buck (O O'Neill) 2014 2303

4 **IVORY HUTCH,** b c Nomination - Gitee (FR) by Carwhite (J S Moore) 604⁷ 793⁴ 1049⁹ 1188

4 **IVY EDITH,** b f Blakeney - Royal Birthday by St Paddy (T G Mills) 2269⁹ 2444² 4172¹

8 **IVY GLEN,** ch m Floriferous - Dame Of St John (F B McGrath) 967 3732

6 **IVY HOUSE(IRE),** b g Orchestra - Gracious View by Sir Herbert (J J O'Neill) 976⁷ 1199² 1406 1502⁸ 1745¹ 2008¹ 2172 2500² 2766

8 **IVYCHURCH(USA),** ch g Sir Ivor - Sunday Purchase (USA) by T V Lark (J Joseph) 687³ 957³ 1136³ 1456⁴ 1718⁵ 3509 3696⁵ 3886 3970⁶ 4064⁴

5 **IZACOMIN(IRE),** b m Ovac (ITY) - Swan Girl by My Swanee (D P Geraghty) 3451 3637⁸

5 **IZITALLWORTHIT,** b m My Dad Tom (USA) - Torlonia by Royal Palace (J Mackie) 524

7 **J BRAND,** b g Persian Bold - Napa Valley by Wolver Hollow (R J Hodges) 2697⁶ 2781⁷ 3020⁵

5 **J J JACKSON(IRE),** b g Strong Statement (USA) - Proud Actress by Pry (Martin Michael Lynch) 2869

10 **J J JIMMY,** b g Lochnager - J J Caroline by Track Spare (S Christian) 1641⁴ 2047

6 **J P MORGAN,** b or br g Law Society (USA) - Queen Of The Brush by Averof (M P Naughton) 912⁴ 1357⁵ 1485⁶ 1961² 2070² 2243³ 2580² 2740⁵

7 **J R JONES,** b g Blakeney - Bonne Baiser by Most Secret (Mrs A R Hewitt) 428⁵ 632⁴ 839⁷ 970⁹

8 **J-TEC BOY,** gr g Orange Reef - Fotostar by Polyfoto (Thomas Kinane) 4408 47⁴ 106⁹ 133⁹ 3955 4190

10 **JAAEZ,** b g Ela-Mana-Mou - Almagest by Dike (USA) (Jon Trice-Rolph) 2456

7 **JACINTA'S BOY,** gr g Roselier (FR) - Longorchard by Linacre (J H Scott) 1609⁷ 1764 1987⁴ 2098⁶

4 **JACK A HOY,** b g Son Of Shaka - Angie's Darling by Milford (R Brotherton) 3208 3832

8 **JACK DANDY,** b g Roi Guillaume (FR) - Give Us A Breeze by Brave Invader (USA) (Mark Jeffrey Millar) 3813⁸

6 **JACK DIAMOND,** ch g Seven Hearts - Barlinnie Blossom by Broadmoor (Mrs R Williams) 983 3043

5 **JACK DREAMING(IRE),** b g Supreme Leader - Dishcloth by Fury Royal (G B Balding) 2509

14 **JACK OF CLUBS,** b g Kinglet - Laughing Stock by Woodcut (Miss Tina Hammond) 3181⁴ 3867⁷

8 **JACK SOUND,** b g Mister Lord (USA) - Dale Road by Le Tricolore (H W Lavis) 3920²

11 **JACK THE HIKER,** b g Rare One - Royal Dress by Perspex (Mrs J G Retter) 154¹ 220³ 385

5 **JACK'S BAR(IRE),** b g Supreme Leader - Jukebox Katie by Jukebox (Eugene M O'Sullivan) 530 692

10 **JACK'S BARN,** b h St Columbus - Dane Hole by Past Petition (J R Bosley) 628⁶ 737⁵

9 **JACKI'S DREAM,** b m Proverb - Cloneen Lady by Master Owen (Gerard Cully) 170

8 **JACKS ARMY,** b g Riot Helmet - Eva Dodd by Orchardist (M P Naughton) 2409

6 **JACKSON FLINT,** b g Nishapour (FR) - Scamperdale by French Beige (T Thomson Jones) 2528⁴ 2778³

6 **JACKSON SQUARE(IRE),** b g Prince Tenderfoot (USA) - Double Habit by Double Form (P R Rodford) 216⁵

4 **JACKSONS BAY,** b g Creetown - Siblette by Persepolis (FR) (R Rowe) 1244⁸ 1885 2275⁶ 2969

4 **JADE SHOON,** b g Green Shoon - Milparinka by King's Equity (J I A Charlton) 1484

6 **JADIDH,** b m Touching Wood (USA) - Petrol by Troy (C P Wildman) 2067⁴ 2131³ 2496²

4 **JAFETICA,** gr f Kalaglow - Rashah by Blakeney (D R Laing) 379 406

6 **JAFFAPPEAL(IRE),** b g Bishop Of Orange - Prairie Stream by Paddy's Steam (J E Mulhern) 3394⁴ 3733

7 **JAILBREAKER,** ch g Prince Of Peace - Last Farewell by Palm Track (B R Millman) 1274² 1520³ 1870² 2416¹ 2648¹ 2861³ 3172 3349² 3633²

7 **JALINGO,** ch g Jalmood (USA) - Linguistic by Porto Bello (P J Makin) 1709 1956 2734¹ 2933⁷ 3100⁴

8 **JALMUSIQUE,** ch g Jalmood (USA) - Rose Music by Luthier (M H Easterby) 915³ 1114⁸

5 **JALORE,** gr g Jalmood (USA) - Lorelene (FR) by Lorenzaccio (S Coathup) 130¹ 197³ 259⁵ 626⁸ 737⁴ 1067

10 **JAMES GIRL,** b f Fidel - Newpark Girl by Lion (Michael Mellett) 4358 1038⁸ 3693⁸ 3812 3944

6 **JAMES IS SPECIAL(IRE),** b g Lyphard's Special (USA) - High Explosive by Mount Hagen (FR) (H J Collingridge) 2646⁵ 2828

14 **JAMES MY BOY,** ch g Jimmy Reppin - College Brief by Lucky Brief (W Clay) 1923² 2639 2836⁶ 2926³ 3223

7 **JAMES PIGG,** b g Lord Ha Ha - Bank Strike by Even Money (David A Kiely) 4370⁷ 44³ 767 134 214⁴ 332⁴ 509⁴ 4150

6 **JAMES THE FIRST,** ch g Wolver Heights - Juliette Mariner by Welsh Pageant (P F Nicholls) 651³ 750³ 958⁵ 1298² 1505² 1947

6 **JAMESTOWN BOY,** b g King Of Clubs - Jhansi Ki Rani (USA) by Far North (CAN) (B Preece) 4393² 226² 370⁴ 447² 662³ 839² 1072¹

10 **JAN-RE,** ch g Deep Run - Khalketta by Khalkis (F Murphy) 2132

6 **JANE'S AFFAIR,** b m Alleging (USA) - Blue Jane by Blue Cashmere (Mrs A Swinbank) 2152 2581

8 **JANET SCIBS,** b m Dubassoff (USA) - Luckley Brake by Quiet Fling (USA) (N G Ayliffe) 1272 1468⁴ 1707 2421⁷ 2841 3051³ 3253⁵ 3713²

9 **JANUARY DON,** b h Hold Your Peace (USA) - Meg's Pride by Sparkler (J S Warner) 4392 3948⁵

4 **JANZOE(IRE),** ch f Phardante (FR) - Roof Garden by Thatch (USA) (A P O'Brien) 3246

4 **JAPACADA,** b g Celtic Cone - Bird's Custard by Birdbrook (S Mellor) 2996⁹ 3227⁵

7 **JARROW LAD,** b g Lochnager - Domino Smith by White Speck (A J Le Blond) 3539

6 **JARRWAH,** ch m Niniski (USA) - Valiancy by Grundy (J L Spearing) 1772 2067¹ 2131² 2544⁶ 2862⁵

6 **JARZON DANCER,** br g Lidhame - Long Valley by Ribero (D A Wilson) 4331⁵ 465³

4 **JASON'S BOY,** b g Librate - Misty Glen by Leander (J M Bradley) 3079⁹ 3458

4 **JASPER ONE,** b g Jalmood (USA) - First Pleasure by Dominion (R D E Woodhouse) 790⁸ 1408⁷ 1767 2083²

4 **JASSU,** br g Strong Gale - Princess Charmere by Tepukei (J E Kiely) 2755¹ 3324⁸ 3933¹ 4168¹

5 **JATHAAB(IRE),** b g Ajdal (USA) - Etoile de Nuit by Troy (I Campbell) 4383²

4 **JATINGA(IRE),** b m Bulldozer - Lady Talisman by Continuation (J F C Maxwell) 804⁵ 1016⁴ 2023⁴

8 **JAUNTY GIG,** b g Dunphy - Hazel Gig by Captain's Gig (USA) (J J Birkett) 3927⁹ 4074⁴ 4134²

INDEX TO NATIONAL HUNT RESULTS 1993-94

7 **KELLY'S PEARL,** br m Miner's Lamp - Gallant Blade by Fine Blade (USA) (A P O'Brien) 2682² 2986 3199⁷

8 **KELLYMOUNT,** b g Strong Gale - Serenade Lady by Pry (W P Mullins) 2158² 2278 2607 2940 4192

7 **KEMALS DELIGHT,** ch m Kemal (FR) - Sheena's Delight by Whistling Top (C D Broad) 1948⁷ 2118⁸ 3478² 3751⁵

7 **KEMMY DARLING,** b m Kemal (FR) - Dream Away by Dusky Boy (M P Muggeridge) 593 774⁶ 1107 1527 1700 2344³ 2558 2799⁷ 3337³ 3917

6 **KENILWORTH(IRE),** b g Kemal (FR) - Araglin Dora by Green Shoon (J G FitzGerald) 1406² 3620⁶

6 **KENILWORTH LAD,** br g Ring Bidder - Lucky Joker by Cawston's Clown (Mrs M Reveley) 721² 869² 1099² 2106² 2262² 2447² 2970¹ 3126¹ 3359² 3472⁴ 4090¹

7 **KENMAC,** ch g Golden Love - Coquito by Go Match (Michael Hourigan) 10³ 43 79³ 97⁴ 120⁶ 173⁶ 302³ 527

7 **KENMORE-SPEED,** gr g Scallywag - Quick Exit by David Jack (Mrs S J Smith) 1133¹ 1548² 1736¹ 1872⁵ 2871⁴ 3023 3284¹

9 **KENNEL HILL,** b g Dunphy - Zameen (FR) by Armistice III (W P Mullins) 4369

4 **KENNINGTON KUWAIT,** ch g Bairn (USA) - Mylotta by Hotfoot (R T Juckes) 2407 3833

4 **KENNINGTON PROTON,** br f Interrex (CAN) - Supper Party by He Loves Me (R T Juckes) 193⁶ 1049 1522

9 **KENTISH PIPER,** br g Black Minstrel - Toombeola by Raise You Ten (N A Gaselee) 615⁴ 842⁵ 1162 2174¹ 2598¹ 3041⁹ 3405²

4 **KEPPOLS HARRIER(IRE),** b or br g Phardante (FR) - Keppols by Furry Glen (Norman Cassidy) 3793 3993

7 **KEPPOLS PRINCE,** b or br h Kampala - Keppols by Furry Glen (John Houghton) 136 123⁹ 1234⁷ 1765³ 1894⁸ 2079 2279⁹ 3654

9 **KERFONTAINE,** b m Lafontaine (USA) - Kero Code by Straight Lad (P Mullins) 938⁵ 1235⁴ 1380 1580⁶ 1851⁶ 1980⁵ 2078⁸

4 **KERKY(IRE),** ch g Stalker - Blinky by Salvo (Martyn J McEnery) 2663⁹ 2868⁶ 4078

5 **KERMESINA(IRE),** b m Lancastrian - Little Quince by Laurence O (J S Cullen) 3469⁹

5 **KERNEL GRAIN(IRE),** b g Double Schwartz - Weavers' Tack by Weavers' Hall (D Moffatt) 2373⁵ 2573 3459 3674⁵ 3907⁶

8 **KERRY HILL,** ch g Scallywag - Katie Fare by Ritudyr (R B Davies) 3335

7 **KERRY MY HOME,** ch g Le Moss - Sno-Sleigh by Bargello (B J Curley) 3441

8 **KERRY TO CLARE,** gr m Step Together (USA) - Creagh by Sky Boy (T M Gibson) 2583 3177 4050⁸

4 **KERRYHEAD GIRL(IRE),** b or br f Be My Native (USA) - Dedham Vale by Dike (USA) (Patrick Joseph Flynn) 2663⁴ 3250² 3616¹

10 **KERRYS EYE,** b g Gladden - Swinging Time (P R Rodford) 3361 3575

4 **KESANTA,** b f The Dissident - Nicaline by High Line (W G M Turner) 128²

5 **KESS(IRE),** b m Kafu - Joanns Goddess by Godswalk (USA) (W T Bourke) 638³ 1039 3712

7 **KETFORD BRIDGE,** ch g Hardboy - Unsinkable Sarah by Mon Capitaine (R Dickin) 2204 2404 3110 3758⁴ 3827⁶

9 **KETTI,** br m Hotfoot - Nigrel by Sovereign Path (D L Williams) 1513⁶ 1667⁵ 1947 2146⁵ 2251³ 2458³ 2693⁶ 2851⁵ 3135 3426² 3614⁶ 3823⁴ 3960⁶

6 **KEV'S LASS(IRE),** ch m Kemal (FR) - Nelly's Dream by Over The River (FR) (G A Hub-

bard) 591⁸ 750⁷ 849⁸ 981 1491⁴ 1631³ 1836³ 2293³ 2417 2668 2733 2879⁹

7 **KEY DEAR(FR),** ch g Darly (FR) - Keep Happy (FR) by Red Vagabonde (R T Juckes) 181³ 226⁵ 307⁸ 485⁶ 549 1071 1149² 1427⁴ 3751⁸ 3926

5 **KEY WEST(IRE),** b g Hard Fought - Twaddle II by Tim Tam (Patrick Mooney) 3⁴ 39⁴ 1762 2024 2309⁹ 2465⁹ 2775¹ 3276⁶ 3448⁵ 3793³

5 **KEYLU,** b m Sula Bula - Key Biscayne by Deep Run (G W Giddings) 3114⁴ 3543

6 **KHAKI LIGHT,** b g Lighter - Blue Speckle by Tom Noddy (M J Charles) 1354⁷ 3009 3191

5 **KHALIDI(IRE),** b g Shernazar - Khaiyla by Mill Reef (USA) (D R Gandolfo) 705¹ 809 964³ 1085² 1341 3549² 3767⁵ 4021⁴

5 **KHALLOOF(IRE),** b g Ballad Rock - Tapiola by Tap On Wood (Denys Smith) 1202

4 **KHARASAR(IRE),** b g Standaan (FR) - Khatima by Relko (Anthony Mullins) 2614³ 2864¹ 3246² 3656⁵ 3732¹ 3836⁶ 3973¹

10 **KHATTAF,** b g Kris - Hanna Alta (FR) by Busted (K Cumings) 3480⁴ 3918³

6 **KHAZARI(USA),** ch g Shahrastani (USA) - Kozana by Kris (R Brotherton) 4305⁶ 2⁸ 63⁶ 493⁴ 805⁶ 3020¹ 3398⁴ 3561⁴ 4054⁵

7 **KHOJOHN,** ch g Chief Singer - Pirate Lass (USA) by Cutlass (USA) (Mrs V A Aconley) 222⁷ 3802⁶

7 **KHULM,** b g Kafu - Little Wild Duck by Great Heron (USA) (R Evans) 574

8 **KIARA DEE,** b m Bulldozer - Nice One Jackie by Prince Tenderfoot (USA) (P J Deegan) 104⁹ 234⁴ 265⁶ 503⁹

5 **KIBBY BANK,** gr g Pragmatic - Alcide Inn by Alcide (J H Johnson) 3284

7 **KIBREET,** ch g Try My Best (USA) - Princess Pageant by Welsh Pageant (R H Alner) 1348⁵ 1525¹ 1947¹ 2087³ 2511³ 3024 3194³ 3303⁵ 3513² 3847³ 3979² 4105⁴

5 **KICK ON MAJESTIC(IRE),** b g Mister Majestic - Avebury Ring by Auction Ring (USA) (N Bycroft) 244⁷

8 **KICKALONG,** b m Taufan (USA) - Green Idol by Green God (Liam McAteer) 4306⁶ 39³ 61³ 343¹ 476³

7 **KICKING BIRD,** b m Bold Owl - Sodina by Saulingo (K C Bailey) 524⁹ 715⁵ 883³ 1252⁴ 2042

7 **KIL KIL CASTLE,** ch g Carlingford Castle - Miss Pooh by Deep Run (P J Healy) 4338⁵ 18³ 894 1775 507 690 1499⁷ 2100⁵ 2618⁹ 2922 3200⁶ 4042³

5 **KILADANTE(IRE),** b m Phardante (FR) - Marble Cloud by Hard Tack (A P O'Brien) 292¹ 476¹ 1076⁷ 1903³ 2080¹

7 **KILARA,** b g Pollerton - Misty Boosh by Tarboosh (USA) (Michael O'Connor) 3791² 3888²

4 **KILBRICKEN DANCER(IRE),** br f Lord Chancellor (USA) - Arcticmars by Arctic Chevalier (G T Hourigan) 3245 3552⁹ 3842

4 **KILBRICKEN MAID(IRE),** b f Meneval (USA) - Kilbricken Bay by Salluceva (Derek O'Keeffe) 3245⁸

7 **KILBRICKEN STAR,** b m Mandalus - Kilbricken Bay by Salluceva (Derek O'Keeffe) 618¹

4 **KILCARBERY(IRE),** b f Mandalus - Miss Dunbrody by Le Prince (W P Mullins) 2663⁵ 2943⁸ 3245⁷ 3372 3971⁵

6 **KILCASH(IRE),** b g Salmon Leap (USA) - Roblanna by Roberto (USA) (P R Hedger) 1559⁶ 1755³ 1842² 2079 3269⁹ 3422

12 **KILCLOONEY FORREST,** b g King's Equity - Carrig-An-Neady by Orchardist (Mrs S J Smith) 727

7 **KILCOLGAN,** ch g Le Bavard (FR) - Katula by Khalkis (Mrs J D Goodfellow) 1723 2103⁴ 2809⁵ 2952⁵ 3599⁵

7 **KILDERIHEEN,** ch g Le Bavard (FR) - Meneleck Queen by Menelek (Michael J O'Connor) 903⁷

14 **KILDIMO,** b g Le Bavard (FR) - Leuze by Vimy (Mrs S J Smith) 1789

8 **KILDOWNEY HILL,** b g Kemal (FR) - Nadine's Pride by Double Jay (J J O'Neill) 139⁵ 455² 660² 2325⁴ 2764

6 **KILFINNY CROSS(IRE),** ch g Mister Lord (USA) - Anvil Chorus by Levanter (Miss C Saunders) 2669¹ 2885¹ 3216 3951²

8 **KILGARIFF,** ch g Le Bavard (FR) - Negrada by Nelcius (R A Fahey) 2243¹ 2403⁶ 3028³ 3408 3622³

11 **KILHALLON CASTLE,** b g Town And Country - Castell Memories by Tacitus (G M Moore) 449² 579³

11 **KILIAN MY BOY,** b g Green Shoon - My Puttens by David Jack (Patrick G Kelly) 69⁸ 123 135 254² 376⁵ 410² 557⁵ 689¹ 854¹ 927⁵

12 **KILKILMARTIN,** b g Rarity - Kilkilwell by Harwell (H J Manners) 521⁶ 960

5 **KILLANNA LASS(IRE),** b m Bishop Of Orange - Hilarys Mark by On Your Mark (T J O'Mara) 3791⁷ 3956

12 **KILLBANON,** b g Imperius - Flail by Hill Gail (C C Trietline) 661³ 1083⁷ 1302 3260⁵

6 **KILLEEN COUNTESS(IRE),** b m Torus - Gay Countess by Master Buck (Edward P Mitchell) 4409 41 71 327⁵ 475⁶

12 **KILLELAN LAD,** br g Kambalda - Dusky Glory by Dusky Boy (D F Bassett) 682⁷

8 **KILLESHIN,** bl g Al Sirat (USA) - Spin Off by Wrekin Rambler (H J Manners) 2482 2889¹ 3155¹ 3412¹

7 **KILLIMOR LAD,** b g Tina's Pet - Jeldi by Tribal Chief (G T Lynch) 2918 3243⁹ 3291 3789 3872 4034⁶

5 **KILLINEY GAYLE(IRE),** b m Lancastrian - Killiney Lady by Lord Gayle (USA) (W P Mullins) 3124³ 3250⁵ 3469⁸ 4152⁴

8 **KILLINEY GRADUATE,** b g Wolverlife - Kilima by Mount Hagen (FR) (F Lennon) 831⁹ 940³ 1382 1552³ 1847

6 **KILLINISKY(IRE),** ch g Decent Fellow - Shady Tree by Three Wishes (A P O'Brien) 4400⁷ 469⁶ 536

5 **KILLONE ABBOT(IRE),** ch g The Parson - Outdoor Girl by Blue Chariot (J A B Old) 2339² 2677³ 3042⁵

7 **KILLOSKEHAN QUEEN,** b m Bustineto - Diana Harwell by Harwell (L Young) 4343 2616 3466⁷ 3550³ 3811¹ 3944⁹

5 **KILSHANDRA(IRE),** b m Heraldiste (USA) - Gulistan by Sharpen Up (Mrs Barbara Waring) 2414

8 **KILLTUBBER HOUSE,** ch g Deep Run - Astrella Celeste by Menelek (R Lee) 2762⁵ 3008⁹ 3315⁶ 3682⁸

7 **KILLULA CHIEF,** b g Strong Gale - Lolos Run Vii (J G M O'Shea) 4344² 168³ 223¹ 286¹ 436¹ 566¹ 661 813¹ 2368¹ 2576¹ 3039

6 **KILLURA(IRE),** b g Royal Fountain - Hill Side Glen by Goldhill (K C Bailey) 2295⁶ 3215³ 3340⁸

4 **KILLY'S FILLY,** b f Lochnager - May Kells by Artaius (USA) (J M Bradley) 2857

5 **KILLYMADDY(IRE),** ch m Boyne Valley - Sing Song Girl (Mrs S C Bradburne) 273

7 **KILMACREW,** br g Bulldozer - Chartreuse by Ionian (J G Cosgrave) 81

5 **KILMESSAN JUNCTION(IRE),** b g Fine Blade (USA) - Another Cirrus by Laurence O (C W Thornton) 2490

7 **KILMINFOYLE,** b g Furry Glen - Loreto Lady by Brave Invader (USA) (Mrs M Reveley) 639² 770² 1060⁶ 2252 2358⁷ 2561⁴

6 **KILMOUNTAIN DAWN(IRE),** b m Kemal (FR) - Andy's Pet by Laurence O (P D FitzGerald) 15

7 **KILMOYLER,** b g Fidel - Connor's Queen by Avocat (Daniel O'Connell) 2278

8 **KILMYSHALL,** b h Hard Fought - Run Swift (J T Gifford) 2535⁹ 3724 4097⁴

10 **KILN COPSE,** b g Celtic Cone - Blast's Queen by Blast (P R Chamings) 3860¹

4 **KILNAMARTYRA GIRL,** b f Arkan - Star Cove by Porto Bello (J Parkes) 3347 3832

8 **KILSHANNON SPRINGS,** b g Palm Track - Khotso by Alcide (A L T Moore) 108¹ 158⁴ 807

11 **KILSHEELAN LAD,** ch g Kambalda - Lady Ashton by Anthony (H W Lavis) 44 3950³

7 **KILTONGA,** b or br g Indian King (USA) - Miss Teto by African Sky (P Leach) 1087⁶ 1274 1427 3533 3769

4 **KIMANICKY(IRE),** b g Phardante (FR) - Kitty Frisk by Prince Tenderfoot (USA) (D P Kelly) 2290⁶ 3124⁴ 3372⁹

4 **KIMBERLEY BOY,** b g Mtoto - Diamond House by Habitat (G F H Charles-Jones) 2245 3002

7 **KIMBOLTON KRACKER,** ch m Gabitat - One Sharper by Dublin Taxi (Mrs P Sly) 1929

5 **KIMS SELECTION(IRE),** b g Red Sunset - Restless Lady by Sandford Lad (R D E Woodhouse) 1917 429

4 **KINCADE,** gr g Starch Reduced - Hunters Glen by Tiger Shark (B R Cambidge) 453 1416

5 **KINCOR(IRE),** b m Asir - Aureoletta (FR) by Aureole (Michael J Carroll) 4409 32 94 236

9 **KIND'A SMART,** ch g Kind Of Hush - Treasure Seeker by Deep Diver (K A Morgan) 591⁹ 2151⁴ 2563² 2738¹ 2832¹ 3091 3473⁵

5 **KINDA GROOVY,** b g Beveled (USA) - Tory Blues by Final Straw (I Park) 915⁸ 1129² 1574⁶ 2252⁶ 2409⁷ 2583⁵ 3061⁴ 3236¹ 3641⁶ 3787⁵ 3964¹ 4037¹ 4138¹

7 **KINDERSLEIGH,** br m King Persian - Emyvale by Furry Glen (T F Lacy) 4305² 25⁶ 51¹ 131⁴ 232⁴ 574

6 **KINDLE'S DELIGHT,** b g Idiot's Delight - Kindled Spirit by Little Buskins (Miss H C Knight) 1126 1490 2426⁵ 2728⁸ 3502 3825⁶

10 **KINDLY KING,** b g King's Ride - Kindly by Tarqogan (M Keane) 87⁹ 119 1850 2025 3081

6 **KINDLY LADY,** b m Kind Of Hush - Welcome Honey by Be Friendly (Mrs J G Retter) 773

6 **KING ATHELSTAN(USA),** b h Sovereign Dancer (USA) - Wimbledon Star (USA) by Hoist The Flag (USA) (K A Morgan) 2154⁴ 2430⁵ 2741¹ 2874 3281⁹

4 **KING BRIAN(IRE),** gr g Dara Monarch - Cut The Ribbon by Sharp Edge (E J O'Grady) 1377 1575⁷ 1853

8 **KING CASH,** b g Kambalda - Lisgarvan Highway by Dusky Boy (Mrs S A Bramall) 874

9 **KING CREDO,** b g Kinglet - Credo's Daughter by Credo (S Woodman) 1347¹ 1663 1888⁵ 2376 3025

5 **KING CREOLE(IRE),** b g King's Ride - Lugnagullagh by Pitpan (J Berry) 1084 1779⁶ 2074⁴

4 **KING FOWLER(IRE),** gr g King's Ride - Chicchick by Smartset (A J McNamara) 3842 3971

5 **KING LUCIFER(IRE),** b g King's Ride - Cahore by Quayside (D Nicholson) 2387⁷ 2749 2950² 3264³

8 **KING MELODY,** ch g Black Minstrel - Ardglass Belle by Carnival Night (G Richards) 823[7] 2445

5 **KING OF NORMANDY(IRE),** ch g King Of Clubs - Miss Deauville by Sovereign Path (S G Chadwick) 4318 543 787[6] 2929[5] 3029

7 **KING OF SHADOWS,** b or br g Connaught - Rhiannon by Welsh Pageant (F M Barton) 2425 3224 3445[3] 3776[4] 3966[5]

5 **KING OF SHERWOOD(IRE),** ch g King Persian - Sevens Wild by Malinowski (USA) (Donal Hassett) 530

8 **KING OF STEEL,** b g Kemal (FR) - Black Spangle by Black Tarquin (M D Hammond) 1184

7 **KING OF THE GALES,** br g Strong Gale - Paulas Fancy by Lucky Guy (J E Kiely) 855[1] 1381[1] 1611[1] 1850[1] 2259

8 **KING OF THE GLEN,** b g King's Ride - Anabore by Darantus (A J McNamara) 1178[9] 1498[7] 1825 2055[1]

11 **KING OF THE LOT,** br g Space King - Nicola Lisa by Dumbarnie (D Nicholson) 1001[1] 1207[1]

4 **KING OF THE MICKS,** ch g Revlow - Gypsy Lea by Gambling Debt (P Wakely) 3257[5] 3458

9 **KING OF THE WOOD,** br g Chukaroo - Amore (ITY) by Kashmir II (W G M Turner) 1306

6 **KING OF THE WORLD(IRE),** ch g King Of Clubs - Larch by Busted (D G O'Gorman) 43[4] 88[2] 124[7] 536[2] 675[6] 858[4] 1178[4] 1495

6 **KING RUST,** ch g Rustingo - Lyricist by Averof (R L Brown) 743[5] 901 1108 1800 2327

5 **KING SCORPIO(IRE),** b g King's Ride - Ballyholland Star by Laurence O (C R Egerton) 1626 1835[7] 2167[3]

7 **KING TASMAN(NZ),** b g King Delamere (NZ) - Lady Tasman (NZ) by Battle-Waggon (Mrs J Renfree-Barons) 1624 3163

5 **KING TYRANT(IRE),** ch g Mummy's Luck - Lady Thatch by Tyrant (USA) (P Meany) 3088

5 **KING UBAD(USA),** ch h Trempolino (USA) - Glitter (FR) by Reliance (K O Cunningham-Brown) 483[1] 715 772[3] 889 1344[4]

5 **KING WAH GLORY(IRE),** b g Phardante (FR) - Rose's Best by Caribo (P Burke) 255[1] 1397 1815[6] 2155[8] 2278

9 **KING WILLIAM,** b g Dara Monarch - Norman Delight (USA) by Val de L'orne (FR) (J L Spearing) 280[2] 499[1] 3499[5] 3634[5] 4080[5]

5 **KING'S COURTIER(IRE),** b g King's Ride - Glamorous Night by Sir Herbert (M C Pipe) 2509 2916

10 **KING'S CURATE,** b g King's Ride - Parnessa by The Parson (M C Pipe) 2173[4] 2474 2824[4]

5 **KING'S DECREE(IRE),** b g King's Ride - Rose de Lema by Beau Tudor (A J McNamara) 530[9] 1610[6] 2353[1] 2918[3] 3197[6]

4 **KING'S FROLIC(IRE),** b g King's Ride - Castle Creeper by Royal Buck (A J McNamara) 3839[7] 3971 4059

4 **KING'S GOLD,** b g King Of Spain - Goldyke by Bustino (T M Jones) 2335 2857 3145

5 **KING'S GUEST(IRE),** b g Tender King - Saintly Guest by What A Guest (G M Moore) 1092[5] 1404[4] 1738[3] 1961

6 **KING'S MAVERICK(IRE),** b g King's Ride - Lawless Secret by Meadsville (M C Pipe) 1871 2315 2556[6]

8 **KING'S RARITY,** b g King's Ride - Kilim by Weavers' Hall (C L Popham) 326[6] 710[4] 1058[5] 1511 1615[4] 3004[7] 3361 3479[7] 3533[9]

7 **KING'S SHILLING(USA),** b g Fit To Fight (USA) - Pride's Crossing (USA) by Riva Ridge (USA) (C D Broad) 4349[3] 4377[4] 3702[4] 4371[4]

629[4] 998 1298 1422 1650[7] 1799[7] 3499[4] 3594[7] 3755[6] 4054[1] 4141[3]

5 **KING'S TREASURE(USA),** b g King Of Clubs - Crown Treasure (USA) by Graustark (I A Balding) 605[1] 772[1] 1082[4] 1539[5] 2440[5] 3270[4] 3543[5] 3713[1]

9 **KINGFISHER BAY,** b g Try My Best (USA) - Damiya (FR) by Direct Flight (J White) 669[1] 1026[4] 1302[4] 1796[3] 2001 2410[6]

6 **KINGFISHER BLUES(IRE),** ch g Quayside - Night Spot by Midsummer Night II (J White) 778 3530[6]

7 **KINGLY LOOK,** br g Roi Guillaume (FR) - Give Us A Breeze by Brave Invader (USA) (C R Beever) 1469 1861 2409

7 **KINGOFSPANCILHILL,** b or br g King's Ride - Cappahard by Record Run (Mrs Edward Crow) 4340 22 79[9] 137[7]

5 **KINGQUILLO(IRE),** b g Henbit (USA) - Friendly Polly by Be Friendly (M Halford) 95 4145

8 **KINGS BROMPTON,** b g Latest Model - Idson Lass by Levanter (J R Payne) 1717

7 **KINGS CHARIOT,** b g King's Ride - Royalement by Little Buskins (Lady Eliza Mays-Smith) 815[6] 1329[2] 2014[2] 2250[3]

6 **KINGS CHERRY(IRE),** b g King's Ride - Another Cherry by Le Bavard (FR) (T Costello) 4404[5] 41 56[9] 108

5 **KINGS DECREE(IRE),** b g King's Ride - Rose de Lema by Beau Tudor (A J McNamara) 36[4] 887

8 **KINGS ENGLISH,** b g Seymour Hicks (FR) - Zarella by Bustino (A L T Moore) 940[2] 1382[6] 1847 2159[6] 2466[2] 3389[1] 3612[3]

11 **KINGS FOUNTAIN,** br g Royal Fountain - K-King by Fury Royal (K C Bailey) 884[3] 1436[5]

6 **KINGS GAL,** b m King Of Spain - Outward's Gal by Ashmore (FR) (R Hollinshead) 3707 4023

4 **KINGS GAMBLE,** b g Lightning Dealer - Sussex Queen by Music Boy (M F Barraclough) 3114 3457 3833 4159[7]

7 **KINGS GUNNER,** ch g Kings Lake (USA) - Resooka by Godswalk (USA) (W G Gooden) 2765[5] 2949 3947[9]

8 **KINGS HATCH,** ch g Down The Hatch - Lady Hapsburg by Perhapsburg (H J Hopper) 3856

12 **KINGS HILL,** b g Pitpan - Prime Mistress by Skymaster (Michael Butler) 4405[2] 807[7] 1035[5] 1402[2] 2036[5] 2235[5] 2847[3] 2984 3551[8] 3790[1] 4042[6]

5 **KINGS LANE,** b g Majestic Streak - Gala Lane by Gala Performance (USA) (G R Dun) 2931[8] 3488 3868[6]

8 **KINGS LAW,** br g Regular Guy - Loughehoe Star by Sandyman Star (D Scott) 3238 3438[6] 3863

7 **KINGS LORD,** b or br g King's Ride - Yankee View by Yankee Gold (V T O'Brien) 571 689

6 **KINGS PEARL(IRE),** b m King's Ride - Lorna Doone by Raise You Ten (Cecil Ross) 4360[7] 3450

9 **KINGS RANK,** br g Tender King - Jhansi Ki Rani (USA) by Far North (CAN) (R Barber) 4335 4367[5]

10 **KINGS RIVER LAD,** b g Beau Charmeur (FR) - Monasootha by Paddy's Stream (R J Whitford) 4409[9] 10

8 **KINGS THYNE,** b f Good Thyne (USA) - Kingstown Girl by Bright Will (R K Aston) 2898[3] 3157[5] 3399

4 **KINGS VENTURE(IRE),** b g King Luthier - Never Intended by Sayyaf (A P O'Brien) 3937[9] 4148[8]

10 **KINGS VICTORY,** ch g What A Guest - Directrice (GER) by Zank (Mrs Julie Read) 3093[1]

13 **KINGS WILD,** b g Mandalus - Queens Trip by Mon Capitaine (A P Jones) 4332

5 **KINGSFOLD PET,** b g Tina's Pet - Bella Lisa by River Chanter (M J Haynes) 2111[5] 2343[5] 2544[4] 2762[4] 3119[1]

6 **KINGSLEY SINGER,** b g Chief Singer - Yelming by Thatch (USA) (Nick Burd) 3049

8 **KINGSTON WAY,** gr g Crash Course - Miragold by Grey Mirage (Francis M O'Brien) 4380[5] 14[2] 42[5] 83[2] 119[5] 306[4] 364[4] 1499[8] 2698[4] 3648[4] 3746[6] 3841[3] 4033[1]

14 **KINGSWOOD KITCHENS,** b g General Ironside - Tyrone Typhoon by Typhoon (S Bruce) 4311[7]

6 **KINLET VISION(IRE),** b m Vision (USA) - Verandah by Jaazeiro (USA) (W Jenks) 126[3] 307[2] 425[5]

10 **KINNESTON,** b g Night Porter - Dysie Mary by Apollonius (J Barclay) 3181[3]

5 **KINO'S CROSS,** b g Relkino - Coral Delight by Idiot's Delight (A J Wilson) 4172[6]

6 **KINOKO,** ch g Bairn (USA) - Octavia by Sallust (K W Hogg) 719[2] 767[3]

6 **KINON-PENNY,** b g Relkino - Great Aunt Emily by Traditionalist (USA) (B Stevens) 3010 3306 3547

7 **KINROSS,** ch f Nearly A Hand - Moonbreaker by Twilight Alley (I R Ferguson) 1832[8] 2197 2311[9] 2587 3072[7] 3654

9 **KINROYAL,** br g Royal Fountain - Most Kind by Tudenham (F Jestin) 3143 3474[9] 4014

6 **KINTARO,** b g Glint Of Gold - Tzarina (USA) by Gallant Romeo (USA) (S G Griffiths) 1057[3] 2142

6 **KIR(IRE),** ch g M Double M (USA) - Wolver Rose by Wolver Hollow (V Thompson) 2222 2449[6] 2740 3057[2] 3240 3678

6 **KIRBY OPPORTUNITY,** ch m Mummy's Game - Empress Catherine by Welsh Pageant (P Leach) 883 3496 3765[4]

6 **KIRCHWYN LAD,** b g Kirchner - Gowyn by Goldhill (S J Leadbetter) 821

5 **KIRKCALDY(IRE),** b g Glad Dancer - Rosabuskins by Little Buskins (Mrs S C Bradburne) 1582 2104 2739[3] 2952[4] 3428[3] 3554

5 **KIRKTON GLEN,** br g Scorpio (FR) - Chocolate Drop by Goldhill (C Parker) 723[9] 2951[8]

7 **KIRKTON GREY,** gr g Scallywag - Chocolate Drop by Goldhill (C Parker) 1726[4] 1938[7] 2367 3179

7 **KIRSTENBOSCH,** b g Caerleon (USA) - Flower Petals by Busted (L Lungo) 4299[4] 1583

11 **KIRSTY'S BOY,** b g Majestic Streak - Cute Peach by Hardicanute (Miss L A Perratt) 4353[1] 127[3] 271[4] 449[5] 544[4] 655[6] 720[2] 822 876[3]

5 **KISMET DANCER(IRE),** b m Lancastrian - Bedouin Dancer by Lorenzaccio (Victor Bowens) 747

4 **KISMETIM,** b g Dowsing (USA) - Naufrage by Main Reef (B J Meehan) 1510

4 **KISS IN THE DARK,** b f Starry Night (USA) - Hasty Sarah by Gone Native (Mrs M Reveley) 247[7] 320[4] 497 578[1] 732[4] 3125[6] 3826 4012 4086[6]

13 **KISSANE,** br g Kemal (FR) - Chamowen by Master Owen (R J Deake) 3335 3501 3951[7]

7 **KISU KALI,** ch g Kris - Evita by Reform (B P J Baugh) 602[5] 761[2] 1044[2] 1138[4] 1260[3] 1466[2] 1689[4] 2397 3452[7]

7 **KITES HARDWICKE,** b g Sunyboy - Kitty Stobling by Goldhill (Niall Madden) 1159[7] 1830[6] 2036[4] 2235[7] 2312[3] 2619[9] 3274[5]

6 **KITSBEL,** ro g Belfort (FR) - Fair Kitty by Saucy Kit (T P McGovern) 2430 2621[7] 2914[4]

13 **KITTINGER,** b g Crash Course - Mandaloch by Mandamus (P A Pritchard) 198[2] 700[4]

4 **KITZBUHEL(IRE),** br f Buckskin (FR) - Fairogan by Tarqogan (F Lennon) 2081[8]

5 **KIVETON TYCOON(IRE),** b g Last Tycoon - Zillionaire (USA) by Vaguely Noble (J A Glover) 1256[3] 1874[4] 2385[4] 2480[2] 2994 3413[4] 3820

5 **KIWI CRYSTAL(NZ),** b m Blanco (USA) - Rhine Valley (NZ) by Val Du Fier (FR) (D H Barons) 3176

8 **KIWI L'EGLISE(NZ),** br g Church Parade - Llantilly Lass (NZ) by Llananthony (NZ) (D H Barons) 2991 3215

7 **KIWI VELOCITY(NZ),** b m Veloso (NZ) - Eumenides (NZ) by Head Hunter (P J Hobbs) 1441 1866[2] 2017 2146 2362[2] 2654 3135[2] 3175[1] 3351[2] 3532[3] 3896[2]

7 **KIZZY ROSE,** br m Celtic Cone - Constant Rose by Confusion (Michael Hourigan) 79[6] 201[5] 292 414[4] 538[6] 2311[6] 2616

5 **KLAIRON DAVIS(FR),** b or br h Rose Laurel - Styrene (FR) by Trenel (A L T Moore) 1077[1] 1397[1] 1781[1] 2097[1] 2391[1] 3323[1] 3613[1]

7 **KLICKITAT,** br m Seclude (USA) - Mount St Helen by Mount Hagen (FR) (Victor Bowens) 69 135 293

5 **KLINGON(IRE),** b g Formidable (USA) - Melbourne Miss by Chaparral (FR) (L A Snook) 1173[3] 1303[8] 1622[3]

7 **KNAVE OF CLUBS,** ch g King Of Clubs - La Calera (GER) by Caracol (FR) (J G M O'Shea) 2084[3] 2209[2] 2514

6 **KNIFEBOARD,** b g Kris - Catalpa by Reform (Paul O J Hosgood) 2898[1] 3216 3717[3] 4182

8 **KNIGHT IN SIDE,** ch g Tachypous - Miss Saddler by St Paddy (R Callow) 687[6] 887[9] 1795[7] 3098 3773[4] 3853[2] 4052[3] 4096[5]

11 **KNIGHT OIL,** b g Miner's Lamp - Fair Argument by No Argument (O Sherwood) 518[3] 696[2] 792[3] 1026[3]

7 **KNIGHT'S SPUR(USA),** b g Diesis - Avoid (USA) by Buckpasser (J Webber) 444[5] 676 1022

7 **KNIGHTLY ARGUS,** ch g Le Moss - Cala San Vicente by Gala Performance (USA) (S E Sherwood) 264[2] 390[1] 439[1] 605[3] 1057[9] 3623

8 **KNIGHTON COOMBE(NZ),** ch g The Expatriate - Sashay (NZ) by Showoff (S A Bowen) 351[4] 455 646 1711

8 **KNIGHTS(NZ),** br g Vice Regal (NZ) - Montrose Lass (AUS) by Gay Gambler (USA) (C D Broad) 2403 2540[6] 2862 3895 4064 4181[8]

5 **KNIGHTSBRIDGE STAR(IRE),** br g Good Thyne (USA) - Sparkling Cherry by Sparkler (D Nicholson) 3234[1]

9 **KNOCK KNOCK,** ch g Tap On Wood - Ruby River by Red God (I A Balding) 3574[8]

9 **KNOCK RANK,** b g Ranksborough - Knockabitoff by Raise You Ten (E H Owen Jun) 1200[5] 1288[3] 1477

6 **KNOCKAVERRY(IRE),** b m Kemal (FR) - Ballinlough by Prince Hansel (M J Wilkinson) 4403[6] 1174[4] 2599[2] 2802[5] 2997[1] 3167[1] 3253[2] 3509[1] 3583[4]

7 **KNOCKAVILLA,** b g Rontino - Grannie No by Brave Invader (USA) (Donal Hassett) 3088[2] 3296

14 **KNOCKBRACK,** b g Pitpan - Highway Mistress by Royal Highway (M C Denning) 3951

14 **KNOCKELLY CASTLE,** ch g Deep Run - Laganore by Will Somers (T E Hyde) 170[5]

9 **KNOCKGRAFFON,** b g Smooth Stepper - Northern Rose by Northern Value (USA) (Miss Ursula Ryan) 4368 4403

6 **LADY POLY,** b m Dunbeath (USA) - First Temptation (USA) by Mr Leader (USA) (J E Long) 4389[5] 2113[4]

6 **LADY QUAKER,** b m Oats - Sweet Optimist by Energist (B S Rothwell) 1374

7 **LADY RASHEE,** ch m Le Bavard (FR) - Plumuck by Master Buck (Irwin Kirkpatrick) 746

4 **LADY RELKO,** b f Sizzling Melody - Rosalka (ITY) by Relko (R Voorspuy) 1049[8] 1261[4] 2130[7]

6 **LADY ROMANCE(IRE),** b m Brewery Boy (AUS) - Romantic Rhapsody by Ovac (ITY) (B J Llewellyn) 1935 2461

5 **LADY SALLY(IRE),** b m Seclude (USA) - Lady Mountcashel by Propeller (J L Rothwell) 31

6 **LADY'S ISLAND(IRE),** br m Over The River (FR) - Banner Lady by Milan (J I A Charlton) 1115[2] 1530[2] 1937[3]

4 **LADYS BID(IRE),** b f Auction Ring (USA) - Miss Spencer by Imperial Fling (USA) (Capt D G Swan) 2349[9] 2750

6 **LADYSIBELOU,** gr m Alias Smith (USA) - Bargello's Lady by Bargello (Mrs A Hamilton) 1938 2068 2500

5 **LAFANTA(IRE),** b g Lancastrian - Infanta Helena by Pollerton (J Wade) 482 622[9] 823 1152[5] 1425[2] 1809[1] 1926[3] 2212[3] 2896[4] 3061

5 **LAFFAN'S BRIDGE(IRE),** br m Mandalus - Kimin by Kibenka (H de Bromhead) 73 102 236

6 **LAFHEEN(IRE),** b g Lafontaine (USA) - Curraheen by Crash Course (Miss R J Patman) 1456[5] 1595 2630[4]

7 **LAFKADIO,** b g Gay Mecene (USA) - Lakonia by Kris (M C Chapman) 4301

5 **LAGGARD'S QUEST,** br h Daring March - Doubtful Request by Cheveley Lad (A P Jones) 1546

4 **LAID BACK BEN,** ch g Starch Reduced - Mrs Dumbfounded by Adropejo (B Palling) 486

4 **LAKE CHARLES(IRE),** b g Kings Lake (USA) - Lady Angela by Sallust (J A O'Connell) 1182

5 **LAKE DOMINION,** b g Primo Dominie - Piney Lake by Sassafras (FR) (J White) 2065[3] 3899[2] 4179[1]

5 **LAKE HOTEL(IRE),** br g Nashamaa - Killyhevlin by Green God (W M Roper) 102[6] 274[5] 671[5]

9 **LAKE MISSION,** b g Blakeney - Missed Blessing by So Blessed (S E Sherwood) 595[1] 700[1]

4 **LAKE OF LOUGHREA(IRE),** ch g Kings Lake (USA) - Polynesian Charm (USA) by What A Pleasure (USA) (Kevin Prendergast) 1454[5] 1983 2099 3993[1]

4 **LAKE POWELL(FR),** 3679[3]

9 **LAKE TEEREEN,** ch g Callernish - Gusserane Lark by Napoleon Bonaparte (R Rowe) 1171 1520[1] 1693[4] 2013[2] 2462[1] 2726[2] 3132[3] 3669

8 **LAKENHEATHER(NZ),** b g Lakenheath (USA) - Monanne by Pharamond (Mrs Pat Mullen) 4103

12 **LAKINO,** b g Relkino - Lake Naivasha by Blakeney (K A Morgan) 4394

4 **LAMBAST,** b f Relkino - Lambay by Lorenzaccio (D Nicholson) 1229 1473[9] 1705[5]

5 **LANCANA(IRE),** b m Lancastrian - Sky Is The Limit by Diamonds Are Trumps (USA) (Victor Bowens) 1076 1230 1397

5 **LANCASTER COURT(IRE),** ch m Lancastrian - Torus Court by Torus (J S Cullen) 2039 2944

5 **LANCASTER LADY(IRE),** b m Lancastrian - Chancy Gal by Al Sirat (USA) (Capt D G Swan) 1180

4 **LANCASTER PILOT,** ch g Crofthall - Spinner by Blue Cashmere (J L Eyre) 2401[8] 2741[9]

5 **LANCASTRIANS DREAM(IRE),** ch f Lancastrian - Silver Gala by Gala Performance (USA) (A P O'Brien) 2620[4] 2919 2983[9] 3122 3197[9] 3731[4]

7 **LAND AFAR,** b g Dominion - Jouvencelle by Rusticaro (FR) (J Webber) 827[1] 1106[4] 1559[1] 2079 2595[5] 3025 3422[2]

5 **LAND OF THE FREE,** b m Valiyar - L'americaine (USA) by Verbatim (USA) (R J Baker) 2082[6] 2366[9] 2528 2801[5] 3020[4] 3174[5] 3338[4] 3517[7] 3671[4] 3844[6]

5 **LANDED GENTRY(USA),** b h Vaguely Noble - Phydilla (FR) by Lyphard (USA) (C D Broad) 1206 2862

6 **LANDENSTOWN(IRE),** br g Furry Glen - Divine Drapes by Divine Gift (J Weld) 400[6] 513[1] 1016[9]

5 **LANDSKER MISSILE,** b m Cruise Missile - Gemmerly Jane by Bally Russe (M C Pipe) 3832 4023

5 **LANDSKER PRYDE,** b m Nearly A Hand - Blonde Pryncesse by Pry (M C Pipe) 1779[2] 2176[3]

12 **LANIGANS WINE,** br g Laurence O - Little Dotia by Giolla Mear Or Proverb (V T O'Brien) 1683[9] 1784 1901[6] 2125 2984 3249

5 **LANLAU(IRE),** b g Lancastrian - Laurenca by Laurence O (T R George) 1806

4 **LANSBOROUGH,** gr g Uncle Pokey - Young Lamb by Sea Hawk II (G Richards) 3488

6 **LANSDOWNE,** b g High Top - Fettle by Relkino (G A Ham) 1645[5] 1775[4] 1869[3] 2208[2] 2483[1] 2657[1] 3109[4] 3535

6 **LANTERN LUCK(IRE),** b or br m The Parson - Cahernane Girl by Bargello (Michael Hourigan) 4339[5] 423 723 875 1228 1995 3302 4151[7]

4 **LANZAMAR,** b f Buzzards Bay - Maravista by Swing Easy (USA) (R T Phillips) 1705 1965

10 **LAPIAFFE,** b g Piaffer (USA) - Laval by Cheval (A Harrison) 4365[3] 4387 245 324[4] 477 518[1] 579[5] 726[2] 911[4] 1375[3] 1679[1] 1789[4] 2064[8] 2151[2] 2437[6] 2737 2973[3] 3237[2] 3437 3784[2] 3908 4175[4]

6 **LARA'S BABY(IRE),** ch m Valiyar - Tapiola by Tap On Wood (P D Evans) 1370 1801

6 **LARAPINTA(IRE),** b g Montelimar (USA) - Shapely by Parthia (J H Johnson) 639[1] 770[1] 1181[1] 1607

6 **LARGE ACTION(IRE),** b g The Parson - Ballyadam Lass by Menelek (O Sherwood) 1010[2] 1442[1] 1661[1] 1992[1] 2595[1] 3025[3] 3409[3]

6 **LARGE PROFILE,** b g Town And Country - Madam Chesty by English Prince (Thomas Carberry) 2

4 **LARKSPUR LEGEND,** ch g Legend Of France (USA) - Remainder Tip by Remainder Man (J Mackie) 588 1253 1404

10 **LARLOCH,** br g Young Generation - Black Fire by Firestreak (D A Nolan) 3536[9] 3864[4]

7 **LARNACA,** b g Shernazar - Checkers by Habat (B V Kelly) 1159

5 **LARRY'S LEGACY(IRE),** b or br g Buckskin (FR) - Anaglogs Daughter by Above Suspicion (Martin Michael Lynch) 2394[8]

5 **LARRYS PENNY(IRE),** b m Huckster (USA) - Taca (USA) by Sovereign Dancer (USA) (Laurence Murphy) 73 709 908[5] 1039

9 **LASATA,** b g Buckskin (FR) - De Lafield by No Argument (M F Morris) 878[3] 992[6] 1336[2] 1382[4] 1682[2] 1847[1] 2280[1] 2466[6] 2698[3] 3423 3612

5 **LASSIE(IRE),** ch m Moulin - Miss Brodie (FR) by Margouillat (FR) (K O Cunningham-Brown) 3362[1] 3514 3831[7] 3980[4] 4098[2]

10 **LAST 'O' THE BUNCH,** ch g Meldrum - Golden Royalty by Royalty (G Richards) 780[4] 1056[2] 1294[2] 1618[1] 1876

5 **LAST APPEARANCE,** b m Slip Anchor - Thespian by Ile de Bourbon (USA) (R T Phillips) 1794[9]

5 **LAST CONQUEST(IRE),** b g Slip Anchor - Migiyas by Kings Lake (USA) (R J O'Sullivan) 310

6 **LAST DECADE(IRE),** ch g Leap High (USA) - Another Decade by Daring Display (USA) (George Stewart) 3813[9]

6 **LAST MATCH,** b g Final Straw - Light Duty by Queen's Hussar (D H Barons) 3543 3713[8] 3975[3]

6 **LAST OF MOHICANS,** b g Warpath - Gemima Tenderfoot by Prince Tenderfoot (USA) (C L Popham) 4319

5 **LAST REFUGE(IRE),** b g Lancastrian - Newland's Bloom by Lucifer (USA) (T J Carr) 2140[5] 2367 2500[5] 3431[8] 3687[4]

8 **LASTING MEMORY,** b m Ardross - Irreprochable by Mount Hagen (FR) (R H Alner) 459[4] 701[6] 1139[5] 1777[3] 2862[6] 3350[4] 3771[5]

9 **LASTOFTHEVIKINGS,** ch g Cisto (FR) - Vivyiki by Kirtonian (J L Needham) 845[7] 996 1527[3] 1805 1952[3] 2206[6] 2524[3] 2858[1] 3040[8] 3442 3621

10 **LATE SESSION,** ch g Enchantment - Treatise by Bold Lad (IRE) (R W Savery) 2800 3412 3877[4] 3951

10 **LATENT TALENT,** b g Celtic Cone - Fra Mau by Wolver Hollow (S E Sherwood) 1011[1] 1540[4] 1757[2] 2747

6 **LATOSKY,** br g Teenoso (USA) - Patosky by Skymaster (J Norton) 2870[8] 2997 3317

6 **LAUDER SQUARE,** gr g Pragmatic - Royal Ruby by Rubor (T D C Dun) 1200[4]

12 **LAUDERDALE LAD,** b g Politico (USA) - Cannes Beach by Canadel II (J S King) 696[6] 865[4] 1083[3] 1326[4] 3512[2]

5 **LAUGHING GAS(IRE),** ch g Lord Ha Ha - Magic Deer by Whistling Deer (John R Upson) 1210[3] 1533[9] 1775 2034[5] 2657[5]

4 **LAUNCH INTO SONG(IRE),** b c Fayruz - Launch The Raft by Home Guard (USA) (Patrick Phelan) 529

11 **LAUNDRYMAN,** b g Celtic Cone - Lovely Laura by Lauso (M Bradstock) 1887[5] 2307[4]

5 **LAURA,** gr m Never So Bold - Cottage Pie by Kalamoun (R Brotherton) 3745[6] 3928[8] 4101[4]

5 **LAURA GALE(IRE),** b m Strong Gale - Laurentino by Laurence O (F Warren) 1020 1820 2056[6] 2869 3469

10 **LAURA'S BEAU,** b g Beau Charmeur (FR) - Laurabeg by Laurence O (Francis Berry) 539 855[3] 992[5] 1381 1553[6] 1611[4] 1850[9] 2701[6] 3249[8] 3425 3524

5 **LAURA'S PURSUIT(IRE),** b m Meneval (USA) - Laurabeg by Laurence O (J L Rothwell) 3295 3652[4] 3994 4118

6 **LAURAS TEEARA(IRE),** b m Torus - Dusky Glory by Dusky Boy (P Beaumont) 3862

7 **LAUREL VALLEY,** ch m Decent Fellow - Donna Chimene by Royal Gunner (USA) (A P O'Brien) 274[3]

9 **LAUREL WALK,** br m Buckskin (FR) - Lady Conkers (W P Mullins) 4370

5 **LAURETTA BLUE(IRE),** b m Bluebird (USA) - Lauretta by Relko (W J Burke) 1333 1610

10 **LAURIE-O,** b g Deep Run - Eight Of Diamonds by Silent Spring (R R Lamb) 822 911[7] 1185[5]

8 **LAVA FALLS(USA),** b or br h Riverman (USA) - In Triumph (USA) by Hoist The Flag (USA) (M C Banks) 4333[5] 2168[1] 2330[5] 2532[3]

7 **LAVALIGHT,** b g Lighter - Laval by Cheval (R J Hodges) 607[6] 774 1008[5] 1189 1411 3545 3769 3899[8]

8 **LAVINS THATCH,** b m Buckskin (FR) - Siba Vione by Dusky Boy (J A Berry) 28

7 **LAW BRIDGE,** b g Law Society (USA) - Rhein Bridge by Rheingold (M J P O'Brien) 1235[1] 1378[2] 1683[2] 1896[3] 2587[7] 3322

6 **LAW COURSE(IRE),** b m Crash Course - Penny Buskins by Little Buskins (Patrick J McCarthy) 251[8] 327

5 **LAW FACULTY(IRE),** b g Law Society (USA) - Ask The Wind by Run The Gauntlet (G A Ham) 592[5] 699[3] 891[2] 1167[9] 1366[7] 1546[6] 3632

12 **LAWLEY,** br g Humdoleila - Cloudari by Pindari (Mrs Angus Campbell) 3638

4 **LAWNSWOOD QUAY,** ch g Bairn (USA) - Miss Quay by Quayside (D W Whillans) 2003

7 **LAWYER'S BRIEF(FR),** ch g Sky Lawyer (FR) - Autumn Leaves (FR) by Sole Mio (USA) (P D Osborne) 4357[7] 1551[7] 2024[3] 2155[1] 2552[6] 2703 2866 3789[9] 3955[5]

5 **LAY IT OFF(IRE),** br m Strong Gale - Give Her The Boot by Little Buskins (J G O'Neill) 1109[9] 1568[7] 1974[3] 2558[6] 3515[4] 3762[1] 4004[5]

6 **LAY ONE ON YA(IRE),** b g Trimmingham - Lougharue by Deep Run (E J O'Grady) 20[5]

8 **LAZY RHYTHM(USA),** gr g Drone - Ritual Dance by Godswalk (USA) (J L Eyre) 821 1613 1865[9]

5 **LB'S GIRL,** gr m My Treasure Chest - Barley Fire by Prince Barle (J C Poulton) 2494 2621 3145 3543 3938

5 **LE BARON PERCHE(FR),** b h Vayrann - Dayira by Sparkler (C James) 1729[8] 2244[5] 2599[6] 2914 3119[2]

8 **LE BRAVE,** b g Le Bavard (FR) - Country Scene by Brave Invader (USA) (J H Scott) 124[4] 201[1] 258[3] 618[2] 746[3] 903[9] 1156[3] 1829[3] 2157[9] 2282 2390[4] 2661 3648[8]

8 **LE BUCHERON,** b g Vaigly Great - Couteau by Nelcius (M J Ryan) 2668 2879[3] 3090 3341[3] 3774[1] 4161

11 **LE CHAT NOIR,** b g Paico - June by Pendragon (Mrs D M Grissell) 2456[4] 2669

10 **LE CLOS MARVILLE(FR),** b or br g Mistigri - Soie Royale (A E Gareau) 2677

7 **LE DENSTAN,** b g Valuta - Sweet Canyon (NZ) by Headland II (P R Hedger) 3115[9] 3575 3827[5]

9 **LE GERARD,** ch g Le Bavard (FR) - Pauline Blue by Majority Blue (P J Lally) 65[3] 112 231[5] 510[5]

7 **LE GINNO(FR),** ch g Concorde Jr (USA) - Fromentel (FR) by Timour II (C P E Brooks) 743[1] 1108[1] 1745 2897[1] 3036

7 **LE HACHETTE,** ch m Torus - Crossboyne by Polyfoto (Jeremiah Ryan) 46

5 **LE MEILLE(IRE),** ch g Le Bavard (FR) - Glens Princess by Prince Hansel (A P Jarvis) 2877[3] 3190[4]

6 **LE METAYER(FR),** b g Le Nain Jaune (FR) - Tawendo (FR) by Tamelo (FR) (K C Bailey) 662[2] 1249

5 **LE MINTER(IRE),** b m Le Moss - Cherry Token by Prince Hansel (Peter McCreery) 3450[8]

10 **LE PICCOLAGE,** b g The Parson - Daithis Coleen by Carnival Night (N J Henderson) 1340[4] 1889 3821[3] 4007[9]

5 **LE QUARANTIEME,** b m Looking Glass - Theresa by Tanfirion (A Bailey) 4057

5 **LE ROI THIBAULT(FR),** b g Rahotep (FR) - Psathoura by Direct Flight (G Doleuze) 2121[1]

7 **LE SEPT,** b m Le Bavard (FR) - Colour Clown by Random Shot (P D FitzGerald) 7[5] 29 4152

8 **LE TEMERAIRE,** b h Top Ville - La Mirande (FR) by Le Fabuleux (Don Enrico Incisa) 2480[5]

INDEX TO NATIONAL HUNT RESULTS 1993-94

709

5 **LINTON ROCKS,** b g Town And Country - Top Soprano by High Top (T Thomson Jones) 1996⁸ 2114¹ 2890¹ 3042 3476³

11 **LINVAR,** b g Le Bavard (FR) - Super Cailin by Brave Invader (USA) (Francis Berry) 1234 1554 1980⁴ 2160⁶ 2618 2774⁵ 2984 3274⁷ 3996

5 **LINWOOD LADY(IRE),** gr m Auction Ring (USA) - Fraudulant (T A Regan) 4378³ 276⁸

7 **LION OF VIENNA,** b g Bulldozer - Lucky Favour by Ballyciptic (T J Carr) 2487⁸ 3287⁴ 3622²

6 **LION ROCK(IRE),** ch g Quayside - Magar's Prde by No Time (C R Egerton) 3509

7 **LIRELLA,** ch m Lir - Barry's Girl by Silly Answer (P R Rodford) 1716 1948 2195

5 **LISAHANE VILLE,** b g Top Ville - La Carlotta (USA) by J O Tobin (USA) (P R Hedger) 3234³ 3589⁵

7 **LISALEEN RIVER,** ch m Over The River (FR) - Chestnut Fire by Deep Run (Michael Hourigan) 1902⁴

7 **LISCAHILL HIGHWAY,** b h Mandalus - Carlow Highway by Royal Highway (James McLoughney) 159⁶ 258 536 877⁵ 1330³ 1401⁷ 1687 1827 3528⁴ 3913⁹ 4078 4192

7 **LISMEEN JOY,** ch m Carlingford Castle - Blue Apron by Bluerullah (J P Kavanagh) 4338

5 **LISMORE LAD,** b g Full Extent (USA) - Highlands Park by Gunner B (R Allan) 3489 3868

7 **LISNABOY PRINCE,** bl g Prince Regent (FR) - Paiukiri by Ballyciptic (A P O'Brien) 993 1332 2203⁸ 2389 2588 2661

5 **LISNAGAR LADY(IRE),** br m Supreme Leader - Galteemore Lady Vii (Denis FitzGerald) 1858

6 **LISNAGREE BOY(IRE),** b g Baragoi - Legal Bells by London Bells (CAN) (S J Treacy) 6 92⁶ 235³ 2517

6 **LISNAGREE PRINCESS(IRE),** b m Whistling Deer - Sasscombe by Sahib (Thomas Cooper) 1608

4 **LISNATIERNEY(IRE),** ch f Denel (FR) - Winadoon by Knotty Pine (Mayne Kidd) 4078

8 **LISNAVARAGH,** b g Kemal (FR) - Weaver's Fool by Weaver's Hall (J T Gorman) 2235 2619 3655

5 **LISSADELL LADY,** gr m Sharrood (USA) - Clouded Vision by So Blessed (Mrs M E Long) 864 1040 1137

6 **LISSELAN PRINCE(IRE),** b g Kemal (FR) - Princess Menelek by Menelek (Fergus Sutherland) 3529⁷

7 **LISTEN MAN,** ch g Viking (USA) - Tara Gold by Yankee Gold (T I Duggan) 3795

6 **LITMORE DANCER,** br m Mashhor Dancer (USA) - Daring Charm by Daring March (J M Bradley) 146²

5 **LITTLE AND OFTEN(IRE),** gr m Roselier (FR) - Lady Perry by David Jack (James Joseph O'Connor) 4378 692⁹ 798⁹ 902⁸

6 **LITTLE BALLYWOODEN(IRE),** b f Leap High (USA) - Valsong (FR) by Sanctus II (J K Magee) 343⁷ 491⁵ 2314 3276 3796⁷

5 **LITTLE BERTHA,** ch m Nearly A Hand - General's Daughter by Spartan General (P F Nicholls) 2114³

7 **LITTLE BIG,** b g Indian King (USA) - Route Royale by Roi Soleil (C D Broad) 125¹ 222⁴ 730² 1474⁶ 2528⁶ 2792⁵ 3003⁴ 3337 3545

7 **LITTLE BROMLEY,** ch m Riberetto - Bromley Rose by Rubor (A Eubank) 2445⁵ 2903¹ 3179⁹

6 **LITTLE BUCK(IRE),** b g Buckskin (FR) - Little Quince by Laurence O (J S Cullen) 31⁵ 2236⁸ 2869² 3327⁴ 3694³ 3712⁴ 3936⁶

7 **LITTLE BUCKSKIN,** ch m Buckskin (FR) - Madam Torus by Torus (N A Twiston-Davies) 883

7 **LITTLE CLARE,** b m Oats - County Clare by Vimadee (C R Barwell) 2946 3204⁵ 3497 3509⁷ 3970 4144

6 **LITTLE CONKER,** ch g All Systems Go - L'irondelle by On Your Mark (A Smith) 728 970 1356 1485⁴

5 **LITTLE FREDDIE,** ch g Roman Warrior - Dawns Ballad by Balidar (J I A Charlton) 1482⁵ 2741 3470² 3565⁴ 3905

11 **LITTLE GENERAL,** ch g General Ironside - Coolentallagh by Perhapsburg (R Rowe) 886 1140⁴ 1388² 1512⁷ 1769² 2429² 2690⁴ 2880⁴ 3437 3808³ 3939⁴

6 **LITTLE GLEN,** b g Germont - Glendyke by Elvis (A B Crozier) 3158

4 **LITTLE GUNNER,** ch c Gunner B - Love Of Kings by Golden Love (P D Evans) 1290⁵ 1473⁶ 1634³

8 **LITTLE ISLAND,** b m Noble Imp - Island Serenade by Easter Island (H Rowsell) 3860⁹

5 **LITTLE JOE(IRE),** br g Cataldi - Linanbless by So Blessed (C Collins) 2203

7 **LITTLE MAHARANEE,** b m Majestic Maharaj - Lady Redhaven by Red Man (C J Mann) 3922

5 **LITTLE MOON,** ch m Little Wolf - Moonbreaker by Twilight Alley (I R Ferguson) 343

5 **LITTLE NOD,** ch g Domynsky - Vikris by Viking (USA) (J White) 4336² 355¹ 434²

4 **LITTLE PORKY,** b g Dreams To Reality (USA) - Wrekinianne by Reform (Mrs H Parrott) 606⁷ 702⁵ 1237⁷

4 **LITTLE SERENA,** b f Primitive Rising (USA) - Navos by Tyrnavos (J W Walmsley) 2909⁴ 3457⁸

9 **LITTLE THYNE,** br g Good Thyne (USA) - You Never Know by Brave Invader (USA) (Dr P Pritchard) 227⁹ 325 525 920³ 1837⁶ 2033¹ 2208 2418⁵

4 **LITTLE TINCTURE(IRE),** ch g Meneval (USA) - Lakefield Lady by Over The River (FR) (A L T Moore) 1377 1575⁹ 1846 2122

9 **LITTLE TOM,** b g Nearly A Hand - Lost In Silence by Silent Spring (J S King) 52 198¹ 457² 615² 860¹ 1041¹ 1363 1489⁶ 2981² 3268¹ 3397² 3500⁵ 3830⁵

4 **LITTLE TOWN(IRE),** br f Strong Gale - Lowtown by Camden Town (J Weld) 3070⁶

10 **LITTLE WENLOCK,** b g Tycoon II - Oujarater by Adropejo (Mrs D S C Gibson) 3157 4084⁴

6 **LITTLE WISHFUL,** b g Dutch Treat - Waveney Wish by Crooner (R Dickin) 1277

8 **LITTLEDALE(USA),** b h Lypheor - Smeralda by Grey Sovereign (M J Wilkinson) 4348⁴

5 **LIVE A LITTLE,** ch m Nearly A Hand - Royal Rushes by Royal Palace (J H Peacock) 743

5 **LIVELY KNIGHT(IRE),** b g Remainder Man - Love The Irish by Irish Love (J T Gifford) 3234²

5 **LIVING ON THE EDGE(IRE),** ch g Callernish - Clashdermot Lady by Shackleton (C R Egerton) 3823⁸

4 **LIVONIAN,** b g Kris - Air Distingue (USA) by Sir Ivor (O Sherwood) 2381 3231⁸ 3597⁹

5 **LIXWM,** b m Scorpio (FR) - Connaughts' Trump by Connaught (N J Henderson) 3522

5 **LIZZIE DRIPPIN(CAN),** b m Artichoke (USA) - Adieu (FR) by Tompion (USA) (M D I Usher) 1353 1717 2797

9 **LIZZIES LASS,** br m Sandalay - Kiltegan by Charlottesvilles Flyer (F Gray) 593 751 862 1169 2543² 2642² 3204¹

INDEX TO NATIONAL HUNT RESULTS 1993-94

5 **LLAMA LADY,** b m Puget (USA) - Miss Inigo by Sagaro (H J M Webb) 2176 2546⁵ 2716³

6 **LLANTHONY ABBEY(IRE),** br m Hardboy - Aerial Orchid by Perspex (P F Nicholls) 1779

6 **LLES LE BUCFLOW,** ch h Little Wolf - Elsell by Grey Mirage (F Jordan) 2789 3008 3564⁹ 3682⁶

5 **LLOYDS DREAM,** b g Lidhame - Christines Lady by Roman Warrior (J J Sheehan) 2335⁷ 2521⁵ 3098 3725⁵ 3878³ 3970 4098⁴

8 **LO STREGONE,** b g The Parson - Somers Castle by Will Somers (T P Tate) 1091¹ 1288¹ 1615² 2010² 2497¹ 2784³ 3358³ 3554³

9 **LOANINGDALE,** ch g Lomond (USA) - Aliceva by Alcide (R Akehurst) 4333³

6 **LOAVES AND FISHES,** ch g Oats - River Belle by Divine Gift (Norman Cassidy) 489⁴ 746¹ 1157² 1453⁹ 1977 2468 2751⁴ 2988³ 3506⁶ 3719⁴ 3812⁶ 4058⁷

5 **LOBILIO(USA),** b h Robellino (USA) - Nabila (USA) by Foolish Pleasure (USA) (D Burchell) 3189⁴

9 **LOBRIC,** b g Electric - Light O'Battle by Queen's Hussar (J R Jenkins) 1405² 1704³ 2223² 2338 2706³ 2999² 3154² 3621² 3750² 3901

9 **LOCAL CUSTOMER,** b g Le Bavard (FR) - Penny Bar by Bargello (P Bradley) 4387² 3171 458² 501¹

6 **LOCAL DEALER,** ch g Scottish Reel - Green Pool by Whistlefield (D T Garraton) 4336⁶ 2891⁸ 3125⁷ 3222

6 **LOCAL FLYER,** b g Local Suitor (USA) - Noirmont Girl by Skymaster (J E Banks) 949⁴ 1154⁶ 1632⁵

7 **LOCAL MANOR,** ch g Le Bavard (FR) - Blackrath Girl by Bargello (O Sherwood) 1490 2030² 2249² 2603³ 2872 3510

5 **LOCAL SILK(IRE),** b m Fayruz - Instanter by Morston (FR) (F Flood) 469 638 3793 3953

10 **LOCAL WHISPER,** b g Deep Run - Dream Toi by Carlburg (D R C Elsworth) 1520 3041

12 **LOCH BLUE,** b g Lochnager - La Sinope (FR) by Thatch (USA) (S Dow) 1216¹ 1600⁵ 2246⁴ 2536² 2824³ 3260

8 **LOCH DUICH,** ch h Kris - Sleat by Santa Claus (R J Hodges) 144⁴ 297⁵ 1187² 1597⁵

6 **LOCH GARANNE,** br m Lochnager - Raperon by Rapid River (M J Camacho) 1571⁷ 1863⁹ 3376⁵

5 **LOCH SCAVAIG(IRE),** b m The Parson - Regent Star by Prince Regent (FR) (D Moffatt) 731 821⁴ 1099¹ 1938⁴ 2220² 2785 2905¹ 3230³ 3583² 3737¹ 4072¹ 4178²

7 **LOCHEART LADY,** b m Lochnager - Cross Your Heart by Busted (J Berry) 1143 1313

9 **LOCHINGALL,** br g Mljet - Petite Doutelle by Percy Dear (Miss P Morris) 2526 2793

6 **LOCHNAGRAIN(IRE),** b or br g Strong Gale - Mountain Sedge by Goldhill (Mrs M Reveley) 2834⁷ 2976¹ 3284²

9 **LOCHNDOM,** b m Lochnager - Domino Smith by White Speck (A J Le Blond) 289 368

4 **LOCHORE,** b c Nordico (USA) - Hound Song by Jukebox (R Ingram) 1125⁷ 1244³

11 **LOCKWOOD PRINCE,** b g Tanfirion - Mink Fur (CAN) by Victoria Park (R G Frost) 3477 3978² 4083³

10 **LODATO,** b g Ela-Mana-Mou - Kye-Hye by Habitat (P G Bruen) 20 57 66 122 134 178⁶ 254

4 **LODESTONE LAD(IRE),** br g Norwick (USA) - Gentle Star by Comedy Star (USA) (R Dickin) 1705³ 2083 2503³ 2676⁶ 2991³ 3228⁷

6 **LODGE PARTY(IRE),** br m Strong Gale - Verenda (J R H Fowler) 45⁹

7 **LODGING,** ch g Longleat (USA) - Mollified by Lombard (GER) (B Ellison) 3435 3635 4082¹ 4176

8 **LOGAMIMO,** br g Lord Gayle (USA) - Miss Morgan by Native Prince (J A Hellens) 769¹ 871 1001⁴ 1144⁴ 2139

4 **LOGANI,** b f Domynsky - Vidette by Billion (USA) (D A Nolan) 3489 3868 4004⁴

6 **LOGICAL FUN,** b g Nishapour (FR) - Thimblerigger by Sharpen Up (J J O'Neill) 1940 2222 2792⁴ 2974⁴ 3287³ 4176⁶

5 **LOMOND SPRINGS(IRE),** b g Kambalda - Fast And Clever by Clever Fella (J Barclay) 2003 2220 2500⁹ 3641

10 **LONDON EXPRESS,** ch m True Song - Loophole by London Gazette (P J Hobbs) 202³ 287 567⁸

6 **LONDON HILL,** b g Little Wolf - Bambag by Goldhill (Mrs T J McInnes Skinner) 547⁹ 734⁸ 1582⁸ 1724⁵ 1787 3179⁵ 3429⁴ 3542¹ 3641³

6 **LONE WOLF,** ch m Little Wolf - Sober Sue by Tudor Treasure (Miss A E Broyd) 1957

6 **LONESOME GLORY(USA),** ch g Transworld (USA) - Stronghold (FR) by Green Dancer (USA) (F Bruce Miller) 817¹

5 **LONESOME TRAIN(USA),** ch g Crafty Prospector (USA) - Alaki Miss (USA) by Olden Times (C Weedon) 3736⁴ 3924⁶

6 **LONG FURLONG,** b g Castle Keep - Myrtlegrove by Scottish Rifle (R Akehurst) 151⁶

5 **LONG GUE(FR),** b h Lightning (FR) - Alamosa (FR) by Wildsun (A L T Moore) 803 1230

6 **LONG REACH,** br g Reach - Peperino by Relko (N A Twiston-Davies) 664⁸ 1194

6 **LONG'S EXPRESS(IRE),** b m Mandalus - Banross by Allangrange (K C Bailey) 114 236⁶ 536 675⁸ 747² 1456 1946⁸ 2225⁶ 2341⁷

7 **LONGSHOREMAN,** gr g Longleat (USA) - Cabotage by Sea Hawk II (Mrs A Barclay) 527⁶ 3992¹ 4124⁶

12 **LONTANO(GER),** b g Pentathlon - Lodina (GER) by Hodell (M J Ryan) 4348⁵

5 **LONZA VALLEY,** b g Pragmatic - Nautical Step by Julio Mariner (D R Gandolfo) 901

5 **LOOK NONCHALANT(IRE),** ch m Fayruz - Gobolino by Don (Norman Cassidy) 803 1681 1815 2607

6 **LOOKOUT MOUNTAIN(IRE),** b g Mandalus - Addies Lass by Little Buskins (J T Gifford) 2991⁵

6 **LOOPIN'S BOY(IRE),** b g King's Ride - Cherryville by Bowling Pin (H Eastwood) 3469

8 **LOOSE WHEELS,** b g Strong Gale - Kylogue Daisy by Little Buskins (Mrs P Sly) 770⁴ 917⁵ 1194³ 1563⁵ 3510⁴ 3802⁴

14 **LOR MOSS,** ch g Mossberry - Lor Darnie by Dumbarnie (S G Griffiths) 2650² 3212⁷ 3335 3501⁴ 3661⁷ 3852¹ 3929³ 4102¹ 4164²

6 **LORD ADVOCATE,** br g Law Society (USA) - Kereolle by Riverman (USA) (F Jestin) 1478 1677⁷

4 **LORD BARNARD(IRE),** gr g Toca Madera - Avital by Pitskelly (J E Mulhern) 2290 4010

6 **LORD BERTRAM(IRE),** b g Teofane - Satlan by Milan (J A Hellens) 974 2497 3431

6 **LORD CAMBERLEY(IRE),** br g Sandhurst Prince - Sally Gal by Lord Gayle (USA) (S G Griffiths) 2890³ 3190⁵ 3387

8 **LORD DIAMOND,** b g Lord Ha Ha - Santa Jo by Pitpan (J T R Dreaper) 1549 1760 1814

4 **LORD DORCET(IRE),** b g Remainder Man - Lady Dorcet by Condorcet (FR) (J I A Charlton) 3079² 3427⁸

9 **LORD FAWSLEY,** b or br g St Columbus - Ducal Gold by Solar Duke (G J Tarry) 4366² 3900⁴

712

INDEX TO NATIONAL HUNT RESULTS 1993-94

5 **LUCK OF A LADY(IRE),** b m Trojan Fen - Ounovarra by Homeric (Peter McCreery) 1230⁹ 1455⁹

6 **LUCKNAM DREAMER,** b g Macmillion - River Damsel by Forlorn River (Mrs Barbara Waring) 715⁷ 1085⁶ 2640⁶

7 **LUCKY AGAIN,** br h Ile de Bourbon (USA) - Soft Pedal by Hotfoot (C L Popham) 665² 840³ 1022⁷ 1165² 1328 1758 2645⁶ 2825 3116⁴ 3301 3573⁸ 3697⁵

7 **LUCKY BLUE,** b g Blue Cashmere - Cooling by Tycoon II (N B Thomson) 1245 1526⁵ 2110⁵ 2142⁵ 2841¹ 3020² 3340² 3574⁴ 3685⁵ 3804⁶

4 **LUCKY BUST(IRE),** b c Amazing Bust - Perpetue by Proverb (W Harney) 3842⁷

5 **LUCKY DAWN(IRE),** b g Lancastrian - Slave Light by Arctic Slave (C D Broad) 1277⁷ 1524⁵

4 **LUCKY DOMINO,** b c Primo Dominie - Ruff's Luck (USA) by Ruffinal (USA) (N Waggott) 3488 3868 4040⁷

9 **LUCKY ENOUGH,** b m Furry Glen - Friend In Town by Be Friendly (I J Keeling) 1⁸ 64⁹ 176⁶ 256⁷ 342⁵

4 **LUCKY HOLLY,** ch f General David - Holly Doon by Doon (R S Wood) 3169 3489 4040⁹

6 **LUCKY LANCER(IRE),** br g Seclude (USA) - Kova's Daughter by Brave Invader (USA) (Fergus Sutherland) 2774

9 **LUCKYLANDERS,** ch g Ascendant - Chetsford Water by Sir Lark (N A Twiston-Davies) 3309

10 **LUCKY LANE,** b g Mart Lane - O Token by Laurence O (P J Hobbs) 962³ 1411¹ 1537 1700² 2017² 2264⁴ 2493¹ 2647⁵ 3133

6 **LUCKY LORENZO,** b m Enchantment - Love Beach by Lorenzaccio (P R Hedger) 1688 2048

6 **LUCKY MINSTREL(IRE),** ch m Black Minstrel - Nautilus by Deep Run (Eugene M O'Sullivan) 90 472⁷ 535⁹

8 **LUCKY OAK,** ch g Tap On Wood - Zalinndia (FR) by Brigadier Gerard (R Rowe) 2400⁹ 2781⁸ 3156⁸ 3545 3698⁶ 3940⁶ 4096

5 **LUCKY SALUTE(IRE),** b g Mandalus - Addies Lass by Little Buskins (A P O'Brien) 3749³ 3936³

5 **LUCKY WEDSONG,** b g Lucky Wednesday - Hannah's Song by Saintly Song (W J Smith) 976 1103⁸ 1813⁸

8 **LUCY SOMERS,** ch m Bright Will - Gwen Gale by Lucifer (J E B Jobson) 3611⁵

5 **LUCY TWO SHOES(IRE),** b m Tumble Gold - Jet Black by Moyrath Jet (Andrew McCarren) 3071 4186

11 **LUCY'S CYGNET,** b g Le Bavard (FR) - Lucy Swan by Orchardist (John Stirling) 2773³

8 **LUCYS LAW,** b m Rymer - Shahzadeh by Menelek (James Joseph Mangan) 6 72

6 **LUGER(IRE),** b g Farhaan - Divine Wonder by Divine Gift (W S Cunningham) 626⁹ 787⁷ 1094 3429 3570 3864

5 **LUGHNASA'S DANCE(IRE),** ch m Ovac (ITY) - Rugged Cop by Rugged Man (Andrew Lee) 3694

6 **LUKS AKURA,** b g Dominion - Pacificus (USA) by Northern Dancer (M Johnston) 273² 395³

4 **LULA RIDGE,** ch f Sula Bula - Lapleigh Ridge by Sir Lark (M R Keenor) 3387 3880

10 **LUMBERJACK(USA),** b g Big Spruce (USA) - Snip by Shantung (C R Egerton) 842 2359⁵ 2513⁷ 3041 3132¹ 3318¹ 3500 3705⁶ 4001⁴

7 **LUMINOUS LIGHT,** ch m Cardinal Flower - Luminous Lady by Girandole (Michael O'Connor) 903³ 1074² 1332⁵ 1401⁵ 1899¹ 2160² 2392⁹ 2660⁵

6 **LUNABELLE,** b m Idiot's Delight - Barbella by Barolo (I A Balding) 603¹

12 **LUPO NERO,** b g Sallust - Lady Beck by Sir Gaylord (Ralph Hirons) 3385⁵ 3761³

9 **LUPY MINSTREL,** br g Black Minstrel - Lupreno by Hugh Lupus (C Parker) 1222⁸ 1606¹

7 **LUSTREMAN,** ch g Sallust - Miss Speak Easy (USA) by Sea-Bird II (J H Peacock) 195² 240¹ 326¹ 450¹ 629 3930

4 **LUSTRINO(USA),** b g Irish River (FR) - Sequins by Be My Guest (USA) (D K Weld) 290³ 375³ 529³ 706¹ 1111¹ 3656 3957¹

9 **LUSTY LAD,** b g Decoy Boy - Gluhwein by Ballymoss (M J Haynes) 384³ 499⁶ 601³ 961³ 1890² 2109³ 2643

8 **LUSTY LIGHT,** b g Strong Gale - Pale Maid by Rise'n Shine II (Mrs J Pitman) 649¹ 774² 1205 1770¹ 2514⁴ 2999 3408 3562⁹

5 **LUV-U-FRANK(IRE),** b g Good Thyne (USA) - Callula by Crash Course (M C Pipe) 3113³ 3386¹

6 **LUVLY BUBBLY,** b g Carlingford Castle - Mill Shine by Milan (M D Hammond) 1475⁷ 1918 2252⁸

5 **LYCIAN MOON,** b m Norwick (USA) - Brigannie Moon by Brigadier Gerard (A G Foster) 2717 2808 3019⁵ 3395

4 **LYFORD CAY(IRE),** ch g Waajib - Island Goddess by Godswalk (USA) (D W Chapman) 1767⁶ 2115³ 2224⁹ 2364⁴

5 **LYME GOLD(IRE),** ch g Phardante (FR) - Mad For Her Beer by Proverb (O Sherwood) 1494⁴ 2509⁷

5 **LYN'S RETURN(IRE),** b g Nordico (USA) - Salmas (FR) by Right Royal V (R Simpson) 149

6 **LYNCH LAW(IRE),** b or br h Law Society (USA) - Hogan's Sister (USA) by Speak John (M C Pipe) 2379⁴ 2655⁸ 2856² 3038 3214¹ 3413³ 3625² 4006¹ 4072² 4183¹

7 **LYNDON ROSE,** ch f Boreen (FR) - Emma James (Eugene M O'Sullivan) 3791

8 **LYPH(USA),** b g Lypheor - Scottish Lass by Scotland (P R Hedger) 2715² 3014 3574

5 **LYPHANTASTIC(USA),** b h Lyphard's Wish (FR) - Tango Five Juliet (USA) by Fappiano (USA) (C J Mann) 1773⁴ 2828⁴ 3044

10 **LYPHENTO(USA),** b h Lyphard's Wish (FR) - Hasty Viento (USA) by Gallant Man (J T Gifford) 1465⁸ 1653⁸ 1995³ 2246⁵

4 **LYRICAL SEAL,** b f Dubassoff (USA) - Sea-Rosemary by Seaepic (USA) (Miss A J Whitfield) 3208 3522 3855⁶

9 **M I BABE,** ch m Celtic Cone - Cover Your Money by Precipice Wood (Mrs I McKie) 4102²

5 **M MACG(IRE),** ch g M Double M (USA) - Temarie (FR) by Exbury (Daniel J Murphy) 42⁷ 66⁶ 91⁸ 169⁵ 251³

6 **M T POCKETS(IRE),** b g Flash Of Steel - Singing Away by Welsh Pageant (W P Mullins) 1383⁷ 1555⁷ 1897

5 **MA BELLA LUNA,** b m Jalmood (USA) - Macarte (FR) by Gift Card (FR) (J S Moore) 2430⁸ 2599 2881⁶ 3925⁹

6 **MAAMUR(USA),** gr g Robellino (USA) - Tiger Trap (USA) by Al Hattab (USA) (D Burchell) 1106⁵ 1559⁴ 1882²

4 **MAASTRICHT,** b g Common Grounds - Awatef by Ela-Mana-Mou (D Burchell) 702⁴ 1094

6 **MABES TOWN(IRE),** b g Horage - Mothers Blessing by Wollow Hollow (Laurence Skelly) 1 25⁷ 46⁶ 63² 113 161 232⁵ 392 493¹ 805 880⁵ 4077⁷

714

6 **MABTHUL(USA)**, b g Northern Baby (CAN) - Persuadable (USA) by What A Pleasure (USA) (F J O'Mahony) 4331¹ 183³ 344² 552⁴ 685² 837 959⁵ 1488 1810

7 **MAC RAMBLER**, b g Hotfoot - Arkengarthdale by Sweet Story (N Bycroft) 1924 2108 2321 2498⁷ 2686⁴ 2891³

6 **MAC THE BAT(IRE)**, gr g Court Macsherry - Grey Willow by Willowick (USA) (W A Murphy) 4336⁴ 565⁸

4 **MAC TOMB**, b g Valiyar - Elaine Ann by Garda's Revenge (USA) (R J Price) 3211 3444

5 **MAC'S BOY**, b g Macmillion - Tender Manx by Owen Dudley (B Palling) 3113 3503

10 **MAC'S GLEN**, ch g Furry Glen - Graham Dieu by Three Dons (Michael Cunningham) 52⁴ 75⁴ 119 132³ 303³ 422

6 **MAC'S LEAP**, ch g Homeboy - Miss Sunblest by Whistler (Mrs I McKie) 844⁶ 1309⁸ 2333 2762 3825

8 **MACAMORE GALE**, b g Strong Gale - Not At All by Royal Highway (Thomas Foley) 2183⁵ 2662

8 **MACAMORE STAR**, b g Callernish - Lucy Ladybird by Menelek (Thomas Foley) 2351¹ 2681⁴ 2865⁷ 3241³

7 **MACCONACHIE**, b h Good Times (ITY) - High Point Lady (CAN) by Knightly Dawn (USA) (M Dods) 2218 2251⁶ 2565⁷ 2971² 3178⁶

6 **MACEDONAS**, b h Niniski (USA) - Miss Saint-Cloud by Nonoalco (USA) (C P E Brooks) 936 1135⁵ 1508¹ 3338¹ 3420 3548⁶ 3706² 3966¹

9 **MACHO MAN**, b g Mummy's Game - Shoshoni by Ballymoss (T J Etherington) 1600⁷ 1943 2191⁷ 2396⁵

7 **MACK A DAY**, b g Niels - Soothamona by Beau Charmeur (FR) (Michael Condon) 101³ 121¹ 214² 306² 539 800⁶ 3294 3524 3890⁵

5 **MACKABEE(IRE)**, b or br g Supreme Leader - Donegal Queen by Quayside (Mrs J Pitman) 2339⁷ 2834⁹

9 **MACKINNON**, b g Broadsword (USA) - Salambos by Doon (G Richards) 2501

9 **MACMURPHY**, ch g Deep Run - Millymeeta by New Brig (A M Thomson) 4388⁷ 656 770 874

5 **MACS MISS(IRE)**, ch m Le Moss - Sweet Start by Candy Cane (Patrick J F Gillespie) 1766 1820

9 **MAD CASANOVA**, b g Scorpio (FR) - Parveen (FR) by Kouban (FR) (R J O'Sullivan) 1395

4 **MAD MYTTON**, b g Crowning Honors (CAN) - Vynz Girl by Tower Walk (A Bailey) 188 406⁹ 448⁶ 1749

7 **MAD THYME**, b g Idiot's Delight - Another Breeze by Deep Run (N A Gaselee) 1108⁴ 1539³ 1878³ 2263³ 2505² 3036 3215² 3518

9 **MAD TOM**, b g Furry Glen - Artic Leap by Arctic Slave (J T R Dreaper) 1382⁵ 1761² 1985¹ 2159⁵ 2466⁵ 2698⁹ 3123⁶ 3693⁴

4 **MADAM GYMCRAK**, b f Celestial Storm (USA) - Finlandaise (FR) by Arctic Tern (USA) (G Holmes) 790⁴ 3661¹

5 **MADAM MARGEAUX(IRE)**, b m Ardross - Madam Slaney by Prince Tenderfoot (USA) (Mrs J G Retter) 3176 3256⁷

7 **MADAM NODDY**, b f Welsh Term - Hatha (USA) by Bold Reason (Cecil Mahon) 39

5 **MADAM PICASSO(IRE)**, gr m Anita's Prince - Perbury by Grisaille (N R Mitchell) 1502⁴ 1701³

4 **MADAM ROSE(IRE)**, b f Cardinal Flower - Misquested by Lord Ha Ha (J W Mullins) 3833

6 **MADDYDOO(IRE)**, ch g Stalker - Lengua Franca by St Chad (Robin Marrs) 4094⁹

4 **MADISON COUNTY(IRE)**, b g The Parson - Lucie Fort by Lucifer (USA) (D K Weld) 3936⁷

6 **MADRAJ(IRE)**, b or br h Double Schwartz - Poka Poka (FR) by King Of Macedon (R J Hodges) 300³ 358¹ 420³ 522⁵ 667² 826⁶ 1188⁶

5 **MADRIKO(FR)**, b g Iron Duke - Madrina by Pen Mane 621³

8 **MAESTRO PAUL**, b g Petorius - Muligatawny by Malacate (USA) (J T Gifford) 2366⁴ 2649⁴ 2727² 3038 3363¹ 3535¹

5 **MAESTROSO(IRE)**, b g Mister Majestic - That's Easy by Swing Easy (USA) (R F Johnson Houghton) 1804 2263⁶

6 **MAGELLAN BAY(IRE)**, b g Orchestra - Kintullagh by Crash Course (Mrs J Pitman) 2269 2860⁴ 3164

6 **MAGENTA BOY**, b g Belfort (FR) - Krugerrand by Goldhill (G M Moore) 1199 1872 1959 2239⁸

6 **MAGGIE TEE**, b m Lepanto (GER) - Grey Receipt by Rugantino (N R Mitchell) 1626 2147 2426 2950⁹ 3151 3630

6 **MAGGIES LAD**, b g Red Johnnie - Busted Love by Busted (K R Burke) 2760 3584⁸ 3755⁸ 3998³ 4086⁷

7 **MAGGOTS GREEN**, ch m Pas de Seul - Fabled Lady by Bold Lad (IRE) (J M Bradley) 705⁹ 988 1109 1301 1413⁴ 1525⁴ 1718¹ 1795¹ 2030⁴ 2146⁴ 2486⁵ 3585² 3664⁴ 3847 3882⁴

8 **MAGIC BLOOM**, br m Full Of Hope - Mantavella by Andrea Mantegna (A P Stringer) 4350¹ 4385⁴ 972⁸ 1127⁴ 1746 3538⁹ 3819⁷

4 **MAGIC FAN(IRE)**, b g Taufan (USA) - Magic Gold by Sallust (Mrs A Swinbank) 128⁵ 285⁸

4 **MAGIC FEELING(IRE)**, ch f Magical Wonder (USA) - Papsie's Pet by Busted (A P O'Brien) 1264¹ 1454² 1816³ 2156¹ 2608³ 2699² 3656² 3836²

5 **MAGIC GLOW(IRE)**, br g Glow (USA) - Manela Lady by Ela-Mana-Mou (Thomas Bergin) 51

8 **MAGIC MILLION**, b g Gorytus (USA) - Beach Light by Bustino (M A O'Toole) 492² 806² 878¹ 1019 1268² 1382¹ 1433³ 2159⁴

4 **MAGIC MOONBEAM(IRE)**, b f Decent Fellow - Alice Johnston by Majetta (Mrs J A Morgan) 3372⁴ 3616

9 **MAGIC SOLDIER**, br g Mandrake Major - Dior Queen by Manacle (J Gilbert) 366² 500³ 676³ 810⁸

4 **MAGICAL MINSTER**, b f Wonderful Surprise - Lingdale Lady by Sandford Lad (B A McMahon) 3401⁵

12 **MAGICAL MORRIS**, ch g Balinger - River Spell by Spartan General (W R Hacking) 3155⁴ 3856² 4095

6 **MAGNIFICENT OAK(NZ)**, b g Oak Ridge (FR) - Hine Maia (NZ) by Heir Presumptive (USA) (C Kinane) 4404 41 98² 201⁶

10 **MAGNOLIA EXPRESS**, b h Magnolia Lad - Wasdale by Psidium (D E Probert) 3947

5 **MAGNUM STAR(IRE)**, b g Damister (USA) - North Telstar by Sallust (Basil King) 944⁷ 2348⁶ 3468 3731 3834⁴ 3840 4030⁶ 4115⁶

5 **MAGS SUPER TOI(IRE)**, b g Supreme Leader - Mags Toi by Prince Hansel (K Riordan) 3720

9 **MAGSOOD**, ch g Mill Reef (USA) - Shark Song by Song (S Mellor) 237³

10 **MAHANA**, b g Tepukei - Easby Saint by Saintly Song (J J Coates) 3846⁷ 4073

5 **MAHANKHALI(IRE)**, br g Mandalus - Simbella by Simbir (Niall Madden) 1581 3508 3653 3891⁹ 4171⁷

7 **MAHATMACOAT**, ch g Prince Of Peace - Avec Amour by Jolly Jet (Mrs J G Retter) 1946⁶ 2144 2362 2657³ 2799

7 **MAHON RIVER,** b g Callernish - River Farm by Over The River (FR) (David A Kiely) 4396⁹

6 **MAHONG,** gr g Petong - Balearica by Bustino (Mrs H Parrott) 1751³ 1867⁸ 2606³ 3144⁹ 3340 3716 3773⁹ 4003³ 4107⁶

6 **MAI PEN RAI,** ch g All Systems Go - Jersey Maid by On Your Mark (R J Hodges) 1414⁷

5 **MAIASAURA(IRE),** b g Head For Heights - Mursuma by Rarity (P F Graffin) 3813 4091

5 **MAID FOR DANCING(IRE),** b m Crash Course - La Flamenca by Brave Invader (USA) (J R H Fowler) 3393³ 3694⁵

6 **MAID OF GLENDURAGH(IRE),** b m Ya Zaman (USA) - Mazzola (FR) by Val de Loir (J F C Maxwell) 2197 3388 3647

9 **MAID TO MATCH,** b f Matching Pair - Millies Last by Cheval (Mrs Helen Mobley) 3920

8 **MAILCOM,** b g Strong Gale - Poll's Turn by Le Tricolore (Mrs J Pitman) 1206⁴ 1491¹ 1704¹ 1973² 2193¹ 2514² 3039

4 **MAJA GRADDNOS,** b f Glint Of Gold - Tzarina (USA) by Gallant Romeo (USA) (J K Magee) 2771³ 3069⁸ 3448⁶ 3719

5 **MAJAL(IRE),** b g Caerleon (USA) - Park Special by Relkino (J S Wainwright) 915⁶ 1100⁶ 1811¹ 2057⁵ 2645¹ 3755² 3898⁴

5 **MAJBOOR(IRE),** b g Wassl - Mashteen (USA) by Majestic Prince (Daniel J Murphy) 1610

6 **MAJED(IRE),** b h Wolverlife - Martin Place by Martinmas (Mrs M Reveley) 1571¹ 2850²

14 **MAJESTIC BUCK,** b g Majestic Streak - Young Katie by Drumbeg (Mrs J Sidebottom) 2301 2526⁹

6 **MAJESTIC GOLD,** b g Majestic Maharaj - Balas by Goldfella (F Jordan) 315 1301 3745⁵

5 **MAJESTIC MAIGUE(IRE),** gr m Standaan (FR) - Countess Decima (USA) by Sir Gaylord (John Brassil) 997

9 **MAJESTIC PARK,** ch g Majestic Guard - Naughton Park by Lorenzaccio (Mrs Ann Ferris) 92

7 **MAJESTIC QUEEN,** b m Morston's Heir - Royal Guest by Guest Of Honour (G H Barber) 3729⁸ 3886⁹

10 **MAJESTIC RIDE,** b g Palm Track - Lakeland Lady by Leander (Major Malcolm Wallace) 2889

9 **MAJIC RAIN,** bl g Northern Value (USA) - Dinsdale by Menelek (G M R Coatsworth) 4327⁴ 4387 2253⁹ 2448 3437

6 **MAJIRIYOUN(IRE),** b g Darshaan - Majanada by Tap On Wood (Declan Gillespie) 83¹

6 **MAJOR BELL,** br g Silly Prices - Melaura Belle by Meldrum (A C Whillans) 1478⁴ 1677¹ 2008² 2237¹ 2367³ 2740⁷ 2812⁵ 3140² 3472¹

6 **MAJOR BERT(IRE),** b g Kemal (FR) - African Nelly by Pitpan (James Joseph Mangan) 1786⁸ 2128 3551 3709⁹ 3789 3872⁸ 3972

5 **MAJOR BUGLER(IRE),** b g Thatching - Bugle Sound by Bustino (G B Balding) 648⁵ 898⁸ 1755⁵ 2175⁹

7 **MAJOR BUSH,** b g Julio Mariner - Peperino by Relko (Mrs J Pitman) 4362

8 **MAJOR CUT,** b g Furry Glen - Quetta's Dual (R H Buckler) 962⁶ 1527² 1795³ 2206

9 **MAJOR EFFORT,** ro g General Ironside - Julie's Gi-Gi by Brave Invader (USA) (J Allen) 1168 1409 1461 2254

9 **MAJOR ELSTON,** b g Record Run - Glanfield by Eborneezer (M J Bolton) 957 1463 2780⁵ 3260⁹

8 **MAJOR FOUNTAIN,** br g Royal Fountain - Singing Span by Crooner (W L Barker) 625

5 **MAJOR GALE(IRE),** b g Strong Gale - Cailin Rialta by Royal Match (J Morrison) 530⁷ 709

8 **MAJOR INQUIRY(USA),** b g The Minstrel (CAN) - Hire A Brain (USA) by Seattle Slew (USA) (J T Gifford) 762⁶ 1120⁶ 2043⁶ 2319⁴ 2622¹ 3305⁴ 3548 3724⁴

4 **MAJOR JACK,** br g Uncle Pokey - Streakella by Firestreak (Mrs S C Bradburne) 3557 3892

9 **MAJOR KINSMAN,** b g Nepotism - Noon Hunting by Green Shoon (R Lee) 650 737⁷ 1171 2174

7 **MAJOR MAC,** b g Mandalus - Ullard Lady by Official (D L Williams) 1027

12 **MAJOR MATCH(NZ),** b g Frassino - Burks Rainbow (NZ) by Weyand (USA) (Capt T A Forster) 354¹ 457⁴ 566 684³

6 **MAJOR MINER(IRE),** b g Miner's Lamp - Chiminee Bee by Bluerullah (G B Balding) 2144⁸

5 **MAJOR RISK,** ch g Risk Me (FR) - Brampton Grace by Tachypous (J A Harris) 227 369³ 1810

6 **MAJOR RUMPUS,** b g Politico (USA) - Premier Susan by Murrayfield (A L T Moore) 2607² 2849² 3393¹

4 **MAJOR TRIUMPH(IRE),** ch f Hatim (USA) - Hetty Green by Bay Express (G C Bravery) 851 1253⁸

5 **MAJOR TROOP,** br g State Trooper - Highflyer Park by Midsummer Night II (N B Mason) 541²

5 **MAJOR'S LAW(IRE),** b g Law Society (USA) - Maryinsky (USA) by Northern Dancer (J White) 662 849 2395² 2628³

9 **MAJORITY HOLDING,** b g Mandrake Major - Kirkby by Midsummer Night II (J White) 1488⁹

5 **MAJORITY MAJOR(IRE),** b g Cheval - La Perla by Majority Blue (P Cheesbrough) 728 1181² 1574⁷ 1745² 2104³ 3126² 3359³ 3646¹ 4050²

14 **MAJUBA ROAD,** ch m Scottish Rifle - Cleo Baby by Dicta Drake (John Morley) 3989 4130

6 **MAKE A LINE,** b g High Line - Another Packet by Main Reef (S E Sherwood) 43⁶ 55³ 150³ 302 441³ 934 1152 1926⁵

9 **MAKE ME AN ISLAND,** br m Creative Plan (USA) - Bali by Ballymoss (Patrick G Kelly) 131 200⁴ 293 554³ 635⁹ 690⁷ 928¹ 1179³ 1761³ 1826⁵ 2235² 2659 2922 3873¹ 4042

5 **MAKE ME PROUD(IRE),** b m Be My Native (USA) - Miami Life by Miami Springs (W Bentley) 757³ 1066⁷ 1186⁶ 1485⁷ 1633² 1740² 1963⁵ 2256⁷ 2502⁶ 2894

6 **MAKES ME GOOSEY(IRE),** b g Roselier (FR) - Clonmeen Official by Official (Mrs I McKie) 1327⁴ 1729⁵ 1998² 2208⁸ 2428 2936¹ 3514

9 **MAKES YOU WONDER(IRE),** ch g Beau Charmeur (FR) - Rosie Josie by Trombone (P F Graffin) 124⁵ 378³ 513⁶ 1016⁸

7 **MAKING TIME,** gr m Furry Glen - Arctic Border by Arctic Slave (G L Humphrey) 883⁹ 1040³ 1263⁷ 1536 1734⁴ 2187³ 2361 2705⁷ 3571⁹ 3729⁷ 3917

4 **MALACHITE GREEN,** b g Lochnager - Rhiannon by Welsh Pageant (R Hollinshead) 2534³ 3035¹ 3183⁵

10 **MALACHYS BAR,** b g Habyom - Dainty Eden by Orbit (Patrick J F Hassett) 134⁵ 178 293¹ 364² 468⁵ 799⁷ 966² 1402

4 **MALAIA(IRE),** b f Commanche Run - Spartan Helen by Troy (J A B Old) 2652¹ 2857¹

8 **MALAMUTE SALOON(USA),** ch g Arctic Tern (USA) - Square Generation (USA) by Olden Times (C D Broad) 1033

12 **MALAQUETTE,** gr m Jellaby - Alpha Tor by Great Nephew (J Norton) 2094

4 **MALAWI,** ch g Northern State (USA) - Nyeri by Saint Crespin III (W A Bethell) 784⁵ 2135⁶ 2404

718

INDEX TO NATIONAL HUNT RESULTS 1993-94

5 **MIDDLEHAM CASTLE,** b g Lafontaine (USA) - Superfina (USA) by Fluorescent Light (USA) (V Thompson) 2687 429 2735 2927

9 **MIDDLEWICK,** b g Ballacashtal (CAN) - Thunder Bay by Canisbay (S Christian) 43771 32064 34554 38319 40162

8 **MIDFIELDER,** ch g Formidable (USA) - Pampas Flower by Pampered King (P J Hobbs) 1483 4592 7501 8293 10252 12068 31941 35001 37052 39231 41562

4 **MIDGET GEM,** ch g Midyan (USA) - Nafla (FR) by Arctic Tern (USA) (Mrs A Knight) 3765

11 **MIDLAND EXPRESS,** ch g Midland Gayle - Queens County by Harewell (Denys Smith) 14818 27409 28157 29745 3287

6 **MIDNIGHT AT MAY'S(IRE),** b m King's Ride - Brave Express by Brave Invader (USA) (Donal Hassett) 18581 20507

8 **MIDNIGHT CALLER,** br g Callernish - Miss Pitpan by Pitpan (S E Sherwood) 12731 16251 1993 2085 2318 35031

11 **MIDNIGHT COURT(USA),** b g Alleged (USA) - Lassie Dear by Buckpasser (A Butler) 251

8 **MIDNIGHT FLOTILLA,** b m Balinger - Foglet by Foggy Bell (P Beaumont) 27858 30302 32369 3440 3751 40452

5 **MIDNIGHT HOUR(IRE),** gr g Roselier (FR) - Shirowen by Master Owen (D T Hughes) 1230 16811 18488 20563 25869 2863 41895

6 **MIDNIGHT JESTOR(IRE),** b m Jester - Midnight Patrol by Ashmore (FR) (G E Jones) 3829

10 **MIDNIGHT MISS(NZ),** br m Princes Gate - Princess Jane (NZ) by Head Hunter (Michael Robinson) 265

5 **MIDNIGHT SERVICE(IRE),** b g The Parson - Stringfellows (M F Morris) 3366

9 **MIDNIGHT STORY,** gr g Pragmatic - Midnight Oil by Menelek (Mrs M E Long) 960 14442 20434

10 **MIDNIGHT STRIKE(USA),** b g Topsider (USA) - Revels End by Welsh Pageant (M Williams) 5696 687

6 **MIDORI,** b m State Diplomacy (USA) - Predora by Premonition (Mrs A Tomkinson) 2409 2785 2905 33595

5 **MIDVALE GRADUATE(IRE),** ch g Pennine Walk - Red Jade by Red God (T Thomson Jones) 31833

9 **MIG,** b m Sagaro - Lady Gaylord by Double Jump (N B Mason) 2793 2887 3160 34624 35585 3867

4 **MIGAVON,** b f Sharrood (USA) - Migoletty by Oats (L A Snook) 2494 26855 28817 35311 37673

5 **MIGHTY EXPRESS,** b g Bay Express - Astral Suite by On Your Mark (I Park) 1674

8 **MIGHTY FALCON,** b g Comedy Star (USA) - Lettuce by So Blessed (D R C Elsworth) 1887 2143 22664 2513 26484 2824 32613 3425 35197 39393

7 **MIGHTY FROLIC,** b m Oats - Mighty Nice by Vimadee (Miss S Edwards) 41821

7 **MIGHTY HAGGIS,** b g Glen Quaich - Willie Pat by Pitpan (Daniel Lordan) 9937 18276 22364 23553 26209 3837

15 **MIGHTY MARK,** b g Rebel Prince - White Net by Monet (F T Walton) 43924

5 **MIGHTY MAURICE(IRE),** b g Carlingford Castle - Cooladerry Lassy by Laurence O (A G Foster) 21342 25463

7 **MIGHTY PRINCE,** ch g Pharly (FR) - Anne Stuart (FR) by Bolkonski (P D Evans) 523

5 **MIGHTY PROFILE(IRE),** b g Over The River (FR) - Nice An' Fluffy by Furry Glen (R O'Leary) 28775

11 **MIINNEHOMA,** b or br g Kambalda - Mrs Cairns by Choral Society (M C Pipe) 28521 30647 34251

7 **MILDRED SOPHIA,** b m Crooner - Glanfield by Eborneezer (N R Mitchell) 8597 1519 16991 1719 18621 22967 2400 24966 27177 27815 31503 32545 33484 38534 4064

5 **MILENKEH(IRE),** b g Salluceva - Petite Fee by Cut Above (M J Home) 1786 3087

7 **MILEY SWEENEY,** ch g Le Moss - Abbeyside by Paddy's Stream (Bryan F Murphy) 39568 40609

6 **MILFORD MATCH(IRE),** b m Millfontaine - Another Match by Sovereign Path (W P Mullins) 7 508 90 115 2361 2958 574

9 **MILITARY HONOUR,** b g Shirley Heights - Princess Tiara by Crowned Prince (USA) (J E Swiers) 13606 2136 22423 22551 24121 25631 27872 30322 32882 3582 3865

8 **MILITARY SECRET,** ch g Tug Of War - Leeann by Pitpan (Mrs E Moscrop) 4792 11452 13193

12 **MILITARY TWO STEP,** b g Rarity - Jasusa by Cantab (Mrs Teresa Elwell) 4374

5 **MILIYEL,** ch m Rousillon (USA) - Amalee by Troy (Miss Gay Kelleway) 43071 2482

11 **MILK QUOTA,** br g Healaugh Fox - Gina by Teme Valley (B J Eckley) 525 1302

5 **MILL BELLE(IRE),** b m Orchestra - Asinara by Julio Mariner (J A O'Connell) 266

5 **MILL BURN,** ch g Precocious - Northern Ballerina by Dance In Time (CAN) (A L Forbes) 664 13703 1627 20656 21304 22243 23434 26412 27131 36354 41608

9 **MILL DE LEASE,** b h Milford - Melting Snows by High Top (J Dooler) 6237 7677 16394 1740 2256

12 **MILL KNOCK,** b g Park Row - Barlocco Bay by Cantab (J D Thompson) 31574 3430 35816

5 **MILL O'THE RAGS(IRE),** b g Strong Gale - Lady Rag by Ragapan (Anthony Mullins) 37929

6 **MILLBROOK LAD(IRE),** gr g Roselier (FR) - Skinana by Buckskin (FR) (William Patton) 1016

6 **MILLENIUM LASS(IRE),** ch m Viking (USA) - Sandford Star by Sandford Lad (W M Roper) 292 512 2323 3922 2703 2774 3526

7 **MILLER'S CHAP,** br g Teofane - Millar's Gayle (Ms Rosemary Rooney) 15771

7 **MILLER'S CROSSING,** b m Mandalus - Somelli by Candy Cane (D Carroll) 43382 158 795 1758 2296 1902 2232 34694 3837 39741 41133

4 **MILLERS MILL(IRE),** ch g Shy Groom (USA) - Millers Lady by Mill Reef (USA) (E McNamara) 3751 6172 19113

8 **MILLHAVEN PRINCESS,** br f Mandalus - Bunty Noggan by Current Coin (Mark Jeffrey Millar) 18326 21828 30718 3447 4091

6 **MILLIE(USA),** ch m Master Willie - La Zonga (USA) by Run The Gantlet (USA) (J Mooney) 1252 13715 16283 1812 1863 21654 30297 33427 39266 40707

8 **MILLIE BELLE,** ch m Milford - Charter Belle by Runnymede (P G Warner) 43135 1494 3573 4613 6005 38544 39877

6 **MILLIES GIRL(IRE),** b m Millfontaine - Perennial Twinkle by Continuation (A J McNamara) 4402 32 418 1117

7 **MILLIES OWN,** ch g Deep Run - The Cardy by Chou Chin Chow (S Mellor) 6957 7943 960 10933 13161 15353 18092 2117 2264

5 **MILLION IN MIND(IRE),** ch g Lomond (USA) - Klairlone by Klairon (J White) 12835 24093 31023

723

1334⁶ 1826 1915 2100 2200 2282 2847 2922 3200 3504 3655 3954

10 **MONEY SAVED,** b g Torenaga - Mascarita by Final Problem (S Braddish) 1898 2158⁵

6 **MONGARD(IRE),** ch g Monksfield - Lyngard by Balliol (Desmond McDonogh) 1555 1609⁸ 1764

5 **MONGIE(IRE),** b h Blazing Saddles (AUS) - Femme de Fer (USA) by Mr Leader (USA) (R W T Brabazon) 233 469

7 **MONKEY AGO,** b g Black Minstrel - Arctic Sue by Arctic Slave (P Mullins) 4398² 1580³ 1780³ 1894⁶ 2052³ 2201² 2390 2588 2700⁴ 2987 3198¹ 3465⁵ 3614³ 3789⁴ 4032¹

7 **MONKS AIR,** ch m Monksfield - Merton Air by Prince Hansel (Eugene M O'Sullivan) 554 1399 1857 2351⁴ 2550⁵ 2661⁹ 3293⁷ 3551⁷ 3790³ 3835 3911 3972⁶ 4042¹

7 **MONKS DEAR VI,** b m Monksfield - No Dear (Peter McCreery) 808 3720

5 **MONKS JAY(IRE),** br g Monksfield - Boro Penny by Normandy (C T Nash) 4023 4172

6 **MONKS SOHAM(IRE),** b g The Parson - Kadaga by Linacre (G A Hubbard) 2916 3264⁸

8 **MONKSANDER,** b g Monksfield - Maudie's Choice by Nebbiolo (P C Ritchens) 1023³ 1341⁴ 1469 1994 3007 3361³ 3510¹ 3844

9 **MONKSLAND,** b g Monksfield - Very Much by Bluerullah (A P Mannerings) 1916⁶ 1989⁹

6 **MONKTON(IRE),** ch g The Parson - Poula Scawla by Pollerton (Capt T A Forster) 1109⁴ 1567 1715 3453

8 **MONSIEUR LE CURE,** b g The Parson - Caramore Lady by Deep Run (J A C Edwards) 1291² 1547 1754⁴ 1844² 2264¹ 2378¹ 2746¹ 3039¹ 3411¹

8 **MONT MIRAIL,** b g Buckskin (FR) - Woodcliffe by Harwell (G Richards) 2217⁹

10 **MONTAGNARD,** b g Strong Gale - Louisa Stuart (FR) by Ruysdael II (M Bradstock) 1972² 2172 3028 3491

5 **MONTAGNE,** br m Midyan (USA) - La Masse by High Top (M W Eckley) 126⁸ 1079 1323³

11 **MONTALINO,** br g Neltino - Montage by Polyfoto (G L Humphrey) 1489⁵ 1641³ 1887⁴

7 **MONTE FIGO,** ch g Wolver Heights - Algarve by Alcide (A L T Moore) 1987⁷ 2279⁷ 2590 2842⁶ 3693² 3935 4030²

4 **MONTEJUSTICE(IRE),** b f Montelimar (USA) - Wild Justice by Sweet Revenge (P J Casserly) 253⁷ 2750 3505

13 **MONTGOMERY,** b g Push On - Mirror Back by Master Owen (W G McKenzie-Coles) 3171⁹

8 **MONTIFIORE AVENUE,** b g Kings Lake (USA) - Lady Of Cornwall (USA) by Cornish Prince (G Fierro) 1292⁴ 1481 3491 3661 3773

7 **MONTPELIER LAD,** br g Elegant Air - Leg Glance by Home Guard (USA) (G Richards) 450² 544

5 **MONTRAVE,** ch g Netherkelly - Streakella by Firestreak (R Allan) 1478 1724⁴ 2148³ 2735⁵ 3144⁷

5 **MONTY ROYALE(IRE),** b h Montelimar (USA) - Atlanta Royale by Prince Tenderfoot (USA) (K C Bailey) 2224² 2525² 2789¹ 3008³

11 **MONUMENTAL LAD,** ro g Jellaby - Monumental Moment by St Paddy (Mrs H Parrott) 1171⁵ 1523²

5 **MONY-GRIT(IRE),** b g Sheer Grit - Lisnacoilla by Beau Chapeau (M D Hammond) 2490⁷

5 **MONY-SKIP(IRE),** b g Strong Gale - Skiporetta by Even Money (M D Hammond) 2931²

5 **MONYMOSS(IRE),** b g Le Moss - El Scarsdale by Furry Glen (Mrs S J Smith) 3590³ 3868⁴

5 **MOOHONO(IRE),** gr m Roselier (FR) - Dawn Shade by Beau Charmeur (FR) (P Kiely) 504⁶

6 **MOON MONKEY(IRE),** b g Derring Rose - Paiukiri by Ballyciptic (Mrs A L M King) 1354⁹ 2837³ 3395⁹

7 **MOON-FROG,** ch g Tesoro Mio - Willya Pauper by Pauper (Patrick John Murphy) 53 95 150 258 433⁶ 505⁵

8 **MOONCAPER,** b g Candy Cane - Any Old Time by Mon Capitaine (A P O'Brien) 1235⁸ 1378⁶ 1496⁹ 1897 2157 2661² 2752¹ 3249³ 3392

8 **MOONLIGHT SHIFT,** ch g Night Shift (USA) - Rana by Welsh Pageant (W Clay) 3597

6 **MOONSHEE(IRE),** ch m Le Moss - Whisper Moon by Chinatown (Capt D G Swan) 1403⁴ 1859⁴ 2038⁹ 2664⁸ 2924¹

4 **MOONSHINE DANCER,** b g Northern State (USA) - Double Birthday by Cavo Doro (Mrs M Reveley) 272¹ 1483⁹ 3034

9 **MOORCROFT BOY,** g Roselier (FR) - Well Mannered by Menelek (D Nicholson) 4374² 1447² 1635² 2011¹ 2173¹ 2748² 3425³

6 **MOORE BONES,** b g Relkino - Hopeful Step by Hopeful Venture (D R Gandolfo) 1626⁸ 2509⁶ 2916⁴

8 **MOORECHURCH GLEN,** b g Furry Glen - Sneem by Rum (USA) (Mrs M Wilson) 4094⁶

5 **MOOREFIELD GIRL(IRE),** ch m Gorytus (USA) - Tracy's Sundown by Red Sunset (A P O'Brien) 12² 266¹ 365² 671 3466 3730 3913 4114⁴

6 **MOORETOWN LAD(IRE),** b g Camden Town - La Lola by Le Levanstell (Hugh McCaffrey) 4061

4 **MOORISH,** b g Dominion - Remoosh by Glint Of Gold (J White) 1473² 2303¹ 2516¹ 3062² 3656⁶

4 **MOORLOUGH BAY(IRE),** ch c Abednego - Monica's Pet by Sovereign Gleam (S A Kirk) 3937

6 **MOORLOUGH VIEW(IRE),** ch m Mirror Boy - Hatha (USA) by Bold Reason (Cecil Mahon) 37

5 **MOPHEAD KELLY,** ch h Netherkelly - Trois Filles by French Marny (W Clay) 2534⁷ 3396 3826

4 **MORAN BRIG,** ch g Bustino - Aunt Judy by Great Nephew (G B Balding) 1244 1464⁴ 1705 2016⁴ 2083⁸ 2428 2878

5 **MORBIDELLI(IRE),** ch g King Persian - Magnanimous by Runnymede (Michael Flynn) 1762 1815

5 **MORCAT,** ch m Morston (FR) - Ancat Girl by Politico (USA) (G P Kelly) 3589 3868

6 **MORCELI(IRE),** gr g Mouktar - Safiah (FR) by St Paddy (J H Johnson) 1289¹ 1661³ 1918¹ 2356⁷ 2812¹ 3036

8 **MORE BUBBLES,** b m Ragapan - Ascot Princess by Prince Hansel (Mrs Edwina Finn) 3912⁷ 3956

6 **MORE DASH(IRE),** b m Strong Gale - Wee Mite by Menelek (James Joseph Mangan) 73¹ 88⁸ 258⁵ 333² 534 558³

4 **MORE DASH THANCASH(IRE),** ch g Stalker - Gobolino by Don (Martyn J McEnery) 2848⁴ 3245³

7 **MORE IMPORTANT,** m m Import - Sponsorship by Sparkler (M A Barnes) 3378

9 **MORE OF IT,** b g Furry Glen - Homewrecker by Wrekin Rambler (M J Roberts) 2400⁸ 2883⁴ 3117 3455⁷ 3728 3883⁴

5 **MORE TO LIFE,** b m Northern Tempest (USA) - Kaloon by Kala Shikari (S W Campion) 2963⁸

4 **MOREOF A GUNNER,** ch g Gunner B - Coliemore by Coliseum (J M Jefferson) 2490⁵ 2931⁴ 3489⁴

8 **MORGANS HARBOUR,** br g Radical - Parsfield by The Parson (Mrs M Reveley) 2325¹ 2635² 3059¹ 3437¹ 3908¹

5 **MORGANS MAN,** b h Morgans Choice - Mandover by Mandamus (Mrs S D Williams) 4319¹ 796 985

7 **MORIARTY,** b g Martinmas - Love Is Blind (USA) by Hasty Road (R J Price) 2048⁸ 2292¹ 2405⁴ 2665³ 2804² 3094² 3281⁵ 3319¹

4 **MORJINSKI,** ch f Myjinski (USA) - Morley by Hotfoot (D J S Ffrench Davis) 4179³

10 **MORLEY STREET,** ch g Deep Run - High Board by High Line (G B Balding) 1226⁹ 1664⁷ 3025

4 **MORNING BLUSH(IRE),** ch f Glow (USA) - Sweetbird by Ela-Mana-Mou (M C Pipe) 3401 3708⁸

7 **MORNING DREAM,** br g Saher - Love Resolved by Dan Cupid (Donal Hassett) 4338 65¹ 135 294 574¹ 690 856 1331⁵ 1399⁸ 1907⁵ 2126

6 **MORNING IN MAY(IRE),** b g General Ironside - Orinda Way by Deep Run (Patrick Prendergast) 1681 1833 3747 4031⁸

7 **MORSHOT,** b g Oats - Duckdown by Blast (C P E Brooks) 1448⁹ 1775⁸ 2420

7 **MOSARAT(IRE),** b m Montelimar (USA) - Choclate Baby (Owen Weldon) 377 102³ 173³ 274² 341⁴

5 **MOSCOW DUKE(IRE),** ch g King Persian - Tamar Di Bulgaria (ITY) by Duke Of Marmalade (USA) (E McNamara) 671⁷ 925 1176⁶ 1609

4 **MOSES PREY(IRE),** ch g Waajib - Simone's Luck by Malinowski (USA) (T M Walsh) 2290⁴ 2868³

4 **MOSHAAJIR(USA),** b c Woodman (USA) - Hidden Trail (USA) by Gleaming (USA) (C Smith) 616⁶ 1007¹ 3734⁸

7 **MOSS BEE,** br g Zambrano - Brown Bee III by Marcus Superbus (W G Reed) 4325⁴ 643⁵ 788⁵ 973⁶ 1095² 1585⁷ 2151⁸ 2242 2787⁴ 2906 3691² 3865¹ 4071³

9 **MOSS CASTLE,** ch g Le Moss - Distant Castle by Deep Run (P Moakley) 3295 3527 3791⁸

4 **MOSS PAGEANT,** b g Then Again - Water Pageant by Welsh Pageant (F T Walton) 2810 3179 3429 3892⁷

6 **MOSSA NOVA(IRE),** b g Le Moss - Rugged Glen by Rugged Man (Miss I T Oakes) 3529

6 **MOSSIMAN(IRE),** b g Le Moss - Suparoli by Super Sam (J Barclay) 1722⁵ 1938 2104 2925⁵ 3287

8 **MOSSY FERN,** b m Le Moss - Deep Fern by Deep Run (O Sherwood) 740¹ 628

5 **MOSSY'S SLAVE(IRE),** ch g Le Moss - Slavesville by Charlottesvilles Flyer (T J O'Mara) 531 925

4 **MOST EQUAL,** ch g Presidium - Dissolution by Henbit (USA) (M C Pipe) 406¹ 588

9 **MOST INTERESTING,** b m Music Boy - Quick Glance by Oats (G H Jones) 4322³ 748 3222 3661² 4052⁷ 4104³

7 **MOTILITY,** b m Yashgan - Fiodoir by Weavers' Hall (Thomas Foley) 4401⁴ 29⁹

5 **MOTORCADE(USA),** b or br g Mac Diarmida (USA) - Society Editor (USA) by Native Royalty (USA) (Joseph D Gillet) 1665⁴

9 **MOTTRAM'S GOLD,** ch g Good Times (ITY) - Speed The Plough by Grundy (S Dow) 1492 1598⁶

5 **MOUGINS(IRE),** ch g Ela-Mana-Mou - Western Goddess by Red God (D R C Elsworth) 888

8 **MOULTON BULL,** ch g Chabrias (FR) - Welsh Cloud by Welsh Saint (M H Easterby) 4325¹ 973 1739³ 1997³ 2253³ 2906⁵

8 **MOUNT AILEY,** b m Final Straw - Dear Heart by Blakeney (L R Lloyd-James) 2630

12 **MOUNT ARGUS,** ch g Don - Pendula by Tamerlane (S A Brookshaw) 2605¹ 2807² 3165² 3991

11 **MOUNT EATON FOX,** b or br g Buckskin (FR) - Town Fox by Continuation (P F Henderson) 4315⁷

7 **MOUNT KINABALU,** b g Head For Heights - Kaisersage (FR) by Exbury (S Christian) 4375³

4 **MOUNT OVAL(IRE),** b g Mister Majestic - Judy's Pinch by Ballymore (Olive M Pearse) 1575

10 **MOUNT PATRICK,** b g Paddy's Stream - Hills Of Fashion by Tarqogan (N W Padfield) 3856⁶

7 **MOUNT SACKVILLE,** ch m Whistling Deer - Sackville Street by Ete Indien (USA) (J G Groome) 58⁸ 107⁹ 159⁷

6 **MOUNT SERRATH(IRE),** b or br g Mandalus - Hopeful Secret by Pry (C R Egerton) 3707⁵ 4023

6 **MOUNTAIN BLOOM(IRE),** b m Shirley Heights - Sally Rose by Sallust (M J P O'Brien) 119⁹ 511¹

8 **MOUNTAIN MASTER,** b g Furry Glen - Leney Girl by Seminole II (Miss H C Knight) 864⁴ 955⁸ 1750⁴ 2428⁵ 2766 3099 3192⁶ 3545⁸

8 **MOUNTAIN RETREAT,** br g Top Ville - Tarrystone by So Blessed (M Williams) 796 1187

8 **MOUNTAIN SKY,** b m Skyliner - Ballymountain Girl by London Gazette (J A Berry) 212⁴

6 **MOUNTAIN STAGE(IRE),** b m Pennine Walk - Stage Lights by Connaught (Mrs John Harrington) 1785 1857

7 **MOUNTAINFOOT GIRL,** b m Zamazaan (FR) - Dream World by Quadrangle (P G Bruen) 61 98 162

10 **MOUNTEBOR,** b g Prince Regent (FR) - Land by Baldric II (P C Haslam) 579⁴ 624³ 1095⁴ 1222³ 1486⁴ 1997¹ 2322³ 2895 3332⁴

6 **MOUNTHENRY STAR(IRE),** b g Kambalda - Rathoe Princess by Never Slip (Augustine Leahy) 4368⁴ 19 71² 120⁴ 158⁵ 291³ 378¹ 505² 557⁷ 3550 3840 4149⁴ 4192⁴

4 **MOUNTMEAD(IRE),** ch f Jamesmead - Countess Christy by Mon Capitaine (I A Duncan) 3450 3797⁸

8 **MOUNTSHANNON,** b g Pry - Tara Ogan by Tarqogan (C C Trietline) 312⁶ 443⁴ 698⁸ 936⁷ 1025 1172³ 1474⁸ 2084 2524 2729⁸ 2900³ 3222⁶ 3317⁷ 3561¹ 3678² 3820⁵ 4106⁵

11 **MOURNE WARRIOR,** b g Le Bavard (FR) - Glenallen by Carnatic (K White) 223³

4 **MOUSE BIRD(IRE),** b c Glow (USA) - Irish Bird (USA) by Sea-Bird II (D R Gandolfo) 453⁴

4 **MOUSSAHIM(USA),** ch c Riverman (USA) - Abeesh (USA) by Nijinsky (CAN) (G A Cusack) 3321⁴ 3656

5 **MOVE A MINUTE(USA),** br g Al Nasr (FR) - Call Me Goddess (USA) by Prince John (J T Gifford) 1010⁴ 1193¹ 1557 2430⁷ 2621⁵

6 **MOVING OUT,** b g Slip Anchor - New Generation by Young Generation (Miss H C Knight) 812³ 1278² 2226⁴ 2432¹ 2883¹ 3193² 3594⁸ 3820¹

10 **MOW CREEK,** b g Pony Express - Vernal Slave by Artic Slave (Mrs S C Bradburne) 1477 1679³ 2069⁵ 2219³ 2497 2736 2809⁷ 2952

9 **MOWTHORPE,** ch g Ballad Rock - Simeonova by Northfields (USA) (M W Easterby) 4352⁶

8 **MOY LINETTA,** ch f Linarius (FR) - Hanseletta by Prince Hansel (R Nevin) 4368

8 **MOYDRUM PRINCE,** ch g Carlingford Castle - Chinese Queen by Tarim (Mrs Amanda Bryan) 4366⁶

INDEX TO NATIONAL HUNT RESULTS 1993-94

INDEX TO NATIONAL HUNT RESULTS 1993-94

7 **NICKLUP,** ch m Netherkelly - Voolin by Jimmy Reppin (Capt T A Forster) 1457 1530 1696 2146¹ 2517² 2816² 3135

9 **NICKNAVAR,** ch g Raga Navarro (ITY) - Bay Girl by Persian Bold (Mrs P A Tetley) 1407

8 **NICKSLINE,** ch g Nicholas Bill - Shanette by Melody Rock (J T Gifford) 1970⁴ 2186² 2455 2706² 2855 3381⁶

9 **NICKY'S BELLE,** ch m Nicholas Bill - Raging Calm by Salvo (Lady Ann Bowlby) 2925

5 **NICKY'S CHOICE,** ch m Baron Blakeney - Mae Mae by Communication (R Brotherton) 3880⁹

7 **NICSAMLYN,** ch m Julio Mariner - Booterstown by Master Owen (C A Smith) 1418⁸ 1622⁶ 1797³ 2308⁷

7 **NIDOMI,** ch g Dominion - Nicholas Grey by Track Spare (G P Enright) 185³ 259¹

6 **NIGEL'S LUCKY GIRL,** gr m Belfort (FR) - Haiti Mill by Free State (R Harris) 1193⁴ 1460 3886⁷ 4112⁷

6 **NIGHT FANCY,** ch g Night Shift (USA) - Smooth Siren (USA) by Sea Bird II (Mrs A M Woodrow) 2263 2599 2723 2881⁴ 3046⁵ 3515⁶ 3628⁵ 3825 3970⁹ 4069⁶

12 **NIGHT GUEST,** br g Northern Guest (USA) - Night Rose by Sovereign Gleam (P Monteith) 4327² 560⁴ 735 973¹ 1144³ 1606² 1921⁴ 3141⁶ 3433⁴ 3777

7 **NIGHT OF MADNESS,** br g Black Minstrel - Margeno's Love by Golden Love (K A Morgan) 2371⁸ 2498⁴ 3125⁴ 3455

6 **NIGHT SERVICE(IRE),** b f Sandalay - Super Slaney by Brave Invader (USA) (James William Cullen) 2664 3388 4063 4169

7 **NIGHT WIND,** b g Strong Gale - Kylogue Lady by London Gazette (Andrew Turnell) 713¹ 887⁶ 1206² 1839⁴

5 **NIGHTMAN,** b g Night Shift (USA) - Freely Given by Petingo (Charles O'Brien) 1076¹ 2281² 3323⁷

4 **NIGHTMARE LADY,** b f Celestial Storm (USA) - Presentable by Sharpen Up (R Harris) 1244 1404

6 **NIJMEGEN,** b g Niniski (USA) - Petty Purse by Petingo (J G FitzGerald) 1106 2175³ 2267¹ 2595⁸ 3068⁸ 3422⁹ 3736⁵

9 **NIKITAS,** b g Touching Wood (USA) - Hi There by High Top (Miss A J Whitfield) 407² 459⁵ 1055² 1364² 1672³ 1991¹ 2480¹ 2595⁹ 3422⁶ 3736

4 **NIKITRIA,** b f Robellino (USA) - Hi There by High Top (Miss A J Whitfield) 406

6 **NILE LODGE(IRE),** ch m Krayyan - Interpretation by Levmoss (Miss Ursula Ryan) 801

7 **NILOUSHA,** b m Darshaan - Nayseen by Sheshoon (Victor Bowens) 807⁵ 1073¹

6 **NIMBLE WIND,** b m Tumble Wind (USA) - Viable by Nagami (Francis M O'Brien) 4378⁴ 4404⁴ 28¹ 85⁷ 175⁴ 249¹ 294² 362³ 413² 467¹ 831

10 **NINE BROTHERS,** gr g Black Minstrel - Teresa Jane by My Swanee (R Thompson) 1503 1776 1864

5 **NINE O THREE(IRE),** b g Supreme Leader - Grenache by Menelek (Michael Hourigan) 431⁶ 530³ 1337² 1455 1822⁷ 2389 2553¹ 2679³ 2919³ 3083⁷ 3294⁴ 3468

6 **NINFA(IRE),** b m The Parson - Lulu's Daughter by Levanter (G Richards) 1181 1475 1734² 2008⁶ 2252² 3641

5 **NIRVANA PRINCE,** ch g Celestial Storm (USA) - Princess Sunshine by Busted (B Preece) 1027¹ 1297¹ 1594¹ 2382² 3046¹

5 **NISHIKI(USA),** b m Brogan (USA) - A Honey Belle (USA) by Son Ange (USA) (Augustine

Leahy) 431¹ 574⁸ 689 854 1176⁴ 1495⁸ 1823 2098 3468 3835 3972⁷ 4041⁵ 4190⁸

6 **NISHKINA,** b g Nishapour (FR) - Varishkina by Derring-Do (M E Sowersby) 139³ 396² 451³ 2875⁵

4 **NITA'S CHOICE,** b f Valiyar - What's The Matter by High Top (A G Newcombe) 1410 1640 2018

7 **NO ASHES,** ch g Noalto - Bryony Ash by Ribero (Mrs V C Ward) 1502

7 **NO BATTERY NEEDED,** b g Doctor Pangloss - Corncrop by Mycropolis (D P Geraghty) 1951⁵ 2295

6 **NO BETTER BUACHAIL(IRE),** b g Strong Gale - Merry Love by Golden Love (F Flood) 1379⁸ 1612 1988⁵ 2233⁶ 2683⁶ 3275² 3709 3795⁷

8 **NO BOUNDARIES,** b g Pitskelly - Santa Chiara by Astec (Mrs Ailsa Russell) 3429

10 **NO DAW,** ch g Al Sirat (USA) - Carmoni Princess by Allangrange (F Sheridan) 488 549 946

6 **NO DEBT,** b m Oats - Deep In Debt by Deep Run (B J Meehan) 1126⁸ 1536 1707 2112⁴ 3215

10 **NO DESERT,** b g Le Bavard (FR) - El Reine by Bargello (Michael J O'Connor) 3648

5 **NO DIPLOMACY(IRE),** ch m Fayruz - Lady Heather by Manado (C P Magnier) 3197

5 **NO DOZING(IRE),** b g Bulldozer - Miss Pet Tina by Choral Society (J F C Maxwell) 620⁸ 747⁶ 1833⁶ 2309 2465 3276² 3797⁵

10 **NO ESCORT,** b g Pitpan - Royal Escort by Royal Highway (Miss C Saunders) 2508 3212 4008

8 **NO FIZZ,** ch m Broadsword (USA) - Blakes Lass by Blakeney (Mrs D M Grissell) 2709¹ 3096 3216⁵ 3859¹

5 **NO FRONTIERS(IRE),** ch g Rhoman Rule (USA) - Auntie Molly by Wishing Star (Brendan W Duke) 2607

10 **NO GRANDAD,** br m Strong Gale - Blue Bleep by Bleep-Bleep (John R Upson) 765 865⁶ 956

7 **NO LIGHT,** gr g Celio Rufo - Lady Templar by Lord Gayle (USA) (Mrs I McKie) 4377 1730 1999 3490

6 **NO MISTAKE VI(IRE),** ch g Duky - Midway Model (Daniel O'Connell) 3611

5 **NO MORE NICE GUY(IRE),** b g Remainder Man - Vaguely Decent by Decent Fellow (G Harwood) 2339⁹ 2996

8 **NO MORE THE FOOL,** ch g Jester - Prima Bella by High Hat (Capt D C Foster) 3721⁵ 4150⁴

8 **NO MORE TRIX,** b g Kemal (FR) - Blue Trix by Blue Chariot (T P Tate) 1486¹ 2384 2582³ 2831 3058³ 3374

4 **NO NEAR MISS,** ch f Nearly A Hand - G W Supermare by Rymer (D R C Elsworth) 3458¹ 3833² 4172³

6 **NO ONE KNOWS(IRE),** ch m Kemal (FR) - No Battle by Khalkis (A J Martin) 1681 2464

6 **NO PAIN NO GAIN(IRE),** ch g Orchestra - Clarrie by Ballyciptic (B J Curley) 2426¹ 2692² 3151¹ 3270¹

10 **NO PANIC,** b g Pitpan - Scirea by Cantab (M J R Bannister) 3159⁴ 3412

4 **NO POSSIBLE DOUBT(IRE),** b f Anita's Prince - Jubilaire by Gala Performance (USA) (Patrick Woods) 1111⁹ 1846

12 **NO REBASSE,** b g Over The River (FR) - Good Surprise by Maelsheachlainn (Michael A Johnson) 3412⁶

4 **NO SHOW(IRE),** ch g Shy Groom (USA) - Captive Audience by Bold Lad (IRE) (K S Bridgwater) 1887 349⁶ 406⁶ 890⁹ 1473 2092² 3685⁶ 4051³ 4139⁶

735

6 **NO SID NO STARS(USA),** ch g Diamond Shoal -
Side Saddle (USA) by Codex (USA) (J H
Johnson) 623 767⁹ 1793
8 **NO SIR ROM,** b g Ragapan - Lady Hansel by
Prince Hansel (R Dickin) 2379 3193
6 **NO TAG(IRE),** b g Torus - Etnas Princess by
The Parson (Patrick G Kelly) 993² 1403 2102⁹
2465³ 2919¹ 3292⁸ 3506² 4058¹
7 **NO TAKERS,** b m Carlingford Castle - La
Perla by Majority Blue (David A Kiely)
4368⁶ 5⁷ 50² 113⁵ 131⁸ 276⁹ 327 432⁶
6 **NO WHEN TO RUN(IRE),** b g Deep Run - Hourly
Rate by Menelek (E J O'Grady) 1383⁴
7 **NO WORD,** b or br g Oats - Rapenna by
Straightdad (J White) 377³ 411 1351⁴ 1587³
2063⁵ 3882 4089
8 **NOBBY,** b g Dalsaan - Parkeen Princess by
He Loves Me (B Beasley) 766⁹ 912 1484⁶ 1923³
2149 3285
6 **NOBLE AUK(NZ),** b g Le Grand Seigneur
(CAN) - Lady Auk (NZ) by Auk (AUS) (D H
Barons) 1110⁸
10 **NOBLE BID,** b h Kings Lake (USA) - First
Round by Primera (Miss S J Wilton) 1084
6 **NOBLE BRONZE,** b m Sonnen Gold - Gouly
Duff by Party Mink (Mrs V A Aconley) 627³
1099⁷ 1362⁴
13 **NOBLE CLANSMAN(USA),** b g Norcliffe (CAN)
- Deed A Double (USA) by No Double (USA)
(P J Healy) 928⁷ 1179⁸ 1826
13 **NOBLE EYRE,** br g Aristocracy - Jane Eyre
by Master Buck (D R Gandolfo) 1884
6 **NOBLE FORESTER(IRE),** b g Lord Ha Ha -
Diana Harwell by Harwell (Major D N Chappell) 3604⁹
7 **NOBLE INSIGHT,** ch g The Noble Player
(USA) - Instanter by Morston (FR) (C P E
Brooks) 4333⁴ 438⁵ 593⁵ 646⁶ 887 2790³ 2992³ 3206³
3408 3635⁵
6 **NOBLE KNIGHT(IRE),** ch g Boyne Valley -
Nano's View by Carnival Night (W Trehy)
1332 2983 3201 4149⁶
6 **NOBLE MADAME(IRE),** b f Tall Noble (USA) -
Ahoy Dolly by Windjammer (USA) (John
Queally) 1978⁸ 2938
7 **NOBLE MINISTER,** gr g Rusticaro (FR) -
Nofert (USA) by Graustark (Francis M
O'Brien) 969⁷ 1500⁵ 2041⁹
5 **NOBLE MONARCH(IRE),** br g Strong Gale -
Perusia by Pirate King (J A Hellens) 1223
6 **NOBLE PEACE(IRE),** b g Tall Noble (USA) -
Bridge Way Peace by Hard Away (J R Cox)
68⁶
4 **NOBLE RISK,** b c Risk Me (FR) - Nativity
(USA) by Native Royalty (USA) (B de Haan)
2503⁶ 2722
6 **NOBLE SOCIETY,** b g Law Society (USA) - Be
Noble by Vaguely Noble (M D I Usher) 2461⁶
10 **NOBLE YEOMAN,** b g King's Ride - Baronston
by Boreen (FR) (R Dickin) 1703 1949² 2082³
7 **NOBLELY(USA),** b g Lyphard (USA) - Non-
oalca (USA) by Nonoalco (N J H Walker)
1192³ 1414¹ 1595⁴ 2129¹ 2229¹ 3806⁴ 3930² 4125¹
6 **NOBODYS FLAME(IRE),** br g Dalsaan - Hamers
Flame by Green Shoon (John Brassil) 71
115⁸ 157² 294 376⁴ 534⁶ 673⁶ 989³ 1334⁵
8 **NOBODYS SON,** gr g Nobody Knows - Fine
Performance by Gala Performance (USA)
(Daniel O'Connell) 4380¹ 14⁵ 52² 82⁵
4 **NOBULL(IRE),** b f Torus - Hansel's Queen by
Prince Hansel (J G Groome) 3082⁴
5 **NOCATCHIM,** b g Shardari - Solar by Hotfoot
(S E Sherwood) 569² 812⁵ 3219¹ 3499⁸ 3736
6 **NODDLE(USA),** ch h Sagace (FR) - Formartin
(USA) by Forli (ARG) (L Lungo) 1619 1740¹
1963¹ 2256¹ 2788

9 **NODDYS EXPRESS,** ch g Pony Express -
Toddy Noddy by Three Wishes (R H Buckler) 1524⁶
7 **NODFORM WONDER,** b g Cut Above - Wonder
by Tekoah (J A Hellens) 873⁷ 1066² 1364⁸ 2385
2740 3555⁹
11 **NODFORMS DILEMMA(USA),** ch g State Din-
ner (USA) - Princess Jo Jo (S A Brookshaw)
3987²
5 **NODFORMS INFERNO,** b g Idiot's Delight -
River Linnet by Forlorn River (P J Hobbs)
3907⁴
5 **NOEL(IRE),** b g Fairy King (USA) - Glenar-
dina by Furry Glen (J G M O'Shea) 434⁴ 640⁵
1646⁶ 1811⁶ 1926⁹
5 **NOELEENS DELIGHT(IRE),** ch m Le Bavard
(FR) - Graham Dieu by Three Dons (Michael Cunningham) 98⁵ 292⁸ 504⁸
4 **NOELS DANCER(IRE),** ch g Nordance (USA) -
Royal Desire by Royal Match (Michael
Cunningham) 2122 2314⁵
4 **NOMADIC FIRE,** b or br g Sharrood (USA) -
Flaming Peace by Queen's Hussar (Mrs N
Macauley) 147² 285⁴ 448² 497⁷
5 **NONAME,** b g Faustus (USA) - Campagna by
Romulus (P J Hobbs) 2728 3826
5 **NONANNO,** b g Noalto - Fortune's Fancy by
Workboy (A J Chamberlain) 809
7 **NONCOMMITAL,** b h Mummy's Pet - Shadow
Play by Busted (J Mackie) 658 1068⁸ 1173²
1353⁹ 1535
8 **NONE SO WISE(USA),** ch g Believe It (USA) -
Nonesuch Bay by Mill Reef (USA) (N R Mitchell) 3850
10 **NOPADDLE,** b g Bulldozer - Canoe by Milesian (W P Mullins) 1910 2041⁸ 2161³ 2236¹ 2704⁴
3712⁶
5 **NORA ANN(IRE),** b m Camden Town - Alone
All Alone by Tanfirion (Francis Ennis) 211¹
252⁶ 558⁸ 671⁶ 1036³ 1155³ 2988 3506
5 **NORA'S ERROR(IRE),** ch g His Turn - Winning
Nora by Northfields (USA) (Denis J Reddan) 671 803 1020⁸ 1681 2124 2310⁹ 3507 3694 3840
3972
5 **NORDANSK,** ch g Nordance (USA) - Free On
Board by Free State (M Madgwick) 1709⁴
5 **NORDEN(IRE),** ch g M Double M (USA) -
Papukeena by Simbir (R J Hodges) 1957 2269
2717 2797⁶ 3173⁴ 3478
5 **NORDIC BEAT(IRE),** b g Nordico (USA) - Pol-
lination by Pentotal (W Clay) 71⁴ 85⁴ 113 173²
658⁶ 724⁶ 1079 1731³ 2033
6 **NORDIC BLUE(IRE),** b m Nordico (USA) -
Gorm by Majority Blue (J P Byrne) 511⁶
7 **NORDIC FLASH,** b g Nordico (USA) - Rosemore by Ashmore (FR) (T J Naughton) 4309³
4377³ 183¹ 3998
6 **NORDIC FLIGHT,** b or br g Julio Mariner -
Last Flight by Saucy Kit (R J Eckley) 441
650 773 1023 3339 3421
4 **NORDIC MINE(IRE),** b c Nordico (USA) -
Tower Belle by Tower Walk (P J Hobbs) 228⁴
802³
7 **NORDIC RACE,** b h Nordico (USA) - Lady
Dulcinea (ARG) by General (FR) (Thomas
Bergin) 49 1174 1549 2232⁵ 4043⁶ 4093⁶
5 **NORDIC SENSATION(IRE),** b g Nordico (USA) -
Royal Sensation by Prince Regent (FR) (J
S Bolger) 3730⁴ 4059¹
5 **NORDIC SIGN(IRE),** b h Nordico (USA) - Lady
Beck (FR) by Sir Gaylord (J S Bolger) 257⁹
555
6 **NORDIC SUN(IRE),** gr g Nordico (USA) - Cie-
lsoleil (USA) by Conquistador Cielo (USA)
(A J Martin) 4378¹ 13¹ 46¹ 84³ 110³ 527 556⁶ 905²
989² 1831¹ 2469 3841⁴ 4062²

4 **NORDIC THORN(IRE),** b g Nordico (USA) - Rosemore by Ashmore (FR) (Martin Brassil) 391³ 529² 617⁴ 3839¹ 3993⁵

6 **NORDROSS,** b m Ardross - Noreena by Non-oalco (USA) (J H Peacock) 814 937⁷ 1280⁶ 1948 3222⁸ 3829 3965⁹

9 **NORMAN CONQUEROR,** br g Royal Fountain - Constant Rose by Confusion (T Thomson Jones) 2648⁶

5 **NORMAN WARRIOR,** gr g Petong - Petulengra by Mummy's Pet (D Morris) 1053⁸ 1353⁸ 1488

4 **NORMAN'S CONVINCED(IRE),** b g Convinced - A Nice Alert by Red Alert (M C Pipe) 2095² 2407³ 3113²

7 **NORMANDY BILL,** br g Golden Love - Billeragh Girl by Normandy (Mrs C J Black) 2838

8 **NORRISMOUNT,** b g Swan's Rock - Laurabeg by Lawrence O (G Richards) 2411⁷ 2497⁴ 3428 3687¹ 4131³

4 **NORSE RAIDER,** gr g Norwick (USA) - Lady Andrea by Andrea Mantegna (P G Murphy) 2749 3234³ 3832⁵

7 **NORSTOCK,** b m Norwick (USA) - Millingdale by Tumble Wind (USA) (J White) 4301² 145¹ 165¹ 223² 357² 1373¹ 2067⁸ 3135¹ 3426 3783 4074

12 **NORSTOWN,** ch g Town And Country - Norsemen's Lady by Habat (P G Murphy) 2968⁵ 3260

9 **NORTH HOLLOW,** b g Tyrnavos - Philigree by Moulton (D McCain) 2029 2291⁷ 2837 3221⁶ 3509⁵

9 **NORTH OF WATFORD,** ch g Jasmine Star - Wallie Girl by Right Tack (Martyn Wane) 582⁸ 912

9 **NORTH PRIDE(USA),** ch h Northjet - Necie's Pride (USA) by Sky High (AUS) (S G Payne) 1481

8 **NORTHANTS,** b g Northern Baby (CAN) - Astania (GER) by Arratos (FR) (W Storey) 1619² 1922¹ 2172² 2487¹ 3028⁸

8 **NORTHERN ACE,** b g Shareef Dancer (USA) - Monaco Melody by Tudor Melody (V T O'Brien) 929 1177⁹

7 **NORTHERN BREGA,** b g Furry Glen - Cool Kitten (Oliver Finnegan) 362⁵ 467² 2842

6 **NORTHERN CONQUEROR(IRE),** ch g Mazaad - Gaylom by Lord Gayle (USA) (T J Naughton) 4312³ 181⁵ 3998 4165⁶

8 **NORTHERN CREST,** ch g Anfield - Contadina by Memling (Mrs S D Williams) 795⁸ 1192² 1415⁵ 2361⁴

12 **NORTHERN DAWN,** gr g General Ironside - Hopeful Dawn (S Hyde) 3501 3665

8 **NORTHERN HIDE,** b g Buckskin (FR) - Lovely Tyrone by Peacock (FR) (A L T Moore) 133¹ 412² 619¹ 879 965³ 1112⁴

11 **NORTHERN JINKS,** b m Piaffer (USA) - Miss Merida by Midsummer Night II (R Dickin) 1461³ 1623⁵ 1975⁷ 2248¹ 3066⁹ 3210² 3500⁸ 3607⁶

4 **NORTHERN JUDY(IRE),** ch f Jareer (USA) - Robin Red Breast by Red Alert (R Hollinshead) 1705⁴ 1927⁸ 2083 2763

7 **NORTHERN MOSS,** b g Le Moss - Blue Pan by Pitpan (Michael Condon) 3259 3888⁹

6 **NORTHERN NATION,** b g Nomination - Ballagarrow Girl by North Stoke (W Clay) 226⁴ 370¹ 682² 949³ 1154² 2062⁵

7 **NORTHERN NIKKI,** ch m Nicholas Bill - Northern Venture by St Alphage (W T Kemp) 3905⁹

6 **NORTHERN OPTIMIST,** b m Northern Tempest (USA) - On A Bit by Mummy's Pet (B J Llewellyn) 1079⁸ 1280⁹ 1519⁵ 2094³ 2328 2461³ 2729 3111⁷ 3706⁴ 3879⁵ 4005³ 4124²

6 **NORTHERN RAINBOW,** b g Rainbow Quest (USA) - Safe House by Lyphard (USA) (R W Emery) 587³ 1188⁹

4 **NORTHERN REEF(IRE),** ch g Orange Reef - Jarat by Habitat (P J P Doyle) 4171⁸

7 **NORTHERN SADDLER,** ch g Norwick (USA) - Miss Saddler by St Paddy (R J Hodges) 713⁶ 936 1051¹ 1521⁴ 1701¹ 1868¹ 1955¹ 2267⁶ 2379² 2649² 2819³ 3068

4 **NORTHERN SINGER,** ch c Norwick (USA) - Be Lyrical by Song (R J Hodges) 1996 2269 2546⁹ 3576

6 **NORTHERN SQUIRE,** b g Uncle Pokey - Kit's Future by Saucy Kit (J M Jefferson) 581² 974² 1214 1469⁵ 1745⁵ 1938¹ 2276² 2500¹ 2927¹ 3374⁵ 3518

6 **NORTHERN TRIAL(USA),** b g Far North (CAN) - Make An Attempt (USA) by Nashua (K R Burke) 402² 429³ 597⁹ 849³ 1070⁴ 1353³ 1632⁶ 2776 2837 3740² 3826¹ 3915² 4000³

7 **NORTHERN VILLAGE,** ch g Norwick (USA) - Merokette by Blast (S Dow) 526¹ 632 1120¹ 1227

7 **NORTHERN VISION,** b g Vision (USA) - Smelter by Prominer (R R Lamb) 820⁴ 909 1182⁶ 2739⁸ 3033⁵ 3642⁵ 3893

8 **NORTHUMBRIAN KING,** b g Indian King (USA) - Tuna by Silver Shark (Mrs K Walton) 1005³ 1119⁷ 2830 3130¹ 3374¹ 3622⁶

6 **NORTINO,** ch g Norwick (USA) - Soft Chinook (USA) by Hitting Away (J I A Charlton) 4352⁵ 1738⁶

8 **NORTON VILLE,** b g Alzao (USA) - Temarie (FR) by Exbury (Daniel J Murphy) 1433⁴ 1578⁵ 1901⁵

11 **NOS NA GAOITHE,** br g Strong Gale - Abroad by Takawalk II (N J H Walker) 2696² 2800 2911³ 3041 3203 3548 3766² 4018⁵ 4102³ 4180²

5 **NOSEABIT(IRE),** b g Nearly A Nose (USA) - Marsabit by Martinmas (John J Walsh) 1039

5 **NOT A BID(IRE),** br m Buckskin (FR) - Wrekenogan by Tarqogan (John A White) 1180 1610 2050

5 **NOT AN INCH(IRE),** br g Roselier (FR) - White's Quay by Quayside (J J McInerney) 1822 2128 3072 3327

5 **NOT GORDONS,** b g All Systems Go - Lady Abernant by Abwah (K C Lewis) 243⁶ 264⁸ 374 483

5 **NOT MY LINE(IRE),** gr g Entre Nous - Uno Navarro by Raga Navarro (ITY) (Daniel O'Connell) 314⁶ 431⁷ 504³ 692⁵ 925⁶ 990⁴ 2924 3197⁴ 3469 3615⁸ 3834² 3953²

5 **NOTABLE EXCEPTION,** b g Top Ville - Shorthouse by Habitat (Mrs M Reveley) 398² 623³ 824² 972¹ 1143² 1292² 1481¹ 2360⁷ 2956⁴ 3130² 3240³ 3475 3678³ 3866⁶ 3959¹ 4127¹

8 **NOTARY-NOWELL,** b g Deep Run - Hamers Flame by Green Shoon (F Murphy) 518 751⁴ 847³ 978⁵ 1216⁸ 1884⁷ 2294 2666³ 2732 2911⁴

6 **NOTED STRAIN(IRE),** b g Gorytus (USA) - Almuadiyeh by Thatching (D F Bassett) 2317⁷ 2439 2743⁹ 3716⁶ 4100⁸

10 **NOTHINGBUTTROUBLE,** ch g Roselier (FR) - Continuity Lass by Continuation (Mrs H Parrott) 988⁵ 1173⁶ 1564⁴

6 **NOTTODAY(IRE),** b g Kambalda - War Queen by Yrrah Jr (Patrick G Kelly) 4405 77

9 **NOTUS,** b g Relkino - Wind Goddess by Whistling Wind (Brian Kennedy) 3693

13 **NOUGAT RUSSE,** b g Sweet Story - Natasha VI by Blue Cliff (A Twiston-Davies) 1459 2363⁵ 2656 3336⁷ 3593⁶ 3875 4143

6 **NOUVELLE CUISINE,** b m Yawa - Radigo by Ragstone (G M Moore) 4326¹ 125² 3819 3960⁵

8 **PABREY,** gr g Pablond - Grey Receipt by Rugantino (N R Mitchell) 607 710 773³ 864⁵ 964⁶ 1090⁶

11 **PACIFIC SOUND,** b g Palm Track - Pacific Dream by Meldrum (Miss C D Richardson) 2484

4 **PACIFIC SPIRIT,** b f Governor General - Mossberry Fair by Mossberry (M Tate) 2478 3826 4009 4139⁹

9 **PACO'S BOY,** b g Good Thyne (USA) - Jeremique by Sunny Way (M C Pipe) 2363 3425 3724³

11 **PACTOLUS(USA),** b g Lydian (FR) - Honey Sand (USA) by Windy Sands (S Christian) 4389³ 3038 3561³

5 **PADASHPAN(USA),** b g Shahrastani (USA) - Palama (USA) by Blushing Groom (FR) (W P Mullins) 257¹ 672² 1175¹ 1554¹ 1906² 2287⁶ 2612⁶ 2702³ 3422⁷ 3650⁷

9 **PADAVENTURE,** b g Belfalas - Cardamine by Indigenous (Mrs M Reveley) 822¹ 1063⁶ 1319¹ 1540¹

5 **PADDITATE(IRE),** b g Supreme Leader - Ballyoran Princess by The Parson (R J Hodges) 3256⁶ 3523

7 **PADDY MORRISSEY,** b g Strong Gale - Reynoldstown Rose by Caribo (J S Haldane) 1726⁶ 2004 2103² 2238⁵ 2497⁶ 2814³ 3286⁶

6 **PADDY RED(IRE),** ch g Bon Sang (FR) - Grangeclare Lady by Menelek (Liam McAteer) 3327 3796⁶ 3958

6 **PADDY'S GOLD(IRE),** b g Kemal (FR) - Thai Nang by Tap On Wood (B Smart) 191 441⁹

5 **PADDY'S PET(IRE),** ch g Le Moss - Avatea by Arctic Slave (C Kinane) 3749

16 **PADDY'S POND,** ch g Paddy's Stream - Clerihan by Immortality (N J Reece) 3563⁷

5 **PADDY'S RAMBO(IRE),** ch g Venetian Gate - Taberna Lady by Paddy's Stream (S J Treacy) 393⁸ 1036

6 **PADDYS TIPP(IRE),** b g Bulldozer - Harp Song by Auction Ring (USA) (S J Treacy) 2940 4166

7 **PADIORD,** ch g Caerleon (USA) - Osmunda by Mill Reef (USA) (Miss L Bower) 601

6 **PADRE MIO(IRE),** b g The Parson - Mwanamio by Sole Mio (USA) (Anthony Mullins) 534¹ 672¹ 937¹ 1175² 1818¹ 2287⁷ 3323⁵

11 **PADRIGAL,** ch m Paddy's Stream - Peaceful Madrigal by Blue Cliff (J N Cheatle) 3165⁶ 3399⁷

4 **PAEANDISPLAY(IRE),** b g Paean - Colonial Line (USA) by Plenty Old (USA) (H de Bromhead) 4171⁴

4 **PAGET,** b g Taufan (USA) - Haco by Trible Chief (M A O'Toole) 4361¹ 10¹ 131 328³ 471⁴ 797⁵ 927⁸

9 **PAID ELATION,** m Pia Fort - Dellation (D E Fletcher) 2885⁴ 3093 3155

4 **PAIR OF JACKS(IRE),** ch g Music Boy - Lobbino by Bustino (D A Wilson) 2541⁹

4 **PAKED(IRE),** b f Treasure Kay - Sales Talk by Auction Ring (USA) (A D Evans) 1432 1846 1983 2349

8 **PAKENHAM,** b g Deep Run - Hazy Dawn by Official (G Richards) 1621 2435⁵ 3460² 3893

5 **PAKOL(IRE),** b m Martin John - Tamen John by African Sky (A D Evans) 4378⁷ 49⁴

10 **PALACE GARDENS,** b g Royal Boxer - Privy Court by Adropejo (J M Bradley) 682⁴

7 **PALACE GEM,** b g Horage - Angela's Gem by My Swallow (Peter Casey) 46⁴ 106⁵ 230⁸ 506⁴ 831 904⁵ 4077⁹

5 **PALACE KING(IRE),** ch g Great Eastern - Fancy Girl by Mon Capitaine (Patrick McAllen) 4371 4041

6 **PALACE MAN(USA),** ch g Island Kingdom (USA) - Palace Maid (USA) by Golden Palace (USA) (P G Murphy) 885

4 **PALACE PARADE(USA),** ch g Cure The Blues (USA) - Parasail (USA) by In Reality (B R Millman) 2624 2722⁶ 3016 3202⁶ 3281 3478⁴ 3629⁵ 3804⁵

10 **PALACE WOLF(NZ),** b g Star Wolf - Castle Star (NZ) by Indian Order (Miss H C Knight) 713⁸ 812⁹ 1213⁸ 3499 3764³ 3931⁶ 4105¹ 4164⁵

5 **PALACEGATE KING,** ch g King Among Kings - Market Blues by Porto Bello (A C Whillans) 1481² 1728⁴ 1922³ 2371⁶ 2929¹ 3078¹ 3182² 3434² 3578³

4 **PALACEGATE SUNSET,** gr g Skyliner - Grey Morley by Pongee (J Berry) 137⁶

12 **PALANQUIN,** ch g Royal Palace - Duresme by Starry Halo (W G Reed) 3142

6 **PALEFOOT(IRE),** b m Gorytus (USA) - Grayfoot by Grundy (Ronald O'Neill) 3529 3974 4044⁶ 4152³

5 **PALLAS CHAMPION(IRE),** ch g White Mill - Soan Abhaile by Trimmingham (Jeremiah Ryan) 2658⁷ 2919 3834

6 **PALLASKENRY(IRE),** ch g Parliament - Lady Margaret by Yellow God (J W Boyers) 4360⁶ 4404⁸ 24⁷ 100⁹ 122 199⁶

7 **PALLASTOWN BREEZE,** br m Le Moss - Bartlemy Hostess by Bargello (W P Mullins) 2041

5 **PALLASTOWN GALE(IRE),** b m Strong Gale - Pallastown Run by Deep Run (W P Mullins) 531

9 **PALM HOUSE,** ch g Coquelin (USA) - Kew Gift by Faraway Son (USA) (G M Moore) 1963 2152⁹ 2321⁸

10 **PALM READER,** b g Palm Track - Carbia by Escart III (N J Henderson) 457 523² 615⁶ 2825⁴ 3210⁷ 3595⁷

5 **PALM SUNDAY,** b m Java Tiger - Palm Cross by Palm Track (Miss J Eaton) 3401

8 **PALM SWIFT,** b m Rabdan - Swiftsand by Sharpen Up (B Smart) 402⁸ 705⁷ 1245⁶ 1470 1525 1947³ 2146⁸ 2653 2803⁵ 3017 3661

8 **PALMO DAYS,** b g Flower Robe - Lucifer's Dream by Lucifer (USA) (D W Browning) 862

7 **PALMROCK DONNA,** b m Quayside - The Race Fly by Pollerton (Martin Higgins) 22⁹ 72 97² 177⁶ 474 674⁸ 941⁷ 2100 2126 2202⁴ 2550⁶ 3507⁹ 4033

10 **PALMRUSH,** b g Tepukei - Vulrusika by Vulgan (M D Hammond) 288³

11 **PAMBER PRIORY,** b g Balinger - Miset by Right Royal V (T Thomson Jones) 1198² 1653⁷ 1845⁸ 2143 2506⁴ 2733

8 **PAMELA'S LAD,** ch g Dalsaan - La Margarite by Bonne Noel (M A Lloyd) 2889³ 3212⁴

6 **PAMPERED GEM,** b m Pitpan - Fidelight by Fidel (T J Carr) 2326⁹

13 **PAMPERING,** b g Pamroy - Crosswise by Firestreak (S J Goodings) 2882⁵

6 **PAMPILLO(FR),** 192²

9 **PANATHINAIKOS(USA),** b g Nodouble (USA) - Faisana (ARG) by Yata Nahuel (G A Ham) 125³ 217

6 **PANDA(IRE),** b m Deep Run - Maestra Gema by Master Buck (P Mullins) 535⁸ 585³ 853⁸ 939² 1074¹ 1453¹ 1551² 1851 2098³ 2277 2392 2550 2682⁴

7 **PANDESSA,** b m Blue Cashmere - Jeanne Du Barry by Dubassoff (USA) (W S Cunningham) 4352¹ 972 1201⁶ 1633⁷ 1793 4138⁴

6 **PANDORA'S FIRE,** ch m Royal Vulcan - Sparkler Superb by Grisaille (P A Pritchard) 3590 4057

8 **PANDORA'S PRIZE,** ch m Royal Vulcan - Semi-Colon by Colonist II (Mrs P M Joynes) 442

8 **PANDY,** b g Thatching - Hot Stone by Hotfoot (G Thorner) 592 3549[6]

4 **PANIC BUTTON(IRE),** br f Simply Great (FR) - Hysteria by Prince Bee (M H Easterby) 1476

9 **PANICSUN,** b g Sunyboy - Midnight Panic by Panco (K S Bridgwater) 263[1]

8 **PANT LLIN,** b g Mummy's Pet - Goosie-Gantlet by Run The Gantlet (USA) (F Jordan) 1068[9] 1325[7] 1590 1805[7] 2206

14 **PANTECHNICON,** b g Pitpan - Avatea by Arctic Slave (A Barrow) 3667

4 **PANTHER(IRE),** ch g Primo Dominie - High Profile by High Top (J Hetherton) 2241

8 **PANTO LADY,** br m Lepanto (GER) - Dusky Damsel by Sahib (Mrs K M Lamb) 1092 1357 1605 1790 2071 2153 2435[6] 3030[7] 3144 3641 3787[6]

13 **PANTO PRINCE,** br g Lepanto (GER) - Native Wings by Al-'alawi (C L Popham) 749[1] 884[1] 1088[1] 2948

9 **PAPAS SURPRISE,** ch g Lighter - Papa's Paradise by Florus (Miss S Horner) 2904[4]

7 **PAPER CRAFT,** b g Formidable (USA) - Civility by Shirley Heights (W H Bissill) 3899 4003[5]

4 **PAPER DAYS,** b g Teenoso (USA) - April Days by Silly Season (P G Murphy) 1504[7] 2014[4] 2300 2471[3] 2638[4] 2969[7] 3062

7 **PAPER STAR,** br m Strong Gale - Lynwood Lady by Malicious (M P Muggeridge) 683 892[6] 1086[3] 1441[3] 2264 2543 2780[6] 3232[4] 3517[5] 3805[4] 4055[4] 4184

9 **PAPERWORK BOY,** ch g Buckskin (FR) - Orinda Way by Deep Run (Miss N Berry) 2265 3156[3]

6 **PAPPA DONT PREACH(IRE),** b g Carlingford Castle - Ballyoran Princess by The Parson (John R Upson) 145[4] 184[4] 347[3] 455[5] 660[4] 751 917[7]

5 **PAPRIKA(IRE),** ch m The Parson - Barhopper by Avocat (M S Saunders) 2560

6 **PAPRS GALE(IRE),** br f Strong Gale - Silkam Sue (Patrick Joseph Flynn) 4381[2] 43[2] 73 124 801[4] 857

6 **PAR-BAR(IRE),** gr m The Parson - Baranee by My Swanee (D Eddy) 18[9] 1722[2] 2104[5] 2322[4] 2367[4] 2894[2]

5 **PARABELLUM(IRE),** b m Roselier (FR) - Deceptive Response by Furry Glen (F Flood) 3197 3290 3937

9 **PARADISE BEACH,** b g Skyliner - Looks A Million by Wollow (Major M R Dangerfield) 2885 3335

6 **PARADISE FOUND,** b g Ilium - Paradise Straits by Derrylin (A L T Moore) 3934

5 **PARADISE NAVY,** b g Slip Anchor - Ivory Waltz (USA) by Sir Ivor (J R Shaw) 2291[2] 2452[1] 2743[5] 3023

5 **PARADISE ROAD,** gr g Teenoso (USA) - Fair Melys (FR) by Welsh Pageant (A L T Moore) 2470 3124[6] 3653[9]

8 **PARALIGHT,** b f The Parson - Light Thrust (M J Byrne) 4338[8] 18[5]

5 **PARAMOUNT,** b g Jupiter Island - Barbella by Barolo (T Thomson Jones) 1428[7] 1957 2269 2802

6 **PARBOLD HILL,** ch g Carwhite - Coppice by Pardao (K R Burke) 350[1] 438[3] 603[4] 1124[3] 1245

8 **PARDON ME MUM,** ch g The Parson - Please Mum by Kabale (K C Bailey) 4324[3] 663[3] 917[1] 1043[3] 2668[5]

10 **PARDON ME SIR,** b g North Summit - Peaceful Pleasure by Silent Whistle (G B Balding) 899[3] 1164

8 **PARGALE,** b or br g Strong Gale - Lady Park by No Argument (A L T Moore) 4397[6] 132 532[4] 799[2] 943 1019[3] 1819

4 **PARIS BY NIGHT(IRE),** b f Slew O' Gold (USA) - I'll Take Paris (USA) by Vaguely Noble (R J Hodges) 2797 3012

4 **PARIS ROBBER,** b c Robellino (USA) - Parisana (FR) by Gift Card (FR) (J S Moore) 896 1049

9 **PARISIAN,** b h Shirley Heights - Miss Paris by Sovereign Path (J A Bennett) 3098 3511 3878[7] 4017[4] 4056[5]

5 **PARK BOREEN(IRE),** br g Boreen (FR) - Regular Maid by Regular Guy (Patrick G Kelly) 73

8 **PARKBHRIDE,** b g Wolver Hollow - Gulistan by Sharpen Up (R K Aston) 2301

7 **PARKBOY LASS,** b m Lafontaine (USA) - Johnnie's Lass by Menelek (Michael J Carroll) 1236 1500[6] 1760 1898[9] 2197[7] 2616 3504

5 **PARLEBIZ,** b m Parliament - That's Show Biz by The Parson (C Parker) 3177[4] 3284[3] 3431[4]

10 **PARLEZVOUSFRANCAIS,** b g Blakeney - Oula-Ka Fu-Fu by Run The Gantlet (USA) (M C Pipe) 2247 2727[3] 3283[7] 3491[8] 3533[1]

8 **PARLIAMENT HALL,** gr g Piling (USA) - Miss Carribean by Sea Hawk II (A P O'Brien) 1400 1686[5] 1855[2] 2124[3] 2280[3] 2590[6] 2698 2754 3651[4] 3746

5 **PARLIAMENTARIAN(IRE),** br g Idiot's Delight - Elect by New Member (T J Etherington) 2477 2991 3637[4]

4 **PARSON FROM HEAVEN(IRE),** ch f The Parson - Flower From Heaven by Baptism (W P Mullins) 3616[6] 4060[7]

10 **PARSON'S CROSS,** b g The Parson - Croom Cross by Menelek (Mrs J P Mayes) 3165[5] 3313 3501[2] 3638[4]

6 **PARSON'S LODGE(IRE),** ch m The Parson - Loge by Orchestra (L Lungo) 3079 3347[7] 3459[3]

8 **PARSON'S QUEST,** ch g The Parson - Gortroe Queen by Simbir (N B Mason) 3157

7 **PARSON'S RUN,** b m The Parson - Free Run by Deep Run (Ms T B O'Neill) 2311[4] 2587[5] 2660[8]

7 **PARSON'S WAY,** b g The Parson - Daithis Coleen by Carnival Night (A P Jones) 778 1108[8] 1406[5] 1621 1866 2822 3007[9] 3309 3510[7] 3750

6 **PARSONS BELLE(IRE),** b f The Parson - Madam Rocket by Tudor Rocket (Michael J Carroll) 1403 1766 2050 2197[6] 2548[7]

8 **PARSONS BRIG,** b g The Parson - Tumlin Brig by New Brig (Michael Hourigan) 1178 1399[7] 1497[3] 1685 1825[3] 2282[4] 3198[2] 3465[7] 3551[3] 3887[5] 4116[3]

6 **PARSONS EYRE(IRE),** b m The Parson - Denys Eyre by Saint Denys (A J McNamara) 17[5] 50 80[2] 174[6] 232[6] 295[3] 489[2] 857

10 **PARSONS GREEN,** b g The Parson - Move Along Gypsy by Menelek (N J Henderson) 1026[1] 1224[6] 1540

11 **PARSONS PLEASURE,** b g Pry - Will Preach by Will Somers (Mrs Amanda Bowlby) 2800[2] 2937 3313

9 **PARSONS SON,** b g The Parson - Ripperidge by Knotty Pine (Gerard Cully) 3873[4] 3945[4]

6 **PARSONS TERM(IRE),** b m The Parson - Zozimus by Rarity (Noel Meade) 2465

9 **PARSONS TOI,** b m The Parson - Mags Toi by Prince Hansel (K Riordan) 4381 79 212 343[8] 503[7]

4 **PARTICULAR(IRE),** br g Nordance (USA) - Mink Fur (CAN) by Victoria Park (Joseph M Canty) 3466

6 **PARTNERS IN CRIME,** b m Crofthall - Waiariki by Condorcet (FR) (Victor Bowens) 46[7] 1400 1551[9] 1765[7] 1894

7 **PARTY GUEST,** ch m What A Guest - Tremiti by Sun Prince (Seamus Fahey) 313[9]

10 **PARTY POLITICS,** br g Politico (USA) - Spin Again by Royalty (N A Gaselee) 1545[1]

4 **PASQUINOBLE(FR),** 3679[2]

12 **PASSAGE TO FREEDOM,** gr m Pals Passage - Arctic Freedom by Arctic Chevalier (Mrs S Lamyman) 4384[2] 729 909 1215

4 **PASSAMEZZO(IRE),** b c Alzao (USA) - Pastel Shade (USA) by Affirmed (USA) (B Preece) 3496[9] 3680[7]

10 **PASTORAL PRIDE(USA),** b g Exceller (USA) - Pastoral Miss by Northfields (USA) (M C Pipe) 1641

11 **PAT'S JESTER,** ch g Orchestra - Owey by Sovereign Gleam (R Allan) 1031[4]

6 **PAT'S VALENTINE(IRE),** b m Balboa - Ditschla (GER) by Le Mas Marvent (FR) (Jeremiah Ryan) 7[8] 88 114 993 1332[8]

4 **PATONG BEACH,** ch f Infantry - Winter Resort by Miami Springs (M P Muggeridge) 379[4] 2430 2797

9 **PATROCLUS,** b g Tyrnavos - Athenia Princess by Athens Wood (J Mackie) 920[6] 1137 2768[1] 2902[1] 3225[1] 3441[4]

5 **PATROL,** b h Shirley Heights - Tender Loving Care by Final Straw (J H Johnson) 875

8 **PATRUSIKA,** b m Full Of Hope - Vulrusika by Vulgan (A J Taylor) 763[6] 862

6 **PATS FAREWELL(IRE),** ch g Bustomi - Mattress by Silver Cloud (Cecil Mahon) 2028[5] 2314[4] 2470 3447[6] 3811[4] 4091

7 **PATS FORGE,** ch m Orchestra - Front Room by Crowded Room (Peter McCreery) 4340

9 **PATS MINSTREL,** b g Black Minstrel - Lohunda Park by Malinowski (USA) (R Champion) 573[1] 1165[4] 1649[3] 3662[5]

7 **PAUL TIMOTHY,** b g Buckskin (FR) - Sea Fog by Menelek (Michael Condon) 4398

7 **PAUL'S PRINCESS,** ch m Town And Country - Go Continental by Royalty (A M Forte) 2950 3170

4 **PAULA'S BOY(IRE),** br g Spin Of A Coin - Bunavoree by Rugged Man (William Patton) 4063

6 **PAULINUS,** b g Nomination - New Ribbons by Ribero (Denys Smith) 4326[8]

7 **PAULMATIC,** gr g Pragmatic - Paulownia by Palestine (Mrs Sue Maude) 108

10 **PAVLARIOS,** b or br g Niels - Sunny Tang by Sunny Way (V T O'Brien) 276

6 **PAVLOVA RUN(IRE),** ch g Commanche Run - Anna Pavlova (USA) by Lyphard (USA) (J F Bailey Jun) 4399 70 107

6 **PAY HOMAGE,** ch g Primo Dominie - Embraceable Slew (USA) by Seattle Slew (USA) (I A Balding) 1085[3] 1283

5 **PEACE FORMULA(IRE),** ch g Thatching - Greatest Pleasure by Be My Guest (USA) (M Tate) 1951[6] 3189 4009 4052 4121[8]

8 **PEACE OFFICER,** br g Strong Gale - Peace Woman by Pitpan (A Barrow) 3152[5] 3282[1] 3500[6] 3766[3] 3968[4]

5 **PEACE TRIBUTE(IRE),** br g Nomination - Olderfleet by Steel Heart (D P Kelly) 1230 1400 1495 4030[4] 4113[4] 4187[4]

6 **PEACEFUL POLLY(IRE),** b m Pollerton - Rule The Waves by Deep Run (M Tate) 4375

5 **PEACEFUL RIVER(IRE),** b m Over The River (FR) - No Battle by Khalkis (Norman Cassidy) 39[2] 59[4]

8 **PEACEMAN,** b g Martinmas - Miss Posy by Pitskelly (Mrs D Haine) 848[1] 1279[2] 1621[3] 2319[2] 2603 2818[3] 3400[1] 3490[1]

6 **PEACOCK FEATHER,** b m Bustino - Wide Of The Mark by Gulf Pearl (K R Burke) 1154 1272[3] 1506[4] 1699 1942[1] 2185 2292

10 **PEAJADE,** b g Buckskin (FR) - Kaminaki by Deep Run (D Nicholson) 2305 2460

8 **PEAK DISTRICT,** b g Beldale Flutter (USA) - Grand Teton by Bustino (R Lee) 424[6] 526[4] 651 936 1592[3] 3545[3] 3801[6] 4121[7]

9 **PEANUTS PET,** b g Tina's Pet - Sinzinbra by Royal Palace (T P Tate) 726 1116[7] 1322[7] 1619[3] 2487[4] 2788[1] 3038 3408[5]

6 **PEARL'S CHOICE(IRE),** b m Deep Run - Vendevar by Pardigras (Michael Purcell) 9[4] 50[4] 61[4] 80[5] 103[2] 150[7] 254[5] 572[5] 3085[8]

7 **PEARLED(USA),** b g Affirmed (USA) - Snow Pearl (USA) by Boldnesian (J R Bostock) 4407

7 **PEARLS BEAU,** b g Beau Charmeur (FR) - Clonamona by Karabas (J R Jenkins) 184[1] 204[1] 281[2] 360[1] 382[2] 521 667

8 **PEARLTWIST,** b m Roi Guillaume (FR) - Tullylust by Private Walk (Jeremiah John O'Neill) 208[1] 42[2] 60[1]

6 **PEARLY CASTLE(IRE),** ch m Carlingford Castle - Bluejama by Windjammer (USA) (I R Ferguson) 37 80

5 **PEARLY WHITE,** b m Petong - White's Pet by Mummy's Pet (D L Williams) 166[3] 454[7] 592[3] 651[5] 932[2] 1079[3] 1731[5] 2225[4] 2424[5] 4107[9] 4160[4] 4179[6]

6 **PEATSWOOD,** ch g Rolfe (USA) - Cathy Jane by Lauso (M R Channon) 1310[1] 1756[6] 1845[1] 2012[3] 2473 3028[7] 3408[7] 3609[4] 3735[3]

9 **PEATY GLEN,** b g Furry Glen - June's Slipper by No Argument (M H Tompkins) 1444[4] 1563

7 **PEBBLE BROOK,** ch g Invited (USA) - Brookland Lass by Mon Capitaine (V T O'Brien) 200

8 **PEBBLE LANE,** br m On Your Mark - Garda's Lane by Garda's Revenge (USA) (Bernard Jones) 1453 1686[3] 1818[3] 2026[1] 2180[5]

6 **PEBBLE ROCK,** b g Uncle Pokey - Hejera by Cantab (Capt T A Forster) 1800 3494

10 **PECCAVI,** ch g Hard Fought - Princess Sinna by Sun Prince (V R Bishop) 4323 325[4] 442 612[5] 703[7] 1525[5] 3879[4] 4105[2] 4161

10 **PECHE D'OR,** ch g Glint Of Gold - Fishermans Bridge by Crepello (H E Haynes) 4324[5] 3454 3510 3921[7] 4005[4] 4105[5] 4161[5]

6 **PECTORUS(IRE),** b g Denel (FR) - Pretty Damsel by Prince Hansel (M C Pipe) 483[6] 1542[9] 2827

4 **PEEDIE PEAT,** gr g Petong - White's Pet by Mummy's Pet (J J O'Neill) 278[4] 742[7] 971[3] 1356[2] 1526[5]

11 **PEGMARINE(USA),** b g Text (USA) - Symbionese (USA) by Bold Reason (Mrs A M Woodrow) 1934[4] 2170

7 **PEGUS GOLD,** br m Strong Gale - Real Pegus by Decent Fellow (Patrick O'Leary) 2553[6] 3296[7] 3469[6]

5 **PEGUS PRINCE(IRE),** br g Mandalus - Flying Pegus by Beau Chapeau (A J McNamara) 4399 4 925 990 1180 1609 1823 2661[7] 3872[7] 3972[5] 4114

7 **PEJAWI,** br m Strong Gale - Beau St by Will Somers (Mrs John Harrington) 71[9] 103[3] 169[9] 410 1785[5] 1857[5] 2035[9] 3655 3790

9 **PELEUS(USA),** b g Irish River (FR) - Pellinora (USA) by King Pellinore (USA) (D T Hughes) 1986[7] 2157 2281[6] 3526

8 **PELOTA,** gr m Petong - Lucky Deal by Floribunda (Neil King) 4158[7]

5 **POKONO TRAIL(IRE), ch** g Aristocracy - Frank's Choice by Whistling Deer (F Flood) 3122³ 3891

6 **POLAR HAT, ch** g Norwick (USA) - Sky Bonnet by Sky Gipsy (M C Pipe) 3300 3530 3977⁴ 4144

8 **POLAR REGION, br** g Alzao (USA) - Bonny Hollow by Wolver Hollow (J G FitzGerald) 1486 1670⁴ 1864⁵ 2305

5 **POLAR RHAPSODY(IRE), b** g Orchestra - Arctic Vista by Deep Run (Miss H C Knight) 2210⁷

6 **POLDEN PRIDE, b** g Vital Season - Bybrook by Border Chief (G B Balding) 1717 1946⁷ 2950⁸ 3549

8 **POLDER, b** g Lochnager - Dutch Girl by Workboy (D L Williams) 4323³ 153³ 225² 374 500⁶ 643⁸ 810⁶ 3959⁹ 4109⁵ 4164⁶

11 **POLECROFT, b** g Crofter (USA) - Grange Kova by Allangrange (G W Davies) 1299² 1740

5 **POLICEMANS PRIDE(FR), bl** g Policeman (FR) - Proud Pet by Petingo (M Madgwick) 901 1161 1392⁶ 2048⁶ 2426 2728⁷ 3151⁵ 3365 3547⁶

6 **POLISH RIDER(USA), ch** h Danzig Connection (USA) - Missy T (USA) by Lt Stevens (Mrs D Haine) 3094 3342⁵ 3549¹ 3756 3848² 3938³ 4110⁴

7 **POLISHING, ch** g Touching Wood (USA) - Loveshine (USA) by Gallant Romeo (USA) (M D Hammond) 1119² 1561⁹ 2403 2830³ 3028 3142¹ 3461⁴ 3622⁸ 4006⁸

10 **POLITICAL MAN, b** g Mandalus - Worth A Vote by Vilmoray (Mrs T J Hills) 3947

7 **POLITICAL TOWER, b** g Politico (USA) - Crosby Waves by Bing II (M A Barnes) 734³ 875 1096⁴ 1484² 1735¹ 1958¹ 2007 2218¹ 2832⁸

5 **POLK(FR), b** g Jefferson - Dark Light (FR) by Dark Tiger (M C Pipe) 1068 1187 1404 1519⁴ 3572⁶

10 **POLLANEDIN, b** g Paico - Lady Mell (P J Deegan) 124 252⁹ 708

6 **POLLEROO(IRE), ch** m Pollerton - Oriental Roo by Amazon (J Collins) 2919⁸ 3466⁹ 3550 3788⁷

7 **POLLERTON'S PRIDE, b** m Pollerton - Arctic Snow Cat by Raise You Ten (W Clay) 4347⁶ 948⁴ 1080³ 1311 2600⁶ 2766 3192⁴ 3278⁶ 3562 3901⁵

10 **POLLIBRIG, br** m Politico (USA) - Taras Brig by New Brig (William Hamilton) 2451⁴

8 **POLLITTS PRIDE, ch** m Crash Course - Fotopan by Polyfoto (J L Eyre) 4328⁴ 2561

4 **POLLY LEACH, b** f Pollerton - Come On Gracie by Hardiran (G A Ham) 606³ 890⁸ 1007 2300

7 **POLLY MINOR, b** m Sunley Builds - Polly Major by Politico (USA) (G P Enright) 380 764⁸ 863³ 1252⁵ 1734⁷ 2133³ 3151² 3547³

6 **POLLY PLUM, ch** m Pollerton - Rosie Probert by Captain's Gig (USA) (R Coonan) 4378 80⁴ 174² 295⁶ 508³ 4044

6 **POLLYKENDU(IRE), b** or br g Pollerton - Moykendu by Tudor Music (Patrick Heffernan) 393 435⁵ 536⁸ 993⁵ 1113³

6 **POLLYTICKLE, gr** m Politico (USA) - No Don't by Don't Look (C T Nash) 883

4 **POLY VISION(IRE), b** g Vision (USA) - Beechwood (USA) by Blushing Groom (FR) (M Tate) 3108⁸ 3451 3559² 4004

4 **POLYGAR, b** g Pollerton - Sugar Pea by Bold As Brass (C L Popham) 3855

8 **POLYNOGAN, b** g Pollerton - Wrekenogan by Tarqogan (R H Buckler) 869 1248 3360

5 **POND HOUSE(IRE), b** g Phardante (FR) - Arctic Tack by Arctic Slave (M C Pipe) 2916⁷ 3458

10 **PONDERED BID, b** or br g Auction Ring (USA) - Ponca by Jim French (USA) (J Dooler) 1485 1963⁹

4 **PONDERING, br** g Another Realm - Fishpond by Homing (M C Pipe) 1504¹ 1710¹ 2262¹ 3036⁹

8 **PONENTINO, b** g Strong Gale - Milan United by Milan (G P Kelly) 4350 4384

5 **PONGO WARING(IRE), b** g Strong Gale - Super Cailin by Brave Invader (USA) (Miss H C Knight) 2210⁵ 3113⁷ 3680⁸

13 **PONTEUS PILOT, ch** g Levanter - Quelle Pas by Kelling (R J Down) 4315⁴

7 **PONTOON BRIDGE, ch** g Carlingford Castle - Lumax by Maximilian (G Harwood) 601¹ 894² 3068 3698⁵ 3943 4098¹

6 **PONTYNYSWEN, b** g Ballacashtal (CAN) - Tropingay by Cawston's Clown (D Burchell) 1755⁶ 2258⁴ 2833³ 3269² 3383¹ 3736⁷ 4019⁷

6 **POOR MOTHER(IRE), b** f The Parson - Deceptive Response by Furry Glen (F Flood) 1760 2050⁵ 2155⁴ 2311² 2660 2921⁸ 3504⁹ 3719⁵

6 **POOR TIMES(IRE), ch** m Roselier (FR) - Try Me Again by Push On (Thomas Noonan) 432⁴ 571⁴ 689⁷ 798⁴ 991⁹ 3467³ 3731⁵ 3869⁵ 4115⁷

7 **POORS WOOD, b** g Martinmas - Lyaaric by Privy Seal (J T Gifford) 829⁷

9 **POP ABROAD, b** or br m Broadsword (USA) - Lady Poppy by Sahib (P J Bevan) 4347 664⁷

5 **POP FESTIVAL, b** m Electric - Vino Festa by Nebbiolo (P T Dalton) 4344⁹ 1707 2117 3583 4004

6 **POP IN THERE(IRE), br** g Monksfield - Why Don't Ye by Illa Laudo (John Stirling) 4337

10 **POP SONG, b** g High Season - Top Of The Pops II by Hanover (G L Roe) 1273³ 1643 4006

7 **POPESHALL, b** g Mufrij - Allez Stanwick by Goldhill (Miss Sally Williamson) 3157¹ 3377⁴

11 **POPESWOOD, b** g Nicholas Bill - Villarrica (FR) by Dan Cupid (W G R Wightman) 615⁷ 3480

5 **POPEYE THE GUY(IRE), b** g Regular Guy - Debonair Dolly by Cidrax (FR) (David McBratney) 3813³

5 **POPPEA(IRE), br** m Strong Gale - Lepida by Royal Match (J T R Dreaper) 2989²

7 **POPPETS PET, b** g Native Bazaar - Imperial Miss by Philip Of Spain (J W Mullins) 981² 1298⁴ 1441 1457¹ 1754³ 1844³ 2145⁵ 2378⁵ 2693⁵ 2978³ 3426 3726⁵

5 **PORT IN A STORM, b** h Blakeney - Crusader's Dream by St Paddy (N Tinkler) 932⁵ 1079⁴ 1237² 1370¹ 1472¹ 1655⁷ 1731¹ 1961¹ 2108⁶ 2354⁵ 2401⁵

5 **PORT PRINCESS(IRE), b** m Dance Of Life (USA) - Nelly Gail by Mount Hagen (FR) (F X Doyle) 2231 2615⁴

5 **PORT RISING(IRE), ch** g Rising - Portal Lady by Pals Passage (R Donoghue) 4396² 55⁴ 67⁸ 2317 431³

6 **PORT SUNLIGHT(IRE), ch** g Tate Gallery (USA) - Nana's Girl by Tin Whistle (R Hannon) 2250⁶

7 **PORT TIME, b** g Good Thyne (USA) - Portal Lady by Pals Passage (Michael Purcell) 557 3198³ 3325³

10 **PORTAVOGIE, b** g Kambalda - Mary's Honour by Honour Bound (Mrs Jean Brown) 4300⁵ 4387 544 677⁴ 789¹ 975⁴ 2605

13 **PORTER'S SONG, ch** g True Song - Spartan Clover by Spartan General (H Hutsby) 2482⁴ 2669⁹

9 **PORTLAND LAD, b** g Balboa - Ravella by Raeburn II (M McDonagh) 26³ 101 132⁸ 468 532 3873 4033

10 **PORTONIA, b** m Ascertain (USA) - Hardwick Sun by Dieu Soleil (Mrs M Reveley) 1028⁷

INDEX TO NATIONAL HUNT RESULTS 1993-94

8 **PURRIT THERE,** ch g Don - Glencoe Lights by Laser Light (Philip Brolan) 1910 2128 2664

5 **PUSH GENTLY(IRE),** ch m Ovac (ITY) - Miss Pushover by Push On (Peter McCreery) 709 3610⁶ 3794 4113

4 **PUSH THE BUTTON(IRE),** ch f Shardari - Offshore Boom by Be My Guest (USA) (M J P O'Brien) 3246³ 3321² 3466³ 3656 3934² 3993⁴ 4167²

8 **PUSHY PARSON,** b g Push On - Maries Party by The Parson (T W Donnelly) 1169

13 **PYJAMAS,** ch g Lighter - Arctic Dawn by Arctic Slave (Mrs D A Whitaker) 4130

9 **PYLON SPARKS,** b g Electric - Fancy Work by Sparkler (Miss Suzy Barkley) 63 1015⁴ 1269

7 **PYR FOUR,** b g Strong Gale - Distant Castle by Deep Run (J T R Dreaper) 2 967⁴ 1232 1907²

4 **PYRAMIS PRINCE(IRE),** b g Fairy King (USA) - Midnight Patrol by Ashmore (FR) (Miss H C Knight) 406⁷ 1350¹

9 **PYRO PENNANT,** b g Official - Courtney Pennant by Angus (D Burchell) 1298⁵ 1527 1926 2057⁶ 2329 2900 3315⁴ 3682⁷

4 **PYRRHIC DANCE,** b g Sovereign Dancer (USA) - Cherubim (USA) by Stevward (C J Mann) 356¹ 462³ 611 742² 997¹ 1166 2874 3330 3715¹ 3932³ 4110⁶

4 **QAFFAL(USA),** b g Seattle Dancer (USA) - Samalex by Ela-Mana-Mou (R T Phillips) 2115⁴

5 **QUADRAPOL,** br m Pollerton - Dream World by Quadrangle (S Christian) 2677⁹ 3208⁶ 3832⁴ 4040¹

5 **QUADRIREME,** b g Rousillon (USA) - Bireme by Grundy (J A B Old) 4344¹

6 **QUAGO,** ch m New Member - Spiritus Miss by Master Spiritus (R H Buckler) 778⁸ 2141 2558⁷ 3005⁹ 3213⁴ 3671⁸

9 **QUAI D'ORSAY,** b g Be My Guest (USA) - Noblanna (USA) by Vaguely Noble (F J O'Mahony) 3696

5 **QUAINT HONOUR,** b m Niniski (USA) - Red Nanda by Status Seeker (Francis V Kiernan) 98⁹ 709

4 **QUAKER WALTZ,** br f Faustus (USA) - Silent Dancer by Quiet Fling (USA) (J C Tuck) 3208⁷ 3523

5 **QUALITAIR IDOL,** b m Dreams To Reality (USA) - Village Idol by Blakeney (Mrs A Knight) 1519 1749

5 **QUALITAIR MEMORY(IRE),** ch g Don't Forget Me - Whist Awhile by Caerleon (USA) (J Akehurst) 4345³ 1597³ 2067² 2165¹ 2346⁶ 2711⁴ 3014² 3308⁷ 3545⁴ 4121

6 **QUALITAIR SOUND(IRE),** b g Mazaad - A Nice Alert by Red Alert (J F Bottomley) 4354 318⁵

9 **QUALITY ASSURED,** gr g Grey Ghost - Rosamond by Spiritus (T J Carr) 1792⁵ 2069

4 **QUANTUM LEADER(IRE),** b g Supreme Leader - Papapatch by Patch (R O'Leary) 3589

6 **QUARRY HOUSE(IRE),** b g The Parson - April Sal by Sallust (Major D N Chappell) 1768² 2728² 3380 3518

6 **QUARTER MARKER(IRE),** br g Celio Rufo - Palatine Lady by Pauper (Thomas Foley) 107 215⁴ 276 508¹ 636

6 **QUARTZ(FR),** ch g Saint Estephe - Quintefolle by Luthier 621²

11 **QUAYSIDE BUOY,** br g Quayside - Ivernia by Golden Vision (Declan Queally) 33² 92¹ 116² 214⁶ 306 1980⁷ 4032 4168⁷

6 **QUAYSIDE COTTAGE(IRE),** b or br g Quayside - Polly's Cottage by Pollerton (James Joseph Mangan) 3956⁹ 4193⁴

8 **QUE BELLA,** b m Hello Handsome - Waterbeck by Weathercock (Mrs J P Gabb) 3950

6 **QUEEN BUZZARD,** b m Buzzards Bay - Cabaletta by Double Jump (E Weymes) 2909 3079⁵ 3590²

5 **QUEEN KAM(IRE),** ch m Kambalda - War Queen by Yrrah Jr (Thomas Bergin) 4406 31⁶ 94² 179⁴ 292

4 **QUEEN MARIANA,** b f King Of Spain - Duck Soup by Decoy Boy (R T Phillips) 3832

5 **QUEEN OF THE CELTS,** b m Celtic Cone - Run In Tune by Deep Run (R Simpson) 2860

4 **QUEEN OF THE LAKES(IRE),** b f Supreme Leader - Pollettia by Pollerton (Michael Hourigan) 3871⁷

4 **QUEEN OF THE QUORN,** b f Governor General - Alumia by Great Nephew (G M Moore) 1483⁷ 2783⁷ 3103

6 **QUEEN OF THE ROCK(IRE),** b m The Parson - Driella by Even Money (J E Kiely) 4402⁷ 1330 1687 1859²

10 **QUEEN OF THE SWANS,** b m Floriferous - Swanee Lady by My Swanee (Mrs Edwina Finn) 21⁹ 170⁹ 306 532

7 **QUEEN PERSIAN,** ch m King Persian - Edansa (J O'Dowd) 2590 3747 4093⁸

5 **QUEEN'S AWARD(IRE),** ch g Bishop Of Orange - Demelza Carne by Woodville II (R Champion) 1494 2042 2991

10 **QUEEN'S CHAPLAIN,** b g The Parson - Reginasway by Flair Path (Mrs M Morris) 4363⁵ 2605⁴ 2782¹ 2888⁴ 3165³ 3313

4 **QUEENFORD BELLE,** ch f Celtic Cone - Belle Bavard by Le Bavard (FR) (P J Hobbs) 2546² 3138¹ 3476

7 **QUEENIES CHILD,** b or br m Seymour Hicks (FR) - Mystery Queen by Martinmas (C P Donoghue) 4361² 79¹ 88³ 576² 858⁵ 1236⁸ 1576⁹ 1766⁵ 1986⁴ 2197⁵

5 **QUEENLIER(IRE),** gr m Roselier (FR) - Kindly Miss by Master Buck (S G Walsh) 2394 2684

4 **QUEENS CONTRACTOR,** b g Formidable (USA) - Salazie by Ile de Bourbon (USA) (S Mellor) 188⁸ 221⁵

7 **QUEENS CURATE,** b m Bustineto - Bright Gail by Levanter (Mrs E B Scott) 593 751 954 3148³ 3420³

6 **QUEENS HALL(IRE),** b m Orchestra - Legal Argument by No Argument (J T R Dreaper) 39⁷ 179⁷

9 **QUEENS TOUR,** b h Sweet Monday - On Tour by Queen's Hussar (E H Owen Jun) 4388 730⁷ 3928⁹

6 **QUEENS WALK,** ch m Brando - Quiet Queen by Richboy (P G Murphy) 1169

5 **QUEENSEAL(IRE),** ch m King Persian - Seal Beach by Tarboosh (USA) (Eamon Gibney) 495⁹

4 **QUENIE TWO(IRE),** b f Taufan (USA) - Requena by Dom Racine (FR) (M Quaid) 1853

8 **QUENTIN DURWOOD,** gr g Mr Fluorocarbon - Donallan by No Mercy (B de Haan) 2043³ 2272 2538⁵ 2822⁴ 3338⁵ 3575³ 3750⁴

5 **QUICK LEARNER(IRE),** b g Crash Course - Rifflealp by Sterling Bay (SWE) (Francis Berry) 2863 2983

5 **QUICK RAISE(FR),** b g In Fijar (USA) - Borjana (USA) by To The Quick (USA) (Peter Casey) 2203 3810

9 **QUICK RAPOR,** b g Rapid Pass - Dark Sensation by Thriller (Richard Barber) 2966¹ 3263

11 **QUICK REACTION,** b g Main Reef - Swift Response by No Argument (Mrs E H Heath) 3265⁸

4 **QUICK SILVER BOY,** gr g Kalaglow - Safidar by Roan Rocket (D Burchell) 830⁶ 1059² 1297² 1927¹ 2422 2977³

752

5 **RATHCARRICK LASS(IRE),** b m Le Bavard (FR) - Tepukei River by Tepukei (S F Maye) 4360⁹ 98 233⁷ 469 3934

7 **RATHCORE,** b g King's Ride - Lady Willma by Reformed Character (Michael Kiernan) 464⁴ 538 672⁶ 1156² 1609¹ 1782⁴ 1823² 2098² 2158¹ 2590⁷ 2617³ 3085⁴ 3242⁸

5 **RATHER AINNIS(IRE),** ch m Great Eastern - Venture Wild by Deep Run (P J P Doyle) 1766

8 **RATHER SHARP,** b g Green Shoon - Rather Special by Varano (C L Popham) 946⁵ 1275³ 1463⁸ 1923¹ 2240¹ 2255⁴ 2397 2798 3017³ 3185³ 3312⁶ 3456

6 **RATHFARDON(IRE),** b g Callernish - Our June by Tarqogan (N J Tector) 1549 1892 2123 2863 3366 3747⁶ 3954 4077⁶

6 **RATHNAGEERA GIRL(IRE),** b m Asir - Meneleks Daughter by Menelek (Thomas Foley) 4410⁴ 17⁸ 45

6 **RATHNURE LADY(IRE),** b or br m Step Together (USA) - Knocknahour Windy Vii (Dermot Day) 433 638 1018 1265 1501 2035² 2234³ 2940 3465

7 **RATHVINDEN HOUSE(USA),** b g Hostage (USA) - Great Verdict (USA) by Le Fabuleux (J White) 792¹ 886² 1993² 2593² 3027

7 **RATIFY,** br g Shirley Heights - Rattle (FR) by Riverman (USA) (K A Morgan) 1101 1389² 1746⁶ 2360⁵ 2580¹ 2670 2833¹ 3092¹ 3422⁸ 3736

7 **RATTLE AND HUM,** br g Vision (USA) - Geraldville by Lord Gayle (M J Grassick) 4357³ 2⁵ 25²

5 **RAVEN'S ROCK(IRE),** b g Good Thyne (USA) - Fanlight Fanny by Sky Gipsy (Martin Michael Lynch) 1230 1815 2199 2348

4 **RAVENSPUR(IRE),** b c Reference Point - Royal Nugget (USA) by Mr Prospector (USA) (J Parkes) 1476⁸ 1655 2068 2271⁶ 2420⁴ 2530⁷

10 **RAWHIDE,** ch g Buckskin (FR) - Shuil Eile by Deep Run (Mrs J G Retter) 4391⁷ 2982⁵

11 **RAWYARDS BRIG,** b g New Brig - Moonbreaker by Twilight Alley (Mrs D Thomson) 1585 2105 3537⁸

5 **RAYLEO(IRE),** ch g Gorytus (USA) - Vagrant Maid (USA) by Honest Pleasure (USA) (Capt J Wilson) 723⁶ 976⁹ 3183⁴ 3345⁶ 3497 3640

7 **RAYMYLETTE,** ch g Le Moss - Myralette by Deep Run (N J Henderson) 2293¹ 2504¹ 3067¹

9 **RAYSULID,** b g Caerleon (USA) - Ramanouche (FR) by Riverman (USA) (Patrick Phelan) 63⁷

6 **RBF ARIANNE,** b m Cruise Missile - Boherash by Boreen (FR) (Ms Jackie McKeand) 695 795 883⁸

5 **REACH FOR GLORY,** b g Reach - Carlton Glory by Blakeney (W G M Turner) 137⁷ 1602 3632 3876² 4160²

5 **REACH ME NOT(IRE),** ch m Reach - Injaz by Golden Act (USA) (Mrs N S Sharpe) 4322

4 **REACTED(IRE),** b f Entitled - Rosecrea by Ballymore (J P Kavanagh) 4145

8 **READY OR NOT,** ch g Sunyboy - Flammula by Wrekin Rambler (Andrew Turnell) 847 1107 1417

12 **READY STEADY,** ch g Bivouac - Very Merry by Lord Of Verona (S Friar) 2451

11 **REAL CLASS,** b g Deep Run - Our Cherry by Tarqogan (R K Aston) 3927

5 **REAL GLEE(IRE),** ch g Phardante (FR) - Richest by Richboy (O Sherwood) 2876⁵ 3386

8 **REAL HARMONY,** ch g Le Bavard (FR) - Winning Wink by Milan (R J O'Sullivan) 1714⁴ 2223 3764⁶ 4097

6 **REAL PROGRESS(IRE),** ch g Ashford (USA) - Dulcet Dido by Dike (USA) (P J Hobbs) 701 984² 1058⁴ 1805⁶ 2725⁵ 3605¹ 3706⁶

7 **REALLY A RASCAL,** b g Scallywag - Rockefillee by Tycoon II (D R Gandolfo) 683

8 **REALLY NEAT,** gr m Alias Smith (USA) - Tiddley by Filiberto (USA) (L Waring) 953⁴ 1272⁷ 1516 1716⁹ 1950⁶ 3478⁸

4 **REASILVIA(IRE),** b f Supreme Leader - Quiteamazing by Flair Path (E J O'Grady) 1983⁷ 2156⁴ 2391⁶ 2703

5 **REASKA SURPRISE(IRE),** b m Huntingdale - Santa Maria (GER) by Literat (M McDonagh) 4360 4406⁸ 98

5 **REASON TO BELIEVE(IRE),** b m Kafu - Stoirin by Mart Lane (Desmond McDonogh) 472⁶ 671 1036 1400 1551

7 **REBAH(FR),** b g Lou Piguet - Pasuk by Kalamoun 4132²

4 **REBEL KING,** b g Doc Marten - Cape Farewell by Record Run (M A Barnes) 732⁵ 1217 2217⁴ 2369³ 2783⁸ 2903² 3373⁹

8 **RECIDIVIST,** b m Royben - On Remand by Reform (R J Hodges) 794⁹ 931⁷

7 **RECORD BILLY,** b g Mummy's Treasure - Miss Tudy Green by Pals Passage (Charles King) 17

4 **RECORD LOVER(IRE),** b g Alzao (USA) - Spun Gold by Thatch (USA) (M C Chapman) 406² 516⁸ 890⁶ 1097² 1188¹ 1317³ 1865³ 2528⁹ 4072⁵ 4088⁴ 4178⁴

5 **RECTORY GARDEN(IRE),** b g The Parson - Peace Run by Deep Run (Capt T A Forster) 1957 2333 3170

8 **RED AMBER,** ch g The Parson - April Sal by Sallust (S E Sherwood) 835² 956⁵ 1459² 1720⁷ 3168 3512

5 **RED BARONS LADY(IRE),** b m Electric - Tour Nobel (FR) by Habitat (P Mullins) 3⁹ 531⁶ 620 692 908⁷

7 **RED BEACON,** b g Red Sunset - Mount Of Light by Sparkler (J L Goulding) 717 910⁹

6 **RED BEAN,** ch g Ginger Boy - Pharona by Pharaoh Hophra (J O'Donoghue) 2400⁶ 2649⁵ 3117⁵ 3728

5 **RED BRANCH(IRE),** ch g Remainder Man - Run With Rosie by Deep Run (K R Burke) 2404 3102

8 **RED CARDINAL,** b g Cardinal Flower - Deep Bonnie by Deep Run (T Thomson Jones) 553² 1314¹

13 **RED COLUMBIA,** ch g St Columbus - Red Tan by Crespin Rouge (F Coton) 4310² 4387⁹ 1151² 1423 1606⁵ 2424¹ 2630

5 **RED DUST,** ch m Saxon Farm - Gentle Madam by Camden Town (E H Owen Jun) 3457

9 **RED EXPRESS VI,** b g Red Field - Dam Unknown (O J Roche) 3295² 3527² 3722¹ 3888 3994

4 **RED FAN(IRE),** b g Taufan (USA) - The Woman In Red by Red Regent (M Dods) 1920 2241

5 **RED FOUNTAIN(IRE),** b g Lafontaine (USA) - Red For Go by Tanfirion (James Joseph O'Connor) 234 3911

8 **RED INDIAN,** ch g Be My Native (USA) - Martialette by Welsh Saint (W W Haigh) 662¹ 781² 1055¹ 1364⁶ 1735³ 2833 3446²

5 **RED INK,** ch g Blushing Scribe (USA) - Pink Robber (USA) by No Robbery (J R Jenkins) 244³ 454¹ 1708 1741⁹ 2342⁴ 2542⁴ 2641³

5 **RED JACK(IRE),** b g Red Sunset - Rockeater by Roan Rocket (J Akehurst) 1562⁷ 1931⁵ 2317⁴

INDEX TO NATIONAL HUNT RESULTS 1993-94

7 **ROLLESTON BLADE,** ch g Broadsword (USA) - Pearl Bride by Spartan General (H J Jarvis) 3860⁶

11 **ROLLING BALL(FR),** b g Quart de Vin (FR) - Etoile Du Berger III by Farabi (M C Pipe) 1439 1843

5 **ROLLING THE BONES(USA),** b g Green Dancer (USA) - Davelle's Bid (USA) by Bold Bidder (P S Felgate) 639⁷

5 **ROLSTER PRINCESS,** ch m Right Regent - Sharp Lass by Sharpen Up (A M Forte) 775⁸

5 **ROLY PRIOR,** b g Celtic Cone - Moonduster by Sparkler (Miss L C Plater) 2931⁶ 3079⁴ 3868

5 **ROLY WALLACE,** b g Primo Dominie - Ethel Knight by Thatch (USA) (A L Forbes) 1079 1353⁷ 1472 3635

4 **ROMALITO,** b g Robellino (USA) - Princess Zita by Manado (M Blanshard) 606⁴ 3314³ 3444² 3734⁹

10 **ROMAN DART,** b g Roman Warrior - Angodeen by Aberdeen (M Scudamore) 834 1022

6 **ROMAN FORUM(IRE),** b g Rhoman Rule (USA) - Bodelle by Falcon (Victor Bowens) 4398⁸ 1269³ 1400 1746⁶ 1818 2988⁸

6 **ROMAN SWORD,** br m Broadsword (USA) - Winnetka by Buckskin (FR) (S J Leadbetter) 2106 2447

12 **ROMAN WOOD,** b m St Columbus - Weywood by Coliseum (Mrs T J Hill) 3947⁶ 4103

5 **ROMANY BLUES,** b m Oats - Romany Serenade by Romany Air (A P Jones) 1126⁶ 1536 1994

5 **ROMANY CREEK(IRE),** b g Trimmingham - Rare Picture by Pollerton (G B Balding) 1567 2170 2299

10 **ROMANY KING,** br g Crash Course - Winsome Lady by Tarqogan (G B Balding) 828³ 2377⁶ 2747⁷ 3132⁴ 3258 3425

9 **ROMANY SPLIT,** b g Official - Romany Park by Romany Air (J G M O'Shea) 1469⁶ 1770 1926⁸ 3764⁵ 3850

6 **ROMANY TRAVELLER,** b m Impecunious - Romany Serenade by Romany Air (R Barton) 1734⁸

11 **ROMFUL PRINCE,** b g White Prince (USA) - Romfultears by Romany Air (C W Mitchell) 986

6 **ROMOLA NIJINSKY,** b m Bustino - Verchinina by Star Appeal (P D Evans) 522¹ 730

6 **RONEO(USA),** ch g Secretariat (USA) - Zaizafon (USA) by The Minstrel (CAN) (Miss Jacqueline S Doyle) 1167 1425

12 **RONOCCO,** ch g Baptism - Kilteelagh Lady by King's Leap (Mrs S D Williams) 1547³ 309³ 366³

7 **ROOKS ROCK,** b g Tesoro Mio - Fancy Girl by Mon Capitaine (Thomas F Walshe) 79⁴ 124 258⁶

5 **ROONA,** ch m Ra Nova - The Muskerry Lady by Golden Gorden (J White) 3547

4 **ROOTSMAN(IRE),** b g Glenstal (USA) - Modena by Sassafras (FR) (Mrs Merrita Jones) 228⁶ 253⁴ 2722 3597⁶

4 **ROOUAN GIRL(IRE),** ch f Tremblant - Kimangao by Garda's Revenge (USA) (L Young) 3946 4152

8 **ROPE,** b g Rolfe (USA) - Mountain Rescue by Mountain Call (A L Forbes) 838⁴

6 **RORY JOHN,** ch g Country Classic - Rasimareem by Golden Mallard (J Mulhall) 3598 3800 3903

5 **ROSCEEN BUI(IRE),** b m Phardante (FR) - Tullow Performance by Gala Performance (USA) (Michael Hourigan) 535 3912⁹

12 **ROSCOE HARVEY,** br g Roscoe Blake - Hunter's Treasure by Tudor Treasure (C P E Brooks) 777 921³ 1121 2328⁴ 3512

10 **ROSCOE'S GEMMA,** b m Roscoe Blake - Ash Copse by Golden Love (N K Thick) 2899 3278² 3498 4020⁵

4 **ROSCOMMON JOE(IRE),** b g Simply Great (FR) - Kilvarnet by Furry Glen (J J O'Neill) 247³ 285⁷ 1147¹ 1473³ 1584²

6 **ROSDEMON(IRE),** gr g Roselier (FR) - Castle Demon by Tiepolo II (J T R Dreaper) 1910⁸ 2161⁵ 3747

8 **ROSE APPEAL,** ch g Star Appeal - Rose And The Ring by Welsh Pageant (P Mullins) 209¹ 1331³ 1576⁸ 1686⁷ 1824⁶ 2097

7 **ROSE KING,** b g King's Ride - Choral Rose by Blue Refrain (J T Gifford) 1309 2477¹ 2671⁷

11 **ROSE TABLEAU,** ch m Ballymore - Princess Pageant by Welsh Pageant (J J O'Neill) 2153 2954⁴ 3287 3688² 3783⁴

8 **ROSEATE LODGE,** b g Habitat - Elegant Tern (USA) by Sea-Bird II (K R Burke) 1283 1448

5 **ROSEBERRY TOPPING,** gr g Nicholas Bill - Habitab by Sovereign Path (Mrs M Reveley) 815⁴ 1103³ 1376² 1482⁴ 2239 2905⁸

9 **ROSEHIP,** b g Derring Rose - Fairy Island by Prince Hansel (P Cheesbrough) 4363⁴ 2736⁴

5 **ROSEL WALK(IRE),** gr g Roselier (FR) - Winawalk by Private Walk (Francis M O'Brien) 2944 3550 3730 3834

5 **ROSEMARY MAC(IRE),** b m Supreme Leader - Show Business by Auction Ring (USA) (A P O'Brien) 508 530

4 **ROSEMARY'S MEMORY(IRE),** ch f Convinced - Corvina by Ardoon (J S Moore) 207 296⁹ 381⁴

7 **ROSEMOSS,** ch m Le Moss - Roseitess by Royal And Regal (USA) (M C Pipe) 3630³

6 **ROSEN THE BEAU(IRE),** gr g Roselier (FR) - Dunderry Class by Dusky Boy (N A Gaselee) 983 1196⁶ 1392⁴ 2208 3213⁶ 3575

6 **ROSENTHAL,** b m Green Ruby (USA) - Demetria (GER) by Basalt (GER) (W G M Turner) 1626 1797⁵ 2117

6 **ROSEPERRIE(IRE),** gr m Roselier (FR) - Lady Perry by David Jack (A D Evans) 636⁷ 798⁸ 967⁶ 1075 1782 1980⁶ 2050⁶ 2232⁴

4 **ROSES RED(IRE),** ch f Exhibitioner - Marsh Benham by Dragonara Palace (USA) (G M Lyons) 4078

4 **ROSES WISH(IRE),** gr f Roselier (FR) - Brave Wish by Brave Invader (USA) (Michael Hourigan) 3946 4148²

8 **ROSGILL,** ch g Mill Reef (USA) - Speedy Rose by On Your Mark (J White) 248⁶ 1278³ 1561 2418¹ 3131²

4 **ROSIE-B,** b f Gunner B - Saucy Mop by Saucy Kit (R M Stronge) 3138³ 3458

6 **ROSIES SISTER(IRE),** ch f Deep Run - Raise A Queen by Raise You Ten (J R Walsh) 4368

5 **ROSIN THE BOW(IRE),** gr g Roselier (FR) - Pastinas Lass by Bargello (David McBratney) 1828¹ 2201⁶ 2310 2590⁵ 2846 3273 3812⁹ 4093⁹

5 **ROSINA MAE,** b m Rousillon (USA) - Dame Ashfield by Grundy (D Burchell) 3494

11 **ROSITARY(FR),** b m Trenel - Houri V (FR) by Vieux Chateau (P Winkworth) 1445 1759 2047 2184⁴ 2247 2495² 2758¹ 2911² 3146

10 **ROSLAVAN LAD,** b g Trimmingham - Mightylikearose by Deep Run (Donal Hassett) 2352 2551

6 **ROSS GRAHAM,** gr g Macmillion - Play It Sam by Mandamus (Mrs Barbara Waring) 773⁹ 1010⁵ 1344³ 1557³ 2874⁵ 3184³ 3496⁴ 3604⁷

9 **ROSS VENTURE,** b g Monksfield - Fitz's Buck by Master Buck (L Lungo) 1063⁵ 1220³ 2791³

760

INDEX TO NATIONAL HUNT RESULTS 1993-94

7 **ROSSBEIGH CREEK,** ch g Crash Course - Smile Away by Never Slip (F Flood) 93³ 170¹ 178¹ 332⁵ 468³ 532² 800² 906¹ 4062⁶

4 **ROSSCOYNE,** b f Ardross - Banking Coyne by Deep Diver (Miss B Sanders) 971 1284

11 **ROSSI NOVAE,** gr g Roselier (FR) - The Blazing Star by Proverb (P J Stokes) 1037⁸ 1178 1402 2619⁷ 2662⁷ 2984⁴ 3249⁷ 3524⁹ 4042

5 **ROSSMANAGHER(IRE),** b g Baillamont (USA) - Lady Is A Tramp by Mr Prospector (USA) (P M Lynch) 56 115⁴ 257⁶

5 **ROSTARR(IRE),** gr m Roselier (FR) - Alice Starr by Windjammer (USA) (A P O'Brien) 3124¹ 3276⁵ 3653⁴ 3958⁷

11 **ROSY PROSPECT,** ch g Abednego - Swift Maid by Giolla Mear (Simon J Robinson) 2889

6 **ROUBABAY(IRE),** b g Darshaan - Rosy Moon (FR) by Sheshoon (P Mullins) 1236⁷ 1379³ 1500⁴ 1681² 1908² 2076³ 2278² 2465¹ 2986 3242 4077⁵

9 **ROUCHEAL,** gr g Rough Lad - Cheal Rose by Pony Express (Miss Julia Cleeland) 218 525 686

7 **ROUGH LEA,** b g Tudor Diver - Fodderlee by Cagirama (B Mactaggart) 4079

8 **ROUGH QUEST,** b g Crash Course - Our Quest by Private Walk (T J Etherington) 1507⁶ 2266² 2513² 2747 2948² 3405

9 **ROUGHSIDE,** b g Black Minstrel - Glazing Lady by Beau Chapeau (A H Mactaggart) 1477 2103

5 **ROUNDWOOD(IRE),** ch g Orchestra - Another Bless by Random Shot (D T Hughes) 3327⁵ 4063³

6 **ROUSITTO,** ch g Rousillon (USA) - Helenetta by Troy (R Hollinshead) 1773³ 1951

6 **ROUTING,** b g Rousillon (USA) - Tura by Northfields (USA) (N G Ayliffe) 716 885 1192⁵ 1642² 3574¹ 3806² 4019²

6 **ROUYAN,** b g Akarad (FR) - Rosy Moon (FR) by Sheshoon (Mrs J Pitman) 2293² 2479¹ 2601² 3039 3483³

6 **ROVANIEMI(IRE),** b g Fidel - Janey Fly by Grange Melody (I R Ferguson) 74 115 208 341⁶ 489⁸

7 **ROVING REPORT,** gr g Celio Rufo - Black Rapper by Le Tricolore (H Wellstead) 2800 3096⁵

6 **ROVULENKA,** b g Royal Vulcan - Natenka by Native Prince (M C Pipe) 1172⁵ 2034

9 **ROWAN REX,** b g Furry Glen - Glenreigh by Double-U-Jay (V Kennedy) 708⁸ 1232 3247

8 **ROWHEDGE,** ch g Tolomeo - Strident Note by The Minstrel (CAN) (Miss Jacqueline S Doyle) 195¹ 217² 307³ 344⁴

4 **ROWLANDSONS GOLD(IRE),** ch f Jamesmead - Rowlandsons Ruby by Nearly A Hand (M R Channon) 296⁷ 1885⁶ 2189⁴ 2492³ 3153¹ 3441 3698

6 **ROWSERSTOWN(IRE),** b h Asir - Samosa by Sexton Blake (A J Martin) 3694

10 **ROXALL CLUMP,** b g Neltino - Wyn-Bank by Green God (Mrs J M Bailey) 2888³ 3263⁶ 3501⁶

9 **ROXTON HILL,** b g Croghan Hill - Norhamina by Tyrone (C P E Brooks) 1321¹ 3297³

5 **ROXY RIVER,** ch m Ardross - Royal Yacht (USA) by Riverman (USA) (J L Spearing) 1414 1646 1929¹ 2244⁶ 3209⁵ 3680² 3745¹

9 **ROYAL ACCLAIM,** ch g Tender King - Glimmer by Hot Spark (J M Bradley) 1325⁹ 1589

4 **ROYAL ALBERT(IRE),** b g Mandalus - Sparkling Stream by Paddy's Stream (P Mullins) 3327² 3694¹

11 **ROYAL APPROVAL,** ch g Privy Seal - Delilah Dell by The Dell (Miss D B Stanhope) 4374⁵ 3884⁴

11 **ROYAL ATHLETE,** ch g Roselier (FR) - Darjoy by Darantus (Mrs J Pitman) 1011⁵ 1224¹ 1439

11 **ROYAL BATTERY(NZ),** br g Norfolk Air - All At Sea (NZ) by Man The Rail (D H Barons) 1720

6 **ROYAL BATTLE,** b m Broadsword (USA) - Non Such Valley by Colonist II (Mrs J Bloom) 1040 1215 1628

7 **ROYAL CHANCE(FR),** ch g Lightning (FR) - Volcanute by Hardicanute (Y Porzier) 816²

5 **ROYAL CIRCUS,** b g Kris - Circus Ring by High Top (J G M O'Shea) 1801 2065¹ 2229⁶ 2346¹ 2544³ 2644¹ 2715¹

5 **ROYAL COUP,** b g Relkino - Royal Snip by Royal Highway (Capt T A Forster) 3833⁶

13 **ROYAL CRAFTSMAN,** b or br g Workboy - Royal Huntress by Royal Avenue (A J K Dunn) 167²

8 **ROYAL DAY,** ch g Deep Run - Lady Perkins by Little Buskins (Miss C Saunders) 2456 2959²

9 **ROYAL DERBI,** b g Derrylin - Royal Birthday by St Paddy (N A Callaghan) 827² 1256⁴ 1663⁵ 1906³ 2079 2719² 3422³ 3650⁵

4 **ROYAL EXECUTIVE(IRE),** b g Waajib - Royal Episode by Royal Match (K S Bridgwater) 1097 1532 3559

10 **ROYAL EXHIBITION,** ch g Le Bavard (FR) - The Brown Link by Rugged Man (R Curtis) 4343 2336 2479

8 **ROYAL FIFE,** br m Royal Fountain - Aunt Bertha by Blandford Lad (Mrs S C Bradburne) 4326⁶ 1202⁸ 1677⁶ 1790 2436 2925⁷ 3076 3431 3542⁹

7 **ROYAL FIREWORKS,** ch g Royal Vulcan - Bengal Lady by Celtic Cone (D L Williams) 3611⁶

8 **ROYAL FLAMINGO,** gr m Deep Run - Crown Bird by Birdbrook (G C Bravery) 2666 2966 3091 3308¹ 3578² 3760

6 **ROYAL GAIT(NZ),** b g Gaiter (NZ) - Heather Carlyle (NZ) by Faux Tirage (D H Barons) 901 1108 1747 1994 2762⁶ 3009⁹

5 **ROYAL GARDEN,** ch g Royal Vulcan - Park Covert by On Your Mark (G B Balding) 1542

8 **ROYAL GIOTTO,** br g Royal Fountain - Mount Fairy VI by Prefairy (J L W Foster) 772

5 **ROYAL GLINT,** b m Glint Of Gold - Princess Matilda by Habitat (H E Haynes) 4319² 2430 3088³ 3571 3878² 4009⁴

12 **ROYAL GREEK,** ch g Royal Captive - Greek Empress by Royal Buck (P H Morris) 2605

5 **ROYAL GREENWOOD(IRE),** b or br m Radical - Rathcolman by Royal Buck (David J McGrath) 3912¹ 4060

7 **ROYAL HOFSA,** br m Royal Fountain - The Hofsa by Varano (B Mactaggart) 1475

6 **ROYAL HONEY BEE,** ch m Royal Match - Honey Gamble by Gambling Debt (P Wakely) 3252 3630

10 **ROYAL IRISH,** ch g Le Bavard (FR) - Leuze by Vimy (G B Balding) 2477⁵

10 **ROYAL JESTER,** b g Royal Fountain - Tormina by Tormento (Mrs Jane Storey) 3181¹ 3432¹ 3645¹

4 **ROYAL MANOEVRE,** b g Slip Anchor - Lady Regent by Wolver Hollow (S E Kettlewell) 2485

6 **ROYAL MOUNTBROWNE,** b g Royal Vulcan - Star Shell by Queen's Hussar (Patrick G Kelly) 1177¹ 1763¹ 1825² 2469¹ 2755³ 3474⁶ 3746

6 **ROYAL OAK LADY(IRE),** b or br m Brewery Boy (AUS) - Buffy by French Beige (Mrs Edwina Finn) 990³ 1496

10 **ROYAL OPTIMIST,** b m Prince Regent (FR) - Port Magee by Royal Highway (Capt D G Swan) 4398⁴

761

10 **SACROSANCT,** b g The Parson - Cahernane Girl by Bargello (K C Bailey) 4367¹ 1405 1511⁸

9 **SADDLER'S CHOICE,** b g Buckskin (FR) - Lady Perry by David Jack (J A C Edwards) 1273⁴ 1512⁶ 1769 3417⁵ 3495

9 **SADDLESTOWN GLEN,** b g Furry Glen - Cushlabawn by Space King (T G McCourt) 1764⁵ 1828⁵ 1980³ 2160⁷ 2590¹ 2772⁵ 2986 3242 3507 3693⁶

8 **SAFARI KEEPER,** b g Longleat (USA) - Garden Party by Reform (J Norton) 659⁷ 770⁵ 970 1812

5 **SAFARI PARK,** ch m Absalom - Nyeri by Saint Crespin III (W A Bethell) 138¹ 243² 368² 587² 728⁴ 1100⁵ 1239² 3583⁵ 3932⁴ 4029⁴ 4123

6 **SAFE ARRIVAL(USA),** gr m Shadeed (USA) - Flyingtrip (USA) by Vaguely Noble (P D Evans) 1639⁵

7 **SAFETY(USA),** b g Topsider (USA) - Flare Pass (USA) by Buckpasser (J White) 4302³ 4376⁷ 146¹ 182⁴ 353² 680² 2342² 2641⁶

7 **SAFFAAH(USA),** ch g Secreto (USA) - Somebody Noble (USA) by Vaguely Noble (W R Muir) 841⁶ 2829 3479¹

12 **SAFFRON LORD,** b g Idiot's Delight - Saffron Princess by Thriller (M J Ryan) 3563³ 3684³

4 **SAFFRON MOSS,** ch g Le Moss - Saffron's Daughter by Prince Hansel (Mrs S M Farr) 3523 3855

6 **SAFRANE,** b g Broadsword (USA) - Saucy Linda by Saucy Kit (J P N Parker) 675 1236 2863

8 **SAGAMILL(USA),** b g Sagace (FR) - Lequilla by Mill Reef (USA) (N J Henderson) 3880¹

8 **SAGARO BELLE,** ch m Sagaro - La Chunga by Queen's Hussar (A M Crow) 3486⁶ 3577³ 3689⁶ 3896

8 **SAGARO SUN,** b g Sagaro - Star Alert by Red Alert (M A J Anthony) 2555 2687⁴

14 **SAGART AROON,** b g The Parson - Mountain Bell by Pyrenean (Miss S Pitman) 1137³

7 **SAGASTINI(USA),** br g Sagace (FR) - Martessana (USA) (M J Grassick) 804⁷ 1076 1449⁶

5 **SAHEL SAND(IRE),** br m Buckskin (FR) - Flashy Money by Even Money (John A White) 1333 1608

5 **SAIBOT(USA),** ch g Riverman (USA) - Arabev (USA) by Damascus (D K Weld) 1815²

5 **SAIF AL ADIL(IRE),** b g Reference Point - Hardihostess by Be My Guest (USA) (Mrs M Williams) 1974 2910⁵ 3184⁸ 3757 3881⁸

5 **SAIL BY THE STARS,** b m Celtic Cone - Henry's True Love by Random Shot (Capt T A Forster) 1215² 2808⁹

7 **SAILIN BISHOP,** b g Bishop Of Orange - Sailin Lass by Golden Love (John Brassil) 3837⁷ 4192

7 **SAILOR BLUE,** b g Julio Mariner - Blue Delphinium by Quorum (Andrew Turnell) 796³ 1198 1884⁶ 3254² 3514³ 3760

8 **SAILOR BOY,** b g Main Reef - Main Sail by Blakeney (A S Reid) 149⁵ 312⁹ 348

7 **SAILOR JIM,** gr g Scallywag - Madge Hill by Spartan General (D R Bloor) 3824¹ 3992

10 **SAILOR'S DELIGHT,** b g Idiot's Delight - Sarasail by Hitting Away (Mrs P M Joynes) 143⁶ 262 322⁴ 946 1328³ 1534³ 2116⁵ 3017⁵

5 **SAILOR'S ROSE,** ch m Julio Mariner - Roseitess by Royal And Regal (USA) (M C Pipe) 3191⁵

9 **SAILORS LUCK,** b g Idiot's Delight - Sarasail by Hitting Away (P G Murphy) 931 1022⁴ 1168¹ 1446¹ 1461 1975⁵ 2365 2481¹ 2696¹ 2798⁵ 3066 3312⁵ 3595⁵

6 **SAINT BENE'T(IRE),** b g Glenstal (USA) - Basilea (FR) by Frere Basile (FR) (George Prodromou) 4307³ 4372² 140⁴ 3329

6 **SAINT CIEL(USA),** b h Skywalker (USA) - Holy Tobin (USA) by J O Tobin (USA) (F Jordan) 242² 988³ 1173¹ 1448⁵ 1751² 2606¹ 2708⁶

4 **SAINT HILDA(IRE),** br f Doulab (USA) - Suba (GER) by Limbo (GER) (A P O'Brien) 1432 1853⁵ 2099⁵ 2349³

6 **SAKIL(IRE),** b g Vision (USA) - Sciambola by Great Nephew (S Dow) 149² 185² 465¹ 553³ 1137¹ 1601⁵ 1711⁷ 1942⁵ 2064⁴

6 **SALAR'S SPIRIT,** ch g Salmon Leap (USA) - Indigine (USA) by Raise A Native (W G M Turner) 181² 238² 260¹ 297³ 3740⁴ 3826⁷

6 **SALBYNG,** b g Night Shift (USA) - Hsian by Shantung (J W Hills) 885

10 **SALCOMBE HARBOUR(NZ),** ch g English Harbour - Faux Leigh (NZ) by Harleigh (H M Irish) 2301² 2508⁴

5 **SALDA,** b g Bustino - Martinova by Martinmas (P Bradley) 2445⁹ 3539⁵ 4112²

7 **SALESMAN,** b g Starch Reduced - Miss Purchase by Sterling Bay (SWE) (B Palling) 703

8 **SALINA BAY,** b m Furry Glen - Miss Fion by He Loves Me (J P Byrne) 343 489⁹ 744² 1159 1831

6 **SALINGER,** b g Rousillon (USA) - Scholastika (GER) by Alpenkonig (GER) (J Parkes) 1295 1773⁹ 1930 2686

5 **SALISONG,** gr g Song - Sylvanecte (FR) by Silver Shark (John Whyte) 666² 2665⁶ 2743

8 **SALLOW GLEN,** b g Furry Glen - Bargain Bid by Run The Gantlet (USA) (Thomas Carberry) 1³ 38 66 135

4 **SALLY OF THE ALLEY,** b f Kala Shikari - The Dupecat by Javelot (Mrs S J Smith) 516 754⁶ 872⁴ 1032⁶ 1243⁴ 1532⁴ 3601³ 3702³ 3864³

6 **SALLY SOHAM(IRE),** b or br m Kambalda - Riseaway by Raise You Ten (F Murphy) 3467 502⁸ 725⁴ 1215⁷ 2734

9 **SALLY'S GEM,** b g Hasty Word - China Bank by Wrekin Rambler (J White) 2479⁴ 2668² 3104¹ 3351¹ 3608

4 **SALLY'S PRINCESS,** b f Rakaposhi King - Rigton Sally by Joshua (Mrs P A Barker) 2909 3553

8 **SALMAN(USA),** b g Nain Bleu (FR) - H M S Pellinore (USA) by King Pellinore (USA) (Mrs V C Ward) 129² 239 326 407³ 591⁶ 849⁵ 1213 3594² 3904⁴ 4162⁴

5 **SALMON DANCER(IRE),** b g Salmon Leap (USA) - Welsh Walk by Welsh Saint (J Barlow) 1811 2957

8 **SALMON PRINCE,** ch g Salmon Leap (USA) - Princesse Anglaise by Crepello (C R Barwell) 2044 3363² 3514

7 **SALMON TRAIL,** b g Salmon Leap (USA) - Miss Morgan by Native Prince (E P Hickey) 3243

8 **SALMONID,** ch h Salmon Leap (USA) - Persian Polly by Persian Bold (R Barber) 181⁶

5 **SALMOOSKY(IRE),** b m Salmon Leap (USA) - Favant by Faberge II (Anthony Mullins) 2620 2944⁹

6 **SALTHORSE DELIGHT,** b m Idiot's Delight - Lucys Willing by Will Hays (USA) (R H Buckler) 2560

5 **SALTY SNACKS(IRE),** b g Callernish - Salty Sea by Sir Herbert (Augustine Leahy) 1827 2041 2615⁵

10 **SALVAGER,** b g Balinger - Mahnaz by Deep Diver (J C Poulton) 1511 1712 3149

7 **SALVATION,** b h Formidable (USA) - Major Barbara by Tambourine II (W Rock) 4306⁴ 3 37 64 74⁵ 256⁵ 489⁶

8 **SAM PEPPER,** ch g Turn Back The Time (USA) - Haselbech by Spartan General (Mrs S M Farr) 1527 1879 3850

12 **SAM SHORROCK,** b or br g Vivadari - To Windward by Hard Tack (G Thorner) 600⁴ 726 921⁶ 1713⁴ 2184¹ 2363 2733 3006

5 **SAM VAUGHAN(IRE),** ch g Milk Of The Barley - Kentstown Girl by Prince Tenderfoot (USA) (Eugene M O'Sullivan) 1077¹ 1180⁶ 1397⁸ 1610¹ 2096¹ 2391³ 2552⁴ 3083⁴ 3294² 3468² 3871⁴

9 **SAM WELLER,** ch g Be My Guest (USA) - Chalon by Habitat (Victor Bowens) 75⁹ 134

8 **SAMANTHA'S FLUTTER,** b g Beldale Flutter (USA) - Wimosa by Mossborough (John J Walsh) 939⁵ 1330

7 **SAMANTHABROWNTHORN,** b m Mandalus - Alice Redmink by Party Mink (Michael Hourigan) 540 801 969

4 **SAMANTHAS JOY,** b f Marching On - Sister Racine by Dom Racine (FR) (A W Potts) 3965

6 **SAME DIFFERENCE(IRE),** b g Seymour Hicks (FR) - Santa Fe (GER) by Orsini (Thomas Kinane) 114³ 266³ 304² 536 881⁸ 1833⁸ 3243⁸ 3466 4031 4193⁶

5 **SAMJAMALIFRAN,** b m Blakeney - Royal Shoe by Hotfoot (M C Pipe) 2642 2808⁷ 3108⁷ 3395² 3751⁶

6 **SAMMIES DOZER(IRE),** b m Bulldozer - Sinead's Princess by Sun Prince (G Murphy) 638⁵ 908⁶ 1501

4 **SAMOT(IRE),** ch g Exhibitioner - Sister Dympna by Grundy (C D Broad) 1377

10 **SAMS HERITAGE,** b g National Trust - Taberella by Aberdeen (P G Warner) 3171¹ 3563¹ 3846³ 4163⁵

5 **SAMS QUEEN,** b m Another Sam - Star Shell by Queen's Hussar (John R Upson) 1797⁴ 3108 3396⁷

6 **SAMS-THE-MAN,** ch g Marching On - Bath Miss by Appiani II (R Gray) 1918 2106 3140 3435 3959

8 **SAMSMEDAD,** b m Another Sam - Chez Pauline by Paniko (Anthony Mullins) 469

12 **SAMSUN,** b g Sunyboy - Etoile de Lune by Apollo Eight (R Champion) 167 220⁴ 299⁴ 386 525⁵ 669³ 947⁵ 1302 2162³ 2437 2718 2813³

5 **SAN GIORGIO,** b g Lighter - Gold Willow by Goldfella (C A Smith) 2877⁹ 3183⁹

6 **SAN LORENZO(USA),** b g El Gran Senor (USA) - Wising Up (USA) by Smarten (USA) (K C Bailey) 729 933³ 1071² 1245² 1413¹ 1803¹ 1886¹ 2357¹ 2511² 3066 3479² 3683¹ 3923²

7 **SAN PIER NICETO,** b g Norwick (USA) - Langton Herring by Nearly A Hand (M D Hammond) 125⁸

7 **SAN REMO,** b g Sexton Blake - Rockwood Lady by Aeolian (Patrick Heffernan) 105

9 **SANCREED,** b g Shaab - St Barbe by Galeopsis (Terry Long) 3171

11 **SAND-DOLLAR,** ch g Persian Bold - Late Spring by Silly Season (J A B Old) 1342¹ 1650¹ 4125²

8 **SANDAIG,** b g Kemal (FR) - Pride Of Croghan by Raise You Ten (K C Bailey) 703² 847¹ 996¹ 1150 1394² 1590⁷ 1968³ 3006⁵ 3336³ 3477² 3562⁶ 3844⁴

10 **SANDBROOK,** b g Golden Love - Spinnys Love by Saulingo (R W J Willcox) 2793⁴ 3021 3854³ 3948

4 **SANDCHORUS(IRE),** b c Wind And Wuthering (USA) - Faye by Monsanto (FR) (Bernard Lawlor) 802

7 **SANDEDGE,** b m Major Domo - Hallo Cheeky by Flatbush (G F White) 482⁹ 627⁴ 786² 1091⁷ 1477⁶ 1605 2149⁷ 2219⁵ 3474³

7 **SANDEMALL,** ch g Kemal (FR) - Stormy Sandra (Lindsay Woods) 1156⁷ 1829

11 **SANDMOOR PRINCE,** b g Grundy - Princesse Du Seine (FR) by Val de Loir (Dr P Pritchard) 262⁷ 368⁶ 628⁵ 1108 1415⁸ 1630⁵ 1811⁵ 1933⁵ 2032³

5 **SANDRIFT,** ch m Glint Of Gold - Olivian by Hotfoot (Miss H C Knight) 4023³

5 **SANDRO,** b g Niniski (USA) - Miller's Creek (USA) by Star de Naskra (USA) (R J Baker) 887 1063³ 1154³ 1395⁴ 1521⁹ 1719¹ 1867⁴ 2132⁵ 2523 3348 3572⁹ 3853⁹ 4052⁵ 4179²

11 **SANDSTONE ARCH,** b g Niels - War Rain by Bahrain (T H Caldwell) 4387 127⁴ 3412 3684 3989⁹

8 **SANDY ANDY,** ch g Sandalay - Fort Etna by Be Friendly (J K M Oliver) 874¹ 1033⁵ 1477

5 **SANDY SHACK(IRE),** b f Sandalay - Caddy Shack by Precipice Wood (J A Berry) 4169⁷

9 **SANDY'S BEACON,** b g Foggy Bell - Ditchling Beacon by High Line (J G FitzGerald) 2895⁴

9 **SANDY-BRANDY,** gr g Scallywag - Rose Of Daveen by Proverb (F Murphy) 1771⁴ 2913

9 **SANDYBRAES,** ch g Kambalda - Kinsella's Choice by Middle Temple (D Nicholson) 677³ 811² 947¹ 1151¹ 1326¹ 1512³ 2666²

8 **SANSOOL,** b g Dominion - Young Diana by Young Generation (A C Whillans) 1936² 2108² 2296⁶ 2502⁵ 2954 3287¹ 3603²

7 **SANTA PONSA BAY,** b g Kemal (FR) - Kasperova by He Loves Me (Mrs L C Jewell) 4305¹ 63⁴ 69⁶ 113 849⁷ 1045³ 1474 1597 1812 2119⁶ 2214³ 2423² 2627⁴ 3635 3926³ 4121⁵

4 **SANTA STELLAR,** b f Celestial Storm (USA) - Santa Magdalena by Hard Fought (C R Beever) 1504

7 **SANTAMORE,** bl m Buckskin (FR) - Santa Jo by Pitpan (James Joseph Mangan) 929 1073⁶ 1857 1914⁴ 2126⁵ 2234⁵

8 **SANTANO,** gr g Monsanto (FR) - Stance by Habat (N J Pewter) 4308

8 **SANTARAY,** ch g Formidable (USA) - Stockingful by Santa Claus (T W Donnelly) 3048⁵

9 **SANTELLA BOBKES(USA),** b g Solford (USA) - Ambiente (USA) by Tentam (USA) (M A Barnes) 789 1145⁵ 1936

6 **SAOIRSE(IRE),** b m Horage - Teletype by Guillaume Tell (USA) (D Moffatt) 334¹ 654⁵ 818⁴ 1487⁸ 1633⁹ 1961⁴ 2070⁷ 2152⁵ 3584² 3895⁸ 4045⁴ 4086² 4176⁴

6 **SARACEN'S BOY(IRE),** gr g Thatching - Leukas (GER) by Pentathlon (M R Churches) 61 111⁹ 2141 2671 2779 3051

8 **SARAEMMA,** b m Wolver Hollow - Star Vision by Golden Vision (J H Scott) 1552⁵ 1682¹ 1847² 2077 2159⁷ 2549 2698⁷ 3621¹

5 **SARAG(FR),** br g Saratoga Six (USA) - Lady B Gay by Sir Gaylord 1134²

4 **SARAH BLUE(IRE),** b f Bob Back (USA) - Blue Lookout by Cure The Blues (USA) (M J Grassick) 2314²

9 **SARAH'S WROATH,** b g Morston (FR) - All Our Yesterdays by Jimsun (M Scudamore) 2841⁹ 3109 3441

9 **SARAKAYA,** gr m Dalsaan - Safaya (FR) by Zeddaan (Francis Berry) 4371⁷ 1236 1500⁹

6 **SARAKIN(IRE),** ch m Buckskin (FR) - Softly Sarah by Hardboy (Miss M T Condon) 535 857 1898 2278 2660

5 **SARANNPOUR(IRE),** b g Darshaan - Safita by Habitat (N Tinkler) 268⁹ 502⁵ 664³ 728² 823³ 1060⁹ 1142 3395 3584⁵ 3798⁴

7 **SARAVILLE,** ch m Kemal (FR) - Golden Ingot by Prince Hansel (M C Pipe) 2416² 2656³ 3052² 3318 4038¹ 4184¹

5 **SARAZAR(USA),** ch g Shahrastani (USA) - Sarshara by Habitat (R Akehurst) 1622⁹ 2910⁷ 3115⁷

INDEX TO NATIONAL HUNT RESULTS 1993-94

7 **SCOTTISH REFORM,** b g Night Shift (USA) -
Molvitesse by Molvedo (J J O'Neill) 4325²
4386 548 726 1204

4 **SCOTTISH TEMPTRESS,** ch f Northern Tempest (USA) - Scotch Rocket by Roan
Rocket (Mrs A Knight) 1522 1749 2797

5 **SCOTTON BANKS(IRE),** b g Le Moss - Boher-
deel by Boreen (FR) (M H Easterby) 1574³
1726² 1241¹ 2252¹ 2459 3140⁵

5 **SCRABBLE,** ch m Scallywag - Word Game by
Hasty Word (Mrs S J Smith) 1133³ 1768 2326³
2573 2785²

6 **SCRABO VIEW(IRE),** ch g Denel (FR) - Patri-
cias Choice by Laurence O (J W Curtis) 81³
1289 1478⁵ 1736³ 2213² 2327³ 2629⁵ 2905⁴ 3344⁹

9 **SCRAGGED OAK LASS,** ch m Hell's Gate -
Iris's Wish by Prince Of Norway (R Dean)
4318⁷

6 **SCREEN PRINTER(IRE),** ch m Torus - Dulcet
Dido by Dike (USA) (Michael Hourigan)
116⁶ 430⁴ 506³ 797⁸ 3791⁴ 3835⁶ 3955

8 **SCRIBBLER,** ch g The Parson - Chapter Four
by Shackleton (A L T Moore) 929² 1451² 1988¹
2282² 2681 2865² 3391 3649⁹ 3746⁴

9 **SCRUMPY COUNTRY,** b g Country Retreat -
Windfall VI by Master Owen (Major C Marriott) 3260² 3950

5 **SCRUTINEER(USA),** b g Danzig Connection
(USA) - Script Approval (USA) by Silent
Screen (USA) (D Nicholson) 1104²

11 **SEA BARN,** ch g Julio Mariner - Zakyna by
Charlottesville (M J Coombe) 3533 3853 4052⁸

6 **SEA BREAKER(IRE),** b g Glow (USA) - Surfing
by Grundy (A Hide) 248³ 348³ 917⁶ 1080⁵ 1214⁵
3328 4121¹ 4176¹

6 **SEA BRIGHT(IRE),** b m King's Ride - Lovely
London by London Gazette (J R Cox) 1378⁸
1434⁸

8 **SEA BUCK,** b g Simply Great (FR) - Heather-
side by Hethersett (H Candy) 1206⁵ 1474⁹
1759² 1971³ 2172 2515⁷ 2674⁶ 3028 3384⁸ 3520³ 3609²
3771⁴ 3943⁷ 4006⁷

6 **SEA GALE(IRE),** b m Strong Gale - Sea Scope
by Deep Run (E J O'Grady) 993⁶ 1174² 1332²
1608¹ 3654⁸ 3935¹

7 **SEA PATROL,** b g Shirley Heights - Boat-
house by Habitat (M C Pipe) 2086⁴

5 **SEA PET,** b m Dubassoff (USA) - Palace Pet
by Dragonara Palace (USA) (J J Birkett)
2970⁶ 3139 3580⁶ 3690⁵ 4045⁵

5 **SEA PRODIGY,** b g Precocious - Aunt Judy by
Great Nephew (M Blanshard) 402⁹ 520 592 775³
932 1315⁴

5 **SEA SCAMP(IRE),** b g Crash Course - Smile
Away by Never Slip (W Jenks) 2210

4 **SEA-AYR(IRE),** ch f Magical Wonder (USA) -
Kunuz by Ela-Mana-Mou (Mrs S M Austin)
724 1094⁹

4 **SEABURN,** b g State Trooper - Star Display
by Sparkler (N B Mason) 2373⁹ 2573 2789 3236

5 **SEACHANGE,** gr g Neltino - Maytide by
Vimadee (M J Wilkinson) 3458²

5 **SEAGULL HOLLOW(IRE),** b g Taufan (USA) -
Marthe Meynet by Welsh Pageant (M H
Easterby) 781³ 1746 2360³ 2480⁴ 3193

8 **SEAHAWK RETRIEVER,** ch g Treasure Hunter
- Sister Claire by Quayside (J G FitzGerald)
1813² 2074⁹ 3183⁶

7 **SEANS SHOON,** ch m Green Shoon - More
Than Words by Proverb (M Keane) 857 1035
1177 1857

9 **SEARCHER,** br g Furry Glen - Pollys Flake
by Will Somers (D M Kemp-Gee) 3021⁶

6 **SEARCHLIGHT(IRE),** ch g Seymour Hicks
(FR) - Night Caller by Middle Temple (Mrs

John Harrington) 4402² 28³ 57³ 199² 275³ 392³
673⁴

6 **SEARCY,** b g Good Times (ITY) - Fee by Mandamus (S Christian) 3225³ 3496⁵ 3762 4014³
4173²

7 **SEASAMACAMILE,** b m Lafontaine (USA) -
Crisp Star by Star Moss (R H Buckler) 3278³

4 **SEASIDE DREAMER,** b g Electric - Guilty
Guest (USA) by Be My Guest (USA) (A A
Hambly) 870⁵ 1032 1243 1408⁵ 1504⁸ 1927⁴

6 **SEASIDE MINSTREL,** ch g Song - Blackpool
Belle by The Brianstan (D L Williams) 216
567

4 **SEATTLE AFFAIR(IRE),** b f Seattle Dancer
(USA) - Affair by Bold Lad (IRE) (C H
Jones) 3314

7 **SEATTLE BRAVE,** b g Seattle Song (USA) -
Oraston by Morston (FR) (G Harwood) 3215

5 **SEATWIST,** gr g Pragmatic - March At Dawn
by Nishapour (FR) (J A Pickering) 1674⁶
1957⁹ 2333 2790 2957⁹ 3211

11 **SEATYRN,** b g Tyrnavos - Windy Sea by Sea
Hawk II (Michael Hourigan) 2941³ 3295

5 **SEBASTOPOL,** b g Royal Match - Saucy
Sprite by Balliol (P F Nicholls) 1329³ 1548
2444¹ 2950

11 **SEBEL HOUSE,** b g Buckskin (FR) - Lulu Dee
by Straight Deal (D McCain) 2886⁴

10 **SECOND ATTEMPT,** b g Julio Mariner - Maria
Da Gloria by St Chad (M J McGovern) 269
281⁴ 319³ 396³ 563² 653⁴ 756⁵ 874 3160³ 3439 3645

5 **SECOND CALL,** ch m Kind Of Hush -
Matinata by Dike (USA) (Capt T A Forster)
2175² 2402 2721 2992⁴

8 **SECOND FIDDLE VI,** b g Fidel - Unknown
(Miss Suzy Barkley) 4304

9 **SECOND SCHEDUAL,** b g Golden Love - Billeragh Girl by Normandy (Miss A M
McMahon) 537¹ 584¹ 1226 1664⁵ 2474¹ 2720³ 3659⁶

5 **SECOND SLIP,** b g Slip Anchor - Bahamas
Princess by Sharpen Up (N Tinkler) 2490⁸
2749⁹ 3459⁶ 3592

11 **SECOND TIME ROUND,** bl g Genuine - Brinny
River (Miss J C Arthur) 2968 3860

6 **SECRET CASTLE,** b g Castle Keep - Excava-
tor Lady by Most Secret (B P J Baugh) 1633
2062 2713 3222 3773 4086⁸

5 **SECRET COURSE(IRE),** b m Crash Course -
Hazy Rule by Will Hays (USA) (G Hackett)
2470 2775 4148

4 **SECRET FORMULA,** b g Sulaafah (USA) -
Bidula by Manacle (T R Greathead) 1705⁶
2016⁹ 3337 3572 3702⁶ 3823³ 3965⁴ 4069⁴

7 **SECRET GALE,** br m Strong Gale - Never No
by No Argument (Thomas Bergin) 97 176

8 **SECRET LIASON,** b g Ballacashtal (CAN) -
Midnight Mistress by Midsummer Night II
(K S Bridgwater) 4385³ 3109 347⁴ 679³ 1279⁵
1427³ 2214²

7 **SECRET MISSILE,** ch g Cruise Missile - Peggy
W by Nulli Secundus (W P Mullins) 1687 2394
3528⁵ 3936⁴ 4043³ 4078

11 **SECRET RITE,** ch g Kambalda - Deepdecend-
ing by Deep Run (C Weedon) 1262⁴ 1739¹ 2453⁴
2622⁵

7 **SECRET SCEPTRE,** ch g Kambalda - Secret
Suspicion by Above Suspicion (I R Ferguson) 746² 1017¹ 1201⁴ 1782⁷ 1828³ 2078⁴ 2284⁹
3449⁸

8 **SECRET SUMMIT(USA),** b g Diamond Shoal -
Ygraine by Blakeney (A L Forbes) 550² 677⁵
1025⁴ 1257⁵ 3636⁴ 4125⁶ 4164¹

8 **SECRET TURN(USA),** b g Secreto (USA) -
Changing (USA) by Forli (ARG) (Andrew
Turnell) 826

767

5 **SHARP PRINCE,** ch g Sharpo - Jungle Queen by Twilight Alley (J H Peacock) 4056 4165

4 **SHARP SENSATION,** ch g Crofthall - Pink Sensation by Sagaro (D Nicholls) 394² 481² 732² 1059⁶

4 **SHARP TOUCH,** b g Grey Desire - Kindling by Psidium (D McCain) 3227

10 **SHARPRIDGE,** ch g Nearly A Hand - Maria's Piece by Rose Knight (M B Mawhinney) 485³ 607

7 **SHARPSIDE,** b g Broadsword (USA) - Moll by Rugantino (P J Hobbs) 1303 1516 2308⁵ 2606² 2841⁷ 3022⁴ 3395³ 3531⁵ 3682¹ 3826⁵

5 **SHARRIBA,** gr m Sharrood (USA) - Alsiba by Northfields (USA) (G L Humphrey) 1755⁷ 1842⁸ 2480⁷ 3156⁵ 3408 3574⁹

9 **SHASTON,** ch g Rolfe (USA) - Nicaline by High Line (W G M Turner) 1262³ 1394³ 1600⁴ 1943³ 2143⁶ 2363 2453¹ 2758³ 3146² 3364 3477⁴ 3631⁶

6 **SHATRAVIV,** b m Meadowbrook - M-N-Ms Lass by Workboy (J I A Charlton) 1959⁸ 2148⁹ 2500 2628

8 **SHATTERED ILLUSION,** b g Ballymore - Rose by Sterling Bay (SWE) (Charles Black) 3794⁶

6 **SHAURNI GIRL,** ch m Precocious - Crockfords Green by Roan Rocket (R Harris) 346 1247

5 **SHAWAR(IRE),** ch h Shernazar - Sharmada (FR) by Zeddaan (J H Scott) 671⁴ 803³ 1155¹

5 **SHAWIYA(IRE),** b m Lashkari - Shaiyra by Relko (M J P O'Brien) 1554³ 2287³ 3025⁸ 3424⁶ 3650⁴

7 **SHAWWELL,** ro g Alias Smith (USA) - Besciamella by Foggy Bell (J I A Charlton) 875¹ 1131² 1726 3144¹ 3487⁴ 3817⁵

9 **SHAYISTA,** b m Tap On Wood - Shayina by Run The Gantlet (USA) (Ronald O'Neill) 230³ 291⁶

5 **SHAYNA MAIDEL,** ch m Scottish Reel - Revisit by Busted (J J Birkett) 4298³ 191⁶ 287 334² 394 7178 970 1356⁸ 3907⁵ 3981³

4 **SHE KNEW THE RULES(IRE),** ch f Jamesmead - Falls Of Lora by Scottish Rifle (D N Carey) 1271⁸ 1522⁸

7 **SHE'S NO NUN,** b m The Parson - Last Alliance by Honour Bound (S Christian) 3922⁸

6 **SHEAMY'S DREAM(IRE),** br g Yashgan - Maybird by Royalty (J G Coogan) 8¹ 84² 123 135⁶ 293³ 575³ 807³ 1399

6 **SHEAN ALAINN(IRE),** b m Le Moss - Stable Lass by Golden Love (Mrs M Reveley) 4347⁹ 914

4 **SHEAN HILL(IRE),** br f Bar Dexter (USA) - Gentle Lass by Cardinal Flower (Christopher Kenneally) 3946²

7 **SHEARMAC STEEL,** b g Le Moss - Shahzadeh by Menelek (P J Hobbs) 934³ 2802³ 2964⁵ 3188¹ 3442³ 3562⁵

7 **SHEBA'S PAL,** b m Claude Monet (USA) - Bread 'n Honey by Goldhills Pride (P Delaney) 257

6 **SHEELIN LAD(IRE),** ch m Orchestra - Aryumad by Goldhill (L Lungo) 675⁷ 808⁷ 939

6 **SHEEP STEALER,** gr g Absalom - Kilroe's Calin by Be Friendly (M C Pipe) 3754 3931³

6 **SHEEP WALK(IRE),** b m Deep Run - Bucks Princess by Buckskin (FR) (R M Collins) 2664

10 **SHEEPHAVEN,** b g Relkino - Suffolk Broads by Moulton (T J Etherington) 1197 1600⁶ 2294⁹ 2764² 2935 4065

8 **SHEER ABILITY,** b g Carlingford Castle - Auburn Queen by Kinglet (C J Mann) 1282¹ 1545 1720¹ 1966¹ 2396¹ 2602¹ 2820¹ 3187¹

7 **SHEER INDULGENCE,** ch g Starlan - Dolan by Milan (S A Kirk) 3811

9 **SHEER JEST,** b g Mummy's Game - Tabasheer (USA) by Indian Chief II (W J Warner) 4392² 3385¹ 3521¹

9 **SHEER MIRTH,** b g Sheer Grit - Merry Mirth by Menelek (A J Martin) 70² 112 804² 969¹ 1431

7 **SHEER MIST,** b m Norwick (USA) - Narnia by Le Moss (P A Fahy) 3526⁹ 3710⁵ 4077 4191²

5 **SHEER POWER(IRE),** b g Exhibitioner - Quality Blake by Blakeney (Miss Joli Smith) 4336⁸

6 **SHEHEREZADE(IRE),** br m Asir - Alhamdulillah by Pry (Francis M O'Brien) 4406⁷ 50

8 **SHEILA NA GIG,** br m Crash Course - Asile by David Jack (J R H Fowler) 856⁸ 941 1266⁵ 1451 1785 2157

5 **SHEILA'S SUPRISE,** ch m Little Wolf - Burley Hill Lass by Crimson Beau (Miss S J Wilton) 3401

8 **SHEILAS HILLCREST,** b g Hotfoot - Be Honest by Klairon (N B Mason) 768³ 948² 1146¹ 1358³ 1861¹ 2372⁴ 2577⁵ 3143³ 3689⁸

6 **SHELLHOUSE(IRE),** ch g Deep Run - Miss Curraghmore by Little Buskins (K C Bailey) 1460 1930 3898²

5 **SHELLY'S DELIGHT(IRE),** b f Mandalus - Rathsallagh by Mart Lane (F Flood) 3290

6 **SHELTERED(IRE),** br m Strong Gale - Shady Doorknocker by Mon Capitaine (J T R Dreaper) 2177

8 **SHELTON ABBEY,** br g The Parson - Herald Holidolly by New Member (J Wade) 644² 759⁴ 1201⁵ 1603⁸ 1928⁴ 2137² 2325⁵ 2497 3059 3343 3461⁵ 3578⁴ 3678⁶ 3863 4037⁵

8 **SHEPHERDS KATE(IRE),** b m Royal Auction (USA) - Shepherds Bush by Shooting Chant (Wilbert Tolerton) 2770⁹ 3071

6 **SHERE(IRE),** b g Shernazar - Top Mouse by High Top (J H Scott) 1786² 1910¹ 2080⁵

4 **SHEREGORI(IRE),** b g Darshaan - Sherzana by Great Nephew (M J P O'Brien) 1575 2388⁵ 2608⁵ 2678 2750¹ 2864²

12 **SHERMAGO,** b m Humdoleila - Tartarbee by Charlottesville (Mrs J D Goodfellow) 580⁵

4 **SHERS DELIGHT(IRE),** b g Anita's Prince - Valiant Light (FR) by Luthier (A P O'Brien) 3797³ 4094¹

5 **SHERWOOD BOY,** ch g Seclude (USA) - Madame Persian by Persian Bold (K C Bailey) 815⁵ 1247 3476⁵ 3530 3680⁶

7 **SHERWOOD FOX,** b g Sallust - Nicholette (S C Horn) 1869 3713⁴ 3977⁶ 4139⁴

6 **SHERWOOD GRANGE(IRE),** ch g Ovac (ITY) - Leebrook Lass by Allangrange (O Brennan) 2407⁸ 3190 4027⁵

4 **SHES A STAR(IRE),** br f Supreme Leader - Cill Dara by Lord Gayle (USA) (E Bolger) 4031⁵ 4186⁴

5 **SHESAHUNNY(IRE),** b m Heraldiste (USA) - Lisahunny by Pitskelly (Kevin McQuillan) 233

9 **SHIFNAL,** ch g Tower Walk - Leitha by Vienna (P D Evans) 1325

7 **SHIKARI KID,** b g Kala Shikari - Muffet by Matador (R Thompson) 1068 1299 2600 2729 3111⁵ 3690

6 **SHILDON(IRE),** b h Ovac (ITY) - Hal's Pauper by Official (Denys Smith) 2074

12 **SHILGROVE PLACE,** ch g Le Bavard (FR) - Petmon by Eudaemon (Mrs S A Bramall) 3165 3558³ 4068⁶

6 **SHIMBA HILLS,** b g Scorpio (FR) - Leading Line by Leading Man (Mrs J G Retter) 1626⁵ 2021⁷ 3170⁶

8 **SHIMMERETTO,** b f Bustineto - Shimmering by Privy Councilor (B Lalor) 1608 2038⁵ 2123 2311 2616 2920⁷ 4043 4192

INDEX TO NATIONAL HUNT RESULTS 1993-94

9 **SINGING SAM,** b g Tudor Rhythm - Saxon Slave by Be Friendly (W S Cunningham) 676 913⁵ 1095 1203⁵ 1360 2240⁶ 3357⁷ 3673⁷ 3964

9 **SINGLESOLE,** ch g Celtic Cone - Milly Kelly by Murrayfield (Mrs P Sly) 1151³ 1388 1629 2256

5 **SIOBHAILIN DUBH(IRE),** b m Seclude (USA) - Curraheen Rose by Roselier (FR) (A P O'Brien) 692 907 1039² 1180⁴ 1501⁴ 2353⁵ 2586 2616² 2775³ 2918¹ 3084⁴ 3273⁷ 3449⁴ 3647 3840³ 3887² 3944⁴

8 **SIOBHAN MARIE,** b m Lochnagar - Kilroe's Calin by Be Friendly (F M O'Donnell) 1577

12 **SIR CRUSTY,** br g Gunner B - Brazen by Cash And Courage (O O'Neill) 526⁶ 613⁴ 2172 2512⁴ 2766⁶ 3166 3283⁶ 3520⁸

5 **SIR GREGORY(IRE),** ch h Soughaan (USA) - Lilac Lass by Virginia Boy (G A Cusack) 3953

5 **SIR HENRY KNYVET(IRE),** b h Reference Point - La Mer (NZ) by Copenhagen (D T Hughes) 115⁹ 150² 3388⁷

5 **SIR JOHN(IRE),** gr g Roselier (FR) - Dame Of St John by Counsel (Michael Butler) 2944 3290 3366 3953⁵

10 **SIR L MUNNY,** ch g Torus - Ard Money (Donal Hassett) 4118⁶

7 **SIR MOSS,** ch g Le Moss - Trojan Lady by Lucifer (USA) (S A Kirk) 1833⁵ 2024² 2863¹ 3080⁴ 3367

11 **SIR NODDY,** ch g Tom Noddy - Pinzarose by Pinzan (J Groucott) 3927¹

5 **SIR PAGEANT,** b g Pharly (FR) - National Dress by Welsh Pageant (K S Bridgwater) 4319³ 402⁵ 456⁶ 514² 737¹ 889⁵ 1456¹ 1755⁷

7 **SIR PETER LELY,** b g Teenoso (USA) - Picture by Lorenzaccio (M D Hammond) 643⁶ 758¹ 1029 1286³ 1789¹ 2437¹ 2832 3141¹ 3473⁶

5 **SIR SOOJE(IRE),** b h Mansooj - Green Bird by Pitskelly (Augustine Leahy) 4409⁴ 56⁷ 3085⁵ 3197⁷ 3711 3788⁹

4 **SIR THOMAS BEECHAM,** b g Daring March - Balinese by Balidar (S Dow) 668¹ 830³ 1032⁴ 3010³

5 **SIRAJAO(IRE),** gr m Kings Lake (USA) - Seat Of Wisdom by Try My Best (USA) (F J Lacy) 56 102 208⁵ 803 1380

8 **SIRANA,** br f Al Sirat (USA) - Anna Harwell by Harwell (L G Doyle) 635 906

10 **SIRISAT,** ch g Cisto (FR) - Gay Ruin by Master Spiritus (Kerry Hollowell) 195⁵ 299⁶ 386⁵

4 **SIRKA(FR),** b g Sirk - La Basilica (FR) by Margouillat (FR) (M C Pipe) 3826² 3965⁷ 4036³

14 **SIRRAH JAY,** b or br g Tug Of War - Dellasville by Trouville (K R Burke) 663⁶ 850³ 884⁵ 1121³ 1365⁴ 1732 1932⁴ 3001² 3105³ 3405³ 3636⁵ 3753² 3852⁶

5 **SIRRONS DEAL,** b m Rymer - Sybil by Harwell (Mrs Ailsa Russell) 1582

10 **SIRTA(FR),** 16⁴ 1250⁴

6 **SISTER ALICE(IRE),** gr f The Parson - Etrenne by Happy New Year (M J Byrne) 1858² 2394⁴ 2943² 3088³

4 **SISTER CARMEL(IRE),** b f Carmelite House (USA) - Press Luncheon by Be Friendly (J A O'Connell) 494⁶ 617⁶ 3793⁸

4 **SISTER ELLY,** b f Bairn (USA) - Arbor Lane by Wolverlife (B Preece) 4172⁷

7 **SISTER EMU,** b m Buckskin (FR) - Hill Master by Master Owen (Mrs Edward Crow) 4399⁸ 538

6 **SISTER NORA(IRE),** b m The Parson - Nora Grany by Menelek (J D Cosgrave) 2203 2311⁵ 2586 2770² 2985 3271⁸

6 **SISTER ROSZA(IRE),** b m Roselier (FR) - Glentoran Valley by Little Buskins (Timothy O'Callaghan) 3974⁸ 4192⁸

5 **SISTER STEPHANIE(IRE),** b or br m Phardante (FR) - Soul Lucy by Lucifer (USA) (Mrs M McCourt) 3176¹ 3386³

8 **SISTERLY,** b m Brotherly (USA) - Wee Jennie by Vimadee (J W E Weaver) 4321⁵

4 **SITE DEVELOPMENT(IRE),** b g Mazaad - Watermark by Henry Vii (F W Pennicott) 3616

6 **SIXTH IN LINE(IRE),** ch g Deep Run - Yellow Lotus by Majority Blue (T R George) 1109 1301 3337

5 **SKEHANAGH BRIDGE(IRE),** b g Strong Gale - Natasha Ann by Allanagrange (W P Mullins) 4078

11 **SKELETOR,** b g Scallywag - Wayside Dancer by Road House II (W S Cunningham) 1149 1422¹ 1604

5 **SKELTON LASS(IRE),** ch m Lord Chancellor (USA) - Juleith by Guillaume Tell (USA) (J Parkes) 2834 3379⁹ 3583

6 **SKEOUGH(IRE),** b or br g Tanfirion - Birchwood by Fordham (USA) (J Webber) 4343⁶ 4371⁴ 4382⁴ 304¹ 409¹ 1648 2263 3277³ 3494⁵ 3680³ 3825

10 **SKERRY MEADOW,** b g Anfield - Mi Tia by Great Nephew (O J Carter) 4392⁵ 3171 3501³ 3532² 3669¹ 3808 3990⁴ 4065 4182

11 **SKETCHER(NZ),** b g Candyboy (NZ) - Jezebel (NZ) by Ardistan (D H Barons) 2948 3175⁶ 3336 3477 3532 3669²

6 **SKI LADY,** b m Myjinski (USA) - Lady Jay by Double Jump (J I A Charlton) 1129⁴ 1707 2970 3429

7 **SKI NUT,** b g Sharpo - Saint Cynthia by Welsh Saint (A J Martin) 4339 3449

5 **SKI PATH,** ch m Celtic Cone - Obergurgl by Warpath (N Bycroft) 2490 3079⁷ 3347

5 **SKIDDAW CALYPSO,** b m Grey Desire - Wyn-Bank by Green God (M A Barnes) 976 1114 1582 1724

5 **SKIDDAW SAMBA,** b m Viking (USA) - Gavea by African Sky (Mrs M Reveley) 1660² 2909⁵ 3035³ 3674¹

5 **SKIDDER,** ro g Van Der Linden (FR) - Skiddy River by Saratoga Skiddy (S G Smith) 1376 1813 3589 3800⁹ 4025⁸ 4178

5 **SKIMMER HAWK,** b g Buzzards Bay - Song To Singo by Master Sing (Bob Jones) 1193⁹ 1655³ 1942⁴ 2760⁶ 3770⁵ 4107⁵

8 **SKIN GRAFT,** b m Buckskin (FR) - Grafton Fashions by Dikusa (P J Mackin) 70 235 256 511⁵

10 **SKINNHILL,** b g Final Straw - Twenty Two (FR) by Busted (Mrs Sarah Clarke) 2669⁴ 2882³ 3412 3857⁵ 4022³ 4095⁸

4 **SKIPO(USA),** ro g Theatrical - Paloma Blanca (USA) by Blushing Groom (FR) (D K Weld) 1816⁴ 1983² 2285⁵

9 **SKIPPING GALE,** b g Strong Gale - Skiporetta by Even Money (Richard Barber) 3807³

15 **SKIPPING TIM,** b g Deep Run - Skiporetta by Even Money (M C Pipe) 4346³ 143¹ 220² 299² 525¹ 589¹ 3669 3978⁸

9 **SKIRCOAT GREEN,** ch g Buckskin (FR) - Little Exchange by Laurence O (P Beaumont) 767⁸ 1361⁶ 2502 2766⁹ 2894⁶ 3603¹ 4050³ 4181¹

8 **SKITTLE ALLEY,** b g Adonijah - Skittish (USA) by Far North (CAN) (W Clay) 642¹ 693¹

10 **SKOLERN,** b g Lochnager - Piethorne by Fine Blade (USA) (A Harrison) 543⁴ 812 1357⁴ 1583² 1788⁹ 2152⁴

773

9 **SKY RANGE,** b g Skyliner - Dixir Girl by Realm (A P O'Brien) 134² 306⁷ 422⁸ 509² 532

10 **SKY VENTURE,** b g Paddy's Stream - Mijette by Pauper (C C Trietline) 310⁶ 502

5 **SKY VISION(IRE),** b m Roselier (FR) - Dusky Sky by Dusky Boy (Kevin O'Donnell) 1455⁶ 1581⁸ 2102⁸ 2128⁴ 2684⁷ 3292 3467⁴ 3525⁷ 4041¹ 4149⁵

4 **SKY WISH,** b g Skyliner - On The Record by Record Token (Mrs V A Aconley) 971 2241

5 **SKYE DUCK,** ch m Adonijah - Sule Skerry by Scottish Rifle (R J Baker) 815 952⁷ 1110

13 **SKYGRANGE,** b g Al Sirat (USA) - Lady Rois by Prince Rois (J M Turner) 3329

4 **SKYVAL,** ch f Domynsky - Derry Island by Varano (R Robinson) 3079

4 **SLAINTA(IRE),** b g Dromod Hill - Rose Violet by Kings Lake (USA) (John Monroe) 290⁹ 706 1264

11 **SLANEY ABBEY,** b g Billion (USA) - Gambling Girl by Raise You Ten (Dermot Day) 4342

6 **SLANEY AGAIN(IRE),** b g Kemal (FR) - Julie's Gi-Gi by Brave Invader (USA) (P J P Doyle) 2041⁷ 2347⁵ 3788 4114⁸

7 **SLANEY BACON,** b g Corvaro (USA) - Davy's Hall by Weavers' Hall (Francis Berry) 2770⁴ 2983⁷ 3275 3325⁶ 3709²

6 **SLANEY FAYRE(IRE),** ch g Sheer Grit - Merry Mirth by Menelek (P J P Doyle) 157⁶ 534 2236² 4043

7 **SLANEY FOOD,** br g Strong Gale - Martones Chance by Golden Love (P J P Doyle) 476⁵ 2231 2389

7 **SLANEY GENT(IRE),** b g Red Johnnie - Euromey by Runnett (P J P Doyle) 393⁷ 531⁵ 2944 3792 4171

6 **SLANEY LAMB(IRE),** b g Baragoi - Miss Breta Vii (P J P Doyle) 2038¹ 2231⁸ 4058⁴

5 **SLANEY PEACE(IRE),** b g Lancastrian - Natanya by Menelek (P J P Doyle) 4119⁷

6 **SLANEY SAUCE(IRE),** ch g Hawaiian Return (USA) - Bohemian Girl by Pardao (P J P Doyle) 409⁷ 472²·⁵ 535

7 **SLANEY SPECIAL,** b or br g Decent Fellow - Chestnut Choice by Prince Hansel (P J P Doyle) 3710⁶

5 **SLANEY STAR(IRE),** b or br g M Double M (USA) - Weapon by Prince Ippi (GER) (Francis Berry) 4189³

6 **SLANEY VISON(IRE),** b or br m Kemal (FR) - Young's Pride by Golden Vision (Dermot Day) 94⁸ 124

8 **SLANG,** b g Lucifer (USA) - Artistic Gold by Preciptic (Patrick Griffin) 1580⁹ 1782

6 **SLAUGHT SON(IRE),** b g Roselier (FR) - Stream Flyer by Paddy's Stream (R F Fisher) 2074³ 2358³ 2435³ 3030⁴

8 **SLAVE TRAIN,** br g Green Shoon - Lou by Arctic Chevalier (Garrett Verling) 4399

9 **SLAVOMER,** b g Caribo - Biddy McGee by Major Point (Patrick Martin) 490⁶ 493⁶ 745² 966⁹ 1158⁶

7 **SLEAVEEN HILL,** ch m Salmon Leap (USA) - Compliment (P Cluskey) 1549 1978⁹

8 **SLEMISH MINSTREL,** b g Swan's Rock - Blue Native by Tudor Music (William Johnston) 36 53⁷ 61⁷ 105⁹ 159² 215⁵ 266⁶ 393⁴ 433 969

7 **SLEMISH MIST,** ch f Beau Charmeur (FR) - Uisce Geal by Sovereign Gleam (J F Sleator) 1549 1902⁵ 2236³ 2470 2943 3243 3869

5 **SLIABH BLOOM(IRE),** b f Spanish Place (USA) - Western Starlight Vii (A P O'Brien) 2620

7 **SLICK CHERRY,** b m Noalto - Slick Chick by Shiny Tenth (K O Cunningham-Brown) 859⁶ 1259⁴ 1519⁷ 2653⁵ 2912⁶ 3853⁷

5 **SLIEVE LEAGUE(IRE),** gr m Roselier (FR) - Advantage by Perspex (J Webber) 2419⁵ 2558 2731⁷ 3225

8 **SLIEVENAMON MIST,** ch g Thatching - La Generale by Brigadier Gerard (K C Bailey) 2386² 2436¹ 2761 3828¹

8 **SLIM-N-LITE,** b m Furry Glen - Tara Dream by Tarqogan (Brian Kennedy) 4306⁷ 37 59 489 510³ 4063 4091

5 **SLIPMATIC,** b m Pragmatic - Slipalong by Slippered (P J Jones) 1548⁹ 2333³ 2671² 2979⁴ 3230

10 **SLIPPERY MAX,** b g Nicholas Bill - Noammo by Realm (R T Juckes) 4300 182⁷ 457⁵ 589² 749³ 810⁵ 3773⁷ 3929⁷

7 **SLIPPITT,** b g Slippered - Nevada Run by Deep Run (G M R Coatsworth) 721

8 **SLOE HILL,** ch m Le Moss - Donna Chimene by Royal Gunner (USA) (W J Burke) 4369⁶ 929

6 **SLY PROSPECT(USA),** ch g Barachois (CAN) - Miss Sly (USA) by Diamond Prospect (USA) (K White) 126⁹ 592

5 **SMALL TALK(IRE),** ch m Roselier (FR) - Ortygia by St Paddy (Gerard Quirk) 2465 2679 2983 3525³ 3792 4043⁹

7 **SMALLMEAD LAD,** b g Teofane - Raise The Clouds by Silver Cloud (D R Gandolfo) 451 517³ 996

5 **SMART CASANOVA,** br g Oats - I'm Smart by Menelek (M J Wilkinson) 3233⁶

4 **SMART DAISY,** b f Elegant Air - Michaelmas by Silly Season (Mrs L C Jewell) 1464 1710 2422 3702⁸

5 **SMART DEBUTANTE(IRE),** b m Glenstal (USA) - Cecily by Prince Regent (FR) (Miss S J Wilton) 520¹ 658⁹ 839³ 988 1448 1528 1931⁷ 2214 3131⁷ 3317⁴

6 **SMART DECISION(IRE),** b m Le Moss - Condonstown Rose by Giolla Mear (Ronald Curran) 4409⁵ 7 28⁴ 857⁷

9 **SMART DRESSER,** b g Buckskin (FR) - Cinderwood by Laurence O (Mrs L C Jewell) 667⁴ 763⁵

7 **SMART IN SABLE,** br g Roscoe Blake - Cool Down by Warpath (P R Hedger) 1929² 3151⁸ 3543⁷ 3809² 3914⁴

9 **SMART PAL,** b g Balinger - Smart Bird by Stephen George (Mrs Anthea L Farrell) 3799⁵

4 **SMART ROOKIE(IRE),** b or br g King's Ride - Jim's Honey by Reformed Character (D Nicholson) 2749³ 3190¹ 3427²

12 **SMARTIE EXPRESS,** b or br g Pony Express - Spick And Span by Smartie (R J Hodges) 884⁴ 1089² 1343² 1394 1641¹ 1887² 2557⁴ 2852⁴ 2948¹ 3041³ 3268² 3500³

7 **SMARTIE LEE,** ch m Dominion - Nosy Parker (FR) by Kashmir II (J White) 312⁴ 1299 2094⁴

6 **SMILES AHEAD,** ch g Primo Dominie - Baby's Smile by Shirley Heights (P J Bevan) 222² 424⁴ 1533⁸ 1812³ 2293 2636 2872⁶

6 **SMILING CHIEF(IRE),** b g Montelimar (USA) - Victa by Northfields (USA) (R J Hodges) 887⁷ 1087³ 1342 1643² 2086⁶ 2366⁶ 2655⁷ 2710⁵ 3014¹ 3308⁶ 3535³

6 **SMITH TOO(IRE),** br g Roselier (FR) - Beau St by Will Somers (Mrs J Pitman) 1025¹ 1198⁵ 2209³ 2792¹ 3136 3398³ 3561⁶

6 **SMITH'S BAND(IRE),** b g Orchestra - Pollys Flake by Will Somers (Mrs J Pitman) 1624² 2144 2404 2606⁴ 2731⁵ 2997³ 3623

8 **SMOKE,** gr m Rusticaro (FR) - Fire Screen by Roan Rocket (W G Reed) 582⁵ 656 771

8 **SMOOTH COUP,** b m Smooth Stepper - Another Coup by Le Patron (P Budds) 6 1608 2616

10 **SMOOTH ESCORT,** b g Beau Charmeur (FR) - Wishing Trout by Three Wishes (Mrs D Haine) 518⁵ 726³ 986² 1281⁴ 1565⁴ 2011 2173 2305³ 2623³ 2733³ 2935³ 3260⁶ 3544

9 **SMOOTH START,** b g Smooth Stepper - Ardmoyne by Le Bavard (FR) (A P James) 847⁴ 1041

6 **SMOULDER(USA),** b g Glow (USA) - Whitethroat by Artaius (USA) (Anthony Mullins) 4339⁶ 4408¹ 13⁴ 46²

4 **SMUGGLER'S POINT(USA),** b g Lyphard (USA) - Smugly (USA) by Caro (J J Bridger) 1710⁹ 3557¹ 3734³ 3874²

12 **SNAPPIT,** b g Billion (USA) - Snippet by Ragstone (D McCain) 3665 3896⁴ 4154

6 **SNEEK,** gr g Belfort (FR) - Gold Duchess by Sonnen Gold (Mrs G Moore) 4352

6 **SNICKERSNEE,** b g Kris - Cat Girl (USA) by Grey Dawn II (K Bishop) 772⁵ 1515 1950⁷ 2361 3337 3632 3765 3977⁵ 4104⁵

4 **SNIPE'S BRIDGE(IRE),** b g Phardante (FR) - Noel's Flash by Deep Run (Philip McCartan) 3508⁷ 3997⁶

8 **SNITTON LANE,** b m Cruise Missile - Cala Di Volpe by Hardiran (W Clay) 1069⁴ 1419³ 1706³ 2359⁴ 2832² 3066¹ 3423⁴ 3627²

6 **SNITTON STILE,** b m Cruise Missile - Cala Di Volpe by Hardiran (D Burchell) 2890⁵

7 **SNOOK POINT,** b g Bybicello - Tarisma by Most Secret (R R Lamb) 2814 3143⁵ 3486 3554⁶

11 **SNOOKER TABLE,** b g Ballymore - Northern Twilight by English Prince (A M Forte) 168 217 425¹

7 **SNOWDRIFTER,** br m Strong Gale - Prancer by Santa Claus (Patrick Joseph Flynn) 5⁶

5 **SNOWSHILL SHAKER,** b g Son Of Shaka - Knight Hunter by Skyliner (N A Twiston-Davies) 616 1108 3008 3231⁵

6 **SNOWY LANE(IRE),** ch g Commanche Run - Lassalia by Sallust (M C Pipe) 2298⁶ 2559¹

13 **SNOWY RUN,** ch g Deep Run - Snow Sweet (Miss J Thomas) 3824 3947⁵ 4084⁵

6 **SNUGLET(IRE),** ch g Torus - Deep Spa by Deep Run (P R Lenihan) 1174

6 **SO AUDACIOUS,** ch g Stanford - Be Malicious by Malicious (N A Gaselee) 1161⁸ 1390⁸ 1646⁷ 2692⁴ 3020 3196⁶ 3509⁴ 3623³

6 **SO DISCREET(USA),** b g Secreto (USA) - I'll Be Around (USA) by Isgala (J White) 1280² 2354¹ 2535¹ 2870¹ 3696

5 **SO HOPEFUL(NZ),** b g Little Brown Jug (NZ) - Red Highland (NZ) by Beau Diable (D H Barons) 2210⁴ 2677

5 **SO PINK(IRE),** ch m Deep Run - Saffron's Daughter by Prince Hansel (P Mullins) 637⁵ 854² 991³ 1176³ 1609² 1899⁶ 2351³ 2617⁶ 2845⁴ 3293⁸ 3551 3614 3835 3955² 4041³ 4188⁷

9 **SO PROUD,** b g Idiot's Delight - Deep Pride by Deep Run (M C Pipe) 2540² 2806 2982¹ 3038² 3136⁷

5 **SOBER ISLAND,** b g Little Wolf - Sea Countess by Ercolano (USA) (N A Twiston-Davies) 2339 2444⁶ 3190

10 **SOCIAL CLIMBER,** b or br g Crash Course - What A Duchess by Bargello (Andrew Turnell) 694¹ 899⁵ 1197⁹ 1531³ 1834² 3255² 3513⁴ 3758

8 **SOCIETY BAY(USA),** b g Alleged (USA) - Meadow Blue (USA) by Raise A Native (Oliver Finnegan) 1765⁸ 1818⁵ 2026² 2180⁴ 2846⁴ 3322

8 **SOCIETY GUEST,** ch g High Line - Welcome Break by Wollow (Andrew Turnell) 1955³ 2142 2366³

15 **SOCKS DOWNE,** b or br g Paddy's Stream - Kincsem by Nelcius (A J Chamberlain) 322² 487⁴ 700⁶ 1216 1302⁷ 2020 3727³ 3847⁷ 4102⁸

6 **SODA POPINSKI(USA),** b g Sir Ivor - Four Runs (USA) by Reviewer (USA) (I Campbell) 2306 2423

6 **SOFT WINTER(IRE),** b g Kemal (FR) - Ballyheda's Love by Golden Love (Anthony Mullins) 2128³ 2664⁴

11 **SOHAIL(USA),** ch g Topsider (USA) - Your Nuts (USA) by Creme Dela Creme (J White) 154³

5 **SOL ROUGE(IRE),** ch m Red Sunset - Grace de Bois by Tap On Wood (R Thompson) 1810 2061 3965⁵

5 **SOLAR FLASH(IRE),** ch m Shy Groom (USA) - Solar Jinks by Delirium/immortality (Victor Bowens) 574

9 **SOLAR GREEN,** ch g Green Shoon - Solaranda by Green God (S A Brookshaw) 4073¹

6 **SOLAR KESTREL(IRE),** b g Decent Fellow - The Tonne by Raise You Ten (N J Henderson) 634⁴ 869 3231⁴

4 **SOLAR KNIGHT,** gr f Le Solaret (FR) - Knightly Dia (USA) by Diamond Prospect (USA) (K S Bridgwater) 193⁵ 497⁶ 724 1702

6 **SOLAR NOVA,** b m Sunley Builds - Damascus Star by Mandamus (I Park) 1736 3598 3815 3959 4035⁹

8 **SOLAR SYMPHONY,** ch f Orchestra - Sunshot by Candy Cane (J A O'Connell) 1231 1381

5 **SOLBA(USA),** b g Solford (USA) - Pabapa by Patch (Augustine Leahy) 4409³ 4¹ 131 537⁷ 798 3889¹ 4058⁵

9 **SOLDIER BANK,** b g Soldier Rose - Ladybank by Dear Gazelle (Stephen Bush) 3501 3824⁶ 3947

8 **SOLDIER EVE,** ch m Soldier Rose - Jubilee Eve by Royalty (M J Wilkinson) 660

4 **SOLDIER-B,** ch c Gunner B - Meldon Lady by Ballymoss (T B Hallett) 2021

6 **SOLE CONTROL,** b m Jupiter Island - Maureen Mhor by Taj Dewan (R T Phillips) 705⁴ 885⁷

6 **SOLEIL DANCER(IRE),** b g Fairy King (USA) - Cooliney Dancer by Dancer's Image (USA) (D M Grissell) 977² 1249² 1395³ 1709² 1945⁴ 2457² 2697⁴ 3099¹ 3548² 3841⁴

11 **SOLENT LAD,** b g Undulate (USA) - River Palace by Royal Palace (B Stevens) 1042⁶ 1458 1600 2225⁹ 2317⁶

11 **SOLICITOR'S CHOICE,** b g Cagirama - Girostar by Drumbeg (R T Juckes) 4363³ 139² 189⁶ 223⁴ 366 2526

6 **SOLID(IRE),** b g Glenstal (USA) - Reine de Chypre (FR) by Habitat (D J S Cosgrove) 1389⁶ 1474 1562⁸ 1810

8 **SOLID FUEL,** ch g Le Bavard (FR) - Twilight Spring by Cantab (D Moffatt) 1296³ 1533

12 **SOLIDASAROCK,** ch g Hardboy - Limefield Rita by Mon Capitaine (R Akehurst) 1340¹ 2747 2995³ 3229² 3772⁶

6 **SOLMUS(IRE),** b f Sexton Blake - Enslavement by Arctic Slave (Mrs John Harrington) 2464⁷ 3082

8 **SOLO BUCK,** b m Buckskin (FR) - Go-It-Alone by Linacre (Mrs V A Aconley) 1861 2238

4 **SOLO CHARTER,** b g Chief Singer - Royal Agreement (USA) by Vaguely Noble (J W Mullins) 1767 1880 2112⁷ 3825⁴

9 **SOLO CORNET,** br g Furry Glen - Royal Willow by Royal Buck (P Bradley) 1068 1448⁶ 1589² 1708⁷ 1947 2251 2581 2790 3770 4107

8 **SOUTHEND UNITED,** b g Black Minstrel - Diamond Panes by Lock Diamond (John R Upson) 4323

11 **SOUTHERLY BUSTER,** b g Strong Gale - Southern Slave by Arctic Slave (O Sherwood) 501

7 **SOUTHERLY GALE,** b g Strong Gale - Chestnut Belle by Even Money (M C Pipe) 1169² 1715² 2141⁶

6 **SOUTHERN DEALER,** b g Lightning Dealer - Southern Bird by Shiny Tenth (J White) 2860⁶ 3191⁸

11 **SOUTHERN MINSTREL,** ch g Black Minstrel - Jadida (FR) by Yelapa (FR) (P Cheesbrough) 1029³ 1365² 1572² 2013¹ 2377³ 2748⁷ 3425 3626⁵

6 **SOUTHOLT(IRE),** b g Deep Run - Girseach by Furry Glen (G A Hubbard) 922¹ 1100¹ 1289² 2244³ 2538¹ 3024³ 3411⁴

11 **SOUTHOVER LAD(NZ),** b g Frassino - Tarea (NZ) by Balios (D H Barons) 1474 2947 3174 3545⁷

6 **SOUVAROV,** 267⁴

4 **SOVEREIGN CHOICE(IRE),** b g Shernazar - Florentink (USA) by The Minstrel (CAN) (D K Weld) 2290¹ 3042⁸

6 **SOVEREIGN NICHE(IRE),** gr g Nishapour (FR) - Sovereign Flash (FR) by Busted (M C Pipe) 4372⁶ 4393 2653² 2804¹ 2912² 3348¹ 3773¹ 3904⁶ 4086

4 **SOVIET CHOICE(IRE),** b f Soviet Star (USA) - Miracle Drug (USA) by Seattle Slew (USA) (T Stack) 2388² 3839³

4 **SOVIET EXPRESS,** br g Siberian Express (USA) - Our Shirley by Shirley Heights (C P E Brooks) 2422 2541⁴

6 **SPA KELLY,** br h Netherkelly - Tarkon Spa by Tarqogan (J A Pickering) 1674⁹ 1957 2407⁶ 3503

7 **SPACE CAPTAIN,** b g Star Appeal - Dovey by Welsh Pageant (G M Moore) 641 729³ 1034³ 1219⁵ 1746⁵ 2153⁸

11 **SPACE FAIR,** b g Space King - Katie Fare by Ritudyr (R Lee) 631² 1084² 1226⁶ 1440 1666³ 2744³ 3037⁶ 3627³ 4018⁴ 4180⁴

11 **SPACE MAN,** ch g True Song - Perfect Day by Roan Rocket (A J Mason) 2884

5 **SPACE MOLLY,** b m Capitano - Space Speaker by Space King (J Webber) 934 1023

13 **SPACE PRINCE,** b g Space King - Queens Purse by Lucky Sovereign (R A Phillips) 2526⁸ 3596⁷ 3854

10 **SPECIAL(USA),** b g Star Appeal - Abeer (USA) by Dewan (USA) (Mrs B Hill) 4320⁵ 3717⁴

13 **SPANDULAY(USA),** b m Arts And Letters - Objectivity by Bald Eagle (W J Warner) 3093³

5 **SPANISH ARCH(IRE),** ch g Ovac (ITY) - Castile's Rose by Ballyciptic (Michael Hourigan) 4192

6 **SPANISH BLAZE(IRE),** b g Spanish Place (USA) - The Blazing Star by Proverb (N J Henderson) 1490 1729 2014 2428 3762⁴

6 **SPANISH FAIR(IRE),** b g Spanish Place (USA) - Bonne Fair by Bonne Noel (Mrs S A Bramall) 654⁷ 1221⁴ 1671³ 2007³ 2260⁴

6 **SPANISH HERO,** bl g Heres - Native Senorita by Indigenous (G B Balding) 3880

5 **SPANISH STORM(IRE),** b g King Of Spain - Storm Chest by Lord Gayle (USA) (S P C Woods) 916⁷

7 **SPANISH WHISPER,** b g Aragon - Whisper Gently by Pitskelly (J R Bostock) 4307⁴ 287⁸ 846² 949² 1426⁵ 1485² 1801⁵ 2165³ 2214¹ 2408² 3092⁴ 3328⁴ 3998⁴ 4176⁸

5 **SPANKERS HILL(IRE),** b h Monksfield - Pindas by Bargello (S J Treacy) 1337 2869 2944¹ 3290⁹ 3525 3653

8 **SPARKLER GEBE,** b g Be My Native (USA) - Siliferous by Sandy Creek (R J O'Sullivan) 401¹ 670⁵ 1187³ 1711 2064² 2225¹ 2441² 2713² 3696

8 **SPARKLING BLAKE,** ch g Sexton Blake - Edenacan by Cantab (George Stewart) 2313³ 2774⁴ 3275⁵ 3795⁴

5 **SPARKLING CONE,** gr g Celtic Cone - Sparkling Time (USA) by Olden Times (M C Pipe) 2560¹ 3042

10 **SPARKLING FLAME,** b g Beau Charmeur (FR) - Shreelane by Laurence O (N J Henderson) 1745⁶ 2141² 2448⁴ 2747⁹ 2995 3280³ 3541⁵ 3567⁴

6 **SPARKLING SUNSET(IRE),** br g Strong Gale - Cherry Jubilee by Le Bavard (FR) (N J Henderson) 1688¹ 2263⁴

4 **SPARKY GAYLE(IRE),** b g Strong Gale - Baybush by Boreen (FR) (C Parker) 3488² 3797¹

7 **SPARROW HALL,** b g Fine Blade (USA) - Churchtown Breeze by Tarqogan (J G FitzGerald) 799⁵ 1295¹ 1574⁴ 2561⁶

8 **SPARTAN FLAPJACK,** ch g Oats - Miss Spartan by Spartan General (D F Bassett) 962 1467 1651⁵ 1776 1796 2316

13 **SPARTAN RAFT,** ch g Lighter - Tanaway by Spartan General (John Whyte) 3090² 3332 3546 3799⁶ 3999

9 **SPARTAN RANGER,** b g Lochnager - Spartan Flutter by Spartan General (Miss Kate Milligan) 2687² 2955³ 3158³ 3377² 3462³

10 **SPARTAN TIMES,** b g Official - Pillbox by Spartan General (Capt T A Forster) 2507 2766⁸ 2967⁹ 3166⁷

4 **SPARTS FAULT(IRE),** ch g King Persian - Clonross Lady by Red Alert (S E Sherwood) 3476⁶

7 **SPEAK OF THE DEVIL,** ch g Le Bavard (FR) - Lucifer's Way by Lucifer (USA) (Miss Anne Collen) 618⁹ 708⁹ 945⁵ 1018 2289⁷ 3082⁵ 3913 4145⁹

5 **SPEAKER WEATHERILL(IRE),** b g Strong Gale - Arctic Verb by Proverb (O Brennan) 2387

5 **SPEAKER'S HOUSE(USA),** b g Lear Fan (USA) - Bring Me Flowers (FR) by Dancer's Image (USA) (P F I Cole) 1515⁸

11 **SPEAKERS CORNER,** ch g Politico (USA) - Gusty Lucy by White Speck (M E Sowersby) 2875⁴ 3065⁴ 3990² 4130²

6 **SPEAKING TOUR(USA),** br g Verbatim (USA) - Tour Verte (FR) by Green Dancer (James Joseph O'Connor) 528 904 1073⁷ 1498² 1826⁷ 1901¹ 2037 2126³ 2701 3649 3659⁹ 4171⁵

5 **SPEARHEAD AGAIN(IRE),** b g Strong Gale - Affordthe Queen by Pitpan (S Christian) 1674 3707⁴

8 **SPECIAL ACCOUNT,** b g Le Moss - Liffey's Choice by Little Buskins (C R Barwell) 687² 867¹ 1274 1643⁷ 2044³ 2879⁵ 3192³ 3309 3442² 3609⁷ 4006⁴ 4155¹

6 **SPECIAL CORNER(IRE),** b g Millfontaine - Ellette by Le Levanstell (D T Hughes) 113 1997

4 **SPECIAL OFFER(IRE),** b f Shy Groom (USA) - Big Bugs Bomb by Skymaster (W M Roper) 2678⁷ 2771 2917⁷

4 **SPECTACLE(IRE),** gr g Peacock (FR) - Aunty Babs by Sexton Blake (J R Cox) 3947 4148

5 **SPECTACULAR STAR(IRE),** ch g Good Thyne (USA) - Cailin Alainn by Sweet Revenge (Joseph G Murphy) 1383⁸ 1581 1821⁸ 2465⁶ 3327⁷

4 **SPECTRE BROWN,** b g Respect - My Goddess by Palm Track (F Jestin) 3907

INDEX TO NATIONAL HUNT RESULTS 1993-94

12 **SPECULATION,** ch g New Member - Stockley Crystal by Dairialatan (C E Ward) 3093[5] 3329[5]

11 **SPEECH,** ch g Salluceva - Malone by Politico (Miss J L Rae) 544 624[6] 911 1145[6] 1585[9] 1679[2] 1789[7] 3676[5]

5 **SPEEDY SIOUX,** ch m Mandrake Major - Sioux Be It by Warpath (S G Chadwick) 4299[9] 477[9] 580[4] 755[7] 1066[6] 1603 3926 3982[7] 4070

8 **SPERRIN VIEW,** ch m Fidel - Baroness Vimy by Barrons Court (M F Loggin) 4362 4388

4 **SPICE AND SUGAR,** ch f Chilibang - Pretty Miss by So Blessed (B R Cambidge) 2522[8]

6 **SPIDERS DELIGHT,** ch g Sula Bula - Spiders Web by Big Deal (T A K Cuthbert) 910 1199[4] 3617

4 **SPIKE,** b g Good Times (ITY) - Distant Sound by Faraway Times (USA) (C J Hemsley) 3314 3874 4101

4 **SPIKEIE ROSE,** b f Derring Rose - Ms Largesse by Goldhill (G H Jones) 3256[8]

8 **SPIKEY(NZ),** b g Valuta - Sweet Canyon (NZ) by Headland II (J R Jenkins) 1346[1] 1537[2] 1841[3] 2193 2514[3] 2647[2] 2913[4] 3608[2]

5 **SPIN ECHO(IRE),** b g The Parson - Swanee Mistress by My Swanee (R Waley-Cohen) 3234

8 **SPIN THE COIN,** b g Scallywag - Furstin by Furry Glen (N Marmont) 4347[8] 3563 3824

7 **SPINNING STEEL,** b g Kinglet - Lasses Nightshade by Deadly Nightshade (K Bishop) 1525[6] 2319 3338[3] 3479 3605[2]

5 **SPIRIT IN THE NITE(IRE),** b g Orchestra - Haut Lafite by Tamerlane (J T Gifford) 1515[1] 2556 2692[5] 3191[4] 3380[3] 3518

6 **SPIRIT LEVEL,** ch m Sunley Builds - Tuneful Flutter by Orchestra (J R Payne) 1272[8] 1519[8] 1716 1867[7] 2799[8] 3055[6] 3253[4] 3300[2]

9 **SPIRIT OF KIBRIS,** ch g Quayside - Golden Shuil by Master Owen (Mrs J Pitman) 4334[3] 813[3] 917[3] 1352[2] 1441[1] 1657[5]

9 **SPIRITED HOLME(FR),** b g Gay Mecene (USA) - Lyphard's Holme (USA) (D L Williams) 127 372

8 **SPIRITUALIST,** ch g Simply Great (FR) - Parima by Pardao (Mrs G S Plowright) 3046[8] 3354[3] 4107[1]

6 **SPITFIRE GIRL,** b m Glint Of Gold - Premiere Danseuse by Saritamer (USA) (James Dunne) 804

4 **SPLEODRACH(IRE),** b or br f Supreme Leader - Grey Duchy by Sexton Blake (Patrick G Kelly) 3749[8] 3997[7]

5 **SPLIT SECOND,** b g Damister (USA) - Moment In Time by Without Fear (FR) (Mrs V A Aconley) 1287 3438 3778 4039[3]

6 **SPONTANEOUS PRIDE,** b g Belfort (FR) - Seaknot by Perhapsburg (K C Bailey) 2834 3362

8 **SPOONHILL WOOD,** ch m Celtic Cone - My Darling by Arctic Slave (J Wharton) 1385[2] 1530[3] 1834[4] 2270[4] 2486[1] 2636[4] 2872[5] 3116[1] 3346[1] 3585[8]

5 **SPORT OF FOOLS(IRE),** b m Trojan Fen - Senouire by Shirley Heights (W J Reed) 3769[4]

9 **SPORTING IDOL,** b g Mummy's Game - Village Idol by Blakeney (J G M O'Shea) 2790 3131 3222

12 **SPORTING MARINER,** b g Julio Mariner - Ma Griffe by Indian Ruler (D R Bloor) 2301 2456 2605 2724[5] 2887[4] 3165[4] 3439[2] 4008[1] 4065[5] 4184[6]

5 **SPORTS VIEW,** b g Mashhor Dancer (USA) - Persian Express by Persian Bold (R J Hodges) 1192[4]

4 **SPORTSTYLE(IRE),** b g Commanche Run - Toast Of The Town by Prince Tenderfoot (USA) (M Halford) 968 1377[5] 1432 3246 3321 3505[4] 3748[3] 3934

10 **SPOTTED HEUGH,** gr g Montreal Boy - Zo-Zo by Hamood (Christopher Graham) 3157

5 **SPOUT HOUSE(IRE),** b m Flash Of Steel - Otterhill by Brigadier Gerard (Michael Purcell) 292[4] 3550

6 **SPOUTING INSPECTOR(IRE),** b g Leap High (USA) - Renewal by Dual (A L T Moore) 39 881[9]

5 **SPRAY OF ORCHIDS,** ch m Pennine Walk - Mana (GER) by Windwurf (GER) (R A Fahey) 1655[6] 1810

6 **SPREAD YOUR WINGS(IRE),** ch m Decent Fellow - The Wren's Nest by Wrekin Rambler (D R Gandolfo) 1196[3] 2029[2] 2141 2558[3] 2692[1] 2808[2]

8 **SPREE CROSS,** b g Kemal (FR) - Danger Lady by Commando (Mrs D Haine) 450[8] 1098 1212[2] 1489[2] 1733[3] 1975[1] 2248 2337[2] 2825[1] 3262[1] 3607[2]

4 **SPRING CALL(IRE),** br g Mandalus - Miss Cuckoo by Never Slip (M H Easterby) 2490[3]

11 **SPRING FUN,** b g Over The River (FR) - Russian Fun by Zabeg (David Young) 3918[1] 4095[2]

6 **SPRING GRASS,** br m Pardigras - Spring River by Silly Season (B J M Ryall) 815[3]

4 **SPRING MARATHON(USA),** b c Topsider (USA) - April Run by Run The Gantlet (USA) (Mrs P N Dutfield) 1229[1] 1647[3] 1880[5] 2806[1] 3036[5] 3414

5 **SPRING SAINT,** ch g Midyan (USA) - Lady Of Chalon (USA) by Young Emperor (Miss C Horler) 3365[4]

5 **SPRING SPIRIT(IRE),** b g Commanche Run - Rosserk by Roan Rocket (K C Bailey) 934 1068

4 **SPRING SUNRISE,** b f Robellino (USA) - Saniette by Crystal Palace (FR) (B de Haan) 3576[5]

7 **SPRING TO GLORY,** b h Teenoso (USA) - English Spring (USA) by Grey Dawn II (P Hayward) 569[3] 662[4] 796[1] 1395[2] 1513[5] 2247[2]

9 **SPRINGALEAK,** b or br m Lafontaine (USA) - Union Rules by Workboy (C A Smith) 661[1] 1011[2] 1224 3026 4001[5]

5 **SPRINGFIELD-BARON,** b g Baron Blakeney - Viceroy Lass by Certingo (J Mackie) 1806[9]

6 **SPRINGFIELDS JILL(IRE),** b f Ovac (ITY) - Jupiters Jill by Jupiter Pluvius (Patrick Mooney) 150

10 **SPRINGMOUNT,** b g Mandalus - Jadini by Gombos (FR) (J S Swindells) 2793

6 **SPRINTFAYRE,** b g Magnolia Lad - Headliner by Pampered King (Mrs M E Long) 1126[1] 1548[8] 3386

11 **SPROWSTON BOY,** ch g Dominion - Cavalier's Blush by King's Troop (M C Chapman) 1322[9] 2273[7] 2385[6] 2487[6] 2830[8] 3136[5] 3344[6] 3622[9]

4 **SPRUNG RHYTHM(IRE),** ch g Remainder Man - Creation Lady by Cavo Doro (Patrick Joseph Flynn) 2750[4] 3616

6 **SPUFFINGTON,** b g Sula Bula - Pita by Raffingora (J T Gifford) 1542[3] 2144[4] 2505[3] 2705[2] 3115[2] 3530[1]

7 **SPUR BAY,** b g Deep Run - Sweet Slievenamon by Arctic Slave (B Stevens) 773[4] 1067

7 **SPUR OF THE MOMENT,** b m Montelimar (USA) - Alitos Choice by Baptism (J P Kavanagh) 941[6] 1451[1] 1893[2] 2101[3] 2390 2751 3274[6] 3326[5] 3933[2]

8 **SPURIOUS,** b g The Parson - Lady Of Desmond by Polly's Jet (William Patton) 70

8 **SUPERIOR FINISH,** br g Oats - Emancipated by Mansingh (USA) (Mrs J Pitman) 1208⁵ 1447⁴ 1652⁵ 2506¹ 3134 3485³ 3591

6 **SUPERVISION,** b g Superlative - Something Casual by Good Times (ITY) (Mrs M A Kendall) 2931 3079

6 **SUPPOSIN,** b g Enchantment - Misty Rocket by Roan Rocket (Mrs S J Smith) 587⁵ 639³ 779⁶ 874³ 1033⁴ 1184⁶ 1770² 1862³ 2238⁷ 2489¹ 2958⁴ 3133 3354² 3492⁹

5 **SUPREME ARCTIC(IRE),** b f Supreme Leader - All Profit by Deep Run (P Moakley) 3953

7 **SUPREME BLUSHER,** ch m Blushing Scribe (USA) - Yashama by Supreme Red (W T Kemp) 1604 1792⁸ 2069 2164⁵

4 **SUPREME MASTER,** b g Primo Dominie - French Surprise by Hello Gorgeous (USA) (R Hannon) 1510² 1990 2245⁴ 2853³

5 **SUPREME RAMBLER(IRE),** b g Supreme Leader - Panel Pin by Menelek (Miss H C Knight) 3833¹

4 **SUPREME SOVIET,** ch c Presidium - Sylvan Song by Song (J S Haldane) 2148 2433⁵ 3553 3892⁴ 4085⁶

4 **SUPREME WONDER(IRE),** b f Supreme Leader - Cauriedator by Laurence O (Anthony Mullins) 3082³ 3245¹ 3372³

7 **SURCOAT,** b g Bustino - Mullet by Star Appeal (R J Baker) 1884 2086² 2338⁵ 2496³ 2655 3053² 3535² 3919² 3980⁶

5 **SURE HAVEN(IRE),** b g Sure Blade (USA) - Tea House by Sassafras (FR) (R J Hodges) 1509³ 1930³

6 **SURE PRIDE(USA),** b g Bates Motel (USA) - Coquelicot (CAN) by L'enjoleur (CAN) (A Moore) 1163⁶ 1561 1945³ 2697⁵ 3117⁷

5 **SURE SHOT NORMAN,** b h Song - Angel Drummer by Dance In Time (CAN) (G H Jones) 3277 3682

8 **SUREST DANCER(USA),** b g Green Dancer (USA) - Oopsie Daisy (USA) by Dewan (W L Barker) 1963⁸ 2252⁷

4 **SURGICAL SPIRIT,** b f Lighter - Sheba Queen by Pongee (J W Mullins) 2444 2996 3101²

8 **SURREY DANCER,** b g Shareef Dancer (USA) - Juliette Marny by Blakeney (Mrs M Reveley) 1202¹ 1478² 2356³ 2445¹ 3464¹ 4048²

4 **SUSSEX MAESTRO,** ch g Executive Man - Badsworth Girl by Arch Sculptor (F Gray) 3095⁹ 3898

7 **SUSTENANCE,** ch m Torus - Laurelann by Sir Herbert (J P Rossiter) 4379² 103¹ 158³

5 **SUTR-MAKE(IRE),** b g Mansooj - Side Step by Double Jump (J P Byrne) 881⁷ 1015³ 1267⁵ 1397

6 **SUTTON CENTENARY(IRE),** br m Godswalk (USA) - Glorino by Bustino (D G McArdle) 1157⁹

6 **SUVLA BAY(IRE),** b g Kemal (FR) - Miss Lacemore by Red Alert (O Brennan) 2339 2905⁵ 3046 3756⁷ 3928⁵

5 **SUZY BLUE,** br m Relkino - Sally Blue by Bluerullah (T R George) 1626 2426

6 **SWALLOW REEF(IRE),** b m Decent Fellow - Soldier's Friend by King's Troop (Mrs J A Morgan) 3201 3528 3837⁶

7 **SWALLOWS NEST,** ch g Kemal (FR) - Slave Trade by African Sky (John W Nicholson) 160² 274 305² 363² 571¹ 929³ 965²

6 **SWAN WALK(IRE),** gr g Godswalk (USA) - Garland Song by My Swanee (Mrs N Macauley) 2665⁷ 3089³ 3635³ 4017⁶

5 **SWANING AROUND(IRE),** ch g Burslem - Masina by Current Coin (J T Gorman) 675⁵ 2289 3388 3934

8 **SWANK GILBERT,** b h Balliol - Song To Singo by Master Sing (T A K Cuthbert) 287⁹ 316⁴ 6267 642⁶ 787⁵ 912 3078³ 4047⁵ 4082⁶ 4136⁶

5 **SWEET CALLERNISH(IRE),** br g Callernish - Winsome Doe by Buckskin (FR) (A P O'Brien) 2470⁷ 2944⁵

11 **SWEET CHARMER,** ch g Beau Charmeur (FR) - Shreelane by Laurence O (W M Halley) 57

9 **SWEET CITY,** ch g Sweet Monday - City's Sister by Maystreak (G Richards) 662⁹ 819² 1057 1186² 1728⁸ 1940¹ 2222⁴ 2437⁴ 2815⁴ 2974¹ 3475⁸ 3541¹ 4050⁶

9 **SWEET DEMOND,** br g Belfalas - Miss Tiepolo VI (R Goulding) 638 853 1174 1496

13 **SWEET DOWNS,** ch g Persian Bold - Pigeon's Nest by Sovereign Gleam (P J Lally) 122 135 291

7 **SWEET DUKE(FR),** b g Iron Duke (FR) - Sweet Virginia (FR) by Tapioca (FR) (N A Twiston-Davies) 1030² 1347² 1438² 1756¹ 2012¹ 2257³ 2376² 2473⁴ 3063⁵ 3267⁴ 3384⁶

6 **SWEET FRIENDSHIP,** b m Alleging (USA) - Child Of Grace by King's Leap (E T Buckley) 1428⁸ 1996 2204 2525

7 **SWEET GEORGE,** b g Ardross - Madam Slaney by Prince Tenderfoot (USA) (D Burchell) 1643⁸ 2425⁴ 2798

7 **SWEET GLOW(FR),** b g Crystal Glitters (USA) - Very Sweet by Bellypha (M C Pipe) 54 2257⁷ 2376⁵ 3063⁶ 3267¹ 3735²

7 **SWEET KILDARE,** ch m Parole - Lady Royal by Sharpen Up (David Wynne Evans) 17 61 80⁹

10 **SWEET LIBERTY,** b m Gleason (USA) - Belle Fillette by Beau Chapeau (R Brotherton) 3494 3680

7 **SWEET MANATTE,** b m Teamwork - Seal Marine by Harwell (B Palling) 2419⁴ 2723

4 **SWEET MARTINI,** gr f Belfort (FR) - High Run (HOL) by Runnymede (R Lee) 3590⁶ 3833⁷ 4159⁶

5 **SWEET NOBLE(IRE),** ch g The Noble Player (USA) - Penny Candy by Tamerlane (J G FitzGerald) 639 1287¹ 1588³ 2358⁸ 2896³ 3166⁸ 3555³ 3922²

8 **SWEET ON WILLIE(USA),** ch m Master Willie - Maryland Cookie (USA) by Bold Hour (Miss M J Turner) 3768⁵

4 **SWEET PEACH(IRE),** b f Glenstal (USA) - Peach Stone by Mourne (Eugene M O'Sullivan) 228⁹ 290⁶ 688

7 **SWEET PETEL,** b m Cardinal Flower - Findabair by Sunny Way (Noel Henley) 942⁷ 2664 3837⁹ 3946 4044

5 **SWEET REVELATION,** ch m Revlow - Honey Beam by Heswall Honey (M C Pipe) 3176³ 3401³

5 **SWEET SCIMITAR,** b m Broadsword (USA) - Saucy Linda by Saucy Kit (P J Jones) 1509

8 **SWEET THUNDER,** ch m Le Bavard (FR) - Raheny by Sir Herbert (W M Roper) 4338 256⁴ 400¹

5 **SWEET VALLEY HIGH(IRE),** br m Strong Gale - Erne Gold Vii (David Fenton) 4170

9 **SWEETING,** b g Lighter - Snare by Poaching (J White) 4073

4 **SWEETWATER MOON,** b f Jupiter Island - Troy Moon by Troy (Mrs A Swinbank) 1749

6 **SWERVIN MERVIN,** ch g Dominion - Brilliant Rosa by Luthier (J M Carr) 4178⁶

12 **SWIFT ASCENT(USA),** b g Crow (FR) - Barely Flying (USA) by Fleet Nasrullah (A Barrow) 260 387⁶

8 **SWIFT CARRIAGE,** br m Carriage Way - River Petterill by Another River (M A Barnes) 3864⁵

4 **TENDER RIVER(IRE)**, b g Tender King - Still River by Kings Lake (USA) (C Collins) 4078

6 **TENDERENE(IRE)**, b m Tender King - Fun Frolic by Sexton Blake (Mrs Helen O'Keeffe Daly) 85

6 **TENDRESSE(IRE)**, b m Tender King - Velinowski by Malinowski (USA) (R J Hodges) 1794⁴ 1950⁴ 2461² 2801⁶ 3098⁴ 3559⁵ 3765¹ 3915⁴

7 **TENELORD**, ch g True Song - Tenella by Wrekin Rambler (Miss C Saunders) 2889 3761

7 **TENESA**, gr f Teenoso (USA) - Be Easy by Be Friendly (John Daly) 4406⁹ 414⁵

14 **TENNESSEE PASS**, b g Pry - Tennessee Bell by David Jack (Michael Butler) 1231⁹ 2755⁷ 3121⁴

5 **TENPENCE PRINCESS(IRE)**, b m Prince Bee - Tax Code by Workboy (Capt D G Swan) 2553

6 **TERINGETTE(HUN)**, br m Masetta (HUN) - Terilen (HUN) by Indikator (Michael Robinson) 4399³ 50¹ 91¹ 175³

12 **TERRA DI SIENA**, ch g Manor Farm Boy - Paddys Tern by St Paddy (Mrs N Mackay) 3021 3171

9 **TERRIBLE GEL(FR)**, b g Raisingelle (USA) - Ina Du Soleil (FR) by Or de Chine (Mrs M Reveley) 919 987 1168² 1409 1727¹ 2107 2272 2563⁵ 3032³ 3239³ 3346 3556²

9 **TERRIFORN**, br g Northern Value (USA) - Sparkling Bell by Spartan General (Mrs T J Hill) 2889⁴ 3155 3501 3988

4 **TERRINGTON**, ch g Local Suitor (USA) - Salala by Connaught (M W Easterby) 2490⁹ 3347⁵ 3620 3781⁴ 3800 4126⁶

8 **TERRY'S PRIDE**, ch m Good Thyne (USA) - Fethard Lady (John J Walsh) 71 108 169

7 **TERZIA**, b m Elegant Air - The Yellow Girl by Yellow God (P Hughes) 4339³ 11¹ 25¹ 87¹ 122¹ 291 2468 2682⁶ 2751⁷ 2846

7 **TESALIA(SPA)**, b or br m Finissimo (SPA) - Cartama by Sagaro (Capt D C Foster) 108

7 **TESEKKUREDERIM**, b or br g Blazing Saddles (AUS) - Rhein Symphony by Rheingold (W Clay) 1315³ 1526⁴ 2058² 2116⁴ 2631⁴

7 **TEST MATCH**, ch g Glenstal (USA) - Reprint by Kampala (W Clay) 1773⁸ 2029⁴ 2303⁵ 2897³ 3315¹ 3496¹ 3967⁶

6 **TEX MEX(IRE)**, b g Deep Run - Polar Bee by Gunner B (D Nicholson) 2731 3756⁴

6 **TEXAN BABY(BEL)**, b g Baby Turk - Texan Rose (FR) by Margouillat (FR) (N A Twiston-Davies) 683¹ 934⁶ 1524¹ 2515³ 2936²

6 **TEXAN TYCOON**, b g Last Tycoon - High Move by High Top (R Akehurst) 1010¹ 1442 3736

4 **TEXAS FRIDAY(IRE)**, b g Vision (USA) - Reine Dagobert (Patrick O'Leary) 2285⁶ 2678⁴ 4059⁸

7 **TEXASIAN(USA)**, 2049²

4 **THALEROS**, b c Green Desert (USA) - Graecia Magna (USA) by Private Account (USA) (G M Moore) 1920⁶ 2154 3179⁷

9 **THAMESDOWN TOOTSIE**, b m Comedy Star (USA) - Lizzie Lightfoot by Hotfoot (A P Jones) 1625³ 1838⁵ 2429⁴ 3006⁶ 3307¹ 3544⁷ 4065⁷

8 **THANKS A MILLION**, ch m Simply Great (FR) - Friendly Thoughts (USA) by Al Hattab (USA) (N B Thomson) 3767 3998 4104¹ 4185²

7 **THANKS ALOT(IRE)**, b g Double Schwartz - Silver Heart by Yankee Gold (A P O'Brien) 393

6 **THANKSFORTHEOFFER**, b or br g Buzzards Bay - Raise The Offer by Auction Ring (USA) (I R Jones) 775⁵ 1280⁷ 1801 1948⁵ 2094 2215⁷ 2729⁷ 2790⁶ 2912⁴ 3111³ 3298⁵ 3478

6 **THARIF**, b g Green Desert (USA) - Mrs Bacon by Balliol (N J Pewter) 151⁷ 260⁸ 323⁸ 567 608⁶

9 **THARSIS**, ch g What A Guest - Grande Promesse (FR) by Sea Hawk II (W J Smith) 4352² 4385¹ 226⁶ 270²

4 **THAT'S GOSPEL(IRE)**, b f Strong Gale - Panalee by Pitpan (Thomas Bergin) 2943⁹ 3245⁹ 3508 3842⁶ 3997² 4170¹

5 **THAT'S POLITICS(IRE)**, b g Mister Lord (USA) - Glenadore by Furry Glen (Anthony Mullins) 3388³ 3749⁶

5 **THAT'S SPECIAL**, gr g B M C Special - That's It by Adropejo (R Harris) 346 983⁷ 1251

6 **THATCH AND GOLD(IRE)**, b g Thatching - Tuck by Artaius (USA) (Patrick Joseph Flynn) 40⁴ 854³ 1400⁴ 1894² 2079⁶ 2201¹ 2610⁴ 2754³ 2986

4 **THATCHED(IRE)**, b c Thatching - Shadia (USA) by Naskra (USA) (R E Barr) 1655 2241 2433⁷ 2783 2907³ 3139⁹

9 **THATCHER ROCK(NZ)**, b g Le Grand Seigneur (CAN) - Lady Joelyn (NZ) by Noble Bijou (USA) (P F Nicholls) 647 1171⁴ 1343¹ 1507² 1698¹ 1995

6 **THATS A SECRET**, b g Crofthall - Elbeam by Hornbeam (Thomas Foley) 277⁵ 801³ 908¹ 1435⁵ 2283⁴ 2704¹ 3243⁶ 3291⁶ 3660⁵ 3788² 4166

4 **THATS FAR ENOUGH(IRE)**, b g Carlingford Castle - Love And Idleness by Malinowski (USA) (Peter McCreery) 3937 4078

6 **THATS MY BOY(IRE)**, ch g Deep Run - Regency View by Royal Highway (Victor Bowens) 798 877⁸ 1018⁶ 1555⁵ 1687² 1814

9 **THATS THE LIFE**, ch g Wolverlife - Culleenamore by Northfields (USA) (T R George) 4380⁸ 35¹ 121² 631⁶ 840¹ 1168³ 1363² 2696³ 3210⁴ 3548

6 **THATSTHEFASHION(IRE)**, gr m Roselier (FR) - Theinthing by Harwell (Michael Donohoe) 4118⁸

6 **THE ADJUTANT(IRE)**, ch g Deep Run - Inagh's Image by Menelek (G Richards) 1003 1582

8 **THE APPRENTICE**, ch g Torus - Bog View by African Sky (James Joseph Mangan) 102 927 993

10 **THE ARTFUL RASCAL**, b g Scallywag - Quick Exit by David Jack (R K Aston) 2605 2838 3665 3927⁸

6 **THE BARGEMAN(NZ)**, b g Lanfranco - Stevadette (NZ) by Even Stevens (Mrs J Renfree-Barons) 1626⁵ 3164³

8 **THE BARREN ARCTIC**, br g Baron Blakeney - Arctic Granada by Arctic Slave (R H Buckler) 165

11 **THE BATCHLOR**, b g Sparkler - Proxy by Quorum (J M B Pugh) 3951

4 **THE BERUKI(IRE)**, ch f Stalker - Connaught Rose by Connaught (S J Treacy) 228¹ 1264⁵ 1454¹ 1816² 2608

6 **THE BLACK MEADOW(IRE)**, ch f Cardinal Flower - Badly Stung (Michael Aherne) 36 43

6 **THE BLACK MONK(IRE)**, ch g Sexton Blake - Royal Demon by Tarboosh (USA) (M C Pipe) 4324¹ 4391³ 324² 1633⁶

6 **THE BLUE BOY(IRE)**, ch g Tate Gallery (USA) - Blue Lookout by Cure The Blues (USA) (P Bowen) 4372 4393⁸

5 **THE BLUEBELL POLKA(IRE)**, b m Regular Guy - Daisy Spring by Straight Rule (F Flood) 1455² 1687⁴ 1766² 2028² 2943¹ 3291¹ 3647

5 **THE BOBTAIL FOX(IRE)**, b g Supreme Leader - Tiepoless by Tiepolo II (Noel Meade) 1820⁸ 2199⁷ 3508⁴ 3723¹ 4060¹

6 **THE BOLD FOAL(IRE)**, ch g Avocat - Little Ann by Little Buskins (J R Cox) 231 808⁹

6 **THE BOOLYA(IRE)**, b g Bowling Pin - Dontlike by Amazon (Ms Rosemary Rooney) 3747⁵

6 **THE PIPE FITTER(IRE),** b g Decent Fellow - Watch The Birdie by Polyfoto (J J O'Neill) 1223 1779⁷ 1938 2220⁸ 2633 3144

7 **THE PLEDGER,** b m Strong Gale - My Halo by Be Friendly (Thomas N FitzGerald) 30 1902

9 **THE POD'S REVENGE,** b g Pollerton - Fair People by Varano (E J Alston) 1204⁹ 1321⁴ 1776 1952⁴ 2206³ 2325³ 2908 3075² 3608³

7 **THE POINT IS,** ch g Major Point - Babble by Forlorn River (P S Hewitt) 4344³

7 **THE PORTSOY LOON,** b g Miami Springs - Glittering Gem by Silly Season (G Thorner) 1729⁶ 2208⁷ 2693⁴ 2980¹ 3442

5 **THE POWER OF ONE,** b g Bellypha - Biding by Habat (M C Pipe) 888 2910

4 **THE PREMIER EXPRES,** gr g Siberian Express (USA) - Home And Away by Home Guard (USA) (B Beasley) 790² 872² 1147² 1408⁸ 1483³ 1634² 2241¹ 2371³ 2685³

8 **THE PRIOR,** b g Monksfield - Merry Rambler by Wrekin Rambler (Mrs P A Barker) 3536⁴

8 **THE PRUSSIAN(USA),** b h Danzig (USA) - Miss Secretariat (USA) by Secretariat (USA) (K G Wingrove) 3637¹ 3903² 4110¹

8 **THE PUB,** br g Riki Lash - Melerings by Tudor Melody (L R Lloyd-James) 2386 2497 2637 2903

8 **THE PUNTERS PAL(IRE),** b g Torus - Tullac Maig by Lucky Brief (K J McGrath) 1820

8 **THE QUAKER,** ch m Oats - Malford Lass by Paveh Star (R Hawker) 1878⁷ 2263⁸ 2428⁶ 2808⁵ 3022³ 3189⁷

10 **THE QUIET MAN,** ch g Buckskin (FR) - Saint Audrey by Cracksman (James Joseph O'Connor) 4380 2942 3326⁴ 3648⁹ 3945² 4033³

7 **THE RAMBLING MAN,** b g Pitpan - Chammyville by Chamier (G Richards) 269³ 319 755 2955 3558⁴

5 **THE REAL ARTICLE(IRE),** gr g Tate Gallery (USA) - Pasadena Girl by Busted (Gerard Stack) 1180² 1989² 2161¹ 2607⁵ 2983² 3122¹ 3367³ 3615⁵

4 **THE REAL BAVARD(IRE),** b g Le Bavard (FR) - Bishopswood Lady by Tarqogan (Peter McCreery) 3997

6 **THE REAL GAEL(IRE),** b f Strong Gale - Gaelic Sport by Pollerton (Daniel O'Connell) 798 990 1330 1898 2050

5 **THE REAL JOKER(IRE),** b g Orchestra - Mother Cluck by Energist (J R H Fowler) 2849 4063

9 **THE REAL UNYOKE,** b or br g Callernish - Tudor Dancer by Balidar (J A Berry) 2280⁷ 2591³ 2755⁶ 2867³ 3081⁷ 3524⁴ 3648 3890 3945⁷

6 **THE REGAL ROYAL(IRE),** b g Sandhurst Prince - Blue Regalia by Royal And Regal (USA) (W P Mullins) 58⁴ 109³ 150⁹

5 **THE REPROBATE(IRE),** ch g Orchestra - Heather-Can by Cantab (C R Egerton) 3523¹

6 **THE REVEREND BERT(IRE),** b g Decent Fellow - Best Of Kin by Pry (G B Balding) 3386⁹ 3604²

10 **THE RIDGE BOREEN,** b g Boreen (FR) - Slave Trade by African Sky (Gerard Farrell) 1327 3123 3937²

6 **THE ROCKING CHAIR(IRE),** b h Cataldi - Lady Kimberley by Salvo (Martin Higgins) 421⁷ 472³ 536 620 2394⁷ 2470 3122 3244

4 **THE SALTY FROG(IRE),** ch g Salt Dome (USA) - Sweet Shop by Sweet Revenge (Thomas Carmody) 1377 1575⁵ 1853¹ 2156³ 2285⁴ 2864⁸

4 **THE SECRET SEVEN,** ch f Balidar - Will Be Wanton by Palm Track (J K Cresswell) 448⁴ 1350⁶ 1705

8 **THE SHAUGHRAUN,** b g Alzao (USA) - Light Jumper by Red God (P Hughes) 2124⁹ 2610¹ 2754⁴ 2866⁴ 3369 3654 3710⁴ 3836⁸ 3944⁷

5 **THE SHAW TRADER,** ch g Noalto - Relkusa by Relkino (N A Twiston-Davies) 1624⁹ 1800 3277²

6 **THE SHIRALEE(IRE),** ch h Denel (FR) - Maud Gonne by Laser Light (Patrick Mooney) 2314 3694

5 **THE SHY PADRE(IRE),** br g The Parson - Kenodon by Menelek (R Lee) 3707²

6 **THE SILVER ROLLS,** gr g Carwhite - Sagora by Sagaro (M O Cullinane) 534 675 853⁵ 3295

9 **THE SLATER,** ch g Town And Country - Yashama by Supreme Red (W G M Turner) 1022¹

4 **THE SNOUT,** b f Good Times (ITY) - Kimble Blue by Blue Refrain (C J Hemsley) 896⁶

7 **THE STING,** b g Today And Tomorrow - Alexzena by Upper Case (USA) (D C O'Brien) 1027

5 **THE SUBBIE(IRE),** br g Good Thyne (USA) - Huntoon by Gay Fandango (USA) (Francis Ennis) 530¹ 832¹ 1230 2613³ 2753⁵ 3080⁵ 3660⁹

10 **THE TARTAN SPARTAN,** ch g McIndoe - Themopolli by Spartan General (M J Wilkinson) 1242⁵ 1769¹ 1925¹ 2294⁶ 2518⁴ 3120¹ 3307⁴

7 **THE TENANT,** ch g Creative Plan (USA) - The Music Lady by Tudor Music (Capt D G Swan) 4371⁵ 43⁵ 79² 124 171⁵ 258² 305³ 433² 536⁵

5 **THE THIRD MAN(IRE),** ch g Jamesmead - Maid Of Antrim by Arapaho (I A Duncan) 1833 2314⁸ 2771 3072⁴ 3276⁸ 3447 3723⁷ 3793⁵ 4091⁷

7 **THE TOASTER,** b g Furry Glen - Foolish Lady by Signa Infesta (Victor Bowens) 1076 2314⁹ 2607³ 3448¹ 3719² 3812³

7 **THE VERY MAN,** b g Bulldozer - Sinead's Princess by Sun Prince (P Mullins) 17⁴ 45¹ 135 213¹ 291

11 **THE VIBES,** ch g Le Bavard (FR) - So Called (Lady Sarah Barry) 176

6 **THE VICARETTE(IRE),** b m The Parson - Men's Fun by Menelek (Liam Cashman) 3295⁴ 3527⁴ 3652 3835⁵

11 **THE WALTZING MOUSE,** b g Strong Gale - Tip Your Toes by Prince Tenderfoot (USA) (Mrs L J Leggat) 4351³ 542 653³ 756³ 786⁴ 911

6 **THE WEATHERMAN,** b g Official - Deep Depression by Weathercock (A E Jessop) 645² 735⁵ 1181 2925⁸ 3435⁶ 3690² 3862³

9 **THE WEST'S ASLEEP,** ch f Mr Fordette - Ballinphonta by Tepukei (P M Lynch) 977 116³ 575 635 941⁸ 1177⁷ 1334⁴ 1399⁵ 1915² 2101⁴ 2282⁶ 2683³ 2984⁹ 3507²

7 **THE WHIP,** ch g Fine Blade (USA) - Phayre Vulgan by Vulgan (D M Grissell) 864³ 1263² 1715⁴ 2320² 2708 3011¹ 3727²

6 **THE WHIRLIE WEEVIL,** gr m Scallywag - Primrose Wood by Precipice Wood (G Richards) 1060⁵ 1724³ 2003⁸ 2220³ 2367⁵ 2578⁵

5 **THE WICKED CHICKEN(IRE),** b m Saher - Glad Rain by Bahrain (P Mullins) 7² 12³ 48 107⁴ 136⁵ 171² 236³ 292 3197² 3290¹ 3647 3889 4030 4093

8 **THE WIDGET MAN,** b g Callernish - Le Tricolore Token (J T Gifford) 1050⁴ 1693¹ 2513² 2673¹

11 **THE WOODEN HUT,** ch g Windjammer (USA) - Bunduq by Scottish Rifle (Mrs A Price) 998⁸ 1774

8 **THE YANK,** b or br g Deroulede - Determined Lady by Distinctly (USA) (M D Hammond) 3566⁴ 4013

8 **THE YOKEL,** b g Hays - Some Dame by Will Somers (W Clay) 1081⁷ 1311 1621 3454⁴ 3774² 3929 3966⁴

9 **THEKINDWORD VI,** b g Rowlandson - Rakish Lass by Tarqogan (Edward Martin) 231⁸ 510⁴ 746 3747

8 **THEM AND US,** b g Gleason (USA) - Mainham by Boreen (FR) (Peter McCreery) 3795

8 **TOP VILLAIN,** b g Top Ville - Swan Ann by My Swanee (C H P Bell) 623 914⁹ 1148⁶ 3139 3357⁵ 3959

6 **TOP WAVE,** br g High Top - Sea Fret by Habat (N J Henderson) 977³ 1342 1389³ 1709¹ 1839² 2192¹ 2267⁸ 2626³ 2992⁶ 3311⁸ 3464⁸

7 **TOPFORMER,** gr g Highlands - Umtali by Boreen (FR) (F Watson) 273¹

5 **TOPICAL TIP(IRE),** b g Tip Moss (FR) - Sami (FR) by Sukawa (FR) (J E Mulhern) 2469 2588⁶ 3694

4 **TOPKAR(FR),** b f Arokar (FR) - Tophole by High Top (J P Delaporte) 3679¹

5 **TOPPING TOM(IRE),** br g King's Ride - Jeanarie by Reformed Character (N A Twiston-Davies) 547² 743³ 1028⁶ 1490⁷ 1622¹ 1951³ 2380⁴ 2671

9 **TOPPING-THE-BILL,** b g Nicholas Bill - Top-N-Tale by Sweet Story (Mrs Emma Coveney) 3013⁴

11 **TOPSHAM BAY,** b g Proverb - Biowen by Master Owen (D H Barons) 647³ 1011³ 1652³ 2011 2720 3064 3425 3591⁷

4 **TOR,** b c Reference Point - Devon Defender by Home Guard (M F Morris) 3749

10 **TORANFIELD,** b g Monksfield - Toranquine (FR) by Right Royal V (F Lennon) 1554 2466⁴ 2755⁴

4 **TORC MOUNTAIN(IRE),** ch g Simply Great (FR) - Toll Teller by Sharpman (G Barnett) 617⁵ 688⁵ 802⁸ 1243⁶

10 **TORENAGA HILL,** b m Torenaga - Halidon Hill by Mugatpura (Eamonn Finn) 4342⁷ 377⁵ 496⁴ 879⁵ 1019⁵

9 **TORLOUGH,** b g Torus - Summer Again by Arctic Chevalier (A J Kennedy) 79⁸ 89⁶ 177⁴

6 **TORMORE LADY(IRE),** gr m Celio Rufo - Wind Over Spain by Tumble Wind (USA) (M Brew) 211

6 **TORONTO TELEGRAM,** br f Torus - Kiltegan by Charlottesvilles Flyer (B Lalor) 1500 3201⁴ 3296⁵ 3529² 3946⁹ 3974³

9 **TORSTAR,** b g Torus - Star Luck by Star Signal (Miss Suzy Barkley) 746 969 1577⁵

10 **TORT,** b g Le Moss - Steady Flow by Reliance II (P T Dalton) 4394⁹ 696¹ 1254¹ 1565

5 **TORTULA,** ch m Good Times (ITY) - Bristle-Moss by Brigadier Gerard (R O'Leary) 2876 3169

5 **TORY LAD(IRE),** gr g Torus - Flower Dust by Wind Drift (S G Walsh) 2869

5 **TOSS UP(IRE),** b g Spin Of A Coin - Edenacan by Cantab (J R Cox) 3720⁹

7 **TOT EM UP,** gr m Strong Gale - Myra Grey by Upper Case (USA) (Michael O'Connor) 877 1018³ 1330⁵ 1496³ 1823⁶ 1913⁶ 3242⁷ 3292⁹ 3731⁶

7 **TOTAL CONFUSION,** b g Pollerton - Black Crash by Crash Course (Norman Cassidy) 2182⁴ 2394³ 2664² 2849¹ 3393⁷ 3870⁴ 4060⁵

5 **TOTAL UP(IRE),** b g Kafu - Sarah Van Fleet by Cracksman (T H Caldwell) 547⁴ 3209

6 **TOTHEWOODS,** b g The Parson - Elsea Wood by Eborneezer (N A Twiston-Davies) 753⁷ 888 1568¹ 1994² 2295¹ 2459⁴ 3036 3264 3396⁴ 3518⁴

7 **TOUCH OF WINTER,** b or br g Strong Gale - Ballyhoura Lady by Green Shoon (K C Bailey) 3398² 3491⁶ 3845 3919⁶ 4054⁶ 4181⁷

4 **TOUCH SILVER,** ch g Local Suitor (USA) - Octavia Girl by Octavo (USA) (H J Manners) 611⁷ 760⁶ 870⁹ 1523¹ 1702 1965¹

7 **TOUCHDOWN,** ch m Hard Fought - Forest Fortune by Fortino II (D T Hughes) 8 106 1907⁶

4 **TOUCHEE BOUCHEE,** b f Then Again - Sweet Move by Corvaro (USA) (D J S Ffrench Davis) 3233

6 **TOUCHER(IRE),** ch g Fidel - Lealies Pride by Knotty Pine (William Patton) 4360 39

4 **TOUCHING MOMENT(IRE),** b c Pennine Walk - Sea Mistress by Habitat (A L T Moore) 494² 802⁶ 1853⁸ 2122⁶ 2750⁵ 3246⁶ 3839² 3993²

9 **TOUCHING STAR,** b g Touching Wood (USA) - Beaufort Star by Great Nephew (P J Hobbs) 4317² 143³ 206³ 288¹ 405¹ 458³ 566⁴ 714¹ 1394¹ 1512¹ 1720⁵ 1889 2966³ 3260⁴ 3808⁵ 4007⁸ 4184⁴

6 **TOUCHING TIMES,** b g Touching Wood - Pagan Deity by Brigadier Gerard (R Rowe) 670 2132⁹

6 **TOUGH DEAL(IRE),** b g Sheer Grit - Ballyeel by Girandole (P Bradley) 743 1376⁹ 1773 1961⁵

4 **TOUGHNUTOCRACK,** b g Morston (FR) - Capel Lass by The Brianstan (J F Panvert) 2444

5 **TOUR LEADER(NZ),** ch g Nassipour (USA) - Colleen (NZ) by Karyar (R H Buckler) 795² 982² 1414⁴ 1804⁵

9 **TOURAQUE(FR),** b g Caerleon (USA) - Ange Gris (USA) by Grey Dawn II (Mrs D F Culham) 3139 3285⁵ 3553 3570⁷

7 **TOUREEN GIRL,** b m Star Appeal - Storm Foot by Import (W P Mullins) 12⁴ 53¹ 89³ 113⁶ 230¹ 294⁵ 392⁶ 528⁴ 556³

4 **TOUREEN LODGE(IRE),** b g Phardante (FR) - Storm Foot by Import (F Flood) 3997

11 **TOUREEN PRINCE,** b g Cheval - Lauregreen by Laurence O (Miss H C Knight) 663²

7 **TOURIG LE MOSS,** ch m Le Moss - Hogan's Cherry by General Ironside (Michael C Walsh) 36 48⁶ 86⁹ 162² 229⁷ 907⁴ 2943 5533

6 **TOURIST ATTRACTION(IRE),** b f Pollerton - Sayanarra by King's Leap (W P Mullins) 2056¹ 2283 3276³ 3393² 3653¹ 4010⁶

8 **TOUSHTARI(USA),** b g Youth (USA) - Taduska (FR) by Daring Display (USA) (W R Hacking) 2709

6 **TOUT VA BIEN,** b g Town And Country - Sans Blague by Above Suspicion (Thomas Carberry) 1234⁴ 1453 1764³ 1988³

6 **TRADER TYE(IRE),** b g Buckskin (FR) - Hunter's Pet by Cracksman (G A Hubbard) 1490

6 **TRADESPARK,** b m Vital Season - Trade Only by Andrea Mantegna (A J Williams) 1110 1301 1642 3630

7 **TRAIN ROBBER,** b g Sharp Deal - Biggsie's Bird by Even Money (W G McKenzie-Coles) 774⁸ 892⁵ 1043⁴ 1248⁵ 1511⁹ 1644 2964⁹ 3174⁶ 3623⁴ 3804³ 3980¹

7 **TRANSCRIBER(USA),** b h Transworld (USA) - Scrabbler (USA) by Verbatim (USA) (H de Bromhead) 86 133 575 905

6 **TRAP DANCER,** gr g Mashhor Dancer (USA) - Patraana by Nishapour (FR) (B Mactaggart) 4131⁷

6 **TRAP ONE(IRE),** b g Trojan Fen - Seldovia by Charlottetown (Francis Berry) 39⁶ 58 179⁸ 2465 2586 2939

10 **TRAPPER JOHN,** b g The Parson - Blueola by Blue Ruler (M F Morris) 584⁶

7 **TRASSEY BRIDGE,** b m Strong Gale - Flying Pegus by Beau Chapeau (Raymund S Martin) 22 2774⁷ 2987⁴ 3325⁴ 3507⁸ 3795³ 4033² 4116² 4188¹

8 **TRAVADO,** br g Strong Gale - Adelina by Athenius (N J Henderson) 1048¹ 1387¹ 1560⁴ 1843 3037² 3410²

9 **TRAVEL BOUND,** b g Belfalas - Sugar Shaker by Quisling (J Parkes) 1740 2071⁴ 2149² 3224⁷ 3343² 3442⁵ 3602²

13 **TRAVELLER'S TRIP,** ch g Royal Trip - Bohemian Girl by Pardao (J Mackie) 4384

INDEX TO NATIONAL HUNT RESULTS 1993-94

5 **TULLYKYNE BELLS,** gr g Le Solaret (FR) - Cowbells by Mountain Call (L A Snook) 2779⁶ 3051⁷ 3453 3632² 3849⁵

8 **TUMBLED BRIDE,** b m Tumble Wind (USA) - Bridewell Belle by Saulingo (V G Greenway) 2717 3055³ 3300¹ 3502

5 **TURALITY(IRE),** ch g Seclude (USA) - Natural Majority by Majority Blue (Michael G Holden) 4402 102 1578¹ 1075³ 1333⁶ 1495 2039³ 2232³ 2348⁴ 2679⁷ 3290⁶ 3506⁵ 3732

7 **TURBULENT WIND,** b m Strong Gale - Knock Off by Arctic Slave (A L T Moore) 332² 573³ 800⁴ 966¹ 1268 1985⁵ 2183³ 2550⁴

7 **TURF RUN,** br g Deep Run - Tranquil Love by Ardoon (D Nicholson) 988⁴ 1308 2637 3756⁵

4 **TURFMANS VISION,** b g Vision (USA) - Persian Alexandra by Persian Bold (R Hollinshead) 742⁸ 1021⁴

9 **TURKISH STAR,** b m Star Appeal - Latakia by Morston (FR) (G A Ham) 1168⁵ 1518 1718 2146 2361 2461 2717

8 **TURNBERRY LAKE,** b g Kings Lake (USA) - Miss Turnberry by Mummy's Pet (Francis M O'Brien) 4397 35⁵ 52⁷ 116⁵

7 **TURNING TRIX,** b g Buckskin (FR) - Merry Run by Deep Run (S E Sherwood) 710²

9 **TUROLDUS(FR),** b g Toujours Pret (USA) - Katy Collonge (FR) by Trenel (S A Brookshaw) 3992

6 **TURTANE CHOICE(IRE),** ch m Over The River (FR) - Well Mannered by Menelek (Thomas Foley) 3552

7 **TURTURILLA(FR),** b m Jefferson - La Vegre by Rose Laurel 267³

5 **TUSCANY HIGHWAY(IRE),** ch g Aristocracy - Johnnie's Lass by Menelek (Michael J Carroll) 1786 2056⁸

9 **TUSKER LADY,** bl m Callernish - Chiminee Bee by Bluerullah (Patrick Day) 4380⁴ 6¹ 52³ 170²

6 **TUSKY,** ch g Prince Sabo - Butosky by Busted (G M Moore) 2413⁵ 2585⁸ 2828³ 2998¹ 3225² 3494¹ 3817 3932⁶

6 **TV PITCH(FR),** b m Fast Topaze (USA) - Allatum (USA) by Alleged (USA) (D Lee) 4352⁴ 3057⁶

6 **TWABLADE(IRE),** gr f Strong Gale - Grey Duchy by Sexton Blake (W P Mullins) 3797⁷ 4044⁴

7 **TWELTH MAN,** b g Remainder Man - Merry Cherry by Deep Run (J J O'Neill) 1288⁴

7 **TWICE AS LUCKY(IRE),** b m Denel (FR) - Lisgarvan by Walshford (John Turley) 3796

5 **TWICE IN ONE NIGHT,** b g Pitpan - Again Kathleen by Status Seeker (S W Campion) 1376 2963⁹

5 **TWICE WEEKLY,** b m Young Man (FR) - My Goddess by Palm Track (F Jestin) 3488

7 **TWIN RAINBOW,** ch g Ragapan - Tangmalangaloo by Laurence O (P D Osborne) 1576 1897⁶ 2123⁸ 2389⁶ 2863² 3366¹ 3657

5 **TWIN STATES,** b g State Diplomacy (USA) - Malmo by Free State (J R Turner) 482⁴ 577⁷ 1181⁶ 1362 2239¹ 2308 3378⁶ 3440¹ 3580 3817³ 3932

7 **TWINKLE BRIGHT(USA),** b or br m Star de Naskra (USA) - Lady May (FR) by Luthier (John J Harding) 4368 4409

6 **TWIST 'N' SCU,** ch g Prince Sabo - Oranella by Orange Bay (N A Twiston-Davies) 541¹ 1090 1621 2196³ 2405⁹ 3685

6 **TWISTALL(IRE),** b g Callernish - Irish Beauty by Even Money (G A Hubbard) 1494

6 **TWISTED BAR,** ch g Sergeant Drummer (USA) - Evening Bar by Pardigras (P J Hobbs) 1027⁴

10 **TWO BOB,** gr g Colinstable - Unknown (I O'Leary) 6⁶ 33

7 **TWO COVERS,** ch g Arapahos (FR) - Jennifer Jane by Woodville II (Patrick J F Hassett) 3722⁴ 4118

7 **TWO HILLS,** ch m Muscatite - June Goddess (L Skehan) 3243 3291 3954

5 **TWO HILLS FOLLY(IRE),** b m Pollerton - Pirgo by Sweet Revenge (James Joseph Mangan) 692⁷ 1077⁶ 1858 2231⁷ 2616⁸

6 **TWO IN TUNE(IRE),** br g Beau Charmeur (FR) - Flying Shadow by Charlottesvilles Flyer (Daniel Lordan) 7⁷ 1555 1859⁷

5 **TWO JOHN'S(IRE),** b or br g King's Ride - No Honey by Dual (P F Nicholls) 1251⁵

7 **TWO MAGPIES,** ch m Doulab (USA) - Captive Audience by Bold Lad (IRE) (M J Grassick) 249 376⁸

8 **TYARA,** b m Buckskin (FR) - Young's Pride by Golden Vision (W J Burke) 71 3912

10 **TYDELMORE,** b g Tycoon II - Delcombe by Cracksman (NZ) (B Preece) 4312

5 **TYDFIL LASS,** b m Scallywag - Roadway Mistress by Mandamus (D Burchell) 3114⁹ 3680

6 **TYLERS CABIN(IRE),** ch g Kambalda - Last Wish by Three Wishes (John J Harding) 535

6 **TYMOOLE(IRE),** b g Henbit (USA) - Song Beam by Song (Noel Meade) 4340⁶

5 **TYNRON DOON,** b g Cragador - Bel Esprit by Sagaro (Mrs N Macauley) 1472² 1731¹⁴ 1965² 2196² 2308⁶ 2401¹ 2670⁴ 3094⁴ 3897⁴

6 **TYPHOON JOE(IRE),** b g Strong Gale - Chestnut Belle by Even Money (W P Mullins) 540 675 1270 1501

8 **TYRO DOMANI,** b h Ginger Boy - Tyrotina by Tyrone (G P Enright) 1108

8 **TYRONE BRIDGE,** b g Kings Lake (USA) - Rhein Bridge by Rheingold (N J H Walker) 1339

10 **TZAMBUKO(FR),** 16

8 **UBU III(FR),** b g Maiymad - Isis (FR) by Or de Chine (FR) (F Doumen) 54¹

8 **UBU VAL(FR),** b g Kashneb (FR) - Lady Val (FR) by Credit Man (W A Bethell) 2884⁵

9 **UCELLO II(FR),** b g Quart de Vin (FR) - Judy by Laniste (F Doumen) 4356¹ 16¹ 816¹ 1252²

8 **UFANO(FR),** b g Toujours Pret (USA) - Osca (FR) by Taj Dewan (Capt T A Forster) 1457⁷ 1776⁵ 2999¹ 3175¹⁴ 3744³

8 **UGOLIN DE LA WERA(FR),** ch g Faucon Noir (FR) - Only One (FR) by Sangioveto (FR) (D T Hughes) 4306⁵ 4399 45² 112 158⁸ 832⁹

8 **ULLSWATER,** b g Waffl - Dignified Air (FR) by Wolver Hollow (A S Reid) 140³ 307⁶ 347¹ 625 917⁸

7 **ULTRA FLUTTER,** b g Beldale Flutter (USA) - Ultra Vires by High Line (Michael Hourigan) 2700³ 3040 3244¹ 3292¹ 3657¹

7 **ULTRA MAGIC,** b m Magic Mirror - Cardane (FR) by Dan Cupid (T A Kent) 4378⁸ 46³ 57⁵ 113¹ 230⁵ 313² 528¹ 556⁴

4 **ULTRAKAY(IRE),** b g Treasure Kay - Ultra by Stanford (J J O'Neill) 1290 1416

6 **ULURU(IRE),** b g Kris - Mountain Lodge by Blakeney (C T Nash) 934² 1067¹ 1341⁵ 1458¹ 1759³ 2009⁴ 2597⁶ 2823 2967⁵ 3186³ 3283⁵ 3967³

6 **UNA'S CHOICE(IRE),** b g Beau Charmeur (FR) - Laurabeg by Laurence O (F Flood) 1681 1897¹ 2278⁶ 3366²

6 **UNCERTAIN,** ch h Noalto - Paridance by Doudance (M C Pipe) 1646

7 **UNCERTAIN TIMES,** ch g Sunley Builds - Winter Gala by Monksfield (R Rowe) 1957⁸ 2315 2494

798

6 **VIAGGIO,** b g High Line - Al Washl (USA) by The Minstrel (CAN) (A L Forbes) 190⁴ 324³ 693³ 839⁴ 932⁴ 1248 1393⁵ 1463⁴ 1718⁴ 1967¹

5 **VIARDOT(IRE),** b g Sadler's Wells (USA) - Vive La Reine by Vienna (Mrs M Reveley) 2385 2487⁵ 2788³ 2967¹ 3038⁴ 3374⁴

7 **VICAR OF BRAY,** b g The Parson - Fanfare Beauty by Le Prince (G B Balding) 1536 1708⁶ 1804⁹ 2596⁶ 2732 2978⁴ 3336⁸ 3562³ 3844³ 4108¹

7 **VICARIDGE,** b g The Parson - Streamon by Rapid River (R Brewis) 3129⁴

5 **VICOSA(IRE),** gr g General View - Mesena by Pals Passage (T F Lacy) 37¹ 209² 329⁴ 533⁵ 805³ 880⁶ 1176¹ 1855⁸ 2279

7 **VICTOR BRAVO(NZ),** br g War Hawk - Regal Command (NZ) by First Consul (USA) (N A Gaselee) 2507⁴ 2727⁵ 3283³ 3520¹ 4006²

8 **VICTORIOUS KING,** b g Petorius - Petit Secret by Petingo (M C Pipe) 165³ 202

8 **VICTORY ANTHEM,** ch g Tug Of War - Anvil Chorus by Levanter (P C Clarke) 4309² 1632⁸ 2065⁴ 2229⁴ 2545² 3548⁸ 3758¹ 3879³ 4000⁵ 4109³

9 **VICTORY GATE(USA),** b g English (FR) - Pago Miss (USA) by Pago Pago (A Moore) 1164 2491² 3099⁷ 3546⁵ 3699³ 3942³

5 **VICTORY TOAST(IRE),** ch m Glow (USA) - Toast Of The Town by Prince Tenderfoot (USA) (Edward Lynam) 4 62⁴

9 **VICTORY WIND,** ch g Asdic - Cool Wind by Windjammer (USA) (Mrs E Kulbicki) 264

6 **VIENNA SHOP(IRE),** b g Le Johnstan - Pai-Collect by Paico (J F Bailey Jun) 4409¹

7 **VIKING FLAGSHIP,** b g Viking (USA) - Fourth Degree by Oats (D Nicholson) 1618² 1995² 2171¹ 2594¹ 3037¹ 3423²

12 **VILLA PARK,** b g Varano - Fethard Flirt by Furry Glen (G Wareham) 2338⁷ 2496⁵ 2710⁶ 3150² 3545⁶ 3943

9 **VILLA RECOS,** b g Deep Run - Lovely Colour by Shantung (A Barrow) 1701⁶ 1947² 2084⁵ 2458 2596¹ 3054³ 3175³ 3338 3477 3534

9 **VILLA TARANTO,** b m Ashmore (FR) - Gun-nard by Gunner B (Mrs B Brunt) 3354

7 **VILLAGE REINDEER(NZ),** b g Le Grand Seig-neur (CAN) - Riggane (NZ) by Reindeer (P Calver) 948¹

5 **VILLAINS BRIEF(IRE),** b g Torus - Larrys Glen by Laurence O (M G Meagher) 2210⁶

9 **VINCERO,** b g River Knight (FR) - Kilbride Madam by Mandalus (D T Hughes) 1017⁷ 1178 1380 1453

4 **VINEY(USA),** b g Trempolino (USA) - Fille Du Nord (FR) by Northern Treat (USA) (C Weedon) 1261³ 3661³

8 **VINEYARD SPECIAL,** b g Good Thyne (USA) - Right Chimes by Even Money (W J Burke) 4379 11 47² 91² 122³ 176² 410 430¹ 856³ 928⁶ 1179² 3241 3657 3732⁶ 4058 4150⁷

7 **VIOLET'S BOY,** b g Starch Reduced - Otterden by Crooner (P J Hobbs) 715 795¹ 1046⁴

7 **VIRGINIA'S BAY,** b g Uncle Pokey - Carnation by Runnymede (John Prangley) 286³ 350⁴ 485⁴ 612⁶ 810⁷

9 **VIRIDIAN,** b g Green Shoon - Cahermone Ivy by Perspex (E T Buckley) 749 842⁴ 1026² 1459 3519⁸ 4018² 4143¹ 4156⁴

5 **VIS-A-VIS,** gr g Efisio - River Vixen by Sagaro (D W P Arbuthnot) 486⁸

8 **VISAGA,** b g King's Ride - Subiacco by Yel-low River (N A Twiston-Davies) 1527¹ 1750³ 2017⁴ 3562¹

9 **VISCOUNT TULLY,** b g Blakeney - Cymbel by Ribero (C F C Jackson) 2839⁴ 2982⁴ 3186⁶ 3398¹

8 **VISIBLE DIFFERENCE,** b g Carlingford Castle - Pitalina by Pitpan (Patrick Heffernan)

496¹ 619² 879¹ 1233 1334¹ 1430¹ 1817⁵ 2286⁴ 3391² 3651¹

4 **VISIMOTION(USA),** ch g Imp Society (USA) - Ditdad (USA) by Tudor Grey (Mrs J Cecil) 2422³ 2624³ 2821³ 3700³

6 **VISION OF FREEDOM(IRE),** b g Vision (USA) - Captive Audience by Bold Lad (IRE) (W J Reed) 3672³

10 **VISION OF WONDER,** b g Tyrnavos - Valeur by Val de Loir (J S King) 1081 1248 1324⁶ 3154 3510⁹ 3805 3976

6 **VISIONARY(IRE),** b or br g Vision (USA) - Tithe Barn by Zarathustra (J P Kavanagh) 341 636

7 **VISIONS PRIDE,** gr h Vision (USA) - Danielle Delight by Song (Noel Meade) 1765⁹ 1818

6 **VISTAGE(IRE),** b g Vision (USA) - Something Swift by Rarity (D G McArdle) 939 1904⁵ 2155 2309 2607⁹ 3506

8 **VITAL SCORE,** b g Vital Season - Tia Song by Acrania (J S King) 1730 1973 2263 2479 2729

9 **VITAL SINGER,** br g Vital Season - Tia Song by Acrania (G W Davies) 2631

7 **VITAL TRIX,** b m Torus - Beatrix by Escart III (Thomas Matthews) 2863 3244⁸ 3366 4113¹

7 **VITAL TYCOON,** b m Vital Season - Tycoons Belle by Tycoon II (D C Tucker) 1519 3740

7 **VITAL WITNESS(CAN),** b g Val de L'orne (FR) - Friendly Witness (USA) by Northern Dancer (K A Morgan) 2402³ 2668⁴ 3043² 3374 3622

6 **VITAL WONDER,** ch g Vital Season - Honey Wonder by Winden (D R C Elsworth) 885⁴ 1840⁷ 2671⁴ 3476² 3670³ 3914⁸

5 **VITAMAN(IRE),** b g King's Ride - Sea Cygnet by Menelek (Mrs J Pitman) 3522¹

7 **VIVA BELLA(FR),** b g Cap Martin (FR) - Moldau (FR) by Francois Saubaber (FR) (Mrs S A Bramall) 720⁴ 876 947⁶ 1254³ 1486⁷ 1941¹ 2294² 2499² 2635¹ 2733¹ 2935 3077¹ 3512¹

5 **VLADIMIR'S WAY(IRE),** b h Don't Forget Me - Susan's Way by Red God (J C Hayden) 3957⁷ 4093³

4 **VLADIVOSTOK,** gr g Siberian Express (USA) - Tsungani by Cure The Blues (USA) (R Lee) 688

9 **VODKA FIZZ,** ch g Don - Doon Royal by Ardoon (J T Gifford) 761

8 **VOLCANIC DANCER(USA),** b g Northern Baby (CAN) - Salva (USA) by Secretariat (USA) (Mrs N Macauley) 526⁷ 660 833³ 948⁸ 1081 3283 3398 3801 3895⁷ 4064⁵ 4121³ 4176

4 **VOLCANIC ROC,** b g Rustingo - La Chica by El Cid (G W Davies) 2332 3190⁹

7 **VOLDI,** br g Tumble Gold - Annie Sue VI by Snuff Matter (Andrew McCarren) 3994⁶

5 **VOLLEYBALL(IRE),** b g Montelimar (USA) - Ingrid Volley (ITY) by Romolo Augusto (USA) (G L Humphrey) 2916

4 **VOLUNTEER POINT(IRE),** b g Mister Majestic - Lola Sharp by Sharpen Up (Mrs S A Bra-mall) 1990⁴ 2291⁸ 2638⁶ 2783⁴ 3074² 3289³ 3444³ 3536

4 **VON CARTY(IRE),** b m Supreme Leader - Nicat by Wolver Hollow (A J McNamara) 4381³ 58³ 109⁶ 236² 292² 431² 531¹ 854 1036² 1333 1608⁷ 2039⁴ 3086⁴

10 **VORETIN(FR),** b g Cap Martin (FR) - Kren-eldore by Trenel 16³

7 **VULPIN DE LAUGERE(FR),** b g Olmeto - Quisl-ing II (FR) by Trenel (FR) (Mrs S A Bra-mall) 718 874 1218⁹ 1587² 2434 2497²

16 **VULRORY'S CLOWN,** b g Idiot's Delight - Vul-rory by Vulgan (O Brennan) 4376³ 500² 5894 946² 1656³ 2563⁴ 3968²

5 **WAAZA(USA),** b g Danzig Connection (USA) - Nishig (USA) by Naskra (USA) (M F Barraclough) 522⁸ 288l 3572 3725¹² 3822¹ 4165⁹

4 **WADABLAST(IRE),** ch f Milk Of The Barley - Shining Green by Green Shoon (Graham T Morrow) 3271

8 **WADI RUM,** b g Buckskin (FR) - Hansel's Princess by Prince Hansel (John A White) 1035 1179 1612 2942

4 **WAIPIRO,** ch g Doulab (USA) - Kundrie (GER) by Luciano (Mrs S D Williams) 2426

8 **WAIT NO LONGER,** b g Le Bavard (FR) - Knockaville by Crozier (P Hughes) 4342¹ 573⁴

9 **WAIT YOU THERE(USA),** b g Nureyev (USA) - Ma Mere L'oie (FR) by Lightning (FR) (H Alexander) 3239⁶ 3375⁴ 3676¹ 3816¹ 4013 4137⁵

7 **WAKE UP,** ch g Night Shift (USA) - Astonishing by Jolly Good (R O'Leary) 781⁵ 972 1055³ 1571 1671⁷ 1777⁶ 2138⁸ 2243² 2371⁴ 2566² 3344¹ 3475 3578 3618³

9 **WAKE UP LUV,** ch g Some Hand - Arctic Ander by Leander (Gerard Cully) 4397 928⁹ 3241⁵ 3790 3945 4117⁴

7 **WAKEUP LITTLESUSIE,** ch m Bulldozer - Sousheen by Ballymore (P J Deegan) 1916⁷ 2128 2353

8 **WAKT,** b f Akarad (FR) - Nasara (FR) by Home Guard (USA) (J White) 2478⁷ 3770 4021⁷ 4185⁴

8 **WALDORF T BEAGLE,** b g Buckskin (FR) - Arctic Alice by Brave Invader (USA) (F Coton) 1152⁶ 1603

4 **WALID'S PRINCESS(IRE),** b f Waajib - Glomach (USA) by Majestic Light (USA) (R G Frost) 2652 2945⁴ 3531 3765² 3915⁹ 4011⁴

13 **WALK IN RHYTHM,** b g Tower Walk - Maiden D'Or by Songedor (Mrs A Price) 811

7 **WALK IN THE WOODS,** b m Elegant Air - Red Roses (FR) by Roi Dagobert (Bob Baldry) 2800³ 3049²

5 **WALK RITE BACK(IRE),** gr g Bob Back (USA) - Nephrite by Godswalk (USA) (J S Bolger) 71¹ 113⁸ 329

6 **WALKERS LADY(IRE),** b m Strong Gale - Macapple by Tug Of War (John O'Callaghan) 30⁹ 90⁴ 169⁶ 302⁵ 572⁷ 3888

8 **WALKERS POINT,** b g Le Moss - Saltee Star by Arapaho (Miss R J Patman) 2380⁷ 2483

7 **WALKING SAINT,** b m Godswalk (USA) - Saintly Tune by Welsh Saint (Graeme Roe) 1526

5 **WALKING THE PLANK,** b g Daring March - Pirate Maid by Auction Ring (USA) (N Tinkler) 1084⁶ 1675⁷ 1872

7 **WALLISTRANO,** br g Indian King (USA) - Kilistrano by Capistrano (John R Upson) 703⁶ 833 954³ 1311³ 1511 2308 3400³

4 **WALLS COURT,** ch g Cardinal Flower - Anega by Run The Gantlet (USA) (V T O'Brien) 941⁵ 1266⁴ 1499³ 1819 2025³ 2200⁴ 3392 3648³

11 **WALLY WREKIN,** ch g Peter Wrekin - Winning Venture by Eastern Venture (Mrs P A Powley) 2526⁶

7 **WALLYS RUN,** ch g Deep Run - Peg Cooney by Menelek (W J Lanigan) 2683² 3325

5 **WALNEY ISLAND,** b h Midyan (USA) - Character Builder by African Sky (E J O'Grady) 71³ 108 157⁴ 797 923⁵ 1039

4 **WALSHAM WITCH,** b f Music Maestro - Makinlau by Lauso (C Smith) 247 285 588⁹ 724⁵

11 **WALTINGO,** b g Certingo - Honeyglen by Tynwald (S B Clark) 2887 3962²

6 **WALTON THORNS,** b g Leading Man - Jacqueline Jane by David Jack (C R Egerton) 864⁷ 1715⁵ 2117

4 **WAMDHA(IRE),** b f Thatching - Donya by Mill Reef (USA) (K A Morgan) 1243³ 1510⁷ 1865¹ 2150⁴ 3002¹ 3333⁶ 3482⁸ 3925⁶

7 **WANDERLINE,** ch g Tug Of War - Carrigal by Deep Run (C C Trietline) 664 1023⁷ 1169⁶ 1524

6 **WANDERWEG(FR),** ch g The Wonder (FR) - Sharpclad (FR) by Sharpman (P Leach) 882⁵ 1393² 1637² 1754 2767⁶

6 **WANG HOW,** b g Nishapour (FR) - Killifreth by Jimmy Reppin (C W Thornton) 976⁸ 2573 2960⁶ 3102⁴ 3801

6 **WANOVOWERS(IRE),** b g Reasonable (FR) - Sisterhood by Malinowski (USA) (G A Pritchard-Gordon) 1549⁸ 3145

4 **WANZA,** b g Petoski - Lovers Light by Grundy (M D Hammond) 285¹ 561² 971⁸ 3373⁸ 3617³ 3897³

7 **WAPITI,** ch g Whistling Deer - Gaelic Lady by Guillaune Tell (USA) (James Augustine O'Brien) 1270 1500 1687

6 **WAR BEAT,** b g Wolver Heights - Branitska by Mummy's Pet (B P J Baugh) 1897 312⁸ 425⁴ 1280 1485³ 1592⁸ 2606⁴ 2711

8 **WAR DEVIL,** b m Tug Of War - Purdey Good by Welsh Saint (E Lacey) 4398⁶ 42 291 330⁶ 528⁶ 584 689

6 **WAR FLOWER(IRE),** ch m Cardinal Flower - Purdey Good by Welsh Saint (E McNamara) 4190

5 **WAR LADY,** ch m War Hero - Fast Lady by Push On (M A Barnes) 3079

7 **WAR OFFICE,** b m Tug Of War - Purdy Good by Welsh Saint (E McNamara) 475⁵ 690⁸ 1035⁹ 1451

8 **WARASH,** b g Ashford (USA) - War Rain by Bahrain (J R H Fowler) 807 903

8 **WAREZ(IRE),** b g Seclude (USA) - Fawnock by Push On (W T Murphy) 3072 3124 3528 3694

7 **WARFIELD,** b g Glint Of Gold - Alys by Blakeney (P F Nicholls) 1524 1747³ 2015⁸ 2361¹ 2483² 2657² 3053¹ 3363³ 3487⁵

13 **WARLEGGAN,** br g Star Appeal - Dauphiness by Supreme Sovereign (S A Brookshaw) 3212⁶ 3927² 4022¹ 4182⁴

4 **WARM SPELL,** b g Northern State (USA) - Warm Wind by Tumble Wind (USA) (G L Moore) 3095¹ 3228²

5 **WARNER FOR SPORT,** b g Mandalus - Joy Travel by Ete Indien (USA) (P J Hobbs) 2749 3739⁵

8 **WARNER FOR WINNERS,** b g Roman Warrior - Cala Conta by Deep Run (P J Hobbs) 1459¹ 1796⁴ 2047² 2143⁸ 2791 2880¹ 3417¹ 3703¹

13 **WARNER'S END,** ch g Legal Tender - Yoriet by Hornet (J Webber) 935⁷ 1197 1706⁶ 1966⁴ 3260

6 **WARREN HOUSE,** b g Crofthall - Gay Ribbon by Ribero (M D Hammond) 2387 3079⁸

4 **WARREN STREET(IRE),** b g Wassl - Key To The Door by Patch (B V Kelly) 529⁷ 3793⁹ 4091⁴

4 **WARSPITE,** b g Slip Anchor - Valkyrie by Bold Lad (IRE) (R Akehurst) 1510

12 **WARWICK SUITE,** b g Orchestra - Place To Place (USA) by No Robbery (J L Eyre) 755 818

5 **WASHINGTON HEIGHTS(USA),** br g Linkage (USA) - Refill by Mill Reef (USA) (J H Scott) 930⁸ 1180

8 **WASHINGTONCROSSING,** ch g Over The River (FR) - Rather Grand by Will Somers (Andrew Turnell) 995² 1208⁴

8 **WASSLS MILLION,** b h Wassl - Black Crow by Sea Hawk II (T Morton) 130

7 **WASTEOFTIME,** ch m Le Bavard (FR) - Pirgo by Sweet Revenge (E T Buckley) 699 1456

8 **WICK POUND,** b g Niniski (USA) - Hors Serie (USA) by Vaguely Noble (J A B Old) 1396⁵ 1561² 3038 4017² 4183²

9 **WICKET,** b m Deep Run - Knock Off by Arctic Slave (M J Wilkinson) 1772⁴ 1972³ 2528⁷ 2674

9 **WICKET KEEPER,** b g Green Shoon - Penthouse Pet by Deep Run (I R Ferguson) 1013² 1159⁶ 1579 1831 2179³

11 **WICKFIELD LAD,** gr g Owen Anthony - Dumbella by Dumbarnie (N M Babbage) 4376 946¹ 1044⁵ 1189⁴ 1463² 1659³ 3210¹ 3595⁴ 3776³ 4102

4 **WICKLOW WAY(IRE),** b f Pennine Walk - Faraway Places by Flair Path (Desmond McDonogh) 1432⁴ 2547² 2678² 2864⁶ 3321⁵ 4076³

12 **WIDE BOY,** b g Decoy Boy - Wide Of The Mark by Gulf Pearl (P J Hobbs) 684² 1638¹ 1883³ 2174⁶ 2377⁵ 2602⁴

4 **WIDE-EYED,** ch f Funny Man - Smooth Talk by Rhodomantade (R H Alner) 2339

11 **WIGTOWN BAY,** br g Young Nelson - Bonnie Bladnoch by Lord Of Verona (J Mackie) 4365² 426⁶ 663⁴ 1069⁶ 1144⁵ 1407³ 1503⁶ 1656⁴

4 **WILBURY WONDER,** ch f Precious Metal - Bridgett Ann by Keep The Peace (R Brotherton) 1473 1705

11 **WILD ATLANTIC,** b g Welsh Saint - Stonebow Lady by Windjammer (S G Payne) 581¹ 788³ 1128⁵ 1604⁴ 1790² 3784⁴

6 **WILD BRAMBLE(IRE),** ch m Deep Run - Bramble Leaf by Even Money (Mrs M Reveley) 813⁴

4 **WILD EXPRESSION,** ch g Then Again - Pleasure Island by Dalsaan (J H Johnson) 3373 3580

6 **WILD FANTASY(IRE),** b m Cataldi - Sea Shrub by Ballymore (A P O'Brien) 48¹ 136³ 636² 942¹ 1174¹ 1851³ 2181 2548⁴

12 **WILD FORTUNE,** b g Free Boy - Hopeful Fortune by Autre Prince (P Baring) 1467 1651³ 2206 3744 3850⁶

10 **WILD ILLUSION,** ch g True Song - Fused Light by Fury Royal (Miss Jennifer Pidgeon) 2570 2968² 3212¹ 3399¹ 3563² 3638¹ 3858¹ 4182⁷

8 **WILD SALLY,** ch m Boreen Beag - Lady Cardigan by Light Brigade (Robert O'Brien) 4370⁹

5 **WILD STRAWBERRY,** ro m Ballacashtal (CAN) - Pts Fairway by Runnymede (Miss B Sanders) 616² 964² 2112¹ 2345¹

6 **WILD VENTURE(IRE),** ch m Le Bavard (FR) - Fast Adventure by Deep Run (J R H Fowler) 638² 857² 1265⁶ 1401⁶ 1683⁸ 2050¹ 2181¹ 2468⁶ 2844³ 3322

10 **WILDNITE,** b g Whealden - Melinite by Milesian (Miss L Robbins) 3947² 4163

5 **WILKINS,** b g Master Willie - Segos by Runnymede (R J O'Sullivan) 1646² 2014 2525⁴ 3209⁸ 3339³

7 **WILL BONNY(NZ),** br g Val Dansant (CAN) - Tobacco Road (NZ) by Crown Lease (Mrs A E Jermy) 567⁶ 666⁹ 950³ 1153 1313³ 3365 3977

4 **WILL HYDE,** b c Coquelin (USA) - Debutante Ball by Cut Above (C Weedon) 180³

8 **WILL JAMES,** ch g Raga Navarro (ITY) - Sleekit by Blakeney (C J Drewe) 1249⁶ 2883³ 3048⁶ 3574² 3806³ 3924¹ 4162³

8 **WILL PHONE,** br m Buckskin (FR) - Scottish Maid by Giolla Mear (M J P O'Brien) 392⁴ 473³ 554 707¹ 1112¹ 1430 1579³ 3081¹

11 **WILL YOU STOP VI,** b g Roselier (FR) - Pedigree Unknown (Michael Aherne) 42 52

11 **WILL'S BOUNTY,** b g Tudor Treasure - Silva by Spartan General (J Colston) 187³ 323⁴ 441⁵ 565⁵ 753⁶ 988² 2380⁶ 3825

7 **WILLCHRIS,** b h Fidel - Culkeern by Master Buck (David McBratney) 4304⁸ 3 38 3811² 4091⁶

9 **WILLIE MCGARR(USA),** ch g Master Willie - Pay T V (USA) by T V Commercial (USA) (Mrs D Thomas) 649² 774³ 933⁶ 2084⁶ 2299³ 2458 3007⁸ 3175

8 **WILLIE SPARKLE,** b g Roi Guillaume (FR) - Adamay by Florescence (Mrs S C Bradburne) 873³ 1106⁷ 1219³ 2436²

7 **WILLOW GALE,** b m Strong Gale - Tric Willow by Le Tricolore (P Butler) 1973 2427³ 2725³ 2854³ 3232²

11 **WILLSFORD,** b g Beau Charmeur (FR) - Wish Again by Three Wishes (Mrs J Pitman) 1281² 1543⁴ 1881⁴ 2172 2403⁵ 2602³ 2805⁵ 3485⁹

5 **WILLUBELONG,** ch g Move Off - Scally's Girl by Scallywag (W Raw) 915

6 **WILTOSKI,** b g Petoski - Cojean (USA) by Prince John (R R Ledger) 4307² 4372³ 181⁴ 194 347 861 1562⁴ 2067 2496⁹ 3014⁹ 3696⁴ 3843² 4096³

14 **WILTSHIRE YEOMAN,** ch g Derrylin - Ribo Pride by Ribero (P Hayward) 936 1759

4 **WIN A HAND,** b f Nearly A Hand - Mariban by Mummy's Pet (B J M Ryall) 2269 2916⁸ 3458

8 **WIN ELECTRIC,** br m Down The Hatch - Claddagh Pride by Bargello (Mrs R G Henderson) 218

11 **WINABUCK,** ch g Buckskin (FR) - Mistic Breeze by Master Owen (R Dickin) 935 1057 1458⁸ 1643⁴ 2044⁶ 2674 3187⁴ 3280² 3593⁴ 3828⁶ 4122⁴

9 **WINCHLING,** br g Broadsword (USA) - Blakes Lass by Blakeney (A J Maxwell) 28 95⁵ 161¹ 313⁵ 467⁴ 674

9 **WIND FORCE,** br g Strong Gale - Richest by Richboy (G Richards) 661² 3626⁴

10 **WIND ZING,** b c Hittite Glory - Head Scarf by Tumble Wind (Francis M O'Brien) 376⁶ 557 797

4 **WINDERMERE TERRACE,** ch f Scorpio (FR) - Rainbow Lady by Jaazeiro (USA) (M G Meagher) 3401

7 **WINDMILL CROSS,** b g Farhaan - All Class by Laurence O (Thomas Cooper) 79 112

6 **WINDOVER(IRE),** b g Deep Run - Home And Dry by Crash Course (J R Cox) 1379⁵ 1549² 1760² 1832² 2309³

7 **WINDOVER LODGE,** ch g Don - Arabian Squaw (J H Scott) 1 8³ 37⁸ 47⁷ 107 115⁵ 124 208² 489³ 745³ 805 989⁶ 3722⁶ 3794⁴

9 **WINDS OF WAR,** br g Strong Gale - Kind Rose by Royal And Regal (USA) (M F Morris) 575 635² 905¹ 1825 3371⁴ 3465³ 3658⁴ 3746³

4 **WINDSOR FOX(IRE),** b f Mandalus - Foxy Jane by Pollerton (R Rowe) 2176

8 **WINDSOR PARK(USA),** br g Bold Forbes (USA) - Round Tower by High Top (C D Broad) 148⁵ 153⁴ 168² 298 325¹ 404³ 568³ 703⁵

5 **WINDSWEPT LADY(IRE),** br m Strong Gale - Smithstown Lady by Tarqogan (Mrs M Reveley) 3169⁵ 3489⁶

8 **WINDWARD ARIOM,** ch g Pas de Seul - Deja Vu (FR) by Be My Guest (USA) (K R Burke) 499⁷ 662⁷ 1238⁷ 1474 1721⁶ 2998³ 3254⁷ 3743¹ 3924⁷ 4047¹ 4141⁴

9 **WINDY WAYS,** br g Strong Gale - Woodville Grove by Harwell (N J Henderson) 1447⁵ 1757⁴ 2506 3027⁴ 3519³

9 **WINGCOMMANDER EATS,** b g Nishapour (FR) - Rhodie Blake by Blakeney (P J Hobbs) 1169

5 **WINGED WHISPER(USA),** ch g Air Forbes Won (USA) - Soft Reply (USA) by Personality (USA) (J A Pickering) 323² 402⁴ 622⁶ 837² 1079⁹ 1456 1741³ 2538⁶ 2803⁷

National Hunt Speed Ratings 1993-94

● THIS list derived from Sporting Life Average Times, represents the optimum time-rating of a horse after taking into account varying ground conditions, adjusted to 12st. To qualify for inclusion a horse must earn a speed rating of over 30. Supplementary information after the name and figure contains the distance, course, going based on times and date when the rating was achieved.

HURDLERS

Aal El Aal 34[1] (2m, Winc, Y, Feb 10, *H*)
Abbot Of Furness 46[3] (2m, Weth, S, Dec 27, *H*)
Abjar 28[2] (2m 1½f, Mark, Y, Jan 22)
Absalom's Lady 69[3] (2m, Kemp, S, Dec 28)
Absent Relative 54[1] (2m 2f, Font, G, Oct 27, *H*)
Act Of Parliament (IRE) 35[2] (2m 4f, Donc, G, Mar 5)
Admiral's Well (IRE) 30[1] (2m, Hayd, F, May 2, *H*)
Admiralty Way 35[3] (2m, Catt, G, Dec 1, *H*)
Aiybak (IRE) 43 (2m ½f, Chel, Y, Mar 15)
Al Skeet (USA) 26[2] (2m, Sout, Hrd, May 11, *H*)
Aljadeer (USA) 32[2] (2m, Weth, S, Dec 27)
All Greek To Me (IRE) 25[1] (2m 1f, Bang, S, Mar 26, *H*)
All Welcome 31[3] (2m ½f, Hunt, G, Oct 23, *H*)
Allegation 37[3] (2m, Utto, Hvy, Apr 2, *H*)
Almamzar (USA) 25[2] (2m, Worc, G, Mar 30, *H*)
Alosaili 25[3] (2m, Winc, Y, Jan 13, *H*)
Always Remember 28[2] (2m, Winc, G, Nov 18, *H*)
Amazon Express 61[3] (2m ½f, Chel, Y, Nov 12)
American Hero 40[1] (2m, Edin, G, Dec 11)
Anabatic (IRE) 43[1] (2m, Leop, S, Feb 13, *M*)
Andante (IRE) 26[4] (2m, Leop, S, Mar 6)
Angareb (IRE) 42[3] (2m, Leop, S, Dec 27, *M*)
Any Dream Would Do 34[3] (2m, Sout, Hrd, May 11, *H*)
Arabian Bold (IRE) 62[2] (2m ½f, Chel, Y, Nov 12)
Aragon Ayr 35[2] (2m, Ayr, G, Apr 14, *H*)
Arcot 63[1] (2m 1f, Chel, G, Apr 20, *H*)
Arctic Course (IRE) 32[4] (2m 5f, Newb, S, Jan 1, *G*)
Arctic Kinsman 69[1] (2m ½f, Chel, Y, Mar 15)
Arctic Weather (IRE) 34[2] (2m, Leop, S, Jan 8, *L*)
Arfer Mole (IRE) 29[1] (2m 1f, Chel, Hvy, Jan 3)
Ariadler (IRE) 28[1] (2m 6½f, Kels, S, Nov 3)
Aslan (IRE) 46[4] (2m 4f, Live, Hvy, Apr 8, *G*)
Assert Star 28[4] (2m, Leop, F, Nov 6)
Atone 65[3] (2m, Leop, Y, Dec 28, *H*)
Atours (USA) 49[2] (2m, Ayr, G, Apr 16, *G*)
Attadale 64[1] (2m 6½f, Utto, S, Mar 19, *H*)
Avro Anson 69[2] (2m 4½f, Chep, Y, Nov 6, *H*)
Azureus (IRE) 26[2] (2m, Hexh, G, Aug 23, *H*)
Badrakhani (FR) 33 (2m 1f, Chel, Hvy, Jan 29, *H*)
Balaat (USA) 25[2] (2m 1½f, Mark, G, Sep 25, *H*)
Balasani (FR) 43[1] (3m ½f, Chel, G, Mar 17, *G*)
Ballet Royal (USA) 43[1] (2m 1½f, Folk, S, Feb 16)
Ballon 31[1] (2m ½f, Newc, G, Mar 19, *H*)
Bally Clover 35[6] (2m ½f, Newb, G, Oct 22, *H*)
Ballyhyland (IRE) 25[1] (2m, Worc, Y, Apr 13)
Barna Boy (IRE) 55[2] (2m, Kemp, Hvy, Feb 26)
Bas de Laine (FR) 54[2] (2m 6f, Sand, G, Nov 6, *H*)
Basilicus (FR) 26[3] (2m, Warw, S, Jan 8, *H*)
Bass Rock 29[1] (2m 2f, Devo, S, Mar 23)
Batabanoo 66[1] (2m ½f, Newc, G, Nov 6, *H*)
Bay Mischief (IRE) 37[1] (2m 4½f, Chep, Hvy, Dec 28)
Beaucadeau 57[3] (2m ½f, Newc, G, Nov 6, *H*)
Beauchamp Grace 51[4] (2m ½f, Newc, G, Nov 6, *H*)
Bell Staffboy (IRE) 42[2] (2m 4½f, Utto, Y, Nov 4)
Bells Life (IRE) 42[2] (2m, Leop, S, Dec 27, *M*)
Ben Zabeedy 31[3] (2m, Towc, Y, Oct 6, *H*)
Bend Sable (IRE) 26[2] (2m, Edin, G, Feb 3, *C*)
Bertone (IRE) 46[1] (2m 4½f, Utto, Y, Nov 4)
Bibendum 30[5] (2m ½f, Newb, G, Oct 22, *H*)
Bickerman 33[1] (2m 4½f, Leic, S, Nov 30, *H*)
Big Beat (USA) 48[3] (2m ½f, Asco, G, Oct 30, *H*)
Big Matt (IRE) 43[1] (2m, Leop, F, Oct 25, *L*)
Billy Boru 26[2] (2m, Worc, F, Sep 11)
Billygoat Gruff 33[2] (2m ½f, Chep, Hvy, Mar 19)
Blazon Of Troy 28[2] (2m, Ludl, G, Oct 7)
Blue Grotto (IRE) 46[4] (2m 1f, Chel, G, Mar 17, *G*)
Bo Knows Best (IRE) 59[1] (2m 4f, Donc, Y, Jan 29, *H*)
Bold Stroke 36[1] (2m 1f, Newt, Hvy, Dec 13)
Bollin Magdalene 52[1] (2m 5½f, Nott, Hvy, Feb 1, *H*)
Bollin William 71[2] (2m 5½f, Chel, Hvy, Jan 3)
Bonanza 38[1] (2m 5½f, Sedg, S, Nov 9, *H*)
Bond Jnr (IRE) 30[4] (2m 1f, Newt, Hvy, Dec 13)
Book Of Music (IRE) 46[2] (3m, Chep, Hvy, Feb 5)
Bottles (USA) 57[1] (2m, Warw, G, May 21, *H*)
Brambleberry 32[1] (2m ½f, Hunt, S, Feb 10, *H*)
Brandon Prince (IRE) 32[5] (2m ½f, Newb, G, Nov 27)
Brave Highlander (IRE) 27 (2m ½f, Newb, G, Nov 27)
Brief Gale 54[5] (2m 5f, Newb, Y, Mar 26, *H*)
Broad Steane 26[5] (2m 5f, Kemp, S, Jan 22)
Brodessa 35[1] (2m ½f, Kels, G, Oct 16)
Browned Off 34[1] (2m 1f, Here, Y, Apr 4)
Brownside Brig 25[3] (2m, Hexh, G, Apr 30, *H*)
Buonarroti 45[5] (2m 6f, Sand, S, Feb 5, *H*)
Burgoyne 61[3] (3m 1f, Weth, G, Oct 30)
Burnt Imp (USA) 44[2] (2m ½f, Newb, S, Feb 11)
Butler's Twitch 42[1] (2m ½f, Stra, S, Dec 29)
Cabin Hill 37[1] (2m, Winc, F, Nov 4, *H*)
Cabochon 43[3] (2m 2f, Font, S, Nov 30, *H*)
Cairncastle 35[3] (3m ½f, Kemp, G, Oct 28, *H*)
Caithness Cloud 27[1] (2m, Ayr, Hvy, Mar 11, *M*)
Caliandak (IRE) 38[2] (2m ½f, Newb, S, Mar 5)
Cambo (USA) 26[2] (2m 4½f, Leic, Hvy, Dec 31, *H*)
Canoscan 32[1] (2m 4f, Plum, S, Oct 19, *H*)
Captain Dolford 37[1] (3m, Chep, Hvy, Jan 25, *H*)
Captain Khedive 43[2] (2m, Ludl, Y, Apr 6)
Captains Bar 34[4] (2m, Leop, S, Feb 13, *M*)
Cardinal Red 36 (3m ½f, Chel, G, Mar 17, *G*)
Caribbean Prince 33[1] (2m, Warw, G, May 21)
Cariboo Gold (USA) 56[2] (2m 4½f, Utto, G, Apr 30, *G*)
Carnetto 35[1] (2m ½f, Kels, Hvy, Jan 12)
Caspian Beluga 25[2] (2m 1f, Newt, G, May 13)
Castigliero (FR) 54[2] (3m, Asco, S, Apr 6, *H*)
Castle Courageous 46[1] (2m 5f, Kemp, G, Oct 16, *H*)
Castle Court (IRE) 27[2] (2m 5f, Newb, S, Mar 4, *H*)
Castle Diamond 27[2] (2m 2f, Worc, F, Aug 7, *H*)
Castle Secret 46[2] (2m 1f, Chel, G, Apr 20, *H*)
Celcius 34[1] (2m 1f, Newt, Hvy, Mar 28, *H*)
Celtic Shot 27[5] (2m, Hayd, Hvy, Jan 22)
Chadwick's Ginger 26[3] (2m ½f, Newc, G, Mar 21, *H*)
Chance Coffey 45[3] (2m 5f, Chel, G, Mar 16, *H*)
Change The Act 59[2] (2m 2f, Font, S, Nov 30, *H*)
Charlycia 26[1] (2m 1½f, Mark, S, Apr 4, *H*)
Cheeky Pot 26[2] (2m, Edin, F, Dec 6, *H*)
Chief Celt 28[2] (2m 6½f, Wind, S, Jan 3, *H*)
Chief Minister (IRE) 46[1] (2m ½f, Pert, F, Apr 20, *H*)
Chief Raider (IRE) 41[1] (2m 4½f, Weth, G, Apr 5, *H*)
Chief's Song 29[2] (2m ½f, Ling, Y, Mar 18, *M*)
Child Of The Mist 49[2] (2m ½f, Newb, S, Mar 5, *H*)
Chuck Curley (USA) 35[1] (2m ½f, Hunt, S, Dec 1, *H*)
Cloghans Bay (IRE) 48[3] (2m 5½f, Chel, F, Oct 20)
Clurican (IRE) 42[3] (2m ½f, Sand, S, Feb 17, *H*)
Cock Cockburn 42[5] (2m, Leop, S, Feb 13, *H*)
Cockney Lad (IRE) 50[6] (2m, Hayd, F, May 2, *H*)
Coiled Spring 25[1] (2m 5f, Fake, Y, Feb 18)
Col Buckmore (IRE) 25[2] (2m, Hayd, G, Nov 3)
Collier Bay 45[1] (2m 1f, Newt, Hvy, Apr 4)
Cool Dude 25[3] (2m, Catt, G, Oct 23, *S*)
Coq Hardi Affair (IRE) 52[4] (2m 5f, Chel, G, Mar 16, *G*)
Coqui Lane 27[2] (2m 6½f, Kels, S, Nov 3)
Corrin Hill 27[5] (2m, Winc, Y, Feb 10, *H*)
Corrouge (USA) 61[1] (2m 4½f, Utto, G, Apr 30, *G*)
Coulton 26[3] (2m, Nott, S, Feb 19, *H*)
Court Circular 31[3] (3m 3f, Stra, G, May 20, *H*)
Court Master (IRE) 48[3] (2m, Ayr, G, Apr 16, *G*)

Couture Stockings 27[1] (2m 4½f, Weth, S, Apr 26, *H*)
Crabby Bill 25[2] (2m 4f, Asco, Y, Feb 9, *H*)
Crank Shaft 35[1] (2m 4½f, Weth, G, May 30, *H*)
Crystal Bear (NZ) 44[3] (3m, Asco, S, Apr 6, *H*)
Cultured 59[4] (2m, Kemp, G, Oct 16)
Cumbrian Challenge (IRE) 58[1] (2m ½f, Donc, G, Jan 28, *G*)
Cunninghams Ford (IRE) 39[1] (2m 4½f, Warw, S, Feb 8)
Cyborgo (FR) 50[1] (2m 4f, Live, Hvy, Apr 8, *G*)
Dagobertin (FR) 31[5] (2m ½f, Newc, G, Oct 20, *H*)
Damier Blanc (FR) 38[2] (2m, Winc, F, Nov 4, *H*)
Dancing Paddy 68[1] (2m ½f, Newb, S, Mar 5, *H*)
Danoli (IRE) 81[1] (2m 4f, Live, Hvy, Apr 9, *G*)
Daring Past 32[1] (2m ½f, Newb, Y, Mar 26, *H*)
Dark Den (USA) 46[1] (2m ½f, Asco, G, Apr 26, *H*)
Dark Honey 58[1] (2m 6f, Sand, S, Feb 5, *H*)
Deb's Ball 60[1] (3m 1f, Weth, G, Oct 30)
Deep Inagh 51[3] (2m, Leop, S, Feb 13, *H*)
Derrymoss 26[1] (2m 2f, Devo, Hvy, Jan 3, *H*)
Derrymoyle (IRE) 31[4] (2m, Leop, S, Jan 8, *L*)
Desert Force (IRE) 36[1] (2m, Sout, Hrd, May 11, *H*)
Destriero 69[4] (2m, Leop, S, Dec 29, *L*)
Diplomatic 57[2] (2m 1f, Chel, G, Mar 17, *G*)
Divine Chance (IRE) 26[4] (2m, Warw, S, Jan 8, *H*)
Dizzy (USA) 57[1] (2m 1f, Chel, G, Mar 17, *G*)
Djebel Prince 30[2] (2m 1f, Here, S, Dec 21, *H*)
Do Be Have (IRE) 31[2] (2m, Wind, Hvy, Feb 2)
Doctoor (USA) 27 (2m ½f, Asco, G, Mar 30, *H*)
Dominant Serenade 57[2] (2m 6f, Sand, S, Feb 5, *H*)
Dominant Force 38[2] (2m ½f, Sand, S, Dec 4, *H*)
Don't Forget Marie (IRE) 28[1] (2m 1f, Bang, G, Apr 29, *H*)
Double Sherry 27[2] (2m 4½f, Hexh, S, Nov 5)
Double The Stakes (USA) 28[1] (2m, Worc, G, May 18)
Dreams End 71[1] (2m, Hayd, F, May 2, *H*)
Dual Image 25[4] (2m 2f, Kels, S, Nov 11, *H*)
Duveen (IRE) 32 (2m 1f, Chel, G, Mar 17, *G*)
Ealing Court 33[2] (2m 5f, Kemp, Hvy, Feb 25)
Easby Joker 26[3] (2m 4½f, Carl, S, Dec 30)
Easthorpe 45[1] (2m, Nott, S, Jan 1, *H*)
Eden's Close 51 (2m 1f, Chel, G, Mar 17, *G*)
Edimbourg 55[1] (2m ½f, Sand, S, Feb 17, *H*)
El Volador 37[1] (2m, Winc, F, Oct 21, *H*)
Elaine Tully (IRE) 34[1] (2m 6f, Newt, Hvy, Mar 28)
Elementary 44[3] (2m 1f, Chel, Hvy, Jan 29, *H*)
Empire Blue 35[1] (2m, Ludl, Y, Jan 19)
Erckule 27[4] (2m ½f, Newb, Y, Mar 26, *H*)
Everaldo (FR) 56[4] (2m 5½f, Chel, Hvy, Jan 3)
Exarch (USA) 26[3] (2m 6½f, Stra, G, May 20, *H*)
Fairfields Cone 40[6] (2m 4½f, Chep, Y, Nov 6, *H*)
Fairways On Target 36[1] (2m 5½f, Hunt, F, Aug 30, *H*)
Family Line 35[4] (2m ½f, Newc, F, May 7, *H*)
Fantasy World 32[1] (2m 6f, Font, G, May 16, *H*)
Fast Thoughts 42[1] (2m 6½f, Stra, Hvy, Mar 5, *H*)
Fatack 52[2] (2m ½f, Newb, G, Nov 27)
Father Dan (IRE) 27[2] (2m ½f, Hunt, G, Oct 23, *H*)
Faux Pavillon 25[5] (2m 2f, Devo, Y, Dec 3, *H*)
Ferrycarrig Hotel (IRE) 44[1] (2m, Leop, S, Dec 27, *M*)
Fired Earth (IRE) 37[1] (2m 4½f, Leic, Hvy, Dec 31, *H*)
Firm Price 39[1] (2m 5½f, Sedg, Y, Nov 19, *H*)
First Avenue 28[1] (2m, Wind, Hvy, Feb 2)
Five To Seven (USA) 47[1] (2m, Catt, G, Feb 12)
Flakey Dove 76[1] (2m ½f, Chel, Y, Mar 15, *G*)
Flash Of Realm (FR) 29[1] (2m ½f, Newc, G, Mar 19)
Flight Lieutenant (USA) 36[4] (2m ½f, Newb, G, Nov 27)
Fling In Spring 26[2] (2m ½f, Kels, S, Nov 11, *H*)
Flowing River (USA) 26[3] (2m ½f, Pert, G, Sep 22, *H*)
Fontanays (IRE) 33[4] (2m ½f, Ling, Hvy, Mar 19, *H*)
For Reg (IRE) 75[2] (2m, Hayd, F, May 2, *H*)
Formal Affair 30[2] (2m, Winc, S, Feb 24, *M*)
Fortune And Fame 80[1] (2m, Leop, S, Dec 29, *L*)
Fortune's Girl 26[2] (2m, Edin, G, Jan 14, *H*)
Fortunes Course (IRE) 26[6] (2m 5f, Newb, Y, Mar 26, *H*)
Fotoexpress 39[2] (2m 2f, Font, G, Sep 27, *H*)
Four Deep (IRE) 40[1] (2m 4½f, Hexh, S, Nov 5)
Fox Chapel 40[2] (2m 3½f, Mark, Y, Dec 27, *H*)
Free Transfer (IRE) 25[3] (2m 1½f, Cart, F, May 28)
Friendly Fellow 38[3] (2m 5f, Kemp, Hvy, Feb 25)
Front Street 33[3] (2m 2f, Devo, Y, Dec 3, *H*)
Fuzzy Logic (IRE) 47[1] (2m 5½f, Chel, F, Oct 20)
Galaxy High 30 (2m ½f, Sand, S, Feb 17, *H*)
Gales Cavalier (IRE) 43[1] (2m ½f, Hunt, S, Jan 27)
Gandouge Glen 26[6] (2m ½f, Asco, G, Mar 30, *H*)
Gayloire (IRE) 33[3] (2m, Leic, Hvy, Jan 24)
General Mouktar 34[3] (2m, Winc, S, Feb 24, *M*)
General Wolfe 36[1] (2m 6½f, Folk, Hvy, Feb 9)
Genseric (FR) 28[5] (2m ½f, Newc, G, Mar 19, *H*)
Gesnera 26[1] (2m 1f, Here, G, Mar 14)
Giordano (IRE) 32[2] (2m, Nott, S, Dec 18)
Giventime 56[3] (2m ½f, Newb, G, Oct 22, *H*)
Glaisdale (IRE) 42[1] (2m 5f, Newb, S, Dec 31)
Glenstal Flagship (IRE) 42[6] (2m 1f, Chel, G, Mar 17, *G*)
Glentower (IRE) 30[1] (2m 5f, Newb, S, Mar 4, *H*)
Go Mary 40[1] (2m 5f, Newb, Y, Mar 26, *H*)
Golden Isle 27[5] (2m ½f, Pert, G, Sep 22, *H*)
Goldingo 34[1] (2m ½f, Stra, S, Mar 24, *H*)
Good Insight (IRE) 26[3] (2m, Kemp, G, Nov 17)
Googly 41[1] (2m 1f, Plum, Hvy, Mar 21)
Gospel (IRE) 38[2] (2m 5f, Newb, Y, Mar 26, *H*)
Gotta Be Joking 32[2] (2m 1f, Here, S, Mar 5)
Grand Applause (IRE) 28[1] (2m ½f, Newb, Y, Nov 10)
Grand Tour (NZ) 34[1] (2m, Leop, S, Dec 29, *H*)
Granville Again 64 (2m ½f, Chel, Y, Mar 15, *G*)
Gray's Ellergy 37[3] (3m, Chep, Hvy, Feb 5)
Great Mill 36[1] (2m 4f, Bang, G, May 14, *C*)
Grenagh 44[2] (2m 4½f, Chep, Hvy, Dec 28, *H*)
Grey Power 58[1] (2m ½f, Kels, S, Feb 4)
Ground Nut (IRE) 36[1] (2m, Winc, S, Feb 24, *M*)
Gymcrak Sovereign 35[4] (2m ½f, Donc, G, Mar 5, *H*)
Gymcrak Stardom 57[3] (2m ½f, Pert, F, Apr 20, *H*)
Habasha (IRE) 28[3] (2m 1f, Taun, Hvy, Feb 17)
Halkopous 78[2] (2m 1f, Chel, Y, Dec 11)
Hallo Mam (IRE) 29[1] (2m 1½f, Sedg, S, Nov 9, *H*)
Happy Horse (NZ) 38[2] (2m 6½f, Stra, Hvy, Mar 5, *H*)
Hawaiian Youth (IRE) 37[1] (2m ½f, Sand, S, Feb 18)
Hawkfield (IRE) 25[5] (2m 3½f, Mark, Y, Sep 18, *H*)
Hebridean 51[2] (2m 5f, Kemp, G, Oct 16, *H*)
Hedgehopper (IRE) 37[1] (2m ½f, Stra, F, May 13, *H*)
Heist 50[1] (2m, Leop, S, Jan 8)
Her Honour 64[5] (2m 1f, Chel, G, Mar 17, *G*)
Here He Comes 65[2] (2m ½f, Newb, S, Jan 1, *H*)
High Alltitude (IRE) 63[2] (2m 4f, Donc, Y, Jan 29, *H*)
High Baron 75[1] (2m ½f, Asco, G, Mar 30, *H*)
High Mind (FR) 25[2] (2m 1f, Taun, Y, Nov 25)
Highbrook (USA) 56[2] (2m ½f, Sand, S, Dec 4, *G*)
Highland Spirit 39[4] (2m ½f, Newb, S, Mar 5, *H*)
His Way (IRE) 38[2] (2m, Leop, F, May 18, *H*)
Holy Joe 25[1] (2m 4½f, Chep, F, May 10, *H*)
Holy Wanderer (USA) 45[4] (2m ½f, Newb, S, Jan 1, *H*)
Home Counties (IRE) 52[5] (2m ½f, Sand, Y, Mar 12, *H*)
Homile 25[1] (2m, Worc, Y, Oct 9, *H*)
Honest Word 37[6] (2m, Kemp, Y, Dec 27, *H*)
Hostile Witness (IRE) 32[1] (2m, Warw, S, Feb 8)
Hotdiggity 30[1] (2m 4½f, Hexh, F, May 31, *S*)
Hypnotist 25[1] (2m ½f, Newc, F, May 7, *H*)
Ice Strike (USA) 41[3] (2m, Hayd, F, May 2, *H*)
Imperial Bid (FR) 29[2] (2m, Edin, G, Dec 11)
Indian Quest 42[5] (2m ½f, Asco, G, Mar 30, *H*)
Integrity Boy 25[2] (3m ½f, Carl, Y, Feb 8, *H*)
Isabeau 30[3] (2m 6½f, Utto, S, Mar 19, *H*)
Isaiah 27[3] (2m ½f, Stra, Y, Apr 16, *H*)
Island Jewel 34[1] (2m, Wind, S, Feb 19, *H*)
It's The Pits 37[1] (2m, Hayd, Hvy, Dec 8, *H*)
Iveagh House 30[5] (2m ½f, Newb, S, Jan 1, *H*)
Ivor's Flutter 45[2] (2m 5f, Newb, S, Mar 5, *G*)
Jawani (IRE) 27[2] (3m ½f, Kemp, G, Oct 28, *H*)
Jazilah (FR) 58[1] (2m, Kemp, Hvy, Feb 26)
Jeassu 55[3] (2m ½f, Chel, S, Nov 13, *H*)
Jefferby 27[2] (3m 4f, Nott, S, Dec 3, *H*)
Jehol 25[2] (2m 2f, Font, G, Apr 21)
Jinxy Jack 60[6] (2m ½f, Newc, G, Nov 6, *H*)
Johns The Boy 27[4] (2m 4½f, Weth, G, Oct 29)
Johnsted 27[4] (2m 1f, Here, Y, May 26, *H*)
Jopanini 46 (2m 6f, Sand, S, Mar 11, *H*)
Judges Fancy 28 (2m 5½f, Nott, Hvy, Feb 1, *H*)
Judicial Field (IRE) 42[5] (2m, Leop, Y, Dec 28, *H*)
Jump Start 30[2] (2m, Winc, Y, Feb 10, *H*)
Jupiter Jimmy 45[1] (2m, Leop, Y, Dec 28, *H*)
Just You Dare (IRE) 30[4] (2m, Winc, S, Feb 24, *M*)
Kabayil 43[1] (2m ½f, Hunt, Y, Nov 12, *H*)
Kadastrof (FR) 52[2] (2m ½f, Live, S, Apr 7, *G*)
Kadi (GER) 57[5] (2m 5f, Chel, G, Mar 16, *H*)

Kalko 28[1] (2m, Nott, S, Nov 13, *S*)
Kanndabil 31[3] (2m, Weth, S, Jan 13, *H*)
Kano Warrior 30[1] (3m ½f, Kemp, G, Oct 28, *H*)
Karar (IRE) 28[2] (2m 2f, Font, Hvy, Jan 17)
Kaytak (FR) 31[2] (2m, Worc, G, May 7, *H*)
Keep Me In Mind (IRE) 44[1] (2m, Winc, S, Apr 4)
Kenilworth Lad 42[2] (2m 5½f, Chel, F, Oct 20)
Kenmore-Speed 30[5] (2m, Weth, S, Dec 27)
Khalidi (IRE) 29[1] (2m, Ludl, G, Oct 7)
Kharasar (IRE) 37[1] (2m, Leop, S, Mar 6)
Kilcash (IRE) 69[6] (2m ½f, Sand, S, Dec 4, *G*)
Kilgariff 40[1] (2m, Catt, Y, Jan 21, *H*)
King Credo 79[1] (2m 4f, Asco, G, Nov 19, *G*)
King's Shilling (USA) 27[4] (2m ½f, Stra, F, Sep 4, *H*)
King's Treasure (USA) 38[4] (2m ½f, Asco, G, Mar 30, *H*)
Kings Chariot 29[2] (2m 1f, Chel, Hvy, Jan 3)
Kingsfold Pet 29[1] (2m ½f, Ling, Hvy, Mar 19, *H*)
Kinoko 26[3] (2m 5½f, Sedg, S, Oct 12, *H*)
Kiveton Tycoon (IRE) 41[4] (2m 4f, Donc, Y, Jan 29, *H*)
Knockaverry (IRE) 27[2] (2m 6f, Newt, Hvy, Mar 28)
Konvekta Control 32[1] (2m 4f, Bang, G, May 14, *H*)
Konvekta King (IRE) 45[1] (2m, Ludl, Y, Jan 19)
Kovalevskia 29[1] (2m 2f, Font, Hvy, Mar 2, *H*)
Kytton Castle 37 (2m 5f, Newb, Y, Mar 26, *H*)
Lady Donoghue (USA) 30[1] (2m 1½f, Cart, F, May 28)
Land Afar 70[1] (2m ½f, Sand, S, Dec 4, *G*)
Large Action (IRE) 78[3] (2m ½f, Chel, Y, Mar 15, *G*)
Le Ginno (FR) 31[1] (2m 1f, Bang, S, Mar 9)
Leading Prospect 32[3] (3m, Newc, G, Mar 21, *H*)
Leavenworth 30[2] (2m 6f, Sand, S, Mar 11, *H*)
Legal Profession (IRE) 31[4] (2m, Leop, F, May 18, *H*)
Legatissimo (IRE) 26[4] (2m 2f, Leop, Y, Dec 26, *M*)
Legitim 25[4] (2m ½f, Pert, F, Apr 20, *H*)
Lemon's Mill (USA) 62[2] (3m ½f, Chel, G, Apr 20, *H*)
Leotard 67[3] (2m ½f, Sand, Y, Mar 12, *H*)
Lesbet 28[3] (2m 4½f, Leic, Hvy, Dec 31, *H*)
Lexus (IRE) 29[2] (2m 1½f, Mark, S, Nov 20)
Life Saver (IRE) 54[4] (2m, Leop, Y, Dec 28, *H*)
Linkside 35[1] (3m ½f, Ayr, G, Nov 12, *H*)
Linngate 37[1] (2m ½f, Kels, Hvy, Dec 16)
Lion Of Vienna 25[4] (3m ½f, Carl, S, Apr 2, *H*)
Loch Scavaig (IRE) 31[2] (2m 3½f, Mark, Y, Apr 23)
Lodestone Lad (IRE) 25[3] (2m ½f, Sand, Y, Mar 12)
Lonesome Train (USA) 41[4] (2m, Hayd, F, May 2, *H*)
Lovely Run 33[2] (2m 2f, Leop, Y, Dec 26, *M*)
Lustreman 30[1] (2m 1f, Bang, G, Sep 11, *H*)
Lustrino (USA) 41[1] (2m, Leop, F, May 18, *H*)
Lusty Lad 36[3] (2m 2f, Font, G, Oct 27, *H*)
Lynch Law (IRE) 49[1] (3m 3f, Stra, G, May 20, *H*)
Maamur (USA) 63[4] (2m ½f, Sand, S, Dec 4, *G*)
Mad Thyme 44[3] (2m 5f, Kemp, S, Jan 22)
Maestro Paul 33[4] (2m ½f, Sand, S, Feb 17, *H*)
Mailcom 26[4] (2m 5f, Chel, Y, Nov 12, *H*)
Majal (IRE) 30[2] (2m, Sout, Hrd, May 2, *C*)
Majed (IRE) 73[2] (2m ½f, Newb, S, Mar 5, *H*)
Major Bell 29[1] (2m 4f, Ayr, G, Apr 15)
Major Bugler (IRE) 48[5] (2m ½f, Asco, Y, Dec 18)
Major Rumpus 45[2] (2m, Leop, S, Feb 13, *M*)
Malaia (IRE) 33[1] (2m ½f, Stra, Hvy, Mar 5)
Mames Boy 27[1] (2m ½f, Ling, S, Jan 26)
Man For All Season (USA) 30[2] (2m 4½f, Chep, Hvy, Mar 12, *H*)
Man To Man (NZ) 40[4] (2m, Kemp, Y, Dec 27)
Maneree 33[2] (2m ½f, Hunt, S, Dec 1, *H*)
Manhattan Boy 30[3] (2m 4f, Plum, S, Oct 19, *H*)
Manhattan Castle (IRE) 31[5] (2m, Leop, S, Jan 8)
Marchwood 39[3] (2m 2f, Kels, S, Mar 4)
Marra's Roscoe 25[3] (2m 7½f, Chel, F, Oct 20, *H*)
Marros Mill 36[2] (2m, Utto, Hvy, Apr 2, *H*)
Marsh's Law 34[1] (2m 3½f, Mark, G, May 6, *H*)
Martha's Son 46[4] (2m ½f, Newb, G, Oct 22, *H*)
Masroug 26[2] (2m 2f, Font, G, Oct 27, *H*)
Master Of Troy 31[2] (2m 1f, Carl, S, Dec 30, *H*)
Mathal (USA) 40[1] (2m 1f, Taun, Y, Dec 9)
Mediane (USA) 35[3] (3m 4f, Nott, S, Dec 3, *H*)
Meditator 38[1] (2m 4½f, Chep, Hvy, Dec 4, *H*)
Mega Blue 34[6] (2m ½f, Donc, G, Jan 28, *G*)
Menebuck 49[1] (2m 6f, Font, G, Nov 9, *H*)
Merlins Wish (USA) 40[1] (2m 1f, Bang, G, May 14, *H*)
Merry Nutkin 39[2] (2m, Ayr, Y, Jan 3)
Miami Splash 40[3] (2m ½f, Newb, S, Jan 1, *H*)
Micks Delight (IRE) 35[3] (2m, Leop, S, Mar 6)
Middle Marker (IRE) 42[1] (2m ½f, Newb, G, Oct 22)
Midfielder 25[3] (2m 5f, Kemp, G, Oct 16, *H*)
Minella Lad 40[3] (3m ½f, Chel, G, Mar 17, *G*)
Miss Equilia (USA) 28[1] (2m, Winc, Y, Jan 13, *H*)
Missy-S (IRE) 36[1] (2m, Sout, F, May 21)
Mister Major 26[4] (2m 5½f, Nott, Hvy, Feb 1, *H*)
Mizyan (IRE) 31[3] (2m 3½f, Mark, Y, Dec 27, *H*)
Moat Garden (USA) 30[1] (2m 1½f, Mark, S, Nov 20)
Mohana 55[2] (2m 1f, Newt, Hvy, Dec 27, *H*)
Mole Board 74[4] (2m ½f, Chel, Y, Mar 15, *G*)
Monalee River (IRE) 59[2] (2m 4f, Live, Hvy, Apr 8, *G*)
Monday Club 42[3] (2m ½f, Hunt, Y, Nov 12, *H*)
Montagnard 32[2] (3m ½f, Newb, S, Dec 31, *H*)
Montpelier Lad 55[2] (2m 1f, Bang, G, Sep 11, *H*)
Monty Royale (IRE) 33[1] (2m, Ludl, S, Mar 3)
Moorish 52[2] (2m 1f, Chel, G, Mar 17, *G*)
Morceli (IRE) 57[1] (2m 2f, Kels, S, Mar 4)
Move A Minute (USA) 37[1] (2m, Towc, Y, Nov 11)
Moving Out 44[1] (2m, Wind, S, Mar 7, *H*)
Mr Flutts 26[3] (2m 4½f, Leic, S, Nov 30, *H*)
Mr Matt (IRE) 44[3] (2m 4f, Plum, Hvy, Jan 31, *H*)
Mr Pickpocket (IRE) 25[1] (2m, Leic, Hvy, Jan 3)
Mrs Mayhew (IRE) 28[4] (2m ½f, Hunt, Y, Nov 12, *H*)
Mubadir (USA) 58[2] (2m, Leop, F, Oct 25, *L*)
Mulciber 33[1] (2m, Winc, Hrd, May 6, *H*)
Muse 80[1] (2m, Kemp, S, Dec 28)
My Wizard 42[3] (2m, Kemp, Y, Dec 27)
Mysilv 51[1] (2m 1f, Chel, G, Mar 17, *G*)
Mystic Memory 31[2] (2m 4½f, Pert, F, May 19, *H*)
Nadjati (USA) 26[4] (2m 5f, Kemp, Hvy, Feb 25)
Nahar 64[4] (2m 1f, Chel, G, Mar 17, *G*)
Naiysari (IRE) 36[4] (2m, Utto, F, May 30, *H*)
Native Chieftan 41[2] (2m ½f, Newb, G, Oct 22)
Nawar (FR) 28[1] (2m, Leic, S, Nov 30)
Nazzaro 29[2] (2m 2f, Devo, S, Mar 23)
Ned The Hall (IRE) 26[3] (2m ½f, Stra, G, Oct 28)
Newton Point 38[1] (3m ½f, Chel, Y, Dec 10, *H*)
Nick The Dreamer 32[3] (2m 4½f, Chep, Hvy, Mar 12, *H*)
Night Wind 31[1] (2m, Winc, G, Oct 7, *H*)
Nijmegen 54 (2m 1f, Chel, G, Mar 17, *G*)
Nikitas 45[1] (2m ½f, Newb, S, Jan 1, *H*)
Nirvana Prince 41[2] (2m 4f, Donc, Y, Jan 29)
No Pain No Gain (IRE) 38[1] (2m ½f, Asco, G, Mar 30, *H*)
Noblely (USA) 39[2] (2m 1f, Bang, G, May 14, *H*)
Nocatchim 50[1] (2m ½f, Newb, Y, Mar 25, *H*)
Nodform Wonder 31 (2m ½f, Newc, G, Oct 20, *H*)
Northern Village 40[1] (2m 6f, Sand, G, Nov 6, *H*)
Northern Saddler 45[1] (2m, Warw, S, Dec 30, *H*)
Northern Squire 36[1] (2m 4½f, Carl, S, Mar 10)
Notable Exception 30[2] (2m 1½f, Sedg, S, Nov 9, *H*)
Oh So Risky 89[2] (2m ½f, Newb, S, Feb 12, *H*)
Olympian 57[3] (2m 6f, Sand, S, Feb 5, *H*)
Oneupmanship 34[2] (2m 4½f, Chep, Hvy, Dec 4, *H*)
Otter Bush 33[2] (2m, Weth, S, Apr 26)
Ourownfellow (IRE) 28[2] (2m 4f, Plum, Hvy, Feb 28)
Outset (IRE) 40[3] (2m ½f, Newc, G, Mar 19, *H*)
Overlord 32[1] (2m 1f, Taun, G, Apr 15)
Padashpan (USA) 66[2] (2m, Leop, S, Dec 29, *L*)
Palace Wolf (NZ) 25 (2m ½f, Hunt, Y, Nov 12, *H*)
Palacegate King 32[2] (2m 2f, Kels, Hvy, Mar 23, *H*)
Pamber Priory 26[2] (2m 5f, Towc, Y, Nov 11, *H*)
Paradise Navy 35[2] (2m, Leic, Hvy, Jan 24)
Peanuts Pet 52[1] (2m 4½f, Weth, Hvy, Mar 2, *H*)
Peatswood 60[3] (2m 5½f, Chel, Hvy, Jan 3)
Persian Halo (IRE) 34[3] (2m, Leop, S, Dec 29, *H*)
Persuasive 50[4] (2m, Weth, Y, Dec 4, *H*)
Pipers Copse 44[3] (2m 2f, Font, S, Oct 11, *H*)
Polishing 47[1] (3m, Newc, G, Mar 21, *H*)
Pondering 41[1] (2m 1½f, Folk, S, Dec 14)
Pontoon Bridge 27[1] (2m 2f, Font, F, May 30, *H*)
Pontynyswen 55[3] (2m ½f, Donc, G, Mar 5, *H*)
Powleyvale 32[1] (2m 4f, Hayd, S, Nov 18)
Precious Boy 68[1] (2m ½f, Sand, Y, Mar 12, *H*)
Prerogative 36[1] (2m ½f, Stra, S, Feb 5)
Pridwell 53[2] (2m ½f, Chel, Y, Mar 15)
Prime Of Life (IRE) 28[2] (2m, Warw, S, Feb 8)
Principal Player (USA) 26[2] (2m ½f, Pert, F, Apr 21)
Pyr Four 29[2] (2m, Leop, S, Dec 29, *H*)
Rafters 27[1] (2m, Weth, Hvy, Feb 5)
Ramallah 28[2] (2m ½f, Hunt, S, Jan 27)

Ramstar 27[2] (2m, Towc, Y, Nov 11)
Ratify 46[1] (2m ½f, Fake, S, Mar 18, *H*)
Red Marauder 27[2] (2m ½f, Newc, S, Dec 29)
Redeemyourself (IRE) 42[2] (2m ½f, Sand, Y, Mar 12)
Regal Aura (IRE) 25[1] (2m 1½f, Sedg, G, Oct 27)
Regal Romper (IRE) 27[1] (2m, Weth, Y, Apr 4, *H*)
Relkeel 44[2] (2m 5½f, Hunt, S, Feb 10)
Reluctant Suitor 49 (2m ½f, Chel, Y, Mar 15)
Res Ipsa Loquitur 45[1] (2m ½f, Stra, G, Jun 3, *H*)
Rich Life (IRE) 34[6] (2m ½f, Newc, G, Mar 19, *H*)
Rimouski 33[3] (3m ½f, Nott, S, Mar 1, *H*)
Rising Waters (IRE) 46[3] (2m, Leop, F, May 18, *H*)
Riva (NZ) 55[2] (2m ½f, Sand, Y, Mar 12, *H*)
River Lossie 49[1] (2m, Leic, Hvy, Feb 2)
Roc Color (FR) 36[1] (2m, Towc, Y, Oct 6, *H*)
Rosgill 45[3] (2m, Warw, G, Nov 16, *H*)
Roubabay (IRE) 40[3] (2m, Leop, S, Jan 8)
Routing 35[2] (2m, Warw, G, May 21, *H*)
Roxy River 30[1] (2m, Ludl, F, May 2)
Royal Derbi 74[3] (2m, Leop, S, Dec 29, *L*)
Royal Flamingo 36[1] (2m 4f, Plum, Hvy, Apr 2, *H*)
Royal Print (IRE) 37[1] (2m ½f, Stra, Y, Apr 16, *H*)
Royal Vacation 32[1] (2m 4½f, Carl, G, Oct 8)
Ruling Dynasty 25[4] (2m 2f, Font, G, Sep 27, *H*)
Rustino 29[1] (3m ½f, Nott, S, Mar 1, *H*)
Sailor Blue 28[2] (2m 1f, Newt, Hvy, Mar 28, *H*)
Saint Ciel (USA) 27[1] (2m, Utto, S, Feb 12, *H*)
Salman (USA) 28[4] (2m, Sout, Hrd, May 11, *H*)
Sand-Dollar 42[2] (2m, Utto, F, May 30, *H*)
Sansool 32[2] (3m, Hexh, Hvy, Apr 25, *H*)
Saskia's Hero 27[2] (2m ½f, Hunt, Y, Nov 12, *H*)
Satin Lover 67[2] (2m ½f, Asco, Y, Dec 18)
Saymore 30[5] (2m, Sout, Hrd, May 11, *H*)
Scobie Boy (IRE) 54[2] (2m ½f, Donc, G, Jan 28, *G*)
See Enough 48[1] (3m, Chep, Hvy, Feb 5)
Seekin Cash (USA) 58[1] (2m 5½f, Hunt, S, Feb 10)
Sendai 55[2] (2m 5½f, Nott, Hvy, Feb 1, *H*)
Sense Of Value 30[5] (2m, Leop, S, Dec 27, *M*)
Seon 47[5] (2m ½f, Newc, G, Nov 6, *H*)
Shaffic (FR) 37[1] (2m 4½f, Weth, G, Oct 29)
Shahgram (IRE) 32[2] (2m 1½f, Sedg, S, Feb 1)
Shamshom Al Arab (IRE) 28[3] (2m ½f, Newc, F, May 7, *H*)
Shanakee 28[2] (2m 1f, Plum, Hvy, Mar 21)
Shannon Glen 41[1] (2m 4f, Plum, Hvy, Feb 28, *H*)
Sharp Dance 27[1] (2m, Warw, F, May 7, *H*)
Sharp Invite 32[5] (2m, Leop, F, Oct 25, *L*)
Shawiya (IRE) 56 (2m ½f, Chel, Y, Mar 15, *G*)
Sheregori (IRE) 41[2] (2m, Leop, S, Mar 6)
Shirley's Delight (IRE) 45[3] (2m 1f, Chel, G, Mar 17, *G*)
Shu Fly (NZ) 32[3] (2m, Warw, G, Nov 27)
Shujan (USA) 53[1] (2m, Kemp, Y, Dec 27)
Sillars Stalker (IRE) 50[2] (3m ½f, Chel, Y, Dec 10, *H*)
Sillian 30[2] (2m ½f, Stra, G, Jun 3, *H*)
Silver Standard 28[1] (2m 2f, Font, Hvy, Jan 17)
Simone's Son (IRE) 26[3] (2m, Utto, F, May 30, *H*)
Simply (IRE) 27[2] (2m 4f, Plum, S, Dec 7)
Simpson 43[2] (2m, Leic, Y, Nov 15)
Slipmatic 26[2] (2m ½f, Sand, S, Feb 18)
Smiling Chief (IRE) 30[3] (2m, Winc, F, Nov 4, *H*)
Smuggler's Point (USA) 35[1] (2m ½f, Pert, F, Apr 21)
So Proud 52[2] (2m 5f, Chel, G, Mar 16, *H*)
Society Guest 29[3] (2m, Warw, S, Dec 30, *H*)
Soothfast (USA) 33[3] (2m, Towc, S, Mar 10, *H*)
Sound Reveille 31[4] (2m ½f, Sand, Y, Mar 12)
Southolt (IRE) 34[2] (2m, Weth, G, Nov 16)
Sparkling Sunset (IRE) 48[4] (2m 5f, Kemp, S, Jan 22)
Special Account 34[1] (2m 7½f, Chel, F, Oct 20, *H*)
Spread Your Wings (IRE) 25[1] (2m, Wind, S, Feb 19)
Spring Marathon (USA) 41[5] (2m 5f, Chel, G, Mar 16, *G*)
Spuffington 31[2] (2m 1½f, Folk, Hvy, Feb 23)
Squire Silk 54[1] (2m, Ludl, Y, Apr 6)
Squire York 30[2] (2m, Ludl, S, Mar 3)
Srivijaya 31[4] (2m ½f, Kels, G, Oct 2, *H*)
Star Of The Glen 51[2] (2m, Winc, G, Oct 7, *H*)
Starstreak 35[3] (2m 2f, Kels, S, Nov 11, *H*)
Staunch Friend (USA) 83[1] (2m 1f, Chel, Y, Dec 11)
Steel Dawn 55[3] (2m 1f, Chel, G, Mar 17, *G*)
Stingray City (USA) 26[3] (2m ½f, Kels, S, Nov 11, *H*)
Stoproveritate 25[2] (2m, Catt, G, Feb 12)
Storm Drum 30[1] (3m ½f, Utto, G, Sep 8, *H*)
Stormhead 54[1] (2m 4½f, Leic, Hvy, Jan 24, *H*)
Straldi (IRE) 49[2] (2m, Leop, S, Jan 8)
Strath Royal 64[1] (2m, Towc, G, May 27, *H*)
Strong Case (IRE) 31[3] (3m ½f, Utto, F, Jun 2, *H*)
Strong Medicine 40[3] (2m 6f, Font, G, Nov 9, *H*)
Style And Class 32[2] (2m 1½f, Devo, S, Oct 13, *H*)
Stylus 46[4] (2m, Hayd, Hvy, Dec 8, *H*)
Sukaab 37[4] (2m 6f, Sand, S, Mar 11, *H*)
Sun Surfer (FR) 39[3] (2m, Winc, Y, Mar 10, *H*)
Sunkala Shine 25[4] (2m, Catt, G, Feb 12)
Sunset And Vine 40[1] (2m ½f, Asco, G, Oct 30, *H*)
Super Coin 52[5] (2m ½f, Chel, Y, Mar 15)
Supreme Master 27[3] (2m ½f, Newb, S, Mar 5)
Sure Haven (IRE) 27[3] (2m, Wind, G, Dec 2)
Surrey Dancer 48[3] (2m ½f, Donc, G, Jan 28, *G*)
Sweet City 37[1] (2m 1f, Carl, S, Dec 30, *H*)
Sweet Duke (FR) 85[1] (2m 5½f, Chel, Hvy, Jan 3)
Sweet Glow (FR) 43[1] (3m, Asco, G, Mar 30, *G*)
Swift Conveyance (IRE) 32[2] (2m ½f, Donc, Y, Dec 11)
Sybillin 41[3] (2m, Hayd, Hvy, Jan 22)
Take The Buckskin 34[2] (2m 4f, Bang, G, Apr 16)
Talbot 36[2] (3m ½f, Nott, S, Mar 1, *H*)
Tapatch (IRE) 40[2] (2m, Catt, G, Dec 1, *H*)
Tarkovsky 29[2] (2m, Ludl, G, Oct 15, *H*)
Taroudant 56[5] (2m ½f, Sand, S, Dec 4, *G*)
Temple Knight 29[1] (2m, Worc, G, Mar 30, *H*)
Templemary Boy (IRE) 32[2] (2m, Leop, F, Nov 6)
Test Match 28[1] (2m, Utto, Hvy, Apr 2, *M*)
Texan Tycoon 45[1] (2m ½f, Asco, G, Oct 30)
Thatch And Gold (IRE) 46[2] (2m, Leop, Y, Dec 28, *H*)
The Bud Club (IRE) 35[3] (2m ½f, Ling, Y, Dec 11)
The Changeling (IRE) 25[3] (2m ½f, Ling, S, Jan 26)
The Frog Prince (IRE) 25[2] (2m, Nott, Hvy, Jan 25)
The Green Fool 29[5] (2m, Edin, F, Dec 6, *H*)
The Mrs 27[2] (2m 4½f, Leic, S, Nov 30, *H*)
The Real Article (IRE) 30[5] (2m, Leop, S, Feb 13, *M*)
The Shaughraun 40[1] (2m, Leop, S, Feb 13, *H*)
The Toaster 36[3] (2m, Leop, S, Feb 13, *M*)
Thumbs Up 58[4] (2m ½f, Newb, S, Feb 12, *H*)
Tiananmen Square (IRE) 53[2] (2m, Hayd, Hvy, Jan 22)
Time For A Run 76[1] (2m 5f, Chel, G, Mar 16, *H*)
Time For A Flutter 37[2] (2m, Worc, S, Nov 29)
Time It Right (IRE) 38[4] (2m, Leop, S, Dec 27, *M*)
Time Won't Wait (IRE) 26[1] (2m 1f, Newt, G, May 13)
Tip It In 28[1] (2m, Catt, G, Dec 1, *H*)
Tissisat (USA) 37[1] (2m, Worc, S, Nov 29)
Too Sharp 25[2] (2m 1f, Here, Y, Apr 4)
Toogood To Be True 45[1] (2m 2f, Kels, S, Nov 11, *H*)
Top Spin 54[2] (2m 5f, Kemp, S, Jan 22)
Top Wave 40[1] (2m 1½f, Folk, S, Jan 18, *H*)
Tothewoods 40[4] (2m, Ludl, Y, Apr 6)
Triple Witching 62[1] (2m 4½f, Chep, Y, Nov 6, *H*)
Tronchetto (IRE) 26[2] (3m ½f, Ayr, G, Nov 12, *H*)
Tropical Lake (IRE) 52[1] (2m ½f, Live, S, Apr 7, *G*)
Trying Again 32[1] (2m 1f, Taun, S, Dec 30)
Tusky 41[1] (2m 4f, Bang, G, Apr 16)
Uncle Ernie 39[6] (2m, Weth, Y, Dec 4, *H*)
Va Utu 32[3] (2m 1½f, Devo, G, Sep 28, *H*)
Vagador (CAN) 36[4] (2m 2f, Font, S, Nov 30, *H*)
Valfinet (FR) 43[1] (2m, Winc, S, Feb 24, *G*)
Valiant Dash 25[1] (2m 4½f, Pert, F, May 19, *H*)
Vanart 26[3] (2m, Catt, G, Mar 9)
Vasiliev 32[3] (2m, Nott, Hvy, Jan 25)
Viardot (IRE) 56[1] (2m 6f, Sand, S, Mar 11, *H*)
Victor Bravo (NZ) 42[1] (3m ½f, Chel, G, Apr 20, *H*)
Warm Spell 41[2] (2m ½f, Newb, Y, Mar 26, *H*)
Weaver George (IRE) 27[2] (2m ½f, Newc, G, Mar 19, *H*)
Wee Wizard (IRE) 32[2] (2m, Hayd, Hvy, Dec 8, *H*)
Welsh Lustre (IRE) 31[4] (2m 5f, Newb, Y, Mar 26, *H*)
Welshman 51[3] (2m ½f, Live, G, Nov 20, *H*)
Westholme (USA) 49[1] (2m ½f, Donc, Y, Dec 11)
What A Question (IRE) 41[6] (2m 5f, Chel, G, Mar 16, *G*)
Whippers Delight (IRE) 29[2] (2m ½f, Newb, Y, Mar 25, *H*)
White Willow 34[1] (2m 1½f, Sedg, S, Feb 1)
Whitechapel (USA) 41[1] (2m ½f, Chep, Hvy, Mar 19)
Who's Tef (IRE) 44[3] (2m 1f, Chel, G, Apr 20, *H*)
Wick Pound 26[2] (2m 6f, Sand, S, Dec 4, *H*)
Wild Strawberry 27[2] (2m ½f, Chel, Hrd, Sep 29)
Willie Sparkle 37[3] (2m ½f, Newc, G, Oct 20, *H*)
Willsford 35[5] (2m 5½f, Nott, Hvy, Feb 1, *H*)

Winnie The Witch 30² (2m, Warw, G, Nov 27)
Winter Belle (USA) 47 (2m ½f, Chel, Y, Mar 15)
Winter Forest (USA) 56² (2m ½f, Asco, G, Apr 26, *H*)
World Without End (USA) 25¹ (2m 5½f, Worc, S, Nov 10)
Yaheeb (USA) 39⁴ (2m 1f, Carl, S, Dec 30, *H*)
Zamirah (IRE) 43¹ (2m ½f, Hunt, S, Dec 27, *H*)
Zealous Kitten (USA) 33² (2m ½f, Fake, S, Mar 18, *H*)

CHASERS

Able Player (USA) 26² (2m 1f, Kels, Hvy, Mar 23)
Abu Muslab 25¹ (2m ½f, Taun, G, Oct 14)
Al Hashimi 52³ (3m 2f, Devo, G, Nov 2, *G*)
Alan Ball 27³ (2m 1½f, Mark, S, Mar 11, *H*)
Algari 36³ (2m 4½f, Pert, G, May 11, *H*)
Alkinor Rex 53¹ (2m, Plum, Y, Oct 4, *H*)
All The Aces 34¹ (2m 5f, Leop, Hvy, Mar 6)
Allezmoss 41³ (2m 6f, Live, Hvy, Apr 8)
Always Remember 32¹ (2m 4½f, Worc, F, May 31)
Among Friends 26⁴ (2m 4½f, Hunt, F, Aug 30, *H*)
Amtrak Express 44¹ (2m 1f, Newb, G, Oct 22)
Andermatt 37¹ (2m 5½f, Nott, Hvy, Mar 22)
Another Excuse (IRE) 33¹ (2m 5f, Wind, S, Mar 7)
Antonin (FR) 73² (3m 5½f, Sand, Y, Apr 23, *G*)
Ardbrin 46⁴ (2m ½f, Hunt, G, Oct 23, *H*)
Ardcroney Chief 38¹ (2m 5½f, Fake, S, Mar 18, *H*)
Armagret 63² (2m 4½f, Weth, G, Oct 13, *H*)
Around The Horn 53¹ (2m, Ayr, G, Apr 15, *H*)
Astings (FR) 28¹ (2m 4f, Mark, S, Dec 17, *H*)
Atlaal 49¹ (2m ½f, Hunt, G, Oct 23, *H*)
Atone 60⁴ (2m, Chel, Y, Mar 15, *G*)
Auction Law (NZ) 46¹ (3m 1½f, Winc, S, Jan 13, *H*)
Avonburn (NZ) 43² (3m, Donc, G, Jan 29, *H*)
Bad Trade 29⁴ (2m 5f, Sedg, Y, Jan 26, *H*)
Bally Parson 27¹ (2m 4f, Ludl, S, Mar 3)
Baltic Brown 29² (2m 6½f, Mark, S, Jan 22, *H*)
Barely Black 26¹ (2m 4½f, Worc, Hvy, Dec 8)
Barkisland 28³ (2m, Nott, S, Nov 25, *H*)
Barton Bank 90¹ (3m, Kemp, Y, Dec 27, *G*)
Bas de Laine (FR) 39³ (2m 4½f, Sand, S, Feb 5)
Basilicus (FR) 27¹ (2m 1f, Kels, Hvy, Mar 23)
Baydon Star 65² (2m, Chel, Y, Mar 15, *G*)
Beachy Head 51¹ (2m 4½f, Carl, S, Mar 10)
Beaucadeau 37² (2m 1½f, Cart, F, May 25, *H*)
Beldine 27¹ (2m ½f, Hexh, G, Apr 30, *H*)
Bellton 36² (2m, Weth, G, Oct 13)
Belstone Fox 44¹ (2m, Sout, S, Oct 4, *H*)
Belvederian 58² (2m 3f, Leop, S, Jan 23, *L*)
Better Times Ahead 41¹ (2m 4½f, Bang, Y, Oct 29, *H*)
Betty Hayes 33¹ (3m 1½f, Plum, Hvy, Mar 21, *H*)
Bibendum 49¹ (2m 5f, Winc, G, Nov 4, *H*)
Big Beat (USA) 54¹ (2m 2f, Devo, Y, Dec 3)
Big Matt (IRE) 32¹ (2m 1f, Newb, S, Dec 31)
Billy Bathgate 61¹ (2m, Asco, Y, Dec 18, *H*)
Bishops Island 54¹ (3m ½f, Bang, S, Mar 9, *H*)
Black Humour 80¹ (3m, Wind, S, Feb 19)
Blitzkreig 27⁴ (2m 1f, Leop, Y, Dec 27, *H*)
Bluff Knoll 34⁴ (3m 1f, Kels, Y, Oct 16, *H*)
Blustery Fellow 30² (2m 4f, Ludl, G, Oct 7, *H*)
Boarding School 31⁴ (2m 3½f, Donc, G, Mar 5, *H*)
Bob Devani 30³ (2m 1f, Leop, Y, Dec 27, *H*)
Bobby Socks 36³ (3m 1½f, Here, F, May 11, *H*)
Bold Choice 25² (2m ½f, Newt, Hvy, Apr 2, *H*)
Boll Weevil 32¹ (2m 5f, Utto, G, Nov 4, *H*)
Bollinger 32² (3m, Stra, S, Feb 5)
Bonanza 41³ (2m 5f, Sedg, Y, Jan 26, *H*)
Bonsai Bud 52² (3m 1½f, Winc, G, Nov 4, *H*)
Born Deep 27³ (2m 5f, Cop, Hvy, Mar 6)
Boro Smackeroo 27⁵ (2m, Weth, Y, Nov 16, *H*)
Boscean Chieftain 64¹ (2m 4½f, Warw, G, May 7)
Boston Rover 45² (2m ½f, Towc, S, Dec 4, *H*)
Boutzdaroff 64³ (2m, Weth, Y, Nov 16, *H*)
Bowl Of Oats 32² (3m, Leic, S, Nov 30, *H*)
Brackenfield 43¹ (2m 4f, Mark, Hvy, Apr 4)
Bradbury Star 90² (2m, Kemp, Y, Dec 27, *G*)
Briggs Builders 27² (2m, Kemp, S, Jan 21, *H*)
Brockley Court 59² (2m 1f, Leop, Y, Dec 26, *L*)
Broughton Manor 48³ (2m ½f, Taun, S, Mar 3, *H*)
Brown Windsor 42² (2m 6f, Live, Hvy, Apr 8)
Buck Willow 48² (3m 2½f, Chel, G, Apr 20, *H*)

Buckboard Bounce 46² (3m, Leop, S, Jan 23, *L*)
Bucks-Choice 49³ (2m 3f, Leop, S, Jan 23, *L*)
Cab On Target 80² (3m ½f, Weth, G, Oct 30)
Cabochon 42¹ (2m, Ling, Hvy, Jan 26)
Cahervillahow 74² (3m 2½f, Newb, G, Nov 27, *G*)
Callmecha 49³ (4m 2f, Utto, Hvy, Mar 19, *G*)
Cambo (USA) 26³ (2m, Folk, S, Jan 18)
Camelot Knight 32² (3m ½f, Bang, S, Oct 9, *H*)
Campsea-Ash 46² (2m, Weth, Y, Nov 16, *H*)
Canoscan 39¹ (2m 5f, Folk, Y, Dec 14)
Capability Brown 56⁴ (2m 7f, Worc, G, Mar 30, *H*)
Captain Brandy 48³ (3m, Leop, S, Mar 17, *H*)
Captain Frisk 43¹ (3m 5f, Warw, S, Mar 3, *H*)
Carbisdale 29¹ (3m, Donc, G, Jan 29, *H*)
Castle Diamond 40¹ (2m, Here, S, Mar 5)
Catch The Cross 27⁵ (2m 4½f, Sand, S, Feb 17, *H*)
Centenary Star 35¹ (2m 4½f, Weth, S, Apr 26, *H*)
Chain Shot 33² (2m, Ludl, Y, Nov 18, *H*)
Change The Act 28² (2m 5f, Newt, S, Mar 16, *H*)
Chatam (USA) 71⁴ (3m, Leop, S, Feb 13, *L*)
Chiasso Forte (ITY) 35³ (2m 4½f, Hunt, Y, Dec 1, *H*)
Chic And Elite 45⁴ (2m 1f, Leop, Y, Dec 26, *L*)
Chichell's Hurst 25² (2m 4½f, Worc, G, Oct 23)
Chirkpar 65¹ (2m 1f, Leop, Y, Dec 26, *L*)
Choice Challange 29² (3m, Pert, G, Apr 20, *H*)
City Kid 48² (2m 6f, Towc, Y, Nov 11, *H*)
Clares Own 36² (2m 1f, Sedg, F, May 18, *H*)
Classic Contact 39¹ (2m 5f, Sedg, G, Oct 27)
Clay County 66¹ (2m ½f, Newc, Y, Nov 30, *H*)
Clyde Ranger 46² (2m 4½f, Carl, S, Mar 10)
Cogent 71¹ (3m 2½f, Newb, G, Nov 27, *G*)
Comedy Road 31¹ (2m 7f, Worc, G, Apr 23, *H*)
Commercial Artist 28⁵ (2m 5f, Leop, Hvy, Mar 6, *H*)
Congregation 29¹ (2m 3f, Devo, S, Oct 13)
Coole Dodger 31⁴ (2m 5f, Newc, Y, Nov 18, *H*)
Coonawara 65¹ (2m ½f, Chep, Hvy, Feb 5)
Copper Mine 41¹ (2m 7f, Worc, G, Aug 9, *H*)
Cornet 39³ (3m, Pert, G, Apr 20, *H*)
Corrarder 40¹ (2m 5½f, Cart, F, May 30, *H*)
Couldnt Be Better 41² (2m 4½f, Ling, Hvy, Mar 19)
Coulton 45¹ (2m, Weth, G, Oct 13)
Country Lad (IRE) 48¹ (2m, Nott, S, Feb 19, *G*)
Crafty Chaplain 25¹ (2m, Utto, G, Apr 30)
Cross Cannon 35² (2m 5f, Sedg, G, Oct 27, *H*)
Crosula 31² (2m 5f, Newt, G, Apr 20, *H*)
Crystal Bear (NZ) 42¹ (2m 4f, Stra, Hvy, Mar 5, *H*)
Crystal Spirit 59² (2m 4½f, Sand, S, Feb 5)
Current Express 55¹ (2m, Kemp, Y, Jan 22)
Cyphrate (USA) 55 (2m, Sand, S, Dec 4, *G*)
Cythere 34⁴ (4m 2f, Utto, Hvy, Mar 19, *G*)
Dakyns Boy 49⁴ (3m ½f, Asco, G, Oct 30, *H*)
Davy Blake 35¹ (3m 1f, Kels, Hvy, Mar 4)
Dawson City 42² (2m 4½f, Weth, G, Oct 30, *H*)
Deadly Charm (USA) 27¹ (2m 4½f, Sand, Y, Dec 3, *H*)
Deep Bramble 80² (3m, Leop, S, Feb 13, *L*)
Deep Dark Dawn 33⁴ (2m ½f, Hunt, F, May 30, *H*)
Deep Sensation 85² (2m, Kemp, S, Feb 26)
Dextra Dove 33² (2m, Folk, S, Feb 23, *H*)
Diamond Fort 32³ (3m 1½f, Here, Y, Apr 9, *H*)
Dis Train 52¹ (2m 5f, Newt, S, Oct 5, *H*)
Do Be Brief 37¹ (2m 7f, Worc, S, Nov 10, *H*)
Docklands Express 75³ (3m 2f, Donc, Y, Dec 11, *H*)
Dolikos 40¹ (2m 4½f, Hunt, Y, Dec 1, *H*)
Don't Light Up 25² (3m 2½f, Newt, S, Nov 16, *H*)
Doradus 29² (2m 1f, Sedg, G, Apr 12)
Double Silk 46¹ (3m 2½f, Chel, G, Mar 17)
Down The Road 33² (2m 4½f, Pert, G, May 11, *H*)
Dr Rocket 37² (2m, Warw, S, Jan 8, *H*)
Dragons Den 34¹ (2m 5½f, Stra, Y, Oct 16, *H*)
Driving Force 41¹ (2m ½f, Hunt, F, May 30, *H*)
Drumstick 56¹ (2m ½f, Chel, G, Apr 27, *H*)
Dubacilla 49² (2m 7f, Worc, S, Nov 10, *H*)
Dublin Flyer 63² (2m 4½f, Chel, G, Mar 16, *H*)
Duo Drom 28¹ (2m 4½f, Hunt, S, Jan 27, *H*)
Durham Sunset 29² (3m 1f, Ayr, G, Apr 16)
Earth Summit 45¹ (2m 5f, Chel, Hvy, Jan 3)
Easy Buck 44¹ (2m, Wind, G, Nov 13)
Ebony Jane 48⁴ (3m, Leop, S, Jan 23, *L*)
Egypt Mill Prince 69¹ (2m, Winc, S, Jan 28, *H*)
Elfast 69¹ (2m 4½f, Chel, G, Mar 16, *H*)
Emsee-H 42³ (2m, Kemp, G, Oct 16, *H*)

Errant Knight 48[1] (2m 4½f, Worc, Y, Apr 13, *H*)
Esha Ness 41[4] (2m 5f, Winc, S, Mar 10, *H*)
Espy 29[6] (3m ½f, Asco, G, Oct 30, *H*)
Explosive Speed (USA) 35[1] (2m 1f, Sedg, G, Apr 12)
Fabricator 58[1] (2m 1f, Leop, Hvy, Jan 8)
Fantasy World 32[3] (2m, Kemp, S, Dec 28)
Fantus 38[2] (3m, Kemp, S, Feb 25)
Far Senior 51[6] (3m 2½f, Chel, G, Apr 20, *H*)
Fardross 32[5] (2m 3½f, Donc, G, Mar 5, *H*)
Fastbit 32[1] (2m ½f, Hunt, G, Sep 17, *C*)
Festival Dreams 33[3] (2m 4½f, Ling, Hvy, Mar 19)
Fighting Words 60[1] (3m, Kemp, S, Dec 28, *H*)
File Concord 48[2] (2m 4½f, Leic, Hvy, Dec 31, *H*)
Flashing Steel 77[4] (3m 2½f, Chel, G, Mar 17, *G*)
Force Seven 69[3] (3m, Leop, S, Feb 13, *L*)
Forest Sun 58[2] (2m 4f, Newb, S, Mar 5, *H*)
Fourth Of July 44[4] (2m 4½f, Chel, G, Mar 16, *H*)
Fragrant Dawn 68[1] (2m 5f, Chel, Y, Dec 11, *H*)
Fred Splendid 27[3] (2m, Folk, S, Feb 23, *H*)
Freeline Finishing 66[3] (2m 5f, Chel, Y, Dec 11, *H*)
French Charmer 42[1] (2m 5f, Newt, G, Apr 20, *H*)
Frickley 33[1] (2m, Catt, G, Dec 1)
Friends Of Gerald 42[1] (2m 3f, Leop, S, Dec 29)
Front Line 47[2] (2m, Nott, S, Feb 19, *G*)
Front Street 30[2] (2m 1f, Newb, S, Dec 31)
Full O'Praise (NZ) 36[1] (2m ½f, Newc, G, Mar 19)
Furry Star 35[5] (2m 1f, Leop, Hvy, Jan 8)
Gaelic Frolic 30[2] (2m 5½f, Stra, Y, Oct 16, *H*)
Galagames (USA) 30[2] (2m ½f, Taun, S, Mar 3, *H*)
Galaxy High 34[2] (2m, Plum, S, Dec 7)
Gale Again 65[1] (2m 5f, Chel, G, Apr 27, *G*)
Gallant Effort (IRE) 31[2] (2m 5f, Folk, S, Feb 16, *H*)
Gallateen 36[2] (2m, Ayr, Y, Jan 3)
Gandouge Glen 30[2] (2m 3f, Font, S, Oct 11)
Garrison Savannah 72[2] (2m 5f, Chel, F, Oct 20, *H*)
General Idea 71[4] (3m, Leop, Hvy, Dec 28, *L*)
General James 26[2] (2m, Kemp, G, Oct 16, *H*)
General Pershing 71[1] (3m ½f, Weth, S, Dec 27, *H*)
Ghia Gneuiagh 33[2] (2m, Chel, S, Nov 13)
Ghofar 34[2] (2m 5f, Newt, G, May 13, *H*)
Gilston Lass 31[2] (3m 1½f, Here, F, Apr 30, *H*)
Ginger Tristan 29[2] (2m 4½f, Sand, Y, Mar 11)
Glemot (IRE) 32[4] (2m ½f, Newc, S, Dec 29, *G*)
Glenbrook D'Or 45[1] (4m 2f, Utto, Hvy, Mar 19, *G*)
Glenshane Lad 47[1] (3m, Pert, G, Apr 20, *H*)
Glove Puppet 35[2] (3m 1½f, Here, F, May 11, *H*)
Gnome's Tycoon 50[3] (3m, Donc, G, Jan 29, *H*)
Golden Isle 27[2] (2m ½f, Newc, G, Mar 19)
Good For A Laugh 49[1] (2m ½f, Donc, G, Jan 29, *H*)
Good For A Loan 26[1] (2m, Ludl, G, Dec 6)
Grange Brake 59[1] (3m 2½f, Chel, G, Apr 20, *H*)
Grazember 27[1] (2m 1f, Sedg, F, May 5, *H*)
Greek Flutter 35[2] (2m, Weth, G, May 4, *H*)
Green Island (USA) 35[2] (2m 3f, Devo, G, Sep 28, *H*)
Greenhill Raffles 39[1] (2m 4f, Ludl, G, Apr 22, *H*)
Guiburn's Nephew 44[3] (2m 4f, Newb, S, Mar 5, *H*)
Guildway 26[1] (2m 4½f, Hunt, F, May 11, *H*)
Gymcrak Stardom 26[1] (2m, Catt, Y, Feb 12)
Handsome Ned 27[2] (2m, Plum, Hvy, Mar 21)
Hangover 29[2] (2m, Plum, S, Feb 28)
He Who Dares Wins 29[3] (3m 1f, Ayr, S, Feb 12, *H*)
Hearts Are Wild 40[1] (2m 4f, Ludl, Y, Nov 18)
High Padre 45[1] (3m 3f, Sedg, S, Nov 9, *H*)
High Peak 43[1] (3m, Leop, S, Jan 23, *L*)
Highland Poacher 25[2] (2m, Here, S, Mar 5)
Hillwalk 34[1] (3m, Stra, S, Mar 24)
Honest Word 41[1] (3m, Kemp, S, Feb 25)
Hops And Pops 37[4] (2m, Nott, S, Feb 19, *G*)
Hot Pursuit 29[2] (2m 1f, Sedg, F, May 5, *H*)
Howaryadoon 33[2] (2m 4½f, Worc, S, Nov 29, *H*)
Howe Street 44[1] (2m 4f, Newc, G, Oct 20, *H*)
In The Navy 47[2] (2m ½f, Chep, Hvy, Feb 5)
Indian Tonic 49[1] (3m 3f 30yds, Live, S, Nov 20, *H*)
Island Gale 27[1] (3m 1f, Kels, Hvy, Jan 12, *H*)
Island Jetsetter 35[2] (2m, Nott, S, Nov 25, *H*)
Issyin 36[2] (2m ½f, Donc, G, Jan 28)
Its A Cracker 48[5] (3m, Leop, Hvy, Dec 28, *L*)
Its Nearly Time 45[1] (2m 1½f, Stra, S, Dec 29, *H*)
Jailbreaker 31[2] (2m 5f, Newt, Hvy, Apr 4, *H*)
James The First 33[2] (2m, Here, G, Nov 17)
Jimmy The Gillie 49[2] (2m, Live, S, Apr 7, *G*)
Jinxy Jack 51[1] (2m, Pert, G, Apr 21, *H*)
Jodami 92[3] (3m, Hayd, S, Jan 22, *H*)
Joe White 28[5] (3m, Leop, S, Mar 17, *H*)
Jumbeau 38[1] (2m 4½f, Bang, S, Nov 26, *H*)
Just Frankie 51[1] (2m, Weth, Y, Nov 16, *H*)
Just So 37[1] (3m 5½f, Chep, Hvy, Feb 5, *H*)
Kalanski 45[1] (2m 5f, Newt, Hvy, Dec 27)
Kambalda Rambler 33[1] (2m, Carl, S, Apr 2, *H*)
Katabatic 46[5] (2m, Chel, G, Mar 16, *G*)
Keep Talking 36[2] (3m ½f, Bang, G, Apr 16, *H*)
Kentish Piper 53[2] (2m 6f, Live, S, Apr 7, *H*)
Kibreet 38[2] (2m ½f, Towc, S, Apr 19, *H*)
Killeshin 44[1] (2m 6f, Live, Hvy, Apr 8)
Killula Chief 33[1] (3m 1f, Ayr, S, Feb 12, *H*)
Kind'a Smart 46[1] (2m 3½f, Donc, G, Mar 5, *H*)
King Of The Lot 82[1] (2m, Chel, Y, Nov 12, *H*)
Kings Fountain 49[3] (2m 5f, Winc, G, Oct 21, *G*)
Kirsty's Boy 31[4] (2m 4½f, Pert, F, Aug 20, *H*)
Kiwi Velocity (NZ) 29[2] (2m 5f, Newt, Hvy, Dec 27)
Knight Oil 31[2] (3m 1f, Towc, Y, Oct 6, *H*)
Kushbaloo 37[2] (2m 4f, Ayr, Y, Nov 13, *H*)
L'uomo Piu 36[1] (2m ½f, Taun, S, Mar 3, *H*)
Lackendara 46[1] (2m, Asco, Y, Feb 9)
Lady Bar 43[2] (3m, Leop, S, Mar 17, *H*)
Lady Ghislaine (FR) 34[1] (2m 2f, Plum, Hvy, Apr 2, *H*)
Lake Mission 40[1] (2m 4f, Ludl, G, Oct 7, *H*)
Lasata 46[1] (2m 1f, Leop, Y, Dec 27, *H*)
Last 'O' The Bunch 63[1] (2m, Hayd, Hvy, Dec 8, *H*)
Latent Talent 71[2] (3m ½f, Asco, Y, Dec 18, *H*)
Light Veneer 52[4] (3m 1½f, Chel, Y, Dec 10, *H*)
Little Tom 31[1] (2m 5f, Plum, G, Nov 1, *H*)
Lo Stregone 37[2] (2m 5f, Chel, Hvy, Jan 3)
Logamimo 46[1] (2m 1f, Sedg, G, Oct 12, *H*)
Lord Relic (NZ) 66[1] (2m 4½f, Ling, Hvy, Feb 4)
Los Buccaneros 31[2] (2m 4½f, Sand, S, Feb 18)
Lucky Again 25 (2m, Warw, F, Oct 30, *H*)
Lucky Lane 28[2] (2m 7½f, Devo, Hvy, Jan 3)
Lusty Light 32[2] (2m 3f, Devo, S, Oct 13)
M I Babe 34[2] (2m 3f, Here, F, May 30, *H*)
Magic Soldier 25[3] (2m ½f, Hunt, G, Sep 17, *C*)
Mailcom 59[2] (3m ½f, Asco, Y, Feb 9, *G*)
Major Match (NZ) 26[3] (2m 5f, Newt, S, Oct 5, *H*)
Man From Mars 25[1] (2m 2f, Font, G, Oct 27, *H*)
Man Of Mystery 35[4] (2m ½f, Chel, G, Apr 27, *H*)
Mandika 27[4] (2m 4½f, Hunt, G, Nov 12)
Marlingford 31[2] (2m 5f, Sedg, Y, Nov 19)
Martha's Son 41[1] (2m ½f, Hunt, S, Mar 16)
Martomick 62[2] (2m 4½f, Warw, G, May 7)
Master Jolson 34[2] (3m, Ludl, Y, Jan 19, *H*)
Master Oats 51[2] (3m 1½f, Winc, S, Jan 13, *H*)
Master Salesman 28[2] (2m 1½f, Cart, F, May 28, *H*)
Maudlins Cross 44[2] (2m 1f, Sedg, Y, Feb 1, *H*)
Mega Blue 36[2] (2m ½f, Donc, G, Dec 10, *H*)
Menebuck 34[1] (2m 4½f, Warw, Y, Dec 13, *H*)
Merapi 25[2] (2m 5f, Leop, Hvy, Mar 6, *H*)
Merry Master 33[6] (3m 2½f, Newb, G, Nov 27, *G*)
Midfielder 25[1] (2m 4f, Stra, S, Mar 24, *H*)
Midnight Caller 41[1] (3m 2½f, Newt, S, Nov 16, *H*)
Miinnehoma 78[1] (2m 4f, Newb, S, Mar 5, *H*)
Military Honour 37[2] (2m, Carl, S, Apr 2, *H*)
Military Secret 33[2] (3m 3f, Sedg, S, Nov 9, *H*)
Mine's An Ace (NZ) 41[2] (2m ½f, Newt, G, May 3)
Miss Fern 27[2] (3m 1½f, Here, Y, Apr 4, *H*)
Mister Ed 53[3] (3m 3f 30yds, Live, S, Nov 20, *H*)
Mister Oddy 32[3] (2m, Plum, S, Feb 28)
Monsieur Le Cure 42[1] (2m 5f, Chel, Hvy, Jan 29, *H*)
Moorcroft Boy 36[1] (4m 1f, Chel, Hvy, Jan 3, *H*)
Morley Street 35 (2m 4½f, Chel, S, Nov 13, *H*)
Mossy Fern 49[1] (3m ½f, Bang, S, Oct 9, *H*)
Mr Boston 61[2] (3m ½f, Weth, S, Dec 27, *H*)
Mr Jamboree 34[2] (2m 4½f, Hunt, S, Jan 27, *H*)
Mr Matt (IRE) 32[2] (3m, Stra, S, Apr 16)
Mr Sunbeam 25[3] (2m 3½f, Devo, G, Oct 22)
Mr Woodcock 27[1] (2m 4f, Mark, S, Nov 20)
Mr-Paw 29[1] (2m 4½f, Hunt, F, Aug 30, *H*)
Mubadir (USA) 45[5] (2m, Chel, Y, Mar 15, *G*)
Mudahim 41[1] (3m, Newb, S, Dec 31)
Mulbank 52[2] (2m, Sand, G, Mar 29, *H*)
Murphy 39 (2m, Warw, F, Oct 30, *H*)
Musthaveaswig 42[2] (2m 4½f, Worc, S, Oct 9, *H*)
My Young Man 56[3] (2m, Live, Hvy, Apr 9, *G*)

NATIONAL HUNT SPEED RATINGS 1993-94

Nakir (FR) 73[1] (2m, Chel, Y, Mar 15, *G*)
Nathir (USA) 31[1] (2m, Plum, S, Jan 31, *H*)
Native Mission 53[1] (2m, Nott, S, Nov 13)
Native Pride 27[6] (3m 1f, Chel, Y, Nov 12, *H*)
Nearco Bay (NZ) 51[1] (3m 1½f, Here, F, May 11, *H*)
Needs Must 27[4] (2m ½f, Newt, G, May 3)
Nevada Gold 55[6] (3m, Kemp, Y, Dec 27, *G*)
New Ghost 28[2] (3m, Wind, S, Feb 2)
New Halen 32[2] (2m 4f, Ludl, S, Dec 22, *H*)
Newlands-General 35[2] (2m ½f, Hunt, S, Feb 10)
Nickle Joe 26[1] (2m 3½f, Chep, Hvy, Mar 19)
Nicklup 30[1] (2m, Winc, S, Jan 13, *H*)
Northern Jinks 38[1] (2m, Kemp, S, Jan 21, *H*)
Northern Squire 25[2] (2m 5f, Sedg, G, Oct 27)
Nos Na Gaoithe 29[2] (2m, Wind, S, Feb 19, *H*)
Oh So Grumpy 43[4] (2m 1f, Leop, Hvy, Jan 8)
Old Eros 35[1] (2m 1f, Kels, Y, Nov 11, *H*)
On The Other Hand 31[2] (3m, Newc, G, Oct 20, *H*)
One For The Pot 44[2] (2m ½f, Hexh, S, Oct 14, *H*)
One Man (IRE) 62[1] (3m ½f, Asco, Y, Feb 9, *G*)
One More Dream 39[1] (2m, Sand, G, Nov 6)
Padaventure 35[1] (3m 1f, Kels, Y, Oct 16, *H*)
Palace Wolf (NZ) 26[3] (2m ½f, Newt, G, May 3)
Palm Reader 29[4] (2m 1f, Newb, S, Mar 4, *H*)
Panto Prince 60[1] (2m 5f, Winc, G, Oct 21, *G*)
Party Politics 75[1] (3m, Chep, Hvy, Dec 4, *H*)
Pat's Jester 56[4] (3m ½f, Weth, G, Oct 30)
Peace Officer 42[1] (2m 4½f, Worc, G, Mar 30, *H*)
Peaceman 46[1] (2m, Ludl, S, Apr 6)
Persian House 48[1] (2m 4½f, Hexh, S, Nov 5, *H*)
Persian Sword 36[1] (2m, Warw, G, Nov 16)
Philip's Woody 32[1] (2m, Plum, S, Feb 28)
Pims Quarter (IRE) 28[2] (2m 4½f, Weth, S, Apr 26, *H*)
Piper O'Drummond 27[1] (3m, Leic, S, Nov 30, *H*)
Political Tower 36[1] (2m, Ayr, S, Jan 20, *H*)
Portonia 47[1] (3m 4f, Sedg, G, Mar 8, *H*)
Positive Action 36[5] (2m, Warw, F, Oct 30, *H*)
Postman's Path 38[1] (2m 6f, Towc, Y, Nov 11, *H*)
Precipice Run 34[1] (2m, Ayr, Y, Apr 14)
Private Audition 37[2] (2m, Folk, S, Mar 9, *H*)
Propero 34[2] (2m, Folk, S, Jan 18)
Prudent Peggy 25[2] (2m, Winc, S, Jan 13, *H*)
Purbeck Dove 30[1] (3m 1½f, Plum, Y, Nov 15, *H*)
Raba Riba 40[1] (2m 4f, Ludl, G, Mar 25)
Radical Lady 36[3] (3m 3f, Sedg, S, Nov 9, *H*)
Rafiki 28[1] (2m 3½f, Chep, Hvy, Jan 25, *H*)
Rakaia River (NZ) 29[1] (3m, Wind, S, Feb 2)
Rathvinden House (USA) 34[2] (3m 2½f, Newb, S, Jan 1, *H*)
Raymylette 48[1] (2m 4½f, Leic, Hvy, Jan 24)
Rejoinus 41[1] (2m ½f, Towc, S, Dec 4, *H*)
Remittance Man 89[1] (2m, Kemp, S, Feb 26)
Richard Hunt 26[1] (3m ½f, Asco, G, Mar 30)
Richville 45[1] (2m 4½f, Ling, S, Dec 11, *H*)
River Bounty 49[5] (2m 4½f, Chel, S, Nov 13, *H*)
River Mandate 36[2] (2m 5½f, Nott, Hvy, Mar 22)
River Pearl 42[1] (2m 4½f, Pert, G, May 11, *H*)
Riverside Boy 68[2] (3m, Chep, Hvy, Dec 4, *G*)
Road To Fame 32[3] (2m 4½f, Hunt, G, Nov 12)
Roc Color (FR) 27[1] (2m, Plum, S, Dec 7)
Roc de Prince (FR) 48[3] (3m 5f, Warw, S, Feb 8, *H*)
Rodeo Star (USA) 45[1] (2m, Ayr, S, Jan 3)
Ross Venture 33[3] (2m 4f, Ayr, Y, Nov 13, *H*)
Rough Quest 47[2] (2m 5f, Winc, S, Mar 10, *H*)
Rouyan 33[1] (3m, Stra, S, Feb 5)
Roxton Hill 37[1] (2m, Hayd, Y, Nov 18)
Royal Athlete 53[5] (3m ½f, Asco, G, Oct 30, *H*)
Run For Free 84[2] (3m, Hayd, S, Jan 22, *H*)
Run Pet Run 34[2] (3m 1f, Kels, Hvy, Jan 12, *H*)
Ryde Again 71[2] (2m 5f, Winc, S, Feb 10)
Saffaah (USA) 33[1] (2m ½f, Taun, G, Apr 15)
Sailors Luck 34[4] (2m, Warw, F, Oct 30, *H*)
San Lorenzo (USA) 42[1] (2m ½f, Donc, G, Jan 28)
Sandybraes 31[1] (3m, Ludl, Y, Nov 18, *H*)
Saraemma 51[2] (2m 1f, Leop, Y, Dec 27, *H*)
Sartorius 45[1] (2m ½f, Towc, S, Apr 19, *H*)
Scotoni 32[2] (2m 4½f, Ling, S, Dec 11, *H*)
Scribbler 31[2] (2m 5f, Leop, Hvy, Mar 6)
Second Schedual 58[5] (2m 5f, Chel, Y, Dec 11, *H*)
See More Indians 34[1] (2m 4½f, Worc, G, Oct 23)
Seon 39[5] (2m, Nott, S, Feb 19, *G*)

Setter Country 39[2] (2m, Winc, S, Jan 28, *H*)
Shaab Turbo 33[2] (2m, Winc, S, Feb 24)
Shaston 29[3] (3m, Wind, G, Nov 24, *H*)
Sheer Ability 54[1] (2m 7f, Worc, Y, Mar 23, *H*)
Sheilas Hillcrest 26[1] (2m 4f, Mark, S, Dec 27)
Shrewd John 34[2] (2m ½f, Donc, G, Mar 5)
Shu Fly (NZ) 52[1] (2m, Ludl, G, Dec 6, *H*)
Sibton Abbey 54[5] (3m ½f, Weth, G, Oct 30)
Sikera Spy 45[2] (3m ½f, Bang, S, Mar 9, *H*)
Simple Pleasure 39[1] (2m 1f, Kels, S, Apr 11, *H*)
Sir Peter Lely 41[1] (2m 4f, Newc, G, Mar 21, *H*)
Sirrah Jay 30[1] (3m 3f 30yds, Live, S, Nov 20, *H*)
Skeletor 29[1] (2m, Sout, Hvy, Nov 26)
Slievenamon Mist 30[1] (2m 7f, Worc, G, May 7, *H*)
Smartie Express 54[3] (2m 4½f, Chel, G, Mar 16, *H*)
Snitton Lane 57[1] (2m ½f, Chel, G, Mar 17, *H*)
Social Climber 28[2] (2m ½f, Hunt, S, Dec 27, *H*)
Soleil Dancer (IRE) 25[1] (2m, Ling, S, Mar 18, *H*)
Son Of War 45[3] (3m, Leop, S, Jan 23, *L*)
Sonsie Mo 44[2] (2m, Edin, G, Feb 26, *H*)
Sorry About That 51[2] (2m 1f, Font, Hvy, Jan 8)
Southern Minstrel 38[2] (3m 3f 30yds, Live, S, Nov 20, *H*)
Southolt (IRE) 63[3] (2m, Chel, Y, Mar 15, *G*)
Space Fair 68[2] (2m ½f, Chel, F, Sep 30, *H*)
Spanish Fair (IRE) 28[3] (2m, Ayr, Y, Jan 3)
Sparkling Flame 39[3] (2m 7f, Worc, G, Mar 30, *H*)
Spikey (NZ) 48[3] (3m ½f, Asco, Y, Feb 9, *H*)
Spree Cross 54[1] (2m, Sand, G, Mar 29, *H*)
Springaleak 58[2] (3m ½f, Asco, G, Oct 30, *H*)
Squeeze Play 33[2] (2m 4½f, Hunt, G, Nov 12)
Squire Jim 28[4] (2m 5f, Chel, G, Apr 20)
St Athans Lad 41[2] (2m 2f, Font, G, Nov 9, *H*)
Star Of The Glen 32[3] (2m 1½f, Stra, G, Oct 28, *H*)
Staunch Rival (USA) 27[1] (3m, Taun, S, Dec 9, *H*)
Stay Awake 45[1] (2m 1½f, Cart, F, May 28, *H*)
Storm Alert 76[3] (2m ½f, Chel, G, Mar 17, *H*)
Storm Flight 32[3] (2m 3f, Taun, S, Nov 25)
Strong Approach 27[5] (2m, Carl, S, Apr 2, *H*)
Strong Sound 28[1] (2m 4½f, Weth, S, Apr 5, *H*)
Strong Views 37[2] (2m, Asco, G, Nov 19, *G*)
Stunning Stuff 43[3] (3m, Kemp, S, Dec 28, *H*)
Sunbeam Talbot 41[4] (2m 6f, Towc, Y, Nov 11, *H*)
Superior Finish 55[1] (3m 5f, Warw, S, Feb 8, *H*)
Sword Beach 54[1] (2m 4½f, Weth, G, Oct 13, *H*)
Sybillin 89[1] (2m, Sand, S, Dec 4, *G*)
Teaplanter 41[2] (3m 2½f, Chel, G, Mar 17)
Terrible Gel (FR) 38[3] (2m 1f, Sedg, F, Mar 26, *H*)
Thatcher Rock (NZ) 42[1] (2m 5f, Winc, G, Nov 18, *H*)
Thats The Life 38[3] (2m, Worc, S, Nov 10, *H*)
The Committee 50[2] (3m 1f, Chel, Y, Mar 15, *H*)
The Country Trader 26[3] (2m ½f, Donc, G, Mar 5)
The Fellow (FR) 84[1] (3m 2½f, Chel, G, Mar 17, *G*)
The Glow (IRE) 38[3] (2m 5f, Chel, Y, Dec 11)
The Green Stuff 41[1] (2m, Sout, S, Oct 16, *H*)
The Real Unyoke 25[3] (2m 5f, Leop, Hvy, Mar 6, *H*)
The Slater 46[1] (2m, Warw, F, Oct 30, *H*)
Third Quarter 34[2] (2m 3f, Leop, S, Dec 29)
Threeoutoffour 50[1] (2m 6½f, Mark, S, Jan 22, *H*)
Thumbs Up 42[1] (2m, Winc, S, Feb 24)
Tinas Lad 31[1] (2m, Ludl, Y, Nov 18, *H*)
Tipp Mariner 32[3] (2m 6f, Towc, Y, Nov 11, *H*)
Tipping Tim 49[3] (2m 5f, Chel, F, Oct 20, *H*)
Tochenka 33[2] (2m 7f, Worc, G, Apr 23, *H*)
Topsham Bay 76[3] (3m 1½f, Chel, Y, Dec 10, *H*)
Touching Star 25[1] (3m, Wind, G, Nov 24, *H*)
Toureen Prince 31[2] (2m 5f, Utto, Y, Oct 2, *H*)
Travado 87[1] (2m 4½f, Hunt, Y, Nov 23, *G*)
Tresidder 40[1] (2m 1f, Sedg, G, Mar 16, *H*)
Tri Folene (FR) 46[1] (3m, Stra, S, Dec 29, *H*)
Trimlough 49[2] (2m, Warw, G, Nov 27, *H*)
Tudor Fable (IRE) 43[1] (2m, Here, G, Nov 17)
Uncle Ernie 77[1] (2m, Live, Hvy, Apr 9, *G*)
Unholy Alliance 36[1] (2m, Here, F, May 11)
Ushers Island 62[1] (3m 5½f, Sand, Y, Apr 23, *H*)
Valiant Boy 55[6] (2m, Sand, S, Dec 4, *G*)
Valiant Warrior 29[1] (2m 4½f, Bang, G, Sep 11)
Vayrua (FR) 29[1] (2m 4½f, Leic, Hvy, Jan 3)
Vazon Bay 28[1] (2m 4f, Ludl, S, Mar 3)
Very Very Ordinary 53[5] (3m ½f, Asco, Y, Dec 18, *H*)
Viking Flagship 89[1] (2m 1f, Newb, S, Feb 12)

Visible Difference 50[5] (2m 1f, Leop, Y, Dec 26, *L*)
Wait You There (USA) 27[1] (2m 5f, Sedg, G, Apr 29, *H*)
Wanderweg (FR) 29[2] (2m 4f, Hayd, Hvy, Dec 9)
Warner For Winners 37[1] (3m 1½f, Here, Y, Apr 9, *H*)
Washingtoncrossing 41[4] (3m 1f, Chel, Y, Nov 12, *H*)
Waterloo Boy 86[3] (2m, Sand, S, Dec 4, *G*)
Welknown Character 45[3] (3m 1½f, Winc, G, Nov 4, *H*)
Well Briefed 34[1] (2m 3½f, Asco, Y, Apr 6, *H*)
Welsh Bard 29[2] (2m ½f, Taun, Y, Mar 14, *C*)
Whaat Fettle 40[5] (3m 1f, Kels, Hvy, Jan 12, *H*)
What's In Orbit 45[1] (2m ½f, Newt, G, May 3)
Whispering Steel 60[1] (2m 4f, Ayr, Y, Nov 13, *H*)
Whitwood 35[1] (2m 1½f, Mark, S, Mar 11, *H*)
Wide Boy 46[2] (2m 5f, Newt, S, Oct 5, *H*)
Wild Atlantic 28[4] (2m 1f, Sedg, F, May 5, *H*)
Will Phone 50[1] (3m, Leop, S, Mar 17, *H*)
Willie McGarr (USA) 28[2] (2m 3½f, Chep, Y, Oct 2)
Winabuck 32[2] (2m 7f, Worc, G, Mar 30, *H*)
Wind Force 30[4] (2m 5f, Chel, G, Apr 27, *G*)
Windy Ways 52[3] (3m 2½f, Chel, G, Apr 20, *H*)
Wings Of Freedom (IRE) 25[3] (2m 5f, Chel, Hvy, Jan 3)
Wingspan (USA) 42[2] (2m ½f, Newt, F, Apr 29, *H*)
Wonder Man (FR) 79[2] (2m 1f, Newb, S, Feb 12)
Yellow Spring 44[1] (2m 4½f, Ling, Hvy, Mar 19)
Yorkshire Gale 34[1] (2m 4½f, Sand, Y, Mar 11)
Yorkshireman (USA) 34[2] (2m 4½f, Hunt, F, Aug 30, *H*)
Young Benz 67[1] (2m 4½f, Weth, S, Dec 4, *H*)
Young Hustler 83[1] (3m ½f, Asco, Y, Dec 18, *H*)
Young Miner 32[1] (3m 1½f, Catt, S, Mar 9, *H*)
Young Snugfit 79[2] (2m, Chel, Y, Nov 12, *H*)
Zamil (USA) 30[3] (2m 4½f, Ling, S, Dec 11, *H*)
Zeta's Lad 80[1] (3m, Hayd, S, Jan 22, *H*)

NOTES

NOTES

NOTES

NOTES

NOTES

NOTES

NOTES

NOTES

NOTES

NOTES

NOTES

NOTES

NOTES

NOTES

NOTES

NOTES

NOTES

NOTES

NOTES

NOTES

NOTES

NOTES